FAITH *in* ACTION

STUDY BIBLE

● **LIVING GOD'S WORD IN A CHANGING WORLD**

NEW
INTERNATIONAL
VERSION

FAITH in ACTION
STUDY BIBLE

LIVING GOD'S WORD
IN A CHANGING WORLD

ZONDERVAN™

GRAND RAPIDS, MICHIGAN 49530 USA

Table of Contents

Alphabetical Order
of the Books of the Bible, vi

Abbreviations, vii

Introduction
by Richard Stearns
of World Vision, viii

About World Vision, ix

About This Bible, x

Acknowledgements, xii

Preface to the NIV, xv

THE OLD TESTAMENT, 1

THE NEW TESTAMENT, 1553

Table of Weights
and Measures, 2111

Reading Tracks, 2112

Study Guides, 2120

Subject Index, 2132

Index to Charts, 2141

Index to Articles, 2144

Index to Snapshots, 2146

Bibliography, 2148

Concordance, 2150

Colophon, 2316

THE OLD TESTAMENT

Genesis 1
Exodus 82
Leviticus 151
Numbers 195
Deuteronomy 258
Joshua 315
Judges 353
Ruth 390
1 Samuel 398
2 Samuel 444
1 Kings 487
2 Kings 537
1 Chronicles 585
2 Chronicles 639
Ezra 691
Nehemiah 711
Esther 736
Job 751
Psalms 808
Proverbs 974
Ecclesiastes 1032
Song of Songs 1054
Isaiah 1070
Jeremiah 1194
Lamentations 1295
Ezekiel 1310
Daniel 1387
Hosea 1413
Joel 1434
Amos 1445
Obadiah 1464
Jonah 1468
Micah 1475
Nahum 1491
Habakkuk 1498
Zephaniah 1506
Haggai 1516
Zechariah 1522
Malachi 1542

THE NEW TESTAMENT

Matthew 1553
Mark 1624
Luke 1668
John 1737
Acts 1787
Romans 1845
1 Corinthians 1874
2 Corinthians 1900
Galatians 1918
Ephesians 1929
Philippians 1941
Colossians 1952
1 Thessalonians 1961
2 Thessalonians 1969
1 Timothy 1975
2 Timothy 1985
Titus 1993
Philemon 1999
Hebrews 2004
James 2027
1 Peter 2037
2 Peter 2048
1 John 2054
2 John 2064
3 John 2067
Jude 2070
Revelation 2074

Alphabetical Order
of the Books of the Bible

The books of the New Testament are indicated by *italics*.

Acts *1787*	*James* *2027*	Nehemiah 711
Amos 1445	Jeremiah 1194	Numbers 195
1 Chronicles 585	Job 751	Obadiah 1464
2 Chronicles 639	Joel 1434	*1 Peter* *2037*
Colossians *1952*	*John* *1737*	*2 Peter* *2048*
1 Corinthians *1874*	*1 John* *2054*	*Philemon* *1999*
2 Corinthians *1900*	*2 John* *2064*	*Philippians* *1941*
Daniel 1387	*3 John* *2067*	Proverbs 974
Deuteronomy 258	Jonah 1468	Psalms 808
Ecclesiastes 1032	Joshua 315	*Revelation* *2074*
Ephesians *1929*	*Jude* *2070*	*Romans* *1845*
Esther 736	Judges 353	Ruth 390
Exodus 82	1 Kings 487	1 Samuel 398
Ezekiel 1310	2 Kings 537	2 Samuel 444
Ezra 691	Lamentations 1295	Song of Songs 1054
Galatians *1918*	Leviticus 151	*1 Thessalonians* *1961*
Genesis 1	*Luke* *1668*	*2 Thessalonians* *1969*
Habakkuk 1498	Malachi 1542	*1 Timothy* *1975*
Haggai 1516	*Mark* *1624*	*2 Timothy* *1985*
Hebrews *2004*	*Matthew* *1553*	*Titus* *1993*
Hosea 1413	Micah 1475	Zechariah 1522
Isaiah 1070	Nahum 1491	Zephaniah 1506

Abbreviations

**Abbreviations Used
in Parentheses in Study Notes:**

c.	*about, approximately*
cf.	*compare, confer*
ch., chs.	*chapter, chapters*
e.g.	*for example*
esp.	*especially*
etc.	*and so on*
ff.	*and following (and the verses following)*
i.e.	*that is*
lit.	*literal, literally*
lit. tr.	*literally translated, literal translation*
NT	*New Testament*
OT	*Old Testament*
p., pp.	*page, pages*
v., vv.	*verse, verses*

Bible book names are designated within parentheses in study notes as follows:

Genesis	Gen.	*Matthew*	Matt.
Exodus	Ex.	*Mark*	Mark
Leviticus	Lev.	*Luke*	Luke
Numbers	Num.	*John*	John
Deuteronomy	Deut.	*Acts*	Acts
Joshua	Josh.	*Romans*	Rom.
Judges	Judg.	*1 Corinthians*	1 Cor.
Ruth	Ruth	*2 Corinthians*	2 Cor.
1 Samuel	1 Sam.	*Galatians*	Gal.
2 Samuel	2 Sam.	*Ephesians*	Eph.
1 Kings	1 Kings	*Philippians*	Phil.
2 Kings	2 Kings	*Colossians*	Col.
1 Chronicles	1 Chron.	*1 Thessalonians*	1 Thess.
2 Chronicles	2 Chron.	*2 Thessalonians*	2 Thess.
Ezra	Ezra	*1 Timothy*	1 Tim.
Nehemiah	Neh.	*2 Timothy*	2 Tim.
Esther	Est.	*Titus*	Titus
Job	Job	*Philemon*	Philem.
Psalms	Ps.	*Hebrews*	Heb.
Proverbs	Prov.	*James*	James
Ecclesiastes	Eccl.	*1 Peter*	1 Peter
Song of Songs	Song	*2 Peter*	2 Peter
Isaiah	Isa.	*1 John*	1 Jn.
Jeremiah	Jer.	*2 John*	2 Jn.
Lamentations	Lam.	*3 John*	3 Jn.
Ezekiel	Ezek.	*Jude*	Jude
Daniel	Dan.	*Revelation*	Rev.
Hosea	Hos.		
Joel	Joel		
Amos	Amos		
Obadiah	Obad.		
Jonah	Jonah		
Micah	Mic.		
Nahum	Nah.		
Habakkuk	Hab.		
Zephaniah	Zeph.		
Haggai	Hag.		
Zechariah	Zech.		
Malachi	Mal.		

Introduction

Dear Friend,

A friend of mine once said he had seen a Bible from which all of the passages that related to helping the poor, standing up for justice, and giving generously had been removed with a razor blade. The result, he said, was a book in tatters, barely held together, because so much had been slashed out. That is because the faith described in the Bible is inseparable from the actions that flow naturally from it. The Christian faith is a faith of bold and revolutionary action. It was revolutionary in Jesus' time, and it is still revolutionary in ours.

In today's world, wracked by terrorism, poverty, lawlessness, disease, and violence, the message of the gospel and the need for Christians who put their faith into action has never been more acute. We, the followers of Jesus Christ, are an integral part of God's plan for the world—the same world that God loved so much "that he gave his one and only Son, that whoever believes in him shall not perish but have everlasting life" (John 3:16). In this famous verse we see the depth of God's love for our world. It was not a passive and sentimental love but rather a dynamic, active, and sacrificial love. For God so loved the world *that he acted!*

It was with this spirit that *World Vision* sought to partner with *Zondervan* to produce a truly unique study Bible, one that would amplify God's love for the world and energize followers of Jesus Christ to put their faith into action. The result is a Bible that ignites in our hearts the desire to follow Christ with our faith and with our deeds.

The Christian life is a journey of faith that begins when we accept God's free gift of salvation.

"For it is by grace you have been saved, through faith—and this not from yourselves, it is the gift of God—not by works, so that no one can boast."

Ephesians 2:8–9

But after our salvation we begin our journey of discipleship as we seek to become fully committed followers of Jesus Christ.

"For we are God's workmanship, created in Christ Jesus to do good works, which God prepared in advance for us to do."

Ephesians 2:10

The *Faith in Action Study Bible* is dedicated to helping us in this journey of discipleship. It amplifies with commentary the great passages of discipleship and lays out study tracks on issues like poverty, justice, stewardship, and evangelism. It is filled with essays by leading Christian thinkers who wrestle with the great questions of what it means to be a Christian in our 21st-century world, and it offers up real-life stories of men, women, and children who have put their faith into action in dynamic ways.

More than 50 years ago Bob Pierce, the founder of World Vision, wrote a prayer in the flyleaf of his Bible that has motivated our organization ever since: *"Let my heart be broken by the things that break the heart of God."* World Vision is nothing more than a partnership of Christians worldwide who are committed wholeheartedly to demonstrating God's love to a hurting world. We are grateful for all who have joined us on this journey. It is our prayer that the *Faith in Action Study Bible* will better equip all of us to love our neighbors as ourselves and will motivate a new generation of Christians in their journey of discipleship.

Rich Stearns
President, World Vision United States
October 2004

About World Vision

WORLD VISION—BUILDING A BETTER WORLD FOR CHILDREN

World Vision is a Christian relief and development organization dedicated to helping children and their communities worldwide reach their full potential by tackling the causes of poverty. Motivated by our faith in Jesus, we seek to serve the poor as a demonstration of God's unconditional love for all people. We provide emergency assistance to those affected by natural disasters and civil conflict, work with communities to develop long-term solutions to poverty, and advocate for justice on behalf of the poor.

The ability of children to reach their God-given potential depends on the physical, social, and spiritual strength of their families and communities. To help secure a better future for each child we focus on lasting, community-based access to clean water, food supplies, spiritual nurture, health care, education, and economic opportunities. We believe these efforts are a witness to Jesus Christ through life, word, sign, and deed, and encourage individuals to respond to the gospel.

IT IS OUR FATHER'S WORLD

As Christians, we believe we are caretakers of all that God has created and are committed to use his gifts responsibly, being good stewards of the resources that are entrusted to us. World Vision strives to keep overhead low and optimizes and distributes resources where they are needed most.

We use donations and grants for their intended purposes and look for ways to leverage every dollar entrusted to World Vision, monitoring project progress and evaluating our performance in order to ensure that programs are having the maximum benefit for the children and families we serve. These practices have earned the trust and support of more than one million donors, thousands of churches, and hundreds of corporations, institutions, and government agencies around the globe.

WITH GOD, ALL THINGS ARE POSSIBLE

World Vision cares for the well-being of poor and distressed people in difficult places in the world—partnering with churches and other Christian organizations for the glory of God. Our staff includes experts in child-related issues, community development, and business operations. These extraordinary individuals—the majority of whom work in their native regions—seek to demonstrate the example set by Jesus, living side-by-side with those they serve. We believe that by working hand-in-hand with community members we can effectively tackle the devastating effects as well as the causes of poverty.

With God, all things are possible. So even in the face of difficult circumstances, our ongoing grassroots development work and community partnerships allow us to achieve what might seem impossible without God's undergirding strength and help.

www.worldvision.org

About This Bible

The *Faith in Action Study Bible* is a complete, comprehensive study Bible with a strong central message: We're not here for ourselves. Its goal is to help Christians better understand the Bible and discover how their faith can impact their family, community, and world. This Bible focuses on the question "What is God doing?" with the intention that the reader will enter in and join him there. As James 1:22 puts it, "Do not merely listen to the word, and so deceive yourselves. Do what it says." Humanitarian content in the notes and features appears in conjunction with the many passages from which it naturally flows.

The following descriptions will help familiarize you with the features of this Bible:

There and Then — Jesus went to regarding oaths when swear "at all." He was name, or substitutes fo statement. His follower integrity of character a whatever they say is ab able—without the bacl

Here and Now — Jesus didn't say testified under oath at h son operates under the

STUDY NOTES

"Commentary style" notes, divided into "There and Then" and "Here and Now" segments (denoted by scroll and laptop icons), cover not individual verses but sections between NIV sectional headings. "There and Then" notes supply background information and/or explain some aspect of the passage. "Here and Now" application notes explore a variety of contexts, both personal and social/cultural, in which the passage may be applied today. Their goal is to coach, encourage, and inspire. Many include open-ended questions and invitations for reflection. While an important focus of this Bible is the working out of faith through action to alleviate the plight of the least, last, and lost, notes cover many other issues, as the text invites.

FULL-PAGE ARTICLES

Interspersed throughout the text are full-page articles from a wide variety of contemporary and classic authors (see indexes to charts, articles, and Snapshots on pages 2145–2150 at the back of this Bible). These fall into three categories: (1) thematic articles tied to relevant passages, (2) profiles of well-known people who have moved from looking at Christianity as a *view* of life to embracing it as a *way* of life, and (3) classic material applicable to a particular Scripture portion.

BOOK INTRODUCTIONS

Introductions provide detail regarding the background and content of each book, including at-a-glance style timelines and outlines. Included are thought-provoking discussions of themes and Biblical role models from the book, as well as action-oriented challenges for the reader.

CHARTS AND GRAPHS

Individually designed, eye-catching charts and graphs are scattered throughout the text. "Thumbtacks" tie in the topics to particular texts. Many of these were inspired directly by Scripture, but the tie-in for others is indirect but equally relevant (e.g., statistical or other information of a psycho-social nature, most often related to a humanitarian theme).

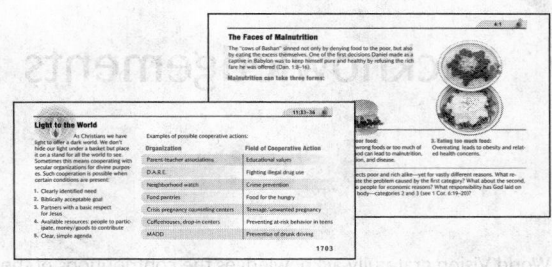

SNAPSHOTS

The content for many of the brief inspirational stories and profiles ("Snapshots") sprinkled throughout the Bible was selected from the extensive World Vision archives. These snippets, focusing on well-known or anonymous "heroes" and "heroines" of the faith, as well as of recipients of their assistance from various continents and cultures, aim straight for the heart.

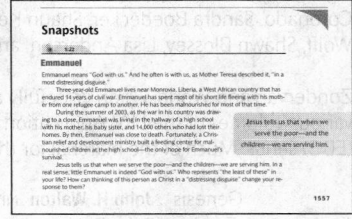

SIDE-COLUMN CROSS REFERENCES

This feature helps you locate with a minimum of effort other Biblical material related to the passage or subject matter at hand.

READING TRACKS

Approximately 30 sets of reading tracks under the categories of "heart shaping," "mind building," "action producing," and "building tools," lead the reader through the stages of the Christian life, beginning with God and ending with his followers acting on his behalf in the world.

STUDY GUIDES

Short, suggestive study guides based on the material in the reading tracks are ideal for use in church school classes, small group discussions, and personal Bible study.

SUBJECT INDEX

This handy resource allows you to locate articles, stories, charts, and graphs related to specific themes.

INDEX TO CHARTS, ARTICLES, AND SNAPSHOTS

This location-finder for all charts, articles, and stories provides a broad picture of the scope of their subject matter and allows for easy location of articles by favorite authors.

CONCORDANCE

Complementary to the side-column cross-reference system described above, this feature provides an alternate approach for locating texts and passages (1) by featuring key words to help the reader pinpoint specific texts and (2) by identifying key passages related to particular themes.

Acknowledgements

World Vision gratefully acknowledges the contributions of the following individuals: Rich Stearns, Atul Tandon, Bryant Myers, Tim Dearborn, Mark Rhode, John Jensen, Denise Koenig, Timothy Beals, Steve Haas, Shelly Ngo, George Marhad, Nathalie Overland, Brian Sytsma, Cam-vien Ha, Arlene Mitsui, Selena Koosmann, Robert Coronado, Sandra Boedecker, Shaun Kempston, Rae Tapia, Joan Mussa, Barry Swindon, Jane Sutton, Rachel Wolff, Shawn Blossey, Lisa Anderson, and Amy Parodi.

Zondervan and World Vision gratefully acknowledge the contributions of the following scholars, authors of various volumes of the NIV Application Commentary (NIVAC) series and the Expositor's Bible Commentary (EBC) series. Much of the material for the study notes in this NIV Bible was adapted from their work, as follows:

Genesis	**John H. Walton** NIVAC		Jonah	**James K. Bruckner** NIVAC
Exodus	**Peter Enns** NIVAC		Micah	**Gary Smith** NIVAC
Leviticus	**Roy E. Gane** NIVAC		Nahum	**James K. Bruckner** NIVAC
Numbers	**Roy E. Gane** NIVAC		Habakkuk	**James K. Bruckner** NIVAC
Deuteronomy	**Earl S. Kalland** EBC		Zephaniah	**James K. Bruckner** NIVAC
Joshua	**Donald H. Madvig** EBC		Haggai	**Mark J. Boda** NIVAC
Judges	**K. Lawson Younger, Jr.** NIVAC		Zechariah	**Mark J. Boda** NIVAC
Ruth	**K. Lawson Younger, Jr.** NIVAC		Malachi	**Robert L. Alden** EBC
1 Samuel	**Bill T. Arnold** NIVAC		Matthew	**Michael J. Wilkins** NIVAC
2 Samuel	**Bill T. Arnold** NIVAC		Mark	**David E. Garland** NIVAC
1 Kings	**Gus Konkel** NIVAC		Luke	**Darrell L. Bock** NIVAC
2 Kings	**Gus Konkel,** NIVAC		John	**Gary M. Burge** NIVAC
	Richard D. Patterson, EBC		Acts	**Ajith Fernando** NIVAC
	and Hermann J. Austel EBC		Romans	**Douglas J. Moo** NIVAC
1 Chronicles	**Andrew E. Hill** NIVAC		1 Corinthians	**Craig Blomberg** NIVAC
2 Chronicles	**Andrew E. Hill** NIVAC		2 Corinthians	**Scott J. Hafemann** NIVAC
Ezra	**Edwin Yamauchi** EBC		Galatians	**Scot McKnight** NIVAC
Nehemiah	**Edwin Yamauchi** EBC		Ephesians	**Klyne Snodgrass** NIVAC
Esther	**Karen Jobes** NIVAC		Philippians	**Frank Thielman** NIVAC
Job	**Elmer B. Smick** EBC		Colossians	**David E. Garland** NIVAC
Psalms First Half	**Gerald H. Wilson** NIVAC		1 Thessalonians	**Michael W. Holmes** NIVAC
Psalms Second Half	**Willem A. VanGemeren** EBC		2 Thessalonians	**Michael W. Holmes** NIVAC
Proverbs	**Paul E. Koptak** NIVAC		1 Timothy	**Walter L. Liefeld** NIVAC
Ecclesiastes	**Iain Provan** NIVAC		2 Timothy	**Walter L. Liefeld** NIVAC
Song of Songs	**Dennis F. Kinlaw** EBC		Titus	**Walter L. Liefeld** NIVAC
	and Iain Provan NIVAC		Philemon	**David E. Garland** NIVAC
Isaiah	**John Oswalt** NIVAC		Hebrews	**George H. Guthrie** NIVAC
Jeremiah	**J. Andrew Dearman** NIVAC		James	**David P. Nystrom** NIVAC
Lamentations	**J. Andrew Dearman** NIVAC		1 Peter	**Scot McKnight** NIVAC
Ezekiel	**Iain Duguid** NIVAC		2 Peter	**Douglas J. Moo** NIVAC
Daniel	**Tremper Longman III** NIVAC		1 John	**Gary M. Burge** NIVAC
Hosea	**Gary Smith** NIVAC		2 John	**Gary M. Burge** NIVAC
Joel	*Richard D. Patterson* EBC		3 John	**Gary M. Burge** NIVAC
Amos	**Gary Smith** NIVAC		Jude	**Douglas J. Moo** NIVAC
Obadiah	**Carl E. Armerding** EBC		Revelation	**Craig S. Keener** NIVAC

ARTICLE AUTHORS

Thomas à Kempis, German mystic and religious author

Frances Adeney, professor of mission at Louisville Presbyterian Theological Seminary in Louisville, Kentucky

Timothy J. Beals, publisher of World Vision Press in Federal Way, Washington

David R. Befus, president of Latin America Mission in Miami, Florida

Kenneth Boa, president of Reflections Ministries in Atlanta, Georgia

Susan Power Bratton, chair of environmental studies at Baylor University in Waco, Texas

John Calvin, French theologian, church reformer, and pastor

Tony Campolo, professor emeritus of sociology at Eastern College in St. Davids, Pennsylvania

Jimmy Carter, former president of the United States

Michael Cassidy, founder and international team leader of African Enterprise in Monrovia, California

Ellen Charry, professor of theology at Princeton Theological Seminary in Princeton, New Jersey

Jayakumar Christian, country director of World Vision India

Maxie Dunnam, chancellor of Asbury Theological Seminary in Wilmore, Kentucky

William Dyrness, professor of theology and culture at Fuller Theological Seminary in Pasadena, California

Ted Engstrom, former president of World Vision U.S. in Federal Way, Washington

William Enright, pastor of Central Presbyterian Church in Indianapolis, Indiana

Ajith Fernando, national director of Youth for Christ in Sri Lanka

Richard J. Foster, writer on Christian spirituality

Millard Fuller, founder and president of Habitat for Humanity International in Americus, Georgia

Steve Haas, vice president of World Vision U.S. in Federal Way, Washington

Gary A. Haugen, president of the International Justice Mission in Washington, D.C.

Carl F. H. Henry, founding editor of *Christianity Today* magazine and former lecturer at-large for World Vision U.S. in Federal Way, Washington

George G. Hunter III, professor of evangelism and church growth at Asbury Theological Seminary in Wilmore, Kentucky

Bill Hybels, pastor of Willow Creek Community Church in Barrington, Illinois

Thomas R. Kelly, devotional author

Terry LeBlanc, director of aboriginal programs at World Vision Canada in Mississauga, Ontario

C.S. Lewis, writer, novelist and critic, and former chair of Medieval and Renaissance studies at Cambridge University in Cambridge, United Kingdom

Max Lucado, pulpit minister of Oak Hills Church of Christ in San Antonio, Texas, and author of over 30 books

Scot McKnight, Karl A. Olsson Professor of Religious Studies at North Park University in Chicago, Illinois

Richard Mouw, president of Fuller Theological Seminary in Pasadena, California

Bryant L. Myers, vice president of World Vision International in Monrovia, California

John Ortberg, teaching pastor at Menlo Park Presbyterian Church in Menlo Park, California

Bill Pannell, professor of urban studies at Fuller Theological Seminary in Pasadena, California

Christine D. Pohl, professor of social ethics at Asbury Theological Seminary in Wilmore, Kentucky

Dana L. Robert, Truman Collins Professor of World Mission at Boston University School of Theology in Boston, Massachusetts

Robert Seiple, former U.S. Ambassador of Religious Freedom, former president of World Vision U.S., and founder and chairman of the board of the Institute for Global Engagement in St. David's, Pennsylvania

Marshall Shelley, vice president of Christianity Today International in Carol Stream, Illinois

ACKNOWLEDGEMENTS

Ronald J. Sider, professor of theology, holistic ministry, and public policy at Eastern Seminary in Philadelphia and president of Evangelicals for Social Action in Wynnewood, Pennsylvania

Howard Snyder, professor of the history and theology of mission at Asbury Theological Seminary in Wilmore, Kentucky

Marion L. Soards, professor of New Testament at Louisville Presbyterian Theological Seminary in Louisville, Kentucky

Richard Stearns, president of World Vision U.S. in Federal Way, Washington

John Stott, preacher, evangelist, leader of evangelicals worldwide, and principal framer of the landmark Lausanne Covenant (1974)

Joni Eareckson Tada, president of Joni and Friends in Agura Hills, California

Teresa, Mother, Roman Catholic nun and founder of the Sisters of Charity in Calcutta, India

Ted Ward, professor emeritus of Trinity International University in Deerfield, Illinois, and Michigan State University in East Lansing, Michigan

Dolphus Weary, executive director of Mission Mississippi, a faith-based program in Jackson, Mississippi, that cultivates racial tolerance by facilitating church-to-church dialogue

John W. Whitehead, president of the Rutherford Institute based in Charlottesville, Virginia

Darrell Whiteman, dean of the E. Stanley Jones School of World Mission and Evangelism at Asbury Theological Seminary in Wilmore, Kentucky

Philip Yancey, Christian author and editor-at-large for *Christianity Today* magazine in Carol Stream, Illinois

Hwa Yung, director of the Centre for the Study of Christianity in Asia at Trinity Theological College in Singapore

H. Matthew Zahniser, professor emeritus of mission and world religions at Asbury Theological Seminary in Wilmore, Kentucky

Preface to the NIV

THE NEW INTERNATIONAL VERSION is a completely new translation of the Holy Bible made by over a hundred scholars working directly from the best available Hebrew, Aramaic and Greek texts. It had its beginning in 1965 when, after several years of exploratory study by committees from the Christian Reformed Church and the National Association of Evangelicals, a group of scholars met at Palos Heights, Illinois, and concurred in the need for a new translation of the Bible in contemporary English. This group, though not made up of official church representatives, was transdenominational. Its conclusion was endorsed by a large number of leaders from many denominations who met in Chicago in 1966.

Responsibility for the new version was delegated by the Palos Heights group to a self-governing body of fifteen, the Committee on Bible Translation, composed for the most part of biblical scholars from colleges, universities and seminaries. In 1967 the New York Bible Society (now the International Bible Society) generously undertook the financial sponsorship of the project—a sponsorship that made it possible to enlist the help of many distinguished scholars. The fact that participants from the United States, Great Britain, Canada, Australia and New Zealand worked together gave the project its international scope. That they were from many denominations—including Anglican, Assemblies of God, Baptist, Brethren, Christian Reformed, Church of Christ, Evangelical Free, Lutheran, Mennonite, Methodist, Nazarene, Presbyterian, Wesleyan and other churches—helped to safeguard the translation from sectarian bias.

How it was made helps to give the New International Version its distinctiveness. The translation of each book was assigned to a team of scholars. Next, one of the Intermediate Editorial Committees revised the initial translation, with constant reference to the Hebrew, Aramaic or Greek. Their work then went to one of the General Editorial Committees, which checked it in detail and made another thorough revision. This revision in turn was carefully reviewed by the Committee on Bible Translation, which made further changes and then released the final version for publication. In this way the entire Bible underwent three revisions, during each of which the translation was examined for its faithfulness to the original languages and for its English style.

All this involved many thousands of hours of research and discussion regarding the meaning of the texts and the precise way of putting them into English. It may well be that no other translation has been made by a more thorough process of review and revision from committee to committee than this one.

From the beginning of the project, the Committee on Bible Translation held to certain goals for the New International Version: that it would be an accurate translation and one that would have clarity and literary quality and so prove suitable for public and private reading, teaching, preaching, memorizing and liturgical use. The Committee also sought to preserve some measure of continuity with the long tradition of translating the Scriptures into English.

In working toward these goals, the translators were united in their commitment to the authority and infallibility of the Bible as God's Word in written form. They believe that it contains the divine answer to the deepest needs of humanity, that it sheds unique light on our path in a dark world, and that it sets forth the way to our eternal well-being.

The first concern of the translators has been the accuracy of the translation and its fidelity to the thought of the biblical writers. They have weighed the significance of the lexical and grammatical details of the Hebrew, Aramaic and Greek texts. At the same time, they have striven for more than a word-for-word translation. Because thought patterns and syntax differ from language to language, faithful communication of the meaning of the writers of the Bible demands frequent modifications in sentence structure and constant regard for the contextual meanings of words.

A sensitive feeling for style does not always accompany scholarship. Accordingly the Committee on Bible Translation submitted the developing version to a number of stylistic consultants. Two of them read every book of both Old and New Testaments twice—once before and once after the last major revision—and made invaluable suggestions. Samples of the translation were tested for clarity and ease of reading by various kinds of people—young and old, highly educated and less well educated, ministers and laymen.

Concern for clear and natural English—that the New International Version should be idiomatic but not idiosyncratic, contemporary but not dated—motivated the translators and consultants. At the same time, they tried to reflect the differing styles of the biblical writers. In view of the international use of English, the translators sought to avoid obvious Americanisms on the one hand and obvious Anglicisms on the other. A British edition reflects the comparatively few differences of significant idiom and of spelling.

As for the traditional pronouns "thou," "thee" and "thine" in reference to the Deity, the translators judged that to use these archaisms (along with the old verb forms such as "doest," "wouldest" and "hadst") would violate accuracy in translation. Neither Hebrew, Aramaic nor Greek uses special pronouns for the persons of the Godhead. A present-day translation is not enhanced by forms that in the time of the King James Version were used in everyday speech, whether referring to God or man.

For the Old Testament the standard Hebrew text, the Masoretic Text as published in the latest editions of *Biblia Hebraica*, was used throughout. The Dead Sea Scrolls contain material bearing on an earlier stage of the Hebrew text. They were consulted, as were the Samaritan Pentateuch and the ancient scribal traditions relating to textual changes. Sometimes a variant Hebrew reading in the margin of the Masoretic Text was followed instead of the text itself. Such instances, being variants within the Masoretic tradition, are not specified by footnotes. In rare cases, words in the consonantal text were divided differently from the way they appear in the Masoretic Text. Footnotes indicate this. The translators also consulted the more important early versions—the Septuagint; Aquila, Symmachus and Theodotion; the Vulgate; the Syriac Peshitta; the Targums; and for the Psalms the *Juxta Hebraica* of Jerome. Readings from these versions were occasionally followed where the Masoretic Text seemed doubtful and where accepted principles of textual criticism showed that one or more of these textual witnesses appeared to provide the correct reading. Such instances are footnoted. Sometimes vowel letters and vowel signs did not, in the judgment of the translators, represent the correct vowels for the original consonantal text. Accordingly some words were read with a different set of vowels. These instances are usually not indicated by footnotes.

The Greek text used in translating the New Testament was an eclectic one. No other piece of ancient literature has such an abundance of manuscript witnesses as does the New Testament. Where existing manuscripts differ, the translators made their choice of readings according to accepted principles of New Testament textual criticism. Footnotes call attention to places where there was uncertainty about what the original text was. The best current printed texts of the Greek New Testament were used.

There is a sense in which the work of translation is never wholly finished. This applies to all great literature and uniquely so to the Bible. In 1973 the New Testament in the New International Version was published. Since then, suggestions for corrections and revisions have been received from various sources. The Committee on Bible Translation carefully considered the suggestions and adopted a number of them. These were incorporated in the first printing of the entire Bible in 1978. Additional revisions were made by the Committee on Bible Translation in 1983 and appear in printings after that date.

As in other ancient documents, the precise meaning of the biblical texts is sometimes uncertain. This is more often the case with the Hebrew and Aramaic texts than with the Greek text. Although archaeological and linguistic discoveries in this century aid in understanding difficult passages, some uncertainties remain. The more significant of these have been called to the reader's attention in the footnotes.

In regard to the divine name *YHWH,* commonly referred to as the *Tetragrammaton,* the translators adopted the device used in most English versions of rendering that name as "Lord" in capital letters to distinguish it from *Adonai,* another Hebrew word rendered "Lord," for which small letters are used. Wherever the two names stand together in the Old Testament as a compound name of God, they are rendered "Sovereign Lord."

Because for most readers today the phrases "the Lord of hosts" and "God of hosts" have little meaning, this version renders them "the Lord Almighty" and "God Almighty." These renderings convey the sense of the Hebrew, namely, "he who is sovereign over all the 'hosts' (powers) in heaven and on earth, especially over the 'hosts' (armies) of Israel." For readers unacquainted with Hebrew this does not make clear the distinction between *Sabaoth* ("hosts" or "Almighty") and *Shaddai* (which can also be translated "Almighty"), but the latter occurs infrequently and is always footnoted. When *Adonai* and *YHWH Sabaoth* occur together, they are rendered "the Lord, the Lord Almighty."

As for other proper nouns, the familiar spellings of the King James Version are generally retained. Names traditionally spelled with "ch," except where it is final, are usually spelled in this translation with "k" or "c," since the biblical languages do not have the sound that "ch" frequently indicates in English—for example, in *chant.* For well-known names such as Zechariah, however, the traditional spelling has been retained. Variation in the spelling of names in the original languages has usually not been indicated. Where a person or place has

two or more different names in the Hebrew, Aramaic or Greek texts, the more familiar one has generally been used, with footnotes where needed.

To achieve clarity the translators sometimes supplied words not in the original texts but required by the context. If there was uncertainty about such material, it is enclosed in brackets. Also for the sake of clarity or style, nouns, including some proper nouns, are sometimes substituted for pronouns, and vice versa. And though the Hebrew writers often shifted back and forth between first, second and third personal pronouns without change of antecedent, this translation often makes them uniform, in accordance with English style and without the use of footnotes.

Poetical passages are printed as poetry, that is, with indentation of lines and with separate stanzas. These are generally designed to reflect the structure of Hebrew poetry. This poetry is normally characterized by parallelism in balanced lines. Most of the poetry in the Bible is in the Old Testament, and scholars differ regarding the scansion of Hebrew lines. The translators determined the stanza divisions for the most part by analysis of the subject matter. The stanzas therefore serve as poetic paragraphs.

As an aid to the reader, italicized sectional headings are inserted in most of the books. They are not to be regarded as part of the NIV text, are not for oral reading, and are not intended to dictate the interpretation of the sections they head.

The footnotes in this version are of several kinds, most of which need no explanation. Those giving alternative translations begin with "Or" and generally introduce the alternative with the last word preceding it in the text, except when it is a single-word alternative; in poetry quoted in a footnote a slant mark indicates a line division. Footnotes introduced by "Or" do not have uniform significance. In some cases two possible translations were considered to have about equal validity. In other cases, though the translators were convinced that the translation in the text was correct, they judged that another interpretation was possible and of sufficient importance to be represented in a footnote.

In the New Testament, footnotes that refer to uncertainty regarding the original text are introduced by "Some manuscripts" or similar expressions. In the Old Testament, evidence for the reading chosen is given first and evidence for the alternative is added after a semicolon (for example: Septuagint; Hebrew *father*). In such notes the term "Hebrew" refers to the Masoretic Text.

It should be noted that minerals, flora and fauna, architectural details, articles of clothing and jewelry, musical instruments and other articles cannot always be identified with precision. Also measures of capacity in the biblical period are particularly uncertain (see the table of weights and measures following the text).

Like all translations of the Bible, made as they are by imperfect man, this one undoubtedly falls short of its goals. Yet we are grateful to God for the extent to which he has enabled us to realize these goals and for the strength he has given us and our colleagues to complete our task. We offer this version of the Bible to him in whose name and for whose glory it has been made. We pray that it will lead many into a better understanding of the Holy Scriptures and a fuller knowledge of Jesus Christ the incarnate Word, of whom the Scriptures so faithfully testify.

The Committee on Bible Translation

June 1978
(Revised Aug 1983)

Names of the translators and editors may be secured from the
International Bible Society, translation sponsors of the New International Version,
1820 Jet Stream Drive, Colorado Springs, Colorado 80921-3696 U.S.A.

The Old Testament

INTRODUCTION TO
Genesis

AUTHOR

Though Genesis doesn't identify its author, Scripture and church tradition ascribe authorship to Moses. Moses, using some earlier written sources and oral traditions, as well as material directly revealed to him by God, gave Genesis its essential form and content. But like the rest of the Pentateuch (the first five books of the OT), there is evidence of some later editorial updating with regard to grammar and place-name modernizations (see also the list of kings in 36:31–43).

DATE WRITTEN

Genesis was probably written between 1446 and 1406 B.C.

ORIGINAL READERS

Genesis was written to the Israelites to show that though God created a good world, sin corrupted that creation, and God initiated a plan of salvation to restore it.

TIMELINE

	2200BC	2100	2000	1900	1800	1700	1600	1500	1400
Creation, Fall									
The Flood									
The Tower of Babel									
Abraham's life (c. 2166-1991 B.C.)									
Isaac's life (c. 2066-1886 B.C.)									
Jacob's life (c. 2006-1859 B.C.)									
Joseph's life (c. 1915-1805 B.C.)									
Book of Genesis written (c. 1446-1406 B.C.)									

THEMES

Genesis is the book of beginnings—the beginning of the cosmos and the beginning of humanity. It includes the following themes:

1. *Creation.* God created the world "very good" (1:31). There was harmony between God and his human creatures and between human beings. Indeed, all of creation was whole and at peace.

2. *Sin.* Sin entered the world through one man, Adam (3:1–19; Rom. 5:12). Unbelief, human conflict, sickness, and environmental degradation are its result. The present condition of the planet isn't the result of creation but of sin's corrupting effects.

3. *The image of God.* All human beings are created in the image of God; each person *is* God's likeness as a personal, rational, creative, moral being. Accordingly, everyone is to be treated with respect. Men and women were created equal, as both were made in God's image. The fact that Eve was created second, as a "helper" to man (2:18–23), doesn't indicate her subservience. In fact, in other contexts God himself is called the "helper" of Israel (Ex. 18:4; Deut. 33:29; Hos. 13:9), as is the Holy Spirit (John 14:16; 16:7).

4. *God's global plan of redemption.* Though God chose to work through one ethnic group in the Old Testament, his divine intention from the beginning was that all nations would come to know him through Abraham's descendants (Gen. 12:1–3). Abraham was chosen because of his faith, making him the father of all who come to God on the same basis. Genesis shows God's concern not just for Abraham, Isaac, and Jacob, but also for Ishmael and Esau, who fathered other family groups.

FAITH IN ACTION

The pages of Genesis are filled with life lessons and role models of faith—people who challenge believers to put their faith in action.

Role Models

- NOAH (6:22) obeyed God by building an ark in an area where the threat of a flood seemed ludicrous. Is God calling you to do something that seems absurd?

- ABRAHAM (12:1–4) obeyed God by leaving his home and family to travel to a foreign country. Is God asking you to do something difficult or risky?

- REBEKAH (24:1–67) practiced unusually generous hospitality to a stranger, thereby showing her "fit-ness" to be a wife for Isaac. Would people describe you as generous or hospitable? Do you go the "extra mile"?

- JACOB (32:22–30) was a deceptive, manipulative man whom God graciously transformed into "Israel" (32:28), the namesake of God's people. Is there an improbable or impossible case in your life—someone you feel is unlikely to become a person of faith? Is it difficult for you to put your faith into action? Are the changes slow in coming?

- JOSEPH (50:15–21) chose forgiveness, not revenge. Is there someone you need to forgive?

Challenges

- As a steward of God's creation, you do well to periodically review your lifestyle. What can you do to protect and nurture what God has made?

- Treat every individual with dignity and respect because each person reflects God's image.

- Seek God's guidance, asking him to help you choose his ways. Resist the temptation to take matters into your own hands (16:1–6), but trust God to accomplish his purpose in his own time.

- Study the family conflicts mentioned in Genesis (e.g., Abraham and Lot, Sarah and Hagar, Jacob and Esau, Rachel and Leah, Joseph and his brothers). Determine to live at peace with your relatives, and be responsive to God if he calls you to initiate reconciliation.

- Don't foster family turmoil by favoring one child over another (25:27; 37:3).

- The next time you are tempted to pass judgment on someone else, remember Judah (38:1–30), as well as Jesus' words (Matt. 7:3–5). Seek God's mercy for those who deserve judgment, as Abraham did (18:16–32).

- Your status or position is irrelevant when it comes to serving God. God can use you whether you are a prisoner (39:20–40:8) or a national leader (41:39–49).

- Resolve to be a blessing to the hungry (47:13–26), meeting their need from the abundance you possess.

OUTLINE

I. Primeval History: Four Great Events (1:1—11:26)
  A. The Creation of the Universe; Adam and Eve (1–2)
  B. The Fall and the Results of Sin (3–5)
  C. The Flood (6–9)
  D. The Scattering of the Nations (10:1—11:26)

II. Patriarchal History: Four Great Characters (11:27—50:26)
  A. Abraham (11:27—20:18)
  B. Isaac (21—26)
  C. Jacob (27:1—37:1)
  D. Joseph (37:2—50:26)

The Beginning

1 In the beginning[a] God created the heavens and the earth.[b] 2 Now the earth was[a] formless and empty,[c] darkness was over the surface of the deep, and the Spirit of God[d] was hovering over the waters.

3 And God said,[e] "Let there be light," and there was light.[f] 4 God saw that the light was good, and he separated the light from the darkness. 5 God called the light

---

a 2 Or possibly *became*

1:1
a Jn 1:1-2
b Job 38:4; Ps 90:2; Isa 42:5; 44:24; 45:12,18; Ac 17:24; Heb 11:3; Rev 4:11
1:2
c Jer 4:23
d Ps 104:30
1:3
e Ps 33:6,9; 148:5; Heb 11:3
f 2Co 4:6*

Genesis 1:1—2:3

The Scriptures begin with the bold affirmation that the entire creation is purposeful, intentional, and ordered. Rather than creation having been a random accident, God created the matter of which the cosmos is composed (Col. 1:16–17; Heb. 11:3). That which God has made is good, is owned by him, and is to be guarded by people. God is referred to in the plural, "Let us," believed by the church to refer to his triune nature. He's relational in his inner being, and people are made in his image. We are most fully human when we live in intimate community with God and with each other.

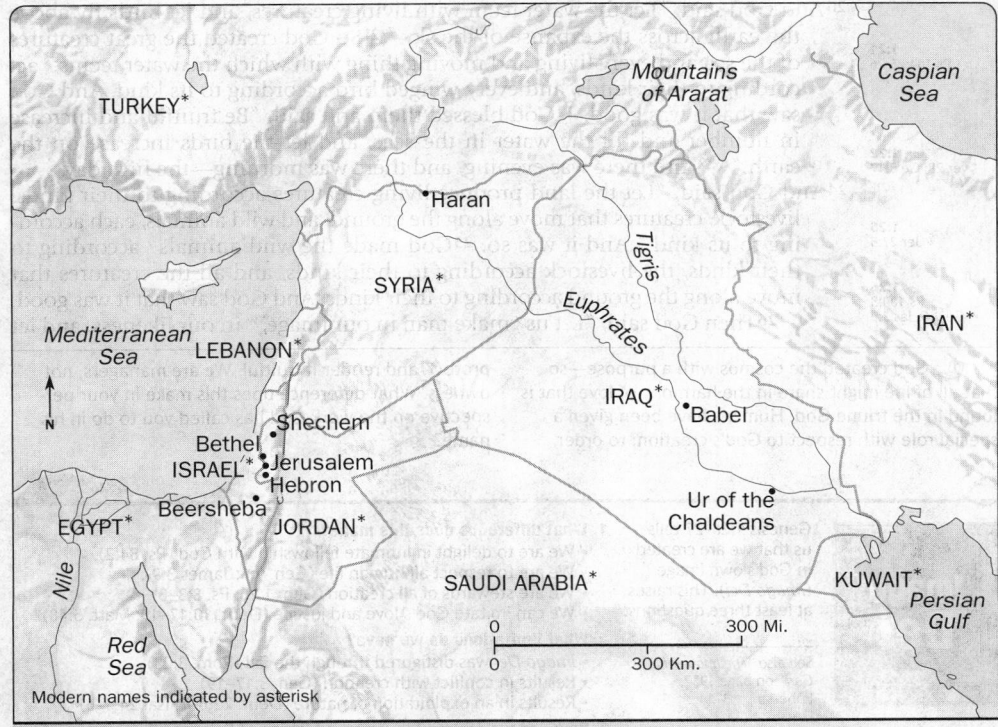

Setting of Genesis (1:1)
Then: The events of Genesis took place in Eden, Babel, the region only much later known as Palestine, and Egypt.
Now: The Garden of Eden was probably located at the head of the Persian Gulf, at the confluence of the Tigris and Euphrates Rivers in modern Iraq.

1:5
g Ps 74:16

1:6
h Jer 10:12

1:7
i Job 38:8-11,16;
Ps 148:4

1:9
j Job 38:8-11;
Ps 104:6-9; Pr 8:29;
Jer 5:22; 2Pe 3:5

1:11
k Ps 65:9-13;
104:14

1:14
l Ps 74:16
m Jer 10:2
n Ps 104:19

1:16
o Ps 136:8
p Ps 136:9
q Job 38:7,31-32;
Ps 8:3; Isa 40:26
1:18
r Jer 33:20,25

1:21
s Ps 104:25-26

1:22
t ver 28; Ge 8:17

1:25
u Jer 27:5

1:26
v Ps 100:3
w Ge 9:6; Jas 3:9

"day," and the darkness he called "night." g And there was evening, and there was morning—the first day.

6 And God said, "Let there be an expanse h between the waters to separate water from water." 7 So God made the expanse and separated the water under the expanse from the water above it. i And it was so. 8 God called the expanse "sky." And there was evening, and there was morning—the second day.

9 And God said, "Let the water under the sky be gathered to one place, j and let dry ground appear." And it was so. 10 God called the dry ground "land," and the gathered waters he called "seas." And God saw that it was good.

11 Then God said, "Let the land produce vegetation: k seed-bearing plants and trees on the land that bear fruit with seed in it, according to their various kinds." And it was so. 12 The land produced vegetation: plants bearing seed according to their kinds and trees bearing fruit with seed in it according to their kinds. And God saw that it was good. 13 And there was evening, and there was morning—the third day.

14 And God said, "Let there be lights l in the expanse of the sky to separate the day from the night, and let them serve as signs m to mark seasons n and days and years, 15 and let them be lights in the expanse of the sky to give light on the earth." And it was so. 16 God made two great lights—the greater light to govern o the day and the lesser light to govern p the night. He also made the stars. q 17 God set them in the expanse of the sky to give light on the earth, 18 to govern the day and the night, r and to separate light from darkness. And God saw that it was good. 19 And there was evening, and there was morning—the fourth day.

20 And God said, "Let the water teem with living creatures, and let birds fly above the earth across the expanse of the sky." 21 So God created the great creatures of the sea and every living and moving thing with which the water teems, s according to their kinds, and every winged bird according to its kind. And God saw that it was good. 22 God blessed them and said, "Be fruitful and increase in number and fill the water in the seas, and let the birds increase on the earth." t 23 And there was evening, and there was morning—the fifth day.

24 And God said, "Let the land produce living creatures according to their kinds: livestock, creatures that move along the ground, and wild animals, each according to its kind." And it was so. 25 God made the wild animals u according to their kinds, the livestock according to their kinds, and all the creatures that move along the ground according to their kinds. And God saw that it was good. 26 Then God said, "Let us v make man in our image, w in our likeness, and let

📖 God created the cosmos with a purpose—so that all of life might share in the harmony of love that is found in the triune God. Humans have been given a special role with respect to God's creation: to order, protect, and render it fruitful. We are managers, not owners. What difference does this make in your perspective on the work God has called you to do in his name?

1:26

Imago Dei

Genesis 1:26–27 tells us that we are created in God's own image (*imago Dei*). This raises at least three questions:

See also *"The Image of God"* on page 1932, Ephesians 1:3–14.

1. What difference does this make?
- We are to delight in intimate fellowship with God (Ps. 84:2).
- We are to respect all human life (Gen. 9:6; James 3:9).
- We are stewards of all creation (Gen. 1:26; Ps. 8:3–8).
- We can imitate God's love and justice (Deut. 10:17–19; Matt. 5:48).

2. What limitations do we have?
- *Imago Dei* was disfigured through the fall (Rom. 3:23).
- Results in conflict with creation (Gen. 3:17–19)
- Results in an exploitation of nature (Deut. 22:6–7; Isa. 24:4–6)

3. How can we restore the damaged image of God in us?
- Jesus Christ is the perfect image of God (Phil. 2:6; Col. 1:15).
- Jesus Christ is the faultless human being (2 Cor. 5:21; Heb. 1:3).
- God's image is renewed in those united with Jesus by faith (Rom. 8:29).
- Complete restoration will occur in the future (1 Cor. 15:49).
- Christian life is a process of transformation (2 Cor. 3:18).

them rule[x] over the fish of the sea and the birds of the air, over the livestock, over all the earth,[a] and over all the creatures that move along the ground."

27 So God created man in his own image,[y]
in the image of God he created him;
male and female[z] he created them.

28 God blessed them and said to them, "Be fruitful and increase in number; fill the earth[a] and subdue it. Rule over the fish of the sea and the birds of the air and over every living creature that moves on the ground."

29 Then God said, "I give you every seed-bearing plant on the face of the whole earth and every tree that has fruit with seed in it. They will be yours for food.[b] 30 And to all the beasts of the earth and all the birds of the air and all the creatures that move on the ground—everything that has the breath of life in it—I give every green plant for food.[c]" And it was so.
31 God saw all that he had made,[d] and it was very good.[e] And there was evening, and there was morning—the sixth day.

2 Thus the heavens and the earth were completed in all their vast array.

2 By the seventh day God had finished the work he had been doing; so on the seventh day he rested[b] from all his work.[f] 3 And God blessed the seventh day and made it holy,[g] because on it he rested from all the work of creating that he had done.

Adam and Eve

4 This is the account of the heavens and the earth when they were created.

When the LORD God made the earth and the heavens— 5 and no shrub of the field had yet appeared on the earth[c] and no plant of the field had yet sprung up,[h] for the LORD God had not sent rain on the earth[c][i] and there was no man to work the ground, 6 but streams[d] came up from the earth and watered the whole surface of the ground— 7 the LORD God formed the man[e] from the dust[j] of the ground[k] and breathed into his nostrils the breath[l] of life,[m] and the man became a living being.[n]

8 Now the LORD God had planted a garden in the east, in Eden;[o] and there he put the man he had formed. 9 And the LORD God made all kinds of trees grow out of the ground—trees that were pleasing to the eye and good for food. In the middle of the garden were the tree of life[p] and the tree of the knowledge of good and evil.[q]

10 A river watering the garden flowed from Eden; from there it was separated into four headwaters. 11 The name of the first is the Pishon; it winds through the entire land of Havilah, where there is gold. 12 (The gold of that land is good; aromatic resin[f] and onyx are also there.) 13 The name of the second river is the Gihon; it winds through the entire land of Cush.[g] 14 The name of the third river is the Tigris;[r] it runs along the east side of Asshur. And the fourth river is the Euphrates.

---

a 26 Hebrew; Syriac *all the wild animals*   b 2 Or *ceased*; also in verse 3   c 5 Or *land*; also in verse 6
d 6 Or *mist*   e 7 The Hebrew for *man (adam)* sounds like and may be related to the Hebrew for *ground (adamah)*; it is also the name *Adam* (see Gen. 2:20).   f 12 Or *good; pearls*   g 13 Possibly southeast Mesopotamia

1:26
x Ps 8:6-8
1:27
y 1Co 11:7
z Ge 5:2; Mt 19:4*;
Mk 10:6*
1:28
a Ge 9:1,7;
Lev 26:9
1:29
b Ps 104:14
1:30
c Ps 104:14,27;
145:15
1:31
d Ge 1:31
e 1Ti 4:4
2:2
f Ex 20:11; 31:17;
Heb 4:4*
2:3
g Lev 23:3;
Isa 58:13
2:5
h Ge 1:11
i Ps 65:9-10
2:7
j Ge 3:19
k Ps 103:14
l Job 33:4
m Ac 17:25
n 1Co 15:45*
2:8
o Ge 3:23,24;
Isa 51:3
2:9
p Ge 3:22,24;
Rev 2:7; 22:2,14,19
q Eze 47:12
2:14
r Da 10:4

Genesis 2:4–25

While the first creation account in Genesis 1 stresses creation as God's good gift, this one emphasizes life's interdependency. Adam's life was mutually interwoven with that of the animals, whom he named in his role as their guardian. But Adam needed a companion (the meaning of the word "helper" in this context is companion, as opposed to assistant). Eve's origin from Adam's rib expresses their interdependence. It's striking that God commanded the man to leave his own family to become one with his wife (v. 24). This concept contrasts to the common cultural practice of the woman being "given away" to join the man's family.

When Adam identified the roles and functions of each animal, he realized that none could serve as his partner in the functions of subduing, ruling, serving and preserving the garden, or being fruitful and multiplying. Eve became his companion in all these areas. Genesis 2 pictures man and woman serving together in mutual interdependence. We are all members of God's family, and we are called to respect one another as joint heirs of God's grace.

Be Fruitful and Increase

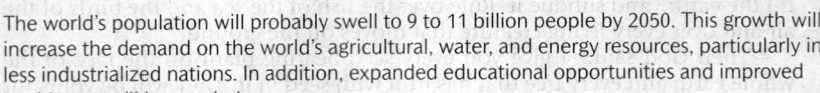

1:28

The world's population will probably swell to 9 to 11 billion people by 2050. This growth will increase the demand on the world's agricultural, water, and energy resources, particularly in less industrialized nations. In addition, expanded educational opportunities and improved health care will be needed.

The expansion of the human population has produced numerous blessings, including a readily available work force to staff growing industrial economies. But the sudden upsurge in human numbers in the last century has exacerbated social and environmental problems, such as land shortages for farming families; excessive gathering of fuel wood in tropical regions; overgrazing of semi-arid lands; and the expansion of mega cities, with their associated slums and squatters' districts. Population growth is a major factor in the clearing of the world's rainforests, the degradation of the world's lakes and rivers via human pollution, and the extinction of hundreds of animal and plant species.

> God intended children to be one of the great joys and experiences of human life—a blessing to be shared with all the living.

What does a Christian response look like? Genesis 1 and 2 highlight the importance of biological reproduction to God's plan for the cosmos. God said, "Let the land produce vegetation" (Gen. 1:11), thereby linking plants to soil. In Genesis 1:24–25 God directed the land to produce living creatures, tying animals to their habitats.

Most world religions offer an explanation for the origins of sex in their stories about the beginnings of the universe. Many describe a divine couple or a sexual act as producing the incipient earth, oceans, and sky. But in Genesis, the cosmos didn't arise from a sexual act or the conjugation of two deities but from a conscious, creative act of God. Once God had created the birds and the "great creatures of the sea," he blessed them and instructed them to be fruitful and increase in numbers (Gen. 1:22). This blessing was given first to the animals, who joyfully responded. In Genesis 1:28, God repeated the directive to Adam and Eve.

Christians have often treated Genesis 1:28 as an ethical imperative. Assuming that more is better, they have used the passage to justify large families. Genesis 1 suggests, though, that God's original design for the cosmos had built-in boundaries. The stars and planets had their places, as did day and night and the various animal species in their habitats. Genesis 1:28 was in the form of a blessing for humans to share with all living creatures (Gen. 1:21).

God's universe also was structured so that humans were dependent on the earth, plants, and animals for sustenance. God intended children to be one of the great joys and experiences of human life—a blessing to be shared with all the living. If we steal the blessing of reproduction from other creatures, eventually we will find it's fled from us as well, as natural environments and resources deteriorate. The fruits of God's providence, including both natural resources and our own reproductive blessings, also are to be shared among human beings.

The earth can support more people than it did a century ago. Yet speedy and unrelenting population growth often exceeds the capacity of both human infrastructure and the natural environment. As we read the first chapters of Genesis, we do well to contemplate not just the wealth of resources God has made available to us through the creation but also our obligation to care for and share them. Our reproductive decisions, from the level of national healthcare policies to individual family childbearing choices, will ultimately determine whether we actualize God's admonition to "be fruitful and increase" as a blessing or as a destructive struggle for damaged and inadequate basic resources.

Susan Power Bratton, chair of environmental studies at Baylor University in Waco, Texas

15The LORD God took the man and put him in the Garden of Eden to work it and take care of it. 16And the LORD God commanded the man, "You are free to eat from any tree in the garden; 17but you must not eat from the tree of the knowledge of good and evil, for when you eat of it you will surely die." *s*

18The LORD God said, "It is not good for the man to be alone. I will make a helper suitable for him." *t*

19Now the LORD God had formed out of the ground all the beasts of the field *u* and all the birds of the air. He brought them to the man to see what he would name them; and whatever the man called each living creature, *v* that was its name. 20So the man gave names to all the livestock, the birds of the air and all the beasts of the field.

But for Adam *a* no suitable helper was found. 21So the LORD God caused the man to fall into a deep sleep; and while he was sleeping, he took one of the man's ribs *b* and closed up the place with flesh. 22Then the LORD God made a woman from the rib *c w* he had taken out of the man, and he brought her to the man.

23The man said,

"This is now bone of my bones
  and flesh of my flesh; *x*

a 20 Or *the man*   *b* 21 Or *took part of the man's side*   *c* 22 Or *part*

2:17
s Dt 30:15,19;
Ro 5:12; 6:23;
Jas 1:15
2:18
t 1Co 11:9
2:19
u Ps 8:7 *v* Ge 1:24

2:22
w 1Co 11:8,9,12

2:23
x Ge 29:14;
Eph 5:28-30

2:1–2

Days of Creation

1 The Hebrew words most logically refer not to the creation of light as a physical entity but to the creation of a period of light. In other words, on day one God created *time*.

2 The ancients pictured the "firmament" (atmosphere) as a solid dome, to which the heavenly lights were affixed and which restrained the waters above the earth, the source of precipitation.

3 Soil and water sources and the reproduction of plants through seed together represent the crucial ingredients for vegetation. The description focuses on how God set up the agricultural system to function.

Days 1–3 present three functions God set up as he brought the ordered cosmos into operation: time, weather, and agriculture. He deemed these functions "good" (operating according to purpose). Had the Biblical text stated its message in terms of structure, it would have required constant revision. Understanding it in terms of function allows it to communicate clearly to peoples of all time.

4 God once again *spoke*, with the result that the celestial bodies were assigned their functions in the newly operational cosmos. The text doesn't address how or when the bodies originated. Instead, it describes the assignment of functions.

5 We might immediately identify the sea creatures as whales, sharks, and the like, but the Hebrew word (*tannin*) is associated with "chaos monsters" believed to inhabit the waters (e.g., "Leviathan" of Ps. 74:13–14). Such creatures were living beings given functions like any others.

6 The earth brought forth the animals that inhabited the dry land in the same way it "brought forth" vegetation in verse 12. In keeping with the functional emphasis, this didn't describe a biological process but a functional relationship.

Days 4–6 discuss *functionaries*, not functions. Celestial bodies (day four) carry out their functions in the sphere of day and night (day one). Birds and fish (day five) populate the sphere of sky and water (day two). And animals and people (day six) rely on dry land vegetation (day three). These functionaries populate their spheres and carry out their own functions within it. The recognition that people are functionaries in no way diminishes our importance in God's sight. The fact that we bear his image endows us with dignity and establishes the sanctity of human life (see "*Imago Dei*" at Gen. 1:26, p. 4).

7 The seventh day was marked by God's ceasing the work of the previous six days and settling into the stability of the cosmos, perhaps experiencing refreshment as he did so. By blessing the creation, he extended his favor to it.

Day 7 Sabbath observance requires a worldview in which worship has an appropriate role. Certainly recognition of God's place in the cosmos and his role in history inspires worship. But observing the Sabbath also means stepping away from a self-focus and the needs that drive people's existence six days a week and thereby resting in God's provision for us. It offers a reset button in life that allows us to regain God's perspective.

Source: NIV Application Commentary Genesis (2001)

> she shall be called 'woman,'[a]
> for she was taken out of man."

2:24
y Mal 2:15
z Mt 19:5*;
Mk 10:7-8*;
1Co 6:16*;
Eph 5:31*
2:25
a Ge 3:7,10-11

24For this reason a man will leave his father and mother and be united[y] to his wife, and they will become one flesh.[z]

25The man and his wife were both naked,[a] and they felt no shame.

The Fall of Man

3:1
b 2Co 11:3;
Rev 12:9; 20:2

3 Now the serpent[b] was more crafty than any of the wild animals the LORD God had made. He said to the woman, "Did God really say, 'You must not eat from any tree in the garden'?"

2The woman said to the serpent, "We may eat fruit from the trees in the garden, 3but God did say, 'You must not eat fruit from the tree that is in the middle of the garden, and you must not touch it, or you will die.'"

3:4
c Jn 8:44; 2Co 11:3
3:5
d Isa 14:14;
Eze 28:2

4"You will not surely die," the serpent said to the woman.[c] 5"For God knows that when you eat of it your eyes will be opened, and you will be like God,[d] knowing good and evil."

3:6
e Jas 1:14-15;
1Jn 2:16 f 1Ti 2:14

6When the woman saw that the fruit of the tree was good for food and pleasing to the eye, and also desirable[e] for gaining wisdom, she took some and ate it. She also gave some to her husband, who was with her, and he ate it.[f] 7Then the eyes of both of them were opened, and they realized they were naked; so they sewed fig leaves together and made coverings for themselves.

3:8
g Dt 23:14
h Job 31:33;
Ps 139:7-12;
Jer 23:24

8Then the man and his wife heard the sound of the LORD God as he was walking[g] in the garden in the cool of the day, and they hid[h] from the LORD God among the trees of the garden. 9But the LORD God called to the man, "Where are you?"

10He answered, "I heard you in the garden, and I was afraid because I was naked; so I hid."

11And he said, "Who told you that you were naked? Have you eaten from the tree that I commanded you not to eat from?"

12The man said, "The woman you put here with me—she gave me some fruit from the tree, and I ate it."

3:13
i 2Co 11:3;
1Ti 2:14

13Then the LORD God said to the woman, "What is this you have done?"

The woman said, "The serpent deceived me,[i] and I ate."

14So the LORD God said to the serpent, "Because you have done this,

3:14
j Dt 28:15-20
k Isa 65:25;
Mic 7:17

> "Cursed[j] are you above all the livestock
>   and all the wild animals!
> You will crawl on your belly
>   and you will eat dust[k]
>   all the days of your life.
> 15And I will put enmity
>   between you and the woman,

a 23 The Hebrew for *woman* sounds like the Hebrew for *man*.

Genesis 3:1–24

Genesis 3 describes the rupture of the harmonious interdependence God intended for creation. Adam and Eve doubted God's goodness and distrusted him. As a result, hostility and strife became characteristic of the relations among humans and between people and the creation. Adam and Eve hid from God, certain that he meant them harm. Labor—both in child bearing and garden tending—became harsh rather than joyous. But still God provided. He clothed Adam and Eve, protecting them in their new experience of shame. Even their expulsion from the garden expressed God's provision; he was protecting them from living eternally with struggle and conflict.

Which concept sounds more comforting to you—dependence on or independence from God? Inde-pendence and *freedom* aren't synonyms. God offered Adam and Eve the privilege of the freedom and the joy found only in trusting God. In rejecting dependence upon God, we humans choose a far more costly dependence—on ourselves and our own deficient resources.

The consequences are pain, conflict, and struggle. The evil one continually tempts people to doubt God's goodness. Yet even in their distrust and shame, God still provided for Adam and Eve. God calls Christ's followers to continue to show his goodness and trustworthiness to people in their suffering. Globally, Christian mission and humanitarian organizations can witness to the truth and demonstrate Christ's love to the poor, sick, and oppressed. What role(s) do you play in this endeavor?

and between your offspring[a][l] and hers;[m]
he will crush[b] your head,[n]
and you will strike his heel."

16To the woman he said,

"I will greatly increase your pains in childbearing;
with pain you will give birth to children.
Your desire will be for your husband,
and he will rule over you.[o]"

17To Adam he said, "Because you listened to your wife and ate from the tree about which I commanded you, 'You must not eat of it,'

"Cursed[p] is the ground because of you;
through painful toil you will eat of it
all the days of your life.[q]
18It will produce thorns and thistles for you,
and you will eat the plants of the field.[r]
19By the sweat of your brow
you will eat your food[s]
until you return to the ground,
since from it you were taken;
for dust you are
and to dust you will return."[t]

20Adam[c] named his wife Eve,[d] because she would become the mother of all the living.
21The LORD God made garments of skin for Adam and his wife and clothed them. 22And the LORD God said, "The man has now become like one of us, knowing good and evil. He must not be allowed to reach out his hand and take also from the tree of life[u] and eat, and live forever." 23So the LORD God banished him from the Garden of Eden[v] to work the ground[w] from which he had been taken. 24After he drove the man out, he placed on the east side[e] of the Garden of Eden cherubim[x] and a flaming sword[y] flashing back and forth to guard the way to the tree of life.[z]

Cain and Abel

4 Adam[c] lay with his wife Eve, and she became pregnant and gave birth to Cain.[f] She said, "With the help of the LORD I have brought forth[g] a man." 2Later she gave birth to his brother Abel.[a]

Now Abel kept flocks, and Cain worked the soil. 3In the course of time Cain brought some of the fruits of the soil as an offering to the LORD.[b] 4But Abel brought fat portions[c] from some of the firstborn of his flock.[d] The LORD looked with favor on Abel and his offering,[e] 5but on Cain and his offering he did not look with favor. So Cain was very angry, and his face was downcast.
6Then the LORD said to Cain, "Why are you angry? Why is your face downcast? 7If

Side references:

3:15
l Jn 8:44; Ac 13:10;
1Jn 3:8 *m* Isa 7:14;
Mt 1:23; Rev 12:17
n Ro 16:20;
Heb 2:14

3:16
o 1Co 11:3;
Eph 5:22

3:17
p Ge 5:29;
Ro 8:20-22
q Job 5:7; 14:1;
Ecc 2:23

3:18
r Ps 104:14

3:19
s 2Th 3:10 *t* Ge 2:7;
Ps 90:3; 104:29;
Ecc 12:7

3:22
u Rev 22:14
3:23
v Ge 2:8 *w* Ge 4:2
3:24
x Ex 25:18-22
y Ps 104:4 *z* Ge 2:9

4:2
a Lk 11:51

4:3
b Nu 18:12
4:4
c Lev 3:16
d Ex 13:2,12
e Heb 11:4

---

a 15 Or *seed*   *b 15* Or *strike*   *c 20* Or *The man*   *d 20* *Eve* probably means *living.*
e 24 Or *placed in front*   *f 1* *Cain* sounds like the Hebrew for *brought forth* or *acquired.*   *g 1* Or *have acquired*

Genesis 4:1–26

Though childbirth was now painful, Eve's joy over Cain's birth expressed the restoration of her trust in God (v. 1). Whatever the cause of God's rejection of Cain's offering, the text is more interested in Cain's response. God encouraged Cain to do the right thing, and his favor was apparently still available. Our own distrust of God not only produces conflict with creation but also leads us to distrust one another.

Sin brings internal strife to families and alienation among their members. The subtleties of the problem are revealed in part by Cain's tragic, rhetorical question, "Am I my brother's keeper?"

The mark placed on Cain is like the clothing provided for Adam and Eve in 3:21—both acts of grace served as God's protective provisions within a changed environment. Both times God responded directly to the sinners' recognition of their vulnerability caused by sin.

4:7
f Nu 32:23
g Ro 6:16
4:8
h Mt 23:35;
1Jn 3:12

4:10
i Ge 9:5; Nu 35:33;
Heb 12:24;
Rev 6:9-10

4:14
j 2Ki 17:18;
Ps 51:11; 139:7-12;
Jer 7:15; 52:3
k Ge 9:6;
Nu 35:19,21,27,33
4:15
l Eze 9:4,6
m ver 24; Ps 79:12
4:16
n Ge 2:8

4:17
o Ps 49:11

4:23
p Ex 20:13;
Lev 19:18
4:24
q Dt 32:35 r ver 15

4:25
s Ge 5:3 t ver 8

4:26
u Ge 12:8;
1Ki 18:24;
Ps 116:17;
Joel 2:32; Zep 3:9;
Ac 2:21; 1Co 1:2

5:1
v Ge 1:27;
Eph 4:24; Col 3:10

you do what is right, will you not be accepted? But if you do not do what is right, sin is crouching at your door;[f] it desires to have you, but you must master it. [g]"

[8]Now Cain said to his brother Abel, "Let's go out to the field."[a] And while they were in the field, Cain attacked his brother Abel and killed him.[h]

[9]Then the LORD said to Cain, "Where is your brother Abel?"

"I don't know," he replied. "Am I my brother's keeper?"

[10]The LORD said, "What have you done? Listen! Your brother's blood cries out to me from the ground.[i] [11]Now you are under a curse and driven from the ground, which opened its mouth to receive your brother's blood from your hand. [12]When you work the ground, it will no longer yield its crops for you. You will be a restless wanderer on the earth."

[13]Cain said to the LORD, "My punishment is more than I can bear. [14]Today you are driving me from the land, and I will be hidden from your presence;[j] I will be a restless wanderer on the earth, and whoever finds me will kill me."[k]

[15]But the LORD said to him, "Not so[b]; if anyone kills Cain,[l] he will suffer vengeance seven times over. [m]" Then the LORD put a mark on Cain so that no one who found him would kill him. [16]So Cain went out from the LORD's presence and lived in the land of Nod,[c] east of Eden.[n]

[17]Cain lay with his wife, and she became pregnant and gave birth to Enoch. Cain was then building a city, and he named it after his son[o] Enoch. [18]To Enoch was born Irad, and Irad was the father of Mehujael, and Mehujael was the father of Methushael, and Methushael was the father of Lamech.

[19]Lamech married two women, one named Adah and the other Zillah. [20]Adah gave birth to Jabal; he was the father of those who live in tents and raise livestock. [21]His brother's name was Jubal; he was the father of all who play the harp and flute. [22]Zillah also had a son, Tubal-Cain, who forged all kinds of tools out of[d] bronze and iron. Tubal-Cain's sister was Naamah.

[23]Lamech said to his wives,

"Adah and Zillah, listen to me;
　wives of Lamech, hear my words.
I have killed[e][p] a man for wounding me,
　a young man for injuring me.
[24]If Cain is avenged[q] seven times,[r]
　then Lamech seventy-seven times."

[25]Adam lay with his wife again, and she gave birth to a son and named him Seth,[f][s] saying, "God has granted me another child in place of Abel, since Cain killed him."[t] [26]Seth also had a son, and he named him Enosh.

At that time men began to call on[g] the name of the LORD.[u]

From Adam to Noah

5 This is the written account of Adam's line.

When God created man, he made him in the likeness of God.[v] [2]He created them

---

[a] 8 Samaritan Pentateuch, Septuagint, Vulgate and Syriac; Masoretic Text does not have "Let's go out to the field."   [b] 15 Septuagint, Vulgate and Syriac; Hebrew Very well   [c] 16 Nod means wandering (see verses 12 and 14).   [d] 22 Or who instructed all who work in   [e] 23 Or I will kill   [f] 25 Seth probably means granted.   [g] 26 Or to proclaim

---

📖 Cain's murder of Abel had consequences. Not only would he be unable to live in harmony with other people, but he would experience disharmony with the ground itself. Cain interpreted these realities as God's rejection of him (v. 14)—something God never suggested. Thus Cain withdrew from God's presence (v. 16), though the text never says that God withdrew from him. God was patient with Cain, still providing for and protecting him. From the hand of God come both justice and mercy.

Genesis 5:1–32

📖 Long life spans in the shadow of Eden shouldn't surprise us. We can speculate that they testify to the gradual penetration of sin (and death) or to the enduring effect of Adam and Eve's pre-fall diet from the tree of life. Such longevity was also necessary to populate the earth.

Genealogies represent continuity and relationship. Birth and death marched on, and the burden of the

male and female[w] and blessed them. And when they were created, he called them "man.[a]"

[3]When Adam had lived 130 years, he had a son in his own likeness, in his own image;[x] and he named him Seth. [4]After Seth was born, Adam lived 800 years and had other sons and daughters. [5]Altogether, Adam lived 930 years, and then he died.[y]

[6]When Seth had lived 105 years, he became the father[b] of Enosh. [7]And after he became the father of Enosh, Seth lived 807 years and had other sons and daughters. [8]Altogether, Seth lived 912 years, and then he died.

[9]When Enosh had lived 90 years, he became the father of Kenan. [10]And after he became the father of Kenan, Enosh lived 815 years and had other sons and daughters. [11]Altogether, Enosh lived 905 years, and then he died.

[12]When Kenan had lived 70 years, he became the father of Mahalalel. [13]And after he became the father of Mahalalel, Kenan lived 840 years and had other sons and daughters. [14]Altogether, Kenan lived 910 years, and then he died.

[15]When Mahalalel had lived 65 years, he became the father of Jared. [16]And after he became the father of Jared, Mahalalel lived 830 years and had other sons and daughters. [17]Altogether, Mahalalel lived 895 years, and then he died.

[18]When Jared had lived 162 years, he became the father of Enoch.[z] [19]And after he became the father of Enoch, Jared lived 800 years and had other sons and daughters. [20]Altogether, Jared lived 962 years, and then he died.

[21]When Enoch had lived 65 years, he became the father of Methuselah. [22]And after he became the father of Methuselah, Enoch walked with God[a] 300 years and had other sons and daughters. [23]Altogether, Enoch lived 365 years. [24]Enoch walked with God;[b] then he was no more, because God took him away.[c]

[25]When Methuselah had lived 187 years, he became the father of Lamech. [26]And after he became the father of Lamech, Methuselah lived 782 years and had other sons and daughters. [27]Altogether, Methuselah lived 969 years, and then he died.

[28]When Lamech had lived 182 years, he had a son. [29]He named him Noah[c] and said, "He will comfort us in the labor and painful toil of our hands caused by the ground the LORD has cursed.[d]" [30]After Noah was born, Lamech lived 595 years and had other sons and daughters. [31]Altogether, Lamech lived 777 years, and then he died.

[32]After Noah was 500 years old, he became the father of Shem, Ham and Japheth.

The Flood

6 When men began to increase in number on the earth[e] and daughters were born to them, [2]the sons of God saw that the daughters of men were beautiful, and they married any of them they chose. [3]Then the LORD said, "My Spirit will not contend with[d] man forever,[f] for he is mortal[e];[g] his days will be a hundred and twenty years."

[4]The Nephilim[h] were on the earth in those days—and also afterward—when the sons of God went to the daughters of men and had children by them. They were the heroes of old, men of renown.

[5]The LORD saw how great man's wickedness on the earth had become, and that every inclination of the thoughts of his heart was only evil all the time.[i] [6]The LORD was grieved[j] that he had made man on the earth, and his heart was filled with pain. [7]So the LORD said, "I will wipe mankind, whom I have created, from the face of the

---

[a] 2 Hebrew *adam*   [b] 6 *Father* may mean *ancestor*; also in verses 7-26.   [c] 29 *Noah* sounds like the Hebrew for *comfort*.   [d] 3 Or *My spirit will not remain in*   [e] 3 Or *corrupt*

Cross references (right margin):

5:2 w Ge 1:27; Mt 19:4; Mk 10:6; Gal 3:28

5:3 x Ge 1:26; 1Co 15:49

5:5 y Ge 3:19

5:18 z Jude 1:14

5:22 a ver 24; Ge 6:9; 17:1; 48:15; Mic 6:8; Mal 2:6
5:24 b ver 22 c 2Ki 2:1,11; Heb 11:5

5:29 d Ge 3:17; Ro 8:20

6:1 e Ge 1:28

6:3 f Isa 57:16 g Ps 78:39

6:4 h Nu 13:33

6:5 i Ge 8:21; Ps 14:1-3
6:6 j 1Sa 15:11,35; Isa 63:10

---

curse on the ground weighed heavily on humanity, living in a hostile world.

📖 Have you found yourself baffled by the paradox of a God who both extends blessing and carries out a curse? God's judgments aren't necessarily punitive. They are also protective: in this instance protecting others

from Cain, but also protecting people from living forever in struggle and pain.

Genesis 6:1—8:22

That God "grieved" (6:6–7) expresses something striking about his character. God isn't remote or indifferent to creation's pain. His love for the creation he

11

earth—men and animals, and creatures that move along the ground, and birds of the air—for I am grieved that I have made them." [8] But Noah found favor in the eyes of the LORD. [k]

[9] This is the account of Noah.

Noah was a righteous man, blameless among the people of his time, [l] and he walked with God. [m] [10] Noah had three sons: Shem, Ham and Japheth. [n]

[11] Now the earth was corrupt in God's sight and was full of violence. [o] [12] God saw how corrupt the earth had become, for all the people on earth had corrupted their ways. [p] [13] So God said to Noah, "I am going to put an end to all people, for the earth is filled with violence because of them. I am surely going to destroy both them and the earth. [q] [14] So make yourself an ark of cypress [a] wood; [r] make rooms in it and coat it with pitch [s] inside and out. [15] This is how you are to build it: The ark is to be 450 feet long, 75 feet wide and 45 feet high. [b] [16] Make a roof for it and finish [c] the ark to within 18 inches [d] of the top. Put a door in the side of the ark and make lower, middle and upper decks. [17] I am going to bring floodwaters on the earth to destroy all life under the heavens, every creature that has the breath of life in it. Everything on earth will perish. [t] [18] But I will establish my covenant with you, [u] and you will enter the ark [v]—you and your sons and your wife and your sons' wives with you. [19] You are to bring into the ark two of all living creatures, male and female, to keep them alive with you. [20] Two [w] of every kind of bird, of every kind of animal and of every kind of creature that moves along the ground will come to you to be kept alive. [21] You are to take every kind of food that is to be eaten and store it away as food for you and for them."

[a] 14 The meaning of the Hebrew for this word is uncertain.   [b] 15 Hebrew *300 cubits long, 50 cubits wide and 30 cubits high* (about 140 meters long, 23 meters wide and 13.5 meters high)   [c] 16 Or *Make an opening for light by finishing*   [d] 16 Hebrew *a cubit* (about 0.5 meter)

Cross-references (margin):
6:8
[k] Ge 19:19;
Ex 33:12,13,17;
Lk 1:30; Ac 7:46
6:9
[l] Ge 7:1; Eze 14:14,
20; Heb 11:7;
2Pe 2:5 [m] Ge 5:22
6:10
[n] Ge 5:32
6:11
[o] Eze 7:23; 8:17
6:12
[p] Ps 14:1-3
6:13
[q] ver 17; Eze 7:2-3
6:14
[r] Heb 11:7;
1Pe 3:20 [s] Ex 2:3
6:17
[t] Ge 7:4,21-23;
2Pe 2:5
6:18
[u] Ge 9:9-16
[v] Ge 7:1,7,13
6:20
[w] Ge 7:15

pronounced as "good" and his dismay over the evil generated by sin were so great that his heart was broken. The Old Testament God is the same God of love and compassion we meet in the New. God couldn't tolerate the beauty and joy of creation continuing to be defiled by sin. To spare creation from ever increasing suffering, he opted to start over.

We may picture pairs of animals entering into the ark (6:20), but God was more specific. His instructions were to take one pair of each unclean animal and seven pairs of each clean animal (7:2–3). This distinction was already in effect, long before God gave Moses his law (Lev. 11:46-47). Ceremonially clean animals would be needed after the flood for Noah's sacrifice (8:20) and possibly also for food (9:2–3).

6:7

Natural Disasters

The Biblical flood is a prototype for all natural disasters. In our sin-damaged world they are always with us. On the right is a comparison of the numbers of people killed in Asia, Africa, Latin America, and North America, respectively, between 1900–1999 by category of disaster:

Factors affecting large regional discrepancies in per capita death tolls

 Wealth: Rich countries better able to protect their citizens

 Urbanization: Housing construction standards lower in poor, densely populated cities

 Isolation: *Higher percentage of population in hard-to-reach areas*

 Conflict: Nations at war less able to muster resources to help disaster victims

Source: "Natural Disasters," *The Economist* (February 7, 2004): 28

Earthquakes	PERSONS KILLED PER MILLION POPULATION
ASIA	23
AFRICA	1
LATIN AMERICA	2.5
NORTH AMERICA	.03

Cyclones, Tornados	
ASIA	53
AFRICA	45
LATIN AMERICA	1
NORTH AMERICA	.86

Floods	
ASIA	14
AFRICA	10
LATIN AMERICA	9
NORTH AMERICA	.09

6:8–9

William Wilberforce (1759–1833), a member of the British parliament at the age of twenty-one, was already destined for political greatness. Then on December 2, 1785, he found himself convicted by the error of his partying lifestyle and was converted to the gospel of Jesus Christ. At this moment Wilberforce was faced with another decision. As Chuck Colson pointed out in an article about him in *Christianity Today*, Wilberforce had to answer this question: Had God seen fit to save him only for the eternal rescue of his own soul, or also to bring God's light to the world around him?

Wilberforce determined to speak for God regarding the despicable practice of human slavery. He opted not to give up political office but to spend whatever political influence he could muster to accomplish these goals.

Strange as it may seem today, the abolition of slavery was at the time supported by very few in Great Britain. The economic case for the institution was strong. As one advocate put it, "Abolition would instantly annihilate a trade which annually employs 5,500 sailors, 160 ships, and where exports amount to 800,000 pounds sterling." God had, it seemed, recruited Wilberforce for a "Mission Impossible" assignment.

We are reminded of a somewhat equivalent Biblical event: God commanding Noah to build a boat large enough to withstand a catastrophic flood and to accommodate a comprehensive sampling of the world's animal population. Noah built the boat. And Wilberforce took on the pro-slavery lobby.

Wilberforce's fight began in the British Parliament in 1788 when at his request his friend, Prime Minister William Pitt, introduced a resolution requiring the House of Commons to discuss the slave trade during its next session. For the next *45 years* Wilberforce and his colleagues assiduously fought for the passage of an anti-slavery bill. Some years they came close. In other terms they were soundly defeated due to economic and/or political fluctuation.

> **D**oing what God calls us to do is a total life commitment.

Finally, on July 26, 1833, passage of the Bill for the Abolition of Slavery sounded the final death blow for slavery in England. The same issue in the United States gave rise to the American Civil War (1861–1865), resulting in societal rifts that still linger today, as well as in a large and tragic loss of human life. Lesson: *Not all good causes find an easy way in this world; a trailblazer needs persistence and patience.*

To sustain themselves and support one another through this long struggle, a number of the Christian parliamentarians supporting Wilberforce decided to live together—an arrangement also facilitating research and strategizing. Henry Thornton, a member of Parliament and a wealthy banker, offered his home, Battersea Rise in Clapham. As more and more Christian abolitionist members of Parliament moved in, Thornton built extra rooms. Eventually, Battersea Rise had 34 bedrooms, as well as a large, airy library designed by Prime Minister Pitt. Lesson: *Doing what God calls us to do is a total life commitment.*

The Clapham Society, as Wilberforce and his colleagues came to be called, had to alter its strategy frequently, sometimes focusing its energies on changing the minds of politicians, sometimes taking the case directly to the people with pamphlets, boycotts, and petitions. The upheaval caused by the French Revolution set back the group's efforts a decade or more. Lesson: *There are many good means to achieve a just cause. A trailblazer is expected to be flexible in searching for ways to help build the kingdom of God.*

6:22
x Ge 7:5,9,16
7:1
y Mt 24:38
z Ge 6:9; Eze 14:14
7:2
a ver 8; Ge 8:20;
Lev 10:10; 11:1-47

7:5
b Ge 6:22

7:11
c Eze 26:19
d Ge 8:2
7:12
e ver 4

7:15
f Ge 6:19

7:17
g ver 4

7:19
h Ps 104:6

7:21
i Ge 6:7,13
7:22
j Ge 1:30

7:23
k Mt 24:39;
Lk 17:27; 1Pe 3:20;
2Pe 2:5 l Heb 11:7
7:24
m Ge 8:3
8:1
n Ge 9:15; 19:29;
Ex 2:24;
1Sa 1:11,19
o Ex 14:21
8:2
p Ge 7:11

22Noah did everything just as God commanded him.[x]

7 The LORD then said to Noah, "Go into the ark, you and your whole family,[y] because I have found you righteous[z] in this generation. 2Take with you seven[a] of every kind of clean[a] animal, a male and its mate, and two of every kind of unclean animal, a male and its mate, 3and also seven of every kind of bird, male and female, to keep their various kinds alive throughout the earth. 4Seven days from now I will send rain on the earth for forty days and forty nights, and I will wipe from the face of the earth every living creature I have made."

5And Noah did all that the LORD commanded him.[b]

6Noah was six hundred years old when the floodwaters came on the earth. 7And Noah and his sons and his wife and his sons' wives entered the ark to escape the waters of the flood. 8Pairs of clean and unclean animals, of birds and of all creatures that move along the ground, 9male and female, came to Noah and entered the ark, as God had commanded Noah. 10And after the seven days the floodwaters came on the earth.

11In the six hundredth year of Noah's life, on the seventeenth day of the second month—on that day all the springs of the great deep[c] burst forth, and the floodgates of the heavens[d] were opened. 12And rain fell on the earth forty days and forty nights.[e]

13On that very day Noah and his sons, Shem, Ham and Japheth, together with his wife and the wives of his three sons, entered the ark. 14They had with them every wild animal according to its kind, all livestock according to their kinds, every creature that moves along the ground according to its kind and every bird according to its kind, everything with wings. 15Pairs of all creatures that have the breath of life in them came to Noah and entered the ark.[f] 16The animals going in were male and female of every living thing, as God had commanded Noah. Then the LORD shut him in.

17For forty days[g] the flood kept coming on the earth, and as the waters increased they lifted the ark high above the earth. 18The waters rose and increased greatly on the earth, and the ark floated on the surface of the water. 19They rose greatly on the earth, and all the high mountains under the entire heavens were covered.[h] 20The waters rose and covered the mountains to a depth of more than twenty feet.[b,c] 21Every living thing that moved on the earth perished—birds, livestock, wild animals, all the creatures that swarm over the earth, and all mankind.[i] 22Everything on dry land that had the breath of life[j] in its nostrils died. 23Every living thing on the face of the earth was wiped out; men and animals and the creatures that move along the ground and the birds of the air were wiped from the earth.[k] Only Noah was left, and those with him in the ark.[l]

24The waters flooded the earth for a hundred and fifty days.[m]

8 But God remembered[n] Noah and all the wild animals and the livestock that were with him in the ark, and he sent a wind over the earth,[o] and the waters receded. 2Now the springs of the deep and the floodgates of the heavens[p] had been closed, and the rain had stopped falling from the sky. 3The water receded steadily from the earth. At the end of the hundred and fifty days the water had gone down, 4and on the seventeenth day of the seventh month the ark came to rest on the mountains of Ararat. 5The waters continued to recede until the tenth month, and on the first day of the tenth month the tops of the mountains became visible.

a 2 Or *seven pairs*; also in verse 3   b 20 Hebrew *fifteen cubits* (about 6.9 meters)   c 20 Or *rose more than twenty feet, and the mountains were covered*

Sometimes we may feel that our lives, our country, and/or our world are overwhelmed by evil and suffering. Do passages like the flood story help strengthen your faith that God is aware and in control? We are invited to share in his grief over creation's suffering, to allow our hearts to be broken by the things that break God's heart. But God isn't merely grieved, sitting back like a helpless spectator. He acts to stop evil and restore his creation.

More than just salvation was at stake here. God looks beyond our sin to see our value as unique and individual persons he's created in his image. He nurtures in each of us the capacity to bring goodness and harmony to bear in the world. What changes do you perceive him working in you?

⁶After forty days Noah opened the window he had made in the ark ⁷and sent out a raven, and it kept flying back and forth until the water had dried up from the earth. ⁸Then he sent out a dove to see if the water had receded from the surface of the ground. ⁹But the dove could find no place to set its feet because there was water over all the surface of the earth; so it returned to Noah in the ark. He reached out his hand and took the dove and brought it back to himself in the ark. ¹⁰He waited seven more days and again sent out the dove from the ark. ¹¹When the dove returned to him in the evening, there in its beak was a freshly plucked olive leaf! Then Noah knew that the water had receded from the earth. ¹²He waited seven more days and sent the dove out again, but this time it did not return to him.

¹³By the first day of the first month of Noah's six hundred and first year, the water had dried up from the earth. Noah then removed the covering from the ark and saw that the surface of the ground was dry. ¹⁴By the twenty-seventh day of the second month the earth was completely dry.

¹⁵Then God said to Noah, ¹⁶"Come out of the ark, you and your wife and your sons and their wives. ⁹ ¹⁷Bring out every kind of living creature that is with you— the birds, the animals, and all the creatures that move along the ground—so they can multiply on the earth and be fruitful and increase in number upon it." ʳ

¹⁸So Noah came out, together with his sons and his wife and his sons' wives. ¹⁹All the animals and all the creatures that move along the ground and all the birds— everything that moves on the earth—came out of the ark, one kind after another.

²⁰Then Noah built an altar to the LORD ˢ and, taking some of all the clean animals and clean ᵗ birds, he sacrificed burnt offerings ᵘ on it. ²¹The LORD smelled the pleasing aroma ᵛ and said in his heart: "Never again will I curse the ground ʷ because of man, even though ᵃ every inclination of his heart is evil from childhood. ˣ And never again will I destroy all living creatures, ʸ as I have done.

> ²² "As long as the earth endures,
>   seedtime and harvest,
>   cold and heat,
>   summer and winter,
>   day and night
>   will never cease." ᶻ

God's Covenant With Noah

9 Then God blessed Noah and his sons, saying to them, "Be fruitful and increase in number and fill the earth. ᵃ ²The fear and dread of you will fall upon all the beasts of the earth and all the birds of the air, upon every creature that moves along the ground, and upon all the fish of the sea; they are given into your hands. ³Everything that lives and moves will be food for you. ᵇ Just as I gave you the green plants, I now give you everything.

⁴"But you must not eat meat that has its lifeblood still in it. ᶜ ⁵And for your lifeblood I will surely demand an accounting. I will demand an accounting from every animal. ᵈ And from each man, too, I will demand an accounting for the life of his fellow man. ᵉ

> ⁶ "Whoever sheds the blood of man,
>   by man shall his blood be shed; ᶠ
> for in the image of God ᵍ
>   has God made man.

ᵃ 21 Or man, for

8:16
ᵍ Ge 7:13

8:17
ʳ Ge 1:22

8:20
ˢ Ge 12:7-8; 13:18; 22:9 ᵗ Ge 7:8; Lev 11:1-47 ᵘ Ge 22:2,13; Ex 10:25
8:21
ᵛ Ge 1:9,13; 2Co 2:15 ʷ Ge 3:17 ˣ Ge 6:5; Ps 51:5; Jer 17:9 ʸ Ge 9:11,15; Isa 54:9

8:22
ᶻ Ge 1:14; Jer 33:20,25

9:1
ᵃ Ge 1:22

9:3
ᵇ Ge 1:29

9:4
ᶜ Lev 3:17; 17:10-14; Dt 12:16, 23-25; 1Sa 14:33
9:5
ᵈ Ex 21:28-32 ᵉ Ge 4:10

9:6
ᶠ Ge 4:14; Ex 21:12, 14; Lev 24:17; Mt 26:52 ᵍ Ge 1:26

Genesis 9:1–17

God promised that sin and its punishment would never again destroy his world (8:21–22) or the steady flow of his blessing (9:11,15). There would be a basic stability in the world, and human life would be ordered by some basic commitments.

This passage mentions "covenant" eight times. A covenant is different from our own legal contracts in that it's not bilateral. God alone initiates it and pledges faithfulness to his promises. In turn, he demands certain commitments from people who long to experience the fullness of his blessing.

15

9:7
h Ge 1:22

7As for you, be fruitful and increase in number; multiply on the earth and increase upon it." *h*

9:9
i Ge 6:18

8Then God said to Noah and to his sons with him: 9"I now establish my covenant with you *i* and with your descendants after you 10and with every living creature that was with you—the birds, the livestock and all the wild animals, all those that came out of the ark with you—every living creature on earth. 11I establish my covenant *j* with you: Never again will all life be cut off by the waters of a flood; never again will there be a flood to destroy the earth. *k* "

9:11
j ver 16; Isa 24:5
k Ge 8:21; Isa 54:9

9:12
l ver 17; Ge 17:11

12And God said, "This is the sign of the covenant *l* I am making between me and you and every living creature with you, a covenant for all generations to come: 13I have set my rainbow in the clouds, and it will be the sign of the covenant between me and the earth. 14Whenever I bring clouds over the earth and the rainbow appears in the clouds, 15I will remember my covenant *m* between me and you and all living creatures of every kind. Never again will the waters become a flood to destroy all life. 16Whenever the rainbow appears in the clouds, I will see it and remember

9:15
m Ex 2:24;
Lev 26:42,45;
Dt 7:9; Eze 16:60

God promised ecological stability in Genesis 8:21–22 and 9:11 and 15. But we have legitimate worries: depletion of the ozone layer, global warming, disappearing rain forests, dwindling fossil-fuel reserves, melting ice caps, dimishing drinking water and food supplies. God called Adam and Eve to "guard" the garden (2:15). Instead we have focused on tilling the ground and exer-

cising dominion over the earth. Our future depends on our obedience to this other aspect of our vocation, on our protection and preservation of creation rather than its use and depletion. *God* won't again wreak mass chaos on the world, but that doesn't guarantee that we ourselves won't bring about Earth's destruction.

9:13–16

Symbols of Christianity

The sign of the rainbow is only the first of a rich list of Biblically based symbols used to express our faith. Here are some of the more common:

ΑΩ	*Alpha* and *Omega* (first and last letters of the Greek alphabet): The eternality of Christ
⚓	**Anchor:** Faith
🍷🍞	**Bread and Wine:** The Lord's Supper or the Eucharist; Christ's atoning death
☧	*Chi-Rho:* First two letters of the name Christ in Greek
✝	**Cross:** Christ's atoning death
🕊	**Dove:** Holy Spirit at Christ's baptism
🔥	**Tongues of fire:** Manifestation of the Holy Spirit on the day of Pentecost
🐟	**Fish:** Initial letters in Greek of "Jesus Christ, God's Son, Savior" (*Icthus* is the Greek word for fish)
🐑	**Lamb:** Christ's self-sacrifice
🧎	**Shepherd:** Christ's care for his people
🍇	**Vine:** Christ's union with his people; the wine of the Eucharist or Lord's Supper

What others can you name? The list could go on and on.
Which symbols are most meaningful to you?

Source: Galindo (2002:112–113)

the everlasting covenant[n] between God and all living creatures of every kind on the earth."

[17] So God said to Noah, "This is the sign of the covenant[o] I have established between me and all life on the earth."

The Sons of Noah

[18] The sons of Noah who came out of the ark were Shem, Ham and Japheth. (Ham was the father of Canaan.)[p] [19] These were the three sons of Noah, and from them came the people who were scattered over the earth.[q]

[20] Noah, a man of the soil, proceeded[a] to plant a vineyard. [21] When he drank some of its wine, he became drunk and lay uncovered inside his tent. [22] Ham, the father of Canaan, saw his father's nakedness and told his two brothers outside. [23] But Shem and Japheth took a garment and laid it across their shoulders; then they walked in backward and covered their father's nakedness. Their faces were turned the other way so that they would not see their father's nakedness.

[24] When Noah awoke from his wine and found out what his youngest son had done to him, [25] he said,

> "Cursed be Canaan![r]
> The lowest of slaves
> will he be to his brothers.[s]"

[26] He also said,

> "Blessed be the LORD, the God of Shem!
> May Canaan be the slave of Shem.[b]
> [27] May God extend the territory of Japheth[c];
> may Japheth live in the tents of Shem,
> and may Canaan be his[d] slave."

[28] After the flood Noah lived 350 years. [29] Altogether, Noah lived 950 years, and then he died.

The Table of Nations

10 This is the account[t] of Shem, Ham and Japheth, Noah's sons, who themselves had sons after the flood.

The Japhethites

[2] The sons[e] of Japheth:

Gomer,[u] Magog,[v] Madai, Javan, Tubal,[w] Meshech and Tiras.

---

a 20 Or *soil, was the first*   b 26 Or *be his slave*   c 27 *Japheth* sounds like the Hebrew for *extend.*
d 27 Or *their*   e 2 *Sons* may mean *descendants* or *successors* or *nations;* also in verses 3, 4, 6, 7, 20-23, 29 and 31.

Cross-references (margin)

9:16
n ver 11;
Ge 17:7, 13, 19;
2Sa 7:13; 23:5
9:17
o ver 12; Ge 17:11

9:18
p ver 25-27;
Ge 10:6, 15
9:19
q Ge 10:32

9:25
r ver 18 s Ge 25:23;
Jos 9:23

10:1
t Ge 2:4

10:2
u Eze 38:6
v Eze 38:2;
Rev 20:8
w Isa 66:19

Genesis 9:18–29

The themes of blessing and sin introduced in the garden appear again after the flood. God restated his blessing in verses 1–3 and 7 (see also vv. 18–19,20). And 8:21 confirms the persistence of sin. Further sad evidence that sin didn't abate with the floodwaters is found in Noah's indiscretion and Ham's subsequent behavior.

Some think that the curse on Canaan was too harsh in light of Ham's offense (whatever it was). It might help to consider that: (1) The curse may have been driven by more than this one event. (2) Noah's statement might have been somewhat irrational, uttered in the heat of the moment. Since the words were Noah's, not God's, God wasn't obligated to fulfill the prophecy. (3) Canaan was one of four brothers (10:6), but for whatever reason the curse didn't extend to Ham's entire family.

Cycles of sin are repeated not just across the span of centuries but also in an individual's habits and thoughts. The repetitive patterns that can be traced through our lives would horrify us if we would allow ourselves to be fully conscious of them. Christ has given us the power to become children of God, breaking our sin cycles and empowering us to live as new creations in him (2 Cor. 5:17). How is his creative power being shown in your life?

Genesis 10:1

Chapter 10 is commonly called the "table of nations." It provides the detail behind 9:18–19 and 10:32, where we simply learn that the nations descended from Noah's three sons. In chapter 11 the narrator will move backward in time to the fascinating account of how these nations first became separated peoples.

10:3
x Jer 51:27
y Eze 27:14; 38:6
10:4
z Eze 27:12,25;
Jnh 1:3

³The sons of Gomer:
Ashkenaz, ^x Riphath and Togarmah. ^y
⁴The sons of Javan:
Elishah, Tarshish, ^z the Kittim and the Rodanim. ^a ⁵(From these the maritime peoples spread out into their territories by their clans within their nations, each with its own language.)

The Hamites

10:6
a ver 15; Ge 9:18

⁶The sons of Ham:
Cush, Mizraim, ^b Put and Canaan. ^a
⁷The sons of Cush:
Seba, Havilah, Sabtah, Raamah and Sabteca.
The sons of Raamah:
Sheba and Dedan.

10:10
b Ge 11:9 c Ge 11:2
10:11
d Ps 83:8; Mic 5:6
e Jnh 1:2; 4:11;
Na 1:1

⁸Cush was the father ^c of Nimrod, who grew to be a mighty warrior on the earth. ⁹He was a mighty hunter before the LORD; that is why it is said, "Like Nimrod, a mighty hunter before the LORD." ¹⁰The first centers of his kingdom were Babylon, ^b Erech, Akkad and Calneh, in ^d Shinar. ^{e c} ¹¹From that land he went to Assyria, ^d where he built Nineveh, ^e Rehoboth Ir, ^f Calah ¹²and Resen, which is between Nineveh and Calah; that is the great city.

10:14
f Ge 21:32,34;
26:1,8
10:15
g ver 6; Ge 9:18

¹³Mizraim was the father of
the Ludites, Anamites, Lehabites, Naphtuhites, ¹⁴Pathrusites, Casluhites (from whom the Philistines ^f came) and Caphtorites.
¹⁵Canaan ^g was the father of

---

^a 4 Some manuscripts of the Masoretic Text and Samaritan Pentateuch (see also Septuagint and 1 Chron. 1:7); most manuscripts of the Masoretic Text *Dodanim*   ^b 6 That is, Egypt; also in verse 13   ^c 8 *Father* may mean *ancestor* or *predecessor* or *founder*; also in verses 13, 15, 24 and 26.   ^d 10 Or *Erech and Akkad—all of them in*   ^e 10 That is, Babylonia   ^f 11 Or *Nineveh with its city squares*

Genesis 10 showcases the continuation of God's blessing. People continued to be fruitful and multiply—beginning once again to "fill" the earth.

How far do you take the human connection? The text's intent is to proclaim that all of us are related. Not only are we to respect all people as God's image bearers (9:6) but to appreciate our common ancestry. It's easy to forget, in our diverse world, millennia removed from this obscure point of ancient history, our essential connectedness—not just with our "brothers and sisters" in Christ, but to each individual within the masses that populate our globe. Our obligation to our fellow citizens on planet Earth brings us closer to home than we realize.

Genesis 10:2–5

The list of Noah's descendants contains 70 names—a number that symbolized for the ancients totality and completion. We may notice, though, that the list is incomplete and apparently representative. The author penetrated selectively into various lines in order to achieve his final number.

Knowledge of the peoples and countries of the world was considered just as much an indication of wisdom as knowledge of plants and animals. The "wisdom" represented by this catalog of known peoples wasn't just academic. The point was that all the known peoples had resulted from God's early blessing. There was zero toler-

ance here for the concept of one pure race, with others being "tainted."

Are you prejudiced? Think carefully before you answer: The indications can be subtle. The origins of such repellent notions as "white supremacy" or a "master race" are clouded in history. But all prejudice based on ethnicity, race, religion, culture, class, gender, physical characteristics, or educational or financial status remain evil at their core. Intolerance seems ingrained in the human psyche.

Genesis 10:6–20

The text offers no explanation of how the different races came to be. While the Bible sheds no light on the origins of ethnic (and other) distinctions, it does offer a definitive standard about how we are to regard them: "There is neither Jew nor Greek, slave nor free, male nor female, for you are all one in Christ Jesus" (Gal. 3:28).

For centuries the curse of Canaan (often called "the curse of Ham"; see 9:25–27) was used to justify the enslavement of African tribes. The "logic" was that Ham was the forefather of the African people and that their slavery was Biblically mandated by the curse. Both points are flawed. (1) There are few families from the line of Ham that ended in dark-skinned people, and none from the line of Canaan. (2) A curse is something for God, not humans, to carry out. Prejudice and oppression have no Biblical justification.

Sidon[h] his firstborn,[a] and of the Hittites,[i] [16]Jebusites,[j] Amorites, Girgashites, [17]Hivites, Arkites, Sinites, [18]Arvadites, Zemarites and Hamathites.

Later the Canaanite[k] clans scattered [19]and the borders of Canaan[l] reached from Sidon[m] toward Gerar as far as Gaza, and then toward Sodom, Gomorrah, Admah and Zeboiim, as far as Lasha.

[20]These are the sons of Ham by their clans and languages, in their territories and nations.

The Semites

[21]Sons were also born to Shem, whose older brother was[b] Japheth; Shem was the ancestor of all the sons of Eber.[n]

[22]The sons of Shem:
Elam,[o] Asshur, Arphaxad,[p] Lud and Aram.
[23]The sons of Aram:
Uz,[q] Hul, Gether and Meshech.[c]
[24]Arphaxad was the father of[d] Shelah,
and Shelah the father of Eber.[r]
[25]Two sons were born to Eber:
One was named Peleg,[e] because in his time the earth was divided; his brother was named Joktan.
[26]Joktan was the father of
Almodad, Sheleph, Hazarmaveth, Jerah, [27]Hadoram, Uzal, Diklah, [28]Obal, Abimael, Sheba, [29]Ophir, Havilah and Jobab. All these were sons of Joktan.

[30]The region where they lived stretched from Mesha toward Sephar, in the eastern hill country.

[31]These are the sons of Shem by their clans and languages, in their territories and nations.

[32]These are the clans of Noah's sons,[s] according to their lines of descent, within their nations. From these the nations spread out over the earth[t] after the flood.

The Tower of Babel

11 Now the whole world had one language and a common speech. [2]As men moved eastward,[f] they found a plain in Shinar[g][u] and settled there. [3]They said to each other, "Come, let's make bricks[v] and bake them thoroughly." They used brick instead of stone, and tar[w] for mortar. [4]Then they said, "Come, let

---

10:15
h Eze 28:21
i Ge 23:3,20
10:16
j 1Ch 11:4
10:18
k Ge 12:6; Ex 13:11
10:19
l Ge 11:31; 13:12; 17:8 m ver 15

10:21
n ver 24; Nu 24:24

10:22
o Jer 49:34
p Lk 3:36
10:23
q Job 1:1

10:24
r ver 21

10:32
s ver 1 t Ge 9:19

11:2
u Ge 10:10
11:3
v Ex 1:14
w Ge 14:10

---

a 15 Or of the Sidonians, the foremost   b 21 Or Shem, the older brother of   c 23 See Septuagint and 1 Chron. 1:17; Hebrew Mash   d 24 Hebrew; Septuagint father of Cainan, and Cainan was the father of   e 25 Peleg means division.   f 2 Or from the east; or in the east   g 2 That is, Babylonia

---

Genesis 10:21–32

The text only accounts for groups the Israelites were aware of, with no hint at a world beyond the ancient Near East. The author (Moses) made no attempt to provide a comprehensive list of all the people(s) descended from Noah but addressed only how the known peoples and nations of his day were related to Israel.

Human beings by nature place themselves at the center of the universe, often concerning themselves with others only as they relate to or impact the self. But our Creator is the master Artist, capable of endless diversity—all of it beautiful in concept and design, despite the obvious flaws brought about by sin. Many people appreciate beautiful paintings, musical pieces, and sculpture. Have you ever sat back to appreciate God's human masterpieces—your family members, your neighbors, your schoolmates, your colleagues, your fellow wor-

shipers, peoples from a totally different ethnic or cultural background?

Genesis 11:1–9

The city during this period was designed for public, not residential, use. It was in effect a temple complex, including a tower (ziggurat), resembling a pyramid. Ziggurats were dedicated to particular deities. Their design made it convenient for a god to "come down" to his temple, receive worship from his people, and bless them. God did come down—and wasn't pleased.

People had begun to think of their gods in human terms with the development of their cities. They weren't trying to be like God but were attempting to bring their gods down to their level. This went beyond mere idolatry. They had degraded God's nature by treating him like one of them.

11:4
x Dt 1:28; 9:1
y Ge 6:4 z Dt 4:27

us build ourselves a city, with a tower that reaches to the heavens,[x] so that we may make a name[y] for ourselves and not be scattered over the face of the whole earth."[z]

11:5
a ver 7; Ge 18:21;
Ex 3:8; 19:11,18,20

5But the LORD came down[a] to see the city and the tower that the men were building. 6The LORD said, "If as one people speaking the same language they have begun to do this, then nothing they plan to do will be im-

11:7
b Ge 1:26
c Ge 42:23

possible for them. 7Come, let us[b] go down and confuse their language so they will not understand each other."[c]

11:8
d Ge 9:19; Lk 1:51

8So the LORD scattered them from there over all the earth,[d] and they stopped building

11:9
e Ge 10:10

the city. 9That is why it was called Babel[a][e]— because there the LORD confused the language of the whole world. From there the LORD scattered them over the face of the whole earth.

From Shem to Abram

10This is the account of Shem.

Two years after the flood, when Shem was 100 years old, he became the father[b]

The Tower of Babel (11:4)

Then: Many towers or ziggurats were built in Babel to pagan gods like Marduk and Ishtar.

Now: Babel is the Hebrew word for Babylon, a modern city in Iraq.

---

a 9 That is, Babylon; *Babel* sounds like the Hebrew for *confused*.   b 10 *Father* may mean *ancestor*; also in verses 11-25.

📖 We often try to water down God's power and identity by (1) relying on him *and* our own strength and abilities; (2) seeing him as being obligated to us; and/or (3) trying to tap into his power to redirect for our purposes. By dividing people through language differences, God acted decisively here against any effort to create a united, human-centered religion that would attempt to harness him as humanity's servant. This division would be sur-

mounted at Pentecost (Acts 2), not by a return to one universal language but by every listener hearing the Good News in his or her own language. The gospel creates a means of unity while preserving cultural particularities.

Genesis 11:10–32

📖 Shem's line leads us to Abram. This isn't a repetition of Shem's descendants from 10:21–31. There the focus was on the representative tribes of Moses' time

11:8–9

Tower of Babel

The Tower of Babel represents the downside of human pride of achievement. In general, when our attempts to achieve anything divide God's people and/or reduce their value to purely material factors, they are "Babel" achievements. Some of the worst:

Babel Achievements

Plato's Ghost:	Descartes Error:	Kant's Divide:	Darwin's Law:	Marx's Revolution:	Freud's Obsession:
reducing reality to nothing more than an ideal in our minds	reduction of the quality/nature of being human to the purely rational	separating "scientific knowledge" from "ethical knowledge"	natural selection as survival of the fittest	reducing history to strictly economic factors	reducing human motivation to a single root: sexual libido

If you are interested in additional detail about any of these intriguing fallacies, the Internet or your local library would be excellent resources.

But there is another side of human achievement: Biblical achievements. These are efforts that can measure up to Biblical standards because they acknowledge the physical, intellectual, emotional, and spiritual nature and intrinsic worth of human beings, as well as their capacity to work together to build God's kingdom. The concept of this kind of achievement is perhaps best captured in the apostle Paul's body-of-Christ metaphor, in which he acknowledged the complementary nature of spiritual gifts (see 1 Cor. 12:12–31).

of Arphaxad. [11]And after he became the father of Arphaxad, Shem lived 500 years and had other sons and daughters.

[12]When Arphaxad had lived 35 years, he became the father of Shelah.[f] [13]And after he became the father of Shelah, Arphaxad lived 403 years and had other sons and daughters.[a]

[14]When Shelah had lived 30 years, he became the father of Eber. [15]And after he became the father of Eber, Shelah lived 403 years and had other sons and daughters.

[16]When Eber had lived 34 years, he became the father of Peleg. [17]And after he became the father of Peleg, Eber lived 430 years and had other sons and daughters.

[18]When Peleg had lived 30 years, he became the father of Reu. [19]And after he became the father of Reu, Peleg lived 209 years and had other sons and daughters.

[20]When Reu had lived 32 years, he became the father of Serug.[g] [21]And after he became the father of Serug, Reu lived 207 years and had other sons and daughters.

[22]When Serug had lived 30 years, he became the father of Nahor. [23]And after he became the father of Nahor, Serug lived 200 years and had other sons and daughters.

[24]When Nahor had lived 29 years, he became the father of Terah.[h] [25]And after he became the father of Terah, Nahor lived 119 years and had other sons and daughters.

[26]After Terah had lived 70 years, he became the father of Abram,[i] Nahor[j] and Haran.

[27]This is the account of Terah.

Terah became the father of Abram, Nahor and Haran. And Haran became the father of Lot.[k] [28]While his father Terah was still alive, Haran died in Ur of the Chaldeans,[l] in the land of his birth. [29]Abram and Nahor both married. The name of Abram's wife was Sarai,[m] and the name of Nahor's wife was Milcah;[n] she was the daughter of Haran, the father of both Milcah and Iscah. [30]Now Sarai was barren; she had no children.[o]

[31]Terah took his son Abram, his grandson Lot son of Haran, and his daughter-in-law Sarai, the wife of his son Abram, and together they set out from Ur of the Chaldeans[p] to go to Canaan.[q] But when they came to Haran, they settled there. [32]Terah lived 205 years, and he died in Haran.

The Call of Abram

12 The LORD had said to Abram, "Leave your country, your people and your father's household and go to the land I will show you.[r]

2 "I will make you into a great nation[s]
and I will bless you;[t]

---

[a] 12,13 Hebrew; Septuagint (see also Luke 3:35, 36 and note at Gen. 10:24) *35 years, he became the father of Cainan. [13]And after he became the father of Cainan, Arphaxad lived 430 years and had other sons and daughters, and then he died. When Cainan had lived 130 years, he became the father of Shelah. And after he became the father of Shelah, Cainan lived 330 years and had other sons and daughters*

---

who could trace their ancestry back to Shem. Here the intention was to trace the line from Noah to Abram as a means of establishing continuity from the blessed line of Shem to the forefather of the Hebrews.

The comment that "Sarai was barren" looks like a disruption in the "story" line. The uninformed ancient reader would have dismissed this family due to Sarai's condition. We don't have to go much further, though, to discover that this apparent point of trivia is important. It prepares us for God's covenant offer and helps us appreciate the faith it took for Abram and Sarai to follow God's instructions.

Though God is sovereign over creation and the nations, he's also attentive to individual people. Human history hinges on the faithfulness of individuals. We move with the end of Genesis 11 from the history of creation and the nations to the story of one couple. The rest of Genesis, and indeed of the Biblical narrative, flows from them. We begin by knowing only their inadequacy—Sarai's infertility. God works out his purposes through individual people and is never thwarted by our weaknesses.

Genesis 12:1–9

The promises God offered Abram were associated with his original blessing to all people (1:28–29).

11:12 [f] Lk 3:35
11:20 [g] Lk 3:35
11:24 [h] Lk 3:34
11:26 [i] Lk 3:34 [j] Jos 24:2
11:27 [k] ver 31; Ge 12:4; 14:12; 19:1; 2Pe 2:7
11:28 [l] ver 31; Ge 15:7
11:29 [m] Ge 17:15 [n] Ge 22:20
11:30 [o] Ge 16:1; 18:11
11:31 [p] Ge 15:7; Ne 9:7; Ac 7:4 [q] Ge 10:19
12:1 [r] Ac 7:3*; Heb 11:8
12:2 [s] Ge 15:5; 17:2,4; 18:18; 22:17; Dt 26:5 [t] Ge 24:1, 35

I will make your name great,
and you will be a blessing.
³ I will bless those who bless you,
and whoever curses you I will
curse; ᵘ
and all peoples on earth
will be blessed through you. ᵛ"

⁴ So Abram left, as the LORD had told him; and Lot went with him. Abram was seventy-five years old when he set out from Haran. ʷ ⁵ He took his wife Sarai, his nephew Lot, all the possessions they had accumulated and the people ˣ they had acquired in Haran, and they set out for the land of Canaan, and they arrived there.

⁶ Abram traveled through the land ʸ as far as the site of the great tree of Moreh ᶻ at Shechem. At that time the Canaanites ᵃ were in the land. ⁷ The LORD appeared to Abram ᵇ and said, "To your offspring ᵃ I will give this land." ᶜ So he built an altar there to the LORD, ᵈ who had appeared to him.

⁸ From there he went on toward the hills east of Bethel ᵉ and pitched his tent, with Bethel on the west and Ai on the east. There he built an altar to the LORD and called on the name of the LORD. ⁹ Then Abram set out and continued toward the Negev. ᶠ

Abram in Egypt

¹⁰ Now there was a famine in the land, and Abram went down to Egypt to live there for a while because the famine was severe. ¹¹ As he was about to enter Egypt, he said to his wife Sarai, "I know what a beautiful woman you are. ¹² When the Egyptians see you, they will say, 'This is his wife.' Then they will kill me but will let you live. ¹³ Say you are my sister, ᵍ so that I will be treated well for your sake and my life will be spared because of you."

ᵃ 7 Or *seed*

12:3
ᵘ Ge 27:29;
Ex 23:22; Nu 24:9
ᵛ Ge 18:18; 22:18;
26:4; Ac 3:25;
Gal 3:8*

12:4
ʷ Ge 11:31

12:5
ˣ Ge 14:14; 17:23

12:6
ʸ Heb 11:9
ᶻ Ge 35:4; Dt 11:30
ᵃ Ge 10:18

12:7
ᵇ Ge 17:1; 18:1;
Ex 6:3 ᶜ Ge 13:15,
17; 15:18; 17:8;
Ps 105:9-11
ᵈ Ge 13:4

12:8
ᵉ Ge 13:3

12:9
ᶠ Ge 13:1,3

12:13
ᵍ Ge 20:2; 26:7

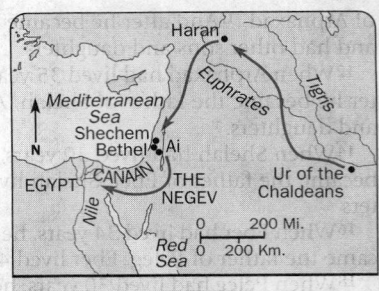

Abram's Journeys (12:4)
Then: God called Abram to journey to Canaan and blessed him with grazing land, peace, and water—a resource in increasingly short supply in Ur of the Chaldeans.
Now: Abram's journey followed the Euphrates River in order to avoid the direct route to Canaan across what remains an inhospitable wilderness.

But in Abram's case God didn't just offer the blessing of being fruitful and multiplying: Abram would become a great *nation*. God didn't just give Abram the promise of food or permission to eat; he promised a *land* that would provide abundant food.

The trip from Haran to Canaan is about 500 miles and takes the better part of a month at normal caravan pace (about 20 miles per day). The rest stops, Shechem and Bethel, located in the central hill country, became major sacred sites in later Israelite history.

📖 What Abram, missionaries, and all disciples of Christ have in common is that they leave something familiar in order to embrace the claims of God on their lives. Jesus doesn't always ask us to physically leave behind what we love, but if he does, we are to be ready. We do well to remember the haunting words of missionary/martyr Jim Elliott (1927–1956): "He is no fool who gives what he cannot keep to gain what he cannot lose." What has God asked you to leave behind for him?

Genesis 12:10–20

🍞 Famine was common in Canaan, since its productivity depended on rainfall. Egypt was less suscepti-ble to drought and famine because of its dependence on the annual flooding of the Nile. Modern archaeologists and geologists have found evidence of a massive, three-hundred-year drought cycle that occurred during the end of the third millennium B.C. and the beginning of the second—the time period to which Abram traditionally is dated.

This is the first of three incidents in which a patriarch attempted to identify his wife as his sister to avoid problems with the region's power establishment (see chs. 12; 20; 26). The sociological realities that prompted this course of action are unknown to us. The original Israelite audience likely knew what advantage was to be gained from this deception, so the author provided no explanation.

📖 Sarai was at least 65 years old by this point. Modern societies aren't as inclined to think of older women as beautiful in an alluring sense. But not every culture was/is as superficial in its assessment of beauty as ours. Sarai's character, dignity, bearing, and clothing all may have contributed to the conclusion that she was striking. What value do you place on people in their retirement years?

[14]When Abram came to Egypt, the Egyptians saw that she was a very beautiful woman. [15]And when Pharaoh's officials saw her, they praised her to Pharaoh, and she was taken into his palace. [16]He treated Abram well for her sake, and Abram acquired sheep and cattle, male and female donkeys, menservants and maidservants, and camels.

[17]But the LORD inflicted serious diseases on Pharaoh and his household[h] because of Abram's wife Sarai. [18]So Pharaoh summoned Abram. "What have you done to me?"[i] he said. "Why didn't you tell me she was your wife? [19]Why did you say, 'She is my sister,' so that I took her to be my wife? Now then, here is your wife. Take her and go!" [20]Then Pharaoh gave orders about Abram to his men, and they sent him on his way, with his wife and everything he had.

Abram and Lot Separate

13 So Abram went up from Egypt to the Negev,[j] with his wife and everything he had, and Lot went with him. [2]Abram had become very wealthy in livestock and in silver and gold.

[3]From the Negev he went from place to place until he came to Bethel,[k] to the place between Bethel and Ai where his tent had been earlier [4]and where he had first built an altar.[l] There Abram called on the name of the LORD.

[5]Now Lot, who was moving about with Abram, also had flocks and herds and tents. [6]But the land could not support them while they stayed together, for their possessions were so great that they were not able to stay together.[m] [7]And quarreling[n] arose between Abram's herdsmen and the herdsmen of Lot. The Canaanites and Perizzites were also living in the land[o] at that time.

[8]So Abram said to Lot, "Let's not have any quarreling between you and me,[p] or between your herdsmen and mine, for we are brothers. [9]Is not the whole land before you? Let's part company. If you go to the left, I'll go to the right; if you go to the right, I'll go to the left."

[10]Lot looked up and saw that the whole plain of the Jordan was well watered, like the garden of the LORD,[r] like the land of Egypt, toward Zoar.[s] (This was before the LORD destroyed Sodom and Gomorrah.)[t] [11]So Lot chose for himself the whole plain of the Jordan and set out toward the east. The two men parted company: [12]Abram lived in the land of Canaan, while Lot lived among the cities of the plain[u] and pitched his tents near Sodom.[v] [13]Now the men of Sodom were wicked and were sinning greatly against the LORD.[w]

[14]The LORD said to Abram after Lot had parted from him, "Lift up your eyes from where you are and look north and south, east and west.[x] [15]All the land that you see I will give to you and your offspring[a] forever.[y] [16]I will make your offspring like the dust of the earth, so that if anyone could count the dust, then your offspring could be counted. [17]Go, walk through the length and breadth of the land,[z] for I am giving it to you."

[18]So Abram moved his tents and went to live near the great trees of Mamre[a] at Hebron,[b] where he built an altar to the LORD.[c]

[a] 15 Or *seed*; also in verse 16

Cross references (margin)

12:17
[h] 1Ch 16:21

12:18
[i] Ge 20:9; 26:10

13:1
[j] Ge 12:9

13:3
[k] Ge 12:8

13:4
[l] Ge 12:7

13:6
[m] Ge 36:7
13:7
[n] Ge 26:20,21
[o] Ge 12:6
13:8
[p] Pr 15:18; 20:3
[q] Ps 133:1

13:10
[r] Ge 2:8-10;
Isa 51:3
[s] Ge 19:22,30
[t] Ge 14:8; 19:17-29
13:12
[u] Ge 19:17,25,29
[v] Ge 14:12

13:13
[w] Ge 18:20;
Eze 16:49-50;
2Pe 2:8
13:14
[x] Ge 28:14; Dt 3:27
13:15
[y] Ge 12:7;
Gal 3:16*
13:17
[z] ver 15;
Nu 13:17-25
13:18
[a] Ge 14:13,24; 18:1
[b] Ge 35:27
[c] Ge 8:20

Genesis 13:1–18

We gain nothing by placing Abram on a pedestal and picturing Lot, who chose first and settled near Sodom, as either villain or victim. Lot would become tangled in Sodom's web of evil, but there is no indication here of any ulterior motive for his choice. Lot was an obstacle to Abram's receiving the land God had promised him—Canaan. Once that obstacle was removed, we see advancement of the covenant. The themes of covenant obstacles and advancements appear throughout Genesis.

There is no textual clue that Abram knew or should have known that Lot was an obstacle. God didn't tell Abram to somehow get Lot out of the way. Instead, God handled the matter. Further, Lot didn't keep Abram from serving God; he was a means by which Abram received the promised blessing. If there are obstacles in our lives that need to be removed or overcome, God may choose to do the job himself or tell us what steps to take. What has been your experience in this regard?

Abram Rescues Lot

14:1
d Ge 10:10
14:2
e Ge 10:19
f Ge 13:10
14:3
g Nu 34:3,12;
Dt 3:17; Jos 3:16;
15:2,5
14:5
h Ge 15:20;
Dt 2:11,20
i Dt 2:10
14:6
j Dt 2:12,22
k Dt 2:1,5,22
l Ge 21:21;
Nu 10:12
14:7
m 2Ch 20:2
14:8
n Ge 13:10; 19:17-
29 o Dt 29:23
14:10
p Ge 19:17,30
14:13
q ver 24; Ge 13:18
14:14
r Ge 15:3 s Dt 34:1;
Jdg 18:29
14:17
t 2Sa 18:18
14:18
u Ps 110:4; Heb 5:6
v Ps 76:2; Heb 7:2
14:19
w Heb 7:6 x ver 22
14:20
y Ge 24:27
z Ge 28:22;
Dt 26:12; Heb 7:4
14:22
a Ex 6:8; Da 12:7;
Rev 10:5-6 b ver 19

14 At this time Amraphel king of Shinar, [a] [d] Arioch king of Ellasar, Kedorlaomer king of Elam and Tidal king of Goiim [2]went to war against Bera king of Sodom, Birsha king of Gomorrah, Shinab king of Admah, Shemeber king of Zeboiim, [e] and the king of Bela (that is, Zoar). [f] [3]All these latter kings joined forces in the Valley of Siddim (the Salt Sea [b] [g]). [4]For twelve years they had been subject to Kedorlaomer, but in the thirteenth year they rebelled.

[5]In the fourteenth year, Kedorlaomer and the kings allied with him went out and defeated the Rephaites [h] in Ashteroth Karnaim, the Zuzites in Ham, the Emites [i] in Shaveh Kiriathaim [6]and the Horites [j] in the hill country of Seir, [k] as far as El Paran [l] near the desert. [7]Then they turned back and went to En Mishpat (that is, Kadesh), and they conquered the whole territory of the Amalekites, as well as the Amorites who were living in Hazazon Tamar. [m]

[8]Then the king of Sodom, the king of Gomorrah, [n] the king of Admah, the king of Zeboiim [o] and the king of Bela (that is, Zoar) marched out and drew up their battle lines in the Valley of Siddim [9]against Kedorlaomer king of Elam, Tidal king of Goiim, Amraphel king of Shinar and Arioch king of Ellasar—four kings against five. [10]Now the Valley of Siddim was full of tar pits, and when the kings of Sodom and Gomorrah fled, some of the men fell into them and the rest fled to the hills. [p] [11]The four kings seized all the goods of Sodom and Gomorrah and all their food; then they went away. [12]They also carried off Abram's nephew Lot and his possessions, since he was living in Sodom.

[13]One who had escaped came and reported this to Abram the Hebrew. Now Abram was living near the great trees of Mamre [q] the Amorite, a brother [c] of Eshcol and Aner, all of whom were allied with Abram. [14]When Abram heard that his relative had been taken captive, he called out the 318 trained men born in his household [r] and went in pursuit as far as Dan. [s] [15]During the night Abram divided his men to attack them and he routed them, pursuing them as far as Hobah, north of Damascus. [16]He recovered all the goods and brought back his relative Lot and his possessions, together with the women and the other people.

[17]After Abram returned from defeating Kedorlaomer and the kings allied with him, the king of Sodom came out to meet him in the Valley of Shaveh (that is, the King's Valley). [t] [18]Then Melchizedek [u] king of Salem [d] [v] brought out bread and wine. He was priest of God Most High, [19]and he blessed Abram, [w] saying,

> "Blessed be Abram by God Most High,
>   Creator [e] of heaven and earth. [x]
> [20]And blessed be [f] God Most High, [y]
>   who delivered your enemies into your hand."

Then Abram gave him a tenth of everything. [z]
[21]The king of Sodom said to Abram, "Give me the people and keep the goods for yourself."
[22]But Abram said to the king of Sodom, "I have raised my hand [a] to the LORD, God Most High, Creator of heaven and earth, [b] and have taken an oath [23]that I will

---

[a] 1 That is, Babylonia; also in verse 9   [b] 3 That is, the Dead Sea   [c] 13 Or *a relative*; or *an ally*
[d] 18 That is, Jerusalem   [e] 19 Or *Possessor*; also in verse 22   [f] 20 Or *And praise be to*

Genesis 14:1–24

Abram set out simply to rescue Lot and his family. Theoretically, though, if he conquered these kings, dominion of the land reverted to him. His victory placed *him in a position to seize power. But was this the way* God intended to give him the promised land?

What do you do when presented with those situations many call "low-hanging fruit"? There is much to be said for "picking" opportunities when they are ripe.

Certainly there are times God wants us to step out in faith. But Abram gave up chances to seize the land either from Lot (ch. 13) or from these kings. Similarly, Jesus relinquished Satan's enticing offer to accept the world's kingdoms (Luke 4:5–8) in favor of the longterm goal of gaining God's kingdom (Rev. 11:15). It can be disastrous to take the easy way toward our goal. Simply grasping what lies before us may be counterproductive to God's will.

accept nothing belonging to you, ^c not even a thread or the thong of a sandal, so that you will never be able to say, 'I made Abram rich.' ²⁴I will accept nothing but what my men have eaten and the share that belongs to the men who went with me—to Aner, Eshcol and Mamre. Let them have their share."

God's Covenant With Abram

15 After this, the word of the LORD came to Abram^d in a vision:

"Do not be afraid,^e Abram.
I am your shield,^a^f
your very great reward.^b"

²But Abram said, "O Sovereign LORD, what can you give me since I remain childless^g and the one who will inherit^c my estate is Eliezer of Damascus?" ³And Abram said, "You have given me no children; so a servant^h in my household will be my heir."

⁴Then the word of the LORD came to him: "This man will not be your heir, but a son coming from your own body will be your heir.ⁱ" ⁵He took him outside and said, "Look up at the heavens and count the stars^j—if indeed you can count them." Then he said to him, "So shall your offspring be."^k

⁶Abram believed the LORD, and he credited it to him as righteousness.^l

⁷He also said to him, "I am the LORD, who brought you out of Ur of the Chaldeans to give you this land to take possession of it."

⁸But Abram said, "O Sovereign LORD, how can I know^m that I will gain possession of it?"

⁹So the LORD said to him, "Bring me a heifer, a goat and a ram, each three years old, along with a dove and a young pigeon."

¹⁰Abram brought all these to him, cut them in two and arranged the halves opposite each other;ⁿ the birds, however, he did not cut in half.^o ¹¹Then birds of prey came down on the carcasses, but Abram drove them away.

¹²As the sun was setting, Abram fell into a deep sleep,^p and a thick and dreadful darkness came over him. ¹³Then the LORD said to him, "Know for certain that your descendants will be strangers in a country not their own, and they will be enslaved^q and mistreated four hundred years.^r ¹⁴But I will punish the nation they serve as slaves, and afterward they will come out^s with great possessions.^t ¹⁵You, however, will go to your fathers in peace and be buried at a good old age.^u ¹⁶In the fourth generation your descendants will come back here, for the sin of the Amorites^v has not yet reached its full measure."

¹⁷When the sun had set and darkness had fallen, a smoking firepot with a blazing torch appeared and passed between the pieces.^w ¹⁸On that day the LORD made a covenant with Abram and said, "To your descendants I give this land,^x from the

^a 1 Or *sovereign*   ^b 1 Or *shield; / your reward will be very great*   ^c 2 The meaning of the Hebrew for this phrase is uncertain.

14:23
c 2Ki 5:16

15:1
d Da 10:1
e Ge 21:17; 26:24; 46:3; 2Ki 6:16; Ps 27:1; Isa 41:10,13-14
f Dt 33:29; 2Sa 22:3,31; Ps 3:3

15:2
g Ac 7:5
15:3
h Ge 24:2,34

15:4
i Gal 4:28
15:5
j Ps 147:4; Jer 33:22
k Ge 12:2; 22:17; Ex 32:13; Ro 4:18*; Heb 11:12
15:6
l Ps 106:31; Ro 4:3*,20-24*; Gal 3:6*; Jas 2:23*
15:8
m Lk 1:18
15:10
n ver 17; Jer 34:18
o Lev 1:17

15:12
p Ge 2:21

15:13
q Ex 1:11 r ver 16; Ex 12:40; Ac 7:6,17
15:14
s Ac 7:7*
t Ex 12:32-38
15:15
u Ge 25:8
15:16
v 1Ki 21:26

15:17
w ver 10
15:18
x Ge 12:7

Genesis 15:1–21

Abram didn't come from a monotheistic family (worshiping only one god; cf. Josh. 24:2,14). Though we have no indication that God explained or demanded this kind of belief, it's clear that exclusive worship of God characterized Abram's later religious experience. By making a break with his land, family, and inheritance, Abram also broke all other religious ties. The Lord filled the void, becoming the "God of Abraham, Isaac and Jacob."

Because Abram took God at his word, God credited him with a legacy based on the "rightness" of his faith, which in turn became the basis for blessing. Abram accepted God's word about his descendants. But when God spoke of giving him the land, he seemed skeptical.

Why the difference? The first promise would begin to see fulfillment in his lifetime—but not the second. God showed no frustration or disappointment at Abram's request for certainty.

"The LORD said to Abram . . ." Have you ever wished God would speak to you that plainly? There are eight recorded conversations between God and Abram—over the course of 100 years. Abram didn't control these conversations, and he often came away more confused than enlightened. Which would you prefer: a brief conversation with God eight times during your lifetime or a book that shows you what God is like and explains his plans and expectations? God has given us far more revelation and guidance through his Word than Abram could have dreamed possible.

15:18
y Nu 34:5

river^a of Egypt^y to the great river, the Euphrates—¹⁹the land of the Kenites, Keniz-zites, Kadmonites, ²⁰Hittites, Perizzites, Rephaites, ²¹Amorites, Canaanites, Girga-shites and Jebusites."

Hagar and Ishmael

16:1
z Ge 11:30;
Gal 4:24-25
a Ge 21:9

16 Now Sarai, Abram's wife, had borne him no children.^z But she had an Egyptian maidservant^a named Hagar; ²so she said to Abram, "The LORD has kept me from having children. Go, sleep with my maidservant; perhaps I can build a family through her."^b

16:2
b Ge 30:3-4,9-10
16:3
c Ge 12:5

Abram agreed to what Sarai said. ³So after Abram had been living in Canaan^c ten years, Sarai his wife took her Egyptian maidservant Hagar and gave her to her hus-band to be his wife. ⁴He slept with Hagar, and she conceived.

16:5
d Ge 31:53

When she knew she was pregnant, she began to despise her mistress. ⁵Then Sa-rai said to Abram, "You are responsible for the wrong I am suffering. I put my ser-vant in your arms, and now that she knows she is pregnant, she despises me. May the LORD judge between you and me."^d

^a 18 Or *Wadi*

Genesis 16:1–16

That Sarai had borne no children for Abram jeopardized the covenant. The privilege of childbearing was appropriately viewed to be in God's hands. Con-versely, the inability to bear children was seen as his punishment. Ancient people often considered a barren woman accursed, and in some cases her condition served as cause for divorce. Marriage contracts of the time stipulated that an infertile wife should provide her husband with a surrogate child-bearer.

The situation in this chapter presented a triple jeop-ardy to the covenant. (1) The absence of an heir created the first challenge. (2) The human attempt to resolve the problem created a competing heir. (3) The makeshift heir was in danger of being lost to Abram and Sarai by Hagar's flight.

Many believe that "the angel of the LORD" who spoke to Hagar was the pre-incarnate Christ (in an appearance prior to his physical birth). While this explanation isn't impossible, many others believe this was the Lord's mes-senger speaking on his behalf.

Through Ishmael's birth, Abram and Sarai be-lieved they were hurdling an obstacle; in fact they were creating one. Considering their cultural reality, does their action suggest a lack of faith? If it was an error, God redeemed it. We don't need to think of our failures as unproductive. God in his sovereignty doesn't waste our experiences. As long as we are not defying him or in-dulging our self-will, we can be confident that he's con-tinuously shaping us for his service. In what ways has he been sculpting you?

15:18

Great Rivers of the Bible

The great rivers of the ancient Near East were, not surprisingly, all sites of great Biblical civilizations:

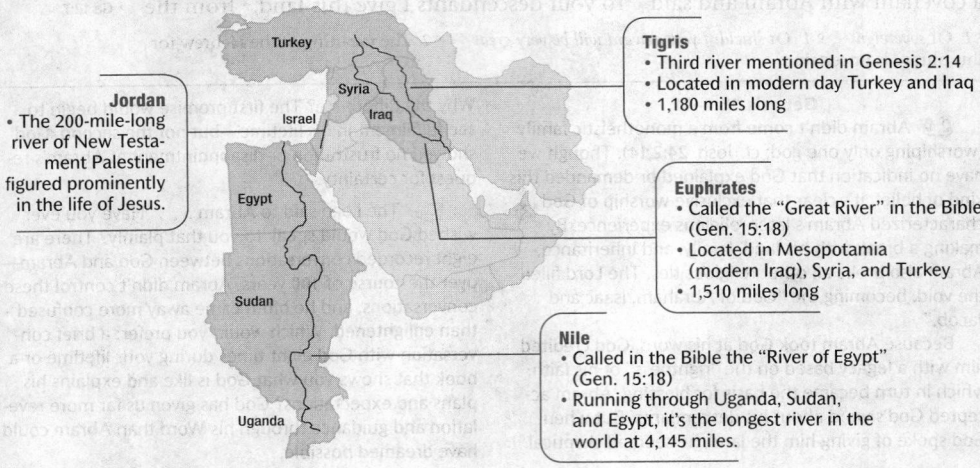

Jordan
• The 200-mile-long river of New Testa-ment Palestine figured prominently in the life of Jesus.

Tigris
• Third river mentioned in Genesis 2:14
• Located in modern day Turkey and Iraq
• 1,180 miles long

Euphrates
• Called the "Great River" in the Bible (Gen. 15:18)
• Located in Mesopotamia (modern Iraq), Syria, and Turkey
• 1,510 miles long

Nile
• Called in the Bible the "River of Egypt" (Gen. 15:18)
• Running through Uganda, Sudan, and Egypt, it's the longest river in the world at 4,145 miles.

6 "Your servant is in your hands," Abram said. "Do with her whatever you think best." Then Sarai mistreated Hagar; so she fled from her.

7 The angel of the LORD *e* found Hagar near a spring in the desert; it was the spring that is beside the road to Shur. *f* 8 And he said, "Hagar, servant of Sarai, where have you come from, and where are you going?"

"I'm running away from my mistress Sarai," she answered.

9 Then the angel of the LORD told her, "Go back to your mistress and submit to her." 10 The angel added, "I will so increase your descendants that they will be too numerous to count." *g*

11 The angel of the LORD also said to her:

> "You are now with child
> and you will have a son.
> You shall name him Ishmael, *a*
> for the LORD has heard of your misery. *h*
> 12 He will be a wild donkey of a man;
> his hand will be against everyone
> and everyone's hand against him,
> and he will live in hostility
> toward *b* all his brothers. *i*"

13 She gave this name to the LORD who spoke to her: "You are the God who sees me," for she said, "I have now seen *c* the One who sees me." *j* 14 That is why the well was called Beer Lahai Roi *d*; it is still there, between Kadesh and Bered.

15 So Hagar bore Abram a son, *k* and Abram gave the name Ishmael to the son she had borne. 16 Abram was eighty-six years old when Hagar bore him Ishmael.

The Covenant of Circumcision

17 When Abram was ninety-nine years old, the LORD appeared to him and said, "I am God Almighty *e;l* walk before me and be blameless. *m* 2 I will confirm my covenant between me and you *n* and will greatly increase your numbers."

3 Abram fell facedown, and God said to him, 4 "As for me, this is my covenant with you: *o* You will be the father of many nations. *p* 5 No longer will you be called Abram *f*; your name will be Abraham, *g q* for I have made you a father of many nations. *r* 6 I will make you very fruitful; *s* I will make nations of you, and kings will come from you. *t* 7 I will establish my covenant as an everlasting covenant between me and you and your descendants after you for the generations to come, to be your God *u* and the God of your descendants after you. *v* 8 The whole land of Canaan, *w* where you are now an alien, *x* I will give as an everlasting possession to you and your descendants after you; *y* and I will be their God."

9 Then God said to Abraham, "As for you, you must keep my covenant, you and your descendants after you for the generations to come. 10 This is my covenant with you and your descendants after you, the covenant you are to keep: Every male among you shall be circumcised. *z* 11 You are to undergo circumcision, *a* and it will be the sign of the covenant *b* between me and you. 12 For the generations

Cross references

16:7
e Ge 21:17; 22:11,15; 31:11
f Ge 20:1

16:10
g Ge 13:16; 17:20

16:11
h Ex 2:24; 3:7,9

16:12
i Ge 25:18

16:13
j Ge 32:30

16:15
k Gal 4:22

17:1
l Ge 28:3; Ex 6:3
m Dt 18:13
17:2
n Ge 15:18
17:4
o Ge 15:18
p ver 16; Ge 12:2; 35:11; 48:19
17:5
q ver 15; Ne 9:7
r Ro 4:17*
17:6
s Ge 35:11 *t* Mt 1:6
17:7
u Ex 29:45,46
v Ro 9:8; Gal 3:16
17:8
w Ps 105:9,11
x Ge 23:4; 28:4; Ex 6:4 *y* Ge 12:7

17:10
z ver 23; Ge 21:4; Jn 7:22; Ac 7:8; Ro 4:11
17:11
a Ex 12:48; Dt 10:16 *b* Ro 4:11

---

a 11 Ishmael means God hears.   *b 12 Or live to the east / of*   *c 13 Or seen the back of*   *d 14 Beer Lahai Roi means well of the Living One who sees me.*   *e 1 Hebrew El-Shaddai*   *f 5 Abram means exalted father.*   *g 5 Abraham means father of many.*

Genesis 17:1–27

The theophany (appearance of God) in this chapter includes the most complete presentation in Genesis of the covenant promises and expectations, as well as specific information about Abram's two sons. There were several new promises: Abram was to father many nations, kings were to come from him, and the covenant was "everlasting." In addition, there were name changes for Abram and Sarai, designation of circumcision as a sign, and reference to keeping the covenant. This was a clear advancement of the covenant.

Circumcision demonstrates the importance of making committed responses to God. Today, communion and baptism are signs of our covenant relationship with Christ. But just as circumcision was only an indication of a deeper, spiritual reality, these signs of the new covenant can't substitute for active faith in Christ. In what shape is your faith?

17:12
c Lev 12:3; Lk 2:21

to come every male among you who is eight days old must be circumcised, [c] including those born in your household or bought with money from a foreigner—those who are not your offspring. [13]Whether born in your household or bought with your money, they must be circumcised. My covenant in your flesh is to be an everlasting covenant. [14]Any uncircumcised male, who has not been circumcised in the flesh, will be cut off from his people; [d] he has broken my covenant."

17:14
d Ex 4:24-26

17:16
e Ge 18:10
f Ge 35:11;
Gal 4:31

[15]God also said to Abraham, "As for Sarai your wife, you are no longer to call her Sarai; her name will be Sarah. [16]I will bless her and will surely give you a son by her. [e] I will bless her so that she will be the mother of nations; [f] kings of peoples will come from her."

17:17
g Ge 18:12; 21:6

[17]Abraham fell facedown; he laughed [g] and said to himself, "Will a son be born to a man a hundred years old? Will Sarah bear a child at the age of ninety?" [18]And Abraham said to God, "If only Ishmael might live under your blessing!"

17:19
h Ge 18:14; 21:2
i Ge 26:3

[19]Then God said, "Yes, but your wife Sarah will bear you a son, [h] and you will call him Isaac. [a] I will establish my covenant with him [i] as an everlasting covenant for his descendants after him. [20]And as for Ishmael, I have heard you: I will surely bless him; I will make him fruitful and will greatly increase his numbers. [j] He will be the father of twelve rulers, [k] and I will make him into a great nation. [l] [21]But my covenant I will establish with Isaac, whom Sarah will bear to you by this time next year." [m] [22]When he had finished speaking with Abraham, God went up from him.

17:20
j Ge 16:10
k Ge 25:12-16
l Ge 21:18

17:21
m Ge 21:2

17:24
n Ro 4:11

[23]On that very day Abraham took his son Ishmael and all those born in his household or bought with his money, every male in his household, and circumcised them, as God told him. [24]Abraham was ninety-nine years old when he was circumcised, [n] [25]and his son Ishmael was thirteen; [26]Abraham and his son Ishmael were both circumcised on that same day. [27]And every male in Abraham's household, including those born in his household or bought from a foreigner, was circumcised with him.

a 19 *Isaac* means *he laughs.*

17:7

2000 BC	1800	1600	1400	1200	1000	800	600	400	200	AD	200

2166–1859 Age of the Patriarchs (Abraham, Isaac, Jacob)
1900 Sojourn into Egypt (Joseph)
1446–1375 Exodus and conquest of Canaan (Moses, Joshua)
1375–1055 Period of the Judges
1050–930 Period of the Kings (Saul, David, Solomon)
930 Divided Kingdom (Israel in North, Judah in South)
722 Kingdom of Israel falls to Assyria
586 Kingdom of Judah falls to Babylonia
538 Jews return to Jerusalem
445 Nehemiah rebuilds the walls of Jerusalem
433–5 Period between Old and New Testaments
332 Greece conquers the Holy Land (Alexander)
167 Maccabees revolt
63 Rome captures Jerusalem (Pompey)
37–4 Herod rules Judea
7 John the Baptist is born
6/5 Jesus of Nazareth is born
26 Jesus begins his ministry
30 Jesus' crucifixion and resurrection
35 Conversion of Paul of Tarsus
46 Paul begins his mission to Gentiles
65 Christians persecuted in Rome
66 Jews revolt against Rome
70 Romans destroy Jerusalem

Chronology
of Bible Events

The Three Visitors

18 The LORD appeared to Abraham near the great trees of Mamre[o] while he was sitting at the entrance to his tent in the heat of the day. [2]Abraham looked up and saw three men[p] standing nearby. When he saw them, he hurried from the entrance of his tent to meet them and bowed low to the ground.

[3]He said, "If I have found favor in your eyes, my lord,[a] do not pass your servant by. [4]Let a little water be brought, and then you may all wash your feet[q] and rest under this tree. [5]Let me get you something to eat,[r] so you can be refreshed and then go on your way—now that you have come to your servant."

"Very well," they answered, "do as you say."

[6]So Abraham hurried into the tent to Sarah. "Quick," he said, "get three seahs[b] of fine flour and knead it and bake some bread." [7]Then he ran to the herd and selected a choice, tender calf and gave it to a servant, who hurried to prepare it. [8]He then brought some curds and milk and the calf that had been prepared, and set these before them.[s] While they ate, he stood near them under a tree.

[9]"Where is your wife Sarah?" they asked him.

"There, in the tent," he said.

[10]Then the LORD[c] said, "I will surely return to you about this time next year, and Sarah your wife will have a son."[t]

Now Sarah was listening at the entrance to the tent, which was behind him. [11]Abraham and Sarah were already old and well advanced in years,[u] and Sarah was past the age of childbearing.[v] [12]So Sarah laughed[w] to herself as she thought, "After I am worn out and my master[d][x] is old, will I now have this pleasure?"

[13]Then the LORD said to Abraham, "Why did Sarah laugh and say, 'Will I really have a child, now that I am old?' [14]Is anything too hard for the LORD?[y] I will return to you at the appointed time next year and Sarah will have a son."

[15]Sarah was afraid, so she lied and said, "I did not laugh."

But he said, "Yes, you did laugh."

Abraham Pleads for Sodom

[16]When the men got up to leave, they looked down toward Sodom, and Abraham walked along with them to see them on their way. [17]Then the LORD said, "Shall I hide from Abraham[z] what I am about to do?[a] [18]Abraham will surely become a great and powerful nation,[b] and all nations on earth will be blessed through him. [19]For I have chosen him, so that he will direct his children[c] and his household af-

---

[a] 3 Or O Lord   [b] 6 That is, probably about 20 quarts (about 22 liters)   [c] 10 Hebrew Then he
[d] 12 Or husband

Cross references

18:1 [o] Ge 13:18; 14:13
18:2 [p] ver 16,22; Ge 32:24; Jos 5:13; Jdg 13:6-11; Heb 13:2
18:4 [q] Ge 19:2; 43:24
18:5 [r] Jdg 13:15
18:8 [s] Ge 19:3
18:10 [t] Ro 9:9*
18:11 [u] Ge 17:17 [v] Ro 4:19
18:12 [w] Ge 17:17; 21:6 [x] 1Pe 3:6
18:14 [y] Jer 32:17,27; Zec 8:6; Mt 19:26; Lk 1:37; Ro 4:21
18:17 [z] Am 3:7 [a] Ge 19:24
18:18 [b] Gal 3:8*
18:19 [c] Dt 4:9-10; 6:7

Genesis 18:1–15

Both Abraham's and Sarah's laughter (17:17; 18:12) expressed a skepticism we can easily understand, given the circumstances. But skepticism isn't lack of faith. Abraham's laughter was immediately followed by a request that shows he accepted the pronouncement: He asked that Ishmael not lose favor (17:18).

Abraham's conduct gave no indication that he recognized the supernatural nature of his visitors. His attentiveness toward his guests—bowing, foot-washing, offer of refreshment in the shade—was standard hospitality. Social protocol required an actual meal to exceed what was first offered. Thus, Abraham ordered fresh bread, a calf, and a mixture of milk and yogurt. The fresh meat was particularly generous—not a normal staple in the ancients' daily diet.

The question of verse 14 ("Is anything too hard for the LORD?") is a basis for faith and hope. When we face hard times, we can't automatically claim this verse as assurance that God will change our circumstances. He can, but he may just as well ask us to accept our situation and grow through it. We are wise not to try to dictate "solutions" to God. He may have answers in mind far beyond our ability to imagine. When have you experienced the unfolding of such an answer?

Genesis 18:16–33

Verses 20–21 show God on a fact-finding mission. His omnipresence and omniscience (traits of being everywhere present and all-knowing) weren't in question, but any fair judge sees evidence firsthand. It's implied in verse 17 and specified in 19:13 that the messengers' mission was to destroy the city. The dialogue between God and Abraham took place, not so Abraham could persuade God to do the right thing, but so Abraham could consider the issue of justice from a godly perspective.

18:19
d Jos 24:15;
Eph 6:4

18:21
e Ge 11:5

18:22
f Ge 19:1

18:23
g Nu 16:22

18:24
h Jer 5:1

18:25
i Job 8:3,20;
Ps 58:11; 94:2;
Isa 3:10-11; Ro 3:6
18:26
j Jer 5:1

18:27
k Ge 2:7; 3:19;
Job 30:19; 42:6

ter him to keep the way of the LORD [d] by doing what is right and just, so that the LORD will bring about for Abraham what he has promised him."

20 Then the LORD said, "The outcry against Sodom and Gomorrah is so great and their sin so grievous 21 that I will go down [e] and see if what they have done is as bad as the outcry that has reached me. If not, I will know."

22 The men turned away and went toward Sodom, [f] but Abraham remained standing before the LORD. [a] 23 Then Abraham approached him and said: "Will you sweep away the righteous with the wicked? [g] 24 What if there are fifty righteous people in the city? Will you really sweep it away and not spare [b] the place for the sake of the fifty righteous people in it? [h] 25 Far be it from you to do such a thing—to kill the righteous with the wicked, treating the righteous and the wicked alike. Far be it from you! Will not the Judge [c] of all the earth do right?" [i]

26 The LORD said, "If I find fifty righteous people in the city of Sodom, I will spare the whole place for their sake. [j]"

27 Then Abraham spoke up again: "Now that I have been so bold as to speak to the Lord, though I am nothing but dust and ashes, [k] 28 what if the number of the righteous is five less than fifty? Will you destroy the whole city because of five people?"

"If I find forty-five there," he said, "I will not destroy it."

29 Once again he spoke to him, "What if only forty are found there?"

> [a] 22 Masoretic Text; an ancient Hebrew scribal tradition *but the LORD remained standing before Abraham*   [b] 24 Or *forgive*; also in verse 26   [c] 25 Or *Ruler*

Whenever we raise questions about God's justice, we suggest that, if given the opportunity, we would be more just than God. Whether we focus on his love, grace, or mercy—or any of God's attributes—if we think we can do better, our view of him is deficient. We never have all the information, and we are never wise enough to apply what information we do have infallibly to whatever issue may be at hand. Yet as Abraham asked rhetorically in this passage, "Will not the Judge of all the earth do right?"

Snapshots

18:18

Henry Martyn

Henry Martyn (1781?–1812) served as an Anglican chaplain and missionary in India. Prevented by personal circumstances from missionary service, Martyn became a chaplain with the East India Company, devoting his 305-day voyage to India to studying the Urdu and Bengali languages. Once there, he assisted in Bible translation efforts.

> His ecumenical openness, desire to implant the gospel in Indian culture, and concern for spiritual exchange with Muslims left a legacy that inspired later missionaries.

Martyn served as chaplain in two locations from 1806 to 1810. His refusal to treat Indians as inferior and his appreciation of Indian culture alienated many of his peers, and he opted to devote his energies to Bible translation work, eventually producing Urdu, Arabic, and Persian versions of Scripture for his audiences. To aid his efforts, Martyn immersed himself in the culture and read "everything [he] could pick up" to help him understand those he served.

In 1810 Martyn traveled through Iran to test his Persian translation and hopefully benefit from a drier climate to alleviate his suffering from tuberculosis. While there, he thoroughly revised the translation, which was presented to the shah. His dream of returning to England to persuade a childhood sweetheart to marry him never materialized.

Martyn died at age 31. His ecumenical openness, desire to implant the gospel in Indian culture, and concern for spiritual exchange with Muslims left a legacy that inspired later missionaries to adopt a more moderate, conciliatory approach to missions efforts.

He said, "For the sake of forty, I will not do it."
30 Then he said, "May the Lord not be angry, but let me speak. What if only thirty can be found there?"
He answered, "I will not do it if I find thirty there."
31 Abraham said, "Now that I have been so bold as to speak to the Lord, what if
only twenty can be found there?"
He said, "For the sake of twenty, I will not destroy it."
32 Then he said, "May the Lord not be angry, but let me speak just once more.[l]
What if only ten can be found there?"
He answered, "For the sake of ten,[m] I will not destroy it."
33 When the LORD had finished speaking with Abraham, he left, and Abraham returned home.

18:32 [l] Jdg 6:39 [m] Jer 5:1

Sodom and Gomorrah Destroyed

19 The two angels arrived at Sodom[n] in the evening, and Lot was sitting in the
gateway of the city.[o] When he saw them, he got up to meet them and
bowed down with his face to the ground. 2 "My lords," he said, "please turn aside
to your servant's house. You can wash your feet[p] and spend the night and then go
on your way early in the morning."
"No," they answered, "we will spend the night in the square."
3 But he insisted so strongly that they did go with him and entered his house. He
prepared a meal for them, baking bread without yeast, and they ate.[q] 4 Before they
had gone to bed, all the men from every part of the city of Sodom—both young and
old—surrounded the house. 5 They called to Lot, "Where are the men who came to
you tonight? Bring them out to us so that we can have sex with them."[r]
6 Lot went outside to meet them[s] and shut the door behind him 7 and said, "No,
my friends. Don't do this wicked thing. 8 Look, I have two daughters who have never slept with a man. Let me bring them out to you, and you can do what you like
with them. But don't do anything to these men, for they have come under the protection of my roof."[t]
9 "Get out of our way," they replied. And they said, "This fellow came here as an
alien, and now he wants to play the judge![u] We'll treat you worse than them." They
kept bringing pressure on Lot and moved forward to break down the door.
10 But the men inside reached out and pulled Lot back into the house and shut
the door. 11 Then they struck the men who were at the door of the house, young and
old, with blindness[v] so that they could not find the door.
12 The two men said to Lot, "Do you have anyone else here—sons-in-law, sons or
daughters, or anyone else in the city who belongs to you?[w] Get them out of here,
13 because we are going to destroy this place. The outcry to the LORD against its people is so great that he has sent us to destroy it."[x]
14 So Lot went out and spoke to his sons-in-law, who were pledged to marry[a] his
daughters. He said, "Hurry and get out of this place, because the LORD is about to
destroy the city![y]" But his sons-in-law thought he was joking.[z]

19:1 [n] Ge 18:22 [o] Ge 18:1
19:2 [p] Ge 18:4; Lk 7:44
19:3 [q] Ge 18:6
19:5 [r] Jdg 19:22; Isa 3:9; Ro 1:24-27
19:6 [s] Jdg 19:23
19:8 [t] Jdg 19:24
19:9 [u] Ex 2:14; Ac 7:27
19:11 [v] Dt 28:28-29; 2Ki 6:18; Ac 13:11
19:12 [w] Ge 7:1
19:13 [x] 1Ch 21:15
19:14 [y] Nu 16:21 [z] Ex 9:21; Lk 17:28

[a] 14 Or *were married to*

Genesis 19:1–29

Lot's response to the men's demand shakes us. Was he truly offering his daughters for gang rape and probable murder? It's possible he was making a psychological appeal: "I would as soon have you violate my own family members as those I have taken in." This would be like saying to a mortgage company about to foreclose on your home, "Why don't you just take the clothes off my kids' backs?"

Jesus may have implied in Luke 17:31–32 that Lot's wife turned, rather than glanced, back toward Sodom. Perhaps an earthquake caused the combustion of natural tars, sulfur deposits, and other chemicals found in the area (Deut. 29:23). If so, many of those engulfed by the fallout could have been described as "pillars of salt."

Can good people make a difference in the world? God-honoring persons will always be a minority. Still, individually and as the church, we are called upon to impact the world however we can—to make a difference for God (James 5:16–18). We can't be result-driven: We may never know our impact on others' lives this side of heaven. Are you motivated by the world's needs and the example of Christ's love to act as he would (Matt. 25:31–46)?

19:15
a Nu 16:26
b Rev 18:4

15With the coming of dawn, the angels urged Lot, saying, "Hurry! Take your wife and your two daughters who are here, or you will be swept away[a] when the city is punished.[b]"

16When he hesitated, the men grasped his hand and the hands of his wife and of his two daughters and led them safely out of the city, for the LORD was merciful

19:17
c Jer 48:6 d ver 26

to them. 17As soon as they had brought them out, one of them said, "Flee for your lives![c] Don't look back,[d] and don't stop anywhere in the plain! Flee to the mountains or you will be swept away!"

18But Lot said to them, "No, my lords,[a] please! 19Your[b] servant has found favor in your[b] eyes, and you[b] have shown great kindness to me in sparing my life. But I can't flee to the mountains; this disaster will overtake me, and I'll die. 20Look, here is a town near enough to run to, and it is small. Let me flee to it—it is very small, isn't it? Then my life will be spared."

21He said to him, "Very well, I will grant this request too; I will not overthrow the town you speak of. 22But flee there quickly, because I cannot do anything until you reach it." (That is why the town was called Zoar.[c])

19:24
e Dt 29:23; Isa 1:9;
13:19 f Lk 17:29;
2Pe 2:6; Jude 7
19:25
g Ps 107:34;
Eze 16:48
19:26
h ver 17 i Lk 17:32
19:27
j Ge 18:22

23By the time Lot reached Zoar, the sun had risen over the land. 24Then the LORD rained down burning sulfur on Sodom and Gomorrah[e]—from the LORD out of the heavens.[f] 25Thus he overthrew those cities and the entire plain, including all those living in the cities—and also the vegetation in the land.[g] 26But Lot's wife looked back,[h] and she became a pillar of salt.[i]

27Early the next morning Abraham got up and returned to the place where he had stood before the LORD.[j] 28He looked down toward Sodom and Gomorrah, toward

19:28
k Rev 9:2; 18:9

all the land of the plain, and he saw dense smoke rising from the land, like smoke from a furnace.[k]

19:29
l 2Pe 2:7

29So when God destroyed the cities of the plain, he remembered Abraham, and he brought Lot out of the catastrophe[l] that overthrew the cities where Lot had lived.

19:30
m ver 19

Lot and His Daughters

30Lot and his two daughters left Zoar and settled in the mountains,[m] for he was afraid to stay in Zoar. He and his two daughters lived in a cave. 31One day the older daughter said to the younger, "Our father is old, and there is no man around here to lie with us, as is the custom all over the earth. 32Let's get our father to drink wine and then lie with him and preserve our family line through our father."

33That night they got their father to drink wine, and the older daughter went in and lay with him. He was not aware of it when she lay down or when she got up.

34The next day the older daughter said to the younger, "Last night I lay with my father. Let's get him to drink wine again tonight, and you go in and lie with him so we can preserve our family line through our father." 35So they got their father to drink wine that night also, and the younger daughter went and lay with him. Again he was not aware of it when she lay down or when she got up.

19:37
n Dt 2:9

36So both of Lot's daughters became pregnant by their father. 37The older daughter had a son, and she named him Moab[d]; he is the father of the Moabites[n] of today. 38The younger daughter also had a son, and she named him Ben-Ammi[e]; he

19:38
o Dt 2:19

is the father of the Ammonites[o] of today.

[a] 18 Or No, Lord; or No, my lord   [b] 19 The Hebrew is singular.   [c] 22 Zoar means small.
[d] 37 Moab sounds like the Hebrew for from father.   [e] 38 Ben-Ammi means son of my people.

Genesis 19:30–38

Lot's daughters are viewed in some quarters as tragic-heroic figures willing to do the unimaginable to achieve the necessary. Their actions may be seen as driven by the desperation of their situation as they evaluated it. They were isolated in virtual exile; their world had been destroyed, and with their promised spouses now dead (19:14), no male counterparts could be found for them. But the text doesn't portray them as heroines. Their scheme to resolve a difficult situation was unacceptable to God.

Do the ends justify the means? The Bible, history, and contemporary society are littered with examples of people excusing their behavior based on circumstances. It's important to guard ourselves against falling into this trap. God is in control and will bring about his desired outcomes. As Christians we are called to live holy and blameless lives. No extenuating circumstances excuse violating the standards of right living.

Abraham and Abimelech

20 Now Abraham moved on from there[p] into the region of the Negev and lived between Kadesh and Shur. For a while he stayed in Gerar,[q] **2**and there Abraham said of his wife Sarah, "She is my sister."[r] Then Abimelech king of Gerar sent for Sarah and took her.[s]

3But God came to Abimelech in a dream[t] one night and said to him, "You are as good as dead because of the woman you have taken; she is a married woman."[u]

4Now Abimelech had not gone near her, so he said, "Lord, will you destroy an innocent nation?[v] **5**Did he not say to me, 'She is my sister,' and didn't she also say, 'He is my brother'? I have done this with a clear conscience and clean hands."

6Then God said to him in the dream, "Yes, I know you did this with a clear conscience, and so I have kept[w] you from sinning against me. That is why I did not let you touch her. **7**Now return the man's wife, for he is a prophet, and he will pray for you[x] and you will live. But if you do not return her, you may be sure that you and all yours will die."

8Early the next morning Abimelech summoned all his officials, and when he told them all that had happened, they were very much afraid. **9**Then Abimelech called Abraham in and said, "What have you done to us? How have I wronged you that you have brought such great guilt upon me and my kingdom? You have done things to me that should not be done."[y] **10**And Abimelech asked Abraham, "What was your reason for doing this?"

11Abraham replied, "I said to myself, 'There is surely no fear of God[z] in this place, and they will kill me because of my wife.'[a] **12**Besides, she really is my sister, the daughter of my father though not of my mother; and she became my wife. **13**And when God had me wander from my father's household, I said to her, 'This is how you can show your love to me: Everywhere we go, say of me, "He is my brother."' "

14Then Abimelech brought sheep and cattle and male and female slaves and gave them to Abraham,[b] and he returned Sarah his wife to him. **15**And Abimelech said, "My land is before you; live wherever you like."[c]

16To Sarah he said, "I am giving your brother a thousand shekels[a] of silver. This is to cover the offense against you before all who are with you; you are completely vindicated."

17Then Abraham prayed to God,[d] and God healed Abimelech, his wife and his slave girls so they could have children again, **18**for the LORD had closed up every womb in Abimelech's household because of Abraham's wife Sarah.[e]

The Birth of Isaac

21 Now the LORD was gracious to Sarah[f] as he had said, and the LORD did for Sarah what he had promised.[g] **2**Sarah became pregnant and bore a son[h] to

[a] *16* That is, about 25 pounds (about 11.5 kilograms)

Cross-references

20:1 p Ge 18:1; q Ge 26:1,6,17
20:2 r ver 12; Ge 12:13; 26:7 s Ge 12:15
20:3 t Job 33:15; Mt 27:19; u Ps 105:14
20:4 v Ge 18:25
20:6 w 1Sa 25:26,34
20:7 x ver 17; 1Sa 7:5; Job 42:8
20:9 y Ge 12:18; 26:10; 34:7
20:11 z Ge 42:18; Ps 36:1 a Ge 12:12; 26:7
20:14 b Ge 12:16
20:15 c Ge 13:9
20:17 d Job 42:9
20:18 e Ge 12:17
21:1 f 1Sa 2:21 g Ge 8:1; 17:16,21; Gal 4:23
21:2 h Ge 17:19

Genesis 20:1–18

The promised son was to be born within the year (18:10). In chapter 12 Abraham was in danger of losing his wife. Here the danger was of losing claim to the heir, since his fathering of a child would have been in question if Sarah had slept with Abimelech.

Gerar as a nation was blessed through Abraham. Through Abraham's intercession, the wombs of every female in Abimelech's house were opened. The twist is that it was also through Abraham that they had been closed. This reflects the covenant clause indicating that those who blessed him would be blessed, while those who cursed him would be cursed (12:3).

Still today, God's people have an impact on the wicked. Abraham, a resident alien, considered this king and his people beyond his influence. The irony was that God used Abraham to make himself known to them. Instead of bringing grace and deliverance, though, Abraham nearly brought destruction. God is able to carry out his blessing program even when we can't see how it can be done—and even when we act in ways that may appear to jeopardize his intended blessing. In what ways have you impacted the attitudes or behavior of nonbelievers?

Genesis 21:1–7

Chapter 21 again reports the covenant's advance. God, as promised, provided Abraham a son. The long-awaited birth, presumably a high point in the plot of Genesis, is reported briefly and without fanfare. The scene had been well set for the conferring of the name Isaac ("laughter"; see 17:17; 18:12–15), but there would be an ill turn on the name in verse 9 (NIV "mocking").

We marvel at the miracle of a child being born to a

21:2
i Gal 4:22;
Heb 11:11
21:3
j Ge 17:19
21:4
k Ge 17:10,12;
Ac 7:8
21:6
l Ge 17:17; Isa 54:1

Abraham in his old age,[i] at the very time God had promised him. [3]Abraham gave the name Isaac[a][j] to the son Sarah bore him. [4]When his son Isaac was eight days old, Abraham circumcised him,[k] as God commanded him. [5]Abraham was a hundred years old when his son Isaac was born to him.

[6]Sarah said, "God has brought me laughter,[l] and everyone who hears about this will laugh with me." [7]And she added, "Who would have said to Abraham that Sarah would nurse children? Yet I have borne him a son in his old age."

Hagar and Ishmael Sent Away

[8]The child grew and was weaned, and on the day Isaac was weaned Abraham held a great feast. [9]But Sarah saw that the son whom Hagar the Egyptian had borne to Abraham[m] was mocking,[n] [10]and she said to Abraham, "Get rid of that slave woman and her son, for that slave woman's son will never share in the inheritance with my son Isaac."[o]

21:9
m Ge 16:15
n Gal 4:29
21:10
o Gal 4:30*

21:11
p Ge 17:18

[11]The matter distressed Abraham greatly because it concerned his son.[p] [12]But God said to him, "Do not be so distressed about the boy and your maidservant. Listen to whatever Sarah tells you, because it is through Isaac that your offspring[b] will be reckoned.[q] [13]I will make the son of the maidservant into a nation[r] also, because he is your offspring."

21:12
q Ro 9:7*;
Heb 11:18*
21:13
r ver 18

[14]Early the next morning Abraham took some food and a skin of water and gave them to Hagar. He set them on her shoulders and then sent her off with the boy. She went on her way and wandered in the desert of Beersheba.[s]

21:14
s ver 31,32

[15]When the water in the skin was gone, she put the boy under one of the bushes. [16]Then she went off and sat down nearby, about a bowshot away, for she thought, "I cannot watch the boy die." And as she sat there nearby, she[c] began to sob.

21:17
t Ex 3:7

[17]God heard the boy crying,[t] and the angel of God called to Hagar from heaven and said to her, "What is the matter, Hagar? Do not be afraid; God has heard the boy crying as he lies there. [18]Lift the boy up and take him by the hand, for I will make him into a great nation.[u]"

21:18
u ver 13
21:19
v Nu 22:31

[19]Then God opened her eyes[v] and she saw a well of water. So she went and filled the skin with water and gave the boy a drink.

21:20
w Ge 26:3,24;
28:15; 39:2,21,23
21:21
x Ge 24:4,38

[20]God was with the boy[w] as he grew up. He lived in the desert and became an archer. [21]While he was living in the Desert of Paran, his mother got a wife for him[x] from Egypt.

---

[a] 3 *Isaac* means *he laughs.*   [b] 12 Or *seed*   [c] 16 Hebrew; Septuagint *the child*

---

woman who had been infertile during her childbearing years and had since passed through menopause. Sarah's womb was twice dead. It's almost as though it were not enough for God to restore fertility to a woman who had been barren. He waited until all hope was apparently gone.

📖 The text has been tracking the obstacle of childlessness for ten chapters, but this report of resolution is so low-key that the understatement captures our attention. *What* God does should never cease to amaze us. But *that* he consistently shows himself capable of doing what he does, without apparent effort, is strikingly commonplace and entirely unremarkable. The text is appropriately nonchalant. Are we to be impressed? By all means. Surprised? Definitely not.

Genesis 21:8–21

📖 For a second time (see 16:7–13) Hagar received a heavenly visitation, this time unquestionably from God himself. He not only comforted her with a promise but provided for her immediate needs. This was another indication of the blessings that surrounded Abraham and

those associated with him.

Verses 15–19 reintroduce a familiar theme: the threat of extinction. Abraham's family had been on the brink of dying off. Lot's similar situation had led to his daughters' actions to preserve the line. Here Ishmael was near death, anticipating the next chapter in which Isaac would be a breath away from an early demise. Both Hagar and Abraham experienced divine encounters, each affirming that the one whose life hung in the balance would produce many descendants. God has the power to preserve life and, in so doing, plot the course of history.

📖 In Luke 1:37 the angel Gabriel expressed a reality that has brought consolation to Christians throughout history: "Nothing is impossible with God." This statement was made in the context of the announcement to Mary that her relative, Elizabeth—who like Sarah had been post-menopausal and infertile—was now unaccountably pregnant. When have you wracked your brain for resolution to a seemingly impossible situation, forgetting that God may have a creative solution beyond your wildest imagination?

The Treaty at Beersheba

22At that time Abimelech and Phicol the commander of his forces said to Abraham, "God is with you in everything you do. 23Now swear[y] to me here before God that you will not deal falsely with me or my children or my descendants. Show to me and the country where you are living as an alien the same kindness I have shown to you."

24Abraham said, "I swear it."

25Then Abraham complained to Abimelech about a well of water that Abimelech's servants had seized.[z] 26But Abimelech said, "I don't know who has done this. You did not tell me, and I heard about it only today."

27So Abraham brought sheep and cattle and gave them to Abimelech, and the two men made a treaty.[a] 28Abraham set apart seven ewe lambs from the flock, 29and Abimelech asked Abraham, "What is the meaning of these seven ewe lambs you have set apart by themselves?"

30He replied, "Accept these seven lambs from my hand as a witness[b] that I dug this well."

31So that place was called Beersheba,[a][c] because the two men swore an oath there.

32After the treaty had been made at Beersheba, Abimelech and Phicol the commander of his forces returned to the land of the Philistines. 33Abraham planted a tamarisk tree in Beersheba, and there he called upon the name of the LORD,[d] the Eternal God.[e] 34And Abraham stayed in the land of the Philistines for a long time.

Abraham Tested

22 Some time later God tested[f] Abraham. He said to him, "Abraham!" "Here I am," he replied.

2Then God said, "Take your son[g], your only son, Isaac, whom you love, and go to the region of Moriah.[h] Sacrifice him there as a burnt offering on one of the mountains I will tell you about."

3Early the next morning Abraham got up and saddled his donkey. He took with him two of his servants and his son Isaac. When he had cut enough wood for the burnt offering, he set out for the place God had told him about. 4On the third day Abraham looked up and saw the place in the distance. 5He said to his servants, "Stay

---

a 31 *Beersheba* can mean *well of seven* or *well of the oath*.

Cross references:
21:23 y ver 31; Jos 2:12
21:25 z Ge 26:15,18, 20-22
21:27 a Ge 26:28,31
21:30 b Ge 31:44,47,48, 50,52
21:31 c Ge 26:33
21:33 d Ge 4:26 e Dt 33:27
22:1 f Dt 8:2,16; Heb 11:17; Jas 1:12-13
22:2 g ver 12,16; Jn 3:16; Heb 11:17; 1Jn 4:9 h 2Ch 3:1

Genesis 21:22–34

In a land of seasonal rainfall, wells were extremely important to the welfare of the human population and their flocks and herds. The area in which Abraham had dug a well was under Abimelech's political control but was owned by no one. Abraham was claiming ownership not of the land, but of the rights to the water in the well. Such squatter's rights were available to a resident alien.

Abraham's worship was expressed in verse 33 in two ways. (1) He planted a tamarisk tree, evidently a significant act like building an altar. (2) He called on God's name, most likely praising God's reputation and attributes. We too easily accept God's blessings without taking the time to thank him when he's resolved a dilemma for us. When things "return to normal," we forget that the problem ever existed and go our way, focused on the next agenda item in our busy lives (cf. Luke 17:12–19). When has this behavior characterized you?

Genesis 22:1–19

Abraham's obedience, as much as it reflected the power of his faith, also suggests that the concept of human sacrifice was familiar to his worldview. However

stricken he may have been, he wasn't dumbfounded by the nature of God's demand. It was culturally logical—only baffling in light of the covenant promises (cf. 17:19).

Many suggestions have been made about God's purpose in this test, among them: (1) to strengthen Abraham's faith; (2) to give Isaac firsthand experience of God; (3) to show the world that God was justified in selecting Abraham as the recipient of his covenant promises; (4) to offer a picture of a father's pain in sacrificing his son, as God would eventually do in offering up Jesus; and (5) to demonstrate that God hates human sacrifice. God knew what Abraham would do, yet Scripture repeatedly evidences that he wants us to act out our faith and worship.

Just when Abraham thought life was back to normal, he found himself back in crisis mode. We can't expect stability and security to define "normal" in a fallen world. "Normal" isn't the smooth, gliding monorail; it's the roller coaster with its tortuous climbs and hurtling drops. This idea is clearly presented in Ecclesiastes 3, where we are told that there are times for all types of experiences. Unlike the monorail, which functions to take us somewhere, the roller coaster is designed with the ride, not the destination, in mind.

here with the donkey while I and the boy go over there. We will worship and then we will come back to you."

6Abraham took the wood for the burnt offering and placed it on his son Isaac,[i] and he himself carried the fire and the knife. As the two of them went on together, 7Isaac spoke up and said to his father Abraham, "Father?"

"Yes, my son?" Abraham replied.

"The fire and wood are here," Isaac said, "but where is the lamb[j] for the burnt offering?"

8Abraham answered, "God himself will provide the lamb for the burnt offering, my son." And the two of them went on together.

9When they reached the place God had told him about, Abraham built an altar there and arranged the wood on it. He bound his son Isaac and laid him on the altar,[k] on top of the wood. 10Then he reached out his hand and took the knife to slay his son. 11But the angel of the LORD called out to him from heaven, "Abraham! Abraham!"

"Here I am," he replied.

12"Do not lay a hand on the boy," he said. "Do not do anything to him. Now I know that you fear God,[l] because you have not withheld from me your son, your only son.[m]"

13Abraham looked up and there in a thicket he saw a ram[a] caught by its horns. He went over and took the ram and sacrificed it as a burnt offering instead of his son.[n] 14So Abraham called that place The LORD Will Provide. And to this day it is said, "On the mountain of the LORD it will be provided.[o]"

15The angel of the LORD called to Abraham from heaven a second time 16and said, "I swear by myself,[p] declares the LORD, that because you have done this and have not withheld your son, your only son, 17I will surely bless you and make your descendants[q] as numerous as the stars in the sky[r] and as the sand on the seashore.[s] Your descendants will take possession of the cities of their enemies,[t] 18and through your offspring[b] all nations on earth will be blessed,[u] because you have obeyed me."[v]

19Then Abraham returned to his servants, and they set off together for Beersheba. And Abraham stayed in Beersheba.

Nahor's Sons

20Some time later Abraham was told, "Milcah is also a mother; she has borne sons to your brother Nahor:[w] 21Uz the firstborn, Buz his brother, Kemuel (the father of Aram), 22Kesed, Hazo, Pildash, Jidlaph and Bethuel." 23Bethuel became the father of Rebekah.[x] Milcah bore these eight sons to Abraham's brother Nahor. 24His concubine, whose name was Reumah, also had sons: Tebah, Gaham, Tahash and Maacah.

22:6
i Jn 19:17

22:7
j Lev 1:10

22:9
k Heb 11:17-19; Jas 2:21

22:12
l 1Sa 15:22; Jas 2:21-22
m ver 2; Jn 3:16

22:13
n Ro 8:32
22:14
o ver 8

22:16
p Lk 1:73; Heb 6:13

22:17
q Heb 6:14*
r Ge 15:5
s Ge 26:24; 32:12
t Ge 24:60
22:18
u Ge 12:2,3;
Ac 3:25*; Gal 3:8*
v ver 10

22:20
w Ge 11:29

22:23
x Ge 24:15

---

[a] 13 Many manuscripts of the Masoretic Text, Samaritan Pentateuch, Septuagint and Syriac; most manuscripts of the Masoretic Text *a ram behind him*   [b] 18 Or *seed*

A test like Abraham's wouldn't be primarily concerned with investigating whether we love our children more than we love God. Nor would it concern whether we trust God with our children. Such a test would seek to uncover the motivating factor in our relationship with God: Is it God himself, or the benefits and hope he provides and offers us?

Genesis 22:20–24

Abraham's brother Nahor (see 11:26) fathered eight sons by his wife and four by his concubine. They would become the ancestors of 12 Aramean tribes, just as Abraham's son Ishmael would become the ancestor of 12 tribes (17:20; 25:12–16) and his grandson Jacob the ancestor of the 12 tribes of Israel (35:22–26; 49:28).

"Some time later" Abraham became aware that his brother Nahor had 12 sons. What a contrast to our age of instant messaging and e-mail. We may marvel at Abraham's willingness to undertake an arduous, three-day trek before he knew for certain the outcome of God's test of faith (vv. 1–4). Today's insta-culture does little to prepare us for the seemingly plodding pace at which we often grow in patience and in our Christian faith and commitment. Have you battled impatience in this area?

The Death of Sarah

23 Sarah lived to be a hundred and twenty-seven years old. [2] She died at Kiriath Arba[y] (that is, Hebron)[z] in the land of Canaan, and Abraham went to mourn for Sarah and to weep over her.

[3] Then Abraham rose from beside his dead wife and spoke to the Hittites.[a] He said, [4] "I am an alien and a stranger[a] among you. Sell me some property for a burial site here so I can bury my dead."

[5] The Hittites replied to Abraham, [6] "Sir, listen to us. You are a mighty prince[b] among us. Bury your dead in the choicest of our tombs. None of us will refuse you his tomb for burying your dead."

[7] Then Abraham rose and bowed down before the people of the land, the Hittites. [8] He said to them, "If you are willing to let me bury my dead, then listen to me and intercede with Ephron son of Zohar[c] on my behalf [9] so he will sell me the cave of Machpelah, which belongs to him and is at the end of his field. Ask him to sell it to me for the full price as a burial site among you."

[10] Ephron the Hittite was sitting among his people and he replied to Abraham in the hearing of all the Hittites who had come to the gate[d] of his city. [11] "No, my lord," he said. "Listen to me; I give[b] [e] you the field, and I give[b] you the cave that is in it. I give[b] it to you in the presence of my people. Bury your dead."

[12] Again Abraham bowed down before the people of the land [13] and he said to Ephron in their hearing, "Listen to me, if you will. I will pay the price of the field. Accept it from me so I can bury my dead there."

[14] Ephron answered Abraham, [15] "Listen to me, my lord; the land is worth four hundred shekels[c] of silver,[f] but what is that between me and you? Bury your dead."

[16] Abraham agreed to Ephron's terms and weighed out for him the price he had named in the hearing of the Hittites: four hundred shekels of silver,[g] according to the weight current among the merchants.

[17] So Ephron's field in Machpelah near Mamre[h]—both the field and the cave in it, and all the trees within the borders of the field—was deeded [18] to Abraham as his property in the presence of all the Hittites who had come to the gate of the city. [19] Afterward Abraham buried his wife Sarah in the cave in the field of Machpelah near Mamre (which is at Hebron) in the land of Canaan. [20] So the field and the cave in it were deeded[i] to Abraham by the Hittites as a burial site.

Isaac and Rebekah

24 Abraham was now old and well advanced in years, and the LORD had blessed him in every way.[j] [2] He said to the chief[d] servant in his household, the one in charge of all that he had,[k] "Put your hand under my thigh.[l] [3] I want you to swear by the LORD, the God of heaven and the God of earth,[m] that you will not get a wife for my son[n] from the daughters of the Canaanites,[o] among whom I am

---

a 3 Or *the sons of Heth; also in verses 5, 7, 10, 16, 18 and 20*   *b 11* Or *sell*   *c 15* That is, about 10 pounds (about 4.5 kilograms)   *d 2* Or *oldest*

Side references:

23:2
y Jos 14:15
z ver 19; Ge 13:18

23:4
a Ge 17:8;
1Ch 29:15;
Ps 105:12;
Heb 11:9,13
23:6
b Ge 14:14-16;
24:35

23:8
c Ge 25:9

23:10
d Ge 34:20-24;
Ru 4:4
23:11
e 2Sa 24:23

23:15
f Eze 45:12

23:16
g Jer 32:9;
Zec 11:12
23:17
h Ge 25:9;
49:30-32; 50:13;
Ac 7:16

23:20
i Jer 32:10

24:1
j ver 35
24:2
k Ge 39:4-6 l ver 9;
Ge 47:29
24:3
m Ge 14:19
n Ge 28:1; Dt 7:3
o Ge 10:15-19

Genesis 23:1–20

Land suitable for farming was so precious in the ancient world that owners typically refused to sell it outside the family. But Abraham wasn't trying to buy farmland, only a burial site. Village cultures used burial chambers. A family tomb was used by several generations. A body was laid on a shelf along with grave goods (food, pottery, trinkets, weapons, tools). Later the skeletal remains were placed in another chamber or box to accommodate another burial.

This passage is comparable to chapter 14 and 21:22–34. Abraham had first refused to gain land or possessions by right of conquest and later secured water rights without land. Attachments to the land were being established, but little that could be called possession. What ownership there was, though, was carefully included to trace the preliminary fulfillment of the covenant promises.

It isn't uncommon to see young couples starting out in homes beyond the wildest dreams of their parents. There may be little concern that these upscale dwellings, along with the accoutrements necessary for success, are mortgaged to the hilt. Cashing in on the good life must for them be instantaneous, or the promise is viewed as empty. How different from God's ancient people, who were content to wait many generations for promise fulfillment. When have you enjoyed anticipation of a dream as much as its realization?

24:4
p Ge 12:1; 28:2

24:7
q Gal 3:16*
r Ge 12:7; 13:15
s Ex 23:20,23

24:9
t ver 2

24:11
u Ex 2:15 v ver 13;
1Sa 9:11
24:12
w ver 27,42,48;
Ge 26:24;
Ex 3:6,15,16

24:14
x Jdg 6:17,37
24:15
y ver 45 z Ge 22:23
a Ge 22:20
b Ge 11:29
24:16
c Ge 26:7

24:18
d ver 14

24:19
e ver 14

24:21
f ver 12
24:22
g ver 47

living, 4but will go to my country and my own relatives p and get a wife for my son Isaac."

5The servant asked him, "What if the woman is unwilling to come back with me to this land? Shall I then take your son back to the country you came from?"

6"Make sure that you do not take my son back there," Abraham said. 7"The LORD, the God of heaven, who brought me out of my father's household and my native land and who spoke to me and promised me on oath, saying, 'To your off-spring a q I will give this land' r—he will send his angel before you s so that you can get a wife for my son from there. 8If the woman is unwilling to come back with you, then you will be released from this oath of mine. Only do not take my son back there." 9So the servant put his hand under the thigh t of his master Abraham and swore an oath to him concerning this matter.

10Then the servant took ten of his master's camels and left, taking with him all kinds of good things from his master. He set out for Aram Naharaim b and made his way to the town of Nahor. 11He had the camels kneel down near the well u outside the town; it was toward evening, the time the women go out to draw water. v

12Then he prayed, "O LORD, God of my master Abraham, w give me success today, and show kindness to my master Abraham. 13See, I am standing beside this spring, and the daughters of the townspeople are coming out to draw water. 14May it be that when I say to a girl, 'Please let down your jar that I may have a drink,' and she says, 'Drink, and I'll water your camels too'—let her be the one you have chosen for your servant Isaac. By this I will know x that you have shown kindness to my master."

15Before he had finished praying, y Rebekah z came out with her jar on her shoulder. She was the daughter of Bethuel son of Milcah, a who was the wife of Abraham's brother Nahor. b 16The girl was very beautiful, c a virgin; no man had ever lain with her. She went down to the spring, filled her jar and came up again.

17The servant hurried to meet her and said, "Please give me a little water from your jar."

18"Drink, d my lord," she said, and quickly lowered the jar to her hands and gave him a drink.

19After she had given him a drink, she said, "I'll draw water for your camels too, e until they have finished drinking." 20So she quickly emptied her jar into the trough, ran back to the well to draw more water, and drew enough for all his camels. 21Without saying a word, the man watched her closely to learn whether or not the LORD had made his journey successful. f

22When the camels had finished drinking, the man took out a gold nose ring g weighing a beka c and two gold bracelets weighing ten shekels. d 23Then he asked, "Whose daughter are you? Please tell me, is there room in your father's house for us to spend the night?"

24She answered him, "I am the daughter of Bethuel, the son that Milcah bore to

---

a 7 Or seed   b 10 That is, Northwest Mesopotamia   c 22 That is, about 1/5 ounce (about 5.5 grams)   d 22 That is, about 4 ounces (about 110 grams)

Genesis 24:1–66

Abraham's insistence that Isaac's wife be chosen from among family was a covenant matter, but his concern wasn't with the worship of God. Abraham's relatives were no more monotheistic (worshiping only one God) than the Canaanites. But intermarriage would risk assimilation into the people of the land and jeopardize the covenant promises of the land to Abraham's descendents.

The prayer of Abraham's servant used an oracle to identify Isaac's bride-to-be. An oracle posed a yes/no question to a deity, and a mechanism (cf. Judg. 6:36–40; 1 Sam. 6:7–12) was given so the deity could answer. A camel that has gone a few days without water can drink as much as 25 gallons (up to 100 drawings from the well for all the servant's camels). Abraham's servant intentionally selected an extreme action as a sign to avoid any doubt that God was controlling the situation.

As much as we like direct and clear guidance on specific issues, we can't approach this passage looking for a formula by which to extract information from God. This doesn't mean that we can't be guided by circumstances. The problem comes when we try to tell God what kinds of circumstances he should arrange. When facing a critical decision, have you asked God to motivate you by what pleases and honors him? Do you think clearly about the decision to be made and allow him to guide you to the right choice?

Nahor."*" 25And she added, "We have plenty of straw and fodder, as well as room for you to spend the night."

26Then the man bowed down and worshiped the Lord, *i* 27saying, "Praise be to the Lord, *j* the God of my master Abraham, who has not abandoned his kindness and faithfulness*k* to my master. As for me, the Lord has led me on the journey*l* to the house of my master's relatives." *m*

28The girl ran and told her mother's household about these things. 29Now Rebekah had a brother named Laban, *n* and he hurried out to the man at the spring. 30As soon as he had seen the nose ring, and the bracelets on his sister's arms, and had heard Rebekah tell what the man said to her, he went out to the man and found him standing by the camels near the spring. 31"Come, you who are blessed by the Lord, " *o* he said. "Why are you standing out here? I have prepared the house and a place for the camels."

32So the man went to the house, and the camels were unloaded. Straw and fodder were brought for the camels, and water for him and his men to wash their feet.*p* 33Then food was set before him, but he said, "I will not eat until I have told you what I have to say."

"Then tell us," ⌊Laban⌋ said.

34So he said, "I am Abraham's servant. 35The Lord has blessed my master abundantly, *q* and he has become wealthy. He has given him sheep and cattle, silver and gold, menservants and maidservants, and camels and donkeys. *r* 36My master's wife Sarah has borne him a son in her*a* old age, *s* and he has given him everything he owns. *t* 37And my master made me swear an oath, and said, 'You must not get a wife for my son from the daughters of the Canaanites, in whose land I live, *u* 38but go to my father's family and to my own clan, and get a wife for my son.' *v*

39"Then I asked my master, 'What if the woman will not come back with me?' *w*

40"He replied, 'The Lord, before whom I have walked, will send his angel with you*x* and make your journey a success, so that you can get a wife for my son from my own clan and from my father's family. 41Then, when you go to my clan, you will be released from my oath even if they refuse to give her to you—you will be released from my oath.' *y*

42"When I came to the spring today, I said, 'O Lord, God of my master Abraham, if you will, please grant success*z* to the journey on which I have come. 43See, I am standing beside this spring; *a* if a maiden comes out to draw water and I say to her, "Please let me drink a little water from your jar," *b* 44and if she says to me, "Drink, and I'll draw water for your camels too," let her be the one the Lord has chosen for my master's son.'

45"Before I finished praying in my heart, *c* Rebekah came out, with her jar on her shoulder. *d* She went down to the spring and drew water, and I said to her, 'Please give me a drink.' *e*

46"She quickly lowered her jar from her shoulder and said, 'Drink, and I'll water your camels too.' *f* So I drank, and she watered the camels also.

47"I asked her, 'Whose daughter are you?' *g*

"She said, 'The daughter of Bethuel son of Nahor, whom Milcah bore to him.' *h*

"Then I put the ring in her nose and the bracelets on her arms, *i* 48and I bowed down and worshiped the Lord. *j* I praised the Lord, the God of my master Abraham, who had led me on the right road to get the granddaughter of my master's brother for his son. *k* 49Now if you will show kindness and faithfulness*l* to my master, tell me; and if not, tell me, so I may know which way to turn."

50Laban and Bethuel answered, "This is from the Lord; *m* we can say nothing to you one way or the other. *n* 51Here is Rebekah; take her and go, and let her become the wife of your master's son, as the Lord has directed."

52When Abraham's servant heard what they said, he bowed down to the ground before the Lord. *o* 53Then the servant brought out gold and silver jewelry and articles of clothing and gave them to Rebekah; he also gave costly gifts*p* to her broth-

a 36 Or *his*

24:24
h ver 15

24:26
i ver 48,52; Ex 4:31
24:27
j Ex 18:10; Ru 4:14;
1Sa 25:32 *k* ver 49;
Ge 32:10; Ps 98:3
l ver 21
m ver 12,48

24:29
n ver 4; Ge 29:5,12,
13

24:31
o Ge 26:29;
Ru 3:10; Ps 115:15

24:32
p Ge 43:24;
Jdg 19:21

24:35
q ver 1 *r* Ge 13:2

24:36
s Ge 21:2,10
t Ge 25:5
24:37
u ver 3
24:38
v ver 4
24:39
w ver 5

24:40
x ver 7

24:41
y ver 8
24:42
z ver 12
24:43
a ver 13 *b* ver 14

24:45
c 1Sa 1:13 *d* ver 15
e ver 17

24:46
f ver 18-19
24:47
g ver 23 *h* ver 24
i Eze 16:11-12

24:48
j ver 26 *k* ver 27

24:49
l Ge 47:29; Jos 2:14

24:50
m Ps 118:23
n Ge 31:7,24,29,42

24:52
o ver 26
24:53
p ver 10,22

er and to her mother. ⁵⁴Then he and the men who were with him ate and drank and

24:54
q ver 56,59

spent the night there.

When they got up the next morning, he said, "Send me on my way^q to my master."

⁵⁵But her brother and her mother replied, "Let the girl remain with us ten days or so; then you^a may go."

⁵⁶But he said to them, "Do not detain me, now that the LORD has granted success to my journey. Send me on my way so I may go to my master."

⁵⁷Then they said, "Let's call the girl and ask her about it." ⁵⁸So they called Rebekah and asked her, "Will you go with this man?"

"I will go," she said.

24:59
r Ge 35:8

⁵⁹So they sent their sister Rebekah on her way, along with her nurse^r and Abraham's servant and his men. ⁶⁰And they blessed Rebekah and said to her,

24:60
s Ge 17:16
t Ge 22:17

"Our sister, may you increase
to thousands upon thousands;^s
may your offspring possess
the gates of their enemies."^t

24:62
u Ge 16:14; 25:11
v Ge 20:1
24:63
w Ps 1:2; 77:12;
119:15,27,48,97,
148; 143:5; 145:5

⁶¹Then Rebekah and her maids got ready and mounted their camels and went back with the man. So the servant took Rebekah and left.

⁶²Now Isaac had come from Beer Lahai Roi,^u for he was living in the Negev.^v ⁶³He went out to the field one evening to meditate,^{b w} and as he looked up, he saw camels approaching. ⁶⁴Rebekah also looked up and saw Isaac. She got down from her camel ⁶⁵and asked the servant, "Who is that man in the field coming to meet us?"

"He is my master," the servant answered. So she took her veil and covered herself.

24:67
x Ge 25:20
y Ge 29:18,20
z Ge 23:1-2

⁶⁶Then the servant told Isaac all he had done. ⁶⁷Isaac brought her into the tent of his mother Sarah, and he married Rebekah.^x So she became his wife, and he loved her;^y and Isaac was comforted after his mother's death.^z

The Death of Abraham

25:2
a 1Ch 1:32,33

25 Abraham took^c another wife, whose name was Keturah. ²She bore him Zimran, Jokshan, Medan, Midian, Ishbak and Shuah.^a ³Jokshan was the father of Sheba and Dedan; the descendants of Dedan were the Asshurites, the Letushites and the Leummites. ⁴The sons of Midian were Ephah, Epher, Hanoch, Abida and Eldaah. All these were descendants of Keturah.

25:5
b Ge 24:36

25:6
c Ge 22:24
d Ge 21:10,14

⁵Abraham left everything he owned to Isaac.^b ⁶But while he was still living, he gave gifts to the sons of his concubines^c and sent them away from his son Isaac^d to the land of the east.

25:8
e Ge 15:15 f ver 17;
Ge 35:29; 49:29,33
25:9
g Ge 35:29
h Ge 50:13
25:10
i Ge 23:16

⁷Altogether, Abraham lived a hundred and seventy-five years. ⁸Then Abraham breathed his last and died at a good old age,^e an old man and full of years; and he was gathered to his people.^f ⁹His sons Isaac and Ishmael buried him^g in the cave of Machpelah near Mamre, in the field of Ephron son of Zohar the Hittite,^h ¹⁰the field Abraham had bought from the Hittites.^{d i} There Abraham was buried with his

---

^a 55 Or she   ^b 63 The meaning of the Hebrew for this word is uncertain.   ^c 1 Or had taken   ^d 10 Or the sons of Heth

---

Genesis 25:1–11

Keturah may have come on the scene at an earlier time (e.g., between Ishmael and Isaac). The narrator picked up the detail here as an appendix to close out the issue of inheritance and other miscellaneous items connected to Abraham and the covenant. Isaac was to be the sole heir of the covenant, and verses 5 and 11, respectively, show Abraham's and God's blessing of Isaac. The in-between verses assure us that the other sons had been compensated and sent on their way.

Old Testament believers had little, if any, concept of an afterlife. So the clause "and [Abraham] was gathered to his people" may strike us as odd. This may have been a euphemistic way of talking about death, like "dust to dust, ashes to ashes." But given the knowledge about eternity we as Christians possess, it's also a beautiful figure of speech. What better way of describing our own deaths in Christ? At that defining moment he gathers us up in his arms and carries us to "our people," our glorified brothers and sisters in him (cf. Heb. 12:1, referring to those faith heroes listed in Heb. 11).

wife Sarah. [11]After Abraham's death, God blessed his son Isaac, who then lived near Beer Lahai Roi.[j]

Ishmael's Sons

[12]This is the account of Abraham's son Ishmael, whom Sarah's maidservant, Hagar[k] the Egyptian, bore to Abraham.[l]

[13]These are the names of the sons of Ishmael, listed in the order of their birth: Nebaioth the firstborn of Ishmael, Kedar, Adbeel, Mibsam, [14]Mishma, Dumah, Massa, [15]Hadad, Tema, Jetur, Naphish and Kedemah. [16]These were the sons of Ishmael, and these are the names of the twelve tribal rulers[m] according to their settlements and camps. [17]Altogether, Ishmael lived a hundred and thirty-seven years. He breathed his last and died, and he was gathered to his people.[n] [18]His descendants settled in the area from Havilah to Shur, near the border of Egypt, as you go toward Asshur. And they lived in hostility toward[a] all their brothers.[o]

Jacob and Esau

[19]This is the account of Abraham's son Isaac.

Abraham became the father of Isaac, [20]and Isaac was forty years old[p] when he married Rebekah[q] daughter of Bethuel the Aramean from Paddan Aram[b] and sister of Laban[r] the Aramean.

[21]Isaac prayed to the LORD on behalf of his wife, because she was barren. The LORD answered his prayer,[s] and his wife Rebekah became pregnant. [22]The babies jostled each other within her, and she said, "Why is this happening to me?" So she went to inquire of the LORD.[t]

[23]The LORD said to her,

"Two nations[u] are in your womb,
    and two peoples from within you will be separated;
one people will be stronger than the other,
    and the older will serve the younger.[v]"

[24]When the time came for her to give birth, there were twin boys in her womb. [25]The first to come out was red, and his whole body was like a hairy garment;[w] so they named him Esau.[c] [26]After this, his brother came out, with his hand grasping

---

a 18 Or *lived to the east of*   *b 20* That is, Northwest Mesopotamia   *c 25 Esau* may mean *hairy;* he was also called Edom, which means *red.*

25:11
j Ge 16:14

25:12
k Ge 16:1
l Ge 16:15

25:16
m Ge 17:20

25:17
n ver 8

25:18
o Ge 16:12

25:20
p ver 26; Ge 26:34
q Ge 24:67
r Ge 24:29

25:21
s 1Ch 5:20;
2Ch 33:13;
Ezr 8:23; Ps 127:3;
Ro 9:10
25:22
t 1Sa 9:9; 10:22

25:23
u Ge 17:4
v Ge 27:29,40;
Mal 1:3;
Ro 9:11-12*

25:25
w Ge 27:11

Genesis 25:12–18

The writer pursued one line (Ishmael's) and drew it to conclusion before coming back to the genealogy he was interested in following (Isaac's). In 16:12 the angel of the Lord had told Hagar that Ishmael would live in hostility to his brothers (see 25:18), and in 21:18 the angel of God had promised that Ishmael would become a great nation. Eight of his twelve sons appear again in Scripture, but only a few times each. The still existing tribes are mostly Bedouin and range the desert areas in Sinai, Arabia, and Syria.

This brief section isn't as interested in removing Ishmael from a position of competition (already done in ch. 21) as in showing that God kept his promises to him. Even in this, we see God as One who overcomes obstacles and fulfills promises. It's interesting that Ishmael and Isaac together buried Abraham, setting aside, at least temporarily, the hostility between them.

Do you believe that God leaves no "loose ends" as he weaves the complex tapestry of history? Or do you sometimes think he made a mistake in creating you? Every human life has a purpose in his plan—and, provided the individual makes a conscious decision to live as closely as possible within his will, a glorious future. There are no secondary characters in God's grand scheme.

Genesis 25:19–34

The "barrenness" obstacle/theme showed up again in this generation: Rebekah conceived but had a problem pregnancy. She inquired of the Lord whether the "jostling" was significant. God's response referred to her sons' descendants, not to the babies themselves. This neither excused Rebekah's preferential treatment of Jacob nor condemned Isaac's favoritism of Esau.

The birthright was the oldest son's share of the family's estate. In the ancient world, the firstborn typically received a double share of the inheritance. This would have been painful enough for a second son, but it must have been substantially more galling when the second-born was a twin, arriving only minutes "late."

25:26
x Hos 12:3
y Ge 27:36

25:27
z Ge 27:3,5
25:28
a Ge 27:19
b Ge 27:6

Esau's heel;[x] so he was named Jacob.[a][y] Isaac was sixty years old when Rebekah gave birth to them.

27The boys grew up, and Esau became a skillful hunter, a man of the open country,[z] while Jacob was a quiet man, staying among the tents. 28Isaac, who had a taste for wild game,[a] loved Esau, but Rebekah loved Jacob.[b]

29Once when Jacob was cooking some stew, Esau came in from the open country, famished. 30He said to Jacob, "Quick, let me have some of that red stew! I'm famished!" (That is why he was also called Edom.[b])

31Jacob replied, "First sell me your birthright."

32"Look, I am about to die," Esau said. "What good is the birthright to me?"

25:33
c Ge 27:36;
Heb 12:16

33But Jacob said, "Swear to me first." So he swore an oath to him, selling his birthright[c] to Jacob.

34Then Jacob gave Esau some bread and some lentil stew. He ate and drank, and then got up and left.

So Esau despised his birthright.

26:1
d Ge 12:10
e Ge 20:1

26:2
f Ge 12:7; 17:1;
18:1 g Ge 12:1

26:3
h Ge 20:1; 28:15
i Ge 12:2; 22:16-18
j Ge 12:7; 13:15;
15:18

26:4
k Ge 15:5; 22:17;
Ex 32:13 l Ge 12:3;
22:18; Gal 3:8

26:5
m Ge 22:16

26:7
n Ge 12:13;
20:2,12;
Pr 29:25

Isaac and Abimelech

26 Now there was a famine in the land[d]—besides the earlier famine of Abraham's time—and Isaac went to Abimelech king of the Philistines in Gerar.[e] 2The LORD appeared[f] to Isaac and said, "Do not go down to Egypt; live in the land where I tell you to live.[g] 3Stay in this land for a while,[h] and I will be with you and will bless you.[i] For to you and your descendants I will give all these lands[j] and will confirm the oath I swore to your father Abraham. 4I will make your descendants as numerous as the stars in the sky[k] and will give them all these lands, and through your offspring[c] all nations on earth will be blessed,[l] 5because Abraham obeyed me[m] and kept my requirements, my commands, my decrees and my laws." 6So Isaac stayed in Gerar.

7When the men of that place asked him about his wife, he said, "She is my sister,[n]" because he was afraid to say, "She is my wife." He thought, "The men of this place might kill me on account of Rebekah, because she is beautiful."

8When Isaac had been there a long time, Abimelech king of the Philistines looked down from a window and saw Isaac caressing his wife Rebekah. 9So Abimelech summoned Isaac and said, "She is really your wife! Why did you say, 'She is my sister'?"

Isaac answered him, "Because I thought I might lose my life on account of her."

26:10
o Ge 20:9

10Then Abimelech said, "What is this you have done to us?[o] One of the men might well have slept with your wife, and you would have brought guilt upon us."

26:11
p Ps 105:15

11So Abimelech gave orders to all the people: "Anyone who molests[p] this man or his wife shall surely be put to death."

a 26 Jacob means he grasps the heel (figuratively, he deceives).   b 30 Edom means red.   c 4 Or seed

---

The verb translated "despised" doesn't reflect Esau's feelings about the birthright but the low value he placed on it. Look at our use of the word *contempt*, which can refer to an emotion or mood but also applies in a legal context ("contempt of court"). If Esau so lightly esteemed his material birthright, what reason was there to believe he would value his spiritual heritage as conveyed by the covenant?

📖 Christians who abandon or neglect their spiritual heritage can waste their years, missing out on blessings, spiritual growth, and opportunities for ministry and service. Even if they repent, their choices may have brought consequences they can't undo: a criminal record, an unbelieving spouse, financial ruin, health ravaged by *self-destructive habits*, children so influenced by their godless example that their course in life is set. How sad to permanently forfeit God's rich blessings for something temporary!

Genesis 26:1–35

🕮 The author used Genesis 26, sandwiched between unsavory stories about Jacob and Esau, to put the activities and attitudes of the brothers in perspective. The wife-sister episode here didn't constitute the obstacle to the covenant it did in Genesis 12 and 20; it was simply a masquerade. The story about the wells shows resolution of conflict resulting from God's blessing. Both themes will be important in coming chapters.

📖 This chapter illustrates how God is able to accomplish his plan, preserve his covenant, and bring blessing in spite of masquerades, jealousy, hostility, and conflict. Genesis 26 hints that everything will work out satisfactorily for the covenant, even in the hands of the likes of Esau and Jacob. Similarly, God can and does work despite and through our weaknesses. What examples can you cite in your own life of God's working in this way?

12Isaac planted crops in that land and the same year reaped a hundredfold, because the LORD blessed him.*q* 13The man became rich, and his wealth continued to grow until he became very wealthy.*r* 14He had so many flocks and herds and servants*s* that the Philistines envied him.*t* 15So all the wells*u* that his father's servants had dug in the time of his father Abraham, the Philistines stopped up,*v* filling them with earth.

16Then Abimelech said to Isaac, "Move away from us; you have become too powerful for us.*w*"

17So Isaac moved away from there and encamped in the Valley of Gerar and settled there. 18Isaac reopened the wells*x* that had been dug in the time of his father Abraham, which the Philistines had stopped up after Abraham died, and he gave them the same names his father had given them.

19Isaac's servants dug in the valley and discovered a well of fresh water there. 20But the herdsmen of Gerar quarreled with Isaac's herdsmen and said, "The water is ours!"*y* So he named the well Esek,*a* because they disputed with him. 21Then they dug another well, but they quarreled over that one also; so he named it Sitnah.*b* 22He moved on from there and dug another well, and no one quarreled over it. He named it Rehoboth,*c* saying, "Now the LORD has given us room and we will flourish*z* in the land."

23From there he went up to Beersheba. 24That night the LORD appeared to him and said, "I am the God of your father Abraham.*a* Do not be afraid,*b* for I am with you; I will bless you and will increase the number of your descendants*c* for the sake of my servant Abraham."*d*

25Isaac built an altar*e* there and called on the name of the LORD. There he pitched his tent, and there his servants dug a well.

26Meanwhile, Abimelech had come to him from Gerar, with Ahuzzath his personal adviser and Phicol the commander of his forces.*f* 27Isaac asked them, "Why have you come to me, since you were hostile to me and sent me away?*g*"

28They answered, "We saw clearly that the LORD was with you;*h* so we said, 'There ought to be a sworn agreement between us'—between us and you. Let us make a treaty with you 29that you will do us no harm, just as we did not molest you but

---

a 20 Esek means dispute.   *b 21 Sitnah means opposition.*   *c 22 Rehoboth means room.*

26:12
q ver 3; Job 42:12
26:13
r Pr 10:22
26:14
s Ge 24:36
t Ge 37:11
26:15
u Ge 21:30
v Ge 21:25
26:16
w Ex 1:9

26:18
x Ge 21:30

26:20
y Ge 21:25

26:22
z Ge 17:6; Ex 1:7

26:24
a Ge 24:12; Ex 3:6
b Ge 15:1 *c* ver 4
d Ge 17:7

26:25
e Ge 12:7,8;
13:4,18; Ps 116:17

26:26
f Ge 21:22
26:27
g ver 16
26:28
h Ge 21:22

Snapshots

  26:19–22

Water for Joateca

For Joateca municipality in El Salvador, water is a scarce commodity. Rufino, fifty-eight, used to walk two kilometers to collect drinking water from a small spring: "I would wake up every day at one A.M. to go to the well, because if I got there after three A.M., there would be a long line of people waiting." Bathing and washing clothes were more problematic, requiring a ten-kilometer trek to the nearest creek.

With the help of a humanitarian aid organization, a water association was formed in 1997. A small spring was donated on a plot of land with a watershed. Pipes were installed to a water storage tank and from there to every house.

But the flow was insufficient, necessitating rationing of water. The land where it was located was arid and sloped, raising concerns about erosion and lack of water infiltration. The work to remedy these issues took more than five years. Every Saturday since 1998, residents have made themselves available to provide maintenance. A year ago, the Joateca City Council declared the land a protected area, prohibiting the cutting of trees in the zone and permitting natural regeneration of the forest.

> "**If** I got [to the spring] after three A.M., there would be a long line of people waiting."

26:29
i Ge 24:31;
Ps 115:15
26:30
j Ge 19:3
26:31
k Ge 21:31

always treated you well and sent you away in peace. And now you are blessed by the LORD." [i]

[30] Isaac then made a feast[j] for them, and they ate and drank. [31] Early the next morning the men swore an oath[k] to each other. Then Isaac sent them on their way, and they left him in peace.

26:33
l Ge 21:14
26:34
m Ge 25:20
n Ge 28:9; 36:2

26:35
o Ge 27:46

[32] That day Isaac's servants came and told him about the well they had dug. They said, "We've found water!" [33] He called it Shibah, [a] and to this day the name of the town has been Beersheba. [b][l]

[34] When Esau was forty years old,[m] he married Judith daughter of Beeri the Hittite, and also Basemath daughter of Elon the Hittite.[n] [35] They were a source of grief to Isaac and Rebekah.[o]

Jacob Gets Isaac's Blessing

27:1
p Ge 48:10; 1Sa 3:2
q Ge 25:25

27 When Isaac was old and his eyes were so weak that he could no longer see,[p] he called for Esau his older son[q] and said to him, "My son."

"Here I am," he answered.

27:2
r Ge 47:29
27:3
s Ge 25:27

[2] Isaac said, "I am now an old man and don't know the day of my death.[r] [3] Now then, get your weapons—your quiver and bow—and go out to the open country[s] to hunt some wild game for me. [4] Prepare me the kind of tasty food I like and bring it to me to eat, so that I may give you my blessing[t] before I die."

27:4
t ver 10,25,31;
Ge 49:28; Dt 33:1;
Heb 11:20
27:6
u Ge 25:28

[5] Now Rebekah was listening as Isaac spoke to his son Esau. When Esau left for the open country to hunt game and bring it back, [6] Rebekah said to her son Jacob,[u] "Look, I overheard your father say to your brother Esau, [7] 'Bring me some game and prepare me some tasty food to eat, so that I may give you my blessing in the presence of the LORD before I die.' [8] Now, my son, listen carefully and do what I tell you:[v]

27:8
v ver 13,43

[9] Go out to the flock and bring me two choice young goats, so I can prepare some tasty food for your father, just the way he likes it. [10] Then take it to your father to eat, so that he may give you his blessing before he dies."

27:11
w Ge 25:25

[11] Jacob said to Rebekah his mother, "But my brother Esau is a hairy man,[w] and I'm a man with smooth skin. [12] What if my father touches me?[x] I would appear to be tricking him and would bring down a curse on myself rather than a blessing."

27:12
x ver 22
27:13
y Mt 27:25 *z* ver 8

[13] His mother said to him, "My son, let the curse fall on me.[y] Just do what I say;[z] go and get them for me."

[14] So he went and got them and brought them to his mother, and she prepared some tasty food, just the way his father liked it. [15] Then Rebekah took the best clothes[a] of Esau her older son, which she had in the house, and put them on her younger son Jacob. [16] She also covered his hands and the smooth part of his neck with the goatskins. [17] Then she handed to her son Jacob the tasty food and the bread she had made.

27:15
a ver 27

[18] He went to his father and said, "My father."

"Yes, my son," he answered. "Who is it?"

---

[a] 33 *Shibah* can mean *oath* or *seven.*   [b] 33 *Beersheba* can mean *well of the oath* or *well of seven.*

Genesis 27:1–40

🔍 Isaac was planning to give the patriarchal blessing, not to be confused with the inheritance (birthright; see Gen. 25). This blessing had nothing to do with possessions or birth order. It also differed from the covenant blessing, though there may have been overlap. The covenant blessing would be passed on to Jacob by Isaac in 28:3–4 and later confirmed by God (e.g., 28:13–15).

What first strikes us as Rebekah's scheme unfolds is its sheer improbability. We must conclude that all of Isaac's senses were dulled, including his common sense and reasoning ability. Jacob again exploited the vulnerability of a relative: Esau was care-less (didn't care about his birthright), and Isaac was sense-less.

A second unusual twist comes with Rebekah's response to Jacob's qualms about being discovered (vv. 11–13). Since a blessing wasn't transferable, why should a curse be? Rebekah was probably referring to the consequences of the curse rather than to the curse itself.

📖 Too many families in our nations and churches are paralyzed by conflict and dysfunction. Brothers and sisters are at odds; children rebel; in-laws find fault; wives nag; husbands disengage. Conflicts run so deep and have existed for so long that they may seem beyond resolution. But God can resolve even the most entrenched and complex discord. Ask him today to work in your relationships. Be prepared to be the one through whom he works reconciliation.

19Jacob said to his father, "I am Esau your firstborn. I have done as you told me.
Please sit up and eat some of my game so that you may give me your blessing."[b]
20Isaac asked his son, "How did you find it so quickly, my son?"
"The LORD your God gave me success,[c]" he replied.
21Then Isaac said to Jacob, "Come near so I can touch you,[d] my son, to know
whether you really are my son Esau or not."
22Jacob went close to his father Isaac, who touched him and said, "The voice is
the voice of Jacob, but the hands are the hands of Esau." 23He did not recognize
him, for his hands were hairy like those of his brother Esau;[e] so he blessed him.
24"Are you really my son Esau?" he asked.
"I am," he replied.
25Then he said, "My son, bring me some of your game to eat, so that I may give
you my blessing."[f]
Jacob brought it to him and he ate; and he brought some wine and he drank.
26Then his father Isaac said to him, "Come here, my son, and kiss me."
27So he went to him and kissed him[g]. When Isaac caught the smell of his
clothes,[h] he blessed him and said,

"Ah, the smell of my son
is like the smell of a field
that the LORD has blessed.[i]
28May God give you of heaven's dew[j]
and of earth's richness[k]—
an abundance of grain and new wine.[l]
29May nations serve you
and peoples bow down to you.[m]
Be lord over your brothers,
and may the sons of your mother bow down to you.[n]
May those who curse you be cursed
and those who bless you be blessed.[o]"

30After Isaac finished blessing him and Jacob had scarcely left his father's presence, his brother Esau came in from hunting. 31He too prepared some tasty food
and brought it to his father. Then he said to him, "My father, sit up and eat some
of my game, so that you may give me your blessing."[p]
32His father Isaac asked him, "Who are you?"[q]
"I am your son," he answered, "your firstborn, Esau."
33Isaac trembled violently and said, "Who was it, then, that hunted game and
brought it to me? I ate it just before you came and I blessed him—and indeed he
will be blessed![r]"
34When Esau heard his father's words, he burst out with a loud and bitter cry[s] and
said to his father, "Bless me—me too, my father!"
35But he said, "Your brother came deceitfully[t] and took your blessing."
36Esau said, "Isn't he rightly named Jacob[a]?[u] He has deceived me these two
times: He took my birthright,[v] and now he's taken my blessing!" Then he asked,
"Haven't you reserved any blessing for me?"
37Isaac answered Esau, "I have made him lord over you and have made all his relatives his servants, and I have sustained him with grain and new wine.[w] So what can
I possibly do for you, my son?"
38Esau said to his father, "Do you have only one blessing, my father? Bless me
too, my father!" Then Esau wept aloud.[x]
39His father Isaac answered him,

"Your dwelling will be
away from the earth's richness,
away from the dew[y] of heaven above.
40You will live by the sword

27:19 [b] ver 4
27:20 [c] Ge 24:12
27:21 [d] ver 12
27:23 [e] ver 16
27:25 [f] ver 4
27:27 [g] Heb 11:20 [h] SS 4:11 [i] Ps 65:9-13
27:28 [j] Dt 33:13 [k] ver 39 [l] Ge 45:18; Nu 18:12; Dt 33:28
27:29 [m] Isa 45:14,23; 49:7,23 [n] Ge 9:25; 25:23; 37:7 [o] Ge 12:3; Nu 24:9; Zep 2:8
27:31 [p] ver 4
27:32 [q] ver 18
27:33 [r] ver 29; Ge 28:3,4; Ro 11:29
27:34 [s] Heb 12:17
27:35 [t] Jer 9:4; 12:6
27:36 [u] Ge 25:26 [v] Ge 25:33
27:37 [w] ver 28
27:38 [x] Heb 12:17
27:39 [y] ver 28

[a] 36 *Jacob* means *he grasps the heel* (figuratively, *he deceives*).

27:40
z 2Sa 8:14
a Ge 25:23
b 2Ki 8:20-22

and you will serve[z] your brother. [a]
But when you grow restless,
    you will throw his yoke
    from off your neck. [b]"

27:41
c Ge 37:4
d Ge 32:11
e Ge 50:4,10
f Ob 1:10

Jacob Flees to Laban

41Esau held a grudge[c] against Jacob[d] because of the blessing his father had given him. He said to himself, "The days of mourning[e] for my father are near; then I will kill my brother Jacob."[f]

42When Rebekah was told what her older son Esau had said, she sent for her younger son Jacob and said to him, "Your brother Esau is consoling himself with the thought of killing you. 43Now then, my son, do what I say: [g] Flee at once to my brother Laban[h] in Haran. [i] 44Stay with him for a while[j] until your brother's fury subsides. 45When your brother is no longer angry with you and forgets what you did to him, [k] I'll send word for you to come back from there. Why should I lose both of you in one day?"

27:43
g ver 8 h Ge 24:29
i Ge 11:31
27:44
j Ge 31:38,41
27:45
k ver 35

46Then Rebekah said to Isaac, "I'm disgusted with living because of these Hittite women. If Jacob takes a wife from among the women of this land, from Hittite women like these, my life will not be worth living."[l]

27:46
l Ge 26:35

28:1
m Ge 24:3
28:2
n Ge 25:20
28:3
o Ge 17:1 p Ge 17:6

28 So Isaac called for Jacob and blessed[a] him and commanded him: "Do not marry a Canaanite woman. [m] 2Go at once to Paddan Aram, [b] to the house of your mother's father Bethuel. [n] Take a wife for yourself there, from among the daughters of Laban, your mother's brother. 3May God Almighty[c][o] bless you and make you fruitful[p] and increase your numbers until you become a community of peoples. 4May he give you and your descendants the blessing given to Abraham, [q] so that you may take possession of the land where you now live as an alien, [r] the land God gave to Abraham." 5Then Isaac sent Jacob on his way, and he went to Paddan Aram, [s] to Laban son of Bethuel the Aramean, the brother of Rebekah, [t] who was the mother of Jacob and Esau.

28:4
q Ge 12:2,3
r Ge 17:8

28:5
s Hos 12:12
t Ge 24:29

6Now Esau learned that Isaac had blessed Jacob and had sent him to Paddan Aram to take a wife from there, and that when he blessed him he commanded him, "Do not marry a Canaanite woman," [u] 7and that Jacob had obeyed his father and mother and had gone to Paddan Aram. 8Esau then realized how displeasing the Canaanite women[v] were to his father Isaac; [w] 9so he went to Ishmael and married Mahalath, the sister of Nebaioth[x] and daughter of Ishmael son of Abraham, in addition to the wives he already had. [y]

28:6
u ver 1

28:8
v Ge 24:3
w Ge 26:35
28:9
x Ge 25:13
y Ge 26:34

Jacob's Dream at Bethel

28:10
z Ge 11:31

10Jacob left Beersheba and set out for Haran. [z] 11When he reached a certain place, he stopped for the night because the sun had set. Taking one of the stones there, he put it under his head and lay down to sleep. 12He had a dream[a] in which he saw a stairway[d] resting on the earth, with its top reaching to heaven, and the angels of God were ascending and descending on it. [b] 13There above it[e] stood the LORD, [c] and

28:12
a Ge 20:3 b Jn 1:51

28:13
c Ge 12:7; 35:7,9;
48:3

a 1 Or greeted   b 2 That is, Northwest Mesopotamia; also in verses 5, 6 and 7   c 3 Hebrew El-Shaddai   d 12 Or ladder   e 13 Or There beside him

---

Genesis 27:41—28:9

Before Jacob's departure, Isaac conferred on him the covenant blessing—the only place this occurred in Genesis. The text doesn't say that Isaac recognized his misplaced favoritism of Esau or that Jacob alone would play a role in God's covenant plan. Note, however, that Isaac pronounced blessings, not promises. The promises were up to God (28:13–15).

Jacob didn't escape "without a scratch." He avoided home for 20 years and never saw his mother again. He suffered appropriate consequences, but God spared him

from the results that would have come had the scheme failed. The consequences of its *success* were worse for Jacob personally—but more productive in the long run for his life.

When has God allowed you success in spite of your sin because he had a later, greater lesson to teach you? His timing is strategic. We don't experience an immediate response from God every time we sin. But at the proper time he will bring each sin to light to serve his purposes in our lives and in his plan. Sin's benefits are short-lived.

he said: "I am the LORD, the God of your father Abraham and the God of Isaac.*d* I will give you and your descendants the land*e* on which you are lying. 14Your descendants will be like the dust of the earth, and you*f* will spread out to the west and to the east, to the north and to the south.*g* All peoples on earth will be blessed through you and your offspring.*h* 15I am with you*i* and will watch over you*j* wherever you go, and I will bring you back to this land. I will not leave you*k* until I have done what I have promised you."*l*

16When Jacob awoke from his sleep, he thought, "Surely the LORD is in this place, and I was not aware of it." 17He was afraid and said, "How awesome is this place!*m* This is none other than the house of God; this is the gate of heaven."

18Early the next morning Jacob took the stone he had placed under his head and set it up as a pillar*n* and poured oil on top of it.*o* 19He called that place Bethel,*a* though the city used to be called Luz.*p*

20Then Jacob made a vow,*q* saying, "If God will be with me and will watch over me*r* on this journey I am taking and will give me food to eat and clothes to wear 21so that I return safely*s* to my father's house, then the LORD*b* will be my God*t* 22and*c* this stone that I have set up as a pillar will be God's house,*u* and of all that you give me I will give you a tenth.*v*"

Jacob Arrives in Paddan Aram

29 Then Jacob continued on his journey and came to the land of the eastern peoples.*w* 2There he saw a well in the field, with three flocks of sheep lying near it because the flocks were watered from that well. The stone over the mouth of the well was large. 3When all the flocks were gathered there, the shepherds would roll the stone away from the well's mouth and water the sheep. Then they would return the stone to its place over the mouth of the well.

4Jacob asked the shepherds, "My brothers, where are you from?"

"We're from Haran,*x*" they replied.

5He said to them, "Do you know Laban, Nahor's grandson?"

"Yes, we know him," they answered.

6Then Jacob asked them, "Is he well?"

"Yes, he is," they said, "and here comes his daughter Rachel with the sheep."

7"Look," he said, "the sun is still high; it is not time for the flocks to be gathered. Water the sheep and take them back to pasture."

---

a 19 Bethel means house of God.   *b* 20,21 Or Since God . . . father's house, the LORD   *c* 21,22 Or house, and the LORD will be my God, 22then

28:13
d Ge 26:24
e Ge 13:15; 35:12
28:14
f Ge 26:4
g Ge 13:14
h Ge 12:3; 18:18; 22:18; Gal 3:8
28:15
i Ge 26:3; 48:21
j Nu 6:24;
Ps 121:5,7-8
k Dt 31:6,8
l Nu 23:19

28:17
m Ex 3:5; Jos 5:15

28:18
n Ge 35:14
o Lev 8:11
28:19
p Jdg 1:23,26
28:20
q Ge 31:13;
Jdg 11:30; 2Sa 15:8
r ver 15
28:21
s Jdg 11:31
t Dt 26:17
28:22
u Ge 35:7,14
v Ge 14:20;
Lev 27:30

29:1
w Jdg 6:3,33

29:4
x Ge 28:10

Genesis 28:10–22

Jacob made a promise to God—with strings attached. If Providence smiled on him, he would recognize God's hand behind it, guiding his destiny. Jacob's vow looked suspiciously like a bargain. He demanded benefits up front, before he delivered on anything. God had stated his intentions, but Jacob demanded proof. He took on the role of tester, putting conditions on God before God could become the "beneficiary" of his promises. This was an intolerable situation that would have to be fixed before God could proceed with Jacob. Jacob was a "work in progress"—another of God's salvage projects.

Too often our requests of God focus on our own material gain, recovery, success, pleasant circumstances, and the like. How do you think God might respond if more of them were to zero in on spiritual gain—a quest for stronger faith, purer thoughts, better attitudes, greater patience, love for the unappealing, sensitivity to his leading, increased commitment to his service? Such requests will achieve his purpose in helping us come to an understanding of our true nature and dependence on him.

Genesis 29:1–14

Jacob's warm greeting and the excitement in the family were understandable; there may have been no news of Rebekah for many decades. It's doubtful that Laban thought right away of profiting from Jacob, but we have a hint of what was to come when he commented that Jacob was his own flesh and blood. The reader has gotten a taste of Jacob's nature and rightly suspects Laban is "cut from the same cloth."

Jacob was no longer an impulsive young man. He was approximately the age Abraham had been when he had responded to God's call to leave his homeland. Sometimes we are prone to give up on ourselves or others as we age. The time spans in Genesis easily escape our notice, but awareness of them may help us to appreciate God's patience in dealing with his flawed people. From God's perspective it's never too late for us to defeat habits and grow spiritually mature. What nonproductive habits in your life have become more entrenched over time? If you have given up working on them, why not invite the Spirit now to help you?

29:9
y Ex 2:16

29:10
z Ex 2:17
29:11
a Ge 33:4
29:12
b Ge 13:8; 14:14,16
c Ge 24:28
29:13
d Ge 24:29

29:14
e Ge 2:23; Jdg 9:2;
2Sa 19:12-13

29:18
f Hos 12:12

29:20
g SS 8:7; Hos 12:12

29:21
h Jdg 15:1
29:22
i Jdg 14:10;
Jn 2:1-2

29:25
j Ge 12:18
k Ge 27:36

29:27
l Jdg 14:12

29:29
m Ge 30:3
n Ge 16:1

29:30
o ver 16 p Ge 31:41

29:31
q Dt 21:15-17
r Ge 11:30; 30:1;
Ps 127:3

8 "We can't," they replied, "until all the flocks are gathered and the stone has been rolled away from the mouth of the well. Then we will water the sheep."

9 While he was still talking with them, Rachel came with her father's sheep, y for she was a shepherdess. 10 When Jacob saw Rachel daughter of Laban, his mother's brother, and Laban's sheep, he went over and rolled the stone away from the mouth of the well and watered his uncle's sheep. z 11 Then Jacob kissed Rachel and began to weep aloud. a 12 He had told Rachel that he was a relative b of her father and a son of Rebekah. So she ran and told her father. c

13 As soon as Laban d heard the news about Jacob, his sister's son, he hurried to meet him. He embraced him and kissed him and brought him to his home, and there Jacob told him all these things. 14 Then Laban said to him, "You are my own flesh and blood." e

Jacob Marries Leah and Rachel

After Jacob had stayed with him for a whole month, 15 Laban said to him, "Just because you are a relative of mine, should you work for me for nothing? Tell me what your wages should be."

16 Now Laban had two daughters; the name of the older was Leah, and the name of the younger was Rachel. 17 Leah had weak a eyes, but Rachel was lovely in form, and beautiful. 18 Jacob was in love with Rachel and said, "I'll work for you seven years in return for your younger daughter Rachel." f

19 Laban said, "It's better that I give her to you than to some other man. Stay here with me." 20 So Jacob served seven years to get Rachel, but they seemed like only a few days to him because of his love for her. g

21 Then Jacob said to Laban, "Give me my wife. My time is completed, and I want to lie with her. h"

22 So Laban brought together all the people of the place and gave a feast. i 23 But when evening came, he took his daughter Leah and gave her to Jacob, and Jacob lay with her. 24 And Laban gave his servant girl Zilpah to his daughter as her maidservant.

25 When morning came, there was Leah! So Jacob said to Laban, "What is this you have done to me? j I served you for Rachel, didn't I? Why have you deceived me? k"

26 Laban replied, "It is not our custom here to give the younger daughter in marriage before the older one. 27 Finish this daughter's bridal week; l then we will give you the younger one also, in return for another seven years of work."

28 And Jacob did so. He finished the week with Leah, and then Laban gave him his daughter Rachel to be his wife. 29 Laban gave his servant girl Bilhah m to his daughter Rachel as her maidservant. n 30 Jacob lay with Rachel also, and he loved Rachel more than Leah. o And he worked for Laban another seven years. p

Jacob's Children

31 When the LORD saw that Leah was not loved, q he opened her womb, r but Rachel was barren. 32 Leah became pregnant and gave birth to a son. She named him

---

a 17 Or delicate

Genesis 29:15–30

The possibility that Jacob was drunk may account for his inability to recognize the substitution of Leah for Rachel. The text offers only a summary statement of what must have been a distraught response from him the morning after. Jacob ended up obligating himself to seven more years of labor, though he was allowed to marry Rachel in short order. The scene was set for the favoritism that would play a major role in the next generation.

How much did the women know about this plot? To what extent were they willing accomplices? How did they feel about it? Why did Laban do it? The text doesn't answer our questions, but it does demonstrate how Jacob was beginning to suffer the consequences of his own behavior. He was being treated the same way he had treated others. This reversal is crucial to our understanding this section.

"Be sure that your sin will find you out" is a good Old Testament caution (Num. 32:23). Paul phrased it, "A man reaps what he sows" (Gal. 6:7). This isn't a guarantee that every person will receive in this life an exact reward or punishment for his or her behavior. But God's nature assures us that our behavior will have consequences as our destiny unfolds. Identify some ways in which you have seen this borne out in your life.

Reuben,[a] for she said, "It is because the LORD has seen my misery.[s] Surely my husband will love me now."

[33]She conceived again, and when she gave birth to a son she said, "Because the LORD heard that I am not loved, he gave me this one too." So she named him Simeon.[b][t]

[34]Again she conceived, and when she gave birth to a son she said, "Now at last my husband will become attached to me,[u] because I have borne him three sons." So he was named Levi.[c][v]

[35]She conceived again, and when she gave birth to a son she said, "This time I will praise the LORD." So she named him Judah.[d][w] Then she stopped having children.

30 When Rachel saw that she was not bearing Jacob any children,[x] she became jealous of her sister.[y] So she said to Jacob, "Give me children, or I'll die!"

[2]Jacob became angry with her and said, "Am I in the place of God, who has kept you from having children?"[z]

[3]Then she said, "Here is Bilhah, my maidservant. Sleep with her so that she can bear children for me and that through her I too can build a family."[a]

[4]So she gave him her servant Bilhah as a wife.[b] Jacob slept with her,[c] [5]and she became pregnant and bore him a son. [6]Then Rachel said, "God has vindicated me;[d] he has listened to my plea and given me a son." Because of this she named him Dan.[e][e]

[7]Rachel's servant Bilhah conceived again and bore Jacob a second son. [8]Then Rachel said, "I have had a great struggle with my sister, and I have won."[f] So she named him Naphtali.[f][g]

[9]When Leah saw that she had stopped having children, she took her maidservant Zilpah and gave her to Jacob as a wife.[h] [10]Leah's servant Zilpah bore Jacob a son. [11]Then Leah said, "What good fortune!"[g] So she named him Gad.[h][i]

[12]Leah's servant Zilpah bore Jacob a second son. [13]Then Leah said, "How happy I am! The women will call me[j] happy."[k] So she named him Asher.[i][l]

[14]During wheat harvest, Reuben went out into the fields and found some mandrake plants,[m] which he brought to his mother Leah. Rachel said to Leah, "Please give me some of your son's mandrakes."

[15]But she said to her, "Wasn't it enough[n] that you took away my husband? Will you take my son's mandrakes too?"

"Very well," Rachel said, "he can sleep with you tonight in return for your son's mandrakes."

[16]So when Jacob came in from the fields that evening, Leah went out to meet him. "You must sleep with me," she said. "I have hired you with my son's mandrakes." So he slept with her that night.

[17]God listened to Leah,[o] and she became pregnant and bore Jacob a fifth son. [18]Then Leah said, "God has rewarded me for giving my maidservant to my husband." So she named him Issachar.[j][p]

---

[a] 32 Reuben sounds like the Hebrew for he has seen my misery; the name means see, a son.
[b] 33 Simeon probably means one who hears.   [c] 34 Levi sounds like and may be derived from the Hebrew for attached.   [d] 35 Judah sounds like and may be derived from the Hebrew for praise.
[e] 6 Dan here means he has vindicated.   [f] 8 Naphtali means my struggle.   [g] 11 Or "A troop is coming!"   [h] 11 Gad can mean good fortune or a troop.   [i] 13 Asher means happy.   [j] 18 Issachar sounds like the Hebrew for reward.

29:32
[s] Ge 16:11; 31:42; Ex 4:31; Dt 26:7; Ps 25:18

29:33
[t] Ge 34:25; 49:5

29:34
[u] Ge 30:20; 1Sa 1:2-4
[v] Ge 49:5-7

29:35
[w] Ge 49:8; Mt 1:2-3
30:1
[x] Ge 29:31; 1Sa 1:5-6
[y] Lev 18:18

30:2
[z] Ge 16:2; 20:18; 29:31
30:3
[a] Ge 16:2
30:4
[b] ver 9,18
[c] Ge 16:3-4
30:6
[d] Ps 35:24; 43:1; La 3:59
[e] Ge 49:16-17

30:8
[f] Hos 12:3-4
[g] Ge 49:21

30:9
[h] ver 4
30:11
[i] Ge 49:19
30:13
[j] Ps 127:3
[k] Pr 31:28; Lk 1:48
[l] Ge 49:20

30:14
[m] SS 7:13

30:15
[n] Nu 16:9,13

30:17
[o] Ge 25:21

30:18
[p] Ge 49:14

Genesis 29:31—30:24

Abraham had responded to Sarah's barrenness with patient faith and Isaac to Rebekah's with prayer. Given the context of tension, conflict, and jealousy, it's no surprise that Rachel's infertility occasioned angry frustration. As had Sarah before her, Rachel encouraged Jacob to resort to her handmaid as a surrogate to provide a child from their marriage.

Why is the text so interested in Leah's status as the unloved wife? In this we find a new level of conflict. Not only do we see Leah unfavored by Jacob; we see Rachel "unfavored" by God (reflected in her barrenness). This in turn would lead to another conflict (30:8). In the next generation favoritism would become central to the relationship between Joseph and his brothers.

God's covenant people aren't exempt from rivalry and discord. But the Genesis story shows God as the One who resolves discord—a lesson we need desperately to learn. What conflicts are negatively affecting your life at this point? What would it take to resolve them?

¹⁹Leah conceived again and bore Jacob a sixth son. ²⁰Then Leah said, "God has presented me with a precious gift. This time my husband will treat me with honor, because I have borne him six sons." So she named him Zebulun. ^{a q}

²¹Some time later she gave birth to a daughter and named her Dinah.

²²Then God remembered Rachel;^r he listened to her and opened her womb.^s ²³She became pregnant and gave birth to a son^t and said, "God has taken away my disgrace."^u ²⁴She named him Joseph,^{b v} and said, "May the Lord add to me another son."^w

Jacob's Flocks Increase

²⁵After Rachel gave birth to Joseph, Jacob said to Laban, "Send me on my way^x so I can go back to my own homeland. ²⁶Give me my wives and children, for whom I have served you,^y and I will be on my way. You know how much work I've done for you."

²⁷But Laban said to him, "If I have found favor in your eyes, please stay. I have learned by divination that^c the Lord has blessed me because of you."^z ²⁸He added, "Name your wages,^a and I will pay them."

²⁹Jacob said to him, "You know how I have worked for you^b and how your livestock has fared under my care.^c ³⁰The little you had before I came has increased greatly, and the Lord has blessed you wherever I have been. But now, when may I do something for my own household?^d"

³¹"What shall I give you?" he asked.

"Don't give me anything," Jacob replied. "But if you will do this one thing for me, I will go on tending your flocks and watching over them: ³²Let me go through all your flocks today and remove from them every speckled or spotted sheep, every dark-colored lamb and every spotted or speckled goat.^e They will be my wages. ³³And my honesty will testify for me in the future, whenever you check on the wages you have paid me. Any goat in my possession that is not speckled or spotted, or any lamb that is not dark-colored, will be considered stolen."

³⁴"Agreed," said Laban. "Let it be as you have said." ³⁵That same day he removed all the male goats that were streaked or spotted, and all the speckled or spotted female goats (all that had white on them) and all the dark-colored lambs, and he placed them in the care of his sons.^f ³⁶Then he put a three-day journey between himself and Jacob, while Jacob continued to tend the rest of Laban's flocks.

³⁷Jacob, however, took fresh-cut branches from poplar, almond and plane trees and made white stripes on them by peeling the bark and exposing the white inner wood of the branches. ³⁸Then he placed the peeled branches in all the watering troughs, so that they would be directly in front of the flocks when they came to

---

^a 20 *Zebulun* probably means *honor.*   ^b 24 *Joseph* means *may he add.*   ^c 27 Or possibly *have become rich and*

Cross-references

30:20 ^q Ge 35:23; 49:13; Mt 4:13

30:22 ^r Ge 8:1; 1Sa 1:19-20 ^s Ge 29:31

30:23 ^t ver 6 ^u Isa 4:1; Lk 1:25

30:24 ^v Ge 35:24; 37:2; 39:1; 49:22-26 ^w Ge 35:17

30:25 ^x Ge 24:54

30:26 ^y Ge 29:20,30; Hos 12:12

30:27 ^z Ge 26:24; 39:3,5

30:28 ^a Ge 29:15

30:29 ^b Ge 31:6 ^c Ge 31:38-40

30:30 ^d 1Ti 5:8

30:32 ^e Ge 31:8,12

30:35 ^f Ge 31:1

Genesis 30:25–43

Laban offered Jacob part ownership of the herd, with the potential to increase his share over time. Ancient shepherding contracts provided for a share of between 10 and 20 percent of the flock, along with a percentage of the wool and milk by-products. Dark and spotted animals typically represented a smaller proportion, giving Laban the better deal. Jacob proposed to remove the designated sheep from Laban's flock for his wages, so Laban's actions (vv. 35–36) appeared to violate the agreement.

Since Jacob insisted in verse 31 that Laban give him nothing, it appears that he intended to separate out the type of animals he had spoken about and perhaps mark them as Laban's. Then any spotted or speckled sheep born from that point would be his wages. Laban reacted by removing all spotted animals from the breeding pool.

Not to be deterred, Jacob countered by combining common sense (strong animals breed strong offspring) and folk tradition (what is in the animals' visual field during breeding affects their offspring). But any level of success Jacob enjoyed was in the end attributable to God.

Society teaches us to "look out for Number One" and take whatever steps are necessary to assure success. Shrewd or cunning strategies that may involve dishonesty are counterproductive to God's work in our lives. Just as God thwarted Jacob's attempts to succeed in order to replace them with his own blessings, God can use failure and frustration in our lives to draw us to depend on him. What have you learned from attempts to make things work out in your favor? We *should* plan and strategize, but it's critical that we acknowledge God as the source of our achievements and successes.

drink. When the flocks were in heat and came to drink, ³⁹they mated in front of the branches. And they bore young that were streaked or speckled or spotted. ⁴⁰Jacob set apart the young of the flock by themselves, but made the rest face the streaked and dark-colored animals that belonged to Laban. Thus he made separate flocks for himself and did not put them with Laban's animals. ⁴¹Whenever the stronger females were in heat, Jacob would place the branches in the troughs in front of the animals so they would mate near the branches, ⁴²but if the animals were weak, he would not place them there. So the weak animals went to Laban and the strong ones to Jacob. ⁴³In this way the man grew exceedingly prosperous and came to own large flocks, and maidservants and menservants, and camels and donkeys.^g

Jacob Flees From Laban

31 Jacob heard that Laban's sons were saying, "Jacob has taken everything our father owned and has gained all this wealth from what belonged to our father." ²And Jacob noticed that Laban's attitude toward him was not what it had been.

³Then the Lord said to Jacob, "Go back^h to the land of your fathers and to your relatives, and I will be with you."ⁱ

⁴So Jacob sent word to Rachel and Leah to come out to the fields where his flocks were. ⁵He said to them, "I see that your father's attitude toward me is not what it was before, but the God of my father has been with me.^j ⁶You know that I've worked for your father with all my strength,^k ⁷yet your father has cheated me by changing my wages ten times.^l However, God has not allowed him to harm me.^m ⁸If he said, 'The speckled ones will be your wages,' then all the flocks gave birth to speckled young; and if he said, 'The streaked ones will be your wages,'ⁿ then all the flocks bore streaked young. ⁹So God has taken away your father's livestock and has given them to me.^o

¹⁰"In breeding season I once had a dream in which I looked up and saw that the male goats mating with the flock were streaked, speckled or spotted. ¹¹The angel of God^p said to me in the dream, 'Jacob.' I answered, 'Here I am.' ¹²And he said, 'Look up and see that all the male goats mating with the flock are streaked, speckled or spotted, for I have seen all that Laban has been doing to you.^q ¹³I am the God of Bethel,^r where you anointed a pillar and where you made a vow to me. Now leave this land at once and go back to your native land.^s'"

¹⁴Then Rachel and Leah replied, "Do we still have any share in the inheritance of our father's estate? ¹⁵Does he not regard us as foreigners? Not only has he sold us, but he has used up what was paid for us.^t ¹⁶Surely all the wealth that God took away from our father belongs to us and our children. So do whatever God has told you."

¹⁷Then Jacob put his children and his wives on camels, ¹⁸and he drove all his livestock ahead of him, along with all the goods he had accumulated in Paddan Aram,^a to go to his father Isaac^u in the land of Canaan.^v

^a 18 That is, Northwest Mesopotamia

Cross references: 30:43 ^g ver 30; Ge 12:16; 13:2; 24:35; 26:13-14 | 31:3 ^h ver 13; Ge 32:9 ⁱ Ge 21:22; 26:3; 28:15 | 31:5 ^j Ge 21:22; 26:3 | 31:6 ^k Ge 30:29 | 31:7 ^l ver 41; Job 19:3 ^m ver 52; Ps 37:28; 105:14 | 31:8 ⁿ Ge 30:32 | 31:9 ^o ver 1,16; Ge 30:42 | 31:11 ^p Ge 16:7; 48:16 | 31:12 ^q Ex 3:7 | 31:13 ^r Ge 28:10-22 ^s ver 3; Ge 32:9 | 31:15 ^t Ge 29:20 | 31:18 ^u Ge 35:27 ^v Ge 10:19

Genesis 31:1–21

Leah and Rachel's willingness to leave was based on an accusation against their father about his handling of their inheritance. The bride price paid by the husband's family was supposed to be held in trust to provide for the wife if she were abandoned or widowed. Jacob had given no bride price, so Laban should have set aside the equivalent of his wages for the women. If their father's house held no economic security for them, the women had no reason to stay.

The household gods were images of either ancestors or patron gods of ancestors. They were believed to bring prosperity and protection. These gods had no temples but were likely provided with a shrine area in the home. Deception and theft had precipitated Jacob's departure from Canaan; now both accompanied his return.

The writer didn't typically conclude his record of an incident with a moralizing summary, but he did here: "Jacob deceived Laban . . . by not telling him he was running away." Despite all Jacob's experiences, he was still a deceiver. Each of us is born with personality traits that show themselves from an early age and often stay with us through life. But God specializes in transformation. How has has he changed you? The rest of Jacob's story shows how God gradually worked change in his character.

31:19
w ver 30,32,34-35;
Ge 35:2; Jdg 17:5;
1Sa 19:13; Hos 3:4
31:20
x Ge 27:36 y ver 27
31:21
z Ge 37:25

[19]When Laban had gone to shear his sheep, Rachel stole her father's household gods. [w] [20]Moreover, Jacob deceived [x] Laban the Aramean by not telling him he was running away. [y] [21]So he fled with all he had, and crossing the River, [a] he headed for the hill country of Gilead. [z]

Laban Pursues Jacob

[22]On the third day Laban was told that Jacob had fled. [23]Taking his relatives with him, he pursued Jacob for seven days and caught up with him in the hill country of Gilead. [24]Then God came to Laban the Aramean in a dream at night and said to him, [a] "Be careful not to say anything to Jacob, either good or bad." [b]

31:24
a Ge 20:3;
Job 33:15
b Ge 24:50

[25]Jacob had pitched his tent in the hill country of Gilead when Laban overtook him, and Laban and his relatives camped there too. [26]Then Laban said to Jacob, "What have you done? You've deceived me, [c] and you've carried off my daughters like captives in war. [d] [27]Why did you run off secretly and deceive me? Why didn't you tell me, so I could send you away with joy and singing to the music of tambourines [e] and harps? [f] [28]You didn't even let me kiss my grandchildren and my daughters good-by. [g] You have done a foolish thing. [29]I have the power to harm you; [h] but last night the God of your father [i] said to me, 'Be careful not to say anything to Jacob, either good or bad.' [30]Now you have gone off because you longed to return to your father's house. But why did you steal my gods? [j]

31:26
c Ge 27:36
d 1Sa 30:2-3
31:27
e Ex 15:20
f Ge 4:21
31:28
g ver 55
31:29
h ver 7 i ver 53
31:30
j ver 19; Jdg 18:24

[31]Jacob answered Laban, "I was afraid, because I thought you would take your daughters away from me by force. [32]But if you find anyone who has your gods, he shall not live. [k] In the presence of our relatives, see for yourself whether there is anything of yours here with me; and if so, take it." Now Jacob did not know that Rachel had stolen the gods.

31:32
k Ge 44:9

[33]So Laban went into Jacob's tent and into Leah's tent and into the tent of the two maidservants, but he found nothing. After he came out of Leah's tent, he entered Rachel's tent. [34]Now Rachel had taken the household gods and put them inside her camel's saddle and was sitting on them. Laban searched [l] through everything in the tent but found nothing.

31:34
l ver 37; Ge 44:12

[35]Rachel said to her father, "Don't be angry, my lord, that I cannot stand up in your presence; [m] I'm having my period." So he searched but could not find the household gods.

31:35
m Ex 20:12;
Lev 19:3,32

[36]Jacob was angry and took Laban to task. "What is my crime?" he asked Laban. "What sin have I committed that you hunt me down? [37]Now that you have searched through all my goods, what have you found that belongs to your household? Put it here in front of your relatives [n] and mine, and let them judge between the two of us.

31:37
n ver 23

[38]"I have been with you for twenty years now. Your sheep and goats have not miscarried, nor have I eaten rams from your flocks. [39]I did not bring you animals torn by wild beasts; I bore the loss myself. And you demanded payment from me for whatever was stolen by day or night. [o] [40]This was my situation: The heat consumed me in the daytime and the cold at night, and sleep fled from my eyes. [41]It was like this for the twenty years I was in your household. I worked for you fourteen years for your two daughters [p] and six years for your flocks, and you changed my wages ten

31:39
o Ex 22:13

31:41
p Ge 29:30

---

a 21 That is, the Euphrates

Genesis 31:22-55

In their meeting Laban and Jacob vented frustration over 20 years of mutually underhanded behavior. Their only point of agreement was that Jacob's God had protected and prospered him. Their covenant was designed to protect each one against the other. It's not unusual to hear verse 49 quoted at the end of a church service or to find it etched on wedding rings. But in Genesis it expressed suspicion. Jacob and Laban had no way of keeping an eye on one another, so they commended each other to God's watchful eye. Accountability is important. Who better to oversee our daily activities than our loving heavenly Father?

One way we suffer the consequences of our behavior is by passing on destructive traits to our children. Suppose a Christian parent cheats on taxes or is privately critical of church leadership. The children witness the hypocrisy firsthand. Everyone else may be surprised when such children become mired in a scandal or are instrumental in causing a church to split, but the seed was planted at home. The good news is that God can halt cycles of sin in our lives and families. If you are a parent, are you using discretion in your daily life and conversations?

times. *q* 42If the God of my father, *r* the God of Abraham and the Fear of Isaac, *s* had not been with me, *t* you would surely have sent me away empty-handed. But God has seen my hardship and the toil of my hands, *u* and last night he rebuked you."

43Laban answered Jacob, "The women are my daughters, the children are my children, and the flocks are my flocks. All you see is mine. Yet what can I do today about these daughters of mine, or about the children they have borne? 44Come now, let's make a covenant, *v* you and I, and let it serve as a witness between us." *w*

45So Jacob took a stone and set it up as a pillar. *x* 46He said to his relatives, "Gather some stones." So they took stones and piled them in a heap, and they ate there by the heap. 47Laban called it Jegar Sahadutha, *a* and Jacob called it Galeed. *b*

48Laban said, "This heap is a witness between you and me today." That is why it was called Galeed. 49It was also called Mizpah, *cy* because he said, "May the LORD keep watch between you and me when we are away from each other. 50If you mistreat my daughters or if you take any wives besides my daughters, even though no one is with us, remember that God is a witness *z* between you and me."

51Laban also said to Jacob, "Here is this heap, and here is this pillar *a* I have set up between you and me. 52This heap is a witness, and this pillar is a witness, *b* that I will not go past this heap to your side to harm you and that you will not go past this heap and pillar to my side to harm me. *c* 53May the God of Abraham *d* and the God of Nahor, the God of their father, judge between us." *e*

So Jacob took an oath *f* in the name of the Fear of his father Isaac. *g* 54He offered a sacrifice there in the hill country and invited his relatives to a meal. After they had eaten, they spent the night there.

55Early the next morning Laban kissed his grandchildren and his daughters *h* and blessed them. Then he left and returned home. *i*

Jacob Prepares to Meet Esau

32 Jacob also went on his way, and the angels of God *j* met him. 2When Jacob saw them, he said, "This is the camp of God!" *k* So he named that place Mahanaim. *d l*

3Jacob sent messengers ahead of him to his brother Esau *m* in the land of Seir, the country of Edom. *n* 4He instructed them: "This is what you are to say to my master Esau: 'Your servant Jacob says, I have been staying with Laban and have remained there till now. 5I have cattle and donkeys, sheep and goats, menservants and maidservants. *o* Now I am sending this message to my lord, that I may find favor in your eyes.' *p* "

6When the messengers returned to Jacob, they said, "We went to your brother Esau, and now he is coming to meet you, and four hundred men are with him." *q*

7In great fear *r* and distress Jacob divided the people who were with him into two groups, *e* and the flocks and herds and camels as well. 8He thought, "If Esau comes and attacks one group, *f* the group *f* that is left may escape."

a 47 The Aramaic *Jegar Sahadutha* means *witness heap.*   *b* 47 The Hebrew *Galeed* means *witness heap.*
c 49 *Mizpah* means *watchtower.*   *d* 2 *Mahanaim* means *two camps.*   *e* 7 Or *camps; also in verse 10*
f 8 Or *camp*

31:41
q ver 7
31:42
r ver 5; Ex 3:15;
1Ch 12:17 *s* ver 53;
Isa 8:13
t Ps 124:1-2
u Ge 29:32

31:44
v Ge 21:27; 26:28
w Jos 24:27
31:45
x Ge 28:18

31:49
y Jdg 11:29;
1Sa 7:5-6

31:50
z Jer 29:23; 42:5
31:51
a Ge 28:18
31:52
b Ge 21:30 *c* ver 7;
Ge 26:29
31:53
d Ge 28:13
e Ge 16:5
f Ge 21:23,27
g ver 42

31:55
h ver 28 *i* Ge 18:33;
30:25

32:1
j Ge 16:11;
2Ki 6:16-17;
Ps 34:7; 91:11;
Heb 1:14
32:2
k Ge 28:17
l 2Sa 2:8,29
32:3
m Ge 27:41-42
n Ge 25:30; 36:8,9
32:5
o Ge 12:16; 30:43
p Ge 33:8,10,15

32:6
q Ge 33:1
32:7
r ver 11

Genesis 32:1–21

Jacob finally resorted to prayer. If concern for God's interest marks a mature prayer, though, his would hardly have registered on the scale. He acknowledged that his skills couldn't assure his family's safety but also did all he could to secure a strategic advantage: (1) His gifts of animals arriving in installments would wear down the military readiness of Esau's men. (2) Esau would have to move more slowly with a larger group of people and animals. (3) Esau's possible military strategies would be less effective with Jacob's household in the mix.

Jacob's tactics exhausted his reserves and left him feeling vulnerable—precisely where God wanted him.

The character flaw in Jacob that needed to be resolved went deeper than his inclination toward deception and manipulation. These were only symptoms of his basic problem: self-sufficiency.

God loves us as we are, but it's his desire and right to transform us. The problem is that most of us aren't motivated to change. Sometimes we pray that God will work on the other person to produce harmony. Is it possible you need to pray that God will help you resolve your own bitterness; overcome your negative habits; re-examine your expectations; and think more highly of others, placing their needs ahead of your own?

32:9
s Ge 28:13; 31:42
t Ge 31:13
32:10
u Ge 24:27

32:11
v Ps 59:2
w Ge 27:41

32:12
x Ge 22:17
y Ge 28:13-15;
Hos 1:10; Ro 9:27
32:13
z Ge 43:11,15,25,
26; Pr 18:16

32:18
a Ge 18:3

32:20
b Ge 33:10;
Pr 21:14

32:22
c Dt 2:37; 3:16;
Jos 12:2
32:24
d Ge 18:2

32:25
e ver 32

32:26
f Hos 12:4

32:28
g Ge 17:5; 35:10;
1Ki 18:31

32:29
h Jdg 13:17
i Jdg 13:18
j Ge 35:9
32:30
k Ge 16:13;
Ex 24:11; Nu 12:8;
Jdg 6:22; 13:22

[9]Then Jacob prayed, "O God of my father Abraham, God of my father Isaac,[s] O LORD, who said to me, 'Go back to your country and your relatives, and I will make you prosper,'[t] [10]I am unworthy of all the kindness and faithfulness[u] you have shown your servant. I had only my staff when I crossed this Jordan, but now I have become two groups. [11]Save me, I pray, from the hand of my brother Esau, for I am afraid he will come and attack me,[v] and also the mothers with their children.[w] [12]But you have said, 'I will surely make you prosper and will make your descendants like the sand[x] of the sea, which cannot be counted.'[y] "

[13]He spent the night there, and from what he had with him he selected a gift[z] for his brother Esau: [14]two hundred female goats and twenty male goats, two hundred ewes and twenty rams, [15]thirty female camels with their young, forty cows and ten bulls, and twenty female donkeys and ten male donkeys. [16]He put them in the care of his servants, each herd by itself, and said to his servants, "Go ahead of me, and keep some space between the herds."

[17]He instructed the one in the lead: "When my brother Esau meets you and asks, 'To whom do you belong, and where are you going, and who owns all these animals in front of you?' [18]then you are to say, 'They belong to your servant[a] Jacob. They are a gift sent to my lord Esau, and he is coming behind us.' "

[19]He also instructed the second, the third and all the others who followed the herds: "You are to say the same thing to Esau when you meet him. [20]And be sure to say, 'Your servant Jacob is coming behind us.' " For he thought, "I will pacify him with these gifts I am sending on ahead; later, when I see him, perhaps he will receive me."[b] [21]So Jacob's gifts went on ahead of him, but he himself spent the night in the camp.

Jacob Wrestles With God

[22]That night Jacob got up and took his two wives, his two maidservants and his eleven sons and crossed the ford of the Jabbok.[c] [23]After he had sent them across the stream, he sent over all his possessions. [24]So Jacob was left alone, and a man[d] wrestled with him till daybreak. [25]When the man saw that he could not overpower him, he touched the socket of Jacob's hip[e] so that his hip was wrenched as he wrestled with the man. [26]Then the man said, "Let me go, for it is daybreak."

But Jacob replied, "I will not let you go unless you bless me."[f]

[27]The man asked him, "What is your name?"

"Jacob," he answered.

[28]Then the man said, "Your name will no longer be Jacob, but Israel,[a][g] because you have struggled with God and with men and have overcome."

[29]Jacob said, "Please tell me your name."[h]

But he replied, "Why do you ask my name?"[i] Then he blessed[j] him there.

[30]So Jacob called the place Peniel,[b] saying, "It is because I saw God face to face,[k] and yet my life was spared."

[31]The sun rose above him as he passed Peniel,[c] and he was limping because of

---

[a] 28 *Israel* means *he struggles with God.* [b] 30 *Peniel* means *face of God.* [c] 31 Hebrew *Penuel*, a variant of *Peniel*

Genesis 32:22–32

Jacob didn't best his opponent physically but refused on a spiritual level to yield. Only when his rival threatened to go without offering assurances of God's help did Jacob show a willingness to negotiate. The turning point came when he insisted that he wouldn't release the stranger until he had received a blessing—an apparent indication that he was willing to submit to God's demands. Jacob first experienced the adversary as "a man" but later acknowledged that he had wrestled with God. In Hosea 12:3–4, the prophet stated that Jacob had struggled with God in the form of an angel.

"Wrestling with an angel" might describe God's actions to reform us. We can resist and stubbornly prevail in our sin, or we can take hold of him and refuse to let go until he grants us blessing—determined to have him work his transforming power in us. It's not good to prevail when wrestling an angel! As Scottish preacher and novelist George MacDonald (1824–1905) observed, "There are victories far worse than defeats, and to overcome an angel too gentle to put out all his strength, and ride away in triumph on the back of a devil, is one of the poorest."

his hip. [32]Therefore to this day the Israelites do not eat the tendon attached to the socket of the hip, because the socket of Jacob's hip was touched near the tendon.

Jacob Meets Esau

33 Jacob looked up and there was Esau, coming with his four hundred men;[l] so he divided the children among Leah, Rachel and the two maidservants. [2]He put the maidservants and their children in front, Leah and her children next, and Rachel and Joseph in the rear. [3]He himself went on ahead and bowed down to the ground[m] seven times as he approached his brother.

[4]But Esau ran to meet Jacob and embraced him; he threw his arms around his neck and kissed him. And they wept.[n] [5]Then Esau looked up and saw the women and children. "Who are these with you?" he asked.

Jacob answered, "They are the children God has graciously given your servant.[o]"

[6]Then the maidservants and their children approached and bowed down. [7]Next, Leah and her children came and bowed down. Last of all came Joseph and Rachel, and they too bowed down.

[8]Esau asked, "What do you mean by all these droves I met?"[p]

"To find favor in your eyes, my lord,"[q] he said.

[9]But Esau said, "I already have plenty, my brother. Keep what you have for yourself."

[10]"No, please!" said Jacob. "If I have found favor in your eyes, accept this gift from me. For to see your face is like seeing the face of God,[r] now that you have received me favorably.[s] [11]Please accept the present[t] that was brought to you, for God has been gracious to me[u] and I have all I need." And because Jacob insisted, Esau accepted it.

[12]Then Esau said, "Let us be on our way; I'll accompany you."

[13]But Jacob said to him, "My lord knows that the children are tender and that I must care for the ewes and cows that are nursing their young. If they are driven hard just one day, all the animals will die. [14]So let my lord go on ahead of his servant, while I move along slowly at the pace of the droves before me and that of the children, until I come to my lord in Seir.[v]"

[15]Esau said, "Then let me leave some of my men with you."

"But why do that?" Jacob asked. "Just let me find favor in the eyes of my lord."[w]

[16]So that day Esau started on his way back to Seir. [17]Jacob, however, went to Succoth,[x] where he built a place for himself and made shelters for his livestock. That is why the place is called Succoth.[a]

[18]After Jacob came from Paddan Aram,[b][y] he arrived safely at the[c] city of Shechem[z] in Canaan and camped within sight of the city. [19]For a hundred pieces of silver,[d] he bought from the sons of Hamor, the father of Shechem,[a] the plot of ground[b] where he pitched his tent. [20]There he set up an altar and called it El Elohe Israel.[e]

Dinah and the Shechemites

34 Now Dinah,[c] the daughter Leah had borne to Jacob, went out to visit the women of the land. [2]When Shechem son of Hamor the Hivite, the ruler of

---

[a] 17 *Succoth* means *shelters.*   [b] 18 That is, Northwest Mesopotamia   [c] 18 Or *arrived at Shalem, a*
[d] 19 Hebrew *hundred kesitahs;* a kesitah was a unit of money of unknown weight and value.
[e] 20 *El Elohe Israel* can mean *God, the God of Israel* or *mighty is the God of Israel.*

Cross references (margin):

33:1 *l* Ge 32:6
33:3 *m* Ge 18:2; 42:6
33:4 *n* Ge 45:14-15
33:5 *o* Ge 48:9; Ps 127:3; Isa 8:18
33:8 *p* Ge 32:14-16 *q* Ge 24:9; 32:5
33:10 *r* Ge 16:13 *s* Ge 32:20
33:11 *t* 1Sa 25:27 *u* Ge 30:43
33:14 *v* Ge 32:3
33:15 *w* Ge 34:11; 47:25; Ru 2:13
33:17 *x* Jos 13:27; Jdg 8:5,6,8,14-16; Ps 60:6
33:18 *y* Ge 25:20; 28:2 *z* Jos 24:1; Jdg 9:1
33:19 *a* Jos 24:32 *b* Jn 4:5
34:1 *c* Ge 30:21

Genesis 33:1–20

His recurring mention of God in his reunion conversation with Esau shows us the new Jacob. Most important were Jacob's words to Esau regarding his nighttime wrestling encounter: "To see your face is like seeing the face of God." The old Jacob had prevailed with God and men; the new Jacob found favor with both. Now that Jacob had become a man of faith, he took his rightful place as covenant heir.

What's necessary in your life for you to see God face-to-face? What reality do you need to learn about yourself? What sacrifice do you have to make in order to stand before God and look him in the eyes? The obstacle may not be self-reliance. In your case it may be vanity, selfishness, greed, or the need for other people's approval. Whatever it is, your usefulness to God depends on your allowing him to change you.

GENESIS 34:3

that area, saw her, he took her and violated her. ³His heart was drawn to Dinah daughter of Jacob, and he loved the girl and spoke tenderly to her. ⁴And Shechem said to his father Hamor, "Get me this girl as my wife."

⁵When Jacob heard that his daughter Dinah had been defiled, his sons were in the fields with his livestock; so he kept quiet about it until they came home.

⁶Then Shechem's father Hamor went out to talk with Jacob. *d* ⁷Now Jacob's sons had come in from the fields as soon as they heard what had happened. They were filled with grief and fury, because Shechem had done a disgraceful thing in*a* Israel*e* by lying with Jacob's daughter—a thing that should not be done.*f*

⁸But Hamor said to them, "My son Shechem has his heart set on your daughter. Please give her to him as his wife. ⁹Intermarry with us; give us your daughters and take our daughters for yourselves. ¹⁰You can settle among us;*g* the land is open to you.*h* Live in it, trade*b* in it,*i* and acquire property in it."

¹¹Then Shechem said to Dinah's father and brothers, "Let me find favor in your eyes, and I will give you whatever you ask. ¹²Make the price for the bride*j* and the gift I am to bring as great as you like, and I'll pay whatever you ask me. Only give me the girl as my wife."

¹³Because their sister Dinah had been defiled, Jacob's sons replied deceitfully as they spoke to Shechem and his father Hamor. ¹⁴They said to them, "We can't do such a thing; we can't give our sister to a man who is not circumcised.*k* That would be a disgrace to us. ¹⁵We will give our consent to you on one condition only: that you become like us by circumcising all your males.*l* ¹⁶Then we will give you our daughters and take your daughters for ourselves. We'll settle among you and become one people with you. ¹⁷But if you will not agree to be circumcised, we'll take our sister*c* and go."

¹⁸Their proposal seemed good to Hamor and his son Shechem. ¹⁹The young man, who was the most honored of all his father's household, lost no time in doing what they said, because he was delighted with Jacob's daughter.*m* ²⁰So Hamor and his son Shechem went to the gate of their city*n* to speak to their fellow townsmen. ²¹"These men are friendly toward us," they said. "Let them live in our land and trade in it; the land has plenty of room for them. We can marry their daughters and they can marry ours. ²²But the men will consent to live with us as one people only on the condition that our males be circumcised, as they themselves are. ²³Won't their livestock, their property and all their other animals become ours? So let us give our consent to them, and they will settle among us."

²⁴All the men who went out of the city gate*o* agreed with Hamor and his son Shechem, and every male in the city was circumcised.

²⁵Three days later, while all of them were still in pain, two of Jacob's sons, Simeon and Levi, Dinah's brothers, took their swords*p* and attacked the unsuspecting city, killing every male. *q* ²⁶They put Hamor and his son Shechem to the sword and took Dinah from Shechem's house and left. ²⁷The sons of Jacob came upon the dead bodies and looted the city where*d* their sister had been defiled. ²⁸They seized their flocks and herds and donkeys and everything else of theirs in the city and out in the fields. ²⁹They carried off all their wealth and all their women and children, taking as plunder everything in the houses.

³⁰Then Jacob said to Simeon and Levi, "You have brought trouble on me by mak-

---

a 7 Or *against*   *b* 10 Or *move about freely*; also in verse 21   *c* 17 Hebrew *daughter*
d 27 Or *because*

Genesis 34:1–31

God was able to continue establishing the covenant despite Jacob's and Esau's character flaws. But Jacob's petty swindling had blossomed into full-fledged violence and brutality in his sons. How could anything be salvaged from such depraved behavior? Thus begins the text's case that God is able to bring good out of evil. This will eventually be summarized in Joseph's comment to his brothers in 50:20.

Simeon's and Levi's inexcusable behavior kept back Jacob's family from assimilating into the surrounding culture. We may think of providence as a fortunate turn of events, but it can operate in the context of sinful behavior. If God can work only through godly behavior, there is little he can do in a sinful world. His sovereignty is demonstrated not just by his overriding wicked choices but by his dovetailing acts of wickedness into his plan. When has God worked good from a sinful episode in your past?

56

ing me a stench[r] to the Canaanites and Perizzites, the people living in this land.[s] We are few in number,[t] and if they join forces against me and attack me, I and my household will be destroyed."

31But they replied, "Should he have treated our sister like a prostitute?"

Jacob Returns to Bethel

35 Then God said to Jacob, "Go up to Bethel[u] and settle there, and build an altar there to God, who appeared to you when you were fleeing from your brother Esau."[v]

2So Jacob said to his household[w] and to all who were with him, "Get rid of the foreign gods[x] you have with you, and purify yourselves and change your clothes.[y] 3Then come, let us go up to Bethel, where I will build an altar to God, who answered me in the day of my distress[z] and who has been with me wherever I have gone.[a]" 4So they gave Jacob all the foreign gods they had and the rings in their ears, and Jacob buried them under the oak at Shechem.[b] 5Then they set out, and the terror of God[c] fell upon the towns all around them so that no one pursued them.

6Jacob and all the people with him came to Luz[d] (that is, Bethel) in the land of Canaan. 7There he built an altar, and he called the place El Bethel,[a] because it was there that God revealed himself to him[e] when he was fleeing from his brother.

8Now Deborah, Rebekah's nurse,[f] died and was buried under the oak below Bethel. So it was named Allon Bacuth.[b]

9After Jacob returned from Paddan Aram,[c] God appeared to him again and blessed him.[g] 10God said to him, "Your name is Jacob,[d] but you will no longer be called Jacob; your name will be Israel.[e]" So he named him Israel.

11And God said to him, "I am God Almighty[f][i] be fruitful and increase in number. A nation[j] and a community of nations will come from you, and kings will come from your body.[k] 12The land I gave to Abraham and Isaac I also give to you, and I will give this land to your descendants after you.[l][m] 13Then God went up from him[n] at the place where he had talked with him.

14Jacob set up a stone pillar at the place where God had talked with him, and he poured out a drink offering on it; he also poured oil on it.[o] 15Jacob called the place where God had talked with him Bethel.[g][p]

The Deaths of Rachel and Isaac

16Then they moved on from Bethel. While they were still some distance from Ephrath, Rachel began to give birth and had great difficulty. 17And as she was having great difficulty in childbirth, the midwife said to her, "Don't be afraid, for you have another son."[q] 18As she breathed her last—for she was dying—she named her son Ben-Oni.[h] But his father named him Benjamin.[i]

---

[a] 7 El Bethel means God of Bethel.   [b] 8 Allon Bacuth means oak of weeping.   [c] 9 That is, Northwest Mesopotamia; also in verse 26   [d] 10 Jacob means he grasps the heel (figuratively, he deceives).   [e] 10 Israel means he struggles with God.   [f] 11 Hebrew El-Shaddai   [g] 15 Bethel means house of God.   [h] 18 Ben-Oni means son of my trouble.   [i] 18 Benjamin means son of my right hand.

34:30
[r] Ex 5:21; 1Sa 13:4
[s] Ge 13:7
[t] Ge 46:27; 1Ch 16:19; Ps 105:12

35:1
[u] Ge 28:19
[v] Ge 27:43

35:2
[w] Ge 18:19; Jos 24:15
[x] Ge 31:19
[y] Ex 19:10,14
35:3
[z] Ge 32:7
[a] Ge 28:15,20-22; 31:3,42
35:4
[b] Jos 24:25-26
35:5
[c] Ex 15:16; 23:27; Jos 2:9
35:6
[d] Ge 28:19; 48:3
35:7
[e] Ge 28:13
35:8
[f] Ge 24:59

35:9
[g] Ge 32:29
35:10
[h] Ge 17:5
35:11
[i] Ge 17:1; Ex 6:3
[j] Ge 28:3; 48:4
[k] Ge 17:6

35:12
[l] Ge 13:15; 28:13
[m] Ge 12:7; 26:3
35:13
[n] Ge 17:22
35:14
[o] Ge 28:18
35:15
[p] Ge 28:19

35:17
[q] Ge 30:24

Genesis 35:1–15

📖 Genesis 35 draws the Jacob storyline to its climax. Personally, he had emerged to take his rightful place among his forefathers as a man of faith. Regardless of what spiritual shortcomings may have been exposed in his vow or of the dangers that accompanied that vow, Jacob had fulfilled it, and it stood as a testimony to his commitment to the Lord. God's patient work in his life had resulted in a character transformation that may have seemed beyond reach in earlier chapters.

📖 God moves each of us along step by step in the process of spiritual maturity. Sometimes we may look back with shame or embarrassment at things we have done that may at the time have seemed spiritual. Hindsight allows us to recognize those actions as naïve, shallow, or self-serving. Or we may regret wasted time, lost opportunities, and sinful choices. But instead of focusing on the negative, why not thank God for his patience in moving you forward in faith, commitment, and service?

Genesis 35:16–29

📖 Rachel's death in childbirth was ironic, considering her demand of Jacob in 30:1, "Give me children, or I'll die!" On her deathbed she named her son in accordance with the misery she faced. Jacob, though, was unwilling to let the name stand as a sad reminder of the circumstances of the birth. Benjamin can mean either "son of the right [hand]," signifying a place of protection and favor, or "son of the south."

35:19
r Ge 48:7;
Ru 1:1,19;
Mic 5:2; Mt 2:16
35:20
s 1Sa 10:2
35:22
t Ge 49:4; 1Ch 5:1
u Ge 29:29;
Lev 18:8

[19]So Rachel died and was buried on the way to Ephrath (that is, Bethlehem[r]). [20]Over her tomb Jacob set up a pillar, and to this day that pillar marks Rachel's tomb. [s]

[21]Israel moved on again and pitched his tent beyond Migdal Eder. [22]While Israel was living in that region, Reuben went in and slept with his father's concubine[t] Bilhah, [u] and Israel heard of it.

Jacob had twelve sons:

35:23
v Ge 46:8
w Ge 29:35
x Ge 30:20

[23]The sons of Leah:

Reuben the firstborn[v] of Jacob,

Simeon, Levi, Judah, [w] Issachar and Zebulun. [x]

35:24
y Ge 30:24 z ver 18

[24]The sons of Rachel:

Joseph[y] and Benjamin. [z]

35:25
a Ge 30:8

[25]The sons of Rachel's maidservant Bilhah:

Dan and Naphtali. [a]

35:26
b Ge 30:11
c Ge 30:13

[26]The sons of Leah's maidservant Zilpah:

Gad[b] and Asher. [c]

These were the sons of Jacob, who were born to him in Paddan Aram.

35:27
d Ge 13:18; 18:1
e Jos 14:15
35:28
f Ge 25:7,20
35:29
g Ge 25:8; 49:33
h Ge 15:15
i Ge 25:9

[27]Jacob came home to his father Isaac in Mamre, [d] near Kiriath Arba[e] (that is, Hebron), where Abraham and Isaac had stayed. [28]Isaac lived a hundred and eighty years. [f] [29]Then he breathed his last and died and was gathered to his people, [g] old and full of years. [h] And his sons Esau and Jacob buried him. [i]

Esau's Descendants

36:1
j Ge 25:30

36

This is the account of Esau (that is, Edom). [j]

36:2
k Ge 28:8-9
l Ge 26:34 m ver 25

[2]Esau took his wives from the women of Canaan: [k] Adah daughter of Elon the Hittite, [l] and Oholibamah daughter of Anah[m] and granddaughter of Zibeon the Hivite— [3]also Basemath daughter of Ishmael and sister of Nebaioth.

36:4
n 1Ch 1:35

[4]Adah bore Eliphaz to Esau, Basemath bore Reuel, [n] [5]and Oholibamah bore Jeush, Jalam and Korah. These were the sons of Esau, who were born to him in Canaan.

36:6
o Ge 12:5

[6]Esau took his wives and sons and daughters and all the members of his household, as well as his livestock and all his other animals and all the goods he had acquired in Canaan, [o] and moved to a land some distance from his brother Jacob. [7]Their possessions were too great for them to remain together; the land where they were staying could not support them both because of their livestock. [p] [8]So Esau[q] (that is, Edom) settled in the hill country of Seir. [r]

36:7
p Ge 13:6; 17:8;
28:4
36:8
q Dt 2:4 r Ge 32:3

[9]This is the account of Esau the father of the Edomites in the hill country of Seir.

Slaves, servants, and concubines were considered part of the inheritance passed along from father to son. The oldest son would with his birthright inherit the human members of the household. When inheritance was seized prior to a father's death, the father's role was usurped (cf. 49:3–4). Bilhah's place as Rachel's maidservant may indicate the vulnerability of Rachel's part of the household after her death. This is the first indication that the jeopardy of the next generation would again concern birthright, inheritance, and favoritism.

Still today, how often don't favoritism and inheritance issues divide families? Have you ever thought of these concerns as jeopardizing the generation to come? Stopping a negative cycle can be one of the most important actions you will ever take with regard to your extended family. What repeated issues come to mind as you think of dysfunctions in your family? What can you

do to free the next generation from the grip of the cycle?

Genesis 36:1–43

Jacob wouldn't die until the end of chapter 49, but the "account of Jacob" beginning in 37:2 actually pertains to his sons—Joseph in particular. Before proceeding, the text disposes of Esau. This is the last chapter in Genesis that mentions him.

God's providence extends beyond the principal characters in the Genesis story to include the peripheral players—the Ishmaels, Leahs, and Esaus of this world. Still today it's important for us as believers to avoid cliquish or snobbish behavior toward those outside our Christian circle. God, said Peter in 2 Peter 3:9, "is patient with [all people], not wanting anyone to perish, but everyone to come to repentance." How does reflection on Peter's words impact your attitude toward that offensive neighbor or obnoxious coworker?

10These are the names of Esau's sons:

Eliphaz, the son of Esau's wife Adah, and Reuel, the son of Esau's wife Basemath.

11The sons of Eliphaz:^s

Teman,^t Omar, Zepho, Gatam and Kenaz.

12Esau's son Eliphaz also had a concubine named Timna, who bore him Amalek.^u These were grandsons of Esau's wife Adah.^v

13The sons of Reuel:

Nahath, Zerah, Shammah and Mizzah. These were grandsons of Esau's wife Basemath.

14The sons of Esau's wife Oholibamah daughter of Anah and granddaughter of Zibeon, whom she bore to Esau:

Jeush, Jalam and Korah.

15These were the chiefs^w among Esau's descendants:

The sons of Eliphaz the firstborn of Esau:

Chiefs Teman,^x Omar, Zepho, Kenaz, 16Korah,^a Gatam and Amalek. These were the chiefs descended from Eliphaz in Edom; they were grandsons of Adah.^y

17The sons of Esau's son Reuel:^z

Chiefs Nahath, Zerah, Shammah and Mizzah. These were the chiefs descended from Reuel in Edom; they were grandsons of Esau's wife Basemath.

18The sons of Esau's wife Oholibamah:

Chiefs Jeush, Jalam and Korah. These were the chiefs descended from Esau's wife Oholibamah daughter of Anah.

19These were the sons of Esau (that is, Edom),^a and these were their chiefs.

20These were the sons of Seir the Horite,^b who were living in the region:

Lotan, Shobal, Zibeon, Anah, 21Dishon, Ezer and Dishan. These sons of Seir in Edom were Horite chiefs.

22The sons of Lotan:

Hori and Homam.^b Timna was Lotan's sister.

23The sons of Shobal:

Alvan, Manahath, Ebal, Shepho and Onam.

24The sons of Zibeon:

Aiah and Anah. This is the Anah who discovered the hot springs^c in the desert while he was grazing the donkeys of his father Zibeon.

25The children of Anah:

Dishon and Oholibamah daughter of Anah.

26The sons of Dishon^d:

Hemdan, Eshban, Ithran and Keran.

27The sons of Ezer:

Bilhan, Zaavan and Akan.

28The sons of Dishan:

Uz and Aran.

29These were the Horite chiefs:

Lotan, Shobal, Zibeon, Anah, 30Dishon, Ezer and Dishan. These were the Horite chiefs, according to their divisions, in the land of Seir.

The Rulers of Edom

31These were the kings who reigned in Edom before any Israelite king^c reigned^e:

32Bela son of Beor became king of Edom. His city was named Dinhabah.

33When Bela died, Jobab son of Zerah from Bozrah^d succeeded him as king.

---

^a 16 Masoretic Text; Samaritan Pentateuch (see also Gen. 36:11 and 1 Chron. 1:36) does not have *Korah*.   ^b 22 Hebrew *Hemam*, a variant of *Homam* (see 1 Chron. 1:39)   ^c 24 Vulgate; Syriac *discovered water;* the meaning of the Hebrew for this word is uncertain.   ^d 26 Hebrew *Dishan*, a variant of *Dishon*   ^e 31 Or *before an Israelite king reigned over them*

36:11
^s ver 15-16;
Job 2:11 ^t Am 1:12;
Hab 3:3
36:12
^u Ex 17:8,16;
Nu 24:20; 1Sa 15:2
^v ver 16

36:15
^w Ex 15:15
^x Job 2:11

36:16
^y ver 12
36:17
^z 1Ch 1:37

36:19
^a Ge 25:30

36:20
^b Ge 14:6;
Dt 2:12,22;
1Ch 1:38

36:31
^c Ge 17:6; 1Ch 1:43

36:33
^d Jer 49:13,22

36:34
e Eze 25:13

34 When Jobab died, Husham from the land of the Temanites[e] succeeded him as king.

36:35
f Ge 19:37;
Nu 22:1; Dt 1:5;
Ru 1:1,6

35 When Husham died, Hadad son of Bedad, who defeated Midian in the country of Moab,[f] succeeded him as king. His city was named Avith.

36 When Hadad died, Samlah from Masrekah succeeded him as king.

37 When Samlah died, Shaul from Rehoboth on the river[a] succeeded him as king.

38 When Shaul died, Baal-Hanan son of Acbor succeeded him as king.

39 When Baal-Hanan son of Acbor died, Hadad[b] succeeded him as king. His city was named Pau, and his wife's name was Mehetabel daughter of Matred, the daughter of Me-Zahab.

40 These were the chiefs descended from Esau, by name, according to their clans and regions:

Timna, Alvah, Jetheth, 41 Oholibamah, Elah, Pinon, 42 Kenaz, Teman, Mibzar, 43 Magdiel and Iram. These were the chiefs of Edom, according to their settlements in the land they occupied.

This was Esau the father of the Edomites.

Joseph's Dreams

37:1
g Ge 17:8
h Ge 10:19

37 Jacob lived in the land where his father had stayed,[g] the land of Canaan.[h]

2 This is the account of Jacob.

37:2
i Ps 78:71
j Ge 35:25
k Ge 35:26
l 1Sa 2:24

Joseph, a young man of seventeen, was tending the flocks[i] with his brothers, the sons of Bilhah[j] and the sons of Zilpah,[k] his father's wives, and he brought their father a bad report[l] about them.

37:3
m Ge 25:28
n Ge 44:20
o 2Sa 13:18-19

3 Now Israel loved Joseph more than any of his other sons,[m] because he had been born to him in his old age;[n] and he made a richly ornamented[c] robe[o] for him. 4 When his brothers saw that their father loved him more than any of them, they hated him[p] and could not speak a kind word to him.

37:4
p Ge 27:41;
49:22-23; Ac 7:9
37:5
q Ge 20:3; 28:12

5 Joseph had a dream,[q] and when he told it to his brothers, they hated him all the more. 6 He said to them, "Listen to this dream I had: 7 We were binding sheaves of grain out in the field when suddenly my sheaf rose and stood upright, while your sheaves gathered around mine and bowed down to it."[r]

37:7
r Ge 42:6,9; 43:26,
28; 44:14; 50:18

8 His brothers said to him, "Do you intend to reign over us? Will you actually rule us?"[s] And they hated him all the more because of his dream and what he had said.

37:8
s Ge 49:26

9 Then he had another dream, and he told it to his brothers. "Listen," he said, "I had another dream, and this time the sun and moon and eleven stars were bowing down to me."

37:10
t ver 5 u ver 7;
Ge 27:29

10 When he told his father as well as his brothers,[t] his father rebuked him and said, "What is this dream you had? Will your mother and I and your brothers actually come and bow down to the ground before you?"[u] 11 His brothers were jealous of him,[v] but his father kept the matter in mind.[w]

37:11
v Ac 7:9
w Lk 2:19,51

a 37 Possibly the Euphrates   b 39 Many manuscripts of the Masoretic Text, Samaritan Pentateuch and Syriac (see also 1 Chron. 1:50); most manuscripts of the Masoretic Text *Hadar*
c 3 The meaning of the Hebrew for *richly ornamented* is uncertain; also in verses 23 and 32.

Genesis 37:1–11

The favoritism of Rebekah for Jacob and of Isaac for Esau had torn apart Jacob's family and threatened its demise. The same issues of favoritism and conflict recurred in the Joseph cycle, bringing renewed jeopardy to the effective operation of the covenant. The first segment of the Joseph account (chs. 37–41; resolved in 42:1–9) opens with the cause of the conflict—Jacob's favoritism of Joseph and his brothers' resulting jealousy.

Envy has been classified as one of the "seven deadly sins." But in our culture envy, along with lust, carries a certain level of prestige. Advertising doesn't say envy is good—but it's good to be envied. If someone tries hard enough to make someone else jealous, that person is likely to eventually succeed. Unfortunately, when we convince ourselves that someone is trying to make us jealous, we start to excuse our sins and see ourselves as victims at someone else's expense.

Joseph Sold by His Brothers

¹²Now his brothers had gone to graze their father's flocks near Shechem, ¹³and Israel said to Joseph, "As you know, your brothers are grazing the flocks near Shechem. Come, I am going to send you to them."

"Very well," he replied.

¹⁴So he said to him, "Go and see if all is well with your brothers and with the flocks, and bring word back to me." Then he sent him off from the Valley of Hebron.ˣ

When Joseph arrived at Shechem, ¹⁵a man found him wandering around in the fields and asked him, "What are you looking for?"

¹⁶He replied, "I'm looking for my brothers. Can you tell me where they are grazing their flocks?"

¹⁷"They have moved on from here," the man answered. "I heard them say, 'Let's go to Dothan.ʸ '"

So Joseph went after his brothers and found them near Dothan. ¹⁸But they saw him in the distance, and before he reached them, they plotted to kill him.ᶻ

¹⁹"Here comes that dreamer!" they said to each other. ²⁰"Come now, let's kill him and throw him into one of these cisternsᵃ and say that a ferocious animal devoured him. Then we'll see what comes of his dreams."ᵇ

²¹When Reuben heard this, he tried to rescue him from their hands. "Let's not take his life," he said.ᶜ ²²"Don't shed any blood. Throw him into this cistern here in the desert, but don't lay a hand on him." Reuben said this to rescue him from them and take him back to his father.

²³So when Joseph came to his brothers, they stripped him of his robe—the richly ornamented robe he was wearing— ²⁴and they took him and threw him into the cistern.ᵈ Now the cistern was empty; there was no water in it.

²⁵As they sat down to eat their meal, they looked up and saw a caravan of Ishmaelites coming from Gilead. Their camels were loaded with spices, balm and myrrh,ᵉ and they were on their way to take them down to Egypt.ᶠ

²⁶Judah said to his brothers, "What will we gain if we kill our brother and cover up his blood?ᵍ ²⁷Come, let's sell him to the Ishmaelites and not lay our hands on him; after all, he is our brother,ʰ our own flesh and blood." His brothers agreed.

²⁸So when the Midianiteⁱ merchants came by, his brothers pulled Joseph up out of the

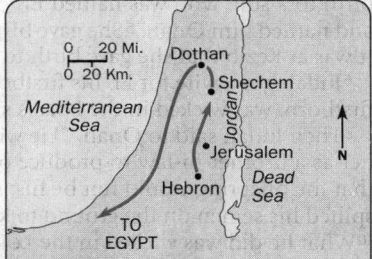

Joseph Sold Into Egypt (37:28)
Then: Sheep and goats had to be grazed where grass grew and water flowed. This meant that Joseph's family was often scattered over a wide range of possible pasture land.
Now: With irrigation and transportation for feed, today's herds of farm animals can stay in one place. Hebron's modern name is el-Khalil ("the friend"). It's located 20 miles southwest of modern Jerusalem.

37:14 ˣ Ge 13:18; 35:27
37:17 ʸ 2Ki 6:13
37:18 ᶻ 1Sa 19:1; Mk 14:1; Ac 23:12
37:20 ᵃ Jer 38:6,9 ᵇ Ge 50:20
37:21 ᶜ Ge 42:22
37:24 ᵈ Jer 41:7
37:25 ᵉ Ge 43:11 ᶠ ver 28
37:26 ᵍ ver 20; Ge 4:10
37:27 ʰ Ge 42:21
37:28 ⁱ Ge 25:2; Jdg 6:1-3

Genesis 37:12–36

The caravan was made up of Midianites and Ishmaelites. Midianites were descendants of Abraham through Keturah and Ishmaelites his descendants through Hagar. The forebears of these two peoples were Jacob's uncles, making these traders second or third cousins to Joseph and his brothers.

God didn't approve of the treachery of Joseph's brothers, nor did he need it to accomplish his plan. But one way or another, Joseph was going to get to Egypt and come to the place at which God's blessing and deliverance would come through him. If God couldn't use the sinful choices people make, his sovereignty would be limited. There would be no hope for any of us.

Do you think you are totally different from Joseph's brothers? Chances are none of us would let our envy go as far as theirs did, but jealousy has far more subtle effects that can be just as damaging. Our resentment of a coworker may not drive us to try to arrange for their dismissal or transfer, but it may lead to a steady onslaught of put-downs, insults, and insinuations behind their back. This is envy's more common face—a face we need to recognize in our mirrors if we hope to overcome it (cf. James 1:19–24).

37:28
i Ge 45:4-5;
Ps 105:17; Ac 7:9
cistern and sold him for twenty shekels[a] of silver to the Ishmaelites, who took him to Egypt.[j]

37:29
k ver 34; Ge 44:13;
Job 1:20
37:30
l ver 22;
Ge 42:13,36
29When Reuben returned to the cistern and saw that Joseph was not there, he tore his clothes.[k] 30He went back to his brothers and said, "The boy isn't there! Where can I turn now?"[l]

37:31
m ver 3,23
37:33
n ver 20
o Ge 44:20,28
31Then they got Joseph's robe,[m] slaughtered a goat and dipped the robe in the blood. 32They took the ornamented robe back to their father and said, "We found this. Examine it to see whether it is your son's robe."

33He recognized it and said, "It is my son's robe! Some ferocious animal[n] has devoured him. Joseph has surely been torn to pieces."[o]

37:34
p ver 29 *q* 2Sa 3:31
r Ge 50:3,10,11
37:35
s Ge 42:38;
44:22,29,31
34Then Jacob tore his clothes,[p] put on sackcloth[q] and mourned for his son many days.[r] 35All his sons and daughters came to comfort him, but he refused to be comforted. "No," he said, "in mourning will I go down to the grave[b s] to my son." So his father wept for him.

37:36
t Ge 39:1
36Meanwhile, the Midianites[c] sold Joseph in Egypt to Potiphar, one of Pharaoh's officials, the captain of the guard.[t]

Judah and Tamar

38:2
u 1Ch 2:3
38:3
v ver 6; Ge 46:12;
Nu 26:19
38 At that time, Judah left his brothers and went down to stay with a man of Adullam named Hirah. 2There Judah met the daughter of a Canaanite man named Shua.[u] He married her and lay with her; 3she became pregnant and gave birth to a son, who was named Er.[v] 4She conceived again and gave birth to a son and named him Onan. 5She gave birth to still another son and named him Shelah. It was at Kezib that she gave birth to him.

38:7
w ver 10; Ge 46:12;
1Ch 2:3
6Judah got a wife for Er, his firstborn, and her name was Tamar. 7But Er, Judah's firstborn, was wicked in the LORD's sight; so the LORD put him to death.[w]

38:8
x Dt 25:5-6;
Mt 22:24-28
8Then Judah said to Onan, "Lie with your brother's wife and fulfill your duty to her as a brother-in-law to produce offspring for your brother."[x] 9But Onan knew that the offspring would not be his; so whenever he lay with his brother's wife, he spilled his semen on the ground to keep from producing offspring for his brother.

38:10
y Ge 46:12;
Dt 25:7-10
10What he did was wicked in the LORD's sight; so he put him to death also.[y]

38:11
z Ru 1:13
11Judah then said to his daughter-in-law Tamar, "Live as a widow in your father's house until my son Shelah grows up."[z] For he thought, "He may die too, just like his brothers." So Tamar went to live in her father's house.

38:12
a ver 14;
Jos 15:10,57
12After a long time Judah's wife, the daughter of Shua, died. When Judah had recovered from his grief, he went up to Timnah,[a] to the men who were shearing his sheep, and his friend Hirah the Adullamite went with him.

38:14
b ver 11
13When Tamar was told, "Your father-in-law is on his way to Timnah to shear his sheep," 14she took off her widow's clothes, covered herself with a veil to disguise herself, and then sat down at the entrance to Enaim, which is on the road to Timnah. For she saw that, though Shelah[b] had now grown up, she had not been given to him as his wife.

15When Judah saw her, he thought she was a prostitute, for she had covered her

---

[a] 28 That is, about 8 ounces (about 0.2 kilogram)   [b] 35 Hebrew *Sheol*   [c] 36 Samaritan Pentateuch, Septuagint, Vulgate and Syriac (see also verse 28); Masoretic Text *Medanites*

Genesis 38:1–30

A Hittite law stipulated that when a widow married her late husband's brother and *he* died, she was to marry his father. That wasn't how the later law of Moses would read, but it was apparently the procedure Tamar was following. When she accepted as guarantee *of payment* Jacob's seal, cord, and staff, she held symbols of his individual and corporate identity—the equivalent of an ancient photo I.D.

In a brief two verses Judah moved from a demand that Tamar be burned to a declaration that she was

more righteous than he. This admission of moral failure was the first hint of a change taking place in Judah.

When Tamar's pregnancy became apparent, Judah's reaction was harsh. But he was made aware of his own guilt when she showed him the things he had left as a pledge. How typical of human behavior to see first and most clearly the sins of another! Consider Jesus' words in Matthew 7:3–5. How willing are you to examine yourself first before trying to correct someone else's faulty behavior?

face. 16Not realizing that she was his daughter-in-law,[c] he went over to her by the
roadside and said, "Come now, let me sleep with you."
"And what will you give me to sleep with you?" she asked.
17"I'll send you a young goat[d] from my flock," he said.
"Will you give me something as a pledge[e] until you send it?" she asked.
18He said, "What pledge should I give you?"
"Your seal[f] and its cord, and the staff in your hand," she answered. So he gave
them to her and slept with her, and she became pregnant by him. 19After she left,
she took off her veil and put on her widow's clothes[g] again.
20Meanwhile Judah sent the young goat by his friend the Adullamite in order to
get his pledge back from the woman, but he did not find her. 21He asked the men
who lived there, "Where is the shrine prostitute[h] who was beside the road at
Enaim?"
"There hasn't been any shrine prostitute here," they said.
22So he went back to Judah and said, "I didn't find her. Besides, the men who
lived there said, 'There hasn't been any shrine prostitute here.' "
23Then Judah said, "Let her keep what she has, or we will become a laughingstock. After all, I did send her this young goat, but you didn't find her."
24About three months later Judah was told, "Your daughter-in-law Tamar is guilty
of prostitution, and as a result she is now pregnant."
Judah said, "Bring her out and have her burned to death!"[i]
25As she was being brought out, she sent a message to her father-in-law. "I am
pregnant by the man who owns these," she said. And she added, "See if you recognize whose seal and cord and staff these are."[j]
26Judah recognized them and said, "She is more righteous than I,[k] since I
wouldn't give her to my son Shelah.[l]" And he did not sleep with her again.
27When the time came for her to give birth, there were twin boys in her womb.[m]
28As she was giving birth, one of them put out his hand; so the midwife took a scarlet thread and tied it on his wrist and said, "This one came out first." 29But when
he drew back his hand, his brother came out, and she said, "So this is how you have
broken out!" And he was named Perez.[a][n] 30Then his brother, who had the scarlet
thread on his wrist, came out and he was given the name Zerah.[b][o]

Joseph and Potiphar's Wife

39 Now Joseph had been taken down to Egypt. Potiphar, an Egyptian who was
one of Pharaoh's officials, the captain of the guard,[p] bought him from the
Ishmaelites who had taken him there.[q]
2The LORD was with Joseph[r] and he prospered, and he lived in the house of his
Egyptian master. 3When his master saw that the LORD was with him[s] and that the
LORD gave him success in everything he did,[t] 4Joseph found favor in his eyes and became his attendant. Potiphar put him in charge of his household, and he entrusted
to his care everything he owned.[u] 5From the time he put him in charge of his household and of all that he owned, the LORD blessed the household of the Egyptian because of Joseph.[v] The blessing of the LORD was on everything Potiphar had, both in
the house and in the field. 6So he left in Joseph's care everything he had; with Joseph
in charge, he did not concern himself with anything except the food he ate.
Now Joseph was well-built and handsome,[w] 7and after a while his master's wife
took notice of Joseph and said, "Come to bed with me!"[x]
8But he refused.[y] "With me in charge," he told her, "my master does not concern
himself with anything in the house; everything he owns he has entrusted to my care.

38:16 [c] Lev 18:15; 20:12
38:17 [d] Eze 16:33 [e] ver 20
38:18 [f] ver 25
38:19 [g] ver 14
38:21 [h] Lev 19:29; Hos 4:14
38:24 [i] Lev 21:9; Dt 22:21,22
38:25 [j] ver 18
38:26 [k] 1Sa 24:17 [l] ver 11
38:27 [m] Ge 25:24
38:29 [n] Ge 46:12; Nu 26:20,21; Ru 4:12,18; 1Ch 2:4; Mt 1:3
38:30 [o] 1Ch 2:4
39:1 [p] Ge 37:36 [q] Ge 37:25; Ps 105:17
39:2 [r] Ge 21:20,22; Ac 7:9
39:3 [s] Ge 21:22; 26:28 [t] Ps 1:3
39:4 [u] ver 8,22; Ge 24:2
39:5 [v] Ge 26:24; 30:27
39:6 [w] 1Sa 16:12
39:7 [x] 2Sa 13:11; Pr 7:15-18
39:8 [y] Pr 6:23-24

[a] 29 *Perez* means *breaking out.* [b] 30 *Zerah* can mean *scarlet* or *brightness.*

Genesis 39:1–23

In the last chapter God had put Judah's sons to death. Here he was with Joseph, and Joseph prospered. Much as Laban had recognized that the Lord's favor was with Jacob (30:27), Potiphar saw the same in Joseph and trusted him with responsibility. As a result, the blessing side of the covenant continued to be realized on a small scale as Potiphar and his house were blessed through Joseph. The success, though, was short-lived.

39:9
z Ge 41:33,40
a Ge 20:6; 42:18;
2Sa 12:13

39:12
b Pr 7:13

39:14
c Dt 22:24,27

39:17
d Ex 23:1,7;
Ps 101:5

39:19
e Pr 6:34
39:20
f Ge 40:3;
Ps 105:18
39:21
g Ex 3:21

39:22
h ver 4

39:23
i ver 3

40:1
j Ne 1:11
40:2
k Pr 16:14,15

40:3
l Ge 39:20
40:4
m Ge 39:4

40:5
n Ge 41:11

40:7
o Ne 2:2

⁹No one is greater in this house than I am.ᶻ My master has withheld nothing from me except you, because you are his wife. How then could I do such a wicked thing and sin against God?"ᵃ ¹⁰And though she spoke to Joseph day after day, he refused to go to bed with her or even be with her.

¹¹One day he went into the house to attend to his duties, and none of the household servants was inside. ¹²She caught him by his cloakᵇ and said, "Come to bed with me!" But he left his cloak in her hand and ran out of the house.

¹³When she saw that he had left his cloak in her hand and had run out of the house, ¹⁴she called her household servants. "Look," she said to them, "this Hebrew has been brought to us to make sport of us! He came in here to sleep with me, but I screamed.ᶜ ¹⁵When he heard me scream for help, he left his cloak beside me and ran out of the house."

¹⁶She kept his cloak beside her until his master came home. ¹⁷Then she told him this story:ᵈ "That Hebrew slave you brought us came to me to make sport of me. ¹⁸But as soon as I screamed for help, he left his cloak beside me and ran out of the house."

¹⁹When his master heard the story his wife told him, saying, "This is how your slave treated me," he burned with anger.ᵉ ²⁰Joseph's master took him and put him in prison,ᶠ the place where the king's prisoners were confined.

But while Joseph was there in the prison, ²¹the LORD was with him; he showed him kindness and granted him favor in the eyes of the prison warden.ᵍ ²²So the warden put Joseph in charge of all those held in the prison, and he was made responsible for all that was done there.ʰ ²³The warden paid no attention to anything under Joseph's care, because the LORD was with Joseph and gave him success in whatever he did.ⁱ

The Cupbearer and the Baker

40 Some time later, the cupbearerʲ and the baker of the king of Egypt offended their master, the king of Egypt. ²Pharaoh was angryᵏ with his two officials, the chief cupbearer and the chief baker, ³and put them in custody in the house of the captain of the guard,ˡ in the same prison where Joseph was confined. ⁴The captain of the guard assigned them to Joseph,ᵐ and he attended them.

After they had been in custody for some time, ⁵each of the two men—the cupbearer and the baker of the king of Egypt, who were being held in prison—had a dream the same night, and each dream had a meaning of its own.ⁿ

⁶When Joseph came to them the next morning, he saw that they were dejected. ⁷So he asked Pharaoh's officials who were in custody with him in his master's house, "Why are your faces so sad today?"ᵒ

📖 God temporarily allows the presence of evil—a fact we may find hard to square with his sovereignty. The Bible doesn't attempt to reconcile these issues through detailed, technical theology. Instead, God's Word supports the reality of his rule, as in the Joseph story, by illustration. Hebrews 11 considers a lineup of prominent faith heroes and the different outcomes of their lives under God's hand. What principles can you learn from comparisons and contrasts in this New Testament chapter?

Genesis 40:1–23

🔍 In the ancient Near East, dream interpretations were sought from experts trained in the techniques and methods of the day. Both the Egyptians and the Babylonians compiled "dream books," which contained sample dreams with a key to their interpretation. These books preserved the data concerning past dreams and interpretations, providing the security of "scientific" documentation. Joseph consulted God, but his interpretation followed the way Egyptian dream literature interpreted comparable symbols.

The difference between the interpretations Joseph gave for the two dreams hinged on the phrase "Pharaoh will lift up/off your head." Ironically, in Hebrew the words are exactly the same; the context determines the different meanings. The king would lift *up* the cupbearer's head by offering him favor and forgiveness. But Pharaoh would lift up the baker's head by lifting it *off*—by executing him.

📖 The value of our service to God isn't just measured by how remarkable the end results might be. God also finds value in our effort, in our journey. Joseph's consistent faithfulness in slavery and in prison was every bit as valuable to God as the deliverance he would later bring as second-in-command in Egypt. Faithfulness is faithfulness, regardless of the scale on which God chooses to use it. Is this a new perspective for you, particularly if you are struggling in a seemingly fruitless effort?

8 "We both had dreams," they answered, "but there is no one to interpret them." *p* Then Joseph said to them, "Do not interpretations belong to God? *q* Tell me your dreams."

9 So the chief cupbearer told Joseph his dream. He said to him, "In my dream I saw a vine in front of me, 10 and on the vine were three branches. As soon as it budded, it blossomed, and its clusters ripened into grapes. 11 Pharaoh's cup was in my hand, and I took the grapes, squeezed them into Pharaoh's cup and put the cup in his hand."

12 "This is what it means, *r*" Joseph said to him. "The three branches are three days. 13 Within three days Pharaoh will lift up your head and restore you to your position, and you will put Pharaoh's cup in his hand, just as you used to do when you were his cupbearer. 14 But when all goes well with you, remember me *s* and show me kindness; *t* mention me to Pharaoh and get me out of this prison. 15 For I was forcibly carried off from the land of the Hebrews, *u* and even here I have done nothing to deserve being put in a dungeon."

16 When the chief baker saw that Joseph had given a favorable interpretation, he said to Joseph, "I too had a dream: On my head were three baskets of bread. *a* 17 In the top basket were all kinds of baked goods for Pharaoh, but the birds were eating them out of the basket on my head."

18 "This is what it means," Joseph said. "The three baskets are three days. *v* 19 Within three days Pharaoh will lift off your head *w* and hang you on a tree. *b* And the birds will eat away your flesh."

20 Now the third day was Pharaoh's birthday, *x* and he gave a feast for all his officials. *y* He lifted up the heads of the chief cupbearer and the chief baker in the presence of his officials: 21 He restored the chief cupbearer to his position, so that he once again put the cup into Pharaoh's hand, *z* 22 but he hanged *c* the chief baker, *a* just as Joseph had said to them in his interpretation. *b*

23 The chief cupbearer, however, did not remember Joseph; he forgot him. *c*

Pharaoh's Dreams

41 When two full years had passed, Pharaoh had a dream: *d* He was standing by the Nile, 2 when out of the river there came up seven cows, sleek and fat, *e* and they grazed among the reeds. *f* 3 After them, seven other cows, ugly and gaunt, came

---

a 16 Or *three wicker baskets*   *b* 19 Or *and impale you on a pole*   *c* 22 Or *impaled*

40:8
p Ge 41:8,15
q Ge 41:16;
Da 2:22,28,47

40:12
r Ge 41:12,15,25;
Da 2:36; 4:19

40:14
s Lk 23:42
t Jos 2:12;
1Sa 20:14,42;
1Ki 2:7
40:15
u Ge 37:26-28

40:18
v ver 12
40:19
w ver 13

40:20
x Mt 14:6-10
y Mk 6:21
40:21
z ver 13
40:22
a ver 19
b Ps 105:19

40:23
c Job 19:14;
Ecc 9:15

41:1
d Ge 20:3
41:2
e ver 26 *f* Isa 19:6

40:20–22

Understanding Genesis

To fully understand the stories in the book of Genesis, it's important for us to appreciate the differences between the ways a person of that day viewed the world and how people in many Western cultures see it today. Some important distinctions:

Modern View	Ancient View	God's View
• Individual centered	Group centered	Cares about individuals and how they interact as a group (John 15:1–17)
• Distinguish the parts	Concentrate on the whole	Concentrates on a whole made up of individual parts (Eph. 4:16)
• Urge uniqueness	Urge conformity	Desires conformity to the Son and to his creative call on people's lives (Rom. 8:29)
• Equality as key value	Hierarchy as key value	Concerned with mutual submission under Christ (Matt. 28:18; Eph. 5:21)
• Self-reliant achievement	Interdependent collaboration	Promotes Spirit-dependent individual and collaborative efforts (Zech. 4:6; 1 Cor. 12:4–6)
• Status achieved	Status ascribed or given	Glory belongs to God alone (1 Cor. 1:30–31; 10:21)

up out of the Nile and stood beside those on the riverbank. [4]And the cows that were ugly and gaunt ate up the seven sleek, fat cows. Then Pharaoh woke up.

[5]He fell asleep again and had a second dream: Seven heads of grain, healthy and good, were growing on a single stalk. [6]After them, seven other heads of grain sprouted—thin and scorched by the east wind. [7]The thin heads of grain swallowed up the seven healthy, full heads. Then Pharaoh woke up; it had been a dream.

[8]In the morning his mind was troubled,[g] so he sent for all the magicians[h] and wise men of Egypt. Pharaoh told them his dreams, but no one could interpret them for him.

[9]Then the chief cupbearer said to Pharaoh, "Today I am reminded of my shortcomings. [10]Pharaoh was once angry with his servants,[i] and he imprisoned me and the chief baker in the house of the captain of the guard.[j] [11]Each of us had a dream the same night, and each dream had a meaning of its own.[k] [12]Now a young Hebrew was there with us, a servant of the captain of the guard. We told him our dreams, and he interpreted them for us, giving each man the interpretation of his dream.[l] [13]And things turned out exactly as he interpreted them to us: I was restored to my position, and the other man was hanged.[a][m]"

[14]So Pharaoh sent for Joseph, and he was quickly brought from the dungeon.[n] When he had shaved and changed his clothes, he came before Pharaoh.

[15]Pharaoh said to Joseph, "I had a dream, and no one can interpret it. But I have heard it said of you that when you hear a dream you can interpret it."[o]

[16]"I cannot do it," Joseph replied to Pharaoh, "but God will give Pharaoh the answer he desires."[p]

[17]Then Pharaoh said to Joseph, "In my dream I was standing on the bank of the Nile, [18]when out of the river there came up seven cows, fat and sleek, and they grazed among the reeds. [19]After them, seven other cows came up—scrawny and very ugly and lean. I had never seen such ugly cows in all the land of Egypt. [20]The lean, ugly cows ate up the seven fat cows that came up first. [21]But even after they ate them, no one could tell that they had done so; they looked just as ugly as before. Then I woke up.

[22]"In my dreams I also saw seven heads of grain, full and good, growing on a single stalk. [23]After them, seven other heads sprouted—withered and thin and scorched by the east wind. [24]The thin heads of grain swallowed up the seven good heads. I told this to the magicians, but none could explain it to me.[q]"

[25]Then Joseph said to Pharaoh, "The dreams of Pharaoh are one and the same. God has revealed to Pharaoh what he is about to do.[r] [26]The seven good cows[s] are seven years, and the seven good heads of grain are seven years; it is one and the same dream. [27]The seven lean, ugly cows that came up afterward are seven years, and so are the seven worthless heads of grain scorched by the east wind: They are seven years of famine.[t]

[28]"It is just as I said to Pharaoh: God has shown Pharaoh what he is about to do. [29]Seven years of great abundance[u] are coming throughout the land of Egypt, [30]but seven years of famine[v] will follow them. Then all the abundance in Egypt will be forgotten, and the famine will ravage the land.[w] [31]The abundance in the land will not be remembered, because the famine that follows it will be so severe. [32]The rea-

---

[a] 13 Or *impaled*

41:8
[g] Da 2:1,3; 4:5,19
[h] Ex 7:11,22; Da 1:20; 2:2,27; 4:7

41:10
[i] Ge 40:2 [j] Ge 39:20

41:11
[k] Ge 40:5

41:12
[l] Ge 40:12

41:13
[m] Ge 40:22
41:14
[n] Ps 105:20; Da 2:25

41:15
[o] Da 5:16

41:16
[p] Ge 40:8; Da 2:30; Ac 3:12; 2Co 3:5

41:24
[q] ver 8

41:25
[r] Da 2:45
41:26
[s] ver 2

41:27
[t] Ge 12:10; 2Ki 8:1

41:29
[u] ver 47
41:30
[v] ver 54; Ge 47:13
[w] ver 56

Genesis 41:1–40

Joseph treated the dream as a message from God but used generic terminology. Pharaoh was left to draw his own conclusion about which deity was responsible. Egypt didn't depend on rainfall for its food production but on the flooding of the Nile, which was much more dependable. Rarely, then, did the country suffer extended famine. The gods connected to the Nile and its annual flooding were considered powerful. Any deity who could impose such a severe famine on Egypt must be exceptionally great.

In today's fast-paced business world, the ability to think quickly, creatively, and proactively is considered indispensable for success. God gives each of us a unique skill-set, and our direction in life—and how far we travel in that direction—depend largely on those skills and our ability to use them. But how often do we stop to recognize God as the Giver of our talents? We are wise to consider Jesus' words as recorded in Luke 12:48: "From everyone who has been given much, much will be demanded."

son the dream was given to Pharaoh in two forms is that the matter has been firmly decided[x] by God, and God will do it soon.

33"And now let Pharaoh look for a discerning and wise man[y] and put him in charge of the land of Egypt. 34Let Pharaoh appoint commissioners over the land to take a fifth[z] of the harvest of Egypt during the seven years of abundance.[a] 35They should collect all the food of these good years that are coming and store up the grain under the authority of Pharaoh, to be kept in the cities for food.[b] 36This food should be held in reserve for the country, to be used during the seven years of famine that will come upon Egypt,[c] so that the country may not be ruined by the famine."

37The plan seemed good to Pharaoh and to all his officials.[d] 38So Pharaoh asked them, "Can we find anyone like this man, one in whom is the spirit of God[a]?"[e] 39Then Pharaoh said to Joseph, "Since God has made all this known to you, there is no one so discerning and wise as you. 40You shall be in charge of my palace, and all my people are to submit to your orders.[f] Only with respect to the throne will I be greater than you."

Joseph in Charge of Egypt

41So Pharaoh said to Joseph, "I hereby put you in charge of the whole land of Egypt."[g] 42Then Pharaoh took his signet ring[h] from his finger and put it on Joseph's finger. He dressed him in robes of fine linen and put a gold chain around his neck.[i] 43He had him ride in a chariot as his second-in-command,[b] and men shouted before him, "Make way[c]!"[j] Thus he put him in charge of the whole land of Egypt.

44Then Pharaoh said to Joseph, "I am Pharaoh, but without your word no one will lift hand or foot in all Egypt."[k] 45Pharaoh gave Joseph the name Zaphenath-Paneah and gave him Asenath daughter of Potiphera, priest of On,[d] to be his wife.[l] And Joseph went throughout the land of Egypt.

46Joseph was thirty years old[m] when he entered the service[n] of Pharaoh king of Egypt. And Joseph went out from Pharaoh's presence and traveled throughout Egypt. 47During the seven years of abundance the land produced plentifully. 48Joseph collected all the food produced in those seven years of abundance in Egypt and stored it in the cities. In each city he put the food grown in the fields surrounding it. 49Joseph stored up huge quantities of grain, like the sand of the sea; it was so much that he stopped keeping records because it was beyond measure.

50Before the years of famine came, two sons were born to Joseph by Asenath daughter of Potiphera, priest of On.[o] 51Joseph named his firstborn[p] Manasseh[e] and said, "It is because God has made me forget all my trouble and all my father's household." 52The second son he named Ephraim[f][q] and said, "It is because God has made me fruitful[r] in the land of my suffering."

53The seven years of abundance in Egypt came to an end, 54and the seven years of famine began,[s] just as Joseph had said. There was famine in all the other lands,

41:32 [x] Nu 23:19; Isa 46:10-11
41:33 [y] ver 39
41:34 [z] 1Sa 8:15 [a] ver 48
41:35 [b] ver 48
41:36 [c] ver 56
41:37 [d] Ge 45:16
41:38 [e] Nu 27:18; Job 32:8; Da 4:8-9,18; 5:11,14
41:40 [f] Ps 105:21-22; Ac 7:10

41:41 [g] Ge 42:6; Da 6:3
41:42 [h] Est 3:10 [i] Da 5:7, 16,29
41:43 [j] Est 6:9
41:44 [k] Ps 105:22
41:45 [l] ver 50; Ge 46:20,27
41:46 [m] Ge 37:2 [n] 1Sa 16:21; Da 1:19

41:50 [o] Ge 46:20; 48:5
41:51 [p] Ge 48:14,18,20
41:52 [q] Ge 48:1,5; 50:23 [r] Ge 17:6; 28:3; 49:22

41:54 [s] ver 30; Ps 105:11; Ac 7:11

---

[a] 38 Or of the gods   [b] 43 Or in the chariot of his second-in-command; or in his second chariot   [c] 43 Or Bow down   [d] 45 That is, Heliopolis; also in verse 50   [e] 51 Manasseh sounds like and may be derived from the Hebrew for forget.   [f] 52 Ephraim sounds like the Hebrew for twice fruitful.

Genesis 41:41–57

The second-in-command in all administrative matters in ancient Egypt was the Grand Vizier. This may have been Joseph's title. But those holding certain other posts could claim to be second-in-command within the area of their own responsibility. One of the most appropriate known titles to describe Joseph's duties was "Overseer of the Granaries of Upper and Lower Egypt." The covenant blessing (12:2–3) echoes through the passage: All nations on Earth were blessed through Joseph's promotion in the Egyptian government.

Joseph was being "made" by Pharaoh. Ironically, though, God's hand, not Pharaoh's, remade Joseph.

Joseph wasn't first and foremost Pharaoh's instrument of economic survival; he was God's instrument of salvation. Pharaoh too was God's instrument. Without his knowledge, his choices carried out God's plan.

Does the title really matter? In God's timetable some people find themselves in important positions after a lifetime of struggling in obscurity. But God's plan for others is that they serve him anonymously for their whole lives, receiving no recognition, gaining no prominence, and enjoying only minimal results. We don't know their stories. But they will be told in eternity, because God doesn't forget. God knows your faithfulness and is doing his work through you as you yield yourself to him.

41:55
t Dt 32:24 u ver 41

41:56
v Ge 12:10
41:57
w Ge 42:5; 47:15

42:1
x Ac 7:12

42:2
y Ge 43:8

42:4
z ver 38
42:5
a Ge 41:57
b Ge 12:10; Ac 7:11
42:6
c Ge 41:41
d Ge 37:7-10
42:7
e ver 30

42:8
f Ge 37:2
42:9
g Ge 37:7

42:13
h Ge 37:30,33;
44:20
42:15
i 1Sa 17:55

42:16
j ver 11
42:17
k Ge 40:4
42:18
l Ge 20:11;
Lev 25:43
42:20
m ver 15,34;
Ge 43:5; 44:23

42:21
n Ge 37:26-28
o Hos 5:15

but in the whole land of Egypt there was food. [55]When all Egypt began to feel the famine,[t] the people cried to Pharaoh for food. Then Pharaoh told all the Egyptians, "Go to Joseph and do what he tells you."[u]

[56]When the famine had spread over the whole country, Joseph opened the storehouses and sold grain to the Egyptians, for the famine[v] was severe throughout Egypt. [57]And all the countries came to Egypt to buy grain from Joseph,[w] because the famine was severe in all the world.

Joseph's Brothers Go to Egypt

42 When Jacob learned that there was grain in Egypt,[x] he said to his sons, "Why do you just keep looking at each other?" [2]He continued, "I have heard that there is grain in Egypt. Go down there and buy some for us, so that we may live and not die."[y]

[3]Then ten of Joseph's brothers went down to buy grain from Egypt. [4]But Jacob did not send Benjamin, Joseph's brother, with the others, because he was afraid that harm might come to him.[z] [5]So Israel's sons were among those who went to buy grain,[a] for the famine was in the land of Canaan also.[b]

[6]Now Joseph was the governor of the land,[c] the one who sold grain to all its people. So when Joseph's brothers arrived, they bowed down to him with their faces to the ground.[d] [7]As soon as Joseph saw his brothers, he recognized them, but he pretended to be a stranger and spoke harshly to them.[e] "Where do you come from?" he asked.

"From the land of Canaan," they replied, "to buy food."

[8]Although Joseph recognized his brothers, they did not recognize him.[f] [9]Then he remembered his dreams[g] about them and said to them, "You are spies! You have come to see where our land is unprotected."

[10]"No, my lord," they answered. "Your servants have come to buy food. [11]We are all the sons of one man. Your servants are honest men, not spies."

[12]"No!" he said to them. "You have come to see where our land is unprotected."

[13]But they replied, "Your servants were twelve brothers, the sons of one man, who lives in the land of Canaan. The youngest is now with our father, and one is no more."[h]

[14]Joseph said to them, "It is just as I told you: You are spies! [15]And this is how you will be tested: As surely as Pharaoh lives,[i] you will not leave this place unless your youngest brother comes here. [16]Send one of your number to get your brother; the rest of you will be kept in prison, so that your words may be tested to see if you are telling the truth.[j] If you are not, then as surely as Pharaoh lives, you are spies!" [17]And he put them all in custody[k] for three days.

[18]On the third day, Joseph said to them, "Do this and you will live, for I fear God:[l] [19]If you are honest men, let one of your brothers stay here in prison, while the rest of you go and take grain back for your starving households. [20]But you must bring your youngest brother to me,[m] so that your words may be verified and that you may not die." This they proceeded to do.

[21]They said to one another, "Surely we are being punished because of our brother.[n] We saw how distressed he was when he pleaded with us for his life, but we would not listen; that's why this distress[o] has come upon us."

Genesis 42:1–38

Again a masquerade (cf. ch. 27) figures in the plot as Joseph pretended to be a stranger. There was also reversal as he treated his brothers harshly—though quite differently from their earlier cruel treatment of him (37:23–28). As he accused them of being spies (cf. 37:2), the situation was heavy with irony. It becomes almost laughable as the brothers protest their honesty, but sad as they remark about their brother who "is no more." Joseph *was* testing his brothers, but his purpose was to see whether they had reformed.

In the 20 or more years since Joseph had seen his brothers, their guilt had enslaved and imprisoned them as much as Joseph's chains. Our own unconfessed sin will fester until the thorn is removed from our hearts through repentance. In Psalm 32:1–7 David used a different analogy to make the same point, immediately afterward breaking forth with irrepressible joy following the release of his guilt and his acceptance of the blessed gift of forgiveness. If you need forgiveness for any behavior, God is waiting to offer you his grace (1 Jn. 1:9).

²²Reuben replied, "Didn't I tell you not to sin against the boy?^p But you wouldn't listen! Now we must give an accounting^q for his blood."^r ²³They did not realize that Joseph could understand them, since he was using an interpreter.

²⁴He turned away from them and began to weep, but then turned back and spoke to them again. He had Simeon taken from them and bound before their eyes.^s

²⁵Joseph gave orders to fill their bags with grain,^t to put each man's silver back in his sack,^u and to give them provisions for their journey.^v After this was done for them, ²⁶they loaded their grain on their donkeys and left.

²⁷At the place where they stopped for the night one of them opened his sack to get feed for his donkey, and he saw his silver in the mouth of his sack.^w ²⁸"My silver has been returned," he said to his brothers. "Here it is in my sack."

Their hearts sank and they turned to each other trembling and said, "What is this that God has done to us?"^x

²⁹When they came to their father Jacob in the land of Canaan, they told him all that had happened to them. They said, ³⁰"The man who is lord over the land spoke harshly to us^y and treated us as though we were spying on the land. ³¹But we said to him, 'We are honest men; we are not spies.^z ³²We were twelve brothers, sons of one father. One is no more, and the youngest is now with our father in Canaan.'

³³"Then the man who is lord over the land said to us, 'This is how I will know whether you are honest men: Leave one of your brothers here with me, and take food for your starving households and go.^a ³⁴But bring your youngest brother to me so I will know that you are not spies but honest men. Then I will give your brother back to you, and you can trade^a in the land.^b'"

³⁵As they were emptying their sacks, there in each man's sack was his pouch of silver! When they and their father saw the money pouches, they were frightened.^c ³⁶Their father Jacob said to them, "You have deprived me of my children. Joseph is no more and Simeon is no more, and now you want to take Benjamin.^d Everything is against me!"

³⁷Then Reuben said to his father, "You may put both of my sons to death if I do not bring him back to you. Entrust him to my care, and I will bring him back."

³⁸But Jacob said, "My son will not go down there with you; his brother is dead^e and he is the only one left. If harm comes to him^f on the journey you are taking, you will bring my gray head down to the grave^{b g} in sorrow.^h"

The Second Journey to Egypt

43 Now the famine was still severe in the land.ⁱ ²So when they had eaten all the grain they had brought from Egypt, their father said to them, "Go back and buy us a little more food."

³But Judah said to him, "The man warned us solemnly, 'You will not see my face again unless your brother is with you.'^j ⁴If you will send our brother along with us, we will go down and buy food for you. ⁵But if you will not send him, we will not go down, because the man said to us, 'You will not see my face again unless your brother is with you.^k'"

⁶Israel asked, "Why did you bring this trouble on me by telling the man you had another brother?"

⁷They replied, "The man questioned us closely about ourselves and our family. 'Is your father still living?'^l he asked us. 'Do you have another brother?'^m We simply answered his questions. How were we to know he would say, 'Bring your brother down here'?"

^a 34 Or *move about freely* ^b 38 Hebrew *Sheol*

Cross references

42:22 ^p Ge 37:21-22 ^q Ge 9:5 ^r 1Ki 2:32; 2Ch 24:22; Ps 9:12

42:24 ^s ver 13; Ge 43:14,23; 45:14-15

42:25 ^t Ge 43:2 ^u Ge 44:1,8 ^v Ro 12:17,20-21

42:27 ^w Ge 43:21-22

42:28 ^x Ge 43:23

42:30 ^y ver 7

42:31 ^z ver 11

42:33 ^a ver 19,20

42:34 ^b Ge 34:10

42:35 ^c Ge 43:12,15,18

42:36 ^d Ge 43:14

42:38 ^e Ge 37:33 ^f ver 4 ^g Ge 37:35 ^h Ge 44:29,34

43:1 ⁱ Ge 12:10; 41:56-57

43:3 ^j Ge 42:15; 44:23

43:5 ^k Ge 42:15; 2Sa 3:13

43:7 ^l ver 27 ^m Ge 42:13

Genesis 43:1–34

The brothers got three surprises: (1) They were invited to the ruler's house for dinner. (2) Their questions of the steward were answered theologically—God, they were told, had given them a treasure. (3) At dinner they were seated in birth order. The older brothers' portions were hearty, but not in comparison to the plate set before Benjamin. By this time they were reeling with astonishment, but Joseph was still setting them up. Would the others respond with jealousy toward Benjamin as they had years before toward Joseph?

43:8
n Ge 42:2;
Ps 33:18-19

43:9
o Ge 42:37; 44:32;
Phm 1:18-19

43:11
p Ge 32:20;
Pr 18:16
q Ge 37:25;
Jer 8:22 r 1Ki 10:2
43:12
s Ge 42:25
43:14
t Ge 17:1; 28:3;
35:11 u Ge 42:24
v Est 4:16

43:15
w Ge 45:9,13
x Ge 47:2,7
43:16
y Ge 44:1,4,12
z ver 31; Lk 15:23

43:18
a Ge 42:35

43:20
b Ge 42:3

43:21
c ver 15;
Ge 42:27,35

43:23
d Ge 42:28
e Ge 42:24

43:24
f ver 16 g Ge 18:4;
24:32

43:26
h Mt 2:11
i Ge 37:7,10

43:27
j ver 7

43:28
k Ge 37:7

43:29
l Ge 42:13
m Nu 6:25; Ps 67:1
43:30
n Jn 11:33,38
o Ge 42:24; 45:2,
14,15; 46:29
43:31
p Ge 45:1

8Then Judah said to Israel his father, "Send the boy along with me and we will go at once, so that we and you and our children may live and not die.ⁿ 9I myself will guarantee his safety; you can hold me personally responsible for him. If I do not bring him back to you and set him here before you, I will bear the blame before you all my life.^o 10As it is, if we had not delayed, we could have gone and returned twice."

11Then their father Israel said to them, "If it must be, then do this: Put some of the best products of the land in your bags and take them down to the man as a gift^p—a little balm^q and a little honey, some spices^r and myrrh, some pistachio nuts and almonds. 12Take double the amount of silver with you, for you must return the silver that was put back into the mouths of your sacks.^s Perhaps it was a mistake. 13Take your brother also and go back to the man at once. 14And may God Almighty^a ^t grant you mercy before the man so that he will let your other brother and Benjamin come back with you.^u As for me, if I am bereaved, I am bereaved."^v

15So the men took the gifts and double the amount of silver, and Benjamin also. They hurried^w down to Egypt and presented themselves^x to Joseph. 16When Joseph saw Benjamin with them, he said to the steward of his house,^y "Take these men to my house, slaughter an animal and prepare dinner;^z they are to eat with me at noon."

17The man did as Joseph told him and took the men to Joseph's house. 18Now the men were frightened^a when they were taken to his house. They thought, "We were brought here because of the silver that was put back into our sacks the first time. He wants to attack us and overpower us and seize us as slaves and take our donkeys."

19So they went up to Joseph's steward and spoke to him at the entrance to the house. 20"Please, sir," they said, "we came down here the first time to buy food.^b 21But at the place where we stopped for the night we opened our sacks and each of us found his silver—the exact weight—in the mouth of his sack. So we have brought it back with us.^c 22We have also brought additional silver with us to buy food. We don't know who put our silver in our sacks."

23"It's all right," he said. "Don't be afraid. Your God, the God of your father, has given you treasure in your sacks;^d I received your silver." Then he brought Simeon out to them.^e

24The steward took the men into Joseph's house,^f gave them water to wash their feet^g and provided fodder for their donkeys. 25They prepared their gifts for Joseph's arrival at noon, because they had heard that they were to eat there.

26When Joseph came home, they presented to him the gifts^h they had brought into the house, and they bowed down before him to the ground.ⁱ 27He asked them how they were, and then he said, "How is your aged father you told me about? Is he still living?"^j

28They replied, "Your servant our father is still alive and well." And they bowed low to pay him honor.^k

29As he looked about and saw his brother Benjamin, his own mother's son, he asked, "Is this your youngest brother, the one you told me about?"^l And he said, "God be gracious to you,^m my son." 30Deeply movedⁿ at the sight of his brother, Joseph hurried out and looked for a place to weep. He went into his private room and wept^o there.

31After he had washed his face, he came out and, controlling himself,^p said, "Serve the food."

32They served him by himself, the brothers by themselves, and the Egyptians who

---

^a 14 Hebrew *El-Shaddai*

📖 What "treasures" do you have that others—even nonbelievers—have to point out to you? Do you value your family? Are you thankful to God for the blessing of a good job? What in your relationship with Christ do you take for granted? Have you considered thanking him for the Bible you hold in your hands? Most of us live with physical comforts and resources billions of people in the rest of the world can only dream about. Yet we often think of them as our right. Why not prayerfully ask the Lord to show you the treasures he's given you.

ate with him by themselves, because Egyptians could not eat with Hebrews, [q] for that is detestable to Egyptians. [r] 33The men had been seated before him in the order of their ages, from the firstborn to the youngest; and they looked at each other in astonishment. 34When portions were served to them from Joseph's table, Benjamin's portion was five times as much as anyone else's. [s] So they feasted and drank freely with him.

A Silver Cup in a Sack

44 Now Joseph gave these instructions to the steward of his house: "Fill the men's sacks with as much food as they can carry, and put each man's silver in the mouth of his sack. [t] 2Then put my cup, the silver one, in the mouth of the youngest one's sack, along with the silver for his grain." And he did as Joseph said.

3As morning dawned, the men were sent on their way with their donkeys. 4They had not gone far from the city when Joseph said to his steward, "Go after those men at once, and when you catch up with them, say to them, 'Why have you repaid good with evil? [u] 5Isn't this the cup my master drinks from and also uses for divination? [v] This is a wicked thing you have done.' "

6When he caught up with them, he repeated these words to them. 7But they said to him, "Why does my lord say such things? Far be it from your servants to do anything like that! 8We even brought back to you from the land of Canaan the silver we found inside the mouths of our sacks. [w] So why would we steal silver or gold from your master's house? 9If any of your servants is found to have it, he will die; [x] and the rest of us will become my lord's slaves."

10"Very well, then," he said, "let it be as you say. Whoever is found to have it will become my slave; the rest of you will be free from blame."

11Each of them quickly lowered his sack to the ground and opened it. 12Then the steward proceeded to search, beginning with the oldest and ending with the youngest. And the cup was found in Benjamin's sack. [y] 13At this, they tore their clothes. [z] Then they all loaded their donkeys and returned to the city.

14Joseph was still in the house when Judah and his brothers came in, and they threw themselves to the ground before him. [a] 15Joseph said to them, "What is this you have done? Don't you know that a man like me can find things out by divination? [b]"

16"What can we say to my lord?" Judah replied. "What can we say? How can we prove our innocence? God has uncovered your servants' guilt. We are now my lord's slaves [c]—we ourselves and the one who was found to have the cup. [d]"

17But Joseph said, "Far be it from me to do such a thing! Only the man who was found to have the cup will become my slave. The rest of you, go back to your father in peace."

18Then Judah went up to him and said: "Please, my lord, let your servant speak a word to my lord. Do not be angry [e] with your servant, though you are equal to Pharaoh himself. 19My lord asked his servants, 'Do you have a father or a brother?' [f] 20And we answered, 'We have an aged father, and there is a young son born to him in his old age. [g] His brother is dead, [h] and he is the only one of his mother's sons left, and his father loves him.' [i]

21"Then you said to your servants, 'Bring him down to me so I can see him for myself.' [j] 22And we said to my lord, 'The boy cannot leave his father; if he leaves him, his father will die.' [k] 23But you told your servants, 'Unless your youngest brother

---

43:32
q Gal 2:12
r Ge 46:34; Ex 8:26

43:34
s Ge 37:3; 45:22

44:1
t Ge 42:25

44:4
u Ps 35:12
44:5
v Ge 30:27;
Dt 18:10-14

44:8
w Ge 42:25; 43:21
44:9
x Ge 31:32

44:12
y ver 2
44:13
z Ge 37:29;
Nu 14:6; 2Sa 1:11
44:14
a Ge 37:7,10

44:15
b ver 5; Ge 30:27

44:16
c ver 9; Ge 43:18
d ver 2

44:18
e Ge 18:30;
Ex 32:22
44:19
f Ge 43:7
44:20
g Ge 37:3
h Ge 37:33
i Ge 42:13

44:21
j Ge 42:15
44:22
k Ge 37:35

Genesis 44:1–34

Joseph finally learned what Jacob had believed all these years about his fate—the "torn to pieces" by a wild animal story. Most important, it became clear that Judah (along with the rest of Joseph's brothers?) had become unselfish, preferring slavery to guilt. This change in the brothers was every bit as miraculous as the transformation in Joseph's status.

Judah's willingness to intercede for Benjamin and to endure horrible, and most likely permanent, punishment in his place, reminds us of Jesus' willingness to suffer a horrendous death—and abandonment by God—in ours. Unlike Benjamin, who was "set up" for this test of his older brothers, each of us is in every sense guilty as charged. Do you still marvel in the face of such a sacrifice?

44:23
l Ge 43:5

44:25
m Ge 43:2

44:27
n Ge 46:19

44:28
o Ge 37:33
44:29
p Ge 42:38

44:30
q 1Sa 18:1

44:32
r Ge 43:9
44:33
s Ge 43:18
t Jn 15:13

44:34
u Est 8:6

comes down with you, you will not see my face again.'*l* 24When we went back to your servant my father, we told him what my lord had said.

25"Then our father said, 'Go back and buy a little more food.'*m* 26But we said, 'We cannot go down. Only if our youngest brother is with us will we go. We cannot see the man's face unless our youngest brother is with us.'

27"Your servant my father said to us, 'You know that my wife bore me two sons.*n* 28One of them went away from me, and I said, "He has surely been torn to pieces."*o* And I have not seen him since. 29If you take this one from me too and harm comes to him, you will bring my gray head down to the grave*a* in misery.'*p*

30"So now, if the boy is not with us when I go back to your servant my father and if my father, whose life is closely bound up with the boy's life,*q* 31sees that the boy isn't there, he will die. Your servants will bring the gray head of our father down to the grave in sorrow. 32Your servant guaranteed the boy's safety to my father. I said, 'If I do not bring him back to you, I will bear the blame before you, my father, all my life!'*r*

33"Now then, please let your servant remain here as my lord's slave*s* in place of the boy,*t* and let the boy return with his brothers. 34How can I go back to my father if the boy is not with me? No! Do not let me see the misery that would come upon my father."*u*

Joseph Makes Himself Known

45:1
v Ge 43:31

45:2
w Ge 29:11
x ver 16; Ge 46:29

45:3
y Ac 7:13 *z* ver 15

45:4
a Ge 37:28
45:5
b Ge 42:21
c Ge 42:22
d ver 7-8; Ge 50:20; Ps 105:17
45:7
e 2Ki 19:4,30,31; Isa 10:20,21; Mic 4:7; Zep 2:7
f Ex 15:2; Est 4:14; Isa 25:9
45:8
g Jdg 17:10
h Ge 41:41
45:9
i Ge 43:10
45:10
j Ge 46:28,34; 47:1
45:11
k Ge 47:12

45 Then Joseph could no longer control himself*v* before all his attendants, and he cried out, "Have everyone leave my presence!" So there was no one with Joseph when he made himself known to his brothers. 2And he wept*w* so loudly that the Egyptians heard him, and Pharaoh's household heard about it.*x*

3Joseph said to his brothers, "I am Joseph! Is my father still living?"*y* But his brothers were not able to answer him,*z* because they were terrified at his presence.

4Then Joseph said to his brothers, "Come close to me." When they had done so, he said, "I am your brother Joseph, the one you sold into Egypt!*a* 5And now, do not be distressed*b* and do not be angry with yourselves for selling me here,*c* because it was to save lives that God sent me ahead of you.*d* 6For two years now there has been famine in the land, and for the next five years there will not be plowing and reaping. 7But God sent me ahead of you to preserve for you a remnant*e* on earth and to save your lives by a great deliverance.*b f*

8"So then, it was not you who sent me here, but God. He made me father*g* to Pharaoh, lord of his entire household and ruler of all Egypt.*h* 9Now hurry back to my father and say to him, 'This is what your son Joseph says: God has made me lord of all Egypt. Come down to me; don't delay.*i* 10You shall live in the region of Goshen*j* and be near me—you, your children and grandchildren, your flocks and herds, and all you have. 11I will provide for you there,*k* because five years of famine are still to come. Otherwise you and your household and all who belong to you will become destitute.'

45:13
l Ac 7:14

12"You can see for yourselves, and so can my brother Benjamin, that it is really I who am speaking to you. 13Tell my father about all the honor accorded me in Egypt and about everything you have seen. And bring my father down here quickly.'*l*

14Then he threw his arms around his brother Benjamin and wept, and Benjamin

---

a 29 Hebrew *Sheol*; also in verse 31   *b* 7 Or *save you as a great band of survivors*

Genesis 45:1–28

The brothers were understandably speechless after Joseph's disclosure. As they cowered in fear and shock, he had to draw them back to himself. Joseph sought to calm them by voicing the truth at the center of his story: God had sovereignly directed these events to accomplish his purposes.

We might wonder at Joseph's question: "Is my father still living?" After all, Judah had just made it clear that the loss of Benjamin would bring about Jacob's death. A couple of observations may clarify the issue. (1) Joseph

was ending his masquerade. His question was less important than his word choice ("my father," not "your father"). (2) The Hebrew word translated "living" may also mean "well." Joseph wanted detailed news of his father.

God's power and blessing can be found in what appear to be the most monstrous crimes and most disastrous circumstances. God doesn't reveal his sovereignty by repressing our bad choices but by demonstrating that no choice we can make can interfere with his plan. In fact, our seemingly foolish choices may end up furthering that plan. Have you ever seen this happen?

embraced him, weeping. [15]And he kissed[m] all his brothers and wept over them. Afterward his brothers talked with him.[n]

[16]When the news reached Pharaoh's palace that Joseph's brothers had come,[o] Pharaoh and all his officials were pleased. [17]Pharaoh said to Joseph, "Tell your brothers, 'Do this: Load your animals and return to the land of Canaan, [18]and bring your father and your families back to me. I will give you the best of the land of Egypt[p] and you can enjoy the fat of the land.'[q]

[19]"You are also directed to tell them, 'Do this: Take some carts[r] from Egypt for your children and your wives, and get your father and come. [20]Never mind about your belongings, because the best of all Egypt will be yours.'"

[21]So the sons of Israel did this. Joseph gave them carts, as Pharaoh had commanded, and he also gave them provisions for their journey.[s] [22]To each of them he gave new clothing, but to Benjamin he gave three hundred shekels[a] of silver and five sets of clothes.[t] [23]And this is what he sent to his father: ten donkeys loaded with the best things of Egypt, and ten female donkeys loaded with grain and bread and other provisions for his journey. [24]Then he sent his brothers away, and as they were leaving he said to them, "Don't quarrel on the way!"[u]

[25]So they went up out of Egypt and came to their father Jacob in the land of Canaan. [26]They told him, "Joseph is still alive! In fact, he is ruler of all Egypt." Jacob was stunned; he did not believe them.[v] [27]But when they told him everything Joseph had said to them, and when he saw the carts[w] Joseph had sent to carry him back, the spirit of their father Jacob revived. [28]And Israel said, "I'm convinced! My son Joseph is still alive. I will go and see him before I die."

Jacob Goes to Egypt

46 So Israel set out with all that was his, and when he reached Beersheba,[x] he offered sacrifices to the God of his father Isaac.[y]

[2]And God spoke to Israel in a vision at night[z] and said, "Jacob! Jacob!"

"Here I am,"[a] he replied.

[3]"I am God, the God of your father,"[b] he said. "Do not be afraid to go down to Egypt, for I will make you into a great nation[c] there.[d] [4]I will go down to Egypt with you, and I will surely bring you back again.[e] And Joseph's own hand will close your eyes.[f]"

[5]Then Jacob left Beersheba, and Israel's sons took their father Jacob and their children and their wives in the carts[g] that Pharaoh had sent to transport him. [6]They also took with them their livestock and the possessions they had acquired in Canaan, and Jacob and all his offspring went to Egypt.[h] [7]He took with him to Egypt his sons and grandsons and his daughters and granddaughters––all his offspring.[i]

[8]These are the names of the sons of Israel[j] (Jacob and his descendants) who went to Egypt:

Reuben the firstborn of Jacob.

[9]The sons of Reuben:[k]

Hanoch, Pallu, Hezron and Carmi.

[10]The sons of Simeon:[l]

[a] 22 That is, about 7 1/2 pounds (about 3.5 kilograms)

45:15
[m] Lk 15:20 [n] ver 3

45:16
[o] Ac 7:13

45:18
[p] Ge 27:28; 46:34; 47:6,11,27; Nu 18:12,29
[q] Ps 37:19

45:19
[r] Ge 46:5

45:21
[s] Ge 42:25

45:22
[t] Ge 37:3; 43:34

45:24
[u] Ge 42:21-22

45:26
[v] Ge 44:28

45:27
[w] ver 19

46:1
[x] Ge 21:14; 28:10
[y] Ge 26:24; 28:13; 31:42

46:2
[z] Ge 15:1; Job 33:14-15
[a] Ge 22:1; 31:11

46:3
[b] Ge 28:13
[c] Ge 12:2; Dt 26:5
[d] Ex 1:7

46:4
[e] Ge 28:15; 48:21; Ex 3:8 [f] Ge 50:1,24

46:5
[g] Ge 45:19

46:6
[h] Dt 26:5; Jos 24:4; Ps 105:23; Isa 52:4; Ac 7:15

46:7
[i] Ge 45:10

46:8
[j] Ex 1:1; Nu 26:4

46:9
[k] 1Ch 5:3

46:10
[l] Ge 29:33; Nu 26:14

Genesis 46:1—47:12

Contrary to Pharaoh's advice (45:20), Jacob left nobody in the family behind to hold the fort and preserve the family holdings in Canaan. The move was a complete act of faith. This would later remind the exodus generation that they should expect to find no kin in the land to which they were going.

Both at the beginning and end of of their conversation, Jacob blessed Pharaoh—another illustration of God's covenant promise to Abram: "All peoples on earth will be blessed through you" (12:3).

Jacob and his family were unwilling to accept Pharaoh's generous proposal that they leave everything behind on faith that he would provide their needs. Some people view Jacob's choice as a compromise of faith (his self-sufficiency rearing its head; cf. 32:1–21). God does at times ask people to abandon the comforts of home to serve him in harsh and primitive surroundings. But more often he asks us to practice generosity and contentment and to make sure our priorities are in order with his kingdom in first place.

Jemuel,[m] Jamin, Ohad, Jakin, Zohar and Shaul the son of a Canaanite woman.

11 The sons of Levi:[n]

Gershon, Kohath and Merari.

12 The sons of Judah:[o]

Er, Onan, Shelah, Perez and Zerah (but Er and Onan had died in the land of Canaan).

The sons of Perez:[p]

Hezron and Hamul.

13 The sons of Issachar:[q]

Tola, Puah,[a][r] Jashub[b] and Shimron.

14 The sons of Zebulun:[s]

Sered, Elon and Jahleel.

15 These were the sons Leah bore to Jacob in Paddan Aram,[c] besides his daughter Dinah. These sons and daughters of his were thirty-three in all.

16 The sons of Gad:[t]

Zephon,[d][u] Haggi, Shuni, Ezbon, Eri, Arodi and Areli.

17 The sons of Asher:[v]

Imnah, Ishvah, Ishvi and Beriah.

Their sister was Serah.

The sons of Beriah:

Heber and Malkiel.

18 These were the children born to Jacob by Zilpah,[w] whom Laban had given to his daughter Leah[x]—sixteen in all.

19 The sons of Jacob's wife Rachel:

Joseph and Benjamin.[y] 20 In Egypt, Manasseh[z] and Ephraim[a] were born to Joseph by Asenath daughter of Potiphera, priest of On.[e]

21 The sons of Benjamin:[b]

Bela, Beker, Ashbel, Gera, Naaman, Ehi, Rosh, Muppim, Huppim and Ard.

22 These were the sons of Rachel who were born to Jacob—fourteen in all.

23 The son of Dan:

Hushim.

24 The sons of Naphtali:

Jahziel, Guni, Jezer and Shillem.

25 These were the sons born to Jacob by Bilhah,[c] whom Laban had given to his daughter Rachel[d]—seven in all.

26 All those who went to Egypt with Jacob—those who were his direct descendants, not counting his sons' wives—numbered sixty-six persons.[e] 27 With the two sons[f] who had been born to Joseph in Egypt, the members of Jacob's family, which went to Egypt, were seventy[g] in all.[f]

28 Now Jacob sent Judah ahead of him to Joseph to get directions to Goshen.[g] When they arrived in the region of Goshen, 29 Joseph had his chariot made ready and went to Goshen to meet his father Israel. As soon as Joseph appeared before him, he threw his arms around his father[h] and wept for a long time.[h]

30 Israel said to Joseph, "Now I am ready to die, since I have seen for myself that you are still alive."

31 Then Joseph said to his brothers and to his father's household, "I will go up and speak to Pharaoh and will say to him, 'My brothers and my father's household, who were living in the land of Canaan, have come to me.[i] 32 The men are shepherds; they

---

Left margin cross-references:

46:10 m Ex 6:15
46:11 n Ge 29:34; Nu 3:17
46:12 o Ge 29:35 p 1Ch 2:5; Mt 1:3
46:13 q Ge 30:18 r 1Ch 7:1
46:14 s Ge 30:20
46:16 t Ge 30:11 u Nu 26:15
46:17 v Ge 30:13; 1Ch 7:30-31
46:18 w Ge 30:10 x Ge 29:24
46:19 y Ge 44:27
46:20 z Ge 41:51 a Ge 41:52
46:21 b Nu 26:38-41; 1Ch 7:6-12; 8:1
46:25 c Ge 30:8 d Ge 29:29
46:26 e ver 5-7; Ex 1:5; Dt 10:22
46:27 f Ac 7:14
46:28 g Ge 45:10
46:29 h Ge 45:14-15; Lk 15:20
46:31 i Ge 47:1

---

a 13 Samaritan Pentateuch and Syriac (see also 1 Chron. 7:1); Masoretic Text *Puvah*
b 13 Samaritan Pentateuch and some Septuagint manuscripts (see also Num. 26:24 and 1 Chron. 7:1); Masoretic Text *Iob*   c 15 That is, Northwest Mesopotamia   d 16 Samaritan Pentateuch and Septuagint (see also Num. 26:15); Masoretic Text *Ziphion*   e 20 That is, Heliopolis   f 27 Hebrew; Septuagint *the nine children*   g 27 Hebrew (see also Exodus 1:5 and footnote); Septuagint (see also Acts 7:14) *seventy-five*   h 29 Hebrew *around him*

tend livestock, and they have brought along their flocks and herds and everything they own.' 33When Pharaoh calls you in and asks, 'What is your occupation?' *j* 34you should answer, 'Your servants have tended livestock from our boyhood on, just as our fathers did.' Then you will be allowed to settle in the region of Goshen, *k* for all shepherds are detestable to the Egyptians.' *l*"

47 Joseph went and told Pharaoh, "My father and brothers, with their flocks and herds and everything they own, have come from the land of Canaan and are now in Goshen." *m* 2He chose five of his brothers and presented them before Pharaoh.

3Pharaoh asked the brothers, "What is your occupation?" *n*

"Your servants are shepherds," they replied to Pharaoh, "just as our fathers were."
4They also said to him, "We have come to live here awhile, *o* because the famine is severe in Canaan *p* and your servants' flocks have no pasture. So now, please let your servants settle in Goshen." *q*

5Pharaoh said to Joseph, "Your father and your brothers have come to you, 6and the land of Egypt is before you; settle your father and your brothers in the best part of the land. *r* Let them live in Goshen. And if you know of any among them with special ability, *s* put them in charge of my own livestock."

7Then Joseph brought his father Jacob in and presented him before Pharaoh. After Jacob blessed *a* Pharaoh, *t* 8Pharaoh asked him, "How old are you?"

9And Jacob said to Pharaoh, "The years of my pilgrimage are a hundred and thirty. *u* My years have been few and difficult, *v* and they do not equal the years of the pilgrimage of my fathers. *w*" 10Then Jacob blessed *b* Pharaoh *x* and went out from his presence.

11So Joseph settled his father and his brothers in Egypt and gave them property in the best part of the land, the district of Rameses, *y* as Pharaoh directed. 12Joseph also provided his father and his brothers and all his father's household with food, according to the number of their children. *z*

Joseph and the Famine

13There was no food, however, in the whole region because the famine was severe; both Egypt and Canaan wasted away because of the famine. *a* 14Joseph collected all the money that was to be found in Egypt and Canaan in payment for the grain they were buying, and he brought it to Pharaoh's palace. *b* 15When the money of the people of Egypt and Canaan was gone, all Egypt came to Joseph and said, "Give us food. Why should we die before your eyes? *c* Our money is used up."

16"Then bring your livestock," said Joseph. "I will sell you food in exchange for your livestock, since your money is gone." 17So they brought their livestock to Joseph, and he gave them food in exchange for their horses, *d* their sheep and goats, their cattle and donkeys. And he brought them through that year with food in exchange for all their livestock.

18When that year was over, they came to him the following year and said, "We cannot hide from our lord the fact that since our money is gone and our livestock belongs to you, there is nothing left for our lord except our bodies and our land. 19Why

---

a 7 Or *greeted*   *b* 10 Or *said farewell to*

46:33
j Ge 47:3

46:34
k Ge 45:10
l Ge 43:32; Ex 8:26

47:1
m Ge 46:31
47:3
n Ge 46:33

47:4
o Ge 15:13; Dt 26:5
p Ge 43:1
q Ge 46:34

47:6
r Ge 45:18
s Ex 18:21,25

47:7
t ver 10; 2Sa 14:22
47:9
u Ge 25:7
v Heb 11:9,13
w Ge 35:28
47:10
x ver 7

47:11
y Ex 1:11; 12:37

47:12
z Ge 45:11

47:13
a Ge 41:30; Ac 7:11

47:14
b Ge 41:56

47:15
c ver 19; Ex 16:3

47:17
d Ex 14:9

Genesis 47:13–31

Joseph's policies may seem economically repressive, but hard times require hard solutions. Theoretically, a prosperous farmer could have rebuilt his wealth when the famine ended, though it's unclear whether he could have bought back his land. In spite of personal hardship and servitude, the people were grateful for their lives.

Verse 27 indicates that the Israelites had become fruitful and multiplied. This draws together the blessing of all humankind from 1:28 and the covenant blessing that Abraham's family would become a great nation. God had granted them covenant-type blessings in Egypt in a partial fulfillment of the promises that would come

to full completion in the return to Canaan. The time in Egypt wasn't an interruption of the covenant but an incubation of the covenant people.

The results of the devastating famine in this story are repeated around the world today. Lack of food pushes regions and nations into grinding poverty. Some of the victims never recover lost wealth, lands, freedom, or personal dignity. How would God have us be a blessing to these people? What can we share of our generosity to help struggling families regain hope for the future? Should we consume less so that there is more to go around? These are serious questions for each representative of God's covenant people to consider.

should we perish before your eyes—we and our land as well? Buy us and our land in exchange for food, and we with our land will be in bondage to Pharaoh. Give us seed so that we may live and not die, and that the land may not become desolate."

20 So Joseph bought all the land in Egypt for Pharaoh. The Egyptians, one and all, sold their fields, because the famine was too severe for them. The land became Pharaoh's, 21 and Joseph reduced the people to servitude,[a] from one end of Egypt to the other. 22 However, he did not buy the land of the priests, because they received a regular allotment from Pharaoh and had food enough from the allotment[e] Pharaoh gave them. That is why they did not sell their land.

23 Joseph said to the people, "Now that I have bought you and your land today for Pharaoh, here is seed for you so you can plant the ground. 24 But when the crop comes in, give a fifth[f] of it to Pharaoh. The other four-fifths you may keep as seed for the fields and as food for yourselves and your households and your children."

25 "You have saved our lives," they said. "May we find favor in the eyes of our lord;[g] we will be in bondage to Pharaoh."

26 So Joseph established it as a law concerning land in Egypt—still in force today—that a fifth of the produce belongs to Pharaoh. It was only the land of the priests that did not become Pharaoh's.[h]

27 Now the Israelites settled in Egypt in the region of Goshen. They acquired property there and were fruitful and increased greatly in number.[i]

28 Jacob lived in Egypt[j] seventeen years, and the years of his life were a hundred and forty-seven. 29 When the time drew near for Israel to die,[k] he called for his son Joseph and said to him, "If I have found favor in your eyes, put your hand under my thigh[l] and promise that you will show me kindness and faithfulness.[m] Do not bury me in Egypt, 30 but when I rest with my fathers, carry me out of Egypt and bury me where they are buried."[n]

"I will do as you say," he said.

31 "Swear to me,"[o] he said. Then Joseph swore to him,[p] and Israel worshiped as he leaned on the top of his staff.[b][q]

Manasseh and Ephraim

48 Some time later Joseph was told, "Your father is ill." So he took his two sons Manasseh and Ephraim[r] along with him. 2 When Jacob was told, "Your son Joseph has come to you," Israel rallied his strength and sat up on the bed.

3 Jacob said to Joseph, "God Almighty[c] appeared to me at Luz[s] in the land of Canaan, and there he blessed me[t] 4 and said to me, 'I am going to make you fruitful and will increase your numbers.[u] I will make you a community of peoples, and I will give this land as an everlasting possession to your descendants after you.'

5 "Now then, your two sons born to you in Egypt[v] before I came to you here will be reckoned as mine; Ephraim and Manasseh will be mine,[w] just as Reuben and Simeon are mine. 6 Any children born to you after them will be yours; in the territory they inherit they will be reckoned under the names of their brothers. 7 As I was returning from Paddan,[d] to my sorrow Rachel died in the land of Canaan while we were still on the way, a little distance from Ephrath. So I buried her there beside the road to Ephrath" (that is, Bethlehem).[x]

---

[a] 21 Samaritan Pentateuch and Septuagint (see also Vulgate); Masoretic Text *and he moved the people into the cities*   [b] 31 Or *Israel bowed down at the head of his bed*   [c] 3 Hebrew *El-Shaddai*   [d] 7 That is, Northwest Mesopotamia

---

Genesis 48:1–22

Jacob "adopted" Ephraim and Manasseh, in a sense replacing Reuben and Simeon (Jacob's oldest sons). A literal translation of the final Hebrew clause in verse 5 might read: "Like Reuben and Simeon they will be to me." Joseph's sons "became" Jacob's firstborn sons. In a roundabout way the double portion of the firstborn's inheritance went to Joseph. Theoretically, Joseph received his portion and Ephraim and Manasseh the portions of Reuben and Simeon, giving Joseph three shares. Judah may have received the double portion, but verse 22 suggests that it went to Joseph (cf. 1 Chron. 5:1–2).

Jacob insisted on favoring Ephraim over his older brother. As surprising as this appearred to Joseph, to the readers of Genesis it occasions only a wry grin (here we go again!). The recurring motif (cf. 25:23) testifies that grace as blessing comes to those with least reason to expect it.

Cross-references (margin):

47:22 e Dt 14:28-29; Ezr 7:24
47:24 f Ge 41:34
47:25 g Ge 32:5
47:26 h ver 22
47:27 i Ge 17:6; 46:3; Ex 1:7
47:28 j Ps 105:23
47:29 k Dt 31:14; l Ge 24:2; m Ge 24:49
47:30 n Ge 49:29-32; 50:5,13; Ac 7:15-16
47:31 o Ge 21:23; p Ge 24:3; q Heb 11:21 fn 1Ki 1:47
48:1 r Ge 41:52
48:3 s Ge 28:19; t Ge 28:13; 35:9-12
48:4 u Ge 17:6
48:5 v Ge 41:50-52; 46:20 w 1Ch 5:1; Jos 14:4
48:7 x Ge 35:19

[8]When Israel saw the sons of Joseph, he asked, "Who are these?" [9]"They are the sons God has given me here," [y] Joseph said to his father. Then Israel said, "Bring them to me so I may bless [z] them."

[10]Now Israel's eyes were failing because of old age, and he could hardly see. [a] So Joseph brought his sons close to him, and his father kissed them [b] and embraced them. [11]Israel said to Joseph, "I never expected to see your face again, and now God has allowed me to see your children too." [c]

[12]Then Joseph removed them from Israel's knees and bowed down with his face to the ground. [13]And Joseph took both of them, Ephraim on his right toward Israel's left hand and Manasseh on his left toward Israel's right hand, [d] and brought them close to him. [14]But Israel reached out his right hand and put it on Ephraim's head, though he was the younger, and crossing his arms, he put his left hand on Manasseh's head, even though Manasseh was the firstborn. [e]

[15]Then he blessed [f] Joseph and said,

"May the God before whom my fathers
   Abraham and Isaac walked,
the God who has been my shepherd [g]
   all my life to this day,
[16]the Angel who has delivered me from all harm
   —may he bless these boys. [h]
May they be called by my name
   and the names of my fathers Abraham and Isaac, [i]
and may they increase greatly
   upon the earth."

[17]When Joseph saw his father placing his right hand on Ephraim's head [j] he was displeased; so he took hold of his father's hand to move it from Ephraim's head to Manasseh's head. [18]Joseph said to him, "No, my father, this one is the firstborn; put your right hand on his head."

[19]But his father refused and said, "I know, my son, I know. He too will become a people, and he too will become great. [k] Nevertheless, his younger brother will be greater than he, [l] and his descendants will become a group of nations." [20]He blessed them that day and said,

"In your [a] name will Israel pronounce this blessing:
   'May God make you like Ephraim [m] and Manasseh. [n]'"

So he put Ephraim ahead of Manasseh.

[21]Then Israel said to Joseph, "I am about to die, but God will be with you [o] and take you [b] back to the land of your [b] fathers. [p] [22]And to you, as one who is over your brothers, [q] I give the ridge of land [c] [r] I took from the Amorites with my sword and my bow."

Jacob Blesses His Sons

49 Then Jacob called for his sons and said: "Gather around so I can tell you what will happen to you in days to come. [s]

[2]"Assemble and listen, sons of Jacob;
   listen to your father Israel. [t]

---

[a] 20 The Hebrew is singular.   [b] 21 The Hebrew is plural.   [c] 22 Or *And to you I give one portion more than to your brothers—the portion*

How would you respond if someone were to say, "I just don't like you"? As later generations of Israelites mused over these stories, they learned that some of their intertribal strife had identifiable causes, like the offenses of Reuben (35:22; 49:4) and Simeon (34:13–30). Other elements made less sense, like the elevation of Ephraim over Manasseh. So too with our situations. Sometimes, but not always, we can pinpoint cause and effect. Our one anchor, no matter what favor we enjoy on a human scale, is God's unmoveable, never-ending love for us (Rom. 8:38–39). That is a sure confidence builder.

48:9
y Ge 33:5 z Ge 27:4

48:10
a Ge 27:1
b Ge 27:27

48:11
c Ge 50:23;
Ps 128:6

48:13
d Ps 110:1

48:14
e Ge 41:51
48:15
f Ge 17:1
g Ge 49:24

48:16
h Heb 11:21
i Ge 28:13

48:17
j ver 14

48:19
k Ge 17:20
l Ge 25:23

48:20
m Nu 2:18
n Nu 2:20; Ru 4:11

48:21
o Ge 26:3; 46:4
p Ge 28:13; 50:24

48:22
q Ge 37:8
r Jos 24:32; Jn 4:5

49:1
s Nu 24:14;
Jer 23:20

49:2
t Ps 34:11

49:3
u Ge 29:32
v Dt 21:17;
Ps 78:51
49:4
w Isa 57:20
x Ge 35:22;
Dt 27:20

3 "Reuben, you are my firstborn, [u]
    my might, the first sign of my strength, [v]
    excelling in honor, excelling in power.
4 Turbulent as the waters, [w] you will no longer excel,
    for you went up onto your father's bed,
    onto my couch and defiled it. [x]

49:5
y Ge 34:25; Pr 4:17

5 "Simeon and Levi are brothers—
    their swords [a] are weapons of violence. [y]

49:6
z Pr 1:15; Eph 5:11
a Ge 34:26

6 Let me not enter their council,
    let me not join their assembly, [z]
    for they have killed men in their anger [a]
    and hamstrung oxen as they pleased.

49:7
b Jos 19:1,9;
21:1-42

7 Cursed be their anger, so fierce,
    and their fury, so cruel!
  I will scatter them in Jacob
    and disperse them in Israel. [b]

49:8
c Dt 33:7; 1Ch 5:2
49:9
d Nu 24:9;
Eze 19:5; Mic 5:8
e Rev 5:5

8 "Judah, [b] your brothers will praise you;
    your hand will be on the neck of your enemies;
    your father's sons will bow down to you. [c]
9 You are a lion's [d] cub, O Judah; [e]
    you return from the prey, my son.
  Like a lion he crouches and lies down,
    like a lioness—who dares to rouse him?

49:10
f Nu 24:17,19;
Ps 60:7 g Ps 2:9;
Isa 42:1,4

10 The scepter will not depart from Judah, [f]
    nor the ruler's staff from between his feet,
  until he comes to whom it belongs [c]
    and the obedience of the nations is his. [g]
11 He will tether his donkey to a vine,
    his colt to the choicest branch;
  he will wash his garments in wine,
    his robes in the blood of grapes.
12 His eyes will be darker than wine,
    his teeth whiter than milk. [d]

49:13
h Ge 30:20;
Dt 33:18-19;
Jos 19:10-11

13 "Zebulun [h] will live by the seashore
    and become a haven for ships;
    his border will extend toward Sidon.

49:14
i Ge 30:18

14 "Issachar [i] is a rawboned [e] donkey
    lying down between two saddlebags. [f]
15 When he sees how good is his resting place
    and how pleasant is his land,
  he will bend his shoulder to the burden
    and submit to forced labor.

---

a 5 The meaning of the Hebrew for this word is uncertain.   b 8 *Judah* sounds like and may be derived from the Hebrew for *praise.*   c 10 Or *until Shiloh comes;* or *until he comes to whom tribute belongs*   d 12 Or *will be dull from wine, / his teeth white from milk*   e 14 Or *strong*
f 14 Or *campfires*

Genesis 49:1–28

Genesis 49 targeted the distant future, when the tribe of Judah would move into a place of leadership among the tribes. Joseph was to be leader among the sons, *Judah among the tribes.* The unfolding of history would eventually realize this in David (1 Sam. 16:12) and Jesus (Matt. 1:1–3).

Some of Jacob's words sounded harsh. We instinctively look for the benefit of the doubt, the letting off the hook. These may have been the patriarch's final words to his sons, and several must have walked away crushed. Jacob had already shown incredible patience with them. Yet the quality of mercy seems strangely absent here. Our own parting words, whether at the school entrance, at bedtime, or at the end of a visit can profoundly affect our children. We owe it to them to be up front about moral and ethical issues, but we can always season our words with grace and unconditional love.

16 "Dan[a][j] will provide justice for his people
    as one of the tribes of Israel.
17 Dan[k] will be a serpent by the roadside,
    a viper along the path,
    that bites the horse's heels
      so that its rider tumbles backward.

18 "I look for your deliverance, O Lord.[l]

19 "Gad[b][m] will be attacked by a band of raiders,
    but he will attack them at their heels.

20 "Asher's[n] food will be rich;
    he will provide delicacies fit for a king.

21 "Naphtali[o] is a doe set free
    that bears beautiful fawns.[c]

22 "Joseph[p] is a fruitful vine,
    a fruitful vine near a spring,
    whose branches climb over a wall.[d]
23 With bitterness archers attacked him;
    they shot at him with hostility.[q]
24 But his bow remained steady,
    his strong arms[r] stayed[e] limber,
because of the hand of the Mighty One of Jacob,[s]
    because of the Shepherd, the Rock of Israel,[t]
25 because of your father's God,[u] who helps you,
    because of the Almighty,[f] who blesses you
with blessings of the heavens above,
    blessings of the deep that lies below,[v]
    blessings of the breast and womb.
26 Your father's blessings are greater
    than the blessings of the ancient mountains,
    than[g] the bounty of the age-old hills.
Let all these rest on the head of Joseph,
    on the brow of the prince among[h] his brothers.[w]

27 "Benjamin[x] is a ravenous wolf;
    in the morning he devours the prey,
    in the evening he divides the plunder."

28 All these are the twelve tribes of Israel, and this is what their father said to them when he blessed them, giving each the blessing appropriate to him.

The Death of Jacob

29 Then he gave them these instructions:[y] "I am about to be gathered to my people.[z] Bury me with my fathers[a] in the cave in the field of Ephron the Hittite, 30 the cave in the field of Machpelah,[b] near Mamre in Canaan, which Abraham bought as a burial place from Ephron the Hittite, along with the field.[c] 31 There Abraham[d]

---

[a] 16 *Dan* here means *he provides justice.*   [b] 19 *Gad* can mean *attack* and *band of raiders.*
[c] 21 Or *free; / he utters beautiful words*   [d] 22 Or *Joseph is a wild colt, / a wild colt near a spring, / a wild donkey on a terraced hill*   [e] 23,24 Or *archers will attack . . . will shoot . . . will remain . . . will stay*
[f] 25 Hebrew *Shaddai*   [g] 26 Or *of my progenitors, / as great as*   [h] 26 Or *the one separated from*

49:16
[j] Ge 30:6; Dt 33:22;
Jdg 18:26-27
49:17
[k] Jdg 18:27

49:18
[l] Ps 119:166,174
49:19
[m] Ge 30:11;
Dt 33:20; 1Ch 5:18

49:20
[n] Ge 30:13;
Dt 33:24

49:21
[o] Ge 30:8; Dt 33:23

49:22
[p] Ge 30:24;
Dt 33:13-17

49:23
[q] Ge 37:24

49:24
[r] Ps 18:34
[s] Ps 132:2,5;
Isa 1:24; 41:10
[t] Isa 28:16

49:25
[u] Ge 28:13
[v] Ge 27:28

49:26
[w] Dt 33:15-16

49:27
[x] Ge 35:18;
Jdg 20:12-13

49:29
[y] Ge 50:16
[z] Ge 25:8
[a] Ge 15:15; 47:30;
50:13
49:30
[b] Ge 23:9
[c] Ge 23:20
49:31
[d] Ge 25:9

Genesis 49:29—50:14
Though it was common practice in Egypt, embalming of Israelites is found only in this chapter. The philosophy behind the Egyptians' practice was a belief that the body was to be preserved as a repository for the soul after death. The Israelites may have been trying to accommodate the Egyptians, but the embalming of the bodies of Jacob and later Joseph also preserved them for later burial in Canaan.

49:31
e Ge 23:19
f Ge 35:29
and his wife Sarah [e] were buried, there Isaac and his wife Rebekah [f] were buried, and there I buried Leah. [32]The field and the cave in it were bought from the Hittites. [a]"

49:33
g ver 29; Ge 25:8; Ac 7:15
50:1
h Ge 46:4
[33]When Jacob had finished giving instructions to his sons, he drew his feet up into the bed, breathed his last and was gathered to his people. [g]

50 Joseph threw himself upon his father and wept over him and kissed him. [h] [2]Then Joseph directed the physicians in his service to embalm his father Is-

50:2
i ver 26; 2Ch 16:14
50:3
j Ge 37:34; Nu 20:29; Dt 34:8
rael. So the physicians embalmed him, [i] [3]taking a full forty days, for that was the time required for embalming. And the Egyptians mourned for him seventy days. [j]

50:5
k Ge 47:31
l 2Ch 16:14; Isa 22:16
m Ge 47:31
[4]When the days of mourning had passed, Joseph said to Pharaoh's court, "If I have found favor in your eyes, speak to Pharaoh for me. Tell him, [5]'My father made me swear an oath [k] and said, "I am about to die; bury me in the tomb I dug for myself [l] in the land of Canaan." [m] Now let me go up and bury my father; then I will return.' "

[6]Pharaoh said, "Go up and bury your father, as he made you swear to do."

[7]So Joseph went up to bury his father. All Pharaoh's officials accompanied him— the dignitaries of his court and all the dignitaries of Egypt— [8]besides all the members of Joseph's household and his brothers and those belonging to his father's household. Only their children and their flocks and herds were left in Goshen. [9]Chariots and horsemen [b] also went up with him. It was a very large company.

50:10
n 2Sa 1:17; Ac 8:2
o 1Sa 31:13; Job 2:13
[10]When they reached the threshing floor of Atad, near the Jordan, they lamented loudly and bitterly; [n] and there Joseph observed a seven-day period [o] of mourning for his father. [11]When the Canaanites who lived there saw the mourning at the threshing floor of Atad, they said, "The Egyptians are holding a solemn ceremony of mourning." That is why that place near the Jordan is called Abel Mizraim. [c]

[12]So Jacob's sons did as he had commanded them: [13]They carried him to the land of Canaan and buried him in the cave in the field of Machpelah, near Mamre, which Abraham had bought as a burial place from Ephron the Hittite, along with the

50:13
p Ge 23:20; Ac 7:16
field. [p] [14]After burying his father, Joseph returned to Egypt, together with his brothers and all the others who had gone with him to bury his father.

Joseph Reassures His Brothers

50:15
q Ge 37:28; 42:21-22
[15]When Joseph's brothers saw that their father was dead, they said, "What if Joseph holds a grudge against us and pays us back for all the wrongs we did to him?" [q] [16]So they sent word to Joseph, saying, "Your father left these instructions before he died: [17]'This is what you are to say to Joseph: I ask you to forgive your brothers the sins and the wrongs they committed in treating you so badly.' Now please forgive the sins of the servants of the God of your father." When their message came to him, Joseph wept.

50:18
r Ge 37:7
s Ge 43:18
[18]His brothers then came and threw themselves down before him. [r] "We are your slaves," [s] they said.

a 32 Or the sons of Heth   b 9 Or charioteers   c 11 Abel Mizraim means mourning of the Egyptians.

When we find ourselves on unfamiliar cultural turf, we may feel obligated to compromise. This can be a sensitive issue in missionary situations, particularly in the early stages of witness, when the native population hasn't yet become sensitized to their own practices that may later appear distasteful in light of their Christian faith. We do well to seek understanding without betraying our consciences and Biblical morality. Their eventual change will be a natural byproduct of Christ's life in them, when reasons for it have become internalized.

Genesis 50:15–21

Joseph's brothers hadn't fully believed his forgiveness. In their possibly manufactured message from their now-deceased father, we find their first acknowledgement of guilt. Even now, they offered it in the context of a message from their father rather than owning up themselves to their crime.

What humans intend for evil, God intends for good. As God reveals this truth about himself, other attributes fall into place. His sovereignty, love, mercy, justice, faithfulness, goodness—all are revealed as we stand on the sidelines of Genesis and watch him at work. Evil can't triumph. Blessings will prevail. Obstacles will melt away. God's revelation of his mastery and control of his creation is the message of Genesis.

Joseph's rhetorical question in verse 19 gives us pause: "Am I in the place of God?" It's one thing for us to recognize God's sovereignty but quite another to keep ourselves and our roles in proper perspective. Joseph not only had a firm picture of who God is but an understanding of what he himself was not. Do you allow God to be God? Being in a position of power is never a license to abuse people. It places us in another important position—of responsibility, under God, to do the right thing.

¹⁹But Joseph said to them, "Don't be afraid. Am I in the place of God? *t* ²⁰You intended to harm me, *u* but God intended *v* it for good *w* to accomplish what is now being done, the saving of many lives. *x* ²¹So then, don't be afraid. I will provide for you and your children. *y*" And he reassured them and spoke kindly to them.

The Death of Joseph

²²Joseph stayed in Egypt, along with all his father's family. He lived a hundred and ten years *z* ²³and saw the third generation *a* of Ephraim's children. Also the children of Makir *b* son of Manasseh were placed at birth on Joseph's knees. *a*

²⁴Then Joseph said to his brothers, "I am about to die. *c* But God will surely come to your aid *d* and take you up out of this land to the land *e* he promised on oath to Abraham, Isaac and Jacob." *f* ²⁵And Joseph made the sons of Israel swear an oath and said, "God will surely come to your aid, and then you must carry my bones up from this place." *g*

²⁶So Joseph died at the age of a hundred and ten. And after they embalmed him, *h* he was placed in a coffin in Egypt.

a 23 That is, were counted as his

50:19
t Ro 12:19; Heb 10:30
50:20
u Ge 37:20
v Mic 4:11-12
w Ro 8:28
x Ge 45:5
50:21
y Ge 45:11; 47:12
50:22
z Ge 25:7; Jos 24:29
50:23
a Job 42:16
b Nu 32:39,40
50:24
c Ge 48:21
d Ex 3:16-17
e Ge 15:14
f Ge 12:7; 26:3; 28:13; 35:12
50:25
g Ge 47:29-30; Ex 13:19; Jos 24:32; Heb 11:22
50:26
h ver 2

Genesis 50:22–26

 In verse 25 Joseph referred to the transportation of his bones. His words probably reflected his upbringing in Canaan more than the Egyptian culture. Nomadic groups often practiced secondary burial, in which survivors transported the skeletal remains of relatives to a traditional site long after death. If Joseph was anticipating mummification, he wouldn't have referred to transportation of just his *bones*.

Joseph died at age 110. Egyptians considered this an ideal length of life, even though mummies have demonstrated that the average life expectancy in Egypt was between 40 and 50 years. To the Egyptians Joseph's ripe old age would have been a witness of divine blessing.

Centuries later Joseph's bones were "buried at Shechem in the tract of land that Jacob bought . . . from the sons of Hamor" (Josh. 24:32; see Gen. 33:19). Considering the spirituality of this patriarch, it's remarkable that the author of Hebrews (11:22) noted Joseph's anticipation of the exodus and instructions about his bones as a great example of faith from his life. It qualified him to stand with the other faith heroes listed in the chapter. Does that surprise you? What act(s) in your life demonstrate most vividly your commitment to Christ?

Snapshots

50:18–21

Geoffrey

Geoffrey, a Rwandan native, spent part of his childhood sleeping and surviving on the streets of Kampala, Uganda. His father left Rwanda in 1959, when the attacks against Tutsis began. He married, but later separated from, a Ugandan woman.

"In 1981 my father joined Museveni's struggle to liberate Uganda, and a year later he died. I suddenly found myself a totally independent child," Geoffrey recalls. Rev. Kefa Sempangi won the confidence of a group of street children to which Geoffrey had attached himself. He convinced them to move into a home he was establishing in a converted school.

> "Maybe I was put on the street like Joseph was put in Egypt to save Israel."

After Geoffrey's college graduation, he returned to the Kampala institution for street children to supervise the work there. In 1994 he joined the effort to free Rwanda from the genocidal government in power at the time, later returning to Kampala.

He didn't stay long in Uganda, though: "I returned to Rwanda in 1998 because people were saying I should come and help . . .

"The problems facing the children in Rwanda go beyond mere poverty. These children are coping with the trauma of the genocide . . . Everyone is struggling to survive, and no one shares . . .

"Maybe I was put on the street like Joseph was put in Egypt to save Israel."

INTRODUCTION TO
Exodus

AUTHOR
Exodus itself (17:14; 24:3–4,7; 34:27), as well as other Scriptures (Josh. 8:31; Mal. 4:4; Mark 7:10; 12:26; Luke 2:22–23; 20:37), identifies Moses as its author.

DATE WRITTEN
Exodus was probably written around 1440 B.C.

ORIGINAL READERS
Exodus was written to the Israelites as a reminder of how God had rescued them from oppression in Egypt and of his standards for their living as his people.

TIMELINE

	2200BC	2100	2000	1900	1800	1700	1600	1500	1400

Moses' birth (c. 1526 B.C.) ——————————————————

The plagues; The Passover (c. 1446 B.C.) ——————————

The exodus (c. 1446 B.C.) —————————————————————

Desert wanderings (c. 1446-1406 B.C.) —————————————

The Ten Commandments (c. 1445 B.C.) ——————————————

Book of Exodus written (c. 1440 B.C.) ——————————————

Moses dies; Joshua becomes leader (c. 1406 B.C.) —————

Israelites enter Canaan (c. 1406 B.C.) ——————————————

THEMES
Exodus describes the beginning of the nation of Israel, including God's deliverance of the Israelites from Egypt and his covenant with them. It includes the following themes:

1. *Deliverance.* Through the deliverance of his people from Egypt (1:1—18:27), God revealed that he's involved in human activity, having entered history to rescue his people. Exodus reveals God's power (6:1; 9:13–16) and compassionate love for people (15:13), attributes that are still evident today as he offers deliverance to everyone from the bondage of sin (John 8:34–36; Rom. 6:20–22).

2. *The covenant.* The Ten Commandments and the Book of the Covenant (19:1—24:18) reveal God's justice and righteousness; basic principles of ethics and morality; people's choices and responsibilities (obedience brings blessing; disobedience brings punishment); and God's concern for the poor, helpless, and oppressed.

3. *The tabernacle.* God's desire to be present among his people is revealed in the construction and regulations regarding the tabernacle and worship of God (25:1—40:38). Exodus emphasizes God's holiness and, by extension, the holiness of the tabernacle (40:9).

4. *Moses.* The central human character of the book is Moses, the mediator between God and his people (20:19). Moses points to Christ, our great Mediator (1 Tim. 2:5; Heb. 9:15).

FAITH IN ACTION
The pages of Exodus are filled with life lessons and role models of faith—people who challenge believers to put their faith in action.

Role Models

• SHIPHRAH AND PUAH (1:15–20) courageously endangered their own lives to protect the lives of unborn children. How can God use you to protect children?

• MOSES (4:19–20) obeyed God, trusting that God would use him in spite of his weaknesses (3:11—4:17). What is God calling you to do that you fear may be beyond your ability?

• JETHRO (18:1–27), Moses' father-in-law, was a gifted troubleshooter whom God used to organize a chaotic situation. What "ordinary" skills do you possess that God wants to use?

• MIRIAM (15:19–21) praised God for coming to the rescue. Do you give God the credit and praise he deserves or tend to chalk up your successes to good luck or hard work?

• JOSHUA (33:11), Moses' aide, served God "outside the camp" (33:7), away from public recognition. Is God calling you to some unnoticed place of service?

Challenges

• Protect the well-being of children, even if risk is involved.

• Believe that God's call on your life is his invitation to participate with him in his work. Despite your flaws, God wants to use you, so resolve to obey him when he calls.

• Show mercy to the oppressed, just as God hears their cries and responds with compassion (22:21–27).

• Evaluate your ethics and morals. Determine to live a life that reflects your love for, and obedience to, God (23:1–9).

• Make a conscious choice to view all people as equal; one isn't worth more than any other (30:11–16).

• Discover your gifts and willingly use them, along with your time and money, to serve your local church and the global cause of Christ (31:1–6; 35:5–10).

• Seek to know God more intimately, as Moses did (33:12–23); the Lord longs for a deep and enduring relationship with you.

OUTLINE

   I. Preparation for Israel's Deliverance From Bondage (1–4)
  II. Israel's Deliverance From Bondage (5–18)
     A. Pharaoh's Resistance and the Lord's Reassurance (5:1—6:27)
     B. Plagues on Egypt (6:28—12:36)
     C. The Exodus From Egypt to Mount Sinai (12:37—18:27)
  III. The Covenant at Sinai (19–24)
  IV. The Tabernacle for Worship (25–40)
     A. Instructions for Tabernacle Construction and Furnishings (25–31)
     B. The Golden Calf (32–34)
     C. Tabernacle Construction (35–40)

The Israelites Oppressed

1:1
a Ge 46:8

1 These are the names of the sons of Israel[a] who went to Egypt with Jacob, each with his family: 2Reuben, Simeon, Levi and Judah; 3Issachar, Zebulun and Benjamin; 4Dan and Naphtali; Gad and Asher. 5The descendants of Jacob numbered seventy[a] in all;[b] Joseph was already in Egypt.

1:5
b Ge 46:26
1:6
c Ge 50:26
1:7
d Ge 46:3; Dt 26:5;
Ac 7:17

6Now Joseph and all his brothers and all that generation died,[c] 7but the Israelites were fruitful and multiplied greatly and became exceedingly numerous,[d] so that the land was filled with them.

1:9
e Ps 105:24-25
1:10
f Ps 83:3
g Ac 7:17-19

8Then a new king, who did not know about Joseph, came to power in Egypt. 9"Look," he said to his people, "the Israelites have become much too numerous[e] for us. 10Come, we must deal shrewdly[f] with them or they will become even more numerous and, if war breaks out, will join our enemies, fight against us and leave the country."[g]

1:11
h Ex 3:7 i Ge 15:13;
Ex 2:11; 5:4; 6:6-7
j Ge 47:11
k 1Ki 9:19; 2Ch 8:4

11So they put slave masters[h] over them to oppress them with forced labor,[i] and they built Pithom and Rameses[j] as store cities[k] for Pharaoh. 12But the more they were oppressed, the more they multiplied and spread; so the Egyptians came to dread the Israelites 13and worked them ruthlessly.[l] 14They made their lives bitter with hard labor in brick and mortar and with all kinds of work in the fields; in all their hard labor the Egyptians used them ruthlessly.[m]

1:13
l Dt 4:20

1:14
m Ex 2:23; 6:9;
Nu 20:15; Ps 81:6;
Ac 7:19

15The king of Egypt said to the Hebrew midwives, whose names were Shiphrah and Puah, 16"When you help the Hebrew women in childbirth and observe them on the delivery stool, if it is a boy, kill him; but if it is a girl, let her live." 17The midwives, however, feared[n] God and did not do what the king of Egypt had told them to do;[o] they let the boys live. 18Then the king of Egypt summoned the midwives and asked them, "Why have you done this? Why have you let the boys live?"

1:17
n ver 21; Pr 16:6
o Da 3:16-18;
Ac 4:18-20; 5:29

19The midwives answered Pharaoh, "Hebrew women are not like Egyptian women; they are vigorous and give birth before the midwives arrive."[p]

1:19
p Jos 2:4-6;
2Sa 17:20

20So God was kind to the midwives[q] and the people increased and became even more numerous. 21And because the midwives feared God, he gave them families[r] of their own.

1:20
q ver 12; Pr 11:18;
Isa 3:10
1:21
r 1Sa 2:35;
2Sa 7:11,27-29;
1Ki 11:38

22Then Pharaoh gave this order to all his people: "Every boy that is born[b] you must throw into the Nile, but let every girl live."[s]

1:22
s Ac 7:19

The Birth of Moses

2:1
t Ex 6:20; Nu 26:59

2 Now a man of the house of Levi married a Levite woman,[t] 2and she became pregnant and gave birth to a son. When she saw that he was a fine child, she hid him for three months.[u] 3But when she could hide him no longer, she got a papyrus basket for him and coated it with tar and pitch. Then she placed the child in it and put it among the reeds along the bank of the Nile. 4His sister[v] stood at a distance to see what would happen to him.

2:2
u Ac 7:20;
Heb 11:23
2:4
v Ex 15:20;
Nu 26:59

5Then Pharaoh's daughter went down to the Nile to bathe, and her attendants

---

a 5 Masoretic Text (see also Gen. 46:27); Dead Sea Scrolls and Septuagint (see also Acts 7:14 and note at Gen. 46:27) *seventy-five*   b 22 Masoretic Text; Samaritan Pentateuch, Septuagint and Targums *born to the Hebrews*

Exodus 1:1–22

The "creation language" of verse 7 reminds us of Genesis 1:28 and 9:1. The Israelites' increasing numbers signified God's presence and blessing. On the other hand, the oppression of the Egyptians, the order for midwives to kill newborns, and the throwing of newborn males into the Nile all worked against the created order. The exodus (deliverance) and Genesis (creation) connection will become more explicit later in the book. God would deliver the Israelites from bondage by unleashing the forces of creation against the Egyptians.

The writer's description of the Israelites' situation in Exodus 1 is one of many Old Testament examples that

force readers to view their present in terms of their past: God is the same yesterday, today, and forever (cf. Heb. 13:8). This outlook provides security now and assurance of what will be.

People are often threatened when ethnic minorities in their midst become affluent and strong. Tyrants may seek to oppress them, and children usually suffer most. This chapter also portrays the first Biblical account of civil disobedience. The midwives refused to obey the authorities, even lying about what they had done, and yet God blessed them. What questions does this raise in your mind regarding appropriate responses to unjust governments?

were walking along the river bank. [w] She saw the basket among the reeds and sent her slave girl to get it. [6]She opened it and saw the baby. He was crying, and she felt sorry for him. "This is one of the Hebrew babies," she said.

[7]Then his sister asked Pharaoh's daughter, "Shall I go and get one of the Hebrew women to nurse the baby for you?"

[8]"Yes, go," she answered. And the girl went and got the baby's mother. [9]Pharaoh's daughter said to her, "Take this baby and nurse him for me, and I will pay you." So the woman took the baby and nursed him. [10]When the child grew older, she took him to Pharaoh's daughter and he became her son. She named him Moses, [a] saying, "I drew him out of the water."

Moses Flees to Midian

[11]One day, after Moses had grown up, he went out to where his own people [x] were and watched them at their hard labor. He saw an Egyptian beating a Hebrew, one of his own people. [12]Glancing this way and that and seeing no one, he killed the Egyptian and hid him in the sand. [13]The next day he went out and saw two Hebrews fighting. He asked the one in the wrong, "Why are you hitting your fellow Hebrew?" [y]

[14]The man said, "Who made you ruler and judge over us? [z] Are you thinking of killing me as you killed the Egyptian?" Then Moses was afraid and thought, "What I did must have become known."

[15]When Pharaoh heard of this, he tried to kill Moses, but Moses fled from Pharaoh and went to live in Midian, [a] where he sat down by a well. [16]Now a priest of Midian [b] had seven daughters, and they came to draw water [c] and fill the troughs to water their father's flock. [17]Some shepherds came along and drove them away, but Moses got up and came to their rescue and watered their flock. [d]

[18]When the girls returned to Reuel [e] their father, he asked them, "Why have you returned so early today?"

[19]They answered, "An Egyptian rescued us from the shepherds. He even drew water for us and watered the flock."

Moses Flees to Midian (2:15)
Then: Midian, located in an inaccessible wilderness area occupied by nomads, provided a refuge for Moses.
Now: Modern Midian is located in northwestern Saudi Arabia, near the eastern shore of the Gulf of Aqaba.

[a] 10 *Moses* sounds like the Hebrew for *draw out.*

2:5
w Ex 7:15; 8:20

2:11
x Ac 7:23; Heb 11:24-26

2:13
y Ac 7:26

2:14
z Ac 7:27*

2:15
a Ac 7:29; Heb 11:27
2:16
b Ex 3:1 c Ge 24:11
2:17
d Ge 29:10
2:18
e Nu 10:29

Exodus 2:1–10

At various critical junctures in the Old Testament the birth of a child was instrumental to God's plan of delivering his people. This theme typically involved a miraculous birth—or an "against the odds" birth or survival. The theme culminated centuries later in a manger in Bethlehem (cf. Luke 2:4–7). It challenges modern thought and practice, in which a child may be viewed as an inconvenience. In the Bible, a baby represented hope: a perspective shared by the wise (cf. Ex. 1:21).

The tendency of the powerful is often to exploit or ignore children. God's way is for people to have compassion on these vulnerable members of society. Sometimes this demands that we defy common practices and with cunning wisdom seek to protect these little ones. God so honored the shrewdness of Moses' mother that she was actually paid by Pharaoh's daughter to nurse her own child! God used Pharaoh's evil decree to deliver his people. What are some ways in which children today need protection from human evil?

Exodus 2:11–25

Moses went out to be with his people (lit., "his brothers"; 2:11). We aren't told how and when Moses became aware of his true heritage, but the New Testament author to the Hebrews (Heb. 11:24–25) indicated that Moses was aware at least by this time of his background. His response to the beating of the Hebrew slave foreshadowed the future deliverance of all the Israelites. Later Moses interceded in another conflict (v. 13), introducing a recurring theme from Exodus through Deuteronomy: Israel's rebellion and rejection of Moses.

In various ways Christ's redemptive work reminds us of themes from this passage. Christ (1) protects his church, though now the sphere of conflict is primarily in the spiritual realm; (2) shepherds his flock (he was born for that very purpose; Matt. 2:6; cf. Mic. 5:2–4); and (3) was rejected by his own (cf. Acts 7:35,39–40,51–53).

2:20
f Ge 31:54
2:21
g Ex 18:2
2:22
h Ex 18:3-4;
Heb 11:13
2:23
i Ac 7:30 / Ex 3:7,9;
Dt 26:7; Jas 5:4
2:24
k Ex 6:5;
Ps 105:10,42
2:25
l Ex 3:7; 4:31

20 "And where is he?" he asked his daughters. "Why did you leave him? Invite him to have something to eat." f

21 Moses agreed to stay with the man, who gave his daughter Zipporah g to Moses in marriage. 22 Zipporah gave birth to a son, and Moses named him Gershom, a saying, "I have become an alien h in a foreign land."

23 During that long period, i the king of Egypt died. The Israelites groaned in their slavery and cried out, and their cry j for help because of their slavery went up to God. 24 God heard their groaning and he remembered his covenant k with Abraham, with Isaac and with Jacob. 25 So God looked on the Israelites and was concerned l about them.

Moses and the Burning Bush

3:1
m Ex 2:18
n 1Ki 19:8 o Ex 18:5
3:2
p Ge 16:7
q Dt 33:16;
Mk 12:26; Ac 7:30

3 Now Moses was tending the flock of Jethro m his father-in-law, the priest of Midian, and he led the flock to the far side of the desert and came to Horeb, n the mountain o of God. 2 There the angel of the LORD p appeared to him in flames of fire from within a bush. q Moses saw that though the bush was on fire it did not burn up. 3 So Moses thought, "I will go over and see this strange sight—why the bush does not burn up."

4 When the LORD saw that he had gone over to look, God called to him from within the bush, "Moses! Moses!"

And Moses said, "Here I am."

3:5
r Ge 28:17;
Jos 5:15; Ac 7:33*
3:6
s Ex 4:5; Mt 22:32*;
Mk 12:26*;
Lk 20:37*; Ac 7:32*
3:7
t Ex 2:25
3:8
u Ge 50:24
v ver 17; Ex 13:5;
Dt 1:25
w Ge 15:18-21

5 "Do not come any closer," God said. "Take off your sandals, for the place where you are standing is holy ground." r 6 Then he said, "I am the God of your father, the God of Abraham, the God of Isaac and the God of Jacob." s At this, Moses hid his face, because he was afraid to look at God.

7 The LORD said, "I have indeed seen the misery of my people in Egypt. I have heard them crying out because of their slave drivers, and I am concerned t about their suffering. 8 So I have come down u to rescue them from the hand of the Egyptians and to bring them up out of that land into a good and spacious land, a land flowing with milk and honey v —the home of the Canaanites, Hittites, Amorites, Perizzites, Hivites and Jebusites. w 9 And now the cry of the Israelites has reached me, and I have seen the way the Egyptians are oppressing x them. 10 So now, go. I am sending you to Pharaoh to bring my people the Israelites out of Egypt." y

3:9
x Ex 1:14; 2:23
3:10
y Mic 6:4
3:11
z Ex 6:12,30;
1Sa 18:18
3:12
a Ge 31:3; Jos 1:5;
Ro 8:31

11 But Moses said to God, "Who am I, z that I should go to Pharaoh and bring the Israelites out of Egypt?"

12 And God said, "I will be with you. a And this will be the sign to you that it is I who have sent you: When you have brought the people out of Egypt, you b will worship God on this mountain."

13 Moses said to God, "Suppose I go to the Israelites and say to them, 'The God of your fathers has sent me to you,' and they ask me, 'What is his name?' Then what shall I tell them?"

---

a 22 *Gershom* sounds like the Hebrew for *an alien there.*   b 12 The Hebrew is plural.

Moses' identification with the suffering of his people foreshadowed Jesus' identification with us (cf. Phil. 2:5–11). Moses was right in seeking to advocate for the Hebrews, but his method was obviously foolish. Christ identified with us in our oppression not by killing our tormentors but by taking our suffering upon himself. What does it mean for you to advocate for others and empathize with their pain? Is it at times necessary for you to enter into their suffering? How?

Exodus 3:1–22

God called, but Moses was reluctant to answer. His hesitation seems to have been a mix of true humility, a recognition of the difficulties that would confront him, and simple stubbornness. We might have expected God's chosen representative for Israel's deliverance to show more resolve and less hesitation. Yet this very human portrayal of Moses is one with which God's people today can identify.

When we seek to apply God's call (cf. Josh. 1:1–9; Judg. 6:11–16; 1 Sam. 3:1–19; Isa. 6:1–10) in general and this passage in particular, we ask ourselves, *What does it mean to be "called" by God?* It means being confronted by his holiness. The holy God calls us into his kingdom and even allows us to participate in his kingdom work. The fact that he chooses to work through imperfect people makes us feel welcomed by and reliant upon God (cf. 2 Cor. 12:9). In what way have you taken off your shoes, acknowledging God's holiness as you worshiped him in a life-altering moment?

Deliverance From Bondage

3:7–10

Moses, as God's agent, delivered Israel from bondage in Egypt. Because of their unique history, Latin American theologians have taken as their theological starting point God's deliverance of Israel from the bondage (and poverty) of Egypt. During the 1960s the failure of postwar development programs and growing poverty led to increasing social unrest in this part of the world. Latin Americans felt estranged from their own colonial (and even religious) past and longed for a better life, as well as freedom from both political and economic oppression.

Influenced by the Second Vatican Council (1961–1965), theologians like Gustavo Gutiérrez began to speak of God's promise of salvation as "liberation" both from the ravages of sin and the effects of poverty. He believed the poor were in a better position than the wealthy to understand God's program of deliverance and needed to be empowered to read and obey Scripture for themselves. Enrique Dussel argued that, reminiscent of Moses' legacy, pastoral theology must reflect on God's work of liberation from bondage. Gutiérrez' bestselling book, *A Theology of Liberation* (1971), became the primary text of a new movement, labeled liberation theology, that also influenced theologians outside of Latin America, especially African Americans in the United States and Blacks in South Africa.

In the following decades there has been a conservative reaction to the more extreme (and political) forms of liberation theology, both on the part of the Roman Catholic church and political authorities, but its influence continues to be profound in Latin America and beyond. Jon Sobrino has sought to apply this way of reading Scripture to Christology, understanding Christ based on his position as a social outsider. Leonardo Boff has formulated an understanding of the church in terms of the Spirit working among the pilgrim people of God, and Paulo Freire has exercised widespread influence on educational theory with his view of education for social transformation.

Protestants traditionally have made up a minority of the Latin American population, but with the explosive growth of Pentecostalism in the last generation this is changing—with *evangelicos*, as they are called, now accounting for 25–35% of the population in some countries. Since these Christians come largely from the poorer classes, they have developed a unique understanding of God's delivering power.

Pentecostals have shown themselves to be adept at addressing both the spiritual and material needs of the poor. Their theology emphasizes the work of the Holy Spirit but sees the Spirit's work as including the provision of food, clothing, and shelter to those in need. Though they speak on behalf of the poor with a different accent, both liberation theology and Pentecostalism remind us of the Biblical call to reach out to the most vulnerable in our midst.

> Though they speak on behalf of the poor with a different accent, both liberation theology and Pentecostalism remind us of the Biblical call to reach out to the most vulnerable in our midst.

William Dyrness, professor of theology and culture at Fuller Theological Seminary in Pasadena, California

14 God said to Moses, "I AM WHO I AM.[a] This is what you are to say to the Israelites: 'I AM[b] has sent me to you.' "
15 God also said to Moses, "Say to the Israelites, 'The LORD,[b] the God of your fathers—the God of Abraham, the God of Isaac and the God of Jacob—has sent me
to you.' This is my name[c] forever, the name by which I am to be remembered from
generation to generation.
16 "Go, assemble the elders[d] of Israel and say to them, 'The LORD, the God of your
fathers—the God of Abraham, Isaac and Jacob—appeared to me and said: I have
watched over you and have seen what has been done to you in Egypt. 17 And I have
promised to bring you up out of your misery in Egypt[e] into the land of the Canaanites, Hittites, Amorites, Perizzites, Hivites and Jebusites—a land flowing with milk
and honey.'
18 "The elders of Israel will listen[f] to you. Then you and the elders are to go to the
king of Egypt and say to him, 'The LORD, the God of the Hebrews, has met with us.
Let us take a three-day journey into the desert to offer sacrifices[g] to the LORD our
God.' 19 But I know that the king of Egypt will not let you go unless a mighty hand[h]
compels him. 20 So I will stretch out my hand[i] and strike the Egyptians with all the
wonders[j] that I will perform among them. After that, he will let you go.[k]
21 "And I will make the Egyptians favorably disposed[l] toward this people, so that
when you leave you will not go empty-handed.[m] 22 Every woman is to ask her
neighbor and any woman living in her house for articles of silver and gold[n] and for
clothing, which you will put on your sons and daughters. And so you will plunder[o]
the Egyptians."

Signs for Moses

4 Moses answered, "What if they do not believe me or listen[p] to me and say, 'The
LORD did not appear to you'?"
2 Then the LORD said to him, "What is that in your hand?"
"A staff,"[q] he replied.
3 The LORD said, "Throw it on the ground."
Moses threw it on the ground and it became a snake, and he ran from it. 4 Then
the LORD said to him, "Reach out your hand and take it by the tail." So Moses
reached out and took hold of the snake and it turned back into a staff in his hand.
5 "This," said the LORD, "is so that they may believe[r] that the LORD, the God of their
fathers—the God of Abraham, the God of Isaac and the God of Jacob—has appeared to you."
6 Then the LORD said, "Put your hand inside your cloak." So Moses put his hand
into his cloak, and when he took it out, it was leprous,[c] like snow.[s]
7 "Now put it back into your cloak," he said. So Moses put his hand back into his
cloak, and when he took it out, it was restored,[t] like the rest of his flesh.
8 Then the LORD said, "If they do not believe you or pay attention to the first miraculous sign, they may believe the second. 9 But if they do not believe these two
signs or listen to you, take some water from the Nile and pour it on the dry ground.
The water you take from the river will become blood[u] on the ground."
10 Moses said to the LORD, "O Lord, I have never been eloquent, neither in the past
nor since you have spoken to your servant. I am slow of speech and tongue."[v]
11 The LORD said to him, "Who gave man his mouth? Who makes him deaf or
mute? Who gives him sight or makes him blind?[w] Is it not I, the LORD? 12 Now go;
I will help you speak and will teach you what to say."[x]

3:14 [b] Ex 6:2-3; Jn 8:58; Heb 13:8
3:15 [c] Ps 135:13; Hos 12:5
3:16 [d] Ex 4:29
3:17 [e] Ge 15:16; Jos 24:11
3:18 [f] Ex 4:1,8,31 [g] Ex 5:1,3
3:19 [h] Ex 4:21; 5:2
3:20 [i] Ex 6:1,6; 9:15 [j] Dt 6:22; Ne 9:10; Ac 7:36 [k] Ex 12:31-33
3:21 [l] Ex 12:36 [m] Ps 105:37
3:22 [n] Ex 11:2 [o] Eze 39:10
4:1 [p] Ex 3:18; 6:30
4:2 [q] ver 17,20
4:5 [r] Ex 19:9
4:6 [s] Nu 12:10; 2Ki 5:1,27
4:7 [t] Nu 12:13-15; Dt 32:39; 2Ki 5:14; Mt 8:3
4:9 [u] Ex 7:17-21
4:10 [v] Ex 6:12; Jer 1:6
4:11 [w] Ps 94:9; Mt 11:5
4:12 [x] Isa 50:4; Jer 1:9; Mt 10:19-20; Mk 13:11; Lk 12:12; 21:14-15

[a] *14* Or *I WILL BE WHAT I WILL BE* [b] *15* The Hebrew for *LORD* sounds like and may be derived from the Hebrew for *I AM* in verse 14. [c] *6* The Hebrew word was used for various diseases affecting the skin—not necessarily leprosy.

Exodus 4:1–17

The dialogue between Moses and God ended abruptly: "Don't forget your staff, Moses." You might envision a number of alternative endings to this dramatic encounter, but it appears that Moses needed some reminding. His shepherd's staff would become important in the plagues. It would humble the world of power and cause the water of the sea to part. God would use this symbol of lowliness to bring about the central act of salvation of the Old Testament.

Rev. Martin Luther King, Jr.

 4:10–11

Martin Luther King, Jr. (1929–1968) led the 1960s civil rights movement in the American South. Through acts of nonviolent resistance, he initiated a movement of African Americans that led to national legislation called the Civil Rights Act. King was an ordained minister, and we can't read two paragraphs of any King speech without running up against a Biblical allusion or Christian truth.

King was a prophet, not a saint. He had personal weaknesses, to be sure, but he knew he was called of God to confront the monstrous evil called racism. Once he clearly heard that call, he never faltered.

In many ways King's life and calling are reminiscent of the life and calling of Moses. Moses too was flawed and questioned whether he was the right one to lead a beleaguered people out of bondage in Egypt. Moses hemmed and hawed—but once God got through to him through a burning bush that wasn't consumed, he never looked back.

Moses succeeded. Why? Because he did what God called him to do. God freed his people, using Moses as his spokesperson. Moses was a model, a hero of the faith, someone we can learn from as we attempt to follow God's call on our lives.

Martin Luther King, Jr. also was a model. He insisted that American society acknowledge its own failures in comparison to God's righteousness. In a 1990 article in *Christianity Today*, Philip Yancey outlined some of the lessons we can learn from King's life.

> "Christianity has always insisted that the cross we bear precedes the crown we wear."

King realized early that if his cause was right and just God would empower him and be with him. King remembered that when he was twenty-six he was already receiving death threats against his wife and young child. He was afraid. He felt powerless—so much so that he informed God he was losing his stomach for the battle. At that moment he heard an inner voice: "Martin Luther, stand up for righteousness. Stand up for justice. Stand up for truth. And, lo, I will be with you, even until the end of the world." It was the voice of Jesus telling him to fight on. Three nights later a bomb thrown on his porch exploded, but no one was injured. And King fought on. *Lesson: God won't empower us to do just anything, but he will empower us to do the right thing.*

King taught his followers that the way to victory was through non-violence, not anarchy. This was a principled stance, costing King many young followers and numerous nights in jail. It exposed his followers to physical abuse and persecution. But it was right, and it produced the right results. "Christianity" he asserted, "has always insisted that the cross we bear precedes the crown we wear." *Lesson: Moral change isn't accomplished through immoral means.*

King inspired hope when any experienced evaluation of the situation at hand would have led anyone else to despair. He lived this truth: No matter how bad things may appear at any given moment, God reigns. He lived it because he believed it. And because he both believed and lived it, anyone associated with King came to believe and begin to live it too. *Lesson: The long view is that God reigns.*

The goal of any Christian social movement isn't defeat of the opponent but reconciliation. King fought evil, but he wanted to live at peace with the white community. That peace is still only partially achieved. We have work to do.

¹³But Moses said, "O Lord, please send someone else to do it."

¹⁴Then the LORD's anger burned against Moses and he said, "What about your brother, Aaron the Levite? I know he can speak well. He is already on his way to meet^y you, and his heart will be glad when he sees you. ¹⁵You shall speak to him and put words in his mouth;^z I will help both of you speak and will teach you what to do. ¹⁶He will speak to the people for you, and it will be as if he were your mouth^a and as if you were God to him. ¹⁷But take this staff^b in your hand so you can perform miraculous signs^c with it."

Moses Returns to Egypt

¹⁸Then Moses went back to Jethro his father-in-law and said to him, "Let me go back to my own people in Egypt to see if any of them are still alive."

Jethro said, "Go, and I wish you well."

¹⁹Now the LORD had said to Moses in Midian, "Go back to Egypt, for all the men who wanted to kill^d you are dead.^e" ²⁰So Moses took his wife and sons, put them on a donkey and started back to Egypt. And he took the staff^f of God in his hand.

²¹The LORD said to Moses, "When you return to Egypt, see that you perform before Pharaoh all the wonders^g I have given you the power to do. But I will harden his heart^h so that he will not let the people go. ²²Then say to Pharaoh, 'This is what the LORD says: Israel is my firstborn son,ⁱ ²³and I told you, "Let my son go,^j so he may worship me." But you refused to let him go; so I will kill your firstborn son.' "^k

²⁴At a lodging place on the way, the LORD met ⌊Moses⌋^a and was about to kill^l him. ²⁵But Zipporah took a flint knife, cut off her son's foreskin^m and touched ⌊Moses'⌋ feet with it.^b "Surely you are a bridegroom of blood to me," she said. ²⁶So the LORD let him alone. (At that time she said "bridegroom of blood," referring to circumcision.)

²⁷The LORD said to Aaron, "Go into the desert to meet Moses." So he met Moses at the mountainⁿ of God and kissed^o him. ²⁸Then Moses told Aaron everything the LORD had sent him to say,^p and also about all the miraculous signs he had commanded him to perform.

²⁹Moses and Aaron brought together all the elders^q of the Israelites, ³⁰and Aaron told them everything the LORD had said to Moses. He also performed the signs before the people, ³¹and they believed.^r And when they heard that the LORD was concerned^s about them and had seen their misery, they bowed down and worshiped.

^a 24 Or ⌊Moses' son⌋; Hebrew him   ^b 25 Or and drew near ⌊Moses'⌋ feet

Cross-reference notes (left margin):

4:14
y ver 27
4:15
z Nu 23:5,12,16
4:16
a Ex 7:1-2
4:17
b ver 2 c Ex 7:9-21
4:19
d Ex 2:15 e Ex 2:23
4:20
f Ex 17:9;
Nu 20:8-9,11
4:21
g Ex 3:19,20
h Ex 7:3,13;
9:12,35; 14:4,8;
Dt 2:30; Isa 63:17;
Jn 12:40; Ro 9:18
4:22
i Isa 63:16; 64:8;
Jer 31:9; Hos 11:1;
Ro 9:4
4:23
j Ex 5:1; 7:16
k Ex 11:5; 12:12,29
4:24
l Nu 22:22
4:25
m Ge 17:14;
Jos 5:2,3
4:27
n Ex 3:1 o ver 14
4:28
p ver 8-9,16
4:29
q Ex 3:16
4:31
r ver 8; Ex 3:18
s Ex 2:25

The Old Testament "call" texts (such as the passages cited in the previous "Here and Now") share common elements. (1) God initiates the contact. (2) The chosen leaders are often engaged in ordinary activities at the time of their callings. (3) Those called are often jolted by the thought of what God intends for them, responding in humility, disbelief, and self-doubt. (4) These leaders learn that "salvation comes from the LORD" (Jonah 2:9).

God's promise to be with Moses has been fulfilled in us to a degree neither Moses nor any other Old Testament believer could have thought possible. Even though we may encounter doubts and struggles with respect to God's call on our lives, the Father gives us the Spirit of Christ. God isn't merely *with* us, but *in* us—and we are *in* Christ (cf. John 14:16–20). This powerful presence of God in our lives doesn't prevent doubt and struggle but serves as the proper setting in which to view our struggle. What difference does this perspective make for you?

Exodus 4:18–31

The connection between 3:19 and 4:21 is lost in English, but "mighty" and "harden" stem from the same Hebrew root. God would not only act mightily and sovereignly in delivering Israel, but his actions also would dictate Pharaoh's response. Israel's coming deliverance would be entirely God's doing and under his control. It would be a play with God as Author, Producer, Director, and principal Actor.

The church, like Israel, is God's "son." This relationship is more intense because the church is united to the true Son. Christ is more than simply the Father's firstborn Son; he's "the firstborn among many brothers" (Rom. 8:29; cf. Col. 1:15,18). We are, to use John's language, "born again" or "born from above" (John 3:3).

God demonstrated his power by how he treated Pharaoh. At times Pharaoh hardened his own heart; at other times God did it for him. This recurring mystery in Scripture is called by various terms: election, predestination, or the sovereignty of God. The tension in Scripture between God's sovereignty and people's free will reminds us of how distant our thoughts are from God's (Isa. 55:8–9). It appears that God doesn't exercise his sovereignty in ways that are contrary to our human desires. How does your understanding of God's sovereignty affect how you live your life?

Bricks Without Straw

5 Afterward Moses and Aaron went to Pharaoh and said, "This is what the LORD, the God of Israel, says: 'Let my people go, so that they may hold a festival[t] to me in the desert.'"

5:1
t Ex 3:18

²Pharaoh said, "Who is the LORD,[u] that I should obey him and let Israel go? I do not know the LORD and I will not let Israel go."[v]

5:2
u 2Ki 18:35;
Job 21:15 v Ex 3:19

³Then they said, "The God of the Hebrews has met with us. Now let us take a three-day journey into the desert to offer sacrifices to the LORD our God, or he may strike us with plagues[w] or with the sword."

5:3
w Ex 3:18

⁴But the king of Egypt said, "Moses and Aaron, why are you taking the people away from their labor?[x] Get back to your work!" ⁵Then Pharaoh said, "Look, the people of the land are now numerous,[y] and you are stopping them from working."

5:4
x Ex 1:11
5:5
y Ex 1:7,9

⁶That same day Pharaoh gave this order to the slave drivers and foremen in charge of the people: ⁷"You are no longer to supply the people with straw for making bricks; let them go and gather their own straw. ⁸But require them to make the same number of bricks as before; don't reduce the quota. They are lazy; that is why they are crying out, 'Let us go and sacrifice to our God.' ⁹Make the work harder for the men so that they keep working and pay no attention to lies."

¹⁰Then the slave drivers and the foremen went out and said to the people, "This is what Pharaoh says: 'I will not give you any more straw. ¹¹Go and get your own straw wherever you can find it, but your work will not be reduced at all.'" ¹²So the people scattered all over Egypt to gather stubble to use for straw. ¹³The slave drivers kept pressing them, saying, "Complete the work required of you for each day, just as when you had straw." ¹⁴The Israelite foremen appointed by Pharaoh's slave drivers were beaten[z] and were asked, "Why didn't you meet your quota of bricks yesterday or today, as before?"

5:14
z Isa 10:24

¹⁵Then the Israelite foremen went and appealed to Pharaoh: "Why have you treated your servants this way? ¹⁶Your servants are given no straw, yet we are told, 'Make bricks!' Your servants are being beaten, but the fault is with your own people."

¹⁷Pharaoh said, "Lazy, that's what you are—lazy![a] That is why you keep saying, 'Let us go and sacrifice to the LORD.' ¹⁸Now get to work. You will not be given any straw, yet you must produce your full quota of bricks."

5:17
a ver 8

¹⁹The Israelite foremen realized they were in trouble when they were told, "You are not to reduce the number of bricks required of you for each day." ²⁰When they left Pharaoh, they found Moses and Aaron waiting to meet them, ²¹and they said, "May the LORD look upon you and judge you! You have made us a stench[b] to Pharaoh and his officials and have put a sword in their hand to kill us."[c]

5:21
b Ge 34:30
c Ex 14:11

God Promises Deliverance

²²Moses returned to the LORD and said, "O Lord, why have you brought trouble upon this people?[d] Is this why you sent me? ²³Ever since I went to Pharaoh to speak

5:22
d Nu 11:11

Exodus 5:1–21

The first pharaoh tried three schemes to reduce the Jewish population (see "There and Then" for 1:1–22). This new pharaoh seemed comfortable with their large numbers but wanted to exploit them for his purposes. Both worked against God's creation mandate—one openly and the other subtly. Pharaoh's current command to increase Israelite labor was calculated to drive a wedge between Moses and the people. How ironic that the Israelites called down God's judgment on the one he had chosen to deliver them.

God doesn't condone oppression or injustice, whether political, cultural, judicial, or private. As the Lord of history, he can't and won't bless nations that oppress others. Harmony with God and with people are interwoven. Exodus isn't only about human freedom. It's

about God calling people back into relationship with himself. Pharaoh's actions pitted him squarely against God; he was demanding the people's worship/allegiance in defiance of the Lord's claim on them.

We as Christians are "Christ's ambassadors"—"God" to the world, speaking on his behalf. The Lord entrusts us to carry out his work, the ministry of reconciliation (2 Cor. 5:18–20). Our speaking God's truth to human powers won't necessarily be received with pleasure. Advocating for the oppressed requires courage, conviction, and wisdom.

Exodus 5:22—6:12

Moses' focus was on the disastrous outcome of his first encounter with Pharaoh, not on the character of the God who had called him. The most vital lesson of

5:23
e Jer 4:10

in your name, he has brought trouble upon this people, and you have not rescued[e] your people at all."

6:1
f Ex 3:19 *g* Ex 3:20
h Ex 12:31,33,39

6 Then the LORD said to Moses, "Now you will see what I will do to Pharaoh: Because of my mighty hand[f] he will let them go;[g] because of my mighty hand he will drive them out of his country."[h]

6:3
i Ge 17:1 *j* Ps 68:4;
83:18; Isa 52:6
k Ex 3:14

²God also said to Moses, "I am the LORD. ³I appeared to Abraham, to Isaac and to Jacob as God Almighty,[a][i] but by my name[j] the LORD[b][k] I did not make myself known to them.[c] ⁴I also established my covenant[l] with them to give them the land of Ca-

6:4
l Ge 15:18
m Ge 28:4,13

naan, where they lived as aliens.[m] ⁵Moreover, I have heard the groaning[n] of the Israelites, whom the Egyptians are enslaving, and I have remembered my covenant.

6:5
n Ex 2:23

⁶"Therefore, say to the Israelites: 'I am the LORD, and I will bring you out from under the yoke of the Egyptians. I will free you from being slaves to them, and I will

6:6
o Dt 7:8; 1Ch 17:21
p Dt 26:8

redeem[o] you with an outstretched arm[p] and with mighty acts of judgment. ⁷I will take you as my own people, and I will be your God.[q] Then you will know[r] that I

6:7
q Dt 4:20; 2Sa 7:24
r Ex 16:12;
Isa 41:20

am the LORD your God, who brought you out from under the yoke of the Egyptians. ⁸And I will bring you to the land[s] I swore with uplifted hand[t] to give to Abraham,

6:8
s Ge 15:18; 26:3
t Ge 14:22
u Ps 136:21-22

to Isaac and to Jacob.[u] I will give it to you as a possession. I am the LORD.' "

⁹Moses reported this to the Israelites, but they did not listen to him because of their discouragement and cruel bondage.

¹⁰Then the LORD said to Moses, ¹¹"Go, tell Pharaoh king of Egypt to let the Israelites go out of his country."

6:12
v ver 30; Ex 4:10;
Jer 1:6

¹²But Moses said to the LORD, "If the Israelites will not listen to me, why would Pharaoh listen to me, since I speak with faltering lips[d]?"[v]

Family Record of Moses and Aaron

¹³Now the LORD spoke to Moses and Aaron about the Israelites and Pharaoh king of Egypt, and he commanded them to bring the Israelites out of Egypt.

6:14
w Ge 46:9

¹⁴These were the heads of their families[e]:[w]

The sons of Reuben the firstborn son of Israel were Hanoch and Pallu, Hez-

6:15
x Ge 46:10;
1Ch 4:24

ron and Carmi. These were the clans of Reuben.

¹⁵The sons of Simeon[x] were Jemuel, Jamin, Ohad, Jakin, Zohar and Shaul the son of a Canaanite woman. These were the clans of Simeon.

---

a 3 Hebrew *El-Shaddai*   *b 3* See note at Exodus 3:15.   *c 3* Or *Almighty, and by my name the LORD did I not let myself be known to them?*   *d 12* Hebrew *I am uncircumcised of lips*; also in verse 30
e 14 The Hebrew for *families* here and in verse 25 refers to units larger than clans.

---

the burning bush experience (3:1—4:17)—"I will be with you"—hadn't sunk in. Moses hadn't yet learned that there was more at stake here than how he was doing. God's character was in the balance; he had a promise to keep to Abraham, Isaac, and Jacob.

The author (Moses) presented a complex picture of himself. He was the chosen instrument of Israel's redemption but also a refugee from justice and a reluctant participant in God's plan. As you read through the Pentateuch (first five OT books), watch for signs of progress in Moses' self-understanding and relationship to God.

📖 Rather than striking Moses dead for the way he had rebuked God in prayer, the Lord responded by revealing more fully to his servant God's character, purposes, and promises. We can take heart in this. Honesty in prayer is far more faithful than pious phrases we don't *really mean. God works with a "mighty hand"* through human weakness, even our weakness in our understanding of him. Often oppression and poverty thwart people's capacity to trust God (v. 9). At such times it may be necessary for others to believe on our behalf.

Exodus 6:13–27

📖 This genealogy focuses on specific descendants of Levi. It extends back to the patriarchal period (Gen. 49:1–28), underscoring the vital connection with the past and highlighting God's plan to redeem Israel. It ends with Aaron's grandson, Phinehas, suggesting that God's purpose reaches both backward and forward. The passage helps establish Aaron, like Moses, as a worthy leader.

📖 Why was it important for the author to establish a pedigree (resume or curricula vitae) for Aaron and Moses? This may seem to have been a concession to human nature, since people tend to be impressed and motivated by achievements, power, and lines of authority. But God is no respecter of persons. The same God who recruited a reclusive, tongue-tied shepherd to be his spokesperson before the mighty pharaoh still chooses people who are insignificant by this world's standards to accomplish his kingdom purposes (1 Cor. 1:26–30). For what work has he chosen you?

16 These were the names of the sons of Levi according to their records: Gershon,[y] Kohath and Merari.[z] Levi lived 137 years.
17 The sons of Gershon, by clans, were Libni and Shimei.[a]
18 The sons of Kohath were Amram, Izhar, Hebron and Uzziel.[b] Kohath
lived 133 years.
19 The sons of Merari were Mahli and Mushi.[c]
These were the clans of Levi according to their records.
20 Amram married his father's sister Jochebed, who bore him Aaron and Moses.[d] Amram lived 137 years.
21 The sons of Izhar[e] were Korah, Nepheg and Zicri.
22 The sons of Uzziel were Mishael, Elzaphan[f] and Sithri.
23 Aaron married Elisheba, daughter of Amminadab[g] and sister of Nahshon, and she bore him Nadab and Abihu,[h] Eleazar[i] and Ithamar.[j]
24 The sons of Korah[k] were Assir, Elkanah and Abiasaph. These were the Korahite clans.
25 Eleazar son of Aaron married one of the daughters of Putiel, and she bore
him Phinehas.[l]

These were the heads of the Levite families, clan by clan.

26 It was this same Aaron and Moses to whom the LORD said, "Bring the Israelites
out of Egypt by their divisions."[m] 27 They were the ones who spoke to Pharaoh king
of Egypt about bringing the Israelites out of Egypt. It was the same Moses and
Aaron.

Aaron to Speak for Moses

28 Now when the LORD spoke to Moses in Egypt, 29 he said to him, "I am the
LORD.[n] Tell Pharaoh king of Egypt everything I tell you."
30 But Moses said to the LORD, "Since I speak with faltering lips,[o] why would Pharaoh listen to me?"

7 Then the LORD said to Moses, "See, I have made you like God[p] to Pharaoh, and
your brother Aaron will be your prophet. 2 You are to say everything I command
you, and your brother Aaron is to tell Pharaoh to let the Israelites go out of his
country. 3 But I will harden Pharaoh's heart,[q] and though I multiply my miraculous
signs and wonders in Egypt, 4 he will not listen[r] to you. Then I will lay my hand on
Egypt and with mighty acts of judgment[s] I will bring out my divisions, my people
the Israelites. 5 And the Egyptians will know that I am the LORD[t] when I stretch out
my hand[u] against Egypt and bring the Israelites out of it."
6 Moses and Aaron did just as the LORD commanded[v] them. 7 Moses was eighty
years old[w] and Aaron eighty-three when they spoke to Pharaoh.

Aaron's Staff Becomes a Snake

8 The LORD said to Moses and Aaron, 9 "When Pharaoh says to you, 'Perform a miracle,[x]' then say to Aaron, 'Take your staff and throw it down before Pharaoh,' and
it will become a snake."[y]
10 So Moses and Aaron went to Pharaoh and did just as the LORD commanded. Aaron threw his staff down in front of Pharaoh and his officials, and it became a snake.
11 Pharaoh then summoned wise men and sorcerers, and the Egyptian magicians[z]

6:16 [y] Ge 46:11 [z] Nu 3:17
6:17 [a] 1Ch 6:17
6:18 [b] 1Ch 6:2,18
6:19 [c] Nu 3:20,33; 1Ch 6:19; 23:21
6:20 [d] Ex 2:1-2; Nu 26:59
6:21 [e] 1Ch 6:38
6:22 [f] Lev 10:4; Nu 3:30
6:23 [g] Ru 4:19,20 [h] Lev 10:1 [i] Nu 3:2,32 [j] Nu 26:60
6:24 [k] Nu 26:11
6:25 [l] Nu 25:7,11; Jos 24:33; Ps 106:30
6:26 [m] Ex 7:4; 12:17,41,51
6:29 [n] ver 11; Ex 7:2
6:30 [o] ver 12; Ex 4:10
7:1 [p] Ex 4:16
7:3 [q] Ex 4:21; 11:9
7:4 [r] Ex 11:9 [s] Ex 3:20; 6:6
7:5 [t] ver 17; Ex 8:19,22 [u] Ex 3:20
7:6 [v] ver 2
7:7 [w] Dt 31:2; 34:7; Ac 7:23,30
7:9 [x] Isa 7:11; Jn 2:18 [y] Ex 4:2-5
7:11 [z] Ge 41:8; 2Ti 3:8

Exodus 6:28—7:7

Exodus 7:1, like 4:16, refers to Moses as "God." (The word "like" in the NIV isn't literally reflected in the Hebrew.) This in no way suggests that Moses actually would become the God of Israel, but he would be God *functionally* both to Pharaoh and the Israelites. In Egypt, the pharaoh was considered to be divine. So by calling Moses "God," the Lord was beating Pharaoh at his own game. Moses was "God" to Pharaoh in that God was acting through him, and Moses would be the one through whom God would bring salvation to Israel.

We have often heard the argument for boldness in our witness to the gospel in life, deed, and word: "You may be the only Bible some people will ever read." Taking your cue from this passage, why not take this a step further: You may be the only, or at least the first, "God" others see. As true image-bearers of God, even though in ourselves we are all too inadequate, we are the means by which the Good News of God's salvation is manifest. What an incredible privilege and responsibility!

7:11
a ver 22; Ex 8:7,18
7:13
b Ex 4:21

also did the same things by their secret arts:[a] 12Each one threw down his staff and it became a snake. But Aaron's staff swallowed up their staffs. 13Yet Pharaoh's heart[b] became hard and he would not listen to them, just as the LORD had said.

The Plague of Blood

7:14
c Ex 8:15,32; 10:1,20,27

14Then the LORD said to Moses, "Pharaoh's heart is unyielding;[c] he refuses to let the people go. 15Go to Pharaoh in the morning as he goes out to the water. Wait on the bank of the Nile to meet him, and take in your hand the staff that was changed into a snake. 16Then say to him, 'The LORD, the God of the Hebrews, has

7:16
d Ex 3:18; 5:1,3

sent me to say to you: Let my people go, so that they may worship[d] me in the desert. But until now you have not listened. 17This is what the LORD says: By this you

7:17
e Ex 5:2 *f* Ex 4:9; Rev 11:6; 16:4

will know that I am the LORD:[e] With the staff that is in my hand I will strike the water of the Nile, and it will be changed into blood.[f] 18The fish in the Nile will die,

7:18
g ver 21,24

and the river will stink; the Egyptians will not be able to drink its water.' "[g]

7:19
h Ex 8:5-6, 16; 9:22; 10:12,21; 14:21

19The LORD said to Moses, "Tell Aaron, 'Take your staff and stretch out your hand[h] over the waters of Egypt—over the streams and canals, over the ponds and all the reservoirs'—and they will turn to blood. Blood will be everywhere in Egypt, even in the wooden buckets and stone jars."

7:20
i Ex 17:5 *j* Ps 78:44; 105:29

20Moses and Aaron did just as the LORD had commanded. He raised his staff in the presence of Pharaoh and his officials and struck the water of the Nile,[i] and all the water was changed into blood.[j] 21The fish in the Nile died, and the river smelled so bad that the Egyptians could not drink its water. Blood was everywhere in Egypt.

7:22
k ver 11

22But the Egyptian magicians did the same things by their secret arts,[k] and Pharaoh's heart became hard; he would not listen to Moses and Aaron, just as the LORD

Exodus 7:8–13

This passage introduces the coming battle between the Lord and Pharaoh, providing a snapshot of the drama to unfold and the victory to be won. More than a display of God flexing his muscles, the plagues against Egypt would be the unleashing of his creative forces against his enemies. We can imagine God using a variety of other means to bring Egypt to its knees, but he chose to fight with weapons only he could command. What defense is possible against the forces of creation itself?

Have you ever felt overwhelmed by the world's "powers that be"? Be comforted. Counterfeit power can't last. It's easy for us to lose sight of this when facing persecution or resistance. Our enemies, the devil and his forces (Eph. 6:12), will ultimately lose their battle against God

(Rev. 20:10). Jesus vanquished demonic powers that held people enslaved (cf. Matt. 8:28–34), and Paul silenced a sorcerer who opposed his ministry (Acts 13:6–12).

Exodus 7:14–24

The first plague was significant in four symbolic senses: (1) Notice the parallel between it and the demise of the Egyptian army in the Red Sea (chs. 14–15). (2) The means by which the first pharaoh had tried to eliminate the Israelite threat—casting their babies into the Nile (1:22)—became a source of trouble for the Egyptians. (3) Egypt's greatness as a civilization depended wholly on the Nile's life-giving waters, so an attack on the Nile was nothing less than an attack on Egypt. (4) The Egyptians worshiped the Nile, so an attack on the river constituted an attack on their gods.

7:1–5

The PLAGUES

The plagues God sent down on the Egyptians were designed to gain freedom for God's people. They directly challenged all that the Egyptians worshiped and held sacred. Today the same types of afflictions plague us, most of them not directly God-sent but the result of human failing.

Plagues That Struck Ancient Egypt	Human "Plagues" Today
• Water turned to blood	25 percent of people have difficulty finding fresh water.
• Frogs, gnats, flies, locusts	Both pests and pesticides the world over create problems for farmers.
• Livestock	Mad cow disease and Avian Influenza (bird flu) threaten modern farm animals.
• Hail, darkness	Drought, wildfires, flooding, earthquakes, hurricanes, monsoons, avalanches, global warming, and mudslides are only some examples of climate/weather related problems threatening our planet today.
• Death of firstborn	Modern epidemics, including AIDS, continue to cause widespread death and devastation.

had said. 23Instead, he turned and went into his palace, and did not take even this to heart. 24And all the Egyptians dug along the Nile to get drinking water, because they could not drink the water of the river.

The Plague of Frogs

8 25Seven days passed after the LORD struck the Nile. 1Then the LORD said to Moses, "Go to Pharaoh and say to him, 'This is what the LORD says: Let my people go, so that they may worship[/] me. 2If you refuse to let them go, I will plague your whole country with frogs. 3The Nile will teem with frogs. They will come up into your palace and your bedroom and onto your bed, into the houses of your officials and on your people,[m] and into your ovens and kneading troughs. 4The frogs will go up on you and your people and all your officials.' "

5Then the LORD said to Moses, "Tell Aaron, 'Stretch out your hand with your staff[n] over the streams and canals and ponds, and make frogs come up on the land of Egypt.' "

6So Aaron stretched out his hand over the waters of Egypt, and the frogs[o] came up and covered the land. 7But the magicians did the same things by their secret arts;[p] they also made frogs come up on the land of Egypt.

8Pharaoh summoned Moses and Aaron and said, "Pray[q] to the LORD to take the frogs away from me and my people, and I will let your people go to offer sacrifices[r] to the LORD."

9Moses said to Pharaoh, "I leave to you the honor of setting the time for me to pray for you and your officials and your people that you and your houses may be rid of the frogs, except for those that remain in the Nile."

10"Tomorrow," Pharaoh said.

Moses replied, "It will be as you say, so that you may know there is no one like the LORD our God.[s] 11The frogs will leave you and your houses, your officials and your people; they will remain only in the Nile."

12After Moses and Aaron left Pharaoh, Moses cried out to the LORD about the frogs he had brought on Pharaoh. 13And the LORD did what Moses asked. The frogs died in the houses, in the courtyards and in the fields. 14They were piled into heaps, and the land reeked of them. 15But when Pharaoh saw that there was relief, he hardened his heart[t] and would not listen to Moses and Aaron, just as the LORD had said.

The Plague of Gnats

16Then the LORD said to Moses, "Tell Aaron, 'Stretch out your staff and strike the dust of the ground,' and throughout the land of Egypt the dust will become gnats." 17They did this, and when Aaron stretched out his hand with the staff and struck the dust of the ground, gnats[u] came upon men and animals. All the dust through-

8:1 / Ex 3:12,18; 4:23
8:3 m Ex 10:6
8:5 n Ex 7:19
8:6 o Ps 78:45; 105:30
8:7 p Ex 7:11
8:8 q ver 28; Ex 9:28; 10:17 r ver 25
8:10 s Ex 9:14; Dt 4:35; 33:26; 2Sa 7:22; 1Ch 17:20; Ps 86:8; Isa 46:9; Jer 10:6
8:15 t Ex 7:14
8:17 u Ps 105:31

The plagues spoke volumes to the average Egyptian, though they didn't move Pharaoh until the bitter end. Still today calamitous events cause people to at least entertain the notion of "God." These situations offer the watching Christian untold opportunities to influence people for the kingdom. Think about the responses of people in the U.S. immediately following the events of September 11, 2001. Though many have returned to pre-9/11 behavior and attitudes about God, others can trace their new birth in Christ directly to this tragedy.

Exodus 7:25—8:15

All the plagues were in a sense creation reversals: Animals harmed rather than served humanity; darkness eradicated light; water became a source of death rather than life. The climax of Genesis 1 was the creation of humans, while the culmination of the plagues would be the destruction of people. The plagues didn't run rampant, though. Each eventually ceased, and each

ending was a fresh display of God's creative power. Again and again he restored order to chaos as he had done "in the beginning."

When we read that old story of frogs, gnats, and rivers turning into blood, scenes from the movie *The Ten Commandments* may come to mind. We are so familiar with the story line that the reality doesn't strike us deeply. At the end of the day, though, when the masks come off and we are left to our own consciences, do we really believe in the God the Biblical text presents to us? Do you believe this God is somehow connected to us—his people thousands of years removed from these events?

Exodus 8:16–19

Dust was the origin of this plague. Is there a connection here with Genesis 3:19? Dust in the present context represented death (see also Job 17:16; 21:26; Ps. 22:29). The gnats, more than a nagging discomfort, were a sign of human mortality. The dust, to which all flesh

8:18
v Ex 9:11; Da 5:8
w Ex 7:11
8:19
x Ex 7:5; 10:7;
Ps 8:3; Lk 11:20

out the land of Egypt became gnats. [18]But when the magicians[v] tried to produce gnats by their secret arts,[w] they could not. And the gnats were on men and animals. [19]The magicians said to Pharaoh, "This is the finger[x] of God." But Pharaoh's heart was hard and he would not listen, just as the LORD had said.

The Plague of Flies

8:20
y Ex 7:15; 9:13
z ver 1; Ex 3:18

[20]Then the LORD said to Moses, "Get up early in the morning[y] and confront Pharaoh as he goes to the water and say to him, 'This is what the LORD says: Let my people go, so that they may worship[z] me. [21]If you do not let my people go, I will send swarms of flies on you and your officials, on your people and into your houses. The houses of the Egyptians will be full of flies, and even the ground where they are.

8:22
a Ex 9:4,6,26;
10:23; 11:7
b Ex 7:5; 9:29

[22]" 'But on that day I will deal differently with the land of Goshen, where my people live;[a] no swarms of flies will be there, so that you will know[b] that I, the LORD, am in this land. [23]I will make a distinction[a] between my people and your people. This miraculous sign will occur tomorrow.' "

8:24
c Ps 78:45; 105:31
8:25
d ver 8; Ex 9:27

[24]And the LORD did this. Dense swarms of flies poured into Pharaoh's palace and into the houses of his officials, and throughout Egypt the land was ruined by the flies. [c]

[25]Then Pharaoh summoned[d] Moses and Aaron and said, "Go, sacrifice to your God here in the land."

8:26
e Ge 43:32; 46:34
8:27
f Ex 3:18

[26]But Moses said, "That would not be right. The sacrifices we offer the LORD our God would be detestable to the Egyptians.[e] And if we offer sacrifices that are detestable in their eyes, will they not stone us? [27]We must take a three-day journey into the desert to offer sacrifices[f] to the LORD our God, as he commands us."

8:28
g ver 8; Ex 9:28;
1Ki 13:6

[28]Pharaoh said, "I will let you go to offer sacrifices to the LORD your God in the desert, but you must not go very far. Now pray[g] for me."

8:29
h ver 15

[29]Moses answered, "As soon as I leave you, I will pray to the LORD, and tomorrow the flies will leave Pharaoh and his officials and his people. Only be sure that Pharaoh does not act deceitfully[h] again by not letting the people go to offer sacrifices to the LORD."

8:30
i ver 12

[30]Then Moses left Pharaoh and prayed to the LORD,[i] [31]and the LORD did what Moses asked: The flies left Pharaoh and his officials and his people; not a fly remained.

8:32
j ver 8,15; Ex 4:21

[32]But this time also Pharaoh hardened his heart[j] and would not let the people go.

The Plague on Livestock

9 Then the LORD said to Moses, "Go to Pharaoh and say to him, 'This is what the LORD, the God of the Hebrews, says: "Let my people go, so that they may worship[k] me." [2]If you refuse to let them go and continue to hold them back, [3]the hand[l] of the LORD will bring a terrible plague on your livestock in the field—on your hors-

9:1
k Ex 8:1
9:3
l Ex 7:4

a 23 Septuagint and Vulgate; Hebrew will put a deliverance

must return, speeded the Egyptians toward that unavoidable end.

The Exodus story isn't alone in linking creation and salvation. In fact, in the pages of the Old Testament creation often turns chaotic when God wants to punish or save. The most obvious example is the flood. This was the first creation reversal, and it appears in Genesis soon after the portrayal of the majesty of creation itself.

The story of the plagues and the exodus wasn't taken for granted by the generations of Israelites living after the events. It was for them a gripping reminder of who God is. This story isn't about what God does to save us, or even so much about how he saved Israel. It's about God—period. The question to ask of this section of Scripture isn't "What does this have to do with me?" but "What does this tell me about God?" Why not stop a moment and try to answer this question?

Exodus 8:20–32

The fourth plague introduced a number of "firsts." (1) No shepherd's staff was involved in bringing about the swarms of flies. A staff is reintroduced in plagues 7, 8, and 9, but it was Moses' rather than Aaron's. (2) This was the first plague in which God made a distinction between his people and Pharaoh's. God unleashed his creation power for Israel's benefit—but Egypt's destruction. (3) The plague brought destruction to the land, taking the Lord's judgment to a new level by previewing the outcome—the destruction of Egypt at the Red Sea.

We can imagine that the Israelites from the time of the exodus onward "applied" the plagues by falling back in awe as they remembered what God had done for them. How regularly do you worship God, not just for his great love, but also for his fearful might? Praising is the goal of redemption itself.

es and donkeys and camels and on your cattle and sheep and goats. 4But the LORD
will make a distinction between the livestock of Israel and that of Egypt,[m] so that
no animal belonging to the Israelites will die.' "
5The LORD set a time and said, "Tomorrow the LORD will do this in the land."
6And the next day the LORD did it: All the livestock[n] of the Egyptians died,[o] but not
one animal belonging to the Israelites died. 7Pharaoh sent men to investigate and
found that not even one of the animals of the Israelites had died. Yet his heart was
unyielding and he would not let the people go.[p]

The Plague of Boils

8Then the LORD said to Moses and Aaron, "Take handfuls of soot from a furnace
and have Moses toss it into the air in the presence of Pharaoh. 9It will become fine
dust over the whole land of Egypt, and festering boils[q] will break out on men and
animals throughout the land."
10So they took soot from a furnace and stood before Pharaoh. Moses tossed it
into the air, and festering boils broke out on men and animals. 11The magicians[r]
could not stand before Moses because of the boils that were on them and on all the
Egyptians. 12But the LORD hardened Pharaoh's heart[s] and he would not listen to
Moses and Aaron, just as the LORD had said to Moses.

The Plague of Hail

13Then the LORD said to Moses, "Get up early in the morning, confront Pharaoh
and say to him, 'This is what the LORD, the God of the Hebrews, says: Let my people go, so that they may worship[t] me, 14or this time I will send the full force of my
plagues against you and against your officials and your people, so you may know[u]
that there is no one like[v] me in all the earth. 15For by now I could have stretched
out my hand and struck you and your people[w] with a plague that would have wiped
you off the earth. 16But I have raised you up[a] for this very purpose,[x] that I might
show you my power[y] and that my name might be proclaimed in all the earth. 17You
still set yourself against my people and will not let them go. 18Therefore, at this time
tomorrow I will send the worst hailstorm[z] that has ever fallen on Egypt, from the
day it was founded till now.[a] 19Give an order now to bring your livestock and ev-

9:4 [m] ver 26; Ex 8:22
9:6 [n] ver 19-21; Ex 11:5 [o] Ps 78:48-50
9:7 [p] Ex 7:14; 8:32
9:9 [q] Dt 28:27,35; Rev 16:2
9:11 [r] Ex 8:18
9:12 [s] Ex 4:21
9:13 [t] Ex 8:20
9:14 [u] Ex 8:10 [v] 2Sa 7:22; 1Ch 17:20; Ps 86:8; Isa 46:9; Jer 10:6
9:15 [w] Ex 3:20
9:16 [x] Pr 16:4 [y] Ro 9:17*
9:18 [z] ver 23 [a] ver 24

[a] 16 Or *have spared you*

Exodus 9:1–7

God's "finger" (8:19) had brought about the plague of gnats. This time the force of his "hand" (9:3) was about to come on the Egyptians. The "hand" of God to deliver the Israelites is a common term in Exodus (e.g., 3:19; 6:1; 13:3), normally associated with some mighty act of judgment. This was the first plague in which the term is used—and also the first directed toward the death of created things. As in the last plague, God's people were protected; their livestock escaped harm.

Some people take a moralistic approach to the plagues—saying, for example, that they warn us against Pharaoh's example of making promises he had no intention of keeping. While true, such a reading falls short. The Israelites came to know God better by what he had done, and this knowledge formed the basis for their morality. To what degree is your knowledge of God based on his historical "record"? If our hearts and minds are filled with a personal knowledge of our Creator, our behavior will follow suit.

Exodus 9:8–12

This was the first real demonstration to the Egyptians that their lives were in danger. Up until now they had encountered only frustrating frogs and insects and plagues on livestock. It's ironic that Moses took soot from a kiln in which the oppressed Israelites baked bricks to initiate this plague. It represented a concrete step toward the ultimate, irrevocable outcome: the deaths of the firstborn and of the Egyptian army in the sea.

We miss something of the wonder of our own personal salvation if we fail to see it in light of the grand scope of God's provision of salvation. In the plagues, God manipulated the created order and thereby reached both back to the dawn of time and ahead to its pinnacle—the death, resurrection, and return of Christ. He did this ultimately for his own glory. (See "Here and Now" to follow.) What implications does this perspective have for you?

Exodus 9:13–35

Weather disturbances, especially hail, are associated in the Bible with God's judgment (Josh. 10:11; Isa. 28:2,17; 30:30; Ezek. 13:11–13; 38:22). Moses let Pharaoh in on a secret from God, saying in effect: "By now I could have wiped you off the face of the earth. The reason I haven't is that I'm using you to spread the word throughout the world that I am God. Understand this well, Pharaoh: You are serving my purpose." The end of verse 16 refers to God's reputation being proclaimed "in all the earth" (cf. vv. 14,29).

erything you have in the field to a place of shelter, because the hail will fall on every man and animal that has not been brought in and is still out in the field, and they will die.' "

9:20
b Pr 13:13

[20]Those officials of Pharaoh who feared[b] the word of the LORD hurried to bring their slaves and their livestock inside. [21]But those who ignored the word of the LORD left their slaves and livestock in the field.

[22]Then the LORD said to Moses, "Stretch out your hand toward the sky so that hail will fall all over Egypt—on men and animals and on everything growing in the fields of Egypt." [23]When Moses stretched out his staff toward the sky, the LORD sent thunder[c] and hail,[d] and lightning flashed down to the ground. So the LORD rained hail on the land of Egypt; [24]hail fell and lightning flashed back and forth. It was the worst storm in all the land of Egypt since it had become a nation. [25]Throughout Egypt hail struck everything in the fields—both men and animals; it beat down everything growing in the fields and stripped every tree.[e] [26]The only place it did not hail was the land of Goshen,[f] where the Israelites were.[g]

9:23
c Ps 18:13
d Jos 10:11;
Ps 78:47; 105:32;
Isa 30:30;
Eze 38:22; Rev 8:7;
16:21

9:25
e Ps 105:32-33

9:26
f ver 4 *g* Ex 8:22;
10:23; 11:7; 12:13

9:27
h Ex 10:16
i 2Ch 12:6;
Ps 129:4; La 1:18

9:28
j Ex 10:17 *k* Ex 8:8

9:29
l 1Ki 8:22,38;
Ps 143:6; Isa 1:15
m Ex 19:5; Ps 24:1;
1Co 10:26

[27]Then Pharaoh summoned Moses and Aaron. "This time I have sinned,"[h] he said to them. "The LORD is in the right,[i] and I and my people are in the wrong. [28]Pray[j] to the LORD, for we have had enough thunder and hail. I will let you go;[k] you don't have to stay any longer."

[29]Moses replied, "When I have gone out of the city, I will spread out my hands[l] in prayer to the LORD. The thunder will stop and there will be no more hail, so you may know that the earth[m] is the LORD's. [30]But I know that you and your officials still do not fear the LORD God."

9:31
n Ru 1:22; 2:23

[31](The flax and barley[n] were destroyed, since the barley had headed and the flax was in bloom. [32]The wheat and spelt, however, were not destroyed, because they ripen later.)

[33]Then Moses left Pharaoh and went out of the city. He spread out his hands toward the LORD; the thunder and hail stopped, and the rain no longer poured down on the land. [34]When Pharaoh saw that the rain and hail and thunder had stopped, he sinned again: He and his officials hardened their hearts. [35]So Pharaoh's heart[o] was hard and he would not let the Israelites go, just as the LORD had said through Moses.

9:35
o Ex 4:21

The Plague of Locusts

10:1
p Ex 4:21 *q* Ex 7:3
10:2
r Ex 12:26-27;
13:8,14; Dt 4:9;
Ps 44:1; 78:4,5;
Joel 1:3

10 Then the LORD said to Moses, "Go to Pharaoh, for I have hardened his heart[p] and the hearts of his officials so that I may perform these miraculous signs[q] of mine among them [2]that you may tell your children[r] and grandchildren how I dealt harshly with the Egyptians and how I performed my signs among them, and that you may know that I am the LORD."

10:3
s 1Ki 21:29;
Jas 4:10; 1Pe 5:6
10:4
t Rev 9:3
10:5
u Ex 9:32; Joel 1:4

[3]So Moses and Aaron went to Pharaoh and said to him, "This is what the LORD, the God of the Hebrews, says: 'How long will you refuse to humble[s] yourself before me? Let my people go, so that they may worship me. [4]If you refuse to let them go, I will bring locusts[t] into your country tomorrow. [5]They will cover the face of the ground so that it cannot be seen. They will devour what little you have left[u] after the hail, including every tree that is growing in your fields. [6]They will fill your houses and those of all your officials and all the Egyptians—something neither your fathers nor your forefathers have ever seen from the day they settled in this land till now.' " Then Moses turned and left Pharaoh.

📖 Our redemption is a large piece of a puzzle that extends beyond our personal, eternal state. It's about the restoration or re-creation of what was lost in Eden. This is why salvation, whether in deliverance from Egypt or through Jesus' death and resurrection, is often described in creation language. Jesus came to re-create humanity and to inaugurate a new world order, the kingdom of God. Creation will one day be restored to the glory God intended for it from the beginning. How does your life proclaim this astounding fact to those around you?

Exodus 10:1–20
📖 Like the plague of hail, the plague of locusts brought widespread devastation on people, animals, and crops and represented forms of judgment common to other parts of Scripture. The locust plague brought to light another purpose of the plagues, one that had been hinted at but not yet given clear expression: that future generations of Israelites, as well as the Egyptians, might "know" God. His redemptive purposes reached far beyond the generation living at the time of these events.

7Pharaoh's officials said to him, "How long will this man be a snare[v] to us? Let the people go, so that they may worship the LORD their God. Do you not yet realize that Egypt is ruined?"[w]

8Then Moses and Aaron were brought back to Pharaoh. "Go, worship[x] the LORD your God," he said. "But just who will be going?"

9Moses answered, "We will go with our young and old, with our sons and daughters, and with our flocks and herds, because we are to celebrate a festival to the LORD."

10Pharaoh said, "The LORD be with you—if I let you go, along with your women and children! Clearly you are bent on evil.[a] 11No! Have only the men go; and worship the LORD, since that's what you have been asking for." Then Moses and Aaron were driven out of Pharaoh's presence.

12And the LORD said to Moses, "Stretch out your hand[y] over Egypt so that locusts will swarm over the land and devour everything growing in the fields, everything left by the hail."

13So Moses stretched out his staff over Egypt, and the LORD made an east wind blow across the land all that day and all that night. By morning the wind had brought the locusts;[z] 14they invaded all Egypt and settled down in every area of the country in great numbers. Never before had there been such a plague of locusts,[a] nor will there ever be again. 15They covered all the ground until it was black. They devoured[b] all that was left after the hail—everything growing in the fields and the fruit on the trees. Nothing green remained on tree or plant in all the land of Egypt.

16Pharaoh quickly summoned Moses and Aaron and said, "I have sinned[c] against the LORD your God and against you. 17Now forgive my sin once more and pray[d] to the LORD your God to take this deadly plague away from me."

18Moses then left Pharaoh and prayed to the LORD.[e] 19And the LORD changed the wind to a very strong west wind, which caught up the locusts and carried them into the Red Sea.[b] Not a locust was left anywhere in Egypt. 20But the LORD hardened Pharaoh's heart,[f] and he would not let the Israelites go.

The Plague of Darkness

21Then the LORD said to Moses, "Stretch out your hand toward the sky so that darkness[g] will spread over Egypt—darkness that can be felt." 22So Moses stretched out his hand toward the sky, and total darkness[h] covered all Egypt for three days. 23No one could see anyone else or leave his place for three days. Yet all the Israelites had light in the places where they lived.[i]

24Then Pharaoh summoned Moses and said, "Go, worship the LORD. Even your women and children[j] may go with you; only leave your flocks and herds behind."

25But Moses said, "You must allow us to have sacrifices and burnt offerings to present to the LORD our God. 26Our livestock too must go with us; not a hoof is to be

[a] 10 Or Be careful, trouble is in store for you!   [b] 19 Hebrew Yam Suph; that is, Sea of Reeds

10:7
v Ex 23:33;
Jos 23:13;
1Sa 18:21; Ecc 7:26
w Ex 8:19
10:8
x Ex 8:8

10:12
y Ex 7:19

10:13
z Ps 105:34
10:14
a Ps 78:46;
Joel 2:1-11,25
10:15
b ver 5;
Ps 105:34-35
10:16
c Ex 9:27
10:17
d Ex 8:8

10:18
e Ex 8:30

10:20
f Ex 4:21; 11:10

10:21
g Dt 28:29
10:22
h Ps 105:28;
Rev 16:10
10:23
i Ex 8:22

10:24
j ver 8-10

📖 Who is this God who, rather than fanning Pharaoh's apparently budding obedience into a flame, seemed to force him in a completely opposite direction? Who is this God who chose a people for himself, through no merit of their own, and then determined to mold them into his own image despite their repeated failures and rebellions? An appropriate response to reading this story might be to shake our heads in wonder: God is truly beyond our understanding.

Exodus 10:21–29

📖 The plague of darkness was almost certainly a challenge against Re, an Egyptian sun god. This would have spoken directly to Pharaoh, since Egyptian kings were referred to as sons of Re. Darkness was the first thing God brought under control by introducing light in Genesis 1:2–3. A reintroduction of darkness brought creation back to its chaotic beginnings, a signal to the Egyptians of what awaited them at the Red Sea.

📖 We see in the plagues both God's openness and his hiddenness, a paradox embodied in Christ: The fullness of God dwells in him (Col. 1:19), yet he's like us in every way (Heb. 2:17). All who "have come to share in Christ" (Heb. 3:14) also share in this tension. God is in our midst—yet beyond us. We are dealing with a God of boundless depth, who has creation at his fingertips. Yet he has gone to great lengths to reveal himself to us and invite us into a relationship with himself. How does this realization affect you?

left behind. We have to use some of them in worshiping the LORD our God, and until we get there we will not know what we are to use to worship the LORD."

10:27
k ver 20; Ex 4:21

27But the LORD hardened Pharaoh's heart,[k] and he was not willing to let them go. 28Pharaoh said to Moses, "Get out of my sight! Make sure you do not appear before me again! The day you see my face you will die."

10:29
l Heb 11:27

29"Just as you say," Moses replied, "I will never appear[l] before you again."

The Plague on the Firstborn

11 Now the LORD had said to Moses, "I will bring one more plague on Pharaoh and on Egypt. After that, he will let you go from here, and when he does, he will drive you out completely. 2Tell the people that men and women alike are to ask their neighbors for articles of silver and gold."[m] 3(The LORD made the Egyptians favorably disposed toward the people, and Moses himself was highly regarded[n] in Egypt by Pharaoh's officials and by the people.)

11:2
m Ex 3:21,22
11:3
n Dt 34:11

11:4
o Ex 12:29
11:5
p Ex 4:23; Ps 78:51

4So Moses said, "This is what the LORD says: 'About midnight[o] I will go throughout Egypt. 5Every firstborn[p] son in Egypt will die, from the firstborn son of Pharaoh, who sits on the throne, to the firstborn son of the slave girl, who is at her hand mill, and all the firstborn of the cattle as well. 6There will be loud wailing[q] throughout Egypt—worse than there has ever been or ever will be again. 7But among the Israelites not a dog will bark at any man or animal.' Then you will know that the LORD makes a distinction[r] between Egypt and Israel. 8All these officials of yours will come to me, bowing down before me and saying, 'Go,[s] you and all the people who follow you!' After that I will leave." Then Moses, hot with anger, left Pharaoh.

11:6
q Ex 12:30

11:7
r Ex 8:22
11:8
s Ex 12:31-33

11:9
t Ex 7:4

9The LORD had said to Moses, "Pharaoh will refuse to listen[t] to you—so that my wonders may be multiplied in Egypt." 10Moses and Aaron performed all these wonders before Pharaoh, but the LORD hardened Pharaoh's heart,[u] and he would not let the Israelites go out of his country.

11:10
u Ex 4:21; 10:20,27

The Passover

12:2
v Ex 13:4; Dt 16:1

12 The LORD said to Moses and Aaron in Egypt, 2"This month is to be for you the first month,[v] the first month of your year. 3Tell the whole community of Israel that on the tenth day of this month each man is to take a lamb[a] for his family, one for each household. 4If any household is too small for a whole lamb, they must share one with their nearest neighbor, having taken into account the number of people there are. You are to determine the amount of lamb needed in accordance with what each person will eat. 5The animals you choose must be year-old males without defect,[w] and you may take them from the sheep or the goats.

12:5
w Lev 22:18-21;
Heb 9:14

a 3 The Hebrew word can mean *lamb* or *kid*; also in verse 4.

Exodus 11:1–10

The deaths of the Egyptian firstborn remind us of the first chapter of Exodus. In verses 4–5 Moses warned Pharaoh that God was coming at midnight to kill the firstborn throughout Egypt. This would seem to have been retribution for the earlier pharaoh's attempt to kill Israel's male children in chapter 1. That king's decree was ultimately not against Israel's children, but against God's.

Pharaoh's heart had been hardened by God so that God's "wonders [might] be multiplied in Egypt" (v. 9). What was about to happen would fulfill God's plan on a deeper level than mere retribution for a king's defiance. Pharaoh's actions had been scripted so that God could execute his plan, and God's dealings with Pharaoh remain a deep mystery to us. We will never truly understand until all is explained to us on that great future day.

Have you struggled to reconcile the two "sides" of God's nature? This God of retribution seems a far cry

from the God of love worshiped on so personal a level by Christians today. Revenge is opposite the law of love invoked by Jesus in Matthew 5:38–48. Ironically, the Old Testament law of retaliation (Ex. 21:23–25) was intended to limit punishment to fit the crime. The first pharaoh's genocidal act was unspeakably horrible, and God's retribution, primitive to our "civilized" sensibilities, was in kind. We live in the new era of God's grace but still serve a God who is wholly righteous and just.

Exodus 12:1–30

The Passover celebration is recorded in passages throughout the Old Testament that reflect various stages in Israel's faith journey. Passover and the accompanying Feast of Unleavened Bread remained an abiding feature in Israel's relationship with the God of the exodus, a means whereby the people would remember and reenact what God had done for them. The feasts celebrated the Israelites' redemption from Egypt and the beginning of their existence as a nation.

6Take care of them until the fourteenth day of the month, *x* when all the people of the community of Israel must slaughter them at twilight. *y* 7Then they are to take some of the blood and put it on the sides and tops of the doorframes of the houses where they eat the lambs. 8That same night *z* they are to eat the meat roasted *a* over the fire, along with bitter herbs, *b* and bread made without yeast. *c* 9Do not eat the meat raw or cooked in water, but roast it over the fire—head, legs and inner parts. 10Do not leave any of it till morning; *d* if some is left till morning, you must burn it. 11This is how you are to eat it: with your cloak tucked into your belt, your sandals on your feet and your staff in your hand. Eat it in haste; *e* it is the LORD's Passover. *f*

12"On that same night I will pass through *g* Egypt and strike down every firstborn—both men and animals—and I will bring judgment on all the gods *h* of Egypt. I am the LORD. *i* 13The blood will be a sign for you on the houses where you are; and when I see the blood, I will pass over you. No destructive plague will touch you when I strike Egypt.

14"This is a day you are to commemorate; *j* for the generations to come you shall celebrate it as a festival to the LORD—a lasting ordinance. *k* 15For seven days you are to eat bread made without yeast. *l* On the first day remove the yeast from your houses, for whoever eats anything with yeast in it from the first day through the seventh must be cut off *m* from Israel. 16On the first day hold a sacred assembly, and another one on the seventh day. Do no work at all on these days, except to prepare food for everyone to eat—that is all you may do.

17"Celebrate the Feast of Unleavened Bread, because it was on this very day that I brought your divisions out of Egypt. *n* Celebrate this day as a lasting ordinance for the generations to come. 18In the first month *o* you are to eat bread made without yeast, from the evening of the fourteenth day until the evening of the twenty-first day. 19For seven days no yeast is to be found in your houses. And whoever eats anything with yeast in it must be cut off from the community of Israel, whether he is an alien or native-born. 20Eat nothing made with yeast. Wherever you live, you must eat unleavened bread."

21Then Moses summoned all the elders of Israel and said to them, "Go at once and select the animals for your families and slaughter the Passover *p* lamb. 22Take a bunch of hyssop, dip it into the blood in the basin and put some of the blood *q* on the top and on both sides of the doorframe. Not one of you shall go out the door of his house until morning. 23When the LORD goes through the land to strike down the Egyptians, he will see the blood *r* on the top and sides of the doorframe and will pass over *s* that doorway, and he will not permit the destroyer *t* to enter your houses and strike you down.

24"Obey these instructions as a lasting ordinance for you and your descendants. 25When you enter the land that the LORD will give you as he promised, observe this ceremony. 26And when your children *u* ask you, 'What does this ceremony mean to you?' 27then tell them, 'It is the Passover *v* sacrifice to the LORD, who passed over the houses of the Israelites in Egypt and spared our homes when he struck down the Egyptians.'" Then the people bowed down and worshiped. *w* 28The Israelites did just what the LORD commanded Moses and Aaron.

29At midnight *x* the LORD struck down all the firstborn *y* in Egypt, from the firstborn of Pharaoh, who sat on the throne, to the firstborn of the prisoner, who was in the dungeon, and the firstborn of all the livestock *z* as well. 30Pharaoh and all his officials and all the Egyptians got up during the night, and there was loud wailing *a* in Egypt, for there was not a house without someone dead.

12:6
x Lev 23:5;
Nu 9:1-3,5,11
y Ex 16:12;
Dt 16:4,6
12:8
z Ex 34:25; Nu 9:12
a Dt 16:7 *b* Nu 9:11
c Dt 16:3-4;
1Co 5:8
12:10
d Ex 23:18; 34:25

12:11
e Dt 16:3
f ver 13,21,27,43;
Dt 16:1
12:12
g Ex 11:4; Am 5:17
h Nu 33:4 *i* Ex 6:2

12:14
j Ex 13:9
k ver 17,24;
Ex 13:5,10;
2Ki 23:21
12:15
l Ex 13:6-7; 23:15;
34:18; Lev 23:6;
Dt 16:3
m Ge 17:14;
Nu 9:13

12:17
n ver 41; Ex 13:3
12:18
o ver 2; Lev 23:5-8;
Nu 28:16-25

12:21
p ver 11;
Mk 14:12-16
12:22
q ver 7; Heb 11:28

12:23
r Rev 7:3 *s* ver 13
t 1Co 10:10;
Heb 11:28

12:26
u Ex 10:2;
13:8,14-15; Jos 4:6
12:27
v ver 11 *w* Ex 4:31

12:29
x Ex 11:4 *y* Ex 4:23;
Ps 78:51 *z* Ex 9:6

12:30
a Ex 11:6

The obvious application of the Passover for Christians was instituted by Jesus and concerns the church: the regular celebration of the Lord's Supper by Christians around the world and through all time (Matt. 26:17–30). As we celebrate the feast in our day, we commemorate our redemption and anticipate the glory that awaits us. But the Lord's Supper is also a fulfillment of that Israelite meal. By partaking in Communion, we participate in the effects of God's ancient, liberating work, completed on Easter.

The Exodus

12:31
b Ex 8:8
12:32
c Ex 10:9,26
12:33
d Ps 105:38

31 During the night Pharaoh summoned Moses and Aaron and said, "Up! Leave my people, you and the Israelites! Go, worship*b* the LORD as you have requested. 32 Take your flocks and herds,*c* as you have said, and go. And also bless me."

33 The Egyptians urged the people to hurry and leave*d* the country. "For otherwise," they said, "we will all die!" 34 So the people took their dough before the yeast was added, and carried it on their shoulders in kneading troughs wrapped in clothing.

12:35
e Ex 3:22

35 The Israelites did as Moses instructed and asked the Egyptians for articles of silver and gold*e* and for clothing. 36 The LORD had made the Egyptians favorably disposed toward the people, and they gave them what they asked for; so they plundered*f* the Egyptians.

12:36
f Ex 3:22
12:37
g Nu 33:3-5
h Ex 38:26;
Nu 1:46; 11:13,21
12:38
i Nu 11:4

37 The Israelites journeyed from Rameses to Succoth.*g* There were about six hundred thousand men*h* on foot, besides women and children. 38 Many other people*i* went up with them, as well as large droves of livestock, both flocks and herds. 39 With the dough they had brought from Egypt, they baked cakes of unleavened bread. The dough was without yeast because they had been driven out*j* of Egypt and did not have time to prepare food for themselves.

12:39
j ver 31-33; Ex 6:1;
11:1
12:40
k Ge 15:13; Ac 7:6;
Gal 3:17
12:41
l ver 17; Ex 6:26
m Ex 3:10
12:42
n Ex 13:10;
Dt 16:1,6

40 Now the length of time the Israelite people lived in Egypt*a* was 430 years.*k* 41 At the end of the 430 years, to the very day, all the LORD's divisions*l* left Egypt.*m* 42 Because the LORD kept vigil that night to bring them out of Egypt, on this night all the Israelites are to keep vigil to honor the LORD for the generations to come.*n*

Passover Restrictions

12:43
o ver 11 p ver 48;
Nu 9:14
12:44
q Ge 17:12-13
12:45
r Lev 22:10
12:46
s Nu 9:12;
Jn 19:36*

43 The LORD said to Moses and Aaron, "These are the regulations for the Passover:*o* "No foreigner*p* is to eat of it. 44 Any slave you have bought may eat of it after you have circumcised*q* him, 45 but a temporary resident and a hired worker*r* may not eat of it.

46 "It must be eaten inside one house; take none of the meat outside the house. Do not break any of the bones.*s* 47 The whole community of Israel must celebrate it.

12:48
t Nu 9:14
12:49
u Nu 15:15-16,29;
Gal 3:28

48 "An alien living among you who wants to celebrate the LORD's Passover must have all the males in his household circumcised; then he may take part like one born in the land.*t* No uncircumcised male may eat of it. 49 The same law applies to the native-born and to the alien*u* living among you."

12:51
v ver 41; Ex 6:26

50 All the Israelites did just what the LORD had commanded Moses and Aaron. 51 And on that very day the LORD brought the Israelites out of Egypt by their divisions.*v*

---

a 40 Masoretic Text; Samaritan Pentateuch and Septuagint Egypt and Canaan

---

Exodus 12:31–42

After repeated refusals to release the Israelites, Pharaoh and the Egyptians "urged the people to hurry and leave the country"—but not before the Israelites had "plundered" the Egyptians by asking for valuable possessions (see 3:21–22). Some consider it improper for the Israelites, a holy people, to have plundered anyone. Others believe that any material gain they received was a fitting reward for their years of slavery. At any rate, the Israelites marched out of Egypt through the front door, with dignity, as God's people.

It's easy for us to see the scope and seriousness of a situation and throw up our hands in despair. But in so doing we fail to consider that the God of the impossible is ready to help (cf. Luke 1:37). Surely the God who can escort his people uncontested from the jaws of death is able and willing to rescue souls from the grip of sin; to feed, clothe, and comfort the hungry and hurting; and to lead his children by the hand to safety. What "impossible" thing has this God done for you?

Exodus 12:43–51

Many non-Israelites left Egypt with the Israelites. The Hebrew word translated "other people" in verse 38 likely indicates an ethnic mixture. Non-Israelites weren't excluded from the meal, but the men had to put themselves under the sign of the covenant (i.e., circumcision) to participate. We see here a combination of exclusiveness and inclusiveness—a hint that God's purpose was broader than the deliverance of the Israelites from Egypt.

Our God has a big heart! He's patient with the whole human race, "not wanting anyone to perish, but everyone to come to repentance" (2 Peter 3:9). The gospel is inclusive. Anyone can express faith in Christ. At the same time, though, it's exclusive. Those who choose not to accept salvation in Christ will be excluded from heaven (Eph. 5:5). The ability of any person to participate in his eternal feast (Rev. 19:9) is dependent on one condition—faith in the atoning death of Jesus Christ.

Consecration of the Firstborn

13 The LORD said to Moses, [2]"Consecrate to me every firstborn male.[w] The first offspring of every womb among the Israelites belongs to me, whether man or animal."

[3]Then Moses said to the people, "Commemorate this day, the day you came out of Egypt, out of the land of slavery, because the LORD brought you out of it with a mighty hand.[x] Eat nothing containing yeast.[y] [4]Today, in the month of Abib,[z] you are leaving. [5]When the LORD brings you into the land of the Canaanites, Hittites, Amorites, Hivites and Jebusites[a]—the land he swore to your forefathers to give you, a land flowing with milk and honey—you are to observe this ceremony[b] in this month: [6]For seven days eat bread made without yeast and on the seventh day hold a festival[c] to the LORD. [7]Eat unleavened bread during those seven days; nothing with yeast is to be seen among you, nor shall any yeast be seen anywhere within your borders. [8]On that day tell your son,[d] 'I do this because of what the LORD did for me when I came out of Egypt.' [9]This observance will be for you like a sign on your hand and a reminder on your forehead[e] that the law of the LORD is to be on your lips. For the LORD brought you out of Egypt with his mighty hand. [10]You must keep this ordinance[f] at the appointed time year after year.

[11]"After the LORD brings you into the land of the Canaanites and gives it to you, as he promised on oath to you and your forefathers, [12]you are to give over to the LORD the first offspring of every womb. All the firstborn males of your livestock belong to the LORD.[g] [13]Redeem with a lamb every firstborn donkey, but if you do not redeem it, break its neck.[h] Redeem every firstborn among your sons.[i]

[14]"In days to come, when your son[j] asks you, 'What does this mean?' say to him, 'With a mighty hand the LORD brought us out of Egypt, out of the land of slavery.[k] [15]When Pharaoh stubbornly refused to let us go, the LORD killed every firstborn in Egypt, both man and animal. This is why I sacrifice to the LORD the first male offspring of every womb and redeem each of my firstborn sons.'[l] [16]And it will be like a sign on your hand and a symbol on your forehead[m] that the LORD brought us out of Egypt with his mighty hand."

Crossing the Sea

[17]When Pharaoh let the people go, God did not lead them on the road through the Philistine country, though that was shorter. For God said, "If they face war, they might change their minds and return to Egypt."[n] [18]So God led[o] the people around by the desert road toward the Red Sea.[a] The Israelites went up out of Egypt armed for battle.[p]

[19]Moses took the bones of Joseph[q] with him because Joseph had made the sons

---

[a] 18 Hebrew *Yam Suph*; that is, Sea of Reeds

13:2 w ver 12, 13, 15; Ex 22:29; Nu 3:13; Dt 15:19; Lk 2:23*
13:3 x Ex 3:20; 6:1 y Ex 12:19
13:4 z Ex 12:2
13:5 a Ex 3:8 b Ex 12:25-26
13:6 c Ex 12:15-20
13:8 d ver 14; Ex 10:2; Ps 78:5-6
13:9 e ver 16; Dt 6:8; 11:18
13:10 f Ex 12:24-25
13:12 g Lev 27:26; Lk 2:23*
13:13 h Ex 34:20 i Nu 18:15
13:14 j Ex 10:2; 12:26-27; Dt 6:20 k ver 3, 9
13:15 l Ex 12:29
13:16 m ver 9
13:17 n Ex 14:11; Nu 14:1-4; Dt 17:16
13:18 o Ps 136:16 p Jos 1:14
13:19 q Jos 24:32; Ac 7:16

Exodus 13:1–16

God's divine right to the firstborn extended to all Israel (see 22:29–30); he could have expressed his ownership over Israel by killing its firstborn as well. This is why the consecration of the firstborn is closely related to the Passover celebration. Both the deaths of the Egyptian firstborn (an expression of a redemptive pattern that required death as a means to fuller life) and the blood on the doorposts symbolized God's ownership of the firstborn and his provision to protect his own firstborn son, Israel.

Passover remains a defining element in both Judaism and Christianity. The Gospel writers closely associated the Last Supper, a lasting reminder of God's culminating act of deliverance, with the Passover. Jesus' sacrifice also fulfills the other important theme, the consecration of the firstborn son. But whereas in the Old Testament the

"son" (Israel) was redeemed through the substitution of animal sacrifices, Jesus is the Lamb of God, slain for us. With Christ's death and resurrection the true spiritual pedigree of God's people comes to light. Whether or not you have thought about it, you have *become* firstborn through your union with Christ, the true firstborn Son.

Exodus 13:17—14:31

God caused the wheels to come off of the Egyptians' mighty chariots. Stuck in the middle of the sea, the hapless soldiers realized they were indeed in over their heads. In a tragi-comic confession in light of the preceding 14 chapters, they finally drew the obvious conclusion: "Let's get away from the Israelites! The Lord is fighting for them against Egypt." The fact that the Egyptians' bodies were washed up on the shore, in plain view of all, proved to the Israelites that their escape (redemption) had been accomplished.

13:19
r Ge 50:24-25
13:20
s Nu 33:6
13:21
t Ex 14:19,24;
33:9-10;
Nu 9:16; Dt 1:33;
Ne 9:12,19;
Ps 78:14; 99:7;
105:39; Isa 4:5;
1Co 10:1
14:2
u Nu 33:7; Jer 44:1

14:4
v Ex 4:21
w Ro 9:17,22-23
x Ex 7:5

of Israel swear an oath. He had said, "God will surely come to your aid, and then you must carry my bones up with you from this place." ª ʳ

20After leaving Succoth they camped at Etham on the edge of the desert. ˢ 21By day the LORD went ahead of them in a pillar of cloud ᵗ to guide them on their way and by night in a pillar of fire to give them light, so that they could travel by day or night. 22Neither the pillar of cloud by day nor the pillar of fire by night left its place in front of the people.

14 Then the LORD said to Moses, 2"Tell the Israelites to turn back and encamp near Pi Hahiroth, between Migdol ᵘ and the sea. They are to encamp by the sea, directly opposite Baal Zephon. 3Pharaoh will think, 'The Israelites are wandering around the land in confusion, hemmed in by the desert.' 4And I will harden Pharaoh's heart, ᵛ and he will pursue them. But I will gain glory ʷ for myself through Pharaoh and all his army, and the Egyptians will know that I am the LORD." ˣ So the Israelites did this.

5When the king of Egypt was told that the people had fled, Pharaoh and his officials changed their minds about them and said, "What have we done? We have let the Israelites go and have lost their services!" 6So he had his chariot made ready and

a 19 See Gen. 50:25.

The significance of the exodus lies at the core of what it means to be "in Christ" and is summed up by Jesus' words in John 5:24: We have "*crossed over* from death to life" (emphasis added). The event also affords us a glimpse of the underlying battle between God and evil and its eter-

nal significance. We are not awaiting God's deliverance; it's already come, in Christ. Our Egypt is behind us. We are on the far side of the sea, and our focus is on how we are expected to live as God's redeemed people. What practical, behavioral implications does this have for you?

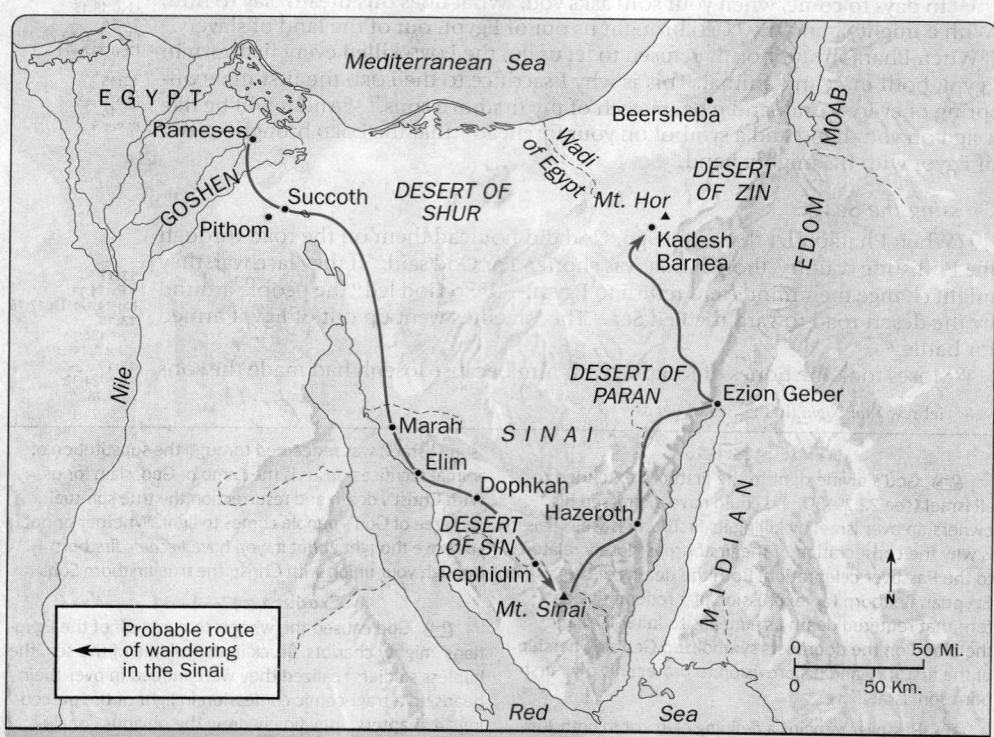

The Exodus (13:17)
Then: The escape, the years of wandering, and the eventual entrance into the land of Canaan all depended on God's miraculous provisions.
Now: The land through which the Israelites tramped is as inhospitable today as it was in Biblical times.

took his army with him. 7He took six hundred of the best chariots, along with all the other chariots of Egypt, with officers over all of them. 8The LORD hardened the heart[y] of Pharaoh king of Egypt, so that he pursued the Israelites, who were marching out boldly.[z] 9The Egyptians—all Pharaoh's horses and chariots, horsemen[a] and troops—pursued the Israelites and overtook[a] them as they camped by the sea near Pi Hahiroth, opposite Baal Zephon.

10As Pharaoh approached, the Israelites looked up, and there were the Egyptians, marching after them. They were terrified and cried[b] out to the LORD. 11They said to Moses, "Was it because there were no graves in Egypt that you brought us to the desert to die?[c] What have you done to us by bringing us out of Egypt? 12Didn't we say to you in Egypt, 'Leave us alone; let us serve the Egyptians'? It would have been better for us to serve the Egyptians than to die in the desert!"

13Moses answered the people, "Do not be afraid.[d] Stand firm and you will see[e] the deliverance the LORD will bring you today. The Egyptians you see today you will never see[f] again. 14The LORD will fight[g] for you; you need only to be still."[h]

15Then the LORD said to Moses, "Why are you crying out to me? Tell the Israelites to move on. 16Raise your staff[i] and stretch out your hand over the sea to divide the water[j] so that the Israelites can go through the sea on dry ground. 17I will harden the hearts of the Egyptians so that they will go in after them.[k] And I will gain glory through Pharaoh and all his army, through his chariots and his horsemen. 18The Egyptians will know that I am the LORD when I gain glory through Pharaoh, his chariots and his horsemen."

a 9 Or *charioteers*; also in verses 17, 18, 23, 26 and 28

14:8
y ver 4; Ex 11:10
z Nu 33:3; Ac 13:17
14:9
a Ex 15:9
14:10
b Jos 24:7; Ne 9:9;
Ps 34:17
14:11
c Ps 106:7-8
14:13
d Ge 15:1
e 2Ch 20:17;
Isa 41:10,13-14
f ver 30
14:14
g ver 25; Ex 15:3;
Dt 1:30; 3:22;
h Ps 37:7; 46:10;
Isa 30:15
14:16
i Ex 4:17;
Nu 20:8-9,11
j Isa 10:26
14:17
k ver 4

13:18

Refugees Then and Now

Moses' band of travelers qualified as emigrants and refugees according to modern definitions. They chose to leave Egypt, making them emigrants. However, their living conditions as slave laborers in Egypt forced their decision, making them refugees.

The number of refugees and asylum seekers has shown some improvement since 1994, when it was estimated to be 16.3 million people. Today some 13 million people are believed to be refugees or asylum seekers. However, the total number of uprooted persons today is approximately 35 million, including refugees, asylum seekers, and internally displaced people.

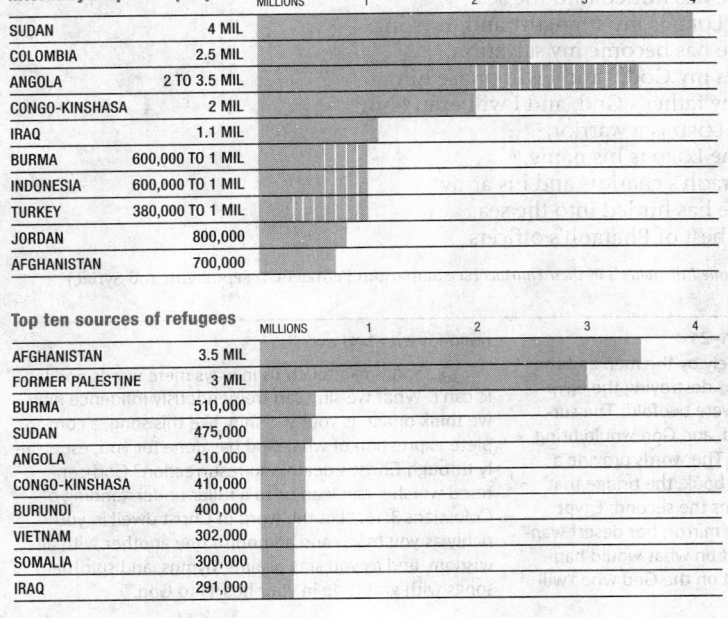

Top ten sources of internally displaced people (MILLIONS)

SUDAN	4 MIL
COLOMBIA	2.5 MIL
ANGOLA	2 TO 3.5 MIL
CONGO-KINSHASA	2 MIL
IRAQ	1.1 MIL
BURMA	600,000 TO 1 MIL
INDONESIA	600,000 TO 1 MIL
TURKEY	380,000 TO 1 MIL
JORDAN	800,000
AFGHANISTAN	700,000

Top ten sources of refugees (MILLIONS)

AFGHANISTAN	3.5 MIL
FORMER PALESTINE	3 MIL
BURMA	510,000
SUDAN	475,000
ANGOLA	410,000
CONGO-KINSHASA	410,000
BURUNDI	400,000
VIETNAM	302,000
SOMALIA	300,000
IRAQ	291,000

Ratio of refugees to host country population (selected)

GAZA STRIP	1:	2
LEBANON	1:	11
IRAN/YUGOSLAVIA	1:	30
ZAMBIA	1:	40
LIBERIA	1:	51
PAKISTAN	1:	95
UGANDA	1:	12
UNITED STATES	1:	450
INDONESIA	1:	7,482
JAPAN	1:	19,538

Source: U.S. Committee for Refugees (*www.refugees.org*), December 31, 2002

14:19
l Ex 13:21

14:21
m Ex 15:8
n Ps 74:13; 114:5;
Isa 63:12
14:22
o Ex 15:19;
Ne 9:11; Ps 66:6;
Heb 11:29
14:24
p Ex 13:21

14:25
q ver 14

14:27
r Jos 4:18
s Ex 15:1,21;
Ps 78:53; 106:11

14:29
t ver 22
14:30
u Ps 106:8,10,21

14:31
v Ps 106:12; Jn 2:11

15:1
w Rev 15:3
x Ps 106:12

15:2
y Ps 59:17
z Ps 18:2,46;
Isa 12:2; Hab 3:18
a Ge 28:21
b Ex 3:6,15-16;
Isa 25:1

15:3
c Ex 14:14; Ps 24:8;
Rev 19:11
d Ex 6:2-3,7-8;
Ps 83:18
15:4
e Ex 14:6-7

[19]Then the angel of God, who had been traveling in front of Israel's army, withdrew and went behind them. The pillar of cloud[l] also moved from in front and stood behind them, [20]coming between the armies of Egypt and Israel. Throughout the night the cloud brought darkness to the one side and light to the other side; so neither went near the other all night long.

[21]Then Moses stretched out his hand over the sea, and all that night the LORD drove the sea back with a strong east wind[m] and turned it into dry land. The waters were divided, [n] [22]and the Israelites went through the sea on dry ground, [o] with a wall of water on their right and on their left.

[23]The Egyptians pursued them, and all Pharaoh's horses and chariots and horsemen followed them into the sea. [24]During the last watch of the night the LORD looked down from the pillar of fire and cloud[p] at the Egyptian army and threw it into confusion. [25]He made the wheels of their chariots come off[a] so that they had difficulty driving. And the Egyptians said, "Let's get away from the Israelites! The LORD is fighting[q] for them against Egypt."

[26]Then the LORD said to Moses, "Stretch out your hand over the sea so that the waters may flow back over the Egyptians and their chariots and horsemen." [27]Moses stretched out his hand over the sea, and at daybreak the sea went back to its place. [r] The Egyptians were fleeing toward[b] it, and the LORD swept them into the sea. [s] [28]The water flowed back and covered the chariots and horsemen—the entire army of Pharaoh that had followed the Israelites into the sea. Not one of them survived.

[29]But the Israelites went through the sea on dry ground, [t] with a wall of water on their right and on their left. [30]That day the LORD saved[u] Israel from the hands of the Egyptians, and Israel saw the Egyptians lying dead on the shore. [31]And when the Israelites saw the great power the LORD displayed against the Egyptians, the people feared the LORD and put their trust[v] in him and in Moses his servant.

The Song of Moses and Miriam

15 Then Moses and the Israelites sang this song[w] to the LORD:

"I will sing[x] to the LORD,
    for he is highly exalted.
The horse and its rider
    he has hurled into the sea.
[2]The LORD is my strength[y] and my song;
    he has become my salvation. [z]
He is my God, [a] and I will praise him,
    my father's God, and I will exalt[b] him.
[3]The LORD is a warrior; [c]
    the LORD is his name. [d]
[4]Pharaoh's chariots and his army[e]
    he has hurled into the sea.
The best of Pharaoh's officers

---

[a] 25 Or *He jammed the wheels of their chariots* (see Samaritan Pentateuch, Septuagint and Syriac)
[b] 27 Or *from*

Exodus 15:1–21

Perhaps sung responsively by the men and the women, this song praised God for destroying the Egyptian army. The practical results were twofold: The surrounding nations would fear God, and God would bring his people safely to his dwelling. The words provide a gateway to the remainder of the book, the bridge that closes the first segment and opens the second. Egypt would remain in Israel's rearview mirror; her desert wandering had begun. The focus isn't on what would happen to Israel or the Egyptians but on the God who "will

reign for ever and ever."

Songs can touch us in ways mere words and logic can't. What we sing can tremendously influence how we think or act. Is your worship, like this song, a complete expression of what God has done for you, especially through Christ's death and resurrection? God-centered worship can lead us to a fuller understanding of Colossians 3:16: "Let the word of Christ dwell in you richly as you teach and admonish one another with all wisdom, and as you sing psalms, hymns, and spiritual songs with gratitude in your hearts to God."

are drowned in the Red Sea. [a]
5 The deep waters have covered them;
  they sank to the depths like a stone. [f]

6 "Your right hand, [g] O LORD,
    was majestic in power.
  Your right hand, O LORD,
    shattered the enemy.
7 In the greatness of your majesty
    you threw down those who opposed you.
  You unleashed your burning anger; [h]
    it consumed them like stubble.
8 By the blast of your nostrils [i]
    the waters piled up. [j]
  The surging waters stood firm like a wall; [k]
    the deep waters congealed in the heart of the sea.

9 "The enemy boasted,
    'I will pursue, [l] I will overtake them.
  I will divide the spoils; [m]
    I will gorge myself on them.
  I will draw my sword
    and my hand will destroy them.'
10 But you blew with your breath,
    and the sea covered them.
  They sank like lead
    in the mighty waters. [n]

11 "Who among the gods is like you, [o] O LORD?
    Who is like you—
    majestic in holiness, [p]
    awesome in glory, [q]
    working wonders?

a 4 Hebrew *Yam Suph*; that is, Sea of Reeds; also in verse 22

15:5
f ver 10; Ne 9:11
15:6
g Ps 118:15

15:7
h Ps 78:49-50

15:8
i Ex 14:21
j Ps 78:13
k Ex 14:22

15:9
l Ex 14:5-9
m Jdg 5:30;
Isa 53:12

15:10
n ver 5; Ex 14:27-28

15:11
o Ex 8:10; Dt 3:24;
Ps 77:13 p Isa 6:3;
Rev 4:8 q Ps 8:1

Snapshots

 15:2

Genet

Genet, age ten, lives in Ambowuha village in Ethiopia. During the recent famine her family received assistance from a Christian ministry's aid center, and soon afterward the organization running the center trained her father as a plumber.

Genet began singing in the Ambowuha Church choir in 2003. "There is nothing on this earth that satisfies me more than singing and praising my Lord. When I turn eighteen," she bubbles, "God-willing, I hope to become a renowned singer in my church. I would like to encourage my two brothers who also sing to keep up their service."

There is a song in her native language Genet loves to sing. Its lyrics: *"Balatsega, Baletsega Hulu Kante Zenda Honelin Zare Ijig Des Yilengal Yante Bemehone,"* roughly translated, "Thou are affluent; all is given to us by thee today. I am extremely delighted for I belong to thee."

Asked why she likes the song so much, Genet responds, "When I see every good thing that God has done for us . . . the song appeals to my soul and I am always touched by it."

> "There is nothing on this earth that satisfies me more than singing and praising my Lord."

12 You stretched out your right hand
and the earth swallowed them.

13 "In your unfailing love you will lead[r]
the people you have redeemed.
In your strength you will guide them
to your holy dwelling.[s]
14 The nations will hear and tremble;[t]
anguish will grip the people of Philistia.
15 The chiefs[u] of Edom will be terrified,
the leaders of Moab will be seized with trembling,[v]
the people[a] of Canaan will melt[w] away;
16   terror[x] and dread will fall upon them.
By the power of your arm
they will be as still as a stone[y]—
until your people pass by, O LORD,
until the people you bought[b][z] pass by.
17 You will bring them in and plant[a] them
on the mountain[b] of your inheritance—
the place, O LORD, you made for your dwelling,
the sanctuary, O Lord, your hands established.
18 The LORD will reign
for ever and ever."

19 When Pharaoh's horses, chariots and horsemen[c] went into the sea,[c] the LORD brought the waters of the sea back over them, but the Israelites walked through the sea on dry ground.[d] 20 Then Miriam[e] the prophetess,[f] Aaron's sister, took a tambourine in her hand, and all the women followed her, with tambourines and dancing.[g] 21 Miriam sang to them:

"Sing to the LORD,
for he is highly exalted.
The horse and its rider
he has hurled into the sea."[h]

The Waters of Marah and Elim

22 Then Moses led Israel from the Red Sea and they went into the Desert of Shur. For three days they traveled in the desert without finding water. 23 When they came to Marah, they could not drink its water because it was bitter. (That is why the place is called Marah.[d][i]) 24 So the people grumbled[j] against Moses, saying, "What are we to drink?"

25 Then Moses cried out[k] to the LORD, and the LORD showed him a piece of wood. He threw it into the water, and the water became sweet.

There the LORD made a decree and a law for them, and there he tested[l] them. 26 He said, "If you listen carefully to the voice of the LORD your God and do what is right in his eyes, if you pay attention to his commands and keep all his decrees,[m] I will

---

a 15 Or rulers   b 16 Or created   c 19 Or charioteers   d 23 Marah means bitter.

Exodus 15:22–27

Here we see another example of God's control over chaotic waters (the first two being the changing of the waters of Egypt into blood and the parting of the Red Sea). The sweetening of the bitter water was the reverse of God's having turned the "sweet" waters of the Nile into blood (7:14–24). By performing an opposite miracle here, he showed his continued faithfulness to his people.

It's easy to condemn the complaining Israelites as faithless, but few of us would have fared better under the same circumstances. Life had been hard in Egypt, but it must have seemed harder still in the uncharted desert through which they now wandered. Their only recourse in a barren land was to trust in God completely. If the Bible teaches us anything about human nature, it's that total trust and obedience are rare, even in the most godly persons. What examples of such trust and obedience can you cite in believers you know? How have they affected your own outlook and behavior?

not bring on you any of the diseases[n] I brought on the Egyptians, for I am the LORD, who heals[o] you."

27Then they came to Elim, where there were twelve springs and seventy palm trees, and they camped[p] there near the water.

Manna and Quail

16 The whole Israelite community set out from Elim and came to the Desert of Sin,[q] which is between Elim and Sinai, on the fifteenth day of the second month after they had come out of Egypt. 2In the desert the whole community grumbled[r] against Moses and Aaron. 3The Israelites said to them, "If only we had died by the LORD's hand in Egypt![s] There we sat around pots of meat and ate all the food[t] we wanted, but you have brought us out into this desert to starve this entire assembly to death."

4Then the LORD said to Moses, "I will rain down bread from heaven[u] for you. The people are to go out each day and gather enough for that day. In this way I will test them and see whether they will follow my instructions. 5On the sixth day they are to prepare what they bring in, and that is to be twice[v] as much as they gather on the other days."

6So Moses and Aaron said to all the Israelites, "In the evening you will know that it was the LORD who brought you out of Egypt,[w] 7and in the morning you will see the glory[x] of the LORD, because he has heard your grumbling[y] against him. Who are we, that you should grumble against us?"[z] 8Moses also said, "You will know that it was the LORD when he gives you meat to eat in the evening and all the bread you want in the morning, because he has heard your grumbling against him. Who are we? You are not grumbling against us, but against the LORD."[a]

Cross references (margin)

15:26 n Dt 28:27,58-60 · o Ex 23:25-26
15:27 p Nu 33:9
16:1 q Nu 33:11,12
16:2 r Ex 14:11; 15:24; 1Co 10:10
16:3 s Ex 17:3 · t Nu 11:4,34
16:4 u Dt 8:3; Jn 6:31*
16:5 v ver 22
16:6 w Ex 6:6
16:7 x ver 10; Isa 35:2; 40:5 y ver 12; Nu 14:2,27,28 z Nu 16:11
16:8 a 1Sa 8:7; Ro 13:2

Exodus 16:1–36

The Israelites brought an absurd charge against their leaders: "You have brought us out into this desert to starve this entire assembly to death." Rather than punishing them, God rained down bread from heaven. Without anger or malice, he provided for his people once again.

Complaint in the Old Testament wasn't necessarily bad. Many psalms are complaints by God's people who wondered why he had apparently abandoned them (see Ps. 64:1; 142:2, cf. Hab. 2:1). But the complaining here was rebellious, unlike that of the psalmists calling to God *on the basis* of their faith. The desert community grumbled to a third party against God (or his chosen leader) because of a lack of faith.

Our view of the world balances our knowledge that it belongs to God with the reality that it isn't our final resting place (cf. Heb. 11:10,13–16). Do you take comfort in the fact that you are a part of God's special people? Is it easy or difficult for you to remember not to become too comfortable in your present surroundings?

16:2–3

Hunger in the Bible

Wandering in the Sinai desert was a sure way to create food insecurity. For the Israelite throngs, God provided manna from heaven. Millions today still drift through a wilderness of malnutrition. The Bible has much to say about physical hunger.

Causes of Hunger
1. Famine (Gen. 41:56; Ps. 37:19; Amos 8:11–12)
2. Desperate circumstances (Deut. 28:53–57; 1 Sam. 21:1–5)
3. Natural human need (Matt. 12:1; 15:32; 21:18; Mark 11:12)
4. Fasting (Ps. 109:24; Matt. 4:2)
5. God's correction (Lev. 26:23–26)

Effects of Hunger
1. Physical and mental deterioration and illness/developmental difficulties in children/death (Job 30:3; Isa. 5:13; 44:12; Lam. 2:19; 4:4,9; 5:10)
2. Mental preoccupation (Prov. 16:26; Isa. 29:8)
3. Impaired judgment (Gen. 25:29–34; Ex. 16:3)
4. Moral degradation/unspeakable atrocities (Lev. 26:29; Deut. 28:53–57; Isa. 9:20; Lam. 2:20; 4:10)
5. Sharpened spiritual sensitivity in fasting (Matt. 4:2–4; Luke 5:35; Acts 14:23)

Provisions for Hunger
1. Natural: "The seed will grow well, the vine will yield its fruit, the ground will produce its crops, and the heavens will drop their dew. I will give all these things as an inheritance to the remnant of this people" (Zech. 8:12).
2. Miraculous: "He humbled you, causing you to hunger and then feeding you with manna, which neither you nor your fathers had known, to teach you that man does not live on bread alone but on every word that comes from the mouth of the LORD" (Deut. 8:3).
3. Spiritual: "Blessed are those who hunger and thirst for righteousness, for they will be filled" (Matt. 5:6).

16:10
b ver 7; Nu 16:19
c Ex 13:21; 1Ki 8:10
16:12
d ver 7

9Then Moses told Aaron, "Say to the entire Israelite community, 'Come before the LORD, for he has heard your grumbling.' "

10While Aaron was speaking to the whole Israelite community, they looked toward the desert, and there was the glory[b] of the LORD appearing in the cloud.[c]

11The LORD said to Moses, 12"I have heard the grumbling[d] of the Israelites. Tell them, 'At twilight you will eat meat, and in the morning you will be filled with bread. Then you will know that I am the LORD your God.' "

16:13
e Nu 11:31;
Ps 78:27-28; 105:40
f Nu 11:9
16:14
g ver 31;
Nu 11:7-9;
Ps 105:40
16:15
h ver 4; Jn 6:31
16:16
i ver 32,36

13That evening quail[e] came and covered the camp, and in the morning there was a layer of dew[f] around the camp. 14When the dew was gone, thin flakes like frost[g] on the ground appeared on the desert floor. 15When the Israelites saw it, they said to each other, "What is it?" For they did not know what it was.

Moses said to them, "It is the bread[h] the LORD has given you to eat. 16This is what the LORD has commanded: 'Each one is to gather as much as he needs. Take an omer[a][i] for each person you have in your tent.' "

16:18
j 2Co 8:15*

17The Israelites did as they were told; some gathered much, some little. 18And when they measured it by the omer, he who gathered much did not have too much, and he who gathered little did not have too little.[j] Each one gathered as much as he needed.

16:19
k ver 23; Ex 12:10;
23:18

19Then Moses said to them, "No one is to keep any of it until morning."[k]

20However, some of them paid no attention to Moses; they kept part of it until morning, but it was full of maggots and began to smell. So Moses was angry with them.

16:22
l ver 5 *m* Ex 34:31

21Each morning everyone gathered as much as he needed, and when the sun grew hot, it melted away. 22On the sixth day, they gathered twice[l] as much—two omers[b] for each person—and the leaders of the community[m] came and reported this to Moses. 23He said to them, "This is what the LORD commanded: 'Tomorrow is to be a day of rest, a holy Sabbath[n] to the LORD. So bake what you want to bake and boil what you want to boil. Save whatever is left and keep it until morning.' "

16:23
n Ge 2:3; Ex 20:8;
23:12; Lev 23:3

24So they saved it until morning, as Moses commanded, and it did not stink or get maggots in it. 25"Eat it today," Moses said, "because today is a Sabbath to the LORD. You will not find any of it on the ground today. 26Six days you are to gather it, but on the seventh day, the Sabbath,[o] there will not be any."

16:26
o Ex 20:9-10

27Nevertheless, some of the people went out on the seventh day to gather it, but they found none. 28Then the LORD said to Moses, "How long will you[c] refuse to keep my commands[p] and my instructions? 29Bear in mind that the LORD has given you the Sabbath; that is why on the sixth day he gives you bread for two days. Everyone is to stay where he is on the seventh day; no one is to go out." 30So the people rested on the seventh day.

16:28
p 2Ki 17:14;
Ps 78:10; 106:13

16:31
q Nu 11:7-9

31The people of Israel called the bread manna.[d][q] It was white like coriander seed and tasted like wafers made with honey. 32Moses said, "This is what the LORD has commanded: 'Take an omer of manna and keep it for the generations to come, so they can see the bread I gave you to eat in the desert when I brought you out of Egypt.' "

16:33
r Heb 9:4

33So Moses said to Aaron, "Take a jar and put an omer of manna[r] in it. Then place it before the LORD to be kept for the generations to come."

16:34
s Ex 25:16,21,22;
40:20; Nu 17:4,10
16:35
t Jn 6:31,49
u Ne 9:21
v Jos 5:12

34As the LORD commanded Moses, Aaron put the manna in front of the Testimony,[s] that it might be kept. 35The Israelites ate manna[t] forty years,[u] until they came to a land that was settled; they ate manna until they reached the border of Canaan.[v] 36(An omer is one tenth of an ephah.)

Water From the Rock

17:1
w Ex 16:1
x Nu 33:14

17 The whole Israelite community set out from the Desert of Sin,[w] traveling from place to place as the LORD commanded. They camped at Rephidim, but there was no water[x] for the people to drink. 2So they quarreled with Moses and said, "Give us water[y] to drink."

17:2
y Nu 20:2

[a] 16 That is, probably about 2 quarts (about 2 liters); also in verses 18, 32, 33 and 36   [b] 22 That is, probably about 4 quarts (about 4.5 liters)   [c] 28 The Hebrew is plural.   [d] 31 *Manna* means *What is it?* (see verse 15).

Moses replied, "Why do you quarrel with me? Why do you put the LORD to the test?"[z]

[3]But the people were thirsty for water there, and they grumbled[a] against Moses. They said, "Why did you bring us up out of Egypt to make us and our children and livestock die of thirst?"

[4]Then Moses cried out to the LORD, "What am I to do with these people? They are almost ready to stone[b] me."

[5]The LORD answered Moses, "Walk on ahead of the people. Take with you some of the elders of Israel and take in your hand the staff with which you struck the Nile,[c] and go. [6]I will stand there before you by the rock at Horeb. Strike the rock, and water[d] will come out of it for the people to drink." So Moses did this in the sight of the elders of Israel. [7]And he called the place Massah[a] and Meribah[b][e] because the Israelites quarreled and because they tested the LORD saying, "Is the LORD among us or not?"

The Amalekites Defeated

[8]The Amalekites[f] came and attacked the Israelites at Rephidim. [9]Moses said to Joshua, "Choose some of our men and go out to fight the Amalekites. Tomorrow I will stand on top of the hill with the staff[g] of God in my hands."

[10]So Joshua fought the Amalekites as Moses had ordered, and Moses, Aaron and Hur[h] went to the top of the hill. [11]As long as Moses held up his hands, the Israelites were winning,[i] but whenever he lowered his hands, the Amalekites were winning. [12]When Moses' hands grew tired, they took a stone and put it under him and he sat on it. Aaron and Hur held his hands up—one on one side, one on the other—so that his hands remained steady till sunset. [13]So Joshua overcame the Amalekite army with the sword.

[14]Then the LORD said to Moses, "Write[j] this on a scroll as something to be remembered and make sure that Joshua hears it, because I will completely blot out the memory of Amalek[k] from under heaven."

[15]Moses built an altar and called it The LORD is my Banner. [16]He said, "For hands were lifted up to the throne of the LORD. The[c] LORD will be at war against the Amalekites from generation to generation."

[a] 7 *Massah* means *testing.*   [b] 7 *Meribah* means *quarreling.*   [c] 16 Or *"Because a hand was against the throne of the LORD, the*

17:2
[z] Dt 6:16;
Ps 78:18,41;
1Co 10:9
17:3
[a] Ex 15:24; 16:2-3

17:4
[b] Nu 14:10;
1Sa 30:6

17:5
[c] Ex 7:20

17:6
[d] Nu 20:11;
Ps 114:8; 1Co 10:4
17:7
[e] Nu 20:13,24;
Ps 81:7

17:8
[f] Ge 36:12;
Dt 25:17-19

17:9
[g] Ex 4:17

17:10
[h] Ex 24:14
17:11
[i] Jas 5:16

17:14
[j] Ex 24:4; 34:27;
Nu 33:2 [k] 1Sa 15:3;
30:17-18

Exodus 17:1–7

Like Pharaoh before them, how many times did the Israelites need to see God work before they understood? Two episodes of complaining about lack of water (cf. 15:22–27) so close together point out the absurdity of Israel's lack of trust in God. His people still failed to see that he had their best interests at heart. The word in verse 2 is "quarrel," which is somewhat stronger than "grumble" used in the other episode and in verse 3. This rebellion against God was both sudden and sustained.

Have you thought something along the lines of "If the Red Sea parted in front of *me*, I wouldn't complain against God ever again"? Christians are called to a higher life, but we tend to accept the "needs" our world tells us to have. We often go through our own desert experiences honed in on our lacks and desires, oblivious to the new creations we are in Christ. First Corinthians 10:1–13 serves as a warning: What happened to the exodus generation provides an example to us of how *not* to respond to God. So before we judge the Israelites too harshly, it's a good idea to inventory our own responses to God.

Exodus 17:8–16

This battle foreshadowed the ultimate goal toward which God was bringing his newly freed people—the conquest of Canaan. Ironically, in Numbers 13–14 the presence of the Amalekites contributed to the Israelites' doubting of God's promise that they could take the land. The defeat of this enemy *now* would have no apparent bearing on their perception of the same adversary two years later.

Why do you think Moses' raised hands had such an effect on how God directed the battle? What do you learn from this passage about God, who pledged the complete destruction of a people for one act of aggression?

The defeat of the Amalekites was an early manifestation of a more basic battle, one that would come to a head when Jesus arose from the grave. In one sense that battle continues today. The Amalekites in our lives are those who can seriously affect our spiritual state. Everyday situations vie for our attention and tempt us away from God. The battle is best seen in the quiet of our own hearts, where two powers fight for control. Read Paul's description of this inner battle in Romans 7:14–25. What strikes you in these verses?

Jethro Visits Moses

18:1
l Ex 2:16; 3:1

18 Now Jethro, the priest of Midian*l* and father-in-law of Moses, heard of everything God had done for Moses and for his people Israel, and how the LORD had brought Israel out of Egypt.

18:2
m Ex 2:21; 4:25
18:3
n Ex 4:20; Ac 7:29
o Ex 2:22
18:4
p 1Ch 23:15

2After Moses had sent away his wife Zipporah,*m* his father-in-law Jethro received her 3and her two sons.*n* One son was named Gershom,*a* for Moses said, "I have become an alien in a foreign land";*o* 4and the other was named Eliezer,*b p* for he said, "My father's God was my helper; he saved me from the sword of Pharaoh."

18:5
q Ex 3:1

5Jethro, Moses' father-in-law, together with Moses' sons and wife, came to him in the desert, where he was camped near the mountain*q* of God. 6Jethro had sent word to him, "I, your father-in-law Jethro, am coming to you with your wife and her two sons."

18:7
r Ge 43:28
s Ge 29:13

7So Moses went out to meet his father-in-law and bowed down*r* and kissed*s* him. They greeted each other and then went into the tent. 8Moses told his father-in-law about everything the LORD had done to Pharaoh and the Egyptians for Israel's sake and about all the hardships they had met along the way and how the LORD had

18:8
t Ex 15:6,16;
Ps 81:7

saved*t* them.

9Jethro was delighted to hear about all the good things the LORD had done for Israel in rescuing them from the hand of the Egyptians. 10He said, "Praise be to the

18:10
u Ge 14:20;
Ps 68:19-20

LORD,*u* who rescued you from the hand of the Egyptians and of Pharaoh, and who rescued the people from the hand of the Egyptians. 11Now I know that the LORD is

18:11
v Ex 12:12; 15:11;
2Ch 2:5 *w* Lk 1:51

greater than all other gods,*v* for he did this to those who had treated Israel arrogantly."*w* 12Then Jethro, Moses' father-in-law, brought a burnt offering and other sacrifices to God, and Aaron came with all the elders of Israel to eat bread with Moses'

18:12
x Dt 12:7

father-in-law in the presence*x* of God.

13The next day Moses took his seat to serve as judge for the people, and they stood around him from morning till evening. 14When his father-in-law saw all that Moses was doing for the people, he said, "What is this you are doing for the people? Why do you alone sit as judge, while all these people stand around you from morning till evening?"

18:15
y Nu 9:6,8;
Dt 17:8-13

15Moses answered him, "Because the people come to me to seek God's will.*y*

18:16
z Lev 24:12

16Whenever they have a dispute, it is brought to me, and I decide between the parties and inform them of God's decrees and laws."*z*

17Moses' father-in-law replied, "What you are doing is not good. 18You and these

18:18
a Nu 11:11,14,17
18:19
b Ex 3:12 *c* Nu 27:5
18:20
d Dt 5:1 *e* Ps 143:8
f Dt 1:18
18:21
g Ac 6:3
h Dt 16:19; Ps 15:5;
Eze 18:8
i Dt 1:13,15;
2Ch 19:5-10

people who come to you will only wear yourselves out. The work is too heavy for you; you cannot handle it alone.*a* 19Listen now to me and I will give you some advice, and may God be with you.*b* You must be the people's representative before God and bring their disputes*c* to him. 20Teach them the decrees and laws,*d* and show them the way to live*e* and the duties they are to perform.*f* 21But select capable men*g* from all the people—men who fear God, trustworthy men who hate dishonest gain*h*—and appoint them as officials*i* over thousands, hundreds, fifties and

---

a 3 Gershom sounds like the Hebrew for *an alien there.*   *b 4 Eliezer* means *my God is helper.*

Exodus 18:1–27

  Neither the Egyptians nor the Amalekites got it, but Jethro, the Midianite, had learned the lesson of the exodus: "The LORD is greater than all other gods" (v. 11). This non-Israelite's insight served as an example of how the nations ought to have responded to Israel's God, as well as an indication that God's reach was, and is, broader than Israel. The nations are always on God's mind.

There is more to any Biblical story than meets the eye. The people came to Moses to "seek God's will" (v. 15). Jethro gave Moses a solution to the demands he was facing. The problem, though, wasn't just Moses' weakness, but the people's. They needed to become personally aware of God's standards. God was in the

process of raising a people, as a father raises his child, to know him so well that his law was in their hearts.

  Nothing more needs to be done for the accomplishment of God's purpose to bring the gospel to all the world—Christ's saving work is complete. This isn't to say that missionary activity can cease! The nations are still being called into God's kingdom, and we can help bring this about. What specific role is God calling *you* to play?

What's written on your heart? To have God's law written on our hearts is a primary goal of the Christian life. Psalm 78 helps broaden our understanding of the word *law.* It goes beyond commandments to everything God has done to and through his people.

tens. 22Have them serve as judges for the people at all times, but have them bring
every difficult case[j] to you; the simple cases they can decide themselves. That will
make your load lighter, because they will share[k] it with you. 23If you do this and
God so commands, you will be able to stand the strain, and all these people will
go home satisfied."

18:22 [j] Dt 1:17-18 [k] Nu 11:17

24Moses listened to his father-in-law and did everything he said. 25He chose capable men from all Israel and made them leaders of the people, officials over thousands, hundreds, fifties and tens.[l] 26They served as judges for the people at all
times. The difficult cases they brought to Moses, but the simple ones they decided
themselves.[m]

18:25 [l] Dt 1:13-15
18:26 [m] ver 22

27Then Moses sent his father-in-law on his way, and Jethro returned to his own
country.[n]

18:27 [n] Nu 10:29-30

At Mount Sinai

19 In the third month after the Israelites left Egypt—on the very day—they
came to the Desert of Sinai. 2After they set out from Rephidim,[o] they entered the Desert of Sinai, and Israel camped there in the desert in front of the
mountain.[p]

19:2 [o] Ex 17:1 [p] Ex 3:1

3Then Moses went up to God, and the LORD called[q] to him from the mountain
and said, "This is what you are to say to the house of Jacob and what you are to tell
the people of Israel: 4'You yourselves have seen what I did to Egypt,[r] and how I carried you on eagles' wings[s] and brought you to myself. 5Now if you obey me fully[t]

19:3 [q] Ex 3:4; Ac 7:38
19:4 [r] Dt 29:2 [s] Isa 63:9
19:5 [t] Ex 15:26

Exodus 19:1–25

The first phase of Moses' assignment was complete: He had led God's people out of Egypt to the foot of the mountain. Now the second stage had begun: bringing God's message to the people. Not only were the Israelites to remember God' saving activity, but that memory was to motivate them to obey. This scene and the subsequent laws were built on what God had done. People don't earn their salvation, but once saved, they are obligated to behave in a manner worthy of their calling (see Eph. 4:1; 2 Thess. 1:11).

In God's first official encounter with his redeemed people, he referred to them as a treasured possession, a kingdom of priests, and a holy nation (cf. 1 Peter 2:9). God had chosen a people to be separate from the rest of the world, not just so they could belong to him in some private sense, but so he could use them for a special purpose. Exodus 19:5–6 established a pattern that would come to fuller expression as Israel's story, in its triumphs and failures, continued to unfold.

Snapshots

18:20

Salih Abdul Masih

Salih Abdul Masih (c. 1772?–1827) was an early Indian Muslim convert to Christianity and one of the most influential indigenous Christians to shape mission efforts in early 19th-century India. As a Muslim scholar, teacher, and religious *shaykh*, Abdul Masih befriended Henry Martyn, a chaplain of the British East India Company who was devoted to evangelism. Abdul Masih studied Martyn's Urdu translation of the New Testament and received instruction from two other company chaplains, David Brown and Daniel Corrie.

Converted and baptized in 1811, he moved to Agra to avoid unrest. There he labored as an itinerant preacher and healer, assisting in the early development of the Church Missionary Society in that city. Abdul Masih was instrumental in winning both Muslim and Hindu converts. He temporarily became a Lutheran, returning to the Anglican Church in 1825 as the first Indian-ordained minister under Bishop Heber of Calcutta. Abdul Masah's background afforded him influence in both Anglican and Lutheran missionary endeavors. His work paved the way for German evangelist Karl Gottlieb Pfander.

Abdul Masih was instrumental in winning both Muslim and Hindu converts.

19:5
u Dt 5:2 v Dt 14:2;
Ps 135:4 w Ex 9:29;
Dt 10:14
19:6
x 1Pe 2:5 y Isa 7:6;
26:19; Isa 62:12
19:8
z Ex 24:3,7; Dt 5:27
19:9
a ver 16;
Ex 24:15-16
b Dt 4:12,36
19:10
c Lev 11:44;
Heb 10:22
d Ge 35:2
19:11
e ver 16
19:13
f Heb 12:20*
19:16
g Heb 12:18-19;
Rev 4:1
h Heb 12:21
19:18
i Ps 104:32 j Ex 3:2;
24:17; Dt 4:11;
2Ch 7:1; Ps 18:8;
Heb 12:18
k Ge 19:28
l Jdg 5:5; Ps 68:8;
Jer 4:24
19:19
m Ne 9:13
n Ps 81:7
19:21
o Ex 3:5; 1Sa 6:19
19:22
p Lev 10:3
q 2Sa 6:7
19:23
r ver 12
19:24
s Ex 24:1,9
20:2
t Ex 13:3

and keep my covenant,[u] then out of all nations you will be my treasured possession.[v] Although the whole earth[w] is mine, [6]you[a] will be for me a kingdom of priests[x] and a holy nation.'[y] These are the words you are to speak to the Israelites."

[7]So Moses went back and summoned the elders of the people and set before them all the words the Lord had commanded him to speak. [8]The people all responded together, "We will do everything the Lord has said."[z] So Moses brought their answer back to the Lord.

[9]The Lord said to Moses, "I am going to come to you in a dense cloud,[a] so that the people will hear me speaking[b] with you and will always put their trust in you." Then Moses told the Lord what the people had said.

[10]And the Lord said to Moses, "Go to the people and consecrate[c] them today and tomorrow. Have them wash their clothes[d] [11]and be ready by the third day,[e] because on that day the Lord will come down on Mount Sinai in the sight of all the people. [12]Put limits for the people around the mountain and tell them, 'Be careful that you do not go up the mountain or touch the foot of it. Whoever touches the mountain shall surely be put to death. [13]He shall surely be stoned[f] or shot with arrows; not a hand is to be laid on him. Whether man or animal, he shall not be permitted to live.' Only when the ram's horn sounds a long blast may they go up to the mountain."

[14]After Moses had gone down the mountain to the people, he consecrated them, and they washed their clothes. [15]Then he said to the people, "Prepare yourselves for the third day. Abstain from sexual relations."

[16]On the morning of the third day there was thunder and lightning, with a thick cloud over the mountain, and a very loud trumpet blast.[g] Everyone in the camp trembled.[h] [17]Then Moses led the people out of the camp to meet with God, and they stood at the foot of the mountain. [18]Mount Sinai was covered with smoke,[i] because the Lord descended on it in fire.[j] The smoke billowed up from it like smoke from a furnace,[k] the whole mountain[b] trembled[l] violently, [19]and the sound of the trumpet grew louder and louder. Then Moses spoke and the voice[m] of God answered[n] him.[c]

[20]The Lord descended to the top of Mount Sinai and called Moses to the top of the mountain. So Moses went up [21]and the Lord said to him, "Go down and warn the people so they do not force their way through to see[o] the Lord and many of them perish. [22]Even the priests, who approach[p] the Lord, must consecrate themselves, or the Lord will break out against them."[q]

[23]Moses said to the Lord, "The people cannot come up Mount Sinai, because you yourself warned us, 'Put limits[r] around the mountain and set it apart as holy.' "

[24]The Lord replied, "Go down and bring Aaron[s] up with you. But the priests and the people must not force their way through to come up to the Lord, or he will break out against them."

[25]So Moses went down to the people and told them.

The Ten Commandments

20

And God spoke all these words:

[2]"I am the Lord your God, who brought you out of Egypt, out of the land of slavery.[t]

---

[a] 5,6 Or possession, for the whole earth is mine. 6You   [b] 18 Most Hebrew manuscripts; a few Hebrew manuscripts and Septuagint all the people   [c] 19 Or and God answered him with thunder

---

As detailed in 1 Peter 2:4–12, the church as the new Israel is to exhibit irreproachable behavior. By fulfilling this mandate to be holy, we show ourselves to be different from the world, so that the world will be drawn to "glorify God on the day he visits us" (1 Peter 2:12). God's intention to reconcile the world to himself through a select and holy people, first announced in Genesis 12:1–3, came to a climax in Jesus' death and resurrection, but God is still working out the details. How is he acting in and through you?

Exodus 20:1–21

The Ten Commandments were given to a people *already* redeemed. The law of God wasn't a condition for salvation—"do this and you will be saved"—but its consequence—"I have delivered you. Now continue to stay out of slavery by living this way." These commandments enabled the Israelites to manifest God's character and purposes as they lived among the nations of the world and protected them from being ensnared once again by sin and evil.

3 "You shall have no other gods before[a] me.[u]

4 "You shall not make for yourself an idol[v] in the form of anything in heaven above or on the earth beneath or in the waters below. 5You shall not bow down to them or worship[w] them; for I, the LORD your God, am a jealous God,[x] punishing the children for the sin of the fathers to the third and fourth generation[y] of those who hate me, 6but showing love to a thousand[z] ⌊generations⌋ of those who love me and keep my commandments.

7 "You shall not misuse the name of the LORD your God, for the LORD will not hold anyone guiltless who misuses his name.[a]

8 "Remember the Sabbath[b] day by keeping it holy. 9Six days you shall labor and do all your work,[c] 10but the seventh day is a Sabbath to the LORD your God. On it you shall not do any work, neither you, nor your son or daughter, nor your manservant or maidservant, nor your animals, nor the alien within your gates. 11For in six days the LORD made the heavens and the earth, the sea, and all that is in them, but he rested[d] on the seventh day. Therefore the LORD blessed the Sabbath day and made it holy.

12 "Honor your father and your mother,[e] so that you may live long in the land the LORD your God is giving you.

13 "You shall not murder.[f]

14 "You shall not commit adultery.[g]

15 "You shall not steal.[h]

16 "You shall not give false testimony against your neighbor.[i]

17 "You shall not covet[j] your neighbor's house. You shall not covet your neighbor's wife, or his manservant or maidservant, his ox or donkey, or anything that belongs to your neighbor."

18When the people saw the thunder and lightning and heard the trumpet[k] and saw the mountain in smoke, they trembled with fear. They stayed at a distance 19and said to Moses, "Speak to us yourself and we will listen. But do not have God speak to us or we will die."[l]

20Moses said to the people, "Do not be afraid. God has come to test you, so that the fear[m] of God will be with you to keep you from sinning."[n]

21The people remained at a distance, while Moses approached the thick darkness[o] where God was.

Idols and Altars

22Then the LORD said to Moses, "Tell the Israelites this: 'You have seen for yourselves that I have spoken to you from heaven:[p] 23Do not make any gods to be alongside me;[q] do not make for yourselves gods of silver or gods of gold.[r]

24 "'Make an altar of earth for me and sacrifice on it your burnt offerings and fellowship offerings,[b] your sheep and goats and your cattle. Wherever I cause my name[s] to be honored, I will come to you and bless[t] you. 25If you make an altar of stones for me, do not build it with dressed stones, for you will defile it if you use a

---

20:3
[u] Dt 6:14; Jer 35:15
20:4
[v] Lev 26:1;
Dt 4:15-19,23;
27:15
20:5
[w] Isa 44:15,17,19
[x] Ex 34:14; Dt 4:24
[y] Nu 14:18;
Jer 32:18
20:6
[z] Dt 7:9
20:7
[a] Lev 19:12;
Mt 5:33
20:8
[b] Ex 31:13-16;
Lev 26:2
20:9
[c] Ex 34:21;
Lk 13:14

20:11
[d] Ge 2:2

20:12
[e] Mt 15:4*;
Mk 7:10*; Eph 6:2
20:13
[f] Mt 5:21*;
Ro 13:9*
20:14
[g] Mt 19:18*
20:15
[h] Lev 19:11,13;
Mt 19:18*
20:16
[i] Ex 23:1,7;
Mt 19:18*
20:17
[j] Ro 7:7*; 13:9*;
Eph 5:3
20:18
[k] Ex 19:16-19;
Heb 12:18-19

20:19
[l] Dt 5:5,23-27;
Gal 3:19
20:20
[m] Dt 4:10; Isa 8:13
[n] Pr 16:6
20:21
[o] Dt 5:22

20:22
[p] Ne 9:13
20:23
[q] ver 3
[r] Ex 32:4,8,31
20:24
[s] Dt 12:5; 16:6,11;
2Ch 6:6 [t] Ge 12:2

---

[a] 3 Or *besides*   [b] 24 Traditionally *peace offerings*

📖 Why do you as a 21st-century Christian obey these commandments? Not to demonstrate your worth before God or to earn your salvation, but to show the world the kind of God you worship and to stay free from bondage to sin.

Exodus 20:22—21:1

📖 This passage begins the section from Exodus 20:22—23:19 known as the Book of the Covenant (see 24:7). Many of these laws expanded on the Ten Commandments. This passage relates to the first and second commandments (20:3,4). Proper worship of God wasn't left to Israel's whim. Listen again to the refrain of the exodus story: "Let my people go, so that they may worship

me." Israel was a worshiping community, and the Book of the Covenant contained the stipulations directing God's people in this area.

📖 The law has no place for Christ's followers either as a means of salvation or as a standard for separating us from non-believers (e.g., Rom. 10:4). Yet the law isn't irrelevant. Jesus said he had come to fulfill the Law and the Prophets (Matt. 5:17-20), and in his Sermon on the Mount he pushed the implications of the law from actions to attitudes. And Paul stated that we uphold the law by putting our faith in Christ (Rom. 3:21-31). As the life of Christ is lived out in us by the Spirit's power, our lives will express Christ's fulfillment of the law in action *and* in attitude.

20:25
u Dt 27:5-6

tool[u] on it. 26And do not go up to my altar on steps, lest your nakedness be exposed on it.'

21:1
v Dt 4:14

21 "These are the laws[v] you are to set before them:

Hebrew Servants

21:2
w Jer 34:8,14

2 "If you buy a Hebrew servant, he is to serve you for six years. But in the seventh year, he shall go free,[w] without paying anything. 3If he comes alone, he is to go free alone; but if he has a wife when he comes, she is to go with him. 4If his master gives him a wife and she bears him sons or daughters, the woman and her children shall belong to her master, and only the man shall go free.

21:5
x Dt 15:16
21:6
y Ex 22:8-9
z Ne 5:5

5 "But if the servant declares, 'I love my master and my wife and children and do not want to go free,'[x] 6then his master must take him before the judges.[a][y] He shall take him to the door or the doorpost and pierce his ear with an awl. Then he will be his servant for life.[z]

7 "If a man sells his daughter as a servant, she is not to go free as menservants do. 8If she does not please the master who has selected her for himself,[b] he must let her be redeemed. He has no right to sell her to foreigners, because he has broken faith with her. 9If he selects her for his son, he must grant her the rights of a daughter. 10If he marries another woman, he must not deprive the first one of her food, clothing and marital rights.[a] 11If he does not provide her with these three things, she is to go free, without any payment of money.

21:10
a 1Co 7:3-5

Personal Injuries

21:12
b Ge 9:6; Mt 26:52
21:13
c Nu 35:10-34;
Dt 19:2-13;
Jos 20:9;
1Sa 24:4,10,18
21:14
d Heb 10:26
e Dt 19:11-12;
1Ki 2:28-34
21:16
f Ge 37:28
g Ex 22:4; Dt 24:7
21:17
h Lev 20:9-10;
Mt 15:4*; Mk 7:10*

12 "Anyone who strikes a man and kills him shall surely be put to death.[b] 13However, if he does not do it intentionally, but God lets it happen, he is to flee to a place[c] I will designate. 14But if a man schemes and kills another man deliberately,[d] take him away from my altar and put him to death.[e]

15 "Anyone who attacks[c] his father or his mother must be put to death.

16 "Anyone who kidnaps another and either sells[f] him or still has him when he is caught must be put to death.[g]

17 "Anyone who curses his father or mother must be put to death.[h]

---

[a] 6 Or before God   [b] 8 Or master so that he does not choose her   [c] 15 Or kills

---

Exodus 21:2–11

It seems ironic that a recently emancipated Israelite could be owned by another Israelite. But the focus of this passage was on the proper treatment of such slaves. In a world where the powerful exercised no restraint on their control of others, and where revenge and retaliation could be disproportionate to the offense, God was sowing in Israel the seeds of a better way. Even the poor and marginalized had a right to respect. There was no perpetual or permanent slavery among the Israelites.

Our worship of God is intimately related to how we treat others. It's striking that following the "thunder and lightning" in the worship of chapter 20, the ordinances for how the Israelites were to live out their salvation began with regulations regarding the worst form of human relations—slavery. But the Book of the Covenant teaches us that God requires his people to behave properly toward himself and others. God commands us how to live, not in an ideal situation but in a broken and fallen world, a world of slavery.

21:1

LAYERS
of Legislation

The Ten Commandments are the most basic law code of the Bible, the first four dealing with relationship to God and the last six with relationships between people. But they are followed by three chapters of more specific laws and commandments. Together, these chapters are often called the Book of the Covenant.

Societies often have several layers of regulations dealing with relationships between people, formal and informal, and institutions that support/ enforce them (rows below are not intended to align across):

Institutions	Standards	Means of Change
• Government agencies	• Regulations	• Vote
• Civic organizations	• Laws	• Custom
• Police	• Procedures	• Legislation
• Courts	• Constitutions	• Societal agreement
• Religions	• Revealed morality	• Consensus

18 "If men quarrel and one hits the other with a stone or with his fist[a] and he does not die but is confined to bed, 19 the one who struck the blow will not be held responsible if the other gets up and walks around outside with his staff; however, he must pay the injured man for the loss of his time and see that he is completely healed.

20 "If a man beats his male or female slave with a rod and the slave dies as a direct result, he must be punished, 21 but he is not to be punished if the slave gets up after a day or two, since the slave is his property.[i]

22 "If men who are fighting hit a pregnant woman and she gives birth prematurely[b] but there is no serious injury, the offender must be fined whatever the woman's husband demands[j] and the court allows. 23 But if there is serious injury, you are to take life for life,[k] 24 eye for eye, tooth for tooth,[l] hand for hand, foot for foot, 25 burn for burn, wound for wound, bruise for bruise.

26 "If a man hits a manservant or maidservant in the eye and destroys it, he must let the servant go free to compensate for the eye. 27 And if he knocks out the tooth of a manservant or maidservant, he must let the servant go free to compensate for the tooth.

28 "If a bull gores a man or a woman to death, the bull must be stoned to death,[m] and its meat must not be eaten. But the owner of the bull will not be held responsible. 29 If, however, the bull has had the habit of goring and the owner has been warned but has not kept it penned up and it kills a man or woman, the bull must be stoned and the owner also must be put to death. 30 However, if payment is demanded of him, he may redeem his life by paying whatever is demanded.[n] 31 This law also applies if the bull gores a son or daughter. 32 If the bull gores a male or female slave, the owner must pay thirty shekels[c][o] of silver to the master of the slave, and the bull must be stoned.

33 "If a man uncovers a pit or digs one and fails to cover it and an ox or a donkey falls into it, 34 the owner of the pit must pay for the loss; he must pay its owner, and the dead animal will be his.

35 "If a man's bull injures the bull of another and it dies, they are to sell the live one and divide both the money and the dead animal equally. 36 However, if it was known that the bull had the habit of goring, yet the owner did not keep it penned up, the owner must pay, animal for animal, and the dead animal will be his.

Protection of Property

22 "If a man steals an ox or a sheep and slaughters it or sells it, he must pay back[p] five head of cattle for the ox and four sheep for the sheep.

2 "If a thief is caught breaking in[q] and is struck so that he dies, the defender is not guilty of bloodshed;[r] 3 but if it happens[d] after sunrise, he is guilty of bloodshed.

"A thief must certainly make restitution, but if he has nothing, he must be sold[s] to pay for his theft.

a 18 Or with a tool   b 22 Or she has a miscarriage   c 32 That is, about 12 ounces (about 0.3 kilogram)   d 3 Or if he strikes him

21:21 i Lev 25:44-46
21:22 j ver 30; Dt 22:18-19
21:23 k Lev 24:19; Dt 19:21
21:24 l Mt 5:38*
21:28 m ver 32; Ge 9:5
21:30 n ver 22; Nu 35:31
21:32 o Zec 11:12-13; Mt 26:15; 27:3,9
22:1 p 2Sa 12:6; Pr 6:31; Lk 19:8
22:2 q Mt 6:19-20; 24:43 r Nu 35:27
22:3 s Ex 21:2; Mt 18:25

Exodus 21:12–36
Like the previous passage, this one deals with proper treatment of fellow Israelites—this time focusing on personal injury in general. Since verses 20–21 and 26–27 deal with situations specifically related to slaves, we must assume the other laws held for all Israelites. Rather than disproportionate revenge, which was the common custom, the Israelites were to practice restraint and permit only punishment proportionate to an offense.

The Book of the Covenant contains regulations for Israel's worship (see "There and Then" notes for 20:22—21:1 and 23:14–19). Interwoven with those "vertically" oriented stipulations are the "horizontal" laws like those we find in this passage—laws about social conduct. The Book of the Covenant is one body of law. Its structure is an expression of Jesus' words in Matthew 22:37–40, where he summarized the law's intent as love for God and neighbor.

Exodus 22:1–15
These laws are based on the eighth commandment (20:15). In general, they concern property protection, but a variety of scenarios are described. The basic categories are theft, carelessness leading to property damage, and the safekeeping of one person's property by another. Negligence, like stealing, was a crime, and restitution was required. Many of these principles still underlie laws governing social interaction and influence public opinion on what's considered fair or just.

117

Amy Carmichael

Amy Carmichael (1867–1951) wanted to serve God in Belfast, Ireland, 15 miles west of her father's mill. She discovered that she had a special gift for working with poor children at the Belfast City Mission. Amy taught them hygiene and etiquette, Bible stories, and how to pray. And she raised money to build a welcome hall where they could meet. It was so successful that a group in Manchester, England, asked her to come and construct a similar hall for them. She did.

Amy's world was getting wider and wider. Then she began to study the lives of great missionaries: William Carey in India, Hudson Taylor in China, David Livingstone in Africa. Amy learned that there are millions of unsaved people in the world who need to hear the gospel of Jesus Christ.

> Amy Carmichael lived her life as a testimony to what service to the teachings of the Bible can do.

Carmichael wanted to bring the Good News to these people but recognized that she was already doing important work with the children of Belfast and Great Britain. Was it in God's will for her to give up this effort in order to go halfway around the world with the words of salvation? The answer, she learned, was yes. After a short time in Japan, she traveled to Dohnavur, India, where she founded the Donhavur Fellowship, a sanctuary for thousands of children who would otherwise have faced a life of poverty and desperation. She labored there for 56 years.

Amy Carmichael's secret? She believed that doctrinal distinctions, while important, can be a distraction. She knew intuitively that to be a good servant of Christ demands first of all humility and sanctity. All bitterness and animosity need to be put away. Only then can the self be freed for service to God. For Amy that service meant taking seriously Jesus' admonition in Matthew to let the children come to him (Matt. 19:14).

Amy Carmichael lived her life as a testimony to what service to the teachings of the Bible can do. She didn't overemphasize "religious" talk and traditions but was wholly committed to the gospel spiritually. *Lesson: The most powerful evangelistic "method" is a life in Christ.*

There were times in Amy's life when she became discouraged. Her response? She just kept working. She developed a philosophy of life that focused on the positive and the hope that is in all of us because of the work of Christ in our lives and in the world. *Lesson: If the day ends in what seems failure, don't succumb to despondency. Discouragement never comes from God.*

When she first arrived in Dohnavur, India, Carmichael discovered a group of women already trying to live lives dedicated to Christ and to helping orphaned children. She pitched in to help with a work already in process. *Lesson: We don't need to suggest to God what to do—he already knows.*

4 "If the stolen animal is found alive in his possession—whether ox or donkey or sheep—he must pay back double. [t]

5 "If a man grazes his livestock in a field or vineyard and lets them stray and they graze in another man's field, he must make restitution from the best of his own field or vineyard.

6 "If a fire breaks out and spreads into thornbushes so that it burns shocks of grain or standing grain or the whole field, the one who started the fire must make restitution.

7 "If a man gives his neighbor silver or goods for safekeeping and they are stolen from the neighbor's house, the thief, if he is caught, must pay back double. [u] 8 But if the thief is not found, the owner of the house must appear before the judges [a] [v] to determine whether he has laid his hands on the other man's property. 9 In all cases of illegal possession of an ox, a donkey, a sheep, a garment, or any other lost property about which somebody says, 'This is mine,' both parties are to bring their cases before the judges. [w] The one whom the judges declare [b] guilty must pay back double to his neighbor.

10 "If a man gives a donkey, an ox, a sheep or any other animal to his neighbor for safekeeping and it dies or is injured or is taken away while no one is looking, 11 the issue between them will be settled by the taking of an oath [x] before the LORD that the neighbor did not lay hands on the other person's property. The owner is to accept this, and no restitution is required. 12 But if the animal was stolen from the neighbor, he must make restitution to the owner. 13 If it was torn to pieces by a wild animal, he shall bring in the remains as evidence and he will not be required to pay for the torn animal. [y]

14 "If a man borrows an animal from his neighbor and it is injured or dies while the owner is not present, he must make restitution. 15 But if the owner is with the animal, the borrower will not have to pay. If the animal was hired, the money paid for the hire covers the loss.

Social Responsibility

16 "If a man seduces a virgin [z] who is not pledged to be married and sleeps with her, he must pay the bride-price, and she shall be his wife. 17 If her father absolutely refuses to give her to him, he must still pay the bride-price for virgins.

18 "Do not allow a sorceress [a] to live.

19 "Anyone who has sexual relations with an animal [b] must be put to death.

20 "Whoever sacrifices to any god other than the LORD must be destroyed. [c] [c]

21 "Do not mistreat an alien [d] or oppress him, for you were aliens [e] in Egypt.

22 "Do not take advantage of a widow or an orphan. [f] 23 If you do and they cry out [g] to me, I will certainly hear their cry. [h] 24 My anger will be aroused, and I will kill you with the sword; your wives will become widows and your children fatherless. [i]

25 "If you lend money to one of my people among you who is needy, do not be like a moneylender; charge him no interest. [d] [j] 26 If you take your neighbor's cloak

a 8 Or *before God*; also in verse 9   b 9 Or *whom God declares*   c 20 The Hebrew term refers to the irrevocable giving over of things or persons to the LORD, often by totally destroying them.   d 25 Or *excessive interest*

Cross-references

22:4 t Ge 43:12
22:7 u ver 4
22:8 v Ex 21:6; Dt 17:8-9; 19:17
22:9 w ver 28; Dt 25:1
22:11 x Heb 6:16
22:13 y Ge 31:39
22:16 z Dt 22:28
22:18 a Lev 20:27; Dt 18:11; 1Sa 28:3
22:19 b Lev 18:23; Dt 27:21
22:20 c Dt 17:2-5
22:21 d Lev 19:33   e Dt 10:19
22:22 f Dt 24:6,10,12,17
22:23 g Lk 18:7 h Dt 15:9; Ps 69:24; 109:9
22:24 i Ps 69:24; 109:9
22:25 j Lev 25:35-37; Dt 23:20; Ps 15:5

📖 A thread common to many of these commands is restoration above and beyond the minimum (cf. Luke 19:1–10). Some Christians respond negatively to the concept of lawsuits, characterizing claimants as greedy opportunists (indeed, many awards do seem to exceed common sense). But this isn't the kind of justice God asks of his people. If we have wronged someone else, he asks us to allow the law of love to motivate us to step beyond fairness in making amends.

Exodus 22:16–31
📖 This passage demonstrates the close association between "secular" or social concerns and matters of proper worship. For ancient Israel, all of life was rooted in worship, and the quality of people's worship was shown in part by their conduct toward others.

Many of these laws (like killing a sorceress or idol worshiper) sound harsh to our ears, sensitized by the acceptance and tolerance so ingrained in our culture. But God's words in verse 31 catch our attention: "You are to be my holy people." Tight reins were needed to keep the Israelites—who were "set apart" as God's own people—in check.

📖 It's easy to take advantage of the already disadvantaged—the poor, young, ignorant, addicted, mentally

22:26
k Dt 24:6
22:27
l Ex 34:6
22:28
m Lev 24:11,16
n Ecc 10:20;
Ac 23:5*
22:29
o Ex 23:15,16,19
p Ex 13:2
22:30
q Ex 13:12;
Dt 15:19
r Lev 22:27
22:31
s Lev 19:2
t Eze 4:14

23:1
u Ex 20:16;
Ps 101:5 v Ps 35:11;
Ac 6:11

23:2
w Dt 16:19

23:4
x Dt 22:1-3
23:5
y Dt 22:4
23:6
z ver 2
23:7
a Eph 4:25

23:8
b Dt 10:17; 16:19;
Pr 15:27
23:9
c Ex 22:21

23:12
d Ex 20:9

as a pledge, k return it to him by sunset, 27because his cloak is the only covering he has for his body. What else will he sleep in? When he cries out to me, I will hear, for I am compassionate. l

28"Do not blaspheme God a m or curse the ruler of your people. n

29"Do not hold back offerings o from your granaries or your vats. b

"You must give me the firstborn of your sons. p 30Do the same with your cattle and your sheep. q Let them stay with their mothers for seven days, but give them to me on the eighth day. r

31"You are to be my holy people. s So do not eat the meat of an animal torn by wild beasts; t throw it to the dogs.

Laws of Justice and Mercy

23 "Do not spread false reports. u Do not help a wicked man by being a malicious witness. v

2"Do not follow the crowd in doing wrong. When you give testimony in a lawsuit, do not pervert justice w by siding with the crowd, 3and do not show favoritism to a poor man in his lawsuit.

4"If you come across your enemy's ox or donkey wandering off, be sure to take it back to him. x 5If you see the donkey y of someone who hates you fallen down under its load, do not leave it there; be sure you help him with it.

6"Do not deny justice z to your poor people in their lawsuits. 7Have nothing to do with a false charge a and do not put an innocent or honest person to death, for I will not acquit the guilty.

8"Do not accept a bribe, b for a bribe blinds those who see and twists the words of the righteous.

9"Do not oppress an alien; c you yourselves know how it feels to be aliens, because you were aliens in Egypt.

Sabbath Laws

10"For six years you are to sow your fields and harvest the crops, 11but during the seventh year let the land lie unplowed and unused. Then the poor among your people may get food from it, and the wild animals may eat what they leave. Do the same with your vineyard and your olive grove.

12"Six days do your work, d but on the seventh day do not work, so that your ox

---

a 28 Or *Do not revile the judges*   b 29 The meaning of the Hebrew for this phrase is uncertain.

---

or physically challenged, or refugees. Just as God had rescued the Israelites from captivity, so they were now to show special care for foreigners living among them, as well as for widows and orphans (vv. 21–24). God still hears the cries of the oppressed—and the prayers of those who advocate for them. Proper conduct toward God and others constitutes true religion (cf. James 1:27). James made a strong statement that paralleled God's promised wrath against his people if they didn't care for foreigners and the marginalized. How seriously do you take this command?

Exodus 23:1–9

Most of the laws in this passage relate to the ninth commandment (20:16) pertaining to matters of legal justice. Verse 3 is to be read in conjunction with verses 6 and 9. The Israelites were to remember what it was like to be poor, enslaved foreigners. People who didn't possess the power of wealth and social status were to be *defended by the law and by those* in power. Even enemies were to be treated with the same respect they would like to have received (vv. 4–5).

When it comes to justice, the majority doesn't

rule. In fact, God calls us not to "follow a majority in wrongdoing" (23:2). In our day, as in Moses', it's tempting to follow the crowd. If we are called upon to testify in a trial, justice can't be served if we give in to social pressure and automatically side with the popular and/or the powerful. In what ways does our culture try to entrap believers into going along with the group? How does it try to keep us from following Christ's commands, especially in our care of the poor and oppressed?

Exodus 23:10–13

These Sabbath laws expand on the fourth commandment (20:8–11). The Israelites weren't to offer the produce of the seventh year to God, but to leave it for the poor. The emphasis on protecting the disadvantaged throughout the Book of the Covenant (20:22—23:19) is strikingly evident here. Provision for allowing even wild animals to eat of the produce may indicate a broader concern in this law for the well-being of all creation. Even animals, slaves, and foreigners were to enjoy the benefit of a Sabbath. One day a week, and one year in every seven, all of creation was to rest from its labors and be refreshed.

and your donkey may rest and the slave born in your household, and the alien as well, may be refreshed.

¹³"Be careful[e] to do everything I have said to you. Do not invoke the names of other gods; do not let them be heard on your lips.

The Three Annual Festivals

¹⁴"Three times[f] a year you are to celebrate a festival to me.

¹⁵"Celebrate the Feast of Unleavened Bread;[g] for seven days eat bread made without yeast, as I commanded you. Do this at the appointed time in the month of Abib, for in that month you came out of Egypt.

"No one is to appear before me empty-handed.[h]

¹⁶"Celebrate the Feast of Harvest with the firstfruits[i] of the crops you sow in your field.

"Celebrate the Feast of Ingathering at the end of the year, when you gather in your crops from the field.[j]

¹⁷"Three times[k] a year all the men are to appear before the Sovereign LORD.

¹⁸"Do not offer the blood of a sacrifice to me along with anything containing yeast.[l]

"The fat of my festival offerings must not be kept until morning.[m]

¹⁹"Bring the best of the firstfruits[n] of your soil to the house of the LORD your God.

"Do not cook a young goat in its mother's milk.[o]

God's Angel to Prepare the Way

²⁰"See, I am sending an angel[p] ahead of you to guard you along the way and to bring you to the place I have prepared.[q] ²¹Pay attention to him and listen[r] to what he says. Do not rebel against him; he will not forgive your rebellion,[s] since my Name is in him. ²²If you listen carefully to what he says and do all that I say, I will be an enemy[t] to your enemies and will oppose those who oppose you. ²³My angel will go ahead of you and bring you into the land of the Amorites, Hittites, Perizzites, Canaanites, Hivites and Jebusites,[u] and I will wipe them out. ²⁴Do not bow down before their gods or worship[v] them or follow their practices.[w] You must demolish[x] them and break their sacred stones to pieces. ²⁵Worship the LORD your God,[y] and his blessing[z] will be on your food and water. I will take away sickness[a]

23:13 e 1Ti 4:16
23:14 f Ex 34:23,24
23:15 g Ex 12:17 h Ex 34:20
23:16 i Ex 34:22 j Dt 16:13
23:17 k Dt 16:16
23:18 l Ex 34:25 m Dt 16:4
23:19 n Ex 22:29; Dt 26:2,10 o Dt 14:21
23:20 p Ex 14:19; 32:34 q Ge 15:17
23:21 r Nu 14:11; Dt 18:19 s Ps 78:8, 40,56
23:22 t Ge 12:3; Dt 30:7
23:23 u ver 20; Jos 24:8,11
23:24 v Ex 20:5 w Dt 12:30-31 x Ex 34:13; Nu 33:52
23:25 y Dt 6:13; Mt 4:10 z Dt 7:12-15; 28:1-14 a Ex 15:26

God's judgment against Israel for failing to keep the Sabbath was severe. Sabbath-breaking is a form of idolatry, of failing to trust God to provide all that is necessary and instead placing our confidence in the work of our own hands. It also keeps the poor and powerless, as well as creation itself, from needed rest. Deliberately and regularly ceasing from work and setting aside a block of time for physical and spiritual refreshment is vital. What are your convictions—and track record—in that regard? How could you arrange and make good use of a mini "sabbatical"—for your own sake as well as for the poor?

Exodus 23:14–19

It was fitting to end the Book of the Covenant (20:22—23:19) with a reminder to the Israelites that they were a worshiping community, a reality that extended to every area of life but was most clearly seen in the ceremonies by which they worshiped God. The three annual feasts corresponded to three different stages in Israel's agricultural year.

We, too, engage in annual celebrations, in which we commemorate Jesus' birth, crucifixion, resurrection, and ascension, as well as the outpouring of the Holy Spirit. Nowhere does the Bible prescribe how we are to celebrate such occasions (except for the Lord's Supper). As Christians we are wise to exercise caution, particularly with regard to Christmas and Easter, and to avoid commercialism. Have you tried including the needy on your shopping list? How has this helped you keep in perspective what Jesus has done for you?

A convicting statement in this passage is God's injunction that "no one is to appear before me empty-handed." This impacts our pocketbook, but for those of us living in relative affluence, it requires more. We are not to come empty-hearted either. We are to be prepared to give our very lives, not just in love to God, but in open willingness to serve in his name wherever and whenever he calls us (Rom. 12:1).

Exodus 23:20–33

This isn't the first time the angel of the Lord appeared in Exodus. His presence was mentioned interchangeably with that of God himself at the burning bush (3:1–4). He was at hand at Israel's redemption at the sea (14:19)—closely associated with the cloud (cf. 13:21–22). Despite the mystery surrounding his precise identity, the angel was clearly a tangible manifestation of God's presence with his people. To say that the angel would command the people meant that God himself would address them.

23:26
b Dt 7:14; Mal 3:11
c Job 5:26
23:27
d Ex 15:14; Dt 2:25
e Dt 7:23
23:28
f Dt 7:20; Jos 24:12

23:29
g Dt 7:22

23:31
h Ge 15:18
i Jos 21:44;
24:12,18
23:32
j Ex 34:12; Dt 7:2
23:33
k Dt 7:16;
Ps 106:36

24:1
l Ex 6:23;
Lev 10:1-2
m Nu 11:16

24:3
n Ex 19:8; Dt 5:27
24:4
o Dt 31:9
p Ge 28:18

24:6
q Heb 9:18

24:7
r Heb 9:19

24:8
s Heb 9:20*;
1Pe 1:2

24:9
t ver 1
24:10
u Mt 17:2; Jn 1:18;
6:46 v Eze 1:26
w Rev 4:3
24:11
x Ge 32:30;
Ex 19:21

from among you, 26and none will miscarry or be barren b in your land. I will give you a full life span. c

27 "I will send my terror d ahead of you and throw into confusion e every nation you encounter. I will make all your enemies turn their backs and run. 28I will send the hornet f ahead of you to drive the Hivites, Canaanites and Hittites out of your way. 29But I will not drive them out in a single year, because the land would become desolate and the wild animals g too numerous for you. 30Little by little I will drive them out before you, until you have increased enough to take possession of the land.

31 "I will establish your borders from the Red Sea a to the Sea of the Philistines, b and from the desert to the River. c h I will hand over to you the people who live in the land and you will drive them out i before you. 32Do not make a covenant j with them or with their gods. 33Do not let them live in your land, or they will cause you to sin against me, because the worship of their gods will certainly be a snare k to you."

The Covenant Confirmed

24 Then he said to Moses, "Come up to the LORD, you and Aaron, Nadab and Abihu, l and seventy of the elders m of Israel. You are to worship at a distance, 2but Moses alone is to approach the LORD; the others must not come near. And the people may not come up with him."

3When Moses went and told the people all the LORD's words and laws, they responded with one voice, "Everything the LORD has said we will do." n 4Moses then wrote o down everything the LORD had said.

He got up early the next morning and built an altar at the foot of the mountain and set up twelve stone pillars p representing the twelve tribes of Israel. 5Then he sent young Israelite men, and they offered burnt offerings and sacrificed young bulls as fellowship offerings d to the LORD. 6Moses took half of the blood q and put it in bowls, and the other half he sprinkled on the altar. 7Then he took the Book of the Covenant r and read it to the people. They responded, "We will do everything the LORD has said; we will obey."

8Moses then took the blood, sprinkled it on the people and said, "This is the blood of the covenant s that the LORD has made with you in accordance with all these words."

9Moses and Aaron, Nadab and Abihu, and the seventy elders t of Israel went up 10and saw u the God of Israel. Under his feet was something like a pavement made of sapphire, e v clear as the sky w itself. 11But God did not raise his hand against these leaders of the Israelites; they saw x God, and they ate and drank.

---

a 31 Hebrew *Yam Suph*; that is, Sea of Reeds   b 31 That is, the Mediterranean   c 31 That is, the Euphrates   d 5 Traditionally *peace offerings*   e 10 Or *lapis lazuli*

📖 The Holy Spirit is with us at every step in our journey. He was there at our redemption—not with arms folded, waiting to see whether we had made the right choice, but calling us into his presence. And having called us, he walks ahead to guard us and guide us home. Such personal application of the angel's presence and activity is hinted at in the Psalms (see Ps. 34:7; 35:5–6). Imagine yourself being personally led by a cloud or fire. Do these images make the Holy Spirit's role in your life seem more real?

Exodus 24:1–18

🔁 Exodus 24 revisits the covenant, confirmed through worship, personal dedication, and the writing of the law. But the chapter also looks ahead. Moses was called to ascend the mountain still again. This time he received instructions on a number of issues that will dominate the rest of Exodus, as well as of the Pentateuch (first five books of the Bible) and much of the rest of the Old Testament: the building of the tabernacle, the

priesthood, and Sabbath regulations.

How do you reconcile the claim that Israel's leaders "saw" God (vv. 10–11) with his words in 33:20: "You cannot see my face, for no one may see me and live"? Evidently these individuals truly witnessed God in some fashion, but not in the fullness of his glory. Since no human being can see God as he really is, they must have seen him in a form he took upon himself temporarily.

📖 We can't "see" God if we bypass the only means by which he's made this possible—his Son, Jesus Christ. As Jesus said to Philip, "Anyone who has seen me has seen the Father" (John 14:9). Yet John wrote elsewhere that "no one has ever seen God; but if we love one another, God lives in us and his love is made complete in us" (1 Jn. 4:12). If we love one another, we see God reflected in each other. Can you recall a time when loving concern from God's people provided a spiritual lift when you needed it most?

¹²The LORD said to Moses, "Come up to me on the mountain and stay here, and I will give you the tablets of stone,*y* with the law and commands I have written for their instruction."

¹³Then Moses set out with Joshua*z* his aide, and Moses went up on the mountain*a* of God. ¹⁴He said to the elders, "Wait here for us until we come back to you. Aaron and Hur are with you, and anyone involved in a dispute can go to them."

¹⁵When Moses went up on the mountain, the cloud*b* covered it, ¹⁶and the glory*c* of the LORD settled on Mount Sinai. For six days the cloud covered the mountain, and on the seventh day the LORD called to Moses from within the cloud.*d* ¹⁷To the Israelites the glory of the LORD looked like a consuming fire*e* on top of the mountain. ¹⁸Then Moses entered the cloud as he went on up the mountain. And he stayed on the mountain forty*f* days and forty nights.*g*

Offerings for the Tabernacle

25 The LORD said to Moses, ²"Tell the Israelites to bring me an offering. You are to receive the offering for me from each man whose heart prompts*h* him to give. ³These are the offerings you are to receive from them: gold, silver and bronze; ⁴blue, purple and scarlet yarn and fine linen; goat hair; ⁵ram skins dyed red and hides of sea cows*a*; acacia wood; ⁶olive oil*i* for the light; spices for the anointing oil and for the fragrant incense; ⁷and onyx stones and other gems to be mounted on the ephod*j* and breastpiece.*k*

⁸"Then have them make a sanctuary*l* for me, and I will dwell*m* among them. ⁹Make this tabernacle and all its furnishings exactly like the pattern*n* I will show you.

The Ark

¹⁰"Have them make a chest*o* of acacia wood—two and a half cubits long, a cubit and a half wide, and a cubit and a half high.*b* ¹¹Overlay it with pure gold, both inside and out, and make a gold molding around it. ¹²Cast four gold rings for it and fasten them to its four feet, with two rings on one side and two rings on the other. ¹³Then make poles of acacia wood and overlay them with gold. ¹⁴Insert the poles into the rings on the sides of the chest to carry it. ¹⁵The poles are to remain in the rings of this ark; they are not to be removed.*p* ¹⁶Then put in the ark the Testimony,*q* which I will give you.

¹⁷"Make an atonement cover*c r* of pure gold—two and a half cubits long and a cubit and a half wide.*d* ¹⁸And make two cherubim out of hammered gold at the ends of the cover. ¹⁹Make one cherub on one end and the second cherub on the other;

---

a 5 That is, dugongs   *b* 10 That is, about 3 3/4 feet (about 1.1 meters) long and 2 1/4 feet (about 0.7 meter) wide and high   *c* 17 Traditionally *a mercy seat*   *d* 17 That is, about 3 3/4 feet (about 1.1 meters) long and 2 1/4 feet (about 0.7 meter) wide

---

24:12 *y* Ex 32:15-16
24:13 *z* Ex 17:9 *a* Ex 3:1
24:15 *b* Ex 19:9
24:16 *c* Ex 16:10 *d* Ps 99:7
24:17 *e* Ex 3:2; Dt 4:36; Heb 12:18,29
24:18 *f* Dt 9:9 *g* Ex 34:28

25:2 *h* Ex 35:21; 1Ch 29:5,7,9; Ezr 2:68; 2Co 8:11-12; 9:7
25:6 *i* Ex 27:20; 30:22-32
25:7 *j* Ex 28:4,6-14 *k* Ex 28:15-30
25:8 *l* Ex 36:1-5; Heb 9:1-2 *m* Ex 29:45; 1Ki 6:13; 2Co 6:16; Rev 21:3
25:9 *n* ver 40; Ac 7:44; Heb 8:5
25:10 *o* Dt 10:1-5; Heb 9:4

25:15 *p* 1Ki 8:8
25:16 *q* Dt 31:26; Heb 9:4
25:17 *r* Ro 3:25

Exodus 25:1–9

🔲 God commanded Moses to build the tabernacle according to a precise pattern. The reason? "I will dwell among them" (v. 8). God intended to be present with his people in a new way. The tabernacle was to be an earthly symbol of a greater, heavenly reality.

The clause "the LORD said to Moses" occurs seven times in chapters 25–31. The first six concern the building of the tabernacle and its furnishings (v. 1; 30:11,17, 22,34; 31:1), while the seventh introduces the Sabbath command (31:12). We are immediately reminded of creation, which also involved six creative acts culminating in a seventh-day rest.

🔲 The building materials for the tabernacle were donated by the people. Undoubtedly the items themselves came from what they had received as they left Egypt (12:35–36). Freewill gifts were pleasing to God and

appropriate for building a tabernacle for his presence. Our wholehearted devotion to and worship of God also are fitting responses to the gift of salvation he offers us through his Son. How do you express your devotion? In gifts? In service? In worship?

Exodus 25:10–22

🔲 The actual building of the ark in 37:1–9 followed that of the tabernacle. Here in the instruction stage the sequence was reversed—possibly to stress the ark's importance as the central point of contact between heaven and the tabernacle. Since any image of God was forbidden, the best Israel could do to emphasize God's holiness was to make an image of those closest to him—the cherubim. The "Testimony" refers to the stone tablets inscribed with the Ten Commandments, God's supreme self-revelation. These tablets were kept inside the ark, making it the central reminder of God's presence.

25:20
s 1Ki 8:7;
1Ch 28:18; Heb 9:5
25:21
t Ex 26:34 u ver 16
25:22
v Nu 7:89; 1Sa 4:4;
2Sa 6:2; 2Ki 19:15;
Ps 80:1; Isa 37:16
w Ex 29:42-43

make the cherubim of one piece with the cover, at the two ends. 20The cherubim are to have their wings spread upward, overshadowing⁵ the cover with them. The cherubim are to face each other, looking toward the cover. 21Place the cover on top of the ark ᵗ and put in the ark the Testimony, ᵘ which I will give you. 22There, above the cover between the two cherubim ᵛ that are over the ark of the Testimony, I will meet ʷ with you and give you all my commands for the Israelites.

The Table

25:23
x Heb 9:2

23"Make a table ˣ of acacia wood—two cubits long, a cubit wide and a cubit and a half high. ᵃ 24Overlay it with pure gold and make a gold molding around it. 25Also make around it a rim a handbreadth ᵇ wide and put a gold molding on the rim. 26Make four gold rings for the table and fasten them to the four corners, where the four legs are. 27The rings are to be close to the rim to hold the poles used in carrying the table. 28Make the poles of acacia wood, overlay them with gold and carry the table with them. 29And make its plates and dishes of pure gold, as well as its pitchers and bowls for the pouring out of offerings. ʸ 30Put the bread of the Presence ᶻ on this table to be before me at all times.

25:29
y Nu 4:7
25:30
z Lev 24:5-9

The Lampstand

25:31
a 1Ki 7:49; Zec 4:2;
Heb 9:2; Rev 1:12

31"Make a lampstand ᵃ of pure gold and hammer it out, base and shaft; its flowerlike cups, buds and blossoms shall be of one piece with it. 32Six branches are to extend from the sides of the lampstand—three on one side and three on the other. 33Three cups shaped like almond flowers with buds and blossoms are to be on one branch, three on the next branch, and the same for all six branches extending from the lampstand. 34And on the lampstand there are to be four cups shaped like almond flowers with buds and blossoms. 35One bud shall be under the first pair of branches extending from the lampstand, a second bud under the second pair, and a third bud under the third pair—six branches in all. 36The buds and branches shall all be of one piece with the lampstand, hammered out of pure gold.

25:37
b Ex 27:21;
Lev 24:3-4; Nu 8:2

37"Then make its seven lamps ᵇ and set them up on it so that they light the space

ᵃ 23 That is, about 3 feet (about 0.9 meter) long and 1 1/2 feet (about 0.5 meter) wide and 2 1/4 feet (about 0.7 meter) high   ᵇ 25 That is, about 3 inches (about 8 centimeters)

What picture of God do you see in the tabernacle? (1) It represented creation. God lived on Earth in a structure intended to reflect the perfect created order—a piece of heaven on Earth. (2) In the later, climactic stage of redemptive history, God took up residence in Christ, the "temple" who "tabernacled," or lived, among his people (cf. John 1:14; 2:19–21). (3) The God of creation has built us up to be his house and has taken up residence in us (cf. 1 Cor. 3:16–17; 6:19). We are worthy of the Spirit's indwelling because we have been re-created by God's power into beings made righteous by Christ's sacrifice.

Exodus 25:23–30

The table was constructed for the apparent purpose of holding the bread of the "Presence" (the presence of God). Its dimensions were 3' long by 1'6" wide and 2'3" high. It was made of acacia wood overlaid with pure gold. Like the ark, it had a system of rings and poles for carrying it. It would be placed in the Holy Place along with the lampstand and the incense altar. See also "There and Then" for 37:10–16.

There are at least two ways in which we, as tabernacles, can reflect God's order amid chaos: how we worship and how we live. Worship is the place where heaven and Earth meet. Still today, God's saints worship in holy time and space. We also reflect divine order by how we live day to day in a fallen world. When you think of your body as a "temple of the Holy Spirit" (1 Cor. 6:19–20), does the concept put sinning in a different perspective? How does your identity as a "transporter" of divinity affect your attitudes and behavior?

Exodus 25:31–40

The lampstand and its lamps were small enough to be made of pure gold with no wood, though a talent of gold (about 75 pounds) was needed. Beyond the practical function of providing light, there is no clear indication of their symbolic meaning. Tending the lamps was serious business; the high priest did so "from evening until morning, continually" (Lev. 24:3–4). The priest's function was likely ritualistic and symbolic, though precisely what it involved we don't know.

Christ's coming didn't dull the tabernacle's majesty but reinforced what it stood for. The ornate decorations and furnishings are gone, but something far better has taken their place. The tabernacle was an earthly representation of a heavenly reality (Heb. 9:23–24). How much more so is Christ, who "came from the Father, full of grace and truth" (John 1:14)! Christ fulfills the purpose for which the tabernacle and its accessories were built.

in front of it. 38Its wick trimmers and trays are to be of pure gold. 39A talent a of pure gold is to be used for the lampstand and all these accessories. 40See that you make them according to the pattern c shown you on the mountain.

25:40
c Ex 26:30; Nu 8:4;
Ac 7:44; Heb 8:5*

The Tabernacle

26 "Make the tabernacle with ten curtains of finely twisted linen and blue, purple and scarlet yarn, with cherubim worked into them by a skilled craftsman. 2All the curtains are to be the same size—twenty-eight cubits long and four cubits wide. b 3Join five of the curtains together, and do the same with the other five. 4Make loops of blue material along the edge of the end curtain in one set, and do the same with the end curtain in the other set. 5Make fifty loops on one curtain and fifty loops on the end curtain of the other set, with the loops opposite each other. 6Then make fifty gold clasps and use them to fasten the curtains together so that the tabernacle is a unit.

7"Make curtains of goat hair for the tent over the tabernacle—eleven altogether. 8All eleven curtains are to be the same size—thirty cubits long and four cubits wide. c 9Join five of the curtains together into one set and the other six into another set. Fold the sixth curtain double at the front of the tent. 10Make fifty loops along the edge of the end curtain in one set and also along the edge of the end curtain in the other set. 11Then make fifty bronze clasps and put them in the loops to fasten the tent together as a unit. 12As for the additional length of the tent curtains, the half curtain that is left over is to hang down at the rear of the tabernacle. 13The tent curtains will be a cubit d longer on both sides; what is left will hang over the sides of the tabernacle so as to cover it. 14Make for the tent a covering of ram skins dyed red, and over that a covering of hides of sea cows. e d

26:14
d Ex 36:19; Nu 4:25

15"Make upright frames of acacia wood for the tabernacle. 16Each frame is to be ten cubits long and a cubit and a half wide, f 17with two projections set parallel to each other. Make all the frames of the tabernacle in this way. 18Make twenty frames for the south side of the tabernacle 19and make forty silver bases to go under them—two bases for each frame, one under each projection. 20For the other side, the north side of the tabernacle, make twenty frames 21and forty silver bases—two under each frame. 22Make six frames for the far end, that is, the west end of the tabernacle, 23and make two frames for the corners at the far end. 24At these two corners they must be double from the bottom all the way to the top, and fitted into a single ring; both shall be like that. 25So there will be eight frames and sixteen silver bases—two under each frame.

26"Also make crossbars of acacia wood: five for the frames on one side of the tabernacle, 27five for those on the other side, and five for the frames on the west, at the far end of the tabernacle. 28The center crossbar is to extend from end to end at the middle of the frames. 29Overlay the frames with gold and make gold rings to hold the crossbars. Also overlay the crossbars with gold.

30"Set up the tabernacle according to the plan e shown you on the mountain.

31"Make a curtain f of blue, purple and scarlet yarn and finely twisted linen, with

26:30
e Ex 25:9,40;
Ac 7:44; Heb 8:5
26:31
f 2Ch 3:14;
Mt 27:51; Heb 9:3

a 39 That is, about 75 pounds (about 34 kilograms)   b 2 That is, about 42 feet (about 12.5 meters) long and 6 feet (about 1.8 meters) wide   c 8 That is, about 45 feet (about 13.5 meters) long and 6 feet (about 1.8 meters) wide   d 13 That is, about 1 1/2 feet (about 0.5 meter)   e 14 That is, dugongs   f 16 That is, about 15 feet (about 4.5 meters) long and 2 1/4 feet (about 0.7 meter) wide

---

Exodus 26:1–37

The tabernacle was to be a series of curtains and frames. A curtain was to divide it into two rooms, the Holy Place and the Most Holy Place (half the size of the Holy Place, and probably a perfect cube, 15' by 15' by 15'). The Most Holy place contained the ark and represented God's throne room. The Holy Place was his royal guest chamber, where his people symbolically came before him.

Under the old covenant only the high priest could go behind the curtain separating the Holy Place from the Most Holy Place, and then only once a year on the Day of Atonement. The moment Christ died the curtain was torn, giving believers direct access to God's presence (see Mark 15:38; Heb. 10:19–22). Our souls' security rests in the eternal, high-priestly work of Christ, who entered God's presence on our behalf and made a way for us to follow (see Heb. 6:19–20). Are you following boldly and eagerly (Heb. 4:16)?

26:31
g Ex 36:35
26:33
h Ex 40:3,21;
Lev 16:2
i Heb 9:2-3
26:34
j Ex 25:21; 40:20;
Heb 9:5
26:35
k Heb 9:2
l Ex 40:22,24

cherubim ^{g} worked into it by a skilled craftsman. ^{32} Hang it with gold hooks on four posts of acacia wood overlaid with gold and standing on four silver bases. ^{33} Hang the curtain from the clasps and place the ark of the Testimony behind the curtain. ^{h} The curtain will separate the Holy Place from the Most Holy Place. ^{i} ^{34} Put the atonement cover ^{j} on the ark of the Testimony in the Most Holy Place. ^{35} Place the table ^{k} outside the curtain on the north side of the tabernacle and put the lampstand ^{l} opposite it on the south side.

^{36} "For the entrance to the tent make a curtain of blue, purple and scarlet yarn and finely twisted linen—the work of an embroiderer. ^{37} Make gold hooks for this curtain and five posts of acacia wood overlaid with gold. And cast five bronze bases for them.

The Altar of Burnt Offering

27 "Build an altar ^{m} of acacia wood, three cubits ^{a} high; it is to be square, five cubits long and five cubits wide. ^{b} ^{2} Make a horn ^{n} at each of the four corners, so that the horns and the altar are of one piece, and overlay the altar with bronze. ^{3} Make all its utensils of bronze—its pots to remove the ashes, and its shovels, sprinkling bowls, meat forks and firepans. ^{4} Make a grating for it, a bronze network, and make a bronze ring at each of the four corners of the network. ^{5} Put it under the ledge of the altar so that it is halfway up the altar. ^{6} Make poles of acacia wood for the altar and overlay them with bronze. ^{7} The poles are to be inserted into the rings so they will be on two sides of the altar when it is carried. ^{8} Make the altar hollow, out of boards. It is to be made just as you were shown ^{o} on the mountain.

The Courtyard

^{9} "Make a courtyard for the tabernacle. The south side shall be a hundred cubits ^{c} long and is to have curtains of finely twisted linen, ^{10} with twenty posts and twenty bronze bases and with silver hooks and bands on the posts. ^{11} The north side shall also be a hundred cubits long and is to have curtains, with twenty posts and twenty bronze bases and with silver hooks and bands on the posts.

^{12} "The west end of the courtyard shall be fifty cubits ^{d} wide and have curtains, with ten posts and ten bases. ^{13} On the east end, toward the sunrise, the courtyard shall also be fifty cubits wide. ^{14} Curtains fifteen cubits ^{e} long are to be on one side of the entrance, with three posts and three bases, ^{15} and curtains fifteen cubits long are to be on the other side, with three posts and three bases.

---

^{a} 1 That is, about 4 1/2 feet (about 1.3 meters) high ^{b} 1 That is, about 7 1/2 feet (about 2.3 meters) long and wide ^{c} 9 That is, about 150 feet (about 46 meters); also in verse 11 ^{d} 12 That is, about 75 feet (about 23 meters); also in verse 13 ^{e} 14 That is, about 22 1/2 feet (about 6.9 meters); also in verse 15

Exodus 27:1–8

The altar of burnt offering measured 7'6" square and was 4'6" tall. A curious characteristic of the altar was the horn at each corner. We read in 29:12 and Leviticus 4:7 that blood, symbolizing redemption (cf. Gen. 22:13; Ex. 30:10), was to be put on the horns. Clinging to the horns was a way to seek refuge in God's presence from harm (1 Kings 1:50–51; 2:28). The horns, then, represented help and refuge as well as atoning power—and were the practical means by which the sacrifice was bound to the altar. See also "There and Then" for 38:1–7.

This altar was the first and largest item an Israelite encountered upon entering the court. Just inside the gate, it was accessible, unavoidable, and unmistakable. The continuous sacrifices made on it were a constant and vivid reminder that the people could approach God only by means of a sacrifice. There was only one altar, just as there is now only one way of salvation—Jesus (see

John 1:29; 14:6)! The perfect sacrifice Jesus offered was made "once for all" (Heb. 7:27; 9:12; 9:26; 10:10). How are you reminded regularly of Jesus' perfect and complete sacrifice?

Exodus 27:9–19

The courtyard was a rectangle measuring 150' on the north and south ends and 75' on the east and west. The entrance was to be positioned on the east side, 30' long. Most of the description concerns the making of curtains and the system of posts, bases, and hooks for keeping the structure together.

The tabernacle, despite having been built as a perfect rectangle, was never intended to be a "box" in which God could be stored away and called upon to serve the people's purpose. If anything, the many allusions to creation in its construction reminded Israel of the opposite: The God worshiped within was the Creator of heaven and Earth.

16 "For the entrance to the courtyard, provide a curtain twenty cubits[a] long, of blue, purple and scarlet yarn and finely twisted linen—the work of an embroiderer—with four posts and four bases. 17 All the posts around the courtyard are to have silver bands and hooks, and bronze bases. 18 The courtyard shall be a hundred cubits long and fifty cubits wide,[b] with curtains of finely twisted linen five cubits[c] high, and with bronze bases. 19 All the other articles used in the service of the tabernacle, whatever their function, including all the tent pegs for it and those for the courtyard, are to be of bronze.

Oil for the Lampstand

20 "Command the Israelites to bring you clear oil of pressed olives for the light so that the lamps may be kept burning. 21 In the Tent of Meeting,[p] outside the curtain that is in front of the Testimony,[q] Aaron and his sons are to keep the lamps[r] burning before the LORD from evening till morning. This is to be a lasting ordinance[s] among the Israelites for the generations to come.

The Priestly Garments

28 "Have Aaron[t] your brother brought to you from among the Israelites, along with his sons Nadab and Abihu, Eleazar and Ithamar, so they may serve me as priests.[u] 2 Make sacred garments[v] for your brother Aaron, to give him dignity and honor. 3 Tell all the skilled men[w] to whom I have given wisdom[x] in such matters that they are to make garments for Aaron, for his consecration, so he may serve me as priest. 4 These are the garments they are to make: a breastpiece,[y] an ephod, a robe,[z] a woven tunic,[a] a turban and a sash. They are to make these sacred garments for your brother Aaron and his sons, so they may serve me as priests. 5 Have them use gold, and blue, purple and scarlet yarn, and fine linen.

The Ephod

6 "Make the ephod of gold, and of blue, purple and scarlet yarn, and of finely twisted linen—the work of a skilled craftsman. 7 It is to have two shoulder pieces

27:21
p Ex 28:43
q Ex 26:31,33
r Ex 25:37; 30:8; 1Sa 3:3; 2Ch 13:11
s Ex 29:9; Lev 3:17; 16:34; Nu 18:23; 19:21
28:1
t Heb 5:4
u Nu 18:1-7; Heb 5:1
28:2
v Ex 29:5,29; 31:10; 39:1; Lev 8:7-9,30
28:3
w Ex 31:6; 36:1
x Ex 31:3
28:4
y ver 15-30
z ver 31-35 a ver 39

---

a 16 That is, about 30 feet (about 9 meters)   b 18 That is, about 150 feet (about 46 meters) long and 75 feet (about 23 meters) wide   c 18 That is, about 7 1/2 feet (about 2.3 meters)

The notion that God—a spirit being—can be confined to a specific location is absurd. That God chose to meet with Israel in a "box" doesn't mean we can confine him to one. His ways and being are wholly "outside the box"—beyond our capacity to understand while we remain on Earth (cf. Isa. 55:8–9). When were you surprised at God's ability to exceed the imaginary barriers your mind had constructed around him? Reflect for a moment on the statement "Your God is too small." Is it true of you today?

Exodus 27:20–21

It's unclear why the instructions for the oil weren't given immediately after those for the lampstand (25:31–40). Clear olive oil was to be used; it produced little smoke and gave off good light. We don't know where the Israelites got the olives, but they may have brought the oil from Egypt. The lamps were to be kept burning by Aaron (cf. Lev. 24:1–4), though here Aaron's sons were included. The lamps were lit every evening (Ex. 30:8) and evidently extinguished every morning.

Here for the first time the tabernacle was referred to as "the Tent of Meeting," though the term would be used another 32 times before the end of Exodus. The term doesn't describe what the Israelites did (met for corporate worship) but what God did (made

himself known). Referring to the Tent of Meeting, God said in 29:42–43, "There I will meet you and speak to you . . . and the place will be consecrated by my glory." As a "temple of the Holy Spirit" (1 Cor. 6:19), how do you make yourself available for God to "meet" you?

Exodus 28:1–5

This entire chapter pertains to the garments Aaron (vv. 1–39), Israel's first high priest, and his sons (vv. 40–43) were to wear when ministering in the tabernacle. Though the description of the garments may not be entirely clear, their purpose is spelled out in verses 2 and 40: to give the priests "dignity and honor." No doubt this dignity and honor were conferred by the use of expensive materials—not just costly but parallel to those used to make the tabernacle itself.

On the one hand, the New Testament teaches "the priesthood of all believers" (cf. 1 Peter 2:5,9; Rev. 5:10). All Christians have direct access to God's presence and can minister to others on his behalf. But Paul asserted that "the elders who direct the affairs of the church well are worthy of double honor, especially those whose work is preaching and teaching" (1 Tim. 5:17). The author of Hebrews instructed, "Obey your leaders . . . so that their work will be a joy, not a burden" (Heb. 13:17–18). Are you giving "dignity and honor" to the spiritual leaders God has placed in your life?

attached to two of its corners, so it can be fastened. ⁸Its skillfully woven waistband is to be like it—of one piece with the ephod and made with gold, and with blue, purple and scarlet yarn, and with finely twisted linen.

⁹"Take two onyx stones and engrave on them the names of the sons of Israel ¹⁰in the order of their birth—six names on one stone and the remaining six on the other. ¹¹Engrave the names of the sons of Israel on the two stones the way a gem cutter engraves a seal. Then mount the stones in gold filigree settings ¹²and fasten them on the shoulder pieces of the ephod as memorial stones for the sons of Israel. Aaron is to bear the names on his shoulders as a memorial before the LORD. ¹³Make gold filigree settings ¹⁴and two braided chains of pure gold, like a rope, and attach the chains to the settings.

The Breastpiece

¹⁵"Fashion a breastpiece for making decisions—the work of a skilled craftsman. Make it like the ephod: of gold, and of blue, purple and scarlet yarn, and of finely twisted linen. ¹⁶It is to be square—a span ᵃ long and a span wide—and folded double. ¹⁷Then mount four rows of precious stones on it. In the first row there shall be a ruby, a topaz and a beryl; ¹⁸in the second row a turquoise, a sapphire ᵇ and an emerald; ¹⁹in the third row a jacinth, an agate and an amethyst; ²⁰in the fourth row a chrysolite, an onyx and a jasper. ᶜ Mount them in gold filigree settings. ²¹There are to be twelve stones, one for each of the names of the sons of Israel, each engraved like a seal with the name of one of the twelve tribes.

²²"For the breastpiece make braided chains of pure gold, like a rope. ²³Make two gold rings for it and fasten them to two corners of the breastpiece. ²⁴Fasten the two gold chains to the rings at the corners of the breastpiece, ²⁵and the other ends of the chains to the two settings, attaching them to the shoulder pieces of the ephod at the front. ²⁶Make two gold rings and attach them to the other two corners of the breastpiece on the inside edge next to the ephod. ²⁷Make two more gold rings and attach them to the bottom of the shoulder pieces on the front of the ephod, close to the seam just above the waistband of the ephod. ²⁸The rings of the breastpiece are to be tied to the rings of the ephod with blue cord, connecting it to the waistband, so that the breastpiece will not swing out from the ephod.

28:29
ᵇ ver 12

²⁹"Whenever Aaron enters the Holy Place, ᵇ he will bear the names of the sons of Israel over his heart on the breastpiece of decision as a continuing memorial before

---

ᵃ 16 That is, about 9 inches (about 22 centimeters)   ᵇ 18 Or *lapis lazuli*   ᶜ 20 The precise identification of some of these precious stones is uncertain.

Exodus 28:6–14

The priests, whose garments were made of the same materials as the tabernacle, were its bodily representations. Its purpose—to connect the people with God—also was fulfilled by the priests as they performed their duties in that tent. Like a priest, Christ also embodies the tabernacle, not by how he's dressed but by who he is. As both God *and* a human, he himself is the manifestation of the heavenly reality. That which the tabernacle and priesthood together could symbolize only partially is personified fully in Christ alone.

The apostle Paul often used the metaphor of clothing in relation to the spiritual life, referring to believers as those who "have clothed [themselves] with Christ" (Gal. 3:27). As we would shed dirty clothes in favor of clean ones, so we are called to turn from the old ways of the sinful nature to the new ways of the Spirit (cf. Rom. 13:12–14; Col. 3:5–14). If you could take a really good look at your spirit in a mirror, what do you suspect would need to happen for you to be fully "clothed" with Christ?

Exodus 28:15–30

Fitted into Aaron's ephod was "a breastpiece for making decisions" (v. 15). The means of doing this were the "Urim and Thummim" (v. 30). The high priest functioned not only in a sacrificial role but also as a conduit of God's revelation to the people. The Urim and Thummim have fascinated the curious for centuries. The act of decision making likely involved the casting of lots or stones to determine a yes or no answer. This process was used in crises to discern God's will (cf. Num. 27:21; 1 Sam. 23:9–12; 30:7–8).

Today, finding God's will isn't so mysterious a matter. Scripture clearly expresses his desire for us, and we enjoy direct access to God through prayer. He's given us the community of believers to guide us, and we have the inner witness of the Holy Spirit. These sources can combine in powerful ways to bring us to understand God's general and specific will for our lives. How successful do you feel you have been in finding—and following—God's will for you? The process isn't always simple, but neither is God trying to trick us!

the LORD. [30]Also put the Urim and the Thummim[c] in the breastpiece, so they may be over Aaron's heart whenever he enters the presence of the LORD. Thus Aaron will always bear the means of making decisions for the Israelites over his heart before the LORD.

Other Priestly Garments

[31]"Make the robe of the ephod entirely of blue cloth, [32]with an opening for the head in its center. There shall be a woven edge like a collar[a] around this opening, so that it will not tear. [33]Make pomegranates of blue, purple and scarlet yarn around the hem of the robe, with gold bells between them. [34]The gold bells and the pomegranates are to alternate around the hem of the robe. [35]Aaron must wear it when he ministers. The sound of the bells will be heard when he enters the Holy Place before the LORD and when he comes out, so that he will not die.

[36]"Make a plate of pure gold and engrave on it as on a seal: HOLY TO THE LORD.[d] [37]Fasten a blue cord to it to attach it to the turban; it is to be on the front of the turban. [38]It will be on Aaron's forehead, and he will bear the guilt[e] involved in the sacred gifts the Israelites consecrate, whatever their gifts may be. It will be on Aaron's forehead continually so that they will be acceptable to the LORD.

[39]"Weave the tunic of fine linen and make the turban of fine linen. The sash is to be the work of an embroiderer. [40]Make tunics, sashes and headbands for Aaron's sons,[f] to give them dignity and honor. [41]After you put these clothes on your brother Aaron and his sons, anoint[g] and ordain them. Consecrate them so they may serve me as priests.[h]

[42]"Make linen undergarments[i] as a covering for the body, reaching from the waist to the thigh. [43]Aaron and his sons must wear them whenever they enter the Tent of Meeting[j] or approach the altar to minister in the Holy Place, so that they will not incur guilt and die.[k]

"This is to be a lasting ordinance[l] for Aaron and his descendants.

Consecration of the Priests

29 "This is what you are to do to consecrate them, so they may serve me as priests: Take a young bull and two rams without defect. [2]And from fine wheat flour, without yeast, make bread, and cakes mixed with oil, and wafers spread with oil.[m] [3]Put them in a basket and present them in it—along with the bull and the two rams. [4]Then bring Aaron and his sons to the entrance to the Tent of Meeting and wash them with water.[n] [5]Take the garments[o] and dress Aaron with the tunic, the robe of the ephod, the ephod itself and the breastpiece. Fasten the ephod on him by its skillfully woven waistband.[p] [6]Put the turban on his head and attach

---

[a] 32 The meaning of the Hebrew for this word is uncertain.

Cross-references

28:30 [c] Lev 8:8; Nu 27:21; Dt 33:8; Ezr 2:63; Ne 7:65
28:36 [d] Zec 14:20
28:38 [e] Lev 10:17; 22:9, 16; Nu 18:1; Heb 9:28; 1Pe 2:24
28:40 [f] ver 4; Ex 39:41
28:41 [g] Ex 29:7; Lev 10:7
[h] Ex 29:7-9; 30:30; 40:15; Lev 8:1-36; Heb 7:28
28:42 [i] Lev 6:10; 16:4,23; Eze 44:18
28:43 [j] Ex 27:21
[k] Ex 20:26
[l] Lev 17:7
29:2 [m] Lev 2:1,4; 6:19-23
29:4 [n] Ex 40:12; Heb 10:22
29:5 [o] Ex 28:2; Lev 8:7
[p] Ex 28:8

Exodus 28:31–43

First an ephod and a breastpiece. Now robes, tunics, turbans, sashes, headbands, and undergarments. The end of this passage states that neglecting to wear the undergarments would bring "guilt and death." Exodus 20:26 provides insight as to why. There the Lord said, "Do not go up to my altar on steps, lest your nakedness be exposed on it." By wearing the undergarments, the priests avoided this shame.

Though our culture may seem to anesthetize us to the fact, Scripture equates nakedness, after the fall, with shame (Gen. 2:25; 3:7; 9:20–23; Isa. 47:1–3; Rev. 16:15). But ever since the fall, God has continually provided for our release from shame. He made "garments of skin" to clothe Adam and Eve (Gen. 3:21)—necessitating, in a sense, the very first animal sacrifice. Our shame is ultimately and completely covered through the gift of Christ's sacrifice, which allows us to be clothed in his righteousness (cf. Gal. 3:26–27).

Exodus 29:1–46

The ordination process took seven days—beginning with creation, the Biblical number for completeness. Exodus as a whole and the tabernacle in particular are full of creation imagery, so it seems appropriate to suggest a connection. The ordination ceremony prepared the priests for service in the tabernacle—the microcosm, or symbol in miniature, of creation.

The final three verses of chapter 29 tie together the tabernacle and priesthood with the exodus itself. The tabernacle and priests would be consecrated, and God would live with his people. They were to think back to God's initiative in bringing them out of Egypt. God's purpose in the exodus wasn't just freedom for slaves. He wanted to bring his people into a covenant relationship with himself through the law, tabernacle, and priesthood.

29:6
a Lev 8:9
29:7
r Ex 30:25,30,31;
Lev 8:12; 21:10;
Nu 35:25; Ps 133:2
29:9
s Ex 28:40
t Ex 40:15; Nu 3:10;
18:7; 25:13; Dt 18:5
29:12
u Ex 27:2

29:13
v Lev 3:3,5,9

29:14
w Lev 4:11-12,21;
Heb 13:11

29:18
x Ge 8:21
29:19
y ver 3

29:21
z Heb 9:22
a Ex 30:25,31
b ver 1

29:24
c Lev 7:30

29:26
d Lev 7:31-34

29:27
e Lev 7:31,34;
Dt 18:3
29:28
f Lev 10:15

29:29
g Nu 20:26,28
29:30
h Nu 20:28

29:32
i Mt 12:4
29:33
j Lev 10:14;
22:10,13
29:34
k Ex 12:10

29:36
l Heb 10:11
m Ex 40:10

29:37
n Ex 30:28-29;
40:10; Mt 23:19

the sacred diadem[q] to the turban. [7]Take the anointing oil[r] and anoint him by pouring it on his head. [8]Bring his sons and dress them in tunics [9]and put headbands on them. Then tie sashes on Aaron and his sons. [a][s] The priesthood is theirs by a lasting ordinance.[t] In this way you shall ordain Aaron and his sons.

[10]"Bring the bull to the front of the Tent of Meeting, and Aaron and his sons shall lay their hands on its head. [11]Slaughter it in the LORD's presence at the entrance to the Tent of Meeting. [12]Take some of the bull's blood and put it on the horns[u] of the altar with your finger, and pour out the rest of it at the base of the altar. [13]Then take all the fat[v] around the inner parts, the covering of the liver, and both kidneys with the fat on them, and burn them on the altar. [14]But burn the bull's flesh and its hide and its offal outside the camp.[w] It is a sin offering.

[15]"Take one of the rams, and Aaron and his sons shall lay their hands on its head. [16]Slaughter it and take the blood and sprinkle it against the altar on all sides. [17]Cut the ram into pieces and wash the inner parts and the legs, putting them with the head and the other pieces. [18]Then burn the entire ram on the altar. It is a burnt offering to the LORD, a pleasing aroma,[x] an offering made to the LORD by fire.

[19]"Take the other ram,[y] and Aaron and his sons shall lay their hands on its head. [20]Slaughter it, take some of its blood and put it on the lobes of the right ears of Aaron and his sons, on the thumbs of their right hands, and on the big toes of their right feet. Then sprinkle blood against the altar on all sides. [21]And take some of the blood[z] on the altar and some of the anointing oil[a] and sprinkle it on Aaron and his garments and on his sons and their garments. Then he and his sons and their garments will be consecrated.[b]

[22]"Take from this ram the fat, the fat tail, the fat around the inner parts, the covering of the liver, both kidneys with the fat on them, and the right thigh. (This is the ram for the ordination.) [23]From the basket of bread made without yeast, which is before the LORD, take a loaf, and a cake made with oil, and a wafer. [24]Put all these in the hands of Aaron and his sons and wave them before the LORD as a wave offering.[c] [25]Then take them from their hands and burn them on the altar along with the burnt offering for a pleasing aroma to the LORD, an offering made to the LORD by fire. [26]After you take the breast of the ram for Aaron's ordination, wave it before the LORD as a wave offering, and it will be your share.[d]

[27]"Consecrate those parts of the ordination ram that belong to Aaron and his sons:[e] the breast that was waved and the thigh that was presented. [28]This is always to be the regular share from the Israelites for Aaron and his sons. It is the contribution the Israelites are to make to the LORD from their fellowship offerings.[b][f]

[29]"Aaron's sacred garments will belong to his descendants so that they can be anointed and ordained in them.[g] [30]The son[h] who succeeds him as priest and comes to the Tent of Meeting to minister in the Holy Place is to wear them seven days.

[31]"Take the ram for the ordination and cook the meat in a sacred place. [32]At the entrance to the Tent of Meeting, Aaron and his sons are to eat the meat of the ram and the bread[i] that is in the basket. [33]They are to eat these offerings by which atonement was made for their ordination and consecration. But no one else may eat[j] them, because they are sacred. [34]And if any of the meat of the ordination ram or any bread is left over till morning,[k] burn it up. It must not be eaten, because it is sacred.

[35]"Do for Aaron and his sons everything I have commanded you, taking seven days to ordain them. [36]Sacrifice a bull each day[l] as a sin offering to make atonement. Purify the altar by making atonement for it, and anoint it to consecrate[m] it. [37]For seven days make atonement for the altar and consecrate it. Then the altar will be most holy, and whatever touches it will be holy.[n]

a 9 Hebrew; Septuagint *on them*   b 28 Traditionally *peace offerings*

📖 How different from this rigid formality our situation is today. Jesus Christ has become our high priest, and each believer now serves in the role of priest. The apostle John, overwhelmed by this reality, burst forth with praise in Revelation 1:5–6: "To him who loves us and has freed us from our sins by his blood, and has made us to be a kingdom and priests to serve his God and Father—to him be glory and power for ever and ever! Amen." Do you echo the enthusiasm of John's exuberant praise?

38 "This is what you are to offer on the altar regularly each day: [o] two lambs a year old. 39 Offer one in the morning and the other at twilight. [p] 40 With the first lamb offer a tenth of an ephah [a] of fine flour mixed with a quarter of a hin [b] of oil from pressed olives, and a quarter of a hin of wine as a drink offering. 41 Sacrifice the other lamb at twilight with the same grain offering and its drink offering as in the morning—a pleasing aroma, an offering made to the LORD by fire.

42 "For the generations to come [q] this burnt offering is to be made regularly at the entrance to the Tent of Meeting before the LORD. There I will meet you and speak to you; [r] 43 there also I will meet with the Israelites, and the place will be consecrated by my glory. [s]

44 "So I will consecrate the Tent of Meeting and the altar and will consecrate Aaron and his sons to serve me as priests. [t] 45 Then I will dwell [u] among the Israelites and be their God. [v] 46 They will know that I am the LORD their God, who brought them out of Egypt so that I might dwell among them. I am the LORD their God. [w]

The Altar of Incense

30 "Make an altar [x] of acacia wood for burning incense. [y] 2 It is to be square, a cubit long and a cubit wide, and two cubits high [c]—its horns [z] of one piece with it. 3 Overlay the top and all the sides and the horns with pure gold, and make a gold molding around it. 4 Make two gold rings for the altar below the molding—two on opposite sides—to hold the poles used to carry it. 5 Make the poles of acacia wood and overlay them with gold. 6 Put the altar in front of the curtain that is before the ark of the Testimony—before the atonement cover [a] that is over the Testimony—where I will meet with you.

7 "Aaron must burn fragrant incense [b] on the altar every morning when he tends the lamps. 8 He must burn incense again when he lights the lamps at twilight so incense will burn regularly before the LORD for the generations to come. 9 Do not offer on this altar any other incense [c] or any burnt offering or grain offering, and do not pour a drink offering on it. 10 Once a year Aaron shall make atonement [d] on its horns. This annual atonement must be made with the blood of the atoning sin offering for the generations to come. It is most holy to the LORD."

Atonement Money

11 Then the LORD said to Moses, 12 "When you take a census [e] of the Israelites to count them, each one must pay the LORD a ransom [f] for his life at the time he is counted. Then no plague [g] will come on them when you number them. 13 Each one who crosses over to those already counted is to give a half shekel, [d] according to the sanctuary shekel, [h] which weighs twenty gerahs. This half shekel is an offering to the LORD. 14 All who cross over, those twenty years old or more, are to give an offering

---

29:38
o Nu 28:3-8;
1Ch 16:40;
Da 2:11
29:39
p Eze 46:13-15

29:42
q Ex 30:8 r Ex 25:22

29:43
s 1Ki 8:11

29:44
t Lev 21:15
29:45
u Ex 25:8;
Lev 26:12;
Zec 2:10; Jn 14:17
v 2Co 6:16;
Rev 21:3
29:46
w Ex 20:2
30:1
x Ex 37:25
y Rev 8:3
30:2
z Ex 27:2

30:6
a Ex 25:22; 26:34

30:7
b ver 34-35;
Ex 27:21; 1Sa 2:28

30:9
c Lev 10:1
30:10
d Lev 16:18-19,30

30:12
e Ex 38:25; Nu 1:2,
49; 2Sa 24:1
f Nu 31:50;
Mt 20:28
g 2Sa 24:13

30:13
h Nu 3:47;
Mt 17:24

---

a 40 That is, probably about 2 quarts (about 2 liters)   b 40 That is, probably about 1 quart (about 1 liter)   c 2 That is, about 1 1/2 feet (about 0.5 meter) long and wide and about 3 feet (about 0.9 meter) high   d 13 That is, about 1/5 ounce (about 6 grams); also in verse 15

Exodus 30:1–10

We might have expected descriptions of all the tabernacle items before the instruction on consecrating the priests in chapter 29. Perhaps the altar of incense is mentioned afterward to emphasize the importance of this consecration. The tabernacle and priesthood are twin concepts in Exodus. Chapters 25–40 are about the institution of an entire system. See also "There and Then" for 37:25–29.

The fragrant smoke of incense is a symbol of the prayers of God's people (cf. Luke 1:8–11). In the book of Revelation, the hosts of heaven lift up incense to God as "the prayers of the saints" (Rev. 5:8; 8:3–5). Take encouragement in the fact that your accumulating prayers are recognized, honored, and powerful in heav-en! And take a moment to make the psalmist's prayer your own: "May my prayer be set before you like incense; may the lifting up of my hands be like the evening sacrifice" (Ps. 141:2).

Exodus 30:11–16

This passage calls to mind 2 Samuel 24:1–17, where David was punished for taking a census of his fighting men. If this later episode is relevant to understanding Exodus 30:11–16, it would seem more reasonable to have stated, "Don't take a census—it's wrong to do so." The assumption seems to have been that a census *would* be taken from time to time. Usually it was equivalent to mustering troops; that is why it was so dangerous in David's case. The ransom may have reminded Israel not to rely on its own strength.

30:15
i Pr 22:2; Eph 6:9

30:16
j Ex 38:25-28

30:18
k Ex 38:8; 40:7,30

30:19
l Ex 40:31-32;
Isa 52:11 *m* Ps 26:6

30:21
n Ex 27:21; 28:43

30:23
o Ge 37:25
30:24
p Ps 45:8

30:25
q Ex 37:29 *r* Ex 40:9
30:26
s Ex 40:9; Lev 8:10;
Nu 7:1

30:29
t Ex 29:37
30:30
u Ex 29:7;
Lev 8:2,12,30

to the LORD. 15The rich are not to give more than a half shekel and the poor are not to give less *i* when you make the offering to the LORD to atone for your lives. 16Receive the atonement money from the Israelites and use it for the service of the Tent of Meeting.*j* It will be a memorial for the Israelites before the LORD, making atonement for your lives."

Basin for Washing

17Then the LORD said to Moses, 18"Make a bronze basin,*k* with its bronze stand, for washing. Place it between the Tent of Meeting and the altar, and put water in it. 19Aaron and his sons are to wash their hands and feet *l* with water *m* from it. 20Whenever they enter the Tent of Meeting, they shall wash with water so that they will not die. Also, when they approach the altar to minister by presenting an offering made to the LORD by fire, 21they shall wash their hands and feet so that they will not die. This is to be a lasting ordinance *n* for Aaron and his descendants for the generations to come."

Anointing Oil

22Then the LORD said to Moses, 23"Take the following fine spices: 500 shekels *a* of liquid myrrh,*o* half as much (that is, 250 shekels) of fragrant cinnamon, 250 shekels of fragrant cane, 24500 shekels of cassia*p*—all according to the sanctuary shekel—and a hin*b* of olive oil. 25Make these into a sacred anointing oil, a fragrant blend, the work of a perfumer.*q* It will be the sacred anointing oil.*r* 26Then use it to anoint*s* the Tent of Meeting, the ark of the Testimony, 27the table and all its articles, the lampstand and its accessories, the altar of incense, 28the altar of burnt offering and all its utensils, and the basin with its stand. 29You shall consecrate them so they will be most holy, and whatever touches them will be holy.*t* 30"Anoint Aaron and his sons and consecrate*u* them so they may serve me as priests. 31Say to the Israelites, 'This is to be my sacred anointing oil for the genera-

a 23 That is, about 12 1/2 pounds (about 6 kilograms)   *b 24* That is, probably about 4 quarts (about 4 liters)

📖 The atonement money was to be used for "the service of the Tent of Meeting." We as modern Christians are reminded of the need to provide adequately for our church's "general" or operating fund, as well as to be generous in our giving for special causes.

The ransom money was an extension of 13:13–15: Firstborn sons belonged to the Lord and had to be redeemed by a sacrifice. Notice here that in verse 15 the rich were instructed not to give more than a half shekel and the poor not to give less. Everyone redeemed by God is of equal worth; God isn't a respecter of persons.

Exodus 30:17–21

📖 The basin was to be placed in the courtyard between the curtain to the Holy Place and the altar of burnt offering. As with other tabernacle furnishings and their intended use, there was no room for negotiation: If the priests failed to wash, they would die. This washing likely had a practical as well as a ceremonial function. The slaughter that took place at the altar would certainly have left the priests bloodied. Washing would have made them more presentable, as well as reducing the possibility of contamination. The washing also may symbolize cleansing from sin (cf. 29:1–4).

📖 Paul in his letter to Titus talked about Jesus saving us "through the washing of rebirth and renewal by the Holy Spirit" (Titus 3:5). Similarly, Peter referred to those in Noah's ark who were saved through water,

adding that "this water symbolizes baptism that now saves you also—not the removal of dirt from the body but the pledge of a good conscience toward God" (1 Peter 3:21). These verses remind us of the important role water plays both for everyday life and for religious purposes. Think about the rich "water" imagery throughout both Testaments. What symbol means the most to you?

Exodus 30:22–33

📖 The anointing oil, as well as the incense (v. 37), was to be reserved for religious functions, not used for self-adornment or merchandizing. The penalty was being "cut off from [the] people" (cf. this same phrase in 12:15,19, regarding the keeping of the Passover). We can infer from 31:14 that being "cut off" may have meant death. Elsewhere in Scripture, oil is symbolic of the Holy Spirit (cf. Zech. 4).

📖 Paul told his young protégé Timothy that "everything God created is good, and nothing is to be rejected if it is received with thanksgiving, because it is consecrated by the word of God and prayer" (1 Tim. 4:4–5). To consecrate means to dedicate for a sacred purpose—the function of the anointing oil and of God's Spirit. All of creation, despite its imperfections caused by sin, is sacred to God. One day he will usher in his new heaven and new Earth, perfect in every way. But for now he asks us to treat his world with the respect it deserves. What are some immediate, practical implications for you?

tions to come. 32Do not pour it on men's bodies and do not make any oil with the same formula. It is sacred, and you are to consider it sacred.*v* 33Whoever makes perfume like it and whoever puts it on anyone other than a priest must be cut off*w* from his people.' "

Incense

34Then the LORD said to Moses, "Take fragrant spices—gum resin, onycha and galbanum—and pure frankincense, all in equal amounts, 35and make a fragrant blend of incense, the work of a perfumer.*x* It is to be salted and pure and sacred. 36Grind some of it to powder and place it in front of the Testimony in the Tent of Meeting, where I will meet with you. It shall be most holy*y* to you. 37Do not make any incense with this formula for yourselves; consider it holy*z* to the LORD. 38Whoever makes any like it to enjoy its fragrance must be cut off*a* from his people."

Bezalel and Oholiab

31 Then the LORD said to Moses, 2"See, I have chosen Bezalel*b* son of Uri, the son of Hur, of the tribe of Judah, 3and I have filled him with the Spirit of God, with skill, ability and knowledge in all kinds of crafts*c*— 4to make artistic designs for work in gold, silver and bronze, 5to cut and set stones, to work in wood, and to engage in all kinds of craftsmanship. 6Moreover, I have appointed Oholiab son of Ahisamach, of the tribe of Dan, to help him. Also I have given skill to all the craftsmen to make everything I have commanded you: 7the Tent of Meeting,*d* the ark of the Testimony*e* with the atonement cover*f* on it, and all the other furnishings of the tent— 8the table*g* and its articles, the pure gold lampstand*h* and all its accessories, the altar of incense, 9the altar of burnt offering and all its utensils, the basin with its stand— 10and also the woven garments*i*, both the sacred garments for Aaron the priest and the garments for his sons when they serve as priests, 11and the anointing oil*j* and fragrant incense for the Holy Place. They are to make them just as I commanded you."

The Sabbath

12Then the LORD said to Moses, 13"Say to the Israelites, 'You must observe my Sab-

---

30:32
v ver 25,37
30:33
w ver 38; Ge 17:14

30:35
x ver 25

30:36
y ver 32; Ex 29:37; Lev 2:3
30:37
z ver 32
30:38
a ver 33

31:2
b Ex 36:1,2; 1Ch 2:20
31:3
c 1Ki 7:14

31:7
d Ex 36:8-38
e Ex 37:1-5
f Ex 37:6
31:8
g Ex 37:10-16
h Ex 37:17-24
31:10
i Ex 28:2; 39:1,41

31:11
j Ex 30:22-32

Exodus 30:34–38	Exodus 31:1–11
It's interesting to read the recipe for the incense and to note that the blend was to be prepared by a skilled perfumer. This mixture was designed specifically and solely for the altar of incense in the Holy Place (cf. 30:7–9), but such fragrances were important to ancient peoples—particularly for burials. In John 12:3 we are told that Jesus' friend Mary "took about a pint of pure nard, an expensive perfume; she poured it on Jesus' feet and wiped his feet with her hair." Jesus indicated that she had rightly reserved the perfume for his burial.	Two men were singled out for the task of compiling the information and building the tabernacle, its furnishings, and the other elements. They were filled with the Spirit of God. The seriousness of the matter might have discouraged most people from even attempting such a task, were it not for special, divine appointment and gifting. By God naming these men, Moses was spared the search for talented individuals and, perhaps, arguments or political maneuvering.
The apostle John tells us that we "have an anointing from the Holy One" (1 Jn. 2:20), going on to say: "The anointing you received from him remains in you . . . As his anointing teaches you about all things and as that anointing is real, not counterfeit—just as it has taught you, remain in him" (v. 27). We as Christians are called and anointed by God's Spirit to serve as priests under our great high priest, Christ himself. As priests of the new covenant, we live with great privilege but also great responsibility. What are some of those privileges and responsibilities? Have you taken them seriously?	God continues today through the working of the Holy Spirit to distribute varying gifts to his people. The apostle Paul mentioned a point easily missed: "To each one the manifestation of the Spirit is given *for the common good*" (1 Cor. 12:7, emphasis added). Just as these two individuals labored in humble and selfless obedience, each of us is called to find our niche in the kingdom and work diligently for the good of all.
	Some of us may be artistically inclined, while others may relate well to young children or older adults. Still others may be able to donate money and/or time for the needs of others. Like Bezalel and Oholiab, we may be assured that God has a special role for each of us as uniquely functioning members of his body, the church.

31:13
k Ex 20:8;
Lev 19:3,30
l Eze 20:12,20
m Lev 11:44
31:14
n Nu 15:32-36
31:15
o Ex 20:8-11
p Ge 2:3; Ex 16:23
31:17
q ver 13 r Ge 2:2-3

31:18
s Ex 24:12
t Ex 32:15-16; 34:1,
28; Dt 4:13; 5:22

32:1
u Ex 24:18;
Dt 9:9-12
v Ac 7:40*
32:2
w Ex 35:22

32:4
x Dt 9:16; Ne 9:18;
Ps 106:19; Ac 7:41

32:5
y Lev 23:2,37;
2Ki 10:20
32:6
z Nu 25:2; Ac 7:41
a ver 17-19;
1Co 10:7*
32:7
b ver 4,11
c Ge 6:11-12;
Dt 9:12
32:8
d Ex 20:4
e Ex 22:20
f 1Ki 12:28
32:9
g Ex 33:3,5; 34:9;
Isa 48:4; Ac 7:51
32:10
h Nu 14:12; Dt 9:14
32:11
i Dt 9:18 j Dt 9:26

baths.[k] This will be a sign[l] between me and you for the generations to come, so you may know that I am the LORD, who makes you holy.[a][m]

14 " 'Observe the Sabbath, because it is holy to you. Anyone who desecrates it must be put to death;[n] whoever does any work on that day must be cut off from his people. 15 For six days, work[o] is to be done, but the seventh day is a Sabbath of rest,[p] holy to the LORD. Whoever does any work on the Sabbath day must be put to death. 16 The Israelites are to observe the Sabbath, celebrating it for the generations to come as a lasting covenant. 17 It will be a sign[q] between me and the Israelites forever, for in six days the LORD made the heavens and the earth, and on the seventh day he abstained from work and rested.'[r] "

18 When the LORD finished speaking to Moses on Mount Sinai, he gave him the two tablets of the Testimony, the tablets of stone[s] inscribed by the finger of God.[t]

The Golden Calf

32 When the people saw that Moses was so long in coming down from the mountain,[u] they gathered around Aaron and said, "Come, make us gods[b] who will go before us. As for this fellow Moses who brought us up out of Egypt, we don't know what has happened to him."[v]

2 Aaron answered them, "Take off the gold earrings[w] that your wives, your sons and your daughters are wearing, and bring them to me." 3 So all the people took off their earrings and brought them to Aaron. 4 He took what they handed him and made it into an idol cast in the shape of a calf,[x] fashioning it with a tool. Then they said, "These are your gods,[c] O Israel, who brought you up out of Egypt."

5 When Aaron saw this, he built an altar in front of the calf and announced, "Tomorrow there will be a festival[y] to the LORD." 6 So the next day the people rose early and sacrificed burnt offerings and presented fellowship offerings.[d][z] Afterward they sat down to eat and drink and got up to indulge in revelry.[a]

7 Then the LORD said to Moses, "Go down, because your people, whom you brought up out of Egypt,[b] have become corrupt.[c] 8 They have been quick to turn away from what I commanded them and have made themselves an idol[d] cast in the shape of a calf. They have bowed down to it and sacrificed[e] to it and have said, 'These are your gods, O Israel, who brought you up out of Egypt.'[f]

9 "I have seen these people," the LORD said to Moses, "and they are a stiff-necked[g] people. 10 Now leave me alone so that my anger may burn against them and that I may destroy them. Then I will make you into a great nation."[h]

11 But Moses sought the favor[i] of the LORD his God. "O LORD," he said, "why should your anger burn against your people, whom you brought out of Egypt with great power and a mighty hand?[j] 12 Why should the Egyptians say, 'It was with evil intent that he brought them out, to kill them in the mountains and to wipe them

---

a 13 Or who sanctifies you; or who sets you apart as holy   b 1 Or a god; also in verses 23 and 31
c 4 Or This is your god; also in verse 8   d 6 Traditionally peace offerings

---

Exodus 31:12–18

📖 The Old Testament Sabbath commandments were grounded in two activities of God: creation and the exodus. In their redemption from bondage in Egypt, God's people were enabled to join him in the rest established in creation. By their pattern of work and rest they exhibited God's image. To find God's rest means to fulfill our place as human beings in the created order. We see here what Jesus meant when he said, "The Sabbath was made for man, not man for the Sabbath" (Mark 2:27). Sabbath-keeping benefits us, helping us to better understand who God is.

💻 As St. Augustine noted long ago, rest comes to realization only as wanderers find it in God. True rest involves ceasing from our own work as God did at creation, rightly relating to God through faith and obedi-

ence to his Word. Only by joining him in his creation rest and humbling ourselves in light of his Son's atoning sacrifice can we experience the Sabbath celebration reserved for God's people. See Hebrews 4:1–13.

Exodus 32:1–33:6

📖 The ancients saw in an idol an earthly representation of a god—not the god itself. It was widely thought that calves or bulls functioned as pedestals for the gods. The Israelites likely viewed the calf as the place above which God was enthroned, thus ensuring his presence with them. By constructing the calf and reciting what God had spoken when introducing the Ten Commandments (cf. 32:4 with 20:2), the Israelites weren't only breaking the second commandment (20:4–5) but fashioning a new, false religion according to the very pattern God had earlier revealed to them.

off the face of the earth'?[k] Turn from your fierce anger; relent and do not bring disaster on your people. [13]Remember[l] your servants Abraham, Isaac and Israel, to whom you swore by your own self:[m] 'I will make your descendants as numerous as the stars[n] in the sky and I will give your descendants all this land[o] I promised them, and it will be their inheritance forever.' " [14]Then the LORD relented[p] and did not bring on his people the disaster he had threatened.

[15]Moses turned and went down the mountain with the two tablets of the Testimony[q] in his hands.[r] They were inscribed on both sides, front and back. [16]The tablets were the work of God; the writing was the writing of God, engraved on the tablets.[s]

[17]When Joshua heard the noise of the people shouting, he said to Moses, "There is the sound of war in the camp."

[18]Moses replied:

> "It is not the sound of victory,
>   it is not the sound of defeat;
>   it is the sound of singing that I hear."

[19]When Moses approached the camp and saw the calf[t] and the dancing, his anger burned and he threw the tablets out of his hands, breaking them to pieces[u] at the foot of the mountain. [20]And he took the calf they had made and burned it in the fire; then he ground it to powder, scattered it on the water[v] and made the Israelites drink it.

[21]He said to Aaron, "What did these people do to you, that you led them into such great sin?"

[22]"Do not be angry, my lord," Aaron answered. "You know how prone these people are to evil.[w] [23]They said to me, 'Make us gods who will go before us. As for this fellow Moses who brought us up out of Egypt, we don't know what has happened to him.'[x] [24]So I told them, 'Whoever has any gold jewelry, take it off.' Then they gave me the gold, and I threw it into the fire, and out came this calf!"[y]

[25]Moses saw that the people were running wild and that Aaron had let them get out of control and so become a laughingstock to their enemies. [26]So he stood at the entrance to the camp and said, "Whoever is for the LORD, come to me." And all the Levites rallied to him.

[27]Then he said to them, "This is what the LORD, the God of Israel, says: 'Each man strap a sword to his side. Go back and forth through the camp from one end to the other, each killing his brother and friend and neighbor.' "[z] [28]The Levites did as Moses commanded, and that day about three thousand of the people died. [29]Then Moses said, "You have been set apart to the LORD today, for you were against your own sons and brothers, and he has blessed you this day."

[30]The next day Moses said to the people, "You have committed a great sin.[a] But now I will go up to the LORD; perhaps I can make atonement[b] for your sin."

[31]So Moses went back to the LORD and said, "Oh, what a great sin these people have committed![c] They have made themselves gods of gold.[d] [32]But now, please forgive their sin—but if not, then blot me[e] out of the book[f] you have written."

[33]The LORD replied to Moses, "Whoever has sinned against me I will blot out[g] of my book. [34]Now go, lead the people to the place[h] I spoke of, and my angel[i] will go before you. However, when the time comes for me to punish,[j] I will punish them for their sin."

[35]And the LORD struck the people with a plague because of what they did with the calf[k] Aaron had made.

Cross references:

32:12
[k] Nu 14:13-16; Dt 9:28
32:13
[l] Ex 2:24
[m] Ge 22:16; Heb 6:13
[n] Ge 15:5; 26:4
[o] Ge 12:7
32:14
[p] 2Sa 24:16; Ps 106:45
32:15
[q] Ex 31:18 [r] Dt 9:15
32:16
[s] Ex 31:18
32:19
[t] Dt 9:16 [u] Dt 9:17
32:20
[v] Dt 9:21
32:22
[w] Dt 9:24
32:23
[x] ver 1
32:24
[y] ver 4
32:27
[z] Nu 25:3,5; Dt 33:9
32:30
[a] 1Sa 12:20
[b] Lev 1:4; Nu 25:13
32:31
[c] Dt 9:18
[d] Ex 20:23
32:32
[e] Ro 9:3 [f] Ps 69:28; Da 12:1; Php 4:3; Rev 3:5; 21:27
32:33
[g] Dt 29:20; Ps 9:5
32:34
[h] Ex 3:17 [i] Ex 23:20
[j] Dt 32:35; Ps 99:8; Ro 2:5-6
32:35
[k] ver 4

For Israel prior to the tabernacle rituals and regulations, the means of atoning for sin was still in the future. But for us, the church, the complete, once-for-all atonement for sin has already happened. The means of atonement Moses offered (32:30,32)—substituting himself for his people—was precisely what Christ was able to do for us on the cross. Hebrews 10:26–29 reminds us that no other sacrifice is available for someone who has rejected Christ's accomplishment. That is a pretty serious reality. Enough to make you want to enlighten the uninformed?

33

Then the LORD said to Moses, "Leave this place, you and the people you brought up out of Egypt, and go up to the land I promised on oath to Abraham, Isaac and Jacob, saying, 'I will give it to your descendants.'[l] [2]I will send an angel[m] before you and drive out the Canaanites, Amorites, Hittites, Perizzites, Hivites and Jebusites.[n] [3]Go up to the land flowing with milk and honey.[o] But I will not go with you, because you are a stiff-necked[p] people and I might destroy[q] you on the way."

[4]When the people heard these distressing words, they began to mourn[r] and no one put on any ornaments. [5]For the LORD had said to Moses, "Tell the Israelites, 'You are a stiff-necked people. If I were to go with you even for a moment, I might destroy you. Now take off your ornaments and I will decide what to do with you.' " [6]So the Israelites stripped off their ornaments at Mount Horeb.

The Tent of Meeting

[7]Now Moses used to take a tent and pitch it outside the camp some distance away, calling it the "tent of meeting."[s] Anyone inquiring of the LORD would go to the tent of meeting outside the camp. [8]And whenever Moses went out to the tent, all the people rose and stood at the entrances to their tents,[t] watching Moses until he entered the tent. [9]As Moses went into the tent, the pillar of cloud[u] would come down and stay at the entrance, while the LORD spoke[v] with Moses. [10]Whenever the people saw the pillar of cloud standing at the entrance to the tent, they all stood and worshiped, each at the entrance to his tent. [11]The LORD would speak to Moses face to face,[w] as a man speaks with his friend. Then Moses would return to the camp, but his young aide Joshua son of Nun did not leave the tent.

Moses and the Glory of the LORD

[12]Moses said to the LORD, "You have been telling me, 'Lead these people,'[x] but you have not let me know whom you will send with me. You have said, 'I know you by name[y] and you have found favor with me.' [13]If you are pleased with me, teach me your ways[z] so I may know you and continue to find favor with you. Remember that this nation is your people."[a]

[14]The LORD replied, "My Presence[b] will go with you, and I will give you rest."[c]

[15]Then Moses said to him, "If your Presence does not go with us, do not send us up from here. [16]How will anyone know that you are pleased with me and with your people unless you go with us?[d] What else will distinguish me and your people from all the other people on the face of the earth?"[e]

Side references

33:1
l Ge 12:7
33:2
m Ex 32:34
n Ex 23:27-31; Jos 24:11
33:3
o Ex 3:8 p Ex 32:9
q Ex 32:10
33:4
r Nu 14:39

33:7
s Ex 29:42-43

33:8
t Nu 16:27
33:9
u Ex 13:21
v Ex 31:18; Ps 99:7

33:11
w Nu 12:8; Dt 34:10

33:12
x Ex 3:10 y ver 17; Jn 10:14-15; 2Ti 2:19

33:13
z Ps 25:4; 86:11; 119:33 a Ex 34:9; Dt 9:26,29
33:14
b Isa 63:9
c Jos 21:44; 22:4
33:16
d Nu 14:14
e Ex 34:10

Exodus 33:7–11

This tent was different from the tabernacle, or "Tent of Meeting" (cf. 27:21), with its ark and other furniture. Unlike the tabernacle, this temporary "tent of meeting" was outside the camp. The people could go there to consult the Lord, and Moses could meet there with him, until the more permanent structure was constructed. The verbs in verse 7 show that Moses customarily and regularly pitched this tent.

In the tent the Lord spoke to Moses "face to face." This is an expression of intimacy, not to be understood literally (see v. 20 and "There and Then" for 24:1–18). It's striking, though, that whenever Moses entered the tent, the people had to remain at a respectful distance and engage in worship. What a contrast to our situation today, in which we can approach God on a heart-to-heart basis anytime and anywhere. In fact, we carry God's presence within us in the form of the indwelling Holy Spirit. How often do you stop to appreciate this amazing reality?

Exodus 33:12–23

As the time approached for Moses to give up his leadership position, he became concerned about the identity of the companion God had promised him (32:34; 33:2–3). He believed that no mere angel could substitute for God's presence. And he knew that God's presence was essential to Israel's testimony, in order to keep his people distinct from the rest of the world. That was the response God was waiting for, but Moses sought one more thing: God's "glory." The Lord complied, but since no human can see his face, he promised that Moses could see his "back"—the afterglow of his radiant glory, after he had passed by.

It's encouraging to note Moses' spiritual growth. When he first met the Lord at the burning bush, he had been "afraid to look at God" (3:6) and inquired concerning his name (3:13). Now he asked to be shown God's glory unveiled. God's response was that he had asked too much—that he had to be content with the fuller proclamation of God's name (33:19; 34:5–7). Let's be bold enough to pray with Moses, "Teach me your ways so I may know you and continue to find favor with you . . . Show me your glory."

17And the LORD said to Moses, "I will do the very thing you have asked, because I am pleased with you and I know you by name."

18Then Moses said, "Now show me your glory."

19And the LORD said, "I will cause all my goodness to pass in front of you, and I will proclaim my name, the LORD, in your presence. I will have mercy on whom I will have mercy, and I will have compassion on whom I will have compassion.[f] 20But," he said, "you cannot see my face, for no one may see[g] me and live."

21Then the LORD said, "There is a place near me where you may stand on a rock. 22When my glory passes by, I will put you in a cleft in the rock and cover you with my hand[h] until I have passed by. 23Then I will remove my hand and you will see my back; but my face must not be seen."

The New Stone Tablets

34 The LORD said to Moses, "Chisel out two stone tablets like the first ones, and I will write on them the words that were on the first tablets,[i] which you broke.[j] 2Be ready in the morning, and then come up on Mount Sinai.[k] Present yourself to me there on top of the mountain. 3No one is to come with you or be seen anywhere on the mountain;[l] not even the flocks and herds may graze in front of the mountain."

4So Moses chiseled out two stone tablets like the first ones and went up Mount Sinai early in the morning, as the LORD had commanded him; and he carried the two stone tablets in his hands. 5Then the LORD came down in the cloud and stood there with him and proclaimed his name, the LORD.[m] 6And he passed in front of Moses, proclaiming, "The LORD, the LORD, the compassionate[n] and gracious God, slow to anger,[o] abounding in love[p] and faithfulness,[q] 7maintaining love to thousands,[r] and forgiving wickedness, rebellion and sin.[s] Yet he does not leave the guilty unpunished;[t] he punishes the children and their children for the sin of the fathers to the third and fourth generation."

8Moses bowed to the ground at once and worshiped. 9"O Lord, if I have found favor in your eyes," he said, "then let the Lord go with us.[u] Although this is a stiff-necked people, forgive our wickedness and our sin, and take us as your inheritance."[v]

10Then the LORD said: "I am making a covenant[w] with you. Before all your people I will do wonders never before done in any nation in all the world.[x] The people you live among will see how awesome is the work that I, the LORD, will do for you. 11Obey what I command you today. I will drive out before you the Amorites, Canaanites, Hittites, Perizzites, Hivites and Jebusites.[y] 12Be careful not to make a treaty with those who live in the land where you are going, or they will be a snare[z] among you. 13Break down their altars, smash their sacred stones and cut down their Asherah poles.[a a] 14Do not worship any other god,[b] for the LORD, whose name is Jealous, is a jealous God.[c]

15"Be careful not to make a treaty with those who live in the land; for when they prostitute[d] themselves to their gods and sacrifice to them, they will invite you and you will eat their sacrifices.[e] 16And when you choose some of their daughters as

a 13 That is, symbols of the goddess Asherah

33:19
f Ro 9:15*
33:20
g Ge 32:30; Isa 6:5

33:22
h Ps 91:4

34:1
i Dt 10:2,4
j Ex 32:19
34:2
k Ex 19:11
34:3
l Ex 19:12-13,21

34:5
m Ex 33:19
34:6
n Ps 86:15
o Nu 14:18; Ro 2:4
p Ne 9:17;
Ps 103:8; Joel 2:13
q Ps 108:4
34:7
r Ex 20:6
s Ps 103:3; 130:4,8;
Da 9:9; 1Jn 1:9
t Job 10:14; Na 1:3
34:9
u Ex 33:15
v Ps 33:12

34:10
w Dt 5:2-3
x Ex 33:16; Dt 4:32

34:11
y Ex 33:2
34:12
z Ex 23:32-33

34:13
a Ex 23:24; Dt 12:3;
2Ki 18:4
34:14
b Ex 20:3 *c* Ex 20:5;
Dt 4:24
34:15
d Jdg 2:17
e Nu 25:2; 1Co 8:4

Exodus 34:1–28

This revelation was indeed God's response to Moses' request in 33:18: "Now show me your glory." But the Lord's revelation of his *character* also was an answer to Moses' prayer in 33:13: "Teach me your ways so I may know you." This experience humbled Moses and caused him to once more plead for God's grace to be given to his people, even though they were stubborn and wicked. God's statement, "I am making a covenant with you," doesn't mean he was instituting a second covenant in verses 10–27. This passage is best seen as a renewing of

the original covenant after the events of Exodus 32–33.

Do you sometimes find yourself compelled to pray as your heart breaks over the sins and needs of others? We read in Hebrews 7:25 that Christ "always lives to intercede" for his people. Moses did the same (34:9; cf. 32:11–14,30–34; 33:12–17; Deut. 9:18–29). Like Christ's, his intercession was continual and relentless. We don't know what form Christ's heavenly intercession takes, but we do know that it's perfectly effective. How does this knowledge affect your prayer life?

34:16
f Dt 7:3 g 1Ki 11:4

34:17
h Ex 32:8

34:18
i Ex 12:17
j Ex 12:15 k Ex 12:2

34:19
l Ex 13:2

34:20
m Ex 13:13,15
n Ex 23:15;
Dt 16:16

34:21
o Ex 20:9; Lk 13:14

34:22
p Ex 23:16
34:23
q Ex 23:14
34:24
r Ex 23:28; 33:2;
Ps 78:55

34:25
s Ex 23:18
t Ex 12:8,10

34:26
u Ex 23:19
34:27
v Ex 17:14; 24:4

34:28
w Ge 7:4; Ex 24:18;
Mt 4:2 x ver 1;
Ex 31:18 y Dt 4:13;
10:4

34:29
z Ex 32:15
a Ps 34:5; Mt 17:2;
2Co 3:7,13

34:32
b Ex 24:3

34:33
c 2Co 3:13

wives f for your sons and those daughters prostitute themselves to their gods, g they will lead your sons to do the same.

17 "Do not make cast idols. h

18 "Celebrate the Feast of Unleavened Bread. i For seven days eat bread made without yeast, j as I commanded you. Do this at the appointed time in the month of Abib, k for in that month you came out of Egypt.

19 "The first offspring l of every womb belongs to me, including all the firstborn males of your livestock, whether from herd or flock. 20 Redeem the firstborn donkey with a lamb, but if you do not redeem it, break its neck. m Redeem all your firstborn sons.

"No one is to appear before me empty-handed. n

21 "Six days you shall labor, but on the seventh day you shall rest; o even during the plowing season and harvest you must rest.

22 "Celebrate the Feast of Weeks with the firstfruits of the wheat harvest, and the Feast of Ingathering p at the turn of the year. a 23 Three times q a year all your men are to appear before the Sovereign LORD, the God of Israel. 24 I will drive out nations r before you and enlarge your territory, and no one will covet your land when you go up three times each year to appear before the LORD your God.

25 "Do not offer the blood of a sacrifice to me along with anything containing yeast, s and do not let any of the sacrifice from the Passover Feast remain until morning. t

26 "Bring the best of the firstfruits of your soil to the house of the LORD your God.

"Do not cook a young goat in its mother's milk." u

27 Then the LORD said to Moses, "Write v down these words, for in accordance with these words I have made a covenant with you and with Israel." 28 Moses was there with the LORD forty days and forty nights w without eating bread or drinking water. And he wrote on the tablets x the words of the covenant—the Ten Commandments. y

The Radiant Face of Moses

29 When Moses came down from Mount Sinai with the two tablets of the Testimony in his hands, z he was not aware that his face was radiant a because he had spoken with the LORD. 30 When Aaron and all the Israelites saw Moses, his face was radiant, and they were afraid to come near him. 31 But Moses called to them; so Aaron and all the leaders of the community came back to him, and he spoke to them. 32 Afterward all the Israelites came near him, and he gave them all the commands b the LORD had given him on Mount Sinai.

33 When Moses finished speaking to them, he put a veil c over his face. 34 But whenever he entered the LORD's presence to speak with him, he removed the veil until he came out. And when he came out and told the Israelites what he had been

a 22 That is, in the fall

Exodus 34:29–35

📖 Once again, after 40 days on Mount Sinai, Moses returned with the Ten Commandments (cf. 24:18; 32:15–19). This time, though, he entered the camp filled with radiance, not wrath. Just as the people couldn't enter the Most Holy Place to behold God's glory, they couldn't look upon the glory of God reflected on Moses' face. He had become the embodiment, or image, of the coming tabernacle.

Moses saw and reflected God's glory imperfectly. The intimacy he enjoyed with God was unique in the Old Testament, but the *fullness* of God's glory lives only in Christ. Note Hebrews 1:3: "The Son is the radiance of God's glory." Christ reflected God's glory to his people

completely because he *fully* contained the Father's glory. That fullness is best expressed in Jesus' own words, "I and the Father are one" (John 10:30).

📖 In 2 Corinthians 3:7–18 Paul pointed out why Moses wore the veil: so the Israelites wouldn't see the glory *as it faded away*. Moses' fading glory was like that of the law (vv. 14–16)—real but temporary. The refusal of the Jews of Paul's day to observe the law's fading glory was due to the "veil" over their hearts that kept them from seeing that law for what it was. We, like Moses, both see and reflect God's glory—with "unveiled faces." But the glory we reflect won't fade away because, unlike Moses, we are "being transformed into [Christ's] likeness with ever-increasing glory."

commanded, 35they saw that his face was radiant. Then Moses would put the veil back over his face until he went in to speak with the LORD.

Sabbath Regulations

35 Moses assembled the whole Israelite community and said to them, "These are the things the LORD has commanded[d] you to do: 2For six days, work is to be done, but the seventh day shall be your holy day, a Sabbath[e] of rest to the LORD. Whoever does any work on it must be put to death. 3Do not light a fire in any of your dwellings on the Sabbath day.[f]"

Materials for the Tabernacle

4Moses said to the whole Israelite community, "This is what the LORD has commanded: 5From what you have, take an offering for the LORD. Everyone who is willing is to bring to the LORD an offering of gold, silver and bronze; 6blue, purple and scarlet yarn and fine linen; goat hair; 7ram skins dyed red and hides of sea cows[a]; acacia wood; 8olive oil for the light; spices for the anointing oil and for the fragrant incense; 9and onyx stones and other gems to be mounted on the ephod and breastpiece.

10"All who are skilled among you are to come and make everything the LORD has commanded:[g] 11the tabernacle[h] with its tent and its covering, clasps, frames, crossbars, posts and bases; 12the ark[i] with its poles and the atonement cover and the curtain that shields it; 13the table[j] with its poles and all its articles and the bread of the Presence; 14the lampstand[k] that is for light with its accessories, lamps and oil for the light; 15the altar[l] of incense with its poles, the anointing oil[m] and the fragrant incense;[n] the curtain for the doorway at the entrance to the tabernacle; 16the altar[o] of burnt offering with its bronze grating, its poles and all its utensils; the bronze basin with its stand; 17the curtains of the courtyard with its posts and bases, and the

35:1
d Ex 34:32
35:2
e Ex 20:9-10; 34:21; Lev 23:3
35:3
f Ex 16:23

35:10
g Ex 31:6
35:11
h Ex 26:1-37
35:12
i Ex 25:10-22
35:13
j Ex 25:23-30; Lev 24:5-6
35:14
k Ex 25:31
35:15
l Ex 30:1-6
m Ex 30:25
n Ex 30:34-38
35:16
o Ex 27:1-8

---

a 7 That is, dugongs; also in verse 23

Exodus 35:1–3

If the tabernacle represented holy space, the Sabbath was holy time. There was no more holy spot on the face of the earth than the tabernacle on the Sabbath. We can see how important the tabernacle, and later the temple, were to Israel's identity as God's people. We also can see how devastating the destruction of the temple by the Babylonians would later be. By entering the tabernacle, Israel stepped into God's house; by keeping the Sabbath, his people entered God's rest.

Jesus Christ, in whom God's glory resides, is himself holy space or ground. But with the spread of the gospel, God's glory can now be seen in new temples everywhere—wherever individuals repent and come to

know God, wherever people gather for worship. God's sacred space is no longer restricted to one building or only embodied in his Son, as it was for a brief time 2,000 years ago. By the work of the Holy Spirit, that space has spread over the whole earth—in the form of the church, both collectively (1 Cor. 3:16–17) and individually (1 Cor. 6:19).

Exodus 35:4–29

Exodus 35:4–9 corresponds directly with 25:1–7. The first passage records God's preliminary instructions and the second the repeated directions at the time they were to be carried out. Chapters 25–40 follow a basic structure, with chapters 25–31 recording God's instructions and 35–40 the actual construction. The story of the golden calf intervenes.

35:5

GIFTS
TO GOD

The tabernacle was built with the people's voluntary gifts. These offerings were the best they had, items that reflected their lives.

Why do people give?
• Because God gives to us (John 3:16; Rom. 8:32)
• To obey God (Num. 18:25–26)
• To manage the church (Acts 6:1–6)
• To manage households (2 Sam. 16:1)
• To be accountable to God (Luke 16:1–12)
• To help others (Acts 20:25)
• To express thanks to God (Luke 19:1–10)
• To express devotion to Jesus (John 11:2)

What can you give?
Here are some examples:
• Money
• "In-kind" gifts, like food, clothing, or other material goods
• Time
• Talents or abilities
• Care for creation
• Care for people
• Management or leadership
• Prayer
• Spiritual nurture

Symbols and Ceremonies

God chose symbols and ceremonies as means for forming Israel into a faithful community. Modern projects of community development, reconciliation, and formation also will be more effective if accompanied by relevant Christian symbols and ceremonies.

Exodus 35:20—40:38 chronicles the carrying out of God's detailed directions to Moses regarding tabernacle construction. By devoting a large portion of his instruction to the creation of worship symbols, God indicated their importance for liberating and forming his people.

Bruce Bradshaw, an expert on Christian community development, reports that Western Christians engaged in community development projects tend not to see a direct spiritual component to their efforts. Traditional religious societies, in contrast, interpret everything in relation to the spiritual world. Furthermore, people from such cultures readily express the interrelationship of their world's spiritual and physical aspects through symbol and ceremony.

Symbols can aid in the process of communal reconciliation. Lisa Schirch of Eastern Mennonite University's Conflict Transformation Program helped Greek and Turkish Cypriots—traditional enemies—to act out the concept of peace together through song and dance. Some of Schirch's suggestions apply to any holistic mission project: (1) Look for shared symbols and metaphors. (2) Use common cultural features to facilitate interaction. (3) Recognize the potential force of Christian symbols and stories like foot-washing and Biblical dramas.

St. Martin's Community Church of Melbourne, Australia, and its holistic mission organization Care and Communication Concern find symbols and ceremonies foundational for their work. A St. Martin's project called "Hand Brake Turn" virtually eliminated teenage car theft in Melbourne. The project provided instruction and experience in auto body and mechanical work for former teenage thieves too poor to expect automobile ownership. St. Martin's made symbols a vital part of its mission for several reasons: (1) Symbols and ceremonies bonded new converts and the church's own children. (2) Festivals help believers maintain awareness of their pilgrim status. (3) Ceremonies of incorporation enable believers to make the radical commitment necessary for sustaining their ministry to the poor.

> The Lord's Supper or Eucharist celebrated by early Christians commemorated the Pass-over of humanity from sin to salvation through Christ's death and resurrection.

God didn't limit Israel's guidance to oral instruction. Its content was literally recorded on the bodies and dwellings of his people (Deut. 6:8ff). The festival of Passover (Ex. 12:14–20,43–49; 13:1–16; Lev. 23:4–14; Deut. 16:1–8; Ezek. 45:18–24) employed symbolic objects, stories, and actions to establish moods and motivations for living a communal life of faith. Other festivals and holy days, like Pentecost (Deut. 16:9–12), Booths (Deut. 16:13–17), the Day of Atonement (Lev. 16:1–34), and the Sabbath (Deut. 5:13–14), also used symbols for spiritual formation.

The mission of Christ's followers to make disciples of all nations involves a symbolic act of incorporation into Christ's body (Matt. 28:18–20; 1 Cor. 12:27). The Lord's Supper or Eucharist celebrated by early Christians commemorated the Pass-over of humanity from sin to salvation through Christ's death and resurrection (Matt. 26:17–29; Mark 14:16–26; Luke 22:7–20). It acknowledged God's presence in the faith community and foreshadowed his future return (1 Cor. 11:23–26). Baptism and the Eucharist brought symbols to bear on creating a community capable of witness and service in a frequently hostile world.

Consider the role symbols and ceremonies can play in any mission activity you are involved in. Consider as well your gifts in the visual and performing arts. They will help imbue projects of mercy, justice, and development with deep and abiding Christian significance.

H. Matthew Zahniser, professor emeritus of mission and world religions at Asbury Theological Seminary in Wilmore, Kentucky

curtain for the entrance to the courtyard;[p] 18 the tent pegs for the tabernacle and for
the courtyard, and their ropes; 19 the woven garments worn for ministering in the
sanctuary—both the sacred garments[q] for Aaron the priest and the garments for his
sons when they serve as priests."
20 Then the whole Israelite community withdrew from Moses' presence, 21 and everyone who was willing and whose heart moved him came and brought an offering to the LORD for the work on the Tent of Meeting, for all its service, and for the
sacred garments. 22 All who were willing, men and women alike, came and brought
gold jewelry of all kinds: brooches, earrings, rings and ornaments. They all presented their gold as a wave offering to the LORD. 23 Everyone who had blue, purple or
scarlet yarn[r] or fine linen, or goat hair, ram skins dyed red or hides of sea cows
brought them. 24 Those presenting an offering of silver or bronze brought it as an
offering to the LORD, and everyone who had acacia wood for any part of the work
brought it. 25 Every skilled woman[s] spun with her hands and brought what she had
spun—blue, purple or scarlet yarn or fine linen. 26 And all the women who were
willing and had the skill spun the goat hair. 27 The leaders[t] brought onyx stones and
other gems to be mounted on the ephod and breastpiece. 28 They also brought spices and olive oil for the light and for the anointing oil and for the fragrant incense.[u]
29 All the Israelite men and women who were willing[v] brought to the LORD freewill
offerings[w] for all the work the LORD through Moses had commanded them to do.

Bezalel and Oholiab

30 Then Moses said to the Israelites, "See, the LORD has chosen Bezalel son of Uri,
the son of Hur, of the tribe of Judah, 31 and he has filled him with the Spirit of God,
with skill, ability and knowledge in all kinds of crafts[x]— 32 to make artistic designs
for work in gold, silver and bronze, 33 to cut and set stones, to work in wood and
to engage in all kinds of artistic craftsmanship. 34 And he has given both him and
Oholiab[y] son of Ahisamach, of the tribe of Dan, the ability to teach[z] others. 35 He
has filled them with skill to do all kinds of work[a] as craftsmen, designers, embroi-
derers in blue, purple and scarlet yarn and fine linen, and weavers—all of them
36 master craftsmen and designers. 1 So Bezalel, Oholiab and every skilled
person[b] to whom the LORD has given skill and ability to know how to carry out all the work of constructing the sanctuary[c] are to do the work just as the LORD
has commanded."
2 Then Moses summoned Bezalel[d] and Oholiab[e] and every skilled person to
whom the LORD had given ability and who was willing[f] to come and do the work.
3 They received from Moses all the offerings[g] the Israelites had brought to carry out
the work of constructing the sanctuary. And the people continued to bring freewill
offerings morning after morning. 4 So all the skilled craftsmen who were doing all
the work on the sanctuary left their work 5 and said to Moses, "The people are bringing more than enough[h] for doing the work the LORD commanded to be done."
6 Then Moses gave an order and they sent this word throughout the camp: "No
man or woman is to make anything else as an offering for the sanctuary." And so

35:17 [p] Ex 27:9
35:19 [q] Ex 28:2; 31:10; 39:1
35:23 [r] 1Ch 29:8
35:25 [s] Ex 28:3
35:27 [t] 1Ch 29:6; Ezr 2:68
35:28 [u] Ex 25:6
35:29 [v] ver 21; 1Ch 29:9 [w] ver 4-9; Ex 25:1-7; 36:3; 2Ki 12:4
35:31 [x] ver 35; 2Ch 2:7,14
35:34 [y] Ex 31:6 [z] 2Ch 2:14
35:35 [a] ver 31; Ex 31:3,6; 1Ki 7:14
36:1 [b] Ex 28:3 [c] Ex 25:8
36:2 [d] Ex 31:2 [e] Ex 31:6 [f] Ex 25:2; 35:21,26; 1Ch 29:5
36:3 [g] Ex 35:29
36:5 [h] 2Ch 24:14; 31:10; 2Co 8:2-3

Verses 10–19 review what the Israelites were to make, and verses 20–29 recount the collecting of the necessary materials. The emphasis seems to have been on the willingness of the Israelites to give and the participation of both men and women.

While verse 5 directed "everyone who [was] willing" to bring an offering, verse 10 asked "all who [were] skilled" to come and work. God wants us to give of ourselves willingly, and he welcomes both our money and our time and skill. The former is easier for well-to-do Christians, but both reap untold rewards. God can use each of us in his kingdom. He may call us to a ministry of food preparation and delivery for the sick and grieving or to regular intercessory prayer. Every contribution is welcome. To what is he calling you?

Exodus 35:30—36:7

God provided Bezalel and Oholiab not only with artistic skill but also with the ability to teach others. Both would lead the army of volunteers (36:2) in doing the work necessary to complete the tabernacle and its implements. Anyone in a similar position can appreciate the huge undertaking these men oversaw. Teaching and leading volunteers remain critical ministries in the church today.

Whether from guilt over the golden calf incident or truly from hearts turned to God, the people gave until nothing else was needed. Moses ordered the offerings to stop because there was "more than enough."

36:7
i 1Ki 7:47

the people were restrained from bringing more, 7because what they already had was more*i* than enough to do all the work.

The Tabernacle

8All the skilled men among the workmen made the tabernacle with ten curtains of finely twisted linen and blue, purple and scarlet yarn, with cherubim worked into them by a skilled craftsman. 9All the curtains were the same size—twenty-eight cubits long and four cubits wide. a 10They joined five of the curtains together and did the same with the other five. 11Then they made loops of blue material along the edge of the end curtain in one set, and the same was done with the end curtain in the other set. 12They also made fifty loops on one curtain and fifty loops on the end curtain of the other set, with the loops opposite each other. 13Then they made fifty gold clasps and used them to fasten the two sets of curtains together so that the tabernacle was a unit.*j*

36:13
j ver 18

14They made curtains of goat hair for the tent over the tabernacle—eleven altogether. 15All eleven curtains were the same size—thirty cubits long and four cubits wide. b 16They joined five of the curtains into one set and the other six into another set. 17Then they made fifty loops along the edge of the end curtain in one set and also along the edge of the end curtain in the other set. 18They made fifty bronze clasps to fasten the tent together as a unit.*k* 19Then they made for the tent a covering of ram skins dyed red, and over that a covering of hides of sea cows. c

36:18
k ver 13

20They made upright frames of acacia wood for the tabernacle. 21Each frame was ten cubits long and a cubit and a half wide, d 22with two projections set parallel to each other. They made all the frames of the tabernacle in this way. 23They made twenty frames for the south side of the tabernacle 24and made forty silver bases to go under them—two bases for each frame, one under each projection. 25For the other side, the north side of the tabernacle, they made twenty frames 26and forty silver bases—two under each frame. 27They made six frames for the far end, that is, the west end of the tabernacle, 28and two frames were made for the corners of the tabernacle at the far end. 29At these two corners the frames were double from the bottom all the way to the top and fitted into a single ring; both were made alike. 30So there were eight frames and sixteen silver bases—two under each frame.

31They also made crossbars of acacia wood: five for the frames on one side of the tabernacle, 32five for those on the other side, and five for the frames on the west, at the far end of the tabernacle. 33They made the center crossbar so that it extended from end to end at the middle of the frames. 34They overlaid the frames with gold and made gold rings to hold the crossbars. They also overlaid the crossbars with gold.

a 9 That is, about 42 feet (about 12.5 meters) long and 6 feet (about 1.8 meters) wide   b 15 That is, about 45 feet (about 13.5 meters) long and 6 feet (about 1.8 meters) wide   c 19 That is, dugongs   d 21 That is, about 15 feet (about 4.5 meters) long and 2 1/4 feet (about 0.7 meter) wide

---

📖 The church is no place for grandstanders. Those skilled in any given area are to stand ready and willing to mentor others who may show promise in the same area.

Exodus 36:3–7 offers encouragement and motivation for Christians who may feel that the little they have to offer will be insignificant in view of the overwhelming needs around them. God accepts and uses every gift, in many instances to the point that a particular need is met and exceeded. As we offer our seeming trickle of resources for the kingdom cause, he pours out his abundant blessing on both the recipients and the givers.

Exodus 36:8–38

📖 In this passage the workers made the framework and coverings of the tabernacle. In the midst of a fallen world, in exile from the Garden of Eden—the original "heaven on earth"—God undertook another act of creation, a building project representing a return to pre-fall splendor. The tabernacle was laden with redemptive significance, not just because of the sacrifices and offerings within its walls, but as a piece of holy ground in a world that had lost its way.

📖 The execution of God's instructions by a skilled group of laborers is a beautiful example of coordination and cooperation. Each Christian has the option of doing his or her own thing in terms of giving and service, and God may call his children to unique opportunities. But most projects undertaken by churches or ministry organizations yield better results if they are executed with prayer, meticulous planning, fiscal responsibility, and careful coordination. What has your own experience taught you in this regard?

[35]They made the curtain[l] of blue, purple and scarlet yarn and finely twisted linen, with cherubim worked into it by a skilled craftsman. [36]They made four posts of acacia wood for it and overlaid them with gold. They made gold hooks for them and cast their four silver bases. [37]For the entrance to the tent they made a curtain of blue, purple and scarlet yarn and finely twisted linen—the work of an embroiderer;[m] [38]and they made five posts with hooks for them. They overlaid the tops of the posts and their bands with gold and made their five bases of bronze.

The Ark

37 Bezalel[n] made the ark[o] of acacia wood—two and a half cubits long, a cubit and a half wide, and a cubit and a half high.[a] [2]He overlaid it with pure gold,[p] both inside and out, and made a gold molding around it. [3]He cast four gold rings for it and fastened them to its four feet, with two rings on one side and two rings on the other. [4]Then he made poles of acacia wood and overlaid them with gold. [5]And he inserted the poles into the rings on the sides of the ark to carry it.

[6]He made the atonement cover[q] of pure gold—two and a half cubits long and a cubit and a half wide.[b] [7]Then he made two cherubim[r] out of hammered gold at the ends of the cover. [8]He made one cherub on one end and the second cherub on the other; at the two ends he made them of one piece with the cover. [9]The cherubim had their wings spread upward, overshadowing[s] the cover with them. The cherubim faced each other, looking toward the cover.[t]

The Table

[10]They[c] made the table[u] of acacia wood—two cubits long, a cubit wide, and a cubit and a half high.[d] [11]Then they overlaid it with pure gold[v] and made a gold molding around it. [12]They also made around it a rim a handbreadth[e] wide and put a gold molding on the rim. [13]They cast four gold rings for the table and fastened them to the four corners, where the four legs were. [14]The rings[w] were put close to the rim to hold the poles used in carrying the table. [15]The poles for carrying the table were made of acacia wood and were overlaid with gold. [16]And they made from pure gold the articles for the table—its plates and dishes and bowls and its pitchers for the pouring out of drink offerings.

[a] 1 That is, about 3 3/4 feet (about 1.1 meters) long and 2 1/4 feet (about 0.7 meter) wide and high
[b] 6 That is, about 3 3/4 feet (about 1.1 meters) long and 2 1/4 feet (about 0.7 meter) wide
[c] 10 Or He; also in verses 11-29   [d] 10 That is, about 3 feet (about 0.9 meter) long, 1 1/2 feet (about 0.5 meter) wide, and 2 1/4 feet (about 0.7 meter) high   [e] 12 That is, about 3 inches (about 8 centimeters)

36:35 l Ex 39:38; Mt 27:51; Lk 23:45; Heb 9:3
36:37 m Ex 27:16
37:1 n Ex 31:2 o Ex 30:6; 39:35; Dt 10:3
37:2 p ver 11,26
37:6 q Ex 26:34; 31:7; Heb 9:5
37:7 r Eze 41:18
37:9 s Heb 9:5 t Dt 10:3
37:10 u Heb 9:2
37:11 v ver 2
37:14 w ver 27

Exodus 37:1–9
While skilled workers labored on the rest of the tabernacle and its implements, Bezalel himself built the ark of the covenant according to the instructions given to Moses by God. As we read in the well-known story of Uzzah, to touch the ark—an object holy to God—meant death (2 Sam. 6:6–7; 1 Chron. 13:9–10). A person couldn't just walk up to it, pick it up, and move it as we might a basketful of laundry. A system of rings and poles was necessary to transport it.

Imagine how Bezalel felt as he constructed the most sacred object of the tabernacle—essentially the earthly throne of the great heavenly King. These few verses reflect wonderful preparation for meeting God. We as Christians can have audience with him on a regular basis. But how seriously do we take our obligation to prepare to meet him—in prayer, communion, meditation on his Word, or some other avenue? God wants us to approach him fearlessly, but not nonchalantly. Reflect on ways in which you can re-establish awed reverence for God in your own heart and life.

Exodus 37:10–16
Twelve loaves of fresh bread, symbolizing the twelve tribes of Israel, were baked each Sabbath and placed on this table. This offering was continually kept in the Holy Place. By it Israel dedicated to God the fruits of its labors, and at the same time acknowledged that all such fruit had been provided by God's blessing. Each week, when new bread was put before the Lord, the priests were allowed to eat the old bread (see Lev. 24:5–9). See also "There and Then" for 25:23–30.

In the Lord's Supper, Jesus meets his family for dinner on a regular basis, offering us "the gifts of God for the people of God." As we celebrate Holy Communion, we can take the time to reflect on the implications of this meal for our Christian lives. As we come to the Lord's "table," we not only share in Christ's sacrifice but also share an intimate meal with our brothers and sisters in him. How meaningful is this celebration in your experience?

The Lampstand

37:17
x Heb 9:2; Rev 1:12

17They made the lampstand* of pure gold and hammered it out, base and shaft; its flowerlike cups, buds and blossoms were of one piece with it. 18Six branches extended from the sides of the lampstand—three on one side and three on the other. 19Three cups shaped like almond flowers with buds and blossoms were on one branch, three on the next branch and the same for all six branches extending from the lampstand. 20And on the lampstand were four cups shaped like almond flowers with buds and blossoms. 21One bud was under the first pair of branches extending from the lampstand, a second bud under the second pair, and a third bud under the third pair—six branches in all. 22The buds and the branches were all of one piece with the lampstand, hammered out of pure gold. *y*

37:22
y ver 17; Nu 8:4
37:23
z Ex 40:4,25

23They made its seven lamps, *z* as well as its wick trimmers and trays, of pure gold. 24They made the lampstand and all its accessories from one talent*a* of pure gold.

The Altar of Incense

37:25
a Ex 30:34-36;
Lk 1:11; Heb 9:4;
Rev 8:3 b Ex 27:2;
Rev 9:13

25They made the altar of incense*a* out of acacia wood. It was square, a cubit long and a cubit wide, and two cubits high*b*—its horns*b* of one piece with it. 26They overlaid the top and all the sides and the horns with pure gold, and made a gold molding around it.

37:27
c ver 14

27They made two gold rings*c* below the molding—two on opposite sides—to hold the poles used to carry it. 28They made the poles of acacia wood and overlaid them with gold. *d*

37:28
d Ex 25:13
37:29
e Ex 31:11
f Ex 30:1,25; 39:38

29They also made the sacred anointing oil*e* and the pure, fragrant incense*f*—the work of a perfumer.

The Altar of Burnt Offering

38 They*c* built the altar of burnt offering of acacia wood, three cubits*d* high; it was square, five cubits long and five cubits wide. *e* 2They made a horn at each of the four corners, so that the horns and the altar were of one piece, and they overlaid the altar with bronze. *g* 3They made all its utensils*h* of bronze—its pots, shovels, sprinkling bowls, meat forks and firepans. 4They made a grating for the altar, a

38:2
g 2Ch 1:5
38:3
h Ex 31:9

a 24 That is, about 75 pounds (about 34 kilograms)   *b 25* That is, about 1 1/2 feet (about 0.5 meter) long and wide, and about 3 feet (about 0.9 meter) high   *c 1* Or *He*; also in verses 2-9   *d 1* That is, about 4 1/2 feet (about 1.3 meters)   *e 1* That is, about 7 1/2 feet (about 2.3 meters) long and wide

---

Exodus 37:17–24

That the lampstand and its lamps were surrounded by mystery (see "There and Then" for 25:31–40) may have been precisely the point—God may not have wanted to reveal what they represented. The bottom line was that the lampstand was made and the light was to be kept burning. It was possible that the mystery would be further revealed as Israel continued to obey God's command. But for the time being, the instructions were straightforward: "See that you make them according to the pattern shown you on the mountain" (25:40).

The lampstand, with its budding branches, may remind readers of one of Jesus' well-known "I am" statements in John: "I am the vine; you are the branches. If [you remain] in me and I in [you, you] will bear much fruit; apart from me you can do nothing" (John 15:5). Similarly, its continuous light may call to mind another of Jesus' statements: "I am the light of the world. Whoever follows me will never walk in darkness, but will have the light of life" (John 8:12). Why not take the time to thank Jesus today for who he is!

Exodus 37:25–29

The altar of incense was located in the Holy Place just in front of the curtain leading to the Most Holy Place and the ark of the covenant (see also 30:1–10). What purpose did the incense serve? Did it counter the smell of dead animals permeating the tabernacle? Perhaps the placement of the altar immediately between the priest and the Most Holy Place indicated that the incense performed a protective function: Its smoke concealed the atonement cover from the priest so that he wouldn't die (cf. Lev. 16:11–13). This was a barrier the high priest crossed only once each year on the Day of Atonement (30:10).

Our very lives are a sweet-smelling incense, wafting upward toward God and saturating the world with his presence and message. In Paul's words in 2 Corinthians 2:14–16, "Thanks be to God, who . . . through us spreads everywhere the fragrance of the knowledge of him. For we are to God the aroma of Christ among those who are being saved and those who are perishing. To the one we are the smell of death; to the other, the fragrance of life." Are you letting God spread this life-giving fragrance through you to others—regardless of whether they receive or reject the Good News?

bronze network, to be under its ledge, halfway up the altar. ⁵They cast bronze rings to hold the poles for the four corners of the bronze grating. ⁶They made the poles of acacia wood and overlaid them with bronze. ⁷They inserted the poles into the rings so they would be on the sides of the altar for carrying it. They made it hollow, out of boards.

Basin for Washing

⁸They made the bronze basin ⁱ and its bronze stand from the mirrors of the women ʲ who served at the entrance to the Tent of Meeting.

The Courtyard

⁹Next they made the courtyard. The south side was a hundred cubits ᵃ long and had curtains of finely twisted linen, ¹⁰with twenty posts and twenty bronze bases, and with silver hooks and bands on the posts. ¹¹The north side was also a hundred cubits long and had twenty posts and twenty bronze bases, with silver hooks and bands on the posts.

¹²The west end was fifty cubits ᵇ wide and had curtains, with ten posts and ten bases, with silver hooks and bands on the posts. ¹³The east end, toward the sunrise, was also fifty cubits wide. ¹⁴Curtains fifteen cubits ᶜ long were on one side of the entrance, with three posts and three bases, ¹⁵and curtains fifteen cubits long were on the other side of the entrance to the courtyard, with three posts and three bases. ¹⁶All the curtains around the courtyard were of finely twisted linen. ¹⁷The bases for the posts were bronze. The hooks and bands on the posts were silver, and their tops were overlaid with silver; so all the posts of the courtyard had silver bands.

ᵃ 9 That is, about 150 feet (about 46 meters)   ᵇ 12 That is, about 75 feet (about 23 meters)
ᶜ 14 That is, about 22 1/2 feet (about 6.9 meters)

38:8
ⁱ Ex 30:18; 40:7
ʲ Dt 23:17;
1Sa 2:22; 1Ki 14:24

Exodus 38:1–7

🔲 The worlds of Biblical study and archaeology come together with respect to altars. The Israelites' altar of burnt offering from the tabernacle hasn't been found, but others like it have been. A horned altar was discovered in Tel Dan in 1974. An altar located in Arad not only has horns but also is five cubits square, like the one here. Another horned altar was found in Beersheba. The presence of horned altars in antiquity is thus well established, suggesting the authenticity of the one described here. See also "There and Then" for 27:1–8.

🔲 In contrast to the ornate Israelite altar of burnt offering, Jesus' "old rugged cross" was rude indeed. And yet it was upon this splintery crossbeam that the Son of God made the ultimate sacrifice in our stead, doing away forever with the cumbersome and repetitive Jewish sacrificial system. The writer to the Hebrews concluded that the blood of Christ's sacrifice has opened up a "new and living way" for us to approach God—with the awesome benefit that we have been cleansed "from a guilty conscience" (Heb. 10:19–22).

Exodus 38:8

🔲 This information byte about the basin isn't found in the passage's counterpart in 30:17–21. Mirrors in the ancient world weren't made of glass but of polished bronze. Hence, this verse explains the source of the bronze. But who were these women and in what capacity did they serve? Perhaps they were greeters or helped direct the people assembled in what was undoubtedly a noisy and bustling place. The closest analogy in our experience may be that of someone collecting

tickets; handing out programs; and/or offering directions for a concert, sports event, or other public occasion.

🔲 The lack of detail in this passage can remind us that ultimately we serve God alone. What we do in ministry may never receive the notice or praise of others, but that doesn't make it less meaningful to our Master or to the work of the kingdom. For acts great and small, all believers can look forward to hearing, "Well done, good and faithful servant" (cf. Matt. 25:21,23). What kinds of service are you offering your Lord?

Exodus 38:9–20

🔲 Ancient Egypt was known as the center for trading linen. It came in many grades and textures, as evidenced by the different Hebrew words for this cloth. God didn't ask the Israelites to use materials that would have required traveling long distances or become a hardship to acquire. He asked them to donate materials for his tabernacle from the items they had received as bounty when leaving Egypt (12:35–36).

🔲 It's interesting to compare this passage with 27:9–19. In that earlier section God gave Moses the blueprint for the tabernacle. Here we read about the actual building. Many of these parallel passages are nearly identical, but with the verbs in the later section primarily in the past rather than the future tense and the topics arranged in a different order. Such repetition was common in ancient literature and was intended to fix the details in the reader's or listener's mind. Do you have a strategy—such as a Scripture-reading or memorization plan—for riveting and reinforcing God's Word in your own heart and mind?

38:20
k Ex 35:18

[18]The curtain for the entrance to the courtyard was of blue, purple and scarlet yarn and finely twisted linen—the work of an embroiderer. It was twenty cubits[a] long and, like the curtains of the courtyard, five cubits[b] high, [19]with four posts and four bronze bases. Their hooks and bands were silver, and their tops were overlaid with silver. [20]All the tent pegs[k] of the tabernacle and of the surrounding courtyard were bronze.

The Materials Used

38:21
l Nu 1:50,53; 8:24;
9:15; 10:11; 17:7;
1Ch 23:32;
2Ch 24:6; Ac 7:44;
Rev 15:5
m Nu 4:28,33
38:22
n Ex 31:2
38:23
o Ex 31:6
38:24
p Ex 30:16
18:16
Lev 27:25; Nu 3:47;
38:25
r Ex 30:12
38:26
s Ex 30:12
t Ex 30:13
u Ex 30:14
v Ex 12:37; Nu 1:46
38:27
w Ex 26:19

[21]These are the amounts of the materials used for the tabernacle, the tabernacle of the Testimony,[l] which were recorded at Moses' command by the Levites under the direction of Ithamar[m] son of Aaron, the priest. [22](Bezalel[n] son of Uri, the son of Hur, of the tribe of Judah, made everything the LORD commanded Moses; [23]with him was Oholiab[o] son of Ahisamach, of the tribe of Dan—a craftsman and designer, and an embroiderer in blue, purple and scarlet yarn and fine linen.) [24]The total amount of the gold from the wave offering used for all the work on the sanctuary[p] was 29 talents and 730 shekels,[c] according to the sanctuary shekel.[q]

[25]The silver obtained from those of the community who were counted in the census[r] was 100 talents and 1,775 shekels,[d] according to the sanctuary shekel— [26]one beka per person,[s] that is, half a shekel,[e] according to the sanctuary shekel,[t] from everyone who had crossed over to those counted, twenty years old or more,[u] a total of 603,550 men.[v] [27]The 100 talents[f] of silver were used to cast the bases[w] for the sanctuary and for the curtain—100 bases from the 100 talents, one talent for each base. [28]They used the 1,775 shekels[g] to make the hooks for the posts, to overlay the tops of the posts, and to make their bands.

[29]The bronze from the wave offering was 70 talents and 2,400 shekels.[h] [30]They used it to make the bases for the entrance to the Tent of Meeting, the bronze altar with its bronze grating and all its utensils, [31]the bases for the surrounding courtyard and those for its entrance and all the tent pegs for the tabernacle and those for the surrounding courtyard.

The Priestly Garments

39:1
x Ex 35:23
y Ex 35:19 z ver 41;
Ex 28:2

39 From the blue, purple and scarlet yarn[x] they made woven garments for ministering in the sanctuary.[y] They also made sacred garments[z] for Aaron, as the LORD commanded Moses.

a 18 That is, about 30 feet (about 9 meters)   b 18 That is, about 7 1/2 feet (about 2.3 meters)   c 24 The weight of the gold was a little over one ton (about 1 metric ton).   d 25 The weight of the silver was a little over 3 3/4 tons (about 3.4 metric tons).   e 26 That is, about 1/5 ounce (about 5.5 grams)   f 27 That is, about 3 3/4 tons (about 3.4 metric tons)   g 28 That is, about 45 pounds (about 20 kilograms)   h 29 The weight of the bronze was about 2 1/2 tons (about 2.4 metric tons).

Exodus 38:21–31

We have here a list not only of the materials used but also of their weights. To put the matter in perspective, the total weight in precious metals the Israelites carried out of Egypt was about 15,000 pounds. This may seem like an excessively heavy amount in the abstract, but it comes to only approximately .025 pounds for every adult male—pocket change.

It's difficult for us today to visualize the complexity of the tabernacle combined with its portability. When we think of other nomadic peoples, such as desert Bedouins or 19th-century Native Americans, we picture small, lightweight tents that were packed and moved with little effort and at times on very short notice. Precisely how the tabernacle and its furnishings were moved from place to place isn't explained in the Exodus narrative.

A little in God's hands truly does become a lot! The 15,000 pounds of precious metals needed for God's tabernacle could indeed have been gleaned through a

gathering of pennies, nickels, dimes, and quarters—small change many of us wouldn't bother to stoop down and pick up from the sidewalk. Even the seemingly insignificant offerings of church school children, carefully collected and enthusiastically saved for a period of months, can provide encouragement to the recipients beyond their monetary value. To what organization could you and your family make a point of regularly contributing pocket change?

Exodus 39:1

By being decked out with the same blue, purple, and scarlet yarn used for the tabernacle itself (26:1), the priest became the focus of God's presence for God's people—a mini-tabernacle, as it were. We hesitate to extend the analogy to say that God's Spirit resided "in" the priest as the priest did in the Most Holy Place. These garments, rather, reflected the holiness of the place in which the priests were called to minister. How else would we expect them to dress? In everyday clothes? Out of the question!

The Ephod

2They[a] made the ephod of gold, and of blue, purple and scarlet yarn, and of finely twisted linen. 3They hammered out thin sheets of gold and cut strands to be worked into the blue, purple and scarlet yarn and fine linen—the work of a skilled craftsman. 4They made shoulder pieces for the ephod, which were attached to two of its corners, so it could be fastened. 5Its skillfully woven waistband was like it—of one piece with the ephod and made with gold, and with blue, purple and scarlet yarn, and with finely twisted linen, as the LORD commanded Moses.

6They mounted the onyx stones in gold filigree settings and engraved them like a seal with the names of the sons of Israel. 7Then they fastened them on the shoulder pieces of the ephod as memorial[a] stones for the sons of Israel, as the LORD commanded Moses.

39:7
a Lev 24:7; Jos 4:7

The Breastpiece

8They fashioned the breastpiece[b]—the work of a skilled craftsman. They made it like the ephod: of gold, and of blue, purple and scarlet yarn, and of finely twisted linen. 9It was square—a span[b] long and a span wide—and folded double. 10Then they mounted four rows of precious stones on it. In the first row there was a ruby, a topaz and a beryl; 11in the second row a turquoise, a sapphire[c] and an emerald; 12in the third row a jacinth, an agate and an amethyst; 13in the fourth row a chrysolite, an onyx and a jasper.[d] They were mounted in gold filigree settings. 14There were twelve stones, one for each of the names of the sons of Israel, each engraved like a seal with the name of one of the twelve tribes.[c]

39:8
b Lev 8:8

39:14
c Rev 21:12

15For the breastpiece they made braided chains of pure gold, like a rope. 16They made two gold filigree settings and two gold rings, and fastened the rings to two of the corners of the breastpiece. 17They fastened the two gold chains to the rings at the corners of the breastpiece, 18and the other ends of the chains to the two settings, attaching them to the shoulder pieces of the ephod at the front. 19They made two gold rings and attached them to the other two corners of the breastpiece on the inside

a 2 Or He; also in verses 7, 8 and 22   b 9 That is, about 9 inches (about 22 centimeters)
c 11 Or lapis lazuli   d 13 The precise identification of some of these precious stones is uncertain.

📖 Christians might not want to "dress for success" or "dress to impress" for worship services, but it's appropriate to give God our best at all times. This may include presenting ourselves before him for worship in our "Sunday best": wide awake, well-groomed, and with our hearts prepared to stand in his presence and offer our lives as living sacrifices to him (cf. Rom. 12:1). On the other hand, James calls us in James 2:1–4 to embrace and dignify the poor, unkempt, or downtrodden individual who might find his or her way into our assembly, not judging on the basis of appearance.

Exodus 39:2–7

📖 We can't help but be impressed by the artistry needed for construction of the ephod, a sleeveless vest, right down to the thin sheets of hammered gold to be worked into its strands. If we allow our imaginations to wander, though, we come to the shocking realization that this apron-like garment would be repeatedly spattered with animal blood during the execution of the priest's sacrificial duties.

📖 Many today are offended by Biblical references to blood and by God's requirement of sacrifices to pay for sin. But sin is a serious matter; its "wages" are death (Rom. 6:23). Out of God's mercy he accepted the substitute sacrifice of animals, and ultimately of his Son, instead of requiring the death of the individual sinner. The apostle John referred in Revelation 7:14 to the saints of God who have "washed their robes and made them white in the blood of the Lamb." And we can pray with the psalmist, "Wash me, and I will be whiter than snow" (Ps. 51:7).

Exodus 39:8–21

📖 The breastpiece, fitted into Aaron's ephod, held four rows each of three precious stones. Each stone was engraved with the name of one of the tribes of Israel. This signified that the high priest represented all the people when he ministered in the tabernacle. In addition, on the shoulder pieces of the ephod were two onyx stones with six tribal names engraved on each one (28:9–12; 39:6–7). The Israelites were doubly represented before the Lord. The high priest carried the burden for them both on his shoulders and "over his heart" (28:29).

📖 Much as the twelve precious stones were "each engraved like a seal with the name of one of the twelve tribes" (v. 14), so, the apostle Paul reminded us in 2 Corinthians 1:22 (cf. Eph. 1:13–14), Christ has "set his seal of ownership on us, and put his Spirit in our hearts as a deposit, guaranteeing what is to come." Each individual believer is as precious to God as one of the tribes of ancient Israel. Each of us is "engraved . . . on the palms of [God's] hands" (Isa. 49:16). And each of us can carry, through intercessory prayer, those who are close to our hearts. Who are you lifting daily in this way?

edge next to the ephod. 20Then they made two more gold rings and attached them to the bottom of the shoulder pieces on the front of the ephod, close to the seam just above the waistband of the ephod. 21They tied the rings of the breastpiece to the rings of the ephod with blue cord, connecting it to the waistband so that the breastpiece would not swing out from the ephod—as the LORD commanded Moses.

Other Priestly Garments

22They made the robe of the ephod entirely of blue cloth—the work of a weaver— 23with an opening in the center of the robe like the opening of a collar,a and a band around this opening, so that it would not tear. 24They made pomegranates of blue, purple and scarlet yarn and finely twisted linen around the hem of the robe. 25And they made bells of pure gold and attached them around the hem between the pomegranates. 26The bells and pomegranates alternated around the hem of the robe to be worn for ministering, as the LORD commanded Moses.

27For Aaron and his sons, they made tunics of fine linend—the work of a weaver— 28and the turbane of fine linen, the linen headbands and the undergarments of finely twisted linen. 29The sash was of finely twisted linen and blue, purple and scarlet yarn—the work of an embroiderer—as the LORD commanded Moses.

30They made the plate, the sacred diadem, out of pure gold and engraved on it, like an inscription on a seal: HOLY TO THE LORD. 31Then they fastened a blue cord to it to attach it to the turban, as the LORD commanded Moses.

Moses Inspects the Tabernacle

32So all the work on the tabernacle, the Tent of Meeting, was completed. The Israelites did everything just as the LORD commanded Moses.f 33Then they brought the tabernacle to Moses: the tent and all its furnishings, its clasps, frames, crossbars, posts and bases; 34the covering of ram skins dyed red, the covering of hides of sea cowsb and the shielding curtain; 35the ark of the Testimonyg with its poles and the atonement cover; 36the table with all its articles and the bread of the Presence; 37the pure gold lampstandh with its row of lamps and all its accessories, and the oil for the light; 38the gold altar,i the anointing oil, the fragrant incense, and the curtainj for the entrance to the tent; 39the bronze altar with its bronze grating, its poles and all its utensils; the basin with its stand; 40the curtains of the courtyard with its posts and bases, and the curtain for the entrance to the courtyard;k the ropes and tent pegs for the courtyard; all the furnishings for the tabernacle, the Tent of Meeting; 41and

Margin references
39:27 d Lev 6:10
39:28 e Ex 28:4
39:32 f ver 42-43; Ex 25:9
39:35 g Ex 30:6
39:37 h Ex 25:31
39:38 i Ex 30:1-10
j Ex 36:35
39:40 k Ex 27:9-19

---

a 23 The meaning of the Hebrew for this word is uncertain.   b 34 That is, dugongs

---

Exodus 39:22–31

📖 Aaron was to wear a robe beneath the ephod, decorated with, among other things, gold bells (v. 25; cf. 28:33). Their purpose was apparently to ring when Aaron entered or left the Most Holy Place "so that he [would] not die" (28:35). This warning most likely pertained not only to the bells but to all the strict demands of the priestly ritual. The suggestion is that omission of any one of the details would have had fatal consequences.

📘 No longer do we approach God's house with trembling. Yet it has become all too easy for us to miss the sacred context of meeting together to worship. Our casual style of dress, openness to light-hearted conversation, and penchant for prayers characterized primarily by personal requests, while not wrong in themselves, can detract from the sacredness of the moment in which we meet God in worship. Fear should never characterize our worship, but a lack of respect for God may cause us to miss the essence of true worship. Does your church's worship style enhance your reverence for God?

Exodus 39:32–43

📖 We see once again in this passage a number of creation connections. (1) In verse 32, the work was "completed." The same Hebrew root is used in Genesis 2:2 for the completion of God's creative work. (2) Moses inspected the work and saw that it had been completed well, according to plan. We are reminded of God's inspecting his creative work and pronouncing it "good" (e.g., Gen. 1:31). (3) Moses blessed the people after they had finished the work, just as God had blessed his creation (Gen. 1:22,28; 2:3).

📘 Many of us are good starters. Unfortunately, we may be easily sidetracked in our kingdom efforts and fail to finish well. How are you progressing toward your spiritual and servant goal(s)? Do you need to make any course corrections? How can you see to it that you aren't easily distracted in the future? If you have gotten off course, be encouraged to get back on track. Ask for God's help—and move forward.

the woven garments worn for ministering in the sanctuary, both the sacred garments for Aaron the priest and the garments for his sons when serving as priests.

[42] The Israelites had done all the work just as the LORD had commanded Moses.[l] [43] Moses inspected the work and saw that they had done it just as the LORD had commanded. So Moses blessed[m] them.

Setting Up the Tabernacle

40 Then the LORD said to Moses: [2] "Set up the tabernacle, the Tent of Meeting,[n] on the first day of the first month.[o] [3] Place the ark[p] of the Testimony in it and shield the ark with the curtain. [4] Bring in the table and set out what belongs on it.[q] Then bring in the lampstand[r] and set up its lamps. [5] Place the gold altar[s] of incense in front of the ark of the Testimony and put the curtain at the entrance to the tabernacle.

[6] "Place the altar of burnt offering in front of the entrance to the tabernacle, the Tent of Meeting; [7] place the basin[t] between the Tent of Meeting and the altar and put water in it. [8] Set up the courtyard around it and put the curtain at the entrance to the courtyard.

[9] "Take the anointing oil and anoint[u] the tabernacle and everything in it; consecrate it and all its furnishings, and it will be holy. [10] Then anoint the altar of burnt offering and all its utensils; consecrate[v] the altar, and it will be most holy. [11] Anoint the basin and its stand and consecrate them.

[12] "Bring Aaron and his sons to the entrance to the Tent of Meeting and wash them with water.[w] [13] Then dress Aaron in the sacred garments,[x] anoint him and consecrate[y] him so he may serve me as priest. [14] Bring his sons and dress them in tunics. [15] Anoint them just as you anointed their father, so they may serve me as priests. Their anointing will be to a priesthood that will continue for all generations to come.[z]" [16] Moses did everything just as the LORD commanded him.

[17] So the tabernacle[a] was set up on the first day of the first month[b] in the second year. [18] When Moses set up the tabernacle, he put the bases in place, erected the frames, inserted the crossbars and set up the posts. [19] Then he spread the tent over the tabernacle and put the covering over the tent, as the LORD commanded him.

[20] He took the Testimony[c] and placed it in the ark, attached the poles to the ark and put the atonement cover over it. [21] Then he brought the ark into the tabernacle and hung the shielding curtain[d] and shielded the ark of the Testimony, as the LORD commanded him.

[22] Moses placed the table[e] in the Tent of Meeting on the north side of the tabernacle outside the curtain [23] and set out the bread[f] on it before the LORD, as the LORD commanded him.

[24] He placed the lampstand[g] in the Tent of Meeting opposite the table on the south side of the tabernacle [25] and set up the lamps[h] before the LORD, as the LORD commanded him.

[26] Moses placed the gold altar[i] in the Tent of Meeting in front of the curtain [27] and burned fragrant incense on it, as the LORD commanded[j] him. [28] Then he put up the curtain[k] at the entrance to the tabernacle.

[29] He set the altar of burnt offering near the entrance to the tabernacle, the Tent of Meeting, and offered on it burnt offerings and grain offerings,[l] as the LORD commanded him.

39:42
[l] Ex 25:9

39:43
[m] Lev 9:22,23; Nu 6:23-27; 2Sa 6:18; 1Ki 8:14, 55; 2Ch 30:27

40:2
[n] Nu 1:1 o ver 17; Ex 12:2

40:3
[p] ver 21; Nu 4:5; Ex 26:33

40:4
[q] Ex 25:30 r ver 22-25; Ex 26:35

40:5
[s] ver 26; Ex 30:1

40:7
[t] ver 30; Ex 30:18

40:9
[u] Ex 30:26; Lev 8:10

40:10
[v] Ex 29:36

40:12
[w] Lev 8:1-13

40:13
[x] Ex 28:41
[y] Lev 8:12

40:15
[z] Ex 29:9; Nu 25:13

40:17
[a] Nu 7:1 b ver 2

40:20
[c] Ex 16:34; 25:16; Dt 10:5; 1Ki 8:9; Heb 9:4

40:21
[d] Ex 26:33

40:22
[e] Ex 26:35

40:23
[f] ver 4

40:24
[g] Ex 26:35

40:25
[h] ver 4; Ex 25:37

40:26
[i] ver 5; Ex 30:6

40:27
[j] Ex 30:7

40:28
[k] Ex 26:36

40:29
[l] ver 6; Ex 29:38-42

Exodus 40:1–33

As God instructed in verse 2, the tabernacle was set up "on the first day of the first month in the second year" (v. 17). As indicated in 12:2, the exodus inaugurated a new calendar in Israelite life: The month in which it took place was to be the first month of the year. The deliverance of Israel from Egypt marked a new beginning for God's people, a "new creation." It's no surprise, then, that the tabernacle was set up one year later on the first day of the first month. It, too, was a new creation.

Just as the tabernacle was a new creation, so, "if anyone is in Christ, he [or she] is a new creation; the old has gone, the new has come!" (2 Cor. 5:17). The day of our conversion is, in a very real sense, the "first day of the rest of our lives," a new beginning that makes our old existence pale by comparison. Reflect back on your own conversion experience. What became new immediately? What's still in process?

40:30
m ver 7

40:32
n Ex 30:20
40:33
o Ex 27:9 *p* ver 8

40:34
q Nu 9:15-23;
1Ki 8:12
40:35
r 1Ki 8:11;
2Ch 5:13-14

40:36
s Nu 9:17-23;
10:13; Ne 9:19
40:38
t Ex 13:21; Nu 9:15;
1Co 10:1

30He placed the basin*m* between the Tent of Meeting and the altar and put water in it for washing, 31and Moses and Aaron and his sons used it to wash their hands and feet. 32They washed whenever they entered the Tent of Meeting or approached the altar,*n* as the LORD commanded Moses.

33Then Moses set up the courtyard*o* around the tabernacle and altar and put up the curtain*p* at the entrance to the courtyard. And so Moses finished the work.

The Glory of the LORD

34Then the cloud*q* covered the Tent of Meeting, and the glory of the LORD filled the tabernacle. 35Moses could not enter the Tent of Meeting because the cloud had settled upon it, and the glory of the LORD filled the tabernacle.*r*

36In all the travels of the Israelites, whenever the cloud lifted from above the tabernacle, they would set out;*s* 37but if the cloud did not lift, they did not set out—until the day it lifted. 38So the cloud*t* of the LORD was over the tabernacle by day, and fire was in the cloud by night, in the sight of all the house of Israel during all their travels.

Exodus 40:34–38

📖 This brief passage prepares us for what will become a dominant theme in Numbers and Deuteronomy: the relentless push toward Canaan. These closing verses explain how this would happen. When God moved, the people moved. When he stayed put, so did they. After all, God's plan and purpose were being fulfilled. Israel's eventual arrival in the promised land would be solely by God's guidance and direction, according to his will and in his time.

The God who had brought the Israelites out of Egypt was at the same time both holy (apart) and nearby. Verses 34–35 remind us of his sanctity. There was a point even Moses couldn't cross, a boundary set by God that

kept even his chosen redeemer at a distance. The guiding function of the cloud and fire, on the other hand, tell us that God was very near his people—with them every step of the way.

📖 We, too, have been delivered and are waiting to arrive at our final destination, poised to reach our rest. On this journey, we follow our holy Redeemer as he guides us to our promised land. There is no cloud overhead, but we have Christ's Spirit dwelling within us and bringing us to the goal of our salvation, just as surely as the cloud guided the Israelites to their ultimate destination. God is present with his people wherever we go. He still leads and guides us, not to an earthly destination but to "a better country—a heavenly one" (Heb. 11:16).

Leviticus

AUTHOR

Leviticus states that its contents were given to Moses by God at Mount Sinai (1:1; 27:34). Other Scripture passages (e.g., Matt. 8:4; Luke 2:22–24; John 7:22; Rom. 10:5) also attribute authorship of Leviticus to Moses.

DATE WRITTEN

Leviticus was probably written around 1440 B.C.

ORIGINAL READERS

Leviticus was written to the Levites specifically and to the Israelites in general. It addresses religious issues of worship: the sacrificial system and the people's responsibility to maintain moral and ceremonial holiness—a requirement for the worship of God.

TIMELINE

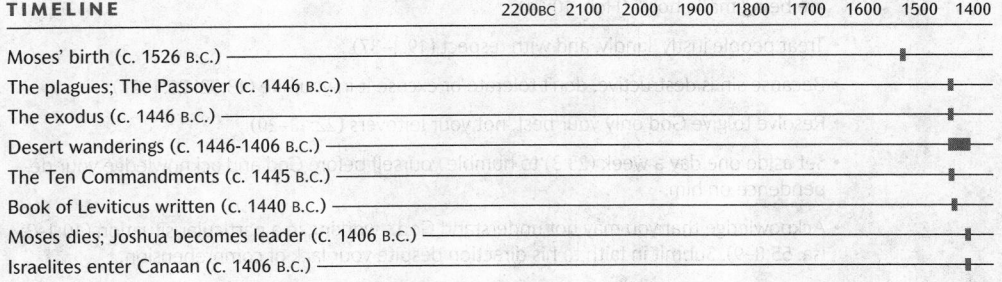

	2200BC 2100 2000 1900 1800 1700 1600 1500 1400
Moses' birth (c. 1526 B.C.)	
The plagues; The Passover (c. 1446 B.C.)	
The exodus (c. 1446 B.C.)	
Desert wanderings (c. 1446-1406 B.C.)	
The Ten Commandments (c. 1445 B.C.)	
Book of Leviticus written (c. 1440 B.C.)	
Moses dies; Joshua becomes leader (c. 1406 B.C.)	
Israelites enter Canaan (c. 1406 B.C.)	

THEMES

Leviticus means "matters pertaining to the Levites," the priestly tribe of Israel. Accordingly, topics such as sacrifice and ceremonial laws that deal with food, skin disease, mildew, and incest are prominent. The book contains the following themes:

1. *Holiness.* "Be holy because I, the LORD your God, am holy" (19:2) is the overwhelming message of this book. In Leviticus spiritual holiness is symbolized by physical perfection, or purity, and separation from the world. The Old Testament ceremonial laws functioned as a means of separating the Israelites from the surrounding tribes. The wall dividing Jewish and Christian worship was removed by God's invitation to faith in Christ and his work on the cross (Gal. 3:28; Eph. 2:11–22), so these laws are no longer observed. But the moral principles they espouse still apply today (Matt. 5:1—7:29; 12:11–12; Mark 2:23–28).

2. *Sin, sacrifice, atonement.* Since no human being is perfect, God provided the Old Testament sacrificial system as a means of atonement (forgiveness of sin). In this system, a life was to be given for a life. This temporary arrangement is no longer necessary, for Jesus' death paid the penalty for sin once for all (Heb. 9:23–28).

3. *Worship.* Leviticus reveals God's desire to be present with his people and enjoy fellowship with them. Through worship God's people acknowledge who he is and what he has done by expressing their love, honor, thanks, and praise to him. While the mode of worship has changed from that practiced in the Old Testament, the requirement that God's worshipers "must worship in spirit and in truth" (John 4:24) has not.

FAITH IN ACTION

The pages of Leviticus contain life lessons and role models of faith—people who challenge believers to put their faith in action.

Role Models

- THE ISRAELITES were given high standards to obey. Jesus claimed that the whole law could be summed up in two commands: Love God wholeheartedly and love your neighbor in the same way and to the same degree as you love yourself (Matt. 22:37–39). This is the basic ethic required of God's people. Do these two principles guide your actions?

- AARON (10:1–3), in spite of his grief, accepted God's judgment on his sons when they flagrantly disobeyed God's instructions for worship. Are you unjustifiably angry at God for something he has justly done? What would be your proper response?

- MOSES (10:12–20) understood that extenuating circumstances sometimes call for a relaxing of "required" behavior. Are you able to set aside what you think is "required" when unusual circumstances arise?

Challenges

- God demands holiness (11:44), but trying to be "good enough" to earn his favor is an exhausting, fruitless endeavor. Surrender yourself to Christ and depend on his perfection (Heb. 4:15) to make you righteous. By his "one sacrifice he has made perfect forever those who are being made holy" (Heb. 10:14).

- Treat people justly, kindly, and with respect (19:1–37).

- Because sin is destructive, don't tolerate or excuse it in your life (13:52; 20:1–27).

- Resolve to give God only your best, not your leftovers (22:18–20).

- Set aside one day a week (23:3) to humble yourself before God and acknowledge your dependence on him.

- Acknowledge that you may not understand God's working in a particular situation (10:1–3; Isa. 55:8–9). Submit in faith to his direction despite your lack of comprehension.

OUTLINE

    I. Laws and Instructions for Offerings (1–7)
   II. Aaron and His Sons as God's Priests (8–10)
  III. Rules for Holy Living (11–15)
  IV. The Day of Atonement (16)
   V. Practical Holiness (17–22)
  VI. The Sabbath, Feasts, and Seasons (23–25)
 VII. Conditions for God's Blessing (26–27)

The Burnt Offering

1 The LORD called to Moses[a] and spoke to him from the Tent of Meeting.[b] He said, 2 "Speak to the Israelites and say to them: 'When any of you brings an offering to the LORD, bring as your offering an animal from either the herd or the flock.[c]

3 " 'If the offering is a burnt offering from the herd, he is to offer a male without defect.[d] He must present it at the entrance to the Tent[e] of Meeting so that it[a] will be acceptable to the LORD. 4 He is to lay his hand on the head[f] of the burnt offer-

a 3 Or *he*

1:1
a Ex 19:3; 25:22
b Nu 7:89

1:2
c Lev 22:18-19

1:3
d Ex 12:5; Dt 15:21; Heb 9:14; 1Pe 1:19
e Lev 17:9

1:4
f Ex 29:10,15; Lev 3:2

Leviticus 1:1–17

According to Exodus 19:1, the Israelites came to Sinai three months after leaving Egypt. The tabernacle was set up "on the first day of the first month in the second year" (Ex. 40:17). Numbers 1:1 begins one month later—"on the first day of the second month of the second year." Leviticus, sandwiched in between, presents a highly concentrated dose of divine revelation.

God wasted no time launching into a series of commands regarding the heart of worship: sacrifice. The goal of the burnt offering was to present God with a gift—a pleasing aroma. God could accept a gift of food (Lev. 1:4,9) but didn't visibly take it unless he chose to appear in human form (Gen. 18:1–8) or send fire to consume a sacrifice (Lev. 9:24; 1 Kings 18:38). Through the ritual of burnt offering, the people gave God a token food gift, receiving in response removal of their sin.

Ancient Israel and its culture were part of the worldwide web of humanity, to which we also belong. More importantly, through our "new covenant" naturalization into the stream of Abraham's heirs, Israel's promises and salvation history are ours. Through this sensory, visual book we can experience the awe of approaching God's Presence, feel the weight of the life-and-death consequences of sin, and rejoice in the release from guilt and fear through the animal sacrifices God provided.

1:1–2

Offerings

Sacrifice	Scripture	Elements	Purpose
• Burnt Offering	Lev. 1; 6:8–13; 8:18–21; 16:24	Bull, ram, or male bird (dove or young pigeon for the poor); wholly consumed; no defect	Voluntary act of worship; atonement for unintentional sin in general; expression of devotion, commitment, and complete surrender to God
• Grain Offering	Lev. 2; 6:14–23	Grain, fine flour, olive oil, incense, baked bread (cakes or wafers), salt; no yeast or honey; accompanied burnt offering and fellowship offering (along with drink offering)	Voluntary act of worship; recognition of God's goodness and provisions; devotion to God
• Fellowship Offering	Lev. 3; 7:11–34	Any animal without defect from herd or flock; variety of breads	Voluntary act of worship; thanksgiving and fellowship (it included a communal meal)
• Sin Offering	Lev. 4:1—5:13; 6:24–30; 8:14–17; 16:3–22	1. Young bull: for high priest and congregation 2. Male goat: for leader 3. Female goat or lamb: for common person 4. Dove or pigeon: for the poor 5. Tenth of an ephah of fine flour: for the very poor	Mandatory atonement for specific, unintentional sin; confession of sin; forgiveness of sin; cleansing from defilement
• Guilt Offering	Lev. 5:14—6:7; 7:1–6	Ram	Mandatory atonement for unintentional sin requiring restitution; cleansing from defilement; making restitution; 20% fine

When more than one kind of offering was presented (as in Num. 7:16,17), the order was usually as follows: (1) sin offering or guilt offering, (2) burnt offering, (3) fellowship offering and grain offering (along with a drink offering). This sequence furnishes part of the spiritual significance of the sacrificial system. First, sin had to be dealt with (sin offering or guilt offering). Second, the worshipers committed themselves completely to God (burnt offering and grain offering). Third, fellowship or communion between the Lord, the priest, and the worshiper (fellowship offering) was established. To state it another way, there were sacrifices of expiation (sin offerings and guilt offerings), consecration (burnt offerings and grain offerings), and communion (fellowship offerings—these included vow offerings, thank offerings, and freewill offerings).

1:4
g 2Ch 29:23-24
1:5
h Lev 3:2,8
i Heb 12:24;
1Pe 1:2
1:6
j Lev 7:8
1:7
k Lev 6:12
1:8
l ver 12
1:9
m Ex 29:18
n ver 13; Ge 8:21;
Nu 15:8-10;
Eph 5:2
1:10
o ver 3; Ex 12:5
1:11
p ver 5

1:14
q Ge 15:9; Lev 5:7;
Lk 2:24
1:15
r Lev 5:9
1:16
s Lev 6:10
1:17
t Ge 15:10
u Lev 5:8

2:1
v Lev 6:14-18
w Nu 15:4
2:2
x Lev 5:11
y Lev 6:15; Isa 66:3
z ver 9,16;
Lev 5:12; 6:15;
24:7; Ac 10:4
2:3
a ver 10; Lev 6:16;
10:12,13
2:4
b Ex 29:2
2:7
c Lev 7:9
2:9
d ver 2 e Ex 29:18;
Lev 6:15
2:10
f ver 3

ing, and it will be accepted on his behalf to make atonement[g] for him. [5]He is to slaughter[h] the young bull before the LORD, and then Aaron's sons the priests shall bring the blood and sprinkle it against the altar on all sides[i] at the entrance to the Tent of Meeting. [6]He is to skin[j] the burnt offering and cut it into pieces. [7]The sons of Aaron the priest are to put fire on the altar and arrange wood[k] on the fire. [8]Then Aaron's sons the priests shall arrange the pieces, including the head and the fat,[l] on the burning wood that is on the altar. [9]He is to wash the inner parts and the legs with water, and the priest is to burn all of it on the altar.[m] It is a burnt offering, an offering made by fire, an aroma pleasing to the LORD.[n]

[10]" 'If the offering is a burnt offering from the flock, from either the sheep or the goats,[o] he is to offer a male without defect. [11]He is to slaughter it at the north side of the altar before the LORD, and Aaron's sons the priests shall sprinkle its blood against the altar on all sides.[p] [12]He is to cut it into pieces, and the priest shall arrange them, including the head and the fat, on the burning wood that is on the altar. [13]He is to wash the inner parts and the legs with water, and the priest is to bring all of it and burn it on the altar. It is a burnt offering, an offering made by fire, an aroma pleasing to the LORD.

[14]" 'If the offering to the LORD is a burnt offering of birds, he is to offer a dove or a young pigeon.[q] [15]The priest shall bring it to the altar, wring off the head and burn it on the altar; its blood shall be drained out on the side of the altar.[r] [16]He is to remove the crop with its contents[a] and throw it to the east side of the altar, where the ashes[s] are. [17]He shall tear it open by the wings, not severing it completely,[t] and then the priest shall burn it on the wood[u] that is on the fire on the altar. It is a burnt offering, an offering made by fire, an aroma pleasing to the LORD.

The Grain Offering

2 " 'When someone brings a grain offering[v] to the LORD, his offering is to be of fine flour. He is to pour oil[w] on it, put incense on it [2]and take it to Aaron's sons the priests. The priest shall take a handful of the fine flour[x] and oil, together with all the incense,[y] and burn this as a memorial portion[z] on the altar, an offering made by fire, an aroma pleasing to the LORD. [3]The rest of the grain offering belongs to Aaron and his sons;[a] it is a most holy part of the offerings made to the LORD by fire.

[4]" 'If you bring a grain offering baked in an oven, it is to consist of fine flour: cakes made without yeast and mixed with oil, or[b] wafers made without yeast and spread with oil.[b] [5]If your grain offering is prepared on a griddle, it is to be made of fine flour mixed with oil, and without yeast. [6]Crumble it and pour oil on it; it is a grain offering. [7]If your grain offering is cooked in a pan,[c] it is to be made of fine flour and oil. [8]Bring the grain offering made of these things to the LORD; present it to the priest, who shall take it to the altar. [9]He shall take out the memorial portion[d] from the grain offering and burn it on the altar as an offering made by fire, an aroma pleasing to the LORD.[e] [10]The rest of the grain offering belongs to Aaron and his sons;[f] it is a most holy part of the offerings made to the LORD by fire.

[a] 16 Or *crop and the feathers*; the meaning of the Hebrew for this word is uncertain.   [b] 4 Or *and*

Rituals, like baptism and the Lord's Supper, move beyond the boundary between the seen and unseen. So does prayer. Prayer is communication, while ritual is interaction. Through prayer and ritual, we can reach out and touch God. Like language, ritual communicates through symbols. But it packs a special punch because its meanings are acted out.

Leviticus 2:1–16

Leviticus 2 gives instructions for grain offerings. Like burnt offerings, they involved turning offering material into smoke for the Lord on the outer altar. Two major categories were uncooked and cooked grain offerings. A special category was the firstfruits offering, which acknowledged the harvest as having come from God. Verses 11–13 state rules regarding certain ingredients of grain offerings in general, as well as of all other kinds of sacrifices.

Bloodless Israelite grain offerings help us understand that we can truly offer ourselves to God as "living sacrifices" (Rom. 12:1–2). By meeting other people's needs, we can give gifts that are "a fragrant offering, an acceptable sacrifice, pleasing to God" (Phil. 4:18). "Through Jesus, therefore, let us continually offer to God a sacrifice of praise—the fruit of lips that confess his name. And do not forget to do good and to share with others, for which such sacrifices God is pleased" (Heb. 13:15–16).

11 " 'Every grain offering you bring to the LORD must be made without yeast, *g* for you are not to burn any yeast or honey in an offering made to the LORD by fire. 12You may bring them to the LORD as an offering of the firstfruits, *h* but they are not to be offered on the altar as a pleasing aroma. 13Season all your grain offerings with salt. Do not leave the salt of the covenant*i* of your God out of your grain offerings; add salt to all your offerings.

14 " 'If you bring a grain offering of firstfruits*j* to the LORD, offer crushed heads of new grain roasted in the fire. 15Put oil and incense on it; it is a grain offering. 16The priest shall burn the memorial portion*k* of the crushed grain and the oil, together with all the incense, as an offering made to the LORD by fire.

The Fellowship Offering

3 " 'If someone's offering is a fellowship offering,*a l* and he offers an animal from the herd, whether male or female, he is to present before the LORD an animal without defect.*m* 2He is to lay his hand on the head*n* of his offering and slaughter it*o* at the entrance to the Tent of Meeting. Then Aaron's sons the priests shall sprinkle the blood against the altar on all sides. 3From the fellowship offering he is to bring a sacrifice made to the LORD by fire: all the fat*p* that covers the inner parts or is connected to them, 4both kidneys with the fat on them near the loins, and the covering of the liver, which he will remove with the kidneys. 5Then Aaron's sons*q* are to burn it on the altar on top of the burnt offering*r* that is on the burning wood, as an offering made by fire, an aroma pleasing to the LORD.

6 " 'If he offers an animal from the flock as a fellowship offering*s* to the LORD, he is to offer a male or female without defect. 7If he offers a lamb, he is to present it before the LORD.*t* 8He is to lay his hand on the head of his offering and slaughter it*u* in front of the Tent of Meeting. Then Aaron's sons shall sprinkle its blood against the altar on all sides. 9From the fellowship offering he is to bring a sacrifice made to the LORD by fire: its fat, the entire fat tail cut off close to the backbone, all the fat that covers the inner parts or is connected to them, 10both kidneys with the fat on them near the loins, and the covering of the liver, which he will remove with the kidneys. 11The priest shall burn them on the altar*v* as food,*w* an offering made to the LORD by fire.

12 " 'If his offering is a goat, he is to present it before the LORD. 13He is to lay his hand on its head and slaughter it in front of the Tent of Meeting. Then Aaron's sons shall sprinkle*x* its blood against the altar on all sides. 14From what he offers he is to make this offering to the LORD by fire: all the fat that covers the inner parts or is connected to them, 15both kidneys with the fat on them near the loins, and the covering of the liver, which he will remove with the kidneys. 16The priest shall burn them on the altar as food, an offering made by fire, a pleasing aroma. All the fat is the LORD's.*y*

17 " 'This is a lasting ordinance for the generations to come,*z* wherever you live: You must not eat any fat or any blood.*a' * "

The Sin Offering

4 The LORD said to Moses, 2"Say to the Israelites: 'When anyone sins unintentionally*b* and does what is forbidden in any of the LORD's commands—

3 " 'If the anointed priest sins, bringing guilt on the people, he must bring to the

---

a 1 Traditionally *peace offering*; also in verses 3, 6 and 9

2:11
g Ex 23:18; 34:25;
Lev 6:16
2:12
h Lev 7:13; 23:10
2:13
i Nu 18:19;
Eze 43:24
2:14
j Lev 23:10
2:16
k ver 2

3:1
l Lev 7:11-34
m Lev 1:3; 22:21
3:2
n Ex 29:10,15
o Lev 1:5

3:3
p Ex 29:13
3:5
q Lev 7:29-34
r Ex 29:13,38-42
3:6
s ver 1
3:7
t Lev 17:8-9
3:8
u ver 2; Lev 1:5

3:11
v ver 5 *w* ver 16;
Lev 21:6,17

3:13
x Ex 24:6

3:16
y 1Sa 2:16
3:17
z Lev 6:18; 17:7
a Ge 9:4;
Lev 7:25-26;
17:10-16; Dt 12:16;
Ac 15:20

4:2
b Lev 5:15-18;
Ps 19:12; Heb 9:7

Leviticus 3:1–17

📖 The suet (fat) of a "fellowship" (or "well-being") offering was burned for God. The breast and thigh went to the priests (7:31–36), and the rest of the meat was eaten by the person making the offering. Such offerings didn't involve atonement for sin and could be given in thanksgiving (7:12–15), to confirm a vow (7:16), or simply as a freewill offering. The harvest Festival of Booths (like our Thanksgiving) involved more sacrifices than any other festival (Num. 29:12–38). The sacrificial system was solemn, not morbid—and it could be joyful.

📖 Healthy interaction with God doesn't have to focus on problems, including the need to get rid of sins that separate us from him. How do you like it when all your communication with another person centers around that person's troubles? We can joyfully thank God in all kinds of ways, including prayer, praise through music, and gifts of service to others. We can also fulfill vows of commitment, resources, or service—and express our love and devotion to God, for no "special" reason, anytime we want!

4:3
c ver 14; Ps 66:15
d Lev 9:2-22;
Heb 9:13-14
4:4
e Lev 1:3
4:5
f Lev 16:14

4:7
g ver 34; Lev 8:15
h ver 18, 30;
Lev 5:9; 9:9; 16:18
4:8
i Lev 3:3-5
4:9
j Lev 3:4

4:11
k Ex 29:14;
Lev 9:11; Nu 19:5
4:12
l Heb 13:11
m Lev 6:11
4:13
n ver 2; Lev 5:2-4,
17; Nu 15:24-26

4:14
o ver 3 p ver 23,28
4:15
q Lev 1:4; 8:14,22;
Nu 8:10

4:16
r ver 5
4:17
s ver 6

4:18
t ver 7

4:19
u ver 8
4:20
v Heb 10:10-12
w Nu 15:25

4:21
x Lev 16:5,15

4:22
y Nu 31:13 z ver 2

LORD a young bull[c] without defect as a sin offering[d] for the sin he has committed. [4]He is to present the bull at the entrance to the Tent of Meeting before the LORD.[e] He is to lay his hand on its head and slaughter it before the LORD. [5]Then the anointed priest shall take some of the bull's blood[f] and carry it into the Tent of Meeting. [6]He is to dip his finger into the blood and sprinkle some of it seven times before the LORD, in front of the curtain of the sanctuary. [7]The priest shall then put some of the blood on the horns of the altar of fragrant incense that is before the LORD in the Tent of Meeting. The rest of the bull's blood he shall pour out at the base of the altar[g] of burnt offering[h] at the entrance to the Tent of Meeting. [8]He shall remove all the fat[i] from the bull of the sin offering—the fat that covers the inner parts or is connected to them, [9]both kidneys with the fat on them near the loins, and the covering of the liver, which he will remove with the kidneys[j]— [10]just as the fat is removed from the ox[a] sacrificed as a fellowship offering.[b] Then the priest shall burn them on the altar of burnt offering. [11]But the hide of the bull and all its flesh, as well as the head and legs, the inner parts and offal[k]— [12]that is, all the rest of the bull—he must take outside the camp[l] to a place ceremonially clean,[m] where the ashes are thrown, and burn it in a wood fire on the ash heap.

[13]" 'If the whole Israelite community sins unintentionally[n] and does what is forbidden in any of the LORD's commands, even though the community is unaware of the matter, they are guilty. [14]When they become aware of the sin they committed, the assembly must bring a young bull[o] as a sin offering[p] and present it before the Tent of Meeting. [15]The elders of the community are to lay their hands on the bull's head[q] before the LORD, and the bull shall be slaughtered before the LORD. [16]Then the anointed priest is to take some of the bull's blood[r] into the Tent of Meeting. [17]He shall dip his finger into the blood and sprinkle it before the LORD[s] seven times in front of the curtain. [18]He is to put some of the blood on the horns of the altar that is before the LORD[t] in the Tent of Meeting. The rest of the blood he shall pour out at the base of the altar of burnt offering at the entrance to the Tent of Meeting. [19]He shall remove all the fat[u] from it and burn it on the altar, [20]and do with this bull just as he did with the bull for the sin offering. In this way the priest will make atonement[v] for them, and they will be forgiven.[w] [21]Then he shall take the bull outside the camp and burn it as he burned the first bull. This is the sin offering for the community.[x]

[22]" 'When a leader[y] sins unintentionally[z] and does what is forbidden in any of the commands of the LORD his God, he is guilty. [23]When he is made aware of the sin he committed, he must bring as his offering a male goat without defect. [24]He

---

a [10] The Hebrew word can include both male and female.   b [10] Traditionally *peace offering*; also in verses 26, 31 and 35

Leviticus 4:1—5:13

Whereas chapters 1–3 give instructions for voluntary offerings, chapters 4:1—6:7 deal with mandatory sacrifices. "Sin" or "purification" offerings atoned for involuntary or inadvertent sins (once the sinners realized what they had done) and removed ritual impurities incompatible with the divine holiness living among the Israelites. These offerings included a much wider variety of rituals than any of the other types.

Chapter 5:1–13 still concerns sin offerings but differs from chapter 4: (1) Chapter 4 covers unintentional violation of any divine command; 5:1–13 moves into the more serious aspects of omission or neglect (still without a defiant attitude). (2) In 5:1–13, the sinner was required to confess before bringing a sacrifice. (3) In chapter 4 sacrificial animals of different values were required based on the sinner's status; in 5:1–13 the offering was based on what he or she could afford.

Forgiveness can't be handed out like candy or compliments. To for*give* means to *give* up something. It has a cost, even for God—especially for God! We are called to forgive as Jesus did from the cross (Luke 23:34). But it's not to be an unthinking, "knee-jerk" or "feel good" reaction. Forgiveness is a transaction—a process involving two parties. God made it possible, but the Old Testament sinner was only "forgiven" when he or she accepted God's provision by offering a sacrifice.

Leviticus established equal opportunities in terms of gender, economic position, and social status. Women offered sacrifices, and offerings included male and female animals. In line with Biblical teaching (see Gal. 3:28), the church is to lead the way to wholesome equality based on unity—not to get bogged down with political collisions (like "gender benders" of prejudice). Leviticus 5:1–13 also established equal liability for people of different means. Before the divine King, worldly status shrinks to insignificance.

is to lay his hand on the goat's head and slaughter it at the place where the burnt offering is slaughtered before the LORD. It is a sin offering. [25]Then the priest shall take some of the blood of the sin offering with his finger and put it on the horns of the altar of burnt offering and pour out the rest of the blood at the base of the altar. [a] [26]He shall burn all the fat on the altar as he burned the fat of the fellowship offering. In this way the priest will make atonement for the man's sin, and he will be forgiven. [b]

[27] "'If a member of the community sins unintentionally[c] and does what is forbidden in any of the LORD's commands, he is guilty. [28]When he is made aware of the sin he committed, he must bring as his offering[d] for the sin he committed a female goat[e] without defect. [29]He is to lay his hand on the head[f] of the sin offering[g] and slaughter it at the place of the burnt offering. [30]Then the priest is to take some of the blood with his finger and put it on the horns of the altar of burnt offering[h] and pour out the rest of the blood at the base of the altar. [31]He shall remove all the fat, just as the fat is removed from the fellowship offering, and the priest shall burn it on the altar as an aroma pleasing to the LORD. [i] In this way the priest will make atonement for him, and he will be forgiven.

[32] "'If he brings a lamb as his sin offering, he is to bring a female without defect.[j] [33]He is to lay his hand on its head and slaughter it for a sin offering at the place where the burnt offering is slaughtered.[k] [34]Then the priest shall take some of the blood of the sin offering with his finger and put it on the horns of the altar of burnt offering and pour out the rest of the blood at the base of the altar.[l] [35]He shall remove all the fat, just as the fat is removed from the lamb of the fellowship offering, and the priest shall burn it on the altar[m] on top of the offerings made to the LORD by fire. In this way the priest will make atonement for him for the sin he has committed, and he will be forgiven.

5 "'If a person sins because he does not speak up when he hears a public charge to testify[n] regarding something he has seen or learned about, he will be held responsible.[o]

[2] "'Or if a person touches anything ceremonially unclean—whether the carcasses of unclean wild animals or of unclean livestock or of unclean creatures that move along the ground[p]—even though he is unaware of it, he has become unclean and is guilty.

[3] "'Or if he touches human uncleanness[q]—anything that would make him unclean—even though he is unaware of it, when he learns of it he will be guilty.

[4] "'Or if a person thoughtlessly takes an oath[r] to do anything, whether good or evil—in any matter one might carelessly swear about—even though he is unaware of it, in any case when he learns of it he will be guilty.

[5] "'When anyone is guilty in any of these ways, he must confess[s] in what way he has sinned [6]and, as a penalty for the sin he has committed, he must bring to the LORD a female lamb or goat from the flock as a sin offering;[t] and the priest shall make atonement for him for his sin.

[7] "'If he cannot afford[u] a lamb, he is to bring two doves or two young pigeons to the LORD as a penalty for his sin—one for a sin offering and the other for a burnt offering. [8]He is to bring them to the priest, who shall first offer the one for the sin offering. He is to wring its head from its neck,[v] not severing it completely,[w] [9]and is to sprinkle some of the blood of the sin offering against the side of the altar; the rest of the blood must be drained out at the base of the altar.[x] It is a sin offering. [10]The priest shall then offer the other as a burnt offering in the prescribed way[y] and make atonement for him for the sin he has committed, and he will be forgiven.[z]

[11] "'If, however, he cannot afford two doves or two young pigeons, he is to bring as an offering for his sin a tenth of an ephah[a] of fine flour[a] for a sin offering. He must not put oil or incense on it, because it is a sin offering. [12]He is to bring it to the priest, who shall take a handful of it as a memorial portion and burn it on the altar on top of the offerings made to the LORD by fire. It is a sin offering. [13]In this

---

[a] *11* That is, probably about 2 quarts (about 2 liters)

4:25
a ver 7,18,30,34;
Lev 9:9
4:26
b Lev 5:10
4:27
c ver 2; Nu 15:27
4:28
d ver 23 *e* ver 3
4:29
f ver 4,24 *g* Lev 1:4
4:30
h ver 7
4:31
i Ge 8:21
4:32
j ver 28
4:33
k ver 29
4:34
l ver 7
4:35
m ver 26,31
5:1
n Pr 29:24 *o* ver 17
5:2
p Lev 11:11,24-40;
Dt 14:8
5:3
q Nu 19:11-16
5:4
r Nu 30:6,8
5:5
s Lev 16:21; 26:40;
Nu 5:7; Pr 28:13
5:6
t Lev 4:28
5:7
u Lev 12:8; 14:21
5:8
v Lev 1:15
w Lev 1:17
5:9
x Lev 4:7,18
5:10
y Lev 1:14-17
z Lev 4:26
5:11
a Lev 2:1

5:13
b Lev 4:26 c Lev 2:3
way the priest will make atonement[b] for him for any of these sins he has committed, and he will be forgiven. The rest of the offering will belong to the priest,[c] as in the case of the grain offering.' "

The Guilt Offering

5:15
d Lev 22:14
e Nu 5:8 f Ex 30:13
14The LORD said to Moses: 15"When a person commits a violation and sins unintentionally in regard to any of the LORD's holy things, he is to bring to the LORD as a penalty[d] a ram[e] from the flock, one without defect and of the proper value in silver, according to the sanctuary shekel. [a][f] It is a guilt offering. 16He must make restitution[g] for what he has failed to do in regard to the holy things, add a fifth of the value[h] to that and give it all to the priest, who will make atonement for him with the ram as a guilt offering, and he will be forgiven.

5:16
g Lev 6:4
h Lev 22:14; Nu 5:7

5:17
i ver 15; Lev 4:2
17"If a person sins and does what is forbidden in any of the LORD's commands, even though he does not know it,[i] he is guilty and will be held responsible. 18He is to bring to the priest as a guilt offering a ram from the flock, one without defect and of the proper value. In this way the priest will make atonement for him for the wrong he has committed unintentionally, and he will be forgiven.[j] 19It is a guilt offering; he has been guilty of[b] wrongdoing against the LORD."

5:18
j ver 15

6:2
k Nu 5:6; Ac 5:4; Col 3:9 l Pr 24:28
m Ex 22:7

6:3
n Dt 22:1-3

6:4
o Lk 19:8

6:5
p Nu 5:7 q Lev 5:15

6:6
r Lev 5:15

6:7
s Lev 4:26

6 The LORD said to Moses: 2"If anyone sins and is unfaithful to the LORD[k] by deceiving his neighbor[l] about something entrusted to him or left in his care[m] or stolen, or if he cheats him, 3or if he finds lost property and lies about it,[n] or if he swears falsely, or if he commits any such sin that people may do— 4when he thus sins and becomes guilty, he must return[o] what he has stolen or taken by extortion, or what was entrusted to him, or the lost property he found, 5or whatever it was he swore falsely about. He must make restitution[p] in full, add a fifth of the value to it and give it all to the owner on the day he presents his guilt offering. [q] 6And as a penalty he must bring to the priest, that is, to the LORD, his guilt offering,[r] a ram from the flock, one without defect and of the proper value. 7In this way the priest will make atonement[s] for him before the LORD, and he will be forgiven for any of these things he did that made him guilty."

The Burnt Offering

6:10
t Ex 28:39-42,43; 39:28
8The LORD said to Moses: 9"Give Aaron and his sons this command: 'These are the regulations for the burnt offering: The burnt offering is to remain on the altar hearth throughout the night, till morning, and the fire must be kept burning on the altar. 10The priest shall then put on his linen clothes, with linen undergarments next to his body,[t] and shall remove the ashes of the burnt offering that the fire has consumed on the altar and place them beside the altar. 11Then he is to take off these

---

[a] 15 That is, about 2/5 ounce (about 11.5 grams)   [b] 19 Or *has made full expiation for his*

Leviticus 5:14—6:7

Under certain circumstances, an Israelite was to offer a sacrifice labeled a "guilt" or "reparation" (amends or compensation) offering. Such offerings were required for offenses that created measurable, provable debt that could be repaid. Instructions for the ritual procedure appear later, in 7:1–7. The debtor was to repay the debt before the offering was performed. The sin offering, by contrast, applied to sin to which no price tag could be attached.

Like Humpty Dumpty, we can't fix our brokenness. Even when we acknowledge that we have done damage and patch things up as best we can, we need to depend on the sacrifice of the King's Son to put everything back together again. His atoning death did for us what the ancient "repair-ation" offering did for the Israelite who had wronged a neighbor and tried with only partial success to put things right.

Leviticus 6:8–13

Here we find additional instructions for burnt offerings. This would be followed by similar directions for grain (vv. 14–23), sin (purification; vv. 24–30), and guilt (reparation; 7:1–7) offerings. No portion of a burnt offering was to be eaten by a human being, so these instructions to "Aaron and his sons" concerned maintenance of the altar fire. Keeping the fire going was critical, and Leviticus 9:24 will tell us why: God himself had lit it!

God's ministers today are still keepers of the flame, not lighters of the fire or inventors of their own doctrines. We can still expect that where God is present, we will find divine fire that illuminates our dark pathways, protects us from evil, and purifies us from sin. Like the Olympic torch, God's gospel fire is to be relayed around the world in all kinds of ways, but it must come from the Source—the sacred, eternal Flame.

clothes and put on others, and carry the ashes outside the camp to a place that is ceremonially clean.[u] [12]The fire on the altar must be kept burning; it must not go out. Every morning the priest is to add firewood and arrange the burnt offering on the fire and burn the fat of the fellowship offerings[a] on it. [13]The fire must be kept burning on the altar continuously; it must not go out.

The Grain Offering

[14]" 'These are the regulations for the grain offering:[v] Aaron's sons are to bring it before the LORD, in front of the altar. [15]The priest is to take a handful of fine flour and oil, together with all the incense on the grain offering,[w] and burn the memorial portion[x] on the altar as an aroma pleasing to the LORD. [16]Aaron and his sons[y] shall eat the rest[z] of it, but it is to be eaten without yeast[a] in a holy place;[b] they are to eat it in the courtyard of the Tent of Meeting. [17]It must not be baked with yeast; I have given it as their share of the offerings made to me by fire. Like the sin offering and the guilt offering, it is most holy.[c] [18]Any male descendant of Aaron may eat it.[d] It is his regular share of the offerings made to the LORD by fire for the generations to come. Whatever touches them will become holy.[b] ' "

[19]The LORD also said to Moses, [20]"This is the offering Aaron and his sons are to bring to the LORD on the day he[c] is anointed: a tenth of an ephah[d] [f] of fine flour as a regular grain offering,[g] half of it in the morning and half in the evening. [21]Prepare it with oil on a griddle;[h] bring it well-mixed and present the grain offering broken[e] in pieces as an aroma pleasing to the LORD. [22]The son who is to succeed him as anointed priest shall prepare it. It is the LORD's regular share and is to be burned completely. [23]Every grain offering of a priest shall be burned completely; it must not be eaten."

The Sin Offering

[24]The LORD said to Moses, [25]"Say to Aaron and his sons: 'These are the regulations for the sin offering: The sin offering is to be slaughtered before the LORD[i] in the place[j] the burnt offering is slaughtered; it is most holy. [26]The priest who offers it shall eat it; it is to be eaten in a holy place,[k] in the courtyard[l] of the Tent of Meeting. [27]Whatever touches any of the flesh will become holy,[m] and if any of the blood is spattered on a garment, you must wash it in a holy place. [28]The clay pot[n] the meat is cooked in must be broken; but if it is cooked in a bronze pot, the pot is to be scoured and rinsed with water. [29]Any male in a priest's family may eat it;[o] it is most holy.[p] [30]But any sin offering whose blood is brought into the Tent of Meeting to make atonement in the Holy Place[q] must not be eaten; it must be burned.[r]

6:11
u Lev 4:12

6:14
v Lev 2:1; 15:4
6:15
w Lev 2:9 x Lev 2:2
6:16
y Lev 2:3
z Eze 44:29
a Lev 2:11
b Lev 10:13

6:17
c ver 29; Ex 40:10; Nu 18:9,10
6:18
d ver 29; Nu 18:9-10
e ver 27
6:20
f Ex 16:36 g Ex 29:2

6:21
h Lev 2:5

6:25
i Lev 1:3 j Lev 1:5, 11
6:26
k ver 16
l Lev 10:17-18
6:27
m Ex 29:37
6:28
n Lev 11:33; 15:12
6:29
o ver 18 p ver 17
6:30
q Lev 4:18
r Lev 4:12

---

[a] 12 Traditionally *peace offerings*   [b] 18 Or *Whoever touches them must be holy*; similarly in verse 27   [c] 20 Or *each*   [d] 20 That is, probably about 2 quarts (about 2 liters)   [e] 21 The meaning of the Hebrew for this word is uncertain.

Leviticus 6:14–23

The first section of this passage specifies how priests were to eat their portions of the grain offerings brought by laypersons (vv. 14–18). The second gives directions for grain offerings brought by priests themselves (vv. 19–23). This kind of mandatory grain offering wasn't included in chapter 2, which dealt with voluntary grain offerings. Because the priests sacrificed their grain offerings on their own behalf, they were to be wholly burned up; no portion needed to be left over.

The high priest made his grain offering twice daily, according to the way people ate. It wasn't his gift to God; it was "the Lord's eternal due." In much the same way, the priests were entitled to eat the people's grain offerings.

What do you offer God regularly as his "eternal due"? What do you feel he most wants from you?

Leviticus 6:24–30

Chapter 4 doesn't say what was to happen to the remaining meat of an "outer altar" sin (purification) offering. Chapter 6 fills in the blank: It belonged to the priest. The meat was "most holy" and therefore restricted: The priest was to eat it in the tabernacle courtyard, though he could share it with any male priestly family members.

Through sin (purification) offerings and through Christ's ministry, God has allowed the unthinkable—holiness contacted by corruption—to help those who would otherwise be without help. Christians are to be "a chosen people, a royal priesthood, a holy nation, a people belonging to God" (2 Peter 2:9). And Christ has commanded his holy people to go out into the dark, polluted environment from which they came to praise God by serving as he did through contact with everyone in need—which is *everyone!*

The Guilt Offering

7:1
s Lev 5:14-6:7

7:3
t Ex 29:13;
Lev 3:4,9

7:6
u Lev 6:18;
Nu 18:9-10
v Lev 2:3

7:7
w Lev 6:17,26;
1Co 9:13
7:9
x Lev 2:5

7 " 'These are the regulations for the guilt offering, [s] which is most holy: [2]The guilt offering is to be slaughtered in the place where the burnt offering is slaughtered, and its blood is to be sprinkled against the altar on all sides. [3]All its fat[t] shall be offered: the fat tail and the fat that covers the inner parts, [4]both kidneys with the fat on them near the loins, and the covering of the liver, which is to be removed with the kidneys. [5]The priest shall burn them on the altar as an offering made to the LORD by fire. It is a guilt offering. [6]Any male in a priest's family may eat it, [u] but it must be eaten in a holy place; it is most holy. [v]

[7] " 'The same law applies to both the sin offering and the guilt offering: They belong to the priest[w] who makes atonement with them. [8]The priest who offers a burnt offering for anyone may keep its hide for himself. [9]Every grain offering baked in an oven or cooked in a pan or on a griddle[x] belongs to the priest who offers it, [10]and every grain offering, whether mixed with oil or dry, belongs equally to all the sons of Aaron.

The Fellowship Offering

7:12
y ver 13,15
z Lev 2:4; Nu 6:15

7:13
a Lev 23:17;
Am 4:5

7:15
b Lev 22:30

7:16
c Lev 19:5-8

7:18
d Lev 19:7
e Nu 18:27

[11] " 'These are the regulations for the fellowship offering[a] a person may present to the LORD:

[12] " 'If he offers it as an expression of thankfulness, then along with this thank offering[y] he is to offer cakes of bread made without yeast and mixed with oil, wafers[z] made without yeast and spread with oil, and cakes of fine flour well-kneaded and mixed with oil. [13]Along with his fellowship offering of thanksgiving he is to present an offering with cakes of bread made with yeast. [a] [14]He is to bring one of each kind as an offering, a contribution to the LORD; it belongs to the priest who sprinkles the blood of the fellowship offerings. [15]The meat of his fellowship offering of thanksgiving must be eaten on the day it is offered; he must leave none of it till morning. [b]

[16] " 'If, however, his offering is the result of a vow or is a freewill offering, the sacrifice shall be eaten on the day he offers it, but anything left over may be eaten on the next day. [c] [17]Any meat of the sacrifice left over till the third day must be burned up. [18]If any meat of the fellowship offering is eaten on the third day, it will not be accepted. [d] It will not be credited[e] to the one who offered it, for it is impure; the person who eats any of it will be held responsible.

[19] " 'Meat that touches anything ceremonially unclean must not be eaten; it must

---

[a] 11 Traditionally *peace offering*; also in verses 13-37

Leviticus 7:1–10

🔲 As with the sin (purification) offering, the meat of a guilt (reparation) offering was to be eaten by a male priest in the sacred precincts. Along the same vein, verses 8–10 summarize priestly privileges with regard to burnt and grain offerings.

🔲 Christian ministers aren't priests who receive portions of sacrifices for which we need their intervention to carry out spiritual transactions with God. But they do contribute some of the same vital services: worship leadership, discipline, and teaching people how to live holy lives. Jesus told his disciples that they could expect support from those who benefited from their ministry (Matt. 10:10; Luke 10:7), and Paul taught that pastors deserve material support for theirs (1 Cor. 9:4–11; cf. 1 Tim. 5:18).

Leviticus 7:11–21

🔲 *The motivation of thanksgiving affected a "fellowship" (or "well-being") offering in a way not specified in chapter 3. A person had to offer special grain items, aside from the usual grain and wine specified in Num-

bers 15:1–12. After giving one of each kind of cake or wafer as a "contribution to the LORD" (for consumption by the priest), the offerer, with any guests he may have invited, could enjoy a thanksgiving feast with the leftover meat and grain items.

To preserve the sacredness of the meat from "well-being" offerings, God restricted its consumption. The last ban (ritually impure persons couldn't eat sacrificial flesh) carried a most severe penalty: being "cut off from his people." This was a fate worse than death. In fact, it could go *beyond* death: A person stoned (killed) for Molech worship *also* could be "cut off" by God (e.g., 20:2–3).

🔲 Well-being offerings were occasions for joy, but as *slain* offerings they pointed to the future heavy cost God would pay for the complete joy we will one day experience. C.S. Lewis, a beloved 20th-century author, expressed this concept well: "All joy (as distinct from mere pleasure, still more amusement) emphasizes our pilgrim status; always reminds, beckons, awakens desire. Our best havings are wantings." What blessings do you already *have* in the sense that you *want* them and know they will one day be yours?

be burned up. As for other meat, anyone ceremonially clean may eat it. 20But if anyone who is unclean eats any meat of the fellowship offering belonging to the LORD, that person must be cut off from his people. f 21If anyone touches something unclean g—whether human uncleanness or an unclean animal or any unclean, detestable thing—and then eats any of the meat of the fellowship offering belonging to the LORD, that person must be cut off from his people.' "

Eating Fat and Blood Forbidden

22The LORD said to Moses, 23"Say to the Israelites: 'Do not eat any of the fat of cattle, sheep or goats. h 24The fat of an animal found dead or torn by wild animals i may be used for any other purpose, but you must not eat it. 25Anyone who eats the fat of an animal from which an offering by fire may be a made to the LORD must be cut off from his people. 26And wherever you live, you must not eat the blood j of any bird or animal. 27If anyone eats blood, k that person must be cut off from his people.' "

The Priests' Share

28The LORD said to Moses, 29"Say to the Israelites: 'Anyone who brings a fellowship offering to the LORD is to bring part of it as his sacrifice to the LORD. 30With his own hands he is to bring the offering made to the LORD by fire; he is to bring the fat, together with the breast, and wave the breast before the LORD as a wave offering. l 31The priest shall burn the fat on the altar, but the breast belongs to Aaron and his sons. m 32You are to give the right thigh of your fellowship offerings to the priest as a contribution. n 33The son of Aaron who offers the blood and the fat of the fellowship offering shall have the right thigh as his share. 34From the fellowship offerings of the Israelites, I have taken the breast that is waved and the thigh o that is presented and have given them to Aaron the priest and his sons p as their regular share from the Israelites.' "

35This is the portion of the offerings made to the LORD by fire that were allotted to Aaron and his sons on the day they were presented to serve the LORD as priests. 36On the day they were anointed, q the LORD commanded that the Israelites give this to them as their regular share for the generations to come.

37These, then, are the regulations for the burnt offering, r the grain offering, s the sin offering, the guilt offering, the ordination offering t and the fellowship offering, 38which the LORD gave Moses on Mount Sinai on the day he commanded the Israelites to bring their offerings to the LORD, u in the Desert of Sinai.

a 25 Or fire is

7:20
f Lev 22:3-7
7:21
g Lev 5:2; 11:24,28

7:23
h Lev 3:17; 17:13-14
7:24
i Ex 22:31
7:26
j Ge 9:4
7:27
k Lev 17:10-24; Ac 15:20,29

7:30
l Ex 29:24; Nu 6:20
7:31
m ver 34
7:32
n ver 34; Lev 9:21; Nu 6:20
7:34
o Lev 10:15
p Ex 29:27; Nu 18:18-19

7:36
q Ex 40:13,15; Lev 8:12,30

7:37
r Lev 6:9 s Lev 6:14
t ver 1,11

7:38
u Lev 1:2

Leviticus 7:22–27

The rule against eating suet/fat only applied to sacrificeable species, even if the animal died from something other than slaughter by a human being. Because all suet of such animals belonged to God, for a human to eat it was sacrilege—punishable by being cut off. The ban against eating meat from which the blood hadn't been drained applied to *all* animals except fish. This command was rooted in the instructions God gave Noah after the flood (Gen. 9:3–4). It had nothing to do with God's *ownership* of the blood.

Have you ever reflected on the importance God places on life blood? The shed blood was certainly sacred, a symbol of life that had to be treated with respect (Gen. 9:5–6). Atonement involved substituting one life for another: "Without the shedding of blood there is no forgiveness" (Heb. 9:12). The blood of the Old Testament sacrifices pointed ahead to that of the Lamb of God. Jesus' shed blood didn't *belong* to him; he willingly *gave it away* for our salvation. What other insights come to mind?

Leviticus 7:28–38

The priestly portions of a "well-being" offering consisted of the breast (dedicated through a ritual gesture) and the right thigh (set apart as a "contribution").

Verses 37–38 conclude the first major portion of Leviticus. The summary of sacrifices lists the types in order of their treatment in 6:8—7:36, except that it inserts "the ordination offering" before the well-being or fellowship offering. The ordination offering was part of the series of rituals through which priests were consecrated as God's special agents (Ex. 29; Lev. 8).

Only Christ is now qualified for high priesthood in God's heavenly temple (Heb. 7). Today, instead of praying horizontally toward the altar in the Jerusalem temple (e.g., 1 Kings 8:30,35; Dan. 6:10), we as Christians are invited to pray vertically to the place where Christ is always available to intercede for us (Heb. 7:25). We no longer need special agents to act as go-betweens: Our prayers shoot straight to the throne of grace, the control center of the universe (Heb. 4:14–16; cf. Rev. 4–5).

The Ordination of Aaron and His Sons

8:2
v Ex 30:23-25,30
w Ex 29:2-3
8:3
x Nu 8:9

8 The Lord said to Moses, 2"Bring Aaron and his sons, their garments, the anointing oil, *v* the bull for the sin offering, the two rams and the basket containing bread made without yeast, *w* 3and gather the entire assembly*x* at the entrance to the Tent of Meeting." 4Moses did as the Lord commanded him, and the assembly gathered at the entrance to the Tent of Meeting.

5Moses said to the assembly, "This is what the Lord has commanded to be done." 6Then Moses brought Aaron and his sons forward and washed them with water. *y* 7He put the tunic on Aaron, tied the sash around him, clothed him with the robe and put the ephod on him. He also tied the ephod to him by its skillfully woven waistband; so it was fastened on him. *z* 8He placed the breastpiece on him and put the Urim and Thummim*a* in the breastpiece. 9Then he placed the turban on Aaron's head and set the gold plate, the sacred diadem, *b* on the front of it, as the Lord commanded Moses.

8:6
y Ex 29:4; 30:19;
Ps 26:6; Ac 22:16;
1Co 6:11; Eph 5:26
8:7
z Ex 28:4
8:8
a Ex 28:30
8:9
b Ex 28:36
8:10
c ver 2 d Ex 30:26

10Then Moses took the anointing oil*c* and anointed*d* the tabernacle and everything in it, and so consecrated them. 11He sprinkled some of the oil on the altar seven times, anointing the altar and all its utensils and the basin with its stand, to consecrate them. *e* 12He poured some of the anointing oil on Aaron's head and anointed*f* him to consecrate him. *g* 13Then he brought Aaron's sons forward, put tunics on them, tied sashes around them and put headbands on them, as the Lord commanded Moses.

8:11
e Ex 30:29
8:12
f Lev 21:10,12
g Ex 30:30

14He then presented the bull*h* for the sin offering, *i* and Aaron and his sons laid their hands on its head. 15Moses slaughtered the bull and took some of the blood, and with his finger he put it on all the horns of the altar*j* to purify the altar. *k* He poured out the rest of the blood at the base of the altar. So he consecrated it to make atonement for it. *l* 16Moses also took all the fat around the inner parts, the covering of the liver, and both kidneys and their fat, and burned it on the altar. 17But the bull with its hide and its flesh and its offal*m* he burned up outside the camp, *n* as the Lord commanded Moses.

8:14
h Lev 4:3
i Ps 66:15;
Eze 43:19
8:15
j Lev 4:7
k Heb 9:22
l Eze 43:20
8:17
m Lev 4:11
n Lev 4:12
8:18
o ver 2

18He then presented the ram*o* for the burnt offering, and Aaron and his sons laid their hands on its head. 19Then Moses slaughtered the ram and sprinkled the blood against the altar on all sides. 20He cut the ram into pieces and burned the head, the pieces and the fat. 21He washed the inner parts and the legs with water and burned the whole ram on the altar as a burnt offering, a pleasing aroma, an offering made to the Lord by fire, as the Lord commanded Moses.

8:22
p ver 2

22He then presented the other ram, the ram for the ordination, *p* and Aaron and his sons laid their hands on its head. 23Moses slaughtered the ram and took some of its blood and put it on the lobe of Aaron's right ear, on the thumb of his right hand and on the big toe of his right foot. 24Moses also brought Aaron's sons forward and put some of the blood on the lobes of their right ears, on the thumbs of their right hands and on the big toes of their right feet. Then he sprinkled blood against the altar on all sides. *q* 25He took the fat, the fat tail, all the fat around the inner parts, the covering of the liver, both kidneys and their fat and the right thigh. 26Then from the basket of bread made without yeast, which was before the Lord, he took a cake of bread, and one made with oil, and a wafer; he put these on the fat portions and on the right thigh. 27He put all these in the hands of Aaron and his sons and waved them before the Lord as a wave offering. 28Then Moses took

8:24
q Heb 9:18-22

Leviticus 8:1–36

Leviticus 8–10 tells a single story in three sections: consecration (ch. 8) and service of the new priests (ch. 9) and the disastrous aftermath (ch. 10). Chapter 8 describes in detail the ceremonial rituals Moses performed to consecrate the sanctuary and its priesthood and to ordain the priests.

God called the entire ancient Israelite community to be "a kingdom of priests and a holy nation" (Ex 19:6), and Christians today live under the New Testament model of the "priesthood of all believers" (see 1 Peter 2:9). We are called and consecrated to go into the world to praise God. Jesus instructed a man released from demon possession, "Go home to your family and tell them how much the Lord has done for you" (Mark 5:19). What a simple but powerful testimony—something even the angels can't claim: God healed *me*! Are you busy spreading the wonderful News?

them from their hands and burned them on the altar on top of the burnt offering as an ordination offering, a pleasing aroma, an offering made to the LORD by fire. ²⁹He also took the breast—Moses' share of the ordination ram ʳ—and waved it before the LORD as a wave offering, as the LORD commanded Moses.

³⁰Then Moses took some of the anointing oil and some of the blood from the altar and sprinkled them on Aaron and his garments ˢ and on his sons and their garments. So he consecrated ᵗ Aaron and his garments and his sons and their garments. ³¹Moses then said to Aaron and his sons, "Cook the meat at the entrance to the Tent of Meeting and eat it there with the bread from the basket of ordination offerings, as I commanded, saying, ᵃ 'Aaron and his sons are to eat it.' ³²Then burn up the rest of the meat and the bread. ³³Do not leave the entrance to the Tent of Meeting for seven days, until the days of your ordination are completed, for your ordination will last seven days. ³⁴What has been done today was commanded by the LORD ᵘ to make atonement for you. ³⁵You must stay at the entrance to the Tent of Meeting day and night for seven days and do what the LORD requires, ᵛ so you will not die; for that is what I have been commanded." ³⁶So Aaron and his sons did everything the LORD commanded through Moses.

The Priests Begin Their Ministry

9 On the eighth day ʷ Moses summoned Aaron and his sons and the elders of Israel. ²He said to Aaron, "Take a bull calf for your sin offering and a ram for your burnt offering, both without defect, and present them before the LORD. ³Then say to the Israelites: 'Take a male goat for a sin offering, a calf and a lamb—both a year old and without defect—for a burnt offering, ⁴and an ox ᵇ and a ram for a fellowship offering ᶜ to sacrifice before the LORD, together with a grain offering mixed with oil. For today the LORD will appear to you. ˣ ' "

⁵They took the things Moses commanded to the front of the Tent of Meeting, and the entire assembly came near and stood before the LORD. ⁶Then Moses said, "This is what the LORD has commanded you to do, so that the glory of the LORD ʸ may appear to you."

⁷Moses said to Aaron, "Come to the altar and sacrifice your sin offering and your burnt offering and make atonement for yourself and the people; sacrifice the offering that is for the people and make atonement for them, as the LORD has commanded. ᶻ "

⁸So Aaron came to the altar and slaughtered the calf as a sin offering ᵃ for himself. ⁹His sons brought the blood to him, ᵇ and he dipped his finger into the blood and put it on the horns of the altar; the rest of the blood he poured out at the base of the altar. ᶜ ¹⁰On the altar he burned the fat, the kidneys and the covering of the liver from the sin offering, as the LORD commanded Moses; ¹¹the flesh and the hide ᵈ he burned up outside the camp. ᵉ

¹²Then he slaughtered the burnt offering. His sons handed him the blood, and he sprinkled it against the altar on all sides. ¹³They handed him the burnt offering piece by piece, including the head, and he burned them on the altar. ᶠ ¹⁴He washed

---

8:29
ʳ Lev 7:31-34

8:30
ˢ Ex 28:2 ᵗ Nu 3:3

8:34
ᵘ Heb 7:16
8:35
ᵛ Nu 3:7; 9:19; Dt 11:1; 1Ki 2:3; Eze 48:11

9:1
ʷ Eze 43:27

9:4
ˣ Ex 29:43

9:6
ʸ ver 23; Ex 24:16

9:7
ᶻ Heb 5:1,3; 7:27
9:8
ᵃ Lev 4:1-12
9:9
ᵇ ver 12,18
ᶜ Lev 4:7

9:11
ᵈ Lev 4:11
ᵉ Lev 4:12; 8:17

9:13
ᶠ Lev 1:8

ᵃ 31 Or *I was commanded:*   ᵇ 4 The Hebrew word can include both male and female; also in verses 18 and 19.   ᶜ 4 Traditionally *peace offering;* also in verses 18 and 22

Leviticus 9:1–24

After Moses had issued preliminary instructions, Aaron approached the altar to make his debut as Israel's high priest, assisted by his newly ordained sons. Aaron & Sons officiated in all the inaugural sacrifices, first for themselves and then for the rest of the people. The end of Leviticus 9 records the glorious and miraculous climax of the first Aaronic service. When God's fire flashed forth to vaporize in an instant the animal pieces that would have burned for many hours (cf. 6:9),

the people were jubilant and awestruck.

If God loves us (John 3:16), why do we need a mediator to interact with him? Christ's sacrifice and intercession don't *make* God love us; they *result* from his love. We need a go-between (Heb. 4:15–16) because sin has separated us from God's holy Presence (e.g., Gen. 3; Ex. 33:20). Christ's sacrifice uniquely empowers him to separate us from that sin (Heb. 9:14–15). Hebrews invites us as Christians to approach God through the avenue of access Christ has made available (10:19–22).

the inner parts and the legs and burned them on top of the burnt offering on the altar.

15Aaron then brought the offering that was for the people. *g* He took the goat for the people's sin offering and slaughtered it and offered it for a sin offering as he did with the first one.

16He brought the burnt offering and offered it in the prescribed way. *h* 17He also brought the grain offering, took a handful of it and burned it on the altar in addition to the morning's burnt offering. *i*

18He slaughtered the ox and the ram as the fellowship offering for the people. *j* His sons handed him the blood, and he sprinkled it against the altar on all sides. 19But the fat portions of the ox and the ram—the fat tail, the layer of fat, the kidneys and the covering of the liver— 20these they laid on the breasts, and then Aaron burned the fat on the altar. 21Aaron waved the breasts and the right thigh before the LORD as a wave offering, *k* as Moses commanded.

22Then Aaron lifted his hands toward the people and blessed them. *l* And having sacrificed the sin offering, the burnt offering and the fellowship offering, he stepped down.

23Moses and Aaron then went into the Tent of Meeting. When they came out, they blessed the people; and the glory of the LORD *m* appeared to all the people. 24Fire *n* came out from the presence of the LORD and consumed the burnt offering and the fat portions on the altar. And when all the people saw it, they shouted for joy and fell facedown. *o*

The Death of Nadab and Abihu

10 Aaron's sons Nadab and Abihu *p* took their censers, put fire in them *q* and added incense; and they offered unauthorized fire before the LORD, contrary to his command. *r* 2So fire came out from the presence of the LORD and consumed them, *s* and they died before the LORD. 3Moses then said to Aaron, "This is what the LORD spoke of when he said:

" 'Among those who approach me *t*
I will show myself holy; *u*
in the sight of all the people
I will be honored. *v* ' "

Aaron remained silent.

4Moses summoned Mishael and Elzaphan, *w* sons of Aaron's uncle Uzziel, *x* and said to them, "Come here; carry your cousins outside the camp, *y* away from the front of the sanctuary." 5So they came and carried them, still in their tunics, *z* outside the camp, as Moses ordered.

6Then Moses said to Aaron and his sons Eleazar and Ithamar, "Do not let your hair become unkempt, *a a* and do not tear your clothes, or you will die and the LORD will be angry with the whole community. *b* But your relatives, all the house of Isra-

---

a 6 Or *Do not uncover your heads*

9:15
g Lev 4:27-31

9:16
h Lev 1:1-13

9:17
i Lev 2:1-2; 3:5
9:18
j Lev 3:1-11

9:21
k Ex 29:24,26;
Lev 7:30-34
9:22
l Nu 6:23; Dt 21:5;
Lk 24:50

9:23
m ver 6
9:24
n Jdg 6:21; 2Ch 7:1
o 1Ki 18:39

10:1
p Ex 24:1; Nu 3:2-4;
26:61 *q* Lev 16:12
r Ex 30:9

10:2
s Nu 3:4; 16:35;
26:61

10:3
t Ex 19:22
u Ex 30:29;
Lev 21:6; Eze 28:22
v Isa 49:3

10:4
w Ex 6:22 *x* Ex 6:18
y Ac 5:6,9,10

10:5
z Lev 8:13

10:6
a Lev 21:10
b Nu 1:53; 16:22;
Jos 7:1; 22:18;
2Sa 24:1

Leviticus 10:1–20

🔲🔲 Nadab and Abihu may have had "good reasons" for what they did, just as Uzzah would later have a good reason to grasp the ark of the covenant to steady it when the cart jolted (2 Sam. 6:6–7). But these reasons weren't good enough to prevent their sudden deaths. For those who came this close to the "nuclear reactor" of the divine Presence, there was no leeway for deviations from protocol.

On the other hand, Aaron's decision not to eat the meat wasn't a careless ritual mistake but a careful, considered choice. The priests, he felt, were unworthy to bear the guilt of others on the very day their family had fallen under divine condemnation. Moses' approval im-

plied that the sacrifice remained valid in spite of this departure from the norm.

🔲 God expected Aaron, Eleazar, and Ithamar to carry on for others despite their pain. Don and Helen Thomas buried their four-year-old Margaret in the Congo after she died of cerebral malaria, but stayed on as missionaries. Father Damien De Veuster, a Belgian Catholic priest, devoted his life to a colony of hopeless lepers banished to a remote peninsula of Molokai, Hawaii. Eventually he succumbed to the disease but stayed on with those to whom he now belonged. When have other people become "your own" to the extent that you felt compelled to live out God's mandate to "carry each other's burdens"?

el, may mourn for those the LORD has destroyed by fire. [7]Do not leave the entrance to the Tent of Meeting or you will die, because the LORD's anointing oil[c] is on you." So they did as Moses said.

[8]Then the LORD said to Aaron, [9]"You and your sons are not to drink wine[d] or other fermented drink[e] whenever you go into the Tent of Meeting, or you will die. This is a lasting ordinance for the generations to come. [10]You must distinguish between the holy and the common, between the unclean and the clean,[f] [11]and you must teach[g] the Israelites all the decrees the LORD has given them through Moses.[h]"

[12]Moses said to Aaron and his remaining sons, Eleazar and Ithamar, "Take the grain offering left over from the offerings made to the LORD by fire and eat it prepared without yeast beside the altar,[i] for it is most holy. [13]Eat it in a holy place, because it is your share and your sons' share of the offerings made to the LORD by fire; for so I have been commanded. [14]But you and your sons and your daughters may eat the breast that was waved and the thigh that was presented. Eat them in a ceremonially clean place;[j] they have been given to you and your children as your share of the Israelites' fellowship offerings.[a] [15]The thigh[k] that was presented and the breast that was waved must be brought with the fat portions of the offerings made by fire, to be waved before the LORD as a wave offering. This will be the regular share for you and your children, as the LORD has commanded."

[16]When Moses inquired about the goat of the sin offering[l] and found that it had been burned up, he was angry with Eleazar and Ithamar, Aaron's remaining sons, and asked, [17]"Why didn't you eat the sin offering[m] in the sanctuary area? It is most holy; it was given to you to take away the guilt of the community by making atonement for them before the LORD. [18]Since its blood was not taken into the Holy Place,[n] you should have eaten the goat in the sanctuary area, as I commanded."

[19]Aaron replied to Moses, "Today they sacrificed their sin offering and their burnt offering[o] before the LORD, but such things as this have happened to me. Would the LORD have been pleased if I had eaten the sin offering today?" [20]When Moses heard this, he was satisfied.

Clean and Unclean Food

11 The LORD said to Moses and Aaron, [2]"Say to the Israelites: 'Of all the animals that live on land, these are the ones you may eat:[p] [3]You may eat any animal that has a split hoof completely divided and that chews the cud.

[4]"There are some that only chew the cud or only have a split hoof, but you must not eat them. The camel, though it chews the cud, does not have a split hoof; it is ceremonially unclean for you. [5]The coney,[b] though it chews the cud, does not have a split hoof; it is unclean for you. [6]The rabbit, though it chews the cud, does not have a split hoof; it is unclean for you. [7]And the pig,[q] though it has a split hoof completely divided, does not chew the cud; it is unclean for you. [8]You must not eat their meat or touch their carcasses; they are unclean for you.[r]

[9]"'Of all the creatures living in the water of the seas and the streams, you may eat any that have fins and scales. [10]But all creatures in the seas or streams that do not have fins and scales—whether among all the swarming things or among all the other living creatures in the water—you are to detest.[s] [11]And since you are to de-

---

[a] 14 Traditionally *peace offerings*   [b] 5 That is, the hyrax or rock badger

---

Marginal references:

10:7 c Ex 28:41; Lev 21:12
10:9 d Hos 4:11 e Pr 20:1; Isa 28:7; Eze 44:21; Lk 1:15; Eph 5:18; 1Ti 3:3; Tit 1:7
10:10 f Lev 11:47; 20:25; Eze 22:26
10:11 g Mal 2:7 h Dt 24:8
10:12 i Lev 6:14-18; 21:22
10:14 j Ex 29:24,26-27; Lev 7:31,34; Nu 18:11
10:15 k Lev 7:34
10:16 l Lev 9:3
10:17 m Lev 6:24-30
10:18 n Lev 6:26,30
10:19 o Lev 9:12
11:2 p Ac 10:12-14
11:7 q Isa 65:4; 66:3,17
11:8 r Isa 52:11; Heb 9:10
11:10 s Lev 7:18

Leviticus 11:1–47

The conclusion in verses 43–45 emphasizes the point of the chapter: Observing God's dietary regulations allowed an individual Israelite to imitate God's holiness, which is utterly opposed to impurity. If God's people were to have made themselves repulsive by what they ate, they would have misrepresented him. Living according to the dietary regulations outlined in chapter 11 was vital for maintaining a healthy divine-human relationship.

Why wasn't a spring or cistern affected by the carcass of an impure creature? Because, as a pure source, it couldn't be defiled. The same applies to Jesus, who could touch and heal lepers without becoming impure (e.g., Matt. 8:2–3). We can come to him, contaminated as we are by all kinds of faults that creep and crawl into every corner of our lives. Yet when he touches us with his healing power and cleanses us with his "living water" of life (cf. John 4:10,13–14; Rev. 7:17; 21:6,17), he has just as much purity and power to give as he had before.

test them, you must not eat their meat and you must detest their carcasses. ¹²Anything living in the water that does not have fins and scales is to be detestable to you.

¹³ " 'These are the birds you are to detest and not eat because they are detestable: the eagle, the vulture, the black vulture, ¹⁴the red kite, any kind of black kite, ¹⁵any kind of raven, ¹⁶the horned owl, the screech owl, the gull, any kind of hawk, ¹⁷the little owl, the cormorant, the great owl, ¹⁸the white owl, the desert owl, the osprey, ¹⁹the stork, any kind of heron, the hoopoe and the bat. ᵃ

²⁰ " 'All flying insects that walk on all fours are to be detestable to you. ᵗ ²¹There are, however, some winged creatures that walk on all fours that you may eat: those that have jointed legs for hopping on the ground. ²²Of these you may eat any kind of locust, ᵘ katydid, cricket or grasshopper. ²³But all other winged creatures that have four legs you are to detest.

²⁴ " 'You will make yourselves unclean by these; whoever touches their carcasses will be unclean till evening. ²⁵Whoever picks up one of their carcasses must wash his clothes, ᵛ and he will be unclean till evening. ʷ

²⁶ " 'Every animal that has a split hoof not completely divided or that does not chew the cud is unclean for you; whoever touches the carcass of any of them will be unclean. ²⁷Of all the animals that walk on all fours, those that walk on their paws are unclean for you; whoever touches their carcasses will be unclean till evening. ²⁸Anyone who picks up their carcasses must wash his clothes, and he will be unclean till evening. They are unclean for you.

²⁹ " 'Of the animals that move about on the ground, these are unclean for you: the weasel, the rat, ˣ any kind of great lizard, ³⁰the gecko, the monitor lizard, the wall lizard, the skink and the chameleon. ³¹Of all those that move along the ground, these are unclean for you. Whoever touches them when they are dead will be unclean till evening. ³²When one of them dies and falls on something, that article, whatever its use, will be unclean, whether it is made of wood, cloth, hide or sackcloth. ʸ Put it in water; it will be unclean till evening, and then it will be clean. ³³If one of them falls into a clay pot, everything in it will be unclean, and you must break the pot. ᶻ ³⁴Any food that could be eaten but has water on it from such a pot is unclean, and any liquid that could be drunk from it is unclean. ³⁵Anything that one of their carcasses falls on becomes unclean; an oven or cooking pot must be broken up. They are unclean, and you are to regard them as unclean. ³⁶A spring, however, or a cistern for collecting water remains clean, but anyone who touches one of these carcasses is unclean. ³⁷If a carcass falls on any seeds that are to be planted, they remain clean. ³⁸But if water has been put on the seed and a carcass falls on it, it is unclean for you.

³⁹ " 'If an animal that you are allowed to eat dies, anyone who touches the carcass will be unclean till evening. ⁴⁰Anyone who eats some of the carcass must wash his clothes, and he will be unclean till evening. ᵃ Anyone who picks up the carcass must wash his clothes, and he will be unclean till evening.

⁴¹ " 'Every creature that moves about on the ground is detestable; it is not to be eaten. ⁴²You are not to eat any creature that moves about on the ground, whether it moves on its belly or walks on all fours or on many feet; it is detestable. ⁴³Do not defile yourselves by any of these creatures. ᵇ Do not make yourselves unclean by means of them or be made unclean by them. ⁴⁴I am the LORD your God; ᶜ consecrate yourselves ᵈ and be holy, ᵉ because I am holy. ᶠ Do not make yourselves unclean by any creature that moves about on the ground. ⁴⁵I am the LORD who brought you up out of Egypt ᵍ to be your God; ʰ therefore be holy, because I am holy. ⁱ

⁴⁶ " 'These are the regulations concerning animals, birds, every living thing that *moves in the water* and every creature that moves about on the ground. ⁴⁷You must distinguish between the unclean and the clean, between living creatures that may be eaten and those that may not be eaten. ʲ' "

ᵃ 19 The precise identification of some of the birds, insects and animals in this chapter is uncertain.

11:20
ᵗ Ac 10:14

11:22
ᵘ Mt 3:4; Mk 1:6

11:25
ᵛ Lev 14:8,47; 15:5
ʷ ver 40; Nu 31:24

11:29
ˣ Isa 66:17

11:32
ʸ Lev 15:12

11:33
ᶻ Lev 6:28; 15:12

11:40
ᵃ Lev 17:15; 22:8;
Eze 44:31

11:43
ᵇ Lev 20:25
11:44
ᶜ Ex 6:2,7; Isa 43:3;
51:15 ᵈ Lev 20:7
ᵉ Ex 19:6
ᶠ Lev 19:2; Ps 99:3;
Eph 1:4; 1Th 4:7;
1Pe 1:15,16*
11:45
ᵍ Lev 25:38,55;
Ex 6:7; 20:2
ʰ Ge 17:7 ⁱ Ex 19:6;
1Pe 1:16*

11:47
ʲ Lev 10:10

Purification After Childbirth

12 The LORD said to Moses, [2] "Say to the Israelites: 'A woman who becomes pregnant and gives birth to a son will be ceremonially unclean for seven days, just as she is unclean during her monthly period.[k] [3] On the eighth day the boy is to be circumcised.[l] [4] Then the woman must wait thirty-three days to be purified from her bleeding. She must not touch anything sacred or go to the sanctuary until the days of her purification are over. [5] If she gives birth to a daughter, for two weeks the woman will be unclean, as during her period. Then she must wait sixty-six days to be purified from her bleeding.

[6] "'When the days of her purification for a son or daughter are over,[m] she is to bring to the priest at the entrance to the Tent of Meeting a year-old lamb[n] for a burnt offering and a young pigeon or a dove for a sin offering.[o] [7] He shall offer them before the LORD to make atonement for her, and then she will be ceremonially clean from her flow of blood.

"'These are the regulations for the woman who gives birth to a boy or a girl.' [8] If she cannot afford a lamb, she is to bring two doves or two young pigeons,[p] one for a burnt offering and the other for a sin offering.[q] In this way the priest will make atonement for her, and she will be clean.'[r] "

Regulations About Infectious Skin Diseases

13 The LORD said to Moses and Aaron, [2] "When anyone has a swelling[s] or a rash or a bright spot[t] on his skin that may become an infectious skin disease,[a][u] he must be brought to Aaron the priest[v] or to one of his sons[b] who is a priest. [3] The priest is to examine the sore on his skin, and if the hair in the sore has turned white and the sore appears to be more than skin deep,[c] it is an infectious skin disease. When the priest examines him, he shall pronounce him ceremonially unclean.[w] [4] If the spot[x] on his skin is white but does not appear to be more than skin deep and the hair in it has not turned white, the priest is to put the infected person in isolation for seven days.[y] [5] On the seventh day[z] the priest is to examine him,[a] and if he sees that the sore is unchanged and has not spread in the skin, he is to keep him in isolation another seven days. [6] On the seventh day the priest is to examine him again, and if the sore has faded and has not spread in the skin, the priest shall pronounce him clean;[b] it is only a rash. The man must wash his clothes,[c] and he will be clean.[d] [7] But if the rash does spread in his skin after he has shown himself to the

---

[a] 2 Traditionally *leprosy*; the Hebrew word was used for various diseases affecting the skin—not necessarily leprosy; also elsewhere in this chapter.   [b] 2 Or *descendants*   [c] 3 Or *be lower than the rest of the skin*; also elsewhere in this chapter

---

Leviticus 12:1–8
The translation "sin" offering (as opposed to "purification" offering) begs the question how a woman has sinned in giving birth. She hasn't. Nor is she sick. Childbirth and regular menstruation are healthy processes, in spite of a sign at the office of a doctor in Rome: "Specialist in Women and Other Diseases." The goal/meaning of the ritual procedure was to remove physical, ritual impurity from the woman, not to remove moral fault in preparation for divine forgiveness.

Even though sin offerings didn't always relate to sins, they had to do with the state of human mortality (the inevitability of death) resulting from sin. It's no accident that Christ offered forgiveness with healing during his earthly ministry. This was a foretaste of the gift provided by his final sacrifice—the ultimate sin/purification offering. We think of Jesus' death as a sacrifice for sin, and so it was (John 1:29). But it went further, eliminating eternal death as a result of the inborn, sinful nature of all people.

Leviticus 13:1–46
The familiar but incorrect translation "leprosy" for the scaly skin disease referred to here arose from confusion regarding translation of a Greek word in the Septuagint (Greek translation of the Hebrew OT). *Lepra* isn't leprosy (Hansen's Disease). The mix-up began in A.D. 777–857, when a doctor, John of Damascus, misused the term. But because Leviticus deals in religious ritual, not medicine, scientific identification of the disease isn't critical.

The Biblical stigma of scale disease had to do with *ritual* impurity. Diseases like AIDS can result from specific sins, but three truths can help us: (1) A diseased result doesn't automatically imply a sinful cause in the sense of one person's particular sin. (2) Only God can judge the heart. (3) God can both forgive and heal. As an example to us, Jesus gave the paralyzed man in Mark 2 the combination he needed: healing grace. When have you as his representative offered this dynamic formula to a hurting person?

13:7
e Lk 5:14

priest to be pronounced clean, he must appear before the priest again. [e] [8]The priest is to examine him, and if the rash has spread in the skin, he shall pronounce him unclean; it is an infectious disease.

[9]"When anyone has an infectious skin disease, he must be brought to the priest. [10]The priest is to examine him, and if there is a white swelling in the skin that has turned the hair white and if there is raw flesh in the swelling, [11]it is a chronic skin disease[f] and the priest shall pronounce him unclean. He is not to put him in isolation, because he is already unclean.

13:11
f Ex 4:6; Lev 14:8;
Nu 12:10; Mt 8:2

[12]"If the disease breaks out all over his skin and, so far as the priest can see, it covers all the skin of the infected person from head to foot, [13]the priest is to examine him, and if the disease has covered his whole body, he shall pronounce that person clean. Since it has all turned white, he is clean. [14]But whenever raw flesh appears on him, he will be unclean. [15]When the priest sees the raw flesh, he shall pronounce him unclean. The raw flesh is unclean; he has an infectious disease. [g] [16]Should the raw flesh change and turn white, he must go to the priest. [17]The priest is to examine him, and if the sores have turned white, the priest shall pronounce the infected person clean;[h] then he will be clean.

13:15
g ver 2

13:17
h ver 6
13:18
i Ex 9:9
13:19
j ver 24,42;
Lev 14:37 k ver 2

[18]"When someone has a boil[i] on his skin and it heals, [19]and in the place where the boil was, a white swelling or reddish-white[j] spot[k] appears, he must present himself to the priest. [20]The priest is to examine it, and if it appears to be more than skin deep and the hair in it has turned white, the priest shall pronounce him unclean. It is an infectious skin disease[l] that has broken out where the boil was. [21]But if, when the priest examines it, there is no white hair in it and it is not more than skin deep and has faded, then the priest is to put him in isolation for seven days. [22]If it is spreading in the skin, the priest shall pronounce him unclean; it is infectious. [23]But if the spot is unchanged and has not spread, it is only a scar from the boil, and the priest shall pronounce him clean.[m]

13:20
l ver 2

13:23
m ver 6

[24]"When someone has a burn on his skin and a reddish-white or white spot appears in the raw flesh of the burn, [25]the priest is to examine the spot, and if the hair in it has turned white, and it appears to be more than skin deep, it is an infectious disease that has broken out in the burn. The priest shall pronounce him unclean; it is an infectious skin disease.[n] [26]But if the priest examines it and there is no white hair in the spot and if it is not more than skin deep and has faded, then the priest is to put him in isolation for seven days.[o] [27]On the seventh day the priest is to examine him,[p] and if it is spreading in the skin, the priest shall pronounce him unclean; it is an infectious skin disease. [28]If, however, the spot is unchanged and has not spread in the skin but has faded, it is a swelling from the burn, and the priest shall pronounce him clean; it is only a scar from the burn.[q]

13:25
n ver 11

13:26
o ver 4
13:27
p ver 5

13:28
q ver 2
13:29
r ver 43,44

[29]"If a man or woman has a sore on the head[r] or on the chin, [30]the priest is to examine the sore, and if it appears to be more than skin deep and the hair in it is yellow and thin, the priest shall pronounce that person unclean; it is an itch, an infectious disease of the head or chin. [31]But if, when the priest examines this kind of sore, it does not seem to be more than skin deep and there is no black hair in it, then the priest is to put the infected person in isolation for seven days.[s] [32]On the seventh day the priest is to examine the sore,[t] and if the itch has not spread and there is no yellow hair in it and it does not appear to be more than skin deep, [33]he must be shaved except for the diseased area, and the priest is to keep him in isolation another seven days. [34]On the seventh day the priest is to examine the itch,[u] and if it has not spread in the skin and appears to be no more than skin deep, the priest

13:31
s ver 4
13:32
t ver 5

13:34
u ver 5

Leviticus 13:47–59

In verses 2–44 the diagnostic procedure for skin disease is logical. In verses 47–59 a roughly parallel procedure for priestly examination at one-week intervals was applied to fabrics affected by mold. Treating these phenomena as a unified problem was a remarkably holistic approach. Not only are humans affected by sin; so is our environment (see Rom. 8:21–22).

We are the ultimate ecological disaster. But we have the choice to accept the solution from God, who alone can put us and everything around us back together again. Meanwhile, it's right and in our best interest that we nurture our environment to the best of our ability. Do you see the environment as something you can impact positively for the kingdom?

shall pronounce him clean. He must wash his clothes, and he will be clean. ^v ³⁵But if the itch does spread in the skin after he is pronounced clean, ³⁶the priest is to examine him, and if the itch has spread in the skin, the priest does not need to look for yellow hair; the person is unclean. ^w ³⁷If, however, in his judgment it is unchanged and black hair has grown in it, the itch is healed. He is clean, and the priest shall pronounce him clean.

³⁸"When a man or woman has white spots on the skin, ³⁹the priest is to examine them, and if the spots are dull white, it is a harmless rash that has broken out on the skin; that person is clean.

⁴⁰"When a man has lost his hair and is bald, ^x he is clean. ⁴¹If he has lost his hair from the front of his scalp and has a bald forehead, he is clean. ⁴²But if he has a reddish-white sore on his bald head or forehead, it is an infectious disease breaking out on his head or forehead. ⁴³The priest is to examine him, and if the swollen sore on his head or forehead is reddish-white like an infectious skin disease, ⁴⁴the man is diseased and is unclean. The priest shall pronounce him unclean because of the sore on his head.

⁴⁵"The person with such an infectious disease must wear torn clothes, ^y let his hair be unkempt, ^a cover the lower part of his face ^z and cry out, 'Unclean! Unclean!' ^a ⁴⁶As long as he has the infection he remains unclean. He must live alone; he must live outside the camp. ^b

Regulations About Mildew

⁴⁷"If any clothing is contaminated with mildew—any woolen or linen clothing, ⁴⁸any woven or knitted material of linen or wool, any leather or anything made of leather— ⁴⁹and if the contamination in the clothing, or leather, or woven or knitted material, or any leather article, is greenish or reddish, it is a spreading mildew and must be shown to the priest. ^c ⁵⁰The priest is to examine the mildew ^d and isolate the affected article for seven days. ⁵¹On the seventh day he is to examine it, ^e and if the mildew has spread in the clothing, or the woven or knitted material, or the leather, whatever its use, it is a destructive mildew; the article is unclean. ^f ⁵²He must burn up the clothing, or the woven or knitted material of wool or linen, or any leather article that has the contamination in it, because the mildew is destructive; the article must be burned up. ^g

⁵³"But if, when the priest examines it, the mildew has not spread in the clothing, or the woven or knitted material, or the leather article, ⁵⁴he shall order that the contaminated article be washed. Then he is to isolate it for another seven days. ⁵⁵After the affected article has been washed, the priest is to examine it, and if the mildew has not changed its appearance, even though it has not spread, it is unclean. Burn it with fire, whether the mildew has affected one side or the other. ⁵⁶If, when the priest examines it, the mildew has faded after the article has been washed, he is to tear the contaminated part out of the clothing, or the leather, or the woven or knitted material. ⁵⁷But if it reappears in the clothing, or in the woven or knitted material, or in the leather article, it is spreading, and whatever has the mildew must be burned with fire. ⁵⁸The clothing, or the woven or knitted material, or any leather article that has been washed and is rid of the mildew, must be washed again, and it will be clean."

⁵⁹These are the regulations concerning contamination by mildew in woolen or linen clothing, woven or knitted material, or any leather article, for pronouncing them clean or unclean.

Cleansing From Infectious Skin Diseases

14 The LORD said to Moses, ²"These are the regulations for the diseased person at the time of his ceremonial cleansing, when he is brought to the priest: ^h ³The priest is to go outside the camp and examine him. ⁱ If the person has been healed of his infectious skin disease, ^b ⁴the priest shall order that two live clean birds

---

^a 45 Or *clothes, uncover his head*   ^b 3 Traditionally *leprosy*; the Hebrew word was used for various diseases affecting the skin—not necessarily leprosy; also elsewhere in this chapter.

13:34
v Lev 11:25

13:36
w ver 30

13:40
x Lev 21:5;
2Ki 2:23; Isa 3:24;
15:2; 22:12;
Eze 27:31; 29:18;
Am 8:10; Mic 1:16

13:45
y Lev 10:6
z Eze 24:17,22;
Mic 3:7 a Lev 5:2;
La 4:15; Lk 17:12
13:46
b Nu 5:1-4; 12:14;
2Ki 7:3; 15:5;
Lk 17:12

13:49
c Mk 1:44
13:50
d Eze 44:23
13:51
e ver 5 f Lev 14:44

13:52
g ver 55,57

14:2
h Mt 8:2-4;
Mk 1:40-44;
Lk 5:12-14; 17:14
14:3
i Lev 13:46

Outdated Laws?

13:47–59

One of the major weaknesses of modern culture is our loss of morality. We misconstrue the nature of laws, rules, and command(ment)s, calling them "legalisms." Then, based on this misunderstanding, we reject them out of hand.

Similar reasoning may lead us to avoid the Biblical books of Leviticus and Numbers. We don't like reading what appear to be the outdated dictates of a "grouchy" God who seems to have gotten up on the wrong side of bed.

Yet, if we read Leviticus and Numbers faithfully, our squeamishness about morality itself begins to disappear. There are two reasons why:

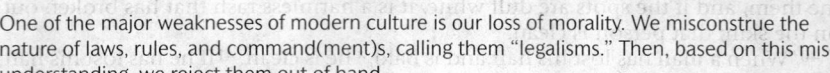

Is it any wonder that the New Testament so often references Levitical laws to explain the morality of people in God's kingdom?

First, the laws of Leviticus are effective because they were intended for groups of people, not for individuals. These laws are only secondarily about safety, health, order, and good manners. Make no mistake, they address these issues—but only secondarily, after they speak about the worship of God. Worship is the precondition, the setting, of all the Levitical laws. Why are we to love our neighbor (19:18)? Because we can't worship God effectively unless we do. Once this principle has been established, we discover that loving our neighbor makes for good, safe, healthy relationships, both vertically and horizontally.

We live in a culture where we tend to understand laws, rules, and commands primarily as they relate to us as individuals. Because we live in an individualistic age, it takes deliberate effort to recognize that individual morality is rooted in communal morality. In the Bible this isn't always made explicit because in Biblical times it was assumed that community core values preceded individual values. Today the order's been reversed.

Second, the laws of Leviticus only make sense to us if we are able to transpose their meaning from a cultural context three millennia in time and half a world in distance from our own. The content of many, if not most, of these laws seems strange and, not unexpectedly, absolutely foreign.

The discussions of mildew in chapter 13, for example, can only be understood by someone living in a humid zone where mildew remains a problem. And the solution to "destructive mildew"—to have the priest adjudicate whether or not the article in question is to be destroyed—isn't something most modern church leaders would appreciate encountering in their job description. On the other hand, the implications of this law in the context of the Old Testament Israelite community are evident. Still today, any destructive force with the potential to spread throughout the body of Christ is something we are all to be concerned with corralling.

Is it any wonder that the New Testament so often references Levitical laws to explain the morality of people in God's kingdom? They are, in the final analysis, laws sent to *us* by God through Moses. That means that, like it or not, they are important. They are prohibitions that ordered the lives of a holy, tribal community centered in the divine presence. Since that is what we long for the church at large (and individual congregations) to be, we could do worse than to try to live by the general principles promoted by these laws.

God's call to holiness isn't a summons to be embraced by hermits. It's a call that is always to be lived out in relation to a community, a group of people centered in and around the worship of God.

and some cedar wood, scarlet yarn and hyssop be brought for the one to be cleansed.[j] [5]Then the priest shall order that one of the birds be killed over fresh water in a clay pot. [6]He is then to take the live bird and dip it, together with the cedar wood, the scarlet yarn and the hyssop, into the blood of the bird that was killed over the fresh water.[k] [7]Seven times he shall sprinkle[l] the one to be cleansed of the infectious disease and pronounce him clean. Then he is to release the live bird in the open fields.

[8]"The person to be cleansed must wash his clothes,[m] shave off all his hair and bathe with water;[n] then he will be ceremonially clean.[o] After this he may come into the camp,[p] but he must stay outside his tent for seven days. [9]On the seventh day he must shave off all his hair; he must shave his head, his beard, his eyebrows and the rest of his hair. He must wash his clothes and bathe himself with water, and he will be clean.

[10]"On the eighth day[q] he must bring two male lambs and one ewe lamb a year old, each without defect, along with three-tenths of an ephah[a] of fine flour mixed with oil for a grain offering,[r] and one log[b] of oil.[s] [11]The priest who pronounces him clean shall present both the one to be cleansed and his offerings before the LORD at the entrance to the Tent of Meeting.

[12]"Then the priest is to take one of the male lambs and offer it as a guilt offering,[t] along with the log of oil; he shall wave them before the LORD as a wave offering.[u] [13]He is to slaughter the lamb in the holy place[v] where the sin offering and the burnt offering are slaughtered. Like the sin offering, the guilt offering belongs to the priest;[w] it is most holy. [14]The priest is to take some of the blood of the guilt offering and put it on the lobe of the right ear of the one to be cleansed, on the thumb of his right hand and on the big toe of his right foot.[x] [15]The priest shall then take some of the log of oil, pour it in the palm of his own left hand, [16]dip his right forefinger into the oil in his palm, and with his finger sprinkle some of it before the LORD seven times. [17]The priest is to put some of the oil remaining in his palm on the lobe of the right ear of the one to be cleansed, on the thumb of his right hand and on the big toe of his right foot, on top of the blood of the guilt offering. [18]The rest of the oil in his palm the priest shall put on the head of the one to be cleansed and make atonement for him before the LORD.

[19]"Then the priest is to sacrifice the sin offering and make atonement for the one to be cleansed from his uncleanness. After that, the priest shall slaughter the burnt offering [20]and offer it on the altar, together with the grain offering, and make atonement for him, and he will be clean.[y]

[21]"If, however, he is poor[z] and cannot afford these,[a] he must take one male lamb as a guilt offering to be waved to make atonement for him, together with a tenth of an ephah[c] of fine flour mixed with oil for a grain offering, a log of oil, [22]and two doves or two young pigeons,[b] which he can afford, one for a sin offering and the other for a burnt offering.

---

[a] 10 That is, probably about 6 quarts (about 6.5 liters)   [b] 10 That is, probably about 2/3 pint (about 0.3 liter); also in verses 12, 15, 21 and 24   [c] 21 That is, probably about 2 quarts (about 2 liters)

Leviticus 14:1–32

📖 The good news was that scale disease could run its course. Leviticus 14 tells us about the ritual restoration of a person or house if the physical condition ceased. The text doesn't say why the disease might stop. Its concern was with how to move people or things from the "impure" to the "pure" category so that they would no longer impact the sacred realm negatively.

In Mark 8:22–25 Jesus healed a blind man in stages. By allowing the "patient" to experience healing as a process, he demonstrated the extent of the change. So it was with purification from scale disease. The complex, phased process that returned a person to normal taught the people that it was a long way back. Why? Because of the enormity of the fall from purity that had occurred at Eden.

📖 God could heal our moral nature in one zap. But in so doing he would destroy our free choice, the element of our human nature that allows us to love him. He would annihilate the human race, because we would no longer *be* human. God wants people, not pets or robots—people who love him freely, in thanks for what he's done. If he were to raise us too quickly to face his holiness, we would die (Ex. 33:20), just like a scuba diver coming up too fast. When has God's grace restored you through a process?

14:4 [j] ver 6,49,51,52; Nu 19:6; Ps 51:7

14:6 [k] ver 4
14:7 [l] 2Ki 5:10,14; Isa 52:15; Eze 36:25
14:8 [m] Lev 11:25; 13:6 [n] ver 9 [o] ver 20 [p] Nu 5:2,3; 12:14,15; 2Ch 26:21

14:10 [q] Mt 8:4; Mk 1:44; Lk 5:14 [r] Lev 2:1 [s] ver 12,15,21,24

14:12 [t] Lev 5:18; 6:6-7 [u] Ex 29:24
14:13 [v] Ex 29:11 [w] Lev 6:24-30; 7:7

14:14 [x] Ex 29:20; Lev 8:23

14:20 [y] ver 8
14:21 [z] Lev 5:7; 12:8 [a] ver 22,32

14:22 [b] Lev 5:7

14:23
c ver 10,11
14:24
d Nu 6:14 e ver 10
f ver 12

14:25
g ver 14; Ex 29:20
14:26
h ver 15

14:29
i ver 18
14:30
j Lev 5:7
14:31
k ver 22; Lev 5:7;
15:15,30
l ver 18,19
14:32
m Lev 13:2 n ver 21

14:34
o Ge 12:5; Ex 6:4;
Nu 13:2 p Ge 17:8;
48:4; Nu 27:12;
32:22; Dt 3:27; 7:1;
32:49

14:37
q Lev 13:19

14:38
r Lev 13:4
14:39
s Lev 13:5

14:40
t ver 45

14:44
u Lev 13:51

14:46
v Lev 11:24
14:47
w Lev 11:25
14:48
x Lev 13:6

14:49
y ver 4; 1Ki 4:33;
ver 4

23 "On the eighth day he must bring them for his cleansing to the priest at the entrance to the Tent of Meeting, before the LORD. c 24 The priest is to take the lamb for the guilt offering, d together with the log of oil, e and wave them before the LORD as a wave offering. f 25 He shall slaughter the lamb for the guilt offering and take some of its blood and put it on the lobe of the right ear of the one to be cleansed, on the thumb of his right hand and on the big toe of his right foot. g 26 The priest is to pour some of the oil into the palm of his own left hand, h 27 and with his right forefinger sprinkle some of the oil from his palm seven times before the LORD. 28 Some of the oil in his palm he is to put on the same places he put the blood of the guilt offering—on the lobe of the right ear of the one to be cleansed, on the thumb of his right hand and on the big toe of his right foot. 29 The rest of the oil in his palm the priest shall put on the head of the one to be cleansed, to make atonement for him before the LORD. i 30 Then he shall sacrifice the doves or the young pigeons, which the person can afford, j 31 one a as a sin offering and the other as a burnt offering, k together with the grain offering. In this way the priest will make atonement before the LORD on behalf of the one to be cleansed. l"

32 These are the regulations for anyone who has an infectious skin disease m and who cannot afford the regular offerings n for his cleansing.

Cleansing From Mildew

33 The LORD said to Moses and Aaron, 34 "When you enter the land of Canaan, o which I am giving you as your possession, p and I put a spreading mildew in a house in that land, 35 the owner of the house must go and tell the priest, 'I have seen something that looks like mildew in my house.' 36 The priest is to order the house to be emptied before he goes in to examine the mildew, so that nothing in the house will be pronounced unclean. After this the priest is to go in and inspect the house. 37 He is to examine the mildew on the walls, and if it has greenish or reddish q depressions that appear to be deeper than the surface of the wall, 38 the priest shall go out the doorway of the house and close it up for seven days. r 39 On the seventh day s the priest shall return to inspect the house. If the mildew has spread on the walls, 40 he is to order that the contaminated stones be torn out and thrown into an unclean place outside the town. t 41 He must have all the inside walls of the house scraped and the material that is scraped off dumped into an unclean place outside the town. 42 Then they are to take other stones to replace these and take new clay and plaster the house.

43 "If the mildew reappears in the house after the stones have been torn out and the house scraped and plastered, 44 the priest is to go and examine it and, if the mildew has spread in the house, it is a destructive mildew; the house is unclean. u 45 It must be torn down—its stones, timbers and all the plaster—and taken out of the town to an unclean place.

46 "Anyone who goes into the house while it is closed up will be unclean till evening. v 47 Anyone who sleeps or eats in the house must wash his clothes. w

48 "But if the priest comes to examine it and the mildew has not spread after the house has been plastered, he shall pronounce the house clean, x because the mildew is gone. 49 To purify the house he is to take two birds and some cedar wood, scarlet yarn and hyssop. y 50 He shall kill one of the birds over fresh water in a clay

a 31 Septuagint and Syriac; Hebrew 31 such as the person can afford, one

---

Leviticus 14:33–57

📖 Verses 33–53 switch to fungus in houses. This law would apply after the Israelites had settled in Canaan and lived in houses rather than tents. It included provisions for diagnosis and remedies. A house restored from impure mildew required an elimination ritual using two birds (vv. 49–53), modeled after the first-day purification ritual for a healed person (vv. 4–7).

💬 If asked, most Christians would say they want to see Christ's kingdom advance by leaps and bounds. But most human progress happens in steps—a baby's first steps, Neil Armstrong's "one small step" onto the moon in 1969, and software upgrades. A leap can even be undesirable. Severe illness can make people so weak that rapid progress through surgery or medications can be harmful or fatal. How might you cultivate an appreciation for progress that comes in increments or small stages?

pot.ᶻ 51Then he is to take the cedar wood, the hyssop,ᵃ the scarlet yarn and the live bird, dip them into the blood of the dead bird and the fresh water, and sprinkle the house seven times.ᵇ 52He shall purify the house with the bird's blood, the fresh water, the live bird, the cedar wood, the hyssop and the scarlet yarn. 53Then he is to release the live bird in the open fieldsᶜ outside the town. In this way he will make atonement for the house, and it will be clean.ᵈ

54These are the regulations for any infectious skin disease,ᵉ for an itch, 55for mildewᶠ in clothing or in a house, 56and for a swelling, a rash or a bright spot,ᵍ 57to determine when something is clean or unclean.

These are the regulations for infectious skin diseases and mildew.ʰ

Discharges Causing Uncleanness

15 The Lord said to Moses and Aaron, 2"Speak to the Israelites and say to them: 'When any man has a bodily discharge,ⁱ the discharge is unclean. 3Whether it continues flowing from his body or is blocked, it will make him unclean. This is how his discharge will bring about uncleanness:

4" 'Any bed the man with a discharge lies on will be unclean, and anything he sits on will be unclean. 5Anyone who touches his bed must wash his clothesʲ and bathe with water,ᵏ and he will be unclean till evening.ˡ 6Whoever sits on anything that the man with a discharge sat on must wash his clothes and bathe with water, and he will be unclean till evening.

7" 'Whoever touches the manᵐ who has a dischargeⁿ must wash his clothes and bathe with water, and he will be unclean till evening.

8" 'If the man with the discharge spitsᵒ on someone who is clean, that person must wash his clothes and bathe with water, and he will be unclean till evening.

9" 'Everything the man sits on when riding will be unclean, 10and whoever touches any of the things that were under him will be unclean till evening; whoever picks up those thingsᵖ must wash his clothes and bathe with water, and he will be unclean till evening.

11" 'Anyone the man with a discharge touches without rinsing his hands with water must wash his clothes and bathe with water, and he will be unclean till evening.

12" 'A clay potᵍ that the man touches must be broken, and any wooden articleʳ is to be rinsed with water.

13" 'When a man is cleansed from his discharge, he is to count off seven daysˢ for his ceremonial cleansing; he must wash his clothes and bathe himself with fresh water, and he will be clean.ᵗ 14On the eighth day he must take two doves or two young pigeonsᵘ and come before the Lord to the entrance to the Tent of Meeting and give them to the priest. 15The priest is to sacrifice them, the one for a sin offeringᵛ and the other for a burnt offering.ʷ In this way he will make atonement before the Lord for the man because of his discharge.ˣ

16" 'When a man has an emission of semen,ʸ he must bathe his whole body with water, and he will be unclean till evening.ᶻ 17Any clothing or leather that has semen on it must be washed with water, and it will be unclean till evening. 18When a man lies with a woman and there is an emission of semen,ᵃ both must bathe with water, and they will be unclean till evening.

19" 'When a woman has her regular flow of blood, the impurity of her monthly periodᵇ will last seven days, and anyone who touches her will be unclean till evening.

20" 'Anything she lies on during her period will be unclean, and anything she sits on will be unclean. 21Whoever touches her bed must wash his clothes and bathe

14:50 z ver 5
14:51 a ver 6; Ps 51:7 b ver 4,7
14:53 c ver 7 d ver 20
14:54 e Lev 13:2,30
14:55 f Lev 13:47-52
14:56 g Lev 13:2
14:57 h Lev 10:10
15:2 i ver 16,32; Lev 22:4; Nu 5:2; 2Sa 3:29; Mt 9:20
15:5 j Lev 11:25 k Lev 14:8 l Lev 11:24
15:7 m ver 19; Lev 22:5 n ver 16; Lev 22:4
15:8 o Nu 12:14
15:10 p Nu 19:10
15:12 q Lev 6:28 r Lev 11:32
15:13 s Lev 8:33 t ver 5
15:14 u Lev 14:22
15:15 v Lev 5:7 w Lev 14:31 x Lev 14:18,19
15:16 y ver 2; Lev 22:4; Dt 23:10 z ver 5; Dt 23:11
15:18 a 1Sa 21:4
15:19 b ver 24; Lev 12:2

Leviticus 15:1–33

Discharges from genital organs are private matters, and some are healthy rather than abnormal. Thus, in Leviticus 15, determination of ritual impurities from these sources required no examination by priests. Individuals were accountable before God to take proper precautions, notify each other as necessary, and make use of any required ritual remedies.

The fall (Gen. 3) adversely affected human sexuality. With female reproductive potential or fulfillment comes loss of blood, which represents life. With male fertility comes loss of semen, another "life liquid." These healthy discharges are mimicked by diseases involving the same genital areas that contribute to reproduction.

15:21
c ver 27

15:24
d ver 19; Lev 12:2;
18:19; 20:18;
Eze 18:6

15:25
e Mt 9:20; Mk 5:25;
Lk 8:43

15:29
f Lev 14:22

15:30
g Lev 5:10; 14:20,
31; 18:19; 2Sa 11:4;
Mk 5:25; Lk 8:43
15:31
h Lev 15:2; Nu 5:3;
19:13,20;
2Sa 15:25; 2Ki 21:7;
Ps 33:14; 74:7;
76:2; Eze 5:11;
23:38
15:32
i ver 2
15:33
j ver 19,24,25

with water, and he will be unclean till evening. c 22Whoever touches anything she sits on must wash his clothes and bathe with water, and he will be unclean till evening. 23Whether it is the bed or anything she was sitting on, when anyone touches it, he will be unclean till evening.

24 " 'If a man lies with her and her monthly flow d touches him, he will be unclean for seven days; any bed he lies on will be unclean.

25 " 'When a woman has a discharge of blood for many days at a time other than her monthly period e or has a discharge that continues beyond her period, she will be unclean as long as she has the discharge, just as in the days of her period. 26Any bed she lies on while her discharge continues will be unclean, as is her bed during her monthly period, and anything she sits on will be unclean, as during her period. 27Whoever touches them will be unclean; he must wash his clothes and bathe with water, and he will be unclean till evening.

28 " 'When she is cleansed from her discharge, she must count off seven days, and after that she will be ceremonially clean. 29On the eighth day she must take two doves or two young pigeons f and bring them to the priest at the entrance to the Tent of Meeting. 30The priest is to sacrifice one for a sin offering and the other for a burnt offering. In this way he will make atonement for her before the LORD for the uncleanness of her discharge. g

31 " 'You must keep the Israelites separate from things that make them unclean, so they will not die in their uncleanness for defiling my dwelling place, a h which is among them.' "

32These are the regulations for a man with a discharge, for anyone made unclean by an emission of semen, i 33for a woman in her monthly period, for a man or a woman with a discharge, and for a man who lies with a woman who is ceremonially unclean. j

The Day of Atonement

16:1
k Lev 10:1
16:2
l Ex 30:10; Heb 9:7
m Heb 9:25; 10:19
n Ex 25:22
o Ex 40:34
16:3
p Heb 9:24,25

16 The LORD spoke to Moses after the death of the two sons of Aaron who died when they approached the LORD. k 2The LORD said to Moses: "Tell your brother Aaron not to come whenever he chooses l into the Most Holy Place m behind the curtain in front of the atonement cover on the ark, or else he will die, because I appear n in the cloud o over the atonement cover.

3"This is how Aaron is to enter the sanctuary area: p with a young bull for a sin offering and a ram for a burnt offering. 4He is to put on the sacred linen tunic, with linen undergarments next to his body; he is to tie the linen sash around him and put on the linen turban. q These are sacred garments; r so he must bathe himself with water s before he puts them on. 5From the Israelite community t he is to take two male goats u for a sin offering and a ram for a burnt offering.

16:4
q Ex 28:39
r Ex 28:42 s ver 24;
Heb 10:22
16:5
t Lev 4:13-21
u 2Ch 29:23
16:6
v Lev 9:7; Heb 5:3;
7:27; 9:7,12

6"Aaron is to offer the bull for his own sin offering to make atonement for himself and his household. v 7Then he is to take the two goats and present them before the LORD at the entrance to the Tent of Meeting. 8He is to cast lots for the two goats—one lot for the LORD and the other for the scapegoat. b 9Aaron shall bring the goat whose lot falls to the LORD and sacrifice it for a sin offering. 10But the goat chosen by lot as the scapegoat shall be presented alive before the LORD to be used for making atonement w by sending it into the desert as a scapegoat.

16:10
w Isa 53:4-10;
Ro 3:25; 1Jn 2:2

a 31 Or my tabernacle   b 8 That is, the goat of removal; Hebrew azazel; also in verses 10 and 26

Leviticus 16:1–34

The rituals of the annual Day of Atonement led to cleansing, not forgiveness. Throughout the year sin offerings removed evils from the people and left them to accumulate—moving *into* the sanctuary. This first stage resulted in forgiveness or physical cleansing for the offerers. But what goes in must come out! On the Day of Atonement, special sin offerings removed these accumulated evils *from* the sanctuary and camp. This resulted in moral cleansing for the Israelites. The effect was a dramatic reversal in the flow of evil.

Sin and death, represented by ritual impurity, have spread *to* each of us (cf. Rom. 5:12). But our ultimate Sin (Purification) Offering (John 1:29) allowed them to penetrate him (2 Cor. 5:21) so that he could cleanse these evils *out of* us who accept his sacrifice: "If we confess our sins, he is faithful and just and will forgive us our sins and purify us from all unrighteousness" (1 Jn. 1:9).

11 "Aaron shall bring the bull for his own sin offering to make atonement for himself and his household, *x* and he is to slaughter the bull for his own sin offering. 12 He is to take a censer full of burning coals *y* from the altar before the LORD and two handfuls of finely ground fragrant incense *z* and take them behind the curtain. 13 He is to put the incense on the fire before the LORD, and the smoke of the incense will conceal the atonement cover above the Testimony, so that he will not die. *a* 14 He is to take some of the bull's blood *b* and with his finger sprinkle it on the front of the atonement cover; then he shall sprinkle some of it with his finger seven times before the atonement cover. *c*

15 "He shall then slaughter the goat for the sin offering for the people *d* and take its blood behind the curtain *e* and do with it as he did with the bull's blood: He shall sprinkle it on the atonement cover and in front of it. 16 In this way he will make atonement *f* for the Most Holy Place because of the uncleanness and rebellion of the Israelites, whatever their sins have been. He is to do the same for the Tent of Meeting, which is among them in the midst of their uncleanness. 17 No one is to be in the Tent of Meeting from the time Aaron goes in to make atonement in the Most Holy Place until he comes out, having made atonement for himself, his household and the whole community of Israel.

18 "Then he shall come out to the altar *g* that is before the LORD and make atonement for it. He shall take some of the bull's blood and some of the goat's blood and put it on all the horns of the altar. *h* 19 He shall sprinkle some of the blood on it with his finger seven times to cleanse it and to consecrate it from the uncleanness of the Israelites. *i*

20 "When Aaron has finished making atonement for the Most Holy Place, the Tent of Meeting and the altar, he shall bring forward the live goat. 21 He is to lay both hands on the head of the live goat and confess *j* over it all the wickedness and rebellion of the Israelites—all their sins—and put them on the goat's head. He shall send the goat away into the desert in the care of a man appointed for the task. 22 The goat will carry on itself all their sins *k* to a solitary place; and the man shall release it in the desert.

23 "Then Aaron is to go into the Tent of Meeting and take off the linen garments he put on before he entered the Most Holy Place, and he is to leave them there. *l* 24 He shall bathe himself with water in a holy place and put on his regular garments. *m* Then he shall come out and sacrifice the burnt offering for himself and the burnt offering for the people, to make atonement for himself and for the people. 25 He shall also burn the fat of the sin offering on the altar.

26 "The man who releases the goat as a scapegoat must wash his clothes *n* and bathe himself with water; afterward he may come into the camp. 27 The bull and the goat for the sin offerings, whose blood was brought into the Most Holy Place to make atonement, must be taken outside the camp; *o* their hides, flesh and offal are to be burned up. 28 The man who burns them must wash his clothes and bathe himself with water; afterward he may come into the camp.

29 "This is to be a lasting ordinance for you: On the tenth day of the seventh month you must deny yourselves *a p* and not do any work—whether native-born or an alien living among you— 30 because on this day atonement will be made for you, to cleanse you. Then, before the LORD, you will be clean from all your sins. *q* 31 It is a sabbath of rest, and you must deny yourselves; *r* it is a lasting ordinance. 32 The priest who is anointed and ordained to succeed his father as high priest is to make atonement. He is to put on the sacred linen garments *s* 33 and make atonement for the Most Holy Place, for the Tent of Meeting and the altar, and for the priests and all the people of the community. *t*

34 "This is to be a lasting ordinance for you: Atonement is to be made once a year *u* for all the sins of the Israelites."

And it was done, as the LORD commanded Moses.

---

a 29 Or *must fast;* also in verse 31

16:11
x Heb 7:27; 9:7
16:12
y Lev 10:1
z Ex 30:34-38

16:13
a Ex 28:43;
Lev 22:9
16:14
b Lev 4:5; Heb 9:7,
13,25 *c* Lev 4:6

16:15
d Heb 9:7,12
e Heb 9:3

16:16
f Ex 29:36

16:18
g Lev 4:7
h Lev 4:25

16:19
i Eze 43:20

16:21
j Lev 5:5

16:22
k Isa 53:12

16:23
l Eze 42:14; 44:19

16:24
m ver 3-5

16:26
n Lev 11:25

16:27
o Lev 4:12,21;
Heb 13:11

16:29
p Lev 23:27,32;
Nu 29:7; Isa 58:3
16:30
q Jer 33:8;
Eph 5:26
16:31
r Isa 58:3,5
16:32
s ver 4; Nu 20:26,
28

16:33
t ver 11,16-18
16:34
u Heb 9:7,25

Eating Blood Forbidden

17 The LORD said to Moses, 2"Speak to Aaron and his sons and to all the Israelites and say to them: 'This is what the LORD has commanded: 3Any Israelite who sacrifices an ox,ᵃ a lamb or a goat in the camp or outside of it 4instead of bringing it to the entrance to the Tent of Meeting to present it as an offering to the LORD in front of the tabernacle of the LORDᵛ—that man shall be considered guilty of bloodshed; he has shed blood and must be cut off from his people.ʷ 5This is so the Israelites will bring to the LORD the sacrifices they are now making in the open fields. They must bring them to the priest, that is, to the LORD, at the entrance to the Tent of Meeting and sacrifice them as fellowship offerings.ᵇ 6The priest is to sprinkle the blood against the altar of the LORDˣ at the entrance to the Tent of Meeting and burn the fat as an aroma pleasing to the LORD.ʸ 7They must no longer offer any of their sacrifices to the goat idolsᶜᶻ to whom they prostitute themselves.ᵃ This is to be a lasting ordinance for them and for the generations to come.'

8"Say to them: 'Any Israelite or any alien living among them who offers a burnt offering or sacrifice 9and does not bring it to the entrance to the Tent of Meetingᵇ to sacrifice it to the LORD—that man must be cut off from his people.

10" 'Any Israelite or any alien living among them who eats any blood—I will set my face against that person who eats bloodᶜ and will cut him off from his people. 11For the life of a creature is in the blood,ᵈ and I have given it to you to make atonement for yourselves on the altar; it is the blood that makes atonement for one's life.ᵉ 12Therefore I say to the Israelites, "None of you may eat blood, nor may an alien living among you eat blood."

13" 'Any Israelite or any alien living among you who hunts any animal or bird that

---

Marginal cross-references:

17:4
v Dt 12:5-21
w Ge 17:14

17:6
x Lev 3:2
y Nu 18:17
17:7
z Ex 22:20;
2Ch 11:15
a Ex 32:8; 34:15;
Dt 32:17;
1Co 10:20
17:9
b ver 4

17:10
c Ge 9:4; Lev 3:17;
Dt 12:16,23;
1Sa 14:33
17:11
d ver 14; Ge 9:4
e Heb 9:22

ᵃ 3 The Hebrew word can include both male and female.   ᵇ 5 Traditionally *peace offerings*
ᶜ 7 Or *demons*

Leviticus 17:1–16

Leviticus 17 looked back at the ritual laws in chapters 1–16 and forward to the instructions for holy living in chapters 18–27. Addressed to all Israelites, chapter 17 issued three sharp warnings against violation of divine commands recorded earlier in Leviticus. (1) They concerned offering sacrifices at the sanctuary (nowhere else) to God (no one else) throughout the year. And they related to diet: (2) no eating blood with

meat, and (3) ritual purification when eating meat from animals not slaughtered by human beings.

Do Old Testament laws apply to us today? Is there a simple rule of thumb? Yes. A law should be kept if its principles still apply (i.e., unless the NT has removed the reason for its application). The principles— but not necessarily the particular applications—underlying the Old Testament are valid and authoritative for Christians.

17:8,10,13,15

Love Your Neighbor

Loving your neighbor who isn't like you—perhaps foreign born or from a different cultural, social, or religious background—is becoming more and more a requirement for modern Christian living (cf. Ezek. 47:22–23). Increasingly, countries around the world are welcoming large numbers of immigrants. In eight countries, 5 percent or more of the labor force is made up of these "strangers."

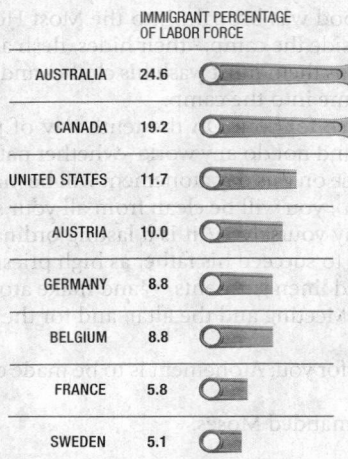

IMMIGRANT PERCENTAGE OF LABOR FORCE		25	50%
AUSTRALIA	24.6		
CANADA	19.2		
UNITED STATES	11.7		
AUSTRIA	10.0		
GERMANY	8.8		
BELGIUM	8.8		
FRANCE	5.8		
SWEDEN	5.1		

How open are we, in tough economic times, about really "welcoming" these newcomers who are taking so many jobs? This can be a hot button issue among Christians, as well as others in society. Some positions (i.e., bussers and dishwashers in many restaurants) are disproportionately filled by such workers. In addition, many telemarketers and even medical practitioners have foreign backgrounds.

How do we treat the "poor among us" in light of Scriptural instructions to welcome the "alien and stranger"? What is your one-on-one approach?

Source: "The Longest Journey," *The Economist* (November 2, 2002): 4

may be eaten must drain out the blood and cover it with earth, *f* 14because the life of every creature is its blood. That is why I have said to the Israelites, "You must not eat the blood of any creature, because the life of every creature is its blood; anyone who eats it must be cut off." *g*

15 " 'Anyone, whether native-born or alien, who eats anything found dead or torn by wild animals *h* must wash his clothes and bathe with water, and he will be ceremonially unclean till evening; then he will be clean. 16But if he does not wash his clothes and bathe himself, he will be held responsible.' "

Unlawful Sexual Relations

18 The LORD said to Moses, 2 "Speak to the Israelites and say to them: 'I am the LORD your God. *i* 3You must not do as they do in Egypt, where you used to live, and you must not do as they do in the land of Canaan, where I am bringing you. Do not follow their practices. *j* 4You must obey my laws and be careful to follow my decrees. I am the LORD your God. *k* 5Keep my decrees and laws, for the man who obeys them will live by them.' *l* I am the LORD.

6 " 'No one is to approach any close relative to have sexual relations. I am the LORD.

7 " 'Do not dishonor your father *m* by having sexual relations with your mother. *n* She is your mother; do not have relations with her.

8 " 'Do not have sexual relations with your father's wife; *o* that would dishonor your father. *p*

9 " 'Do not have sexual relations with your sister, *q* either your father's daughter or your mother's daughter, whether she was born in the same home or elsewhere.

10 " 'Do not have sexual relations with your son's daughter or your daughter's daughter; that would dishonor you.

11 " 'Do not have sexual relations with the daughter of your father's wife, born to your father; she is your sister.

12 " 'Do not have sexual relations with your father's sister; *r* she is your father's close relative.

13 " 'Do not have sexual relations with your mother's sister, because she is your mother's close relative.

14 " 'Do not dishonor your father's brother by approaching his wife to have sexual relations; she is your aunt. *s*

15 " 'Do not have sexual relations with your daughter-in-law. *t* She is your son's wife; do not have relations with her.

16 " 'Do not have sexual relations with your brother's wife; *u* that would dishonor your brother.

17 " 'Do not have sexual relations with both a woman and her daughter. *v* Do not have sexual relations with either her son's daughter or her daughter's daughter; they are her close relatives. That is wickedness.

18 " 'Do not take your wife's sister as a rival wife and have sexual relations with her while your wife is living.

17:13
f Lev 7:26; Dt 12:16
17:14
g ver 11; Ge 9:4
17:15
h Ex 22:31; Dt 14:21

18:2
i Ex 6:7; Lev 11:44; Eze 20:5
18:3
j ver 24-30; Ex 23:24; Lev 20:23
18:4
k ver 2
18:5
l Eze 20:11; Ro 10:5*; Gal 3:12*
18:7
m Lev 20:11
n Eze 22:10
18:8
o 1Co 5:1
p Lev 20:11
18:9
q Lev 20:17

18:12
r Lev 20:19

18:14
s Lev 20:20
18:15
t Lev 20:12
18:16
u Lev 20:21
18:17
v Lev 20:14

Leviticus 18:1–30

Moving from ritual matters (ch. 17) to a focus on moral holiness, Leviticus 18 begins with a call to obey God's laws rather than to follow the practices of Egypt or Canaan. God contrasted his approach to sexuality with that of Egypt, where incest was common, and Canaan, a hotbed of promiscuity.

Verse 5 had to do with life in the promised land, not eternal salvation. The Israelites didn't earn eternal life by doing works of the law: Salvation was and is his to give. God had already saved his people from slavery and was about to give them the land of Canaan. They couldn't earn it. But he couldn't bless his people with life and prosperity in that land if they violated laws of cause and effect and broke their covenant connection with him by revolting behavior.

In the first marriage (Gen. 2:20–25), we see God's continuing ideal for human sexuality: a (1) permanent, (2) monogamous (one man/one woman), (3) heterosexual relationship (4) between people. Deviations from this ideal offend God to varying degrees. For instance, he tolerates divorce as a concession to weakness under certain circumstances, regulates it to minimize its worst effects, and warns against divorcing without justification. Leviticus 18 (cf. ch. 20) established a fifth standard: Close relatives could no longer be sexual partners.

18:19
w Lev 15:24; 20:18
18:20
x Ex 20:14;
Lev 20:10; Mt 5:27,
28; 1Co 6:9;
Heb 13:4
18:21
y Dt 12:31
z Lev 20:2-5
a Lev 19:12; 21:6;
Eze 36:20
18:22
b Lev 20:13;
Dt 23:18; Ro 1:27
18:23
c Ex 22:19;
Lev 20:15; Dt 27:21
18:24
d ver 3,27,30
e Dt 18:12
18:25
f Lev 20:23; Dt 9:5;
18:12 g ver 28;
Lev 20:22

19 " 'Do not approach a woman to have sexual relations during the uncleanness of her monthly period. w

20 " 'Do not have sexual relations with your neighbor's wife x and defile yourself with her.

21 " 'Do not give any of your children y to be sacrificed a to Molech, z for you must not profane the name of your God. a I am the LORD.

22 " 'Do not lie with a man as one lies with a woman; b that is detestable.

23 " 'Do not have sexual relations with an animal and defile yourself with it. A woman must not present herself to an animal to have sexual relations with it; that is a perversion. c

24 " 'Do not defile yourselves in any of these ways, because this is how the nations that I am going to drive out before you d became defiled. e 25 Even the land was defiled; so I punished it for its sin, f and the land vomited out its inhabitants. g 26 But you must keep my decrees and my laws. The native-born and the aliens living among you must not do any of these detestable things, 27 for all these things were done by the people who lived in the land before you, and the land became defiled. 28 And if you defile the land, it will vomit you out as it vomited out the nations that were before you.

18:30
h Dt 11:1 i ver 2

29 " 'Everyone who does any of these detestable things—such persons must be cut off from their people. 30 Keep my requirements h and do not follow any of the detestable customs that were practiced before you came and do not defile yourselves with them. I am the LORD your God. i' "

Various Laws

19:2
j 1Pe 1:16*;
Lev 11:44
19:3
k Ex 20:12
l Lev 11:44
19:4
m Ex 20:4,23;
34:17; Lev 26:1;
Ps 96:5; 115:4-7

19 The LORD said to Moses, 2 "Speak to the entire assembly of Israel and say to them: 'Be holy because I, the LORD your God, am holy. j

3 " 'Each of you must respect his mother and father, k and you must observe my Sabbaths. I am the LORD your God. l

4 " 'Do not turn to idols or make gods of cast metal for yourselves. m I am the LORD your God.

5 " 'When you sacrifice a fellowship offering b to the LORD, sacrifice it in such a way that it will be accepted on your behalf. 6 It shall be eaten on the day you sacrifice it or on the next day; anything left over until the third day must be burned up. 7 If any of it is eaten on the third day, it is impure and will not be accepted. 8 Whoever eats it will be held responsible because he has desecrated what is holy to the LORD; that person must be cut off from his people.

19:9
n Lev 23:10,22;
Dt 24:19-22

9 " 'When you reap the harvest of your land, do not reap to the very edges of your field or gather the gleanings of your harvest. n 10 Do not go over your vineyard a second time or pick up the grapes that have fallen. Leave them for the poor and the alien. I am the LORD your God.

19:11
o Ex 20:15
p Eph 4:25

11 " 'Do not steal. o

" 'Do not lie. p

" 'Do not deceive one another.

19:12
q Ex 20:7; Mt 5:33

12 " 'Do not swear falsely by my name q and so profane the name of your God. I am the LORD.

---

a 21 Or to be passed through the fire   b 5 Traditionally peace offering

---

Leviticus 19:1–37

It's easy for us to underestimate the contribution of Leviticus 19: Its principle is that relationships between human beings are to be based on love (v. 18). Not on power, greed, a self-serving desire for a good image, or self-preservation, but love. It's normal to love those within a person's immediate circle, but God extended the Israelites' grasp. They were to love the poor and alien (v. 10), their neighbors and employees (v. 13), and the deaf and blind (v. 14). The reason was simple. It's re-

peated 12 times: because "I am the LORD your God"! (vv. 10,12,13,16,18,23,26,30,31,32,34,37).

In Leviticus 19 God tells us as human beings what aspect of God's character we are to reflect most strongly: his active, righteous love, expressed especially toward those we don't naturally love. Expressed simply, we love because God loves. Is love your overarching motivation in life? Jesus commanded the disciples to love each other and identified this as a hallmark of his followers (John 13:34–35). How do your relationships measure up?

People in Need of Christian Care and Protection

Leviticus 19–20 and Deuteronomy 23:9—25:19 list miscellaneous laws God's people were to follow. They delineate certain elements of nature, people, or groups to be protected, taken care of, or given special consideration. Other Scriptures reinforce and add to the list.

Groups/individuals	Scripture
• All creation	Gen. 1:28; 2:15; 1 Kings 4:33; Ps. 145:13,17
• Animals	Gen. 2:19–20; Ex. 20:10; 23:11; 1 Kings 4:33; Prov. 12:10
• People in general/the unsaved	Ex. 1:20–21; Lev. 19:16; Matt. 25:40; Gal. 6:10; Phil. 2:14–16
• Your own family/household	Gen. 7:1; Prov. 31:15; 1 Tim. 5:8
• Your parents	Gen. 44:30–31,34; Lev. 19:3; 20:9; Deut. 27:16; Eph. 6:1–3
• Your spouse	Prov. 31:10–31; Gal. 5:22–33; 1 Peter 3:1–7
• Your children	Lev. 20:2–5; Ps. 139:13–16; Matt. 7:11; Eph. 6:4
• Your daughters	Lev. 19:29
• Your sons	2 Sam. 12:15–23; 18:33
• Your sisters	Gen. 34; 2 Sam. 13; John 11:28–29
• Your brothers	Gen. 44:30–31,34
• Your neighbors	Lev. 19:13,16–18; 20:10
• Widows	Deut. 27:19; Ps. 68:5; Jer. 30:7; 1 Tim. 5:3–5; James 1:27
• Orphans/fatherless/disadvantaged children	Deut. 27:19; Ps. 68:5; Jer. 30:7; James 1:27
• Elderly people	Lev. 19:32; Zech. 8:4; 1 Tim. 5:1–2
• Aliens/refugees/strangers	Lev. 19:33; Matt. 25:35
• Sick/disabled/mentally ill	Lev. 19:14; Matt. 25:36
• Innocent	Deut. 25:1; Prov. 18:5; 24:23–25
• Imprisoned	Ps. 146:7; Matt. 25:36
• Slaves/employees	Lev. 19:13,20–22; Eph. 6:9
• Employers/authority figures	Eph. 6:5–8; 1 Tim. 6:1–2; 1 Peter 2:13–21
• The poor	Lev 19:15; Prov. 19:17; 22:22; Isa. 25:4; James 2:1–6
• The oppressed	Ps. 146:7–8
• The hungry/thirsty	Prov. 22:4; Matt. 25:35
• Women	John 19:25–27; Phil. 4:3
• Pregnant/nursing women	Ex. 21:22–24; Matt. 24:19–20
• Infertile women	1 Sam. 1:1–20
• The unborn	2 Kings 8:12; Ps. 139:13–16; Jer. 1:5; 31:8
• Christian workers/missionaries	1 Cor. 9:13–14; Phil. 4:10–19; 3 Jn. 5–8
• Needy churches	1 Cor. 16:1–4; 2 Cor. 8:1–15; 9:12–14
• Fellow Christians	Gal. 6:10; Eph. 4:1–6; Phil. 2:1–11; 1 Jn. 3:11–24

19:13
r Ex 22:15, 25-27
s Dt 24:15; Jas 5:4
19:14
t Dt 27:18

19:15
u Ex 23:2,6
v Dt 1:17
19:16
w Ps 15:3; Eze 22:9
x Ex 23:7

19:17
y 1Jn 2:9; 3:15
z Mt 18:15; Lk 17:3
19:18
a Ro 12:19
b Ps 103:9
c Mt 5:43*; 19:16*;
22:39*; Mk 12:31*;
Lk 10:27*;
Jn 13:34; Ro 13:9*;
Gal 5:14*; Jas 2:8*
19:19
d Dt 22:9
e Dt 22:11

19:21
f Lev 5:15

19:24
g Pr 3:9

19:26
h Lev 17:10
i Dt 18:10

19:27
j Lev 21:5

19:29
k Dt 23:18

19:30
l Lev 26:2
19:31
m Lev 20:6;
Isa 8:19
19:32
n 1Ti 5:1

19:34
o Ex 12:48
p Dt 10:19

19:36
q Dt 25:13-15

20:3
r Lev 15:31
s Lev 18:21

13 " 'Do not defraud your neighbor or rob him. r

" 'Do not hold back the wages of a hired man overnight. s

14 " 'Do not curse the deaf or put a stumbling block in front of the blind, t but fear your God. I am the LORD.

15 " 'Do not pervert justice; u do not show partiality v to the poor or favoritism to the great, but judge your neighbor fairly.

16 " 'Do not go about spreading slander w among your people.

" 'Do not do anything that endangers your neighbor's life. x I am the LORD.

17 " 'Do not hate your brother in your heart. y Rebuke your neighbor frankly z so you will not share in his guilt.

18 " 'Do not seek revenge a or bear a grudge b against one of your people, but love your neighbor as yourself. c I am the LORD.

19 " 'Keep my decrees.

" 'Do not mate different kinds of animals.

" 'Do not plant your field with two kinds of seed. d

" 'Do not wear clothing woven of two kinds of material. e

20 " 'If a man sleeps with a woman who is a slave girl promised to another man but who has not been ransomed or given her freedom, there must be due punishment. Yet they are not to be put to death, because she had not been freed. 21 The man, however, must bring a ram to the entrance to the Tent of Meeting for a guilt offering to the LORD. f 22 With the ram of the guilt offering the priest is to make atonement for him before the LORD for the sin he has committed, and his sin will be forgiven.

23 " 'When you enter the land and plant any kind of fruit tree, regard its fruit as forbidden. a For three years you are to consider it forbidden a; it must not be eaten. 24 In the fourth year all its fruit will be holy, g an offering of praise to the LORD. 25 But in the fifth year you may eat its fruit. In this way your harvest will be increased. I am the LORD your God.

26 " 'Do not eat any meat with the blood still in it. h

" 'Do not practice divination or sorcery. i

27 " 'Do not cut the hair at the sides of your head or clip off the edges of your beard. j

28 " 'Do not cut your bodies for the dead or put tattoo marks on yourselves. I am the LORD.

29 " 'Do not degrade your daughter by making her a prostitute, k or the land will turn to prostitution and be filled with wickedness.

30 " 'Observe my Sabbaths and have reverence for my sanctuary. I am the LORD. l

31 " 'Do not turn to mediums or seek out spiritists, m for you will be defiled by them. I am the LORD your God.

32 " 'Rise in the presence of the aged, show respect for the elderly n and revere your God. I am the LORD.

33 " 'When an alien lives with you in your land, do not mistreat him. 34 The alien living with you must be treated as one of your native-born. o Love him as yourself, for you were aliens in Egypt. p I am the LORD your God.

35 " 'Do not use dishonest standards when measuring length, weight or quantity. 36 Use honest scales and honest weights, an honest ephah b and an honest hin. c q I am the LORD your God, who brought you out of Egypt.

37 " 'Keep all my decrees and all my laws and follow them. I am the LORD.' "

Punishments for Sin

20 The LORD said to Moses, 2 "Say to the Israelites: 'Any Israelite or any alien living in Israel who gives d any of his children to Molech must be put to death. The people of the community are to stone him. 3 I will set my face against that man and I will cut him off from his people; for by giving his children to Molech, he has defiled my sanctuary r and profaned my holy name. s 4 If the people of the commu-

a 23 Hebrew *uncircumcised*   b 36 An ephah was a dry measure.   c 36 A hin was a liquid measure.
d 2 Or *sacrifices*; also in verses 3 and 4

nity close their eyes when that man gives one of his children to Molech and they fail to put him to death,[t] [5]I will set my face against that man and his family and will cut off from their people both him and all who follow him in prostituting themselves to Molech.

[6]" 'I will set my face against the person who turns to mediums and spiritists to prostitute himself by following them, and I will cut him off from his people.[u]

[7]" 'Consecrate yourselves and be holy,[v] because I am the LORD your God. [8]Keep my decrees and follow them. I am the LORD, who makes you holy.[a][w]

[9]" 'If anyone curses his father or mother,[x] he must be put to death.[y] He has cursed his father or his mother, and his blood will be on his own head.[z]

[10]" 'If a man commits adultery with another man's wife[a]—with the wife of his neighbor—both the adulterer and the adulteress must be put to death.

[11]" 'If a man sleeps with his father's wife, he has dishonored his father.[b] Both the man and the woman must be put to death; their blood will be on their own heads.

[12]" 'If a man sleeps with his daughter-in-law,[c] both of them must be put to death. What they have done is a perversion; their blood will be on their own heads.

[13]" 'If a man lies with a man as one lies with a woman, both of them have done what is detestable.[d] They must be put to death; their blood will be on their own heads.

[14]" 'If a man marries both a woman and her mother,[e] it is wicked. Both he and they must be burned in the fire, so that no wickedness will be among you.[f]

[15]" 'If a man has sexual relations with an animal,[g] he must be put to death, and you must kill the animal.

[16]" 'If a woman approaches an animal to have sexual relations with it, kill both the woman and the animal. They must be put to death; their blood will be on their own heads.

[17]" 'If a man marries his sister[h], the daughter of either his father or his mother, and they have sexual relations, it is a disgrace. They must be cut off before the eyes of their people. He has dishonored his sister and will be held responsible.

[18]" 'If a man lies with a woman during her monthly period[i] and has sexual relations with her, he has exposed the source of her flow, and she has also uncovered it. Both of them must be cut off from their people.

[19]" 'Do not have sexual relations with the sister of either your mother or your father,[j] for that would dishonor a close relative; both of you would be held responsible.

[20]" 'If a man sleeps with his aunt,[k] he has dishonored his uncle. They will be held responsible; they will die childless.

[21]" 'If a man marries his brother's wife,[l] it is an act of impurity; he has dishonored his brother. They will be childless.

[22]" 'Keep all my decrees and laws and follow them, so that the land[m] where I am bringing you to live may not vomit you out. [23]You must not live according to the customs of the nations[n] I am going to drive out before you.[o] Because they did all

---

[a] 8 Or *who sanctifies you*; or *who sets you apart as holy*

20:4
[t] Dt 17:2-5
20:6
[u] Lev 19:31
20:7
[v] Eph 1:4; 1Pe 1:16*
20:8
[w] Ex 31:13
20:9
[x] Dt 27:16
[y] Ex 21:17; Mt 15:4*; Mk 7:10*
[z] ver 11; 2Sa 1:16
20:10
[a] Ex 20:14; Dt 5:18; 22:22
20:11
[b] Lev 18:7; Dt 27:23
20:12
[c] Lev 18:15
20:13
[d] Lev 18:22
20:14
[e] Lev 18:17
[f] Dt 27:23
20:15
[g] Lev 18:23
20:17
[h] Lev 18:9
20:18
[i] Lev 15:24; 18:19
20:19
[j] Lev 18:12-13
20:20
[k] Lev 18:14
20:21
[l] Lev 18:16
20:22
[m] Lev 18:25-28
20:23
[n] Lev 18:3
[o] Lev 18:24,27,30

Leviticus 20:1–27

Holy living isn't optional for those who want to live as God's people. So Leviticus 20 lays out terminal penalties for serious moral offenses, paralleling chapter 18 in prohibiting specific sexual practices and Molech worship, including child sacrifice.

In the modern West, it has become politically incorrect to attach shame to behaviors previously viewed as immoral. Anything that threatens self-esteem is shunned—except being critical of someone else's behavior, which is considered shameful beyond measure. The Lord is rigorous regarding sexual relations because as people created in the image of the triune God, we affront his very nature and violate our essential humanness when we do anything that violates relational intimacy.

In some countries today impoverished parents still sell their sons and daughters into sex slavery or bonded labor. Others jeopardize their children's nurture in order to pursue their own professional and financial advancement. This isn't far from Molech worship: sacrifice of one's child for personal gain. These children may easily become slaves to addictive behaviors and fall prey to many kinds of sin due to their parents' absence. Is there something you can do to save even one child from being sacrificed to these modern gods?

these things, I abhorred them. 24But I said to you, "You will possess their land; I will give it to you as an inheritance, a land flowing with milk and honey."*p* I am the LORD your God, who has set you apart from the nations.*q*

25 " 'You must therefore make a distinction between clean and unclean animals and between unclean and clean birds.*r* Do not defile yourselves by any animal or bird or anything that moves along the ground—those which I have set apart as unclean for you. 26You are to be holy to me*a* because I, the LORD, am holy,*s* and I have set you apart from the nations to be my own.

27 " 'A man or woman who is a medium or spiritist among you must be put to death.*t* You are to stone them; their blood will be on their own heads.' "

Rules for Priests

21 The LORD said to Moses, "Speak to the priests, the sons of Aaron, and say to them: 'A priest must not make himself ceremonially unclean for any of his people who die,*u* 2except for a close relative, such as his mother or father, his son or daughter, his brother, 3or an unmarried sister who is dependent on him since she has no husband—for her he may make himself unclean. 4He must not make himself unclean for people related to him by marriage,*b* and so defile himself.

21:5
v Eze 44:20
w Lev 19:28;
Dt 14:1
21:6
x Lev 18:21
y Lev 3:11
5 " 'Priests must not shave their heads or shave off the edges of their beards*v* or cut their bodies.*w* 6They must be holy to their God and must not profane the name of their God.*x* Because they present the offerings made to the LORD by fire,*y* the food of their God, they are to be holy.

7 " 'They must not marry women defiled by prostitution or divorced from their husbands,*z* because priests are holy to their God.*a* 8Regard them as holy,*b* because they offer up the food of your God. Consider them holy, because I the LORD am holy—I who make you holy.*c*

9 " 'If a priest's daughter defiles herself by becoming a prostitute, she disgraces her father; she must be burned in the fire.*c*

21:10
d Lev 16:32
e Lev 10:6
21:11
f Nu 19:11,13,14
g Lev 19:28
21:12
h Ex 29:6-7;
Lev 10:7
21:13
i Eze 44:22
10 " 'The high priest, the one among his brothers who has had the anointing oil poured on his head and who has been ordained to wear the priestly garments,*d* must not let his hair become unkempt*d* or tear his clothes.*e* 11He must not enter a place where there is a dead body.*f* He must not make himself unclean,*g* even for his father or mother, 12nor leave the sanctuary of his God or desecrate it, because he has been dedicated by the anointing oil*h* of his God. I am the LORD.

13 " 'The woman he marries must be a virgin.*i* 14He must not marry a widow, a divorced woman, or a woman defiled by prostitution, but only a virgin from his own people, 15so he will not defile his offspring among his people. I am the LORD, who makes him holy.*e* "

16The LORD said to Moses, 17"Say to Aaron: 'For the generations to come none of your descendants who has a defect may come near to offer the food of his God.*j* 18No man who has any defect*k* may come near: no man who is blind or lame, dis-

---

a 26 Or *be my holy ones*   *b 4* Or *unclean as a leader among his people*   *c 8* Or *who sanctify you;* or
who set you apart as holy   *d 10* Or *not uncover his head*   *e 15* Or *who sanctifies him;* or *who sets him*
apart as holy

Leviticus 21:1—22:16

The exclusion of "defective" priests from ceremonial roles grates against our inclusive sensitivities. But because an officiating priest served as an ideal Israelite with special access to God, freedom from serious physical defects was even more essential than it would be today for an NBA basketball player.

Both officiating priests and sacrificial victims had to be unblemished in a limited sense. In the New Testament, the completely unblemished Christ fused *both* roles in himself. As priest, he was free from *the* underlying physical blemish that limited the effectiveness of the Aaronic priesthood: human mortality (Heb. 7). And he

was free from the moral blemish of sin (Heb. 4:15) that required priests to offer unblemished animal sacrifices for their own sins (Heb. 5:3; 7:27).

Privilege and influence meant responsibility for Israelite priests—and their families. PKs (priest's kids) were expected to be well-behaved. The laypersons were in turn expected to help members of priestly families bear the burden of exemplary living. Christian ministers and their families, as God's representatives, carry the same responsibilities. Congregations benefit themselves, their communities, and God's cause by upholding dedicated leaders and their families in prayer and walking with them on the path of holiness.

figured or deformed; [19]no man with a crippled foot or hand, [20]or who is hunchbacked or dwarfed, or who has any eye defect, or who has festering or running sores or damaged testicles. [l] [21]No descendant of Aaron the priest who has any defect is to come near to present the offerings made to the LORD by fire. He has a defect; he must not come near to offer the food of his God. [22]He may eat the most holy food of his God, [m] as well as the holy food; [23]yet because of his defect, he must not go near the curtain or approach the altar, and so desecrate my sanctuary. I am the LORD, who makes them holy. [a] "

[24]So Moses told this to Aaron and his sons and to all the Israelites.

22 The LORD said to Moses, [2]"Tell Aaron and his sons to treat with respect the sacred offerings the Israelites consecrate to me, so they will not profane my holy name. I am the LORD.

[3]"Say to them: 'For the generations to come, if any of your descendants is ceremonially unclean and yet comes near the sacred offerings that the Israelites consecrate to the LORD, that person must be cut off from my presence. [n] I am the LORD.

[4]" 'If a descendant of Aaron has an infectious skin disease[b] or a bodily discharge, [o] he may not eat the sacred offerings until he is cleansed. He will also be unclean if he touches something defiled by a corpse[p] or by anyone who has an emission of semen, [5]or if he touches any crawling thing[q] that makes him unclean, or any person[r] who makes him unclean, whatever the uncleanness may be. [6]The one who touches any such thing will be unclean till evening. He must not eat any of the sacred offerings unless he has bathed himself with water. [7]When the sun goes down, he will be clean, and after that he may eat the sacred offerings, for they are his food. [s] [8]He must not eat anything found dead[t] or torn by wild animals, [u] and so become unclean[v] through it. I am the LORD.

[9]" 'The priests are to keep my requirements so that they do not become guilty and die[w] for treating them with contempt. I am the LORD, who makes them holy. [c]

[10]" 'No one outside a priest's family may eat the sacred offering, nor may the guest of a priest or his hired worker eat it. [11]But if a priest buys a slave with money, or if a slave is born in his household, that slave may eat his food. [x] [12]If a priest's daughter marries anyone other than a priest, she may not eat any of the sacred contributions. [13]But if a priest's daughter becomes a widow or is divorced, yet has no children, and she returns to live in her father's house as in her youth, she may eat of her father's food. No unauthorized person, however, may eat any of it.

[14]" 'If anyone eats a sacred offering by mistake, he must make restitution to the priest for the offering and add a fifth of the value[y] to it. [15]The priests must not desecrate the sacred offerings the Israelites present to the LORD[z] [16]by allowing them to eat the sacred offerings and so bring upon them guilt requiring payment. [a] I am the LORD, who makes them holy.' "

21:20 / Dt 23:1; Isa 56:3
21:22 m 1Co 9:13
22:3 n Lev 7:20,21; Nu 19:13
22:4 o Lev 14:1-32; 15:2-15 p Lev 11:24-28,39
22:5 q Lev 11:24-28,43 r Lev 15:7
22:7 s Nu 18:11
22:8 t Lev 11:39 u Ex 22:31; Lev 17:15 v Lev 11:40
22:9 w ver 16; Ex 28:43
22:11 x Ge 17:13; Ex 12:44
22:14 y Lev 5:15
22:15 z Nu 18:32
22:16 a ver 9

---

[a] 23 Or *who sanctifies them*; or *who sets them apart as holy*   [b] 4 Traditionally *leprosy*; the Hebrew word was used for various diseases affecting the skin—not necessarily leprosy.   [c] 9 Or *who sanctifies them*; or *who sets them apart as holy*; also in verse 16

Paul's appeal "to offer [our] bodies as living sacrifices, holy and pleasing to God" (Rom. 12:1) means that we are to strive to live without moral blemish. Paul referred to the total dedication of our physical and mental energies to God and to transformation "by the renewing of [our] mind" (Rom. 12:2). Our transformation is a gift from God through his Spirit (Titus 3:4–7), who brings divine love into our hearts (Rom. 5:5).

Leviticus 22:17—23:2

An Israelite with a defective animal couldn't pass on the problem to God by offering the animal to him (v. 25). Treating God with respect called for giving him something of quality. While he helps the needy

(e.g., Isa. 45:22; Heb. 4:14–16) and accepts a widow's mite (Mark 12:42–44), this didn't mean that God's people should dump on him "gifts" nobody else wanted.

Do you devote your best to God in terms of time, energy, and other resources? Or do you offer leftover bits of the day, spare time (what's that?), and spare change, as though he were a beggar? Speaking of beggars, Jesus said, "Whatever you did for one of the least of these brothers of mine, you did for me" (Matt. 25:40). Obviously everyone's resources are limited. But are you in the habit of truly "sacrificing" for others? Or do you generally give away what you might otherwise have sold at a garage sale?

Unacceptable Sacrifices

22:18
b Lev 1:2
22:19
c Lev 1:3
22:20
d Dt 15:21; 17:1;
Mal 1:8,14;
Heb 9:14; 1Pe 1:19
22:21
e Lev 3:6;
Nu 15:3,8

[17]The LORD said to Moses, [18]"Speak to Aaron and his sons and to all the Israelites and say to them: 'If any of you—either an Israelite or an alien living in Israel—presents a gift[b] for a burnt offering to the LORD, either to fulfill a vow or as a freewill offering, [19]you must present a male without defect[c] from the cattle, sheep or goats in order that it may be accepted on your behalf. [20]Do not bring anything with a defect, [d] because it will not be accepted on your behalf. [21]When anyone brings from the herd or flock a fellowship offering[a][e] to the LORD to fulfill a special vow or as a freewill offering, it must be without defect or blemish to be acceptable. [22]Do not offer to the LORD the blind, the injured or the maimed, or anything with warts or festering or running sores. Do not place any of these on the altar as an offering made to the LORD by fire. [23]You may, however, present as a freewill offering an ox[b] or a sheep that is deformed or stunted, but it will not be accepted in fulfillment of a vow. [24]You must not offer to the LORD an animal whose testicles are bruised, crushed, torn or cut.[f] You must not do this in your own land, [25]and you must not accept such animals from the hand of a foreigner and offer them as the food of your God.[g] They will not be accepted on your behalf, because they are deformed and have defects.' "

22:24
f Lev 21:20
22:25
g Lev 21:6

22:27
h Ex 22:30
22:28
i Dt 22:6,7
22:29
j Lev 7:12;
Ps 107:22
22:30
k Lev 7:15
22:31
l Dt 4:2,40;
Ps 105:45
22:32
m Lev 18:21
n Lev 10:3
22:33
o Lev 11:45

[26]The LORD said to Moses, [27]"When a calf, a lamb or a goat is born, it is to remain with its mother for seven days.[h] From the eighth day on, it will be acceptable as an offering made to the LORD by fire. [28]Do not slaughter a cow or a sheep and its young on the same day.[i]

[29]"When you sacrifice a thank offering[j] to the LORD, sacrifice it in such a way that it will be accepted on your behalf. [30]It must be eaten that same day; leave none of it till morning.[k] I am the LORD.

[31]"Keep[l] my commands and follow them. I am the LORD. [32]Do not profane my holy name.[m] I must be acknowledged as holy by the Israelites.[n] I am the LORD, who makes[c] you holy[d] [33]and who brought you out of Egypt to be your God.[o] I am the LORD."

23:2
p ver 4,37,44;
Nu 29:39
q ver 21,27

23

The LORD said to Moses, [2]"Speak to the Israelites and say to them: 'These are my appointed feasts,[p] the appointed feasts of the LORD, which you are to proclaim as sacred assemblies.[q]

The Sabbath

23:3
r Ex 20:9
s Ex 20:10; 31:13-
17; Lev 19:3;
Dt 5:13;
Heb 4:9,10

[3]" 'There are six days when you may work,[r] but the seventh day is a Sabbath of rest,[s] a day of sacred assembly. You are not to do any work; wherever you live, it is a Sabbath to the LORD.

The Passover and Unleavened Bread

23:5
t Ex 12:18-19;
Nu 28:16-17;
Dt 16:1-8
23:7
u ver 3,8

[4]" 'These are the LORD's appointed feasts, the sacred assemblies you are to proclaim at their appointed times: [5]The LORD's Passover begins at twilight on the fourteenth day of the first month.[t] [6]On the fifteenth day of that month the LORD's Feast of Unleavened Bread begins; for seven days you must eat bread made without yeast. [7]On the first day hold a sacred assembly[u] and do no regular work. [8]For sev-

---

[a] 21 Traditionally *peace offering*   [b] 23 The Hebrew word can include both male and female.   [c] 32 Or *made*   [d] 32 Or *who sanctifies you; or who sets you apart as holy*

Leviticus 23:3

By blessing the seventh day and making it holy (Gen. 2:3), God gave it a special relationship to himself—the only fundamentally holy being (cf. 1 Sam. 2:2). God never intended for human beings to work while he rested. The blessing of the Sabbath was from "Day One" for the benefit of people, as Jesus later declared (Mark 2:27). In order to receive the blessing, humans made in God's image (Gen. 2:26–127) imitate him,

consecrating the day as he did: by resting.

One of the blessings we receive from the command to rest on the Sabbath is the very fact that God *requires* it. A workaholic needs it to be a command from God himself, or he or she will rest-lessly continue to work, risking ill health and burnout. It can be an immense relief to halt work for 24 peaceful hours to enjoy God through church, family, and walks in the park—without having to feel the slightest twinge of guilt!

en days present an offering made to the LORD by fire. And on the seventh day hold a sacred assembly and do no regular work.' "

Firstfruits

⁹The LORD said to Moses, ¹⁰"Speak to the Israelites and say to them: 'When you enter the land I am going to give you and you reap its harvest, bring to the priest a sheaf ᵛ of the first grain you harvest. ¹¹He is to wave the sheaf before the LORD ʷ so it will be accepted on your behalf; the priest is to wave it on the day after the Sabbath. ¹²On the day you wave the sheaf, you must sacrifice as a burnt offering to the LORD a lamb a year old without defect, ¹³together with its grain offering ˣ of two-tenths of an ephah ᵃ of fine flour mixed with oil—an offering made to the LORD by fire, a pleasing aroma—and its drink offering of a quarter of a hin ᵇ of wine. ¹⁴You must not eat any bread, or roasted or new grain, until the very day you bring this

23:10
ᵛ Ex 23:16,19; 34:26
23:11
ʷ Ex 29:24
23:13
ˣ Lev 2:14-16; 6:20

ᵃ *13* That is, probably about 4 quarts (about 4.5 liters); also in verse 17   ᵇ *13* That is, probably about 1 quart (about 1 liter)

Leviticus 23:4–8

Verses 5–8 reminded the Israelites to celebrate Passover on the fourteenth day of the first month (Nissan); the seven-day festival of Unleavened Bread immediately followed (cf. Ex. 12–13; 23:15; 34:18). Exodus 12:16 established a model for Leviticus 23 by labeling the first and seventh days of the festival "proclamations of holiness," when work was forbidden except for food preparation.

Paul stated in 1 Corinthians 5:7: "Christ, our Passover lamb, has been sacrificed." Notice three aspects of his statement: (1) He used the familiar ritual of Passover to explain Christ's sacrifice. (2) Christ is "our Passover lamb," the ultimate Lamb for all Christians. An animal sacrifice, by contrast, served only one household (Ex. 12:3). (3) Jesus died at the Passover season. What associations come to your mind when you think of him as your sacrificial Lamb?

Leviticus 23:9–14

Elevating the sheaf was tied to the beginning of harvest, which fluctuated. But by the Second Temple period, tradition had connected this rite to the first part of the festival of Unleavened Bread. A fierce controversy raged over whether "the day after the Sabbath" meant the first weekly Sabbath after Passover or the ceremonial Sabbath on the first day of Unleavened Bread. The timing of the sheaf ritual was the basis for calculating the date for the festival of Weeks (v. 15). Hence the fuss!

Paul claimed in 1 Corinthians 15:20: "Christ has indeed been raised from the dead, the firstfruits of those who have fallen asleep." The apostle explained Christ's resurrection by referring to a familiar scenario: the ritual offering of new grain at the beginning of the harvest. His point was that Christ's one resurrection preceded the resurrection of many people, just as the firstfruits offering of a sheaf of grain at the beginning of the barley harvest came before the harvest of countless other sheaves. What traditions in your Christian life are dear to you for the associations they bring to mind?

23:1

Ancient Israelite and Contemporary Christian Feasts

Several Old Testament feasts have some relationship to modern Christian commemorations:

Old Testament Feasts	Modern Christian Commemorations	Purpose
• Atonement	Lent, Good Friday	Remember our cleansing from sin
• Passover	Maundy Thursday, Easter	Remember God's deliverance
• Tabernacles	Thanksgiving	Celebrate God's harvest/blessings
• Trumpets	New Year's Day	Celebrate new beginnings

Other Old Testament Feasts had important functions—but no modern equivalents:

• Year of Jubilee	Help for poor; stabilization of society
• Sabbath Year	Rest for land
• Remembrance Feasts: (Unleavened Bread, First Fruits, Purim, etc.)	Remember God's gracious acts

In addition to other Christian holidays, like Ascension Day and Pentecost, we celebrate national holidays, holidays of questionable origin, and holidays with purely commercial intent.

23:14
y Ex 34:26
z Nu 15:21

offering to your God. *y* This is to be a lasting ordinance for the generations to come, *z* wherever you live.

Feast of Weeks

15 " 'From the day after the Sabbath, the day you brought the sheaf of the wave offering, count off seven full weeks. 16Count off fifty days up to the day after the sev-

23:16
a Nu 28:26; Ac 2:1

enth Sabbath, *a* and then present an offering of new grain to the LORD. 17From wher-

23:17
b Ex 34:22;
Lev 2:12

ever you live, bring two loaves made of two-tenths of an ephah of fine flour, baked with yeast, as a wave offering of firstfruits *b* to the LORD. 18Present with this bread seven male lambs, each a year old and without defect, one young bull and two rams. They will be a burnt offering to the LORD, together with their grain offerings and drink offerings—an offering made by fire, an aroma pleasing to the LORD. 19Then sacrifice one male goat for a sin offering and two lambs, each a year old, for a fellowship offering. *a* 20The priest is to wave the two lambs before the LORD as a wave offering, together with the bread of the firstfruits. They are a sacred offering

23:21
c ver 2 d ver 3

to the LORD for the priest. 21On that same day you are to proclaim a sacred assembly *c* and do no regular work. *d* This is to be a lasting ordinance for the generations to come, wherever you live.

23:22
e Lev 19:9
f Lev 19:10;
Dt 24:19-21;
Ru 2:15

22 " 'When you reap the harvest *e* of your land, do not reap to the very edges of your field or gather the gleanings of your harvest. *f* Leave them for the poor and the alien. I am the LORD your God.' "

Feast of Trumpets

23The LORD said to Moses, 24"Say to the Israelites: 'On the first day of the seventh month you are to have a day of rest, a sacred assembly commemorated with trumpet

23:24
g Lev 25:9;
Nu 10:9, 10; 29:1
23:25
h ver 21

blasts. *g* 25Do no regular work, *h* but present an offering made to the LORD by fire.' "

Day of Atonement

23:27
i Lev 16:29
/ Ex 30:10
k Nu 29:7

26The LORD said to Moses, 27"The tenth day of this seventh month *i* is the Day of Atonement. *j* Hold a sacred assembly *k* and deny yourselves, *b* and present an offering made to the LORD by fire. 28Do no work on that day, because it is the Day of Atonement, when atonement is made for you before the LORD your God. 29Anyone

23:29
l Ge 17:14; Nu 5:2
23:30
m Lev 20:3

who does not deny himself on that day must be cut off from his people. *l* 30I will destroy from among his people *m* anyone who does any work on that day. 31You shall do no work at all. This is to be a lasting ordinance for the generations to come, wherever you live. 32It is a sabbath of rest for you, and you must deny yourselves.

a 19 Traditionally *peace offering*　　b 27 Or *and fast*; also in verses 29 and 32

Leviticus 23:15–22

Because the festival of Weeks had to do with harvest, verse 22 adds a reminder to leave something behind for the poor and the foreigner to glean (cf. 19:9–10). At the heart of Leviticus 23, God commanded his people not to get so focused on their religious duties that they neglected human beings in need (cf. Luke 10:20–32). In the vernacular of a decade or two ago, they weren't to be so heavenly minded as to be of no earthly use.

Fifty days after elevation of the first barley sheaf came the festival of Weeks. So it's no surprise that fifty days after Christ's resurrection the next great event for the early church—the outpouring of the Holy Spirit as a gift from the new heavenly high priest (cf. Eph. 4:8), as well as the beginning of a great "harvest" of conversions—came precisely on the festival of Weeks, which coincided with the day of Pentecost (Acts 2:41).

Leviticus 23:23–25

In Numbers 10:9 trumpet blasts meant battle.

Why would God command a war signal here? Numbers 23:21 clues us in. Balaam blessed Israel: "The LORD their God is with them; the shout of the King is among them." The word "shout" functioned like trumpet blasts (cf. 2 Chron. 13:12–16). When the people heard this signal, they remembered that their King was with them. This feast came ten days before the Day of Atonement, when God judged between his loyal and disloyal subjects (16:29–31; 23:26–32). So the short blasts also implied the importance of repentance and reformation.

Long after the destruction of the temple, blowing a ram's horn shofar still ushers in the Jewish "days of awe," the high holy days of the seventh month when it's believed that all humankind must seek repentance in order to be saved. Because the first day of this month heralds renewal of life with God, it has become Rosh Ha-Shanah—"New Year" in Jewish tradition today. How might this festival's intent be meaningful for you? Do you as a Christian see value in familiarizing yourself with the significance of the Jewish holy days?

From the evening of the ninth day of the month until the following evening you are to observe your sabbath."

Feast of Tabernacles

33The LORD said to Moses, 34"Say to the Israelites: 'On the fifteenth day of the seventh month the LORD's Feast of Tabernacles[n] begins, and it lasts for seven days. 35The first day is a sacred assembly; do no regular work. 36For seven days present offerings made to the LORD by fire, and on the eighth day hold a sacred assembly[o] and present an offering made to the LORD by fire. It is the closing assembly; do no regular work.

37(" 'These are the LORD's appointed feasts, which you are to proclaim as sacred assemblies for bringing offerings made to the LORD by fire—the burnt offerings and grain offerings, sacrifices and drink offerings[p] required for each day. 38These offerings are in addition to those for the LORD's Sabbaths[q] and[a] in addition to your gifts and whatever you have vowed and all the freewill offerings you give to the LORD.)

39" 'So beginning with the fifteenth day of the seventh month, after you have gathered the crops of the land, celebrate the festival to the LORD for seven days;[r] the first day is a day of rest, and the eighth day also is a day of rest. 40On the first day you are to take choice fruit from the trees, and palm fronds, leafy branches and poplars,[s] and rejoice before the LORD your God for seven days. 41Celebrate this as a festival to the LORD for seven days each year. This is to be a lasting ordinance for the generations to come; celebrate it in the seventh month. 42Live in booths[t] for seven days: All native-born Israelites are to live in booths 43so your descendants will know[u] that I had the Israelites live in booths when I brought them out of Egypt. I am the LORD your God.' "

44So Moses announced to the Israelites the appointed feasts of the LORD.

Oil and Bread Set Before the LORD

24 The LORD said to Moses, 2"Command the Israelites to bring you clear oil of pressed olives for the light so that the lamps may be kept burning continually. 3Outside the curtain of the Testimony in the Tent of Meeting, Aaron is to tend

---

a 38 Or These feasts are in addition to the LORD's Sabbaths, and these offerings are

Cross-references

23:34
n Ex 23:16;
Dt 16:13; Ezr 3:4;
Ne 8:14; Zec 14:16;
Jn 7:2
23:36
o 2Ch 7:9; Ne 8:18;
Jn 7:37

23:37
p ver 2,4
23:38
q Eze 45:17

23:39
r Ex 23:16;
Dt 16:13

23:40
s Ne 8:14-17

23:42
t Ne 8:14-16

23:43
u Dt 31:13; Ps 78:5

Leviticus 23:26–32

This passage repeats the commands of 16:29–31 to practice self-denial and abstain from work on the Day of Atonement, adding three elements: (1) It names the day. (2) It condemns violators to divine "cutting off" and destruction. (3) The commands of self-denial and keeping total Sabbath (complete rest) apply from evening on the ninth day to the next evening. The purpose of self-denial appears to have been humble acknowledgement of total dependence upon God at a time of special need.

Hebrews 10:26–30 warns Christians who have received sanctification through Christ's blood of the (new) covenant against the deadly danger of apostasy (abandoning the faith; cf. Num. 15:30–31). Our post-forgiveness experience, like that of the Israelites, involves accountability to God for choosing him rather than sin.

Ongoing loyalty to God isn't just an attitude. Doing things for Christ by doing them for others doesn't buy salvation. But serving others is the inevitable outflow of true, living faith that expresses itself through love (Gal. 5:6). If there is a source, there will be a river. If there is no river, James says that the source is dead (James 2:26). How is your "river" flowing?

Leviticus 23:33–44

This third festival of the seventh (harvest) month is also called the festival of Booths or Ingathering. Living in booths meant that the Israelites did more than rejoice in God's power over agriculture: They relived his historical redemption, also accomplished by his creative power. Both God's creative and redemptive roles are motives for Sabbath keeping (Ex. 20:11; Deut. 5:15).

This festival, like Thanksgiving, celebrated God's goodness at the end of the agricultural year. No doubt you as a Christian give special thanks to God on Thanksgiving, Christmas, and New Years Day. But do you thank him for his faithfulness and favor at the end of your company's (or country's) fiscal year? Do you thank him for an abundant harvest, whether or not you are personally involved in farming? Proceeds from God's grace and generosity make your life satisfying but also filter down to satisfy the hunger of millions around the globe.

Leviticus 24:1–9

After instructions for holy times in chapter 23, chapter 24 has to do with other holy things. Regular rituals at the sanctuary reinforced the concept that the divine King (cf. Num. 23:21) was in residence and treated him to a significant extent the way a human king would

24:4
v Ex 25:31; 31:8
24:5
w Ex 25:30
24:6
x Ex 25:23-30;
1Ki 7:48
24:7
y Lev 2:2
24:8
z Nu 4:7; 1Ch 9:32;
2Ch 2:4 a Mt 12:5
24:9
b Lev 8:31;
Mt 12:4; Mk 2:26;
Lk 6:4

the lamps before the LORD from evening till morning, continually. This is to be a lasting ordinance for the generations to come. [4]The lamps on the pure gold lampstand [v] before the LORD must be tended continually.

[5]"Take fine flour and bake twelve loaves of bread, [w] using two-tenths of an ephah [a] for each loaf. [6]Set them in two rows, six in each row, on the table of pure gold [x] before the LORD. [7]Along each row put some pure incense as a memorial portion [y] to represent the bread and to be an offering made to the LORD by fire. [8]This bread is to be set out before the LORD regularly, [z] Sabbath after Sabbath, [a] on behalf of the Israelites, as a lasting covenant. [9]It belongs to Aaron and his sons, [b] who are to eat it in a holy place, because it is a most holy part of their regular share of the offerings made to the LORD by fire."

A Blasphemer Stoned

[10]Now the son of an Israelite mother and an Egyptian father went out among the Israelites, and a fight broke out in the camp between him and an Israelite. [11]The son

24:11
c Ex 3:15

of the Israelite woman blasphemed the Name [c] with a curse; so they brought him to Moses. (His mother's name was Shelomith, the daughter of Dibri the Danite.)

24:12
d Ex 18:16;
Nu 15:34

[12]They put him in custody until the will of the LORD should be made clear to them. [d]

[13]Then the LORD said to Moses: [14]"Take the blasphemer outside the camp. All those who heard him are to lay their hands on his head, and the entire assembly

24:14
e Lev 20:27;
Dt 13:9; 17:5,7;
21:21
24:15
f Ex 22:28
24:16
g 1Ki 21:10,13;
Mt 26:66
24:17
h Ge 9:6; Ex 21:12;
Nu 35:30-31;
Dt 27:24
24:18
i ver 21
24:20
j Ex 21:24;
Mt 5:38*
24:21
k ver 17
24:22
l Ex 12:49
m Nu 9:14; 15:16

is to stone him. [e] [15]Say to the Israelites: 'If anyone curses his God, [f] he will be held responsible; [16]anyone who blasphemes the name of the LORD must be put to death. [g] The entire assembly must stone him. Whether an alien or native-born, when he blasphemes the Name, he must be put to death.

[17]" 'If anyone takes the life of a human being, he must be put to death. [h] [18]Anyone who takes the life of someone's animal must make restitution [i]—life for life. [19]If anyone injures his neighbor, whatever he has done must be done to him: [20]fracture for fracture, eye for eye, tooth for tooth. [j] As he has injured the other, so he is to be injured. [21]Whoever kills an animal must make restitution, but whoever kills a man must be put to death. [k] [22]You are to have the same law for the alien [l] and the native-born. [m] I am the LORD your God.' "

[23]Then Moses spoke to the Israelites, and they took the blasphemer outside the camp and stoned him. The Israelites did as the LORD commanded Moses.

The Sabbath Year

25 The LORD said to Moses on Mount Sinai, [2]"Speak to the Israelites and say to them: 'When you enter the land I am going to give you, the land itself must observe a sabbath to the LORD. [3]For six years sow your fields, and for six years

a 5 That is, probably about 4 quarts (about 4.5 liters)

---

have been served. God "enjoyed" altar sacrifices in a nonhuman way through the smoke alone, but in his outer "living room" the "bread of the Presence" was laid out before him on the golden table (Ex. 25:30) the way it would have been for a human king.

📖 Manna ("bread" from heaven) fed the Israelites in the wilderness (Ex. 16:14–18). It sustained their physical lives in a way they acknowledged by keeping a sample of manna with the ark of the covenant (vv. 33–34; Heb. 9:4) and also by offering the "bread of the Presence." But the life Christ makes available through the sacrifice of his own flesh ("living bread") is eternal (John 6:51).

Leviticus 24:10–23

📖 As in chapter 10, regarding Nadab and Abihu, this passage reports a person's sin against the sphere of holiness, resulting in death. Each of these accounts (the

only story portions in Leviticus) is accompanied by additional legislation. The problem here started when a half-Israelite, who would have been expected to camp with the mixed multitude of non-Israelites (cf. Ex. 12:38; Deut. 23:7–8), strayed from his area into the Israelite encampment. A fight ensued, likely due to the fact that the man was in the wrong neighborhood.

📖 Using the power of speech against God, who created the world for the human species through the process of speaking (Gen. 1), is the height of ingratitude and rebellion. It's also ultimate arrogance to suppose that we can engage in a verbal slugfest with the Almighty. This is an implied claim to divine power—an attitude not protected by a right of "free speech" under God's constitution. You may never have fallen into this serious verbal sin, but how careful are you in other areas to keep your tongue in check (see James 3:1–12)?

prune your vineyards and gather their crops. [n] 4But in the seventh year the land is to have a sabbath of rest, a sabbath to the LORD. Do not sow your fields or prune your vineyards. 5Do not reap what grows of itself or harvest the grapes of your untended vines. The land is to have a year of rest. 6Whatever the land yields during the sabbath year[o] will be food for you—for yourself, your manservant and maidservant, and the hired worker and temporary resident who live among you, 7as well as for your livestock and the wild animals in your land. Whatever the land produces may be eaten.

The Year of Jubilee

8 " 'Count off seven sabbaths of years—seven times seven years—so that the seven sabbaths of years amount to a period of forty-nine years. 9Then have the trumpet[p] sounded everywhere on the tenth day of the seventh month; on the Day of Atonement sound the trumpet throughout your land. 10Consecrate the fiftieth year and proclaim liberty[q] throughout the land to all its inhabitants. It shall be a jubilee[r] for you; each one of you is to return to his family property and each to his own clan. 11The fiftieth year shall be a jubilee for you; do not sow and do not reap what grows of itself or harvest the untended vines. 12For it is a jubilee and is to be holy for you; eat only what is taken directly from the fields.

13 " 'In this Year of Jubilee[s] everyone is to return to his own property.

14 " 'If you sell land to one of your countrymen or buy any from him, do not take advantage of each other.[t] 15You are to buy from your countryman on the basis of the number of years[u] since the Jubilee. And he is to sell to you on the basis of the number of years left for harvesting crops. 16When the years are many, you are to increase the price, and when the years are few, you are to decrease the price,[v] because what he is really selling you is the number of crops. 17Do not take advantage of each other,[w] but fear your God.[x] I am the LORD your God.[y]

18 " 'Follow my decrees and be careful to obey my laws, and you will live safely in the land.[z] 19Then the land will yield its fruit,[a] and you will eat your fill and live there in safety. 20You may ask, "What will we eat in the seventh year[b] if we do not plant or harvest our crops?" 21I will send you such a blessing[c] in the sixth year that the land will yield enough for three years. 22While you plant during the eighth year, you will eat from the old crop and will continue to eat from it until the harvest of the ninth year comes in.[d]

23 " 'The land must not be sold permanently, because the land is mine[e] and you

25:3
[n] Ex 23:10

25:6
[o] ver 20

25:9
[p] Lev 23:24

25:10
[q] Isa 61:1; Jer 34:8, 15, 17; Lk 4:19
[r] Nu 36:4

25:13
[s] ver 10
25:14
[t] Lev 19:13; 1Sa 12:3,4
25:15
[u] Lev 27:18,23
25:16
[v] ver 27,51,52
25:17
[w] Pr 22:22; Jer 7:5, 6; 1Th 4:6
[x] Lev 19:14
[y] Lev 19:32
25:18
[z] Lev 26:4,5; Dt 12:10; Ps 4:8; Jer 23:6
25:19
[a] Lev 26:4
25:20
[b] ver 4
25:21
[c] Dt 28:8,12; Hag 2:19; Mal 3:10
25:22
[d] Lev 26:10
25:23
[e] Ex 19:5

Leviticus 25:1–7

The Sabbath of the land in the seventh year was "to the LORD," so letting the land revert to its natural state carried religious significance. According to Exodus 23:11 there was also a humanitarian purpose: "Then the poor among your people may get food from it, and the wild animals may eat what they leave." Whatever grew by itself from kernels spilled during the previous harvest would belong to any, human or animal, who needed it. Because there would be no reaping, the whole population would live off the land from day to day.

While it's important that the church not try to take over functions of the state, the church isn't exempt from addressing social problems, like poverty and inequality, or ecological concerns just because the state is working on the same problems in its own way. Leviticus 25 teaches us that faith and ethics both impact the lives of believers in significant ways. In what ways are church and government cooperating in your locality to assist those in need?

Leviticus 25:8–55

Every 50 years Israel was to observe a "super-Sabbatical." Not only would the land rest; it would return to its original owner. Not only would agricultural workers rest from planting or harvesting; they would return to their own clans and land. Not only would the economy rest; debts that had kept people under obligation would claim them no more. This legislation stressed the desirability of economic self-sufficiency and the need to treat people experiencing economic hardship with kindness and respect.

"Developing" nations today are strapped with colossal debts. Banks, businesses, governments, and the International Monetary Fund provide bailouts, but always with big "strings" attached. Some of these are necessary to ensure that help goes where it's needed, not into "black holes" of poor management and corruption. But there is a widespread craving for some kind of "Jubilee" relief. In all likelihood nothing this drastic will ever happen (we have no knowledge that Israel ever actually celebrated a Jubilee year either!). If you held an influential, advisory position to your government, what "solutions" might you recommend?

are but aliens^f and my tenants. ^{24}Throughout the country that you hold as a possession, you must provide for the redemption of the land.

^{25} " 'If one of your countrymen becomes poor and sells some of his property, his nearest relative^g is to come and redeem^h what his countryman has sold. ^{26}If, however, a man has no one to redeem it for him but he himself prospers and acquires sufficient means to redeem it, ^{27}he is to determine the value for the years since he sold it and refund the balance to the man to whom he sold it; he can then go back to his own property. ^{28}But if he does not acquire the means to repay him, what he sold will remain in the possession of the buyer until the Year of Jubilee. It will be returned in the Jubilee, and he can then go back to his property.^{i}

^{29} " 'If a man sells a house in a walled city, he retains the right of redemption a full year after its sale. During that time he may redeem it. ^{30}If it is not redeemed before a full year has passed, the house in the walled city shall belong permanently to the buyer and his descendants. It is not to be returned in the Jubilee. ^{31}But houses in villages without walls around them are to be considered as open country. They can be redeemed, and they are to be returned in the Jubilee.

^{32} " 'The Levites always have the right to redeem their houses in the Levitical towns,^{j} which they possess. ^{33}So the property of the Levites is redeemable—that is, a house sold in any town they hold—and is to be returned in the Jubilee, because the houses in the towns of the Levites are their property among the Israelites. ^{34}But the pastureland belonging to their towns must not be sold; it is their permanent possession.^{k}

^{35} " 'If one of your countrymen becomes poor^l and is unable to support himself among you, help him^m as you would an alien or a temporary resident, so he can continue to live among you. ^{36}Do not take interest^n of any kind^a from him, but fear your God, so that your countryman may continue to live among you. ^{37}You must not lend him money at interest or sell him food at a profit. ^{38}I am the LORD your God, who brought you out of Egypt to give you the land of Canaan and to be your God.^{o}

^{39} " 'If one of your countrymen becomes poor among you and sells himself to you, do not make him work as a slave.^{p} ^{40}He is to be treated as a hired worker or a temporary resident among you; he is to work for you until the Year of Jubilee. ^{41}Then he and his children are to be released, and he will go back to his own clan and to the property^q of his forefathers. ^{42}Because the Israelites are my servants, whom I brought out of Egypt, they must not be sold as slaves. ^{43}Do not rule over them ruthlessly,^{r} but fear your God.

^{44} " 'Your male and female slaves are to come from the nations around you; from them you may buy slaves. ^{45}You may also buy some of the temporary residents living among you and members of their clans born in your country, and they will become your property. ^{46}You can will them to your children as inherited property and can make them slaves for life, but you must not rule over your fellow Israelites ruthlessly.

^{47} " 'If an alien or a temporary resident among you becomes rich and one of your countrymen becomes poor and sells himself to the alien living among you or to a member of the alien's clan, ^{48}he retains the right of redemption after he has sold himself. One of his relatives^s may redeem him: ^{49}An uncle or a cousin or any blood relative in his clan may redeem him. Or if he prospers,^{t} he may redeem himself. ^{50}He and his buyer are to count the time from the year he sold himself up to the Year of Jubilee. The price for his release is to be based on the rate paid to a hired man^u for that number of years. ^{51}If many years remain, he must pay for his redemption a larger share of the price paid for him. ^{52}If only a few years remain until the Year of Jubilee, he is to compute that and pay for his redemption accordingly. ^{53}He is to be treated as a man hired from year to year; you must see to it that his owner does not rule over him ruthlessly.

^{54} " 'Even if he is not redeemed in any of these ways, he and his children are to be released in the Year of Jubilee, ^{55}for the Israelites belong to me as servants. They are my servants, whom I brought out of Egypt. I am the LORD your God.

^{a} 36 Or *take excessive interest*; similarly in verse 37

25:23
^{f} Ge 23:4;
1Ch 29:15;
Ps 39:12;
Heb 11:13;
1Pe 2:11
25:25
^{g} Ru 2:20; Jer 32:7
^{h} Lev 27:13,19,31;
Ru 4:4

25:28
^{i} ver 10

25:32
^{j} Nu 35:1-8;
Jos 21:2

25:34
^{k} Nu 35:2-5
25:35
^{l} Dt 24:14,15
^{m} Dt 15:8;
Ps 37:21,26;
Lk 6:35
25:36
^{n} Ex 22:25;
Dt 23:19-20

25:38
^{o} Ge 17:7;
Lev 11:45
25:39
^{p} Ex 21:2; Dt 15:12;
1Ki 9:22

25:41
^{q} ver 28

25:43
^{r} Ex 1:13; Eze 34:4;
Col 4:1

25:48
^{s} Ne 5:5
25:49
^{t} ver 26

25:50
^{u} Job 7:1;
Isa 16:14; 21:16

Reward for Obedience

26 " 'Do not make idols[v] or set up an image or a sacred stone[w] for yourselves, and do not place a carved stone[x] in your land to bow down before it. I am the LORD your God.

2 " 'Observe my Sabbaths and have reverence for my sanctuary.[y] I am the LORD.

3 " 'If you follow my decrees and are careful to obey[z] my commands, 4I will send you rain[a] in its season, and the ground will yield its crops and the trees of the field their fruit.[b] 5Your threshing will continue until grape harvest and the grape harvest will continue until planting, and you will eat all the food you want[c] and live in safety in your land.[d]

6 " 'I will grant peace in the land,[e] and you will lie down[f] and no one will make you afraid.[g] I will remove savage beasts[h] from the land, and the sword will not pass through your country. 7You will pursue your enemies, and they will fall by the sword before you. 8Five of you will chase a hundred, and a hundred of you will chase ten thousand, and your enemies will fall by the sword before you.[i]

9 " 'I will look on you with favor and make you fruitful and increase your num-

26:1
v Ex 20:4; Lev 19:4;
Dt 5:8 w Ex 23:24
x Nu 33:52
26:2
y Lev 19:30
26:3
z Dt 7:12; 11:13,22;
28:1,9
26:4
a Dt 11:14
b Ps 67:6
26:5
c Dt 11:15;
Joel 2:19,26;
Am 9:13
d Lev 25:18
26:6
e Ps 29:11; 85:8;
147:14 f Ps 4:8
g Zep 3:13 h ver 22
26:8
i Dt 32:30;
Jos 23:10

Leviticus 26:1–13

Leviticus 26 provides a dramatic climax to the book. It consists mainly of a series of conditional covenant blessings—if the Israelites obeyed the Lord, and curses—if they disobeyed his commands.

The blessings in verses 3–13 touch the major aspects of life that would have been dear to an ancient Israelite: agricultural prosperity, plenty of food, peace and safety from human and animal enemies, military victory against overwhelming odds, freedom with dignity under the kindly rule of a resident, covenant God.

In the United States Declaration of Independence, the *pursuit* of happiness (not happiness itself) is cited as an inalienable right. A democratic country can provide freedom to seek well-being and fulfillment, but whether or not such desires are achieved depends on all kinds of factors. One thing is certain: Our pursuit of happiness will be successful only if we allow it to pursue us! As the ancient Israelites found out, chasing happiness will only chase it away. We get it to pursue us by pursuing a positive relationship with God, the Source of all blessings. Are you actively pursuing God?

Snapshots

26:3–6

New Beginnings in Francisco de Opalaca

Farmers in the isolated, rural district of San Francisco de Opalaca in Honduras have been struggling for generations to eke out a living from the land. Traditional agricultural habits have left it unproductive, resulting in widespread malnutrition and sickness.

A Christian ministry has been working with farmers to change this picture. The project has trained 100 small farmers in basic grain production and vegetable growing techniques. In addition, approximately 50 coffee growers have been helped to grow highland coffee for export.

The organization's work is centered in Monte Verde, which has around 11,500 inhabitants, many from the Lenca tribe, a people of Mayan origin and the country's oldest indigenous group. The Lenca are marginalized, suffering from poverty and neglect. But the Lenca tribes here are struggling to overcome these drawbacks—without abandoning their culture, for which they demand acknowledgement and respect.

Municipal authorities and the public agree that education is key. They are working to promote learning, from kindergarten through adult literacy classes. The project coordinates its health-related activities with the Public Health Ministry of Honduras and other aid groups. Together they have instituted medical and dental evaluations, massive vaccine campaigns, and provision for special attention for unique cases.

> The Lenca tribes . . . are struggling to overcome . . . drawbacks—without abandoning their culture, for which they demand acknowledgement and respect.

26:9
j Ge 17:6; Ne 9:23
k Ge 17:7
26:10
l Lev 25:22
26:11
m Ex 25:8; Ps 76:2;
Eze 37:27
26:12
n Ge 3:8
o 2Co 6:16*
26:13
p Eze 34:27
26:14
q Dt 28:15-68;
Mal 2:2

26:16
r Dt 28:22,35
s 1Sa 2:33
t Job 31:8
26:17
u Lev 17:10
v Ps 106:41
w ver 36,37;
Dt 28:7,25; Ps 53:5
26:18
x ver 21
26:19
y Isa 25:11
z Dt 28:23
26:20
a Ps 127:1;
Isa 17:11
b Dt 11:17
26:21
c ver 18
26:22
d Dt 32:24

26:23
e Jer 2:30; 5:3

26:25
f Nu 14:12;
Eze 5:17

26:26
g Ps 105:16; Isa 3:1;
Mic 6:14

26:29
h Dt 28:53
26:30
i 2Ch 34:3; Eze 6:3
j Eze 6:6 k Eze 6:13
26:31
l Ps 74:3-7
26:32
m Jer 9:11
26:33
n Dt 4:27;
Eze 12:15; 20:23;
Zec 7:14
26:34
o ver 43; 2Ch 36:21

bers,^{j} and I will keep my covenant^k with you. ^{10}You will still be eating last year's harvest when you will have to move it out to make room for the new.^{l} ^{11}I will put my dwelling place^{a}^{m} among you, and I will not abhor you. ^{12}I will walk^n among you and be your God, and you will be my people.^{o} ^{13}I am the LORD your God, who brought you out of Egypt so that you would no longer be slaves to the Egyptians; I broke the bars of your yoke^p and enabled you to walk with heads held high.

Punishment for Disobedience

^{14} 'But if you will not listen to me and carry out all these commands,^{q} ^{15}and if you reject my decrees and abhor my laws and fail to carry out all my commands and so violate my covenant, ^{16}then I will do this to you: I will bring upon you sudden terror, wasting diseases and fever^r that will destroy your sight and drain away your life.^{s} You will plant seed in vain, because your enemies will eat it.^{t} ^{17}I will set my face^u against you so that you will be defeated by your enemies; those who hate you will rule over you,^{v} and you will flee even when no one is pursuing you.^{w}

^{18} 'If after all this you will not listen to me, I will punish you for your sins seven times over.^{x} ^{19}I will break down your stubborn pride^y and make the sky above you like iron and the ground beneath you like bronze.^{z} ^{20}Your strength will be spent in vain,^{a} because your soil will not yield its crops, nor will the trees of the land yield their fruit.^{b}

^{21} 'If you remain hostile toward me and refuse to listen to me, I will multiply your afflictions seven times over,^{c} as your sins deserve. ^{22}I will send wild animals^d against you, and they will rob you of your children, destroy your cattle and make you so few in number that your roads will be deserted.

^{23} 'If in spite of these things you do not accept my correction^e but continue to be hostile toward me, ^{24}I myself will be hostile toward you and will afflict you for your sins seven times over. ^{25}And I will bring the sword upon you to avenge the breaking of the covenant. When you withdraw into your cities, I will send a plague^f among you, and you will be given into enemy hands. ^{26}When I cut off your supply of bread,^{g} ten women will be able to bake your bread in one oven, and they will dole out the bread by weight. You will eat, but you will not be satisfied.

^{27} 'If in spite of this you still do not listen to me but continue to be hostile toward me, ^{28}then in my anger I will be hostile toward you, and I myself will punish you for your sins seven times over. ^{29}You will eat the flesh of your sons and the flesh of your daughters.^{h} ^{30}I will destroy your high places,^{i} cut down your incense altars^j and pile your dead bodies on the lifeless forms of your idols,^{k} and I will abhor you. ^{31}I will turn your cities into ruins and lay waste your sanctuaries,^{l} and I will take no delight in the pleasing aroma of your offerings. ^{32}I will lay waste the land,^{m} so that your enemies who live there will be appalled. ^{33}I will scatter you among the nations^n and will draw out my sword and pursue you. Your land will be laid waste, and your cities will lie in ruins. ^{34}Then the land will enjoy its sabbath years all the time that it lies desolate and you are in the country of your enemies;^{o} then the land

---

^{a} 11 Or *my tabernacle*

Leviticus 26:14–46

The contrast between blessings and curses is shocking—and meant to be that way. The threatened curses were much more extensive than the blessings. Did negative motivation need to be more substantial to serve as an effective deterrent? Compare Deuteronomy 31:15–29, which is pessimistic regarding Israel's future. Curses would predominate in her later history.

After all these horrible things had happened, would anyone survive? Verses 40–45 pry open a door of hope at what looked like a dead end: *But if* the Israelites would "confess their sins" . . . That's it—only confess. At the time of their return from exile there would be no elaborate ceremonies. Only humbling themselves before God and putting themselves at his mercy.

Like the ancient Israelites, we can benefit from a dose of "covenant consciousness." Like the prodigal son, who finally came to his senses in a pigsty (Luke 15:17), we need awareness of who our Father is and what he's been offering us all along. It's not necessary to wait until our life is in ruins. We can offer a covenant prayer anytime, anywhere: "Our Father in heaven, hallowed by your name, your kingdom come, your will be done on earth as it is in heaven . . ." (Matt. 6:9–10). How fully do you avail yourself of God's promised blessings?

will rest and enjoy its sabbaths. 35All the time that it lies desolate, the land will have the rest it did not have during the sabbaths you lived in it.

36 " 'As for those of you who are left, I will make their hearts so fearful in the lands of their enemies that the sound of a windblown leaf will put them to flight. *p* They will run as though fleeing from the sword, and they will fall, even though no one is pursuing them. 37They will stumble over one another as though fleeing from the sword, even though no one is pursuing them. So you will not be able to stand before your enemies. *q* 38You will perish among the nations; the land of your enemies will devour you. *r* 39Those of you who are left will waste away in the lands of their enemies because of their sins; also because of their fathers' sins they will waste away. *s*

40 " 'But if they will confess their sins and the sins of their fathers*t*—their treachery against me and their hostility toward me, 41which made me hostile toward them so that I sent them into the land of their enemies—then when their uncircumcised hearts *u* are humbled and they pay for their sin, 42I will remember my covenant with Jacob *v* and my covenant with Isaac *w* and my covenant with Abraham, and I will remember the land. 43For the land will be deserted by them and will enjoy its sabbaths while it lies desolate without them. They will pay for their sins because they rejected my laws and abhorred my decrees. 44Yet in spite of this, when they are in the land of their enemies, I will not reject them or abhor *x* them so as to destroy them completely, *y* breaking my covenant *z* with them. I am the LORD their God. 45But for their sake I will remember *a* the covenant with their ancestors whom I brought out of Egypt *b* in the sight of the nations to be their God. I am the LORD.' "

46These are the decrees, the laws and the regulations that the LORD established on Mount Sinai between himself and the Israelites through Moses. *c*

Redeeming What Is the LORD's

27 The LORD said to Moses, 2"Speak to the Israelites and say to them: 'If anyone makes a special vow *d* to dedicate persons to the LORD by giving equivalent values, 3set the value of a male between the ages of twenty and sixty at fifty shekels *a* of silver, according to the sanctuary shekel *b;* *e* 4and if it is a female, set her value at thirty shekels. *c* 5If it is a person between the ages of five and twenty, set the value of a male at twenty shekels *d* and of a female at ten shekels. *e* 6If it is a person between one month and five years, set the value of a male at five shekels *f;f* of silver and that of a female at three shekels *g* of silver. 7If it is a person sixty years old or more, set the value of a male at fifteen shekels *h* and of a female at ten shekels. 8If anyone making the vow is too poor to pay *g* the specified amount, he is to present the person to the priest, who will set the value *h* for him according to what the man making the vow can afford.

9 " 'If what he vowed is an animal that is acceptable as an offering to the LORD, such an animal given to the LORD becomes holy. 10He must not exchange it or substitute a good one for a bad one, or a bad one for a good one; *i* if he should substitute one animal for another, both it and the substitute become holy. 11If what he vowed is a ceremonially unclean animal—one that is not acceptable as an offering to the LORD—the animal must be presented to the priest, 12who will judge its quality as good or bad. Whatever value the priest then sets, that is what it will be. 13If the owner wishes to redeem *j* the animal, he must add a fifth to its value.

a 3 That is, about 1 1/4 pounds (about 0.6 kilogram); also in verse 16   *b 3* That is, about 2/5 ounce (about 11.5 grams); also in verse 25   *c 4* That is, about 12 ounces (about 0.3 kilogram)
d 5 That is, about 8 ounces (about 0.2 kilogram)   *e 5* That is, about 4 ounces (about 110 grams); also in verse 7   *f 6* That is, about 2 ounces (about 55 grams)   *g 6* That is, about 1 1/4 ounces (about 35 grams)   *h 7* That is, about 6 ounces (about 170 grams)

26:36
p Eze 21:7

26:37
q Jos 7:12
26:38
r Dt 4:26
26:39
s Eze 4:17
26:40
t Jer 3:12-15;
Lk 15:18; 1Jn 1:9

26:41
u Eze 44:7,9;
Ac 7:51
26:42
v Ge 22:15-18;
28:15 *w* Ge 26:5

26:44
x Ro 11:2 *y* Dt 4:31;
Jer 30:11
z Jer 33:26
26:45
a Ge 17:7 *b* Ex 6:8;
Lev 25:38

26:46
c Lev 7:38; 27:34

27:2
d Nu 6:2

27:3
e Ex 30:13;
Nu 3:47; 18:16

27:6
f Nu 18:16

27:8
g Lev 5:11
h ver 12,14

27:10
i ver 33

27:13
j ver 15,19;
Lev 25:25

Leviticus 27:1–34

Leviticus 27, regulating gifts to the sanctuary, seems tacked on after the more dramatic chapter 26. But its focus on holy things links it with earlier portions of the book. Placement of the climax of Leviticus in chapter 26 rather than at the very end of the book may seem strange to us, but this approach would have been understood by ancient Hebrews, who often put their most weighty expressions at the centers of literary pieces.

14 " 'If a man dedicates his house as something holy to the LORD, the priest will judge its quality as good or bad. Whatever value the priest then sets, so it will remain. 15 If the man who dedicates his house redeems it,[k] he must add a fifth to its value, and the house will again become his.

16 " 'If a man dedicates to the LORD part of his family land, its value is to be set according to the amount of seed required for it—fifty shekels of silver to a homer[a] of barley seed. 17 If he dedicates his field during the Year of Jubilee, the value that has been set remains. 18 But if he dedicates his field after the Jubilee, the priest will determine the value according to the number of years that remain[l] until the next Year of Jubilee, and its set value will be reduced. 19 If the man who dedicates the field wishes to redeem it, he must add a fifth to its value, and the field will again become his. 20 If, however, he does not redeem the field, or if he has sold it to someone else, it can never be redeemed. 21 When the field is released in the Jubilee,[m] it will become holy, like a field devoted to the LORD;[n] it will become the property of the priests.[b]

22 " 'If a man dedicates to the LORD a field he has bought, which is not part of his family land, 23 the priest will determine its value up to the Year of Jubilee, and the man must pay its value on that day as something holy to the LORD. 24 In the Year of Jubilee the field will revert to the person from whom he bought it,[o] the one whose land it was. 25 Every value is to be set according to the sanctuary shekel,[p] twenty gerahs[q] to the shekel.

26 " 'No one, however, may dedicate the firstborn of an animal, since the firstborn already belongs to the LORD;[r] whether an ox[c] or a sheep, it is the LORD's. 27 If it is one of the unclean animals,[s] he may buy it back at its set value, adding a fifth of the value to it. If he does not redeem it, it is to be sold at its set value.

28 " 'But nothing that a man owns and devotes[d][t] to the LORD—whether man or animal or family land—may be sold or redeemed; everything so devoted is most holy to the LORD.

29 " 'No person devoted to destruction[e] may be ransomed; he must be put to death.

30 " 'A tithe[u] of everything from the land, whether grain from the soil or fruit from the trees, belongs to the LORD; it is holy to the LORD. 31 If a man redeems any of his tithe, he must add a fifth of the value to it. 32 The entire tithe of the herd and flock—every tenth animal that passes under the shepherd's rod[v]—will be holy to the LORD. 33 He must not pick out the good from the bad or make any substitution.[w] If he does make a substitution, both the animal and its substitute become holy and cannot be redeemed.' "

34 These are the commands the LORD gave Moses on Mount Sinai for the Israelites.[x]

a 16 That is, probably about 6 bushels (about 220 liters)   b 21 Or priest   c 26 The Hebrew word can include both male and female.   d 28 The Hebrew term refers to the irrevocable giving over of things or persons to the LORD.   e 29 The Hebrew term refers to the irrevocable giving over of things or persons to the LORD, often by totally destroying them.

Cross references:
27:15 k ver 13,20
27:18 l Lev 25:15
27:21 m Lev 25:10; n ver 28; Nu 18:14; Eze 44:29
27:24 o Lev 25:28
27:25 p Ex 30:13; Nu 18:16; q Nu 3:47; Eze 45:12
27:26 r Ex 13:2,12
27:27 s ver 11
27:28 t Nu 18:14; Jos 6:17-19
27:30 u Ge 28:22; 2Ch 31:6; Mal 3:8
27:32 v Jer 33:13; Eze 20:37
27:33 w ver 10
27:34 x Lev 26:46; Dt 4:5

The idea of vowing the monetary worth of a human being (vv. 1–8) goes against our grain. It appears that this system had to do with the benefit the sanctuary would receive if the vowed person were to belong to it as a servant. This begs a perennial question: What is a person really worth? We as Christians know that every human being is made in God's image (Gen. 1:26; 9:6). How can anyone put a price tag on that? Our individual value can't be calculated! Life that comes from the holy Creator is sacred. How does this reality affect your concern for others, including the needy?

15:15 "THE COMMUNITY IS TO HAVE THE SAME RULES FOR YOU
AND FOR THE ALIEN LIVING AMONG YOU . . . YOU AND THE
ALIEN SHALL BE THE SAME BEFORE THE LORD."

INTRODUCTION TO

Numbers

AUTHOR

Moses has traditionally been identified as the author of Numbers. He was commanded by God in 33:1–2 to keep a detailed record of Israel's journey, and as the leader of the Israelites, he was the most qualified person to write this account. Though later editors may have added information from Israel's later history, it's reasonable to assume that Moses wrote the book's essential content.

DATE WRITTEN

Numbers was probably written around 1406 B.C., just before Moses' death and as the Israelites were poised to enter Canaan.

ORIGINAL READERS

Numbers was written to the Israelites as a reminder of God's faithful commitment to his people in spite of their failures. It calls its readers to fulfill their responsibility to God's call for holy living.

TIMELINE

	2200BC	2100	2000	1900	1800	1700	1600	1500	1400
Moses' birth (c. 1526 B.C.)									
The plagues; The Passover (c. 1446 B.C.)									
The exodus (c. 1446 B.C.)									
Desert wanderings (c. 1446-1406 B.C.)									
Exploration of Canaan (c. 1443 B.C.)									
Book of Numbers written (c. 1406 B.C.)									
Moses dies; Joshua becomes leader (c. 1406 B.C.)									
Israelites enter Canaan (c. 1406 B.C.)									

THEMES

Numbers describes the Israelites' wandering in the desert. It contains the following themes:

1. *God's mercy and faithfulness.* Numbers shows God guiding (9:17) and comforting his people as he offers forgiveness, reconciliation, and hope. The rebellion and unfaithfulness of the Israelites is contrasted with God's ever faithful love for his people (14:18).

2. *God's justice.* Numbers describes the grumbling, complaining, and rebellion of the people (11:1,4–6; 13:1—14:45) and their leaders (12:1–2; 16:1–11; 20:1–13) against God and his provision. Though God is merciful, judgment follows repeated rebellion (11:1,33; 12:4–10; 14:11–37; 16:25–49; 20:12–13,24) and unbelief (14:1–38; Heb. 3:16–19).

3. *Hope.* Disobedience brings judgment and pain (11:1,33; 14:39–45; 16:31–35), but repentance (11:2; 12:13–15; 16:22,46–48) and obedience (13:30; 14:24) result in forgiveness and hope (14:20; 15:25–26). Even after their repeated failures, God didn't leave the Israelites to die

in the desert. He protected them from Balak's plan to curse them by turning Balaam's prophecies into blessings (23:1—24:25). God also prepared the second generation for the conquest of the promised land. Through these events Numbers displays the truth that God is sovereign and his plan will be accomplished.

FAITH IN ACTION

The pages of Numbers contain life lessons and role models of faith—people who challenge believers to put their faith in action.

Role Models

- FAMILY LEADERS (7:1–89) brought offerings for the dedication of the tabernacle. Do you set aside appropriate offerings to the Lord for his gracious presence in your life?

- MOSES (9:8), in times of uncertainty, asked God for direction and then waited for his leading. Are you quick to ask for God's guidance when you are unsure of what to do?

- ELDAD AND MEDAD (11:24–30) were representatives of the 70 elders who prophesied as the Spirit of God rested on Israel's leaders. Is the Lord asking you to be a leader in the body of Christ?

- JOSHUA AND CALEB (14:6–9) put their trust in the all-powerful God, believing that he could defeat any enemy. What enemies do you fear? Who can you trust?

- PHINEHAS (25:11) put God's honor first. How can you do the same as you live in this world?

- ZELOPHEHAD'S DAUGHTERS (27:1–11; 36:1–12; cf. Josh. 17:3–4) sought legal recourse to keep their father's land in the family since he had no sons. Is there an unjust issue or circumstance you can address with the Lord's help?

Challenges

- Resolve to accept whatever task God assigns to you, no matter how insignificant or menial it may seem (4:4–33). All service to God has significance.

- View any wrong you commit against another person as an act of unfaithfulness to God (5:5).

- Give generously to your local church, as well as to Christ's global cause, viewing your gift as a way to celebrate and join in God's work (7:1–10).

- Determine to be content with God's provision for you (11:4–33).

- Step up to a role of spiritual leadership at whatever level if the Lord asks of you (11:24–30).

- Resolve that racism will have no place in your life or heart (12:1).

- Guard against grumbling and criticizing, behaviors that often evidence a rebellious spirit (14:1–9).

- Respect those in positions of leadership as those who have been placed in their positions by God (17:1–10; 1 Thess. 5:12–13; Heb. 13:17).

- Determine never to rob God of glory by taking credit for his actions (20:1–13; Isa. 42:8).

- Seek to right injustice through appropriate channels (27:1–11).

OUTLINE

I. Israel at Sinai, Preparing to Leave for Canaan (1:1—10:10)
II. From Sinai to Kadesh (10:11—12:16)
III. Israel at Kadesh, the Delay Resulting From Rebellion (13:1—20:13)
IV. From Kadesh to the Plains of Moab (20:14—22:1)
V. Israel on the Plains of Moab, Anticipating the Taking of Canaan (22:2—32:42)
VI. Supplements Dealing With Various Matters (33–36)

The Census

1 The LORD spoke to Moses in the Tent of Meeting[a] in the Desert of Sinai[b] on the first day of the second month[c] of the second year after the Israelites came out of Egypt. He said: 2"Take a census[d] of the whole Israelite community by their clans and families, listing every man by name, one by one. 3You and Aaron are to number by their divisions all the men in Israel twenty years old or more[e] who are able to serve in the army. 4One man from each tribe, each the head of his family,[f] is to help you. [g] 5These are the names of the men who are to assist you:

from Reuben,[h] Elizur son of Shedeur;
6from Simeon, Shelumiel son of Zurishaddai;
7from Judah,[i] Nahshon son of Amminadab;[j]
8from Issachar,[k] Nethanel son of Zuar;
9from Zebulun,[l] Eliab son of Helon;
10from the sons of Joseph:
   from Ephraim,[m] Elishama son of Ammihud;
   from Manasseh, Gamaliel son of Pedahzur;
11from Benjamin, Abidan son of Gideoni;
12from Dan,[n] Ahiezer son of Ammishaddai;
13from Asher,[o] Pagiel son of Ocran;
14from Gad, Eliasaph son of Deuel;[p]
15from Naphtali,[q] Ahira son of Enan."

16These were the men appointed from the community, the leaders[r] of their ancestral tribes. They were the heads of the clans of Israel.[s]

17Moses and Aaron took these men whose names had been given, 18and they called the whole community together on the first day of the second month.[t] The people indicated their ancestry[u] by their clans and families, and the men twenty years old or more were listed by name, one by one, 19as the LORD commanded Moses. And so he counted them in the Desert of Sinai:

20From the descendants of Reuben[v] the firstborn son of Israel:
   All the men twenty years old or more who were able to serve in the army were listed by name, one by one, according to the records of their clans and families. 21The number from the tribe of Reuben was 46,500.

22From the descendants of Simeon:[w]
   All the men twenty years old or more who were able to serve in the army were counted and listed by name, one by one, according to the records of their clans and families. 23The number from the tribe of Simeon was 59,300.

24From the descendants of Gad:[x]
   All the men twenty years old or more who were able to serve in the army were listed by name, according to the records of their clans and families. 25The number from the tribe of Gad was 45,650.

26From the descendants of Judah:[y]
   All the men twenty years old or more who were able to serve in the army

Cross references
1:1 [a] Ex 40:2 [b] Ex 19:1 [c] Ex 40:17
1:2 [d] Ex 30:11-16; Nu 26:2
1:3 [e] Ex 30:14
1:4 [f] ver 16 [g] Ex 18:21; Dt 1:15
1:5 [h] Ge 29:32; Dt 33:6; Rev 7:5
1:7 [i] Ge 29:35; Ps 78:68 [j] Ru 4:20; 1Ch 2:10; Lk 3:32
1:8 [k] Ge 30:18
1:9 [l] ver 30
1:10 [m] ver 32
1:12 [n] ver 38
1:13 [o] ver 40
1:14 [p] Nu 2:14
1:15 [q] ver 42
1:16 [r] Ex 18:25 [s] ver 4; Ex 18:21; Nu 7:2
1:18 [t] ver 1 [u] Ezr 2:59; Heb 7:3
1:20 [v] Nu 26:5-11; Rev 7:5
1:22 [w] Nu 26:12-14; Rev 7:7
1:24 [x] Ge 30:11; Nu 26:15-18; Rev 7:5
1:26 [y] Ge 29:35; Nu 26:19-22; Mt 1:2; Rev 7:5

Numbers 1:1–54

The book of Numbers begins 13 months after the exodus from Egypt. During the past year, the Israelites had been in the vicinity of Mount Sinai receiving the law and setting up the tabernacle. Before they resumed their journey, God commanded them to take a military census (lit., "lift the head") of men twenty years old or older who could serve as soldiers. This was preliminary to conscription and organization of an army able to exert maximum force to conquer Canaan. This heralded dramatic events leading to fulfillment of God's promise to give his people a permanent home in the promised land.

God directed the Israelite army to be organized by family units, so that each soldier would train and fight alongside his relatives. A casualty wouldn't simply be a fellow private first class, sergeant, or lieutenant, but a brother, cousin, or uncle! Like the Israelites, we fight our spiritual battles alongside our spiritual family—those dear and precious to us. We have life-and-death motivation not just to win, but to help each other win. What difference has the eternal well-being of those you love made in your motivation to Christian life and service?

were listed by name, according to the records of their clans and families. [27]The number from the tribe of Judah was 74,600.

[28]From the descendants of Issachar: [z]
All the men twenty years old or more who were able to serve in the army were listed by name, according to the records of their clans and families. [29]The number from the tribe of Issachar was 54,400.

[30]From the descendants of Zebulun: [a]
All the men twenty years old or more who were able to serve in the army were listed by name, according to the records of their clans and families. [31]The number from the tribe of Zebulun was 57,400.

[32]From the sons of Joseph:
From the descendants of Ephraim: [b]
All the men twenty years old or more who were able to serve in the army were listed by name, according to the records of their clans and families. [33]The number from the tribe of Ephraim was 40,500.

[34]From the descendants of Manasseh: [c]
All the men twenty years old or more who were able to serve in the army were listed by name, according to the records of their clans and families. [35]The number from the tribe of Manasseh was 32,200.

[36]From the descendants of Benjamin: [d]
All the men twenty years old or more who were able to serve in the army were listed by name, according to the records of their clans and families. [37]The number from the tribe of Benjamin was 35,400.

[38]From the descendants of Dan: [e]
All the men twenty years old or more who were able to serve in the army were listed by name, according to the records of their clans and families. [39]The number from the tribe of Dan was 62,700.

[40]From the descendants of Asher: [f]
All the men twenty years old or more who were able to serve in the army were listed by name, according to the records of their clans and families. [41]The number from the tribe of Asher was 41,500.

[42]From the descendants of Naphtali: [g]
All the men twenty years old or more who were able to serve in the army were listed by name, according to the records of their clans and families. [43]The number from the tribe of Naphtali was 53,400.

[44]These were the men counted by Moses and Aaron [h] and the twelve leaders of Israel, each one representing his family. [45]All the Israelites twenty years old or more who were able to serve in Israel's army were counted according to their families. [46]The total number was 603,550. [i]

[47]The families of the tribe of Levi, [j] however, were not counted [k] along with the others. [48]The LORD had said to Moses: [49]"You must not count the tribe of Levi or include them in the census of the other Israelites. [50]Instead, appoint the Levites to be in charge of the tabernacle of the Testimony [l]—over all its furnishings and everything belonging to it. They are to carry the tabernacle and all its furnishings; they are to take care of it and encamp around it. [51]Whenever the tabernacle is to move, the Levites are to take it down, and whenever the tabernacle is to be set up, the Levites shall do it. [m] Anyone else who goes near it shall be put to death. [52]The Israelites are to set up their tents by divisions, each man in his own camp under his own standard. [n] [53]The Levites, however, are to set up their tents around the tabernacle of the Testimony so that wrath will not fall [o] on the Israelite community. The Levites are to be responsible for the care of the tabernacle of the Testimony. [p]"

[54]The Israelites did all this just as the LORD commanded Moses.

1:28
z Nu 26:23-25; Rev 7:7

1:30
a Nu 26:26-27; Rev 7:8

1:32
b Nu 26:35-37

1:34
c Nu 26:28-34; Rev 7:6

1:36
d Nu 26:38-41; 2Ch 17:17; Rev 7:8

1:38
e Ge 30:6; Nu 26:42-43

1:40
f Nu 26:44-47; Rev 7:6

1:42
g Nu 26:48-50; Rev 7:6

1:44
h Nu 26:64

1:46
i Ex 12:37; 38:26; Nu 2:32; 26:51
1:47
j Nu 2:33; 26:57
k Nu 4:3,49

1:50
l Ex 38:21; Ac 7:44

1:51
m Nu 3:38; 4:1-33

1:52
n Nu 2:2; Ps 20:5
1:53
o Lev 10:6; Nu 16:46; 18:5
p Nu 18:2-4

The Arrangement of the Tribal Camps

2 The LORD said to Moses and Aaron: 2 "The Israelites are to camp around the Tent of Meeting some distance from it, each man under his standard[q] with the banners of his family."

3 On the east, toward the sunrise, the divisions of the camp of Judah are to encamp under their standard. The leader of the people of Judah is Nahshon son of Amminadab.[r] 4 His division numbers 74,600.

5 The tribe of Issachar will camp next to them. The leader of the people of Issachar is Nethanel son of Zuar.[s] 6 His division numbers 54,400.

7 The tribe of Zebulun will be next. The leader of the people of Zebulun is Eliab son of Helon.[t] 8 His division numbers 57,400.

9 All the men assigned to the camp of Judah, according to their divisions, number 186,400. They will set out first.[u]

10 On the south will be the divisions of the camp of Reuben under their standard. The leader of the people of Reuben is Elizur son of Shedeur.[v] 11 His division numbers 46,500.

12 The tribe of Simeon will camp next to them. The leader of the people of Simeon is Shelumiel son of Zurishaddai.[w] 13 His division numbers 59,300.

14 The tribe of Gad will be next. The leader of the people of Gad is Eliasaph son of Deuel.[a][x] 15 His division numbers 45,650.

16 All the men assigned to the camp of Reuben,[y] according to their divisions, number 151,450. They will set out second.

17 Then the Tent of Meeting and the camp of the Levites[z] will set out in the middle of the camps. They will set out in the same order as they encamp, each in his own place under his standard.

18 On the west will be the divisions of the camp of Ephraim[a] under their standard. The leader of the people of Ephraim is Elishama son of Ammihud.[b] 19 His division numbers 40,500.

20 The tribe of Manasseh will be next to them. The leader of the people of Manasseh is Gamaliel son of Pedahzur.[c] 21 His division numbers 32,200.

22 The tribe of Benjamin will be next. The leader of the people of Benjamin is Abidan son of Gideoni.[d] 23 His division numbers 35,400.

24 All the men assigned to the camp of Ephraim,[e] according to their divisions, number 108,100. They will set out third.[f]

25 On the north will be the divisions of the camp of Dan, under their standard. The leader of the people of Dan is Ahiezer son of Ammishaddai.[g] 26 His division numbers 62,700.

27 The tribe of Asher will camp next to them. The leader of the people of Asher is Pagiel son of Ocran.[h] 28 His division numbers 41,500.

29 The tribe of Naphtali will be next. The leader of the people of Naphtali is Ahira son of Enan.[i] 30 His division numbers 53,400.

2:2
q Nu 1:52; Ps 74:4; Isa 31:9

2:3
r Nu 10:14; Ru 4:20; 1Ch 2:10
2:5
s Nu 1:8

2:7
t Nu 1:9

2:9
u Nu 10:14

2:10
v Nu 1:5

2:12
w Nu 1:6

2:14
x Nu 1:14
2:16
y Nu 10:18

2:17
z Nu 1:53; 10:21

2:18
a Ge 48:20; Jer 31:18-20
b Nu 1:10

2:20
c Nu 1:10

2:22
d Nu 1:11; Ps 68:27
2:24
e Nu 10:22
f Ps 80:2

2:25
g Nu 1:12

2:27
h Nu 1:13

2:29
i Nu 1:15

---

a 14 Many manuscripts of the Masoretic Text, Samaritan Pentateuch and Vulgate (see also Num. 1:14); most manuscripts of the Masoretic Text *Reuel*

Numbers 2:1–34

🔲 If the Israelite men were to be organized into an army, their camp would be a military camp. The tribes were to be arranged in a square like the Egyptian war camp of Pharaoh Rameses II (13th century B.C.). While the similarity is striking, so is a crucial difference: The center of the Israelite war camp was occupied by God's sanctuary, not the tent of Pharaoh, a human god-king. As the pagan prophet Balaam would later observe, the Israelites enjoyed the power and protection of a Leader in their midst who wasn't just royal but truly divine (Num. 23:21)!

🔲 How important to you is personal independence? Our culture revels in it. Commercials bombard us with what we already "know": We are the center of the universe, and our desires govern it. Numbers 2 disagrees. God, in the middle of the camp, was its Source of strength, its "nuclear reactor." His people weren't individual islands of destiny, but a community under and accountable to God. We are *not* the center of our own religion if it's that of the Bible.

2:31
i Nu 10:25

[31]All the men assigned to the camp of Dan number 157,600. They will set out last,[i] under their standards.

2:32
k Ex 38:26; Nu 1:46
2:33
l Nu 1:47; 26:57-62

[32]These are the Israelites, counted according to their families. All those in the camps, by their divisions, number 603,550.[k] [33]The Levites, however, were not counted[l] along with the other Israelites, as the LORD commanded Moses.

[34]So the Israelites did everything the LORD commanded Moses; that is the way they encamped under their standards, and that is the way they set out, each with his clan and family.

The Levites

3:1
m Ex 6:27

3 This is the account of the family of Aaron and Moses[m] at the time the LORD talked with Moses on Mount Sinai.

3:2
n Ex 6:23; Nu 26:60
3:3
o Ex 28:41
3:4
p Lev 10:2
q Lev 10:1
r 1Ch 24:1
3:6
s Dt 10:8; 31:9;
1Ch 15:2 *t* Nu 8:6-
22; 18:1-7;
2Ch 29:11
3:7
u Lev 8:35; Nu 1:50

[2]The names of the sons of Aaron were Nadab the firstborn and Abihu, Eleazar and Ithamar.[n] [3]Those were the names of Aaron's sons, the anointed priests,[o] who were ordained to serve as priests. [4]Nadab and Abihu, however, fell dead before the LORD[p] when they made an offering with unauthorized fire before him in the Desert of Sinai.[q] They had no sons; so only Eleazar and Ithamar served as priests during the lifetime of their father Aaron.[r]

[5]The LORD said to Moses, [6]"Bring the tribe of Levi[s] and present them to Aaron the priest to assist him.[t] [7]They are to perform duties for him and for the whole community at the Tent of Meeting by doing the work[u] of the tabernacle. [8]They are to take care of all the furnishings of the Tent of Meeting, fulfilling the obligations of the Israelites by doing the work of the tabernacle.

3:9
v Nu 8:19; 18:6
3:10
w Ex 29:9 *x* Nu 1:51

[9]Give the Levites to Aaron and his sons;[v] they are the Israelites who are to be given wholly to him.[a] [10]Appoint Aaron and his sons to serve as priests;[w] anyone else who approaches the sanctuary must be put to death."[x]

3:12
y Mal 2:4 *z* ver 41;
Nu 8:16,18
a Ex 13:2
3:13
b Ex 13:12

[11]The LORD also said to Moses, [12]"I have taken the Levites[y] from among the Israelites in place of the first male offspring[z] of every Israelite woman. The Levites are mine,[a] [13]for all the firstborn are mine.[b] When I struck down all the firstborn in Egypt, I set apart for myself every firstborn in Israel, whether man or animal. They are to be mine. I am the LORD."

3:15
c ver 39 *d* Nu 26:62

[14]The LORD said to Moses in the Desert of Sinai, [15]"Count[c] the Levites by their families and clans. Count every male a month old or more."[d] [16]So Moses counted them, as he was commanded by the word of the LORD.

3:17
e Ge 46:11
f Ex 6:16

[17]These were the names of the sons of Levi:[e]

Gershon, Kohath and Merari.[f]

3:18
g Ex 6:17

[18]These were the names of the Gershonite clans:

Libni and Shimei.[g]

3:19
h Ex 6:18
3:20
i Ge 46:11 *j* Ex 6:19

[19]The Kohathite clans:

Amram, Izhar, Hebron and Uzziel.[h]

[20]The Merarite clans:[i]

Mahli and Mushi.[j]

These were the Levite clans, according to their families.

3:21
k Ex 6:17

[21]To Gershon belonged the clans of the Libnites and Shimeites;[k] these were the Gershonite clans. [22]The number of all the males a month old or more who were counted was 7,500. [23]The Gershonite clans were to camp on the west, behind the taberna-

---

[a] 9 Most manuscripts of the Masoretic Text; some manuscripts of the Masoretic Text, Samaritan Pentateuch and Septuagint (see also Num. 8:16) *to me*

Numbers 3:1–51

The Levites belonged to God. He had given them to the priests (Aaron and his descendants, also from the tribe of Levi). They were to assist in place of the Israelite firstborn—whom he had consecrated to himself, along with firstborn animals, when he had spared them at the time he struck the firstborn in Egypt (vv. 11–13; cf. Ex. 13:2,11–16). Rather than using the firstborn of every tribe for lifelong sanctuary service, which would have removed people from their families, God chose one tribe to maintain and guard the tabernacle (later the temple) precincts.

cle. ²⁴The leader of the families of the Gershonites was Eliasaph son of Lael. ²⁵At the Tent of Meeting the Gershonites were responsible for the care of the tabernacle^l and tent, its coverings,^m the curtain at the entranceⁿ to the Tent of Meeting, ²⁶the curtains of the courtyard^o, the curtain at the entrance to the courtyard surrounding the tabernacle and altar, and the ropes^p—and everything related to their use.

²⁷To Kohath belonged the clans of the Amramites, Izharites, Hebronites and Uzzielites;^q these were the Kohathite clans. ²⁸The number of all the males a month old or more was 8,600.^a The Kohathites were responsible for the care of the sanctuary. ²⁹The Kohathite clans were to camp on the south side^r of the tabernacle. ³⁰The leader of the families of the Kohathite clans was Elizaphan son of Uzziel. ³¹They were responsible for the care of the ark,^s the table,^t the lampstand,^u the altars,^v the articles of the sanctuary used in ministering, the curtain,^w and everything related to their use.^x ³²The chief leader of the Levites was Eleazar son of Aaron, the priest. He was appointed over those who were responsible for the care of the sanctuary.

³³To Merari belonged the clans of the Mahlites and the Mushites;^y these were the Merarite clans. ³⁴The number of all the males a month old or more who were counted was 6,200. ³⁵The leader of the families of the Merarite clans was Zuriel son of Abihail; they were to camp on the north side of the tabernacle.^z ³⁶The Merarites were appointed^a to take care of the frames of the tabernacle, its crossbars, posts, bases, all its equipment, and everything related to their use, ³⁷as well as the posts of the surrounding courtyard with their bases, tent pegs and ropes.

³⁸Moses and Aaron and his sons were to camp to the east^b of the tabernacle, toward the sunrise, in front of the Tent of Meeting.^c They were responsible for the care of the sanctuary^d on behalf of the Israelites. Anyone else who approached the sanctuary was to be put to death.^e

³⁹The total number of Levites counted at the LORD's command by Moses and Aaron according to their clans, including every male a month old or more, was 22,000.^f

⁴⁰The LORD said to Moses, "Count all the firstborn Israelite males who are a month old or more^g and make a list of their names. ⁴¹Take the Levites for me in place of all the firstborn of the Israelites,^h and the livestock of the Levites in place of all the firstborn of the livestock of the Israelites. I am the LORD."

⁴²So Moses counted all the firstborn of the Israelites, as the LORD commanded him. ⁴³The total number of firstborn males a month old or more, listed by name, was 22,273.ⁱ

⁴⁴The LORD also said to Moses, ⁴⁵"Take the Levites in place of all the firstborn of Israel, and the livestock of the Levites in place of their livestock. The Levites are to be mine. I am the LORD. ⁴⁶To redeem^j the 273 firstborn Israelites who exceed the number of the Levites, ⁴⁷collect five shekels^b ^k for each one, according to the sanctuary shekel,^l which weighs twenty gerahs.^m ⁴⁸Give the money for the redemption of the additional Israelites to Aaron and his sons."

⁴⁹So Moses collected the redemption money from those who exceeded the number redeemed by the Levites. ⁵⁰From the firstborn of the Israelites he collected silver weighing 1,365 shekels,^c ⁿ according to the sanctuary shekel. ⁵¹Moses gave the redemption money to Aaron and his sons, as he was commanded by the word of the LORD.

---

^a 28 Hebrew; some Septuagint manuscripts 8,300   ^b 47 That is, about 2 ounces (about 55 grams)
^c 50 That is, about 35 pounds (about 15.5 kilograms)

God values family life. Just as the conscripted soldiers had been assigned to divisions based on family, clan, and tribe (see "Here and Now" for 1:1–54), he now saw to it that family units throughout Israel could remain intact despite the need for individuals to be set apart for exclusive tabernacle service. How has God blessed you, not just individually, but as a family? Has he called you, like the Levite clans, to family service in his name? What have you done together for him as a unit? How has each of you benefited?

Side references:
3:25 l Ex 25:9; m Ex 26:14; n Ex 26:36; Nu 4:25
3:26 o Ex 27:9; p Ex 35:18
3:27 q 1Ch 26:23
3:29 r Nu 1:53
3:31 s Ex 25:10-22; t Ex 25:23; u Ex 25:31; v Ex 27:1; 30:1; w Ex 26:33; x Nu 4:15
3:33 y Ex 6:19
3:35 z Nu 1:53; 2:25
3:36 a Nu 4:32
3:38 b Nu 2:3 c Nu 1:53; d ver 7; Nu 18:5; e ver 10; Nu 1:51
3:39 f Nu 26:62
3:40 g ver 15
3:41 h ver 12
3:43 i ver 39
3:46 j Ex 13:13; Nu 18:15; k Lev 27:6; l Ex 30:13; m Lev 27:25
3:50 n ver 46-48

The Kohathites

4:2
o Ex 30:12

4:3
p ver 23; Nu 8:25;
1Ch 23:3,24,27;
Ezr 3:8

4:4
q ver 19

4:5
r Ex 26:31,33
s Ex 25:10,16

4:6
t Ex 25:13-15;
1Ki 8:7; 2Ch 5:8

4:7
u Ex 25:23,29;
Lev 24:6 v Ex 25:30

4:9
w Ex 25:31,37,38

4 The LORD said to Moses and Aaron: 2 "Take a census[o] of the Kohathite branch of the Levites by their clans and families. 3 Count all the men from thirty to fifty years of age[p] who come to serve in the work in the Tent of Meeting.

4 "This is the work of the Kohathites in the Tent of Meeting: the care of the most holy things.[q] 5 When the camp is to move, Aaron and his sons are to go in and take down the shielding curtain[r] and cover the ark of the Testimony with it.[s] 6 Then they are to cover this with hides of sea cows,[a] spread a cloth of solid blue over that and put the poles[t] in place.

7 "Over the table of the Presence[u] they are to spread a blue cloth and put on it the plates, dishes and bowls, and the jars for drink offerings; the bread that is continually there[v] is to remain on it. 8 Over these they are to spread a scarlet cloth, cover that with hides of sea cows and put its poles in place.

9 "They are to take a blue cloth and cover the lampstand that is for light, together with its lamps, its wick trimmers and trays,[w] and all its jars for the oil used to sup-

---

[a] 6 That is, dugongs; also in verses 8, 10, 11, 12, 14 and 25

Numbers 4:1-20

The census of Levite males a month old or older in chapter 3 had been for the purpose of calculating their substitution for the firstborn of the other tribes. Here in chapter 4 another census was needed to determine the number of Levites available for actual tabernacle work. They were to be men thirty through fifty years of age—mature but in their physical prime. God filled out the job descriptions of the three Levite groups (cf.

3:25–26,31,36–37), particularly in terms of procedures for moving the portable sanctuary.

The job description of the Kohathites was by far the longest and most complicated because it involved careful coordination with the priests, who were to cover the sacred objects before the Kohathites could carry them. Only the priests could touch or even look at these holy things—on pain of death (4:15,20).

4:1–3

Census Time

God asked Moses to count the people. There are nearly endless ways of slicing and dicing when it comes to counting most anything, people included. Moses counted by tribe. Two of the many methods we use today are by religion (see chart titled "Unity in the Body of Christ" on page 1935 at Eph. 4:2–6) and by income (see below):

$1 REPRESENTS $10,000 PER YEAR

PERCENTAGE OF WORLD'S POPULATION

The Affluent (9%); Per capita income over $5,000 per year
500 billionaires
75,000 multimillionaires
3,000,000 millionaires

9%

The Well-off (35%); Per capita income up to $5,000 per year
Third world elites own $1.5 trillion in Western banks.

35%

The Just-Coping (10%); Per capita income up to $1,000 per year

10%

The Needy (28%); Per capita income up to $100 per year
1.4 billion urban poor
500 million orphans
100 million people subsisting on garbage

28%

The Desperately Poor (18%); Per capita income up to $10 per year
500 million on verge of starvation
150 million with no shelter whatsoever
120 million street children
45 million poverty-induced deaths per year

18%

Source: Barrett and Johnson (2001:34)

ply it. 10Then they are to wrap it and all its accessories in a covering of hides of sea cows and put it on a carrying frame.

11 "Over the gold altar[x] they are to spread a blue cloth and cover that with hides of sea cows and put its poles in place.

12 "They are to take all the articles used for ministering in the sanctuary, wrap them in a blue cloth, cover that with hides of sea cows and put them on a carrying frame.

13 "They are to remove the ashes from the bronze altar[y] and spread a purple cloth over it. 14Then they are to place on it all the utensils used for ministering at the altar, including the firepans, meat forks,[z] shovels and sprinkling bowls.[a] Over it they are to spread a covering of hides of sea cows and put its poles[b] in place.

15 "After Aaron and his sons have finished covering the holy furnishings and all the holy articles, and when the camp is ready to move, the Kohathites are to come to do the carrying.[c] But they must not touch the holy things or they will die.[d] The Kohathites are to carry those things that are in the Tent of Meeting.

16 "Eleazar[e] son of Aaron, the priest, is to have charge of the oil for the light,[f] the fragrant incense, the regular grain offering[g] and the anointing oil. He is to be in charge of the entire tabernacle and everything in it, including its holy furnishings and articles."

17The LORD said to Moses and Aaron, 18 "See that the Kohathite tribal clans are not cut off from the Levites. 19So that they may live and not die when they come near the most holy things,[h] do this for them: Aaron and his sons are to go into the sanctuary and assign to each man his work and what he is to carry. 20But the Kohathites must not go in to look[i] at the holy things, even for a moment, or they will die."

The Gershonites

21The LORD said to Moses, 22 "Take a census also of the Gershonites by their families and clans. 23Count all the men from thirty to fifty years of age[j] who come to serve in the work at the Tent of Meeting.

24 "This is the service of the Gershonite clans as they work and carry burdens: 25They are to carry the curtains of the tabernacle,[k] the Tent of Meeting,[l] its covering[m] and the outer covering of hides of sea cows, the curtains for the entrance to the Tent of Meeting, 26the curtains of the courtyard surrounding the tabernacle and altar, the curtain for the entrance, the ropes and all the equipment used in its service. The Gershonites are to do all that needs to be done with these things. 27All their service, whether carrying or doing other work, is to be done under the direction of Aaron and his sons. You shall assign to them as their responsibility all they are to carry. 28This is the service of the Gershonite clans[n] at the Tent of Meeting. Their duties are to be under the direction of Ithamar son of Aaron, the priest.

4:11
x Ex 30:1

4:13
y Ex 27:1-8
4:14
z 2Ch 4:16
a Jer 52:18
b Ex 27:6

4:15
c Nu 7:9 d Nu 1:51;
2Sa 6:6,7
4:16
e Lev 10:6 f Ex 25:6
g Ex 29:41;
Lev 6:14-23

4:19
h ver 15

4:20
i Ex 19:21; 1Sa 6:19

4:23
j ver 3; 1Ch 23:3,
24,27

4:25
k Ex 27:10-18;
Nu 3:26 l Nu 3:25
m Ex 26:14

4:28
n Nu 7:7

In verses 18–19 God made clear that his warning to the Kohathites allowed them to survive when they came near the most sacred items. Reflective of God's character, this wasn't a matter of arbitrary vindictiveness. He was protecting his servants so they wouldn't get hurt.

Why didn't God authorize everyone, instead of just the priests? Could it have been that he didn't want his people to become so familiar with him that they would lose their sense of reverence? We as Christians can "enter the Most Holy Place" (Heb. 10:19), but is there still a sense in which the divine Presence is a mystery to—and an "other than"—ourselves?

Numbers 4:21–28

Moses and the priests (Aaron and his sons) were Kohathites, which explains why God gave this branch of the tribe of Levi the more privileged responsi-

bilities. When the Kohathites had emptied the sanctuary of its furniture and utensils, the Gershonites were to pack up and carry away all the fabric and skin coverings of the tabernacle and its court, including the ropes, etc. The one fabric for which they weren't responsible was the inner veil, used to cover the ark of the covenant during transportation (v. 5; cf. 3:31).

At the ancient Israelite sanctuary the Levites performed menial labor. But the work was honorable and vital because it was for the divine King. Similarly today, the smallest, least significant task that contributes to God's work is important: cleaning the church, changing its light bulbs, overseeing the nursery committee, preparing food for a social event, visiting a sick person, teaching a Scripture song to a child, encouraging a neighbor . . . To what such special roles has God called you?

The Merarites

4:29
o Ge 46:11

29 "Count the Merarites by their clans and families. o 30 Count all the men from thirty to fifty years of age who come to serve in the work at the Tent of Meeting.

4:31
p Nu 3:36

31 This is their duty as they perform service at the Tent of Meeting: to carry the frames of the tabernacle, its crossbars, posts and bases, p 32 as well as the posts of the surrounding courtyard with their bases, tent pegs, ropes, all their equipment and everything related to their use. Assign to each man the specific things he is to carry. 33 This is the service of the Merarite clans as they work at the Tent of Meeting under the direction of Ithamar son of Aaron, the priest."

The Numbering of the Levite Clans

4:34
q ver 2

34 Moses, Aaron and the leaders of the community counted the Kohathites q by their clans and families. 35 All the men from thirty to fifty years of age who came to

4:37
r Nu 3:27

serve in the work in the Tent of Meeting, 36 counted by clans, were 2,750. 37 This was the total of all those in the Kohathite clans r who served in the Tent of Meeting. Moses and Aaron counted them according to the LORD's command through Moses.

4:38
s Ge 46:11

38 The Gershonites s were counted by their clans and families. 39 All the men from thirty to fifty years of age who came to serve in the work at the Tent of Meeting, 40 counted by their clans and families, were 2,630. 41 This was the total of those in the Gershonite clans who served at the Tent of Meeting. Moses and Aaron counted them according to the LORD's command.

42 The Merarites were counted by their clans and families. 43 All the men from thirty to fifty years of age who came to serve in the work at the Tent of Meeting,

4:45
t ver 29

44 counted by their clans, were 3,200. 45 This was the total of those in the Merarite clans. t Moses and Aaron counted them according to the LORD's command through Moses.

4:47
u ver 3
4:48
v Nu 3:39

46 So Moses, Aaron and the leaders of Israel counted all the Levites by their clans and families. 47 All the men from thirty to fifty years of age u who came to do the work of serving and carrying the Tent of Meeting 48 numbered 8,580. v 49 At the LORD's command through Moses, each was assigned his work and told what to carry.

4:49
w Nu 1:47

Thus they were counted, w as the LORD commanded Moses.

The Purity of the Camp

5:2
x Lev 13:46
y Lev 15:2; Mt 9:20
z Lev 13:3;
Nu 9:6-10

5 The LORD said to Moses, 2 "Command the Israelites to send away from the camp anyone who has an infectious skin disease a x or a discharge y of any kind, or who is ceremonially unclean z because of a dead body. 3 Send away male and female alike; send them outside the camp so they will not defile their camp, where

---

a 2 Traditionally *leprosy*; the Hebrew word was used for various diseases affecting the skin—not necessarily leprosy.

Numbers 4:29–33

After the Gershonites had stripped the portable sanctuary down to its skeleton, the Merarites were to carry the disassembled pieces of the framework and everything pertaining to it. Their work was as important as that of any other family group. Without it the more desirable, prestigious work of the tabernacle couldn't be done.

For the person who seeks to do everything to God's glory (cf. 1 Cor. 10:31), life is holy. It's as though every meal is a sacrament, every word a prayer, every deed an act of worship. What a difference this perspective can make as we go about our often mundane routines!

Numbers 4:34–49

The remainder of chapter 4 reports on the carrying out of God's instructions, again in the order of the Kohathites, Gershonites, and Merarites. In verses 46–49 notice was given of compliance on the part of the lead-

ers. Such summary texts allow the reader to enjoy a sense of going full circle.

Understanding God's will, as expressed in Scripture, is one thing. Doing it is quite another. The census of the Levite clans was carried out "as the LORD commanded Moses" (v. 49). This kind of obedience is the initial benchmark of the book of Numbers. But as the book progresses we will find that on more than one occasion the people did *everything but* what God had commanded through Moses. To what extent are you executing your daily accountabilities as the Lord has commanded you?

Numbers 5:1–4

Having described the process of organizing the Israelite camp (chs. 1–4), Numbers 5 addresses concerns of ritual impurity (vv. 1–4) and moral faults (vv. 5–31) from the perspective of community relations. This legislation supplemented rules given earlier in Leviticus.

I dwell among them. *a* " 4The Israelites did this; they sent them outside the camp. They did just as the LORD had instructed Moses.

5:3
a Lev 26:12; Nu 35:34; 2Co 6:16

Restitution for Wrongs

5The LORD said to Moses, 6"Say to the Israelites: 'When a man or woman wrongs another in any way*a* and so is unfaithful*b* to the LORD, that person is guilty*c* 7and must confess*d* the sin he has committed. He must make full restitution*e* for his wrong, add one fifth to it and give it all to the person he has wronged. 8But if that person has no close relative to whom restitution can be made for the wrong, the restitution belongs to the LORD and must be given to the priest, along with the ram with which atonement is made for him.*f* 9All the sacred contributions the Israelites bring to a priest will belong to him.*g* 10Each man's sacred gifts are his own, but what he gives to the priest will belong to the priest.*h* ' "

5:6
b Lev 6:2
c Lev 5:14-6:7
5:7
d Lev 5:5; 26:40; Jos 7:19; Lk 19:8
e Lev 6:5

5:8
f Lev 6:6,7; 7:7
5:9
g Lev 6:17; 7:6-14
5:10
h Lev 10:13

The Test for an Unfaithful Wife

11Then the LORD said to Moses, 12"Speak to the Israelites and say to them: 'If a man's wife goes astray*i* and is unfaithful to him 13by sleeping with another man,*j* and this is hidden from her husband and her impurity is undetected (since there is no witness against her and she has not been caught in the act), 14and if feelings of jealousy*k* come over her husband and he suspects his wife and she is impure—or if he is jealous and suspects her even though she is not impure— 15then he is to take his wife to the priest. He must also take an offering of a tenth of an ephah*b l* of barley flour*m* on her behalf. He must not pour oil on it or put incense on it, because it is a grain offering for jealousy, a reminder*n* offering to draw attention to guilt.

16" 'The priest shall bring her and have her stand before the LORD. 17Then he shall take some holy water in a clay jar and put some dust from the tabernacle floor into

5:12
i Ex 20:14
5:13
j Lev 18:20; 20:10

5:14
k Pr 6:34; SS 8:6

5:15
l Ex 16:36
m Lev 6:20
n Eze 29:16

---

a 6 Or *woman commits any wrong common to mankind*   *b* 15 That is, probably about 2 quarts (about 2 liters)

The primary reason for sending "unclean" persons away wasn't to avoid the spread of sickness but to prevent defiling the holy camp in which God dwelt with his people. Around the sanctuary, with its three levels of holiness (inner sanctum, outer sanctum, and court), there was a fourth gradation: the camp.

Sometimes a rebellious individual who is hurting the church may need to be "sent out of the camp" for the ultimate benefit of all concerned, including the potential salvation of that person (1 Cor. 5). But we are not to excommunicate or shun believers just because they are struggling. To the contrary, our role is to strengthen and encourage one another (Gal. 6:1; 1 Thess. 5:11; Heb. 3:13; 10:25; 2 Tim. 4:2). Christ's church is exactly where weak people belong.

Numbers 5:5–10

Verses 5–10 supplemented the law of compensation for ethical wrongs spelled out in Leviticus 6:1–7. The new information byte came in verse 8, which deals with a situation in which the wronged person died, leaving no relative ("kinsman-redeemer") to whom damages could be paid. The person who had committed the wrong was to pay the reparation to the priest, as God's representative. The connection of this paragraph to the previous is that of moving from the outward and visible to the inward, more secret faults that mar community.

In ancient times people were acutely aware that they couldn't survive on their own. There was safety in belonging to a group. This is still true, but we don't like

to admit it. In modern times our individuality has asserted itself at the expense of community solidarity. What can you do—in your family, neighborhood, church, place of employment, etc.—to promote unity, mutual accountability, and caring? Specifically, when you wrong someone, do you take initiative to make restitution? When you are wronged by another, do you seek restoration—or revenge?

Numbers 5:11–31

This passage progresses from public, obvious impurity to private, hidden sins. The language regarding the woman's thigh wasting away and abdomen swelling speaks figuratively of an inability to conceive—or of miscarriage (see vv. 21,22,27 and NIV text notes). Bearing children validated a woman's worth in the ancient world, so this was serious punishment.

Why was the suspected adultery ritual only for women? In clear cases of adultery, the penalty for both man and woman was death (Lev. 20:10). But to protect innocent women from false accusation by a jealous husband within a male-dominated court system, God removed their fates from human jurisdiction. He could be fair because he alone knew the facts. This was the only instance in which God promised to judge and render a verdict himself by supernatural means. The right to a Supreme Court trial belonged only to women.

In the book of Proverbs, on the issue of marital unfaithfulness, Foolishness enticingly calls out: "Stolen water is sweet; food eaten in secret is delicious!" (Prov.

5:18
o Lev 10:6;
1Co 11:6

5:19
p ver 12,29

5:20
q ver 12

5:21
r Jos 6:26;
1Sa 14:24;
Ne 10:29
5:22
s Ps 109:18 *t* ver 18
u Dt 27:15

5:23
v Jer 45:1

5:25
w Lev 8:27

5:27
x Isa 43:28; 65:15;
Jer 26:6; 29:18;
42:18; 44:12,22;
Zec 8:13
5:29
y ver 19

5:31
z Lev 5:1; 20:17

6:2
a Ge 28:20;
Ac 21:23
b Jdg 13:5; 16:17;
Am 2:11,12
6:3
c Lk 1:15 *d* Ru 2:14;
Ps 69:21; Pr 10:26

6:5
e Ps 52:2; 57:4;
59:7; Isa 7:20;
Eze 5:1 *f* 1Sa 1:11

the water. [18]After the priest has had the woman stand before the Lord, he shall loosen her hair[o] and place in her hands the reminder offering, the grain offering for jealousy, while he himself holds the bitter water that brings a curse. [19]Then the priest shall put the woman under oath and say to her, "If no other man has slept with you and you have not gone astray[p] and become impure while married to your husband, may this bitter water that brings a curse not harm you. [20]But if you have gone astray[q] while married to your husband and you have defiled yourself by sleeping with a man other than your husband"— [21]here the priest is to put the woman under this curse of the oath[r]—"may the Lord cause your people to curse and denounce you when he causes your thigh to waste away and your abdomen to swell. [a] [22]May this water[s] that brings a curse[t] enter your body so that your abdomen swells and your thigh wastes away. [b]"

" 'Then the woman is to say, "Amen. So be it.[u]"

[23] " 'The priest is to write these curses on a scroll[v] and then wash them off into the bitter water. [24]He shall have the woman drink the bitter water that brings a curse, and this water will enter her and cause bitter suffering. [25]The priest is to take from her hands the grain offering for jealousy, wave it before the Lord[w] and bring it to the altar. [26]The priest is then to take a handful of the grain offering as a memorial offering and burn it on the altar; after that, he is to have the woman drink the water. [27]If she has defiled herself and been unfaithful to her husband, then when she is made to drink the water that brings a curse, it will go into her and cause bitter suffering; her abdomen will swell and her thigh waste away, [c] and she will become accursed[x] among her people. [28]If, however, the woman has not defiled herself and is free from impurity, she will be cleared of guilt and will be able to have children.

[29] " 'This, then, is the law of jealousy when a woman goes astray[y] and defiles herself while married to her husband, [30]or when feelings of jealousy come over a man because he suspects his wife. The priest is to have her stand before the Lord and is to apply this entire law to her. [31]The husband will be innocent of any wrongdoing, but the woman will bear the consequences[z] of her sin.' "

The Nazirite

6 The Lord said to Moses, [2]"Speak to the Israelites and say to them: 'If a man or woman wants to make a special vow[a], a vow of separation to the Lord as a Nazirite,[b] [3]he must abstain from wine[c] and other fermented drink and must not drink vinegar[d] made from wine or from other fermented drink. He must not drink grape juice or eat grapes or raisins. [4]As long as he is a Nazirite, he must not eat anything that comes from the grapevine, not even the seeds or skins.

[5] " 'During the entire period of his vow of separation no razor[e] may be used on his head.[f] He must be holy until the period of his separation to the Lord is over;

---

[a] 21 Or *causes you to have a miscarrying womb and barrenness*   [b] 22 Or *body and cause you to be barren and have a miscarrying womb*   [c] 27 Or *suffering; she will have barrenness and a miscarrying womb*

9:17). The result may be an initial rush of exciting chemistry. But when lustful curiosity is sated, adultery is shallow, boring, and leaves an aftertaste of guilt. It can't begin to compare with the emotional and spiritual depth of "[our] own cistern" (Prov. 5:15). If you are married, do you enjoy this sense of deep and enduring satisfaction with your spouse?

Numbers 6:1–21

From the Hebrew term for "separated one"—*nazir*—comes the label "Nazirite." A man or woman *from any tribe could be separated or consecrated to God* for a specified period of time, occasionally even for life (e.g., Judg. 13:5; 1 Sam. 1:11). We tend to focus on the prohibitions imposed on a Nazirite, but more important to God was the positive separation (see Num. 6:8).

Why would someone choose to become a Nazirite? The text leaves open a range of possibilities that could suit a variety of individuals and circumstances. Like other voluntary vows and dedications to the Lord (cf. Lev. 27), this commitment could simply be an expression of devotion or gratitude to God. Or it could be tied to a request for some kind of tangible or spiritual benefit.

The story of Samson, the lifelong Nazirite (Judg. 13–16), illustrates the fact that the greatest danger to our own holiness and godly power comes from ourselves: our own pride, hardheartedness, materialism, and self-gratification, which separate us from the Source of sacredness. But if we focus on God and maintain our separation *to* him, "who shall separate us *from* the love of Christ?" (Rom. 8:35, emphasis added).

he must let the hair of his head grow long. [6]Throughout the period of his separation to the LORD he must not go near a dead body. [g] [7]Even if his own father or mother or brother or sister dies, he must not make himself ceremonially unclean[h] on account of them, because the symbol of his separation to God is on his head. [8]Throughout the period of his separation he is consecrated to the LORD.

[9]" 'If someone dies suddenly in his presence, thus defiling the hair he has dedicated,[i] he must shave his head on the day of his cleansing[j]—the seventh day. [10]Then on the eighth day he must bring two doves or two young pigeons[k] to the priest at the entrance to the Tent of Meeting. [11]The priest is to offer one as a sin offering and the other as a burnt offering[l] to make atonement[m] for him because he sinned by being in the presence of the dead body. That same day he is to consecrate his head. [12]He must dedicate himself to the LORD for the period of his separation and must bring a year-old male lamb as a guilt offering. The previous days do not count, because he became defiled during his separation.

[13]" 'Now this is the law for the Nazirite when the period of his separation is over.[n] He is to be brought to the entrance to the Tent of Meeting. [14]There he is to present his offerings to the LORD: a year-old male lamb without defect for a burnt offering, a year-old ewe lamb without defect for a sin offering,[o] a ram without defect for a fellowship offering,[a] [15]together with their grain offerings and drink offerings,[p] and

a 14 Traditionally *peace offering*; also in verses 17 and 18

6:6
g Lev 21:1-3;
Nu 19:11-22
6:7
h Nu 9:6

6:9
i ver 18 j Lev 14:9
6:10
k Lev 5:7; 14:22

6:11
l Ge 8:20
m Ex 29:36

6:13
n Ac 21:26

6:14
o Lev 14:10;
Nu 15:27
6:15
p Nu 15:1-7

6:1–8

Nazirite Vow

The purpose of the Nazirite vow was to purify oneself for intensive service to God. Biblical Nazirites took the vow, often for a limited time period but sometimes for life, to address problems in their world. Would something like the Nazirite vow (the Roman Catholic Church is a good example of modern use of vows of devotion to God and service) help Christians today to address the structures of sin we encounter (see below)?

STRUCTURES OF SIN

Global Mega-Problems

- Invasive surveillance: 86 restricted-access countries; 43 closed-access countries

- Exploitation of women: 2.5 million reported rapes and 250 million battered women each year

- Debt: $100 billion tied up per year to service debt

- Financial crime: $3 trillion per year

- Pollution: 33% of Earth's surface endangered

- Manipulation: 3 billion people denied freedom to travel, assemble, or teach new ideas

Mega-Evils

- Pornography: 70 million pornography readers/viewers/users

- Warfare: 1 million people killed annually in wars (25 wars in 2000 alone)

- Financial fraud: $932 million removed fraudulently from circulation each year

- Corruption: 1.2 billion victims of corruption each year

- Crime: 73.6 million identified crimes each year

- Drugs: $250 billion spent/made on illegal drugs each year

- Terrorism: 4,000 terrorist acts committed each year

- Assassination: 975,000 politically motivated murders each year

- Murder: 975,000 each year

- Genocide: 50,000 average per year since 1947

Source: Barrett and Johnson (2001:35)

6:15
q Ex 29:2; Lev 2:4
a basket of bread made without yeast—cakes made of fine flour mixed with oil, and wafers spread with oil. *q*

16 " 'The priest is to present them before the LORD and make the sin offering and the burnt offering. 17 He is to present the basket of unleavened bread and is to sacrifice the ram as a fellowship offering to the LORD, together with its grain offering and drink offering.

6:18
r ver 9; Ac 21:24
18 " 'Then at the entrance to the Tent of Meeting, the Nazirite must shave off the hair that he dedicated. *r* He is to take the hair and put it in the fire that is under the sacrifice of the fellowship offering.

19 " 'After the Nazirite has shaved off the hair of his dedication, the priest is to place in his hands a boiled shoulder of the ram, and a cake and a wafer from the basket, both made without yeast. 20 The priest shall then wave them before the LORD as a wave offering; they are holy and belong to the priest, together with the breast that

6:20
s Ecc 9:7
was waved and the thigh that was presented. After that, the Nazirite may drink wine. *s*

21 " 'This is the law of the Nazirite who vows his offering to the LORD in accordance with his separation, in addition to whatever else he can afford. He must fulfill the vow he has made, according to the law of the Nazirite.' "

The Priestly Blessing

6:23
t Dt 21:5;
1Ch 23:13
6:24
u Dt 28:3-6; Ps 28:9
v 1Sa 2:9; Ps 17:8
22 The LORD said to Moses, 23 "Tell Aaron and his sons, 'This is how you are to bless *t* the Israelites. Say to them:

24 " ' "The LORD bless you *u*
 and keep you; *v*

6:25
w Job 29:24;
Ps 31:16; 80:3;
119:135
x Ge 43:29;
Ps 25:16; 86:16
6:26
y Ps 4:6; 44:3
z Ps 29:11; 37:11,
37; Jn 14:27
6:27
a Dt 28:10;
2Sa 7:23; 2Ch 7:14;
Ne 9:10; Jer 25:29
25 the LORD make his face shine upon you *w*
 and be gracious to you; *x*
26 the LORD turn his face *y* toward you
 and give you peace. *z* " '

27 "So they will put my name *a* on the Israelites, and I will bless them."

Offerings at the Dedication of the Tabernacle

7:1
b Ex 40:17
c Ex 40:9 *d* ver 84,
88; Ex 40:10
7:2
e Nu 1:5-16
7 When Moses finished setting up the tabernacle, *b* he anointed it and consecrated it and all its furnishings. *c* He also anointed and consecrated the altar and all its utensils. *d* 2 Then the leaders of Israel, *e* the heads of families who were the tribal leaders in charge of those who were counted, made offerings. 3 They brought as their gifts before the LORD six covered carts and twelve oxen—an ox from each leader and a cart from every two. These they presented before the tabernacle.

4 The LORD said to Moses, 5 "Accept these from them, that they may be used in the work at the Tent of Meeting. Give them to the Levites as each man's work requires."

7:7
f Nu 4:24-26,28
7:8
g Nu 4:31-33
6 So Moses took the carts and oxen and gave them to the Levites. 7 He gave two carts and four oxen to the Gershonites, *f* as their work required, 8 and he gave four carts and eight oxen to the Merarites, *g* as their work required. They were all under

---

Numbers 6:22–27

Israelites have long found comfort in these cherished words. A shortened form of the priestly blessing appears on two small amulets of silver leaf found in the tomb chambers of a cave outside ancient Jerusalem. Discovered in 1979, the miniature scrolls with words scratched into their surfaces had apparently been worn around the neck on cords. Dated about 600 B.C., they are among the earliest known written quotations of any Scripture passage.

The priestly blessing provides special assurance because its requests were formulated by the divine Giver himself. This implies an invitation like the one later extended by Jesus: "Ask and it will be given to you; seek and you will find; knock and the door will be opened to you" (Matt. 7:7). So why don't we ask more? If your prayers are real to God, are they real to you? Are you confident that your praises and petitions, feeble and unfocused as they may be, are successfully transmitted to him through the Spirit (Rom. 8:26)?

Numbers 7:1–89

A new house calls for celebration, including "housewarming gifts." Just as modern neighbors may shower recently installed residents with presents, ancient Israelites gave useful items to the Owner of the freshly completed "mansion" at the center of their neighborhood. The offerings of the tribal leaders over 12 days were all the same. The list of items is fully repeated 12 times, sacrificing the economy of "ditto" to the grand impact of a public record in which each leader was acknowledged.

the direction of Ithamar son of Aaron, the priest. ⁹But Moses did not give any to the Kohathites, because they were to carry on their shoulders ʰ the holy things, for which they were responsible.

7:9
ʰ Nu 4:15

¹⁰When the altar was anointed, ⁱ the leaders brought their offerings for its dedication ʲ and presented them before the altar. ¹¹For the Lᴏʀᴅ had said to Moses, "Each day one leader is to bring his offering for the dedication of the altar."

7:10
ⁱ ver 1 / 2Ch 7:9

¹²The one who brought his offering on the first day was Nahshon son of Amminadab of the tribe of Judah.

¹³His offering was one silver plate weighing a hundred and thirty shekels, ᵃ and one silver sprinkling bowl weighing seventy shekels, ᵇ both according to the sanctuary shekel, ᵏ each filled with fine flour mixed with oil as a grain offering; ˡ ¹⁴one gold dish weighing ten shekels, ᶜ filled with incense; ᵐ ¹⁵one young bull, ⁿ one ram and one male lamb a year old, for a burnt offering; ᵒ ¹⁶one male goat for a sin offering; ᵖ ¹⁷and two oxen, five rams, five male goats and five male lambs a year old, to be sacrificed as a fellowship offering. ᵈ �q This was the offering of Nahshon son of Amminadab. ʳ

7:13
ᵏ Ex 30:13; Nu 3:47
ˡ Lev 2:1
7:14
ᵐ Ex 30:34
7:15
ⁿ Ex 24:5; 29:3;
Nu 28:11 ᵒ Lev 1:3
7:16
ᵖ Lev 4:3,23
7:17
q Lev 3:1 ʳ Nu 1:7
7:18
ˢ Nu 1:8

¹⁸On the second day Nethanel son of Zuar, ˢ the leader of Issachar, brought his offering.

¹⁹The offering he brought was one silver plate weighing a hundred and thirty shekels, and one silver sprinkling bowl weighing seventy shekels, both according to the sanctuary shekel, each filled with fine flour mixed with oil as a grain offering; ²⁰one gold dish ᵗ weighing ten shekels, filled with incense; ²¹one young bull, one ram and one male lamb a year old, for a burnt offering; ²²one male goat for a sin offering; ²³and two oxen, five rams, five male goats and five male lambs a year old, to be sacrificed as a fellowship offering. This was the offering of Nethanel son of Zuar.

7:20
ᵗ ver 14

²⁴On the third day, Eliab son of Helon, ᵘ the leader of the people of Zebulun, brought his offering.

²⁵His offering was one silver plate weighing a hundred and thirty shekels, and one silver sprinkling bowl weighing seventy shekels, both according to the sanctuary shekel, each filled with fine flour mixed with oil as a grain offering; ²⁶one gold dish weighing ten shekels, filled with incense; ²⁷one young bull, one ram and one male lamb a year old, for a burnt offering; ²⁸one male goat for a sin offering; ²⁹and two oxen, five rams, five male goats and five male lambs a year old, to be sacrificed as a fellowship offering. This was the offering of Eliab son of Helon.

7:24
ᵘ Nu 1:9

³⁰On the fourth day Elizur son of Shedeur, ᵛ the leader of the people of Reuben, brought his offering.

³¹His offering was one silver plate weighing a hundred and thirty shekels, and one silver sprinkling bowl weighing seventy shekels, both according to the sanctuary shekel, each filled with fine flour mixed with oil as a grain offering; ³²one gold dish weighing ten shekels, filled with incense; ³³one young bull, one ram and one male lamb a year old, for a burnt offering; ³⁴one male goat for a sin offering; ³⁵and two oxen, five rams, five male goats and five male

7:30
ᵛ Nu 1:5

ᵃ 13 That is, about 3 1/4 pounds (about 1.5 kilograms); also elsewhere in this chapter   ᵇ 13 That is, about 1 3/4 pounds (about 0.8 kilogram); also elsewhere in this chapter   ᶜ 14 That is, about 4 ounces (about 110 grams); also elsewhere in this chapter   ᵈ 17 Traditionally *peace offering*; also elsewhere in this chapter

---

Like the Israelite chieftains, who brought gifts to God at the sanctuary, and the Magi, who paid rich homage to the newborn King (Matt. 2:11), we have the privilege of joyfully acknowledging him with material gifts, prayers, songs, and testimonies. When Christians today initiate the use of a church and provide it with a van, kitchen utensils, and food for God's work in their community, they are following in the worthy footsteps of Nahshon, Nethanel, Eliab, and their fellow leaders. As always, though, it's not the size of the gift that counts in the King's eyes, but the spirit in which it's offered.

lambs a year old, to be sacrificed as a fellowship offering. This was the offering of Elizur son of Shedeur.

7:36
w Nu 1:6

36On the fifth day Shelumiel son of Zurishaddai, w the leader of the people of Simeon, brought his offering.
37His offering was one silver plate weighing a hundred and thirty shekels, and one silver sprinkling bowl weighing seventy shekels, both according to the sanctuary shekel, each filled with fine flour mixed with oil as a grain offering; 38one gold dish weighing ten shekels, filled with incense; 39one young bull, one ram and one male lamb a year old, for a burnt offering; 40one male goat for a sin offering; 41and two oxen, five rams, five male goats and five male lambs a year old, to be sacrificed as a fellowship offering. This was the offering of Shelumiel son of Zurishaddai.

7:42
x Nu 1:14

42On the sixth day Eliasaph son of Deuel, x the leader of the people of Gad, brought his offering.
43His offering was one silver plate weighing a hundred and thirty shekels, and one silver sprinkling bowl weighing seventy shekels, both according to the sanctuary shekel, each filled with fine flour mixed with oil as a grain offering; 44one gold dish weighing ten shekels, filled with incense; 45one young bull, one ram and one male lamb a year old, for a burnt offering; 46one male goat for a sin offering; 47and two oxen, five rams, five male goats and five male lambs a year old, to be sacrificed as a fellowship offering. This was the offering of Eliasaph son of Deuel.

7:48
y Nu 1:10

48On the seventh day Elishama son of Ammihud, y the leader of the people of Ephraim, brought his offering.
49His offering was one silver plate weighing a hundred and thirty shekels, and one silver sprinkling bowl weighing seventy shekels, both according to the sanctuary shekel, each filled with fine flour mixed with oil as a grain offering; 50one gold dish weighing ten shekels, filled with incense; 51one young bull, one ram and one male lamb a year old, for a burnt offering; 52one male goat for a sin offering; 53and two oxen, five rams, five male goats and five male lambs a year old, to be sacrificed as a fellowship offering. This was the offering of Elishama son of Ammihud. z

7:53
z Nu 1:10

7:54
a Nu 1:10; 2:20

54On the eighth day Gamaliel son of Pedahzur, a the leader of the people of Manasseh, brought his offering.
55His offering was one silver plate weighing a hundred and thirty shekels, and one silver sprinkling bowl weighing seventy shekels, both according to the sanctuary shekel, each filled with fine flour mixed with oil as a grain offering; 56one gold dish weighing ten shekels, filled with incense; 57one young bull, one ram and one male lamb a year old, for a burnt offering; 58one male goat for a sin offering; 59and two oxen, five rams, five male goats and five male lambs a year old, to be sacrificed as a fellowship offering. This was the offering of Gamaliel son of Pedahzur.

7:60
b Nu 1:11

60On the ninth day Abidan son of Gideoni, b the leader of the people of Benjamin, brought his offering.
61His offering was one silver plate weighing a hundred and thirty shekels, and one silver sprinkling bowl weighing seventy shekels, both according to the sanctuary shekel, each filled with fine flour mixed with oil as a grain offering; 62one gold dish weighing ten shekels, filled with incense; 63one young bull, one ram and one male lamb a year old, for a burnt offering; 64one male goat for a sin offering; 65and two oxen, five rams, five male goats and five male lambs a year old, to be sacrificed as a fellowship offering. This was the offering of Abidan son of Gideoni.

7:66
c Nu 1:12; 2:25

66On the tenth day Ahiezer son of Ammishaddai, c the leader of the people of Dan, brought his offering.

67His offering was one silver plate weighing a hundred and thirty shekels, and one silver sprinkling bowl weighing seventy shekels, both according to the sanctuary shekel, each filled with fine flour mixed with oil as a grain offering; 68one gold dish weighing ten shekels, filled with incense; 69one young bull, one ram and one male lamb a year old, for a burnt offering; 70one male goat for a sin offering; 71and two oxen, five rams, five male goats and five male lambs a year old, to be sacrificed as a fellowship offering. This was the offering of Ahiezer son of Ammishaddai.

72On the eleventh day Pagiel son of Ocran,*d* the leader of the people of Asher, brought his offering.

7:72
d Nu 1:13

73His offering was one silver plate weighing a hundred and thirty shekels, and one silver sprinkling bowl weighing seventy shekels, both according to the sanctuary shekel, each filled with fine flour mixed with oil as a grain offering; 74one gold dish weighing ten shekels, filled with incense; 75one young bull, one ram and one male lamb a year old, for a burnt offering; 76one male goat for a sin offering; 77and two oxen, five rams, five male goats and five male lambs a year old, to be sacrificed as a fellowship offering. This was the offering of Pagiel son of Ocran.

78On the twelfth day Ahira son of Enan,*e* the leader of the people of Naphtali, brought his offering.

7:78
e Nu 1:15; 2:29

79His offering was one silver plate weighing a hundred and thirty shekels, and one silver sprinkling bowl weighing seventy shekels, both according to the sanctuary shekel, each filled with fine flour mixed with oil as a grain offering; 80one gold dish weighing ten shekels, filled with incense; 81one young bull, one ram and one male lamb a year old, for a burnt offering; 82one male goat for a sin offering; 83and two oxen, five rams, five male goats and five male lambs a year old, to be sacrificed as a fellowship offering. This was the offering of Ahira son of Enan.

84These were the offerings of the Israelite leaders for the dedication of the altar when it was anointed:*f* twelve silver plates, twelve silver sprinkling bowls*g* and twelve gold dishes.*h* 85Each silver plate weighed a hundred and thirty shekels, and each sprinkling bowl seventy shekels. Altogether, the silver dishes weighed two thousand four hundred shekels,*a* according to the sanctuary shekel. 86The twelve gold dishes filled with incense weighed ten shekels each, according to the sanctuary shekel. Altogether, the gold dishes weighed a hundred and twenty shekels.*b* 87The total number of animals for the burnt offering came to twelve young bulls, twelve rams and twelve male lambs a year old, together with their grain offering. Twelve male goats were used for the sin offering. 88The total number of animals for the sacrifice of the fellowship offering came to twenty-four oxen, sixty rams, sixty male goats and sixty male lambs a year old. These were the offerings for the dedication of the altar after it was anointed.*i*

7:84
f ver 1,10
g Nu 4:14 *h* ver 14

89When Moses entered the Tent of Meeting to speak with the Lord,*j* he heard the voice speaking to him from between the two cherubim above the atonement cover*k* on the ark of the Testimony. And he spoke with him.

7:88
i ver 1,10
7:89
j Ex 25:21,22; 33:9, 11 *k* Ps 80:1; 99:1

Setting Up the Lamps

8 The Lord said to Moses, 2"Speak to Aaron and say to him, 'When you set up the seven lamps, they are to light the area in front of the lampstand.'"

8:2
l Ex 25:37;
Lev 24:2,4

a 85 That is, about 60 pounds (about 28 kilograms)   *b* 86 That is, about 3 pounds (about 1.4 kilograms)

Numbers 8:1–4

Aside from the practical benefit of supplying light for the priests to properly perform their duties at the incense altar and the golden table, the lamps were God's light. He didn't need a human source of illumina-

tion, but the light symbolized that the tabernacle was his residence and that Somebody was home! God's light burned all night (Ex. 27:21; Lev. 24:3). What a boon for Israel to have a divine Protector who was always present!

3 Aaron did so; he set up the lamps so that they faced forward on the lampstand,
just as the LORD commanded Moses. 4 This is how the lampstand was made: It was
made of hammered gold[m]—from its base to its blossoms. The lampstand was
made exactly like the pattern[n] the LORD had shown Moses.

The Setting Apart of the Levites

5 The LORD said to Moses: 6 "Take the Levites from among the other Israelites and
make them ceremonially clean.[o] 7 To purify them, do this: Sprinkle the water of
cleansing[p] on them; then have them shave their whole bodies[q] and wash their
clothes,[r] and so purify themselves. 8 Have them take a young bull with its grain offering of fine flour mixed with oil;[s] then you are to take a second young bull for a
sin offering. 9 Bring the Levites to the front of the Tent of Meeting[t] and assemble the
whole Israelite community.[u] 10 You are to bring the Levites before the LORD, and the
Israelites are to lay their hands on them.[v] 11 Aaron is to present the Levites before
the LORD as a wave offering[w] from the Israelites, so that they may be ready to do the
work of the LORD.

12 "After the Levites lay their hands on the heads of the bulls,[x] use the one for a
sin offering to the LORD and the other for a burnt offering, to make atonement[y] for
the Levites. 13 Have the Levites stand in front of Aaron and his sons and then present them as a wave offering to the LORD. 14 In this way you are to set the Levites
apart from the other Israelites, and the Levites will be mine.[z]

15 "After you have purified the Levites and presented them as a wave offering,[a]
they are to come to do their work at the Tent of Meeting. 16 They are the Israelites
who are to be given wholly to me. I have taken them as my own in place of the firstborn, the first male offspring[b] from every Israelite woman. 17 Every firstborn male
in Israel, whether man or animal,[c] is mine. When I struck down all the firstborn in
Egypt, I set them apart for myself.[d] 18 And I have taken the Levites in place of all the
firstborn sons in Israel.[e] 19 Of all the Israelites, I have given the Levites as gifts to Aaron and his sons[f] to do the work at the Tent of Meeting on behalf of the Israelites[g]
and to make atonement for them[h] so that no plague will strike the Israelites when
they go near the sanctuary."

20 Moses, Aaron and the whole Israelite community did with the Levites just as
the LORD commanded Moses. 21 The Levites purified themselves and washed their
clothes.[i] Then Aaron presented them as a wave offering before the LORD and made
atonement for them to purify them.[j] 22 After that, the Levites came to do their
work at the Tent of Meeting under the supervision of Aaron and his sons. They did
with the Levites just as the LORD commanded Moses.

23 The LORD said to Moses, 24 "This applies to the Levites: Men twenty-five years
old or more[k] shall come to take part in the work at the Tent of Meeting,[l] 25 but at
the age of fifty, they must retire from their regular service and work no longer.
26 They may assist their brothers in performing their duties at the Tent of Meeting,

8:4 [m] Ex 25:18,36; 25:18 [n] Ex 25:9
8:6 [o] Lev 22:2; Isa 1:16; 52:11
8:7 [p] Nu 19:9,17 [q] Lev 14:9; Dt 21:12 [r] Lev 14:8
8:8 [s] Lev 2:1; Nu 15:8-10
8:9 [t] Ex 40:12 [u] Lev 8:3
8:10 [v] Ac 6:6
8:11 [w] Lev 7:30
8:12 [x] Ex 29:10 [y] Ex 29:36
8:14 [z] Nu 3:12
8:15 [a] Ex 29:24
8:16 [b] Nu 3:12
8:17 [c] Ex 4:23 [d] Ex 13:2; Lk 2:23
8:18 [e] Nu 3:12
8:19 [f] Nu 3:9 [g] Nu 1:53 [h] Nu 16:46
8:21 [i] ver 7 [j] ver 12
8:24 [k] 1Ch 23:3 [l] Ex 38:21; Nu 4:3

Do you take the Lord's presence with you for granted (Matt. 28:20: Heb. 13:5)? His aren't empty promises or marketing slogans. He's always there, with us in our darkest moments and also on the days that vibrate with joy. Light and "voltage" come from above, but we as Christians are to stay "plugged in" to our divine Source.

Numbers 8:5–26

The Levites in general weren't priests, and their authorization service didn't include consecration with anointing oil. But they did belong to God, to serve the *priests in place of the firstborn males of all the other* tribes (see 3:6–9,12–13,41,45 and "There and Then" for 3:1–51). They were to do the work of the sanctuary on behalf of the rest of the Israelites.

What did it mean for the Levites to make atonement for the Israelites so that no plague would strike them (v. 19)? The Levites were responsible for guarding the tabernacle against encroachment, literally with their lives (1:51; 18:23). If they failed to stop such evil, they would bear the guilt.

The end of this passage talks about granting men over age fifty retirement from Levitical work, but they still could assist the younger men. What a model for honoring years of service while still passing the baton to those better equipped to carry a heavy, manual workload! In our everyone-for-themselves, expendable culture, this kind of respect seems a lost value. How, in your workplace or church fellowship, can you implement the spirit of these verses on behalf of those nearing or entering retirement years? Could you personally offer to mow a lawn or clean rain gutters for an older neighbor?

but they themselves must not do the work. This, then, is how you are to assign the responsibilities of the Levites."

The Passover

9 The LORD spoke to Moses in the Desert of Sinai in the first month[m] of the second year after they came out of Egypt.[n] He said, [2]"Have the Israelites celebrate the Passover at the appointed time. [3]Celebrate it at the appointed time, at twilight on the fourteenth day of this month, in accordance with all its rules and regulations.[o]"

[4]So Moses told the Israelites to celebrate the Passover, [5]and they did so in the Desert of Sinai at twilight on the fourteenth day of the first month.[p] The Israelites did everything just as the LORD commanded Moses.

[6]But some of them could not celebrate the Passover on that day because they were ceremonially unclean[q] on account of a dead body. So they came to Moses and Aaron[r] that same day [7]and said to Moses, "We have become unclean because of a dead body, but why should we be kept from presenting the LORD's offering with the other Israelites at the appointed time?"

[8]Moses answered them, "Wait until I find out what the LORD commands concerning you."[s]

[9]Then the LORD said to Moses, [10]"Tell the Israelites: 'When any of you or your descendants are unclean because of a dead body or are away on a journey, they may still celebrate[t] the LORD's Passover. [11]They are to celebrate it on the fourteenth day of the second month at twilight. They are to eat the lamb, together with unleavened bread and bitter herbs.[u] [12]They must not leave any of it till morning[v] or break any of its bones.[w] When they celebrate the Passover, they must follow all the regulations. [13]But if a man who is ceremonially clean and not on a journey fails to celebrate the Passover, that person must be cut off from his people[x] because he did not present the LORD's offering at the appointed time. That man will bear the consequences of his sin.

[14]" 'An alien[y] living among you who wants to celebrate the LORD's Passover must do so in accordance with its rules and regulations. You must have the same regulations for the alien and the native-born.' "

The Cloud Above the Tabernacle

[15]On the day the tabernacle, the Tent of the Testimony, was set up, the cloud[z] covered it. From evening till morning the cloud above the tabernacle looked like fire.[a] [16]That is how it continued to be; the cloud covered it, and at night it looked like fire. [17]Whenever the cloud lifted from above the Tent, the Israelites set out; wherever the cloud settled, the Israelites encamped.[b] [18]At the LORD's command the Israelites set out, and at his command they encamped. As long as the cloud stayed over the tabernacle, they remained in camp. [19]When the cloud remained over the tabernacle a long time, the Israelites obeyed the LORD's order and did not set out.

9:1 m Ex 40:2 n Nu 1:1

9:3 o Ex 12:2-11,43-49; Lev 23:5-8; Dt 16:1-8
9:5 p Ex 12:1-13; Jos 5:10

9:6 q Lev 5:3 r Ex 18:15; Nu 27:2

9:8 s Ex 18:15; Nu 27:5,21; Ps 85:8

9:10 t 2Ch 30:2

9:11 u Ex 12:8
9:12 v Ex 12:10,43 w Ex 12:46; Jn 19:36*
9:13 x Ge 17:14; Ex 12:15

9:14 y Ex 12:48,49

9:15 z Ex 40:34 a Ex 13:21

9:17 b Ex 40:36-38; Nu 10:11,12; 1Co 10:1

Numbers 9:1–14

It's clear that the impure Israelites didn't arrange to be disqualified from the Passover so that they could skip it. They expressed frustration that circumstances beyond their control had prevented them from participating. Theirs was a refreshing kind of complaint. God's solution was to establish a second date, one month later, for those who had been unclean because of contact with a corpse. He added to this concession those who had been away on a journey. Presumably this provision would go into effect once the Israelites were settled in Canaan.

Whether we are raising our children, interacting with coworkers, or socializing, we do well to imitate aspects of God's character at work in this passage. Based

on this text, we might use such adjectives to describe him as *considerate, reasonable, fair, flexible, generous, organized, firm,* and *farsighted.* What other words come to mind? Do you attempt to demonstrate these same qualities? How can learning to follow God's example in specific situations improve your life and the lives of those around you?

Numbers 9:15–23

The cloud first appeared in Exodus 13:21, where God went ahead of the Israelites "in a pillar of cloud to guide them on their way and by night in a pillar of fire to give them light, so that they could travel by day or night." In addition to providing guidance and illumination, God in his cloud had protected his people from the Egyptians at the Red Sea (Ex. 14:19–24).

20Sometimes the cloud was over the tabernacle only a few days; at the LORD's command they would encamp, and then at his command they would set out. 21Sometimes the cloud stayed only from evening till morning, and when it lifted in the morning, they set out. Whether by day or by night, whenever the cloud lifted, they set out. 22Whether the cloud stayed over the tabernacle for two days or a month or a year, the Israelites would remain in camp and not set out; but when it lifted, they would set out. 23At the LORD's command they encamped, and at the LORD's command they set out. They obeyed the LORD's order, in accordance with his command through Moses.

The Silver Trumpets

10 The LORD said to Moses: 2"Make two trumpets[c] of hammered silver, and use them for calling the community[d] together and for having the camps set out. 3When both are sounded, the whole community is to assemble before you at the entrance to the Tent of Meeting. 4If only one is sounded, the leaders[e]—the heads of the clans of Israel—are to assemble before you. 5When a trumpet blast is sounded, the tribes camping on the east are to set out.[f] 6At the sounding of a second blast, the camps on the south are to set out.[g] The blast will be the signal for setting out. 7To gather the assembly, blow the trumpets,[h] but not with the same signal.[i]

8"The sons of Aaron, the priests, are to blow the trumpets. This is to be a lasting ordinance for you and the generations to come.[j] 9When you go into battle in your own land against an enemy who is oppressing you,[k] sound a blast on the trumpets. Then you will be remembered[l] by the LORD your God and rescued from your enemies.[m] 10Also at your times of rejoicing—your appointed feasts and New Moon festivals[n]—you are to sound the trumpets[o] over your burnt offerings and fellowship offerings,[a] and they will be a memorial for you before your God. I am the LORD your God."

The Israelites Leave Sinai

11On the twentieth day of the second month of the second year,[p] the cloud lifted[q] from above the tabernacle of the Testimony. 12Then the Israelites set out from the Desert of Sinai and traveled from place to place until the cloud came to rest in the Desert of Paran. 13They set out, this first time, at the LORD's command through Moses.[r] 14The divisions of the camp of Judah went first, under their standard.[s] Nahshon

---

a 10 Traditionally peace offerings

10:2 c Ne 12:35; Ps 47:5 d Jer 4:5,19; 6:1; Hos 5:8; Joel 2:1,15; Am 3:6 **10:4** e Ex 18:21; Nu 1:16; 7:2 **10:5** f ver 14 **10:6** g ver 18 **10:7** h Eze 33:3; Joel 2:1 i 1Co 14:8 **10:8** j Nu 31:6 **10:9** k Jdg 2:18; 6:9; 1Sa 10:18; Ps 106:42 l Ge 8:1 m Ps 106:4 **10:10** n Ps 81:3 o Lev 23:24 **10:11** p Ex 40:17 q Nu 9:17 **10:13** r Dt 1:6 **10:14** s Nu 2:3-9

For the Israelites to remain with God's resident Presence, they had to move with him. No use lingering to worship at the spot where he had been! Nor trying to guess where he might go next and running ahead to wait for him there. God offered no rationale for his movements. The important thing was to know where his cloud was and follow.

Divine leading doesn't replace decisions and risks. But God's guidance does serve as a Global Positioning System, a reference point for navigating the challenges of our way. God doesn't give us a detailed map of our journey. He is that map. To avoid getting lost, we can find out where he's leading and follow him. We have no visible, divine cloud to follow, but we can discern his will through a variety of ways. Among them are his Spirit, our consciences, the Bible, providence, and the balanced counsel of mature believers.

Numbers 10:1–10

When the divine cloud over the tabernacle rose from its resting place, the Israelites were to prepare for travel (9:17). But what if people were inside their tents and didn't see the cloud's movement? No problem. As with other people in the ancient world (e.g., Egyptians,

Romans armies), signal sounds would get their attention.

Different types of trumpet blasts would signal a variety of activities, to which a wide range of emotions would be associated. Variables in trumpet calls included one or two trumpets, long or short blasts, and differences in the numbers of blasts.

What if the Israelites had decided not to blow the trumpets, pack up, and move out? What if they had chosen to stay at Mount Sinai and pray for God to miraculously transport them to the promised land? Cooperation with God requires first learning what he wants and then doing it. If our prayers are one-way monologues from us to him, without listening for his voice or "trumpet" or looking for his "cloud," we miss opportunities for his direction for our lives. How has God guided you?

Numbers 10:11–36

After almost a year in the vicinity of Mount Sinai, the Israelites set out. Moses' brother-in-law Hobab was an experienced desert dweller with connections to the people who controlled wilderness regions on the way to Canaan. But why did the Israelites need his guidance (v. 31) when they had God's ark and cloud to perform the same function? God can and does bring about

son of Amminadab ^{t} was in command. ¹⁵Nethanel son of Zuar was over the division of the tribe of Issachar, ¹⁶and Eliab son of Helon was over the division of the tribe of Zebulun. ¹⁷Then the tabernacle was taken down, and the Gershonites and Merarites, who carried it, set out. ^{u}

¹⁸The divisions of the camp of Reuben went next, under their standard. ^{v} Elizur son of Shedeur was in command. ¹⁹Shelumiel son of Zurishaddai was over the division of the tribe of Simeon, ²⁰and Eliasaph son of Deuel was over the division of the tribe of Gad. ²¹Then the Kohathites set out, carrying the holy things. ^{w} The tabernacle was to be set up before they arrived. ^{x}

²²The divisions of the camp of Ephraim ^{y} went next, under their standard. Elishama son of Ammihud was in command. ²³Gamaliel son of Pedahzur was over the division of the tribe of Manasseh, ²⁴and Abidan son of Gideoni was over the division of the tribe of Benjamin.

²⁵Finally, as the rear guard ^{z} for all the units, the divisions of the camp of Dan set out, under their standard. Ahiezer son of Ammishaddai was in command. ²⁶Pagiel son of Ocran was over the division of the tribe of Asher, ²⁷and Ahira son of Enan was over the division of the tribe of Naphtali. ²⁸This was the order of march for the Israelite divisions as they set out.

²⁹Now Moses said to Hobab ^{a} son of Reuel ^{b} the Midianite, Moses' father-in-law, ^{c} "We are setting out for the place about which the LORD said, 'I will give it to you.' ^{d} Come with us and we will treat you well, for the LORD has promised good things to Israel."

³⁰He answered, "No, I will not go; ^{e} I am going back to my own land and my own people."

³¹But Moses said, "Please do not leave us. You know where we should camp in the desert, and you can be our eyes. ^{f} ³²If you come with us, we will share with you ^{g} whatever good things the LORD gives us. ^{h}"

³³So they set out ^{i} from the mountain of the LORD and traveled for three days. The ark of the covenant of the LORD ^{j} went before them during those three days to find them a place to rest. ³⁴The cloud of the LORD was over them by day when they set out from the camp. ^{k}

³⁵Whenever the ark set out, Moses said,

"Rise up, O LORD!
May your enemies be scattered; ^{l}
may your foes flee before you. ^{m}"

³⁶Whenever it came to rest, he said,

"Return, ^{n} O LORD,
to the countless thousands of Israel. ^{o}"

Fire From the LORD

11 Now the people complained about their hardships in the hearing of the LORD, and when he heard them his anger was aroused. Then fire from the LORD burned among them ^{p} and consumed some of the outskirts of the camp. ²When the people cried out to Moses, he prayed to the LORD ^{q} and the fire died

10:14 ^{t} Nu 1:7
10:17 ^{u} Nu 4:21-32
10:18 ^{v} Nu 2:10-16
10:21 ^{w} Nu 4:20 ^{x} ver 17
10:22 ^{y} Nu 2:24
10:25 ^{z} Nu 2:31; Jos 6:9
10:29 ^{a} Jdg 4:11 ^{b} Ex 2:18 ^{c} Ex 3:1 ^{d} Ge 12:7
10:30 ^{e} Mt 21:29
10:31 ^{f} Job 29:15
10:32 ^{g} Dt 10:18 ^{h} Ps 22:27-31; 67:5-7
10:33 ^{i} ver 12; Dt 1:33 ^{j} Jos 3:3
10:34 ^{k} Nu 9:15-23
10:35 ^{l} Ps 68:1 ^{m} Dt 7:10; 32:41; Ps 68:2; Isa 17:12-14
10:36 ^{n} Isa 63:17 ^{o} Dt 1:10
11:1 ^{p} Lev 10:2
11:2 ^{q} Nu 21:7

his purposes through human activity (cf. Gen. 45:5–8). Moses saw Hobab's potential for enhancing the quality of the Israelites' journey. He could instill confidence and help them plan ahead by telling them what to expect (cf. Num. 13:17–20).

Why does God have human beings do anything, no matter how small, when he wants to do something amazing for them? Obviously, it's not because he can't do these things—and far more efficiently, too. But human activity is an expression of faith. When has God asked you to do something in preparation for his acting

in the situation in a wonderful way?

Numbers 11:1–3

We have made it through ten chapters of Numbers without encountering anyone with a bad attitude! But the first verse of chapter 11 hits a sour note of *déjà vu* (see Ex. 15:22—17:7). The divine cloud had been appearing like fire at night to protect the Israelites (9:15–16), but now God answered grumbling with destructive fire at the outskirts of the camp. The text doesn't say what the fire consumed, but it seems likely that some people were hurt. The warning came through hot and clear.

11:3
r Dt 9:22
11:4
s Ex 12:38
t Ps 78:18;
1Co 10:6
11:5
u Ex 16:3
11:7
v Ex 16:31
w Ge 2:12
11:9
x Ex 16:13
11:11
y Ex 5:22
11:12
z Isa 40:11; 49:23
a Ex 13:5
11:13
b Jn 6:5-9
11:14
c Ex 18:18
11:15
d Ex 32:32
e 1Ki 19:4; Jnh 4:3
11:17
f ver 25,29;
1Sa 10:6; 2Ki 2:9,
15; Joel 2:28
g Ex 18:18
11:18
h Ex 19:10 i Ex 16:7
j ver 5; Ac 7:39
11:20
k Ps 78:29; 106:14,
15 l Jos 24:27;
1Sa 10:19
11:21
m Ex 12:37

down. ³So that place was called Taberah,ᵃʳ because fire from the LORD had burned among them.

Quail From the LORD

⁴The rabble with them began to crave other food,ˢ and again the Israelites started wailingᵗ and said, "If only we had meat to eat! ⁵We remember the fish we ate in Egypt at no cost—also the cucumbers, melons, leeks, onions and garlic.ᵘ ⁶But now we have lost our appetite; we never see anything but this manna!"

⁷The manna was like coriander seedᵛ and looked like resin.ʷ ⁸The people went around gathering it, and then ground it in a handmill or crushed it in a mortar. They cooked it in a pot or made it into cakes. And it tasted like something made with olive oil. ⁹When the dewˣ settled on the camp at night, the manna also came down.

¹⁰Moses heard the people of every family wailing, each at the entrance to his tent. The LORD became exceedingly angry, and Moses was troubled. ¹¹He asked the LORD, "Why have you brought this trouble on your servant? What have I done to displease you that you put the burden of all these people on me?ʸ ¹²Did I conceive all these people? Did I give them birth? Why do you tell me to carry them in my arms, as a nurse carries an infant,ᶻ to the land you promised on oath to their forefathers?ᵃ ¹³Where can I get meat for all these people?ᵇ They keep wailing to me, 'Give us meat to eat!' ¹⁴I cannot carry all these people by myself; the burden is too heavy for me.ᶜ ¹⁵If this is how you are going to treat me, put me to deathᵈ right nowᵉ—if I have found favor in your eyes—and do not let me face my own ruin."

¹⁶The LORD said to Moses: "Bring me seventy of Israel's elders who are known to you as leaders and officials among the people. Have them come to the Tent of Meeting, that they may stand there with you. ¹⁷I will come down and speak with you there, and I will take of the Spirit that is on you and put the Spirit on them.ᶠ They will help you carry the burden of the people so that you will not have to carry it alone.ᵍ

¹⁸"Tell the people: 'Consecrate yourselvesʰ in preparation for tomorrow, when you will eat meat. The LORD heard you when you wailed,ⁱ "If only we had meat to eat! We were better off in Egypt!"ʲ Now the LORD will give you meat, and you will eat it. ¹⁹You will not eat it for just one day, or two days, or five, ten or twenty days, ²⁰but for a whole month—until it comes out of your nostrils and you loathe itᵏ—because you have rejected the LORD,ˡ who is among you, and have wailed before him, saying, "Why did we ever leave Egypt?" ' "

²¹But Moses said, "Here I am among six hundred thousand menᵐ on foot, and you say, 'I will give them meat to eat for a whole month!' ²²Would they have

ᵃ 3 *Taberah* means *burning*.

Faith has a learning curve. After giving the Israelites evidence on which to base their faith, God expected them to trust him and held them accountable for the quality of their faith in his goodness. He had to cure them of their rebellious attitude in a wilderness boot camp. After all, they couldn't survive a military assault on fortified Canaan without implicit trust in miracles only he could provide. Where do you see yourself on your faith learning curve?

Numbers 11:4–35

The divine King didn't take kindly to insulting rejection of the heavenly bounty he daily provided. Contributing to the seriousness of the situation was Moses' *burnout. Just as the people were sick and tired of manna,* Moses was sick and tired of them! God first addressed Moses' need, instructing him to gather 70 others to help shoulder his load. Then, when it sounded as though the people were to enjoy an all-you-can-eat meal, their

wish-come-true turned to appropriate punishment.

Large numbers of quail migrate each year across the Sinai Peninsula from Africa on their way to Europe and Asia. Since these birds have heavy bodies and don't fly well, they partly depend on prevailing winds to assist their flight and become exhausted by long journeys. During the 1900s, Arabs living in northern Sinai used nets to catch 1–2 million low-flying quail.

Complaining is alive and well today, especially with regard to little aggravations, inconveniences, aches, and pains. Obviously there is a place for directing legitimate grievances to those who have caused our problems or can do something about them. But grumbling behind someone's back—including God's—is destructive. Instead, we can take our concerns directly to him, correctly believing that he will hear us (cf. Ps. 142:1–3). A complaint voiced as a faith petition can strengthen us and others when God answers.

enough if flocks and herds were slaughtered for them? Would they have enough if all the fish in the sea were caught for them?"[n]

[23]The LORD answered Moses, "Is the LORD's arm too short?[o] You will now see whether or not what I say will come true for you.[p]"

[24]So Moses went out and told the people what the LORD had said. He brought together seventy of their elders and had them stand around the Tent. [25]Then the LORD came down in the cloud[q] and spoke with him,[r] and he took of the Spirit[s] that was on him and put the Spirit on the seventy elders.[t] When the Spirit rested on them, they prophesied,[u] but they did not do so again.[a]

[26]However, two men, whose names were Eldad and Medad, had remained in the camp. They were listed among the elders, but did not go out to the Tent. Yet the Spirit also rested on them, and they prophesied in the camp. [27]A young man ran and told Moses, "Eldad and Medad are prophesying in the camp."

[28]Joshua son of Nun, who had been Moses' aide[v] since youth, spoke up and said, "Moses, my lord, stop them!"[w]

[29]But Moses replied, "Are you jealous for my sake? I wish that all the LORD's people were prophets[x] and that the LORD would put his Spirit on them!" [30]Then Moses and the elders of Israel returned to the camp.

[31]Now a wind went out from the LORD and drove quail[y] in from the sea. It brought them[b] down all around the camp to about three feet[c] above the ground, as far as a day's walk in any direction. [32]All that day and night and all the next day the people went out and gathered quail. No one gathered less than ten homers.[d] Then they spread them out all around the camp. [33]But while the meat was still between their teeth[z] and before it could be consumed, the anger of the LORD burned against the people, and he struck them with a severe plague.[a] [34]Therefore the place was named Kibroth Hattaavah,[e][b] because there they buried the people who had craved other food.

[35]From Kibroth Hattaavah the people traveled to Hazeroth[c] and stayed there.

Miriam and Aaron Oppose Moses

12 Miriam and Aaron began to talk against Moses because of his Cushite wife,[d] for he had married a Cushite. [2]"Has the LORD spoken only through Moses?" they asked. "Hasn't he also spoken through us?"[e] And the LORD heard this.[f]

[3](Now Moses was a very humble man,[g] more humble than anyone else on the face of the earth.)

[4]At once the LORD said to Moses, Aaron and Miriam, "Come out to the Tent of Meeting, all three of you." So the three of them came out. [5]Then the LORD came down in a pillar of cloud;[h] he stood at the entrance to the Tent and summoned Aaron and Miriam. When both of them stepped forward, [6]he said, "Listen to my words:

"When a prophet of the LORD is among you,
    I reveal myself to him in visions,[i]

---

[a] 25 Or *prophesied and continued to do so*   [b] 31 Or *They flew*   [c] 31 Hebrew *two cubits* (about 1 meter)   [d] 32 That is, probably about 60 bushels (about 2.2 kiloliters)   [e] 34 *Kibroth Hattaavah* means *graves of craving.*

11:22
[n] Mt 15:33
11:23
[o] Isa 50:2; 59:1
[p] Nu 23:19;
Eze 12:25; 24:14

11:25
[q] Nu 12:5 [r] ver 17
[s] 1Sa 10:6 [t] Ac 2:17
[u] 1Sa 10:10

11:28
[v] Ex 33:11; Jos 1:1
[w] Mk 9:38-40

11:29
[x] 1Co 14:5

11:31
[y] Ex 16:13;
Ps 78:26-28

11:33
[z] Ps 78:30
[a] Ps 106:15
11:34
[b] Dt 9:22
11:35
[c] Nu 33:17

12:1
[d] Ex 2:21
12:2
[e] Nu 16:3 [f] Nu 11:1
12:3
[g] Mt 11:29

12:5
[h] Nu 11:25

12:6
[i] Ge 15:1; 46:2

Numbers 12:1–16

We are not sure of the identity of Moses' wife here. She may have been Zipporah, his Midianite wife (see Ex. 2:15–21). Or perhaps Moses had married a second woman, a "Cushite" (scholars aren't sure what people group "Cushite" refers to). Miriam and Aaron's criticism of Moses' non-Israelite wife was the pretext for a deeper issue: jealousy over their brother's leadership and reputation.

Moses didn't defend himself, but God took decisive action, summoning a "family meeting" at the Tent of Meeting. He didn't deny Miriam and Aaron's claim to prophetic inspiration but rebuked them for speaking against Moses. After wishing to socially exclude Moses' wife, in the end Miriam (evidently the instigator) herself was physically excluded from the camp for a time.

Racism is always about status and control—and always insults God. Putting people down for their genetic makeup implies that God creates inferior products in his image (cf. Gen. 1:26). Racism is grossly unfair for exactly the same reason it's attractive to those attempting to gain the upper hand at any cost: People are born with their race and can't change it (see Jer. 13:23). Can you honestly say you have never voiced condemning stereotypes based on race or ethnicity? If you have, it's not too late to seek the Lord for forgiveness.

12:6
j Ge 31:10; 1Ki 3:5;
Heb 1:1
12:7
k Jos 1:1-2;
Ps 105:26
l Heb 3:2,5
12:8
m Dt 34:10
n Ex 20:4; Ps 17:15

12:9
o Ge 17:22

12:10
p Ex 4:6; Dt 24:9
q 2Ki 5:1,27

12:11
r 2Sa 19:19; 24:10

12:13
s Isa 30:26;
Jer 17:14
12:14
t Dt 25:9; Job 17:6;
30:9-10; Isa 50:6
u Lev 13:46;
Nu 5:2-3
12:16
v Nu 11:35

13:2
w Dt 1:22

13:6
x ver 30; Nu 14:6,
24; 34:19;
Jdg 1:12-15

13:16
y ver 8 z Dt 32:44
13:17
a Ge 12:9 b Jdg 1:9

I speak to him in dreams. [j]
7 But this is not true of my servant Moses; [k]
  he is faithful in all my house. [l]
8 With him I speak face to face,
  clearly and not in riddles; [m]
  he sees the form of the LORD. [n]
Why then were you not afraid
  to speak against my servant Moses?"

9 The anger of the LORD burned against them, and he left them. [o]
10 When the cloud lifted from above the Tent, there stood Miriam—leprous, [a] like snow. [p] Aaron turned toward her and saw that she had leprosy; [q] 11 and he said to Moses, "Please, my lord, do not hold against us the sin we have so foolishly committed. [r] 12 Do not let her be like a stillborn infant coming from its mother's womb with its flesh half eaten away."

13 So Moses cried out to the LORD, "O God, please heal her! [s]"

14 The LORD replied to Moses, "If her father had spit in her face, [t] would she not have been in disgrace for seven days? Confine her outside the camp [u] for seven days; after that she can be brought back." 15 So Miriam was confined outside the camp for seven days, and the people did not move on till she was brought back.

16 After that, the people left Hazeroth [v] and encamped in the Desert of Paran.

Exploring Canaan

13 The LORD said to Moses, 2 "Send some men to explore [w] the land of Canaan, which I am giving to the Israelites. From each ancestral tribe send one of its leaders."

3 So at the LORD's command Moses sent them out from the Desert of Paran. All of them were leaders of the Israelites. 4 These are their names:

  from the tribe of Reuben, Shammua son of Zaccur;
  5 from the tribe of Simeon, Shaphat son of Hori;
  6 from the tribe of Judah, Caleb son of Jephunneh; [x]
  7 from the tribe of Issachar, Igal son of Joseph;
  8 from the tribe of Ephraim, Hoshea son of Nun;
  9 from the tribe of Benjamin, Palti son of Raphu;
  10 from the tribe of Zebulun, Gaddiel son of Sodi;
  11 from the tribe of Manasseh (a tribe of Joseph), Gaddi son of Susi;
  12 from the tribe of Dan, Ammiel son of Gemalli;
  13 from the tribe of Asher, Sethur son of Michael;
  14 from the tribe of Naphtali, Nahbi son of Vophsi;
  15 from the tribe of Gad, Geuel son of Maki.

16 These are the names of the men Moses sent to explore the land. (Moses gave Hoshea son of Nun [y] the name Joshua.) [z]

17 When Moses sent them to explore Canaan, he said, "Go up through the Negev [a] and on into the hill country. [b] 18 See what the land is like and whether the people who live there are strong or weak, few or many. 19 What kind of land do they live in? Is it good or bad? What kind of towns do they live in? Are they unwalled or for-

---

[a] 10 The Hebrew word was used for various diseases affecting the skin—not necessarily leprosy.

Numbers 13:1–25

Numbers 13–14 recounts a major turning point in Israel's journey: the spy expedition and the impact of the scouts' reports on the people's willingness to trust God's promise about the land. Deuteronomy 1:22–23 describes the idea of the detective operation as having come from the people, not God. But the two accounts aren't mutually exclusive. Surely Moses would have approached the Lord for approval regarding any such un-

dertaking if members of the community had suggested it. Numbers and Deuteronomy single out different aspects: divine and human initiative, respectively.

When have you sensed confirmation of God's will for a venture you thought you had initiated? On the other hand, when has God surprised you with plans for your life you would never have imagined? As long as we are yielded to God's will and ready to follow wherever he leads, his will and ours often work in tandem.

tified? [20]How is the soil? Is it fertile or poor? Are there trees on it or not? Do your best to bring back some of the fruit of the land. [c]" (It was the season for the first ripe grapes.)

[21]So they went up and explored the land from the Desert of Zin[d] as far as Rehob, [e] toward Lebo[a] Hamath. [f] [22]They went up through the Negev and came to Hebron, where Ahiman, Sheshai and Talmai, [g] the descendants of Anak, [h] lived. (Hebron had been built seven years before Zoan in Egypt.)[i] [23]When they reached the Valley of Eshcol, [b] they cut off a branch bearing a single cluster of grapes. Two of them carried it on a pole between them, along with some pomegranates and figs. [24]That place was called the Valley of Eshcol because of the cluster of grapes the Israelites cut off there. [25]At the end of forty days they returned from exploring the land.

Report on the Exploration

[26]They came back to Moses and Aaron and the whole Israelite community at Kadesh in the Desert of Paran. There they reported to them[j] and to the whole assembly and showed them the fruit of the land. [27]They gave Moses this account: "We went into the land to which you sent us, and it does flow with milk and honey![k] Here is its fruit. [l] [28]But the people who live there are powerful, and the cities are fortified and very large. [m] We even saw descendants of Anak there. [29]The Amalekites live in the Negev; the Hittites, Jebusites and Amorites live in the hill country; and the Canaanites live near the sea and along the Jordan."

[a] 21 Or toward the entrance to   [b] 23 Eshcol means cluster; also in verse 24.

13:20
c Dt 1:25
13:21
d Nu 20:1; 27:14; 33:36; Jos 15:1
e Jos 19:28
f Jos 13:5
13:22
g Jos 15:14
h Jos 15:13
i Ps 78:12,43; Isa 19:11,13
13:26
j Nu 32:8
13:27
k Ex 3:8 l Dt 1:25
13:28
m Dt 1:28; 9:1,2

Numbers 13:26–33

When the spies reached the military portion of their report, optimism vaporized. Matching the promised land's abundant, lush fruits were its numerous, powerful peoples. The scouts exaggerated by characterizing the oversized inhabitants as Nephilim, descended from daunting men who had lived before the flood (Gen. 6:4). It's unclear how they supposed these Nephilim might have survived this catastrophe (cf. Gen. 7:21–23). The spies succumbed to paralyzing fear, having bought into the idea that the Canaanites were a vastly superior class of human beings.

In the opposing attitudes of Caleb and the ten scouts (Joshua would weigh in with Caleb in the next chapter), we see two basic orientations at work: faith in God to overcome "unbeatable" odds versus unbelief that makes people think they have to save themselves. Faith is courage that conquers. Disbelief is cowardice that (perhaps correctly) assesses the "impossibility" of a situation but fails to take God into account. For the person of faith, obstacles are temporary because God is real. But for the disbeliever, obstacles are permanent because God isn't real enough. Do you believe, act, and live as though he's alive and involved?

13:17–20

God had promised extensive and productive real estate to his wandering people. Moses sent out leaders from each of the 12 tribes to explore the promised land (13:3). What did Moses ask them to look for?

Question	Issue	Report
1. What's the land like?	Geography	Good land
2. Are the people strong or weak?	Military capabilities	Good fighters
3. Are there many or few?	Demography	Many people
4. What kinds of towns are already there?	Urbanization	Populous, fortified
5. How's the soil?	Fertility	Good soil
6. Are there trees on it?	Forestation	No report; perhaps not too many trees
7. What kind of produce is being grown?	Agriculture	Land "flowing with milk [Moses mentioned grapes] and honey"

Result of exploration:
Good land, worth taking. God had promised victory. Yet . . .

Recommendation:
The majority report (10 of 12) claimed the Israelites couldn't overcome such powerful people. Only Joshua and Caleb protested. What difference does vision make?

30Then Caleb silenced the people before Moses and said, "We should go up and take possession of the land, for we can certainly do it."

31But the men who had gone up with him said, "We can't attack those people; they are stronger than we are."n 32And they spread among the Israelites a bad report o about the land they had explored. They said, "The land we explored devours p those living in it. All the people we saw there are of great size. q 33We saw the Nephilim r there (the descendants of Anak s come from the Nephilim). We seemed like grasshoppers in our own eyes, and we looked the same to them."

The People Rebel

14 That night all the people of the community raised their voices and wept aloud. 2All the Israelites grumbled against Moses and Aaron, and the whole assembly said to them, "If only we had died in Egypt! Or in this desert! t 3Why is the LORD bringing us to this land only to let us fall by the sword? Our wives and children will be taken as plunder. Wouldn't it be better for us to go back to Egypt?" 4And they said to each other, "We should choose a leader and go back to Egypt. u"

5Then Moses and Aaron fell facedown v in front of the whole Israelite assembly gathered there. 6Joshua son of Nun and Caleb son of Jephunneh, who were among those who had explored the land, tore their clothes 7and said to the entire Israelite assembly, "The land we passed through and explored is exceedingly good. w 8If the LORD is pleased with us, x he will lead us into that land, a land flowing with milk and honey, y and will give it to us. 9Only do not rebel z against the LORD. And do not be afraid of the people of the land, a because we will swallow them up. Their protection is gone, but the LORD is with us. Do not be afraid of them."

10But the whole assembly talked about stoning b them. Then the glory of the LORD c appeared at the Tent of Meeting to all the Israelites. 11The LORD said to Moses, "How long will these people treat me with contempt? How long will they refuse to believe in me, d in spite of all the miraculous signs I have performed among them? 12I will strike them down with a plague and destroy them, but I will make you into a nation e greater and stronger than they."

13Moses said to the LORD, "Then the Egyptians will hear about it! By your power you brought these people up from among them. f 14And they will tell the inhabitants of this land about it. They have already heard g that you, O LORD, are with these people and that you, O LORD, have been seen face to face, that your cloud stays over them, and that you go before them in a pillar of cloud by day and a pillar of fire by night. h 15If you put these people to death all at one time, the nations who have heard this report about you will say, 16'The LORD was not able to bring these people into the land he promised them on oath; so he slaughtered them in the desert.' i

17"Now may the Lord's strength be displayed, just as you have declared: 18'The LORD is slow to anger, abounding in love and forgiving sin and rebellion. j Yet he does not leave the guilty unpunished; he punishes the children for the sin of the fathers to the third and fourth generation.' k 19In accordance with your great love, forgive l the sin of these people, m just as you have pardoned them from the time they left Egypt until now." n

20The LORD replied, "I have forgiven them, o as you asked. 21Nevertheless, as surely as I live p and as surely as the glory of the LORD fills the whole earth, q 22not one of the men who saw my glory and the miraculous signs I performed in Egypt and in the desert but who disobeyed me and tested me ten times r— 23not one of them

Side references:

13:31
n Dt 1:28; 9:1;
Jos 14:8
13:32
o Nu 14:36,37
p Eze 36:13,14
q Am 2:9
13:33
r Ge 6:4 s Dt 1:28

14:2
t Nu 11:1

14:4
u Ne 9:17
14:5
v Nu 16:4,22,45

14:7
w Nu 13:27;
Dt 1:25
14:8
x Dt 10:15
y Nu 13:27
14:9
z Dt 1:26; 9:7,23,
24 a Dt 1:21; 7:18;
20:1
14:10
b Ex 17:4 c Lev 9:23

14:11
d Ps 78:22; 106:24

14:12
e Ex 32:10

14:13
f Ex 32:11-14;
Ps 106:23
14:14
g Ex 15:14
h Ex 13:21

14:16
i Jos 7:7
14:18
j Ex 34:6; Ps 145:8;
Jnh 4:2 k Ex 20:5
14:19
l Ex 34:9
m Ps 106:45
n Ps 78:38
14:20
o Ps 106:23;
Mic 7:18-20
14:21
p Dt 32:40;
Isa 49:18
q Ps 72:19; Isa 6:3;
Hab 2:14
14:22
r Ex 14:11; 32:1;
1Co 10:5

Numbers 14:1–45

Persuaded by the negative scouts that it was hopeless to attempt to overcome Canaan, the Israelites concluded that God was their enemy and that their best option was to mutiny against Moses and return to Egypt. Preempting the fulfillment of their murderous threats, God's glory appeared at the Tent of Meeting. This manifestation of his presence and wrath must have been staggering, turning rampaging rage into trembling terror.

Amazingly, Moses pled for the lives of those who had heaped abuse on him. Rather than citing any redeeming or redeemable quality in this miserable people, Moses appealed to the preservation of God's reputation and clung to the Lord's own declaration of his character (vv. 14:17–19; cf. Ex. 34:6–7). God did forgive Israel but didn't ignore the wrong or erase its consequences. He refused to bestow the promised land on rebels, who would only use it to defame his Name.

will ever see the land I promised on oath[s] to their forefathers. No one who has treated me with contempt will ever see it.[t] 24But because my servant Caleb has a different spirit and follows me wholeheartedly,[u] I will bring him into the land he went to, and his descendants will inherit it.[v] 25Since the Amalekites and Canaanites are living in the valleys, turn[w] back tomorrow and set out toward the desert along the route to the Red Sea.[a]"

26The LORD said to Moses and Aaron: 27"How long will this wicked community grumble against me? I have heard the complaints of these grumbling Israelites.[x] 28So tell them, 'As surely as I live,[y] declares the LORD, I will do to you the very things I heard you say: 29In this desert your bodies will fall[z]—every one of you twenty years old or more[a] who was counted in the census and who has grumbled against me. 30Not one of you will enter the land I swore with uplifted hand to make your home, except Caleb son of Jephunneh and Joshua son of Nun. 31As for your children that you said would be taken as plunder, I will bring them in to enjoy the land you have rejected.[b] 32But you—your bodies will fall[c] in this desert. 33Your children will be shepherds here for forty years, suffering for your unfaithfulness, until the last of your bodies lies in the desert. 34For forty years—one year for each of the forty days you explored the land[d]—you will suffer for your sins and know what it is like to have me against you.' 35I, the LORD, have spoken, and I will surely do these things[e] to this whole wicked community, which has banded together against me. They will meet their end in this desert; here they will die."

36So the men Moses had sent[f] to explore the land, who returned and made the whole community grumble against him by spreading a bad report[g] about it— 37these men responsible for spreading the bad report[h] about the land were struck down and died of a plague[i] before the LORD. 38Of the men who went to explore the land, only Joshua son of Nun and Caleb son of Jephunneh survived.[j]

39When Moses reported this to all the Israelites, they mourned[k] bitterly. 40Early the next morning they went up toward the high hill country. "We have sinned[l]," they said. "We will go up to the place the LORD promised."

41But Moses said, "Why are you disobeying the LORD's command? This will not succeed![m] 42Do not go up, because the LORD is not with you. You will be defeated by your enemies,[n] 43for the Amalekites and Canaanites will face you there. Because you have turned away from the LORD, he will not be with you and you will fall by the sword."

44Nevertheless, in their presumption they went up[o] toward the high hill country, though neither Moses nor the ark of the LORD's covenant moved from the camp.[p] 45Then the Amalekites and Canaanites who lived in that hill country came down and attacked them and beat them down all the way to Hormah.[q]

Supplementary Offerings

15 The LORD said to Moses, 2"Speak to the Israelites and say to them: 'After you enter the land I am giving you[r] as a home 3and you present to the LORD offerings made by fire, from the herd or the flock,[s] as an aroma pleasing to the LORD[t]—whether burnt offerings[u] or sacrifices, for special vows or freewill offerings[v] or festival offerings[w]— 4then the one who brings his offering shall present to the

[a] 25 Hebrew *Yam Suph*; that is, Sea of Reeds

14:23
[s] Nu 32:11
[t] Heb 3:18
14:24
[u] ver 6-9;
Jos 14:8, 14
[v] Nu 32:12
14:25
[w] Dt 1:40

14:27
[x] Ex 16:12
14:28
[y] ver 21
14:29
[z] Nu 26:65
[a] Nu 1:45

14:31
[b] Ps 106:24
14:32
[c] 1Co 10:5
14:34
[d] Nu 13:25

14:35
[e] Nu 23:19

14:36
[f] Nu 13:4-16
[g] Nu 13:32
14:37
[h] 1Co 10:10
[i] Nu 16:49
14:38
[j] Jos 14:6
14:39
[k] Ex 33:4
14:40
[l] Dt 1:41

14:41
[m] 2Ch 24:20
14:42
[n] Dt 1:42

14:44
[o] Dt 1:43 [p] Nu 31:6

14:45
[q] Nu 21:3; Dt 1:44;
Jdg 1:17

15:2
[r] Lev 23:10
15:3
[s] Lev 1:2 [t] ver 24;
Ge 8:21; Ex 29:18
[u] Nu 28:19,27
[v] Lev 22:18,21;
Ezr 1:4
[w] Lev 23:1-44

If we ask God to forgive someone else, as Moses and Jesus did (see Luke 23:34), we are asking him to give them an opportunity to make a better choice. If we pray for those who have wronged us, we relinquish our right to divine justice against them on our behalf. "Lord," we might say, "I'm not pressing charges. Please don't punish them for my sake." When, if ever, have you prayed like this? Might such a request be appropriate now?

Numbers 15:1–21

After the breathtaking drama of chapter 14,

Numbers 15 introduces an eerie calm. We are in the tranquil eye of a hurricane that will strike again with full fury in chapter 16. The fact that God was willing to continue as Israel's Lawgiver and to accept sacrificial gifts was a good sign. So was clear application of these laws to future life in the promised land (vv. 2,18), where the people would be privileged to offer him its bounty, like grain and wine. This affirmed God's promise in 14:31 to bring the younger generation into the promised land.

15:4
x Lev 2:1; 6:14
15:5
y Nu 28:7,14
15:6
z Lev 5:15
a Nu 28:12
b Eze 46:14

LORD a grain offering[x] of a tenth of an ephah[a] of fine flour mixed with a quarter of a hin[b] of oil. [5]With each lamb for the burnt offering or the sacrifice, prepare a quarter of a hin of wine[y] as a drink offering.

[6] " 'With a ram[z] prepare a grain offering[a] of two-tenths of an ephah[c] of fine flour mixed with a third of a hin[d] of oil, [b] [7]and a third of a hin of wine as a drink offering. Offer it as an aroma pleasing to the LORD.

15:8
c Lev 1:3; 3:1
15:9
d Lev 14:10

[8] " 'When you prepare a young bull as a burnt offering or sacrifice, for a special vow or a fellowship offering[ec] to the LORD, [9]bring with the bull a grain offering of three-tenths of an ephah[fd] of fine flour mixed with half a hin[g] of oil. [10]Also bring half a hin of wine as a drink offering. It will be an offering made by fire, an aroma pleasing to the LORD. [11]Each bull or ram, each lamb or young goat, is to be prepared in this manner. [12]Do this for each one, for as many as you prepare.

15:13
e Lev 16:29

[13] " 'Everyone who is native-born[e] must do these things in this way when he brings an offering made by fire as an aroma pleasing to the LORD. [14]For the generations to come, whenever an alien or anyone else living among you presents an offering made by fire as an aroma pleasing to the LORD, he must do exactly as you do.

15:15
f ver 29; Nu 9:14
15:16
g Nu 9:14

[15]The community is to have the same rules for you and for the alien living among you; this is a lasting ordinance for the generations to come. [f] You and the alien shall be the same before the LORD: [16]The same laws and regulations will apply both to you and to the alien living among you. [g] ' "

15:19
h Jos 5:11,12
15:20
i Ex 34:26;
Lev 23:14;
Dt 26:2,10
j Lev 2:14
15:21
k Ro 11:16

[17]The LORD said to Moses, [18]"Speak to the Israelites and say to them: 'When you enter the land to which I am taking you [19]and you eat the food of the land, [h] present a portion as an offering to the LORD. [20]Present a cake from the first of your ground meal[i] and present it as an offering from the threshing floor. [j] [21]Throughout the generations to come you are to give this offering to the LORD from the first of your ground meal. [k]

Offerings for Unintentional Sins

15:22
l Lev 4:2
15:24
m Lev 5:15
n Lev 4:14 o Lev 4:3

[22] " 'Now if you unintentionally fail to keep any of these commands the LORD gave Moses[l]— [23]any of the LORD's commands to you through him, from the day the LORD gave them and continuing through the generations to come— [24]and if this is done unintentionally without the community being aware of it, [m] then the whole community is to offer a young bull for a burnt offering[n] as an aroma pleasing to the LORD, along with its prescribed grain offering and drink offering, and a male goat for a sin offering. [o] [25]The priest is to make atonement for the whole Israelite

15:25
p Lev 4:20; Ro 3:25;
Heb 2:17

community, and they will be forgiven, [p] for it was not intentional and they have brought to the LORD for their wrong an offering made by fire and a sin offering.

15:26
q ver 24

[26]The whole Israelite community and the aliens living among them will be forgiven, because all the people were involved in the unintentional wrong. [q]

[a] 4 That is, probably about 2 quarts (about 2 liters)   [b] 4 That is, probably about 1 quart (about 1 liter); also in verse 5   [c] 6 That is, probably about 4 quarts (about 4.5 liters)   [d] 6 That is, probably about 1 1/4 quarts (about 1.2 liters); also in verse 7   [e] 8 Traditionally *peace offering*   [f] 9 That is, probably about 6 quarts (about 6.5 liters)   [g] 9 That is, probably about 2 quarts (about 2 liters); also in verse 10

God provided ritual remedies for his people's imperfections as long as they remained loyal to him. Loyalty is a matter of relationship, not just performance. God focuses on the health of the relationship, not on some scorecard. His ideal for each of us, as illustrated by Christ and empowered by his Spirit (2 Cor. 3; Phil. 2:5; 1 Peter 2:21), is far above what we could assume by looking around at each other. Are you gazing upward— or glancing at others from the corner of your eye—to determine how well you are doing?

Numbers 15:22–31

Verses 22–29 repeat part of the Leviticus 4 legislation regarding purification offerings for unintentional sins, either of the community or of an individual. The

text goes on to contrast this kind of inadvertent sin with defiant, deliberately rebellious acts. For such sins there was no sacrificial remedy—only the punishment of being "cut off" from God's people, either by execution or banishment.

The warnings against defiant sin (vv. 30–31) sound harsh, unless we think of them in a preventative sense. God's incredible mercy should bring hope to any sinner who desires salvation. But it shouldn't lead anyone to slide down the slippery slope of apostasy with the assurance of finding a sure footing at any given time. The problem isn't for God to be willing to forgive but for a sinner to want to be forgiven. Who do you know who simply doesn't care to be saved?

27 " 'But if just one person sins unintentionally,^{r} he must bring a year-old female goat for a sin offering. 28 The priest is to make atonement before the LORD for the one who erred by sinning unintentionally, and when atonement has been made for him, he will be forgiven.^{s} 29 One and the same law applies to everyone who sins unintentionally, whether he is a native-born Israelite or an alien.

30 " 'But anyone who sins defiantly,^{t} whether native-born or alien,^{u} blasphemes the LORD, and that person must be cut off from his people. 31 Because he has despised the LORD's word and broken his commands,^{v} that person must surely be cut off; his guilt remains on him.^{w} ' "

The Sabbath-Breaker Put to Death

32 While the Israelites were in the desert, a man was found gathering wood on the Sabbath day.^{x} 33 Those who found him gathering wood brought him to Moses and Aaron and the whole assembly, 34 and they kept him in custody, because it was not clear what should be done to him.^{y} 35 Then the LORD said to Moses, "The man must die.^{z} The whole assembly must stone him outside the camp.^{a} " 36 So the assembly took him outside the camp and stoned him to death, as the LORD commanded Moses.

Tassels on Garments

37 The LORD said to Moses, 38 "Speak to the Israelites and say to them: 'Throughout the generations to come you are to make tassels on the corners of your garments,^{b} with a blue cord on each tassel. 39 You will have these tassels to look at and so you will remember^c all the commands of the LORD, that you may obey them and not prostitute yourselves by going after the lusts of your own hearts and eyes. 40 Then you will remember to obey all my commands and will be consecrated to your God.^{d} 41 I am the LORD your God, who brought you out of Egypt to be your God. I am the LORD your God.' "

Korah, Dathan and Abiram

16 Korah^e son of Izhar, the son of Kohath, the son of Levi, and certain Reubenites—Dathan and Abiram, sons of Eliab,^{f} and On son of Peleth—became insolent^a 2 and rose up against Moses. With them were 250 Israelite men, well-known community leaders who had been appointed members of the council.^{g} 3 They came as a group to oppose Moses and Aaron^h and said to them, "You have gone too far! The whole community is holy,^{i} every one of them, and the LORD is with them.^{j} Why then do you set yourselves above the LORD's assembly?"^{k}

4 When Moses heard this, he fell facedown.^{l} 5 Then he said to Korah and all his followers: "In the morning the LORD will show who belongs to him and who is holy,^{m} and he will have that person come near him. The man he chooses^n he will

---

^{a} 1 Or *Peleth—took ⌐men.⌐*

15:27
^{r} Lev 4:27
15:28
^{s} Lev 4:35
15:30
^{t} Nu 14:40-44;
Dt 1:43; 17:13;
Ps 19:13 ^{u} ver 14
15:31
^{v} 2Sa 12:9;
Ps 119:126;
Pr 13:13 ^{w} Lev 5:1;
Eze 18:20
15:32
^{x} Ex 31:14,15;
35:2,3
15:34
^{y} Nu 9:8
15:35
^{z} Ex 31:14,15;
Dt 21:21
^{a} Lev 20:2; 24:14;
Ac 7:58
15:38
^{b} Dt 22:12; Mt 23:5
15:39
^{c} Dt 4:23; 6:12;
Ps 73:27
15:40
^{d} Lev 11:44;
Ro 12:1; Col 1:22;
1Pe 1:15
16:1
^{e} Jude 1:11
^{f} Nu 26:8; Dt 11:6
16:2
^{g} Nu 1:16; 26:9
16:3
^{h} ver 7; Ps 106:16
^{i} Ex 19:6 / Nu 14:14
^{k} Nu 12:2
16:4
^{l} Nu 14:5
16:5
^{m} Lev 10:3;
2Ti 2:19*
^{n} Nu 17:5; Ps 65:4

Numbers 15:32-36

🕮 This man seemed to be going out of his way to violate the Sabbath command (Ex. 20:8–11), of which the people were reminded every weekend when they received a double portion of manna on Friday to tide them over through it (Ex. 16:22–30). God had clearly communicated that breaking the Sabbath by working was punishable by death (Ex. 31:15; 35:2).

📖 Have you ever known someone who seemed to revel in sinning? To do it deliberately when you or another Christian was within sight or hearing? To brag about it in your presence? What possible explanation(s) can you think of for such flagrant defiance? How have you responded?

Numbers 15:37-41

🕮 The fate of the wood gatherer no doubt helped the people remember the Sabbath commandment. In addition, verses 37–41 prescribe an ongoing strategy to jog their memory regarding all the commandments. The tassels would remind them to obey and be consecrated to God, as opposed to exploring and committing spiritual promiscuity by going wherever their hearts or eyes should lead them.

📖 The swirling tassels would serve as practical memory aids to obey God's commands, and the blue color of the cords would likely remind the Israelites of their royal relationship with God. Can you think of modern equivalents to these tassels? How about wearing a cross necklace or a WWJD bracelet? Attaching a "fish" symbol to your car bumper or a Bible verse to the front of your refrigerator? Have such customs helped you?

cause to come near him. 6You, Korah, and all your followers are to do this: Take censers 7and tomorrow put fire and incense in them before the LORD. The man the LORD chooses will be the one who is holy. You Levites have gone too far!"

8Moses also said to Korah, "Now listen, you Levites! 9Isn't it enough for you that the God of Israel has separated you from the rest of the Israelite community and brought you near himself to do the work at the LORD's tabernacle and to stand before the community and minister to them?*o* 10He has brought you and all your fellow Levites near himself, but now you are trying to get the priesthood too.*p* 11It is against the LORD that you and all your followers have banded together. Who is Aaron that you should grumble*q* against him?*r*"

12Then Moses summoned Dathan and Abiram, the sons of Eliab. But they said, "We will not come! 13Isn't it enough that you have brought us up out of a land flowing with milk and honey to kill us in the desert?*s* And now you also want to lord it over us?*t* 14Moreover, you haven't brought us into a land flowing with milk and honey*u* or given us an inheritance of fields and vineyards.*v* Will you gouge out the eyes of*a* these men?*w* No, we will not come!"

15Then Moses became very angry and said to the LORD, "Do not accept their offering. I have not taken so much as a donkey*x* from them, nor have I wronged any of them."

16Moses said to Korah, "You and all your followers are to appear before the LORD tomorrow—you and they and Aaron.*y* 17Each man is to take his censer and put incense in it—250 censers in all—and present it before the LORD. You and Aaron are to present your censers also." 18So each man took his censer, put fire and incense in it, and stood with Moses and Aaron at the entrance to the Tent of Meeting. 19When Korah had gathered all his followers in opposition to them*z* at the entrance to the Tent of Meeting, the glory of the LORD*a* appeared to the entire assembly. 20The LORD said to Moses and Aaron, 21"Separate yourselves from this assembly so I can put an end to them at once."*b*

22But Moses and Aaron fell facedown*c* and cried out, "O God, God of the spirits of all mankind,*d* will you be angry with the entire assembly when only one man sins?"*e*

23Then the LORD said to Moses, 24"Say to the assembly, 'Move away from the tents of Korah, Dathan and Abiram.'"

25Moses got up and went to Dathan and Abiram, and the elders of Israel followed him. 26He warned the assembly, "Move back from the tents of these wicked men!*f* Do not touch anything belonging to them, or you will be swept away*g* because of all their sins." 27So they moved away from the tents of Korah, Dathan and Abiram. Dathan and Abiram had come out and were standing with their wives, children and little ones at the entrances to their tents.

28Then Moses said, "This is how you will know that the LORD has sent me*h* to do all these things and that it was not my idea: 29If these men die a natural death and experience only what usually happens to men, then the LORD has not sent me.*i* 30But if the LORD brings about something totally new, and the earth opens its mouth and swallows them, with everything that belongs to them, and they go down alive into the grave,*b i* then you will know that these men have treated the LORD with contempt." 31As soon as he finished saying all this, the ground under them split apart*k* 32and

---

16:9
o Nu 3:6; Dt 10:8
16:10
p Nu 3:10; 18:7
16:11
q 1Co 10:10
r Ex 16:7
16:13
s Nu 14:2 *t* Ac 7:27, 35
16:14
u Lev 20:24
v Ex 22:5; 23:11; Nu 20:5
w Jdg 16:21; 1Sa 11:2
16:15
x 1Sa 12:3
16:16
y ver 6
16:19
z ver 42 *a* Ex 16:7; Nu 14:10; 20:6
16:21
b Ex 32:10
16:22
c Nu 14:5
d Nu 27:16; Job 12:10; Heb 12:9
e Ge 18:23
16:26
f Isa 52:11
g Ge 19:15
16:28
h Ex 3:12; Jn 5:36; 6:38
16:29
i Ecc 3:19
16:30
j ver 33; Ps 55:15
16:31
k Mic 1:3-4

---

a 14 Or *you make slaves of*; or *you deceive*   *b 30* Hebrew *Sheol*; also in verse 33

Numbers 16:1–50

Burning incense to God, a priestly function, was off limits to all but Aaron and his descendants. Even the rest of the tribe of Levi, though privileged to serve at the tabernacle, hadn't been given priestly authorization. Lacking divine appointment, Israelites acting like priests couldn't survive any more than unprotected people today working with radioactive materials. In the process of destroying themselves, Korah and Company nearly triggered a catastrophic "meltdown" that would have wiped out their entire nation.

Later, when the Israelites deliberately attributed God's work to the powers of darkness, as though Moses and Aaron had killed the rebels by some sort of black magic, God's fuse was extremely short. The people had cut themselves off from any avenue of appeal (cf. Matt. 12:24–32; Heb. 10:26–27).

the earth opened its mouth and swallowed them,[l] with their households and all Korah's men and all their possessions. [33]They went down alive into the grave, with everything they owned; the earth closed over them, and they perished and were gone from the community. [34]At their cries, all the Israelites around them fled, shouting, "The earth is going to swallow us too!"

[35]And fire came out from the LORD[m] and consumed[n] the 250 men who were offering the incense.

[36]The LORD said to Moses, [37]"Tell Eleazar son of Aaron, the priest, to take the censers out of the smoldering remains and scatter the coals some distance away, for the censers are holy— [38]the censers of the men who sinned at the cost of their lives.[o] Hammer the censers into sheets to overlay the altar, for they were presented before the LORD and have become holy. Let them be a sign[p] to the Israelites."

[39]So Eleazar the priest collected the bronze censers brought by those who had been burned up, and he had them hammered out to overlay the altar, [40]as the LORD directed him through Moses. This was to remind the Israelites that no one except a descendant of Aaron should come to burn incense[q] before the LORD,[r] or he would become like Korah and his followers.[s]

[41]The next day the whole Israelite community grumbled against Moses and Aaron. "You have killed the LORD's people," they said.

[42]But when the assembly gathered in opposition[t] to Moses and Aaron and turned toward the Tent of Meeting, suddenly the cloud covered it and the glory of the LORD appeared. [43]Then Moses and Aaron went to the front of the Tent of Meeting, [44]and the LORD said to Moses, [45]"Get away from this assembly so I can put an end to them at once." And they fell facedown.

[46]Then Moses said to Aaron, "Take your censer and put incense in it, along with fire from the altar, and hurry to the assembly[u] to make atonement[v] for them. Wrath has come out from the LORD; the plague[w] has started." [47]So Aaron did as Moses said, and ran into the midst of the assembly. The plague had already started among the people,[x] but Aaron offered the incense and made atonement for them. [48]He stood between the living and the dead, and the plague stopped.[y] [49]But 14,700 people died from the plague, in addition to those who had died because of Korah.[z] [50]Then Aaron returned to Moses at the entrance to the Tent of Meeting, for the plague had stopped.

The Budding of Aaron's Staff

17 The LORD said to Moses, [2]"Speak to the Israelites and get twelve staffs from them, one from the leader of each of their ancestral tribes. Write the name of each man on his staff. [3]On the staff of Levi write Aaron's name,[a] for there must be one staff for the head of each ancestral tribe. [4]Place them in the Tent of Meeting in front of the Testimony,[b] where I meet with you.[c] [5]The staff belonging to the man I choose[d] will sprout, and I will rid myself of this constant grumbling against you by the Israelites."

16:32
l Nu 26:11; Dt 11:6;
Ps 106:17

16:35
m Nu 11:1-3; 26:10
n Lev 10:2

16:38
o Pr 20:2
p Nu 26:10;
Eze 14:8; 2Pe 2:6

16:40
q Ex 30:7-10;
Nu 1:51
r 2Ch 26:18
s Nu 3:10

16:42
t ver 19; Nu 20:6

16:46
u Lev 10:6
v Nu 18:5; 25:13;
Dt 9:22 w Nu 8:19;
Ps 106:29
16:47
x Nu 25:6-8
16:48
y Nu 25:8;
Ps 106:30
16:49
z ver 32

17:3
a Nu 1:3

17:4
b ver 7 c Ex 25:22
17:5
d Nu 16:5

Occasionally a piece of ground in Florida collapses into a massive pit called a "sinkhole." A sinkhole develops when an underground stream dries up and fails to support the ground above it. With impressive credentials, forceful personalities, and powerful political support, Korah, Dathan, and Abiram were outwardly strong. But they lacked the inner support of a spiritual connection with God. They were already sunk before they sank. How can you maintain your inner, spiritual strength?

God didn't satisfy or save the adult Israelites he had so gloriously redeemed from slavery. Taking our cue from his example, we are to love people consistently and persistently, with everything we have. But if they choose to reject us and our God, we need to let them go. Like Moses and Aaron, we are accountable for the quality of service we give, not for the responses we get.

Numbers 17:1–13

After the events of Numbers 16, it should have been crystal clear that Aaron was the one God had chosen to approach him as Israel's priest and intercessor (see 16:5,16–17,39–40). To hammer the final nail in the coffin of opposition to Aaron's divine election, God set up a further test, this time a peaceful one. He then exceeded the demands of his own test, causing Aaron's staff not only to sprout but to blossom and produce ripe almonds—all overnight! There was no doubt that Aaron's staff was the one that had sprouted; his name was written on it. Nor was there uncertainty about God's actions or intentions.

225

17:7
e Ex 38:21; Ac 7:44

6So Moses spoke to the Israelites, and their leaders gave him twelve staffs, one for the leader of each of their ancestral tribes, and Aaron's staff was among them. 7Moses placed the staffs before the LORD in the Tent of the Testimony. e

17:8
f Eze 17:24; Heb 9:4

8The next day Moses entered the Tent of the Testimony and saw that Aaron's staff, which represented the house of Levi, had not only sprouted but had budded, blossomed and produced almonds. f 9Then Moses brought out all the staffs from the LORD's presence to all the Israelites. They looked at them, and each man took his own staff.

17:10
g Dt 9:24

10The LORD said to Moses, "Put back Aaron's staff in front of the Testimony, to be kept as a sign to the rebellious. g This will put an end to their grumbling against me, so that they will not die." 11Moses did just as the LORD commanded him.

17:12
h Isa 6:5
17:13
i Nu 1:51

12The Israelites said to Moses, "We will die! We are lost, we are all lost! h 13Anyone who even comes near the tabernacle of the LORD will die. i Are we all going to die?"

Duties of Priests and Levites

18:1
j Ex 28:38

18 The LORD said to Aaron, "You, your sons and your father's family are to bear the responsibility for offenses against the sanctuary, j and you and your sons alone are to bear the responsibility for offenses against the priesthood. 2Bring your fellow Levites from your ancestral tribe to join you and assist you when you and your sons minister k before the Tent of the Testimony. 3They are to be responsible to you and are to perform all the duties of the Tent, l but they must not go near the furnishings of the sanctuary or the altar, or both they and you will die. m 4They are to join you and be responsible for the care of the Tent of Meeting—all the work at the Tent—and no one else may come near where you are.

18:2
k Nu 3:10
18:3
l Nu 1:51 m ver 7; Nu 4:15

18:5
n Nu 16:46

5"You are to be responsible for the care of the sanctuary and the altar, n so that wrath will not fall on the Israelites again. 6I myself have selected your fellow Levites from among the Israelites as a gift to you, o dedicated to the LORD to do the work at the Tent of Meeting. 7But only you and your sons may serve as priests in connection with everything at the altar and inside the curtain. p I am giving you the service of the priesthood as a gift. q Anyone else who comes near the sanctuary must be put to death. r"

18:6
o Nu 3:9

18:7
p Heb 9:3,6
q ver 20; Ex 29:9
r Nu 3:10

Offerings for Priests and Levites

18:8
s Lev 6:16; 7:6,31-34,36
18:9
t Lev 2:1 u Lev 6:25
v Lev 5:15; 7:7

8Then the LORD said to Aaron, "I myself have put you in charge of the offerings presented to me; all the holy offerings the Israelites give me I give to you and your sons as your portion and regular share. s 9You are to have the part of the most holy offerings that is kept from the fire. From all the gifts they bring me as most holy offerings, whether grain t or sin u or guilt offerings, v that part belongs to you and your

---

How do we apply to the church age the reality of God's choice of only one man and his descendants to be priests for all of Israel? The New Testament definitely makes the case for "the priesthood of all believers" (1 Peter 2:5,9; Rev. 1:6). But it also indicates that not every believer is a leader (Eph. 4:11–13) and that those who are deserve respect and support (1 Tim. 5:17–20; Heb. 13:17). Is there "tension" in your congregation about the "priesthood" of all members alongside the functioning of designated leadership? If so, is that tension generally healthy and creative?

Numbers 18:1–7

Aaron & Sons, chosen by God as Israel's priests, shouldered a heavy responsibility. The people's cry in 17:12–13 was real: Trespasses against God's tabernacle would result in death. God's authorization of a priesthood was actually a provision of his grace, Israel's only

hope for deliverance from judgment. The priests were to be assisted by the rest of the tribe of Levi; but these assistants weren't to move beyond their serving role. If they did, they would die—as would the responsible priests.

The service of the priesthood was a gift from God (v. 7)—to priests and people. Today we can be thankful for the fulfillment of this gift in several ways: (1) As our great high priest, Jesus has provided the way for us to enter the Most Holy Place by his own blood (Heb. 9:11–12; 10:19–22). (2) The risen Christ has given every believer gifts for ministry (1 Cor. 12:4–7; 1 Peter 4:10). (3) Christ has given us church leaders to build us up and make us mature (Eph. 4:11–16; see also previous "Here and Now"). Take a moment to thank God for each of these gifts.

sons. [10]Eat it as something most holy; every male shall eat it. [w] You must regard it as holy.

[11] "This also is yours: whatever is set aside from the gifts of all the wave offerings [x] of the Israelites. I give this to you and your sons and daughters as your regular share. Everyone in your household who is ceremonially clean [y] may eat it.

[12] "I give you all the finest olive oil and all the finest new wine and grain they give the LORD as the firstfruits of their harvest. [z] [13]All the land's firstfruits that they bring to the LORD will be yours. [a] Everyone in your household who is ceremonially clean may eat it.

[14] "Everything in Israel that is devoted [a] to the LORD [b] is yours. [15]The first offspring of every womb, both man and animal, that is offered to the LORD is yours. [c] But you must redeem [d] every firstborn son and every firstborn male of unclean animals. [e] [16]When they are a month old, you must redeem them at the redemption price set at five shekels [b][f] of silver, according to the sanctuary shekel, [g] which weighs twenty gerahs.

[17] "But you must not redeem the firstborn of an ox, a sheep or a goat; they are holy. [h] Sprinkle their blood [i] on the altar and burn their fat as an offering made by fire, an aroma pleasing to the LORD. [18]Their meat is to be yours, just as the breast of the wave offering [j] and the right thigh are yours. [19]Whatever is set aside from the holy offerings the Israelites present to the LORD I give to you and your sons and daughters as your regular share. It is an everlasting covenant of salt [k] before the LORD for both you and your offspring."

[20]The LORD said to Aaron, "You will have no inheritance in their land, nor will you have any share among them; [l] I am your share and your inheritance [m] among the Israelites.

[21] "I give to the Levites all the tithes [n] in Israel as their inheritance [o] in return for the work they do while serving at the Tent of Meeting. [22]From now on the Israelites must not go near the Tent of Meeting, or they will bear the consequences of their sin and will die. [p] [23]It is the Levites who are to do the work at the Tent of Meeting and bear the responsibility for offenses against it. This is a lasting ordinance for the generations to come. They will receive no inheritance [q] among the Israelites. [24]Instead, I give to the Levites as their inheritance the tithes that the Israelites present as an offering to the LORD. That is why I said concerning them: 'They will have no inheritance among the Israelites.' "

[25]The LORD said to Moses, [26] "Speak to the Levites and say to them: 'When you receive from the Israelites the tithe I give you [r] as your inheritance, you must present a tenth of that tithe as the LORD's offering. [s] [27]Your offering will be reckoned to you as grain from the threshing floor or juice from the winepress. [28]In this way you also will present an offering to the LORD from all the tithes [t] you receive from the Israelites. From these tithes you must give the LORD's portion to Aaron the priest. [29]You must present as the LORD's portion the best and holiest part of everything given to you.'

[30] "Say to the Levites: 'When you present the best part, it will be reckoned to you

---

[a] 14 The Hebrew term refers to the irrevocable giving over of things or persons to the LORD.
[b] 16 That is, about 2 ounces (about 55 grams)

18:10
[w] Lev 6:16
18:11
[x] Ex 29:26
[y] Lev 22:1-16

18:12
[z] Ex 23:19; Ne 10:35
18:13
[a] Ex 22:29; 23:19
18:14
[b] Lev 27:28
18:15
[c] Ex 13:2 [d] Nu 3:46
[e] Ex 13:13

18:16
[f] Lev 27:6
[g] Ex 30:13

18:17
[h] Dt 15:19 [i] Lev 3:2

18:18
[j] Lev 7:30

18:19
[k] Lev 2:13; 2Ch 13:5

18:20
[l] Dt 12:12
[m] Dt 10:9; 14:27; 18:1-2; Jos 13:33; Eze 44:28
18:21
[n] Dt 14:22; Mal 3:8
[o] Lev 27:30-33; Heb 7:5
18:22
[p] Lev 22:9; Nu 1:51

18:23
[q] ver 20

18:26
[r] ver 21 [s] Ne 10:38

18:28
[t] Mal 3:8

Numbers 18:8–32

This passage details the portions of sacred gifts for the priests and Levites. In lieu of a separate tribal territory in the promised land, the priests and other Levites would receive agricultural tithes so they could devote themselves to God's service rather than supporting themselves through farming. Placement of this legislation here accomplished two things: (1) God reaffirmed his choice of the Aaronic priests and their Levite assistants. (2) He rewarded them for their potentially hazardous work at the sanctuary.

It's easy to see how the tithe principle can be applied for maintaining a stable source of support for God's work (1 Tim. 5:17–18). And Christians are encouraged to "excel in the grace of giving" (2 Cor. 8:7). Some individuals who feel especially blessed voluntarily add a second tithe, which they also give their churches. In addition to giving to their church, some set aside a portion of their incomes for helping disadvantaged people, as the Israelites were to do every third year (Deut. 14:28–29; 26:12). What is your system for giving to God's work? More importantly, what's your attitude as you give (2 Cor. 9:6–7)?

18:30
u ver 27
18:32
v Lev 22:15
w Lev 19:8

as the product of the threshing floor or the winepress. [u] 31 You and your households may eat the rest of it anywhere, for it is your wages for your work at the Tent of Meeting. 32 By presenting the best part [v] of it you will not be guilty in this matter; then you will not defile the holy offerings [w] of the Israelites, and you will not die.' "

The Water of Cleansing

19:2
x Ge 15:9;
Heb 9:13
y Lev 22:19-25
z Dt 21:3; 1Sa 6:7
19:3
a Nu 3:4
b Lev 4:12,21;
Heb 13:11
19:4
c Lev 4:17
19:5
d Ex 29:14
19:6
e ver 18; Ps 51:7
f Lev 14:4
19:7
g Lev 11:25; 16:26,
28; 22:6
19:9
h Heb 9:13 i ver 13;
Nu 8:7

19 The Lord said to Moses and Aaron: 2 "This is a requirement of the law that the Lord has commanded: Tell the Israelites to bring you a red heifer [x] without defect or blemish [y] and that has never been under a yoke. [z] 3 Give it to Eleazar [a] the priest; it is to be taken outside the camp [b] and slaughtered in his presence. 4 Then Eleazar the priest is to take some of its blood on his finger and sprinkle [c] it seven times toward the front of the Tent of Meeting. 5 While he watches, the heifer is to be burned—its hide, flesh, blood and offal. [d] 6 The priest is to take some cedar wood, hyssop [e] and scarlet wool [f] and throw them onto the burning heifer. 7 After that, the priest must wash his clothes and bathe himself with water. [g] He may then come into the camp, but he will be ceremonially unclean till evening. 8 The man who burns it must also wash his clothes and bathe with water, and he too will be unclean till evening.

9 "A man who is clean shall gather up the ashes of the heifer [h] and put them in a ceremonially clean place outside the camp. They shall be kept by the Israelite community for use in the water of cleansing; [i] it is for purification from sin. 10 The man who gathers up the ashes of the heifer must also wash his clothes, and he too will be unclean till evening. This will be a lasting ordinance both for the Israelites and for the aliens living among them.

19:11
j Lev 21:1; Nu 5:2
k Lev 31:19
19:12
l ver 19; Nu 31:19
19:13
m Lev 20:3
n Lev 15:31;
2Ch 36:14
o Lev 7:20; 22:3
p Hag 2:13

11 "Whoever touches the dead body [j] of anyone will be unclean for seven days. [k] 12 He must purify himself with the water on the third day and on the seventh day; [l] then he will be clean. But if he does not purify himself on the third and seventh days, he will not be clean. 13 Whoever touches the dead body [m] of anyone and fails to purify himself defiles the Lord's tabernacle. [n] That person must be cut off from Israel. [o] Because the water of cleansing has not been sprinkled on him, he is unclean; [p] his uncleanness remains on him.

14 "This is the law that applies when a person dies in a tent: Anyone who enters the tent and anyone who is in it will be unclean for seven days, 15 and every open container without a lid fastened on it will be unclean.

19:16
q Nu 31:19
r Mt 23:27
19:17
s ver 9

16 "Anyone out in the open who touches someone who has been killed with a sword or someone who has died a natural death, [q] or anyone who touches a human bone or a grave, [r] will be unclean for seven days.

17 "For the unclean person, put some ashes [s] from the burned purification offering into a jar and pour fresh water over them. 18 Then a man who is ceremonially clean is to take some hyssop, [t] dip it in the water and sprinkle the tent and all the furnishings and the people who were there. He must also sprinkle anyone who has touched a human bone or a grave or someone who has been killed or someone who has died a natural death. 19 The man who is clean is to sprinkle the unclean

19:18
t ver 6

19:19
u Eze 36:25;
Heb 10:22

person on the third and seventh days, and on the seventh day he is to purify him. [u] The person being cleansed must wash his clothes and bathe with water, and that evening he will be clean. 20 But if a person who is unclean does not purify himself, he must be cut off from the community, because he has defiled the sanctuary of the

---

Numbers 19:1–22

The death of a red cow gave the Israelites ongoing assurance of freedom from corpse contamination. The cow provided a ready supply of ashes to be mixed with water and sprinkled on impure persons whenever *burial or other contact with the dead had occurred.* There was no need to bring an animal to the sanctuary and sacrifice it as a purification offering. The sacrifice had already taken place. Its benefit just needed to be applied.

Hebrews 9:13–14 compares Christ's sacrifice to the ceremony associated with the heifer's ashes. If this procedure could effect cleansing from physical, ritual impurity, which was associated with mortality and death, how much more does Christ's shed blood make abundant, *ongoing* provision for cleansing us—morally, spiritually, and ultimately from physical death itself (cf. 1 Cor. 15:51–54)? The purifying effect of his sacrifice is continuously available today, and it's no less potent than it was two millennia ago!

LORD. The water of cleansing has not been sprinkled on him, and he is unclean. 21This is a lasting ordinance for them.

"The man who sprinkles the water of cleansing must also wash his clothes, and anyone who touches the water of cleansing will be unclean till evening. 22Anything that an unclean v person touches becomes unclean, and anyone who touches it becomes unclean till evening."

Water From the Rock

20 In the first month the whole Israelite community arrived at the Desert of Zin, w and they stayed at Kadesh. x There Miriam y died and was buried.

2Now there was no water for the community, z and the people gathered in opposition a to Moses and Aaron. 3They quarreled b with Moses and said, "If only we had died when our brothers fell dead before the LORD! c 4Why did you bring the LORD's community into this desert, that we and our livestock should die here? d 5Why did you bring us up out of Egypt to this terrible place? It has no grain or figs, grapevines or pomegranates. e And there is no water to drink!"

6Moses and Aaron went from the assembly to the entrance to the Tent of Meeting and fell facedown, f and the glory of the LORD g appeared to them. 7The LORD said to Moses, 8"Take the staff, h and you and your brother Aaron gather the assembly together. Speak to that rock before their eyes and it will pour out its water. i You will bring water out of the rock for the community so they and their livestock can drink."

19:22
v Lev 5:2; Hag 2:13,14

20:1
w Nu 13:21
x Nu 33:36
y Ex 15:20
20:2
z Ex 17:1
a Nu 16:19
20:3
b Ex 17:2
c Nu 14:2; 16:31-35
20:4
d Ex 14:11; 17:3; Nu 14:3; 16:13
20:5
e Nu 16:14
20:6
f Nu 14:5
g Nu 16:19
20:8
h Ex 4:17,20
i Ex 17:6; Isa 43:20

Numbers 20:1–13

 By failing to follow directions, Moses acted as though the miracle were his doing. "Must we bring you water out of this rock?" (v. 10, emphasis added) he cried in unrestrained exasperation. God supplied water for the people's benefit, but by punishing Moses and Aaron corrected their dangerous misimpression about who was in charge.

Moses and Aaron were understandably upset by the people's words and attitude, and their assessment of them as "rebels" (v. 10) was accurate. But in their reaction the brothers tragically became rebellious too (cf. v. 24). The Israelites had cast contempt on God's holiness, but only Moses and Aaron suffered the penalty. This may seem unfair, but as those closest to God they bore the highest responsibility before him (cf. 18:1).

Snapshots

19:7–8

Water for Ethiopia

Yetisha has worked as a public health and sanitation specialist since 1984, the height of the infamous drought that killed tens of thousands throughout Ethiopia. Over the past 15 years, thousands of rural villagers have experienced improved health and food security as a result of his efforts.

"I remember when a pregnant woman here had to fetch water three hours away," recalls an elderly man. "It so happened that the lady gave birth to her child on her way back home . . . . Praise the Lord she survived." One elder in the community noted that since the 1984/1985 drought, the people could only wash their clothes once a year.

A few years ago, Yetisha proposed to the local government two new water projects that would benefit 68,000 rural people. At first local officials resisted. The regional government had already tried to establish water projects but had failed due to difficult landscape and prohibitive costs.

But Yetisha moved ahead, with the help of a Christian international aid organization. His substantial contributions to the health and well-being of Ethiopia's rural poor haven't been without sacrifice. Yet Yetisha harbors no resentment: "There is nothing better than serving the poor and seeing God glorified at the end."

> "There is nothing better than serving the poor and seeing God glorified at the end."

20:9
i Nu 17:10
20:10
k Ps 106:32,33
20:11
l Ex 17:6; Dt 8:15;
Ps 78:16; Isa 48:2;
1Co 10:4
20:12
m Nu 27:14
n ver 24; Dt 1:37;
3:27
20:13
o Ex 17:7 *d* Dt 33:8;
Ps 95:8; 106:32
20:14
q Jdg 11:16-17
r Dt 2:4 *s* Jos 2:11;
9:9
20:15
t Ge 46:6
u Ge 15:13;
Ex 12:40 *v* Ex 1:11;
Dt 26:6
20:16
w Ex 2:23; 3:7
x Ex 14:19
20:17
y Nu 21:22
20:19
z Ex 12:38
a Dt 2:6,28

9So Moses took the staff from the LORD's presence,*i* just as he commanded him. 10He and Aaron gathered the assembly together in front of the rock and Moses said to them, "Listen, you rebels, must we bring you water out of this rock?"*k* 11Then Moses raised his arm and struck the rock twice with his staff. Water*l* gushed out, and the community and their livestock drank.

12But the LORD said to Moses and Aaron, "Because you did not trust in me enough to honor me as holy*m* in the sight of the Israelites, you will not bring this community into the land I give them."*n*

13These were the waters of Meribah,ªᵒ where the Israelites quarreled*p* with the LORD and where he showed himself holy among them.

Edom Denies Israel Passage

14Moses sent messengers from Kadesh*q* to the king of Edom,*r* saying:

"This is what your brother Israel says: You know*s* about all the hardships that have come upon us. 15Our forefathers went down into Egypt,*t* and we lived there many years.*u* The Egyptians mistreated*v* us and our fathers, 16but when we cried out to the LORD, he heard our cry*w* and sent an angel*x* and brought us out of Egypt.

"Now we are here at Kadesh, a town on the edge of your territory. 17Please let us pass through your country. We will not go through any field or vineyard, or drink water from any well. We will travel along the king's highway and not turn to the right or to the left until we have passed through your territory.*y*"

18But Edom answered:

"You may not pass through here; if you try, we will march out and attack you with the sword."

19The Israelites replied:

"We will go along the main road, and if we or our livestock*z* drink any of your water, we will pay for it.*a* We only want to pass through on foot—nothing else."

ª 13 *Meribah* means *quarreling*.

📖 Without God's authorization we have no right to personally dish out to even the most wicked people a fraction of the punishment they deserve. He has said, "It is mine to avenge; I will repay" (Deut. 32:35; Rom. 12:19). Our job is to do what God says and let him be God. It can be excruciating to exercise such restraint. But we have a towering example in Christ (see 1 Peter 2:23).

No amount of human merit stored up through past obedience can atone for even one sin (see Luke 17:10). Responsibility for living and responding to God at a high level as an example to other people is one of the duties of being his servant.

Numbers 20:14–21

📖 After 38 years, the Israelites were back at Kadesh (cf. 13:26) for another shot at entering the promised land, this time from the east. But they needed to pass through Edom, which lay directly in their path. Moses diplomatically appealed to the sympathies of these relatives through Esau (cf. Gen. 25,36), pledging to respect their resources, but their king resoundingly refused to grant safe passage. This forced a long detour around Edom (Num. 21:4).

📖 The community was gearing up for movement after nearly 40 years of stagnation, funerals, and seemingly endless waiting. Poised on the Edomite border, the new generation of travelers must have experienced heart-thumping exhilaration. They were so close—but, as it turned out, "yet so far." When have you experienced this kind of frustration in your Christian life? How did you handle the situation? Did you sense that God was trying to teach or prepare you for something?

Numbers 20:22–29

📖 Aaron had shared in Moses' rebellion against God (v. 12), and his demise signaled Moses' approaching death as well (cf. 27:12–14; Deut. 34). After the people had seen Aaron for the last time, but before he breathed his last, his son Eleazar accompanied him and Moses up the mountain so Moses could transfer Aaron's high priestly garments to Eleazar. Presumably this avoided corpse contamination of the sacred vestments. Moses, not the new high priest (cf. Lev. 21:10–12), buried his brother.

📖 The deaths of Miriam and Aaron frame a dispute over water and the Edomite refusal to let the people pass through their territory. The gloom is only slightly relieved by the fact that Israel and its high priestly office would survive to see better days. What seasons of grief have punctuated your life? Were you able at the time to identify blessings that *did* continue? In retrospect, can you trace God's loving hand at work?

20Again they answered:

"You may not pass through."

Then Edom came out against them with a large and powerful army. 21Since Edom refused to let them go through their territory, Israel turned away from them.[b]

The Death of Aaron

22The whole Israelite community set out from Kadesh and came to Mount Hor.[c] 23At Mount Hor, near the border of Edom,[d] the LORD said to Moses and Aaron, 24"Aaron will be gathered to his people.[e] He will not enter the land I give the Israelites, because both of you rebelled against my command[f] at the waters of Meribah. 25Get Aaron and his son Eleazar and take them up Mount Hor.[g] 26Remove Aaron's garments and put them on his son Eleazar, for Aaron will be gathered to his people;[h] he will die there."

27Moses did as the LORD commanded: They went up Mount Hor in the sight of the whole community. 28Moses removed Aaron's garments and put them on his son Eleazar.[i] And Aaron died there[j] on top of the mountain. Then Moses and Eleazar came down from the mountain, 29and when the whole community learned that Aaron had died, the entire house of Israel mourned for him[k] thirty days.

Arad Destroyed

21 When the Canaanite king of Arad,[l] who lived in the Negev,[m] heard that Israel was coming along the road to Atharim, he attacked the Israelites and captured some of them. 2Then Israel made this vow to the LORD: "If you will deliver these people into our hands, we will totally destroy[a] their cities." 3The LORD listened to Israel's plea and gave the Canaanites over to them. They completely destroyed them and their towns; so the place was named Hormah.[b]

The Bronze Snake

4They traveled from Mount Hor[n] along the route to the Red Sea,[c] to go around Edom. But the people grew impatient on the way;[o] 5they spoke against God[p] and

Marginal references:
20:21 b Dt 2:8; Jdg 11:18
20:22 c Nu 33:37
20:23 d Nu 33:37
20:24 e Ge 25:8 f ver 10
20:25 g Nu 33:38
20:26 h ver 24
20:28 i Ex 29:29
j Nu 33:38; Dt 10:6; 32:50
20:29 k Dt 34:8
21:1 l Nu 33:40; Jos 12:14 m Jdg 1:9,16
21:4 n Nu 20:22 o Dt 2:8; Jdg 11:18
21:5 p Ps 78:19

a 2 The Hebrew term refers to the irrevocable giving over of things or persons to the LORD, often by totally destroying them; also in verse 3.   b 3 *Hormah* means *destruction.*   c 4 Hebrew *Yam Suph*; that is, Sea of Reeds

---

Numbers 21:1–3

The Israelites had backed down in the face of an armed threat from the Edomites (20:20–21). Why did they respond so differently now? Unlike the Edomites, the Canaanites weren't relatives. They inhabited part of the land promised to Israel, and they actually attacked the Israelites rather than merely threatening to do so.

After a series of tragedies in Numbers 20, chapter 21 shows what a transition from losing to winning looks like. The road would be bumpy. And it can be the same for us. If we are still in "basic training," we may find ourselves repeating the same testing points from various angles. We will finally "get it" when we learn to give up on our own strength and wisdom and to rely on God.

Numbers 21:4–9

Particularly in light of Israel's victory over Arad, Moses' determination not to engage Edom in battle, but to add extra travel instead, resulted in growing impatience and rebellion. When the people confessed their sin and called for help, God didn't just call off the

21:4–9

The Bronze Snake

People bitten by snakes were instructed to gaze up at a bronze snake erected on a pole in the center of the camp. Result? Instant antivenom. God still makes provision for healing sick, disabled, disturbed, and wounded people—a message we (and they) need to hear in a world rife with disease and suffering. A few statistics:

1.2 million poisonous snake bites per year; 50,000 deaths per year

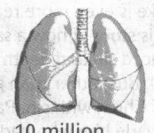

10 million tuberculosis cases; 2.9 million deaths per year

700 million tobacco smokers; 3 million tobacco-related deaths each year

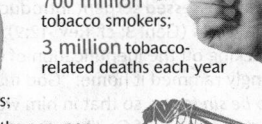

450 million new malaria cases per year; by some accounts, as many as 2.7 million people die each year.

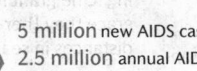

5 million new AIDS cases per year; 2.5 million annual AIDS deaths

Source: Barrett and Johnson (2001:34)

against Moses, and said, "Why have you brought us up out of Egypt to die in the desert? *q* There is no bread! There is no water! And we detest this miserable food!" *r*

6Then the LORD sent venomous snakes *s* among them; they bit the people and many Israelites died. *t* 7The people came to Moses *u* and said, "We sinned when we spoke against the LORD and against you. Pray that the LORD *v* will take the snakes away from us." So Moses prayed *w* for the people.

8The LORD said to Moses, "Make a snake and put it up on a pole; *x* anyone who is bitten can look at it and live." 9So Moses made a bronze snake *y* and put it up on a pole. Then when anyone was bitten by a snake and looked at the bronze snake, he lived. *z*

The Journey to Moab

10The Israelites moved on and camped at Oboth. *a* 11Then they set out from Oboth and camped in Iye Abarim, in the desert that faces Moab *b* toward the sunrise. 12From there they moved on and camped in the Zered Valley. *c* 13They set out from there and camped alongside the Arnon *d*, which is in the desert extending into Amorite territory. The Arnon is the border of Moab, between Moab and the Amorites. 14That is why the Book of the Wars of the LORD says:

> ". . . Waheb in Suphah *a* and the ravines,
>   the Arnon 15and *b* the slopes of the ravines
> that lead to the site of Ar *e*
>   and lie along the border of Moab."

16From there they continued on to Beer, *f* the well where the LORD said to Moses, "Gather the people together and I will give them water."

17Then Israel sang this song: *g*

> "Spring up, O well!
>   Sing about it,
> 18about the well that the princes dug,
>   that the nobles of the people sank—
>   the nobles with scepters and staffs."

Then they went from the desert to Mattanah, 19from Mattanah to Nahaliel, from Nahaliel to Bamoth, 20and from Bamoth to the valley in Moab where the top of Pisgah overlooks the wasteland.

Defeat of Sihon and Og

21Israel sent messengers to say to Sihon *h* king of the Amorites:

---

a 14 The meaning of the Hebrew for this phrase is uncertain.   *b 14,15* Or *"I have been given from Suphah and the ravines / of the Arnon 15to*

Marginal references

21:5
q Nu 14:2,3
r Nu 11:6
21:6
s Dt 8:15; Jer 8:17
t 1Co 10:9
21:7
u Ps 78:34;
Hos 5:15 *v* Ex 8:8;
Ac 8:24 *w* Nu 11:2
21:8
x Jn 3:14
21:9
y 2Ki 18:4
z Jn 3:14-15

21:10
a Nu 33:43
21:11
b Nu 33:44
21:12
c Dt 2:13,14
21:13
d Nu 22:36;
Jdg 11:13,18

21:15
e ver 28; Dt 2:9,18

21:16
f Jdg 9:21

21:17
g Ex 15:1

21:21
h Dt 1:4; 2:26-27;
Jdg 11:19-21

---

snakes. He commanded Moses to use a visual anti-venom. The bronze snake was symbolic, not magical. To confront the serpent sculpture was to face one's own sin. It was the spiritual equivalent of looking in the mirror. That unspoken confession was all it took to live.

📖 We might find it disturbing that Jesus identified himself, in John 3:14–15, with Moses' snake, which symbolized sin and death. The snake is even more repulsive when we remember the Genesis story of how a satanically possessed serpent introduced sin and death into the world (Gen. 3; cf. Rev. 12:9). But rather than gently backing off the identification of Christ with sin, Paul jarringly rammed it home: "God made him who had no sin to *be sin* for us, so that in him we might become the righteousness of God" (2 Cor. 5:21, emphasis added).

Numbers 21:10–20

Another potential water crisis (cf. 20:2–13) turned into a refreshing example of divine-human cooperation when the Israelites dug a well at God's direction. The words "Spring up, O well!" (v. 17) celebrated their claiming of the divine promise. It was as though they were saying, "We know you are down there, water, so just get on up here as God said you would!" This is the second recorded occasion on which the Israelites sang for joy upon receiving divine assistance (see Ex. 14–15).

📖 Do you appreciate the clean water available in your community? In places where water is scarce or too polluted for consumption, celebrations like this emerge when a well is drilled and a clean water source becomes available. Recently, a Ghanian teenager was the first to pump out a spout of water, fetching it in a symbolic calabash. The village women and children burst into dancing. One grandmother voiced her gratitude: "By God's grace they [her grandchildren] won't have to walk long distances in search of water. I thank . . . God."

22 "Let us pass through your country. We will not turn aside into any field or vineyard, or drink water from any well. We will travel along the king's highway until we have passed through your territory. ^{i}"

23 But Sihon would not let Israel pass through his territory.^{j} He mustered his entire army and marched out into the desert against Israel. When he reached Jahaz,^{k} he fought with Israel. 24 Israel, however, put him to the sword^l and took over his land from the Arnon to the Jabbok, but only as far as the Ammonites,^{m} because their border was fortified. 25 Israel captured all the cities of the Amorites^n and occupied them, including Heshbon and all its surrounding settlements. 26 Heshbon was the city of Sihon^o king of the Amorites, who had fought against the former king of Moab and had taken from him all his land as far as the Arnon.

27 That is why the poets say:

"Come to Heshbon and let it be rebuilt;
　　let Sihon's city be restored.

28 "Fire went out from Heshbon,
　　a blaze from the city of Sihon.^{p}
　It consumed Ar^q of Moab,
　　the citizens of Arnon's heights.^{r}
29 Woe to you, O Moab!^{s}
　　You are destroyed, O people of Chemosh!^{t}
　He has given up his sons as fugitives^u
　　and his daughters as captives^v
　　to Sihon king of the Amorites.

30 "But we have overthrown them;
　　Heshbon is destroyed all the way to Dibon.^{w}
　We have demolished them as far as Nophah,
　　which extends to Medeba."

31 So Israel settled in the land of the Amorites.

32 After Moses had sent spies to Jazer,^{x} the Israelites captured its surrounding settlements and drove out the Amorites who were there. 33 Then they turned and went up along the road toward Bashan^{y,z} and Og king of Bashan and his whole army marched out to meet them in battle at Edrei.^{a}

34 The LORD said to Moses, "Do not be afraid of him, for I have handed him over to you, with his whole army and his land. Do to him what you did to Sihon king of the Amorites, who reigned in Heshbon.^{b}"

35 So they struck him down, together with his sons and his whole army, leaving them no survivors. And they took possession of his land.

Balak Summons Balaam

22 Then the Israelites traveled to the plains of Moab and camped along the Jordan across from Jericho.$^{a c}$

2 Now Balak son of Zippor^d saw all that Israel had done to the Amorites, 3 and

^{a} 1 Hebrew *Jordan of Jericho*; possibly an ancient name for the Jordan River

Cross references
21:22 ^{i} Nu 20:17
21:23 ^{j} Nu 20:21; ^{k} Dt 2:32; Jdg 11:20
21:24 ^{l} Dt 2:33; Ps 135:10-11; Am 2:9 ^{m} Dt 2:37
21:25 ^{n} Nu 13:29; Jdg 10:11; Am 2:10
21:26 ^{o} Dt 29:7; Ps 135:11
21:28 ^{p} Jer 48:45 ^{q} ver 15 ^{r} Nu 22:41; Isa 15:2
21:29 ^{s} Isa 25:10; Jer 48:46 ^{t} Jdg 11:24; 1Ki 11:7,33; 2Ki 23:13; Jer 48:7, 46 ^{u} Isa 15:5 ^{v} Isa 16:2
21:30 ^{w} Nu 32:3; Isa 15:2; Jer 48:18,22
21:32 ^{x} Nu 32:1,3,35; Jer 48:32
21:33 ^{y} Dt 3:3 ^{z} Dt 3:4 ^{a} Dt 1:4; 3:1,10; Jos 13:12,31
21:34 ^{b} Dt 3:2
22:1 ^{c} Nu 33:48
22:2 ^{d} Jdg 11:25

Numbers 21:21–35

God gave Israel victory over two nations east of the Jordan River: the kingdoms of Sihon of the Amorites and Og further to the north. According to other passages, Og's people were also Amorites (Deut. 4:47; Josh. 2:10). Since the Israelites weren't related to the Amorites (see "There and Then" for 21:1–3), there were no restrictions against crushing them and seizing their territory. This wasn't part of Canaan, but it was the first land the Israelites occupied and was to become a permanent part of their holdings.

The Israelites at long last were on a roll. Not coincidentally, it was soon after their triumph at the well (vv. 16–18) that they won the lands of Sihon and Og. When they could trust God to provide their daily needs, they were ready to trust him in battle. When they were willing to dig for his gift in a desert land, they were on the way toward receiving their own promised land. The same is true of us. Small challenges prepare us for bigger ones. Our trust needs constant renewal. Think about your "journey" so far. How has this been true?

22:3
e Ex 15:15

22:5
f Dt 23:4;
Jos 13:22; 24:9;
Ne 13:2; Mic 6:5;
2Pe 2:15
22:6
g ver 12,17;
Nu 23:7,11,13

22:7
h Nu 23:23; 24:1

22:8
i ver 19
22:9
j Ge 20:3 k ver 20

22:12
l Ge 12:2; 22:17;
Nu 23:20

22:17
m ver 37; Nu 24:11
n ver 6

22:18
o ver 38; Nu 23:12,
26; 24:13;
1Ki 22:14;
2Ch 18:13; Jer 42:4
22:19
p ver 8
22:20
q Ge 20:3
r ver 35,38;
Nu 23:5,12,16,26;
24:13; 2Ch 18:13

Moab was terrified because there were so many people. Indeed, Moab was filled with dread e because of the Israelites.

4 The Moabites said to the elders of Midian, "This horde is going to lick up everything around us, as an ox licks up the grass of the field."

So Balak son of Zippor, who was king of Moab at that time, 5 sent messengers to summon Balaam son of Beor, f who was at Pethor, near the River, a in his native land. Balak said:

"A people has come out of Egypt; they cover the face of the land and have settled next to me. 6 Now come and put a curse g on these people, because they are too powerful for me. Perhaps then I will be able to defeat them and drive them out of the country. For I know that those you bless are blessed, and those you curse are cursed."

7 The elders of Moab and Midian left, taking with them the fee for divination. h When they came to Balaam, they told him what Balak had said.

8 "Spend the night here," Balaam said to them, "and I will bring you back the answer the LORD gives me. i" So the Moabite princes stayed with him.

9 God came to Balaam j and asked, k "Who are these men with you?"

10 Balaam said to God, "Balak son of Zippor, king of Moab, sent me this message: 11 'A people that has come out of Egypt covers the face of the land. Now come and put a curse on them for me. Perhaps then I will be able to fight them and drive them away.' "

12 But God said to Balaam, "Do not go with them. You must not put a curse on those people, because they are blessed. l"

13 The next morning Balaam got up and said to Balak's princes, "Go back to your own country, for the LORD has refused to let me go with you."

14 So the Moabite princes returned to Balak and said, "Balaam refused to come with us."

15 Then Balak sent other princes, more numerous and more distinguished than the first. 16 They came to Balaam and said:

"This is what Balak son of Zippor says: Do not let anything keep you from coming to me, 17 because I will reward you handsomely m and do whatever you say. Come and put a curse n on these people for me."

18 But Balaam answered them, "Even if Balak gave me his palace filled with silver and gold, I could not do anything great or small to go beyond the command of the LORD my God. o 19 Now stay here tonight as the others did, and I will find out what else the LORD will tell me. p"

20 That night God came to Balaam q and said, "Since these men have come to summon you, go with them, but do only what I tell you." r

Balaam's Donkey

21 Balaam got up in the morning, saddled his donkey and went with the princes

a 5 That is, the Euphrates

Numbers 22:1–20

Not accepting Balaam's divinely directed "no" for an answer, desperate Balak offered him a blank check. The first part of Balaam's answer (v. 18) would have made him a Biblical model of loyalty to God—were it not for the rest of the story. Inviting the messengers to stay so he could see what else God might have to say strikes us as odd. Why would Balaam think God might change his mind? Why would he *hope* this might happen? Balak had upped the ante to a point Balaam couldn't resist.

Since God gave Balaam permission (v. 22), why was he angry with him for going to Moab? Why would

God hold Balaam to his earlier "no" answer (v. 12)? Do such tests reveal whether we will show restraint based on what we know to be right? In Balaam's case there was another factor: He was setting out to enrich himself at the expense of God's people. Do you at times find yourself tempted to go beyond limits you know to be right or to enrich yourself at another's expense?

Numbers 22:21–41

Balaam valued his own insight and wisdom, but his life was saved by the lowly beast of burden he mistreated for irritating him. She was his greatest asset. When God uncovered Balaam's eyes and he saw what the donkey had done, he reacted similarly by prostrating

of Moab. 22But God was very angry[s] when he went, and the angel of the LORD[t] stood in the road to oppose him. Balaam was riding on his donkey, and his two servants were with him. 23When the donkey saw the angel of the LORD standing in the road with a drawn sword[u] in his hand, she turned off the road into a field. Balaam beat her[v] to get her back on the road.

24Then the angel of the LORD stood in a narrow path between two vineyards, with walls on both sides. 25When the donkey saw the angel of the LORD, she pressed close to the wall, crushing Balaam's foot against it. So he beat her again.

26Then the angel of the LORD moved on ahead and stood in a narrow place where there was no room to turn, either to the right or to the left. 27When the donkey saw the angel of the LORD, she lay down under Balaam, and he was angry[w] and beat her with his staff. 28Then the LORD opened the donkey's mouth,[x] and she said to Balaam, "What have I done to you to make you beat me these three times?[y]"

29Balaam answered the donkey, "You have made a fool of me! If I had a sword in my hand, I would kill you right now.[z]"

30The donkey said to Balaam, "Am I not your own donkey, which you have always ridden, to this day? Have I been in the habit of doing this to you?"

"No," he said.

31Then the LORD opened Balaam's eyes,[a] and he saw the angel of the LORD standing in the road with his sword drawn. So he bowed low and fell facedown.

32The angel of the LORD asked him, "Why have you beaten your donkey these three times? I have come here to oppose you because your path is a reckless one before me.[a] 33The donkey saw me and turned away from me these three times. If she had not turned away, I would certainly have killed you by now,[b] but I would have spared her."

34Balaam said to the angel of the LORD, "I have sinned.[c] I did not realize you were standing in the road to oppose me. Now if you are displeased, I will go back."

35The angel of the LORD said to Balaam, "Go with the men, but speak only what I tell you." So Balaam went with the princes of Balak.

36When Balak heard that Balaam was coming, he went out to meet him at the Moabite town on the Arnon[d] border, at the edge of his territory. 37Balak said to Balaam, "Did I not send you an urgent summons? Why didn't you come to me? Am I really not able to reward you?"

38"Well, I have come to you now," Balaam replied. "But can I say just anything? I must speak only what God puts in my mouth."[e]

39Then Balaam went with Balak to Kiriath Huzoth. 40Balak sacrificed cattle and sheep,[f] and gave some to Balaam and the princes who were with him. 41The next morning Balak took Balaam up to Bamoth Baal,[g] and from there he saw part of the people.[h]

Balaam's First Oracle

23 Balaam said, "Build me seven altars here, and prepare seven bulls and seven rams[i] for me." 2Balak did as Balaam said, and the two of them offered a bull and a ram on each altar.[j]

3Then Balaam said to Balak, "Stay here beside your offering while I go aside. Perhaps the LORD will come to meet with me.[k] Whatever he reveals to me I will tell you." Then he went off to a barren height.

---

[a] 32 The meaning of the Hebrew for this clause is uncertain.

Side references

22:22 [s] Ex 4:14 [t] Ge 16:7; Ex 23:20; Jdg 13:3, 6,13

22:23 [u] Jos 5:13 [v] ver 25,27

22:27 [w] Nu 11:1; Jas 1:19
22:28 [x] 2Pe 2:16 [y] ver 32

22:29 [z] Dt 25:4; Pr 12:10; 27:23-27; Mt 15:19

22:31 [a] Ge 21:19

22:33 [b] ver 29
22:34 [c] Ge 39:9; Nu 14:40; 1Sa 15:24,30; 2Sa 12:13; 24:10; Job 33:27; Ps 51:4

22:36 [d] Nu 21:13

22:38 [e] Nu 23:5,16,26

22:40 [f] Nu 23:1,14,29; Eze 45:23
22:41 [g] Nu 21:28
22:42 [h] Nu 23:13

23:1 [i] Nu 22:40
23:2 [j] ver 14,30
23:3 [k] ver 15

---

himself before the awesome angel with the drawn sword blocking his way (cf. Gen. 3:24).

Balaam saw himself as superior to the donkey, but this day she could have felt superior to him. Whether we are male or female, young or old, rich or poor, educated or ignorant, asking who is superior to whom misses the point. God can use whomever or whatever he chooses, including stones if necessary (Luke 19:40; cf. Luke 3:8). He's superior, and none of us are excluded from service to him.

Here's a call for humility and for treating each other with respect (cf. Rom. 12:10; 1 Cor. 12:21–25).

Numbers 23:1–12
Balak had hired Balaam as a master sorcerer, a powerful practitioner of black magic (cf. Ex. 7:11–12,22), but Balaam wasn't even a sorcerer's apprentice. He was just a pagan diviner who was mastered by divinity to heap divine blessing on his enemy. Balaam was playing a dicey game between God's interest in Israel and Balak's

23:4
/ ver 16
23:5
m Dt 18:18; Jer 1:9
n Nu 22:20
23:6
o ver 17
23:7
p Nu 22:5 q ver 18;
Nu 24:3,21
r Nu 22:6; Dt 23:4
23:8
s Nu 22:12
23:9
t Ex 33:16; Dt 32:8;
33:28
23:10
u Ge 13:16
v Ps 116:15;
Isa 57:1 w Ps 37:37
23:11
x Nu 24:10;
Ne 13:2
23:12
y Nu 22:20,38
23:14
z ver 2
23:16
a Nu 22:38

⁴God met with him,/ and Balaam said, "I have prepared seven altars, and on each altar I have offered a bull and a ram."

⁵The LORD put a message in Balaam's mouth*m* and said, "Go back to Balak and give him this message."*n*

⁶So he went back to him and found him standing beside his offering, with all the princes of Moab.*o* ⁷Then Balaam*p* uttered his oracle:*q*

"Balak brought me from Aram,
    the king of Moab from the eastern mountains.
'Come,' he said, 'curse Jacob for me;
    come, denounce Israel.'*r*
⁸How can I curse
    those whom God has not cursed?*s*
How can I denounce
    those whom the LORD has not denounced?
⁹From the rocky peaks I see them,
    from the heights I view them.
I see a people who live apart
    and do not consider themselves one of the nations.*t*
¹⁰Who can count the dust of Jacob*u*
    or number the fourth part of Israel?
Let me die the death of the righteous,*v*
    and may my end be like theirs!*w*"

¹¹Balak said to Balaam, "What have you done to me? I brought you to curse my enemies, but you have done nothing but bless them!"*x*

¹²He answered, "Must I not speak what the LORD puts in my mouth?"*y*

Balaam's Second Oracle

¹³Then Balak said to him, "Come with me to another place where you can see them; you will see only a part but not all of them. And from there, curse them for me." ¹⁴So he took him to the field of Zophim on the top of Pisgah, and there he built seven altars and offered a bull and a ram on each altar.*z*

¹⁵Balaam said to Balak, "Stay here beside your offering while I meet with him over there."

¹⁶The LORD met with Balaam and put a message in his mouth*a* and said, "Go back to Balak and give him this message."

¹⁷So he went to him and found him standing beside his offering, with the princes of Moab. Balak asked him, "What did the LORD say?"

¹⁸Then he uttered his oracle:

"Arise, Balak, and listen;
    hear me, son of Zippor.

---

antagonism toward the same nation. But Balaam had his escape clause ready: He could only speak God's words.

📖 God's resolve to bless Abraham's children applies to Christians: "If you belong to Christ, then you are Abraham's seed, and heirs according to the promise" (Gal. 3:29). That promise includes adoption as spiritual descendants of Abraham, the patriarch who set the pattern for our faith (cf. Heb. 11:10–12). With the divine King in our camp, we have ultimate "social security." This doesn't mean we will never suffer persecution. But God sorts out our final destinies according to his will. What comfort does this provide you in uncertain times?

Numbers 23:13–26
📖 Balak hoped that moving the curser (like a cursor!) to a different location would delete Balaam's bless-

ings. So he took Balaam to another spot, where a narrower field of vision would hopefully help him retain his focus. Curses and narrow outlooks often go together! Balaam affirmed that no divination would be effective against Israel. The point wasn't what Israel could do, but "what God [had] done!" (v. 23).

📖 God has always had a vested interest in his people who do his work in the world. As in ancient times, whoever touches his modern people "touches the apple [pupil] of his eye" (Zech. 2:8; cf. Deut. 32:10)—that is, touches him in a sensitive spot. Consequently, he rewards us with blessing and takes it personally when anyone mistreats us. Does this infuse you with confidence as you step out of your comfort zone to accomplish the work he's called you to do?

19 God is not a man, [b] that he should lie,
  nor a son of man, that he should change his mind. [c]
Does he speak and then not act?
  Does he promise and not fulfill?
20 I have received a command to bless;
  he has blessed, [d] and I cannot change it. [e]

21 "No misfortune is seen in Jacob, [f]
  no misery observed in Israel. [a][g]
The LORD their God is with them; [h]
  the shout of the King [i] is among them.
22 God brought them out of Egypt; [j]
  they have the strength of a wild ox. [k]
23 There is no sorcery against Jacob,
  no divination [l] against Israel.
It will now be said of Jacob
  and of Israel, 'See what God has done!'
24 The people rise like a lioness; [m]
  they rouse themselves like a lion [n]
that does not rest till he devours his prey
  and drinks the blood of his victims."

25 Then Balak said to Balaam, "Neither curse them at all nor bless them at all!"
26 Balaam answered, "Did I not tell you I must do whatever the LORD says?"

Balaam's Third Oracle

27 Then Balak said to Balaam, "Come, let me take you to another place. [o] Perhaps it will please God to let you curse them for me from there." 28 And Balak took Balaam to the top of Peor, [p] overlooking the wasteland.

29 Balaam said, "Build me seven altars here, and prepare seven bulls and seven rams for me." 30 Balak did as Balaam had said, and offered a bull and a ram on each altar.

24 Now when Balaam saw that it pleased the LORD to bless Israel, he did not resort to sorcery [q] as at other times, but turned his face toward the desert. [r] 2 When Balaam looked out and saw Israel encamped tribe by tribe, the Spirit of God came upon him [s] 3 and he uttered his oracle:

  "The oracle of Balaam son of Beor,
    the oracle of one whose eye sees clearly,
4 the oracle of one who hears the words of God, [t]
    who sees a vision from the Almighty, [b][u]
    who falls prostrate, and whose eyes are opened:

5 "How beautiful are your tents, O Jacob,
    your dwelling places, O Israel!

6 "Like valleys they spread out,
    like gardens beside a river,

a 21 Or He has not looked on Jacob's offenses / or on the wrongs found in Israel. b 4 Hebrew Shaddai; also in verse 16

Cross references

23:19
b Isa 55:9; Hos 11:9
c 1Sa 15:29; Mal 3:6; Tit 1:2; Jas 1:17

23:20
d Ge 22:17; Nu 22:12
e Isa 43:13

23:21
f Ps 32:2,5; Ro 4:7-8 g Isa 40:2; Jer 50:20
h Ex 29:45,46; Ps 145:18 i Dt 33:5; Ps 89:15-18

23:22
j Nu 24:8
k Dt 33:17; Job 39:9

23:23
l Nu 24:1; Jos 13:22

23:24
m Na 2:11
n Ge 49:9

23:27
o ver 13

23:28
p Ps 106:28

24:1
q Nu 23:23
r Nu 23:28

24:2
s Nu 11:25,26; 1Sa 10:10; 19:20; 2Ch 15:1

24:4
t Nu 22:20
u Ge 15:1

Numbers 23:27—24:14

At the top of Peor, Balaam gave up seeking omens/divinations. To short-circuit God's control, he skipped going off by himself and simply set his face in the direction of the desert, where Israel was encamped. Balaam, wanting to claim his reward, was bent on sorcery without interference by the Source. Since he didn't come to God, though, God came to him (cf. 11:26) with some short-circuiting of his own: He overpowered the prophet's ability to say anything contrary to the divine will.

Balaam's words were impressive, but he had "heart trouble." God had blessed him with rare privilege as a prophet of extraordinary insight and foresight, but we can and must be spiritually closer to God than Balaam was. As the apostle Paul put it so eloquently (and disturbingly), "If I have the gift of prophecy and can fathom all mysteries and all knowledge, and if I have a faith that can move mountains, but have not love, I am nothing" (1 Cor. 13:2). What will it take for you to be something for God—or better, someone he can trust?

like aloes[v] planted by the LORD,
　like cedars beside the waters.[w]
[7] Water will flow from their buckets;
　their seed will have abundant water.

"Their king will be greater than Agag;[x]
　their kingdom will be exalted.[y]

[8] "God brought them out of Egypt;
　they have the strength of a wild ox.
They devour hostile nations
　and break their bones in pieces;[z]
　with their arrows they pierce them.[a]
[9] Like a lion they crouch and lie down,
　like a lioness[b]—who dares to rouse them?

"May those who bless you be blessed
　and those who curse you be cursed!"[c]

[10] Then Balak's anger burned against Balaam. He struck his hands together[d] and said to him, "I summoned you to curse my enemies, but you have blessed them[e] these three times.[f] [11] Now leave at once and go home! I said I would reward you handsomely,[g] but the LORD has kept you from being rewarded." [12] Balaam answered Balak, "Did I not tell the messengers you sent me,[h] [13] 'Even if Balak gave me his palace filled with silver and gold, I could not do anything of my own accord, good or bad, to go beyond the command of the LORD[i]—and I must say only what the LORD says'?[j] [14] Now I am going back to my people, but come, let me warn you of what this people will do to your people in days to come."[k]

Balaam's Fourth Oracle

[15] Then he uttered his oracle:

"The oracle of Balaam son of Beor,
　the oracle of one whose eye sees clearly,
[16] the oracle of one who hears the words of God,
　who has knowledge from the Most High,
who sees a vision from the Almighty,
　who falls prostrate, and whose eyes are opened:

[17] "I see him, but not now;
　I behold him, but not near.[l]
A star will come out of Jacob;[m]
　a scepter will rise out of Israel.[n]
He will crush the foreheads of Moab,[o]
　the skulls[a] of[b] all the sons of Sheth.[c]
[18] Edom[p] will be conquered;

---

[a] 17 Samaritan Pentateuch (see also Jer. 48:45); the meaning of the word in the Masoretic Text is uncertain.　[b] 17 Or possibly Moab, / batter　[c] 17 Or all the noisy boasters

---

Numbers 24:15–19

Before leaving, Balaam delivered unsolicited divine counsel regarding what the Israelites would do to the Moabites in the distant future (v. 14; cf. Gen. 49:1; Deut. 31:29; and Jer. 48:47—on Moab's restoration). Verses 17–19 are startling. Balaam saw a future ruler, a "star" or "scepter" that would originate from Israel and strike the heads of the Moabites. Unlike Balaam's third oracle, this wasn't a conditional threat that the Moabites would be defeated if they disturbed Israel (see vv. 8–9). It was a prediction.

As revealed by Christ, the divine mind is characterized by humility and unselfish love for other people, not by conceit and selfish ambition (Phil. 2:1–8). At this point Balaam was less invested in his own words than his donkey had been (22:21–35). God's reluctant prophet was mouthing words God had given him. When have you experienced God speaking truth or doing good through the unwilling words or actions of an uncommitted agent? If you are yielded and willing, just imagine what he can do through you!

Seir, his enemy, will be conquered,
but Israel will grow strong.
19 A ruler will come out of Jacob q
and destroy the survivors of the city."

Balaam's Final Oracles

20 Then Balaam saw Amalek r and uttered his oracle:

"Amalek was first among the nations,
but he will come to ruin at last."

21 Then he saw the Kenites s and uttered his oracle:

"Your dwelling place is secure,
your nest is set in a rock;
22 yet you Kenites will be destroyed
when Asshur t takes you captive."

23 Then he uttered his oracle:

"Ah, who can live when God does this? a
24 Ships will come from the shores of Kittim; u
they will subdue Asshur and Eber, v
but they too will come to ruin. w"

25 Then Balaam x got up and returned home and Balak went his own way.

Moab Seduces Israel

25 While Israel was staying in Shittim, y the men began to indulge in sexual immorality z with Moabite women, a 2 who invited them to the sacrifices b to their gods. c The people ate and bowed down before these gods. 3 So Israel joined in worshiping the Baal of Peor. d And the LORD's anger burned against them.

4 The LORD said to Moses, "Take all the leaders of these people, kill them and expose them in broad daylight before the LORD, e so that the LORD's fierce anger f may turn away from Israel."

5 So Moses said to Israel's judges, "Each of you must put to death g those of your men who have joined in worshiping the Baal of Peor."

6 Then an Israelite man brought to his family a Midianite woman right before the eyes of Moses and the whole assembly of Israel while they were weeping at the entrance to the Tent of Meeting. 7 When Phinehas son of Eleazar, the son of Aaron, the priest, saw this, he left the assembly, took a spear in his hand 8 and followed the Israelite into the tent. He drove the spear through both of them—through the Isra-

a 23 Masoretic Text; with a different word division of the Hebrew A people will gather from the north.

Cross references

24:19 q Ge 49:10; Mic 5:2
24:20 r Ex 17:14
24:21 s Ge 15:19
24:22 t Ge 10:22
24:24 u Ge 10:4; v Ge 10:21 w ver 20
24:25 x Nu 31:8
25:1 y Jos 2:1; Mic 6:5 z 1Co 10:8; Rev 2:14 a Nu 31:16
25:2 b Ex 34:15
c Ex 20:5; Dt 32:38; 1Co 10:20
25:3 d Ps 106:28; Hos 9:10
25:4 e Dt 4:3 f Dt 13:17
25:5 g Ex 32:27

Numbers 24:20–25

Balaam concluded his verbal barrage with three brief oracles against other nations. Numbers 24 ends rather anticlimactically by reporting that Balaam went home and Balak went on his way. We might assume their threat to Israel was over. But such a conclusion would be premature.

The forces of evil can be determined and relentless—and they don't engage in a fair fight. They often attack right after we have laid down our armor and let down our guard, thinking a crisis has passed. Have you personally experienced such a surprise confrontation? How, with God's help, were you able to respond?

Numbers 25:1–18

At Shittim, across the Jordan River opposite Jericho, the Israelite men were lured by Moabite (and Midianite; see vv. 16–18) women into erotic fertility rites associated with Baal worship. The resulting death toll of 24,000 was the highest ever suffered by the Israelites for any rebellion during their passage from Egypt to Canaan. We learn later (Num. 31:8,16) that Balaam had advised this seductive plot. He evidently came up with the scheme and returned to counsel the Moabites and Midianites to use their women to incite Israel to apostasy.

By shrewdly exploiting his understanding of the relationship between God and his people, in a sense Balaam succeeded in cursing Israel after all—probably in order to acquire the fee he had been denied (24:10–11). The apostle Peter referred to this prophet for profit as a paradigm of later false teachers who were immoral and greedy: "They have left the straight way and wandered off to follow the way of Balaam son of Beor, who loved the wages of wickedness" (2 Peter 2:15; cf. Rev. 2:14).

25:8
h Nu 16:46-48;
Ps 106:30
25:9
i Nu 14:37;
1Co 10:8
j Nu 31:16
25:11
k Ps 106:30
l Ex 20:5; Dt 32:16,
21; Ps 78:58
25:12
m Isa 54:10;
Eze 34:25;
Mal 2:4,5
25:13
n Ex 29:9
o Nu 16:46
25:15
p ver 18 q Nu 31:8;
Jos 13:21
25:17
r Nu 31:1-3
25:18
s Nu 31:16

elite and into the woman's body. Then the plague against the Israelites was stopped;[h] 9but those who died in the plague[i] numbered 24,000.[j]

10The LORD said to Moses, 11"Phinehas son of Eleazar, the son of Aaron, the priest, has turned my anger away from the Israelites;[k] for he was as zealous as I am for my honor[l] among them, so that in my zeal I did not put an end to them. 12Therefore tell him I am making my covenant of peace[m] with him. 13He and his descendants will have a covenant of a lasting priesthood,[n] because he was zealous for the honor of his God and made atonement[o] for the Israelites."

14The name of the Israelite who was killed with the Midianite woman was Zimri son of Salu, the leader of a Simeonite family. 15And the name of the Midianite woman who was put to death was Cozbi[p] daughter of Zur, a tribal chief of a Midianite family.[q]

16The LORD said to Moses, 17"Treat the Midianites[r] as enemies and kill them, 18because they treated you as enemies when they deceived you in the affair of Peor[s] and their sister Cozbi, the daughter of a Midianite leader, the woman who was killed when the plague came as a result of Peor."

The Second Census

26:2
t Ex 30:11-16;
38:25-26; Nu 1:2
u Nu 1:3
26:3
v Nu 33:48
w Nu 22:1

26 After the plague the LORD said to Moses and Eleazar son of Aaron, the priest, 2"Take a census[t] of the whole Israelite community by families—all those twenty years old or more who are able to serve in the army[u] of Israel." 3So on the plains of Moab[v] by the Jordan across from Jericho,[a][w] Moses and Eleazar the priest spoke with them and said, 4"Take a census of the men twenty years old or more, as the LORD commanded Moses."

These were the Israelites who came out of Egypt:

26:5
x Ge 46:9 y 1Ch 5:3

5The descendants of Reuben, the firstborn son of Israel, were:
   through Hanoch,[x] the Hanochite clan;
   through Pallu,[y] the Palluite clan;
   6through Hezron, the Hezronite clan;
   through Carmi, the Carmite clan.

26:9
z Nu 16:1
a Nu 1:16
b Nu 16:2

7These were the clans of Reuben; those numbered were 43,730.

8The son of Pallu was Eliab, 9and the sons of Eliab[z] were Nemuel, Dathan and Abiram. The same Dathan and Abiram were the community[a] officials who rebelled against Moses and Aaron and were among Korah's followers when they rebelled against the LORD.[b] 10The earth opened its mouth and swallowed them along with Korah, whose followers died when the fire devoured the 250 men. And they served as a warning sign.[c] 11The line of Korah,[d] however, did not die out.[e]

26:10
c Nu 16:35,38
26:11
d Ex 6:24
e Nu 16:33;
Dt 24:16
26:12
f 1Ch 4:24
26:13
g Ge 46:10

12The descendants of Simeon by their clans were:
   through Nemuel, the Nemuelite clan;
   through Jamin,[f] the Jaminite clan;
   through Jakin, the Jakinite clan;
13through Zerah,[g] the Zerahite clan;
   through Shaul, the Shaulite clan.

a 3 Hebrew Jordan of Jericho; possibly an ancient name for the Jordan River; also in verse 63

Severe as our tests may be in this dot-com world—with its idolatrous allurements, like lust and greed, that invite us to follow "the way of Balaam"—we can hold on to the promise of 1 Corinthians 10:13: "God is faithful; he will not let you be tempted beyond what you can bear. But when you are tempted, he will also provide a way out so that you can stand up under it." Temptations are screened by the watchful eye of the One who doesn't want any to perish (2 Peter 3:9). God provides ways of escape—but we choose to take them.

Numbers 26:1–65

About to conquer Canaan, the Israelites were back to the situation at the time of their first census (ch. 1)—after having lost nearly four decades. The second census determined the strength of the military and the Levite forces, assessed the growth or decline of the various tribes, and established a basis for division of the land. But it had one other important purpose: to make sure the entire generation excluded from Canaan due to rebellion at Kadesh (ch. 14), with the exceptions of Joshua and Caleb, had died.

14These were the clans of Simeon; there were 22,200 men. [h]

15The descendants of Gad by their clans were:
through Zephon, [i] the Zephonite clan;
through Haggi, the Haggite clan;
through Shuni, the Shunite clan;
16through Ozni, the Oznite clan;
through Eri, the Erite clan;
17through Arodi, [a] the Arodite clan;
through Areli, the Arelite clan.
18These were the clans of Gad; [j] those numbered were 40,500.

19Er and Onan were sons of Judah, but they died [k] in Canaan.
20The descendants of Judah by their clans were:
through Shelah, [l] the Shelanite clan;
through Perez, the Perezite clan;
through Zerah, the Zerahite clan. [m]
21The descendants of Perez were:
through Hezron, [n] the Hezronite clan;
through Hamul, the Hamulite clan.
22These were the clans of Judah; [o] those numbered were 76,500.

23The descendants of Issachar by their clans were:
through Tola, [p] the Tolaite clan;
through Puah, the Puite [b] clan;
24through Jashub, [q] the Jashubite clan;
through Shimron, the Shimronite clan.
25These were the clans of Issachar; [r] those numbered were 64,300.

26The descendants of Zebulun by their clans were:
through Sered, the Seredite clan;
through Elon, the Elonite clan;
through Jahleel, the Jahleelite clan.
27These were the clans of Zebulun; [s] those numbered were 60,500.

28The descendants of Joseph by their clans through Manasseh and Ephraim were:

29The descendants of Manasseh:
through Makir, [t] the Makirite clan (Makir was the father of Gilead [u]);
through Gilead, the Gileadite clan.
30These were the descendants of Gilead:
through Iezer, [v] the Iezerite clan;
through Helek, the Helekite clan;
31through Asriel, the Asrielite clan;
through Shechem, the Shechemite clan;
32through Shemida, the Shemidaite clan;
through Hepher, the Hepherite clan.

[a] 17 Samaritan Pentateuch and Syriac (see also Gen. 46:16); Masoretic Text *Arod*   [b] 23 Samaritan Pentateuch, Septuagint, Vulgate and Syriac (see also 1 Chron. 7:1); Masoretic Text *through Puvah, the Punite*

26:14
h Nu 1:23

26:15
i Ge 46:16

26:18
j Nu 1:25; Jos 13:24-28
26:19
k Ge 38:2-10; 46:12
26:20
l 1Ch 2:3
m Jos 7:17

26:21
n Ru 4:19; 1Ch 2:9

26:22
o Nu 1:27

26:23
p Ge 46:13; 1Ch 7:1

26:24
q Ge 46:13

26:25
r Nu 1:29

26:27
s Nu 1:31

26:29
t Jos 17:1
u Jdg 11:1

26:30
v Jos 17:2; Jdg 6:11

📖 When the previous generation of Israelites had lamented that any attempted invasion of Canaan would result in their children being taken captive by the enemy (14:3), God had responded by saying he would give the promised land to those same defenseless children (14:31–33). If God "can't" use some people to carry out his purposes, he turns to others—even if they seem inadequate.

We are privileged to participate in God's plan, but our realization that its success doesn't depend on us provides rest and security. We are to bear each other's burdens (Gal. 6:2), but the real weight of responsibility never rests on our shoulders. Another carries it, and he's indispensable because he's not an ordinary human being: "For to us a child is born, to us a son is given, *and the government will be on his shoulders*" (Isa. 9:6, emphasis added). What a tremendous source of comfort as we seek to fill God's chosen role for us!

26:33
w Nu 27:1
x Nu 36:11
26:34
y Nu 1:35

33 (Zelophehad[w] son of Hepher had no sons; he had only daughters, whose names were Mahlah, Noah, Hoglah, Milcah and Tirzah.)[x]

34 These were the clans of Manasseh; those numbered were 52,700.[y]

35 These were the descendants of Ephraim by their clans:

through Shuthelah, the Shuthelahite clan;

through Beker, the Bekerite clan;

through Tahan, the Tahanite clan.

36 These were the descendants of Shuthelah:

26:37
z Nu 1:33

through Eran, the Eranite clan.

37 These were the clans of Ephraim;[z] those numbered were 32,500.

These were the descendants of Joseph by their clans.

26:38
a Ge 46:21; 1Ch 7:6

38 The descendants of Benjamin[a] by their clans were:

through Bela, the Belaite clan;

through Ashbel, the Ashbelite clan;

through Ahiram, the Ahiramite clan;

39 through Shupham,[a] the Shuphamite clan;

through Hupham, the Huphamite clan.

26:40
b Ge 46:21; 1Ch 8:3

40 The descendants of Bela through Ard[b] and Naaman were:

through Ard,[b] the Ardite clan;

through Naaman, the Naamite clan.

26:41
c Nu 1:37

41 These were the clans of Benjamin;[c] those numbered were 45,600.

26:42
d Ge 46:23

42 These were the descendants of Dan by their clans:

through Shuham,[d] the Shuhamite clan.

These were the clans of Dan: 43 All of them were Shuhamite clans; and those numbered were 64,400.

44 The descendants of Asher by their clans were:

through Imnah, the Imnite clan;

through Ishvi, the Ishvite clan;

through Beriah, the Beriite clan;

45 and through the descendants of Beriah:

through Heber, the Heberite clan;

through Malkiel, the Malkielite clan.

26:47
e Nu 1:41

46 (Asher had a daughter named Serah.)

47 These were the clans of Asher;[e] those numbered were 53,400.

26:48
f Ge 46:24; 1Ch 7:13

48 The descendants of Naphtali[f] by their clans were:

through Jahzeel, the Jahzeelite clan;

through Guni, the Gunite clan;

49 through Jezer, the Jezerite clan;

26:50
g Nu 1:43

through Shillem, the Shillemite clan.

50 These were the clans of Naphtali;[g] those numbered were 45,400.

26:51
h Ex 12:37; 38:26; Nu 1:46; 11:21

51 The total number of the men of Israel was 601,730.[h]

26:53
i Jos 11:23; 14:1; Eze 45:8
26:54
j Nu 33:54
26:55
k Nu 34:14

52 The LORD said to Moses, 53 "The land is to be allotted to them as an inheritance based on the number of names.[i] 54 To a larger group give a larger inheritance, and to a smaller group a smaller one; each is to receive its inheritance according to the number[j] of those listed. 55 Be sure that the land is distributed by lot.[k] What each group inherits will be according to the names for its ancestral tribe. 56 Each inheritance is to be distributed by lot among the larger and smaller groups."

26:57
l Ge 46:11; Ex 6:16-19

57 These were the Levites[l] who were counted by their clans:

a 39 A few manuscripts of the Masoretic Text, Samaritan Pentateuch, Vulgate and Syriac (see also Septuagint); most manuscripts of the Masoretic Text *Shephupham*   b 40 Samaritan Pentateuch and Vulgate (see also Septuagint); Masoretic Text does not have *through Ard*.

through Gershon, the Gershonite clan;
through Kohath, the Kohathite clan;
through Merari, the Merarite clan.
58 These also were Levite clans:
the Libnite clan,
the Hebronite clan,
the Mahlite clan,
the Mushite clan,
the Korahite clan.
(Kohath was the forefather of Amram;*m* 59 the name of Amram's wife was Jochebed,*n* a descendant of Levi, who was born to the Levites*a* in Egypt. To Amram she bore Aaron, Moses*o* and their sister Miriam. 60 Aaron was the father of Nadab and Abihu, Eleazar and Ithamar.*p* 61 But Nadab and Abihu*q* died when they made an offering before the LORD with unauthorized fire.)*r*

62 All the male Levites a month old or more numbered 23,000.*s* They were not counted*t* along with the other Israelites because they received no inheritance*u* among them.*v*

63 These are the ones counted by Moses and Eleazar the priest when they counted the Israelites on the plains of Moab*w* by the Jordan across from Jericho. 64 Not one of them was among those counted*x* by Moses and Aaron the priest when they counted the Israelites in the Desert of Sinai. 65 For the LORD had told those Israelites they would surely die in the desert,*y* and not one of them was left except Caleb son of Jephunneh and Joshua son of Nun.*z*

Zelophehad's Daughters

27 The daughters of Zelophehad*a* son of Hepher,*b* the son of Gilead, the son of Makir,*c* the son of Manasseh, belonged to the clans of Manasseh son of Joseph. The names of the daughters were Mahlah, Noah, Hoglah, Milcah and Tirzah. They approached 2 the entrance to the Tent of Meeting and stood before Moses, Eleazar the priest, the leaders and the whole assembly, and said, 3 "Our father died in the desert.*d* He was not among Korah's followers, who banded together against the LORD,*e* but he died for his own sin and left no sons.*f* 4 Why should our father's name disappear from his clan because he had no son? Give us property among our father's relatives."

5 So Moses brought their case*g* before the LORD*h* 6 and the LORD said to him, 7 "What Zelophehad's daughters are saying is right. You must certainly give them property as an inheritance*i* among their father's relatives and turn their father's inheritance over to them.*j*

8 "Say to the Israelites, 'If a man dies and leaves no son, turn his inheritance over to his daughter. 9 If he has no daughter, give his inheritance to his brothers. 10 If he has no brothers, give his inheritance to his father's brothers. 11 If his father had no brothers, give his inheritance to the nearest relative in his clan, that he may possess it. This is to be a legal requirement*k* for the Israelites, as the LORD commanded Moses.' "

a 59 Or *Jochebed, a daughter of Levi, who was born to Levi*

26:58
m Ex 6:20
26:59
n Ex 2:1 o Ex 6:20
26:60
p Nu 3:2
26:61
q Lev 10:1-2
r Nu 3:4
26:62
s Nu 3:39 t Nu 1:47
u Nu 18:23
v Nu 2:33; Dt 10:9

26:63
w ver 3
26:64
x Nu 14:29;
Dt 2:14-15;
Heb 3:17
26:65
y Nu 14:28;
1Co 10:5
z Jos 14:6-10

27:1
a Nu 26:33
b Jos 17:2,3
c Nu 36:1

27:3
d Nu 26:65
e Nu 16:2
f Nu 26:33

27:5
g Ex 18:19 h Nu 9:8

27:7
i Job 42:15
j Jos 17:4

27:11
k Nu 35:29

Numbers 27:1–11

The solution for Zelophehad's daughters would elevate their status to that of property owners, but this was only to bridge the gap in the male line for the sake of their father's honor. They didn't need to inherit property for their own survival and prosperity, since they were to be supported by the families into which they would marry (cf. ch. 36). But, no matter the reason, for women to inherit land broke all social customs of the day. This new legislation created a more equitable inheritance structure.

In some countries today women still can't own or inherit land or obtain a bank loan without a male cosignor. Business transactions can only be accomplished with the help of willing men, and girls can be forced into marriage by male relatives. Just as Zelophehad's daughters sought social justice, numerous Christians and Christian organizations work behind the scenes to influence legislation to help poor women and children worldwide improve their situations.

Joshua to Succeed Moses

27:12
l Nu 33:47;
Jer 22:20
m Dt 3:23-27;
32:48-52
27:13
n Nu 31:2
o Nu 20:28
27:14
p Nu 20:12
q Ex 17:7; Dt 32:51;
Ps 106:32
27:16
r Nu 16:22
27:17
s Dt 31:2;
1Ki 22:17;
Eze 34:5; Zec 10:2;
Mt 9:36; Mk 6:34
27:18
t Ge 41:38;
Nu 11:25-29
u ver 23; Dt 34:9
27:19
v Dt 3:28; 31:14,23
w Dt 31:7
27:20
x Jos 1:16,17
27:21
y Jos 9:14
z Ex 28:30

12Then the LORD said to Moses, "Go up this mountain in the Abarim range[l] and see the land[m] I have given the Israelites. 13After you have seen it, you too will be gathered to your people,[n] as your brother Aaron[o] was, 14for when the community rebelled at the waters in the Desert of Zin, both of you disobeyed my command to honor me as holy[p] before their eyes." (These were the waters of Meribah[q] Kadesh, in the Desert of Zin.)

15Moses said to the LORD, 16"May the LORD, the God of the spirits of all mankind,[r] appoint a man over this community 17to go out and come in before them, one who will lead them out and bring them in, so the LORD's people will not be like sheep without a shepherd."[s]

18So the LORD said to Moses, "Take Joshua son of Nun, a man in whom is the spirit,[t] and lay your hand on him.[u] 19Have him stand before Eleazar the priest and the entire assembly and commission him[v] in their presence.[w] 20Give him some of your authority so the whole Israelite community will obey him.[x] 21He is to stand before Eleazar the priest, who will obtain decisions for him by inquiring[y] of the Urim[z] before the LORD. At his command he and the entire community of the Israelites will go out, and at his command they will come in."

22Moses did as the LORD commanded him. He took Joshua and had him stand before Eleazar the priest and the whole assembly. 23Then he laid his hands on him and commissioned him, as the LORD instructed through Moses.

Daily Offerings

28:2
a Lev 3:11

28:3
b Ex 29:38

28:5
c Lev 2:1; Nu 15:4
28:6
d Ex 19:3
28:7
e Ex 29:41 f Lev 3:7

28:8
g Lev 1:9

28 The LORD said to Moses, 2"Give this command to the Israelites and say to them: 'See that you present to me at the appointed time the food[a] for my offerings made by fire, as an aroma pleasing to me.' 3Say to them: 'This is the offering made by fire that you are to present to the LORD: two lambs a year old without defect, as a regular burnt offering each day.[b] 4Prepare one lamb in the morning and the other at twilight, 5together with a grain offering of a tenth of an ephah[b] of fine flour mixed with a quarter of a hin[c] of oil[c] from pressed olives. 6This is the regular burnt offering instituted at Mount Sinai[d] as a pleasing aroma, an offering made to the LORD by fire. 7The accompanying drink offering[e] is to be a quarter of a hin of fermented drink with each lamb. Pour out the drink offering to the LORD at the sanctuary.[f] 8Prepare the second lamb at twilight, along with the same kind of grain offering and drink offering that you prepare in the morning. This is an offering made by fire, an aroma pleasing to the LORD.[g]

---

a 18 Or *Spirit*   b 5 That is, probably about 2 quarts (about 2 liters); also in verses 13, 21 and 29
c 5 That is, probably about 1 quart (about 1 liter); also in verses 7 and 14

Numbers 27:12–23

📖 By commissioning Joshua, Moses shared leadership while he was still alive to ensure a smooth transition after his death. Not until the end of Deuteronomy would Moses climb to the top of Pisgah, there identified as Mount Nebo (Deut. 34:1; cf. Deut. 3:27; 32:49), to view the promised land and die there. Most of Deuteronomy consists of Moses' final speeches to the Israelites before God called him up a mountain for the last time.

📖 This approach to leadership is a model for us today. While it was the smart thing to do, can you imagine the humility it took for Moses to co-lead this group for whom he had for so long (with Aaron's assistance) carried primary responsibility? How difficult it must have been for him to step back and let Joshua begin to exercise his leadership. Moses had mentored Joshua. How might this have helped or hindered their new working relationship? In what modern situations might this example be helpful?

Numbers 28:1–8

📖 In the ritual calendar of Leviticus 23, the emphasis was on overall observance of sacred times. The parallel calendar in Numbers 28–29 provides a comprehensive list of public sacrifices that were to be performed at regular and festival occasions. Numbers 28:1–8 repeats the instructions given earlier at Sinai (Ex. 29:38–42) for daily burnt offerings—the foundation of the sacrificial system.

📖 The earthly sanctuary and its sacrifices are gone, but there remains the need for everyone who enjoys a "new covenant" relationship with God to maintain it on a daily basis. The point isn't that God is dependent on our service or will reject us if we miss a day. But *we need* frequent and regular connection with him. By maintaining our line of communication with God, we refresh our assurance that we belong to him.

Sabbath Offerings

9 " 'On the Sabbath[h] day, make an offering of two lambs a year old without defect, together with its drink offering and a grain offering of two-tenths of an ephah[a][i] of fine flour mixed with oil. 10This is the burnt offering for every Sabbath, in addition to the regular burnt offering[j] and its drink offering.

Monthly Offerings

11 " 'On the first of every month,[k] present to the LORD a burnt offering of two young bulls, one ram and seven male lambs a year old, all without defect.[l] 12With each bull there is to be a grain offering[m] of three-tenths of an ephah[b][n] of fine flour mixed with oil; with the ram, a grain offering of two-tenths of an ephah of fine flour mixed with oil; 13and with each lamb, a grain offering[o] of a tenth of an ephah of fine flour mixed with oil. This is for a burnt offering, a pleasing aroma, an offering made to the LORD by fire. 14With each bull there is to be a drink offering[p] of half a hin[c] of wine; with the ram, a third of a hin[d]; and with each lamb, a quarter of a hin. This is the monthly burnt offering to be made at each new moon[q] during the year. 15Besides the regular burnt offering[r] with its drink offering, one male goat is to be presented to the LORD as a sin offering.[s]

The Passover

16 " 'On the fourteenth day of the first month the LORD's Passover[t] is to be held. 17On the fifteenth day of this month there is to be a festival; for seven days[u] eat bread made without yeast.[v] 18On the first day hold a sacred assembly and do no regular work.[w] 19Present to the LORD an offering made by fire, a burnt offering of two young bulls, one ram and seven male lambs a year old, all without defect. 20With each bull prepare a grain offering of three-tenths of an ephah[x] of fine flour mixed with oil; with the ram, two-tenths; 21and with each of the seven lambs, one-

28:9
h Ex 20:10
i Lev 23:13
28:10
j ver 3

28:11
k Nu 10:10
l Lev 1:3
28:12
m Nu 15:6
n Nu 15:9
28:13
o Lev 6:14
28:14
p Nu 15:7 q Ezr 3:5

28:15
r ver 3,23,24
s Lev 4:3

28:16
t Ex 12:6,18;
Lev 23:5; Dt 16:1
28:17
u Ex 12:19
v Ex 23:15; 34:18;
Lev 23:6; Dt 16:3-8
28:18
w Ex 12:16;
Lev 23:7
28:20
x Lev 14:10

---

a 9 That is, probably about 4 quarts (about 4.5 liters); also in verses 12, 20 and 28   b 12 That is, probably about 6 quarts (about 6.5 liters); also in verses 20 and 28   c 14 That is, probably about 2 quarts (about 2 liters)   d 14 That is, probably about 1 1/4 quarts (about 1.2 liters)

Numbers 28:9–10

It's not surprising that the Sabbath was to be honored with additional offerings, along with renewal of the "bread of the Presence" (Ex. 25:30; Lev. 24:8). In addition to its function as a celebration of creation (Ex. 20:11), the Sabbath took on further meaning for the Israelites as a reminder of their divine deliverance from Egypt (Deut. 5:15). God had accomplished the redemption from Egypt by his creative power—which he had displayed in the plagues on Egypt, salvation from Pharaoh's army at the Red Sea, and miraculous provision for his people in the wilderness.

For most Christians, the Sabbath doesn't commemorate the deliverance of our physical ancestors from Egypt. But its honored place in Israel's worship system doesn't nullify its foundational significance as the ongoing celebration of creation and redemption for all peoples. As you set aside a day of worship in the coming weeks, remember that you are doing so in honor of *your* "Maker, Defender, Redeemer, and Friend"!

Numbers 28:11–15

These beginning-of-the-month sacrifices were important, marked by celebration and the blowing of trumpets (see 10:10) to prepare the people to meet God. Later, David would expand the instruments to include a full orchestra (see, e.g., 1 Chron. 25). Again notice the extensiveness of sacrifice in the life of the peo-

ple and the magnitude of the priests' responsibilities.

Daily, monthly, and festival sacrifices at the Israelite sanctuary, with their smoke ascending heavenward, showed that a healthy relationship with God was available. Now our prayers ascend to where our sacrificial Lamb is pictured as if he had just been slaughtered (Rev. 5:6). It's as though he carries his cross with him to continually offer its healing to all who will accept it. Yes, you have been healed once for all time, but regular remembering opens the way for regular renewal.

Numbers 28:16–25

The priests were instructed about the proper preparations for the Passover, to be celebrated during the first month of the year. Passover also was associated with the Feast of Unleavened Bread (see Ex. 12:15; Lev. 23:4–8). The sacred number seven, and its multiple fourteen, appears frequently in this section.

The exodus from Pharaoh's Egypt foresaw a universal "exodus" from bondage to sin and Satan through Christ, our Passover Lamb (1 Cor. 5:7). Christ transformed a Passover celebration into the Lord's Supper (Matt. 26:26–29; 1 Cor. 11:23–26). Because this commemoration uses only bread and wine and requires no temple priesthood, it's perfectly suited for ongoing observance. We don't need to use our ingenuity to figure out how to adapt this Israelite festival. Christ himself adapted the observance he commanded us to keep.

28:22
y Ro 8:3 z Nu 15:28

tenth. 22Include one male goat as a sin offering[y] to make atonement for you.[z] 23Prepare these in addition to the regular morning burnt offering. 24In this way prepare the food for the offering made by fire every day for seven days as an aroma pleasing to the Lord; it is to be prepared in addition to the regular burnt offering and its drink offering. 25On the seventh day hold a sacred assembly and do no regular work.

Feast of Weeks

28:26
a Ex 34:22
b Ex 23:16 c ver 18;
Dt 16:10

26 " 'On the day of firstfruits,[a] when you present to the Lord an offering of new grain during the Feast of Weeks,[b] hold a sacred assembly and do no regular work.[c] 27Present a burnt offering of two young bulls, one ram and seven male lambs a year old as an aroma pleasing to the Lord. 28With each bull there is to be a grain offering of three-tenths of an ephah of fine flour mixed with oil; with the ram, two-

28:29
d ver 13

tenths; 29and with each of the seven lambs, one-tenth.[d] 30Include one male goat to make atonement for you. 31Prepare these together with their drink offerings, in

28:31
e ver 3,19

addition to the regular burnt offering[e] and its grain offering. Be sure the animals are without defect.

Feast of Trumpets

29:1
f Lev 23:24
29:2
g Nu 28:2
h Nu 28:3

29 " 'On the first day of the seventh month hold a sacred assembly and do no regular work.[f] It is a day for you to sound the trumpets. 2As an aroma pleasing to the Lord,[g] prepare a burnt offering of one young bull, one ram and seven male lambs a year old, all without defect.[h] 3With the bull prepare a grain offering of three-tenths of an ephah[a] of fine flour mixed with oil; with the ram, two-

29:5
i Nu 28:15
29:6
j Nu 28:11
k Nu 28:3

tenths[b]; 4and with each of the seven lambs, one-tenth.[c] 5Include one male goat[i] as a sin offering to make atonement for you. 6These are in addition to the monthly[j] and daily burnt offerings[k] with their grain offerings and drink offerings as specified. They are offerings made to the Lord by fire—a pleasing aroma.

Day of Atonement

29:7
l Ac 27:9
m Ex 31:15;
Lev 16:29; 23:26-32
29:9
n ver 3,18

7 " 'On the tenth day of this seventh month hold a sacred assembly. You must deny yourselves[d][l] and do no work.[m] 8Present as an aroma pleasing to the Lord a burnt offering of one young bull, one ram and seven male lambs a year old, all without defect. 9With the bull prepare a grain offering[n] of three-tenths of an ephah of fine flour mixed with oil; with the ram, two-tenths; 10and with each of the sev-

---

[a] 3 That is, probably about 6 quarts (about 6.5 liters); also in verses 9 and 14   [b] 3 That is, probably about 4 quarts (about 4.5 liters); also in verses 9 and 14   [c] 4 That is, probably about 2 quarts (about 2 liters); also in verses 10 and 15   [d] 7 Or *must fast*

Numbers 28:26–31

The Feast of Weeks was so named because it was celebrated seven weeks after the Feast of Unleavened Bread (see Lev. 23:9–22). Because of this 50-day span, the festival was known in the New Testament as Pentecost (see Acts 2:1), which means "fifty." It was also referred to as the Feast of Harvest (Ex. 23:16), since the Israelites were to bring a firstfruits offering of new grain from the wheat harvest.

The yearly festivals were temporary in the sense that they were tied to ancient Israel's historical and agricultural setting. Today it would be nearly impossible for us to fulfill the festival requirements. From the New Testament onward, the focus of Christian worship has shifted from an earthly place of God's presence—with its human priests, animal sacrifices, etc.—to the heavenly tabernacle where Christ ministers (Heb. 7–10). Do you regularly take advantage of your standing invitation to enter that sanctuary (see Heb. 10:19–22)?

Numbers 29:1–6

The Feast of Trumpets was to be celebrated at the beginning of the seventh month—a busy month for holy festivals, as all three events of chapter 29 occurred then. Today this feast commemorates the Jewish New Year (Rosh Hashanah). The sounding of trumpets across the land signaled the end of the agricultural year and the beginning of a new season.

When was the last time you took a spiritual "day off"—dedicated to your relationship with God? Such a day can be especially meaningful in times of transition or new "seasons" in our lives. Why not get out your calendar and block off a day for a personal retreat? The Israelites made extra animal and grain sacrifices on this sacred day. The greatest sacrifice for most of us today is an offering of our time.

Numbers 29:7–11

The Feast of Trumpets would lead into the Day

en lambs, one-tenth. *o* **11**Include one male goat as a sin offering, in addition to the sin offering for atonement and the regular burnt offering*p* with its grain offering, and their drink offerings.

Feast of Tabernacles

12 " 'On the fifteenth day of the seventh*q* month,*r* hold a sacred assembly and do no regular work. Celebrate a festival to the LORD for seven days. **13**Present an offering made by fire as an aroma pleasing to the LORD, a burnt offering of thirteen young bulls, two rams and fourteen male lambs a year old, all without defect. **14**With each of the thirteen bulls prepare a grain offering*s* of three-tenths of an ephah of fine flour mixed with oil; with each of the two rams, two-tenths; **15**and with each of the fourteen lambs, one-tenth. **16**Include one male goat as a sin offering, in addition to the regular burnt offering with its grain offering and drink offering.*t*

17 " 'On the second day*u* prepare twelve young bulls, two rams and fourteen male lambs a year old, all without defect.*v* **18**With the bulls, rams and lambs, prepare their grain offerings*w* and drink offerings*x* according to the number specified.*y* **19**Include one male goat as a sin offering,*z* in addition to the regular burnt offering with its grain offering, and their drink offerings.

20 " 'On the third day prepare eleven bulls, two rams and fourteen male lambs a year old, all without defect.*a* **21**With the bulls, rams and lambs, prepare their grain offerings and drink offerings according to the number specified.*b* **22**Include one male goat as a sin offering, in addition to the regular burnt offering with its grain offering and drink offering.

23 " 'On the fourth day prepare ten bulls, two rams and fourteen male lambs a year old, all without defect. **24**With the bulls, rams and lambs, prepare their grain offerings and drink offerings according to the number specified. **25**Include one male goat as a sin offering, in addition to the regular burnt offering with its grain offering and drink offering.

26 " 'On the fifth day prepare nine bulls, two rams and fourteen male lambs a year old, all without defect. **27**With the bulls, rams and lambs, prepare their grain offerings and drink offerings according to the number specified. **28**Include one male goat as a sin offering, in addition to the regular burnt offering with its grain offering and drink offering.

29 " 'On the sixth day prepare eight bulls, two rams and fourteen male lambs a year old, all without defect. **30**With the bulls, rams and lambs, prepare their grain offerings and drink offerings according to the number specified. **31**Include one male goat as a sin offering, in addition to the regular burnt offering with its grain offering and drink offering.

32 " 'On the seventh day prepare seven bulls, two rams and fourteen male lambs a year old, all without defect. **33**With the bulls, rams and lambs, prepare their grain

---

29:10
o Nu 28:13
29:11
p Lev 16:3; Nu 28:3

29:12
q 1Ki 8:2
r Lev 23:24

29:14
s ver 3

29:16
t ver 6
29:17
u Lev 23:36
v Nu 28:3
29:18
w ver 9 *x* Nu 28:7
y Nu 15:4-12
29:19
z Nu 28:15

29:20
a ver 17
29:21
b ver 18

---

of Atonement, a time of confession, repentance, and celebration (see "There and Then" for Lev. 16:1–34 and "Here and Now" for Ex. 26:1–37).

📖 Christians aren't obligated to keep the festivals (see "Here and Now" for 28:26–31). But any of us privileged to participate in a Jewish holiday (holy day) will likely experience rich blessing and an enhanced understanding of our common heritage. In so doing, we can grow spiritually in three important ways. We can (1) symbolically enact our *experience* of God's deliverance from evil; (2) gain appreciation for the *community* dimension of our redemption; and (3) participate meaningfully in the joy of expressing *thanksgiving* to God.

Numbers 29:12–40

📖 The last of Israel's three annual pilgrim festivals was called the Feast of Tabernacles because the Israelites were to remember the desert wanderings by living in temporary booths or tents ("tabernacles"). It was also known as the Feast of Ingathering (Ex. 23:16) since it celebrated the end of harvest. Each day of the festival had its own order for sacrifice. The large number of sacrifices acknowledged God's blessings at the thanksgiving season of harvest.

📖 Just as God appointed yearly times of thanksgiving for the Israelites, it's good for us to schedule regular intervals of gratitude that we celebrate even when we might not otherwise be in a joyful mood. Did the United States cancel Thanksgiving in November of 2001 because it came so soon after September 11? No. That Thanksgiving commemoration drew on and strengthened a richer dimension of faith. If less bright, it was deeper. Have you ever felt closer to the Lord on Thanksgiving, Christmas, or Easter because you were going through or emerging from a difficult time?

offerings and drink offerings according to the number specified. 34Include one male goat as a sin offering, in addition to the regular burnt offering with its grain offering and drink offering.

35 " 'On the eighth day hold an assembly[c] and do no regular work. 36Present an offering made by fire as an aroma pleasing to the LORD,[d] a burnt offering of one bull, one ram and seven male lambs a year old,[e] all without defect. 37With the bull, the ram and the lambs, prepare their grain offerings and drink offerings according to the number specified. 38Include one male goat as a sin offering, in addition to the regular burnt offering with its grain offering and drink offering.

39 " 'In addition to what you vow[f] and your freewill offerings, prepare these for the LORD at your appointed feasts:[g] your burnt offerings,[h] grain offerings, drink offerings and fellowship offerings.[a] ' "

40Moses told the Israelites all that the LORD commanded him.

Vows

30 Moses said to the heads of the tribes of Israel:[i] "This is what the LORD commands: 2When a man makes a vow to the LORD or takes an oath to obligate himself by a pledge, he must not break his word but must do everything he said.[j]

3 "When a young woman still living in her father's house makes a vow to the LORD or obligates herself by a pledge 4and her father hears about her vow or pledge but says nothing to her, then all her vows and every pledge by which she obligated herself will stand.[k] 5But if her father forbids her when he hears about it, none of her vows or the pledges by which she obligated herself will stand; the LORD will release her because her father has forbidden her.

6 "If she marries after she makes a vow[l] or after her lips utter a rash promise by which she obligates herself 7and her husband hears about it but says nothing to her, then her vows or the pledges by which she obligated herself will stand. 8But if her husband[m] forbids her when he hears about it, he nullifies the vow that obligates her or the rash promise by which she obligates herself, and the LORD will release her.

9 "Any vow or obligation taken by a widow or divorced woman will be binding on her.

10 "If a woman living with her husband makes a vow or obligates herself by a pledge under oath 11and her husband hears about it but says nothing to her and does not forbid her, then all her vows or the pledges by which she obligated herself will stand. 12But if her husband nullifies them when he hears about them, then none of the vows or pledges that came from her lips will stand.[n] Her husband has nullified them, and the LORD will release her. 13Her husband may confirm or nullify any vow she makes or any sworn pledge to deny herself. 14But if her husband says nothing to her about it from day to day, then he confirms all her vows or the pledges binding on her. He confirms them by saying nothing to her when he hears about them. 15If, however, he nullifies them some time after he hears about them, then he is responsible for her guilt."

16These are the regulations the LORD gave Moses concerning relationships be-

---

a 39 Traditionally *peace offerings*

Numbers 30:1–16

The main concern of Numbers 30 wasn't the binding nature of vows and oaths taken by men. It was the tension that could arise if dependent women bound themselves by obligations to God that conflicted with the will of their fathers or husbands—to whom they were legally subordinate if they were either still living with their parents or married. The vows and obligations of widowed or divorced women, who were independent, were binding like those of men. God waived his right to receive fulfillment of a dependent woman's vow in favor of preserving something highly valuable to him: harmony in the home.

Modern Western culture is much different from ancient Israelite society. But Numbers 30 contains important principles that go beyond cultural differences. (1) Promises to God are serious. (2) We are wise to consider the effects our promises may have on others and undertake binding obligations carefully. (3) Family harmony isn't to be disturbed unless necessary. (4) By waiving his own rights, God taught us that we don't always need to insist on ours. (5) If you are in a position of authority and override someone else's decision, you owe that person a good and consistent reason.

29:35
c Lev 23:36
29:36
d Lev 1:9 e ver 2

29:39
f Nu 6:2 g Lev 23:2
h Lev 1:3;
1Ch 23:31;
2Ch 31:3

30:1
i Nu 1:4

30:2
j Dt 23:21-23;
Jdg 11:35;
Job 22:27;
Ps 22:25; 50:14;
116:14; Pr 20:25;
Ecc 5:4,5; Jnh 1:16
30:4
k ver 7

30:6
l Lev 5:4

30:8
m Ge 3:16

30:12
n Eph 5:22;
Col 3:18

tween a man and his wife, and between a father and his young daughter still living in his house.

Vengeance on the Midianites

31 The LORD said to Moses, ²"Take vengeance on the Midianites⁰ for the Israelites. After that, you will be gathered to your people.ᵖ"

³So Moses said to the people, "Arm some of your men to go to war against the Midianites and to carry out the LORD's vengeance۹ on them. ⁴Send into battle a thousand men from each of the tribes of Israel." ⁵So twelve thousand men armed for battle, a thousand from each tribe, were supplied from the clans of Israel. ⁶Moses sent them into battle, a thousand from each tribe, along with Phinehas son of Eleazar, the priest, who took with him articles from the sanctuaryʳ and the trumpetsˢ for signaling.

⁷They fought against Midian, as the LORD commanded Moses, and killed every man.ᵗ ⁸Among their victims were Evi, Rekem, Zur, Hur and Rebaᵘ—the five kings of Midian.ᵛ They also killed Balaam son of Beor with the sword.ʷ ⁹The Israelites captured the Midianite women and children and took all the Midianite herds, flocks and goods as plunder. ¹⁰They burned all the towns where the Midianites had settled, as well as all their camps.ˣ ¹¹They took all the plunder and spoils, including the people and animals,ʸ ¹²and brought the captives, spoils and plunder to Moses and Eleazar the priest and the Israelite assemblyᶻ at their camp on the plains of Moab, by the Jordan across from Jericho.ᵃ

¹³Moses, Eleazar the priest and all the leaders of the community went to meet them outside the camp. ¹⁴Moses was angry with the officers of the armyᵃ—the commanders of thousands and commanders of hundreds—who returned from the battle.

¹⁵"Have you allowed all the women to live?" he asked them. ¹⁶"They were the ones who followed Balaam's adviceᵇ and were the means of turning the Israelites away from the LORD in what happened at Peor,ᶜ so that a plague struck the LORD's people. ¹⁷Now kill all the boys. And kill every woman who has slept with a man,ᵈ ¹⁸but save for yourselves every girl who has never slept with a man.

¹⁹"All of you who have killed anyone or touched anyone who was killedᵉ must stay outside the camp seven days. On the third and seventh days you must purify yourselvesᶠ and your captives. ²⁰Purify every garmentᵍ as well as everything made of leather, goat hair or wood."

²¹Then Eleazar the priest said to the soldiers who had gone into battle, "This is the

---

ᵃ 12 Hebrew *Jordan of Jericho*; possibly an ancient name for the Jordan River

31:2
⁰ Ge 25:2
ᵖ Nu 20:26; 27:13

31:3
۹ Jdg 11:36; 1Sa 24:12; 2Sa 4:8; 22:48; Ps 94:1; 149:7

31:6
ʳ Nu 14:44
ˢ Nu 10:9

31:7
ᵗ Dt 20:13; Jdg 21:11; 1Ki 11:15,16
31:8
ᵘ Jos 13:21
ᵛ Nu 25:15
ʷ Jos 13:22
31:10
ˣ Ge 25:16; 1Ch 6:54; Ps 69:25; Eze 25:4
31:11
ʸ Dt 20:14
31:12
ᶻ Nu 27:2
31:14
ᵃ ver 48; Ex 18:21; Dt 1:15

31:16
ᵇ 2Pe 2:15; Rev 2:14
ᶜ Nu 25:1-9
31:17
ᵈ Dt 7:2; 20:16-18; Jdg 21:11
31:19
ᵉ Nu 19:16
ᶠ Nu 19:12
31:20
ᵍ Nu 19:19

Numbers 31:1–24

Moses had a major piece of unfinished business to complete: carrying out "the LORD's vengeance" (v. 3) on the Midianites for their role in seducing Israel to engage in sexual immorality and Baal worship (see 25:16–18). The Israelites enjoyed total victory, killing every Midianite man (v. 7) without suffering a single casualty (v. 49). They also killed Balaam, the pagan diviner who had advised the plot at Peor (vv. 8,16; see "There and Then" for 25:1–18).

But when the triumphant Israelite warriors returned with women and children as captives, Moses became angry. It had been the women of Midian (and Moab) who had infiltrated the Israelite camp like a Trojan horse. Whether or not the army officers had received explicit orders regarding these women, Moses thought they should have known what to do. He ordered the execution of all the female captives except virgins and of all boys (who could potentially have threatened the inheritance rights of Israelite men).

Instead of destroying the Canaanites by fire as he had done at Sodom and Gomorrah (Gen. 19:24–28), God used the Israelites as his instrument (see also "There and Then" for Deut. 7:1–26). Some people refuse to accept the possibility that God could have commanded genocide under any circumstances. But it's pointless for us who accept the entire Bible as his Word to either defend or condemn God (cf. Job 40:1–5). In the final analysis we can only stand back and let him be God. Ultimately, our acceptance of his character is a matter of faith. He's given us plenty of evidence to trust him, but not enough insight to penetrate all the mysteries of his ways (cf. Deut. 29:29).

Nor does this passage give modern nations the nod to sanction ethnic cleansing, which is too often used by the powerful to annihilate an enemy or group of people for past wrongs or economic advantage. Christ asks his followers to pray for their enemies and turn the other cheek, leaving punishment to him.

31:22
h Jos 6:19; 22:8
31:23
i 1Co 3:13
j Nu 19:9,17

31:24
k Lev 11:25

requirement of the law that the LORD gave Moses: 22Gold, silver, bronze, iron,h tin, lead 23and anything else that can withstand fire must be put through the fire,i and then it will be clean. But it must also be purified with the water of cleansing.j And whatever cannot withstand fire must be put through that water. 24On the seventh day wash your clothes and you will be clean.k Then you may come into the camp."

Dividing the Spoils

31:26
l Nu 1:19
31:27
m Jos 22:8;
1Sa 30:24
31:28
n Nu 18:21

25The LORD said to Moses, 26"You and Eleazar the priest and the family heads of the community are to count all the peoplel and animals that were captured. 27Dividem the spoils between the soldiers who took part in the battle and the rest of the community. 28From the soldiers who fought in the battle, set apart as tribute for the LORDn one out of every five hundred, whether persons, cattle, donkeys, sheep or goats. 29Take this tribute from their half share and give it to Eleazar the priest as the LORD's part. 30From the Israelites' half, select one out of every fifty, whether persons,

31:30
o Nu 3:7; 18:3

cattle, donkeys, sheep, goats or other animals. Give them to the Levites, who are responsible for the care of the LORD's tabernacle.o" 31So Moses and Eleazar the priest did as the LORD commanded Moses.

32The plunder remaining from the spoils that the soldiers took was 675,000 sheep, 3372,000 cattle, 3461,000 donkeys 35and 32,000 women who had never slept with a man.

36The half share of those who fought in the battle was:

31:37
p ver 38-41

337,500 sheep, 37of which the tribute for the LORDp was 675;
38 36,000 cattle, of which the tribute for the LORD was 72;
39 30,500 donkeys, of which the tribute for the LORD was 61;
40 16,000 people, of which the tribute for the LORD was 32.

31:41
q Nu 5:9; 18:8

41Moses gave the tribute to Eleazar the priest as the LORD's part,q as the LORD commanded Moses.

42The half belonging to the Israelites, which Moses set apart from that of the fighting men— 43the community's half—was 337,500 sheep, 4436,000 cattle, 4530,500 donkeys 46and 16,000 people. 47From the Israelites' half, Moses selected one out of every fifty persons and animals, as the LORD commanded him, and gave them to the Levites, who were responsible for the care of the LORD's tabernacle.

31:49
r Jer 23:4

48Then the officers who were over the units of the army—the commanders of thousands and commanders of hundreds—went to Moses 49and said to him, "Your servants have counted the soldiers under our command, and not one is missing.r

31:50
s Ex 30:16

50So we have brought as an offering to the LORD the gold articles each of us acquired—armlets, bracelets, signet rings, earrings and necklaces—to make atonement for ourselvess before the LORD."

51Moses and Eleazar the priest accepted from them the gold—all the crafted articles. 52All the gold from the commanders of thousands and commanders of hundreds that Moses and Eleazar presented as a gift to the LORD weighed 16,750 shek-

31:53
t Dt 20:14

els.a 53Each soldier had taken plundert for himself. 54Moses and Eleazar the priest

a 52 That is, about 420 pounds (about 190 kilograms)

Numbers 31:25–54

The captured girls and animals were to be divided equally between the soldiers and the community. Part of each of these half portions was to be set apart for the Lord: 1/500th from the soldiers and 1/50th from the community. Presumably the animals were offered as sacrifices, while the girls were to serve at the tabernacle (cf. Ex. 38:8).

All other plunder belonged to the soldiers. But the army officers were so grateful to God that their casualties had amounted to a miraculous zero that they presented the gold they had seized. This was similar to the ransom or atonement money mentioned in Exodus 30:11–16.

What gave the Israelites any more right to massacre and/or enslave entire populations than other "holy warriors" or crusaders through the centuries? Ancient Israel's holy wars were unique in history. The nation was a true theocracy (under God's direct rule), acting on the basis of direct revelation from God and carrying out justice on his behalf.

If we could agree that, because theocracy no longer exists on Planet Earth, there is no such thing as "holy war" in the 21st century, making indiscriminate slaughter or enslavement unconscionable—we would have a solid basis for conflict resolution.

accepted the gold from the commanders of thousands and commanders of hundreds and brought it into the Tent of Meeting as a memorial[u] for the Israelites before the LORD.

The Transjordan Tribes

32 The Reubenites and Gadites, who had very large herds and flocks, saw that the lands of Jazer[v] and Gilead were suitable for livestock.[w] 2So they came to Moses and Eleazar the priest and to the leaders of the community, and said, 3"Ataroth,[x] Dibon, Jazer, Nimrah,[y] Heshbon, Elealeh,[z] Sebam, Nebo and Beon[a]— 4the land the LORD subdued[b] before the people of Israel—are suitable for livestock,[c] and your servants have livestock. 5If we have found favor in your eyes," they said, "let this land be given to your servants as our possession. Do not make us cross the Jordan."

6Moses said to the Gadites and Reubenites, "Shall your countrymen go to war while you sit here? 7Why do you discourage the Israelites from going over into the land the LORD has given them?[d] 8This is what your fathers did when I sent them from Kadesh Barnea to look over the land.[e] 9After they went up to the Valley of Eshcol[f] and viewed the land, they discouraged the Israelites from entering the land the LORD had given them. 10The LORD's anger was aroused[g] that day and he swore this oath: 11'Because they have not followed me wholeheartedly, not one of the men twenty years old or more[h] who came up out of Egypt will see the land I promised on oath[i] to Abraham, Isaac and Jacob[j]— 12not one except Caleb son of Jephunneh the Kenizzite and Joshua son of Nun, for they followed the LORD wholeheartedly.'[k] 13The LORD's anger burned against Israel[l] and he made them wander in the desert forty years, until the whole generation of those who had done evil in his sight was gone.[m]

14"And here you are, a brood of sinners, standing in the place of your fathers and making the LORD even more angry with Israel.[n] 15If you turn away from following him, he will again leave all this people in the desert, and you will be the cause of their destruction.[o]"

16Then they came up to him and said, "We would like to build pens here for our livestock[p] and cities for our women and children. 17But we are ready to arm ourselves and go ahead of the Israelites[q] until we have brought them to their place.[r] Meanwhile our women and children will live in fortified cities, for protection from the inhabitants of the land. 18We will not return to our homes until every Israelite has received his inheritance.[s] 19We will not receive any inheritance with them on the other side of the Jordan, because our inheritance has come to us on the east side of the Jordan."[t]

20Then Moses said to them, "If you will do this—if you will arm yourselves before the LORD for battle,[u] 21and if all of you will go armed over the Jordan before the LORD until he has driven his enemies out before him— 22then when the land is subdued before the LORD, you may return[v] and be free from your obligation to the LORD and to Israel. And this land will be your possession before the LORD.[w]

23"But if you fail to do this, you will be sinning against the LORD; and you may be sure that your sin will find you out.[x] 24Build cities for your women and children, and pens for your flocks,[y] but do what you have promised.[z]"

25The Gadites and Reubenites said to Moses, "We your servants will do as our lord

31:54
u Ex 28:12

32:1
v Nu 21:32
w Ex 12:38
32:3
x ver 34 v ver 36
z ver 37; Isa 15:4;
16:9; Jer 48:34
a ver 38; Jos 13:17;
Eze 25:9
32:4
b Nu 21:34
c Ex 12:38

32:7
d Nu 13:27-14:4
32:8
e Nu 13:3,26;
Dt 1:19-25
32:9
f Nu 13:23; Dt 1:24
32:10
g Nu 11:1
32:11
h Ex 30:14
i Nu 14:23
j Nu 14:28-30
32:12
k Nu 14:24,30;
Dt 1:36; Ps 63:8
32:13
l Ex 4:14
m Nu 14:28-35;
26:64,65

32:14
n ver 10; Dt 1:34;
Ps 78:59
32:15
o Dt 30:17-18;
2Ch 7:20

32:16
p Ex 12:38; Dt 3:19
32:17
q Jos 4:12,13
r Nu 22:4; Dt 3:20

32:18
s Jos 22:1-4

32:19
t Jos 12:1

32:20
u Dt 3:18

32:22
v Jos 22:4
w Dt 3:18-20

32:23
x Ge 4:7; 44:16;
Isa 59:12
32:24
y ver 1,16
z Nu 30:2

Numbers 32:1–42

When the Israelites conquered the lands east of the Jordan River (21:21–35), they didn't intend to permanently occupy them. But the tribes of Reuben and Gad asked to settle in this fertile, productive area. Because they ended their request with "Do not make us cross the Jordan" (v. 5), Moses assumed they were trying to get out of fighting for Canaan and accused them of discouraging the rest of the people from crossing over into the promised land. To Moses, the situation felt like a *déjà vu* of Israel's earlier refusal to take the land (chs. 13–14).

The Reubenites and Gadites clarified their intentions, outlining a plan for their men not just to go *with* their fellow Israelites, but to be deployed *in advance* of them. Moses approved, provided they would follow through. These tribes—along with half the tribe of Manasseh, who joined them—made good on their pledge (Josh. 4:12), after which their fighting men returned to the land God had given them (Josh. 22:9).

32:26
a Jos 1:14

32:28
b Dt 3:18-20;
Jos 1:13

32:31
c ver 29

32:33
d Jos 13:24-28;
1Sa 13:7 e Dt 2:26
f Nu 21:24;
Jos 12:6

32:34
g Dt 2:36;
Jdg 11:26
32:35
h ver 3
32:36
i ver 3
32:38
j ver 3; Isa 15:2;
Jer 48:1,22
32:39
k Ge 50:23
32:40
l Dt 3:15; Jos 17:1

32:41
m Dt 3:14;
Jos 13:30; Jdg 10:4;
1Ch 2:23
32:42
n 2Sa 18:18;
Ps 49:11

33:1
o Mic 6:4
p Ps 77:20

33:3
q Ex 13:4 r Ex 14:8

33:4
s Ex 12:12

commands. 26Our children and wives, our flocks and herds will remain here in the cities of Gilead. *a* 27But your servants, every man armed for battle, will cross over to fight before the LORD, just as our lord says."

28Then Moses gave orders about them *b* to Eleazar the priest and Joshua son of Nun and to the family heads of the Israelite tribes. 29He said to them, "If the Gadites and Reubenites, every man armed for battle, cross over the Jordan with you before the LORD, then when the land is subdued before you, give them the land of Gilead as their possession. 30But if they do not cross over with you armed, they must accept their possession with you in Canaan."

31The Gadites and Reubenites answered, "Your servants will do what the LORD has said. *c* 32We will cross over before the LORD into Canaan armed, but the property we inherit will be on this side of the Jordan."

33Then Moses gave to the Gadites, *d* the Reubenites and the half-tribe of Manasseh son of Joseph the kingdom of Sihon king of the Amorites *e* and the kingdom of Og king of Bashan—the whole land with its cities and the territory around them. *f*

34The Gadites built up Dibon, Ataroth, Aroer, *g* 35Atroth Shophan, Jazer, *h* Jogbehah, 36Beth Nimrah *i* and Beth Haran as fortified cities, and built pens for their flocks. 37And the Reubenites rebuilt Heshbon, Elealeh and Kiriathaim, 38as well as Nebo *j* and Baal Meon (these names were changed) and Sibmah. They gave names to the cities they rebuilt.

39The descendants of Makir *k* son of Manasseh went to Gilead, captured it and drove out the Amorites who were there. 40So Moses gave Gilead to the Makirites, *l* the descendants of Manasseh, and they settled there. 41Jair, a descendant of Manasseh, captured their settlements and called them Havvoth Jair. *a m* 42And Nobah captured Kenath and its surrounding settlements and called it Nobah after himself. *n*

Stages in Israel's Journey

33 Here are the stages in the journey of the Israelites when they came out of Egypt *o* by divisions under the leadership of Moses and Aaron. *p* 2At the LORD's command Moses recorded the stages in their journey. This is their journey by stages:

3The Israelites set out from Rameses on the fifteenth day of the first month, the day after the Passover. *q* They marched out boldly *r* in full view of all the Egyptians, 4who were burying all their firstborn, whom the LORD had struck down among them; for the LORD had brought judgment on their gods. *s*

a 41 Or *them the settlements of Jair*

📖 "Possession is nine-tenths of the law." Modern law protects a lender from a borrower's default by enforcing the right of repossession or seizure of collateral. But how could Israel foreclose on two tribes if they refused to help their brothers? Recognizing the danger in loaning them land they already possessed, Moses warned them of a higher authority with power to enforce the contract (v. 23). If they reneged, their sin would boomerang back to haunt them. Still today, God holds people accountable by completing the consequences of their own actions. When have you seen this principle in action?

Numbers 33:1–56

🔎 The summary in Numbers 33 is more complete than the accounts in Exodus and earlier in Numbers, which concentrate on places where memorable events occurred. Scholars haven't been able to locate all the places mentioned here. The Israelites were camping in an uninhabited area, without building anything perma-

nent. More important than its geography is this travelogue's value as a litany of God's deliverance of and care for his people.

The survey of past journeys returned to the present on the plains of Moab, where the Israelites were encamped. There God instructed them on how to treat the Canaanites when they crossed the Jordan: Drive them out, destroy all their objects of worship, and settle in their land, dividing it up by casting lots.

📖 God's people maintain a balanced perspective by reviewing their journey and remembering how he has led them, step by step and day by day. In this way we reinforce our sense of dependence on and confidence in him. As one member of an urban church replied when her pastor asked how she was getting along: "I find myself living somewhere between 'thank you, Lord' and 'help me, Jesus.'" Do you sense this kind of closeness in your daily walk with God?

Moses had just warned the Gadites and Reubenites

5 The Israelites left Rameses and camped at Succoth.[t]
6 They left Succoth and camped at Etham, on the edge of the desert.[u]
7 They left Etham, turned back to Pi Hahiroth, to the east of Baal Zephon,[v]
and camped near Migdol.[w]
8 They left Pi Hahiroth[a] and passed through the sea[x] into the desert, and
when they had traveled for three days in the Desert of Etham, they camped at
Marah.[y]
9 They left Marah and went to Elim, where there were twelve springs and seventy palm trees, and they camped[z] there.
10 They left Elim and camped by the Red Sea.[b]
11 They left the Red Sea and camped in the Desert of Sin.[a]
12 They left the Desert of Sin and camped at Dophkah.
13 They left Dophkah and camped at Alush.
14 They left Alush and camped at Rephidim, where there was no water for the
people to drink.
15 They left Rephidim[b] and camped in the Desert of Sinai.[c]
16 They left the Desert of Sinai and camped at Kibroth Hattaavah.[d]
17 They left Kibroth Hattaavah and camped at Hazeroth.[e]
18 They left Hazeroth and camped at Rithmah.
19 They left Rithmah and camped at Rimmon Perez.
20 They left Rimmon Perez and camped at Libnah.[f]
21 They left Libnah and camped at Rissah.
22 They left Rissah and camped at Kehelathah.
23 They left Kehelathah and camped at Mount Shepher.
24 They left Mount Shepher and camped at Haradah.
25 They left Haradah and camped at Makheloth.
26 They left Makheloth and camped at Tahath.
27 They left Tahath and camped at Terah.
28 They left Terah and camped at Mithcah.
29 They left Mithcah and camped at Hashmonah.
30 They left Hashmonah and camped at Moseroth.[g]
31 They left Moseroth and camped at Bene Jaakan.
32 They left Bene Jaakan and camped at Hor Haggidgad.
33 They left Hor Haggidgad and camped at Jotbathah.[h]
34 They left Jotbathah and camped at Abronah.
35 They left Abronah and camped at Ezion Geber.[i]
36 They left Ezion Geber and camped at Kadesh, in the Desert of Zin.[j]
37 They left Kadesh and camped at Mount Hor,[k] on the border of Edom.[l] 38 At
the LORD's command Aaron the priest went up Mount Hor, where he died[m] on
the first day of the fifth month of the fortieth year after the Israelites came out
of Egypt.[n] 39 Aaron was a hundred and twenty-three years old when he died on
Mount Hor.
40 The Canaanite king of Arad,[o] who lived in the Negev of Canaan, heard
that the Israelites were coming.
41 They left Mount Hor and camped at Zalmonah.
42 They left Zalmonah and camped at Punon.
43 They left Punon and camped at Oboth.[p]
44 They left Oboth and camped at Iye Abarim, on the border of Moab.[q]
45 They left Iyim[c] and camped at Dibon Gad.

33:5 [t] Ex 12:37
33:6 [u] Ex 13:20
33:7 [v] Ex 14:9 [w] Ex 14:2
33:8 [x] Ex 14:22 [y] Ex 15:23
33:9 [z] Ex 15:27
33:11 [a] Ex 16:1
33:15 [b] Ex 17:1 [c] Ex 19:1
33:16 [d] Nu 11:34
33:17 [e] Nu 11:35
33:20 [f] Jos 10:29
33:30 [g] Dt 10:6
33:33 [h] Dt 10:7
33:35 [i] Dt 2:8; 1Ki 9:26; 22:48
33:36 [j] Nu 20:1
33:37 [k] Nu 20:22 [l] Nu 20:16; 21:4
33:38 [m] Dt 10:6 [n] Nu 20:25-28
33:40 [o] Nu 21:1
33:43 [p] Nu 21:10
33:44 [q] Nu 21:11

[a] *8* Many manuscripts of the Masoretic Text, Samaritan Pentateuch and Vulgate; most manuscripts of the Masoretic Text *left from before Hahiroth* [b] *10* Hebrew *Yam Suph*; that is, Sea of Reeds; also in verse 11 [c] *45* That is, Iye Abarim

that their sin would find them out if they were unfaithful (see 32:23 and "Here and Now" for 32:1–42). Now he cautioned the nation as a whole: If they chose to bond to the Canaanites instead of displacing them, they would eventually also bond to their sins. What does this say to you about living faithfully in a fallen world (see James 4:4; 1 Jn. 2:15–17)?

33:47
r Nu 27:12

33:48
s Nu 22:1
33:49
t Nu 25:1

33:51
u Jos 3:17
33:52
v Ex 23:24; 34:13;
Lev 26:1; Dt 7:2,5;
12:3; Jos 11:12;
Ps 106:34-36
33:53
w Dt 11:31;
Jos 21:43
33:54
x Nu 26:54
33:55
y Jos 23:13;
Jdg 2:3; Ps 106:36

46They left Dibon Gad and camped at Almon Diblathaim.

47They left Almon Diblathaim and camped in the mountains of Abarim, r near Nebo.

48They left the mountains of Abarim and camped on the plains of Moab by the Jordan across from Jericho. a s 49There on the plains of Moab they camped along the Jordan from Beth Jeshimoth to Abel Shittim. t

50On the plains of Moab by the Jordan across from Jericho the LORD said to Moses, 51"Speak to the Israelites and say to them: 'When you cross the Jordan into Canaan, u 52drive out all the inhabitants of the land before you. Destroy all their carved images and their cast idols, and demolish all their high places. v 53Take possession of the land and settle in it, for I have given you the land to possess. w 54Distribute the land by lot, according to your clans. x To a larger group give a larger inheritance, and to a smaller group a smaller one. Whatever falls to them by lot will be theirs. Distribute it according to your ancestral tribes.

55 " 'But if you do not drive out the inhabitants of the land, those you allow to remain will become barbs in your eyes and thorns y in your sides. They will give you trouble in the land where you will live. 56And then I will do to you what I plan to do to them.' "

Boundaries of Canaan

34:2
z Ge 17:8; Dt 1:7-8;
Ps 78:54-55
a Eze 47:15

34 The LORD said to Moses, 2"Command the Israelites and say to them: 'When you enter Canaan, the land that will be allotted to you as an inheritance z will have these boundaries: a

34:3
b Jos 15:1-3
c Ge 14:3

3 " 'Your southern side will include some of the Desert of Zin b along the border of Edom. On the east, your southern boundary will start from the end of the Salt Sea, b c 4cross

34:4
d Jos 15:3
e Nu 32:8

south of Scorpion c Pass, d continue on to Zin and go south of Kadesh Barnea. e Then it will go to Hazar Addar and over to Azmon,

34:5
f Ge 15:18; Jos 15:4

5where it will turn, join the Wadi of Egypt f and end at the Sea. d

6 " 'Your western boundary will be the coast of the Great Sea. This will be your boundary on the west.

34:7
g Eze 47:15-17
34:8
h Nu 13:21;
Jos 13:5

7 " 'For your northern boundary, g run a line from the Great Sea to Mount Hor 8and from Mount Hor to Lebo e Hamath. h Then the boundary will go to Zedad, 9continue to Ziphron and end at Hazar Enan. This will be your boundary on the north.

34:11
i 2Ki 23:33;
Jer 39:5 j Dt 3:17;
Jos 11:2; 13:27

10 " 'For your eastern boundary, run a line from Hazar Enan to Shepham. 11The boundary will go down from Shepham to Riblah i on the east side of Ain and continue along the slopes east of the Sea of Kinnereth. f j 12Then the boundary will go down along the Jordan and end at the Salt Sea.

34:13
k Jos 14:1-5

" 'This will be your land, with its boundaries on every side.' "

13Moses commanded the Israelites: "Assign this land by lot as an inheritance. k The LORD has ordered that it be given to the nine and a half tribes, 14because the

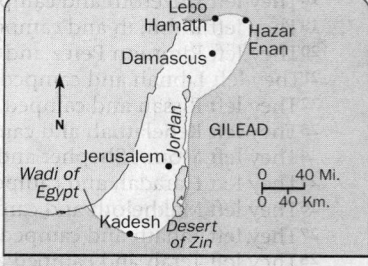

Boundaries of Canaan (34:2)

Then: The careful description of the boundaries of the land (34:3–12) sounds more like modern legalese than the manner in which land was typically occupied and used in Biblical times.

Now: The modern state of Israel is substantially smaller than the land these boundaries describe.

---

a 48 Hebrew *Jordan of Jericho*; possibly an ancient name for the Jordan River; also in verse 50   b 3 That is, the Dead Sea; also in verse 12   c 4 Hebrew *Akrabbim*   d 5 That is, the Mediterranean; also in verses 6 and 7   e 8 Or *to the entrance to*   f 11 That is, Galilee

---

Numbers 34:1–29

The described boundaries of the promised land demonstrate the great gift God was giving his people. At no time in their history, even during the golden age of David and Solomon, did the Israelites ever realize the full extent of the area this passage presents. Chapter 34 also lists the leaders who would be responsible for dividing up the land. The tribes of Reuben and Gad weren't represented because their inheritance was to be on the other side of the Jordan.

families of the tribe of Reuben, the tribe of Gad and the half-tribe of Manasseh have received their inheritance. [l] 15These two and a half tribes have received their inheritance on the east side of the Jordan of Jericho, [a] toward the sunrise."

16The Lᴏʀᴅ said to Moses, 17 "These are the names of the men who are to assign the land for you as an inheritance: Eleazar the priest and Joshua[m] son of Nun. 18And appoint one leader from each tribe to help[n] assign the land. 19These are their names:

Caleb[o] son of Jephunneh,
    from the tribe of Judah;[p]
20Shemuel son of Ammihud,
    from the tribe of Simeon;[q]
21Elidad son of Kislon,
    from the tribe of Benjamin;[r]
22Bukki son of Jogli,
    the leader from the tribe of Dan;
23Hanniel son of Ephod,
    the leader from the tribe of Manasseh son of Joseph;
24Kemuel son of Shiphtan,
    the leader from the tribe of Ephraim son of Joseph;
25Elizaphan son of Parnach,
    the leader from the tribe of Zebulun;
26Paltiel son of Azzan,
    the leader from the tribe of Issachar;
27Ahihud son of Shelomi,
    the leader from the tribe of Asher;[s]
28Pedahel son of Ammihud,
    the leader from the tribe of Naphtali."

29These are the men the Lᴏʀᴅ commanded to assign the inheritance to the Israelites in the land of Canaan.

Towns for the Levites

35 On the plains of Moab by the Jordan across from Jericho,[b] the Lᴏʀᴅ said to Moses, 2 "Command the Israelites to give the Levites towns to live in[t] from the inheritance the Israelites will possess. And give them pasturelands around the towns. 3Then they will have towns to live in and pasturelands for their cattle, flocks and all their other livestock.

4 "The pasturelands around the towns that you give the Levites will extend out fifteen hundred feet[c] from the town wall. 5Outside the town, measure three thousand

---

34:14
[l] Nu 32:33; Jos 14:3

34:17
[m] Jos 14:1
34:18
[n] Nu 1:4,16

34:19
[o] Nu 26:65
[p] Ge 29:35; Dt 33:7

34:20
[q] Ge 49:5

34:21
[r] Ge 49:27;
Ps 68:27

34:27
[s] Nu 1:40

35:2
[t] Lev 25:32-34;
Jos 14:3,4

---

[a] 15 *Jordan of Jericho* was possibly an ancient name for the Jordan River.   [b] 1 Hebrew *Jordan of Jericho*; possibly an ancient name for the Jordan River   [c] 4 Hebrew *a thousand cubits* (about 450 meters)

📖 There are two ways to look at the gap between the promised boundaries and the reality of Israel's history. Do you think God's generosity overreached his people's capabilities? Or did Israel's lack of faithfulness result in underachievement? Maybe both are true. All of us can identify with the lavishness of God's gifts and love on the one hand (cf. Eph. 1:7–8; 3:20; 1 Jn. 3:1), and our own failures and shortfalls on the other (cf. Rom. 7:14–25; Phil. 3:12–14).

Numbers 35:1–5

⚖ Because the Levites were to receive tithes instead of territory (18:20–24; cf. 26:62), they wouldn't have a part in the division of the promised land. But they would have to live somewhere. Chapter 35 provided for the other tribes to give the Levites 48 towns distributed throughout their territories and surrounded by pasturelands (vv. 1–8). Spreading out the Levite ministers of the Lord in this way was designed to help maintain the spiritual devotion of the other tribes who would be geographically distant from the tabernacle and eventual temple.

📖 This promise to the Levites found fulfillment in Joshua 21, just before the two-and-a-half eastern tribes returned home, having fulfilled their obligation (Josh. 22). No, the Israelites hadn't conquered *all* the Canaanite peoples as God had commanded (cf. Josh. 23:4–5), but he was apparently satisfied at this juncture. Take a moment to read Joshua 21:44–45. What a beautiful and comforting summary of a (temporarily) peaceful situation! Can you affirm the reflection that not one of all God's good promises *to you* has failed?

feet[a] on the east side, three thousand on the south side, three thousand on the west and three thousand on the north, with the town in the center. They will have this area as pastureland for the towns.

Cities of Refuge

35:6
u Jos 20:7-9;
21:3,13

6 "Six of the towns you give the Levites will be cities of refuge, to which a person who has killed someone may flee. [u] In addition, give them forty-two other towns. 7 In all you must give the Levites forty-eight towns, together with their pasturelands. 8 The towns you give the Levites from the land the Israelites possess are to be given

35:8
v Nu 26:54; 33:54;
Jos 21:1-42

in proportion to the inheritance of each tribe: Take many towns from a tribe that has many, but few from one that has few." [v]

35:10
w Jos 20:2
35:11
x ver 22-25
y Ex 21:13; Dt 19:1-
13
35:12
z Dt 19:6; Jos 20:3

9 Then the LORD said to Moses: 10 "Speak to the Israelites and say to them: 'When you cross the Jordan into Canaan, [w] 11 select some towns to be your cities of refuge, to which a person who has killed someone[x] accidentally[y] may flee. 12 They will be places of refuge from the avenger,[z] so that a person accused of murder may not die before he stands trial before the assembly. 13 These six towns you give will be your cities of refuge. 14 Give three on this side of the Jordan and three in Canaan as cities of refuge. 15 These six towns will be a place of refuge for Israelites, aliens and any other people living among them, so that anyone who has killed another accidentally can flee there.

35:16
a Ex 21:12;
Lev 24:17

16 " 'If a man strikes someone with an iron object so that he dies, he is a murderer; the murderer shall be put to death. [a] 17 Or if anyone has a stone in his hand that could kill, and he strikes someone so that he dies, he is a murderer; the murderer shall be put to death. 18 Or if anyone has a wooden object in his hand that could kill, and he hits someone so that he dies, he is a murderer; the murderer shall be

35:19
b ver 21

put to death. 19 The avenger of blood shall put the murderer to death; when he meets him, he shall put him to death. [b] 20 If anyone with malice aforethought

35:20
c Ge 4:8; Ex 21:14;
Dt 19:11; 2Sa 3:27;
20:10

shoves another or throws something at him intentionally[c] so that he dies 21 or if in hostility he hits him with his fist so that he dies, that person shall be put to death; he is a murderer. The avenger of blood shall put the murderer to death when he meets him.

35:22
d ver 11; Ex 21:13

22 " 'But if without hostility someone suddenly shoves another or throws something at him unintentionally[d] 23 or, without seeing him, drops a stone on him that could kill him, and he dies, then since he was not his enemy and he did not intend to harm him, 24 the assembly[e] must judge between him and the avenger of blood

35:24
e ver 12; Jos 20:6

according to these regulations. 25 The assembly must protect the one accused of murder from the avenger of blood and send him back to the city of refuge to which he fled. He must stay there until the death of the high priest, who was anointed with

35:25
f Ex 29:7

the holy oil.[f]

26 " 'But if the accused ever goes outside the limits of the city of refuge to which he has fled 27 and the avenger of blood finds him outside the city, the avenger of blood may kill the accused without being guilty of murder. 28 The accused must stay in his city of refuge until the death of the high priest; only after the death of the high

35:29
g Nu 27:11

priest may he return to his own property.

29 " 'These are to be legal requirements[g] for you throughout the generations to come, wherever you live.

---

[a] 5 Hebrew *two thousand cubits* (about 900 meters)

Numbers 35:6–34

A person guilty of unintentional manslaughter was free to leave a city of refuge only after the high priest's death (vv. 25,28). Why? The killer wasn't guilty of first degree murder but had still taken the life of a human being. Only the life of another person could purify him or her in God's sight, and only a priest could bear the guilt of others (cf. Ex. 28:38; Lev. 10:17). Instead of calling for the legal/ritual slaughter of a priest in place

of the accused killer, God accepted the natural death of the high priest as satisfying the demand of justice.

Christ is our heavenly high priest (Heb. 7–10). His death on behalf of sinners wasn't a natural one. But by bearing human sin as priest and then dying for that sin as sacrificial victim (e.g., Heb. 7:27; 9:12–15; 10:5–14), he has united in himself the roles by which we are freed from blame—and free to go Home!

30 " 'Anyone who kills a person is to be put to death as a murderer only on the testimony of witnesses. But no one is to be put to death on the testimony of only one witness. [h]

31 " 'Do not accept a ransom for the life of a murderer, who deserves to die. He must surely be put to death.

32 " 'Do not accept a ransom for anyone who has fled to a city of refuge and so allow him to go back and live on his own land before the death of the high priest.

33 " 'Do not pollute the land where you are. Bloodshed pollutes the land, [i] and atonement cannot be made for the land on which blood has been shed, except by the blood of the one who shed it. 34 Do not defile the land [j] where you live and where I dwell, [k] for I, the LORD, dwell among the Israelites.' "

Inheritance of Zelophehad's Daughters

36 The family heads of the clan of Gilead [l] son of Makir, the son of Manasseh, who were from the clans of the descendants of Joseph, came and spoke before Moses and the leaders, [m] the heads of the Israelite families. 2 They said, "When the LORD commanded my lord to give the land as an inheritance to the Israelites by lot, he ordered you to give the inheritance of our brother Zelophehad [n] to his daughters. 3 Now suppose they marry men from other Israelite tribes; then their inheritance will be taken from our ancestral inheritance and added to that of the tribe they marry into. And so part of the inheritance allotted to us will be taken away. 4 When the Year of Jubilee [o] for the Israelites comes, their inheritance will be added to that of the tribe into which they marry, and their property will be taken from the tribal inheritance of our forefathers."

5 Then at the LORD's command Moses gave this order to the Israelites: "What the tribe of the descendants of Joseph is saying is right. 6 This is what the LORD commands for Zelophehad's daughters: They may marry anyone they please as long as they marry within the tribal clan of their father. 7 No inheritance [p] in Israel is to pass from tribe to tribe, for every Israelite shall keep the tribal land inherited from his forefathers. 8 Every daughter who inherits land in any Israelite tribe must marry someone in her father's tribal clan, [q] so that every Israelite will possess the inheritance of his fathers. 9 No inheritance may pass from tribe to tribe, for each Israelite tribe is to keep the land it inherits."

10 So Zelophehad's daughters did as the LORD commanded Moses. 11 Zelophehad's daughters—Mahlah, Tirzah, Hoglah, Milcah and Noah [r]—married their cousins on their father's side. 12 They married within the clans of the descendants of Manasseh son of Joseph, and their inheritance remained in their father's clan and tribe.

13 These are the commands and regulations the LORD gave through Moses [s] to the Israelites on the plains of Moab by the Jordan across from Jericho. [a][t]

[a] 13 Hebrew *Jordan of Jericho*; possibly an ancient name for the Jordan River

35:30 [h] ver 16; Dt 17:6; 19:15; Mt 18:16; Jn 7:51; 2Co 13:1; Heb 10:28

35:33 [i] Ge 9:6; Ps 106:38; Mic 4:11

35:34 [j] Lev 18:24,25 [k] Ex 29:45

36:1 [l] Nu 26:29 [m] Nu 27:2

36:2 [n] Nu 26:33; 27:1,7

36:4 [o] Lev 25:10

36:7 [p] 1Ki 21:3

36:8 [q] 1Ch 23:22

36:11 [r] Nu 26:33; 27:1

36:13 [s] Lev 26:46; 27:34 [t] Nu 22:1

Numbers 36:1–13

Numbers 36 is a postscript to 27:1–11, where God had allowed Zelophehad's daughters to inherit his property. The heads of Zelophehad's clan detected a potential problem. If his daughters were to marry men from another tribe, they would join that tribe and take his property with them—thereby diminishing the allotted territory of their own clan and tribe. God's solution was simple: An heiress would be required to marry within her father's clan. Zelophehad's daughters complied, and that was the end of the story. This gentle resolution of a problem reminds us of the report of Israelite compli-ance that set the standard for faithfulness at the beginning of the book (1:54).

Thanks to these noble women, the book of Numbers—which so often recounts the rebellion of God's people against his grace and goodness—ends as it began: on a positive note. It's too bad that so much in between was negative! The apostle Paul stated that God's acts of punishment upon the Israelites during this period of their history "happened to them as examples and were written down as warnings for us" (1 Cor. 10:11). In what way do these stories most impress you as a personal warning? What will you do about it?

INTRODUCTION TO
Deuteronomy

AUTHOR

Deuteronomy itself identifies Moses as its author (1:5; 31:9,22,24), and other Scripture passages concur (2 Kings 14:6; Matt. 19:7–8; Luke 24:27; John 7:19; Rom. 10:5–8,19; 1 Cor. 9:9). It's apparent that some portions of the book were later additions (34:1–12) or underwent later editing.

DATE WRITTEN

Deuteronomy was probably written about 1400 B.C., just prior to Moses' death and as the Israelites prepared to enter Canaan.

ORIGINAL READERS

Deuteronomy was written to the Israelites to challenge them to obey God and reject idolatry.

TIMELINE

	2200BC	2100	2000	1900	1800	1700	1600	1500	1400

Moses' birth (c. 1526 B.C.)

The plagues; The Passover (c. 1446 B.C.)

The exodus (c. 1446 B.C.)

Desert wanderings (c. 1446-1406 B.C.)

The Ten Commandments (c. 1445 B.C.)

Book of Deuteronomy written (c. 1400 B.C.)

Moses dies; Joshua becomes leader (c. 1406 B.C.)

Israelites enter Canaan (c. 1406 B.C.)

THEMES

Deuteronomy records three speeches given by Moses at the end of his life and calling the Israelites to renew their covenant with God. The book contains the following themes:

1. *The covenant.* The major theme of Deuteronomy is the covenant relationship between God and his people. God's unmerited love (7:6–9) is the basis not only of the covenant, but also of our trust in him. His faithfulness in the past (his provision and protection) encourages faith in him for the future. Covenants, a central focus in Scripture, take on a historical progression: the Noahic covenant (Gen. 9:8–17), the Abrahamic covenant (Gen. 15:9–21), the Sinaitic covenant (Ex. 19:5–6), the Levitical covenant (Num. 25:10–13), the Davidic covenant (2 Sam. 7:5–16), and the new covenant (Jer. 31:31–34).

2. *Choices.* The covenant exhorts God's people to teach, remember, and obey (6:6–25). God promised that obedience would bring blessing (28:1–14) but warned that disobedience would result in harm (28:15–68). Christians today are called to love God (Matt. 22:36–37) and obey him (John 14:23). As was true of the Israelites, our choices affect our future (Ps. 62:12; Matt. 16:27; Rom. 2:6).

3. *The poor.* As a reflection of God's love for society's socially vulnerable (10:18–19), Deuteronomy designates special protections and commands involving the inclusion of widows, orphans, resident foreigners, the disabled, and the elderly (5:14; 14:29; 15:7–11; 16:11,14; 24:10–21; 26:12–13; 27:19).

FAITH IN ACTION
The pages of Deuteronomy are filled with life lessons and role models of faith—people who challenge believers to put their faith in action.

Role Models

• JOSHUA (3:28; 31:14,23; 34:9) was called by God to be a leader, and God blessed him with the strength, courage, and wisdom he needed for the job. What challenge are you facing? Can you trust God to provide you with the tools necessary to accomplish what he's placed before you?

• THE PEOPLE OF ISRAEL (9:1–3) were encouraged to trust in the Lord and his promises when faced with strong resistance. To whom do you turn when you encounter what appears to be overwhelming opposition?

• GOD (10:18–19) loves the fatherless, the widow, the alien, and the poor. How does his love motivate your care for others, especially those who are vulnerable?

• MOSES (33:1) was called "the man of God," even though he made some serious mistakes during his life (32:48–52). How does this encourage you as you attempt to live with integrity?

Challenges

• Have you ever thought that God didn't love (or even that he hated) you (1:27)? Use the concordance in the back of this Bible to look up verses about God's love. Make a list of your favorites. In times of doubt, consult your list to strengthen your trust in God.

• Choose to accept God's discipline (4:21–31), resist the temptation to shift the blame, learn from your mistakes, and warn others to avoid the same pitfalls.

• Take your authority as a pastor, parent, or friend seriously when you see those you love being disobedient to God. They need your encouragement and intercessory prayers (9:12–29).

• Imitate God in his defense of the fatherless and the widow and in his love for the poor (10:18). Provide generously for their needs (14:29; 15:7–11), exhibiting mercy and compassion (24:10–21).

• Evaluate the influences your family members and friends have on you. Are they leading you away from God or toward him (13:1–18; 1 Cor. 15:33)?

• Do you have regrets? Be encouraged by the concluding words of Deuteronomy (34:10–12). Despite Moses' sin and its consequence (32:48–52), his life and character were praised. Determine to live your own life so that its *summary* will be worthy of praise.

OUTLINE

  I. Preamble (1:1–5)
  II. Historical Prologue (1:6—4:43)
  III. Stipulations of the Covenant (4:44—26:19)
     A. Primary Demands (4:44—11:32)
     B. Supplementary Requirements (12–26)
  IV. Ratification; Curses, and Blessings (27–30)
  V. Leadership Succession Under the Covenant (31–34)

The Command to Leave Horeb

1 These are the words Moses spoke to all Israel in the desert east of the Jordan—that is, in the Arabah—opposite Suph, between Paran and Tophel, Laban, Hazeroth and Dizahab. ²(It takes eleven days to go from Horeb*ᵃ* to Kadesh Barnea*ᵇ* by the Mount Seir road.)

³In the fortieth year,*ᶜ* on the first day of the eleventh month, Moses proclaimed*ᵈ* to the Israelites all that the LORD had commanded him concerning them. ⁴This was after he had defeated Sihon*ᵉ* king of the Amorites, who reigned in Heshbon,*ᶠ* and at Edrei had defeated Og*ᵍ* king of Bashan, who reigned in Ashtaroth.

⁵East of the Jordan in the territory of Moab, Moses began to expound this law, saying:

⁶The LORD our God said to us*ʰ* at Horeb,*ⁱ* "You have stayed long enough at this mountain. ⁷Break camp and advance into the hill country of the Amorites; go to all the neighboring peoples in the Arabah, in the mountains, in the western foothills, in the Negev*ʲ* and along the coast, to the land of the Canaanites and to Lebanon,*ᵏ* as far as the great river, the Euphrates. ⁸See, I have given you this land. Go in and take possession of the land that the LORD swore*ˡ* he would give to your fathers—to Abraham, Isaac and Jacob—and to their descendants after them."

The Appointment of Leaders

⁹At that time I said to you, "You are too heavy a burden for me to carry alone.*ᵐ* ¹⁰The LORD your God has increased your numbers so that today you are as many*ⁿ* as the stars in the sky.*ᵒ* ¹¹May the LORD, the God of your fathers, increase you a thousand times and bless you as he has promised!*ᵖ* ¹²But how can I bear your problems and your burdens and your disputes all by myself? ¹³Choose some wise, understanding and respected men*ᵠ* from each of your tribes, and I will set them over you."

Margin references
1:2 *ᵃ* Ex 3:1 *ᵇ* Nu 13:26; Dt 9:23
1:3 *ᶜ* Nu 33:38 *ᵈ* Dt 4:1-2
1:4 *ᵉ* Nu 21:21-26 *ᶠ* Nu 21:25 *ᵍ* Nu 21:33-35; Jos 13:12
1:6 *ʰ* Nu 10:13 *ⁱ* Ex 3:1
1:7 *ʲ* Jos 10:40 *ᵏ* Dt 11:24
1:8 *ˡ* Ge 12:7; 15:18; 17:7-8; 26:4; 28:13
1:9 *ᵐ* Ex 18:18
1:10 *ⁿ* Ge 15:5 *ᵒ* Dt 10:22; 28:62
1:11 *ᵖ* Ge 22:17; Ex 32:13
1:13 *ᵠ* Ex 18:21

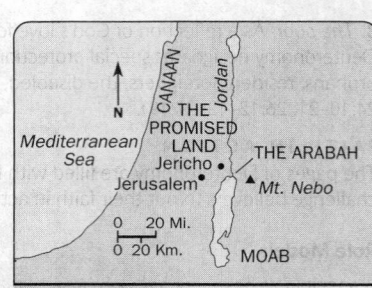

Setting of Deuteronomy (1:1)
Then: The desert east of the Jordan was called the Arabah, meaning "dry" or "burnt up."
Now: The Arabah is located in the modern nation of Jordan.

Deuteronomy 1:1–8

The book of Deuteronomy records Moses' words to the Israelites when they were east of the Jordan River, near the Dead Sea. The places mentioned are locations on Israel's journey from Mount Sinai (usually referred to as Horeb in Deut.) to their current encampment. The 40 years include the time (1) spent on the journey from Egypt to Sinai, (2) spent at Sinai, and (3) that had elapsed on the journey to Kadesh Barnea.

God's command to the Israelites to enter and possess the land began here but would be repeated and emphasized again and again throughout Deuteronomy. The promised land was God's gift—free and clear—but their possession of it had definite contingencies.

Forty years sounds like a long time, especially to us who are often impatient even in our instant-culture. But consider that the church has waited more than two millennia for the fulfillment of an even greater promise, Christ's return. God and Moses were concerned about the people's readiness for the conquest and occupation of the land. Are you ready for Jesus' return, for that day when he will grant us as believers "possession" of our eternal home?

Deuteronomy 1:9–18

Moses didn't mention his father-in-law's role in instigating this procedure (Ex. 18:13–26), stating simply that he had seen the need for leaders to assist him in political and judicial matters. In Exodus it would seem that Moses himself had appointed these leaders. But verse 13 specifies that the people had selected them as representative of the various tribes, after which Moses delegated their specific tasks. The leaders were to be characterized by wisdom, understanding, and experience.

Four specifics are mentioned with regard to the new judges: (1) Disputes between Israelites or with foreigners were to be arbitrated. (2) Partiality wasn't to be tolerated. (3) They weren't to fear others, realizing that "judgment belongs to God" (v. 17). (4) Cases too difficult for them were to be referred to Moses.

Have you ever been so overwhelmed by responsibilities that you felt you would be crushed by their weight? Moses couldn't lead the nation of Israel without help. But he was willing to share his leadership and entrust responsibility to others. Is it hard for you to trust others enough to delegate accountability? How willing are you to ask for help—to spread the load and share

14You answered me, "What you propose to do is good."

15So I took[r] the leading men of your tribes, wise and respected men, and appointed them to have authority over you—as commanders of thousands, of hundreds, of fifties and of tens and as tribal officials. 16And I charged your judges at that time: Hear the disputes between your brothers and judge fairly,[s] whether the case is between brother Israelites or between one of them and an alien.[t] 17Do not show partiality[u] in judging; hear both small and great alike. Do not be afraid of any man,[v] for judgment belongs to God. Bring me any case too hard for you, and I will hear it.[w] 18And at that time I told you everything you were to do.

Spies Sent Out

19Then, as the LORD our God commanded us, we set out from Horeb and went toward the hill country of the Amorites through all that vast and dreadful desert[x] that you have seen, and so we reached Kadesh Barnea.[y] 20Then I said to you, "You have reached the hill country of the Amorites, which the LORD our God is giving us. 21See, the LORD your God has given you the land. Go up and take possession of it as the LORD, the God of your fathers, told you. Do not be afraid;[z] do not be discouraged."

22Then all of you came to me and said, "Let us send men ahead to spy out the land for us and bring back a report about the route we are to take and the towns we will come to."

23The idea seemed good to me; so I selected[a] twelve of you, one man from each tribe. 24They left and went up into the hill country, and came to the Valley of Eshcol[b] and explored it. 25Taking with them some of the fruit of the land, they brought it down to us and reported,[c] "It is a good land that the LORD our God is giving us."

Rebellion Against the LORD

26But you were unwilling to go up;[d] you rebelled against the command of the LORD your God. 27You grumbled[e] in your tents and said, "The LORD hates us; so he brought us out of Egypt to deliver us into the hands of the Amorites to destroy us. 28Where can we go? Our brothers have made us lose heart. They say, 'The people are stronger and taller[f] than we are; the cities are large, with walls up to the sky. We even saw the Anakites[g] there.'"

29Then I said to you, "Do not be terrified; do not be afraid of them. 30The LORD your God, who is going before you, will fight[h] for you, as he did for you in Egypt, before your very eyes, 31and in the desert. There you saw how the LORD your God carried[i] you, as a father carries his son, all the way you went until you reached this place."

32In spite of this, you did not trust[j] in the LORD your God, 33who went ahead of you on your journey, in fire by night and in a cloud by day,[k] to search[l] out places for you to camp and to show you the way you should go.

34When the LORD heard what you said, he was angry and solemnly swore:[m] 35"Not a man of this evil generation shall see the good land[n] I swore to give your

---

1:15
r Ex 18:25

1:16
s Dt 16:18; Jn 7:24
t Lev 24:22

1:17
u Lev 19:15;
Dt 16:19; Pr 24:23;
Jas 2:1 v 2Ch 19:6
w Ex 18:26

1:19
x Dt 8:15; Jer 2:2,6
y ver 2; Nu 13:26

1:21
z Jos 1:6,9,18

1:23
a Nu 13:1-3
1:24
b Nu 13:21-25
1:25
c Nu 13:27

1:26
d Nu 14:1-4
1:27
e Dt 9:28;
Ps 106:25

1:28
f Nu 13:32
g Nu 13:33;
Dt 9:1-3
1:30
h Ex 14:14; Dt 3:22;
Ne 4:20
1:31
i Dt 32:10-12;
Isa 46:3-4; 63:9;
Hos 11:3; Ac 13:18
1:32
j Ps 106:24;
Jude 1:5
1:33
k Ex 13:21;
Ps 78:14 l Nu 10:33
1:34
m Nu 14:23,28-30
1:35
n Ps 95:11

---

the burden? The New Testament confirms that life in the kingdom is a community experience where responsibilities and joys are shared (Acts 4:32–35).

Deuteronomy 1:19–25

Moses recalled the Israelites' arrival in Kadesh Barnea, south of the promised land, some 38 years earlier. There he had repeated God's command to take possession of the land, challenging the people not to be afraid. But they were afraid, as evidenced by their suggestion to send out spies.

Their request and Moses' implementation of the idea seem to conflict with Numbers 13:1–3, which states that God ordered the reconnaissance mission. It's possible that the people first suggested the plan, after which Moses approved of it and referred the request to the

Lord—who agreed and instructed each tribe to send a representative.

The accounts here and in Numbers 13, which seem contradictory on the surface, tell us something about divine-human interaction. Have you ever made a decision and recognized, then or later, that you had been prompted by God? Hindsight, the perspective of Deuteronomy, often shows us God's guiding hand at work through circumstances or conversations that may have tipped the scales one way or another.

Deuteronomy 1:26–46

The Israelites had added to their rebellion against God by misinterpreting his attitude toward them and their unbelief in his promises (v. 26). "The LORD hates us," they grumbled (v. 27), when in truth he loved them.

forefathers, [36]except Caleb son of Jephunneh. He will see it, and I will give him and his descendants the land he set his feet on, because he followed the LORD whole-heartedly. [o]"

[37]Because of you the LORD became angry[p] with me also and said, "You shall not enter[q] it, either. [38]But your assistant, Joshua[r] son of Nun, will enter it. Encourage[s] him, because he will lead[t] Israel to inherit it. [39]And the little ones that you said would be taken captive,[u] your children who do not yet know[v] good from bad—they will enter the land. I will give it to them and they will take possession of it. [40]But as for you, turn around and set out toward the desert along the route to the Red Sea.[a w]"

[41]Then you replied, "We have sinned against the LORD. We will go up and fight, as the LORD our God commanded us." So every one of you put on his weapons, thinking it easy to go up into the hill country.

[42]But the LORD said to me, "Tell them, 'Do not go up and fight, because I will not be with you. You will be defeated by your enemies.' "[x]

[43]So I told you, but you would not listen. You rebelled against the LORD's command and in your arrogance you marched up into the hill country. [44]The Amorites who lived in those hills came out against you; they chased you like a swarm of bees[y] and beat you down from Seir all the way to Hormah. [45]You came back and wept before the LORD, but he paid no attention to your weeping and turned a deaf ear to you. [46]And so you stayed in Kadesh[z] many days—all the time you spent there.

Wanderings in the Desert

2 Then we turned back and set out toward the desert along the route to the Red Sea,[a a] as the LORD had directed me. For a long time we made our way around the hill country of Seir.

[2]Then the LORD said to me, [3]"You have made your way around this hill country long enough; now turn north. [4]Give the people these orders:[b] 'You are about to pass through the territory of your brothers the descendants of Esau, who live in Seir. They will be afraid of you, but be very careful. [5]Do not provoke them to war, for I will not give you any of their land, not even enough to put your foot on. I have given Esau the hill country of Seir as his own.[c] [6]You are to pay them in silver for the food you eat and the water you drink.' "

[7]The LORD your God has blessed you in all the work of your hands. He has watched[d] over your journey through this vast desert. These forty years the LORD your God has been with you, and you have not lacked anything.

[8]So we went on past our brothers the descendants of Esau, who live in Seir. We

Cross references (left margin):

1:36 o Nu 14:24; Jos 14:9
1:37 p Dt 3:26; 4:21 q Nu 20:12
1:38 r Nu 14:30 s Dt 31:7 t Dt 3:28
1:39 u Nu 14:3 v Isa 7:15-16
1:40 w Nu 14:25
1:42 x Nu 14:41-43
1:44 y Ps 118:12
1:46 z Nu 20:1; Jdg 11:17
2:1 a Nu 21:4
2:4 b Nu 20:14-21
2:5 c Ge 36:8; Jos 24:4
2:7 d Dt 8:2-4

---

[a] 40,1 Hebrew *Yam Suph*; that is, Sea of Reeds

The Israelites had gone on to complain that God had brought them out of Egypt to destroy them by Amorite hands. The contrary was true; when they later advanced in obedience, God gave them victory over the Amorites (2:26—3:11). But their complaint, in the short run, became a self-fulfilling prophecy: When they presumptuously attacked the Amorites after their rebellion, the Israelites were routed (1:41–44).

Did you as a child ever accuse your parents of "hating" you following discipline or disappointment? Have you ever accused God of the same thing? In some sense the word *grown-up* is a misnomer. As we mature physically, most of us also develop intellectually, emotionally, and spiritually. But if we look honestly in the mirror, we are likely to see a remnant of our younger selves pouting over some perceived injustice. Why not take a moment, right now, to tell God how much you appreciate his love and care—and how deeply you love him in return!

Deuteronomy 2:1–23

The Lord instructed Moses not to engage the Edomites, Moabites, and Ammonites in battle as Israel passed through or near their territories. These nations were ancient relatives of Israel—Edom through Jacob's brother Esau, Moab and Ammon through the two sons of Abraham's nephew Lot. God had given the descendants of Esau and Lot their lands, just as he was giving the Israelites the land of Canaan.

Throughout their 40-year journey, the Lord had supplied the Israelites with manna and water as needed. Now they were to buy food and water as they moved through Edomite territory (v. 6). God's provision of manna wouldn't completely cease until the day after the first celebration of the Passover at Gilgal in Canaan under Joshua (Josh. 5:10–12), but he may have gradually phased it out. Exodus 16:35 says that the people ate manna "until they reached the border of Canaan."

turned from the Arabah road, which comes up from Elath and Ezion Geber, *e* and traveled along the desert road of Moab. *f*

⁹Then the LORD said to me, "Do not harass the Moabites or provoke them to war, for I will not give you any part of their land. I have given Ar *g* to the descendants of Lot *h* as a possession."

¹⁰(The Emites *i* used to live there—a people strong and numerous, and as tall as the Anakites. *j* ¹¹Like the Anakites, they too were considered Rephaites, but the Moabites called them Emites. ¹²Horites used to live in Seir, but the descendants of Esau drove them out. They destroyed the Horites from before them and settled in their place, just as Israel did *k* in the land the LORD gave them as their possession.)

¹³And the LORD said, "Now get up and cross the Zered Valley." So we crossed the valley.

¹⁴Thirty-eight years passed from the time we left Kadesh Barnea *l* until we crossed the Zered Valley. By then, that entire generation *m* of fighting men had perished from the camp, as the LORD had sworn to them. *n* ¹⁵The LORD's hand was against them until he had completely eliminated *o* them from the camp.

¹⁶Now when the last of these fighting men among the people had died, ¹⁷the LORD said to me, ¹⁸"Today you are to pass by the region of Moab at Ar. ¹⁹When you come to the Ammonites, *p* do not harass them or provoke them to war, for I will not give you possession of any land belonging to the Ammonites. I have given it as a possession to the descendants of Lot. *q*"

²⁰(That too was considered a land of the Rephaites, who used to live there; but the Ammonites called them Zamzummites. ²¹They were a people strong and numerous, and as tall as the Anakites. *r* The LORD destroyed them from before the Ammonites, who drove them out and settled in their place. ²²The LORD had done the same for the descendants of Esau, who lived in Seir, *s* when he destroyed the Horites from before them. They drove them out and have lived in their place to this day. ²³And as for the Avvites *t* who lived in villages as far as Gaza, the Caphtorites *u* coming out from Caphtor *a v* destroyed them and settled in their place.)

Defeat of Sihon King of Heshbon

²⁴"Set out now and cross the Arnon Gorge. *w* See, I have given into your hand Sihon the Amorite, king of Heshbon, and his country. Begin to take possession of it and engage him in battle. ²⁵This very day I will begin to put the terror *x* and fear *y* of you on all the nations under heaven. They will hear reports of you and will tremble *z* and be in anguish because of you."

²⁶From the desert of Kedemoth I sent messengers to Sihon king of Heshbon of-

a 23 That is, Crete

Cross references (margin)

2:8 *e* 1Ki 9:26 *f* Jdg 11:18
2:9 *g* Nu 21:15 *h* Ge 19:36-38
2:10 *i* Ge 14:5 *j* Nu 13:22,33
2:12 *k* ver 22
2:14 *l* Nu 13:26 *m* Nu 14:29-35 *n* Dt 1:34-35
2:15 *o* Ps 106:26
2:19 *p* Ge 19:38 *q* ver 9
2:21 *r* ver 10
2:22 *s* Ge 36:8
2:23 *t* Jos 13:3 *u* Ge 10:14 *v* Am 9:7
2:24 *w* Nu 21:13-14; Jdg 11:13,18
2:25 *x* Dt 11:25 *y* Jos 2:9,11 *z* Ex 15:14-16

📖 When has God unexpectedly, even miraculously, supplied you with some sort of "manna"—something you urgently needed, exactly when you needed it? Conversely, how can you relate to the Israelites' transition to Canaan, as they were in a sense "weaned" from God's miraculous provision? Is there an area of your life in which God currently may be developing maturity in you along these lines?

Deuteronomy 2:24–37

📖 Israel wasn't to disturb the Edomites, Moabites, or Ammonites (see previous "There and Then"), but this prohibition didn't extend to the Amorites. Sihon of his own conscious will refused Israel passage, though God "had made his spirit stubborn and his heart obstinate" (v. 30). Moses was certain that God would, in his own way, give his people victory over the Amorites. In this instance God allowed them to take plunder. Later on he would, in certain situations, demand total destruction (cf. the stories of Achan in Josh. 7 and Saul in 1 Sam. 15).

📖 Many Christians today find it hard to identify the God of the Old Testament with the God of the New (except perhaps in rare NT instances like the deaths of Ananias and Sapphira and Herod; Acts 5:1–11; 12:19–23). The complete annihilation of a people group like the Amorites, including women and children, strikes them as unfair.

Yet we know from other Old Testament sources that such destruction was generally the result of long-delayed judgment. In fact, 400 years earlier God had promised Abraham that his descendants would possess the land of the Amorites when the Amorites' sin had "reached its full measure" (Gen. 15:16–21). This hostile people's idolatrous practices included religious prostitution and human sacrifice—sometimes even of their own children. Still, as God said through Ezekiel, "I take no pleasure in the death of the wicked, but rather that they turn from their ways and live" (Ezek. 33:11; cf. 2 Peter 3:9; see also "There and Then" for 7:1–26).

2:27
a Nu 21:21-22
2:28
b Nu 20:19

2:30
c Jos 11:20
d Ex 4:21;
Nu 21:23; Ro 9:18

2:31
e Dt 1:8
2:32
f Nu 21:23
2:33
g Dt 29:7

2:34
h Dt 3:6; 7:2

2:36
i Dt 3:12; 4:48;
Jos 13:9 / Ps 44:3

2:37
k ver 18-19
l Nu 21:24
m Ge 32:22;
Dt 3:16

3:1
n Nu 21:33
3:2
o Nu 21:34

3:3
p Nu 21:35

3:4
q 1Ki 4:13

3:6
r Dt 2:24,34

3:9
s Dt 4:48; Ps 29:6
t 1Ch 5:23
3:10
u Jos 13:11
3:11
v Ge 14:5
w 2Sa 12:26;
Jer 49:2

fering peace and saying, 27"Let us pass through your country. We will stay on the main road; we will not turn aside to the right or to the left. a 28Sell us food to eat and water to drink for their price in silver. Only let us pass through on foot b— 29as the descendants of Esau, who live in Seir, and the Moabites, who live in Ar, did for us—until we cross the Jordan into the land the LORD our God is giving us." 30But Sihon king of Heshbon refused to let us pass through. For the LORD c your God had made his spirit stubborn d and his heart obstinate in order to give him into your hands, as he has now done.

31The LORD said to me, "See, I have begun to deliver Sihon and his country over to you. Now begin to conquer and possess his land." e

32When Sihon and all his army came out to meet us in battle f at Jahaz, 33the LORD our God delivered him over to us and we struck him down, g together with his sons and his whole army. 34At that time we took all his towns and completely destroyed a h them—men, women and children. We left no survivors. 35But the livestock and the plunder from the towns we had captured we carried off for ourselves. 36From Aroer i on the rim of the Arnon Gorge, and from the town in the gorge, even as far as Gilead, not one town was too strong for us. The LORD our God gave j us all of them. 37But in accordance with the command of the LORD our God, k you did not encroach on any of the land of the Ammonites, l neither the land along the course of the Jabbok m nor that around the towns in the hills.

Defeat of Og King of Bashan

3 Next we turned and went up along the road toward Bashan, and Og king of Bashan with his whole army marched out to meet us in battle at Edrei. n 2The LORD said to me, "Do not be afraid o of him, for I have handed him over to you with his whole army and his land. Do to him what you did to Sihon king of the Amorites, who reigned in Heshbon."

3So the LORD our God also gave into our hands Og king of Bashan and all his army. We struck them down, leaving no survivors. p 4At that time we took all his cities. There was not one of the sixty cities that we did not take from them—the whole region of Argob, Og's kingdom in Bashan. q 5All these cities were fortified with high walls and with gates and bars, and there were also a great many unwalled villages. 6We completely destroyed a them, as we had done with Sihon king of Heshbon, destroying a r every city—men, women and children. 7But all the livestock and the plunder from their cities we carried off for ourselves.

8So at that time we took from these two kings of the Amorites the territory east of the Jordan, from the Arnon Gorge as far as Mount Hermon. 9(Hermon is called Sirion s by the Sidonians; the Amorites call it Senir.) t 10We took all the towns on the plateau, and all Gilead, and all Bashan as far as Salecah u and Edrei, towns of Og's kingdom in Bashan. 11(Only Og king of Bashan was left of the remnant of the Rephaites. v His bed b was made of iron and was more than thirteen feet long and six feet wide. c It is still in Rabbah w of the Ammonites.)

a 34,6 The Hebrew term refers to the irrevocable giving over of things or persons to the LORD, often by totally destroying them.   b 11 Or sarcophagus   c 11 Hebrew nine cubits long and four cubits wide (about 4 meters long and 1.8 meters wide)

Deuteronomy 3:1–11

Israel's advance continued by pressing north to engage a second Amorite king, the king of Bashan. The 60 cities "fortified with high walls and with gates and bars" (v. 5) were formidable obstacles. They were later referred to as "large walled cities" (1 Kings 4:13), implying that this area was heavily populated. The remarkable success of their capture was fixed in Israel's memory (see Num. 32:33; Josh. 9:10; Ps. 135:10–11; 136:18–22), no doubt giving the people courage as they

undertook the conquest of Canaan.

When has God given you remarkable success in a particular venture? Has the event fed your ego—or nurtured your love and trust for your heavenly Provider? As Paul reminded the Corinthians, "Let him who boasts boast in the Lord" (1 Cor. 1:31). Paul was quoting God's words through the prophet Jeremiah, who went on to say: "Let him who boasts boast about this: that he understands and knows me" (Jer. 9:24). Ultimately, only our relationship with God is worth bragging about!

Division of the Land

12Of the land that we took over at that time, I gave the Reubenites and the Gadites the territory north of Aroer[x] by the Arnon Gorge, including half the hill country of Gilead, together with its towns. 13The rest of Gilead and also all of Bashan, the kingdom of Og, I gave to the half-tribe of Manasseh. (The whole region of Argob in Bashan used to be known as a land of the Rephaites. 14Jair,[y] a descendant of Manasseh, took the whole region of Argob as far as the border of the Geshurites and the Maacathites; it was named after him, so that to this day Bashan is called Havvoth Jair.[a]) 15And I gave Gilead to Makir.[z] 16But to the Reubenites and the Gadites I gave the territory extending from Gilead down to the Arnon Gorge (the middle of the gorge being the border) and out to the Jabbok River,[a] which is the border of the Ammonites. 17Its western border was the Jordan in the Arabah, from Kinnereth[b] to the Sea of the Arabah (the Salt Sea[b c]), below the slopes of Pisgah.

18I commanded you at that time: "The LORD your God has given you this land to take possession of it. But all your able-bodied men, armed for battle, must cross over ahead of your brother Israelites.[d] 19However, your wives, your children and your livestock (I know you have much livestock) may stay in the towns I have given you, 20until the LORD gives rest to your brothers as he has to you, and they too have taken over the land that the LORD your God is giving them, across the Jordan. After that, each of you may go back to the possession I have given you."

Moses Forbidden to Cross the Jordan

21At that time I commanded Joshua: "You have seen with your own eyes all that the LORD your God has done to these two kings. The LORD will do the same to all the kingdoms over there where you are going. 22Do not be afraid[e] of them; the LORD your God himself will fight[f] for you."

23At that time I pleaded with the LORD: 24"O Sovereign LORD, you have begun to show to your servant your greatness[g] and your strong hand. For what god[h] is there in heaven or on earth who can do the deeds and mighty works[i] you do?[j] 25Let me go over and see the good land[k] beyond the Jordan—that fine hill country and Lebanon. 26But because of you the LORD was angry[l] with me and would not listen to me. "That is enough," the LORD said. "Do not speak to me anymore about this matter. 27Go up to the top of Pisgah and look west and north and south and east. Look at the land with your own eyes, since you are not going to cross this Jordan.[m] 28But commission[n] Joshua, and encourage and strengthen him, for he will lead this peo-

[a] 14 Or called the settlements of Jair   [b] 17 That is, the Dead Sea

3:12 [x] Nu 32:32-38; Dt 2:36; Jos 13:8-13
3:14 [y] Nu 32:41; 1Ch 2:22
3:15 [z] Nu 32:39-40
3:16 [a] Nu 21:24
3:17 [b] Nu 34:11; Jos 13:27 [c] Ge 14:3; Jos 12:3
3:18 [d] Nu 32:17
3:22 [e] Dt 1:29 [f] Ex 14:14; Dt 20:4
3:24 [g] Dt 11:2 [h] Ex 15:11; Ps 86:8 [i] Ps 71:16,19 [j] 2Sa 7:22
3:25 [k] Dt 4:22
3:26 [l] Dt 1:37; 31:2
3:27 [m] Nu 27:12
3:28 [n] Nu 27:18-23

Deuteronomy 3:12–20

We know from Numbers 32 that the tribes of Reuben and Gad and half the tribe of Manasseh desired to settle in the lands taken from the Amorites rather than proceed into Canaan proper. Moses affirmed that God had given them this territory east of the Jordan but reminded them of their responsibility to help the rest of the Israelites win their land. All the "able-bodied men, armed for battle" (v. 18) apparently represented a special body of soldiers. Some armed men no doubt remained in Transjordan to protect the women and children.

Beyond your immediate family, with whom do you identify most closely? Is your "community"—the group to whom you belong—primarily your church family, your neighborhood, your extended family, your circle of friends? Are you fiercely loyal to your country? Does the family of God (the worldwide church) hold a special place in your heart? Is your perspective global, in that you love all human beings created in God's image? Chances are, several of the above apply. How much are you willing to sacrifice for others?

Deuteronomy 3:21–29

Two subjects are intertwined in these verses: the commissioning and encouragement of Joshua and God's denial of Moses' plea to enter the land. The Lord directed Moses to climb to the top of Pisgah to get an "aerial view" of the promised land. Moses would do so after he had delivered the messages of Deuteronomy to prepare the people for life in the land and entrusted Israel's leadership to Joshua.

So close, and yet so far! Do you view God's act of allowing Moses to see the land as a reluctant concession, a reminder of the cost of disobedience—or as a loving touch of God's grace? Deuteronomy 34:1–5 gives a brief account of Moses' climb up Mount Nebo "to the top of Pisgah," his glimpse of the awesome panorama laid out before him, and his death. Indications are that Moses was at least resigned to God's decision; he continued to function until the end as the great prophet/leader he was.

3:28
o Dt 31:3,23
3:29
p Dt 4:46; 34:6

ple across[o] and will cause them to inherit the land that you will see." [29]So we stayed in the valley near Beth Peor.[p]

Obedience Commanded

4:1
q Dt 5:33; 8:1;
16:20; 30:15-20;
Eze 20:11; Ro 10:5
4:2
r Dt 12:32; Jos 1:7;
Rev 22:18-19
4:3
s Nu 25:1-9;
Ps 106:28

4 Hear now, O Israel, the decrees and laws I am about to teach you. Follow them so that you may live[q] and may go in and take possession of the land that the LORD, the God of your fathers, is giving you. [2]Do not add[r] to what I command you and do not subtract from it, but keep the commands of the LORD your God that I give you.

[3]You saw with your own eyes what the LORD did at Baal Peor.[s] The LORD your God destroyed from among you everyone who followed the Baal of Peor, [4]but all of you who held fast to the LORD your God are still alive today.

4:6
t Dt 30:19-20;
Ps 19:7; Pr 1:7
u Job 28:28
4:7
v 2Sa 7:23
w Ps 46:1; Isa 55:6

[5]See, I have taught you decrees and laws as the LORD my God commanded me, so that you may follow them in the land you are entering to take possession of it. [6]Observe them carefully, for this will show your wisdom[t] and understanding to the nations, who will hear about all these decrees and say, "Surely this great nation is a wise and understanding people."[u] [7]What other nation is so great[v] as to have their gods near[w] them the way the LORD our God is near us whenever we pray to him? [8]And what other nation is so great as to have such righteous decrees and laws as this body of laws I am setting before you today?

4:9
x Pr 4:23
y Ge 18:19; Eph 6:4
z Ps 78:5-6

[9]Only be careful,[x] and watch yourselves closely so that you do not forget the things your eyes have seen or let them slip from your heart as long as you live. Teach[y] them to your children[z] and to their children after them. [10]Remember the day you stood before the LORD your God at Horeb,[a] when he said to me, "Assemble the people before me to hear my words so that they may learn to revere me as long as they live in the land and may teach them to their children." [11]You came near and stood at the foot of the mountain while it blazed with fire[b] to the very heavens, with black clouds and deep darkness. [12]Then the LORD spoke[c] to you out of the fire. You heard the sound of words but saw no form; there was only a voice. [13]He declared to you his covenant,[d] the Ten Commandments,[e] which he commanded you to follow and then wrote them on two stone tablets. [14]And the LORD directed me at that time to teach you the decrees and laws you are to follow in the land that you are crossing the Jordan to possess.

4:10
a Ex 19:9,16

4:11
b Ex 19:18;
Heb 12:18-19
4:12
c Ex 20:22; Dt 5:4,
22
4:13
d Dt 9:9,11
e Ex 24:12; 31:18;
34:28

Deuteronomy 4:1–14

Moses was concerned not only that the generation before him learn the conditions of their covenant with the Lord (vv. 1–2,14) but that his hearers pass along these commands to the generations to come (vv. 9–10). Knowledge wouldn't be enough. The people had to "follow" God's requirements (vv. 1,5,13–14) and "observe them

carefully" (v. 6). Active obedience—then as now—is key.

What does God expect of us with respect to the church's upcoming generations? Whether or not you are currently in an active parenting role, what are you doing to facilitate the spiritual education and well-being of the younger members of your congregation and extended family?

4:1–2

Obedience

Deuteronomy is in many ways a law book. When Christians approach such a book, there is a "pre-law" requirement: obedience. Rather than reading Moses' first five books with a critical or skeptical attitude, we are to comply with what God tells us to do through them. Why?

Because God tells us to
• "Follow my decrees and be careful to obey my laws" (Lev. 25:18).
• "Though you used to be slaves to sin, you wholeheartedly obeyed" (Rom. 6:17).

In imitation of Jesus Christ
• "Not as I will, but as you will" (Matt. 26:39).

Because obedience is a sign of love and faith
• "If you love me, you will obey what I command" (John 14:15).
• "By faith Abraham . . . obeyed and went" (Heb. 11:8).

Because Jesus quoted Deuteronomy 6:5 as a foundational summary of the law

Because we will be rewarded
• "If you obey me fully and keep my covenant, then out of all nations you will be my treasured possession" (Ex. 19:5).

Because the Bible exalts those who obey God. Some examples:
• Noah, who built a big boat (Gen. 6:9)
• Abraham, who uprooted his family and home (Gen. 12:1–4)
• The psalmist, who wanted to follow God's laws (Ps. 119:30,100–106)
• Paul, who considered everything a loss, except what he did for God (Phil. 3:7–14)

Idolatry Forbidden

¹⁵You saw no form[f] of any kind the day the LORD spoke to you at Horeb out of the fire. Therefore watch yourselves very carefully,[g] ¹⁶so that you do not become corrupt and make for yourselves an idol,[h] an image of any shape, whether formed like a man or a woman, ¹⁷or like any animal on earth or any bird that flies in the air, ¹⁸or like any creature that moves along the ground or any fish in the waters below. ¹⁹And when you look up to the sky and see the sun,[i] the moon and the stars—all the heavenly array[j]—do not be enticed into bowing down to them and worshiping things the LORD your God has apportioned to all the nations under heaven. ²⁰But as for you, the LORD took you and brought you out of the iron-smelting furnace,[k] out of Egypt, to be the people of his inheritance,[l] as you now are.

²¹The LORD was angry with me[m] because of you, and he solemnly swore that I would not cross the Jordan and enter the good land the LORD your God is giving you as your inheritance. ²²I will die in this land; I will not cross the Jordan; but you are about to cross over and take possession of that good land.[n] ²³Be careful not to forget the covenant[o] of the LORD your God that he made with you; do not make for yourselves an idol[p] in the form of anything the LORD your God has forbidden. ²⁴For the LORD your God is a consuming fire,[q] a jealous God.

²⁵After you have had children and grandchildren and have lived in the land a long

4:15
f Isa 40:18
g Jos 23:11
4:16
h Ex 20:4-5; 32:7; Dt 5:8; Ro 1:23
4:19
i Dt 17:3; Job 31:26
j 2Ki 17:16; 21:3; Ro 1:25
4:20
k 1Ki 8:51; Jer 11:4
l Ex 19:5; Dt 9:29
4:21
m Nu 20:12; Dt 1:37
4:22
n Dt 3:25
4:23
o ver 9, 16 p Ex 20:4
4:24
q Ex 24:17; Dt 9:3; Heb 12:29

Deuteronomy 4:15–31

For the third time Moses referred to God's refusal to let him cross the Jordan and enter Canaan proper (1:37; 3:23–27). Each time he spoke of God's anger toward him "because of you." Moses had been punished for failing to honor the Lord before the people when he struck the rock twice to produce water (God had commanded him to speak to the rock; Num. 20:2–13). While not denying his own sin, Moses reasoned that the people's accusations about his bringing them to the desert to die of thirst were to blame for his action.

How easy is it for you to redirect the blame when God confronts you with your disobedience? This trend appears early in human history (cf. Gen. 3:1–13, noticing Eve's final stab in v. 13—the soon-to-become-classic "the devil made me do it!"). There is always a *reason* when we disobey. But in God's eyes there is never an *excuse*. It's critical that we as God's people understand the distinction.

Snapshots

 4:9

Grace

Grace facilitates the training of church leaders and Child Evangelism Fellowship teachers at local, cluster, and district levels, also gathering grassroots information on evangelism and leadership activities in project communities in Ghana. She runs a tight work schedule, yet still finds time to maintain contact with regional, district, and local heads of churches, as well as with evangelists and paraprofessional groups.

A typical working day for Grace begins with organizing morning devotions with her staff. A lover of children, she attends school outreach programs and later in the day monitors Bible clubs for children.

"O'Gra", as friends call her, started in her position in January, 2001. "It is God who gave me this job because he knows this is the type of work I like doing," she enthuses. "Child evangelism is my calling!" Grace also has been a Sunday school teacher for eight years at the Presbyterian church where she worships. She's taught religious and moral education at a training college and holds a bachelor's degree in education from the University of Cape Coast.

"My vision is to help build the capacity of rural church leaders and women in leadership skills and vocational training and that I would not be daunted by the challenges before me," Grace concludes.

> "My vision is to help build the capacity of rural church leaders and women in leadership skills and vocational training."

4:25
r 2Ki 17:2,17

4:26
s Dt 30:18-19;
Isa 1:2; Mic 6:2

4:27
t Lev 26:33;
Dt 28:36,64; Ne 1:8

4:28
u Dt 28:36,64;
1Sa 26:19;
Jer 16:13
v Ps 115:4-8;
135:15-18

4:29
w 2Ch 15:4;
Isa 55:6 x Jer 29:13
y Dt 30:1-3,10

4:30
z Dt 31:29;
Jer 23:20; Hos 3:5

4:31
a 2Ch 30:9;
Ne 9:31; Ps 116:5;
Jnh 4:2

4:32
b Dt 32:7; Job 8:8
c Ge 1:27
d Mt 24:31

4:33
e Ex 20:22; Dt 5:24-
26

4:34
f Ex 6:6 g Ex 7:3
h Dt 7:19; 26:8
i Ex 13:3 j Dt 34:12

4:35
k Dt 32:39; 1Sa 2:2;
Isa 45:5,18

4:36
l Ex 19:9,19

4:37
m Dt 10:15
n Ex 13:3,9,14

4:38
o Dt 7:1; 9:5

4:39
p ver 35; Jos 2:11

4:40
q Lev 22:31;
Dt 5:33 r Dt 5:16
s Dt 6:3,18;
Eph 6:2-3

time—if you then become corrupt and make any kind of idol, doing evil[r] in the eyes of the LORD your God and provoking him to anger, [26]I call heaven and earth as witnesses against you[s] this day that you will quickly perish from the land that you are crossing the Jordan to possess. You will not live there long but will certainly be destroyed. [27]The LORD will scatter[t] you among the peoples, and only a few of you will survive among the nations to which the LORD will drive you. [28]There you will worship man-made gods[u] of wood and stone, which cannot see or hear or eat or smell.[v] [29]But if from there you seek[w] the LORD your God, you will find him if you look for him with all your heart[x] and with all your soul.[y] [30]When you are in distress and all these things have happened to you, then in later days[z] you will return to the LORD your God and obey him. [31]For the LORD your God is a merciful[a] God; he will not abandon or destroy you or forget the covenant with your forefathers, which he confirmed to them by oath.

The LORD Is God

[32]Ask[b] now about the former days, long before your time, from the day God created man on the earth;[c] ask from one end of the heavens to the other.[d] Has anything so great as this ever happened, or has anything like it ever been heard of? [33]Has any other people heard the voice of God[a] speaking out of fire, as you have, and lived?[e] [34]Has any god ever tried to take for himself one nation out of another nation,[f] by testings, by miraculous signs[g] and wonders,[h] by war, by a mighty hand and an outstretched arm,[i] or by great and awesome deeds,[j] like all the things the LORD your God did for you in Egypt before your very eyes?

[35]You were shown these things so that you might know that the LORD is God; besides him there is no other.[k] [36]From heaven he made you hear his voice[l] to discipline you. On earth he showed you his great fire, and you heard his words from out of the fire. [37]Because he loved[m] your forefathers and chose their descendants after them, he brought you out of Egypt by his Presence and his great strength,[n] [38]to drive out before you nations greater and stronger than you and to bring you into their land to give it to you for your inheritance,[o] as it is today.

[39]Acknowledge and take to heart this day that the LORD is God in heaven above and on the earth below. There is no other.[p] [40]Keep[q] his decrees and commands, which I am giving you today, so that it may go well[r] with you and your children after you and that you may live long[s] in the land the LORD your God gives you for all time.

Cities of Refuge

[41]Then Moses set aside three cities east of the Jordan, [42]to which anyone who had killed a person could flee if he had unintentionally killed his neighbor without malice aforethought. He could flee into one of these cities and save his life. [43]The cities were these: Bezer in the desert plateau, for the Reubenites; Ramoth in Gilead, for the Gadites; and Golan in Bashan, for the Manassites.

---

a 33 Or of a god

Deuteronomy 4:32-40

God's love for his people finds expression in verse 37. The reference to his choice of the Israelites, based on his love for their forefathers, as well as to his gift of Canaan as an inheritance, goes back to his covenant with Abraham and its promises (Gen. 12:1-3; 17:4-8; 18:18-19). This love theme will be developed further in Deuteronomy 7:8-9, 10:15, and 23:5. Deuteronomy also urges love for God from his people (6:5; 7:9; 10:12; 11:1,13,22; 13:3; 19:9; 30:6,16,20).

Moses' mention of God's covenant love in verse 37 reminds us of the apostle John's writings—such as "We love because [God] first loved us" (1 Jn. 4:19) and

Jesus' words, "If you love me, you will obey what I command" (John 14:15). What's the basis for your obedience to God?

Deuteronomy 4:41-43

These verses are a historical observation sandwiched between two addresses by Moses, probably because the cities were chosen at this particular time. Each side of the Jordan was given three cities of refuge. These six cities were among those also assigned to the Levites, where the intent of God's law would hopefully be known and followed. Regulations regarding appropriate use of these cities are spelled out in 19:1-13 and Numbers 35:9-34.

Introduction to the Law

44This is the law Moses set before the Israelites. **45**These are the stipulations, decrees and laws Moses gave them when they came out of Egypt **46**and were in the valley near Beth Peor east of the Jordan, in the land of Sihon[t] king of the Amorites, who reigned in Heshbon and was defeated by Moses and the Israelites as they came out of Egypt. **47**They took possession of his land and the land of Og king of Bashan, the two Amorite kings east of the Jordan. **48**This land extended from Aroer[u] on the rim of the Arnon Gorge to Mount Siyon[a][v] (that is, Hermon), **49**and included all the Arabah east of the Jordan, as far as the Sea of the Arabah,[b] below the slopes of Pisgah.

The Ten Commandments

5 Moses summoned all Israel and said:
Hear, O Israel, the decrees and laws I declare in your hearing today. Learn them and be sure to follow them. **2**The LORD our God made a covenant[w] with us at Horeb. **3**It was not with our fathers that the LORD made this covenant, but with us, with all of us who are alive here today.[x] **4**The LORD spoke[y] to you face to face out of the fire on the mountain. **5**(At that time I stood between[z] the LORD and you to declare to you the word of the LORD, because you were afraid[a] of the fire and did not go up the mountain.) And he said:

6"I am the LORD your God, who brought you out of Egypt, out of the land of slavery.

7"You shall have no other gods before[c] me.

8"You shall not make for yourself an idol in the form of anything in heaven above or on the earth beneath or in the waters below. **9**You shall not bow down to them or worship them; for I, the LORD your God, am a jealous God, punishing the children for the sin of the fathers to the third and fourth generation of those who hate me,[b] **10**but showing love to a thousand ⌊generations⌋ of those who love me and keep my commandments.[c]

11"You shall not misuse the name of the LORD your God, for the LORD will not hold anyone guiltless who misuses his name.[d]

12"Observe the Sabbath day by keeping it holy,[e] as the LORD your God has commanded you. **13**Six days you shall labor and do all your work, **14**but the seventh day[f] is a Sabbath to the LORD your God. On it you shall not do any work, neither you, nor your son or daughter, nor your manservant or

4:46 [t] Nu 21:26; Dt 3:29
4:48 [u] Dt 2:36 [v] Dt 3:9
5:2 [w] Ex 19:5
5:3 [x] Heb 8:9
5:4 [y] Dt 4:12,33,36
5:5 [z] Gal 3:19 [a] Ex 20:18,21
5:9 [b] Ex 34:7
5:10 [c] Jer 32:18
5:11 [d] Lev 19:12; Mt 5:33-37
5:12 [e] Ex 20:8
5:14 [f] Ge 2:2; Heb 4:4

[a] 48 Hebrew; Syriac (see also Deut. 3:9) *Sirion*   [b] 49 That is, the Dead Sea   [c] 7 Or *besides*

The cities of refuge were God's provision of mercy for those responsible for accidental deaths. Yet God was and is just as concerned about justice, and no culture can lay claim to an unblemished track record of consistently protecting its innocent or punishing the guilty. We do well to remember that it's just as unfair to ignore misconduct as it is to make unfounded presumptions about guilt. Are matters of justice and mercy priorities for you (Matt. 23:23)?

Deuteronomy 4:44–49

As reflected in the NIV heading, this passage may have been an introduction to the law as Moses would outline it in chapters 5–26. But it may also have been a summary of what he had already stated. The material in this short passage relates both to what Moses had said and would say. The book of Deuteronomy tends to repeat itself (e.g., cf. this paragraph with 1:1–5)—probably for emphasis and instruction. It may help us to remember that these details were being passed along orally, not in a written form for easy reference.

Does your mind "boggle" when you think of the amount of information the Israelites were expected to remember? Yet how many of the laws of your own land do you find it necessary to "look up"? Other than a possible quick review for the written test to renew your driver's license, probably none. Ignorance of the law has never been an excuse, but the repetitions in the Pentateuch clue us in to the fact that God made whatever provisions were necessary to ensure that his people didn't sin based on lack of knowledge. Then as now, many specific laws are based on overriding principles of humane behavior that make sense either universally or in a particular culture.

Deuteronomy 5:1–33

The already familiar Ten Commandments (cf. Ex. 20:1–17) sit appropriately at the beginning of Moses' explanation of God's basic legislation for the Israelites. These commands weren't just to be learned but also to be obeyed. They came directly from the Lord—the same God who had brought his people up from Egypt, the land of slavery. Their relationship with God was rooted in history, a history of his intervention on their behalf.

maidservant, nor your ox, your donkey or any of your animals, nor the alien within your gates, so that your manservant and maidservant may rest, as you do. [15]Remember that you were slaves in Egypt and that the LORD your God brought you out of there with a mighty hand and an outstretched arm.[g] Therefore the LORD your God has commanded you to observe the Sabbath day.

[16]"Honor your father and your mother,[h] as the LORD your God has commanded you, so that you may live long[i] and that it may go well with you in the land the LORD your God is giving you.

[17]"You shall not murder.[j]

[18]"You shall not commit adultery.[k]

[19]"You shall not steal.

[20]"You shall not give false testimony against your neighbor.

[21]"You shall not covet your neighbor's wife. You shall not set your desire on your neighbor's house or land, his manservant or maidservant, his ox or donkey, or anything that belongs to your neighbor."[l]

[22]These are the commandments the LORD proclaimed in a loud voice to your whole assembly there on the mountain from out of the fire, the cloud and the deep darkness; and he added nothing more. Then he wrote them on two stone tablets[m] and gave them to me.

[23]When you heard the voice out of the darkness, while the mountain was ablaze with fire, all the leading men of your tribes and your elders came to me. [24]And you said, "The LORD our God has shown us his glory and his majesty, and we have heard his voice from the fire. Today we have seen that a man can live even if God speaks with him.[n] [25]But now, why should we die? This great fire will consume us, and we will die if we hear the voice of the LORD our God any longer.[o] [26]For what mortal man has ever heard the voice of the living God speaking out of fire, as we have, and survived?[p] [27]Go near and listen to all that the LORD our God says. Then tell us whatever the LORD our God tells you. We will listen and obey."

[28]The LORD heard you when you spoke to me and the LORD said to me, "I have heard what this people said to you. Everything they said was good.[q] [29]Oh, that their hearts would be inclined to fear me[r] and keep all my commands[s] always, so that it might go well with them and their children forever![t]

[30]"Go, tell them to return to their tents. [31]But you stay here[u] with me so that I may give you all the commands, decrees and laws you are to teach them to follow in the land I am giving them to possess."

[32]So be careful to do what the LORD your God has commanded you; do not turn aside to the right or to the left.[v] [33]Walk in all the way that the LORD your God has commanded you,[w] so that you may live and prosper and prolong your days[x] in the land that you will possess.

Love the LORD Your God

6 These are the commands, decrees and laws the LORD your God directed me to teach you to observe in the land that you are crossing the Jordan to possess, [2]so

---

Cross references (margin)

5:15
g Dt 4:34

5:16
h Ex 20:12;
Lev 19:3; Dt 27:16;
Eph 6:2-3*;
Col 3:20 / Dt 4:40

5:17
i Mt 5:21-22*

5:18
k Mt 5:27-30;
Lk 18:20*;
Jas 2:11*

5:21
l Ro 7:7*; 13:9*

5:22
m Ex 24:12; 31:18;
Dt 4:13

5:24
n Ex 19:19
5:25
o Dt 18:16

5:26
p Dt 4:33

5:28
q Dt 18:17
5:29
r Ps 81:8,13
s Dt 11:1; Isa 48:18
t Dt 4:1,40
5:31
u Ex 24:12

5:32
v Dt 17:11,20;
28:14; Jos 1:7;
23:6; Pr 4:27
5:33
w Jer 7:23
x Dt 4:40

⌨ "He added nothing more" (v. 22) refers to the Ten Commandments that were spoken and then written by God on two stone tablets. They constitute the basic behavioral code that would determine the people's loyalty and lifestyle—for all succeeding generations. No other short list of commands begins to compare with the effect these have had on world history. In spite of being constantly broken, they stand as the moral code gold standard. Think about the scope of the laws of your land. How many find their moral basis in one or another of these ten directives?

Deuteronomy 6:1–25

🔗 The shades of meaning of the Hebrew word for "fear" (vv. 2,13,24) may confuse readers. Being afraid is sometimes a factor—as in the Israelites' experience at Mount Sinai with its thunder, lightning, earthquake, and darkness (cf. 5:22–25). But the sensation of standing in awe of God and then of holding him in the highest reverence and respect is essential to an understanding of "fearing God" in Deuteronomy. In Israelite literature, the "fear of the LORD" denotes a right relationship with God. The same idea is here—though not developed as fully as, for example, in Psalms and Proverbs.

that you, your children and their children after them may fear[y] the LORD your God as long as you live by keeping all his decrees and commands that I give you, and so that you may enjoy long life. [3]Hear, O Israel, and be careful to obey so that it may go well with you and that you may increase greatly[z] in a land flowing with milk and honey,[a] just as the LORD, the God of your fathers, promised you.

[4]Hear, O Israel: The LORD our God, the LORD is one.[a][b] [5]Love[c] the LORD your God with all your heart and with all your soul and with all your strength.[d] [6]These commandments that I give you today are to be upon your hearts.[e] [7]Impress them on your children. Talk about them when you sit at home and when you walk along the road, when you lie down and when you get up.[f] [8]Tie them as symbols on your hands and bind them on your foreheads.[g] [9]Write them on the doorframes of your houses and on your gates.[h]

[10]When the LORD your God brings you into the land he swore to your fathers, to Abraham, Isaac and Jacob, to give you—a land with large, flourishing cities you did not build,[i] [11]houses filled with all kinds of good things you did not provide, wells you did not dig, and vineyards and olive groves you did not plant—then when you eat and are satisfied,[j] [12]be careful that you do not forget the LORD, who brought you out of Egypt, out of the land of slavery.

[13]Fear the LORD[k] your God, serve him only[l] and take your oaths in his name. [14]Do not follow other gods, the gods of the peoples around you; [15]for the LORD your God[m], who is among you, is a jealous God and his anger will burn against you, and he will destroy you from the face of the land. [16]Do not test the LORD your God[n] as you did at Massah. [17]Be sure to keep the commands of the LORD your God and the stipulations and decrees he has given you.[o] [18]Do what is right and good in the LORD's sight, so that it may go well[p] with you and you may go in and take over the good land that the LORD promised on oath to your forefathers, [19]thrusting out all your enemies before you, as the LORD said.

[20]In the future, when your son asks you,[q] "What is the meaning of the stipulations, decrees and laws the LORD our God has commanded you?" [21]tell him: "We were slaves of Pharaoh in Egypt, but the LORD brought us out of Egypt with a mighty hand. [22]Before our eyes the LORD sent miraculous signs and wonders—great and terrible—upon Egypt and Pharaoh and his whole household. [23]But he brought us out from there to bring us in and give us the land that he promised on oath to our forefathers. [24]The LORD commanded us to obey all these decrees and to fear the LORD our God,[r] so that we might always prosper and be kept alive, as is the case today.[s] [25]And if we are careful to obey all this law before the LORD our God, as he has commanded us, that will be our righteousness.[t]"

Driving Out the Nations

7 When the LORD your God brings you into the land you are entering to possess and drives out before you many nations[u]—the Hittites, Girgashites, Amorites, Canaanites, Perizzites, Hivites and Jebusites, seven nations larger and stronger than you— [2]and when the LORD your God has delivered them over to you and you have

[a] 4 Or *The LORD our God is one LORD*; or *The LORD is our God, the LORD is one*; or *The LORD is our God, the LORD alone*

Verse 4 (the well-known *Shema*; lit., "hear") declared that there is only one true God. God couldn't be known or acknowledged in other forms like the Canaanite Baals. There was only one Lord, and he alone was God. He was *Israel's* God, the God with whom Israel had entered into a covenant.

The Israelites were to love God totally—with all their heart, soul, mind, and strength. Verse 5 doesn't invite us to dissect and analyze the intellectual, emotional, and physical dimensions of people. The three Hebrew words (and their NT Greek counterparts) all point to the

totality of human experience. Together they represent relating to God with our whole selves. We might express such "no holds barred" commitment in terms like giving everything we have got or putting our heart and soul into a relationship or endeavor.

Deuteronomy 7:1–26

God would drive out the Canaanites and "deliver them over to" Israel, but the Israelite army would be his usual instrument. An exception would be the "hornet" of verse 20, which was likely a symbolic reference to a sense of fear, panic, or discouragement the Lord

---

Cross references (margin):

6:2 y Ex 20:20; Dt 10:12-13
6:3 z Dt 5:33 a Ex 3:8
6:4 b Mk 12:29*; 1Co 8:4
6:5 c Mt 22:37*; Mk 12:30*; Lk 10:27* d Dt 10:12
6:6 e Dt 11:18
6:7 f Dt 4:9; 11:19; Eph 6:4
6:8 g Ex 13:9,16; Dt 11:18
6:9 h Dt 11:20
6:10 i Jos 24:13
6:11 j Dt 8:10
6:13 k Dt 10:20 l Mt 4:10*; Lk 4:8*
6:15 m Dt 4:24
6:16 n Ex 17:7; Mt 4:7*; Lk 4:12*
6:17 o Dt 11:22; Ps 119:4
6:18 p Dt 4:40
6:20 q Ex 13:14
6:24 r Dt 10:12; Jer 32:39 s Ps 41:2
6:25 t Dt 24:13; Ro 10:3,5
7:1 u Dt 31:3; Ac 13:19

7:2
v Ex 23:32
w Dt 13:8
7:3
x Ex 34:15-16;
Ezr 9:2
7:4
y Dt 6:15

7:5
z Ex 23:24;
Dt 12:2-3
7:6
a Ex 19:5-6; 1Pe 2:9
b Ps 50:5; Jer 2:3
c Dt 14:2
7:7
d Dt 10:22
7:8
e Dt 10:15
f Ex 32:13
g Ex 13:14

7:9
h Dt 4:35 i 1Co 1:9;
2Ti 2:13 j Ne 1:5;
Da 9:4

defeated them, then you must destroy them totally.^a Make no treaty^v with them, and show them no mercy.^w ³Do not intermarry with them.^x Do not give your daughters to their sons or take their daughters for your sons, ⁴for they will turn your sons away from following me to serve other gods, and the LORD's anger will burn against you and will quickly destroy^y you. ⁵This is what you are to do to them: Break down their altars, smash their sacred stones, cut down their Asherah poles^b and burn their idols in the fire.^z ⁶For you are a people holy^a to the LORD your God.^b The LORD your God has chosen^c you out of all the peoples on the face of the earth to be his people, his treasured possession.

⁷The LORD did not set his affection on you and choose you because you were more numerous than other peoples, for you were the fewest of all peoples.^d ⁸But it was because the LORD loved^e you and kept the oath he swore^f to your forefathers that he brought you out with a mighty hand and redeemed you from the land of slavery,^g from the power of Pharaoh king of Egypt. ⁹Know therefore that the LORD your God is God;^h he is the faithful God,ⁱ keeping his covenant of love^j to a thousand generations of those who love him and keep his commands. ¹⁰But

> those who hate him he will repay to their face by destruction;
> he will not be slow to repay to their face those who hate him.

¹¹Therefore, take care to follow the commands, decrees and laws I give you today.

7:12
k Lev 26:3-13;
Dt 28:1-14;
Ps 105:8-9
7:13
l Jn 14:21
m Dt 28:4

7:14
n Ex 23:26
7:15
o Ex 15:26

¹²If you pay attention to these laws and are careful to follow them, then the LORD your God will keep his covenant of love with you, as he swore to your forefathers.^k ¹³He will love you and bless you^l and increase your numbers. He will bless the fruit of your womb, the crops of your land—your grain, new wine and oil—the calves of your herds and the lambs of your flocks in the land that he swore to your forefathers to give you.^m ¹⁴You will be blessed more than any other people; none of your men or women will be childless, nor any of your livestock without young.ⁿ ¹⁵The LORD will keep you free from every disease.^o He will not inflict on you the horrible diseases you knew in Egypt, but he will inflict them on all who hate you. ¹⁶You must destroy all the peoples the LORD your God gives over to you. Do not look on them with pity^p and do not serve their gods, for that will be a snare^q to you.

7:16
p ver 2; Ex 23:33
q Jdg 8:27
7:17
r Nu 33:53
7:18
s Dt 31:6 t Ps 105:5

7:19
u Dt 4:34
7:20
v Ex 23:28;
Jos 24:12
7:21
w Jos 3:10
x Dt 10:17; Ne 9:32
7:22
y Ex 23:28-30

¹⁷You may say to yourselves, "These nations are stronger than we are. How can we drive them out?^r" ¹⁸But do not be afraid^s of them; remember well what the LORD your God did to Pharaoh and to all Egypt.^t ¹⁹You saw with your own eyes the great trials, the miraculous signs and wonders, the mighty hand and outstretched arm, with which the LORD your God brought you out. The LORD your God will do the same to all the peoples you now fear.^u ²⁰Moreover, the LORD your God will send the hornet^v among them until even the survivors who hide from you have perished. ²¹Do not be terrified by them, for the LORD your God, who is among you,^w is a great and awesome God.^x ²²The LORD your God will drive out those nations before you, little by little.^y You will not be allowed to eliminate them all at once, or the wild animals will multiply around you. ²³But the LORD your God will deliver them over to you, throwing them into great confusion until they are destroyed. ²⁴He will give their kings into your hand, and you will wipe out their names from under heaven.

---

^a 2 The Hebrew term refers to the irrevocable giving over of things or persons to the LORD, often by totally destroying them; also in verse 26.   ^b 5 That is, symbols of the goddess Asherah; here and elsewhere in Deuteronomy

---

would inflict on the Canaanites. Compare verses 1, 22a, and 23 (emphasizing God's work) with 2, 16, 17, 22b, and 24 (emphasizing Israel's work—at God's initiation).

Why would the Lord command the Israelites to destroy the peoples of Canaan totally, showing them no mercy (v. 2; cf. v. 16)? God appointed the Israelites to be his instruments of judgment on the sinful Canaanites and their pagan idolatry, so they were to reflect his zeal and determination. Anything less might have jeopardized their own spiritual purity and commitment to God's

purposes. See also the notes for 2:24–37.

📖 Israel's driving out of the Canaanites would happen little by little so that the land wouldn't become desolate, allowing wild animals to multiply to the people's detriment (v. 22; cf. Ex. 23:29–30). Is this a contingency you would have thought of? Looking back on your own life, can you identify instances in which God has worked a change over time rather than immediately or instantly? Can you think of some possible reasons for his timetable?

No one will be able to stand up against you;[z] you will destroy them. [25]The images of their gods you are to burn[a] in the fire. Do not covet[b] the silver and gold on them, and do not take it for yourselves, or you will be ensnared[c] by it, for it is detestable[d] to the LORD your God. [26]Do not bring a detestable thing into your house or you, like it, will be set apart for destruction.[e] Utterly abhor and detest it, for it is set apart for destruction.

Do Not Forget the LORD

8 Be careful to follow every command I am giving you today, so that you may live[f] and increase and may enter and possess the land that the LORD promised on oath to your forefathers. [2]Remember how the LORD your God led[g] you all the way in the desert these forty years, to humble you and to test you in order to know what was in your heart, whether or not you would keep his commands. [3]He humbled you, causing you to hunger and then feeding you with manna,[h] which neither you nor your fathers had known, to teach you that man does not live on bread alone but on every word that comes from the mouth of the LORD.[i] [4]Your clothes did not wear out and your feet did not swell during these forty years.[j] [5]Know then in your heart that as a man disciplines his son, so the LORD your God disciplines you.[k]

[6]Observe the commands of the LORD your God, walking in his ways and revering him.[l] [7]For the LORD your God is bringing you into a good land—a land with streams and pools of water, with springs flowing in the valleys and hills;[m] [8]a land with wheat and barley, vines and fig trees, pomegranates, olive oil and honey; [9]a land where bread will not be scarce and you will lack nothing; a land where the rocks are iron and you can dig copper out of the hills.

[10]When you have eaten and are satisfied,[n] praise the LORD your God for the good land he has given you. [11]Be careful that you do not forget the LORD your God, failing to observe his commands, his laws and his decrees that I am giving you this day. [12]Otherwise, when you eat and are satisfied, when you build fine houses and settle down,[o] [13]and when your herds and flocks grow large and your silver and gold increase and all you have is multiplied, [14]then your heart will become proud and you will forget[p] the LORD your God, who brought you out of Egypt, out of the land of slavery. [15]He led you through the vast and dreadful desert,[q] that thirsty and waterless land, with its venomous snakes[r] and scorpions. He brought you water out of hard rock.[s] [16]He gave you manna to eat in the desert, something your fathers had never known,[t] to humble and to test you so that in the end it might go well with you. [17]You may say to yourself,[u] "My power and the strength of my hands have produced this wealth for me." [18]But remember the LORD your God, for it is he who gives you the ability to produce wealth,[v] and so confirms his covenant, which he swore to your forefathers, as it is today.

[19]If you ever forget the LORD your God and follow other gods and worship and bow down to them, I testify against you today that you will surely be destroyed.[w] [20]Like the nations the LORD destroyed before you, so you will be destroyed for not obeying the LORD your God.

7:24 [z] Jos 23:9
7:25 [a] Ex 32:20; 1Ch 14:12 [b] Jos 7:21 [c] Jdg 8:27 [d] Dt 17:1
7:26 [e] Lev 27:28-29
8:1 [f] Dt 4:1
8:2 [g] Am 2:10
8:3 [h] Ex 16:12,14,35 [i] Ex 16:2-3; Mt 4:4*; Lk 4:4*
8:4 [j] Dt 29:5; Ne 9:21
8:5 [k] 2Sa 7:14; Pr 3:11-12; Heb 12:5-11; Rev 3:19
8:6 [l] Dt 5:33
8:7 [m] Dt 11:9-12
8:10 [n] Dt 6:10-12
8:12 [o] Hos 13:6
8:14 [p] Ps 106:21
8:15 [q] Jer 2:6 [r] Nu 21:6 [s] Nu 20:11; Ps 78:15; 114:8
8:16 [t] Ex 16:15
8:17 [u] Dt 9:4,7,24
8:18 [v] Pr 10:22; Hos 2:8
8:19 [w] Dt 4:26; 30:18

Deuteronomy 8:1–20

Chapter 8 reaffirms the admonitions and warnings God through Moses had already given his people. The chapter covers the discipline of the prior 40 years, which they were to remember and from which they were to learn humility and reliance on the Lord. Moses also spoke again of Canaan's natural benefits, for which the Israelites were to praise God. The tendency would be strong to forget him in their coming prosperity, to attribute their wealth to their own abilities instead of to God's fulfillment of his covenant promises to them.

Those of us living in Westernized nations are inordinately wealthy compared to those in developing countries. It might be easy to attribute our resources to education, drive, or acquired skills and to fail to remember that it's only by God's grace that we were born into such a land. Our skills, intellect, and abilities are gifts from his hand. He gives the "power" to acquire wealth, and we ignore that fact to our peril. Thank the Lord today for where you live, what you have, and any skills or abilities he's given you. Acknowledge his gracious provision and honor him through faithful stewardship of your resources.

Not Because of Israel's Righteousness

9:1
x Dt 4:38; 11:23,31
y Dt 1:28

9 Hear, O Israel. You are now about to cross the Jordan to go in and dispossess nations greater and stronger than you,[x] with large cities that have walls up to the sky.[y] 2The people are strong and tall—Anakites! You know about them and have

9:2
z Nu 13:22,28,32-33

heard it said: "Who can stand up against the Anakites?"[z] 3But be assured today that

9:3
a Dt 31:3; Jos 3:11
b Dt 4:24;
Heb 12:29
c Ex 23:31; Dt 7:23-24

the LORD your God is the one who goes across ahead of you[a] like a devouring fire.[b] He will destroy them; he will subdue them before you. And you will drive them out and annihilate them quickly,[c] as the LORD has promised you.

9:4
d Dt 8:17
e Lev 18:21,24-30;
Dt 18:9-14

4After the LORD your God has driven them out before you, do not say to yourself,[d] "The LORD has brought me here to take possession of this land because of my righteousness." No, it is on account of the wickedness of these nations[e] that the LORD is going to drive them out before you. 5It is not because of your righteousness or

9:5
f Tit 3:5 g Ge 12:7;
13:15; 15:7; 17:8;
26:4

your integrity[f] that you are going in to take possession of their land; but on account of the wickedness of these nations, the LORD your God will drive them out before you, to accomplish what he swore[g] to your fathers, to Abraham, Isaac and Jacob.

9:6
h ver 13; Ex 32:9;
Dt 31:27

6Understand, then, that it is not because of your righteousness that the LORD your God is giving you this good land to possess, for you are a stiff-necked people.[h]

The Golden Calf

7Remember this and never forget how you provoked the LORD your God to anger in the desert. From the day you left Egypt until you arrived here, you have been rebellious against the LORD. 8At Horeb you aroused the LORD's wrath so that he was

9:8
i Ex 32:7-10;
Ps 106:19

angry enough to destroy you.[i] 9When I went up on the mountain to receive the tab-

9:9
j Ex 24:12,15,18;
34:28

lets of stone, the tablets of the covenant that the LORD had made with you, I stayed on the mountain forty days and forty nights; I ate no bread and drank no water.[j]

9:10
k Ex 31:18; Dt 4:13

10The LORD gave me two stone tablets inscribed by the finger of God.[k] On them were all the commandments the LORD proclaimed to you on the mountain out of the fire, on the day of the assembly.

11At the end of the forty days and forty nights, the LORD gave me the two stone tablets, the tablets of the covenant. 12Then the LORD told me, "Go down from here at once, because your people whom you brought out of Egypt have become cor-

9:12
l Ex 32:7-8;
Dt 31:29
m Jdg 2:17

rupt.[l] They have turned away quickly[m] from what I commanded them and have made a cast idol for themselves."

9:13
n ver 6; Ex 32:9;
Dt 10:16

13And the LORD said to me, "I have seen this people[n], and they are a stiff-necked people indeed! 14Let me alone,[o] so that I may destroy them and blot out[p] their

9:14
o Ex 32:10
p Nu 14:12;
Dt 29:20

name from under heaven. And I will make you into a nation stronger and more numerous than they."

15So I turned and went down from the mountain while it was ablaze with fire.

Deuteronomy 9:1–6

Earlier Moses had made it clear that God's selection of the Israelites wasn't due to their superiority in numbers (7:7). Now he broke the news that it wasn't because of their righteousness, either. Canaanite wickedness, not Israelite righteousness, caused the Canaanites' dispossession. Leviticus 18 gives more detail on what Moses called here "the wickedness of these nations" (v. 4). Still, Israel would prevail because God *chose* to subdue the Canaanites by empowering his people.

When has God helped you through a difficult situation despite odds to the contrary? If God has allowed you to use your own faculties to come out on top, were you *aware, at the time or afterward,* of his role as instigator and enabler? Have you thanked him? It's never too late.

Deuteronomy 9:7–29

When God spoke to Moses about the people's sin, he called the Israelites "*your* people whom *you* brought out of Egypt" (v. 12, emphasis added). But when Moses prayed, he referred to them as "*your* people, *your* (own) inheritance" (vv. 26,29, emphasis added). What was behind this interplay of pronouns? God may have been trying to stir up Moses' concern for the Israelites by identifying them as Moses' people. Moses did show his concern by his great intercessory prayer.

When have you approached God in distress concerning an issue involving the church in general, a group of believers, or an individual Christian? Did you remind God that they belonged to him (not that he needed a reminder but to acknowledge his incomparable power and love)? Do you think your "ownership" of fellow members of the body of Christ, while on an entirely different level from God's supreme ownership of everyone and everything, is important to God? How does your personal commitment both to God and to other Christians impact your discipleship and service?

And the two tablets of the covenant were in my hands. [a][q] [16]When I looked, I saw that you had sinned against the LORD your God; you had made for yourselves an idol cast in the shape of a calf. [r] You had turned aside quickly from the way that the LORD had commanded you. [17]So I took the two tablets and threw them out of my hands, breaking them to pieces before your eyes.

[18]Then once again I fell [s] prostrate before the LORD for forty days and forty nights; I ate no bread and drank no water, because of all the sin you had committed, doing what was evil in the LORD's sight and so provoking him to anger. [19]I feared the anger and wrath of the LORD, for he was angry enough with you to destroy you. [t] But again the LORD listened to me. [u] [20]And the LORD was angry enough with Aaron to destroy him, but at that time I prayed for Aaron too. [21]Also I took that sinful thing of yours, the calf you had made, and burned it in the fire. Then I crushed it and ground it to powder as fine as dust and threw the dust into a stream that flowed down the mountain. [v]

[22]You also made the LORD angry at Taberah, [w] at Massah [x] and at Kibroth Hattaavah. [y]

[23]And when the LORD sent you out from Kadesh Barnea, he said, "Go up and take possession of the land I have given you." But you rebelled against the command of the LORD your God. You did not trust [z] him or obey him. [24]You have been rebellious against the LORD ever since I have known you. [a]

[25]I lay prostrate before the LORD those forty days and forty nights because the LORD had said he would destroy you. [b] [26]I prayed to the LORD and said, "O Sovereign LORD, do not destroy your people, your own inheritance that you redeemed by your great power and brought out of Egypt with a mighty hand. [c] [27]Remember your servants Abraham, Isaac and Jacob. Overlook the stubbornness of this people, their wickedness and their sin. [28]Otherwise, the country from which you brought us will say, 'Because the LORD was not able to take them into the land he had promised them, and because he hated them, he brought them out to put them to death in the desert.' [d] [29]But they are your people, your inheritance [e] that you brought out by your great power and your outstretched arm. [f]"

Tablets Like the First Ones

10 At that time the LORD said to me, "Chisel out two stone tablets [g] like the first ones and come up to me on the mountain. Also make a wooden chest. [b] [2]I will write on the tablets the words that were on the first tablets, which you broke. Then you are to put them in the chest." [h]

[3]So I made the ark out of acacia wood [i] and chiseled [j] out two stone tablets like the first ones, and I went up on the mountain with the two tablets in my hands. [4]The LORD wrote on these tablets what he had written before, the Ten Commandments he had proclaimed [k] to you on the mountain, out of the fire, on the day of the assembly. And the LORD gave them to me. [5]Then I came back down the mountain [l] and put the tablets in the ark [m] I had made, as the LORD commanded me, and they are there now. [n]

---

[a] 15 Or *And I had the two tablets of the covenant with me, one in each hand*   [b] 1 That is, an ark

---

9:15
[q] Ex 19:18; 32:15
9:16
[r] Ex 32:19

9:18
[s] Ex 34:28

9:19
[t] Ex 32:10-11,14
[u] Dt 10:10

9:21
[v] Ex 32:20
9:22
[w] Nu 11:3 [x] Ex 17:7
[y] Nu 11:34

9:23
[z] Ps 106:24
9:24
[a] ver 7; Dt 31:27
9:25
[b] ver 18

9:26
[c] Ex 32:11

9:28
[d] Ex 32:12;
Nu 14:16
9:29
[e] Dt 4:20; 1Ki 8:51
[f] Dt 4:34; Ne 1:10

10:1
[g] Ex 25:10; 34:1-2

10:2
[h] Ex 25:16,21;
Dt 4:13
10:3
[i] Ex 25:5,10; 37:1-9
[j] Ex 34:4

10:4
[k] Ex 20:1

10:5
[l] Ex 34:29
[m] Ex 40:20
[n] 1Ki 8:9

Deuteronomy 10:1–11

In verses 1–5 Moses recounted his second experience regarding the two stone tablets of the covenant. The order of events doesn't match the initial, longer account in Exodus 34–37. Verses 3 and 5 imply that Moses made the chest (or ark) himself before climbing Mount Sinai the second time and then immediately after descending the mountain put the tablets in it. We know from Exodus 37:1–9 that the ark was built by Bezalel after Moses' return, during the course of tabernacle construction. It isn't unusual in the Old Testament for events to be reported out of chronological order—or for

a leader to be credited with doing something actually accomplished by someone else.

Do you ever find yourself disturbed by apparent contradictions in the Bible, either from one book to another or even within a single book? A couple of points might help to resolve this issue in your mind. (1) Literary standards change drastically from one period to another. Our modern concern for "instant replay" reporting might not have been an issue in an earlier day. (2) The Bible's infallibility assures us that its words, gleaned from whatever passage or book, will never mislead us (cf. 2 Tim. 3:16).

10:6
o Nu 33:30-31,38
p Nu 20:25-28
10:7
q Nu 33:32-34
10:8
r Nu 3:6 s Dt 18:5
t Dt 21:5

10:9
u Nu 18:20;
Dt 18:1-2;
Eze 44:28
10:10
v Ex 33:17; 34:28;
Dt 9:18-19,25

10:12
w Mic 6:8
x Dt 5:33; 6:13;
Mt 22:37 y Dt 6:5

10:14
z 1Ki 8:27 a Ex 19:5

10:15
b Dt 4:37
10:16
c Jer 4:4 d Dt 9:6
10:17
e Jos 22:22;
Da 2:47 f Ac 10:34;
Ro 2:11; Eph 6:9
10:18
g Ps 68:5
10:19
h Lev 19:34
10:20
i Mt 4:10 / Dt 11:22
k Ps 63:11
10:21
l Ex 15:2; Jer 17:14
m Ps 106:21-22
10:22
n Ge 46:26-27
o Ge 15:5; Dt 1:10

11:1
p Dt 10:12
q Zec 3:7

11:2
r Dt 5:24; 8:5

11:4
s Ex 14:27

6(The Israelites traveled from the wells of the Jaakanites to Moserah.[o] There Aaron died and was buried, and Eleazar his son succeeded him as priest.[p] 7From there they traveled to Gudgodah and on to Jotbathah, a land with streams of water.[q] 8At that time the LORD set apart the tribe of Levi[r] to carry the ark of the covenant of the LORD, to stand before the LORD to minister[s] and to pronounce blessings[t] in his name, as they still do today. 9That is why the Levites have no share or inheritance among their brothers; the LORD is their inheritance,[u] as the LORD your God told them.)

10Now I had stayed on the mountain forty days and nights, as I did the first time, and the LORD listened to me at this time also. It was not his will to destroy you.[v] 11"Go," the LORD said to me, "and lead the people on their way, so that they may enter and possess the land that I swore to their fathers to give them."

Fear the LORD

12And now, O Israel, what does the LORD your God ask of you[w] but to fear the LORD your God, to walk in all his ways, to love him,[x] to serve the LORD your God with all your heart[y] and with all your soul, 13and to observe the LORD's commands and decrees that I am giving you today for your own good?

14To the LORD your God belong the heavens, even the highest heavens,[z] the earth and everything in it.[a] 15Yet the LORD set his affection on your forefathers and loved[b] them, and he chose you, their descendants, above all the nations, as it is today. 16Circumcise[c] your hearts, therefore, and do not be stiff-necked[d] any longer. 17For the LORD your God is God of gods[e] and Lord of lords, the great God, mighty and awesome, who shows no partiality[f] and accepts no bribes. 18He defends the cause of the fatherless and the widow,[g] and loves the alien, giving him food and clothing. 19And you are to love those who are aliens, for you yourselves were aliens in Egypt.[h] 20Fear the LORD your God and serve him.[i] Hold fast[j] to him and take your oaths in his name.[k] 21He is your praise;[l] he is your God, who performed for you those great and awesome wonders[m] you saw with your own eyes. 22Your forefathers who went down into Egypt were seventy in all,[n] and now the LORD your God has made you as numerous as the stars in the sky.[o]

Love and Obey the LORD

11 Love[p] the LORD your God and keep his requirements, his decrees, his laws and his commands always.[q] 2Remember today that your children were not the ones who saw and experienced the discipline of the LORD your God:[r] his majesty, his mighty hand, his outstretched arm; 3the signs he performed and the things he did in the heart of Egypt, both to Pharaoh king of Egypt and to his whole country; 4what he did to the Egyptian army, to its horses and chariots, how he overwhelmed them with the waters of the Red Sea[a][s] as they were pursuing you, and how

a 4 Hebrew Yam Suph; that is, Sea of Reeds

Deuteronomy 10:12–22

God's relationship with his people is based on his being. His greatness is portrayed by the characteristics and acts attributed to him. His majesty extends to his righteous behavior: The Lord shows no partiality and accepts no bribes. He defends the fatherless and widows and loves aliens, providing for their needs. The Israelites were to be like him. They of all people were to love refugees/immigrants and foreigners, for they had been in the same position in Egypt.

You may never have experienced many—or any—of the devastating events that have shaped the lives of the lost, the least, or the last. Yet the hurting people in your neighborhood and throughout the world need your empathy (your feeling *with* them in their pain), not just your sympathy (your feeling *for* them).

You may never have been a refugee or an immigrant, but you have experienced similar human emotions, like loneliness, isolation, confusion, alienation, and fear. Your care and concern for those in similar straits demonstrates your faith in profound ways.

Deuteronomy 11:1–32

The echoing of ideas, words, and phrases in this section characterizes the messages of Deuteronomy. Chapter 11 illustrates Moses' hammer-like, repetitive style. His exhortations to love, remember, observe, worship (serve), obey, teach, and walk in the Lord's ways are all here. So are the words used to describe the basic content of the messages: requirements, decrees, laws, commands, words, and symbols. Moses literally hammered home the consequences of right and wrong behavior.

Climaxing the repetitive directions in chapter 11 is

the LORD brought lasting ruin on them. [5]It was not your children who saw what he did for you in the desert until you arrived at this place, [6]and what he did [t] to Dathan and Abiram, sons of Eliab the Reubenite, when the earth opened its mouth right in the middle of all Israel and swallowed them up with their households, their tents and every living thing that belonged to them. [7]But it was your own eyes that saw all these great things the LORD has done.

[8]Observe therefore all the commands I am giving you today, so that you may have the strength to go in and take over the land that you are crossing the Jordan to possess, [u] [9]and so that you may live long [v] in the land that the LORD swore [w] to your forefathers to give to them and their descendants, a land flowing with milk and honey. [x] [10]The land you are entering to take over is not like the land of Egypt, from which you have come, where you planted your seed and irrigated it by foot as in a vegetable garden. [11]But the land you are crossing the Jordan to take possession of is a land of mountains and valleys that drinks rain from heaven. [y] [12]It is a land the LORD your God cares for; the eyes [z] of the LORD your God are continually on it from the beginning of the year to its end.

[13]So if you faithfully obey [a] the commands I am giving you today—to love [b] the LORD your God and to serve him with all your heart and with all your soul— [14]then I will send rain [c] on your land in its season, both autumn and spring rains, [d] so that you may gather in your grain, new wine and oil. [15]I will provide grass [e] in the fields for your cattle, and you will eat and be satisfied. [f]

[16]Be careful, or you will be enticed to turn away and worship other gods and bow down to them. [g] [17]Then the LORD's anger [h] will burn against you, and he will shut [i] the heavens so that it will not rain and the ground will yield no produce, and you will soon perish [j] from the good land the LORD is giving you. [18]Fix these words of mine in your hearts and minds; tie them as symbols on your hands and bind them on your foreheads. [k] [19]Teach them to your children, [l] talking about them when you sit at home and when you walk along the road, when you lie down and when you get up. [m] [20]Write them on the doorframes of your houses and on your gates, [n] [21]so that your days and the days of your children may be many [o] in the land that the LORD swore to give your forefathers, as many as the days that the heavens are above the earth. [p]

[22]If you carefully observe [q] all these commands I am giving you to follow—to love the LORD your God, to walk in all his ways and to hold fast [r] to him— [23]then the LORD will drive out all these nations before you, and you will dispossess nations larger and stronger than you. [s] [24]Every place where you set your foot will be yours: [t] Your territory will extend from the desert to Lebanon, and from the Euphrates River to the western sea. [a] [25]No man will be able to stand against you. The LORD your God, as he promised you, will put the terror and fear of you on the whole land, wherever you go. [u]

[26]See, I am setting before you today a blessing and a curse [v]— [27]the blessing [w] if you obey the commands of the LORD your God that I am giving you today; [28]the curse if you disobey [x] the commands of the LORD your God and turn from the way that I command you today by following other gods, which you have not known. [29]When the LORD your God has brought you into the land you are entering to pos-

---

[a] 24 That is, the Mediterranean

---

the blessing and curse recital to be proclaimed from Mounts Gerizim and Ebal (vv. 26–32; cf. chs. 27–28). Blessings and curses are essential to the covenant conditions that make up Deuteronomy. Here they conclude the first section of the book and introduce what follows: a more detailed delineation of God's decrees. Simply put, the blessing would be Israel's for obedience—and the curse for disobedience (vv. 26–28).

📖 If you are involved with children, you may use a system of rewards and natural consequences to instill principles of right and acceptable behavior. As the child develops, the repetition of good behavior over time is internalized and usually becomes his or her standard for living. Similarly, God no longer holds us under a strict blessing-and-curse formula as he did the ancient Israelites. Through the life of Jesus in us, his Holy Spirit helps us to internalize the law of God, writing it "on our hearts" (Jer. 31:33; Rom. 8:9–11). Energized by the Spirit, our new nature desires to please God (Gal. 5:16–18).

11:6
[t] Nu 16:1-35

11:8
[u] Jos 1:7
11:9
[v] Dt 4:40; Pr 10:27
[w] Dt 9:5 [x] Ex 3:8

11:11
[y] Dt 8:7
11:12
[z] 1Ki 9:3

11:13
[a] Dt 6:17
[b] Dt 10:12
11:14
[c] Lev 26:4; Dt 28:12
[d] Joel 2:23; Jas 5:7
11:15
[e] Ps 104:14
[f] Dt 6:11
11:16
[g] Dt 8:19; 29:18; Job 31:9,27
11:17
[h] Dt 6:15
[i] 1Ki 8:35; 2Ch 6:26
[j] Dt 4:26

11:18
[k] Dt 6:6-8
11:19
[l] Dt 6:7 [m] Dt 4:9-10
11:20
[n] Dt 6:9
11:21
[o] Pr 3:2; 4:10
[p] Ps 72:5

11:22
[q] Dt 6:17
[r] Dt 10:20

11:23
[s] Dt 4:38; 9:1
11:24
[t] Ge 15:18; Ex 23:31; Jos 1:3; 14:9

11:25
[u] Ex 23:27; Dt 7:24
11:26
[v] Dt 30:1,15,19
11:27
[w] Dt 28:1-14
11:28
[x] Dt 28:15

11:29
y Dt 27:12-13;
Jos 8:33
11:30
z Ge 12:6
a Jos 4:19
11:31
b Dt 9:1; Jos 1:11

sess, you are to proclaim on Mount Gerizim the blessings, and on Mount Ebal the curses.[y] [30]As you know, these mountains are across the Jordan, west of the road,[a] toward the setting sun, near the great trees of Moreh,[z] in the territory of those Canaanites living in the Arabah in the vicinity of Gilgal.[a] [31]You are about to cross the Jordan to enter and take possession[b] of the land the LORD your God is giving you. When you have taken it over and are living there, [32]be sure that you obey all the decrees and laws I am setting before you today.

The One Place of Worship

12:1
c Dt 4:9-10;
1Ki 8:40
12:2
d 2Ki 16:4; 17:10
12:3
e Nu 33:52; Dt 7:5;
Jdg 2:2

12 These are the decrees and laws you must be careful to follow in the land that the LORD, the God of your fathers, has given you to possess—as long as you live in the land.[c] [2]Destroy completely all the places on the high mountains and on the hills and under every spreading tree[d] where the nations you are dispossessing worship their gods. [3]Break down their altars, smash[e] their sacred stones and burn their Asherah poles in the fire; cut down the idols of their gods and wipe out their names from those places.

12:5
f ver 11,13;
2Ch 7:12,16
12:6
g Dt 14:22-23
12:7
h ver 12,18;
Lev 23:40; Dt 14:26

[4]You must not worship the LORD your God in their way. [5]But you are to seek the place the LORD your God will choose from among all your tribes to put his Name there for his dwelling.[f] To that place you must go; [6]there bring your burnt offerings and sacrifices, your tithes[g] and special gifts, what you have vowed to give and your freewill offerings, and the firstborn of your herds and flocks. [7]There, in the presence of the LORD your God, you and your families shall eat and shall rejoice[h] in everything you have put your hand to, because the LORD your God has blessed you.

[8]You are not to do as we do here today, everyone as he sees fit, [9]since you have not yet reached the resting place and the inheritance the LORD your God is giving you. [10]But you will cross the Jordan and settle in the land the LORD your God is giving[i] you as an inheritance, and he will give you rest from all your enemies around you so that you will live in safety. [11]Then to the place the LORD your God will choose as a dwelling for his Name[j]—there you are to bring everything I command you: your burnt offerings and sacrifices, your tithes and special gifts, and all the choice possessions you have vowed to the LORD. [12]And there rejoice[k] before the LORD your God, you, your sons and daughters, your menservants and maidservants, and the Levites from your towns, who have no allotment or inheritance[l] of their own. [13]Be careful not to sacrifice your burnt offerings anywhere you please. [14]Offer them only at the place the LORD will choose[m] in one of your tribes, and there observe everything I command you.

12:10
i Dt 11:31
12:11
j ver 5; Dt 15:20;
16:2
12:12
k ver 7 l Dt 10:9;
14:29

12:14
m ver 11

[15]Nevertheless, you may slaughter your animals in any of your towns and eat as much of the meat as you want, as if it were gazelle or deer,[n] according to the blessing the LORD your God gives you. Both the ceremonially unclean and the clean may eat it. [16]But you must not eat the blood;[o] pour it out on the ground like water.[p] [17]You must not eat in your own towns the tithe of your grain and new wine and oil, or the firstborn of your herds and flocks, or whatever you have vowed to give, or your freewill offerings or special gifts. [18]Instead, you are to eat[q] them in the presence of the LORD your God at the place the LORD your God will choose[r]—you, your sons and daughters, your menservants and maidservants, and the Levites from your towns—

12:15
n ver 20-23;
Dt 14:5; 15:22
12:16
o Ge 9:4; Lev 7:26;
17:10-12 p Dt 15:23

12:18
q Dt 14:23 r ver 5

---

a 30 Or *Jordan, westward*

Deuteronomy 12:1–32

Chapter 12 opens a new section of Moses' address, presenting crucial elements for the Israelites' national and individual spiritual lives. (1) They were to worship God in the place where he chose to put his Name and reveal his presence. (2) They were to destroy places and articles related to the worship of Canaanite gods. (3) They weren't to worship the Lord in the way the Canaanites worshiped their gods. (4) The people's sacrifices and offerings were to be brought to the place where God chose to put his Name.

While sacrificial offerings were to be brought to the central sanctuary, the regular butchering and eating of meat could take place anywhere—though the people were prohibited from eating the blood. Blood, the symbol of life, was sacred, because the giving of life brought atonement. This central characteristic of the Old Testament sacrificial system becomes all-important in the New Testament. All aspects of Old Testament sacrifices were permanently fulfilled in Christ by the shedding of his blood on the cross for sin (see Acts 20:28; Rom. 3:25; 5:9; Eph. 1:7; Col. 1:20; Heb. 9:11–28; 10:19–20; Rev. 1:5).

and you are to rejoice[s] before the LORD your God in everything you put your hand to. [19]Be careful not to neglect the Levites[t] as long as you live in your land.

[20]When the LORD your God has enlarged your territory[u] as he promised[v] you, and you crave meat and say, "I would like some meat," then you may eat as much of it as you want. [21]If the place where the LORD your God chooses to put his Name is too far away from you, you may slaughter animals from the herds and flocks the LORD has given you, as I have commanded you, and in your own towns you may eat as much of them as you want. [22]Eat them as you would gazelle or deer.[w] Both the ceremonially unclean and the clean may eat. [23]But be sure you do not eat the blood,[x] because the blood is the life, and you must not eat the life with the meat. [24]You must not eat the blood; pour it out on the ground like water. [25]Do not eat it, so that it may go well[y] with you and your children after you, because you will be doing what is right[z] in the eyes of the LORD.

[26]But take your consecrated things and whatever you have vowed to give,[a] and go to the place the LORD will choose. [27]Present your burnt offerings[b] on the altar of the LORD your God, both the meat and the blood. The blood of your sacrifices must be poured beside the altar of the LORD your God, but you may eat the meat. [28]Be careful to obey all these regulations I am giving you, so that it may always go well[c] with you and your children after you, because you will be doing what is good and right in the eyes of the LORD your God.

[29]The LORD your God will cut off[d] before you the nations you are about to invade and dispossess. But when you have driven them out and settled in their land, [30]and after they have been destroyed before you, be careful not to be ensnared by inquiring about their gods, saying, "How do these nations serve their gods? We will do the same." [31]You must not worship the LORD your God in their way, because in worshiping their gods, they do all kinds of detestable things the LORD hates.[e] They even burn their sons[f] and daughters in the fire as sacrifices to their gods.

[32]See that you do all I command you; do not add[g] to it or take away from it.

Worshiping Other Gods

13 If a prophet,[h] or one who foretells by dreams, appears among you and announces to you a miraculous sign or wonder, [2]and if the sign or wonder of which he has spoken takes place, and he says, "Let us follow other gods"[i] (gods you

---

Cross references (right margin):

12:18
s ver 7,12
12:19
t Dt 14:27
12:20
u Dt 19:8
v Ge 15:18;
Dt 11:24

12:22
w ver 15
12:23
x ver 16; Ge 9:4;
Lev 17:11,14

12:25
y Dt 4:40; Isa 3:10
z Ex 15:26;
Dt 13:18; 1Ki 11:38
12:26
a ver 17; Nu 5:9-10
12:27
b Lev 1:5,9,13

12:28
c ver 25; Dt 4:40

12:29
d Jos 23:4

12:31
e Dt 9:5 f Dt 18:10;
Jer 32:35

12:32
g Dt 4:2; Jos 1:7;
Rev 22:18-19

13:1
h Mt 24:24;
Mk 13:22; 2Th 2:9
13:2
i ver 6,13

 Where has God chosen to put his Name today? A place is no longer significant because his "temples" are multiple and mobile (Eph. 2:19-22). As his children move about, we infiltrate culture with his message and spread love in his Name. What an incredible privilege and responsibility to bear the name Christian (Christ-one) as his direct representatives on Earth! How are you participating in his kingdom and bearing his message today?

Deuteronomy 13:1–18

 Moses cautioned the people not to be seduced to the worship of other gods—not only by false prophets but also by close family members or friends. They weren't to yield to, listen to, pity, spare, or shield an enticer (v. 8). Not only was the defector to be stoned to death (v. 10), but the first stone was to be thrown by the near relative or friend the individual had attempted to drive from the Lord (v. 9).

12:23

Shed Blood

Blood has always been essential to life. Throughout the Bible it functioned as a strong symbol of spiritual life, and it still has that connotation today, through our celebration of communion. But with the advent of modern medicine, the role of blood for prolonging and enhancing physical life has come increasingly to the fore. Christ shed his blood for our eternal spiritual and physical salvation. Now you as his servant may have opportunity to "shed" yours for others' physical "salvation."

Biblical roles of blood: an essential to life and the seat of life's power

- In Old Testament sacrifices, an eradicator of personal and corporate sin
- In the New Testament, Jesus' shed blood eradicated sin.
- In the Old Testament, a ritual tool to set apart priests
- In the New Testament, a symbol of God's promises, especially in communion

Modern roles of blood: a necessity of physical life

- There is an 85 percent chance you or a family member will need a blood transfusion within your/their lifetime.
- 6 percent of the population gives blood on a regular basis; 16 percent donate once a year, while 76 percent never do so.
- 43 percent of all donated blood is used by people over age 65.
- A person is eligible to donate blood every 56 days (eight weeks).

13:3
j Dt 8:2,16
13:4
k 2Ki 23:3;
2Ch 34:31
l Dt 10:20
13:5
m Dt 17:7,12;
1Co 5:13
13:6
n Dt 17:2-7; 29:18
13:8
o Pr 1:10
13:9
p Dt 17:5,7
13:11
q Dt 19:20
13:13
r ver 2,6; 1Jn 2:19
13:16
s Jos 6:24
t Jos 8:28; Jer 49:2
13:17
u Nu 25:4 *v* Dt 30:3
w Dt 7:13
x Ge 22:17; 26:4,
24; 28:14
13:18
y Dt 12:25,28
14:1
z Lev 19:28; 21:5;
Jer 16:6; 41:5;
Ro 8:14; 9:8;
Gal 3:26
14:2
a Lev 20:26
b Dt 7:6; 26:18-19
14:3
c Eze 4:14
14:4
d Lev 11:2-45;
Ac 10:14

have not known) "and let us worship them," [3]you must not listen to the words of that prophet or dreamer. The LORD your God is testing[j] you to find out whether you love him with all your heart and with all your soul. [4]It is the LORD your God you must follow,[k] and him you must revere. Keep his commands and obey him; serve him and hold fast[l] to him. [5]That prophet or dreamer must be put to death, because he preached rebellion against the LORD your God, who brought you out of Egypt and redeemed you from the land of slavery; he has tried to turn you from the way the LORD your God commanded you to follow. You must purge the evil[m] from among you.

[6]If your very own brother, or your son or daughter, or the wife you love, or your closest friend secretly entices[n] you, saying, "Let us go and worship other gods" (gods that neither you nor your fathers have known, [7]gods of the peoples around you, whether near or far, from one end of the land to the other), [8]do not yield[o] to him or listen to him. Show him no pity. Do not spare him or shield him. [9]You must certainly put him to death.[p] Your hand must be the first in putting him to death, and then the hands of all the people. [10]Stone him to death, because he tried to turn you away from the LORD your God, who brought you out of Egypt, out of the land of slavery. [11]Then all Israel will hear and be afraid,[q] and no one among you will do such an evil thing again.

[12]If you hear it said about one of the towns the LORD your God is giving you to live in [13]that wicked men[r] have arisen among you and have led the people of their town astray, saying, "Let us go and worship other gods" (gods you have not known), [14]then you must inquire, probe and investigate it thoroughly. And if it is true and it has been proved that this detestable thing has been done among you, [15]you must certainly put to the sword all who live in that town. Destroy it completely,[a] both its people and its livestock. [16]Gather all the plunder of the town into the middle of the public square and completely burn the town and all its plunder as a whole burnt offering to the LORD your God.[s] It is to remain a ruin[t] forever, never to be rebuilt. [17]None of those condemned things[a] shall be found in your hands, so that the LORD will turn from his fierce anger;[u] he will show you mercy, have compassion[v] on you, and increase your numbers,[w] as he promised[x] on oath to your forefathers, [18]because you obey the LORD your God, keeping all his commands that I am giving you today and doing what is right[y] in his eyes.

Clean and Unclean Food

14 You are the children[z] of the LORD your God. Do not cut yourselves or shave the front of your heads for the dead, [2]for you are a people holy to the LORD your God.[a] Out of all the peoples on the face of the earth, the LORD has chosen you to be his treasured possession.[b]

[3]Do not eat any detestable thing.[c] [4]These are the animals you may eat:[d] the ox, the sheep, the goat, [5]the deer, the gazelle, the roe deer, the wild goat, the ibex, the antelope and the mountain sheep.[b] [6]You may eat any animal that has a split hoof

---

[a] 15,17 The Hebrew term refers to the irrevocable giving over of things or persons to the LORD, often by totally destroying them.   [b] 5 The precise identification of some of the birds and animals in this chapter is uncertain.

Our loyalty to God overrides every other allegiance in importance. How would you deal with a situation in which someone close to you—maybe even a spouse or best friend—were drawing you further and further into some form of sin? Could you maintain a relationship but still extricate yourself from the trap? How?

A modern application of this Old Testament principle is for us to avoid forming intimate relationships (marriage, e.g.) with people who aren't believers or would influence us away from Christ (see 2 Cor. 6:14–18).

Deuteronomy 14:1–21

The Israelites were to distinguish themselves from the surrounding peoples, who stood in opposition to the holiness of God and his children. The reason for prohibitions against eating "unclean" animals was basically spiritual, though there may have been psychological and health considerations as well. Some of these animals were associated with Canaanite religions. Some were hazardous to the health of any who ate them. Eating anything found dead also related to the restriction against eating blood (12:16,24), since the blood wouldn't have been properly drained.

Rules, rules, rules. Even those of us living in a free society are bound by seeming rivers of restrictions, some of which are necessary and appropriate and others that just keep the system flowing. Many of us chafe at

divided in two and that chews the cud. [7]However, of those that chew the cud or that have a split hoof completely divided you may not eat the camel, the rabbit or the coney.[a] Although they chew the cud, they do not have a split hoof; they are ceremonially unclean for you. [8]The pig is also unclean; although it has a split hoof, it does not chew the cud. You are not to eat their meat or touch their carcasses.[e]

[9]Of all the creatures living in the water, you may eat any that has fins and scales. [10]But anything that does not have fins and scales you may not eat; for you it is unclean.

[11]You may eat any clean bird. [12]But these you may not eat: the eagle, the vulture, the black vulture, [13]the red kite, the black kite, any kind of falcon, [14]any kind of raven, [15]the horned owl, the screech owl, the gull, any kind of hawk, [16]the little owl, the great owl, the white owl, [17]the desert owl, the osprey, the cormorant, [18]the stork, any kind of heron, the hoopoe and the bat.

[19]All flying insects that swarm are unclean to you; do not eat them. [20]But any winged creature that is clean you may eat.

[21]Do not eat anything you find already dead.[f] You may give it to an alien living in any of your towns, and he may eat it, or you may sell it to a foreigner. But you are a people holy to the LORD your God.[g]

Do not cook a young goat in its mother's milk.[h]

Tithes

[22]Be sure to set aside a tenth[i] of all that your fields produce each year. [23]Eat the tithe of your grain, new wine and oil, and the firstborn of your herds and flocks in the presence of the LORD your God at the place he will choose as a dwelling for his Name,[j] so that you may learn[k] to revere the LORD your God always. [24]But if that place is too distant and you have been blessed by the LORD your God and cannot carry your tithe (because the place where the LORD will choose to put his Name is so far away), [25]then exchange your tithe for silver, and take the silver with you and go to the place the LORD your God will choose. [26]Use the silver to buy whatever you like: cattle, sheep, wine or other fermented drink, or anything you wish. Then you and your household shall eat there in the presence of the LORD your God and rejoice.[l] [27]And do not neglect the Levites[m] living in your towns, for they have no allotment or inheritance of their own.[n]

[28]At the end of every three years, bring all the tithes of that year's produce and store it in your towns,[o] [29]so that the Levites (who have no allotment[p] or inheritance of their own) and the aliens,[q] the fatherless and the widows who live in your towns may come and eat and be satisfied, and so that the LORD your God may bless[r] you in all the work of your hands.

The Year for Canceling Debts

15 At the end of every seven years you must cancel debts.[s] [2]This is how it is to be done: Every creditor shall cancel the loan he has made to his fellow Is-

---

[a] 7 That is, the hyrax or rock badger

Side notes

14:8
[e] Lev 11:26-27

14:21
[f] Lev 17:15; 22:8
[g] ver 2 [h] Ex 23:19; 34:26

14:22
[i] Lev 27:30; Dt 12:6,17; Ne 10:37

14:23
[j] Dt 12:5 [k] Dt 4:10

14:26
[l] Dt 12:7-8
14:27
[m] Dt 12:19
[n] Nu 18:20
14:28
[o] Dt 26:12
14:29
[p] ver 27 [q] Dt 26:12
[r] Dt 15:10; Mal 3:10

15:1
[s] Dt 31:10

---

the regulations we don't understand, much as the Israelites did. Yet we still abide by the law. How much more gladly should we obey God's Word—the truth revealed in Jesus Christ—given wholly for our benefit?

Deuteronomy 14:22–29

Every year the people were to offer a tithe of their harvest at the central sanctuary. They would eat part of the tithe, but the great majority would go to the Levites. Every three years the tithes were to be brought to towns where they would be stored for use by the Levites, aliens, and the poor. This care for those who didn't own land would lead to God's blessing on the work of the people's hands. After the sixth year, the sabbatical

year was to be observed as a period during which the fields would lie fallow. Then the cycle would begin again.

Ever notice how systematic God was in making sure the needy were remembered? Had he left this critical area to the goodwill or best intentions of individual Israelites, many powerless, low-profile people would have fallen through the cracks. "Civilized" societies have systems in place as well, though too many destitute people—especially those without addresses—still exist without aid. What systems does your church have in place to help the needy? Do you personally seek them out, whether in your own congregation or locality or in the world at large? Does your routine include regular service activities?

15:3
t Dt 23:20

15:4
u Dt 28:8
15:5
v Dt 28:1

15:6
w Dt 28:12-13,44

15:7
x 1Jn 3:17
15:8
y Mt 5:42; Lk 6:34

15:9
z ver 1 a Mt 20:15
b Dt 24:15

15:10
c 2Co 9:5
d Dt 14:29; 24:19

15:11
e Mt 26:11;
Mk 14:7; Jn 12:8

15:12
f Ex 21:2;
Lev 25:39;
Jer 34:14

15:15
g Dt 5:15
h Dt 16:12

raelite. He shall not require payment from his fellow Israelite or brother, because the LORD's time for canceling debts has been proclaimed. 3You may require payment from a foreigner,[t] but you must cancel any debt your brother owes you. 4However, there should be no poor among you, for in the land the LORD your God is giving you to possess as your inheritance, he will richly bless[u] you, 5if only you fully obey the LORD your God and are careful to follow[v] all these commands I am giving you today. 6For the LORD your God will bless you as he has promised, and you will lend to many nations but will borrow from none. You will rule over many nations but none will rule over you.[w]

7If there is a poor man among your brothers in any of the towns of the land that the LORD your God is giving you, do not be hardhearted or tightfisted[x] toward your poor brother. 8Rather be openhanded[y] and freely lend him whatever he needs. 9Be careful not to harbor this wicked thought: "The seventh year, the year for canceling debts,[z] is near," so that you do not show ill will[a] toward your needy brother and give him nothing. He may then appeal to the LORD against you, and you will be found guilty of sin.[b] 10Give generously to him and do so without a grudging heart;[c] then because of this the LORD your God will bless[d] you in all your work and in everything you put your hand to. 11There will always be poor people in the land. Therefore I command you to be openhanded toward your brothers and toward the poor and needy in your land.[e]

Freeing Servants

12If a fellow Hebrew, a man or a woman, sells himself to you and serves you six years, in the seventh year you must let him go free.[f] 13And when you release him, do not send him away empty-handed. 14Supply him liberally from your flock, your threshing floor and your winepress. Give to him as the LORD your God has blessed you. 15Remember that you were slaves[g] in Egypt and the LORD your God redeemed you.[h] That is why I give you this command today.

16But if your servant says to you, "I do not want to leave you," because he loves you and your family and is well off with you, 17then take an awl and push it through his ear lobe into the door, and he will become your servant for life. Do the same for your maidservant.

18Do not consider it a hardship to set your servant free, because his service to you these six years has been worth twice as much as that of a hired hand. And the LORD your God will bless you in everything you do.

Deuteronomy 15:1–11

The statement in verse 4 that "there should be no poor among you" seems to conflict with verse 7 ("If there is a poor man among your brothers . . .") and especially verse 11 ("There will always be poor people in the land"). The same kind of apparent contradiction appears in 1 John 2:1, emphasis added: "I write this to you so that you will not sin. *But if anybody does sin . . .*" Both Moses and John proclaimed and urged the ideal situation—apparently doubtful that it could be fully realized. Maybe Jesus was thinking of verse 11 when he commented, "The poor you will always have with you" (Matt. 26:11; Mark 14:7; John 12:8).

Why must we always have the poor among us? Centuries and millennia have passed since Moses first pronounced this to be the case, and it has certainly proven true. The obvious answer is that we live in a *world of sin*—*the essential problem behind all of poverty's root causes.* But might God also want to provide opportunity for us to represent him in service to the world (no matter how small or large that contribution may be for a given individual)?

Deuteronomy 15:12–18

Concern for the poor (see notes for previous two passages) also related to an Israelite's attitude toward fellow Hebrews who had sold themselves into servitude, a situation usually caused by poverty. That such persons should go free after no more than six years had already been spelled out in Exodus 21:2–6. But Israelite masters needed to go beyond liberation to liberal generosity. Remembering that they had been redeemed from Egyptian slavery, they were to give freely of their possessions to released servants.

From dysfunctional relationships and alcoholism to prostitution and massive credit card debt, people in the 21st century are as enslaved as the ancient Israelites who sold themselves into servitude. And they don't have the option of freedom (with farewell gifts in the bargain) after x number of years. The common denominator in all these situations is sin—the ultimate taskmaster. The Good News is that Christ, through his representatives, offers freedom—physical, emotional, and spiritual. Sadly, not every "servant" will choose freedom, and not every person will have opportunity to hear the gospel. But that

The Firstborn Animals

19 Set apart for the LORD your God every firstborn male[i] of your herds and flocks. Do not put the firstborn of your oxen to work, and do not shear the firstborn of your sheep. 20 Each year you and your family are to eat them in the presence of the LORD your God at the place he will choose.[j] 21 If an animal has a defect, is lame or blind, or has any serious flaw, you must not sacrifice it to the LORD your God.[k] 22 You are to eat it in your own towns. Both the ceremonially unclean and the clean may eat it, as if it were gazelle or deer.[l] 23 But you must not eat the blood; pour it out on the ground like water.[m]

Passover

16 Observe the month of Abib[n] and celebrate the Passover of the LORD your God, because in the month of Abib he brought you out of Egypt by night. 2 Sacrifice as the Passover to the LORD your God an animal from your flock or herd at the place the LORD will choose as a dwelling for his Name.[o] 3 Do not eat it with bread made with yeast, but for seven days eat unleavened bread, the bread of affliction,[p] because you left Egypt in haste[q]—so that all the days of your life you may remember the time of your departure from Egypt.[r] 4 Let no yeast be found in your possession in all your land for seven days. Do not let any of the meat you sacrifice on the evening of the first day remain until morning.[s]

5 You must not sacrifice the Passover in any town the LORD your God gives you 6 except in the place he will choose as a dwelling for his Name. There you must sacrifice the Passover in the evening, when the sun goes down, on the anniversary[a][t] of your departure from Egypt. 7 Roast[u] it and eat it at the place the LORD your God will choose. Then in the morning return to your tents. 8 For six days eat unleavened bread and on the seventh day hold an assembly[v] to the LORD your God and do no work.

Feast of Weeks

9 Count off seven weeks[w] from the time you begin to put the sickle to the standing grain.[x] 10 Then celebrate the Feast of Weeks to the LORD your God by giving a freewill offering in proportion to the blessings the LORD your God has given you. 11 And

[a] 6 Or *down, at the time of day*

15:19 [i] Ex 13:2
15:20 [j] Dt 12:5-7,17,18; 14:23
15:21 [k] Lev 22:19-25
15:22 [l] Dt 12:15,22
15:23 [m] Dt 12:16
16:1 [n] Ex 12:2; 13:4
16:2 [o] Dt 12:5,26
16:3 [p] Ex 12:8,39; 34:18 [q] Ex 12:11,15,19 [r] Ex 13:3,6-7
16:4 [s] Ex 12:10; 34:25
16:6 [t] Ex 12:6; Dt 12:5
16:7 [u] Ex 12:8; 2Ch 35:13
16:8 [v] Ex 12:16; 13:6; Lev 23:8
16:9 [w] Ex 34:22; Lev 23:15 [x] Ex 23:16; Nu 28:26

---

doesn't mean we aren't to labor untiringly toward that end. Are you working to secure someone else's freedom, giving freely from the riches you have received in Christ?

Deuteronomy 15:19–23

Numbers 18:8–19 specifies that certain parts of firstborn animals were to be given to the priests and their families. Nothing is said there about all the people eating and rejoicing together at the annual festivals, as seen in verse 20 of this passage. That Deuteronomy would have this expanded focus isn't surprising. Generally speaking, the regulations in Deuteronomy were given to all the people, including the priests. And the "tithe" could be used for corporate worship celebrations but wasn't to be used for secular purposes or private gain.

These verses illustrate the axiom "You can't outgive God." While the people gave animals for sacrifices and for use by the tribe of Levi (since the Levites were charged with serving in the Tent of Meeting and not with "secular" work), when it came time to celebrate everyone participated in eating from what they had given in worship. Think about the ways in which you have given to the Lord's work. How have your contributions been multiplied or given back to you? Have these been times of celebration for you?

Deuteronomy 16:1–8

The Israelites had been celebrating the Passover for the past 40 years. Moses stressed the importance of centralizing the place of worship as he prepared the people for settlement in the promised land. Whereas the Canaanites had many places of worship, the tabernacle, God's dwelling place during the desert journey, would be located in the city in Canaan where God would choose to dwell.

"All the days of your life" (v. 3) was a phrase representing the lifetime of an individual as well as the nation's entire existence. In this context Moses called the people to celebrate the Passover as they "remembered" their deliverance from slavery in Egypt, a common theme in Deuteronomy.

In the New Testament, the last Passover Jesus ate with his disciples became the Lord's Supper (Matt. 26:17–29; Mark 14:12–25; Luke 22:7–22). And Christ's death on the cross became the Passover sacrifice to take away sin (1 Cor. 5:7–8; cf. John 1:29). Increasingly, many Christians are taking steps to "remember" their Jewish roots. What benefits do you see for Christians to familiarize themselves with and appreciate Old Testament Jewish traditions, especially those associated with Passover?

16:11
y Dt 12:7
z Dt 12:12

rejoice[y] before the LORD your God at the place he will choose as a dwelling for his Name—you, your sons and daughters, your menservants and maidservants, the Levites[z] in your towns, and the aliens, the fatherless and the widows living among you.

16:12
a Dt 15:15

12Remember that you were slaves in Egypt,[a] and follow carefully these decrees.

Feast of Tabernacles

16:13
b Lev 23:34
c Ex 23:16
16:14
d ver 11

13Celebrate the Feast of Tabernacles for seven days after you have gathered the produce of your threshing floor[b] and your winepress.[c] 14Be joyful[d] at your Feast— you, your sons and daughters, your menservants and maidservants, and the Levites, the aliens, the fatherless and the widows who live in your towns. 15For seven days celebrate the Feast to the LORD your God at the place the LORD will choose. For the LORD your God will bless you in all your harvest and in all the work of your hands, and your joy[e] will be complete.

16:15
e Lev 23:39

16Three times a year all your men must appear before the LORD your God at the place he will choose: at the Feast of Unleavened Bread, the Feast of Weeks and the Feast of Tabernacles.[f] No man should appear before the LORD empty-handed:[g] 17Each of you must bring a gift in proportion to the way the LORD your God has blessed you.

16:16
f Ex 23:14,16
g Ex 34:20

Judges

16:18
h Dt 1:16

18Appoint judges[h] and officials for each of your tribes in every town the LORD your God is giving you, and they shall judge the people fairly. 19Do not pervert jus-

---

Deuteronomy 16:9–12

This festival was called the Feast of Weeks because it came seven weeks after the harvesting that began with the offering of the first barley sheaf during Passover (Lev. 23:15; Num. 28:26). Because of its connection to harvest, it was also known as the Feast of Harvest (Ex. 23:16). The miracle of the outpouring of the Holy Spirit recorded centuries later in Acts 2:1–13 occurred during this festival, known then as Pentecost (which means "fifty"), since it was celebrated fifty days after Passover (Lev. 23:16).

This was one of the three great pilgrim festivals of Judaism, along with the Passover/Feast of Unleavened Bread and the Feast of Tabernacles (see Deut. 16:16). By the 1st Christian century, Pentecost was also considered the anniversary of the giving of the law at Mount Sinai and viewed as a time for renewal of the Mosaic covenant. Pentecost was for Judaism the day of the giving of the law. For Christians it celebrates the coming of the Spirit. What is significant in this connection in terms of salvation history?

Deuteronomy 16:13–17

The Feast of Tabernacles or Booths (cf. Lev. 23:42–43), also called the Feast of Ingathering (Ex. 23:16; 34:22), was celebrated for seven days after the processing of grain and grapes. The people were urged to be joyful at the feast. In fact, because of God's blessing on the work of their hands, their joy was to be "complete"! The closing summary (vv. 16–17) reminded the Israelite men that they weren't to attend any of the three annual

16:18–20

Nations

By giving the Israelites a land, God made his people the Biblical equivalent of a nation, complete with laws, a king (eventually), courts, and an army. We can learn much from Scripture about being a godly nation, especially since nations have become increasingly important in world history:

REPRESENTS 10 NATIONS

Modern Nations		
COUNTRIES IN THE WORLD	238	
UNITED NATIONS MEMBERS	185	
MULTI-PARTY DEMOCRACIES	82	
ONE-PARTY STATES	50	
DICTATORSHIPS	40	
DEPENDENCIES	39	
MILITARY REGIMES	35	

Source: Barrett and Johnson (2001:8)

We have no statistics about godly nations, and this is too subjective a subject to quantify. Can you cite some particular nations you view as fitting this description? What about your own?

tice[i] or show partiality.[j] Do not accept a bribe,[k] for a bribe blinds the eyes of the wise and twists the words of the righteous. 20Follow justice and justice alone, so that you may live and possess the land the LORD your God is giving you.

Worshiping Other Gods

21Do not set up any wooden Asherah pole[a][l] beside the altar you build to the LORD your God,[m] 22and do not erect a sacred stone,[n] for these the LORD your God hates.

17 Do not sacrifice to the LORD your God an ox or a sheep that has any defect[o] or flaw in it, for that would be detestable to him.[p]

2If a man or woman living among you in one of the towns the LORD gives you is found doing evil in the eyes of the LORD your God in violation of his covenant,[q] 3and contrary to my command[r] has worshiped other gods, bowing down to them or to the sun[s] or the moon or the stars of the sky, 4and this has been brought to your attention, then you must investigate it thoroughly. If it is true and it has been proved that this detestable thing has been done in Israel,[t] 5take the man or woman who has done this evil deed to your city gate and stone that person to death. [u] 6On the testimony of two or three witnesses a man shall be put to death, but no one shall be put to death on the testimony of only one witness. [v] 7The hands of the witnesses must be the first in putting him to death, and then the hands of all the people. You must purge the evil[w] from among you.

Law Courts

8If cases come before your courts that are too difficult for you to judge—wheth-

a 21 Or Do not plant any tree dedicated to Asherah

16:19
i Ex 23:2,8
j Lev 19:15; Dt 1:17
k Ecc 7:7

16:21
l Dt 7:5 m Ex 34:13; 2Ki 17:16; 21:3; 2Ch 33:3
16:22
n Lev 26:1
17:1
o Mal 1:8,13
p Dt 15:21
17:2
q Dt 13:6-11
17:3
r Jer 7:22-23
s Job 31:26

17:4
t Dt 13:12-14
17:5
u Lev 24:14
17:6
v Nu 35:30; Dt 19:15; Jos 7:25; Mt 18:16; Jn 8:17; 2Co 13:1; 1Ti 5:19; Heb 10:28
17:7
w Dt 13:5,9

festivals empty-handed. Each was to bring a contribution proportionate to God's blessing on his labor.

Our celebration of "Thanksgiving" is quite similar to the feast in this passage. And many Christians use the Thanksgiving holiday as a time to bring gifts to their church or for the poor in honor of God's goodness to them. How might this tradition make the celebration more meaningful to you and your family? Ask the Lord to show you other creative ways to bring meaning and add "complete" joy to your appreciation of his blessings.

Deuteronomy 16:18–20

At first Moses was the sole judge for the people. At Sinai other judges were provided as assistants (1:9–18; Ex. 18:13–26). Now, however, when the nation was contemplating settlement in Canaan, further arrangements were necessary. Every town would need "judges" (civil magistrates) and "officials" (subordinates who would implement the judges' decisions). The ethical commands of verses 19–20 were for the judges in particular and the populace in general—as seen in the promised reward of continuing to live as a nation in possession of the land.

Every follower of God is called to imitate the Lord's integrity—as the One "who shows no partiality and accepts no bribes" (10:17; cf. 16:19). How careful are you to avoid favoritism in your relationships? To refuse to be "bought" in business dealings or in your own workplace? Do you "follow justice and justice alone" (16:20)? For God that included defending the cause of the fatherless, widows, and aliens (10:18). How are these concerns integrated into your life as a disciple?

If you are in a position of some authority—like a manager or parent—how good are you at delegating? It's not uncommon for Christians to have a strong work ethic—itself a Biblical trait. But when compulsion to work closes the door to accepting help, the system begins to fall apart. The apostle Paul made a powerful statement in Ephesians 4:16: "From [Christ] the whole body [of believers], joined and held together by every supporting ligament, grows and builds itself up in love, as each part does its work." To what degree are you accepting of supporting ligaments? Or how do you fill this critical role? Do you see it as a valuable ministry?

Deuteronomy 16:21—17:7

The Israelites weren't to worship sun, moon, or stars either as physical entities or as representations of pagan deities. In Old Testament theology the sun, moon, and stars, along with other natural elements—like mountains and seas—showcased God's glory, as they do today. But they weren't to be made into physical or idolatrous representations of God (Ps. 8:3; 19:1–6; 148:3–6; Jer. 10:10–13; see also Rom. 1:20). Contemplating the heavenly lights on a clear, dark night might have inspired the Israelites to praise their Creator—not the lights themselves.

People differ in the degree to which they are moved by the artistry of nature, or by visual images in general. But when we are willing to pause before a breathtaking sunset, twinkling night sky, soaring mountain range, or array of wildflowers, we open ourselves up to the possibility of a meaningful worship experience. How often do you allow yourself simply to contemplate God's greatness, whether you are moved by his Word, music, the arts, or God's constantly changing outdoor documentary of himself?

17:8
x 2Ch 19:10
y Dt 12:5; Hag 2:11
17:9
z Dt 19:17;
Eze 44:24

er bloodshed, lawsuits or assaults^x—take them to the place the LORD your God will choose.^y 9Go to the priests, who are Levites, and to the judge who is in office at that time. Inquire of them and they will give you the verdict.^z 10You must act according to the decisions they give you at the place the LORD will choose. Be careful to do everything they direct you to do. 11Act according to the law they teach you and the decisions they give you. Do not turn aside from what they tell you, to the right or to

17:11
a Dt 25:1
17:12
b Nu 15:30
17:13
c Dt 13:11; 19:20

the left.^a 12The man who shows contempt^b for the judge or for the priest who stands ministering there to the LORD your God must be put to death. You must purge the evil from Israel. 13All the people will hear and be afraid, and will not be contemptuous again.^c

The King

17:14
d Dt 11:31; 1Sa 8:5,
19-20
17:15
e Jer 30:21
17:16
f 1Ki 4:26; 10:26
g Isa 31:1; Hos 11:5
h 1Ki 10:28;
Eze 17:15
i Ex 13:17
17:17
j 1Ki 11:3
17:18
k Dt 31:22,24
17:19
l Jos 1:8

14When you enter the land the LORD your God is giving you and have taken possession of it and settled in it, and you say, "Let us set a king over us like all the nations around us,"^d 15be sure to appoint over you the king the LORD your God chooses. He must be from among your own brothers.^e Do not place a foreigner over you, one who is not a brother Israelite. 16The king, moreover, must not acquire great numbers of horses for himself^f or make the people return to Egypt^g to get more of them,^h for the LORD has told you, "You are not to go back that way again."ⁱ 17He must not take many wives,^j or his heart will be led astray. He must not accumulate large amounts of silver and gold.

18When he takes the throne of his kingdom, he is to write^k for himself on a scroll a copy of this law, taken from that of the priests, who are Levites. 19It is to be with him, and he is to read it all the days of his life^l so that he may learn to revere the LORD his God and follow carefully all the words of this law and these decrees 20and

17:20
m 1Ki 15:5
n Dt 5:32

not consider himself better than his brothers and turn from the law^m to the right or to the left.ⁿ Then he and his descendants will reign a long time over his kingdom in Israel.

Offerings for Priests and Levites

18:1
o Dt 10:9; 1Co 9:13

18 The priests, who are Levites—indeed the whole tribe of Levi—are to have no allotment or inheritance with Israel. They shall live on the offerings made to the LORD by fire, for that is their inheritance.^o 2They shall have no inheritance among their brothers; the LORD is their inheritance, as he promised them.

Deuteronomy 17:8–13

All cases too difficult for lower local court decision were to be taken to the priests and the current judge at the chosen center for decisions, which were final and binding. The local judges would then implement the higher court's ruling. Contempt of court, whether by a judge who didn't want to exact the punishment handed down or by a judged citizen, was a capital offense.

The priest or judge deciding matters of law between people was seen as "ministering before the LORD." Contempt of court was serious because the individual was showing contempt for God. God is merciful and kind, but he doesn't tolerate disrespect. What practices, values, and attitudes of our society show lack of respect for the Lord? In what areas might laxness in these matters have seeped into your own life?

Deuteronomy 17:14–20

The king was to copy the law onto a scroll, keeping the copy for his personal and regular use. Sound impractical? Perhaps, but this activity would have impressed God's law on the king's heart. This emphasis on the "words of this law" had three purposes: The king would (1) learn to serve the Lord, (2) follow carefully all

the words of the law and its decrees, and (3) stay on the same level as his fellow citizens before the law of God. The result would be a long reign and the success of future generations.

Fortunately, today we have enough Bibles that most Western believers possess several different versions and copies. And some Christians work to make copies of a Gospel available to people of another language who have never before had access to Scripture. Determine not to take God's Word for granted. Pray and give sacrificially so that Bible translation work can continue. Present and future generations of believers around the world depend on our faithfulness and generosity today.

Deuteronomy 18:1–8

The Levites weren't to have a tribal allotment in Canaan. *God* himself was their inheritance. Their special relationship to him brought with it a share of what belonged to the Lord in the Israelite economy. They were to have specified cities within the boundaries of the other tribes. Under certain circumstances, Levites also could possess private holdings (see v. 8; Num. 35:1–5; Josh. 21). The Levites' daily provision for living came from the offerings made to the Lord and from the firstfruits.

3 This is the share due the priests from the people who sacrifice a bull or a sheep:
the shoulder, the jowls and the inner parts.[p] 4 You are to give them the firstfruits of
your grain, new wine and oil, and the first wool from the shearing of your sheep,[q]
5 for the LORD your God has chosen them[r] and their descendants out of all your
tribes to stand and minister[s] in the LORD's name always.
6 If a Levite moves from one of your towns anywhere in Israel where he is living,
and comes in all earnestness to the place the LORD will choose,[t] 7 he may minister
in the name of the LORD his God like all his fellow Levites who serve there in the
presence of the LORD. 8 He is to share equally in their benefits, even though he has
received money from the sale of family possessions.[u]

Detestable Practices

9 When you enter the land the LORD your God is giving you, do not learn to imitate[v] the detestable ways of the nations there. 10 Let no one be found among you
who sacrifices his son or daughter in[a] the fire, who practices divination[w] or sorcery,
interprets omens, engages in witchcraft,[x] 11 or casts spells, or who is a medium or
spiritist or who consults the dead. 12 Anyone who does these things is detestable to
the LORD, and because of these detestable practices the LORD your God will drive out
those nations before you.[y] 13 You must be blameless before the LORD your God.

The Prophet

14 The nations you will dispossess listen to those who practice sorcery or divination. But as for you, the LORD your God has not permitted you to do so. 15 The LORD
your God will raise up for you a prophet like me from among your own brothers.[z]
You must listen to him. 16 For this is what you asked of the LORD your God at Horeb on the day of the assembly when you said, "Let us not hear the voice of the LORD
our God nor see this great fire anymore, or we will die."[a]
17 The LORD said to me: "What they say is good. 18 I will raise up for them a prophet like you from among their brothers; I will put my words[b] in his mouth, and he
will tell them everything I command him.[c] 19 If anyone does not listen to my words
that the prophet speaks in my name, I myself will call him to account.[d] 20 But a

18:3 [p] Lev 7:28-34
18:4 [q] Ex 22:29; Nu 18:12
18:5 [r] Ex 28:1 [s] Dt 10:8
18:6 [t] Nu 35:2-3
18:8 [u] 2Ch 31:4; Ne 12:44,47
18:9 [v] Dt 12:29-31
18:10 [w] Dt 12:31 [x] Lev 19:31
18:12 [y] Lev 18:24; Dt 9:4
18:15 [z] Jn 1:21; Ac 3:22*; 7:37*
18:16 [a] Ex 20:19; Dt 5:23-27
18:18 [b] Isa 51:16; Jn 17:8 [c] Jn 4:25-26; 8:28; 12:49-50
18:19 [d] Ac 3:23*

[a] 10 *Or who makes his son or daughter pass through*

No modern equivalent to the Levites exists in our culture. Yet general comparisons with the pastorate and church leadership may be appropriate. The financial support of pastors varies widely, with many expected to live sacrificial lives in terms of material possessions. Struggling congregations, to their credit, often do the best they can. How seriously does yours take its commitment to your pastor(s) and family(ies)?

Deuteronomy 18:9–13

The evil practices listed here were the reason God was going to drive the Canaanites out of the land. God's people were to shun not only the false gods of Canaan but the means by which the inhabitants of the land attempted to communicate with them. Both the objects and methods of Canaanite religious life were to be rejected, and this rejection was to be total and complete.

"You must be blameless before the LORD your God" sounds like a tall order, even for redeemed sinners. But such a seemingly audacious claim comes up repeatedly in the Psalms (e.g., Ps. 18:23; 19:13; 26:1,11; 101:2). Jesus himself instructed his hearers in the Sermon on the Mount, "Be perfect . . . as your heavenly Father is perfect" (Matt. 5:48). The apostle Paul put it in perspective: "Not that I have already obtained all this, or have already been made perfect, but I press on to take hold of that for which Christ Jesus took hold of me" (Phil. 3:12). How do this passage and its New Testament counterparts challenge you?

Deuteronomy 18:14–22

Israel had been given a written covenant as a revelation from God. Priests had been provided to implement its religious aspect. Judges and possible future kings were to care for legislative and executive matters. But how would people know God's will in day-to-day circumstances? The prophets, as spokespersons for the Lord (like Moses), would supply this lack. Though Moses promised a series of prophets for future generations, he also looked ahead to the ultimate revealer of God—Jesus (see John 1:45; 5:46; Acts 3:22–23).

When many Christians think about prophets, they think first of predictions of the future. But prediction is only one element of Biblical prophecy. In 1 Corinthians 14:3–4, Paul asserted that the one who prophesies also strengthens, encourages, comforts, and edifies the church. God still uses prophets—representatives who reveal his will and word. Most aren't dedicated to prophecy on a "full-time" basis. They are surrendered people used by God as his willing servants where and when he needs them. When have you served in a prophetic role? Did you recognize your function at the time?

prophet who presumes to speak in my name anything I have not commanded him to say, or a prophet who speaks in the name of other gods, *e* must be put to death." *f* 21You may say to yourselves, "How can we know when a message has not been spoken by the LORD?" 22If what a prophet proclaims in the name of the LORD does not take place or come true, that is a message the LORD has not spoken. *g* That prophet has spoken presumptuously. *h* Do not be afraid of him.

Cities of Refuge

19 When the LORD your God has destroyed the nations whose land he is giving you, and when you have driven them out and settled in their towns and houses, *i* 2then set aside for yourselves three cities centrally located in the land the LORD your God is giving you to possess. 3Build roads to them and divide into three parts the land the LORD your God is giving you as an inheritance, so that anyone who kills a man may flee there.

4This is the rule concerning the man who kills another and flees there to save his life—one who kills his neighbor unintentionally, without malice aforethought. 5For instance, a man may go into the forest with his neighbor to cut wood, and as he swings his ax to fell a tree, the head may fly off and hit his neighbor and kill him. That man may flee to one of these cities and save his life. 6Otherwise, the avenger of blood *j* might pursue him in a rage, overtake him if the distance is too great, and kill him even though he is not deserving of death, since he did it to his neighbor without malice aforethought. 7This is why I command you to set aside for yourselves three cities.

8If the LORD your God enlarges your territory, as he promised on oath to your forefathers, and gives you the whole land he promised them, 9because you carefully follow all these laws I command you today—to love the LORD your God and to walk always in his ways *k*—then you are to set aside three more cities. 10Do this so that innocent blood will not be shed in your land, which the LORD your God is giving you as your inheritance, and so that you will not be guilty of bloodshed. *l*

11But if a man hates his neighbor and lies in wait for him, assaults and kills him, *m* and then flees to one of these cities, 12the elders of his town shall send for him, bring him back from the city, and hand him over to the avenger of blood to die. 13Show him no pity. *n* You must purge from Israel the guilt of shedding innocent blood, *o* so that it may go well with you.

14Do not move your neighbor's boundary stone set up by your predecessors in the inheritance you receive in the land the LORD your God is giving you to possess. *p*

Witnesses

15One witness is not enough to convict a man accused of any crime or offense he may have committed. A matter must be established by the testimony of two or three witnesses. *q*

Deuteronomy 19:1–14

The establishment of cities of refuge for those who unintentionally committed murder was a radical innovation. The cycle of revenge was to be broken. The guarantee of property rights outlined in verse 14 also was innovative. Possession wasn't determined by power but by the right of ownership.

Endless cycles of revenge and disrespect for others' legitimate claims to property have been major contributors to the wars of the past century. God's regard for harmony is so utterly basic and practical that it pertains to these details of life. Many nations confiscate the lands of minority ethnic and religious groups or political opponents. Widows and especially orphans worldwide are often victims of property theft, even by close family members. Wars arise over boundary disputes. These abuses dishonor God and his will for how people are to treat one another. Women, children, and the extremely poor are often held captive in their poverty by others' control of their land. Pray today for people whose lands have been stolen, and ask the Lord to sensitize your heart to this kind of injustice.

Deuteronomy 19:15–21

A "malicious" witness (v. 16) was one whose intent was to harm, especially by using particularly harsh or injurious language. When one accused another in this fashion, both the accused and the accuser were to stand before the higher court (see "There and Then" for 17:8–13). The investigation was to be "thorough" (v. 18; cf. 13:14; 17:4). If the accuser proved to be a liar, the punishment sought for the accused would be meted out to the accuser—certainly a radical deterrent against slander or libel.

The so-called law of retaliation in verse 21 (also cited

16If a malicious witness[r] takes the stand to accuse a man of a crime, 17the two men involved in the dispute must stand in the presence of the LORD before the priests and the judges[s] who are in office at the time. 18The judges must make a thorough investigation, and if the witness proves to be a liar, giving false testimony against his brother, 19then do to him as he intended to do to his brother.[t] You must purge the evil from among you. 20The rest of the people will hear of this and be afraid,[u] and never again will such an evil thing be done among you. 21Show no pity:[v] life for life, eye for eye, tooth for tooth, hand for hand, foot for foot.[w]

Going to War

20 When you go to war against your enemies and see horses and chariots and an army greater than yours,[x] do not be afraid[y] of them,[z] because the LORD your God, who brought you up out of Egypt, will be with you. 2When you are about to go into battle, the priest shall come forward and address the army. 3He shall say: "Hear, O Israel, today you are going into battle against your enemies. Do not be fainthearted[a] or afraid; do not be terrified or give way to panic before them. 4For the LORD your God is the one who goes with you to fight[b] for you against your enemies to give you victory."

5The officers shall say to the army: "Has anyone built a new house and not dedicated[c] it? Let him go home, or he may die in battle and someone else may dedicate it. 6Has anyone planted a vineyard and not begun to enjoy it? Let him go home, or he may die in battle and someone else enjoy it. 7Has anyone become pledged to a woman and not married her? Let him go home, or he may die in battle and someone else marry her.[d]" 8Then the officers shall add, "Is any man afraid or fainthearted? Let him go home so that his brothers will not become disheartened too."[e] 9When the officers have finished speaking to the army, they shall appoint commanders over it.

10When you march up to attack a city, make its people an offer of peace.[f] 11If they accept and open their gates, all the people in it shall be subject to forced labor[g] and shall work for you. 12If they refuse to make peace and they engage you in battle, lay siege to that city. 13When the LORD your God delivers it into your hand, put to the sword all the men in it.[h] 14As for the women, the children, the livestock[i] and everything else in the city, you may take these as plunder for yourselves. And you may use the plunder the LORD your God gives you from your enemies. 15This is how you are to treat all the cities that are at a distance from you and do not belong to the nations nearby.

16However, in the cities of the nations the LORD your God is giving you as an in-

19:16
r Ex 23:1; Ps 27:12

19:17
s Dt 17:9

19:19
t Pr 19:5,9

19:20
u Dt 17:13; 21:21
19:21
v ver 13
w Ex 21:24;
Lev 24:20; Mt 5:38*

20:1
x Ps 20:7; Isa 31:1
y Dt 31:6,8
z 2Ch 32:7-8

20:3
a Jos 23:10
20:4
b Dt 1:30; 3:22;
Jos 23:10

20:5
c Ne 12:27

20:7
d Dt 24:5
20:8
e Jdg 7:3

20:10
f Lk 14:31-32
20:11
g 1Ki 9:21

20:13
h Nu 31:7
20:14
i Jos 8:2; 22:8

---

in Ex. 21:23–25; Lev. 24:18–20) was given as the guideline for punishing offenders. "Show no pity," God instructed through Moses. Mitigating circumstances and legal loopholes weren't to be tolerated in the Israelite justice system. However, the punishment could only be proportionate to the crime.

In Matthew 5:38–42 Jesus commanded his followers not to apply the principle of Deuteronomy 19:21 in protection of their own rights but to substitute the radical new concept of turning the other cheek. The laws in Deuteronomy were designed to protect the public, punish offenders, and deter crime. Jesus, on the other hand, was speaking to individuals about violence against themselves personally. When you consider how the Sanhedrin violated these basic laws during Jesus' trial (Mark 14:55–59), what do you think of his request that God forgive them (Luke 23:34)?

Deuteronomy 20:1–20
The rules for warfare outlined in this chapter were another radical innovation of the Deuteronomic

law. In the future, when Israel would attack a city beyond the boundaries of Canaan proper (vv. 10–15), different rules would apply than for the conquest of the promised land (vv. 16–18). As opposed to being offered peace, the cities of Canaan were subject to total destruction so that the Israelites wouldn't be enticed into the supreme sin of defecting from the Lord and worshiping other gods (see also "There and Then" for 7:1–26).

The military officers were to speak to potential inductees in a most extraordinary way: spelling out ways to be excused from service (vv. 5–8). Only the ready and willing were wanted for battle. If a man didn't fit any of the specific categories of exemption, the last—"Is anyone afraid?"—would relieve him of duty if he so desired.

Discipleship—service in the "Lord's army"—carries a cost. In Luke 14:15–35 Jesus paralleled Deuteronomy 20:5–8 in his remarks to those who would enlist disciples in the kingdom of God. How do the principles in Deuteronomy about military service correlate? Differ? Do we in the church make discipleship too light a matter?

20:16
_j_ Ex 23:31-33;
Nu 21:2-3; Dt 7:2;
Jos 11:14
20:18
_k_ Ex 34:16; Dt 7:4;
12:30-31 _l_ Ex 23:33

heritance, do not leave alive anything that breathes._j_ [17]Completely destroy[a] them—the Hittites, Amorites, Canaanites, Perizzites, Hivites and Jebusites—as the LORD your God has commanded you. [18]Otherwise, they will teach you to follow all the detestable things they do in worshiping their gods,_k_ and you will sin_l_ against the LORD your God.

[19]When you lay siege to a city for a long time, fighting against it to capture it, do not destroy its trees by putting an ax to them, because you can eat their fruit. Do not cut them down. Are the trees of the field people, that you should besiege them?[b] [20]However, you may cut down trees that you know are not fruit trees and use them to build siege works until the city at war with you falls.

Atonement for an Unsolved Murder

21 If a man is found slain, lying in a field in the land the LORD your God is giving you to possess, and it is not known who killed him, [2]your elders and judges shall go out and measure the distance from the body to the neighboring towns. [3]Then the elders of the town nearest the body shall take a heifer that has never been worked and has never worn a yoke [4]and lead her down to a valley that has not been plowed or planted and where there is a flowing stream. There in the valley they are to break the heifer's neck. [5]The priests, the sons of Levi, shall step forward, for the LORD your God has chosen them to minister and to pronounce blessings_m_ in the name of the LORD and to decide all cases of dispute and assault._n_ [6]Then all the elders of the town nearest the body shall wash their hands_o_ over the heifer whose neck was broken in the valley, [7]and they shall declare: "Our hands did not shed this blood, nor did our eyes see it done. [8]Accept this atonement for your people Israel, whom you have redeemed, O LORD, and do not hold your people guilty of the blood of an innocent man." And the bloodshed will be atoned for._p_ [9]So you will purge_q_ from yourselves the guilt of shedding innocent blood, since you have done what is right in the eyes of the LORD.

21:5
_m_ 1Ch 23:13
_n_ Dt 17:8-11
21:6
_o_ Mt 27:24

21:8
_p_ Nu 35:33-34
21:9
_q_ Dt 19:13

Marrying a Captive Woman

21:10
_r_ Jos 21:44

[10]When you go to war against your enemies and the LORD your God delivers them into your hands_r_ and you take captives, [11]if you notice among the captives a beau-

---

[a] 17 The Hebrew term refers to the irrevocable giving over of things or persons to the LORD, often by totally destroying them.   [b] 19 Or _down to use in the siege, for the fruit trees are for the benefit of man._

Deuteronomy 21:1–9

📖 When murder or manslaughter had been committed, God's justice was affronted. The unidentified criminal was connected with both the land and the people. Unless the perpetrator of the crime was punished, justice couldn't be met (Num. 35:33). When the murderer's identity couldn't be determined, some method for removal of the guilt that had fallen on the land and people needed to be secured. The procedure given here provided the means for satisfying God's justice by the removal of corporate (community) guilt.

📖 Atonement was made for the bloodshed when the elders broke the heifer's neck and washed their hands over its body, declaring their own innocence and that of the people. This action purged them from the guilt of spilling innocent blood. This atonement was outside the sacrificial system. But the heifer died in place of the criminal, to clear the land of guilt. Much of the unresolved conflict that divides communities in our world today stems from the failure to recognize corporate guilt and conduct ceremonies to affirm forgiveness and reconciliation. What similarities to Christ's death do you see in this passage?

Deuteronomy 21:10–14

📖 These verses relate to the marriage of an Israelite man to an unmarried woman captured in warfare "at a distance" from Canaan (see 20:10–15). Because of the distance, she wouldn't be under the ban of total destruction (see 20:16–18), and the couple would be subject to all rules pertaining to Israelite marriage. Cleansing rites (cf. Lev. 14:8; Num. 8:7; 2 Sam. 19:24) would initiate her into the family, but she was to be granted one month to mourn her parents. As the God of the oppressed and powerless, the Lord insisted that even these captive women were to have rights. If the husband later dishonored such a woman by rejecting her, she was to go free rather than be treated as a slave.

📖 This passage is shocking to us, but still today women are often the sexually exploited victims of war. This law created boundaries for men's lust and promoted a standard of respect for women that is too often violated today in combat situations. Pray for the ministries that seek to bring healing and wholeness to the women and girls who are the victims of wars' brutal sexual exploitation in places like Kosovo, Sierra Leone, Afghanistan, and Iraq.

tiful woman and are attracted to her, you may take her as your wife. [12]Bring her into your home and have her shave her head, [s] trim her nails [13]and put aside the clothes she was wearing when captured. After she has lived in your house and mourned her father and mother for a full month, [t] then you may go to her and be her husband and she shall be your wife. [14]If you are not pleased with her, let her go wherever she wishes. You must not sell her or treat her as a slave, since you have dishonored her. [u]

The Right of the Firstborn

[15]If a man has two wives, and he loves one but not the other, and both bear him sons but the firstborn is the son of the wife he does not love, [v] [16]when he wills his property to his sons, he must not give the rights of the firstborn to the son of the wife he loves in preference to his actual firstborn, the son of the wife he does not love. [w] [17]He must acknowledge the son of his unloved wife as the firstborn by giving him a double share of all he has. That son is the first sign of his father's strength. [x] The right of the firstborn belongs to him. [y]

A Rebellious Son

[18]If a man has a stubborn and rebellious son who does not obey his father and mother [z] and will not listen to them when they discipline him, [19]his father and mother shall take hold of him and bring him to the elders at the gate of his town. [20]They shall say to the elders, "This son of ours is stubborn and rebellious. He will not obey us. He is a profligate and a drunkard." [21]Then all the men of his town shall stone him to death. You must purge the evil [a] from among you. All Israel will hear of it and be afraid. [b]

Various Laws

[22]If a man guilty of a capital offense [c] is put to death and his body is hung on a tree, [23]you must not leave his body on the tree overnight. [d] Be sure to bury him that same day, because anyone who is hung on a tree is under God's curse. [e] You must not desecrate [f] the land the LORD your God is giving you as an inheritance.

21:12 [s] Lev 14:9; Nu 6:9

21:13 [t] Ps 45:10

21:14 [u] Ge 34:2

21:15 [v] Ge 29:33

21:16 [w] 1Ch 26:10

21:17 [x] Ge 49:3 [y] Ge 25:31

21:18 [z] Pr 1:8; Isa 30:1; Eph 6:1-3

21:21 [a] Dt 19:19; 1Co 5:13* [b] Dt 13:11

21:22 [c] Dt 22:26; Mk 14:64; Ac 23:29

21:23 [d] Jos 8:29; 10:27; Jn 19:31 [e] Gal 3:13* [f] Lev 18:25; Nu 35:34

Deuteronomy 21:15–17

Though it wasn't God's ideal will, he tolerated polygamy and created innovative laws to regulate the abuse and injustice it often creates. How many Old Testament family dysfunctions can be traced directly back to polygamy? While not officially approved in ancient Biblical times, the practice was allowed. The stories of Jacob, Leah, and Rachel in particular show how custom and favoritism could adversely affect life in the polygamous family (Gen. 29:15—30:24). Elkanah's rival wives, Hannah and Peninnah, also each suffered bitterly (1 Sam. 1:1–20), and David's family was devastated by polygamy's disastrous results (2 Sam. 13–19; 1 Kings 1).

While not members of a polygamous society, Westerners have been accused of practicing serial monogamy—having multiple marriages, one after the other. What consequences have we reaped in our society as a result? How have children and families been affected? How might the Lord be asking you to respond personally or with regard to your own family? What kinds of legal, relational, and emotional safeguards need to be created in order to protect children and women in such situations?

Deuteronomy 21:18–21

The son in mind here wasn't just stubborn and rebellious but irredeemably and defiantly disobedient. We can assume that his parents had tried everything to turn the situation around before resorting to this desperate, permanent measure. The punishment of being stoned to death was intended to purge the evil from among the people (13:5; 17:7,12). Fear of it was expected to restrain such rebellion, which was strictly forbidden by the fifth commandment (5:16; Ex. 20:12; cf. Ex. 21:15). Happily, the Old Testament doesn't contain a single recorded instance of this consequence being applied.

Several insights are striking in this passage. The expressions of rebellion portrayed here were gluttony and drunkenness. For parents to judge this behavior must have implied that they themselves weren't gluttons. Otherwise, the evil they were seeking to purge would still be among them. The discipline of children wasn't merely the parents' responsibility but that of the community. This both protected children from irrational parents and called the community to a high quality of moral living. To what extent are the adults in your faith community living as exemplary models to all children and seeking together to raise them in the holiness of the Lord?

Deuteronomy 21:22—22:12

Lifestyle legislation in the land of promise went beyond rules about wrongdoing. Involvement in a fellow citizen's plight (or that of his animal) demanded that assistance be given—without reward, except for the satisfaction of having helped.

Concern for "being kind to animals" and for ensuring

22:1
g Ex 23:4-5

22 If you see your brother's ox or sheep straying, do not ignore it but be sure to take it back to him. *g* 2If the brother does not live near you or if you do not know who he is, take it home with you and keep it until he comes looking for it. Then give it back to him. 3Do the same if you find your brother's donkey or his cloak or anything he loses. Do not ignore it.

22:4
h Ex 23:5

4If you see your brother's donkey *h* or his ox fallen on the road, do not ignore it. Help him get it to its feet.

5A woman must not wear men's clothing, nor a man wear women's clothing, for the LORD your God detests anyone who does this.

22:6
i Lev 22:28
22:7
j Dt 4:40

6If you come across a bird's nest beside the road, either in a tree or on the ground, and the mother is sitting on the young or on the eggs, do not take the mother with the young. *i* 7You may take the young, but be sure to let the mother go, so that it may go well with you and you may have a long life. *j*

8When you build a new house, make a parapet around your roof so that you may not bring the guilt of bloodshed on your house if someone falls from the roof.

22:9
k Lev 19:19

9Do not plant two kinds of seed in your vineyard; *k* if you do, not only the crops you plant but also the fruit of the vineyard will be defiled. *a*

22:10
l 2Co 6:14
22:11
m Lev 19:19
22:12
n Nu 15:37-41;
Mt 23:5

10Do not plow with an ox and a donkey yoked together. *l*

11Do not wear clothes of wool and linen woven together. *m*

12Make tassels on the four corners of the cloak you wear. *n*

Marriage Violations

22:13
o Dt 24:1

13If a man takes a wife and, after lying with her *o*, dislikes her 14and slanders her and gives her a bad name, saying, "I married this woman, but when I approached her, I did not find proof of her virginity," 15then the girl's father and mother shall bring proof that she was a virgin to the town elders at the gate. 16The girl's father will say to the elders, "I gave my daughter in marriage to this man, but he dislikes her. 17Now he has slandered her and said, 'I did not find your daughter to be a virgin.' But here is the proof of my daughter's virginity." Then her parents shall display

22:18
p Ex 18:21

the cloth before the elders of the town, 18and the elders *p* shall take the man and punish him. 19They shall fine him a hundred shekels of silver *b* and give them to

a 9 Or be forfeited to the sanctuary   *b 19 That is, about 2 1/2 pounds (about 1 kilogram)*

---

species propagation (as in modern hunting laws) may have been in mind in 22:6–7. God had instructed Adam and Eve to "rule over the fish of the sea and the birds of the air and over every living creature that moves on the ground" (Gen. 1:28). The covenant God had made with Noah and his descendants after the flood also included every living creature in the ark (Gen. 9:8–11). Moses tied long life and well-being to obedience to this command—the same promise as for honoring father and mother (Deut. 5:16).

📖 Common decency and thoughtfulness toward others aren't legislated in our society. Nor are they expected to the degree they were just a generation or two ago. "Rules" of etiquette have been lost in recent decades. Stranded motorists are more likely to receive glares than assistance. What forms of decency do you practice? If you are training children, what "manners" do you teach? What differences do small kindnesses make for life in a care-less, hectic world?

Deuteronomy 22:13–30

📖 The "proof" of virginity (v. 17) was probably a bloodstained bed sheet or garment, resulting from the new wife's first experience of intercourse. Though not

infallible, such items were widely accepted in the ancient Near East as indications of prior virginity.

Marital fidelity looms large in the Law of Moses. Even though Jesus would later say that Moses allowed divorce "because your hearts were hard" (Mark 10:5), divorce was subject to a number of restrictions. It's noteworthy that the formula "You must purge the evil from among you" (or "from Israel") occurs three times (vv. 21,22,24) in this series of capital offenses—an indication of the seriousness of crimes against marital fidelity.

📖 Certain cultures today go beyond the Biblical evidence required for virginity, enforcing a practice called female circumcision, thought to "ensure" virginity. This mutilation of an elementary-aged girl's vaginal area is carried out by tribal women under the most brutal circumstances, without the benefit of anesthesia. Besides the psychological scars, the results for the girl are extreme difficulty in later childbirth, sometimes resulting in death of the mother and/or child. Other post-childbirth consequences include fistulas, torn internal areas that leak bodily waste uncontrollably. One hospital founded by Christian medical missionaries performs surgeries to repair fistulas. Other ministries work at a grassroots level to eradicate female circumcision entirely.

the girl's father, because this man has given an Israelite virgin a bad name. She shall continue to be his wife; he must not divorce her as long as he lives.

20If, however, the charge is true and no proof of the girl's virginity can be found, 21she shall be brought to the door of her father's house and there the men of her town shall stone her to death. She has done a disgraceful thing*q* in Israel by being promiscuous while still in her father's house. You must purge the evil from among you.

22If a man is found sleeping with another man's wife, both the man who slept with her and the woman must die.*r* You must purge the evil from Israel.

23If a man happens to meet in a town a virgin pledged to be married and he sleeps with her, 24you shall take both of them to the gate of that town and stone them to death—the girl because she was in a town and did not scream for help, and the man because he violated another man's wife. You must purge the evil from among you.*s*

25But if out in the country a man happens to meet a girl pledged to be married and rapes her, only the man who has done this shall die. 26Do nothing to the girl; she has committed no sin deserving death. This case is like that of someone who attacks and murders his neighbor, 27for the man found the girl out in the country, and though the betrothed girl screamed, there was no one to rescue her.

28If a man happens to meet a virgin who is not pledged to be married and rapes her and they are discovered,*t* 29he shall pay the girl's father fifty shekels of silver.*a* He must marry the girl, for he has violated her. He can never divorce her as long as he lives.

30A man is not to marry his father's wife; he must not dishonor his father's bed.*u*

Exclusion From the Assembly

23 No one who has been emasculated by crushing or cutting may enter the assembly of the LORD.

2No one born of a forbidden marriage*b* nor any of his descendants may enter the assembly of the LORD, even down to the tenth generation.

3No Ammonite or Moabite or any of his descendants may enter the assembly of the LORD, even down to the tenth generation.*v* 4For they did not come to meet you with bread and water on your way when you came out of Egypt, and they hired Balaam*w* son of Beor from Pethor in Aram Naharaim*c* to pronounce a curse on you. 5However, the LORD your God would not listen to Balaam but turned the curse*x* into a blessing for you, because the LORD your God loves you. 6Do not seek a treaty of friendship with them as long as you live.*y*

7Do not abhor an Edomite, for he is your brother.*z* Do not abhor an Egyptian, because you lived as an alien in his country.*a* 8The third generation of children born to them may enter the assembly of the LORD.

Uncleanness in the Camp

9When you are encamped against your enemies, keep away from everything im-

Margin references:
22:21 *q* Ge 34:7; Dt 13:5; 23:17-18; Jdg 20:6; 2Sa 13:12
22:22 *r* Lev 20:10; Jn 8:5
22:24 *s* ver 21-22; 1Co 5:13*
22:28 *t* Ex 22:16
22:30 *u* Lev 18:8; 20:11; Dt 27:20; 1Co 5:1
23:3 *v* Ne 13:2
23:4 *w* Nu 22:5-6; 23:7; 2Pe 2:15
23:5 *x* Pr 26:2
23:6 *y* Ezr 9:12
23:7 *z* Ge 25:26; Ob 1:10,12 *a* Ex 22:21; 23:9; Lev 19:34; Dt 10:19

---

a 29 That is, about 1 1/4 pounds (about 0.6 kilogram) *b 2* Or *one of illegitimate birth* *c 4* That is, Northwest Mesopotamia

---

Deuteronomy 23:1–8

Three categories of persons were to be excluded from "the assembly of the LORD"—i.e., from participation in Israel's religious rites. Those mentioned first had probably been made eunuchs deliberately. If so, this rule was directed particularly toward men who had been emasculated in dedication to foreign gods.

Which individuals fell into the second category isn't clear. While "one born of a forbidden marriage" (v. 2) could mean all children born out of wedlock (see NIV text note), some contend that a "forbidden marriage" meant an incestuous affair or a sexual union with a cult prostitute.

Ammonites and Moabites were excluded because of their sins of omission (failing to show concern when the Israelites moved toward Canaan) and commission (hiring Balaam to curse Israel).

Excluding descendants "to the tenth generation" for the fault of their ancestors seems extreme; thus some scholars see this as a figure of speech (hyperbole). This penalty on the Moabites didn't prevent Ruth from becoming a convert to Judaism and an ancestor in the Messiah's family line (Ruth 1:16; 4:17). And because of the Messiah, all eunuchs, illegitimate children, and foreigners are welcome in God's new "assembly" (cf. Isa. 56:3–8; Luke 5:29–31; Acts 8:26–39; Rev. 5:9–10).

23:10
b Lev 15:16

pure. [10]If one of your men is unclean because of a nocturnal emission, he is to go outside the camp and stay there. [b] [11]But as evening approaches he is to wash himself, and at sunset he may return to the camp.

[12]Designate a place outside the camp where you can go to relieve yourself. [13]As part of your equipment have something to dig with, and when you relieve yourself, dig a hole and cover up your excrement. [14]For the LORD your God moves[c] about in your camp to protect you and to deliver your enemies to you. Your camp must be holy, [d] so that he will not see among you anything indecent and turn away from you.

23:14
c Lev 26:12 d Ex 3:5

Miscellaneous Laws

23:15
e 1Sa 30:15

[15]If a slave has taken refuge with you, do not hand him over to his master. [e] [16]Let him live among you wherever he likes and in whatever town he chooses. Do not oppress[f] him.

23:16
f Ex 22:21
23:17
g Ge 19:25;
2Ki 23:7
h Lev 19:29;
Dt 22:21

[17]No Israelite man[g] or woman is to become a shrine prostitute. [h] [18]You must not bring the earnings of a female prostitute or of a male prostitute[a] into the house of the LORD your God to pay any vow, because the LORD your God detests them both.

23:19
i Ex 22:25;
Lev 25:35-37
23:20
j Dt 15:10; 28:12

[19]Do not charge your brother interest, whether on money or food or anything else that may earn interest. [i] [20]You may charge a foreigner interest, but not a brother Israelite, so that the LORD your God may bless[j] you in everything you put your hand to in the land you are entering to possess.

23:21
k Nu 30:1-2;
Ecc 5:4-5; Mt 5:33

[21]If you make a vow to the LORD your God, do not be slow to pay it, for the LORD your God will certainly demand it of you and you will be guilty of sin. [k] [22]But if you refrain from making a vow, you will not be guilty. [23]Whatever your lips utter you must be sure to do, because you made your vow freely to the LORD your God with your own mouth.

[24]If you enter your neighbor's vineyard, you may eat all the grapes you want, but do not put any in your basket. [25]If you enter your neighbor's grainfield, you may pick kernels with your hands, but you must not put a sickle to his standing grain.[l]

23:25
l Mt 12:1; Mk 2:23;
Lk 6:1
24:1
m Dt 22:13
n Mt 5:31*; 19:7-9;
Mk 10:4-5

24

If a man marries a woman who becomes displeasing to him[m] because he finds something indecent about her, and he writes her a certificate of divorce, [n] gives it to her and sends her from his house, [2]and if after she leaves his house she becomes the wife of another man, [3]and her second husband dislikes her and writes her a certificate of divorce, gives it to her and sends her from his house, or if he dies, [4]then her first husband, who divorced her, is not allowed to marry her again after she has been defiled. That would be detestable in the eyes of the LORD. Do not bring sin upon the land the LORD[o] your God is giving you as an inheritance.

24:4
o Jer 3:1

[5]If a man has recently married, he must not be sent to war or have any other duty laid on him. For one year he is to be free to stay at home and bring happiness to the wife he has married.[p]

24:5
p Dt 20:7

---

a 18 Hebrew *of a dog*

Deuteronomy 23:9–14

"Cleanliness is next to godliness" isn't an Old Testament quote, as some think, but the concept does have a Biblical basis. For the ancient Israelites, holiness was indeed identified with cleanliness. Only the ritually clean person could approach the Lord in worship (Ex. 19:10–11; 30:18–21; Josh. 3:5; Ps. 51:7,10).

What do you do to "clean yourself up" before attending a worship service? For many Christians today, the concept of "Sunday best" no longer holds meaning. This reduces competition, places everyone on an equal footing, and discourages us from putting on airs to impress fellow church members. Avoiding legalism and show, most of us would agree, are good things. While acknowledging that we can't make ourselves right before God, how can we in a positive sense prepare our hearts and minds for worship in his presence?

Deuteronomy 23:15—25:19

Divorce in the books of Moses (24:1–4; Lev. 21:7,14; 22:13; Num. 30:9) was a fact of life—permitted under some circumstances but regulated. Its basis couldn't be frivolous or trivial. The phrase "something indecent" (24:1) possibly referred to something less than adultery, which was punishable by death (22:22–27; Lev. 20:10).

Concern for the underprivileged appears again and again in this section of miscellaneous laws, as well as in the rest of Deuteronomy (e.g., 10:18–19; 14:28–29; 16:11; 27:19). That concern was in part based on the Israelites' slavery in Egypt, which should have made them sensitive to the needs of the less fortunate, as stated twice in 24:17–22 (see also 15:12–15).

⁶Do not take a pair of millstones—not even the upper one—as security for a debt, because that would be taking a man's livelihood as security.

⁷If a man is caught kidnapping one of his brother Israelites and treats him as a slave or sells him, the kidnapper must die. ⁹ You must purge the evil from among you.

⁸In cases of leprousᵃ diseases be very careful to do exactly as the priests, who are Levites, instruct you. You must follow carefully what I have commanded them.ʳ ⁹Remember what the LORD your God did to Miriam along the way after you came out of Egypt.ˢ

¹⁰When you make a loan of any kind to your neighbor, do not go into his house to get what he is offering as a pledge. ¹¹Stay outside and let the man to whom you are making the loan bring the pledge out to you. ¹²If the man is poor, do not go to sleep with his pledge in your possession. ¹³Return his cloak to him by sunsetᵗ so that he may sleep in it. Then he will thank you, and it will be regarded as a righteous act in the sight of the LORD your God.ᵘ

¹⁴Do not take advantage of a hired man who is poor and needy, whether he is a brother Israelite or an alien living in one of your towns.ᵛ ¹⁵Pay him his wages each day before sunset, because he is poorʷ and is counting on it.ˣ Otherwise he may cry to the LORD against you, and you will be guilty of sin.ʸ

¹⁶Fathers shall not be put to death for their children, nor children put to death for their fathers; each is to die for his own sin.ᶻ

¹⁷Do not deprive the alien or the fatherless of justice,ᵃ or take the cloak of the widow as a pledge. ¹⁸Remember that you were slaves in Egypt and the LORD your God redeemed you from there. That is why I command you to do this.

ᵃ 8 The Hebrew word was used for various diseases affecting the skin—not necessarily leprosy.

24:7
⁹ Ex 21:16
24:8
ʳ Lev 13:1-46; 14:2
24:9
ˢ Nu 12:10
24:13
ᵗ Ex 22:26
ᵘ Dt 6:25; Da 4:27
24:14
ᵛ Lev 25:35-43; Dt 15:12-18
24:15
ʷ Jer 22:13
ˣ Lev 19:13
ʸ Dt 15:9; Jas 5:4
24:16
ᶻ 2Ki 14:6; 2Ch 25:4; Jer 31:29-30; Eze 18:20
24:17
ᵃ Dt 1:17; 10:17-18; 16:19

📖 Compassionate action is often the result of suffering. The annals of faith are filled with those who have allowed past experiences to become the impetus for ministry to others. Paul affirmed in 2 Corinthians 1:3–11 that our suffering can be used by God to minister comfort to others who find themselves in similar circumstances. What have you learned through suffering? Have you experienced trial, adverse circumstances, or challenges that God may be asking you to share for others' benefit? Be courageous and take the first step of faith today!

Snapshots

 24:17

Lee

The Phnom Penh Street Children Centre in Cambodia is a place where children can learn, meet new friends, receive food and clothing, and escape violence.

Lee is among them. Son of a prostitute mother and soldier father, Lee was stigmatized and unwanted. He lived for a time with his grandmother and his aunt's family in a soldier camp, where he learned a lot—but not love. Family violence was a top-down affair. Being youngest, Lee was first to be abused and last to be fed.

Lee and his grandmother escaped and lived on the street. She decided to take him to the PPSC, convinced that his life would change for the better.

> "**I receive a lot of love and care from mothers.**"

Established in 1993, the PPSC has significantly addressed the most acute problems faced by street children. It acts as an informal drop-in center, offering short-, medium-, and long-term accommodations. Children are helped to enroll in school, trained in vocational skills, and offered engaging activities. The center coordinates family reunification or foster placement.

"I receive a lot of love and care from mothers [house-parents at the centre]," asserts Lee, aware of his own improvement. "I have enough food and many friends. I want to show to my grandma how my life has changed."

24:19
b Lev 19:9; 23:22
c Pr 19:17
24:20
d Lev 19:10

[19]When you are harvesting in your field and you overlook a sheaf, do not go back to get it. [b] Leave it for the alien, the fatherless and the widow, so that the LORD your God may bless[c] you in all the work of your hands. [20]When you beat the olives from your trees, do not go over the branches a second time. [d] Leave what remains for the alien, the fatherless and the widow. [21]When you harvest the grapes in your vineyard, do not go over the vines again. Leave what remains for the alien, the fatherless and

24:22
e ver 18

the widow. [22]Remember that you were slaves in Egypt. That is why I command you to do this. [e]

25:1
f Dt 19:17
g Dt 1:16-17
25:2
h Lk 12:47-48
25:3
i 2Co 11:24
j Job 18:3
25:4
k Pr 12:10;
1Co 9:9*; 1Ti 5:18*

25 When men have a dispute, they are to take it to court and the judges will decide the case, [f] acquitting the innocent and condemning the guilty. [g] [2]If the guilty man deserves to be beaten, [h] the judge shall make him lie down and have him flogged in his presence with the number of lashes his crime deserves, [3]but he must not give him more than forty lashes. [i] If he is flogged more than that, your brother will be degraded in your eyes. [j]

[4]Do not muzzle an ox while it is treading out the grain. [k]

25:5
l Mt 22:24;
Mk 12:19; Lk 20:28
25:6
m Ge 38:9; Ru 4:5,
10

[5]If brothers are living together and one of them dies without a son, his widow must not marry outside the family. Her husband's brother shall take her and marry her and fulfill the duty of a brother-in-law to her. [l] [6]The first son she bears shall carry on the name of the dead brother so that his name will not be blotted out from Israel. [m]

25:7
n Ru 4:1-2,5-6

[7]However, if a man does not want to marry his brother's wife, she shall go to the elders at the town gate and say, "My husband's brother refuses to carry on his brother's name in Israel. He will not fulfill the duty of a brother-in-law to me." [n] [8]Then the elders of his town shall summon him and talk to him. If he persists in

25:9
o Ru 4:7-8,11

saying, "I do not want to marry her," [9]his brother's widow shall go up to him in the presence of the elders, take off one of his sandals, [o] spit in his face and say, "This is what is done to the man who will not build up his brother's family line." [10]That man's line shall be known in Israel as The Family of the Unsandaled.

[11]If two men are fighting and the wife of one of them comes to rescue her husband from his assailant, and she reaches out and seizes him by his private parts,

25:12
p Dt 19:13
25:13
q Lev 19:35-37;
Pr 11:1; Eze 45:10;
Mic 6:11
25:15
r Ex 20:12

[12]you shall cut off her hand. Show her no pity. [p]

[13]Do not have two differing weights in your bag—one heavy, one light. [q] [14]Do not have two differing measures in your house—one large, one small. [15]You must have accurate and honest weights and measures, so that you may live long[r] in the land the LORD your God is giving you. [16]For the LORD your God detests anyone who does

25:16
s Pr 11:1
25:17
t Ex 17:8

these things, anyone who deals dishonestly. [s]

[17]Remember what the Amalekites[t] did to you along the way when you came out of Egypt. [18]When you were weary and worn out, they met you on your journey and

25:18
u Ps 36:1; Ro 3:18

cut off all who were lagging behind; they had no fear of God. [u] [19]When the LORD your God gives you rest from all the enemies around you in the land he is giving

25:19
v 1Sa 15:2-3

you to possess as an inheritance, you shall blot out the memory of Amalek[v] from under heaven. Do not forget!

Firstfruits and Tithes

26:2
w Ex 22:29; 23:16,
19; Nu 18:13;
Pr 3:9 x Dt 12:5

26 When you have entered the land the LORD your God is giving you as an inheritance and have taken possession of it and settled in it, [2]take some of the firstfruits[w] of all that you produce from the soil of the land the LORD your God is giving you and put them in a basket. Then go to the place the LORD your God will choose as a dwelling for his Name[x] [3]and say to the priest in office at the time, "I declare today to the LORD your God that I have come to the land the LORD swore to our forefathers to give us." [4]The priest shall take the basket from your hands and

---

Deuteronomy 26:1–15

Verses 1–11 prepared the people for the special occasion of bringing to God the firstfruits of the promised land when they would first settle in it. Every year thereafter the firstfruits were to be offered in support of the priests and Levites (18:4–5). Verses 12–15 address the tithe given every three years to the Levites and the less fortunate (see "There and Then" for 14:22–29). It wasn't a secular tax for the welfare of the poor but an act inspired by God. Both giving and receiving this "sacred portion" (v. 13) were spiritual acts, and the tithe itself was to be recognized as holy, set apart for the Lord.

set it down in front of the altar of the LORD your God. 5Then you shall declare before the LORD your God: "My father was a wandering Aramean,^{y} and he went down into Egypt with a few people^z and lived there and became a great nation, powerful and numerous. 6But the Egyptians mistreated us and made us suffer,^{a} putting us to hard labor. 7Then we cried out to the LORD, the God of our fathers, and the LORD heard our voice^b and saw^c our misery, toil and oppression. 8So the LORD brought us out of Egypt with a mighty hand and an outstretched arm, with great terror and with miraculous signs and wonders.^{d} 9He brought us to this place and gave us this land, a land flowing with milk and honey;^{e} 10and now I bring the firstfruits of the soil that you, O LORD, have given me." Place the basket before the LORD your God and bow down before him. 11And you and the Levites^f and the aliens among you shall rejoice^g in all the good things the LORD your God has given to you and your household.

12When you have finished setting aside a tenth^h of all your produce in the third year, the year of the tithe,^{i} you shall give it to the Levite, the alien, the fatherless and the widow, so that they may eat in your towns and be satisfied. 13Then say to the LORD your God: "I have removed from my house the sacred portion and have given it to the Levite, the alien, the fatherless and the widow, according to all you commanded. I have not turned aside from your commands nor have I forgotten any of them.^{j} 14I have not eaten any of the sacred portion while I was in mourning, nor have I removed any of it while I was unclean,^{k} nor have I offered any of it to the dead. I have obeyed the LORD my God; I have done everything you commanded me. 15Look down from heaven,^{l} your holy dwelling place, and bless your people Israel and the land you have given us as you promised on oath to our forefathers, a land flowing with milk and honey."

Follow the LORD's Commands

16The LORD your God commands you this day to follow these decrees and laws; carefully observe them with all your heart and with all your soul.^{m} 17You have declared this day that the LORD is your God and that you will walk in his ways, that you will keep his decrees, commands and laws, and that you will obey him. 18And the LORD has declared this day that you are his people, his treasured possession^n as he promised, and that you are to keep all his commands. 19He has declared that he will set you in praise, fame and honor high above all the nations^o he has made and that you will be a people holy^p to the LORD your God, as he promised.

The Altar on Mount Ebal

27 Moses and the elders of Israel commanded the people: "Keep all these commands that I give you today. 2When you have crossed the Jordan into the land the LORD your God is giving you, set up some large stones and coat them with plaster.^{q} 3Write on them all the words of this law when you have crossed over to enter the land the LORD your God is giving you, a land flowing with milk and

---

26:5
^{y} Hos 12:12
^{z} Ge 43:1-2; 45:7, 11; 46:27; Dt 10:22
26:6
^{a} Ex 1:11,14
26:7
^{b} Ex 2:23-25
^{c} Ex 3:9
26:8
^{d} Dt 4:34
26:9
^{e} Ex 3:8
26:11
^{f} Dt 12:7 ^{g} Dt 16:11

26:12
^{h} Lev 27:30
^{i} Nu 18:24; Dt 14:28-29; Heb 7:5,9

26:13
^{j} Ps 119:141,153, 176
26:14
^{k} Lev 7:20; Hos 9:4
26:15
^{l} Isa 63:15; Zec 2:13

26:16
^{m} Dt 4:29

26:18
^{n} Ex 6:7; 19:5; Dt 7:6; 14:2; 28:9
26:19
^{o} Dt 4:7-8; 28:1,13,44
^{p} Ex 19:6; Dt 7:6; 1Pe 2:9

27:2
^{q} Jos 8:31

How do you believe Christians today should respond to the Old Testament principle of the tithe? While the New Testament doesn't answer this question directly, it does point toward the results we see in Deuteronomy. As in the case of the priests and Levites, the church's ministers were provided for (Gal. 6:6; 1 Tim. 5:17–18). And Paul addressed believers able to share with those in need: "At the present time your plenty will supply what they need, so that in turn their plenty will supply what you need" (2 Cor. 8:14). As in Old Testament Israel, the result in principle would be equality. How do you and your church "excel in this grace of giving" (2 Cor. 8:7)?

Deuteronomy 26:16–19

Chapter 26—and this whole section of

Deuteronomy (12:1—26:19)—concludes with an exhortation to adhere carefully to the stipulations of the covenant between God and Israel. "This day" (v. 16) points to a particular day when the command to follow God's decrees and laws was repeated on the plains of Moab—when the people declared that the Lord was their God and he in turn claimed them as his own (vv. 17–18).

Under God's new covenant (unfolded in the NT), you too can be one of God's special people—his own child, to be more precise. Using the concordance at the back of this Bible, locate some passages that tell you so. Have you acknowledged to the Lord that he is your God? Have you made promises to him? What are some of his promises to you?

27:3
r Dt 26:9
27:4
s Dt 11:29
27:5
t Jos 8:31
u Ex 20:25

honey,^{r} just as the LORD, the God of your fathers, promised you. ⁴And when you have crossed the Jordan, set up these stones on Mount Ebal,^{s} as I command you today, and coat them with plaster. ⁵Build there an altar^t to the LORD your God, an altar of stones. Do not use any iron tool^u upon them. ⁶Build the altar of the LORD your God with fieldstones and offer burnt offerings on it to the LORD your God. ⁷Sacrifice fellowship offerings^a there, eating them and rejoicing in the presence of the LORD your God. ⁸And you shall write very clearly all the words of this law on these stones you have set up."

^{a} 7 Traditionally *peace offerings*

Deuteronomy 27:1–8

Upon entering Canaan, the Israelites were to set up on Mount Ebal inscribed stones and an altar. Writing laws on stones (or even mountainsides) was common in the ancient Near East. Large writing stones, some eight feet tall, from before Moses' time have been found. This altar wouldn't replace the tabernacle altar but was for use on special occasions.

26:16–19

Major Social Concerns in the Covenant

1. Personhood	Everyone's person was to be secure (Ex. 20:13; 21:16-21,26-32; Lev. 19:14; Deut. 5:17; 24:7; 27:18).
2. False Accusation	Everyone was to be secure against slander and false accusation (Ex. 20:16; 23:1-3,6-8; Lev. 19:16; Deut. 5:20; 19:15-21).
3. Women	No woman was to be taken advantage of within her subordinate status in society (Ex. 21:7-11,20,26-32; 22:16-17; Deut. 21:10-14; 22:13-30; 24:1-5).
4. Punishment	Punishment for wrongdoing wasn't to be excessive to the point that the culprit was dehumanized (Deut. 25:1-5).
5. Dignity	Every Israelite's dignity and right to be God's servant were to be honored and safeguarded (Ex. 21:2,5-6; Lev. 25; Deut. 15:12-18).
6. Inheritance	Every Israelite's inheritance in the promised land was to be secure (Lev. 25; Num. 27:5-7; 36:1-9; Deut. 25:5-10).
7. Property	Everyone's property was to be secure (Ex. 20:15; 21:33-36; 22:1-15; 23:4-5; Lev. 19:35-36; Deut. 5:19; 22:1-4; 25:13-15).
8. Fruit of Labor	Everyone was to receive the fruit of his or her labors (Lev. 19:13; Deut. 24:14; 25:4).
9. Fruit of the Ground	Everyone was to share the fruit of the ground (Ex. 23:10-11; Lev. 19:9-10; 23:22; 25:3-55; Deut. 14:28-29; 24:19-21).
10. Rest on Sabbath	Everyone, down to the humblest servant and the resident alien, was to share in the weekly rest of God's Sabbath (Ex. 20:8-11; 23:12; Deut. 5:12-15).
11. Marriage	The marriage relationship was to be kept inviolate (Ex. 20:14; Deut. 5:18; see also Lev. 18:6-23; 20:10-21; Deut. 22:13-30).
12. Exploitation	No one, however disabled, impoverished, or powerless, was to be oppressed or exploited (Ex. 22:21-27; Lev. 19:14,33-34; 25:35-36; Deut. 23:19; 24:6,12-15,17; 27:18).
13. Fair Trial	Everyone was to have free access to the courts and be afforded a fair trial (Ex. 23:6-8; Lev. 19:15; Deut. 1:17; 10:17-18; 16:18-20; 17:8-13; 19:15-21).
14. Social Order	Every person's God-given place in the social order was to be honored (Ex. 20:12; 21:15,17; 22:28; Lev. 19:3,32; 20:9; Deut. 5:16; 17:8-13; 21:15-21; 27:16).
15. Law	No one was to be above the law, not even the king (Deut. 17:18-20).
16. Animals	Concern for the welfare of all creatures was to be extended to the animal world (Ex. 23:5,11; Lev. 25:7; Deut. 22:4,6-7; 25:4).

Curses From Mount Ebal

⁹Then Moses and the priests, who are Levites, said to all Israel, "Be silent, O Israel, and listen! You have now become the people of the LORD your God. ⱽ ¹⁰Obey the LORD your God and follow his commands and decrees that I give you today."

¹¹On the same day Moses commanded the people:

¹²When you have crossed the Jordan, these tribes shall stand on Mount Gerizim ʷ to bless the people: Simeon, Levi, Judah, Issachar, Joseph and Benjamin. ˣ ¹³And these tribes shall stand on Mount Ebal to pronounce curses: Reuben, Gad, Asher, Zebulun, Dan and Naphtali.

¹⁴The Levites shall recite to all the people of Israel in a loud voice:

¹⁵"Cursed is the man who carves an image or casts an idol ʸ—a thing detestable to the LORD, the work of the craftsman's hands—and sets it up in secret."

Then all the people shall say, "Amen!"

¹⁶"Cursed is the man who dishonors his father or his mother." ᶻ

Then all the people shall say, "Amen!"

¹⁷"Cursed is the man who moves his neighbor's boundary stone." ᵃ

Then all the people shall say, "Amen!"

¹⁸"Cursed is the man who leads the blind astray on the road." ᵇ

Then all the people shall say, "Amen!"

¹⁹"Cursed is the man who withholds justice from the alien, ᶜ the fatherless or the widow." ᵈ

Then all the people shall say, "Amen!"

²⁰"Cursed is the man who sleeps with his father's wife, for he dishonors his father's bed." ᵉ

Then all the people shall say, "Amen!"

²¹"Cursed is the man who has sexual relations with any animal." ᶠ

Then all the people shall say, "Amen!"

²²"Cursed is the man who sleeps with his sister, the daughter of his father or the daughter of his mother." ᵍ

Then all the people shall say, "Amen!"

²³"Cursed is the man who sleeps with his mother-in-law." ʰ

Then all the people shall say, "Amen!"

²⁴"Cursed is the man who kills ⁱ his neighbor secretly."

Then all the people shall say, "Amen!"

²⁵"Cursed is the man who accepts a bribe to kill an innocent person." ʲ

Then all the people shall say, "Amen!"

27:9
v Dt 26:18
27:12
w Dt 11:29
x Jos 8:35
27:15
y Ex 20:4; 34:17;
Lev 19:4; 26:1;
Dt 4:16,23; 5:8;
Isa 44:9
27:16
z Ex 20:12; 21:17;
Lev 19:3; 20:9
27:17
a Dt 19:14;
Pr 22:28
27:18
b Lev 19:14
27:19
c Ex 22:21;
Dt 24:19 d Dt 10:18
27:20
e Lev 18:7;
Dt 22:30
27:21
f Lev 18:23
27:22
g Lev 18:9; 20:17
27:23
h Lev 20:14
27:24
i Lev 24:17;
Nu 35:31
27:25
j Ex 23:7-8;
Dt 10:17; Eze 22:12

What is meant by "all the words of this law" (v. 3) can't definitely be determined. Some think this may mean the laws of chapters 12–26. Others suggest a reference to the curses of verses 15–26, since the laws were written on stones to be erected in the same place where the curses were pronounced (vv. 4,13).

📖 Are you a list maker, dependent on "writing it down" when you want to remember something? Does this free your mind to concentrate on other things? Oral traditions are alien to us but have prevailed in many cultures until recent centuries. They are still the rule in much of the world. God had much to say to his Old Testament people—and still has endless wisdom to communicate to us. Why not pause a moment to thank him for his messages, available to you daily in his written Word?

Deuteronomy 27:9–26

📖 "You have now become the people of the LORD your God" (v. 9). Not only was God the Creator of each Israelite individually; he was the Creator of them as a na-

tion—a special nation whose laws related to the people's personal commitment to him as their God, as well as to their behavior and its motivation. Rewards and punishments, blessings and curses, stemmed from that relationship.

The curses were warnings not to break the law, given with the intent that paying heed to the warning would keep Israel in good relationship with the Lord. Those living in Old Testament times who were faithful to God had the witness of God's Spirit that they were acceptable to him.

📖 Do you ever worry about whether or not you are acceptable to God, about whether you are good enough or doing enough—even though you don't specifically doubt your salvation? What would it take to convince you of your precious status in God's sight? Ephesians 1:3–14 is a hallmark passage describing the believer's life "in Christ" (you will find this phrase repeated in these verses). This section of Scripture should erase any doubts about your place in God's family.

27:26
k Jer 11:3;
Gal 3:10*

26 "Cursed is the man who does not uphold the words of this law by carrying them out." k

Then all the people shall say, "Amen!"

Blessings for Obedience

28:1
l Ex 15:26;
Lev 26:3;
Dt 7:12-26
m Dt 26:19
28:2
n Zec 1:6

28 If you fully obey the LORD your God and carefully follow all his commands l I give you today, the LORD your God will set you high above all the nations on earth. m 2 All these blessings will come upon you n and accompany you if you obey the LORD your God:

28:3
o Ps 128:1,4
p Ge 39:5

3 You will be blessed o in the city and blessed in the country. p

4 The fruit of your womb will be blessed, and the crops of your land and the young of your livestock—the calves of your herds and the lambs of your flocks. q

28:4
q Ge 49:25;
Pr 10:22
28:6
r Ps 121:8

5 Your basket and your kneading trough will be blessed.

6 You will be blessed when you come in and blessed when you go out. r

28:7
s Lev 26:8,17

7 The LORD will grant that the enemies who rise up against you will be defeated before you. They will come at you from one direction but flee from you in seven. s

8 The LORD will send a blessing on your barns and on everything you put your hand to. The LORD your God will bless you in the land he is giving you.

28:9
t Ex 19:6; Dt 7:6

9 The LORD will establish you as his holy people, t as he promised you on oath, if you keep the commands of the LORD your God and walk in his ways. 10 Then all the peoples on earth will see that you are called by the name u of the LORD, and they will fear you. 11 The LORD will grant you abundant prosperity—in the fruit of your womb, the young of your livestock and the crops of your ground—in the land he swore to your forefathers to give you. v

28:10
u 2Ch 7:14

28:11
v Dt 30:9; Pr 10:22
28:12
w Lev 26:4
x Dt 15:3,6

12 The LORD will open the heavens, the storehouse of his bounty, to send rain w on your land in season and to bless all the work of your hands. You will lend to many nations but will borrow from none. x 13 The LORD will make you the head, not the tail. If you pay attention to the commands of the LORD your God that I give you this day and carefully follow them, you will always be at the top, never at the bottom.

28:14
y Dt 5:32

14 Do not turn aside from any of the commands I give you today, to the right or to the left, y following other gods and serving them.

Curses for Disobedience

28:15
z Lev 26:14
a Jos 23:15;
Da 9:11; Mal 2:2

15 However, if you do not obey z the LORD your God and do not carefully follow all his commands and decrees I am giving you today, all these curses will come upon you and overtake you: a

16 You will be cursed in the city and cursed in the country.

17 Your basket and your kneading trough will be cursed.

Deuteronomy 28:1–14

Two sections on blessings and curses (generalizations or specific areas of blessings or curses representing all of life) balance each other in verses 3–6 as over against 16–19 (see notes to follow). After the section on blessing (vv. 3–6), the nature of the blessed state that results from obedience is portrayed. Similarly, after the curses (vv. 16–19) the condition of disobedient Israel is described. These weren't the blessings and curses to be repeated on Gerizim and Ebal. Moses was giving a fuller explanation in a prophetic vein of the options Israel faced.

As New Testament Christians, we are no longer under the threat of curses for our sinful actions (Gal. 3:10-13,23–25), though we are to strive continuously to reach the goal of perfection (see "Here and Now" for

18;9–13). Why? Out of gratitude for God's blessings and a desire to demonstrate our love through faithful service. Can you name identifiable, quantifiable blessings you believe you have received as a direct result of that service? Thank God today that Jesus bore the curse for your sins on the cross.

Deuteronomy 28:15–68

After basic coverage of the curse (vv. 16–19), following the same plan as that of the blessings (vv. 3–6), Moses developed—at about six times the length—a description of the disaster to follow disobedient Israel. Curses, confusion, and rebuke would fall on everything her people did, until destruction and sudden ruin would envelop her. Disobeying God was comparable to forsaking him. National and personal commitment to him was the central command—and forsaking him the central evil.

¹⁸The fruit of your womb will be cursed, and the crops of your land, and the calves of your herds and the lambs of your flocks.

¹⁹You will be cursed when you come in and cursed when you go out.

²⁰The LORD will send on you curses, [b] confusion and rebuke [c] in everything you put your hand to, until you are destroyed and come to sudden ruin [d] because of the evil you have done in forsaking him. [a] ²¹The LORD will plague you with diseases until he has destroyed you from the land you are entering to possess. [e] ²²The LORD will strike you with wasting disease, with fever and inflammation, with scorching heat and drought, [f] with blight and mildew, which will plague you until you perish. [g] ²³The sky over your head will be bronze, the ground beneath you iron. [h] ²⁴The LORD will turn the rain of your country into dust and powder; it will come down from the skies until you are destroyed.

²⁵The LORD will cause you to be defeated before your enemies. You will come at them from one direction but flee from them in seven, [i] and you will become a thing of horror to all the kingdoms on earth. [j] ²⁶Your carcasses will be food for all the birds of the air and the beasts of the earth, and there will be no one to frighten them away. [k] ²⁷The LORD will afflict you with the boils of Egypt [l] and with tumors, festering sores and the itch, from which you cannot be cured. ²⁸The LORD will afflict you with madness, blindness and confusion of mind. ²⁹At midday you will grope [m] about like a blind man in the dark. You will be unsuccessful in everything you do; day after day you will be oppressed and robbed, with no one to rescue you.

³⁰You will be pledged to be married to a woman, but another will take her and ravish her. [n] You will build a house, but you will not live in it. [o] You will plant a vineyard, but you will not even begin to enjoy its fruit. [p] ³¹Your ox will be slaughtered before your eyes, but you will eat none of it. Your donkey will be forcibly taken from you and will not be returned. Your sheep will be given to your enemies, and no one will rescue them. ³²Your sons and daughters will be given to another nation, [q] and you will wear out your eyes watching for them day after day, powerless to lift a hand. ³³A people that you do not know will eat what your land and labor produce, and you will have nothing but cruel oppression all your days. [r] ³⁴The sights you see will drive you mad. ³⁵The LORD will afflict your knees and legs with painful boils [s] that cannot be cured, spreading from the soles of your feet to the top of your head.

³⁶The LORD will drive you and the king [t] you set over you to a nation unknown to you or your fathers. [u] There you will worship other gods, gods of wood and stone. [v] ³⁷You will become a thing of horror and an object of scorn and ridicule to all the nations where the LORD will drive you. [w]

³⁸You will sow much seed in the field but you will harvest little, [x] because locusts will devour [y] it. ³⁹You will plant vineyards and cultivate them but you will not drink the wine or gather the grapes, because worms will eat them. [z] ⁴⁰You will have olive trees throughout your country but you will not use the oil, because the olives will drop off. [a] ⁴¹You will have sons and daughters but you will not keep them, because they will go into captivity. [b] ⁴²Swarms of locusts will take over all your trees and the crops of your land.

⁴³The alien who lives among you will rise above you higher and higher, but you will sink lower and lower. [c] ⁴⁴He will lend to you, but you will not lend to him. [d] He will be the head, but you will be the tail. [e]

⁴⁵All these curses will come upon you. They will pursue you and overtake you until you are destroyed, [f] because you did not obey the LORD your God and observe the commands and decrees he gave you. ⁴⁶They will be a sign and a wonder to you and

---

^a 20 Hebrew *me*

28:20
[b] Mal 2:2
[c] Isa 51:20; 66:15
[d] Dt 4:26
28:21
[e] Lev 26:25; Jer 24:10
28:22
[f] Lev 26:16
[g] Am 4:9
28:23
[h] Lev 26:19

28:25
[i] Isa 30:17
[j] Jer 15:4; 24:9; Eze 23:46
28:26
[k] Jer 7:33; 16:4; 34:20
28:27
[l] ver 60-61; 1Sa 5:6
28:29
[m] Job 5:14; Isa 59:10

28:30
[n] Job 31:10; Jer 8:10 [o] Am 5:11
[p] Jer 12:13

28:32
[q] ver 41

28:33
[r] Jer 5:15-17
28:35
[s] ver 27

28:36
[t] 2Ki 17:4,6; 24:12, 14; 25:7,11
[u] Jer 16:13
[v] Dt 4:28
28:37
[w] Jer 24:9
28:38
[x] Mic 6:15; Hag 1:6,9
[y] Joel 1:4
28:39
[z] Isa 5:10; 17:10-11
28:40
[a] Mic 6:15
28:41
[b] ver 32

28:43
[c] ver 13
28:44
[d] ver 12 [e] ver 13

28:45
[f] ver 15

📖 The piling of curse on curse overwhelms us. The low point of this passage may be the unthinkable, graphic image of a ravenous woman (known to be sensitive and gentle) waiting for an opportunity to secretly devour the afterbirth following delivery of her child—followed by the starveling infant itself (vv. 56–57). Such hideous scenes might be imagined in desperate situations of famine today. But who would *choose* them? Think of the millions in our day who, aware of Christ's salvation offer, deliberately reject it. Pray for someone right now who has rejected the gospel—that their heart might be softened and that they might repent.

28:46
g Isa 8:18; Eze 14:8
28:47
h Dt 32:15
i Ne 9:35
28:48
j Jer 28:13-14

28:49
k Jer 5:15; 6:22
l La 4:19; Hos 8:1
28:50
m Isa 47:6

28:51
n ver 33
28:52
o Jer 10:18;
Zep 1:14-16,17

28:53
p Lev 26:29;
2Ki 6:28-29;
Jer 19:9; La 2:20;
4:10

28:56
q ver 54

28:58
r Mal 1:14 s Ex 6:3

28:60
t ver 27

28:61
u Dt 4:25-26
28:62
v Dt 4:27; 10:22;
Ne 9:23
28:63
w Jer 32:41
x Pr 1:26
y Jer 12:14; 45:4
28:64
z Lev 26:33;
Dt 4:27 a Ne 1:8

28:65
b Lev 26:16,36

28:67
c ver 34; Job 7:4

29:1
d Dt 5:2-3

your descendants forever.[g] [47]Because you did not serve[h] the LORD your God joyfully and gladly[i] in the time of prosperity, [48]therefore in hunger and thirst, in nakedness and dire poverty, you will serve the enemies the LORD sends against you. He will put an iron yoke[j] on your neck until he has destroyed you.

[49]The LORD will bring a nation against you from far away, from the ends of the earth,[k] like an eagle[l] swooping down, a nation whose language you will not understand, [50]a fierce-looking nation without respect for the old[m] or pity for the young. [51]They will devour the young of your livestock and the crops of your land until you are destroyed. They will leave you no grain, new wine or oil, nor any calves of your herds or lambs of your flocks until you are ruined.[n] [52]They will lay siege to all the cities throughout your land until the high fortified walls in which you trust fall down. They will besiege all the cities throughout the land the LORD your God is giving you.[o]

[53]Because of the suffering that your enemy will inflict on you during the siege, you will eat the fruit of the womb, the flesh of the sons and daughters the LORD your God has given you.[p] [54]Even the most gentle and sensitive man among you will have no compassion on his own brother or the wife he loves or his surviving children, [55]and he will not give to one of them any of the flesh of his children that he is eating. It will be all he has left because of the suffering your enemy will inflict on you during the siege of all your cities. [56]The most gentle and sensitive[q] woman among you—so sensitive and gentle that she would not venture to touch the ground with the sole of her foot—will begrudge the husband she loves and her own son or daughter [57]the afterbirth from her womb and the children she bears. For she intends to eat them secretly during the siege and in the distress that your enemy will inflict on you in your cities.

[58]If you do not carefully follow all the words of this law, which are written in this book, and do not revere[r] this glorious and awesome name[s]—the LORD your God— [59]the LORD will send fearful plagues on you and your descendants, harsh and prolonged disasters, and severe and lingering illnesses. [60]He will bring upon you all the diseases of Egypt[t] that you dreaded, and they will cling to you. [61]The LORD will also bring on you every kind of sickness and disaster not recorded in this Book of the Law, until you are destroyed.[u] [62]You who were as numerous as the stars in the sky[v] will be left but few in number, because you did not obey the LORD your God. [63]Just as it pleased[w] the LORD to make you prosper and increase in number, so it will please[x] him to ruin and destroy you. You will be uprooted[y] from the land you are entering to possess.

[64]Then the LORD will scatter[z] you among all nations,[a] from one end of the earth to the other. There you will worship other gods—gods of wood and stone, which neither you nor your fathers have known. [65]Among those nations you will find no repose, no resting place for the sole of your foot. There the LORD will give you an anxious mind, eyes weary with longing, and a despairing heart.[b] [66]You will live in constant suspense, filled with dread both night and day, never sure of your life. [67]In the morning you will say, "If only it were evening!" and in the evening, "If only it were morning!"—because of the terror that will fill your hearts and the sights that your eyes will see.[c] [68]The LORD will send you back in ships to Egypt on a journey I said you should never make again. There you will offer yourselves for sale to your enemies as male and female slaves, but no one will buy you.

Renewal of the Covenant

29 These are the terms of the covenant the LORD commanded Moses to make with the Israelites in Moab, in addition to the covenant he had made with them at Horeb.[d]

[2]Moses summoned all the Israelites and said to them:

Deuteronomy 29:1–29

📖 As Moses began the final addresses of Deuteronomy and of his life, he identified the people with their past history. This historical perspective was all-important. It had been 40 years since God had miraculously delivered Israel from Egypt. Many in Moses' audience had been born in the desert—after the exodus— or would have been young children at the time of their

Your eyes have seen all that the LORD did in Egypt to Pharaoh, to all his officials and to all his land. [e] 3With your own eyes you saw those great trials, those miraculous signs and great wonders. [f] 4But to this day the LORD has not given you a mind that understands or eyes that see or ears that hear. [g] 5During the forty years that I led you through the desert, your clothes did not wear out, nor did the sandals on your feet. [h] 6You ate no bread and drank no wine or other fermented drink. I did this so that you might know that I am the LORD your God. [i]

7When you reached this place, Sihon[j] king of Heshbon and Og king of Bashan came out to fight against us, but we defeated them. [k] 8We took their land and gave it as an inheritance to the Reubenites, the Gadites and the half-tribe of Manasseh. [l]

9Carefully follow[m] the terms of this covenant, so that you may prosper in everything you do. [n] 10All of you are standing today in the presence of the LORD your God—your leaders and chief men, your elders and officials, and all the other men of Israel, 11together with your children and your wives, and the aliens living in your camps who chop your wood and carry your water. [o] 12You are standing here in order to enter into a covenant with the LORD your God, a covenant the LORD is making with you this day and sealing with an oath, 13to confirm you this day as his people, [p] that he may be your God[q] as he promised you and as he swore to your fathers, Abraham, Isaac and Jacob. 14I am making this covenant, [r] with its oath, not only with you 15who are standing here with us today in the presence of the LORD our God but also with those who are not here today. [s]

16You yourselves know how we lived in Egypt and how we passed through the countries on the way here. 17You saw among them their detestable images and idols of wood and stone, of silver and gold. [t] 18Make sure there is no man or woman, clan or tribe among you today whose heart turns away from the LORD our God to go and worship the gods of those nations; make sure there is no root among you that produces such bitter poison. [u]

19When such a person hears the words of this oath, he invokes a blessing on himself and therefore thinks, "I will be safe, even though I persist in going my own way." This will bring disaster on the watered land as well as the dry. [a] 20The LORD will never be willing to forgive him; his wrath and zeal[v] will burn[w] against that man. All the curses written in this book will fall upon him, and the LORD will blot[x] out his name from under heaven. 21The LORD will single him out from all the tribes of Israel for disaster, according to all the curses of the covenant written in this Book of the Law.

22Your children who follow you in later generations and foreigners who come from distant lands will see the calamities that have fallen on the land and the diseases with which the LORD has afflicted it. [y] 23The whole land will be a burning waste[z] of salt[a] and sulfur—nothing planted, nothing sprouting, no vegetation growing on it. It will be like the destruction of Sodom and Gomorrah, [b] Admah and Zeboiim, which the LORD overthrew in fierce anger. 24All the nations will ask: "Why has the LORD done this to this land? [c] Why this fierce, burning anger?"

25And the answer will be: "It is because this people abandoned the covenant of the LORD, the God of their fathers, the covenant he made with them when he brought them out of Egypt. 26They went off and worshiped other gods and bowed down to them, gods they did not know, gods he had not given them. 27Therefore the LORD's anger burned against this land, so that he brought on it all the curses written in this book. [d] 28In furious anger and in great wrath the LORD uprooted[e] them from their land and thrust them into another land, as it is now."

---

[a] 19 Or way, in order to add drunkenness to thirst."

Cross references (right margin):

29:2
e Ex 19:4
29:3
f Dt 4:34; 7:19
29:4
g Isa 6:10; Ac 28:26-27; Ro 11:8*; Eph 4:18
29:5
h Dt 8:4
29:6
i Dt 8:3
29:7
j Dt 2:32; 3:1
k Nu 21:21-24,33-35
29:8
l Nu 32:33; Dt 3:12-13
29:9
m Dt 4:6; Jos 1:7
n 1Ki 2:3
29:11
o Jos 9:21,23,27

29:13
p Dt 28:9
q Ge 17:7; Ex 6:7
29:14
r Jer 31:31
29:15
s Ac 2:39

29:17
t Dt 28:36

29:18
u Dt 11:16; Heb 12:15

29:20
v Eze 23:25
w Ps 74:1; 79:5
x Ex 32:33; Dt 9:14

29:22
y Jer 19:8
29:23
z Isa 34:9 a Jer 17:6
b Ge 19:24,25; Zep 2:9

29:24
c 1Ki 9:8; Jer 22:8-9

29:27
d Da 9:11,13,14
29:28
e 1Ki 14:15; 2Ch 7:20; Ps 52:5; Pr 2:22

---

deliverance. Yet Moses could say they had seen God's wonders with their "own eyes" (v. 3; cf. v. 2): His message was directed to the people as a nation.

Just as God viewed all the current Israelites as participants in the exodus and the Sinai covenant (5:3), in verses 14–15 Moses declared that not only those

standing before him but also those in later generations would be involved in renewing the covenant. Peter would make a similar statement in his Pentecost address to another crowd: "The promise is for you and your children and for all who are far off—for all whom the Lord our God will call" (Acts 2:39). What implications does this insight and reality have for you?

²⁹The secret things belong to the LORD our God, but the things revealed belong to us and to our children forever, that we may follow all the words of this law.

Prosperity After Turning to the LORD

30 When all these blessings and curses^f I have set before you come upon you and you take them to heart wherever the LORD your God disperses you among the nations,^g ²and when you and your children return^h to the LORD your God and obey him with all your heart and with all your soul according to everything I command you today, ³then the LORD your God will restore your fortunes^aⁱ and have compassion on you and gather^j you again from all the nations where he scattered you.^k ⁴Even if you have been banished to the most distant land under the heavens, from there the LORD your God will gather you and bring you back.^l ⁵He will bring^m you to the land that belonged to your fathers, and you will take possession of it. He will make you more prosperous and numerous than your fathers. ⁶The LORD your God will circumcise your hearts and the hearts of your descendants,ⁿ so that you may love him with all your heart and with all your soul, and live. ⁷The LORD your God will put all these curses on your enemies who hate and persecute you.^o ⁸You will again obey the LORD and follow all his commands I am giving you today. ⁹Then the LORD your God will make you most prosperous in all the work of your hands and in the fruit of your womb, the young of your livestock and the crops of your land.^p The LORD will again delight in you and make you prosperous, just as he delighted in your fathers, ¹⁰if you obey the LORD your God and keep his commands and decrees that are written in this Book of the Law and turn to the LORD your God with all your heart and with all your soul.^q

The Offer of Life or Death

¹¹Now what I am commanding you today is not too difficult for you or beyond your reach.^r ¹²It is not up in heaven, so that you have to ask, "Who will ascend into heaven to get it and proclaim it to us so we may obey it?"^s ¹³Nor is it beyond the sea, so that you have to ask, "Who will cross the sea to get it and proclaim it to us so we may obey it?" ¹⁴No, the word is very near you; it is in your mouth and in your heart so you may obey it.

¹⁵See, I set before you today life and prosperity, death and destruction.^t ¹⁶For I command you today to love the LORD your God, to walk in his ways, and to keep

^a 3 Or *will bring you back from captivity*

Side references:
30:1 f ver 15,19; Dt 11:26; g Lev 26:40-45; Dt 28:64; 29:28; 1Ki 8:47
30:2 h Dt 4:30; Ne 1:9
30:3 i Ps 126:4; j Ps 147:2; Jer 32:37; Eze 34:13; k Jer 29:14
30:4 l Ne 1:8-9; Isa 43:6
30:5 m Jer 29:14
30:6 n Dt 10:16; Jer 32:39
30:7 o Dt 7:15
30:9 p Dt 28:11; Jer 31:28; 32:41
30:10 q Dt 4:29
30:11 r Isa 45:19,23
30:12 s Ro 10:6*
30:15 t Dt 11:26

Deuteronomy 30:1–10

In 29:22 Moses' speech had turned predictive, demonstrating that he wasn't optimistic about all of Israel's future. God's prophet foresaw the "curse" of exile. But when the people returned to the Lord with all their heart and soul, God would have compassion and regather them from among the nations (30:1–3). The Hebrew phrase translated "restore your fortunes" (v. 3; see NIV text note) signifies a total change, a return to a former state, an indication that the Israelites would return to the position of being under God's blessing in their own land.

Even when the Israelites had messed up so badly that God would have to banish them from the promised land, they would be able to repent and return to him. God, in his grace and mercy, still welcomes repentant sinners. Jesus' message and ministry were permeated by this truth, as illustrated in the parable of the lost son (Luke 15:11–32). In what ways can you identify with the Biblical theme of exile and restoration (being "lost" and then "found"; Luke 15:32)?

Deuteronomy 30:11–20

Moses stressed the availability of the resources for responding affirmatively to the commands he was giving the people. These commands (all of God's revelation through Moses in the covenant) were neither too difficult to achieve nor beyond the people's reach. In fact, the word was in their mouth (they could repeat it) and in their heart (they could understand and react to it). Obedience was possible. The choice was theirs, and it was clear—life or death.

When have you been so overwhelmed by the requirements of a needed change that you felt powerless to even begin? It may have been a time when you needed to "return to the Lord" (see previous "Here and Now"). Or perhaps the situation involved lifestyle modifications due to the onset of a chronic illness or budgetary considerations due to a change in your economic circumstances. In the back of your mind you realized that failure to change wasn't optional, but you needed someone to convince you that change was not only possible but quite achievable. How did you feel after that "breakthrough" moment? What difference has it made since?

his commands, decrees and laws; then you will live and increase, and the LORD your God will bless you in the land you are entering to possess.

¹⁷But if your heart turns away and you are not obedient, and if you are drawn away to bow down to other gods and worship them, ¹⁸I declare to you this day that you will certainly be destroyed. You will not live long in the land you are crossing the Jordan to enter and possess.

¹⁹This day I call heaven and earth as witnesses against you that I have set before you life and death, blessings and curses. Now choose life, so that you and your children may live ²⁰and that you may love the LORD your God, listen to his voice, and hold fast to him. For the LORD is your life, and he will give you many years in the land he swore to give to your fathers, Abraham, Isaac and Jacob.

Joshua to Succeed Moses

31 Then Moses went out and spoke these words to all Israel: ²"I am now a hundred and twenty years old and I am no longer able to lead you. The LORD has said to me, 'You shall not cross the Jordan.' ³The LORD your God himself will cross over ahead of you. He will destroy these nations before you, and you will take possession of their land. Joshua also will cross over ahead of you, as the LORD said. ⁴And the LORD will do to them what he did to Sihon and Og, the kings of the Amorites, whom he destroyed along with their land. ⁵The LORD will deliver them to you, and you must do to them all that I have commanded you. ⁶Be strong and courageous. Do not be afraid or terrified because of them, for the LORD your God goes with you; he will never leave you nor forsake you."

Deuteronomy 31:1–8

Most of the material in chapter 31 had been given elsewhere in Deuteronomy. This chapter appears to be a summary with some specific additions—much as someone who knows that that his ministry is nearing its end repeats, for emphasis' sake, things he or she has said before.

Moses' exhortation to "be strong and courageous,"

given first to the people (v. 6) and then specifically to Joshua (v. 7), would be repeated by God to Joshua after Moses' death (Josh. 1:6,9) and also urged on Joshua by the people (Josh. 1:18). Joshua would in turn later exhort them to be strong and courageous (Josh. 10:25). David also would pick up these words to urge Solomon to follow the decrees God had given Moses (1 Chron. 22:13; 28:20).

30:19–20

Blessings and Curses

The Christian church in our day is blessed with almost unlimited resources but functions in a world cursed with seemingly limitless evils. The overall annual cost of fighting them is shocking:

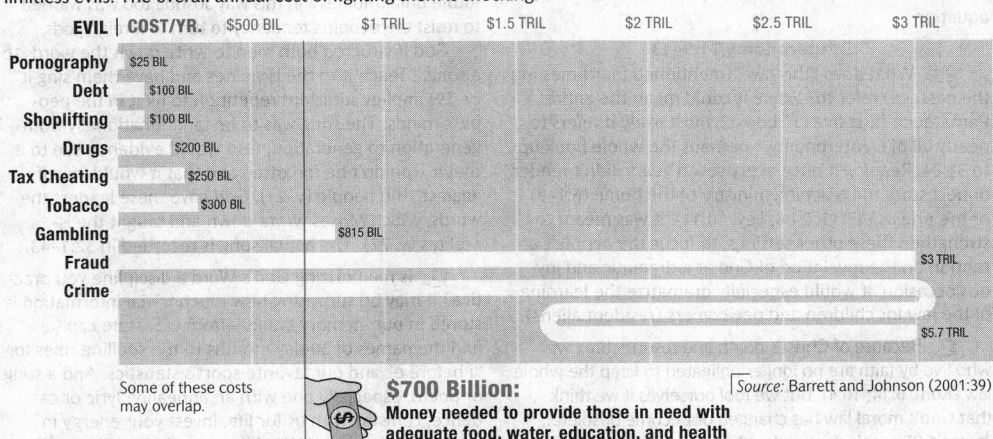

Source: Barrett and Johnson (2001:39)

$700 Billion: Money needed to provide those in need with adequate food, water, education, and health

Some of these costs may overlap.

When it comes to money, billions and trillions probably don't compute in your mind. But singles, fives, tens, twenties, fifties, and hundred dollar bills are the currency of your life. Which causes are close to your heart? Which of these staggering figures are you using your resources to fight? All Christians can do their best to ensure that their taxes are figured correctly.

31:7
l Dt 1:38; 3:28

31:8
m Ex 13:21; 33:14

[7]Then Moses summoned Joshua and said[l] to him in the presence of all Israel, "Be strong and courageous, for you must go with this people into the land that the LORD swore to their forefathers to give them, and you must divide it among them as their inheritance. [8]The LORD himself goes before you and will be with you;[m] he will never leave you nor forsake you. Do not be afraid; do not be discouraged."

The Reading of the Law

31:9
n ver 25; Nu 4:15; Jos 3:3

31:10
o Dt 15:1
p Lev 23:34

31:11
q Dt 16:16
r Jos 8:34-35; 2Ki 23:2

31:12
s Dt 4:10

31:13
t Dt 11:2; Ps 78:6-7

[9]So Moses wrote down this law and gave it to the priests, the sons of Levi, who carried[n] the ark of the covenant of the LORD, and to all the elders of Israel. [10]Then Moses commanded them: "At the end of every seven years, in the year for canceling debts,[o] during the Feast of Tabernacles,[p] [11]when all Israel comes to appear[q] before the LORD your God at the place he will choose, you shall read this law[r] before them in their hearing. [12]Assemble the people—men, women and children, and the aliens living in your towns—so they can listen and learn[s] to fear the LORD your God and follow carefully all the words of this law. [13]Their children,[t] who do not know this law, must hear it and learn to fear the LORD your God as long as you live in the land you are crossing the Jordan to possess."

Israel's Rebellion Predicted

31:14
u Nu 27:13; Dt 32:49-50

31:15
v Ex 33:9

31:16
w Jdg 2:12
x Jdg 10:6,13

31:17
y Jdg 2:14,20
z Jdg 6:13; 2Ch 15:2
a Dt 32:20; Isa 1:15; 8:17

[14]The LORD said to Moses, "Now the day of your death[u] is near. Call Joshua and present yourselves at the Tent of Meeting, where I will commission him." So Moses and Joshua came and presented themselves at the Tent of Meeting.

[15]Then the LORD appeared at the Tent in a pillar of cloud, and the cloud stood over the entrance to the Tent.[v] [16]And the LORD said to Moses: "You are going to rest with your fathers, and these people will soon prostitute[w] themselves to the foreign gods of the land they are entering. They will forsake[x] me and break the covenant I made with them. [17]On that day I will become angry[y] with them and forsake[z] them; I will hide[a] my face from them, and they will be destroyed. Many disasters

📖 Has someone urged you in some particularly challenging situation to be strong and courageous? Probably not in those exact words, but more likely in spirit. The beauty for us as Christians is that this kind of advice isn't an unrealistic cliché. Why? Because God has given us the reasons—and the means—to be strong and brave, no matter what circumstances we may face (see previous "Here and Now"). What are some of those reasons and means? How does the Holy Spirit factor into the equation?

Deuteronomy 31:9–13

📖 What does "this law" (mentioned four times in the passage) refer to? While it could mean the entire Pentateuch (first five OT books), most likely it refers to nearly all of Deuteronomy—perhaps the whole book up to 31:24. Reading it once every seven years didn't render unnecessary the teaching ministry of the home (6:1–9) or the priests (17:11; 24:8; Lev. 10:11). It was meant to strengthen these other settings, to focus the people's attention on the revelation of God at a dramatic and joyous occasion. It would especially dramatize the learning of the law for children and newcomers (resident aliens).

📖 Because of Christ's death and resurrection, we who live by faith are no longer obligated to keep the whole law (Rom. 6:14; 10:4). But we fool ourselves if we think that God's moral law has changed or become obsolete. James 1:25 extols the "perfect law that gives freedom." James meant the moral and ethical teaching of Christianity based on the Old Testament moral codes, as embodied by the Ten Commandments, and the summarizing law of love

as voiced by Jesus in Matthew 22:37–40. How can the church ensure that its members, including children and new believers, know God's expectations—standards that in reality free us to be who we were created to be?

Deuteronomy 31:14–29

📖 At Joshua's commissioning, Moses and Joshua presented themselves before the Lord at the Tent of Meeting. God spoke to Moses, in Joshua's hearing, about Israel's future unfaithfulness. In this way Joshua too was warned to resist the people's tendency to turn to foreign gods.

God instructed both men to write down the words to a song. "Teach it to the Israelites and have them sing it" (v. 19) implies sufficient repetition to fix it in the people's minds. The song was to be taught nationally from generation to generation. God would evidently see to it that it wouldn't be forgotten and that it would "testify against" the people (v. 21). God gave these leaders the words, which Moses wrote down and taught the Israelites (v. 22). The actual song is recorded in 32:1–43.

📖 Is memorizing God's Word a discipline you practice? It may be surprising how much trivial information is stored in our memory banks—from U.S. state capitals and the names of 30-day months to the spelling rules for "i before e" and our favorite sport's statistics. And a song or poem, especially one with an appealing lyric or cadence, can stay with us for life. Invest your energy in storing God's eternal Word in your mind and heart. Take time to memorize one or more verses today. Many current worship choruses are taken directly from the Bible's pages and can be an easy entry point.

and difficulties will come upon them, and on that day they will ask, 'Have not these disasters come upon us because our God is not with us?' [b] 18And I will certainly hide my face on that day because of all their wickedness in turning to other gods.

19 "Now write down for yourselves this song and teach it to the Israelites and have them sing it, so that it may be a witness for me against them. 20When I have brought them into the land flowing with milk and honey, the land I promised on oath to their forefathers, [c] and when they eat their fill and thrive, they will turn to other gods [d] and worship them, rejecting me and breaking my covenant. [e] 21And when many disasters and difficulties come upon them, [f] this song will testify against them, because it will not be forgotten by their descendants. I know what they are disposed to do, [g] even before I bring them into the land I promised them on oath." 22So Moses wrote [h] down this song that day and taught it to the Israelites.

23The LORD gave this command [i] to Joshua son of Nun: "Be strong and courageous, [j] for you will bring the Israelites into the land I promised them on oath, and I myself will be with you."

24After Moses finished writing in a book the words of this law from beginning to end, 25he gave this command to the Levites who carried the ark of the covenant of the LORD: 26"Take this Book of the Law and place it beside the ark of the covenant of the LORD your God. There it will remain as a witness against you. [k] 27For I know how rebellious and stiff-necked [l] you are. If you have been rebellious against the LORD while I am still alive and with you, how much more will you rebel after I die! 28Assemble before me all the elders of your tribes and all your officials, so that I can speak these words in their hearing and call heaven and earth to testify against them. [m] 29For I know that after my death you are sure to become utterly corrupt [n] and to turn from the way I have commanded you. In days to come, disaster [o] will fall upon you because you will do evil in the sight of the LORD and provoke him to anger by what your hands have made."

The Song of Moses

30And Moses recited the words of this song from beginning to end in the hearing of the whole assembly of Israel:

32 Listen, O heavens, [p] and I will speak;
hear, O earth, the words of my mouth.
2 Let my teaching fall like rain
and my words descend like dew, [q]
like showers [r] on new grass,
like abundant rain on tender plants.

3 I will proclaim the name of the LORD. [s]
Oh, praise the greatness [t] of our God!
4 He is the Rock, [u] his works are perfect, [v]
and all his ways are just.
A faithful God [w] who does no wrong,
upright and just is he.

5 They have acted corruptly toward him;

Side references

31:17
b Nu 14:42

31:20
c Dt 6:10-12
d Dt 32:15-17
e ver 16
31:21
f ver 17 g Hos 5:3
31:22
h ver 19
31:23
i ver 7 j Jos 1:6

31:26
k ver 19
31:27
l Ex 32:9; Dt 9:6, 24

31:28
m Dt 4:26; 30:19; 32:1
31:29
n Dt 32:5; Jdg 2:19
o Dt 28:15

32:1
p Isa 1:2

32:2
q Isa 55:11
r Ps 72:6

32:3
s Ex 33:19 t Dt 3:24

32:4
u ver 15,18,30
v 2Sa 22:31
w Dt 7:9

Deuteronomy 31:30—32:47

After teaching the Israelites this song that would serve as a "witness for [the LORD] against them" (31:19), Moses charged the people not to take God's words lightly, as though they could either follow them or disregard them with no great effect on their welfare one way or the other (32:46–47). The revelation of the covenant was to be obeyed in every detail, with a willing devotion to the words and spirit of the law and to its Giver. God was their life (see 30:20)—as were his words (32:47). Commitment to God and his Word would ensure a long national life for Israel in the promised land.

Urgent! Rush! ASAP! Immediate attention! Priority! The sheer volume of communications we receive today, along with their purported urgency, can distract us from prioritizing God's words. Moses' charge—to be devoted to God in heart and action—is the call of discipleship. Based on your behavior over the last few weeks, have God's communications been more important than your office memos, mail, e-mail, phone calls, and text-messaging? How do you plan to live out Moses' charge in these verses from today forward?

to their shame they are no longer his children,
but a warped and crooked generation.[a][x]
6 Is this the way you repay[y] the LORD,
O foolish and unwise people?[z]
Is he not your Father,[a] your Creator,[b]
who made you and formed you?[b]

7 Remember the days of old;
consider the generations long past.
Ask your father and he will tell you,
your elders, and they will explain to you.[c]
8 When the Most High gave the nations their inheritance,
when he divided all mankind,[d]
he set up boundaries for the peoples
according to the number of the sons of Israel.[c]
9 For the LORD's portion[e] is his people,
Jacob his allotted inheritance.[f]
10 In a desert[g] land he found him,
in a barren and howling waste.
He shielded him and cared for him;
he guarded him as the apple of his eye,[h]
11 like an eagle that stirs up its nest
and hovers over its young,[i]
that spreads its wings to catch them
and carries them on its pinions.
12 The LORD alone led him;
no foreign god was with him.[j]

13 He made him ride on the heights[k] of the land
and fed him with the fruit of the fields.
He nourished him with honey from the rock,
and with oil[l] from the flinty crag,
14 with curds and milk from herd and flock
and with fattened lambs and goats,
with choice rams of Bashan
and the finest kernels of wheat.[m]
You drank the foaming blood of the grape.[n]

15 Jeshurun[d] grew fat[o] and kicked;
filled with food, he became heavy and sleek.
He abandoned[p] the God who made him
and rejected the Rock[q] his Savior.
16 They made him jealous[r] with their foreign gods
and angered[s] him with their detestable idols.
17 They sacrificed to demons, which are not God—
gods they had not known,[t]
gods that recently appeared,[u]
gods your fathers did not fear.
18 You deserted the Rock, who fathered you;
you forgot[v] the God who gave you birth.

19 The LORD saw this and rejected them[w]
because he was angered by his sons and daughters.[x]
20 "I will hide my face[y] from them," he said,
"and see what their end will be;

32:5 [x] Dt 31:29
32:6 [y] Ps 116:12 [z] Ps 74:2 [a] Dt 1:31; Isa 63:16 [b] ver 15
32:7 [c] Ex 13:14
32:8 [d] Ge 11:8; Ac 17:26
32:9 [e] Jer 10:16 [f] 1Ki 8:51,53
32:10 [g] Jer 2:6 [h] Ps 17:8; Zec 2:8
32:11 [i] Ex 19:4
32:12 [j] ver 39
32:13 [k] Isa 58:14 [l] Job 29:6
32:14 [m] Ps 81:16; 147:14 [n] Ge 49:11
32:15 [o] Dt 31:20 [p] ver 6; Isa 1:4,28 [q] ver 4
32:16 [r] 1Co 10:22 [s] Ps 78:58
32:17 [t] Dt 28:64 [u] Jdg 5:8
32:18 [v] Isa 17:10
32:19 [w] Jer 44:21-23 [x] Ps 106:40
32:20 [y] Dt 31:17,29

[a] 5 Or *Corrupt are they and not his children, / a generation warped and twisted to their shame*
[b] 6 Or *Father, who bought you*   [c] 8 Masoretic Text; Dead Sea Scrolls (see also Septuagint) *sons of God*
[d] 15 *Jeshurun* means *the upright one,* that is, Israel.

for they are a perverse generation, [z]
 children who are unfaithful.
21 They made me jealous [a] by what is no god
 and angered me with their worthless idols. [b]
 I will make them envious by those who are not a people;
 I will make them angry by a nation that has no understanding. [c]
22 For a fire has been kindled by my wrath,
 one that burns to the realm of death [a] below. [d]
 It will devour the earth and its harvests
 and set afire the foundations of the mountains.

23 "I will heap calamities [e] upon them
 and spend my arrows [f] against them.
24 I will send wasting famine against them,
 consuming pestilence [g] and deadly plague; [h]
 I will send against them the fangs of wild beasts, [i]
 the venom of vipers [j] that glide in the dust.
25 In the street the sword will make them childless;
 in their homes terror will reign. [k]
 Young men and young women will perish,
 infants and gray-haired men. [l]
26 I said I would scatter [m] them
 and blot out their memory from mankind, [n]
27 but I dreaded the taunt of the enemy,
 lest the adversary misunderstand
 and say, 'Our hand has triumphed;
 the LORD has not done all this.' " [o]

28 They are a nation without sense,
 there is no discernment in them.
29 If only they were wise and would understand this [p]
 and discern what their end will be!
30 How could one man chase a thousand,
 or two put ten thousand to flight, [q]
 unless their Rock had sold them,
 unless the LORD had given them up? [r]
31 For their rock is not like our Rock,
 as even our enemies concede.
32 Their vine comes from the vine of Sodom
 and from the fields of Gomorrah.
 Their grapes are filled with poison,
 and their clusters with bitterness.
33 Their wine is the venom of serpents,
 the deadly poison of cobras. [s]

34 "Have I not kept this in reserve
 and sealed it in my vaults? [t]
35 It is mine to avenge; I will repay. [u]
 In due time their foot will slip; [v]
 their day of disaster is near
 and their doom rushes upon them. [w]"

36 The LORD will judge his people
 and have compassion on his servants [x]
 when he sees their strength is gone
 and no one is left, slave or free.
37 He will say: "Now where are their gods,
 the rock they took refuge in, [y]

[a] 22 Hebrew to Sheol

32:20
z ver 5
32:21
a 1Co 10:22
b 1Ki 16:13,26
c Ro 10:19*

32:22
d Ps 18:7-8;
Jer 15:14; La 4:11

32:23
e Dt 29:21
f Ps 7:13; Eze 5:16

32:24
g Dt 28:22
h Ps 91:6
i Lev 26:22
j Am 5:18-19

32:25
k Eze 7:15
l 2Ch 36:17;
La 2:21

32:26
m Dt 4:27
n Ps 34:16

32:27
o Isa 10:13

32:29
p Dt 5:29; Ps 81:13

32:30
q Lev 26:8
r Ps 44:12

32:33
s Ps 58:4

32:34
t Jer 2:22;
Hos 13:12
32:35
u Ro 12:19*;
Heb 10:30*
v Jer 23:12
w Eze 7:8-9

32:36
x Dt 30:1-3;
Ps 135:14;
Joel 2:14

32:37
y Jdg 10:14;
Jer 2:28

³⁸ the gods who ate the fat of their sacrifices
and drank the wine of their drink offerings?
Let them rise up to help you!
Let them give you shelter!

32:39
z Isa 41:4 a Isa 45:5
b 1Sa 2:6; Ps 68:20
c Hos 6:1
d Ps 50:22

³⁹ "See now that I myself am He!^z
There is no god besides me.^a
I put to death and I bring to life,^b
I have wounded and I will heal,^c
and no one can deliver out of my hand.^d
⁴⁰ I lift my hand to heaven and declare:
As surely as I live forever,

32:41
e Isa 34:6; 66:16;
Eze 21:9-10
f Jer 50:29

⁴¹ when I sharpen my flashing sword^e
and my hand grasps it in judgment,
I will take vengeance on my adversaries
and repay those who hate me.^f

32:42
g ver 23
h Jer 46:10,14

⁴² I will make my arrows drunk with blood,^g
while my sword devours flesh:^h
the blood of the slain and the captives,
the heads of the enemy leaders."

32:43
i Ro 15:10* k Ps 65:3;
j 2Ki 9:7 85:1; Rev 19:2

⁴³ Rejoice,ⁱ O nations, with his people,^{a, b}
for he will avenge the blood of his servants;^j
he will take vengeance on his enemies
and make atonement for his land and people.^k

32:44
l Nu 13:8,16

⁴⁴ Moses came with Joshua^c^l son of Nun and spoke all the words of this song in the hearing of the people. ⁴⁵When Moses finished reciting all these words to all Israel, ⁴⁶he said to them, "Take to heart all the words I have solemnly declared to you

32:46
m Eze 40:4
32:47
n Dt 30:20

this day,^m so that you may command your children to obey carefully all the words of this law. ⁴⁷They are not just idle words for you—they are your life.ⁿ By them you will live long in the land you are crossing the Jordan to possess."

Moses to Die on Mount Nebo

32:49
o Nu 27:12

⁴⁸ On that same day the LORD told Moses, ⁴⁹"Go up into the Abarim^o Range to Mount Nebo in Moab, across from Jericho, and view Canaan, the land I am giving the Israelites as their own possession. ⁵⁰There on the mountain that you have

32:50
p Ge 25:8

climbed you will die^p and be gathered to your people, just as your brother Aaron died on Mount Hor and was gathered to his people. ⁵¹This is because both of you broke faith with me in the presence of the Israelites at the waters of Meribah Kadesh

32:51
q Nu 20:11-13

in the Desert of Zin^q and because you did not uphold my holiness among the Is-

---

^a 43 Or *Make his people rejoice, O nations*   ^b 43 Masoretic Text; Dead Sea Scrolls (see also Septuagint) *people, / and let all the angels worship him /*   ^c 44 Hebrew *Hoshea,* a variant of *Joshua*

Deuteronomy 32:48–52

The reason for God's ban against Moses' entry into the promised land is stated more explicitly here than for Aaron in Numbers 20:24. There we are told simply that the two had rebelled against God's command at the waters of Meribah. Here we read that they "broke faith" with God in Israel's presence, failing to uphold his holiness among the people (v. 51). The brothers were guilty because they hadn't properly conveyed God's message or followed the way he intended to supply water to the thirsty Israelites, instead speaking and acting with rash anger (see Num. 20:7–12; Ps. 106:32–33). By God's grace Moses was permitted to see the land—but only "from a distance" (Deut. 32:52).

Does the phrase "from a distance" sound familiar? These words appear in Hebrews 11, a well-loved chapter on Old Testament heroes of faith. Verse 13 reads in part: "All these people were still living by faith when they died. They did not receive the things promised; they only saw them and welcomed them from a distance." Though we are privileged to live in the era of salvation through faith in Christ (cf. Heb. 11:39–40), in what ways do you experience the complete fulfillment of your salvation only "from a distance"? Moses may not have set foot in the earthly promised land, but his presence on the Mount of Transfiguration (Matt. 17:1–13) confirmed that he had indeed entered the greater promised land to which we all look forward.

raelites.^r ⁵²Therefore, you will see the land only from a distance;^s you will not enter^t the land I am giving to the people of Israel."

Moses Blesses the Tribes

33 This is the blessing that Moses the man of God^u pronounced on the Israelites before his death. ²He said:

> "The LORD came from Sinai^v
>   and dawned over them from Seir;^w
> he shone forth from Mount Paran.^x
> He came with^a myriads of holy ones^y
>   from the south, from his mountain slopes.^b
> ³Surely it is you who love^z the people;
>   all the holy ones are in your hand.^a
> At your feet they all bow down,^b
>   and from you receive instruction,
> ⁴the law that Moses gave us,^c
>   the possession of the assembly of Jacob.^d
> ⁵He was king over Jeshurun^c
>   when the leaders of the people assembled,
>   along with the tribes of Israel.

> ⁶"Let Reuben live and not die,
>   nor^d his men be few."

⁷And this he said about Judah:^e

> "Hear, O LORD, the cry of Judah;
>   bring him to his people.
> With his own hands he defends his cause.
> Oh, be his help against his foes!"

⁸About Levi he said:

> "Your Thummim and Urim^f belong
>   to the man you favored.
> You tested him at Massah;
>   you contended with him at the waters of Meribah.^g
> ⁹He said of his father and mother,^h
>   'I have no regard for them.'
> He did not recognize his brothers
>   or acknowledge his own children,

---

^a 2 Or *from*   ^b 2 The meaning of the Hebrew for this phrase is uncertain.   ^c 5 *Jeshurun* means *the upright one,* that is, Israel; also in verse 26.   ^d 6 Or *but let*

Side references

32:51
^r Nu 27:14
32:52
^s Dt 34:1-3
^t Dt 1:37

33:1
^u Jos 14:6

33:2
^v Ex 19:18; Ps 68:8
^w Jdg 5:4 · Hab 3:3
^y Da 7:10; Ac 7:53; Rev 5:11

33:3
^z Hos 11:1
^a Dt 14:2
^b Lk 10:39

33:4
^c Jn 1:17
^d Ps 119:111

33:7
^e Ge 49:10

33:8
^f Ex 28:30 ^g Ex 17:7

33:9
^h Ex 32:26-29

Deuteronomy 33:1–29

Moses' blessings on the tribes appear after the Song of Moses, between God's instructions to him regarding his death and the account of that death. Chapter 33 presents these blessings as recorded by someone other than Moses (as was ch. 34, of course).

Moses' final blessing turned to Israel as a whole—beginning in verse 26 with praise to the Lord as the God of "Jeshurun" (righteous Israel; see v. 5 and NIV text note there). This God is uniquely great, riding on the clouds in his majesty to help his people (cf. Ps. 18:9; 68:33; Isa. 19:1).

God, Moses declared, was his people's dwelling; his everlasting arms were beneath them to keep them from harm, discouragement, and failure. They wouldn't be left to rely on their own strength. The Lord would drive out their enemy before them with the command "Destroy!" His promise to go before Israel to conquer the land, though, always implied the people's obedient participation. That participation would be effective only as God worked with and through them.

Are you already a Christian committed to *doing* God's word (James 1:22)—to participating with him as a willing partner in his work on Earth? Have you done your homework—laid careful plans, done your research, and gathered your resources in preparation? In this light, the final point of "There and Then," above, bears repeating: Your participation will be effective only as God, through his Spirit, works through you. The impetus and empowerment come from him. God's work in the world is a cooperative effort; he still today uses yielded servants.

33:9
i Mal 2:5

but he watched over your word
and guarded your covenant.*i*

33:10
j Lev 10:11;
Dt 31:9-13
k Ps 51:19

10 He teaches your precepts to Jacob
and your law to Israel.*j*
He offers incense before you
and whole burnt offerings on your altar.*k*

33:11
l 2Sa 24:23

11 Bless all his skills, O LORD,
and be pleased with the work of his hands.*l*
Smite the loins of those who rise up against him;
strike his foes till they rise no more."

12 About Benjamin he said:

33:12
m Dt 12:10
n Ex 28:12

"Let the beloved of the LORD rest secure in him,*m*
for he shields him all day long,
and the one the LORD loves rests between his shoulders.*n*

33:13
o Ge 49:25
p Ge 27:28

13 About Joseph*o* he said:

"May the LORD bless his land
with the precious dew from heaven above
and with the deep waters that lie below;*p*

14 with the best the sun brings forth
and the finest the moon can yield;

33:15
q Hab 3:6

15 with the choicest gifts of the ancient mountains*q*
and the fruitfulness of the everlasting hills;

33:16
r Ex 3:2

16 with the best gifts of the earth and its fullness
and the favor of him who dwelt in the burning bush.*r*
Let all these rest on the head of Joseph,
on the brow of the prince among*a* his brothers.

33:17
s Nu 23:22
t 1Ki 22:11; Ps 44:5

17 In majesty he is like a firstborn bull;
his horns are the horns of a wild ox.*s*
With them he will gore*t* the nations,
even those at the ends of the earth.
Such are the ten thousands of Ephraim;
such are the thousands of Manasseh."

33:18
u Ge 49:13-15

18 About Zebulun*u* he said:

"Rejoice, Zebulun, in your going out,
and you, Issachar, in your tents.

33:19
v Ex 15:17; Isa 2:3
w Ps 4:5
x Isa 60:5,11

19 They will summon peoples to the mountain*v*
and there offer sacrifices of righteousness;*w*
they will feast on the abundance of the seas,*x*
on the treasures hidden in the sand."

33:20
y Ge 49:19

20 About Gad*y* he said:

"Blessed is he who enlarges Gad's domain!
Gad lives there like a lion,
tearing at arm or head.

33:21
z Nu 32:1-5,31-32
a Jos 4:12; 22:1-3

21 He chose the best land for himself;*z*
the leader's portion was kept for him.
When the heads of the people assembled,
he carried out the LORD's righteous will,*a*
and his judgments concerning Israel."

33:22
b Ge 49:16

22 About Dan*b* he said:

"Dan is a lion's cub,
springing out of Bashan."

a 16 Or *of the one separated from*

312

23About Naphtali he said:

"Naphtali is abounding with the favor of the LORD
 and is full of his blessing;
 he will inherit southward to the lake."

24About Asher[c] he said:

"Most blessed of sons is Asher;
 let him be favored by his brothers,
 and let him bathe his feet in oil.[d]
25The bolts of your gates will be iron and bronze,
 and your strength will equal your days.[e]

26"There is no one like the God of Jeshurun,[f]
 who rides on the heavens to help you[g]
 and on the clouds in his majesty.
27The eternal God is your refuge,[h]
 and underneath are the everlasting arms.
He will drive out your enemy before you,[i]
 saying, 'Destroy him!'[j]
28So Israel will live in safety alone;[k]
 Jacob's spring is secure
in a land of grain and new wine,
 where the heavens drop dew.[l]
29Blessed are you, O Israel![m]
 Who is like you,[n]
 a people saved by the LORD?[o]
He is your shield and helper[p]
 and your glorious sword.
Your enemies will cower before you,
 and you will trample down their high places.[a][q]"

The Death of Moses

34 Then Moses climbed Mount Nebo from the plains of Moab to the top of Pisgah, across from Jericho.[r] There the LORD showed[s] him the whole land— from Gilead to Dan, 2all of Naphtali, the territory of Ephraim and Manasseh, all the land of Judah as far as the western sea,[b][t] 3the Negev and the whole region from the Valley of Jericho, the City of Palms,[u] as far as Zoar. 4Then the LORD said to him, "This is the land I promised on oath[v] to Abraham, Isaac and Jacob when I said, 'I will give it[w] to your descendants.' I have let you see it with your eyes, but you will not cross[x] over into it."

5And Moses the servant of the LORD[y] died[z] there in Moab, as the LORD had said. 6He buried him[c] in Moab, in the valley opposite Beth Peor,[a] but to this day no one knows where his grave is.[b] 7Moses was a hundred and twenty years old[c] when he died, yet his eyes were not weak[d] nor his strength gone. 8The Israelites grieved for Moses in the plains of Moab thirty days, until the time of weeping and mourning[e] was over.

9Now Joshua son of Nun was filled with the spirit[d] of wisdom[f] because Moses

---

a 29 Or *will tread upon their bodies*   b 2 That is, the Mediterranean   c 6 Or *He was buried*
d 9 Or *Spirit*

33:24
c Ge 49:21
d Ge 49:20;
Job 29:6

33:25
e Dt 4:40; 32:47
33:26
f Ex 15:11
g Ps 104:3

33:27
h Ps 90:1
i Jos 24:18 j Dt 7:2

33:28
k Nu 23:9; Jer 23:6
l Ge 27:28

33:29
m Ps 144:15
n Ps 18:44
o 2Sa 7:23
p Ps 115:9-11
q Dt 32:13

34:1
r Dt 32:49
s Dt 32:52
34:2
t Dt 11:24
34:3
u Jdg 1:16; 3:13;
2Ch 28:15
34:4
v Ge 28:13
w Ge 12:7 x Dt 3:27
34:5
y Nu 12:7
z Dt 32:50;
Jos 1:1-2
34:6
a Dt 3:29
b Jude 1:9
34:7
c Dt 31:2 d Ge 27:1
34:8
e Ge 50:3, 10;
2Sa 11:27
34:9
f Ge 41:38;
Isa 11:2; Da 6:3

Deuteronomy 34:1–12

What a sense of accomplishment mixed with disappointment must have been in Moses' mind as he surveyed the promised land! Egyptian bondage had faded into history. The painful formative years of the new nation's desert experience were past. The promised land lay before Moses—but his mission was over. His desire had led him to plead that God would relent, but this final report makes no mention of that kind of prayer. Had Moses at last accepted God's will and bowed to the inevitable?

Deuteronomy closes by eulogizing Moses as the greatest of all prophets, the one whom God knew intimately, and the greatest miracle worker. Not until Jesus came (the One whom Moses had spoken about; John 5:46) was anyone greater than Moses—Israel's emancipator, prophet, lawgiver, and spiritual father.

34:9
g Nu 27:18,23

had laid his hands on him. *g* So the Israelites listened to him and did what the LORD had commanded Moses.

34:10
h Dt 18:15,18
i Ex 33:11;
Nu 12:6,8; Dt 5:4

34:11
j Dt 4:34 *k* Dt 7:19

¹⁰Since then, no prophet has risen in Israel like Moses, *h* whom the LORD knew face to face, *i* ¹¹who did all those miraculous signs and wonders *j* the LORD sent him to do in Egypt—to Pharaoh and to all his officials *k* and to his whole land. ¹²For no one has ever shown the mighty power or performed the awesome deeds that Moses did in the sight of all Israel.

Passing the torch is seldom easy. Retirement celebrations for leaders may have satisfying, memorable moments, but how often are they tinged with regret in the face of declining physical and/or intellectual powers? Couldn't I have done or given a *little more?* What could I have done better? Reflect on verses 10–12 of this closing passage. Moses had made mistakes, but God didn't demonstrate mixed feelings about his honor. These three verses reverberate with the words we all long one day to hear: "Well done, good and faithful servant!" (Matt. 25:21).

34:5

THE TOP 24 CAUSES OF CHRISTIAN DEATHS

1. Poverty
2. Natural causes
3. Pollution and dirty water
4. Starvation, hunger
5. Parasitic diseases
6. Childhood diseases (including pneumonia)
7. Circulatory and cardiovascular diseases
8. Infant mortality, perinatal diseases
9. Cancer
10. Injury and accident
11. Malaria
12. Diarrhea
13. AIDS
14. Pneumonia
15. Tuberculosis
16. Tobacco
17. Homicide
18. Manmade disaster, pesticides
19. Suicide
20. Martydom
21. Motor vehicle crashes
22. Natural disasters: earthquakes, floods
23. War, torture, execution
24. Terrorism

Source: Barrett and Johnson (2001:34)

Which of these directly affect your culture, and which are completely foreign to your personal experience? Are you surprised by some of them? Which lie to some degree within your direct sphere of influence? Which could benefit from your personal involvement or financial generosity?

24:15 "CHOOSE FOR YOURSELVES THIS DAY WHOM YOU WILL
SERVE . . . BUT AS FOR ME AND MY HOUSEHOLD, WE WILL SERVE
THE LORD."

INTRODUCTION TO

Joshua

AUTHOR

The author of Joshua is unknown. Evidence points to Joshua's having written at least a portion of it (24:26), but the book as we now have it was probably completed by someone else,
perhaps the high priest Phinehas or a later compiler in the postexilic period (see 15:13–19;
19:47; 24:29–33). The phrase "to this day" (e.g., 4:9; 9:27; 16:10) indicates that some portions
were written at a later date.

DATE WRITTEN

If Joshua wrote the book, it was probably written around 1390 B.C., just before his death.

ORIGINAL READERS

Joshua was written to the Israelites to remind them of God's faithfulness and to encourage
them to commit themselves to the Lord.

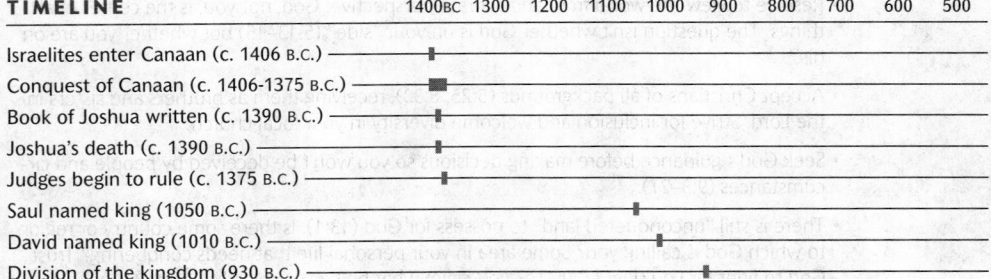

TIMELINE	1400BC	1300	1200	1100	1000	900	800	700	600	500
Israelites enter Canaan (c. 1406 B.C.)										
Conquest of Canaan (c. 1406-1375 B.C.)										
Book of Joshua written (c. 1390 B.C.)										
Joshua's death (c. 1390 B.C.)										
Judges begin to rule (c. 1375 B.C.)										
Saul named king (1050 B.C.)										
David named king (1010 B.C.)										
Division of the kingdom (930 B.C.)										

THEMES

Joshua describes Israel's conquest and settlement of Canaan, the promised land. It contains
the following themes:

1. *God, the great warrior.* Joshua depicts God as a warrior who rescues his people from their
enemies (1:1—12:24; Ex. 15:3). The Israelites understood that their victories were due not to
their own strength and wisdom, but to his presence with them. When they trusted and
obeyed God, they won (5:13—6:27; 8:1–29; 10:1—12:24), but when they depended on their
own judgment and disobeyed him, they lost (7:1–12; 9:1–21). God's people are still at war today. Indeed, we are engaged in a much more dangerous confrontation—an ongoing battle
against spiritual powers and authorities, against evil itself (Eph. 6:12). But God has given us
powerful spiritual weapons (Eph. 6:10–18), and we enter this battle because Jesus Christ has
already assured the final outcome by his victory (Col. 2:13–15; Rev. 19:11–21).

2. *God's faithfulness.* The second half of Joshua (13:1—24:33) portrays God's faithfulness to
his promises (21:45; 23:14). As Israel took possession of the land, the ancient promises to
Abraham (Gen. 12:1–3) became concrete realities. God's promises were being fulfilled. God is

a promise keeper, and Christians today have been given "great and precious promises" (2 Peter 1:4), every one of which is fulfilled in Jesus (2 Cor. 1:20). It's out of gratitude for God's faithfulness that we offer ourselves into his service.

FAITH IN ACTION

The pages of Joshua contain life lessons and role models of faith—people who challenge believers to put their faith in action.

Role Models

• THE ISRAELITES (4:20–24) were to remind their children of all that God had done for them. When was the last time you shared your story of God's goodness to you?

• RAHAB (2:1–21; 6:25) was saved from death because of her faith in God (Heb. 11:31), which she exhibited by hiding the spies. Is God calling you to do something dangerous or risky for him?

• ACSAH (15:16–19) asked for water rights for the desert land awarded to her husband/family. Do you ask God to supply the practical and spiritual needs of yourself and your family?

• ZELOPHEHAD'S DAUGHTERS (17:3-4; cf. Num. 27:1–11; 36:1–12) followed through with Joshua and Eleazar to receive their land allotment as promised by Moses. Do you persevere to see the fulfillment of the promises of God in your life?

• JOSHUA (24:15) chose to live for and obey God. Whom have you chosen as the master of your life? Does your life reflect your choice?

Challenges

• "Be strong and very courageous. Be careful to obey" (1:7).

• Exhibit your faith in God despite dangerous or uncomfortable circumstances (6:25).

• Resolve to view the world from an accurate perspective: God, not you, is the center of all things. The question isn't whether God is on your "side" (5:13–15) but whether you are on his.

• Accept Christians of all backgrounds (5:25; 8:33), receiving them as brothers and sisters in the Lord. Strive for inclusion and welcome diversity in your local church.

• Seek God's guidance before making decisions so you won't be deceived by people and circumstances (9:3–27).

• There is still "unconquered land" to possess for God (13:1). Is there some country or region to which God is calling you? Some area in your personal life that needs conquering? Trust God to fight for you (Deut. 20:4) as you claim what he has promised (17:3-4; 23:5).

OUTLINE

I. Preparation and Entrance Into Canaan (1:1—5:12)
II. Conquest of the Land (5:13—12:24)
   A. Jericho and Ai (5:13—8:35)
   B. Gibeonites, Amorites, and Southern Cities (9–10)
   C. Northern Kings (11)
   D. List of Defeated Kings (12)
III. The Division of the Land by Tribes (13–21)
IV. Joshua's Farewell and Death (22–24)

The LORD Commands Joshua

1 After the death of Moses the servant of the LORD, [a] the LORD said to Joshua [b] son of Nun, Moses' aide: [2] "Moses my servant is dead. Now then, you and all these people, get ready to cross the Jordan River [c] into the land I am about to give to them—to the Israelites. [3] I will give you every place where you set your foot, [d] as I promised Moses. [4] Your territory will extend from the desert to Lebanon, and from the great river, the Euphrates [e] —all the Hittite country—to the Great Sea [a] on the west. [f] [5] No one will be able to stand up against you [g] all the days of your life. As I was with [h] Moses, so I will be with you; I will never leave you nor forsake [i] you.

[6] "Be strong and courageous, because you will lead these people to inherit the land I swore to their forefathers [j] to give them. [7] Be strong and very courageous. Be careful to obey all the law my servant Moses gave you; do not turn from it to the right or to the left, [k] that you may be successful wherever you go. [l] [8] Do not let this Book of the Law depart from your mouth; meditate on it day and night, so that you may be careful to do everything written in it. Then you will be prosperous and successful. [m] [9] Have I not commanded you? Be strong and courageous. Do not be terrified; [n] do not be discouraged, for the LORD your God will be with you wherever you go." [o]

[10] So Joshua ordered the officers of the people: [11] "Go through the camp and tell the people, 'Get your supplies ready. Three days from now you will cross the Jordan here to go in and take possession [p] of the land the LORD your God is giving you for your own.' "

[12] But to the Reubenites, the Gadites and the half-tribe of Manasseh, [q] Joshua said, [13] "Remember the command that Moses the servant of the LORD gave you:

[a] 4 That is, the Mediterranean

1:1
[a] Nu 12:7; Dt 34:5
[b] Ex 24:13; Dt 1:38

1:2
[c] ver 11

1:3
[d] Dt 11:24

1:4
[e] Ge 15:18
[f] Nu 34:2-12

1:5
[g] Dt 7:24 [h] Jos 3:7; 6:27 [i] Dt 31:6-8

1:6
[j] Dt 31:23

1:7
[k] Dt 5:32; 28:14
[l] Jos 11:15

1:8
[m] Dt 29:9; Ps 1:1-3
1:9
[n] Ps 27:1 [o] ver 7; Dt 31:7-8; Jer 1:8

1:11
[p] Joel 3:2

1:12
[q] Nu 32:20-22

Joshua 1:1–18

Crossing the Jordan marked the Israelites' entrance into the promised land, just as crossing the Red Sea had marked their departure from Egypt. Flood conditions and the presence of the enemy on the other shore made this a formidable undertaking. God's promise of the land, first given to Abraham in Genesis 12:7, was a major theme throughout patriarchal history and the exodus, especially in the book of Deuteronomy. The fulfillment of that promise is a major theme of Joshua.

The command to "be strong and courageous" is repeated three times in God's charge to Joshua (vv. 6–9) and again in the people's reply to Joshua (v. 18). Joshua may have been intimidated by the greatness of his predecessor, Moses, and the awesomeness of his own responsibility. This passage introduces the two major parts of the book: the conquest (chs. 1–12) and division (chs. 13–21) of the land.

Verse 8 is the theme verse of Joshua. God blesses his people when they obey him. The phrase "from your mouth" refers to the custom of muttering while studying or reflecting. In fact, the Hebrew word translated "meditate" means "mutter." Whether or not moving your lips when in deep concentration is your style, all of Scripture, especially its exhortations and commands, is worthy of that level of concentration. Meditating on God's Word leads us "to *do* everything written in it" (v. 8, emphasis added; cf. James 1:22–25). Does the Word of God control both your thoughts and your actions?

1:6–11

BE **STRONG** AND **COURAGEOUS**

Joshua 1:6–11 is the classic Biblical statement of courage. But the rest of the Bible isn't silent about this important Christian virtue. It records many situations calling for courage:

When we are asked to obey
- King David challenged his son Solomon (1 Chron. 22:11–13).
- Jesus was asked to sacrifice his life (Matt. 26:39).

When we are faced with wrongdoing
- Nathan challenged King David (2 Sam. 12:7–9).
- John the Baptist challenged King Herod (Mark 6:18).

When we are under pressure
- Isaiah encouraged the exiles of Israel (Isa. 12:2).
- Paul cheered up his shipwrecked companions (Acts 27:22).

When we confront an enemy
- Jael cunningly executed Sisera (Judg. 4:21).

- David prevailed in a showdown with Goliath (1 Sam. 17).
- Christians of all ages have stood firm against spiritual wickedness (Eph. 6:10–13).

When we are asked to deny faith
- The three Hebrews wouldn't bow to Nebuchadnezzar's idol (Dan. 3:13–15).
- Stephen boldly confronted religious leaders (Acts 7:51–60).

When we are asked to witness to our faith
- Peter and John testified before the Sanhedrin (Acts 4:18–20).
- Peter challenged us all (1 Peter 3:15).

When we pray
- Abraham asked God to spare more people in Sodom (Gen. 18:27–28).
- We can approach Jesus with confidence (Heb. 4:14–16).

Courage

Joshua, son of Nun and Moses' aide and successor, epitomized the virtue of courage. He needed it. When Moses died on the doorstep of the promised land, Joshua was left to lead the Israelite army in its conquest of the land of the giants—Canaan. God gave him the command position with instructions to "be strong and courageous" in carrying it out.

Similarly, it's courage that enables each of us to hear God's voice and obey. It's courage that moves us from thinking that teaching fourth-grade boys' church school is a good idea to actually doing it. It's courage that enables us to face a possibly terminal illness. It's courage that makes us finally decide to go on that short-term mission trip to help build houses in Latin America.

Courage is the quality that enables us to face danger with self-possession, confidence, and resolution. Without courage we are armchair Christians. With it, we become world Christians.

> **Courageous Christians are fearless only in the sense that they don't act afraid or . . . fail to act.**

So where do we get courage? Well, where did Joshua get his? At least four possible answers have been suggested.

The first is that for some reason Joshua was born brave. Courage was part of a whole bundle of innate predispositions that together characterized this newborn. In this view some are born brave and some aren't.

The second answer is that Mr. and Mrs. Nun taught Joshua the meaning of courage. Joshua listened and learned, and as a result he became gutsy.

The third answer is that Joshua was required as a young man to perform tasks that developed courage. Though he might have been fearful in doing them, the habit of doing brave things eventually made him a self-assured man.

The fourth answer is that God made Joshua courageous. The Lord needed a brave warrior, so he filled Joshua with the valor necessary to do the job.

Trying to pick the right answer isn't just an intellectual game. If we want to be trailblazing Christians, we need courage to act according to God's call. Where does courage really come from? How can each of us develop and/or enhance the quality?

The answer the best thinkers in our Western and Christian tradition have given is that all four of the answers above contribute to our individual store of resolve. If children can learn about their own ability to be brave and choose to develop it through habit, so can we as God's children. Two things to think about as you undertake a courage-building program:

1. Courage is important. In the first chapter of the book of Joshua, the phrase "be strong and courageous" is repeated four times. It appears twice in the specific charge of God to Joshua in verses 6–7: "Be strong and courageous, because you will lead these people to inherit the land I swore to their forefathers to give them. Be strong and very courageous."

2. Being courageous doesn't equate to being unafraid. Courageous Christians throughout history haven't necessarily been fearless Christians. But they have acted in spite of their fears, not in their absence. The opposite of courage isn't necessarily cowardice. It may be discouragement, becoming paralyzed by our fear or overwhelmed by negative conditions. Courageous Christians are fearless only in the sense that they don't act afraid or, more importantly, fail to act at all.

To what courageous venture has God been calling you?

'The LORD your God is giving you rest[r] and has granted you this land.' [14] Your wives, your children and your livestock may stay in the land that Moses gave you east of the Jordan, but all your fighting men, fully armed, must cross over ahead of your brothers. You are to help your brothers [15] until the LORD gives them rest, as he has done for you, and until they too have taken possession of the land that the LORD your God is giving them. After that, you may go back and occupy your own land, which Moses the servant of the LORD gave you east of the Jordan toward the sunrise."[s]

[16] Then they answered Joshua, "Whatever you have commanded us we will do, and wherever you send us we will go. [17] Just as we fully obeyed Moses, so we will obey you.[t] Only may the LORD your God be with you as he was with Moses. [18] Whoever rebels against your word and does not obey your words, whatever you may command them, will be put to death. Only be strong and courageous!"

Rahab and the Spies

2 Then Joshua son of Nun secretly sent two spies[u] from Shittim.[v] "Go, look over the land," he said, "especially Jericho." So they went and entered the house of a prostitute[a] named Rahab[w] and stayed there.

[2] The king of Jericho was told, "Look! Some of the Israelites have come here tonight to spy out the land." [3] So the king of Jericho sent this message to Rahab: "Bring out the men who came to you and entered your house, because they have come to spy out the whole land."

[4] But the woman had taken the two men and hidden them.[x] She said, "Yes, the men came to me, but I did not know where they had come from. [5] At dusk, when it was time to close the city gate, the men left. I don't know which way they went. Go after them quickly. You may catch up with them." [6] (But she had taken them up to the roof and hidden them under the stalks of flax[y] she had laid out on the roof.)[z] [7] So the men set out in pursuit of the spies on the road that leads to the fords of the Jordan, and as soon as the pursuers had gone out, the gate was shut.

[8] Before the spies lay down for the night, she went up on the roof [9] and said to them, "I know that the LORD has given this land to you and that a great fear[a] of you has fallen on us, so that all who live in this country are melting in fear because of you. [10] We have heard how the LORD dried up[b] the water of the Red Sea[b] for you when you came out of Egypt,[c] and what you did to Sihon and Og,[d] the two kings of the Amorites east of the Jordan, whom you completely destroyed.[c] [11] When we heard of it, our hearts melted and everyone's courage failed because of you,[e] for the LORD your God is God in heaven above and on the earth[f] below. [12] Now then, please swear to me by the LORD that you will show kindness to my family, because I have shown kindness to you. Give me a sure sign[g] [13] that you will spare the lives of my father and mother, my brothers and sisters, and all who belong to them, and that you will save us from death."

Cross-references (margin)

1:13 r Dt 3:18-20

1:15 s Jos 22:1-4

1:17 t ver 5,9

2:1 u Jas 2:25; v Nu 25:1; Jos 3:1; w Heb 11:31

2:4 x 2Sa 17:19-20

2:6 y Jas 2:25; z Ex 1:17,19; 2Sa 17:19

2:9 a Ge 35:5; Ex 23:27; Dt 2:25

2:10 b Ex 14:21; c Nu 23:22; d Nu 21:21,24,34-35

2:11 e Ex 15:14; Jos 5:1; 7:5; Ps 22:14; Isa 13:7; f Dt 4:39

2:12 g ver 18

---

a 1 Or possibly *an innkeeper*   b 10 Hebrew *Yam Suph*; that is, Sea of Reeds   c 10 The Hebrew term refers to the irrevocable giving over of things or persons to the LORD, often by totally destroying them.

Joshua 2:1–24

It's remarkable how much Rahab knew about Israel's history and God's plans for his people's future. One of God's great purposes in the exodus had been to make these same facts known to Pharaoh and the Egyptians (Ex. 7:5). Rahab spoke of the takeover of the land as though it were an already accomplished fact (v. 9). The "great fear" that had fallen on all the people had been predicted in Exodus 15:15b–16.

Verse 11 underscores the reality that morale is a major factor in warfare. Gideon would later excuse the fearful from armed service (Judg. 7:3). Fear is contagious and can even lead to the defeat of an army superior in all other respects. Verse 11 is also the high point of this chapter, as it records Rahab's confession of faith. This testimony, amazing from a pagan, evidenced her conversion to faith in Israel's God.

Deception is an important strategy in warfare; without it espionage would be impossible. When Rahab hid the spies and lied, she sided with Israel against her own people—an act of treason! God takes his law seriously, but the Bible includes examples of infractions that were apparently excused or overlooked due to extenuating circumstances. These instances confuse us; we can only fall back on the reality that God knows best. Can you identify some contemporary situations in which disobedience (in some cases civil disobedience) seems to have been the best course of action?

2:14
h Jdg 1:24; Mt 5:7
2:15
i Ac 9:25
2:16
j Jas 2:25
k Heb 11:31
2:17
l Ge 24:8
2:18
m ver 12; Jos 6:23
2:19
n Eze 33:4
o Mt 27:25
2:24
p ver 9; Jos 6:2
3:1
q Jos 2:1
3:2
r Jos 1:11
3:3
s Nu 10:33
t Dt 31:9
3:5
u Ex 19:10,14;
Lev 20:7; Jos 7:13;
1Sa 16:5; Joel 2:16
3:7
v Jos 4:14;
1Ch 29:25
w Jos 1:5
3:8
x ver 3
3:10
y Dt 5:26;
1Sa 17:26,36;
2Ki 19:4,16;
Hos 1:10; Mt 16:16;
1Th 1:9

[14] "Our lives for your lives!" the men assured her. "If you don't tell what we are doing, we will treat you kindly and faithfully[h] when the LORD gives us the land."

[15] So she let them down by a rope through the window,[i] for the house she lived in was part of the city wall. [16] Now she had said to them, "Go to the hills so the pursuers will not find you. Hide yourselves there three days[j] until they return, and then go on your way."[k]

[17] The men said to her, "This oath[l] you made us swear will not be binding on us [18] unless, when we enter the land, you have tied this scarlet cord in the window through which you let us down, and unless you have brought your father and mother, your brothers and all your family[m] into your house. [19] If anyone goes outside your house into the street, his blood will be on his own head;[n] we will not be responsible. As for anyone who is in the house with you, his blood will be on our head[o] if a hand is laid on him. [20] But if you tell what we are doing, we will be released from the oath you made us swear."

[21] "Agreed," she replied. "Let it be as you say." So she sent them away and they departed. And she tied the scarlet cord in the window.

[22] When they left, they went into the hills and stayed there three days, until the pursuers had searched all along the road and returned without finding them. [23] Then the two men started back. They went down out of the hills, forded the river and came to Joshua son of Nun and told him everything that had happened to them. [24] They said to Joshua, "The LORD has surely given the whole land into our hands;[p] all the people are melting in fear because of us."

Crossing the Jordan

3 Early in the morning Joshua and all the Israelites set out from Shittim[q] and went to the Jordan, where they camped before crossing over. [2] After three days the officers went throughout the camp,[r] [3] giving orders to the people: "When you see the ark of the covenant[s] of the LORD your God, and the priests,[t] who are Levites, carrying it, you are to move out from your positions and follow it. [4] Then you will know which way to go, since you have never been this way before. But keep a distance of about a thousand yards[a] between you and the ark; do not go near it."

[5] Joshua told the people, "Consecrate yourselves,[u] for tomorrow the LORD will do amazing things among you."

[6] Joshua said to the priests, "Take up the ark of the covenant and pass on ahead of the people." So they took it up and went ahead of them.

[7] And the LORD said to Joshua, "Today I will begin to exalt you[v] in the eyes of all Israel, so they may know that I am with you as I was with Moses.[w] [8] Tell the priests[x] who carry the ark of the covenant: 'When you reach the edge of the Jordan's waters, go and stand in the river.'"

[9] Joshua said to the Israelites, "Come here and listen to the words of the LORD your God. [10] This is how you will know that the living God[y] is among you and that he

---

[a] 4 Hebrew *about two thousand cubits* (about 900 meters)

Joshua 3:1—4:24

📖 The ark of the covenant is the most prominent feature in these two chapters. Its presence indicates that crossing the Jordan was much more than a military maneuver: It was a religious procession. The ark symbolized God's presence among his people. The Lord was marching in to claim his land.

The crossings of the Red Sea (Ex. 14) and the Jordan were mighty miracles to be celebrated by Israel forever (cf. Ps. 114). They marked Israel's exodus from the land of bondage and entrance into the land of promise, signaling the nation's transition from slavery to freedom.

📖 The priests were commanded to take up the ark and head for the Jordan, but they weren't told how they would cross the river, which was overflowing its banks

(3:15). God had earlier led the previous generation of Israelites to the Red Sea without indicating how they would get across (Ex. 14). Still today, he often waits for us to step out in faith before removing all obstacles or opening the way for us. When have you experienced this? Is there a step you need to take right now?

Stone monuments were a common means in the Old Testament to allow future generations to remember—and participate in—the great acts God had accomplished for his people (Gen. 28:18–22; 31:45–46; Josh. 24:26–27; 1 Sam. 7:12). Do you look for opportunities to tell others, particularly your children, about your "memorial stones"—your own stories of how God brought you spiritual freedom or did something else of particular significance in your life?

will certainly drive out before you the Canaanites, Hittites, Hivites, Perizzites, Girgashites, Amorites and Jebusites.^z ¹¹See, the ark of the covenant of the Lord of all the earth^a will go into the Jordan ahead of you. ¹²Now then, choose twelve men^b from the tribes of Israel, one from each tribe. ¹³And as soon as the priests who carry the ark of the LORD—the Lord of all the earth^c—set foot in the Jordan, its waters flowing downstream^d will be cut off and stand up in a heap.^e"

¹⁴So when the people broke camp to cross the Jordan, the priests carrying the ark of the covenant^f went ahead^g of them. ¹⁵Now the Jordan is at flood stage^h all during harvest. Yet as soon as the priests who carried the ark reached the Jordan and their feet touched the water's edge, ¹⁶the water from upstream stopped flowing.ⁱ It piled up in a heap a great distance away, at a town called Adam in the vicinity of Zarethan,^j while the water flowing down^k to the Sea of the Arabah^l (the Salt Sea^{a m}) was completely cut off. So the people crossed over opposite Jericho. ¹⁷The priests who carried the ark of the covenant of the LORD stood firm on dry ground in the middle of the Jordan, while all Israel passed by until the whole nation had completed the crossing on dry ground.ⁿ

4 When the whole nation had finished crossing the Jordan,^o the LORD said to Joshua, ²"Choose twelve men^p from among the people, one from each tribe, ³and tell them to take up twelve stones^q from the middle of the Jordan from right where the priests stood and to carry them over with you and put them down at the place where you stay tonight.^r"

⁴So Joshua called together the twelve men he had appointed from the Israelites, one from each tribe, ⁵and said to them, "Go over before the ark of the LORD your God into the middle of the Jordan. Each of you is to take up a stone on his shoulder, according to the number of the tribes of the Israelites, ⁶to serve as a sign among you. In the future, when your children ask you, 'What do these stones mean?'^s ⁷tell them that the flow of the Jordan was cut off^t before the ark of the covenant of the LORD. When it crossed the Jordan, the waters of the Jordan were cut off. These stones are to be a memorial^u to the people of Israel forever."

⁸So the Israelites did as Joshua commanded them. They took twelve stones from the middle of the Jordan, according to the number of the tribes of the Israelites, as the LORD had told Joshua;^v and they carried them over with them to their camp, where they put them down. ⁹Joshua set up the twelve stones^w that had been^b in the middle of the Jordan at the spot where the priests who carried the ark of the covenant had stood. And they are there to this day.

¹⁰Now the priests who carried the ark remained standing in the middle of the Jordan until everything the LORD had commanded Joshua was done by the people, just as Moses had directed Joshua. The people hurried over, ¹¹and as soon as all of them had crossed, the ark of the LORD and the priests came to the other side while the people watched. ¹²The men of Reuben, Gad and the half-tribe of Manasseh crossed over, armed, in front of the Israelites,^x as Moses had directed them. ¹³About forty thousand armed for battle crossed over before the LORD to the plains of Jericho for war.

¹⁴That day the LORD exalted^y Joshua in the sight of all Israel; and they revered him all the days of his life, just as they had revered Moses.

¹⁵Then the LORD said to Joshua, ¹⁶"Command the priests carrying the ark of the Testimony^z to come up out of the Jordan."

¹⁷So Joshua commanded the priests, "Come up out of the Jordan."

¹⁸And the priests came up out of the river carrying the ark of the covenant of the LORD. No sooner had they set their feet on the dry ground than the waters of the Jordan returned to their place and ran at flood stage^a as before.

¹⁹On the tenth day of the first month the people went up from the Jordan and camped at Gilgal^b on the eastern border of Jericho. ²⁰And Joshua set up at Gilgal the twelve stones^c they had taken out of the Jordan. ²¹He said to the Israelites, "In the future when your descendants ask their fathers, 'What do these stones mean?'^d ²²tell them, 'Israel crossed the Jordan on dry ground.'^e ²³For the LORD your God dried up the Jordan before you until you had crossed over. The LORD your God did

---

^a 16 That is, the Dead Sea   ^b 9 Or Joshua also set up twelve stones

Cross references (margin)

3:10 z Ex 33:2; Dt 7:1
3:11 a ver 13; Job 41:11; Zec 6:5
3:12 b Jos 4:2,4
3:13 c ver 11 d ver 16 e Ex 15:8; Ps 78:13
3:14 f Ps 132:8 g Ac 7:44-45
3:15 h Jos 4:18; 1Ch 12:15
3:16 i Ps 66:6; 74:15 j 1Ki 4:12; 7:46 k ver 13 l Dt 1:1 m Ge 14:3
3:17 n Ex 14:22,29
4:1 o Dt 27:2
4:2 p Jos 3:12
4:3 q ver 20 r ver 19
4:6 s ver 21; Ex 12:26; 13:14
4:7 t Jos 3:13 u Ex 12:14
4:8 v ver 20
4:9 w Ge 28:18; Jos 24:26; 1Sa 7:12
4:12 x Nu 32:27
4:14 y Jos 3:7
4:16 z Ex 25:22
4:18 a Jos 3:15
4:19 b Jos 5:9
4:20 c ver 3,8
4:21 d ver 6
4:22 e Jos 3:17

4:23
f Ex 14:21
4:24
g 1Ki 8:42-43;
2Ki 19:19; Ps 106:8;
Jer 10:7 h Ex 15:16;
1Ch 29:12;
Ps 89:13 i Ex 14:31

5:1
j Nu 13:29
k Jos 2:9-11
5:2
l Ex 4:25

5:4
m Dt 2:14

5:6
n Dt 2:7
o Nu 14:23,29-35;
Dt 2:14 p Ex 3:8

5:8
q Ge 34:25

5:10
r Ex 12:6

5:11
s Nu 15:19
t Lev 23:14

5:12
u Ex 16:35

5:13
v Ge 18:2; 32:24

to the Jordan just what he had done to the Red Sea[a] when he dried it up before us until we had crossed over.[f] 24He did this so that all the peoples of the earth might know[g] that the hand of the LORD is powerful[h] and so that you might always fear the LORD your God.[i]"

Circumcision at Gilgal

5 Now when all the Amorite kings west of the Jordan and all the Canaanite kings along the coast[j] heard how the LORD had dried up the Jordan before the Israelites until we had crossed over, their hearts melted[k] and they no longer had the courage to face the Israelites.

2At that time the LORD said to Joshua, "Make flint knives[l] and circumcise the Israelites again." 3So Joshua made flint knives and circumcised the Israelites at Gibeath Haaraloth.[b]

4Now this is why he did so: All those who came out of Egypt—all the men of military age—died in the desert on the way after leaving Egypt.[m] 5All the people that came out had been circumcised, but all the people born in the desert during the journey from Egypt had not. 6The Israelites had moved about in the desert forty years[n] until all the men who were of military age when they left Egypt had died, since they had not obeyed the LORD. For the LORD had sworn to them that they would not see the land that he had solemnly promised their fathers to give us,[o] a land flowing with milk and honey.[p] 7So he raised up their sons in their place, and these were the ones Joshua circumcised. They were still uncircumcised because they had not been circumcised on the way. 8And after the whole nation had been circumcised, they remained where they were in camp until they were healed.[q]

9Then the LORD said to Joshua, "Today I have rolled away the reproach of Egypt from you." So the place has been called Gilgal[c] to this day.

10On the evening of the fourteenth day of the month,[r] while camped at Gilgal on the plains of Jericho, the Israelites celebrated the Passover. 11The day after the Passover, that very day, they ate some of the produce of the land:[s] unleavened bread and roasted grain.[t] 12The manna stopped the day after[d] they ate this food from the land; there was no longer any manna for the Israelites, but that year they ate of the produce of Canaan.[u]

The Fall of Jericho

13Now when Joshua was near Jericho, he looked up and saw a man[v] standing in

---

a 23 Hebrew *Yam Suph*; that is, Sea of Reeds   b 3 *Gibeath Haaraloth* means *hill of foreskins.*
c 9 *Gilgal* sounds like the Hebrew for *roll.*   d 12 Or *the day*

Joshua 5:1–12

Israel couldn't claim the covenant land until the sign of the covenant had been restored. We see here one of numerous parallels between Moses and Joshua. When called to lead the covenant people out of Egypt, Moses had restored the covenant of circumcision in his own family (Ex. 4:24–26). No uncircumcised males had been allowed to participate in the original Passover meal (Ex. 12:48–49). Circumcision was practiced by other nations (e.g., as a puberty rite), but not for covenantal reasons (see Gen. 17:9–14).

The Israelites celebrated the Passover in the land of promise on the same day of the year they had first done so before leaving the land of slavery. Though observed at Sinai (Num. 9:1–5), the Passover—like the rite of circumcision—had been neglected during the years of wandering.

Of course, only males could be circumcised, but Israelites of both genders and all ages were included in the covenant community and celebrated Passover (Ex.

12:3–4,24–27). Many years later another "Joshua" (the Greek form of the name, meaning "the LORD saves," is *Jesus*) would eat the Passover with his disciples and constitute them as the new people of God under the new covenant in which we still live (Matt. 26:26–28). Here there is no circumcision or uncircumcision, no male or female—because we are all one in Christ (Gal. 3:28; Col. 3:11).

God had been gradually weaning his people from manna (see "There and Then" for Deut. 2:1–23). But when they began to eat produce from the promised land this daily, miraculous provision abruptly stopped (Josh. 5:12). Many Christians, during a time of need, have received from God on a daily basis exactly what they needed from some unusual source—only to have that provision "dry up" exactly when it was no longer needed. Do you know of such a situation, or have you experienced this yourself? How has this affected your trust in God's willingness and ability to provide?

front of him with a drawn sword^w in his hand. Joshua went up to him and asked, "Are you for us or for our enemies?"

14"Neither," he replied, "but as commander of the army of the LORD I have now come." Then Joshua fell facedown^x to the ground in reverence, and asked him, "What message does my Lord^a have for his servant?"

15The commander of the LORD's army replied, "Take off your sandals, for the place where you are standing is holy."^{y} And Joshua did so.

6 Now Jericho^z was tightly shut up because of the Israelites. No one went out and no one came in.

2Then the LORD said to Joshua, "See, I have delivered^a Jericho into your hands, along with its king and its fighting men. 3March around the city once with all the armed men. Do this for six days. 4Have seven priests carry trumpets of rams' horns in front of the ark. On the seventh day, march around the city seven times, with the priests blowing the trumpets.^{b} 5When you hear them sound a long blast^c on the trumpets, have all the people give a loud shout;^{d} then the wall of the city will collapse and the people will go up, every man straight in."

6So Joshua son of Nun called the priests and said to them, "Take up the ark of the covenant of the LORD and have seven priests carry trumpets in front of it." 7And he ordered the people, "Advance^e! March around the city, with the armed guard going ahead of the ark of the LORD."

8When Joshua had spoken to the people, the seven priests carrying the seven trumpets before the LORD went forward, blowing their trumpets, and the ark of the LORD's covenant followed them. 9The armed guard marched ahead of the priests who blew the trumpets, and the rear guard^f followed the ark. All this time the trumpets were sounding. 10But Joshua had commanded the people, "Do not give a war cry, do not raise your voices, do not say a word until the day I tell you to shout. Then shout!"^{g} 11So he had the ark of the LORD carried around the city, circling it once. Then the people returned to camp and spent the night there.

12Joshua got up early the next morning and the priests took up the ark of the LORD. 13The seven priests carrying the seven trumpets went forward, marching before the ark of the LORD and blowing the trumpets. The armed men went ahead of them and the rear guard followed the ark of the LORD, while the trumpets kept sounding. 14So on the second day they marched around the city once and returned to the camp. They did this for six days.

15On the seventh day, they got up at daybreak and marched around the city seven times in the same manner, except that on that day they circled the city seven times.^{h} 16The seventh time around, when the priests sounded the trumpet blast, Joshua commanded the people, "Shout! For the LORD has given you the city! 17The city and all that is in it are to be devoted$^{b\,i}$ to the LORD. Only Rahab the prostitute^c and all who are with her in her house shall be spared, because she hid^j the spies we sent. 18But keep away from the devoted things,^{k} so that you will not bring about your own destruction by taking any of them. Otherwise you will make the camp of Israel liable to destruction^l and bring trouble^m on it. 19All the silver and gold and

---

^{a} 14 Or lord ^{b} 17 The Hebrew term refers to the irrevocable giving over of things or persons to the LORD, often by totally destroying them; also in verses 18 and 21. ^{c} 17 Or possibly innkeeper; also in verses 22 and 25

Joshua 5:13—6:27

The stranger (5:13) was a heavenly being who fought behind the scenes in the spiritual realm. His presence was a sign that God was the real military leader of the conquest. Many identify this figure as the angel of the Lord, sometimes indistinguishable from God himself (cf. Ex. 3: 1–4; Judg. 6:11–23). The army of the Lord was an angelic host assuring victory to an obedient Israel (cf. 2 Kings 6:15–17).

The repetition of the number seven (representing divine perfection or completeness), the use of ceremonial trumpets, the presence of priests, and the prominence of the ark all identify the conquest of Jericho as a religious event. The ban placed on Jericho called for all the city's residents, livestock, and plunder to be destroyed (see 6:17 and NIV text note, and "There and Then" for 8:1–29). Metal articles that couldn't be burned were to be removed from common use and placed in the Lord's house (6:19,24). Moses had instructed Israel to annihilate the inhabitants of Canaan upon entering the land (Deut. 7:1–2; regarding ethical issues of the conquest, see "There and Then" for Deut. 7:1–26).

6:19
n ver 24; Nu 31:22
6:20
o Jdg 6:34;
Jer 4:21; Am 2:2
p ver 5 *q* Heb 11:30

6:21
r Dt 20:16

6:22
s Jos 2:14;
Heb 11:31
6:23
t Jos 2:13

6:24
u ver 19
6:25
v Heb 11:31
w Jos 2:6

6:26
x 1Ki 16:34

6:27
y Ge 39:2; Jos 1:5
z Jos 9:1

7:1
a Jos 6:18
b Jos 22:20

7:2
c Jos 18:12;
1Sa 13:5; 14:23

the articles of bronze and iron[n] are sacred to the LORD and must go into his treasury."

20When the trumpets sounded,[o] the people shouted, and at the sound of the trumpet, when the people gave a loud shout,[p] the wall collapsed; so every man charged straight in, and they took the city. [q] 21They devoted the city to the LORD and destroyed[r] with the sword every living thing in it—men and women, young and old, cattle, sheep and donkeys.

22Joshua said to the two men who had spied out the land, "Go into the prostitute's house and bring her out and all who belong to her, in accordance with your oath to her.[s]" 23So the young men who had done the spying went in and brought out Rahab, her father and mother and brothers and all who belonged to her.[t] They brought out her entire family and put them in a place outside the camp of Israel.

24Then they burned the whole city and everything in it, but they put the silver and gold and the articles of bronze and iron[u] into the treasury of the LORD's house. 25But Joshua spared Rahab the prostitute,[v] with her family and all who belonged to her, because she hid the men Joshua had sent as spies to Jericho[w]—and she lives among the Israelites to this day.

26At that time Joshua pronounced this solemn oath: "Cursed before the LORD is the man who undertakes to rebuild this city, Jericho:

"At the cost of his firstborn son
    will he lay its foundations;
at the cost of his youngest
    will he set up its gates."[x]

27So the LORD was with Joshua,[y] and his fame spread[z] throughout the land.

Achan's Sin

7 But the Israelites acted unfaithfully in regard to the devoted things[a];[a] Achan son of Carmi, the son of Zimri,[b] the son of Zerah,[b] of the tribe of Judah, took some of them. So the LORD's anger burned against Israel.

2Now Joshua sent men from Jericho to Ai, which is near Beth Aven[c] to the east of Bethel, and told them, "Go up and spy out the region." So the men went up and spied out Ai.

3When they returned to Joshua, they said, "Not all the people will have to go up against Ai. Send two or three thousand men to take it and do not weary all the people, for only a few men are there." 4So about three thousand men went up; but they

---

[a] *1* The Hebrew term refers to the irrevocable giving over of things or persons to the LORD, often by totally destroying them; also in verses 11, 12, 13 and 15.   [b] *1* See Septuagint and 1 Chron. 2:6; Hebrew *Zabdi*; also in verses 17 and 18.

Joshua's oath in 6:26 shows that Jericho was to remain an object lesson of God's great victory in Israel's first battle. The city was soon resettled (18:21; Judg. 3:13; 2 Sam. 10:5) but remained without a wall. The curse was fulfilled during the reign of the evil King Ahab, when Hiel rebuilt the wall around Jericho (1 Kings 16:34). It's unclear whether fulfillment came via a plague or accident or whether Hiel offered his sons as sacrifices.

Rahab must have abandoned her profession as a prostitute before being assimilated into Israel (6:25) and marrying into what would become the royal family, the lineage of David and Jesus (Matt. 1:5). Her occupation is mentioned repeatedly (6:17,22,25), emphasizing the unlikely nature of her conversion. The New Testament interprets Rahab's action of hiding the spies as evidence of her faith (cf. Heb. 11:32; James 2:25). What unlikely converts can you cite as surprising trophies of God's grace?

Joshua 7:1–26

Only one Israelite sinned in regard to the "devoted things" (see second paragraph of "There and Then" for 5:13—6:27), but all Israel was considered guilty. The nation could be absolved of guilt only when the guilty party had been ferreted out and punished. As head of his family, Achan also involved its members in his crime (cf. Deut. 5:9). We can assume that he couldn't have hidden his loot in the ground under his tent without their knowledge. After execution by stoning, their bodies were burned to purge the land of evil.

God's judgment on the Canaanites was the consequence of their own sin. Now, when God's chosen people sinned, they too would be judged. This is the reverse side of the book's theme (see "Here and Now" for 1:1–18): God's disobedient people won't succeed.

Achan confessed his sin but wasn't forgiven. Why? Apparently at least in part because he didn't con-

were routed by the men of Ai, [d] [5]who killed about thirty-six of them. They chased the Israelites from the city gate as far as the stone quarries [a] and struck them down on the slopes. At this the hearts of the people melted [e] and became like water.

[6]Then Joshua tore his clothes [f] and fell facedown to the ground before the ark of the LORD, remaining there till evening. The elders of Israel did the same, and sprinkled dust [g] on their heads. [7]And Joshua said, "Ah, Sovereign LORD, why did you ever bring this people across the Jordan to deliver us into the hands of the Amorites to destroy us? [h] If only we had been content to stay on the other side of the Jordan! [8]O Lord, what can I say, now that Israel has been routed by its enemies? [9]The Canaanites and the other people of the country will hear about this and they will surround us and wipe out our name from the earth. [i] What then will you do for your own great name?"

[10]The LORD said to Joshua, "Stand up! What are you doing down on your face? [11]Israel has sinned; they have violated my covenant, [j] which I commanded them to keep. They have taken some of the devoted things; they have stolen, they have lied, [k] they have put them with their own possessions. [12]That is why the Israelites cannot stand against their enemies; [l] they turn their backs and run because they have been made liable to destruction. [m] I will not be with you anymore unless you destroy whatever among you is devoted to destruction.

[13]"Go, consecrate the people. Tell them, 'Consecrate yourselves [n] in preparation for tomorrow; for this is what the LORD, the God of Israel, says: That which is devoted is among you, O Israel. You cannot stand against your enemies until you remove it.

[14]"'In the morning, present yourselves tribe by tribe. The tribe that the LORD takes [o] shall come forward clan by clan; the clan that the LORD takes shall come forward family by family; and the family that the LORD takes shall come forward man by man. [15]He who is caught with the devoted things shall be destroyed by fire, along with all that belongs to him. [p] He has violated the covenant [q] of the LORD and has done a disgraceful thing in Israel!'" [r]

[16]Early the next morning Joshua had Israel come forward by tribes, and Judah was taken. [17]The clans of Judah came forward, and he took the Zerahites. [s] He had the clan of the Zerahites come forward by families, and Zimri was taken. [18]Joshua had his family come forward man by man, and Achan son of Carmi, the son of Zimri, the son of Zerah, of the tribe of Judah, was taken.

[19]Then Joshua said to Achan, "My son, give glory [t] to the LORD, [b] the God of Israel, and give him the praise. [c] Tell [u] me what you have done; do not hide it from me."

[20]Achan replied, "It is true! I have sinned against the LORD, the God of Israel. This is what I have done: [21]When I saw in the plunder a beautiful robe from Babylonia, [d] two hundred shekels [e] of silver and a wedge of gold weighing fifty shekels, [f] I coveted [v] them and took them. They are hidden in the ground inside my tent, with the silver underneath."

[22]So Joshua sent messengers, and they ran to the tent, and there it was, hidden in his tent, with the silver underneath. [23]They took the things from the tent, brought them to Joshua and all the Israelites and spread them out before the LORD.

[24]Then Joshua, together with all Israel, took Achan son of Zerah, the silver, the robe, the gold wedge, his sons and daughters, his cattle, donkeys and sheep, his tent and all that he had, to the Valley of Achor. [w] [25]Joshua said, "Why have you brought this trouble [x] on us? The LORD will bring trouble on you today."

Then all Israel stoned him, [y] and after they had stoned the rest, they burned them. [26]Over Achan they heaped up a large pile of rocks, which remains to this day.

---

[a] 5 Or as far as Shebarim   [b] 19 A solemn charge to tell the truth   [c] 19 Or and confess to him
[d] 21 Hebrew Shinar   [e] 21 That is, about 5 pounds (about 2.3 kilograms)   [f] 21 That is, about
1 1/4 pounds (about 0.6 kilogram)

---

fess willingly (cf. Ps. 32; 1 Jn. 1:9). As the selection process came closer and closer to implicating him, he apparently still hoped to avoid detection. True confession goes beyond the admission of wrongdoing to include recognition of our guilt and true remorse. When have you been "caught red-handed"? What thoughts and feelings were foremost in your mind and heart as you faced the consequences?

7:4
d Lev 26:17;
Dt 28:25
7:5
e Lev 26:36;
Jos 2:9, 11;
Eze 21:7; Na 2:10
7:6
f Ge 37:29
g 1Sa 4:12;
2Sa 13:19; Ne 9:1;
Job 2:12; La 2:10;
Rev 18:19
7:7
h Ex 5:22

7:9
i Ex 32:12; Dt 9:28

7:11
j Jos 6:17-19
k Ac 5:1-2

7:12
l Nu 14:45;
Jdg 2:14 m Jos 6:18

7:13
n Jos 3:5; 6:18

7:14
o Pr 16:33

7:15
p 1Sa 14:39
q ver 11 r Ge 34:7

7:17
s Nu 26:20

7:19
t Isa 6:5; Jer 13:16;
Jn 9:24*
u 1Sa 14:43

7:21
v Dt 7:25; Eph 5:5;
1Ti 6:10

7:24
w ver 26; Jos 15:7
7:25
x Jos 6:18 y Dt 17:5

Then the LORD turned from his fierce anger. z Therefore that place has been called the Valley of Achor[a] ever since.

Ai Destroyed

8 Then the LORD said to Joshua, "Do not be afraid;[b] do not be discouraged.[c] Take the whole army[d] with you, and go up and attack Ai. For I have delivered[e] into your hands the king of Ai, his people, his city and his land. 2You shall do to Ai and its king as you did to Jericho and its king, except that you may carry off their plunder and livestock for yourselves.[f] Set an ambush behind the city."

3So Joshua and the whole army moved out to attack Ai. He chose thirty thousand of his best fighting men and sent them out at night 4with these orders: "Listen carefully. You are to set an ambush behind the city. Don't go very far from it. All of you be on the alert. 5I and all those with me will advance on the city, and when the men come out against us, as they did before, we will flee from them. 6They will pursue us until we have lured them away from the city, for they will say, 'They are running away from us as they did before.' So when we flee from them, 7you are to rise up from ambush and take the city. The LORD your God will give it into your hand.[g] 8When you have taken the city, set it on fire.[h] Do what the LORD has commanded.[i] See to it; you have my orders."

9Then Joshua sent them off, and they went to the place of ambush[j] and lay in wait between Bethel and Ai, to the west of Ai—but Joshua spent that night with the people.

10Early the next morning[k] Joshua mustered his men, and he and the leaders of Israel[l] marched before them to Ai. 11The entire force that was with him marched up and approached the city and arrived in front of it. They set up camp north of Ai, with the valley between them and the city. 12Joshua had taken about five thousand men and set them in ambush between Bethel and Ai, to the west of the city. 13They had the soldiers take up their positions—all those in the camp to the north of the city and the ambush to the west of it. That night Joshua went into the valley.

14When the king of Ai saw this, he and all the men of the city hurried out early in the morning to meet Israel in battle at a certain place overlooking the Arabah.[m] But he did not know[n] that an ambush had been set against him behind the city. 15Joshua and all Israel let themselves be driven back[o] before them, and they fled toward the desert.[p] 16All the men of Ai were called to pursue them, and they pursued Joshua and were lured away[q] from the city. 17Not a man remained in Ai or Bethel who did not go after Israel. They left the city open and went in pursuit of Israel.

18Then the LORD said to Joshua, "Hold out toward Ai the javelin[r] that is in your hand,[s] for into your hand I will deliver the city." So Joshua held out his javelin[t] toward Ai. 19As soon as he did this, the men in the ambush rose quickly[u] from their position and rushed forward. They entered the city and captured it and quickly set it on fire.[v]

20The men of Ai looked back and saw the smoke of the city rising against the sky,[w] but they had no chance to escape in any direction, for the Israelites who had been fleeing toward the desert had turned back against their pursuers. 21For when Joshua and all Israel saw that the ambush had taken the city and that smoke was going up

a 26 Achor means trouble.

Joshua 8:1–29

Unlike Jericho, only the king and the people of Ai were to be destroyed. The plunder and livestock from this and all subsequent cities could be kept by the Israelites as their means of support through the years of conquest. Jericho had been Israel's first conquest in the land of Canaan, a kind of firstfruits. Everything in it—people, animals, and property—was devoted to the Lord (6:17–19,24). The battle of Jericho, not that of Ai, was unique.

Joshua and all Israel had been demoralized by their initial defeat at Ai. Now that Achan's sin had been dealt with, God assured Israel of his presence and help. The interplay of miracle and human effort is hard to unravel in the book of Joshua. Even with God's help, common sense and military strategy couldn't be neglected. A generation or so ago this reality might have been stated as "God helps those who help themselves." He doesn't help us as an afterthought, once we have formulated our best laid plans. But neither does he expect us to sit back and allow him to do all the hard work—or even the hard thinking.

from the city, they turned around and attacked the men of Ai. 22 The men of the ambush also came out of the city against them, so that they were caught in the middle,
with Israelites on both sides. Israel cut them down, leaving them neither survivors
nor fugitives.[x] 23 But they took the king of Ai alive[y] and brought him to Joshua.
24 When Israel had finished killing all the men of Ai in the fields and in the desert where they had chased them, and when every one of them had been put to the
sword, all the Israelites returned to Ai and killed those who were in it. 25 Twelve
thousand men and women fell that day—all the people of Ai.[z] 26 For Joshua did not
draw back the hand that held out his javelin until he had destroyed[a][a] all who lived
in Ai.[b] 27 But Israel did carry off for themselves the livestock and plunder of this city,
as the LORD had instructed Joshua.[c]
28 So Joshua burned[d] Ai[e] and made it a permanent heap of ruins,[f] a desolate place
to this day.[g] 29 He hung the king of Ai on a tree and left him there until evening. At
sunset,[h] Joshua ordered them to take his body from the tree and throw it down at
the entrance of the city gate. And they raised a large pile of rocks[i] over it, which remains to this day.

The Covenant Renewed at Mount Ebal

30 Then Joshua built on Mount Ebal[j] an altar[k] to the LORD, the God of Israel, 31 as
Moses the servant of the LORD had commanded the Israelites. He built it according
to what is written in the Book of the Law of Moses—an altar of uncut stones, on
which no iron tool[l] had been used. On it they offered to the LORD burnt offerings
and sacrificed fellowship offerings.[b][m] 32 There, in the presence of the Israelites,
Joshua copied on stones the law of Moses, which he had written.[n] 33 All Israel, aliens
and citizens[o] alike, with their elders, officials and judges, were standing on both
sides of the ark of the covenant of the LORD, facing those who carried it—the
priests, who were Levites.[p] Half of the people stood in front of Mount Gerizim and
half of them in front of Mount Ebal,[q] as Moses the servant of the LORD had formerly commanded when he gave instructions to bless the people of Israel.
34 Afterward, Joshua read all the words of the law—the blessings and the curses—
just as it is written in the Book of the Law.[r] 35 There was not a word of all that Moses had commanded that Joshua did not read to the whole assembly of Israel, including the women and children, and the aliens who lived among them.[s]

The Gibeonite Deception

9 Now when all the kings west of the Jordan heard about these things—those in
the hill country, in the western foothills, and along the entire coast of the
Great Sea[c][t] as far as Lebanon (the kings of the Hittites, Amorites, Canaanites, Perizzites, Hivites and Jebusites)[u]— 2 they came together to make war against Joshua
and Israel.
3 However, when the people of Gibeon[v] heard what Joshua had done to Jericho
and Ai, 4 they resorted to a ruse: They went as a delegation whose donkeys were

8:22 [x] Dt 7:2; Jos 10:1
8:23 [y] 1Sa 15:8
8:25 [z] Dt 20:16-18
8:26 [a] Nu 21:2 [b] Ex 17:12
8:27 [c] ver 2
8:28 [d] Nu 31:10 [e] Jos 7:2; Jer 49:3 [f] Dt 13:16; Jos 10:1 [g] Ge 35:20
8:29 [h] Dt 21:23; Jn 19:31 [i] 2Sa 18:17
8:30 [j] Dt 11:29 [k] Ex 20:24
8:31 [l] Ex 20:25 [m] Dt 27:6-7
8:32 [n] Dt 27:8
8:33 [o] Lev 16:29 [p] Dt 31:12 [q] Dt 11:29; 27:11-14
8:34 [r] Dt 28:61; 31:11; Jos 1:8
8:35 [s] Ex 12:38; Dt 31:12
9:1 [t] Nu 34:6 [u] Ex 3:17; Jos 3:10
9:3 [v] ver 17; Jos 10:2; 2Sa 2:12; 2Ch 1:3; Isa 28:21

[a] *26* The Hebrew term refers to the irrevocable giving over of things or persons to the LORD, often by totally destroying them. [b] *31* Traditionally *peace offerings* [c] *1* That is, the Mediterranean

Joshua 8:30–35

The building of this altar and the ceremony that followed had been commanded by Moses (Deut. 27–28). By this act Joshua acknowledged God as the source of every victory and blessing. Like Abraham, who had built altars wherever he traveled throughout the land, Joshua claimed this territory in God's name. It was an appropriate time to worship: Israel had established a foothold in the central highlands that divided north from south. In both the conquest and possession of the land, God's people were to recognize their relationship with and obedience to him. "Aliens and citizens" alike participated in the covenant renewal (v. 33).

God intended Israel's religion to be a missionary religion (cf. 1 Kings 8:41–43). From the exodus on, aliens who chose to live with Israel and worship her God had been assimilated into the nation. Rahab and her family are one example (Josh. 6:25). Can you think of others? What does this say to you about God's later inclusion of the Gentiles into his new covenant in Christ? About the mission of the church in all ages to reach out to any and all who will hear and believe? About the need for inclusiveness within a given congregation or Christian family—or in the heart of an individual believer like you?

loaded[a] with worn-out sacks and old wineskins, cracked and mended. 5The men put worn and patched sandals on their feet and wore old clothes. All the bread of their food supply was dry and moldy. 6Then they went to Joshua in the camp at Gilgal[w] and said to him and the men of Israel, "We have come from a distant country; make a treaty with us."

7The men of Israel said to the Hivites,[x] "But perhaps you live near us. How then can we make a treaty[y] with you?"

8"We are your servants,[z] they said to Joshua.

But Joshua asked, "Who are you and where do you come from?"

9They answered: "Your servants have come from a very distant country[a] because of the fame of the LORD your God. For we have heard reports[b] of him: all that he did in Egypt, 10and all that he did to the two kings of the Amorites east of the Jordan—Sihon king of Heshbon, and Og king of Bashan,[c] who reigned in Ashtaroth.[d] 11And our elders and all those living in our country said to us, 'Take provisions for your journey; go and meet them and say to them, "We are your servants; make a treaty with us." ' 12This bread of ours was warm when we packed it at home on the day we left to come to you. But now see how dry and moldy it is. 13And these wineskins that we filled were new, but see how cracked they are. And our clothes and sandals are worn out by the very long journey."

14The men of Israel sampled their provisions but did not inquire[e] of the LORD. 15Then Joshua made a treaty of peace[f] with them to let them live, and the leaders of the assembly ratified it by oath.

16Three days after they made the treaty with the Gibeonites, the Israelites heard that they were neighbors, living near them. 17So the Israelites set out and on the third day came to their cities: Gibeon, Kephirah, Beeroth[g] and Kiriath Jearim.[h]

[a] 4 Most Hebrew manuscripts; some Hebrew manuscripts, Vulgate and Syriac (see also Septuagint) *They prepared provisions and loaded their donkeys*

Margin references:
9:6 w Jos 5:10
9:7 x ver 1; Jos 11:19 y Ex 23:32; Dt 7:2
9:8 z Dt 20:11; 2Ki 10:5
9:9 a Dt 20:15 b ver 24; Jos 2:9
9:10 c Nu 21:33 d Nu 21:24,35
9:14 e Nu 27:21
9:15 f Ex 23:32; Jos 11:19; 2Sa 21:2
9:17 g Jos 18:25 h 1Sa 7:1-2

Joshua 9:1–27

Somehow the people of Gibeon knew that God had forbidden Israel to make any treaties or to save alive any of the inhabitants of the land (Deut. 7:1–3; 20:16–18). Israel should have been suspicious. The Gibeonites would have had little reason to seek a treaty had they really come from a distant country.

The Gibeonites' statement that they had come "because of the fame of the LORD your God" (v. 9) is key. "Fame" here translates a Hebrew word commonly rendered as "name." It included the idea of fame but was a much richer concept. A person's name stood for his or her character (7:9). Their actions were deceitful, but the Gibeonites were drawn by their knowledge of God—and were spared (cf. Josh. 2:8–13). In the prophet Joel's words, "Everyone who calls on the name of the LORD will be saved" (Joel 2:32).

How tragic that God's people were so impressed by the Gibeonites' stale provisions that they failed to seek his guidance! Of all people, Joshua should have known to inquire of the Lord. He had climbed up the mountain of revelation with Moses (Ex. 24:12–13) and been trained in the use of the Urim and Thummim for determining God's will (Num. 27:18–21). How easy it is even in God's service to take his guidance and blessing for granted! When has this been a pitfall for you?

9:1–2

Wars

The Israelites took over the promised land through warfare. Unfortunately, war has always been a feature of human existence:

There have been 500 major wars since A.D. 1700.

100 of these have been fought since 1960. What do you think accounts for this startling proliferation?

There were 25 wars underway in 2000.

In our day over 1 million people are killed each year in wars.

WAR
ONE MILLION
PEOPLE PER YEAR

Currently about 60 countries are engaged in armed conflict, either internally or externally.

150 nations have signed disarmament treaties.

The maintenance and activities of international peacekeeping forces cost $250 million each year.

Source: Barrett and Johnson (2001:35)

18But the Israelites did not attack them, because the leaders of the assembly had sworn an oath[i] to them by the LORD, the God of Israel.

The whole assembly grumbled[j] against the leaders, 19but all the leaders answered, "We have given them our oath by the LORD, the God of Israel, and we cannot touch them now. 20This is what we will do to them: We will let them live, so that wrath will not fall on us for breaking the oath we swore to them." 21They continued, "Let them live,[k] but let them be woodcutters and water carriers[l] for the entire community." So the leaders' promise to them was kept.

22Then Joshua summoned the Gibeonites and said, "Why did you deceive us by saying, 'We live a long way[m] from you,' while actually you live near[n] us? 23You are now under a curse:[o] You will never cease to serve as woodcutters and water carriers for the house of my God."

24They answered Joshua, "Your servants were clearly told[p] how the LORD your God had commanded his servant Moses to give you the whole land and to wipe out all its inhabitants from before you. So we feared for our lives because of you, and that is why we did this. 25We are now in your hands.[q] Do to us whatever seems good and right to you."

26So Joshua saved them from the Israelites, and they did not kill them. 27That day he made the Gibeonites woodcutters and water carriers for the community and for the altar of the LORD at the place the LORD would choose.[r] And that is what they are to this day.

The Sun Stands Still

10 Now Adoni-Zedek king of Jerusalem[s] heard that Joshua had taken Ai[t] and totally destroyed[a][u] it, doing to Ai and its king as he had done to Jericho and its king, and that the people of Gibeon had made a treaty of peace[v] with Israel and were living near them. 2He and his people were very much alarmed at this, because Gibeon was an important city, like one of the royal cities; it was larger than Ai, and all its men were good fighters. 3So Adoni-Zedek king of Jerusalem appealed to Hoham king of Hebron,[w] Piram king of Jarmuth, Japhia king of Lachish[x] and Debir king of Eglon. 4"Come up and help me attack Gibeon," he said, "because it has made peace[y] with Joshua and the Israelites."

5Then the five kings of the Amorites[z]—the kings of Jerusalem, Hebron, Jarmuth, Lachish and Eglon—joined forces. They moved up with all their troops and took up positions against Gibeon and attacked it.

6The Gibeonites then sent word to Joshua in the camp at Gilgal: "Do not abandon your servants. Come up to us quickly and save us! Help us, because all the Amorite kings from the hill country have joined forces against us."

7So Joshua marched up from Gilgal with his entire army,[a] including all the best fighting men. 8The LORD said to Joshua, "Do not be afraid[b] of them; I have given them into your hand. Not one of them will be able to withstand you."

9After an all-night march from Gilgal, Joshua took them by surprise. 10The LORD threw them into confusion before Israel,[c] who defeated them in a great victory at Gibeon. Israel pursued them along the road going up to Beth Horon[d] and cut them down all the way to Azekah[e] and Makkedah. 11As they fled before Israel on the road

---

a 1 The Hebrew term refers to the irrevocable giving over of things or persons to the LORD, often by totally destroying them; also in verses 28, 35, 37, 39 and 40.

9:18
i Ps 15:4 / Ex 15:24

9:21
k ver 15 / Dt 29:11

9:22
m ver 6 n ver 16
9:23
o Ge 9:25

9:24
p ver 9

9:25
q Ge 16:6

9:27
r Dt 12:5

10:1
s Jdg 1:7 t Jos 8:1
u Dt 20:16;
Jos 8:22 v Jos 9:15

10:3
w Ge 13:18
x 2Ch 11:9; 25:27;
Ne 11:30; Isa 36:2;
37:8; Jer 34:7;
Mic 1:13
10:4
y Jos 9:15
10:5
z Nu 13:29

10:7
a Jos 8:1
10:8
b Dt 3:2; Jos 1:9

10:10
c Dt 7:23
d Jos 16:3,5
e Jos 15:35

The Gibeonites lived peaceably in Israel for many years. Nehemiah 3:7 and 7:25 suggest that ultimately they were fully assimilated into the nation. God's divine purpose was served even by his people's foolish error. What other examples of this outcome, either Biblical or in later history, come to mind for you? Have you experienced this in your own life?

Joshua 10:1–15
When God intervened on behalf of his people

with large hailstones, the accomplishments of Israel's army were dwarfed by comparison. Unquestionably, the Lord won the victory. The Canaanites, who worshiped nature deities, must have thought their own gods were aiding Israel. Commentators disagree on the exact nature of the miracle often referred to as Joshua's "long day" (vv. 12–13), but verse 14 leaves no doubt that something spectacular occurred that elevated Joshua as a man of God: His prayers were unusually effective.

10:11
f Ps 18:12; Isa 28:2,
17
10:12
g Am 2:9
h Jdg 1:35; 12:12

down from Beth Horon to Azekah, the LORD hurled large hailstones[f] down on them from the sky, and more of them died from the hailstones than were killed by the swords of the Israelites.

12 On the day the LORD gave the Amorites[g] over to Israel, Joshua said to the LORD in the presence of Israel:

> "O sun, stand still over Gibeon,
>   O moon, over the Valley of Aijalon.[h]"

10:13
i Hab 3:11
j 2Sa 1:18
k Isa 38:8

> 13 So the sun stood still,[i]
>   and the moon stopped,
>   till the nation avenged itself on[a] its enemies,

as it is written in the Book of Jashar.[j]

The sun stopped[k] in the middle of the sky and delayed going down about a full day. 14 There has never been a day like it before or since, a day when the LORD lis-

10:14
l ver 42; Ex 14:14;
Dt 1:30; Ps 106:43;
136:24
10:15
m ver 43

tened to a man. Surely the LORD was fighting[l] for Israel! 15 Then Joshua returned with all Israel to the camp at Gilgal.[m]

Five Amorite Kings Killed

16 Now the five kings had fled and hidden in the cave at Makkedah. 17 When Joshua was told that the five kings had been found hiding in the cave at Makkedah, 18 he said, "Roll large rocks up to the mouth of the cave, and post some men there to guard it. 19 But don't stop! Pursue your enemies, attack them from the rear and don't let them reach their cities, for the LORD your God has given them into your hand."

10:20
n Dt 20:16

20 So Joshua and the Israelites destroyed them completely[n]—almost to a man—but the few who were left reached their fortified cities. 21 The whole army then returned safely to Joshua in the camp at Makkedah, and no one uttered a word against the Israelites.

22 Joshua said, "Open the mouth of the cave and bring those five kings out to me." 23 So they brought the five kings out of the cave—the kings of Jerusalem, Hebron, Jarmuth, Lachish and Eglon. 24 When they had brought these kings to Joshua, he

10:24
o Mal 4:3
p Ps 110:1

summoned all the men of Israel and said to the army commanders who had come with him, "Come here and put your feet[o] on the necks of these kings." So they came forward and placed their feet[p] on their necks.

10:25
q Dt 31:6

25 Joshua said to them, "Do not be afraid; do not be discouraged. Be strong and courageous.[q] This is what the LORD will do to all the enemies you are going to fight." 26 Then Joshua struck and killed the kings and hung them on five trees, and they were left hanging on the trees until evening.

10:27
r Dt 21:23;
Jos 8:9,29

27 At sunset[r] Joshua gave the order and they took them down from the trees and threw them into the cave where they had been hiding. At the mouth of the cave they placed large rocks, which are there to this day.

---

a 13 Or nation triumphed over

The second half of the opening sentence of verse 14, like the first part, invites a second reading: "a day when the LORD listened to a man." God listens to us all the time, doesn't he? But is it possible that the uncommon denominator here might have been the strength of Joshua's faith in making his unusual request? Might he have been experiencing a "mustard-seed moment" in terms of his faith (see Jesus' words in Matt. 17:20)? In times of great need or opportunity, how hard has it been for you to make an "audacious" request of God, fully trusting him to honor it?

Joshua 10:16–28

The five kings were humiliated before they were killed. Joshua did all he could to bolster the morale of his troops. When the officers placed their feet on the necks of these great and powerful kings, they recognized

them as frail human beings like everyone else. This practice was widespread in ancient times and is pictured in the artwork of Egypt and Assyria.

The concept of putting one's enemies under one's feet is found both elsewhere in the Old Testament (1 Kings 5:3; Ps. 110:1) and in the New. The apostle Paul proclaimed that God the Father raised Christ from the dead, seated him at his right hand in heaven, and "placed all things under his feet and appointed him to be head over everything for the church" (Eph. 1:20–22). Paul also wrote that Christ will "reign until he has put all his enemies under his feet. The last enemy to be destroyed is death" (1 Cor. 15:25–26; cf. Heb. 10:11–14). What a comfort as we direct our own feet along life's often difficult path!

28That day Joshua took Makkedah. He put the city and its king to the sword and totally destroyed everyone in it. He left no survivors.⁵ And he did to the king of Makkedah as he had done to the king of Jericho.ᵗ

Southern Cities Conquered

29Then Joshua and all Israel with him moved on from Makkedah to Libnah and attacked it. 30The LORD also gave that city and its king into Israel's hand. The city and everyone in it Joshua put to the sword. He left no survivors there. And he did to its king as he had done to the king of Jericho.

31Then Joshua and all Israel with him moved on from Libnah to Lachish; he took up positions against it and attacked it. 32The LORD handed Lachish over to Israel, and Joshua took it on the second day. The city and everyone in it he put to the sword, just as he had done to Libnah. 33Meanwhile, Horam king of Gezerᵘ had come up to help Lachish, but Joshua defeated him and his army—until no survivors were left.

34Then Joshua and all Israel with him moved on from Lachish to Eglon; they took up positions against it and attacked it. 35They captured it that same day and put it to the sword and totally destroyed everyone in it, just as they had done to Lachish.

36Then Joshua and all Israel with him went up from Eglon to Hebronᵛ and attacked it. 37They took the city and put it to the sword, together with its king, its villages and everyone in it. They left no survivors. Just as at Eglon, they totally destroyed it and everyone in it.

38Then Joshua and all Israel with him turned around and attacked Debir.ʷ 39They took the city, its king and its villages, and put them to the sword. Everyone in it they totally destroyed. They left no survivors. They did to Debir and its king as they had done to Libnah and its king and to Hebron.

40So Joshua subdued the whole region, including the hill country, the Negev,ˣ the western foothills and the mountain slopes,ʸ together with all their kings.ᶻ He left no survivors. He totally destroyed all who breathed, just as the LORD, the God of Israel, had commanded.ᵃ 41Joshua subdued them from Kadesh Barneaᵇ to Gazaᶜ and from the whole region of Goshenᵈ to Gibeon. 42All these kings and their lands Joshua conquered in one campaign, because the LORD, the God of Israel, foughtᵉ for Israel.

43Then Joshua returned with all Israel to the camp at Gilgal.ᶠ

Northern Kings Defeated

11 When Jabinᵍ king of Hazorʰ heard of this, he sent word to Jobab king of Madon, to the kings of Shimronⁱ and Acshaph, 2and to the northern kings who were in the mountains, in the Arabah ʲ south of Kinnereth,ᵏ in the western foothills and in Naphoth Dorᵃ ˡ on the west; 3to the Canaanites in the east and west; to

ᵃ 2 Or in the heights of Dor

Side references

10:28
ˢ Dt 20:16
ᵗ Jos 6:21

10:33
ᵘ Jos 16:3,10; Jdg 1:29; 1Ki 9:15

10:36
ᵛ Jos 14:13; 15:13; Jdg 1:10

10:38
ʷ Jos 15:15; Jdg 1:11

10:40
ˣ Ge 12:9; Jos 12:8
ʸ Dt 1:7 ᶻ Dt 7:24
ᵃ Dt 20:16-17

10:41
ᵇ Ge 14:7
ᶜ Ge 10:19
ᵈ Jos 11:16; 15:51

10:42
ᵉ ver 14

10:43
ᶠ ver 15; Jos 5:9

11:1
ᵍ Jdg 4:2,7,23
ʰ ver 10; 1Sa 12:9
ⁱ Jos 19:15

11:2
ʲ Jos 12:3
ᵏ Nu 34:11
ˡ Jos 17:11; Jdg 1:27; 1Ki 4:11

Joshua 10:29–43

📖 With monotonous regularity we are reminded that Joshua faithfully carried out the command to devote all the inhabitants of the land to the Lord by annihilating them. Verse 40 suggests that the accounts of the capture of a few cities comprise only a sketchy summary of victories in a far more extensive campaign. The conquest was wide-ranging enough to give Israel control of the area but not possession of every city (Jerusalem, e.g., wasn't taken at this time). The Israelites didn't occupy these cities immediately, returning instead to their families and livestock in their base camp at Gilgal.

🔲 Many Christians are deeply troubled by the role warfare and genocide play in the book of Joshua. Some ascribe the author's perspective to a pre-Christian (and now sub-Christian) stage of moral development that we, in light of Jesus' teaching, are to renounce. But this is the story of how God, to whom the whole world belongs, at one stage in redemption history re-conquered a portion of the earth that the powers of this world had, in reliance on false gods, claimed for themselves.

War is a terrible curse that the human race brings on itself as it seeks to possess the earth by its own unrighteous ways. But it pales before the curse that awaits those who don't heed God's testimony to himself, those who oppose his rule and reject his offer of grace. The God of the second Joshua—Jesus (the Greek form of the Hebrew *Joshua*)—also is the God of the first. Though now for a time he reaches out to the whole world with the gospel, his sword of judgment waits in the wings—and his second Joshua will wield it (Rev. 19:11–16).

11:3
m Dt 7:1; Jdg 3:3,5;
1Ki 9:20
n Ge 31:49;
Jos 15:38; 18:26
11:4
o Jdg 7:12;
1Sa 13:5
11:5
p Jdg 5:19
11:6
q Jos 10:8 r 2Sa 8:4

11:8
s Jos 13:6

11:11
t Dt 20:16-17

11:12
u Nu 33:50-52;
Dt 7:2

11:14
v Nu 31:11-12

11:15
w Ex 34:11; Jos 1:7

11:16
x Jos 10:41

11:17
y Jos 12:7 z Dt 7:24

11:19
a Jos 9:3

11:20
b Ex 14:17; Ro 9:18
c Dt 7:16; Jdg 14:4

11:21
d Nu 13:22,33;
Dt 9:2

11:22
e 1Sa 17:4;
1Ki 2:39; 1Ch 8:13
f 1Sa 5:1; Isa 20:1

the Amorites, Hittites, Perizzites and Jebusites in the hill country; and to the Hivites[m] below Hermon in the region of Mizpah.[n] 4They came out with all their troops and a large number of horses and chariots—a huge army, as numerous as the sand on the seashore.[o] 5All these kings joined forces[p] and made camp together at the Waters of Merom, to fight against Israel.

6The LORD said to Joshua, "Do not be afraid of them, because by this time tomorrow I will hand all of them over[q] to Israel, slain. You are to hamstring[r] their horses and burn their chariots."

7So Joshua and his whole army came against them suddenly at the Waters of Merom and attacked them, 8and the LORD gave them into the hand of Israel. They defeated them and pursued them all the way to Greater Sidon, to Misrephoth Maim,[s] and to the Valley of Mizpah on the east, until no survivors were left. 9Joshua did to them as the LORD had directed: He hamstrung their horses and burned their chariots.

10At that time Joshua turned back and captured Hazor and put its king to the sword. (Hazor had been the head of all these kingdoms.) 11Everyone in it they put to the sword. They totally destroyed[a] them, not sparing anything that breathed,[t] and he burned up Hazor itself.

12Joshua took all these royal cities and their kings and put them to the sword. He totally destroyed them, as Moses the servant of the LORD had commanded.[u] 13Yet Israel did not burn any of the cities built on their mounds—except Hazor, which Joshua burned. 14The Israelites carried off for themselves all the plunder and livestock of these cities, but all the people they put to the sword until they completely destroyed them, not sparing anyone that breathed.[v] 15As the LORD commanded his servant Moses, so Moses commanded Joshua, and Joshua did it; he left nothing undone of all that the LORD commanded Moses.[w]

16So Joshua took this entire land: the hill country, all the Negev, the whole region of Goshen, the western foothills,[x] the Arabah and the mountains of Israel with their foothills, 17from Mount Halak, which rises toward Seir, to Baal Gad in the Valley of Lebanon[y] below Mount Hermon. He captured all their kings and struck them down, putting them to death.[z] 18Joshua waged war against all these kings for a long time. 19Except for the Hivites living in Gibeon,[a] not one city made a treaty of peace with the Israelites, who took them all in battle. 20For it was the LORD himself who hardened their hearts[b] to wage war against Israel, so that he might destroy them totally, exterminating them without mercy, as the LORD had commanded Moses.[c]

21At that time Joshua went and destroyed the Anakites[d] from the hill country: from Hebron, Debir and Anab, from all the hill country of Judah, and from all the hill country of Israel. Joshua totally destroyed them and their towns. 22No Anakites were left in Israelite territory; only in Gaza, Gath[e] and Ashdod[f] did any survive. 23So

---

a 11 The Hebrew term refers to the irrevocable giving over of things or persons to the LORD, often by totally destroying them; also in verses 12, 20 and 21.

Joshua 11:1–23

Canaan was at this time made up of independent, hostile city-states, but a common enemy led them to combine forces. The northern coalition was Israel's most formidable foe to date. Horses and chariots posed an awesome challenge to the Israelites, whose army was made up of foot soldiers. Disabling the horses and burning the chariots showed Israel's disdain for modern weapons. Her confidence was in God alone (cf. Ps. 20:7). Early Israelite tradition was consistently negative toward the use of horses and chariots (cf. Deut. 17:16; 2 Sam. 8:4; Isa. 31:1).

The last of the Canaanites weren't subdued until the reign of David. The style of the narrative gives the impression of a lightning-quick campaign, but the conquest actually took "a long time" (v. 18). God hardened the Canaanites' hearts (v. 20), not to keep them from repenting but to prevent them from surrendering without repentance.

Rahab and the Gibeonites demonstrate God's unchanging promise that "everyone who calls on the name of the Lord will be saved" (Rom. 10:13; see notes for Josh. 9:1–27). God does harden hearts—of those who harden their own (cf. Ex. 8:32 with Ex. 9:12). He's patient as long as there is hope of repentance (Rom. 2:4). But the sin of the Amorites (representing the inhabitants of Canaan) had reached its full measure (Gen. 15:16). Offensive as it may seem to us, the writer celebrated their annihilation: There was no other way God's promise could be fulfilled. How does the reality that God's purpose has a "breaking point" impact your attitude toward missions?

Joshua took the entire land, *g* just as the LORD had directed Moses, and he gave it as an inheritance *h* to Israel according to their tribal divisions. *i*

Then the land had rest from war. *j*

List of Defeated Kings

12 These are the kings of the land whom the Israelites had defeated and whose territory they took over east of the Jordan, from the Arnon Gorge to Mount Hermon, *k* including all the eastern side of the Arabah:

²Sihon king of the Amorites,

who reigned in Heshbon. He ruled from Aroer on the rim of the Arnon Gorge—from the middle of the gorge—to the Jabbok River, which is the bor-

11:23
g Jos 21:43-45
h Dt 1:38; 12:9-10; 25:19 *i* Nu 26:53
j Jos 14:15

12:1
k Dt 3:8

Joshua 12:1–24

The conquest is summarized by listing the kings Israel defeated. East of the Jordan were only two kings, each of whom ruled a wide area with many cities. The land west of the Jordan was divided into individual city-states. Israel's conquests on both sides of the river are mentioned together to emphasize the nation's unity. Moses is mentioned at the end of verses 1–6 and Joshua at the beginning of verses 7–24 to highlight the way Joshua's work complemented Moses'.

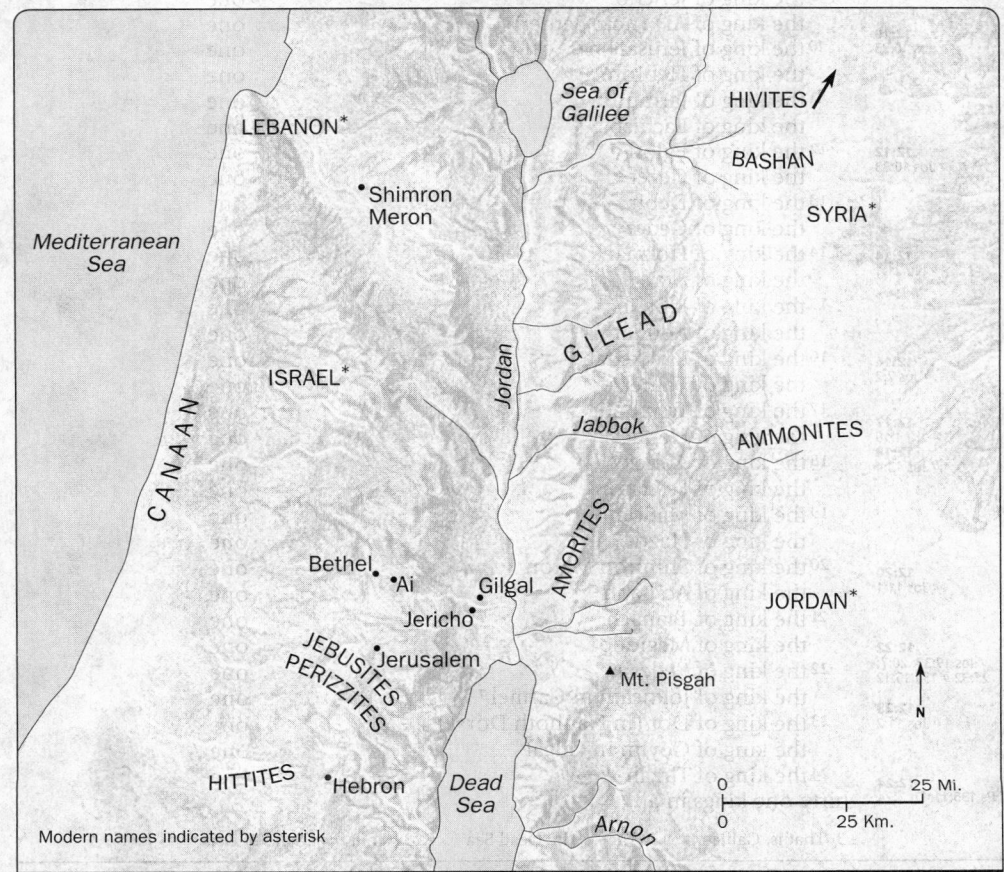

Conquest of Canaan (12:1)

Then: In many ways the conquest of Canaan by a relatively small and ill-equipped band of Hebrews was remarkable; in other ways it was incomplete.

Now: The regions not conquered by the Hebrews (despite God's command to do so) remain problem areas for the modern state of Israel. See "The Unconquered Land" map on page 335.

12:2
l Dt 2:36
12:3
m Jos 11:2
n Jos 13:20
12:4
o Nu 21:21,33;
Dt 3:11 p Dt 1:4
12:5
q Dt 3:10 r 1Sa 27:8
s Dt 3:14
12:6
t Nu 32:29,33;
Jos 13:8
12:7
u Jos 11:17
12:8
v Jos 11:16
12:9
w Jos 6:2 x Jos 8:29
12:10
y Jos 10:23
12:12
z Jos 10:33
12:14
a Nu 21:1
12:16
b Jos 7:2
12:17
c 1Ki 4:10
12:18
d Jos 13:4
12:20
e Jos 11:1
12:22
f Jos 19:37; 20:7;
21:32 g 1Sa 15:12
12:23
h Jos 11:2
12:24
i Ps 135:11; Dt 7:24

der of the Ammonites. This included half of Gilead.[l] [3]He also ruled over the eastern Arabah from the Sea of Kinnereth[a][m] to the Sea of the Arabah (the Salt Sea[b]), to Beth Jeshimoth,[n] and then southward below the slopes of Pisgah.

[4]And the territory of Og king of Bashan,[o]
one of the last of the Rephaites, who reigned in Ashtaroth[p] and Edrei. [5]He ruled over Mount Hermon, Salecah,[q] all of Bashan to the border of the people of Geshur[r] and Maacah,[s] and half of Gilead to the border of Sihon king of Heshbon.

[6]Moses, the servant of the LORD, and the Israelites conquered them. And Moses the servant of the LORD gave their land to the Reubenites, the Gadites and the half-tribe of Manasseh to be their possession.[t]

[7]These are the kings of the land that Joshua and the Israelites conquered on the west side of the Jordan, from Baal Gad in the Valley of Lebanon[u] to Mount Halak, which rises toward Seir (their lands Joshua gave as an inheritance to the tribes of Israel according to their tribal divisions— [8]the hill country, the western foothills, the Arabah, the mountain slopes, the desert and the Negev[v]—the lands of the Hittites, Amorites, Canaanites, Perizzites, Hivites and Jebusites):

[9]the king of Jericho[w]	one
the king of Ai[x] (near Bethel)	one
[10]the king of Jerusalem[y]	one
the king of Hebron	one
[11]the king of Jarmuth	one
the king of Lachish	one
[12]the king of Eglon	one
the king of Gezer[z]	one
[13]the king of Debir	one
the king of Geder	one
[14]the king of Hormah	one
the king of Arad[a]	one
[15]the king of Libnah	one
the king of Adullam	one
[16]the king of Makkedah	one
the king of Bethel[b]	one
[17]the king of Tappuah	one
the king of Hepher[c]	one
[18]the king of Aphek[d]	one
the king of Lasharon	one
[19]the king of Madon	one
the king of Hazor	one
[20]the king of Shimron Meron	one
the king of Acshaph[e]	one
[21]the king of Taanach	one
the king of Megiddo	one
[22]the king of Kedesh[f]	one
the king of Jokneam in Carmel[g]	one
[23]the king of Dor (in Naphoth Dor[c][h])	one
the king of Goyim in Gilgal	one
[24]the king of Tirzah	one

thirty-one kings in all.[i]

[a] 3 That is, Galilee   [b] 3 That is, the Dead Sea   [c] 23 Or *in the heights of Dor*

Compared with what we have become accustomed to in the books preceding Joshua, we have read little so far in this book about Israel's stubbornness or disobedience. True, this was a new generation, a group of vigorous individuals who had learned unreserved trust, discipline, teamwork, and patience during a nearly 40-year stopover in the inhospitable desert. Still, what a welcome relief to read of seemingly uninterrupted cooperation and compliance with God's instructions. What has your experience been like in this regard? Can you attest to the difference solidarity and a willing spirit make when there is work to be done?

Land Still to Be Taken

13 When Joshua was old and well advanced in years,[j] the LORD said to him, "You are very old, and there are still very large areas of land to be taken over.

2 "This is the land that remains: all the regions of the Philistines and Geshurites: 3from the Shihor River[k] on the east of Egypt to the territory of Ekron[l] on the north, all of it counted as Canaanite (the territory of the five Philistine rulers[m] in Gaza, Ashdod, Ashkelon, Gath and Ekron—that of the Avvites);[n] 4from the south, all the land of the Canaanites, from Arah of the Sidonians as far as Aphek,[o] the region of the Amorites,[p] 5the area of the Gebalites[a];[q] and all Lebanon[r] to the east, from Baal Gad below Mount Hermon to Lebo[b] Hamath.

6 "As for all the inhabitants of the mountain regions from Lebanon to Misrephoth Maim,[s] that is, all the Sidonians, I myself will drive them out before the Israelites. Be sure to allocate this land to Israel for an inheritance, as I have instructed you,[t] 7and divide it as an inheritance[u] among the nine tribes and half of the tribe of Manasseh."

Division of the Land East of the Jordan

8The other half of Manasseh,[c] the Reubenites and the Gadites had received the inheritance that Moses had given them east of the Jordan, as he, the servant of the LORD, had assigned[v] it to them.

9It extended from Aroer[w] on the rim of the Arnon Gorge, and from the town in the middle of the gorge, and included the whole plateau[x] of Medeba as far as Dibon,[y] 10and all the towns of Sihon king of the Amorites, who ruled in Heshbon, out to the border of the Ammonites.[z] 11It also included Gilead, the territory of the people of Geshur and Maacah, all of Mount Hermon and all

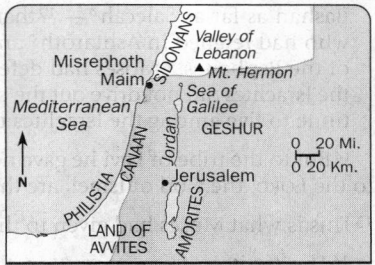

The Unconquered Land (13:1)
Then: The Israelites failed to defeat completely the Sidonians, Philistines, and Avvites.
Now: These unconquered tribes occupied modern Lebanon, the Golan Heights, the West Bank of the Jordan, and the Gaza Strip, all familiar trouble spots in the modern Middle East.

13:1 j Ge 24:1; Jos 14:10
13:3 k Jer 2:18 l Jdg 1:18 m Jdg 3:3 n Dt 2:23
13:4 o Jos 12:18; 19:30 p Am 2:10
13:5 q 1Ki 5:18; Ps 83:7; Eze 27:9 r Jos 12:7
13:6 s Jos 11:8 t Nu 33:54
13:7 u Jos 11:23; Ps 78:55
13:8 v Jos 12:6
13:9 w ver 16; Jdg 11:26 x Jer 48:8,21 y Nu 21:30
13:10 z Nu 21:24

a 5 That is, the area of Byblos   b 5 Or *to the entrance to*   c 8 Hebrew *With it* (that is, with the other half of Manasseh)

Joshua 13:1–7

It seems that Israel had experienced a letdown after the widespread victories recorded in the first part of this book. God reminded Joshua of his unfinished task. The division of the land (v. 7) was a part of his original commission (Deut. 31:7), and it had to be completed before Joshua died.

God reaffirmed his promise to drive out the inhabitants of the land (cf. Josh. 3:10). From this point on, though, further conquests would be the concern of individual tribes. God's promise was conditional and would never wholly be fulfilled due to the incompleteness of Israel's obedience (cf. 13:13). Joshua was to divide all the land promised to Israel, whether or not Israel possessed it at the time.

Joshua was in his nineties at this time. Though some individuals in his day lived longer than people do today, the Lord described Joshua as "very old" (v. 1). Yet God still had work for this senior citizen to do. How

would Joshua likely be treated by our society—a culture that idolizes the young and the beautiful? Does your church mobilize—or set aside—older members? What about your own attitude toward the elderly? Do you believe that God will still have work for you when you are "very old"?

Joshua 13:8–33

After delineation of the area assigned to the two-and-a-half tribes east of the Jordan (vv. 8–13), a slightly more detailed description is recorded of the inheritance given to each of them (vv. 14–32). It may seem that the Transjordanian tribes receive a disproportionate amount of attention in this book that records the conquest and division of the land *west* of the Jordan (cf. 1:12–15; 4:12; 12:1–6; 22:1–34). The author may have been eager to uphold the unity of the 12 tribes despite the geographic separation. There may also have been an undercurrent of feeling that only the territory west of the Jordan was truly the promised land.

13:11
a Jos 12:5
13:12
b Dt 3:11 c Jos 12:4
d Ge 14:5
13:13
e Jos 12:5 f Dt 3:14

Bashan as far as Salecah[a]— [12]that is, the whole kingdom of Og in Bashan,[b] who had reigned in Ashtaroth[c] and Edrei and had survived as one of the last of the Rephaites.[d] Moses had defeated them and taken over their land. [13]But the Israelites did not drive out the people of Geshur[e] and Maacah,[f] so they continue to live among the Israelites to this day.

13:14
g ver 33; Dt 18:1-2

[14]But to the tribe of Levi he gave no inheritance, since the offerings made by fire to the LORD, the God of Israel, are their inheritance, as he promised them.[g]

13:16
h ver 9; Jos 12:2
i Nu 21:30
13:17
j Nu 32:3 k 1Ch 5:8
13:18
l Nu 21:23
m Jer 48:21
13:19
n Nu 32:37
13:20
o Dt 3:29
13:21
p Nu 25:15
q Nu 31:8
13:22
r Nu 22:5; 31:8

[15]This is what Moses had given to the tribe of Reuben, clan by clan:

[16]The territory from Aroer[h] on the rim of the Arnon Gorge, and from the town in the middle of the gorge, and the whole plateau past Medeba[i] [17]to Heshbon and all its towns on the plateau, including Dibon,[j] Bamoth Baal, Beth Baal Meon,[k] [18]Jahaz,[l] Kedemoth, Mephaath,[m] [19]Kiriathaim,[n] Sibmah, Zereth Shahar on the hill in the valley, [20]Beth Peor,[o] the slopes of Pisgah, and Beth Jeshimoth [21]—all the towns on the plateau and the entire realm of Sihon king of the Amorites, who ruled at Heshbon. Moses had defeated him and the Midianite chiefs,[p] Evi, Rekem, Zur, Hur and Reba[q]—princes allied with Sihon—who lived in that country. [22]In addition to those slain in battle, the Israelites had put to the sword Balaam son of Beor,[r] who practiced divination. [23]The boundary of the Reubenites was the bank of the Jordan. These towns and their villages were the inheritance of the Reubenites, clan by clan.

[24]This is what Moses had given to the tribe of Gad, clan by clan:

13:25
s Nu 21:32;
Jos 21:39
13:26
t Nu 21:25; Jer 49:3
u Jos 10:3
13:27
v Ge 33:17
w Nu 34:11
13:28
x Nu 32:33

[25]The territory of Jazer,[s] all the towns of Gilead and half the Ammonite country as far as Aroer, near Rabbah; [26]and from Heshbon[t] to Ramath Mizpah and Betonim, and from Mahanaim to the territory of Debir;[u] [27]and in the valley, Beth Haram, Beth Nimrah, Succoth[v] and Zaphon with the rest of the realm of Sihon king of Heshbon (the east side of the Jordan, the territory up to the end of the Sea of Kinnereth[a w]). [28]These towns and their villages were the inheritance of the Gadites,[x] clan by clan.

[29]This is what Moses had given to the half-tribe of Manasseh, that is, to half the family of the descendants of Manasseh, clan by clan:

13:30
y Ge 32:2
z Nu 32:41

[30]The territory extending from Mahanaim[y] and including all of Bashan, the entire realm of Og king of Bashan—all the settlements of Jair[z] in Bashan, sixty towns, [31]half of Gilead, and Ashtaroth and Edrei (the royal cities of Og in Bashan). This was for the descendants of Makir[a] son of Manasseh—for half of the sons of Makir, clan by clan.

13:31
a Ge 50:23

13:33
b Nu 18:20
c ver 14; Jos 18:7

[32]This is the inheritance Moses had given when he was in the plains of Moab across the Jordan east of Jericho. [33]But to the tribe of Levi, Moses had given no inheritance; the LORD, the God of Israel, is their inheritance,[b] as he promised them.[c]

Division of the Land West of the Jordan

14 Now these are the areas the Israelites received as an inheritance in the land of Canaan, which Eleazar the priest, Joshua son of Nun and the heads of the

---

[a] 27 That is, Galilee

📖 Over the course of generations many have viewed the Western church as Christianity's hub—a bit like those Israelites who had settled west of the Jordan. The church in the third world does indeed owe much today to its Western counterpart. But the irony is that Christ's body in many places outside the West is strong and growing, while in Europe and America the church (and culture's moral fabric) is declining at an alarming rate. American Christians do well to resist the assump-

tion that we are living under God's blessing in the land of promise. How long before we begin to rely on the rest of the world for evangelistic efforts on our soil?

Joshua 14:1–5

🔗 Following the description of the land allotments on the east side of the Jordan (ch. 13), this passage introduces the allotment of Canaan proper (chs. 14–21). At the beginning of the nation's existence, Jacob (renamed "Israel" in Gen. 32:28) had gathered together his

tribal clans of Israel allotted to them. [d] 2Their inheritances were assigned by lot [e] to the nine-and-a-half tribes, as the LORD had commanded through Moses. 3Moses had granted the two-and-a-half tribes their inheritance east of the Jordan [f] but had not granted the Levites an inheritance among the rest, [g] 4for the sons of Joseph had become two tribes—Manasseh and Ephraim. [h] The Levites received no share of the land but only towns to live in, with pasturelands for their flocks and herds. 5So the Israelites divided the land, just as the LORD had commanded Moses. [i]

Hebron Given to Caleb

6Now the men of Judah approached Joshua at Gilgal, and Caleb son of Jephunneh [j] the Kenizzite said to him, "You know what the LORD said to Moses the man of God at Kadesh Barnea [k] about you and me. 7I was forty years old when Moses the servant of the LORD sent me from Kadesh Barnea to explore the land. [l] And I brought him back a report according to my convictions, [m] 8but my brothers who went up with me made the hearts of the people melt with fear. [n] I, however, followed the LORD my God wholeheartedly. [o] 9So on that day Moses swore to me, 'The land on which your feet have walked will be your inheritance and that of your children [p] forever, because you have followed the LORD my God wholeheartedly.' [a]

10"Now then, just as the LORD promised, [q] he has kept me alive for forty-five years since the time he said this to Moses, while Israel moved about in the desert. So here I am today, eighty-five years old! 11I am still as strong [r] today as the day Moses sent me out; I'm just as vigorous to go out to battle now as I was then. 12Now give me this hill country that the LORD promised me that day. You yourself heard then that the Anakites [s] were there and their cities were large and fortified, [t] but, the LORD helping me, I will drive them out just as he said."

13Then Joshua blessed [u] Caleb son of Jephunneh and gave him Hebron [v] as his inheritance. [w] 14So Hebron has belonged to Caleb son of Jephunneh the Kenizzite ever since, because he followed the LORD, the God of Israel, wholeheartedly. 15(Hebron used to be called Kiriath Arba [x] after Arba, [y] who was the greatest man among the Anakites.)

Then the land had rest [z] from war.

[a] 9 Deut. 1:36

14:1 [d] Nu 34:17-18
14:2 [e] Nu 26:55
14:3 [f] Nu 32:33 [g] Jos 13:14
14:4 [h] Ge 41:52; 48:5
14:5 [i] Nu 34:13; 35:2; Jos 21:2
14:6 [j] Nu 13:6; 14:30 [k] Nu 13:26
14:7 [l] Nu 13:17 [m] Nu 13:30; 14:6-9
14:8 [n] Nu 13:31 [o] Nu 14:24
14:9 [p] Nu 14:24; Dt 1:36
14:10 [q] Nu 14:30
14:11 [r] Dt 34:7
14:12 [s] Nu 13:33 [t] Nu 13:28
14:13 [u] Jos 22:6,7 [v] Jos 10:36 [w] Jdg 1:20; 1Ch 6:56
14:15 [x] Ge 23:2 [y] Jos 15:13 [z] Jos 11:23

---

sons to bless them before he died (Gen. 49:1–28). Much of Jacob's poetic and prophetic blessing was remarkably fulfilled in the division of the promised land.

Though the tribe of Levi was honored to serve at the Lord's tabernacle and receive the people's offerings as its inheritance (13:14; cf. Deut. 18:1–8), Jacob's words that Levi's descendants would be "scattered" as punishment for Levi's violence, anger, and cruelty (Gen. 49:5–7) were also fulfilled. Since Jacob had adopted Joseph's sons, Manasseh and Ephraim, as his own (Gen. 48:5), they were treated as two separate tribes to preserve the full number of 12. In fulfillment of Jacob's blessing, Judah (Gen. 49:8–12), Manasseh, and Ephraim (Gen. 49:22–26) were given prominence in the south and north, respectively.

The land was to be "assigned by lot" (v. 2). Jewish rabbis have a tradition that the names of the tribes were placed in one bowl and slips describing sections of land in another. These were supposedly matched up by drawing one slip from each bowl. It's quite possible, though, that Eleazar used the Urim and Thummim (cf. Num. 27:21; 34:17). Christians today are leery of relying on "chance," and rightly so. In reality, though, the use of lots in this and other Old Testament contexts placed everything in God's hands—making sure everyone knew that chance *didn't* come into the picture!

Joshua 14:6–15

Caleb and Joshua were the two faithful spies who had believed that God was able to give Israel the land (Num. 13:30; 14:6–9,30). The receiving of their inheritances frames the story of the dividing of the land among the nine-and-a-half tribes, with Caleb's here at the beginning and Joshua's at the end (19:49–50). Caleb and Joshua were living examples of God's faithfulness in fulfilling his promises made more than 40 years earlier.

Of all who were twenty years old and older when Israel left Egypt, only Caleb and Joshua lived to enter the promised land. From Caleb's twice noting his age we can calculate that the conquest lasted approximately seven years.

Some form of the statement that Caleb "followed the LORD his God wholeheartedly" appears three times in this brief passage (vv. 8,9,14). It describes Caleb as one who really lived out the theme of this book (see 1:8). In fact, this was the reason he was still alive and would inherit part of the land. None of us is perfect, but can you make the general statement that you have followed the Lord your God wholeheartedly as a result of committing your life to Christ? If so, God has a wonderful inheritance waiting for you. Some day you will hear blessed words from Jesus' own lips: "Well done, good and faithful servant!" (Matt. 25:21).

Allotment for Judah

15:1
a Nu 34:3
b Nu 33:36

15:3
c Nu 34:4

15:4
d Nu 34:5
e Ge 15:18
15:5
f Nu 34:10
g Jos 18:15-19

15:6
h Jos 18:19,21
i Jos 18:17
15:7
j Jos 7:24
k 2Sa 17:17; 1Ki 1:9

15:8
l ver 63; Jos 18:16,
28; Jdg 1:21; 19:10

15:9
m Jos 18:15
n 1Ch 13:6

15:10
o Ge 38:12;
Jdg 14:1

15:11
p Jos 19:33
15:12
q Nu 34:6

15:13
r Jos 14:13-15
15:14
s Nu 13:33
t Nu 13:22
u Jdg 1:10,20
15:16
v Jdg 1:12
15:17
w Jdg 3:9,11

15 The allotment for the tribe of Judah, clan by clan, extended down to the territory of Edom,^{a} to the Desert of Zin^b in the extreme south.

²Their southern boundary started from the bay at the southern end of the Salt Sea,^{a} ³crossed south of Scorpion^b Pass,^{c} continued on to Zin and went over to the south of Kadesh Barnea. Then it ran past Hezron up to Addar and curved around to Karka. ⁴It then passed along to Azmon^d and joined the Wadi of Egypt,^{e} ending at the sea. This is their^c southern boundary.

⁵The eastern boundary^f is the Salt Sea as far as the mouth of the Jordan.

The northern boundary^g started from the bay of the sea at the mouth of the Jordan, ⁶went up to Beth Hoglah^h and continued north of Beth Arabah to the Stone of Bohan^i son of Reuben. ⁷The boundary then went up to Debir from the Valley of Achor^j and turned north to Gilgal, which faces the Pass of Adummim south of the gorge. It continued along to the waters of En Shemesh and came out at En Rogel.^{k} ⁸Then it ran up the Valley of Ben Hinnom along the southern slope of the Jebusite^l city (that is, Jerusalem). From there it climbed to the top of the hill west of the Hinnom Valley at the northern end of the Valley of Rephaim. ⁹From the hilltop the boundary headed toward the spring of the waters of Nephtoah,^{m} came out at the towns of Mount Ephron and went down toward Baalah^n (that is, Kiriath Jearim). ¹⁰Then it curved westward from Baalah to Mount Seir, ran along the northern slope of Mount Jearim (that is, Kesalon), continued down to Beth Shemesh and crossed to Timnah.^{o} ¹¹It went to the northern slope of Ekron, turned toward Shikkeron, passed along to Mount Baalah and reached Jabneel.^{p} The boundary ended at the sea.

¹²The western boundary is the coastline of the Great Sea.$^{d\,q}$ These are the boundaries around the people of Judah by their clans.

¹³In accordance with the LORD's command to him, Joshua gave to Caleb son of Jephunneh a portion in Judah—Kiriath Arba, that is, Hebron. (Arba was the forefather of Anak.)^r ¹⁴From Hebron Caleb drove out the three Anakites^s—Sheshai, Ahiman and Talmai^t—descendants of Anak.^{u} ¹⁵From there he marched against the people living in Debir (formerly called Kiriath Sepher). ¹⁶And Caleb said, "I will give my daughter Acsah^v in marriage to the man who attacks and captures Kiriath Sepher." ¹⁷Othniel^w son of Kenaz, Caleb's brother, took it; so Caleb gave his daughter Acsah to him in marriage.

¹⁸One day when she came to Othniel, she urged him^e to ask her father for a field. When she got off her donkey, Caleb asked her, "What can I do for you?"

¹⁹She replied, "Do me a special favor. Since you have given me land in the Negev, give me also springs of water." So Caleb gave her the upper and lower springs.

---

^{a} 2 That is, the Dead Sea; also in verse 5 ^{b} 3 Hebrew *Akrabbim* ^{c} 4 Hebrew *your* ^{d} 12 That is, the Mediterranean; also in verse 47 ^{e} 18 Hebrew and some Septuagint manuscripts; other Septuagint manuscripts (see also note at Judges 1:14) *Othniel, he urged her*

Joshua 15:1–63

📖 God had commanded that the size of each territory should correspond to the size of the respective tribe or clan (Num. 33:54). But Joshua gave Judah a territory larger than her numbers merited (19:9). No explanation is given (but see "There and Then" for 14:1–5). Having the "Great Sea" (i.e., the Mediterranean) as her western boundary (v. 12) meant that Judah's allotment included as yet unconquered Philistine and Geshurite territory (cf. 13:1–3). This was in conformity with God's command that the entire land be allotted in the confidence that some day all would belong to Israel (13:6).

The Hebrew word for "a special favor" (v. 19) is commonly translated "blessing." Perhaps Caleb's daughter was asking her father for a wedding gift. Land in the Negev is of little value without water but highly productive when irrigated. Othniel recognized the validity of her request. "She urged him" may alternatively be read as "he urged her" (see NIV footnote on v. 18).

📖 The long list of towns allotted to Judah (vv. 20–63) evidences the historical, down-to-earth nature of God's redemptive program. The sending of the Savior— "the Lion of the tribe of Judah" (Rev. 5:5; cf. Gen. 49:9–10)—was also, quite literally, "down to earth": "The Word became flesh and made his dwelling among us" (John 1:14). Still today, God doesn't require us to embark on a lengthy and dangerous pilgrimage to meet himself through his Son. He's so close that his Spirit resides *in* us. How much more down to earth can we get than Immanuel, *God with—and even within— us* (Matt. 1:23)?

²⁰This is the inheritance of the tribe of Judah, clan by clan:

²¹The southernmost towns of the tribe of Judah in the Negev toward the boundary of Edom were:

Kabzeel, Eder, ^x Jagur, ²²Kinah, Dimonah, Adadah, ²³Kedesh, Hazor, Ithnan, ²⁴Ziph, ^y Telem, Bealoth, ²⁵Hazor Hadattah, Kerioth Hezron (that is, Hazor), ²⁶Amam, Shema, Moladah, ^z ²⁷Hazar Gaddah, Heshmon, Beth Pelet, ²⁸Hazar Shual, Beersheba, ^a Biziothiah, ²⁹Baalah, ^b Iim, Ezem, ³⁰Eltolad, ^c Kesil, Hormah, ³¹Ziklag, ^d Madmannah, Sansannah, ³²Lebaoth, Shilhim, Ain and Rimmon ^e—a total of twenty-nine towns and their villages.

³³In the western foothills:

Eshtaol, ^f Zorah, Ashnah, ³⁴Zanoah, ^g En Gannim, Tappuah, Enam, ³⁵Jarmuth, ^h Adullam, ⁱ Socoh, Azekah, ³⁶Shaaraim, Adithaim and Gederah ^j (or Gederothaim) ^a—fourteen towns and their villages.

³⁷Zenan, Hadashah, Migdal Gad, ³⁸Dilean, Mizpah, Joktheel, ^k ³⁹Lachish, ^l Bozkath, ^m Eglon, ⁴⁰Cabbon, Lahmas, Kitlish, ⁴¹Gederoth, Beth Dagon, Naamah and Makkedah ⁿ—sixteen towns and their villages.

⁴²Libnah, Ether, Ashan, ^o ⁴³Iphtah, Ashnah, Nezib, ⁴⁴Keilah, Aczib ^p and Mareshah ^q—nine towns and their villages.

⁴⁵Ekron, with its surrounding settlements and villages; ⁴⁶west of Ekron, all that were in the vicinity of Ashdod, together with their villages; ⁴⁷Ashdod, ^r its surrounding settlements and villages; and Gaza, its settlements and villages, as far as the Wadi of Egypt ^s and the coastline of the Great Sea. ^t

⁴⁸In the hill country:

Shamir, Jattir, ^u Socoh, ⁴⁹Dannah, Kiriath Sannah (that is, Debir ^v), ⁵⁰Anab, Eshtemoh, ^w Anim, ⁵¹Goshen, ^x Holon and Giloh—eleven towns and their villages.

⁵²Arab, Dumah, ^y Eshan, ⁵³Janim, Beth Tappuah, Aphekah, ⁵⁴Humtah, Kiriath Arba (that is, Hebron) and Zior—nine towns and their villages.

^a 36 Or *Gederah and Gederothaim*

Snapshots

 15:16–19

A Life Source

Mwajuma deftly balances a bucketful of water on her head. She carries the twenty-liter bucket from the dam, about 300 meters from her home in Tanzania. On her left hand perches her one-year-old son, Ally Abdallah, while her right cradles the pumpkin mug for fetching water.

Clusters of tattered, barefoot, tired-looking women approach the well. Yet their joviality indicates the community's hope for a prosperous future. The new dam has become a source of life, providing water for drinking, cooking, washing, and bathing. "We don't use salty water any more," Mwajuma enthuses. "Thank God that now I no longer have to worry about the availability of water."

> "We spent almost half the day looking for water."

In the past, Ngerengere residents were preoccupied with this issue. "We spent almost half the day looking for water," recalls Mwajuma. The time saved is now used in productive activities, like farming and small scale business. And children can attend school continuously.

The community has adopted a sense of ownership and responsibility for the project. Five years since being handed over to them, the dam is still operational. And the project has fostered equality: The committees boast equal male and female representation. "[The project] has brought more self-esteem to women in a male-dominated world," asserts Mwajuma.

15:55 [z] Jos 12:22
15:56 [a] Jos 17:16
15:57 [b] Jos 18:28; Jdg 19:12
15:58 [c] 1Ch 2:45
15:60 [d] Jos 18:14 [e] Dt 3:11
15:62 [f] 1Sa 23:29
15:63 [g] Jdg 1:21 [h] 2Sa 5:6
16:1 [i] Jos 8:15; 18:12
16:2 [j] Jos 18:13
16:3 [k] 2Ch 8:5 [l] Jos 10:33; 1Ki 9:15
16:4 [m] Jos 17:14
16:5 [n] Jos 18:13
16:6 [o] Jos 17:7
16:7 [p] 1Ch 7:28
16:8 [q] Jos 17:9
16:10 [r] Jos 17:13; Jdg 1:28-29; 1Ki 9:16
17:1 [s] Ge 41:51 [t] Ge 50:23
17:2 [u] Nu 26:30; 1Ch 7:18
17:3 [v] Nu 27:1 [w] Nu 26:33
17:4 [x] Nu 27:5-7

55 Maon, Carmel,[z] Ziph, Juttah, 56 Jezreel,[a] Jokdeam, Zanoah, 57 Kain, Gibeah[b] and Timnah—ten towns and their villages.

58 Halhul, Beth Zur,[c] Gedor, 59 Maarath, Beth Anoth and Eltekon—six towns and their villages.

60 Kiriath Baal (that is, Kiriath Jearim[d]) and Rabbah[e]—two towns and their villages.

61 In the desert:

Beth Arabah, Middin, Secacah, 62 Nibshan, the City of Salt and En Gedi[f]—six towns and their villages.

63 Judah could not[g] dislodge the Jebusites[h], who were living in Jerusalem; to this day the Jebusites live there with the people of Judah.

Allotment for Ephraim and Manasseh

16 The allotment for Joseph began at the Jordan of Jericho,[a] east of the waters of Jericho, and went up from there through the desert[i] into the hill country of Bethel. 2 It went on from Bethel (that is, Luz[j]),[b] crossed over to the territory of the Arkites in Ataroth, 3 descended westward to the territory of the Japhletites as far as the region of Lower Beth Horon[k] and on to Gezer,[l] ending at the sea.

4 So Manasseh and Ephraim, the descendants of Joseph, received their inheritance.[m]

5 This was the territory of Ephraim, clan by clan:

The boundary of their inheritance went from Ataroth Addar[n] in the east to Upper Beth Horon 6 and continued to the sea. From Micmethath[o] on the north it curved eastward to Taanath Shiloh, passing by it to Janoah on the east. 7 Then it went down from Janoah to Ataroth[p] and Naarah, touched Jericho and came out at the Jordan. 8 From Tappuah the border went west to the Kanah Ravine[q] and ended at the sea. This was the inheritance of the tribe of the Ephraimites, clan by clan. 9 It also included all the towns and their villages that were set aside for the Ephraimites within the inheritance of the Manassites.

10 They did not dislodge the Canaanites living in Gezer; to this day the Canaanites live among the people of Ephraim but are required to do forced labor.[r]

17 This was the allotment for the tribe of Manasseh as Joseph's firstborn,[s] that is, for Makir,[t] Manasseh's firstborn. Makir was the ancestor of the Gileadites, who had received Gilead and Bashan because the Makirites were great soldiers. 2 So this allotment was for the rest of the people of Manasseh—the clans of Abiezer,[u] Helek, Asriel, Shechem, Hepher and Shemida. These are the other male descendants of Manasseh son of Joseph by their clans.

3 Now Zelophehad son of Hepher,[v] the son of Gilead, the son of Makir, the son of Manasseh, had no sons but only daughters,[w] whose names were Mahlah, Noah, Hoglah, Milcah and Tirzah. 4 They went to Eleazar the priest, Joshua son of Nun, and the leaders and said, "The LORD commanded Moses to give us an inheritance among our brothers." So Joshua gave them an inheritance along with the brothers of their father, according to the LORD's command.[x] 5 Manasseh's share consisted of

[a] *1 Jordan of Jericho* was possibly an ancient name for the Jordan River. [b] *2* Septuagint; Hebrew *Bethel to Luz*

Joshua 16:1—17:18

"The allotment for Joseph" was divided between the tribe of Ephraim (16:5–10) and the half-tribe of Manasseh (17:1–13). The other half-tribe of Manasseh had already received its land east of the Jordan River (13:8–13,29–31). The tribe of Joseph had been divided *into two tribes to compensate for the tribe* of Levi, which received no territorial allotment (14:3–4). See also "There and Then" for 14:1–5.

Surviving Canaanites were conscripted to "forced labor" (16:10; 17:13; cf. Judg. 1:28–30,33,35). The entire native population was supposed to have been put to death without pity or exception (Deut. 20:10–18). As a result of this failure, the Israelites would be corrupted by intermarrying with these pagans and repeatedly engage in their perverse and idolatrous worship (see Judg. 2:1–3; 3:5–6; 10:6).

The daughters of Zelophehad based their claim on what "the LORD commanded Moses" (17:4; cf. Num. 27:5–7). Whether the rights of the father or of the daughters were primarily being protected, an unusual privilege and remarkable measure of equality were granted to these women.

ten tracts of land besides Gilead and Bashan east of the Jordan, ⁶because the daughters of the tribe of Manasseh received an inheritance among the sons. The land of Gilead belonged to the rest of the descendants of Manasseh.

⁷The territory of Manasseh extended from Asher to Micmethath[y] east of Shechem.[z] The boundary ran southward from there to include the people living at En Tappuah. ⁸(Manasseh had the land of Tappuah, but Tappuah[a] itself, on the boundary of Manasseh, belonged to the Ephraimites.) ⁹Then the boundary continued south to the Kanah Ravine.[b] There were towns belonging to Ephraim lying among the towns of Manasseh, but the boundary of Manasseh was the northern side of the ravine and ended at the sea. ¹⁰On the south the land belonged to Ephraim, on the north to Manasseh. The territory of Manasseh reached the sea and bordered Asher on the north and Issachar[c] on the east.

¹¹Within Issachar and Asher, Manasseh also had Beth Shan,[d] Ibleam and the people of Dor,[e] Endor,[f] Taanach and Megiddo,[g] together with their surrounding settlements (the third in the list is Naphoth[a]).

¹²Yet the Manassites were not able[h] to occupy these towns, for the Canaanites were determined to live in that region. ¹³However, when the Israelites grew stronger, they subjected the Canaanites to forced labor but did not drive them out completely.[i]

¹⁴The people of Joseph said to Joshua, "Why have you given us only one allotment and one portion for an inheritance? We are a numerous people and the LORD has blessed us abundantly."[j]

¹⁵"If you are so numerous," Joshua answered, "and if the hill country of Ephraim is too small for you, go up into the forest and clear land for yourselves there in the land of the Perizzites and Rephaites.[k]"

¹⁶The people of Joseph replied, "The hill country is not enough for us, and all the Canaanites who live in the plain have iron chariots,[l] both those in Beth Shan and its settlements and those in the Valley of Jezreel."

¹⁷But Joshua said to the house of Joseph—to Ephraim and Manasseh—"You are numerous and very powerful. You will have not only one allotment ¹⁸but the forested hill country as well. Clear it, and its farthest limits will be yours; though the Canaanites have iron chariots[m] and though they are strong, you can drive them out."

Division of the Rest of the Land

18 The whole assembly of the Israelites gathered at Shiloh[n] and set up the Tent of Meeting[o] there. The country was brought under their control, ²but there were still seven Israelite tribes who had not yet received their inheritance.

³So Joshua said to the Israelites: "How long will you wait before you begin to take possession of the land that the LORD, the God of your fathers, has given you? ⁴Appoint three men from each tribe. I will send them out to make a survey of the land and to write a description of it, according to the inheritance of each.[p] Then they will return to me. ⁵You are to divide the land into seven parts. Judah is to remain in its

---

17:7
y Jos 16:6
z Ge 12:6;
Jos 21:21
17:8
a Jos 16:8
17:9
b Jos 16:8
17:10
c Ge 30:18
17:11
d 1Sa 31:10;
1Ki 4:12; 1Ch 7:29
e Jos 11:2
f 1Sa 28:7; Ps 83:10
g 1Ki 9:15
17:12
h Jdg 1:27
17:13
i Jos 16:10
17:14
j Nu 26:28-37
17:15
k Ge 14:5
17:16
l Jdg 1:19; 4:3,13
17:18
m ver 16
18:1
n Jos 19:51; 21:2;
Jdg 18:31; 21:12,
19; 1Sa 1:3; 4:3;
Jer 7:12; 26:6
o Ex 27:21
18:4
p Mic 2:5

---

a *11* That is, Naphoth Dor

The territory allotted to the Joseph tribes, like Judah's, seems excessively large. Their difficulty wasn't the size of their allotment, nor the forested condition of the highlands, but the presence of inhabitants they felt unable to drive out (17:16). Joshua reminded them that they themselves were "numerous and very powerful" (17:17), able to provide for their needs within the area already assigned to them. When have you felt intimidated by the task you felt called to do, so much so that you underestimated the ample resources God had provided? How did he open your eyes to reality? Second Kings 6:8–23 is a memorable and even delightful account of God's provision. Take time to read it the next time you feel demoralized.

Joshua 18:1–10

Though the Israelites had the land "under their control," they still didn't possess it all. They hadn't subdued all the Canaanites. That "there were still seven Israelite tribes who had not yet received their inheritance" implies that a significant amount of time had elapsed. Throughout the book of Joshua, events that took a considerable amount of time are compressed into a few verses. Apparently the remaining tribes had grown complacent. Satisfied with nomadic life in the fertile land of Ephraim and Manasseh, they weren't anxious to be involved in the warfare required to claim their own territories.

18:5
q Jos 15:1
r Jos 16:1-4
18:6
s Jos 14:2
territory on the south[q] and the house of Joseph in its territory on the north.[r] 6After you have written descriptions of the seven parts of the land, bring them here to me and I will cast lots[s] for you in the presence of the LORD our God. 7The Levites,

18:7
t Jos 13:33
u Jos 13:8
however, do not get a portion among you, because the priestly service of the LORD is their inheritance.[t] And Gad, Reuben and the half-tribe of Manasseh have already received their inheritance on the east side of the Jordan. Moses the servant of the LORD gave it to them.[u]"

8As the men started on their way to map out the land, Joshua instructed them, "Go and make a survey of the land and write a description of it. Then return to me,

18:8
v ver 1
and I will cast lots for you here at Shiloh[v] in the presence of the LORD." 9So the men left and went through the land. They wrote its description on a scroll, town by town, in seven parts, and returned to Joshua in the camp at Shiloh. 10Joshua then cast

18:10
w Nu 34:13 x ver 1;
Jer 7:12
y Nu 33:54;
Jos 19:51
lots[w] for them in Shiloh in the presence[x] of the LORD, and there he distributed the land to the Israelites according to their tribal divisions.[y]

Allotment for Benjamin

11The lot came up for the tribe of Benjamin, clan by clan. Their allotted territory lay between the tribes of Judah and Joseph:

12On the north side their boundary began at the Jordan, passed the northern slope of Jericho and headed west into the hill country, coming out at the

18:12
z Jos 16:1 a Jos 7:2
18:13
b Ge 28:19
c Jdg 1:23
d Jos 16:5
18:14
e Jos 10:10
desert[z] of Beth Aven.[a] 13From there it crossed to the south slope of Luz[b] (that is, Bethel[c]) and went down to Ataroth Addar[d] on the hill south of Lower Beth Horon.

14From the hill facing Beth Horon[e] on the south the boundary turned south along the western side and came out at Kiriath Baal (that is, Kiriath Jearim), a town of the people of Judah. This was the western side.

18:15
f Jos 15:9
15The southern side began at the outskirts of Kiriath Jearim on the west, and the boundary came out at the spring of the waters of Nephtoah.[f] 16The bound-

18:16
g Jos 15:8;
2Ki 23:10
h Jos 15:7
ary went down to the foot of the hill facing the Valley of Ben Hinnom, north of the Valley of Rephaim. It continued down the Hinnom Valley[g] along the southern slope of the Jebusite city and so to En Rogel.[h] 17It then curved north,

18:17
i Jos 15:6
18:18
j Jos 15:6
went to En Shemesh, continued to Geliloth, which faces the Pass of Adummim, and ran down to the Stone of Bohan[i] son of Reuben. 18It continued to the northern slope of Beth Arabah[a][j] and on down into the Arabah. 19It then

18:19
k Ge 14:3
went to the northern slope of Beth Hoglah and came out at the northern bay of the Salt Sea,[b][k] at the mouth of the Jordan in the south. This was the southern boundary.

20The Jordan formed the boundary on the eastern side.

These were the boundaries that marked out the inheritance of the clans of Benja-

18:20
l Jos 21:4,17;
1Sa 9:1
min on all sides.[l]

---

[a] 18 Septuagint; Hebrew *slope facing the Arabah*   [b] 19 That is, the Dead Sea

---

Joshua was eager to complete his commission, which included not only the conquest of the land but also its division among the tribes. He reproved these seven tribes for the ingratitude and unbelief manifested in their failure to take the territory God had already given them. Do you think God was impatient with you over your reluctance to test and claim his promises? When were you satisfied with a little, when God stood ready and eager to hand you a lot? When did you resist the effort required of you to claim his blessing?

Joshua 18:11–28

Benjamin wasn't the largest of the seven tribes receiving their allotments, yet its territory is described in greater detail than that of the others. The areas given to Benjamin and Dan (19:40–48) constituted a buffer zone

between Judah to the south and Ephraim to the north, the two tribes that would later become dominant in Israel.

Nothing in our direct experience begins to correspond to Israel's conquest and occupation of assigned tribal territories. Perhaps the closest parallel in American history relates to the rush to establish homesteads in the "wild west" of 19th-century frontier days. "The sky's the limit" concept of "eminent domain" and the siren call of "Go west, young man" drove heady idealists to give up all they knew of security and stability to claim their prize. But not everyone shared this hearty pioneer spirit. Try to put yourself in the sandals of the average Israelite during this time of excitement and upheaval. What role would faith have played as you ventured forward?

21The tribe of Benjamin, clan by clan, had the following cities:
Jericho, Beth Hoglah, Emek Keziz, 22Beth Arabah, Zemaraim, Bethel,[m] 23Av-
vim, Parah, Ophrah, 24Kephar Ammoni, Ophni and Geba[n]—twelve towns
and their villages.
25Gibeon,[o] Ramah,[p] Beeroth,[q] 26Mizpah,[r] Kephirah, Mozah, 27Rekem, Ir-
peel, Taralah, 28Zelah,[s] Haeleph, the Jebusite city[t] (that is, Jerusalem[u]), Gibeah[v] and Kiriath—fourteen towns and their villages.
This was the inheritance of Benjamin for its clans.

Allotment for Simeon

19 The second lot came out for the tribe of Simeon, clan by clan. Their inheritance lay within the territory of Judah.[w] 2It included:
Beersheba[x] (or Sheba),[a] Moladah, 3Hazar Shual, Balah, Ezem, 4Eltolad,
Bethul, Hormah, 5Ziklag, Beth Marcaboth, Hazar Susah, 6Beth Lebaoth and
Sharuhen—thirteen towns and their villages;
7Ain, Rimmon, Ether and Ashan[y]—four towns and their villages— 8and all
the villages around these towns as far as Baalath Beer (Ramah in the Negev).[z]
This was the inheritance of the tribe of the Simeonites, clan by clan. 9The inheritance of the Simeonites was taken from the share of Judah,[a] because Judah's portion was more than they needed. So the Simeonites received their inheritance within the territory of Judah.[b]

Allotment for Zebulun

10The third lot came up for Zebulun,[c] clan by clan:
The boundary of their inheritance went as far as Sarid. 11Going west it ran
to Maralah, touched Dabbesheth, and extended to the ravine near Jokneam.[d]
12It turned east from Sarid toward the sunrise to the territory of Kisloth Tabor
and went on to Daberath and up to Japhia. 13Then it continued eastward to
Gath Hepher and Eth Kazin; it came out at Rimmon[e] and turned toward

18:22 [m] Jos 16:1
18:24 [n] Isa 10:29
18:25 [o] Jos 9:3 [p] Jdg 4:5 [q] Jos 9:17
18:26 [r] Jos 11:3
18:28 [s] 2Sa 21:14 [t] Jos 15:8 [u] Jos 10:1 [v] Jos 15:57
19:1 [w] ver 9; Ge 49:7
19:2 [x] Ge 21:14; 1Ki 19:3
19:7 [y] Jos 15:42
19:8 [z] Jos 10:40
19:9 [a] Ge 49:7 [b] Eze 48:24
19:10 [c] Jos 21:7,34
19:11 [d] Jos 12:22
19:13 [e] Jos 15:32

[a] 2 Or *Beersheba, Sheba;* 1 Chron. 4:28 does not have *Sheba.*

Joshua 19:1–9

Simeon's allotment was an adjustment, as Judah's original portion was too large. When Jacob blessed his sons before his death, he stated that the descendants of Simeon and Levi were destined to be scattered among the other tribes as punishment for their violent revenge against the Shechemites (Gen. 49:7; cf. Gen. 34; see also "There and Then" for Josh. 14:1–5). All the towns assigned to Simeon were located within the borders of Judah, and Simeon was soon absorbed by Judah. Apparently 1 Kings 19:3 reflects a period when Simeon's assimilation into Judah was complete: Beersheba, which had been given to Simeon, is there called Beersheba in Judah.

Inheritance was a basic right in Israelite society. A piece of real estate became a family's inalienable possession. Numerous Old Testament laws were dedicated to regulating and protecting the rights of inheritance (cf. 17:3–6).

The New Testament stresses inheritance too—of a different kind (see Matt. 5:5; 19:29; 25:34; Eph. 1:13–14; Col. 1:12; 3:24): "Christ is the mediator of a new covenant, that those who are called may receive the promised inheritance—now that he has died as a ransom to set them free from the sins committed under the first covenant" (Heb. 9:15). The Simeonites eventually lost their inheritance, but we as believers have "an inheritance that can never perish, spoil or fade—kept in heaven for [us]" (1 Peter 1:4).

Joshua 19:10–16

Zebulun and Issachar were the last of Jacob's six sons through Leah (Gen. 30:14–20; 35:23) and were mentioned together in Moses' blessing of the tribes (Deut. 33:18–19). Though Zebulun was the younger brother of Issachar, he received his inheritance first (Josh. 19:10–23). The same had been true of Ephraim, Joseph's younger son and the younger brother of Manasseh (Josh. 16:5–17:11). The prominence of Ephraim over Manasseh isn't surprising in light of the fact that Jacob favored Ephraim when he adopted and blessed these two grandsons (Gen. 48).

Bethlehem (v. 15) is Beth Lahm east of Mount Carmel—not to be confused with Bethlehem in Judah.

What other Biblical examples can you think of in which younger brothers received blessing or favoritism exceeding that of older? Identify some New Testament examples of the same principle at work, particularly in terms of Jesus' "topsy-turvy" assessments of values on the human plane. What do the unchurched of our age make of a system in which the first are last (Mark 9:35; 10:31) and the meek are heirs and heiresses (Matt. 5:5)? How successful have you been in attempting to explain these concepts? Check out 1 Corinthians 1:18–31 for an explanation.

19:15
f Ge 35:19
19:16
g ver 10; Jos 21:7
h Eze 48:26

19:17
i Ge 30:18
19:18
j Jos 15:56
k 1Sa 28:4; 2Ki 4:8

19:22
l Jdg 4:6, 12;
Ps 89:12
m Jos 15:10
19:23
n Jos 17:10
o Ge 49:15;
Eze 48:25

19:24
p Jos 17:7

19:26
q Jos 12:22
19:27
r ver 10 s 1Ki 9:13

19:28
t Jdg 1:31
u 1Ch 6:76
v Ge 10:19;
Jos 11:8
19:29
w Jos 18:25
x 2Sa 5:11; 24:7;
Isa 23:1; Jer 25:22;
Eze 26:2 y Jdg 1:31
19:31
z Ge 30:13;
Eze 48:2

19:35
a Jos 11:2

Neah. [14]There the boundary went around on the north to Hannathon and ended at the Valley of Iphtah El. [15]Included were Kattath, Nahalal, Shimron, Idalah and Bethlehem.[f] There were twelve towns and their villages. [16]These towns and their villages were the inheritance of Zebulun,[g] clan by clan.[h]

Allotment for Issachar

[17]The fourth lot came out for Issachar,[i] clan by clan. [18]Their territory included:
Jezreel,[j] Kesulloth, Shunem,[k] [19]Hapharaim, Shion, Anaharath, [20]Rabbith, Kishion, Ebez, [21]Remeth, En Gannim, En Haddah and Beth Pazzez. [22]The boundary touched Tabor,[l] Shahazumah and Beth Shemesh,[m] and ended at the Jordan. There were sixteen towns and their villages. [23]These towns and their villages were the inheritance of the tribe of Issachar,[n] clan by clan.[o]

Allotment for Asher

[24]The fifth lot came out for the tribe of Asher,[p] clan by clan. [25]Their territory included:
Helkath, Hali, Beten, Acshaph, [26]Allammelech, Amad and Mishal. On the west the boundary touched Carmel[q] and Shihor Libnath. [27]It then turned east toward Beth Dagon, touched Zebulun[r] and the Valley of Iphtah El, and went north to Beth Emek and Neiel, passing Cabul[s] on the left. [28]It went to Abdon,[a] Rehob,[t] Hammon[u] and Kanah, as far as Greater Sidon.[v] [29]The boundary then turned back toward Ramah[w] and went to the fortified city of Tyre,[x] turned toward Hosah and came out at the sea in the region of Aczib,[y] [30]Ummah, Aphek and Rehob. There were twenty-two towns and their villages. [31]These towns and their villages were the inheritance of the tribe of Asher,[z] clan by clan.

Allotment for Naphtali

[32]The sixth lot came out for Naphtali, clan by clan:
[33]Their boundary went from Heleph and the large tree in Zaanannim, passing Adami Nekeb and Jabneel to Lakkum and ending at the Jordan. [34]The boundary ran west through Aznoth Tabor and came out at Hukkok. It touched Zebulun on the south, Asher on the west and the Jordan[b] on the east. [35]The fortified cities were Ziddim, Zer, Hammath, Rakkath, Kinnereth,[a] [36]Adamah,

---

a 28 Some Hebrew manuscripts (see also Joshua 21:30); most Hebrew manuscripts *Ebron*
b 34 Septuagint; Hebrew *west, and Judah, the Jordan,*

Joshua 19:17–23

📖 No description is given of the borders of Issachar, only a list of towns. This tribe's inheritance lay southwest of the Sea of Galilee and was bounded on the west by Zebulun, on the north by Naphtali, on the east by the Jordan River, and on the south by Manasseh.

📖 If you have one or more siblings, how sensitive have you been to perceived favoritism (see "There and Then" for vv. 10–16)? Barring the possibility of deliberate unfairness on the part of your parents, are you willing to respect their judgment and accept on faith that they have reasons for their choices? A truth many today find unpalatable is that people *aren't* created equal in terms of their endowments and abilities (value and worth in God's eyes are quite another story!). And treating them as such wouldn't necessarily be fair. Read and reflect on Paul's words about equality in 1 Corinthians 12:12–31.

Joshua 19:24–31

📖 Asher's allotment was along the Mediterranean Sea in the extreme northwestern area of the promised

land. The fertile farmlands near the coast fulfilled Jacob's ages-old blessing: "Asher's food will be rich" (Gen. 49:20).

Once again, the account of the outcome of the lot for this tribe is matter-of-fact. We are not aware of any problem with the allocation, but neither do we read of a complaint like that voiced by the Joseph tribes in 17:14–18.

📖 How true in your experience is the maxim that the squeaky wheel gets the grease? In the case of the grievances of Ephraim and the half-tribe of Manasseh (above), Joshua—and presumably God—weren't impressed. When you voice protests, are you typically speaking on your own behalf or as a representative of voiceless people—like those in the tribe of Asher?

Joshua 19:32–39

📖 The allotment for Naphtali extended from the Sea of Galilee into the hill country well to the north. Jesus would spend most of his public ministry in Galilee, in the area of Naphtali and Zebulun. The gospel of Matthew points out that this reality was in fulfillment of a Messianic prophecy from Isaiah (Matt. 4:12–16; cf. Isa. 9:1–2).

Ramah,[b] Hazor,[c] 37Kedesh, Edrei,[d] En Hazor, 38Iron, Migdal El, Horem, Beth Anath and Beth Shemesh. There were nineteen towns and their villages. 39These towns and their villages were the inheritance of the tribe of Naphtali, clan by clan.[e]

Allotment for Dan

40The seventh lot came out for the tribe of Dan, clan by clan. 41The territory of their inheritance included:

Zorah, Eshtaol, Ir Shemesh, 42Shaalabbin, Aijalon,[f] Ithlah, 43Elon, Timnah,[g] Ekron, 44Eltekeh, Gibbethon, Baalath, 45Jehud, Bene Berak, Gath Rimmon,[h] 46Me Jarkon and Rakkon, with the area facing Joppa.[i]

47(But the Danites had difficulty taking possession of their territory,[j] so they went up and attacked Leshem,[k] took it, put it to the sword and occupied it. They settled in Leshem and named it Dan after their forefather.)[l]

48These towns and their villages were the inheritance of the tribe of Dan,[m] clan by clan.

Allotment for Joshua

49When they had finished dividing the land into its allotted portions, the Israelites gave Joshua son of Nun an inheritance among them, 50as the LORD had commanded. They gave him the town he asked for—Timnath Serah[a][n] in the hill country of Ephraim. And he built up the town and settled there.

51These are the territories that Eleazar the priest, Joshua son of Nun and the heads of the tribal clans of Israel assigned by lot at Shiloh in the presence of the LORD at the entrance to the Tent of Meeting. And so they finished dividing the land.[o]

Cities of Refuge

20 Then the LORD said to Joshua: 2"Tell the Israelites to designate the cities of refuge, as I instructed you through Moses, 3so that anyone who kills a person accidentally and unintentionally[p] may flee there and find protection from the avenger of blood.[q]

a 50 Also known as *Timnath Heres* (see Judges 2:9)

19:36
b Jos 18:25
c Jos 11:1
19:37
d Nu 21:33
19:39
e Dt 33:23; Eze 48:3

19:42
f Jdg 1:35
19:43
g Ge 38:12
19:45
h Jos 21:24; 1Ch 6:69
19:46
i 2Ch 2:16; Jnh 1:3
19:47
j Jdg 18:1
k Jdg 18:7,14
l Jdg 18:27,29
19:48
m Ge 30:6

19:50
n Jos 24:30

19:51
o Jos 14:1; 18:10; Ac 13:19

20:3
p Lev 4:2
q Nu 35:12

Do all these allotments seem like "a lot" of irrelevant data to you? A central theme in the book of Joshua is the fulfillment of God's promise: He would give Israel the land (Ex. 23:20–33; Deut. 7:18–24; Josh. 21:43–45). These geographical details help us appreciate the Lord's faithfulness, and remembering that faithfulness encourages us to trust him more fully.

Joshua 19:40–48

Dan's allotment, together with Benjamin's, served as a buffer zone between Judah and Ephraim (see "There and Then" for 18:11–28). The Danites were unsuccessful in displacing the Amorites, who "confined the Danites to the hill country, not allowing them to come down into the plain" (Judg. 1:34). Therefore most of the tribe migrated about 100 miles to the north, where they destroyed Leshem (or Laish)—rebuilding the city and renaming it Dan (Judg. 18). This became Israel's northernmost settlement.

A number of Danites made an end run around God's plan for their tribe. Rather than trusting God to help them drive out the inhabitants of the territory he had given them, they attacked "a peaceful and unsuspecting people" (Judg. 18:27). It's a lot easier to trust God when life's challenges seem manageable, isn't it? When have you devised a Plan B when you felt inca-

pable of handling a responsibility given to you by God? If you are facing that kind of dilemma now, you can call out to the God of promises to help you "take the land."

Joshua 19:49–51

The descriptions of the inheritances allotted to Caleb (14:6–15) and Joshua, the two faithful spies, provide the "bookends" for the accounts of the distribution of Canaan to the tribes (see notes for 14:6–15). Since they were men of faith, this arrangement symbolizes the spiritual truth that the gift of the promised land to Israel was based on faith. Both received what they asked for—and, fittingly, Joshua the servant of the Lord (cf. 5:14; 24:29) received his inheritance last (see Mark 10:42–45).

The author of the New Testament book of Hebrews would centuries later pen the well-loved "faith hall of fame" regarding Old Testament heroes of faith. Yet this author was quick to acknowledge that "none of them received what had been promised. God had planned something better for us so that only together with us would they be made perfect" (Heb. 11: 39–40). The book of Proverbs establishes the principle that faithful living often does yield material rewards. But not always. The best promises are spiritual—and eternal. On what sure promises are you basing your life?

20:4
r Ru 4:1; Jer 38:7
s Jos 7:6

4 "When he flees to one of these cities, he is to stand in the entrance of the city gate[r] and state his case before the elders[s] of that city. Then they are to admit him into their city and give him a place to live with them. 5If the avenger of blood pursues him, they must not surrender the one accused, because he killed his neighbor unintentionally and without malice aforethought. 6He is to stay in that city until he has stood trial before the assembly[t] and until the death of the high priest who is serving at that time. Then he may go back to his own home in the town from which he fled."

20:6
t Nu 35:12

20:7
u Jos 21:32;
1Ch 6:76 v Ge 12:6
w Jos 10:36; 21:11
x Lk 1:39
20:8
y Jos 21:36;
1Ch 6:78 z Jos 12:2

7So they set apart Kedesh[u] in Galilee in the hill country of Naphtali, Shechem[v] in the hill country of Ephraim, and Kiriath Arba (that is, Hebron[w]) in the hill country of Judah.[x] 8On the east side of the Jordan of Jericho[a] they designated Bezer[y] in the desert on the plateau in the tribe of Reuben, Ramoth in Gilead[z] in the tribe of Gad, and Golan in Bashan in the tribe of Manasseh. 9Any of the Israelites or any alien living among them who killed someone accidentally could flee to these designated cities and not be killed by the avenger of blood prior to standing trial before the assembly.[a]

20:9
a Ex 21:13;
Nu 35:15

Towns for the Levites

21 Now the family heads of the Levites approached Eleazar the priest, Joshua son of Nun, and the heads of the other tribal families of Israel[b] 2at Shiloh[c] in Canaan and said to them, "The LORD commanded through Moses that you give us towns to live in, with pasturelands for our livestock."[d] 3So, as the LORD had commanded, the Israelites gave the Levites the following towns and pasturelands out of their own inheritance:

21:1
b Jos 14:1
21:2
c Jos 18:1
d Nu 35:2-3

4The first lot came out for the Kohathites, clan by clan. The Levites who were descendants of Aaron the priest were allotted thirteen towns from the tribes of Judah, Simeon and Benjamin.[e] 5The rest of Kohath's descendants were allotted ten towns from the clans of the tribes of Ephraim, Dan and half of Manasseh.[f]

21:4
e ver 19
21:5
f ver 26

6The descendants of Gershon were allotted thirteen towns from the clans of the tribes of Issachar,[g] Asher, Naphtali and the half-tribe of Manasseh in Bashan.

7The descendants of Merari,[h] clan by clan, received twelve towns from the tribes of Reuben, Gad and Zebulun.[i]

21:6
g Ge 30:18
21:7
h Ex 6:16
i Jos 19:10

---

a 8 Jordan of Jericho was possibly an ancient name for the Jordan River.

Cities of Refuge (20:2)

Then: The six cities of refuge were designated as safe havens where accused murderers could go to escape vigilante justice.

Now: Cities of refuge no longer exist as such; modern Israel relies instead on systematic courts of law.

Joshua 20:1-9

Blood vengeance was an ancient custom traceable all the way back to Cain's expectation that he would be killed in revenge for murdering his brother Abel (Gen. 4:13–14). It was still in force during the time of the monarchy (cf. 2 Sam. 3:27; 14:6–7). Though the right of sanctuary was respected widely in the ancient Near East, the provision of "cities of refuge" was a practice without parallel. The goal was to distinguish between murder and accidental killing (manslaughter) and to grant the right of trial to suspected murderers.

Asylum in the cities of refuge was offered to "any alien" living within Israel's borders (v. 9). The care shown to aliens testified to God's care for all humanity. Though the Israelites stood against the pagan societies around them, their hearts were to be open to receive any foreigner who would adopt their religion and customs. How open are you to "receiving" refugees and other immigrants into your locality, including your church and immediate social circle? Do you expect from them a quick acclimation to Western ways, or are you willing to respect and learn from their customs—even to some extent from their religious practices?

Joshua 21:1-45

It's generally believed that the Levites lived in these towns without actually owning them, possibly side by side with members of the particular tribe from whose territory the town had been selected. The Levitical towns were selected from every tribe, but they weren't evenly distributed throughout the land. They seem to have been clustered on the frontiers and in other endangered areas.

8So the Israelites allotted to the Levites these towns and their pasturelands, as the LORD had commanded through Moses.

9From the tribes of Judah and Simeon they allotted the following towns by name 10(these towns were assigned to the descendants of Aaron who were from the Kohathite clans of the Levites, because the first lot fell to them):

11They gave them Kiriath Arba (that is, Hebron*j*), with its surrounding pastureland, in the hill country of Judah. (Arba was the forefather of Anak.) 12But the fields and villages around the city they had given to Caleb son of Jephunneh as his possession.

13So to the descendants of Aaron the priest they gave Hebron (a city of refuge for one accused of murder), Libnah,*k* 14Jattir,*l* Eshtemoa,*m* 15Holon,*n* Debir, 16Ain, Juttah*o* and Beth Shemesh,*p* together with their pasturelands—nine towns from these two tribes.

17And from the tribe of Benjamin they gave them Gibeon, Geba,*q* 18Anathoth and Almon, together with their pasturelands—four towns.

19All the towns for the priests, the descendants of Aaron, were thirteen, together with their pasturelands.

20The rest of the Kohathite clans of the Levites were allotted towns from the tribe of Ephraim:

21In the hill country of Ephraim they were given Shechem*r* (a city of refuge for one accused of murder) and Gezer, 22Kibzaim and Beth Horon,*s* together with their pasturelands—four towns.*t*

23Also from the tribe of Dan they received Eltekeh, Gibbethon, 24Aijalon and Gath Rimmon,*u* together with their pasturelands—four towns.

25From half the tribe of Manasseh they received Taanach and Gath Rimmon, together with their pasturelands—two towns.

26All these ten towns and their pasturelands were given to the rest of the Kohathite clans.

27The Levite clans of the Gershonites were given:

from the half-tribe of Manasseh,

Golan in Bashan*v* (a city of refuge for one accused of murder*w*) and Be Eshtarah, together with their pasturelands—two towns;

28from the tribe of Issachar,*x*

Kishion, Daberath, 29Jarmuth and En Gannim, together with their pasturelands—four towns;

30from the tribe of Asher,*y*

Mishal, Abdon, 31Helkath and Rehob, together with their pasturelands—four towns;

32from the tribe of Naphtali,

Kedesh*z* in Galilee (a city of refuge for one accused of murder*a*), Hammoth Dor and Kartan, together with their pasturelands—three towns.

33All the towns of the Gershonite*b* clans were thirteen, together with their pasturelands.

21:11
j Jos 15:13;
1Ch 6:55

21:13
k Jos 15:42;
1Ch 6:57
21:14
l Jos 15:48
m Jos 15:50
21:15
n Jos 15:51
21:16
o Jos 15:55
p Jos 15:10
21:17
q Jos 18:24

21:21
r Jos 17:7; 20:7
21:22
s Jos 10:10
t 1Sa 1:1

21:24
u Jos 19:45

21:27
v Jos 12:5
w Nu 35:6

21:28
x Ge 30:18

21:30
y Jos 17:7

21:32
z Jos 12:22
a Nu 35:6; Jos 20:7

21:33
b ver 6

"The LORD gave Israel" (v. 43) emphasizes God's sovereign action. His people's obedient participation was essential, but always secondary. The land was God's gift. Not all of Canaan was yet in Israel's possession, nor were all her enemies destroyed, but Israel was basically in control of "all the land." The promise of the land is a prominent theme in the history of the patriarchs, beginning with the call of Abraham (Gen. 12:1–7). God's oath to Abraham had now been fulfilled.

The "rest" God gave his people (v. 44) was a ter-mination of hostilities, allowing them to live securely in the land (cf. Deut. 12:9–10). This theme would be taken up centuries later by the writer of Hebrews (Heb. 4:1–11), who pointed to a deeper rest that can only be fulfilled in Christ. "Not one of all the LORD's good promises . . . failed" (v. 45): On this note of victory and celebration, the story of the conquest and division of the land is completed. Are you finding rejuvenation in Christ's deeper rest? Can you attest personally to his unfailing promise-keeping? Are you sharing the news?

21:34
c Jos 19:10;
1Ch 6:77

[34]The Merarite clans (the rest of the Levites) were given:

from the tribe of Zebulun,[c]

Jokneam, Kartah, [35]Dimnah and Nahalal, together with their pasturelands—four towns;

[36]from the tribe of Reuben,

21:36
d Jos 20:8

Bezer,[d] Jahaz, [37]Kedemoth and Mephaath, together with their pasturelands—four towns;

[38]from the tribe of Gad,

21:38
e Dt 4:43 f Ge 32:2

Ramoth[e] in Gilead (a city of refuge for one accused of murder), Mahanaim,[f] [39]Heshbon and Jazer, together with their pasturelands—four towns in all.

[40]All the towns allotted to the Merarite clans, who were the rest of the Levites, were twelve.

21:41
g Nu 35:7

[41]The towns of the Levites in the territory held by the Israelites were forty-eight in all, together with their pasturelands.[g] [42]Each of these towns had pasturelands surrounding it; this was true for all these towns.

21:43
h Dt 34:4 i Dt 11:31
j Dt 17:14
21:44
k Ex 33:14; Jos 1:13
l Dt 6:19
m Ex 23:31
n Dt 7:24; 21:10
21:45
o Jos 23:14; Ne 9:8

[43]So the LORD gave Israel all the land he had sworn to give their forefathers,[h] and they took possession[i] of it and settled there.[j] [44]The LORD gave them rest[k] on every side, just as he had sworn to their forefathers. Not one of their enemies[l] withstood them; the LORD handed all their enemies[m] over to them.[n] [45]Not one of all the LORD's good promises[o] to the house of Israel failed; every one was fulfilled.

Eastern Tribes Return Home

22:2
p Nu 32:25

22 Then Joshua summoned the Reubenites, the Gadites and the half-tribe of Manasseh [2]and said to them, "You have done all that Moses the servant of the LORD commanded,[p] and you have obeyed me in everything I commanded. [3]For a long time now—to this very day—you have not deserted your brothers but have carried out the mission the LORD your God gave you. [4]Now that the LORD your God has given your brothers rest as he promised, return to your homes[q] in the land that Moses the servant of the LORD gave you on the other side of the Jordan.[r] [5]But be very careful to keep the commandment[s] and the law that Moses the servant of the LORD gave you: to love the LORD your God, to walk in all his ways, to obey his commands,[t] to hold fast to him and to serve him with all your heart and all your soul.[u]"

22:4
q Nu 32:22; Dt 3:20
r Nu 32:18;
Jos 1:13-15
22:5
s Isa 43:22 t Dt 5:29
u Dt 6:6,17

22:6
v Ex 39:43
22:7
w Nu 32:33;
Jos 12:5
x Jos 17:2,5

[6]Then Joshua blessed[v] them and sent them away, and they went to their homes. [7](To the half-tribe of Manasseh Moses had given land in Bashan,[w] and to the other half of the tribe Joshua gave land on the west side[x] of the Jordan with their brothers.) When Joshua sent them home, he blessed them, [8]saying, "Return to your homes with your great wealth—with large herds of livestock,[y] with silver, gold, bronze and iron, and a great quantity of clothing—and divide[z] with your brothers the plunder[a] from your enemies."

22:8
y Dt 20:14
z Nu 31:27
a Ge 49:27;
1Sa 30:16; Isa 9:3

22:9
b Nu 32:26,29

[9]So the Reubenites, the Gadites and the half-tribe of Manasseh left the Israelites at Shiloh in Canaan to return to Gilead,[b] their own land, which they had acquired in accordance with the command of the LORD through Moses.

Joshua 22:1–34

The zeal of the nine-and-a-half tribes for God's honor and for pure worship might have ended disastrously had they disregarded his command to always investigate carefully before taking action (Deut. 13:14). Pressing for repentance and reconciliation before declaring war gave the two-and-a-half tribes an opportunity to explain. Note that those west of the Jordan didn't accuse their countrymen of serving other gods but of deviating from God's revealed will. Even sacrifices offered in his name had to be given on an approved altar.

"Defiled" (v. 19) was a term for ritual uncleanness; it didn't necessarily imply something sinful. It's clear that the nine-and-a-half tribes viewed only the land of

Canaan as the promised land (cf. Num. 32:6–9). The presence of the tabernacle on their side of the river confirmed for them that this land was especially blessed. Their willingness to "share the land" revealed a beautifully generous spirit and proved the sincerity of their concern for orthodox worship.

Joshua seemed to be afraid that the isolation caused by the formidable barrier of the Jordan might lead the two-and-a-half tribes to turn from God (vv. 4–5). On the other hand, they feared this separation might cause their descendants to be rejected by the rest of Israel (vv. 24–25). Neither apprehension was unfounded. The altar was intended as a witness that the Lord was God of all the tribes.

10When they came to Geliloth near the Jordan in the land of Canaan, the Reuben-ites, the Gadites and the half-tribe of Manasseh built an imposing altar there by the Jordan. 11And when the Israelites heard that they had built the altar on the border of Canaan at Geliloth near the Jordan on the Israelite side, 12the whole assembly of Israel gathered at Shiloh c to go to war against them.

13So the Israelites sent Phinehas d son of Eleazar, e the priest, to the land of Gile-ad—to Reuben, Gad and the half-tribe of Manasseh. 14With him they sent ten of the chief men, one for each of the tribes of Israel, each the head of a family divi-sion among the Israelite clans. f

15When they went to Gilead—to Reuben, Gad and the half-tribe of Manasseh—they said to them: 16"The whole assembly of the LORD says: 'How could you break faith g with the God of Israel like this? How could you turn away from the LORD and build yourselves an altar in rebellion h against him now? 17Was not the sin of Peor i enough for us? Up to this very day we have not cleansed ourselves from that sin, even though a plague fell on the community of the LORD! 18And are you now turn-ing away from the LORD?

" 'If you rebel against the LORD today, tomorrow he will be angry with the whole community j of Israel. 19If the land you possess is defiled, come over to the LORD's land, where the LORD's tabernacle stands, and share the land with us. But do not re-bel against the LORD or against us by building an altar for yourselves, other than the altar of the LORD our God. 20When Achan son of Zerah acted unfaithfully regard-ing the devoted things, a k did not wrath l come upon the whole community of Isra-el? He was not the only one who died for his sin.' " m

21Then Reuben, Gad and the half-tribe of Manasseh replied to the heads of the clans of Israel: 22"The Mighty One, God, the LORD! The Mighty One, God, n the LORD! o He knows! p And let Israel know! If this has been in rebellion or disobedi-ence to the LORD, do not spare us this day. 23If we have built our own altar to turn away from the LORD and to offer burnt offerings and grain offerings, q or to sacri-fice fellowship offerings b on it, may the LORD himself call us to account. r

24"No! We did it for fear that some day your descendants might say to ours, 'What do you have to do with the LORD, the God of Israel? 25The LORD has made the Jor-dan a boundary between us and you—you Reubenites and Gadites! You have no share in the LORD.' So your descendants might cause ours to stop fearing the LORD.

26"That is why we said, 'Let us get ready and build an altar—but not for burnt of-ferings or sacrifices.' 27On the contrary, it is to be a witness s between us and you and the generations that follow, that we will worship the LORD at his sanctuary with our burnt offerings, sacrifices and fellowship offerings. t Then in the future your descen-dants will not be able to say to ours, 'You have no share in the LORD.'

28"And we said, 'If they ever say this to us, or to our descendants, we will answer: Look at the replica of the LORD's altar, which our fathers built, not for burnt offer-ings and sacrifices, but as a witness between us and you.'

29"Far be it from us to rebel u against the LORD and turn away from him today by building an altar for burnt offerings, grain offerings and sacrifices, other than the altar of the LORD our God that stands before his tabernacle. v"

30When Phinehas the priest and the leaders of the community—the heads of the clans of the Israelites—heard what Reuben, Gad and Manasseh had to say, they were pleased. 31And Phinehas son of Eleazar, the priest, said to Reuben, Gad and Manas-seh, "Today we know that the LORD is with us, w because you have not acted unfaith-

a 20 The Hebrew term refers to the irrevocable giving over of things or persons to the LORD, often by totally destroying them.   b 23 Traditionally peace offerings; also in verse 27

22:12
c Jos 18:1
22:13
d Nu 25:7
e Nu 3:32;
Jos 24:33
22:14
f Nu 1:4

22:16
g Dt 13:14
h Dt 12:13-14
22:17
i Nu 25:1-9
22:18
j Lev 10:6;
Nu 16:22

22:20
k Jos 7:1 l Ps 7:11
m Jos 7:5

22:22
n Dt 10:17
o Ps 50:1
p 1Ki 8:39;
Job 10:7; Ps 44:21;
Jer 17:10
22:23
q Jer 41:5
r Dt 12:11; 18:19;
1Sa 20:16

22:27
s Ge 21:30;
Jos 24:27 t Dt 12:6

22:29
u Jos 24:16
v Dt 12:13-14

22:31
w Lev 26:11-12;
2Ch 15:2

What about the church today? When we look at en-trenched denominational and theological partitions and isolation—and the resulting suspicions and misunder-standings—we might find cause to despair. A single or-ganizational structure may not be possible or even desir-able. But the memory of a single cross must be the sym-bol of unity that will destroy all divisions. To what extent today does that cross function as "A Witness Between Us that the LORD is God" (v. 34)?

fully toward the LORD in this matter. Now you have rescued the Israelites from the LORD's hand."

³²Then Phinehas son of Eleazar, the priest, and the leaders returned to Canaan from their meeting with the Reubenites and Gadites in Gilead and reported to the Israelites. ³³They were glad to hear the report and praised God. ^x And they talked no more about going to war against them to devastate the country where the Reubenites and the Gadites lived.

³⁴And the Reubenites and the Gadites gave the altar this name: A Witness^y Between Us that the LORD is God.

Joshua's Farewell to the Leaders

23 After a long time had passed and the LORD had given Israel rest^z from all their enemies around them, Joshua, by then old and well advanced in years,^a ²summoned all Israel—their elders,^b leaders, judges and officials^c—and said to them: "I am old and well advanced in years. ³You yourselves have seen everything the LORD your God has done to all these nations for your sake; it was the LORD your God who fought for you.^d ⁴Remember how I have allotted^e as an inheritance for your tribes all the land of the nations that remain—the nations I conquered—between the Jordan and the Great Sea^a^f in the west. ⁵The LORD your God himself will drive them out of your way. He will push them out before you, and you will take possession of their land, as the LORD your God promised you.^g

⁶"Be very strong; be careful to obey all that is written in the Book of the Law of Moses, without turning aside to the right or to the left.^h ⁷Do not associate with these nations that remain among you; do not invoke the names of their gods or swearⁱ by them. You must not serve them or bow down^j to them. ⁸But you are to hold fast to the LORD^k your God, as you have until now.

⁹"The LORD has driven out before you great and powerful nations;^l to this day no one has been able to withstand you.^m ¹⁰One of you routs a thousand,ⁿ because the LORD your God fights for you,^o just as he promised. ¹¹So be very careful to love the LORD^p your God.

¹²"But if you turn away and ally yourselves with the survivors of these nations that remain among you and if you intermarry with them^q and associate with them,^r ¹³then you may be sure that the LORD your God will no longer drive out these nations before you. Instead, they will become snares^s and traps for you, whips on your backs and thorns in your eyes,^t until you perish from this good land, which the LORD your God has given you.

¹⁴"Now I am about to go the way of all the earth.^u You know with all your heart and soul that not one of all the good promises the LORD your God gave you has failed. Every promise has been fulfilled; not one has failed.^v ¹⁵But just as every good promise of the LORD your God has come true, so the LORD will bring on you all the evil he has threatened, until he has destroyed you from this good land he has

---

22:33
^x 1Ch 29:20; Da 2:19; Lk 2:28

22:34
^y Ge 21:30

23:1
^z Dt 12:9; Jos 21:44
^a Jos 13:1

23:2
^b Jos 7:6 ^c Jos 24:1

23:3
^d Ex 14:14
23:4
^e Jos 19:51
^f Nu 34:6

23:5
^g Ex 23:30; Nu 33:53
23:6
^h Dt 5:32; Jos 1:7

23:7
ⁱ Ex 23:13; Ps 16:4; Jer 5:7 ^j Ex 20:5
23:8
^k Dt 10:20
23:9
^l Dt 11:23
^m Dt 7:24
23:10
ⁿ Lev 26:8
^o Ex 14:14; Dt 3:22
23:11
^p Jos 22:5
23:12
^q Dt 7:3 ^r Ex 34:16; Ps 106:34-35
23:13
^s Ex 23:33
^t Nu 33:55

23:14
^u 1Ki 2:2
^v Jos 21:45

---

^a 4 That is, the Mediterranean

Joshua 23:1–16

The events of chapters 23 and 24 probably occurred shortly before Joshua's death at age 110 (24:29). The theme of Joshua's address in chapter 23 was a call for loyalty to the Lord because of all he had done for Israel. The Israelites had been eyewitnesses of God's mighty acts (v. 3; cf. 24:31). Ultimately *he* had defeated and dispossessed the Canaanites. The Israelites had participated in this holy war, but the victory was credited to God alone (cf. Deut. 1:30; 3:22; 20:4).

God's faithfulness to his promises was proof positive that he would "keep" his threats as well. The Israelites weren't to suppose that being the recipients of God's blessings made them immune to his judgment (v. 15). The threat contained in verses 15 and 16 would eventu-

ally be fulfilled in the Assyrian and Babylonian exiles of the northern and southern kingdoms, respectively.

The Hebrew word translated "hold fast" in verse 8 also is used in Genesis 2:24 to describe the intimate and binding relationship between husband and wife. The same term appears several times in Deuteronomy to describe a close relationship between God and his people (4:4; 10:20; 11:22; 13:4). In verse 12, "ally yourselves" translates the same word; the devotion that belongs exclusively to God isn't to be directed to any other.

In spite of occasional lapses, Israel's behavior in the book of Joshua was characterized as holding fast to the Lord (v. 8). What words, phrases, or images might best describe your relationship with God?

given you.[w] [16]If you violate the covenant of the LORD your God, which he commanded you, and go and serve other gods and bow down to them, the LORD's anger will burn against you, and you will quickly perish from the good land he has given you.[x]"

The Covenant Renewed at Shechem

24 Then Joshua assembled all the tribes of Israel at Shechem. He summoned the elders, leaders, judges and officials of Israel,[y] and they presented themselves before God.

[2]Joshua said to all the people, "This is what the LORD, the God of Israel, says: 'Long ago your forefathers, including Terah the father of Abraham and Nahor, lived beyond the River[a] and worshiped other gods.[z] [3]But I took your father Abraham from the land beyond the River and led him throughout Canaan[a] and gave him many descendants.[b] I gave him Isaac,[c] [4]and to Isaac I gave Jacob and Esau.[d] I assigned the hill country of Seir[e] to Esau, but Jacob and his sons went down to Egypt.[f]

[5]"Then I sent Moses and Aaron,[g] and I afflicted the Egyptians by what I did there, and I brought you out. [6]When I brought your fathers out of Egypt, you came to the sea, and the Egyptians pursued them with chariots and horsemen[b][h] as far as the Red Sea.[c] [7]But they cried to the LORD for help, and he put darkness[i] between you and the Egyptians; he brought the sea over them and covered them.[j] You saw with your own eyes what I did to the Egyptians. Then you lived in the desert for a long time.[k]

[8]"'I brought you to the land of the Amorites who lived east of the Jordan. They fought against you, but I gave them into your hands. I destroyed them from before you, and you took possession of their land.[l] [9]When Balak son of Zippor,[m] the king of Moab, prepared to fight against Israel, he sent for Balaam son of Beor to put a curse on you.[n] [10]But I would not listen to Balaam, so he blessed you[o] again and again, and I delivered you out of his hand.

[11]"'Then you crossed the Jordan[p] and came to Jericho.[q] The citizens of Jericho fought against you, as did also the Amorites, Perizzites, Canaanites, Hittites, Girgashites, Hivites and Jebusites, but I gave them into your hands.[r] [12]I sent the hornet[s] ahead of you, which drove them out before you—also the two Amorite kings. You did not do it with your own sword and bow. [13]So I gave you a land on which you did not toil and cities you did not build; and you live in them and eat from vineyards and olive groves that you did not plant.'[t]

[14]"Now fear the LORD and serve him with all faithfulness.[u] Throw away the gods[v] your forefathers worshiped beyond the River and in Egypt,[w] and serve the LORD. [15]But if serving the LORD seems undesirable to you, then choose for yourselves this day whom you will serve, whether the gods your forefathers served beyond the River, or the gods of the Amorites,[x] in whose land you are living. But as for me and my household, we will serve the LORD."[y]

[16]Then the people answered, "Far be it from us to forsake the LORD to serve oth-

---

[a] 2 That is, the Euphrates; also in verses 3, 14 and 15   [b] 6 Or *charioteers*   [c] 6 Hebrew *Yam Suph*; that is, Sea of Reeds

23:15
w Lev 26:17;
Dt 28:15
23:16
x Dt 4:25-26

24:1
y Jos 23:2

24:2
z Ge 11:32
24:3
a Ge 12:1 b Ge 15:5
c Ge 21:3
24:4
d Ge 25:26 e Dt 2:5
f Ge 46:5-6
24:5
g Ex 3:10

24:6
h Ex 14:9
24:7
i Ex 14:20
j Ex 14:28 k Dt 1:46

24:8
l Nu 21:31
24:9
m Nu 22:2
n Nu 22:6
24:10
o Nu 23:11; Dt 23:5
24:11
p Jos 3:16-17
q Jos 6:1
r Ex 23:23; Dt 7:1
24:12
s Ex 23:28; Dt 7:20;
Ps 44:3,6-7

24:13
t Dt 6:10-11
24:14
u Dt 10:12; 18:13;
1Sa 12:24;
2Co 1:12 v ver 23
w Eze 23:3

24:15
x Jdg 6:10; Ru 1:15
y Ru 1:16;
1Ki 18:21

Joshua 24:1–27

The ceremony of covenant renewal is similar to the suzerainty treaties common in the ancient Near East (a suzerain was a feudal lord or overlord). As in those covenants, the past history of how the suzerain (God) had benefited his subjects (Israel) was recounted (vv. 2–13). After stating the stipulations demanded of the subject nation (v. 14), Joshua professed his own commitment—hoping the people would do the same (v. 15).

The fertility cult of the Amorites with its many corrupt and immoral practices held a special appeal to the Israelites, who were settling down to agricultural life after so many years of wandering. Though Joshua instructed the people to "choose for yourselves" (v. 15), he didn't intend to encourage idolatry. The very thought of making a commitment to an idol should have been so abhorrent that they would take a stand against all such worship.

Joshua's statement in verse 19, "You are not able to serve the LORD," is unexpected. After encouraging the Israelites to make a commitment to God, he told them they couldn't keep it. Joshua didn't want to discourage the people but to lead them to count the cost and mean what they said (cf. Luke 14:25–35). In one sense his statement was true: The people were fallen, sinful human beings. They needed New Testament grace. God did give them a measure of grace that allowed them to serve him faithfully for many years (cf. v. 31). What is qualitatively different about the grace we enjoy today?

er gods! [17]It was the LORD our God himself who brought us and our fathers up out of Egypt, from that land of slavery, and performed those great signs before our eyes. He protected us on our entire journey and among all the nations through which we traveled. [18]And the LORD drove out before us all the nations, including the Amorites, who lived in the land. We too will serve the LORD, because he is our God."

[19]Joshua said to the people, "You are not able to serve the LORD. He is a holy God;[z] he is a jealous God.[a] He will not forgive your rebellion[b] and your sins. [20]If you forsake the LORD[c] and serve foreign gods, he will turn[d] and bring disaster on you and make an end of you,[e] after he has been good to you."

[21]But the people said to Joshua, "No! We will serve the LORD."

[22]Then Joshua said, "You are witnesses against yourselves that you have chosen[f] to serve the LORD."

"Yes, we are witnesses," they replied.

[23]"Now then," said Joshua, "throw away the foreign gods[g] that are among you and yield your hearts[h] to the LORD, the God of Israel."

[24]And the people said to Joshua, "We will serve the LORD our God and obey him."[i]

[25]On that day Joshua made a covenant[j] for the people, and there at Shechem he drew up for them decrees and laws.[k] [26]And Joshua recorded these things in the Book of the Law of God.[l] Then he took a large stone[m] and set it up there under the oak near the holy place of the LORD.

[27]"See!" he said to all the people. "This stone will be a witness[n] against us. It has heard all the words the LORD has said to us. It will be a witness against you if you are untrue to your God."

Buried in the Promised Land

[28]Then Joshua sent the people away, each to his own inheritance.

[29]After these things, Joshua son of Nun, the servant of the LORD, died at the age of a hundred and ten.[o] [30]And they buried him in the land of his inheritance, at Timnath Serah[a][p] in the hill country of Ephraim, north of Mount Gaash.

[31]Israel served the LORD throughout the lifetime of Joshua and of the elders[q] who outlived him and who had experienced everything the LORD had done for Israel.

[32]And Joseph's bones, which the Israelites had brought up from Egypt,[r] were buried at Shechem in the tract of land[s] that Jacob bought for a hundred pieces of silver[b] from the sons of Hamor, the father of Shechem. This became the inheritance of Joseph's descendants.

[33]And Eleazar son of Aaron[t] died and was buried at Gibeah, which had been allotted to his son Phinehas[u] in the hill country of Ephraim.

[a] 30 Also known as *Timnath Heres* (see Judges 2:9)   [b] 32 Hebrew *hundred kesitahs*; a kesitah was a unit of money of unknown weight and value.

Marginal references

24:19
z Lev 19:2; 20:26
a Ex 20:5
b Ex 23:21
24:20
c 1Ch 28:9,20
d Ac 7:42
e Jos 23:15
24:22
f Ps 119:30,173

24:23
g ver 14 h 1Ki 8:58;
Ps 119:36; 141:4

24:24
i Ex 19:8; 24:3,7;
Dt 5:27
24:25
j Ex 24:8 k Ex 15:25

24:26
l Dt 31:24
m Ge 28:18

24:27
n Jos 22:27

24:29
o Jdg 2:8
24:30
p Jos 19:50
24:31
q Jdg 2:7

24:32
r Ge 50:25;
Ex 13:19
s Ge 33:19; Jn 4:5;
Ac 7:16

24:33
t Jos 22:13
u Ex 6:25

Joshua 24:28–33

That the people were faithful "throughout the lifetime of Joshua" (v. 31) was eloquent testimony to the power of his influence and the effectiveness of personal experience. The memorials, confessions, and rituals of covenant renewal were designed to keep the people loyal, but they weren't adequate forever. The tragic reality of what happened in the next generation is described in Judges 2:10–15.

These three burials marked both the conclusion of this story and the fact that God had indeed been faithful to establish his people in the promised land. When Joseph gave instructions for his bones to be buried in Canaan, he manifested great faith in God's promises (Gen. 50:24–25; Ex. 13:19; Heb. 11:22). The burial of Joseph's remains symbolized the completion of an era and the fulfillment of God's promises to the patriarchs. When did you last experience the satisfaction of closure regarding some area of your life? Did you see and acknowledge God's hand in it?

INTRODUCTION TO

Judges

AUTHOR
The author of Judges is unknown. Jewish tradition attributes the book to the prophet Samuel, but it may have been written by one of Samuel's associates or by a compiler during the post-exilic period.

DATE WRITTEN
Judges was probably written around 1000 B.C., during the time of the monarchy (see 17:6; 18:1; 19:1; 21:25).

ORIGINAL READERS
Judges was written to the Israelites to recount Israel's history after the conquest of Canaan but prior to the time of its first king.

TIMELINE

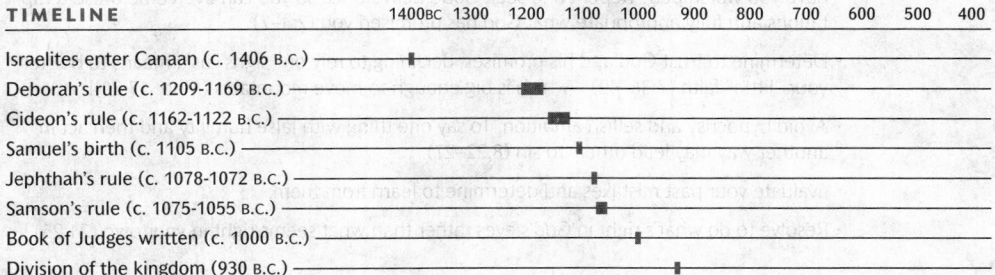

	1400BC	1300	1200	1100	1000	900	800	700	600	500	400
Israelites enter Canaan (c. 1406 B.C.)											
Deborah's rule (c. 1209-1169 B.C.)											
Gideon's rule (c. 1162-1122 B.C.)											
Samuel's birth (c. 1105 B.C.)											
Jephthah's rule (c. 1078-1072 B.C.)											
Samson's rule (c. 1075-1055 B.C.)											
Book of Judges written (c. 1000 B.C.)											
Division of the kingdom (930 B.C.)											

THEMES
Judges describes the life of Israel from the death of Joshua to the rise of the monarchy. The period of the judges was a time of great moral, spiritual, and political confusion and failure. Even so, it was also a time when God demonstrated his continuing love toward his people. Judges contains the following themes:

1. *God's faithfulness.* Through the repeated cycle of disobedience, oppression, repentance, and deliverance (e.g., 2:11–19), Judges portrays God as a God of both judgment and forgive-ness. When the people sinned, they found their lives becoming more and more difficult as God punished them. When they repented, God was quick to send them aid. While Judges en-courages a life of obedience and repentance, other books (like Job and Ecclesiastes) point out that obedience doesn't guarantee a problem-free life.

2. *Compromise.* Judges illustrates that compromise with the world brings disaster. The particu-lar sin of the Israelites at this time was their conformity to the beliefs and cultural practices of the Canaanites (2:11–12; 3:7; 8:33; 10:6,10). The temptation to be like secular society is still powerful today, and Judges reminds its readers to resist the urge to conform to a culture hos-tile to God.

3. *Need for godly leadership.* The period of the judges was a time of political fragmentation. These judges weren't operating throughout Israel but were more or less local leaders, many of whom were far from paragons of virtue. The failures of Israel's leaders—parents (2:6–10), priests (17:1–13), and judges (8:27)—pointed out the importance of godly leadership, which came later in the form of Davidic kingship and ultimately in the kingship of Christ.

FAITH IN ACTION

The pages of Judges contain life lessons and role models of faith—people who challenge believers to put their faith in action.

Role Models

- OTHNIEL (3:7–11) was filled with the Spirit and overpowered Israel's enemy, bringing peace to the land for 40 years. How can God use an ordinary person like you to do great things?

- DEBORAH (4:1—5:31) used her strategic skills, wisdom, and prophetic abilities to lead the Israelites. How can you make use of your God-given gifts to serve God's people?

- GIDEON (6:12) was called by God a "mighty warrior" before he had done anything noteworthy or courageous. He went on with God's help to defeat Israel's enemy with only a handful of men and no weapons (7:1–25). What potential does God see in you that has yet to be displayed?

- SAMSON (13:1—16:31) was used by God and fulfilled God's purposes for his life (Heb. 11:32–34) in spite of moral failures. How can you learn from his example to avoid temptation? How does God's grace to Samson encourage you?

Challenges

- What compromises and alliances have you made with secular society (2:2)? What "idols" have you worshiped? Repent and seek God's deliverance so you can overcome these temptations and fully appropriate what God has promised you (2:4–7).

- Determine to trust God and his promises, declining to rely on "signs" as a means to bolster your "little" faith (7:36–40)—which is big enough to move mountains (Matt. 17:20)!

- Avoid hypocrisy and selfish ambition. To say one thing with false humility and then act in another way may lead others to sin (8:22–27).

- Evaluate your past mistakes and determine to learn from them.

- Resolve to do what's right in God's eyes rather than what seems right in your own (21:25).

OUTLINE

   I. Introduction: Incomplete Conquest and Apostasy (1:1—3:6)
      A. First Episode (1:1—2:5)
      B. Second Episode (2:6—3:6)
  II. Oppression by Enemies and Deliverance by Judges (3:7—16:31)
      A. Othniel (3:7–11)
      B. Ehud and Shamgar (3:12–31)
      C. Deborah (4–5)
      D. Gideon, Tola, and Jair (6:1—10:5)
      E. Jephthah, Ibzan, Elon, and Abdon (10:6—12:15)
      F. Samson (13–16)
 III. Epilogue: Religious and Moral Disorder (17–21)
      A. First Episode (17–18)
      B. Second Episode (19–21)

Israel Fights the Remaining Canaanites

1 After the death[a] of Joshua, the Israelites asked the LORD, "Who will be the first[b] to go up and fight for us against the Canaanites?[c]"

2 The LORD answered, "Judah[d] is to go; I have given the land into their hands.[e]"

3 Then the men of Judah said to the Simeonites their brothers, "Come up with us into the territory allotted to us, to fight against the Canaanites. We in turn will go with you into yours." So the Simeonites[f] went with them.

4 When Judah attacked, the LORD gave the Canaanites and Perizzites[g] into their hands and they struck down ten thousand men at Bezek.[h] 5 It was there that they found Adoni-Bezek and fought against him, putting to rout the Canaanites and Perizzites. 6 Adoni-Bezek fled, but they chased him and caught him, and cut off his thumbs and big toes.

7 Then Adoni-Bezek said, "Seventy kings with their thumbs and big toes cut off have picked up scraps under my table. Now God has paid me back[i] for what I did to them." They brought him to Jerusalem, and he died there.

8 The men of Judah attacked Jerusalem[j] also and took it. They put the city to the sword and set it on fire.

9 After that, the men of Judah went down to fight against the Canaanites living in the hill country,[k] the Negev[l] and the western foothills. 10 They advanced against the Canaanites living in Hebron[m] (formerly called Kiriath Arba[n]) and defeated Sheshai, Ahiman and Talmai.[o]

11 From there they advanced against the people living in Debir[p] (formerly called Kiriath Sepher). 12 And Caleb said, "I will give my daughter Acsah in marriage to the man who attacks and captures Kiriath Sepher." 13 Othniel son of Kenaz, Caleb's younger brother, took it; so Caleb gave his daughter Acsah to him in marriage.

14 One day when she came to Othniel, she urged him[a] to ask her father for a field. When she got off her donkey, Caleb asked her, "What can I do for you?"

15 She replied, "Do me a special favor. Since you have given me land in the Negev, give me also springs of water." Then Caleb gave her the upper and lower springs.

16 The descendants of Moses' father-in-law,[q] the Kenite,[r] went up from the City of Palms[b][s] with the men of Judah to live among the people of the Desert of Judah in the Negev near Arad.[t]

17 Then the men of Judah went with the Simeonites[u] their brothers and attacked the Canaanites living in Zephath, and they totally destroyed[c] the city. Therefore it was called Hormah.[d][v] 18 The men of Judah also took[e] Gaza,[w] Ashkelon and Ekron—each city with its territory.

19 The LORD was with[x] the men of Judah. They took possession of the hill country, but they were unable to drive the people from the plains, because they had iron

---

a 14 Hebrew; Septuagint and Vulgate Othniel, he urged her *b 16 That is, Jericho* *c 17 The Hebrew term refers to the irrevocable giving over of things or persons to the LORD, often by totally destroying them.* *d 17 Hormah means destruction.* *e 18 Hebrew; Septuagint Judah did not take*

Judges 1:1–36

📖 Judges repeats and expands on the story of the Israelites taking possession of the land of Canaan. Readers learn the details to some events only hinted at in Joshua. We see the general success of Judah and the increasing failure of the other tribes in driving out the Canaanites from their territories.

We see in Acsah an image of the ideal woman—a hero's daughter who took the initiative to provide for her husband and children. She had already received from her father land in the arid Negev as a dowry. Now she bolstered its value by obtaining adequate water rights.

📖 Like ancient Israel, Christians are in a covenant with God—a "better" covenant (Heb. 7:22). But its terms—"the law of love" (Rom. 13:10; Gal. 5:14)—still require obedience. Our warfare is spiritual, not physical. It's a battle won or lost by our answer to this question: Are we willing to follow Christ's example in the way we live?

Acsah's story speaks to countless women and girls in the developing world, who spend as much as seven hours daily carrying water for their families. They understand her foresight, as well as the tremendous blessing she received in response—land with a clean, available water supply. Acsah was a woman who wouldn't be denied her full inheritance. She resembles the women of the Gospels, who sought out Jesus and refused to be turned back by the crowds and by Jesus' own disciples. As a result, they found salvation, healing, and blessing for themselves and their families (see Matt. 15:21–28; 26:6–13; Luke 7:36–50; 18:1–5).

1:1
a Jos 24:29
b Nu 27:21
c ver 27; Jdg 3:1-6
1:2
d Ge 49:8 a ver 4; Jdg 3:28
1:3
f ver 17
1:4
g Ge 13:7; Jos 3:10
h 1Sa 11:8
1:7
i Lev 24:19
1:8
j ver 21; Jos 15:63
1:9
k Nu 13:17
l Nu 21:1
1:10
m Ge 13:18
n Ge 35:27
o Jos 15:14
1:11
p Jos 15:15
1:16
q Nu 10:29
r Ge 15:19; Jdg 4:11 s Dt 34:3; Jdg 3:13 t Nu 21:1
1:17
u ver 3 v Nu 21:3
1:18
w Jos 11:22
1:19
x ver 2

1:19
y Jos 17:16
1:20
z Jos 14:9; 15:13-14
a ver 10; Jos 14:13
1:21
b Jos 15:63 c ver 8

1:23
d Ge 28:19

1:24
e Jos 2:12,14
1:25
f Jos 6:25

1:27
g Jos 17:11 h ver 1

1:29
i 1Ki 9:16
j Jos 16:10

1:31
k Jdg 10:6

1:33
l Jos 19:38

1:34
m Ex 3:17

1:35
n Jos 19:42

1:36
o Jos 15:3

2:1
p Jdg 6:11 q ver 5
r Ex 20:2 s Ge 17:8
t Lev 26:42-44;
Dt 7:9
2:2
u Ex 23:32; 34:12;
Dt 7:2 v Ex 34:13

2:3
w Jos 23:13
x Nu 33:55
y Dt 7:16; Jdg 3:6;
Ps 106:36

chariots.[y] [20]As Moses had promised, Hebron[z] was given to Caleb, who drove from it the three sons of Anak.[a] [21]The Benjamites, however, failed[b] to dislodge the Jebusites, who were living in Jerusalem;[c] to this day the Jebusites live there with the Benjamites.

[22]Now the house of Joseph attacked Bethel, and the LORD was with them. [23]When they sent men to spy out Bethel (formerly called Luz),[d] [24]the spies saw a man coming out of the city and they said to him, "Show us how to get into the city and we will see that you are treated well.[e]" [25]So he showed them, and they put the city to the sword but spared[f] the man and his whole family. [26]He then went to the land of the Hittites, where he built a city and called it Luz, which is its name to this day.

[27]But Manasseh did not drive out the people of Beth Shan or Taanach or Dor or Ibleam[g] or Megiddo and their surrounding settlements, for the Canaanites[h] were determined to live in that land. [28]When Israel became strong, they pressed the Canaanites into forced labor but never drove them out completely. [29]Nor did Ephraim drive out the Canaanites living in Gezer,[i] but the Canaanites continued to live there among them.[j] [30]Neither did Zebulun drive out the Canaanites living in Kitron or Nahalol, who remained among them; but they did subject them to forced labor. [31]Nor did Asher drive out those living in Acco or Sidon or Ahlab or Aczib[k] or Helbah or Aphek or Rehob, [32]and because of this the people of Asher lived among the Canaanite inhabitants of the land. [33]Neither did Naphtali drive out those living in Beth Shemesh or Beth Anath[l]; but the Naphtalites too lived among the Canaanite inhabitants of the land, and those living in Beth Shemesh and Beth Anath became forced laborers for them. [34]The Amorites[m] confined the Danites to the hill country, not allowing them to come down into the plain. [35]And the Amorites were determined also to hold out in Mount Heres, Aijalon[n] and Shaalbim, but when the power of the house of Joseph increased, they too were pressed into forced labor. [36]The boundary of the Amorites was from Scorpion[a] Pass[o] to Sela and beyond.

The Angel of the LORD at Bokim

2 The angel of the LORD[p] went up from Gilgal to Bokim[q] and said, "I brought you up out of Egypt[r] and led you into the land that I swore to give to your forefathers.[s] I said, 'I will never break my covenant with you,[t] [2]and you shall not make a covenant with the people of this land,[u] but you shall break down their altars.'[v] Yet you have disobeyed me. Why have you done this? [3]Now therefore I tell you that I will not drive them out before you;[w] they will be ⌊thorns⌋[x] in your sides and their gods will be a snare[y] to you."

[4]When the angel of the LORD had spoken these things to all the Israelites, the people wept aloud, [5]and they called that place Bokim.[b] There they offered sacrifices to the LORD.

Disobedience and Defeat

[6]After Joshua had dismissed the Israelites, they went to take possession of the

---

a 36 Hebrew *Akrabbim*   b 5 *Bokim* means *weepers.*

Judges 2:1–5

📖 The Israelites weren't judged for failing to remove all the Canaanites but for entering into covenant (treaty) with them. Complete occupation of the land would have occurred quickly had they fulfilled their obligations to God. The question at the end of verse 2 might be paraphrased "What in the world have you done?"

📖 God wasn't as concerned with the elimination of *Canaanite culture* as with the *rejection of Canaanite religion.* Most people assume that a modern secular society doesn't have idols, when in reality they are woven into the fabric of our culture. How often have we compromised and forgotten the apostle John's admonition not

to "love the world or anything in the world" (1 Jn. 2:15)? Judges 1:1—2:5 warns us of the dangers of failing to trust in God's Word or follow his instructions. Are you listening?

Judges 2:6—3:6

📖 Any distinct ethnicity of the Israelites is almost impossible to determine from archaeological records from the period 1200–1000 B.C. They intermarried with the Canaanites and served their gods. In religious and social matters, most were indistinguishable from their neighbors.

Judges 2:11–19 introduces the repeating, downward spiral of history that characterizes the book. There were

land, each to his own inheritance. 7The people served the LORD throughout the lifetime of Joshua and of the elders who outlived him and who had seen all the great things the LORD had done for Israel.

8Joshua son of Nun, the servant of the LORD, died at the age of a hundred and ten. 9And they buried him in the land of his inheritance, at Timnath Heres[a][z] in the hill country of Ephraim, north of Mount Gaash.

10After that whole generation had been gathered to their fathers, another generation grew up, who knew neither the LORD nor what he had done for Israel.[a] 11Then the Israelites did evil in the eyes of the LORD[b] and served the Baals.[c] 12They forsook the LORD, the God of their fathers, who had brought them out of Egypt. They followed and worshiped various gods[d] of the peoples around them.[e] They provoked the LORD to anger 13because they forsook him and served Baal and the Ashtoreths.[f] 14In his anger[g] against Israel the LORD handed them over[h] to raiders who plundered them. He sold them[i] to their enemies all around, whom they were no longer able to resist.[j] 15Whenever Israel went out to fight, the hand of the LORD was against them to defeat them, just as he had sworn to them. They were in great distress.

16Then the LORD raised up judges,[b][k] who saved[l] them out of the hands of these raiders. 17Yet they would not listen to their judges but prostituted[m] themselves to other gods and worshiped them. Unlike their fathers, they quickly turned from the way in which their fathers had walked, the way of obedience to the LORD's commands.[n] 18Whenever the LORD raised up a judge for them, he was with the judge and saved them out of the hands of their enemies as long as the judge lived; for the LORD had compassion[o] on them as they groaned[p] under those who oppressed and afflicted them. 19But when the judge died, the people returned to ways even more corrupt[q] than those of their fathers, following other gods and serving and worshiping them.[r] They refused to give up their evil practices and stubborn ways.

20Therefore the LORD was very angry[s] with Israel and said, "Because this nation has violated the covenant that I laid down for their forefathers and has not listened to me, 21I will no longer drive out[t] before them any of the nations Joshua left when he died. 22I will use them to test[u] Israel and see whether they will keep the way of the LORD and walk in it as their forefathers did." 23The LORD had allowed those nations to remain; he did not drive them out at once by giving them into the hands of Joshua.

3 These are the nations the LORD left to test[v] all those Israelites who had not experienced any of the wars in Canaan 2(he did this only to teach warfare to the descendants of the Israelites who had not had previous battle experience): 3the five[w] rulers of the Philistines, all the Canaanites, the Sidonians, and the Hivites living in the Lebanon mountains from Mount Baal Hermon to Lebo[c] Hamath. 4They were left to test[x] the Israelites to see whether they would obey the LORD's commands, which he had given their forefathers through Moses.

5The Israelites lived[y] among the Canaanites, Hittites, Amorites, Perizzites, Hivites and Jebusites. 6They took their daughters in marriage and gave their own daughters to their sons, and served their gods.[z]

Othniel

7The Israelites did evil in the eyes of the LORD; they forgot the LORD[a] their God

---

[a] 9 Also known as *Timnath Serah* (see Joshua 19:50 and 24:30)   [b] 16 Or *leaders*; similarly in verses 17-19   [c] 3 Or *to the entrance to*

2:9
z Jos 19:50

2:10
a Ex 5:2; 1Sa 2:12; 1Ch 28:9; Gal 4:8
2:11
b Jdg 3:12; 4:1; 6:1; 10:6 c Jdg 3:7; 8:33
2:12
d Ps 106:36
e Dt 31:16; Jdg 10:6
2:13
f Jdg 10:6
2:14
g Dt 31:17
h Ps 106:41
i Dt 32:30; Jdg 3:8
j Dt 28:25
2:16
k Ac 13:20
l Ps 106:43
2:17
m Ex 34:15 n ver 7

2:18
o Dt 32:36; Jos 1:5
p Ps 106:44
2:19
q Jdg 3:12
r Jdg 4:1; 8:33

2:20
s ver 14; Jos 23:16
2:21
t Jos 23:13
2:22
u Dt 8:2,16; Jdg 3:1,14

3:1
v Jdg 2:21-22

3:3
w Jos 13:3

3:4
x Dt 8:2; Jdg 2:22

3:5
y Ps 106:35

3:6
z Ex 34:16; Dt 7:3-4

3:7
a Dt 4:9

---

three distinct and repeated stages: Israel's apostasy (abandonment of the faith); God's anger and Israel's resulting punishment (the nations wouldn't be driven out but would stay to frustrate and torment God's people); and his compassion, evidenced by his raising up of judges.

It isn't surprising that God became angry with the Israelites, but his anger isn't unrighteous like ours can be. It's always consistent with his character and at-tributes—and it's his just response to spiritual unfaithfulness. His constant desire is to bring repentance, not to punish.

The two-pronged statement that the people "knew neither the LORD nor what he had done for Israel" (2:10) raises questions for us as followers of Christ to consider. Do you really know the Lord? How well are you acquainted with the Bible and God's revelation of himself through its pages?

3:7
b Ex 34:13;
Jdg 2:11,13
3:8
c Jdg 2:14
3:9
d ver 15; Jdg 6:6,7;
10:10; Ps 106:44
e Jdg 1:13
3:10
f Nu 11:25,29;
24:2; Jdg 6:34;
11:29; 13:25; 14:6,
19; 1Sa 11:6

3:12
g Jdg 2:11,14
h 1Sa 12:9

3:13
i Jdg 1:16

3:15
j ver 9; Ps 78:34;
107:13

3:17
k ver 12

and served the Baals and the Asherahs.[b] [8]The anger of the LORD burned against Israel so that he sold[c] them into the hands of Cushan-Rishathaim king of Aram Naharaim,[a] to whom the Israelites were subject for eight years. [9]But when they cried out[d] to the LORD, he raised up for them a deliverer, Othniel[e] son of Kenaz, Caleb's younger brother, who saved them. [10]The Spirit of the LORD came upon him,[f] so that he became Israel's judge[b] and went to war. The LORD gave Cushan-Rishathaim king of Aram into the hands of Othniel, who overpowered him. [11]So the land had peace for forty years, until Othniel son of Kenaz died.

Ehud

[12]Once again the Israelites did evil in the eyes of the LORD,[g] and because they did this evil the LORD gave Eglon king of Moab[h] power over Israel. [13]Getting the Ammonites and Amalekites to join him, Eglon came and attacked Israel, and they took possession of the City of Palms.[c] [i] [14]The Israelites were subject to Eglon king of Moab for eighteen years.

[15]Again the Israelites cried out to the LORD, and he gave them a deliverer[j]—Ehud, a left-handed man, the son of Gera the Benjamite. The Israelites sent him with tribute to Eglon king of Moab. [16]Now Ehud had made a double-edged sword about a foot and a half[d] long, which he strapped to his right thigh under his clothing. [17]He presented the tribute to Eglon king of Moab, who was a very fat man.[k] [18]After Ehud had presented the tribute, he sent on their way the men who had carried it. [19]At the idols[e] near Gilgal he himself turned back and said, "I have a secret message for you, O king."

The king said, "Quiet!" And all his attendants left him.

[20]Ehud then approached him while he was sitting alone in the upper room of his summer palace[f] and said, "I have a message from God for you." As the king rose from his seat, [21]Ehud reached with his left hand, drew the sword from his right thigh and plunged it into the king's belly. [22]Even the handle sank in after the blade, which came out his back. Ehud did not pull the sword out, and the fat closed

---

a 8 That is, Northwest Mesopotamia   b 10 Or *leader*   c 13 That is, Jericho   d 16 Hebrew *a cubit*
(about 0.5 meter)   e 19 Or *the stone quarries*; also in verse 26   f 20 The meaning of the Hebrew
for this phrase is uncertain.

Judges 3:7–11

🔗 The gods Baal and Asherah were part of a fertility religion. Worshipers were concerned with success and materialism: securing for themselves a large family, ample flocks and herds, and abundant crops. At the heart of this idolatry was the idea that the deity magically took up residence within the manmade idol. Idols were produced using precise methods and specific materials to ensure that this "magic indwelling" would take place.

In a world with a scarcity of godly role models, Othniel served as a breath of fresh air: (1) He married a godly woman (1:13). (2) As a Kenizzite, he overcame a non-Israelite background that might have been considered limiting. (3) Othniel prevailed over a prime example of the worst of Israel's oppressors (Cushan-Rishathaim probably meant "doubly wicked Cushan"). (4) He performed this deliverance in tandem with God.

📖 Scripture provides numerous examples of men and women who walked with God, but Othniel stands out because of his simplicity. This first account of Israel's judges is brief, including no dialogue or dramatization—and no description of character flaws. Background should never hinder our service to Christ. No matter what our human limitations, we can be faithful to God's calling in our lives. Have you bought into the deception that your background predetermines your effectiveness for God?

Judges 3:12–30

🔗 Ehud, the left-handed hero, was ironically a Benjamite ("son of the right hand"). Left-handedness was common in this tribe (see 20:16; cf. 1 Chron. 12:2) and may have been artificially induced by binding the right arms of young boys to produce superior warriors. Ehud's left-handedness explains how he smuggled in his dagger. The palace guards would likely have checked only his left side for weapons.

Ehud resorted to a complex process of deception to accomplish his task of deliverance. As we go deeper into the cycles of judges, we see the heroes demonstrating an intensifying mixture of good and bad qualities. The Ehud story introduces a tension that will tighten as the book of Judges proceeds—between the character and actions of the judge and God's presumed involvement or approval.

📖 Christian warfare is spiritual, and following Christ's example in faith is our only hope of victory. We are not asked to fashion our own daggers as Ehud did (cf. 2 Cor. 10:3–4), but we are called to engage the world with a better weapon, already supplied for us—the sword of the Spirit, the Word of God (Eph. 6:17). Are you practiced in wielding this sword (cf. 2 Tim. 2:15)?

in over it. 23Then Ehud went out to the porch[a]; he shut the doors of the upper room behind him and locked them.

24After he had gone, the servants came and found the doors of the upper room locked. They said, "He must be relieving himself[l] in the inner room of the house." 25They waited to the point of embarrassment,[m] but when he did not open the doors of the room, they took a key and unlocked them. There they saw their lord fallen to the floor, dead.

26While they waited, Ehud got away. He passed by the idols and escaped to Seirah. 27When he arrived there, he blew a trumpet[n] in the hill country of Ephraim, and the Israelites went down with him from the hills, with him leading them. 28"Follow me," he ordered, "for the LORD has given Moab, your enemy, into your hands.[o]" So they followed him down and, taking possession of the fords of the Jordan[p] that led to Moab, they allowed no one to cross over. 29At that time they struck down about ten thousand Moabites, all vigorous and strong; not a man escaped. 30That day Moab was made subject to Israel, and the land had peace[q] for eighty years.

Shamgar

31After Ehud came Shamgar son of Anath,[r] who struck down six hundred[s] Philistines with an oxgoad. He too saved Israel.

Deborah

4 After Ehud died, the Israelites once again did evil[t] in the eyes of the LORD. 2So the LORD sold them into the hands of Jabin, a king of Canaan, who reigned in Hazor.[u] The commander of his army was Sisera,[v] who lived in Harosheth Haggoyim. 3Because he had nine hundred iron chariots[w] and had cruelly oppressed[x] the Israelites for twenty years, they cried to the LORD for help.

4Deborah, a prophetess, the wife of Lappidoth, was leading[b] Israel at that time. 5She held court under the Palm of Deborah between Ramah and Bethel[y] in the hill country of Ephraim, and the Israelites came to her to have their disputes decided. 6She sent for Barak son of Abinoam[z] from Kedesh in Naphtali and said to him, "The LORD, the God of Israel, commands you: 'Go, take with you ten thousand men of Naphtali and Zebulun and lead the way to Mount Tabor. 7I will lure Sisera, the

---

[a] 23 The meaning of the Hebrew for this word is uncertain.   [b] 4 Traditionally judging

Cross references
3:24 l 1Sa 24:3
3:25 m 2Ki 2:17; 8:11
3:27 n Jdg 6:34; 1Sa 13:3
3:28 o Jos 7:9,15 p Jos 2:7; Jdg 7:24; 12:5
3:30 q ver 11
3:31 r Jdg 5:6 s Jos 23:10
4:1 t Jdg 2:19
4:2 u Jos 11:1 v ver 13, 16; 1Sa 12:9; Ps 83:9
4:3 w Jdg 1:19 x Ps 106:42
4:5 y Ge 35:8
4:6 z Heb 11:32

Judges 3:31

This brief account introduces the first minor judge (cf. 10:1–5; 12:8–15). In the tradition of Ehud, Shamgar delivered Israel through a single-handed act, this time with an agricultural tool, an oxgoad (similar to a modern-day cattle prod). Again the enemy wasn't just defeated but made to look ridiculous. "Oxgoad" literally means "an instrument of learning." To be sure, Shamgar "taught" the Philistines a thing or two. It's clear that Shamgar—again a non-Israelite—saved the day.

The minor judges, like their "major" counterparts, evidenced a spiritual and moral degeneration—with later leaders being worse than earlier ones. Shamgar, like Othniel (a major judge), was the first in a chain. He's presented in a positive light, but the character of future minor judges would continue to deteriorate. As a Christian disciple, how carefully do you consider the influence of your attitudes and actions on younger generations who may be watching you?

Judges 4:1–24

Deborah wasn't what, or who, we would have expected. A woman in a man's world, she pronounced legal decisions, governed Israel, and stood as God's mes-

senger, through whom he issued his call to General Barak. Deborah anticipated Barak's reluctance to follow her instructions. He apparently took her words ("This is the day the LORD has given Sisera into your hands") literally, vainly pursuing Sisera to the end. But neither Sisera nor Barak would control the outcome. Another woman, Jael, conquered both. In this round, God's choice fell not on an Israelite woman, but on "Jael, the wife of Heber the Kenite."

The cast of characters: two men and two women. In both cases the men lost out when they made demands on the women. Throughout the Bible we see counter-cultural examples of God using women in amazing ways. Women may be encouraged today as they seek to determine where they fit in God's plan.

Ultimately God was the One raising generals, deploying armies, dictating strategy, and effecting victory. This passage encourages us to see his sovereignty—in the world and in our lives. Whether in his discipline, deliverance, provision, or guidance with our decision-making, God is continuously at work bringing his plan to fulfillment. What comfort does this afford you in your day-to-day living?

4:7
a Ps 83:9

4:9
b ver 21; Jdg 2:14
4:10
c ver 14;
Jdg 5:15,18
4:11
d Jdg 1:16
e Nu 10:29
f Jos 19:33

4:13
g ver 3

4:14
h Dt 9:3; 2Sa 5:24;
Ps 68:7
4:15
i Jos 10:10;
Ps 83:9-10
4:16
j Ps 83:9

4:19
k Jdg 5:25

4:21
l Jdg 5:26

4:23
m Ne 9:24;
Ps 18:47

commander of Jabin's army, with his chariots and his troops to the Kishon River[a] and give him into your hands.' "

⁸Barak said to her, "If you go with me, I will go; but if you don't go with me, I won't go."

⁹"Very well," Deborah said, "I will go with you. But because of the way you are going about this,[a] the honor will not be yours, for the LORD will hand Sisera over to a woman." So Deborah went with Barak to Kedesh,[b] ¹⁰where he summoned[c] Zebulun and Naphtali. Ten thousand men followed him, and Deborah also went with him.

¹¹Now Heber the Kenite had left the other Kenites,[d] the descendants of Hobab,[e] Moses' brother-in-law,[b] and pitched his tent by the great tree in Zaanannim[f] near Kedesh.

¹²When they told Sisera that Barak son of Abinoam had gone up to Mount Tabor, ¹³Sisera gathered together his nine hundred iron chariots[g] and all the men with him, from Harosheth Haggoyim to the Kishon River.

¹⁴Then Deborah said to Barak, "Go! This is the day the LORD has given Sisera into your hands. Has not the LORD gone ahead[h] of you?" So Barak went down Mount Tabor, followed by ten thousand men. ¹⁵At Barak's advance, the LORD routed[i] Sisera and all his chariots and army by the sword, and Sisera abandoned his chariot and fled on foot. ¹⁶But Barak pursued the chariots and army as far as Harosheth Haggoyim. All the troops of Sisera fell by the sword; not a man was left.[j]

¹⁷Sisera, however, fled on foot to the tent of Jael, the wife of Heber the Kenite, because there were friendly relations between Jabin king of Hazor and the clan of Heber the Kenite.

¹⁸Jael went out to meet Sisera and said to him, "Come, my lord, come right in. Don't be afraid." So he entered her tent, and she put a covering over him.

¹⁹"I'm thirsty," he said. "Please give me some water." She opened a skin of milk,[k] gave him a drink, and covered him up.

²⁰"Stand in the doorway of the tent," he told her. "If someone comes by and asks you, 'Is anyone here?' say 'No.' "

²¹But Jael, Heber's wife, picked up a tent peg and a hammer and went quietly to him while he lay fast asleep, exhausted. She drove the peg through his temple into the ground, and he died.[l]

²²Barak came by in pursuit of Sisera, and Jael went out to meet him. "Come," she said, "I will show you the man you're looking for." So he went in with her, and there lay Sisera with the tent peg through his temple—dead.

²³On that day God subdued[m] Jabin, the Canaanite king, before the Israelites. ²⁴And the hand of the Israelites grew stronger and stronger against Jabin, the Canaanite king, until they destroyed him.

a 9 Or *But on the expedition you are undertaking*   b 11 Or *father-in-law*

4:4–5

Women in the Military

Deborah was a prophetess who led Israel to military victories over her enemies. Along with another woman, Jael (Judg. 4:17–23), she won victories that secured the central and northern portions of the promised land against the Canaanites. In Israel today both genders are eligible for military service, but exemptions are granted. How unusual is it today to have women in the armed forces?

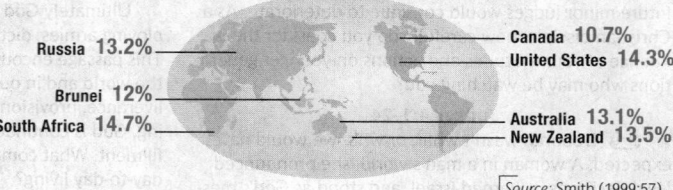

Countries whose total armed forces are comprised of over 10% women:

Russia 13.2%

Brunei 12%

South Africa 14.7%

Canada 10.7%

United States 14.3%

Australia 13.1%

New Zealand 13.5%

Source: Smith (1999:57)

The Song of Deborah

5 On that day Deborah and Barak son of Abinoam sang this song: [n]

2 "When the princes in Israel take the lead,
    when the people willingly offer[o] themselves—
    praise the LORD![p]

3 "Hear this, you kings! Listen, you rulers!
    I will sing to[a] the LORD, I will sing;
    I will make music to[b] the LORD, the God of Israel.[q]

4 "O LORD, when you went out from Seir,[r]
    when you marched from the land of Edom,
the earth shook, the heavens poured,
    the clouds poured down water.[s]
5 The mountains quaked[t] before the LORD, the One of Sinai,
    before the LORD, the God of Israel.

6 "In the days of Shamgar son of Anath,[u]
    in the days of Jael,[v] the roads[w] were abandoned;
    travelers took to winding paths.
7 Village life[c] in Israel ceased,
    ceased until I,[d] Deborah, arose,
    arose a mother in Israel.
8 When they chose new gods,[x]
    war came to the city gates,
and not a shield or spear was seen
    among forty thousand in Israel.
9 My heart is with Israel's princes,
    with the willing volunteers[y] among the people.
    Praise the LORD!

10 "You who ride on white donkeys,[z]
    sitting on your saddle blankets,
    and you who walk along the road,
consider 11 the voice of the singers[e] at the watering places.
    They recite the righteous acts[a] of the LORD,
    the righteous acts of his warriors[f] in Israel.

"Then the people of the LORD
    went down to the city gates.[b]
12 'Wake up,[c] wake up, Deborah!
    Wake up, wake up, break out in song!
Arise, O Barak!
    Take captive your captives,[d] O son of Abinoam.'

[a] 3 Or *of* [b] 3 Or */ with song I will praise* [c] 7 Or *Warriors* [d] 7 Or *you* [e] 11 Or *archers*; the meaning of the Hebrew for this word is uncertain. [f] 11 Or *villagers*

5:1 [n] Ex 15:1
5:2 [o] 2Ch 17:16; Ps 110:3 [p] ver 9
5:3 [q] Ps 27:6
5:4 [r] Dt 33:2 [s] Ps 68:8
5:5 [t] Ex 19:18; Ps 68:8; 97:5; Isa 64:3
5:6 [u] Jdg 3:31 [v] Jdg 4:17 [w] Isa 33:8
5:8 [x] Dt 32:17
5:9 [y] ver 2
5:10 [z] Jdg 10:4; 12:14
5:11 [a] 1Sa 12:7; Mic 6:5 [b] ver 8
5:12 [c] Ps 57:8 [d] Ps 68:18; Eph 4:8

Judges 5:1–31

Chapter 5 retells the story of chapter 4 in poetic form—a common technique in the ancient Near East. Chapter 4 is a logical account with a carefully constructed point. Chapter 5, a song, presents an emotional, figurative version with special themes. Its purpose was to acknowledge and praise God and those who participated in the battle.

The Song of Deborah emphasizes the positive involvement of some of the tribes and of Jael. The negative evaluation of the non-participating tribes comments on God's outlook and expectations for his people. The non-partici-

pants were guilty of indirect support of God's enemies.

The Lord calls for his people—across all time periods—to participate in his kingdom's advancement. When God wants to use us, he expects us to be willing, no matter how inadequate we might feel. When Christians fail to trust him in these situations, they lose out on the opportunity for him to work through them. We may find ourselves expending time and energy hopelessly trying to make up the difference—wanting up-front guarantees of success. But God has already given us assurance in his Word; he wants our participation in accomplishing *his* plan. How willing are you?

13 "Then the men who were left
    came down to the nobles;
 the people of the LORD
    came to me with the mighty.

5:14
e Jdg 3:13

14 Some came from Ephraim, whose roots were in Amalek; e
    Benjamin was with the people who followed you.
 From Makir captains came down,
    from Zebulun those who bear a commander's staff.

5:15
f Jdg 4:10

15 The princes of Issachar were with Deborah; f
    yes, Issachar was with Barak,
    rushing after him into the valley.
 In the districts of Reuben
    there was much searching of heart.

5:16
g Nu 32:1

16 Why did you stay among the campfires a
    to hear the whistling for the flocks? g
 In the districts of Reuben
    there was much searching of heart.

5:17
h Jos 19:29

17 Gilead stayed beyond the Jordan.
    And Dan, why did he linger by the ships?
 Asher remained on the coast h
    and stayed in his coves.

5:18
i Jdg 4:6,10

18 The people of Zebulun risked their very lives;
    so did Naphtali on the heights of the field. i

5:19
j Jos 11:5; Jdg 4:13
k Jdg 1:27 l ver 30

19 "Kings came j, they fought;
    the kings of Canaan fought
 at Taanach by the waters of Megiddo, k
    but they carried off no silver, no plunder. l

5:20
m Jos 10:11

20 From the heavens m the stars fought,
    from their courses they fought against Sisera.

5:21
n Jdg 4:7

21 The river Kishon n swept them away,
    the age-old river, the river Kishon.
    March on, my soul; be strong!

22 Then thundered the horses' hoofs—
    galloping, galloping go his mighty steeds.

23 'Curse Meroz,' said the angel of the LORD.
    'Curse its people bitterly,
 because they did not come to help the LORD,
    to help the LORD against the mighty.'

5:24
o Jdg 4:17

24 "Most blessed of women be Jael, o
    the wife of Heber the Kenite,
    most blessed of tent-dwelling women.

5:25
p Jdg 4:19

25 He asked for water, and she gave him milk; p
    in a bowl fit for nobles she brought him curdled milk.

26 Her hand reached for the tent peg,
    her right hand for the workman's hammer.

5:26
q Jdg 4:21

 She struck Sisera, she crushed his head,
    she shattered and pierced his temple. q

27 At her feet he sank,
    he fell; there he lay.
 At her feet he sank, he fell;
    where he sank, there he fell—dead.

5:28
r Pr 7:6

28 "Through the window peered Sisera's mother;
    behind the lattice she cried out, r
 'Why is his chariot so long in coming?

a 16 Or saddlebags

Why is the clatter of his chariots delayed?'
²⁹ The wisest of her ladies answer her;
indeed, she keeps saying to herself,
³⁰ 'Are they not finding and dividing the spoils: ^s
a girl or two for each man,
colorful garments as plunder for Sisera,
colorful garments embroidered,
highly embroidered garments for my neck—
all this as plunder?'

³¹ "So may all your enemies perish, O Lord!
But may they who love you be like the sun ^t
when it rises in its strength."

Then the land had peace ^u forty years.

Gideon

6 Again the Israelites did evil in the eyes of the Lord, ^v and for seven years he gave them into the hands of the Midianites. ^w ² Because the power of Midian was so oppressive, ^x the Israelites prepared shelters for themselves in mountain clefts, caves and strongholds. ^y ³ Whenever the Israelites planted their crops, the Midianites, Amalekites ^z and other eastern peoples invaded the country. ⁴ They camped on the land and ruined the crops ^a all the way to Gaza and did not spare a living thing for Israel, neither sheep nor cattle nor donkeys. ⁵ They came up with their livestock and their tents like swarms of locusts. ^b It was impossible to count the men and their

5:30
s Ex 15:9; 1Sa 30:24

5:31
t 2Sa 23:4; Ps 19:4; 89:36 u Jdg 3:11

6:1
v Jdg 2:11
w Nu 25:15-18; 31:1-3
6:2
x 1Sa 13:6; Isa 8:21
y Heb 11:38
6:3
z Jdg 3:13
6:4
a Lev 26:16; Dt 28:30,51

6:5
b Jdg 7:12

Judges 6:1–40

 God picked a panicked, cowering Gideon to lead his people out of Midianite oppression. But this reluctant appointee rebutted the angel messenger, throwing objections in God's face. After asking for a sign confirming that the message really was from God, Gideon received his first assurance. In a moment of temporary inspiration, he built an altar to the Lord.

Snapshots

5:24–25

Milk Money

Doxer, age twelve, squats behind the family cow as he milks it. His father, Aggrey, holds out a basin of elephant grass to divert the animal. Even so, the angry calf struggles to break lose from the post to which it's tied. Doxer works on, unfazed.

"This morning we have got five liters. In the evening we might get about the same," estimates Doxer, a round boy. He hands the milk to his mother, Anna, who will keep three liters for breakfast tea and sell the rest.

Not everybody in Kamwezi village, Uganda, enjoys milk tea. Few have cows. But a Christian organization provided 17 heifers to 17 families. The animals have multiplied to 31. When a cow produces her first calf, it's passed along to another beneficiary.

These families are experiencing a higher standard of living. With milk revenue they can purchase commodities like paraffin, soap, sugar, salt, rice, and fish.

Aggrey observes solemnly: "We experience famine in Kamwezi often. If you don't have money to buy food, you starve."

"From milk we pay tuition fees and buy exercise books, uniforms, and pens for the children. We want them to get a good education," Anna adds.

> **"W**e experience famine in Kamwezi often. If you don't have money to buy food, you starve."

camels;[c] they invaded the land to ravage it. [6]Midian so impoverished the Israelites that they cried out[d] to the LORD for help.

[7]When the Israelites cried to the LORD because of Midian, [8]he sent them a prophet, who said, "This is what the LORD, the God of Israel, says: I brought you up out of Egypt,[e] out of the land of slavery. [9]I snatched you from the power of Egypt and from the hand of all your oppressors. I drove them from before you and gave you their land.[f] [10]I said to you, 'I am the LORD your God; do not worship[g] the gods of the Amorites,[h] in whose land you live.' But you have not listened to me."

[11]The angel of the LORD[i] came and sat down under the oak in Ophrah that belonged to Joash the Abiezrite,[j] where his son Gideon[k] was threshing wheat in a winepress to keep it from the Midianites. [12]When the angel of the LORD appeared to Gideon, he said, "The LORD is with you,[l] mighty warrior."

[13]"But sir," Gideon replied, "if the LORD is with us, why has all this happened to us? Where are all his wonders that our fathers told[m] us about when they said, 'Did not the LORD bring us up out of Egypt?' But now the LORD has abandoned[n] us and put us into the hand of Midian."

[14]The LORD turned to him and said, "Go in the strength you have[o] and save Israel out of Midian's hand. Am I not sending you?"

[15]"But Lord,[a]" Gideon asked, "how can I save Israel? My clan is the weakest in Manasseh, and I am the least in my family.[p]"

[16]The LORD answered, "I will be with you[q], and you will strike down all the Midianites together."

[17]Gideon replied, "If now I have found favor in your eyes, give me a sign[r] that it is really you talking to me. [18]Please do not go away until I come back and bring my offering and set it before you."

And the LORD said, "I will wait until you return."

[19]Gideon went in, prepared a young goat, and from an ephah[b] of flour he made bread without yeast. Putting the meat in a basket and its broth in a pot, he brought them out and offered them to him under the oak.[s]

---

[a] 15 Or sir   [b] 19 That is, probably about 3/5 bushel (about 22 liters)

Side references
6:5 c Jdg 8:10
6:6 d Jdg 3:9
6:8 e Jdg 2:1
6:9 f Ps 44:2
6:10 g 2Ki 17:35 h Jer 10:2
6:11 i Ge 16:7 j Jos 17:2 k Heb 11:32
6:12 l Jos 1:5; Jdg 13:3; Lk 1:11,28
6:13 m Ps 44:1 n 2Ch 15:2
6:14 o Heb 11:34
6:15 p Ex 3:11; 1Sa 9:21
6:16 q Ex 3:12; Jos 1:5
6:17 r ver 36-37; Ge 24:14; Isa 38:7-8
6:19 s Ge 18:7-8

Gideon's problems lay in his lack of knowledge of God's word (he and his family had added Baal and Asherah worship to their worship of the Lord), his inaccurate perception of God's involvement in Israel's life, his hesitancy to serve, and his lack of faith. Gideon, who should already have been convinced, begged for and received two more "signs." Those who see this as a "how to" passage for determining God's will misapply Scripture: God isn't obligated to respond to requests based on unbelief. If he does, it's only by his grace.

Christians may still offer objections when God calls them to do something. We crave rock-solid assurances of success. How often, despite a clear signal, don't we still doubt, coming up with yet another reason to hold back? Ask yourself: How many "signs" do I need before I will trust God? Has waiting for the "next" (or a "clearer") one become an excuse for you to sit back and ignore his call?

It's difficult, if not impossible, to have faith in someone you hardly know. Gideon's ignorance and misconceptions about the Lord had a lot to do with his inability to trust him. If we don't take in God's Word, if it doesn't become part of who we are, we will likely demonstrate the same unbelief and stubbornness Gideon did.

6:14

Gideons Bibles

Gideon defeated a superior force of Midianites with only 300 men. It's no wonder his name was chosen to represent an effort to make God's Word available to all travelers stopping over in hotel rooms.

Source: Gideons International (www.gideons.org)

When? Founded by three traveling Wisconsin salesmen in 1899

What? Place Bibles in hotel rooms bedside table drawers

Who? Gideons International has 235,000 members.

How many? Distributes more than 60 million Scriptures each year

Where? Active in more than 175 countries around the world

Statistic: Somewhere in the world, Gideons are placing 112 Bibles per minute.

Challenge: Other religions have begun imitating Gideons by placing copies of their scriptures in hotels: *The Teachings of the Buddha, Bhagavad Gita, Quran, Book of Mormon,* and *Jehovah the First God-Father.*

20The angel of God said to him, "Take the meat and the unleavened bread, place them on this rock,[t] and pour out the broth." And Gideon did so. 21With the tip of the staff that was in his hand, the angel of the LORD touched the meat and the unleavened bread.[u] Fire flared from the rock, consuming the meat and the bread. And the angel of the LORD disappeared. 22When Gideon realized[v] that it was the angel of the LORD, he exclaimed, "Ah, Sovereign LORD! I have seen the angel of the LORD face to face!"[w]

23But the LORD said to him, "Peace! Do not be afraid.[x] You are not going to die."

24So Gideon built an altar to the LORD there and called[y] it The LORD is Peace. To this day it stands in Ophrah[z] of the Abiezrites.

25That same night the LORD said to him, "Take the second bull from your father's herd, the one seven years old.[a] Tear down your father's altar to Baal and cut down the Asherah pole[b][a] beside it. 26Then build a proper kind of[c] altar to the LORD your God on the top of this height. Using the wood of the Asherah pole that you cut down, offer the second[d] bull as a burnt offering."

27So Gideon took ten of his servants and did as the LORD told him. But because he was afraid of his family and the men of the town, he did it at night rather than in the daytime.

28In the morning when the men of the town got up, there was Baal's altar,[b] demolished, with the Asherah pole beside it cut down and the second bull sacrificed on the newly built altar!

29They asked each other, "Who did this?"

When they carefully investigated, they were told, "Gideon son of Joash did it."

30The men of the town demanded of Joash, "Bring out your son. He must die, because he has broken down Baal's altar and cut down the Asherah pole beside it."

31But Joash replied to the hostile crowd around him, "Are you going to plead Baal's cause? Are you trying to save him? Whoever fights for him shall be put to death by morning! If Baal really is a god, he can defend himself when someone breaks down his altar." 32So that day they called Gideon "Jerub-Baal,[e][c]" saying, "Let Baal contend with him," because he broke down Baal's altar.

33Now all the Midianites, Amalekites and other eastern peoples[d] joined forces and crossed over the Jordan and camped in the Valley of Jezreel.[e] 34Then the Spirit of the LORD came upon[f] Gideon, and he blew a trumpet,[g] summoning the Abiezrites to follow him. 35He sent messengers throughout Manasseh, calling them to arms, and also into Asher, Zebulun and Naphtali,[h] so that they too went up to meet them.

36Gideon said to God, "If you will save[i] Israel by my hand as you have promised— 37look, I will place a wool fleece on the threshing floor.[j] If there is dew only on the fleece and all the ground is dry, then I will know[k] that you will save Israel by my hand, as you said." 38And that is what happened. Gideon rose early the next day; he squeezed the fleece and wrung out the dew—a bowlful of water.

39Then Gideon said to God, "Do not be angry with me. Let me make just one more request.[l] Allow me one more test with the fleece. This time make the fleece dry and the ground covered with dew." 40That night God did so. Only the fleece was dry; all the ground was covered with dew.

Gideon Defeats the Midianites

7 Early in the morning, Jerub-Baal[m] (that is, Gideon) and all his men camped at the spring of Harod. The camp of Midian was north of them in the valley near the hill of Moreh.[n] 2The LORD said to Gideon, "You have too many men for me to deliver Midian into their hands. In order that Israel may not boast against me that

Side references:

6:20 t Jdg 13:19
6:21 u Lev 9:24
6:22 v Jdg 13:16,21 w Ge 32:30; Ex 33:20; Jdg 13:22
6:23 x Da 10:19
6:24 y Ge 22:14 z Jdg 8:32
6:25 a Ex 34:13; Dt 7:5
6:28 b 1Ki 16:32
6:32 c Jdg 7:1; 8:29,35; 1Sa 12:11
6:33 d ver 3 e Jos 17:16
6:34 f Jdg 3:10; 1Ch 12:18; 2Ch 24:20 g Jdg 3:27
6:35 h Jdg 4:6
6:36 i ver 14
6:37 j Ex 4:3-7 k Ge 24:14
6:39 l Ge 18:32
7:1 m Jdg 6:32 n Ge 12:6

a 25 Or Take a full-grown, mature bull from your father's herd   b 25 That is, a symbol of the goddess Asherah; here and elsewhere in Judges   c 26 Or build with layers of stone an   d 26 Or full-grown; also in verse 28   e 32 Jerub-Baal means let Baal contend.

Judges 7:1–25

God gave in to Gideon's request for a sign, only to immediately put him in an even more defenseless position through troop reductions. The message? God alone would get the glory for the coming victory.

A direct promise from God didn't convince Gideon

Catherine Booth

Catherine Booth (1829–1890), co-founder of the Salvation Army, preached a gospel of a Savior who wasn't only willing to pardon sinners but empowered them to put away their sins and live a Christian life. "Tell a man the truth about himself, then the truth about God, then the truth about his obligation to others," she counseled.

Booth's interest in others was wide-ranging. She managed to fight against child prostitution and animal suffering, as well as for evangelistic missions, all at the same time, making them seem like natural extensions of one another.

Catherine, though, had to do preparatory work before she could engage in ministry with her husband, William Booth. She had to earn her right, as a woman, to do ministry. Even though she was dogged by ill health all her life, Catherine was a woman of clear convictions, which she preferred to call "settled views." One of her most settled views was the absolute equality of women with men. Catherine set about convincing her husband-to-be and co-founder of the Salvation Army, William Booth, of this reality.

> "Tell a man the truth about himself, then the truth about God, then the truth about his obligation to others."

She did so with the semi-military discipline that would come to characterize the Army—the same kind of discipline demanded by Gideon as he prepared an under-matched army to fight the Midianites in Judges 7. Contrary to all apparent reason, God informed Gideon that his pitiful army was too large. So Gideon reduced the number from 32,000 to 10,000 by offering an honorable discharge to anyone who was afraid. He then hand-picked 300 of the 10,000 troops to actually carry out the campaign against the formidable Midianite army. Thus the first lesson the Booths learned about ministry: *A few good people can effectively minister to much larger numbers*.

The semi-military structure of the Salvation Army served another purpose. The ranks and uniforms gave a sense of "set-apartness" to those who joined and served. When fighting an uphill ministry battle, sometimes an extra sense of calling is required, and this can be enhanced by the physical and social trappings of ministry. Lesson: *Don't overlook the importance of dress, social standing, and other vehicles that might serve to inspire future trailblazers.*

Such an emphasis on separation can be overdone and must be balanced by Christian charity (love). Catherine Booth exemplified this. Early in her career, her pastor, David Thomas, gave a series of sermons on the moral and intellectual inferiority of women. Catherine sent him a public letter debating the issue. Yet she refused to let the disagreement sever their personal friendship—Thomas later officiated at her marriage to William Booth. Lesson: *Relationships are key to ministry.*

A large factor in ministry relationships is encouragement of others in their work. Catherine Booth was a master at this skill. Her own encouragement was rooted in prayer, and she often advised others to "pray more and talk less." She followed her own advice, especially in her final years of sickness. From her sickbed she wrote upbeat letters to other Army officers, especially women. Roger Green, in his book *Catherine Booth*, recorded a letter she wrote one year prior to her death from cancer in 1890 to Captain Polly Ashton: "I lie here in a corner of the battlefield, helpless to do more than send out a counsel or two, and give my blessing, and cry to my Father that His presence may be with these who are in the thick of the fight." Lesson: *"Fighting" in ministry has to do with exerting great energy on God's behalf in spite of opposition or great trial.*

her own strength[o] has saved her, [3]announce now to the people, 'Anyone who trembles with fear may turn back and leave Mount Gilead.[p]' " So twenty-two thousand men left, while ten thousand remained.

[4]But the LORD said to Gideon, "There are still too many[q] men. Take them down to the water, and I will sift them for you there. If I say, 'This one shall go with you,' he shall go; but if I say, 'This one shall not go with you,' he shall not go."

[5]So Gideon took the men down to the water. There the LORD told him, "Separate those who lap the water with their tongues like a dog from those who kneel down to drink." [6]Three hundred men lapped with their hands to their mouths. All the rest got down on their knees to drink.

[7]The LORD said to Gideon, "With the three hundred men that lapped I will save you and give the Midianites into your hands. Let all the other men go, each to his own place."[r] [8]So Gideon sent the rest of the Israelites to their tents but kept the three hundred, who took over the provisions and trumpets of the others.

Now the camp of Midian lay below him in the valley. [9]During that night the LORD said to Gideon, "Get up, go down against the camp, because I am going to give it into your hands.[s] [10]If you are afraid to attack, go down to the camp with your servant Purah [11]and listen to what they are saying. Afterward, you will be encouraged to attack the camp." So he and Purah his servant went down to the outposts of the camp. [12]The Midianites, the Amalekites[t] and all the other eastern peoples had settled in the valley, thick as locusts.[u] Their camels[v] could no more be counted than the sand on the seashore.[w]

[13]Gideon arrived just as a man was telling a friend his dream. "I had a dream," he was saying. "A round loaf of barley bread came tumbling into the Midianite camp. It struck the tent with such force that the tent overturned and collapsed."

[14]His friend responded, "This can be nothing other than the sword of Gideon son of Joash, the Israelite. God has given the Midianites and the whole camp into his hands."

[15]When Gideon heard the dream and its interpretation, he worshiped God.[x] He returned to the camp of Israel and called out, "Get up! The LORD has given the Midianite camp into your hands." [16]Dividing the three hundred men[y] into three companies,[z] he placed trumpets and empty jars in the hands of all of them, with torches inside.

[17]"Watch me," he told them. "Follow my lead. When I get to the edge of the camp, do exactly as I do. [18]When I and all who are with me blow our trumpets,[a] then from all around the camp blow yours and shout, 'For the LORD and for Gideon.' "

[19]Gideon and the hundred men with him reached the edge of the camp at the beginning of the middle watch, just after they had changed the guard. They blew their trumpets and broke the jars that were in their hands. [20]The three companies blew the trumpets and smashed the jars. Grasping the torches in their left hands and holding in their right hands the trumpets they were to blow, they shouted, "A sword[b] for the LORD and for Gideon!" [21]While each man held his position around the camp, all the Midianites ran, crying out as they fled.[c]

[22]When the three hundred trumpets sounded,[d] the LORD caused the men throughout the camp to turn on each other[e] with their swords. The army fled to Beth Shittah toward Zererah as far as the border of Abel Meholah[f] near Tabbath. [23]Israelites from Naphtali, Asher and all Manasseh were called out,[g] and they pursued the Midianites. [24]Gideon sent messengers throughout the hill country of Ephraim, saying, "Come down against the Midianites and seize the waters of the Jordan[h] ahead of them as far as Beth Barah."

7:2
o Dt 8:17; 2Co 4:7
7:3
p Dt 20:8
7:4
q 1Sa 14:6

7:7
r 1Sa 14:6

7:9
s Jos 2:24; 10:8; 11:6

7:12
t Jdg 8:10 u Jdg 6:5
v Jer 49:29
w Jos 11:4

7:15
x 1Sa 15:31

7:16
y Ge 14:15
z 2Sa 18:2

7:18
a Jdg 3:27

7:20
b ver 14
7:21
c 2Ki 7:7
7:22
d Jdg 6:20
e 1Sa 14:20;
2Ch 20:23
f 1Ki 4:12; 19:16
7:23
g Jdg 6:35

7:24
h Jdg 3:28

(his fleece tests didn't either), but hearing the truth from the lips of a Midianite soldier *did* persuade him. After this final "sign" of encouragement, all conversation between God and Gideon stopped. Gideon worshiped God because of the sign—but we don't read about him doing so again. Instead, he seized the glory for his unlikely victory.

The narrator leaves us with a gripping message: God may bring us to a moment when all our human confidence is stripped away, when we can only sit silently before the One who is totally sufficient against all odds to accomplish whatever he desires. Gideon and his puny three hundred weren't the reason for the victory in this battle; they were simply used by God to achieve *his* victory.

So all the men of Ephraim were called out and they took the waters of the Jordan as far as Beth Barah. [25]They also captured two of the Midianite leaders, Oreb and Zeeb. [i] They killed Oreb at the rock of Oreb, [j] and Zeeb at the winepress of Zeeb. They pursued the Midianites and brought the heads of Oreb and Zeeb to Gideon, who was by the Jordan. [k]

7:25
i Jdg 8:3; Ps 83:11
j Isa 10:26 *k* Jdg 8:4

Zebah and Zalmunna

8 Now the Ephraimites asked Gideon, "Why have you treated us like this? Why didn't you call us when you went to fight Midian?" [l] And they criticized him sharply. [m]

8:1
l Jdg 12:1
m 2Sa 19:41

[2]But he answered them, "What have I accomplished compared to you? Aren't the gleanings of Ephraim's grapes better than the full grape harvest of Abiezer? [3]God gave Oreb and Zeeb, [n] the Midianite leaders, into your hands. What was I able to do compared to you?" At this, their resentment against him subsided.

8:3
n Jdg 7:25; Pr 15:1

[4]Gideon and his three hundred men, exhausted yet keeping up the pursuit, came to the Jordan [o] and crossed it. [5]He said to the men of Succoth, [p] "Give my troops some bread; they are worn out, and I am still pursuing Zebah and Zalmunna, [q] the kings of Midian."

8:4
o Jdg 7:25
8:5
p Ge 33:17
q Ps 83:11

[6]But the officials of Succoth said, "Do you already have the hands of Zebah and Zalmunna in your possession? Why should we give bread [r] to your troops?" [s]

8:6
r 1Sa 25:11 *s* ver 15

[7]Then Gideon replied, "Just for that, when the LORD has given Zebah and Zalmunna [t] into my hand, I will tear your flesh with desert thorns and briers."

8:7
t Jdg 7:15

[8]From there he went up to Peniel [a] [u] and made the same request of them, but they answered as the men of Succoth had. [9]So he said to the men of Peniel, "When I return in triumph, I will tear down this tower." [v]

8:8
u Ge 32:30;
1Ki 12:25
8:9
v ver 17

[10]Now Zebah and Zalmunna were in Karkor with a force of about fifteen thousand men, all that were left of the armies of the eastern peoples; a hundred and twenty thousand swordsmen had fallen. [w] [11]Gideon went up by the route of the nomads east of Nobah [x] and Jogbehah [y] and fell upon the unsuspecting army. [12]Zebah and Zalmunna, the two kings of Midian, fled, but he pursued them and captured them, routing their entire army.

8:10
w Jdg 6:5; 7:12;
Isa 9:4
8:11
x Nu 32:42
y Nu 32:35

[13]Gideon son of Joash then returned from the battle by the Pass of Heres. [14]He caught a young man of Succoth and questioned him, and the young man wrote down for him the names of the seventy-seven officials of Succoth, the elders of the town. [15]Then Gideon came and said to the men of Succoth, "Here are Zebah and Zalmunna, about whom you taunted me by saying, 'Do you already have the hands of Zebah and Zalmunna in your possession? Why should we give bread to your exhausted men?' " [z] [16]He took the elders of the town and taught the men of Succoth a lesson [a] by punishing them with desert thorns and briers. [17]He also pulled down the tower of Peniel and killed the men of the town. [b]

8:15
z ver 6
8:16
a ver 7
8:17
b ver 9

[18]Then he asked Zebah and Zalmunna, "What kind of men did you kill at Tabor? [c]"

"Men like you," they answered, "each one with the bearing of a prince."

8:18
c Jos 19:22; Jdg 4:6

[19]Gideon replied, "Those were my brothers, the sons of my own mother. As surely as the LORD lives, if you had spared their lives, I would not kill you." [20]Turn-

---

a 8 Hebrew *Penuel*, a variant of *Peniel*; also in verses 9 and 17

Judges 8:1–21

Had the story ended at verse 3, Gideon still would have appeared heroic. But Judges documents his degeneration. Driven by revenge, he pursued retaliation first against his own countrymen and then against Zebah and Zalmunna. His retribution against Succoth and Peniel was an excessive response to people who doubted his ability to achieve victory and feared reprisals from Zebah and Zalmunna. True, these people should have helped Gideon and his men. But Gideon's actions were the opposite of how God had earlier acted toward him when he was full of doubt and fear.

There are still situations today in which generations gloatingly wait for the prime opportunity to execute "justice" on those who have oppressed them—going back to their adversaries' long-deceased relatives. The problem is that human nature is sinful; we can't make things "right" with revenge fueled by hatred. Our motives matter to God. Is there someone you long to repay for some offense? What will it take for you to let it go?

ing to Jether, his oldest son, he said, "Kill them!" But Jether did not draw his sword, because he was only a boy and was afraid. [21]Zebah and Zalmunna said, "Come, do it yourself. 'As is the man, so is his strength.' " So Gideon stepped forward and killed them, and took the ornaments[d] off their camels' necks.

8:21
d ver 26; Ps 83:11

Gideon's Ephod

[22]The Israelites said to Gideon, "Rule over us—you, your son and your grandson—because you have saved us out of the hand of Midian."

[23]But Gideon told them, "I will not rule over you, nor will my son rule over you. The LORD will rule[e] over you." [24]And he said, "I do have one request, that each of you give me an earring from your share of the plunder." (It was the custom of the Ishmaelites[f] to wear gold earrings.)

8:23
e Ex 16:8; 1Sa 8:7; 10:19; 12:12
8:24
f Ge 25:13

[25]They answered, "We'll be glad to give them." So they spread out a garment, and each man threw a ring from his plunder onto it. [26]The weight of the gold rings he asked for came to seventeen hundred shekels,[a] not counting the ornaments, the pendants and the purple garments worn by the kings of Midian or the chains that were on their camels' necks. [27]Gideon made the gold into an ephod,[g] which he placed in Ophrah, his town. All Israel prostituted themselves by worshiping it there, and it became a snare[h] to Gideon and his family.

8:27
g Jdg 17:5; 18:14
h Dt 7:16;
Ps 106:39

Gideon's Death

[28]Thus Midian was subdued before the Israelites and did not raise its head again. During Gideon's lifetime, the land enjoyed peace[i] forty years.

[29]Jerub-Baal[j] son of Joash went back home to live. [30]He had seventy sons[k] of his own, for he had many wives. [31]His concubine, who lived in Shechem, also bore him a son, whom he named Abimelech.[l] [32]Gideon son of Joash died at a good old age[m] and was buried in the tomb of his father Joash in Ophrah of the Abiezrites.

[33]No sooner had Gideon died than the Israelites again prostituted themselves to the Baals.[n] They set up Baal-Berith[o] as their god[p] and [34]did not remember[q] the LORD their God, who had rescued them from the hands of all their enemies on every side. [35]They also failed to show kindness to the family of Jerub-Baal (that is, Gideon) for all the good things he had done for them.[r]

8:28
i Jdg 5:31
8:29
j Jdg 7:1
8:30
k Jdg 9:2,5,18,24
8:31
l Jdg 9:1
8:32
m Ge 25:8
8:33
n Jdg 2:11,13,19
o Jdg 9:4
p Jdg 9:27,46
8:34
q Jdg 3:7; Dt 4:9;
Ps 78:11,42
8:35
r Jdg 9:16

a 26 That is, about 43 pounds (about 19.5 kilograms)

Judges 8:22–27

When God has performed a mighty act on someone's behalf, the glory belongs to him alone. No other judge demanded a donation from each Israelite—from the loot of battle—and Gideon had no right making this request. He had answered the Israelites correctly about kingship, but his request for earrings contradicted his response.

Gideon's construction of an ephod (a high priestly garment, and perhaps also the image it was draped on) from the Midianites' golden earrings reminds us of Aaron casting the golden calf from the Egyptians' earrings (Ex. 32:1–8). Both Gideon's and Aaron's idols were illegitimate objects for Israel to worship. Gideon was somewhat like Moses in his calling, but more like Aaron in this act.

We can have our beliefs right and still live as hypocrites. Nothing causes people to turn away from Christianity more quickly than the double standards of some who profess Christ. Our words and actions too often contradict each other—and beg for attention. People form enough excuses not to trust in Christ without

church members providing ammunition! How does your life look to the unbelieving world?

Judges 8:28–35

Gideon returned home to live, which would seem to imply that he retired into private life to honor his commitment that God, not he, was to rule Israel. But even though he declined kingship outwardly (v. 23), his actions show that he craved this honor. His accumulation of wives specifically violated the kingship model in Deuteronomy 17:14–20. Additionally, to support such a harem and its many children, he would have had to enjoy the resources of a king!

Those called to leadership/labor in God's kingdom often struggle with personal ambition. Ironically, the more impressive the achievements for God, the greater the temptation. Gideon at first resisted the temptation to rule over Israel, but he fell prey to more subtle ambition—with the same end result. Often it's not the obvious enticement, but the hidden, more-sophisticated temptation that trips us up. How closely do you pay attention to the seemingly minor temptations in your life or ministry?

Abimelech

9:1
s Jdg 8:31

9 Abimelech *s* son of Jerub-Baal went to his mother's brothers in Shechem and said to them and to all his mother's clan, 2"Ask all the citizens of Shechem, 'Which is better for you: to have all seventy of Jerub-Baal's sons rule over you, or just one man?' Remember, I am your flesh and blood. *t*"

9:2
t Ge 29:14;
Jdg 8:30

3When the brothers repeated all this to the citizens of Shechem, they were inclined to follow Abimelech, for they said, "He is our brother." 4They gave him seventy shekels *a* of silver from the temple of Baal-Berith, *u* and Abimelech used it to hire reckless adventurers, *v* who became his followers. 5He went to his father's home in Ophrah and on one stone murdered his seventy brothers, *w* the sons of Jerub-Baal. But Jotham, the youngest son of Jerub-Baal, escaped by hiding. *x* 6Then all the citizens of Shechem and Beth Millo gathered beside the great tree at the pillar in Shechem to crown Abimelech king.

9:4
u Jdg 8:33
v Jdg 11:3;
2Ch 13:7

9:5
w ver 2; Jdg 8:30
x 2Ki 11:2

7When Jotham was told about this, he climbed up on the top of Mount Gerizim *y* and shouted to them, "Listen to me, citizens of Shechem, so that God may listen to you. 8One day the trees went out to anoint a king for themselves. They said to the olive tree, 'Be our king.'

9:7
y Dt 11:29; 27:12;
Jn 4:20

9"But the olive tree answered, 'Should I give up my oil, by which both gods and men are honored, to hold sway over the trees?'

10"Next, the trees said to the fig tree, 'Come and be our king.'

11"But the fig tree replied, 'Should I give up my fruit, so good and sweet, to hold sway over the trees?'

12"Then the trees said to the vine, 'Come and be our king.'

9:13
z Ecc 2:3

13"But the vine answered, 'Should I give up my wine, *z* which cheers both gods and men, to hold sway over the trees?'

14"Finally all the trees said to the thornbush, 'Come and be our king.'

9:15
a Isa 30:2 *b* ver 20
c Isa 2:13

15"The thornbush said to the trees, 'If you really want to anoint me king over you, come and take refuge in my shade; *a* but if not, then let fire come out *b* of the thornbush and consume the cedars of Lebanon!' *c*

16"Now if you have acted honorably and in good faith when you made Abimelech king, and if you have been fair to Jerub-Baal and his family, and if you have treated him as he deserves— 17and to think that my father fought for you, risked his life to rescue you from the hand of Midian 18(but today you have revolted

a 4 That is, about 1 3/4 pounds (about 0.8 kilogram)

Judges 9:1–57

Abimelech shrewdly sought power by playing the family card for trust. Once he received it, he promptly turned around and murdered his 70 brothers—not counting on Jotham's escape. Jotham, using a parable, tried to convince the Shechemites of the truth. When his audience didn't "get it," he was forced into hiding. The people were perfectly content with their evil ruler.

8:33–35

Apostasy

Joshua was a book of revival and growth. Sadly, Judges is about regression and decline. The people of God practiced apostasy and engaged in idolatry of all sorts. Apostasy can mean believing wrong things, failing to do right things, and/or rejecting God's way. There are at least four active approaches people can take with regard to Scripture:

	Response to Scripture	Teaching	Effect on Church
1. Orthodoxy	True to Scripture	Affirm right teaching	Appoint faithful leaders (concerned enough with truth to choose and nurture leaders who will teach truth and can identify and avoid "false teachers")
2. Orthopraxy	Act on basis of Scripture	Act on implications of Scriptural teachings	Build God's church
3. Heresy	Teach against Scripture	Endorse false teaching	Ignore the church
4. Apostasy	Turn against Scripture	Counter true teachings	Work against the church

against my father's family, murdered his seventy sons *d* on a single stone, and made Abimelech, the son of his slave girl, king over the citizens of Shechem because he is your brother)— ¹⁹if then you have acted honorably and in good faith toward Jerub-Baal and his family today, may Abimelech be your joy, and may you be his, too! ²⁰But if you have not, let fire come out *e* from Abimelech and consume you, citizens of Shechem and Beth Millo, and let fire come out from you, citizens of Shechem and Beth Millo, and consume Abimelech!"

²¹Then Jotham fled, escaping to Beer, and he lived there because he was afraid of his brother Abimelech.

²²After Abimelech had governed Israel three years, ²³God sent an evil spirit *f* between Abimelech and the citizens of Shechem, who acted treacherously against Abimelech. ²⁴God did this in order that the crime against Jerub-Baal's seventy sons, the shedding *g* of their blood, might be avenged *h* on their brother Abimelech and on the citizens of Shechem, who had helped him *i* murder his brothers. ²⁵In opposition to him these citizens of Shechem set men on the hilltops to ambush and rob everyone who passed by, and this was reported to Abimelech.

²⁶Now Gaal son of Ebed moved with his brothers into Shechem, and its citizens put their confidence in him. ²⁷After they had gone out into the fields and gathered the grapes and trodden *j* them, they held a festival in the temple of their god. *k* While they were eating and drinking, they cursed Abimelech. ²⁸Then Gaal son of Ebed said, "Who *l* is Abimelech, and who is Shechem, that we should be subject to him? Isn't he Jerub-Baal's son, and isn't Zebul his deputy? Serve the men of Hamor, *m* Shechem's father! Why should we serve Abimelech? ²⁹If only this people were under my command! *n* Then I would get rid of him. I would say to Abimelech, 'Call out your whole army!' " *a*

³⁰When Zebul the governor of the city heard what Gaal son of Ebed said, he was very angry. ³¹Under cover he sent messengers to Abimelech, saying, "Gaal son of

a 29 Septuagint; Hebrew *him.*" Then he said to Abimelech, "Call out your whole army!"

9:18 *d* ver 5-6; Jdg 8:30

9:20 *e* ver 15

9:23 *f* 1Sa 16:14,23; 18:10; 1Ki 22:22; Isa 19:14; 33:1

9:24 *g* Nu 35:33; 1Ki 2:32 *h* ver 56-57 *i* Dt 27:25

9:27 *j* Am 9:13 *k* Jdg 8:33

9:28 *l* 1Sa 25:10; 1Ki 12:16 *m* Ge 34:2,6

9:29 *n* 2Sa 15:4

After Gideon's death, the Israelites failed to show covenant faithfulness to God or to other humans (see 8:33-35; 9:4,16-18). God withdrew his gracious hand, giving them the king they deserved—and Abimelech the people he deserved. What characterized the Israelites in general also distinguished their leader, who continued to show no regard for family loyalty—and certainly none for God. The further slaughter and destruction in chapter 9 directly resulted from Gideon's sins in 8:27-31—sins that would impact the next generation of his family in ways he could never have predicted.

Speaking out against wrongdoing takes courage. How much easier it would have been for Jotham to have

blended in and let it go. On the surface it didn't appear that Jotham made much difference. But at the very least he presented the truth. How willing are you to do this in tough situations, even when you know you can't control others' reactions?

An individual's abandonment of the faith never cancels out God's sovereignty. He's in control, whether or not we acknowledge him. He's the Truth, whether or not we believe him. The Lord moves events along to his intended outcome. Whatever "gods" we have chosen to replace him will prove to be worthless in the day of trouble, just as Baal-Berith, or El-Berith, proved to be for the Shechemites who took refuge in their false god's temple (cf. vv. 4,46-49).

8:35

Showing Gratitude

For what are we to be grateful? Traditionally, Christians have been taught to be thankful for seven things, to demonstrate that gratitude to God (through worship, song, and service), and to respond to others in ways that imitate that for which we are grateful:

How thankful are you? Does your gratitude encompass all these areas?

1. God's goodness	Ps. 11:4-5
2. God's provision	Ps. 147:7-9
3. Jesus Christ	2 Cor. 9:15
4. Deliverance from sin and danger	Ps. 35:9-10
5. Answered prayer	Ps. 30:1-12
6. Other people	Neh. 11:17
7. The world	Ps. 68:19

Ebed and his brothers have come to Shechem and are stirring up the city against you. ³²Now then, during the night you and your men should come and lie in wait ᵒ in the fields. ³³In the morning at sunrise, advance against the city. When Gaal and his men come out against you, do whatever your hand finds to do. ᵖ"

³⁴So Abimelech and all his troops set out by night and took up concealed positions near Shechem in four companies. ³⁵Now Gaal son of Ebed had gone out and was standing at the entrance to the city gate just as Abimelech and his soldiers came out from their hiding place. �q

³⁶When Gaal saw them, he said to Zebul, "Look, people are coming down from the tops of the mountains!"

Zebul replied, "You mistake the shadows of the mountains for men."

³⁷But Gaal spoke up again: "Look, people are coming down from the center of the land, and a company is coming from the direction of the soothsayers' tree."

³⁸Then Zebul said to him, "Where is your big talk now, you who said, 'Who is Abimelech that we should be subject to him?' Aren't these the men you ridiculed? ʳ Go out and fight them!"

³⁹So Gaal led out ᵃ the citizens of Shechem and fought Abimelech. ⁴⁰Abimelech chased him, and many fell wounded in the flight—all the way to the entrance to the gate. ⁴¹Abimelech stayed in Arumah, and Zebul drove Gaal and his brothers out of Shechem.

⁴²The next day the people of Shechem went out to the fields, and this was reported to Abimelech. ⁴³So he took his men, divided them into three companies ˢ and set an ambush in the fields. When he saw the people coming out of the city, he rose to attack them. ⁴⁴Abimelech and the companies with him rushed forward to a position at the entrance to the city gate. Then two companies rushed upon those in the fields and struck them down. ⁴⁵All that day Abimelech pressed his attack against the city until he had captured it and killed its people. Then he destroyed the city ᵗ and scattered salt ᵘ over it.

⁴⁶On hearing this, the citizens in the tower of Shechem went into the stronghold of the temple ᵛ of El-Berith. ⁴⁷When Abimelech heard that they had assembled there, ⁴⁸he and all his men went up Mount Zalmon. ʷ He took an ax and cut off some branches, which he lifted to his shoulders. He ordered the men with him, "Quick! Do what you have seen me do!" ⁴⁹So all the men cut branches and followed Abimelech. They piled them against the stronghold and set it on fire over the people inside. So all the people in the tower of Shechem, about a thousand men and women, also died.

⁵⁰Next Abimelech went to Thebez ˣ and besieged it and captured it. ⁵¹Inside the city, however, was a strong tower, to which all the men and women—all the people of the city—fled. They locked themselves in and climbed up on the tower roof. ⁵²Abimelech went to the tower and stormed it. But as he approached the entrance to the tower to set it on fire, ⁵³a woman dropped an upper millstone on his head and cracked his skull. ʸ

ᵃ 39 Or Gaal went out in the sight of

Cross-references (margin)

9:32
o Jos 8:2
9:33
p 1Sa 10:7

9:35
q Ps 32:7; Jer 49:10

9:38
r ver 28-29

9:43
s Jdg 7:16

9:45
t ver 20; 2Ki 3:25
u Dt 29:23

9:46
v Jdg 8:33
9:48
w Ps 68:14

9:50
x 2Sa 11:21

9:53
y 2Sa 11:21

9:56–57

God's Anger

Judges as a book talks about Israel's shortcomings and God's resulting anger. It answers these basic questions:

Why does God get angry?	What is it about God that makes him get angry?	What happens when God gets angry?	How can we be saved from God's anger?
• Disobedience (Isa. 5:24–25)	• His holiness (Ps. 7:11)	• Death (Deut. 9:8)	• Humility (Zeph. 2:3)
• Sinfulness (Eph. 2:1–3)	• His jealousy (1 Kings 14:22)	• Present judgment (Lam. 2:2)	• Repentance (Gen. 18:30–32)
• Idolatry (Num. 25:3)	• His role as judge (Ps. 79:6)	• Future judgment (Isa. 13:9)	• Love (Hos. 11:9)
		• Rejection (Jer. 7:29)	• Acceptance of the finished work of Jesus Christ on the cross (Rom. 5:9)

54Hurriedly he called to his armor-bearer, "Draw your sword and kill me,ᶻ so that they can't say, 'A woman killed him.' " So his servant ran him through, and he died. 55When the Israelites saw that Abimelech was dead, they went home.

56Thus God repaid the wickedness that Abimelech had done to his father by murdering his seventy brothers. 57God also made the men of Shechem pay for all their wickedness.ᵃ The curse of Jotham son of Jerub-Baal came on them.

Tola

10 After the time of Abimelech a man of Issachar,ᵇ Tola son of Puah,ᶜ the son of Dodo, rose to saveᵈ Israel. He lived in Shamir, in the hill country of Ephraim. 2He ledᵃ Israel twenty-three years; then he died, and was buried in Shamir.

Jair

3He was followed by Jair of Gilead, who led Israel twenty-two years. 4He had thirty sons, who rode thirty donkeys. They controlled thirty towns in Gilead, which to this day are called Havvoth Jair.ᵇ ᵉ 5When Jair died, he was buried in Kamon.

Jephthah

6Again the Israelites did evil in the eyes of the LORD.ᶠ They served the Baals and the Ashtoreths,ᵍ and the gods of Aram, the gods of Sidon, the gods of Moab, the gods of the Ammonites and the gods of the Philistines.ʰ And because the Israelites forsook the LORDⁱ and no longer served him, 7he became angryʲ with them. He sold themᵏ into the hands of the Philistines and the Ammonites, 8who that year shattered and crushed them. For eighteen years they oppressed all the Israelites on the east side of the Jordan in Gilead, the land of the Amorites. 9The Ammonites also crossed the Jordan to fight against Judah, Benjamin and the house of Ephraim; and Israel was in great distress. 10Then the Israelites cried out to the LORD, "We have sinned against you, forsaking our God and serving the Baals."ˡ

11The LORD replied, "When the Egyptians,ᵐ the Amorites, the Ammonites,ⁿ the Philistines,ᵒ 12the Sidonians, the Amalekites and the Maonitesᶜ oppressed youᵖ and

---

ᵃ 2 Traditionally *judged*; also in verse 3   ᵇ 4 Or *called the settlements of Jair*   ᶜ 12 Hebrew; some Septuagint manuscripts *Midianites*

Side references

9:54
z 1Sa 31:4; 2Sa 1:9

9:57
a ver 20

10:1
b Ge 30:18
c Ge 46:13
d Jdg 2:16; 6:14

10:4
e Nu 32:41

10:6
f Jdg 2:11
g Jdg 2:13
h Jdg 2:12
i Dt 32:15
10:7
j Dt 31:17
k Dt 32:30;
Jdg 2:14; 1Sa 12:9

10:10
l 1Sa 12:10
10:11
m Ex 14:30
n Nu 21:21;
Jdg 3:13 o Jdg 3:31
10:12
p Ps 106:42

Judges 10:1-2

Why was a man from Issachar living outside the area God had allotted this tribe? Apparently certain clans of Issachar had given up on occupying their own land (cf. Josh. 19:17–23) and moved to another, more easily conquerable site. Often in the Old Testament, a genealogical statement gives hints about social status. Tola may have been a wealthy figure with some stature in the region. From whom did he save Israel? The text isn't definite. But his career reminds us of Deborah's, who "arose" when Israel was in disorder (5:6–7). Tola also "rose" from among his generation.

We might wish the text supplied more information. But "all Scripture is God-breathed"—and useful for our spiritual growth (2 Tim. 3:16). One idea to consider: Have we, like the tribe of Issachar, moved over to something easily achievable instead of pursuing God's will for us? Have we abandoned a tough goal for something more manageable? Have we chosen familiarity over God-honoring adventure, ease over faith-building challenges?

Judges 10:3-5

Jair was a powerful man. In order to have 30 sons, he must have had a harem. Reminiscent of the Gideon/Abimelech story (Judg. 6–9), the kingship issue seems again to have been in view. Jair's accumulation of

wives, as well as his need to support such a large family, required kingly resources. He and his sons possessed or controlled 30 cities—in an area that had attained its regional name from Jair himself.

Jair seemed to have been trying to build a power base for himself through his sons. Many fathers dream of their children following in their footsteps. But God has a plan for each life—and it may not conform to our ideas for our children's futures. We create conflict within them when we seek to impose our will on them with regard to their careers or other important decisions. It also sets us up to compete with God for influence in their hearts. If you have children, are you assisting them in following God's plan for their lives?

Judges 10:6—11:40

It would seem that Jephthah had been adopted by his father, Gilead (otherwise the issue of inheritance wouldn't have existed). Apparently after his father died, his brothers went to court—to the elders—to sue on the grounds that his adoption wasn't valid. In their opinion, the son of a prostitute couldn't be adopted. Jephthah at first rejected the elders' request because they had earlier sided with his brothers and rejected him, and because he saw through their offer to make him "commander," not "head."

you cried to me for help, did I not save you from their hands? [13]But you have forsaken me and served other gods, so I will no longer save you. [14]Go and cry out to the gods you have chosen. Let them save you when you are in trouble! [q]"

[15]But the Israelites said to the LORD, "We have sinned. Do with us whatever you think best,[r] but please rescue us now." [16]Then they got rid of the foreign gods among them and served the LORD.[s] And he could bear Israel's misery[t] no longer.[u]

[17]When the Ammonites were called to arms and camped in Gilead, the Israelites assembled and camped at Mizpah.[v] [18]The leaders of the people of Gilead said to each other, "Whoever will launch the attack against the Ammonites will be the head[w] of all those living in Gilead."

11 Jephthah[x] the Gileadite was a mighty warrior.[y] His father was Gilead; his mother was a prostitute. [2]Gilead's wife also bore him sons, and when they were grown up, they drove Jephthah away. "You are not going to get any inheritance in our family," they said, "because you are the son of another woman." [3]So Jephthah fled from his brothers and settled in the land of Tob,[z] where a group of adventurers[a] gathered around him and followed him.

[4]Some time later, when the Ammonites[b] made war on Israel, [5]the elders of Gilead went to get Jephthah from the land of Tob. [6]"Come," they said, "be our commander, so we can fight the Ammonites."

[7]Jephthah said to them, "Didn't you hate me and drive me from my father's house?[c] Why do you come to me now, when you're in trouble?"

[8]The elders of Gilead said to him, "Nevertheless, we are turning to you now; come with us to fight the Ammonites, and you will be our head[d] over all who live in Gilead."

[9]Jephthah answered, "Suppose you take me back to fight the Ammonites and the LORD gives them to me—will I really be your head?"

[10]The elders of Gilead replied, "The LORD is our witness;[e] we will certainly do as you say." [11]So Jephthah went with the elders of Gilead, and the people made him head and commander over them. And he repeated all his words before the LORD in Mizpah.[f]

[12]Then Jephthah sent messengers to the Ammonite king with the question: "What do you have against us that you have attacked our country?"

[13]The king of the Ammonites answered Jephthah's messengers, "When Israel came up out of Egypt, they took away my land from the Arnon to the Jabbok,[g] all the way to the Jordan. Now give it back peaceably."

[14]Jephthah sent back messengers to the Ammonite king, [15]saying:

"This is what Jephthah says: Israel did not take the land of Moab[h] or the land of the Ammonites.[i] [16]But when they came up out of Egypt, Israel went through the desert to the Red Sea[a][j] and on to Kadesh.[k] [17]Then Israel sent messengers[l] to the king of Edom, saying, 'Give us permission to go through your country,'[m] but the king of Edom would not listen. They sent also to the king of Moab, and he refused.[n] So Israel stayed at Kadesh.

---

[a] 16 Hebrew *Yam Suph*; that is, Sea of Reeds

Side references (left margin):

10:14
q Dt 32:37

10:15
r 1Sa 3:18;
2Sa 15:26

10:16
s Jos 24:23;
Jer 18:8 *t* Isa 63:9
u Dt 32:36;
Ps 106:44-45

10:17
v Ge 31:49;
Jdg 11:29

10:18
w Jdg 11:8,9

11:1
x Heb 11:32
y Jdg 6:12

11:3
z 2Sa 10:6,8
a Jdg 9:4

11:4
b Jdg 10:9

11:7
c Ge 26:27

11:8
d Jdg 10:18

11:10
e Ge 31:50;
Jer 42:5

11:11
f Jos 11:3;
Jdg 10:17; 20:1;
1Sa 10:17

11:13
g Ge 32:22;
Nu 21:24

11:15
h Dt 2:9 *i* Dt 2:19

11:16
j Nu 14:25; Dt 1:40
k Nu 20:1

11:17
l Nu 20:14
m Nu 20:18,21
n Jos 24:9

The Spirit's empowerment for military leadership (11:29) didn't make Jephthah spiritually mature. He tried to manipulate God by his poorly considered vow. Jephthah delivered Israel from the Ammonites, who sacrificed their children to their gods—and then sacrificed his own daughter to the Lord, who didn't accept human sacrifice. It was a sin to break a vow (Num. 30:2), but God had made provision for release from rash vows. Had he been better informed, Jephthah could have "redeemed" his daughter (see Lev. 27:1–8).

Have you ever found yourself in a position of making a rash vow, or promise, to God? Such maneuverings are unnecessary; we know that God orders events according to his will. Until we recognize that he isn't obligated by our words or actions to do anything on our behalf, we will experience frustrations in our relationship with him. We are not to worship him because of what we can get out of him—but because he's our God.

Jephthah's heartless sacrifice of his daughter is paralleled by societies today that allow intolerable acts against children, including abortion, slavery, forced military service, prostitution, or abandonment (Matt. 18:5–6). Abused children sometimes become abusers. But a relationship with Christ can free a person from a past that might otherwise have led to destructive behaviors (John 8:32).

18 "Next they traveled through the desert, skirted the lands of Edom[o] and Moab, passed along the eastern side[p] of the country of Moab, and camped on the other side of the Arnon.[q] They did not enter the territory of Moab, for the Arnon was its border.

19 "Then Israel sent messengers to Sihon king of the Amorites, who ruled in Heshbon, and said to him, 'Let us pass through your country to our own place.'[r] 20 Sihon, however, did not trust Israel[a] to pass through his territory. He mustered all his men and encamped at Jahaz and fought with Israel.[s]

21 "Then the LORD, the God of Israel, gave Sihon and all his men into Israel's hands, and they defeated them. Israel took over all the land of the Amorites who lived in that country, 22 capturing all of it from the Arnon to the Jabbok and from the desert to the Jordan.[t]

23 "Now since the LORD, the God of Israel, has driven the Amorites out before his people Israel, what right have you to take it over? 24 Will you not take what your god Chemosh[u] gives you? Likewise, whatever the LORD our God has given us, we will possess. 25 Are you better than Balak son of Zippor,[v] king of Moab? Did he ever quarrel with Israel or fight with them?[w] 26 For three hundred years Israel occupied[x] Heshbon, Aroer, the surrounding settlements and all the towns along the Arnon. Why didn't you retake them during that time? 27 I have not wronged you, but you are doing me wrong by waging war against me. Let the LORD, the Judge,[b][y] decide[z] the dispute this day between the Israelites and the Ammonites."

28 The king of Ammon, however, paid no attention to the message Jephthah sent him.

29 Then the Spirit[a] of the LORD came upon Jephthah. He crossed Gilead and Manasseh, passed through Mizpah of Gilead, and from there he advanced against the Ammonites. 30 And Jephthah made a vow[b] to the LORD: "If you give the Ammonites into my hands, 31 whatever comes out of the door of my house to meet me when I return in triumph from the Ammonites will be the LORD's, and I will sacrifice it as a burnt offering."

32 Then Jephthah went over to fight the Ammonites, and the LORD gave them into his hands. 33 He devastated twenty towns from Aroer to the vicinity of Minnith,[c] as far as Abel Keramim. Thus Israel subdued Ammon.

34 When Jephthah returned to his home in Mizpah, who should come out to meet him but his daughter, dancing to the sound of tambourines![d] She was an only child. Except for her he had neither son nor daughter. 35 When he saw her, he tore his clothes and cried, "Oh! My daughter! You have made me miserable and wretched, because I have made a vow to the LORD that I cannot break.[e]

36 "My father," she replied, "you have given your word to the LORD. Do to me just as you promised,[f] now that the LORD has avenged you of your enemies,[g] the Ammonites. 37 But grant me this one request," she said. "Give me two months to roam the hills and weep with my friends, because I will never marry."

38 "You may go," he said. And he let her go for two months. She and the girls went into the hills and wept because she would never marry. 39 After the two months, she returned to her father and he did to her as he had vowed. And she was a virgin. From this comes the Israelite custom 40 that each year the young women of Israel go out for four days to commemorate the daughter of Jephthah the Gileadite.

Jephthah and Ephraim

12 The men of Ephraim called out their forces, crossed over to Zaphon and said to Jephthah, "Why did you go to fight the Ammonites without calling us to go with you?[h] We're going to burn down your house over your head."

---

[a] 20 Or *however, would not make an agreement for Israel*   [b] 27 Or *Ruler*

Side references

11:18
o Nu 21:4 p Dt 2:8
q Nu 21:13

11:19
r Nu 21:21-22;
Dt 2:26-27
11:20
s Nu 21:23; Dt 2:32

11:22
t Dt 2:36

11:24
u Nu 21:29;
Jos 3:10; 1Ki 11:7
11:25
v Nu 22:2
w Jos 24:9
11:26
x Nu 21:25

11:27
y Ge 18:25
z Ge 16:5; 31:53;
1Sa 24:12,15

11:29
a Nu 11:25;
Jdg 3:10; 6:34;
14:6,19; 15:14;
1Sa 11:6; 16:13;
Isa 11:2
11:30
b Ge 28:20

11:33
c Eze 27:17

11:34
d Ex 15:20; Jer 31:4

11:35
e Nu 30:2;
Ecc 5:2,4,5
11:36
f Lk 1:38
g 2Sa 18:19

12:1
h Jdg 8:1

Judges 12:1–7

The Ephraimites should have congratulated Jephthah on his accomplishment and thanked him for delivering them from the Ammonite threat. Instead, in their jealousy and wounded pride they were determined to destroy the deliverer. Jephthah's tribal "brothers," like

---

12:3
i 1Sa 19:5; 28:21;
Job 13:14

2Jephthah answered, "I and my people were engaged in a great struggle with the Ammonites, and although I called, you didn't save me out of their hands. 3When I saw that you wouldn't help, I took my life in my hands[i] and crossed over to fight the Ammonites, and the LORD gave me the victory over them. Now why have you come up today to fight me?"

4Jephthah then called together the men of Gilead and fought against Ephraim. The Gileadites struck them down because the Ephraimites had said, "You Gilead-ites are renegades from Ephraim and Manasseh." 5The Gileadites captured the fords of the Jordan[j] leading to Ephraim, and whenever a survivor of Ephraim said, "Let me cross over," the men of Gilead asked him, "Are you an Ephraimite?" If he replied, "No," 6they said, "All right, say 'Shibboleth.' " If he said, "Sibboleth," be-cause he could not pronounce the word correctly, they seized him and killed him at the fords of the Jordan. Forty-two thousand Ephraimites were killed at that time.

12:5
j Jos 22:11;
Jdg 3:28

7Jephthah led[a] Israel six years. Then Jephthah the Gileadite died, and was buried in a town in Gilead.

Ibzan, Elon and Abdon

8After him, Ibzan of Bethlehem led Israel. 9He had thirty sons and thirty daugh-ters. He gave his daughters away in marriage to those outside his clan, and for his sons he brought in thirty young women as wives from outside his clan. Ibzan led Israel seven years. 10Then Ibzan died, and was buried in Bethlehem.

11After him, Elon the Zebulunite led Israel ten years. 12Then Elon died, and was buried in Aijalon in the land of Zebulun.

13After him, Abdon son of Hillel, from Pirathon, led Israel. 14He had forty sons and thirty grandsons,[k] who rode on seventy donkeys.[l] He led Israel eight years. 15Then Abdon son of Hillel died, and was buried at Pirathon in Ephraim, in the hill country of the Amalekites.[m]

12:14
k Jdg 10:4
l Jdg 5:10
12:15
m Jdg 5:14

The Birth of Samson

13 Again the Israelites did evil in the eyes of the LORD, so the LORD delivered them into the hands of the Philistines[n] for forty years.

2A certain man of Zorah,[o] named Manoah, from the clan of the Danites, had a wife who was sterile and remained childless. 3The angel of the LORD[p] appeared to her[q] and said, "You are sterile and childless, but you are going to conceive and have a son.[r] 4Now see to it that you drink no wine or other fermented drink and that you

13:1
n Jdg 2:11;
1Sa 12:9
13:2
o Jos 15:33; 19:41
13:3
p ver 6,8; Jdg 6:12
q ver 10 r Lk 1:13

a 7 Traditionally *judged*; also in verses 8-14

his half brothers (11:1–2), rejected him. The implications of the Ephraimite taunt (12:4) weren't lost on the man who had suffered most of his life from the tag "illegiti-mate," nor on his fellow Gileadites. They answered by putting their neighboring tribe to a shameful rout.

Jealousy, envy, and other evils (James 3:13–18) can consume God's people. Think about the petty, unim-portant, unnecessary fights that destroy many churches. The long-term internal damage can be massive—not to mention the harm done to the church's witness (John 13:35)! What a contrast with Jesus, who was despised, rejected, betrayed, and utterly abandoned. Our suffering Savior serves as the ultimate model for overcoming every dysfunction. What harmful or hurt-filled incidents are you seeking, with his help, to overcome?

Judges 12:8–15

Ibzan arranged marriages for all his children to individuals outside his clan. In a tribal context, this would appear to have been a means of building and se-curing his power base. From the little information given, these three minor judges, along with Jair (10:3–5), seem

to have been motivated by ambitions for power and wealth. There is no mention of them delivering Israel from oppressors.

Rather than living up to their responsibilities in "saving" Israel and stimulating the people to godly living, the minor judges, with the exceptions of Shamgar (3:31) and Tola (10:1–2), are essentially portrayed as power-hun-gry, self-interested materialists. This negative characteri-zation serves as a warning for us today. Living in a culture that promotes materialistic self-interest and worships power, are you prone to give in to this mentality—or do you recognize that it fails to reflect the works of God?

Judges 13:1–25

Samson had a special status. Two visits from the angel of the Lord to his parents, his Nazirite calling from conception, and his miraculous birth stressed this stand-ing. Moreover, Samson had God's Spirit "stirring" him as he grew up. All this created the highest level of expecta-tion for this deliverer, since he had so much spiritual ad-vantage. But this only heightened the tragedy of his lost potential, squandered gifts, and failure to achieve.

do not eat anything unclean, [s] [5]because you will conceive and give birth to a son. No razor[t] may be used on his head, because the boy is to be a Nazirite, [u] set apart to God from birth, and he will begin[v] the deliverance of Israel from the hands of the Philistines."

[6]Then the woman went to her husband and told him, "A man of God[w] came to me. He looked like an angel of God, [x] very awesome. I didn't ask him where he came from, and he didn't tell me his name. [7]But he said to me, 'You will conceive and give birth to a son. Now then, drink no wine or other fermented drink and do not eat anything unclean, because the boy will be a Nazirite of God from birth until the day of his death.'"

[8]Then Manoah prayed to the LORD: "O Lord, I beg you, let the man of God you sent to us come again to teach us how to bring up the boy who is to be born."

[9]God heard Manoah, and the angel of God came again to the woman while she was out in the field; but her husband Manoah was not with her. [10]The woman hurried to tell her husband, "He's here! The man who appeared to me the other day!"

[11]Manoah got up and followed his wife. When he came to the man, he said, "Are you the one who talked to my wife?"

"I am," he said.

[12]So Manoah asked him, "When your words are fulfilled, what is to be the rule for the boy's life and work?"

[13]The angel of the LORD answered, "Your wife must do all that I have told her. [14]She must not eat anything that comes from the grapevine, nor drink any wine or other fermented drink[y] nor eat anything unclean.[z] She must do everything I have commanded her."

[15]Manoah said to the angel of the LORD, "We would like you to stay until we prepare a young goat[a] for you."

[16]The angel of the LORD replied, "Even though you detain me, I will not eat any of your food. But if you prepare a burnt offering,[b] offer it to the LORD." (Manoah did not realize that it was the angel of the LORD.)

[17]Then Manoah inquired of the angel of the LORD, "What is your name,[c] so that we may honor you when your word comes true?"

[18]He replied, "Why do you ask my name?[d] It is beyond understanding.[a]" [19]Then Manoah took a young goat, together with the grain offering, and sacrificed it on a rock[e] to the LORD. And the LORD did an amazing thing while Manoah and his wife watched: [20]As the flame[f] blazed up from the altar toward heaven, the angel of the LORD ascended in the flame. Seeing this, Manoah and his wife fell with their faces to the ground.[g] [21]When the angel of the LORD did not show himself again to Manoah and his wife, Manoah realized[h] that it was the angel of the LORD.

[22]"We are doomed[i] to die!" he said to his wife. "We have seen[j] God!"

[23]But his wife answered, "If the LORD had meant to kill us, he would not have accepted a burnt offering and grain offering from our hands, nor shown us all these things or now told us this."[k]

[24]The woman gave birth to a boy and named him Samson.[l] He grew[m] and the LORD blessed him,[n] [25]and the Spirit of the LORD began to stir[o] him while he was in Mahaneh Dan,[p] between Zorah and Eshtaol.

Samson's Marriage

14 Samson went down to Timnah[q] and saw there a young Philistine woman. [2]When he returned, he said to his father and mother, "I have seen a Philistine woman in Timnah; now get her for me as my wife."[r]

[a] 18 Or is wonderful

We live in an exciting time in that there are so many opportunities for the spread of the gospel. The potential with the many resources at the disposal of Christians—spiritual and otherwise—is immense. What will we do with these? What will you do as an individual?

Judges 14:1–20

Samson followed his sensual instincts—instincts that found foreign women more intriguing than those of Israel. Gideon had been ruled by logic, Jephthah by uninformed belief. Samson was motivated by lust, which over-

Cross-references (right margin)

13:4
s ver 14; Nu 6:2-4; Lk 1:15
13:5
t Nu 6:5; 1Sa 1:11
u Nu 6:2, 13
v 1Sa 7:13
13:6
w ver 8; 1Sa 2:27; 9:6 x ver 17-18; Mt 28:3

13:14
y Nu 6:4 z ver 4

13:15
a ver 3; Jdg 6:19

13:16
b Jdg 6:20

13:17
c Ge 32:29

13:18
d Isa 9:6

13:19
e Jdg 6:20
13:20
f Lev 9:24
g 1Ch 21:16; Eze 1:28; Mt 17:6

13:21
h ver 16; Jdg 6:22
13:22
i Dt 5:26
j Ge 32:30; Jdg 6:22
13:23
k Ps 25:14
13:24
l Heb 11:32
m 1Sa 3:19
n Lk 1:80
13:25
o Jdg 3:10
p Jdg 18:12

14:1
q Ge 38:12
14:2
r Ge 21:21; 34:4

14:3
s Ge 24:4 t Dt 7:3
u Ex 34:16

3His father and mother replied, "Isn't there an acceptable woman among your relatives or among all our people?[s] Must you go to the uncircumcised[t] Philistines to get a wife?[u]"

But Samson said to his father, "Get her for me. She's the right one for me." 4(His parents did not know that this was from the LORD, who was seeking an occasion to confront the Philistines;[v] for at that time they were ruling over Israel.)[w] 5Samson went down to Timnah together with his father and mother. As they approached the vineyards of Timnah, suddenly a young lion came roaring toward him. 6The Spirit of the LORD came upon him in power[x] so that he tore the lion apart with his bare hands as he might have torn a young goat. But he told neither his father nor his mother what he had done. 7Then he went down and talked with the woman, and he liked her.

14:4
v Jos 11:20
w Jdg 13:1

14:6
x Jdg 3:10; 13:25

8Some time later, when he went back to marry her, he turned aside to look at the lion's carcass. In it was a swarm of bees and some honey, 9which he scooped out with his hands and ate as he went along. When he rejoined his parents, he gave them some, and they too ate it. But he did not tell them that he had taken the honey from the lion's carcass.

10Now his father went down to see the woman. And Samson made a feast there, as was customary for bridegrooms. 11When he appeared, he was given thirty companions.

14:12
y 1Ki 10:1; Ecc 17:2
z Ge 29:27
a Ge 45:22; 2Ki 5:5

12"Let me tell you a riddle,[y]" Samson said to them. "If you can give me the answer within the seven days of the feast,[z] I will give you thirty linen garments and thirty sets of clothes.[a] 13If you can't tell me the answer, you must give me thirty linen garments and thirty sets of clothes."

"Tell us your riddle," they said. "Let's hear it."

14He replied,

> "Out of the eater, something to eat;
> out of the strong, something sweet."

For three days they could not give the answer.

14:15
b Jdg 16:5; Ecc 7:26
c Jdg 15:6

15On the fourth[a] day, they said to Samson's wife, "Coax[b] your husband into explaining the riddle for us, or we will burn you and your father's household to death.[c] Did you invite us here to rob us?"

14:16
d Jdg 16:15

16Then Samson's wife threw herself on him, sobbing, "You hate me! You don't really love me.[d] You've given my people a riddle, but you haven't told me the answer."

14:17
e Est 1:5

"I haven't even explained it to my father or mother," he replied, "so why should I explain it to you?" 17She cried the whole seven days[e] of the feast. So on the seventh day he finally told her, because she continued to press him. She in turn explained the riddle to her people.

18Before sunset on the seventh day the men of the town said to him,

14:18
f ver 14

> "What is sweeter than honey?
> What is stronger than a lion?"[f]

Samson said to them,

> "If you had not plowed with my heifer,
> you would not have solved my riddle."

14:19
g Nu 11:25;
Jdg 3:10; 6:34;
11:29; 13:25; 15:14;
1Sa 11:6; 16:13;
1Ki 18:46;
2Ch 24:20; Isa 11:2

19Then the Spirit of the LORD came upon him in power.[g] He went down to Ashkelon, struck down thirty of their men, stripped them of their belongings and gave

---

a 15 Some Septuagint manuscripts and Syriac; Hebrew *seventh*

---

rode for him all reason and faith. In addition, his demand to his parents revealed a total disregard for authority.

God's "seeking" in verse 4 didn't mean that he caused Samson's lustful desire for the Philistine woman. It does suggest that Samson's sinful actions happened to

coincide with a task God wanted to accomplish. God used Samson in spite of Samson's wrong motives and actions (cf. Gen. 50:20). This is still frequently God's modus operandi. Do you recognize it, either in your own life or in that of someone else you know?

their clothes to those who had explained the riddle. Burning with anger,[h] he went up to his father's house. [20]And Samson's wife was given to the friend[i] who had attended him at his wedding.

Samson's Vengeance on the Philistines

15 Later on, at the time of wheat harvest, Samson took a young goat[j] and went to visit his wife. He said, "I'm going to my wife's room." But her father would not let him go in.

[2]"I was so sure you thoroughly hated her," he said, "that I gave her to your friend.[k] Isn't her younger sister more attractive? Take her instead."

[3]Samson said to them, "This time I have a right to get even with the Philistines; I will really harm them." [4]So he went out and caught three hundred foxes and tied them tail to tail in pairs. He then fastened a torch to every pair of tails, [5]lit the torches and let the foxes loose in the standing grain of the Philistines. He burned up the shocks and standing grain, together with the vineyards and olive groves.

[6]When the Philistines asked, "Who did this?" they were told, "Samson, the Timnite's son-in-law, because his wife was given to his friend."

So the Philistines went up and burned her and her father to death.[l] [7]Samson said to them, "Since you've acted like this, I won't stop until I get my revenge on you." [8]He attacked them viciously and slaughtered many of them. Then he went down and stayed in a cave in the rock of Etam.

[9]The Philistines went up and camped in Judah, spreading out near Lehi.[m] [10]The men of Judah asked, "Why have you come to fight us?"

"We have come to take Samson prisoner," they answered, "to do to him as he did to us."

[11]Then three thousand men from Judah went down to the cave in the rock of Etam and said to Samson, "Don't you realize that the Philistines are rulers over us?[n] What have you done to us?"

He answered, "I merely did to them what they did to me."

[12]They said to him, "We've come to tie you up and hand you over to the Philistines."

Samson said, "Swear to me that you won't kill me yourselves."

[13]"Agreed," they answered. "We will only tie you up and hand you over to them. We will not kill you." So they bound him with two new ropes and led him up from the rock. [14]As he approached Lehi, the Philistines came toward him shouting. The Spirit of the LORD came upon him in power.[o] The ropes on his arms became like charred flax, and the bindings dropped from his hands. [15]Finding a fresh jawbone of a donkey, he grabbed it and struck down a thousand men.[p]

[16]Then Samson said,

"With a donkey's jawbone
 I have made donkeys of them.[a]
With a donkey's jawbone
 I have killed a thousand men."

[17]When he finished speaking, he threw away the jawbone; and the place was called Ramath Lehi.[b]

[18]Because he was very thirsty, he cried out to the LORD,[q] "You have given your ser-

---

[a] 16 Or *made a heap or two*; the Hebrew for *donkey* sounds like the Hebrew for *heap*.   [b] 17 *Ramath Lehi* means *jawbone hill*.

Cross references

14:19
[h] 1Sa 11:6
14:20
[i] Jdg 15:2,6; Jn 3:29

15:1
[j] Ge 38:17

15:2
[k] Jdg 14:20

15:6
[l] Jdg 14:15

15:9
[m] ver 14,17,19

15:11
[n] Jdg 13:1; 14:4; Ps 106:40-42

15:14
[o] Jdg 3:10; 14:19; 1Sa 11:6
15:15
[p] Lev 26:8; Jos 23:10; Jdg 3:31

15:18
[q] Jdg 16:28

Judges 15:1–20

In matters of motivation, Samson was no different from the Philistines. This section is all about retaliation and counter-retaliation. Sadly, God's appointed deliverer exhibited the same behavior as the unbelieving Philistines.

The world encourages us to live like Samson—to "just do it," to "go for it." Ads target our senses, and appearance is everything. If we don't have the right stuff, we are told, we have, and are, nothing. Samson lived in a style our culture would endorse. But those who follow the code "Whatever's right in my eyes is what I will do" will answer to God one day. How do you see this mentality demonstrated in the choices of Christians? In your own personal decisions and values?

15:19
r Ge 45:27;
Isa 40:29
15:20
s Jdg 13:1; 16:31;
Heb 11:32

vant this great victory. Must I now die of thirst and fall into the hands of the uncircumcised?" [19]Then God opened up the hollow place in Lehi, and water came out of it. When Samson drank, his strength returned and he revived.[r] So the spring was called En Hakkore,[a] and it is still there in Lehi.

[20]Samson led[b] Israel for twenty years[s] in the days of the Philistines.

Samson and Delilah

16 One day Samson went to Gaza, where he saw a prostitute. He went in to spend the night with her. [2]The people of Gaza were told, "Samson is here!" So they surrounded the place and lay in wait for him all night at the city gate.[t] They made no move during the night, saying, "At dawn we'll kill him."

16:2
t 1Sa 23:26;
Ps 118:10-12;
Ac 9:24

[3]But Samson lay there only until the middle of the night. Then he got up and took hold of the doors of the city gate, together with the two posts, and tore them loose, bar and all. He lifted them to his shoulders and carried them to the top of the hill that faces Hebron.[u]

16:3
u Jos 10:36
16:4
v Ge 24:67
16:5
w Jos 13:3
x Ex 10:7;
Jdg 14:15 y ver 18

[4]Some time later, he fell in love[v] with a woman in the Valley of Sorek whose name was Delilah. [5]The rulers of the Philistines[w] went to her and said, "See if you can lure[x] him into showing you the secret of his great strength and how we can overpower him so we may tie him up and subdue him. Each one of us will give you eleven hundred shekels[c] of silver."[y]

[6]So Delilah said to Samson, "Tell me the secret of your great strength and how you can be tied up and subdued."

[7]Samson answered her, "If anyone ties me with seven fresh thongs[d] that have not been dried, I'll become as weak as any other man."

[8]Then the rulers of the Philistines brought her seven fresh thongs that had not been dried, and she tied him with them. [9]With men hidden in the room,[z] she called to him, "Samson, the Philistines are upon you!" But he snapped the thongs as easily as a piece of string snaps when it comes close to a flame. So the secret of his strength was not discovered.

16:9
z ver 12

[10]Then Delilah said to Samson, "You have made a fool of me;[a] you lied to me. Come now, tell me how you can be tied."

16:10
a ver 13

[11]He said, "If anyone ties me securely with new ropes[b] that have never been used, I'll become as weak as any other man."

16:11
b Jdg 15:13

[12]So Delilah took new ropes and tied him with them. Then, with men hidden in the room, she called to him, "Samson, the Philistines are upon you!" But he snapped the ropes off his arms as if they were threads.

[13]Delilah then said to Samson, "Until now, you have been making a fool of me and lying to me. Tell me how you can be tied."

He replied, "If you weave the seven braids of my head into the fabric ⌞on the loom⌟ and tighten it with the pin, I'll become as weak as any other man." So while he was sleeping, Delilah took the seven braids of his head, wove them into the fabric [14]and[e] tightened it with the pin.

---

[a] 19 En Hakkore means caller's spring.   [b] 20 Traditionally judged   [c] 5 That is, about 28 pounds (about 13 kilograms)   [d] 7 Or bowstrings; also in verses 8 and 9   [e] 13,14 Some Septuagint manuscripts; Hebrew "I can; if you weave the seven braids of my head into the fabric ⌞on the loom⌟." [14]So she

---

Judges 16:1–22

The last chapter of Samson's life involves, again, Philistine women. While Samson may have been able to uproot the gates of Gaza and carry them a great distance uphill, he couldn't withstand his own lust. Delilah's tightening of the hairpin reminds us of Jael's striking the tent peg into Sisera's temple (4:21). Both scenes took place in a woman's private quarters while a man slept. Delilah, like Samson, was driven by self-interest. "Love" was the last thing on her mind. Instead, money motivated her betrayal.

Samson's lust led him to abuse and exploit women. In a real, though different, sense, Delilah also viewed Samson as an object to be used. Biblical standards call for the highest respect for others, who are equally created in God's image and endowed with dignity. Biblical texts regard sex as sacred, reserved for a man and a woman within the context of marriage. Anything less is inherently wrong, demeaning, and exploitive. How do our standards within the Christian community measure up? What about your personal principles?

Again she called to him, "Samson, the Philistines are upon you!"[c] He awoke from his sleep and pulled up the pin and the loom, with the fabric.

[15]Then she said to him, "How can you say, 'I love you,'[d] when you won't confide in me? This is the third time[e] you have made a fool of me and haven't told me the secret of your great strength.[f]" [16]With such nagging she prodded him day after day until he was tired to death.

[17]So he told her everything.[g] "No razor has ever been used on my head," he said, "because I have been a Nazirite[h] set apart to God since birth. If my head were shaved, my strength would leave me, and I would become as weak as any other man."

[18]When Delilah saw that he had told her everything, she sent word to the rulers of the Philistines[i], "Come back once more; he has told me everything." So the rulers of the Philistines returned with the silver in their hands. [19]Having put him to sleep on her lap, she called a man to shave off the seven braids of his hair, and so began to subdue him.[a] And his strength left him.[j]

[20]Then she called, "Samson, the Philistines are upon you!"

He awoke from his sleep and thought, "I'll go out as before and shake myself free." But he did not know that the LORD had left him.[k]

[21]Then the Philistines[l] seized him, gouged out his eyes[m] and took him down to Gaza. Binding him with bronze shackles, they set him to grinding[n] in the prison. [22]But the hair on his head began to grow again after it had been shaved.

The Death of Samson

[23]Now the rulers of the Philistines assembled to offer a great sacrifice to Dagon[o] their god and to celebrate, saying, "Our god has delivered Samson, our enemy, into our hands."

[24]When the people saw him, they praised their god,[p] saying,

"Our god has delivered our enemy
 into our hands,[q]
the one who laid waste our land
 and multiplied our slain."

[25]While they were in high spirits,[r] they shouted, "Bring out Samson to entertain us." So they called Samson out of the prison, and he performed for them.

When they stood him among the pillars, [26]Samson said to the servant who held his hand, "Put me where I can feel the pillars that support the temple, so that I may lean against them." [27]Now the temple was crowded with men and women; all the rulers of the Philistines were there, and on the roof[s] were about three thousand men and women watching Samson perform. [28]Then Samson prayed to the LORD,[t] "O Sovereign LORD, remember me. O God, please strengthen me just once more, and let me with one blow get revenge[u] on the Philistines for my two eyes." [29]Then Samson reached toward the two central pillars on which the temple stood. Bracing himself against them, his right hand on the one and his left hand on the other, [30]Samson said, "Let me die with the Philistines!" Then he pushed with all his might, and down came the temple on the rulers and all the people in it. Thus he killed many more when he died than while he lived.

[a] 19 Hebrew; some Septuagint manuscripts *and he began to weaken*

Cross references

16:14
c ver 9,20

16:15
d Jdg 14:16
e Nu 24:10 f ver 5

16:17
g Mic 7:5 h Nu 6:2, 5; Jdg 13:5

16:18
i Jos 13:3; 1Sa 5:8

16:19
j Pr 7:26-27

16:20
k Nu 14:42; Jos 7:12; 1Sa 16:14; 18:12; 28:15
16:21
l Jer 47:1
m Nu 16:14
n Job 31:10; Isa 47:2

16:23
o 1Sa 5:2; 1Ch 10:10

16:24
p Da 5:4
q 1Sa 31:9; 1Ch 10:9

16:25
r Jdg 9:27; Ru 3:7; Est 1:10

16:27
s Dt 22:8; Jos 2:8
16:28
t Jdg 15:18
u Jer 15:15

Judges 16:23–31

Samson's prayer was self-centered, peppered with first-person pronouns. He expressed no thought for the nation he was supposed to be delivering, let alone for the Lord, whose name and reputation had been defamed. Samson killed more Philistines (and accomplished more in general) in his death than during his life. This was especially true since the "dead" in the temple included a god! Thus, in spite of Samson's personal motive of revenge, God used him to begin to deliver Israel. There could be no doubt as to who was the true and living God.

Samson wasn't, as has been suggested, a "type" or representation of Christ. Nowhere is this implied in either the Old or New Testament. There were similarities (e.g., saving people in death), but the contrasts were much greater—and the similarities highlight the contrasts all the more.

Many divinely called and exceptionally gifted Christian leaders have given in to sin. No matter what your role or stature, what are you doing to protect yourself from temptation or spiritual laziness?

31Then his brothers and his father's whole family went down to get him. They brought him back and buried him between Zorah and Eshtaol in the tomb of Manoah v his father. He had led a w Israel twenty years. x

Micah's Idols

17 Now a man named Micah y from the hill country of Ephraim 2said to his mother, "The eleven hundred shekels b of silver that were taken from you and about which I heard you utter a curse—I have that silver with me; I took it."

Then his mother said, "The LORD bless you, z my son!"

3When he returned the eleven hundred shekels of silver to his mother, she said, "I solemnly consecrate my silver to the LORD for my son to make a carved image and a cast idol. a I will give it back to you."

4So he returned the silver to his mother, and she took two hundred shekels c of silver and gave them to a silversmith, who made them into the image and the idol. b And they were put in Micah's house.

5Now this man Micah had a shrine, c and he made an ephod d and some idols e and installed f one of his sons as his priest. g 6In those days Israel had no king; h everyone did as he saw fit. i

17:5
c Isa 44:13;
Eze 8:10 d Jdg 8:27
e Ge 31:19;
Jdg 18:14
f Nu 16:10
g Ex 29:9;
Jdg 18:24
17:6
h Jdg 18:1; 19:1;
21:25 i Dt 12:8

7A young Levite from Bethlehem in Judah, j who had been living within the clan of Judah, 8left that town in search of some other place to stay. On his way d he came to Micah's house in the hill country of Ephraim.

9Micah asked him, "Where are you from?"

"I'm a Levite from Bethlehem in Judah," he said, "and I'm looking for a place to stay."

10Then Micah said to him, "Live with me and be my father and priest, k and I'll give you ten shekels e of silver a year, your clothes and your food." 11So the Levite agreed to live with him, and the young man was to him like one of his sons. 12Then Micah installed l the Levite, and the young man became his priest and lived in his house. 13And Micah said, "Now I know that the LORD will be good to me, since this Levite has become my priest."

Danites Settle in Laish

18 In those days Israel had no king. m And in those days the tribe of the Danites was seeking a place of their own where they might settle, because they had not yet come into an inheritance among the tribes of Israel. n 2So the Danites o sent five warriors from Zorah and Eshtaol to spy out the land and explore it. These men represented all their clans. They told them, "Go, explore the land." p

The men entered the hill country of Ephraim and came to the house of Micah, q

---

a 31 Traditionally *judged*   b 2 That is, about 28 pounds (about 13 kilograms)   c 4 That is, about 5 pounds (about 2.3 kilograms)   d 8 Or *To carry on his profession*   e 10 That is, about 4 ounces (about 110 grams)

Judges 17:1–13

Disregard for parental well-being, theft, homemade idols of stolen silver, private shrines, personal priests, self-made religious paraphernalia—hardly appropriate for someone whose name meant "Who is like God?"! Thinking they were doing right, both Micah and his mother acted contrary to God's requirements in Deuteronomy 12.

The Levite was a wandering opportunist. But having a genuine Levite as his priest gave Micah's shrine an air of legitimacy. The setting was disturbing: the hill country of Ephraim—the tribal area where God's true tabernacle was located (i.e., in Shiloh; 18:31).

As we see in this story, which continues through Judges 18, one sin leads to another. Is there an area

where you are in danger of taking that first or next destructive step? Reflecting on this interlocking nature of sin may help us see how we have gotten to where we are personally. We are wise to call out to the Lord in repentance and seek his forgiveness, to invite him to intervene to break the destructive power and pattern of sin.

Judges 18:1–31

It's almost amusing that the Danites bothered to inquire about God's will when God had already revealed it in the tribal allotments. Micah's illegitimate ephod and household gods ruled out any favor from God. The Levite's message, declared in God's name, was just what they wanted to hear, but it obviously wasn't from God, who condemned such practices.

where they spent the night. 3When they were near Micah's house, they recognized the voice of the young Levite; so they turned in there and asked him, "Who brought you here? What are you doing in this place? Why are you here?"

4He told them what Micah had done for him, and said, "He has hired me and I am his priest.*r*"

5Then they said to him, "Please inquire of God*s* to learn whether our journey will be successful."

6The priest answered them, "Go in peace.*t* Your journey has the LORD's approval."

7So the five men left and came to Laish,*u* where they saw that the people were living in safety, like the Sidonians, unsuspecting and secure. And since their land lacked nothing, they were prosperous.*a* Also, they lived a long way from the Sidonians*v* and had no relationship with anyone else.*b*

8When they returned to Zorah and Eshtaol, their brothers asked them, "How did you find things?"

9They answered, "Come on, let's attack them! We have seen that the land is very good. Aren't you going to do something? Don't hesitate to go there and take it over.*w* 10When you get there, you will find an unsuspecting people and a spacious land that God has put into your hands, a land that lacks nothing*x* whatever.*y*"

11Then six hundred men*z* from the clan of the Danites,*a* armed for battle, set out from Zorah and Eshtaol. 12On their way they set up camp near Kiriath Jearim in Judah. This is why the place west of Kiriath Jearim is called Mahaneh Dan*c b* to this day. 13From there they went on to the hill country of Ephraim and came to Micah's house.

14Then the five men who had spied out the land of Laish said to their brothers, "Do you know that one of these houses has an ephod, other household gods, a carved image and a cast idol?*c* Now you know what to do." 15So they turned in there and went to the house of the young Levite at Micah's place and greeted him. 16The six hundred Danites,*d* armed for battle, stood at the entrance to the gate. 17The five men who had spied out the land went inside and took the carved image, the ephod, the other household gods*e* and the cast idol while the priest and the six hundred armed men stood at the entrance to the gate.

18When these men went into Micah's house and took*f* the carved image, the ephod, the other household gods and the cast idol, the priest said to them, "What are you doing?"

19They answered him, "Be quiet!*g* Don't say a word. Come with us, and be our father and priest.*h* Isn't it better that you serve a tribe and clan in Israel as priest rather than just one man's household?" 20Then the priest was glad. He took the ephod, the other household gods and the carved image and went along with the people. 21Putting their little children, their livestock and their possessions in front of them, they turned away and left.

22When they had gone some distance from Micah's house, the men who lived near Micah were called together and overtook the Danites. 23As they shouted after them, the Danites turned and said to Micah, "What's the matter with you that you called out your men to fight?"

24He replied, "You took the gods I made, and my priest, and went away. What else do I have? How can you ask, 'What's the matter with you?' "

25The Danites answered, "Don't argue with us, or some hot-tempered men will attack you, and you and your family will lose your lives." 26So the Danites went their way, and Micah, seeing that they were too strong for him,*i* turned around and went back home.

27Then they took what Micah had made, and his priest, and went on to Laish,

18:4
r Jdg 17:12
18:5
s 1Ki 22:5
18:6
t 1Ki 22:6
18:7
u Jos 19:47 *v* ver 28

18:9
w Nu 13:30;
1Ki 22:3
18:10
x ver 7,27; Dt 8:9
y 1Ch 4:40
18:11
z ver 16,17
a Jdg 13:2
18:12
b Jdg 13:25

18:14
c Ge 31:19;
Jdg 17:5
18:16
d ver 11

18:17
e Ge 31:19;
Mic 5:13
18:18
f Isa 46:2;
Jer 43:11; Hos 10:5
18:19
g Job 21:5; 29:9;
40:4; Mic 7:16
h Jdg 17:10

18:26
i Ps 18:17; 35:10

---

a 7 The meaning of the Hebrew for this clause is uncertain.   *b* 7 Hebrew; some Septuagint manuscripts *with the Arameans*   *c* 12 Mahaneh Dan means *Dan's camp.*

People's efforts today to put all kinds of things in God's place also appear foolish in the light of Scripture. All the things our society seeks as God-substitutes are illusions—meaningless props. How can we as Christians communicate the truth to a misguided world?

18:27
j ver 7,10
k Ge 49:17;
Jos 19:47
18:28
l ver 7 m Nu 13:21;
2Sa 10:6
18:29
n Ge 14:14
o Jos 19:47;
1Ki 15:20
18:30
p Ex 2:22;
Jdg 17:3,5
18:31
q Jdg 19:18
r Jos 18:1; Jer 7:14

against a peaceful and unsuspecting people.^j They attacked them with the sword and burned down their city. ^k 28There was no one to rescue them because they lived a long way from Sidon^l and had no relationship with anyone else. The city was in a valley near Beth Rehob.^m

The Danites rebuilt the city and settled there. 29They named it Danⁿ after their forefather Dan, who was born to Israel—though the city used to be called Laish.^o 30There the Danites set up for themselves the idols, and Jonathan son of Gershom,^p the son of Moses,^a and his sons were priests for the tribe of Dan until the time of the captivity of the land. 31They continued to use the idols Micah had made, all the time the house of God^q was in Shiloh.^r

A Levite and His Concubine

19:1
s Jdg 18:1 t Ru 1:1

19 In those days Israel had no king.

Now a Levite who lived in a remote area in the hill country of Ephraim^s took a concubine from Bethlehem in Judah.^t 2But she was unfaithful to him. She left him and went back to her father's house in Bethlehem, Judah. After she had been there four months, 3her husband went to her to persuade her to return. He had with him his servant and two donkeys. She took him into her father's house, and when her father saw him, he gladly welcomed him. 4His father-in-law, the girl's father, prevailed upon him to stay; so he remained with him three days, eating and

19:4
u Ex 32:6

drinking,^u and sleeping there.

19:5
v ver 8; Ge 18:5
19:6
w ver 9,22;
Jdg 16:25

5On the fourth day they got up early and he prepared to leave, but the girl's father said to his son-in-law, "Refresh yourself^v with something to eat; then you can go." 6So the two of them sat down to eat and drink together. Afterward the girl's father said, "Please stay tonight and enjoy yourself.^w" 7And when the man got up to go, his father-in-law persuaded him, so he stayed there that night. 8On the morning of the fifth day, when he rose to go, the girl's father said, "Refresh yourself. Wait till afternoon!" So the two of them ate together.

9Then when the man, with his concubine and his servant, got up to leave, his father-in-law, the girl's father, said, "Now look, it's almost evening. Spend the night here; the day is nearly over. Stay and enjoy yourself. Early tomorrow morning you

19:10
x Ge 10:16;
Jos 15:8;
1Ch 11:4-5

can get up and be on your way home." 10But, unwilling to stay another night, the man left and went toward Jebus^x (that is, Jerusalem), with his two saddled donkeys and his concubine.

19:11
y Jos 3:10

11When they were near Jebus and the day was almost gone, the servant said to his master, "Come, let's stop at this city of the Jebusites^y and spend the night."

19:13
z Jos 18:25
19:14
a 1Sa 10:26;
Isa 10:29
19:15
b Ge 19:2
19:16
c Ps 104:23 d ver 1

12His master replied, "No. We won't go into an alien city, whose people are not Israelites. We will go on to Gibeah." 13He added, "Come, let's try to reach Gibeah or Ramah^z and spend the night in one of those places." 14So they went on, and the sun set as they neared Gibeah in Benjamin.^a 15There they stopped to spend the night. They went and sat in the city square,^b but no one took them into his home for the night.

16That evening^c an old man from the hill country of Ephraim,^d who was living in Gibeah (the men of the place were Benjamites), came in from his work in the fields. 17When he looked and saw the traveler in the city square, the old man

19:17
e Ge 29:4

asked, "Where are you going? Where did you come from?"^e

18He answered, "We are on our way from Bethlehem in Judah to a remote area

^a 30 An ancient Hebrew scribal tradition, some Septuagint manuscripts and Vulgate; Masoretic Text *Manasseh*

Judges 19:1–30

The old man, the "model host," came up with the idea of throwing the concubine (and his own daughter!) to the horde at the door. Amazingly, the Levite complied. The scene reminds us of Lot in Sodom (cf. Gen. 19:1–11) and underscores Israel's moral decline.

The Levite's casual "getting up," almost at the same time as his concubine's collapse, chills us. He appears to

have given no thought to her until he practically tripped over her at the door. With unbelievable coldness he commanded her to "get up"—he was ready to go. The two returned to Ephraim—with the jarring twist that she was dead.

The story beginning with a minor problem ended with a major one; the Levite parted with his concubine by cutting her up and sending her body parts to the tribes of

in the hill country of Ephraim where I live. I have been to Bethlehem in Judah and now I am going to the house of the LORD.*f* No one has taken me into his house. ¹⁹We have both straw and fodder*g* for our donkeys and bread and wine*h* for ourselves your servants—me, your maidservant, and the young man with us. We don't need anything."

²⁰"You are welcome at my house," the old man said. "Let me supply whatever you need. Only don't spend the night in the square." ²¹So he took him into his house and fed his donkeys. After they had washed their feet, they had something to eat and drink.*i*

²²While they were enjoying themselves,*j* some of the wicked men*k* of the city surrounded the house. Pounding on the door, they shouted to the old man who owned the house, "Bring out the man who came to your house so we can have sex with him.*l*"

²³The owner of the house went outside*m* and said to them, "No, my friends, don't be so vile. Since this man is my guest, don't do this disgraceful thing.*n* ²⁴Look, here is my virgin daughter,*o* and his concubine. I will bring them out to you now, and you can use them and do to them whatever you wish. But to this man, don't do such a disgraceful thing."

²⁵But the men would not listen to him. So the man took his concubine and sent her outside to them, and they raped her and abused her*p* throughout the night, and at dawn they let her go. ²⁶At daybreak the woman went back to the house where her master was staying, fell down at the door and lay there until daylight.

²⁷When her master got up in the morning and opened the door of the house and stepped out to continue on his way, there lay his concubine, fallen in the doorway of the house, with her hands on the threshold. ²⁸He said to her, "Get up; let's go." But there was no answer. Then the man put her on his donkey and set out for home.

²⁹When he reached home, he took a knife*q* and cut up his concubine, limb by limb, into twelve parts and sent them into all the areas of Israel.*r* ³⁰Everyone who saw it said, "Such a thing has never been seen or done, not since the day the Israelites came up out of Egypt.*s* Think about it! Consider it! Tell us what to do!*t*"

Israelites Fight the Benjamites

20 Then all the Israelites*u* from Dan to Beersheba*v* and from the land of Gilead came out as one man*w* and assembled*x* before the LORD in Mizpah. ²The leaders of all the people of the tribes of Israel took their places in the assembly of the people of God, four hundred thousand soldiers*y* armed with swords. ³(The Benjamites heard that the Israelites had gone up to Mizpah.) Then the Israelites said, "Tell us how this awful thing happened."

⁴So the Levite, the husband of the murdered woman, said, "I and my concubine came to Gibeah*z* in Benjamin to spend the night.*a* ⁵During the night the men of Gibeah came after me and surrounded the house, intending to kill me.*b* They raped my concubine, and she died.*c* ⁶I took my concubine, cut her into pieces and sent one

Margin references

19:18
f Jdg 18:31
19:19
g Ge 24:25
h Ge 14:18

19:21
i Ge 24:32-33; Lk 7:44
19:22
j Jdg 16:25
k Dt 13:13
l Ge 19:4-5; Jdg 20:5; Ro 1:26-27
19:23
m Ge 19:6
n Ge 34:7; Lev 19:29; Dt 22:21; Jdg 20:6; 2Sa 13:12; Ro 1:27
19:24
o Ge 19:8; Dt 21:14

19:25
p 1Sa 31:4

19:29
q Ge 22:6
r Jdg 20:6; 1Sa 11:7

19:30
s Hos 9:9
t Jdg 20:7; Pr 13:10

20:1
u Jdg 21:5
v 1Sa 3:20; 2Sa 3:10; 1Ki 4:25
w 1Sa 11:7
x 1Sa 7:5
20:2
y Jdg 8:10

20:4
z Jos 15:57
a Jdg 19:15
20:5
b Jdg 19:22
c Jdg 19:25-26

Israel. The intention of the dismemberment seems to have been to awaken Israel from her moral lethargy and to stimulate justice. But this act was in effect a call to arms, a summons to an outrageous response.

📖 There are many victims like the concubine today—ill-fated casualties of a world that ignores or rejects God. They are often those whom society deems "least important"—women, children, minorities, vagrants, the homeless, the disabled, the poor—those powerless to defend themselves. If we as Christians fail to demonstrate Christ's love for such people, we have become more like our calloused, violent world than like our Savior. What one thing can you do to reverse this trend?

Judges 20:1–48

👥 This nameless Levite became a self-appointed judge, earning the greatest response from the greatest number of tribes in Judges! He gave a distorted account, implying that his life had been threatened, that he had escaped, but that his concubine had been caught and raped. In reality, he had sacrificed her to save his neck and was now willing to sacrifice the "sons of Israel" in personal revenge.

While the situation was a moral outrage, Israel's leaders should have been equally upset with Micah, his Levite "priest," and the Danites (cf. 17:1—18:31). They also ignored God's requirement that godly leadership should "inquire, probe and investigate (a matter) thoroughly" (Deut. 13:14).

piece to each region of Israel's inheritance,[d] because they committed this lewd and disgraceful act[e] in Israel. [7]Now, all you Israelites, speak up and give your verdict.[f]"

[8]All the people rose as one man, saying, "None of us will go home. No, not one of us will return to his house. [9]But now this is what we'll do to Gibeah: We'll go up against it as the lot directs.[g] [10]We'll take ten men out of every hundred from all the tribes of Israel, and a hundred from a thousand, and a thousand from ten thousand, to get provisions for the army. Then, when the army arrives at Gibeah[a] in Benjamin, it can give them what they deserve for all this vileness done in Israel." [11]So all the men of Israel got together and united as one man[h] against the city.

[12]The tribes of Israel sent men throughout the tribe of Benjamin, saying, "What about this awful crime that was committed among you? [13]Now surrender those wicked men[i] of Gibeah so that we may put them to death and purge the evil from Israel.[j]"

But the Benjamites would not listen to their fellow Israelites. [14]From their towns they came together at Gibeah to fight against the Israelites. [15]At once the Benjamites mobilized twenty-six thousand swordsmen from their towns, in addition to seven hundred chosen men from those living in Gibeah. [16]Among all these soldiers there were seven hundred chosen men who were left-handed,[k] each of whom could sling a stone at a hair and not miss.

[17]Israel, apart from Benjamin, mustered four hundred thousand swordsmen, all of them fighting men.

[18]The Israelites went up to Bethel[b] and inquired of God.[l] They said, "Who of us shall go first to fight[m] against the Benjamites?"

The LORD replied, "Judah shall go first."

[19]The next morning the Israelites got up and pitched camp near Gibeah. [20]The men of Israel went out to fight the Benjamites and took up battle positions against them at Gibeah. [21]The Benjamites came out of Gibeah and cut down twenty-two thousand Israelites[n] on the battlefield that day. [22]But the men of Israel encouraged one another and again took up their positions where they had stationed themselves the first day. [23]The Israelites went up and wept before the LORD until evening,[o] and they inquired of the LORD. They said, "Shall we go up again to battle[p] against the Benjamites, our brothers?"

The LORD answered, "Go up against them."

[24]Then the Israelites drew near to Benjamin the second day. [25]This time, when the Benjamites came out from Gibeah to oppose them, they cut down another eighteen thousand Israelites,[q] all of them armed with swords.

[26]Then the Israelites, all the people, went up to Bethel, and there they sat weeping before the LORD.[r] They fasted that day until evening and presented burnt offerings and fellowship offerings[c] to the LORD.[s] [27]And the Israelites inquired of the LORD. (In those days the ark of the covenant of God[t] was there, [28]with Phinehas son of Eleazar,[u] the son of Aaron, ministering before it.)[v] They asked, "Shall we go up again to battle with Benjamin our brother, or not?"

The LORD responded, "Go, for tomorrow I will give them into your hands.[w]"

[29]Then Israel set an ambush[x] around Gibeah. [30]They went up against the Benjamites on the third day and took up positions against Gibeah as they had done before. [31]The Benjamites came out to meet them and were drawn away[y] from the city. They began to inflict casualties on the Israelites as before, so that about thirty men

Cross references

20:6
[d] Jdg 19:29
[e] Jos 7:15; Jdg 19:23
20:7
[f] Jdg 19:30
20:9
[g] Lev 16:8

20:11
[h] ver 1

20:13
[i] Dt 13:13; Jdg 19:22
[j] Dt 17:12

20:16
[k] Jdg 3:15; 1Ch 12:2

20:18
[l] ver 26-27; Nu 27:21 [m] ver 23, 28

20:21
[n] ver 25

20:23
[o] Jos 7:6 [p] ver 18

20:25
[q] ver 21

20:26
[r] ver 23 [s] Jdg 21:4

20:27
[t] Jos 18:1

20:28
[u] Jos 24:33
[v] Dt 18:5 [w] Jdg 7:9

20:29
[x] Jos 8:2,4

20:31
[y] Jos 8:16

---

[a] 10 One Hebrew manuscript; most Hebrew manuscripts *Geba*, a variant of *Gibeah*   [b] 18 Or *to the house of God*; also in verse 26   [c] 26 Traditionally *peace offerings*

It isn't uncommon for religious charlatans or spiritual quacks to draw large crowds and influence unknowledgeable Christians. Such individuals inspire many to sacrifice their hard-earned money to support ministries motivated by self-interest (Titus 1:11). How can you tell the difference between a godly leader and an impostor?

The Benjamites fought in blind loyalty—protecting men guilty of a despicable act. Christians, too, sometimes act as if loyalty is a greater virtue than defending what's right. God holds evildoers accountable before restoring them. But some religious leaders reverse the order—never making it to the accountability part. How can you make sure you will seek God's way of truth and accountability, not convenience and scandal-avoidance?

fell in the open field and on the roads—the one leading to Bethel and the other to Gibeah.

³²While the Benjamites were saying, "We are defeating them as before," ᶻ the Israelites were saying, "Let's retreat and draw them away from the city to the roads."

³³All the men of Israel moved from their places and took up positions at Baal Tamar, and the Israelite ambush charged out of its place ᵃ on the west ᵃ of Gibeah. ᵇ ³⁴Then ten thousand of Israel's finest men made a frontal attack on Gibeah. The fighting was so heavy that the Benjamites did not realize ᵇ how near disaster was. ᶜ ³⁵The LORD defeated Benjamin ᵈ before Israel, and on that day the Israelites struck down 25,100 Benjamites, all armed with swords. ³⁶Then the Benjamites saw that they were beaten.

Now the men of Israel had given way ᵉ before Benjamin, because they relied on the ambush they had set near Gibeah. ³⁷The men who had been in ambush made a sudden dash into Gibeah, spread out and put the whole city to the sword. ᶠ ³⁸The men of Israel had arranged with the ambush that they should send up a great cloud of smoke ᵍ from the city, ³⁹and then the men of Israel would turn in the battle.

The Benjamites had begun to inflict casualties on the men of Israel (about thirty), and they said, "We are defeating them as in the first battle." ʰ ⁴⁰But when the column of smoke began to rise from the city, the Benjamites turned and saw the smoke of the whole city going up into the sky. ⁱ ⁴¹Then the men of Israel turned on them, and the men of Benjamin were terrified, because they realized that disaster had come upon them. ⁴²So they fled before the Israelites in the direction of the desert, but they could not escape the battle. And the men of Israel who came out of the towns cut them down there. ⁴³They surrounded the Benjamites, chased them and easily ᶜ overran them in the vicinity of Gibeah on the east. ⁴⁴Eighteen thousand Benjamites fell, all of them valiant fighters. ʲ ⁴⁵As they turned and fled toward the desert to the rock of Rimmon, ᵏ the Israelites cut down five thousand men along the roads. They kept pressing after the Benjamites as far as Gidom and struck down two thousand more.

⁴⁶On that day twenty-five thousand Benjamite swordsmen fell, all of them valiant fighters. ⁴⁷But six hundred men turned and fled into the desert to the rock of Rimmon, where they stayed four months. ⁴⁸The men of Israel went back to Benjamin and put all the towns to the sword, including the animals and everything else they found. All the towns they came across they set on fire. ˡ

Wives for the Benjamites

21 The men of Israel had taken an oath ᵐ at Mizpah: ⁿ "Not one of us will give ᵒ his daughter in marriage to a Benjamite."

²The people went to Bethel, ᵈ where they sat before God until evening, raising their voices and weeping bitterly. ³"O LORD, the God of Israel," they cried, "why has this happened to Israel? Why should one tribe be missing from Israel today?"

⁴Early the next day the people built an altar and presented burnt offerings and fellowship offerings. ᵉ ᵖ

⁵Then the Israelites asked, "Who from all the tribes of Israel �q has failed to assemble before the LORD?" For they had taken a solemn oath that anyone who failed to assemble before the LORD at Mizpah should certainly be put to death.

⁶Now the Israelites grieved for their brothers, the Benjamites. "Today one tribe is

20:32 ᶻ ver 39

20:33 ᵃ Jos 8:19
20:34 ᵇ Jos 8:14
ᶜ Isa 47:11
20:35 ᵈ 1Sa 9:21

20:36 ᵉ Jos 8:15

20:37 ᶠ Jos 8:19

20:38 ᵍ Jos 8:20

20:39 ʰ ver 32

20:40 ⁱ Jos 8:20

20:44 ʲ Ps 76:5
20:45 ᵏ Jos 15:32; Jdg 21:13

20:48 ˡ Jdg 21:23

21:1 ᵐ Jos 9:18
ⁿ Jdg 20:1 ᵒ ver 7, 18

21:4 ᵖ Jdg 20:26; 2Sa 24:25
21:5 q Jdg 5:23; 20:1

ᵃ 33 Some Septuagint manuscripts and Vulgate; the meaning of the Hebrew for this word is uncertain.   ᵇ 33 Hebrew *Geba*, a variant of *Gibeah*   ᶜ 43 The meaning of the Hebrew for this word is uncertain.   ᵈ 2 Or *to the house of God*   ᵉ 4 Traditionally *peace offerings*

Judges 21:1–25

📖 The elders did, in principle, the same kind of thing the old man and the Levite had done in Gibeah. The abduction of the daughters of Shiloh sadly resembled the earlier treatment of the concubine, just as the campaign against Jabesh Gilead was disturbingly similar to the war against Benjamin. Not only had justice *not* been served, but many injustices occurred and no rights were truly championed. The final line of Judges captures the essence of the times: "In those days . . . everyone did as he saw fit."

21:7
r ver 1
21:8
s 1Sa 11:1; 31:11

cut off from Israel," they said. ⁷"How can we provide wives for those who are left, since we have taken an oath ʳ by the LORD not to give them any of our daughters in marriage?" ⁸Then they asked, "Which one of the tribes of Israel failed to assemble before the LORD at Mizpah?" They discovered that no one from Jabesh Gilead ˢ had come to the camp for the assembly. ⁹For when they counted the people, they found that none of the people of Jabesh Gilead were there.

21:11
t Nu 31:17-18

¹⁰So the assembly sent twelve thousand fighting men with instructions to go to Jabesh Gilead and put to the sword those living there, including the women and children. ¹¹"This is what you are to do," they said. "Kill every male and every woman who is not a virgin.ᵗ" ¹²They found among the people living in Jabesh Gilead four hundred young women who had never slept with a man, and they took them to the camp at Shiloh ᵘ in Canaan.

21:12
u Jos 18:1
21:13
v Dt 20:10
w Jdg 20:47

¹³Then the whole assembly sent an offer of peace ᵛ to the Benjamites at the rock of Rimmon. ʷ ¹⁴So the Benjamites returned at that time and were given the women of Jabesh Gilead who had been spared. But there were not enough for all of them.

21:15
x ver 6

¹⁵The people grieved for Benjamin, ˣ because the LORD had made a gap in the tribes of Israel. ¹⁶And the elders of the assembly said, "With the women of Benjamin destroyed, how shall we provide wives for the men who are left? ¹⁷The Benjamite survivors must have heirs," they said, "so that a tribe of Israel will not be wiped out. ¹⁸We can't give them our daughters as wives, since we Israelites have taken this oath: 'Cursed be anyone who gives ʸ a wife to a Benjamite.' ¹⁹But look, there is the annual festival of the LORD in Shiloh, ᶻ to the north of Bethel, and east of the road that goes from Bethel to Shechem, and to the south of Lebonah."

21:18
y ver 1
21:19
z Jos 18:1;
Jdg 18:31; 1Sa 1:3

²⁰So they instructed the Benjamites, saying, "Go and hide in the vineyards ²¹and

---

In a sense Judges is the opposite of Joshua: In Joshua, the Israelites had attempted to overcome Canaan; in Judges they Canaanized themselves. There's no "Hollywood" ending to the final chapter. When the book ends, we breathe a sigh—more because the uncomfortable story is finished than because we have experienced positive resolution.

The Israelites were influenced by Canaan, but the source of the problem lay in their own hearts, in their sinful rebellion, which the Canaanite influences only amplified. The root of the church's problem isn't culture either. It's our unwillingness to believe, to take God at his Word, and to obey. Have you truly submitted yourself to God's transforming work in your life (Rom. 12:1–2)? Or do you ultimately do whatever seems appropriate to you?

21:25

Freedom

The degree of anarchy present in Israel during the days of the judges may shock us. Chapters 19–21 are particularly graphic and gruesome in their presentation of the people's daily life. The modern form of democracy with which we're familiar requires participation in the political process. There are signs that this kind of political freedom is expanding around the globe—and signs that much still needs to be done:

125 countries, with 62 percent of the world's population, have a free or partly free press.
And yet, in 2001, 37 journalists died in the line of duty and an additional 118 were imprisoned.

57% OF WORLD'S POPULATION IS FULLY DEMOCRATIC

Since 1980, 81 countries have taken significant steps toward democracy, with 33 military regimes having been replaced by civilian governments. **And yet,** only 82 countries (57% of the world's population) are fully democratic.

In 10 countries, more than 30 percent of legislators are women.
And yet, worldwide only 14 percent of legislators are women. Ten countries have no female governmental representation.

MEN / WOMEN
14%
WORLDWIDE LEGISLATORS

In 2000, there were 37,000 registered international NGOs (nongovernmental organizations, whose charter is to help poor people worldwide with relief and developmental aid), one-fifth more than in 1990.
And yet, only 20 percent are based in developing countries.

1990
2000   20%   37,000

Source: United Nations Development Programme, *Human Development Report 2002* (2002:10)

watch. When the girls of Shiloh come out to join in the dancing, [a] then rush from the vineyards and each of you seize a wife from the girls of Shiloh and go to the land of Benjamin. [22]When their fathers or brothers complain to us, we will say to them, 'Do us a kindness by helping them, because we did not get wives for them during the war, and you are innocent, since you did not give [b] your daughters to them.' "

[23]So that is what the Benjamites did. While the girls were dancing, each man caught one and carried her off to be his wife. Then they returned to their inheritance and rebuilt the towns and settled in them. [c]

[24]At that time the Israelites left that place and went home to their tribes and clans, each to his own inheritance.

[25]In those days Israel had no king; everyone did as he saw fit. [d]

21:21
a Ex 15:20;
Jdg 11:34

21:22
b ver 1,18

21:23
c Jdg 20:48

21:25
d Dt 12:8; Jdg 17:6;
18:1; 19:1

2:15 "AS [RUTH] GOT UP TO GLEAN, BOAZ GAVE ORDERS TO HIS
MEN, 'EVEN IF SHE GATHERS AMONG THE SHEAVES, DON'T
EMBARRASS HER.'"

INTRODUCTION TO
Ruth

AUTHOR

The author of the book of Ruth is unknown. Jewish tradition holds that the prophet Samuel
wrote Ruth, but there is little evidence to support this view.

DATE WRITTEN

The events in Ruth probably occurred during the period of the judges (1375–1050 B.C.), but
the book was likely written after 1000 B.C.

ORIGINAL READERS

The book of Ruth was written to the people of Israel to demonstrate the legitimacy of David's
kingship despite the presence of a Moabite woman in his ancestry.

TIMELINE

	1400BC	1300	1200	1100	1000	900	800	700	600	500	400
Israelites enter Canaan (c. 1406 B.C.)											
Judges begin to rule (c. 1375 B.C.)											
Deborah's rule (c. 1209-1169 B.C.)											
Samuel's birth (c. 1105 B.C.)											
Samson's rule (c. 1075-1055 B.C.)											
David named king (c. 1010 B.C.)											
Book of Ruth written (c. 1000 B.C.)											
Division of the kingdom (930 B.C.)											

THEMES

Ruth describes the self-sacrificing devotion of a Moabitess named Ruth. The book contains
the following themes:

1. *Acceptance.* Ruth demonstrates the truth that participation in the family of God isn't based
on birth or nationality but on faith in, and obedience to, God. The people of Israel accepted
Ruth as one of their own (4:11–15), and God accepted her as his own, giving her the privilege
of a place in the ancestral line of Jesus Christ (4:18–22; Matt. 1:5–16).

2. *Kindness and faithfulness.* Naomi's transformation from a woman in despair (1:20) into a
joyful person (4:14–16) through the selfless loyalty and kindness of Ruth and Boaz reflects
that God's provision often comes to us through the kindness and faithfulness of his obedient
people (2:20; 3:10; Lev. 19:9–10; Deut. 24:19–22).

3. *Redemption.* Boaz's actions to redeem the land (Lev. 25:25–29), marry Ruth (Deut. 25:5–10),
and father a child to keep Naomi's family line alive (Deut. 25:6) are symbolic of Christ's redemption of his bride, the church (Eph. 5:25–27; Rev. 19:1–8; 22:17), and his people (Titus 2:14).

FAITH IN ACTION

The pages of Ruth contain life lessons and role models of faith—people who challenge believers to put their faith in action.

Role Models

- NAOMI (1:20; 4:13–17) was transformed from a woman of bitterness to one of blessing through her trust and faith in God. What needs transformation in your life? How might you help someone else experience God's transforming power?

- RUTH (1:16–17) didn't abandon her mother-in-law but was faithful despite a life of hardship in a foreign land. Her faithfulness was rewarded (4:13–17) with a son whose descendant was Jesus. Do you believe that your faithfulness will be rewarded?

- BOAZ (2:8–16) showed kindness to Ruth, an outsider, by providing her with food and security. What kindness can you show to those in need?

Challenges

- Surrender your prejudices to God, accepting those from outside your social, economic, or cultural group. They, too, are loved by God.

- Find new ways to help the impoverished in your community: Work at a homeless shelter or soup kitchen, support a needy child through an aid or mentoring organization, and/or volunteer for a literacy group.

- Be a loyal friend and family member, modeling love, acceptance, and kindness to those around you.

OUTLINE

I. Introduction: Naomi Emptied (1:1–5)
II. Naomi Returns From Moab (1:6–22)
III. Ruth and Boaz Meet in the Harvest Fields (2)
IV. Ruth Goes to Boaz (3)
V. Boaz Arranges to Marry Ruth (4:1–12)
VI. Conclusion: Naomi Filled (4:13–17)
VII. Epilogue: Genealogy of David (4:18–22)

Naomi and Ruth

1 In the days when the judges ruled,[a][a] there was a famine in the land,[b] and a man from Bethlehem in Judah, together with his wife and two sons, went to live for a while in the country of Moab.[c] 2The man's name was Elimelech, his wife's

1:1
a Jdg 2:16-18
b Ge 12:10;
Ps 105:16
c Jdg 3:30

a 1 Traditionally *judged*

Ruth 1:1–22

📖 Naomi must have had mixed feelings as she urged her daughters-in-law to turn back. To the calamity of losing home, husband, and sons, she thought she needed to add a self-inflicted wound: returning home alone. Ruth's unexpected and determined commitment to Naomi transcended the bonds of race and religion—as well as of human logic and reason.

Believing that God was out to get her, Naomi wanted people to shun her to avoid their being sucked into the vortex of her misfortune. In response to the delighted, welcoming cries of the women of Bethlehem, she remained detached and negative, failing to acknowledge Ruth's presence, let alone her loyal support. Naomi was open about her complaint against God. But pain and anxiety had blurred her perception. Her anguished, re-active speech to the women demonstrates a sad, universal truth about suffering: When people are in pain, suffering can blind them to God's goodness and plan.

📖 Naomi represents millions of women and children, both in the developing world and closer to home, who find themselves in desperate circumstances through no fault of their own. Particularly in Africa, HIV/AIDS is ravaging families. In some countries, children are sold into prostitution or bonded labor as a source of family income. The problems seem insurmountable, but it may help us to recognize that Ruth's stirring response to Naomi represented one person's commitment to another. God calls us to stand alongside people in their suffering. How can you be a Ruth for one hurting person, either close by or far away?

name Naomi, and the names of his two sons were Mahlon and Kilion. They were Ephrathites from Bethlehem,[d] Judah. And they went to Moab and lived there.

1:2
d Ge 35:19

³Now Elimelech, Naomi's husband, died, and she was left with her two sons. ⁴They married Moabite women, one named Orpah and the other Ruth.[e] After they had lived there about ten years, ⁵both Mahlon and Kilion also died, and Naomi was left without her two sons and her husband.

1:4
e Mt 1:5

⁶When she heard in Moab that the LORD had come to the aid of his people[f] by providing food[g] for them, Naomi and her daughters-in-law prepared to return home from there. ⁷With her two daughters-in-law she left the place where she had been living and set out on the road that would take them back to the land of Judah.

1:6
f Ex 4:31; Jer 29:10; Zep 2:7
g Ps 132:15; Mt 6:11

⁸Then Naomi said to her two daughters-in-law, "Go back, each of you, to your mother's home. May the LORD show kindness[h] to you, as you have shown to your dead[i] and to me. ⁹May the LORD grant that each of you will find rest[j] in the home of another husband."

1:8
h Ru 2:20; 2Ti 1:16
i ver 5
1:9
j Ru 3:1

Then she kissed them and they wept aloud ¹⁰and said to her, "We will go back with you to your people."

¹¹But Naomi said, "Return home, my daughters. Why would you come with me? Am I going to have any more sons, who could become your husbands?[k] ¹²Return home, my daughters; I am too old to have another husband. Even if I thought there was still hope for me—even if I had a husband tonight and then gave birth to sons— ¹³would you wait until they grew up? Would you remain unmarried for them? No, my daughters. It is more bitter for me than for you, because the LORD's hand has gone out against me![l]"

1:11
k Ge 38:11; Dt 25:5

1:13
l Jdg 2:15; Job 4:5; 19:21; Ps 32:4
1:14
m Ru 2:11
n Pr 17:17; 18:24

¹⁴At this they wept again. Then Orpah kissed her mother-in-law[m] good-by, but Ruth clung to her.[n]

¹⁵"Look," said Naomi, "your sister-in-law is going back to her people and her gods.[o] Go back with her."

1:15
o Jos 24:14; Jdg 11:24
1:16
p 2Ki 2:2 ✡ Ru 2:11, 12

¹⁶But Ruth replied, "Don't urge me to leave you[p] or to turn back from you. Where you go I will go, and where you stay I will stay. Your people will be my people and your God my God.[q] ¹⁷Where you die I will die, and there I will be buried. May the LORD deal with me, be it ever so severely,[r] if anything but death separates you and me." ¹⁸When Naomi realized that Ruth was determined to go with her, she stopped urging her.[s]

1:17
r 1Sa 3:17; 25:22; 2Sa 19:13; 2Ki 6:31

1:18
s Ac 21:14

¹⁹So the two women went on until they came to Bethlehem. When they arrived in Bethlehem, the whole town was stirred[t] because of them, and the women exclaimed, "Can this be Naomi?"

1:19
t Mt 21:10

Setting of Ruth (1:1)
Then: The Moabites, occupants of a non-Israelite land east of the Dead Sea, were distant relatives of the Israelites (descendants of Lot, Abraham's nephew).
Now: The equivalent travel today would be between the nations of Israel and Jordan.

1:22

Discerning GOD'S WILL

Ruth, a Moabitess, didn't have Israelite culture to guide her actions. She had to rely totally on God for wisdom when:

Deciding what to do: She stayed with Naomi (ch. 1; see also Phil. 1:9–10).

Following Naomi's advice

Telling the difference between right and wrong: She went to Boaz on the threshing floor (ch. 2; see also 2 Sam. 14:17).

Seeing through appearances: She was able to perceive Boaz's character (ch. 4; see also Prov. 28:11).

Understanding the importance of events: She decided to marry Boaz (ch. 5; see also Deut. 32:29–30).

20"Don't call me Naomi,[a]" she told them. "Call me Mara,[b] because the Almighty[c][u] has made my life very bitter.[v] 21I went away full, but the LORD has brought me back empty.[w] Why call me Naomi? The LORD has afflicted[d] me; the Almighty has brought misfortune upon me."

22So Naomi returned from Moab accompanied by Ruth the Moabitess, her daughter-in-law, arriving in Bethlehem as the barley harvest[x] was beginning.[y]

Ruth Meets Boaz

2 Now Naomi had a relative[z] on her husband's side, from the clan of Elimelech,[a] a man of standing, whose name was Boaz.[b]

2And Ruth the Moabitess said to Naomi, "Let me go to the fields and pick up the leftover grain[c] behind anyone in whose eyes I find favor."

Naomi said to her, "Go ahead, my daughter." 3So she went out and began to glean in the fields behind the harvesters. As it turned out, she found herself working in a field belonging to Boaz, who was from the clan of Elimelech.

4Just then Boaz arrived from Bethlehem and greeted the harvesters, "The LORD be with you![d]"

"The LORD bless you![e]" they called back.

5Boaz asked the foreman of his harvesters, "Whose young woman is that?"

6The foreman replied, "She is the Moabitess[f] who came back from Moab with Naomi. 7She said, 'Please let me glean and gather among the sheaves behind the harvesters.' She went into the field and has worked steadily from morning till now, except for a short rest in the shelter."

8So Boaz said to Ruth, "My daughter, listen to me. Don't go and glean in another field and don't go away from here. Stay here with my servant girls. 9Watch the field where the men are harvesting, and follow along after the girls. I have told the

---

[a] 20 *Naomi* means *pleasant*; also in verse 21.   [b] 20 *Mara* means *bitter*.   [c] 20 Hebrew *Shaddai*; also in verse 21   [d] 21 Or *has testified against*

1:20
[u] Ex 6:3 [v] ver 13; Job 6:4
1:21
[w] Job 1:21
1:22
[x] Ex 9:31; Ru 2:23 [y] 2Sa 21:9
2:1
[z] Ru 3:2,12 [a] Ru 1:2 [b] Ru 4:21
2:2
[c] ver 7; Lev 19:9; 23:22; Dt 24:19
2:4
[d] Jdg 6:12; Lk 1:28; 2Th 3:16 [e] Ps 129:7-8
2:6
[f] Ru 1:22

Ruth 2:1–23

The law (Lev. 19:9–10; 23:22; Deut. 24:19–21) gave resident aliens, widows, and orphans the right to glean, but permission wasn't guaranteed. Ruth's words in verse 2 ("behind anyone in whose eyes I find favor") suggest her anxiety. Her social status in the field was tenuous without connection to a male provider. If God hadn't intervened through Boaz's unexpected interest, she might have walked away to try another field.

Following Boaz's surprising instructions to his workers, the beginning of verse 17 telescopes the rest of the day into a single sentence. The irony is rich. Ruth had received extraordinary favor from a "stranger" who had treated her like family. So Naomi's revelation of Boaz's actual relationship to them creates anticipation of events to come. Naomi, who had questioned God's good will in chapter 1, now exclaimed of Boaz, "The LORD bless him!"

2:8

Hunger

Most people in Ruth's time and social circle were involved in agriculture. Barring famine due to drought, siege, or other factors beyond their control, they could produce enough to feed themselves, their families, and the poor (like Ruth and Naomi) in their communities. Fewer and fewer people in the world today engage in the kind of subsistence farming so common in Biblical times. As a result:

Despite the facts that the world produces more than enough food for every man, woman, and child, and an average of 2,790 calories of food could be available daily to every human on the planet . . .

850 million people go to bed **hungry** every night.

THAT IS ABOUT 1 IN 7.5 PEOPLE

The number of **malnourished people**

increases **by 5 million** every year.

Access to available food is **deterred** by poverty, profit, and politics.

Malnutrition (caused by lack of food, improper nourishment, and/or disease) *is rampant on the planet.*

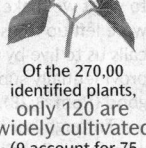

Of the 270,00 identified plants, only 120 are widely cultivated (9 account for 75 percent of our food).

Source: World Bank, *World Development Indicators 2002* (2002:7,16,39–47)

2:10
g 1Sa 25:23
h Ps 41:1 i Dt 15:3

2:11
j Ru 1:14
k Ru 1:16-17

2:12
l 1Sa 24:19
m Ps 17:8; 36:7;
57:1; 61:4; 63:7;
91:4 n Ru 1:16

2:14
o ver 18

2:18
p ver 14

2:19
q ver 10; Ps 41:1

2:20
r Ru 3:10; 2Sa 2:5;
Pr 17:17
s Ru 3:9,12;
4:1,14

2:23
t Dt 16:9

3:1
u Ru 1:9
3:2
v Dt 25:5-10;
Ru 2:1
3:3
w 2Sa 14:2

men not to touch you. And whenever you are thirsty, go and get a drink from the water jars the men have filled."

10At this, she bowed down with her face to the ground.g She exclaimed, "Why have I found such favor in your eyes that you notice me h—a foreigner? i"

11Boaz replied, "I've been told all about what you have done for your mother-in-law j since the death of your husband—how you left your father and mother and your homeland and came to live with a people you did not know before.k 12May the LORD repay you for what you have done. May you be richly rewarded by the LORD,l the God of Israel, under whose wings m you have come to take refuge.n"

13"May I continue to find favor in your eyes, my lord," she said. "You have given me comfort and have spoken kindly to your servant—though I do not have the standing of one of your servant girls."

14At mealtime Boaz said to her, "Come over here. Have some bread and dip it in the wine vinegar."

When she sat down with the harvesters, he offered her some roasted grain. She ate all she wanted and had some left over.o 15As she got up to glean, Boaz gave orders to his men, "Even if she gathers among the sheaves, don't embarrass her. 16Rather, pull out some stalks for her from the bundles and leave them for her to pick up, and don't rebuke her."

17So Ruth gleaned in the field until evening. Then she threshed the barley she had gathered, and it amounted to about an ephah.a 18She carried it back to town, and her mother-in-law saw how much she had gathered. Ruth also brought out and gave her what she had left over p after she had eaten enough.

19Her mother-in-law asked her, "Where did you glean today? Where did you work? Blessed be the man who took notice of you!q"

Then Ruth told her mother-in-law about the one at whose place she had been working. "The name of the man I worked with today is Boaz," she said.

20"The LORD bless him!" Naomi said to her daughter-in-law. "He has not stopped showing his kindness r to the living and the dead." She added, "That man is our close relative; he is one of our kinsman-redeemers.s"

21Then Ruth the Moabitess said, "He even said to me, 'Stay with my workers until they finish harvesting all my grain.'"

22Naomi said to Ruth her daughter-in-law, "It will be good for you, my daughter, to go with his girls, because in someone else's field you might be harmed."

23So Ruth stayed close to the servant girls of Boaz to glean until the barley and wheat harvests t were finished. And she lived with her mother-in-law.

Ruth and Boaz at the Threshing Floor

3 One day Naomi her mother-in-law said to her, "My daughter, should I not try to find a home b u for you, where you will be well provided for? 2Is not Boaz, with whose servant girls you have been, a kinsman v of ours? Tonight he will be winnowing barley on the threshing floor. 3Wash and perfume yourself,w and put on your best clothes. Then go down to the threshing floor, but don't let him know you

a 17 That is, probably about 3/5 bushel (about 22 liters)   b 1 Hebrew find rest (see Ruth 1:9)

In a world that denies God's sovereignty, where events are seen as random occurrences or the results of the independent actions of "free" agents, life is reduced to what we make of it. But Ruth 2 demonstrates that, if it were left up to us, we most likely wouldn't make it. God calls us to live by his Word, but at the same time he providentially supplies our needs and orders our lives for good (Rom. 8:28).

Through her hard work and determination, combined with Boaz's generosity, Ruth helped feed Naomi physically. But in so doing, she also began to nourish Naomi's soul. Simple acts of kindness can make a big difference in a person's life, exchanging a disagreeable outlook for a willingness to hope and praise. In what ways is the Spirit nudging you to supply someone's need?

Ruth 3:1–18

Naomi saw, and seized, an opportunity. She counseled Ruth to take the initiative to encourage Boaz to act on the principle of the kinsman-redeemer and marry her (see Deut. 25:5–10). The symbolic change in Ruth's appearance would signal to Boaz both her availability and her serious intentions. Uncovering a man's feet and lying down was a customary, nonverbal means of requesting marriage. But it wasn't without risk.

are there until he has finished eating and drinking. ⁴When he lies down, note the place where he is lying. Then go and uncover his feet and lie down. He will tell you what to do."

⁵"I will do whatever you say," ˣ Ruth answered. ⁶So she went down to the threshing floor and did everything her mother-in-law told her to do.

⁷When Boaz had finished eating and drinking and was in good spirits, ʸ he went over to lie down at the far end of the grain pile. Ruth approached quietly, uncovered his feet and lay down. ⁸In the middle of the night something startled the man, and he turned and discovered a woman lying at his feet.

⁹"Who are you?" he asked.

"I am your servant Ruth," she said. "Spread the corner of your garment ᶻ over me, since you are a kinsman-redeemer. ᵃ"

¹⁰"The LORD bless you, my daughter," he replied. "This kindness is greater than that which you showed earlier: You have not run after the younger men, whether rich or poor. ¹¹And now, my daughter, don't be afraid. I will do for you all you ask. All my fellow townsmen know that you are a woman of noble character. ᵇ ¹²Although it is true that I am near of kin, there is a kinsman-redeemer ᶜ nearer than ᵈ I. ¹³Stay here for the night, and in the morning if he wants to redeem, ᵉ good; let him redeem. But if he is not willing, as surely as the LORD lives ᶠ I will do it. Lie here until morning."

¹⁴So she lay at his feet until morning, but got up before anyone could be recognized; and he said, "Don't let it be known that a woman came to the threshing floor." ᵍ

¹⁵He also said, "Bring me the shawl you are wearing and hold it out." When she did so, he poured into it six measures of barley and put it on her. Then he ᵃ went back to town.

¹⁶When Ruth came to her mother-in-law, Naomi asked, "How did it go, my daughter?"

Then she told her everything Boaz had done for her ¹⁷and added, "He gave me these six measures of barley, saying, 'Don't go back to your mother-in-law empty-handed.' "

¹⁸Then Naomi said, "Wait, my daughter, until you find out what happens. For the man will not rest until the matter is settled today." ʰ

ᵃ 15 Most Hebrew manuscripts; many Hebrew manuscripts, Vulgate and Syriac *she*

3:5
ˣ Eph 6:1; Col 3:20

3:7
ʸ Jdg 19:6,9,22; 2Sa 13:28; 1Ki 21:7; Est 1:10

3:9
ᶻ Eze 16:8 ᵃ ver 12; Ru 2:20

3:11
ᵇ Pr 12:4; 31:10
3:12
ᶜ ver 9 ᵈ Ru 4:1
3:13
ᵉ Dt 25:5; Ru 4:5; Mt 22:24
ᶠ Jdg 8:19; Jer 4:2

3:14
ᵍ Ro 14:16; 2Co 8:21

3:18
ʰ Ps 37:3-5

Boaz's action in verse 15 paralleled his generosity in 2:14–17. It's clear that his gift symbolized his commitment to the relationship: He would do what was right. The narrator went on to note Boaz's immediate attention to the matter at hand: "Then he went back to town." Upon Ruth's return to Naomi, she quoted Boaz's words exactly: "Don't go back to your mother-in-law empty-handed." We begin to see the reversal of Naomi's "emptiness," expressed in 1:21.

Chapter 3 displays three individuals acting on behalf of others with no obligation to do so. Each one acts honorably and with integrity even in difficult or tempting contexts. This speaks volumes in our world today, where integrity seems to be a forgotten character quality—where people seem more concerned with liability than with doing the right thing. Have you ever hesitated to help someone for fear of legal repercussions? Many people today believe in indulging every oppor-

3:17–18

Malnutrition

What factors can reduce malnutrition? Food obviously is the *most important. The problem* would be reduced by 43% if enough food were accessible. But even with enough food, other factors (or their absence) increase the likelihood of malnutrition. These physical and social indicators in a society can either worsen a bad situation or help rectify distribution inequalities and make available food more useful:

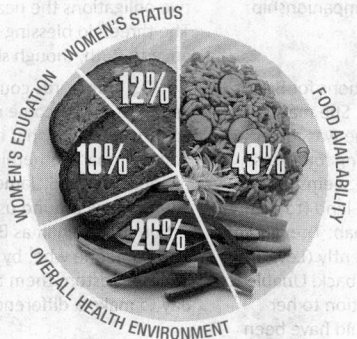

WOMEN'S STATUS
WOMEN'S EDUCATION
12%
19%
43%
FOOD AVAILABILITY
26%
OVERALL HEALTH ENVIRONMENT

How do women's education and status affect food? When women are educated and acknowledged as contributing members of society, they will use their incomes to ensure that their families are fed and their own children attend school. Children who are educated have more opportunities to find good jobs as adults and thus support their families. A beneficial cycle is born in that community.

Source: World Bank, *World Development Indicators 2002* (2002:46)

Boaz Marries Ruth

4:1
i Ru 3:12

4 Meanwhile Boaz went up to the town gate and sat there. When the kinsman-redeemer he had mentioned[i] came along, Boaz said, "Come over here, my friend, and sit down." So he went over and sat down.

4:2
j 1Ki 21:8; Pr 31:23

2Boaz took ten of the elders[j] of the town and said, "Sit here," and they did so. 3Then he said to the kinsman-redeemer, "Naomi, who has come back from Moab, is selling the piece of land that belonged to our brother Elimelech. 4I thought I should bring the matter to your attention and suggest that you buy it in the presence of these seated here and in the presence of the elders of my people. If you will redeem it, do so. But if you[a] will not, tell me, so I will know. For no one has the right to do it except you,[k] and I am next in line."

4:4
k Lev 25:25; Jer 32:7-8

"I will redeem it," he said.

4:5
l Ge 38:8; Dt 25:5-6; Ru 3:13; Mt 22:24

5Then Boaz said, "On the day you buy the land from Naomi and from Ruth the Moabitess, you acquire[b] the dead man's widow, in order to maintain the name of the dead with his property."[l]

4:6
m Lev 25:25; Ru 3:13

6At this, the kinsman-redeemer said, "Then I cannot redeem[m] it because I might endanger my own estate. You redeem it yourself. I cannot do it."

4:7
n Dt 25:7-9

7(Now in earlier times in Israel, for the redemption and transfer of property to become final, one party took off his sandal and gave it to the other. This was the method of legalizing transactions in Israel.)[n]

8So the kinsman-redeemer said to Boaz, "Buy it yourself." And he removed his sandal.

9Then Boaz announced to the elders and all the people, "Today you are witnesses that I have bought from Naomi all the property of Elimelech, Kilion and Mahlon.

4:10
o Dt 25:6

10I have also acquired Ruth the Moabitess, Mahlon's widow, as my wife, in order to maintain the name of the dead with his property, so that his name will not disappear from among his family or from the town records.[o] Today you are witnesses!"

4:11
p Dt 25:9
q Ps 127:3; 128:3
r Ge 35:16

11Then the elders and all those at the gate said, "We are witnesses.[p] May the LORD make the woman who is coming into your home like Rachel and Leah,[q] who together built up the house of Israel. May you have standing in Ephrathah[r] and be famous in Bethlehem. 12Through the offspring the LORD gives you by this young woman, may your family be like that of Perez,[s] whom Tamar bore to Judah."

4:12
s ver 18; Ge 38:29

The Genealogy of David

4:13
t Ge 29:31; 33:5; Ru 3:11

13So Boaz took Ruth and she became his wife. Then he went to her, and the LORD enabled her to conceive,[t] and she gave birth to a son. 14The women[u] said to Nao-

4:14
u Lk 1:58

---

[a] 4 Many Hebrew manuscripts, Septuagint, Vulgate and Syriac; most Hebrew manuscripts *he*
[b] 5 Hebrew; Vulgate and Syriac *Naomi, you acquire Ruth the Moabitess,*

---

tunity for personal gratification. But these verses point to a higher standard. Men: What can you learn from Boaz, a man who discovered an alluring young woman in his sleeping quarters but refused to take advantage of the situation? Women: What can you learn from Ruth, a woman who revealed her desire for companionship without trying to sexualize it too soon?

Ruth 4:1–12

There are two possible explanations for Boaz's words that Naomi was "selling" the field. She may have owned the land but been so poor that she was forced to sell it. Through Boaz, Naomi was appealing for a kinsman to buy it and keep it in the family. It seems more likely that Naomi's husband had sold the land (to an unnamed third party) before leaving for Moab. The land of a family or clan couldn't be sold permanently (Lev. 25:23–28). Naomi had the right to buy it back. Unable to do so, she transferred this right or obligation to her nearest kinsman. In this case, Naomi would have been "selling" the right of redemption.

The nearer kinsman-redeemer had taken no initiative to help the widows and now declined his voluntary family option/responsibility to marry Ruth. Calling the entire assembly as witnesses, Boaz formally declared the two obligations the nearer redeemer had ceded to him. The threefold blessing began and ended with a reference to Ruth, though she wasn't specifically named.

Our words count. Consider how powerfully spoken blessings become reality in this story (2:12; 3:10; 4:11–12,16–17). What can you *say* to bless someone today, to impart something of God's grace to a hurting individual (Col. 4:6; James 3:1–12)? Our actions also count. Many around us desperately need someone to act on their behalf as Boaz did for Ruth, or Ruth for Naomi—someone who, by treating them with kindness, can begin to restore them to wholeness. What will you *do* today to make a difference?

mi: "Praise be to the LORD, who this day has not left you without a kinsman-redeemer. May he become famous throughout Israel! ¹⁵He will renew your life and sustain you in your old age. For your daughter-in-law, who loves you and who is better to you than seven sons,ᵛ has given him birth."

¹⁶Then Naomi took the child, laid him in her lap and cared for him. ¹⁷The women living there said, "Naomi has a son." And they named him Obed. He was the father of Jesse,ʷ the father of David.

¹⁸This, then, is the family line of Perezˣ:

Perez was the father of Hezron,
¹⁹Hezron the father of Ram,
Ram the father of Amminadab,ʸ
²⁰Amminadab the father of Nahshon,
Nahshon the father of Salmon,ᵃ
²¹Salmon the father of Boaz,ᶻ
Boaz the father of Obed,
²²Obed the father of Jesse,
and Jesse the father of David.

ᵃ 20 A few Hebrew manuscripts, some Septuagint manuscripts and Vulgate (see also verse 21 and Septuagint of 1 Chron. 2:11); most Hebrew manuscripts *Salma*

4:15
ᵛ Ru 1:16-17;
2:11-12; 1Sa 1:8

4:17
ʷ ver 22;
1Sa 16:1,18;
1Ch 2:12,13
4:18
ˣ Mt 1:3-6

4:19
ʸ Ex 6:23

4:21
ᶻ Ru 2:1

Ruth 4:13–22

 This section compresses about a year into a few verses in order to resolve the book's main problem: Naomi's emptiness. After years of infertility in Moab, Ruth, through the Lord's intervention, conceived shortly after her marriage to Boaz. The women of Bethlehem celebrated the baby as the one who had restored life and fullness to Naomi (cf. 1:19–21).

The theme of family continuity became that of national continuity. The book of Ruth is the bridge between Israel as family or tribe and Israel as nation. In God's providence, the covenantal loyalty seen in Boaz, Ruth, and Naomi laid the foundation for a salvation that now extends to the ends of the earth. It's striking that this covenant faithfulness to the nations begins with the nations.

Ruth stands out as an individual of integrity and noble character (2:11; 3:11) during a period—in many ways parallel to ours—in which the people habitually disobeyed God and acted in their own self-interest (cf. 1:1; Judg. 2:10–19). Ruth was an outsider to Israelite faith and culture, an unassuming young woman who avoided the limelight. In the end, she became the great-grandmother of David and an ancestor of Jesus (cf. Matt. 1:5). As Lord of the nations, Jesus had the blood of the nations in this veins.

Snapshots

4:14–16

Vali

Vali has been an orphanage caregiver in Bucharest, Romania, since 1997.

"At the beginning it was a little difficult for me to split my care and attention to all the children, because up until then all my love was focused in only one direction—my own child. But in time I learned how to love and care for every child. My greatest reward was the smiles the children gave me every day," remembers Vali.

At first, she recalls, "I had only five children to care for, so I could spend more time with them. Because of that I saw a difference in the children's behavior and development. They learned to walk, talk, and eat properly. We used to spend time in the garden and park, playing with the children and showing them the outside world." Now she cares for ten children. But she manages to share her love and attention with all of them.

> "My greatest reward was the smiles the children gave me every day."

"I thank God for my colleagues," she reflects, "because we are united and all have the same goal. Children are the most wonderful gift in the world; they are beautiful, innocent, and helpless."

16:7 "THE LORD DOES NOT LOOK AT THE THINGS MAN LOOKS AT. MAN LOOKS AT THE OUTWARD APPEARANCE, BUT THE LORD LOOKS AT THE HEART."

INTRODUCTION TO

1 Samuel

AUTHOR

The author of 1 Samuel is unknown. Scripture mentions the records of the prophets Samuel, Nathan, and Gad (see 1 Chron. 29:29) as sources that may have been incorporated into this written history of Israel.

DATE WRITTEN

The two books of Samuel were originally one book that was probably written around 925 B.C., shortly after the division of the nation into the northern and southern kingdoms (930 B.C.).

ORIGINAL READERS

First Samuel was written to the people of Israel to demonstrate God's continuing relationship with them and to provide an accurate history of the development of Israel's monarchy.

TIMELINE

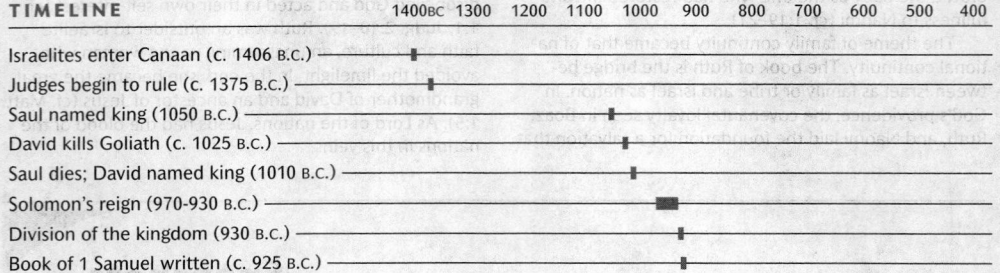

TIMELINE	1400BC	1300	1200	1100	1000	900	800	700	600	500	400
Israelites enter Canaan (c. 1406 B.C.)											
Judges begin to rule (c. 1375 B.C.)											
Saul named king (1050 B.C.)											
David kills Goliath (c. 1025 B.C.)											
Saul dies; David named king (1010 B.C.)											
Solomon's reign (970-930 B.C.)											
Division of the kingdom (930 B.C.)											
Book of 1 Samuel written (c. 925 B.C.)											

THEMES

First Samuel describes the transition of Israel's leadership from judges to kings. Its prominent characters are Samuel (Israel's last judge), Saul (Israel's first king), and David (later to become Israel's second—and greatest—king). Its themes include:

1. *Kingship.* For Israel, kingship held great promise as well as tremendous danger. The wrong type of king might rape and pillage not only the land, but also the people he was supposed to support, protect, and help (8:10–18). More importantly, the wrong type of king might turn the people's hearts from their covenant relationship with God (8:7). First Samuel demonstrates that human leaders aren't the most powerful force in the universe. God is the sovereign King, and he can remove human leaders to protect the well-being of his people, as evidenced in the decline of Saul and the rise of David.

2. *Obedience.* For Israel, a king wasn't autonomous in his authority and power but was an instrument of God's rule (12:14–15; 15:11). The king's ultimate duty was obedience to God (15:11,20). If he disobeyed God, he would be removed from his position of power (13:13–14; 15:23,26). First Samuel emphasizes the truth that obedience, not ritual or tradition, pleases God (15:22). All leaders are flawed, but wholehearted devotion to God is an essential characteristic of any good leader (13:14).

3. *Friendship and loyalty.* David and Jonathan maintained a friendship that withstood tremendous forces. Jonathan would have been king had Saul not been rejected by God for his disobedience. And David should logically have been Jonathan's rival since God had chosen him to be king after Saul. Despite Saul's campaign of terror against David, Jonathan remained true to their friendship, protecting David from his father's wrath and repeated plots on his life (18:1–4; 19:1–10; 20:1–42). David remained loyal to King Saul, not assuming the throne until the Lord had delivered it to him (24:1–22; 26:1–25).

FAITH IN ACTION

The pages of 1 Samuel contains life lessons and role models of faith—people who challenge believers to put their faith in action.

Role Models

- HANNAH (2:11,20,27–28) prayed for a child, and God heard and answered her. What's your heart's desire? Have you brought your request to God?

- SAMUEL (12:1–5) was a faithful and honest leader. No one could say a bad thing about him. What kind of reputation do you have?

- JONATHAN (18:1) displayed loyal, loving friendship to David, putting David's well-being before his own. How do your friendships reveal your character and faith?

- ABIGAIL (25:1–42) was a peacemaker who diffused an explosive situation. How can you promote peace in your relationships?

- DAVID (26:7–24) respected those in leadership and waited for God's timing. Do you show respect for leaders with whom you may disagree, recognizing that they have been given authority by God? How can David's example motivate you?

Challenges

- Resolve not to value God's blessings more than you value God himself. Everything both comes from him and belongs to him (1:27–28; Deut. 8:18; Ps. 50:10).

- If you are a parent, determine not to honor your children above God by condoning their wrongdoing or allowing them to continue in sin (2:29). Verbal confrontation may not be enough (2:23–25); decisive action may be required.

- Reverence for God is essential (6:19–20; see Num. 4:20). Do not take his holiness seriously?

- Fight God's enemies in his strength and in his name (17:1–58).

- Be a trusted and loyal friend (18:1–4).

- Reject society's implicit claim that you should be like everyone else (8:5). Acknowledge God as the ruler of your life.

- Determine to fully obey God as you accomplish the tasks and acts of service to which he has called you. God seeks people whose hearts are aligned with his own (13:13–14).

- Resolve to accept responsibility for your own actions (Rom. 14:12) rather than making excuses or blaming others for your failures (15:15,20–21).

- Reject the temptation to participate in revenge, rebellion, or retaliation, especially with regard to those in authority (24:1–13).

- Accept wise counsel, even if it comes from an unexpected source (25:32–34).

- Be a peacemaker whenever you have the opportunity (25:22–31).

OUTLINE

   I. Background for the Establishment of Kingship in Israel (1–7)
  II. Establishment of Kingship in Israel (8–12)
 III. Saul Fails as King (13–15)
 IV. David's Rise to the Throne and Conflict With Saul (16–30)
  V. The Death of Saul (31)

1:1
a Jos 17:17-18
b 1Ch 6:27,34
1:2
c Dt 21:15-17;
Lk 2:36
1:3
d ver 21; Ex 23:14;
34:23; Lk 2:41
e Dt 12:5-7
f Jos 18:1
1:4
g Dt 12:17-18
1:5
h Ge 16:1; 30:2
1:6
i Job 24:21
1:8
j Ru 4:15
1:9
k 1Sa 3:3
1:10
l Job 7:11
1:11
m Ge 8:1; 28:20;
29:32 n Nu 6:1-21;
Jdg 13:5
1:15
o Ps 42:4; 62:8;
La 2:19
1:17
p Jdg 18:6;
1Sa 25:35; 2Ki 5:19;
Mk 5:34 q Ps 20:3-5
1:18
r Ru 2:13 s Ecc 9:7;
Ro 15:13
1:19
t Ge 4:1; 30:22
1:20
u Ge 41:51-52;
Ex 2:10,22; Mt 1:21
1:21
v ver 3

The Birth of Samuel

1 There was a certain man from Ramathaim, a Zuphite[a] from the hill country[a] of Ephraim, whose name was Elkanah[b] son of Jeroham, the son of Elihu, the son of Tohu, the son of Zuph, an Ephraimite. 2He had two wives;[c] one was called Hannah and the other Peninnah. Peninnah had children, but Hannah had none.

3Year after year[d] this man went up from his town to worship[e] and sacrifice to the LORD Almighty at Shiloh,[f] where Hophni and Phinehas, the two sons of Eli, were priests of the LORD. 4Whenever the day came for Elkanah to sacrifice,[g] he would give portions of the meat to his wife Peninnah and to all her sons and daughters. 5But to Hannah he gave a double portion because he loved her, and the LORD had closed her womb.[h] 6And because the LORD had closed her womb, her rival kept provoking her in order to irritate her.[i] 7This went on year after year. Whenever Hannah went up to the house of the LORD, her rival provoked her till she wept and would not eat. 8Elkanah her husband would say to her, "Hannah, why are you weeping? Why don't you eat? Why are you downhearted? Don't I mean more to you than ten sons?[j]"

9Once when they had finished eating and drinking in Shiloh, Hannah stood up. Now Eli the priest was sitting on a chair by the doorpost of the LORD's temple.[b][k] 10In bitterness of soul[l] Hannah wept much and prayed to the LORD. 11And she made a vow, saying, "O LORD Almighty, if you will only look upon your servant's misery and remember[m] me, and not forget your servant but give her a son, then I will give him to the LORD for all the days of his life, and no razor[n] will ever be used on his head."

12As she kept on praying to the LORD, Eli observed her mouth. 13Hannah was praying in her heart, and her lips were moving but her voice was not heard. Eli thought she was drunk 14and said to her, "How long will you keep on getting drunk? Get rid of your wine."

15"Not so, my lord," Hannah replied, "I am a woman who is deeply troubled. I have not been drinking wine or beer; I was pouring[o] out my soul to the LORD. 16Do not take your servant for a wicked woman; I have been praying here out of my great anguish and grief."

17Eli answered, "Go in peace,[p] and may the God of Israel grant you what you have asked of him.[q]"

18She said, "May your servant find favor in your eyes.[r]" Then she went her way and ate something, and her face was no longer downcast.[s]

19Early the next morning they arose and worshiped before the LORD and then went back to their home at Ramah. Elkanah lay with Hannah his wife, and the LORD remembered[t] her. 20So in the course of time Hannah conceived and gave birth to a son. She named[u] him Samuel,[c] saying, "Because I asked the LORD for him."

Hannah Dedicates Samuel

21When the man Elkanah went up with all his family to offer the annual[v] sacri-

a 1 Or *from Ramathaim Zuphim*   b 9 That is, tabernacle   c 20 *Samuel* sounds like the Hebrew for *heard of God.*

---

1 Samuel 1:1–20

When Samuel was born, Israelite society was idolatrous and people were doing whatever seemed right to them (Judg. 17:6). First Samuel introduces Samuel by relating the unique circumstances of his birth. The narrative emphasizes the devotion and ethical character of his parents—a stark contrast to the apostate and immoral nation of Israel at this time. Samuel's birth *was a momentous event in salvation history,* separating the period of the judges from that of the kings.

Humans have never been especially creative in expressing their rebellion against God. For example, compare the context of the time of Samuel's birth with America's striving to become a secular, non-religious society. God's answer is the same today as it was then: the appearance of godly individuals, both in national leadership and among ordinary citizens, who will allow him to work through them. Are you among their ranks?

1 Samuel 1:21–28

In remarkable faithfulness to her vow and in one of the most sobering scenes of devotion in this book, Hannah found it possible to return to God what he had so graciously given to her. Having come to God with nothing, she returned to Shiloh to give back that which meant everything.

fice to the LORD and to fulfill his vow,*w* 22Hannah did not go. She said to her husband, "After the boy is weaned, I will take him and present*x* him before the LORD, and he will live there always."

23"Do what seems best to you," Elkanah her husband told her. "Stay here until you have weaned him; only may the LORD make good*y* his*a* word." So the woman stayed at home and nursed her son until she had weaned him.

24After he was weaned, she took the boy with her, young as he was, along with a three-year-old bull,*b z* an ephah*c* of flour and a skin of wine, and brought him to the house of the LORD at Shiloh. 25When they had slaughtered the bull, they brought the boy to Eli, 26and she said to him, "As surely as you live, my lord, I am the woman who stood here beside you praying to the LORD. 27I prayed*a* for this child, and the LORD has granted me what I asked of him. 28So now I give him to the LORD. For his whole life*b* he will be given over to the LORD." And he worshiped the LORD there.

Hannah's Prayer

2 Then Hannah prayed and said:*c*

"My heart rejoices*d* in the LORD;
    in the LORD my horn*d e* is lifted high.
My mouth boasts over my enemies,
    for I delight in your deliverance.

2 "There is no one holy*e f* like the LORD;
    there is no one besides you;
    there is no Rock*g* like our God.

3 "Do not keep talking so proudly
    or let your mouth speak such arrogance,*h*
for the LORD is a God who knows,
    and by him deeds*i* are weighed.*j*

4 "The bows of the warriors are broken,*k*
    but those who stumbled are armed with strength.
5 Those who were full hire themselves out for food,
    but those who were hungry hunger no more.
She who was barren*l* has borne seven children,
    but she who has had many sons pines away.
6 "The LORD brings death and makes alive;*m*
    he brings down to the grave*f* and raises up.*n*

---

a 23 Masoretic Text; Dead Sea Scrolls, Septuagint and Syriac *your*   *b* 24 Dead Sea Scrolls, Septuagint and Syriac; Masoretic Text *with three bulls*   *c* 24 That is, probably about 3/5 bushel (about 22 liters)
d 1 *Horn* here symbolizes strength; also in verse 10.   *e* 2 Or *no Holy One*   *f* 6 Hebrew *Sheol*

1:21 *w* Dt 12:11
1:22 *x* ver 11,28; Lk 2:22
1:23 *y* ver 17; Nu 30:7
1:24 *z* Nu 15:8-10; Dt 12:5; Jos 18:1
1:27 *a* ver 11-13; Ps 66:19-20
1:28 *b* ver 11,22; Ge 24:26,52
2:1 *c* Lk 1:46-55 *d* Ps 9:14; 13:5 *e* Ps 89:17,24; 92:10; Isa 12:2-3
2:2 *f* Ex 15:11; Lev 19:2 *g* Dt 32:30-31; 2Sa 22:2,32
2:3 *h* Pr 8:13 *i* 1Sa 16:7; 1Ki 8:39 *j* Pr 16:2; 24:11-12
2:4 *k* Ps 37:15
2:5 *l* Ps 113:9; Jer 15:9
2:6 *m* Dt 32:39 *n* Isa 26:19

God continually works out his purposes through the affairs of righteous people. In Hannah he found a woman he could trust. God provided Israel's future deliverer through her, illustrating how he uses the weakness and barrenness of people to demonstrate his might. In what area of life do you feel weak or "barren"? Like Hannah, you can offer up your pain and prayer to the Lord. And you can take encouragement from God's intervention on her behalf.

1 Samuel 2:1–11

The exalted horn probably represented the horns and head of an animal held high in victory and power (see Dan. 8:3,5,9). Just as God would some day exalt the horn of his anointed king (v. 10), so Hannah could rejoice in her own exalted horn. God had lifted

her head because she had trusted in him. This exaltation of the meek sets the tone for 1–2 Samuel. We will read of the elevation of Samuel, Saul, and David. Their rise from humility to power and distinction set the pattern for what was about to happen to Israel as a nation.

Hannah just had to sing! By drawing on the repertoire of Israel's hymns, she invited the nation to join her. Our own hymns and songs of worship are vital components of our church services, along with the reading and explanation of Scripture and prayer. Whether through Bible choruses or classic hymns of the faith, such singing of theology helps shape our thinking and prepares us for the day when we too will find it impossible *not* to sing. What place do music and song have in your worship experience?

2:7
o Dt 8:18
p Job 5:11; Ps 75:7
2:8
q Ps 113:7-8
r Job 36:7
s Job 38:4

2:9
t Ps 91:12
u Mt 8:12
v Ps 33:16-17

2:10
w Ps 2:9 x Ps 18:13
y Ps 96:13 z Ps 21:1
a Ps 89:24

2:11
b ver 18; 1Sa 3:1

2:12
c Jer 2:8; 9:6

2:13
d Lev 7:29-34

7 The LORD sends poverty and wealth; o
  he humbles and he exalts. p
8 He raises q the poor from the dust
  and lifts the needy from the ash heap;
he seats them with princes
  and has them inherit a throne of honor. r

"For the foundations s of the earth are the LORD's;
  upon them he has set the world.
9 He will guard the feet t of his saints,
  but the wicked will be silenced in darkness. u

"It is not by strength v that one prevails;
10   those who oppose the LORD will be shattered. w
He will thunder x against them from heaven;
  the LORD will judge y the ends of the earth.

"He will give strength z to his king
  and exalt the horn a of his anointed."

11 Then Elkanah went home to Ramah, but the boy ministered b before the LORD under Eli the priest.

Eli's Wicked Sons

12 Eli's sons were wicked men; they had no regard c for the LORD. 13 Now it was the practice of the priests with the people that whenever anyone offered a sacrifice and while the meat d was being boiled, the servant of the priest would come with a three-pronged fork in his hand. 14 He would plunge it into the pan or kettle or caldron or pot, and the priest would take for himself whatever the fork brought up. This is how they treated all the Israelites who came to Shiloh. 15 But even before the fat was burned, the servant of the priest would come and say to the man who was sacrificing, "Give the priest some meat to roast; he won't accept boiled meat from you, but only raw."

---

1 Samuel 2:12–26

The contrasting of two paths of life in this text is a chilling lesson on the importance of individual responsibility. Hophni, Phinehas, and Samuel had similar backgrounds. But the sons of Eli had become "great" in their sins (v. 17)—while Samuel had become great in his faith. When people continuously choose sinful attitudes and actions, they gradually become hardhearted. But those who persist in the faith grow stronger and stand firm to the end (Heb. 3:12–15).

2:18

Child Labor

"Samuel was ministering before the LORD—a boy wearing a linen ephod" (1 Sam. 2:18). From time immemorial children have been employed—but not always "gainfully" or in the protected environment Samuel enjoyed. Our minds might wander to pictures of the semi-starved working waifs from Charles Dickens' novels. And Job 24:9–11 gives a picture of child labor that compares with today's grim picture:

Worldwide, one in six children (ages 5–17) is exploited for child labor.

The cost of ending this evil (by constructing schools and replacing lost income to families) would be $760 billion.

Non-quantified benefits of eliminating child labor:

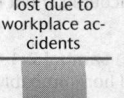

Increased adult job opportunity

Improved child health

Fewer lives lost due to workplace accidents

Child labor decreases education and wider skill development, a future drain on a country's chance for economic growth.

Source: "Sickness or Symptom?" *The Economist* (February 7, 2004): 69

16If the man said to him, "Let the fat be burned up first, and then take whatever you want," the servant would then answer, "No, hand it over now; if you don't, I'll take it by force."

17This sin of the young men was very great in the LORD's sight, for they[a] were treating the LORD's offering with contempt.[e]

18But Samuel was ministering[f] before the LORD—a boy wearing a linen ephod.[g] 19Each year his mother made him a little robe and took it to him when she went up with her husband to offer the annual[h] sacrifice. 20Eli would bless Elkanah and his wife, saying, "May the LORD give you children by this woman to take the place of the one she prayed[i] for and gave to the LORD." Then they would go home. 21And the LORD was gracious to Hannah;[j] she conceived and gave birth to three sons and two daughters. Meanwhile, the boy Samuel grew[k] up in the presence of the LORD.

22Now Eli, who was very old, heard about everything his sons were doing to all Israel and how they slept with the women[l] who served at the entrance to the Tent of Meeting. 23So he said to them, "Why do you do such things? I hear from all the people about these wicked deeds of yours. 24No, my sons; it is not a good report that I hear spreading among the LORD's people. 25If a man sins against another man, God[b] may mediate for him; but if a man sins against the LORD, who will[m] intercede[n] for him?" His sons, however, did not listen to their father's rebuke, for it was the LORD's will to put them to death.

26And the boy Samuel continued to grow[o] in stature and in favor with the LORD and with men.

Prophecy Against the House of Eli

27Now a man of God[p] came to Eli and said to him, "This is what the LORD says: 'Did I not clearly reveal myself to your father's house when they were in Egypt under Pharaoh? 28I chose[q] your father out of all the tribes of Israel to be my priest, to

---

a 17 Or *men*   b 25 Or *the judges*

Cross references:
2:17 e Mal 2:7-9
2:18 f ver 11; 1Sa 3:1   g ver 28
2:19 h 1Sa 1:3
2:20 i 1Sa 1:11,27-28; Lk 2:34
2:21 j Ge 21:1 k ver 26; Jdg 13:24; 1Sa 3:19; Lk 2:40
2:22 l Ex 38:8
2:25 m Nu 15:30; Jos 11:20 n Dt 1:17; 1Sa 3:14; Heb 10:26
2:26 o ver 21; Lk 2:52
2:27 p Ex 4:14-16; 1Ki 13:1
2:28 q Ex 28:1

It's entirely possible to handle the things of God regularly and still fail to have a heart sensitive to God's will. In fact, familiarity can breed disrespect and/or smugness. So what profit is there in assisting in the children's worship program, directing the choir, or even pastoring the congregation? These types of service are commendable. But without the receptive heart of a young Samuel, they are also useless. Are you in need of a heart examination today?

1 Samuel 2:27–36

Eli's entire house/family would suffer the consequences of its present wickedness. Every male would die prematurely, making Eli the last old man in his priestly line. But the immediate and personal application for Eli related to his two sons, who would die on the same day. The good news for Israel as a whole was that God would raise up in their place a faithful priest.

2:26

Educational Opportunity

The boy Samuel was instructed in the temple by Eli. He was privileged to have access to such an education. In today's world education is still too often only for the privileged.

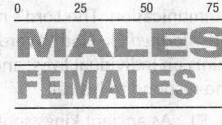

0 25 50 75 100%

83 percent of males and
69 percent of female adults can read and write.[2]

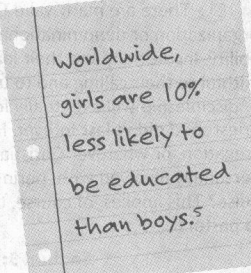

Worldwide, girls are 10% less likely to be educated than boys.[5]

More than 20 percent of primary school-aged children in developing countries aren't in school.[1]

Some 250 million children are forced to work instead of attending school.[3]

One third of all births aren't registered (with a birth certificate), putting those children at risk of losing the chance for an education.[4]

Sources: [1] "Primary School Attendance," *The Economist* (December 14, 2002): 98 [2] Smith (1999:71) [3] World Bank, *World Development Indicators 2002* (2002:77) [4] World Bank, *World Development Indicators 2002* (2002:8) [5] World Bank, *World Bank Atlas 2002* (2002:27)

2:28
r Lev 8:7-8

2:29
s ver 12-17
t Dt 12:5; Mt 10:37

2:30
u Ex 29:9
v Ps 50:23; 91:15
w Mal 2:9

2:31
x 1Sa 4:11-18;
22:16-20
2:32
y 1Ki 2:26-27;
Zec 8:4

2:34
z 1Sa 4:11
a 1Ki 13:3
2:35
b 1Sa 12:3; 1Ki 2:35
c 1Sa 16:13;
2Sa 7:11,27;
1Ki 11:38

2:36
d 1Ki 2:27

3:1
e 1Sa 2:11 f Ps 74:9
g Am 8:11

3:2
h 1Sa 4:15
3:3
i Lev 24:1-4

3:4
j Isa 6:8

3:7
k Ac 19:12

go up to my altar, to burn incense, and to wear an ephod[r] in my presence. I also gave your father's house all the offerings made with fire by the Israelites. [29]Why do you[a] scorn my sacrifice and offering[s] that I prescribed for my dwelling?[t] Why do you honor your sons more than me by fattening yourselves on the choice parts of every offering made by my people Israel?'

[30]"Therefore the LORD, the God of Israel, declares: 'I promised that your house and your father's house would minister before me forever.[u] But now the LORD declares: 'Far be it from me! Those who honor me I will honor,[v] but those who despise[w] me will be disdained. [31]The time is coming when I will cut short your strength and the strength of your father's house, so that there will not be an old man in your family line[x] [32]and you will see distress in my dwelling. Although good will be done to Israel, in your family line there will never be an old man.[y] [33]Every one of you that I do not cut off from my altar will be spared only to blind your eyes with tears and to grieve your heart, and all your descendants will die in the prime of life.

[34]" 'And what happens to your two sons, Hophni and Phinehas, will be a sign to you—they will both die[z] on the same day.[a] [35]I will raise up for myself a faithful priest,[b] who will do according to what is in my heart and mind. I will firmly establish his house, and he will minister before my anointed[c] one always. [36]Then everyone left in your family line will come and bow down before him for a piece of silver and a crust of bread and plead, "Appoint me to some priestly office so I can have food to eat.[d]" ' "

The LORD Calls Samuel

3 The boy Samuel ministered[e] before the LORD under Eli. In those days the word of the LORD was rare;[f] there were not many visions.[g]

[2]One night Eli, whose eyes[h] were becoming so weak that he could barely see, was lying down in his usual place. [3]The lamp[i] of God had not yet gone out, and Samuel was lying down in the temple[b] of the LORD, where the ark of God was. [4]Then the LORD called Samuel.

Samuel answered, "Here I am.[j] [5]And he ran to Eli and said, "Here I am; you called me."

But Eli said, "I did not call; go back and lie down." So he went and lay down.

[6]Again the LORD called, "Samuel!" And Samuel got up and went to Eli and said, "Here I am; you called me."

"My son," Eli said, "I did not call; go back and lie down."

[7]Now Samuel did not yet know the LORD: The word of the LORD had not yet been revealed[k] to him.

[8]The LORD called Samuel a third time, and Samuel got up and went to Eli and said, "Here I am; you called me."

Then Eli realized that the LORD was calling the boy. [9]So Eli told Samuel, "Go and

---

a 29 The Hebrew is plural.   b 3 That is, tabernacle

📖 There are many valid Christian ministries, but no organization or denominational group is above accountability. Institutions and their leaders that fail to remain faithful to their calling and to uphold Biblical principles of discipleship will eventually lose God's favor. Eli's priesthood didn't last forever. How can your local congregation, or whatever Christian organization you are personally involved with, periodically take its leadership pulse? This applies, of course, to office bearers as well as *to pastors.*

1 Samuel 3:1—4:1a

📖 Israel had been doing without God's preserving and revitalizing word through a messenger for some time. But with this episode he reopened the lines of communication. The Lord's message *transformed* Samuel and *informed* Eli. God's Word is true and certain, makes claims on individual lives, and renews and changes all who respond to his call.

📖 As ancient kings spoke for two purposes—to enact laws and to link themselves to their people—so God's Word refers to circumstances around us but also relates to us directly. He speaks both to *inform* and to *form* us. The Word God addresses to modern believers is both an instrument of government, advising us how to live, and a means of fellowship, inviting us into personal relationship with himself. When you pick up your Bible, are you typically looking for information or formation/transformation? How has God sometimes surprised you?

lie down, and if he calls you, say, 'Speak, LORD, for your servant is listening.' " So
Samuel went and lay down in his place.
10The LORD came and stood there, calling as at the other times, "Samuel! Samuel!"
Then Samuel said, "Speak, for your servant is listening."
11And the LORD said to Samuel: "See, I am about to do something in Israel that
will make the ears of everyone who hears of it tingle.[l] 12At that time I will carry out
against Eli everything[m] I spoke against his family—from beginning to end. 13For I
told him that I would judge his family forever because of the sin he knew about;
his sons made themselves contemptible,[a] and he failed to restrain[n] them. 14There-
fore, I swore to the house of Eli, 'The guilt of Eli's house will never be atoned[o] for
by sacrifice or offering.' "
15Samuel lay down until morning and then opened the doors of the house of the
LORD. He was afraid to tell Eli the vision, 16but Eli called him and said, "Samuel,
my son."
Samuel answered, "Here I am."
17"What was it he said to you?" Eli asked. "Do not hide it from me. May God deal
with you, be it ever so severely,[p] if you hide from me anything he told you." 18So
Samuel told him everything, hiding nothing from him. Then Eli said, "He is the
LORD; let him do what is good in his eyes."[q]
19The LORD was with[r] Samuel as he grew[s] up, and he let none[t] of his words fall
to the ground. 20And all Israel from Dan to Beersheba[u] recognized that Samuel was
attested as a prophet of the LORD. 21The LORD continued to appear at Shiloh, and
there he revealed[v] himself to Samuel through his word.
4 And Samuel's word came to all Israel.

The Philistines Capture the Ark

Now the Israelites went out to fight against the Philistines. The Israelites camped
at Ebenezer,[w] and the Philistines at Aphek.[x] 2The Philistines deployed their forces
to meet Israel, and as the battle spread, Israel was defeated by the Philistines, who
killed about four thousand of them on the battlefield. 3When the soldiers returned
to camp, the elders of Israel asked, "Why[y] did the LORD bring defeat upon us today

3:11 [l] 2Ki 21:12; Jer 19:3
3:12 [m] 1Sa 2:27-36
3:13 [n] 1Sa 2:12,17,22, 29-31
3:14 [o] Lev 15:30-31; 1Sa 2:25; Isa 22:14
3:17 [p] Ru 1:17; 2Sa 3:35
3:18 [q] Job 2:10; Isa 39:8
3:19 [r] Ge 21:22; 39:2 [s] 1Sa 2:21 [t] 1Sa 9:6
3:20 [u] Jdg 20:1
3:21 [v] ver 10
4:1 [w] 1Sa 7:12 [x] Jos 12:18; 1Sa 29:1
4:3 [y] Jos 7:7

[a] 13 Masoretic Text; an ancient Hebrew scribal tradition and Septuagint *sons blasphemed God*

1 Samuel 4:1b–11

The decision to bring the ark of the covenant to the battle line was apparently an attempt to recreate the holy wars of Moses and Joshua. As such, it was a useless exercise in self-dependence. The Israelites thought military victory depended on their ability to arouse God's wrath and power to defeat their enemies. This episode was a manipulative attempt to predetermine the outcome of battle for the purpose of self-preservation.

3:19–20

Spiritual Formation

"Spiritual formation," a familiar term in many Christian circles, refers to that process by which we grow in our relationship with God and become conformed to Jesus Christ. Other traditions might be more comfortable with a term like "sanctification," referring to the state of growing in divine grace as a result of Christian commitment after baptism or conversion. Semantics aside, Christians desire spiritual growth.

Why do Christians want to grow spiritually?
Because God desires it (Matt. 5:48).

What's the goal of spiritual formation?
To become more like Jesus (Rom. 8:29; Eph. 4:15).

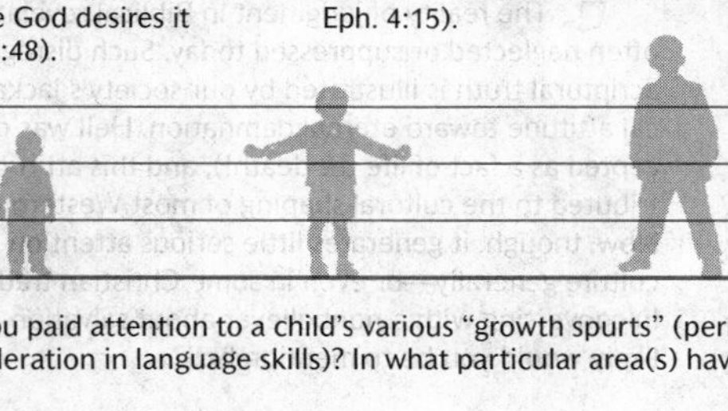

What are the facets of spiritual formation?
1. Growth in grace and in knowledge of Jesus Christ (2 Peter 3:18)
2. Growth in faith (2 Thess. 1:3)
3. Growth in love (1 Thess. 3:12)
4. Growth in understanding (Ps. 119:27)
5. Growth in holiness (2 Cor. 7:1)
6. Growth in fruitfulness (John 15:16)
7. Growth in contentment (Phil. 4:11–12)

Have you paid attention to a child's various "growth spurts" (perhaps a period of rapid physical development followed by an acceleration in language skills)? In what particular area(s) have you been experiencing unusual spiritual growth lately?

4:3
z Nu 10:35; Jos 6:7

before the Philistines? Let us bring the ark[z] of the LORD's covenant from Shiloh, so that it[a] may go with us and save us from the hand of our enemies."

4:4
a Ex 25:22; 2Sa 6:2

4So the people sent men to Shiloh, and they brought back the ark of the covenant of the LORD Almighty, who is enthroned between the cherubim.[a] And Eli's two sons, Hophni and Phinehas, were there with the ark of the covenant of God.

4:5
b Jos 6:5,10

5When the ark of the LORD's covenant came into the camp, all Israel raised such a great shout[b] that the ground shook. 6Hearing the uproar, the Philistines asked, "What's all this shouting in the Hebrew camp?"

4:7
c Ex 15:14

When they learned that the ark of the LORD had come into the camp, 7the Philistines were afraid.[c] "A god has come into the camp," they said. "We're in trouble! Nothing like this has happened before. 8Woe to us! Who will deliver us from the hand of these mighty gods? They are the gods who struck the Egyptians with all kinds of plagues in the desert. 9Be strong, Philistines! Be men, or you will be subject to the Hebrews, as they[d] have been to you. Be men, and fight!"

4:9
d Jdg 13:1; 1Co 16:13
4:10
e ver 2; Dt 28:25; 2Sa 18:17; 2Ki 14:12
4:11
f 1Sa 2:34; Ps 78:61,64

10So the Philistines fought, and the Israelites were defeated[e] and every man fled to his tent. The slaughter was very great; Israel lost thirty thousand foot soldiers. 11The ark of God was captured, and Eli's two sons, Hophni and Phinehas, died.[f]

Death of Eli

4:12
g Jos 7:6; 2Sa 1:2; 15:32; Ne 9:1; Job 2:12
4:13
h ver 18; 1Sa 1:9

12That same day a Benjamite ran from the battle line and went to Shiloh, his clothes torn and dust[g] on his head. 13When he arrived, there was Eli[h] sitting on his chair by the side of the road, watching, because his heart feared for the ark of God. When the man entered the town and told what had happened, the whole town sent up a cry.

4:15
i 1Sa 3:2

14Eli heard the outcry and asked, "What is the meaning of this uproar?"

The man hurried over to Eli, 15who was ninety-eight years old and whose eyes[i] were set so that he could not see. 16He told Eli, "I have just come from the battle line; I fled from it this very day."

a 3 Or he

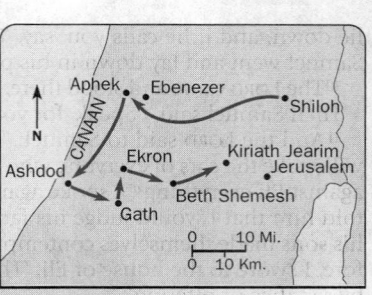

Travels of the Ark (4:3)
Then: The ark of the covenant was a sign of God's protection, though it didn't itself protect—only God can do that.
Now: A modern, secular equivalent might be a symbol such as a nation's flag. The Liberty Bell in the United States carries similar associations for many.

📖 Christians, and "Christian nations," can assume an arrogant posture of righteousness in the face of opposition. But Christ seeks followers who humbly acknowledge their lack of righteousness apart from their relationship with him. Living for Jesus doesn't mean we are always right or will always "win." We can never assume that God owes us something. Nor can we control the outcome of personal or national conflict by appealing to our relationship with him. After all, our life with God is all of grace.

1 Samuel 4:12–22

📖 The back-to-back placement of the stories of Eli's death and Ichabod's birth is significant. The prophetic condemnation of Eli's family line had been confirmed by the anonymous "man of God" in 2:27–36 and by God's words to Samuel in 3:11–14. This passage dramatically confirms the divine pronouncements. The punishment against Hophni and Phinehas already

affected two additional generations.

As Phinehas's wife stated in verses 21–22, God was gone. He had reluctantly accepted the reality of Israel's sin and responded accordingly. Divine judgment isn't so much the vengeful presence of an angry deity as the imposed absence of a loving and protecting God. He had been driven away by the sin of his people, and with his departure the nation had also lost his grace.

📖 The reality of judgment in Biblical revelation is often neglected or suppressed today. Such disregard for Scriptural truth is illustrated by our society's lackadaisical attitude toward eternal damnation. Hell was once accepted as a fact of life (or death!), and this attitude contributed to the cultural shaping of most Western nations. Now, though, it generates little serious attention in our culture generally—or even in some Christian traditions. In conversing with a nonbeliever about salvation, how likely would you be to mention hell?

Eli asked, "What happened, my son?"

[17]The man who brought the news replied, "Israel fled before the Philistines, and the army has suffered heavy losses. Also your two sons, Hophni and Phinehas, are dead, and the ark of God has been captured."

[18]When he mentioned the ark of God, Eli fell backward off his chair by the side of the gate. His neck was broken and he died, for he was an old man and heavy. He had led[a][j] Israel forty years.

[19]His daughter-in-law, the wife of Phinehas, was pregnant and near the time of delivery. When she heard the news that the ark of God had been captured and that her father-in-law and her husband were dead, she went into labor and gave birth, but was overcome by her labor pains. [20]As she was dying, the women attending her said, "Don't despair; you have given birth to a son." But she did not respond or pay any attention.

[21]She named the boy Ichabod,[b][k] saying, "The glory[l] has departed from Israel"— because of the capture of the ark of God and the deaths of her father-in-law and her husband. [22]She said, "The glory has departed from Israel, for the ark of God has been captured."

The Ark in Ashdod and Ekron

5 After the Philistines had captured the ark of God, they took it from Ebenezer[m] to Ashdod.[n] [2]Then they carried the ark into Dagon's temple and set it beside Dagon.[o] [3]When the people of Ashdod rose early the next day, there was Dagon, fallen[p] on his face on the ground before the ark of the LORD! They took Dagon and put him back in his place. [4]But the following morning when they rose, there was Dagon, fallen on his face on the ground before the ark of the LORD! His head and hands had been broken[q] off and were lying on the threshold; only his body remained. [5]That is why to this day neither the priests of Dagon nor any others who enter Dagon's temple at Ashdod step on the threshold.[r]

[6]The LORD's hand[s] was heavy upon the people of Ashdod and its vicinity; he brought devastation[t] upon them and afflicted them with tumors.[c][u] [7]When the men of Ashdod saw what was happening, they said, "The ark of the god of Israel must not stay here with us, because his hand is heavy upon us and upon Dagon our god." [8]So they called together all the rulers of the Philistines and asked them, "What shall we do with the ark of the god of Israel?"

They answered, "Have the ark of the god of Israel moved to Gath.[v]" So they moved the ark of the God of Israel.

[9]But after they had moved it, the LORD's hand was against that city, throwing it into a great panic.[w] He afflicted the people of the city, both young and old, with an outbreak of tumors.[d] [10]So they sent the ark of God to Ekron.

As the ark of God was entering Ekron, the people of Ekron cried out, "They have brought the ark of the god of Israel around to us to kill us and our people." [11]So

[a] 18 Traditionally *judged*   [b] 21 *Ichabod* means *no glory.*   [c] 6 Hebrew; Septuagint and Vulgate *tumors. And rats appeared in their land, and death and destruction were throughout the city*   [d] 9 Or *with tumors in the groin* (see Septuagint)

Marginal references: 4:18 [j] ver 13 · 4:21 [k] Ge 35:18 [l] Ps 26:8; Jer 2:11 · 5:1 [m] 1Sa 4:1; 7:12 [n] Jos 13:3 · 5:2 [o] Jdg 16:23 · 5:3 [p] Isa 19:1; 46:7 · 5:4 [q] Eze 6:6; Mic 1:7 · 5:5 [r] Zep 1:9 · 5:6 [s] ver 7; Ex 9:3; Ps 32:4; Ac 13:11 [t] ver 11; Ps 78:66 [u] Dt 28:27; 1Sa 6:5 · 5:8 [v] ver 11 · 5:9 [w] ver 6,11; Dt 2:15; 1Sa 7:13; Ps 78:66

1 Samuel 5:1–12

God didn't let Israel use the ark as a magic wand (4:4–8), but neither did he allow the Philistines to demean it as a victory trophy. He is sovereign and free, bigger than the Israelite or Philistine theological conception of him. Both peoples had grossly underestimated his power and holiness.

Idolatry was central to the ancient worldview, and the idol was considered an extension of a deity's essence. Placing the Lord's ark beside Dagon's idol symbolized for the Philistines Dagon's victory. But the loss of Dagon's hands and head turned the tables. Wherever the ark traveled in Philistia, God worked his power, teaching the Philistines that the Lord was all-powerful, even in their own backyard.

This text illustrates the inadequacy of the Philistine worldview—similar to today's New Age perspective. God is neither equivalent to the forces of nature nor created in our image. He's not susceptible to magic or idolatry. He can't be manipulated or pressed into service whenever we feel threatened or at risk. He can't be placed alongside or among gods of our making. The fact is, our God is all-powerful and in control, victorious over the forces of our world. Do you proclaim this fearlessly to those around you?

they called together all the rulers[x] of the Philistines and said, "Send the ark of the god of Israel away; let it go back to its own place, or it[a] will kill us and our people." For death had filled the city with panic; God's hand was very heavy upon it. [12]Those who did not die were afflicted with tumors, and the outcry of the city went up to heaven.

The Ark Returned to Israel

6 When the ark of the LORD had been in Philistine territory seven months, [2]the Philistines called for the priests and the diviners[y] and said, "What shall we do with the ark of the LORD? Tell us how we should send it back to its place."

[3]They answered, "If you return the ark of the god of Israel, do not send it away empty,[z] but by all means send a guilt offering[a] to him. Then you will be healed, and you will know why his hand[b] has not been lifted from you."

[4]The Philistines asked, "What guilt offering should we send to him?"

They replied, "Five gold tumors and five gold rats, according to the number[c] of the Philistine rulers, because the same plague has struck both you and your rulers. [5]Make models of the tumors[d] and of the rats that are destroying the country, and pay honor[e] to Israel's god. Perhaps he will lift his hand from you and your gods and your land. [6]Why do you harden[f] your hearts as the Egyptians and Pharaoh did? When he[b] treated them harshly, did they[g] not send the Israelites out so they could go on their way?

[7]"Now then, get a new cart[h] ready, with two cows that have calved and have never been yoked.[i] Hitch the cows to the cart, but take their calves away and pen them up. [8]Take the ark of the LORD and put it on the cart, and in a chest beside it put the gold objects you are sending back to him as a guilt offering. Send it on its way, [9]but keep watching it. If it goes up to its own territory, toward Beth Shemesh,[j] then the LORD has brought this great disaster on us. But if it does not, then we will know that it was not his hand that struck us and that it happened to us by chance."

[10]So they did this. They took two such cows and hitched them to the cart and penned up their calves. [11]They placed the ark of the LORD on the cart and along with it the chest containing the gold rats and the models of the tumors. [12]Then the cows went straight up toward Beth Shemesh, keeping on the road and lowing all the way; they did not turn to the right or to the left. The rulers of the Philistines followed them as far as the border of Beth Shemesh.

[13]Now the people of Beth Shemesh were harvesting their wheat in the valley, and when they looked up and saw the ark, they rejoiced at the sight. [14]The cart came to the field of Joshua of Beth Shemesh, and there it stopped beside a large rock. The people chopped up the wood of the cart and sacrificed the cows as a burnt offering[k] to the LORD. [15]The Levites[l] took down the ark of the LORD, together with the chest containing the gold objects, and placed them on the large rock. On that day the people of Beth Shemesh offered burnt offerings and made sacrifices to the LORD. [16]The five rulers of the Philistines saw all this and then returned that same day to Ekron.

[17]These are the gold tumors the Philistines sent as a guilt offering to the LORD— one each[m] for Ashdod, Gaza, Ashkelon, Gath and Ekron. [18]And the number of the

6:2
y Ge 41:8; Ex 7:11; Isa 2:6
6:3
z Ex 23:15; Dt 16:16 a Lev 5:15 b ver 9
6:4
c ver 17-18; Jos 13:3; Jdg 3:3
6:5
d 1Sa 5:6-11 e Jos 7:19; Isa 42:12; Jn 9:24; Rev 14:7
6:6
f Ex 7:13; 8:15; 9:34; 14:17 g Ex 12:31,33
6:7
h 2Sa 6:3 i Nu 19:2
6:9
j ver 3; Jos 15:10; 21:16
6:14
k 2Sa 24:22; 1Ki 19:21
6:15
l Jos 3:3
6:17
m ver 4

---

a 11 Or he   b 6 That is, God

---

1 Samuel 6:1—7:1

The Philistines learned from their ark experience. They didn't want to repeat the errors of the hard-hearted Egyptians they had heard about (6:5–6). Though their use of golden images as offerings to God was inappropriate, they seemed to realize that Israel's God *couldn't be manipulated. Tragically, the* events at Beth Shemesh revealed that *Israel* hadn't fully learned this lesson. First the people failed to treat the ark with respect, and then they reacted to God's judgment much as the Philistines had earlier (5:6–11).

The events related to the ark speak to the world and the church today. They show the world that God cares—enough to offer himself to the "Philistines" of our day in a full and beautiful revelation of his nature. He cared enough to become vulnerable (taking on human flesh), to be captured by the enemy and treated on the cross as a trophy. As Christians, we are called to recognize and shun all forms of idolatry and to celebrate God's freedom to move in our lives as he wills. Do you need to repent of an incorrect or inappropriate view of God or for something that has taken his place in your affections?

gold rats was according to the number of Philistine towns belonging to the five rulers—the fortified towns with their country villages. The large rock, on which[a] they set the ark of the LORD, is a witness to this day in the field of Joshua of Beth Shemesh.

[19]But God struck down[n] some of the men of Beth Shemesh, putting seventy[b] of them to death because they had looked[o] into the ark of the LORD. The people mourned because of the heavy blow the LORD had dealt them, [20]and the men of Beth Shemesh asked, "Who can stand[p] in the presence of the LORD, this holy[q] God? To whom will the ark go up from here?"

[21]Then they sent messengers to the people of Kiriath Jearim,[r] saying, "The Philistines have returned the ark of the LORD. Come down and take it up to your place."

7 [1]So the men of Kiriath Jearim came and took up the ark of the LORD. They took it to Abinadab's[s] house on the hill and consecrated Eleazar his son to guard the ark of the LORD.

Samuel Subdues the Philistines at Mizpah

[2]It was a long time, twenty years in all, that the ark remained at Kiriath Jearim, and all the people of Israel mourned and sought after the LORD. [3]And Samuel said to the whole house of Israel, "If you are returning[t] to the LORD with all your hearts, then rid[u] yourselves of the foreign gods and the Ashtoreths[v] and commit[w] yourselves to the LORD and serve him only,[x] and he will deliver you out of the hand of the Philistines." [4]So the Israelites put away their Baals and Ashtoreths, and served the LORD only.

[5]Then Samuel said, "Assemble all Israel at Mizpah[y] and I will intercede with the LORD for you." [6]When they had assembled at Mizpah, they drew water and poured[z] it out before the LORD. On that day they fasted and there they confessed, "We have sinned against the LORD." And Samuel was leader[c][a] of Israel at Mizpah.

[7]When the Philistines heard that Israel had assembled at Mizpah, the rulers of the Philistines came up to attack them. And when the Israelites heard of it, they were afraid[b] because of the Philistines. [8]They said to Samuel, "Do not stop crying[c] out to the LORD our God for us, that he may rescue us from the hand of the Philistines." [9]Then Samuel[d] took a suckling lamb and offered it up as a whole burnt offering to the LORD. He cried out to the LORD on Israel's behalf, and the LORD answered him.[e]

[10]While Samuel was sacrificing the burnt offering, the Philistines drew near to engage Israel in battle. But that day the LORD thundered[f] with loud thunder against the Philistines and threw them into such a panic[g] that they were routed before the Israelites. [11]The men of Israel rushed out of Mizpah and pursued the Philistines, slaughtering them along the way to a point below Beth Car.

---

[a] 18 A few Hebrew manuscripts (see also Septuagint); most Hebrew manuscripts *villages as far as Greater Abel, where*   [b] 19 A few Hebrew manuscripts; most Hebrew manuscripts and Septuagint *50,070*   [c] 6 Traditionally *judge*

6:19
[n] 2Sa 6:7
[o] Ex 19:21;
Nu 4:5,15,20

6:20
[p] 2Sa 6:9; Mal 3:2;
Rev 6:17
[q] Lev 11:45
6:21
[r] Jos 9:17; 15:9,60;
1Ch 13:5-6

7:1
[s] 2Sa 6:3

7:3
[t] Dt 30:10; Isa 55:7;
Hos 6:1 [u] Ge 35:2;
Jos 24:14
[v] Jdg 2:12-13;
1Sa 31:10
[w] Joel 2:12
[x] Dt 6:13; Mt 4:10;
Lk 4:8
7:5
[y] Jdg 20:1
7:6
[z] Ps 62:8; La 2:19
[a] Jdg 10:10;
Ne 9:1; Ps 106:6

7:7
[b] 1Sa 17:11
7:8
[c] 1Sa 12:19,23;
Isa 37:4; Jer 15:1
7:9
[d] Ps 99:6 [e] Jer 15:1

7:10
[f] 1Sa 2:10;
2Sa 22:14-15
[g] Jos 10:10

---

1 Samuel 7:2–17

Genuine confession and repentance is to be accompanied by three acts: (1) Reject all other gods—"rid yourselves of the foreign gods." (2) Be loyal and remain faithful to God—"commit yourselves to the LORD." And (3) worship the Lord exclusively—"serve him only."

Samuel's stone monument continued an old and sacred tradition of marking the time and place where God had touched his people in a significant way. Christianity is a historical religion. Its origins in Old Testament faith and its beginnings in Jesus teach us to celebrate what God has done. The Old Testament Passover and Jesus' Last Supper mark the momentous events that stand as central, saving acts of God.

Do you find it easier to listen to a public prayer of confession than to acknowledge and confront your personal sin and guilt? German martyr Dietrich Bonhoeffer, who opposed Nazism, stated forcefully the inconsistency of a gospel without a call to repentance: "Cheap grace means the justification of sin without the justification of the sinner." This watered-down version, he pointed out, is "the deadly enemy of the church."

Most of us have specific and personal ways of commemorating and acknowledging God's work in our lives. We associate those special moments when he has touched us with certain times and places—our personal Ebenezer stones. Such reminders also can inspire us to raise new memorials and to join with the body of believers everywhere to celebrate the saving work of Jesus. What "monuments" or milestones mark your Christian life?

7:12
h Ge 35:14; Jos 4:9

7:13
i Jdg 13:1,5;
1Sa 13:5

7:15
j ver 6; 1Sa 12:11

7:17
k 1Sa 1:19; 8:4
l Jdg 21:4

8:1
m Dt 16:18-19

8:2
n Ge 22:19;
1Ki 19:3; Am 5:4-5
8:3
o Ex 23:8; Dt 16:19;
Ps 15:5
8:4
p 1Sa 7:17
8:5
q Dt 17:14-20
8:6
r 1Sa 15:11
8:7
s Ex 16:8; 1Sa 10:19

8:9
t ver 11-18;
1Sa 10:25

8:11
u 1Sa 10:25; 14:52
v Dt 17:16;
2Sa 15:1
8:12
w 1Sa 22:7

8:14
x Eze 46:18
y 1Ki 21:7,15

8:18
z Pr 1:28; Isa 1:15;
Mic 3:4
8:19
a Isa 66:4;
Jer 44:16
8:20
b ver 5
8:21
c Jdg 11:11
8:22
d ver 7

12Then Samuel took a stone[h] and set it up between Mizpah and Shen. He named it Ebenezer,[a] saying, "Thus far has the LORD helped us." 13So the Philistines were subdued[i] and did not invade Israelite territory again.

Throughout Samuel's lifetime, the hand of the LORD was against the Philistines. 14The towns from Ekron to Gath that the Philistines had captured from Israel were restored to her, and Israel delivered the neighboring territory from the power of the Philistines. And there was peace between Israel and the Amorites.

15Samuel[j] continued as judge over Israel all the days of his life. 16From year to year he went on a circuit from Bethel to Gilgal to Mizpah, judging Israel in all those places. 17But he always went back to Ramah,[k] where his home was, and there he also judged Israel. And he built an altar[l] there to the LORD.

Israel Asks for a King

8 When Samuel grew old, he appointed[m] his sons as judges for Israel. 2The name of his firstborn was Joel and the name of his second was Abijah, and they served at Beersheba.[n] 3But his sons did not walk in his ways. They turned aside after dishonest gain and accepted bribes[o] and perverted justice.

4So all the elders of Israel gathered together and came to Samuel at Ramah.[p] 5They said to him, "You are old, and your sons do not walk in your ways; now appoint a king[q] to lead[b] us, such as all the other nations have."

6But when they said, "Give us a king to lead us," this displeased[r] Samuel; so he prayed to the LORD. 7And the LORD told him: "Listen to all that the people are saying to you; it is not you they have rejected, but they have rejected me as their king.[s] 8As they have done from the day I brought them up out of Egypt until this day, forsaking me and serving other gods, so they are doing to you. 9Now listen to them; but warn them solemnly and let them know[t] what the king who will reign over them will do."

10Samuel told all the words of the LORD to the people who were asking him for a king. 11He said, "This is what the king who will reign over you will do: He will take[u] your sons and make them serve with his chariots and horses, and they will run in front of his chariots.[v] 12Some he will assign to be commanders[w] of thousands and commanders of fifties, and others to plow his ground and reap his harvest, and still others to make weapons of war and equipment for his chariots. 13He will take your daughters to be perfumers and cooks and bakers. 14He will take the best of your[x] fields and vineyards[y] and olive groves and give them to his attendants. 15He will take a tenth of your grain and of your vintage and give it to his officials and attendants. 16Your menservants and maidservants and the best of your cattle[c] and donkeys he will take for his own use. 17He will take a tenth of your flocks, and you yourselves will become his slaves. 18When that day comes, you will cry out for relief from the king you have chosen, and the LORD will not answer[z] you in that day."

19But the people refused[a] to listen to Samuel. "No!" they said. "We want a king over us. 20Then we will be like all the other nations,[b] with a king to lead us and to go out before us and fight our battles."

21When Samuel heard all that the people said, he repeated[c] it before the LORD. 22The LORD answered, "Listen[d] to them and give them a king."

Then Samuel said to the men of Israel, "Everyone go back to his town."

---

a 12 *Ebenezer* means *stone of help.*   b 5 Traditionally *judge*; also in verses 6 and 20
c 16 Septuagint; Hebrew *young men*

---

1 Samuel 8:1–22

God set out to create a nation in his image (Ex. 19:5–6), but Israel wanted a king in hers. The Lord wasn't opposed in principle to an Israelite monarchy (cf. Gen. 17:6,17; 49:10; Num. 24:7,17; Deut. 17:17:14–20), but only to the *kind* of king the people requested. Their demand was: (1) sinful in its motives—As Adam and Eve had longed to become "like God" (Gen. 3:5), the elders of Israel wanted to be "like the other nations." (2) Selfish

in its timing—Impatiently demanding "now" may be as disobedient as saying "no" to God (see Isa. 40:31; James 1:4). And (3) cowardly in its spirit—It's hard to trust God alone with the enemy at the border.

We as Christians can be more like Israel than we care to admit. Do you at times catch yourself seeking security by conforming to the spirit of the times rather than serving the world as a representative of God's counterculture—as you were created to do?

Samuel Anoints Saul

9 There was a Benjamite, a man of standing, whose name was Kish[e] son of Abiel, the son of Zeror, the son of Becorath, the son of Aphiah of Benjamin. [2]He had a son named Saul, an impressive young man without equal[f] among the Israelites—a head taller[g] than any of the others.

[3]Now the donkeys belonging to Saul's father Kish were lost, and Kish said to his son Saul, "Take one of the servants with you and go and look for the donkeys." [4]So he passed through the hill[h] country of Ephraim and through the area around Shalisha,[i] but they did not find them. They went on into the district of Shaalim, but the donkeys were not there. Then he passed through the territory of Benjamin, but they did not find them.

[5]When they reached the district of Zuph,[j] Saul said to the servant who was with him, "Come, let's go back, or my father will stop thinking about the donkeys and start worrying[k] about us."

[6]But the servant replied, "Look, in this town there is a man of God;[l] he is highly respected, and everything[m] he says comes true. Let's go there now. Perhaps he will tell us what way to take."

[7]Saul said to his servant, "If we go, what can we give the man? The food in our sacks is gone. We have no gift[n] to take to the man of God. What do we have?"

[8]The servant answered him again. "Look," he said, "I have a quarter of a shekel[a] of silver. I will give it to the man of God so that he will tell us what way to take." [9](Formerly in Israel, if a man went to inquire of God, he would say, "Come, let us go to the seer," because the prophet of today used to be called a seer.)[o]

[10]"Good," Saul said to his servant. "Come, let's go." So they set out for the town where the man of God was.

[11]As they were going up the hill to the town, they met some girls coming out to draw[p] water, and they asked them, "Is the seer here?"

[12]"He is," they answered. "He's ahead of you. Hurry now; he has just come to our town today, for the people have a sacrifice[q] at the high place.[r] [13]As soon as you enter the town, you will find him before he goes up to the high place to eat. The people will not begin eating until he comes, because he must bless the sacrifice; afterward, those who are invited will eat. Go up now; you should find him about this time."

[14]They went up to the town, and as they were entering it, there was Samuel, coming toward them on his way up to the high place.

[15]Now the day before Saul came, the LORD had revealed this to Samuel: [16]"About this time tomorrow I will send you a man from the land of Benjamin. Anoint[s] him leader over my people Israel; he will deliver[t] my people from the hand of the Philistines. I have looked upon my people, for their cry has reached me."

[17]When Samuel caught sight of Saul, the LORD said to him, "This[u] is the man I spoke to you about; he will govern my people."

[18]Saul approached Samuel in the gateway and asked, "Would you please tell me where the seer's house is?"

[19]"I am the seer," Samuel replied. "Go up ahead of me to the high place, for today you are to eat with me, and in the morning I will let you go and will tell you all that is in your heart. [20]As for the donkeys[v] you lost three days ago, do not worry about them; they have been found. And to whom is all the desire[w] of Israel turned, if not to you and all your father's family?"

---

[a] 8 That is, about 1/10 ounce (about 3 grams)

Cross-references

9:1 e 1Sa 14:51; 1Ch 8:33; 9:39

9:2 f 1Sa 10:24 g 1Sa 10:23

9:4 h Jos 24:33 i 2Ki 4:42

9:5 j 1Sa 1:1 k 1Sa 10:2

9:6 l Dt 33:1; 1Ki 13:1 m 1Sa 3:19

9:7 n 1Ki 14:3; 2Ki 5:5,15; 8:8

9:9 o 2Sa 24:11; 2Ki 17:13; 1Ch 9:22; 26:28; 29:29; Isa 30:10; Am 7:12

9:11 p Ge 24:11,13

9:12 q Nu 28:11-15; 1Sa 7:17 r Ge 31:54; 1Sa 10:5; 1Ki 3:2

9:16 s 1Sa 10:1 t Ex 3:7-9

9:17 u 1Sa 16:12

9:20 v ver 3 w 1Sa 8:5; 12:13

---

1 Samuel 9:1—10:8

This story isn't just a slice in the history of Israel's kingship. It's first and foremost about God, not Saul or Samuel or even Israel. God was the guiding hand behind all that occurred. Beyond the significance of Israelite kingship in general, this text invites us to consider the relationship between God's hand on our lives and the influence of his Spirit in changing our characters (see 10:5–7).

This passage represents a significant step in salvation history: Through Israel's kings God would eventually provide the great King, the Savior of the whole world. The Bible continues to trace the story until the close of the age. In the meantime, an awareness in the world today that God is at work can make us as believers more sensitive to his unexpected and unseen influence in our everyday lives. Are you tuned in?

9:21

21Saul answered, "But am I not a Benjamite, from the smallest tribe[x] of Israel, and is not my clan the least of all the clans of the tribe of Benjamin?[y] Why do you say such a thing to me?"

22Then Samuel brought Saul and his servant into the hall and seated them at the head of those who were invited—about thirty in number. 23Samuel said to the cook, "Bring the piece of meat I gave you, the one I told you to lay aside."

9:24
z Lev 7:32-34; Nu 18:18

24So the cook took up the leg[z] with what was on it and set it in front of Saul. Samuel said, "Here is what has been kept for you. Eat, because it was set aside for you for this occasion, from the time I said, 'I have invited guests.' " And Saul dined with Samuel that day.

9:25
a Dt 22:8; Ac 10:9

25After they came down from the high place to the town, Samuel talked with Saul on the roof[a] of his house. 26They rose about daybreak and Samuel called to Saul on the roof, "Get ready, and I will send you on your way." When Saul got ready, he and Samuel went outside together. 27As they were going down to the edge of the town, Samuel said to Saul, "Tell the servant to go on ahead of us"—and the servant did so—"but you stay here awhile, so that I may give you a message from God."

10:1
b 1Sa 16:13; 2Ki 9:1,3,6
c Ps 2:12 d Dt 32:9; Ps 78:62,71
10:2
e Ge 35:20 f 1Sa 9:4
g 1Sa 9:5

10 Then Samuel took a flask[b] of oil and poured it on Saul's head and kissed him, saying, "Has not the LORD anointed[c] you leader over his inheritance?[a][d] 2When you leave me today, you will meet two men near Rachel's tomb,[e] at Zelzah on the border of Benjamin. They will say to you, 'The donkeys[f] you set out to look for have been found. And now your father has stopped thinking about them and is worried[g] about you. He is asking, "What shall I do about my son?" '

10:3
h Ge 28:22; 35:7-8

3"Then you will go on from there until you reach the great tree of Tabor. Three men going up to God at Bethel[h] will meet you there. One will be carrying three young goats, another three loaves of bread, and another a skin of wine. 4They will greet you and offer you two loaves of bread, which you will accept from them.

10:5
i 1Sa 13:3
j 1Sa 9:12
k 2Ki 3:15
l 1Sa 19:20; 1Co 14:1
10:6
m ver 10; 1Sa 19:23-24
10:7
n Ecc 9:10
o Jos 1:5; Jdg 6:12; Heb 13:5
10:8
p 1Sa 11:14-15

5"After that you will go to Gibeah of God, where there is a Philistine outpost.[i] As you approach the town, you will meet a procession of prophets coming down from the high place[j] with lyres, tambourines, flutes and harps[k] being played before them, and they will be prophesying.[l] 6The Spirit[m] of the LORD will come upon you in power, and you will prophesy with them; and you will be changed into a different person. 7Once these signs are fulfilled, do whatever[n] your hand finds to do, for God is with[o] you.

8"Go down ahead of me to Gilgal.[p] I will surely come down to you to sacrifice burnt offerings and fellowship offerings,[b] but you must wait seven days until I come to you and tell you what you are to do."

Saul Made King

10:9
q ver 6

9As Saul turned to leave Samuel, God changed[q] Saul's heart, and all these signs were fulfilled that day. 10When they arrived at Gibeah, a procession of prophets met him; the Spirit of God came upon him in power, and he joined in their prophesying.[r] 11When all those who had formerly known him saw him prophesying with the prophets, they asked each other, "What is this[s] that has happened to the son of Kish? Is Saul also among the prophets?"[t]

10:10
r ver 5-6; 1Sa 19:20
10:11
s Mt 13:54; Jn 7:15
t 1Sa 19:24

a 1 Hebrew; Septuagint and Vulgate *over his people Israel? You will reign over the LORD's people and save them from the power of their enemies round about. And this will be a sign to you that the LORD has anointed you leader over his inheritance:* b 8 Traditionally *peace offerings*

---

1 Samuel 10:9–27

The question at the end of verse 11 expected a negative answer. Saul's prophesying affirmed his new spiritual gifts—not because he belonged to the band of prophets but because he was the legitimate new ruler of Israel. And it confirmed his anointing by Samuel. This provoked questions from his uncle. Saul's reluctance to answer was appropriate, given the private nature of his encounter with Samuel.

This story contains the Bible's earliest specific reference to the inner changes God works through the ministry of his Spirit. Saul's transformation realigned his worldview so that his former perceptions of himself and his role in Israel were replaced by openness to God. He was now prepared to follow whatever path God directed, and he shared the Lord's perceptions of Israel and of himself as her new king.

¹²A man who lived there answered, "And who is their father?" So it became a saying: "Is Saul also among the prophets?" ¹³After Saul stopped prophesying, he went to the high place.

¹⁴Now Saul's uncle*ᵘ* asked him and his servant, "Where have you been?"

"Looking for the donkeys," he said. "But when we saw they were not to be found, we went to Samuel."

¹⁵Saul's uncle said, "Tell me what Samuel said to you."

¹⁶Saul replied, "He assured us that the donkeys*ᵛ* had been found." But he did not tell his uncle what Samuel had said about the kingship.

¹⁷Samuel summoned the people of Israel to the LORD at Mizpah*ʷ* ¹⁸and said to them, "This is what the LORD, the God of Israel, says: 'I brought Israel up out of Egypt, and I delivered you from the power of Egypt and all the kingdoms that oppressed*ˣ* you.' ¹⁹But you have now rejected your God, who saves you out of all your calamities and distresses. And you have said, 'No, set a king*ʸ* over us.' So now present*ᶻ* yourselves before the LORD by your tribes and clans."

²⁰When Samuel brought all the tribes of Israel near, the tribe of Benjamin was chosen. ²¹Then he brought forward the tribe of Benjamin, clan by clan, and Matri's clan was chosen. Finally Saul son of Kish was chosen. But when they looked for him, he was not to be found. ²²So they inquired*ᵃ* further of the LORD, "Has the man come here yet?"

And the LORD said, "Yes, he has hidden himself among the baggage."

²³They ran and brought him out, and as he stood among the people he was a head taller*ᵇ* than any of the others. ²⁴Samuel said to all the people, "Do you see the man the LORD has chosen?*ᶜ* There is no one like him among all the people."

Then the people shouted, "Long live*ᵈ* the king!"

²⁵Samuel explained to the people the regulations*ᵉ* of the kingship. He wrote them down on a scroll and deposited it before the LORD. Then Samuel dismissed the people, each to his own home.

²⁶Saul also went to his home in Gibeah,*ᶠ* accompanied by valiant men whose hearts God had touched. ²⁷But some troublemakers*ᵍ* said, "How can this fellow save us?" They despised him and brought him no gifts.*ʰ* But Saul kept silent.

10:14
ᵘ 1Sa 14:50

10:16
ᵛ 1Sa 9:20

10:17
ʷ Jdg 20:1; 1Sa 7:5

10:18
ˣ Jdg 6:8-9
10:19
ʸ 1Sa 8:5-7; 12:12
ᶻ Jos 7:14; 24:1

10:22
ᵃ 1Sa 23:2,4,9-11

10:23
ᵇ 1Sa 9:2
10:24
ᶜ Dt 17:15; 2Sa 21:6
ᵈ 1Ki 1:25,34,39
10:25
ᵉ Dt 17:14-20; 1Sa 8:11-18
10:26
ᶠ 1Sa 11:4
10:27
ᵍ Dt 13:13
ʰ 1Ki 10:25; 2Ch 17:5

📖 Saul is a good example of personal transformation through the inner working of God's Spirit—even though God would eventually withdraw his approval and blessing from this chosen leader. Our personal conduct and moral character are central not only in our standing before God but also for our service among his people. Are you eager to launch into service for your Lord? Wonderful! Have you taken the equivalent steps to prepare your heart and align your behavior?

10:25 🔖

Six Firsts of the Jewish People

Being chosen by God seemed to catapult the Jewish people into a diversity of creative accomplishments:

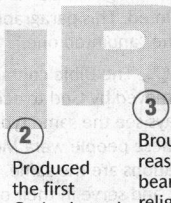

1 Wrote the first history

2 Produced the first God-oriented law code

3 Brought reason to bear on religion

4 Believed in an ethical God

5 Consented (for a while) to let God control politics

6 Produced the modern moral furniture of the mind:
• equality before the law
• sanctity of life
• individual conscience
• collective conscience
• peace as an abstract ideal
• love as a foundation of justice

To what degree have you been shaped by Jewish thought and accomplishment?

Source: Johnson (1987)

Saul Rescues the City of Jabesh

11 Nahash[i] the Ammonite went up and besieged Jabesh Gilead.[j] And all the men of Jabesh said to him, "Make a treaty[k] with us, and we will be subject to you."
²But Nahash the Ammonite replied, "I will make a treaty with you only on the condition that I gouge[l] out the right eye of every one of you and so bring disgrace[m] on all Israel."

³The elders of Jabesh said to him, "Give us seven days so we can send messengers throughout Israel; if no one comes to rescue us, we will surrender to you."

⁴When the messengers came to Gibeah[n] of Saul and reported these terms to the people, they all wept[o] aloud. ⁵Just then Saul was returning from the fields, behind his oxen, and he asked, "What is wrong with the people? Why are they weeping?" Then they repeated to him what the men of Jabesh had said.

⁶When Saul heard their words, the Spirit[p] of God came upon him in power, and he burned with anger. ⁷He took a pair of oxen, cut them into pieces, and sent the pieces by messengers throughout Israel,[q] proclaiming, "This is what will be done to the oxen of anyone[r] who does not follow Saul and Samuel." Then the terror of the LORD fell on the people, and they turned out as one man. ⁸When Saul mustered[s] them at Bezek,[t] the men of Israel numbered three hundred thousand and the men of Judah thirty thousand.

⁹They told the messengers who had come, "Say to the men of Jabesh Gilead, 'By the time the sun is hot tomorrow, you will be delivered.' " When the messengers went and reported this to the men of Jabesh, they were elated. ¹⁰They said to the Ammonites, "Tomorrow we will surrender[u] to you, and you can do to us whatever seems good to you."

¹¹The next day Saul separated his men into three divisions;[v] during the last watch of the night they broke into the camp of the Ammonites and slaughtered them until the heat of the day. Those who survived were scattered, so that no two of them were left together.

Saul Confirmed as King

¹²The people then said to Samuel, "Who[w] was it that asked, 'Shall Saul reign over us?' Bring these men to us and we will put them to death."

¹³But Saul said, "No one shall be put to death today,[x] for this day the LORD has rescued[y] Israel."

¹⁴Then Samuel said to the people, "Come, let us go to Gilgal[z] and there reaffirm the kingship.[a]" ¹⁵So all the people went to Gilgal[b] and confirmed Saul as king in the presence of the LORD. There they sacrificed fellowship offerings[a] before the LORD, and Saul and all the Israelites held a great celebration.

[a] 15 Traditionally *peace offerings*

Side references

11:1
[i] 1Sa 12:12
[j] Jdg 21:8
[k] 1Ki 20:34; Eze 17:13
11:2
[l] Nu 16:14
[m] 1Sa 17:26

11:4
[n] 1Sa 10:5,26; 15:34 [o] Jdg 2:4; 1Sa 30:4

11:6
[p] Jdg 3:10; 6:34; 13:25; 14:6; 1Sa 10:10; 16:13
11:7
[q] Jdg 19:29
[r] Jdg 21:5

11:8
[s] Jdg 20:2 [t] Jdg 1:4

11:10
[u] ver 3

11:11
[v] Jdg 7:16

11:12
[w] 1Sa 10:27; Lk 19:27

11:13
[x] 2Sa 19:22
[y] Ex 14:13; 1Sa 19:5
11:14
[z] 1Sa 10:8
[a] 1Sa 10:25
11:15
[b] 1Sa 10:8,17

---

1 Samuel 11:1–11

God's people depend on him totally for resources and strength. He miraculously multiplies our skills and talents to use them—and us—for his purposes. The rest of Saul's story would unfortunately illustrate what happens when those who are prepared and called by God decide they no longer need to serve under his inspiration.

Do you sometimes find it hard to tell whether you have been moved by God's Spirit or by your own instincts or ambitions? The fact is, no amount of preparation or calling can substitute for a heart that's open to the leading and empowerment of God's Spirit. We are presented here with an Old Testament example of a chosen servant of God, prepared in many ways to fulfill God's mission for his life and open and responsive to God's prodding, direction, and timing.

1 Samuel 11:12–15

Troublemakers (cf. 10:27) had despised and slandered Saul, the Lord's anointed. In so doing, they had despised God himself. Saul was able to pardon them only through his power and authority as the Lord's anointed. This paragraph illustrates the role of the king as the "anointed one."

The Bible contains numerous examples of people moved by God to accomplish his purposes. We don't always see the same type of "Spirit language," and not all these people were Messianic-type kings, but the implications are the same. When God's servants try to minister and serve in their own strength or timing, the results are mixed at best. But when they are open to God's leading and inspiration, the outcomes are uniformly effective. Are you at times tempted to launch into ministry without first checking the pulse of God's leading?

Samuel's Farewell Speech

12 Samuel said to all Israel, "I have listened[c] to everything you said to me and have set a king[d] over you. [2]Now you have a king as your leader.[e] As for me, I am old and gray, and my sons are here with you. I have been your leader from my youth until this day. [3]Here I stand. Testify against me in the presence of the LORD and his anointed.[f] Whose ox have I taken? Whose donkey[g] have I taken? Whom have I cheated? Whom have I oppressed? From whose hand have I accepted a bribe[h] to make me shut my eyes? If I have done[i] any of these, I will make it right."

[4]"You have not cheated or oppressed us," they replied. "You have not taken anything from anyone's hand."

[5]Samuel said to them, "The LORD is witness against you, and also his anointed is witness this day, that you have not found anything[j] in my hand.[k]"

"He is witness," they said.

[6]Then Samuel said to the people, "It is the LORD who appointed Moses and Aaron and brought[l] your forefathers up out of Egypt. [7]Now then, stand here, because I am going to confront[m] you with evidence before the LORD as to all the righteous acts performed by the LORD for you and your fathers.

[8]"After Jacob entered Egypt, they cried[n] to the LORD for help, and the LORD sent[o] Moses and Aaron, who brought your forefathers out of Egypt and settled them in this place.

[9]"But they forgot[p] the LORD their God; so he sold them into the hand of Sisera,[q] the commander of the army of Hazor, and into the hands of the Philistines[r] and the king of Moab,[s] who fought against them. [10]They cried out to the LORD and said, 'We have sinned; we have forsaken[t] the LORD and served the Baals and the Ashtoreths.[u] But now deliver us from the hands of our enemies, and we will serve you.' [11]Then the LORD sent Jerub-Baal,[a][v] Barak,[b][w] Jephthah[x] and Samuel,[c] and he delivered you from the hands of your enemies on every side, so that you lived securely.

[12]"But when you saw that Nahash[y] king[z] of the Ammonites was moving against you, you said to me, 'No, we want a king to rule[a] over us'—even though the LORD your God was your king. [13]Now here is the king[b] you have chosen, the one you asked[c] for; see, the LORD has set a king over you. [14]If you fear[d] the LORD and serve and obey him and do not rebel against his commands, and if both you and the king who reigns over you follow the LORD your God—good! [15]But if you do not obey the LORD, and if you rebel against[e] his commands, his hand will be against you, as it was against your fathers.

[16]"Now then, stand still and see[f] this great thing the LORD is about to do before your eyes! [17]Is it not wheat harvest[g] now? I will call[h] upon the LORD to send thunder and rain.[i] And you will realize what an evil[j] thing you did in the eyes of the LORD when you asked for a king."

[a] 11 Also called *Gideon*   [b] 11 Some Septuagint manuscripts and Syriac; Hebrew *Bedan*
[c] 11 Hebrew; some Septuagint manuscripts and Syriac *Samson*

Cross references

12:1
c 1Sa 8:7
d 1Sa 10:24; 11:15
12:2
e 1Sa 8:5

12:3
f 1Sa 10:1; 24:6; 2Sa 1:14
g Nu 16:15
h Dt 16:19
i Ac 20:33

12:5
j Ac 23:9; 24:20
k Ex 22:4

12:6
l Ex 6:26; Mic 6:4
12:7
m Isa 1:18; Mic 6:1-5
12:8
n Ex 2:23 o Ex 3:10; 4:16

12:9
p Jdg 3:7 q Jdg 4:2
r Jdg 10:7; 13:1
s Jdg 3:12

12:10
t Jdg 10:10,15
u Jdg 2:13
12:11
v Jdg 6:14,32
w Jdg 4:6
x Jdg 11:1
12:12
y 1Sa 11:1 z 1Sa 8:5
a Jdg 8:23;
1Sa 8:6,19
12:13
b 1Sa 8:5;
Hos 13:11
c 1Sa 10:24
12:14
d Jos 24:14
12:15
e ver 9; Jos 24:20;
Isa 1:20

12:16
f Ex 14:13
12:17
g 1Sa 7:9-10
h Jas 5:18 i Pr 26:1
j 1Sa 8:6-7

---

1 Samuel 12:1–25

Samuel forced the people to face the new reality of a human king as opposed to the divinely provided judge-deliverers they had experienced. The nation would have a new political structure, but the people were to continue serving the Lord. They also needed to understand the role of prophets in the new government. To make a lasting impression, Samuel called for a thunderstorm at wheat harvest—when it scarcely ever rained. This demonstration reinforced that Israel was never to neglect the word of God's prophets.

Samuel's sermon has been called a "farewell" address, but the prophet lived for many years afterward. It actually represented the final step in making Saul king. Samuel offered the Israelites a second chance. God had incorporated their failures into his plans. Each time Israel botched an opportunity or began a new venture, the Lord reestablished the covenant and recommitted himself never to abandon his people.

God still transforms our rebellions and frail attempts to serve him into something useful for his kingdom. His ultimate act of forgiveness and redemption for humankind also represented the most hideous of sinful human acts—the torturous, unjust execution of Jesus on a cross. In God's sovereign goodness, our service, no matter how flawed, can become an ocean of love and grace in his hands (Rom. 8:28). What an awesome motivation, particularly in those times we feel we have "precious" little to offer!

12:18
k Ex 14:31
12:19
l ver 23; Ex 9:28;
Jas 5:18; 1Jn 5:16

[18]Then Samuel called upon the LORD, and that same day the LORD sent thunder and rain. So all the people stood in awe[k] of the LORD and of Samuel.

[19]The people all said to Samuel, "Pray[l] to the LORD your God for your servants so that we will not die, for we have added to all our other sins the evil of asking for a king."

12:21
m Isa 41:24,29;
Jer 16:19; Hab 2:18
n Dt 11:16
12:22
o Ps 106:8 p Jos 7:9
q 1Ki 6:13 r Dt 7:7;
1Pe 2:9
12:23
s Ro 1:9-10;
Col 1:9; 2Ti 1:3
t 1Ki 8:36;
Ps 34:11; Pr 4:11
12:24
u Ecc 12:13
v Isa 5:12
w Dt 10:21
12:25
x 1Sa 31:1-5
y Jos 24:20

[20]"Do not be afraid," Samuel replied. "You have done all this evil; yet do not turn away from the LORD, but serve the LORD with all your heart. [21]Do not turn away after useless[m] idols.[n] They can do you no good, nor can they rescue you, because they are useless. [22]For the sake[o] of his great name[p] the LORD will not reject[q] his people, because the LORD was pleased to make[r] you his own. [23]As for me, far be it from me that I should sin against the LORD by failing to pray[s] for you. And I will teach[t] you the way that is good and right. [24]But be sure to fear[u] the LORD and serve him faithfully with all your heart; consider[v] what great[w] things he has done for you. [25]Yet if you persist[x] in doing evil, both you and your king will be swept[y] away."

Samuel Rebukes Saul

13 Saul was ⌊thirty⌋[a] years old when he became king, and he reigned over Israel ⌊forty-⌋[b] two years.

13:2
z 1Sa 10:26
13:3
a 1Sa 10:5

[2]Saul[c] chose three thousand men from Israel; two thousand were with him at Micmash and in the hill country of Bethel, and a thousand were with Jonathan at Gibeah[z] in Benjamin. The rest of the men he sent back to their homes.

13:4
b Ge 34:30

[3]Jonathan attacked the Philistine outpost[a] at Geba, and the Philistines heard about it. Then Saul had the trumpet blown throughout the land and said, "Let the Hebrews hear!" [4]So all Israel heard the news: "Saul has attacked the Philistine outpost, and now Israel has become a stench[b] to the Philistines." And the people were summoned to join Saul at Gilgal.

13:5
c Jos 11:4

[5]The Philistines assembled to fight Israel, with three thousand[d] chariots, six thousand charioteers, and soldiers as numerous as the sand[c] on the seashore. They went up and camped at Micmash, east of Beth Aven. [6]When the men of Israel saw that their situation was critical and that their army was hard pressed, they hid in caves and thickets, among the rocks, and in pits and cisterns. [7]Some Hebrews even crossed the Jordan to the land of Gad[e] and Gilead.

13:6
d Jdg 6:2
13:7
e Nu 32:33

Saul remained at Gilgal, and all the troops with him were quaking with fear. [8]He waited seven[f] days, the time set by Samuel; but Samuel did not come to Gilgal, and Saul's men began to scatter. [9]So he said, "Bring me the burnt offering and the fellowship offerings.[e]" And Saul offered[g] up the burnt offering. [10]Just as he finished making the offering, Samuel[h] arrived, and Saul went out to greet him.

13:8
f 1Sa 10:8
13:9
g 2Sa 24:25; 1Ki 3:4
13:10
h 1Sa 15:13

[11]"What have you done?" asked Samuel.

Saul replied, "When I saw that the men were scattering, and that you did not

---

a 1 A few late manuscripts of the Septuagint; Hebrew does not have *thirty*.   b 1 See the round number in Acts 13:21; Hebrew does not have *forty-*.   c 1,2 Or *and when he had reigned over Israel two years,* [2]*he*   d 5 Some Septuagint manuscripts and Syriac; Hebrew *thirty thousand*   e 9 Traditionally *peace offerings*

---

1 Samuel 13:1–15

The Lord remained Israel's king, but he was represented by his prophet, who in turn directed God's anointed one. Saul's sin wasn't so much in offering the sacrifice as in disobeying Samuel. The term "heart" in verse 14 suggests "will" or "choice" in this context. It emphasizes God's freedom in selecting a replacement for Saul. The phrase also hints at something positive about David's character: He would genuinely act according to God's wishes.

Saul's behavior pattern illustrates the anatomy of sin. First comes the tyranny of the urgent, pressure from prevailing circumstances. This is followed by insecurity and self-doubt arising from a lack of reliance on God. Finally comes the rebellion itself—the human attempt to take matters into our own hands. This is equivalent to usurping, or at least presuming upon, God's authority.

Saul's punishment may seem harsh and unfair. But Samuel recognized a trait in Saul that would recur in subsequent episodes: Saul was content to depend on his own resources rather than on God's word. This text is about learning to trust God when we see our own resources slipping away. But it's also about learning to trust him when we think our own assets and qualities are sufficient, when we believe we are quite capable of going it alone. When are you most open to God? to temptation?

come at the set time, and that the Philistines were assembling at Micmash,[i] 12I thought, 'Now the Philistines will come down against me at Gilgal, and I have not sought the LORD's favor.' So I felt compelled to offer the burnt offering."

13"You acted foolishly,[k]" Samuel said. "You have not kept[l] the command the LORD your God gave you; if you had, he would have established your kingdom over Israel for all time. 14But now your kingdom[m] will not endure; the LORD has sought out a man after his own heart[n] and appointed[o] him leader of his people, because you have not kept the LORD's command."

15Then Samuel left Gilgal[a] and went up to Gibeah[p] in Benjamin, and Saul counted the men who were with him. They numbered about six hundred.

Israel Without Weapons

16Saul and his son Jonathan and the men with them were staying in Gibeah[b] in Benjamin, while the Philistines camped at Micmash. 17Raiding[q] parties went out from the Philistine camp in three detachments. One turned toward Ophrah[r] in the vicinity of Shual, 18another toward Beth Horon,[s] and the third toward the borderland overlooking the Valley of Zeboim[t] facing the desert.

19Not a blacksmith[u] could be found in the whole land of Israel, because the Philistines had said, "Otherwise the Hebrews will make swords or spears!" 20So all Israel went down to the Philistines to have their plowshares, mattocks, axes and sickles[c] sharpened. 21The price was two thirds of a shekel[d] for sharpening plowshares and mattocks, and a third of a shekel[e] for sharpening forks and axes and for repointing goads.

22So on the day of the battle not a soldier with Saul and Jonathan[v] had a sword or spear[w] in his hand; only Saul and his son Jonathan had them.

Jonathan Attacks the Philistines

23Now a detachment of Philistines had gone out to the pass[x] at Micmash.
14 1One day Jonathan son of Saul said to the young man bearing his armor, "Come, let's go over to the Philistine outpost on the other side." But he did not tell his father.

2Saul was staying on the outskirts of Gibeah[y] under a pomegranate tree in Mig-

---

13:11 [i] ver 2,5,16,23
13:12 [j] Jer 26:19
13:13 [k] 2Ch 16:9 [l] 1Sa 15:23,24
13:14 [m] 1Sa 15:28 [n] Ac 7:46; 13:22 [o] 2Sa 6:21
13:15 [p] 1Sa 14:2
13:17 [q] 1Sa 14:15 [r] Jos 18:23
13:18 [s] Jos 18:13-14 [t] Ne 11:34
13:19 [u] 2Ki 24:14; Jer 24:1
13:22 [v] 1Ch 9:39 [w] Jdg 5:8
13:23 [x] 1Sa 14:4
14:2 [y] 1Sa 13:15

---

[a] 15 Hebrew; Septuagint *Gilgal and went his way; the rest of the people went after Saul to meet the army, and they went out of Gilgal*   [b] 16 Two Hebrew manuscripts; most Hebrew manuscripts *Geba,* a variant of *Gibeah*   [c] 20 Septuagint; Hebrew *plowshares*   [d] 21 Hebrew *pim*; that is, about 1/4 ounce (about 8 grams)   [e] 21 That is, about 1/8 ounce (about 4 grams)

---

1 Samuel 13:16–22

📖 The Philistines held decisive military superiority. They substantially outnumbered Israel's troops and could send out raiding parties in different directions to seal off Saul's forces, preventing reinforcements from arriving to help. They also had the upper hand in military equipment. By controlling a monopoly in metallurgical technology, the Philistines limited Israel's arsenal. The result: Only Saul and Jonathan were properly armed, and the Israelite forces were in danger of annihilation.

In chapter 11 Israel also had confronted a threatening neighbor. But in that conflict, Saul had been empowered by the Spirit and had led his army to a courageous and decisive victory. Here in chapter 13 we have no "Spirit-language." We are not explicitly told that the Spirit had departed, but we are left to wonder.

📖 God had promised victory over the Philistines (9:16), but the circumstances of the moment had swallowed Saul and his vision of what God had in store for him. Today we engage in spiritual warfare armed with an arsenal of Biblical promises that may still appear weak or insufficient when compared to the weapons of our enemies (2 Cor. 10:4; Eph. 6:10–13). Are you confident that God is more powerful than your circumstances, hopeless though they may at times appear?

1 Samuel 13:23—14:14

📖 The tragedy of Saul's loss as pronounced by Samuel in 13:13–14 becomes apparent in chapter 14. The story spotlights Jonathan and his surpassing leadership qualities. In the opening sortie, he and his armor-bearer single-handedly killed approximately 20 Philistines in a small area. What a fine king he would have made! The author apparently described and defended the rejection of Saul by contrasting Saul with Jonathan.

The presence of Ahijah, a member of the rejected priestly family of Eli (see 2:30–36), is significant. The implication is that Saul had stopped listening to Samuel altogether—an action apparently matched by Samuel's willingness to stop speaking (13:15). God's word and direction through Samuel had become dissatisfying or threatening to Saul, who had turned in another direction.

14:2
z Isa 10:28
14:3
a 1Sa 4:21
b 1Sa 22:11,20
c 1Sa 2:28
14:4
d 1Sa 13:23

14:6
e 1Sa 17:26,36;
Jer 9:26
f Heb 11:34
g Jdg 7:4
h 1Sa 17:46-47

14:10
i Ge 24:14;
Jdg 6:36-37

14:11
j 1Sa 13:6

14:12
k 1Sa 17:43-44
l 2Sa 5:24

14:15
m Ge 35:5;
2Ki 7:5-7
n 1Sa 13:17

14:16
o 2Sa 18:24

14:18
p 1Sa 30:7

14:19
q Nu 27:21

ron.ᶻ With him were about six hundred men, ³among whom was Ahijah, who was wearing an ephod. He was a son of Ichabod'sᵃ brother Ahitubᵇ son of Phinehas, the son of Eli,ᶜ the LORD's priest in Shiloh. No one was aware that Jonathan had left.

⁴On each side of the passᵈ that Jonathan intended to cross to reach the Philistine outpost was a cliff; one was called Bozez, and the other Seneh. ⁵One cliff stood to the north toward Micmash, the other to the south toward Geba.

⁶Jonathan said to his young armor-bearer, "Come, let's go over to the outpost of those uncircumcisedᵉ fellows. Perhaps the LORD will act in our behalf. Nothingᶠ can hinder the LORD from saving, whether by manyᵍ or by few.ʰ"

⁷"Do all that you have in mind," his armor-bearer said. "Go ahead; I am with you heart and soul."

⁸Jonathan said, "Come, then; we will cross over toward the men and let them see us. ⁹If they say to us, 'Wait there until we come to you,' we will stay where we are and not go up to them. ¹⁰But if they say, 'Come up to us,' we will climb up, because that will be our signⁱ that the LORD has given them into our hands."

¹¹So both of them showed themselves to the Philistine outpost. "Look!" said the Philistines. "The Hebrews are crawling out of the holes they were hidingʲ in." ¹²The men of the outpost shouted to Jonathan and his armor-bearer, "Come up to us and we'll teach you a lesson.ᵏ"

So Jonathan said to his armor-bearer, "Climb up after me; the LORD has given them into the handˡ of Israel."

¹³Jonathan climbed up, using his hands and feet, with his armor-bearer right behind him. The Philistines fell before Jonathan, and his armor-bearer followed and killed behind him. ¹⁴In that first attack Jonathan and his armor-bearer killed some twenty men in an area of about half an acre.ᵃ

Israel Routs the Philistines

¹⁵Then panicᵐ struck the whole army—those in the camp and field, and those in the outposts and raidingⁿ parties—and the ground shook. It was a panic sent by God.ᵇ

¹⁶Saul's lookoutsᵒ at Gibeah in Benjamin saw the army melting away in all directions. ¹⁷Then Saul said to the men who were with him, "Muster the forces and see who has left us." When they did, it was Jonathan and his armor-bearer who were not there.

¹⁸Saul said to Ahijah, "Bringᵖ the ark of God." (At that time it was with the Israelites.)ᶜ ¹⁹While Saul was talking to the priest, the tumult in the Philistine camp increased more and more. So Saul said to the priest,�q "Withdraw your hand."

ᵃ 14 Hebrew *half a yoke*; a "yoke" was the land plowed by a yoke of oxen in one day.   ᵇ 15 Or *a terrible panic*   ᶜ 18 Hebrew; Septuagint *"Bring the ephod."* (At that time he wore the ephod before the Israelites.)

📖 Most of us accept individual freedom as a fundamental right. Unfortunately, we at times assume that this liberty gives us permission to set our own course. But those who love God are incapable of self-rule because, by definition, God's people are created to look beyond themselves for his word to set their course. Do you listen to his way—because no other will satisfy?

1 Samuel 14:15–23

When Saul saw what was happening in the Philistine camp, he called for Ahijah to bring "the ark of God" (v. 18). But the Septuagint (Greek translation of the Hebrew OT) perhaps preserves the original text: Saul may instead have called for the high priest's ephod (cf. v. 3), which contained the Urim and Thummim used to discern God's will (cf. Ex. 28:30). He at first determined to ask for God's guidance but suddenly stopped the inquiry and rushed to the battlefield. Such sudden

reversals exposed Saul's uncertainty and remind us of his earlier failure to wait for Samuel's arrival.

A destructive darkness in Saul's life slowly but relentlessly wells up in the narrative. The text answers one of the book's leading questions: Who could serve suitably as Israel's king? Saul began to function as a negative answer to that question. In so doing he became the foil for David, the future ideal—though by no means perfect—king.

📖 Do you allow God to communicate to you any message he wants you to hear in order to correct or reprimand you? Or have you replaced a Samuel with an Ahijah in your life? Have you turned from the dependable and true to hear another word that is more pleasing? Or one that is better attuned to your personal ambitions or desires? The Bible consistently shows the folly of opting for such a course (cf. 2 Tim. 4:3–5).

20Then Saul and all his men assembled and went to the battle. They found the Philistines in total confusion, striking[r] each other with their swords. 21Those Hebrews who had previously been with the Philistines and had gone up with them to their camp went[s] over to the Israelites who were with Saul and Jonathan. 22When all the Israelites who had hidden[t] in the hill country of Ephraim heard that the Philistines were on the run, they joined the battle in hot pursuit. 23So the LORD rescued[u] Israel that day, and the battle moved on beyond Beth Aven.[v]

Jonathan Eats Honey

24Now the men of Israel were in distress that day, because Saul had bound the people under an oath,[w] saying, "Cursed be any man who eats food before evening comes, before I have avenged myself on my enemies!" So none of the troops tasted food.

25The entire army[a] entered the woods, and there was honey on the ground. 26When they went into the woods, they saw the honey oozing out, yet no one put his hand to his mouth, because they feared the oath. 27But Jonathan had not heard that his father had bound the people with the oath, so he reached out the end of the staff that was in his hand and dipped it into the honeycomb.[x] He raised his hand to his mouth, and his eyes brightened.[b] 28Then one of the soldiers told him, "Your father bound the army under a strict oath, saying, 'Cursed be any man who eats food today!' That is why the men are faint."

29Jonathan said, "My father has made trouble[y] for the country. See how my eyes brightened[c] when I tasted a little of this honey. 30How much better it would have been if the men had eaten today some of the plunder they took from their enemies. Would not the slaughter of the Philistines have been even greater?"

31That day, after the Israelites had struck down the Philistines from Micmash to Aijalon,[z] they were exhausted. 32They pounced on the plunder[a] and, taking sheep, cattle and calves, they butchered them on the ground and ate them, together with the blood.[b] 33Then someone said to Saul, "Look, the men are sinning against the LORD by eating meat that has blood in it."

"You have broken faith," he said. "Roll a large stone over here at once." 34Then he said, "Go out among the men and tell them, 'Each of you bring me your cattle and sheep, and slaughter them here and eat them. Do not sin against the LORD by eating meat with blood still in it.' "

So everyone brought his ox that night and slaughtered it there. 35Then Saul built an altar[c] to the LORD; it was the first time he had done this.

36Saul said, "Let us go down after the Philistines by night and plunder them till dawn, and let us not leave one of them alive."

"Do whatever seems best to you," they replied.

But the priest said, "Let us inquire of God here."

37So Saul asked God, "Shall I go down after the Philistines? Will you give them into Israel's hand?" But God did not answer[d] him that day.

38Saul therefore said, "Come here, all you who are leaders of the army, and let us

---

a 25 Or Now all the people of the land   b 27 Or his strength was renewed   c 29 Or my strength was renewed

---

Cross references

14:20 r Jdg 7:22; 2Ch 20:23
14:21 s 1Sa 29:4
14:22 t 1Sa 13:6
14:23 u Ex 14:30; Ps 44:6-7   v 1Sa 13:5
14:24 w Jos 6:26
14:27 x ver 43; 1Sa 30:12
14:29 y Jos 7:25; 1Ki 18:18
14:31 z Jos 10:12
14:32 a 1Sa 15:19   b Ge 9:4; Lev 3:17; 7:26; 17:10-14; 19:26; Dt 12:16,23-24
14:35 c 1Sa 7:17
14:37 d 1Sa 10:22; 28:6,15

---

1 Samuel 14:24–48

Saul placed an unnecessary and unreasonable burden on his troops by refusing to let them eat on the day of battle. Jonathan, unaware of his father's foolish ban, didn't hesitate to refresh himself with honey. His "brightened" condition proved that he understood God's will better than his father did.

Saul had alienated himself first from Samuel, then from his army with the foolish ban against eating, and finally from his own son. The result was a lost opportunity. The day that had begun with prospects of a decisive victory didn't end that way.

Missed opportunities can be forever lost. In his grace Christ offers us forgiveness, but we can't assume that he will fix or cancel the results of our willful disobedience. His love and commitment to our character development may require us to experience fully the consequences of our sin so that we can become more like Christ. How attuned are you to the lessons God's correction intends to teach you? Are you specifically listening for his voice in the affairs of your life?

e Jos 7:11;
1Sa 10:19
14:39
f 2Sa 12:5

find out what sin has been committed[e] today. 39As surely as the Lord who rescues Israel lives,[f] even if it lies with my son Jonathan, he must die." But not one of the men said a word.

40Saul then said to all the Israelites, "You stand over there; I and Jonathan my son will stand over here."

"Do what seems best to you," the men replied.

14:41
g Ac 1:24
h Pr 16:33

41Then Saul prayed to the Lord, the God of Israel, "Give[g] me the right[h] answer."[a] And Jonathan and Saul were taken by lot, and the men were cleared. 42Saul said, "Cast the lot between me and Jonathan my son." And Jonathan was taken.

14:43
i Jos 7:19 j ver 27

43Then Saul said to Jonathan, "Tell me what you have done."[i]

So Jonathan told him, "I merely tasted a little honey[j] with the end of my staff. And now must I die?"

14:44
k Ru 1:17 l ver 39

44Saul said, "May God deal with me, be it ever so severely,[k] if you do not die, Jonathan.[l]"

14:45
m 1Ki 1:52;
Lk 21:18; Ac 27:34
n 2Sa 14:11

45But the men said to Saul, "Should Jonathan die—he who has brought about this great deliverance in Israel? Never! As surely as the Lord lives, not a hair[m] of his head will fall to the ground, for he did this today with God's help." So the men rescued[n] Jonathan, and he was not put to death.

46Then Saul stopped pursuing the Philistines, and they withdrew to their own land.

14:47
o 1Sa 11:1-13
p ver 52; 2Sa 10:6
14:48
q 1Sa 15:2,7

47After Saul had assumed rule over Israel, he fought against their enemies on every side: Moab, the Ammonites,[o] Edom, the kings[b] of Zobah,[p] and the Philistines. Wherever he turned, he inflicted punishment on them.[c] 48He fought valiantly and defeated the Amalekites,[q] delivering Israel from the hands of those who had plundered them.

Saul's Family

14:49
r 1Sa 31:2;
1Ch 8:33
s 1Sa 18:17-20

49Saul's sons were Jonathan, Ishvi and Malki-Shua.[r] The name of his older daughter was Merab, and that of the younger was Michal.[s] 50His wife's name was Ahinoam daughter of Ahimaaz. The name of the commander of Saul's army was Abner

14:51
t 1Sa 9:1

son of Ner, and Ner was Saul's uncle. 51Saul's father Kish[t] and Abner's father Ner were sons of Abiel.

14:52
u 1Sa 8:11

52All the days of Saul there was bitter war with the Philistines, and whenever Saul saw a mighty or brave man, he took[u] him into his service.

The Lord Rejects Saul as King

15:1
v 1Sa 9:16

15:2
w Ex 17:8-14;
Nu 24:20;
Dt 25:17-19

15 Samuel said to Saul, "I am the one the Lord sent to anoint[v] you king over his people Israel; so listen now to the message from the Lord. 2This is what the Lord Almighty says: 'I will punish the Amalekites[w] for what they did to Israel when they waylaid them as they came up from Egypt. 3Now go, attack the Amalek-

---

[a] 41 Hebrew; Septuagint *"Why have you not answered your servant today? If the fault is in me or my son Jonathan, respond with Urim, but if the men of Israel are at fault, respond with Thummim."*
[b] 47 Masoretic Text; Dead Sea Scrolls and Septuagint *king*   [c] 47 Hebrew; Septuagint *he was victorious*

---

1 Samuel 14:49-52

Unlike the summary of David's reign (2 Sam. 8), Saul's includes no mention of God. Twice we read that "The Lord gave David victory wherever he went" (2 Sam. 8:6,14). Especially important in light of Saul's failure to inflict a decisive blow against the Philistines is the concluding verse. The Philistine threat was Saul's reason for serving as king (9:16). But the final suppression of Philistia would await a greater monarch (2 Sam. 8:1).

Scholars have tried to analyze Saul's personality and behavior. He did exhibit some evidence of paranoia or bipolar illness. But whatever mental challenges Saul may have experienced, the text emphasizes a deeper

and more troubling development: a decaying spiritual character. Finding excuses and blaming behavior on disease, mental weakness, or other outside factors have become the norm today. But Scripture doesn't let us off so easily. Each of us is responsible before God for our actions (cf. Rom. 14:11–12).

1 Samuel 15:1–35

The author strategically placed Saul's rejection as a transition point from Saul to David. Saul continued as king until his death (ch. 31), but his fate was sealed by his own sin. The writer's apparent purpose wasn't to recount the details of Saul's wars with the Amalekites but to explain his rejection by God.

ites and totally[x] destroy[a] everything that belongs to them. Do not spare them; put to death men and women, children and infants, cattle and sheep, camels and donkeys.' "

⁴So Saul summoned the men and mustered them at Telaim—two hundred thousand foot soldiers and ten thousand men from Judah. ⁵Saul went to the city of Amalek and set an ambush in the ravine. ⁶Then he said to the Kenites,[y] "Go away, leave the Amalekites so that I do not destroy you along with them; for you showed kindness to all the Israelites when they came up out of Egypt." So the Kenites moved away from the Amalekites.

⁷Then Saul attacked the Amalekites[z] all the way from Havilah to Shur,[a] to the east of Egypt. ⁸He took Agag king of the Amalekites alive,[b] and all his people he totally destroyed with the sword. ⁹But Saul and the army spared[c] Agag and the best of the sheep and cattle, the fat calves[b] and lambs—everything that was good. These they were unwilling to destroy completely, but everything that was despised and weak they totally destroyed.

¹⁰Then the word of the LORD came to Samuel: ¹¹"I am grieved[d] that I have made Saul king, because he has turned[e] away from me and has not carried out my instructions."[f] Samuel was troubled,[g] and he cried out to the LORD all that night.

¹²Early in the morning Samuel got up and went to meet Saul, but he was told, "Saul has gone to Carmel.[h] There he has set up a monument in his own honor and has turned and gone on down to Gilgal."

¹³When Samuel reached him, Saul said, "The LORD bless you! I have carried out the LORD's instructions."

¹⁴But Samuel said, "What then is this bleating of sheep in my ears? What is this lowing of cattle that I hear?"

¹⁵Saul answered, "The soldiers brought them from the Amalekites; they spared the best of the sheep and cattle to sacrifice to the LORD your God, but we totally destroyed the rest."

¹⁶"Stop!" Samuel said to Saul. "Let me tell you what the LORD said to me last night."

"Tell me," Saul replied.

¹⁷Samuel said, "Although you were once small[i] in your own eyes, did you not become the head of the tribes of Israel? The LORD anointed you king over Israel. ¹⁸And he sent you on a mission, saying, 'Go and completely destroy those wicked people, the Amalekites; make war on them until you have wiped them out.' ¹⁹Why did you not obey the LORD? Why did you pounce on the plunder[j] and do evil in the eyes of the LORD?"

²⁰"But I did obey[k] the LORD," Saul said. "I went on the mission the LORD assigned me. I completely destroyed the Amalekites and brought back Agag their king. ²¹The soldiers took sheep and cattle from the plunder, the best of what was devoted to God, in order to sacrifice them to the LORD your God at Gilgal."

²²But Samuel replied:

"Does the LORD delight in burnt offerings and sacrifices
    as much as in obeying the voice of the LORD?
To obey is better than sacrifice,[l]

---

[a] 3 The Hebrew term refers to the irrevocable giving over of things or persons to the LORD, often by totally destroying them; also in verses 8, 9, 15, 18, 20 and 21.   [b] 9 Or *the grown bulls*; the meaning of the Hebrew for this phrase is uncertain.

15:3
[x] Nu 24:20;
Dt 20:16-18;
Jos 6:17; 1Sa 22:19

15:6
[y] Ex 18:10,19;
Nu 10:29-32; 24:22;
Jdg 1:16; 4:1

15:7
[z] 1Sa 14:48
[a] Ge 16:7;
25:17-18;
Ex 15:22
15:8
[b] 1Sa 30:1
15:9
[c] ver 3,15

15:11
[d] Ge 6:6; 2Sa 24:16
[e] Jos 22:16
[f] 1Sa 13:13;
1Ki 9:6-7 [g] ver 35

15:12
[h] Jos 15:55

15:17
[i] 1Sa 9:21

15:19
[j] 1Sa 14:32

15:20
[k] ver 13

15:22
[l] Ps 40:6-8; 51:16;
Isa 1:11-15;
Jer 7:22; Hos 6:6;
Mic 6:6-8; Mt 12:7;
Mk 12:33;
Heb 10:6-9

Note Saul's rationalizations and attempts to divert the blame (vv. 15,20–21). Finally he changed his strategy: We hear what sounds like a confession, but it was hollow and motivated by self-interest. His concern was saving face before the people, not finding forgiveness before God. Contrast this with David's fitting response when confronted by Nathan with his sins (2 Sam. 12:13–18). David didn't try to defend himself or offer a contrived confession. Unlike Saul, he was a broken man (Ps. 51).

Samuel's question is a powerful wake-up call for all of us: "What then is this bleating of sheep in my ears?" The prophet stands boldly before all who sin and raises the question we can't avoid. The sheep are there; anyone can hear them. All that remains is our reaction. Will you respond as a Saul or a David?

421

15:23
m Dt 18:10
n 1Sa 13:13

and to heed is better than the fat of rams.
23 For rebellion is like the sin of divination, m
   and arrogance like the evil of idolatry.
Because you have rejected n the word of the LORD,
   he has rejected you as king."

15:24
o 2Sa 12:13
p Pr 29:25;
Isa 51:12-13
15:25
q Ex 10:17
15:26
r 1Sa 13:14
15:27
s 1Ki 11:11,31
15:28
t 1Sa 28:17;
1Ki 11:31

24 Then Saul said to Samuel, "I have sinned. o I violated the LORD's command and your instructions. I was afraid p of the people and so I gave in to them. 25 Now I beg you, forgive q my sin and come back with me, so that I may worship the LORD."

26 But Samuel said to him, "I will not go back with you. You have rejected r the word of the LORD, and the LORD has rejected you as king over Israel!"

27 As Samuel turned to leave, Saul caught hold of the hem of his robe, and it tore. s 28 Samuel said to him, "The LORD has torn t the kingdom of Israel from you today and has given it to one of your neighbors—to one better than you. 29 He who is the Glory of Israel does not lie u or change v his mind; for he is not a man, that he should change his mind."

15:29
u 1Ch 29:11; Tit 1:2
v Nu 23:19;
Eze 24:14
15:30
w Isa 29:13;
Jn 5:44; 12:43

30 Saul replied, "I have sinned. But please honor w me before the elders of my people and before Israel; come back with me, so that I may worship the LORD your God." 31 So Samuel went back with Saul, and Saul worshiped the LORD.

32 Then Samuel said, "Bring me Agag king of the Amalekites."

Agag came to him confidently, a thinking, "Surely the bitterness of death is past." 33 But Samuel said,

15:33
x Ge 9:6; Jdg 1:7

"As your sword has made women childless,
   so will your mother be childless among women." x

15:34
y 1Sa 7:17
z 1Sa 11:4
15:35
a 1Sa 19:24
b 1Sa 16:1

And Samuel put Agag to death before the LORD at Gilgal.

34 Then Samuel left for Ramah, y but Saul went up to his home in Gibeah z of Saul. 35 Until the day Samuel a died, he did not go to see Saul again, though Samuel mourned b for him. And the LORD was grieved that he had made Saul king over Israel.

Samuel Anoints David

16:1
c 1Sa 15:35
d 1Sa 15:23
e 2Ki 9:1 f Ru 4:17;
1Sa 9:16
g Ps 78:70;
Ac 13:22

16 The LORD said to Samuel, "How long will you mourn c for Saul, since I have rejected d him as king over Israel? Fill your horn with oil e and be on your way; I am sending you to Jesse f of Bethlehem. I have chosen g one of his sons to be king."

2 But Samuel said, "How can I go? Saul will hear about it and kill me."

The LORD said, "Take a heifer with you and say, 'I have come to sacrifice to the LORD.'

16:3
h Ex 4:15
i Dt 17:15; 1Sa 9:16

3 Invite Jesse to the sacrifice, and I will show h you what to do. You are to anoint i for me the one I indicate."

16:4
j Ge 48:7; Lk 2:4
k 1Ki 2:13; 2Ki 9:17

4 Samuel did what the LORD said. When he arrived at Bethlehem, j the elders of the town trembled when they met him. They asked, "Do you come in peace? k"

16:5
l Ex 19:10,22

5 Samuel replied, "Yes, in peace; I have come to sacrifice to the LORD. Consecrate l yourselves and come to the sacrifice with me." Then he consecrated Jesse and his sons and invited them to the sacrifice.

a 32 Or him trembling, yet

---

1 Samuel 16:1–13

📖 From this point on David is central, though he doesn't become king until the early chapters of 2 Samuel. We finally meet the man after God's own heart (as foretold in 13:14)—here hardly more than a boy. He had become the ideal king of Israel with whom *all future rulers would be compared and who would pave the way for the Messiah's coming.*

God sees in people things we are prone to overlook. Because he has superior vision, we are frequently sur-

prised by his choices. In ancient Israel, for example, he often chose the youngest son or an infertile woman.

📖 God often uses the uneducated, poor, and disenfranchised (cf. 1 Cor. 1:26–29). Since we can't know in advance who will answer his call or be effective in his service, we are wise to avoid prejudging others. On the other hand, we have no business devaluing our own abilities and gifts for service. We may feel as though we have little to offer. But when God calls, he also empowers. Don't underestimate his ability to work through you.

[6]When they arrived, Samuel saw Eliab[m] and thought, "Surely the LORD's anointed stands here before the LORD."

[7]But the LORD said to Samuel, "Do not consider his appearance or his height, for I have rejected him. The LORD does not look at the things man looks at. Man looks at the outward appearance,[n] but the LORD looks at the heart."[o]

[8]Then Jesse called Abinadab[p] and had him pass in front of Samuel. But Samuel said, "The LORD has not chosen this one either." [9]Jesse then had Shammah pass by, but Samuel said, "Nor has the LORD chosen this one." [10]Jesse had seven of his sons pass before Samuel, but Samuel said to him, "The LORD has not chosen these." [11]So he asked Jesse, "Are these all[q] the sons you have?"

"There is still the youngest," Jesse answered, "but he is tending the sheep."

Samuel said, "Send for him; we will not sit down[a] until he arrives."

[12]So he[r] sent and had him brought in. He was ruddy, with a fine appearance and handsome[s] features.

Then the LORD said, "Rise and anoint him; he is the one."

[13]So Samuel took the horn of oil and anointed him in the presence of his brothers, and from that day on the Spirit of the LORD[t] came upon David in power.[u] Samuel then went to Ramah.

David in Saul's Service

[14]Now the Spirit of the LORD had departed[v] from Saul, and an evil[b] spirit[w] from the LORD tormented him.

[15]Saul's attendants said to him, "See, an evil spirit from God is tormenting you. [16]Let our lord command his servants here to search for someone who can play the harp.[x] He will play when the evil spirit from God comes upon you, and you will feel better."

[17]So Saul said to his attendants, "Find someone who plays well and bring him to me."

[18]One of the servants answered, "I have seen a son of Jesse of Bethlehem who knows how to play the harp. He is a brave man and a warrior. He speaks well and is a fine-looking man. And the LORD is with[y] him."

[19]Then Saul sent messengers to Jesse and said, "Send me your son David, who is with the sheep." [20]So Jesse took a donkey loaded with bread,[z] a skin of wine and a young goat and sent them with his son David to Saul.

[21]David came to Saul and entered his service.[a] Saul liked him very much, and David became one of his armor-bearers. [22]Then Saul sent word to Jesse, saying, "Allow David to remain in my service, for I am pleased with him."

[23]Whenever the spirit from God came upon Saul, David would take his harp and play. Then relief would come to Saul; he would feel better, and the evil spirit[b] would leave him.

---

[a] 11 Some Septuagint manuscripts; Hebrew *not gather around*   [b] 14 Or *injurious*; also in verses 15, 16 and 23

16:6
m 1Sa 17:13

16:7
n Ps 147:10
o 1Ki 8:39;
1Ch 28:9; Isa 55:8
16:8
p 1Sa 17:13

16:11
q 1Sa 17:12

16:12
r 1Sa 9:17
s Ge 39:6;
1Sa 17:42

16:13
t Nu 27:18;
Jdg 11:29
u 1Sa 10:1,6,9-10;
11:6

16:14
v Jdg 16:20
w Jdg 9:23;
1Sa 18:10

16:16
x ver 23; 1Sa 18:10;
19:9; 2Ki 3:15

16:18
y 1Sa 3:19;
17:32-37
16:20
z 1Sa 10:27;
Pr 18:16

16:21
a Ge 41:46;
Pr 22:29

16:23
b ver 14-16

---

1 Samuel 16:14–23

Saul and David had met for the first time. The rest of 1 Samuel narrates, in alternating fashion, Saul's fall and David's rise. Their stories crisscross, at times intersecting and at other times moving in separate directions. Verses 18–23 introduce three themes: Saul was in decline; David was prospering because "the LORD [was] with him"; and Saul was deeply attached to David.

Not only is this chapter the center of the book, but its transition at verses 13 and 14 marks a turning point in the stories of the anointed ones. In verse 13 David received God's Spirit, and in verse 14 Saul lost it. This pivotal passage relates the shift of political and spiritual power from Saul to David.

Little did David realize what using his musical talents in the royal court would mean for him later in life. As Christians, we are committed to the idea that God is at work in our lives, but we aren't always consciously aware of the specifics of his involvement. And we are often confused about how it all fits together. David was left, as we frequently are, to do his best without the benefit of the big picture. At what junctions in your life have you begun to see that picture coming together? If you don't see anything yet, stay on course, confident of his work in you (Phil. 1:6)!

423

17:1
c 1Sa 13:5
d Jos 15:35;
2Ch 28:18
17:2
e 1Sa 21:9

17:4
f Jos 11:21-22;
2Sa 21:19

17:6
g ver 45
17:7
h 2Sa 21:19 i ver 41

17:8
j 1Sa 8:17

17:10
k ver 26,45;
2Sa 21:21

17:12
l Ru 4:17;
1Ch 2:13-15
m Ge 35:19
n 1Sa 16:11
17:13
o 1Sa 16:6
p 1Sa 16:9

17:15
q 1Sa 16:19

17:17
r 1Sa 25:18

17:18
s Ge 37:14

17:23
t ver 8-10

17:25
u Jos 15:16;
1Sa 18:17

17:26
v 1Sa 11:2
w 1Sa 14:6 x ver 10
y Dt 5:26

David and Goliath

17 Now the Philistines gathered their forces for war and assembled c at Socoh in Judah. They pitched camp at Ephes Dammim, between Socoh d and Azekah. ²Saul and the Israelites assembled and camped in the Valley of Elah e and drew up their battle line to meet the Philistines. ³The Philistines occupied one hill and the Israelites another, with the valley between them.

⁴A champion named Goliath, f who was from Gath, came out of the Philistine camp. He was over nine feet a tall. ⁵He had a bronze helmet on his head and wore a coat of scale armor of bronze weighing five thousand shekels b; ⁶on his legs he wore bronze greaves, and a bronze javelin g was slung on his back. ⁷His spear shaft was like a weaver's rod, h and its iron point weighed six hundred shekels. c His shield bearer i went ahead of him.

⁸Goliath stood and shouted to the ranks of Israel, "Why do you come out and line up for battle? Am I not a Philistine, and are you not the servants of Saul? Choose j a man and have him come down to me. ⁹If he is able to fight and kill me, we will become your subjects; but if I overcome him and kill him, you will become our subjects and serve us." ¹⁰Then the Philistine said, "This day I defy k the ranks of Israel! Give me a man and let us fight each other." ¹¹On hearing the Philistine's words, Saul and all the Israelites were dismayed and terrified.

¹²Now David was the son of an Ephrathite named Jesse, l who was from Bethlehem m in Judah. Jesse had eight n sons, and in Saul's time he was old and well advanced in years. ¹³Jesse's three oldest sons had followed Saul to the war: The firstborn was Eliab; o the second, Abinadab; and the third, Shammah. p ¹⁴David was the youngest. The three oldest followed Saul, ¹⁵but David went back and forth from Saul to tend his father's sheep q at Bethlehem.

¹⁶For forty days the Philistine came forward every morning and evening and took his stand.

¹⁷Now Jesse said to his son David, "Take this ephah d of roasted grain r and these ten loaves of bread for your brothers and hurry to their camp. ¹⁸Take along these ten cheeses to the commander of their unit. e See how your brothers s are and bring back some assurance f from them. ¹⁹They are with Saul and all the men of Israel in the Valley of Elah, fighting against the Philistines."

²⁰Early in the morning David left the flock with a shepherd, loaded up and set out, as Jesse had directed. He reached the camp as the army was going out to its battle positions, shouting the war cry. ²¹Israel and the Philistines were drawing up their lines facing each other. ²²David left his things with the keeper of supplies, ran to the battle lines and greeted his brothers. ²³As he was talking with them, Goliath, the Philistine champion from Gath, stepped out from his lines and shouted his usual t defiance, and David heard it. ²⁴When the Israelites saw the man, they all ran from him in great fear.

²⁵Now the Israelites had been saying, "Do you see how this man keeps coming out? He comes out to defy Israel. The king will give great wealth to the man who kills him. He will also give him his daughter u in marriage and will exempt his father's family from taxes in Israel."

²⁶David asked the men standing near him, "What will be done for the man who kills this Philistine and removes this disgrace v from Israel? Who is this uncircumcised w Philistine that he should defy x the armies of the living y God?"

---

a 4 Hebrew *was six cubits and a span* (about 3 meters)   b 5 That is, about 125 pounds (about 57 kilograms)   c 7 That is, about 15 pounds (about 7 kilograms)   d 17 That is, probably about 3/5 bushel (about 22 liters)   e 18 Hebrew *thousand*   f 18 Or *some token; or some pledge of spoils*

---

1 Samuel 17:1–58

The NIV's translation of "over nine feet tall" represents the Hebrew text. A Greek translation reads that Goliath was around seven feet tall. Either way, his size and strength remind readers of another leader who was "a head taller than any of the others" (10:23). Saul was evidently the best match for Goliath and would have been expected not only to motivate his troops but to lead them. In contrast, David couldn't have looked more vulnerable and less significant. But superior strength and military resources were useless against God's representative.

27They repeated to him what they had been saying and told him, "This is what will be done for the man who kills him."

28When Eliab, David's oldest brother, heard him speaking with the men, he burned with anger[z] at him and asked, "Why have you come down here? And with whom did you leave those few sheep in the desert? I know how conceited you are and how wicked your heart is; you came down only to watch the battle."

29"Now what have I done?" said David. "Can't I even speak?" 30He then turned away to someone else and brought up the same matter, and the men answered him as before. 31What David said was overheard and reported to Saul, and Saul sent for him.

32David said to Saul, "Let no one lose heart[a] on account of this Philistine; your servant will go and fight him."

33Saul replied,[b] "You are not able to go out against this Philistine and fight him; you are only a boy, and he has been a fighting man from his youth."

34But David said to Saul, "Your servant has been keeping his father's sheep. When a lion[c] or a bear came and carried off a sheep from the flock, 35I went after it, struck it and rescued the sheep from its mouth. When it turned on me, I seized it by its hair, struck it and killed it. 36Your servant has killed both the lion and the bear; this uncircumcised Philistine will be like one of them, because he has defied the armies of the living God. 37The LORD who delivered[d] me from the paw of the lion[e] and the paw of the bear will deliver me from the hand of this Philistine."

Saul said to David, "Go, and the LORD be with[f] you."

38Then Saul dressed David in his own tunic. He put a coat of armor on him and a bronze helmet on his head. 39David fastened on his sword over the tunic and tried walking around, because he was not used to them.

"I cannot go in these," he said to Saul, "because I am not used to them." So he took them off. 40Then he took his staff in his hand, chose five smooth stones from the stream, put them in the pouch of his shepherd's bag and, with his sling in his hand, approached the Philistine.

41Meanwhile, the Philistine, with his shield bearer in front of him, kept coming closer to David. 42He looked David over and saw that he was only a boy, ruddy and handsome,[g] and he despised[h] him. 43He said to David, "Am I a dog,[i] that you come at me with sticks?" And the Philistine cursed David by his gods. 44"Come here," he said, "and I'll give your flesh to the birds of the air and the beasts of the field![j]"

45David said to the Philistine, "You come against me with sword and spear and javelin, but I come against you in the name[k] of the LORD Almighty, the God of the armies of Israel, whom you have defied.[l] 46This day the LORD will hand you over to me, and I'll strike you down and cut off your head. Today I will give the carcasses[m] of the Philistine army to the birds of the air and the beasts of the earth, and the whole world[n] will know that there is a God in Israel.[o] 47All those gathered here will know that it is not by sword[p] or spear that the LORD saves;[q] for the battle[r] is the LORD's, and he will give all of you into our hands."

48As the Philistine moved closer to attack him, David ran quickly toward the battle line to meet him. 49Reaching into his bag and taking out a stone, he slung it and struck the Philistine on the forehead. The stone sank into his forehead, and he fell facedown on the ground.

50So David triumphed over the Philistine with a sling[s] and a stone; without a sword in his hand he struck down the Philistine and killed him.

51David ran and stood over him. He took hold of the Philistine's sword and drew it from the scabbard. After he killed him, he cut[t] off his head with the sword.[u]

When the Philistines saw that their hero was dead, they turned and ran. 52Then the men of Israel and Judah surged forward with a shout and pursued the Philistines

---

17:28 [z] Ge 37:4,8,11; Pr 18:19; Mt 10:36
17:32 [a] Dt 20:3; 1Sa 16:18
17:33 [b] Nu 13:31
17:34 [c] Jer 49:19; Am 3:12
17:37 [d] 2Co 1:10 [e] 2Ti 4:17 [f] 1Sa 20:13; 1Ch 22:11,16
17:42 [g] 1Sa 16:12 [h] Ps 123:3-4; Pr 16:18
17:43 [i] 1Sa 24:14; 2Sa 3:8; 9:8; 2Ki 8:13
17:44 [j] 1Ki 20:10-11
17:45 [k] 2Sa 22:33,35; 2Ch 32:8; Ps 124:8; Heb 11:32-34 [l] ver 10
17:46 [m] Dt 28:26 [n] Jos 4:24; 1Ki 8:43; Isa 52:10 [o] 2Ki 18:36
17:47 [p] Hos 1:7; Zec 4:6 [q] 1Sa 14:6; 2Ch 14:11 [r] 2Ch 20:15; Ps 44:6-7
17:50 [s] 2Sa 23:21
17:51 [t] Heb 11:34 [u] 1Sa 21:9

📖 The account of David's dramatic victory over Goliath is a classic—one of the Bible's best loved stories, illustrating God's ability to provide victory in the face of overwhelming odds. It contains all the elements of great literature and has inspired faith over the centuries precisely because it portrays purity and right as victorious over might. How has this truth been borne out in your experience?

17:52
v Jos 15:11
w Jos 15:36

to the entrance of Gath[a] and to the gates of Ekron.[v] Their dead were strewn along the Shaaraim[w] road to Gath and Ekron. 53When the Israelites returned from chasing the Philistines, they plundered their camp. 54David took the Philistine's head and brought it to Jerusalem, and he put the Philistine's weapons in his own tent.

17:55
x 1Sa 16:21

55As Saul watched David[x] going out to meet the Philistine, he said to Abner, commander of the army, "Abner, whose son is that young man?"

Abner replied, "As surely as you live, O king, I don't know."

56The king said, "Find out whose son this young man is."

57As soon as David returned from killing the Philistine, Abner took him and brought him before Saul, with David still holding the Philistine's head.

17:58
y ver 12

58"Whose son are you, young man?" Saul asked him.

David said, "I am the son of your servant Jesse[y] of Bethlehem."

Saul's Jealousy of David

18:1
z 2Sa 1:26
a Ge 44:30

18:3
b 1Sa 20:8,16,17, 42

18:4
c Ge 41:42

18 After David had finished talking with Saul, Jonathan became one in spirit with David, and he loved[z] him as himself.[a] 2From that day Saul kept David with him and did not let him return to his father's house. 3And Jonathan made a covenant[b] with David because he loved him as himself. 4Jonathan took off the robe[c] he was wearing and gave it to David, along with his tunic, and even his sword, his bow and his belt.

5Whatever Saul sent him to do, David did it so successfully[b] that Saul gave him a high rank in the army. This pleased all the people, and Saul's officers as well.

18:6
d Ex 15:20
e Jdg 11:34; Ps 68:25

18:7
f Ex 15:21
g 1Sa 21:11; 29:5

6When the men were returning home after David had killed the Philistine, the women came out from all the towns of Israel to meet King Saul with singing and dancing,[d] with joyful songs and with tambourines[e] and lutes. 7As they danced, they sang:[f]

> "Saul has slain his thousands,
>   and David his tens[g] of thousands."

18:8
h 1Sa 15:8

18:10
i 1Sa 16:14
j 1Sa 19:7

18:11
k 1Sa 20:7,33
l 1Sa 19:10

18:12
m ver 15,29
n 1Sa 16:13
o 1Sa 28:15

18:13
p ver 16; Nu 27:17
q 2Sa 5:2

18:14
r Ge 39:3
s Ge 39:2,23; Jos 6:27; 1Sa 16:18

18:16
t ver 5

8Saul was very angry; this refrain galled him. "They have credited David with tens of thousands," he thought, "but me with only thousands. What more can he get but the kingdom?"[h] 9And from that time on Saul kept a jealous eye on David.

10The next day an evil[c] spirit[i] from God came forcefully upon Saul. He was prophesying in his house, while David was playing the harp, as he usually[j] did. Saul had a spear in his hand 11and he hurled it, saying to himself,[k] "I'll pin David to the wall." But David eluded[l] him twice.

12Saul was afraid[m] of David, because the LORD[n] was with[o] David but had left Saul. 13So he sent David away from him and gave him command over a thousand men, and David led[p] the troops in their campaigns.[q] 14In everything he did he had great success,[d][r] because the LORD was with[s] him. 15When Saul saw how successful[e] he was, he was afraid of him. 16But all Israel and Judah loved David, because he led them in their campaigns.[t]

a 52 Some Septuagint manuscripts; Hebrew a valley   b 5 Or wisely   c 10 Or injurious
d 14 Or he was very wise   e 15 Or wise

---

1 Samuel 18:1–30

The prickly issue that drives the rest of 1 Samuel is the coexistence of two anointed ones in Israel. Since the historian had already alerted us that David was God's choice, he was left now to narrate the details of Saul's fall and David's rise. The text takes us through twists and turns in a way that beautifully demonstrates God's sovereign work in the world among humans who are free to follow or resist.

The relationship between Jonathan and David was one of deep and abiding friendship—enough to lead the crown prince to renounce the throne. This section continues an interesting sub-theme in which lesser persons passed their weapons to David. King Saul had done so (17:38–39), Goliath's sword had been passed on to him (17:51,54), and here Jonathan gave David his sword and bow.

Christians are called to refuse retaliation, to live in such a way as to overcome and transform their oppressors. Even though Saul had set his course and wouldn't be deterred, David remained faithful, and God was with him. As Christians, we bear testimony to God's grace in our lives in good and bad times. And we remember that a loving response to opposition can transform and reform both our enemies and ourselves. Does an incident come to mind in which this was true for you?

17Saul said to David, "Here is my older daughter[u] Merab. I will give her to you in marriage; only serve me bravely and fight the battles[v] of the LORD." For Saul said to himself,[w] "I will not raise a hand against him. Let the Philistines do that!"

18But David said to Saul, "Who am I,[x] and what is my family or my father's clan in Israel, that I should become the king's son-in-law?"[y] 19So[a] when the time came for Merab,[z] Saul's daughter, to be given to David, she was given in marriage to Adriel of Meholah.[a]

20Now Saul's daughter Michal[b] was in love with David, and when they told Saul about it, he was pleased. 21"I will give her to him," he thought, "so that she may be a snare[c] to him and so that the hand of the Philistines may be against him." So Saul said to David, "Now you have a second opportunity to become my son-in-law."

22Then Saul ordered his attendants: "Speak to David privately and say, 'Look, the king is pleased with you, and his attendants all like you; now become his son-in-law.'"

23They repeated these words to David. But David said, "Do you think it is a small matter to become the king's son-in-law? I'm only a poor man and little known."

24When Saul's servants told him what David had said, 25Saul replied, "Say to David, 'The king wants no other price[d] for the bride than a hundred Philistine foreskins, to take revenge on his enemies.'" Saul's plan[e] was to have David fall by the hands of the Philistines.

26When the attendants told David these things, he was pleased to become the king's son-in-law. So before the allotted time elapsed, 27David and his men went out and killed two hundred Philistines. He brought their foreskins and presented the full number to the king so that he might become the king's son-in-law. Then Saul gave him his daughter Michal[f] in marriage.

28When Saul realized that the LORD was with David and that his daughter Michal loved David, 29Saul became still more afraid of him, and he remained his enemy the rest of his days.

30The Philistine commanders continued to go out to battle, and as often as they did, David met with more success[b][g] than the rest of Saul's officers, and his name became well known.

Saul Tries to Kill David

19 Saul told his son Jonathan[h] and all the attendants to kill[i] David. But Jonathan was very fond of David 2and warned him, "My father Saul is looking for a chance to kill you. Be on your guard tomorrow morning; go into hiding and stay there. 3I will go out and stand with my father in the field where you are. I'll speak[j] to him about you and will tell you what I find out."

4Jonathan spoke[k] well of David to Saul his father and said to him, "Let not the king do wrong[l] to his servant David; he has not wronged you, and what he has done has benefited you greatly. 5He took his life in his hands when he killed the Philistine. The LORD won a great victory[m] for all Israel, and you saw it and were glad. Why then would you do wrong to an innocent[n] man like David by killing him for no reason?"

6Saul listened to Jonathan and took this oath: "As surely as the LORD lives, David will not be put to death."

[a] 19 Or However,   [b] 30 Or David acted more wisely

Cross-references:
18:17 u 1Sa 17:25; v Nu 21:14; 1Sa 25:28 w ver 25
18:18 x 1Sa 9:21; 2Sa 7:18 y ver 23
18:19 z 2Sa 21:8 a Jdg 7:22
18:20 b ver 28
18:21 c ver 17,26
18:25 d Ge 34:12; Ex 22:17; 1Sa 14:24 e ver 17
18:27 f ver 13; 2Sa 3:14
18:30 g ver 5; 2Sa 11:1
19:1 h 1Sa 18:1 i 1Sa 18:9
19:3 j 1Sa 20:12
19:4 k 1Sa 20:32; Pr 31:8,9; Jer 18:20 l Ge 42:22; Pr 17:13
19:5 m 1Sa 11:13; 17:15-50; 1Ch 11:14 n Dt 19:10-13; 1Sa 20:32; Mt 27:4

1 Samuel 19:1–24

The Bible clearly teaches that disobeying authority and lying are wrong. But the Hebrew midwives disobeyed Pharaoh's order to kill baby boys (Ex. 1:15–21), and Rahab lied to the king of Jericho to save two Israelite spies (Josh. 2:1–7; James 2:25). Jonathan and Michal likewise chose a higher good and were willing to accept the consequences of their choices in order to help an innocent person.

It's enlightening to read verses 23–24 in light of Saul's first experience with God's Spirit in 10:1–13. The terminology is only slightly dissimilar, but the context and results are vastly different. While the first Spirit-anointing signaled the beginning of Saul's career, this one marked its end. The Spirit prevented Saul from harming David.

19:7
o 1Sa 16:21; 18:2, 13

19:9
p 1Sa 16:14; 18:10-11

19:10
q 1Sa 18:11

19:11
r Ps 59 Title

19:12
s Jos 2:15; Ac 9:25

19:14
t Jos 2:4

19:18
u 1Sa 7:17

19:20
v ver 11,14; Jn 7:32,45
w Nu 11:25
x 1Sa 10:5; Joel 2:28

19:23
y 1Sa 10:13
19:24
z 2Sa 6:20; Isa 20:2; Mic 1:8 a 1Sa 10:11

20:1
b 1Sa 24:9

7So Jonathan called David and told him the whole conversation. He brought him to Saul, and David was with Saul as before. o

8Once more war broke out, and David went out and fought the Philistines. He struck them with such force that they fled before him.

9But an evil a spirit p from the LORD came upon Saul as he was sitting in his house with his spear in his hand. While David was playing the harp, 10Saul tried to pin him to the wall with his spear, but David eluded q him as Saul drove the spear into the wall. That night David made good his escape.

11Saul sent men to David's house to watch r it and to kill him in the morning. But Michal, David's wife, warned him, "If you don't run for your life tonight, tomorrow you'll be killed." 12So Michal let David down through a window, s and he fled and escaped. 13Then Michal took an idol b and laid it on the bed, covering it with a garment and putting some goats' hair at the head.

14When Saul sent the men to capture David, Michal said, t "He is ill."

15Then Saul sent the men back to see David and told them, "Bring him up to me in his bed so that I may kill him." 16But when the men entered, there was the idol in the bed, and at the head was some goats' hair.

17Saul said to Michal, "Why did you deceive me like this and send my enemy away so that he escaped?"

Michal told him, "He said to me, 'Let me get away. Why should I kill you?' "

18When David had fled and made his escape, he went to Samuel at Ramah u and told him all that Saul had done to him. Then he and Samuel went to Naioth and stayed there. 19Word came to Saul: "David is in Naioth at Ramah"; 20so he sent men to capture him. But when they saw a group of prophets v prophesying, with Samuel standing there as their leader, the Spirit of God came upon w Saul's men and they also prophesied. x 21Saul was told about it, and he sent more men, and they prophesied too. Saul sent men a third time, and they also prophesied. 22Finally, he himself left for Ramah and went to the great cistern at Secu. And he asked, "Where are Samuel and David?"

"Over in Naioth at Ramah," they said.

23So Saul went to Naioth at Ramah. But the Spirit of God came even upon him, and he walked along prophesying y until he came to Naioth. 24He stripped z off his robes and also prophesied in Samuel's presence. He lay that way all that day and night. This is why people say, "Is Saul also among the prophets?" a

David and Jonathan

20 Then David fled from Naioth at Ramah and went to Jonathan and asked, "What have I done? What is my crime? How have I wronged b your father, that he is trying to take my life?"

2"Never!" Jonathan replied. "You are not going to die! Look, my father doesn't do anything, great or small, without confiding in me. Why would he hide this from me? It's not so!"

a 9 Or injurious   b 13 Hebrew teraphim; also in verse 16

Have you ever told or implied an untruth to achieve a higher good? It may be argued that Corrie ten Boom, confronted by the policies of a madman, was justified in lying to protect innocent Jews during the Nazi occupation (see article on page 558). In such circumstances, we have to trust that God will evaluate our behavior and throw ourselves on the mercy of the court. He is, after all, aware of our motives and understands our human frailties (cf. Ps. 103:13–14; Heb. 4:12–13).

We can't live today on the spiritual blessings of yesterday. And no generation can afford to enjoy the spiritual benefits of its ancestors without giving thought to its own responsibility in service and ministry. It's up to us to continually live according to the Spirit (cf. Rom. 8:5).

1 Samuel 20:1–42

The essence of the relationship between David and Jonathan was a covenant involving promises of mutual protection. They were committed to looking out for one another. Jonathan acknowledged that David would succeed his father as king—and pledged to David his allegiance (vv. 13,16). Jonathan would do what he could to protect David, who would likewise look after Jonathan and his offspring. The arrangement depended completely on the covenant relationship with its fierce loyalty.

³But David took an oath[c] and said, "Your father knows very well that I have found favor in your eyes, and he has said to himself, 'Jonathan must not know this or he will be grieved.' Yet as surely as the LORD lives and as you live, there is only a step between me and death."

⁴Jonathan said to David, "Whatever you want me to do, I'll do for you."

⁵So David said, "Look, tomorrow is the New Moon festival,[d] and I am supposed to dine with the king; but let me go and hide[e] in the field until the evening of the day after tomorrow. ⁶If your father misses me at all, tell him, 'David earnestly asked my permission to hurry to Bethlehem,[f] his hometown, because an annual[g] sacrifice is being made there for his whole clan.' ⁷If he says, 'Very well,' then your servant is safe. But if he loses his temper,[h] you can be sure that he is determined to harm me. ⁸As for you, show kindness to your servant, for you have brought him into a covenant[i] with you before the LORD. If I am guilty, then kill[j] me yourself! Why hand me over to your father?"

⁹"Never!" Jonathan said. "If I had the least inkling that my father was determined to harm you, wouldn't I tell you?"

¹⁰David asked, "Who will tell me if your father answers you harshly?"

¹¹"Come," Jonathan said, "let's go out into the field." So they went there together.

¹²Then Jonathan said to David: "By the LORD, the God of Israel, I will surely sound out my father by this time the day after tomorrow! If he is favorably disposed toward you, will I not send you word and let you know? ¹³But if my father is inclined to harm you, may the LORD deal with me, be it ever so severely,[k] if I do not let you know and send you away safely. May the LORD be with[l] you as he has been with my father. ¹⁴But show me unfailing kindness like that of the LORD as long as I live, so that I may not be killed, ¹⁵and do not ever cut off your kindness from my family[m]—not even when the LORD has cut off every one of David's enemies from the face of the earth."

¹⁶So Jonathan made a covenant[n] with the house of David, saying, "May the LORD call David's enemies to account." ¹⁷And Jonathan had David reaffirm his oath[o] out of love for him, because he loved him as he loved himself.

¹⁸Then Jonathan said to David: "Tomorrow is the New Moon festival. You will be missed, because your seat will be empty.[p] ¹⁹The day after tomorrow, toward evening, go to the place where you hid[q] when this trouble began, and wait by the stone Ezel. ²⁰I will shoot three arrows to the side of it, as though I were shooting at a target. ²¹Then I will send a boy and say, 'Go, find the arrows.' If I say to him, 'Look, the arrows are on this side of you; bring them here,' then come, because, as surely as the LORD lives, you are safe; there is no danger. ²²But if I say to the boy, 'Look, the arrows are beyond[r] you,' then you must go, because the LORD has sent you away. ²³And about the matter you and I discussed—remember, the LORD is witness[s] between you and me forever."

²⁴So David hid in the field, and when the New Moon festival came, the king sat down to eat. ²⁵He sat in his customary place by the wall, opposite Jonathan,[a] and Abner sat next to Saul, but David's place was empty.[t] ²⁶Saul said nothing that day, for he thought, "Something must have happened to David to make him ceremonially unclean—surely he is unclean.[u]" ²⁷But the next day, the second day of the month, David's place was empty again. Then Saul said to his son Jonathan, "Why hasn't the son of Jesse come to the meal, either yesterday or today?"

²⁸Jonathan answered, "David earnestly asked me for permission[v] to go to Bethlehem. ²⁹He said, 'Let me go, because our family is observing a sacrifice in the town

---

ᵃ 25 Septuagint; Hebrew *wall. Jonathan arose*

20:3
c Dt 6:13

20:5
d Nu 10:10; 28:11
e 1Sa 19:2

20:6
f 1Sa 17:58
g Dt 12:5

20:7
h 1Sa 25:17

20:8
i 1Sa 18:3; 23:18
j 2Sa 14:32

20:13
k Ru 1:17; 1Sa 3:17
l Jos 1:5; 1Sa 17:37;
18:12;
1Ch 22:11,16

20:15
m 2Sa 9:7

20:16
n 1Sa 25:22

20:17
o 1Sa 18:3

20:18
p ver 5,25
20:19
q 1Sa 19:2

20:22
r ver 37
20:23
s ver 14-15;
Ge 31:50

20:25
t ver 18

20:26
u Lev 7:20-21; 15:5;
1Sa 16:5

20:28
v ver 6

The Bible teaches us to be committed to our fellow human beings so that everyone—not just those who look and sound like us—can enjoy security and prosperity. A Christian application of covenant relationships will consider, for example, not just the effects of greed and materialism on our families and friends, but our broader commitment to society and the world at large. What priority does this wider global concern play in your Christian life?

and my brother has ordered me to be there. If I have found favor in your eyes, let me get away to see my brothers.' That is why he has not come to the king's table."

30Saul's anger flared up at Jonathan and he said to him, "You son of a perverse and rebellious woman! Don't I know that you have sided with the son of Jesse to your own shame and to the shame of the mother who bore you? 31As long as the son of Jesse lives on this earth, neither you nor your kingdom will be established. Now send and bring him to me, for he must die!"

20:32
w 1Sa 19:4;
Mt 27:23
x Ge 31:36;
Lk 23:22
20:33
y ver 7;
1Sa 18:11,17

32"Whyw should he be put to death? Whatx has he done?" Jonathan asked his father. 33But Saul hurled his spear at him to kill him. Then Jonathan knew that his father intendedy to kill David.

34Jonathan got up from the table in fierce anger; on that second day of the month he did not eat, because he was grieved at his father's shameful treatment of David.

35In the morning Jonathan went out to the field for his meeting with David. He had a small boy with him, 36and he said to the boy, "Run and find the arrows I shoot." As the boy ran, he shot an arrow beyond him. 37When the boy came to the place where Jonathan's arrow had fallen, Jonathan called out after him, "Isn't the arrow beyondz you?" 38Then he shouted, "Hurry! Go quickly! Don't stop!" The boy picked up the arrow and returned to his master. 39(The boy knew nothing of all this; only Jonathan and David knew.) 40Then Jonathan gave his weapons to the boy and said, "Go, carry them back to town."

20:37
z ver 22

41After the boy had gone, David got up from the south side ⌊of the stone⌋ and bowed down before Jonathan three times, with his face to the ground. Then they kissed each other and wept together—but David wept the most.

20:42
a ver 22; 1Sa 1:17
b 2Sa 1:26;
Pr 18:24

42Jonathan said to David, "Go in peace,a for we have sworn friendshipb with each other in the name of the LORD, saying, 'The LORD is witness between you and me, and between your descendants and my descendants forever.' " Then David left, and Jonathan went back to the town.

David at Nob

21 David went to Nob,c to Ahimelech the priest. Ahimelech trembledd when he met him, and asked, "Why are you alone? Why is no one with you?"

21:1
c 1Sa 14:3; 22:9,19;
Ne 11:32; Isa 10:32
d 1Sa 16:4

2David answered Ahimelech the priest, "The king charged me with a certain matter and said to me, 'No one is to know anything about your mission and your instructions.' As for my men, I have told them to meet me at a certain place. 3Now then, what do you have on hand? Give me five loaves of bread, or whatever you can find."

4But the priest answered David, "I don't have any ordinary breade on hand; however, there is some consecratedf bread here—provided the men have keptg themselves from women."

21:4
e Lev 24:8-9
f Ex 25:30; Mt 12:4
g Ex 19:15

5David replied, "Indeed women have been kept from us, as usual whenevera I set out. The men's thingsb are holyh even on missions that are not holy. How much

21:5
h 1Th 4:4

a 5 Or *from us in the past few days since*   b 5 Or *bodies*

---

1 Samuel 21:1–9

Why did David answer dishonestly in verse 2? Maybe he wasn't sure he could confide in this priest (Eli's great-grandson; 14:3; 22:11) and used deception to avoid revealing the entire situation. Or maybe David was trying to protect Ahimelech from being accused of aiding his escape from Saul. On the run, David was in immediate need of food, arms, and shelter. Ahimelech offered him "the bread of the Presence" and the sword of Goliath—unique in its ability to prompt images of *strength and victory in God's cause.*

Earlier David had received aid from the old prophet Samuel; now he obtained assistance from a priest in the old tradition. The reminder of his victory over Goliath in

his youth, together with his contacts with the prophet and the priest, helped David cling to the faith of his adolescence. In his hour of need, here and in the challenges to come, he was reminded that God had been his help in time of trouble (cf. Ps. 34; 52; 56).

Centuries later, Paul encouraged Timothy to "fan into flame" the gift of God he had received earlier (2 Tim. 1:5–7; cf. 1 Tim. 4:14). It takes effort to reflect back on the patterns by which God has been working in and through our circumstances to accomplish his purposes. But this can inspire us to faith in his continued work during stressful times. Looking back at your own Christian life, what broad-stroke patterns of God's work can you identify?

more so today!" 6So the priest gave him the consecrated bread,[i] since there was no bread there except the bread of the Presence that had been removed from before the LORD and replaced by hot bread on the day it was taken away.

7Now one of Saul's servants was there that day, detained before the LORD; he was Doeg[j] the Edomite,[k] Saul's head shepherd.

8David asked Ahimelech, "Don't you have a spear or a sword here? I haven't brought my sword or any other weapon, because the king's business was urgent."

9The priest replied, "The sword[l] of Goliath the Philistine, whom you killed in the Valley of Elah,[m] is here; it is wrapped in a cloth behind the ephod. If you want it, take it; there is no sword here but that one."

David said, "There is none like it; give it to me."

David at Gath

10That day David fled from Saul and went[n] to Achish king of Gath. 11But the servants of Achish said to him, "Isn't this David, the king of the land? Isn't he the one they sing about in their dances:

> " 'Saul has slain his thousands,
> and David his tens of thousands'?"[o]

12David took these words to heart and was very much afraid of Achish king of Gath. 13So he pretended to be insane[p] in their presence; and while he was in their hands he acted like a madman, making marks on the doors of the gate and letting saliva run down his beard.

14Achish said to his servants, "Look at the man! He is insane! Why bring him to me? 15Am I so short of madmen that you have to bring this fellow here to carry on like this in front of me? Must this man come into my house?"

David at Adullam and Mizpah

22 David left Gath and escaped to the cave[q] of Adullam. When his brothers and his father's household heard about it, they went down to him there. 2All those who were in distress or in debt or discontented gathered[r] around him, and he became their leader. About four hundred men were with him.

3From there David went to Mizpah in Moab and said to the king of Moab, "Would you let my father and mother come and stay with you until I learn what

David on the Run (21:10)
Then: David became in effect a guerilla warlord in opposition to Saul's men.
Now: Political and military power is as ephemeral today as it was in David's day.

21:6
[i] Lev 24:8-9; Mt 12:3-4; Mk 2:25-28; Lk 6:1-5

21:7
[j] 1Sa 22:9,22
[k] 1Sa 14:47; Ps 52 Title

21:9
[l] 1Sa 17:51
[m] 1Sa 17:2

21:10
[n] 1Sa 27:2

21:11
[o] 1Sa 18:7; 29:5; Ps 56 Title
21:13
[p] Ps 34 Title

22:1
[q] 2Sa 23:13; Ps 57 Title; 142 Title

22:2
[r] 1Sa 23:13; 25:13; 2Sa 15:20

---

1 Samuel 21:10–15
David continued to distance himself from Saul. This passage relates his failed attempt to join up with the Philistines (though an important coalition would be formed later with Achish; see chs. 27–29).

The servants of Achish identified David as "king of the land." They probably thought of him as a local chieftain, while still recognizing Saul as Israel's king. At any rate, they were unaware of David's status as a refugee on the run from Saul. Their early acknowledgement of David as "king" of any kind was ironic. Frequently throughout Scripture enemies and minor characters inadvertently blurt out the truth about God's plan before it comes to fulfillment. It's as though the reality is impossible to squelch.

This incident is a humorous indictment of the Philistines, who were easily duped by the quick-thinking David. Also prevalent in the Bible is the humor that characterizes our God and enhances our delight in life through its expressions in people (his image bearers) and even animals. Laughter, fun, and creativity can be God's gracious gifts in difficult times. When have you experienced sadness and comic relief in close conjunction? Family reunions at the time of a funeral, for example, often become occasions for humorous reflections on the past.

1 Samuel 22:1–5
Driven off by the Philistines, David withdrew to Adullam, some 13 miles southwest of his home in Bethlehem. He was met by family members and 400 malcontents, who joined forces with him. From this motley

22:5
s 2Sa 24:11;
1Ch 21:9; 29:29;
2Ch 29:25

22:6
t Jdg 4:5
u Ge 21:33

22:7
v 1Sa 8:14
22:8
w 1Sa 18:3; 20:16
x 1Sa 23:21

22:9
y 1Sa 21:7; Ps 52
Title z 1Sa 21:1
22:10
a Nu 27:21;
1Sa 10:22
b 1Sa 21:6

22:13
c ver 8

22:14
d 1Sa 19:4

God will do for me?" ⁴So he left them with the king of Moab, and they stayed with him as long as David was in the stronghold.

⁵But the prophet Gad⁵ said to David, "Do not stay in the stronghold. Go into the land of Judah." So David left and went to the forest of Hereth.

Saul Kills the Priests of Nob

⁶Now Saul heard that David and his men had been discovered. And Saul, spear in hand, was seatedᵗ under the tamariskᵘ tree on the hill at Gibeah, with all his officials standing around him. ⁷Saul said to them, "Listen, men of Benjamin! Will the son of Jesse give all of you fields and vineyards? Will he make all of you commandersᵛ of thousands and commanders of hundreds? ⁸Is that why you have all conspired against me? No one tells me when my son makes a covenantʷ with the son of Jesse. None of you is concernedˣ about me or tells me that my son has incited my servant to lie in wait for me, as he does today."

⁹But Doegʸ the Edomite, who was standing with Saul's officials, said, "I saw the son of Jesse come to Ahimelech son of Ahitub at Nob.ᶻ ¹⁰Ahimelech inquiredᵃ of the LORD for him; he also gave him provisionsᵇ and the sword of Goliath the Philistine."

¹¹Then the king sent for the priest Ahimelech son of Ahitub and his father's whole family, who were the priests at Nob, and they all came to the king. ¹²Saul said, "Listen now, son of Ahitub."

"Yes, my lord," he answered.

¹³Saul said to him, "Why have you conspiredᶜ against me, you and the son of Jesse, giving him bread and a sword and inquiring of God for him, so that he has rebelled against me and lies in wait for me, as he does today?"

¹⁴Ahimelech answered the king, "Whoᵈ of all your servants is as loyal as David, the king's son-in-law, captain of your bodyguard and highly respected in your household? ¹⁵Was that day the first time I inquired of God for him? Of course not! Let not the king accuse your servant or any of his father's family, for your servant knows nothing at all about this whole affair."

¹⁶But the king said, "You will surely die, Ahimelech, you and your father's whole family."

¹⁷Then the king ordered the guards at his side: "Turn and kill the priests of the LORD, because they too have sided with David. They knew he was fleeing, yet they did not tell me."

---

band he began to form a fiercely loyal inner circle of followers, which would become an army. This group would grow to at least 600 (see 23:13) and become an important factor for the rest of his rule over Israel (see 2 Sam. 23:8–39).

While he was on the run, David's family was likely in danger. When it became necessary to seek refuge outside Saul's reach and therefore outside Judah's borders, it seemed logical for his parents to turn to the homeland of David's great-grandmother, Ruth the Moabitess (Ruth 4:17). Once again we see God orchestrating the small details to facilitate his larger plan.

📖 Like Jesus, David surrounded himself with (or was surrounded by) society's riffraff—those outside the mainstream of the respectable and conventional (cf. Matt. 9:9–13; Luke 4:18–19). This "rabble" became leaders in Israel's army—David's mighty men. Still today the gospel holds a special appeal for the disenfranchised and the unpresentable, the fringe population who "don't fit" in our churches. How can you as a Christian deliberately nurture a sensitivity for all people, regardless of their race, appearance, status, rank, or educational level?

1 Samuel 22:6–23

📖 This scene opens with Saul surrounded by the trappings of power—yet powerless to do anything about David. When Saul accused his court officials of conspiring against him, only Doeg responded. Doeg, an Edomite with no vested interest in sparing David or the priests, saw this as an opportunity to turn his good fortune into political advantage. When the Israelite officials uniformly refused to carry out Saul's death sentence, Doeg was conscripted to perform the ghastly service.

📖 Priests and diviners were sometimes forced, under penalty of death, to take oaths of loyalty to the king—committing to serve as his informants. We couldn't imagine doing what Saul and Doeg did. But are you completely above climbing the career (or ministry) ladder by squelching a rival? Are you ever tempted to play the part of "Doeg the Snitch"—maybe even committing "character assassination"? And when you witness injustice, do you ever act like Saul's officials: not doing the dirty work, but standing by in silence?

But the king's officials were not willing[e] to raise a hand to strike the priests of the LORD.

[22:17] [e] Ex 1:17

[18]The king then ordered Doeg, "You turn and strike down the priests." So Doeg the Edomite turned and struck them down. That day he killed eighty-five men who wore the linen ephod.[f] [19]He also put to the sword[g] Nob, the town of the priests, with its men and women, its children and infants, and its cattle, donkeys and sheep.

[22:18] [f] 1Sa 2:18,31
[22:19] [g] 1Sa 15:3

[20]But Abiathar,[h] a son of Ahimelech son of Ahitub, escaped and fled to join David.[i] [21]He told David that Saul had killed the priests of the LORD. [22]Then David said to Abiathar: "That day, when Doeg[j] the Edomite was there, I knew he would be sure to tell Saul. I am responsible for the death of your father's whole family. [23]Stay with me; don't be afraid; the man who is seeking your life[k] is seeking mine also. You will be safe with me."

[22:20] [h] 1Sa 23:6,9; 30:7; 1Ki 2:22,26,27
[i] 1Sa 2:32
[22:22] [j] 1Sa 21:7

[22:23] [k] 1Ki 2:26

David Saves Keilah

23 When David was told, "Look, the Philistines are fighting against Keilah[l] and are looting the threshing floors," [2]he inquired[m] of the LORD, saying, "Shall I go and attack these Philistines?"

The LORD answered him, "Go, attack the Philistines and save Keilah."

[3]But David's men said to him, "Here in Judah we are afraid. How much more, then, if we go to Keilah against the Philistine forces!"

[4]Once again David inquired of the LORD, and the LORD answered him, "Go down to Keilah, for I am going to give the Philistines into your hand."[n] [5]So David and his men went to Keilah, fought the Philistines and carried off their livestock. He inflicted heavy losses on the Philistines and saved the people of Keilah. [6](Now Abiathar[o] son of Ahimelech had brought the ephod down with him when he fled to David at Keilah.)

[23:1] [l] Jos 15:44
[23:2] [m] ver 4,12; 1Sa 30:8; 2Sa 5:19, 23

[23:4] [n] Jos 8:7; Jdg 7:7

[23:6] [o] 1Sa 22:20

Saul Pursues David

[7]Saul was told that David had gone to Keilah, and he said, "God has handed him over to me, for David has imprisoned himself by entering a town with gates and bars." [8]And Saul called up all his forces for battle, to go down to Keilah to besiege David and his men.

[9]When David learned that Saul was plotting against him, he said to Abiathar[p] the priest, "Bring the ephod." [10]David said, "O LORD, God of Israel, your servant has heard definitely that Saul plans to come to Keilah and destroy the town on account

[23:9] [p] ver 6; 1Sa 22:20; 30:7

---

1 Samuel 23:1–6

🕮 David used Abiathar the priest to discern God's will about going to Keilah. When his men balked because of the Philistines' superior strength, David checked again to confirm God's message. The phrase used here, "inquired of the LORD," will become an important theme here and at other points in David's story. The reference to the priestly ephod indicates that David's inquiries were answered by the sacred lots, the Urim and Thummim (cf. Num. 27:21).

📖 As much as we long for clear messages from God, it isn't always easy for us to perceive his will. Dramatic means of communication are possible today, but God generally speaks to us through Scripture. The Bible isn't a dead letter; it's alive and active, "sharper than any double-edged sword" (Heb. 4:12). Nor do we separate the work of the Holy Spirit from the role of Scripture, because the Bible also is "the sword of the Spirit" (Eph. 6:17). The Spirit leads within and through, not beyond, the words of the Word.

1 Samuel 23:7–29

🕮 The same God who had delivered the Philistines into David's hands in the previous passage now protected David from Saul. Just as Saul was closing in on David and felt he had him trapped at long last, word came of another Philistine raid, forcing Saul to abandon his pursuit.

David again received guidance through divine disclosure (Abiathar's ephod; cf. v. 6), as well as human confirmation (Jonathan's encouragement). In contrast to David, Saul relied on espionage and subterfuge, leaving him helpless and vulnerable to attack by the Philistines. Saul failed to inquire of the Lord until it was too late. Even then he was wrongly motivated and ill-advised (28:6–7).

📖 We as Christians can be more like Saul than we care to admit. Some believers make unwarranted assumptions about God's will and rely too often on human wisdom. God wants us "to be conformed to the likeness of his Son" (Rom. 8:29)—to be Christlike in all our behavior. Most of us are painfully aware of our failures, but we can allow the Holy Spirit's work to bring to completion what he has begun in us (Phil. 1:6; 1 Thess. 5:23–24).

of me. ¹¹Will the citizens of Keilah surrender me to him? Will Saul come down, as your servant has heard? O Lᴏʀᴅ, God of Israel, tell your servant."

And the Lᴏʀᴅ said, "He will."

23:12
ᵃ ver 20

¹²Again David asked, "Will the citizens of Keilah surrender ᵠ me and my men to Saul?"

And the Lᴏʀᴅ said, "They will."

23:13
ʳ 1Sa 22:2; 25:13

¹³So David and his men, ʳ about six hundred in number, left Keilah and kept moving from place to place. When Saul was told that David had escaped from Keilah, he did not go there.

23:14
ˢ Jos 15:24,55
ᵗ Ps 54:3-4
ᵘ Ps 32:7

¹⁴David stayed in the desert strongholds and in the hills of the Desert of Ziph. ˢ Day after day Saul searched ᵗ for him, but God did not ᵘ give David into his hands.

23:16
ᵛ 1Sa 30:6
23:17
ʷ 1Sa 20:31; 24:20
23:18
ˣ 1Sa 18:3;
20:16,42;
2Sa 9:1; 21:7
23:19
ʸ 1Sa 26:1 *ᶻ* Ps 54
Title *ᵃ* 1Sa 26:3

¹⁵While David was at Horesh in the Desert of Ziph, he learned that Saul had come out to take his life. ¹⁶And Saul's son Jonathan went to David at Horesh and helped him find strength ᵛ in God. ¹⁷"Don't be afraid," he said. "My father Saul will not lay a hand on you. You will be king ʷ over Israel, and I will be second to you. Even my father Saul knows this." ¹⁸The two of them made a covenant ˣ before the Lᴏʀᴅ. Then Jonathan went home, but David remained at Horesh.

23:20
ᵇ ver 12
23:21
ᶜ 1Sa 22:8

¹⁹The Ziphites ʸ went up to Saul at Gibeah and said, "Is not David hiding among us ᶻ in the strongholds at Horesh, on the hill of Hakilah, ᵃ south of Jeshimon? ²⁰Now, O king, come down whenever it pleases you to do so, and we will be responsible for handing ᵇ him over to the king."

²¹Saul replied, "The Lᴏʀᴅ bless you for your concern ᶜ for me. ²²Go and make further preparation. Find out where David usually goes and who has seen him there. They tell me he is very crafty. ²³Find out about all the hiding places he uses and come back to me with definite information. ᵃ Then I will go with you; if he is in the area, I will track him down among all the clans of Judah."

23:24
ᵈ Jos 15:55;
1Sa 25:2

²⁴So they set out and went to Ziph ahead of Saul. Now David and his men were in the Desert of Maon, ᵈ in the Arabah south of Jeshimon. ²⁵Saul and his men began the search, and when David was told about it, he went down to the rock and stayed in the Desert of Maon. When Saul heard this, he went into the Desert of Maon in pursuit of David.

23:26
ᵉ Ps 17:9

²⁶Saul ᵉ was going along one side of the mountain, and David and his men were on the other side, hurrying to get away from Saul. As Saul and his forces were closing in on David and his men to capture them, ²⁷a messenger came to Saul, saying, "Come quickly! The Philistines are raiding the land." ²⁸Then Saul broke off his pursuit of David and went to meet the Philistines. That is why they call this place Sela Hammahlekoth. ᵇ ²⁹And David went up from there and lived in the strongholds of En Gedi. ᶠ

23:29
ᶠ 2Ch 20:2

David Spares Saul's Life

24:1
ᵍ 1Sa 23:28-29
24:2
ʰ 1Sa 26:2
24:3
ⁱ Ps 57 Title; 142
Title *ʲ* Jdg 3:24
24:4
ᵏ 1Sa 25:28-30

24 After Saul returned from pursuing the Philistines, he was told, "David is in the Desert of En Gedi. ᵍ" ²So Saul took three thousand chosen men from all Israel and set out to look ʰ for David and his men near the Crags of the Wild Goats.

³He came to the sheep pens along the way; a cave ⁱ was there, and Saul went in to relieve ʲ himself. David and his men were far back in the cave. ⁴The men said, "This is the day the Lᴏʀᴅ spoke ᵏ of when he said ᶜ to you, 'I will give your enemy

---

ᵃ *23* Or *me at Nacon*   ᵇ *28 Sela Hammahlekoth* means *rock of parting.*   ᶜ *4* Or *"Today the Lᴏʀᴅ is saying*

---

1 Samuel 24:1–22

📖 David's cutting off of a corner of Saul's robe was probably more than a means of proving his goodwill toward Saul. To grasp the hem of a garment symbolized loyalty. Cutting off a piece of a person's robe, on the other hand, signified disloyalty and rebellion. That is why David felt guilty for doing so.

David was motivated by genuine devotion to God and to the office of Israel's king. By contrast, Saul was obsessed with destroying his (perceived) enemy, unjustifiably pursuing David instead of protecting the people from the Philistines. This pattern only heightened David's legitimacy as Saul's successor—a fact even Saul acknowledged.

into your hands for you to deal with as you wish.' " [l] Then David crept up unnoticed and cut off a corner of Saul's robe.

5 Afterward, David was conscience-stricken[m] for having cut off a corner of his robe. 6 He said to his men, "The LORD forbid that I should do such a thing to my master, the LORD's anointed,[n] or lift my hand against him; for he is the anointed of the LORD." 7 With these words David rebuked his men and did not allow them to attack Saul. And Saul left the cave and went his way.

8 Then David went out of the cave and called out to Saul, "My lord the king!" When Saul looked behind him, David bowed down and prostrated himself with his face to the ground.[o] 9 He said to Saul, "Why do you listen when men say, 'David is bent on harming you'? 10 This day you have seen with your own eyes how the LORD delivered you into my hands in the cave. Some urged me to kill you, but I spared you; I said, 'I will not lift my hand against my master, because he is the LORD's anointed.' 11 See, my father, look at this piece of your robe in my hand! I cut off the corner of your robe but did not kill you. Now understand and recognize that I am not guilty[p] of wrongdoing or rebellion. I have not wronged you, but you are hunting[q] me down to take my life. 12 May the LORD judge[r] between you and me. And may the LORD avenge[s] the wrongs you have done to me, but my hand will not touch you. 13 As the old saying goes, 'From evildoers come evil deeds,'[t] so my hand will not touch you.

14 "Against whom has the king of Israel come out? Whom are you pursuing? A dead dog?[u] A flea?[v] 15 May the LORD be our judge[w] and decide between us. May he consider my cause and uphold[x] it; may he vindicate[y] me by delivering[z] me from your hand."

16 When David finished saying this, Saul asked, "Is that your voice,[a] David my son?" And he wept aloud. 17 "You are more righteous than I,"[b] he said. "You have treated me well,[c] but I have treated you badly. 18 You have just now told me of the good you did to me; the LORD delivered[d] me into your hands, but you did not kill me. 19 When a man finds his enemy, does he let him get away unharmed? May the LORD reward you well for the way you treated me today. 20 I know that you will surely be king[e] and that the kingdom[f] of Israel will be established in your hands. 21 Now swear[g] to me by the LORD that you will not cut off my descendants or wipe out my name from my father's family.[h]"

22 So David gave his oath to Saul. Then Saul returned home, but David and his men went up to the stronghold.[i]

David, Nabal and Abigail

25 Now Samuel died,[j] and all Israel assembled and mourned[k] for him; and they buried him at his home in Ramah.[l]

Then David moved down into the Desert of Maon.[a] 2 A certain man in Maon,[m] who had property there at Carmel, was very wealthy. He had a thousand goats and three thousand sheep, which he was shearing in Carmel. 3 His name was Nabal and his wife's name was Abigail.[n] She was an intelligent and beautiful woman, but her husband, a Calebite,[o] was surly and mean in his dealings.

[a] 1 Some Septuagint manuscripts; Hebrew *Paran*

24:4 l 1Sa 23:17; 26:8
24:5 m 2Sa 24:10
24:6 n 1Sa 26:11
24:8 o 1Sa 25:23-24
24:11 p Ps 7:3 q 1Sa 23:14,23; 26:20
24:12 r Ge 16:5; 31:53; Job 5:8 s Jdg 11:27; 1Sa 26:10
24:13 t Mt 7:20
24:14 u 1Sa 17:43; 2Sa 9:8 v 1Sa 26:20
24:15 w ver 12 x Ps 35:1,23; Mic 7:9 y Ps 43:1 z Ps 119:134,154
24:16 a 1Sa 26:17
24:17 b Ps 38:26; 1Sa 26:21 c Mt 5:44
24:18 d 1Sa 26:23
24:20 e 1Sa 23:17 f 1Sa 13:14
24:21 g Ge 21:23; 2Sa 21:1-9 h 1Sa 20:14-15
24:22 i 1Sa 23:29
25:1 j 1Sa 28:3 k Nu 20:29; Dt 34:8 l Ge 21:21; 2Ch 33:20
25:2 m Jos 15:55; 1Sa 23:24
25:3 n Pr 31:10 o Jos 15:13

What's your attitude toward persons in authority? Reverence for the Lord and his anointed one involves more than respect for pastor and church. It's a deep-seated regard for all people, good or bad, whom God allows to govern us, even temporarily. David refused to resort to a "bloody" solution to his problems. We too are to resist participation in rebellion, revenge, retaliation, and other ineffective, negative actions. Under what circumstances is it legitimate to resist authority? Can you cite Biblical examples?

1 Samuel 25:1–44

Before being confronted by Abigail, David's mind was made up; he was determined to take violent action. After her speech, he not only changed his mind but recognized God as the source of her instruction—a remarkable insight for a man from a male-dominated society. It's astounding that David acknowledged God's use of Abigail to further his understanding of his own calling as the anointed one.

The text illustrates a characteristic present in all the exemplary saints of the Old Testament: They were individuals with a capacity for correction and change. David was open to hearing and responding to an entirely unexpected word from God.

25:6
p Ps 122:7; Lk 10:5
q 1Ch 12:18

25:7
r ver 15

25:8
s Ne 8:10

25:10
t Jdg 9:28

25:11
u Jdg 8:6

25:13
v 1Sa 23:13
w 1Sa 30:24

25:14
x 1Sa 13:10
25:15
y ver 7 z ver 21
25:16
a Ex 14:22;
Job 1:10

25:17
b 1Sa 20:7

25:18
c 1Ch 12:40
d 2Sa 16:1

25:19
e Ge 32:20

25:21
f Ps 109:5
25:22
g 1Sa 3:17; 20:13
h 1Ki 14:10; 21:21;
2Ki 9:8

25:23
i 1Sa 20:41

25:25
j Pr 14:16

25:26
k ver 33
l Heb 10:30
m 2Sa 18:32

25:27
n Ge 33:11;
1Sa 30:26
25:28
o ver 24
p 2Sa 7:11,26
q 1Sa 18:17
r 1Sa 24:11

4While David was in the desert, he heard that Nabal was shearing sheep. 5So he sent ten young men and said to them, "Go up to Nabal at Carmel and greet him in my name. 6Say to him: 'Long life to you! Good health[p] to you and your household! And good health to all that is yours![q]

7" 'Now I hear that it is sheep-shearing time. When your shepherds were with us, we did not mistreat[r] them, and the whole time they were at Carmel nothing of theirs was missing. 8Ask your own servants and they will tell you. Therefore be favorable toward my young men, since we come at a festive time. Please give your servants and your son David whatever[s] you can find for them.' "

9When David's men arrived, they gave Nabal this message in David's name. Then they waited.

10Nabal answered David's servants, "Who[t] is this David? Who is this son of Jesse? Many servants are breaking away from their masters these days. 11Why should I take my bread[u] and water, and the meat I have slaughtered for my shearers, and give it to men coming from who knows where?"

12David's men turned around and went back. When they arrived, they reported every word. 13David said to his men, "Put on your swords!" So they put on their swords, and David put on his. About four hundred men went[v] up with David, while two hundred stayed with the supplies.[w]

14One of the servants told Nabal's wife Abigail: "David sent messengers from the desert to give our master his greetings,[x] but he hurled insults at them. 15Yet these men were very good to us. They did not mistreat[y] us, and the whole time we were out in the fields near them nothing was missing.[z] 16Night and day they were a wall[a] around us all the time we were herding our sheep near them. 17Now think it over and see what you can do, because disaster is hanging over our master and his whole household. He is such a wicked[b] man that no one can talk to him."

18Abigail lost no time. She took two hundred loaves of bread, two skins of wine, five dressed sheep, five seahs[a] of roasted grain, a hundred cakes of raisins[c] and two hundred cakes of pressed figs, and loaded them on donkeys.[d] 19Then she told her servants, "Go on ahead;[e] I'll follow you." But she did not tell her husband Nabal.

20As she came riding her donkey into a mountain ravine, there were David and his men descending toward her, and she met them. 21David had just said, "It's been useless—all my watching over this fellow's property in the desert so that nothing of his was missing. He has paid[f] me back evil for good. 22May God deal with David,[b] be it ever so severely,[g] if by morning I leave alive one male[h] of all who belong to him!"

23When Abigail saw David, she quickly got off her donkey and bowed down before David with her face to the ground.[i] 24She fell at his feet and said: "My lord, let the blame be on me alone. Please let your servant speak to you; hear what your servant has to say. 25May my lord pay no attention to that wicked man Nabal. He is just like his name—his name is Fool,[j] and folly goes with him. But as for me, your servant, I did not see the men my master sent.

26"Now since the LORD has kept you, my master, from bloodshed[k] and from avenging[l] yourself with your own hands, as surely as the LORD lives and as you live, may your enemies and all who intend to harm my master be like Nabal.[m] 27And let this gift,[n] which your servant has brought to my master, be given to the men who follow you. 28Please forgive[o] your servant's offense, for the LORD will certainly make a lasting[p] dynasty for my master, because he fights the LORD's battles.[q] Let no wrongdoing[r] be found in you as long as you live. 29Even though someone is pur-

---

a 18 That is, probably about a bushel (about 37 liters)   b 22 Some Septuagint manuscripts; Hebrew with David's enemies

---

📖 Like David, each of us is on a journey somewhere. We are all in the process of becoming someone. Christian discipleship adopts a certain understanding of the nature of growth in grace. In one sense, growth doesn't change a person's essential nature. An oak seedling, for instance, can't grow into a maple tree. But it will grow, developing thick bark, strong branches, and an extended root system. So a new Christian, immature in faith at first, may be expected to grow naturally into a mature believer.

suing you to take your life, the life of my master will be bound securely in the bundle of the living by the LORD your God. But the lives of your enemies he will hurl[s] away as from the pocket of a sling. 30When the LORD has done for my master every good thing he promised concerning him and has appointed him leader[t] over Israel, 31my master will not have on his conscience the staggering burden of needless bloodshed or of having avenged himself. And when the LORD has brought my master success, remember[u] your servant."

32David said to Abigail, "Praise[v] be to the LORD, the God of Israel, who has sent you today to meet me. 33May you be blessed for your good judgment and for keeping me from bloodshed[w] this day and from avenging myself with my own hands. 34Otherwise, as surely as the LORD, the God of Israel, lives, who has kept me from harming you, if you had not come quickly to meet me, not one male belonging to Nabal would have been left alive by daybreak."

35Then David accepted from her hand what she had brought him and said, "Go home in peace. I have heard your words and granted[x] your request."

36When Abigail went to Nabal, he was in the house holding a banquet like that of a king. He was in high[y] spirits and very drunk.[z] So she told[a] him nothing until daybreak. 37Then in the morning, when Nabal was sober, his wife told him all these things, and his heart failed him and he became like a stone. 38About ten days later, the LORD struck[b] Nabal and he died.

39When David heard that Nabal was dead, he said, "Praise be to the LORD, who has upheld my cause against Nabal for treating me with contempt. He has kept his servant from doing wrong and has brought Nabal's wrongdoing down on his own head."

Then David sent word to Abigail, asking her to become his wife. 40His servants went to Carmel and said to Abigail, "David has sent us to you to take you to become his wife."

41She bowed down with her face to the ground and said, "Here is your maidservant, ready to serve you and wash the feet of my master's servants." 42Abigail[c] quickly got on a donkey and, attended by her five maids, went with David's messengers and became his wife. 43David had also married Ahinoam[d] of Jezreel, and they both were his wives.[e] 44But Saul had given his daughter Michal, David's wife, to Paltiel[a][f] son of Laish, who was from Gallim.[g]

David Again Spares Saul's Life

26 The Ziphites[h] went to Saul at Gibeah and said, "Is not David hiding[i] on the hill of Hakilah, which faces Jeshimon?"

2So Saul went down to the Desert of Ziph, with his three thousand chosen men of Israel, to search[j] there for David. 3Saul made his camp beside the road on the hill of Hakilah facing Jeshimon, but David stayed in the desert. When he saw that Saul had followed him there, 4he sent out scouts and learned that Saul had definitely arrived.[b]

5Then David set out and went to the place where Saul had camped. He saw

a 44 Hebrew Palti, a variant of Paltiel   b 4 Or had come to Nacon

1 Samuel 26:1–25

The two episodes in which David spared Saul's life (here and in ch. 24) are recorded in close proximity, separated only by the Nabal-Abigail object lesson. They help us measure David's character development based on his responses to similar sets of circumstances. David matured and became more confident in his role as king-in-waiting—while Saul was rejected. The distance between the two continued to increase. As surely as David was to become Israel's king, Saul was hurtling toward destruction.

We never know on this side of eternity when we are saying "goodbye" to someone forever. David could rest assured that in his final meeting with Saul he had acted with honor. How many Christians live with regrets over relationships unhealed or conflicts unresolved after the untimely death of a rival, family member, colleague, or friend? Jesus taught his disciples to forgive (Matt. 6:14). How can you maintain your integrity as a believer without being reconciled to someone who has offended you (cf. Rom. 14:19)? Is there some unfinished business on your agenda?

26:5
k 1Sa 14:50; 17:55

26:6
l Jdg 7:10-11;
1Ch 2:16

where Saul and Abner[k] son of Ner, the commander of the army, had lain down. Saul was lying inside the camp, with the army encamped around him.

[6]David then asked Ahimelech the Hittite and Abishai son of Zeruiah,[l] Joab's brother, "Who will go down into the camp with me to Saul?"

"I'll go with you," said Abishai.

[7]So David and Abishai went to the army by night, and there was Saul, lying asleep inside the camp with his spear stuck in the ground near his head. Abner and the soldiers were lying around him.

[8]Abishai said to David, "Today God has delivered your enemy into your hands. Now let me pin him to the ground with one thrust of my spear; I won't strike him twice."

26:9
m 2Sa 1:14
n 1Sa 24:5
26:10
o 1Sa 25:38;
Ro 12:19
p Ge 47:29;
Dt 31:14; Ps 37:13
q 1Sa 31:6; 2Sa 1:1

26:12
r Ge 2:21; 15:12

[9]But David said to Abishai, "Don't destroy him! Who can lay a hand on the LORD's anointed[m] and be guiltless?[n] [10]As surely as the LORD lives," he said, "the LORD himself will strike[o] him; either his time[p] will come and he will die,[q] or he will go into battle and perish. [11]But the LORD forbid that I should lay a hand on the LORD's anointed. Now get the spear and water jug that are near his head, and let's go."

[12]So David took the spear and water jug near Saul's head, and they left. No one saw or knew about it, nor did anyone wake up. They were all sleeping, because the LORD had put them into a deep sleep.[r]

[13]Then David crossed over to the other side and stood on top of the hill some distance away; there was a wide space between them. [14]He called out to the army and to Abner son of Ner, "Aren't you going to answer me, Abner?"

Abner replied, "Who are you who calls to the king?"

[15]David said, "You're a man, aren't you? And who is like you in Israel? Why didn't you guard your lord the king? Someone came to destroy your lord the king. [16]What you have done is not good. As surely as the LORD lives, you and your men deserve to die, because you did not guard your master, the LORD's anointed. Look around you. Where are the king's spear and water jug that were near his head?"

26:17
s 1Sa 24:16

[17]Saul recognized David's voice and said, "Is that your voice,[s] David my son?"

David replied, "Yes it is, my lord the king." [18]And he added, "Why is my lord pursuing his servant? What have I done, and what wrong[t] am I guilty of? [19]Now let my lord the king listen to his servant's words. If the LORD has incited you against me, then may he accept an offering.[u] If, however, men have done it, may they be cursed before the LORD! They have now driven me from my share in the LORD's inheritance[v] and have said, 'Go, serve other gods.' [20]Now do not let my blood fall to the ground far from the presence of the LORD. The king of Israel has come out to look for a flea[w]—as one hunts a partridge in the mountains."

26:18
t 1Sa 24:9,11-14

26:19
u 2Sa 16:11
v 2Sa 14:16

26:20
w 1Sa 24:14
26:21
x Ex 9:27;
1Sa 15:24
y 1Sa 24:17

[21]Then Saul said, "I have sinned.[x] Come back, David my son. Because you considered my life precious[y] today, I will not try to harm you again. Surely I have acted like a fool and have erred greatly."

26:23
z Ps 62:12 a Ps 7:8;
18:20,24

26:24
b Ps 54:7

[22]"Here is the king's spear," David answered. "Let one of your young men come over and get it. [23]The LORD rewards[z] every man for his righteousness[a] and faithfulness. The LORD delivered you into my hands today, but I would not lay a hand on the LORD's anointed. [24]As surely as I valued your life today, so may the LORD value my life and deliver[b] me from all trouble."

[25]Then Saul said to David, "May you be blessed, my son David; you will do great things and surely triumph."

So David went on his way, and Saul returned home.

David Among the Philistines

27 But David thought to himself, "One of these days I will be destroyed by the hand of Saul. The best thing I can do is to escape to the land of the Philis-

---

1 Samuel 27:1–12

David's time spent with the Philistines accomplished two objectives. He sought and found protection because Saul was still trying to kill him. And he devoted himself to warring against the potential enemies of Ju-

dah—while convincing Achish that he was fighting Philistine enemies. Thus he endeared himself to both the Philistines and the Judahites, whom he would one day rule as king.

David negotiated his way through tricky circum-

tines. Then Saul will give up searching for me anywhere in Israel, and I will slip out
of his hand."
2So David and the six hundred men[c] with him left and went[d] over to Achish[e] son
of Maoch king of Gath. 3David and his men settled in Gath with Achish. Each man
had his family with him, and David had his two wives:[f] Ahinoam of Jezreel and Abigail of Carmel, the widow of Nabal. 4When Saul was told that David had fled to
Gath, he no longer searched for him.
5Then David said to Achish, "If I have found favor in your eyes, let a place be assigned to me in one of the country towns, that I may live there. Why should your
servant live in the royal city with you?"
6So on that day Achish gave him Ziklag,[g] and it has belonged to the kings of Judah ever since. 7David lived[h] in Philistine territory a year and four months.
8Now David and his men went up and raided the Geshurites,[i] the Girzites and
the Amalekites.[j] (From ancient times these peoples had lived in the land extending to Shur[k] and Egypt.) 9Whenever David attacked an area, he did not leave a man
or woman alive,[l] but took sheep and cattle, donkeys and camels, and clothes. Then
he returned to Achish.
10When Achish asked, "Where did you go raiding today?" David would say,
"Against the Negev of Judah" or "Against the Negev of Jerahmeel[m]" or "Against the
Negev of the Kenites.[n]" 11He did not leave a man or woman alive to be brought to
Gath, for he thought, "They might inform on us and say, 'This is what David did.' "
And such was his practice as long as he lived in Philistine territory. 12Achish trusted David and said to himself, "He has become so odious to his people, the Israel-
ites, that he will be my servant forever."

Saul and the Witch of Endor

28 In those days the Philistines gathered[o] their forces to fight against Israel.
Achish said to David, "You must understand that you and your men will accompany me in the army."
2David said, "Then you will see for yourself what your servant can do."
Achish replied, "Very well, I will make you my bodyguard for life."
3Now Samuel was dead,[p] and all Israel had mourned for him and buried him in
his own town of Ramah.[q] Saul had expelled the mediums and spiritists[r] from the
land.
4The Philistines assembled and came and set up camp at Shunem,[s] while Saul
gathered all the Israelites and set up camp at Gilboa.[t] 5When Saul saw the Philistine army, he was afraid; terror filled his heart. 6He inquired[u] of the LORD, but the
LORD did not answer him by dreams[v] or Urim[w] or prophets. 7Saul then said to his
attendants, "Find me a woman who is a medium,[x] so I may go and inquire of her."
"There is one in Endor,[y]" they said.
8So Saul disguised[z] himself, putting on other clothes, and at night he and two

27:2 [c] 1Sa 25:13 [d] 1Sa 21:10 [e] 1Ki 2:39
27:3 [f] 1Sa 25:43; 30:3
27:6 [g] Jos 15:31; 19:5; Ne 11:28
27:7 [h] 1Sa 29:3
27:8 [i] Jos 13:2,13 [j] Ex 17:8; 1Sa 15:7-8 [k] Ex 15:22
27:9 [l] 1Sa 15:3
27:10 [m] 1Sa 30:29; 1Ch 2:9,25 [n] Jdg 1:16
28:1 [o] 1Sa 29:1
28:3 [p] 1Sa 25:1 [q] 1Sa 7:17 [r] Ex 22:18; Lev 19:31; 20:27; Dt 18:10-11; 1Sa 15:23
28:4 [s] Jos 19:18; 2Ki 4:8 [t] 1Sa 31:1,3
28:6 [u] 1Sa 14:37; 1Ch 10:13-14; Pr 1:28 [v] Nu 12:6 [w] Ex 28:30; Nu 27:21
28:7 [x] Ac 16:16 [y] Jos 17:11
28:8 [z] 2Ch 18:29; 35:22

---

stances without obvious assurance of God's guidance. He needed to rely on faith, remembering past instances of God's faithfulness. This text illustrates how believers in all generations have often been forced to make important decisions without the benefit of a specific word from God.

Reflecting on important decisions after the fact is easy. Seeking to determine the "right" decision at the time, though, can leave us feeling helpless. Our perception of circumstances often guides us in the decision-making process. But as believers we are to acknowledge that God is working in a different dimension, behind the scenes. Our faith helps us to discern his guidance in and through our everyday circumstances. It's vital that we remain open to the possibility that he will step in to change those circumstances to alter our choices.

1 Samuel 28:1–25

With the Philistines and Israelites facing off in the Jezreel Valley, Saul was seized by terror. In his despair, he resorted to consulting a spiritual medium. He turned to the forbidden use of the occult as a means of seeking guidance, all the while closing his ears to the prophetic word. Ironically, the magic confirmed the prophetic voice he had scorned. The prophecies about Saul and David had been fulfilled and couldn't be rescinded.

Severe crisis has a way of bringing to the surface what we really believe. Saul's trip to Endor belied the king's real commitments. His failure to nurture his relationship with God during his lifetime meant he was unprepared for death. Christians do well to attend to that most important of all relationships. Then in our own crises we can face God with confidence and hope.

28:8
a Dt 18:10-11;
1Ch 10:13; Isa 8:19

28:9
b ver 3

28:14
c 1Sa 15:27; 24:8

28:15
d ver 6; 1Sa 18:12

28:17
e 1Sa 15:28
28:18
f 1Sa 15:20
g 1Ki 20:42

28:19
h 1Sa 31:2

28:21
i Jdg 12:3;
1Sa 19:5; Job 13:14

28:23
j 2Ki 5:13

29:1
k 1Sa 28:1
l Jos 12:18; 1Sa 4:1
m 2Ki 9:30
29:2
n 1Sa 28:2

men went to the woman. "Consult*a* a spirit for me," he said, "and bring up for me the one I name."

9 But the woman said to him, "Surely you know what Saul has done. He has cut off*b* the mediums and spiritists from the land. Why have you set a trap for my life to bring about my death?"

10 Saul swore to her by the LORD, "As surely as the LORD lives, you will not be punished for this."

11 Then the woman asked, "Whom shall I bring up for you?"

"Bring up Samuel," he said.

12 When the woman saw Samuel, she cried out at the top of her voice and said to Saul, "Why have you deceived me? You are Saul!"

13 The king said to her, "Don't be afraid. What do you see?"

The woman said, "I see a spirit*a* coming up out of the ground."

14 "What does he look like?" he asked.

"An old man wearing a robe*c* is coming up," she said.

Then Saul knew it was Samuel, and he bowed down and prostrated himself with his face to the ground.

15 Samuel said to Saul, "Why have you disturbed me by bringing me up?"

"I am in great distress," Saul said. "The Philistines are fighting against me, and God has turned*d* away from me. He no longer answers me, either by prophets or by dreams. So I have called on you to tell me what to do."

16 Samuel said, "Why do you consult me, now that the LORD has turned away from you and become your enemy? 17 The LORD has done what he predicted through me. The LORD has torn*e* the kingdom out of your hands and given it to one of your neighbors—to David. 18 Because you did not obey*f* the LORD or carry out his fierce wrath*g* against the Amalekites, the LORD has done this to you today. 19 The LORD will hand over both Israel and you to the Philistines, and tomorrow you and your sons*h* will be with me. The LORD will also hand over the army of Israel to the Philistines."

20 Immediately Saul fell full length on the ground, filled with fear because of Samuel's words. His strength was gone, for he had eaten nothing all that day and night.

21 When the woman came to Saul and saw that he was greatly shaken, she said, "Look, your maidservant has obeyed you. I took my life*i* in my hands and did what you told me to do. 22 Now please listen to your servant and let me give you some food so you may eat and have the strength to go on your way."

23 He refused*j* and said, "I will not eat."

But his men joined the woman in urging him, and he listened to them. He got up from the ground and sat on the couch.

24 The woman had a fattened calf at the house, which she butchered at once. She took some flour, kneaded it and baked bread without yeast. 25 Then she set it before Saul and his men, and they ate. That same night they got up and left.

Achish Sends David Back to Ziklag

29 The Philistines gathered*k* all their forces at Aphek,*l* and Israel camped by the spring in Jezreel.*m* 2 As the Philistine rulers marched with their units of hundreds and thousands, David and his men were marching at the rear*n* with Achish. 3 The commanders of the Philistines asked, "What about these Hebrews?"

Achish replied, "Is this not David, who was an officer of Saul king of Israel? He

a 13 Or *see spirits;* or *see gods*

1 Samuel 29:1–11

Saul was as good as dead, since he was dying from the inside out. But how would David's dilemma be resolved? Would he be able to escape the consequences of his double-crossing of Achish? His future as the anointed king of Israel was once again in jeopardy.

We marvel at God's care but also at the ironic, al-most humorous way David "came out smelling like a rose." In a single turn his predicament, which had seemed so hopeless, became an opportunity to avoid conflict with either Saul or the Philistines. As the next passage shows, it was providential that the Philistine generals had rejected David; he had other business to attend to at Ziklag.

has already been with me for over a year,[o] and from the day he left Saul until now, I have found no fault in him."

4 But the Philistine commanders were angry with him and said, "Send[p] the man back, that he may return to the place you assigned him. He must not go with us into battle, or he will turn[q] against us during the fighting. How better could he regain his master's favor than by taking the heads of our own men? 5 Isn't this the David they sang about in their dances:

" 'Saul has slain his thousands,
    and David his tens of thousands'?"[r]

6 So Achish called David and said to him, "As surely as the LORD lives, you have been reliable, and I would be pleased to have you serve with me in the army. From the day[s] you came to me until now, I have found no fault in you, but the rulers[t] don't approve of you. 7 Turn back and go in peace; do nothing to displease the Philistine rulers."

8 "But what have I done?" asked David. "What have you found against your servant from the day I came to you until now? Why can't I go and fight against the enemies of my lord the king?"

9 Achish answered, "I know that you have been as pleasing in my eyes as an angel[u] of God; nevertheless, the Philistine commanders[v] have said, 'He must not go up with us into battle.' 10 Now get up early, along with your master's servants who have come with you, and leave[w] in the morning as soon as it is light."

11 So David and his men got up early in the morning to go back to the land of the Philistines, and the Philistines went up to Jezreel.

David Destroys the Amalekites

30 David and his men reached Ziklag[x] on the third day. Now the Amalekites[y] had raided the Negev and Ziklag. They had attacked Ziklag and burned it, 2 and had taken captive the women and all who were in it, both young and old. They killed none of them, but carried them off as they went on their way.

3 When David and his men came to Ziklag, they found it destroyed by fire and their wives and sons and daughters taken captive. 4 So David and his men wept aloud until they had no strength left to weep. 5 David's two wives[z] had been captured—Ahinoam of Jezreel and Abigail, the widow of Nabal of Carmel. 6 David was greatly distressed because the men were talking of stoning[a] him; each one was bitter in spirit because of his sons and daughters. But David found strength[b] in the LORD his God.

7 Then David said to Abiathar[c] the priest, the son of Ahimelech, "Bring me the

Cross-references

29:3
o 1Sa 27:7; Da 6:5

29:4
p 1Ch 12:19
q 1Sa 14:21

29:5
r 1Sa 18:7; 21:11

29:6
s 1Sa 27:8-12
t ver 3

29:9
u 2Sa 14:17,20; 19:27 v ver 4
29:10
w 1Ch 12:19

30:1
x 1Sa 29:4,11
y 1Sa 15:7; 27:8

30:5
z 1Sa 25:43; 2Sa 2:2

30:6
a Ex 17:4; Jn 8:59
b Ps 27:14; 56:3-4,11; Ro 4:20
30:7
c 1Sa 22:20

When David's worst-case scenario developed, the Philistine military commanders became God's instrument for delivering him from a "lose-lose" situation. And so it often is in our lives. God's ways are higher in every way than ours. He's more than able—no matter what the obstacles from a human perspective—to deliver us. His rescue may not come in packaging you recognize, so expect the unexpected!

1 Samuel 30:1–31

All David's actions after verse 8 were decisive, confident, and gracious. He took bold steps without hesitation because he accepted the divine word of assurance. David sought God's word—and having found it he never looked back. The text portrays him as a great leader, whose strength arose from a deep reservoir of personal faith and a conviction that the Lord would win his victories for him.

As Christians today we establish patterns of seeking advice and help: either from Endor (28:7) or from Abiathar (30:7). That is, we find answers outside our faith or from the God of heaven and Earth, who has revealed his truth in Scripture. These are the only options. What's your typical modus operandi? Does it depend on the gravity of the situation? Do you tend to seek God only when all else fails?

The text points out David's care for an Egyptian slave left to die in the desert. How ready are you to stop, for instance, for a stranded motorist? Our culture tends to overlook the vulnerable and even blame them for their circumstances. A prophecy concerning the Messiah reads, "A bruised reed he will not break, and a smoldering wick he will not snuff out" (Isa. 42:3). Followers of Jesus have the opportunity to be like him by demonstrating care for those who need our help spiritually, emotionally, and physically.

30:7
d 1Sa 23:9
30:8
e 1Sa 23:2 *f* ver 18

30:9
g 1Sa 27:2
30:10
h ver 9,21

30:12
i Jdg 15:19

30:14
j 2Sa 8:18; 1Ki 1:38,
44; Eze 25:16;
Zep 2:5 *k* ver 16;
Jos 14:13; 15:13
l ver 1

30:16
m Lk 12:19 *n* ver 14
30:17
o 1Sa 11:11
p 1Sa 15:3
30:18
q Ge 14:16

30:21
r ver 10

30:24
s Nu 31:27;
Jos 22:8
30:27
t Jos 7:2 *u* Jos 19:8
v Jos 15:48
30:28
w Jos 13:16
x Jos 15:50
30:29
y 1Sa 27:10
z Jdg 1:16; 1Sa 15:6
30:30
a Nu 14:45;
Jdg 1:17
b Jos 15:42
30:31
c Jos 14:13;
2Sa 2:1,4
31:1
d 1Sa 28:4;
1Ch 10:1-12

ephod. *d*" Abiathar brought it to him, [8]and David inquired*e* of the LORD, "Shall I pursue this raiding party? Will I overtake them?"

"Pursue them," he answered. "You will certainly overtake them and succeed*f* in the rescue."

[9]David and the six hundred men*g* with him came to the Besor Ravine, where some stayed behind, [10]for two hundred men were too exhausted*h* to cross the ravine. But David and four hundred men continued the pursuit.

[11]They found an Egyptian in a field and brought him to David. They gave him water to drink and food to eat— [12]part of a cake of pressed figs and two cakes of raisins. He ate and was revived, *i* for he had not eaten any food or drunk any water for three days and three nights.

[13]David asked him, "To whom do you belong, and where do you come from?"

He said, "I am an Egyptian, the slave of an Amalekite. My master abandoned me when I became ill three days ago. [14]We raided the Negev of the Kerethites*j* and the territory belonging to Judah and the Negev of Caleb.*k* And we burned*l* Ziklag."

[15]David asked him, "Can you lead me down to this raiding party?"

He answered, "Swear to me before God that you will not kill me or hand me over to my master, and I will take you down to them."

[16]He led David down, and there they were, scattered over the countryside, eating, drinking and reveling*m* because of the great amount of plunder*n* they had taken from the land of the Philistines and from Judah. [17]David fought*o* them from dusk until the evening of the next day, and none of them got away, except four hundred young men who rode off on camels and fled.*p* [18]David recovered*q* everything the Amalekites had taken, including his two wives. [19]Nothing was missing: young or old, boy or girl, plunder or anything else they had taken. David brought everything back. [20]He took all the flocks and herds, and his men drove them ahead of the other livestock, saying, "This is David's plunder."

[21]Then David came to the two hundred men who had been too exhausted*r* to follow him and who were left behind at the Besor Ravine. They came out to meet David and the people with him. As David and his men approached, he greeted them. [22]But all the evil men and troublemakers among David's followers said, "Because they did not go out with us, we will not share with them the plunder we recovered. However, each man may take his wife and children and go."

[23]David replied, "No, my brothers, you must not do that with what the LORD has given us. He has protected us and handed over to us the forces that came against us. [24]Who will listen to what you say? The share of the man who stayed with the supplies is to be the same as that of him who went down to the battle. All will share alike.*s*" [25]David made this a statute and ordinance for Israel from that day to this.

[26]When David arrived in Ziklag, he sent some of the plunder to the elders of Judah, who were his friends, saying, "Here is a present for you from the plunder of the LORD's enemies."

[27]He sent it to those who were in Bethel,*t* Ramoth*u* Negev and Jattir;*v* [28]to those in Aroer,*w* Siphmoth, Eshtemoa*x* [29]and Racal; to those in the towns of the Jerahmeelites*y* and the Kenites;*z* [30]to those in Hormah,*a* Bor Ashan,*b* Athach [31]and Hebron;*c* and to those in all the other places where David and his men had roamed.

Saul Takes His Life

31 Now the Philistines fought against Israel; the Israelites fled before them, and many fell slain on Mount Gilboa.*d* [2]The Philistines pressed hard after Saul

---

1 Samuel 31:1–13

🔗 Saul died in battle against the very enemies he was supposed to have subdued (cf. 9:15–16). His body was dismembered and desecrated in a way that seemed especially appalling to ancient peoples. Finally, his remains were burned and given an ignoble burial. The book closes with an emphatic answer to its underlying question: Who could serve suitably as Israel's king?

First Samuel ends in a cemetery near Jabesh, with a group of loyal subjects paying homage to their fallen king. But it also ends in expectation. We are not left with a theme of judgment without hope, but with a quiet sense of expectation, an anticipation of fulfillment in 2 Samuel. The storyteller had carefully prepared his audience for the second anointed one—ready and waiting in the wings to fulfill his role in history and in God's plan.

and his sons, and they killed his sons Jonathan, Abinadab and Malki-Shua. ³The fighting grew fierce around Saul, and when the archers overtook him, they woundedᵉ him critically.

⁴Saul said to his armor-bearer, "Draw your sword and run me through,ᶠ or these uncircumcisedᵍ fellows will come and run me through and abuse me."

But his armor-bearer was terrified and would not do it; so Saul took his own sword and fell on it. ⁵When the armor-bearer saw that Saul was dead, he too fell on his sword and died with him. ⁶So Saul and his three sons and his armor-bearer and all his men died together that same day.

⁷When the Israelites along the valley and those across the Jordan saw that the Israelite army had fled and that Saul and his sons had died, they abandoned their towns and fled. And the Philistines came and occupied them.

⁸The next day, when the Philistines came to strip the dead, they found Saul and his three sons fallen on Mount Gilboa. ⁹They cut off his head and stripped off his armor, and they sent messengers throughout the land of the Philistines to proclaim the newsʰ in the temple of their idols and among their people.ⁱ ¹⁰They put his armor in the temple of the Ashtorethsʲ and fastened his body to the wall of Beth Shan.ᵏ

¹¹When the people of Jabesh Gileadˡ heard of what the Philistines had done to Saul, ¹²all their valiant men journeyed through the night to Beth Shan. They took down the bodies of Saul and his sons from the wall of Beth Shan and went to Jabesh, where they burnedᵐ them. ¹³Then they took their bonesⁿ and buried them under a tamariskᵒ tree at Jabesh, and they fastedᵖ seven days.�q

31:3
ᵉ 2Sa 1:6
31:4
ᶠ Jdg 9:54;
2Sa 1:6,10
ᵍ 1Sa 14:6

31:9
ʰ 2Sa 1:20
ⁱ Jdg 16:24
31:10
ʲ Jdg 2:12-13;
1Sa 7:3 ᵏ Jos 17:11;
2Sa 21:12
31:11
ˡ 1Sa 11:1
31:12
ᵐ 2Sa 2:4-7;
2Ch 16:14;
Am 6:10
31:13
ⁿ 2Sa 21:12-14
ᵒ 1Sa 22:6
ᵖ 2Sa 1:12
q Ge 50:10

📖 Death isn't the end of our story, either. Contemporary believers can read 1 Samuel 31 in the same way ancient readers did—with hope for the future. We know there is more to come. David's greater son, Jesus, has given us reason to hope that a new day will dawn—a day in which death will no longer claim its wretched price (1 Cor. 15:54–57). The gospel offers hope and peace in this life. And by rightly relating to God now, we prepare for loving him in eternity.

INTRODUCTION TO
2 Samuel

AUTHOR

Second Samuel's author is unknown, but it was compiled from the records of Samuel, Nathan, and Gad (see 1 Chron. 29:29) and another source called "the book of Jashar" (1:18).

DATE WRITTEN

The two books of Samuel were originally one book that was probably written around 925 B.C., shortly after the division of the nation into the northern and southern kingdoms (930 B.C.).

ORIGINAL READERS

Second Samuel was written to the people of Israel as a record of the reign of David, Israel's greatest king. It provides the history of David's great successes and tragic failures.

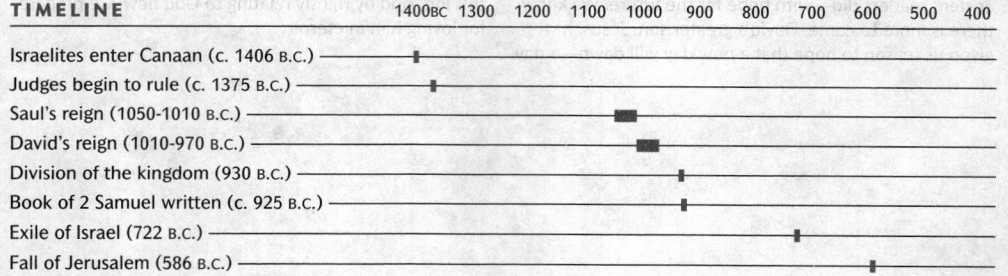

TIMELINE	1400BC 1300 1200 1100 1000 900 800 700 600 500 400
Israelites enter Canaan (c. 1406 B.C.)	
Judges begin to rule (c. 1375 B.C.)	
Saul's reign (1050-1010 B.C.)	
David's reign (1010-970 B.C.)	
Division of the kingdom (930 B.C.)	
Book of 2 Samuel written (c. 925 B.C.)	
Exile of Israel (722 B.C.)	
Fall of Jerusalem (586 B.C.)	

THEMES

Second Samuel describes the rise of David's kingship after the death of Saul. It portrays David as the ideal, though imperfect, king. It includes the following themes:

1. *The Davidic covenant.* The apex of David's life came when God entered into a covenant relationship with him, promising to establish a dynasty through his descendants (7:5–16). This covenant had a conditional element associated with it, since it warned that unfaithful kings in David's line would receive God's punishment (7:14).

2. *Consequences of sin.* David's sin of adultery and murder (11:1–21) was the turning point in his reign. Though David's repentance was genuine and God's forgiveness immediate (12:13), his sin still had consequences (12:10–12). His family life became one disaster after another, with negative consequences for the kingdom, including civil war for a time. By the end of the narrative, David was an elderly king whose kingdom, though intact, was diminished. Nonetheless God was gracious to him, and David's wholehearted devotion to God became his most memorable attribute (2 Kings 18:3; 22:2; Acts 13:22).

3. *Abuse of power.* Several narratives describe the terrible effects of people's abuse of power, notably Joab's murder of Abner, David's arrangements for Uriah's death in battle, Amnon's rape of Tamar, Absalom's murder of Amnon, and Absalom's rebellion. These incidents warn

believers today to use whatever power or authority they have as parents, employers, church leaders, etc., for good and not to aggrandize themselves or succumb to malicious purposes.

FAITH IN ACTION
The pages of 2 Samuel contain life lessons and role models of faith—people who challenge believers to put their faith in action.

Role Models

• DAVID (6:14–22) worshiped God passionately, oblivious to the sometimes negative responses of people around him. His love for God was such that God called David "a man after [his] own heart" (Acts 13:22). How are you doing in the "worship department"?

• NATHAN (12:1–14) fearlessly confronted King David with the truth, despite the possibility that the confrontation could have cost him his life. Does someone in power or someone you love need to be challenged with the truth about their sin? How can Nathan's example encourage you?

• A WISE WOMAN (14:1–20) helped convince David to resolve inflammatory issues with Absalom. Can you help bring healing or reconciliation to a hurting family?

• ITTAI (15:16-22), a foreigner, took David's side when it might have been easier to side with Absalom in his rebellion. Do you consistently do what's right rather than gravitating toward the easier or more convenient path?

• A WISE WOMAN (20:15–22) saved her city. Is there a situation in which you can intervene to bring peace?

• DAVID'S MIGHTY MEN (23:20–39) were fiercely devoted to him, and their exploits were renowned. How can loyalty to a person of integrity reflect your character?

Challenges

• Refuse, as David did (1:1–16), to celebrate the fall of your opponent. Make every effort to see the good in others (1:17–27).

• Determine to seek God's will before you act (2:1; 5:19,23).

• Exhibit integrity in your workplace, rejecting "office politics" and backstabbing (3:22–37).

• Imitate David's humility, trust, and obedience to God (7:18–29).

• Model kindness to those around you—even those who may be perceived as your "enemies" (9:1–11)—regardless of whether your kindness can or will be repaid.

• Choose not to abuse your God-given power (11:1–24), but faithfully serve him in whatever position he places you.

• Confront a sinning Christian in a loving manner (12:1–14), with the goal of repentance and restoration. But beware of making judgments concerning someone else's heart or motives (16:5–14; Matt. 7:1–5; 1 Cor. 4:5).

• Compassionately aid victims of rape, incest, sexual assault, or abuse (13:1–22). Love them and lead them toward healing in Christ, so that their sense of dignity and worth can be restored.

• Don't allow convenience or ease to make your choices for you.

• Be an agent of reconciliation wherever and whenever you are able.

OUTLINE

I. David Becomes King Over Judah (1–4)
II. David Becomes King Over All Israel (5:1–5)
III. David's Kingship in Its Accomplishments and Glory (5:6—9:13)
IV. David's Kingship in Its Weaknesses and Failures (10–20)
V. Final Reflections on David's Reign (21–24)

David Hears of Saul's Death

1:1 *a* 1Sa 31:6 *b* 1Sa 30:17
1:2 *c* 2Sa 4:10 *d* 1Sa 4:12

1 After the death[a] of Saul, David returned from defeating[b] the Amalekites and stayed in Ziklag two days. ²On the third day a man[c] arrived from Saul's camp, with his clothes torn and with dust on his head.[d] When he came to David, he fell to the ground to pay him honor.

³"Where have you come from?" David asked him.

He answered, "I have escaped from the Israelite camp."

⁴"What happened?" David asked. "Tell me."

He said, "The men fled from the battle. Many of them fell and died. And Saul and his son Jonathan are dead."

⁵Then David said to the young man who brought him the report, "How do you know that Saul and his son Jonathan are dead?"

1:6 *e* 1Sa 28:4; 31:2-4

⁶"I happened to be on Mount Gilboa,[e]" the young man said, "and there was Saul, leaning on his spear, with the chariots and riders almost upon him. ⁷When he turned around and saw me, he called out to me, and I said, 'What can I do?'

⁸"He asked me, 'Who are you?'

1:8 *f* 1Sa 15:2; 30:13,17

"'An Amalekite,[f]' I answered.

⁹"Then he said to me, 'Stand over me and kill me! I am in the throes of death, but I'm still alive.'

1:10 *g* Jdg 9:54; 2Ki 11:12
1:11 *h* Ge 37:29; 2Sa 3:31; 13:31

¹⁰"So I stood over him and killed him, because I knew that after he had fallen he could not survive. And I took the crown[g] that was on his head and the band on his arm and have brought them here to my lord."

¹¹Then David and all the men with him took hold of their clothes and tore[h] them. ¹²They mourned and wept and fasted till evening for Saul and his son Jonathan, and for the army of the LORD and the house of Israel, because they had fallen by the sword.

1:13 *i* ver 8

¹³David said to the young man who brought him the report, "Where are you from?"

"I am the son of an alien, an Amalekite,[i]" he answered.

1:14 *j* 1Sa 24:6; 26:9
1:15 *k* 2Sa 4:12 *l* 2Sa 4:10

¹⁴David asked him, "Why were you not afraid to lift your hand to destroy the LORD's anointed?[j]"

¹⁵Then David called one of his men and said, "Go, strike him down!"[k] So he struck him down, and he died.[l] ¹⁶For David had said to him, "Your blood be on your own head.[m] Your own mouth testified against you when you said, 'I killed the LORD's anointed.'"

1:16 *m* Lev 20:9; 2Sa 3:28-29; 1Ki 2:32; Mt 27:24-25; Ac 18:6

David's Lament for Saul and Jonathan

1:17 *n* 2Ch 35:25

¹⁷David took up this lament[n] concerning Saul and his son Jonathan, ¹⁸and or-

---

2 Samuel 1:1–16

The Amalekite messenger's account of Saul's death differs from the report in 1 Samuel 31, in which Saul is said to have taken his own life. The Amalekite may have made up his own involvement in Saul's death to receive a reward for bringing the "good news" to Saul's evident successor (cf. 4:10). David wouldn't have known yet that the Amalekite was lying. But he himself had twice refused to strike down Saul (1 Sam. 24; 26) and wasn't about to condone someone else taking this liberty against the Lord's anointed one.

Tragically, Saul fell because he had taken his position of power personally, abused his role as king to persecute David, and lost sight of his mission and of God's calling on his life.

Power struggles within social groups, including churches and Christian groups, are sometimes unavoidable. Power in and of itself isn't evil, but the way people use it often is, and its heartbreaking consequences can

be told by many. David didn't take opportunities for personal gain if the result would entail losses for God's people or his anointed; he refused to play power politics. This is a good position for Christians to adopt (cf. Rom. 14:19) as a life practice.

2 Samuel 1:17–27

David's pain comes through clearly in this moving scene. He repeated his lament three times: "How the mighty have fallen." His words convince the reader that David would have been incapable of leading a coup against Saul. His love and admiration for God's anointed one and for Jonathan made such subversive behavior out of the question.

The word "love" used to describe David's covenantal relationship with Jonathan has no sexual connotation (see "There and Then" for 1 Sam. 18:1–30). David was probably emphasizing Jonathan's amazing sacrificial commitment. Jonathan acknowledged David as God's choice to be Israel's next king (cf. 1 Sam. 20:13–17).

dered that the men of Judah be taught this lament of the bow (it is written in the Book of Jashar):*o*

19 "Your glory, O Israel, lies slain on your heights.
   How the mighty have fallen!*p*

20 "Tell it not in Gath,*q*
   proclaim it not in the streets of Ashkelon,
lest the daughters of the Philistines*r* be glad,
   lest the daughters of the uncircumcised rejoice.*s*

21 "O mountains of Gilboa,*t*
   may you have neither dew nor rain,
   nor fields that yield offerings*u* ⌞of grain⌟.
For there the shield of the mighty was defiled,
   the shield of Saul—no longer rubbed with oil.*v*

22 From the blood*w* of the slain,
   from the flesh of the mighty,
the bow*x* of Jonathan did not turn back,
   the sword of Saul did not return unsatisfied.

23 "Saul and Jonathan—
   in life they were loved and gracious,
   and in death they were not parted.
They were swifter than eagles,*y*
   they were stronger than lions.*z*

24 "O daughters of Israel,
   weep for Saul,
who clothed you in scarlet and finery,
   who adorned your garments with ornaments of gold.

25 "How the mighty have fallen in battle!
   Jonathan lies slain on your heights.
26 I grieve for you, Jonathan my brother;*a*
   you were very dear to me.
Your love for me was wonderful,*b*
   more wonderful than that of women.

27 "How the mighty have fallen!
   The weapons of war have perished!"*c*

David Anointed King Over Judah

2 In the course of time, David inquired*d* of the LORD. "Shall I go up to one of the towns of Judah?" he asked.
The LORD said, "Go up."
David asked, "Where shall I go?"
"To Hebron,"*e* the LORD answered.

Cross references

1:18
o Jos 10:13;
1Sa 31:3

1:19
p ver 27

1:20
q Mic 1:10
r 1Sa 31:8
s Ex 15:20; 1Sa 18:6

1:21
t ver 6; 1Sa 31:1
u Eze 31:15
v Isa 21:5

1:22
w Isa 34:3,7
x Dt 32:42;
1Sa 18:4

1:23
y Dt 28:49; Jer 4:13
z Jdg 14:18

1:26
a 1Sa 20:42
b 1Sa 18:1

1:27
c ver 19,25; 1Sa 2:4

2:1
d 1Sa 23:2,11-12
e Ge 13:18;
1Sa 30:31

📖 Our situation isn't parallel, but we can learn much from David's respect for God's appointed servants. The New Testament instructs believers, "Obey your leaders and submit to their authority . . . so that their work will be a joy, not a burden, for that would be of no advantage to you" (Heb. 13:17). But respect is a two-way street for Christians. Believers' mutual submission to each other under Christ brings unity of purpose and direction (cf. Eph. 5:21).

2 Samuel 2:1–7
🔁 David's rise to kingship had reached its turning point. The way for him to proceed was clear in theory,

but it also was fraught with danger. Now was the time to claim God's promise for his life. But it can be difficult to know precisely when to take action. So David "inquired of the LORD." He became king in the south through God's direction—in contrast to Ish-Bosheth, who had taken over the reins in the north through political scheming (vv. 8–11). David relied only on God's power and timing, while Ish-Bosheth would be a puppet in the hands of human power structures.

📖 We have the potential to be more faithful than the greatest Old Testament characters! David relied on the priestly ephod, with its Urim and Thummim (see

2:2
f 1Sa 25:43; 30:5
g 1Sa 25:42
2:3
h 1Sa 27:2; 30:9
2:4
i 1Sa 30:31
j 1Sa 2:35;
2Sa 5:3-5
k 1Sa 31:11-13
2:5
l 1Sa 23:21
2:6
m Ex 34:6; 1Ti 1:16

[2] So David went up there with his two wives, [f] Ahinoam of Jezreel and Abigail, [g] the widow of Nabal of Carmel. [3] David also took the men who were with him, [h] each with his family, and they settled in Hebron and its towns. [4] Then the men of Judah came to Hebron [i] and there they anointed [j] David king over the house of Judah.

When David was told that it was the men of Jabesh Gilead [k] who had buried Saul, [5] he sent messengers to the men of Jabesh Gilead to say to them, "The LORD bless [l] you for showing this kindness to Saul your master by burying him. [6] May the LORD now show you kindness and faithfulness, [m] and I too will show you the same favor because you have done this. [7] Now then, be strong and brave, for Saul your master is dead, and the house of Judah has anointed me king over them."

War Between the Houses of David and Saul

2:8
n 1Sa 14:50
o Ge 32:2
2:9
p Nu 32:26
q Jdg 1:32
r 1Ch 12:29

[8] Meanwhile, Abner [n] son of Ner, the commander of Saul's army, had taken Ish-Bosheth son of Saul and brought him over to Mahanaim. [o] [9] He made him king over Gilead, [p] Ashuri [a][q] and Jezreel, and also over Ephraim, Benjamin and all Israel. [r]

2:11
s 2Sa 5:5

[10] Ish-Bosheth son of Saul was forty years old when he became king over Israel, and he reigned two years. The house of Judah, however, followed David. [11] The length of time David was king in Hebron over the house of Judah was seven years and six months. [s]

2:12
t Jos 18:25
2:13
u 2Sa 8:16;
1Ch 2:16; 11:6

[12] Abner son of Ner, together with the men of Ish-Bosheth son of Saul, left Mahanaim and went to Gibeon. [t] [13] Joab [u] son of Zeruiah and David's men went out and met them at the pool of Gibeon. One group sat down on one side of the pool and one group on the other side.

[14] Then Abner said to Joab, "Let's have some of the young men get up and fight hand to hand in front of us."

"All right, let them do it," Joab said.

[15] So they stood up and were counted off—twelve men for Benjamin and Ish-Bosheth son of Saul, and twelve for David. [16] Then each man grabbed his opponent by the head and thrust his dagger into his opponent's side, and they fell down together. So that place in Gibeon was called Helkath Hazzurim. [b]

2:17
v 2Sa 3:1
2:18
w 2Sa 3:39
x 2Sa 3:30
y 1Sa 26:6
z 1Ch 2:16
a 1Ch 12:8

[17] The battle that day was very fierce, and Abner and the men of Israel were defeated [v] by David's men.

[18] The three sons of Zeruiah [w] were there: Joab, [x] Abishai [y] and Asahel. [z] Now Asahel was as fleet-footed as a wild gazelle. [a] [19] He chased Abner, turning neither to the right nor to the left as he pursued him. [20] Abner looked behind him and asked, "Is that you, Asahel?"

"It is," he answered.

[21] Then Abner said to him, "Turn aside to the right or to the left; take on one of the young men and strip him of his weapons." But Asahel would not stop chasing him.

2:22
b 2Sa 3:27

[22] Again Abner warned Asahel, "Stop chasing me! Why should I strike you down? How could I look your brother Joab in the face?" [b]

---

[a] 9 Or *Asher*   [b] 16 *Helkath Hazzurim* means *field of daggers* or *field of hostilities.*

---

1 Sam. 23:1–6 and note on Ex. 28:15–30), to "inquire of the LORD." But we have far superior resources. Instead of limited yes or no answers from God, we have the complete revelation of his plan as revealed in his Word. True, it's often difficult to determine what direction to take in specific situations. But with obedience to God's revealed Word and a heart that takes the time to "inquire of the LORD," we can't fail to find the best path.

2 Samuel 2:8—3:5

The death of Asahel, brother of David's general, Joab, at the hand of Abner (Saul's, and now Ish-Bosheth's, general) sickened both sides (see 2:23). Like the American Civil War, this was a conflict between soldiers who often knew each other. The situation resulted in a temporary

truce. Hostility between Joab and Abner continued and would characterize both David's and Solomon's militaries. David gradually gained strength, while Ish-Bosheth weakened (3:1).

David and Jesus model for us what it means to be real children of God. Jesus, son of David and Son of God, fulfills all that was right about David. He could have chosen the wrong way to accomplish his divine mission. In fact, Satan tempted him to do just that (Matt. 4:1–11). But Jesus is the ideal King of Israel because he became king in the right way: through submission to his divine calling and through patient waiting and service (Heb. 5:7–9). To what extent do you follow these examples?

²³But Asahel refused to give up the pursuit; so Abner thrust the butt of his spear into Asahel's stomach, ᶜ and the spear came out through his back. He fell there and died on the spot. And every man stopped when he came to the place where Asahel had fallen and died. ᵈ

²⁴But Joab and Abishai pursued Abner, and as the sun was setting, they came to the hill of Ammah, near Giah on the way to the wasteland of Gibeon. ²⁵Then the men of Benjamin rallied behind Abner. They formed themselves into a group and took their stand on top of a hill.

²⁶Abner called out to Joab, "Must the sword devourᵉ forever? Don't you realize that this will end in bitterness? How long before you order your men to stop pursuing their brothers?"

²⁷Joab answered, "As surely as God lives, if you had not spoken, the men would have continued the pursuit of their brothers until morning. ᵃ"

²⁸So Joabᶠ blew the trumpet, ᵍ and all the men came to a halt; they no longer pursued Israel, nor did they fight anymore.

²⁹All that night Abner and his men marched through the Arabah. They crossed the Jordan, continued through the whole Bithronᵇ and came to Mahanaim. ʰ

³⁰Then Joab returned from pursuing Abner and assembled all his men. Besides Asahel, nineteen of David's men were found missing. ³¹But David's men had killed three hundred and sixty Benjamites who were with Abner. ³²They took Asahel and buried him in his father's tombⁱ at Bethlehem. Then Joab and his men marched all night and arrived at Hebron by daybreak.

3 The war between the house of Saul and the house of David lasted a long time.ʲ David grew stronger and stronger,ᵏ while the house of Saul grew weaker and weaker.ˡ

²Sons were born to David in Hebron:

His firstborn was Amnon the son of Ahinoamᵐ of Jezreel;

³his second, Kileab the son of Abigailⁿ the widow of Nabal of Carmel;

the third, Absalomᵒ the son of Maacah daughter of Talmai king of Geshur; ᵖ

⁴the fourth, Adonijahᑫ the son of Haggith;

the fifth, Shephatiah the son of Abital;

⁵and the sixth, Ithream the son of David's wife Eglah.

These were born to David in Hebron.

Abner Goes Over to David

⁶During the war between the house of Saul and the house of David, Abner had been strengthening his own position in the house of Saul. ⁷Now Saul had had a concubineʳ named Rizpahˢ daughter of Aiah. And Ish-Bosheth said to Abner, "Why did you sleep with my father's concubine?"

ᵃ 27 Or *spoken this morning, the men would not have taken up the pursuit of their brothers*; or *spoken, the men would have given up the pursuit of their brothers by morning*   ᵇ 29 Or *morning*; or *ravine*; the meaning of the Hebrew for this word is uncertain.

---

2 Samuel 3:6–21

Having sexual relations with a king's concubine amounted to a claim to the throne. In his weakness, Ish-Bosheth suspected that Abner, the real power in the northern kingdom, would use his advantage to take the throne. Insulted by Ish-Bosheth's accusation, Abner defected to David. He moved quickly to exert his influence on the elders of Israel, specifically on Saul's tribe of Benjamin. In so doing, he effectively laid the foundation for David to be king of a unified Israel.

Ish-Bosheth's concubine became a political pawn, and Michal (Saul's daughter) was treated as an object of royal barter. The injustices of ancient Near Eastern culture are often reflected in Biblical texts without commentary. But rather than being seen as acceptable in the context of the times, these narratives are to be read in light of their meaning for the extended story. Ish-Bosheth's rash accusation about the concubine illustrated his weakness. And Michal's return to David reflects David's legitimacy as Saul's successor.

Do you sometimes find yourself offended by the roles of Old Testament women? It may help to recognize that the Old Testament's view of women (as well as of violent bloodshed) was consistently at odds with its cultural context. In these early years God initiated a process (continued in the NT and still today) of liberating women and other vulnerable groups. Committed Christians can find ways to advocate justice for those living under oppressive practices in our society and world.

3:8
t 1Sa 24:14;
2Sa 9:8; 16:9

3:9
u 1Sa 15:28;
1Ki 19:2
3:10
v Jdg 20:1; 1Sa 3:20

3:13
w Ge 43:5;
1Sa 18:20
3:14
x 1Sa 18:27
3:15
y Dt 24:1-4
z 1Sa 25:44
3:16
a 2Sa 16:5; 19:16
3:17
b Jdg 11:11

3:18
c 1Sa 9:16
d 1Sa 15:28;
2Sa 8:6

3:19
e 1Sa 10:20-21;
1Ch 12:2, 16,29

3:21
f ver 10,12
g 1Ki 11:37

3:27
h 2Sa 2:8
i 2Sa 2:22; 20:9-10;
1Ki 2:5

[8] Abner was very angry because of what Ish-Bosheth said and he answered, "Am I a dog's head[t]—on Judah's side? This very day I am loyal to the house of your father Saul and to his family and friends. I haven't handed you over to David. Yet now you accuse me of an offense involving this woman! [9] May God deal with Abner, be it ever so severely, if I do not do for David what the LORD promised[u] him on oath [10] and transfer the kingdom from the house of Saul and establish David's throne over Israel and Judah from Dan to Beersheba."[v] [11] Ish-Bosheth did not dare to say another word to Abner, because he was afraid of him.

[12] Then Abner sent messengers on his behalf to say to David, "Whose land is it? Make an agreement with me, and I will help you bring all Israel over to you."

[13] "Good," said David. "I will make an agreement with you. But I demand one thing of you: Do not come into my presence unless you bring Michal daughter of Saul when you come to see me."[w] [14] Then David sent messengers to Ish-Bosheth son of Saul, demanding, "Give me my wife Michal,[x] whom I betrothed to myself for the price of a hundred Philistine foreskins."

[15] So Ish-Bosheth gave orders and had her taken away from her husband[y] Paltiel[z] son of Laish. [16] Her husband, however, went with her, weeping behind her all the way to Bahurim.[a] Then Abner said to him, "Go back home!" So he went back.

[17] Abner conferred with the elders[b] of Israel and said, "For some time you have wanted to make David your king. [18] Now do it! For the LORD promised David, 'By my servant David I will rescue my people Israel from the hand of the Philistines[c] and from the hand of all their enemies.[d]' "

[19] Abner also spoke to the Benjamites in person. Then he went to Hebron to tell David everything that Israel and the whole house of Benjamin[e] wanted to do. [20] When Abner, who had twenty men with him, came to David at Hebron, David prepared a feast for him and his men. [21] Then Abner said to David, "Let me go at once and assemble all Israel for my lord the king, so that they may make a compact[f] with you, and that you may rule over all that your heart desires."[g] So David sent Abner away, and he went in peace.

Joab Murders Abner

[22] Just then David's men and Joab returned from a raid and brought with them a great deal of plunder. But Abner was no longer with David in Hebron, because David had sent him away, and he had gone in peace. [23] When Joab and all the soldiers with him arrived, he was told that Abner son of Ner had come to the king and that the king had sent him away and that he had gone in peace.

[24] So Joab went to the king and said, "What have you done? Look, Abner came to you. Why did you let him go? Now he is gone! [25] You know Abner son of Ner; he came to deceive you and observe your movements and find out everything you are doing."

[26] Joab then left David and sent messengers after Abner, and they brought him back from the well of Sirah. But David did not know it. [27] Now when Abner[h] returned to Hebron, Joab took him aside into the gateway, as though to speak with him privately. And there, to avenge the blood of his brother Asahel, Joab stabbed him in the stomach, and he died.[i]

[28] Later, when David heard about this, he said, "I and my kingdom are forever in-

---

2 Samuel 3:22–39

The narrator went to great lengths to emphasize David's innocence in Abner's murder. Three times he stated that David sent the general away "in peace" (vv. 21,22,23). When Joab summoned Abner to kill him, "David did not know it." David personally led the throng at the funeral, weeping aloud, fasting, and singing a lament for Abner. The people accepted David's innocence and were pleased by his actions. Joab's actions, on the other hand, eventually resulted in his own death (1 Kings 2:5–6,32–34).

Workplace politics can result in character assassination or the loss of someone's job. We can be thought guilty by association if a colleague takes an action calculated to please us or to ingratiate himself or herself in our eyes. David condemned and distanced himself from Joab's sin. How you respond to a coworker's maneuvering speaks volumes about your faith and serves as a gauge of your spiritual maturity. Can you recall a situation in which workplace politics affected you? Did you respond in a Christlike manner?

nocent[j] before the LORD concerning the blood of Abner son of Ner. [29]May his blood[k] fall upon the head of Joab and upon all his father's house![l] May Joab's house never be without someone who has a running sore[m] or leprosy[a] or who leans on a crutch or who falls by the sword or who lacks food."

[30](Joab and his brother Abishai murdered Abner because he had killed their brother Asahel in the battle at Gibeon.)

[31]Then David said to Joab and all the people with him, "Tear your clothes and put on sackcloth[n] and walk in mourning[o] in front of Abner." King David himself walked behind the bier. [32]They buried Abner in Hebron, and the king wept[p] aloud at Abner's tomb. All the people wept also.

[33]The king sang this lament[q] for Abner:

> "Should Abner have died as the lawless die?
> [34]   Your hands were not bound,
>   your feet were not fettered.
> You fell as one falls before wicked men."

And all the people wept over him again.

[35]Then they all came and urged David to eat something while it was still day; but David took an oath, saying, "May God deal with me, be it ever so severely,[r] if I taste bread[s] or anything else before the sun sets!"

[36]All the people took note and were pleased; indeed, everything the king did pleased them. [37]So on that day all the people and all Israel knew that the king had no part[t] in the murder of Abner son of Ner.

[38]Then the king said to his men, "Do you not realize that a prince and a great man has fallen[u] in Israel this day? [39]And today, though I am the anointed king, I am weak, and these sons of Zeruiah[v] are too strong for me.[w] May the LORD repay[x] the evildoer according to his evil deeds!"

Ish-Bosheth Murdered

4 When Ish-Bosheth son of Saul heard that Abner[y] had died in Hebron, he lost courage, and all Israel became alarmed. [2]Now Saul's son had two men who were leaders of raiding bands. One was named Baanah and the other Recab; they were sons of Rimmon the Beerothite from the tribe of Benjamin—Beeroth[z] is considered part of Benjamin, [3]because the people of Beeroth fled to Gittaim[a] and have lived there as aliens to this day.

[4](Jonathan[b] son of Saul had a son who was lame in both feet. He was five years old when the news[c] about Saul and Jonathan came from Jezreel. His nurse picked him up and fled, but as she hurried to leave, he fell and became crippled.[d] His name was Mephibosheth.)[e]

[5]Now Recab and Baanah, the sons of Rimmon the Beerothite, set out for the house of Ish-Bosheth,[f] and they arrived there in the heat of the day while he was taking his noonday rest. [6]They went into the inner part of the house as if to get

---

[a] 29 The Hebrew word was used for various diseases affecting the skin—not necessarily leprosy.

---

2 Samuel 4:1–12

David determined that Ish-Bosheth's two assassins should be executed. They had made wrong assumptions about the king in Israel, and their use of power and violence was self-incriminating. Once again, David was innocent of violent acts that nevertheless benefited his rise to power.

After Ish-Bosheth's coming death there would be no other viable successor to the throne from Saul's family (v. 4). Just as impressive physical features confirmed the right of both Saul and David to rule (1 Sam. 9:2; 10:23; 16:12), so Mephibosheth's impairment made him an un-

likely choice. Ancient cultures viewed disability as a sign of sin or of God's disfavor.

We would like to think we are more enlightened than the ancients. Yet consider the importance of a political candidate's persona and appearance to the outcome of an election. What cultural prejudices and social stigmas do you accept and, perhaps unintentionally, perpetuate through your thoughts and actions? We can use our comfort zones to insulate ourselves from social interaction with people different from ourselves. Or we can demonstrate true love, care, and respect that go beyond court-imposed, equal access policies.

Marginal cross-references:

3:28 / ver 37; Dt 21:9
3:29 k Lev 20:9 l 1Ki 2:31-33 m Lev 15:2
3:31 n 2Sa 1:2,11; Ps 30:11; Isa 20:2 o Ge 37:34
3:32 p Nu 14:1; Pr 24:17
3:33 q 2Sa 1:17
3:35 r Ru 1:17; 1Sa 3:17 s 1Sa 31:13; 2Sa 1:12; 12:17; Jer 16:7
3:37 t ver 28
3:38 u 2Sa 1:19
3:39 v 2Sa 2:18 w 2Sa 19:5-7 x 1Ki 2:5-6,33-34; Ps 41:10; 101:8
4:1 y 2Sa 3:27; Ezr 4:4
4:2 z Jos 9:17; 18:25
4:3 a Ne 11:33
4:4 b 1Sa 18:1 c 1Sa 31:1-4 d Lev 21:18 e 2Sa 9:3,6; 1Ch 8:34; 9:40
4:5 f 2Sa 2:8

4:6
g 2Sa 2:23

some wheat, and they stabbed[g] him in the stomach. Then Recab and his brother Baanah slipped away.

[7]They had gone into the house while he was lying on the bed in his bedroom. After they stabbed and killed him, they cut off his head. Taking it with them, they traveled all night by way of the Arabah. [8]They brought the head of Ish-Bosheth to David at Hebron and said to the king, "Here is the head of Ish-Bosheth son of Saul,[h] your enemy, who tried to take your life. This day the LORD has avenged my lord the king against Saul and his offspring."

4:8
h 1Sa 24:4; 25:29

[9]David answered Recab and his brother Baanah, the sons of Rimmon the Beerothite, "As surely as the LORD lives, who has delivered[i] me out of all trouble, [10]when a man told me, 'Saul is dead,' and thought he was bringing good news, I seized him and put him to death in Ziklag.[j] That was the reward I gave him for his news! [11]How much more—when wicked men have killed an innocent man in his own house and on his own bed—should I not now demand his blood[k] from your hand and rid the earth of you!"

4:9
i Ge 48:16; 1Ki 1:29

4:10
j 2Sa 1:2-16

4:11
k Ge 9:5; Ps 9:12

[12]So David gave an order to his men, and they killed them.[l] They cut off their hands and feet and hung the bodies by the pool in Hebron. But they took the head of Ish-Bosheth and buried it in Abner's tomb at Hebron.

4:12
l 2Sa 1:15

David Becomes King Over Israel

5 All the tribes of Israel[m] came to David at Hebron and said, "We are your own flesh and blood.[n] [2]In the past, while Saul was king over us, you were the one who led Israel on their military campaigns.[o] And the LORD said to you, 'You will shepherd[p] my people Israel, and you will become their ruler.[q]' "

5:1
m 2Sa 19:43
n 1Ch 11:1

5:2
o 1Sa 18:5,13,16
p 1Sa 16:1; 2Sa 7:7
q 1Sa 25:30

[3]When all the elders of Israel had come to King David at Hebron, the king made a compact[r] with them at Hebron before the LORD, and they anointed[s] David king over Israel.

5:3
r 2Sa 3:21 s 2Sa 2:4

[4]David was thirty years old[t] when he became king, and he reigned[u] forty[v] years. [5]In Hebron he reigned over Judah seven years and six months,[w] and in Jerusalem he reigned over all Israel and Judah thirty-three years.

5:4
t Lk 3:23
u 1Ki 2:11; 1Ch 3:4
v 1Ch 26:31; 29:27

5:5
w 2Sa 2:11; 1Ch 3:4

David Conquers Jerusalem

[6]The king and his men marched to Jerusalem[x] to attack the Jebusites,[y] who lived there. The Jebusites said to David, "You will not get in here; even the blind and the lame can ward you off." They thought, "David cannot get in here." [7]Nevertheless, David captured the fortress of Zion, the City of David.[z]

5:6
x Jdg 1:8 y Jos 15:8

5:7
z 2Sa 6:12,16; 1Ki 2:10

[8]On that day, David said, "Anyone who conquers the Jebusites will have to use the water shaft[a] to reach those 'lame and blind' who are David's enemies.[b]" That is why they say, "The 'blind and lame' will not enter the palace."

[9]David then took up residence in the fortress and called it the City of David. He

---

[a] 8 Or use scaling hooks   [b] 8 Or are hated by David

---

2 Samuel 5:1–5

Historically, Abner had paved the way for northern support, while Ish-Bosheth was weak. *Sociologically*, the northern tribes entered into a covenant agreeing to the terms of David's kingship. *Psychologically*, David was a powerful figure who commanded loyalty. Beyond these factors, the writer argued for David's kingship based on a *theological* cause: God had chosen him. Here the elders of "all the tribes of Israel" affirmed that choice.

Do we search for God's choice in leaders for our churches and ministries? Most "help wanted" ads stress experience. Certainly, as with David, circumstances can point to the one God has selected. But appearances can be deceiving. It's a true test of spiritual maturity to allow the Lord to lead important decision-making processes

rather than to trust the obvious criteria of education or experience. Would your denomination or church likely have approved a candidate like Peter as a primary leader of the early church?

2 Samuel 5:6–16

The references to the "water shaft" and to "the blind and the lame" are unclear, but the main points of the story are transparent. David couldn't rule a newly unified nation from a southern base at Hebron. Jerusalem was ideal for its natural defenses, central location, and lack of previous attachment to the tribes of Israel (though it was in the territory of Benjamin). David cleverly devised a means of attack and turned the venerable old fortress into his own possession—the "City of David."

built up the area around it, from the supporting terraces[a][a] inward. [10]And he became more and more powerful,[b] because the LORD God Almighty was with him.

[11]Now Hiram[c] king of Tyre sent messengers to David, along with cedar logs and carpenters and stonemasons, and they built a palace for David. [12]And David knew that the LORD had established him as king over Israel and had exalted his kingdom for the sake of his people Israel.

[13]After he left Hebron, David took more concubines and wives[d] in Jerusalem, and more sons and daughters were born to him. [14]These are the names of the children born to him there:[e] Shammua, Shobab, Nathan, Solomon, [15]Ibhar, Elishua, Nepheg, Japhia, [16]Elishama, Eliada and Eliphelet.

David Defeats the Philistines

[17]When the Philistines heard that David had been anointed king over Israel, they went up in full force to search for him, but David heard about it and went down to the stronghold.[f] [18]Now the Philistines had come and spread out in the Valley of Rephaim;[g] [19]so David inquired[h] of the LORD, "Shall I go and attack the Philistines? Will you hand them over to me?"

The LORD answered him, "Go, for I will surely hand the Philistines over to you."

[20]So David went to Baal Perazim, and there he defeated them. He said, "As waters break out, the LORD has broken out against my enemies before me." So that place was called Baal Perazim.[b][i] [21]The Philistines abandoned their idols there, and David and his men carried them off.[j]

[22]Once more the Philistines came up and spread out in the Valley of Rephaim; [23]so David inquired of the LORD, and he answered, "Do not go straight up, but circle around behind them and attack them in front of the balsam trees. [24]As soon as you hear the sound[k] of marching in the tops of the balsam trees, move quickly, because that will mean the LORD has gone out in front[l] of you to strike the Philistine army." [25]So David did as the LORD commanded him, and he struck down the Philistines all the way from Gibeon[c][m] to Gezer.[n]

The Ark Brought to Jerusalem

6 David again brought together out of Israel chosen men, thirty thousand in all. [2]He and all his men set out from Baalah[o] of Judah[d] to bring up from there the

(Right margin cross-references)
5:9 *a* ver 7; 1Ki 9:15,24
5:10 *b* 2Sa 3:1
5:11 *c* 1Ki 5:1,18; 1Ch 14:1
5:13 *d* Dt 17:17; 1Ch 3:9
5:14 *e* 1Ch 3:5
5:17 *f* 2Sa 23:14; 1Ch 11:16
5:18 *g* Jos 15:8; 17:15; 18:16
5:19 *h* 1Sa 23:2; 2Sa 2:1
5:20 *i* Isa 28:21
5:21 *j* Dt 7:5; 1Ch 14:12; Isa 46:2
5:24 *k* 2Ki 7:6 *l* Jdg 4:14
5:25 *m* Isa 28:21 *n* 1Ch 14:16
6:2 *o* Jos 15:9

---

a 9 Or the Millo   *b* 20 *Baal Perazim* means *the lord who breaks out.*   *c* 25 Septuagint (see also 1 Chron. 14:16); Hebrew *Geba*   *d* 2 That is, Kiriath Jearim; Hebrew *Baale Judah,* a variant of *Baalah of Judah*

Likely the most contested piece of real estate in the world, Jerusalem today is still a location much desired by Arabs, Palestinians, Israelis, Jews, Muslims, and Christians. Ancient Israelites believed strongly in "Zion theology"—the belief that God, the great King, had chosen Jerusalem as his dwelling place. The apostle John's vision concluded with a description of "the new Jerusalem" that would become God's eternal dwelling place with humanity. We, too, look forward to this city where "God himself will be with [humankind] and be their God" (Rev. 21:3).

2 Samuel 5:17–25

The significance of these victories is highlighted by subtle references. (1) The Philistines' abandonment of their idols reversed the defeat at Ebenezer, when the Philistines had captured the ark of the covenant (1 Sam. 4:1–11). (2) The Israelites in that earlier battle had recklessly attempted to create the circumstances of holy war. Here the imagery of divine armies marching in the balsam trees and of God going out in front of Israel's army does depict spiritual intervention. (3) Once again, "David inquired of the LORD"

(see notes for 1 Sam. 23:1–6 and 2 Sam. 2:1–7).

Victories unite and ignite people. Especially dramatic or emotional triumphs can remain imprinted on a nation's psyche for generations. Think of Gettysburg during the U.S. Civil War and D-Day or the Battle of Midway during WWII. In this text, the victories constituted a realization of David's dream for a consolidated territorial state and emphasized God's faithfulness to promises he had made to Abraham, Jacob, and David. What God has promised, he will do! Have you experienced a spiritual victory that still extends ripples of blessing today?

2 Samuel 6:1–23

Chapters 5–6 describe David's accomplishments that brought his national goals to realization. He captured and then transformed Jerusalem into a new capital city, constructed a palace, drove the Philistines out of Judah's heartland, and instituted religious reforms. The ark of the covenant was the most important symbol of God's approval among the unified tribes of Israel. Its presence in Jerusalem represented the most powerful sign of God's support for David's kingship.

6:2
p 1Sa 4:4; 7:1
q Lev 24:16;
Isa 63:14 *r* Ps 99:1
s Ex 25:22;
1Ch 13:5-6
6:3
t Nu 7:4-9; 1Sa 6:7
6:5
u 1Sa 18:6-7;
Ezr 3:10; Ps 150:5
6:6
v Nu 4:15,19-20;
1Ch 13:9
6:7
w 1Ch 15:13-15
x Ex 19:22;
1Sa 6:19
6:8
y Ps 7:11
z Ge 38:29
6:9
a Ps 119:120
6:10
b 1Ch 13:13; 26:4-5
6:11
c Ge 30:27; 39:5
6:12
d 1Ki 8:1;
1Ch 15:25
6:13
e 1Ki 8:5,62
6:14
f Ex 19:6; 1Sa 2:18
g Ex 15:20
6:15
h Ps 47:5; 98:6
6:16
i 2Sa 5:7
6:17
j 1Ch 15:1; 2Ch 1:4
k Lev 1:1-17;
1Ki 8:62-64
6:18
l 1Ki 8:22
6:19
m Hos 3:1
n Ne 8:10
6:20
o ver 14,16
6:21
p 1Sa 13:14; 15:28

ark[p] of God, which is called by the Name, [a][q] the name of the LORD Almighty, who is enthroned[r] between the cherubim[s] that are on the ark. [3]They set the ark of God on a new cart[t] and brought it from the house of Abinadab, which was on the hill. Uzzah and Ahio, sons of Abinadab, were guiding the new cart [4]with the ark of God on it,[b] and Ahio was walking in front of it. [5]David and the whole house of Israel were celebrating with all their might before the LORD, with songs[c] and with harps, lyres, tambourines, sistrums and cymbals.[u]

[6]When they came to the threshing floor of Nacon, Uzzah reached out and took hold of[v] the ark of God, because the oxen stumbled. [7]The LORD's anger burned against Uzzah because of his irreverent act;[w] therefore God struck him down[x] and he died there beside the ark of God.

[8]Then David was angry because the LORD's wrath[y] had broken out against Uzzah, and to this day that place is called Perez Uzzah.[d][z]

[9]David was afraid of the LORD that day and said, "How[a] can the ark of the LORD ever come to me?" [10]He was not willing to take the ark of the LORD to be with him in the City of David. Instead, he took it aside to the house of Obed-Edom[b] the Gittite. [11]The ark of the LORD remained in the house of Obed-Edom the Gittite for three months, and the LORD blessed him and his entire household.[c]

[12]Now King David[d] was told, "The LORD has blessed the household of Obed-Edom and everything he has, because of the ark of God." So David went down and brought up the ark of God from the house of Obed-Edom to the City of David with rejoicing. [13]When those who were carrying the ark of the LORD had taken six steps, he sacrificed[e] a bull and a fattened calf. [14]David, wearing a linen ephod,[f] danced[g] before the LORD with all his might, [15]while he and the entire house of Israel brought up the ark of the LORD with shouts and the sound of trumpets.[h]

[16]As the ark of the LORD was entering the City of David,[i] Michal daughter of Saul watched from a window. And when she saw King David leaping and dancing before the LORD, she despised him in her heart.

[17]They brought the ark of the LORD and set it in its place inside the tent that David had pitched for it,[j] and David sacrificed burnt offerings[k] and fellowship offerings[e] before the LORD. [18]After he had finished sacrificing[l] the burnt offerings and fellowship offerings, he blessed the people in the name of the LORD Almighty. [19]Then he gave a loaf of bread, a cake of dates and a cake of raisins[m] to each person in the whole crowd of Israelites, both men and women.[n] And all the people went to their homes.

[20]When David returned home to bless his household, Michal daughter of Saul came out to meet him and said, "How the king of Israel has distinguished himself today, disrobing[o] in the sight of the slave girls of his servants as any vulgar fellow would!"

[21]David said to Michal, "It was before the LORD, who chose me rather than your father or anyone from his house when he appointed[p] me ruler over the LORD's people Israel—I will celebrate before the LORD. [22]I will become even more undignified than this, and I will be humiliated in my own eyes. But by these slave girls you spoke of, I will be held in honor."

[23]And Michal daughter of Saul had no children to the day of her death.

---

[a] 2 Hebrew; Septuagint and Vulgate do not have *the Name.*   [b] 3,4 Dead Sea Scrolls and some Septuagint manuscripts; Masoretic Text *cart* [4]*and they brought it with the ark of God from the house of Abinadab, which was on the hill*   [c] 5 See Dead Sea Scrolls, Septuagint and 1 Chronicles 13:8; Masoretic Text *celebrating before the LORD with all kinds of instruments made of pine.*   [d] 8 *Perez Uzzah* means *outbreak against Uzzah.*   [e] 17 Traditionally *peace offerings*; also in verse 18

David wasn't simply building an earthly nation but *God's kingdom.* The LORD had chosen David's city—Jerusalem—as his dwelling place. People who lived in the city with David had to meet God's standards of holiness (Ps. 24:3–4; Isa. 33:13–16). But they also could count on a secure and abundant life in his presence. We as Christians recognize that David was laying the foundation for Zion, the city of our salvation and the kingdom of God described in Revelation 21:1—22:5. Do you thank God regularly for your residence and citizenship within its boundaries?

God's Promise to David

7 After the king was settled in his palace[q] and the LORD had given him rest from all his enemies around him, [2]he said to Nathan the prophet, "Here I am, living in a palace[r] of cedar, while the ark of God remains in a tent."[s]

[3]Nathan replied to the king, "Whatever you have in mind, go ahead and do it, for the LORD is with you."

[4]That night the word of the LORD came to Nathan, saying:

[5]"Go and tell my servant David, 'This is what the LORD says: Are you[t] the one to build me a house to dwell in?[u] [6]I have not dwelt in a house from the day I brought the Israelites up out of Egypt to this day. I have been moving from place to place with a tent[v] as my dwelling. [w] [7]Wherever I have moved with all the Israelites,[x] did I ever say to any of their rulers whom I commanded to shepherd[y] my people Israel, "Why have you not built me a house of cedar?[z]" '

[8]"Now then, tell my servant David, 'This is what the LORD Almighty says: I took you from the pasture and from following the flock[a] to be ruler[b] over my people Israel. [c] [9]I have been with you wherever you have gone, [d] and I have cut off all your enemies from before you. [e] Now I will make your name great, like the names of the greatest men of the earth. [10]And I will provide a place for my people Israel and will plant[f] them so that they can have a home of their own and no longer be disturbed. Wicked[g] people will not oppress them anymore, [h] as they did at the beginning [11]and have done ever since the time I appointed leaders[a][i] over my people Israel. I will also give you rest from all your enemies.[j]

" 'The LORD declares to you that the LORD himself will establish[k] a house[l] for you: [12]When your days are over and you rest[m] with your fathers, I will raise up your offspring to succeed you, who will come from your own body,[n] and I will establish his kingdom. [13]He is the one who will build a house for my Name, [o] and I will establish the throne of his kingdom forever.[p] [14]I will be his father, and he will be my son. [q] When he does wrong, I will punish him with the rod[r] of men, with floggings inflicted by men. [15]But my love will never be taken away from him, as I took it away from Saul, [s] whom I removed from before you. [16]Your house and your kingdom will endure forever before me[b]; your throne[t] will be established forever.[u] ' "

[17]Nathan reported to David all the words of this entire revelation.

David's Prayer

[18]Then King David went in and sat before the LORD, and he said:

"Who am I, [v] O Sovereign LORD, and what is my family, that you have

---

[a] 11 Traditionally *judges*   [b] 16 Some Hebrew manuscripts and Septuagint; most Hebrew manuscripts *you*

7:1 [q] 1Ch 17:1
7:2 [r] 2Sa 5:11 [s] Ex 26:1; Ac 7:45-46
7:5 [t] 1Ki 8:19; 1Ch 22:8 [u] 1Ki 5:3-5
7:6 [v] Ex 40:18,34 [w] 1Ki 8:16
7:7 [x] Dt 23:14 [y] 2Sa 5:2 [z] Lev 26:11-12
7:8 [a] 1Sa 16:11 [b] 2Sa 6:21 [c] Ps 78:70-72; 2Co 6:18*
7:9 [d] 2Sa 5:10 [e] Ps 18:37-42
7:10 [f] Ex 15:17; Isa 5:1-7 [g] Ps 89:22-23 [h] Isa 60:18
7:11 [i] Jdg 2:16; 1Sa 12:9-11 / ver 1 [k] 1Sa 25:28 / ver 27
7:12 [m] 1Ki 2:1 [n] Ps 132:11-12
7:13 [o] 1Ki 5:5; 8:19,29 [p] Isa 9:7
7:14 [q] Ps 89:26; Heb 1:5* [r] Ps 89:30-33
7:15 [s] 1Sa 15:23,28
7:16 [t] Ps 89:36-37 [u] ver 13
7:18 [v] Ex 3:11; 1Sa 18:18

---

2 Samuel 7:1–17

This is one of the Bible's most important chapters. God rejected David's plan to build a temple, but he didn't reject David. He had something greater in store for him. God made a covenant with David, a promise to establish his dynasty in Jerusalem eternally. In later Israelite thinking, this chapter became a constitutional text. Like the Magna Carta of Britain or the Declaration of Independence of the United States, it inspired a people and engendered a national identity.

As Christians we accept the new covenant of Christ as the fulfillment, culmination, and extension of the chain of Old Testament covenants with Abraham, Moses, and David. God's revelation of himself unfolded over time, so the differences in covenants are of degree, not type. That is why Jesus could boil down all the covenant commands into two basic guidelines: Love God with all your heart, and love your neighbor as yourself (cf. Matt. 22:35–40). Are these apparently simple requirements easier for you to keep than a lengthy list of technical demands?

2 Samuel 7:18–29

This chapter showed David to be a paragon of virtue and a model of faith. He was closely related to the people and institutions that became God's means of communication and direction in his life. He listened to Nathan and quickly complied with the prophetic word. Overwhelmed by God's message, he prayed before the ark of the covenant. David expressed a sense of overwhelming unworthiness, at the same time boldly asking the Lord to fulfill his promises.

brought me this far? ¹⁹And as if this were not enough in your sight, O Sovereign LORD, you have also spoken about the future of the house of your servant. Is this your usual way of dealing with man, ʷ O Sovereign LORD?

²⁰"What more can David say to you? For you knowˣ your servant, ʸ O Sovereign LORD. ²¹For the sake of your word and according to your will, you have done this great thing and made it known to your servant.

²²"How greatᶻ you are, ᵃ O Sovereign LORD! There is no one like you, and there is no Godᵇ but you, as we have heard with our own ears. ᶜ ²³And who is like your people Israelᵈ—the one nation on earth that God went out to redeem as a people for himself, and to make a name for himself, and to perform great and awesome wondersᵉ by driving out nations and their gods from before your people, whom you redeemedᶠ from Egypt?ᵃ ²⁴You have established your people Israel as your very ownᵍ forever, and you, O LORD, have become their God. ʰ

²⁵"And now, LORD God, keep forever the promise you have made concerning your servant and his house. Do as you promised, ²⁶so that your name will be great forever. Then men will say, 'The LORD Almighty is God over Israel!' And the house of your servant David will be established before you.

²⁷"O LORD Almighty, God of Israel, you have revealed this to your servant, saying, 'I will build a house for you.' So your servant has found courage to offer you this prayer. ²⁸O Sovereign LORD, you are God! Your words are trustworthy, ⁱ and you have promised these good things to your servant. ²⁹Now be pleased to bless the house of your servant, that it may continue forever in your

7:19
ʷ Isa 55:8-9
7:20
ˣ Jn 21:17
ʸ 1Sa 16:7

7:22
ᶻ Ps 48:1; 86:10; Jer 10:6 ᵃ Dt 3:24
ᵇ Ex 15:11
ᶜ Ex 10:2; Ps 44:1
7:23
ᵈ Dt 4:32-38
ᵉ Dt 10:21
ᶠ Dt 9:26; 15:15

7:24
ᵍ Dt 26:18
ʰ Ex 6:6-7; Ps 48:14

7:28
ⁱ Ex 34:6; Jn 17:17

ᵃ 23 See Septuagint and 1 Chron. 17:21; Hebrew *wonders for your land and before your people, whom you redeemed from Egypt, from the nations and their gods.*

David functions as a model for all of us who worship the "son of David" today. We do well to take every opportunity to receive God's grace through church attendance, Bible study, prayer, giving, involvement in missions and outreach, commitment to serve the poor, etc. Just as David in his time lived close to the means of God's grace, so we can learn to experience the different ways he speaks today. What are some of the means God has chosen to communicate with you?

Snapshots

7:10

Bamboo Shoots Street Children's Center

Leab, eighteen, was a glue-sniffing boy on the streets of Phnom Penh, Cambodia, only two and a half years ago. After years of living on the streets, he met a man who told him about the Bamboo Shoots Street Children's Center. Leab became one of the miracle children. Placed in a loving foster home for almost two years, he recently "graduated" from the program and became a peer counselor.

> The center's aim is to break the cycle of homelessness and vulnerability.

The center's aim is to break the cycle of homelessness and vulnerability by encouraging children to leave the streets and rehabilitating them within the community. Workers comb the area on bikes at night, looking for kids in trouble. They invite them and wait for their response. Access to education, skills training, sports, and cultural activities, including medical assistance, family tracing, and care, also are provided.

Since the center opened in 1992, over 360 children have gone through the program and been reconciled with their families. Another 145 were placed in foster homes. The workers invest a great deal of time researching family situations to make sure placement back in the home is the best solution for a particular child. Often they provide financial assistance to the families so they can better care for their children.

sight; for you, O Sovereign LORD, have spoken, and with your blessing[j] the house of your servant will be blessed forever."

7:29
[j] Nu 6:23-27

David's Victories

8 In the course of time, David defeated the Philistines and subdued them, and he took Metheg Ammah from the control of the Philistines.

[2] David also defeated the Moabites.[k] He made them lie down on the ground and measured them off with a length of cord. Every two lengths of them were put to death, and the third length was allowed to live. So the Moabites became subject to David and brought tribute.

8:2
[k] Ge 19:37;
Nu 24:17

[3] Moreover, David fought Hadadezer[l] son of Rehob, king of Zobah,[m] when he went to restore his control along the Euphrates River. [4] David captured a thousand of his chariots, seven thousand charioteers[a] and twenty thousand foot soldiers. He hamstrung[n] all but a hundred of the chariot horses.

8:3
[l] 2Sa 10:16,19
[m] 1Sa 14:47

8:4
[n] Jos 11:9

[5] When the Arameans of Damascus[o] came to help Hadadezer king of Zobah, David struck down twenty-two thousand of them. [6] He put garrisons in the Aramean kingdom of Damascus, and the Arameans became subject to him and brought tribute. The LORD gave David victory wherever he went.[p]

8:5
[o] 1Ki 11:24

8:6
[p] ver 14; 2Sa 3:18;
7:9

[7] David took the gold shields[q] that belonged to the officers of Hadadezer and brought them to Jerusalem. [8] From Tebah[b] and Berothai,[r] towns that belonged to Hadadezer, King David took a great quantity of bronze.

8:7
[q] 1Ki 10:16
8:8
[r] Eze 47:16
8:9
[s] 1Ki 8:65; 2Ch 8:4

[9] When Tou[c] king of Hamath[s] heard that David had defeated the entire army of Hadadezer, [10] he sent his son Joram[d] to King David to greet him and congratulate him on his victory in battle over Hadadezer, who had been at war with Tou. Joram brought with him articles of silver and gold and bronze.

[11] King David dedicated[t] these articles to the LORD, as he had done with the silver and gold from all the nations he had subdued: [12] Edom[e] and Moab,[u] the Ammonites[v] and the Philistines,[w] and Amalek.[x] He also dedicated the plunder taken from Hadadezer son of Rehob, king of Zobah.

8:11
[t] 1Ki 7:51;
1Ch 26:26
8:12
[u] ver 2 [v] 2Sa 10:14
[w] 2Sa 5:25
[x] 1Sa 27:8
8:13
[y] 2Sa 7:9
[z] 2Ki 14:7;
1Ch 18:12
8:14
[a] Nu 24:17-18
[b] Ge 27:29,37-40
[c] ver 6

[13] And David became famous[y] after he returned from striking down eighteen thousand Edomites[f] in the Valley of Salt.[z]

[14] He put garrisons throughout Edom, and all the Edomites[a] became subject to David.[b] The LORD gave David victory wherever he went.[c]

David's Officials

[15] David reigned over all Israel, doing what was just and right for all his people. [16] Joab[d] son of Zeruiah was over the army; Jehoshaphat[e] son of Ahilud was record-

8:16
[d] 2Sa 19:13;
1Ch 11:6
[e] 2Sa 20:24; 1Ki 4:3

---

[a] 4 Septuagint (see also Dead Sea Scrolls and 1 Chron. 18:4); Masoretic Text *captured seventeen hundred of his charioteers*   [b] 8 See some Septuagint manuscripts (see also 1 Chron. 18:8); Hebrew *Betah*.   [c] 9 Hebrew *Toi*, a variant of *Tou*; also in verse 10   [d] 10 A variant of *Hadoram*   [e] 12 Some Hebrew manuscripts, Septuagint and Syriac (see also 1 Chron. 18:11); most Hebrew manuscripts *Aram*   [f] 13 A few Hebrew manuscripts, Septuagint and Syriac (see also 1 Chron. 18:12); most Hebrew manuscripts *Aram* (that is, Arameans)

---

2 Samuel 8:1–14

In staccato-like repetition, chapter 8 narrates David's military successes, primarily near Israel's borders to the north and across the Jordan to the east. David embodied God's rule on Earth. As God's chosen, anointed one, he ruled as the Lord wanted his people to be governed.

It's a mistake to evaluate David's actions in warfare and treatment of prisoners and animals by today's standards. David didn't live in a time even remotely similar to ours. The text's true significance lies in its recurring theme: "The LORD gave David victory wherever he went" (vv. 6,14).

This catalog of victories inspires us. God is faithful to his Word and strengthens his people for the tasks

to which he has called us. He has already won our victory and promised to empower us for the ministries he asks us to perform in the church and world. We as believers can expect to accomplish successfully our God-given, God-ordained mission—with the help of his Holy Spirit (Acts 1:8). To what has the Spirit led you? Do you feel a tug toward some new kingdom assignment?

2 Samuel 8:15–18

With this list of royal officials, the historian takes us a step further in understanding the new Israelite monarchy. The organization of the state under the new government differed from the tribal organization at the beginning of 1 Samuel under Samuel's able leadership. The previous social arrangement, based on kinship, had given way to a structure based more on skill and ability,

8:17
f 2Sa 15:24,29;
1Ch 16:39; 24:3
g 1Ki 4:3; 2Ki 12:10
8:18
h 2Sa 20:23;
1Ki 1:8,38;
1Ch 18:17
i 1Sa 30:14

9:1
j 1Sa 20:14-17,42
9:2
k 2Sa 16:1-4;
19:17,26,29

9:3
l 1Sa 20:14
m 2Sa 4:4

9:4
n 2Sa 17:27-29

9:6
o 2Sa 16:4;
19:24-30

9:7
p ver 1,3; 2Sa 12:8;
19:28; 1Ki 2:7;
2Ki 25:29
9:8
q 2Sa 16:9

9:10
r ver 7,11,13;
2Sa 19:28

9:11
s Job 36:7; Ps 113:8

9:12
t 1Ch 8:34

er; [17]Zadok[f] son of Ahitub and Ahimelech son of Abiathar were priests; Seraiah was secretary; [g] [18]Benaiah [h] son of Jehoiada was over the Kerethites [i] and Pelethites; and David's sons were royal advisers. [a]

David and Mephibosheth

9 David asked, "Is there anyone still left of the house of Saul to whom I can show kindness for Jonathan's sake?" [j]

[2]Now there was a servant of Saul's household named Ziba. [k] They called him to appear before David, and the king said to him, "Are you Ziba?"

"Your servant," he replied.

[3]The king asked, "Is there no one still left of the house of Saul to whom I can show God's kindness?"

Ziba answered the king, "There is still a son of Jonathan; [l] he is crippled [m] in both feet."

[4]"Where is he?" the king asked.

Ziba answered, "He is at the house of Makir [n] son of Ammiel in Lo Debar."

[5]So King David had him brought from Lo Debar, from the house of Makir son of Ammiel.

[6]When Mephibosheth son of Jonathan, the son of Saul, came to David, he bowed down to pay him honor. [o]

David said, "Mephibosheth!"

"Your servant," he replied.

[7]"Don't be afraid," David said to him, "for I will surely show you kindness for the sake of your father Jonathan. I will restore to you all the land that belonged to your grandfather Saul, and you will always eat at my table." [p]

[8]Mephibosheth bowed down and said, "What is your servant, that you should notice a dead dog [q] like me?"

[9]Then the king summoned Ziba, Saul's servant, and said to him, "I have given your master's grandson everything that belonged to Saul and his family. [10]You and your sons and your servants are to farm the land for him and bring in the crops, so that your master's grandson [r] may be provided for. And Mephibosheth, grandson of your master, will always eat at my table." (Now Ziba had fifteen sons and twenty servants.)

[11]Then Ziba said to the king, "Your servant will do whatever my lord the king commands his servant to do." So Mephibosheth ate at David's [b] table like one of the king's sons. [s]

[12]Mephibosheth had a young son named Mica, and all the members of Ziba's household were servants of Mephibosheth. [t] [13]And Mephibosheth lived in Jerusalem, because he always ate at the king's table, and he was crippled in both feet.

[a] 18 Or *were priests*   [b] 11 Septuagint; Hebrew *my*

much the way a family business might change when transitioning today to a publicly traded corporation.

In summary form, the narrator assessed the new monarchy: "David reigned over all Israel, doing what was just and right for all his people." He became the example and standard by which all future Israelite and Judahite kings would be evaluated. Today, justice remains the hallmark of good government. How people are treated in a nation is history's test of world leaders. In the same way, how a Christian treats others demonstrates her or his allegiance to God's kingdom and leadership. If you were being graded today, how do you suspect you would fare?

2 Samuel 9:1–13

David's "kindness" had covenantal implications. This is clear from 1 Samuel 18, 20, and 23, in which David and Jonathan swore to remember each other in faithfulness. In ancient times, the family of a king replaced by another didn't expect consideration. New dynasties routinely killed the families of the old order to solidify a power base. It was risky for David to grant access to the royal palace and financial freedom to a grandson of Saul (see 16:3). David's kindness to Mephibosheth certainly surpassed his obligation to allow the young man merely to stay alive.

Integrity as modeled here by David implies the determination to exercise justice even when the only compelling reason is the sheer "rightness" of the act. We may be tempted to "show kindness" to people only when it's convenient or when we detect a promise of return. Among your family members, friends, colleagues, classmates, and fellow believers, do you keep your promises whether or not you can reasonably expect repayment?

David Defeats the Ammonites

10 In the course of time, the king of the Ammonites died, and his son Hanun succeeded him as king. ²David thought, "I will show kindness to Hanun son of Nahash, *u* just as his father showed kindness to me." So David sent a delegation to express his sympathy to Hanun concerning his father.

When David's men came to the land of the Ammonites, ³the Ammonite nobles said to Hanun their lord, "Do you think David is honoring your father by sending men to you to express sympathy? Hasn't David sent them to you to explore the city and spy it out and overthrow it?" ⁴So Hanun seized David's men, shaved off half of each man's beard, *v* cut off their garments in the middle at the buttocks, *w* and sent them away.

⁵When David was told about this, he sent messengers to meet the men, for they were greatly humiliated. The king said, "Stay at Jericho till your beards have grown, and then come back."

⁶When the Ammonites realized that they had become a stench *x* in David's nostrils, they hired twenty thousand Aramean *y* foot soldiers from Beth Rehob *z* and Zobah, as well as the king of Maacah *a* with a thousand men, and also twelve thousand men from Tob.

10:2
u 1Sa 11:1

10:4
v Lev 19:27;
Isa 15:2; Jer 48:37
w Isa 20:4

10:6
x Ge 34:30
y 2Sa 8:5
z Jdg 18:28
a Dt 3:14

---

2 Samuel 10:1–19

Most likely Nahash, an old adversary of Saul (cf. 1 Sam. 11), had been David's ally during the difficult days of Saul's reign. Just as David had been faithful to his covenant with Jonathan by treating Mephibosheth with generosity and kindness, he now logically sought to be loyal to Hanun, Nahash's son.

Hanun's humiliation of David's men was in effect a declaration of war. The beard was the pride and joy of an Israelite male, cut only for periods of mourning or as an act of self-humiliation. Since garments often reflected status, power, or identity, the insult of cutting the ambassadors' clothes at their hips was a further humiliation to David's men.

When have you jumped to the wrong conclusion without bothering to gather all the facts? Hanun's ill-considered response says much to us about accepting bad advice and assuming the worst about others. Such reactions can stir up trouble and make enemies of potential friends or allies. Improving our communication skills and following Scriptural advice (Prov. 6:2–5; 12:18; 15:1) can save us from us such unnecessary mistakes.

Snapshots

9:1–13

Mirza

Twelve-year-old Mirza of Boznia-Herzegovina speaks a little English, quite an accomplishment considering that he's mentally challenged. Mirza learned English from watching movies. In fact, he's learned a lot from observation. It's taught him what he wants to be—a good young man who can make a living and be happy. "When I grow up I would like to . . . maybe be a butcher," Mirza explains. Like his father. Mirza and his schoolmates idolize their dads.

With extra effort special needs kids can flourish and contribute to their communities. A special program run by Christians in Mirza's area helps such children develop through art, drama, music, and sports.

Mirza is painfully self-aware: "People . . . say I'm stupid." His mother cries quietly. "Conversations are normal until Mirza mentions the special school, and then the teasing starts."

But Mirza and his classmates have hurdles to overcome beyond verbal insults. Beyond some secondary education, there is no access to training for special needs children here.

"I like this place. You can find a lot of bad places," he notes, meaning institutions for children like himself. "God loves all people equally . . . He doesn't divide them the way some people do."

> "**G**od loves all people equally . . . He doesn't divide them the way some people do."

7On hearing this, David sent Joab out with the entire army of fighting men. 8The Ammonites came out and drew up in battle formation at the entrance to their city gate, while the Arameans of Zobah and Rehob and the men of Tob and Maacah were by themselves in the open country.

9Joab saw that there were battle lines in front of him and behind him; so he selected some of the best troops in Israel and deployed them against the Arameans. 10He put the rest of the men under the command of Abishai his brother and deployed them against the Ammonites. 11Joab said, "If the Arameans are too strong for me, then you are to come to my rescue; but if the Ammonites are too strong for you, then I will come to rescue you. 12Be strong[b] and let us fight bravely for our people and the cities of our God. The LORD will do what is good in his sight."[c]

13Then Joab and the troops with him advanced to fight the Arameans, and they fled before him. 14When the Ammonites saw that the Arameans were fleeing, they fled before Abishai and went inside the city. So Joab returned from fighting the Ammonites and came to Jerusalem.

15After the Arameans saw that they had been routed by Israel, they regrouped. 16Hadadezer had Arameans brought from beyond the River[a]; they went to Helam, with Shobach the commander of Hadadezer's army leading them.

17When David was told of this, he gathered all Israel, crossed the Jordan and went to Helam. The Arameans formed their battle lines to meet David and fought against him. 18But they fled before Israel, and David killed seven hundred of their charioteers and forty thousand of their foot soldiers.[b] He also struck down Shobach the commander of their army, and he died there. 19When all the kings who were vassals of Hadadezer saw that they had been defeated by Israel, they made peace with the Israelites and became subject[d] to them.

So the Arameans[e] were afraid to help the Ammonites anymore.

David and Bathsheba

11 In the spring,[f] at the time when kings go off to war, David sent Joab[g] out with the king's men and the whole Israelite army.[h] They destroyed the Ammonites and besieged Rabbah.[i] But David remained in Jerusalem.

2One evening David got up from his bed and walked around on the roof[j] of the palace. From the roof he saw[k] a woman bathing. The woman was very beautiful, 3and David sent someone to find out about her. The man said, "Isn't this Bathsheba,[l] the daughter of Eliam[m] and the wife of Uriah[n] the Hittite?" 4Then David sent messengers to get her.[o] She came to him, and he slept[p] with her. (She had purified herself from her uncleanness.)[q] Then[c] she went back home. 5The woman conceived and sent word to David, saying, "I am pregnant."

6So David sent this word to Joab: "Send me Uriah[r] the Hittite." And Joab sent him to David. 7When Uriah came to him, David asked him how Joab was, how the soldiers were and how the war was going. 8Then David said to Uriah, "Go down to your house and wash your feet."[s] So Uriah left the palace, and a gift from the king

Cross references (margin)

10:12
b Dt 31:6;
1Co 16:13;
Eph 6:10
c Jdg 2:8;
1Sa 3:18; Ne 4:14

10:19
d 2Sa 8:6
e 1Ki 11:25; 2Ki 5:1

11:1
f 1Ki 20:22,26
g 2Sa 2:18
h 1Ch 20:1
i 2Sa 12:26-28
11:2
j Dt 22:8; Jos 2:8
k Mt 5:28

11:3
l 1Ch 3:5
m 2Sa 23:34
n 2Sa 23:39
11:4
o Lev 20:10; Ps 51
Title; Jas 1:14-15
p Dt 22:22
q Lev 15:25-30;
18:19
11:6
r 1Ch 11:41
11:8
s Ge 18:4; 43:24;
Lk 7:44

---

a 16 That is, the Euphrates   b 18 Some Septuagint manuscripts (see also 1 Chron. 19:18); Hebrew horsemen   c 4 Or with her. When she purified herself from her uncleanness,

---

2 Samuel 11:1–27

The tragic events here can be characterized by the word "send." David *sent* someone to inquire about Bathsheba, exercising his right as king. He *sent* again, to bring her to the palace in a clear misuse of his power. Bathsheba *sent* David a message about her pregnancy, and he was forced to deal with the power of his own sin. David *sent* a decree to Joab, who *sent* Uriah into a dangerous battlefield position. David repeatedly *sent*—and *took*. Ultimately, God, though, would *send*, and David would yield (12:1).

Abuse of God-given power is a root cause of poverty and suffering worldwide. Whether the scenario

involves a trans-national corporation raping a country of its natural resources, a slumlord oppressing tenants, or a corrupt government allowing bribery and embezzling of a nation's wealth, the results are tragic. How often don't we see, whether first- or second-hand, children and families existing well below a healthy standard of living?

The way we ourselves use power reflects either our faithfulness to God or our treason against him. No matter how close we live to God, no matter how much responsibility we have been given in his kingdom, we too are vulnerable to falling. What kinds of power do you exercise? What can you do to guard against letting it "go to your head"?

was sent after him. 9But Uriah slept at the entrance to the palace with all his master's servants and did not go down to his house.

10When David was told, "Uriah did not go home," he asked him, "Haven't you just come from a distance? Why didn't you go home?"

11Uriah said to David, "The ark[t] and Israel and Judah are staying in tents, and my master Joab and my lord's men are camped in the open fields. How could I go to my house to eat and drink and lie with my wife? As surely as you live, I will not do such a thing!"

12Then David said to him, "Stay here one more day, and tomorrow I will send you back." So Uriah remained in Jerusalem that day and the next. 13At David's invitation, he ate and drank with him, and David made him drunk. But in the evening Uriah went out to sleep on his mat among his master's servants; he did not go home.

14In the morning David wrote a letter[u] to Joab and sent it with Uriah. 15In it he wrote, "Put Uriah in the front line where the fighting is fiercest. Then withdraw from him so he will be struck down[v] and die.[w]"

16So while Joab had the city under siege, he put Uriah at a place where he knew the strongest defenders were. 17When the men of the city came out and fought against Joab, some of the men in David's army fell; moreover, Uriah the Hittite died.

18Joab sent David a full account of the battle. 19He instructed the messenger: "When you have finished giving the king this account of the battle, 20the king's anger may flare up, and he may ask you, 'Why did you get so close to the city to fight? Didn't you know they would shoot arrows from the wall? 21Who killed Abimelech[x] son of Jerub-Besheth[a]? Didn't a woman throw an upper millstone on him from the wall,[y] so that he died in Thebez? Why did you get so close to the wall?' If he asks you this, then say to him, 'Also, your servant Uriah the Hittite is dead.' "

22The messenger set out, and when he arrived he told David everything Joab had sent him to say. 23The messenger said to David, "The men overpowered us and came out against us in the open, but we drove them back to the entrance to the city gate. 24Then the archers shot arrows at your servants from the wall, and some of the king's men died. Moreover, your servant Uriah the Hittite is dead."

25David told the messenger, "Say this to Joab: 'Don't let this upset you; the sword devours one as well as another. Press the attack against the city and destroy it.' Say this to encourage Joab."

26When Uriah's wife heard that her husband was dead, she mourned for him. 27After the time of mourning was over, David had her brought to his house, and she became his wife and bore him a son. But the thing David had done displeased[z] the LORD.

Nathan Rebukes David

12 The LORD sent Nathan[a] to David.[b] When he came to him,[c] he said, "There were two men in a certain town, one rich and the other poor. 2The rich man had a very large number of sheep and cattle, 3but the poor man had nothing except one little ewe lamb he had bought. He raised it, and it grew up with him and his children. It shared his food, drank from his cup and even slept in his arms. It was like a daughter to him.

4"Now a traveler came to the rich man, but the rich man refrained from taking one of his own sheep or cattle to prepare a meal for the traveler who had come to him. Instead, he took the ewe lamb that belonged to the poor man and prepared it for the one who had come to him."

[a] 21 Also known as Jerub-Baal (that is, Gideon)

11:11
[t] 2Sa 7:2

11:14
[u] 1Ki 21:8

11:15
[v] 2Sa 12:9
[w] 2Sa 12:12

11:21
[x] Jdg 8:31
[y] Jdg 9:50-54

11:27
[z] 2Sa 12:9;
Ps 51:4-5

12:1
[a] 2Sa 7:2;
1Ki 20:35-41
[b] Ps 51 Title
[c] 2Sa 14:4

---

2 Samuel 12:1–31

📖 Chapters 11–12 follow one of Scripture's great heroes of the faith through the stages of sin, repentance, and forgiveness. David's "I have sinned against the LORD" was spoken without any attempt to blame or dodge. It's possible that he was so overcome with guilt that he welcomed Nathan's rebuke.

Some might conclude that the child died in David's place, atoning for his sin. More likely, the natural consequences of that sin resulted somehow in the baby's death. Long-term, recurring trauma in David's family life would complete his punishment.

12:5
d 1Ki 20:40

12:6
e Ex 22:1; Lk 19:8

12:7
f 1Sa 16:13
g 1Ki 20:42
12:8
h 2Sa 9:7

12:9
i Nu 15:31;
1Sa 15:19
j 2Sa 11:15

12:10
k 2Sa 13:28;
18:14-15;
1Ki 2:25

12:11
l Dt 28:30;
2Sa 16:21-22
12:12
m 2Sa 11:4-15
n 2Sa 16:22
12:13
o Ge 13:13;
Nu 22:34;
1Sa 15:24;
2Sa 24:10
p Ps 32:1-5; 51:1,9;
103:12; Zec 3:4,9
q Pr 28:13;
Mic 7:18-19
r Lev 20:10; 24:17
12:14
s Isa 52:5; Ro 2:24
12:15
t 1Sa 25:38
12:16
u 2Sa 13:31; Ps 5:7
12:17
v 2Sa 3:35

5 David *d* burned with anger against the man and said to Nathan, "As surely as the LORD lives, the man who did this deserves to die! 6 He must pay for that lamb four times over, *e* because he did such a thing and had no pity."

7 Then Nathan said to David, "You are the man! This is what the LORD, the God of Israel, says: 'I anointed *f* you *g* king over Israel, and I delivered you from the hand of Saul. 8 I gave your master's house to you, *h* and your master's wives into your arms. I gave you the house of Israel and Judah. And if all this had been too little, I would have given you even more. 9 Why did you despise *i* the word of the LORD by doing what is evil in his eyes? You struck down *j* Uriah the Hittite with the sword and took his wife to be your own. You killed him with the sword of the Ammonites. 10 Now, therefore, the sword *k* will never depart from your house, because you despised me and took the wife of Uriah the Hittite to be your own.'

11 "This is what the LORD says: 'Out of your own household I am going to bring calamity upon you. *l* Before your very eyes I will take your wives and give them to one who is close to you, and he will lie with your wives in broad daylight. 12 You did it in secret, *m* but I will do this thing in broad daylight *n* before all Israel.' "

13 Then David said to Nathan, "I have sinned *o* against the LORD."

Nathan replied, "The LORD has taken away *p* your sin. *q* You are not going to die. *r* 14 But because by doing this you have made the enemies of the LORD show utter contempt, *a s* the son born to you will die."

15 After Nathan had gone home, the LORD struck *t* the child that Uriah's wife had borne to David, and he became ill. 16 David pleaded with God for the child. He fasted and went into his house and spent the nights lying *u* on the ground. 17 The elders of his household stood beside him to get him up from the ground, but he refused, and he would not eat any food with them. *v*

a 14 Masoretic Text; an ancient Hebrew scribal tradition *this you have shown utter contempt for the LORD*

📖 Our culture has pushed to the limit an emphasis on tolerance and reluctance to judge others. Many Christians, too, have a hard time taking a firm stand on moral issues clearly addressed in the Bible. Even the church often is affected by fuzzy thinking about sin and its consequences. But Scripture teaches that only a full recognition of destructive actions can lead to genuine repentance. Confronting others in love may open the door for them to receive God's forgiveness and restoration. Have you found the courage to challenge a fellow believer in humble Christian love?

12:11–12,14

Relationships

In the Bible relationships aren't strictly defined by one-on-one associations or interactions, but in wider and wider patterns of love/lovelessness. Consider these examples:

Family:
Solomon observed that a greedy man brings trouble not just upon himself but on his entire family (Prov. 15:27).

Community:
God made provision in his law for the unintentional sinning of an entire community. Error can spread like gangrene, but we have to presume that it starts somewhere, probably with one individual (Lev. 4:13).

Country:
David's sin with Bathsheba affected his whole kingdom (2 Sam. 12:11–12,14).

Enemies:
Jonah's gripe wasn't just with God, but also with the Ninevites (Jonah 4:1–3).

Friends:
Jonathan's love for David led him to relinquish the throne, altering the course of Israelite history and making room for the Davidic kingdom (1 Sam. 23:16–18).

Church:
Paul observed how divisions within the church affect the whole body of believers (1 Cor. 1:10).

Self:
The sin of one man and one woman drastically and irreversibly changed the shape of human history (Gen. 3:16–19,24).

Humanity:
All people are created in God's image; all are witnesses to God in some way (Col. 3:9–10).

World:
Noah didn't just save his own skin, or his family's; his obedience made possible the continuation of the human race (Gen. 9:1).

Any single relationship affects all the others represented on this list. The poet John Donne observed that no man is an island—totally alone. But he might have gone on to say that no single relationship is independent of a whole network of other relationships.

¹⁸On the seventh day the child died. David's servants were afraid to tell him that the child was dead, for they thought, "While the child was still living, we spoke to David but he would not listen to us. How can we tell him the child is dead? He may do something desperate."

¹⁹David noticed that his servants were whispering among themselves and he realized the child was dead. "Is the child dead?" he asked.

"Yes," they replied, "he is dead."

²⁰Then David got up from the ground. After he had washed, ʷ put on lotions and changed his clothes, ˣ he went into the house of the LORD and worshiped. Then he went to his own house, and at his request they served him food, and he ate.

²¹His servants asked him, "Why are you acting this way? While the child was alive, you fasted and wept, ʸ but now that the child is dead, you get up and eat!"

²²He answered, "While the child was still alive, I fasted and wept. I thought, 'Who knows? ᶻ The LORD may be gracious to me and let the child live.' ᵃ ²³But now that he is dead, why should I fast? Can I bring him back again? I will go to him, ᵇ but he will not return to me." ᶜ

²⁴Then David comforted his wife Bathsheba, ᵈ and he went to her and lay with her. She gave birth to a son, and they named him Solomon. ᵉ The LORD loved him; ²⁵and because the LORD loved him, he sent word through Nathan the prophet to name him Jedidiah. ᵃᶠ

²⁶Meanwhile Joab fought against Rabbah ᵍ of the Ammonites and captured the royal citadel. ²⁷Joab then sent messengers to David, saying, "I have fought against Rabbah and taken its water supply. ²⁸Now muster the rest of the troops and besiege the city and capture it. Otherwise I will take the city, and it will be named after me."

²⁹So David mustered the entire army and went to Rabbah, and attacked and captured it. ³⁰He took the crown ʰ from the head of their king ᵇ—its weight was a talent ᶜ of gold, and it was set with precious stones—and it was placed on David's head. He took a great quantity of plunder from the city ³¹and brought out the people who were there, consigning them to labor with saws and with iron picks and axes, and he made them work at brickmaking. ᵈ He did this to all the Ammonite ⁱ towns. Then David and his entire army returned to Jerusalem.

Amnon and Tamar

13 In the course of time, Amnon ʲ son of David fell in love with Tamar, ᵏ the beautiful sister of Absalom ˡ son of David.

²Amnon became frustrated to the point of illness on account of his sister Tamar, for she was a virgin, and it seemed impossible for him to do anything to her.

³Now Amnon had a friend named Jonadab son of Shimeah, ᵐ David's brother. Jonadab was a very shrewd man. ⁴He asked Amnon, "Why do you, the king's son, look so haggard morning after morning? Won't you tell me?"

Amnon said to him, "I'm in love with Tamar, my brother Absalom's sister."

⁵"Go to bed and pretend to be ill," Jonadab said. "When your father comes to see you, say to him, 'I would like my sister Tamar to come and give me something to eat. Let her prepare the food in my sight so I may watch her and then eat it from her hand.' "

ᵃ *25* *Jedidiah* means *loved by the LORD.*   ᵇ *30* Or *of Milcom* (that is, Molech)   ᶜ *30* That is, about 75 pounds (about 34 kilograms)   ᵈ *31* The meaning of the Hebrew for this clause is uncertain.

12:20
ʷ Mt 6:17
ˣ Job 1:20

12:21
ʸ Jdg 20:26

12:22
ᶻ Jnh 3:9
ᵃ Isa 38:1-5
12:23
ᵇ Ge 37:35
ᶜ 1Sa 31:13;
2Sa 13:39;
Job 7:10; 10:21
12:24
ᵈ 1Ki 1:11
ᵉ 1Ki 1:10;
1Ch 22:9; 28:5;
Mt 1:6
12:25
ᶠ Ne 13:26
12:26
ᵍ Dt 3:11;
1Ch 20:1-3

12:30
ʰ 1Ch 20:2;
Est 8:15; Ps 21:3;
132:18

12:31
ⁱ 1Sa 14:47

13:1
ʲ 2Sa 3:2
ᵏ 2Sa 14:27;
1Ch 3:9 ˡ 2Sa 3:3

13:3
ᵐ 1Sa 16:9

---

2 Samuel 13:1–22

Amnon summoned his forbidden sister with abusive intent—much as David had called for another man's wife. Amnon dehumanized and then ravaged Tamar, leaving her "a desolate woman." David's sin had come to rest in his immediate family. Some speculate about his failure to defend Tamar and punish Amnon. Did David's own guilt paralyze him when it came to disciplining his children?

The personal consequences of sexual brutality are as devastating today as then. Like Tamar, some people never recover their sense of dignity following such a trauma. Our natural response may be to avoid people who have been damaged in this way. Yet the church has much to offer those suffering the effects of rape or incest. Healing for body, mind, and spirit can be found in Christ and through the compassionate help of those of us who bear his name. How open are you to helping people dealing with "sensitive" emotional or mental issues?

6So Amnon lay down and pretended to be ill. When the king came to see him, Amnon said to him, "I would like my sister Tamar to come and make some special bread in my sight, so I may eat from her hand."

7David sent word to Tamar at the palace: "Go to the house of your brother Amnon and prepare some food for him." 8So Tamar went to the house of her brother Amnon, who was lying down. She took some dough, kneaded it, made the bread in his sight and baked it. 9Then she took the pan and served him the bread, but he refused to eat.

"Send everyone out of here,"n Amnon said. So everyone left him. 10Then Amnon said to Tamar, "Bring the food here into my bedroom so I may eat from your hand." And Tamar took the bread she had prepared and brought it to her brother Amnon in his bedroom. 11But when she took it to him to eat, he grabbedo her and said, "Come to bed with me, my sister."p

12"Don't, my brother!" she said to him. "Don't force me. Such a thing should not be done in Israel!q Don't do this wicked thing.r 13What about me?s Where could I get rid of my disgrace? And what about you? You would be like one of the wicked fools in Israel. Please speak to the king; he will not keep me from being married to you." 14But he refused to listen to her, and since he was stronger than she, he raped her.t

15Then Amnon hated her with intense hatred. In fact, he hated her more than he had loved her. Amnon said to her, "Get up and get out!"

16"No!" she said to him. "Sending me away would be a greater wrong than what you have already done to me."

But he refused to listen to her. 17He called his personal servant and said, "Get this woman out of here and bolt the door after her." 18So his servant put her out and bolted the door after her. She was wearing a richly orname/nteda robe,u for this was the kind of garment the virgin daughters of the king wore. 19Tamar put ashesv on her head and tore the ornamentedb robe she was wearing. She put her hand on her head and went away, weeping aloud as she went.

20Her brother Absalom said to her, "Has that Amnon, your brother, been with you? Be quiet now, my sister; he is your brother. Don't take this thing to heart." And Tamar lived in her brother Absalom's house, a desolate woman.

21When King David heard all this, he was furious.w 22Absalom never said a word to Amnon, either good or bad;x he hatedy Amnon because he had disgraced his sister Tamar.

Absalom Kills Amnon

23Two years later, when Absalom's sheepshearersz were at Baal Hazor near the border of Ephraim, he invited all the king's sons to come there. 24Absalom went to the king and said, "Your servant has had shearers come. Will the king and his officials please join me?"

25"No, my son," the king replied. "All of us should not go; we would only be a burden to you." Although Absalom urged him, he still refused to go, but gave him his blessing.

26Then Absalom said, "If not, please let my brother Amnon come with us."

---

a 18 The meaning of the Hebrew for this phrase is uncertain.   b 19 The meaning of the Hebrew for this word is uncertain.

13:9
n Ge 45:1

13:11
o Ge 39:12
p Ge 38:16

13:12
q Lev 20:17;
Jdg 20:6 r Ge 34:7;
Jdg 19:23
13:13
s Ge 20:12;
Lev 18:9;
Dt 22:21,23-24
13:14
t Ge 34:2; Dt 22:25;
Eze 22:11

13:18
u Ge 37:23;
Jdg 5:30
13:19
v Jos 7:6; 1Sa 4:12;
2Sa 1:2; Est 4:1;
Da 9:3

13:21
w Ge 34:7
13:22
x Ge 31:24
y Lev 19:17-18;
1Jn 2:9-11

13:23
z 1Sa 25:7

---

2 Samuel 13:23–39

Absalom's two-year wait, during which he nursed his hatred and plotted his revenge, culminated in Amnon's murder. Rape was condemned in the Old Testament, but the punishment wasn't murder. Absalom's extreme action was unjustified and cold-blooded—reminding us of David's murder of Uriah. The story here reaches an impasse: David was incapable of administering justice in his own family, and Absalom was unable to return home.

The 20th century was history's most violent, and the trend hasn't slowed into the 21st. The post-Cold War period has been characterized by reemerging tribal hatreds—the same ones that have divided humankind for centuries over race, faith, and nationality. Individuals contribute with their own prejudices to the hatred that threatens to erupt at any moment. But we as Christians are called to reflect God's love for all people by adopting his heart and purpose for the nations (cf. Rev. 22:1–2).

The king asked him, "Why should he go with you?" ²⁷But Absalom urged him, so he sent with him Amnon and the rest of the king's sons.

²⁸Absalom^a ordered his men, "Listen! When Amnon is in high^b spirits from drinking wine and I say to you, 'Strike Amnon down,' then kill him. Don't be afraid. Have not I given you this order? Be strong and brave.^c" ²⁹So Absalom's men did to Amnon what Absalom had ordered. Then all the king's sons got up, mounted their mules and fled.

³⁰While they were on their way, the report came to David: "Absalom has struck down all the king's sons; not one of them is left." ³¹The king stood up, tore^d his clothes and lay down on the ground; and all his servants stood by with their clothes torn.

³²But Jonadab son of Shimeah, David's brother, said, "My lord should not think that they killed all the princes; only Amnon is dead. This has been Absalom's expressed intention ever since the day Amnon raped his sister Tamar. ³³My lord the king should not be concerned about the report that all the king's sons are dead. Only Amnon is dead."

³⁴Meanwhile, Absalom had fled.

Now the man standing watch looked up and saw many people on the road west of him, coming down the side of the hill. The watchman went and told the king, "I see men in the direction of Horonaim, on the side of the hill." ^a

³⁵Jonadab said to the king, "See, the king's sons are here; it has happened just as your servant said."

³⁶As he finished speaking, the king's sons came in, wailing loudly. The king, too, and all his servants wept very bitterly.

³⁷Absalom fled and went to Talmai^e son of Ammihud, the king of Geshur. But King David mourned for his son every day.

³⁸After Absalom fled and went to Geshur, he stayed there three years. ³⁹And the spirit of the king^b longed to go to Absalom,^f for he was consoled^g concerning Amnon's death.

Absalom Returns to Jerusalem

14 Joab^h son of Zeruiah knew that the king's heart longed for Absalom. ²So Joab sent someone to Tekoaⁱ and had a wise woman^j brought from there. He said to her, "Pretend you are in mourning. Dress in mourning clothes, and don't use any cosmetic lotions.^k Act like a woman who has spent many days grieving for the dead. ³Then go to the king and speak these words to him." And Joab^l put the words in her mouth.

⁴When the woman from Tekoa went^c to the king, she fell with her face to the ground to pay him honor, and she said, "Help me, O king!"

⁵The king asked her, "What is troubling you?"

She said, "I am indeed a widow; my husband is dead. ⁶I your servant had two sons. They got into a fight with each other in the field, and no one was there to separate them. One struck the other and killed him. ⁷Now the whole clan has risen up against your servant; they say, 'Hand over the one who struck his brother down, so that we may put him to death^m for the life of his brother whom he killed; then we will get rid of the heirⁿ as well.' They would put out the only burning coal I have left,^o leaving my husband neither name nor descendant on the face of the earth."

Cross references

13:28
^a 2Sa 3:3
^b Jdg 19:6,9,22;
Ru 3:7; 1Sa 25:36
^c 2Sa 12:10

13:31
^d Nu 14:6;
2Sa 1:11; 12:16

13:37
^e ver 34; 2Sa 3:3;
14:23,32

13:39
^f 2Sa 14:13
^g 2Sa 12:19-23

14:1
^h 2Sa 2:18
14:2
ⁱ 2Ch 11:6; Ne 3:5;
Jer 6:1; Am 1:1
^j 2Sa 20:16
^k Ru 3:3; 2Sa 12:20;
Isa 1:6
14:3
^l ver 19

14:7
^m Nu 35:19
ⁿ Mt 21:38
^o Dt 19:10-13

---

^a 34 Septuagint; Hebrew does not have this sentence. ^b 39 Dead Sea Scrolls and some Septuagint manuscripts; Masoretic Text But the spirit of David the king ^c 4 Many Hebrew manuscripts, Septuagint, Vulgate and Syriac; most Hebrew manuscripts spoke

---

2 Samuel 14:1–33

📖 Joab needed this gifted and eloquent actress to persuade David to take action. Just as Nathan's parable in 12:1–4 had drawn out a judgment from the king, so this ruse evoked David's good sense. In both cases, the king unwittingly indicted himself.

David relented and allowed Absalom to return to Jerusalem (unpunished). Absalom's treatment of Joab warns us of a darker side to the king's son that didn't bode well for the future. The father/son reconciliation was brief and formal, but the exile had left its mark on Absalom.

8 The king said to the woman, "Go home,[p] and I will issue an order in your behalf."
9 But the woman from Tekoa said to him, "My lord the king, let the blame[q] rest
on me and on my father's family,[r] and let the king and his throne be without
guilt.[s]"
10 The king replied, "If anyone says anything to you, bring him to me, and he will
not bother you again."
11 She said, "Then let the king invoke the LORD his God to prevent the avenger[t] of
blood from adding to the destruction, so that my son will not be destroyed."
"As surely as the LORD lives," he said, "not one hair[u] of your son's head will fall
to the ground.[v]"
12 Then the woman said, "Let your servant speak a word to my lord the king."
"Speak," he replied.
13 The woman said, "Why then have you devised a thing like this against the people of God? When the king says this, does he not convict himself,[w] for the king has
not brought back his banished son?[x] 14 Like water[y] spilled on the ground, which
cannot be recovered, so we must die.[z] But God does not take away life; instead, he
devises ways so that a banished person[a] may not remain estranged from him.
15 "And now I have come to say this to my lord the king because the people have
made me afraid. Your servant thought, 'I will speak to the king; perhaps he will do
what his servant asks. 16 Perhaps the king will agree to deliver his servant from the
hand of the man who is trying to cut off both me and my son from the inheritance[b]
God gave us.'
17 "And now your servant says, 'May the word of my lord the king bring me rest,
for my lord the king is like an angel[c] of God in discerning[d] good and evil. May the
LORD your God be with you.' "
18 Then the king said to the woman, "Do not keep from me the answer to what I
am going to ask you."
"Let my lord the king speak," the woman said.
19 The king asked, "Isn't the hand of Joab[e] with you in all this?"
The woman answered, "As surely as you live, my lord the king, no one can turn
to the right or to the left from anything my lord the king says. Yes, it was your servant Joab who instructed me to do this and who put all these words into the
mouth of your servant. 20 Your servant Joab did this to change the present situation.
My lord has wisdom[f] like that of an angel of God—he knows everything that happens in the land.[g]"
21 The king said to Joab, "Very well, I will do it. Go, bring back the young man Absalom."
22 Joab fell with his face to the ground to pay him honor, and he blessed the
king.[h] Joab said, "Today your servant knows that he has found favor in your eyes,
my lord the king, because the king has granted his servant's request."
23 Then Joab went to Geshur and brought Absalom back to Jerusalem. 24 But the
king said, "He must go to his own house; he must not see my face." So Absalom
went to his own house and did not see the face of the king.
25 In all Israel there was not a man so highly praised for his handsome appearance
as Absalom. From the top of his head to the sole of his foot there was no blemish
in him. 26 Whenever he cut the hair of his head[i]—he used to cut his hair from time
to time when it became too heavy for him—he would weigh it, and its weight was
two hundred shekels[a] by the royal standard.

14:8 p 1Sa 25:35 **14:9** q 1Sa 25:24 r Mt 27:25 s 1Sa 25:28; 1Ki 2:33 **14:11** t Nu 35:12,21 u Mt 10:30 v 1Sa 14:45 **14:13** w 2Sa 12:7; 1Ki 20:40 x 2Sa 13:38-39 **14:14** y Job 14:11; Ps 58:7; Isa 19:5 z Job 10:8; 17:13; 30:23; Ps 22:15; Heb 9:27 a Nu 35:15,25-28; Job 34:15 **14:16** b Ex 34:9; 1Sa 26:19 **14:17** c ver 20; 1Sa 29:9; 2Sa 19:27 d 1Ki 3:9; Da 2:21 **14:19** e ver 3 **14:20** f 1Ki 3:12,28; Isa 28:6 g ver 17; 2Sa 18:13; 19:27 **14:22** h Ge 47:7 **14:26** i 2Sa 18:9; Eze 44:20

[a] *26* That is, about 5 pounds (about 2.3 kilograms)

A repeated theme in 1 and 2 Samuel involves *tragedy caused by lack of parental discipline*. The situation with regard to Samuel and his sons is mentioned in passing (1 Sam. 8:1–5), but the repercussions of a father's neglect with regard to the households of Eli (1 Sam. 2:27–36) and David affected generations to come. Old Testament wisdom literature, especially Proverbs, repeatedly warns parents not to ignore this crucial aspect of child rearing. Destructive peer influences, a permissive society, and the reluctance of parents to alienate their kids can have devastating consequences. If you are a parent, how are you doing in this area?

[27]Three sons[j] and a daughter were born to Absalom. The daughter's name was Tamar,[k] and she became a beautiful woman.

[28]Absalom lived two years in Jerusalem without seeing the king's face. [29]Then Absalom sent for Joab in order to send him to the king, but Joab refused to come to him. So he sent a second time, but he refused to come. [30]Then he said to his servants, "Look, Joab's field is next to mine, and he has barley[l] there. Go and set it on fire." So Absalom's servants set the field on fire.

[31]Then Joab did go to Absalom's house and he said to him, "Why have your servants set my field on fire?[m]"

[32]Absalom said to Joab, "Look, I sent word to you and said, 'Come here so I can send you to the king to ask, "Why have I come from Geshur?[n] It would be better for me if I were still there!" ' Now then, I want to see the king's face, and if I am guilty of anything, let him put me to death."[o]

[33]So Joab went to the king and told him this. Then the king summoned Absalom, and he came in and bowed down with his face to the ground before the king. And the king kissed[p] Absalom.

Absalom's Conspiracy

15 In the course of time,[q] Absalom provided himself with a chariot[r] and horses and with fifty men to run ahead of him. [2]He would get up early and stand by the side of the road leading to the city gate. Whenever anyone came with a complaint to be placed before the king for a decision, Absalom would call out to him, "What town are you from?" He would answer, "Your servant is from one of the tribes of Israel." [3]Then Absalom would say to him, "Look, your claims are valid and proper, but there is no representative of the king to hear you."[t] [4]And Absalom would add, "If only I were appointed judge in the land![u] Then everyone who has a complaint or case could come to me and I would see that he gets justice."

[5]Also, whenever anyone approached him to bow down before him, Absalom would reach out his hand, take hold of him and kiss him. [6]Absalom behaved in this way toward all the Israelites who came to the king asking for justice, and so he stole the hearts[v] of the men of Israel.

[7]At the end of four[a] years, Absalom said to the king, "Let me go to Hebron and fulfill a vow I made to the LORD. [8]While your servant was living at Geshur[w] in Aram, I made this vow:[x] 'If the LORD takes me back to Jerusalem, I will worship the LORD in Hebron.[b]'"

[9]The king said to him, "Go in peace." So he went to Hebron.

[10]Then Absalom sent secret messengers throughout the tribes of Israel to say, "As soon as you hear the sound of the trumpets,[y] then say, 'Absalom is king in Hebron.' " [11]Two hundred men from Jerusalem had accompanied Absalom. They had been invited as guests and went quite innocently, knowing nothing about the matter. [12]While Absalom was offering sacrifices, he also sent for Ahithophel[z] the Gilonite, David's counselor,[a] to come from Giloh,[b] his hometown. And so the conspiracy gained strength, and Absalom's following kept on increasing.[c]

---

[a] 7 Some Septuagint manuscripts, Syriac and Josephus; Hebrew *forty*   [b] 8 Some Septuagint manuscripts; Hebrew does not have *in Hebron*.

Cross references

14:27
[j] 2Sa 18:18
[k] 2Sa 13:1

14:30
[l] Ex 9:31

14:31
[m] Jdg 15:5

14:32
[n] 2Sa 3:3
[o] 1Sa 20:8

14:33
[p] Ge 33:4; Lk 15:20

15:1
[q] 2Sa 12:11
[r] 1Sa 8:11; 1Ki 1:5

15:2
[s] Ge 23:10; 2Sa 19:8

15:3
[t] Pr 12:2
15:4
[u] Jdg 9:29

15:6
[v] Ro 16:18

15:8
[w] 2Sa 3:3; 13:37-38
[x] Ge 28:20

15:10
[y] 1Ki 1:34,39; 2Ki 9:13

15:12
[z] ver 31,34; 2Sa 16:15,23; 1Ch 27:33
[a] Job 19:14; Ps 41:9; 55:13; Jer 9:4 [b] Jos 15:51
[c] Ps 3:1

---

2 Samuel 15:1–12

Absalom, as crown prince, had legitimate power at his disposal, and he might have been expected one day to become king. But he saw no reason to wait for God's timing. The "heart" in Old Testament Hebrew referred to the seat of intellect as well as of emotion. Rather than merely winning the affections of the Israelites, Absalom "stole their hearts" (v. 6) by duping their minds. This was clearly the situation with regard to the 200 men accompanying him to Hebron. Once there, they would be indelibly marked as rebels.

Have you ever been tempted to justify rebellion as a way to accomplish something you were genuinely called to do? Many of David's psalms speak of waiting for the Lord (e.g., 33:20; 40:1), an attitude and behavior he had learned earlier in life (see "There and Then" for 1 Sam. 25:1–44). Such "waiting" is the same quality the New Testament calls "patience"—a characteristic of the spiritually mature. Christians don't use manipulation or rebellion to achieve their goals. Rather, we are to "imitate those who through faith and patience inherit what has been promised" (Heb. 6:12).

David Flees

13A messenger came and told David, "The hearts of the men of Israel are with Absalom."

15:14
d 2Sa 12:11;
1Ki 2:26; Ps 3 Title;
132:1 e 2Sa 19:9

14Then David said to all his officials who were with him in Jerusalem, "Come! We must flee, *d* or none of us will escape from Absalom. *e* We must leave immediately, or he will move quickly to overtake us and bring ruin upon us and put the city to the sword."

15The king's officials answered him, "Your servants are ready to do whatever our lord the king chooses."

15:16
f 2Sa 16:21-22; 20:3

16The king set out, with his entire household following him; but he left ten concubines*f* to take care of the palace. 17So the king set out, with all the people following him, and they halted at a place some distance away. 18All his men marched past

15:18
g 1Sa 30:14;
2Sa 8:18; 20:7,23;
1Ki 1:38,44;
1Ch 18:17
15:19
h 2Sa 18:2
i Ge 31:15
15:20
j 1Sa 23:13
k 2Sa 2:6

him, along with all the Kerethites*g* and Pelethites; and all the six hundred Gittites who had accompanied him from Gath marched before the king.

19The king said to Ittai*h* the Gittite, "Why should you come along with us? Go back and stay with King Absalom. You are a foreigner, *i* an exile from your homeland. 20You came only yesterday. And today shall I make you wander*j* about with us, when I do not know where I am going? Go back, and take your countrymen. May kindness and faithfulness*k* be with you."

15:21
l Ru 1:16-17;
Pr 17:17

21But Ittai replied to the king, "As surely as the LORD lives, and as my lord the king lives, wherever my lord the king may be, whether it means life or death, there will your servant be."*l*

22David said to Ittai, "Go ahead, march on." So Ittai the Gittite marched on with all his men and the families that were with him.

15:23
m 2Ch 29:16
15:24
n 2Sa 8:17
o Nu 4:15
p 1Sa 22:20

23The whole countryside wept aloud as all the people passed by. The king also crossed the Kidron Valley, *m* and all the people moved on toward the desert.

24Zadok*n* was there, too, and all the Levites who were with him were carrying the ark*o* of the covenant of God. They set down the ark of God, and Abiathar*p* offered sacrifices*a* until all the people had finished leaving the city.

15:25
q Ex 15:13; Ps 43:3;
Jer 25:30
15:26
r 1Sa 3:18;
2Sa 22:20; 1Ki 10:9
15:27
s 1Sa 9:9
t 2Sa 17:17
15:28
u 2Sa 17:16

25Then the king said to Zadok, "Take the ark of God back into the city. If I find favor in the LORD's eyes, he will bring me back and let me see it and his dwelling place*q* again. 26But if he says, 'I am not pleased with you,' then I am ready; let him do to me whatever seems good to him.*r*"

27The king also said to Zadok the priest, "Aren't you a seer?*s* Go back to the city in peace, with your son Ahimaaz and Jonathan*t* son of Abiathar. You and Abiathar take your two sons with you. 28I will wait at the fords*u* in the desert until word comes from you to inform me." 29So Zadok and Abiathar took the ark of God back to Jerusalem and stayed there.

15:30
v 2Sa 19:4; Ps 126:6
w Est 6:12;
Isa 20:2-4
15:31
x ver 12; 2Sa 16:23;
17:14,23

30But David continued up the Mount of Olives, weeping*v* as he went; his head *w* was covered and he was barefoot. All the people with him covered their heads too and were weeping as they went up. 31Now David had been told, "Ahithophel*x* is among the conspirators with Absalom." So David prayed, "O LORD, turn Ahithophel's counsel into foolishness."

32When David arrived at the summit, where people used to worship God, Hushai

---

a 24 Or Abiathar went up

---

2 Samuel 15:13–37

The text emphasizes the foreign troops who had remained loyal to David over the years. The Kerethites and Pelethites constituted a royal bodyguard of crack troops he had assembled while in exile. David's magnanimous spirit is illustrated in his exchange with *Ittai the Gittite (cf. 18:2). David released Ittai and his fellow Philistines from further commitment. Ittai's moving statement of devotion to David, in life or in death, reminds us of Ruth's classic expression of loyalty to Naomi (Ruth 1:16–17).*

How seriously do you take your allegiance to Christ? Loyalty is in short supply in our fickle world. We, as individuals and as the church, can be easily swayed by the winds of opportunity and advantage. Giving of ourselves for an apparently dying cause runs counter to all our instincts. But this kind of fierce loyalty is precisely what Jesus demands of his followers. Like David's passionately loyal foreign troops, we are to attach ourselves personally to our Leader and, from the deepest recesses of our love and appreciation, offer him our undying faithfulness.

the Arkite[y] was there to meet him, his robe torn and dust[z] on his head. 33David said to him, "If you go with me, you will be a burden[a] to me. 34But if you return to the city and say to Absalom, 'I will be your servant, O king; I was your father's servant in the past, but now I will be your servant,'[b] then you can help me by frustrating Ahithophel's advice. 35Won't the priests Zadok and Abiathar be there with you? Tell them anything you hear in the king's palace.[c] 36Their two sons, Ahimaaz son of Zadok and Jonathan[d] son of Abiathar, are there with them. Send them to me with anything you hear."

37So David's friend Hushai[e] arrived at Jerusalem as Absalom[f] was entering the city.

David and Ziba

16 When David had gone a short distance beyond the summit, there was Ziba,[g] the steward of Mephibosheth, waiting to meet him. He had a string of donkeys saddled and loaded with two hundred loaves of bread, a hundred cakes of raisins, a hundred cakes of figs and a skin of wine.[h]

2The king asked Ziba, "Why have you brought these?"

Ziba answered, "The donkeys are for the king's household to ride on, the bread and fruit are for the men to eat, and the wine is to refresh[i] those who become exhausted in the desert."

3The king then asked, "Where is your master's grandson?"[j]

Ziba said to him, "He is staying in Jerusalem, because he thinks, 'Today the house of Israel will give me back my grandfather's kingdom.' "

4Then the king said to Ziba, "All that belonged to Mephibosheth is now yours."

"I humbly bow," Ziba said. "May I find favor in your eyes, my lord the king."

Shimei Curses David

5As King David approached Bahurim,[k] a man from the same clan as Saul's family came out from there. His name was Shimei[l] son of Gera, and he cursed[m] as he came out. 6He pelted David and all the king's officials with stones, though all the troops and the special guard were on David's right and left. 7As he cursed, Shimei said, "Get out, get out, you man of blood, you scoundrel! 8The LORD has repaid you for all the blood you shed in the household of Saul, in whose place you have reigned.[n] The LORD has handed the kingdom over to your son Absalom. You have come to ruin because you are a man of blood!"

9Then Abishai[o] son of Zeruiah said to the king, "Why should this dead dog curse my lord the king? Let me go over and cut off his head."[p]

10But the king said, "What do you and I have in common, you sons of Zeruiah?[q]

15:32
y Jos 16:2 z 2Sa 1:2
15:33
a 2Sa 19:35
15:34
b 2Sa 16:19
15:35
c 2Sa 17:15-16
15:36
d ver 27; 2Sa 17:17
15:37
e 2Sa 16:16-17;
1Ch 27:33
f 2Sa 16:15

16:1
g 2Sa 9:1-13
h 1Sa 25:18

16:2
i 2Sa 17:27-29

16:3
j 2Sa 9:9-10;
19:26-27

16:5
k 2Sa 3:16
l 2Sa 19:16-23;
1Ki 2:8-9,36,44
m Ex 22:28

16:8
n 2Sa 21:9

16:9
o 2Sa 9:8
p Ex 22:28; Lk 9:54
16:10
q 2Sa 19:22

---

2 Samuel 16:1–4

Chapter 9 has prepared us for this encounter. Ziba, the steward of Saul's house, was responsible for Mephibosheth's welfare (9:9–11). The motives for his support of David during the crisis are unclear. He may have seen the insurrection as an opportunity to ingratiate himself to David at Mephibosheth's expense. Mephibosheth himself would deny the charges in 19:24–28, and it does seem likely that Ziba was the real scoundrel.

Absalom's rebellion forced many characters in chapters 15–19 to choose sides. Sometimes life's circumstances require us to take a position about a church leader, boss, or friend. When the arrows are flying, it's often as hard for us to decide what to do as it was for the ancients. But a politically safe choice may not be ethically or morally correct. Ask for wisdom in these situations; God has offered guidance to anyone who asks (cf. James 1:2–5). Then be prepared to follow his direction, no matter what the personal cost.

2 Samuel 16:5–14

Shimei, Saul's relative, may have been expressing resentment over what he saw as David's illegitimate rise to power (including the ascendancy of Judah over Benjamin). But 1 and 2 Samuel have been partially devoted to contradicting such a claim. Shimei was right that David was accursed, but wrong about the reasons. The rebellion resulted from David's sins of adultery and murder—not from any wrongdoing regarding Saul. Nor was Shimei justified in pronouncing the curse himself, an action he would later regret (19:18–20; see 1 Kings 2:8–9,36–46).

Judgers beware! We as Christians are justified in exposing and condemning actions and practices in the church we know to be sinful (this is indeed a *requirement*; cf. Eph. 5:11). But we are to exercise extreme caution in assessing someone else's heart and motives. Jesus warned his followers repeatedly about the folly of such presumption (e.g., Matt. 7:1–5). One day in heaven we will know all things. One of our responses will no doubt be shocked surprise at our own grave miscalculations (cf. 1 Cor. 4:5).

16:10
r Ro 9:20
16:11
s 2Sa 12:11
t Ge 45:5

16:12
u Ps 4:1; 25:18
v Dt 23:5; Ro 8:28
w Ps 109:28

16:14
x 2Sa 17:2

16:15
y 2Sa 15:37
z 2Sa 15:12
16:16
a 2Sa 15:37

16:17
b 2Sa 19:25

16:19
c 2Sa 15:34

16:22
d 2Sa 12:11-12; 15:16
16:23
e 2Sa 17:14,23
f 2Sa 15:12

17:2
g 2Sa 16:14
h 1Ki 22:31; Zec 13:7

17:5
i 2Sa 15:32

17:8
j Hos 13:8
k 1Sa 16:18

17:9
l Jer 41:9

If he is cursing because the LORD said to him, 'Curse David,' who can ask, 'Why do you do this?' " r

11 David then said to Abishai and all his officials, "My son, s who is of my own flesh, is trying to take my life. How much more, then, this Benjamite! Leave him alone; let him curse, for the LORD has told him to. t 12 It may be that the LORD will see my distress u and repay me with good v for the cursing I am receiving today. w"

13 So David and his men continued along the road while Shimei was going along the hillside opposite him, cursing as he went and throwing stones at him and showering him with dirt. 14 The king and all the people with him arrived at their destination exhausted. x And there he refreshed himself.

The Advice of Ahithophel and Hushai

15 Meanwhile, Absalom y and all the men of Israel came to Jerusalem, and Ahithophel z was with him. 16 Then Hushai a the Arkite, David's friend, went to Absalom and said to him, "Long live the king! Long live the king!"

17 Absalom asked Hushai, "Is this the love you show your friend? Why didn't you go with your friend?" b

18 Hushai said to Absalom, "No, the one chosen by the LORD, by these people, and by all the men of Israel—his I will be, and I will remain with him. 19 Furthermore, whom should I serve? Should I not serve the son? Just as I served your father, so I will serve you." c

20 Absalom said to Ahithophel, "Give us your advice. What should we do?"

21 Ahithophel answered, "Lie with your father's concubines whom he left to take care of the palace. Then all Israel will hear that you have made yourself a stench in your father's nostrils, and the hands of everyone with you will be strengthened." 22 So they pitched a tent for Absalom on the roof, and he lay with his father's concubines in the sight of all Israel. d

23 Now in those days the advice e Ahithophel gave was like that of one who inquires of God. That was how both David f and Absalom regarded all of Ahithophel's advice.

17 Ahithophel said to Absalom, "I would a choose twelve thousand men and set out tonight in pursuit of David. 2 I would b attack him while he is weary and weak. g I would b strike him with terror, and then all the people with him will flee. I would b strike down only the king h 3 and bring all the people back to you. The death of the man you seek will mean the return of all; all the people will be unharmed." 4 This plan seemed good to Absalom and to all the elders of Israel.

5 But Absalom said, "Summon also Hushai i the Arkite, so we can hear what he has to say." 6 When Hushai came to him, Absalom said, "Ahithophel has given this advice. Should we do what he says? If not, give us your opinion."

7 Hushai replied to Absalom, "The advice Ahithophel has given is not good this time. 8 You know your father and his men; they are fighters, and as fierce as a wild bear robbed of her cubs. j Besides, your father is an experienced fighter; k he will not spend the night with the troops. 9 Even now, he is hidden in a cave or some other place. l If he should attack your troops first, c whoever hears about it will say, 'There has been a slaughter among the troops who follow Absalom.' 10 Then even the

a 1 Or *Let me*   b 2 Or *will*   c 9 Or *When some of the men fall at the first attack*

---

2 Samuel 16:15—17:29

Ahithophel, Bathsheba's grandfather (cf. 11:3; 23:34), may have joined Absalom's conspiracy in retaliation for David's treatment of Bathsheba and Uriah. His first bit of advice sounds strange to modern ears. Yet royal women played a significant political role in ancient societies. Sexual relations with a king's wife or concubine *constituted a claim on the throne—a common practice* when a king was replaced with a new dynasty. Absalom's follow-through on this suggestion represented an irreversible break between himself and David and would have devastating consequences for the women (20:3).

Ahithophel's military strategy for eliminating David and securing Absalom's rule was "good advice" (17:14) that would likely have been successful. But God saw to it that Ahithophel's advice was overruled by Hushai's. Many people today still speak with "worldly" wisdom (see 1 Cor. 2:1–10). As Christians in a complex society we are to carefully weigh the competing voices that bombard our ears, remaining open to truth from whatever source God may provide it. Sensitivity to the Spirit and knowledge of God's Word will keep us from following bad advice (cf. Ps. 119:24).

bravest soldier, whose heart is like the heart of a lion,[m] will melt[n] with fear, for all Israel knows that your father is a fighter and that those with him are brave.[o]

[11] "So I advise you: Let all Israel, from Dan to Beersheba[p]—as numerous as the sand[q] on the seashore—be gathered to you, with you yourself leading them into battle. [12]Then we will attack him wherever he may be found, and we will fall on him as dew settles on the ground. Neither he nor any of his men will be left alive. [13]If he withdraws into a city, then all Israel will bring ropes to that city, and we will drag it down to the valley[r] until not even a piece of it can be found."

[14]Absalom and all the men of Israel said, "The advice[s] of Hushai the Arkite is better than that of Ahithophel."[t] For the LORD had determined to frustrate[u] the good advice of Ahithophel in order to bring disaster[v] on Absalom.[w]

[15]Hushai told Zadok and Abiathar, the priests, "Ahithophel has advised Absalom and the elders of Israel to do such and such, but I have advised them to do so and so. [16]Now send a message immediately and tell David, 'Do not spend the night at the fords in the desert;[x] cross over without fail, or the king and all the people with him will be swallowed up.[y]'"

[17]Jonathan[z] and Ahimaaz were staying at En Rogel.[a] A servant girl was to go and inform them, and they were to go and tell King David, for they could not risk being seen entering the city. [18]But a young man saw them and told Absalom. So the two of them left quickly and went to the house of a man in Bahurim.[b] He had a well in his courtyard, and they climbed down into it. [19]His wife took a covering and spread it out over the opening of the well and scattered grain over it. No one knew anything about it.[c]

[20]When Absalom's men came to the woman[d] at the house, they asked, "Where are Ahimaaz and Jonathan?"

The woman answered them, "They crossed over the brook."[a] The men searched but found no one, so they returned to Jerusalem.

[21]After the men had gone, the two climbed out of the well and went to inform King David. They said to him, "Set out and cross the river at once; Ahithophel has advised such and such against you." [22]So David and all the people with him set out and crossed the Jordan. By daybreak, no one was left who had not crossed the Jordan.

[23]When Ahithophel saw that his advice[e] had not been followed, he saddled his donkey and set out for his house in his hometown. He put his house in order[f] and then hanged himself. So he died and was buried in his father's tomb.

[24]David went to Mahanaim,[g] and Absalom crossed the Jordan with all the men of Israel. [25]Absalom had appointed Amasa[h] over the army in place of Joab. Amasa was the son of a man named Jether,[b][i] an Israelite[c] who had married Abigail,[d] the daughter of Nahash and sister of Zeruiah the mother of Joab. [26]The Israelites and Absalom camped in the land of Gilead.

[27]When David came to Mahanaim, Shobi son of Nahash[j] from Rabbah[k] of the Ammonites, and Makir[l] son of Ammiel from Lo Debar, and Barzillai[m] the Gileadite[n] from Rogelim [28]brought bedding and bowls and articles of pottery. They also brought wheat and barley, flour and roasted grain, beans and lentils,[e] [29]honey and curds, sheep, and cheese from cows' milk for David and his people to eat.[o] For they said, "The people have become hungry and tired and thirsty in the desert.[p]"

Absalom's Death

18 David mustered the men who were with him and appointed over them commanders of thousands and commanders of hundreds. [2]David sent the troops out[q]—a third under the command of Joab, a third under Joab's brother Abishai[r] son of Zeruiah, and a third under Ittai[s] the Gittite. The king told the troops, "I myself will surely march out with you."

[3]But the men said, "You must not go out; if we are forced to flee, they won't care

---

[a] **20** Or *"They passed by the sheep pen toward the water."*   [b] **25** Hebrew *Ithra*, a variant of *Jether*
[c] **25** Hebrew and some Septuagint manuscripts; other Septuagint manuscripts (see also 1 Chron. 2:17) *Ishmaelite* or *Jezreelite*   [d] **25** Hebrew *Abigal*, a variant of *Abigail*   [e] **28** Most Septuagint manuscripts and Syriac; Hebrew *lentils, and roasted grain*

17:10
[m] 1Ch 12:8
[n] Jos 2:9,11;
Eze 21:15
[o] 2Sa 23:8;
1Ch 11:11
17:11
[p] Jdg 20:1
[q] Ge 12:2; 22:17;
Jos 11:4
17:13
[r] Mic 1:6
17:14
[s] 2Sa 16:23
[t] 2Sa 15:12
[u] 2Sa 15:34;
Ne 4:15 [v] Ps 9:16
[w] 2Ch 10:8

17:16
[x] 2Sa 15:28
[y] 2Sa 15:35
17:17
[z] 2Sa 15:27,36
[a] Jos 15:7; 18:16
17:18
[b] 2Sa 3:16; 16:5

17:19
[c] Jos 2:6
17:20
[d] Ex 1:19;
Jos 2:3-5;
1Sa 19:12-17

17:23
[e] 2Sa 15:12; 16:23
[f] 2Ki 20:1; Mt 27:5

17:24
[g] Ge 32:2; 2Sa 2:8
17:25
[h] 2Sa 19:13;
20:4,9-12;
1Ki 2:5,32;
1Ch 12:18
[i] 1Ch 2:13-17

17:27
[j] 1Sa 11:1
[k] Dt 3:11;
2Sa 10:1-2;
12:26,29 [l] 2Sa 9:4
[m] 2Sa 19:31-39;
1Ki 2:7 [n] 2Sa 19:31;
Ezr 2:61
17:29
[o] 1Ch 12:40
[p] 2Sa 16:2;
Ro 12:13

18:2
[q] Jdg 7:16;
1Sa 11:11
[r] 1Sa 26:6
[s] 2Sa 15:19

18:3
t 1Sa 18:7
u 2Sa 21:17

about us. Even if half of us die, they won't care; but you are worth ten[t] thousand of us.[a] It would be better now for you to give us support from the city."[u]

⁴The king answered, "I will do whatever seems best to you."

So the king stood beside the gate while all the men marched out in units of hundreds and of thousands. ⁵The king commanded Joab, Abishai and Ittai, "Be gentle with the young man Absalom for my sake." And all the troops heard the king giving orders concerning Absalom to each of the commanders.

18:6
v Jos 17:18

⁶The army marched into the field to fight Israel, and the battle took place in the forest[v] of Ephraim. ⁷There the army of Israel was defeated by David's men, and the casualties that day were great—twenty thousand men. ⁸The battle spread out over the whole countryside, and the forest claimed more lives that day than the sword.

18:9
w 2Sa 14:26

⁹Now Absalom happened to meet David's men. He was riding his mule, and as the mule went under the thick branches of a large oak, Absalom's head[w] got caught in the tree. He was left hanging in midair, while the mule he was riding kept on going.

¹⁰When one of the men saw this, he told Joab, "I just saw Absalom hanging in an oak tree."

18:11
x 2Sa 3:39
y 1Sa 18:4

¹¹Joab said to the man who had told him this, "What! You saw him? Why didn't you strike[x] him to the ground right there? Then I would have had to give you ten shekels[b] of silver and a warrior's belt.[y]"

¹²But the man replied, "Even if a thousand shekels[c] were weighed out into my hands, I would not lift my hand against the king's son. In our hearing the king commanded you and Abishai and Ittai, 'Protect the young man Absalom for my sake.[d]'

18:13
z 2Sa 14:19-20

¹³And if I had put my life in jeopardy[e]—and nothing is hidden from the king[z]— you would have kept your distance from me."

18:14
a 2Sa 2:18; 14:30

¹⁴Joab[a] said, "I'm not going to wait like this for you." So he took three javelins in his hand and plunged them into Absalom's heart while Absalom was still alive in the oak tree. ¹⁵And ten of Joab's armor-bearers surrounded Absalom, struck him and killed him.[b]

18:15
b 2Sa 12:10
18:16
c 2Sa 2:28; 20:22

¹⁶Then Joab[c] sounded the trumpet, and the troops stopped pursuing Israel, for Joab halted them. ¹⁷They took Absalom, threw him into a big pit in the forest and piled up[d] a large heap of rocks[e] over him. Meanwhile, all the Israelites fled to their homes.

18:17
d Jos 7:26
e Jos 8:29

¹⁸During his lifetime Absalom had taken a pillar and erected it in the King's Valley[f] as a monument[g] to himself, for he thought, "I have no son[h] to carry on the memory of my name." He named the pillar after himself, and it is called Absalom's Monument to this day.

18:18
f Ge 14:17
g Ge 50:5;
Nu 32:42;
1Sa 15:12
h 2Sa 14:27

---

a 3 Two Hebrew manuscripts, some Septuagint manuscripts and Vulgate; most Hebrew manuscripts *care; for now there are ten thousand like us*   b 11 That is, about 4 ounces (about 115 grams)
c 12 That is, about 25 pounds (about 11 kilograms)   d 12 A few Hebrew manuscripts, Septuagint, Vulgate and Syriac; most Hebrew manuscripts may be translated *Absalom, whoever you may be.*
e 13 Or *Otherwise, if I had acted treacherously toward him*

---

2 Samuel 18:1–18

Hushai's delaying tactics had given David enough time to reach Mahanaim (17:24), which was probably well fortified, and to organize his troops into three companies. The forest was difficult terrain for fighting, giving the advantage to David's men who, though in the minority, specialized in guerilla warfare.

This passage is rich in symbolism. The mule was the usual mount for princes and kings. As Absalom lost his mule from under him, so he lost his royal "seat." His suspension "in midair" indicates that the rebellion had left him without ground beneath his feet, powerless to defend himself, much less lead a nation. Most interpreters feel that he was caught in the tree by his luxuriant hair (cf. 14:25–26). Here was a promising young man entangled by his own pride.

Verse 18 seems an incongruous lull in a live action picture. But if we pause at this still frame, we find the break worthwhile. Absalom had experienced consternation over the lack of a son to carry on his legacy. We know from 14:27 that three sons had been born to him, but evidently they had died in infancy or childhood. How often don't we, when faced with life's disappointments, erect our own private self-monuments? How much better to take our hurts to the Healer for his touch! You need no monument to promote "the memory of [your] name." God never forgets his own (Isa. 49:14–16).

2 Samuel 18:19—19:8a

When David forced Ahimaaz to "stand aside" and wait for the Cushite to deliver the vital piece of missing information, the reader is left waiting for the moment when David learns of Absalom's death. Joab

David Mourns

[19]Now Ahimaaz[i] son of Zadok said, "Let me run and take the news to the king that the LORD has delivered him from the hand of his enemies.[j]"

[20]"You are not the one to take the news today," Joab told him. "You may take the news another time, but you must not do so today, because the king's son is dead."

[21]Then Joab said to a Cushite, "Go, tell the king what you have seen." The Cushite bowed down before Joab and ran off.

[22]Ahimaaz son of Zadok again said to Joab, "Come what may, please let me run behind the Cushite."

But Joab replied, "My son, why do you want to go? You don't have any news that will bring you a reward."

[23]He said, "Come what may, I want to run."

So Joab said, "Run!" Then Ahimaaz ran by way of the plain[a] and outran the Cushite.

[24]While David was sitting between the inner and outer gates, the watchman[k] went up to the roof of the gateway by the wall. As he looked out, he saw a man running alone. [25]The watchman called out to the king and reported it.

The king said, "If he is alone, he must have good news." And the man came closer and closer.

[26]Then the watchman saw another man running, and he called down to the gatekeeper, "Look, another man running alone!"

The king said, "He must be bringing good news,[l] too."

[27]The watchman said, "It seems to me that the first one runs like[m] Ahimaaz son of Zadok."

"He's a good man," the king said. "He comes with good news."

[28]Then Ahimaaz called out to the king, "All is well!" He bowed down before the king with his face to the ground and said, "Praise be to the LORD your God! He has delivered up the men who lifted their hands against my lord the king."

[29]The king asked, "Is the young man Absalom safe?"

Ahimaaz answered, "I saw great confusion just as Joab was about to send the king's servant and me, your servant, but I don't know what it was."

[30]The king said, "Stand aside and wait here." So he stepped aside and stood there.

[31]Then the Cushite arrived and said, "My lord the king, hear the good news! The LORD has delivered you today from all who rose up against you."

[32]The king asked the Cushite, "Is the young man Absalom safe?"

The Cushite replied, "May the enemies of my lord the king and all who rise up to harm you be like that young man."[n]

[33]The king was shaken. He went up to the room over the gateway and wept. As he went, he said: "O my son Absalom! My son, my son Absalom! If only I had died[o] instead of you—O Absalom, my son, my son!"[p]

19 Joab was told, "The king is weeping and mourning for Absalom." [2]And for the whole army the victory that day was turned into mourning, because on that day the troops heard it said, "The king is grieving for his son." [3]The men stole into the city that day as men steal in who are ashamed when they flee from battle. [4]The king covered his face and cried aloud, "O my son Absalom! O Absalom, my son, my son!"

---

[a] 23 That is, the plain of the Jordan

Marginal cross-references

18:19 [i] 2Sa 15:36 [j] ver 31; Jdg 11:36

18:24 [k] 1Sa 14:16; 2Sa 19:8; 2Ki 9:17; Jer 51:12

18:26 [l] 1Ki 1:42; Isa 52:7; 61:1
18:27 [m] 2Ki 9:20

18:32 [n] Jdg 5:31; 1Sa 25:26

18:33 [o] Ex 32:32 [p] Ge 43:14;

---

and David's military may have anticipated a mixed response from the king to the rebellion's end, but there was no joy here—only bitter grief.

David's sense of loss dominates the account. His anguished "my son" is repeated five times in 18:33 and another three in 19:4. He seems to have gathered the past, with all his own sins and those of his family, into one defining moment of remorse and sorrow.

📖 The Bible draws us in by capturing the bittersweet essence of being human. But the real pull of its pages is the reality that God's Word provides the ultimate answers to life's devastations. Life for David would go on, even if he couldn't bear to imagine it without Absalom. When have you experienced grief so profound that you despaired of your ability to go on? Was your own misguided course of action a factor in the equation? How has God met your need?

⁵Then Joab went into the house to the king and said, "Today you have humiliated all your men, who have just saved your life and the lives of your sons and daughters and the lives of your wives and concubines. ⁶You love those who hate you and hate those who love you. You have made it clear today that the commanders and their men mean nothing to you. I see that you would be pleased if Absalom were alive today and all of us were dead. ⁷Now go out and encourage your men. I swear by the LORD that if you don't go out, not a man will be left with you by nightfall. This will be worse for you than all the calamities that have come upon you from your youth till now." *q*

⁸So the king got up and took his seat in the gateway. When the men were told, "The king is sitting in the gateway, *r*" they all came before him.

David Returns to Jerusalem

Meanwhile, the Israelites had fled to their homes. ⁹Throughout the tribes of Israel, the people were all arguing with each other, saying, "The king delivered us from the hand of our enemies; he is the one who rescued us from the hand of the Philistines. *s* But now he has fled the country because of Absalom; *t* ¹⁰and Absalom, whom we anointed to rule over us, has died in battle. So why do you say nothing about bringing the king back?"

¹¹King David sent this message to Zadok *u* and Abiathar, the priests: "Ask the elders of Judah, 'Why should you be the last to bring the king back to his palace, since what is being said throughout Israel has reached the king at his quarters? ¹²You are my brothers, my own flesh and blood. So why should you be the last to bring back the king?' ¹³And say to Amasa, *v* 'Are you not my own flesh and blood? *w* May God deal with me, be it ever so severely, *x* if from now on you are not the commander of my army in place of Joab.' *y* "

¹⁴He won over the hearts of all the men of Judah as though they were one man. They sent word to the king, "Return, you and all your men." ¹⁵Then the king returned and went as far as the Jordan.

Now the men of Judah had come to Gilgal *z* to go out and meet the king and bring him across the Jordan. ¹⁶Shimei *a* son of Gera, the Benjamite from Bahurim, hurried down with the men of Judah to meet King David. ¹⁷With him were a thousand Benjamites, along with Ziba, *b* the steward of Saul's household, *c* and his fifteen sons and twenty servants. They rushed to the Jordan, where the king was. ¹⁸They crossed at the ford to take the king's household over and to do whatever he wished.

When Shimei son of Gera crossed the Jordan, he fell prostrate before the king ¹⁹and said to him, "May my lord not hold me guilty. Do not remember how your servant did wrong on the day my lord the king left Jerusalem. *d* May the king put it out of his mind. ²⁰For I your servant know that I have sinned, but today I have come here as the first of the whole house of Joseph to come down and meet my lord the king."

²¹Then Abishai *e* son of Zeruiah said, "Shouldn't Shimei be put to death for this? He cursed *f* the LORD's anointed." *g*

²²David replied, "What do you and I have in common, you sons of Zeruiah? *h* This day you have become my adversaries! Should anyone be put to death in Israel today? *i* Do I not know that today I am king over Israel?" ²³So the king said to Shimei, "You shall not die." And the king promised him on oath. *j*

²⁴Mephibosheth, *k* Saul's grandson, also went down to meet the king. He had not taken care of his feet or trimmed his mustache or washed his clothes from the day the king left until the day he returned safely. ²⁵When he came from Jerusalem to meet the king, the king asked him, "Why didn't you go with me, *l* Mephibosheth?"

2 Samuel 19:8b–43
The end of Absalom's conspiracy didn't end David's troubles. The shaky union in Israel threatened to dissolve into intertribal conflict at the slightest provocation. The northern Israelites complained that Judah had been given pride of place in the parade across the river. The Judahites responded with an appeal to their closer relationship to David, to which the Israelites countered that they had more tribes. The narrator leaves us with the alarming note that the debate only escalated. The stage was set for open conflict—again fulfilling Nathan's prophecy (12:10).

26He said, "My lord the king, since I your servant am lame,[m] I said, 'I will have my donkey saddled and will ride on it, so I can go with the king.' But Ziba[n] my servant betrayed me. 27And he has slandered your servant to my lord the king. My lord the king is like an angel[o] of God; so do whatever pleases you. 28All my grandfather's descendants deserved nothing but death[p] from my lord the king, but you gave your servant a place among those who eat at your table.[q] So what right do I have to make any more appeals to the king?"

29The king said to him, "Why say more? I order you and Ziba to divide the fields."

30Mephibosheth said to the king, "Let him take everything, now that my lord the king has arrived home safely."

31Barzillai[r] the Gileadite also came down from Rogelim to cross the Jordan with the king and to send him on his way from there. 32Now Barzillai was a very old man, eighty years of age. He had provided for the king during his stay in Mahanaim, for he was a very wealthy[s] man. 33The king said to Barzillai, "Cross over with me and stay with me in Jerusalem, and I will provide for you."

34But Barzillai answered the king, "How many more years will I live, that I should go up to Jerusalem with the king? 35I am now eighty[t] years old. Can I tell the difference between what is good and what is not? Can your servant taste what he eats and drinks? Can I still hear the voices of men and women singers?[u] Why should your servant be an added[v] burden to my lord the king? 36Your servant will cross over the Jordan with the king for a short distance, but why should the king reward me in this way? 37Let your servant return, that I may die in my own town near the tomb of my father[w] and mother. But here is your servant Kimham.[x] Let him cross over with my lord the king. Do for him whatever pleases you."

38The king said, "Kimham shall cross over with me, and I will do for him whatever pleases you. And anything you desire from me I will do for you."

39So all the people crossed the Jordan, and then the king crossed over. The king kissed Barzillai and gave him his blessing,[y] and Barzillai returned to his home.

40When the king crossed over to Gilgal, Kimham crossed with him. All the troops of Judah and half the troops of Israel had taken the king over.

41Soon all the men of Israel were coming to the king and saying to him, "Why did our brothers, the men of Judah, steal the king away and bring him and his household across the Jordan, together with all his men?"[z]

42All the men of Judah answered the men of Israel, "We did this because the king is closely related to us. Why are you angry about it? Have we eaten any of the king's provisions? Have we taken anything for ourselves?"

43Then the men of Israel[a] answered the men of Judah, "We have ten shares in the king; and besides, we have a greater claim on David than you have. So why do you treat us with contempt? Were we not the first to speak of bringing back our king?"

But the men of Judah responded even more harshly than the men of Israel.

Sheba Rebels Against David

20 Now a troublemaker named Sheba son of Bicri, a Benjamite, happened to be there. He sounded the trumpet and shouted,

"We have no share[b] in David,[c]
no part in Jesse's son![d]
Every man to his tent, O Israel!"

Cross-references

19:26 m Lev 21:18; n 2Sa 9:2
19:27 o 1Sa 29:9; 2Sa 14:17,20
19:28 p 2Sa 16:8; 21:6-9; q 2Sa 9:7,13
19:31 r 2Sa 17:27-29; 1Ki 2:7
19:32 s 1Sa 25:2; 2Sa 17:27
19:35 t Ps 90:10; u 2Ch 35:25; Ezr 2:65; Ecc 2:8; 12:1; Isa 5:11-12; v 2Sa 15:33
19:37 w Ge 49:29; 1Ki 2:7; x ver 40; Jer 41:17
19:39 y Ge 31:55; 47:7
19:41 z Jdg 8:1; 12:1
19:43 a 2Sa 5:1
20:1 b Ge 31:14; c Ge 29:14; 1Ki 12:16; d 1Sa 22:7-8; 2Ch 10:16

The bickering between the northern and southern tribes reminds us of how petty our power struggles must appear in God's eyes. Whether our conflict is on a personal front, in the political arena, or in a church/ministry setting, infighting can escalate into bitter rivalry and degenerate into demoralizing "win/lose" scenarios. Consider Jesus' response to James and John's request to receive favored positions in his kingdom (Mark 10:35–45). The principle still stands that humility and service are the means to true greatness.

2 Samuel 20:1–26

David rightly understood the seriousness of the northern revolt. He had held north and south together

475

20:3
e 2Sa 15:16;
16:21-22

20:4
f 2Sa 17:25; 19:13

20:6
g 2Sa 21:17

20:7
h 1Sa 30:14;
2Sa 8:18; 15:18;
1Ki 1:38

20:8
i Jos 9:3 j 2Sa 2:18

20:10
k Jdg 3:21;
2Sa 2:23; 3:27
l 1Ki 2:5

20:12
m 2Sa 2:23

20:14
n Nu 21:16
20:15
o 1Ki 15:20;
2Ki 15:29
p 2Ki 19:32;
Isa 37:33; Jer 6:6;
32:24
20:16
q 2Sa 14:2

20:19
r Dt 2:26
s 1Sa 26:19;
2Sa 21:3

2So all the men of Israel deserted David to follow Sheba son of Bicri. But the men of Judah stayed by their king all the way from the Jordan to Jerusalem.

3When David returned to his palace in Jerusalem, he took the ten concubines[e] he had left to take care of the palace and put them in a house under guard. He provided for them, but did not lie with them. They were kept in confinement till the day of their death, living as widows.

4Then the king said to Amasa,[f] "Summon the men of Judah to come to me within three days, and be here yourself." 5But when Amasa went to summon Judah, he took longer than the time the king had set for him.

6David said to Abishai,[g] "Now Sheba son of Bicri will do us more harm than Absalom did. Take your master's men and pursue him, or he will find fortified cities and escape from us." 7So Joab's men and the Kerethites[h] and Pelethites and all the mighty warriors went out under the command of Abishai. They marched out from Jerusalem to pursue Sheba son of Bicri.

8While they were at the great rock in Gibeon,[i] Amasa came to meet them. Joab[j] was wearing his military tunic, and strapped over it at his waist was a belt with a dagger in its sheath. As he stepped forward, it dropped out of its sheath.

9Joab said to Amasa, "How are you, my brother?" Then Joab took Amasa by the beard with his right hand to kiss him. 10Amasa was not on his guard against the dagger[k] in Joab's[l] hand, and Joab plunged it into his belly, and his intestines spilled out on the ground. Without being stabbed again, Amasa died. Then Joab and his brother Abishai pursued Sheba son of Bicri.

11One of Joab's men stood beside Amasa and said, "Whoever favors Joab, and whoever is for David, let him follow Joab!" 12Amasa lay wallowing in his blood in the middle of the road, and the man saw that all the troops came to a halt[m] there. When he realized that everyone who came up to Amasa stopped, he dragged him from the road into a field and threw a garment over him. 13After Amasa had been removed from the road, all the men went on with Joab to pursue Sheba son of Bicri.

14Sheba passed through all the tribes of Israel to Abel Beth Maacah[a] and through the entire region of the Berites,[n] who gathered together and followed him. 15All the troops with Joab came and besieged Sheba in Abel Beth Maacah.[o] They built a siege ramp[p] up to the city, and it stood against the outer fortifications. While they were battering the wall to bring it down, 16a wise woman[q] called from the city, "Listen! Listen! Tell Joab to come here so I can speak to him." 17He went toward her, and she asked, "Are you Joab?"

"I am," he answered.

She said, "Listen to what your servant has to say."

"I'm listening," he said.

18She continued, "Long ago they used to say, 'Get your answer at Abel,' and that settled it. 19We are the peaceful[r] and faithful in Israel. You are trying to destroy a city that is a mother in Israel. Why do you want to swallow up the Lord's inheritance?"[s]

20"Far be it from me!" Joab replied, "Far be it from me to swallow up or destroy! 21That is not the case. A man named Sheba son of Bicri, from the hill country of Ephraim, has lifted up his hand against the king, against David. Hand over this one man, and I'll withdraw from the city."

---

a 14 Or *Abel, even Beth Maacah*; also in verse 15

---

through the sheer force of his personality, but after Absalom's rebellion he returned a weakened monarch. Sheba's revolt threatened to tear apart the kingdom.

While Joab, the famous commander, brought his considerable military might to bear against the city of Abel, the unnamed woman used only words of wisdom in negotiating with Joab and her own village. The text seems to lift the two as examples of power used in different ways. In the end, the reader may conclude that the wise woman exceeded the general in power.

Our society faces multiple issues that threaten to tear apart families, churches, governments, businesses—sometimes our very souls. We are bombarded by persuasive messages, and the power of words, for good or evil, is far-reaching (James 3:3–9). We as Christians are wise to speak carefully and season our words with compassion and courage, especially in the face of conflict. God has, after all, given us the solemn responsibility of relaying his "message of reconciliation" (2 Cor. 5:18–19). What peace-making role are you playing?

The woman said to Joab, "His head ^{t} will be thrown to you from the wall."
^{22}Then the woman went to all the people with her wise advice, ^{u} and they cut off the head of Sheba son of Bicri and threw it to Joab. So he sounded the trumpet, and his men dispersed from the city, each returning to his home. And Joab went back to the king in Jerusalem.

^{23}Joab ^{v} was over Israel's entire army; Benaiah son of Jehoiada was over the Kerethites and Pelethites; ^{24}Adoniram $^{a\,w}$ was in charge of forced labor; Jehoshaphat ^{x} son of Ahilud was recorder; ^{25}Sheva was secretary; Zadok ^{y} and Abiathar were priests; ^{26}and Ira the Jairite was David's priest.

The Gibeonites Avenged

21 During the reign of David, there was a famine ^{z} for three successive years; so David sought ^{a} the face of the LORD. The LORD said, "It is on account of Saul and his blood-stained house; it is because he put the Gibeonites to death."

^{2}The king summoned the Gibeonites ^{b} and spoke to them. (Now the Gibeonites were not a part of Israel but were survivors of the Amorites; the Israelites had sworn to ⌊spare⌋ them, but Saul in his zeal for Israel and Judah had tried to annihilate them.) ^{3}David asked the Gibeonites, "What shall I do for you? How shall I make amends so that you will bless the LORD's inheritance?" ^{c}

^{4}The Gibeonites answered him, "We have no right to demand silver or gold from Saul or his family, nor do we have the right to put anyone in Israel to death." ^{d}

"What do you want me to do for you?" David asked.

^{5}They answered the king, "As for the man who destroyed us and plotted against us so that we have been decimated and have no place anywhere in Israel, ^{6}let seven of his male descendants be given to us to be killed and exposed ^{e} before the LORD at Gibeah of Saul—the LORD's chosen ^{f} one."

So the king said, "I will give them to you."

^{7}The king spared Mephibosheth ^{g} son of Jonathan, the son of Saul, because of the oath ^{h} before the LORD between David and Jonathan son of Saul. ^{8}But the king took Armoni and Mephibosheth, the two sons of Aiah's daughter Rizpah, ^{i} whom she had borne to Saul, together with the five sons of Saul's daughter Merab, ^{b} whom she had borne to Adriel son of Barzillai the Meholathite. ^{i} ^{9}He handed them over to the Gibeonites, who killed and exposed them on a hill before the LORD. All seven of them fell together; they were put to death ^{k} during the first days of the harvest, just as the barley harvest was beginning. ^{l}

^{10}Rizpah daughter of Aiah took sackcloth and spread it out for herself on a rock. From the beginning of the harvest till the rain poured down from the heavens on the bodies, she did not let the birds of the air touch them by day or the wild animals by night. ^{m} ^{11}When David was told what Aiah's daughter Rizpah, Saul's concubine, had done, ^{12}he went and took the bones of Saul ^{n} and his son Jonathan from the citizens of Jabesh Gilead. (They had taken them secretly from the public square at Beth Shan, ^{o} where the Philistines had hung ^{p} them after they struck Saul

---

^{a} 24 Some Septuagint manuscripts (see also 1 Kings 4:6 and 5:14); Hebrew *Adoram*
^{b} 8 Two Hebrew manuscripts, some Septuagint manuscripts and Syriac (see also 1 Samuel 18:19); most Hebrew and Septuagint manuscripts *Michal*

---

2 Samuel 21:1–14

The last four chapters of 2 Samuel form an epilogue pertaining to David's overall reign. Here David prayed fervently to determine the cause of a plague. God revealed to him that the famine was the result of Saul's hostilities against the Gibeonites. The text assumes knowledge of Joshua 9:3–27, in which the Gibeonites, non-Israelite residents of Canaan, had tricked Joshua into a peace treaty. We don't know the circumstances of Saul's attempt to destroy the Gibeonites in violation of this treaty. David sought restitution as a means of removing the guilt of Saul's actions.

David, concerned both with justice for the Gibeonites and loyalty to the house of Saul, faced a hard decision. Today our leaders are often pressured by competing interests and priorities. The best answer is a just compromise. Yet there is often a price to be paid: A layoff may save a company from going under, or higher taxes may fund programs to help poor families. As believers, our confidence rests in God to work for our good, even if the immediate result brings us loss (Rom. 8:28). When have you voted (in government or church) with the greater good—not your personal benefit—in view?

20:21 *t* 2Sa 4:8
20:22 *u* Ecc 9:13
20:23 *v* 2Sa 2:28; 8:16-18; 24:2
20:24 *w* 1Ki 4:6; 5:14; 12:18; 2Ch 10:18 *x* 2Sa 8:16; 1Ki 4:3
20:25 *y* 1Sa 2:35; 2Sa 8:17
21:1 *z* Ge 12:10; Dt 32:24 *a* Ex 32:11
21:2 *b* Jos 9:15
21:3 *c* 1Sa 26:19; 2Sa 20:19
21:4 *d* Nu 35:33-34
21:6 *e* Nu 25:4 *f* 1Sa 10:24
21:7 *g* 2Sa 4:4 *h* 1Sa 18:3; 20:8,15; 2Sa 9:7
21:8 *i* 2Sa 3:7 *j* 1Sa 18:19
21:9 *k* 2Sa 16:8 *l* Ru 1:22
21:10 *m* ver 8; Dt 21:23; 1Sa 17:44
21:12 *n* 1Sa 31:11-13 *o* Jos 17:11 *p* 1Sa 31:10

down on Gilboa.) **13**David brought the bones of Saul and his son Jonathan from there, and the bones of those who had been killed and exposed were gathered up.

14They buried the bones of Saul and his son Jonathan in the tomb of Saul's father Kish, at Zela^q in Benjamin, and did everything the king commanded. After that,^r God answered prayer^s in behalf of the land.

Wars Against the Philistines

15Once again there was a battle between the Philistines^t and Israel. David went down with his men to fight against the Philistines, and he became exhausted. **16**And Ishbi-Benob, one of the descendants of Rapha, whose bronze spearhead weighed three hundred shekels^a and who was armed with a new ᴸswordᴶ, said he would kill David. **17**But Abishai^u son of Zeruiah came to David's rescue; he struck the Philistine down and killed him. Then David's men swore to him, saying, "Never again will you go out with us to battle, so that the lamp^v of Israel will not be extinguished.^w"

18In the course of time, there was another battle with the Philistines, at Gob. At that time Sibbecai^x the Hushathite killed Saph, one of the descendants of Rapha.

19In another battle with the Philistines at Gob, Elhanan son of Jaare-Oregim^b the Bethlehemite killed Goliath^c the Gittite, who had a spear with a shaft like a weaver's rod.^y

20In still another battle, which took place at Gath, there was a huge man with six fingers on each hand and six toes on each foot—twenty-four in all. He also was descended from Rapha. **21**When he taunted Israel, Jonathan son of Shimeah,^z David's brother, killed him.

22These four were descendants of Rapha in Gath, and they fell at the hands of David and his men.

David's Song of Praise

22 David sang^a to the LORD the words of this song when the LORD delivered him from the hand of all his enemies and from the hand of Saul. **2**He said:

"The LORD is my rock,^b my fortress^c and my deliverer;^d
3 my God is my rock, in whom I take refuge,^e
my shield^f and the horn^{d g} of my salvation.
He is my stronghold,^h my refuge and my savior—
from violent men you save me.
4I call to the LORD, who is worthyⁱ of praise,
and I am saved from my enemies.

---

^a 16 That is, about 7 1/2 pounds (about 3.5 kilograms)   ^b 19 Or *son of Jair the weaver*
^c 19 Hebrew and Septuagint; 1 Chron. 20:5 *son of Jair killed Lahmi the brother of Goliath*   ^d 3 *Horn* here symbolizes strength.

---

2 Samuel 21:15–22

These four episodes, which occurred at various times in David's wars with the Philistines, are held together by two common threads (see v. 22). In each episode one of David's soldiers is credited with the execution of one of the "descendants of Rapha." In light of the weight and size of their spears, we can surmise that these adversaries were giants like Goliath (see 1 Sam. 17)—making this a list of David's "giant-killers." Abishai's rescue of David may signify other situations in which David didn't personally lead his troops in battle.

Have you ever, in the awkwardness of a transition period, tried to relive the high points of your past? Like David, we may exhaust ourselves trying to take on "giants" that are no longer ours to fight. There is no shame in admitting exhaustion or allowing someone else

to find success in "our" area of ministry or expertise. Maybe God is using us to train or inspire other "giant killers" so we can receive needed rest. Or he may want to protect us from failure during a vulnerable season. We can't recapture our past, but we can move into our future with confidence in God's continued blessing.

2 Samuel 22:1–51

The poems at the beginning and end of the books of Samuel (Hannah's prayer in 1 Sam. 2:1–10 and David's psalm and "last words" in 2 Sam. 22:1—23:7) frame the whole. The extended stories in 1–2 Samuel have instructed us about the nature and purpose of Israel's monarchy. The poetic frame articulates more directly the books' core theological points (see "There and Then" to follow). This praise song (repeated in Ps. 18) can be taken as a theological commentary on David's history.

Cross references: 21:14 *q* Jos 18:28 *r* Jos 7:26 *s* 2Sa 24:25 | 21:15 *t* 2Sa 5:25 | 21:17 *u* 2Sa 20:6 *v* 1Ki 11:36 *w* 2Sa 18:3 | 21:18 *x* 1Ch 11:29; 20:4; 27:11 | 21:19 *y* 1Sa 17:7 | 21:21 *z* 1Sa 16:9 | 22:1 *a* Ex 15:1; Jdg 5:1; Ps 18:2-50 | 22:2 *b* Dt 32:4; Ps 71:3 *c* Ps 31:3; 91:2 *d* Ps 144:2 | 22:3 *e* Dt 32:37; Jer 16:19 *f* Ge 15:1 *g* Lk 1:69 *h* Ps 9:9 | 22:4 *i* Ps 48:1; 96:4

5 "The waves[j] of death swirled about me;
  the torrents of destruction overwhelmed me.
6 The cords of the grave[a][k] coiled around me;
  the snares of death confronted me.
7 In my distress[l] I called[m] to the LORD;
  I called out to my God.
  From his temple he heard my voice;
  my cry came to his ears.

8 "The earth[n] trembled and quaked,[o]
  the foundations[p] of the heavens[b] shook;
  they trembled because he was angry.
9 Smoke rose from his nostrils;
  consuming fire[q] came from his mouth,
  burning coals blazed out of it.
10 He parted the heavens and came down;
  dark clouds[r] were under his feet.
11 He mounted the cherubim and flew;
  he soared[c] on the wings of the wind.[s]
12 He made darkness his canopy around him—
  the dark[d] rain clouds of the sky.
13 Out of the brightness of his presence
  bolts of lightning[t] blazed forth.
14 The LORD thundered[u] from heaven;
  the voice of the Most High resounded.
15 He shot arrows[v] and scattered ⌊the enemies⌋,
  bolts of lightning and routed them.
16 The valleys of the sea were exposed
  and the foundations of the earth laid bare
  at the rebuke[w] of the LORD,
  at the blast of breath from his nostrils.

17 "He reached down from on high[x] and took hold of me;
  he drew[y] me out of deep waters.
18 He rescued me from my powerful enemy,
  from my foes, who were too strong for me.
19 They confronted me in the day of my disaster,
  but the LORD was my support.[z]
20 He brought me out into a spacious[a] place;
  he rescued[b] me because he delighted[c] in me.[d]

21 "The LORD has dealt with me according to my righteousness;[e]
  according to the cleanness of my hands[f] he has rewarded me.
22 For I have kept[g] the ways of the LORD;
  I have not done evil by turning from my God.
23 All his laws are before me;[h]
  I have not turned[i] away from his decrees.
24 I have been blameless[j] before him
  and have kept myself from sin.

a 6 Hebrew *Sheol*   b 8 Hebrew; Vulgate and Syriac (see also Psalm 18:7) *mountains*   c 11 Many
Hebrew manuscripts (see also Psalm 18:10); most Hebrew manuscripts *appeared*   d 12 Septuagint
and Vulgate (see also Psalm 18:11); Hebrew *massed*

The books of Samuel have established David as
the ideal king, God's anointed one. This theme would be
refined and developed later on in royal psalms, prophetic
literature, and the New Testament. Jesus came to establish the kingdom of God, as David had established and
built the kingdom in Israel. Jesus is God's "Anointed

One," the Messiah, who rules his people in justice and
truth. He prods each of us with the question of Mark 8:29:
"Who do you say I am?" That "Jesus is the Christ" affirms
the Messianic expectations developed in 1–2 Samuel (see
"Here and Now" to follow). How would you describe
Jesus to an interested but uninformed individual?

Cross references:

22:5 / Ps 69:14-15; 93:4; Jnh 2:3
22:6 k Ps 116:3
22:7 / Ps 120:1 m Ps 34:6,15; 116:4
22:8 n Jdg 5:4; Ps 97:4 o Ps 77:18 p Job 26:11
22:9 q Ps 97:3; Heb 12:29
22:10 r 1Ki 8:12; Na 1:3
22:11 s Ps 104:3
22:13 t ver 9
22:14 u 1Sa 2:10
22:15 v Dt 32:23
22:16 w Na 1:4
22:17 x Ps 144:7 y Ex 2:10
22:19 z Ps 23:4
22:20 a Ps 31:8 b Ps 118:5 c Ps 22:8 d 2Sa 15:26
22:21 e 1Sa 26:23 f Ps 24:4
22:22 g Ge 18:19; Ps 128:1; Pr 8:32
22:23 h Dt 6:4-9; Ps 119:30-32 i Ps 119:102
22:24 j Ge 6:9; Eph 1:4

25 The LORD has rewarded me according to my righteousness, [k]
  according to my cleanness[a] in his sight.

26 "To the faithful you show yourself faithful,
  to the blameless you show yourself blameless,

22:27
l Mt 5:8
m Lev 26:23-24
22:28
n Ex 3:8;
Ps 72:12-13
o Isa 2:12,17; 5:15
22:29
p Ps 27:1

27 to the pure[l] you show yourself pure,
  but to the crooked you show yourself shrewd. [m]

28 You save the humble, [n]
  but your eyes are on the haughty to bring them low. [o]

29 You are my lamp, [p] O LORD;
  the LORD turns my darkness into light.

30 With your help I can advance against a troop[b];
  with my God I can scale a wall.

31 "As for God, his way is perfect;[q]
  the word of the LORD is flawless.[r]
He is a shield
  for all who take refuge in him.

32 For who is God besides the LORD?
  And who is the Rock[s] except our God?

33 It is God who arms me with strength[c]
  and makes my way perfect.

34 He makes my feet like the feet of a deer;[t]
  he enables me to stand on the heights. [u]

35 He trains my hands[v] for battle;
  my arms can bend a bow of bronze.

36 You give me your shield[w] of victory;
  you stoop down to make me great.

37 You broaden the path[x] beneath me,
  so that my ankles do not turn.

38 "I pursued my enemies and crushed them;
  I did not turn back till they were destroyed.

39 I crushed[y] them completely, and they could not rise;
  they fell beneath my feet.

40 You armed me with strength for battle;
  you made my adversaries bow at my feet. [z]

41 You made my enemies turn their backs[a] in flight,
  and I destroyed my foes.

42 They cried for help, [b] but there was no one to save them—[c]
  to the LORD, but he did not answer.

22:43
d Mic 7:10
e Isa 10:6; Mic 7:10
22:44
f 2Sa 3:1 g Dt 28:13
h 2Sa 8:1-14;
Isa 55:3-5

43 I beat them as fine as the dust of the earth;
  I pounded and trampled[d] them like mud[e] in the streets.

44 "You have delivered[f] me from the attacks of my people;
  you have preserved[g] me as the head of nations.
People[h] I did not know are subject to me,

45   and foreigners come cringing[i] to me;
  as soon as they hear me, they obey me.

46 They all lose heart;
  they come trembling[d][j] from their strongholds.

47 "The LORD lives! Praise be to my Rock!
  Exalted be God, the Rock, my Savior![k]

48 He is the God who avenges me, [l]
  who puts the nations under me,

---

a 25 Hebrew; Septuagint and Vulgate (see also Psalm 18:24) *to the cleanness of my hands*
b 30 Or *can run through a barricade*   c 33 Dead Sea Scrolls, some Septuagint manuscripts, Vulgate
and Syriac (see also Psalm 18:32); Masoretic Text *who is my strong refuge*   d 46 Some Septuagint
manuscripts and Vulgate (see also Psalm 18:45); Masoretic Text *they arm themselves.*

49 who sets me free from my enemies.[m]
You exalted me above my foes;
from violent men you rescued me.
50 Therefore I will praise you, O LORD, among the nations;
I will sing praises to your name.[n]
51 He gives his king great victories;[o]
he shows unfailing kindness to his anointed,[p]
to David[q] and his descendants forever."[r]

The Last Words of David

23 These are the last words of David:

"The oracle of David son of Jesse,
the oracle of the man exalted[s] by the Most High,
the man anointed[t] by the God of Jacob,
Israel's singer of songs[a]:

2 "The Spirit[u] of the LORD spoke through me;
his word was on my tongue.
3 The God of Israel spoke,
the Rock[v] of Israel said to me:
'When one rules over men in righteousness,[w]
when he rules in the fear of God,[x]
4 he is like the light of morning at sunrise[y]
on a cloudless morning,
like the brightness after rain
that brings the grass from the earth.'

---

a 1 Or Israel's beloved singer

Side references column:

22:49
m Ps 140:1,4

22:50
n Ro 15:9*

22:51
o Ps 144:9-10
p Ps 89:20
q 2Sa 7:13
r Ps 89:24,29

23:1
s 2Sa 7:8-9;
Ps 78:70-71; 89:27
t 1Sa 16:12-13;
Ps 89:20

23:2
u Mt 22:43;
2Pe 1:21

23:3
v Dt 32:4;
2Sa 22:2,32
w Ps 72:2
x 2Ch 19:7,9;
Isa 11:1-5
23:4
y Jdg 5:31; Ps 89:36

---

2 Samuel 23:1–7

In his thanksgiving psalm, David had looked back at God's mercy and faithfulness during his life and reign. Here in his "last words" he looked forward, trusting in the promises he had received from God. David extolled the virtues and benefits of a righteous kingship. His had been such a kingship; God had made "an everlasting covenant" with him. David's conviction that God had promised such a perpetual covenant no doubt depended on Nathan's prophecy in 7:5–16. The concepts from David's last words became foundational for Israel's Messianic hopes—for the kind of king Israel would long for.

23:3–4

Stress

King David had a stressful job. Yet he recognized that his only legitimate "fear" was the fear of the Lord—a lesson we could well use today.

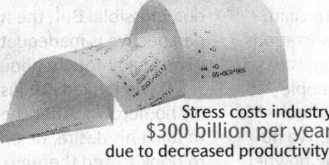

Stress costs industry
$300 billion per year
due to decreased productivity.

Causes of workplace stress:
uncertainty over job future, lack of recognition, lack of control in areas of responsibility

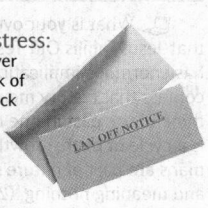

Every day, one million U.S. workers miss work due to stress-related complaints.

80 percent of all workers claim job-related **STRESS**

Americans work one month longer each year than Japanese, three months longer than Germans.

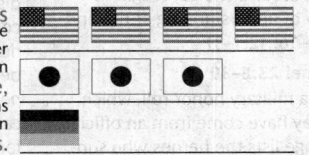

Physical symptoms of stress: chronic headaches, back pain, obesity, insomnia, depression, many others

14 percent of all workers say they have felt like striking a coworker.

20 workers are murdered each year by coworkers due to desk rage.

Source: American Institute of Stress (www.stress.org/job)

5 "Is not my house right with God?
  Has he not made with me an everlasting covenant, z
  arranged and secured in every part?
Will he not bring to fruition my salvation
  and grant me my every desire?

6 But evil men are all to be cast aside like thorns, a
  which are not gathered with the hand.
7 Whoever touches thorns
  uses a tool of iron or the shaft of a spear;
  they are burned up where they lie."

David's Mighty Men

8 These are the names of David's mighty men:

Josheb-Basshebeth, a a Tahkemonite, b was chief of the Three; he raised his spear against eight hundred men, whom he killed c in one encounter.

9 Next to him was Eleazar son of Dodai b the Ahohite. c As one of the three mighty men, he was with David when they taunted the Philistines gathered ⌊at Pas Dam-mim⌋ d for battle. Then the men of Israel retreated, 10 but he stood his ground and struck down the Philistines till his hand grew tired and froze to the sword. The LORD brought about a great victory that day. The troops returned to Eleazar, but only to strip the dead.

11 Next to him was Shammah son of Agee the Hararite. When the Philistines banded together at a place where there was a field full of lentils, Israel's troops fled from them. 12 But Shammah took his stand in the middle of the field. He defended it and struck the Philistines down, and the LORD brought about a great victory.

23:13
d 1Sa 22:1
e 2Sa 5:18
23:14
f 1Sa 22:4-5
g Ru 1:19

13 During harvest time, three of the thirty chief men came down to David at the cave of Adullam, d while a band of Philistines was encamped in the Valley of Rephaim. e 14 At that time David was in the stronghold, f and the Philistine garrison was at Beth-lehem. g 15 David longed for water and said, "Oh, that someone would get me a drink of water from the well near the gate of Bethlehem!" 16 So the three mighty men broke through the Philistine lines, drew water from the well near the gate of Bethlehem and

carried it back to David. But he refused to drink it; instead, he poured h it out before the LORD. 17 "Far be it from me, O LORD, to do this!" he said. "Is it not the blood i of men who went at the risk of their lives?" And David would not drink it.

---

a 8 Hebrew; some Septuagint manuscripts suggest *Ish-Bosheth,* that is, *Esh-Baal* (see also 1 Chron. 11:11 *Jashobeam*).   b 8 Probably a variant of *Hacmonite* (see 1 Chron. 11:11)   c 8 Some Septuagint manuscripts (see also 1 Chron. 11:11); Hebrew and other Septuagint manuscripts *Three; it was Adino the Eznite who killed eight hundred men*   d 9 See 1 Chron. 11:13; Hebrew *gathered there.*

📖 What is your overall view of history? To claim that Jesus fulfills Old Testament Messianic expectations has enormous implications for our faith, forcing us to confess that history means something. Most people think of the past in one of two ways: (1) As a wheel—life is a cycle of birth, growth, maturity, and death. We humans are part of nature's endless cycles—going nowhere and meaning nothing. (2) Or as a road—inviting us to a pilgrimage that defines our life experiences as events leading toward a goal. This second choice, taught in Scripture, results in the joy of understanding at the end of the journey (Heb. 11:13–16; 12:1–3).

2 Samuel 23:8–39

📖 We now come to a military honor roll, which, like the list at 21:15–22, may have come from an official military archive. This passage lists the heroes who supported David, along with a few of their more spectacular exploits. From a human perspective, these were the valiant and loyal soldiers who had made David's king-

dom possible. But, the narrator reminds us, the human perspective is inadequate to explain their successes: "The LORD brought about a great victory" (vv. 10,12).

David longed not just for water, but for water from his hometown. After the unnamed men risked their lives to fulfill his desire, he poured out the water. By declining to drink it, and thereby offering it to God as a sacrifice, he honored their loyalty and love.

📖 The books of Samuel led Israel, and later Jesus' disciples, to expect from David's line a king and a military conqueror. They didn't anticipate someone who would defeat Satan in a victory disguised by death in order to become the ruler of their hearts. How often do you suspect that you have missed Christ's "coming" to you because he didn't fulfill your expectations? Have you looked for deliverance, when in reality he may have come to help you get *through* a trial? Eventually Christ will set up his enduring kingdom (Rev. 11:15). Until then, we are to look for his coming in unlikely places and unexpected ways.

Such were the exploits of the three mighty men.

[18]Abishai[j] the brother of Joab son of Zeruiah was chief of the Three.[a] He raised his spear against three hundred men, whom he killed, and so he became as famous as the Three. [19]Was he not held in greater honor than the Three? He became their commander, even though he was not included among them.

[20]Benaiah[k] son of Jehoiada was a valiant fighter from Kabzeel,[l] who performed great exploits. He struck down two of Moab's best men. He also went down into a pit on a snowy day and killed a lion. [21]And he struck down a huge Egyptian. Although the Egyptian had a spear in his hand, Benaiah went against him with a club. He snatched the spear from the Egyptian's hand and killed him with his own spear. [22]Such were the exploits of Benaiah son of Jehoiada; he too was as famous as the three mighty men. [23]He was held in greater honor than any of the Thirty, but he was not included among the Three. And David put him in charge of his bodyguard.

[24]Among the Thirty were:
Asahel[m] the brother of Joab,
Elhanan son of Dodo from Bethlehem,
[25]Shammah the Harodite,[n]
Elika the Harodite,
[26]Helez[o] the Paltite,
Ira son of Ikkesh from Tekoa,
[27]Abiezer from Anathoth,[p]
Mebunnai[b] the Hushathite,
[28]Zalmon the Ahohite,
Maharai[q] the Netophathite,[r]
[29]Heled[c] son of Baanah the Netophathite,
Ithai son of Ribai from Gibeah[s] in Benjamin,
[30]Benaiah the Pirathonite,[t]
Hiddai[d] from the ravines of Gaash,[u]
[31]Abi-Albon the Arbathite,
Azmaveth the Barhumite,[v]
[32]Eliahba the Shaalbonite,
the sons of Jashen,
Jonathan [33]son of[e] Shammah the Hararite,
Ahiam son of Sharar[f] the Hararite,
[34]Eliphelet son of Ahasbai the Maacathite,
Eliam[w] son of Ahithophel[x] the Gilonite,
[35]Hezro the Carmelite,[y]
Paarai the Arbite,
[36]Igal son of Nathan from Zobah,[z]
the son of Hagri,[g]
[37]Zelek the Ammonite,
Naharai the Beerothite, the armor-bearer of Joab son of Zeruiah,
[38]Ira the Ithrite,[a]
Gareb the Ithrite,
[39]and Uriah[b] the Hittite.
There were thirty-seven in all.

David Counts the Fighting Men

24 Again[c] the anger of the LORD burned against Israel, and he incited David against them, saying, "Go and take a census of[d] Israel and Judah."

[a] 18 Most Hebrew manuscripts (see also 1 Chron. 11:20); two Hebrew manuscripts and Syriac *Thirty*   [b] 27 Hebrew; some Septuagint manuscripts (see also 1 Chron. 11:29) *Sibbecai*   [c] 29 Some Hebrew manuscripts and Vulgate (see also 1 Chron. 11:30); most Hebrew manuscripts *Heleb*   [d] 30 Hebrew; some Septuagint manuscripts (see also 1 Chron. 11:32) *Hurai*   [e] 33 Some Septuagint manuscripts (see also 1 Chron. 11:34); Hebrew does not have *son of*.   [f] 33 Hebrew; some Septuagint manuscripts (see also 1 Chron. 11:35) *Sacar*   [g] 36 Some Septuagint manuscripts (see also 1 Chron. 11:38); Hebrew *Haggadi*

23:18 / 2Sa 10:10,14; 1Ch 11:20
23:20 k 2Sa 8:18; 20:23 / Jos 15:21
23:24 m 2Sa 2:18
23:25 n Jdg 7:1; 1Ch 11:27
23:26 o 1Ch 27:10
23:27 p Jos 21:18
23:28 q 1Ch 27:13 r 2Ki 25:23; Ne 7:26
23:29 s Jos 15:57
23:30 t Jdg 12:13 u Jos 24:30
23:31 v 2Sa 3:16
23:34 w 2Sa 11:3 x 2Sa 15:12
23:35 y Jos 12:22
23:36 z 1Sa 14:47
23:38 a 2Sa 20:26; 1Ch 2:53
23:39 b 2Sa 11:3
24:1 c Jos 9:15 d 1Ch 27:23

Abraham Lincoln

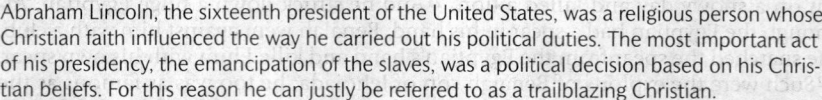

24:1–4

Abraham Lincoln, the sixteenth president of the United States, was a religious person whose Christian faith influenced the way he carried out his political duties. The most important act of his presidency, the emancipation of the slaves, was a political decision based on his Christian beliefs. For this reason he can justly be referred to as a trailblazing Christian.

But the minute we attempt to draw lessons from the way Lincoln's faith influenced his politics we run into problems. Lincoln's understanding of religion didn't neatly fit into our modern categories. He spoke much of God but little of Jesus. Dreams and visions were as important to him as creeds and theology. Second, Lincoln's walk was less precise than his talk. He fit well in the rough and tumble, sometimes bawdy, political arena of his day. Third, the idealism of religion and the realities of politics were and are difficult for anyone to meld into a consistent, character-shaping whole.

In many ways Lincoln reminds us of the Biblical hero David, whose faith in God was unquestioned. But even David struggled to live a consistently holy life (remember Bathsheba?) and too often chose the politically expedient over the spiritually faithful.

> From the trivial to the momentous, [Lincoln's] life was shot through with a moral consciousness rare in a person of power.

Yet unquestionably David did great things. We name our children after him. We see him as a model of how to be a person of faith in a less-than-perfect, highly politicized world.

Similarly, Lincoln was a model to follow, a genuine hero of the faith. In a 1985 article in *Christianity Today*, Mark Noll listed four reasons why Lincoln deserves a place today on a roster of effective Christian heroes:

Lincoln knew the Bible. In his well-publicized debates with Stephen Douglas in 1858, Lincoln on several occasions corrected his opponent's inaccurate quotation or application of God's Word. Lesson: *A hero of the faith bases his or her actions in the words of Scripture and only secondarily uses public opinion polls and social science findings to guide his or her decisions.*

Lincoln was a man of prayer. As Noll noted, Lincoln "came to prayer more regularly and devoutly as he moved through life." Lesson: *Making difficult decisions can't be left to instinct but must result from intentional conversations with God.*

Lincoln was a man of personal integrity. From the trivial to the momentous, his life was shot through with a moral consciousness rare in a person of power. We all remember stories of the unusual energy Lincoln expended as a youth to pay back pennies or return borrowed books. As an adult he brought that same moral force to bear on matters of state, not the least of which was his opposition to slavery. Lesson: *Moral action best springs from a moral foundation. Though none of us is perfect—and like both David and Lincoln we may fail miserably at times—a fundamental commitment to moral integrity is non-negotiable.*

Lincoln was able to navigate the narrow channel between moral ideals and political realism because, in his mind, he could distinguish between the ideals of American democracy and the imperfect way these ideals were lived out in the political process. As Noll put it, "To Lincoln the ideals of the country, rather than the political compromises that had been necessary to establish the government, became the beacon lights for his abolitionist efforts." Lesson: *Not all ideals are just or right. A trailblazing Christian needs the ability to discern righteous ideals and believe they can guide moral actions.*

²So the king said to Joab*ᵉ* and the army commanders*ᵃ* with him, "Go throughout the tribes of Israel from Dan to Beersheba*ᶠ* and enroll the fighting men, so that I may know how many there are."

³But Joab replied to the king, "May the LORD your God multiply the troops a hundred times over,*ᵍ* and may the eyes of my lord the king see it. But why does my lord the king want to do such a thing?"

⁴The king's word, however, overruled Joab and the army commanders; so they left the presence of the king to enroll the fighting men of Israel.

⁵After crossing the Jordan, they camped near Aroer,*ʰ* south of the town in the gorge, and then went through Gad and on to Jazer.*ⁱ* ⁶They went to Gilead and the region of Tahtim Hodshi, and on to Dan Jaan and around toward Sidon.*ʲ* ⁷Then they went toward the fortress of Tyre*ᵏ* and all the towns of the Hivites and Canaanites. Finally, they went on to Beersheba*ˡ* in the Negev*ᵐ* of Judah.

⁸After they had gone through the entire land, they came back to Jerusalem at the end of nine months and twenty days.

⁹Joab reported the number of the fighting men to the king: In Israel there were eight hundred thousand able-bodied men who could handle a sword, and in Judah five hundred thousand.*ⁿ*

¹⁰David was conscience-stricken*ᵒ* after he had counted the fighting men, and he said to the LORD, "I have sinned*ᵖ* greatly in what I have done. Now, O LORD, I beg you, take away the guilt of your servant. I have done a very foolish thing.* q*"

¹¹Before David got up the next morning, the word of the LORD had come to Gad*ʳ* the prophet, David's seer:*ˢ* ¹²"Go and tell David, 'This is what the LORD says: I am giving you three options. Choose one of them for me to carry out against you.'"

ᵃ 2 Septuagint (see also verse 4 and 1 Chron. 21:2); Hebrew *Joab the army commander*

24:2
ᵉ 2Sa 20:23
ᶠ Jdg 20:1; 2Sa 3:10

24:3
ᵍ Dt 1:11

24:5
ʰ Dt 2:36; Jos 13:9
ⁱ Nu 21:32
24:6
ʲ Ge 10:19; Jos 19:28; Jdg 1:31
24:7
ᵏ Jos 19:29
ˡ Ge 21:22-33
ᵐ Dt 1:7; Jos 11:3

24:9
ⁿ Nu 1:44-46; 1Ch 21:5
24:10
ᵒ 1Sa 24:5
ᵖ 2Sa 12:13
q Nu 12:11; 1Sa 13:13

24:11
ʳ 1Sa 22:5
ˢ 1Sa 9:9; 1Ch 29:29

---

2 Samuel 24:1–17

The census reflected a shift in David's object of faith—from God to military might. But this final episode in 2 Samuel reinforces the picture of David as a repentant king. After nearly ten months of hard work, Joab gave his report. But then David had a change of heart. His confession was nearly identical to his words when Nathan had confronted him about his sins of adultery and murder (12:13). But this time David expressed remorse without the need for a prophetic prompt ("You are the man!"; 12:7) to expose his sin.

Do you ever find yourself reluctant to bring your failings before God? Why or why not? This time around David confessed *before* the prophet came; then he thrust himself and the nation on God's mercy. We as Christians, too, are called to live with an open heart before God, confessing and receiving forgiveness early, rather than waiting for confrontation or discovery (1 Jn. 1:9). There may be consequences for sinful actions, but God "delight[s] to show mercy" (Mic. 7:18).

24:10

Bad Counting, Good Counting

Counting (our money, resources, or feathers in our cap) on the basis of pride is wrong. But good stewardship of kingdom resources is a challenge for churches and Christian organizations. Some statistics:

In an average year in the 1990s,

25.2 million
people were added to the Christian church:
22.7 million by birth, 2.5 million by conversion (net gain, subtracting 16,500,000 from 19,000,000, below).[1]

+ 19,000,000
− 16,500,000
In 2000, 19 million people converted to Christianity, while 16.5 million defected.[1]

Christianity declined in the 20th century from 34.5 percent of world population in 1990 to 33 percent in 2000.[1]

33%

Of all world religions, only Christianity has adherents among every one of the world's 238 countries.[1]

In 2000, 419,000 Christian workers were serving God outside of their home countries.[1]

33,200 → → 218,000

The United States sent out 218,000 mission workers in 2000—and (does this statistic surprise you?) received 33,200.[1]

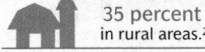
65 percent of all Christians live in cities,

35 percent in rural areas.[2]

Source: [1] Barrett and Johnson (2001:59) [2] Gallagher (2004:144–156)

24:13
t Dt 28:38-42,48;
Eze 14:21
u Lev 26:25

24:14
v Ne 9:28; Ps 51:1;
103:8,13; 130:4

24:15
w 1Ch 27:24

24:16
x Ge 6:6; 1Sa 15:11
y Ex 12:23;
Ac 12:23

24:17
z Ps 74:1 *a* Jnh 1:12

24:21
b Nu 16:44-50

24:22
c 1Sa 6:14;
1Ki 19:21
24:23
d Eze 20:40-41

24:24
e Mal 1:13-14

24:25
f 1Sa 7:17
g 2Sa 21:14

[13] So Gad went to David and said to him, "Shall there come upon you three[a] years of famine[t] in your land? Or three months of fleeing from your enemies while they pursue you? Or three days of plague[u] in your land? Now then, think it over and decide how I should answer the one who sent me."

[14] David said to Gad, "I am in deep distress. Let us fall into the hands of the Lord, for his mercy[v] is great; but do not let me fall into the hands of men."

[15] So the Lord sent a plague on Israel from that morning until the end of the time designated, and seventy thousand of the people from Dan to Beersheba died.[w] [16] When the angel stretched out his hand to destroy Jerusalem, the Lord was grieved[x] because of the calamity and said to the angel who was afflicting the people, "Enough! Withdraw your hand." The angel of the Lord[y] was then at the threshing floor of Araunah the Jebusite.

[17] When David saw the angel who was striking down the people, he said to the Lord, "I am the one who has sinned and done wrong. These are but sheep.[z] What have they done? Let your hand fall upon me and my family."[a]

David Builds an Altar

[18] On that day Gad went to David and said to him, "Go up and build an altar to the Lord on the threshing floor of Araunah the Jebusite." [19] So David went up, as the Lord had commanded through Gad. [20] When Araunah looked and saw the king and his men coming toward him, he went out and bowed down before the king with his face to the ground.

[21] Araunah said, "Why has my lord the king come to his servant?"

"To buy your threshing floor," David answered, "so I can build an altar to the Lord, that the plague on the people may be stopped."[b]

[22] Araunah said to David, "Let my lord the king take whatever pleases him and offer it up. Here are oxen[c] for the burnt offering, and here are threshing sledges and ox yokes for the wood. [23] O king, Araunah gives[d] all this to the king." Araunah also said to him, "May the Lord your God accept you."

[24] But the king replied to Araunah, "No, I insist on paying you for it. I will not sacrifice to the Lord my God burnt offerings that cost me nothing."[e]

So David bought the threshing floor and the oxen and paid fifty shekels[b] of silver for them. [25] David built an altar[f] to the Lord there and sacrificed burnt offerings and fellowship offerings.[c] Then the Lord answered prayer[g] in behalf of the land, and the plague on Israel was stopped.

---

[a] 13 Septuagint (see also 1 Chron. 21:12); Hebrew *seven*   [b] 24 That is, about 1 1/4 pounds (about 0.6 kilogram)   [c] 25 Traditionally *peace offerings*

---

2 Samuel 24:18–25

Threshing floors, normally on hills, were traditional sites for receiving divine messages. The text emphasizes that the plague ceased at this spot. The Chronicler (2 Chron. 3:1) added that this site, north of David's city, was eventually chosen for Solomon's temple (having been purchased with David's money and made sacred by his offerings). David understood the necessity of sacrificing a portion of his personal wealth to honor God. Otherwise his worship would have been cheap and meaningless.

This final lesson from 2 Samuel may be the hardest to understand. Ritual sacrifices aren't necessary today because Christ became the Lamb of God who cleansed us from our sins by his death. But we consequently lack the experience of watching an animal die in our place. Our salvation "costs" us nothing (cf. v. 24 with Eph. 2:8–9)—yet it cost Jesus everything. What will you give back to God? Only what's convenient, easy, or leftover? Or will you offer him your absolute best—a real sacrifice of your life, involving your time, talent, and treasure (cf. Rom. 12:1)?

INTRODUCTION TO

1 Kings

AUTHOR

The books of 1 and 2 Kings were originally one book, the author of which is unknown. Although Jewish tradition attributes the work to Jeremiah, few scholars today agree. Whoever wrote 1 and 2 Kings relied upon a variety of other written sources (11:41; 14:19,29; 1 Chron. 29:29; 2 Chron. 9:29; 12:15; 20:34; 24:27; 26:22; 32:32) to compile this history of the monarchy.

DATE WRITTEN

First Kings was probably written between 560 and 550 B.C., during the Babylonian exile of the Jews (586–538 B.C.).

ORIGINAL READERS

The book of Kings (1 and 2 Kings) was originally written for the Jews living in exile in Babylon to preserve a detailed history of Israel and Judah—from the last days of King David (c. 970 B.C.) to the exile to Babylon (c. 586 B.C.). First Kings includes the history of the united kingdom under King Solomon (1:1—11:43), as well as that of the first 80 years of the divided kingdom of Israel and Judah (12:1—22:53).

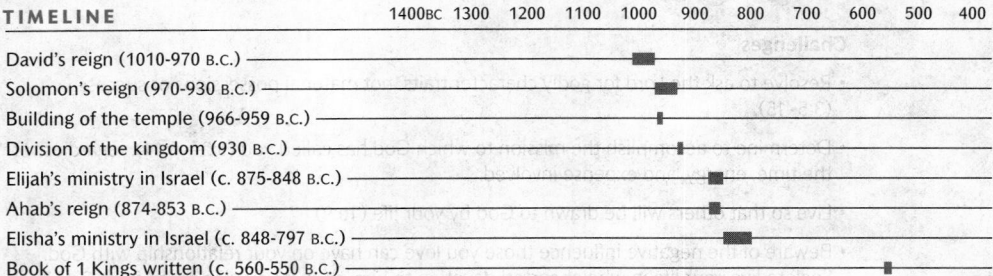

TIMELINE	1400BC	1300	1200	1100	1000	900	800	700	600	500	400
David's reign (1010-970 B.C.)											
Solomon's reign (970-930 B.C.)											
Building of the temple (966-959 B.C.)											
Division of the kingdom (930 B.C.)											
Elijah's ministry in Israel (c. 875-848 B.C.)											
Ahab's reign (874-853 B.C.)											
Elisha's ministry in Israel (c. 848-797 B.C.)											
Book of 1 Kings written (c. 560-550 B.C.)											

THEMES

First Kings describes the history of the kings of Israel and Judah in the context of the Mosaic and Davidic covenants. Israel's welfare depended on the obedience of its kings to God and their fidelity to the Mosaic covenant. First Kings includes the following themes:

1. *The Mosaic covenant.* The history of Israel's kings is presented from a covenantal, rather than from a social, political, or economic viewpoint. Assessments of the various kings were based on their obedience to the Mosaic covenant (see Deut. 17:14–20). The book's major premise is that obedience brings blessing and disobedience results in judgment.

2. *The Davidic covenant.* The historical significance of the Davidic covenant is demonstrated by references to God's promise to David (8:20,25; 11:36) and the use of David's life and reign as the standard by which to measure later kings (9:4; 11:4,6; 14:8; 15:3–5,11; 2 Kings 16:2; 18:3; 22:2).

3. *One true God.* There was to be one central place of worship (Deut. 12:1–14), the temple in Jerusalem (9:3; 2 Kings 21:4,7). The importance of this is seen in the writer's repeated statements of abhorrence for "the sin of the house of Jeroboam" (13:34; see 15:34; 16:2,19,26; 21:22; 22:52), which involved setting up two alternate places of worship in the northern kingdom (12:25–33). The single, official place of worship emphasized the truth that there is but one God. The failure to obey this command led to idolatry, which was the major reason for the defeats of both Israel and Judah (2 Kings 17:7–8,16,19; 21:3–5).

FAITH IN ACTION

The pages of 1 Kings contain life lessons and role models of faith—people who challenge believers to put their faith in action.

Role Models

- BENAIAH (1:8) was a great warrior (see 2 Sam. 23:20–22) whose loyalty to King David eventually earned him the position of commander in chief of Solomon's army (2:35; 4:4). Do you believe that God rewards us for our loyalty to others?

- DAVID (2:1–4) charged his son Solomon to obey God and walk in his ways. What do you want your own legacy to be?

- SOLOMON (3:12) was the wisest, most discerning man who ever lived. His request for wisdom (3:9) pleased God (3:10). What are the desires of your heart? Do you suspect that they are pleasing to God?

- THE QUEEN OF SHEBA (10:9) heard of Solomon's renown, came to see for herself, and praised God for this great king's righteous and just reign. Do you seek godly friends and influences? How does your life encourage seekers to encounter God?

- THE WIDOW OF ZAREPHATH (17:7–24) shared with Elijah the last of her food during a famine. Are you actively concerned for those experiencing famine today? Has someone with meager resources ever taught you a valuable lesson?

- ELIJAH (18:16–39) performed incredible miracles, but one of his most profound experiences of God came not in a display of power but in God's "gentle whisper" (19:12). What is your most cherished experience of God's presence?

Challenges

- Resolve to ask the Lord for godly character traits, not material possessions or success (3:5–15).

- Determine to accomplish the mission to which God has called you (5:2—6:14), regardless of the time, energy, and expense involved.

- Live so that others will be drawn to God by your life (10:9).

- Beware of the negative influence those you love can have on your relationship with God. Seek to live your life in wholehearted devotion to him, so that you won't turn from God in later years (11:4).

- Take to heart the warning that disobedience brings judgment—even to those who at one time were especially close to God (11:6–11). Faithfulness is measured by time.

- Be considerate of those under your authority, serving their needs rather than oppressing them for your own selfish ends (12:1–14).

- Share what you have (17:23–25).

- Seek to discern God's hand in the circumstances around you, because nothing is "random" (22:34). God is always at work bringing his plan to fruition (22:29–38).

OUTLINE

I. Solomon's Reign (1:1—12:24)
II. Israel and Judah From Jeroboam I/Rehoboam to Ahab/Asa (12:25—16:34)
III. Elijah and King Ahab (17:1—22:40)
IV. Jehoshaphat, King of Judah (22:41–50)
V. Ahaziah, King of Israel (22:51–53)

Adonijah Sets Himself Up as King

1 When King David was old and well advanced in years, he could not keep warm even when they put covers over him. ²So his servants said to him, "Let us look for a young virgin to attend the king and take care of him. She can lie beside him so that our lord the king may keep warm."

³Then they searched throughout Israel for a beautiful girl and found Abishag, a Shunammite, *a* and brought her to the king. ⁴The girl was very beautiful; she took care of the king and waited on him, but the king had no intimate relations with her.

⁵Now Adonijah, *b* whose mother was Haggith, put himself forward and said, "I will be king." So he got chariots *c* and horses *c* ready, with fifty men to run ahead of him. ⁶(His father had never interfered *d* with him by asking, "Why do you behave as you do?" He was also very handsome and was born next after Absalom.)

⁷Adonijah conferred with Joab *e* son of Zeruiah and with Abiathar *f* the priest, and they gave him their support. ⁸But Zadok *g* the priest, Benaiah *h* son of Jehoiada, Nathan *i* the prophet, Shimei *j* and Rei *b* and David's special guard *k* did not join Adonijah.

⁹Adonijah then sacrificed sheep, cattle and fattened calves at the Stone of Zoheleth near En Rogel. *l* He invited all his brothers, the king's sons, and all the men of Judah who were royal officials, ¹⁰but he did not invite Nathan the prophet or Benaiah or the special guard or his brother Solomon. *m*

¹¹Then Nathan asked Bathsheba, *n* Solomon's mother, "Have you not heard that Adonijah, *o* the son of Haggith, has become king without our lord David's knowing it? ¹²Now then, let me advise *p* you how you can save your own life and the life of your son Solomon. ¹³Go in to King David and say to him, 'My lord the king, did you not swear *q* to me your servant: "Surely Solomon your son shall be king after me, and he will sit on my throne"? Why then has Adonijah become king?' ¹⁴While you are still there talking to the king, I will come in and confirm what you have said."

¹⁵So Bathsheba went to see the aged king in his room, where Abishag *r* the Shunammite was attending him. ¹⁶Bathsheba bowed low and knelt before the king.

a 5 Or *charioteers*   *b 8* Or *and his friends*

1:3
a Jos 19:18

1:5
b 2Sa 3:4 *c* 2Sa 15:1

1:6
d 2Sa 3:3-4

1:7
e 1Ki 2:22,28;
1Ch 11:6
f 1Sa 22:20;
2Sa 20:25
1:8
g 2Sa 20:25
h 2Sa 8:18
i 2Sa 12:1 / 1Ki 4:18
k 2Sa 23:8
1:9
l 2Sa 17:17
1:10
m 2Sa 12:24
1:11
n 2Sa 12:24
o 2Sa 3:4
1:12
p Pr 15:22

1:13
q ver 30;
1Ch 22:9-13

1:15
r ver 1

---

1 Kings 1:1–27

📖 The book of Kings begins with the rather sad circumstances surrounding the accession of Solomon to the throne of his father, David. Two primary factors are involved: (1) David's feebleness and apparent laissez-faire attitude toward government in his later years and (2) Adonijah's self-willed ambition to succeed his father, based on the fact that he was the oldest of David's surviving sons. In this ambition Adonijah was supported by some influential members of David's government, despite David's clearly expressed designation of Solomon.

David had proven to be in some areas an indecisive king, unable to control his own family, as seen in his dealings with Amnon and Absalom (2 Sam. 13–15). The observation here in verse 6 that David "had never interfered with" Adonijah reinforces David's consistent negligence in disciplining his sons.

📖 Like David, those of us who follow Christ and choose his kingdom don't always have a track record of living up to our potential or ideals. But this doesn't deny the reality of God's kingdom. We too may have to be called to account for our failures and suffer the consequences of our sins. But we can receive a pure and cleansed heart and restoration of the joy of our salvation (see Ps. 51:10–12).

The consequences of a lack of parental discipline can be severe. The effects show up in families, businesses, and communities, and, as with David's family, can last for generations. If you are a parent, how do you implement godly discipline into your family life? In what areas do you see a need for improvement?

"What is it you want?" the king asked.

1:17
s ver 13,30

[17] She said to him, "My lord, you yourself swore[s] to me your servant by the LORD your God: 'Solomon your son shall be king after me, and he will sit on my throne.'

1:19
t ver 9

[18] But now Adonijah has become king, and you, my lord the king, do not know about it. [19] He has sacrificed[t] great numbers of cattle, fattened calves, and sheep, and has invited all the king's sons, Abiathar the priest and Joab the commander of the army, but he has not invited Solomon your servant. [20] My lord the king, the eyes of all Israel are on you, to learn from you who will sit on the throne of my lord the king after him.

1:21
u Dt 31:16;
1Ki 2:10

[21] Otherwise, as soon as my lord the king is laid to rest[u] with his fathers, I and my son Solomon will be treated as criminals."

[22] While she was still speaking with the king, Nathan the prophet arrived. [23] And they told the king, "Nathan the prophet is here." So he went before the king and bowed with his face to the ground.

[24] Nathan said, "Have you, my lord the king, declared that Adonijah shall be king after you, and that he will sit on your throne? [25] Today he has gone down and sacrificed great numbers of cattle, fattened calves, and sheep. He has invited all the king's sons, the commanders of the army and Abiathar the priest. Right now they are eating and drinking with him and saying, 'Long live King Adonijah!' [26] But me your servant,

1:26
v ver 8,10

and Zadok the priest, and Benaiah son of Jehoiada, and your servant Solomon he did not invite.[v] [27] Is this something my lord the king has done without letting his servants know who should sit on the throne of my lord the king after him?"

David Makes Solomon King

[28] Then King David said, "Call in Bathsheba." So she came into the king's presence and stood before him.

1:29
w 2Sa 4:9
1:30
x ver 13,17

[29] The king then took an oath: "As surely as the LORD lives, who has delivered me out of every trouble,[w] [30] I will surely carry out today what I swore[x] to you by the LORD, the God of Israel: Solomon your son shall be king after me, and he will sit on my throne in my place."

[31] Then Bathsheba bowed low with her face to the ground and, kneeling before the king, said, "May my lord King David live forever!"

[32] King David said, "Call in Zadok the priest, Nathan the prophet and Benaiah son of Jehoiada." When they came before the king, [33] he said to them: "Take your lord's

1:33
y 2Sa 20:6-7
z 2Ch 32:30; 33:14
1:34
a 1Sa 10:1; 16:3,12;
1Ki 19:16;
2Ki 9:3,13
b ver 25; 2Sa 5:3;
15:10

servants with you and set Solomon my son on my own mule[y] and take him down to Gihon.[z] [34] There have Zadok the priest and Nathan the prophet anoint[a] him king over Israel. Blow the trumpet[b] and shout, 'Long live King Solomon!' [35] Then you are to go up with him, and he is to come and sit on my throne and reign in my place. I have appointed him ruler over Israel and Judah."

1:37
c Jos 1:5,17;
1Sa 20:13 d ver 47

[36] Benaiah son of Jehoiada answered the king, "Amen! May the LORD, the God of my lord the king, so declare it. [37] As the LORD was with my lord the king, so may he be with[c] Solomon to make his throne even greater[d] than the throne of my lord King David!"

---

1 Kings 1:28–53

David summoned priest, prophet, and general—namely Nathan, Zakok, and Benaiah—and ordered them to immediately carry out Solomon's public anointing. Adonijah had underestimated those loyal to Solomon; his deliberate exclusion of these individuals (v. 10) indicated that he didn't intend to function with a peaceful coalition.

David directed that Solomon be mounted on the king's own private mule, dramatic and visual evidence that royal authority had been turned over to Solomon. The tumult of the coronation reached the ears of those celebrating with Adonijah just down the valley. This effectively put an end to Adonijah's plot, as his supporters quickly scattered. Adonijah himself sought asylum in the sanctuary. He apparently feared death at the hands of Solomon, since no doubt that was what he had planned for Solomon had he been successful.

The idea of David being a "man after God's own heart" expresses God's choice, not David's qualifications. When God chooses a person "after his own heart," it means "according to his criteria"—not someone else's. Saul had been selected according to the people's standards but David by God's, which aren't enumerated. It's typical of the Bible that the reasons underlying God's decisions aren't publicized (e.g., his choice of Abraham, Israel, or any of us). This places the focus on God's wisdom, not on David's—or our own—piety or righteousness.

38 So Zadok the priest, Nathan the prophet, Benaiah son of Jehoiada, the Kerethites and the Pelethites went down and put Solomon on King David's mule and escorted him to Gihon. **39** Zadok the priest took the horn of oil from the sacred tent and anointed Solomon. Then they sounded the trumpet and all the people shouted, "Long live King Solomon!" **40** And all the people went up after him, playing flutes and rejoicing greatly, so that the ground shook with the sound.

41 Adonijah and all the guests who were with him heard it as they were finishing their feast. On hearing the sound of the trumpet, Joab asked, "What's the meaning of all the noise in the city?"

42 Even as he was speaking, Jonathan son of Abiathar the priest arrived. Adonijah said, "Come in. A worthy man like you must be bringing good news."

43 "Not at all!" Jonathan answered. "Our lord King David has made Solomon king. **44** The king has sent with him Zadok the priest, Nathan the prophet, Benaiah son of Jehoiada, the Kerethites and the Pelethites, and they have put him on the king's mule, **45** and Zadok the priest and Nathan the prophet have anointed him king at Gihon. From there they have gone up cheering, and the city resounds with it. That's the noise you hear. **46** Moreover, Solomon has taken his seat on the royal throne. **47** Also, the royal officials have come to congratulate our lord King David, saying, 'May your God make Solomon's name more famous than yours and his throne greater than yours!' And the king bowed in worship on his bed **48** and said, 'Praise be to the LORD, the God of Israel, who has allowed my eyes to see a successor on my throne today.' "

49 At this, all Adonijah's guests rose in alarm and dispersed. **50** But Adonijah, in fear of Solomon, went and took hold of the horns of the altar. **51** Then Solomon was told, "Adonijah is afraid of King Solomon and is clinging to the horns of the altar. He says, 'Let King Solomon swear to me today that he will not put his servant to death with the sword.' "

52 Solomon replied, "If he shows himself to be a worthy man, not a hair of his head will fall to the ground; but if evil is found in him, he will die." **53** Then King Solomon sent men, and they brought him down from the altar. And Adonijah came and bowed down to King Solomon, and Solomon said, "Go to your home."

David's Charge to Solomon

2 When the time drew near for David to die, he gave a charge to Solomon his son.

2 "I am about to go the way of all the earth," he said. "So be strong, show yourself a man, **3** and observe what the LORD your God requires: Walk in his ways, and keep his decrees and commands, his laws and requirements, as written in the Law of Moses, so that you may prosper in all you do and wherever you go, **4** and that the LORD may keep his promise to me: 'If your descendants watch how they live, and if they walk faithfully before me with all their heart and soul, you will never fail to have a man on the throne of Israel.'

5 "Now you yourself know what Joab son of Zeruiah did to me—what he did to

1:38 e ver 8 f 2Sa 8:18
g ver 33
1:39 h Ex 30:23-32; Ps 89:20 i ver 34; 1Sa 10:24
1:42 j 2Sa 15:27,36 k 2Sa 18:26
1:45 l ver 40
1:47 m ver 37; Ge 47:31
1:48 n 2Sa 7:12; 1Ki 3:6
1:50 o 1Ki 2:28
1:52 p 1Sa 14:45; 2Sa 14:11
2:1 q Ge 47:29; Dt 31:14
2:2 r Jos 23:14 s Dt 31:7,23; Jos 1:6
2:3 t Dt 17:14-20; Jos 1:7 u 1Ch 22:13
2:4 v 2Sa 7:13,25; 1Ki 8:25 w 2Ki 20:3; Ps 132:12
2:5 x 2Sa 2:18; 18:5,12,14

Like other human institutions, government/politics has been corrupted by the fall. Many cases of political conflict are almost purely a matter of individual aggression. Seldom are they primarily the result of self-sacrificing service for the well-being of others. People's drive for personal prominence can tempt them to violate the most sacred of relationships, including that among parents, siblings, and children. How do you respond when human politics negatively influences kingdom ministries?

1 Kings 2:1–12

David's last recorded words were his charge to Solomon. Covenant faithfulness was to be the single factor in determining whether future kings were good or bad. David's words regarding loyalty to the Lord expressed the commitment that would be required of every new king if succession to the throne were to continue as God had promised (v. 4).

The second part of David's final words pertained to matters he considered unfinished business. Though to us it may seem that David was motivated by selfish revenge, he undoubtedly was focused both on the justice involved in these situations and the need to prevent a recurrence of the kind of conflict that had just taken place with Adonijah. Joab had murdered not only Abner and Amasa (v. 5; cf. 2 Sam. 3:27; 20:10), but also Absalom (2 Sam. 18:14–15), and had participated in Adonijah's conspiracy (1 Kings 1:7,19). Shimei had been guilty of cursing a ruler (2 Sam. 16:5–13; cf. Ex. 22:28; 1 Kings 21:10).

2:5
y 2Sa 3:27
z 2Sa 20:10
2:6
a ver 9
2:7
b 2Sa 17:27;
19:31-39
c 2Sa 9:7
2:8
d 2Sa 16:5-13
e 2Sa 19:18-23
2:9
f ver 6
2:10
g Ac 2:29; 13:36
h 2Sa 5:7
2:11
i 2Sa 5:4,5
2:12
j 1Ch 29:23
k 2Ch 1:1
2:13
l 1Sa 16:4
2:17
m 1Ki 1:3
2:19
n 1Ki 15:13
o Ps 45:9

the two commanders of Israel's armies, Abner[y] son of Ner and Amasa[z] son of Jether. He killed them, shedding their blood in peacetime as if in battle, and with that blood stained the belt around his waist and the sandals on his feet. 6Deal with him according to your wisdom,[a] but do not let his gray head go down to the grave[a] in peace.

7"But show kindness to the sons of Barzillai[b] of Gilead and let them be among those who eat at your table.[c] They stood by me when I fled from your brother Absalom.

8"And remember, you have with you Shimei[d] son of Gera, the Benjamite from Bahurim, who called down bitter curses on me the day I went to Mahanaim. When he came down to meet me at the Jordan, I swore[e] to him by the LORD: 'I will not put you to death by the sword.' 9But now, do not consider him innocent. You are a man of wisdom;[f] you will know what to do to him. Bring his gray head down to the grave in blood."

10Then David rested with his fathers and was buried[g] in the City of David.[h] 11He had reigned[i] forty years over Israel—seven years in Hebron and thirty-three in Jerusalem. 12So Solomon sat on the throne[j] of his father David, and his rule was firmly established.[k]

Solomon's Throne Established

13Now Adonijah, the son of Haggith, went to Bathsheba, Solomon's mother. Bathsheba asked him, "Do you come peacefully?"[l]

He answered, "Yes, peacefully." 14Then he added, "I have something to say to you."

"You may say it," she replied.

15"As you know," he said, "the kingdom was mine. All Israel looked to me as their king. But things changed, and the kingdom has gone to my brother; for it has come to him from the LORD. 16Now I have one request to make of you. Do not refuse me."

"You may make it," she said.

17So he continued, "Please ask King Solomon—he will not refuse you—to give me Abishag[m] the Shunammite as my wife."

18"Very well," Bathsheba replied, "I will speak to the king for you."

19When Bathsheba went to King Solomon to speak to him for Adonijah, the king stood up to meet her, bowed down to her and sat down on his throne. He had a throne brought for the king's mother,[n] and she sat down at his right hand.[o]

20"I have one small request to make of you," she said. "Do not refuse me."

a 6 Hebrew *Sheol*; also in verse 9

📖 David's spirituality had powerfully influenced Solomon. Loyalty and faithfulness to the Lord were David's themes in his last charge to his son. Have you taken to heart the words of encouragement or godly advice you have been given? But, like Solomon, have you allowed their influence to wane as the years have passed? How do you plan to pass along your spiritual legacy to the next generation of believers?

1 Kings 2:13–46

⚖️ Solomon understood Adonijah's request to marry Abishag as another attempt to gain the throne. Though Abishag had remained a virgin while caring for David (1:1–4), the people would have regarded her as a member of David's harem—which would have strengthened Adonijah's claim to be the rightful king. On the other hand, Abishag's role was somewhat ambiguous since she hadn't "officially" become a part of David's harem (no sexual relations). It's hard to tell whether Solomon or Adonijah or both were trying to exploit that ambiguity to their own purposes.

Solomon surely also recognized the popular support Adonijah would have enjoyed as the older son (v. 22), along with his having been the choice of a leading priest (Abiathar) and military leader (Joab). The elimination of Adonijah, in addition to the actions Solomon took in fulfillment of David's charge in verses 5–9, resulted in the kingdom being "firmly established in Solomon's hands" (v. 46).

📖 Assassinations, coups, and revolts have been the way of many nations, and too often family members have been prime targets. But there is a distinct prophetic dimension in this account: Solomon's succession wasn't just a matter of resolving family, priestly, and military rivalries. The prophetic word concerning David's promised ongoing dynasty through Solomon was being realized (see 1 Chron. 22:7–10). Even though Christians are wise to exercise caution in interpreting predictive prophecy, world events can reassure us of God's sovereignty. What recent situations have served this purpose for you?

The king replied, "Make it, my mother; I will not refuse you."
²¹So she said, "Let Abishag*ᵖ* the Shunammite be given in marriage to your brother Adonijah."

²²King Solomon answered his mother, "Why do you request Abishag*ᵠ* the Shunammite for Adonijah? You might as well request the kingdom for him—after all, he is my older brother*ʳ*—yes, for him and for Abiathar the priest and Joab son of Zeruiah!"

²³Then King Solomon swore by the LORD: "May God deal with me, be it ever so severely,*ˢ* if Adonijah does not pay with his life for this request! ²⁴And now, as surely as the LORD lives—he who has established me securely on the throne of my father David and has founded a dynasty for me as he promised*ᵗ*—Adonijah shall be put to death today!" ²⁵So King Solomon gave orders to Benaiah*ᵘ* son of Jehoiada, and he struck down Adonijah and he died.

²⁶To Abiathar*ᵛ* the priest the king said, "Go back to your fields in Anathoth.*ʷ* You deserve to die, but I will not put you to death now, because you carried the ark*ˣ* of the Sovereign LORD before my father David and shared all my father's hardships."*ʸ* ²⁷So Solomon removed Abiathar from the priesthood of the LORD, fulfilling*ᶻ* the word the LORD had spoken at Shiloh about the house of Eli.

²⁸When the news reached Joab, who had conspired with Adonijah though not with Absalom, he fled to the tent of the LORD and took hold of the horns*ᵃ* of the altar. ²⁹King Solomon was told that Joab had fled to the tent of the LORD and was beside the altar. Then Solomon ordered Benaiah*ᵇ* son of Jehoiada, "Go, strike him down!"

³⁰So Benaiah entered the tent of the LORD and said to Joab, "The king says, 'Come out!*ᶜ* '"

But he answered, "No, I will die here."

Benaiah reported to the king, "This is how Joab answered me."

³¹Then the king commanded Benaiah, "Do as he says. Strike him down and bury him, and so clear me and my father's house of the guilt of the innocent blood*ᵈ* that Joab shed. ³²The LORD will repay*ᵉ* him for the blood he shed,*ᶠ* because without the knowledge of my father David he attacked two men and killed them with the sword. Both of them—Abner son of Ner, commander of Israel's army, and Amasa*ᵍ* son of Jether, commander of Judah's army—were better*ʰ* men and more upright than he. ³³May the guilt of their blood rest on the head of Joab and his descendants forever. But on David and his descendants, his house and his throne, may there be the LORD's peace forever."

³⁴So Benaiah son of Jehoiada went up and struck down Joab and killed him, and he was buried on his own land*ᵃ* in the desert. ³⁵The king put Benaiah*ⁱ* son of Jehoiada over the army in Joab's position and replaced Abiathar with Zadok*ʲ* the priest.

³⁶Then the king sent for Shimei*ᵏ* and said to him, "Build yourself a house in Jerusalem and live there, but do not go anywhere else. ³⁷The day you leave and cross the Kidron Valley,*ˡ* you can be sure you will die; your blood will be on your own head."*ᵐ*

³⁸Shimei answered the king, "What you say is good. Your servant will do as my lord the king has said." And Shimei stayed in Jerusalem for a long time.

³⁹But three years later, two of Shimei's slaves ran off to Achish*ⁿ* son of Maacah, king of Gath, and Shimei was told, "Your slaves are in Gath." ⁴⁰At this, he saddled his donkey and went to Achish at Gath in search of his slaves. So Shimei went away and brought the slaves back from Gath.

⁴¹When Solomon was told that Shimei had gone from Jerusalem to Gath and had returned, ⁴²the king summoned Shimei and said to him, "Did I not make you swear by the LORD and warn you, 'On the day you leave to go anywhere else, you can be sure you will die'? At that time you said to me, 'What you say is good. I will obey.' ⁴³Why then did you not keep your oath to the LORD and obey the command I gave you?"

⁴⁴The king also said to Shimei, "You know in your heart all the wrong*ᵒ* you did

---

ᵃ 34 Or *buried in his tomb*

2:21
ᵖ 1Ki 1:3
2:22
ᵠ 2Sa 12:8; 1Ki 1:3
ʳ 1Ch 3:2
2:23
ˢ Ru 1:17
2:24
ᵗ 2Sa 7:11; 1Ch 22:10
2:25
ᵘ 2Sa 8:18
2:26
ᵛ 1Sa 22:20
ʷ Jos 21:18
ˣ 2Sa 15:24
ʸ 1Sa 23:6
2:27
ᶻ 1Sa 2:27-36
2:28
ᵃ 1Ki 1:7,50
2:29
ᵇ ver 25
2:30
ᶜ Ex 21:14
2:31
ᵈ Nu 35:33; Dt 19:13; 21:8-9
2:32
ᵉ Jdg 9:57; Ps 7:16
ᶠ Jdg 9:24
ᵍ 2Sa 3:27; 20:10
ʰ 2Ch 21:13
2:35
ⁱ 1Ki 4:4 *ʲ* ver 27; 1Ch 29:22
2:36
ᵏ ver 8; 2Sa 16:5
2:37
ˡ 2Sa 15:23
ᵐ Lev 20:9; Jos 2:19; 2Sa 1:16
2:39
ⁿ 1Sa 27:2
2:44
ᵒ 1Sa 25:39; 2Sa 16:5-13; Eze 17:19

2:45
p 2Sa 7:13; Pr 25:5

to my father David. Now the LORD will repay you for your wrongdoing. ⁴⁵But King Solomon will be blessed, and David's throne will remain secure*ᵖ* before the LORD forever."

⁴⁶Then the king gave the order to Benaiah son of Jehoiada, and he went out and struck Shimei down and killed him.

2:46
q ver 12; 2Ch 1:1

The kingdom was now firmly established*�q* in Solomon's hands.

Solomon Asks for Wisdom

3:1
r 1Ki 7:8 *s* 1Ki 9:24
t 2Sa 5:7 *u* 1Ki 7:1;
9:15,19
3:2
v Lev 17:3-5;
Dt 12:2,4-5;
1Ki 22:43
3:3
w Dt 6:5; Ps 31:23;
1Co 8:3 *x* 1Ki 2:3;
9:4; 11:4,6,38
3:4
y 1Ch 16:39

3 Solomon made an alliance with Pharaoh king of Egypt and married*ʳ* his daughter. ⁵ He brought her to the City of David*ᵗ* until he finished building his palace*ᵘ* and the temple of the LORD, and the wall around Jerusalem. ²The people, however, were still sacrificing at the high places,*ᵛ* because a temple had not yet been built for the Name of the LORD. ³Solomon showed his love*ʷ* for the LORD by walking according to the statutes*ˣ* of his father David, except that he offered sacrifices and burned incense on the high places.

3:5
z 1Ki 9:2 *a* Nu 12:6;
Mt 1:20

⁴The king went to Gibeon*ʸ* to offer sacrifices, for that was the most important high place, and Solomon offered a thousand burnt offerings on that altar. ⁵At Gibeon the LORD appeared*ᶻ* to Solomon during the night in a dream,*ᵃ* and God said, "Ask for whatever you want me to give you."

3:6
b 1Ki 2:4; 9:4
c 1Ki 1:48

⁶Solomon answered, "You have shown great kindness to your servant, my father David, because he was faithful*ᵇ* to you and righteous and upright in heart. You have continued this great kindness to him and have given him a son*ᶜ* to sit on his throne this very day.

3:7
d Nu 27:17;
1Ch 29:1
3:8
e Dt 7:6 *f* Ge 15:5
3:9
g 2Sa 14:17; Jas 1:5
h Pr 2:3-9;
Heb 5:14
i Ps 72:1-2

⁷"Now, O LORD my God, you have made your servant king in place of my father David. But I am only a little child*ᵈ* and do not know how to carry out my duties. ⁸Your servant is here among the people you have chosen,*ᵉ* a great people, too numerous to count or number.*ᶠ* ⁹So give your servant a discerning*ᵍ* heart to govern your people and to distinguish*ʰ* between right and wrong. For who is able*ⁱ* to govern this great people of yours?"

3:11
j Jas 4:3
3:12
k 1Jn 5:14-15
l 1Ki 4:29,30,31;
5:12; 10:23;
Ecc 1:16
3:13
m Mt 6:33;
Eph 3:20
n 1Ki 4:21-24;
Pr 3:1-2,16
o 1Ki 10:23

¹⁰The Lord was pleased that Solomon had asked for this. ¹¹So God said to him, "Since you have asked*ʲ* for this and not for long life or wealth for yourself, nor have asked for the death of your enemies but for discernment in administering justice, ¹²I will do what you have asked.*ᵏ* I will give you a wise*ˡ* and discerning heart, so that there will never have been anyone like you, nor will there ever be. ¹³Moreover, I will give you what you have not*ᵐ* asked for—both riches and honor*ⁿ*—so that in your lifetime you will have no equal*ᵒ* among kings. ¹⁴And if you walk*ᵖ* in my ways and obey my statutes and commands as David your father did, I will give you a long life."*�q* ¹⁵Then Solomon awoke*ʳ*—and he realized it had been a dream.

3:14
p ver 6; Pr 3:1-2,16
q Ps 61:6; 91:16
3:15
r Ge 41:7 *s* 1Ki 8:65
t Mk 6:21
u Est 1:3,9; Da 5:1

He returned to Jerusalem, stood before the ark of the Lord's covenant and sacrificed burnt offerings*ˢ* and fellowship offerings.*ᵃᵗ* Then he gave a feast*ᵘ* for all his court.

A Wise Ruling

¹⁶Now two prostitutes came to the king and stood before him. ¹⁷One of them said, "My lord, this woman and I live in the same house. I had a baby while she was

---

ᵃ 15 Traditionally *peace offerings*

---

1 Kings 3:1–15

Solomon had been appointed and anointed by God, and he loved the Lord. Yet he couldn't on his own establish the life of the covenant for the nation. His alliance with Egypt and provisions for continued worship at the high places (as opposed to Jerusalem) already compromised his devotion. When God appeared to him, though, Solomon based his request on the covenant relationship God had established with David (v. 6). The new king had the people's well-being at heart and wisely asked for the ability to rule with justice.

Wisdom goes beyond the ability to make right decisions. And it's not the intelligence to know all the right things. It's a choice of the right life values, coupled with a willingness to learn to live by those values. It's learning how to live so that life can be good. What truly wise people do you know? In terms of the Biblical view (the book of Proverbs is a good source), how would you realistically assess your own WQ (wisdom quotient)?

1 Kings 3:16–28

Most ancient prostitutes were slaves, often daughters who had been sold by their parents. Or they

3:16–28

Solomon demonstrated prudence when he devised a strategy for determining the identity of the true mother in 1 Kings 3. You remember the story. Two mothers, two newborns sharing their beds. One infant accidentally smothered in the night. Both mothers claiming the remaining child as their own. The unique case was brought to Solomon for judgment.

Which baby was which? Solomon could have decided the case based on scientific evidence, had he had access to modern testing procedures. But neither he nor anyone else had the luxury of this benefit. No DNA tests were available. Yet first-hand knowledge was available to both of the mothers. Solomon had to dig deeper, to resort to a more difficult, internal characteristic: wisdom.

Solomon was obligated to decide the case using a particular kind of wisdom, often called prudence or practical wisdom. "Street smarts" is a slang term we sometimes use today to refer to *phronesis* (Aristotle) or *prudentia* (Aquinas). Prudence is more than knowledge; it's knowledge in action.

Solomon capably applied prudence in deciding this case. "Bring me a sword," he instructed curtly. "Cut the living child in two and give half to one and half to the other." The mother of the living child couldn't bear the image. "Give her the living baby," she pleaded in urgent distress. "Whatever you do, don't kill him." Solomon recognized her as the true mother and awarded her the child.

Yet even though Solomon could make wise judgments about other people's situations, he seemed unable to apply prudence to his own affairs. Solomon was extravagant with his wealth and notoriously excessive in his love life. He married 700 women and kept an additional 300 concubines ("wives" of a lesser status). True, the king loved God, but he capitulated to pressure from his foreign wives to build altars to honor their gods, too. To fund his immoderations, as well as a growing government bureaucracy, Solomon instituted an oppressive taxation system.

Why was this wisest of all men so completely blindsided when it came to his own life? Perhaps he was, at least in later years, in short supply of another virtue, humility. Solomon, the favorite son of the powerful King David, had been born into unquestioned privilege. From infancy on, he epitomized the picture of the "silver spoon" child.

When everyone around you acknowledges that you are the wisest person in the world, and when your every word is law in the land, humility is a hard virtue to come by or hold on to. Solomon's lack of prudence with respect to his own life led to his personal downfall and that of his nation.

> **E**ven though Solomon could make wise judgments about other people's situations, he seemed unable to apply prudence to his own affairs.

This lack of humility inevitably led to another serious shortcoming. The more Solomon reveled in his own gifts, the more he demanded that the people of Israel do likewise. They had realized that their king was a stand-in for God, who had claimed their ultimate allegiance. But Solomon damaged that paradigm. The focus shifted to himself. Solomon's wisdom. Solomon's palace. Solomon's temple. Solomon's wives. Solomon's lecture series. Solomon's proverbs. Solomon's horses. Solomon's love of nature. Solomon's wealth. The king in Jerusalem became the center of attention, both within Israel and far beyond its borders (cf. 1 Kings 10:23–29). The outcome was tragically predictable: "So Solomon did evil in the eyes of the LORD; he did not follow the LORD completely as David his father had done (11:6)."

there with me. [18]The third day after my child was born, this woman also had a baby. We were alone; there was no one in the house but the two of us.

[19]"During the night this woman's son died because she lay on him. [20]So she got up in the middle of the night and took my son from my side while I your servant was asleep. She put him by her breast and put her dead son by my breast. [21]The next morning, I got up to nurse my son—and he was dead! But when I looked at him closely in the morning light, I saw that it wasn't the son I had borne."

[22]The other woman said, "No! The living one is my son; the dead one is yours." But the first one insisted, "No! The dead one is yours; the living one is mine." And so they argued before the king.

[23]The king said, "This one says, 'My son is alive and your son is dead,' while that one says, 'No! Your son is dead and mine is alive.' "

[24]Then the king said, "Bring me a sword." So they brought a sword for the king. [25]He then gave an order: "Cut the living child in two and give half to one and half to the other."

[26]The woman whose son was alive was filled with compassion[v] for her son and said to the king, "Please, my lord, give her the living baby! Don't kill him!"

But the other said, "Neither I nor you shall have him. Cut him in two!"

[27]Then the king gave his ruling: "Give the living baby to the first woman. Do not kill him; she is his mother."

[28]When all Israel heard the verdict the king had given, they held the king in awe, because they saw that he had wisdom[w] from God to administer justice.

Solomon's Officials and Governors

4 So King Solomon ruled over all Israel. [2]And these were his chief officials:

Azariah[x] son of Zadok—the priest;
[3]Elihoreph and Ahijah, sons of Shisha—secretaries;
Jehoshaphat[y] son of Ahilud—recorder;
[4]Benaiah[z] son of Jehoiada—commander in chief;
Zadok[a] and Abiathar—priests;
[5]Azariah son of Nathan—in charge of the district officers;
Zabud son of Nathan—a priest and personal adviser to the king;
[6]Ahishar—in charge of the palace;
Adoniram son of Abda—in charge of forced labor.

3:26
[v] Ge 43:30; Isa 49:15; Jer 31:20; Hos 11:8

3:28
[w] ver 9,11-12; Col 2:3

4:2
[x] 1Ch 6:10

4:3
[y] 2Sa 8:16

4:4
[z] 1Ki 2:35
[a] 1Ki 2:27

---

were poor women who had never married or had lost their husbands. Once Solomon ingeniously determined the identity of the true mother he didn't pronounce further punishments, either to deal with the cause of the first baby's death or the subsequent criminal action of switching the children. Justice was best served with mercy. Solomon's wise judgment preserved the life of a child, restored the bond of motherhood, and offered renewed opportunity to make the best of a bad situation (i.e., the circumstances of prostitution).

The church tends to ignore prostitution, but the Bible doesn't. Would you have thrown out this case on the basis of the women's professions? We would like to think our societies today have evolved from ancient times, but little has changed. Many girls and women in developing countries are still sold by their families into prostitution; others worldwide are forced into it by poverty or the death of a provider. Solomon didn't further oppress these women caught in difficult circumstances, and Jesus demonstrated similar compassion to the woman taken in adultery (John 8:1–11). How can we in the church show wise compassion to those trapped by sexual sin or in the sex trade?

1 Kings 4:1–19

This passage records Solomon's officials, chief administrators, and district governors. Verses 11 and 15 indicate that the list was compiled at about the midpoint of Solomon's reign, since two of the officials were his sons-in-law. The 12 district governors were responsible on a rotating basis for taxation and provision of food for Solomon's court and animals (vv. 27–28). The geographical divisions reflected social and political realities rather than traditional tribal boundaries, apparently resulting in satisfaction for all (v. 20).

Solomon was exceptionally capable as a resource manager. An irony of wisdom, though, is that its success in one area can endanger its application and function in another. When have you found yourself blindsided in one area *because* you excelled in another? The wisdom of the Israelites was embodied in the teaching they had received through the covenant. All nations would marvel at their knowledge of life (Deut. 4:5–8). The danger was that they would forget the source of their knowledge and undermine those blessings (Deut. 4:9–10).

7Solomon also had twelve district governors over all Israel, who supplied provisions for the king and the royal household. Each one had to provide supplies for one month in the year. 8These are their names:

Ben-Hur—in the hill country[b] of Ephraim;
9Ben-Deker—in Makaz, Shaalbim,[c] Beth Shemesh[d] and Elon Bethhanan;
10Ben-Hesed—in Arubboth (Socoh[e] and all the land of Hepher[f] were his);
11Ben-Abinadab—in Naphoth Dor[a g] (he was married to Taphath daughter of Solomon);
12Baana son of Ahilud—in Taanach and Megiddo, and in all of Beth Shan[h] next to Zarethan[i] below Jezreel, from Beth Shan to Abel Meholah[j] across to Jokmeam;[k]
13Ben-Geber—in Ramoth Gilead (the settlements of Jair[l] son of Manasseh in Gilead were his, as well as the district of Argob in Bashan and its sixty large walled cities[m] with bronze gate bars);
14Ahinadab son of Iddo—in Mahanaim;[n]
15Ahimaaz[o]—in Naphtali (he had married Basemath daughter of Solomon);
16Baana son of Hushai[p]—in Asher and in Aloth;
17Jehoshaphat son of Paruah—in Issachar;
18Shimei[q] son of Ela—in Benjamin;
19Geber son of Uri—in Gilead (the country of Sihon king of the Amorites and the country of Og[r] king of Bashan). He was the only governor over the district.

Solomon's Daily Provisions

20The people of Judah and Israel were as numerous as the sand[s] on the seashore; they ate, they drank and they were happy. 21And Solomon ruled[t] over all the kingdoms from the River[b u] to the land of the Philistines, as far as the border of Egypt.[v] These countries brought tribute[w] and were Solomon's subjects all his life.

22Solomon's daily provisions were thirty cors[c] of fine flour and sixty cors[d] of meal, 23ten head of stall-fed cattle, twenty of pasture-fed cattle and a hundred sheep and goats, as well as deer, gazelles, roebucks and choice fowl. 24For he ruled over all the kingdoms west of the River, from Tiphsah[x] to Gaza, and had peace[y] on all sides. 25During Solomon's lifetime Judah and Israel, from Dan to Beersheba,[z] lived in safety,[a] each man under his own vine and fig tree.[b]

26Solomon had four[e] thousand stalls for chariot horses,[c] and twelve thousand horses.[f]

27The district officers,[d] each in his month, supplied provisions for King Solomon and all who came to the king's table. They saw to it that nothing was lacking. 28They also brought to the proper place their quotas of barley and straw for the chariot horses and the other horses.

---

[a] 11 Or *in the heights of Dor*   [b] 21 That is, the Euphrates; also in verse 24   [c] 22 That is, probably about 185 bushels (about 6.6 kiloliters)   [d] 22 That is, probably about 375 bushels (about 13.2 kiloliters)   [e] 26 Some Septuagint manuscripts (see also 2 Chron. 9:25); Hebrew *forty*
[f] 26 Or *charioteers*

4:8
[b] Jos 24:33
4:9
[c] Jdg 1:35
[d] Jos 21:16
4:10
[e] Jos 15:35
[f] Jos 12:17
4:11
[g] Jos 11:2
4:12
[h] Jos 17:11; Jdg 5:19 [i] Jos 3:16
[j] 1Ki 19:16
[k] 1Ch 6:68
4:13
[l] Nu 32:41 [m] Dt 3:4
4:14
[n] Jos 13:26
4:15
[o] 2Sa 15:27
4:16
[p] 2Sa 15:32
4:18
[q] 1Ki 1:8
4:19
[r] Dt 3:8-10
4:20
[s] Ge 22:17; 32:12; 1Ki 3:8
4:21
[t] 2Ch 9:26; Ps 72:11 [u] Jos 1:4; Ps 72:8 [v] Ge 15:18
[w] Ps 68:29
4:24
[x] Ps 72:11
[y] 1Ch 22:9
4:25
[z] Jdg 20:1
[a] Jer 23:6
[b] Mic 4:4; Zec 3:10
4:26
[c] 1Ki 10:26; 2Ch 1:14
4:27
[d] ver 7

---

1 Kings 4:20–28

The extent of Solomon's kingdom and the prosperity of the people were fulfillments of God's covenant with Abraham (Gen. 15:18). Solomon reigned from the Euphrates River to the border of Egypt. The territory from Tiphsah, on the southern bend of the Euphrates, to Gaza on the southeastern Mediterranean coast included Syria, the region only much later known as Palestine, and Sinai and probably territory east of the Jordan as well. That all the nations of this vast region brought tribute and were submissive to Solomon all the days of his life serves as an ideal description of his kingdom.

Living by Biblical wisdom doesn't assure us of prosperity. Ancient wisdom tradition made this connection, and it's still alive today in many circles. But the writer of the book of Job understood that there is another side to wisdom: It provides resources to deal with the failure of health and prosperity. Life is one long lesson in learning the fear of the Lord, discovering what it means to trust God as a child of "dust and ashes" (Job 30:19; 42:6). When has God enhanced your wisdom through understandings gleaned during difficult times?

Solomon's Wisdom

4:29
e 1Ki 3:12
4:30
f Ge 25:6 *g* Ac 7:22
4:31
h 1Ki 3:12; 1Ch 2:6;
6:33; 15:19;
Ps 89 Title
4:32
i Pr 1:1; Ecc 12:9
j SS 1:1

4:34
k 1Ki 10:1;
2Ch 9:23

²⁹God gave Solomon wisdom*e* and very great insight, and a breadth of understanding as measureless as the sand on the seashore. ³⁰Solomon's wisdom was greater than the wisdom of all the men of the East,*f* and greater than all the wisdom of Egypt. *g* ³¹He was wiser*h* than any other man, including Ethan the Ezrahite—wiser than Heman, Calcol and Darda, the sons of Mahol. And his fame spread to all the surrounding nations. ³²He spoke three thousand proverbs*i* and his songs*j* numbered a thousand and five. ³³He described plant life, from the cedar of Lebanon to the hyssop that grows out of walls. He also taught about animals and birds, reptiles and fish. ³⁴Men of all nations came to listen to Solomon's wisdom, sent by all the kings*k* of the world, who had heard of his wisdom.

Preparations for Building the Temple

5:1
l ver 10, 18;
2Sa 5:11; 1Ch 14:1

5 When Hiram*l* king of Tyre heard that Solomon had been anointed king to succeed his father David, he sent his envoys to Solomon, because he had always been on friendly terms with David. ²Solomon sent back this message to Hiram:

5:3
m 1Ch 22:8; 28:3

³"You know that because of the wars*m* waged against my father David from all sides, he could not build a temple for the Name of the LORD his God until the LORD put his enemies under his feet. ⁴But now the LORD my God has given me rest*n* on every side, and there is no adversary or disaster. ⁵I intend, therefore, to build a temple*o* for the Name of the LORD my God, as the LORD told my father David, when he said, 'Your son whom I will put on the throne in your place will build the temple for my Name.'*p*

5:4
n 1Ki 4:24;
1Ch 22:9
5:5
o 1Ch 17:12
p 2Sa 7:13;
1Ch 22:10

⁶"So give orders that cedars of Lebanon be cut for me. My men will work with yours, and I will pay you for your men whatever wages you set. You know that we have no one so skilled in felling timber as the Sidonians."

⁷When Hiram heard Solomon's message, he was greatly pleased and said, "Praise be to the LORD today, for he has given David a wise son to rule over this great nation."

⁸So Hiram sent word to Solomon:

5:9
q Ezr 3:7
r Eze 27:17;
Ac 12:20

"I have received the message you sent me and will do all you want in providing the cedar and pine logs. ⁹My men will haul them down from Lebanon to the sea,*q* and I will float them in rafts by sea to the place you specify. There I will separate them and you can take them away. And you are to grant my wish by providing food*r* for my royal household."

---

1 Kings 4:29–34

📖 In addition to the wisdom required to govern a vast kingdom, Solomon had a breadth of knowledge unrivaled in his time. Ancient wisdom included music, poetry, proverbial sayings for wise conduct, and what we would now call science. Solomon's interest in nature went beyond its basis for proverbs. Such knowledge also provided a perspective for understanding life in this world. Solomon's classification of creatures into the categories of animals, birds, reptiles, and fish revealed another aspect of his comprehensive knowledge.

📖 The fear of the Lord is the beginning of wisdom (Prov. 1:7; 9:10), but the search for wisdom also leads us to fear God (Prov. 2:1–6). Those of us who search for wisdom as a treasure find that God doesn't merely grant us treasure; he gives us more wisdom. How have you seen this circular process at work in your life?

The life of Solomon was a complete contrast to that of Job. Job started with much but lost it all. Solomon was given a great kingdom. Job through his loss came to know and understand the fear of the Lord. Solomon

through his gain found his heart turned away from God and the work of his life a loss. The united kingdom didn't survive after his reign. How has your Christian life been affected, positively or negatively, by losses and gains?

1 Kings 5:1–18

📖 The account of Solomon's preparations for building the temple divides into two sections. The first (vv. 1–12) explains the alliance between Solomon and Hiram, through which Solomon acquired the necessary materials and craftsmen. The diplomatic exchange is recounted in terms that specifically recalled the promise to David (e.g., cf. v. 5 with 2 Sam. 7:13). The second section (vv. 13–18) describes the workforce Solomon marshaled to accomplish his building projects.

The alliance between Solomon and Hiram in building the temple is an example of making God's presence known in the world. Hiram's statement in verse 7 obviously demonstrated acknowledgment of the God of Israel, though it didn't likely mean he had chosen Solomon's religion over his own. It was common for the people of one nation to recognize the deities of another (cf. 10:9).

[10]In this way Hiram kept Solomon supplied with all the cedar and pine logs he wanted, [11]and Solomon gave Hiram twenty thousand cors[a] of wheat as food for his household, in addition to twenty thousand baths[b, c] of pressed olive oil. Solomon continued to do this for Hiram year after year. [12]The LORD gave Solomon wisdom,[s] just as he had promised him. There were peaceful relations between Hiram and Solomon, and the two of them made a treaty.[t]

[13]King Solomon conscripted laborers[u] from all Israel—thirty thousand men. [14]He sent them off to Lebanon in shifts of ten thousand a month, so that they spent one month in Lebanon and two months at home. Adoniram[v] was in charge of the forced labor. [15]Solomon had seventy thousand carriers and eighty thousand stonecutters in the hills, [16]as well as thirty-three hundred[d] foremen[w] who supervised the project and directed the workmen. [17]At the king's command they removed from the quarry[x] large blocks of quality stone[y] to provide a foundation of dressed stone for the temple. [18]The craftsmen of Solomon and Hiram and the men of Gebal[e z] cut and prepared the timber and stone for the building of the temple.

Solomon Builds the Temple

6 In the four hundred and eightieth[f] year after the Israelites had come out of Egypt, in the fourth year of Solomon's reign over Israel, in the month of Ziv, the second month, he began to build the temple of the LORD.[a]

[2]The temple[b] that King Solomon built for the LORD was sixty cubits long, twenty wide and thirty high.[g] [3]The portico at the front of the main hall of the temple extended the width of the temple, that is twenty cubits,[h] and projected ten cubits[i] from the front of the temple. [4]He made narrow clerestory windows[c] in the temple. [5]Against the walls of the main hall and inner sanctuary he built a structure around the building, in which there were side rooms.[d] [6]The lowest floor was five cubits[j] wide, the middle floor six cubits[k] and the third floor seven.[l] He made offset ledges around the outside of the temple so that nothing would be inserted into the temple walls.

[7]In building the temple, only blocks dressed[e] at the quarry were used, and no hammer, chisel or any other iron tool[f] was heard at the temple site while it was being built.

[8]The entrance to the lowest[m] floor was on the south side of the temple; a stairway led up to the middle level and from there to the third. [9]So he built the temple and completed it, roofing it with beams and cedar[g] planks. [10]And he built the side rooms all along the temple. The height of each was five cubits, and they were attached to the temple by beams of cedar.

[11]The word of the LORD came to Solomon: [12]"As for this temple you are building, if you follow my decrees, carry out my regulations and keep all my commands and obey them, I will fulfill through you the promise[h] I gave to David your father. [13]And I will live among the Israelites and will not abandon[i] my people Israel."

Cross references (margin)

5:12 s 1Ki 3:12 t Am 1:9
5:13 u 1Ki 9:15
5:14 v 1Ki 4:6; 2Ch 10:18
5:16 w 1Ki 9:23
5:17 x 1Ki 6:7 y 1Ch 22:2
5:18 z Jos 13:5
6:1 a Ac 7:47
6:2 b Eze 41:1
6:4 c Eze 40:16; 41:16
6:5 d ver 16,19-21; Eze 41:5-6
6:7 e Ex 20:25 f Dt 27:5
6:9 g ver 14,38
6:12 h 2Sa 7:12-16; 1Ki 2:4; 9:5
6:13 i Ex 25:8; Lev 26:11; Dt 31:6; Heb 13:5

---

[a] 11 That is, probably about 125,000 bushels (about 4,400 kiloliters)   [b] 11 Septuagint (see also 2 Chron. 2:10); Hebrew *twenty cors*   [c] 11 That is, about 115,000 gallons (about 440 kiloliters)   [d] 16 Hebrew; some Septuagint manuscripts (see also 2 Chron. 2:2, 18) *thirty-six hundred*   [e] 18 That is, Byblos   [f] 1 Hebrew; Septuagint *four hundred and fortieth*   [g] 2 That is, about 90 feet (about 27 meters) long and 30 feet (about 9 meters) wide and 45 feet (about 13.5 meters) high   [h] 3 That is, about 30 feet (about 9 meters)   [i] 3 That is, about 15 feet (about 4.5 meters)   [j] 6 That is, about 7 1/2 feet (about 2.3 meters); also in verses 10 and 24   [k] 6 That is, about 9 feet (about 2.7 meters)   [l] 6 That is, about 10 1/2 feet (about 3.1 meters)   [m] 8 Septuagint; Hebrew *middle*

God doesn't want us to be isolated from people of other religions (or from those without religion). They may not share our worldview, but it's still possible to have mutually satisfactory relationships. Such involvement in the world is necessary and desirable, with certain cautions. The apostle Paul warned that marital unions with unbelievers (2 Cor. 6:14–16) can lead to compromises of value and conduct. It's never easy to maintain a presence in the world without becoming part of it, but that is the calling of the church. What does this distinction mean in a practical sense for you?

1 Kings 6:1–38

The temple itself couldn't represent God's glory. This could only happen when a people of faith understood its significance as representing the God of the covenant—and kept that covenant out of respect for him. But history has sadly shown that the Israelites again and again reinvented God in their own image and twisted the terms of his covenant to suit themselves, bringing the covenant curses on their heads. The destruction of the temple by the Babylonians would evidence that it had ceased to represent God's rule.

6:14
j ver 9,38
6:15
k 1Ki 7:7

6:16
l Ex 26:33;
Lev 16:2; 1Ki 8:6
6:18
m 1Ki 7:24; Ps 74:6
6:19
n 1Ki 8:6 *o* 1Sa 3:3
6:20
p Eze 41:3-4

6:23
q Ex 37:1-9

6:27
r Ex 25:20; 37:9;
1Ki 8:7; 2Ch 5:8

6:29
s ver 32,35

6:36
t 1Ki 7:12; Ezr 6:4

6:38
u Heb 8:5

7:1
v 1Ki 9:10; 2Ch 8:1
7:2
w 2Sa 7:2
x 1Ki 10:17;
2Ch 9:16

14So Solomon built the temple and completed*j* it. 15He lined its interior walls with cedar boards, paneling them from the floor of the temple to the ceiling, *k* and covered the floor of the temple with planks of pine. 16He partitioned off twenty cubits*a* at the rear of the temple with cedar boards from floor to ceiling to form within the temple an inner sanctuary, the Most Holy Place.*l* 17The main hall in front of this room was forty cubits*b* long. 18The inside of the temple was cedar,*m* carved with gourds and open flowers. Everything was cedar; no stone was to be seen.

19He prepared the inner sanctuary*n* within the temple to set the ark of the covenant*o* of the LORD there. 20The inner sanctuary*p* was twenty cubits long, twenty wide and twenty high. *c* He overlaid the inside with pure gold, and he also overlaid the altar of cedar. 21Solomon covered the inside of the temple with pure gold, and he extended gold chains across the front of the inner sanctuary, which was overlaid with gold. 22So he overlaid the whole interior with gold. He also overlaid with gold the altar that belonged to the inner sanctuary.

23In the inner sanctuary he made a pair of cherubim*q* of olive wood, each ten cubits*d* high. 24One wing of the first cherub was five cubits long, and the other wing five cubits—ten cubits from wing tip to wing tip. 25The second cherub also measured ten cubits, for the two cherubim were identical in size and shape. 26The height of each cherub was ten cubits. 27He placed the cherubim*r* inside the innermost room of the temple, with their wings spread out. The wing of one cherub touched one wall, while the wing of the other touched the other wall, and their wings touched each other in the middle of the room. 28He overlaid the cherubim with gold.

29On the walls all around the temple, in both the inner and outer rooms, he carved cherubim, *s* palm trees and open flowers. 30He also covered the floors of both the inner and outer rooms of the temple with gold.

31For the entrance of the inner sanctuary he made doors of olive wood with five-sided jambs. 32And on the two olive wood doors he carved cherubim, palm trees and open flowers, and overlaid the cherubim and palm trees with beaten gold. 33In the same way he made four-sided jambs of olive wood for the entrance to the main hall. 34He also made two pine doors, each having two leaves that turned in sockets. 35He carved cherubim, palm trees and open flowers on them and overlaid them with gold hammered evenly over the carvings.

36And he built the inner courtyard of three courses*t* of dressed stone and one course of trimmed cedar beams.

37The foundation of the temple of the LORD was laid in the fourth year, in the month of Ziv. 38In the eleventh year in the month of Bul, the eighth month, the temple was finished in all its details according to its specifications.*u* He had spent seven years building it.

Solomon Builds His Palace

7 It took Solomon thirteen years, however, to complete the construction of his palace.*v* 2He built the Palace*w* of the Forest of Lebanon*x* a hundred cubits long, fifty wide and thirty high, *e* with four rows of cedar columns supporting

---

a 16 That is, about 30 feet (about 9 meters)   *b* 17 That is, about 60 feet (about 18 meters)
c 20 That is, about 30 feet (about 9 meters) long, wide and high   *d* 23 That is, about 15 feet (about 4.5 meters)   *e* 2 That is, about 150 feet (about 46 meters) long, 75 feet (about 23 meters) wide and 45 feet (about 13.5 meters) high

---

Jesus' disciples would belatedly realize that Jesus himself had replaced the temple in significance (John 2:20–22). He was in bodily form the very presence of God in their midst, everything the temple had represented. The book of Hebrews develops this theme in detail. Jesus' ascension didn't mean that God's presence could no longer be seen in the world. The church is now Christ's body, representing his presence and rule in this world (Eph. 1:18–23). Christ expects his body (believers)—his temple (Eph. 2:19–22)—around the globe to live as an active, vibrant covenant community. What is your own congregation doing to fulfill this mission?

1 Kings 7:1–12
The Palace of the Forest of Lebanon was so named because its many pillars were made from the cedars of Lebanon and gave the appearance of a great forest. It was much larger than the temple and appears to have served as both a great assembly hall and an armory (10:16–17,21; Isa. 22:8). It's unclear whether the Hall of Justice (v. 7), Solomon's own living quarters

trimmed cedar beams. ³It was roofed with cedar above the beams that rested on the columns—forty-five beams, fifteen to a row. ⁴Its windows were placed high in sets of three, facing each other. ⁵All the doorways had rectangular frames; they were in the front part in sets of three, facing each other.ᵃ

⁶He made a colonnade fifty cubits long and thirty wide.ᵇ In front of it was a portico, and in front of that were pillars and an overhanging roof.

⁷He built the throne hall, the Hall of Justice, where he was to judge,ʸ and he covered it with cedar from floor to ceiling.ᶜᶻ ⁸And the palace in which he was to live, set farther back, was similar in design. Solomon also made a palace like this hall for Pharaoh's daughter, whom he had married.ᵃ

⁹All these structures, from the outside to the great courtyard and from foundation to eaves, were made of blocks of high-grade stone cut to size and trimmed with a saw on their inner and outer faces. ¹⁰The foundations were laid with large stones of good quality, some measuring ten cubitsᵈ and some eight.ᵉ ¹¹Above were high-grade stones, cut to size, and cedar beams. ¹²The great courtyard was surrounded by a wall of three coursesᵇ of dressed stone and one course of trimmed cedar beams, as was the inner courtyard of the temple of the LORD with its portico.

The Temple's Furnishings

¹³King Solomon sent to Tyre and brought Huram,ᶠᶜ ¹⁴whose mother was a widow from the tribe of Naphtali and whose father was a man of Tyre and a craftsman in bronze. Huram was highly skilledᵈ and experienced in all kinds of bronze work. He came to King Solomon and did allᵉ the work assigned to him.

¹⁵He cast two bronze pillars,ᶠ each eighteen cubits high and twelve cubits around,ᵍ by line. ¹⁶He also made two capitalsᵍ of cast bronze to set on the tops of the pillars; each capital was five cubitsʰ high. ¹⁷A network of interwoven chains festooned the capitals on top of the pillars, seven for each capital. ¹⁸He made pomegranates in two rowsⁱ encircling each network to decorate the capitals on top of the pillars.ʲ He did the same for each capital. ¹⁹The capitals on top of the pillars in the portico were in the shape of lilies, four cubitsᵏ high. ²⁰On the capitals of both pillars, above the bowl-shaped part next to the network, were the two hundred pomegranatesʰ in rows all around. ²¹He erected the pillars at the portico of the temple. The pillar to the

Cross references (margin)

7:7 ʸ Ps 122:5; Pr 20:8 ᶻ 1Ki 6:15
7:8 ᵃ 1Ki 3:1; 2Ch 8:11
7:12 ᵇ 1Ki 6:36
7:13 ᶜ 2Ch 2:13
7:14 ᵈ Ex 31:2-5; 35:31; 36:1; 2Ch 2:14 ᵉ 2Ch 4:11,16
7:15 ᶠ 2Ki 25:17; 2Ch 3:15; 4:12; 52:17,21
7:16 ᵍ 2Ki 25:17
7:20 ʰ 2Ch 3:16; 4:13; Jer 52:23

ᵃ 5 The meaning of the Hebrew for this verse is uncertain.   ᵇ 6 That is, about 75 feet (about 23 meters) long and 45 feet (about 13.5 meters) wide   ᶜ 7 Vulgate and Syriac; Hebrew *floor*
ᵈ 10 That is, about 15 feet (about 4.5 meters)   ᵉ 10 That is, about 12 feet (about 3.6 meters)
ᶠ 13 Hebrew *Hiram*, a variant of *Huram*; also in verses 40 and 45   ᵍ 15 That is, about 27 feet (about 8.1 meters) high and 18 feet (about 5.4 meters) around   ʰ 16 That is, about 7 1/2 feet (about 2.3 meters); also in verse 23   ⁱ 18 Two Hebrew manuscripts and Septuagint; most Hebrew manuscripts *made the pillars, and there were two rows*   ʲ 18 Many Hebrew manuscripts and Syriac; most Hebrew manuscripts *pomegranates*   ᵏ 19 That is, about 6 feet (about 1.8 meters); also in verse 38

(v. 8), and the palace for Pharaoh's daughter (v. 8) were separate buildings or locations within the Palace of the Forest of Lebanon.

📖 It took Solomon almost twice as long to build the palace complex as the temple (cf. v. 1 with 6:38). In addition to the larger size of the palace complex, this was also likely due to David's extensive advanced planning and acquisition of materials for the temple, which wasn't the case for the palace. Yet these contrasts may well reflect that the author of Kings was subtly criticizing Solomon's priorities. As the king's wealth and power grew, his love for God began to wane. How tempting is it for you to place greater priority on your own "house" than on the Lord's (see Hag. 1:2–4)?

1 Kings 7:13–51

📖 One of the most remarkable aspects of the temple's construction was the attention to detail. This was

obviously of enormous interest, not only to the craftsmen but to all the people. Even practical items like the ten water basins and their stands in the temple court, used to wash portions of the sacrificial animals (vv. 27–39; cf. Lev. 1:9,13; 2 Chron. 4:6), were ornately crafted to contribute to the overall effect.

📖 Clearly church buildings today need to be functional and serviceable, and we as Christians are to be good stewards of our financial resources. But is creativity in craftsmanship a legitimate part of the way we express the beauty of creation and the presence of God within the church? For instance, do you consider it wasteful to highlight a sanctuary's lofty purposes through the art of stained-glass windows, bells, steeples, and similar artistic/architectural features? True, the function of our church buildings is vastly different from that of the temple, but the issue is still worth reflection.

7:21
i 1Ki 6:3; 2Ch 3:17
7:23
j 2Ki 25:13;
1Ch 18:8; Jer 52:17

7:25
k 2Ch 4:4-5;
Jer 52:20

7:27
l ver 38; 2Ch 4:14

7:30
m 2Ki 16:17

7:38
n Ex 30:18; 2Ch 4:6

7:42
o ver 20

7:45
p Ex 27:3

7:46
q 2Ch 4:17
r Ge 33:17;
Jos 13:27 *s* Jos 3:16

south he named Jakin[a] and the one to the north Boaz.[b] [i] 22The capitals on top were in the shape of lilies. And so the work on the pillars was completed.

23He made the Sea[j] of cast metal, circular in shape, measuring ten cubits[c] from rim to rim and five cubits high. It took a line of thirty cubits[d] to measure around it. 24Below the rim, gourds encircled it—ten to a cubit. The gourds were cast in two rows in one piece with the Sea.

25The Sea stood on twelve bulls,[k] three facing north, three facing west, three facing south and three facing east. The Sea rested on top of them, and their hindquarters were toward the center. 26It was a handbreadth[e] in thickness, and its rim was like the rim of a cup, like a lily blossom. It held two thousand baths.[f]

27He also made ten movable stands[l] of bronze; each was four cubits long, four wide and three high.[g] 28This is how the stands were made: They had side panels attached to uprights. 29On the panels between the uprights were lions, bulls and cherubim—and on the uprights as well. Above and below the lions and bulls were wreaths of hammered work. 30Each stand[m] had four bronze wheels with bronze axles, and each had a basin resting on four supports, cast with wreaths on each side. 31On the inside of the stand there was an opening that had a circular frame one cubit[h] deep. This opening was round, and with its basework it measured a cubit and a half.[i] Around its opening there was engraving. The panels of the stands were square, not round. 32The four wheels were under the panels, and the axles of the wheels were attached to the stand. The diameter of each wheel was a cubit and a half. 33The wheels were made like chariot wheels; the axles, rims, spokes and hubs were all of cast metal.

34Each stand had four handles, one on each corner, projecting from the stand. 35At the top of the stand there was a circular band half a cubit[j] deep. The supports and panels were attached to the top of the stand. 36He engraved cherubim, lions and palm trees on the surfaces of the supports and on the panels, in every available space, with wreaths all around. 37This is the way he made the ten stands. They were all cast in the same molds and were identical in size and shape.

38He then made ten bronze basins,[n] each holding forty baths[k] and measuring four cubits across, one basin to go on each of the ten stands. 39He placed five of the stands on the south side of the temple and five on the north. He placed the Sea on the south side, at the southeast corner of the temple. 40He also made the basins and shovels and sprinkling bowls.

So Huram finished all the work he had undertaken for King Solomon in the temple of the LORD:

41 the two pillars;

the two bowl-shaped capitals on top of the pillars;

the two sets of network decorating the two bowl-shaped capitals on top of the pillars;

42 the four hundred pomegranates for the two sets of network (two rows of pomegranates for each network, decorating the bowl-shaped capitals[o] on top of the pillars);

43 the ten stands with their ten basins;

44 the Sea and the twelve bulls under it;

45 the pots, shovels and sprinkling bowls.[p]

All these objects that Huram made for King Solomon for the temple of the LORD were of burnished bronze. 46The king had them cast in clay molds in the plain[q] of the Jordan between Succoth[r] and Zarethan.[s] 47Solomon left all these things un-

---

[a] 21 *Jakin* probably means *he establishes.*   [b] 21 *Boaz* probably means *in him is strength.*   [c] 23 That is, about 15 feet (about 4.5 meters)   [d] 23 That is, about 45 feet (about 13.5 meters)   [e] 26 That is, about 3 inches (about 8 centimeters)   [f] 26 That is, probably about 11,500 gallons (about 44 kiloliters); the Septuagint does not have this sentence.   [g] 27 That is, about 6 feet (about 1.8 meters) long and wide and about 4 1/2 feet (about 1.3 meters) high   [h] 31 That is, about 1 1/2 feet (about 0.5 meter)   [i] 31 That is, about 2 1/4 feet (about 0.7 meter); also in verse 32   [j] 35 That is, about 3/4 foot (about 0.2 meter)   [k] 38 That is, about 230 gallons (about 880 liters)

weighed,[t] because there were so many; the weight of the bronze was not determined.

48 Solomon also made all the furnishings that were in the LORD's temple:

the golden altar;

the golden table[u] on which was the bread of the Presence;[v]
49 the lampstands[w] of pure gold (five on the right and five on the left, in front of the inner sanctuary);

the gold floral work and lamps and tongs;
50 the pure gold basins, wick trimmers, sprinkling bowls, dishes and censers;[x]
and the gold sockets for the doors of the innermost room, the Most Holy Place, and also for the doors of the main hall of the temple.

51 When all the work King Solomon had done for the temple of the LORD was finished, he brought in the things his father David had dedicated[y]—the silver and gold and the furnishings—and he placed them in the treasuries of the LORD's temple.

The Ark Brought to the Temple

8 Then King Solomon summoned into his presence at Jerusalem the elders of Israel, all the heads of the tribes and the chiefs[z] of the Israelite families, to bring up the ark[a] of the LORD's covenant from Zion, the City of David.[b] 2 All the men of Israel came together to King Solomon at the time of the festival[c] in the month of Ethanim, the seventh month.[d]

3 When all the elders of Israel had arrived, the priests[e] took up the ark, 4 and they brought up the ark of the LORD and the Tent of Meeting[f] and all the sacred furnishings in it. The priests and Levites carried them up, 5 and King Solomon and the entire assembly of Israel that had gathered about him were before the ark, sacrificing[g] so many sheep and cattle that they could not be recorded or counted.

6 The priests then brought the ark of the LORD's covenant[h] to its place in the inner sanctuary of the temple, the Most Holy Place, and put it beneath the wings of the cherubim.[i] 7 The cherubim spread their wings over the place of the ark and overshadowed the ark and its carrying poles. 8 These poles were so long that their ends could be seen from the Holy Place in front of the inner sanctuary, but not from outside the Holy Place; and they are still there today.[j] 9 There was nothing in the ark except the two stone tablets[k] that Moses had placed in it at Horeb, where the LORD made a covenant with the Israelites after they came out of Egypt.

10 When the priests withdrew from the Holy Place, the cloud[l] filled the temple of the LORD. 11 And the priests could not perform their service because of the cloud, for the glory of the LORD filled his temple.

12 Then Solomon said, "The LORD has said that he would dwell in a dark cloud;[m] 13 I have indeed built a magnificent temple for you, a place for you to dwell[n] forever."

7:47
t 1Ch 22:3

7:48
u Ex 37:10
v Ex 25:30
7:49
w Ex 25:31-38

7:50
x 2Ki 25:13

7:51
y 2Sa 8:11

8:1
z Nu 7:2 a 2Sa 6:17
b 2Sa 5:7
8:2
c 2Ch 7:8
d Lev 23:34

8:3
e Nu 7:9; Jos 3:3
8:4
f 1Ki 3:4; 2Ch 1:3

8:5
g 2Sa 6:13

8:6
h 2Sa 6:17
i 1Ki 6:19,27

8:8
j Ex 25:13-15

8:9
k Ex 24:7-8; 25:21; 40:20; Dt 10:2-5; Heb 9:4
8:10
l Ex 40:34-35; 2Ch 7:1-2

8:12
m Ps 18:11; 97:2
8:13
n Ex 15:17; 2Sa 7:13; Ps 132:13

1 Kings 8:1–21

Along with all the treasures of David (7:51), Solomon brought to the temple complex the ark of the covenant and the other sacred furnishings of the tabernacle, or "Tent of Meeting" (v. 4). When the ark was put in place, the glory of the Lord filled the temple (vv. 10–11)—just as had happened at the completion of the tabernacle (Ex. 40:34–35).

Solomon, as king and shepherd, blessed the people on God's authority, as his representative. The blessing (vv. 15–21) took the form of praise to God for fulfilling his promise to David. Notice the expressions "with his own hand" and "with his own mouth." What God had promised he also carried out.

Without God's presence Israel's possession of

the land would have been an empty blessing. The scene in verses 10–11 is described with a reporter's concise terminology, but the event must have been a spectacle. All sacrificial activity ceased; the priests couldn't do their work when God revealed his presence. How is God's presence real and meaningful in your life?

One gospel song advises each of us to "count your many blessings, see what God has done." Do you mentally rehearse God's work in your life on a regular basis? Solomon recounted God's faithfulness to his promises, implying that God would continue to be trustworthy. The verb *remember* plays an important part in Scripture and is essential for our faith. You might find it helpful to look up some of the verses for it and related words (like *remembrance*) in the concordance at the back of this Bible.

¹⁴While the whole assembly of Israel was standing there, the king turned around and blessed^o them. ¹⁵Then he said:

"Praise be to the LORD,^p the God of Israel, who with his own hand has fulfilled what he promised with his own mouth to my father David. For he said, ¹⁶'Since the day I brought my people Israel out of Egypt, I have not chosen a city in any tribe of Israel to have a temple built for my Name^q to be there, but I have chosen^r David^s to rule my people Israel.'

¹⁷"My father David had it in his heart to build a temple^t for the Name of the LORD, the God of Israel. ¹⁸But the LORD said to my father David, 'Because it was in your heart to build a temple for my Name, you did well to have this in your heart. ¹⁹Nevertheless, you^u are not the one to build the temple, but your son, who is your own flesh and blood—he is the one who will build the temple for my Name.'^v

²⁰"The LORD has kept the promise he made: I have succeeded David my father and now I sit on the throne of Israel, just as the LORD promised, and I have built^w the temple for the Name of the LORD, the God of Israel. ²¹I have provided a place there for the ark, in which is the covenant of the LORD that he made with our fathers when he brought them out of Egypt."

Solomon's Prayer of Dedication

²²Then Solomon stood before the altar of the LORD in front of the whole assembly of Israel, spread out his hands^x toward heaven ²³and said:

"O LORD, God of Israel, there is no God like^y you in heaven above or on

Cross references (left margin):
8:14
o 2Sa 6:18
8:15
p 2Sa 7:12-13; 1Ch 29:10,20; Ne 9:5; Lk 1:68
8:16
q Dt 12:5 r 1Sa 16:1
s 2Sa 7:4-6,8
8:17
t 2Sa 7:2; 1Ch 17:1
8:19
u 2Sa 7:5
v 2Sa 7:13; 1Ki 5:3,5
8:20
w 1Ch 28:6
8:22
x Ex 9:29; Ezr 9:5
8:23
y 1Sa 2:2; 2Sa 7:22

---

1 Kings 8:22–61

After beginning with a focus on God's promise to David (vv. 23–26), Solomon's lengthy dedication prayer majored on the need for forgiveness in times of failure (vv. 27–53). The *promise* depended on obedience—but the *people* depended on forgiveness. The temple itself was of no account apart from the loyalty of a people destined by their human nature to fail (v. 46)! But this isn't to pour cold water on a great celebration. *Grace* was the means by which the celebration could truly be joyful.

8:22–53

Types of Prayer

The establishment of Solomon's temple in Jerusalem brought a renewed emphasis on prayer to Israelite religious thought and life. Solomon's prayer of dedication for the temple placed great importance on prayer in maintaining Israel's covenant relationship with God (cf. 1 Kings 8:22–53 with 2 Chron. 6:12–42).

Whether we express homage to God or disclose a need, both types of prayer demonstrate dependence on God and glorify him as the One who has answered prayer in the past and has the compassion and ability to do so again in the future. Distinct but related expressions of prayer can be seen as follows:

Worship: ascribing to God the glory due his name (Ps. 29:1–2)	**Devotion:** expression of dedication or commitment; in an Old Testament context, prayer resulting in a vow (1 Sam. 1:11)	**Petition or supplication:** presenting personal needs, concerns, cares, and/or complaints to God (1 Sam. 1:17; Ps. 20:5)
Praise: occupying ourselves with who God is and what he has done (Ps. 135:1–7)	**Communion:** emphasizing relationship with God and two-way communication and fellowship in prayer (Ps. 5:3; 42:8; 94:19)	**Intercession:** petitioning on behalf of another individual or group (Ex. 32:11; 1 Sam. 12:16)
Thanksgiving: specifically appreciating God's goodness (Ps. 136:1)	**Confession:** admitting sin and guilt individually or corporately before God, a necessary prerequisite for prayer and worship (Ezra 9:6–15; Neh. 9:1–3)	**Imprecation:** calling for the application of divine justice against God's enemies (Ps. 137:8). Christ's new covenant emphasizes love and forgiveness of people, so this is considered by some a form of warfare prayer today (cf. 2 Cor. 10:4–6; Eph. 6:12).
Adoration: personal, loving worship (Ps. 73:25)		

Jesus demonstrated a life of prayer and taught his disciples to pray. How is this discipline of prayer being cultivated in your life?

Source: NIV Application Commentary, 1 & 2 Chronicles (2003:425)

earth below—you who keep your covenant of love[z] with your servants who continue wholeheartedly in your way. 24You have kept your promise to your servant David my father; with your mouth you have promised and with your hand you have fulfilled it—as it is today.

25"Now LORD, God of Israel, keep for your servant David my father the promises[a] you made to him when you said, 'You shall never fail to have a man to sit before me on the throne of Israel, if only your sons are careful in all they do to walk before me as you have done.' 26And now, O God of Israel, let your word that you promised[b] your servant David my father come true.

27"But will God really dwell[c] on earth? The heavens, even the highest heaven, cannot contain[d] you. How much less this temple I have built! 28Yet give attention to your servant's prayer and his plea for mercy, O LORD my God. Hear the cry and the prayer that your servant is praying in your presence this day. 29May your eyes be open[e] toward[f] this temple night and day, this place of which you said, 'My Name[g] shall be there,' so that you will hear the prayer your servant prays toward this place. 30Hear the supplication of your servant and of your people Israel when they pray toward this place. Hear from heaven, your dwelling place, and when you hear, forgive.[h]

31"When a man wrongs his neighbor and is required to take an oath and he comes and swears the oath[i] before your altar in this temple, 32then hear from heaven and act. Judge between your servants, condemning the guilty and bringing down on his own head what he has done. Declare the innocent not guilty, and so establish his innocence.[j]

33"When your people Israel have been defeated[k] by an enemy because they have sinned[l] against you, and when they turn back to you and confess your name, praying and making supplication to you in this temple, 34then hear

8:23
z Dt 7:9,12; Ne 1:5; 9:32; Da 9:4

8:25
a 1Ki 2:4

8:26
b 2Sa 7:25
8:27
c Ac 7:48
d 2Ch 2:6; Ps 139:7-16; Isa 66:1; Jer 23:24

8:29
e 2Ch 7:15; Ne 1:6
f Da 6:10
g Dt 12:11

8:30
h Ps 85:2

8:31
i Ex 22:11

8:32
j Dt 25:1

8:33
k Lev 26:17; Dt 28:25
l Lev 26:39

The expression "may your eyes be open toward" (v. 29) an object is a common way of signifying care (cf. Ps. 31:22; 34:15; 101:6). This verse forms the core of the whole prayer. God had allowed a temple to be built in his name (5:5), thereby identifying himself with his people. He provided through the temple a place of contact between the people and himself, a way for sinful humans to approach a holy God, receive forgiveness, and live in fellowship with him.

We too may recognize conceptually the need for forgiveness for our sinful behavior. But we are not always aware when our prayers are coming from a compromised position. It's difficult for Christians in an affluent society to learn the kind of trust and commitment a relationship with God demands. God grants us ample provisions, and we are responsible to use them wisely. But there is a constant danger that we may become dependent upon material resources and technologies. God is all we need, but we don't always grasp that until he's all we have.

Jesus fulfilled for us the promise of the temple. He fully identified with us by "taking the very nature of a servant, being made in human likeness" (Phil. 2:7). He became the point of contact for us as sinful humans to encounter the living God and find forgiveness (Heb. 10:19–22).

8:27

Three Heavens

The word *heaven* means "that which is above." *Heaven* is a word used often in the Bible, but not always in the same sense. Three meanings predominate:

1. Atmospheric Heaven:	2. Celestial Heaven:	3. Believers' Heaven:
Refers to the atmosphere, no more than 20 miles deep, surrounding planet Earth. "The land you are crossing . . . is a land of mountains and valleys that drinks rain from heaven" (Deut. 11:11).	Refers to what we commonly call outer space. It's the realm of the sun, moon, and stars, of the seemingly infinite expanse of galaxies and solar systems. "The heavens declare the glory of God; the skies proclaim the work of his hands" (Ps. 19:1).	Refers to a state of communion with God: "I live in a high and holy place, but also with him who is contrite and lowly in spirit" (Isa. 57:15).

God doesn't "live" in any of these places. The first two simply aren't big enough: "The heavens, even the highest heaven, cannot contain [God]" (1 Kings 8:27). The third, communion with God, is our reward for obedience. We enjoy this fellowship in a limited way now, but one day we will live in full intimacy with God in the new heavens and the new earth (Rev. 21:1–5).

505

from heaven and forgive the sin of your people Israel and bring them back to the land you gave to their fathers.

³⁵ "When the heavens are shut up and there is no rain ^m because your people have sinned against you, and when they pray toward this place and confess your name and turn from their sin because you have afflicted them, ³⁶then hear from heaven and forgive the sin of your servants, your people Israel. Teachⁿ them the right way^o to live, and send rain on the land you gave your people for an inheritance.

³⁷ "When famine^p or plague comes to the land, or blight^q or mildew, locusts or grasshoppers, or when an enemy besieges them in any of their cities, whatever disaster or disease may come, ³⁸and when a prayer or plea is made by any of your people Israel—each one aware of the afflictions of his own heart, and spreading out his hands toward this temple— ³⁹then hear from heaven, your dwelling place. Forgive and act; deal with each man according to all he does, since you know^r his heart (for you alone know the hearts of all men), ⁴⁰so that they will fear^s you all the time they live in the land you gave our fathers.

⁴¹ "As for the foreigner who does not belong to your people Israel but has come from a distant land because of your name— ⁴²for men will hear of your great name and your mighty hand^t and your outstretched arm—when he comes and prays toward this temple, ⁴³then hear from heaven, your dwelling place, and do whatever the foreigner asks of you, so that all the peoples of the earth may know^u your name and fear^v you, as do your own people Israel, and may know that this house I have built bears your Name.

⁴⁴ "When your people go to war against their enemies, wherever you send them, and when they pray to the LORD toward the city you have chosen and the temple I have built for your Name, ⁴⁵then hear from heaven their prayer and their plea, and uphold their cause.

⁴⁶ "When they sin against you—for there is no one who does not sin^w—and you become angry with them and give them over to the enemy, who takes them captive^x to his own land, far away or near; ⁴⁷and if they have a change of heart in the land where they are held captive, and repent and plead^y with you in the land of their conquerors and say, 'We have sinned, we have done wrong, we have acted wickedly';^z ⁴⁸and if they turn back to you with all their heart^a and soul in the land of their enemies who took them captive, and pray^b to you toward the land you gave their fathers, toward the city you have chosen and the temple^c I have built for your Name; ⁴⁹then from heaven, your dwelling place, hear their prayer and their plea, and uphold their cause. ⁵⁰And forgive your people, who have sinned against you; forgive all the offenses they have committed against you, and cause their conquerors to show them mercy;^d ⁵¹for they are your people and your inheritance,^e whom you brought out of Egypt, out of that iron-smelting furnace.^f

⁵² "May your eyes be open to your servant's plea and to the plea of your people Israel, and may you listen to them whenever they cry out to you. ⁵³For you singled them out from all the nations of the world to be your own inheritance,^g just as you declared through your servant Moses when you, O Sovereign LORD, brought our fathers out of Egypt."

⁵⁴When Solomon had finished all these prayers and supplications to the LORD, he rose from before the altar of the LORD, where he had been kneeling with his hands spread out toward heaven. ⁵⁵He stood and blessed^h the whole assembly of Israel in a loud voice, saying:

⁵⁶ "Praise be to the LORD, who has given restⁱ to his people Israel just as he promised. Not one word has failed of all the good promises^j he gave through his servant Moses. ⁵⁷May the LORD our God be with us as he was with our fathers; may he never leave us nor forsake^k us. ⁵⁸May he turn our hearts^l to him, to walk in all his ways and to keep the commands, decrees and regulations he gave our fathers. ⁵⁹And may these words of mine, which I have prayed before

---

8:35
^m Lev 26:19;
Dt 28:24
8:36
ⁿ 1Sa 12:23;
Ps 25:4; 94:12
^o Ps 5:8; 27:11;
Jer 6:16
8:37
^p Lev 26:26
^q Dt 28:22

8:39
^r 1Sa 16:7;
1Ch 28:9; Ps 11:4;
Jer 17:10; Jn 2:24;
Ac 1:24
8:40
^s Ps 130:4
8:42
^t Dt 3:24

8:43
^u 1Sa 17:46;
2Ki 19:19
^v Ps 102:15

8:46
^w Pr 20:9; Ecc 7:20;
Ro 3:9; 1Jn 1:8-10
^x Lev 26:33-39;
Dt 28:64
8:47
^y Lev 26:40; Ne 1:6
^z Ps 106:6; Da 9:5
8:48
^a Dt 4:29;
Jer 29:12-14
^b Da 6:10 ^c Jnh 2:4

8:50
^d 2Ch 30:9;
Ps 106:46
8:51
^e Dt 4:20; 9:29;
Ne 1:10 ^f Jer 11:4

8:53
^g Ex 19:5;
Dt 9:26-29

8:55
^h ver 14; 2Sa 6:18

8:56
ⁱ Dt 12:10
^j Jos 21:45; 23:15

8:57
^k Dt 31:6; Jos 1:5;
Heb 13:5
8:58
^l Ps 119:36

the LORD, be near to the LORD our God day and night, that he may uphold the cause of his servant and the cause of his people Israel according to each day's need, ⁶⁰so that all the peoples ᵐ of the earth may know that the LORD is God and that there is no other. ⁿ ⁶¹But your hearts must be fully committed ᵒ to the LORD our God, to live by his decrees and obey his commands, as at this time."

The Dedication of the Temple

⁶²Then the king and all Israel with him offered sacrifices before the LORD. ⁶³Solomon offered a sacrifice of fellowship offerings ᵃ to the LORD: twenty-two thousand cattle and a hundred and twenty thousand sheep and goats. So the king and all the Israelites dedicated the temple of the LORD.

⁶⁴On that same day the king consecrated the middle part of the courtyard in front of the temple of the LORD, and there he offered burnt offerings, grain offerings and the fat of the fellowship offerings, because the bronze altar ᵖ before the LORD was too small to hold the burnt offerings, the grain offerings and the fat of the fellowship offerings.

⁶⁵So Solomon observed the festival ᵠ at that time, and all Israel with him—a vast assembly, people from Lebo ᵇ Hamath ʳ to the Wadi of Egypt. ˢ They celebrated it before the LORD our God for seven days and seven days more, fourteen days in all. ⁶⁶On the following day he sent the people away. They blessed the king and then went home, joyful and glad in heart for all the good things the LORD had done for his servant David and his people Israel.

The LORD Appears to Solomon

9 When Solomon had finished ᵗ building the temple of the LORD and the royal palace, and had achieved all he had desired to do, ²the LORD appeared ᵘ to him a second time, as he had appeared to him at Gibeon. ³The LORD said to him:

"I have heard ᵛ the prayer and plea you have made before me; I have consecrated this temple, which you have built, by putting my Name there forever. My eyes ʷ and my heart will always be there.

⁴"As for you, if you walk before me in integrity of heart ˣ and uprightness, as David ʸ your father did, and do all I command and observe my decrees and laws, ⁵I will establish ᶻ your royal throne over Israel forever, as I promised David your father when I said, 'You shall never fail ᵃ to have a man on the throne of Israel.'

⁶"But if you ᶜ or your sons turn away ᵇ from me and do not observe the commands and decrees I have given you ᶜ and go off to serve other gods and worship them, ⁷then I will cut off Israel from the land ᶜ I have given them and will reject this temple I have consecrated for my Name. ᵈ Israel will then become a byword ᵉ and an object of ridicule ᶠ among all peoples. ⁸And though this tem-

---

ᵃ 63 Traditionally *peace offerings*; also in verse 64   ᵇ 65 Or *from the entrance to*   ᶜ 6 The Hebrew is plural.

8:60 ᵐ Jos 4:24; 1Sa 17:46 ⁿ Dt 4:35; 1Ki 18:39; Jer 10:10-12 **8:61** ᵒ 1Ki 11:4; 15:3,14; 2Ki 20:3
8:64 ᵖ 2Ch 4:1
8:65 ᵠ ver 2; Lev 23:34 ʳ Nu 34:8; Jos 13:5; Jdg 3:3; 2Ki 14:25 ˢ Ge 15:18
9:1 ᵗ 1Ki 7:1; 2Ch 8:6 **9:2** ᵘ 1Ki 3:5
9:3 ᵛ 2Ki 20:5; Ps 10:17 ʷ Dt 11:12; 1Ki 8:29
9:4 ˣ Ge 17:1 ʸ 1Ki 15:5
9:5 ᶻ 1Ch 22:10 ᵃ 2Sa 7:15; 1Ki 2:4
9:6 ᵇ 2Sa 7:14
9:7 ᶜ 2Ki 17:23; 25:21 ᵈ Jer 7:14 ᵉ Ps 44:14 ᶠ Dt 28:37

---

1 Kings 8:62–66

The temple was dedicated at the time of the Feast of Tabernacles in the seventh month (v. 1). The closing (vv. 65–66) brings the account back to the events in the introduction (vv. 1–2), with added details. The celebration for the dedication of the temple lasted seven days, with an additional seven days for commemoration of the feast (cf. 2 Chron. 7:9–10). Countless sacrifices were offered during the time of the installation of the ark (1 Kings 8:5) and continuously throughout the dedication celebration and the festival.

The people went home rejoicing, deeply satisfied in the realization that God's blessing was on the king and on the nation as a whole. Worshiping God with a whole congregation has an uplifting effect. It raises our hearts to contemplate God's presence and great love for us. It also puts us in contact with others who may need our encouragement or who can encourage us in life's difficult times. Is worshiping God with other believers a regular component of your practice of the spiritual disciplines?

1 Kings 9:1–9

God's promise of an eternal house of David would always be contingent upon the absolute faithfulness of the Davidic kings. This wasn't to dismiss the possibility of grace and forgiveness. The problem lay in the potential for expecting grace while compromising the covenant. This was the warning of the vision: No majestic building or eloquent prayer could substitute for obedience.

9:8
g Dt 29:24;
Jer 22:8-9

ple is now imposing, all who pass by will be appalled and will scoff and say, 'Why has the LORD done such a thing to this land and to this temple?'g 9People will answer, 'Because they have forsaken the LORD their God, who brought their fathers out of Egypt, and have embraced other gods, worshiping and serving them—that is why the LORD brought all this disaster on them.' "

Solomon's Other Activities

10At the end of twenty years, during which Solomon built these two buildings—the temple of the LORD and the royal palace— 11King Solomon gave twenty towns in Galilee to Hiram king of Tyre, because Hiram had supplied him with all the ce-

9:11
h 2Ch 8:2

dar and pine and goldh he wanted. 12But when Hiram went from Tyre to see the towns that Solomon had given him, he was not pleased with them. 13"What kind of towns are these you have given me, my brother?" he asked. And he called them

9:13
i Jos 19:27

the Land of Cabul,a i a name they have to this day. 14Now Hiram had sent to the king 120 talentsb of gold.

9:15
j Jos 16:10;
1Ki 5:13 k ver 24;
2Sa 5:9 l Jos 19:36
m Jos 17:11

15Here is the account of the forced labor King Solomon conscriptedj to build the LORD's temple, his own palace, the supporting terraces,c k the wall of Jerusalem, and Hazor,l Megiddo and Gezer.m 16(Pharaoh king of Egypt had attacked and captured Gezer. He had set it on fire. He killed its Canaanite inhabitants and then gave it as a wedding gift to his daughter, Solomon's wife. 17And Solomon rebuilt Gezer.)

9:17
n Jos 16:3; 2Ch 8:5
9:18
o Jos 19:44
9:19
p ver 1 q 1Ki 4:26

He built up Lower Beth Horon,n 18Baalath,o and Tadmord in the desert, within his land, 19as well as all his store citiesp and the towns for his chariotsq and for his horsese—whatever he desired to build in Jerusalem, in Lebanon and throughout all the territory he ruled.

9:21
r Ge 9:25-26
s Jos 15:63; 17:12;
Jdg 1:21,27,29
t Ezr 2:55,58
9:22
u Lev 25:39

20All the people left from the Amorites, Hittites, Perizzites, Hivites and Jebusites (these peoples were not Israelites), 21that is, their descendantsr remaining in the land, whom the Israelites could not exterminatef s—these Solomon conscripted for his slave labor force,t as it is to this day. 22But Solomon did not make slavesu of any of the Israelites; they were his fighting men, his government officials, his officers,

9:23
v 1Ki 5:16

his captains, and the commanders of his chariots and charioteers. 23They were also the chief officialsv in charge of Solomon's projects—550 officials supervising the men who did the work.

---

a 13 Cabul sounds like the Hebrew for good-for-nothing.   b 14 That is, about 4 1/2 tons (about 4 metric tons)   c 15 Or the Millo; also in verse 24   d 18 The Hebrew may also be read Tamar.
e 19 Or charioteers   f 21 The Hebrew term refers to the irrevocable giving over of things or persons to the LORD, often by totally destroying them.

📖 Worshiping a God who is only our Father or friend isn't truly worshiping the God of Scripture. After all, the Lord of the temple and the Christ of the cosmos will bring all powers to submission to their authority (cf. 1 Cor. 15:24–26). Situations like drought, famine, and war (1 Kings 8:33–40) are all matters of personal concern, but they are not limited to personal concerns. God is a personal God—but never just a personal God. In terms of this passage, who else is he, and what does he expect from you? From your nation? From his body, the church?

1 Kings 9:10–28

📖 Solomon's payments of cities to Hiram should probably be seen as a separate transaction (territory for gold; v. 14). Payment for building materials and wages had already been made in annual contributions of grain and oil (5:6,10–11). The weight of a talent varied in different systems and times, but at minimum Hiram had given Solomon several tons of gold (see NIV text note for v. 14). He thought the 20 settlements in northern Galilee a miserly return on his investment.

The author of Kings presents both the positive and negative aspects of Solomon's lifestyle and reign. This passage affirms how Solomon led the way in honoring the Lord during Israel's three great annual festivals (v. 25). But we also see Solomon breaking three rules God had given Israel's kings in Deuteronomy 17:14–17: He accumulated large amounts of gold (v. 14; cf. 10:14 and notes for 10:14–29); acquired great numbers of horses (v. 19; cf. 4:26; 10:26); and had multiple wives—many of them idol worshiping non-Israelites (v. 24; cf. 11:1–3 and notes for 11:1–13).

📖 Like Solomon, do you at times repay your debts with the least possible effort? How diligent are you at work? Christians are to live and work "so that [our] daily life may win the respect of outsiders and so that [we] will not be dependent on anybody" (1 Thess. 4:12). Solomon's example shows how easy it is to be influenced by the habits and customs of others and of society in general. How do you relate to the mixed bag of Solomon's character and spiritual life (cf. Rom. 7:15)? Are you as a Christian moving in the right (God-ordained) direction?

²⁴After Pharaoh's daughter^w had come up from the City of David to the palace Solomon had built for her, he constructed the supporting terraces.^x

²⁵Three^y times a year Solomon sacrificed burnt offerings and fellowship offerings^a on the altar he had built for the LORD, burning incense before the LORD along with them, and so fulfilled the temple obligations.

²⁶King Solomon also built ships^z at Ezion Geber,^a which is near Elath in Edom, on the shore of the Red Sea.^b ²⁷And Hiram sent his men—sailors^b who knew the sea—to serve in the fleet with Solomon's men. ²⁸They sailed to Ophir^c and brought back 420 talents^c of gold, which they delivered to King Solomon.

The Queen of Sheba Visits Solomon

10 When the queen of Sheba^d heard about the fame of Solomon and his relation to the name of the LORD, she came to test him with hard questions.^e ²Arriving at Jerusalem with a very great caravan—with camels carrying spices, large quantities of gold, and precious stones—she came to Solomon and talked with him about all that she had on her mind. ³Solomon answered all her questions; nothing was too hard for the king to explain to her. ⁴When the queen of Sheba saw all the wisdom of Solomon and the palace he had built, ⁵the food on his table,^f the seating of his officials, the attending servants in their robes, his cupbearers, and the burnt offerings he made at^d the temple of the LORD, she was overwhelmed.

⁶She said to the king, "The report I heard in my own country about your achievements and your wisdom is true. ⁷But I did not believe these things until I came and saw with my own eyes. Indeed, not even half was told me; in wisdom and wealth^g you have far exceeded the report I heard. ⁸How happy your men must be! How happy your officials, who continually stand before you and hear^h your wisdom! ⁹Praiseⁱ be to the LORD your God, who has delighted in you and placed you on the throne of Israel. Because of the LORD's eternal love for Israel, he has made you king, to maintain justice^j and righteousness."

¹⁰And she gave the king 120 talents^e of gold,^k large quantities of spices, and precious stones. Never again were so many spices brought in as those the queen of Sheba gave to King Solomon.

¹¹(Hiram's ships brought gold from Ophir;^l and from there they brought great cargoes of almugwood^f and precious stones. ¹²The king used the almugwood to make supports for the temple of the LORD and for the royal palace, and to make harps and lyres for the musicians. So much almugwood has never been imported or seen since that day.)

¹³King Solomon gave the queen of Sheba all she desired and asked for, besides

---

^a 25 Traditionally *peace offerings*   ^b 26 Hebrew *Yam Suph*; that is, Sea of Reeds   ^c 28 That is, about 16 tons (about 14.5 metric tons)   ^d 5 Or *the ascent by which he went up to*   ^e 10 That is, about 4 1/2 tons (about 4 metric tons)   ^f 11 Probably a variant of *algumwood*; also in verse 12

Cross references (margin):

9:24 w 1Ki 3:1; 7:8 / x 2Sa 5:9; 1Ki 11:27; 2Ch 32:5
9:25 y Ex 23:14; 2Ch 8:12-13,16
9:26 z 1Ki 22:48 / a Nu 33:35; Dt 2:8
9:27 b 1Ki 10:11; Eze 27:8
9:28 c 1Ch 29:4
10:1 d Ge 10:7,28; Mt 12:42; Lk 11:31 / e Jdg 14:12
10:5 f 1Ch 26:16
10:7 g 1Ch 29:25
10:8 h Pr 8:34
10:9 i 1Ki 5:7 / 2Sa 8:15; Ps 33:5; 72:2
10:10 k ver 2
10:11 l Ge 10:29; 1Ki 9:27-28

---

1 Kings 10:1–13

Sheba was in southwest Arabia, present-day Yemen. Though it was the best-watered and most fertile area of Arabia, its chief strength was as a center of trade. Solomon's fame had reached the queen, probably through the caravan traders who regularly passed through Israel on their way to Damascus or Gaza. She came to see for herself whether the glowing reports had been exaggerated. No doubt the "hard questions" (v. 1) or riddles posed by the queen were more than frivolous tests of mental agility. They represented a genuine seeking for truths hidden in some of his sayings known to her or related to problems encountered in her rule.

Jesus would later use this incident to rebuke the Pharisees and teachers of the law for their refusal to give him a fair hearing (Matt. 12:42). The queen of Sheba traveled a great distance to listen to Solomon's wisdom. Yet the scribes, who because of their acquaintance with Scripture should have been interested in learning whether Jesus' claims were true, refused to listen—and Christ is far greater than Solomon. How "far" did you travel in your spiritual journey to discover the wisdom of Christ? How much effort are you exerting now to tap into that limitless supply?

1 Kings 10:14–29

The account of Solomon's wealth and wisdom wasn't included here to provide an illustration of how God expected the Israelites to live, or even to demonstrate an ideal living standard each subsequent king was to try to achieve. The single objective of this account was to show that Solomon was superior to the greatest kings of his time (vv. 23–25).

what he had given her out of his royal bounty. Then she left and returned with her retinue to her own country.

Solomon's Splendor

10:14
m 1Ki 9:28

14 The weight of the gold[m] that Solomon received yearly was 666 talents,[a] 15 not including the revenues from merchants and traders and from all the Arabian kings and the governors of the land.

10:16
n 1Ki 14:26-28

16 King Solomon made two hundred large shields[n] of hammered gold; six hundred bekas[b] of gold went into each shield. 17 He also made three hundred small shields of hammered gold, with three minas[c] of gold in each shield. The king put them in the Palace of the Forest of Lebanon.[o]

10:17
o 1Ki 7:2

18 Then the king made a great throne inlaid with ivory and overlaid with fine gold. 19 The throne had six steps, and its back had a rounded top. On both sides of the seat were armrests, with a lion standing beside each of them. 20 Twelve lions stood on the six steps, one at either end of each step. Nothing like it had ever been made for any other kingdom. 21 All King Solomon's goblets were gold, and all the household articles in the Palace of the Forest of Lebanon were pure gold. Nothing was made of silver, because silver was considered of little value in Solomon's days.

10:22
p 1Ki 9:26

22 The king had a fleet of trading ships[d][p] at sea along with the ships of Hiram. Once every three years it returned, carrying gold, silver and ivory, and apes and baboons.

10:23
q 1Ki 3:13
r 1Ki 4:30
10:24
s 1Ki 3:9, 12, 28

23 King Solomon was greater in riches[q] and wisdom[r] than all the other kings of the earth. 24 The whole world sought audience with Solomon to hear the wisdom[s] God had put in his heart. 25 Year after year, everyone who came brought a gift—articles of silver and gold, robes, weapons and spices, and horses and mules.

10:26
t Dt 17:16;
1Ki 4:26; 9:19;
2Ch 1:14; 9:25
10:27
u Dt 17:17

26 Solomon accumulated chariots and horses;[t] he had fourteen hundred chariots and twelve thousand horses,[e] which he kept in the chariot cities and also with him in Jerusalem. 27 The king made silver as common[u] in Jerusalem as stones, and cedar as plentiful as sycamore-fig trees in the foothills. 28 Solomon's horses were imported from Egypt[f] and from Kue[g]—the royal merchants purchased them from Kue.

10:29
v 2Ki 7:6-7

29 They imported a chariot from Egypt for six hundred shekels[h] of silver, and a horse for a hundred and fifty.[i] They also exported them to all the kings of the Hittites[v] and of the Arameans.

Solomon's Wives

11:1
w Dt 17:17;
Ne 13:26

11 King Solomon, however, loved many foreign women[w] besides Pharaoh's daughter—Moabites, Ammonites, Edomites, Sidonians and Hittites. 2 They

---

a 14 That is, about 25 tons (about 23 metric tons)   b 16 That is, about 7 1/2 pounds (about 3.5 kilograms)   c 17 That is, about 3 3/4 pounds (about 1.7 kilograms)   d 22 Hebrew *of ships of Tarshish*   e 26 Or *charioteers*   f 28 Or possibly *Muzur*, a region in Cilicia; also in verse 29   g 28 Probably *Cilicia*   h 29 That is, about 15 pounds (about 7 kilograms)   i 29 That is, about 3 3/4 pounds (about 1.7 kilograms)

It was important to make this statement, because the king who served the Most High God wasn't to be perceived as inferior to those who served other gods. This description of Solomon was proof that the Lord had entered into a saving relationship with the Israelites in order that they might be his people and he their God.

📖 Wealth can be an evidence of God's blessing. But not all riches result from God's blessing, and affluence itself isn't necessarily a blessing. Great wealth is a great responsibility (it proved too great for Solomon). Most Westerners have considerable material well-being compared to others in the world. We are wise to recognize the vulnerable spiritual situation financial security brings. Are you up to the responsibility of handling your resources in a God-honoring way?

On the other hand, those without prosperity don't

need to fear that the opportunity for goodness in life has passed them by. After all, the King of kings who would fulfill God's promise to David (and therefore to Solomon) would have "no place to lay his head" (Luke 9:58).

1 Kings 11:1–13

⚓ Of all the kings in Israel's history, Solomon received the most mixed review in terms of covenant faithfulness. In his old age his devotion turned from God (v. 4). But the process had begun much earlier. Solomon had married Pharaoh's daughter sometime during the first four years of his rule when he allied himself with Egypt against the Philistines (3:1; 9:16). Like other great ancient monarchs, he had numerous wives and concubines, who retained their cultural and religious affiliations. Solomon built shrines to their gods, a detestable compromise to God's temple and his exclusive claims to worship.

were from nations about which the LORD had told the Israelites, "You must not intermarry[x] with them, because they will surely turn your hearts after their gods." Nevertheless, Solomon held fast to them in love. [3]He had seven hundred wives of royal birth and three hundred concubines, and his wives led him astray. [4]As Solomon grew old, his wives turned his heart after other gods, and his heart was not fully devoted[y] to the LORD his God, as the heart of David his father had been. [5]He followed Ashtoreth[z] the goddess of the Sidonians, and Molech[a][a] the detestable god of the Ammonites. [6]So Solomon did evil in the eyes of the LORD; he did not follow the LORD completely, as David his father had done.

[7]On a hill east[b] of Jerusalem, Solomon built a high place for Chemosh[c] the detestable god of Moab, and for Molech[d] the detestable god of the Ammonites. [8]He did the same for all his foreign wives, who burned incense and offered sacrifices to their gods.

[9]The LORD became angry with Solomon because his heart had turned away from the LORD, the God of Israel, who had appeared[e] to him twice. [10]Although he had forbidden Solomon to follow other gods,[f] Solomon did not keep the LORD's command.[g] [11]So the LORD said to Solomon, "Since this is your attitude and you have not kept my covenant and my decrees, which I commanded you, I will most certainly tear[h] the kingdom away from you and give it to one of your subordinates. [12]Nevertheless, for the sake of David your father, I will not do it during your lifetime. I will tear it out of the hand of your son. [13]Yet I will not tear the whole kingdom from him, but will give him one tribe[i] for the sake[j] of David my servant and for the sake of Jerusalem, which I have chosen."[k]

Solomon's Adversaries

[14]Then the LORD raised up against Solomon an adversary, Hadad the Edomite, from the royal line of Edom. [15]Earlier when David was fighting with Edom, Joab the commander of the army, who had gone up to bury the dead, had struck down all the men in Edom.[l] [16]Joab and all the Israelites stayed there for six months, until they had destroyed all the men in Edom. [17]But Hadad, still only a boy, fled to Egypt with some Edomite officials who had served his father. [18]They set out from Midian and went to Paran.[m] Then taking men from Paran with them, they went to Egypt, to Pharaoh king of Egypt, who gave Hadad a house and land and provided him with food.

[19]Pharaoh was so pleased with Hadad that he gave him a sister of his own wife, Queen Tahpenes, in marriage. [20]The sister of Tahpenes bore him a son named Genubath, whom Tahpenes brought up in the royal palace. There Genubath lived with Pharaoh's own children.

[21]While he was in Egypt, Hadad heard that David rested with his fathers and that

[a] 5 Hebrew *Milcom*; also in verse 33

11:2
[x] Ex 34:16; Dt 7:3-4

11:4
[y] 1Ki 8:61; 9:4
11:5
[z] ver 33; Jdg 2:13; 2Ki 23:13 [a] ver 7

11:7
[b] 2Ki 23:13
[c] Nu 21:29; Jdg 11:24
[d] Lev 20:2-5; Ac 7:43

11:9
[e] ver 2-3; 1Ki 3:5; 9:2
11:10
[f] 1Ki 9:6 [g] 1Ki 6:12

11:11
[h] ver 31; 1Ki 12:15-16; 2Ki 17:21

11:13
[i] 1Ki 12:20
[j] 2Sa 7:15
[k] Dt 12:11

11:15
[l] Dt 20:13; 2Sa 8:14; 1Ch 18:12

11:18
[m] Nu 10:12

Jesus would point to the beauty of flowers in the field and remind his hearers that not even Solomon in all his glory could compare (Matt. 6:28–29). A great and wise king/person also may be weak and foolish. Wisdom has the power to produce riches, but the seductive power of wealth can erode the wisdom of following God. Solomon's story in a sense calls us all to be greater and wiser than this greatest and wisest of kings. None of us may compare to Solomon in his heyday, but our most critical need is the wisdom of faithfulness to God. Somehow Solomon let go of this link. How can you ensure that you don't?

1 Kings 11:14–25

As the Lord had just said in verses 11–13, the punishment for Solomon's disobedience would be the kingdom's demise. The external threats weren't new.

Hadad's hatred went back to David's time, and Rezon had been an adversary during all of Solomon's reign. But these enemies wouldn't be the root cause of the kingdom's collapse. It would crumble from within, a spiritual demise.

Spirituality is uncompromising loyalty to God. If there ever was an individual with the opportunity to know God with this degree of loyalty, it was Solomon. God appeared to him twice (see v. 9). The first time he had assured him of incredible blessing because of the priorities Solomon had chosen (3:5–15). The fulfillment of this blessing should have motivated Solomon to absolute devotion. The second vision came as a warning, a reminder that God's blessing doesn't assure our continued faithfulness (9:1–9). Neither the blessing nor the warning had been enough for Solomon. Which of the two would more likely motivate you?

Joab the commander of the army was also dead. Then Hadad said to Pharaoh, "Let me go, that I may return to my own country."

22"What have you lacked here that you want to go back to your own country?" Pharaoh asked.

"Nothing," Hadad replied, "but do let me go!"

23And God raised up against Solomon another adversary,[n] Rezon son of Eliada, who had fled from his master, Hadadezer[o] king of Zobah. 24He gathered men around him and became the leader of a band of rebels when David destroyed the forces[a] of Zobah; the rebels went to Damascus,[p] where they settled and took control. 25Rezon was Israel's adversary as long as Solomon lived, adding to the trouble caused by Hadad. So Rezon ruled in Aram[q] and was hostile toward Israel.

Jeroboam Rebels Against Solomon

26Also, Jeroboam son of Nebat rebelled[r] against the king. He was one of Solomon's officials, an Ephraimite from Zeredah, and his mother was a widow named Zeruah.

27Here is the account of how he rebelled against the king: Solomon had built the supporting terraces[b][s] and had filled in the gap in the wall of the city of David his father. 28Now Jeroboam was a man of standing,[t] and when Solomon saw how well[u] the young man did his work, he put him in charge of the whole labor force of the house of Joseph.

29About that time Jeroboam was going out of Jerusalem, and Ahijah[v] the prophet of Shiloh met him on the way, wearing a new cloak. The two of them were alone out in the country, 30and Ahijah took hold of the new cloak he was wearing and tore[w] it into twelve pieces. 31Then he said to Jeroboam, "Take ten pieces for yourself, for this is what the LORD, the God of Israel, says: 'See, I am going to tear[x] the kingdom out of Solomon's hand and give you ten tribes. 32But for the sake of my servant David and the city of Jerusalem, which I have chosen out of all the tribes of Israel, he will have one tribe. 33I will do this because they have[c] forsaken me and worshiped[y] Ashtoreth the goddess of the Sidonians, Chemosh the god of the Moabites, and Molech the god of the Ammonites, and have not walked in my ways, nor done what is right in my eyes, nor kept my statutes[z] and laws as David, Solomon's father, did.

34" 'But I will not take the whole kingdom out of Solomon's hand; I have made him ruler all the days of his life for the sake of David my servant, whom I chose and who observed my commands and statutes. 35I will take the kingdom from his son's hands and give you ten tribes. 36I will give one tribe[a] to his son so that David my servant may always have a lamp[b] before me in Jerusalem, the city where I chose to put my Name. 37However, as for you, I will take you, and you will rule over all that your heart desires;[c] you will be king over Israel. 38If you do whatever I command you and walk in my ways and do what is right in my eyes by keeping my statutes[d] and commands, as David my servant did, I will be with you. I will build you

a 24 Hebrew destroyed them   b 27 Or the Millo   c 33 Hebrew; Septuagint, Vulgate and Syriac because he has

1 Kings 11:26–40

Exactly when and where Ahijah met Jeroboam isn't specified, but it wasn't a coincidental encounter. The prophet had a message for the young leader, which he communicated in a highly dramatic manner.

The influence and power of Israel's prophets were in complete contrast to the situation in the neighboring nations, where political power rested in the hands of the king and army. This was because of the theology of the covenant. The king was under God's direct rule, as was every other Israelite. Kings who violated the covenant forfeited their right to rule (cf. vv. 11,38). Jeroboam's only claim to the throne was the word of the Lord through his prophet. Apart from that, he was a widow's son and the king's servant.

Throughout human history only ancient Israel has existed as a genuine theocracy—a state under God's direct authority and control. Nevertheless, to what degree do you feel that modern politicians can and should be held accountable to Biblical standards? Major election campaigns in the U.S. often focus on religion, with a critical eye trained on the faith commitments of the candidates. To what extent do you think active Christian faith lived out by high officials affects God's approval of a nation? How much does it impact the thinking of the general populace?

a dynasty[e] as enduring as the one I built for David and will give Israel to you. 39I will humble David's descendants because of this, but not forever.'"

40Solomon tried to kill Jeroboam, but Jeroboam fled to Egypt, to Shishak[f] the king, and stayed there until Solomon's death.

Solomon's Death

41As for the other events of Solomon's reign—all he did and the wisdom he displayed—are they not written in the book of the annals of Solomon? 42Solomon reigned in Jerusalem over all Israel forty years. 43Then he rested with his fathers and was buried in the city of David his father. And Rehoboam[g] his son succeeded him as king.

Israel Rebels Against Rehoboam

12 Rehoboam went to Shechem, for all the Israelites had gone there to make him king. 2When Jeroboam son of Nebat heard this (he was still in Egypt, where he had fled[h] from King Solomon), he returned from[a] Egypt. 3So they sent for Jeroboam, and he and the whole assembly of Israel went to Rehoboam and said to him: 4"Your father put a heavy yoke[i] on us, but now lighten the harsh labor and the heavy yoke he put on us, and we will serve you."

5Rehoboam answered, "Go away for three days and then come back to me." So the people went away.

6Then King Rehoboam consulted the elders[j] who had served his father Solomon during his lifetime. "How would you advise me to answer these people?" he asked.

7They replied, "If today you will be a servant to these people and serve them and give them a favorable answer,[k] they will always be your servants."

8But Rehoboam rejected the advice the elders gave him and consulted the young men who had grown up with him and were serving him. 9He asked them, "What is your advice? How should we answer these people who say to me, 'Lighten the yoke your father put on us'?"

10The young men who had grown up with him replied, "Tell these people who have said to you, 'Your father put a heavy yoke on us, but make our yoke lighter'— tell them, 'My little finger is thicker than my father's waist. 11My father laid on you a heavy yoke; I will make it even heavier. My father scourged you with whips; I will scourge you with scorpions.'"

---

a 2 Or *he remained in*

Marginal references

11:38 e Jos 1:5; 2Sa 7:11, 27
11:40 f 2Ch 12:2
11:43 g 1Ki 14:21; Mt 1:7
12:2 h 1Ki 11:40
12:4 i 1Sa 8:11-18; 1Ki 4:20-28
12:6 j 1Ki 4:2
12:7 k Pr 15:1

---

1 Kings 11:41–43

The annals (historical records or chronicles) of Solomon refer to a written source used by the author of Kings. He would later mention the annals of the kings of Israel and of Judah (e.g., 14:19,29). These additional accounts may have been lost when Jerusalem was destroyed.

The assessments of Solomon's reign in 1 Kings are divided. He is presented both as an ideal king (10:23–25) and as a dismal failure (11:11). Solomon was legendary in terms of his wisdom. Distant monarchs sought it out. Much of the book of Proverbs is connected with Solomon. And yet, especially in the end, he failed to exercise the fundamental wisdom of the fear of the Lord. How hard is it for you to always "practice what you preach"? To what extent are you guilty of communicating to those close to you (your children, perhaps), "Do as I say, not as I do"?

1 Kings 12:1–24

Rehoboam's choice not to follow the counsel of the elders was more than just a foolish political decision. This turn of events was "from the LORD," in fulfillment of the declaration of the prophet (v. 15). But this didn't indicate divine control over Rehoboam's mind. Rehoboam had no desire to follow the Lord or the way of the covenant. He made choices based on his own values, which he had to some degree learned from his father, Solomon. Rehoboam voluntarily brought upon himself the judgment that comes with the rejection of covenant loyalty. Prophetic fulfillment throughout the Old Testament was always consistent with human response to God's covenant.

Tempted as we may be to pass the buck (see Gen. 3:13), none of us can default to "the devil made me do it." Even those who claim no theological knowledge know the fallacy of this quip, quoting it in jest when they know they are in the wrong.

Neither can we shift responsibility for our wrongdoing to God. He can and does *use* our actions and decisions, good or bad, to further his cause—but he doesn't *choose* them. He also reins in the devil—and never himself tempts us to do evil (see James 1:13–15). Thankfully, our freedom of choice extends to the option of going to God in repentance for the absolute forgiveness he offers through Christ's victory over sin and death.

12Three days later Jeroboam and all the people returned to Rehoboam, as the king had said, "Come back to me in three days." 13The king answered the people harshly. Rejecting the advice given him by the elders, 14he followed the advice of the young men and said, "My father made your yoke heavy; I will make it even heavier. My father scourged[l] you with whips; I will scourge you with scorpions." 15So the king did not listen to the people, for this turn of events was from the LORD,[m] to fulfill the word the LORD had spoken to Jeroboam son of Nebat through Ahijah[n] the Shilonite.

16When all Israel saw that the king refused to listen to them, they answered the king:

> "What share do we have in David,
>   what part in Jesse's son?
> To your tents, O Israel![o]
>   Look after your own house, O David!"

So the Israelites went home. 17But as for the Israelites who were living in the towns of Judah,[p] Rehoboam still ruled over them.

18King Rehoboam sent out Adoniram,[a][q] who was in charge of forced labor, but all Israel stoned him to death. King Rehoboam, however, managed to get into his chariot and escape to Jerusalem. 19So Israel has been in rebellion against the house of David[r] to this day.

20When all the Israelites heard that Jeroboam had returned, they sent and called him to the assembly and made him king over all Israel. Only the tribe of Judah remained loyal to the house of David.[s]

21When Rehoboam arrived in Jerusalem, he mustered the whole house of Judah and the tribe of Benjamin—a hundred and eighty thousand fighting men—to make war[t] against the house of Israel and to regain the kingdom for Rehoboam son of Solomon.

22But this word of God came to Shemaiah[u] the man of God: 23"Say to Rehoboam son of Solomon king of Judah, to the whole house of Judah and Benjamin, and to the rest of the people, 24'This is what the LORD says: Do not go up to fight against your brothers, the Israelites. Go home, every one of you, for this is my doing.' " So they obeyed the word of the LORD and went home again, as the LORD had ordered.

Golden Calves at Bethel and Dan

25Then Jeroboam fortified Shechem[v] in the hill country of Ephraim and lived there. From there he went out and built up Peniel.[b][w]

26Jeroboam thought to himself, "The kingdom will now likely revert to the house of David. 27If these people go up to offer sacrifices at the temple of the LORD in Jerusalem,[x] they will again give their allegiance to their lord, Rehoboam king of Judah. They will kill me and return to King Rehoboam."

a 18 Some Septuagint manuscripts and Syriac (see also 1 Kings 4:6 and 5:14); Hebrew *Adoram*
b 25 Hebrew *Penuel*, a variant of *Peniel*

Marginal references:

12:14 / Ex 1:14; 5:5-9,16-18
12:15 m ver 24; Dt 2:30; Jdg 14:4; 2Ch 22:7; 25:20 n 1Ki 11:29
12:16 o 2Sa 20:1
12:17 p 1Ki 11:13,36
12:18 q 2Sa 20:24; 1Ki 4:6; 5:14
12:19 r 2Ki 17:21
12:20 s 1Ki 11:13,32
12:21 t 2Ch 11:1
12:22 u 2Ch 12:5-7
12:25 v Jdg 9:45 w Jdg 8:8,17
12:27 x Dt 12:5-6

---

1 Kings 12:25–33

The cult shrines at Bethel and Dan were particularly offensive to God. The problem wasn't just that they were contrary to worshiping at the one place of God's choosing (see Deut. 12:4–7). After all, Shiloh and Gibeon had been legitimate places of worship. It was that they led to a mixing of the worship of God with Canaanite religion.

Jeroboam also instituted a new religious order drawn from non-Levitical sources. Because of this, many priests and Levites from the northern kingdom migrated to Judah (2 Chron. 11:13–16). Completing his religious innovations, Jeroboam instituted an annual feast on the fifteenth day of the eighth month, no doubt rivaling the Feast of Tabernacles in the seventh month in Jerusalem.

"Truth" in post-modern terms has become an individual matter, and spirituality is often related to personal, emotional health—a "what works for me" mentality. These trends compromise Christian faith, much as Jeroboam's calves and calendar and Rehoboam's sacred stones and Asherah poles (14:23) undermined faith in Israel and Judah. If we fail to clearly distinguish Christian beliefs from post-modern thinking, our faith can be compromised to conform to the culture in which we find ourselves. How has your life been affected by such inclusive views of truth and spirituality?

28After seeking advice, the king made two golden calves.*y* He said to the people, "It is too much for you to go up to Jerusalem. Here are your gods, O Israel, who brought you up out of Egypt."*z* 29One he set up in Bethel,*a* and the other in Dan.*b* 30And this thing became a sin;*c* the people went even as far as Dan to worship the one there.

31Jeroboam built shrines*d* on high places and appointed priests*e* from all sorts of people, even though they were not Levites. 32He instituted a festival on the fifteenth day of the eighth*f* month, like the festival held in Judah, and offered sacrifices on the altar. This he did in Bethel, sacrificing to the calves he had made. And at Bethel he also installed priests at the high places he had made. 33On the fifteenth day of the eighth month, a month of his own choosing, he offered sacrifices on the altar he had built at Bethel.*g* So he instituted the festival for the Israelites and went up to the altar to make offerings.

The Man of God From Judah

13 By the word of the LORD a man of God*h* came from Judah to Bethel,*i* as Jeroboam was standing by the altar to make an offering. 2He cried out against the altar by the word of the LORD: "O altar, altar! This is what the LORD says: 'A son named Josiah*j* will be born to the house of David. On you he will sacrifice the priests of the high places who now make offerings here, and human bones will be burned on you.' " 3That same day the man of God gave a sign:*k* "This is the sign the LORD has declared: The altar will be split apart and the ashes on it will be poured out."

4When King Jeroboam heard what the man of God cried out against the altar at Bethel, he stretched out his hand from the altar and said, "Seize him!" But the hand he stretched out toward the man shriveled up, so that he could not pull it back. 5Also, the altar was split apart and its ashes poured out according to the sign given by the man of God by the word of the LORD.

6Then the king said to the man of God, "Intercede*l* with the LORD your God and pray for me that my hand may be restored." So the man of God interceded with the LORD, and the king's hand was restored and became as it was before.

7The king said to the man of God, "Come home with me and have something to eat, and I will give you a gift."*m*

8But the man of God answered the king, "Even if you were to give me half your possessions,*n* I would not go with you, nor would I eat bread*o* or drink water here. 9For I was commanded by the word of the LORD: 'You must not eat bread or drink water or return by the way you came.' " 10So he took another road and did not return by the way he had come to Bethel.

11Now there was a certain old prophet living in Bethel, whose sons came and told him all that the man of God had done there that day. They also told their father what he had said to the king. 12Their father asked them, "Which way did he go?" And his sons showed him which road the man of God from Judah had taken. 13So he said to his sons, "Saddle the donkey for me." And when they had saddled the

1 Kings 13:1–34

Jeroboam's disobedience to God's word led him to the same fate as the man of God from Judah. The faithful man of God became unfaithful—just as Jeroboam, Israel's anointed king, had gone his own way and become faithless. The man of God from Judah proclaimed God's word in declaring Jeroboam's folly but then chose the way of folly himself in disobeying God's word to him. In spite of the signs of a broken altar and a withered hand (vv. 4–6), Jeroboam refused to change his ways (v. 33). Nevertheless, the word of judgment given by the man of God from Judah would stand (v. 32).

The prophet's suspicious death might lead some to conclude that he had been a false prophet. The narrator

in all likelihood recounted the full story so we could understand that his death had to do with disobedience, not false prophecy. Either way, Jeroboam's altar would come to ruin.

Jeroboam's story is a sobering reminder of the danger of conforming to the culture around us, all the while believing that we are living by faith. This wicked king had a supporting cast of priests who viewed their version of the covenant as acceptable expressions of faith. It can be easy for those who choose to distort the truth to find support. How discriminating are you when it comes to questionable beliefs and practices that seem to have solid backing?

donkey for him, he mounted it [14]and rode after the man of God. He found him sitting under an oak tree and asked, "Are you the man of God who came from Judah?"

"I am," he replied.

[15]So the prophet said to him, "Come home with me and eat."

[16]The man of God said, "I cannot turn back and go with you, nor can I eat bread[p] or drink water with you in this place. [17]I have been told by the word of the LORD: 'You must not eat bread or drink water there or return by the way you came.' "

[18]The old prophet answered, "I too am a prophet, as you are. And an angel said to me by the word of the LORD: 'Bring him back with you to your house so that he may eat bread and drink water.' " (But he was lying[q] to him.) [19]So the man of God returned with him and ate and drank in his house.

[20]While they were sitting at the table, the word of the LORD came to the old prophet who had brought him back. [21]He cried out to the man of God who had come from Judah, "This is what the LORD says: 'You have defied[r] the word of the LORD and have not kept the command the LORD your God gave you. [22]You came back and ate bread and drank water in the place where he told you not to eat or drink. Therefore your body will not be buried in the tomb of your fathers.' "

[23]When the man of God had finished eating and drinking, the prophet who had brought him back saddled his donkey for him. [24]As he went on his way, a lion[s] met him on the road and killed him, and his body was thrown down on the road, with both the donkey and the lion standing beside it. [25]Some people who passed by saw the body thrown down there, with the lion standing beside the body, and they went and reported it in the city where the old prophet lived.

[26]When the prophet who had brought him back from his journey heard of it, he said, "It is the man of God who defied the word of the LORD. The LORD has given him over to the lion, which has mauled him and killed him, as the word of the LORD had warned him."

[27]The prophet said to his sons, "Saddle the donkey for me," and they did so. [28]Then he went out and found the body thrown down on the road, with the donkey and the lion standing beside it. The lion had neither eaten the body nor mauled the donkey. [29]So the prophet picked up the body of the man of God, laid it on the donkey, and brought it back to his own city to mourn for him and bury him. [30]Then he laid the body in his own tomb, and they mourned over him and said, "Oh, my brother!"[t]

[31]After burying him, he said to his sons, "When I die, bury me in the grave where the man of God is buried; lay my bones[u] beside his bones. [32]For the message he declared by the word of the LORD against the altar in Bethel and against all the shrines on the high places[v] in the towns of Samaria[w] will certainly come true."[x]

[33]Even after this, Jeroboam did not change his evil ways, but once more appointed priests for the high places from all sorts[y] of people. Anyone who wanted to become a priest he consecrated for the high places. [34]This was the sin[z] of the house of Jeroboam that led to its downfall and to its destruction[a] from the face of the earth.

Ahijah's Prophecy Against Jeroboam

14 At that time Abijah son of Jeroboam became ill, [2]and Jeroboam said to his wife, "Go, disguise yourself, so you won't be recognized as the wife of Jeroboam. Then go to Shiloh. Ahijah[b] the prophet is there—the one who told me I would be king over this people. [3]Take ten loaves of bread[c] with you, some cakes and

Side references (left margin):

13:16
p ver 8

13:18
q Dt 13:3

13:21
r ver 26

13:24
s 1Ki 20:36

13:30
t Jer 22:18

13:31
u 2Ki 23:18

13:32
v ver 2; Lev 26:30
w 1Ki 16:24,28
x 2Ki 23:16
13:33
y 1Ki 12:31;
2Ch 11:15; 13:9
13:34
z 1Ki 12:30
a 1Ki 14:10

14:2
b 1Sa 28:8;
2Sa 14:2; 1Ki 11:29
14:3
c 1Sa 9:7

---

1 Kings 14:1–20

Ahijah the prophet, the man who had promised Jeroboam ten parts of the kingdom (11:31,35), now delivered the message that Jeroboam's dynasty would come to an abrupt end because of his disobedience. In fulfillment of this prophecy, Jeroboam's son Nadab, after only a two-year reign, would be murdered in a coup—

along with Jeroboam's entire family (15:25–29). The only member of Jeroboam's family who would have an honorable burial was the boy who died of illness (14:13,18). Furthermore, Jeroboam's sins became synonymous with Israel's sins and would ultimately lead to the nation's death (see 2 Kings 17:21–23).

a jar of honey, and go to him. He will tell you what will happen to the boy." 4So Jeroboam's wife did what he said and went to Ahijah's house in Shiloh.

Now Ahijah could not see; his sight was gone because of his age. 5But the LORD had told Ahijah, "Jeroboam's wife is coming to ask you about her son, for he is ill, and you are to give her such and such an answer. When she arrives, she will pretend to be someone else."

6So when Ahijah heard the sound of her footsteps at the door, he said, "Come in, wife of Jeroboam. Why this pretense? I have been sent to you with bad news. 7Go, tell Jeroboam that this is what the LORD, the God of Israel, says: 'I raised you up from among the people and made you a leader[d] over my people Israel. 8I tore[e] the kingdom away from the house of David and gave it to you, but you have not been like my servant David, who kept my commands and followed me with all his heart, doing only what was right[f] in my eyes. 9You have done more evil than all who lived before you. You have made for yourself other gods, idols[g] made of metal; you have provoked me to anger and thrust me behind your back.[h]

10 " 'Because of this, I am going to bring disaster on the house of Jeroboam. I will cut off from Jeroboam every last male in Israel—slave or free.[i] I will burn up the house of Jeroboam as one burns dung, until it is all gone.[j] 11Dogs[k] will eat those belonging to Jeroboam who die in the city, and the birds of the air will feed on those who die in the country. The LORD has spoken!'

12"As for you, go back home. When you set foot in your city, the boy will die. 13All Israel will mourn for him and bury him. He is the only one belonging to Jeroboam who will be buried, because he is the only one in the house of Jeroboam in whom the LORD, the God of Israel, has found anything good.[l]

14"The LORD will raise up for himself a king over Israel who will cut off the family of Jeroboam. This is the day! What? Yes, even now.[a] 15And the LORD will strike Israel, so that it will be like a reed swaying in the water. He will uproot[m] Israel from this good land that he gave to their forefathers and scatter them beyond the River,[b] because they provoked[n] the LORD to anger by making Asherah[o] poles.[c] 16And he will give Israel up because of the sins[p] Jeroboam has committed and has caused Israel to commit."

17Then Jeroboam's wife got up and left and went to Tirzah.[q] As soon as she stepped over the threshold of the house, the boy died. 18They buried him, and all Israel mourned for him, as the LORD had said through his servant the prophet Ahijah.

19The other events of Jeroboam's reign, his wars and how he ruled, are written in the book of the annals of the kings of Israel. 20He reigned for twenty-two years and then rested with his fathers. And Nadab his son succeeded him as king.

Rehoboam King of Judah

21Rehoboam son of Solomon was king in Judah. He was forty-one years old when he became king, and he reigned seventeen years in Jerusalem, the city the LORD had chosen out of all the tribes of Israel in which to put his Name. His mother's name was Naamah; she was an Ammonite.[r]

22Judah[s] did evil in the eyes of the LORD. By the sins they committed they stirred

14:7 d 2Sa 12:7-8; 1Ki 16:2
14:8 e 1Ki 11:31,33,38 f 1Ki 15:5
14:9 g Ex 34:17; 1Ki 12:28; 2Ch 11:15 h Ne 9:26; Ps 50:17; Eze 23:35
14:10 i Dt 32:36; 1Ki 21:21; 2Ki 9:8-9; 14:26 j 1Ki 15:29
14:11 k 1Ki 16:4; 21:24
14:13 l 2Ch 12:12; 19:3
14:15 m Dt 29:28; 2Ki 15:29; 17:6; Ps 52:5 n Jos 23:15-16 o Ex 34:13; Dt 12:3
14:16 p 1Ki 12:30; 13:34; 15:30,34; 16:2
14:17 q ver 12; 1Ki 15:33; 16:6-9
14:21 r ver 31; 1Ki 11:1; 2Ch 12:13
14:22 s 2Ch 12:1

a 14 The meaning of the Hebrew for this sentence is uncertain.   b 15 That is, the Euphrates
c 15 That is, symbols of the goddess Asherah; here and elsewhere in 1 Kings

Israel's prophets were enabled to proclaim boldly the work of God in their own history. But Christians today are wise to be cautious in our analysis of God's work in current events. The end will come unexpectedly (Matt. 24:43–44; 1 Thess. 5:1–2; 2 Peter 3:10). Efforts to read prophecy in terms of calamitous events may distract us from the critical issues of participating in kingdom efforts today. The signs of the times in themselves will never tell us just what God is doing in his great work of bringing his kingdom to this world.

1 Kings 14:21–31
As in the northern kingdom, the situation in the southern kingdom of Judah was a failure spiritually and politically. Egypt had been Israel's ally in the days of Solomon, with Pharaoh's daughter becoming his queen. But only five years after Rehoboam began to reign, Shishak, from a new Egyptian dynasty, plundered the gold Solomon had amassed. The kingdom of David disintegrated under Solomon, divided under Rehoboam, and ultimately erupted into chronic fighting between north and south (v. 30; 15:6,16).

14:22
t Dt 32:21;
Ps 78:58;
1Co 10:22
14:23
u Dt 16:22;
2Ki 17:9-10;
Eze 16:24-25
v Dt 12:2; Isa 57:5
14:24
w Dt 23:17;
1Ki 15:12; 2Ki 23:7
14:25
x 1Ki 11:40;
2Ch 12:2
14:26
y 1Ki 15:15,18
z 1Ki 10:17

14:30
a 1Ki 12:21; 15:6

14:31
b ver 21; 2Ch 12:16

15:2
c 2Ch 11:20; 13:2

15:3
d 1Ki 11:4;
Ps 119:80
15:4
e 2Sa 21:17;
1Ki 11:36; 2Ch 21:7
15:5
f 1Ki 9:4; 14:8
g 2Sa 11:2-27; 12:9

15:6
h 1Ki 14:30

up his jealous anger[t] more than their fathers had done. 23They also set up for themselves high places, sacred stones[u] and Asherah poles on every high hill and under every spreading tree.[v] 24There were even male shrine prostitutes[w] in the land; the people engaged in all the detestable practices of the nations the LORD had driven out before the Israelites.

25In the fifth year of King Rehoboam, Shishak king of Egypt attacked[x] Jerusalem. 26He carried off the treasures of the temple[y] of the LORD and the treasures of the royal palace. He took everything, including all the gold shields[z] Solomon had made. 27So King Rehoboam made bronze shields to replace them and assigned these to the commanders of the guard on duty at the entrance to the royal palace. 28Whenever the king went to the LORD's temple, the guards bore the shields, and afterward they returned them to the guardroom.

29As for the other events of Rehoboam's reign, and all he did, are they not written in the book of the annals of the kings of Judah? 30There was continual warfare[a] between Rehoboam and Jeroboam. 31And Rehoboam rested with his fathers and was buried with them in the City of David. His mother's name was Naamah; she was an Ammonite.[b] And Abijah[a] his son succeeded him as king.

Abijah King of Judah

15 In the eighteenth year of the reign of Jeroboam son of Nebat, Abijah[b] became king of Judah, 2and he reigned in Jerusalem three years. His mother's name was Maacah[c] daughter of Abishalom.[c]

3He committed all the sins his father had done before him; his heart was not fully devoted[d] to the LORD his God, as the heart of David his forefather had been. 4Nevertheless, for David's sake the LORD his God gave him a lamp[e] in Jerusalem by raising up a son to succeed him and by making Jerusalem strong. 5For David had done what was right in the eyes of the LORD and had not failed to keep[f] any of the LORD's commands all the days of his life—except in the case of Uriah[g] the Hittite.

6There was war[h] between Rehoboam[d] and Jeroboam throughout ⌐Abijah's⌐ lifetime. 7As for the other events of Abijah's reign, and all he did, are they not written in the book of the annals of the kings of Judah? There was war between Abijah and Jeroboam. 8And Abijah rested with his fathers and was buried in the City of David. And Asa his son succeeded him as king.

---

a 31 Some Hebrew manuscripts and Septuagint (see also 2 Chron. 12:16); most Hebrew manuscripts *Abijam*   b 1 Some Hebrew manuscripts and Septuagint (see also 2 Chron. 12:16); most Hebrew manuscripts *Abijam*; also in verses 7 and 8   c 2 A variant of *Absalom*; also in verse 10   d 6 Most Hebrew manuscripts; some Hebrew manuscripts and Syriac *Abijam* (that is, Abijah)

📖 The stories of Jeroboam and Rehoboam beckon Christians to be vigilant about doing God's will. The prophetic witness as reflected in these accounts should be enough to assure us that God rules in all the world's kingdoms and that his judgment may fall even on those who think they serve him. It's enough to warn us as believers never to be complacent about our life and conduct. If we think we stand, we are wise to be careful we are not in for a fall.

1 Kings 15:1–8

📖 The author of Kings had nothing good to say about Abijah. This new king followed in the idolatry of his father, Rehoboam, and God allowed him to reign only on account of his forefather David.

*The writer of Chronicles reported that Abijah was involved in a war with Jeroboam (2 Chron. 13:1–20), in which Judah's army was outflanked by Israel. Abijah gave a speech emphasizing the legitimacy of the Davidic dynasty and the purity of worship in Judah. The north-

erners rejected this appeal, and God gave Judah victory. The author of Kings acknowledged that Abijah continued his father's policy of war with Israel (15:6–7; cf. 14:30) but didn't present this victory as a sign of divine blessing on his reign.

📖 Both Kings and Chronicles were likely written centuries after these events. The author of Kings, writing presumably during the exile, was dealing with a crisis of faith due to loss of national identity. His message? The exile didn't happen because God's word had failed but because he had been absolutely true to his word (see Zech. 1:2–6). The Chronicler wrote during Judah's postexilic period. His purpose? To instill hope in a discouraged people. He wasn't looking for the results of *faithlessness* but for evidence of the rewards of *faithfulness*. In general, what takeaways/lessons do you see from each perspective as you seek to understand your own past and cope with your present?

Asa King of Judah

⁹In the twentieth year of Jeroboam king of Israel, Asa became king of Judah, ¹⁰and he reigned in Jerusalem forty-one years. His grandmother's name was Maacah[i] daughter of Abishalom.

¹¹Asa did what was right in the eyes of the LORD, as his father David had done. ¹²He expelled the male shrine prostitutes[j] from the land and got rid of all the idols his fathers had made. ¹³He even deposed his grandmother Maacah from her position as queen mother, because she had made a repulsive Asherah pole. Asa cut the pole down[k] and burned it in the Kidron Valley. ¹⁴Although he did not remove the high places, Asa's heart was fully committed[l] to the LORD all his life. ¹⁵He brought into the temple of the LORD the silver and gold and the articles that he and his father had dedicated.[m]

¹⁶There was war[n] between Asa and Baasha king of Israel throughout their reigns. ¹⁷Baasha king of Israel went up against Judah and fortified Ramah[o] to prevent anyone from leaving or entering the territory of Asa king of Judah.

¹⁸Asa then took all the silver and gold that was left in the treasuries of the LORD's temple[p] and of his own palace. He entrusted it to his officials and sent[q] them to Ben-Hadad[r] son of Tabrimmon, the son of Hezion, the king of Aram, who was ruling in Damascus. ¹⁹"Let there be a treaty between me and you," he said, "as there was between my father and your father. See, I am sending you a gift of silver and gold. Now break your treaty with Baasha king of Israel so he will withdraw from me."

²⁰Ben-Hadad agreed with King Asa and sent the commanders of his forces against the towns of Israel. He conquered[s] Ijon, Dan, Abel Beth Maacah and all Kinnereth

15:10
i ver 2

15:12
j 1Ki 14:24; 22:46

15:13
k Ex 32:20
15:14
l ver 3; 1Ki 8:61; 22:43
15:15
m 1Ki 7:51
15:16
n ver 32
15:17
o Jos 18:25; 1Ki 12:27

15:18
p ver 15; 1Ki 14:26
q 2Ki 12:18
r 1Ki 11:23-24

15:20
s Jdg 18:29; 2Sa 20:14; 2Ki 15:29

---

1 Kings 15:9–24

The account of Asa's reign in Chronicles is greatly expanded over the one here. The Chronicler echoed the overall assessment that Asa was a king who, like his forefather David, did what was right in God's eyes; and he went into greater detail concerning Asa's spiritual reforms.

But the Chronicler was also more critical of Asa's response to the threat from Baasha and the northern kingdom. Asa saw no hope for success against Baasha without the assistance provided by a renewal of the old treaty with Aram (v. 19; cf. 2 Chron. 16:3). Though his plan seemed to be successful, it was condemned by Hanani the prophet as a foolish act and a denial of reliance on the Lord (see 2 Chron. 16:7–10 and "There and Then" for 2 Chron. 16:1–14). Israel's king wasn't to fear his enemies but to trust in the God of the covenant for security and protection.

15:20

---

800 BC	700	600	500	400

Assyria 745-727* Tiglath-Pileser III
727-722 Shalmaneser V
721-705 Sargon II
705-681 Sennacherib
681-669 Esarhaddon
669-627 Ashurbanipal

Babylonia 605-562 Nebuchadnezzar II
556-539 Nabonidus
553(?)-539 Belshazzar
Coregency with Nabonidus

Chronology
of Foreign Kings

This is a chronology of selected foreign kings mentioned in the Old Testament.

Persia 559-530 Cyrus the Great
530-522 Cambyses
522-486 Darius I the Great
486-465 Xerxes (Ahasuerus)
465-424 Artaxerxes I
423-404 Darius II

*All dates are B.C. and are those of the kings' reigns.

in addition to Naphtali. 21When Baasha heard this, he stopped building Ramah and withdrew to Tirzah. 22Then King Asa issued an order to all Judah—no one was exempt—and they carried away from Ramah the stones and timber Baasha had been using there. With them King Asa built up Geba*t* in Benjamin, and also Mizpah.

23As for all the other events of Asa's reign, all his achievements, all he did and the cities he built, are they not written in the book of the annals of the kings of Judah? In his old age, however, his feet became diseased. 24Then Asa rested with his fathers and was buried with them in the city of his father David. And Jehoshaphat*u* his son succeeded him as king.

Nadab King of Israel

25Nadab son of Jeroboam became king of Israel in the second year of Asa king of Judah, and he reigned over Israel two years. 26He did evil in the eyes of the LORD, walking in the ways of his father*v* and in his sin, which he had caused Israel to commit.

27Baasha son of Ahijah of the house of Issachar plotted against him, and he struck him down*w* at Gibbethon,*x* a Philistine town, while Nadab and all Israel were besieging it. 28Baasha killed Nadab in the third year of Asa king of Judah and succeeded him as king.

29As soon as he began to reign, he killed Jeroboam's whole family.*y* He did not leave Jeroboam anyone that breathed, but destroyed them all, according to the word of the LORD given through his servant Ahijah the Shilonite— 30because of the sins*z* Jeroboam had committed and had caused Israel to commit, and because he provoked the LORD, the God of Israel, to anger.

31As for the other events of Nadab's reign, and all he did, are they not written in the book of the annals of the kings of Israel? 32There was war*a* between Asa and Baasha king of Israel throughout their reigns.

Baasha King of Israel

33In the third year of Asa king of Judah, Baasha son of Ahijah became king of all Israel in Tirzah, and he reigned twenty-four years. 34He did evil*b* in the eyes of the LORD, walking in the ways of Jeroboam and in his sin, which he had caused Israel to commit.

16 Then the word of the LORD came to Jehu*c* son of Hanani*d* against Baasha: 2"I lifted you up from the dust*e* and made you leader*f* of my people Israel, but you walked in the ways of Jeroboam and caused*g* my people Israel to sin and to provoke me to anger by their sins. 3So I am about to consume Baasha and his house,*h* and I will make your house like that of Jeroboam son of Nebat. 4Dogs*i* will

15:22 *t* Jos 18:24; 21:17
15:24 *u* Mt 1:8
15:26 *v* 1Ki 12:30; 14:16
15:27 *w* 1Ki 14:14 *x* Jos 19:44; 21:23
15:29 *y* 1Ki 14:10,14
15:30 *z* 1Ki 14:9,16
15:32 *a* ver 16
15:34 *b* ver 26; 1Ki 12:28-29; 13:33; 14:16
16:1 *c* ver 7; 2Ch 19:2; 20:34 *d* 2Ch 16:7
16:2 *e* 1Sa 2:8 *f* 1Ki 14:7-9 *g* 1Ki 15:34
16:3 *h* ver 11; 1Ki 14:10; 15:29; 21:22
16:4 *i* 1Ki 14:11

The Chronicler provided another example of how Asa struggled with relying on people rather than on God: We know from Kings that Asa's feet became diseased in his old age (v. 23), but 2 Chronicles 16:12 adds that "even in his illness he did not seek help from the LORD, but only from the physicians." All of us struggle to some extent with relying on people rather than on God. How much of an issue is that for you? Who do you usually turn to first when you are stressed or in trouble?

1 Kings 15:25–32

As the prophet Ahijah had proclaimed, no one from Jeroboam's family would receive the usual burial, except for the sick child who had died (14:13,18). Nadab didn't "rest with his fathers" (cf. 14:20,31; 15:8,24) since he was struck down by an act of treason. This judgment was the result of his promoting worship at Bethel and Dan with the pagan symbols of the calves.

Yes, God can and does at times punish harshly—from an ultimate motivation of love. But the Bible, and the history of our own lives, is full of examples of his pa-

tience, mercy, and kindness. How has God shown his love for you today?

1 Kings 15:33—16:7

The prophetic word of the Lord came to Baasha that his dynasty would end with the same kind of violence he himself had inflicted on the house of Jeroboam. His son Elah would reign for two years, as had Nadab, Jeroboam's son, before he and Baasha's entire family would be killed in a conspiracy (16:8–12).

Baasha didn't have royal connections and wasn't entitled to the throne. Yet God raised him "from the dust" (16:2) to be his instrument of divine punishment against the house of Jeroboam (see 15:27–30). How do you reconcile the negative evaluation of Baasha for the execution of Jeroboam's family (16:7) with the fact that he was acting as God's agent? Can you cite possible modern examples of God working in this way? Note: Acts 2:22–23 sheds some light on the subject of God holding wicked people accountable for their actions that nonetheless accomplish his purposes.

eat those belonging to Baasha who die in the city, and the birds of the air will feed on those who die in the country."

⁵As for the other events of Baasha's reign, what he did and his achievements, are they not written in the book of the annals[j] of the kings of Israel? ⁶Baasha rested with his fathers and was buried in Tirzah.[k] And Elah his son succeeded him as king.

⁷Moreover, the word of the LORD came[l] through the prophet Jehu[m] son of Hanani to Baasha and his house, because of all the evil he had done in the eyes of the LORD, provoking him to anger by the things he did, and becoming like the house of Jeroboam—and also because he destroyed it.

Elah King of Israel

⁸In the twenty-sixth year of Asa king of Judah, Elah son of Baasha became king of Israel, and he reigned in Tirzah two years.

⁹Zimri, one of his officials, who had command of half his chariots, plotted against him. Elah was in Tirzah at the time, getting drunk[n] in the home of Arza, the man in charge[o] of the palace at Tirzah. ¹⁰Zimri came in, struck him down and killed him in the twenty-seventh year of Asa king of Judah. Then he succeeded him as king.

¹¹As soon as he began to reign and was seated on the throne, he killed off Baasha's whole family.[p] He did not spare a single male, whether relative or friend. ¹²So Zimri destroyed the whole family of Baasha, in accordance with the word of the LORD spoken against Baasha through the prophet Jehu— ¹³because of all the sins Baasha and his son Elah had committed and had caused Israel to commit, so that they provoked the LORD, the God of Israel, to anger by their worthless idols.[q]

¹⁴As for the other events of Elah's reign, and all he did, are they not written in the book of the annals of the kings of Israel?

Zimri King of Israel

¹⁵In the twenty-seventh year of Asa king of Judah, Zimri reigned in Tirzah seven days. The army was encamped near Gibbethon,[r] a Philistine town. ¹⁶When the Israelites in the camp heard that Zimri had plotted against the king and murdered him, they proclaimed Omri, the commander of the army, king over Israel that very day there in the camp. ¹⁷Then Omri and all the Israelites with him withdrew from Gibbethon and laid siege to Tirzah. ¹⁸When Zimri saw that the city was taken, he went into the citadel of the royal palace and set the palace on fire around him. So he died, ¹⁹because of the sins he had committed, doing evil in the eyes of the LORD

16:5
[j] 1Ki 14:19; 15:31
16:6
[k] 1Ki 14:17; 15:33
16:7
[l] 1Ki 15:27,29
[m] ver 1

16:9
[n] 2Ki 9:30-33
[o] 1Ki 18:3

16:11
[p] ver 3

16:13
[q] Dt 32:21; 1Sa 12:21; Isa 41:29

16:15
[r] Jos 19:44; 1Ki 15:27

---

1 Kings 16:8–14

The judgment pronounced by the prophet Jehu (vv. 3–4) was fulfilled through Elah's assassination, just as that announced by Ahijah against Jeroboam had been (15:29–30). The offense for which Elah died was false worship. While 16:13 describes the idols as "worthless," the Hebrew word carries the further nuance of "without substance"—having no real existence.

What distracts you from focusing on the worship of God? When you allow your mind to wander during a worship service or prayer, what pet themes dominate your thoughts? In comparison with God's glory, how important can these issues really be? Can you go so far as to call them worthless? Or, worse yet, without substance? God wants us to enjoy the things of life, and he blesses us with material wealth beyond the comprehension of many in our world. Yet we, like Elah, can easily be drawn into worship that is empty—if not downright false.

1 Kings 16:15–20

Zimri is counted as one of the kings of Israel even though his reign only lasted seven days. As soon as

the soldiers heard of Zimri's coup, they proclaimed Omri king. Omri, as commander of the army, held a higher rank than Zimri (see v. 9)—and appeared quite willing to vie for the throne. So Zimri's fiery ambitions went up in smoke: When he saw that his cause was lost he chose suicide in the flames of the palace over execution by Omri.

These are sad chapters in the history of God's people. The cycles of violent intrigue confirm the maxim that "power corrupts." What an amazing breath of fresh air when Jesus came and said things like, "Whoever wants to become great among you must be your servant, and whoever wants to be first must be your slave—just as the Son of Man did not come to be served, but to serve, and to give his life as a ransom for many" (Matt. 20:26–28).

In what overt or covert ways do you see people vying for control in the political arena today? In your workplace? Even in your church or family? You can pray that the example of Christ makes a difference in the hearts of those involved—including your own.

and walking in the ways of Jeroboam and in the sin he had committed and had caused Israel to commit.

20As for the other events of Zimri's reign, and the rebellion he carried out, are they not written in the book of the annals of the kings of Israel?

Omri King of Israel

21Then the people of Israel were split into two factions; half supported Tibni son of Ginath for king, and the other half supported Omri. 22But Omri's followers proved stronger than those of Tibni son of Ginath. So Tibni died and Omri became king.

23In the thirty-first year of Asa king of Judah, Omri became king of Israel, and he reigned twelve years, six of them in Tirzah. *s* 24He bought the hill of Samaria from Shemer for two talents *a* of silver and built a city on the hill, calling it Samaria, *t* after Shemer, the name of the former owner of the hill.

25But Omri did evil *u* in the eyes of the LORD and sinned more than all those before him. 26He walked in all the ways of Jeroboam son of Nebat and in his sin, which he had caused *v* Israel to commit, so that they provoked the LORD, the God of Israel, to anger by their worthless idols. *w*

27As for the other events of Omri's reign, what he did and the things he achieved, are they not written in the book of the annals of the kings of Israel? 28Omri rested with his fathers and was buried in Samaria. And Ahab his son succeeded him as king.

Ahab Becomes King of Israel

29In the thirty-eighth year of Asa king of Judah, Ahab son of Omri became king of Israel, and he reigned in Samaria over Israel twenty-two years. 30Ahab son of Omri did more *x* evil in the eyes of the LORD than any of those before him. 31He not only considered it trivial to commit the sins of Jeroboam son of Nebat, but he also married *y* Jezebel daughter *z* of Ethbaal king of the Sidonians, and began to serve Baal *a* and worship him. 32He set up an altar for Baal in the temple *b* of Baal that he built in Samaria. 33Ahab also made an Asherah pole *c* and did more *d* to provoke the LORD, the God of Israel, to anger than did all the kings of Israel before him.

34In Ahab's time, Hiel of Bethel rebuilt Jericho. He laid its foundations at the cost of his firstborn son Abiram, and he set up its gates at the cost of his youngest son Segub, in accordance with the word of the LORD spoken by Joshua son of Nun. *e*

a 24 That is, about 150 pounds (about 70 kilograms)

Margin references

16:23 *s* 1Ki 15:21
16:24 *t* 1Ki 13:32; Jn 4:4
16:25 *u* Dt 4:25; Mic 6:16
16:26 *v* ver 19 *w* Dt 32:21
16:30 *x* ver 25; 1Ki 14:9
16:31 *y* Dt 7:3; 1Ki 11:2 *z* Jdg 18:7; 2Ki 9:34 *a* 2Ki 10:18; 17:16
16:32 *b* 2Ki 10:21,27; 11:18
16:33 *c* 2Ki 13:6 *d* ver 29,30; 1Ki 14:9; 21:25
16:34 *e* Jos 6:26

---

1 Kings 16:21–28

Omri was unable immediately to claim kingship after Zimri's death. Tibni made a bid for the throne, and the country was divided for about four years (cf. v. 23 with v. 15) before Omri became the undisputed king.

The author of Kings gave only the briefest attention to Omri's reign, in contrast to the international prominence attributed to this ruthless monarch in other historical sources. The one achievement this historian did mention was the establishment of a new capital, neutral to Israel's warring factions. The site provided an ideal location for a nearly impregnable capital city for the northern kingdom. From this time on, the northern kingdom could be designated by the name of the royal city, Samaria (e.g., 21:1), just as the southern kingdom could be referred to by its capital, Jerusalem.

Despite Omri's forward-looking vision for restoring Israel's strength and his many accomplishments, spiritually he was more destitute than all his predecessors. He founded a powerful dynasty—but one that would unleash upon Israel the common pagan practices known to the ancient world (see notes for next passage). Thus the Scriptural record concerning Omri is both brief and condemning. How might God describe your legacy? How much ink would it take to elaborate on your spiritual faithfulness and contributions to his kingdom?

1 Kings 16:29–34

Ahab's reign is introduced with the usual formula (v. 29), but the conclusion occurs several chapters later (22:39–40), since the account of his reign is intertwined with the Elijah stories. Ahab carried Israel's idolatry even further. This wicked king's alliance with the Phoenicians (through his marriage to Jezebel) no doubt smoothed the path for official and exclusive state promotion of the Baal cult.

Ahab might well qualify as one of the Bible's "ten most wanted" villains. It isn't always easy to see how apparently undisguised and unmitigated evil can further God's cause. As you read the accounts of Ahab and Elijah, look for some evidences of God's hand at work. They are not hard to find. There is plenty of evil in our world, too. For more recent examples, look at Osama bin Laden and Pol Pot. How do you see God working in such "real time" situations?

Elijah Fed by Ravens

17 Now Elijah[f] the Tishbite, from Tishbe[a] in Gilead,[g] said to Ahab, "As the LORD, the God of Israel, lives, whom I serve, there will be neither dew nor rain[h] in the next few years except at my word."

2 Then the word of the LORD came to Elijah: 3 "Leave here, turn eastward and hide in the Kerith Ravine, east of the Jordan. 4 You will drink from the brook, and I have ordered the ravens[i] to feed you there."

5 So he did what the LORD had told him. He went to the Kerith Ravine, east of the Jordan, and stayed there. 6 The ravens brought him bread and meat in the morning[j] and bread and meat in the evening, and he drank from the brook.

The Widow at Zarephath

7 Some time later the brook dried up because there had been no rain in the land. 8 Then the word of the LORD came to him: 9 "Go at once to Zarephath[k] of Sidon and stay there. I have commanded a widow[l] in that place to supply you with food." 10 So he went to Zarephath. When he came to the town gate, a widow was there gathering sticks. He called to her and asked, "Would you bring me a little water in a jar so I may have a drink?"[m] 11 As she was going to get it, he called, "And bring me, please, a piece of bread."

12 "As surely as the LORD your God lives," she replied, "I don't have any bread— only a handful of flour in a jar and a little oil[n] in a jug. I am gathering a few sticks to take home and make a meal for myself and my son, that we may eat it—and die."

13 Elijah said to her, "Don't be afraid. Go home and do as you have said. But first make a small cake of bread for me from what you have and bring it to me, and then make something for yourself and your son. 14 For this is what the LORD, the God of Israel, says: 'The jar of flour will not be used up and the jug of oil will not run dry until the day the LORD gives rain on the land.' "

15 She went away and did as Elijah had told her. So there was food every day for Elijah and for the woman and her family. 16 For the jar of flour was not used up and the jug of oil did not run dry, in keeping with the word of the LORD spoken by Elijah.

17 Some time later the son of the woman who owned the house became ill. He grew worse and worse, and finally stopped breathing. 18 She said to Elijah, "What do you have against me, man of God? Did you come to remind me of my sin[o] and kill my son?"

17:1 [f] Mal 4:5; Jas 5:17   [g] Jdg 12:4   [h] Dt 10:8; 1Ki 18:1; 2Ki 3:14; Lk 4:25

17:4 [i] Ge 8:7

17:6 [j] Ex 16:8

17:9 [k] Ob 1:20 [l] Lk 4:26

17:10 [m] Ge 24:17; Jn 4:7

17:12 [n] ver 1; 2Ki 4:2

17:18 [o] 2Ki 3:13; Lk 5:8

---

[a] 1 Or *Tishbite, of the settlers*

---

1 Kings 17:1–6

The message to Ahab was delivered in the form of an oath. As such, it called upon God as the guarantor of the truth of the words spoken. An oath was the most solemn form of binding obligation between parties. In this case it was sanctioned by God, given as his challenge to Baal, who was represented by Ahab. If the Lord withheld the rain, rendering Baal—considered the god of fertility and lord of the rain clouds—powerless, he would be proven the true God and Elijah the true prophet of his word.

The Baal cult was a religion of materialism. Ahab was determined to promote it, believing that this would make Israel prosper. The idea that Elijah could temporarily interfere with the plan only stirred up resistance in Ahab, not a change of mind or heart (cf. 18:16–17). When it comes to matters of faith, it's often difficult to sway people's opinions by arguments or even proofs. When have you encountered someone so opposed to God that "proof" of his power only infuriated him or her? What approach might have been more effective?

1 Kings 17:7–24

Elijah's actions just prior to the child's resuscitation were similar to Babylonian practices involving magic. But the Hebrew worldview prohibited the use of magic. In verse 21, Elijah didn't pray for restoration or the reunification of the boy's "soul" with his body (the Hebrew word *nephesh* indicates the breath or life possessed by animals as well as people; e.g., Gen. 1:20–21, 24). Life was restored to the child, demonstrating to this foreign woman that Elijah truly was a man of God and that God's word operated in him.

Does God value your body, or is it a necessary evil, a temporary repository for the part of you that really counts—your eternal soul? The apostle Paul in 1 Corinthians 6:19–20 had some impressive, perhaps even shocking, things to say about our earthly bodies. Far from being warehouses protecting and confining our immortal souls, they are temples housing God's Spirit! Beyond this, our natural bodies, which will die, will one day be raised as spiritual bodies (1 Cor. 15:42–44). So take care of the body God gave you. He loves it, and it will stay with you, in a glorified form, for eternity.

Elijah and the Widow at Zarephath

17:7–15

After Ahab, King of Israel (874–853 B.C.), had re-instituted Baal worship, a drought fell upon the land. God sent Elijah the prophet, who opposed idolatry, to Sidon for a time. There, he was told, he would find a widow who would supply him with food.

When Elijah met the woman at the town gate, he encountered an unexpected situation. The widow of Zarephath was gathering sticks to build a fire. He requested a drink of water and a bit of bread, as any traveler might. Her response demonstrated the seriousness of her plight—that of a woman with no means of financial support during a time of severe societal deprivation. The widow's poignant response communicated both her need and her despair: "I don't have any bread—only a handful of flour in a jar and a little oil in a jug. I am gathering a few sticks to take home and make a meal for myself and my son, that we may eat it—and die" (v. 12).

> The hope Elijah provided by his request for help and the promise of life that accompanied it enabled the woman to take positive action in following Elijah's directives.

Rather than responding with frustration at this turn of events, Elijah immediately tuned in to the woman's feelings. "Don't be afraid," he counseled her (v. 13). But he didn't retract his request for help from the starving widow. "Go home and do as you have said. *But first* make a small cake of bread for me from what you have and bring it to me, and then make something for yourself and your son" (v. 13, emphasis added). He promised that if she did this, God would ensure that the meager supply of flour and oil wouldn't run out until after the land had again been blessed with rain.

The woman took heart and did what Elijah had asked of her. The jar of flour wasn't used up and the jug of oil didn't run dry, just as the word of the Lord, spoken through Elijah, had predicted (v. 15).

What can we learn from this story about helping those in need?

Elijah's Attitude: Elijah approached the woman with a request that conveyed his respect for her as a contributing member of society. His request for hospitality honored the woman's dignity, despite her lack of resources. And he was alert both to her words and to her demeanor. When she declared her dire predicament and revealed her hopeless assumption, he paid attention to the fear beneath her words, addressing her emotion with compassion.

Elijah's Work: God sent Elijah into hiding in Zarephath to avoid being killed by King Ahab for prophesying a drought. By soliciting the help of a widow, he acknowledged her usefulness to society and her ability to do something well. By affirming the worth of her life and offering her the means to care for herself and her family, Elijah cut through the woman's despair.

The Widow's Response: The hope Elijah provided by his request for help and the promise of life that accompanied it enabled the woman to take positive action in following Elijah's directives. As she responded affirmatively to his faith in her, the widow's daily life was literally transformed for herself and her son. Her response empowered her and set her on a course of positive, productive work.

Frances Adeney, professor of mission at Louisville Presbyterian Theological Seminary in Louisville, Kentucky

19 "Give me your son," Elijah replied. He took him from her arms, carried him to the upper room where he was staying, and laid him on his bed. 20Then he cried out to the LORD, "O LORD my God, have you brought tragedy also upon this widow I am staying with, by causing her son to die?" 21Then he stretched[p] himself out on the boy three times and cried to the LORD, "O LORD my God, let this boy's life return to him!"

22The LORD heard Elijah's cry, and the boy's life returned to him, and he lived. 23Elijah picked up the child and carried him down from the room into the house. He gave him to his mother and said, "Look, your son is alive!"

24Then the woman said to Elijah, "Now I know[q] that you are a man of God and that the word of the LORD from your mouth is the truth."[r]

Elijah and Obadiah

18 After a long time, in the third[s] year, the word of the LORD came to Elijah: "Go and present yourself to Ahab, and I will send rain[t] on the land." 2So Elijah went to present himself to Ahab.

Now the famine was severe in Samaria, 3and Ahab had summoned Obadiah, who was in charge[u] of his palace. (Obadiah was a devout believer[v] in the LORD. 4While Jezebel[w] was killing off the LORD's prophets, Obadiah had taken a hundred prophets and hidden[x] them in two caves, fifty in each, and had supplied them with food and water.) 5Ahab had said to Obadiah, "Go through the land to all the springs and valleys. Maybe we can find some grass to keep the horses and mules alive so we will not have to kill any of our animals." 6So they divided the land they were to cover, Ahab going in one direction and Obadiah in another.

7As Obadiah was walking along, Elijah met him. Obadiah recognized[y] him, bowed down to the ground, and said, "Is it really you, my lord Elijah?"

8"Yes," he replied. "Go tell your master, 'Elijah is here.' "

9"What have I done wrong," asked Obadiah, "that you are handing your servant over to Ahab to be put to death? 10As surely as the LORD your God lives, there is not a nation or kingdom where my master has not sent someone to look[z] for you. And whenever a nation or kingdom claimed you were not there, he made them swear they could not find you. 11But now you tell me to go to my master and say, 'Elijah is here.' 12I don't know where the Spirit[a] of the LORD may carry you when I leave you. If I go and tell Ahab and he doesn't find you, he will kill me. Yet I your servant have worshiped the LORD since my youth. 13Haven't you heard, my lord, what I did while Jezebel was killing the prophets of the LORD? I hid a hundred of the LORD's prophets in two caves, fifty in each, and supplied them with food and water. 14And now you tell me to go to my master and say, 'Elijah is here.' He will kill me!"

15Elijah said, "As the LORD Almighty lives, whom I serve, I will surely present[b] myself to Ahab today."

17:21 p 2Ki 4:34; Ac 20:10

17:24 q Jn 3:2; 16:30 r Ps 119:43; Jn 17:17

18:1 s 1Ki 17:1; Lk 4:25; Jas 5:17 t Dt 28:12

18:3 u 1Ki 16:9 v Ne 7:2
18:4 w 2Ki 9:7 x ver 13; Isa 16:3

18:7 y 2Ki 1:8

18:10 z 1Ki 17:3

18:12 a 2Ki 2:16; Eze 3:14; Ac 8:39

18:15 b 1Ki 17:1

---

1 Kings 18:1–15

Obadiah had risked his life hiding and feeding 100 prophets in caves. Ahab, by contrast, was busy trying to make sure his valuable animals weren't cut off for lack of food and water. There were two droughts in the land. In fact, the famine of food was the result of a famine of the word of the covenant God. The prophets' hunger was caused not by physical famine but by the wiles of a wicked woman. Ahab and Obadiah weren't only going in different directions geographically; they were pursuing opposite values.

There is nothing wrong with taking good care of our animals; Proverbs 12:10 tells us that a righteous person does just that. Yet we can't escape the tragi-comic irony in this passage. While Jezebel was "killing off the LORD's prophets," her husband was combing the land for grass for his horses and mules—no doubt motivated by self-interest. Would you agree that *values* are our most important motivators? What ultimate values drive your day-to-day actions? What values does the society around you promote? How are the two in conflict?

1 Kings 18:16–46

Elijah's actions signaled Israel's restoration. The building of an altar, the forsaking of false gods, and the restoration of the name Israel (vv. 30–31) followed the example of Jacob when he built the altar at Bethel (Gen. 35:1–9). The altar of 12 stones and the 12 dousings with water (four jars each emptied three times) recall the 12 tribes and the crossing of the Jordan into the promised land (Josh. 4:1–7,19–24). The Carmel event was, in a real sense, no less significant for Israel than the exodus.

Elijah on Mount Carmel

18:17
c Jos 7:25;
1Ki 21:20; Ac 16:20
18:18
d 1Ki 16:31,33;
21:25 e 2Ch 15:2
18:19
f Jos 19:26

16So Obadiah went to meet Ahab and told him, and Ahab went to meet Elijah. 17When he saw Elijah, he said to him, "Is that you, you troubler[c] of Israel?"

18"I have not made trouble for Israel," Elijah replied. "But you[d] and your father's family have. You have abandoned[e] the LORD's commands and have followed the Baals. 19Now summon the people from all over Israel to meet me on Mount Carmel.[f] And bring the four hundred and fifty prophets of Baal and the four hundred prophets of Asherah, who eat at Jezebel's table."

18:21
g Jos 24:15;
2Ki 17:41; Mt 6:24

20So Ahab sent word throughout all Israel and assembled the prophets on Mount Carmel. 21Elijah went before the people and said, "How long will you waver[g] between two opinions? If the LORD is God, follow him; but if Baal is God, follow him." But the people said nothing.

18:22
h 1Ki 19:10 i ver 19

22Then Elijah said to them, "I am the only one of the LORD's prophets left,[h] but Baal has four hundred and fifty prophets.[i] 23Get two bulls for us. Let them choose one for themselves, and let them cut it into pieces and put it on the wood but not set fire to it. I will prepare the other bull and put it on the wood but not set fire to it. 24Then you call on the name of your god, and I will call on the name of the LORD.

18:24
j ver 38; 1Ch 21:26

The god who answers by fire[j]—he is God."

Then all the people said, "What you say is good."

25Elijah said to the prophets of Baal, "Choose one of the bulls and prepare it first, since there are so many of you. Call on the name of your god, but do not light the fire." 26So they took the bull given them and prepared it.

18:26
k Ps 115:4-5;
Jer 10:5; 1Co 8:4;
12:2

Then they called on the name of Baal from morning till noon. "O Baal, answer us!" they shouted. But there was no response;[k] no one answered. And they danced around the altar they had made.

18:27
l Hab 2:19
18:28
m Lev 19:28;
Dt 14:1

27At noon Elijah began to taunt them. "Shout louder!" he said. "Surely he is a god! Perhaps he is deep in thought, or busy, or traveling. Maybe he is sleeping and must be awakened."[l] 28So they shouted louder and slashed[m] themselves with swords and spears, as was their custom, until their blood flowed. 29Midday passed, and they continued their frantic prophesying until the time for the evening sacrifice.[n] But there was no response, no one answered, no one paid attention.[o]

18:29
n Ex 29:41 o ver 26

18:30
p 1Ki 19:10

30Then Elijah said to all the people, "Come here to me." They came to him, and he repaired the altar[p] of the LORD, which was in ruins. 31Elijah took twelve stones, one for each of the tribes descended from Jacob, to whom the word of the LORD had come, saying, "Your name shall be Israel."[q] 32With the stones he built an altar in the name[r] of the LORD, and he dug a trench around it large enough to hold two seahs[a] of seed. 33He arranged[s] the wood, cut the bull into pieces and laid it on the wood. Then he said to them, "Fill four large jars with water and pour it on the offering and on the wood."

18:31
q Ge 32:28; 35:10;
2Ki 17:34
18:32
r Col 3:17
18:33
s Ge 22:9; Lev 1:6-8

34"Do it again," he said, and they did it again.

"Do it a third time," he ordered, and they did it the third time. 35The water ran down around the altar and even filled the trench.

18:36
t Ex 3:6; Mt 22:32
u 1Ki 8:43;
2Ki 19:19
v Nu 16:28

36At the time of sacrifice, the prophet Elijah stepped forward and prayed: "O LORD, God of Abraham,[t] Isaac and Israel, let it be known[u] today that you are God in Israel and that I am your servant and have done all these things at your command.[v] 37Answer me, O LORD, answer me, so these people will know that you, O LORD, are God, and that you are turning their hearts back again."

18:38
w Lev 9:24;
Jdg 6:21;
1Ch 21:26;
2Ch 7:1; Job 1:16

38Then the fire[w] of the LORD fell and burned up the sacrifice, the wood, the stones and the soil, and also licked up the water in the trench.

a 32 That is, probably about 13 quarts (about 15 liters)

Biblical history is full of parallels to past events. Much of the time we need to have these pointed out to us in order to appreciate them. Think about some of the better known parallels, like that between Abraham's near-sacrifice of Isaac (Gen. 22:1–19) and God's sacrifice of his only Son. Can you cite other events that seem related in this way? Do you find such correlations encouraging and/or comforting? If so, why? What do they say to you about God's control of human history?

[39] When all the people saw this, they fell prostrate and cried, "The Lord—he is God! The Lord—he is God!" [x]

[40] Then Elijah commanded them, "Seize the prophets of Baal. Don't let anyone get away!" They seized them, and Elijah had them brought down to the Kishon Valley [y] and slaughtered [z] there.

[41] And Elijah said to Ahab, "Go, eat and drink, for there is the sound of a heavy rain." [42] So Ahab went off to eat and drink, but Elijah climbed to the top of Carmel, bent down to the ground and put his face between his knees. [a]

[43] "Go and look toward the sea," he told his servant. And he went up and looked.

"There is nothing there," he said.

Seven times Elijah said, "Go back."

[44] The seventh time the servant reported, "A cloud [b] as small as a man's hand is rising from the sea."

So Elijah said, "Go and tell Ahab, 'Hitch up your chariot and go down before the rain stops you.'"

[45] Meanwhile, the sky grew black with clouds, the wind rose, a heavy rain came on and Ahab rode off to Jezreel. [46] The power [c] of the Lord came upon Elijah and, tucking his cloak into his belt, [d] he ran ahead of Ahab all the way to Jezreel.

Elijah Flees to Horeb

19 Now Ahab told Jezebel everything Elijah had done and how he had killed [e] all the prophets with the sword. [2] So Jezebel sent a messenger to Elijah to say, "May the gods deal with me, be it ever so severely, [f] if by this time tomorrow I do not make your life like that of one of them."

[3] Elijah was afraid [a] and ran [g] for his life. When he came to Beersheba in Judah, he left his servant there, [4] while he himself went a day's journey into the desert. He came to a broom tree, sat down under it and prayed that he might die. "I have had enough, Lord," he said. "Take my life; [h] I am no better than my ancestors." [5] Then he lay down under the tree and fell asleep. [i]

All at once an angel touched him and said, "Get up and eat." [6] He looked around, and there by his head was a cake of bread baked over hot coals, and a jar of water. He ate and drank and then lay down again.

[7] The angel of the Lord came back a second time and touched him and said, "Get up and eat, for the journey is too much for you." [8] So he got up and ate and drank. Strengthened by that food, he traveled forty [j] days and forty nights until he reached Horeb, [k] the mountain of God. [9] There he went into a cave [l] and spent the night.

The Lord Appears to Elijah

And the word of the Lord came to him: "What are you doing here, Elijah?"

[10] He replied, "I have been very zealous [m] for the Lord God Almighty. The Israelites have rejected your covenant, broken down your altars, and put your prophets

---

[a] 3 Or *Elijah saw*

18:39
x ver 24

18:40
y Jdg 4:7 z Dt 13:5; 18:20; 2Ki 10:24-25

18:42
a ver 19-20; Jas 5:18

18:44
b Lk 12:54

18:46
c 2Ki 3:15
d 2Ki 4:29; 9:1

19:1
e 1Ki 18:40

19:2
f 1Ki 20:10; 2Ki 6:31; Ru 1:17
19:3
g Ge 31:21

19:4
h Nu 11:15; Jer 20:18; Jnh 4:8
19:5
i Ge 28:11

19:8
j Ex 24:18; 34:28; Dt 9:9-11,18; Mt 4:2 k Ex 3:1
19:9
l Ex 33:22

19:10
m Nu 25:13

---

1 Kings 19:1–9a

Elijah was twice strengthened by God's provision of food and refreshed by sleep (vv. 5–8) before he continued his journey of 40 days and 40 nights. Forty is a typical number of completion in the Scriptures. Horeb is likely another name for Mount Sinai, in the desert about 250 miles south of Beersheba. Moses had spent 40 days on the same mountain, receiving the instructions of the covenant (Ex. 24:18; 34:28). Here, God not only continued to be with his servant Elijah in flight but prepared him once again to receive his divine commission.

God has given each of us tasks in his kingdom, though sometimes we need to probe in order to identify them. The work we do for God, whether it involves full-time ministry or short-term missions, community service, food preparation, childcare, singing in the choir, giving, or prayer, is significant. But God gives us something more: the physical nourishment, rest, and relaxation—as well as the spiritual replenishment—we need to keep up the pace. The Creator who loves us knows and meets our needs (Matt. 6:25–34; 10:29–31). Have you thanked him lately for his care and concern?

1 Kings 19:9b–18

Elijah was a prophet like Moses (cf. Deut. 18:16–18). Both occupied a position above that of other prophets (cf. Num. 12:6–8). God had spoken to Moses out of the storm, earthquake, and fire face-to-face. All of these elements again were present when Elijah stood

19:10
n 1Ki 18:4,22;
Ro 11:3*
19:11
o Ex 24:12
p Eze 1:4; 37:7
to death with the sword. I am the only one left, [n] and now they are trying to kill me too."

[11] The LORD said, "Go out and stand on the mountain [o] in the presence of the LORD, for the LORD is about to pass by."

Then a great and powerful wind [p] tore the mountains apart and shattered the rocks before the LORD, but the LORD was not in the wind. After the wind there was an earthquake, but the LORD was not in the earthquake. [12] After the earthquake came a fire, but the LORD was not in the fire. And after the fire came a gentle whisper. [q]

19:12
q Job 4:16; Zec 4:6
19:13
r ver 9; Ex 3:6
[13] When Elijah heard it, he pulled his cloak over his face [r] and went out and stood at the mouth of the cave.

Then a voice said to him, "What are you doing here, Elijah?"

[14] He replied, "I have been very zealous for the LORD God Almighty. The Israelites have rejected your covenant, broken down your altars, and put your prophets to death with the sword. I am the only one left, [s] and now they are trying to kill me too."

19:14
s ver 10

19:15
t 2Ki 8:7-15
19:16
u 2Ki 9:1-3,6
v ver 21; 2Ki 2:9,15
[15] The LORD said to him, "Go back the way you came, and go to the Desert of Damascus. When you get there, anoint Hazael [t] king over Aram. [16] Also, anoint [u] Jehu son of Nimshi king over Israel, and anoint Elisha [v] son of Shaphat from Abel Meholah to succeed you as prophet. [17] Jehu will put to death any who escape the sword of Hazael, [w] and Elisha will put to death any who escape the sword of Jehu. [18] Yet I reserve [x] seven thousand in Israel—all whose knees have not bowed down to Baal and all whose mouths have not kissed [y] him."

19:17
w 2Ki 8:12,29;
9:14; 13:3,7,22
19:18
x Ro 11:4*
y Hos 13:2

The Call of Elisha

[19] So Elijah went from there and found Elisha son of Shaphat. He was plowing with twelve yoke of oxen, and he himself was driving the twelfth pair. Elijah went up to him and threw his cloak [z] around him. [20] Elisha then left his oxen and ran after Elijah. "Let me kiss my father and mother good-by," [a] he said, "and then I will come with you."

19:19
z 2Ki 2:8,14
19:20
a Mt 8:21-22;
Lk 9:61

"Go back," Elijah replied. "What have I done to you?"

[21] So Elisha left him and went back. He took his yoke of oxen [b] and slaughtered them. He burned the plowing equipment to cook the meat and gave it to the people, and they ate. Then he set out to follow Elijah and became his attendant. [c]

19:21
b 2Sa 24:22
c ver 16

---

before God on the mountain. In Elijah's case, though, God chose not to speak through the storm, earthquake, or fire but afterward either in a whisper or in the absolute silence that prevailed after the destructive effects had passed. The divine word to Elijah renewed his commission to bring about a renewal.

Yet both Moses (Num. 20:1–13) and Elijah failed at significant points. Elijah's God-given successes had fostered pride (vv. 4,10,14) that made him take his own importance too seriously. Maybe he thought Jezebel would repent. He was needed by God to continue the spiritual revival begun on Carmel, but he ran because of her threats.

The word of the Lord aroused Elijah. The penetrating interrogation called for self-evaluation. Did he understand his failure and God's loving guidance thus far? The prophet's answer indicated that he didn't. Yet God dealt graciously with him and gave him new marching orders. We too sometimes fail after mountaintop experiences. Our pride becomes entangled with God's work through us, and we fail to see his loving provision during difficult circumstances. We might learn from

Elijah's example and expect a moment of weakness following a major victory. We might look more closely for his gracious hand at work through us. David expressed it well: "Search me, O God, and know my heart . . . and lead me in the way everlasting" (Ps. 139:22–24). Only then are we ready for our new assignment.

1 Kings 19:19–21

The transfer of Elijah's cloak to Elisha signified a transmission both of Elijah's mission and of his ability, with God's help, to accomplish it. Elisha's sacrifice of the oxen was a thank offering for his call, in which his neighbors were invited to join. His burning of the farm equipment signified a complete break with his past. From that time on Elisha became Elijah's protégé.

What have your parents or grandparents passed on to you, either in the form of a final inheritance or as individual items on meaningful occasions in your life? What has their legacy meant to you so far? Have you experienced and appreciated a transmission of intangible gifts—like their faith? What difference has this cloak, this "garment of salvation" (Isa. 61:10), made in your life?

Ben-Hadad Attacks Samaria

20 Now Ben-Hadad *d* king of Aram mustered his entire army. Accompanied by thirty-two kings with their horses and chariots, he went up and besieged Samaria and attacked it. ²He sent messengers into the city to Ahab king of Israel, saying, "This is what Ben-Hadad says: ³'Your silver and gold are mine, and the best of your wives and children are mine.'"

⁴The king of Israel answered, "Just as you say, my lord the king. I and all I have are yours."

⁵The messengers came again and said, "This is what Ben-Hadad says: 'I sent to demand your silver and gold, your wives and your children. ⁶But about this time tomorrow I am going to send my officials to search your palace and the houses of your officials. They will seize everything you value and carry it away.'"

⁷The king of Israel summoned all the elders of the land and said to them, "See how this man is looking for trouble! *e* When he sent for my wives and my children, my silver and my gold, I did not refuse him."

⁸The elders and the people all answered, "Don't listen to him or agree to his demands."

⁹So he replied to Ben-Hadad's messengers, "Tell my lord the king, 'Your servant will do all you demanded the first time, but this demand I cannot meet.'" They left and took the answer back to Ben-Hadad.

¹⁰Then Ben-Hadad sent another message to Ahab: "May the gods deal with me, be it ever so severely, if enough dust *f* remains in Samaria to give each of my men a handful."

20:1
d 1Ki 15:18; 22:31; 2Ki 6:24

20:7
e 2Ki 5:7

20:10
f 2Sa 22:43; 1Ki 19:2

---

1 Kings 20:1–12

Aram, Israel's perennial enemy, was located northeast of Israel and is known today as Syria. Ben-Hadad was a common name among Aram's kings. Like "Pharaoh," it may have been a throne name rather than a personal name. Ben-Hadad saw his opportunity to eliminate a famine-weakened Israel. Gathering a coalition of 32 "kings"—tribal chieftains or city-state heads—Ben-Hadad swept southward, quickly putting Samaria under siege.

Ben-Hadad's initial demands (v. 3) called for Ahab to be reduced to a subordinate, vassal status, like that of the 32 kings fighting with Ben-Hadad. But his second demands (v. 6) required the surrender of Israel's capital city. Ahab responded in language at least appearing to concede to Ben-Hadad's superiority (v. 9), but he staunchly refused to surrender the city. Today's version of Ahab's proverbial words in verse 11 might be "Don't count your chickens before they hatch."

20:1–12

Ineffective Ways of Dealing With Conflict

Ahab, king of Israel, needed to cultivate better ways of dealing with potential conflict. Avoidance and appeasement obviously didn't work with the likes of Ben-Hadad, king of Aram. Some strategies to deal with conflict:

Don't: Ignore it.
Instead: Face it directly.

Don't: Avoid it.
Instead: Schedule a time to deal with it.

Don't: Give in to it.
Instead: Refuse to enable inappropriate behavior on the part of others.

Don't: Hold on to the belief that all conflict is bad.
Instead: Recognize that it's part of life and can lead to growth.

Don't: Try to win over your opponents only by being nice.
Instead: Be honest (which might include being nice).

Don't: Attempt to win at any cost.
Instead: Seek resolution, not victory.

Don't: Take it personally.
Instead: Realize that 99 times out of 100 it's not about you.

Don't: Keep it all to yourself.
Instead: Share the pain discreetly with an accountability group or mentor to avoid bitterness.

Don't: Believe that once it's settled, it's settled once and for all.
Instead: Be alert for a recurrence.

Don't: Transport the conflict and the accompanying turbulent emotions home.
Instead: Conflict expression belongs in the place it originates.

Source: Galindo (2002:87)

20:11
g Pr 27:1; Jer 9:23
20:12
h ver 16; 1Ki 16:9

[11]The king of Israel answered, "Tell him: 'One who puts on his armor should not boast[g] like one who takes it off.' "

[12]Ben-Hadad heard this message while he and the kings were drinking[h] in their tents,[a] and he ordered his men: "Prepare to attack." So they prepared to attack the city.

Ahab Defeats Ben-Hadad

[13]Meanwhile a prophet came to Ahab king of Israel and announced, "This is what the LORD says: 'Do you see this vast army? I will give it into your hand today, and then you will know[i] that I am the LORD.' "

20:13
i ver 28; Ex 6:7

[14]"But who will do this?" asked Ahab.

The prophet replied, "This is what the LORD says: 'The young officers of the provincial commanders will do it.' "

20:14
j Jdg 1:1

"And who will start[j] the battle?" he asked.

The prophet answered, "You will."

[15]So Ahab summoned the young officers of the provincial commanders, 232 men. Then he assembled the rest of the Israelites, 7,000 in all. [16]They set out at noon while Ben-Hadad and the 32 kings allied with him were in their tents getting drunk.[k] [17]The young officers of the provincial commanders went out first.

20:16
k ver 12; 1Ki 16:9

Now Ben-Hadad had dispatched scouts, who reported, "Men are advancing from Samaria."

[18]He said, "If they have come out for peace, take them alive; if they have come out for war, take them alive."

[19]The young officers of the provincial commanders marched out of the city with the army behind them [20]and each one struck down his opponent. At that, the Arameans fled, with the Israelites in pursuit. But Ben-Hadad king of Aram escaped on horseback with some of his horsemen. [21]The king of Israel advanced and overpowered the horses and chariots and inflicted heavy losses on the Arameans.

20:22
l ver 13 m ver 26;
2Sa 11:1

[22]Afterward, the prophet[l] came to the king of Israel and said, "Strengthen your position and see what must be done, because next spring[m] the king of Aram will attack you again."

[23]Meanwhile, the officials of the king of Aram advised him, "Their gods are gods[n] of the hills. That is why they were too strong for us. But if we fight them on the plains, surely we will be stronger than they. [24]Do this: Remove all the kings from their commands and replace them with other officers. [25]You must also raise an army like the one you lost—horse for horse and chariot for chariot—so we can fight Israel on the plains. Then surely we will be stronger than they." He agreed with them and acted accordingly.

20:23
n 1Ki 14:23;
Ro 1:21-23

[26]The next spring[o] Ben-Hadad mustered the Arameans and went up to Aphek[p] to fight against Israel. [27]When the Israelites were also mustered and given provi-

20:26
o ver 22
p 2Ki 13:17

---

a 12 Or in Succoth; also in verse 16

The saber-rattling diplomacy in this story shows that both kings were arrogant, impulsive, and seemingly spoiling for a fight. Many in our world, including Christians, find themselves at the mercy of the whims and ambitions of power-hungry heads of state. Even in democratic societies, we have only a limited voice in government. How are Christians to respond when they find themselves drawn into situations and conflicts that are less than God-honoring?

1 Kings 20:13–34

Though Ahab hadn't sought God's help in the crisis confronting the city (vv. 1–12), the Lord graciously chose to reveal himself yet again to the king and people (v. 13; cf. 18:36–37), this time through military victory—

twice. Following the devastating defeat at Aphek (vv. 29–30), Ben-Hadad had no alternative but to beg for mercy. Without consulting the Lord, Ahab gave much more than Ben-Hadad could have hoped for—agreeing to all his political and trade proposals.

In times of crisis—and only then!—Ahab found it convenient to comply with and depend on the prophetic word (vv. 13–14,22,28). Do you see a similar tendency among Christians to follow Christian values most consistently in times of need? Jesus' teachings about treasures on Earth, the greedy eye, and serving money (Matt. 6:19–24) reflect God's absolute claim on the lives of his followers. Our use of the things God has given us and our loyalty to his words are matters of deepest importance.

sions, they marched out to meet them. The Israelites camped opposite them like two small flocks of goats, while the Arameans covered the countryside. *q*

²⁸The man of God came up and told the king of Israel, "This is what the LORD says: 'Because the Arameans think the LORD is a god of the hills and not a god *r* of the valleys, I will deliver this vast army into your hands, and you will know *s* that I am the LORD.' "

²⁹For seven days they camped opposite each other, and on the seventh day the battle was joined. The Israelites inflicted a hundred thousand casualties on the Aramean foot soldiers in one day. ³⁰The rest of them escaped to the city of Aphek, *t* where the wall collapsed on twenty-seven thousand of them. And Ben-Hadad fled to the city and hid *u* in an inner room.

³¹His officials said to him, "Look, we have heard that the kings of the house of Israel are merciful. Let us go to the king of Israel with sackcloth *v* around our waists and ropes around our heads. Perhaps he will spare your life."

³²Wearing sackcloth around their waists and ropes around their heads, they went to the king of Israel and said, "Your servant Ben-Hadad says: 'Please let me live.' "

The king answered, "Is he still alive? He is my brother."

³³The men took this as a good sign and were quick to pick up his word. "Yes, your brother Ben-Hadad!" they said.

"Go and get him," the king said. When Ben-Hadad came out, Ahab had him come up into his chariot.

³⁴"I will return the cities *w* my father took from your father," Ben-Hadad offered. "You may set up your own market areas in Damascus, *x* as my father did in Samaria." Ahab said, "On the basis of a treaty *y* I will set you free." So he made a treaty with him, and let him go.

A Prophet Condemns Ahab

³⁵By the word of the LORD one of the sons of the prophets said to his companion, "Strike me with your weapon," but the man refused. *z*

³⁶So the prophet said, "Because you have not obeyed the LORD, as soon as you leave me a lion *a* will kill you." And after the man went away, a lion found him and killed him.

³⁷The prophet found another man and said, "Strike me, please." So the man struck him and wounded him. ³⁸Then the prophet went and stood by the road waiting for the king. He disguised himself with his headband down over his eyes. ³⁹As the king passed by, the prophet called out to him, "Your servant went into the thick of the battle, and someone came to me with a captive and said, 'Guard this man. If he is missing, it will be your life for his life, *b* or you must pay a talent *a* of silver.' ⁴⁰While your servant was busy here and there, the man disappeared."

"That is your sentence," the king of Israel said. "You have pronounced it yourself."

⁴¹Then the prophet quickly removed the headband from his eyes, and the king of Israel recognized him as one of the prophets. ⁴²He said to the king, "This is what

20:27
q Jdg 6:6; 1Sa 13:6

20:28
r ver 23 *s* ver 13

20:30
t ver 26
u 1Ki 22:25;
2Ch 18:24

20:31
v Ge 37:34

20:34
w 1Ki 15:20
x Jer 49:23-27
y Ex 23:32

20:35
z 1Ki 13:21;
2Ki 2:3-7

20:36
a 1Ki 13:24

20:39
b 2Ki 10:24

---

^a 39 That is, about 75 pounds (about 34 kilograms)

---

1 Kings 20:35–43

Verse 42 shows that God had called for Ben-Hadad's death (see NIV text note; cf. Josh. 6:17). It's not clear whether Ahab violated a previous revelation or erred by simply neglecting to inquire of the Lord before releasing Ben-Hadad.

The battles against Ben-Hadad weren't recorded to show Israelite superiority over the Arameans. They were another example of the function of the covenant. The Israelites were dependent upon God, the land in which they lived was his gift, and they lived there by his grace. Ahab instead was interested in alliances; even when God granted him victory he didn't recognize him. The

message from the prophet, delivered through an enacted parable, established the divine verdict against the rebellious king and his kingdom.

It seems incredible that a king could have so benefited from divine providence and yet have had such scorn for God as Ahab did (see 16:30–33). Yet one of the hardest lessons for us to learn is the absolute nature of serving God. Jesus encountered—and countered—that same spirit of independence and self-reliance. Characteristic of our culture is a lack of loyalty. This makes it all the more challenging—and important—for us as Christians to live out the counterculture of the kingdom as taught by Jesus. What does this mean for you?

20:42
c Jer 48:10
d ver 39; Jos 2:14;
1Ki 22:31-37
20:43
e 1Ki 21:4

the LORD says: 'You have set free a man I had determined should die.[a][c] Therefore it is your life for his life,[d] your people for his people.' " 43Sullen and angry,[e] the king of Israel went to his palace in Samaria.

Naboth's Vineyard

21:1
f 2Ki 9:21
g 1Ki 18:45-46

21 Some time later there was an incident involving a vineyard belonging to Naboth[f] the Jezreelite. The vineyard was in Jezreel,[g] close to the palace of Ahab king of Samaria. 2Ahab said to Naboth, "Let me have your vineyard to use for a vegetable garden, since it is close to my palace. In exchange I will give you a better vineyard or, if you prefer, I will pay you whatever it is worth."

21:3
h Lev 25:23;
Nu 36:7; Eze 46:18
21:4
i 1Ki 20:43

3But Naboth replied, "The LORD forbid that I should give you the inheritance[h] of my fathers."

4So Ahab went home, sullen and angry[i] because Naboth the Jezreelite had said, "I will not give you the inheritance of my fathers." He lay on his bed sulking and refused to eat.

5His wife Jezebel came in and asked him, "Why are you so sullen? Why won't you eat?"

6He answered her, "Because I said to Naboth the Jezreelite, 'Sell me your vineyard; or if you prefer, I will give you another vineyard in its place.' But he said, 'I will not give you my vineyard.' "

21:7
j 1Sa 8:14
21:8
k Ge 38:18;
Est 3:12; 8:8, 10

7Jezebel his wife said, "Is this how you act as king over Israel? Get up and eat! Cheer up. I'll get you the vineyard[j] of Naboth the Jezreelite."

8So she wrote letters in Ahab's name, placed his seal[k] on them, and sent them to the elders and nobles who lived in Naboth's city with him. 9In those letters she wrote:

21:10
l Ac 6:11
m Ex 22:28;
Lev 24:15-16

"Proclaim a day of fasting and seat Naboth in a prominent place among the people. 10But seat two scoundrels[l] opposite him and have them testify that he has cursed[m] both God and the king. Then take him out and stone him to death."

21:12
n Isa 58:4

11So the elders and nobles who lived in Naboth's city did as Jezebel directed in the letters she had written to them. 12They proclaimed a fast[n] and seated Naboth in a prominent place among the people. 13Then two scoundrels came and sat opposite him and brought charges against Naboth before the people, saying, "Naboth has cursed both God and the king." So they took him outside the city and stoned

---

a 42 The Hebrew term refers to the irrevocable giving over of things or persons to the LORD, often by totally destroying them.

---

1 Kings 21:1–29

Because royal power in Israel was limited by covenantal law (Deut. 17:14–20; 1 Sam. 10:25), Ahab was unable simply to confiscate privately held land. Naboth's refusal to give up his property was in the spirit of each family jealously preserving its allotted portion as its permanent inheritance in the promised land (Num. 36:7). Jezebel, a Phoenician, sarcastically asked Ahab, "Is this how you act as king over Israel?" (v. 7), based on first-hand knowledge of the despotic practices of Phoenician and Canaanite kings—who wouldn't hesitate to use their power to satisfy their personal interests (cf. 1 Sam. 8:9–18, esp. v. 14).

Jezebel attempted to create the impression that a disaster threatening the people could be averted only if they would humble themselves before the Lord and remove any person whose sin had brought God's judgment on them (v. 9; cf. Judg. 20:26; 1 Sam. 7:5–6; 2 Chron. 20:2–4). It wasn't difficult for unscrupulous witnesses to bring a death sentence against Naboth (v. 10; cf. Ex.

22:28; Lev. 24:15–16). Yet the ease with which the plot could be accomplished testified to the pervasive corruption of Ahab's reign.

Confiscation of land is perhaps the most common crime of the state against individual citizens. Some victims may be refugees from another country; others may have been robbed by their own government. The story of Naboth is a Biblical example of such injustices, exemplifying how the powerful often take advantage of the weak to add to their own wealth. The actions are done legally because they are within the power of the state, so the victims may not even be able to make a case for their oppression having been unjust.

Ahab and Jezebel temporarily escaped the legal consequences of their crimes. But they couldn't escape the eventual judgment (vv. 19,23) of the Owner who had given the land to Israel so that his people might live with him (cf. Lev. 25:23). What does this mean for current situations of property injustice, and how can we as Christians respond to them?

him to death.[o] [14]Then they sent word to Jezebel: "Naboth has been stoned and is dead."

[15]As soon as Jezebel heard that Naboth had been stoned to death, she said to Ahab, "Get up and take possession of the vineyard[p] of Naboth the Jezreelite that he refused to sell you. He is no longer alive, but dead." [16]When Ahab heard that Naboth was dead, he got up and went down to take possession of Naboth's vineyard.

[17]Then the word of the LORD came to Elijah the Tishbite: [18]"Go down to meet Ahab king of Israel, who rules in Samaria. He is now in Naboth's vineyard, where he has gone to take possession of it. [19]Say to him, 'This is what the LORD says: Have you not murdered a man and seized his property?' Then say to him, 'This is what the LORD says: In the place where dogs licked up Naboth's blood,[q] dogs[r] will lick up your blood—yes, yours!' "

[20]Ahab said to Elijah, "So you have found me, my enemy!"[s]

"I have found you," he answered, "because you have sold[t] yourself to do evil in the eyes of the LORD. [21]I am going to bring disaster on you. I will consume your descendants and cut off from Ahab every last male[u] in Israel—slave or free. [22]I will make your house[v] like that of Jeroboam son of Nebat and that of Baasha son of Ahijah, because you have provoked me to anger and have caused Israel to sin.[w]

[23]"And also concerning Jezebel the LORD says: 'Dogs[x] will devour Jezebel by the wall of[a] Jezreel.'

[24]"Dogs[y] will eat those belonging to Ahab who die in the city, and the birds of the air will feed on those who die in the country."

[25](There was never[z] a man like Ahab, who sold himself to do evil in the eyes of the LORD, urged on by Jezebel his wife. [26]He behaved in the vilest manner by going after idols, like the Amorites[a] the LORD drove out before Israel.)

[27]When Ahab heard these words, he tore his clothes, put on sackcloth[b] and fasted. He lay in sackcloth and went around meekly.

[28]Then the word of the LORD came to Elijah the Tishbite: [29]"Have you noticed how Ahab has humbled himself before me? Because he has humbled himself, I will not bring this disaster in his day, but I will bring it on his house in the days of his son."[c]

Micaiah Prophesies Against Ahab

22 For three years there was no war between Aram and Israel. [2]But in the third year Jehoshaphat king of Judah went down to see the king of Israel. [3]The king of Israel had said to his officials, "Don't you know that Ramoth Gilead[d] belongs to us and yet we are doing nothing to retake it from the king of Aram?"

[4]So he asked Jehoshaphat, "Will you go with me to fight[e] against Ramoth Gilead?"

Jehoshaphat replied to the king of Israel, "I am as you are, my people as your people, my horses as your horses." [5]But Jehoshaphat also said to the king of Israel, "First seek the counsel[f] of the LORD."

[6]So the king of Israel brought together the prophets—about four hundred men—and asked them, "Shall I go to war against Ramoth Gilead, or shall I refrain?"

"Go,"[g] they answered, "for the Lord will give it into the king's hand."

---

[a] 23 Most Hebrew manuscripts; a few Hebrew manuscripts, Vulgate and Syriac (see also 2 Kings 9:26) *the plot of ground at*

21:13
o 2Ki 9:26
21:15
p 1Sa 8:14

21:19
q 2Ki 9:26; Ps 9:12; Isa 14:20
r 1Ki 22:38
21:20
s 1Ki 18:17
t ver 25; 2Ki 17:17; Ro 7:14
21:21
u 1Ki 14:10; 2Ki 9:8
21:22
v 1Ki 15:29; 16:3
w 1Ki 12:30
21:23
x 2Ki 9:10,34-36
21:24
y 1Ki 14:11; 16:4
21:25
z ver 20; 1Ki 16:33
21:26
a Ge 15:16; Lev 18:25-30; 2Ki 21:11
21:27
b Ge 37:34; 2Sa 3:31; 2Ki 6:30
21:29
c 2Ki 9:26

22:3
d Dt 4:43; Jos 21:38
22:4
e 2Ki 3:7
22:5
f Ex 33:7; 2Ki 3:11
22:6
g 1Ki 18:19

---

1 Kings 22:1–28

The false prophets carried out God's will as determined in the heavenly court (vv. 19–22). Divine judgment had already been determined against Ahab. Yet both the prophets and the king were responsible for their actions. Centuries earlier Moses had specified a test for false prophets (Deut. 13:1–8): A word of prophecy given by anyone following a false god wasn't to be trusted. Micaiah confirmed in his vision both the truth of the teaching about false prophets and the fate that would befall Ahab in an attack on Ramoth Gilead.

Israel was a theocracy, under God's direct control.

Ideally, the king represented God and modeled obedience. But Ahab rejected God and the covenant, choosing a different set of values and putting in place his own prophetic support group.

Our post-modern world has no concept of a common set of values. As a result, there is continual conflict over whose values will serve as the basis for law. For many, the one "indisputable" principle, sad to say, is that values based on religion should have no legal bearing. Granted, the issues are complex. What role do you envision for faith in a democratic society?

22:7
h 2Ki 3:11

7 But Jehoshaphat asked, "Is there not a prophet[h] of the LORD here whom we can inquire of?"

22:8
i Am 5:10 / Isa 5:20

8 The king of Israel answered Jehoshaphat, "There is still one man through whom we can inquire of the LORD, but I hate[i] him because he never prophesies anything good[j] about me, but always bad. He is Micaiah son of Imlah."

"The king should not say that," Jehoshaphat replied.

9 So the king of Israel called one of his officials and said, "Bring Micaiah son of Imlah at once."

22:10
k ver 6

10 Dressed in their royal robes, the king of Israel and Jehoshaphat king of Judah were sitting on their thrones at the threshing floor[k] by the entrance of the gate of Samaria, with all the prophets prophesying before them. 11 Now Zedekiah son of Ke-

22:11
l Dt 33:17;
Zec 1:18-21

naanah had made iron horns[l] and he declared, "This is what the LORD says: 'With these you will gore the Arameans until they are destroyed.' "

12 All the other prophets were prophesying the same thing. "Attack Ramoth Gilead and be victorious," they said, "for the LORD will give it into the king's hand."

13 The messenger who had gone to summon Micaiah said to him, "Look, as one man the other prophets are predicting success for the king. Let your word agree with theirs, and speak favorably."

22:14
m Nu 22:18; 24:13;
1Ki 18:10,15

14 But Micaiah said, "As surely as the LORD lives, I can tell him only what the LORD tells me."[m]

15 When he arrived, the king asked him, "Micaiah, shall we go to war against Ramoth Gilead, or shall I refrain?"

"Attack and be victorious," he answered, "for the LORD will give it into the king's hand."

16 The king said to him, "How many times must I make you swear to tell me nothing but the truth in the name of the LORD?"

22:17
n ver 34-36;
Nu 27:17; Mt 9:36

17 Then Micaiah answered, "I saw all Israel scattered on the hills like sheep without a shepherd,[n] and the LORD said, 'These people have no master. Let each one go home in peace.' "

18 The king of Israel said to Jehoshaphat, "Didn't I tell you that he never prophesies anything good about me, but only bad?"

22:19
o Isa 6:1; Eze 1:26;
Da 7:9 p Job 1:6;
2:1; Ps 103:20-21;
Mt 18:10;
Heb 1:7,14

19 Micaiah continued, "Therefore hear the word of the LORD: I saw the LORD sitting on his throne[o] with all the host[p] of heaven standing around him on his right and on his left. 20 And the LORD said, 'Who will entice Ahab into attacking Ramoth Gilead and going to his death there?'

"One suggested this, and another that. 21 Finally, a spirit came forward, stood before the LORD and said, 'I will entice him.'

22 " 'By what means?' the LORD asked.

22:22
q Jdg 9:23;
1Sa 16:14; 18:10;
19:9; Eze 14:9;
2Th 2:11

" 'I will go out and be a lying[q] spirit in the mouths of all his prophets,' he said.

" 'You will succeed in enticing him,' said the LORD. 'Go and do it.'

22:23
r Eze 14:9

23 "So now the LORD has put a lying spirit in the mouths of all these prophets[r] of yours. The LORD has decreed disaster for you."

22:24
s ver 11 t Ac 23:2

24 Then Zedekiah[s] son of Kenaanah went up and slapped[t] Micaiah in the face. "Which way did the spirit from[a] the LORD go when he went from me to speak to you?" he asked.

22:25
u 1Ki 20:30

25 Micaiah replied, "You will find out on the day you go to hide[u] in an inner room."

22:27
v 2Ch 16:10

26 The king of Israel then ordered, "Take Micaiah and send him back to Amon the ruler of the city and to Joash the king's son 27 and say, 'This is what the king says: Put this fellow in prison[v] and give him nothing but bread and water until I return safely.' "

22:28
w Dt 18:22

28 Micaiah declared, "If you ever return safely, the LORD has not spoken[w] through me." Then he added, "Mark my words, all you people!"

Ahab Killed at Ramoth Gilead

29 So the king of Israel and Jehoshaphat king of Judah went up to Ramoth Gile-

a 24 Or *Spirit of*

ad. ³⁰The king of Israel said to Jehoshaphat, "I will enter the battle in disguise,ˣ but you wear your royal robes." So the king of Israel disguised himself and went into battle.

³¹Now the king of Aram had ordered his thirty-two chariot commanders, "Do not fight with anyone, small or great, except the kingʸ of Israel." ³²When the chariot commanders saw Jehoshaphat, they thought, "Surely this is the king of Israel." So they turned to attack him, but when Jehoshaphat cried out, ³³the chariot commanders saw that he was not the king of Israel and stopped pursuing him.

³⁴But someone drew his bowᶻ at random and hit the king of Israel between the sections of his armor. The king told his chariot driver, "Wheel around and get me out of the fighting. I've been wounded." ³⁵All day long the battle raged, and the king was propped up in his chariot facing the Arameans. The blood from his wound ran onto the floor of the chariot, and that evening he died. ³⁶As the sun was setting, a cry spread through the army: "Every man to his town; everyone to his land!"ᵃ

³⁷So the king died and was brought to Samaria, and they buried him there. ³⁸They washed the chariot at a pool in Samaria (where the prostitutes bathed),ᵃ and the dogsᵇ licked up his blood, as the word of the LORD had declared.

ᵃ 38 Or *Samaria and cleaned the weapons*

22:30
ˣ 2Ch 35:32

22:31
ʸ 2Sa 17:2

22:34
ᶻ 2Ch 35:23

22:36
ᵃ 2Ki 14:12

22:38
ᵇ 1Ki 21:19

---

1 Kings 22:29–40

 The king of Israel was hit by a "random" shot that found its mark between Ahab's solid breastplate and his lower armor. Yet this shot wasn't an accident but the realization of the judgment Micaiah had pronounced. The wounded king demanded to be removed from the fighting—the first step in separating his fate from that of his army. The central occurrence of the battle was the king's death. The soldiers went home in peace—minus their leader (v. 36; cf. v. 17).

Many Christians use words like *random, arbi-* *trary, chance, luck,* and *accident* with little or no thought about their implications. During hard times we may be more likely to reflect on God's perfect plan and good purpose in and through all events, clinging to verses like Jeremiah 29:11 and Romans 8:28. But such passages can be a comfort at *all* times, no matter how routine or humdrum our hours may seem. If you have been a Christian for as long as you can remember, try to imagine living without the knowledge of God's sovereignty. If you are a newer believer, why not take a moment to reaffirm your thankfulness to God for his control over your life's events?

Snapshots

22:17

Perine

Perine is the customer service coordinator for a Christian sponsorship program in Sri Lanka. This single woman has always found pleasure in making people smile. She began full-time church ministry at the age of twenty-one and has been led by the Lord to where she is now, 16 years later.

Perine, raised in a conservative Christian home, had little exposure to knowing God in a personal way. She lost both her parents and had to support herself from age fifteen on. Somewhere along life's rugged road Perine happened to meet Christ, the Good Shepherd—whom she decided to follow because she had no one else.

Having attended Lanka Bible College and All Nations Christian Bible College in England through mission sponsorship, Perine has been exposed to rich experiences. She's learned that no matter where in the world we are, God is in control, and that there are creative ways to deliver the gospel message.

> Somewhere along life's rugged road Perine happened to meet Christ, the Good Shepherd—whom she decided to follow because she had no one else.

Perine is dedicated to her work and has excellent communication skills. She loves the extended family God has placed her in to serve: "God made a difference in my life through people. I want to make a difference in people's lives too."

22:39
c 2Ch 9:17;
Am 3:15

22:43
d 2Ch 17:3
e 1Ki 3:2; 15:14;
2Ki 12:3

22:46
f Dt 23:17;
1Ki 14:24; 15:12
22:47
g 2Sa 8:14; 2Ki 3:9;
8:20
22:48
h 1Ki 9:26; 10:22

22:52
i 1Ki 15:26; 21:25
22:53
j Jdg 2:11
k 1Ki 16:30-32

39As for the other events of Ahab's reign, including all he did, the palace he built and inlaid with ivory,c and the cities he fortified, are they not written in the book of the annals of the kings of Israel? 40Ahab rested with his fathers. And Ahaziah his son succeeded him as king.

Jehoshaphat King of Judah

41Jehoshaphat son of Asa became king of Judah in the fourth year of Ahab king of Israel. 42Jehoshaphat was thirty-five years old when he became king, and he reigned in Jerusalem twenty-five years. His mother's name was Azubah daughter of Shilhi. 43In everything he walked in the ways of his father Asad and did not stray from them; he did what was right in the eyes of the LORD. The high places,e however, were not removed, and the people continued to offer sacrifices and burn incense there. 44Jehoshaphat was also at peace with the king of Israel.

45As for the other events of Jehoshaphat's reign, the things he achieved and his military exploits, are they not written in the book of the annals of the kings of Judah? 46He rid the land of the rest of the male shrine prostitutesf who remained there even after the reign of his father Asa. 47There was then no kingg in Edom; a deputy ruled.

48Now Jehoshaphat built a fleet of trading shipsa h to go to Ophir for gold, but they never set sail—they were wrecked at Ezion Geber. 49At that time Ahaziah son of Ahab said to Jehoshaphat, "Let my men sail with your men," but Jehoshaphat refused.

50Then Jehoshaphat rested with his fathers and was buried with them in the city of David his father. And Jehoram his son succeeded him.

Ahaziah King of Israel

51Ahaziah son of Ahab became king of Israel in Samaria in the seventeenth year of Jehoshaphat king of Judah, and he reigned over Israel two years. 52He did evili in the eyes of the LORD, because he walked in the ways of his father and mother and in the ways of Jeroboam son of Nebat, who caused Israel to sin. 53He served and worshiped Baalj and provoked the LORD, the God of Israel, to anger, just as his fatherk had done.

a 48 Hebrew of ships of Tarshish

1 Kings 22:41–50

Jehoshaphat's reign is given only a brief summary in Kings, in contrast to the detailed account of his reforms and conquests in Chronicles (2 Chron. 17:1—21:3). Through the prophet Jehu, however, God did severely criticize Jehoshaphat's alliance with Ahab (2 Chron. 19:1–2). This coalition was sealed by the marriage of Jehoshaphat's son Jehoram to Athaliah, Ahab's daughter (2 Kings 8:18).

After rebuking Jehoshaphat for his alliance with Ahab, Jehu conceded that there was "some good" in Jehoshaphat (2 Chron. 19:3). This may strike us as a bit harsh, considering how much he had accomplished during his reign. Do you sometimes find it easy to rationalize your own disobedience based on what you perceive as an overall track record you would characterize as "pretty good"? The fact is that Jesus calls for perfection from his followers (Matt. 5:48). How grateful we can be that our salvation is based on his perfection, not our own!

1 Kings 22:51–53

Our books of 1 and 2 Kings, like 1 and 2 Samuel and 1 and 2 Chronicles, were originally one literary work. The division into two books was introduced by the translators of the Septuagint (the pre-Christian Greek translation of the OT) and subsequently followed in the Latin Vulgate (c. A.D. 400) and most modern versions. Ahaziah's reign is introduced here. Second Kings will pick up his story.

"Like father, like son!" How often doesn't this observation roll off our tongues? In Ahaziah's case it was certainly true. (And, unfortunately, Ahaziah also was influenced by a wicked mother; v. 52.) But it's interesting to track the Biblical examples that break the cycle, particularly among Judah's kings. Lacking detail, it's impossible for us to always determine what factors contributed to bad kings being followed by good sons or vice versa.

There is no guarantee in our lives, either. But as a general principle, godly parents raise godly children. From your observation, what are some of the more important factors that make this generalization a truth?

INTRODUCTION TO
2 Kings

AUTHOR

The books of 1 and 2 Kings were originally one book, the author of which is unknown. Although Jewish tradition attributes the work to Jeremiah, few scholars today agree. Whoever wrote 1 and 2 Kings made use of a variety of other written sources (11:41; 14:19,29; 1 Chron. 29:29; 2 Chron. 9:29; 12:15; 20:34; 24:27; 26:22; 32:32) to compile this history of the monarchy.

DATE WRITTEN

Second Kings was probably written between 560 and 550 B.C., during the Babylonian exile of the Jews (586–538 B.C.).

ORIGINAL READERS

The book of Kings (1 and 2 Kings) was originally written for the Jews living in exile in Babylon to preserve a detailed history of Israel and Judah from the last days of King David (c. 970 B.C.) to the exile to Babylon (c. 586 B.C.). Second Kings includes the history of the divided kingdom (1:1—17:41), as well as that of the surviving kingdom of Judah (18:1—25:30).

TIMELINE

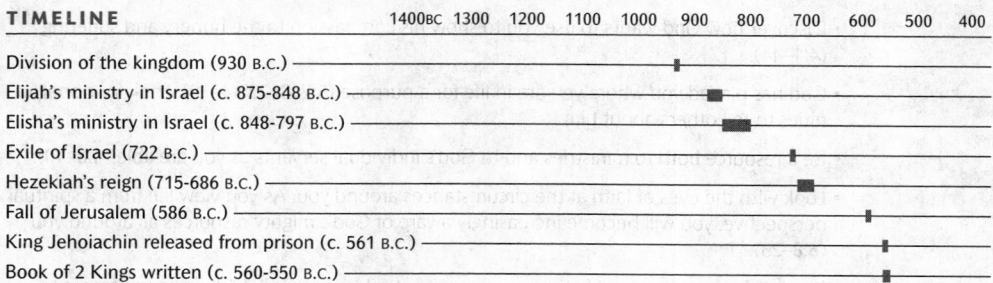

	1400BC	1300	1200	1100	1000	900	800	700	600	500	400
Division of the kingdom (930 B.C.)											
Elijah's ministry in Israel (c. 875-848 B.C.)											
Elisha's ministry in Israel (c. 848-797 B.C.)											
Exile of Israel (722 B.C.)											
Hezekiah's reign (715-686 B.C.)											
Fall of Jerusalem (586 B.C.)											
King Jehoiachin released from prison (c. 561 B.C.)											
Book of 2 Kings written (c. 560-550 B.C.)											

THEMES

Second Kings describes the history of the kings of Israel and Judah in the context of the Mosaic and Davidic covenants. The welfare of the people depended on the obedience of their kings to God and their own fidelity to the Mosaic covenant. Second Kings includes the following themes:

1. *Judgment.* Second Kings explains that the destruction of Samaria and Jerusalem, the exile of the northern kingdom of Israel to Assyria (17:7–23; 18:9–12), and the exile of the southern kingdom of Judah to Babylon (21:1–16; 24:1–4,13–16) were the result of the people's persistent covenant breaking through idolatry. As the spiritual climate declined, so did political and economic conditions. God was patient, but eventually the covenant's curses were realized (Lev. 26:27–43; Deut. 28:64–68).

2. *Prophets.* God used prophets to call his people and their leaders back to a covenant relationship with himself (17:13), warning them of coming judgment if they didn't repent and obey him. The two greatest prophets during this period were Elijah (1 Kings 17–19; 2 Kings 1–2) and Elisha (1 Kings 19; 2 Kings 2–13), both of whom ministered to the northern kingdom of Israel.

FAITH IN ACTION
The pages of 2 Kings contain life lessons and role models of faith—people who challenge believers to put their faith in action.

Role Models

• ELISHA (4:1–7) was used by God to miraculously provide for a poor widow, an act that displayed not only his faith but hers as well. How can you help others in a way that intentionally stretches their faith?

• A WEALTHY SHUNAMMITE WOMAN (4:8–36; 8:1–6) provided a room for Elisha during his travels and saw her son delivered from death and her family preserved during a famine. How do you share your resources with God's servants?

• AN UNNAMED, CAPTIVE ISRAELITE SERVANT GIRL (5:2–3) confided in her Syrian mistress that God's healing power rested with the prophet Elisha, resulting in Naaman's healing. What small thing can you do to bear witness of God's kingdom?

• NAAMAN (5:1–14) overcame his pride and received healing. Is anything holding you back from receiving God's blessings? Does your pride at times trip you up?

• HEZEKIAH (18:5–6) modeled obedience and a close relationship with God. What example are you holding up to those around you?

• JOSIAH (22:11–20) humbled himself before God with a "responsive" (22:19) heart, causing God to delay judgment on the kingdom of Judah. How receptive is your heart to God's calling and claim?

Challenges

• Discover how God wants to use you to show his compassion to the hungry and suffering (4:1–44).

• God has placed you where you are in life for a purpose (5:2–3; 22:14–20). Look for opportunities to tell others about him.

• Be a resource both to ministries and to God's individual servants as you are able (4:8–10).

• Look with the eyes of faith at the circumstances around you. As you view life from a spiritual perspective, you will become increasingly aware of God's mighty resources all around you (6:8–23).

• Be alert for areas in your life that you haven't yet offered to God. Make a commitment to daily reaffirm your wholehearted devotion to him (10:30–31; 12:2–3; 17:33).

• Follow God's ways, not those of the culture around you (17:13–20). Be alert to the negative effects of society's enticements, and refuse to compromise your godly values.

• Take action to change your own life and that of your community and nation (23:1–3). Believe that God can use you to influence others.

OUTLINE

I. Elijah and Elisha (1:1—8:15)
II. Israel and Judah From Joram/Jehoram to Israel's Exile (8:16—17:41)
III. Judah From Hezekiah to the Babylonian Exile (18–25)

The LORD's Judgment on Ahaziah

1 After Ahab's death, Moab[a] rebelled against Israel. [2]Now Ahaziah had fallen through the lattice of his upper room in Samaria and injured himself. So he sent messengers,[b] saying to them, "Go and consult Baal-Zebub,[c] the god of Ekron,[d] to see if I will recover[e] from this injury."

[3]But the angel[f] of the LORD said to Elijah[g] the Tishbite, "Go up and meet the messengers of the king of Samaria and ask them, 'Is it because there is no God in Israel[h] that you are going off to consult Baal-Zebub, the god of Ekron?' [4]Therefore this is what the LORD says: 'You will not leave[i] the bed you are lying on. You will certainly die!' " So Elijah went.

[5]When the messengers returned to the king, he asked them, "Why have you come back?"

[6]"A man came to meet us," they replied. "And he said to us, 'Go back to the king who sent you and tell him, "This is what the LORD says: Is it because there is no God in Israel that you are sending men to consult Baal-Zebub, the god of Ekron? Therefore you will not leave the bed you are lying on. You will certainly die!" ' "

[7]The king asked them, "What kind of man was it who came to meet you and told you this?"

[8]They replied, "He was a man with a garment of hair[j] and with a leather belt around his waist."

The king said, "That was Elijah the Tishbite."

[9]Then he sent[k] to Elijah a captain[l] with his company of fifty men. The captain went up to Elijah, who was sitting on the top of a hill, and said to him, "Man of God, the king says, 'Come down!' "

[10]Elijah answered the captain, "If I am a man of God, may fire come down from heaven and consume you and your fifty men!" Then fire[m] fell from heaven and consumed the captain and his men.

[11]At this the king sent to Elijah another captain with his fifty men. The captain said to him, "Man of God, this is what the king says, 'Come down at once!' "

[12]"If I am a man of God," Elijah replied, "may fire come down from heaven and consume you and your fifty men!" Then the fire of God fell from heaven and consumed him and his fifty men.

[13]So the king sent a third captain with his fifty men. This third captain went up and fell on his knees before Elijah. "Man of God," he begged, "please have respect for my life[n] and the lives of these fifty men, your servants! [14]See, fire has fallen from heaven and consumed the first two captains and all their men. But now have respect for my life!"

[15]The angel[o] of the LORD said to Elijah, "Go down with him; do not be afraid[p] of him." So Elijah got up and went down with him to the king.

[16]He told the king, "This is what the LORD says: Is it because there is no God in Israel for you to consult that you have sent messengers[q] to consult Baal-Zebub, the

1:1 a Ge 19:37; 2Sa 8:2; 2Ki 3:5
1:2 b ver 16 c Mk 3:22 d 1Sa 6:2; Isa 2:6; 14:29; Mt 10:25 e Jdg 18:5; 2Ki 8:7-10
1:3 f ver 15; Ge 16:7 g 1Ki 17:1 h 1Sa 28:8
1:4 i ver 6, 16; Ps 41:8
1:8 j 1Ki 18:7; Zec 13:4; Mt 3:4; Mk 1:6
1:9 k 2Ki 6:14 l Ex 18:25; Isa 3:3
1:10 m 1Ki 18:38; Lk 9:54; Rev 11:5; 13:13
1:13 n 1Sa 26:21; Ps 72:14
1:15 o ver 3 p Isa 51:12; 57:11; Jer 1:17; Eze 2:6
1:16 q ver 2

2 Kings 1:1–18

Ahaziah, who ruled the northern kingdom of Israel from 853–852 B.C., followed in the footsteps of his wicked parents, Ahab and Jezebel (1 Kings 22:52–53). God's judgment against him took at least three forms: (1) Political: Moab found in Ahab's death occasion to rebel against Israel (2 Kings 1:1). (2) Economic: God thwarted Ahaziah's attempted commercial enterprise with Jehoshaphat of Judah (1 Kings 22:48–49; 2 Chron. 20:35–37). (3) Personal: The circumstances of Ahaziah's untimely death are recounted in this passage.

Immersed in the Baal worship of his father, Ahaziah sent messengers to inquire of Baal-Zebub (the name by which Baal was worshiped by the Philistines at Ekron) whether he would recover from his injuries. The pagan people of the time thought the magical power of curses

could be nullified either by forcing the pronouncer of the curse to retract the statement or by killing him or her so the curse would accompany that individual to the netherworld. It appears that Ahaziah shared this view and tried to take Elijah prisoner to counteract his pronouncement of the king's death.

Ahaziah was aware of the seriousness of his worsening physical condition. In such circumstances, a person's basic spiritual temperament will often surface. People who rely on a "deathbed conversion" are often surprised to find that they have no such inclination when that time draws near. What experiences have you had with death and dying? Have you witnessed any dramatic, eleventh-hour changes of heart, or have you found that people either persist in their faith or grow increasingly cynical and/or bitter?

1:16
r ver 4
1:17
s 2Ki 8:15; Jer 20:6;
28:17 t 2Ki 3:1;
8:16

2:1
u Ge 5:24;
Heb 11:5 v ver 11;
1Ki 19:11; Isa 5:28;
66:15; Jer 4:13;
Na 1:3 w 1Ki 19:16,
21 x Dt 11:30;
2Ki 4:38
2:2
y ver 6 z Ru 1:16;
1Sa 1:26; 2Ki 4:30
2:3
a 1Sa 10:5;
2Ki 4:1,38

2:4
b Jos 3:16; 6:26

2:5
c ver 3

2:6
d ver 2 e Jos 3:15
f Ru 1:16

2:8
g 1Ki 19:19
h ver 14 i Ex 14:21
j Ex 14:22,29

2:9
k Dt 21:17
l Nu 11:17

2:11
m 2Ki 6:17;
Ps 68:17; 104:3,4;
Isa 66:15; Hab 3:8;
Zec 6:1 n Ge 5:24
o ver 1
2:12
p 2Ki 6:17; 13:14
q Ge 37:29

god of Ekron? Because you have done this, you will never leave[r] the bed you are lying on. You will certainly die!" [17]So he died,[s] according to the word of the LORD that Elijah had spoken.

Because Ahaziah had no son, Joram[a][t] succeeded him as king in the second year of Jehoram son of Jehoshaphat king of Judah. [18]As for all the other events of Ahaziah's reign, and what he did, are they not written in the book of the annals of the kings of Israel?

Elijah Taken Up to Heaven

2 When the LORD was about to take[u] Elijah up to heaven in a whirlwind,[v] Elijah and Elisha[w] were on their way from Gilgal.[x] [2]Elijah said to Elisha, "Stay here;[y] the LORD has sent me to Bethel."

But Elisha said, "As surely as the LORD lives and as you live, I will not leave you."[z] So they went down to Bethel.

[3]The company[a] of the prophets at Bethel came out to Elisha and asked, "Do you know that the LORD is going to take your master from you today?"

"Yes, I know," Elisha replied, "but do not speak of it."

[4]Then Elijah said to him, "Stay here, Elisha; the LORD has sent me to Jericho.[b]"

And he replied, "As surely as the LORD lives and as you live, I will not leave you." So they went to Jericho.

[5]The company[c] of the prophets at Jericho went up to Elisha and asked him, "Do you know that the LORD is going to take your master from you today?"

"Yes, I know," he replied, "but do not speak of it."

[6]Then Elijah said to him, "Stay here;[d] the LORD has sent me to the Jordan."[e]

And he replied, "As surely as the LORD lives and as you live, I will not leave you."[f] So the two of them walked on.

[7]Fifty men of the company of the prophets went and stood at a distance, facing the place where Elijah and Elisha had stopped at the Jordan. [8]Elijah took his cloak,[g] rolled it up and struck[h] the water with it. The water divided[i] to the right and to the left, and the two of them crossed over on dry[j] ground.

[9]When they had crossed, Elijah said to Elisha, "Tell me, what can I do for you before I am taken from you?"

"Let me inherit a double[k] portion of your spirit,"[l] Elisha replied.

[10]"You have asked a difficult thing," Elijah said, "yet if you see me when I am taken from you, it will be yours—otherwise not."

[11]As they were walking along and talking together, suddenly a chariot of fire[m] and horses of fire appeared and separated the two of them, and Elijah went up to heaven[n] in a whirlwind.[o] [12]Elisha saw this and cried out, "My father! My father! The chariots[p] and horsemen of Israel!" And Elisha saw him no more. Then he took hold of his own clothes and tore[q] them apart.

[13]He picked up the cloak that had fallen from Elijah and went back and stood on

---

a 17 Hebrew *Jehoram*, a variant of *Joram*

---

2 Kings 2:1–18

During the days of Elijah and Elisha, members of a "company of the prophets" (lit., "sons of the prophets"; referred to by some as "school of the prophets") were located at Bethel (v. 3), Jericho (v. 5), and Gilgal (4:38). It appears that Elijah journeyed by divine instruction for a final meeting with each group (vv. 1,2,4).

The reason for Elijah's command to Elisha three times to "stay here" isn't explicitly stated. Elijah knew this was the day God would take him to be with himself (cf. vv. 1,9–10) and that he would leave his work to others—especially to Elisha (1 Kings 19:16). Perhaps he sensed that God wanted to put Elisha to a test to strengthen his faith. Elisha likewise knew that his mentor's ministry was near-

ly finished and his departure near (v. 5). Strongly desirous of God's will for his life and concerned about succeeding Elijah as God's prophet to Israel, Elisha was determined to stay with his tutor until the end.

Elijah knew this would be his last day on Earth, but he humbly and quietly went about his normal duties. It seems that his last concern was for God's work to continue after his passing—so much so that he wanted to assure himself of the continuing progress of his "seminary students." What godly saints in your own experience have remained active in the Lord's work until the very end? How has that work impacted their students or followers? How can you be more of a mentor like Elijah? Or a faithful disciple like Elisha?

the bank of the Jordan. [14]Then he took the cloak[r] that had fallen from him and struck[s] the water with it. "Where now is the LORD, the God of Elijah?" he asked. When he struck the water, it divided to the right and to the left, and he crossed over.

[15]The company[t] of the prophets from Jericho, who were watching, said, "The spirit[u] of Elijah is resting on Elisha." And they went to meet him and bowed to the ground before him. [16]"Look," they said, "we your servants have fifty able men. Let them go and look for your master. Perhaps the Spirit[v] of the LORD has picked him up[w] and set him down on some mountain or in some valley."

"No," Elisha replied, "do not send them."

[17]But they persisted until he was too ashamed[x] to refuse. So he said, "Send them." And they sent fifty men, who searched for three days but did not find him. [18]When they returned to Elisha, who was staying in Jericho, he said to them, "Didn't I tell you not to go?"

Healing of the Water

[19]The men of the city said to Elisha, "Look, our lord, this town is well situated, as you can see, but the water is bad and the land is unproductive."

[20]"Bring me a new bowl," he said, "and put salt in it." So they brought it to him. [21]Then he went out to the spring and threw[y] the salt into it, saying, "This is what the LORD says: 'I have healed this water. Never again will it cause death or make the land unproductive.' " [22]And the water has remained wholesome[z] to this day, according to the word Elisha had spoken.

Elisha Is Jeered

[23]From there Elisha went up to Bethel. As he was walking along the road, some youths came out of the town and jeered[a] at him. "Go on up, you baldhead!" they said. "Go on up, you baldhead!" [24]He turned around, looked at them and called down a curse[b] on them in the name[c] of the LORD. Then two bears came out of the

2:14
r 1Ki 19:19 s ver 8

2:15
t ver 7; 1Sa 10:5
u Nu 11:17

2:16
v 1Ki 18:12
w Ac 8:39

2:17
x 2Ki 8:11

2:21
y Ex 15:25;
2Ki 4:41; 6:6

2:22
z Ex 15:25

2:23
a Ex 22:28;
2Ch 36:16;
Job 19:18; Ps 31:18
2:24
b Ge 4:11;
Ne 13:25-27
c Dt 18:19

---

2 Kings 2:19–22

The chapter closes with two miracles of Elisha. These immediately established the character of his ministry—a helping ministry to those in need, but one that would allow no disrespect for God or his earthly representatives. The "city" here was evidently Jericho (see v. 18). Though Jericho had been rebuilt (with difficulty) in the days of Ahab (1 Kings 16:34), it had remained unproductive. Apparently the water still lay under Joshua's curse

(Josh. 6:26), and both people and land suffered greatly. Elisha's miracle fully removed this older judgment.

Any suggestion of a magical effect of the salt in the purification of the water is excluded by the explicit statement that the Lord himself healed, or purified, the water (v. 21). In this symbolic way Elisha was able, as his first act of ministry, to proclaim to the people that in spite of their disobedience the Lord was merciful, still reaching out to them in his grace (cf. 13:23).

2:23

We can't blame TV for the young Solomon's aggressive ideation in this verse, but we probably could make that case in a similar situation today.

Television Violence

- By age 18, a U.S. youth will have viewed 16,000 simulated murders on television.

- Over 1,000 studies show a causal connection between television violence and aggressive behavior in some children.

- The more "real-life" the televised violence, the greater the likelihood it will be "learned."

- Televised violence may cause aggressive and antisocial behavior, desensitize viewers to future violence, and

increase perceptions that they are living in a mean and dangerous world.

- Televised violence leads to imitation.

- Children who watch televised violence are more likely to strike out at playmates, argue, and disobey authority.

- Reducing the amount of time grade-schoolers spend watching television can make them less aggressive toward peers.

Source: National Institute on Media and the Family (*www.mediafamily.org/facts*)

Add violent video and computer games, as well as R-rated movies and movie previews to the mix, and the situation becomes even more sobering. If you are a parent or otherwise involved with young people, what can you do to minimize the effects of such explosive and suggestive media?

2:25
d 1Ki 18:20;
2Ki 4:25

3:1
e 2Ki 1:17
3:2
f 1Ki 15:26
g 1Ki 16:30-32
h Ex 23:24;
2Ki 10:18,26-28
3:3
i 1Ki 12:28-32;
14:9,16

3:4
j Ge 19:37; 2Ki 1:1
k Ezr 7:17; Isa 16:1
3:5
l 2Ki 1:1

3:7
m 1Ki 22:4

3:9
n 1Ki 22:47

3:11
o Ge 25:22;
1Ki 22:7 p Ge 20:7
q 1Ki 19:16

woods and mauled forty-two of the youths. ²⁵And he went on to Mount Carmel^d and from there returned to Samaria.

Moab Revolts

3 Joram^{a e} son of Ahab became king of Israel in Samaria in the eighteenth year of Jehoshaphat king of Judah, and he reigned twelve years. ²He did evil^f in the eyes of the LORD, but not as his father^g and mother had done. He got rid of the sacred stone^h of Baal that his father had made. ³Nevertheless he clung to the sinsⁱ of Jeroboam son of Nebat, which he had caused Israel to commit; he did not turn away from them.

⁴Now Mesha king of Moab^j raised sheep, and he had to supply the king of Israel with a hundred thousand lambs^k and with the wool of a hundred thousand rams. ⁵But after Ahab died, the king of Moab rebelled^l against the king of Israel. ⁶So at that time King Joram set out from Samaria and mobilized all Israel. ⁷He also sent this message to Jehoshaphat king of Judah: "The king of Moab has rebelled against me. Will you go with me to fight^m against Moab?"

"I will go with you," he replied. "I am as you are, my people as your people, my horses as your horses."

⁸"By what route shall we attack?" he asked.

"Through the Desert of Edom," he answered.

⁹So the king of Israel set out with the king of Judah and the king of Edom.ⁿ After a roundabout march of seven days, the army had no more water for themselves or for the animals with them.

¹⁰"What!" exclaimed the king of Israel. "Has the LORD called us three kings together only to hand us over to Moab?"

¹¹But Jehoshaphat asked, "Is there no prophet of the LORD here, that we may inquire^o of the LORD through him?"

An officer of the king of Israel answered, "Elisha^p son of Shaphat is here. He used to pour water on the hands of Elijah.^{b q}"

---

^a *1* Hebrew *Jehoram*, a variant of *Joram*; also in verse 6   ^b *11* That is, he was Elijah's personal servant.

📖 The miracle of clean water is still needed today. Pollution, contamination, and poor quality ground water plague many worldwide. Christian ministries sometimes participate in well-drilling efforts and other means of bringing clean water to thirsty people. These practical helps can have spiritual effects and ramifications, just as the text demonstrates. A new well, dam, or water catchment provision inaugurated by believers often leads communities to encounter the One who gives the water that satisfies eternally.

2 Kings 2:23–25

📖 Elisha's sweet memories of Jericho were soured at Bethel. The taunt "Go on up" was likely a mocking caricature of Elijah's "going up" to heaven (v. 11). Baldness, uncommon among the ancient Jews, was considered a disgrace (Isa. 3:17,24), while luxuriant hair seems to have been viewed as a sign of strength and vigor (cf. 2 Sam. 14:25–26).

The youths from Bethel expressed that city's utter disdain for the Lord's representative, who, they felt, had no power. Elisha pronounced a curse similar to the covenant curse of Leviticus 26:21–22. The result gave warning of the judgment that would come on the entire nation if it persisted in disobedience and apostasy (cf. 2 Chron. 36:16).

📖 This story can be confusing, with Elisha's stern response appearing to have been motivated by oversensitivity or self-pride. Couldn't he have dismissed this immature taunt and simply walked on, unaffected? When we understand that God's reputation, not Elisha's, was at stake, the puzzle pieces begin to come together. What's your reaction to snide remarks aimed at God (directly or through jabs at Christians)? Are you able to enjoy an adult cartoon, sitcom, or movie that openly flaunts its disrespect for matters of faith?

2 Kings 3:1–27

📖 The Israelite and Edomite armies set up camp in the broad valley (the Arabah) between the highlands of Moab on the east and those of Judah on the west, just south of the Dead Sea. The word of the Lord through Elisha was that every depression in the dry valley bed would become a receptacle for water.

The prophet wasn't commanding the armies to dig ditches (v. 16). It's still common for wadis (dry river beds) in the region to become streams after a cloudburst, leaving behind pools of water. The storm may occur far enough away that no sound of wind or rain can be heard, but the water gathers and rushes down the valleys, often taking travelers by surprise. Though such occurrences weren't infrequent, there was nothing natural about the deliverance experienced by the three armies.

12Jehoshaphat said, "The word[r] of the Lord is with him." So the king of Israel and Jehoshaphat and the king of Edom went down to him.

13Elisha said to the king of Israel, "What do we have to do with each other? Go to the prophets of your father and the prophets of your mother."

"No," the king of Israel answered, "because it was the Lord who called us three kings together to hand us over to Moab."

14Elisha said, "As surely as the Lord Almighty lives, whom I serve, if I did not have respect for the presence of Jehoshaphat king of Judah, I would not look at you or even notice you. 15But now bring me a harpist."[s]

While the harpist was playing, the hand[t] of the Lord came upon Elisha 16and he said, "This is what the Lord says: Make this valley full of ditches. 17For this is what the Lord says: You will see neither wind nor rain, yet this valley will be filled with water,[u] and you, your cattle and your other animals will drink. 18This is an easy[v] thing in the eyes of the Lord; he will also hand Moab over to you. 19You will overthrow every fortified city and every major town. You will cut down every good tree, stop up all the springs, and ruin every good field with stones."

20The next morning, about the time[w] for offering the sacrifice, there it was—water flowing from the direction of Edom! And the land was filled with water.[x]

21Now all the Moabites had heard that the kings had come to fight against them; so every man, young and old, who could bear arms was called up and stationed on the border. 22When they got up early in the morning, the sun was shining on the water. To the Moabites across the way, the water looked red—like blood. 23"That's blood!" they said. "Those kings must have fought and slaughtered each other. Now to the plunder, Moab!"

24But when the Moabites came to the camp of Israel, the Israelites rose up and fought them until they fled. And the Israelites invaded the land and slaughtered the Moabites. 25They destroyed the towns, and each man threw a stone on every good field until it was covered. They stopped up all the springs and cut down every good tree. Only Kir Hareseth[y] was left with its stones in place, but men armed with slings surrounded it and attacked it as well.

26When the king of Moab saw that the battle had gone against him, he took with him seven hundred swordsmen to break through to the king of Edom, but they failed. 27Then he took his firstborn[z] son, who was to succeed him as king, and offered him as a sacrifice on the city wall. The fury against Israel was great; they withdrew and returned to their own land.

The Widow's Oil

4 The wife of a man from the company[a] of the prophets cried out to Elisha, "Your servant my husband is dead, and you know that he revered the Lord. But now his creditor[b] is coming to take my two boys as his slaves."

2Elisha replied to her, "How can I help you? Tell me, what do you have in your house?"

"Your servant has nothing there at all," she said, "except a little oil."[c]

3Elisha said, "Go around and ask all your neighbors for empty jars. Don't ask for just a few. 4Then go inside and shut the door behind you and your sons. Pour oil into all the jars, and as each is filled, put it to one side."

3:12
r Nu 11:17

3:15
s 1Sa 16:23
t Jer 15:17; Eze 1:3

3:17
u Ps 107:35; Isa 32:2; 35:6; 41:18
3:18
v Ge 18:14; 2Ki 20:10; Isa 49:6; Jer 32:17,27; Mk 10:27
3:20
w Ex 29:39-40
x Ex 17:6

3:25
y ver 19; Isa 15:1; 16:7; Jer 48:31,36

3:27
z Dt 12:31; 2Ki 16:3; 21:6; 2Ch 28:3; Ps 106:38; Jer 19:4-5; Am 2:1; Mic 6:7

4:1
a 1Sa 10:5; 2Ki 2:3
b Ex 22:26; Lev 25:39-43; Ne 5:3-5; Job 22:6; 24:9

4:2
c 1Ki 17:12

We as Christians are faced with the task of reconciling the reality of God as the Divine Warrior in the Old Testament with the historical wars we experience. Just as God was active in human affairs in Old Testament times, showing himself to be "sovereign over the kingdoms of men" (Dan. 5:21), so he continues to be involved. When a war seems justified, it's natural for us as believers to assume that God is with our troops in battle. But it's important for us to carefully separate our feelings of nationalism from our Christian faith.

2 Kings 4:1–7

This widow's husband had been a member of one of the companies of the prophets (see "There and Then" for 2:1–18). In addition to having supported Elijah and Elisha, they likely maintained their own properties and families. These followers of the covenant probably paid a high price for their commitment to God in the hostile environment of official support of the Baal cult. The time and sacrifice required to buck the prevailing economic forces would have left little reserve when the family provider died.

5 She left him and afterward shut the door behind her and her sons. They brought the jars to her and she kept pouring. 6 When all the jars were full, she said to her son, "Bring me another one."

But he replied, "There is not a jar left." Then the oil stopped flowing.

7 She went and told the man of God, *d* and he said, "Go, sell the oil and pay your debts. You and your sons can live on what is left."

4:7
d 1Ki 12:22

The Shunammite's Son Restored to Life

4:8
e Jos 19:18

8 One day Elisha went to Shunem. *e* And a well-to-do woman was there, who urged him to stay for a meal. So whenever he came by, he stopped there to eat. 9 She said to her husband, "I know that this man who often comes our way is a holy man of God. 10 Let's make a small room on the roof and put in it a bed and a table, a chair and a lamp for him. Then he can stay *f* there whenever he comes to us."

4:10
f Mt 10:41;
Ro 12:13

11 One day when Elisha came, he went up to his room and lay down there. 12 He said to his servant Gehazi, "Call the Shunammite." *g* So he called her, and she stood before him. 13 Elisha said to him, "Tell her, 'You have gone to all this trouble for us. Now what can be done for you? Can we speak on your behalf to the king or the commander of the army?' "

4:12
g 2Ki 8:1

She replied, "I have a home among my own people."

14 "What can be done for her?" Elisha asked.

Gehazi said, "Well, she has no son and her husband is old."

15 Then Elisha said, "Call her." So he called her, and she stood in the doorway. 16 "About this time *h* next year," Elisha said, "you will hold a son in your arms."

4:16
h Ge 18:10

"No, my lord," she objected. "Don't mislead your servant, O man of God!"

17 But the woman became pregnant, and the next year about that same time she gave birth to a son, just as Elisha had told her.

18 The child grew, and one day he went out to his father, who was with the reapers. *i* 19 "My head! My head!" he said to his father.

4:18
i Ru 2:3

His father told a servant, "Carry him to his mother." 20 After the servant had lifted him up and carried him to his mother, the boy sat on her lap until noon, and then he died. 21 She went up and laid him on the bed *j* of the man of God, then shut the door and went out.

4:21
j ver 32

22 She called her husband and said, "Please send me one of the servants and a donkey so I can go to the man of God quickly and return."

23 "Why go to him today?" he asked. "It's not the New Moon *k* or the Sabbath."

4:23
k Nu 10:10;
1Ch 23:31; Ps 81:3

"It's all right," she said.

24 She saddled the donkey and said to her servant, "Lead on; don't slow down for me unless I tell you." 25 So she set out and came to the man of God at Mount Carmel. *l*

4:25
l 1Ki 18:20;
2Ki 2:25

The woman responded in faith, and, miraculously, all came to pass as Elisha had promised. The fact that she was to act in faith would serve to enlarge her faith. The fact that Elisha wouldn't be present when the miracle took place would display the power of God alone and encourage her to still greater faith. Unreserved obedience can produce bountiful spiritual blessings! What events from your life illustrate this truth?

2 Kings 4:8–37

Childlessness was a great disappointment because it meant that the family's name would cease and its land and possessions would pass on to others. The woman's response in verse 16 revealed the depths of her desire for a son and her fear of disappointment more than a lack of confidence in Elisha's words.

After her beloved son had died, why would the woman say that everything was "all right" (vv. 23,26)? Evidently because she was determined to share her distress with no one but the prophet from whom she had re-

ceived the promise of the birth of her son. Her anguished words in verse 28 demonstrate that she struggled with the question of why the Lord would have taken from her that which she had been given as a special demonstration of his grace and the trustworthiness of his word.

Elisha's actions were similar to Elijah's in reviving the child at Zarephath, though described in greater detail (cf. 1 Kings 17:19–21). Elisha's intensity is reflected in his pacing back and forth, waiting for signs of life to return.

Did you notice the contrast in this chapter? A woman reduced to poverty (v. 1) and a "well-to-do" woman (v. 8) both had needs that God met through his servant. So today, rich and poor alike have needs that we as kingdom ambassadors can help meet—one person at a time. That is key to our ministry: not being overwhelmed by all the needs "out there," but helping where we can with what resources we have. Watch for opportunities to share God's extraordinary love with one person, rich or poor, today.

When he saw her in the distance, the man of God said to his servant Gehazi, "Look! There's the Shunammite! ²⁶Run to meet her and ask her, 'Are you all right? Is your husband all right? Is your child all right?' "

"Everything is all right," she said.

²⁷When she reached the man of God at the mountain, she took hold of his feet. Gehazi came over to push her away, but the man of God said, "Leave her alone! She is in bitter distress,ᵐ but the LORD has hidden it from me and has not told me why."

²⁸"Did I ask you for a son, my lord?" she said. "Didn't I tell you, 'Don't raise my hopes'?"

²⁹Elisha said to Gehazi, "Tuck your cloak into your belt,ⁿ take my staffᵒ in your hand and run. If you meet anyone, do not greet him, and if anyone greets you, do not answer. Lay my staff on the boy's face."

³⁰But the child's mother said, "As surely as the LORD lives and as you live, I will not leave you." So he got up and followed her.

³¹Gehazi went on ahead and laid the staff on the boy's face, but there was no sound or response. So Gehazi went back to meet Elisha and told him, "The boy has not awakened."

³²When Elisha reached the house, there was the boy lying dead on his couch.ᵖ ³³He went in, shut the door on the two of them and prayed�q to the LORD. ³⁴Then he got on the bed and lay upon the boy, mouth to mouth, eyes to eyes, hands to hands. As he stretchedʳ himself out upon him, the boy's body grew warm. ³⁵Elisha turned away and walked back and forth in the room and then got on the bed and stretched out upon him once more. The boy sneezed seven timesˢ and opened his eyes.ᵗ

³⁶Elisha summoned Gehazi and said, "Call the Shunammite." And he did. When she came, he said, "Take your son."ᵘ ³⁷She came in, fell at his feet and bowed to the ground. Then she took her son and went out.

Death in the Pot

³⁸Elisha returned to Gilgalᵛ and there was a famineʷ in that region. While the company of the prophets was meeting with him, he said to his servant, "Put on the large pot and cook some stew for these men."

³⁹One of them went out into the fields to gather herbs and found a wild vine. He gathered some of its gourds and filled the fold of his cloak. When he returned, he cut them up into the pot of stew, though no one knew what they were. ⁴⁰The stew was poured out for the men, but as they began to eat it, they cried out, "O man of God, there is death in the pot!" And they could not eat it.

⁴¹Elisha said, "Get some flour." He put it into the pot and said, "Serve it to the people to eat." And there was nothing harmful in the pot.ˣ

Feeding of a Hundred

⁴²A man came from Baal Shalishah,ʸ bringing the man of God twenty loavesᶻ of

---

4:27 m 1Sa 1:15
4:29 n 1Ki 18:46; 2Ki 2:8,14; 9:1 o Ex 4:2; 7:19; 14:16
4:32 p ver 21
4:33 q 1Ki 17:20; Mt 6:6
4:34 r 1Ki 17:21; Ac 20:10
4:35 s Jos 6:15 t 2Ki 8:5
4:36 u Heb 11:35
4:38 v 2Ki 2:1 w Lev 26:26; 2Ki 8:1
4:41 x Ex 15:25; 2Ki 2:21
4:42 y 1Sa 9:4 z Mt 14:17; 15:36

---

2 Kings 4:38–41

📖 The flour itself didn't make the stew edible (cf. "Here and Now" for 2:19–22). It was simply a means by which the Lord provided for those who were faithful to the covenant, at a time when others suffered under the covenant curse of famine (v. 38; cf. Lev. 26:19–20,26; Deut. 28:18,23–24).

📖 As with Elijah, his teacher, Elisha was led to use flour to demonstrate God's concern for people's daily needs (cf. 1 Kings 17:14–16). Can you think of a modern instance, involving either yourself or someone else, that reflects God's intimate concern for "daily bread" (see Matt. 6:11)? Have you ever, either in your younger days or more recently, faced a bare cupboard and an empty refrigerator with days or weeks before your next paycheck? How did you "survive" the crisis? Could you see God's hand in the details?

2 Kings 4:42–44

📖 The man brought the loaves to Elisha as first-fruits. Normally these portions were reserved for God and the Levitical priests (Lev. 23:15–17,20; Deut. 18:4–5). But because religion in the northern kingdom was apostate, the man brought them to the person he correctly considered to be the true representative of godly religion in Israel.

📖 Does God honor your obedience, even in little things? Does he accept and use your "insignificant" gifts? This brief account—reminiscent of another incident when a young boy's five small barley loaves and two small fish fed thousands (John 6:8–13)—illustrates that he does, often in significant ways.

4:42
a 1Sa 9:7

barley bread*a* baked from the first ripe grain, along with some heads of new grain. "Give it to the people to eat," Elisha said.

4:43
b Lk 9:13
c Mt 14:20; Jn 6:12

43 "How can I set this before a hundred men?" his servant asked.

But Elisha answered, "Give it to the people to eat.*b* For this is what the LORD says: 'They will eat and have some left over.*c* ' " 44 Then he set it before them, and they ate and had some left over, according to the word of the LORD.

Naaman Healed of Leprosy

5:1
d Ge 10:22; 2Sa 10:19 *e* Ex 4:6; Nu 12:10; Lk 4:27

5 Now Naaman was commander of the army of the king of Aram.*d* He was a great man in the sight of his master and highly regarded, because through him the LORD had given victory to Aram. He was a valiant soldier, but he had leprosy.*a e*

5:2
f 2Ki 6:23; 13:20; 24:2

2 Now bands*f* from Aram had gone out and had taken captive a young girl from Israel, and she served Naaman's wife. 3 She said to her mistress, "If only my master

5:3
g Ge 20:7

would see the prophet*g* who is in Samaria! He would cure him of his leprosy."

4 Naaman went to his master and told him what the girl from Israel had said. 5 "By all means, go," the king of Aram replied. "I will send a letter to the king of Israel." So Naaman left, taking with him ten talents*b* of silver, six thousand shekels*c* of gold

5:5
h ver 22; Ge 24:53; Jdg 14:12; 1Sa 9:7

and ten sets of clothing.*h* 6 The letter that he took to the king of Israel read: "With this letter I am sending my servant Naaman to you so that you may cure him of his leprosy."

5:7
i 2Ki 19:14
j Ge 30:2
k Dt 32:39; 1Sa 2:6
l 1Ki 20:7

7 As soon as the king of Israel read the letter,*i* he tore his robes and said, "Am I God?*j* Can I kill and bring back to life?*k* Why does this fellow send someone to me to be cured of his leprosy? See how he is trying to pick a quarrel*l* with me!"

5:8
m 1Ki 22:7

8 When Elisha the man of God heard that the king of Israel had torn his robes, he sent him this message: "Why have you torn your robes? Have the man come to me and he will know that there is a prophet*m* in Israel." 9 So Naaman went with his horses and chariots and stopped at the door of Elisha's house. 10 Elisha sent a mes-

5:10
n Jn 9:7 *o* Ge 33:3; Lev 14:7

senger to say to him, "Go, wash*n* yourself seven times*o* in the Jordan, and your flesh will be restored and you will be cleansed."

5:11
p Ex 7:19

11 But Naaman went away angry and said, "I thought that he would surely come out to me and stand and call on the name of the LORD his God, wave his hand*p* over the spot and cure me of my leprosy. 12 Are not Abana and Pharpar, the rivers of Da-

5:12
q Isa 8:6
r Pr 14:17,29; 19:11; 29:11

mascus, better than any of the waters*q* of Israel? Couldn't I wash in them and be cleansed?" So he turned and went off in a rage.*r*

5:13
s 2Ki 6:21; 13:14

13 Naaman's servants went to him and said, "My father,*s* if the prophet had told you to do some great thing, would you not have done it? How much more, then, when he tells you, 'Wash and be cleansed'!" 14 So he went down and dipped him-

5:14
t Ge 33:3; Lev 14:7; Jos 6:15 *u* Ex 4:7
v Job 33:25; Lk 4:27

self in the Jordan seven times,*t* as the man of God had told him, and his flesh was restored*u* and became clean like that of a young boy.*v*

a 1 The Hebrew word was used for various diseases affecting the skin—not necessarily leprosy; also in verses 3, 6, 7, 11 and 27.   *b 5* That is, about 750 pounds (about 340 kilograms)   *c 5* That is, about 150 pounds (about 70 kilograms)

---

2 Kings 5:1–27

Naaman had become convinced that the Lord alone was God. Accordingly, he asked Elisha for two mule loads of Israelite soil to take back to Aram. In this way, whenever circumstances forced him to bow to the Aramean gods with his king, he might in reality be placing his knees in the soil of the true God of Israel (vv. 17–18). In this way he could be a true, though secret, believer.

Naaman's descent from his chariot to meet Gehazi (v. 21) was the mark of a changed man. No longer haughty and self-important (vv. 9–12), the now grateful (v. 15), reverent (v. 17), and humble (v. 18) Aramean climbed down from his honored place to greet a servant. He who had been a fallen, hopeless sinner displayed the

grace of a true believer. In contrast Gehazi, who had enjoyed all the privileges of his master's/Master's grace, was about to abuse them and fall from that favor.

Servants play important roles in this narrative: One was an evangelist, telling Naaman's wife of Elisha's ministry; others were discerning and encouraging, convincing Naaman to wash in the Jordan; and Gehazi acted dishonorably, falling to the temptation of greed. How do you view those who serve you (restaurant servers, office assistants, etc)? Do you act arrogantly or indifferently toward them? Would you accept advice or counsel from one of them? As a servant of the Lord, have you been tempted to take credit or make extraordinary profit from a ministry effort that blessed a wealthy/influential person?

¹⁵Then Naaman and all his attendants went back to the man of God ʷ. He stood before him and said, "Now I know ˣ that there is no God in all the world except in Israel. Please accept now a gift ʸ from your servant."

¹⁶The prophet answered, "As surely as the Lᴏʀᴅ lives, whom I serve, I will not accept a thing." And even though Naaman urged him, he refused. ᶻ

¹⁷"If you will not," said Naaman, "please let me, your servant, be given as much earth ᵃ as a pair of mules can carry, for your servant will never again make burnt offerings and sacrifices to any other god but the Lᴏʀᴅ. ¹⁸But may the Lᴏʀᴅ forgive your servant for this one thing: When my master enters the temple of Rimmon to bow down and he is leaning ᵇ on my arm and I bow there also—when I bow down in the temple of Rimmon, may the Lᴏʀᴅ forgive your servant for this."

¹⁹"Go in peace," ᶜ Elisha said.

After Naaman had traveled some distance, ²⁰Gehazi, the servant of Elisha the man of God, said to himself, "My master was too easy on Naaman, this Aramean, by not accepting from him what he brought. As surely as the Lᴏʀᴅ ᵈ lives, I will run after him and get something from him."

²¹So Gehazi hurried after Naaman. When Naaman saw him running toward him, he got down from the chariot to meet him. "Is everything all right?" he asked.

²²"Everything is all right," Gehazi answered. "My master sent me to say, 'Two young men from the company of the prophets have just come to me from the hill country of Ephraim. Please give them a talent ᵃ of silver and two sets of clothing.' " ᵉ

²³"By all means, take two talents," said Naaman. He urged Gehazi to accept them, and then tied up the two talents of silver in two bags, with two sets of clothing. He gave them to two of his servants, and they carried them ahead of Gehazi. ²⁴When Gehazi came to the hill, he took the things from the servants and put them away in the house. He sent the men away and they left. ²⁵Then he went in and stood before his master Elisha.

"Where have you been, Gehazi?" Elisha asked.

"Your servant didn't go anywhere," Gehazi answered.

²⁶But Elisha said to him, "Was not my spirit with you when the man got down from his chariot to meet you? Is this the time ᶠ to take money, or to accept clothes, olive groves, vineyards, flocks, herds, or menservants and maidservants? ᵍ ²⁷Naaman's leprosy ʰ will cling to you and to your descendants forever." Then Gehazi ⁱ went from Elisha's presence and he was leprous, as white as snow. ʲ

An Axhead Floats

6 The company ᵏ of the prophets said to Elisha, "Look, the place where we meet with you is too small for us. ²Let us go to the Jordan, where each of us can get a pole; and let us build a place there for us to live."

And he said, "Go."

³Then one of them said, "Won't you please come with your servants?"

"I will," Elisha replied. ⁴And he went with them.

They went to the Jordan and began to cut down trees. ⁵As one of them was cutting down a tree, the iron axhead fell into the water. "Oh, my lord," he cried out, "it was borrowed!"

⁶The man of God asked, "Where did it fall?" When he showed him the place, Eli-

---

ᵃ 22 That is, about 75 pounds (about 34 kilograms)

2 Kings 6:1–7

In contrast to Gehazi, who had received the reward of his unfaithfulness (5:19–27), the account unfolded here demonstrates the reward of faithful labor. Attempts to explain fully—or explain away—this miracle are fruitless. It only needs to be accepted according to the simple statement of the written report.

An iron implement was costly—too much for a

prophet to repay. He would have been forced to work as a bondservant to pay off such a debt.

Are you surprised by God's concern about a man's dismay over the loss of a borrowed tool? Without trying too hard, you can probably think of several comparable situations in your own life. Yet God responded through Elisha with a miracle, recorded for all time in holy Scripture. When has God worked a miracle like this for you?

5:15
ʷ Jos 2:11
ˣ Jos 4:24;
1Sa 17:46; Da 2:47
ʸ 1Sa 9:7; 25:27

5:16
ᶻ ver 20,26;
Ge 14:23; Da 5:17

5:17
ᵃ Ex 20:24

5:18
ᵇ 2Ki 7:2

5:19
ᶜ 1Sa 1:17;
Ac 15:33

5:20
ᵈ Ex 20:7

5:22
ᵉ ver 5; Ge 45:22

5:26
ᶠ ver 16 ᵍ Jer 45:5

5:27
ʰ Nu 12:10;
2Ki 15:5 ⁱ Col 3:5
ʲ Ex 4:6

6:1
ᵏ 1Sa 10:5; 2Ki 4:38

6:6
l Ex 15:25; 2Ki 2:21

sha cut a stick and threw*l* it there, and made the iron float. ⁷"Lift it out," he said. Then the man reached out his hand and took it.

Elisha Traps Blinded Arameans

⁸Now the king of Aram was at war with Israel. After conferring with his officers, he said, "I will set up my camp in such and such a place."

6:9
m ver 12

⁹The man of God sent word to the king*m* of Israel: "Beware of passing that place, because the Arameans are going down there."

6:10
n Jer 11:18

¹⁰So the king of Israel checked on the place indicated by the man of God. Time and again Elisha warned*n* the king, so that he was on his guard in such places.

¹¹This enraged the king of Aram. He summoned his officers and demanded of them, "Will you not tell me which of us is on the side of the king of Israel?"

6:12
o ver 9

¹²"None of us, my lord the king*o*," said one of his officers, "but Elisha, the prophet who is in Israel, tells the king of Israel the very words you speak in your bedroom."

6:13
p Ge 37:17
6:14
q 2Ki 1:9

¹³"Go, find out where he is," the king ordered, "so I can send men and capture him." The report came back: "He is in Dothan."*p* ¹⁴Then he sent*q* horses and chariots and a strong force there. They went by night and surrounded the city.

¹⁵When the servant of the man of God got up and went out early the next morning, an army with horses and chariots had surrounded the city. "Oh, my lord, what shall we do?" the servant asked.

6:16
r Ge 15:1
s 2Ch 32:7;
Ps 55:18; Ro 8:31;
1Jn 4:4

¹⁶"Don't be afraid,"*r* the prophet answered. "Those who are with us are more*s* than those who are with them."

6:17
t 2Ki 2:11,12;
Ps 68:17; Zec 6:1-7

¹⁷And Elisha prayed, "O Lord, open his eyes so he may see." Then the Lord opened the servant's eyes, and he looked and saw the hills full of horses and chariots*t* of fire all around Elisha.

6:18
u Ge 19:11;
Ac 13:11

¹⁸As the enemy came down toward him, Elisha prayed to the Lord, "Strike these people with blindness."*u* So he struck them with blindness, as Elisha had asked.

¹⁹Elisha told them, "This is not the road and this is not the city. Follow me, and I will lead you to the man you are looking for." And he led them to Samaria.

²⁰After they entered the city, Elisha said, "Lord, open the eyes of these men so they can see." Then the Lord opened their eyes and they looked, and there they were, inside Samaria.

6:21
v 2Ki 5:13
6:22
w Dt 20:11;
2Ch 28:8-15;
Ro 12:20

²¹When the king of Israel saw them, he asked Elisha, "Shall I kill them, my father?*v* Shall I kill them?"

²²"Do not kill them," he answered. "Would you kill men you have captured*w* with your own sword or bow? Set food and water before them so that they may eat and drink and then go back to their master."

6:23
x 2Ki 5:2

²³So he prepared a great feast for them, and after they had finished eating and drinking, he sent them away, and they returned to their master. So the bands*x* from Aram stopped raiding Israel's territory.

Famine in Besieged Samaria

6:24
y 1Ki 15:18; 20:1;
2Ki 8:7 *z* Dt 28:52
6:25
a Lev 26:26; Ru 1:1

²⁴Some time later, Ben-Hadad*y* king of Aram mobilized his entire army and marched up and laid siege*z* to Samaria. ²⁵There was a great famine*a* in the city; the

---

2 Kings 6:8–23

Having learned that Elisha had gone to Dothan, the Arameans surrounded the city by night to take him by force. Doubtless Elisha knew about this but allowed himself to be trapped so that the subsequent entrapment of the Arameans might work to God's glory and for everyone's good.

Elisha's intercessions (vv. 18,20) and instructions (vv. 19,22) proved ultimately to be the divine remedy for Israel's *immediate military problem*: The Arameans reported Israel's kindness, and their guerilla raids ceased.

Does God have a sense of humor? He certainly delights in the ironic, the unexpected, the contradictory,

and often the seemingly "illogical" (the reality is that his divine logic is infinitely higher than ours; see Isa. 55:9). Many delightful Old Testament stories, like this one, illustrate God's penchant for paradox. Jesus' words in the Gospels also are full of examples (like the last being first and doing good to those who hate us). Where did your "funny bone" come from? You are created in God's image, you know!

2 Kings 6:24—7:2

Though the author of Kings wasn't specific, this "Ben-Hadad" was probably the same king who had besieged Samaria earlier (see "There and Then" for 1 Kings 20:1–12), and the unnamed king of Israel was

siege lasted so long that a donkey's head sold for eighty shekels[a] of silver, and a quarter of a cab[b] of seed pods[cb] for five shekels.[d]

[6:25]
[b Isa 36:12]

26As the king of Israel was passing by on the wall, a woman cried to him, "Help me, my lord the king!"

27The king replied, "If the LORD does not help you, where can I get help for you? From the threshing floor? From the winepress?" 28Then he asked her, "What's the matter?"

She answered, "This woman said to me, 'Give up your son so we may eat him today, and tomorrow we'll eat my son.' 29So we cooked my son and ate[c] him. The next day I said to her, 'Give up your son so we may eat him,' but she had hidden him."

[6:29]
[c Lev 26:29;]
[Dt 28:53-55]
[6:30]
[d 2Ki 18:37;]
[Isa 22:15]
[e Ge 37:34;]
[1Ki 21:27]

30When the king heard the woman's words, he tore[d] his robes. As he went along the wall, the people looked, and there, underneath, he had sackcloth[e] on his body. 31He said, "May God deal with me, be it ever so severely, if the head of Elisha son of Shaphat remains on his shoulders today!"

32Now Elisha was sitting in his house, and the elders[f] were sitting with him. The king sent a messenger ahead, but before he arrived, Elisha said to the elders, "Don't you see how this murderer[g] is sending someone to cut off my head?[h] Look, when the messenger comes, shut the door and hold it shut against him. Is not the sound of his master's footsteps behind him?"

[6:32]
[f Eze 8:1; 14:1; 20:1]
[g 1Ki 18:4 h ver 31]

33While he was still talking to them, the messenger came down to him. And the king said, "This disaster is from the LORD. Why should I wait[i] for the LORD any longer?"

[6:33]
[i Lev 24:11;]
[Job 2:9; 14:14;]
[Isa 40:31]

7 Elisha said, "Hear the word of the LORD. This is what the LORD says: About this time tomorrow, a seah[e] of flour will sell for a shekel[f] and two seahs[g] of barley for a shekel[j] at the gate of Samaria."

[7:1]
[j ver 16]
[7:2]
[k 2Ki 18:18 l ver 19;]
[Ge 7:11; Ps 78:23;]
[Mal 3:10 m ver 17]

2The officer on whose arm the king was leaning[k] said to the man of God, "Look, even if the LORD should open the floodgates[l] of the heavens, could this happen?"

"You will see it with your own eyes," answered Elisha, "but you will not eat[m] any of it!"

The Siege Lifted

3Now there were four men with leprosy[hn] at the entrance of the city gate. They said to each other, "Why stay here until we die? 4If we say, 'We'll go into the city'— the famine is there, and we will die. And if we stay here, we will die. So let's go over

[7:3]
[n Lev 13:45-46;]
[Nu 5:1-4]

[a] *25* That is, about 2 pounds (about 1 kilogram)   [b] *25* That is, probably about 1/2 pint (about 0.3 liter)   [c] *25* Or *of doves' dung*   [d] *25* That is, about 2 ounces (about 55 grams)   [e] *1* That is, probably about 7 quarts (about 7.3 liters); also in verses 16 and 18   [f] *1* That is, about 2/5 ounce (about 11 grams); also in verses 16 and 18   [g] *1* That is, probably about 13 quarts (about 15 liters); also in verses 16 and 18   [h] *3* The Hebrew word is used for various diseases affecting the skin—not necessarily leprosy; also in verse 8.

---

probably Joram (cf. 2 Kings 3:1–3). Just as Elijah had been held responsible for causing the drought in the days of Ahab (1 Kings 18:17), so Elisha was blamed for the siege that caused this famine. Elisha had confronted Joram harshly in the past (2 Kings 3:13–14), making him a logical target for the frustrations of a powerless, ungodly king. The story moves quickly, highlighting the prophet's control and the king's despair. This disaster was indeed part of God's sovereign purpose. The king could do nothing—not even pray (see 6:33).

📖 This passage is as tragic as the previous one is humorous (see previous "Here and Now"). When it comes to spiritual warfare, our present situation isn't so different from Elisha's tortured, topsy-turvy world. Christians in many places are ravaged by the turbulence of war (and/or famine). Where actual, physical warfare

isn't present, they struggle against ideologies and social forces designed to undermine God's rule.

The faithful everywhere are called to be Elishas. We are called, to the best of our ability, to resist evil and show mercy (see 6:22–23). As with Elisha, our weapon is prayer (see 6:18,20). And our assurance is that the Divine Warrior will act on our behalf (see 6:16–18).

2 Kings 7:3–20

The fulfillment of the word of the Lord through Elisha (vv. 1–2) began with four lepers outside the city gate. According to ritual law, they were quarantined outside the community (Lev. 13:46). Caught in a death trap, no matter the outcome of the siege, they decided to surrender to the Arameans—leaving their fate in the hands of the enemy.

King Joram's unbelief caused him to conclude that

to the camp of the Arameans and surrender. If they spare us, we live; if they kill us, then we die."

5At dusk they got up and went to the camp of the Arameans. When they reached the edge of the camp, not a man was there, 6for the Lord had caused the Arameans to hear the sound⁰ of chariots and horses and a great army, so that they said to one another, "Look, the king of Israel has hiredᵖ the Hittiteᵍ and Egyptian kings to attack us!" 7So they got up and fledʳ in the dusk and abandoned their tents and their horses and donkeys. They left the camp as it was and ran for their lives.

8The men who had leprosyˢ reached the edge of the camp and entered one of the tents. They ate and drank, and carried away silver, gold and clothes, and went off and hid them. They returned and entered another tent and took some things from it and hid them also.

9Then they said to each other, "We're not doing right. This is a day of good news and we are keeping it to ourselves. If we wait until daylight, punishment will overtake us. Let's go at once and report this to the royal palace."

10So they went and called out to the city gatekeepers and told them, "We went into the Aramean camp and not a man was there—not a sound of anyone—only tethered horses and donkeys, and the tents left just as they were." 11The gatekeepers shouted the news, and it was reported within the palace.

12The king got up in the night and said to his officers, "I will tell you what the Arameans have done to us. They know we are starving; so they have left the camp to hideᵗ in the countryside, thinking, 'They will surely come out, and then we will take them alive and get into the city.'"

13One of his officers answered, "Have some men take five of the horses that are left in the city. Their plight will be like that of all the Israelites left here—yes, they will only be like all these Israelites who are doomed. So let us send them to find out what happened."

14So they selected two chariots with their horses, and the king sent them after the Aramean army. He commanded the drivers, "Go and find out what has happened." 15They followed them as far as the Jordan, and they found the whole road strewn with the clothing and equipment the Arameans had thrown away in their headlong flight. So the messengers returned and reported to the king. 16Then the people went out and plunderedᵘ the camp of the Arameans. So a seah of flour sold for a shekel, and two seahs of barley sold for a shekel,ᵛ as the LORD had said.

17Now the king had put the officer on whose arm he leaned in charge of the gate, and the people trampled him in the gateway, and he died,ʷ just as the man of God had foretold when the king came down to his house. 18It happened as the man of God had said to the king: "About this time tomorrow, a seah of flour will sell for a shekel and two seahs of barley for a shekel at the gate of Samaria."

19The officer had said to the man of God, "Look, even if the LORD should open the floodgatesˣ of the heavens, could this happen?" The man of God had replied, "You will see it with your own eyes, but you will not eat any of it!" 20And that is exactly what happened to him, for the people trampled him in the gateway, and he died.

7:6
o Ex 14:24;
2Sa 5:24; Eze 1:24
p 2Sa 10:6;
Jer 46:21
q Nu 13:29
7:7
r Jdg 7:21;
Ps 48:4-6; Pr 28:1;
Isa 30:17
7:8
s Isa 33:23; 35:6

7:12
t Jos 8:4;
2Ki 6:25-29

7:16
u Isa 33:4,23
v ver 1

7:17
w ver 2; 2Ki 6:32

7:19
x ver 2

---

the report of the four leprous men was part of an Aramean ambush (v. 12) rather than evidence of the fulfillment of Elisha's prophecy. But the fulfillment of the prophetic word came with the citizens of Samaria plundering the enemy camp. Food prices became exactly what the prophet had announced (v. 16; cf. v. 1). The death of the officer, who had responded to Elisha's prophecy with unbelief, took place when he was trampled at the gate by the stampede of hungry people (v. 17; cf. v. 2).

The Israelites should have realized that the siege and accompanying famine were the results of covenant curses sent on them because of their sin and unbelief (Deut. 28:15,53–57). But this didn't mean that the covenant God had abandoned his people or his promises. These stories from Elisha's day are examples of God's mercy in rebellious times and show that the will of God can be done on Earth even during times of apostasy, political conflict, suffering, and despair. How can this prompt us to pray—and live—in our day?

The Shunammite's Land Restored

8 Now Elisha had said to the woman[y] whose son he had restored to life, "Go away with your family and stay for a while wherever you can, because the LORD has decreed a famine[z] in the land that will last seven years." [a] 2The woman proceeded to do as the man of God said. She and her family went away and stayed in the land of the Philistines seven years.

3At the end of the seven years she came back from the land of the Philistines and went to the king to beg for her house and land. 4The king was talking to Gehazi, the servant of the man of God, and had said, "Tell me about all the great things Elisha has done." 5Just as Gehazi was telling the king how Elisha had restored[b] the dead to life, the woman whose son Elisha had brought back to life came to beg the king for her house and land.

Gehazi said, "This is the woman, my lord the king, and this is her son whom Elisha restored to life." 6The king asked the woman about it, and she told him.

Then he assigned an official to her case and said to him, "Give back everything that belonged to her, including all the income from her land from the day she left the country until now."

Hazael Murders Ben-Hadad

7Elisha went to Damascus,[c] and Ben-Hadad[d] king of Aram was ill. When the king was told, "The man of God has come all the way up here," 8he said to Hazael,[e] "Take a gift[f] with you and go to meet the man of God. Consult[g] the LORD through him; ask him, 'Will I recover from this illness?' "

9Hazael went to meet Elisha, taking with him as a gift forty camel-loads of all the finest wares of Damascus. He went in and stood before him, and said, "Your son Ben-Hadad king of Aram has sent me to ask, 'Will I recover from this illness?' "

10Elisha answered, "Go and say to him, 'You will certainly recover';[h] but[a] the LORD has revealed to me that he will in fact die." 11He stared at him with a fixed gaze until Hazael felt ashamed.[i] Then the man of God began to weep.[j]

12"Why is my lord weeping?" asked Hazael.

"Because I know the harm[k] you will do to the Israelites," he answered. "You will

8:1
y 2Ki 4:8-37
z Lev 26:26;
Dt 28:22; Ru 1:1
a Ge 12:10;
Ps 105:16;
Hag 1:11

8:5
b 2Ki 4:35

8:7
c 2Sa 8:5; 1Ki 11:24
d 2Ki 6:24
8:8
e 1Ki 19:15
f Ge 32:20; 1Sa 9:7;
2Ki 1:2 g Jdg 18:5

8:10
h Isa 38:1

8:11
i Jdg 3:25
j Lk 19:41

8:12
k 1Ki 19:17;
2Ki 10:32; 12:17;
13:3,7

[a] 10 The Hebrew may also be read *Go and say, 'You will certainly not recover,' for.*

---

2 Kings 8:1–6

Elisha continued to assist his patroness from Shunem (cf. 4:8–37), this time warning her to leave because of the famine (unrelated to that of ch. 6) that was about to devastate the northern kingdom. The legal details of the loss of her land aren't given. It may have been confiscated, possibly by a neighbor or relative. Or in her absence it may have fallen into the king's hands. The time of this encounter is uncertain, but the king's lack of familiarity with Elisha's ministry may indicate that the incident occurred in the early days of Jehu's reign rather than in the time of Joram, who had numerous contacts with Elisha.

This king acted more nobly than his predecessor Ahab, who had shown no hesitation in confiscating the property of Naboth (1 Kings 21). Whether or not he would have been inclined to act justly on his own accord, we may be sure that Elisha's reputation and legacy influenced him to immediately restore the woman's property and revenue. When in your experience has a government official or legislative body been influenced by the legitimate, moral demands of Christian constituents?

2 Kings 8:7–15

Here Elisha fulfilled a task originally given to Elijah: the anointing of Hazael as king of Aram (see 1 Kings 19:15). Elisha's reply to Hazael's question was mysterious, yet truthful. Yes: Under normal circumstances the Aramean king would recover; the illness wouldn't be fatal in itself. And no: Elisha knew this treacherous man would use the king's illness to effect his coup d'état. Elisha's reply and icy stare indicate that Hazael had already plotted the king's death and that Elisha knew his secret thoughts.

Hazael didn't show revulsion at the violent acts Elisha foresaw, but he saw no possibility to gain the power necessary to accomplish them. The "feats," as Hazael called them (v. 13), of smashing children and slashing pregnant women might spell victory to a conquering king—but they wouldn't be great exploits in the eyes of the vulnerable citizens or of God. Too often today such victims are used by the media as decoys to divert attention from the real story, the one about political power. In such circumstances, then and now, the faithful are called to show mercy and to trust that God's sovereignty will ultimately prevail over the world's ruthless powers.

8:12
_l_ Ps 137:9;
Isa 13:16;
Hos 13:16;
Na 3:10; Lk 19:44
_m_ Ge 34:29
_n_ 2Ki 15:16;
Am 1:13
8:13
_o_ 1Sa 17:43;
2Sa 3:8 _p_ 1Ki 19:15
8:15
_q_ 2Ki 1:17

set fire to their fortified places, kill their young men with the sword, dash _l_ their little children _m_ to the ground, and rip open _n_ their pregnant women."

¹³Hazael said, "How could your servant, a mere dog, _o_ accomplish such a feat?"

"The LORD has shown me that you will become king _p_ of Aram," answered Elisha.

¹⁴Then Hazael left Elisha and returned to his master. When Ben-Hadad asked, "What did Elisha say to you?" Hazael replied, "He told me that you would certainly recover." ¹⁵But the next day he took a thick cloth, soaked it in water and spread it over the king's face, so that he died. _q_ Then Hazael succeeded him as king.

Jehoram King of Judah

8:16
_r_ 2Ki 1:17; 3:1
_s_ 2Ch 21:1-4

¹⁶In the fifth year of Joram _r_ son of Ahab king of Israel, when Jehoshaphat was king of Judah, Jehoram _s_ son of Jehoshaphat began his reign as king of Judah. ¹⁷He was thirty-two years old when he became king, and he reigned in Jerusalem eight years.

8:18
_t_ ver 26; 2Ki 11:1
8:19
_u_ Ge 6:13
_v_ 2Sa 21:17; 7:13;
1Ki 11:36;
Rev 21:23

¹⁸He walked in the ways of the kings of Israel, as the house of Ahab had done, for he married a daughter _t_ of Ahab. He did evil in the eyes of the LORD. ¹⁹Nevertheless, for the sake of his servant David, the LORD was not willing to destroy _u_ Judah. He had promised to maintain a lamp _v_ for David and his descendants forever.

8:20
_w_ 1Ki 22:47

²⁰In the time of Jehoram, Edom rebelled against Judah and set up its own king. _w_ ²¹So Jehoram _a_ went to Zair with all his chariots. The Edomites surrounded him and his chariot commanders, but he rose up and broke through by night; his army, however, fled back home. ²²To this day Edom has been in rebellion _x_ against Judah. Libnah _y_ revolted at the same time.

8:22
_x_ Ge 27:40
_y_ Nu 33:20;
Jos 21:13; 2Ki 19:8

²³As for the other events of Jehoram's reign, and all he did, are they not written in the book of the annals of the kings of Judah? ²⁴Jehoram rested with his fathers and was buried with them in the City of David. And Ahaziah his son succeeded him as king.

Ahaziah King of Judah

8:25
_z_ 2Ki 9:29

²⁵In the twelfth _z_ year of Joram son of Ahab king of Israel, Ahaziah son of Jehoram king of Judah began to reign. ²⁶Ahaziah was twenty-two years old when he became king, and he reigned in Jerusalem one year. His mother's name was Athaliah, _a_ a granddaughter of Omri _b_ king of Israel. ²⁷He walked in the ways of the house of Ahab _c_ and did evil _d_ in the eyes of the LORD, as the house of Ahab had done, for he was related by marriage to Ahab's family.

8:26
_a_ ver 18
_b_ 1Ki 16:23
8:27
_c_ 1Ki 16:30
_d_ 1Ki 15:26

8:28
_e_ Dt 4:43;
1Ki 22:3,29

²⁸Ahaziah went with Joram son of Ahab to war against Hazael king of Aram at Ramoth Gilead. _e_ The Arameans wounded Joram; ²⁹so King Joram returned to Jez-

---

_a_ 21 Hebrew _Joram_, a variant of _Jehoram_; also in verses 23 and 24

---

2 Kings 8:16–24

Judah's political history temporarily merged with Israel's. Judah's alliance with Israel through the marriage of Jehoram, son of Jehoshapat, to Athaliah, daughter of Ahab and Jezebel, brought Judah to the same spiritual alienation from God as Israel.

God's mercy preserved David's dynasty in Judah, despite the fact that Jehoram followed in the ways of the house of Ahab. God's promise to David was a light that continued to shine (v. 19; cf. 2 Sam. 21:17; 1 Kings 11:36; 15:4). In Zion God would perpetually keep the lamp of his anointed burning (Ps. 132:17). Though the dynasty was preserved, Judah suffered loss of territory and influence.

What's your track record for keeping promises—especially if the ones to whom you have made them have proven unreliable and undeserving? When we stop to think of the long-term performance of God's Old Testament people, isn't it amazing that God kept his promises at all—when at times few even remembered or acknowl-

edged them? What are some promises God has made to you? For those that haven't been provisional, based on your own obedience, do you rely without doubt on God's impeccable track record in promise keeping?

2 Kings 8:25–29

The queen mother could exercise considerable influence in the affairs of court (e.g., Maacah, who was removed from her position by her grandson Asa because of her idolatry; 1 Kings 15:13). Jezebel's influence in fostering foreign cults in Jerusalem was continued through the equally wicked Athaliah, mother of Ahaziah.

What difference does a godly (or ungodly) spouse make in a leader's performance? The situation varies greatly, of course. But if you pause for a few moments to reflect on recent history (say, from the beginning of the 20th century on), you can no doubt cite notable examples in both directions. What difference does a godly spouse make in the life of an "ordinary" Christian? What strong Christian marriages have influenced you over the course of your life? What role has each partner played?

reel[f] to recover from the wounds the Arameans had inflicted on him at Ramoth[a] in his battle with Hazael[g] king of Aram.

Then Ahaziah son of Jehoram king of Judah went down to Jezreel to see Joram son of Ahab, because he had been wounded.

Jehu Anointed King of Israel

9 The prophet Elisha summoned a man from the company[h] of the prophets and said to him, "Tuck your cloak into your belt,[i] take this flask of oil[j] with you and go to Ramoth Gilead.[k] 2When you get there, look for Jehu son of Jehoshaphat, the son of Nimshi. Go to him, get him away from his companions and take him into an inner room. 3Then take the flask and pour the oil[l] on his head and declare, 'This is what the LORD says: I anoint you king over Israel.' Then open the door and run; don't delay!"

4So the young man, the prophet, went to Ramoth Gilead. 5When he arrived, he found the army officers sitting together. "I have a message for you, commander," he said.

"For which of us?" asked Jehu.

"For you, commander," he replied.

6Jehu got up and went into the house. Then the prophet poured the oil[m] on Jehu's head and declared, "This is what the LORD, the God of Israel, says: 'I anoint you king over the LORD's people Israel. 7You are to destroy the house of Ahab your master, and I will avenge[n] the blood of my servants[o] the prophets and the blood of all the LORD's servants shed by Jezebel.[p] 8The whole house[q] of Ahab will perish. I will cut off from Ahab every last male[r] in Israel—slave or free. 9I will make the house of Ahab like the house of Jeroboam[s] son of Nebat and like the house of Baasha[t] son of Ahijah. 10As for Jezebel, dogs[u] will devour her on the plot of ground at Jezreel, and no one will bury her.' " Then he opened the door and ran.

11When Jehu went out to his fellow officers, one of them asked him, "Is everything all right? Why did this madman[v] come to you?"

"You know the man and the sort of things he says," Jehu replied.

12"That's not true!" they said. "Tell us."

Jehu said, "Here is what he told me: 'This is what the LORD says: I anoint you king over Israel.' "

13They hurried and took their cloaks and spread[w] them under him on the bare steps. Then they blew the trumpet[x] and shouted, "Jehu is king!"

Jehu Kills Joram and Ahaziah

14So Jehu son of Jehoshaphat, the son of Nimshi, conspired against Joram. (Now Joram and all Israel had been defending Ramoth Gilead[y] against Hazael king of Aram, 15but King Joram[b] had returned to Jezreel to recover[z] from the wounds the Arameans had inflicted on him in the battle with Hazael king of Aram.) Jehu said,

a 29 Hebrew *Ramah*, a variant of *Ramoth*   b 15 Hebrew *Jehoram*, a variant of *Joram*; also in verses 17 and 21-24

Cross references (margin)

8:29 f 2Ki 9:15; g 1Ki 19:15,17

9:1 h 1Sa 10:5; i 2Ki 4:29 / 1Sa 10:1; k 2Ki 8:28

9:3 l 1Ki 19:16

9:6 m 1Ki 19:16; 2Ch 22:7

9:7 n Ge 4:24; Rev 6:10; o Dt 32:43; p 1Ki 18:4; 21:15

9:8 q 2Ki 10:17; r Dt 32:36; 1Sa 25:22; 1Ki 21:21; 2Ki 14:26

9:9 s 1Ki 14:10; 15:29; 16:3,11 t 1Ki 16:3

9:10 u ver 35-36; 1Ki 21:23

9:11 v Jer 29:26; Jn 10:20; Ac 26:24

9:13 w Mt 21:8; Lk 19:36; x 2Sa 15:10; 1Ki 1:34,39

9:14 y Dt 4:43; 2Ki 8:28

9:15 z 2Ki 8:29

---

2 Kings 9:1–13

Elisha's appointment of a young prophet to anoint Jehu as Israel's king fulfilled a commission Elisha had received from Elijah (cf. 1 Kings 19:16). (The notation of Jehu's ancestor Nimshi was probably included to distinguish Jehu's father from King Jehoshaphat of Judah.) The demise of Ahab's house had already been declared years earlier by Elijah (1 Kings 21:21–28).

The term "this madman" used by Jehu's fellow officers betrayed their low spiritual condition and contempt for God's prophets. When Jehu revealed the gist of what had happened, their actions probably indicated that, discontented with Joram's reign, they were sporting for insurrection.

Why did Elisha instruct his attendant to run from the house immediately after delivering God's message to Jehu? Elisha was likely concerned about his young associate's safety, as King Joram would have viewed anointing Jehu as an act of treason. But might there also be a lesson here that God's work is often best done and then left to have its own impact? Can you think of other examples, either historical or from your personal experience, when this has been the case?

2 Kings 9:14–29

As Jehu made his wild ride toward Jezreel, three times he was greeted with the question "Do you come in peace?" Though Joram would have been worried about

9:16
a 2Ch 22:7
9:17
b Isa 21:6
c 1Sa 16:4

"If this is the way you feel, don't let anyone slip out of the city to go and tell the news in Jezreel." [16]Then he got into his chariot and rode to Jezreel, because Joram was resting there and Ahaziah*a* king of Judah had gone down to see him.

[17]When the lookout*b* standing on the tower in Jezreel saw Jehu's troops approaching, he called out, "I see some troops coming."

"Get a horseman," Joram ordered. "Send him to meet them and ask, 'Do you come in peace?'*c* "

[18]The horseman rode off to meet Jehu and said, "This is what the king says: 'Do you come in peace?' "

"What do you have to do with peace?" Jehu replied. "Fall in behind me."

The lookout reported, "The messenger has reached them, but he isn't coming back."

[19]So the king sent out a second horseman. When he came to them he said, "This is what the king says: 'Do you come in peace?' "

Jehu replied, "What do you have to do with peace? Fall in behind me."

9:20
d 2Sa 18:27

[20]The lookout reported, "He has reached them, but he isn't coming back either. The driving is like*d* that of Jehu son of Nimshi—he drives like a madman."

9:21
e ver 26;
1Ki 21:1-7,15-19

[21]"Hitch up my chariot," Joram ordered. And when it was hitched up, Joram king of Israel and Ahaziah king of Judah rode out, each in his own chariot, to meet Jehu. They met him at the plot of ground that had belonged to Naboth*e* the Jezreelite. [22]When Joram saw Jehu he asked, "Have you come in peace, Jehu?"

9:22
f 1Ki 16:30-33;
18:19; 2Ch 21:13;
Rev 2:20
9:23
g 2Ki 11:14
9:24
h 1Ki 22:34

"How can there be peace," Jehu replied, "as long as all the idolatry and witchcraft of your mother Jezebel*f* abound?"

[23]Joram turned about and fled, calling out to Ahaziah, "Treachery,*g* Ahaziah!"

[24]Then Jehu drew his bow*h* and shot Joram between the shoulders. The arrow pierced his heart and he slumped down in his chariot. [25]Jehu said to Bidkar, his chariot officer, "Pick him up and throw him on the field that belonged to Naboth the Jezreelite. Remember how you and I were riding together in chariots behind Ahab his father when the LORD made this prophecy*i* about him: [26]'Yesterday I saw the blood of Naboth*j* and the blood of his sons, declares the LORD, and I will surely make you pay for it on this plot of ground, declares the LORD.'*a* Now then, pick him up and throw him on that plot, in accordance with the word of the LORD."*k*

9:25
i 1Ki 21:19-22,
24-29
9:26
j 1Ki 21:19
k 1Ki 21:29

[27]When Ahaziah king of Judah saw what had happened, he fled up the road to Beth Haggan.*b* Jehu chased him, shouting, "Kill him too!" They wounded him in his chariot on the way up to Gur near Ibleam,*l* but he escaped to Megiddo*m* and died there. [28]His servants took him by chariot*n* to Jerusalem and buried him with his fathers in his tomb in the City of David. [29](In the eleventh*o* year of Joram son of Ahab, Ahaziah had become king of Judah.)

9:27
l Jdg 1:27
m 2Ki 23:29
9:28
n 2Ki 14:20; 23:30
9:29
o 2Ki 8:25

Jezebel Killed

9:30
p Jer 4:30;
Eze 23:40

[30]Then Jehu went to Jezreel. When Jezebel heard about it, she painted*p* her eyes, arranged her hair and looked out of a window. [31]As Jehu entered the gate, she asked, "Have you come in peace, Zimri,*q* you murderer of your master?"*c*

9:31
q 1Ki 16:9-10

a 26 See 1 Kings 21:19.   *b 27* Or *fled by way of the garden house*   *c 31* Or *"Did Zimri have peace, who murdered his master?"*

---

peace on the battlefront with the Arameans (see vv. 14–15), the absence of peace was within his own country. Joram's espousal of the idolatry and witchcraft instituted by his mother, Jezebel, had rendered any talk of "peace" impossible (v. 22). Joram realized, too late, that Jehu's reply meant that a coup d'état was taking place.

The murder of Naboth and the confiscation of his land (1 Kings 21:1–16), as well as the resulting prophecy against Ahab and Jezebel (1 Kings 21:17–29), are key to this passage. Jehu was an eyewitness of their crimes (v. 25), Jehu and Joram met at that piece of ground (v. 21), and Joram's dead body was thrown there

(vv. 25–26). Jehu's mission was accomplished by ending the violence of the house of Ahab against the innocent, so that peace and order could be restored to Israel. Once again we see God's concerns for genuine peace for his people and justice for the oppressed (and their oppressors). How are you driven by those concerns (cf. Prov. 29:7)?

2 Kings 9:30–37
When news of Jehu's coup and the assassination of her son Joram reached Jezebel, she arranged herself in queenly fashion and waited for Jehu's arrival. She called tauntingly to Jehu with words calculated to

³²He looked up at the window and called out, "Who is on my side? Who?" Two or three eunuchs looked down at him. ³³"Throw her down!" Jehu said. So they threw her down, and some of her blood spattered the wall and the horses as they trampled her underfoot.ʳ

³⁴Jehu went in and ate and drank. "Take care of that cursed woman," he said, "and bury her, for she was a king's daughter."ˢ ³⁵But when they went out to bury her, they found nothing except her skull, her feet and her hands. ³⁶They went back and told Jehu, who said, "This is the word of the LORD that he spoke through his servant Elijah the Tishbite: On the plot of ground at Jezreel dogsᵗ will devour Jezebel's flesh.ᵃ ᵘ ³⁷Jezebel's body will be like refuseᵛ on the ground in the plot at Jezreel, so that no one will be able to say, 'This is Jezebel.' "

Ahab's Family Killed

10 Now there were in Samariaʷ seventy sonsˣ of the house of Ahab. So Jehu wrote letters and sent them to Samaria: to the officials of Jezreel,ᵇ ʸ to the elders and to the guardiansᶻ of Ahab's children. He said, ²"As soon as this letter reaches you, since your master's sons are with you and you have chariots and horses, a fortified city and weapons, ³choose the best and most worthy of your master's sons and set him on his father's throne. Then fight for your master's house."

⁴But they were terrified and said, "If two kings could not resist him, how can we?" ⁵So the palace administrator, the city governor, the elders and the guardians sent this message to Jehu: "We are your servantsᵃ and we will do anything you say. We will not appoint anyone as king; you do whatever you think best."

⁶Then Jehu wrote them a second letter, saying, "If you are on my side and will obey me, take the heads of your master's sons and come to me in Jezreel by this time tomorrow."

Now the royal princes, seventy of them, were with the leading men of the city, who were rearing them. ⁷When the letter arrived, these men took the princes and slaughtered all seventyᵇ of them. They put their headsᶜ in baskets and sent them to Jehu in Jezreel. ⁸When the messenger arrived, he told Jehu, "They have brought the heads of the princes."

Then Jehu ordered, "Put them in two piles at the entrance of the city gate until morning."

ᵃ 36 See 1 Kings 21:23.   ᵇ 1 Hebrew; some Septuagint manuscripts and Vulgate *of the city*

9:33
ʳ Ps 7:5

9:34
ˢ 1Ki 16:31; 21:25

9:36
ᵗ Ps 68:23; Jer 15:3
ᵘ 1Ki 21:23

9:37
ᵛ Ps 83:10; Isa 5:25; Jer 8:2; 9:22; 16:4; 25:33; Zep 1:17

10:1
ʷ 1Ki 13:32
ˣ Jdg 8:30
ʸ 1Ki 21:1 ᶻ ver 5

10:5
ᵃ Jos 9:8;
1Ki 20:4,32

10:7
ᵇ 1Ki 21:21
ᶜ 2Sa 4:8

---

cut him down to size. The name "Zimri" had become synonymous with "traitor," since Zimri had seized the throne by assassination and destroyed the house of Baasha (cf. 1 Kings 16:8–20). Two of Jezebel's own attendants joined the revolt and threw her to her death. Jehu subsequently rode over her fallen body and went in to dine in the banquet hall of his predecessor.

After reflecting on the day's events, Jehu gave instructions that Jezebel's body be given a proper burial, since she had been a king's daughter. But his second thoughts were too late. The servant found precious little of Jezebel's remains. When this was reported to Jehu, he recognized immediately the full force of fulfilled prophecy (1 Kings 21:23; 2 Kings 9:10).

📖 One dictionary definition of "Jezebel" (or "jezebel") is "an impudent, shameless, or morally unrestrained woman." How many Jezebels (or Judases, for that matter) do you know? How sad when any individual goes down in history with such ignominy that her or his name becomes "marked" for all time! What kind of reputation will you leave behind? Do you think some people might associate your name with the qualities in you that they admire?

2 Kings 10:1–17

❓ Was the pitiless Jehu in God's service or against him? As gruesome as it was, Jehu *was* commissioned to destroy the house of Ahab (9:6–9). But Jehu epitomized the word *overkill!* Beyond the descendants of Ahab, Jehu's bloodbath extended to "all his chief men, his close friends and his priests" (v. 11)—plus 42 members of the royal family of Judah (vv. 13–14). Jehu was later condemned by the prophet Hosea for "the massacre at Jezreel" (Hos. 1:4).

📖 Old Testament Israel was history's only legitimate "theocracy," a nation directly governed by God with every citizen expected to be loyal to his covenant. Christians today aren't commissioned to use armed force against their own societies. If the powers of evil extend beyond the political powers that promote it, our defense must be other than military. Paul urged Christians to take on the armor of faith to stand against the devil's wiles (Eph. 6:10–20). The apostle's most important weapon while in prison was prayer. And his greatest concern in battling the forces that had imprisoned him was his need for courage to witness to his faith. Of what weapons does your spiritual arsenal consist?

9The next morning Jehu went out. He stood before all the people and said, "You are innocent. It was I who conspired against my master and killed him, but who killed all these? 10Know then, that not a word the LORD has spoken against the house of Ahab will fail. The LORD has done what he promised[d] through his servant Elijah."[e] 11So Jehu[f] killed everyone in Jezreel who remained of the house of Ahab, as well as all his chief men, his close friends and his priests, leaving him no survivor.[g]

12Jehu then set out and went toward Samaria. At Beth Eked of the Shepherds, 13he met some relatives of Ahaziah king of Judah and asked, "Who are you?"

They said, "We are relatives of Ahaziah,[h] and we have come down to greet the families of the king and of the queen mother.[i]"

14"Take them alive!" he ordered. So they took them alive and slaughtered them by the well of Beth Eked—forty-two men. He left no survivor.

15After he left there, he came upon Jehonadab[j] son of Recab,[k] who was on his way to meet him. Jehu greeted him and said, "Are you in accord with me, as I am with you?"

"I am," Jehonadab answered.

"If so," said Jehu, "give me your hand."[l] So he did, and Jehu helped him up into the chariot. 16Jehu said, "Come with me and see my zeal[m] for the LORD." Then he had him ride along in his chariot.

17When Jehu came to Samaria, he killed all who were left there of Ahab's family;[n] he destroyed them, according to the word of the LORD spoken to Elijah.

Ministers of Baal Killed

18Then Jehu brought all the people together and said to them, "Ahab served[o] Baal a little; Jehu will serve him much. 19Now summon[p] all the prophets of Baal, all his ministers and all his priests. See that no one is missing, because I am going to hold a great sacrifice for Baal. Anyone who fails to come will no longer live." But Jehu was acting deceptively in order to destroy the ministers of Baal.

20Jehu said, "Call an assembly[q] in honor of Baal." So they proclaimed it. 21Then he sent word throughout Israel, and all the ministers of Baal came; not one stayed away. They crowded into the temple of Baal until it was full from one end to the other. 22And Jehu said to the keeper of the wardrobe, "Bring robes for all the ministers of Baal." So he brought out robes for them.

23Then Jehu and Jehonadab son of Recab went into the temple of Baal. Jehu said to the ministers of Baal, "Look around and see that no servants of the LORD are here with you—only ministers of Baal." 24So they went in to make sacrifices and burnt offerings. Now Jehu had posted eighty men outside with this warning: "If one of you lets any of the men I am placing in your hands escape, it will be your life for his life."[r]

25As soon as Jehu had finished making the burnt offering, he ordered the guards and officers: "Go in and kill[s] them; let no one escape."[t] So they cut them down with the sword. The guards and officers threw the bodies out and then entered the inner shrine of the temple of Baal. 26They brought the sacred stone[u] out of the temple of Baal and burned it. 27They demolished the sacred stone of Baal and tore down the temple[v] of Baal, and people have used it for a latrine to this day.

28So Jehu[w] destroyed Baal worship in Israel. 29However, he did not turn away

Marginal references

10:10
[d] 2Ki 9:7-10
[e] 1Ki 21:29
10:11
[f] Hos 1:4 [g] ver 14;
Job 18:19

10:13
[h] 2Ki 8:24,29;
2Ch 22:8 [i] 1Ki 2:19

10:15
[j] Jer 35:6,14-19
[k] 1Ch 2:55;
Jer 35:2 [l] Ezr 10:19;
Eze 17:18

10:16
[m] Nu 25:13;
1Ki 19:10

10:17
[n] 2Ki 9:8

10:18
[o] Jdg 2:11;
1Ki 16:31-32
10:19
[p] 1Ki 18:19; 22:6

10:20
[q] Ex 32:5; Joel 1:14

10:24
[r] 1Ki 20:39
10:25
[s] Ex 22:20;
2Ki 11:18
[t] 1Ki 18:40

10:26
[u] 1Ki 14:23

10:27
[v] 1Ki 16:32
10:28
[w] 1Ki 19:17

---

2 Kings 10:18–36

In his usual treacherous fashion, Jehu did away with Baal worship in Israel. For this and for eliminating the house of Ahab (though he went beyond the responsibility given him; see previous "There and Then"), God commended Jehu—promising him a royal succession to the fourth generation. In fact, he was the only king of the northern kingdom to receive divine commendation! Yet Jehu would prove a disappointment to God. His reform was motivated by political self-interest more than by any deep concern for the Lord. So God allowed the Arameans to plunder and systematically reduce Israel's size.

Despite his comet-like beginning, Jehu was, spiritually speaking, a falling star. He exercised God's just wrath against the Israelites' compromise with Baalism. But he continued Israel's tradition of worshiping the golden calves at Bethel and Dan (v. 29; see also "There and Then" for 13:1–9)—probably justifying this practice as a point of unification for the northern kingdom. In what ways can you relate to Jehu's flaw of allowing yourself a "little bit" of sin and practicing "just enough" righteousness?

from the sins^x of Jeroboam son of Nebat, which he had caused Israel to commit—the worship of the golden calves^y at Bethel^z and Dan.

³⁰The LORD said to Jehu, "Because you have done well in accomplishing what is right in my eyes and have done to the house of Ahab all I had in mind to do, your descendants will sit on the throne of Israel to the fourth generation."ᵃ ³¹Yet Jehu was not carefulᵇ to keep the law of the LORD, the God of Israel, with all his heart. He did not turn away from the sinsᶜ of Jeroboam, which he had caused Israel to commit.

³²In those days the LORD began to reduceᵈ the size of Israel. Hazaelᵉ overpowered the Israelites throughout their territory ³³east of the Jordan in all the land of Gilead (the region of Gad, Reuben and Manasseh), from Aroerᶠ by the Arnon Gorge through Gilead to Bashan.

³⁴As for the other events of Jehu's reign, all he did, and all his achievements, are they not written in the book of the annalsᵍ of the kings of Israel?

³⁵Jehu rested with his fathers and was buried in Samaria. And Jehoahaz his son succeeded him as king. ³⁶The time that Jehu reigned over Israel in Samaria was twenty-eight years.

Athaliah and Joash

11 When Athaliahʰ the mother of Ahaziah saw that her son was dead, she proceeded to destroy the whole royal family. ²But Jehosheba, the daughter of King Jehoramᵃ and sister of Ahaziah, took Joashⁱ son of Ahaziah and stole him away from among the royal princes, who were about to be murdered. She put him and his nurse in a bedroom to hide him from Athaliah; so he was not killed.ʲ ³He remained hidden with his nurse at the temple of the LORD for six years while Athaliah ruled the land.

⁴In the seventh year Jehoiada sent for the commanders of units of a hundred, the Caritesᵏ and the guards and had them brought to him at the temple of the LORD. He made a covenant with them and put them under oath at the temple of the LORD. Then he showed them the king's son. ⁵He commanded them, saying, "This is what you are to do: You who are in the three companies that are going on duty on the Sabbathˡ—a third of you guarding the royal palace,ᵐ ⁶a third at the Sur Gate, and a third at the gate behind the guard, who take turns guarding the temple— ⁷and you who are in the other two companies that normally go off Sabbath duty are all to guard the temple for the king. ⁸Station yourselves around the king, each man with his weapon in his hand. Anyone who approaches your ranksᵇ must be put to death. Stay close to the king wherever he goes."

⁹The commanders of units of a hundred did just as Jehoiada the priest ordered. Each one took his men—those who were going on duty on the Sabbath and those who were going off duty—and came to Jehoiada the priest. ¹⁰Then he gave the

ᵃ 2 Hebrew *Joram*, a variant of *Jehoram*   ᵇ 8 Or *approaches the precincts*

2 Kings 11:1–21

On the news of the death of her son, Ahaziah, Athaliah took whatever measures were necessary to seize the throne for herself, including the murder of all who remained of the royal family—even her own grandchildren. This attempt to completely destroy the house of David was an attack on God's redemptive plan—a plan that centered in the Messiah, which the Davidic covenant promised. But one grandson was rescued by Jehosheba, Joash's aunt and wife of the high priest, Jehoiada (2 Chron. 22:11).

Jehoiada is the key player of the rest of the chapter. He organized the rebellion, presided over the coronation ceremonies, and ordered the death of the usurping queen and the abolition of her idolatrous cult. The priesthood, army, and populace were united in the

covenant renewal of a Davidic dynasty under God.

Like Joash, whose ascension to the throne restored the Davidic line, the church today functions as the lamp of David (see "There and Then" for 8:16–24). But our times aren't equivalent. Jehoiada took drastic and violent measures to preserve David's lamp and God's covenant against Athaliah's threats. Jesus promised that the gates of hell wouldn't overcome the church (Matt. 16:18); but political and armed conflict aren't the means by which the church will be preserved (see "Here and Now" for 10:1–17).

In contrast, the blood of the martyrs has been the church's seed and strength from its beginnings (2 Tim. 4:6–8; Rev. 2:13; 7:9–14). "Christ suffered for you, leaving you an example, that you should follow in his steps" (1 Peter 2:21). How does his example inspire you?

Corrie ten Boom

Corrie ten Boom (1892–1983) lived in the Netherlands during World War II. An unmarried woman in need of a vocation, she inherited from her father his watchmaking trade. More importantly, she inherited his political activism, particularly his concern for the plight of Europe's Jewish population. Corrie was, in the most basic sense, a Christian in need of a calling—a calling she found in hiding Jews attempting to escape Nazi-inspired pogroms. For this purpose she and her family used a secret room in their home in Haarlem. Thousands of fleeing Jews received, due to the efforts of this courageous family, the gift of temporary refuge on their way to freedom.

Eventually a fellow Dutchman betrayed the operation. Corrie, her sister, and their father were sent to prison, where Mr. ten Boom died. Corrie and her sister were transferred to a concentration camp in Germany, where they endured nearly intolerable conditions. Corrie alone survived.

Corrie ten Boom was a remarkable and noteworthy woman, but she wasn't unique in serving God. We all, like Corrie, are Christians in need of a calling—and we are in various stages of finding it. Familiarizing ourselves with her story can point up a number of key lessons about serving God, among them:

> We all, like Corrie, are Christians in need of a calling—and we are in various stages of finding it.

(1) An organist once came to the ten Booms' church to perform a Bach concert to raise money for a hospital, associated with the work of Albert Schweitzer, in the African jungle. It was a memorable evening, and the family raved about the music. But Betsie, Corrie's sister, protested, "Albert Schweitzer is trying to earn his salvation by doing good works." It was Corrie's turn to object, and she did so with an acute observation she exemplified in attitude all her life: "No. *Being in Christ makes you want to do good works. You can't help yourself.*"

(2) The needless German bombing of Rotterdam, a Dutch city, suggested another lesson about Christian living. The Germans bragged that they didn't need to bomb Rotterdam to occupy it; they did so to erode the resolve of any future Dutch resistance. Corrie took the opposite tack, insisting that *undeserved, excessive loving of the unfortunate instills in them passionate, dedicated love for the One who motivates such action—Jesus Christ.*

(3) When Corrie was finally released from the concentration camp, her first order of business was to help her Dutch compatriots recover and move beyond their war experiences. That meant forgiveness for their oppressors. The Dutchman who had betrayed her family was still alive; with sinking heart Corrie resolved to write him a letter. Realizing that *a righteous act, no matter how reluctantly performed, can capture and change the recipient's heart,* she did so, stating that she forgave him and was sure God would too, based on his repentance. That night Corrie slept for the first time since his betrayal without feeling haunted by bitterness and resentment.

Like the ten Booms, Jehosheba and Jehoiada risked all to shelter a hapless victim of political machinations. Take a moment to compare the gruesome scene at the time of Joash's rescue with the serenity of the ensuing six plus years. Jehosheba and Jehoiada fostered this impressionable future king through infancy, toddlerhood, and early boyhood, immersing him in love and in the things of the Lord, salving his spirit to counteract the effect of losses buried deeply in his subconscious mind from his pre-verbal days.

Corrie ten Boom and Jehosheba stand with thousands of other believing heroines throughout the centuries and millennia in their own unique faith and faithfulness hall of fame.

commanders the spears and shields[n] that had belonged to King David and that were in the temple of the LORD. [11]The guards, each with his weapon in his hand, stationed themselves around the king—near the altar and the temple, from the south side to the north side of the temple.

[12]Jehoiada brought out the king's son and put the crown on him; he presented him with a copy of the covenant[o] and proclaimed him king. They anointed[p] him, and the people clapped their hands[q] and shouted, "Long live the king!"[r]

[13]When Athaliah heard the noise made by the guards and the people, she went to the people at the temple of the LORD. [14]She looked and there was the king, standing by the pillar,[s] as the custom was. The officers and the trumpeters were beside the king, and all the people of the land were rejoicing and blowing trumpets.[t] Then Athaliah tore[u] her robes and called out, "Treason! Treason!"[v]

[15]Jehoiada the priest ordered the commanders of units of a hundred, who were in charge of the troops: "Bring her out between the ranks[a] and put to the sword anyone who follows her." For the priest had said, "She must not be put to death in the temple[w] of the LORD." [16]So they seized her as she reached the place where the horses enter[x] the palace grounds, and there she was put to death.[y]

[17]Jehoiada then made a covenant[z] between the LORD and the king and people that they would be the LORD's people. He also made a covenant between the king and the people. [a] [18]All the people of the land went to the temple[b] of Baal and tore it down. They smashed[c] the altars and idols to pieces and killed Mattan the priest[d] of Baal in front of the altars.

Then Jehoiada the priest posted guards at the temple of the LORD. [19]He took with him the commanders of hundreds, the Carites,[e] the guards and all the people of the land, and together they brought the king down from the temple of the LORD and went into the palace, entering by way of the gate of the guards. The king then took his place on the royal throne, [20]and all the people of the land rejoiced.[f] And the city was quiet, because Athaliah had been slain with the sword at the palace.

[21]Joash[b] was seven years old when he began to reign.

Joash Repairs the Temple

12 In the seventh year of Jehu, Joash[cg] became king, and he reigned in Jerusalem forty years. His mother's name was Zibiah; she was from Beersheba. [2]Joash did what was right in the eyes of the LORD all the years Jehoiada the priest instructed him. [3]The high places,[h] however, were not removed; the people continued to offer sacrifices and burn incense there.

[4]Joash said to the priests, "Collect[i] all the money that is brought as sacred offerings[j] to the temple of the LORD—the money collected in the census,[k] the money received from personal vows and the money brought voluntarily[l] to the temple. [5]Let every priest receive the money from one of the treasurers, and let it be used to repair whatever damage is found in the temple."

[6]But by the twenty-third year of King Joash the priests still had not repaired the

11:10
[n] 2Sa 8:7; 1Ch 18:7

11:12
[o] Ex 25:16; 2Ki 23:3 [p] 1Sa 9:16; 1Ki 1:39 [q] Ps 47:1; 98:8; Isa 55:12 [r] 1Sa 10:24

11:14
[s] 1Ki 7:15; 2Ki 23:3; 2Ch 34:31 [t] 1Ki 1:39 [u] Ge 37:29 [v] 2Ki 9:23

11:15
[w] 1Ki 2:30
11:16
[x] Ne 3:28; Jer 31:40 [y] Ge 4:14
11:17
[z] Ex 24:8; 2Sa 5:3; 2Ch 15:12; 23:3; 29:10; 34:31; Ezr 10:3 [a] 2Ki 23:3; Jer 34:8
11:18
[b] 1Ki 16:32
[d] 1Ki 18:40; 2Ki 10:25; 23:20
11:19
[e] ver 4

11:20
[f] Pr 11:10; 28:12; 29:2

12:1
[g] 2Ki 11:2

12:3
[h] 1Ki 3:3; 2Ki 14:4; 15:35; 18:4

12:4
[i] 2Ki 22:4 [j] Ex 35:5 [k] Ex 30:12 [l] Ex 35:29; 1Ch 29:3-9

---

[a] 15 Or *out from the precincts*   [b] 21 Hebrew *Jehoash*, a variant of *Joash*   [c] 1 Hebrew *Jehoash*, a variant of *Joash*; also in verses 2, 4, 6, 7 and 18

---

2 Kings 12:1–21

The dramatic previous chapter ended with the igniting of the fire of spiritual reform. That fire continued to burn brightly with Joash's restoration of the temple. But the young king's dependence on others, the godly priest Jehoiada in particular, hinted at trouble to come (see v. 2).

We know from 2 Chronicles 24:17–27 that one sad day this promising child's fiery zeal for God would sputter before the chilling winds of apostasy. After Jehoiada's death, Joash would forsake the Lord and turn to idolatry—and even murder Jehoiada's son for confronting him about doing so. The account in 2 Chronicles

makes it clear that the Arameans' military success against Judah and Joash's assassination (2 Kings 12:17–21) were God's judgments on Joash for his later unfaithfulness.

Joash, under Jehoiada's influence, was a shining light. But programmed religion is perilous. Genuine faith must be personal. If you are a parent and/or a teacher or mentor of youth, are you concerned about their continuing Christian commitment once they move beyond your influence? How can you optimize and maximize that influence during their impressionable days? What steps can you take to help them internalize their faith?

temple. ⁷Therefore King Joash summoned Jehoiada the priest and the other priests and asked them, "Why aren't you repairing the damage done to the temple? Take no more money from your treasurers, but hand it over for repairing the temple." ⁸The priests agreed that they would not collect any more money from the people and that they would not repair the temple themselves.

⁹Jehoiada the priest took a chest and bored a hole in its lid. He placed it beside the altar, on the right side as one enters the temple of the LORD. The priests who guarded the entrance ᵐ put into the chest all the money ⁿ that was brought to the temple of the LORD. ¹⁰Whenever they saw that there was a large amount of money in the chest, the royal secretary ᵒ and the high priest came, counted the money that had been brought into the temple of the LORD and put it into bags. ¹¹When the amount had been determined, they gave the money to the men appointed to supervise the work on the temple. With it they paid those who worked on the temple of the LORD—the carpenters and builders, ¹²the masons and stonecutters. ᵖ They purchased timber and dressed stone for the repair of the temple of the LORD, and met all the other expenses of restoring the temple.

¹³The money brought into the temple was not spent for making silver basins, wick trimmers, sprinkling bowls, trumpets or any other articles of gold ᵠ or silver for the temple of the LORD; ¹⁴it was paid to the workmen, who used it to repair the temple. ¹⁵They did not require an accounting from those to whom they gave the money to pay the workers, because they acted with complete honesty. ʳ ¹⁶The money from the guilt offerings ˢ and sin offerings ᵗ was not brought into the temple of the LORD; it belonged ᵘ to the priests.

¹⁷About this time Hazael ᵛ king of Aram went up and attacked Gath and captured it. Then he turned to attack Jerusalem. ¹⁸But Joash king of Judah took all the sacred objects dedicated by his fathers—Jehoshaphat, Jehoram and Ahaziah, the kings of Judah—and the gifts he himself had dedicated and all the gold found in the treasuries of the temple of the LORD and of the royal palace, and he sent ʷ them to Hazael king of Aram, who then withdrew ˣ from Jerusalem.

¹⁹As for the other events of the reign of Joash, and all he did, are they not written in the book of the annals of the kings of Judah? ²⁰His officials ʸ conspired against him and assassinated ᶻ him at Beth Millo, ᵃ on the road down to Silla. ²¹The officials who murdered him were Jozabad son of Shimeath and Jehozabad son of Shomer. He died and was buried with his fathers in the City of David. And Amaziah his son succeeded him as king.

Jehoahaz King of Israel

13 In the twenty-third year of Joash son of Ahaziah king of Judah, Jehoahaz son of Jehu became king of Israel in Samaria, and he reigned seventeen years. ²He did evil ᵇ in the eyes of the LORD by following the sins of Jeroboam son of Nebat, which he had caused Israel to commit, and he did not turn away from them. ³So the LORD's anger ᶜ burned against Israel, and for a long time he kept them under the power ᵈ of Hazael king of Aram and Ben-Hadad ᵉ his son.

⁴Then Jehoahaz sought ᶠ the LORD's favor, and the LORD listened to him, for he saw ᵍ how severely the king of Aram was oppressing ʰ Israel. ⁵The LORD provided a deliverer ⁱ for Israel, and they escaped from the power of Aram. So the Israelites lived in their own homes as they had before. ⁶But they did not turn away from the sins ʲ

Cross references (margin)

12:9
ᵐ Jer 35:4
ⁿ 2Ch 24:8;
Mk 12:41; Lk 21:1
12:10
ᵒ 2Sa 8:17

12:12
ᵖ 2Ki 22:5-6

12:13
ᵠ 1Ki 7:48-51;
2Ch 24:14

12:15
ʳ 2Ki 22:7; 1Co 4:2
12:16
ˢ Lev 5:14-19;
Nu 18:9
ᵗ Lev 4:1-35
ᵘ Lev 7:7
12:17
ᵛ 2Ki 8:12

12:18
ʷ 1Ki 15:18;
2Ch 21:16-17
ˣ 1Ki 15:21

12:20
ʸ 2Ki 14:5
ᶻ 2Ch 24:25
ᵃ Jdg 9:6

13:2
ᵇ 1Ki 12:26-33
13:3
ᶜ Dt 31:17;
Jdg 2:14 ᵈ 1Ki 8:12;
12:17; 19:17
ᵉ ver 24
13:4
ᶠ Dt 4:29; Ps 78:34
ᵍ Ex 3:7; Dt 26:7
ʰ 2Ki 14:26
13:5
ⁱ ver 25;
2Ki 14:25,27
13:6
ʲ 1Ki 12:30

---

2 Kings 13:1–9

📖 Jeroboam's sins are mentioned twice in this account of Jehoahaz (vv. 2,6). Jeroboam had set up golden calves at Bethel and Dan for the people to worship (1 Kings 12:26–30; see also "Here and Now" for 2 Kings 10:18–36 regarding similar motives on the part of Jehoahaz's father, Jehu). The phrase "the sins of Jeroboam," or "the ways of Jeroboam," became a catchall to refer to the sins of Israel in general—appearing 17 times in 1 and 2 Kings.

📖 Jeroboam was honored by God to be selected as king of ten tribes of Israel, and he was given the opportunity to found an enduring dynasty, like David's (1 Kings 11:29–38). Yet well over a century later King Jehoahaz was labeled as perpetuating "the sins of Jeroboam." It's pretty sobering to think that our spiritual faithfulness or unfaithfulness can follow us well past our lifetime. And even if our integrity isn't memorialized by people, we can be sure it will be in the eyes of our Maker and Judge (cf. 2 Cor. 8:21; 1 Peter 3:12).

of the house of Jeroboam, which he had caused Israel to commit; they continued in them. Also, the Asherah pole[a][k] remained standing in Samaria.

[7] Nothing had been left[l] of the army of Jehoahaz except fifty horsemen, ten chariots and ten thousand foot soldiers, for the king of Aram had destroyed the rest and made them like the dust[m] at threshing time.

[8] As for the other events of the reign of Jehoahaz, all he did and his achievements, are they not written in the book of the annals of the kings of Israel? [9] Jehoahaz rested with his fathers and was buried in Samaria. And Jehoash[b] his son succeeded him as king.

Jehoash King of Israel

[10] In the thirty-seventh year of Joash king of Judah, Jehoash son of Jehoahaz became king of Israel in Samaria, and he reigned sixteen years. [11] He did evil in the eyes of the LORD and did not turn away from any of the sins of Jeroboam son of Nebat, which he had caused Israel to commit; he continued in them.

[12] As for the other events of the reign of Jehoash, all he did and his achievements, including his war against Amaziah[n] king of Judah, are they not written in the book of the annals[o] of the kings of Israel? [13] Jehoash rested with his fathers, and Jeroboam[p] succeeded him on the throne. Jehoash was buried in Samaria with the kings of Israel.

[14] Now Elisha was suffering from the illness from which he died. Jehoash king of Israel went down to see him and wept over him. "My father! My father!" he cried. "The chariots[q] and horsemen of Israel!"

[15] Elisha said, "Get a bow and some arrows,"[r] and he did so. [16] "Take the bow in your hands," he said to the king of Israel. When he had taken it, Elisha put his hands on the king's hands.

[17] "Open the east window," he said, and he opened it. "Shoot!"[s] Elisha said, and he shot. "The LORD's arrow of victory, the arrow of victory over Aram!" Elisha declared. "You will completely destroy the Arameans at Aphek."[t]

[18] Then he said, "Take the arrows," and the king took them. Elisha told him, "Strike the ground." He struck it three times and stopped. [19] The man of God was angry with him and said, "You should have struck the ground five or six times; then you would have defeated Aram and completely destroyed it. But now you will defeat it only three times."[u]

[20] Elisha died and was buried.

Now Moabite raiders[v] used to enter the country every spring. [21] Once while some Israelites were burying a man, suddenly they saw a band of raiders; so they threw the man's body into Elisha's tomb. When the body touched Elisha's bones, the man came to life[w] and stood up on his feet.

[22] Hazael king of Aram oppressed[x] Israel throughout the reign of Jehoahaz. [23] But the LORD was gracious to them and had compassion and showed concern for them

13:6
[k] 1Ki 16:33
13:7
[l] 2Ki 10:32-33
[m] 2Sa 22:43

13:12
[n] 2Ki 14:15
[o] 1Ki 15:31
13:13
[p] 2Ki 14:23;
Hos 1:1

13:14
[q] 2Ki 2:12
13:15
[r] 1Sa 20:20

13:17
[s] Jos 8:18
[t] 1Ki 20:26

13:19
[u] ver 25

13:20
[v] 2Ki 3:7; 24:2

13:21
[w] Mt 27:52
13:22
[x] 1Ki 19:17;
2Ki 8:12

---

[a] 6 That is, a symbol of the goddess Asherah; here and elsewhere in 2 Kings   [b] 9 Hebrew *Joash*, a variant of *Jehoash*; also in verses 12-14 and 25

---

2 Kings 13:10–25

Jehoash addressed Elisha with words identical to the prophet's own testimony at the end of Elijah's life (v. 14; cf. 2:12). Jehoash was full of respect, but less than full of faith. Yet because he had at least come to Elisha and addressed him courteously, God used the occasion to attempt to increase the king's slim faith.

Ironically, the final miracle associated with Elisha's life occurred after his death (vv. 20–21). The combination of this event and the preceding prophetic symbolism of the arrows makes clear that the dead man's revival was another divine sign for Jehoash and Israel: God was the God of the living, not the dead (cf. Luke 20:38).

Israel could yet "live" if she would only accept the eternally living God as her own.

Jehoram missed an opportunity to thoroughly rout Israel's enemy (vv. 18–19). Often we too are ill-prepared for coming spiritual battles. It's not a question of God's ability but of our own lack of time spent in prayer and in the Word. Inattention to these daily disciplines weakens us. The weakness may not appear at first (we may win a few skirmishes), but in a particularly long or grueling fight we will become overwhelmed and perhaps fail. Where are you being challenged to grow in your Christian walk today? It may be God's way of preparing you for a coming battle, so use this opportunity wisely.

13:23
y Ge 13:16-17;
Ex 2:24 z Dt 29:20
a Ex 33:15;
2Ki 14:27; 17:18;
24:3,20
13:24
b ver 3
13:25
c ver 18,19
d 2Ki 10:32

because of his covenant[y] with Abraham, Isaac and Jacob. To this day he has been unwilling to destroy[z] them or banish them from his presence.[a]

24Hazael king of Aram died, and Ben-Hadad[b] his son succeeded him as king. 25Then Jehoash son of Jehoahaz recaptured from Ben-Hadad son of Hazael the towns he had taken in battle from his father Jehoahaz. Three times[c] Jehoash defeated him, and so he recovered[d] the Israelite towns.

Amaziah King of Judah

14 In the second year of Jehoash[a] son of Jehoahaz king of Israel, Amaziah son of Joash king of Judah began to reign. 2He was twenty-five years old when he became king, and he reigned in Jerusalem twenty-nine years. His mother's name was Jehoaddin; she was from Jerusalem. 3He did what was right in the eyes of the LORD, but not as his father David had done. In everything he followed the example of his father Joash. 4The high places,[e] however, were not removed; the people continued to offer sacrifices and burn incense there.

14:4
e 2Ki 12:3; 16:4

14:5
f 2Ki 21:24
g 2Ki 12:20
14:6
h Dt 28:61
i Nu 26:11;
Job 21:20;
Jer 31:30; 44:3;
Eze 18:4,20
14:7
j 2Sa 8:13;
2Ch 25:11
k Jdg 1:36

5After the kingdom was firmly in his grasp, he executed[f] the officials[g] who had murdered his father the king. 6Yet he did not put the sons of the assassins to death, in accordance with what is written in the Book of the Law[h] of Moses where the LORD commanded: "Fathers shall not be put to death for their children, nor children put to death for their fathers; each is to die for his own sins."[b][i]

7He was the one who defeated ten thousand Edomites in the Valley of Salt[j] and captured Sela[k] in battle, calling it Joktheel, the name it has to this day.

8Then Amaziah sent messengers to Jehoash son of Jehoahaz, the son of Jehu, king of Israel, with the challenge: "Come, meet me face to face."

14:9
l Jdg 9:8-15

9But Jehoash king of Israel replied to Amaziah king of Judah: "A thistle[l] in Lebanon sent a message to a cedar in Lebanon, 'Give your daughter to my son in marriage.' Then a wild beast in Lebanon came along and trampled the thistle underfoot.

14:10
m Dt 8:14;
2Ch 26:16; 32:25

10You have indeed defeated Edom and now you are arrogant.[m] Glory in your victory, but stay at home! Why ask for trouble and cause your own downfall and that of Judah also?"

14:11
n Jos 15:10
14:12
o 2Sa 18:17

11Amaziah, however, would not listen, so Jehoash king of Israel attacked. He and Amaziah king of Judah faced each other at Beth Shemesh[n] in Judah. 12Judah was routed by Israel, and every man fled to his home.[o] 13Jehoash king of Israel captured Amaziah king of Judah, the son of Joash, the son of Ahaziah, at Beth Shemesh. Then Jehoash went to Jerusalem and broke down the wall[p] of Jerusalem from the Ephraim Gate[q] to the Corner Gate[r]—a section about six hundred feet long.[c] 14He took all the gold and silver and all the articles found in the temple of the LORD and in the treasuries of the royal palace. He also took hostages and returned to Samaria.

14:13
p 1Ki 3:1;
2Ch 33:14; 36:19;
Jer 39:2 q Ne 8:16;
12:39 r 2Ch 25:23;
Jer 31:38;
Zec 14:10

14:15
s 2Ki 13:12

15As for the other events of the reign of Jehoash, what he did and his achievements, including his war[s] against Amaziah king of Judah, are they not written in the book of the annals of the kings of Israel? 16Jehoash rested with his fathers and

---

a 1 Hebrew *Joash*, a variant of *Jehoash*; also in verses 13, 23 and 27   b 6 Deut. 24:16
c 13 Hebrew *four hundred cubits* (about 180 meters)

---

2 Kings 14:1–22

The assessment of Amaziah was clearly mixed. On the one hand, it could be said that "he did what was right in the eyes of the LORD" (v. 3). One example was his response to his father's assassins: In adherence to the Law of Moses, he executed them without extending the payback, as so often happened, to their sons. The parallel account in Chronicles notes that Amaziah was successful against Edom because he obeyed God's prophetic word to go to battle without the help of mercenaries from Israel (2 Chron. 25:5–12).

On the other hand, Amaziah followed in the footsteps of his father, Joash, who succumbed to idolatry (see "There and Then" for 12:1–21), rather than in those

his ancestor David (v. 3). The "high places," though not necessarily used to worship foreign gods rather than the Lord, continued to be tolerated (v. 4). The Chronicler added that Judah was defeated by Israel because Amaziah (amazingly!) defeated the Edomites only to confiscate and worship their gods (2 Chron. 25:14–24). The conspiracy to kill Amaziah was a punishment for his turning away from the Lord (25:27).

How many people, professed Christians or otherwise, do you know who are banking on squeezing into eternity on the strength of phrases like "good enough"? How might you tactfully explain to them the fallacy of their thinking? Have you assessed your own heart for traces of this destructive philosophy?

was buried in Samaria with the kings of Israel. And Jeroboam his son succeeded him as king.

¹⁷Amaziah son of Joash king of Judah lived for fifteen years after the death of Jehoash son of Jehoahaz king of Israel. ¹⁸As for the other events of Amaziah's reign, are they not written in the book of the annals of the kings of Judah?

¹⁹They conspired ᵗ against him in Jerusalem, and he fled to Lachish, ᵘ but they sent men after him to Lachish and killed him there. ²⁰He was brought back by horse ᵛ and was buried in Jerusalem with his fathers, in the City of David.

²¹Then all the people of Judah took Azariah, ᵃʷ who was sixteen years old, and made him king in place of his father Amaziah. ²²He was the one who rebuilt Elath ˣ and restored it to Judah after Amaziah rested with his fathers.

Jeroboam II King of Israel

²³In the fifteenth year of Amaziah son of Joash king of Judah, Jeroboam ʸ son of Jehoash king of Israel became king in Samaria, and he reigned forty-one years. ²⁴He did evil in the eyes of the LORD and did not turn away from any of the sins of Jeroboam son of Nebat, which he had caused Israel to commit. ᶻ ²⁵He was the one who restored the boundaries of Israel from Lebo ᵇ Hamath ᵃ to the Sea of the Arabah, ᶜᵇ in accordance with the word of the LORD, the God of Israel, spoken through his servant Jonah ᶜ son of Amittai, the prophet from Gath Hepher.

²⁶The LORD had seen how bitterly everyone in Israel, whether slave or free, ᵈ was suffering; ᵉ there was no one to help them. ᶠ ²⁷And since the LORD had not said he would blot out ᵍ the name of Israel from under heaven, he saved ʰ them by the hand of Jeroboam son of Jehoash.

²⁸As for the other events of Jeroboam's reign, all he did, and his military achievements, including how he recovered for Israel both Damascus ⁱ and Hamath, ʲ which had belonged to Yaudi, ᵈ are they not written in the book of the annals ᵏ of the kings of Israel? ²⁹Jeroboam rested with his fathers, the kings of Israel. And Zechariah his son succeeded him as king.

Azariah King of Judah

15 In the twenty-seventh year of Jeroboam king of Israel, Azariah ˡ son of Amaziah king of Judah began to reign. ²He was sixteen years old when he became king, and he reigned in Jerusalem fifty-two years. His mother's name was Jecoliah; she was from Jerusalem. ³He did what was right in the eyes of the LORD, just as his father Amaziah had done. ⁴The high places, however, were not removed; the people continued to offer sacrifices and burn incense there.

ᵃ 21 Also called *Uzziah*   ᵇ 25 Or *from the entrance to*   ᶜ 25 That is, the Dead Sea   ᵈ 28 Or *Judah*

Cross references (margin)

14:19
ᵗ 2Ki 12:20
ᵘ Jos 10:3;
2Ki 18:14,17
14:20
ᵛ 2Ki 9:28
14:21
ʷ 2Ki 15:1;
2Ch 26:23
14:22
ˣ 1Ki 9:26; 2Ki 16:6

14:23
ʸ 2Ki 13:13

14:24
ᶻ 1Ki 15:30
14:25
ᵃ Nu 13:21;
1Ki 8:65 ᵇ Dt 3:17
ᶜ Jnh 1:1; Mt 12:39

14:26
ᵈ Dt 32:36
ᵉ 2Ki 13:4
ᶠ Ps 18:41; 22:11;
72:12; 107:12;
Isa 63:5; La 1:7
14:27
ᵍ 2Ki 13:23
ʰ Jdg 6:14
14:28
ⁱ 2Sa 8:5; 1Ki 11:24
ʲ 2Ch 8:3
ᵏ 1Ki 15:31

15:1
ˡ ver 32; 2Ki 14:21

---

2 Kings 14:23–29

The era of Jeroboam II marked a significant change in the fortunes of the northern kingdom. Not since the days of David and Solomon had Israel enjoyed such material and territorial prosperity. But God's blessings are easily taken for granted, and so it would prove in Israel. Jeroboam II continued in the sins of Jeroboam I (v. 24; see also "There and Then" for 13:1–9). As we know from the preaching of Hosea and Amos, who ministered during this time, the lives of God's people degenerated into empty formalism, pagan idolatry, and social injustice.

When Jeroboam II died in 753 B.C., he left behind an outwardly strong kingdom. But its core foundation was so spiritually rotten that the edifice of state wouldn't long withstand the rising tides of international intrigue and pressure. Does this scenario sound frighteningly familiar to you as a concerned Christian living in the early years of the 21ˢᵗ century? If so, how can you join with other Christians to shore up society's compromised foundation?

2 Kings 15:1–7

Azariah was also known as Uzziah (v. 13), likely the name he took when he became king. As with his father, Amaziah, Scripture's assessment of Azariah is mixed (see "There and Then" for 14:1–22). Although Azariah ruled for 52 years (many of those jointly with his father) and was credited with many accomplishments, the author of Kings devoted only seven verses to his legacy.

The much longer account in 2 Chronicles 26 describes Azariah's military, economic, and building project successes—crediting them to the fact that "he sought the LORD" (2 Chron. 26:5). But the Chronicler also filled in the details on why "the LORD afflicted the king with leprosy" (2 Kings 15:5). After Azariah (Uzziah) became famous and powerful, his pride led to his fall: He presumed upon the office of priest and arrogantly strode into the temple to burn incense (2 Chron. 26:16–20).

15:5
m Ge 12:17
n Lev 13:46
o 2Ch 27:1
p Ge 41:40

15:7
q Isa 6:1; 14:28
r ver 5

15:9
s 1Ki 15:26

15:10
t 2Ki 12:20
15:11
u 1Ki 15:31
15:12
v 2Ki 10:30

15:13
w ver 1,8
15:14
x 1Ki 14:17
y 2Ki 12:20

15:15
z 1Ki 15:31
15:16
a 1Ki 4:24
b 2Ki 8:12;
Hos 13:16

5The LORD afflicted[m] the king with leprosy[a] until the day he died, and he lived in a separate house.[b][n] Jotham[o] the king's son had charge of the palace[p] and governed the people of the land.

6As for the other events of Azariah's reign, and all he did, are they not written in the book of the annals of the kings of Judah? 7Azariah rested[q] with his fathers and was buried near them in the City of David. And Jotham[r] his son succeeded him as king.

Zechariah King of Israel

8In the thirty-eighth year of Azariah king of Judah, Zechariah son of Jeroboam became king of Israel in Samaria, and he reigned six months. 9He did evil[s] in the eyes of the LORD, as his fathers had done. He did not turn away from the sins of Jeroboam son of Nebat, which he had caused Israel to commit.

10Shallum son of Jabesh conspired against Zechariah. He attacked him in front of the people,[c] assassinated[t] him and succeeded him as king. 11The other events of Zechariah's reign are written in the book of the annals[u] of the kings of Israel. 12So the word of the LORD spoken to Jehu was fulfilled:[v] "Your descendants will sit on the throne of Israel to the fourth generation."[d]

Shallum King of Israel

13Shallum son of Jabesh became king in the thirty-ninth year of Uzziah king of Judah, and he reigned in Samaria[w] one month. 14Then Menahem son of Gadi went from Tirzah[x] up to Samaria. He attacked Shallum son of Jabesh in Samaria, assassinated[y] him and succeeded him as king.

15The other events of Shallum's reign, and the conspiracy he led, are written in the book of the annals[z] of the kings of Israel.

16At that time Menahem, starting out from Tirzah, attacked Tiphsah[a] and everyone in the city and its vicinity, because they refused to open[b] their gates. He sacked Tiphsah and ripped open all the pregnant women.

Menahem King of Israel

17In the thirty-ninth year of Azariah king of Judah, Menahem son of Gadi became king of Israel, and he reigned in Samaria ten years. 18He did evil in the eyes of the LORD. During his entire reign he did not turn away from the sins of Jeroboam son of Nebat, which he had caused Israel to commit.

a 5 The Hebrew word was used for various diseases affecting the skin—not necessarily leprosy.
b 5 Or in a house where he was relieved of responsibility   c 10 Hebrew; some Septuagint manuscripts in Ibleam   d 12 2 Kings 10:30

A repeated pattern among the kings of Israel and Judah, going back to Saul, the first monarch, was a failure to finish well. Especially those like Azariah, who experienced a measure of political success, had a definite tendency to turn away from the Lord at the height of their achievements. What effect has success had on you? What steps are you taking—and intend to take in the future—in order to finish well on your life's journey as the Lord's disciple?

2 Kings 15:8–12

Little is recorded of Zechariah, the fourth descendant of Jehu to assume Israel's throne, except the familiar evaluation that he did evil in perpetuating the idolatrous sins of Jeroboam I and that he was assassinated. With Zechariah's death, God's prophetic promise to Jehu (10:30) stood fulfilled (cf. Amos 7:9). The shortness of the reigns of both Zechariah and Shallum underscores the decline of the northern kingdom—especially in contrast to its strength and wealth under Jeroboam II.

Why, you might ask, couldn't any of the northern kings get it together? Their depraved reigns remind us of a string of dominoes knocking each other down, one after another in predictable and inevitable succession. Your own observations, both political and personal, can no doubt attest at some level to sin's stranglehold, once it's been allowed to flourish unchecked. Pray for godly leadership in your nation and others around the world. And take the time to thank the Lord for such leadership where it is found in any place and at every level.

2 Kings 15:13–16

Menahem was likely a military commander stationed at Tirzah, the northern kingdom's former capital. After assassinating Shallum and seizing the throne, he launched a savage campaign against Tiphsah for its failure to accept him as Israel's new king. Menahem made this city, whose location is uncertain, a gruesome example of the fact that he would allow no resistance to his self-proclaimed authority.

[19]Then Pul[a][c] king of Assyria invaded the land, and Menahem gave him a thousand talents[b] of silver to gain his support and strengthen his own hold on the kingdom. [20]Menahem exacted this money from Israel. Every wealthy man had to contribute fifty shekels[c] of silver to be given to the king of Assyria. So the king of Assyria withdrew[d] and stayed in the land no longer.

[21]As for the other events of Menahem's reign, and all he did, are they not written in the book of the annals of the kings of Israel? [22]Menahem rested with his fathers. And Pekahiah his son succeeded him as king.

Pekahiah King of Israel

[23]In the fiftieth year of Azariah king of Judah, Pekahiah son of Menahem became king of Israel in Samaria, and he reigned two years. [24]Pekahiah did evil in the eyes of the LORD. He did not turn away from the sins of Jeroboam son of Nebat, which he had caused Israel to commit. [25]One of his chief officers, Pekah[e] son of Remaliah, conspired against him. Taking fifty men of Gilead with him, he assassinated[f] Pekahiah, along with Argob and Arieh, in the citadel of the royal palace at Samaria. So Pekah killed Pekahiah and succeeded him as king.

[26]The other events of Pekahiah's reign, and all he did, are written in the book of the annals of the kings of Israel.

Pekah King of Israel

[27]In the fifty-second year of Azariah king of Judah, Pekah[g] son of Remaliah[h] became king of Israel in Samaria, and he reigned twenty years. [28]He did evil in the eyes of the LORD. He did not turn away from the sins of Jeroboam son of Nebat, which he had caused Israel to commit.

[29]In the time of Pekah king of Israel, Tiglath-Pileser[i] king of Assyria came and

15:19
c 1Ch 5:6,26

15:20
d 2Ki 12:18

15:25
e 2Ch 28:6; Isa 7:1
f 2Ki 12:20

15:27
g 2Ch 28:6; Isa 7:1
h Isa 7:4

15:29
i 2Ki 16:7; 17:6;
1Ch 5:26;
2Ch 28:20;
Jer 50:17

[a] 19 Also called *Tiglath-Pileser*   [b] 19 That is, about 37 tons (about 34 metric tons)   [c] 20 That is, about 1 1/4 pounds (about 0.6 kilogram)

📖 Most of Tiphsah's residents probably had little interest in Menahem's power bid, but they were nonetheless personally affected by his brutal reprisals. How often don't reports of coups, uprisings, and religiously motivated acts of violence dominate the evening news? Depending on where you live, refugees and third-world immigrants may increasingly play a part in your experience. But what of victims left behind in politically troubled countries, languishing in refugee camps or existing in poverty and squalor? How can you make a difference for some of them?

2 Kings 15:17–22

📖 Menahem's decade of rule was characterized by unmitigated sin. In addition to further prostituting Israel's religious experience, he compromised her independence by becoming a vassal to Pul (Tiglath-Pileser III) of Assyria. Menahem's motive wasn't patriotic concern for Israel's survival but hope for an Assyrian alliance to solidify his own hold on the throne. His heavy taxation bought the crown for himself and temporary respite from Assyria. But resulting internal friction likely ignited fires of insurrection soon after Menahem's son, Pekahiah, succeeded him.

📖 Menahem's motivations seem obvious now. But political situations are often complicated, sometimes to the point that the real impetus behind a government's actions may come to light only years after the fact, if at all. Basic human nature may be applied to human governments, simply because they are comprised of people,

often with hidden, or at least personal, agendas. Even in Christian ministries, ambition can drive strategies and goal-setting. Paul noted in his day that some "preach[ed] Christ" from less than stellar motives (Phil. 1:15–18). What motivates your service to the Lord?

2 Kings 15:23–26

📖 This conspiracy and the troubled times that would follow make it clear that an anti-Assyrian party existed during Menahem's fiery rule. The report of a 20-year reign for Pekah (v. 27; see "There and Then" for 15:27–31) suggests that he may have vied for the throne some 12 years earlier and been thwarted by Menahem's swift action in the unsettled times surrounding Shallum's conspiracy (vv. 10–16). Rather than submitting to the encroaching Assyrians, Pekah favored an alliance with the Arameans as a defense against Assyria (cf. 16:5–9; Isa. 7:1).

📖 Do you notice a common thread in the summaries of the reigns of Israel's kings? How about the statement that the king "did evil in the eyes of the LORD. He did not turn away from the sins of Jeroboam son of Nebat, which he had caused Israel to commit" (v. 24; cf. 13:2,11; 14:24; 15:9,18,28)? As Christians we know only too well our sole responsibility for our own sins. Other Scripture passages attest to this again and again. So what might the author of Kings have been trying to say? It might help to ask yourself another question: What influence do your society's values have on you?

15:29
j 1Ki 15:20
k 2Ki 16:9; 17:24;
2Ch 16:4; Isa 9:1
l 2Ki 24:14-16;
1Ch 5:22;
Isa 14:6,17;
36:17; 45:13
15:30
m 2Ki 17:1
n 2Ki 12:20

took Ijon,[j] Abel Beth Maacah, Janoah, Kedesh and Hazor. He took Gilead and Galilee, including all the land of Naphtali,[k] and deported[l] the people to Assyria. [30]Then Hoshea[m] son of Elah conspired against Pekah son of Remaliah. He attacked and assassinated[n] him, and then succeeded him as king in the twentieth year of Jotham son of Uzziah.

[31]As for the other events of Pekah's reign, and all he did, are they not written in the book of the annals of the kings of Israel?

Jotham King of Judah

15:32
o 1Ch 5:17

[32]In the second year of Pekah son of Remaliah king of Israel, Jotham[o] son of Uzziah king of Judah began to reign. [33]He was twenty-five years old when he became

15:34
p ver 3; 1Ki 14:8;
2Ch 26:4-5
15:35
q 2Ki 12:3
r 2Ch 23:20

king, and he reigned in Jerusalem sixteen years. His mother's name was Jerusha daughter of Zadok. [34]He did what was right[p] in the eyes of the LORD, just as his father Uzziah had done. [35]The high places,[q] however, were not removed; the people continued to offer sacrifices and burn incense there. Jotham rebuilt the Upper Gate[r] of the temple of the LORD.

[36]As for the other events of Jotham's reign, and what he did, are they not written

15:37
s 2Ki 16:5; Isa 7:1

in the book of the annals of the kings of Judah? [37](In those days the LORD began to send Rezin[s] king of Aram and Pekah son of Remaliah against Judah.) [38]Jotham rested with his fathers and was buried with them in the City of David, the city of his father. And Ahaz his son succeeded him as king.

16:1
t Isa 1:1; 14:28

Ahaz King of Judah

16:2
u 1Ki 14:8
16:3
v Lev 18:21;
2Ki 21:6
w Lev 18:3; Dt 9:4;
12:31

16 In the seventeenth year of Pekah son of Remaliah, Ahaz[t] son of Jotham king of Judah began to reign. [2]Ahaz was twenty years old when he became king, and he reigned in Jerusalem sixteen years. Unlike David his father, he did not do what was right[u] in the eyes of the LORD his God. [3]He walked in the ways of the kings of Israel and even sacrificed his son[v] in[a] the fire, following the detestable[w] ways of

a 3 Or *even made his son pass through*

---

2 Kings 15:27–31

Attributing to Pekah a 20-year reign (v. 27) is evidently based on the fact that Pekah established essentially a rival government in the region east of the Jordan at the same time Menahem seized power. The account here must include this period of rival rule (see "There and Then" for 15:23–26). The Assyrians dealt Israel heavy blows during Pekah's reign. Hoshea, likely leading a pro-Assyrian party, succeeded in defeating and displacing Pekah. Tiglath-Pileser III, in his annals, claimed to overthrow Pekah and make Hoshea king in his place.

The historical accounts in 2 Kings abound with coups, assassinations, and military intimidation and devastation—illustrations of the maxim that "might makes right." How do you see modern nations and political figures continuing this self-justifying principle? Coming closer to home, are you sure your church, and your own heart, are free of humankind's fallen tendency to grasp and abuse power? If not, what can you do about it?

2 Kings 15:32–38

The reign of Jotham was a continuation of that of his father, Uzziah (Azariah). He had already been coregent with Uzziah for at least a decade, and political and religious conditions remained largely as they had been in Uzziah's day. The country's prosperity continued as well (see 2 Chron. 27 and "There and Then" for

2 Kings 15:1–7). Regrettably, that prosperity was to lead, as it so often does, to spiritual neglect (cf. Isa. 1–5)—a condition that would make Judah ripe for open apostasy in Ahaz's day, as seen in 2 Kings 16.

The luxury and ease of the times of Uzziah and Jotham produced the spiritual laziness in Judah that allowed Ahaz's open sin to flourish. Little compromises and small slips over time can make a big difference—especially when impressionable kids are watching. If you are a parent, what degree of integrity are your children seeing in you? They may be young, but their perception, like their eyesight, is often 20-20. And if you are not a parent, you are not off the hook. People young and old are looking for good Christian role models. Is your walk with Christ one that others will want to follow?

2 Kings 16:1–20

Ahaz inherited a difficult political situation. Judah had been an independent and wealthy nation for more than two generations prior to his reign, and his highest priority was to maintain the standard of living and exercise of power established in the previous regime. The account of Ahaz's wicked reign as presented by the author of Kings centers around his character, his war with Rezin and Pekah, and the further apostasy resulting from his reliance on Tiglath-Pileser III. Supplemental details concerning his life and times are found in 2 Chronicles 28 and Isaiah 7–8.

the nations the LORD had driven out before the Israelites. [4]He offered sacrifices and burned incense at the high places, on the hilltops and under every spreading tree. [x]

[5]Then Rezin[y] king of Aram and Pekah son of Remaliah king of Israel marched up to fight against Jerusalem and besieged Ahaz, but they could not overpower him. [6]At that time, Rezin[z] king of Aram recovered Elath[a] for Aram by driving out the men of Judah. Edomites then moved into Elath and have lived there to this day.

[7]Ahaz sent messengers to say to Tiglath-Pileser[b] king of Assyria, "I am your servant and vassal. Come up and save[c] me out of the hand of the king of Aram and of the king of Israel, who are attacking me." [8]And Ahaz took the silver and gold found in the temple of the LORD and in the treasuries of the royal palace and sent it as a gift[d] to the king of Assyria. [9]The king of Assyria complied by attacking Damascus[e] and capturing it. He deported its inhabitants to Kir[f] and put Rezin to death.

[10]Then King Ahaz went to Damascus to meet Tiglath-Pileser king of Assyria. He saw an altar in Damascus and sent to Uriah[g] the priest a sketch of the altar, with detailed plans for its construction. [11]So Uriah the priest built an altar in accordance with all the plans that King Ahaz had sent from Damascus and finished it before King Ahaz returned. [12]When the king came back from Damascus and saw the altar, he approached it and presented offerings[a][h] on it. [13]He offered up his burnt offering[i] and grain offering, poured out his drink offering, and sprinkled the blood of his fellowship offerings[b][j] on the altar. [14]The bronze altar[k] that stood before the LORD he brought from the front of the temple—from between the new altar and the temple of the LORD—and put it on the north side of the new altar.

[15]King Ahaz then gave these orders to Uriah the priest: "On the large new altar, offer the morning[l] burnt offering and the evening grain offering, the king's burnt offering and his grain offering, and the burnt offering of all the people of the land, and their grain offering and their drink offering. Sprinkle on the altar all the blood of the burnt offerings and sacrifices. But I will use the bronze altar for seeking guidance." [m] [16]And Uriah the priest did just as King Ahaz had ordered.

[17]King Ahaz took away the side panels and removed the basins from the movable stands. He removed the Sea from the bronze bulls that supported it and set it on a stone base.[n] [18]He took away the Sabbath canopy[c] that had been built at the temple and removed the royal entryway outside the temple of the LORD, in deference to the king of Assyria.[o]

[19]As for the other events of the reign of Ahaz, and what he did, are they not written in the book of the annals of the kings of Judah? [20]Ahaz rested with his fathers and was buried with them in the City of David. And Hezekiah his son succeeded him as king.

Hoshea Last King of Israel

17 In the twelfth year of Ahaz king of Judah, Hoshea[p] son of Elah became king of Israel in Samaria, and he reigned nine years. [2]He did evil in the eyes of the LORD, but not like the kings of Israel who preceded him.

[a] 12 Or and went up   [b] 13 Traditionally *peace offerings*   [c] 18 Or *the dais of his throne* (see Septuagint)

16:4 [x] Dt 12:2; Eze 6:13
16:5 [y] 2Ki 15:37; Isa 7:1,4
16:6 [z] Isa 9:12 [a] 2Ki 14:22; 2Ch 26:2
16:7 [b] 2Ki 15:29 [c] Isa 2:6; Jer 2:18; Eze 16:28; Hos 10:6
16:8 [d] 2Ki 12:18
16:9 [e] 2Ki 15:29 [f] Isa 22:6; Am 1:5; 9:7
16:10 [g] Isa 8:2
16:12 [h] 2Ch 26:16
16:13 [i] Lev 6:8-13 [j] Lev 7:11-21
16:14 [k] 2Ch 4:1
16:15 [l] Ex 29:38-41 [m] 1Sa 9:9
16:17 [n] 1Ki 7:27
16:18 [o] Eze 16:28
17:1 [p] 2Ki 15:30

When have you been faced with a hard act to follow? Were you tempted to make compromises so as not to sacrifice accustomed standards—good or bad? Sometimes the most creative thinking takes place in a "nothing to lose" setting. When we can only go "up from here," we are much more likely to take risks. Ahaz's basic character dye was undoubtedly cast by many other factors, but the possibility exists that he might have done a better job had his father and grandfather been a little less "successful"—and laid back about the things of God.

2 Kings 17:1–6
When Tiglath-Pileser III of Assyria died in 727 B.C. and was succeeded by his son Shalmaneser V, the

time seemed ripe for Israel to renounce its vassal status. Egypt seemed like a promising ally. But Hoshea would soon learn (as would King Hezekiah of Judah) that Egypt was a "splintered reed of a staff" that would wound those who leaned on it (18:21). The Assyrian monarch marched quickly into Israel and imprisoned Hoshea. Subsequently he invaded and devastated the land, placing Samaria under siege. Ultimately the Israelite capital fell, in 722 B.C., and its surviving inhabitants were deported to Assyria and Media.

The author's softening of his usual criticism of the Israelite kings (v. 2; cf. "Here and Now" for 15:3–26) may have been an acknowledgement of Hoshea's limited

17:3 [q] 2Ki 18:9-12; Hos 10:14
17:5 [r] Hos 13:16
17:6 [s] Hos 13:16 [t] Dt 28:36,64; 2Ki 18:10-11 [u] 1Ch 5:26

3Shalmaneser[q] king of Assyria came up to attack Hoshea, who had been Shalmaneser's vassal and had paid him tribute. 4But the king of Assyria discovered that Hoshea was a traitor, for he had sent envoys to So[a] king of Egypt, and he no longer paid tribute to the king of Assyria, as he had done year by year. Therefore Shalmaneser seized him and put him in prison. 5The king of Assyria invaded the entire land, marched against Samaria and laid siege[r] to it for three years. 6In the ninth year of Hoshea, the king of Assyria captured Samaria[s] and deported[t] the Israelites to Assyria. He settled them in Halah, in Gozan[u] on the Habor River and in the towns of the Medes.

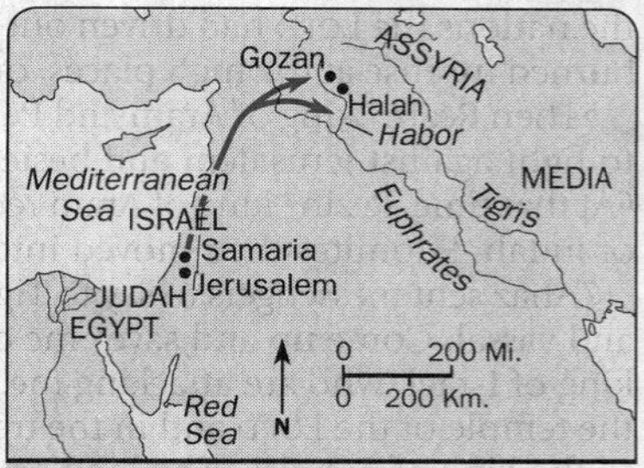

Exile of Israel (17:7)

Then: Between five and fifteen thousand Israelites were relocated to Assyria in the sixth century B.C.

Now: Exile is more than an event for modern Jews; it has become part of a rationale for living in Israel.

Israel Exiled Because of Sin

17:7 [v] Jos 23:16; Jdg 6:10 [w] Ex 14:15-31
17:8 [x] Lev 18:3; Dt 18:9; 2Ki 16:3
17:9 [y] 2Ki 18:8
17:10 [z] Ex 34:13; Mic 5:14 [a] 1Ki 14:23
17:12 [b] Ex 20:4
17:13 [c] 1Sa 9:9 [d] Jer 18:11; 25:5; 35:15
17:14 [e] Ex 32:9; Dt 31:27; Ac 7:51
17:15 [f] Dt 29:25 [g] Dt 32:21; Ro 1:21-23 [h] Dt 12:30-31
17:16 [i] 1Ki 12:28 [j] 1Ki 14:15,23

7All this took place because the Israelites had sinned[v] against the LORD their God, who had brought them up out of Egypt[w] from under the power of Pharaoh king of Egypt. They worshiped other gods 8and followed the practices of the nations[x] the LORD had driven out before them, as well as the practices that the kings of Israel had introduced. 9The Israelites secretly did things against the LORD their God that were not right. From watchtower to fortified city[y] they built themselves high places in all their towns. 10They set up sacred stones and Asherah poles[z] on every high hill and under every spreading tree.[a] 11At every high place they burned incense, as the nations whom the LORD had driven out before them had done. They did wicked things that provoked the LORD to anger. 12They worshiped idols,[b] though the LORD had said, "You shall not do this."[b] 13The LORD warned Israel and Judah through all his prophets and seers:[c] "Turn from your evil ways.[d] Observe my commands and decrees, in accordance with the entire Law that I commanded your fathers to obey and that I delivered to you through my servants the prophets."

14But they would not listen and were as stiff-necked[e] as their fathers, who did not trust in the LORD their God. 15They rejected his decrees and the covenant[f] he had made with their fathers and the warnings he had given them. They followed worthless idols[g] and themselves became worthless. They imitated the nations[h] around them although the LORD had ordered them, "Do not do as they do," and they did the things the LORD had forbidden them to do.

16They forsook all the commands of the LORD their God and made for themselves two idols cast in the shape of calves,[i] and an Asherah[j] pole. They bowed down to

[a] *4* Or *to Sais, to the; So* is possibly an abbreviation for *Osorkon.* [b] *12* Exodus 20:4,5

---

independence. Hoshea's first obligation was to Tiglath-Pileser, who had likely appointed him (see "There and Then" for 15:27–31). Having little time for religious matters, Hoshea's "virtue" (or lack of vice) was born of necessity. How sad a commentary on a human being! Have you ever relied on the rationale that you just didn't have time to do the good you wanted? Hoshea apparently lacked opportunity to do his worst!

2 Kings 17:7–23

A prophetic summary details the sins responsible for the successive falls of Israel and Judah. This sermon, recalling how God had given the land to Israel, condemned idolatrous worship (cf. Josh. 23; Judg. 2:11–23). Conforming to Canaanite ways caused Israel to be sold into the hands of its enemies and expelled from the land God had given. The two main sections (vv. 7–13 and 14–20) are well balanced, each beginning with a general statement of the people's sin followed by a detailed list of their misdeeds. The conclusion recapitulates the sins of Jeroboam that drove Israel into idolatry and then exile (vv. 21–23).

"They followed worthless idols and themselves became worthless" (v. 15). Short, definitely not "sweet"—but telling! What happens to your effectiveness for the cause of the kingdom when you compromise your Christian values? The indulgence may seem so small. *No one will even notice,* you might console yourself, if you even acknowledge the concession to yourself. No matter how you are doing in the matter of Christian integrity, pause to ask yourself one sobering question: How many small compromises does it take to become *worthless?*

all the starry hosts,[k] and they worshiped Baal.[l] [17]They sacrificed[m] their sons and daughters in[a] the fire. They practiced divination and sorcery[n] and sold[o] themselves to do evil in the eyes of the LORD, provoking him to anger.

[18]So the LORD was very angry with Israel and removed them from his presence. Only the tribe of Judah was left, [19]and even Judah did not keep the commands of the LORD their God. They followed the practices Israel had introduced.[p] [20]Therefore the LORD rejected all the people of Israel; he afflicted them and gave them into the hands of plunderers,[q] until he thrust them from his presence.

[21]When he tore[r] Israel away from the house of David, they made Jeroboam son of Nebat their king.[s] Jeroboam enticed Israel away from following the LORD and caused them to commit a great sin. [22]The Israelites persisted in all the sins of Jeroboam and did not turn away from them [23]until the LORD removed them from his presence, as he had warned through all his servants the prophets. So the people of Israel were taken from their homeland into exile in Assyria, and they are still there.

Samaria Resettled

[24]The king of Assyria[t] brought people from Babylon, Cuthah, Avva, Hamath and Sepharvaim[u] and settled them in the towns of Samaria to replace the Israelites. They took over Samaria and lived in its towns. [25]When they first lived there, they did not worship the LORD; so he sent lions[v] among them and they killed some of the people. [26]It was reported to the king of Assyria: "The people you deported and resettled in the towns of Samaria do not know what the god of that country requires. He has sent lions among them, which are killing them off, because the people do not know what he requires."

[27]Then the king of Assyria gave this order: "Have one of the priests you took captive from Samaria go back to live there and teach the people what the god of the land requires." [28]So one of the priests who had been exiled from Samaria came to live in Bethel and taught them how to worship the LORD.

[29]Nevertheless, each national group made its own gods in the several towns[w] where they settled, and set them up in the shrines[x] the people of Samaria had made at the high places.[y] [30]The men from Babylon made Succoth Benoth, the men from Cuthah made Nergal, and the men from Hamath made Ashima; [31]the Avvites made Nibhaz and Tartak, and the Sepharvites burned their children in the fire as sacrifices to Adrammelech[z] and Anammelech, the gods of Sepharvaim.[a] [32]They worshiped the LORD, but they also appointed all sorts[b] of their own people to officiate for them as priests in the shrines at the high places. [33]They worshiped the LORD, but they also served their own gods in accordance with the customs of the nations from which they had been brought.

[34]To this day they persist in their former practices. They neither worship the LORD nor adhere to the decrees and ordinances, the laws and commands that the LORD gave the descendants of Jacob, whom he named Israel.[c] [35]When the LORD

[a] 17 Or *They made their sons and daughters pass through*

17:16
k 2Ki 21:3
l 1Ki 16:31
17:17
m Dt 18:10-12; 2Ki 16:3
n Lev 19:26
o 1Ki 21:20
17:19
p 1Ki 14:22-23; 2Ki 16:3
17:20
q 2Ki 15:29
17:21
r 1Ki 11:11
s 1Ki 12:20
17:24
t Ezr 4:2,10
u 2Ki 18:34
17:25
v Ge 37:20
17:29
w Jer 2:28
x 1Ki 12:31
y Mic 4:5
17:31
z 2Ki 19:37 a ver 24
17:32
b 1Ki 12:31
17:34
c Ge 32:28; 35:10; 1Ki 18:31

---

2 Kings 17:24–41

In accordance with the deportation system used by Tiglath-Pileser III and followed by his successors, a vast transplantation of populaces occurred. Israelites were sent to Assyria, while Babylonians and Arameans were transferred to Israel. One of Israel's exiled priests returned and reinstituted the worship of God at Bethel, the traditional cult center of the northern kingdom. The religion, however, this priest taught was likely the false worship established by Jeroboam I (cf. 1 Kings 12:31–32). The result was a mixture of truth combined with the corrupted experience of Israel and the pagan rites brought in by the deportees.

Such utter confusion continued until the writing of Kings (v. 34) following the fall of Judah in 586 B.C. Later the Samaritans—a mixed race made up of a combination of Israelites who remained in the land and these non-Israelites settlers—came to follow the teachings of Moses, including monotheism (cf. John 4:4–26).

With this summation, the divine case against Israel had been made. Despite all their great Redeemer had done for his people, their thankless, hardened, apostate hearts had led them into spiritual, moral, and social corruption and finally to their own demise. Israel's checkered history should have provided a lesson for Judah and remains an example for the church. Take a moment to review and reflect on Paul's words in 1 Corinthians 10:11–13.

17:35
d Ex 20:5; Jdg 6:10
17:36
e Ex 3:20; 6:6;
Ps 136:12
made a covenant with the Israelites, he commanded them: "Do not worship^d any other gods or bow down to them, serve them or sacrifice to them. ³⁶But the LORD, who brought you up out of Egypt with mighty power and outstretched arm,^e is the one you must worship. To him you shall bow down and to him offer sacrifices.

17:37
f Dt 5:32
17:38
g Dt 4:23; 6:12
³⁷You must always be careful^f to keep the decrees and ordinances, the laws and commands he wrote for you. Do not worship other gods. ³⁸Do not forget^g the covenant I have made with you, and do not worship other gods. ³⁹Rather, worship the LORD your God; it is he who will deliver you from the hand of all your enemies."

17:41
h ver 32-33;
1Ki 18:21; Mt 6:24
⁴⁰They would not listen, however, but persisted in their former practices. ⁴¹Even while these people were worshiping the LORD,^h they were serving their idols. To this day their children and grandchildren continue to do as their fathers did.

Hezekiah King of Judah

18:1
i Isa 1:1; 2Ch 28:27
18 In the third year of Hoshea son of Elah king of Israel, Hezekiahⁱ son of Ahaz king of Judah began to reign. ²He was twenty-five years old when he became king, and he reigned in Jerusalem twenty-nine years.^j His mother's name was Abijah^a daughter of Zechariah. ³He did what was right in the eyes of the LORD, just as his father David^k had done. ⁴He removed^l the high places, smashed the sacred stones^m and cut down the Asherah poles. He broke into pieces the bronze snakeⁿ Moses had made, for up to that time the Israelites had been burning incense to it. (It was called^b Nehushtan. ^c)

18:2
j Isa 38:5
18:3
k Isa 38:5
18:4
l 2Ch 31:1
m Ex 23:24
n Nu 21:9
18:5
o 2Ki 19:10; 23:25
⁵Hezekiah trusted^o in the LORD, the God of Israel. There was no one like him among all the kings of Judah, either before him or after him. ⁶He held fast^p to the LORD and did not cease to follow him; he kept the commands the LORD had given Moses. ⁷And the LORD was with him; he was successful^q in whatever he undertook. He rebelled^r against the king of Assyria and did not serve him. ⁸From watchtower to fortified city,^s he defeated the Philistines, as far as Gaza and its territory.

18:6
p Dt 10:20;
Jos 23:8
18:7
q Ge 39:3;
1Sa 18:14
r 2Ki 16:7
18:8
s 2Ki 17:9;
Isa 14:29
18:9
t Isa 1:1
⁹In King Hezekiah's fourth year,^t which was the seventh year of Hoshea son of Elah king of Israel, Shalmaneser king of Assyria marched against Samaria and laid siege to it. ¹⁰At the end of three years the Assyrians took it. So Samaria was captured in Hezekiah's sixth year, which was the ninth year of Hoshea king of Israel. ¹¹The king^u of Assyria deported Israel to Assyria and settled them in Halah, in Gozan on the Habor River and in towns of the Medes. ¹²This happened because they had not obeyed the LORD their God, but had violated his covenant^v—all that Moses the servant of the LORD commanded. ^w They neither listened to the commands^x nor carried them out.

18:11
u Isa 37:12
18:12
v 2Ki 17:15
w Da 9:6,10
x 1Ki 9:6
18:13
y 2Ch 32:1; Isa 1:7;
Mic 1:9
18:14
z Isa 24:5
¹³In the fourteenth year of King Hezekiah's reign, Sennacherib king of Assyria attacked all the fortified cities of Judah^y and captured them. ¹⁴So Hezekiah king of Judah sent this message to the king of Assyria at Lachish: "I have done wrong.^z

^a 2 Hebrew *Abi*, a variant of *Abijah*   ^b 4 Or *He called it*   ^c 4 *Nehushtan* sounds like the Hebrew for *bronze* and *snake* and *unclean thing*.

---

2 Kings 18:1–16

After the writer of Kings familiarized his readers with Hezekiah's godly character, he immediately turned his attention, beginning in verse 7b, to one of the most critical episodes of Hezekiah's—and Judah's—existence. Hezekiah rebelled against Assyria, to which his father Ahaz had submitted as a vassal (16:7–9). He likely refused to pay the annual tribute sometime shortly after 705 B.C., when Sennacherib became Assyria's king. Hezekiah's example stood in stark contrast to the northern kingdom, which perished because of unbelief and *disobedience* (18:9–12).

Sennacherib was at first occupied with affairs close to home and wasn't free to deal with Hezekiah. But he soon swooped down from the north, capturing key territory that would effectively separate Judah from Egyptian

help. Sensing impending doom, Hezekiah sent a letter of concession to Sennacherib. Hezekiah had "done wrong" (v. 14) from Assyria's perspective. But in the end he was delivered from Sennacherib's retribution by trusting God rather than by handing over silver and gold (cf. vv. 28–30; 19:32–37).

The divine evaluation of Hezekiah, expressed through the author of Kings, is glowing: "There was no one like him among all the kings of Judah, either before him or after him" (v. 5). Hence God was with him and blessed him with success. Hezekiah's character stands as a reminder that living for God's glory is also for *our* good (cf. v. 7a with 2 Chron. 31:20–21). When has standing up for the cause of Christ in the face of seemingly certain doom brought you a surprising victory or reversal of fortune?

Withdraw from me, and I will pay whatever you demand of me." The king of Assyria exacted from Hezekiah king of Judah three hundred talents[a] of silver and thirty talents[b] of gold. [15]So Hezekiah gave[a] him all the silver that was found in the temple of the LORD and in the treasuries of the royal palace.

[16]At this time Hezekiah king of Judah stripped off the gold with which he had covered the doors and doorposts of the temple of the LORD, and gave it to the king of Assyria.

Sennacherib Threatens Jerusalem

[17]The king of Assyria sent his supreme commander,[b] his chief officer and his field commander with a large army, from Lachish to King Hezekiah at Jerusalem. They came up to Jerusalem and stopped at the aqueduct of the Upper Pool,[c] on the road to the Washerman's Field. [18]They called for the king; and Eliakim[d] son of Hilkiah the palace administrator, Shebna[e] the secretary, and Joah son of Asaph the recorder went out to them.

[19]The field commander said to them, "Tell Hezekiah:

" 'This is what the great king, the king of Assyria, says: On what are you basing this confidence of yours? [20]You say you have strategy and military strength—but you speak only empty words. On whom are you depending, that you rebel against me? [21]Look now, you are depending on Egypt,[f] that splintered reed of a staff,[g] which pierces a man's hand and wounds him if he leans on it! Such is Pharaoh king of Egypt to all who depend on him. [22]And if you say to me, "We are depending on the LORD our God"—isn't he the one whose high places and altars Hezekiah removed, saying to Judah and Jerusalem, "You must worship before this altar in Jerusalem"?

[23]" 'Come now, make a bargain with my master, the king of Assyria: I will give you two thousand horses—if you can put riders on them! [24]How can you repulse one officer[h] of the least of my master's officials, even though you are depending on Egypt for chariots and horsemen[c]? [25]Furthermore, have I come to attack and destroy this place without word from the LORD?[i] The LORD himself told me to march against this country and destroy it.' "

[26]Then Eliakim son of Hilkiah, and Shebna and Joah said to the field commander, "Please speak to your servants in Aramaic,[j] since we understand it. Don't speak to us in Hebrew in the hearing of the people on the wall."

[27]But the commander replied, "Was it only to your master and you that my master sent me to say these things, and not to the men sitting on the wall—who, like you, will have to eat their own filth and drink their own urine?"

[28]Then the commander stood and called out in Hebrew: "Hear the word of the great king, the king of Assyria! [29]This is what the king says: Do not let Hezekiah deceive[k] you. He cannot deliver you from my hand. [30]Do not let Hezekiah persuade you to trust in the LORD when he says, 'The LORD will surely deliver us; this city will not be given into the hand of the king of Assyria.'

[31]"Do not listen to Hezekiah. This is what the king of Assyria says: Make peace with me and come out to me. Then every one of you will eat from his own vine and

---

18:15
a 1Ki 15:18;
2Ki 16:8

18:17
b Isa 20:1
c 2Ki 20:20;
2Ch 32:4,30;
Isa 7:3
18:18
d 2Ki 19:2;
Isa 22:20
e Isa 22:15

18:21
f Isa 20:5; Eze 29:6
g Isa 30:5,7

18:24
h Isa 10:8

18:25
i 2Ki 19:6,22

18:26
j Ezr 4:7

18:29
k 2Ki 19:10

---

a 14 That is, about 11 tons (about 10 metric tons)   b 14 That is, about 1 ton (about 1 metric ton)
c 24 Or *charioteers*

---

2 Kings 18:17–37

🔖 The Assyrians' message to Hezekiah and his people was couched in terms of brilliant psychological warfare. Sennacherib's warning was given in two stages. In verses 19–22 he pointed out that Hezekiah's tactics and trust were ill conceived. In verses 23–25 he suggested that the Judahite king's supposed strengths were really weaknesses.

📖 Scare tactics. Intimidation. Spin. How vulnerable

do you suspect you are to psychological manipulation? What role does morale play in your attitude toward current events—both political and personal? Most of us are affected by the media more than we realize, but situations come and go, often at a white-water pace. God's Word is the opposite. It's been there for his people for millennia, and it's as changeless and powerful today as it was when its inspired words were recorded. Next time you need an antidote to disturbing news, try Psalm 90.

18:31
l Nu 13:23;
1Ki 4:25
m Jer 14:3; La 4:4
18:32
n Dt 8:7-9; 30:19
18:33
o 2Ki 19:12;
Isa 10:10-11
18:34
p 2Ki 17:24; 19:13
q Isa 10:9
18:35
r Ps 2:1-2

fig tree[l] and drink water from his own cistern,[m] 32until I come and take you to a land like your own, a land of grain and new wine, a land of bread and vineyards, a land of olive trees and honey. Choose life[n] and not death!

"Do not listen to Hezekiah, for he is misleading you when he says, 'The Lord will deliver us.' 33Has the god[o] of any nation ever delivered his land from the hand of the king of Assyria? 34Where are the gods of Hamath[p] and Arpad?[q] Where are the gods of Sepharvaim, Hena and Ivvah? Have they rescued Samaria from my hand? 35Who of all the gods of these countries has been able to save his land from me? How then can the Lord deliver Jerusalem from my hand?"[r]

36But the people remained silent and said nothing in reply, because the king had commanded, "Do not answer him."

18:37
s 2Ki 6:30

37Then Eliakim son of Hilkiah the palace administrator, Shebna the secretary and Joah son of Asaph the recorder went to Hezekiah, with their clothes torn,[s] and told him what the field commander had said.

Jerusalem's Deliverance Foretold

19:1
t Ge 37:34;
1Ki 21:27;
2Ch 32:20-22

19:2
u Isa 1:1

19 When King Hezekiah heard this, he tore[t] his clothes and put on sackcloth and went into the temple of the Lord. 2He sent Eliakim the palace administrator, Shebna the secretary and the leading priests, all wearing sackcloth, to the prophet Isaiah[u] son of Amoz. 3They told him, "This is what Hezekiah says: This day is a day of distress and rebuke and disgrace, as when children come to the point of birth and there is no strength to deliver them.

19:4
v 2Ki 18:35
w 2Sa 16:12

4It may be that the Lord your God will hear all the words of the field commander, whom his master, the king of Assyria, has sent to ridicule[v] the living God, and that he will rebuke[w] him for the words the Lord your God has heard. Therefore pray for the remnant that still survives."

5When King Hezekiah's officials came to Isaiah, 6Isaiah said to them, "Tell your master, 'This is what the Lord says: Do not be afraid of what you have heard—those

19:6
x 2Ki 18:25

words with which the underlings of the king of Assyria have blasphemed[x] me. 7Lis-

19:7
y ver 37
19:8
z 2Ki 18:14

ten! I am going to put such a spirit in him that when he hears a certain report, he will return to his own country, and there I will have him cut down with the sword.[y] "

8When the field commander heard that the king of Assyria had left Lachish,[z] he withdrew and found the king fighting against Libnah.

9Now Sennacherib received a report that Tirhakah, the Cushite[a] king of Egypt, was marching out to fight against him. So he again sent messengers to Hezekiah with

19:10
a 2Ki 18:5
b 2Ki 18:29

this word: 10"Say to Hezekiah king of Judah: Do not let the god you depend[a] on deceive[b] you when he says, 'Jerusalem will not be handed over to the king of Assyria.' 11Surely you have heard what the kings of Assyria have done to all the countries, destroying them completely. And will you be delivered? 12Did the gods of the nations

19:12
c 2Ki 18:33
d 2Ki 17:6
e Ge 11:31
19:13
f 2Ki 18:34

that were destroyed by my forefathers deliver[c] them: the gods of Gozan,[d] Haran,[e] Rezeph and the people of Eden who were in Tel Assar? 13Where is the king of Hamath, the king of Arpad, the king of the city of Sepharvaim, or of Hena or Ivvah?"[f]

Hezekiah's Prayer

14Hezekiah received the letter from the messengers and read it. Then he went up

___

a 9 That is, from the upper Nile region

---

2 Kings 19:1–13

When Hezekiah heard the report of the Assyrians' demand for Judah's surrender (see 18:31–32), he was filled with grief. Tearing his clothes and donning sackcloth (traditional symbols of mourning), he went with heavy heart to the temple to pour out his soul before God. Desiring to do all within his power to discern the Lord's will, he sent the leading officials and priests, all dressed in sackcloth, to meet with Isaiah so that he might hear God's word through his prophet.

In briefing Isaiah on the emergency, the king's delega-

tion also explained Hezekiah's deep concern. This was (1) a "day of distress," filled with anguish of heart for every true Israelite; (2) a "day of rebuke" (Hezekiah sensed that the Lord was chastising his people); (3) a "day of disgrace" (perhaps God was even now about to reject and cast off his people completely; cf. Deut. 32:15–38; Jer. 14:12).

Hezekiah responded to this crisis with worship, repentance, and prayer (see also vv. 14–19). He also enlisted others to pray and was open to God's guidance through them. How closely does this resemble your typical response to crisis?

to the temple of the LORD and spread it out before the LORD. [15]And Hezekiah prayed to the LORD: "O LORD, God of Israel, enthroned between the cherubim, [g] you alone are God over all the kingdoms of the earth. You have made heaven and earth. [16]Give ear, [h] O LORD, and hear; [i] open your eyes, [j] O LORD, and see; listen to the words Sennacherib has sent to insult the living God.

[17]"It is true, O LORD, that the Assyrian kings have laid waste these nations and their lands. [18]They have thrown their gods into the fire and destroyed them, for they were not gods [k] but only wood and stone, fashioned by men's hands. [l] [19]Now, O LORD our God, deliver us from his hand, so that all kingdoms [m] on earth may know [n] that you alone, O LORD, are God."

Isaiah Prophesies Sennacherib's Fall

[20]Then Isaiah son of Amoz sent a message to Hezekiah: "This is what the LORD, the God of Israel, says: I have heard [o] your prayer concerning Sennacherib king of Assyria. [21]This is the word that the LORD has spoken against him:

" 'The Virgin Daughter [p] of Zion
    despises you and mocks [q] you.
The Daughter of Jerusalem
    tosses her head [r] as you flee.
[22]Who is it you have insulted and blasphemed?
    Against whom have you raised your voice
and lifted your eyes in pride?
    Against the Holy One [s] of Israel!
[23]By your messengers
    you have heaped insults on the Lord.
And you have said, [t]
    "With my many chariots [u]
I have ascended the heights of the mountains,
    the utmost heights of Lebanon.
I have cut down its tallest cedars,
    the choicest of its pines.
I have reached its remotest parts,
    the finest of its forests.
[24]I have dug wells in foreign lands
    and drunk the water there.
With the soles of my feet
    I have dried up all the streams of Egypt."

[25]" 'Have you not heard? [v]
    Long ago I ordained it.

19:15
g Ex 25:22

19:16
h Ps 31:2 i 1Ki 8:29
j ver 4; 2Ch 6:40

19:18
k Isa 44:9-11;
Jer 10:3-10
l Ps 115:4; Ac 17:29
19:19
m 1Ki 8:43
n Ps 83:18

19:20
o 2Ki 20:5

19:21
p Jer 14:17; La 2:13
q Ps 22:7-8
r Job 16:4;
Ps 109:25

19:22
s Ps 71:22; Isa 5:24

19:23
t Isa 10:18
u Ps 20:7

19:25
v Isa 40:21,28

---

2 Kings 19:14–19

Hezekiah's action of spreading out the letter before God in the temple was one of simple faith. As a child bringing a broken toy to a father for repair, so Hezekiah laid out the issues in God's sight for resolution. The Lord was and is the only true God, the One who sovereignly controls the destinies of all nations. He's the Creator—and Consummator—of all things.

Hezekiah pleaded with God to take notice of Sennacherib's blasphemy. His prayer, like Daniel's (Dan. 9:17–19), was concerned most of all with God's reputation. Has this been your main focus as you have approached the Lord in troubled times?

2 Kings 19:20–37

God's answer wasn't long in coming. Isaiah sent a message from God to Hezekiah, assuring him that his prayer had been heard. The major portion of the mes-

sage divides into three poetic sections: (1) a reply to Sennacherib regarding his misguided boasting (vv. 21–28); (2) a sign for Hezekiah that God would deal with Sennacherib and deliver his people (vv. 29–31); and (3) a prophetic declaration for all that Sennacherib wouldn't even begin the battle of Jerusalem, let alone conquer the city (vv. 32–34).

Though Sennacherib would fight yet another five campaigns, he would never again return to Judah. Some 20 years later (681 B.C.), two of Sennacherib's sons assassinated him and another son succeeded him as king. The last vestige of the divine prophecy to Hezekiah finally stood complete (cf. vv. 7,37). God's program may seem to tarry (cf. 2 Peter 3:3–9), but it will be accomplished. When have you been impatient with it? Does it help for you to recognize that time as we know it is only his concession to our human needs?

19:25
w Isa 10:5; 45:7
x Mic 1:6

In days of old I planned[w] it;
    now I have brought it to pass,
that you have turned fortified cities
    into piles of stone.[x]

19:26
y Ps 6:10 z Isa 4:2
a Ps 129:6

26 Their people, drained of power,
    are dismayed[y] and put to shame.
They are like plants in the field,
    like tender green shoots,[z]
like grass sprouting on the roof,
    scorched[a] before it grows up.

19:27
b Ps 139:1-4

27 " 'But I know[b] where you stay
    and when you come and go
    and how you rage against me.
28 Because you rage against me
    and your insolence has reached my ears,
I will put my hook[c] in your nose
    and my bit[d] in your mouth,
and I will make you return[e]
    by the way you came.'

19:28
c Eze 19:9; 29:4
d Isa 30:28 e ver 33

19:29
f 2Ki 20:8-9;
Lk 2:12 g Lev 25:5
h Ps 107:37

29 "This will be the sign[f] for you, O Hezekiah:

"This year you will eat what grows by itself,[g]
    and the second year what springs from that.
But in the third year sow and reap,
    plant vineyards[h] and eat their fruit.

19:30
i 2Ch 32:22-23

30 Once more a remnant of the house of Judah
    will take root[i] below and bear fruit above.
31 For out of Jerusalem will come a remnant,
    and out of Mount Zion a band of survivors.

19:31
j Isa 9:7

The zeal[j] of the LORD Almighty will accomplish this.

32 "Therefore this is what the LORD says concerning the king of Assyria:

"He will not enter this city
    or shoot an arrow here.
He will not come before it with shield
    or build a siege ramp against it.
33 By the way that he came he will return;[k]
    he will not enter this city,

19:33
k ver 28

declares the LORD.

19:34
l 2Ki 20:6
m 1Ki 11:12-13

34 I will defend[l] this city and save it,
    for my sake and for the sake of David[m] my servant."

19:35
n Ex 12:23
o Job 24:24

35 That night the angel of the LORD[n] went out and put to death a hundred and eighty-five thousand men in the Assyrian camp. When the people got up the next morning—there were all the dead bodies![o] 36 So Sennacherib king of Assyria broke camp and withdrew. He returned to Nineveh[p] and stayed there.

19:36
p Ge 10:11; Jnh 1:2

37 One day, while he was worshiping in the temple of his god Nisroch, his sons Adrammelech and Sharezer cut him down with the sword,[q] and they escaped to the land of Ararat.[r] And Esarhaddon[s] his son succeeded him as king.

19:37
q ver 7 r Ge 8:4
s Ezr 4:2

Hezekiah's Illness

20 In those days Hezekiah became ill and was at the point of death. The prophet Isaiah son of Amoz went to him and said, "This is what the LORD says: Put your house in order, because you are going to die; you will not recover."

20:3
t Ne 13:22

2 Hezekiah turned his face to the wall and prayed to the LORD, 3 "Remember,[t]

O Lord, how I have walked before you faithfully[u] and with wholehearted devotion and have done what is good in your eyes." And Hezekiah wept bitterly.

⁴Before Isaiah had left the middle court, the word of the Lord came to him: ⁵"Go back and tell Hezekiah, the leader of my people, 'This is what the Lord, the God of your father David, says: I have heard[v] your prayer and seen your tears;[w] I will heal you. On the third day from now you will go up to the temple of the Lord. ⁶I will add fifteen years to your life. And I will deliver you and this city from the hand of the king of Assyria. I will defend[x] this city for my sake and for the sake of my servant David.' "

⁷Then Isaiah said, "Prepare a poultice of figs." They did so and applied it to the boil,[y] and he recovered.

⁸Hezekiah had asked Isaiah, "What will be the sign that the Lord will heal me and that I will go up to the temple of the Lord on the third day from now?"

⁹Isaiah answered, "This is the Lord's sign[z] to you that the Lord will do what he has promised: Shall the shadow go forward ten steps, or shall it go back ten steps?"

¹⁰"It is a simple matter for the shadow to go forward ten steps," said Hezekiah. "Rather, have it go back ten steps."

¹¹Then the prophet Isaiah called upon the Lord, and the Lord made the shadow go back[a] the ten steps it had gone down on the stairway of Ahaz.

Envoys From Babylon

¹²At that time Merodach-Baladan son of Baladan king of Babylon sent Hezekiah letters and a gift, because he had heard of Hezekiah's illness. ¹³Hezekiah received the messengers and showed them all that was in his storehouses—the silver, the gold, the spices and the fine oil—his armory and everything found among his treasures. There was nothing in his palace or in all his kingdom that Hezekiah did not show them.

¹⁴Then Isaiah the prophet went to King Hezekiah and asked, "What did those men say, and where did they come from?"

"From a distant land," Hezekiah replied. "They came from Babylon."

¹⁵The prophet asked, "What did they see in your palace?"

"They saw everything in my palace," Hezekiah said. "There is nothing among my treasures that I did not show them."

¹⁶Then Isaiah said to Hezekiah, "Hear the word of the Lord: ¹⁷The time will surely come when everything in your palace, and all that your fathers have stored up until this day, will be carried off to Babylon.[b] Nothing will be left, says the Lord. ¹⁸And

20:3 u 2Ki 18:3-6

20:5 v 1Sa 9:16; 1Ki 9:3; 2Ki 19:20 w Ps 39:12; 56:8

20:6 x 2Ki 19:34

20:7 y Isa 38:21

20:9 z Dt 13:2; Jer 44:29

20:11 a Jos 10:13

20:17 b 2Ki 24:13; 25:13; 2Ch 36:10; Jer 27:22; 52:17-23

2 Kings 20:1–11

The events of chapter 20 must have happened before those of 18:13—19:37 (see v. 6 and "There and Then" for 20:12–21). Hezekiah probably wasn't yet forty years old, but his concerns were deeper than any personal desire for added years. This was clear from God's answer to his prayer (vv. 5–6). What was to become of the nation? Hezekiah's reforms were barely yet in progress. Also, at this time Hezekiah still had no male heir. So what would become of the house of David? God's program and person were at stake, and Hezekiah correctly believed he was vitally involved in them.

Not only did Isaiah have spiritual news and instructions for Hezekiah, he also had directions for the king's physical recovery. In accordance with those orders, a poultice of figs was mixed and applied to Hezekiah's ulcerated sore, and he recovered. God chose to work through the accepted medical standards of the day, but there can be no doubt that the healing was brought about by the divine word. When has such a

"medical miracle" affected your own life or that of someone you knew and/or loved? What was the reaction of the medical personnel involved?

2 Kings 20:12–21

God allowed Hezekiah to be put to the test (cf. 2 Chron. 32:31). The stated purpose for Merodach-Baladan's embassy to Hezekiah was delivery of a congratulatory message and gift. But the Babylonian king's checkered career makes clear that his motives were political: He hoped to find in Hezekiah a new ally in his struggles against Assyria.

Hezekiah received the messengers warmly. Doubtless he told them the whole story of his healing and the remarkable incident of the retreating of the sun's shadow. But he went beyond this. To impress his guests still further, he showed them all the vast treasures of the kingdom. The presence of these riches indicates that this event took place before Hezekiah's payment of tribute to Sennacherib in 701 B.C. (2 Kings 18:13–16).

20:18
c 2Ki 24:15;
2Ch 33:11; Da 1:3
some of your descendants, [c] your own flesh and blood, that will be born to you, will be taken away, and they will become eunuchs in the palace of the king of Babylon."

19"The word of the LORD you have spoken is good," Hezekiah replied. For he thought, "Will there not be peace and security in my lifetime?"

20:20
d Ne 3:16
20As for the other events of Hezekiah's reign, all his achievements and how he made the pool[d] and the tunnel by which he brought water into the city, are they not written in the book of the annals of the kings of Judah? 21Hezekiah rested with his fathers. And Manasseh his son succeeded him as king.

Manasseh King of Judah

21:1
e Isa 62:4
21:2
f Jer 15:4
g 2Ki 16:3
21:3
h 2Ki 18:4
i Jdg 6:28;
1Ki 16:32 j Dt 17:3;
2Ki 17:16
21:4
k Jer 32:34
l 2Sa 7:13; 1Ki 8:29
21:5
m 1Ki 7:12;
2Ki 23:12
21:6
n Lev 18:21;
Dt 18:10; 2Ki 16:3;
17:17 o Lev 19:31
21:7
p Dt 16:21;
2Ki 23:4 q 2Sa 7:13;
1Ki 8:29; 9:3;
2Ki 23:27;
Jer 32:34
21:8
r 2Sa 7:10
s 2Ki 18:12
21:9
t Pr 29:12 u Dt 9:4
21:11
v 2Ki 24:3-4
w Ge 15:16;
1Ki 21:26
21:12
x 2Ki 23:26; 24:3;
Jer 15:4 y 1Sa 3:11;
Jer 19:3
21:13
z Isa 34:11; La 2:8;
Am 7:7-9
a 2Ki 23:27
21:14
b Ps 78:58-60
c 2Ki 19:4; Mic 2:12

21 Manasseh was twelve years old when he became king, and he reigned in Jerusalem fifty-five years. His mother's name was Hephzibah. [e] 2He did evil[f] in the eyes of the LORD, following the detestable practices[g] of the nations the LORD had driven out before the Israelites. 3He rebuilt the high places[h] his father Hezekiah had destroyed; he also erected altars to Baal[i] and made an Asherah pole, as Ahab king of Israel had done. He bowed down to all the starry hosts[j] and worshiped them. 4He built altars[k] in the temple of the LORD, of which the LORD had said, "In Jerusalem I will put my Name."[l] 5In both courts[m] of the temple of the LORD, he built altars to all the starry hosts. 6He sacrificed his own son[n] in[a] the fire, practiced sorcery and divination, and consulted mediums and spiritists. [o] He did much evil in the eyes of the LORD, provoking him to anger.

7He took the carved Asherah pole[p] he had made and put it in the temple, of which the LORD had said to David and to his son Solomon, "In this temple and in Jerusalem, which I have chosen out of all the tribes of Israel, I will put my Name[q] forever. 8I will not again[r] make the feet of the Israelites wander from the land I gave their forefathers, if only they will be careful to do everything I commanded them and will keep the whole Law that my servant Moses[s] gave them." 9But the people did not listen. Manasseh led them astray, so that they did more evil[t] than the nations[u] the LORD had destroyed before the Israelites.

10The LORD said through his servants the prophets: 11"Manasseh king of Judah has committed these detestable sins. He has done more evil[v] than the Amorites[w] who preceded him and has led Judah into sin with his idols. 12Therefore this is what the LORD, the God of Israel, says: I am going to bring such disaster[x] on Jerusalem and Judah that the ears of everyone who hears of it will tingle. [y] 13I will stretch out over Jerusalem the measuring line used against Samaria and the plumb line[z] used against the house of Ahab. I will wipe[a] out Jerusalem as one wipes a dish, wiping it and turning it upside down. 14I will forsake[b] the remnant[c] of my inheritance and hand them over to their enemies. They will be looted and plundered by all their

---

a 6 Or *He made his own son pass through*

📖 Hezekiah's foolishness in this instance would contribute to the fulfillment of ancient prophecy (Lev. 26:33; Deut. 28:64–67). His experience stands as a stern warning to all generations against the perils of pride (cf. Prov. 16:5;18; 28:25–26; 29:23). When are you most tempted to "show off"?

2 Kings 21:1–18

📖 Manasseh's great evil understandably provoked God's anger. The king's placement of an Asherah pole within the temple was especially offensive. God had promised to dwell in peace among his people forever (v. 7; cf. 2 Sam. 7:13; 1 Kings 8:16; 9:3) if they would only serve him in righteousness (v. 8; cf. 2 Sam. 7:10; 1 Kings 9:6–9). But instead of listening to their Redeemer, they chose to indulge themselves with unfaithful Manasseh (v. 8). What, we wonder, had come of Hezekiah's far-reaching reforms (cf. 2 Kings 18:3–4)—and why wasn't his son on board?

Manasseh's shedding of "innocent blood" (v. 16) refers not only to human sacrifice but probably also to the martyrdom of God's prophets. The historian Josephus affirmed that Manasseh not only murdered all the righteous men of Judah but also killed prophets daily until Jerusalem "was overflowing with blood." Uniform Jewish and Christian tradition holds that Manasseh arranged to have Isaiah sawn asunder (cf. Heb. 11:37).

📖 Manasseh's Judah exceeded the spiritual degradation of the original Canaanites God had driven out before Israel (v. 9; cf. Deut. 12:29–31; 1 Kings 14:24). What a tragedy! How superficial had been the nation's compliance with Hezekiah's reforms! Without a strong spiritual leader, the people were quickly lured by evil. Based on your knowledge of more recent history, can you cite other instances in which much-needed reform seemed to melt away following the loss or breakdown of strong leadership?

foes, [15]because they have done evil[d] in my eyes and have provoked[e] me to anger from the day their forefathers came out of Egypt until this day."

[16]Moreover, Manasseh also shed so much innocent blood[f] that he filled Jerusalem from end to end—besides the sin that he had caused Judah to commit, so that they did evil in the eyes of the LORD.

[17]As for the other events of Manasseh's reign, and all he did, including the sin he committed, are they not written in the book of the annals of the kings of Judah? [18]Manasseh rested with his fathers and was buried in his palace garden,[g] the garden of Uzza. And Amon his son succeeded him as king.

Amon King of Judah

[19]Amon was twenty-two years old when he became king, and he reigned in Jerusalem two years. His mother's name was Meshullemeth daughter of Haruz; she was from Jotbah. [20]He did evil[h] in the eyes of the LORD, as his father Manasseh had done. [21]He walked in all the ways of his father; he worshiped the idols his father had worshiped, and bowed down to them. [22]He forsook the LORD, the God of his fathers, and did not walk[i] in the way of the LORD.

[23]Amon's officials conspired against him and assassinated[j] the king in his palace. [24]Then the people of the land killed[k] all who had plotted against King Amon, and they made Josiah his son king in his place.

[25]As for the other events of Amon's reign, and what he did, are they not written in the book of the annals of the kings of Judah? [26]He was buried in his grave in the garden[l] of Uzza. And Josiah his son succeeded him as king.

The Book of the Law Found

22 Josiah was eight years old when he became king, and he reigned in Jerusalem thirty-one years. His mother's name was Jedidah daughter of Adaiah; she was from Bozkath.[m] [2]He did what was right[n] in the eyes of the LORD and walked in all the ways of his father David, not turning aside to the right[o] or to the left.

[3]In the eighteenth year of his reign, King Josiah sent the secretary, Shaphan[p] son of Azaliah, the son of Meshullam, to the temple of the LORD. He said: [4]"Go up to Hilkiah the high priest and have him get ready the money that has been brought into the temple of the LORD, which the doorkeepers have collected[q] from the people. [5]Have them entrust it to the men appointed to supervise the work on the temple. And have these men pay the workers who repair[r] the temple of the LORD— [6]the carpenters, the builders and the masons. Also have them purchase timber and dressed stone to repair the temple. [7]But they need not account for the money entrusted to them, because they are acting faithfully."[t]

---

2 Kings 21:19–26

For some reason, the author of Kings didn't include the events late in Manasseh's reign recorded in 2 Chronicles 33:11–17. The Chronicler reported that the Lord humbled Manasseh by allowing him to be taken away as a prisoner by the king of Assyria—which fortunately led to Manasseh's repentance, release, and religious reforms.

Amon's reign was a replay of the earlier period of Manasseh. Amon evidently reinstated the idolatrous practices his father had abolished before he died, since they were in existence again in the time of Amon's son Josiah (see 23:5–7,12).

Amon was assassinated by his own court officials, who were in turn killed by the populace. Jesus much later reminded Peter that "all who draw the sword will die by the sword" (Matt. 26:52). The sad testimony to this truth is seen worldwide. Jesus taught that peace-makers will be called "sons of God" (Matt. 5:9). Many courageous Christians today step into such roles in the aftermath of violent conflict, seeking to bring reconciliation and understanding. Pray today for those working around the world as peacemakers in Jesus' name.

2 Kings 22:1–20

Though it took place in the 18th year of Josiah's reign (when he was twenty-six years old), the author of Kings quickly moved to one of the most outstanding examples of Josiah's godliness: his temple repair. According to 2 Chronicles 34:3–5, this action was preceded by Josiah's firm commitment to God at the age of sixteen and, beginning some four years later, by a thorough purge of idolatry in Judah. In fact, Josiah went so far as to extend his efforts to the territory of the former northern kingdom as well (2 Chron. 34:6–7; cf. 2 Kings 23:15–20). Josiah's action in the 18th year of his reign was fully in keeping with his spiritual character.

22:8
u Dt 31:24

22:10
v Jer 36:21

22:12
w 2Ki 25:22;
Jer 26:24

22:13
x Dt 29:24-28;
31:17

22:16
y Dt 31:29;
Jos 23:15
z Dt 29:27; Da 9:11
22:17
a Dt 29:25-27

22:18
b 2Ch 34:26;
Jer 21:2
22:19
c Ex 10:3;
1Ki 21:29; Ps 51:17;
Isa 57:15; Mic 6:8
d Jer 26:6
e Lev 26:31
22:20
f Isa 57:1

23:2
g Dt 31:11;
2Ki 22:8

8Hilkiah the high priest said to Shaphan the secretary, "I have found the Book of the Law*u* in the temple of the LORD." He gave it to Shaphan, who read it. 9Then Shaphan the secretary went to the king and reported to him: "Your officials have paid out the money that was in the temple of the LORD and have entrusted it to the workers and supervisors at the temple." 10Then Shaphan the secretary informed the king, "Hilkiah the priest has given me a book." And Shaphan read from it in the presence of the king.*v*

11When the king heard the words of the Book of the Law, he tore his robes. 12He gave these orders to Hilkiah the priest, Ahikam*w* son of Shaphan, Acbor son of Micaiah, Shaphan the secretary and Asaiah the king's attendant: 13"Go and inquire of the LORD for me and for the people and for all Judah about what is written in this book that has been found. Great is the LORD's anger*x* that burns against us because our fathers have not obeyed the words of this book; they have not acted in accordance with all that is written there concerning us."

14Hilkiah the priest, Ahikam, Acbor, Shaphan and Asaiah went to speak to the prophetess Huldah, who was the wife of Shallum son of Tikvah, the son of Harhas, keeper of the wardrobe. She lived in Jerusalem, in the Second District.

15She said to them, "This is what the LORD, the God of Israel, says: Tell the man who sent you to me, 16'This is what the LORD says: I am going to bring disaster*y* on this place and its people, according to everything written in the book*z* the king of Judah has read. 17Because they have forsaken*a* me and burned incense to other gods and provoked me to anger by all the idols their hands have made,*a* my anger will burn against this place and will not be quenched.' 18Tell the king of Judah, who sent you to inquire*b* of the LORD, 'This is what the LORD, the God of Israel, says concerning the words you heard: 19Because your heart was responsive and you humbled*c* yourself before the LORD when you heard what I have spoken against this place and its people, that they would become accursed*d* and laid waste,*e* and because you tore your robes and wept in my presence, I have heard you, declares the LORD. 20Therefore I will gather you to your fathers, and you will be buried in peace.*f* Your eyes will not see all the disaster I am going to bring on this place.' "

So they took her answer back to the king.

Josiah Renews the Covenant

23 Then the king called together all the elders of Judah and Jerusalem. 2He went up to the temple of the LORD with the men of Judah, the people of Jerusalem, the priests and the prophets—all the people from the least to the greatest. He read*g* in their hearing all the words of the Book of the Covenant, which had

a 17 Or by everything they have done

The "Book of the Law," called the "Book of the Covenant" in 23:2, was probably either the entire Pentateuch (first five books of the OT) or all or part of the book of Deuteronomy. Josiah's reaction to hearing it read was one of immediate remorse. The king's grief was twofold: over Judah's guilt and her judgment. With sorrowful heart, Josiah sent a commission to the prophetess Huldah (v. 14) to inquire as to God's present intention regarding Jerusalem.

If asked to honestly assess your own spiritual character, what would you say? If you are a committed Christian, this "assignment" might be made more difficult by your natural spiritual humility. Perhaps a more objective approach might be to recall the promises you made at the time of your conversion or rededication to the Lord. How well have you followed through? If life's daily demands and/or the tyranny or the urgent have pushed some commitments into the background, how can you reassess and realign your priorities?

2 Kings 23:1–30

Josiah's spiritual reforms weren't just negative toward Baal; they were positive toward God. He gave instructions that the Passover be observed, in strict accordance with the law (v. 21; cf. 2 Chron. 35:1–19). Still in the 18th year of Josiah's reign (see previous "There and Then"), the Passover was commemorated in Jerusalem—a celebration the likes of which hadn't been seen since Samuel's day (vv. 22–23; cf. 2 Chron. 35:18).

The account of Josiah's life ends, though, on a sad note. Despite all he had done to remove Judah's idolatry, the effects of Manasseh's gross spiritual wickedness were to have a permanent effect on the nation (vv. 26–27). Judah's outward worship experience had been set in order, but the people's confession was superficial. With Josiah's passing, their internal condition would quickly resurface (cf. Jer. 5).

Can a godly leader acting alone really change hearts? Sadly, the answer doesn't require much

been found in the temple of the LORD. 3The king stood by the pillar and renewed
the covenant[h] in the presence of the LORD—to follow[i] the LORD and keep his commands, regulations and decrees with all his heart and all his soul, thus confirming
the words of the covenant written in this book. Then all the people pledged themselves to the covenant.
4The king ordered Hilkiah the high priest, the priests next in rank and the doorkeepers[j] to remove[k] from the temple of the LORD all the articles made for Baal and
Asherah and all the starry hosts. He burned them outside Jerusalem in the fields of
the Kidron Valley and took the ashes to Bethel. 5He did away with the pagan priests
appointed by the kings of Judah to burn incense on the high places of the towns
of Judah and on those around Jerusalem—those who burned incense to Baal, to the
sun and moon, to the constellations and to all the starry hosts.[l] 6He took the
Asherah pole from the temple of the LORD to the Kidron Valley outside Jerusalem
and burned it there. He ground it to powder and scattered the dust over the graves
of the common people.[m] 7He also tore down the quarters of the male shrine prostitutes,[n] which were in the temple of the LORD and where women did weaving for
Asherah.
8Josiah brought all the priests from the towns of Judah and desecrated the high
places, from Geba[o] to Beersheba, where the priests had burned incense. He broke
down the shrines[a] at the gates—at the entrance to the Gate of Joshua, the city governor, which is on the left of the city gate. 9Although the priests of the high places
did not serve[p] at the altar of the LORD in Jerusalem, they ate unleavened bread with
their fellow priests.
10He desecrated Topheth,[q] which was in the Valley of Ben Hinnom,[r] so no one
could use it to sacrifice his son[s] or daughter in[b] the fire to Molech. 11He removed
from the entrance to the temple of the LORD the horses that the kings of Judah had
dedicated to the sun. They were in the court near the room of an official named Na-
than-Melech. Josiah then burned the chariots dedicated to the sun.[t]
12He pulled down the altars the kings of Judah had erected on the roof[u] near the
upper room of Ahaz, and the altars Manasseh had built in the two courts[v] of the
temple of the LORD. He removed them from there, smashed them to pieces and
threw the rubble into the Kidron Valley. 13The king also desecrated the high places that were east of Jerusalem on the south of the Hill of Corruption—the ones Solomon[w] king of Israel had built for Ashtoreth the vile goddess of the Sidonians, for
Chemosh the vile god of Moab, and for Molech[c] the detestable god of the people
of Ammon. 14Josiah smashed[x] the sacred stones and cut down the Asherah poles
and covered the sites with human bones.
15Even the altar[y] at Bethel, the high place made by Jeroboam[z] son of Nebat, who
had caused Israel to sin—even that altar and high place he demolished. He burned
the high place and ground it to powder, and burned the Asherah pole also. 16Then
Josiah[a] looked around, and when he saw the tombs that were there on the hillside,
he had the bones removed from them and burned on the altar to defile it, in accordance with the word of the LORD proclaimed by the man of God who foretold these
things.
17The king asked, "What is that tombstone I see?"
The men of the city said, "It marks the tomb of the man of God who came from
Judah and pronounced against the altar of Bethel the very things you have done
to it."
18"Leave it alone," he said. "Don't let anyone disturb his bones[b]." So they spared
his bones and those of the prophet who had come from Samaria.
19Just as he had done at Bethel, Josiah removed and defiled all the shrines at the
high places that the kings of Israel had built in the towns of Samaria that had pro-

23:3 [h] 2Ki 11:14,17 [i] Dt 13:4
23:4 [j] 2Ki 25:18 [k] 2Ki 21:7
23:5 [l] 2Ki 21:3; Jer 8:2
23:6 [m] Jer 26:23
23:7 [n] 1Ki 14:24; 15:12; Eze 16:16
23:8 [o] 1Ki 15:22
23:9 [p] Eze 44:10-14
23:10 [q] Isa 30:33; Jer 7:31,32; 19:6 [r] Jos 15:8 [s] Lev 18:21; Dt 18:10
23:11 [t] Dt 4:19
23:12 [u] Jer 19:13; Zep 1:5 [v] 2Ki 21:5
23:13 [w] 1Ki 11:7
23:14 [x] Ex 23:24; Dt 7:5, 25
23:15 [y] 1Ki 13:1-3 [z] 1Ki 12:33
23:16 [a] 1Ki 13:2
23:18 [b] 1Ki 13:31

[a] 8 Or *high places* [b] 10 Or *to make his son or daughter pass through* [c] 13 Hebrew *Milcom*

thought. It's easy to get caught up in the momentum a magnetic Christian leader can stir up. But unless the poles of our hearts are truly and permanently attracted to the One to whom that leader points, nothing much will come of the efforts.

23:20
c Ex 22:20;
2Ki 10:25; 11:18
d 1Ki 13:2
23:21
e Ex 12:11; Nu 9:2;
Dt 16:1-8

voked the LORD to anger. [20]Josiah slaughtered[c] all the priests of those high places on the altars and burned human bones[d] on them. Then he went back to Jerusalem.

[21]The king gave this order to all the people: "Celebrate the Passover[e] to the LORD your God, as it is written in this Book of the Covenant." [22]Not since the days of the judges who led Israel, nor throughout the days of the kings of Israel and the kings of Judah, had any such Passover been observed. [23]But in the eighteenth year of King Josiah, this Passover was celebrated to the LORD in Jerusalem.

23:24
f Lev 19:31;
Dt 18:11; 2Ki 21:6
g Ge 31:19

[24]Furthermore, Josiah got rid of the mediums and spiritists,[f] the household gods,[g] the idols and all the other detestable things seen in Judah and Jerusalem. This he did to fulfill the requirements of the law written in the book that Hilkiah the priest had discovered in the temple of the LORD. [25]Neither before nor after Josiah was there a king like him who turned[h] to the LORD as he did—with all his heart and with all his soul and with all his strength, in accordance with all the Law of Moses.

23:25
h 2Ki 18:5

23:26
i 2Ki 21:12;
Jer 15:4
23:27
j 2Ki 21:13
k 2Ki 18:11

[26]Nevertheless, the LORD did not turn away from the heat of his fierce anger, which burned against Judah because of all that Manasseh[i] had done to provoke him to anger. [27]So the LORD said, "I will remove[j] Judah also from my presence[k] as I removed Israel, and I will reject Jerusalem, the city I chose, and this temple, about which I said, 'There shall my Name be.'[a]"

[28]As for the other events of Josiah's reign, and all he did, are they not written in the book of the annals of the kings of Judah?

23:29
l Jer 46:2
m Zec 12:11

[29]While Josiah was king, Pharaoh Neco[l] king of Egypt went up to the Euphrates River to help the king of Assyria. King Josiah marched out to meet him in battle, but Neco faced him and killed him at Megiddo.[m] [30]Josiah's servants brought his body in a chariot[n] from Megiddo to Jerusalem and buried him in his own tomb. And the people of the land took Jehoahaz son of Josiah and anointed him and made him king in place of his father.

23:30
n 2Ki 9:28

Jehoahaz King of Judah

23:31
o 1Ch 3:15;
Jer 22:11
p 2Ki 24:18

[31]Jehoahaz[o] was twenty-three years old when he became king, and he reigned in Jerusalem three months. His mother's name was Hamutal[p] daughter of Jeremiah; she was from Libnah. [32]He did evil in the eyes of the LORD, just as his fathers had done. [33]Pharaoh Neco put him in chains at Riblah[q] in the land of Hamath[b][r] so that he

23:33
q 2Ki 25:6
r 1Ki 8:65

a 27 1 Kings 8:29   b 33 Hebrew; Septuagint (see also 2 Chron. 36:3) *Neco at Riblah in Hamath removed him*

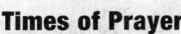

23:30

Times of Prayer

Prayer is first and foremost a matter of the believer's heart before God. The Old Testament mentions appointed times for prayer. Specifically, the Psalms speak of the faithful praying in the morning (Ps. 5:3), sometimes even before dawn (119:147). Elsewhere the psalmists uttered prayers of lament in the morning, at noon, and in the evening (55:17). It seems that morning and evening prayers were common, patterned after the morning and evening sacrifices of the temple liturgy (1 Chron. 23:30). Finally, like the apostle Paul's injunction for believers to "pray continually" (1 Thess. 5:17), the psalmists encouraged recurrent prayer (Ps. 72:15; 105:4).

In the fourth century, Basil of Caesarea drew up a set of monastic rules for Eastern Christianity that included eight daily appointments ("offices") for prayer. Later Benedict of Nursia (c. A.D. 530) developed a similar daily office of prayer for Western Christianity. The daily cycle of prayer, whether in the early church or later monastic practice, was an attempt to follow Paul's instruction to the Thessalonians, above. Eventually a standardized observance of a daily cycle of prayer emerged in the tradition of the Christian church. Following is one example of the standardized format:

Lauds: at daybreak
Prime: in the early morning (after lauds)
Terce: mid morning
Sext: at noon
None: mid afternoon
Vespers: at the end of the working day
Compline: before bedtime
Nocturns (vigils, matins): during the middle of the night

Some Christians today practice some form of daily office of prayer, though for most people the logistics are difficult to arrange around work/school schedules. When do you pray? Is it a regular/daily practice? Have you ever gone on a prayer retreat? How can you more regularly incorporate this vital spiritual discipline into your schedule?

Source: NIV Application Commentary,
1 & 2 Chronicles (2003:425–426)

might not reign in Jerusalem, and he imposed on Judah a levy of a hundred talents^a of silver and a talent^b of gold. ³⁴Pharaoh Neco made Eliakim^s son of Josiah king in place of his father Josiah and changed Eliakim's name to Jehoiakim. But he took Jehoahaz and carried him off to Egypt, and there he died.^t ³⁵Jehoiakim paid Pharaoh Neco the silver and gold he demanded. In order to do so, he taxed the land and exacted the silver and gold from the people of the land according to their assessments.^u

Jehoiakim King of Judah

³⁶Jehoiakim^v was twenty-five years old when he became king, and he reigned in Jerusalem eleven years. His mother's name was Zebidah daughter of Pedaiah; she was from Rumah. ³⁷And he did evil in the eyes of the LORD, just as his fathers had done.

24 During Jehoiakim's reign, Nebuchadnezzar^w king of Babylon invaded the land, and Jehoiakim became his vassal for three years. But then he changed his mind and rebelled against Nebuchadnezzar. ²The LORD sent Babylonian,^c Aramean,^x Moabite and Ammonite raiders against him. He sent them to destroy^y Judah, in accordance with the word of the LORD proclaimed by his servants the prophets. ³Surely these things happened to Judah according to the LORD's command,^z in order to remove them from his presence because of the sins of Manasseh^a and all he had done, ⁴including the shedding of innocent blood.^b For he had filled Jerusalem with innocent blood, and the LORD was not willing to forgive.

⁵As for the other events of Jehoiakim's reign, and all he did, are they not written in the book of the annals of the kings of Judah? ⁶Jehoiakim rested^c with his fathers. And Jehoiachin his son succeeded him as king.

---

^a 33 That is, about 3 3/4 tons (about 3.4 metric tons)   ^b 33 That is, about 75 pounds (about 34 kilograms)   ^c 2 Or *Chaldean*

23:34
^s 1Ch 3:15;
2Ch 36:5-8
^t Jer 22:12;
Eze 19:3-4

23:35
^u ver 33

23:36
^v Jer 26:1

24:1
^w Jer 25:1,9;
Da 1:1

24:2
^x Jer 35:11
^y Jer 25:9

24:3
^z 2Ki 18:25
^a 2Ki 21:12; 23:26
24:4
^b 2Ki 21:16

24:6
^c Jer 22:19

---

2 Kings 23:31–35

At Josiah's death, the people selected as king his son Shallum, who took the throne name Jehoahaz (cf. 1 Chron. 3:15 with Jer. 22:11–12). Josiah's oldest son, Johanan, had probably died much earlier. Eliakim, next in line by age, was passed over, possibly because his mother held a less favored status than Jehoahaz's.

Jehoahaz was no Josiah—nor were any other of Josiah's sons. His downfall was swift in coming. Within three months Egypt's Pharaoh Neco took him captive, replacing him with his brother Eliakim, whom Neco renamed Jehoiakim. A far cry from his godly father, Jehoiakim was to lead Judah into still deeper trouble, both spiritually and politically.

Josiah had been Judah's last gasp. With his passing the nation had lost one of her choicest saints and finest kings. Josiah died tragically (v. 29; cf. 2 Chron. 35:20–24)—though he was thereby spared the greater tragedy of witnessing the death of his nation only 23 years later. It's common today to hear predictions of the demise of the West, the result in large part of corruption and immorality. Yet voices like Josiah's are still being heard around us. Who are some of these courageous and vocal saints? Do you feel that their recommended reforms are having an effect on our culture?

2 Kings 23:36—24:7

Jehoiakim and Judah were soon to change masters. After defeating the combined Assyrian and Egyptian forces at Carchemish in 605 B.C., Nebuchadnezzar and the Babylonians gained control of the eastern Mediterranean world. Jehoiakim served Nebuchadnez-

zar for the next three years (24:1). But when Pharaoh Neco turned back Nebuchadnezzar's forces at the Egyptian border, Jehoiakim rebelled against Nebuchadnezzar, though Jeremiah had warned him against doing so (Jer. 27:7–11).

Nebuchadnezzar's harassment found its ultimate origin in God's command to bring judgment to a wicked Judah that had followed in the train of Manasseh's wickedness. The prophets had repeatedly warned against this very judgment (2 Kings 24:3–4; cf., e.g., Jer. 15:1–9; Hab. 1:2–6; Zeph. 1:4–13; 3:1–7). Jehoiakim died shortly before Jerusalem's surrender to the Babylonians in 597 B.C. (v. 12), but the cause of his death is uncertain (cf. 2 Chron. 36:6).

Chapter 24:3–4 begins and ends with strong—even surprising—language: "Surely these things happened to Judah according to the LORD's command . . . the LORD was not willing to forgive." To the end, the prophets proclaimed God's willingness to forgive—unless his people refused to repent (e.g., Jer. 8:4–5; Ezek. 18:30–32). Based on his covenant with them, the Lord was justified, if not obligated, to ultimately punish the Israelites (cf. Deut. 28).

The situation today, following Christ's once-for-all-time atoning sacrifice, is vastly altered from that of Old Testament days. But we know from New Testament sources that God may still wash his hands of persistently, blatantly impenitent people (cf. Rom. 1:18-32; Heb. 10:26–31; 2 Peter 2:20–22). On what do you base your confidence in God's renewed and repeated forgiveness? How does that knowledge affect your behavior and lifestyle?

24:7
d Ge 15:18
e Jer 37:5-7; 46:2

7The king of Egypt[d] did not march out from his own country again, because the king of Babylon[e] had taken all his territory, from the Wadi of Egypt to the Euphrates River.

Jehoiachin King of Judah

24:8
f 1Ch 3:16

8Jehoiachin[f] was eighteen years old when he became king, and he reigned in Jerusalem three months. His mother's name was Nehushta daughter of Elnathan; she was from Jerusalem. 9He did evil in the eyes of the LORD, just as his father had done.

24:10
g Da 1:1

10At that time the officers of Nebuchadnezzar[g] king of Babylon advanced on Jerusalem and laid siege to it, 11and Nebuchadnezzar himself came up to the city while his officers were besieging it. 12Jehoiachin king of Judah, his mother, his attendants, his nobles and his officials all surrendered[h] to him.

24:12
h 2Ki 25:27;
Jer 22:24-30; 24:1;
25:1; 29:2; 52:28
24:13
i 2Ki 20:17
j 2Ki 25:15; Isa 39:6
k 2Ki 25:14;
Jer 20:5; 1Ki 7:51
24:14
m Jer 24:1; 52:28
n 2Ki 25:12;
Jer 40:7; 52:16

In the eighth year of the reign of the king of Babylon, he took Jehoiachin prisoner. 13As the LORD had declared,[i] Nebuchadnezzar removed all the treasures[j] from the temple of the LORD and from the royal palace, and took away all the gold articles[k] that Solomon[l] king of Israel had made for the temple of the LORD. 14He carried into exile[m] all Jerusalem: all the officers and fighting men, and all the craftsmen and artisans—a total of ten thousand. Only the poorest[n] people of the land were left.

24:15
o Jer 22:24-28
p Est 2:6;
Eze 17:12-14

15Nebuchadnezzar took Jehoiachin captive to Babylon. He also took from Jerusalem to Babylon the king's mother,[o] his wives, his officials and the leading men[p] of the land. 16The king of Babylon also deported to Babylon the entire force of seven thousand fighting men, strong and fit for war, and a thousand craftsmen and artisans.[q] 17He made Mattaniah, Jehoiachin's uncle, king in his place and changed his name to Zedekiah.[r]

24:16
q Jer 52:28
24:17
r 1Ch 3:15;
2Ch 36:11; Jer 37:1

Zedekiah King of Judah

24:18
s Jer 52:1
t 2Ki 23:31

18Zedekiah[s] was twenty-one years old when he became king, and he reigned in Jerusalem eleven years. His mother's name was Hamutal[t] daughter of Jeremiah; she was from Libnah. 19He did evil in the eyes of the LORD, just as Jehoiakim had done.

24:20
u Dt 4:26; 29:27

20It was because of the LORD's anger that all this happened to Jerusalem and Judah, and in the end he thrust[u] them from his presence.

The Fall of Jerusalem

Now Zedekiah rebelled against the king of Babylon.

25:1
v Jer 34:1-7

25 So in the ninth year of Zedekiah's reign, on the tenth day of the tenth month, Nebuchadnezzar[v] king of Babylon marched against Jerusalem with

---

2 Kings 24:8–17

🔑 His father dead, young Jehoiachin faced the specter of Nebuchadnezzar's advancing armies. He could expect no help from Egypt; Pharaoh Neco was in no position to challenge Nebuchadnezzar again (cf. v. 7). And the young king lacked the spiritual commitment and maturity to utilize godly wisdom.

Ultimately, having taken his hostages in charge, Nebuchadnezzar stripped the palace and temple of their treasures as spoils of war. The Babylonian king perpetuated the deportation system made famous by the Assyrians (cf. 17:24), seizing 10,000 of Jerusalem's leaders from every walk of life. With only the poorest, least skilled people of the land remaining, he could assume that Jerusalem would cause no further trouble.

📖 Think about a time in your life when you were backed against a wall. Were you able to extricate yourself "on your own," or did you request (and receive) help from other people—and/or directly from God? In times of personal crisis, our own level of maturity (spiritual, intellectual, and emotional) can make a tremendous difference in terms of our ability to be receptive and responsive to the help God has to offer, either directly or through his agents here on Earth.

2 Kings 24:18–20a

🔑 Nebuchadnezzar installed Josiah's remaining son, Mattaniah (whom he renamed Zedekiah), on the throne (v. 17). Jerusalem had been spared momentarily, but its demise was certain. Not only was Zedekiah no better than Josiah's other descendants (cf. 23:32,37; 24:9), but even this latest judgment of God through the Babylonians had had no effect on his stubbornly apostate people.

📖 Wicked Judah continued to ignore divine chastisement (cf. Jer. 37:1–2). How can you determine whether or not adverse circumstances in your life reflect God's judgment/discipline (cf. Heb. 12:5–11)? The fact is that we don't always know why bad things happen. But God generally gives us liberal cues when something in our lifestyle or decision-making process is counterproductive to our own well-being or to that of others. How well are you listening?

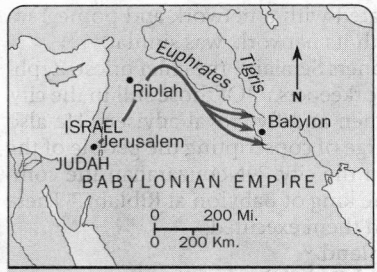

Exile of Judah (25:1)

Then: The fall of Jerusalem, the City of David, and the exile to Babylon were symbolic of total defeat.

Now: Jerusalem occupies the same central place in the hearts of modern Jews as it did for these ancient Judahites.

his whole army. He encamped outside the city and built siege works [w] all around it. [2]The city was kept under siege until the eleventh year of King Zedekiah. [3]By the ninth day of the ⌊fourth⌋[a] month the famine[x] in the city had become so severe that there was no food for the people to eat. [4]Then the city wall was broken through,[y] and the whole army fled at night through the gate between the two walls near the king's garden, though the Babylonians[b] were surrounding[z] the city. They fled toward the Arabah,[c] [5]but the Babylonian[d] army pursued the king and overtook him in the plains of Jericho. All his soldiers were separated from him and scattered,[a] [6]and he was captured.[b] He was taken to the king of Babylon at Riblah,[c] where sentence was pronounced on him. [7]They killed the sons of Zedekiah before his eyes. Then they put out his eyes, bound him with bronze shackles and took him to Babylon.[d]

[8]On the seventh day of the fifth month, in the nineteenth year of Nebuchadnezzar king of Babylon, Nebuzaradan commander of the imperial guard, an official of the king of Babylon, came to Jerusalem. [9]He set fire[e] to the temple of the Lord, the royal palace and all the houses of Jerusalem. Every important building he burned down.[f] [10]The whole Babylonian army, under the commander of the imperial guard, broke down the walls[g] around Jerusalem. [11]Nebuzaradan the commander of the guard carried into exile[h] the people who remained in the city, along with the rest of the populace and those who had gone over to the king of Babylon.[i] [12]But the commander left behind some of the poorest people[j] of the land to work the vineyards and fields.

[13]The Babylonians broke up the bronze pillars, the movable stands and the bronze Sea that were at the temple of the Lord and they carried the bronze to Babylon. [14]They also took away the pots, shovels, wick trimmers, dishes and all the bronze articles[k] used in the temple service. [15]The commander of the imperial guard took away the censers and sprinkling bowls—all that were made of pure gold or silver.

[16]The bronze from the two pillars, the Sea and the movable stands, which Solomon had made for the temple of the Lord, was more than could be weighed. [17]Each pillar[l] was twenty-seven feet[e] high. The bronze capital on top of one pillar

25:1
w Eze 24:2

25:3
x Jer 14:18; La 4:9

25:4
y Eze 33:21
z Jer 4:17

25:5
a Eze 12:14

25:6
b Jer 34:21-22
c 2Ki 23:33

25:7
d Jer 21:7; 32:4-5;
Eze 12:11

25:9
e Isa 60:7
f Ps 74:3-8;
Jer 2:15;
Am 2:5; Mic 3:12
25:10
g Ne 1:3
25:11
h 2Ki 24:14
i 2Ki 24:1
25:12
j 2Ki 24:14

25:14
k Ex 27:3;
1Ki 7:47-50

25:17
l 1Ki 7:15-22

---

a 3 See Jer. 52:6.   b 4 Or *Chaldeans*; also in verses 13, 25 and 26   c 4 Or *the Jordan Valley*   d 5 Or *Chaldean*; also in verses 10 and 24   e 17 Hebrew *eighteen cubits* (about 8.1 meters)

---

2 Kings 24:20b—25:26

One last time a king of Judah was lured into the foolish mistake of rebelling against Babylon. Nebuchadnezzar immediately responded, this time sending the full weight of his mighty army. After setting up headquarters in Riblah, he placed Jerusalem under total siege. Two and a half years later, on July 18, 586 B.C., the city fell.

Zedekiah and his remaining army, attempting to slip through a secluded gate, were overtaken. Before having his eyes gouged out, the king was forced to witness the execution of his own sons; his last sighted memory was the end result of his foolish disobedience. Judah's last king was led captive to Babylon, where he remained a prisoner until his death (cf. Jer. 52:11).

Anticlimactically, to the history of the united and divided kingdoms is added a note about the establishment of a new Judean vassal state. Of Jerusalem's prominent men, only Jeremiah and Gedaliah were left behind (cf. Jer. 39:11–14). Gedaliah, who shared Jeremiah's conviction of cooperating with the Babylonians, was the logical choice of governor over the newly formed district. Tragically, his success would be short-lived.

What kind of people would return to Jerusalem a generation later? A group who would make a lasting difference. Never again would idolatry and gross immorality characterize the Jewish people; Israel's flip-flop history would finally stabilize. Today in the United States we see an unprecedented five living generations: the G.I. Generation, the Silents, the Baby Boomers, the GenXers, and the Millenials. If you are an American, where do you fit in? What kind of legacy will your generation leave? What *lasting good* will result from your influence?

was four and a half feet[a] high and was decorated with a network and pomegranates of bronze all around. The other pillar, with its network, was similar.

25:18
m 1Ch 6:14;
Ezr 7:1; Ne 11:11
n Jer 21:1; 29:25

[18]The commander of the guard took as prisoners Seraiah[m] the chief priest, Zephaniah[n] the priest next in rank and the three doorkeepers. [19]Of those still in the city, he took the officer in charge of the fighting men and five royal advisers. He also took the secretary who was chief officer in charge of conscripting the people of the land and sixty of his men who were found in the city. [20]Nebuzaradan the commander took them all and brought them to the king of Babylon at Riblah. [21]There at Riblah, in the land of Hamath, the king had them executed.

25:21
o Ge 12:7;
Dt 28:64;
Jos 23:13;
2Ki 23:27
25:22
p Jer 39:14; 40:5,7

So Judah went into captivity, away from her land. [o]

[22]Nebuchadnezzar king of Babylon appointed Gedaliah[p] son of Ahikam, the son of Shaphan, to be over the people he had left behind in Judah. [23]When all the army officers and their men heard that the king of Babylon had appointed Gedaliah as governor, they came to Gedaliah at Mizpah—Ishmael son of Nethaniah, Johanan son of Kareah, Seraiah son of Tanhumeth the Netophathite, Jaazaniah the son of the Maacathite, and their men. [24]Gedaliah took an oath to reassure them and their men. "Do not be afraid of the Babylonian officials," he said. "Settle down in the land and serve the king of Babylon, and it will go well with you."

[25]In the seventh month, however, Ishmael son of Nethaniah, the son of Elishama, who was of royal blood, came with ten men and assassinated Gedaliah and also the men of Judah and the Babylonians who were with him at Mizpah. [26]At this, all the people from the least to the greatest, together with the army officers, fled to Egypt[q] for fear of the Babylonians.

25:26
q Isa 30:2; Jer 43:7

Jehoiachin Released

25:27
r 2Ki 24:12;
Jer 52:31-34
25:28
s Ezr 5:5; Ne 2:1;
Da 2:48

[27]In the thirty-seventh year of the exile of Jehoiachin king of Judah, in the year Evil-Merodach[b] became king of Babylon, he released Jehoiachin[r] from prison on the twenty-seventh day of the twelfth month. [28]He spoke kindly to him and gave him a seat of honor[s] higher than those of the other kings who were with him in Babylon. [29]So Jehoiachin put aside his prison clothes and for the rest of his life ate regularly at the king's table. [t] [30]Day by day the king gave Jehoiachin a regular allowance as long as he lived. [u]

25:29
t 2Sa 9:7
25:30
u Est 2:9; Jer 28:4

a 17 Hebrew *three cubits* (about 1.3 meters)   b 27 Also called *Amel-Marduk*

---

2 Kings 25:27–30

The author of Kings drew to a close his account of Judah's (mis)fortunes with this postscript concerning the later lot of Jehoiachin, who would have been considered Judah's last legitimate king. The Lord was disciplining his people through exile, but neither the people of Israel nor the house of David would be completely destroyed (cf. 2 Sam. 7:16).

And so the curtain fell on the drama of the divid-

ed monarchy. What had been a note of dark despair was illuminated by the light of God's gracious concern for his own. Spiritually minded believers might have seen in Jehoiachin's release an assurance of God's greater redemption of those who looked forward to him who gives release and eternal refreshment to all who long for his appearing (cf. 2 Tim. 4:8). Where do we stand in the great unfolding of salvation history? What privileged lives we lead! In what ways are you living out your gratitude?

INTRODUCTION TO

1 Chronicles

AUTHOR

According to Jewish tradition, Ezra wrote the Chronicles, but his authorship has been questioned. Many modern scholars simply refer to the author as "the Chronicler."

DATE WRITTEN

Although a specific date of composition can't be determined, Chronicles was probably written between 450 and 400 B.C.

ORIGINAL READERS

The books of Chronicles (1 and 2 Chronicles) were originally one book written to the post-exilic Jews to give them an accurate historical record and help them recognize their heritage and calling.

TIMELINE

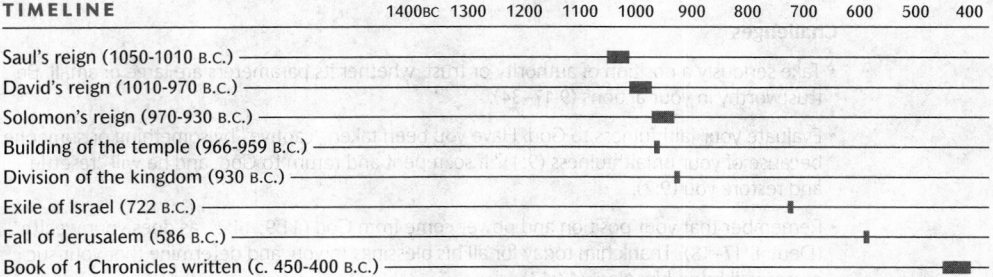

TIMELINE	1400BC	1300	1200	1100	1000	900	800	700	600	500	400
Saul's reign (1050-1010 B.C.)					■						
David's reign (1010-970 B.C.)					■						
Solomon's reign (970-930 B.C.)						■					
Building of the temple (966-959 B.C.)						■					
Division of the kingdom (930 B.C.)						■					
Exile of Israel (722 B.C.)							■				
Fall of Jerusalem (586 B.C.)									■		
Book of 1 Chronicles written (c. 450-400 B.C.)											■

THEMES

First Chronicles describes the reign of David, Israel's greatest king. It includes the following themes:

1. *The Davidic covenant.* The genealogies in 1:1—9:44 emphasize the tribes of Judah and Benjamin because Chronicles is primarily concerned with the Davidic dynasty. God promised David that one day a descendant of David would rule an everlasting kingdom (17:7–14), and Chronicles demonstrates God's continuing faithfulness to that promise.

2. *Preparations for temple worship.* Great emphasis is placed on the detailed preparations David made for construction of the temple by his son Solomon. David brought the ark back to Jerusalem (15:1—16:3) and appointed Levites to attend it (16:4–38). After discovering the temple site (21:18—22:1), he began gathering and stockpiling building materials (22:2–5) and organized the priests and Levites for future temple service (23:2—26:32). David then charged his son Solomon with the building of the temple (22:6–16; 28:9–10) and ordered Israel's leaders to help with its construction (22:17–19; 28:1–8). Near the end of his life, David passed on to Solomon the detailed blueprints for the temple that he had received from God (28:11–19) and

called the people to bring voluntary offerings for its construction (29:1–9). The temple building project was David's dream, and he provided "all [his] resources" (29:2) for its construction.

FAITH IN ACTION

The pages of 1 Chronicles contain life lessons and role models of faith—people who challenge believers to put their faith in action.

Role Models

- GATEKEEPERS (9:17–34) took care of the consecrated articles and furniture and were entrusted with the treasuries. Do you hold a position of trust? Do you carry out your responsibility with integrity?

- DAVID'S WARRIORS (11:10–47) are recorded by name in Scripture as a reminder that faith and loyalty are to be followed up with action. Their loyalty to David was inspired by their devotion to the Lord. How do you demonstrate your commitment to God?

- LEVITE MUSICIANS LED BY KENANIAH (15:16–22) were appointed to lead the congregation in musical celebration when the ark was brought to Jerusalem. Have you been gifted with musical ability? Do you use your skills to enhance your congregational worship?

- DAVID'S (29:1–9) liberality toward the temple building project inspired the people to be openhanded as well. Is your generosity an example to others?

- DAVID'S GOVERNMENT OFFICIALS (18:14–17) did what was "just and right" for all the people. Are you in a government or civil service role? Do you carry out your duties justly? Are you careful not to abuse your authority?

- SOLOMON (28:5–7) was chosen by God to lead the nation of Israel and oversee temple construction. But wholehearted devotion to God was required (28:9). What has God chosen for you to accomplish? What has he required of you?

Challenges

- Take seriously a position of authority or trust, whether its parameters are large or small. Be trustworthy in your actions (9:17–34).

- Evaluate your faithfulness to God. Have you been taken "captive" by something or someone because of your unfaithfulness (9:1)? If so, repent and return to God, and he will "resettle" and restore you (9:2).

- Remember that your position and power come from God (11:9; 14:2), as does your wealth (Deut. 8:17–18). Thank him today for all his blessings to you, and determine that your successes will bring *him* glory (14:17).

- Determine that your actions will reflect your faith and that a right motive doesn't necessarily negate the consequences of a wrong action (13:1–14).

- Respect the worship styles and traditions of all Christians (15:25–29). Broaden your appreciation for worship by visiting Christian congregations that express their worship differently from you.

- Be alert to situations in which Satan is "inciting" you to sin (21:1). Determine to submit to God and resist the devil (James 4:7; 1 Peter 5:8–9).

- Begin now to lay the groundwork for the next generation's successful completion of God's plan (22:1–16; 28:1–19). Remember to give your blessing to their work, pass on to them what you have started, give them the authority they need to complete the work, and enlist others to join them (28:20—29:9).

- Let your generosity be an example to others (29:1–3).

OUTLINE

I.   Genealogies: From Creation to Restoration (1–9)
II. The Reign of David (10–26)
     A. Saul's Death and David's Rise to Power (10–12)
     B. Return of the Ark (13)
     C. David's Reign Established (14–17)
     D. David's Victories and Census (18–21)
     E. Plans for Temple Construction and Organization (22–26)
III. Kingdom Organization and Staffing (27)
IV. Preparations for the Temple; Solomon's Coronation; David's Death (28–29)

Historical Records From Adam to Abraham

To Noah's Sons

1 Adam, [a] Seth, Enosh, 2Kenan, [b] Mahalalel, [c] Jared, [d] 3Enoch, [e] Methuselah, [f] Lamech, [g] Noah. [h]

4The sons of Noah: [a][i]
Shem, Ham and Japheth. [j]

The Japhethites

5The sons [b] of Japheth:
Gomer, Magog, Madai, Javan, Tubal, Meshech and Tiras.
6The sons of Gomer:
Ashkenaz, Riphath [c] and Togarmah.
7The sons of Javan:
Elishah, Tarshish, the Kittim and the Rodanim.

The Hamites

8The sons of Ham:
Cush, Mizraim, [d] Put and Canaan.
9The sons of Cush:
Seba, Havilah, Sabta, Raamah and Sabteca.
The sons of Raamah:
Sheba and Dedan.
10Cush was the father [e] of

---

[a] 4 Septuagint; Hebrew does not have this line.   [b] 5 *Sons* may mean *descendants* or *successors* or *nations*; also in verses 6-10, 17 and 20.   [c] 6 Many Hebrew manuscripts and Vulgate (see also Septuagint and Gen. 10:3); most Hebrew manuscripts *Diphath*   [d] 8 That is, Egypt; also in verse 11   [e] 10 *Father* may mean *ancestor* or *predecessor* or *founder*; also in verses 11, 13, 18 and 20.

Scripture reference column:
1:1 *a* Ge 5:1-32; Lk 3:36-38
1:2 *b* Ge 5:9 *c* Ge 5:12 *d* Ge 5:15
1:3 *e* Ge 5:18; Jude 1:14 *f* Ge 5:21 *g* Ge 5:25 *h* Ge 5:29
1:4 *i* Ge 6:10; 10:1 *j* Ge 5:32

---

1 Chronicles 1:1–27

God is everywhere assumed but nowhere named in the genealogies of 1 Chronicles. The Chronicler took for granted that his audience knew well both the Hebrew Scriptures and the stories and personalities associated with the names. This is important to understanding the rest of Chronicles as well.

Our books of 1 and 2 Chronicles, originally one work, were likely written between 450 and 400 B.C. For hundreds of years, the identity of Judah as a nation had been associated with Davidic kingship. The Babylonian exile of the previous century and its aftermath had disrupted this continuity, resulting in a state of confusion for the Jews concerning their identity as God's people.

The Chronicler's generation had misinterpreted earlier prophetic messages concerning the nature and timing of Israel's restoration. Like the first generation of expatriates who had returned from Babylon, they had expected much but had experienced little (Hag. 1:9).

We sometimes joke about them, but the reality of an identity crisis for an individual or group is no laughing matter—the resulting confusion makes for chaotic living. As believers today, our identity in Christ is secure (Eph. 1:3–14). And we can rest assured that the One who has proven faithful across generations from Adam forward will continue to lead us as well to our eternal destiny.

Nimrod, who grew to be a mighty warrior on earth.

¹¹ Mizraim was the father of
the Ludites, Anamites, Lehabites, Naphtuhites, ¹²Pathrusites, Casluhites
(from whom the Philistines came) and Caphtorites.

¹³ Canaan was the father of
Sidon his firstborn,ᵃ and of the Hittites, ¹⁴Jebusites, Amorites, Girgashites,
¹⁵Hivites, Arkites, Sinites, ¹⁶Arvadites, Zemarites and Hamathites.

The Semites

¹⁷ The sons of Shem:
Elam, Asshur, Arphaxad, Lud and Aram.
The sons of Aram:ᵇ
Uz, Hul, Gether and Meshech.

¹⁸ Arphaxad was the father of Shelah,
and Shelah the father of Eber.

¹⁹ Two sons were born to Eber:
One was named Peleg,ᶜ because in his time the earth was divided; his brother was named Joktan.

²⁰ Joktan was the father of
Almodad, Sheleph, Hazarmaveth, Jerah, ²¹Hadoram, Uzal, Diklah, ²²Obal,ᵈ
Abimael, Sheba, ²³Ophir, Havilah and Jobab. All these were sons of Joktan.

²⁴ Shem,ᵏ Arphaxad,ᵉ Shelah,
²⁵ Eber, Peleg, Reu,
²⁶ Serug, Nahor, Terah
²⁷ and Abram (that is, Abraham).

1:24
ᵏ Ge 10:21-25;
Lk 3:34-36

The Family of Abraham

²⁸ The sons of Abraham:
Isaac and Ishmael.

Descendants of Hagar

²⁹ These were their descendants:
Nebaioth the firstborn of Ishmael, Kedar, Adbeel, Mibsam, ³⁰Mishma, Dumah, Massa, Hadad, Tema, ³¹Jetur, Naphish and Kedemah. These were the
sons of Ishmael.

Descendants of Keturah

1:32
ˡ Ge 22:24
ᵐ Ge 10:7

³² The sons born to Keturah, Abraham's concubine:ˡ
Zimran, Jokshan, Medan, Midian, Ishbak and Shuah.
The sons of Jokshan:
Sheba and Dedan.ᵐ

³³ The sons of Midian:

ᵃ 13 Or *of the Sidonians, the foremost*   ᵇ 17 One Hebrew manuscript and some Septuagint
manuscripts (see also Gen. 10:23); most Hebrew manuscripts do not have this line.   ᶜ 19 *Peleg*
means *division.*   ᵈ 22 Some Hebrew manuscripts and Syriac (see also Gen. 10:28); most Hebrew
manuscripts *Ebal*   ᵉ 24 Hebrew; some Septuagint manuscripts *Arphaxad, Cainan* (see also note at
Gen. 11:10)

---

1 Chronicles 1:28–34

Interestingly, Abraham receives less attention in
the Chronicler's genealogies than Esau. Still, Abraham's
family is located strategically in the middle of the listing
of names from Adam in 1:1 to Jacob ("Israel"; see
"There and Then" for 2:1–2) in 2:1. If we keep in mind
the stories represented by the names, in one sense
Abraham's genealogy is flanked by destruction: Noah
and the flood at the front end and Esau and the eventual
annihilation of the Edomites on the other.

The links to Abraham and Jacob/Israel assured
the postexilic Jewish community that its members were
heirs of the covenant promises God had made to the patriarchs (Gen. 12:1–3; 17:3–14; 26:3–5, etc.). The entire
listing of genealogies is a lesson in God's faithfulness to
his covenant promises. Israel's worth and dignity lay not
in her changing circumstances but in the character and
plan of God. The same holds true today for Christ's
church and for each of us as individual believers.

Ephah, Epher, Hanoch, Abida and Eldaah.
All these were descendants of Keturah.

Descendants of Sarah
34 Abraham[n] was the father of Isaac.[o]
The sons of Isaac:
Esau and Israel.[p]

Esau's Sons
35 The sons of Esau:[q]
Eliphaz, Reuel,[r] Jeush, Jalam and Korah.
36 The sons of Eliphaz:
Teman, Omar, Zepho,[a] Gatam and Kenaz;
by Timna: Amalek.[b][s]
37 The sons of Reuel:[t]
Nahath, Zerah, Shammah and Mizzah.

The People of Seir in Edom
38 The sons of Seir:
Lotan, Shobal, Zibeon, Anah, Dishon, Ezer and Dishan.
39 The sons of Lotan:
Hori and Homam. Timna was Lotan's sister.
40 The sons of Shobal:
Alvan,[c] Manahath, Ebal, Shepho and Onam.
The sons of Zibeon:
Aiah and Anah.[u]
41 The son of Anah:
Dishon.
The sons of Dishon:
Hemdan,[d] Eshban, Ithran and Keran.
42 The sons of Ezer:
Bilhan, Zaavan and Akan.[e]
The sons of Dishan[f]:
Uz and Aran.

The Rulers of Edom
43 These were the kings who reigned in Edom before any Israelite king reigned[g]:
Bela son of Beor, whose city was named Dinhabah.
44 When Bela died, Jobab son of Zerah from Bozrah succeeded him as king.

Marginal references:
1:34 n Lk 3:34; o Ge 21:2-3; Mt 1:2; Ac 7:8; p Ge 17:5; 25:25-26
1:35 q Ge 36:19; r Ge 36:4
1:36 s Ex 17:14
1:37 t Ge 36:17
1:40 u Ge 36:2

---

a 36 Many Hebrew manuscripts, some Septuagint manuscripts and Syriac (see also Gen. 36:11); most Hebrew manuscripts *Zephi*   b 36 Some Septuagint manuscripts (see also Gen. 36:12); Hebrew *Gatam, Kenaz, Timna and Amalek*   c 40 Many Hebrew manuscripts and some Septuagint manuscripts (see also Gen. 36:23); most Hebrew manuscripts *Alian*   d 41 Many Hebrew manuscripts and some Septuagint manuscripts (see also Gen. 36:26); most Hebrew manuscripts *Hamran*   e 42 Many Hebrew and Septuagint manuscripts (see also Gen. 36:27); most Hebrew manuscripts *Zaavan, Jaakan*   f 42 Hebrew *Dishon*, a variant of *Dishan*   g 43 Or *before an Israelite king reigned over them*

---

1 Chronicles 1:35–54

As the text points out, each Edomite king (descendants of Esau) "died." The kings of Judah, of course, died too, but the Judahite people survived the collapse of the Davidic kingship, returned to Jerusalem, and rebuilt the city. The Chronicler's contrasting of Esau's and Israel's (Jacob's) genealogies may point to Malachi's assessment of these twins with respect to their covenant relationship with God: "I have loved [chosen] Jacob, but Esau I have hated [rejected]" (Mal. 1:2–3).

The stories of Abraham and Esau reflect contrasting responses to covenant relationship with the Lord. God wants to relate to us as well, in the terms outlined in his new covenant—clearly revealed to us in the New Testament. Our willingness to accept his invitation and open ourselves up to the intimacy he desires is critical to our spiritual well-being. This covenant relationship is a two-way proposition, involving for us both awesome privilege and serious responsibility.

1:45
v Ge 36:11

45 When Jobab died, Husham from the land of the Temanites [v] succeeded him as king.
46 When Husham died, Hadad son of Bedad, who defeated Midian in the country of Moab, succeeded him as king. His city was named Avith.
47 When Hadad died, Samlah from Masrekah succeeded him as king.
48 When Samlah died, Shaul from Rehoboth on the river [a] succeeded him as king.
49 When Shaul died, Baal-Hanan son of Acbor succeeded him as king.
50 When Baal-Hanan died, Hadad succeeded him as king. His city was named Pau, [b] and his wife's name was Mehetabel daughter of Matred, the daughter of Me-Zahab. 51 Hadad also died.

The chiefs of Edom were:
Timna, Alvah, Jetheth, 52 Oholibamah, Elah, Pinon, 53 Kenaz, Teman, Mibzar, 54 Magdiel and Iram. These were the chiefs of Edom.

Israel's Sons

2 These were the sons of Israel:
Reuben, Simeon, Levi, Judah, Issachar, Zebulun, 2 Dan, Joseph, Benjamin, Naphtali, Gad and Asher.

Judah

2:3
w Ge 29:35;
38:2-10
x Ge 38:5
y Ge 38:2
z Nu 26:19
2:4
a Ge 38:11-30
b Ge 11:31
c Ge 38:29
2:5
d Ge 46:12
e Nu 26:21

To Hezron's Sons

3 The sons of Judah: [w]
Er, Onan and Shelah. [x] These three were born to him by a Canaanite woman, the daughter of Shua. [y] Er, Judah's firstborn, was wicked in the LORD's sight; so the LORD put him to death. [z] 4 Tamar, [a] Judah's daughter-in-law, [b] bore him Perez [c] and Zerah. Judah had five sons in all.

5 The sons of Perez: [d]
Hezron [e] and Hamul.
6 The sons of Zerah:
Zimri, Ethan, Heman, Calcol and Darda [c]—five in all.

2:7
f Jos 7:1 g Jos 6:18

7 The son of Carmi:
Achar, [d][f] who brought trouble on Israel by violating the ban on taking devoted things. [e][g]

---

[a] 48 Possibly the Euphrates   [b] 50 Many Hebrew manuscripts, some Septuagint manuscripts, Vulgate and Syriac (see also Gen. 36:39); most Hebrew manuscripts *Pai*   [c] 6 Many Hebrew manuscripts, some Septuagint manuscripts and Syriac (see also 1 Kings 4:31); most Hebrew manuscripts *Dara*   [d] 7 *Achar* means *trouble*; *Achar* is called *Achan* in Joshua.   [e] 7 The Hebrew term refers to the irrevocable giving over of things or persons to the LORD, often by totally destroying them.

---

1 Chronicles 2:1–2

These two verses list the 12 sons of Jacob, who was later renamed Israel (Gen. 32:28). The Chronicler used only the name "Israel" for the patriarch in retelling the story of God's people. From birth, Jacob's name and character had been associated with deceit (see Gen. 25:26 and NIV text note). Since a name change in the Old Testament often indicated a change in a person's character or station in life, the Chronicler may have been suggesting a similar change for the remnant of Jacob's descendants—the Israelites—after their time in exile.

Can a leopard change its spots? People throughout history have voiced the question. The Chronicler's use of the name "Israel" points to the hope that change, even for scoundrels like Jacob, can be found in relationship with God. Today we rely on the apostle Paul's affirmation: "If anyone is in Christ, he is a new creation: the old has gone, the new has come!" (2 Cor. 5:17). What great news for anyone tired of his or her old, sin-spotted coat!

1 Chronicles 2:3—4:23

The deathbed blessing of Jacob/Israel over his son Judah anticipated Israelite kingship, as the "scepter" was promised to the tribe of Judah (Gen. 49:10). Centuries later this pledge was realized in the covenant of kingship God granted to David and his descendants (2 Sam. 7:4–17; 1 Chron. 17:4–15). Chronicles revived hope for Davidic kingship by setting the tribe of Judah and the family of David as the centerpiece of the genealogical prologue.

8 The son of Ethan:
Azariah.
9 The sons born to Hezron[h] were:
Jerahmeel, Ram and Caleb.[a]

From Ram Son of Hezron

10 Ram[i] was the father of
Amminadab,[j] and Amminadab the father of Nahshon,[k] the leader of the
people of Judah. 11 Nahshon was the father of Salmon,[b] Salmon the father
of Boaz, 12 Boaz[l] the father of Obed and Obed the father of Jesse.[m]
13 Jesse[n] was the father of
Eliab[o] his firstborn; the second son was Abinadab, the third Shimea, 14 the
fourth Nethanel, the fifth Raddai, 15 the sixth Ozem and the seventh David.
16 Their sisters were Zeruiah[p] and Abigail. Zeruiah's[q] three sons were Abishai, Joab[r] and Asahel. 17 Abigail was the mother of Amasa,[s] whose father was
Jether the Ishmaelite.

Caleb Son of Hezron

18 Caleb son of Hezron had children by his wife Azubah (and by Jerioth). These
were her sons: Jesher, Shobab and Ardon. 19 When Azubah died, Caleb[t]
married Ephrath, who bore him Hur. 20 Hur was the father of Uri, and Uri
the father of Bezalel.[u]
21 Later, Hezron lay with the daughter of Makir the father of Gilead[v] (he had married her when he was sixty years old), and she bore him Segub. 22 Segub was the
father of Jair, who controlled twenty-three towns in Gilead. 23 (But Geshur and
Aram captured Havvoth Jair,[c][w] as well as Kenath[x] with its surrounding settlements—sixty towns.) All these were descendants of Makir the father of Gilead.

24 After Hezron died in Caleb Ephrathah, Abijah the wife of Hezron bore him
Ashhur[y] the father[d] of Tekoa.

Jerahmeel Son of Hezron

25 The sons of Jerahmeel the firstborn of Hezron:
Ram his firstborn, Bunah, Oren, Ozem and[e] Ahijah. 26 Jerahmeel had anoth-
er wife, whose name was Atarah; she was the mother of Onam.
27 The sons of Ram the firstborn of Jerahmeel:
Maaz, Jamin and Eker.
28 The sons of Onam:
Shammai and Jada.
The sons of Shammai:
Nadab and Abishur.
29 Abishur's wife was named Abihail, who bore him Ahban and Molid.

a 9 Hebrew *Kelubai,* a variant of *Caleb* *b 11* Septuagint (see also Ruth 4:21); Hebrew *Salma*
c 23 Or *captured the settlements of Jair* *d 24* Father may mean *civic leader* or *military leader*; also in
verses 42, 45, 49-52 and possibly elsewhere. *e 25* Or *Oren and Ozem, by*

2:9
h Nu 26:21

2:10
i Lk 3:32-33
j Ex 6:23 k Nu 1:7

2:12
l Ru 2:1 m Ru 4:17

2:13
n Ru 4:17
o 1Sa 16:6

2:16
p 1Sa 26:6
q 2Sa 2:18
r 2Sa 2:13
2:17
s 2Sa 17:25

2:19
t ver 42,50

2:20
u Ex 31:2
2:21
v Nu 27:1

2:23
w Nu 32:41;
Dt 3:14; Jos 13:30
x Nu 32:42

2:24
y 1Ch 4:5

The Chronicler was intentional about where he wanted to take his audience through the vehicle of Israel's family tree. The genealogical prologue worked for him because his audience was familiar with the story of Hebrew history, in many cases even the names of the cast of thousands participating in that story. All he had to do was mention the names; his audience knew "the rest of the story" (cf. Deut. 6:6–7; Ps. 78:5–6).

Biblical literacy tests given to Christian young people over the past several years reveal the alarming trend of a lack of basic Bible knowledge. Though many youth (and adults) in the church use the Bible on a regu-

lar basis, few seem to know its stories. Small wonder, then, that the genealogies of Chronicles are better known as an antidote for insomnia than a soaring and profound theology of hope for a beleaguered community of faith adrift in a sea of religious and cultural pluralism (the theory that there is more than one brand of ultimate reality).

This is unfortunate for at least two reasons: (1) Today's community of faith is likewise threatened with getting sidetracked, if not shipwrecked, by religious and cultural pluralism; (2) If we want to know where the community of faith is headed, we need to know where it's been.

30 The sons of Nadab:

Seled and Appaim. Seled died without children.

31 The son of Appaim:

Ishi, who was the father of Sheshan.

Sheshan was the father of Ahlai.

32 The sons of Jada, Shammai's brother:

Jether and Jonathan. Jether died without children.

33 The sons of Jonathan:

Peleth and Zaza.

These were the descendants of Jerahmeel.

34 Sheshan had no sons—only daughters.

He had an Egyptian servant named Jarha. 35 Sheshan gave his daughter in marriage to his servant Jarha, and she bore him Attai.

2:36
z 1Ch 11:41

36 Attai was the father of Nathan,

Nathan the father of Zabad,[z]

37 Zabad the father of Ephlal,

Ephlal the father of Obed,

38 Obed the father of Jehu,

Jehu the father of Azariah,

39 Azariah the father of Helez,

Helez the father of Eleasah,

40 Eleasah the father of Sismai,

Sismai the father of Shallum,

41 Shallum the father of Jekamiah,

and Jekamiah the father of Elishama.

2:42
a ver 19

The Clans of Caleb

42 The sons of Caleb[a] the brother of Jerahmeel:

Mesha his firstborn, who was the father of Ziph, and his son Mareshah,[a] who was the father of Hebron.

43 The sons of Hebron:

2:45
b Jos 15:55
c Jos 15:58

Korah, Tappuah, Rekem and Shema. 44 Shema was the father of Raham, and Raham the father of Jorkeam. Rekem was the father of Shammai. 45 The son of Shammai was Maon,[b] and Maon was the father of Beth Zur.[c]

46 Caleb's concubine Ephah was the mother of Haran, Moza and Gazez. Haran was the father of Gazez.

47 The sons of Jahdai:

Regem, Jotham, Geshan, Pelet, Ephah and Shaaph.

2:49
d Jos 15:31
e Jos 15:16

48 Caleb's concubine Maacah was the mother of Sheber and Tirhanah. 49 She also gave birth to Shaaph the father of Madmannah[d] and to Sheva the father of Macbenah and Gibea. Caleb's daughter was Acsah.[e] 50 These were the descendants of Caleb.

2:50
f 1Ch 4:4 g ver 19

The sons of Hur[f] the firstborn of Ephrathah:

Shobal the father of Kiriath Jearim,[g] 51 Salma the father of Bethlehem, and Hareph the father of Beth Gader.

52 The descendants of Shobal the father of Kiriath Jearim were:

2:53
h 2Sa 23:38

Haroeh, half the Manahathites, 53 and the clans of Kiriath Jearim: the Ithrites,[h] Puthites, Shumathites and Mishraites. From these descended the Zorathites and Eshtaolites.

54 The descendants of Salma:

2:54
i Ezr 2:22; Ne 7:26;
12:28

Bethlehem, the Netophathites,[i] Atroth Beth Joab, half the Manahathites, the Zorites, 55 and the clans of scribes[b] who lived at Jabez: the Tirathites, Shimeathites and Sucathites. These are the Kenites[j] who came from Hammath,[k] the father of the house of Recab.[c][l]

2:55
j Ge 15:19;
Jdg 1:16; Jdg 4:11
k Jos 19:35
l 2Ki 10:15,23;
Jer 35:2-19

a 42 The meaning of the Hebrew for this phrase is uncertain.   b 55 Or of the Sopherites   c 55 Or father of Beth Recab

The Sons of David

3 These were the sons of David[m] born to him in Hebron:
  The firstborn was Amnon the son of Ahinoam of Jezreel;[n]
  the second, Daniel the son of Abigail[o] of Carmel;
² the third, Absalom the son of Maacah daughter of Talmai king of Geshur;
  the fourth, Adonijah[p] the son of Haggith;
³ the fifth, Shephatiah the son of Abital;
  and the sixth, Ithream, by his wife Eglah.
⁴ These six were born to David in Hebron,[q] where he reigned seven years and six months.[r]
David reigned in Jerusalem thirty-three years, ⁵ and these were the children born to him there:
  Shammua,[a] Shobab, Nathan and Solomon. These four were by Bathsheba[b][s] daughter of Ammiel. ⁶ There were also Ibhar, Elishua,[c] Eliphelet, ⁷ Nogah, Nepheg, Japhia, ⁸ Elishama, Eliada and Eliphelet—nine in all. ⁹ All these were the sons of David, besides his sons by his concubines. And Tamar[t] was their sister.[u]

The Kings of Judah

¹⁰ Solomon's son was Rehoboam,[v]
  Abijah his son,
  Asa his son,
  Jehoshaphat[w] his son,
¹¹ Jehoram[d][x] his son,
  Ahaziah[y] his son,
  Joash[z] his son,
¹² Amaziah[a] his son,
  Azariah his son,
  Jotham[b] his son,
¹³ Ahaz[c] his son,
  Hezekiah[d] his son,
  Manasseh[e] his son,
¹⁴ Amon[f] his son,
  Josiah[g] his son.
¹⁵ The sons of Josiah:
  Johanan the firstborn,
  Jehoiakim[h] the second son,
  Zedekiah[i] the third,
  Shallum[j] the fourth.
¹⁶ The successors of Jehoiakim:
  Jehoiachin[e][k] his son,
  and Zedekiah.[l]

The Royal Line After the Exile

¹⁷ The descendants of Jehoiachin the captive:
  Shealtiel[m] his son, ¹⁸ Malkiram, Pedaiah, Shenazzar,[n] Jekamiah, Hoshama and Nedabiah.[o]
¹⁹ The sons of Pedaiah:
  Zerubbabel[p] and Shimei.
  The sons of Zerubbabel:
  Meshullam and Hananiah.
  Shelomith was their sister.
²⁰ There were also five others:

3:1
m 1Ch 14:3; 28:5
n Jos 15:56
o 1Sa 25:42

3:2
p 1Ki 2:22

3:4
q 2Sa 5:4; 1Ch 29:27
r 2Sa 2:11; 5:5

3:5
s 2Sa 11:3; 12:24

3:9
t 2Sa 13:1
u 1Ch 14:4

3:10
v 1Ki 11:43; 14:21-31; 2Ch 12:16
w 2Ch 17:1-21:3

3:11
x 2Ki 8:16-24; 2Ch 21:1
y 2Ch 22:1-10
z 2Ki 11:1-12:21

3:12
a 2Ki 14:1-22; 2Ch 25:1-28
b Isa 1:1; Hos 1:1; Mic 1:1

3:13
c 2Ki 16:1-20; 2Ch 28:1; Isa 7:1
d 2Ki 18:1-20:21; 2Ch 29:1; Jer 26:19
e 2Ch 33:1

3:14
f 2Ki 21:19-26; 2Ch 33:21; Zep 1:1
g 2Ki 34:1; Jer 1:2; 3:6; 25:3

3:15
h 2Ki 23:34
i Jer 37:1
j 2Ki 23:31

3:16
k 2Ki 24:6,8; Mt 1:11 l 2Ki 24:18

3:17
m Ezr 3:2
3:18
n Ezr 1:8; 5:14
o Jer 22:30
3:19
p Ezr 2:2; 3:2; 5:2; Ne 7:7; 12:1; Hag 1:1; 2:2; Zec 4:6

---

a 5 Hebrew *Shimea*, a variant of *Shammua*   b 5 One Hebrew manuscript and Vulgate (see also Septuagint and 2 Samuel 11:3); most Hebrew manuscripts *Bathshua*   c 6 Two Hebrew manuscripts (see also 2 Samuel 5:15 and 1 Chron. 14:5); most Hebrew manuscripts *Elishama*   d 11 Hebrew *Joram*, a variant of *Jehoram*   e 16 Hebrew *Jeconiah*, a variant of *Jehoiachin*; also in verse 17

Hashubah, Ohel, Berekiah, Hasadiah and Jushab-Hesed.

21 The descendants of Hananiah:

Pelatiah and Jeshaiah, and the sons of Rephaiah, of Arnan, of Obadiah and of Shecaniah.

22 The descendants of Shecaniah:

3:22
q Ezr 8:2-3

Shemaiah and his sons:

Hattush, *q* Igal, Bariah, Neariah and Shaphat—six in all.

23 The sons of Neariah:

Elioenai, Hizkiah and Azrikam—three in all.

24 The sons of Elioenai:

Hodaviah, Eliashib, Pelaiah, Akkub, Johanan, Delaiah and Anani—seven in all.

4:1
r Ge 29:35; 46:12;
1Ch 2:3 *s* Nu 26:21

Other Clans of Judah

4 The descendants of Judah: *r*

Perez, Hezron, *s* Carmi, Hur and Shobal.

2 Reaiah son of Shobal was the father of Jahath, and Jahath the father of Ahumai and Lahad. These were the clans of the Zorathites.

3 These were the sons *a* of Etam:

Jezreel, Ishma and Idbash. Their sister was named Hazzelelponi. 4 Penuel was the father of Gedor, and Ezer the father of Hushah.

4:4
t 1Ch 2:50
u Ru 1:19

These were the descendants of Hur, *t* the firstborn of Ephrathah and father *b* of Bethlehem. *u*

4:5
v 1Ch 2:24

5 Ashhur *v* the father of Tekoa had two wives, Helah and Naarah.

6 Naarah bore him Ahuzzam, Hepher, Temeni and Haahashtari. These were the descendants of Naarah.

7 The sons of Helah:

Zereth, Zohar, Ethnan, 8 and Koz, who was the father of Anub and Hazzobebah and of the clans of Aharhel son of Harum.

9 Jabez was more honorable than his brothers. His mother had named him Jabez, *c* saying, "I gave birth to him in pain." 10 Jabez cried out to the God of Israel, "Oh, that you would bless me and enlarge my territory! Let your hand be with me, and keep me from harm so that I will be free from pain." And God granted his request.

11 Kelub, Shuhah's brother, was the father of Mehir, who was the father of Eshton. 12 Eshton was the father of Beth Rapha, Paseah and Tehinnah the father of Ir Nahash. *d* These were the men of Recah.

4:13
w Jos 15:17

13 The sons of Kenaz:

Othniel *w* and Seraiah.

The sons of Othniel:

Hathath and Meonothai. *e* 14 Meonothai was the father of Ophrah.

Seraiah was the father of Joab,

the father of Ge Harashim. *f* It was called this because its people were craftsmen.

15 The sons of Caleb son of Jephunneh:

Iru, Elah and Naam.

The son of Elah:

Kenaz.

16 The sons of Jehallelel:

Ziph, Ziphah, Tiria and Asarel.

4:17
x Ex 15:20

17 The sons of Ezrah:

Jether, Mered, Epher and Jalon. One of Mered's wives gave birth to Miriam, *x* Shammai and Ishbah the father of Eshtemoa. 18 (His Judean wife gave birth

---

a 3 Some Septuagint manuscripts (see also Vulgate); Hebrew *father*   *b 4* *Father* may mean *civic leader* or *military leader*; also in verses 12, 14, 17, 18 and possibly elsewhere.   *c 9* *Jabez* sounds like the Hebrew for *pain.*   *d 12* Or *of the city of Nahash*   *e 13* Some Septuagint manuscripts and Vulgate; Hebrew does not have *and Meonothai.*   *f 14* *Ge Harashim* means *valley of craftsmen.*

to Jered the father of Gedor, Heber the father of Soco, and Jekuthiel the father of Zanoah.ʸ) These were the children of Pharaoh's daughter Bithiah, whom Mered had married.
¹⁹The sons of Hodiah's wife, the sister of Naham:
the father of Keilahᶻ the Garmite, and Eshtemoa the Maacathite.ᵃ
²⁰The sons of Shimon:
Amnon, Rinnah, Ben-Hanan and Tilon.
The descendants of Ishi:
Zoheth and Ben-Zoheth.
²¹The sons of Shelahᵇ son of Judah:
Er the father of Lecah, Laadah the father of Mareshah and the clans of the linen workers at Beth Ashbea, ²²Jokim, the men of Cozeba, and Joash and Saraph, who ruled in Moab and Jashubi Lehem. (These records are from ancient times.) ²³They were the potters who lived at Netaim and Gederah; they stayed there and worked for the king.

Simeon

²⁴The descendants of Simeon:ᶜ
Nemuel, Jamin, Jarib,ᵈ Zerah and Shaul;
²⁵Shallum was Shaul's son, Mibsam his son and Mishma his son.
²⁶The descendants of Mishma:
Hammuel his son, Zaccur his son and Shimei his son.
²⁷Shimei had sixteen sons and six daughters, but his brothers did not have many children; so their entire clan did not become as numerous as the people of Judah. ²⁸They lived in Beersheba,ᵉ Moladah,ᶠ Hazar Shual, ²⁹Bilhah, Ezem,ᵍ Tolad, ³⁰Bethuel, Hormah,ʰ Ziklag, ³¹Beth Marcaboth, Hazar Susim, Beth Biri and Shaaraim.ⁱ These were their towns until the reign of David. ³²Their surrounding villages were Etam, Ain,ʲ Rimmon, Token and Ashanᵏ—five towns— ³³and all the villages around these towns as far as Baalath.ᵃ These were their settlements. And they kept a genealogical record.

³⁴Meshobab, Jamlech, Joshah son of Amaziah, ³⁵Joel, Jehu son of Joshibiah, the son of Seraiah, the son of Asiel, ³⁶also Elioenai, Jaakobah, Jeshohaiah, Asaiah, Adiel, Jesimiel, Benaiah, ³⁷and Ziza son of Shiphi, the son of Allon, the son of Jedaiah, the son of Shimri, the son of Shemaiah.

³⁸The men listed above by name were leaders of their clans. Their families increased greatly, ³⁹and they went to the outskirts of Gedorˡ to the east of the valley in search of pasture for their flocks. ⁴⁰They found rich, good pasture, and the land was spacious, peaceful and quiet.ᵐ Some Hamites had lived there formerly.
⁴¹The men whose names were listed came in the days of Hezekiah king of Judah. They attacked the Hamites in their dwellings and also the Meunitesⁿ who were there and completely destroyedᵇ them, as is evident to this day. Then they settled in their place, because there was pasture for their flocks. ⁴²And five hundred of these Sim-

---

ᵃ 33 Some Septuagint manuscripts (see also Joshua 19:8); Hebrew *Baal* ᵇ 41 The Hebrew term refers to the irrevocable giving over of things or persons to the LORD, often by totally destroying them.

---

1 Chronicles 4:24–43

📖 This passage offers insight on genealogical enrollment in ancient Israel—apparently a two-stage process of entering names and then cataloging them according to some type of arrangement. The theme of pastureland for the Simeonites' flocks and herds is repeated three times (vv. 39,40,41). The Chronicler's language here is similar to that of those psalms identifying the Israelites as the sheep of God's pasture (Ps. 37:3; 74:1; 79:13; 95:7, 100:3, etc.). The military tone echoes the prophetic blessing of Jacob over Simeon, who was given to anger and violence (cf. Gen. 49:5–7).

💻 Some in the Chronicler's day no doubt longed for the bygone era of their forefathers. But the genealogies reminded his contemporaries—and reminds us—that the Bible invites reflection on the past not to "take a sentimental journey" but because the act of remembering is educational. We live today, not trying to recapture a nostalgia-enhanced past, but with faith in God to fulfill his promises. Much like Chronicles, the book of Hebrews calls us to follow the example of faithful believers from every generation (cf. Heb. 11:1–40; 12:1).

4:18
ʸ Jos 15:34

4:19
ᶻ Jos 15:44
ᵃ Dt 3:14

4:21
ᵇ Ge 38:5

4:24
ᶜ Ge 29:33
ᵈ Nu 26:12

4:28
ᵉ Ge 21:14
ᶠ Jos 15:26
4:29
ᵍ Jos 15:29
4:30
ʰ Nu 14:45
4:31
ⁱ Jos 15:36
4:32
ʲ Nu 34:11
ᵏ Jos 15:42

4:39
ˡ Jos 15:58

4:40
ᵐ Jdg 18:7-10

4:41
ⁿ 2Ch 20:1; 26:7

4:42
o Ge 14:6
4:43
p 1Sa 15:8; 30:17;
2Sa 8:12; Est 3:1;
9:16

5:1
q Ge 29:32
r Ge 35:22; 49:4
s Ge 48:16,22;
49:26 t Ge 48:5
u 1Ch 26:10
5:2
v Ge 49:10,12
w 1Sa 9:16; 12:12;
2Sa 6:21; 1Ch 11:2;
2Ch 7:18; Ps 60:7;
Mic 5:2; Mt 2:6
x Ge 25:31
5:3
y Ge 29:32; 46:9;
Ex 6:14; Nu 26:5-11
z Nu 26:5

5:6
a ver 26; 2Ki 15:19;
16:10; 2Ch 28:20
5:7
b ver 17

5:8
c Nu 32:34

5:9
d Nu 32:26;
Jos 22:9
5:10
e ver 18-21

5:11
f Jos 13:24-28
g Dt 3:10;
Jos 13:11

eonites, led by Pelatiah, Neariah, Rephaiah and Uzziel, the sons of Ishi, invaded the hill country of Seir. o 43They killed the remaining Amalekites p who had escaped, and they have lived there to this day.

Reuben

5 The sons of Reuben q the firstborn of Israel (he was the firstborn, but when he defiled his father's marriage bed, r his rights as firstborn were given to the sons of Joseph s son of Israel; t so he could not be listed in the genealogical record in accordance with his birthright, u 2and though Judah v was the strongest of his brothers and a ruler w came from him, the rights of the firstborn x belonged to Joseph)— 3the sons of Reuben y the firstborn of Israel:

Hanoch, Pallu, z Hezron and Carmi.

4The descendants of Joel:

Shemaiah his son, Gog his son,

Shimei his son, 5Micah his son,

Reaiah his son, Baal his son,

6and Beerah his son, whom Tiglath-Pileser a a king of Assyria took into exile. Beerah was a leader of the Reubenites.

7Their relatives by clans, b listed according to their genealogical records:

Jeiel the chief, Zechariah, 8and Bela son of Azaz, the son of Shema, the son of Joel. They settled in the area from Aroer c to Nebo and Baal Meon. 9To the east they occupied the land up to the edge of the desert that extends to the Euphrates River, because their livestock had increased in Gilead. d

10During Saul's reign they waged war against the Hagrites e, who were defeated at their hands; they occupied the dwellings of the Hagrites throughout the entire region east of Gilead.

Gad

11The Gadites f lived next to them in Bashan, as far as Salecah: g

12Joel was the chief, Shapham the second, then Janai and Shaphat, in Bashan.

13Their relatives, by families, were:

Michael, Meshullam, Sheba, Jorai, Jacan, Zia and Eber—seven in all.

14These were the sons of Abihail son of Huri, the son of Jaroah, the son of Gilead, the son of Michael, the son of Jeshishai, the son of Jahdo, the son of Buz.

15Ahi son of Abdiel, the son of Guni, was head of their family.

a 6 Hebrew *Tilgath-Pilneser*, a variant of *Tiglath-Pileser*; also in verse 26

---

1 Chronicles 5:1–10

Chapter 5 records the genealogies of the two and a half tribes east of the Jordan River. The Chronicler recalled Reuben's crime of having had sex with his father's concubine in order to explain why Reuben forfeited the rights of the firstborn (v. 1; cf. Gen. 35:22; 49:3–4). This passage also reveals the Chronicler's view of the prominence of Judah over the Joseph tribes (Ephraim and Manasseh), who received the double portion of the firstborn in Reuben's place (2 Chron. 5:1; cf. Gen. 48:5,16,22).

But this passage, and the rest of the chapter, also contributes to the Chronicler's goal of including all the tribes—even those carried away by the Assyrians centuries earlier—in the ideal "all Israel" identity he sought for the postexilic community (cf. 9:1; 11:1–5; 12:38–40). This emphasis on "all Israel" was perhaps based on Ezekiel's prophecy of two sticks (Israel and Judah) being joined after the exile (Ezek. 37:15–23).

The Chronicler subtly warned his audience about spiritual complacency and arrogance based on Israel's status as God's "firstborn" (Ex. 4:22; cf. Deut. 9:5). We as Christians are members of the "church of the firstborn, whose names are written in heaven" (Heb. 12:23). Like Reuben and his tribe, we can be tempted to presume that our redemption is based on external circumstances such as the family we were born into, church membership, or church attendance—while ignoring our covenant obligations to love God and our neighbors (Luke 10:27).

1 Chronicles 5:11–22

As part of the genealogical record of Gad, the Chronicler focused on the theology of warfare. The war with the Hagrites and their allies was God's battle. The men of Reuben, Gad, and East Manasseh trusted in and prayed to God, and he answered their prayers by helping them in battle. The themes of trust in God, prayer in battle, and God's help in gaining victory are repeated throughout Chronicles (e.g., 12:18; 15:26; 2 Chron. 20:15; 25:8; 32:20–21).

16The Gadites lived in Gilead, in Bashan and its outlying villages, and on all the pasturelands of Sharon as far as they extended. 17All these were entered in the genealogical records during the reigns of Jotham[h] king of Judah and Jeroboam[i] king of Israel.

18The Reubenites, the Gadites and the half-tribe of Manasseh had 44,760 men ready for military service[j]—able-bodied men who could handle shield and sword, who could use a bow, and who were trained for battle. 19They waged war against the Hagrites, Jetur,[k] Naphish and Nodab. 20They were helped[l] in fighting them, and God handed the Hagrites and all their allies over to them, because they cried[m] out to him during the battle. He answered their prayers, because they trusted[n] in him. 21They seized the livestock of the Hagrites—fifty thousand camels, two hundred fifty thousand sheep and two thousand donkeys. They also took one hundred thousand people captive, 22and many others fell slain, because the battle[o] was God's. And they occupied the land until the exile.[p]

The Half-Tribe of Manasseh

23The people of the half-tribe of Manasseh were numerous; they settled in the land from Bashan to Baal Hermon, that is, to Senir (Mount Hermon).[q]

24These were the heads of their families: Epher, Ishi, Eliel, Azriel, Jeremiah, Hodaviah and Jahdiel. They were brave warriors, famous men, and heads of their families. 25But they were unfaithful[r] to the God of their fathers and prostituted[s] themselves to the gods of the peoples of the land, whom God had destroyed before them. 26So the God of Israel stirred up the spirit of Pul[t] king of Assyria (that is, Tiglath-Pileser[u] king of Assyria), who took the Reubenites, the Gadites and the half-tribe of Manasseh into exile. He took them to Halah,[v] Habor, Hara and the river of Gozan, where they are to this day.

Levi

6 The sons of Levi:[w]
Gershon, Kohath and Merari.
2The sons of Kohath:
Amram, Izhar, Hebron and Uzziel.
3The children of Amram:
Aaron, Moses and Miriam.
The sons of Aaron:

5:17 h 2Ki 15:32; i 2Ki 14:16,28
5:18 j Nu 1:3
5:19 k ver 10; Ge 25:15; 1Ch 1:31
5:20 l Ps 37:40; m 1Ki 8:44; 2Ch 13:14; 14:11; Ps 20:7-9; 22:5; n Ps 26:1; Da 6:23
5:22 o 2Ch 32:8; p 2Ki 15:29; 17:6
5:23 q Dt 3:8,9; SS 4:8
5:25 r Dt 32:15-18; 2Ki 17:7; 1Ch 9:1; 2Ch 26:16; s Ex 34:15
5:26 t 2Ki 15:19; u 2Ki 15:29; v 2Ki 17:6; 18:11
6:1 w Ge 46:11; Ex 6:16; Nu 26:57; 1Ch 23:6

Paul picked up the military theme in Ephesians 6:10–20, where he reminded his readers, including ourselves, that we wage war against "the powers of this dark world and against the spiritual forces of evil in the heavenly realms." This battle has a conclusion—rest in the land of covenant promise (cf. 1 Chron. 23:25–26; Heb. 4:6–11) and eternal life (Rom. 6:23). The act of prayer reminds us that the battle will be won only in the power of God's Spirit (Eph. 6:18; Phil. 4:13), and the victory proclaims God's glory to those still uncertain about Christianity (cf. Acts 20:24).

1 Chronicles 5:23–26
The seven clan leaders mentioned for East Manasseh are otherwise unknown. The adjectives "brave" and "famous" suggest that these men were also military commanders. The Chronicler contrasted human strength and greatness with the observation that these leaders were "unfaithful" to God. Like the psalmist, he knew that God delights not in human strength but in those who trust in his unfailing love (cf. Ps. 20:7; 147:10–11).
The failure of the Transjordan tribes wasn't so much neglect of prayer and trust as the substitution of foreign

gods as the objects of that prayer and trust. God tolerates no rival (Deut. 4:24), and his only possible response to idolatry among the Israelites was destruction and banishment (Deut. 4:25–27).

Paul ran the race of faith in Christ with vigor, focus, and self-discipline, ensuring that he wouldn't become a "loser," disqualified for the prize (1 Cor. 9:24–27). "Training in godliness" is vital to a spiritual fitness program (1 Tim. 4:7–8). Specific exercises include submitting our minds (Rom. 8:5–7), taming our speech (cf. James 3:7–8), controlling our bodily passions (Rom. 12:1–2), harnessing our emotions (James 1:19–20), maintaining proper motives (Phil. 2:3), and mentoring the next generation (Deut. 4:9–10; Eph. 6:1–4). How well rounded is your spiritual fitness regimen?

1 Chronicles 6:1–81
Along with Judah and Benjamin, Levi was one of three prominent tribes the Chronicler emphasized. Its importance is indicated by its central position in the genealogies and by its length, second only to the register of Judah (2:3—4:23).

6:3
x Lev 10:1
Nadab, Abihu, ˣ Eleazar and Ithamar.

⁴Eleazar was the father of Phinehas,
Phinehas the father of Abishua,
⁵Abishua the father of Bukki,
Bukki the father of Uzzi,
⁶Uzzi the father of Zerahiah,
Zerahiah the father of Meraioth,
⁷Meraioth the father of Amariah,
Amariah the father of Ahitub,

6:8
y 2Sa 8:17; 15:27;
Ezr 7:2
⁸Ahitub the father of Zadok, ʸ
Zadok the father of Ahimaaz,
⁹Ahimaaz the father of Azariah,
Azariah the father of Johanan,

6:10
z 1Ki 4:2; 6:1;
2Ch 3:1; 26:17-18
¹⁰Johanan the father of Azariah ᶻ (it was he who served as priest in the temple
Solomon built in Jerusalem),
¹¹Azariah the father of Amariah,
Amariah the father of Ahitub,
¹²Ahitub the father of Zadok,
Zadok the father of Shallum,

6:13
a 2Ki 22:1-20;
2Ch 34:9; 35:8
¹³Shallum the father of Hilkiah, ᵃ
Hilkiah the father of Azariah,

6:14
b 2Ki 25:18;
Ezr 2:2; Ne 11:11
6:15
c 2Ki 25:18;
Ne 12:1;
Hag 1:1,14; 2:2,4;
Zec 6:11
¹⁴Azariah the father of Seraiah, ᵇ
and Seraiah the father of Jehozadak.
¹⁵Jehozadak ᶜ was deported when the LORD sent Judah and Jerusalem into exile
by the hand of Nebuchadnezzar.

6:16
d Ge 29:34;
Ex 6:16; Nu 3:17-20
e Nu 26:57
¹⁶The sons of Levi: ᵈ
Gershon, ᵃ Kohath and Merari. ᵉ
¹⁷These are the names of the sons of Gershon:
Libni and Shimei.
¹⁸The sons of Kohath:

6:19
f Ge 46:11;
1Ch 23:21; 24:26
Amram, Izhar, Hebron and Uzziel.
¹⁹The sons of Merari: ᶠ
Mahli and Mushi.
These are the clans of the Levites listed according to their fathers:
²⁰Of Gershon:
Libni his son, Jehath his son,
Zimmah his son, ²¹Joah his son,
Iddo his son, Zerah his son
and Jeatherai his son.

6:22
g Ex 6:24
²²The descendants of Kohath:
Amminadab his son, Korah ᵍ his son,
Assir his son, ²³Elkanah his son,
Ebiasaph his son, Assir his son,

6:24
h 1Ch 15:5
²⁴Tahath his son, Uriel ʰ his son,
Uzziah his son and Shaul his son.
²⁵The descendants of Elkanah:

ᵃ 16 Hebrew *Gershom*, a variant of *Gershon*; also in verses 17, 20, 43, 62 and 71

Moses' blessing of the tribes before his death highlights two functions for Levi's descendants: "watching over" God's word through teaching the law and guarding God's covenant with Israel by attending to worship (Deut. 33:8–11). While "their fellow Levites" (1 Chron. 6:48) were called to assist the priests in numerous ways (cf. 23:28–31; 2 Chron. 30:16; 35:11), the sacrificial altar was the exclusive domain of the priests descended from Aaron (cf. Num. 18:1–7).

Originally, the priests and Levites were one of three general categories of Israelite leaders, also including the king and the prophets. The priests and Levites oversaw the sphere of religion; the king became God's anointed agent to rule the people justly, judge in righteousness, defend the poor and needy, and deliver Israel from her enemies; and the prophets functioned as the king and kingdom's spiritual and social conscience.

Amasai, Ahimoth,
26 Elkanah his son,[a] Zophai his son,
Nahath his son, 27 Eliab his son,
Jeroham his son, Elkanah[i] his son
and Samuel[j] his son.[b]
28 The sons of Samuel:
Joel[ck] the firstborn
and Abijah the second son.
29 The descendants of Merari:
Mahli, Libni his son,
Shimei his son, Uzzah his son,
30 Shimea his son, Haggiah his son
and Asaiah his son.

The Temple Musicians

31 These are the men[l] David put in charge of the music[m] in the house of the LORD after the ark came to rest there. 32 They ministered with music before the tabernacle, the Tent of Meeting, until Solomon built the temple of the LORD in Jerusalem. They performed their duties according to the regulations laid down for them.
33 Here are the men who served, together with their sons:
From the Kohathites:
Heman,[n] the musician,
the son of Joel,[o] the son of Samuel,
34 the son of Elkanah,[p] the son of Jeroham,
the son of Eliel, the son of Toah,
35 the son of Zuph, the son of Elkanah,
the son of Mahath, the son of Amasai,
36 the son of Elkanah, the son of Joel,
the son of Azariah, the son of Zephaniah,
37 the son of Tahath, the son of Assir,
the son of Ebiasaph, the son of Korah,[q]
38 the son of Izhar,[r] the son of Kohath,
the son of Levi, the son of Israel;
39 and Heman's associate Asaph,[s] who served at his right hand:
Asaph son of Berekiah, the son of Shimea,[t]
40 the son of Michael, the son of Baaseiah,[d]
the son of Malkijah, 41 the son of Ethni,
the son of Zerah, the son of Adaiah,
42 the son of Ethan, the son of Zimmah,
the son of Shimei, 43 the son of Jahath,
the son of Gershon, the son of Levi;
44 and from their associates, the Merarites, at his left hand:
Ethan son of Kishi, the son of Abdi,
the son of Malluch, 45 the son of Hashabiah,
the son of Amaziah, the son of Hilkiah,
46 the son of Amzi, the son of Bani,
the son of Shemer, 47 the son of Mahli,

6:27 i 1Sa 1:1 / 1Sa 1:20

6:28 k ver 33; 1Sa 8:2

6:31 l 1Ch 25:1; 2Ch 29:25-26; Ne 12:45 m 1Ch 9:33; 15:19; Ezr 3:10; Ps 68:25

6:33 n 1Ki 4:31; 1Ch 15:17; 25:1 o ver 28 **6:34** p 1Sa 1:1

6:37 q Ex 6:24 **6:38** r Ex 6:21

6:39 s 1Ch 25:1,9; 2Ch 29:13; Ne 11:17 t 1Ch 15:17

---

a 26 Some Hebrew manuscripts, Septuagint and Syriac; most Hebrew manuscripts Ahimoth 26 and Elkanah. The sons of Elkanah: b 27 Some Septuagint manuscripts (see also 1 Samuel 1:19,20 and 1 Chron. 6:33,34); Hebrew does not have and Samuel his son.   c 28 Some Septuagint manuscripts and Syriac (see also 1 Samuel 8:2 and 1 Chron. 6:33); Hebrew does not have Joel.   d 40 Most Hebrew manuscripts; some Hebrew manuscripts, one Septuagint manuscript and Syriac Maaseiah

---

📖 The essence of the Levites' ministry was encouraging a right relationship with God—a matter of the "heart" in Chronicles. Today, turning to God in repentance and faith in the word and work of Christ are still the prerequisites for entering the fellowship of God's people (Acts 3:19; Rom. 3:22,25). Our spiritual formation remains a heart issue (cf. Rom. 10:10; Eph. 6:6), and a lifestyle of loving obedience to God is still the true test of our spirituality (cf. 1 Jn. 2:3; 5:3).

the son of Mushi, the son of Merari,
the son of Levi.

6:48
u 1Ch 23:32

⁴⁸Their fellow Levites *u* were assigned to all the other duties of the tabernacle, the house of God. ⁴⁹But Aaron and his descendants were the ones who presented offerings on the altar *v* of burnt offering and on the altar of incense *w* in connection with all that was done in the Most Holy Place, making atonement for Israel, in accordance with all that Moses the servant of God had commanded.

6:49
v Ex 27:1-8
w Ex 30:1-7,10;
2Ch 26:18

⁵⁰These were the descendants of Aaron:
Eleazar his son, Phinehas his son,
Abishua his son, ⁵¹Bukki his son,
Uzzi his son, Zerahiah his son,
⁵²Meraioth his son, Amariah his son,
Ahitub his son, ⁵³Zadok *x* his son
and Ahimaaz his son.

6:53
x 2Sa 8:17

⁵⁴These were the locations of their settlements *y* allotted as their territory (they were assigned to the descendants of Aaron who were from the Kohathite clan, because the first lot was for them):

6:54
y Nu 31:10

⁵⁵They were given Hebron in Judah with its surrounding pasturelands. ⁵⁶But the fields and villages around the city were given to Caleb son of Jephunneh. *z*

6:56
z Jos 14:13; 15:13

⁵⁷So the descendants of Aaron were given Hebron (a city of refuge), and Libnah, *aa* Jattir, *b* Eshtemoa, ⁵⁸Hilen, Debir, *c* ⁵⁹Ashan, *d* Juttah *b* and Beth Shemesh, together with their pasturelands. ⁶⁰And from the tribe of Benjamin they were given Gibeon, *c* Geba, Alemeth and Anathoth, *e* together with their pasturelands.

6:57
a Nu 33:20
b Jos 15:48
6:58
c Jos 10:3
6:59
d Jos 15:42
6:60
e Jer 1:1

These towns, which were distributed among the Kohathite clans, were thirteen in all.

⁶¹The rest of Kohath's descendants were allotted ten towns from the clans of half the tribe of Manasseh.

⁶²The descendants of Gershon, clan by clan, were allotted thirteen towns from the tribes of Issachar, Asher and Naphtali, and from the part of the tribe of Manasseh that is in Bashan.

⁶³The descendants of Merari, clan by clan, were allotted twelve towns from the tribes of Reuben, Gad and Zebulun.

6:64
f Nu 35:1-8;
Jos 21:3,41-42

⁶⁴So the Israelites gave the Levites these towns *f* and their pasturelands. ⁶⁵From the tribes of Judah, Simeon and Benjamin they allotted the previously named towns.

⁶⁶Some of the Kohathite clans were given as their territory towns from the tribe of Ephraim.

⁶⁷In the hill country of Ephraim they were given Shechem (a city of refuge), and Gezer, *dg* ⁶⁸Jokmeam, *h* Beth Horon, *i* ⁶⁹Aijalon *j* and Gath Rimmon, *k* together with their pasturelands.

6:67
g Jos 10:33
6:68
h 1Ki 4:12
i Jos 10:10
6:69
j Jos 10:12
k Jos 19:45

⁷⁰And from half the tribe of Manasseh the Israelites gave Aner and Bileam, together with their pasturelands, to the rest of the Kohathite clans.

⁷¹The Gershonites *l* received the following:
From the clan of the half-tribe of Manasseh
they received Golan in Bashan *m* and also Ashtaroth, together with their pasturelands;

6:71
l 1Ch 23:7
m Jos 20:8

⁷²from the tribe of Issachar
they received Kedesh, Daberath, *n* ⁷³Ramoth and Anem, together with their pasturelands;

6:72
n Jos 19:12

⁷⁴from the tribe of Asher
they received Mashal, Abdon, *o* ⁷⁵Hukok *p* and Rehob, *q* together with their pasturelands;

6:74
o Jos 19:28
6:75
p Jos 19:34
q Nu 13:21

---

a 57 See Joshua 21:13; Hebrew *given the cities of refuge: Hebron, Libnah.*   *b 59* Syriac (see also Septuagint and Joshua 21:16); Hebrew does not have *Juttah.*   *c 60* See Joshua 21:17; Hebrew does not have *Gibeon.*   *d 67* See Joshua 21:21; Hebrew *given the cities of refuge: Shechem, Gezer.*

76 and from the tribe of Naphtali
    they received Kedesh in Galilee, Hammon[r] and Kiriathaim,[s] together with
    their pasturelands.

77 The Merarites (the rest of the Levites) received the following:
    From the tribe of Zebulun
    they received Jokneam, Kartah,[a] Rimmono and Tabor, together with their
    pasturelands;

78 from the tribe of Reuben across the Jordan east of Jericho
    they received Bezer[t] in the desert, Jahzah, 79 Kedemoth[u] and Mephaath, to-
    gether with their pasturelands;

80 and from the tribe of Gad
    they received Ramoth in Gilead,[v] Mahanaim,[w] 81 Heshbon and Jazer,[x] to-
    gether with their pasturelands.[y]

Issachar

7 The sons of Issachar:[z]
    Tola, Puah,[a] Jashub and Shimron—four in all.
2 The sons of Tola:
    Uzzi, Rephaiah, Jeriel, Jahmai, Ibsam and Samuel—heads of their families.
    During the reign of David, the descendants of Tola listed as fighting men in
    their genealogy numbered 22,600.
3 The son of Uzzi:
    Izrahiah.
  The sons of Izrahiah:
    Michael, Obadiah, Joel and Isshiah. All five of them were chiefs. 4 According
    to their family genealogy, they had 36,000 men ready for battle, for they had
    many wives and children.
5 The relatives who were fighting men belonging to all the clans of Issachar, as
    listed in their genealogy, were 87,000 in all.

Benjamin

6 Three sons of Benjamin:[b]
    Bela, Beker and Jediael.
7 The sons of Bela:
    Ezbon, Uzzi, Uzziel, Jerimoth and Iri, heads of families—five in all. Their ge-
    nealogical record listed 22,034 fighting men.
8 The sons of Beker:
    Zemirah, Joash, Eliezer, Elioenai, Omri, Jeremoth, Abijah, Anathoth and Al-

---

a 77 See Septuagint and Joshua 21:34; Hebrew does not have *Jokneam, Kartah.*

6:76
r Jos 19:28
s Nu 32:37

6:78
t Jos 20:8
6:79
u Dt 2:26

6:80
v Jos 20:8
w Ge 32:2
6:81
x Nu 21:32
y 2Ch 11:14

7:1
z Ge 30:18;
Nu 26:23
a Ge 46:13

7:6
b Ge 46:21;
Nu 26:38;
1Ch 8:1-40

---

1 Chronicles 7:1–5

Chapter 7 completes the tribal lists, focusing on the northern tribes. Issachar was the largest tribe in ancient Israel apart from Judah (cf. 21:5). Issachar is often paired with Zebulun (e.g., Deut. 33:18–19), but Zebulun is absent from the Chronicler's tribal register. Zebulun, along with Dan, is included in the list of 12 sons of Israel in 2:1–2; but in order to arrive at the ideal 12 tribes both were likely omitted from the tribal genealogies in favor of Ephraim and the two half-tribes of Manasseh.

Are you experiencing some boredom while poring through these lists of Israel's tribes? No doubt some Israelites also questioned the value of reciting names and stories rehearsing the tribes' departed glory and checkered history. For the Chronicler the unifying principle was the Abrahamic covenant (Gen. 12:1–3; cf.

1 Chron. 1:28), which established a new relationship between God and Israel's ancestors—and with all humanity, seen in the blessing of the nations in Genesis 12:3. We can be thankful that through Christ we have been welcomed into the family of faith begun through these ancient tribes (cf. Rom. 9:4–5).

1 Chronicles 7:6–12

The tribe of Benjamin was transitional in terms of geography, a buffer between Judah to the south and the rest of the tribes to the north. The insertion of the Benjamite genealogy at this juncture serves to introduce the more extensive family tree of Benjamin that follows in chapter 8. Benjamin also was the transitional tribe of Israelite kingship. Israel's first king, Saul, hailed from Benjamin, and the Chronicler would use his genealogy and royal history as a preface to the history of the Davidic dynasty (9:35—10:14).

emeth. All these were the sons of Beker. [9]Their genealogical record listed the heads of families and 20,200 fighting men.

[10]The son of Jediael:

Bilhan.

The sons of Bilhan:

Jeush, Benjamin, Ehud, Kenaanah, Zethan, Tarshish and Ahishahar. [11]All these sons of Jediael were heads of families. There were 17,200 fighting men ready to go out to war.

[12]The Shuppites and Huppites were the descendants of Ir, and the Hushites the descendants of Aher.

Naphtali

7:13
c Ge 30:8; 46:24

[13]The sons of Naphtali:[c]

Jahziel, Guni, Jezer and Shillem[a]—the descendants of Bilhah.

Manasseh

7:14
d Ge 41:51;
Jos 17:1; 1Ch 5:23
e Nu 26:30

[14]The descendants of Manasseh:[d]

Asriel was his descendant through his Aramean concubine. She gave birth to Makir the father of Gilead.[e] [15]Makir took a wife from among the Huppites and Shuppites. His sister's name was Maacah.

7:15
f Nu 26:33; 36:1-12

Another descendant was named Zelophehad,[f] who had only daughters.

[16]Makir's wife Maacah gave birth to a son and named him Peresh. His brother was named Sheresh, and his sons were Ulam and Rakem.

[17]The son of Ulam:

Bedan.

7:17
g Nu 26:30;
1Sa 12:11
7:18
h Jos 17:2

These were the sons of Gilead[g] son of Makir, the son of Manasseh. [18]His sister Hammoleketh gave birth to Ishhod, Abiezer[h] and Mahlah.

[19]The sons of Shemida were:

Ahian, Shechem, Likhi and Aniam.

[a] 13 Some Hebrew and Septuagint manuscripts (see also Gen. 46:24 and Num. 26:49); most Hebrew manuscripts *Shallum*

📖 The inclusive nature of Biblical covenants unifies our two Testaments. At the macro (universal) level, the church does well to reaffirm the "first principles" that define its history: (1) worship that enables all believers to encounter God and serve a needy world; (2) a heart for evangelism; (3) compassion that promotes reconciliation through Christ and heals relationships in disrepair; (4) a vision for ministry that unleashes the gifts of the Spirit for the benefit of the body of Christ; and (5) fellowship rooted in mutual love.

1 Chronicles 7:13

📖 The four clans of Naphtali match the records of Genesis 46:24 and Numbers 26:48–49. The brevity of the genealogy is noteworthy, leading to speculation about the loss of information over time in the sources the Chronicler used. This may also account for the omission of genealogies for Dan and Zebulun (but see "There and Then" for 7:1–5).

📖 At the micro (individual) level, we can learn from the Chronicler's wide heart and open mind (see the previous "Here and Now" and notes for the following passage). Are you as a Christian, and is your particular congregation, "known" for your love for others (John 13:34–35) and your tendency to perform acts of kind-

ness for those who can't repay (Luke 14:12–14)? The Chronicler would have approved of such love in action, as opposed to the gratifying personal experience that too often passes for "love" in our culture.

1 Chronicles 7:14–19

📖 First Chronicles preserves separate genealogies for the Transjordan clans of Manasseh (5:23–26) and the clans that settled west of the Jordan. The sidebar reference to Asriel's Aramean mother (see also 2:34–35 and 4:18) prompts questions, since mixed marriages were outlawed in the reforms of Ezra and Nehemiah (Neh. 13:3,23–30). It seems likely that the Chronicler included these marriages to affirm God's sovereignty in fulfilling the "blessings" clause of the Abrahamic covenant (Gen. 12:3).

📖 The Chronicler grasped the principles behind Christ's inclusive message. He understood that God is no respecter of persons; all humans are created in his image (cf. Deut. 1:17; 10:17; 2 Chron. 19:7). Since the charge to Israel was to be holy as God is holy (Lev. 11:44), it seems only natural that the historian would apply this to human relationships. Likewise, we as Christians are taught not to show favoritism or discrimination when dealing with others (James 2:1; cf. Eph. 6:9; Col. 3:25).

Ephraim

20 The descendants of Ephraim: [i]

Shuthelah, Bered his son,
Tahath his son, Eleadah his son,
Tahath his son, 21 Zabad his son
and Shuthelah his son.

Ezer and Elead were killed by the native-born men of Gath, when they went
down to seize their livestock. 22 Their father Ephraim mourned for them many
days, and his relatives came to comfort him. 23 Then he lay with his wife again,
and she became pregnant and gave birth to a son. He named him Beriah, [a] because there had been misfortune in his family. 24 His daughter was Sheerah,
who built Lower and Upper Beth Horon [j] as well as Uzzen Sheerah.

25 Rephah was his son, Resheph his son, [b]

Telah his son, Tahan his son,
26 Ladan his son, Ammihud his son,
Elishama his son, 27 Nun his son
and Joshua his son.

28 Their lands and settlements included Bethel and its surrounding villages, Na-
aran to the east, Gezer [k] and its villages to the west, and Shechem and its villages all
the way to Ayyah and its villages. 29 Along the borders of Manasseh were Beth
Shan, [l] Taanach, Megiddo and Dor, [m] together with their villages. The descendants
of Joseph son of Israel lived in these towns.

Asher

30 The sons of Asher: [n]

Imnah, Ishvah, Ishvi and Beriah. Their sister was Serah.

31 The sons of Beriah:

Heber and Malkiel, who was the father of Birzaith.

32 Heber was the father of Japhlet, Shomer and Hotham and of their sister Shua.

33 The sons of Japhlet:

Pasach, Bimhal and Ashvath.
These were Japhlet's sons.

34 The sons of Shomer:

Ahi, Rohgah, [c] Hubbah and Aram.

35 The sons of his brother Helem:

Zophah, Imna, Shelesh and Amal.

---

[a] 23 *Beriah* sounds like the Hebrew for *misfortune.*   [b] 25 Some Septuagint manuscripts; Hebrew
does not have *his son.*   [c] 34 Or *of his brother Shomer: Rohgah*

7:20
[i] Ge 41:52;
Nu 1:33; 26:35

7:24
[j] Jos 10:10; 16:3,5

7:28
[k] Jos 10:33; 16:7

7:29
[l] Jos 17:11
[m] Jos 11:2

7:30
[n] Ge 46:17;
Nu 1:40; 26:44

---

1 Chronicles 7:20–29

Ephraim and Manasseh were the Joseph
tribes—adopted by Jacob/Israel as his own sons (Gen.
48:5,15–16). This genealogy concludes with Joshua son
of Nun, descendant of Ephraim and successor of Moses
(cf. Deut. 34:9). This reference is in keeping with the
Chronicler's emphasis on the Israelite conquest and occupation of the promised land.

The historical footnote celebrating Sheerah as the
builder of Beth Horon (v. 24) is noteworthy for the
prominence accorded a woman, but not out of character
for the Chronicler. Her story emphasizes the accomplishments of an individual, encouraging each member of the
postexilic community to become involved in Israel's
restoration. The passing reference to Zelophehad's
daughters (v. 15) also recalled for the Israelites a remarkable story of female initiative (cf. Num. 27:1–11).

Talk about a man ahead of his time! Not only
was the Chronicler open to relationships between Israel

and other nations (see previous "There and Then"), but
now we uncover an emphasis on precedent-setting initiatives by women. Does this wideness of heart and
openness of mind surprise you, coming as it does from
so ancient a background steeped in patriarchy? You
might want to pause here and assess how much progress
we as individual Christians, and the church worldwide,
have really made in the intervening millennia. Can we
do more?

1 Chronicles 7:30–40

As in 2:1–2, Asher concludes the tribal list. Asher was cited after Naphtali and Gad there, but here it's
preceded by Manasseh and Ephraim. This tribe had settled in western Galilee, so it's possible the military census
that served as the Chronicler's primary source cataloged
the tribes on the basis of geographical location from east
to west. The attrition in Asher's muster roll to 26,000 (v.
40) from 41,500 (Num. 1:40–41) and 53,400 (Num. 26:47)
testifies to the misfortunes experienced by this tribe.

36 The sons of Zophah:

Suah, Harnepher, Shual, Beri, Imrah, 37 Bezer, Hod, Shamma, Shilshah, Ithran[a] and Beera.

38 The sons of Jether:

Jephunneh, Pispah and Ara.

39 The sons of Ulla:

Arah, Hanniel and Rizia.

40 All these were descendants of Asher—heads of families, choice men, brave warriors and outstanding leaders. The number of men ready for battle, as listed in their genealogy, was 26,000.

The Genealogy of Saul the Benjamite

8:1
o Ge 46:21;
1Ch 7:6

8 Benjamin[o] was the father of Bela his firstborn,
Ashbel the second son, Aharah the third,
2 Nohah the fourth and Rapha the fifth.

8:3
p Ge 46:21
8:4
q 2Sa 23:9
8:6
r Jdg 3:12-30;
1Ch 2:52

3 The sons of Bela were:

Addar,[p] Gera, Abihud,[b] 4 Abishua, Naaman, Ahoah, [q] 5 Gera, Shephuphan and Huram.

6 These were the descendants of Ehud,[r] who were heads of families of those living in Geba and were deported to Manahath:

7 Naaman, Ahijah, and Gera, who deported them and who was the father of Uzza and Ahihud.

8 Sons were born to Shaharaim in Moab after he had divorced his wives Hushim and Baara. 9 By his wife Hodesh he had Jobab, Zibia, Mesha, Malcam, 10 Jeuz, Sakia and Mirmah. These were his sons, heads of families. 11 By Hushim he had Abitub and Elpaal.

8:12
s Ezr 2:33; Ne 6:2;
7:37; 11:35
8:13
t Jos 10:12
u Jos 11:22

12 The sons of Elpaal:

Eber, Misham, Shemed (who built Ono[s] and Lod with its surrounding villages), 13 and Beriah and Shema, who were heads of families of those living in Aijalon[t] and who drove out the inhabitants of Gath. [u]

14 Ahio, Shashak, Jeremoth, 15 Zebadiah, Arad, Eder, 16 Michael, Ishpah and Joha were the sons of Beriah.

17 Zebadiah, Meshullam, Hizki, Heber, 18 Ishmerai, Izliah and Jobab were the sons of Elpaal.

19 Jakim, Zicri, Zabdi, 20 Elienai, Zillethai, Eliel, 21 Adaiah, Beraiah and Shimrath were the sons of Shimei.

22 Ishpan, Eber, Eliel, 23 Abdon, Zicri, Hanan, 24 Hananiah, Elam, Anthothijah, 25 Iphdeiah and Penuel were the sons of Shashak.

---

a 37 Possibly a variant of Jether   b 3 Or Gera the father of Ehud

---

📖 The Chronicler's wide heart and open mind (seen throughout the genealogies though not expressed in this segment) demonstrates itself in social action as exemplified in Amos. God requires the faithful to act justly and to love mercy (Mic. 6:8) through involvement with the oppressed, including orphans and widows (Isa. 1:17). The New Testament emphasizes providing food and clothing to the needy (Matt. 25:37–40; James 2:14–17). This theme permeates Scripture and can hardly be overlooked by the caring, thinking Christian.

1 Chronicles 8:1—9:1a

📖 The genealogy of Benjamin functions as a sequel to the brief listing of Benjamites found in 7:6–12 and serves as an introduction to that of King Saul in 9:35–44. It includes a report that sons were born to Shaharaim by a third wife, Hodesh, after he had divorced two others (vv. 8–10). The marital problems preceding

the divorces aren't mentioned. This anecdote is in keeping with the Chronicler's evident interest in personalizing these listings with notes that highlighted unusual events or called attention to "marginalized" people (like women and non-Hebrews).

📖 How do you (and your congregation) treat those on the fringes? God hates divorce because it tears families apart (cf. Mal. 2:16). Yet here we see two divorced women and their children preserved in the Biblical record. Our natural tendency is to leave people with messy problems unmentioned and unnoticed on the periphery of our congregations and social circles. This brief note in Chronicles reminds us to include in our lives people who have been sidelined by a variety of problems, including those suffering from HIV/AIDS or struggling with addictions. Read Matthew 9:9–13 for Jesus' perspective.

²⁶Shamsherai, Sheariah, Athaliah, ²⁷Jaareshiah, Elijah and Zicri were the sons of Jeroham.

²⁸All these were heads of families, chiefs as listed in their genealogy, and they lived in Jerusalem.

²⁹Jeiel[a] the father[b] of Gibeon lived in Gibeon.ᵛ

His wife's name was Maacah, ³⁰and his firstborn son was Abdon, followed by Zur, Kish, Baal, Ner,ᶜ Nadab, ³¹Gedor, Ahio, Zeker ³²and Mikloth, who was the father of Shimeah. They too lived near their relatives in Jerusalem.

³³Nerʷ was the father of Kish,ˣ Kish the father of Saul,ʸ and Saul the father of Jonathan, Malki-Shua, Abinadab and Esh-Baal.ᵈ ᶻ

³⁴The son of Jonathan:ᵃ

Merib-Baal,ᵉ ᵇ who was the father of Micah.

³⁵The sons of Micah:

Pithon, Melech, Tarea and Ahaz.

³⁶Ahaz was the father of Jehoaddah, Jehoaddah was the father of Alemeth, Azmaveth and Zimri, and Zimri was the father of Moza. ³⁷Moza was the father of Binea; Raphah was his son, Eleasah his son and Azel his son.

³⁸Azel had six sons, and these were their names:

Azrikam, Bokeru, Ishmael, Sheariah, Obadiah and Hanan. All these were the sons of Azel.

³⁹The sons of his brother Eshek:

Ulam his firstborn, Jeush the second son and Eliphelet the third. ⁴⁰The sons of Ulam were brave warriors who could handle the bow. They had many sons and grandsons—150 in all.

All these were the descendants of Benjamin.ᶜ

9 All Israel was listed in the genealogies recorded in the book of the kings of Israel.

The People in Jerusalem

The people of Judah were taken captive to Babylon because of their unfaithfulness.ᵈ ²Now the first to resettle on their own property in their own townsᵉ were some Israelites, priests, Levites and temple servants.ᶠ

³Those from Judah, from Benjamin, and from Ephraim and Manasseh who lived in Jerusalem were:

⁴Uthai son of Ammihud, the son of Omri, the son of Imri, the son of Bani, a descendant of Perez son of Judah.ᵍ

⁵Of the Shilonites:

Asaiah the firstborn and his sons.

ᵃ 29 Some Septuagint manuscripts (see also 1 Chron. 9:35); Hebrew does not have *Jeiel*.
ᵇ 29 *Father* may mean *civic leader* or *military leader*.   ᶜ 30 Some Septuagint manuscripts (see also 1 Chron. 9:36); Hebrew does not have *Ner*.   ᵈ 33 Also known as *Ish-Bosheth*   ᵉ 34 Also known as *Mephibosheth*

8:29
ᵛ Jos 9:3

8:33
ʷ 1Sa 28:19
ˣ 1Sa 9:1
ʸ 1Sa 14:49
ᶻ 2Sa 2:8
8:34
ᵃ 2Sa 9:12
ᵇ 2Sa 4:4

8:40
ᶜ Nu 26:38

9:1
ᵈ 1Ch 5:25
9:2
ᵉ Jos 9:27; Ezr 2:70
ᶠ Ezr 2:43,58; 8:20; Ne 7:60

9:4
ᵍ Ge 38:29; 46:12

---

1 Chronicles 9:1b–34

The list of families resettling Jerusalem joins the present to the past, directly linking the restoration community to the 12 sons of Israel. The purposes of the extensive genealogical introduction to Chronicles were evidently to legitimize the restoration community as rightful heirs of the promises made to the patriarchs and kings of Israel and to bolster the morale of the returning Hebrews and inspire full participation in the restoration effort.

This postexilic genealogy cites no Judahite connected with King David. The Chronicler, who wrote about a century after the restoration process had begun, seems to have assumed that the fate of postexilic Judah lay in the hands of the priests and Levites until such time as God would raise up a successor to David (cf. Jer. 33:17; Ezek. 34:23–24; 37:25).

The story of Israel, and of the whole Bible, is one of "fresh starts" by God's grace, of God making and remaking, "doing new things" (Isa. 43:19). God repeatedly and lovingly "jump-started" his relationship with his people after covenant failures (cf. Deut. 30:1–3; Jer. 33:25–26). Still today, there is always hope for desperate people in a tired and dismal world to start over. The church's enduring message is that the hope it holds out won't disappoint those who dare to believe (Rom. 5:5).

6 Of the Zerahites:

Jeuel.

The people from Judah numbered 690.

7 Of the Benjamites:

Sallu son of Meshullam, the son of Hodaviah, the son of Hassenuah;

8 Ibneiah son of Jeroham; Elah son of Uzzi, the son of Micri; and Meshullam son of Shephatiah, the son of Reuel, the son of Ibnijah.

9 The people from Benjamin, as listed in their genealogy, numbered 956. All these men were heads of their families.

10 Of the priests:

Jedaiah; Jehoiarib; Jakin;

11 Azariah son of Hilkiah, the son of Meshullam, the son of Zadok, the son of Meraioth, the son of Ahitub, the official in charge of the house of God;

12 Adaiah son of Jeroham, the son of Pashhur, [h] the son of Malkijah; and Maasai son of Adiel, the son of Jahzerah, the son of Meshullam, the son of Meshillemith, the son of Immer.

13 The priests, who were heads of families, numbered 1,760. They were able men, responsible for ministering in the house of God.

14 Of the Levites:

Shemaiah son of Hasshub, the son of Azrikam, the son of Hashabiah, a Merarite; 15 Bakbakkar, Heresh, Galal and Mattaniah [i] son of Mica, the son of Zicri, the son of Asaph; 16 Obadiah son of Shemaiah, the son of Galal, the son of Jeduthun; and Berekiah son of Asa, the son of Elkanah, who lived in the villages of the Netophathites. [j]

17 The gatekeepers: [k]

Shallum, Akkub, Talmon, Ahiman and their brothers, Shallum their chief 18 being stationed at the King's Gate [l] on the east, up to the present time. These were the gatekeepers belonging to the camp of the Levites. 19 Shallum [m] son of Kore, the son of Ebiasaph, the son of Korah, and his fellow gatekeepers from his family (the Korahites) were responsible for guarding the thresholds of the Tent [a] just as their fathers had been responsible for guarding the entrance to the dwelling of the LORD. 20 In earlier times Phinehas [n] son of Eleazar was in charge of the gatekeepers, and the LORD was with him. 21 Zechariah [o] son of Meshelemiah was the gatekeeper at the entrance to the Tent of Meeting.

22 Altogether, those chosen to be gatekeepers [p] at the thresholds numbered 212. They were registered by genealogy in their villages. The gatekeepers had been assigned to their positions of trust by David and Samuel the seer. [q] 23 They and their descendants were in charge of guarding the gates of the house of the LORD—the house called the Tent. 24 The gatekeepers were on the four sides: east, west, north and south. 25 Their brothers in their villages had to come from time to time and share their duties for seven-day [r] periods. 26 But the four principal gatekeepers, who were Levites, were entrusted with the responsibility for the rooms and treasuries [s] in the house of God. 27 They would spend the night stationed around the house of God, [t] because they had to guard it; and they had charge of the key [u] for opening it each morning.

28 Some of them were in charge of the articles used in the temple service; they counted them when they were brought in and when they were taken out. 29 Others were assigned to take care of the furnishings and all the other articles of the sanctuary, [v] as well as the flour and wine, and the oil, incense and spices. 30 But some [w] of the priests took care of mixing the spices. 31 A Levite named Mattithiah, the first-born son of Shallum the Korahite, was entrusted with the responsibility for baking the offering bread. 32 Some of their Kohathite brothers were in charge of preparing for every Sabbath the bread set out on the table. [x]

33 Those who were musicians, [y] heads of Levite families, stayed in the rooms of the temple and were exempt from other duties because they were responsible for the work day and night. [z]

[a] 19 That is, the temple; also in verses 21 and 23

9:12
[h] Ezr 2:38; 10:22;
Ne 10:3; Jer 21:1;
38:1

9:15
[i] 2Ch 20:14;
Ne 11:22

9:16
[j] Ne 12:28
9:17
[k] ver 22; 1Ch 26:1;
2Ch 8:14; 31:14;
Ezr 2:42; Ne 7:45
9:18
[l] 1Ch 26:14;
Eze 43:1; 46:1
9:19
[m] Jer 35:4

9:20
[n] Nu 25:7-13
9:21
[o] 1Ch 26:2,14

9:22
[p] ver 17;
1Ch 26:1-2;
2Ch 31:15,18
[q] 1Sa 9:9

9:25
[r] 2Ki 11:5;
2Ch 23:8
9:26
[s] 1Ch 26:22
9:27
[t] Nu 3:38;
1Ch 23:30-32
[u] Isa 22:22

9:29
[v] Nu 3:28;
1Ch 23:29
9:30
[w] Ex 30:23-25

9:32
[x] Lev 24:5-8;
1Ch 23:29;
2Ch 13:11
9:33
[y] 1Ch 6:31; 25:1-31
[z] Ps 134:1

³⁴All these were heads of Levite families, chiefs as listed in their genealogy, and they lived in Jerusalem.

The Genealogy of Saul

³⁵Jeiel *ª* the father*ª* of Gibeon lived in Gibeon.

His wife's name was Maacah, ³⁶and his firstborn son was Abdon, followed
by Zur, Kish, Baal, Ner, Nadab, ³⁷Gedor, Ahio, Zechariah and Mikloth.
³⁸Mikloth was the father of Shimeam. They too lived near their relatives in
Jerusalem.

³⁹Ner *ᵇ* was the father of Kish, *ᶜ* Kish the father of Saul, and Saul the father of Jonathan, *ᵈ* Malki-Shua, Abinadab and Esh-Baal. *ᵇ ᵉ*

⁴⁰The son of Jonathan:

Merib-Baal, *ᶜ ᶠ* who was the father of Micah.

⁴¹The sons of Micah:

Pithon, Melech, Tahrea and Ahaz. *ᵈ*

⁴²Ahaz was the father of Jadah, Jadah *ᵉ* was the father of Alemeth, Azmaveth
and Zimri, and Zimri was the father of Moza. ⁴³Moza was the father of Binea; Rephaiah was his son, Eleasah his son and Azel his son.

⁴⁴Azel had six sons, and these were their names:

Azrikam, Bokeru, Ishmael, Sheariah, Obadiah and Hanan. These were the
sons of Azel.

Saul Takes His Life

10 Now the Philistines fought against Israel; the Israelites fled before them, and
many fell slain on Mount Gilboa. ²The Philistines pressed hard after Saul and
his sons, and they killed his sons Jonathan, Abinadab and Malki-Shua. ³The fighting grew fierce around Saul, and when the archers overtook him, they wounded him.

⁴Saul said to his armor-bearer, "Draw your sword and run me through, or these
uncircumcised fellows will come and abuse me."

But his armor-bearer was terrified and would not do it; so Saul took his own sword

ª 35 Father may mean *civic leader* or *military leader.*   *ᵇ 39* Also known as *Ish-Bosheth*   *ᶜ 40* Also
known as *Mephibosheth*   *ᵈ 41* Vulgate and Syriac (see also Septuagint and 1 Chron. 8:35); Hebrew
does not have *and Ahaz.*   *ᵉ 42* Some Hebrew manuscripts and Septuagint (see also 1 Chron. 8:36);
most Hebrew manuscripts *Jarah, Jarah*

9:35
ª 1Ch 8:29

9:39
ᵇ 1Ch 8:33
ᶜ 1Sa 9:1
ᵈ 1Sa 13:22
ᵉ 2Sa 2:8

9:40
ᶠ 2Sa 4:4

1 Chronicles 9:35–44

This genealogy repeats the register of Saul's
family tree (with minor variations) found in 8:29–38 as
one segment of the genealogy of Benjamin. Two names
included here, Jeiel and Ner, are found in the previous
passage only in some Septuagint (pre-Christian Greek
translation of the OT) manuscripts (see NIV text notes
for 8:29 and 8:30). And there are variations in the
spellings of five other names recorded in the two genealogies.

These minor differences may have been the result of
scribal errors or of the ongoing process of language
changing over time. Yet we can stand on the elemental
truth that the Bible as the Word of God has accurately
recorded salvation history. Can a minor copying error or
language alteration change the truth or teaching of
God's Word? The answer is an emphatic no!

How will people interpret the archaeological remains of our world thousands of years from now if Christ
hasn't yet returned? Will they figure out that Zaire and
Zimbabwe were at one time the country of Rhodesia?
Or that Vancouver, Washington, and Vancouver, British

Columbia, were two different cities located a few hundred miles apart? Will they discover that "Ashley" and
"Ashleigh" were two ways to spell the same name? Or
that someone named "Steve" in the U.S. might have
been called "Esteban" while traveling in Mexico? Think
about this the next time you run into an apparent discrepancy with names of people or places in the Bible.

1 Chronicles 10:1–14

The abrupt shift from genealogy to story is striking, as is the brevity of the Chronicler's account of Saul's
reign. David was the focus of the Chronicler's retelling of
Israelite history, and Saul's death was a tragic but necessary introduction.

Saul's death served as a grim reminder of God's sovereignty over Israel and all the nations. The Philistines
had merely been agents of God's just punishment of
Saul's disobedience (even as the Babylonians had been
instruments of divine judgment in Judah's exile). The
Chronicler's retelling of this event reminded the returnees that the Israelite kingdom and kingship belonged to God and that God had good reason for transferring that kingdom from Saul's family to David's.

and fell on it. ⁵When the armor-bearer saw that Saul was dead, he too fell on his sword and died. ⁶So Saul and his three sons died, and all his house died together.

⁷When all the Israelites in the valley saw that the army had fled and that Saul and his sons had died, they abandoned their towns and fled. And the Philistines came and occupied them.

⁸The next day, when the Philistines came to strip the dead, they found Saul and his sons fallen on Mount Gilboa. ⁹They stripped him and took his head and his armor, and sent messengers throughout the land of the Philistines to proclaim the news among their idols and their people. ¹⁰They put his armor in the temple of their gods and hung up his head in the temple of Dagon. *g*

¹¹When all the inhabitants of Jabesh Gilead *h* heard of everything the Philistines had done to Saul, ¹²all their valiant men went and took the bodies of Saul and his sons and brought them to Jabesh. Then they buried their bones under the great tree in Jabesh, and they fasted seven days.

¹³Saul died *i* because he was unfaithful *j* to the LORD; he did not keep *k* the word of the LORD and even consulted a medium *l* for guidance, ¹⁴and did not inquire of the LORD. So the LORD put him to death and turned *m* the kingdom *n* over to David son of Jesse.

David Becomes King Over Israel

11 All Israel *o* came together to David at Hebron *p* and said, "We are your own flesh and blood. ²In the past, even while Saul was king, you were the one who led Israel on their military campaigns. *q* And the LORD your God said to you, 'You will shepherd *r* my people Israel, and you will become their ruler.' *s* "

³When all the elders of Israel had come to King David at Hebron, he made a compact with them at Hebron before the LORD, and they anointed *t* David king over Israel, as the LORD had promised through Samuel.

David Conquers Jerusalem

⁴David and all the Israelites marched to Jerusalem (that is, Jebus). The Jebusites *u* who lived there ⁵said to David, "You will not get in here." Nevertheless, David captured the fortress of Zion, the City of David.

⁶David had said, "Whoever leads the attack on the Jebusites will become commander-in-chief." Joab *v* son of Zeruiah went up first, and so he received the command.

10:10
g Jdg 16:23
10:11
h Jdg 21:8

10:13
i 2Sa 1:1
j 1Sa 15:23;
1Ch 5:25
k 1Sa 13:13
l Lev 19:31; 20:6;
Dt 18:9-14;
1Sa 28:7
10:14
m 1Ch 12:23
n 1Sa 13:14; 15:28
11:1
o 1Ch 9:1
p Ge 13:18; 23:19

11:2
q 1Sa 18:5,16
r Ps 78:71; Mt 2:6
s 1Ch 5:2

11:3
t 1Sa 16:1-13

11:4
u Ge 10:16;
15:18-21; Jos 3:10;
15:8; Jdg 1:21;
19:10

11:6
v 2Sa 2:13; 8:16

📖 Timing is important. The Chronicler's restoration community was disillusioned with God, assuming that his Word had failed since no David-like king had arisen to "shepherd Israel" (see 11:2) as God had promised through Jeremiah and Ezekiel (cf. Jer. 33:15; Ezek. 34:23–24). We too live in difficult, violent times, and we understand disillusionment all too well. We wait for what appears to be a delayed fulfillment of Jesus' promised return. But God's timing with regard to Christ's birth was impeccable (Gal. 4:4–5), and we have the assurance that the same will be true for the second coming of the Savior from David's line (2 Peter 3:4,8–9).

1 Chronicles 11:1–3

⚓ The theme of "all Israel's" recognition of David as king unifies 1 Chronicles 11–12. The widespread support of David on the part of the tribes is emphasized both here at the beginning of the section (11:1–3) and at the end (12:38–40). In his account of David's accession to the throne, the Chronicler omitted the fact that David had ruled in Hebron over a separate kingdom of Judah for seven and a half years (2 Sam. 5:5; cf. 1 Chron. 3:4; 29:27). Assuming that his audience knew this, he apparently wanted to emphasize the unity achieved under David,

hoping to instill similar expectations in postexilic Judah.

📖 David's passage from fugitive to king hinged on the principle of loyalty to God. Saul's disloyalty had disqualified him from establishing a royal dynasty (10:13–14). Still today, disloyalty to God inevitably leads to disaster. We live in a time of global unrest, when tensions among nations, even those classified as allies, runs high. As a Christian, do you hold allegiance to God first, above your national or political affiliation? After all, we are strangers and travelers here on Earth; our real citizenship is in heaven (cf. Phil. 3:20).

1 Chronicles 11:4–9

⚓ The Chronicler's agenda at this point was more political than religious; no mention was made of Jerusalem housing the ark of the covenant or as the eventual site of the temple. There was a certain genius in David's annexation of the Jebusite city of Jerusalem. Along with Israel's capturing intact a functioning bureaucratic center, the fact that Jerusalem was situated on the border of Judah and Benjamin—yet controlled by neither tribe—allowed David to secure a neutral site for his capital city as part of his effort to unite the kingdom under his rule.

7David then took up residence in the fortress, and so it was called the City of David. 8He built up the city around it, from the supporting terraces a w to the surrounding wall, while Joab restored the rest of the city. 9And David became more and more powerful, x because the LORD Almighty was with him.

11:8
w 2Sa 5:9; 2Ch 32:5

11:9
x 2Sa 3:1; Est 9:4

David's Mighty Men

10These were the chiefs of David's mighty men—they, together with all Israel, y gave his kingship strong support to extend it over the whole land, as the LORD had promised z— 11this is the list of David's mighty men: a

11:10
y ver 1 z ver 3;
1Ch 12:23

11:11
a 2Sa 17:10

Jashobeam, b a Hacmonite, was chief of the officers c; he raised his spear against three hundred men, whom he killed in one encounter.

12Next to him was Eleazar son of Dodai the Ahohite, one of the three mighty men. 13He was with David at Pas Dammim when the Philistines gathered there for battle. At a place where there was a field full of barley, the troops fled from the Philistines. 14But they took their stand in the middle of the field. They defended it and struck the Philistines down, and the LORD brought about a great victory. b

11:14
b Ex 14:30;
1Sa 11:13
11:15
c 1Ch 14:9; Isa 17:5
11:16
d 2Sa 5:17

15Three of the thirty chiefs came down to David to the rock at the cave of Adullam, while a band of Philistines was encamped in the Valley c of Rephaim. 16At that time David was in the stronghold, d and the Philistine garrison was at Bethlehem. 17David longed for water and said, "Oh, that someone would get me a drink of water from the well near the gate of Bethlehem!" 18So the Three broke through the Philistine lines, drew water from the well near the gate of Bethlehem and carried it back to David. But he refused to drink it; instead, he poured e it out before the LORD. 19"God forbid that I should do this!" he said. "Should I drink the blood of these men who went at the risk of their lives?" Because they risked their lives to bring it back, David would not drink it.

11:18
e Dt 12:16

Such were the exploits of the three mighty men.

20Abishai f the brother of Joab was chief of the Three. He raised his spear against three hundred men, whom he killed, and so he became as famous as the Three. 21He was doubly honored above the Three and became their commander, even though he was not included among them.

11:20
f 1Sa 26:6

22Benaiah son of Jehoiada was a valiant fighter from Kabzeel, g who performed great exploits. He struck down two of Moab's best men. He also went down into a pit on a snowy day and killed a lion. h 23And he struck down an Egyptian who was seven and a half feet d tall. Although the Egyptian had a spear like a weaver's rod i in his hand, Benaiah went against him with a club. He snatched the spear from the Egyptian's hand and killed him with his own spear. 24Such were the exploits of Benaiah son of Jehoiada; he too was as famous as the three mighty men. 25He was

11:22
g Jos 15:21
h 1Sa 17:36

11:23
i 1Sa 17:7

---

a 8 Or the Millo   b 11 Possibly a variant of Jashob-Baal   c 11 Or Thirty; some Septuagint manuscripts Three (see also 2 Samuel 23:8)   d 23 Hebrew five cubits (about 2.3 meters)

The crux of this brief account for us lies in the final clause of verse 9: "because the LORD Almighty was with [David]" (cf. 1 Sam. 16:18; 18:12–14). While we can't help but admire David's political savvy and military prowess, in order for us to bridge the gap to the present we need this critical background information. God's backing was certainly no secret to David as he undertook this venture. We, too, need to be sensitive to the Spirit's leading in our lives. "If God is for us, who can be against us?" (Rom. 8:31).

1 Chronicles 11:10–47

The roster of David's mighty men and the reports of their heroic exploits had been recorded earlier in 2 Samuel 23:8–39. The list in 2 Samuel, though, ended with Uriah the Hittite. The Chronicler obviously had access to additional sources for the 16 names in 11:41b–47.

Joab isn't mentioned, though we may surmise that he was the supreme commander (v. 6; 2 Sam. 8:16). The "Three" probably functioned as generals, while the term "Thirty" designated the complete unit of mighty men, regardless of their exact number at any given time. These elite troops were the equivalent of the United States' "special forces" military units, as well as of its protective "secret service."

Scripture provides ample warning against placing ultimate trust in armies and armaments (e.g., 1 Sam. 17:45–47; Ps. 20:7; 33:16). We live in a day when military might is flaunted, but the security it provides is overrated. Our trust in modern solutions—technology, science, and medicine—to save us from disaster is also misplaced. Nothing and no one but God can be our help in times of trouble. He alone is our rock, fortress, and defense (cf. Ps. 18:2).

held in greater honor than any of the Thirty, but he was not included among the Three. And David put him in charge of his bodyguard.

11:26
j 2Sa 2:18

26 The mighty men were:

Asahel*j* the brother of Joab,

Elhanan son of Dodo from Bethlehem,

11:27
k 1Ch 27:8

27 Shammoth*k* the Harorite,

Helez the Pelonite,

11:28
l 1Ch 27:12
11:29
m 2Sa 21:18

28 Ira son of Ikkesh from Tekoa,

Abiezer*l* from Anathoth,

29 Sibbecai*m* the Hushathite,

Ilai the Ahohite,

30 Maharai the Netophathite,

Heled son of Baanah the Netophathite,

11:31
n 1Ch 27:14
o Jdg 12:13

31 Ithai son of Ribai from Gibeah in Benjamin,

Benaiah*n* the Pirathonite,*o*

32 Hurai from the ravines of Gaash,

Abiel the Arbathite,

33 Azmaveth the Baharumite,

Eliahba the Shaalbonite,

34 the sons of Hashem the Gizonite,

Jonathan son of Shagee the Hararite,

35 Ahiam son of Sacar the Hararite,

Eliphal son of Ur,

36 Hepher the Mekerathite,

Ahijah the Pelonite,

37 Hezro the Carmelite,

Naarai son of Ezbai,

38 Joel the brother of Nathan,

Mibhar son of Hagri,

39 Zelek the Ammonite,

Naharai the Berothite, the armor-bearer of Joab son of Zeruiah,

40 Ira the Ithrite,

Gareb the Ithrite,

11:41
p 2Sa 11:6
q 1Ch 2:36

41 Uriah*p* the Hittite,

Zabad*q* son of Ahlai,

42 Adina son of Shiza the Reubenite, who was chief of the Reubenites, and the thirty with him,

43 Hanan son of Maacah,

Joshaphat the Mithnite,

11:44
r Dt 1:4

44 Uzzia the Ashterathite,*r*

Shama and Jeiel the sons of Hotham the Aroerite,

45 Jediael son of Shimri,

his brother Joha the Tizite,

46 Eliel the Mahavite,

Jeribai and Joshaviah the sons of Elnaam,

Ithmah the Moabite,

47 Eliel, Obed and Jaasiel the Mezobaite.

Warriors Join David

12:1
s Jos 15:31;
1Sa 27:2-6

12 These were the men who came to David at Ziklag,*s* while he was banished from the presence of Saul son of Kish (they were among the warriors who

---

1 Chronicles 12:1–22

📖 Chapter 12 furthers the Chronicler's theme of the wide support David enjoyed from "all Israel." Its purpose seems to have been that of telling the story of the building of David's "great army" (v. 22). Additionally, the Chronicler would seek to demonstrate that David's backing combined the support of the military establishment and the general populace (v. 38). Verses 1–22 concentrate on defectors from Saul's army who joined David, the rival king, while he was a fugitive.

helped him in battle; 2they were armed with bows and were able to shoot arrows or to sling stones right-handed or left-handed;*t* they were kinsmen of Saul*u* from the tribe of Benjamin):

3Ahiezer their chief and Joash the sons of Shemaah the Gibeathite; Jeziel and Pelet the sons of Azmaveth; Beracah, Jehu the Anathothite, 4and Ishmaiah the Gibeonite, a mighty man among the Thirty, who was a leader of the Thirty; Jeremiah, Jahaziel, Johanan, Jozabad the Gederathite,*v* 5Eluzai, Jerimoth, Bealiah, Shemariah and Shephatiah the Haruphite; 6Elkanah, Isshiah, Azarel, Joezer and Jashobeam the Korahites; 7and Joelah and Zebadiah the sons of Jeroham from Gedor.*w*

8Some Gadites*x* defected to David at his stronghold in the desert. They were brave warriors, ready for battle and able to handle the shield and spear. Their faces were the faces of lions,*y* and they were as swift as gazelles*z* in the mountains.

9Ezer was the chief,
Obadiah the second in command, Eliab the third,
10Mishmannah the fourth, Jeremiah the fifth,
11Attai the sixth, Eliel the seventh,
12Johanan the eighth, Elzabad the ninth,
13Jeremiah the tenth and Macbannai the eleventh.

14These Gadites were army commanders; the least was a match for a hundred,*a* and the greatest for a thousand.*b* 15It was they who crossed the Jordan in the first month when it was overflowing all its banks,*c* and they put to flight everyone living in the valleys, to the east and to the west.

16Other Benjamites*d* and some men from Judah also came to David in his stronghold. 17David went out to meet them and said to them, "If you have come to me in peace, to help me, I am ready to have you unite with me. But if you have come to betray me to my enemies when my hands are free from violence, may the God of our fathers see it and judge you."

18Then the Spirit*e* came upon Amasai,*f* chief of the Thirty, and he said:

"We are yours, O David!
We are with you, O son of Jesse!
Success,*g* success to you,
and success to those who help you,
for your God will help you."

So David received them and made them leaders of his raiding bands.

19Some of the men of Manasseh defected to David when he went with the Philistines to fight against Saul. (He and his men did not help the Philistines because, after consultation, their rulers sent him away. They said, "It will cost us our heads if he deserts to his master Saul.")*h* 20When David went to Ziklag,*i* these were the men of Manasseh who defected to him: Adnah, Jozabad, Jediael, Michael, Jozabad, Elihu and Zillethai, leaders of units of a thousand in Manasseh. 21They helped David against raiding bands, for all of them were brave warriors, and they were commanders in his army. 22Day after day men came to help David, until he had a great army, like the army of God.*a*

Others Join David at Hebron

23These are the numbers of the men armed for battle who came to David at Hebron*j* to turn*k* Saul's kingdom over to him, as the Lord had said:*l*

a 22 Or a great and mighty army

12:2 *t* Jdg 3:15; 20:16 *u* 2Sa 3:19
12:4 *v* Jos 15:36
12:7 *w* Jos 15:58
12:8 *x* Ge 30:11 *y* 2Sa 17:10 *z* 2Sa 2:18
12:14 *a* Lev 26:8 *b* Dt 32:30
12:15 *c* Jos 3:15
12:16 *d* 2Sa 3:19
12:18 *e* Jdg 3:10; 6:34; 1Ch 28:12; 2Ch 15:1; 20:14; 24:20 *f* 2Sa 17:25 *g* 1Sa 25:5-6
12:19 *h* 1Sa 29:2-11
12:20 *i* 1Sa 27:6
12:23 *j* 2Sa 2:3-4 *k* 1Ch 10:14 *l* 1Sa 16:1; 1Ch 11:10

David's soldiers were absolutely loyal, though they came from different tribes. An emphasis on tolerance and multicultural awareness has segmented our own society into hundreds of subcultures, creating a new kind of "tribalism." Groups form around addictive behaviors, accumulation of wealth, entertainment preferences, etc. For us as Christians, education and practice in Biblical principles are essential (1) to nurture our loyalty to God and our fellow church members and (2) to disentangle us from our cultural ties.

24 men of Judah, carrying shield and spear—6,800 armed for battle;

25 men of Simeon, warriors ready for battle—7,100;

12:28
m 2Sa 8:17;
1Ch 6:8; 15:11;
16:39; 27:17
12:29
n 2Sa 3:19
o 2Sa 2:8-9

26 men of Levi—4,600, 27 including Jehoiada, leader of the family of Aaron, with 3,700 men, 28 and Zadok, m a brave young warrior, with 22 officers from his family;

29 men of Benjamin, n Saul's kinsmen—3,000, most o of whom had remained loyal to Saul's house until then;

30 men of Ephraim, brave warriors, famous in their own clans—20,800;

31 men of half the tribe of Manasseh, designated by name to come and make David king—18,000;

12:32
p Est 1:13

32 men of Issachar, who understood the times and knew what Israel should do p—200 chiefs, with all their relatives under their command;

33 men of Zebulun, experienced soldiers prepared for battle with every type of weapon, to help David with undivided loyalty—50,000;

34 men of Naphtali—1,000 officers, together with 37,000 men carrying shields and spears;

35 men of Dan, ready for battle—28,600;

36 men of Asher, experienced soldiers prepared for battle—40,000;

37 and from east of the Jordan, men of Reuben, Gad and the half-tribe of Manasseh, armed with every type of weapon—120,000.

12:38
q 2Sa 5:1-3;
1Ch 9:1

38 All these were fighting men who volunteered to serve in the ranks. They came to Hebron fully determined to make David king over all Israel. q All the rest of the Israelites were also of one mind to make David king.

12:39
r 2Sa 3:20;
Isa 25:6-8

39 The men spent three days there with David, eating and drinking, r for their families had supplied provisions for them.

12:40
s 2Sa 16:1; 17:29
t 1Sa 25:18
u 1Ch 29:22

40 Also, their neighbors from as far away as Issachar, Zebulun and Naphtali came bringing food on donkeys, camels, mules and oxen. There were plentiful supplies s of flour, fig cakes, raisin t cakes, wine, oil, cattle and sheep, for there was joy u in Israel.

Bringing Back the Ark

13 David conferred with each of his officers, the commanders of thousands and commanders of hundreds. 2 He then said to the whole assembly of Israel, "If it seems good to you and if it is the will of the LORD our God, let us send word far and wide to the rest of our brothers throughout the territories of Israel, and also to the priests and Levites who are with them in their towns and pasturelands, to come and join us.

13:3
v 1Sa 7:1-2
w 2Ch 1:5

3 Let us bring the ark of our God back to us, v for we did not inquire w of a it b during the reign of Saul." 4 The whole assembly agreed to do this, because it seemed right to all the people.

13:5
x 1Ch 11:1; 15:3
y Jos 13:3

5 So David assembled all the Israelites, x from the Shihor River y in Egypt to Lebo c

---

a 3 Or we neglected   b 3 Or him   c 5 Or to the entrance to

---

1 Chronicles 12:23–40

The tribal muster roll complements the preceding lists of individuals who sided with David prior to Saul's death. The purpose of the gathering at Hebron was the transfer of the kingdom to David. The Chronicler noted that this was done according to the word of the Lord (v. 23). The roll names twelve tribes plus the two half-tribes of Manasseh, the most complete tribal register in the Old Testament—further evidence that "all Israel" had supported David's kingship. It was customary to conclude covenant ceremonies with celebratory meals that ratified the compact—thus the recorded three-day feast.

As human beings, we are prone to celebrate. Celebrations seal in our minds and hearts the significance of an event or a victory won. But as Christians, do we really gather to celebrate the good things the Lord has done, other than at Thanksgiving or during a special church service? David's new kingdom had many obstacles yet to overcome. We can worry excessively about our world and its discouraging realities. A celebration at the appropriate time, like the one in this text, recognizes that there is also cause for joy.

1 Chronicles 13:1–14

An explanation of Uzzah's tragic demise is found in phase two of the record of the transfer of the ark to Jerusalem (15:1–15). Here we learn that David had failed to "inquire" of the Lord as to the proper procedure for moving the ark (15:13). The ark shouldn't have been transported on a cart (13:7). According to Mosaic Law, only the Levites were to carry the holy things of the tabernacle; and even they weren't to touch them, upon threat of death (Num. 4:4–6,15). Accordingly, David directed the Levites to transport the ark by means of the prescribed carrying poles (15:15; cf. Ex. 25:12–15).

Hamath, *z* to bring the ark of God from Kiriath Jearim. *a* 6David and all the Israelites with him went to Baalah *b* of Judah (Kiriath Jearim) to bring up from there the ark of God the LORD, who is enthroned between the cherubim *c*—the ark that is called by the Name.

7They moved the ark of God from Abinadab's *d* house on a new cart, with Uzzah and Ahio guiding it. 8David and all the Israelites were celebrating with all their might before God, with songs and with harps, lyres, tambourines, cymbals and trumpets. *e*

9When they came to the threshing floor of Kidon, Uzzah reached out his hand to steady the ark, because the oxen stumbled. 10The LORD's anger *f* burned against Uzzah, and he struck him down *g* because he had put his hand on the ark. So he died there before God.

11Then David was angry because the LORD's wrath had broken out against Uzzah, and to this day that place is called Perez Uzzah. *a h*

12David was afraid of God that day and asked, "How can I ever bring the ark of God to me?" 13He did not take the ark to be with him in the City of David. Instead, he took it aside to the house of Obed-Edom *i* the Gittite. 14The ark of God remained with the family of Obed-Edom in his house for three months, and the LORD blessed his household *j* and everything he had.

David's House and Family

14 Now Hiram king of Tyre sent messengers to David, along with cedar logs, *k* stonemasons and carpenters to build a palace for him. 2And David knew that the LORD had established him as king over Israel and that his kingdom had been highly exalted *l* for the sake of his people Israel.

3In Jerusalem David took more wives and became the father of more sons *m* and daughters. 4These are the names of the children born to him there: *n* Shammua, Shobab, Nathan, Solomon, 5Ibhar, Elishua, Elpelet, 6Nogah, Nepheg, Japhia, 7Elishama, Beeliada *b* and Eliphelet.

David Defeats the Philistines

8When the Philistines heard that David had been anointed king over all Israel, *o* they went up in full force to search for him, but David heard about it and went out to meet them. 9Now the Philistines had come and raided the Valley *p* of Rephaim; 10so David inquired of God: "Shall I go and attack the Philistines? Will you hand them over to me?"

The LORD answered him, "Go, I will hand them over to you." 11So David and his men went up to Baal Perazim, *q* and there he defeated them.

a 11 Perez Uzzah means outbreak against Uzzah.   *b 7 A variant of Eliada*

13:5
z Nu 13:21
a 1Sa 6:21; 7:2
13:6
b Jos 15:9; 2Sa 6:2
c Ex 25:22;
2Ki 19:15
13:7
d Nu 4:15; 1Sa 7:1

13:8
e 2Sa 6:5;
1Ch 15:16,19,24;
2Ch 5:12; Ps 92:3
13:10
f 1Ch 15:13,15
g Lev 10:2

13:11
h 1Ch 15:13;
Ps 7:11

13:13
i 1Ch 15:18,24;
16:38; 26:4-5,15
13:14
j 2Sa 6:11;
1Ch 26:4-5

14:1
k 2Ch 2:3; Ezr 3:7

14:2
l Nu 24:7; Dt 26:19
14:3
m 1Ch 3:1
14:4
n 1Ch 3:9

14:8
o 1Ch 11:1
14:9
p ver 13; Jos 15:8;
1Ch 11:15

14:11
q Isa 28:21

You may resonate with David's outrage over Uzzah's death. The fact was, though, that God had been explicit in his instructions about transporting his sacred ark, and Uzzah and those with him had taken a cavalier, lackadaisical approach. During the 20th century, the pendulum in Christianity—particularly on an individual level—swung from an emphasis on God's awesome holiness, glory, and justice to a sometimes almost exclusive focus on his forgiveness, mercy, and love.

The Chronicler's report of God's blessing on the household of Obed-Edom during the three months the ark was with them (v. 14) shows that the transgression against God wasn't the transfer of the ark itself but the faulty way in which it was carried out. Our takeaway is that God still requires proper "means" to achieve good and right "ends."

1 Chronicles 14:1–7
Hiram's desire to "build a house" for David

foreshadowed the same theme in chapter 17, where David sought to build a house for God but instead learned of the Lord's desire to "build a house" for him. The Jerusalem birth report and name list assume reader knowledge of the Hebron birth report and name list (2 Sam. 3:2–5). Unlike Saul's dynasty, which died out (1 Chron. 10:6), David's house became a "fruitful vine" (cf. Ps. 128:3).

David rightly interpreted God's extraordinary blessings as a sign of divine approval "for the sake of his people Israel" (v. 2). God still blesses individuals in positions of authority who carry out their responsibilities on behalf of God's people with divine accountability in view. Second Chronicles 7:14 constitutes one of the most memorable Old Testament promises, and it still applies today. God will exercise his power to "heal" a land whose government and citizenry are willing to seek forgiveness and submit to him in humility.

14:12
r Ex 32:20
s Jos 7:15
14:13
t ver 9

He said, "As waters break out, God has broken out against my enemies by my hand." So that place was called Baal Perazim.[a] 12The Philistines had abandoned their gods there, and David gave orders to burn[r] them in the fire.[s]

13Once more the Philistines raided the valley;[t] 14so David inquired of God again, and God answered him, "Do not go straight up, but circle around them and attack them in front of the balsam trees. 15As soon as you hear the sound of marching in the tops of the balsam trees, move out to battle, because that will mean God has gone out in front of you to strike the Philistine army." 16So David did as God commanded him, and they struck down the Philistine army, all the way from Gibeon[u] to Gezer.[v]

14:16
u Jos 9:3
v Jos 10:33
14:17
w Jos 6:27;
2Ch 26:8
x Ex 15:14-16;
Dt 2:25

17So David's fame[w] spread throughout every land, and the LORD made all the nations fear[x] him.

The Ark Brought to Jerusalem

15 After David had constructed buildings for himself in the City of David, he prepared[y] a place for the ark of God and pitched[z] a tent for it. 2Then David said, "No one but the Levites[a] may carry[b] the ark of God, because the LORD chose them to carry the ark of the LORD and to minister[c] before him forever."

15:1
y Ps 132:1-18
z 1Ch 16:1; 17:1
15:2
a Nu 4:15; Dt 10:8;
2Ch 5:5 b Dt 31:9
c 1Ch 23:13
15:3
d 1Ki 8:1; 1Ch 13:5

3David assembled all Israel[d] in Jerusalem to bring up the ark of the LORD to the place he had prepared for it. 4He called together the descendants of Aaron and the Levites:

5From the descendants of Kohath,
Uriel the leader and 120 relatives;
6from the descendants of Merari,
Asaiah the leader and 220 relatives;
7from the descendants of Gershon,[b]
Joel the leader and 130 relatives;
8from the descendants of Elizaphan,[e]
Shemaiah the leader and 200 relatives;
9from the descendants of Hebron,[f]
Eliel the leader and 80 relatives;
10from the descendants of Uzziel,
Amminadab the leader and 112 relatives.

15:8
e Ex 6:22
15:9
f Ex 6:18
15:11
g 1Ch 12:28
h 1Sa 22:20
15:12
i Ex 19:14-15;
Lev 11:44;
2Ch 35:6
15:13
j 1Ki 8:4 k 2Sa 6:3;
1Ch 13:7-10

11Then David summoned Zadok[g] and Abiathar[h] the priests, and Uriel, Asaiah, Joel, Shemaiah, Eliel and Amminadab the Levites. 12He said to them, "You are the heads of the Levitical families; you and your fellow Levites are to consecrate[i] yourselves and bring up the ark of the LORD, the God of Israel, to the place I have prepared for it. 13It was because you, the Levites,[j] did not bring it up the first time that the LORD our God broke out in anger against us.[k] We did not inquire of him about how to do it in the prescribed way." 14So the priests and Levites consecrated them-

a 11 *Baal Perazim* means *the lord who breaks out.*   b 7 Hebrew *Gershom,* a variant of *Gershon*

1 Chronicles 14:8–17

When the Philistines launched a second offensive, God instructed David to circle their army but to wait for the "sound of marching" in the treetops before attacking. The rustling of leaves was most likely God's Spirit, since David was told that the Lord would go before him in battle. The noise, perhaps akin to soldiers' feet rushing into battle, would confuse the enemy (cf. 2 Kings 7:6). The back-to-back victories over the Philistines at the Valley of Rephaim reversed the outcome at Mount Gilboa and avenged the deaths of Saul and Jonathan. They closed the story of that tragic first chapter in the history of Israelite kingship (1 Chron. 10).

The spread of David's fame and the fear of God among the nations were interrelated (v. 17). As God blessed David's faithfulness, so David's success brought glory and honor to God. In a similar way, we as Christians live out our lives before the scrutiny of a watching world. We may to some degree take our faith and lifestyle for granted, but our value systems often are a curiosity to those around us. Do you at times undermine God's glory by offering the world a mixed message?

1 Chronicles 15:1—16:6

The Chronicler was clear that faulty procedure that failed to recognize God's holiness was responsible for the aborted first attempt to transfer the ark (see "There and Then" for 13:1–14). This time David and the religious leaders followed the prescriptions of the Law of Moses. The necessity of obeying God's word—accompanied by God's blessing for obedience and the withholding of his blessing for disobedience—is a recurring theme in Chronicles.

selves in order to bring up the ark of the LORD, the God of Israel. [15]And the Levites carried the ark of God with the poles on their shoulders, as Moses had command-ed[l] in accordance with the word of the LORD.

[16]David told the leaders of the Levites to appoint their brothers as singers[m] to sing joyful songs, accompanied by musical instruments: lyres, harps and cymbals.[n]

[17]So the Levites appointed Heman[o] son of Joel; from his brothers, Asaph[p] son of Berekiah; and from their brothers the Merarites,[q] Ethan son of Kushaiah; [18]and with them their brothers next in rank: Zechariah,[a] Jaaziel, Shemiramoth, Jehiel, Unni, Eliab, Benaiah, Maaseiah, Mattithiah, Eliphelehu, Mikneiah, Obed-Edom[r] and Jeiel,[b] the gatekeepers.

[19]The musicians Heman,[s] Asaph and Ethan were to sound the bronze cymbals; [20]Zechariah, Aziel, Shemiramoth, Jehiel, Unni, Eliab, Maaseiah and Benaiah were to play the lyres according to *alamoth*,[c] [21]and Mattithiah, Eliphelehu, Mikneiah, Obed-Edom, Jeiel and Azaziah were to play the harps, directing according to *shem-inith*.[c] [22]Kenaniah the head Levite was in charge of the singing; that was his respon-sibility because he was skillful at it.

[23]Berekiah and Elkanah were to be doorkeepers for the ark. [24]Shebaniah, Josh-aphat, Nethanel, Amasai, Zechariah, Benaiah and Eliezer the priests were to blow trumpets[t] before the ark of God. Obed-Edom and Jehiah were also to be doorkeep-ers for the ark.

[25]So David and the elders of Israel and the commanders of units of a thousand went to bring up the ark[u] of the covenant of the LORD from the house of Obed-Edom, with rejoicing. [26]Because God had helped the Levites who were carrying the ark of the covenant of the LORD, seven bulls and seven rams[v] were sacrificed. [27]Now David was clothed in a robe of fine linen, as were all the Levites who were carrying the ark, and as were the singers, and Kenaniah, who was in charge of the singing of the choirs. David also wore a linen ephod. [28]So all Israel brought up the ark of the covenant of the LORD with shouts, with the sounding of rams' horns[w] and trumpets, and of cymbals, and the playing of lyres and harps.

[29]As the ark of the covenant of the LORD was entering the City of David, Michal daughter of Saul watched from a window. And when she saw King David dancing and celebrating, she despised him in her heart.

16

They brought the ark of God and set it inside the tent that David had pitched[x] for it, and they presented burnt offerings and fellowship offerings[d] before God. [2]After David had finished sacrificing the burnt offerings and fellowship offerings, he blessed[y] the people in the name of the LORD. [3]Then he gave a loaf of bread, a cake of dates and a cake of raisins to each Israelite man and woman.

[4]He appointed some of the Levites to minister[z] before the ark of the LORD, to make petition, to give thanks, and to praise the LORD, the God of Israel: [5]Asaph was the chief, Zechariah second, then Jeiel, Shemiramoth, Jehiel, Mattithiah, Eliab, Be-naiah, Obed-Edom and Jeiel. They were to play the lyres and harps, Asaph was to sound the cymbals, [6]and Benaiah and Jahaziel the priests were to blow the trum-pets regularly before the ark of the covenant of God.

15:15
l Ex 25:14;
Nu 4:5,15
15:16
m Ps 68:25
n 1Ch 13:8; 25:1;
Ne 12:27,36
15:17
o 1Ch 6:33
p 1Ch 6:39
q 1Ch 6:44
15:18
r 1Ch 26:4-5

15:19
s 1Ch 25:6

15:24
t ver 28; 1Ch 16:6;
2Ch 7:6

15:25
u 1Ch 13:13;
2Ch 1:4

15:26
v Nu 23:1-4,29

15:28
w 1Ch 13:8

16:1
x 1Ch 15:1

16:2
y Ex 39:43

16:4
z 1Ch 15:2

---

[a] 18 Three Hebrew manuscripts and most Septuagint manuscripts (see also verse 20 and 1 Chron. 16:5); most Hebrew manuscripts *Zechariah son and* or *Zechariah, Ben and*   [b] 18 Hebrew; Septuagint (see also verse 21) *Jeiel and Azaziah*   [c] 20,21 Probably a musical term   [d] 1 Traditionally *peace offerings*; also in verse 2

The concluding section of this report showcases the priests and Levites as musicians, another theme in Chronicles. The purpose in David's appointments was simple: The Levitical corps was to provide appropriate music for the processional. The occasion of installing the ark in Jerusalem was to be celebratory and festive.

God's presence is something to celebrate. We can only guess why David's wife Michal "despised [David] in her heart" (15:29). Those of us from every family in Christendom would do well not to make the same mistake about the worship traditions of other parts of the body of Christ. Silence, solemnity, shouting, dancing, instrumental music, singing, liturgy, proces-sions, lifting hands, clapping, kneeling, and other ex-pressions all help us communicate our joy at the pres-ence of the King of kings in our respective traditions. Try visiting another congregation to gain appreciation for a different worship style.

David's Psalm of Thanks

16:7
a 2Sa 23:1

[7]That day David first committed to Asaph and his associates this psalm[a] of thanks to the LORD:

16:8
b ver 34; Ps 136:1
c 2Ki 19:19

[8]Give thanks[b] to the LORD, call on his name;
   make known among the nations[c] what he has done.

16:9
d Ex 15:1

[9]Sing to him, sing praise[d] to him;
   tell of all his wonderful acts.
[10]Glory in his holy name;
   let the hearts of those who seek the LORD rejoice.

16:11
e 1Ch 28:9;
2Ch 7:14; Ps 24:6;
119:2,58
16:12
f Ps 77:11
g Ps 78:43

[11]Look to the LORD and his strength;
   seek[e] his face always.
[12]Remember[f] the wonders he has done,
   his miracles,[g] and the judgments he pronounced,
[13]O descendants of Israel his servant,
   O sons of Jacob, his chosen ones.

16:14
h Isa 26:9

[14]He is the LORD our God;
   his judgments[h] are in all the earth.
[15]He remembers[a] his covenant forever,
   the word he commanded, for a thousand generations,

16:16
i Ge 12:7; 15:18;
17:2; 22:16-18;
26:3; 28:13; 35:11
16:17
j Ge 35:9-12

[16]the covenant[i] he made with Abraham,
   the oath he swore to Isaac.
[17]He confirmed it to Jacob[j] as a decree,
   to Israel as an everlasting covenant:

16:18
k Ge 13:14-17

[18]"To you I will give the land of Canaan[k]
   as the portion you will inherit."

16:19
l Ge 34:30; Dt 7:7

[19]When they were but few in number,[l]
   few indeed, and strangers in it,
[20]they[b] wandered from nation to nation,
   from one kingdom to another.

16:21
m Ge 12:17; 20:3;
Ex 7:15-18
16:22
n Ge 20:7

[21]He allowed no man to oppress them;
   for their sake he rebuked kings:[m]
[22]"Do not touch my anointed ones;
   do my prophets[n] no harm."

[23]Sing to the LORD, all the earth;
   proclaim his salvation day after day.
[24]Declare his glory among the nations,
   his marvelous deeds among all peoples.

16:25
o Ps 48:1 *p* Ps 76:7;
89:7 *q* Dt 32:39

[25]For great is the LORD and most worthy of praise;[o]
   he is to be feared[p] above all gods.[q]
[26]For all the gods of the nations are idols,

a 15 Some Septuagint manuscripts (see also Psalm 105:8); Hebrew *Remember*   *b* 18-20 One Hebrew manuscript, Septuagint and Vulgate (see also Psalm 105:12); most Hebrew manuscripts *inherit,* / [19]*though you are but few in number,* / *few indeed, and strangers in it."* / [20]*They*

1 Chronicles 16:7–43

The installation of the ark in Jerusalem marked the nation's return to God under David's leadership; the ark symbolized the covenant agreement established by the Lord with Israel at Mount Sinai. David's song of praise celebrated God as covenant maker and covenant keeper, a concept central to the Chronicler's theology of hope for postexilic Judah.

The report of David's departure to go home and bless his family concludes the story of the transfer of the ark and introduces the following chapter, since David's action foreshadowed the covenant blessing God would pronounce on the royal family.

In our electronic age of seemingly limitless communication, consumers make reading, listening, and viewing decisions based largely on interest. The emphasis has shifted from facts and explanations to feelings, imagination, and experiences intended to free the spirit and move the heart. Effective Christian education that balances information and experiential application can ensure that all believers are equipped with both adequate knowledge and engaged hearts.

but the LORD made the heavens.[r]

27 Splendor and majesty are before him;
strength and joy in his dwelling place.

28 Ascribe to the LORD, O families of nations,
ascribe to the LORD glory and strength,[s]

29 ascribe to the LORD the glory due his name.
Bring an offering and come before him;
worship the LORD in the splendor of his[a] holiness.[t]

30 Tremble[u] before him, all the earth!
The world is firmly established; it cannot be moved.

31 Let the heavens rejoice, let the earth be glad;[v]
let them say among the nations, "The LORD reigns![w]"

32 Let the sea resound, and all that is in it;[x]
let the fields be jubilant, and everything in them!

33 Then the trees[y] of the forest will sing,
they will sing for joy before the LORD,
for he comes to judge[z] the earth.

34 Give thanks[a] to the LORD, for he is good;[b]
his love endures forever.[c]

35 Cry out, "Save us, O God our Savior;[d]
gather us and deliver us from the nations,
that we may give thanks to your holy name,
that we may glory in your praise."

36 Praise be to the LORD, the God of Israel,[e]
from everlasting to everlasting.

Then all the people said "Amen" and "Praise the LORD."

37 David left Asaph and his associates before the ark of the covenant of the LORD to minister there regularly, according to each day's requirements.[f] 38 He also left Obed-Edom[g] and his sixty-eight associates to minister with them. Obed-Edom son of Jeduthun, and also Hosah,[h] were gatekeepers.

39 David left Zadok[i] the priest and his fellow priests before the tabernacle of the LORD at the high place in Gibeon[j] 40 to present burnt offerings to the LORD on the altar of burnt offering regularly, morning and evening, in accordance with everything written in the Law[k] of the LORD, which he had given Israel. 41 With them were Heman[l] and Jeduthun and the rest of those chosen and designated by name to give thanks to the LORD, "for his love endures forever." 42 Heman and Jeduthun were responsible for the sounding of the trumpets and cymbals and for the playing of the other instruments for sacred song.[m] The sons of Jeduthun were stationed at the gate.

43 Then all the people left, each for his own home, and David returned home to bless his family.

God's Promise to David

17 After David was settled in his palace, he said to Nathan the prophet, "Here I am, living in a palace of cedar, while the ark of the covenant of the LORD is under a tent.[n]"

2 Nathan replied to David, "Whatever you have in mind,[o] do it, for God is with you."

3 That night the word of God came to Nathan, saying:

a 29 Or LORD with the splendor of

Side notes (right column)

16:26
r Lev 19:4;
Ps 102:25

16:28
s Ps 29:1-2

16:29
t Ps 29:1-2
16:30
u Ps 114:7

16:31
v Isa 44:23; 49:13
w Ps 93:1

16:32
x Ps 98:7

16:33
y Isa 55:12
z Ps 96:10; 98:9

16:34
a ver 8 b Na 1:7
c 2Ch 5:13; 7:3;
Ezr 3:11;
Ps 136:1-26;
Jer 33:11
16:35
d Mic 7:7

16:36
e Dt 27:15;
1Ki 8:15;
Ps 72:18-19

16:37
f 2Ch 8:14
16:38
g 1Ch 13:13
h 1Ch 26:10

16:39
i 2Sa 8:17;
1Ch 15:11 / 1Ki 3:4;
2Ch 1:3

16:40
k Ex 29:38;
Nu 28:1-8
16:41
l 1Ch 6:33; 25:1-6;
2Ch 5:13

16:42
m 2Ch 7:6

17:1
n 1Ch 15:1

17:2
o 2Ch 6:7

---

1 Chronicles 17:1-15

Chronicles is the story of two "houses": the house or dynasty of King David and the house or temple of God. David's desire to build a temple for God was typical of royal behavior in the Biblical world. In ancient Egypt and Mesopotamia kings erected monuments and built great temples as an act of homage to the deity they considered responsible for establishing them on the throne. Beyond this, David was ashamed that God as the true King of Israel was confined to a tent while he himself enjoyed the luxury of a palace.

17:4
p 1Ch 28:3

4 "Go and tell my servant David, 'This is what the LORD says: You[p] are not the one to build me a house to dwell in. 5I have not dwelt in a house from the day I brought Israel up out of Egypt to this day. I have moved from one tent site to another, from one dwelling place to another. 6Wherever I have moved with all the Israelites, did I ever say to any of their leaders[a] whom I commanded to shepherd my people, "Why have you not built me a house of cedar?" '

17:7
q 2Sa 6:21

7 "Now then, tell my servant David, 'This is what the LORD Almighty says: I took you from the pasture and from following the flock, to be ruler[q] over my people Israel. 8I have been with you wherever you have gone, and I have cut off all your enemies from before you. Now I will make your name like the names of the greatest men of the earth. 9And I will provide a place for my people Israel and will plant them so that they can have a home of their own and no longer be disturbed. Wicked people will not oppress them anymore, as they

17:10
r Jdg 2:16

did at the beginning 10and have done ever since the time I appointed leaders[r] over my people Israel. I will also subdue all your enemies.

" 'I declare to you that the LORD will build a house for you: 11When your days are over and you go to be with your fathers, I will raise up your offspring to succeed you, one of your own sons, and I will establish his kingdom. 12He is the

17:12
s 1Ki 5:5 t 2Ch 7:18
17:13
u 2Co 6:18
v Lk 1:32; Heb 1:5*
17:14
w 1Ki 2:12;
1Ch 28:5
x Ps 132:11;
Jer 33:17

one who will build[s] a house for me, and I will establish his throne forever.[t] 13I will be his father,[u] and he will be my son.[v] I will never take my love away from him, as I took it away from your predecessor. 14I will set him over my house and my kingdom forever; his throne[w] will be established forever.[x] ' "

15Nathan reported to David all the words of this entire revelation.

David's Prayer

16Then King David went in and sat before the LORD, and he said:

"Who am I, O LORD God, and what is my family, that you have brought me this far? 17And as if this were not enough in your sight, O God, you have spoken about the future of the house of your servant. You have looked on me as though I were the most exalted of men, O LORD God.

17:19
y 2Sa 7:16-17;
2Ki 20:6; Isa 9:7;
37:35; 55:3
z 2Sa 7:25
17:20
a Ex 8:10; 9:14;
15:11; Isa 44:6;
46:9
17:21
b Ex 6:6

18"What more can David say to you for honoring your servant? For you know your servant, 19O LORD. For the sake[y] of your servant and according to your will, you have done this great thing and made known all these great promises.[z] 20"There is no one like you, O LORD, and there is no God but you,[a] as we have heard with our own ears. 21And who is like your people Israel—the one nation on earth whose God went out to redeem[b] a people for himself, and to make a name for yourself, and to perform great and awesome wonders by driv-

---

a 6 Traditionally *judges*; also in verse 10

God's priority to build a house/dynasty for David took precedence over the construction of a permanent sanctuary. Lasting and appropriate Israelite worship of God needed to be founded on righteous leadership. We are accustomed to separation of church and state, but nations like the United States are still profoundly affected by the moral and religious standards of their highest leaders. A president or prime minister who attends church and regularly appeals to the Lord for blessing and direction sets the tone for government—as does the chief executive who plays fast and loose with morality and ethics. What presidents or other top officials have had the greatest impact on your life? Why?

1 Chronicles 17:16–27

These verses constitute the first of several prayers by Israelite kings included in the Chronicler's retelling of Israelite history. The Chronicler wanted to draw the people of postexilic Judah back into conversation with God. His emphasis on prayer fit naturally with his concern for worship renewal. A repeated message in Chronicles is that God both hears and answers the prayers of the righteous by doing great things that bring glory to his name.

His repeated use of the word "forever" indicates that the Chronicler's message was intended for other audiences beyond his own generation. The New Testament recognizes Jesus Christ as the ultimate fulfillment of this prayer. He's the heir of David's throne (Luke 1:32–33)—both the son of David (Matt. 1:1) and the Son of God—charged to build and oversee the very "house" of God (Heb. 3:6). Today God continues to build his "house," the church—a spiritual house that will prevail against the opposition of hell itself (Matt. 16:18; Eph. 2:21; 1 Peter 2:5)!

ing out nations from before your people, whom you redeemed from Egypt? 22You made your people Israel your very own forever, c and you, O LORD, have become their God.

23 "And now, LORD, let the promise d you have made concerning your servant and his house be established forever. Do as you promised, 24so that it will be established and that your name will be great forever. Then men will say, 'The LORD Almighty, the God over Israel, is Israel's God!' And the house of your servant David will be established before you.

25 "You, my God, have revealed to your servant that you will build a house for him. So your servant has found courage to pray to you. 26O LORD, you are God! You have promised these good things to your servant. 27Now you have been pleased to bless the house of your servant, that it may continue forever in your sight; e for you, O LORD, have blessed it, and it will be blessed forever."

David's Victories

18 In the course of time, David defeated the Philistines and subdued them, and he took Gath and its surrounding villages from the control of the Philistines.

2David also defeated the Moabites, f and they became subject to him and brought tribute.

3Moreover, David fought Hadadezer king of Zobah, g as far as Hamath, when he went to establish his control along the Euphrates River. h 4David captured a thousand of his chariots, seven thousand charioteers and twenty thousand foot soldiers. He hamstrung i all but a hundred of the chariot horses.

5When the Arameans of Damascus j came to help Hadadezer king of Zobah, David struck down twenty-two thousand of them. 6He put garrisons in the Aramean kingdom of Damascus, and the Arameans became subject to him and brought tribute. The LORD gave David victory everywhere he went.

7David took the gold shields carried by the officers of Hadadezer and brought them to Jerusalem. 8From Tebah a and Cun, towns that belonged to Hadadezer, David took a great quantity of bronze, which Solomon used to make the bronze Sea, k the pillars and various bronze articles.

9When Tou king of Hamath heard that David had defeated the entire army of Hadadezer king of Zobah, 10he sent his son Hadoram to King David to greet him and congratulate him on his victory in battle over Hadadezer, who had been at war with Tou. Hadoram brought all kinds of articles of gold and silver and bronze.

11King David dedicated these articles to the LORD, as he had done with the silver and gold he had taken from all these nations: Edom l and Moab, the Ammonites and the Philistines, and Amalek. m

12Abishai son of Zeruiah struck down eighteen thousand Edomites n in the Val-

a 8 Hebrew Tibhath, a variant of Tebah

1 Chronicles 18:1–13

The recounting of David's campaigns in chapters 18–20 demonstrates God's blessing on David's reign and the fulfillment of God's promise to subdue David's enemies (17:10). The accounts also provide the background for the explanation that David was prohibited from building God's temple because he had shed so much blood (22:6–8; 28:3). According to Deuteronomy, God would choose a dwelling place for his name once the Israelites had "rest" from their enemies (Deut. 12:10–11). That rest would occur under Solomon (1 Chron. 22:9–10).

The God who "gave David victory" (vv. 6,13) also was the God of the Chronicler and of postexilic Judah. The same blessing of divine approval awaited those who

would dedicate themselves in expectant faith to Jerusalem's spiritual and physical restoration, even as David had dedicated the silver and gold plundered in war to the work of the Lord (v. 11; cf. 22:14).

The war reports in chapters 18–20 are more than stories of the triumph of good over evil. The Chronicler's point: To oppose Israel (God's people) is to oppose God, reminding us that "if God is for us, who can be against us?" (Rom. 8:31). These incidents are stirring examples of God's power to deliver his faithful servants from difficult circumstances. The Chronicler's audience needed to hear that—but no more than do we, who experience stressful and uncertain times of our own (cf. 2 Tim. 3:10–13; James 1:2,12). From what has God delivered you?

ley of Salt. ¹³He put garrisons in Edom, and all the Edomites became subject to David. The LORD gave David victory everywhere he went.

David's Officials

18:14
o 1Ch 29:26
p 1Ch 11:1
18:15
q 2Sa 5:6-8;
1Ch 11:6
18:16
r 2Sa 8:17; 1Ch 6:8
s 1Ch 24:6
18:17
t 1Sa 30:14;
2Sa 8:18; 15:18

19:1
u Ge 19:38;
Jdg 10:17-11:33;
2Ch 20:1-2;
Zep 2:8-11

19:3
v Nu 21:32

19:6
w Ge 34:30
x 1Ch 18:3,5,9

19:7
y Nu 21:30;
Jos 13:9,16

19:11
z 1Sa 26:6

¹⁴David reigned^o over all Israel,^{p} doing what was just and right for all his people. ¹⁵Joab^q son of Zeruiah was over the army; Jehoshaphat son of Ahilud was recorder; ¹⁶Zadok^r son of Ahitub and Ahimelech$^{a\,s}$ son of Abiathar were priests; Shavsha was secretary; ¹⁷Benaiah son of Jehoiada was over the Kerethites and Pelethites;^{t} and David's sons were chief officials at the king's side.

The Battle Against the Ammonites

19 In the course of time, Nahash king of the Ammonites^u died, and his son succeeded him as king. ²David thought, "I will show kindness to Hanun son of Nahash, because his father showed kindness to me." So David sent a delegation to express his sympathy to Hanun concerning his father.

When David's men came to Hanun in the land of the Ammonites to express sympathy to him, ³the Ammonite nobles said to Hanun, "Do you think David is honoring your father by sending men to you to express sympathy? Haven't his men come to you to explore and spy out^v the country and overthrow it?" ⁴So Hanun seized David's men, shaved them, cut off their garments in the middle at the buttocks, and sent them away.

⁵When someone came and told David about the men, he sent messengers to meet them, for they were greatly humiliated. The king said, "Stay at Jericho till your beards have grown, and then come back."

⁶When the Ammonites realized that they had become a stench^w in David's nostrils, Hanun and the Ammonites sent a thousand talents^b of silver to hire chariots and charioteers from Aram Naharaim,^{c} Aram Maacah and Zobah.^{x} ⁷They hired thirty-two thousand chariots and charioteers, as well as the king of Maacah with his troops, who came and camped near Medeba,^{y} while the Ammonites were mustered from their towns and moved out for battle.

⁸On hearing this, David sent Joab out with the entire army of fighting men. ⁹The Ammonites came out and drew up in battle formation at the entrance to their city, while the kings who had come were by themselves in the open country.

¹⁰Joab saw that there were battle lines in front of him and behind him; so he selected some of the best troops in Israel and deployed them against the Arameans. ¹¹He put the rest of the men under the command of Abishai^z his brother, and they

---

^{a} 16 Some Hebrew manuscripts, Vulgate and Syriac (see also 2 Samuel 8:17); most Hebrew manuscripts *Abimelech* ^{b} 6 That is, about 37 tons (about 34 metric tons) ^{c} 6 That is, Northwest Mesopotamia

---

1 Chronicles 18:14–17

The glowing assessment of David's reign in verse 14 both concludes the preceding war report and introduces the list of royal advisers. The fact that David ruled over "all Israel" was important to the Chronicler's message. The statement confirms that David satisfied the Israelites' expectations of the ideal king. Doing what was "just and right" became the standard by which later kings were measured (cf. Jer. 22:15–17).

In his presentation of King David, the Chronicler chose not to include the tarnishing account of David's adultery, murder, and cover-up (cf. 1 Sam. 11–12). The Israelites were no more ignorant of David's moral failures than we are of those of our leaders. Yet Scripture makes a positive overall appraisal of David based on his heart (cf. 1 Sam. 16:7; 1 Kings 3:6; 9:4; Ps. 78:72; Acts 13:22).

Jeremiah's evaluation of Israelite kings (see above)

specifically included their treatment of the needy and oppressed. In a country where the torch of leadership is passed along regularly, American citizens are in a position to make evaluations and comparisons of the candidates. What standards inform your vote?

1 Chronicles 19:1–19

The Arameans originally joined the Ammonites as hired mercenaries, but the resumption of fighting following their early retreat was their response to concern about David's growing military strength. For a second time David was victorious (vv. 17–18). Hadadezer was the king of Zobah (18:3), an Aramean state, and the leader of the Aramean coalition. Hadadezer's vassals (though not Hadadezer himself) entered into a peace treaty with Israel (19:19). The terms apparently included a clause prohibiting the Arameans from partnering with the Ammonites in future campaigns.

were deployed against the Ammonites. 12Joab said, "If the Arameans are too strong for me, then you are to rescue me; but if the Ammonites are too strong for you, then I will rescue you. 13Be strong and let us fight bravely for our people and the cities of our God. The LORD will do what is good in his sight."

14Then Joab and the troops with him advanced to fight the Arameans, and they fled before him. 15When the Ammonites saw that the Arameans were fleeing, they too fled before his brother Abishai and went inside the city. So Joab went back to Jerusalem.

16After the Arameans saw that they had been routed by Israel, they sent messengers and had Arameans brought from beyond the River, a with Shophach the commander of Hadadezer's army leading them.

17When David was told of this, he gathered all Israel a and crossed the Jordan; he advanced against them and formed his battle lines opposite them. David formed his lines to meet the Arameans in battle, and they fought against him. 18But they fled before Israel, and David killed seven thousand of their charioteers and forty thousand of their foot soldiers. He also killed Shophach the commander of their army.

19When the vassals of Hadadezer saw that they had been defeated by Israel, they made peace with David and became subject to him.

So the Arameans were not willing to help the Ammonites anymore.

19:17
a 1Ch 9:1

The Capture of Rabbah

20 In the spring, at the time when kings go off to war, Joab led out the armed forces. He laid waste the land of the Ammonites and went to Rabbah b and besieged it, but David remained in Jerusalem. Joab attacked Rabbah and left it in ruins. c 2David took the crown from the head of their king b—its weight was found to be a talent c of gold, and it was set with precious stones—and it was placed on David's head. He took a great quantity of plunder from the city 3and brought out the people who were there, consigning them to labor with saws and with iron picks and axes. d David did this to all the Ammonite towns. Then David and his entire army returned to Jerusalem.

20:1
b Dt 3:11;
2Sa 12:26
c Am 1:13-15

20:3
d Dt 29:11

War With the Philistines

4In the course of time, war broke out with the Philistines, at Gezer. e At that time Sibbecai the Hushathite killed Sippai, one of the descendants of the Rephaites, f and the Philistines were subjugated.

20:4
e Jos 10:33
f Ge 14:5

a *16* That is, the Euphrates   b *2* Or *of Milcom,* that is, Molech   c *2* That is, about 75 pounds (about 34 kilograms)

At the cross Christ crippled God's enemies, but we still await their decisive defeat. Christians live in the tension between "the now and the yet-to-come." Satan is still on the prowl (1 Peter 5:8), wreaking havoc in a world embroiled in endless conflict. We as individual Christians and as representatives of Christ's church are engaged in constant spiritual warfare, endowed with the "full armor of God" (Eph. 6:12–18). But our armor does us no good unless we wear it (Eph. 6:11).

1 Chronicles 20:1–3

The Chronicler condensed his version of the conclusion of the Ammonite war from the accounts found in the Samuel parallel (2 Sam. 11:1; 12:26–31). Chronicles omits the story of David's tryst with Bathsheba (2 Sam. 11:2—12:25), only hinting at the scandal by referring to David's decision to remain in Jerusalem. The transition between verses 1 and 2 is confusing without knowledge of 2 Samuel 12:26–29. Between these verses David had descended on Rabbah with additional forces

and completed the conquest of the city.

When is it time to move on? As the Chronicler seems to have been implying, once David had repented from (and suffered as a result of) his adultery with Bathsheba, both God and David in a sense put the incident behind them and got back to business as usual. The ramifications of David's sin would be ongoing, but God's forgiveness was final and irrevocable. And so it is with us. We may live with the natural consequences of our sin, but we need not continue to struggle with guilt and shame. We can move forward in confidence that his love for us is unchanged (cf. Rom. 8:1,37–39).

1 Chronicles 20:4–8

The Chronicler returned to the Philistine "problem" to conclude his summary of David's wars. The ongoing conflict stemmed primarily from the fact that Israel was landlocked and needed access to a seaport. The passage here relates to border skirmishes settled by duels between champion warriors more than to full-scale war.

20:5
g 1Sa 17:7
5In another battle with the Philistines, Elhanan son of Jair killed Lahmi the brother of Goliath the Gittite, who had a spear with a shaft like a weaver's rod. g

6In still another battle, which took place at Gath, there was a huge man with six fingers on each hand and six toes on each foot—twenty-four in all. He also was descended from Rapha. 7When he taunted Israel, Jonathan son of Shimea, David's brother, killed him.

8These were descendants of Rapha in Gath, and they fell at the hands of David and his men.

David Numbers the Fighting Men

21:1
h 2Ch 18:21;
Ps 109:6
i 2Ch 14:8; 25:5
21:2
j 1Ch 27:23-24
21:3
k Dt 1:11
21 Satan h rose up against Israel and incited David to take a census i of Israel. 2So David said to Joab and the commanders of the troops, "Go and count j the Israelites from Beersheba to Dan. Then report back to me so that I may know how many there are."

3But Joab replied, "May the LORD multiply his troops a hundred times over. k My lord the king, are they not all my lord's subjects? Why does my lord want to do this? Why should he bring guilt on Israel?"

21:5
l 1Ch 9:1
4The king's word, however, overruled Joab; so Joab left and went throughout Israel and then came back to Jerusalem. 5Joab reported the number of the fighting men to David: In all Israel l there were one million one hundred thousand men who could handle a sword, including four hundred and seventy thousand in Judah.

6But Joab did not include Levi and Benjamin in the numbering, because the king's command was repulsive to him. 7This command was also evil in the sight of God; so he punished Israel.

21:9
m 1Sa 22:5
n 1Sa 9:9
8Then David said to God, "I have sinned greatly by doing this. Now, I beg you, take away the guilt of your servant. I have done a very foolish thing."

9The LORD said to Gad, m David's seer, n 10 "Go and tell David, 'This is what the LORD says: I am giving you three options. Choose one of them for me to carry out against you.' "

21:12
o Dt 32:24
p Eze 30:25
q Ge 19:13
11So Gad went to David and said to him, "This is what the LORD says: 'Take your choice: 12three years of famine, o three months of being swept away a before your enemies, with their swords overtaking you, or three days of the sword p of the LORD q— days of plague in the land, with the angel of the LORD ravaging every part of Israel.' Now then, decide how I should answer the one who sent me."

21:13
r Ps 6:4; 86:15;
130:4,7
21:14
s 1Ch 27:24
21:15
t Ge 32:1
u Ps 125:2 v Ge 6:6;
Ex 32:14
w Ge 19:13
13David said to Gad, "I am in deep distress. Let me fall into the hands of the LORD, for his mercy r is very great; but do not let me fall into the hands of men."

14So the LORD sent a plague on Israel, and seventy thousand men of Israel fell dead. s 15And God sent an angel t to destroy Jerusalem. u But as the angel was doing so, the LORD saw it and was grieved v because of the calamity and said to the angel who was destroying w the people, "Enough! Withdraw your hand." The angel of the LORD was then standing at the threshing floor of Araunah b the Jebusite.

16David looked up and saw the angel of the LORD standing between heaven and

---

a 12 Hebrew; Septuagint and Vulgate (see also 2 Samuel 24:13) of fleeing   b 15 Hebrew Ornan, a variant of Araunah; also in verses 18-28

📖 The New Testament also is full of military terminology. Most Christians today understand Christ's death as a satisfaction of the demands of God's holiness and justice, resulting in redemption and salvation for the individual believer (cf. Rom. 8:32–34; Heb. 7:25). But a more inclusive "warfare worldview" sees the atonement of sinful humanity as one result of Christ's victory over the devil (cf. Heb. 2:14–15). In this broader sense, Jesus' death defeated Satan, enthroned Christ, and liberated the world from bondage to evil. We as individual Christians and as members of Christ's church are truly "more than conquerors" (Rom. 8:37)—in a unique position to infiltrate and influence our world in all areas for good.

1 Chronicles 21:1—22:1

🔄 The Chronicler brought his own unique perspective to bear on the census, one of only two times in which he presented David in a bad light (see also "There and Then" for 13:1–14). His primary concern was the relationship of this story to the Jerusalem temple. The threshing floor David had purchased in order to offer sacrifices to stop God's judgment against Israel had eventually become the site for God's temple. The Chronicler emphasized God's mercy and forgiveness in response to David's prayer and offering as he sought atonement. What better place for God's permanent sanctuary than this site of prayer and pardon?

earth, with a drawn sword in his hand extended over Jerusalem. Then David and the elders, clothed in sackcloth, fell facedown.[x]

[17]David said to God, "Was it not I who ordered the fighting men to be counted? I am the one who has sinned and done wrong. These are but sheep.[y] What have they done? O LORD my God, let your hand fall upon me and my family,[z] but do not let this plague remain on your people."

[18]Then the angel of the LORD ordered Gad to tell David to go up and build an altar to the LORD on the threshing floor[a] of Araunah the Jebusite. [19]So David went up in obedience to the word that Gad had spoken in the name of the LORD.

[20]While Araunah was threshing wheat,[b] he turned and saw the angel; his four sons who were with him hid themselves. [21]Then David approached, and when Araunah looked and saw him, he left the threshing floor and bowed down before David with his face to the ground.

[22]David said to him, "Let me have the site of your threshing floor so I can build an altar to the LORD, that the plague on the people may be stopped. Sell it to me at the full price."

[23]Araunah said to David, "Take it! Let my lord the king do whatever pleases him. Look, I will give the oxen for the burnt offerings, the threshing sledges for the wood, and the wheat for the grain offering. I will give all this."

[24]But King David replied to Araunah, "No, I insist on paying the full price. I will not take for the LORD what is yours, or sacrifice a burnt offering that costs me nothing."

[25]So David paid Araunah six hundred shekels[a] of gold for the site. [26]David built an altar to the LORD there and sacrificed burnt offerings and fellowship offerings.[b] He called on the LORD, and the LORD answered him with fire[c] from heaven on the altar of burnt offering.

[27]Then the LORD spoke to the angel, and he put his sword back into its sheath. [28]At that time, when David saw that the LORD had answered him on the threshing floor of Araunah the Jebusite, he offered sacrifices there. [29]The tabernacle of the LORD, which Moses had made in the desert, and the altar of burnt offering were at that time on the high place at Gibeon.[d] [30]But David could not go before it to inquire of God, because he was afraid of the sword of the angel of the LORD.

22 Then David said, "The house of the LORD God[e] is to be here, and also the altar of burnt offering for Israel."

Preparations for the Temple

[2]So David gave orders to assemble the aliens[f] living in Israel, and from among them he appointed stonecutters[g] to prepare dressed stone for building the house of God. [3]He provided a large amount of iron to make nails for the doors of the gateways and for the fittings, and more bronze than could be weighed.[h] [4]He also pro-

---

[a] 25 That is, about 15 pounds (about 7 kilograms) [b] 26 Traditionally *peace offerings*

21:16
[x] Nu 14:5; Jos 7:6

21:17
[y] 2Sa 7:8; Ps 74:1
[z] Jnh 1:12

21:18
[a] 2Ch 3:1

21:20
[b] Jdg 6:11

21:26
[c] Lev 9:24; Jdg 6:21

21:29
[d] 1Ki 3:4;
1Ch 16:39

22:1
[e] Ge 28:17;
1Ch 21:18-29;
2Ch 3:1

22:2
[f] 1Ki 9:21; Isa 56:6
[g] 1Ki 5:17-18

22:3
[h] ver 14; 1Ki 7:47;
1Ch 29:2-5

📖 This text, particularly the assertion that Satan "incited David" (v. 1) to commit a sin (cf. v. 8), forces us to consider the problem of evil and God's relationship to sin, pain, and suffering. Dark mysteries swirl around this topic, yet a pattern emerges—perhaps expressed most clearly in James 1:13–15.

Each of us is tempted when personal desires, incited by Satan, drag us into sin (v. 14; cf. Matt. 4:1). When we yield to our sinful desires and succumb to Satan's temptation, sin is birthed (v. 15a; cf. Rom. 1:18–25). God has no recourse but to punish sin—though in one sense it punishes itself, in that when sin matures it leads to death (v. 15b; cf. 1 Chron. 21:7,14). Like David, we are without excuse; "God cannot be tempted by evil, nor does he tempt anyone" (v. 13). But the good news is that through his Spirit God still takes up residence at the

site of repentance—in the heart of the forgiven sinner.

1 Chronicles 22:2–19

📖 The events of chapters 22 and 28–29 may have taken place during a brief period of coregency (sharing of the throne) between David and Solomon after Adonijah's coup (1 Kings 1). If so, David's counsel in verses 6–16 was a private charge to Solomon to build God's temple, in anticipation of the later public commissioning of the crown prince in 28:9–10. This section contrasts David, a man of "many wars," with Solomon, a man of "peace and rest" (vv. 8–9). Following the private charge to Solomon, David issued a royal edict to all the leaders of Israel to "help" Solomon—a tacit admission that undertaking a building project of this magnitude demanded the full support of the nation (vv. 17–19).

22:4
i 1Ki 5:6
22:5
j 1Ki 3:7; 1Ch 29:1

vided more cedar logs*i* than could be counted, for the Sidonians and Tyrians had brought large numbers of them to David.

5David said, "My son Solomon is young*j* and inexperienced, and the house to be built for the LORD should be of great magnificence and fame and splendor in the sight of all the nations. Therefore I will make preparations for it." So David made extensive preparations before his death.

22:6
k Ac 7:47
22:7
l 1Ch 17:2
m 2Sa 7:2; 1Ki 8:17
n Dt 12:5,11
22:8
o 1Ki 5:3
p 1Ch 28:3
22:9
q 1Ki 5:4
r 2Sa 12:24
s 1Ki 4:20

6Then he called for his son Solomon and charged him to build*k* a house for the LORD, the God of Israel. 7David said to Solomon: "My son, I had it in my heart*l* to build*m* a house for the Name*n* of the LORD my God. 8But this word of the LORD came to me: 'You have shed much blood and have fought many wars.*o* You are not to build a house for my Name,*p* because you have shed much blood on the earth in my sight. 9But you will have a son who will be a man of peace*q* and rest, and I will give him rest from all his enemies on every side. His name will be Solomon,*ar* and I will grant Israel peace and quiet*s* during his reign. 10He is the one who will

22:10
t 1Ch 17:12
u 2Sa 7:13
v 2Sa 7:14;
2Ch 6:15
22:11
w ver 16
22:12
x 1Ki 3:9-12;
2Ch 1:10

build a house for my Name.*t* He will be my son,*u* and I will be his father. And I will establish the throne of his kingdom over Israel forever.'*v*

11 "Now, my son, the LORD be with*w* you, and may you have success and build the house of the LORD your God, as he said you would. 12May the LORD give you discretion and understanding*x* when he puts you in command over Israel, so that you may keep the law of the LORD your God. 13Then you will have success if you are careful to observe the decrees and laws*y* that the LORD gave Moses for Israel. Be strong and courageous.*z* Do not be afraid or discouraged.

22:13
y 1Ch 28:7
z Dt 31:6;
Jos 1:6-9;
1Ch 28:20

14 "I have taken great pains to provide for the temple of the LORD a hundred thousand talents*b* of gold, a million talents*c* of silver, quantities of bronze and iron too great to be weighed, and wood and stone. And you may add to them.*a* 15You have many workmen: stonecutters, masons and carpenters, as well as men skilled in every kind of work 16in gold and silver, bronze and iron—craftsmen*b* beyond number. Now begin the work, and the LORD be with you."

22:14
a ver 3;
1Ch 29:2-5,19
22:16
b ver 11; 2Ch 2:7

22:17
c 1Ch 28:1-6
22:18
d ver 9; 1Ch 23:25
e 2Sa 7:1

17Then David ordered*c* all the leaders of Israel to help his son Solomon. 18He said to them, "Is not the LORD your God with you? And has he not granted you rest*d* on every side?*e* For he has handed the inhabitants of the land over to me, and the land is subject to the LORD and to his people. 19Now devote your heart and soul to seeking the LORD your God.*f* Begin to build the sanctuary of the LORD God, so that you may bring the ark of the covenant of the LORD and the sacred articles belonging to God into the temple that will be built for the Name of the LORD."

22:19
f ver 7; 1Ki 8:6;
1Ch 28:9; 2Ch 5:7;
7:14

The Levites

23:1
g 1Ki 1:33-39;
1Ch 28:5
h 1Ki 1:30;
1Ch 29:28

23 When David was old and full of years, he made his son Solomon*g* king over Israel.*h*

2He also gathered together all the leaders of Israel, as well as the priests and Le-

---

a 9 *Solomon* sounds like and may be derived from the Hebrew for *peace.*   *b* 14 That is, about 3,750 tons (about 3,450 metric tons)   *c* 14 That is, about 37,500 tons (about 34,500 metric tons)

David readied resources and mentally prepared Solomon to build God's temple in Jerusalem, which would become a symbol of God's covenant faithfulness to Israel. These financial, emotional, political, social, and personal preparations were crucial elements in Solomon's successful temple-building project. How many good ideas, churches, businesses, or organizations have died prematurely or suffered great loss because their leaders failed to plan for a future beyond themselves? David built a bridge through Solomon for centuries beyond his own lifetime. What are you building in those who will follow you in your family, business, or ministry?

1 Chronicles 23:1–6

The census of the Levites isn't to be seen as a contradiction to the ill-advised military census ordered by David in chapter 21. The purpose of this census was to establish a rotation of Levitical service. David organized the Levites according to four distinct categories of labor. The census report provided the background for the subsequent registers of the three sons of Levi.

The characteristics of Old Testament priestly service and ministry have counterparts in the worship and spiritual life of the church today. Though there are differing gifts yielding a diversity of functions or ministries in the church, all are given by the same Spirit for the common good (1 Cor. 12:4–11). Paul reminded us that these gifts are distributed as God determines. Does this reality prompt a like-minded humility in you as you consider God's grace in equipping you for worship and service to the world?

vites. ³The Levites thirty years old or more[i] were counted, and the total number of men was thirty-eight thousand.[j] ⁴David said, "Of these, twenty-four thousand are to supervise[k] the work of the temple of the LORD and six thousand are to be officials and judges.[l] ⁵Four thousand are to be gatekeepers and four thousand are to praise the LORD with the musical instruments[m] I have provided for that purpose."[n]

⁶David divided[o] the Levites into groups corresponding to the sons of Levi: Gershon, Kohath and Merari.

Gershonites

⁷Belonging to the Gershonites:
  Ladan and Shimei.
⁸The sons of Ladan:
  Jehiel the first, Zetham and Joel—three in all.
⁹The sons of Shimei:
  Shelomoth, Haziel and Haran—three in all.
  These were the heads of the families of Ladan.
¹⁰And the sons of Shimei:
  Jahath, Ziza,[a] Jeush and Beriah.
  These were the sons of Shimei—four in all.
¹¹Jahath was the first and Ziza the second, but Jeush and Beriah did not have many sons; so they were counted as one family with one assignment.

Kohathites

¹²The sons of Kohath:[p]
  Amram, Izhar, Hebron and Uzziel—four in all.
¹³The sons of Amram:[q]
  Aaron and Moses.
  Aaron was set apart,[r] he and his descendants forever, to consecrate the most holy things, to offer sacrifices before the LORD, to minister before him and to pronounce blessings[s] in his name forever. ¹⁴The sons of Moses the man[t] of God were counted as part of the tribe of Levi.
¹⁵The sons of Moses:
  Gershom and Eliezer.[u]
¹⁶The descendants of Gershom:[v]
  Shubael was the first.
¹⁷The descendants of Eliezer:
  Rehabiah was the first.
  Eliezer had no other sons, but the sons of Rehabiah were very numerous.
¹⁸The sons of Izhar:
  Shelomith was the first.

a 10 One Hebrew manuscript, Septuagint and Vulgate (see also verse 11); most Hebrew manuscripts Zina

---

Cross references

23:3
i ver 24; Nu 8:24
j Nu 4:3-49
23:4
k Ezr 3:8
l 1Ch 26:29; 2Ch 19:8
23:5
m 1Ch 15:16
n Ne 12:45
23:6
o 2Ch 8:14; 29:25

23:12
p Ex 6:18

23:13
q Ex 6:20; 28:1
r Ex 30:7-10; Dt 21:5 s Nu 6:23

23:14
t Dt 33:1

23:15
u Ex 18:4
23:16
v 1Ch 26:24-28

---

1 Chronicles 23:7–11

The genealogy of Levi (vv. 7–23) is organized according to his three sons, Gershon, Kohath, and Merari, in keeping with the order found elsewhere (cf. Ex. 6:16–19; Num. 3–4; 1 Chron. 6). This genealogical table is repeated in 24:20–31, where some of the family lines mentioned here are expanded. The expression "heads of families" (v. 24) refers to clan leaders or family elders (cf. 27:1).

Solomon would have been unable to meet the demands of temple building without David's foresight and preparatory help (including this careful, advance reassignment of priestly and Levitical duties). This model of intergenerational cooperation was important for the Chronicler's audience and remains so for us as we attempt to serve the Lord in whatever capacity he calls us.

If you are young and energetic, do you appreciate the often unnoticed and behind-the-scenes efforts of an aging generation? If you are part of the older generation, are you helping to mentor and prepare those behind you (see also "Here and Now" for 22:2–19)?

1 Chronicles 23:12–20

Aaron and Moses (of the exodus generation) were "sons" (i.e., descendants) of Amram of the Kohathite clan. As the family "set apart" for priestly service, Aaron's line was excluded from the census and the Levitical duties of verses 4–5. But Moses' family was numbered among the Levites. Its members received no special status despite Moses' standing as a "man of God"—one chosen and sent by God as a prophet and example of holiness.

23:19
w 1Ch 24:23

¹⁹The sons of Hebron: ʷ

Jeriah the first, Amariah the second, Jahaziel the third and Jekameam the fourth.

²⁰The sons of Uzziel:

Micah the first and Isshiah the second.

23:21
x 1Ch 24:26

Merarites

²¹The sons of Merari: ˣ

Mahli and Mushi.

The sons of Mahli:

Eleazar and Kish.

²²Eleazar died without having sons: he had only daughters. Their cousins, the sons of Kish, married them.

²³The sons of Mushi:

Mahli, Eder and Jerimoth—three in all.

23:24
y Nu 4:3; 10:17,21
23:25
z 1Ch 22:9

²⁴These were the descendants of Levi by their families—the heads of families as they were registered under their names and counted individually, that is, the workers twenty years old or moreʸ who served in the temple of the LORD. ²⁵For David had said, "Since the LORD, the God of Israel, has granted restᶻ to his peo-

23:26
a Nu 4:5,15; 7:9;
Dt 10:8

ple and has come to dwell in Jerusalem forever, ²⁶the Levites no longer need to carry the tabernacle or any of the articles used in its service." ᵃ ²⁷According to the last instructions of David, the Levites were counted from those twenty years old or more.

23:28
b 2Ch 29:15;
Ne 13:9; Mal 3:3
23:29
c Ex 25:30
d Lev 2:4-7; 6:20-23
e Lev 19:35-36;
1Ch 9:29,32
23:30
f 1Ch 9:33;
Ps 134:1
23:31
g 2Ki 4:23
h Lev 23:4;
Nu 28:9-29:39;
Isa 1:13-14;
Col 2:16
23:32
i Nu 1:53; 6:48
j Nu 3:6-8,38
k 2Ch 23:18; 31:2;
Eze 44:14

²⁸The duty of the Levites was to help Aaron's descendants in the service of the temple of the LORD: to be in charge of the courtyards, the side rooms, the purification ᵇ of all sacred things and the performance of other duties at the house of God. ²⁹They were in charge of the bread set out on the table, ᶜ the flour for the grain offerings, ᵈ the unleavened wafers, the baking and the mixing, and all measurements of quantity and size. ᵉ ³⁰They were also to stand every morning to thank and praise the LORD. They were to do the same in the eveningᶠ ³¹and whenever burnt offerings were presented to the LORD on Sabbaths and at New Moonᵍ festivals and at appointed feasts. ʰ They were to serve before the LORD regularly in the proper number and in the way prescribed for them.

³²And so the Levitesⁱ carried out their responsibilities for the Tent of Meeting,ʲ for the Holy Place and, under their brothers the descendants of Aaron, for the service of the temple of the LORD. ᵏ

We readily acknowledge that each Christian is equal in God's sight. But how many times do cliques or factions form around one particular leader, a pastor's family members, or ministry assignments in the church? Paul corrected the Corinthian congregation over such a problem (1 Cor. 3). Though Moses is acknowledged as a great leader in Israel, his family is here numbered with everyone else. We can certainly associate freely with others around common interests, but we are wise not to exclude people based on who they are (aren't) or what position they hold (don't hold).

1 Chronicles 23:21–32

The genealogy of Merari is the shortest of Levi's three sons. The reference to Eleazar suggests that his family line, despite the lack of a male heir, was continued through his daughters on the basis of the inheritance regulations decreed by Moses (Num. 27:1–11; 36:6–9).

The census age of twenty follows the standard practice of the numbering of all Israelites established by Moses (cf. Num. 1:3). The age of thirty cited in 1 Chron-

icles 23:3 may have applied to Levites assigned to specific tasks, or those in their twenties may have served apprenticeships.

The shift from a portable to a permanent sanctuary meant that the duties of the Levites had to be reassigned. David anticipated this need, perhaps on the basis of Moses' prediction that one day Israel would worship at a central sanctuary (note David's emphasis on "rest" in v. 25; cf. Deut. 12:10–11).

The joining of "rest" and a designated worship site would come about under the leadership of Solomon—whose name was literally associated with "peace" (see 22:9 and NIV text note there). The Chronicler knew that the citizens of postexilic Jerusalem needed a "post-it note" reminding them of God's faithfulness—a sure word from the God who "remembers his covenant forever" (Ps. 111:5). Those of us who live under the new covenant established in the New Testament need the same reminder. Hebrews 4:1–11 describes the "rest" reserved for the people of God.

The Divisions of Priests

24 These were the divisions[l] of the sons of Aaron:[m] The sons of Aaron were Nadab, Abihu, Eleazar and Ithamar.[n] ²But Nadab and Abihu died before their father did,[o] and they had no sons; so Eleazar and Ithamar served as the priests. ³With the help of Zadok[p] a descendant of Eleazar and Ahimelech a descendant of Ithamar, David separated them into divisions for their appointed order of ministering. ⁴A larger number of leaders were found among Eleazar's descendants than among Ithamar's, and they were divided accordingly: sixteen heads of families from Eleazar's descendants and eight heads of families from Ithamar's descendants. ⁵They divided them impartially by drawing lots,[q] for there were officials of the sanctuary and officials of God among the descendants of both Eleazar and Ithamar.

⁶The scribe Shemaiah son of Nethanel, a Levite, recorded their names in the presence of the king and of the officials: Zadok the priest, Ahimelech[r] son of Abiathar and the heads of families of the priests and of the Levites—one family being taken from Eleazar and then one from Ithamar.

⁷The first lot fell to Jehoiarib,
  the second to Jedaiah,[s]
⁸the third to Harim,[t]
  the fourth to Seorim,
⁹the fifth to Malkijah,
  the sixth to Mijamin,
¹⁰the seventh to Hakkoz,
  the eighth to Abijah,[u]
¹¹the ninth to Jeshua,
  the tenth to Shecaniah,
¹²the eleventh to Eliashib,
  the twelfth to Jakim,
¹³the thirteenth to Huppah,
  the fourteenth to Jeshebeab,
¹⁴the fifteenth to Bilgah,
  the sixteenth to Immer,[v]
¹⁵the seventeenth to Hezir,[w]
  the eighteenth to Happizzez,
¹⁶the nineteenth to Pethahiah,
  the twentieth to Jehezkel,
¹⁷the twenty-first to Jakin,
  the twenty-second to Gamul,
¹⁸the twenty-third to Delaiah
  and the twenty-fourth to Maaziah.

¹⁹This was their appointed order of ministering when they entered the temple of the LORD, according to the regulations prescribed for them by their forefather Aaron, as the LORD, the God of Israel, had commanded him.

The Rest of the Levites

²⁰As for the rest of the descendants of Levi:[x]
  from the sons of Amram: Shubael;

24:1 l 1Ch 23:6; 28:13; 2Ch 5:11; 8:14; 23:8; 31:2; 35:4,5; Ezr 6:18 m Nu 3:2-4 n Ex 6:23
24:2 o Lev 10:1-2; Nu 3:4
24:3 p 2Sa 8:17
24:5 q ver 31; 1Ch 25:8
24:6 r 1Ch 18:16
24:7 s Ezr 2:36; Ne 12:6
24:8 t Ezr 2:39; Ne 10:5
24:10 u Ne 12:4,17; Lk 1:5
24:14 v Jer 20:1
24:15 w Ne 10:20
24:20 x 1Ch 23:6

---

1 Chronicles 24:1–19

The emphasis in this chapter isn't on the liturgical function of the priests but on the organization of their service; the Chronicler assumed that his audience knew the priestly duties associated with temple worship. His concern was twofold: the formal sanctioning of the duty roster by David and the careful ordering of priestly service by lot-casting.

Chapter 24 is part of a larger unit (chs. 23–26) addressing the various groups of Levites and their temple duties. It's healthy for Christians today to acknowledge the priestly role of all believers and to seek to avoid artificial distinctions between ordained clergy and those who sit in the pews in terms of calling and anointing for service (1 Peter 2:5).

24:21
y 1Ch 23:17

from the sons of Shubael: Jehdeiah.
²¹ As for Rehabiah,*ʸ* from his sons:
Isshiah was the first.
²² From the Izharites: Shelomoth;
from the sons of Shelomoth: Jahath.

24:23
z 1Ch 23:19

²³ The sons of Hebron:*ᶻ* Jeriah the first,*ᵃ* Amariah the second, Jahaziel the third
and Jekameam the fourth.
²⁴ The son of Uzziel: Micah;
from the sons of Micah: Shamir.
²⁵ The brother of Micah: Isshiah;
from the sons of Isshiah: Zechariah.

24:26
a 1Ch 6:19; 23:21

²⁶ The sons of Merari:*ᵍ* Mahli and Mushi.
The son of Jaaziah: Beno.
²⁷ The sons of Merari:
from Jaaziah: Beno, Shoham, Zaccur and Ibri.
²⁸ From Mahli: Eleazar, who had no sons.
²⁹ From Kish: the son of Kish:
Jerahmeel.
³⁰ And the sons of Mushi: Mahli, Eder and Jerimoth.

24:31
b ver 5

These were the Levites, according to their families. ³¹ They also cast lots,*ᵇ* just as
their brothers the descendants of Aaron did, in the presence of King David and of
Zadok, Ahimelech, and the heads of families of the priests and of the Levites. The
families of the oldest brother were treated the same as those of the youngest.

The Singers

25:1
c 1Ch 6:39
d 1Ch 6:33
e 1Ch 16:41,42;
Ne 11:17
f 1Sa 10:5; 2Ki 3:15
g 1Ch 15:16
h 1Ch 6:31
i 2Ch 5:12; 8:14;
34:12; 35:15;
Ezr 3:10
25:3
j 1Ch 16:41-42
k Ge 4:21; Ps 33:2

25 David, together with the commanders of the army, set apart some of the
sons of Asaph,*ᶜ* Heman*ᵈ* and Jeduthun*ᵉ* for the ministry of prophesying,*ᶠ*
accompanied by harps, lyres and cymbals.*ᵍ* Here is the list of the men*ʰ* who performed this service:*ⁱ*

² From the sons of Asaph:
Zaccur, Joseph, Nethaniah and Asarelah. The sons of Asaph were under the supervision of Asaph, who prophesied under the king's supervision.
³ As for Jeduthun, from his sons:*ⁱ*
Gedaliah, Zeri, Jeshaiah, Shimei,*ᵇ* Hashabiah and Mattithiah, six in all, under
the supervision of their father Jeduthun, who prophesied, using the harp*ᵏ* in
thanking and praising the LORD.
⁴ As for Heman, from his sons:
Bukkiah, Mattaniah, Uzziel, Shubael and Jerimoth; Hananiah, Hanani, Elia-
thah, Giddalti and Romamti-Ezer; Joshbekashah, Mallothi, Hothir and Maha-

---

ᵃ 23 Two Hebrew manuscripts and some Septuagint manuscripts (see also 1 Chron. 23:19); most
Hebrew manuscripts *The sons of Jeriah:*   *ᵇ 3* One Hebrew manuscript and some Septuagint
manuscripts (see also verse 17); most Hebrew manuscripts do not have *Shimei.*

---

1 Chronicles 24:20–31

📖 This roster of additional Levitical families assigned to assist the priests updates the register found in
23:6–23 and assumes the readers' knowledge of that list.
This section supplements the report of David's organization of the Levites in chapter 23.

📖 The listing of different tasks among priests and
Levites wasn't included to establish a hierarchy of value
in types of service but to underscore the dignity, orderliness, and cooperation characterizing all the service offered to God. In a related manner, Paul instructed the
church that the exercise of the gifts of the Holy Spirit in
Christian worship must "be done in a fitting and orderly
way" (1 Cor. 14:40).

1 Chronicles 25:1–31

📖 This section is devoted to the listing and duties
of the temple musicians. The passage suggests that
singing in the temple liturgy was typically accompanied
by the playing of musical instruments. As in the case of
the priests, the Levitical musicians were ordered in families and arranged in 24 courses (cf. 24:1–18). Verses 1–7
identify the three families comprising the corps of temple musicians and summarize their duties. The rest of
the chapter orders the assignment (and perhaps rotation) of duties by lot-casting.

📖 Are you musically inclined? One way or the other, the New Testament asserts that we all have a music
ministry. We can sing and make melody in our hearts to

zioth. [5]All these were sons of Heman the king's seer. They were given him through the promises of God to exalt him.[a] God gave Heman fourteen sons and three daughters.

[6]All these men were under the supervision of their fathers[l] for the music of the temple of the LORD, with cymbals, lyres and harps, for the ministry at the house of God. Asaph, Jeduthun and Heman[m] were under the supervision of the king.[n] [7]Along with their relatives—all of them trained and skilled in music for the LORD— they numbered 288. [8]Young and old alike, teacher as well as student, cast lots[o] for their duties.

25:6
l 1Ch 15:16
m 1Ch 15:19
n 2Ch 23:18; 29:25

25:8
o 1Ch 26:13

25:9
p 1Ch 6:39

[9]The first lot, which was for Asaph,[p] fell to Joseph,
    his sons and relatives,[b]   12[c]
the second to Gedaliah,
    he and his relatives and sons,   12
[10]the third to Zaccur,
    his sons and relatives,   12
[11]the fourth to Izri,[d]
    his sons and relatives,   12
[12]the fifth to Nethaniah,
    his sons and relatives,   12
[13]the sixth to Bukkiah,
    his sons and relatives,   12
[14]the seventh to Jesarelah,[e]
    his sons and relatives,   12
[15]the eighth to Jeshaiah,
    his sons and relatives,   12
[16]the ninth to Mattaniah,
    his sons and relatives,   12
[17]the tenth to Shimei,
    his sons and relatives,   12
[18]the eleventh to Azarel,[f]
    his sons and relatives,   12
[19]the twelfth to Hashabiah,
    his sons and relatives,   12
[20]the thirteenth to Shubael,
    his sons and relatives,   12
[21]the fourteenth to Mattithiah,
    his sons and relatives,   12
[22]the fifteenth to Jerimoth,
    his sons and relatives,   12
[23]the sixteenth to Hananiah,
    his sons and relatives,   12
[24]the seventeenth to Joshbekashah,
    his sons and relatives,   12
[25]the eighteenth to Hanani,
    his sons and relatives,   12
[26]the nineteenth to Mallothi,
    his sons and relatives,   12
[27]the twentieth to Eliathath,
    his sons and relatives,   12

a 5 Hebrew *exalt the horn*   *b 9* See Septuagint; Hebrew does not have *his sons and relatives.*
c 9 See the total in verse 7; Hebrew does not have *twelve.*   *d 11* A variant of *Zeri*   *e 14* A variant of *Asarelah*   *f 18* A variant of *Uzziel*

the Lord (Eph. 5:19; Col 3:16). And just as the priests were to "thank and praise the LORD" every morning and evening (1 Chron. 23:30), we are to be "always giving thanks to God the Father for everything, in the name of our Lord Jesus Christ" (Eph. 5:20).

²⁸ the twenty-first to Hothir,
his sons and relatives,   12
²⁹ the twenty-second to Giddalti,
his sons and relatives,   12
³⁰ the twenty-third to Mahazioth,
his sons and relatives,   12
³¹ the twenty-fourth to Romamti-Ezer,
his sons and relatives,   12 ^q

25:31
q 1Ch 9:33

The Gatekeepers

26:1
r 1Ch 9:17

26
The divisions of the gatekeepers: ^r

From the Korahites: Meshelemiah son of Kore, one of the sons of Asaph.

26:2
s 1Ch 9:21

² Meshelemiah had sons:
Zechariah ^s the firstborn,
Jediael the second,
Zebadiah the third,
Jathniel the fourth,
³ Elam the fifth,
Jehohanan the sixth
and Eliehoenai the seventh.
⁴ Obed-Edom also had sons:
Shemaiah the firstborn,
Jehozabad the second,
Joah the third,
Sacar the fourth,
Nethanel the fifth,
⁵ Ammiel the sixth,
Issachar the seventh
and Peullethai the eighth.
(For God had blessed Obed-Edom. ^t)

26:5
t 2Sa 6:10;
1Ch 13:13; 16:38

⁶ His son Shemaiah also had sons, who were leaders in their father's family because they were very capable men. ⁷ The sons of Shemaiah: Othni, Rephael, Obed and Elzabad; his relatives Elihu and Semakiah were also able men. ⁸ All these were descendants of Obed-Edom; they and their sons and their relatives were capable men with the strength to do the work—descendants of Obed-Edom, 62 in all.

⁹ Meshelemiah had sons and relatives, who were able men—18 in all.

26:10
u Dt 21:16; 1Ch 5:1

¹⁰ Hosah the Merarite had sons: Shimri the first (although he was not the firstborn, his father had appointed him the first), ^u ¹¹ Hilkiah the second, Tabaliah the third and Zechariah the fourth. The sons and relatives of Hosah were 13 in all.

26:12
v 1Ch 9:22
26:13
w 1Ch 24:5,31;
25:8

¹² These divisions of the gatekeepers, through their chief men, had duties for ministering ^v in the temple of the LORD, just as their relatives had. ¹³ Lots ^w were cast for each gate, according to their families, young and old alike.

---

1 Chronicles 26:1–19

Levitical gatekeepers in the broader sense were a paramilitary security force that played three roles: They oversaw the temple precinct, were responsible for the administration of temple revenues, and were in charge of maintaining the temple. Lot-casting was used to determine gate assignments, as with the previous duty rosters for priests and musicians. This method of selection prevented partiality and emphasized the divine nature of the decision, since the outcome of a lot was from the Lord (Prov. 16:33).

The term *gatekeeper* has come into contemporary usage both in business and in the church. The role of gatekeepers in the church (pastors, typically) is one of spiritual oversight. They protect the sanctity of the church against false teaching and guide or influence the decisions of individual Christians in such areas as morality. You too can be a "gatekeeper" in your family or in other areas of your life. And just as these Levites operated in pairs or teams, you can join with other believers through an accountability partner or group for the purpose of guarding your spiritual life.

[14]The lot for the East Gate[x] fell to Shelemiah.[a] Then lots were cast for his son Zechariah,[y] a wise counselor, and the lot for the North Gate fell to him. [15]The lot for the South Gate fell to Obed-Edom,[z] and the lot for the storehouse fell to his sons. [16]The lots for the West Gate and the Shalleketh Gate on the upper road fell to Shuppim and Hosah.

Guard was alongside of guard: [17]There were six Levites a day on the east, four a day on the north, four a day on the south and two at a time at the storehouse. [18]As for the court to the west, there were four at the road and two at the court itself.

[19]These were the divisions of the gatekeepers who were descendants of Korah and Merari.[a]

The Treasurers and Other Officials

[20]Their fellow Levites[b] were[b] in charge of the treasuries of the house of God and the treasuries for the dedicated things.[c]

[21]The descendants of Ladan, who were Gershonites through Ladan and who were heads of families belonging to Ladan the Gershonite,[d] were Jehieli, [22]the sons of Jehieli, Zetham and his brother Joel. They were in charge of the treasuries[e] of the temple of the LORD.

[23]From the Amramites, the Izharites, the Hebronites and the Uzzielites:[f]

[24]Shubael,[g] a descendant of Gershom son of Moses, was the officer in charge of the treasuries. [25]His relatives through Eliezer: Rehabiah his son, Jeshaiah his son, Joram his son, Zicri his son and Shelomith[h] his son. [26]Shelomith and his relatives were in charge of all the treasuries for the things dedicated[i] by King David, by the heads of families who were the commanders of thousands and commanders of hundreds, and by the other army commanders. [27]Some of the plunder taken in battle they dedicated for the repair of the temple of the LORD. [28]And everything dedicated by Samuel the seer[j] and by Saul son of Kish, Abner son of Ner and Joab son of Zeruiah, and all the other dedicated things were in the care of Shelomith and his relatives.

[29]From the Izharites: Kenaniah and his sons were assigned duties away from the temple, as officials and judges[k] over Israel.

[30]From the Hebronites: Hashabiah[l] and his relatives—seventeen hundred able men—were responsible in Israel west of the Jordan for all the work of the LORD and for the king's service. [31]As for the Hebronites,[m] Jeriah was their chief according to the genealogical records of their families. In the fortieth[n] year of David's reign a search was made in the records, and capable men among the Hebronites were found at Jazer in Gilead. [32]Jeriah had twenty-seven hundred relatives, who were able men and heads of families, and King David put them in charge of the Reubenites, the Gadites and the half-tribe of Manasseh for every matter pertaining to God and for the affairs of the king.

Army Divisions

27 This is the list of the Israelites—heads of families, commanders of thousands and commanders of hundreds, and their officers, who served the

[a] 14 A variant of *Meshelemiah*   [b] 20 Septuagint; Hebrew *As for the Levites, Ahijah was*

Marginal references

26:14
x 1Ch 9:18
y 1Ch 9:21
26:15
z 1Ch 13:13; 2Ch 25:24

26:19
a 2Ch 35:15; Ne 7:1; Eze 44:11

26:20
b 2Ch 24:5
c 1Ch 28:12

26:21
d 1Ch 23:7; 29:8
26:22
e 1Ch 9:26

26:23
f Nu 3:27

26:24
g 1Ch 23:16

26:25
h 1Ch 23:18
26:26
i 2Sa 8:11

26:28
j 1Sa 9:9

26:29
k Dt 17:8-13; 1Ch 23:4; Ne 11:16
26:30
l 1Ch 27:17

26:31
m 1Ch 23:19
n 2Sa 5:4

---

1 Chronicles 26:20–32

The second section of this chapter may be divided into two units: the list of Levites who served as treasurers (vv. 20–28) and those who held administrative posts outside the temple precinct of Jerusalem (vv. 29–32). It's notable that the lines between the ministry of spiritual service and the duties of civil service were fluid.

Today Christian service is regularly performed in the "secular" arenas of our lives. A middle school student speaking up for her beliefs in a science class, a customer service representative performing his repetitive duties with an extra touch of caring, a tutor giving of her time to a literacy program, an employee donating a weekly amount to a local service organization—if such service is done on Christ's behalf, he views the act, no matter how small, as a "cup of cold water" offered in his name (cf. Matt. 10:42; Mark 9:41).

king in all that concerned the army divisions that were on duty month by month throughout the year. Each division consisted of 24,000 men.

27:2
o 2Sa 23:8;
1Ch 11:11

²In charge of the first division, for the first month, was Jashobeam ᵒ son of Zabdiel. There were 24,000 men in his division. ³He was a descendant of Perez and chief of all the army officers for the first month.

27:4
p 2Sa 23:9

⁴In charge of the division for the second month was Dodai ᵖ the Ahohite; Mikloth was the leader of his division. There were 24,000 men in his division.

27:5
q 2Sa 23:20

⁵The third army commander, for the third month, was Benaiah �q son of Jehoiada the priest. He was chief and there were 24,000 men in his division. ⁶This was the Benaiah who was a mighty man among the Thirty and was over the Thirty. His son Ammizabad was in charge of his division.

27:7
r 2Sa 2:18;
1Ch 11:26
27:8
s 1Ch 11:27

⁷The fourth, for the fourth month, was Asahel ʳ the brother of Joab; his son Zebadiah was his successor. There were 24,000 men in his division.

⁸The fifth, for the fifth month, was the commander Shamhuth ˢ the Izrahite. There were 24,000 men in his division.

27:9
t 2Sa 23:26;
1Ch 11:28

⁹The sixth, for the sixth month, was Ira ᵗ the son of Ikkesh the Tekoite. There were 24,000 men in his division.

27:10
u 2Sa 23:26;
1Ch 11:27
27:11
v 2Sa 21:18

¹⁰The seventh, for the seventh month, was Helez ᵘ the Pelonite, an Ephraimite. There were 24,000 men in his division.

¹¹The eighth, for the eighth month, was Sibbecai ᵛ the Hushathite, a Zerahite. There were 24,000 men in his division.

27:12
w 2Sa 23:27;
1Ch 11:28

¹²The ninth, for the ninth month, was Abiezer ʷ the Anathothite, a Benjamite. There were 24,000 men in his division.

27:13
x 2Sa 23:28;
1Ch 11:30
27:14
y 1Ch 11:31

¹³The tenth, for the tenth month, was Maharai ˣ the Netophathite, a Zerahite. There were 24,000 men in his division.

¹⁴The eleventh, for the eleventh month, was Benaiah ʸ the Pirathonite, an Ephraimite. There were 24,000 men in his division.

27:15
z 2Sa 23:29
a Jos 15:17

¹⁵The twelfth, for the twelfth month, was Heldai ᶻ the Netophathite, from the family of Othniel. ᵃ There were 24,000 men in his division.

Officers of the Tribes

¹⁶The officers over the tribes of Israel:

over the Reubenites: Eliezer son of Zicri;
over the Simeonites: Shephatiah son of Maacah;

27:17
b 1Ch 26:30
c 2Sa 8:17;
1Ch 12:28

¹⁷over Levi: Hashabiah ᵇ son of Kemuel;
over Aaron: Zadok; ᶜ

---

1 Chronicles 27:1–15

🐟 Rather than a standing army, the military divisions described here represent a militia or citizen army, something like the U.S. National Guard. David organized his army in 12 divisions, each commanded by a seasoned soldier from his choice corps of "mighty men" (cf. v. 6; 11:10–47). Each division served the king's army for one month in a 12-month relay. The permanent or professional army was comprised of the Three and the Thirty, along with the Kerethites, Pelethites, and Gittites (cf. 2 Sam. 15:18; 23:23).

📖 Are you tempted to question the relevance of the Chronicler's tedious description of David's governmental organization? His own audience may have had similar feelings, given that (a) David lived more than 500 years before them and (b) they were prohibited an organized military presence by their Persian overlords. But these memories were important to the Chronicler, who viewed God as "the LORD Almighty" (cf. 11:9; 17:7,24)—literally, "the LORD of the armies" (cf. Deut. 33:2; Josh. 5:14; 1 Sam.

17:45). Despite their lack of political autonomy or ability to muster an army, the Israelites could still trust God to be a "warrior" for them (cf. Ex. 15:3; Deut. 1:30).

Christians today are in danger when they think of God as fighting on their side in a nationalistic sense. But no thinking Christian can doubt God's might or his concern to act on behalf of what's right and just in the global community.

1 Chronicles 27:16–24

🐟 The exact status of these tribal "officers" is uncertain (typically tribal leaders were called "elders"; cf. 11:3). Perhaps they assisted Joab, the "commander of the royal army" (v. 34), in the census-taking mentioned again in verses 23–24 (see ch. 21 for the full account). God's promise to his people through Abraham "to make Israel as numerous as the stars in the sky" (v. 23; cf. Gen. 15:5; 22:17) was evidently the basis for Joab's objection to the census (cf. 21:3). Joab the general recognized more clearly than David the king that "no king is saved by the size of his army" (Ps. 33:16).

18 over Judah: Elihu, a brother of David;
   over Issachar: Omri son of Michael;
19 over Zebulun: Ishmaiah son of Obadiah;
   over Naphtali: Jerimoth son of Azriel;
20 over the Ephraimites: Hoshea son of Azaziah;
   over half the tribe of Manasseh: Joel son of Pedaiah;
21 over the half-tribe of Manasseh in Gilead: Iddo son of Zechariah;
   over Benjamin: Jaasiel son of Abner;
22 over Dan: Azarel son of Jeroham.
   These were the officers over the tribes of Israel.

23 David did not take the number of the men twenty years old or less, [d] because the LORD had promised to make Israel as numerous as the stars [e] in the sky. 24 Joab son of Zeruiah began to count the men but did not finish. Wrath came on Israel on account of this numbering, [f] and the number was not entered in the book [a] of the annals of King David.

The King's Overseers

25 Azmaveth son of Adiel was in charge of the royal storehouses.
   Jonathan son of Uzziah was in charge of the storehouses in the outlying districts, in the towns, the villages and the watchtowers.
26 Ezri son of Kelub was in charge of the field workers who farmed the land.
27 Shimei the Ramathite was in charge of the vineyards.
   Zabdi the Shiphmite was in charge of the produce of the vineyards for the wine vats.
28 Baal-Hanan the Gederite was in charge of the olive and sycamore-fig [g] trees in the western foothills.
   Joash was in charge of the supplies of olive oil.
29 Shitrai the Sharonite was in charge of the herds grazing in Sharon.
   Shaphat son of Adlai was in charge of the herds in the valleys.
30 Obil the Ishmaelite was in charge of the camels.
   Jehdeiah the Meronothite was in charge of the donkeys.
31 Jaziz the Hagrite [h] was in charge of the flocks.
   All these were the officials in charge of King David's property.

32 Jonathan, David's uncle, was a counselor, a man of insight and a scribe. Jehiel son of Hacmoni took care of the king's sons.
33 Ahithophel [i] was the king's counselor.

---

a 24 Septuagint; Hebrew *number*

27:23
d 1Ch 21:2-5
e Ge 15:5

27:24
f 2Sa 24:15;
1Ch 21:7

27:28
g 1Ki 10:27;
2Ch 1:15

27:31
h 1Ch 5:10

27:33
i 2Sa 15:12

📖 In light of recent events, fears and concerns related to national security are understandable. When the stated purpose of a late-night bombing barrage in Iraq is "shock and awe," we might condone it as a legitimate strategy of psychological warfare with unfortunate but necessary "limited collateral damage." But does the word *awe* used in this context give you pause? Who but our God is worthy of our awe, in the context of battle or otherwise?

1 Chronicles 27:25–34

✒️ A portion of the revenue necessary to meet the expenses of the bureaucracy established by David was generated by income from crown properties. These holdings may have been acquired by military conquest or through formal negotiation (e.g., David's purchase of Araunah's threshing floor in 21:20–25). Naturally the crown properties needed responsible supervision, and the 12 officials named as overseers were in keeping with David's pattern in the administration of both the religious and political sectors.

Material wealth wasn't only necessary to offset expenditures of the centralized government but also enhanced David's prestige. The Old Testament generally saw such wealth as a sign of God's blessing, though the Mosaic provision for kingship prohibited the amassing of large treasuries by the king (Deut. 17:17).

📖 Does the Bible seem to you to give mixed messages regarding wealth? On the one hand we are invited to enjoy God's blessings, while on the other we are cautioned against shifting our allegiance and sense of security from the Giver to the gift. Jesus referred in the Gospels to money more often than to either heaven or hell; this alone alerts us that we are dealing with a difficult subject. Believers are wise to beware of viewing a lack of plentiful resources as a sign of God's disfavor. At the same time, contentment, thankfulness, stewardship, and generosity are appropriate for and expected of those of us who have been given much.

27:33
j 2Sa 15:37
27:34
k 1Ki 1:7 / 1Ch 11:6

Hushai*j* the Arkite was the king's friend. 34Ahithophel was succeeded by Jehoiada son of Benaiah and by Abiathar.*k*

Joab*l* was the commander of the royal army.

David's Plans for the Temple

28:1
m 1Ch 11:10;
27:1-31

28 David summoned all the officials*m* of Israel to assemble at Jerusalem: the officers over the tribes, the commanders of the divisions in the service of the king, the commanders of thousands and commanders of hundreds, and the officials in charge of all the property and livestock belonging to the king and his sons, together with the palace officials, the mighty men and all the brave warriors.

28:2
n 1Ch 17:2
o Ps 99:5; 132:7

2King David rose to his feet and said: "Listen to me, my brothers and my people. I had it in my heart*n* to build a house as a place of rest for the ark of the covenant of the LORD, for the footstool*o* of our God, and I made plans to build it. 3But God

28:3
p 2Sa 7:5
q 1Ch 22:8
r 1Ki 5:3; 1Ch 17:4

said to me,*p* 'You are not to build a house for my Name,*q* because you are a warrior and have shed blood.'*r*

28:4
s 1Ch 17:23,27;
2Ch 6:6 *t*
1Sa 16:1-13
u Ge 49:10;
1Ch 5:2

4"Yet the LORD, the God of Israel, chose me*s* from my whole family*t* to be king over Israel forever. He chose Judah*u* as leader, and from the house of Judah he chose my family, and from my father's sons he was pleased to make me king over all Israel. 5Of all my sons—and the LORD has given me many*v*—he has chosen my son

28:5
v 1Ch 3:1
w 1Ch 22:9; 23:1

Solomon*w* to sit on the throne of the kingdom of the LORD over Israel. 6He said to

28:6
x 2Sa 7:13;
1Ch 22:9-10

me: 'Solomon your son is the one who will build my house and my courts, for I have chosen him to be my son,*x* and I will be his father. 7I will establish his king-

28:7
y 1Ch 22:13

dom forever if he is unswerving in carrying out my commands and laws,*y* as is being done at this time.'

28:8
z Dt 6:1 *a* Dt 4:1

8"So now I charge you in the sight of all Israel and of the assembly of the LORD, and in the hearing of our God: Be careful to follow all the commands*z* of the LORD your God, that you may possess this good land and pass it on as an inheritance to your descendants forever.*a*

28:9
b 1Ch 29:19
c 1Sa 16:7; Ps 7:9
d Ps 40:16;
Jer 29:13
e Jos 24:20;
2Ch 15:2 *f* Ps 44:23

9"And you, my son Solomon, acknowledge the God of your father, and serve him with wholehearted devotion*b* and with a willing mind, for the LORD searches every heart*c* and understands every motive behind the thoughts. If you seek him,*d* he will be found by you; but if you forsake*e* him, he will reject*f* you forever. 10Consider now, for the LORD has chosen you to build a temple as a sanctuary. Be strong and do the work."

28:11
g Ex 25:9

11Then David gave his son Solomon the plans*g* for the portico of the temple, its

28:12
h 1Ch 12:18
i 1Ch 26:20

buildings, its storerooms, its upper parts, its inner rooms and the place of atonement. 12He gave him the plans of all that the Spirit*h* had put in his mind for the courts of the temple of the LORD and all the surrounding rooms, for the treasuries of the temple of God and for the treasuries for the dedicated things.*i* 13He gave him

28:13
j 1Ch 24:1

instructions for the divisions*j* of the priests and Levites, and for all the work of serving in the temple of the LORD, as well as for all the articles to be used in its service.

14He designated the weight of gold for all the gold articles to be used in various kinds of service, and the weight of silver for all the silver articles to be used in var-

28:15
k Ex 25:31

ious kinds of service: 15the weight of gold for the gold lampstands*k* and their

---

1 Chronicles 28:1–21

This chapter reports three speeches by David: a charge to the officials of Israel (vv. 1–8), a charge to Solomon (vv. 9–10), and an additional charge to Solomon (vv. 20–21) after the presentation of written instructions for building the temple (vv. 11–19). David's earlier private commissioning of Solomon to be his successor and build the temple (22:6–16) was now made public.

The emphasis on obedience to God's law and the exhortation to "be strong and courageous" (v. 20) echo Joshua's commissioning by Moses (cf. Deut. 31:7–8; 32:44–47). Two threads tie this chapter together: the

stress on obedience by Israel's leadership, both to God and to Solomon, and the understanding that the temple-building project was a divine initiative.

A lifestyle of obedience was a sign of an Israelite's genuine love for God (Deut. 30:19–20). This willful submission to the authority of divine revelation is still an appropriate response to God. Jesus challenged his disciples: "If you love me, you will obey what I command" (John 14:15). Pretty straightforward, isn't it? And yet its implications can and should be life-changing. Like so many of Jesus' "simple" sayings, this "if/then" statement can be a catalyst for our daily reflection and self-assessment.

lamps, with the weight for each lampstand and its lamps; and the weight of silver for each silver lampstand and its lamps, according to the use of each lampstand; [16] the weight of gold for each table *l* for consecrated bread; the weight of silver for the silver tables; [17] the weight of pure gold for the forks, sprinkling bowls *m* and pitchers; the weight of gold for each gold dish; the weight of silver for each silver dish; [18] and the weight of the refined gold for the altar of incense. *n* He also gave him the plan for the chariot, *o* that is, the cherubim of gold that spread their wings and shelter *p* the ark of the covenant of the LORD.

[19] "All this," David said, "I have in writing from the hand of the LORD upon me, and he gave me understanding in all the details *q* of the plan. *r* "

[20] David also said to Solomon his son, "Be strong and courageous, *s* and do the work. Do not be afraid or discouraged, for the LORD God, my God, is with you. He will not fail you or forsake *t* you until all the work for the service of the temple of the LORD is finished. *u* [21] The divisions of the priests and Levites are ready for all the work on the temple of God, and every willing man skilled *v* in any craft will help you in all the work. The officials and all the people will obey your every command."

Gifts for Building the Temple

29 Then King David said to the whole assembly: "My son Solomon, the one whom God has chosen, is young and inexperienced. *w* The task is great, because this palatial structure is not for man but for the LORD God. [2] With all my resources I have provided for the temple of my God—gold *x* for the gold work, silver for the silver, bronze for the bronze, iron for the iron and wood for the wood, as well as onyx for the settings, turquoise, *a y* stones of various colors, and all kinds of fine stone and marble—all of these in large quantities. *z* [3] Besides, in my devotion to the temple of my God I now give my personal treasures of gold and silver for the temple of my God, over and above everything I have provided *a* for this holy temple: [4] three thousand talents *b* of gold (gold of Ophir) *b* and seven thousand talents *c* of refined silver, *c* for the overlaying of the walls of the buildings, [5] for the gold work and the silver work, and for all the work to be done by the craftsmen. Now, who is willing to consecrate himself today to the LORD?"

[6] Then the leaders of families, the officers of the tribes of Israel, the commanders of thousands and commanders of hundreds, and the officials *d* in charge of the king's work gave willingly. *e* [7] They *f* gave toward the work on the temple of God five thousand talents *d* and ten thousand darics *e* of gold, ten thousand talents *f* of silver, eighteen thousand talents *g* of bronze and a hundred thousand talents *h* of iron. [8] Any who had precious stones *g* gave them to the treasury of the temple of the LORD in the custody of Jehiel the Gershonite. *h* [9] The people rejoiced at the willing re-

Cross references (right column)

28:16
l Ex 25:23
28:17
m Ex 27:3
28:18
n Ex 30:1-10
o Ex 25:18-22
p Ex 25:20
28:19
q 1Ki 6:38 *r* Ex 25:9
28:20
s Dt 31:6;
1Ch 22:13;
2Ch 19:11; Hag 2:4
t Dt 4:31; Jos 24:20
u 1Ki 6:14;
2Ch 7:11
28:21
v Ex 35:25-36:5
29:1
w 1Ki 3:7;
1Ch 22:5; 2Ch 13:7
29:2
x ver 7, 14, 16;
Ezr 1:4; 6:5;
Hag 2:8 *y* Isa 54:11
z 1Ch 22:2-5
29:3
a 2Ch 24:10; 31:3;
35:8
29:4
b Ge 10:29
c 1Ch 22:14
29:6
d 1Ch 27:1; 28:1
e ver 9; Ex 25:1-8;
35:20-29; 36:2;
2Ch 24:10; Ezr 7:15
29:7
f Ex 25:2;
Ne 7:70-71
29:8
g Ex 35:27
h 1Ch 26:21

---

a 2 The meaning of the Hebrew for this word is uncertain. *b* 4 That is, about 110 tons (about 100 metric tons) *c* 4 That is, about 260 tons (about 240 metric tons) *d* 7 That is, about 190 tons (about 170 metric tons) *e* 7 That is, about 185 pounds (about 84 kilograms) *f* 7 That is, about 375 tons (about 345 metric tons) *g* 7 That is, about 675 tons (about 610 metric tons) *h* 7 That is, about 3,750 tons (about 3,450 metric tons)

---

1 Chronicles 29:1–9

David called on the whole assembly, leaders and people alike, to freely offer themselves to God. The issue wasn't the amassing of jewels and precious metals but the pouring out of themselves as God's people into building the temple as a symbol of the wholehearted worship that would soon take place there. This was one way the Israelites could pledge themselves to God as a kingdom of priests (cf. Ex. 19:6).

It's a proven leadership principle that generosity needs an example (e.g., note how often the "matching gift" of a donor is used to spur giving). The open-handed giving of King David and the Israelite leaders served as an inducement for a similar response from the people.

The Chronicler spliced together three related themes that characterized Israel's relationship with God: a *pure heart* (cf. 28:9) that prompted *generous giving*, which resulted in *joy*. J.G. McConville, an Old Testament scholar, noted that "people are closest to God-likeness in self-giving, and the nearer they approach God-likeness the more genuinely and rightly they become capable of rejoicing." We can be examples of generous people. Think about ways you can give more of your "personal treasures" (29:3) to the Lord in terms of your time, talent, and resources.

29:9
i 1Ki 8:61; 2Co 9:7

sponse of their leaders, for they had given freely and wholeheartedly[i] to the LORD. David the king also rejoiced greatly.

David's Prayer

[10]David praised the LORD in the presence of the whole assembly, saying,

> "Praise be to you, O LORD,
>   God of our father Israel,
>   from everlasting to everlasting.

29:11
j Ps 24:8; 59:17; 62:11 *k* Ps 89:11
l Rev 5:12-13

> [11]Yours, O LORD, is the greatness and the power[j]
>   and the glory and the majesty and the splendor,
>   for everything in heaven and earth is yours.[k]
> Yours, O LORD, is the kingdom;
>   you are exalted as head over all.[l]

29:12
m 2Ch 1:12
n 2Ch 20:6; Ro 11:36

> [12]Wealth and honor[m] come from you;
>   you are the ruler[n] of all things.
> In your hands are strength and power
>   to exalt and give strength to all.
> [13]Now, our God, we give you thanks,
>   and praise your glorious name.

29:15
o Ps 39:12; Heb 11:13
p Job 14:2

[14]"But who am I, and who are my people, that we should be able to give as generously as this? Everything comes from you, and we have given you only what comes from your hand. [15]We are aliens and strangers[o] in your sight, as were all our forefathers. Our days on earth are like a shadow,[p] without hope. [16]O LORD our God, as for all this abundance that we have provided for building you a temple for your Holy Name, it comes from your hand, and all of it belongs to you.

29:17
q Ps 139:23; Pr 15:11; 17:3; Jer 11:20; 17:10
r 1Ch 28:9; Ps 15:1-5

[17]I know, my God, that you test the heart[q] and are pleased with integrity. All these things have I given willingly and with honest intent. And now I have seen with joy how willingly your people who are here have given to you.[r] [18]O LORD, God of our fathers Abraham, Isaac and Israel, keep this desire in the hearts of your people forever, and keep their hearts loyal to you.

29:19
s 1Ch 28:9 *t* Ps 72:1
u 1Ch 22:14

[19]And give my son Solomon the wholehearted devotion[s] to keep your commands, requirements and decrees[t] and to do everything to build the palatial structure for which I have provided."[u]

[20]Then David said to the whole assembly, "Praise the LORD your God." So they all praised the LORD, the God of their fathers; they bowed low and fell prostrate before the LORD and the king.

Solomon Acknowledged as King

29:21
v 1Ki 8:62

[21]The next day they made sacrifices to the LORD and presented burnt offerings to him:[v] a thousand bulls, a thousand rams and a thousand male lambs, together with their drink offerings, and other sacrifices in abundance for all Israel.

29:22
w 1Ch 23:1

[22]They ate and drank with great joy[w] in the presence of the LORD that day.

---

1 Chronicles 29:10–20

The repeated word "praise" (Hebrew *barak*; vv. 10,20) may also be rendered "bless." David's act of blessing God showed his gratitude for the bountiful provision that had enabled the people to give generously to the temple building fund. In blessing God, David indirectly blessed the materials freely given and the people responsible for this outpouring of resources. David's blessing closed with a petition for the people: "Keep their hearts loyal to [God]" (v. 18). The Chronicler saw nothing more significant for his own audience. The "heart" is crucial to physical and spiritual life.

As David experienced, God's undeserved and unreserved goodness sparks our gratitude and prompts our joy. And that joy results in loyalty or continued

obedience to God. But this isn't a simple cause-and-effect relationship between the Creator and his creatures. It's the mystery of our faith relationship. Paul marveled that the mystery (unknown to the Chronicler and his generation) had finally been revealed: "Christ in you, the hope of glory" (Col. 1:26–27). We have so much more cause for joy even than those under the old covenant. God's indwelling presence helps our hearts remain loyal to him.

1 Chronicles 29:21–25

If this was the "second time" Solomon was acknowledged as king (v. 22), when was the first time? Perhaps this installation ceremony was the formal and public sequel to the hurried and private appointment in 1 Kings 1:28–40. The Chronicler's account of the

29:10–20

By his words and actions David established the paradigm for Christian stewardship as he gathered resources for the Jerusalem temple. In 1 Chronicles 29:10–20 we discover why stewardship, not ownership, is the teaching of Scripture for Christians.

When it comes to money, American Christians are demonstrating a preference for ownership over stewardship. In 2000, 32 percent of born-again Christians reported that they tithe to the church. An impressive statistic—except that only 12 percent actually do. Forty percent of those who don't, say they would like to start (Barna Research).

David had an answer for these people: "All this abundance . . . comes from [God's] hand, and all of it belongs to [him]" (1 Chron. 29:16). We as Christians own nothing, having relinquished our right to possessions in our commitment to Christ.

How does David's proposition work itself out in practical ways? First, consider our time. We know exactly how much time we have, but somehow we are less careful in managing 24 daily hours than we might be 24 dollars. A good steward of time understands several things: (1) Life is brief (James 4:14). (2) The eternal gives meaning to the temporal (Rom. 13:11; 2 Cor. 4:18). (3) Our time is "owned" by God (Ps. 31:15). (4) We are to make the most of opportunities (Eccl. 8:5; Col. 4:5). (5) Our use of time reflects our priorities (Matt. 6:19–21,34).

Second, we are to be good stewards of talents. Every Christian's cup is brimming with abilities and endowments from God, received freely by grace (Eph. 2:8; 4:8). The good steward uses them to accomplish God's agendas.

Next comes stewardship of treasure. There are over 2,300 Biblical verses dealing with money and possessions—more than those concerning prayer or faith. Jesus said more about money than about any other subject, except for the temporal versus the eternal. The goal of the Christian steward with regard to possessions is contentment (Phil. 4:12; 1 Tim. 6:8; Heb. 13:5). Contentment doesn't mean poverty or passivity in exercising God-given gifts of creativity in sowing and reaping financially. But it does mean recognizing that material things are a means to an end, a tool for accomplishing God's priorities.

> **W**e as Christians own nothing, having relinquished our right to possessions in our commitment to Christ.

We are responsible to manage truth. Truth functions in our lives like the key to a prison (John 8:31–32)—but we are not set free to run wild (Rom. 1:18). Truth is something to be walked in and lived out. Otherwise, a real question can be raised as to whether we know it at all (John 17:17; Eph. 4:1; James 2:17). The Christian steward uses truth to glorify its Author.

Finally, we are to be stewards of relationships. Only two things on Earth will last: God's Word and people's eternal souls (Eccl. 3:11; Isa. 40:8). Our efforts to love and serve people have never-ending consequences. The first relationship the Christian is responsible to cultivate is with Christ (Luke 10:38–42). After that come parents, spouses, children, and neighbors—especially those in peril or need. Since God made Christ "the firstborn among many brothers" (Rom. 8:29), the cultivation of relationships has in view people's eternal as well as temporal needs.

Our personal integrity as Christian stewards is based on three truths: (1) Everything belongs to God (Ps. 24:1). (2) All is at our disposal as a temporary trust (1 Chron. 29:15–16). (3) We are to use everything for God's purposes (Luke 17:7–10).

Kenneth Boa, president of Reflections Ministries in Atlanta, Georgia

29:22
x 1Ki 1:33-39
29:23
y 1Ki 2:12

29:25
z 2Ch 1:1,12
a 1Ki 3:13; Ecc 2:9

29:26
b 1Ch 18:14

29:27
c 2Sa 5:4-5;
1Ki 2:11; 1Ch 3:4
29:28
d Ge 15:15;
Ac 13:36
e 1Ch 23:1
29:29
f 1Sa 9:9 g 2Sa 7:2
h 1Sa 22:5

Then they acknowledged Solomon son of David as king a second time, anointing him before the LORD to be ruler and Zadok[x] to be priest. [23]So Solomon sat on the throne[y] of the LORD as king in place of his father David. He prospered and all Israel obeyed him. [24]All the officers and mighty men, as well as all of King David's sons, pledged their submission to King Solomon.

[25]The LORD highly exalted Solomon in the sight of all Israel and bestowed on him royal splendor[z] such as no king over Israel ever had before.[a]

The Death of David

[26]David son of Jesse was king[b] over all Israel. [27]He ruled over Israel forty years—seven in Hebron and thirty-three in Jerusalem.[c] [28]He died[d] at a good old age, having enjoyed long life, wealth and honor. His son Solomon succeeded him as king.[e] [29]As for the events of King David's reign, from beginning to end, they are written in the records of Samuel the seer,[f] the records of Nathan[g] the prophet and the records of Gad[h] the seer, [30]together with the details of his reign and power, and the circumstances that surrounded him and Israel and the kingdoms of all the other lands.

---

transition of the throne from David to Solomon omits much from 1 Kings 1–2, such as the failed coup of David's son Adonijah and the accompanying palace intrigue. Rather, his selection of material presents a smooth and peaceful transition of power. The David and Solomon of the Chronicler, then, must be seen not only as the David and Solomon of history, but also as typifying the Messianic king of the Chronicler's expectation.

Although the Chronicler himself couldn't foresee this, we can revel in the corresponding image of our promised heavenly banquet—when we will celebrate "with great joy in the presence of the LORD" (v. 22; cf. Matt. 8:11; Luke 22:16; Rev. 19:9). God the Father has "highly exalted" his Son, Jesus Christ, who is the King of kings and Lord of lords (Rev. 17:14; 19:16). It's your incredible privilege to "acknowledge"—this very moment—this King whom every tongue will one day confess as Lord (Phil. 2:9–11).

1 Chronicles 29:26–30

The roles of David and Solomon in solidifying the tribes into a nation can't be overlooked, given the repetition of the phrase "all Israel" for the fourth time in these closing paragraphs (vv. 21,23,25,26). The mention of Solomon succeeding David (v. 28) was a subtle reminder that God had fulfilled his promise to establish a "house" for David (cf. 2 Sam. 7).

Nothing more is known about the "records" of Samuel, Nathan, and Gad. The Chronicler was careful to inform his audience that his account of David's reign was based on the reliable and authoritative word of God's prophets.

We 21st-century Christians have an advantage over the Old Testament Israelites of retrospect on a much longer history of God's faithfulness to his own people—whether to the patriarchs and ancient Israel; the generation of the Chronicler; the Christian church; or, in many cases, our own believing families, traced back through generations of crises and periods of testing. God's mercies, we can testify, are new every morning, fresh with every succeeding generation (Lam. 3:22–23). They remain true through changing regimes and millennia.

INTRODUCTION TO

2 Chronicles

AUTHOR

According to Jewish tradition, Ezra wrote the Chronicles. But his authorship has been questioned, and many modern scholars simply refer to the author as "the Chronicler."

DATE WRITTEN

Although a specific date of composition can't be determined, Chronicles was probably written between 450 and 400 B.C.

ORIGINAL READERS

The books of Chronicles (1 and 2 Chronicles) were originally one book written to the postexilic Jews to give them an accurate historical record and help them recognize their heritage and calling.

TIMELINE

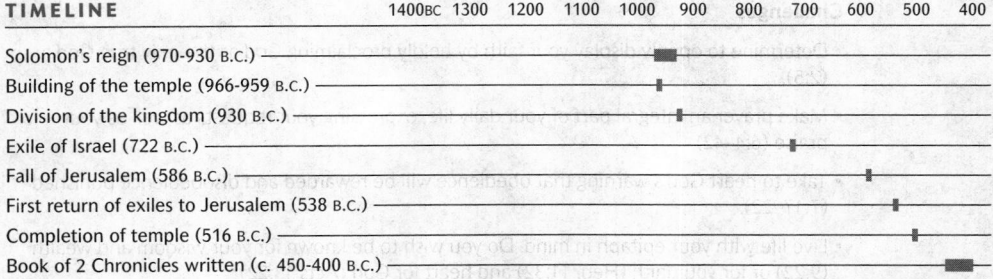

	1400BC	1300	1200	1100	1000	900	800	700	600	500	400
Solomon's reign (970-930 B.C.)											
Building of the temple (966-959 B.C.)											
Division of the kingdom (930 B.C.)											
Exile of Israel (722 B.C.)											
Fall of Jerusalem (586 B.C.)											
First return of exiles to Jerusalem (538 B.C.)											
Completion of temple (516 B.C.)											
Book of 2 Chronicles written (c. 450-400 B.C.)											

THEMES

Second Chronicles describes the reign of Solomon, Israel's wisest and wealthiest king, and records the division of the kingdom. Second Chronicles deals almost exclusively with the kingdom of Judah, describing its spiritual decline and eventual fall. It includes the following themes:

1. *Blessing or judgment.* Second Chronicles emphasizes that God's blessings resulted from obedience to the Mosaic covenant (7:17–18; 15:12–15; 17:3–6; 30:15–20; 31:20–21) but that his judgment followed disobedience (12:1–2; 34:19–21). If the people would humbly repent, God promised to restore them (7:13–14; 12:5–12; 33:10–13).

2. *Worship.* The building and dedication of the temple (2:1—7:22) was the greatest achievement in Solomon's 40-year rule, taking 20 years to complete (8:1). The temple was the central place of worship and symbolized God's presence among his people (7:12,16; 33:7). Its splendor and the joy associated with it (5:12–14; 7:1–6; 29:25–33) emphasize that God is worthy of our wholehearted, exclusive worship—and that he expects nothing less.

FAITH IN ACTION

The pages of 2 Chronicles contain life lessons and role models of faith—people who challenge believers to put their faith in action.

Role Models

• SOLOMON (1:7–12) displayed a heart for God's people by desiring above all else the wisdom and knowledge needed to lead them. God rewarded Solomon with wisdom, knowledge, and great wealth. Are the desires of your heart rooted in selflessness?

• JEHOSHAPHAT (20:2–30) trusted God to fight his enemy, seeking God through prayer and fasting for deliverance. Is the Lord your resource when enemies rear their heads? Do you turn to him in fasting and/or prayer in times of trouble?

• JEHOSHEBA (22:10–12) saved the infant Joash from her aunt's (his grandmother's) murderous rampage. How can you promote the health and well-being of an abused, abandoned, or threatened child?

• JEHOIADA and his wife, Jehosheba, (22:10–12; 24:2) were godly mentors and protectors for the young king Joash, guiding him to obey God. To whom can you be a godly mentor?

• HEZEKIAH (31:20–21) served God wholeheartedly, demonstrating faithfulness in everything he undertook. What is your underlying motivation for service?

• HULDAH (34:22–28) was a brave prophetess who was faithful to communicate God's direction to the king. Has God placed you in a position to convey his direction to someone in leadership? How can Huldah inspire you?

• JOSIAH (34:33) was a godly king who passionately led the people to follow and obey God. How can you use your position of leadership and/or authority to lead others to lives of godly obedience?

Challenges

• Determine to openly display your faith by boldly proclaiming God as the only true God (2:5).

• Make prayer an integral part of your daily life, expressing your requests as well as your praise (6:4–42).

• Take to heart God's warning that obedience will be rewarded and disobedience punished (7:17–22).

• Live life with your epitaph in mind. Do you wish to be known for your wisdom and wealth (9:22) or for your faith (Heb. 11:32) and heart for God (Acts 13:22)?

• Decide to trust God, especially when circumstances seem to be out of control, for every "turn of events [is] from God" (10:15).

• Resolve not to abandon God if he blesses you with power and strength (12:1), for unfaithfulness brings God's punishment (12:5). Remember that repentance results in his forgiveness and mercy (12:6–7) but that forgiveness doesn't necessarily negate sin's natural consequences (12:8).

• While obedience and holiness are commanded (Lev. 11:44–45; Heb. 12:14), rest in the assurance that God knows your heart (15:17); your service won't go unrewarded (Matt. 25:21).

• Fight injustice, favoritism, and bribery (19:6–7), for such evils bring God's judgment on society.

• Children die today from a variety of causes. Commit yourself to promoting a child's health and well-being—perhaps even saving a life (11:1–3)!—through child sponsorship, food assistance, or health care ministry.

• Be a positive role model for the youth in your community (24:2).

• Guard against pride, which leads to unfaithfulness (26:16).

OUTLINE

I. The Reign of Solomon (1–8)
   A. Request for Wisdom (1)
   B. Temple Construction and Dedication (2–7)
   C. Solomon's Activities (8)
II. Visit of the Queen of Sheba and Solomon's Splendor (9:1–28)
III. Solomon's Death (9:29–31)
IV. The Kings of Judah (10:1—36:14)
V. The Destruction of Jerusalem (36:15–23)

Solomon Asks for Wisdom

1 Solomon son of David established[a] himself firmly over his kingdom, for the LORD his God was with[b] him and made him exceedingly great.[c]

2 Then Solomon spoke to all Israel[d]—to the commanders of thousands and commanders of hundreds, to the judges and to all the leaders in Israel, the heads of families— 3 and Solomon and the whole assembly went to the high place at Gibeon, for God's Tent of Meeting[e] was there, which Moses[f] the LORD's servant had made in the desert. 4 Now David had brought up the ark[g] of God from Kiriath Jearim to the place he had prepared for it, because he had pitched a tent[h] for it in Jerusalem. 5 But the bronze altar[i] that Bezalel[j] son of Uri, the son of Hur, had made was in Gibeon in front of the tabernacle of the LORD; so Solomon and the assembly inquired[k] of him there. 6 Solomon went up to the bronze altar before the LORD in the Tent of Meeting and offered a thousand burnt offerings on it.

7 That night God appeared[l] to Solomon and said to him, "Ask for whatever you want me to give you."

8 Solomon answered God, "You have shown great kindness to David my father and have made me[m] king in his place. 9 Now, LORD God, let your promise[n] to my father David be confirmed, for you have made me king over a people who are as numerous as the dust of the earth.[o] 10 Give me wisdom and knowledge, that I may lead[p] this people, for who is able to govern this great people of yours?"

11 God said to Solomon, "Since this is your heart's desire and you have not asked for wealth,[q] riches or honor, nor for the death of your enemies, and since you have not asked for a long life but for wisdom and knowledge to govern my people over whom I have made you king, 12 therefore wisdom and knowledge will be given you. And I will also give you wealth, riches and honor,[r] such as no king who was before you ever had and none after you will have.[s]"

13 Then Solomon went to Jerusalem from the high place at Gibeon, from before the Tent of Meeting. And he reigned over Israel.

1:1
a 1Ki 2:12,26; 2Ch 12:1
b Ge 21:22; 39:2; Nu 14:43
c 1Ch 29:25
1:2
d 1Ch 9:1; 28:1
1:3
e Ex 36:8 / Ex 40:18
1:4
g 2Sa 6:2; 1Ch 15:25
h 2Sa 6:17; 1Ch 15:1
1:5
i Ex 38:2 / Ex 31:2
k 1Ch 13:3
1:7
l 2Ch 7:12
1:8
m 1Ch 23:1; 28:5
1:9
n 2Sa 7:25; 1Ki 8:25
o Ge 12:2
1:10
p Nu 27:17; 2Sa 5:2; Pr 8:15-16
1:11
q Dt 17:17
1:12
r 1Ch 29:12
s 1Ch 29:25; 2Ch 9:22; Ne 13:26

---

2 Chronicles 1:1–17

Solomon's worship at the Tent of Meeting at Gibeon testified publicly that the soon-to-be-built Jerusalem temple would carry on the ancient Mosaic tradition. His presentation of burnt offerings witnessed to his intention to keep his father's charge to obey God's laws and thereby preserve the worship of his ancestors (cf. 1 Chron. 22:11–13).

Solomon didn't approach God as a genie in a bottle. He responded to God's invitation to ask for whatever he wanted by first acknowledging God's covenant promise to David (cf. 1 Chron. 17)—whose legacy he intended to continue—and recalling God's faithfulness in fulfilling covenant promises to Abraham and Jacob (cf. Gen. 13:16; 28:14).

The Chronicler depicted Solomon as the epitome of piety and wisdom—and of riches (cf. 9:13–28). He viewed Solomon's staggering wealth as a demonstration of God's faithfulness in fulfilling his promise in verse 12 and as God's favor resting on David's son.

Like Solomon, the righteous are free to petition God for the desires of their hearts, assuming they do so from a posture of faith and not of doubt or selfish motivation (Ps. 37:3–4; cf. Matt. 7:7–8; Luke 7:9-13; John 15:7–8; James 1:5–6; 4:3). Paul encouraged believers to desire spiritual gifts (1 Cor. 14:1). How free have you been to ask God for the spiritual blessings your heart desires? Do you also pray for him to increase the spiritual endowments of believers worldwide? (cf. Eph. 1:15–22; 3:14–21).

1:14
t 1Sa 8:11;
1Ki 4:26; 9:19
1:15
u 1Ki 9:28; Isa 60:5

1:17
v SS 1:9

[14]Solomon accumulated chariots[t] and horses; he had fourteen hundred chariots and twelve thousand horses,[a] which he kept in the chariot cities and also with him in Jerusalem. [15]The king made silver and gold[u] as common in Jerusalem as stones, and cedar as plentiful as sycamore-fig trees in the foothills. [16]Solomon's horses were imported from Egypt[b] and from Kue[c]—the royal merchants purchased them from Kue. [17]They imported a chariot[v] from Egypt for six hundred shekels[d] of silver, and a horse for a hundred and fifty.[e] They also exported them to all the kings of the Hittites and of the Arameans.

Preparations for Building the Temple

2:1
w Dt 12:5 x Ecc 2:4

2 Solomon gave orders to build a temple[w] for the Name of the LORD and a royal palace for himself.[x] [2]He conscripted seventy thousand men as carriers and eighty thousand as stonecutters in the hills and thirty-six hundred as foremen over them.[y]

2:2
y ver 18; 2Ch 10:4
2:3
z 2Sa 5:11
a 1Ch 14:1

[3]Solomon sent this message to Hiram[f][z] king of Tyre:

2:4
b ver 1; Dt 12:5
c Ex 30:7
d Ex 25:30
e Ex 29:42;
2Ch 13:11
f Nu 28:9-10

"Send me cedar logs[a] as you did for my father David when you sent him cedar to build a palace to live in. [4]Now I am about to build a temple[b] for the Name of the LORD my God and to dedicate it to him for burning fragrant incense[c] before him, for setting out the consecrated bread[d] regularly, and for making burnt offerings[e] every morning and evening and on Sabbaths[f] and New Moons and at the appointed feasts of the LORD our God. This is a lasting ordinance for Israel.

2:5
g 1Ch 22:5;
Ps 135:5
h 1Ch 16:25
2:6
i 1Ki 8:27;
2Ch 6:18; Jer 23:24
j Ex 3:11

[5]"The temple I am going to build will be great,[g] because our God is greater than all other gods.[h] [6]But who is able to build a temple for him, since the heavens, even the highest heavens, cannot contain him?[i] Who then am I[j] to build a temple for him, except as a place to burn sacrifices before him?

2:7
k ver 13-14;
Ex 35:31;
1Ch 22:16

[7]"Send me, therefore, a man skilled to work in gold and silver, bronze and iron, and in purple, crimson and blue yarn, and experienced in the art of engraving, to work in Judah and Jerusalem with my skilled craftsmen,[k] whom my father David provided.

[8]"Send me also cedar, pine and algum[g] logs from Lebanon, for I know that your men are skilled in cutting timber there. My men will work with yours [9]to provide me with plenty of lumber, because the temple I build must be large and magnificent. [10]I will give your servants, the woodsmen who cut the timber, twenty thousand cors[h] of ground wheat, twenty thousand cors of barley, twenty thousand baths[i] of wine and twenty thousand baths of olive oil.[l]"

2:10
l Ezr 3:7

[11]Hiram king of Tyre replied by letter to Solomon:

2:11
m 1Ki 10:9; 2Ch 9:8

"Because the LORD loves[m] his people, he has made you their king."

a 14 Or charioteers   b 16 Or possibly Muzur, a region in Cilicia; also in verse 17   c 16 Probably Cilicia   d 17 That is, about 15 pounds (about 7 kilograms)   e 17 That is, about 3 3/4 pounds (about 1.7 kilograms)   f 3 Hebrew Huram, a variant of Hiram; also in verses 11 and 12   g 8 Probably a variant of almug; possibly juniper   h 10 That is, probably about 125,000 bushels (about 4,400 kiloliters)   i 10 That is, probably about 115,000 gallons (about 440 kiloliters)

---

2 Chronicles 2:1–18

Solomon requested of Hiram a skilled craftsman and Tyre's famous lumber. In return he would provide Hiram with wheat, barley, wine, and olive oil. The foodstuffs were to be sent overland to Tyre, while the timbers would be floated to Joppa on rafts (vv. 15–16). The more significant features of Solomon's letter are his synopsis of temple worship (v. 4) and the claims about God (vv. 5–6) he offered this Baal-worshiping Phoenician king.

The Chronicler specified that the stonecutters and carriers at the quarries in the hills near Jerusalem were to be drawn from among the alien population (vv. 2,17–18; cf. 1 Kings 5:15–17). The parallel account in Kings also mentions the formation of temporary labor gangs of 30,000 Israelites conscripted to cut and dress timber in Lebanon on a rotating basis (1 Kings 5:13–14).

Solomon minced no words about God in addressing his idol-worshiping friend. We might think him insensitive in asserting that "our God is greater than all other gods." He was evidently stating this both as an indisputable fact and as a rationale for the grandeur of the temple to be built. Does Hiram's response in verse 12 surprise you? Christians interested in global welfare and outreach rightly understand the importance of diplomacy, but we need make no apology for the greatness of our God.

12And Hiram added:

"Praise be to the LORD, the God of Israel, who made heaven and earth![n] He has given King David a wise son, endowed with intelligence and discernment, who will build a temple for the LORD and a palace for himself.

13"I am sending you Huram-Abi,[o] a man of great skill, 14whose mother was from Dan[p] and whose father was from Tyre. He is trained[q] to work in gold and silver, bronze and iron, stone and wood, and with purple and blue[r] and crimson yarn and fine linen. He is experienced in all kinds of engraving and can execute any design given to him. He will work with your craftsmen and with those of my lord, David your father.

15"Now let my lord send his servants the wheat and barley and the olive oil[s] and wine he promised, 16and we will cut all the logs from Lebanon that you need and will float them in rafts by sea down to Joppa.[t] You can then take them up to Jerusalem."

17Solomon took a census of all the aliens[u] who were in Israel, after the census[v] his father David had taken; and they were found to be 153,600. 18He assigned[w] 70,000 of them to be carriers and 80,000 to be stonecutters in the hills, with 3,600 foremen over them to keep the people working.

Solomon Builds the Temple

3 Then Solomon began to build[x] the temple of the LORD[y] in Jerusalem on Mount Moriah, where the LORD had appeared to his father David. It was on the threshing floor of Araunah[a][z] the Jebusite, the place provided by David. 2He began building on the second day of the second month in the fourth year of his reign.[a]

3The foundation Solomon laid for building the temple of God was sixty cubits long and twenty cubits wide[b][b] (using the cubit of the old standard). 4The portico at the front of the temple was twenty cubits[c] long across the width of the building and twenty cubits[d] high.

He overlaid the inside with pure gold. 5He paneled the main hall with pine and covered it with fine gold and decorated it with palm tree[c] and chain designs. 6He adorned the temple with precious stones. And the gold he used was gold of Parvaim. 7He overlaid the ceiling beams, doorframes, walls and doors of the temple with gold, and he carved cherubim[d] on the walls.

8He built the Most Holy Place,[e] its length corresponding to the width of the temple—twenty cubits long and twenty cubits wide. He overlaid the inside with six

2:12 [n] Ne 9:6; Ps 8:3; 33:6; 102:25
2:13 [o] 1Ki 7:13
2:14 [p] Ex 31:6 [q] Ex 35:31 [r] Ex 35:35
2:15 [s] ver 10; Ezr 3:7
2:16 [t] Jos 19:46; Jnh 1:3
2:17 [u] 1Ch 22:2 [v] 2Sa 24:2
2:18 [w] ver 2; 1Ch 22:2; 2Ch 8:8
3:1 [x] Ac 7:47 [y] Ge 28:17 [z] 2Sa 24:18; 1Ch 21:18
3:2 [a] Ezr 5:11
3:3 [b] Eze 41:2
3:5 [c] Eze 40:16
3:7 [d] Ge 3:24; 1Ki 6:29-35; Eze 41:18
3:8 [e] Ex 26:33

[a] 1 Hebrew *Ornan*, a variant of *Araunah* [b] 3 That is, about 90 feet (about 27 meters) long and 30 feet (about 9 meters) wide [c] 4 That is, about 30 feet (about 9 meters); also in verses 8, 11 and 13 [d] 4 Some Septuagint and Syriac manuscripts; Hebrew *and a hundred and twenty*

2 Chronicles 3:1–17

The reference to Mount Moriah (v. 1) awakens memories of God's appearance to Abraham at the near sacrifice of his son Isaac (cf. Gen. 22). The Chronicler may have been trying to encourage his own audience. Though the second temple of their experience was less glorious than Solomon's earlier temple, the great sense of history associated with the sacred site offered hope that God's presence might again inhabit his temple.

The extravagant use of gold overlay extended into the Most Holy Place. Like the cherubim guarding the entrance to Eden after the fall (Gen. 3:24), massive sculptures of cherubim guarded the ark of the covenant eventually installed in the Most Holy Place (2 Chron. 5:7–8). This windowless room, enclosed with a veil and doors, was pitch black. Yet in terms of the symbolic divine presence resting there, the Hebrews knew that "darkness is as light" to God (Ps. 139:12).

Moses' close encounter with God at the burning bush at Horeb, "the mountain of God" (Ex. 3:1–6), introduces us to the Old Testament idea of "sacred space"—which culminated in the construction of the temple, housing the Most Holy Place, on God's "holy mountain" (cf. Isa. 2:2; 27:13). Other people groups worshiped at holy sites, often called "high places" (cf. Num. 33:52; Deut. 33:29). These shrines in mountainous or elevated regions were seen as above ordinary life and nearer the gods' dwellings.

Through Christ's incarnation, God ultimately reestablished his presence among the faithful of Israel, all nations, and all creation (John 1:14), reclaiming all space as holy. Our stewardship of and concern for the ecological health of our planet demonstrate our awareness of this reality.

3:9
f Ex 26:32

3:10
g Ex 25:18

3:13
h Ex 25:18

3:14
i Ex 26:31,33;
Heb 9:3 j Ge 3:24
3:15
k 1Ki 7:15;
Rev 3:12 l 1Ki 7:22

3:16
m 1Ki 7:17
n 1Ki 7:20

hundred talents[a] of fine gold. 9The gold nails[f] weighed fifty shekels. [b] He also overlaid the upper parts with gold.

10In the Most Holy Place he made a pair[g] of sculptured cherubim and overlaid them with gold. 11The total wingspan of the cherubim was twenty cubits. One wing of the first cherub was five cubits[c] long and touched the temple wall, while its other wing, also five cubits long, touched the wing of the other cherub. 12Similarly one wing of the second cherub was five cubits long and touched the other temple wall, and its other wing, also five cubits long, touched the wing of the first cherub. 13The wings of these cherubim[h] extended twenty cubits. They stood on their feet, facing the main hall. [d]

14He made the curtain[i] of blue, purple and crimson yarn and fine linen, with cherubim[j] worked into it.

15In the front of the temple he made two pillars, [k] which ⌜together⌟ were thirty-five cubits[e] long, each with a capital[l] on top measuring five cubits. 16He made interwoven chains[f m] and put them on top of the pillars. He also made a hundred pomegranates[n] and attached them to the chains. 17He erected the pillars in the front of the temple, one to the south and one to the north. The one to the south he named Jakin[g] and the one to the north Boaz. [h]

The Temple's Furnishings

4:1
o Ex 20:24; 27:1-2;
40:6; 1Ki 8:64;
2Ki 16:14
4:2
p Rev 4:6; 15:2

4 He made a bronze altar[o] twenty cubits long, twenty cubits wide and ten cubits high. [i] 2He made the Sea[p] of cast metal, circular in shape, measuring ten cubits from rim to rim and five cubits[j] high. It took a line of thirty cubits[k] to measure around it. 3Below the rim, figures of bulls encircled it—ten to a cubit.[l] The bulls were cast in two rows in one piece with the Sea.

4:4
q Nu 2:3-25;
Eze 48:30-34;
Rev 21:13

4The Sea stood on twelve bulls, three facing north, three facing west, three facing south and three facing east. [q] The Sea rested on top of them, and their hindquarters were toward the center. 5It was a handbreadth[m] in thickness, and its rim was like the rim of a cup, like a lily blossom. It held three thousand baths. [n]

4:6
r Ex 30:18
s Ne 13:5,9;
Eze 40:38

6He then made ten basins[r] for washing and placed five on the south side and five on the north. In them the things to be used for the burnt offerings[s] were rinsed, but the Sea was to be used by the priests for washing.

4:7
t Ex 25:31
u Ex 25:40

7He made ten gold lampstands[t] according to the specifications[u] for them and placed them in the temple, five on the south side and five on the north.

4:8
v Ex 25:23
w Nu 4:14
4:9
x 1Ki 6:36;
2Ki 21:5; 2Ch 33:5

8He made ten tables[v] and placed them in the temple, five on the south side and five on the north. He also made a hundred gold sprinkling bowls. [w]

9He made the courtyard[x] of the priests, and the large court and the doors for the court, and overlaid the doors with bronze. 10He placed the Sea on the south side, at the southeast corner.

---

a 8 That is, about 23 tons (about 21 metric tons)   b 9 That is, about 1 1/4 pounds (about 0.6 kilogram)   c 11 That is, about 7 1/2 feet (about 2.3 meters); also in verse 15   d 13 Or facing inward   e 15 That is, about 52 feet (about 16 meters)   f 16 Or possibly made chains in the inner sanctuary; the meaning of the Hebrew for this phrase is uncertain.   g 17 Jakin probably means he establishes.   h 17 Boaz probably means in him is strength.   i 1 That is, about 30 feet (about 9 meters) long and wide, and about 15 feet (about 4.5 meters) high   j 2 That is, about 7 1/2 feet (about 2.3 meters)   k 2 That is, about 45 feet (about 13.5 meters)   l 3 That is, about 1 1/2 feet (about 0.5 meter)   m 5 That is, about 3 inches (about 8 centimeters)   n 5 That is, about 17,500 gallons (about 66 kiloliters)

---

2 Chronicles 4:1—5:1

David had received vast amounts of silver and gold, either as war booty or as tribute from other nations, which he dedicated to temple construction (1 Chron. 18:7–11; 22:2–5,14). The reference here in 5:1 to depositing those objects not used for the production of the temple furnishings into the temple treasuries transitions to the account of the installation of the ark of the covenant. This also recalls the plunder taken from the Egyptians used in tabernacle construction (cf. Ex.

12:35–36; Num. 7). In both cases, the wealth of the nations contributed to the building of God's sanctuaries.

The wealth of the nations—indeed, the resources of the cosmos—belongs solely to our God. It was fitting that Moses' tabernacle and Solomon's temple utilized raw materials from an extensive area. It's equally fitting in our day, when God's Spirit dwells in his people (1 Cor. 3:16), for each of us to play a role in seeing to it that Earth's bounties are distributed equitably, for the enjoyment and well-being of all.

[11] He also made the pots and shovels and sprinkling bowls.

So Huram finished[y] the work he had undertaken for King Solomon in the temple of God:

[12] the two pillars;

the two bowl-shaped capitals on top of the pillars;

the two sets of network decorating the two bowl-shaped capitals on top of the pillars;

[13] the four hundred pomegranates for the two sets of network (two rows of pomegranates for each network, decorating the bowl-shaped capitals on top of the pillars);

[14] the stands[z] with their basins;

[15] the Sea and the twelve bulls under it;

[16] the pots, shovels, meat forks and all related articles.

All the objects that Huram-Abi[a] made for King Solomon for the temple of the LORD were of polished bronze. [17] The king had them cast in clay molds in the plain of the Jordan between Succoth[b] and Zarethan.[a] [18] All these things that Solomon made amounted to so much that the weight of the bronze[c] was not determined.

[19] Solomon also made all the furnishings that were in God's temple:

the golden altar;

the tables[d] on which was the bread of the Presence;

[20] the lampstands[e] of pure gold with their lamps, to burn in front of the inner sanctuary as prescribed;

[21] the gold floral work and lamps and tongs (they were solid gold);

[22] the pure gold wick trimmers, sprinkling bowls, dishes[f] and censers;[g] and the gold doors of the temple: the inner doors to the Most Holy Place and the doors of the main hall.

5 When all the work Solomon had done for the temple of the LORD was finished,[h] he brought in the things his father David had dedicated[i]—the silver and gold and all the furnishings—and he placed them in the treasuries of God's temple.

The Ark Brought to the Temple

[2] Then Solomon summoned to Jerusalem the elders of Israel, all the heads of the tribes and the chiefs of the Israelite families, to bring up the ark[j] of the LORD's covenant from Zion, the City of David. [3] And all the men of Israel[k] came together to the king at the time of the festival in the seventh month.

[4] When all the elders of Israel had arrived, the Levites took up the ark, [5] and they brought up the ark and the Tent of Meeting and all the sacred furnishings in it. The priests, who were Levites,[l] carried them up; [6] and King Solomon and the entire assembly of Israel that had gathered about him were before the ark, sacrificing so many sheep and cattle that they could not be recorded or counted.

[7] The priests then brought the ark[m] of the LORD's covenant to its place in the inner sanctuary of the temple, the Most Holy Place, and put it beneath the wings of the cherubim. [8] The cherubim[n] spread their wings over the place of the ark and cov-

---

[a] 17 Hebrew *Zeredatha*, a variant of *Zarethan*

4:11
y 1Ki 7:14

4:14
z 1Ki 7:27-30

4:16
a 1Ki 7:13
4:17
b Ge 33:17
4:18
c 1Ki 7:23

4:19
d Ex 25:23,30
4:20
e Ex 25:31

4:22
f Nu 7:14
g Lev 10:1

5:1
h 1Ki 6:14
i 2Sa 8:11

5:2
j Nu 3:31; 2Sa 6:12;
1Ch 15:25
5:3
k 1Ch 9:1;
2Ch 7:8-10

5:5
l Nu 3:31; 1Ch 15:2

5:7
m Rev 11:19

5:8
n Ge 3:24

---

2 Chronicles 5:2—6:11

The ark of the covenant was the single most holy object associated with the Mosaic tabernacle. It was a symbol of God's presence among his people and of his special relationship with Israel (cf. 6:41; 1 Chron. 28:2). The installation of the ark and the dedication of the temple were held in conjunction with the Feast of Tabernacles (5:3). The rest of the sacred furniture from the Tent of Meeting, as well as the tent itself, was also transported to the temple precinct. The ark undoubtedly led the proces-

sion from the temporary structure David had erected in Zion to the Jerusalem temple (5:2; cf. 1 Chron. 15:1–3).

Following the pattern of the dedication of the tabernacle, the cloud of God's glory filled the temple after the priests had installed the ark in the Most Holy Place (cf. Ex. 40:34–35). Solomon's expression of praise (6:4–11) underscored the Davidic covenant announced earlier by Nathan (1 Chron. 17:3–14), through which God had provided for righteous leadership and established a place of worship.

ered the ark and its carrying poles. 9These poles were so long that their ends, extending from the ark, could be seen from in front of the inner sanctuary, but not from outside the Holy Place; and they are still there today. 10There was nothing in the ark except[o] the two tablets[p] that Moses had placed in it at Horeb, where the LORD made a covenant with the Israelites after they came out of Egypt.

5:10
o Heb 9:4
p Ex 16:34; Dt 10:2

11The priests then withdrew from the Holy Place. All the priests who were there had consecrated themselves, regardless of their divisions.[q] 12All the Levites who were musicians[r]—Asaph, Heman, Jeduthun and their sons and relatives—stood on the east side of the altar, dressed in fine linen and playing cymbals, harps and lyres. They were accompanied by 120 priests sounding trumpets.[s] 13The trumpeters and singers joined in unison, as with one voice, to give praise and thanks to the LORD. Accompanied by trumpets, cymbals and other instruments, they raised their voices in praise to the LORD and sang:

5:11
q 1Ch 24:1
5:12
r 1Ki 10:12;
1Ch 25:1; Ps 68:25
s 1Ch 13:8; 15:24

"He is good;
  his love endures forever."[t]

Then the temple of the LORD was filled with a cloud, 14and the priests could not perform[u] their service because of the cloud,[v] for the glory[w] of the LORD filled the temple of God.

5:13
t 1Ch 16:34,41;
2Ch 7:3; 20:21;
Ezr 3:11; Ps 100:5;
136:1; Jer 33:11
5:14
u Ex 40:35;
Rev 15:8 v Ex 19:16
w Ex 29:43; 2Ch 7:2
6:1
x Ex 19:9; 1Ki 8:12-
50
6:2
y Ezr 6:12; 7:15;
Ps 135:21

6 Then Solomon said, "The LORD has said that he would dwell in a dark cloud;[x] 2I have built a magnificent temple for you, a place for you to dwell forever.[y]" 3While the whole assembly of Israel was standing there, the king turned around and blessed them. 4Then he said:

"Praise be to the LORD, the God of Israel, who with his hands has fulfilled what he promised with his mouth to my father David. For he said, 5'Since the day I brought my people out of Egypt, I have not chosen a city in any tribe of Israel to have a temple built for my Name to be there, nor have I chosen anyone to be the leader over my people Israel. 6But now I have chosen Jerusalem[z] for my Name[a] to be there, and I have chosen David[b] to rule my people Israel.'

6:6
z Dt 12:5; Isa 14:1
a Ex 20:24;
2Ch 12:13
b 1Ch 28:4
6:7
c 1Sa 10:7;
1Ch 17:2; 28:2;
Ac 7:46

7 "My father David had it in his heart[c] to build a temple for the Name of the LORD, the God of Israel. 8But the LORD said to my father David, 'Because it was in your heart to build a temple for my Name, you did well to have this in your heart. 9Nevertheless, you are not the one to build the temple, but your son, who is your own flesh and blood—he is the one who will build the temple for my Name.'

10 "The LORD has kept the promise he made. I have succeeded David my father and now I sit on the throne of Israel, just as the LORD promised, and I have built the temple for the Name of the LORD, the God of Israel. 11There I have placed the ark, in which is the covenant[d] of the LORD that he made with the people of Israel."

6:11
d Dt 10:2;
2Ch 5:10; Ps 25:10;
50:5

Solomon's Prayer of Dedication

12Then Solomon stood before the altar of the LORD in front of the whole assembly of Israel and spread out his hands. 13Now he had made a bronze platform,[e] five cubits[a] long, five cubits wide and three cubits[b] high, and had placed it in the cen-

6:13
e Ne 8:4

a 13 That is, about 7 1/2 feet (about 2.3 meters)   b 13 That is, about 4 1/2 feet (about 1.3 meters)

The establishment of Solomon's temple brought a renewed emphasis on prayer. For the Israelites, prayer was always a personal encounter with God rooted in his divine self-revelation and covenant relationship with his people—direct communication with a responsive deity. Whether we express praise to God or disclose a need, we demonstrate dependence on him and glory in him as the One who has answered prayer in the past and has the compassion and ability to do so in the future.

2 Chronicles 6:12–42

The fact that Solomon's prayer occupies about as much text as the construction of the temple indicates that the Chronicler was making a theological statement for his own audience about the centrality of prayer in the life of the postexilic community. It seems as though he was calling for the "priests" and "saints" (or "loyal ones") among his contemporaries to reclaim the discipline of prayer, so that the second temple (of their time)

ter of the outer court. He stood on the platform and then knelt down[f] before the whole assembly of Israel and spread out his hands toward heaven. [14]He said:

"O LORD, God of Israel, there is no God like you[g] in heaven or on earth— you who keep your covenant of love[h] with your servants who continue whole-heartedly in your way. [15]You have kept your promise to your servant David my father; with your mouth you have promised[i] and with your hand you have ful-filled it—as it is today.

[16]"Now LORD, God of Israel, keep for your servant David my father the prom-ises you made to him when you said, 'You shall never fail[j] to have a man to sit before me on the throne of Israel, if only your sons are careful in all they do to walk before me according to my law,[k] as you have done.' [17]And now, O LORD, God of Israel, let your word that you promised your servant David come true.

[18]"But will God really dwell[l] on earth with men? The heavens,[m] even the highest heavens, cannot contain you. How much less this temple I have built! [19]Yet give attention to your servant's prayer and his plea for mercy, O LORD my God. Hear the cry and the prayer that your servant is praying in your presence. [20]May your eyes[n] be open toward this temple day and night, this place of which you said you would put your Name[o] there. May you hear[p] the prayer your servant prays toward this place. [21]Hear the supplications of your servant and of your people Israel when they pray toward this place. Hear from heav-en, your dwelling place; and when you hear, forgive.[q]

[22]"When a man wrongs his neighbor and is required to take an oath[r] and he comes and swears the oath before your altar in this temple, [23]then hear from heaven and act. Judge between your servants, repaying[s] the guilty by bringing down on his own head what he has done. Declare the innocent not guilty and so establish his innocence.

[24]"When your people Israel have been defeated[t] by an enemy because they have sinned against you and when they turn back and confess your name, pray-ing and making supplication before you in this temple, [25]then hear from heaven and forgive the sin of your people Israel and bring them back to the land you gave to them and their fathers.

[26]"When the heavens are shut up and there is no rain[u] because your people have sinned against you, and when they pray toward this place and confess your name and turn from their sin because you have afflicted them, [27]then hear from heaven and forgive[v] the sin of your servants, your people Israel. Teach them the right way to live, and send rain on the land you gave your peo-ple for an inheritance.

[28]"When famine[w] or plague comes to the land, or blight or mildew, locusts or grasshoppers, or when enemies besiege them in any of their cities, whatev-er disaster or disease may come, [29]and when a prayer or plea is made by any of your people Israel—each one aware of his afflictions and pains, and spread-ing out his hands toward this temple— [30]then hear from heaven, your dwell-ing place. Forgive,[x] and deal with each man according to all he does, since you know his heart (for you alone know the hearts of men),[y] [31]so that they will fear

6:13
f Ps 95:6

6:14
g Ex 8:10; 15:11
h Dt 7:9

6:15
i 1Ch 22:10

6:16
j 2Sa 7:13,15;
1Ki 2:4; 2Ch 7:18;
23:3 k Ps 132:12

6:18
l Rev 21:3
m 2Ch 2:6; Ps 11:4;
Isa 40:22; 66:1;
Ac 7:49

6:20
n Ex 3:16; Ps 34:15
o Dt 12:11
p 2Ch 7:14; 30:20

6:21
q Ps 51:1; Isa 33:24;
40:1; 43:25; 44:22;
55:7; Mic 7:18
6:22
r Ex 22:11
6:23
s Isa 3:11; 65:6;
Mt 16:27

6:24
t Lev 26:17

6:26
u Lev 26:19;
Dt 11:17; 28:24;
2Sa 1:21; 1Ki 17:1

6:27
v ver 30,39;
2Ch 7:14

6:28
w 2Ch 20:9

6:30
x ver 27 y 1Sa 16:7;
1Ch 28:9; Ps 7:9;
44:21; Pr 16:2; 17:3

---

might become a house of prayer like the first and so that postexilic Israel might experience God's "salvation" and "goodness" (v. 41).

Solomon's temple became the symbolic focal point of God's interest in and care for humanity. It was here that his "eyes" and "ears" were continually open to the suppli-cations of both Israelites and foreigners (e.g., vv. 20–21, 32–33). These qualities differentiated God from the idols of Israel's neighbors, who had eyes but couldn't see and ears but couldn't hear (cf. Ps. 115:4–8; Isa. 44:17–18). God possessed, both then and now, the will, power, and com-passion to respond and intervene in human crises.

Life in Bible times was lived on the "ragged edge" of survival. Childbirth was often fatal to child, mother, or both. A simple infection was potentially lethal. Solomon reminded the faithful of Israel to bring the "stuff of life" to God in penitential prayer—lest na-tional or personal sin be the cause of affliction. Daily sur-vival in much of our world today is fully as precarious. Even in "civilized" countries, life-threatening dangers, though of a different variety, are prevalent. Prayer—both for global needs and for those closer to home—is as es-sential now as ever. And we are assured that our God still hears and answers!

6:31
z Ps 103:11,13;
Pr 8:13

6:32
a 2Ch 9:6;
Jn 12:20; Ac 8:27
b Ex 3:19,20
6:33
c 2Ch 7:14

6:34
d Dt 28:7
e 1Ch 5:20

6:36
f Job 15:14;
Ps 143:2; Ecc 7:20;
Jer 17:9; Jas 3:1;
1Jn 1:8-10
g Lev 26:44
6:37
h 2Ch 7:14;
33:12,19,23;
Jer 29:13

6:40
i 2Ch 7:15;
Ne 1:6,11;
Ps 17:1,6

6:41
j Isa 33:10
k 1Ch 28:2
l Ps 132:16
m Ps 116:12

6:42
n Ps 89:24,28;
Isa 55:3

7:1
o Lev 9:24;
1Ki 18:38
p Ex 16:10
q Ps 26:8
7:2
r 1Ki 8:11
s Ex 29:43; 40:35;
2Ch 5:14

7:3
t 1Ch 16:34;
2Ch 5:13; 20:21

you[z] and walk in your ways all the time they live in the land you gave our fathers.

32 "As for the foreigner who does not belong to your people Israel but has come[a] from a distant land because of your great name and your mighty hand[b] and your outstretched arm—when he comes and prays toward this temple, 33 then hear from heaven, your dwelling place, and do whatever the foreigner[c] asks of you, so that all the peoples of the earth may know your name and fear you, as do your own people Israel, and may know that this house I have built bears your Name.

34 "When your people go to war against their enemies,[d] wherever you send them, and when they pray[e] to you toward this city you have chosen and the temple I have built for your Name, 35 then hear from heaven their prayer and their plea, and uphold their cause.

36 "When they sin against you—for there is no one who does not sin[f]—and you become angry with them and give them over to the enemy, who takes them captive[g] to a land far away or near; 37 and if they have a change of heart[h] in the land where they are held captive, and repent and plead with you in the land of their captivity and say, 'We have sinned, we have done wrong and acted wickedly'; 38 and if they turn back to you with all their heart and soul in the land of their captivity where they were taken, and pray toward the land you gave their fathers, toward the city you have chosen and toward the temple I have built for your Name; 39 then from heaven, your dwelling place, hear their prayer and their pleas, and uphold their cause. And forgive your people, who have sinned against you.

40 "Now, my God, may your eyes be open and your ears attentive[i] to the prayers offered in this place.

41 "Now arise,[j] O Lord God, and come to your resting place,[k]
    you and the ark of your might.
May your priests,[l] O Lord God, be clothed with salvation,
    may your saints rejoice in your goodness.[m]
42 O Lord God, do not reject your anointed one.
    Remember the great love[n] promised to David your servant."

The Dedication of the Temple

7 When Solomon finished praying, fire[o] came down from heaven and consumed the burnt offering and the sacrifices, and the glory of the Lord filled[p] the temple. [q] 2 The priests could not enter[r] the temple of the Lord because the glory[s] of the Lord filled it. 3 When all the Israelites saw the fire coming down and the glory of the Lord above the temple, they knelt on the pavement with their faces to the ground, and they worshiped and gave thanks to the Lord, saying,

"He is good;
    his love endures forever."[t]

---

2 Chronicles 7:1–10

God's issuing fire from heaven on an altar is familiar in the Old Testament. Fire from his presence consumed the burnt offerings as the priests began their tabernacle ministry (Lev. 9:23–24). Fire fell on Elijah's water-drenched altar to prove the Lord's superiority over Baal (1 Kings 18:37–39). Fire from heaven licked up David's offering on the altar at the threshing floor of Araunah as a testimony to God's decision to stop the plague against Israel (1 Chron. 21:26). The fire indicated God's acceptance of these acts of worship. Similarly, the cloud of glory that filled the temple and prevented the priests from entering signaled God's approval of

this new "house of prayer" as his abode among his people.

The prophet Isaiah formalized the understanding of the temple as "a house of prayer for all nations"—not just for Israel (Isa. 56:7). Jesus recognized this when he cleared the temple of those who had turned the sanctuary into a merchandise mart (Mark 11:15–17). The early church continued the discipline of attending daily prayers at the temple (Acts 2:46; 3:1). The Jewish practice of morning and evening rituals gave rise, in part, to the prayer-book tradition within the church of morning and evening prayer. How do you and your church foster disciplines of personal and corporate prayer?

⁴Then the king and all the people offered sacrifices before the LORD. ⁵And King Solomon offered a sacrifice of twenty-two thousand head of cattle and a hundred and twenty thousand sheep and goats. So the king and all the people dedicated the temple of God. ⁶The priests took their positions, as did the Levites ᵘ with the LORD's musical instruments, ᵛ which King David had made for praising the LORD and which were used when he gave thanks, saying, "His love endures forever." Opposite the Levites, the priests blew their trumpets, and all the Israelites were standing.

⁷Solomon consecrated the middle part of the courtyard in front of the temple of the LORD, and there he offered burnt offerings and the fat of the fellowship offerings, ᵃ because the bronze altar he had made could not hold the burnt offerings, the grain offerings and the fat portions.

⁸So Solomon observed the festival ʷ at that time for seven days, and all Israel with him—a vast assembly, people from Lebo ᵇ Hamath to the Wadi of Egypt. ˣ ⁹On the eighth day they held an assembly, for they had celebrated the dedication of the altar for seven days and the festival ʸ for seven days more. ¹⁰On the twenty-third day of the seventh month he sent the people to their homes, joyful and glad in heart for the good things the LORD had done for David and Solomon and for his people Israel.

The LORD Appears to Solomon

¹¹When Solomon had finished the temple of the LORD and the royal palace, and had succeeded in carrying out all he had in mind to do in the temple of the LORD and in his own palace, ¹²the LORD appeared to him at night and said:

"I have heard your prayer and have chosen this place for myself ᶻ as a temple for sacrifices.

¹³"When I shut up the heavens so that there is no rain, ᵃ or command locusts to devour the land or send a plague among my people, ¹⁴if my people, who are called by my name, will humble ᵇ themselves and pray and seek my face ᶜ and turn ᵈ from their wicked ways, then will I hear from heaven and will forgive ᵉ their sin and will heal ᶠ their land. ¹⁵Now my eyes will be open and my ears attentive to the prayers offered in this place. ᵍ ¹⁶I have chosen ʰ and consecrated this temple so that my Name may be there forever. My eyes and my heart will always be there.

¹⁷"As for you, if you walk before me ⁱ as David your father did, and do all I command, and observe my decrees and laws, ¹⁸I will establish your royal throne, as I covenanted with David your father when I said, 'You shall never fail to have a man ʲ to rule over Israel.' ᵏ

¹⁹"But if you ᶜ turn away ˡ and forsake ᵐ the decrees and commands I have given you ᶜ and go off to serve other gods and worship them, ²⁰then I will uproot ⁿ Israel from my land, ᵒ which I have given them, and will reject this temple I have consecrated for my Name. I will make it a byword and an object of ridicule ᵖ among all peoples. ²¹And though this temple is now so imposing, all

---

ᵃ 7 Traditionally *peace offerings*   ᵇ 8 Or *from the entrance to*   ᶜ 19 The Hebrew is plural.

7:6
ᵘ 1Ch 15:16
ᵛ 2Ch 5:12

7:8
ʷ 2Ch 30:26
ˣ Ge 15:18

7:9
ʸ Lev 23:36

7:12
ᶻ Dt 12:5

7:13
ᵃ 2Ch 6:26-28;
Am 4:7
7:14
ᵇ Lev 26:41;
2Ch 6:37; Jas 4:10
ᶜ 1Ch 16:11
ᵈ Isa 55:7; Zec 1:4
ᵉ 2Ch 6:27
ᶠ 2Ch 30:20;
Isa 30:26; 57:18
7:15
ᵍ 2Ch 6:40
7:16
ʰ ver 12; 2Ch 6:6
7:17
ⁱ 1Ki 9:4
7:18
ʲ 2Ch 6:16
ᵏ 2Sa 7:13;
2Ch 13:5
7:19
ˡ Dt 28:15
ᵐ Lev 26:14,33
7:20
ⁿ Dt 29:28
ᵒ 1Ki 14:15
ᵖ Dt 28:37

---

2 Chronicles 7:11–22

The second half of chapter 7 describes God's second dream appearance to Solomon (cf. 1:7–12). Divine approval of Solomon's prayer of dedication and of the temple as the place for God's dwelling was emphasized by the word "chosen" (vv. 12,16), along with the declaration that the temple was "consecrated" (v. 16) as an act of God himself in response to Solomon's dedicatory sacrifices and prayer.

The reference to God's "eyes" and "heart" being connected to the temple is an unusual expression for divine presence. God's eyes and heart symbolize his concern for humanity in that he sees people in distress and has compassion for their plight—as well as the power to intervene and deliver. We can't reflect upon the association of the "eyes" and "heart" of God with the temple and not think ahead to the incarnation of Jesus Christ.

God's "eyes" and "heart" still go out to the hurting—as do our own. But he further asks us to function as his "hands and feet"—which may involve washing one another's dirty feet (John 13:14)! Our intentions with regard to service may be the best, but they do no earthly (or kingdom) good unless and until we act. James 2:15–16 admonishes believers not just to notice needs but to help meet them. How are you putting this challenge into practice?

7:21
q Dt 29:24

who pass by will be appalled and say,*q* 'Why has the LORD done such a thing to this land and to this temple?' 22People will answer, 'Because they have forsaken the LORD, the God of their fathers, who brought them out of Egypt, and have embraced other gods, worshiping and serving them—that is why he brought all this disaster on them.' "

Solomon's Other Activities

8 At the end of twenty years, during which Solomon built the temple of the LORD and his own palace, 2Solomon rebuilt the villages that Hiram*a* had given him, and settled Israelites in them. 3Solomon then went to Hamath Zobah and captured

8:5
r 1Ch 7:24;
2Ch 14:7

it. 4He also built up Tadmor in the desert and all the store cities he had built in Hamath. 5He rebuilt Upper Beth Horon*r* and Lower Beth Horon as fortified cities, with walls and with gates and bars, 6as well as Baalath and all his store cities, and all the cities for his chariots and for his horses*b*—whatever he desired to build in Jerusalem, in Lebanon and throughout all the territory he ruled.

8:7
s Ge 10:16

7All the people left from the Hittites, Amorites, Perizzites, Hivites and Jebusites*s*

8:8
t 1Ki 4:6; 9:21

(these peoples were not Israelites), 8that is, their descendants remaining in the land, whom the Israelites had not destroyed—these Solomon conscripted*t* for his slave labor force, as it is to this day. 9But Solomon did not make slaves of the Israelites for his work; they were his fighting men, commanders of his captains, and commanders of his chariots and charioteers. 10They were also King Solomon's chief officials—two hundred and fifty officials supervising the men.

8:11
u 1Ki 3:1; 7:8

11Solomon brought Pharaoh's daughter*u* up from the City of David to the palace he had built for her, for he said, "My wife must not live in the palace of David king of Israel, because the places the ark of the LORD has entered are holy."

8:12
v 1Ki 8:64; 2Ch 4:1;
15:8
8:13
w Ex 29:38;
Nu 28:3 *x* Nu 28:9
y Ex 23:14;
Dt 16:16 *z* Ex 23:16

12On the altar*v* of the LORD that he had built in front of the portico, Solomon sacrificed burnt offerings to the LORD, 13according to the daily requirement*w* for offerings commanded by Moses for Sabbaths,*x* New Moons and the three*y* annual feasts—the Feast of Unleavened Bread, the Feast of Weeks*z* and the Feast of Tabernacles. 14In keeping with the ordinance of his father David, he appointed the divi-

8:14
a 1Ch 24:1
b 1Ch 25:1
c 1Ch 9:17; 26:1
d Ne 12:24,36
e 1Ch 23:6;
Ne 12:45

sions*a* of the priests for their duties, and the Levites*b* to lead the praise and to assist the priests according to each day's requirement. He also appointed the gatekeepers*c* by divisions for the various gates, because this was what David the man of God*d* had ordered.*e* 15They did not deviate from the king's commands to the priests or to the Levites in any matter, including that of the treasuries.

16All Solomon's work was carried out, from the day the foundation of the temple of the LORD was laid until its completion. So the temple of the LORD was finished.

17Then Solomon went to Ezion Geber and Elath on the coast of Edom. 18And Hiram sent him ships commanded by his own officers, men who knew the sea. These, with Solomon's men, sailed to Ophir and brought back four hundred and fifty tal-

8:18
f 2Ch 9:9

ents*c* of gold,*f* which they delivered to King Solomon.

a 2 Hebrew *Huram*, a variant of *Hiram*; also in verse 18   *b 6* Or *charioteers*   *c 18* That is, about 17 tons (about 16 metric tons)

---

2 Chronicles 8:1–18

More than Solomon's accomplishments, the last segment of the Chronicler's review of his reign (chs. 8–9) celebrates what God achieved through this Davidic king. The emphasis in chapter 8 is on Solomon's faithfulness in following through on David's preparations and seeing the temple building project to completion (cf. 8:16). In chapter 9 God is praised for his faithfulness in making good on his covenant promise to "build David's house" and bless his successor with wisdom (cf. 9:8).

There is irony in the report of Solomon's concern for purity during the first 20 years of his reign (e.g., the displacement of his Egyptian wife from David's palace), since he would later profane Jerusalem by building places of worship for the gods of his foreign wives

(1 Kings 11:4–8). Then, as now, purity wasn't a one-time event (e.g., the ark entering Jerusalem in 2 Chron. 5) but an ongoing process of applying Biblical teaching about God's holiness to daily living (cf. Lev. 11:44; Matt. 5:48).

In Philippians 1:9–10 Paul prayed that the Philippian Christians' love would "abound more and more in knowledge and depth of insight, so that . . . [they] might] be pure and blameless until the day of Christ." Purity sounds like a tall—and naïve—order in today's secular society with its pervasive invitations to evil. But notice the tie-in between love, insight, and purity. If we are guided in our service by the motivation of true Christian love, there is an implied promise here that wisdom and goodness will follow.

The Queen of Sheba Visits Solomon

9 When the queen of Sheba[g] heard of Solomon's fame, she came to Jerusalem to test him with hard questions. Arriving with a very great caravan—with camels carrying spices, large quantities of gold, and precious stones—she came to Solomon and talked with him about all she had on her mind. [2]Solomon answered all her questions; nothing was too hard for him to explain to her. [3]When the queen of Sheba saw the wisdom of Solomon,[h] as well as the palace he had built, [4]the food on his table, the seating of his officials, the attending servants in their robes, the cupbearers in their robes and the burnt offerings he made at[a] the temple of the LORD, she was overwhelmed.

[5]She said to the king, "The report I heard in my own country about your achievements and your wisdom is true. [6]But I did not believe what they said until I came[i] and saw with my own eyes. Indeed, not even half the greatness of your wisdom was told me; you have far exceeded the report I heard. [7]How happy your men must be! How happy your officials, who continually stand before you and hear your wisdom! [8]Praise be to the LORD your God, who has delighted in you and placed you on his throne[j] as king to rule for the LORD your God. Because of the love of your God for Israel and his desire to uphold them forever, he has made you king[k] over them, to maintain justice and righteousness."

[9]Then she gave the king 120 talents[b] of gold,[l] large quantities of spices, and precious stones. There had never been such spices as those the queen of Sheba gave to King Solomon.

[10](The men of Hiram and the men of Solomon brought gold from Ophir;[m] they also brought algumwood[c] and precious stones. [11]The king used the algumwood to make steps for the temple of the LORD and for the royal palace, and to make harps and lyres for the musicians. Nothing like them had ever been seen in Judah.)

[12]King Solomon gave the queen of Sheba all she desired and asked for; he gave her more than she had brought to him. Then she left and returned with her retinue to her own country.

Solomon's Splendor

[13]The weight of the gold that Solomon received yearly was 666 talents,[d] [14]not including the revenues brought in by merchants and traders. Also all the kings of Arabia[n] and the governors of the land brought gold and silver to Solomon.

[15]King Solomon made two hundred large shields of hammered gold; six hundred bekas[e] of hammered gold went into each shield. [16]He also made three hundred

---

9:1
g Ge 10:7;
Eze 23:42;
Mt 12:42; Lk 11:31

9:3
h 1Ki 5:12

9:6
i 2Ch 6:32

9:8
j 1Ki 2:12;
1Ch 17:14; 28:5;
29:23; 2Ch 13:8
k 2Ch 2:11
9:9
l 2Ch 8:18

9:10
m 2Ch 8:18

9:14
n 2Ch 17:11;
Isa 21:13;
Jer 25:24;
Eze 27:21; 30:5

---

[a] 4 Or *the ascent by which he went up to*   [b] 9 That is, about 4 1/2 tons (about 4 metric tons)
[c] 10 Probably a variant of *almugwood*   [d] 13 That is, about 25 tons (about 23 metric tons)
[e] 15 That is, about 7 1/2 pounds (about 3.5 kilograms)

---

2 Chronicles 9:1–12

Declaring God's glory among the nations is a minor theme in Chronicles, and the report of this visit reinforces David's and Asaph's calls to "make God known among the nations" (1 Chron. 16:8,24). It's unclear whether the queen's affirmation in verse 8 was simply acknowledgement of the Israelite God as a local deity or whether it represented a deeper faith commitment to the one true and universal God. Either way, the impression made on this foreigner reflects the power God's children possess to bring God to those who are "far off."

Jesus taught that God's goodness to Solomon is to be viewed as an invitation, not to materialism, but to seeking God's kingdom and righteousness over all else—while trusting that our material needs will be met as well (Matt. 6:28–34). Solomon's send-off of this queen included gifting her with even more than she had given him. This wasn't one-upmanship but an example of uncompromising generosity. Surely we who are so blessed can afford to be open-handed as well.

2 Chronicles 9:13–28

Israel's strategic location connecting the continents of Africa and Asia and Solomon's control of the trade routes generated enormous wealth for him. The 666 talents of gold he received annually equated to approximately 25 tons (see NIV text note on v. 13). The unspecified sum of Solomon's gross yearly income included both money from tributes and tariffs and profits from his own capital ventures (primarily international trade).

The Chronicler indicated that Solomon's wisdom and wealth were the result of God's favor, as foreign potentates came to Jerusalem from all over the world to hear "the wisdom God had put in his heart" (vv. 22–23). This historian wasn't just revisiting the "good old days" but expressing the fondest hopes of many in the restoration community for a return to such an era of righteousness and glory.

9:16
o 2Ch 12:9
p 1Ki 7:2
9:17
q 1Ki 22:39

small shields[o] of hammered gold, with three hundred bekas[a] of gold in each shield. The king put them in the Palace of the Forest of Lebanon.[p]

[17]Then the king made a great throne inlaid with ivory[q] and overlaid with pure gold. [18]The throne had six steps, and a footstool of gold was attached to it. On both sides of the seat were armrests, with a lion standing beside each of them. [19]Twelve lions stood on the six steps, one at either end of each step. Nothing like it had ever been made for any other kingdom. [20]All King Solomon's goblets were gold, and all the household articles in the Palace of the Forest of Lebanon were pure gold. Nothing was made of silver, because silver was considered of little value in Solomon's day. [21]The king had a fleet of trading ships[b] manned by Hiram's[c] men. Once every three years it returned, carrying gold, silver and ivory, and apes and baboons.

9:22
r 1Ki 3:13;
2Ch 1:12
9:23
s 1Ki 4:34
9:24
t 2Ch 32:23;
Ps 45:12; 68:29;
72:10; Isa 18:7
9:25
u 1Sa 8:11; 1Ki 4:26
9:26
v 1Ki 4:21
w Ps 72:8-9
x Ge 15:18-21

[22]King Solomon was greater in riches and wisdom than all the other kings of the earth.[r] [23]All the kings[s] of the earth sought audience with Solomon to hear the wisdom God had put in his heart. [24]Year after year, everyone who came brought a gift[t]— articles of silver and gold, and robes, weapons and spices, and horses and mules.

[25]Solomon had four thousand stalls for horses and chariots,[u] and twelve thousand horses,[d] which he kept in the chariot cities and also with him in Jerusalem. [26]He ruled[v] over all the kings from the River[e w] to the land of the Philistines, as far as the border of Egypt.[x] [27]The king made silver as common in Jerusalem as stones, and cedar as plentiful as sycamore-fig trees in the foothills. [28]Solomon's horses were imported from Egypt[f] and from all other countries.

Solomon's Death

9:29
y 2Sa 7:2;
1Ch 29:29
z 1Ki 11:29
a 2Ch 10:2
9:31
b 1Ki 2:10

[29]As for the other events of Solomon's reign, from beginning to end, are they not written in the records of Nathan[y] the prophet, in the prophecy of Ahijah[z] the Shilonite and in the visions of Iddo the seer concerning Jeroboam[a] son of Nebat? [30]Solomon reigned in Jerusalem over all Israel forty years. [31]Then he rested with his fathers and was buried in the city of David[b] his father. And Rehoboam his son succeeded him as king.

Israel Rebels Against Rehoboam

10:2
c 2Ch 9:29
d 1Ki 11:40
10:3
e 1Ch 9:1

10 Rehoboam went to Shechem, for all the Israelites had gone there to make him king. [2]When Jeroboam[c] son of Nebat heard this (he was in Egypt, where he had fled[d] from King Solomon), he returned from Egypt. [3]So they sent for Jeroboam, and he and all Israel[e] went to Rehoboam and said to him: [4]"Your father

---

[a] 16 That is, about 3 3/4 pounds (about 1.7 kilograms) [b] 21 Hebrew *of ships that could go to Tarshish* [c] 21 Hebrew *Huram*, a variant of *Hiram* [d] 25 Or *charioteers* [e] 26 That is, the Euphrates [f] 28 Or possibly *Muzur*, a region in Cilicia

---

📖 Depending upon our age and experience, many of us can recall a time when life was simpler, safer, and seemingly more innocent. The reality is, though, that since the fall human beings have never been innocent, or conditions ideal. Public norms governing the "acceptable" have little impact on the condition of the human heart. We can present the past to our children and others through rose-tinted glasses, or we can face history honestly, with a willingness to learn from past mistakes.

2 Chronicles 9:29–31

🔖 Though the phrase "rested with his fathers" signifies a peaceful death after a long and prosperous life, the Chronicler wasn't as positive in his remarks about Solomon's death as he had been about David's. In 1 Chronicles 29:28 he had written that David "died at a good old age, having enjoyed long life, wealth and honor." Here he essentially repeated the summary found in 1 Kings 11:41–43 but omitted altogether the unfavorable theological review of Solomon's idolatry-

tainted reign found in 1 Kings 11:1–13, as well as the opposition recorded in 11:14–40.

📖 The Chronicler chose to focus as much as possible on the praiseworthy aspects of the life and reign of Solomon (as well as of David and some other kings of Judah; see notes for 1 Chron. 18:14–17 and "There and Then" for 1 Chron. 29:21–25)—evidently to encourage the postexilic Jewish people regarding God's blessing of their past history and promise of a future Messiah, the perfect son of David. Putting together all the Scriptural record, we see that Solomon's life (as well as David's) was a definite mixture of faithfulness and failure. Is that reality more of an encouragement or discouragement as you reflect on your own life—past, present, and future?

2 Chronicles 10:1—11:4

🔖 A key theological interpretation of developments resulting in the "meltdown" of the united monarchy is found in 10:15: "This turn of events was from God." The Chronicler connected his commentary to

put a heavy yoke on us,[f] but now lighten the harsh labor and the heavy yoke he put on us, and we will serve you."

[5]Rehoboam answered, "Come back to me in three days." So the people went away.

[6]Then King Rehoboam consulted the elders[g] who had served his father Solomon during his lifetime. "How would you advise me to answer these people?" he asked.

[7]They replied, "If you will be kind to these people and please them and give them a favorable answer,[h] they will always be your servants."

[8]But Rehoboam rejected[i] the advice the elders[j] gave him and consulted the young men who had grown up with him and were serving him. [9]He asked them, "What is your advice? How should we answer these people who say to me, 'Lighten the yoke your father put on us'?"

[10]The young men who had grown up with him replied, "Tell the people who have said to you, 'Your father put a heavy yoke on us, but make our yoke lighter'—tell them, 'My little finger is thicker than my father's waist. [11]My father laid on you a heavy yoke; I will make it even heavier. My father scourged you with whips; I will scourge you with scorpions.' "

[12]Three days later Jeroboam and all the people returned to Rehoboam, as the king had said, "Come back to me in three days." [13]The king answered them harshly. Rejecting the advice of the elders, [14]he followed the advice of the young men and said, "My father made your yoke heavy; I will make it even heavier. My father scourged you with whips; I will scourge you with scorpions." [15]So the king did not listen to the people, for this turn of events was from God,[k] to fulfill the word the LORD had spoken to Jeroboam son of Nebat through Ahijah the Shilonite.[l]

[16]When all Israel[m] saw that the king refused to listen to them, they answered the king:

> "What share do we have in David,[n]
> what part in Jesse's son?
> To your tents, O Israel!
> Look after your own house, O David!"

So all the Israelites went home. [17]But as for the Israelites who were living in the towns of Judah, Rehoboam still ruled over them.

[18]King Rehoboam sent out Adoniram,[a][o] who was in charge of forced labor, but the Israelites stoned him to death. King Rehoboam, however, managed to get into his chariot and escape to Jerusalem. [19]So Israel has been in rebellion against the house of David to this day.

11 When Rehoboam arrived in Jerusalem,[p] he mustered the house of Judah and Benjamin—a hundred and eighty thousand fighting men—to make war against Israel and to regain the kingdom for Rehoboam.

---

[a] 18 Hebrew *Hadoram*, a variant of *Adoniram*

10:4
f 2Ch 2:2

10:6
g Job 8:8-9; 12:12; 15:10; 32:7

10:7
h Pr 15:1
10:8
i 2Sa 17:14
j Pr 13:20

10:15
k 2Ch 11:4; 25:16-20
l 1Ki 11:29
10:16
m 1Ch 9:1 n ver 19; 2Sa 20:1

10:18
o 1Ki 5:14

11:1
p 1Ki 12:21

Ahijah's prophecy predicting the split of Solomon's kingdom as punishment for his idolatry (10:15; cf. 1 Kings 11:9–13; 12:29–36). This approach fits a pattern in Chronicles that associates crucial historical moments with what God had said through the prophets in demonstration of his absolute sovereignty as Lord of history (cf. 11:4; but see also notes for 1 Kings 12:1–24).

Following his account of Rehoboam's foolish decision that resulted in schism, the Chronicler focused only on the subsequent history of Judah, omitting that of the northern kingdom unless it had affected Judah. Not only was his audience the restored community of Judah, but his primary concern was to trace God's faithfulness to his promise to give David an unbroken line of descent on Israel's throne.

Yet the Chronicler's emphasis on "all Israel" contin-

ued, as demonstrated by his reference to the tribes of Judah and Benjamin as "Israelites" (11:3). The people of the northern tribes were still their "brothers" (11:4) and together they were still the one people of God—a fact important to the Chronicler's message of hope for God's restoration of postexilic Judah, which was dependent on the unity of all Israelites living in the land.

In difficult times Christians often rely on the promise of Romans 8:23. In this instance, certain factors about Rehoboam's reign weren't good, but God eventually brought good out of a bad situation. Because David's kingly line was unbroken, New Testament writers were able to trace Jesus' lineage back to David (cf. Matt. 1:6–7; Luke 3:31). How does this boost your confidence in God's ability to work "good" out of any situation you are in today?

11:2
q 2Ch 12:5-7, 15

11:4
r 2Ch 28:8-11

2 But this word of the LORD came to Shemaiah[q] the man of God: 3 "Say to Rehoboam son of Solomon king of Judah and to all the Israelites in Judah and Benjamin, 4 'This is what the LORD says: Do not go up to fight against your brothers.[r] Go home, every one of you, for this is my doing.' " So they obeyed the words of the LORD and turned back from marching against Jeroboam.

Rehoboam Fortifies Judah

5 Rehoboam lived in Jerusalem and built up towns for defense in Judah: 6 Bethlehem, Etam, Tekoa, 7 Beth Zur, Soco, Adullam, 8 Gath, Mareshah, Ziph, 9 Adoraim, Lachish, Azekah, 10 Zorah, Aijalon and Hebron. These were fortified cities in Judah and Benjamin. 11 He strengthened their defenses and put commanders in them, with supplies of food, olive oil and wine. 12 He put shields and spears in all the cities, and made them very strong. So Judah and Benjamin were his.

11:14
s Nu 35:2-5
t 2Ch 13:9
11:15
u 1Ki 13:33
v 1Ki 12:31
w Lev 17:7
x 1Ki 12:28;
2Ch 13:8
11:16
y 2Ch 15:9
11:17
z 2Ch 12:1

13 The priests and Levites from all their districts throughout Israel sided with him. 14 The Levites[s] even abandoned their pasturelands and property,[t] and came to Judah and Jerusalem because Jeroboam and his sons had rejected them as priests of the LORD. 15 And he appointed[u] his own priests[v] for the high places and for the goat[w] and calf[x] idols he had made. 16 Those from every tribe of Israel[y] who set their hearts on seeking the LORD, the God of Israel, followed the Levites to Jerusalem to offer sacrifices to the LORD, the God of their fathers. 17 They strengthened[z] the kingdom of Judah and supported Rehoboam son of Solomon three years, walking in the ways of David and Solomon during this time.

Rehoboam's Family

11:20
a 1Ki 15:2
b 2Ch 13:2

11:21
c Dt 17:17
11:22
d Dt 21:15-17

18 Rehoboam married Mahalath, who was the daughter of David's son Jerimoth and of Abihail, the daughter of Jesse's son Eliab. 19 She bore him sons: Jeush, Shemariah and Zaham. 20 Then he married Maacah[a] daughter of Absalom, who bore him Abijah,[b] Attai, Ziza and Shelomith. 21 Rehoboam loved Maacah daughter of Absalom more than any of his other wives and concubines. In all, he had eighteen wives[c] and sixty concubines, twenty-eight sons and sixty daughters.

22 Rehoboam appointed Abijah[d] son of Maacah to be the chief prince among his brothers, in order to make him king. 23 He acted wisely, dispersing some of his sons

---

2 Chronicles 11:5–17

Once again we see the Chronicler's emphasis on "all Israel" (see previous "There and Then"). The migration of priests and Levites from Israel to Judah was precipitated by the false worship centers established in the north by Jeroboam (cf. 1 Kings 12:26–33). Their example prompted other northern Israelites to join them in worshiping God in Jerusalem. These Israelites had "set their hearts on seeking the LORD" (2 Chron. 11:16), something King Rehoboam and his subjects would ultimately refuse to do (12:1,14).

Many Christians and churches in large cities today find themselves fleeing urban blight and crime for worship in the safety and presumably more comfortable atmosphere of suburbia or a better neighborhood. But if such believers have truly "set their hearts on seeking the Lord," it's important that they seek his guidance in this important matter as well.

Unlike the time of ancient Israel, there is no longer just one legitimate place to worship (cf. Deut. 12:5–6; John 4:23). Moreover, if every "light" in our cities were abandoned or moved to another location, how dark would our city neighborhoods become? Fortunately, many great worship centers have been established and are thriving on the opportunities that abound for ministry in the world's great cities. Can you think of one example? Pray for that ministry today.

2 Chronicles 11:18–23

Rehoboam imitated his father's practice of delegation of royal authority by means of district governors (cf. 1 Kings 4:7–19) but made these appointments from among his own sons. This policy prevented infighting among prospective successors to the throne, solidified the king's position, guarded against coup attempts, ensured an heir for the continuation of the dynasty (since housing the princes in one location would have made it easier for a usurper to execute all rivals), and extended the influence of the royal family to outlying districts.

There is nothing wrong—and in some sense "everything" right—with Christian politicians and business people being savvy in their dealings and decisions. An elected official can't be effective if she loses her bid for reelection, nor can a Christian business operate in a competitive environment without sound fiscal policy. The key lies in our attitudes and motivations. Jesus advised the Twelve that he was sending them out "like sheep among wolves" and counseled them to "be as shrewd as snakes and as innocent as doves" (Matt. 10:16). How have you seen wise managerial policies and good stewardship benefit the kingdom?

throughout the districts of Judah and Benjamin, and to all the fortified cities. He gave them abundant provisions and took many wives for them.

Shishak Attacks Jerusalem

12 After Rehoboam's position as king was established[e] and he had become strong,[f] he and all Israel[a] with him abandoned the law of the LORD. [2]Because they had been unfaithful[g] to the LORD, Shishak[h] king of Egypt attacked Jerusalem in the fifth year of King Rehoboam. [3]With twelve hundred chariots and sixty thousand horsemen and the innumerable troops of Libyans, Sukkites and Cushites[b][i] that came with him from Egypt, [4]he captured the fortified cities[j] of Judah and came as far as Jerusalem.

[5]Then the prophet Shemaiah[k] came to Rehoboam and to the leaders of Judah who had assembled in Jerusalem for fear of Shishak, and he said to them, "This is what the LORD says, 'You have abandoned me; therefore, I now abandon[l] you to Shishak.' "

[6]The leaders of Israel and the king humbled themselves and said, "The LORD is just."[m]

[7]When the LORD saw that they humbled themselves, this word of the LORD came to Shemaiah: "Since they have humbled themselves, I will not destroy them but will soon give them deliverance.[n] My wrath will not be poured out on Jerusalem through Shishak. [8]They will, however, become subject[o] to him, so that they may learn the difference between serving me and serving the kings of other lands."

[9]When Shishak king of Egypt attacked Jerusalem, he carried off the treasures of the temple of the LORD and the treasures of the royal palace. He took everything, including the gold shields[p] Solomon had made. [10]So King Rehoboam made bronze shields to replace them and assigned these to the commanders of the guard on duty at the entrance to the royal palace. [11]Whenever the king went to the LORD's temple, the guards went with him, bearing the shields, and afterward they returned them to the guardroom.

[12]Because Rehoboam humbled himself, the LORD's anger turned from him, and he was not totally destroyed. Indeed, there was some good[q] in Judah.

[13]King Rehoboam established himself firmly in Jerusalem and continued as king. He was forty-one years old when he became king, and he reigned seventeen years in Jerusalem, the city the LORD had chosen out of all the tribes of Israel in which to put his Name.[r] His mother's name was Naamah; she was an Ammonite. [14]He did evil because he had not set his heart on seeking the LORD.

[15]As for the events of Rehoboam's reign, from beginning to end, are they not written in the records of Shemaiah[s] the prophet and of Iddo the seer that deal with genealogies? There was continual warfare between Rehoboam and Jeroboam. [16]Rehoboam rested with his fathers and was buried in the City of David. And Abijah[t] his son succeeded him as king.

---

[a] 1 That is, Judah, as frequently in 2 Chronicles   [b] 3 That is, people from the upper Nile region

Side references

12:1 [e] ver 13; [f] 2Ch 11:17

12:2 [g] 1Ki 14:22-24; [h] 1Ki 11:40

12:3 [i] 2Ch 16:8; Na 3:9

12:4 [j] 2Ch 11:10

12:5 [k] 2Ch 11:2; [l] Dt 28:15; 2Ch 15:2

12:6 [m] Ex 9:27; Da 9:14

12:7 [n] 1Ki 21:29; Ps 78:38

12:8 [o] Dt 28:48

12:9 [p] 2Ch 9:16

12:12 [q] 1Ki 14:13; 2Ch 19:3

12:13 [r] Dt 12:5; 2Ch 6:6

12:15 [s] 2Ch 9:29; 11:2

12:16 [t] 2Ch 11:20

---

2 Chronicles 12:1–16

The Chronicler understood Shishak's invasion of Judah as punishment for sin, in that Rehoboam "and all Israel with him abandoned the law of the LORD" (v. 1). By "all Israel" the Chronicler meant all the Israelites living in Judah (the "true" Israel), whether from northern or southern tribal stock. He saw a cause-and-effect relationship in this breach of faithfulness to the Lord and the Egyptian raid—a clear indication of his acknowledgment of God as sovereign.

The statement that God "abandons" those who "abandon" him (v. 5) was basic to the Chronicler's theology (cf. 1 Chron. 28:9,20; 2 Chron. 15:2; 24:20). God accepted the response of Rehoboam and the leaders of Judah as repentance and mercifully decreed a "qualified" deliverance from Shishak—one that would still involve

consequences for disobedience. At times God used whatever means were necessary to teach his people lessons about the nature of his covenant relationship with them.

How often does God respond to our sin in a similar manner as he did with Rehoboam? His forgiveness is certain, so long as we approach him in a spirit of repentance, but natural consequences are nearly inevitable. Have you ever stopped to think of such consequences as blessings? Unpleasant as they may be, they convince us of the seriousness of sin and deter us from repeating the same mistakes. It's important, though, that we not view all difficult circumstances as punishment. God's purposes for suffering—our own or that of the world around us—are often mysterious, but we will one day stand in amazement at the wisdom of the big picture. For more on suffering for doing right, see 1 Peter 4:12–19.

Abijah King of Judah

13 In the eighteenth year of the reign of Jeroboam, Abijah became king of Judah, [2]and he reigned in Jerusalem three years. His mother's name was Maacah,[a] a daughter[b] of Uriel of Gibeah.

There was war between Abijah[u] and Jeroboam.[v] [3]Abijah went into battle with a force of four hundred thousand able fighting men, and Jeroboam drew up a battle line against him with eight hundred thousand able troops.

[4]Abijah stood on Mount Zemaraim,[w] in the hill country of Ephraim, and said, "Jeroboam and all Israel,[x] listen to me! [5]Don't you know that the LORD, the God of Israel, has given the kingship of Israel to David and his descendants forever[y] by a covenant of salt?[z] [6]Yet Jeroboam son of Nebat, an official of Solomon son of David, rebelled[a] against his master. [7]Some worthless scoundrels[b] gathered around him and opposed Rehoboam son of Solomon when he was young and indecisive and not strong enough to resist them.

[8]"And now you plan to resist the kingdom of the LORD, which is in the hands of David's descendants. You are indeed a vast army and have with you the golden calves[c] that Jeroboam made to be your gods. [9]But didn't you drive out the priests of the LORD,[d] the sons of Aaron, and the Levites, and make priests of your own as the peoples of other lands do? Whoever comes to consecrate himself with a young bull[e] and seven rams may become a priest of what are not gods.[f]

[10]"As for us, the LORD is our God, and we have not forsaken him. The priests who serve the LORD are sons of Aaron, and the Levites assist them. [11]Every morning and evening[g] they present burnt offerings and fragrant incense to the LORD. They set out the bread on the ceremonially clean table[h] and light the lamps on the gold lampstand every evening. We are observing the requirements of the LORD our God. But you have forsaken him. [12]God is with us; he is our leader. His priests with their trumpets will sound the battle cry against you.[i] Men of Israel, do not fight against the LORD,[j] the God of your fathers, for you will not succeed."

[13]Now Jeroboam had sent troops around to the rear, so that while he was in front of Judah the ambush[k] was behind them. [14]Judah turned and saw that they were being attacked at both front and rear. Then they cried out[l] to the LORD. The priests blew their trumpets [15]and the men of Judah raised the battle cry. At the sound of their battle cry, God routed Jeroboam and all Israel[m] before Abijah and Judah. [16]The Israelites fled before Judah, and God delivered[n] them into their hands. [17]Abijah and his men inflicted heavy losses on them, so that there were five hundred thousand casualties among Israel's able men. [18]The men of Israel were subdued on that occasion, and the men of Judah were victorious because they relied[o] on the LORD, the God of their fathers.

[19]Abijah pursued Jeroboam and took from him the towns of Bethel, Jeshanah

---

a 2 Most Septuagint manuscripts and Syriac (see also 2 Chron. 11:20 and 1 Kings 15:2); Hebrew *Micaiah* b 2 Or *granddaughter*

Marginal references:

13:2 u 2Ch 11:20; v 1Ki 15:6
13:4 w Jos 18:22; x 1Ch 11:1
13:5 y 2Sa 7:13; z Lev 2:13; Nu 18:19
13:6 a 1Ki 11:26
13:7 b Jdg 9:4
13:8 c 1Ki 12:28; 2Ch 11:15
13:9 d 2Ch 11:14-15; e Ex 29:35-36; f Jer 2:11
13:11 g Ex 29:39; 2Ch 2:4; h Lev 24:5-9
13:12 i Nu 10:8-9; j Ac 5:39
13:13 k Jos 8:9
13:14 l 2Ch 14:11
13:15 m 2Ch 14:12
13:16 n 2Ch 16:8
13:18 o 1Ch 5:20; 2Ch 14:11; Ps 22:5

---

2 Chronicles 13:1—14:1

The accounts of Abijah's reign in Kings and Chronicles are quite different (see notes for 1 Kings 15:1–8). In his brief summary, the author of Kings painted Abijah as a failure because "his heart was not fully devoted to the LORD" (1 Kings 15:3). Rather than contradicting this earlier version, the Chronicler simply reported one of those instances when Abijah's heart *was* devoted to the Lord, even though overall this posture toward God was uncharacteristic of this king.

The plot of this story was larger than Abijah versus Jeroboam. It was a test of the resolve between the two kingdoms over the issue of the Davidic covenant and the question of God's vindication. The punch line of Abijah's speech is in 13:12: "God is with us." Israel could choose to "not fight against the LORD." The Chronicler held out that same option to his own audience. They too could bury their tribal schisms and pursue reconciliation and unity for the good of all the Israelites in postexilic Judah. Only then could "restoration" succeed.

We have the same options as the Israelites, during the days both of the divided kingdom and of the restoration. We can work alongside God and his people to advance his kingdom cause. Or we can "resist the kingdom of the LORD" (13:8) and allow prejudice, greed, or other impediments to hinder our effectiveness in his service. Still today, reconciliation and unity, whether involving individual relationships or people groups, are prerequisites for restoration and kingdom living.

and Ephron, with their surrounding villages. ²⁰Jeroboam did not regain power during the time of Abijah. And the LORD struck him down and he died.

²¹But Abijah grew in strength. He married fourteen wives and had twenty-two sons and sixteen daughters.

²²The other events of Abijah's reign, what he did and what he said, are written in the annotations of the prophet Iddo.

14

And Abijah rested with his fathers and was buried in the City of David. Asa his son succeeded him as king, and in his days the country was at peace for ten years.

Asa King of Judah

²Asa did what was good and right in the eyes of the LORD his God. ³He removed the foreign altars and the high places, smashed the sacred stones and cut down the Asherah poles. ^{a p} ⁴He commanded Judah to seek the LORD, the God of their fathers, and to obey his laws and commands. ⁵He removed the high places and incense altars ^q in every town in Judah, and the kingdom was at peace under him. ⁶He built up the fortified cities of Judah, since the land was at peace. No one was at war with him during those years, for the LORD gave him rest. ^r

⁷"Let us build up these towns," he said to Judah, "and put walls around them, with towers, gates and bars. The land is still ours, because we have sought the LORD our God; we sought him and he has given us rest on every side." So they built and prospered.

⁸Asa had an army of three hundred thousand men from Judah, equipped with large shields and with spears, and two hundred and eighty thousand from Benjamin, armed with small shields and with bows. All these were brave fighting men.

⁹Zerah the Cushite ^s marched out against them with a vast army ^b and three hundred chariots, and came as far as Mareshah. ^t ¹⁰Asa went out to meet him, and they took up battle positions in the Valley of Zephathah near Mareshah.

¹¹Then Asa called ^u to the LORD his God and said, "LORD, there is no one like you to help the powerless against the mighty. Help us, O LORD our God, for we rely ^v on you, and in your name ^w we have come against this vast army. O LORD, you are our God; do not let man prevail ^x against you."

¹²The LORD struck down ^y the Cushites before Asa and Judah. The Cushites fled, ¹³and Asa and his army pursued them as far as Gerar. ^z Such a great number of Cushites fell that they could not recover; they were crushed before the LORD and his forces. The men of Judah carried off a large amount of plunder. ¹⁴They destroyed all the villages around Gerar, for the terror ^a of the LORD had fallen upon them. They plundered all these villages, since there was much booty there. ¹⁵They also attacked the camps of the herdsmen and carried off droves of sheep and goats and camels. Then they returned to Jerusalem.

---

^a 3 That is, symbols of the goddess Asherah; here and elsewhere in 2 Chronicles   ^b 9 Hebrew with an army of a thousand thousands or with an army of thousands upon thousands

14:3
p Ex 34:13; Dt 7:5;
1Ki 15:12-14

14:5
q 2Ch 34:4,7

14:6
r 1Ch 22:9;
2Ch 15:15

14:9
s 2Ch 12:3; 16:8
t 2Ch 11:8

14:11
u 2Ch 13:14
v 2Ch 13:18
w 1Sa 17:45
x 1Sa 14:6; Ps 9:19

14:12
y 2Ch 13:15
14:13
z Ge 10:19

14:14
a Ge 35:5;
2Ch 17:10

---

2 Chronicles 14:2–15

Some form of the expression "seeking the LORD" (vv. 4,7) occurs nine times in the three chapters recounting Asa's kingship (chs. 14–16), setting the theme for the entire section. Asa had fortified Judah's defenses (vv. 6–7) and possessed a large and well-equipped army (v. 8). But Zerah's army was "vast" (lit., "a thousand thousands" or "beyond counting"). In addition, he had chariot forces (the equivalent of the modern tank).

The story turns on Asa's prayer for help from the Lord (v. 11). His prayer seems to have been modeled on Solomon's exhortation for the Israelites to pray toward the temple so that God would hear from heaven and "uphold their cause" (6:34–35). The Chronicler included this story of Judah's victory over Zerah and the Cushites as evidence of the king's faithfulness and reliance on God.

Despite Asa's defensive strategy and military resources, he acknowledged his powerlessness before the foe. His simple but sincere prayer consisted of an affirmation of faith and trust sandwiched between humble pleas to God for deliverance. Such prayer is exemplary, whether for Asa's time, the Chronicler's day, or ours. Are you facing some sort of battle? If so, make Asa's prayer your own.

15:1
b Nu 11:25,26;
24:2; 2Ch 20:14;
24:20
15:2
c ver 4,15;
2Ch 20:17 d Jas 4:8
e Jer 29:13
f 1Ch 28:9;
2Ch 24:20
15:3
g Lev 10:11
h 2Ch 17:9; La 2:9
15:4
i Dt 4:29
15:5
j Jdg 5:6
15:6
k Mt 24:7
15:7
l Jos 1:7,9
m Ps 58:11
15:8
n 2Ch 13:19
o 2Ch 8:12

15:9
p 2Ch 11:16-17

15:11
q 2Ch 14:13
15:12
r 2Ki 11:17;
2Ch 23:16; 34:31
s 1Ch 16:11
15:13
t Ex 22:20;
Dt 13:9-16

15:15
u Dt 4:29
v 1Ch 22:9;
2Ch 14:7
15:16
w Ex 34:13;
2Ch 14:2-5

16:1
x Jer 41:9

Asa's Reform

15 The Spirit of God came upon[b] Azariah son of Oded. 2He went out to meet Asa and said to him, "Listen to me, Asa and all Judah and Benjamin. The LORD is with you[c] when you are with him.[d] If you seek[e] him, he will be found by you, but if you forsake him, he will forsake you.[f] 3For a long time Israel was without the true God, without a priest to teach[g] and without the law.[h] 4But in their distress they turned to the LORD, the God of Israel, and sought him,[i] and he was found by them. 5In those days it was not safe to travel about,[j] for all the inhabitants of the lands were in great turmoil. 6One nation was being crushed by another and one city by another,[k] because God was troubling them with every kind of distress. 7But as for you, be strong[l] and do not give up, for your work will be rewarded."[m]

8When Asa heard these words and the prophecy of Azariah son of[a] Oded the prophet, he took courage. He removed the detestable idols from the whole land of Judah and Benjamin and from the towns he had captured[n] in the hills of Ephraim. He repaired the altar[o] of the LORD that was in front of the portico of the LORD's temple.

9Then he assembled all Judah and Benjamin and the people from Ephraim, Manasseh and Simeon who had settled among them, for large numbers[p] had come over to him from Israel when they saw that the LORD his God was with him.

10They assembled at Jerusalem in the third month of the fifteenth year of Asa's reign. 11At that time they sacrificed to the LORD seven hundred head of cattle and seven thousand sheep and goats from the plunder[q] they had brought back. 12They entered into a covenant[r] to seek the LORD,[s] the God of their fathers, with all their heart and soul. 13All who would not seek the LORD, the God of Israel, were to be put to death,[t] whether small or great, man or woman. 14They took an oath to the LORD with loud acclamation, with shouting and with trumpets and horns. 15All Judah rejoiced about the oath because they had sworn it wholeheartedly. They sought God[u] eagerly, and he was found by them. So the LORD gave them rest[v] on every side.

16King Asa also deposed his grandmother Maacah from her position as queen mother, because she had made a repulsive Asherah pole.[w] Asa cut the pole down, broke it up and burned it in the Kidron Valley. 17Although he did not remove the high places from Israel, Asa's heart was fully committed ⌊to the LORD⌋ all his life. 18He brought into the temple of God the silver and gold and the articles that he and his father had dedicated.

19There was no more war until the thirty-fifth year of Asa's reign.

Asa's Last Years

16 In the thirty-sixth year of Asa's reign Baasha[x] king of Israel went up against Judah and fortified Ramah to prevent anyone from leaving or entering the territory of Asa king of Judah.

a 8 Vulgate and Syriac (see also Septuagint and verse 1); Hebrew does not have *Azariah son of.*

---

2 Chronicles 15:1–19

The theme of Azariah's message was twofold: God rewards obedience and is with those who side with him, and he will be found by those who seek him but forsakes those who abandon him. The sermon ended with a call to continue the good work already begun because God would honor it. The prophet's speech was pertinent to the Chronicler's audience, summarizing the three essentials for sustaining the faith of the restoration community in postexilic Judah: the true God, the teaching priest, and the law (v. 3). Asa's obedience to God's word through Azariah launched sweeping religious reforms.

The Chronicler's evaluation that Asa's "heart was fully committed to the LORD all his life" (v. 17) will be difficult to square with details in chapter 16. This statement is best read as an overall assessment of Asa's life, recog-

nizing the possibility of his eventual repentance as a result of Hanani's rebuke (see 16:7–9).

How comfortable would you be with an outsider's evaluation that your "heart was fully committed to the Lord all your life?" Chances are you would break into a sweat, knowing within the heart in question that this claim couldn't be substantiated. When God searches our hearts, though, he isn't on a quest for perfection. If there were the slightest possibility he would find it, he could have held out for another option rather than sending his own Son to atone for sin. What God evaluates in us is our overall motivation or bent—the driving force that gives purpose to our lives. If we have accepted Jesus as Savior and are sincerely attempting to follow in his steps, God's hearty accolade will be, "Well done, good and faithful servant!"

²Asa then took the silver and gold out of the treasuries of the LORD's temple and of his own palace and sent it to Ben-Hadad king of Aram, who was ruling in Damascus. ³"Let there be a treaty^y between me and you," he said, "as there was between my father and your father. See, I am sending you silver and gold. Now break your treaty with Baasha king of Israel so he will withdraw from me."

⁴Ben-Hadad agreed with King Asa and sent the commanders of his forces against the towns of Israel. They conquered Ijon, Dan, Abel Maim^a and all the store cities of Naphtali. ⁵When Baasha heard this, he stopped building Ramah and abandoned his work. ⁶Then King Asa brought all the men of Judah, and they carried away from Ramah the stones and timber Baasha had been using. With them he built up Geba and Mizpah.

⁷At that time Hanani^z the seer came to Asa king of Judah and said to him: "Because you relied on the king of Aram and not on the LORD your God, the army of the king of Aram has escaped from your hand. ⁸Were not the Cushites^{b a} and Libyans a mighty army with great numbers of chariots and horsemen^c? Yet when you relied on the LORD, he delivered^b them into your hand. ⁹For the eyes^c of the LORD range throughout the earth to strengthen those whose hearts are fully committed to him. You have done a foolish^d thing, and from now on you will be at war."

¹⁰Asa was angry with the seer because of this; he was so enraged that he put him in prison. At the same time Asa brutally oppressed some of the people.

¹¹The events of Asa's reign, from beginning to end, are written in the book of the kings of Judah and Israel. ¹²In the thirty-ninth year of his reign Asa was afflicted with a disease in his feet. Though his disease was severe, even in his illness he did not seek help from the LORD,^e but only from the physicians. ¹³Then in the forty-first year of his reign Asa died and rested with his fathers. ¹⁴They buried him in the tomb that he had cut out for himself in the City of David. They laid him on a bier covered with spices and various blended perfumes,^f and they made a huge fire^g in his honor.

Jehoshaphat King of Judah

17 Jehoshaphat his son succeeded him as king and strengthened himself against Israel. ²He stationed troops in all the fortified cities of Judah and put garrisons in Judah and in the towns of Ephraim that his father Asa had captured.^h

³The LORD was with Jehoshaphat because in his early years he walked in the ways

16:3 y 2Ch 20:35
16:7 z 1Ki 16:1
16:8 a 2Ch 12:3; 14:9 b 2Ch 13:16
16:9 c Pr 15:3; Jer 16:17; Zec 4:10 d 1Sa 13:13
16:12 e Jer 17:5-6
16:14 f Ge 50:2; Jn 19:39-40 g 2Ch 21:19; Jer 34:5
17:2 h 2Ch 15:8

---

^a 4 Also known as *Abel Beth Maacah*   ^b 8 That is, people from the upper Nile region   ^c 8 Or *charioteers*

---

2 Chronicles 16:1–14

The key word in Hanani's speech was "rely." Earlier, Asa had relied on God and Judah had prevailed over the Cushites who had mustered a vast army against them (14:11–13). History should have been Asa's teacher. Yet, instead of relying on God when threatened by the Israelite king Baasha, Asa relied on Ben-Hadad and the kingdom of Aram. Asa shunned divine aid and trusted in his own political savvy and human instincts to deliver Judah.

The consequences of Asa's unbelief were immediate and far-reaching. Somehow Asa had foolishly lost sight of God's sovereignty—hence the reminder that "the eyes of the LORD range throughout the earth" (v. 9; cf. Zech. 4:10). The heart fully committed to God demonstrates such allegiance by relying on him for all things—and God himself works in the faithful to strengthen that resolve. Asa's anger was a sure sign that Hanani's words had hit their mark.

Anger is often a warning sign that something isn't right in our heart. When we get our hackles up for

"no good reason," chances are there is a very good reason, and it may well be the stirrings of conscience. Which makes you angrier: a completely unfounded accusation or an observation that comes too close to a troubling truth for your comfort? Next time you find yourself snapping at everyone around you, take a few moments to take a conscience reading. The Spirit may be prompting you to do just that.

2 Chronicles 17:1–19

The kings of Judah were evaluated against the "gold standard" of kingship, King David himself. Jehoshaphat was compared favorably to David because he was single-minded in his obedience to God (v. 3). Both Testaments teach that the righteous are to love and obey God with their whole heart (Deut. 6:5; 11:13; 26:16; Matt. 22:37; Rom. 1:9; Eph. 6:6). Jehoshaphat's "heart was devoted to the ways of the LORD" (at least "in his early years"); thus, "the LORD was with" him (vv. 3,6). No doubt the Chronicler wanted his audience to see the pattern of divine presence and blessing conditioned by obedience to God's law.

17:3
i 1Ki 22:43
17:4
j 1Ki 12:28;
2Ch 22:9
17:5
k 1Sa 10:27
l 2Ch 18:1
17:6
m 1Ki 8:61;
2Ch 15:17
n 1Ki 15:14;
2Ch 19:3; 20:33
o Ex 34:13
p 2Ch 21:12
17:7
q Lev 10:11;
Dt 6:4-9;
2Ch 15:3; 35:3
17:8
r 2Ch 19:8;
Ne 8:7-8
17:9
s Dt 6:4-9; 28:61
17:10
t Ge 35:5; Dt 2:25;
2Ch 14:14
17:11
u 2Ch 9:14; 26:8
v 2Ch 21:16
17:14
w 2Sa 24:2

17:16
x Jdg 5:9; 1Ch 29:9

17:17
y Nu 1:36

17:19
z 2Ch 11:10
a 2Ch 25:5

18:1
b 2Ch 17:5
c 2Ch 19:1-3; 22:3
d 2Ch 21:6

his father David *i* had followed. He did not consult the Baals 4but sought *j* the God of his father and followed his commands rather than the practices of Israel. 5The LORD established the kingdom under his control; and all Judah brought gifts *k* to Jehoshaphat, so that he had great wealth and honor. *l* 6His heart was devoted *m* to the ways of the LORD; furthermore, he removed the high places *n* and the Asherah poles *o* from Judah. *p*

7In the third year of his reign he sent his officials Ben-Hail, Obadiah, Zechariah, Nethanel and Micaiah to teach *q* in the towns of Judah. 8With them were certain Levites *r*—Shemaiah, Nethaniah, Zebadiah, Asahel, Shemiramoth, Jehonathan, Adonijah, Tobijah and Tob-Adonijah—and the priests Elishama and Jehoram. 9They taught throughout Judah, taking with them the Book of the Law *s* of the LORD; they went around to all the towns of Judah and taught the people.

10The fear *t* of the LORD fell on all the kingdoms of the lands surrounding Judah, so that they did not make war with Jehoshaphat. 11Some Philistines brought Jehoshaphat gifts and silver as tribute, and the Arabs *u* brought him flocks: *v* seven thousand seven hundred rams and seven thousand seven hundred goats.

12Jehoshaphat became more and more powerful; he built forts and store cities in Judah 13and had large supplies in the towns of Judah. He also kept experienced fighting men in Jerusalem. 14Their enrollment *w* by families was as follows:

From Judah, commanders of units of 1,000:
   Adnah the commander, with 300,000 fighting men;
15next, Jehohanan the commander, with 280,000;
16next, Amasiah son of Zicri, who volunteered *x* himself for the service of the LORD, with 200,000.
17From Benjamin: *y*
   Eliada, a valiant soldier, with 200,000 men armed with bows and shields;
18next, Jehozabad, with 180,000 men armed for battle.

19These were the men who served the king, besides those he stationed in the fortified cities *z* throughout Judah. *a*

Micaiah Prophesies Against Ahab

18 Now Jehoshaphat had great wealth and honor, *b* and he allied *c* himself with Ahab *d* by marriage. 2Some years later he went down to visit Ahab in Samaria. Ahab slaughtered many sheep and cattle for him and the people with him and urged him to attack Ramoth Gilead. 3Ahab king of Israel asked Jehoshaphat king of Judah, "Will you go with me against Ramoth Gilead?"

Jehoshaphat replied, "I am as you are, and my people as your people; we will join

---

As part of his spiritual reform package, the king launched an itinerant teaching ministry throughout Judah (vv. 7–9). The verb "to teach" was a common word for instruction in the Old Testament (cf. Deut. 4:10). The program appears to have been one of unrestricted, "tuition-free" access to religious education.

Jehoshaphat's religious education program was innovative, brilliant, and ahead of its time. Though government-sponsored education programs today typically lack religious content, they nevertheless have a lifting effect on those who participate. Education means possibilities for employment and better earnings, which can change people's lives today and into the future. Unfortunately, the blessing of a free basic education is denied to many worldwide, and a majority of the losers are girls. Thank the Lord today for both the spiritual and secular educational opportunities you have been given. Participate in helping someone else achieve his or her learning/academic goals. There are lots of ways to be involved.

2 Chronicles 18:1–27

Micaiah's first vision depicted shepherdless sheep on the hills. Ahab presumed correctly that the prophet was predicting the king's death in battle. But Micaiah's message had a double meaning, in that the Israelites currently had "no master." Ahab's corrupt rule had led them far from God. How tragic that the sheep would have "peace" only when the shepherd was gone!

No one, including Ahab, was fooled by the fraudulent prophets. The king, particularly after his encounters with Elijah, recognized the truth but was determined to suppress it. Ahab's strategy to imprison rather than execute Micaiah was savvy. By keeping him alive, Ahab left open the option of publicly shaming this true prophet and disgracing his message after his own safe return. To kill the prophet might have made the man of God a martyr, should his message have proven accurate.

Ahab was thoroughly corrupt, but he was no fool. It seems safe to conclude that, after the Mount

you in the war." ⁴But Jehoshaphat also said to the king of Israel, "First seek the counsel of the LORD."

⁵So the king of Israel brought together the prophets—four hundred men—and asked them, "Shall we go to war against Ramoth Gilead, or shall I refrain?"

"Go," they answered, "for God will give it into the king's hand."

⁶But Jehoshaphat asked, "Is there not a prophet of the LORD here whom we can inquire of?"

⁷The king of Israel answered Jehoshaphat, "There is still one man through whom we can inquire of the LORD, but I hate him because he never prophesies anything good about me, but always bad. He is Micaiah son of Imlah."

"The king should not say that," Jehoshaphat replied.

⁸So the king of Israel called one of his officials and said, "Bring Micaiah son of Imlah at once."

⁹Dressed in their royal robes, the king of Israel and Jehoshaphat king of Judah were sitting on their thrones at the threshing floor by the entrance to the gate of Samaria, with all the prophets prophesying before them. ¹⁰Now Zedekiah son of Kenaanah had made iron horns, and he declared, "This is what the LORD says: 'With these you will gore the Arameans until they are destroyed.'"

¹¹All the other prophets were prophesying the same thing. "Attack Ramoth Gileadᵉ and be victorious," they said, "for the LORD will give it into the king's hand."

¹²The messenger who had gone to summon Micaiah said to him, "Look, as one man the other prophets are predicting success for the king. Let your word agree with theirs, and speak favorably."

¹³But Micaiah said, "As surely as the LORD lives, I can tell him only what my God says."ᶠ

¹⁴When he arrived, the king asked him, "Micaiah, shall we go to war against Ramoth Gilead, or shall I refrain?"

"Attack and be victorious," he answered, "for they will be given into your hand."

¹⁵The king said to him, "How many times must I make you swear to tell me nothing but the truth in the name of the LORD?"

¹⁶Then Micaiah answered, "I saw all Israelᵍ scattered on the hills like sheep without a shepherd,ʰ and the LORD said, 'These people have no master. Let each one go home in peace.'"

¹⁷The king of Israel said to Jehoshaphat, "Didn't I tell you that he never prophesies anything good about me, but only bad?"

¹⁸Micaiah continued, "Therefore hear the word of the LORD: I saw the LORD sitting on his throneⁱ with all the host of heaven standing on his right and on his left. ¹⁹And the LORD said, 'Who will entice Ahab king of Israel into attacking Ramoth Gilead and going to his death there?'

"One suggested this, and another that. ²⁰Finally, a spirit came forward, stood before the LORD and said, 'I will entice him.'

"'By what means?' the LORD asked.

²¹"'I will go and be a lying spiritʲ in the mouths of all his prophets,' he said.

"'You will succeed in enticing him,' said the LORD. 'Go and do it.'

²²"So now the LORD has put a lying spirit in the mouths of these prophets of yours.ᵏ The LORD has decreed disaster for you."

²³Then Zedekiah son of Kenaanah went up and slappedˡ Micaiah in the face. "Which way did the spirit fromᵃ the LORD go when he went from me to speak to you?" he asked.

ᵃ 23 Or Spirit of

18:11
ᵉ 2Ch 22:5

18:13
ᶠ Nu 22:18,20,35

18:16
ᵍ 1Ch 9:1
ʰ Nu 27:17; Eze 34:5-8

18:18
ⁱ Da 7:9

18:21
ʲ 1Ch 21:1; Job 1:6; Zec 3:1; Jn 8:44

18:22
ᵏ Job 12:16; Isa 19:14; Eze 14:9

18:23
ˡ Jer 20:2; Mk 14:65; Ac 23:2

Carmel showdown (see 1 Kings 18:16–46), this king recognized the truth when he heard it. Otherwise, why would the lone dissenting voice of one inconsequential prophet have irritated him so much? How often do we find ourselves in the same position? If one godly person questions our plans or motivation, isn't our first impulse to seek more advice? To take a survey and close the polls whenever consensus tips in our favor? In such situations we do well to listen to (and ask for) God's guidance, so as to base our decision on something more substantial than majority opinion.

24Micaiah replied, "You will find out on the day you go to hide in an inner room."

25The king of Israel then ordered, "Take Micaiah and send him back to Amon the ruler of the city and to Joash the king's son, 26and say, 'This is what the king says: Put this fellow in prison[m] and give him nothing but bread and water until I return safely.'"

27Micaiah declared, "If you ever return safely, the LORD has not spoken through me." Then he added, "Mark my words, all you people!"

Ahab Killed at Ramoth Gilead

28So the king of Israel and Jehoshaphat king of Judah went up to Ramoth Gilead. 29The king of Israel said to Jehoshaphat, "I will enter the battle in disguise, but you wear your royal robes." So the king of Israel disguised[n] himself and went into battle.

30Now the king of Aram had ordered his chariot commanders, "Do not fight with anyone, small or great, except the king of Israel." 31When the chariot commanders saw Jehoshaphat, they thought, "This is the king of Israel." So they turned to attack him, but Jehoshaphat cried out,[o] and the LORD helped him. God drew them away from him, 32for when the chariot commanders saw that he was not the king of Israel, they stopped pursuing him.

33But someone drew his bow at random and hit the king of Israel between the sections of his armor. The king told the chariot driver, "Wheel around and get me out of the fighting. I've been wounded." 34All day long the battle raged, and the king of Israel propped himself up in his chariot facing the Arameans until evening. Then at sunset he died.[p]

19 When Jehoshaphat king of Judah returned safely to his palace in Jerusalem, 2Jehu[q] the seer, the son of Hanani, went out to meet him and said to the king, "Should you help the wicked[r] and love[a] those who hate the LORD?[s] Because of this, the wrath[t] of the LORD is upon you. 3There is, however, some good[u] in you, for you have rid the land of the Asherah poles[v] and have set your heart on seeking God.[w]"

Jehoshaphat Appoints Judges

4Jehoshaphat lived in Jerusalem, and he went out again among the people from Beersheba to the hill country of Ephraim and turned them back to the LORD, the God of their fathers. 5He appointed judges[x] in the land, in each of the fortified cities of Judah. 6He told them, "Consider carefully what you do,[y] because you are not judging for man[z] but for the LORD, who is with you whenever you give a verdict.

[a] 2 Or and make alliances with

2 Chronicles 18:28—19:3

By engaging in battle against the Arameans, Ahab fulfilled Micaiah's prophecy about the king being lured to his own destruction (vv. 18–22). Though Ahab likely anticipated the Arameans' strategy of targeting him (v. 30), his ploy to disguise himself was also perhaps an attempt to thwart the prophet's word that the king feared might be true. The "random" arrow that pierced a chink in Ahab's armor was certainly God's arrow, verifying that God had indeed spoken through Micaiah (v. 27). Ahab's heroic effort to prop himself up in his chariot to sustain his troops' morale and continue to press the battle was of no avail.

When God closes a door, he does indeed often open a window. But we can't outsmart him by prying open the window ourselves and forging ahead with a slightly revised attempt to achieve our original goal. When God says no, he means precisely that, and he may for reasons known only to himself keep both doors and windows securely locked. This is also true in ministry sit-

uations. Paul, Silas, and Timothy at one point "tried to enter Bithynia, but the Spirit of Jesus would not allow them to" (Acts 16:7). But then God gave Paul a vision of a man from Macedonia begging him to go there. The best laid plans of people are often trumped by God's infinitely better plans, and we need to be willing to listen.

2 Chronicles 19:4–11

The appointment of judges in the cities of Canaan given by God to his people was mandated in the Law of Moses (Deut. 16:18; 17:8–9). Jehoshaphat's decision to place judges and establish forums for legal proceedings in the "fortified cities" was logical. The strategic location of these defensive posts ringing Jerusalem made them accessible to the general population. Jehoshaphat's fervor for judicial reform seems to have been motivated by the pronouncement of God's wrath upon him by the prophet Jehu (2 Chron. 19:2). Jehoshaphat rightly recognized that the judges were agents of God, not the king (v. 6).

Jehoshaphat's appointment of dual "attorneys gener-

⁷Now let the fear of the LORD be upon you. Judge carefully, for with the LORD our God there is no injustice*ᵃ* or partiality*ᵇ* or bribery."

⁸In Jerusalem also, Jehoshaphat appointed some of the Levites, priests and heads of Israelite families to administer*ᶜ* the law of the LORD and to settle disputes. And they lived in Jerusalem. ⁹He gave them these orders: "You must serve faithfully and wholeheartedly in the fear of the LORD. ¹⁰In every case that comes before you from your fellow countrymen who live in the cities—whether bloodshed or other concerns of the law, commands, decrees or ordinances—you are to warn them not to sin against the LORD;*ᵈ* otherwise his wrath will come on you and your brothers. Do this, and you will not sin.

¹¹"Amariah the chief priest will be over you in any matter concerning the LORD, and Zebadiah son of Ishmael, the leader of the tribe of Judah, will be over you in any matter concerning the king, and the Levites will serve as officials before you. Act with courage,*ᵉ* and may the LORD be with those who do well."

Jehoshaphat Defeats Moab and Ammon

20 After this, the Moabites and Ammonites with some of the Meunites*ᵃᶠ* came to make war on Jehoshaphat.

²Some men came and told Jehoshaphat, "A vast army is coming against you from Edom,*ᵇ* from the other side of the Sea.*ᶜ* It is already in Hazazon Tamar*ᵍ*" (that is, En Gedi). ³Alarmed, Jehoshaphat resolved to inquire of the LORD, and he proclaimed a fast*ʰ* for all Judah. ⁴The people of Judah came together to seek help from the LORD; indeed, they came from every town in Judah to seek him.

ᵃ 1 Some Septuagint manuscripts; Hebrew *Ammonites*   *ᵇ 2* One Hebrew manuscript; most Hebrew manuscripts, Septuagint and Vulgate *Aram*   *ᶜ 2* That is, the Dead Sea

---

19:7
ᵃ Ge 18:25; Dt 32:4
ᵇ Dt 10:17;
Job 34:19; Ro 2:11;
Col 3:25
19:8
ᶜ 2Ch 17:8-9

19:10
ᵈ Dt 17:8-13

19:11
ᵉ 1Ch 28:20

20:1
ᶠ 1Ch 4:41

20:2
ᵍ Ge 14:7

20:3
ʰ 1Sa 7:6;
2Ch 19:3; Ezr 8:21;
Jer 36:9; Jnh 3:5,7

---

al" reminds us that tension between "church" and "state" in the administration of public policy has a long history. To ensure some separation of power and introduce a check-and-balance mechanism into the judicial organization, the king gave the chief priest, Amariah, jurisdiction over religious matters, while granting authority for civil matters to Zebadiah, leader of the tribe of Judah.

The injunction against showing favoritism or accepting bribes (v. 7) was foundational to the Mosaic legal tradition (Deut. 1:16–17; 16:19–20) and is still a basic tenet of justice today. Showing partiality in judgment or taking a bribe distorts justice in at least two ways: (1) It puts the poor at a disadvantage for a fair hearing because they are typically unable to afford the bribe to sway a judge's decision. (2) Any deviation from justice in the courts results in *injustice*—the seedbed of social unrest.

2 Chronicles 20:1–30

This holy war narrative is one of the Bible's great stories. Its literary purpose was to contrast Jehoshaphat's *reliance* on God when threatened by an enemy with his earlier *alliance* with Ahab of Israel when faced with a similar situation (ch. 18). The story is another example of "seeking the LORD," a major theme in Chronicles (see also the notes for 2 Chron. 14:2–15). To humble oneself before God in the face of seemingly insurmountable odds and to trust him fully for deliverance is the essence of Biblical faith.

This event was particularly relevant for the Chronicler and his audience, because the postexilic community in Judah was being tormented by descendants of the same peoples who had attacked Jehoshaphat (see Neh. 2:19; 4:1–3,7–9). In retelling the story, the Chronicler

---

19:11

ACT WITH COURAGE

Leadership by its very nature requires courage. When Jehoshaphat appointed judges, his final advice to them was to act with courage. Courage is:

- **Not the absence of fear.** Fear, especially the fear of God, can be productive (Prov. 1:7; see also chart "To Fear God's Name Is Wisdom" at Micah 6:9, page 1487).

- **Not foolhardy recklessness.** Fear, in fact, helps us guard against this (Ps. 46:1).

- **The ability to act—not freeze**—especially when facing enemies or other dangerous situations. This is the most common association of courage in the Old Testament (Josh. 1:6–9).

- **Obedience to God's call** even when the world's pressures to act differently are upon us (2 Sam. 12:7–9).

God gives us courage to act, even when we are afraid. We access courage by asking God for it. Under what circumstances in your life has God enabled you to act courageously?

⁵Then Jehoshaphat stood up in the assembly of Judah and Jerusalem at the temple of the LORD in the front of the new courtyard ⁶and said:

"O LORD, God of our fathers, ^{*i*} are you not the God who is in heaven?^{*j*} You rule over all the kingdoms^{*k*} of the nations. Power and might are in your hand, and no one can withstand you. ⁷O our God, did you not drive out the inhabitants of this land before your people Israel and give it forever to the descendants of Abraham your friend?^{*l*} ⁸They have lived in it and have built in it a sanctuary^{*m*} for your Name, saying, ⁹'If calamity comes upon us, whether the sword of judgment, or plague or famine, ^{*n*} we will stand in your presence before this temple that bears your Name and will cry out to you in our distress, and you will hear us and save us.'

¹⁰"But now here are men from Ammon, Moab and Mount Seir, whose territory you would not allow Israel to invade when they came from Egypt;^{*o*} so they turned away from them and did not destroy them. ¹¹See how they are repaying us by coming to drive us out of the possession^{*p*} you gave us as an inheritance. ¹²O our God, will you not judge them?^{*q*} For we have no power to face this vast army that is attacking us. We do not know what to do, but our eyes are upon you.^{*r*}"

¹³All the men of Judah, with their wives and children and little ones, stood there before the LORD.

¹⁴Then the Spirit^{*s*} of the LORD came upon Jahaziel son of Zechariah, the son of Benaiah, the son of Jeiel, the son of Mattaniah, a Levite and descendant of Asaph, as he stood in the assembly.

¹⁵He said: "Listen, King Jehoshaphat and all who live in Judah and Jerusalem! This is what the LORD says to you: 'Do not be afraid or discouraged^{*t*} because of this vast army. For the battle^{*u*} is not yours, but God's. ¹⁶Tomorrow march down against them. They will be climbing up by the Pass of Ziz, and you will find them at the end of the gorge in the Desert of Jeruel. ¹⁷You will not have to fight this battle. Take up your positions; stand firm and see^{*v*} the deliverance the LORD will give you, O Judah and Jerusalem. Do not be afraid; do not be discouraged. Go out to face them tomorrow, and the LORD will be with you.' "

¹⁸Jehoshaphat bowed^{*w*} with his face to the ground, and all the people of Judah and Jerusalem fell down in worship before the LORD. ¹⁹Then some Levites from the Kohathites and Korahites stood up and praised the LORD, the God of Israel, with a very loud voice.

²⁰Early in the morning they left for the Desert of Tekoa. As they set out, Jehoshaphat stood and said, "Listen to me, Judah and people of Jerusalem! Have faith^{*x*} in the LORD your God and you will be upheld; have faith in his prophets and you will be successful.^{*y*}" ²¹After consulting the people, Jehoshaphat appointed men to sing to the LORD and to praise him for the splendor of his^{*a*} holiness^{*z*} as they went out at the head of the army, saying:

> "Give thanks to the LORD,
> for his love endures forever."^{*a*}

²²As they began to sing and praise, the LORD set ambushes^{*b*} against the men of Ammon and Moab and Mount Seir who were invading Judah, and they were defeated. ²³The men of Ammon^{*c*} and Moab rose up against the men from Mount

---

^{*a*} 21 Or *him with the splendor of*

---

was encouraging his contemporaries to accept Jehoshaphat's challenge to have faith in the Lord and his prophets (2 Chron. 20:20).

📖 Still today government heads, even those of a Christian persuasion, tend to look to allies and coalitions for support prior to entering into armed conflict. Of course, our wars aren't "holy" in the same sense as the Old Testament holy wars, but the motivation for them can be at least partially admirable (e.g., the overthrow of a ruthless, inhumane regime). We are wrong, though, to invoke God in a nationalistic sense (automatically assuming him to be "on our side"). Whether you are a leader or constituent, do you seek his face in sincere prayer in times of national or global conflict?

Cross-references (left margin):

20:6
i Mt 6:9; *j* Dt 4:39
k 1Ch 29:11-12

20:7
l Isa 41:8; Jas 2:23
20:8
m 2Ch 6:20
20:9
n 2Ch 6:28

20:10
o Nu 20:14-21;
Dt 2:4-6,9,18-19
20:11
p Ps 83:1-12
20:12
q Jdg 11:27
r Ps 25:15; 121:1-2

20:14
s 2Ch 15:1

20:15
t 2Ch 32:7
u Ex 14:13-14;
1Sa 17:47

20:17
v Ex 14:13;
2Ch 15:2

20:18
w Ex 4:31

20:20
x Isa 7:9 *y* Ge 39:3;
Pr 16:3

20:21
z 1Ch 16:29;
Ps 29:2 *a* 2Ch 5:13;
Ps 136:1

20:22
b Jdg 7:22;
2Ch 13:13

20:23
c Ge 19:38

Seir[d] to destroy and annihilate them. After they finished slaughtering the men from Seir, they helped to destroy one another.[e] [24]When the men of Judah came to the place that overlooks the desert and looked toward the vast army, they saw only dead bodies lying on the ground; no one had escaped. [25]So Jehoshaphat and his men went to carry off their plunder, and they found among them a great amount of equipment and clothing[a] and also articles of value—more than they could take away. There was so much plunder that it took three days to collect it. [26]On the fourth day they assembled in the Valley of Beracah, where they praised the LORD. This is why it is called the Valley of Beracah[b] to this day.

[27]Then, led by Jehoshaphat, all the men of Judah and Jerusalem returned joyfully to Jerusalem, for the LORD had given them cause to rejoice over their enemies. [28]They entered Jerusalem and went to the temple of the LORD with harps and lutes and trumpets.

[29]The fear[f] of God came upon all the kingdoms of the countries when they heard how the LORD had fought[g] against the enemies of Israel. [30]And the kingdom of Jehoshaphat was at peace, for his God had given him rest[h] on every side.

The End of Jehoshaphat's Reign

[31]So Jehoshaphat reigned over Judah. He was thirty-five years old when he became king of Judah, and he reigned in Jerusalem twenty-five years. His mother's name was Azubah daughter of Shilhi. [32]He walked in the ways of his father Asa and did not stray from them; he did what was right in the eyes of the LORD. [33]The high places,[i] however, were not removed, and the people still had not set their hearts on the God of their fathers.

[34]The other events of Jehoshaphat's reign, from beginning to end, are written in the annals of Jehu[j] son of Hanani, which are recorded in the book of the kings of Israel.

[35]Later, Jehoshaphat king of Judah made an alliance[k] with Ahaziah king of Israel, who was guilty of wickedness.[l] [36]He agreed with him to construct a fleet of trading ships.[c] After these were built at Ezion Geber, [37]Eliezer son of Dodavahu of Mareshah prophesied against Jehoshaphat, saying, "Because you have made an alliance with Ahaziah, the LORD will destroy what you have made." The ships[m] were wrecked and were not able to set sail to trade.[d]

21 Then Jehoshaphat rested with his fathers and was buried with them in the City of David. And Jehoram[n] his son succeeded him as king. [2]Jehoram's brothers, the sons of Jehoshaphat, were Azariah, Jehiel, Zechariah, Azariahu, Michael and Shephatiah. All these were sons of Jehoshaphat king of Israel.[e] [3]Their father had given them many gifts[o] of silver and gold and articles of value, as well as fortified cities[p] in Judah, but he had given the kingdom to Jehoram because he was his firstborn son.

Jehoram King of Judah

[4]When Jehoram established[q] himself firmly over his father's kingdom, he put all

Cross references (margin)

20:23 d 2Ch 21:8; e Jdg 7:22; 1Sa 14:20; Eze 38:21

20:29 f Ge 35:5; Dt 2:25; 2Ch 14:14; 17:10; g Ex 14:14

20:30 h 1Ch 22:9; 2Ch 14:6-7; 15:15

20:33 i 2Ch 17:6; 19:3

20:34 j 1Ki 16:1

20:35 k 2Ch 16:3; l 2Ch 19:1-3

20:37 m 1Ki 9:26; 2Ch 9:21

21:1 n 1Ch 3:11

21:3 o 2Ch 11:23; p 2Ch 11:10

21:4 q 1Ki 2:12

Footnotes

a 25 Some Hebrew manuscripts and Vulgate; most Hebrew manuscripts *corpses*   b 26 *Beracah* means *praise.*   c 36 Hebrew *of ships that could go to Tarshish*   d 37 Hebrew *sail for Tarshish*   e 2 That is, Judah, as frequently in 2 Chronicles

---

2 Chronicles 20:31—21:3

For the second time, Jehoshaphat received prophetic rebuke for entering into a political alliance (20:37; cf. 19:2)—which his father Asa had experienced as well (16:7–9). Also like his father, Jehoshaphat failed to remove completely the high places, vestiges of Canaanite worship still infecting Hebrew religion (20:33; cf. 15:17). Jehoshaphat "walked in the ways of his father Asa" (20:32); but neither father nor son was given the epitaph of Hezekiah and Josiah as one who "walked in the ways of his father David" (29:2; 34:2)—though Jehoshaphat did

receive this tribute for the early years of his reign (17:3).

It's always a temptation for a government or individual to give partial, token allegiance to God. But allowing ourselves to retain even one "innocent vice" sets us on a dangerous, slippery path. Half-hearted attempts to manage sin's symptoms, while allowing the underlying disease to fester, can result in acute, full-blown outbreaks. The particular sin that is especially dear to our hearts needs to be the first to go if we are serious about allowing the Spirit to help us eradicate the contagion holding us back from effective service.

21:4
r Jdg 9:5

21:6
s 1Ki 12:28-30
t 2Ch 18:1; 22:3
21:7
u 2Sa 7:13
v 2Sa 7:15;
2Ch 23:3
w 2Sa 21:17;
1Ki 11:36
21:8
x 2Ch 20:22-23

21:10
y Nu 33:20

21:12
z 2Ki 1:16-17
a 2Ch 17:3-6
b 2Ch 14:2

21:13
c ver 6, 11;
1Ki 16:29-33
d ver 4; 1Ki 2:32

21:15
e ver 18-19;
Nu 12:10

21:16
f 2Ch 17:10-11;
22:1; 26:7

21:17
g 2Ki 12:18;
2Ch 22:1; 25:23;
Joel 3:5

21:19
h 2Ch 16:14

21:20
i 2Ch 24:25; 28:27;
33:20; Jer 22:18,28

22:1
j 2Ch 33:25; 36:1
k 2Ch 23:20-21;
26:1 l 2Ch 21:16-17

his brothers[r] to the sword along with some of the princes of Israel. [5]Jehoram was thirty-two years old when he became king, and he reigned in Jerusalem eight years. [6]He walked in the ways of the kings of Israel,[s] as the house of Ahab had done, for he married a daughter of Ahab.[t] He did evil in the eyes of the LORD. [7]Nevertheless, because of the covenant the LORD had made with David,[u] the LORD was not willing to destroy the house of David.[v] He had promised to maintain a lamp[w] for him and his descendants forever.

[8]In the time of Jehoram, Edom[x] rebelled against Judah and set up its own king. [9]So Jehoram went there with his officers and all his chariots. The Edomites surrounded him and his chariot commanders, but he rose up and broke through by night. [10]To this day Edom has been in rebellion against Judah.

Libnah[y] revolted at the same time, because Jehoram had forsaken the LORD, the God of his fathers. [11]He had also built high places on the hills of Judah and had caused the people of Jerusalem to prostitute themselves and had led Judah astray. [12]Jehoram received a letter from Elijah[z] the prophet, which said:

"This is what the LORD, the God of your father[a] David, says: 'You have not walked in the ways of your father Jehoshaphat or of Asa[b] king of Judah. [13]But you have walked in the ways of the kings of Israel, and you have led Judah and the people of Jerusalem to prostitute themselves, just as the house of Ahab did.[c] You have also murdered your own brothers, members of your father's house, men who were better[d] than you. [14]So now the LORD is about to strike your people, your sons, your wives and everything that is yours, with a heavy blow. [15]You yourself will be very ill with a lingering disease[e] of the bowels, until the disease causes your bowels to come out.' "

[16]The LORD aroused against Jehoram the hostility of the Philistines and of the Arabs[f] who lived near the Cushites. [17]They attacked Judah, invaded it and carried off all the goods found in the king's palace, together with his sons and wives. Not a son was left to him except Ahaziah,[a] the youngest.[g]

[18]After all this, the LORD afflicted Jehoram with an incurable disease of the bowels. [19]In the course of time, at the end of the second year, his bowels came out because of the disease, and he died in great pain. His people made no fire in his honor,[h] as they had for his fathers.

[20]Jehoram was thirty-two years old when he became king, and he reigned in Jerusalem eight years. He passed away, to no one's regret, and was buried[i] in the City of David, but not in the tombs of the kings.

Ahaziah King of Judah

22 The people[j] of Jerusalem[k] made Ahaziah, Jehoram's youngest son, king in his place, since the raiders,[l] who came with the Arabs into the camp, had killed all the older sons. So Ahaziah son of Jehoram king of Judah began to reign.

---

a 17 Hebrew *Jehoahaz*, a variant of *Ahaziah*

---

2 Chronicles 21:4–20

Jehoram was the first king to receive an entirely negative review by the Chronicler. This is especially noticeable in the dark tone set by the murders of his brothers at the onset of his rule and the humiliating, fatal illness that cut short his reign. The affiliation of the house of Judah with the idolatrous house of Ahab of Israel through the marriage of Jehoram and Athaliah (Ahab's daughter) was itself a recipe for self-destruction (cf. Prov. 14:11).

God's faithfulness to the Davidic covenant sets up the conflict that carries the plot of the Biblical story from the monarchy through to the Gospels and the book of Revelation: the continuation of David's line and the fulfillment of the divine promise in the face of wickedness poised to destroy the family. The truth that God is eternally faithful to his covenant word surely instilled hope in the Chronicler's audience (cf. Ps. 111:5,9), reminding them that God's promise remained operative and that the "lamp" of David still burned (2 Chron. 21:7).

An alliance/marriage/partnership between believers and non-believers is as dangerous for us as it was for Jehoram. It can short-circuit ministry opportunities and set a course for destruction in the future (cf. Athaliah's grab for power after Jehoram's death; 2 Chron. 22:10—23:21). For these reasons and others, Paul, in strong language, advised believers to avoid being "unequally yoked" with unbelievers (2 Cor. 6:14–16). How seriously do you take this Scriptural admonition?

²Ahaziah was twenty-two[a] years old when he became king, and he reigned in Jerusalem one year. His mother's name was Athaliah, a granddaughter of Omri.

³He too walked[m] in the ways of the house of Ahab,[n] for his mother encouraged him in doing wrong. ⁴He did evil in the eyes of the LORD, as the house of Ahab had done, for after his father's death they became his advisers, to his undoing. ⁵He also followed their counsel when he went with Joram[b] son of Ahab king of Israel to war against Hazael king of Aram at Ramoth Gilead.[o] The Arameans wounded Joram; ⁶so he returned to Jezreel to recover from the wounds they had inflicted on him at Ramoth[c] in his battle with Hazael[p] king of Aram.

Then Ahaziah[d] son of Jehoram king of Judah went down to Jezreel to see Joram son of Ahab because he had been wounded.

⁷Through Ahaziah's[q] visit to Joram, God brought about Ahaziah's downfall. When Ahaziah arrived, he went out with Joram to meet Jehu son of Nimshi, whom the LORD had anointed to destroy the house of Ahab. ⁸While Jehu was executing judgment on the house of Ahab,[r] he found the princes of Judah and the sons of Ahaziah's relatives, who had been attending Ahaziah, and he killed them. ⁹He then went in search of Ahaziah, and his men captured him while he was hiding[s] in Samaria. He was brought to Jehu and put to death. They buried him, for they said, "He was a son of Jehoshaphat, who sought[t] the LORD with all his heart." So there was no one in the house of Ahaziah powerful enough to retain the kingdom.

Athaliah and Joash

¹⁰When Athaliah the mother of Ahaziah saw that her son was dead, she proceeded to destroy the whole royal family of the house of Judah. ¹¹But Jehosheba,[e] the daughter of King Jehoram, took Joash son of Ahaziah and stole him away from among the royal princes who were about to be murdered and put him and his nurse in a bedroom. Because Jehosheba,[e] the daughter of King Jehoram and wife of the priest Jehoiada, was Ahaziah's sister, she hid the child from Athaliah so she could not kill him. ¹²He remained hidden with them at the temple of God for six years while Athaliah ruled the land.

23 In the seventh year Jehoiada showed his strength. He made a covenant with the commanders of units of a hundred: Azariah son of Jeroham, Ishmael son of Jehohanan, Azariah son of Obed, Maaseiah son of Adaiah, and Elishaphat son of Zicri. ²They went throughout Judah and gathered the Levites[u] and the heads of Israelite families from all the towns. When they came to Jerusalem, ³the whole assembly made a covenant[v] with the king at the temple of God.

Jehoiada said to them, "The king's son shall reign, as the LORD promised concerning the descendants of David.[w] ⁴Now this is what you are to do: A third of you priests and Levites who are going on duty on the Sabbath are to keep watch at the doors, ⁵a third of you at the royal palace and a third at the Foundation Gate, and all the other men are to be in the courtyards of the temple of the LORD. ⁶No one is

---

22:3
[m] 2Ch 18:1
[n] 2Ch 21:6

22:5
[o] 2Ch 18:11,34

22:6
[p] 1Ki 19:15; 2Ki 8:13-15; 9:15

22:7
[q] 2Ki 9:16; 2Ch 10:15

22:8
[r] 2Ki 10:13

22:9
[s] Jdg 9:5 [t] 2Ch 17:4

23:2
[u] Nu 35:2-5

23:3
[v] 2Ki 11:17
[w] 2Sa 7:12; 1Ki 2:4; 2Ch 6:16; 7:18; 21:7

---

[a] 2 Some Septuagint manuscripts and Syriac (see also 2 Kings 8:26); Hebrew *forty-two*   [b] 5 Hebrew *Jehoram*, a variant of *Joram*; also in verses 6 and 7   [c] 6 Hebrew *Ramah*, a variant of *Ramoth*
[d] 6 Some Hebrew manuscripts, Septuagint, Vulgate and Syriac (see also 2 Kings 8:29); most Hebrew manuscripts *Azariah*   [e] 11 Hebrew *Jehoshabeath*, a variant of *Jehosheba*

---

2 Chronicles 22:1–9

The Chronicler bluntly stated that God had "brought about Ahaziah's downfall" (v. 7). Jehu became God's agent of justice in punishing the evil of both Joram of Israel and Ahaziah of Judah (cf. 2 Kings 9:14–29). While 2 Kings 9 relates the parallel destruction of both kings, the Chronicler focused on the house of Judah. The message of the passage is alarmingly clear: God repaid evil for evil on those who failed to imitate David's example of righteous rule.

Though the fiery Jehu was rightly aware of his commission from God to destroy the house of Ahab, it's

questionable whether he was justified in extending his purge to the house of Ahaziah (see "There and Then" for 2 Kings 10:1–17). The Bible offers numerous other examples of "agents" who worked unwittingly to carry out God's eternal purposes (e.g., Pharaoh, Nebuchadnezzar, Judas). While these individuals were wholly responsible for their own actions (not helpless pawns), those actions were at the same time used by God to fulfill his divine plan. Thinking back on recent world history, can you identify one or more "unsavory" characters who you suspect might have worked as God's agents for ultimate good?

23:6
x 1Ch 23:28-29;
Zec 3:7

23:8
y 2Ki 11:9
z 1Ch 24:1

23:11
a Ex 25:16;
Dt 17:18; 1Sa 10:24

23:13
b 1Ki 1:41
c 1Ki 7:15

23:15
d Ne 3:28;
Jer 31:40
23:16
e 2Ch 29:10; 34:31;
Ne 9:38
23:17
f Dt 13:6-9

23:18
g 1Ch 23:28-32;
2Ch 5:5
h 1Ch 23:6; 25:6
23:19
i 1Ch 9:22

23:20
j 2Ki 15:35

23:21
k 2Ch 22:1

to enter the temple of the LORD except the priests and Levites on duty; they may enter because they are consecrated, but all the other men are to guard[x] what the LORD has assigned to them.[a] 7The Levites are to station themselves around the king, each man with his weapons in his hand. Anyone who enters the temple must be put to death. Stay close to the king wherever he goes."

8The Levites and all the men of Judah did just as Jehoiada the priest ordered.[y] Each one took his men—those who were going on duty on the Sabbath and those who were going off duty—for Jehoiada the priest had not released any of the divisions.[z] 9Then he gave the commanders of units of a hundred the spears and the large and small shields that had belonged to King David and that were in the temple of God. 10He stationed all the men, each with his weapon in his hand, around the king—near the altar and the temple, from the south side to the north side of the temple.

11Jehoiada and his sons brought out the king's son and put the crown on him; they presented him with a copy[a] of the covenant and proclaimed him king. They anointed him and shouted, "Long live the king!"

12When Athaliah heard the noise of the people running and cheering the king, she went to them at the temple of the LORD. 13She looked, and there was the king,[b] standing by his pillar[c] at the entrance. The officers and the trumpeters were beside the king, and all the people of the land were rejoicing and blowing trumpets, and singers with musical instruments were leading the praises. Then Athaliah tore her robes and shouted, "Treason! Treason!"

14Jehoiada the priest sent out the commanders of units of a hundred, who were in charge of the troops, and said to them: "Bring her out between the ranks[b] and put to the sword anyone who follows her." For the priest had said, "Do not put her to death at the temple of the LORD." 15So they seized her as she reached the entrance of the Horse Gate[d] on the palace grounds, and there they put her to death.

16Jehoiada then made a covenant[e] that he and the people and the king[c] would be the LORD's people. 17All the people went to the temple of Baal and tore it down. They smashed the altars and idols and killed[f] Mattan the priest of Baal in front of the altars.

18Then Jehoiada placed the oversight of the temple of the LORD in the hands of the priests, who were Levites,[g] to whom David had made assignments in the temple,[h] to present the burnt offerings of the LORD as written in the Law of Moses, with rejoicing and singing, as David had ordered. 19He also stationed doorkeepers[i] at the gates of the LORD's temple so that no one who was in any way unclean might enter.

20He took with him the commanders of hundreds, the nobles, the rulers of the people and all the people of the land and brought the king down from the temple of the LORD. They went into the palace through the Upper Gate[j] and seated the king on the royal throne, 21and all the people of the land rejoiced. And the city was quiet, because Athaliah had been slain with the sword.[k]

---

a 6 Or *to observe the LORD's command ꞁnot to enterꞁ*   b 14 Or *out from the precincts*   c 16 Or *covenant between ꞁthe LORDꞁ and the people and the king that they* (see 2 Kings 11:17)

---

2 Chronicles 22:10—23:21

📖 The report of Athaliah's usurpation of the Judahite throne may be described as a tale of two women. One, Athaliah, sought to destroy David's family (even murdering her own grandchildren) and ruled the land illegitimately for six years. The other, Jehosheba, worked courageously and covertly to preserve the family of David during those same years. The name Jehosheba means "the Lord vows." Fittingly, God used this faithful woman to keep his oath to maintain the lamp of David (cf. 21:7).

Jehoiada's coup was well-planned and carefully orchestrated, and there was no dissension in the ranks. The conspiracy was shrewdly coordinated with Sabbath observance; the commotion of an assembly at the temple wouldn't have been unexpected. The cooperation of priests with army commanders suggests a coalition of religious and military leaders.

Joash's coronation climaxed with a covenant-renewal ceremony led by Jehoiada. Two distinct but related covenants were reaffirmed. The first reestablished the authority of the Davidic kingship (23:3,11; cf. 2 Kings 11:17b), and the second bound king and people in obedience to the Mosaic Law (23:16; cf. 2 Kings 11:17a).

💬 What covenants, either formal (e.g., your baptism or marriage vows) or personal, have you made with God? What has been your track record in upholding your part of the promise? Can you cite specific evidences of God's covenant keeping? Might a covenant renewal between you and God, you and your spouse and God, or you and your church and God be warranted?

Joash Repairs the Temple

24 Joash was seven years old when he became king, and he reigned in Jerusalem forty years. His mother's name was Zibiah; she was from Beersheba. 2Jo-
ash did what was right in the eyes of the LORD[l] all the years of Jehoiada the priest.
3Jehoiada chose two wives for him, and he had sons and daughters.
4Some time later Joash decided to restore the temple of the LORD. 5He called together the priests and Levites and said to them, "Go to the towns of Judah and collect the money[m] due annually from all Israel,[n] to repair the temple of your God.
Do it now." But the Levites[o] did not act at once.
6Therefore the king summoned Jehoiada the chief priest and said to him, "Why
haven't you required the Levites to bring in from Judah and Jerusalem the tax imposed by Moses the servant of the LORD and by the assembly of Israel for the Tent
of the Testimony?"[p]
7Now the sons of that wicked woman Athaliah had broken into the temple of
God and had used even its sacred objects for the Baals.
8At the king's command, a chest was made and placed outside, at the gate of the
temple of the LORD. 9A proclamation was then issued in Judah and Jerusalem that
they should bring to the LORD the tax that Moses the servant of God had required
of Israel in the desert. 10All the officials and all the people brought their contributions gladly,[q] dropping them into the chest until it was full. 11Whenever the chest
was brought in by the Levites to the king's officials and they saw that there was a
large amount of money, the royal secretary and the officer of the chief priest would
come and empty the chest and carry it back to its place. They did this regularly and
collected a great amount of money. 12The king and Jehoiada gave it to the men who
carried out the work required for the temple of the LORD. They hired[r] masons and
carpenters to restore the LORD's temple, and also workers in iron and bronze to repair the temple.
13The men in charge of the work were diligent, and the repairs progressed under
them. They rebuilt the temple of God according to its original design and reinforced
it. 14When they had finished, they brought the rest of the money to the king and
Jehoiada, and with it were made articles for the LORD's temple: articles for the service and for the burnt offerings, and also dishes and other objects of gold and silver. As long as Jehoiada lived, burnt offerings were presented continually in the temple of the LORD.
15Now Jehoiada was old and full of years, and he died at the age of a hundred
and thirty. 16He was buried with the kings in the City of David, because of the good
he had done in Israel for God and his temple.

The Wickedness of Joash

17After the death of Jehoiada, the officials of Judah came and paid homage to the
king, and he listened to them. 18They abandoned[s] the temple of the LORD, the God

24:2 [l] 2Ch 25:2; 26:5
24:5 [m] Ex 30:16; Ne 10:32-33; Mt 17:24 [n] 1Ch 11:1 [o] 1Ch 26:20
24:6 [p] Ex 30:12-16; Nu 1:50
24:10 [q] Ex 25:2; 1Ch 29:3,6,9
24:12 [r] 2Ch 34:11
24:18 [s] ver 4; Jos 24:20; 2Ch 7:19

2 Chronicles 24:1–16

Jehoiada was the model high priest for the Chronicler because of his role as royal guardian and adviser. The ideal of shared power between the civil and religious sectors in the oversight of Israel can be traced back to the leadership of Moses and Aaron after the exodus. In one sense Jehoiada was a prototype for the high priests of the later postexilic period since he wielded considerable civil as well as religious authority. Unlike the priests of the later period, though, Jehoiada showed great concern for the preservation of legitimate kingship in Israel.

The extent of Jehoiada's influence over Joash was amazing, given the king's swift decline following his mentor's death. It's easy to underestimate the degree to which our words and example can affect the lives of the young. Whether we set aside quality time to talk to our own children, commit to teaching a church school class, act as a "Big Brother" or "Big Sister" to a disadvantaged youth, or simply show an interest in a kid from an upcoming generation, our efforts may accomplish far more than we might imagine. Which individuals influenced you in your younger years, and what differences did they make?

2 Chronicles 24:17–27

Ironically, Joash had Zechariah murdered in the temple courtyard, the site where "Jehoiada and his sons" had anointed Joash as king (23:11). Zechariah's dying words aren't to be regarded as a plea for vengeance but as a petition for God to mete out divine justice. This likely was the same Zechariah mentioned by Jesus in reference to Old Testament martyrs (Matt. 23:35; Luke 11:50–51).

24:18
t Ex 34:13;
1Ki 14:23;
2Ch 33:3; Jer 17:2
u Jos 22:20;
2Ch 19:2
24:19
v Nu 11:29;
Jer 7:25; Zec 1:4
24:20
w Jdg 3:10;
1Ch 12:18;
2Ch 20:14
x Mt 23:35;
Lk 11:51
y Nu 14:41
z Dt 31:17;
2Ch 15:2
24:21
a Jos 7:25;
Ac 7:58-59
b Ne 9:26;
Jer 26:21
c Jer 20:2; Mt 23:35
24:22
d Ge 9:5
24:23
e 2Ki 12:17-18
24:24
f 2Ch 14:9; 16:8;
20:2,12
g Lev 26:23-25;
Dt 28:25
24:25
h 2Ch 21:20

of their fathers, and worshiped Asherah poles and idols. t Because of their guilt, God's anger u came upon Judah and Jerusalem. 19Although the LORD sent prophets to the people to bring them back to him, and though they testified against them, they would not listen. v

20Then the Spirit w of God came upon Zechariah x son of Jehoiada the priest. He stood before the people and said, "This is what God says: 'Why do you disobey the LORD's commands? You will not prosper. y Because you have forsaken the LORD, he has forsaken z you.' "

21But they plotted against him, and by order of the king they stoned a him to death b in the courtyard of the LORD's temple. c 22King Joash did not remember the kindness Zechariah's father Jehoiada had shown him but killed his son, who said as he lay dying, "May the LORD see this and call you to account." d

23At the turn of the year, a the army of Aram marched against Joash; it invaded Judah and Jerusalem and killed all the leaders of the people. e They sent all the plunder to their king in Damascus. 24Although the Aramean army had come with only a few men, f the LORD delivered into their hands a much larger army. g Because Judah had forsaken the LORD, the God of their fathers, judgment was executed on Joash. 25When the Arameans withdrew, they left Joash severely wounded. His officials conspired against him for murdering the son of Jehoiada the priest, and they killed him in his bed. So he died and was buried h in the City of David, but not in the tombs of the kings.

24:26
i 2Ki 12:21 j Ru 1:4

26Those who conspired against him were Zabad, b son of Shimeath an Ammonite woman, and Jehozabad, son of Shimrith c i a Moabite woman. j 27The account of his sons, the many prophecies about him, and the record of the restoration of the temple of God are written in the annotations on the book of the kings. And Amaziah his son succeeded him as king.

Amaziah King of Judah

25:2
k ver 14; 1Ki 8:61;
2Ch 24:2
25:4
l Dt 28:61
m Nu 26:11;
Dt 24:16

25 Amaziah was twenty-five years old when he became king, and he reigned in Jerusalem twenty-nine years. His mother's name was Jehoaddin d; she was from Jerusalem. 2He did what was right in the eyes of the LORD, but not wholeheartedly. k 3After the kingdom was firmly in his control, he executed the officials who had murdered his father the king. 4Yet he did not put their sons to death, but acted in accordance with what is written in the Law, in the Book of Moses, l where the LORD commanded: "Fathers shall not be put to death for their children, nor children put to death for their fathers; each is to die for his own sins." e m

a 23 Probably in the spring   b 26 A variant of *Jozabad*   c 26 A variant of *Shomer*   d 1 Hebrew *Jehoaddan*, a variant of *Jehoaddin*   e 4 Deut. 24:16

To remove any doubt that the Aramean invasion was divinely ordained as punishment for Joash and Judah, the Chronicler reported that the small contingent of soldiers was victorious because "the LORD delivered" Judah's larger army into its hands. God's sovereignty as Judge and Lord of history was further highlighted in extensive word plays. For example, even as Joash and the leaders had "abandoned" (v. 18) God, the Arameans "left" (v. 25) the king for dead. All of this came about because Judah had "forsaken" (vv. 20,24) the Lord. In each case, the same Hebrew word was used.

How, we wonder, could Joash (and Amaziah and Uzziah after him, as we will learn) start out so well and yet fail so miserably? In each case success seems to have been a catalyst for decidedly negative changes in attitude and behavior. Success, like its frequent partner wealth, is in and of itself neither bad nor a sign of God's displeasure. Indeed, it may signify his blessing and open doors for service that might otherwise have remained

shut for us. But success can open other doors as well—for abuse, complacency, temptation, and pride, to name a few. With enhanced privilege inevitably comes added responsibility (Luke 12:48). How has any success you have enjoyed affected your spiritual life?

2 Chronicles 25:1–28

Amaziah's military campaign against Edom is summarized in a single verse in the Kings account (2 Kings 14:7). There are two apparent reasons for the expanded account in Chronicles: (1) The ill-fated hiring of Israelite mercenaries (vv. 6,10,13) helps explain Amaziah's subsequent war with Jehoash of Israel (v. 17), and (2) Amaziah's apostasy (v. 27) was directly related to the aftermath of his resounding victory over Edom when he worshiped the Edomite gods (v. 14). Amaziah may have assumed that Judah's defeat of Edom was due in part to a shift in loyalty on the part of the Edomite deities to Judah's cause. This would have explained his desire to placate these gods in some way.

⁵Amaziah called the people of Judah together and assigned them according to their families to commanders of thousands and commanders of hundreds for all Judah and Benjamin. He then mustered ⁿ those twenty years old ᵒ or more and found that there were three hundred thousand men ready for military service, ᵖ able to handle the spear and shield. ⁶He also hired a hundred thousand fighting men from Israel for a hundred talents ᵃ of silver.

⁷But a man of God came to him and said, "O king, these troops from Israel ᵠ must not march with you, for the LORD is not with Israel—not with any of the people of Ephraim. ⁸Even if you go and fight courageously in battle, God will overthrow you before the enemy, for God has the power to help or to overthrow." ʳ

⁹Amaziah asked the man of God, "But what about the hundred talents I paid for these Israelite troops?"

The man of God replied, "The LORD can give you much more than that." ˢ

¹⁰So Amaziah dismissed the troops who had come to him from Ephraim and sent them home. They were furious with Judah and left for home in a great rage. ᵗ

¹¹Amaziah then marshaled his strength and led his army to the Valley of Salt, where he killed ten thousand men of Seir. ¹²The army of Judah also captured ten thousand men alive, took them to the top of a cliff and threw them down so that all were dashed to pieces. ᵘ

¹³Meanwhile the troops that Amaziah had sent back and had not allowed to take part in the war raided Judean towns from Samaria to Beth Horon. They killed three thousand people and carried off great quantities of plunder.

¹⁴When Amaziah returned from slaughtering the Edomites, he brought back the gods of the people of Seir. He set them up as his own gods, ᵛ bowed down to them and burned sacrifices to them. ¹⁵The anger of the LORD burned against Amaziah, and he sent a prophet to him, who said, "Why do you consult this people's gods, which could not save ʷ their own people from your hand?"

¹⁶While he was still speaking, the king said to him, "Have we appointed you an adviser to the king? Stop! Why be struck down?"

So the prophet stopped but said, "I know that God has determined to destroy you, because you have done this and have not listened to my counsel."

¹⁷After Amaziah king of Judah consulted his advisers, he sent this challenge to Jehoash ᵇ son of Jehoahaz, the son of Jehu, king of Israel: "Come, meet me face to face."

¹⁸But Jehoash king of Israel replied to Amaziah king of Judah: "A thistle ˣ in Lebanon sent a message to a cedar in Lebanon, 'Give your daughter to my son in marriage.' Then a wild beast in Lebanon came along and trampled the thistle underfoot. ¹⁹You say to yourself that you have defeated Edom, and now you are arrogant and proud. But stay at home! Why ask for trouble and cause your own downfall and that of Judah also?"

²⁰Amaziah, however, would not listen, for God so worked that he might hand them over to ⌊Jehoash⌋, because they sought the gods of Edom. ʸ ²¹So Jehoash king of Israel attacked. He and Amaziah king of Judah faced each other at Beth Shemesh

25:5
ⁿ 2Sa 24:2
ᵒ Ex 30:14
ᵖ Nu 1:3; 1Ch 21:1;
2Ch 17:14-19

25:7
ᵠ 2Ch 16:2-9;
19:1-3

25:8
ʳ 2Ch 14:11; 20:6

25:9
ˢ Dt 8:18; Pr 10:22

25:10
ᵗ ver 13

25:12
ᵘ Ps 141:6; Ob 1:3

25:14
ᵛ Ex 20:3;
2Ch 28:23;
Isa 44:15

25:15
ʷ Ps 96:5; Isa 36:20

25:18
ˣ Jdg 9:8-15

25:20
ʸ 1Ki 12:15;
2Ch 10:15; 22:7

ᵃ 6 That is, about 3 3/4 tons (about 3.4 metric tons); also in verse 9   ᵇ 17 Hebrew *Joash*, a variant of *Jehoash*; also in verses 18, 21, 23 and 25

Amaziah's worship of Edom's gods set a course of self-destruction that eventually led to his mistreatment of God's prophet (v. 16), revenge against Israel (v. 17), prideful arrogance in his military achievements (v. 19), rebellion against God's word (v. 20), and ultimate death (v. 27).

📖 We don't always get the "cause" of circumstances right. Like Amaziah we sometimes trace human or societal influences to certain results in life. James 1:17 reminds believers that "every good and perfect gift" comes from God. We are wise to acknowledge his loving care instead of the gods of education, a good stock portfolio, a doctor's

life-saving diagnosis, or a brilliant career move.

Most of us have experienced the snowball effect of one sin leading to another . . . and another . . . Chances are that your first encounter came in childhood, when an infraction of one rule "necessitated" a lie, which in turn led to a loss of control when you were confronted with the obvious facts. In most cases, looking back, we would have to say that the whole cycle just wasn't worth the effort—that "fessing" up and taking the consequences in the first place would have been the sensible approach. Has this trap been an issue for you as an adult? If so, ask God to help you break this destructive pattern.

in Judah. ²²Judah was routed by Israel, and every man fled to his home. ²³Jehoash king of Israel captured Amaziah king of Judah, the son of Joash, the son of Ahaziah,ᵃ at Beth Shemesh. Then Jehoash brought him to Jerusalem and broke down the wall of Jerusalem from the Ephraim Gateᶻ to the Corner Gateᵃ—a section about six hundred feetᵇ long. ²⁴He took all the gold and silver and all the articles found in the temple of God that had been in the care of Obed-Edom,ᵇ together with the palace treasures and the hostages, and returned to Samaria.

25:23
z 2Ki 14:13;
Ne 8:16; 12:39
a 2Ch 26:9;
Jer 31:38
25:24
b 1Ch 26:15

²⁵Amaziah son of Joash king of Judah lived for fifteen years after the death of Jehoash son of Jehoahaz king of Israel. ²⁶As for the other events of Amaziah's reign, from beginning to end, are they not written in the book of the kings of Judah and Israel? ²⁷From the time that Amaziah turned away from following the LORD, they conspired against him in Jerusalem and he fled to Lachishᶜ, but they sent men after him to Lachish and killed him there. ²⁸He was brought back by horse and was buried with his fathers in the City of Judah.

25:27
c Jos 10:3

Uzziah King of Judah

26:1
d 2Ch 22:1

26 Then all the people of Judahᵈ took Uzziah,ᶜ who was sixteen years old, and made him king in place of his father Amaziah. ²He was the one who rebuilt Elath and restored it to Judah after Amaziah rested with his fathers.

³Uzziah was sixteen years old when he became king, and he reigned in Jerusalem fifty-two years. His mother's name was Jecoliah; she was from Jerusalem. ⁴He did what was right in the eyes of the LORD, just as his father Amaziah had done. ⁵He sought God during the days of Zechariah, who instructed him in the fearᵈ of God.ᵉ As long as he sought the LORD, God gave him success.ᶠ

26:5
e 2Ch 15:2; 24:2;
Da 1:17 f 2Ch 27:6

26:6
g Isa 2:6; 11:14;
14:29; Jer 25:20
h Am 1:8; 3:9
26:7
i 2Ch 21:16
j 2Ch 20:1
26:8
k Ge 19:38;
2Ch 17:11
26:9
l 2Ki 14:13;
2Ch 25:23
m Ne 2:13; 3:13

⁶He went to war against the Philistinesᵍ and broke down the walls of Gath, Jabneh and Ashdod.ʰ He then rebuilt towns near Ashdod and elsewhere among the Philistines. ⁷God helped him against the Philistines and against the Arabsⁱ who lived in Gur Baal and against the Meunites.ʲ ⁸The Ammonitesᵏ brought tribute to Uzziah, and his fame spread as far as the border of Egypt, because he had become very powerful.

⁹Uzziah built towers in Jerusalem at the Corner Gate,ˡ at the Valley Gateᵐ and at the angle of the wall, and he fortified them. ¹⁰He also built towers in the desert and dug many cisterns, because he had much livestock in the foothills and in the plain. He had people working his fields and vineyards in the hills and in the fertile lands, for he loved the soil.

¹¹Uzziah had a well-trained army, ready to go out by divisions according to their numbers as mustered by Jeiel the secretary and Maaseiah the officer under the direction of Hananiah, one of the royal officials. ¹²The total number of family leaders over the fighting men was 2,600. ¹³Under their command was an army of 307,500 men trained for war, a powerful force to support the king against his ene-

---

ᵃ 23 Hebrew *Jehoahaz*, a variant of *Ahaziah*   ᵇ 23 Hebrew *four hundred cubits* (about 180 meters)
ᶜ 1 Also called *Azariah*   ᵈ 5 Many Hebrew manuscripts, Septuagint and Syriac; other Hebrew manuscripts *vision*

---

2 Chronicles 26:1–23

Though Uzziah's accomplishments during the earlier years of his reign were impressive, the report of his fatal flaw, pride, was the focal point of the Chronicler's review. Ironically, Uzziah's success led to his downfall, resulting in unfaithfulness to the Lord (v. 16; see also "Here and Now" for 24:17–27). "Unfaithfulness" is the single most important term for sin in Chronicles. It could topple a dynasty (1 Chron. 10:13) or sweep a nation away into exile (1 Chron. 5:25; 2 Chron. 36:14).

The priests' challenge to Uzziah's presumption of the priestly role was made at great personal risk (cf. 1 Sam. 22:17–19; 2 Chron. 24:20–22). The divinely ordained division of labor and service had been designed by God to separate political power from religious authority in Israelite society in order to prevent abuse of one office by the other. Uzziah's disregard for the Lord's priests and sanctuary signaled a disregard for God himself, and God wouldn't stand by idly while his holiness was being violated.

The potential for abuse is amplified when individuals wield both religious and political authority. God made provision in Israelite society to separate these powers. How did he intend for the two—religious and civil—to work together to create a just society? How and why do modern governments miss the mark? Is there a role for Christians to play in helping restore a godly perspective? What might God be asking you to do?

mies. [14]Uzziah provided shields, spears, helmets, coats of armor, bows and sling-stones for the entire army.[n] [15]In Jerusalem he made machines designed by skillful men for use on the towers and on the corner defenses to shoot arrows and hurl large stones. His fame spread far and wide, for he was greatly helped until he became powerful.

[16]But after Uzziah became powerful, his pride[o] led to his downfall.[p] He was un-faithful[q] to the LORD his God, and entered the temple of the LORD to burn incense[r] on the altar of incense. [17]Azariah[s] the priest with eighty other courageous priests of the LORD followed him in. [18]They confronted him and said, "It is not right for you, Uzziah, to burn incense to the LORD. That is for the priests,[t] the descendants[u] of Aaron,[v] who have been consecrated to burn incense.[w] Leave the sanctuary, for you have been unfaithful; and you will not be honored by the LORD God."

[19]Uzziah, who had a censer in his hand ready to burn incense, became angry. While he was raging at the priests in their presence before the incense altar in the LORD's temple, leprosy[a][x] broke out on his forehead. [20]When Azariah the chief priest and all the other priests looked at him, they saw that he had leprosy on his forehead, so they hurried him out. Indeed, he himself was eager to leave, because the LORD had afflicted him.

[21]King Uzziah had leprosy until the day he died. He lived in a separate house[b][y]—leprous, and excluded from the temple of the LORD. Jotham his son had charge of the palace and governed the people of the land.

[22]The other events of Uzziah's reign, from beginning to end, are recorded by the prophet Isaiah[z] son of Amoz. [23]Uzziah[a] rested with his fathers and was buried near them in a field for burial that belonged to the kings, for people said, "He had lep-rosy." And Jotham his son succeeded him as king.[b]

[a] 19 The Hebrew word was used for various diseases affecting the skin—not necessarily leprosy; also in verses 20, 21 and 23.   [b] 21 Or *in a house where he was relieved of responsibilities*

26:14
[n] Jer 46:4

26:16
[o] 2Ki 14:10
[p] Dt 32:15;
2Ch 25:19
[q] 1Ch 5:25
[r] 2Ki 16:12
26:17
[s] 1Ki 4:2; 1Ch 6:10
26:18
[t] Nu 16:39
[u] Nu 18:1-7
[v] Ex 30:7
[w] 1Ch 6:49

26:19
[x] Nu 12:10;
2Ki 5:25-27

26:21
[y] Ex 4:6; Lev 13:46;
14:8; Nu 5:2; 19:12

26:22
[z] 2Ki 15:1; Isa 1:1;
6:1
26:23
[a] Isa 1:1; 6:1
[b] 2Ki 14:21; 15:7;
Am 1:1

26:21

HIV/AIDS

There are uncanny parallels between leprosy as described in the Bible and the modern scourge of HIV/AIDS—social contamination and separation, for starters. In the face of such diseases we can learn a negative lesson from King Asa (2 Chron. 16:12), who sought help for his malady only from physicians, not from God. Both are needed to combat the greatest humanitarian challenge of our time.

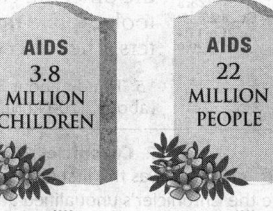

AIDS
3.8
MILLION
CHILDREN

AIDS
22
MILLION
PEOPLE

40 million people worldwide are living with HIV/AIDS.

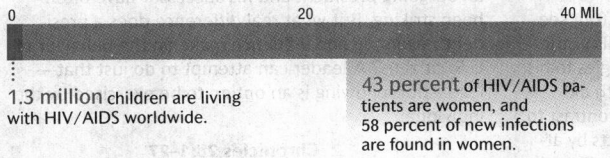

0   20   40 MIL

1.3 million children are living with HIV/AIDS worldwide.

43 percent of HIV/AIDS pa-tients are women, and 58 percent of new infections are found in women.

3.8 million children under the age of 15 have died of AIDS since 1981.

22 million people have died of AIDS since 1981.

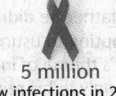

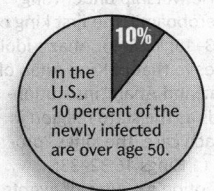

10%

In the U.S., 10 percent of the newly infected are over age 50.

Nations with more than 3 million HIV/AIDS sufferers:

South Africa

India

Ethiopia

Nigeria

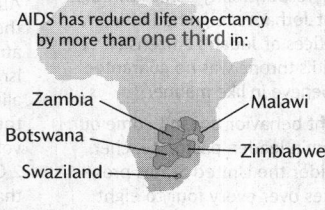

AIDS has reduced life expectancy by more than one third in:

Zambia

Botswana

Swaziland

Malawi

Zimbabwe

5 million new infections in 2001

1,700 children infected each day in 1999

15 million children orphaned by AIDS since 1981

Source: Wright (2003:483)

Jotham King of Judah

27 Jotham ^c was twenty-five years old when he became king, and he reigned in Jerusalem sixteen years. His mother's name was Jerusha daughter of Zadok. ²He did what was right in the eyes of the LORD, just as his father Uzziah had done, but unlike him he did not enter the temple of the LORD. The people, however, continued their corrupt practices. ³Jotham rebuilt the Upper Gate of the temple of the LORD and did extensive work on the wall at the hill of Ophel. ^d ⁴He built towns in the Judean hills and forts and towers in the wooded areas.

⁵Jotham made war on the king of the Ammonites ^e and conquered them. That year the Ammonites paid him a hundred talents ^a of silver, ten thousand cors ^b of wheat and ten thousand cors of barley. The Ammonites brought him the same amount also in the second and third years.

⁶Jotham grew powerful ^f because he walked steadfastly before the LORD his God.

⁷The other events in Jotham's reign, including all his wars and the other things he did, are written in the book of the kings of Israel and Judah. ⁸He was twenty-five years old when he became king, and he reigned in Jerusalem sixteen years. ⁹Jotham rested with his fathers and was buried in the City of David. And Ahaz his son succeeded him as king.

Ahaz King of Judah

28 Ahaz ^g was twenty years old when he became king, and he reigned in Jerusalem sixteen years. Unlike David his father, he did not do what was right in the eyes of the LORD. ²He walked in the ways of the kings of Israel and also made cast idols ^h for worshiping the Baals. ³He burned sacrifices in the Valley of Ben Hinnom ⁱ and sacrificed his sons ^j in the fire, following the detestable ^k ways of the nations the LORD had driven out before the Israelites. ⁴He offered sacrifices and burned incense at the high places, on the hilltops and under every spreading tree.

⁵Therefore the LORD his God handed him over to the king of Aram. ^l The Arameans defeated him and took many of his people as prisoners and brought them to Damascus.

He was also given into the hands of the king of Israel, who inflicted heavy casualties on him. ⁶In one day Pekah ^m son of Remaliah killed a hundred and twenty thousand soldiers in Judah ⁿ—because Judah had forsaken the LORD, the God of their fathers. ⁷Zicri, an Ephraimite warrior, killed Maaseiah the king's son, Azrikam the officer in charge of the palace, and Elkanah, second to the king. ⁸The Israelites took captive from their kinsmen ^o two hundred thousand wives, sons and daughters. They also took a great deal of plunder, which they carried back to Samaria. ^p

---

Cross-references (margin)

27:1 c 2Ki 15:5,32; 1Ch 3:12
27:3 d 2Ch 33:14; Ne 3:26
27:5 e Ge 19:38
27:6 f 2Ch 26:5

28:1 g 1Ch 3:13; Isa 1:1
28:2 h Ex 34:17; 2Ch 22:3
28:3 i Jos 15:8; 2Ki 23:10 j Lev 18:21; 2Ki 3:27; 2Ch 33:6; Eze 20:26 k Dt 18:9; 2Ch 33:2
28:5 l Isa 7:1
28:6 m 2Ki 15:25,27 n ver 8; Isa 9:21; 11:13
28:8 o Dt 28:25-41; 2Ch 11:4 p 2Ch 29:9

---

^a 5 That is, about 3 3/4 tons (about 3.4 metric tons)   ^b 5 That is, probably about 62,000 bushels (about 2,200 kiloliters)

---

2 Chronicles 27:1–9

Jotham was the first king since Abijah to receive the Chronicler's unqualified affirmation (but see "There and Then" for 2 Chron. 13:1—14:1). His virtue was illustrated by positive and negative analogies to his father. He was compared favorably in that both did "right in the eyes of the LORD" (v. 2a), but in contrast to his father he didn't violate the temple precincts by attempting to usurp the priestly role (v. 2b). The Chronicler's theme of individual responsibility comes through strongly in his report that Jotham's reign had little impact on the corrupt practices of Judah's citizens (v. 2c). A righteous king on David's throne was no guarantee that his subjects would behave in like manner.

Goodness or right behavior doesn't come our way through osmosis from a leader, pastor, teacher, parent, or mentor. Consider the United States presidency. A new leader takes over every four to eight years, and the moral and religious contrasts between an outgoing president and his successor have often been striking. But what real difference does a president's example and influence make on the behavior of U.S. citizens? A leader can attempt to do just that—lead—but following is an option to be exercised by the individual.

2 Chronicles 28:1–27

The proliferation of false worship under King Ahaz echoed the apostasy of Jeroboam I, the first king of the northern kingdom (cf. 11:13–15; 13:8–9). Ahaz's idolatry had even greater similarities to that of King Ahab of Israel, though, in that both Ahaz and Ahab "institutionalized" the worship of false gods as the state religion in their respective kingdoms. In each case, the kings "provoke[d] the the LORD to anger" (1 Kings 16:32–33; 2 Chron. 28:24–25) and set in motion a course of events that inevitably culminated in exile.

9But a prophet of the LORD named Oded was there, and he went out to meet the
army when it returned to Samaria. He said to them, "Because the LORD, the God of
your fathers, was angry[q] with Judah, he gave them into your hand. But you have
slaughtered them in a rage that reaches to heaven.[r] 10And now you intend to make
the men and women of Judah and Jerusalem your slaves.[s] But aren't you also guilty
of sins against the LORD your God? 11Now listen to me! Send back your fellow countrymen you have taken as prisoners, for the LORD's fierce anger rests on you.[t]"
12Then some of the leaders in Ephraim—Azariah son of Jehohanan, Berekiah son
of Meshillemoth, Jehizkiah son of Shallum, and Amasa son of Hadlai—confronted those who were arriving from the war. 13"You must not bring those prisoners
here," they said, "or we will be guilty before the LORD. Do you intend to add to our
sin and guilt? For our guilt is already great, and his fierce anger rests on Israel."
14So the soldiers gave up the prisoners and plunder in the presence of the officials and all the assembly. 15The men designated by name took the prisoners, and
from the plunder they clothed all who were naked. They provided them with
clothes and sandals, food and drink,[u] and healing balm. All those who were weak
they put on donkeys. So they took them back to their fellow countrymen at Jericho,
the City of Palms,[v] and returned to Samaria.
16At that time King Ahaz sent to the king[a] of Assyria[w] for help. 17The Edomites[x]
had again come and attacked Judah and carried away prisoners,[y] 18while the Philistines[z] had raided towns in the foothills and in the Negev of Judah. They captured
and occupied Beth Shemesh, Aijalon[a] and Gederoth, as well as Soco, Timnah and
Gimzo, with their surrounding villages. 19The LORD had humbled Judah because of
Ahaz king of Israel,[b] for he had promoted wickedness in Judah and had been most
unfaithful[b] to the LORD. 20Tiglath-Pileser[c][c] king of Assyria came to him, but he gave
him trouble instead of help.[d] 21Ahaz took some of the things from the temple of
the LORD and from the royal palace and from the princes and presented them to the
king of Assyria, but that did not help him.
22In his time of trouble King Ahaz became even more unfaithful[e] to the LORD.
23He offered sacrifices to the gods[f] of Damascus, who had defeated him; for he
thought, "Since the gods of the kings of Aram have helped them, I will sacrifice to
them so they will help me."[g] But they were his downfall and the downfall of all
Israel.
24Ahaz gathered together the furnishings from the temple of God[h] and took them
away.[d] He shut the doors[i] of the LORD's temple and set up altars[j] at every street corner in Jerusalem. 25In every town in Judah he built high places to burn sacrifices
to other gods and provoked the LORD, the God of his fathers, to anger.
26The other events of his reign and all his ways, from beginning to end, are written in the book of the kings of Judah and Israel. 27Ahaz rested[k] with his fathers and
was buried[l] in the city of Jerusalem, but he was not placed in the tombs of the kings
of Israel. And Hezekiah his son succeeded him as king.

Hezekiah Purifies the Temple

29 Hezekiah[m] was twenty-five years old when he became king, and he reigned
in Jerusalem twenty-nine years. His mother's name was Abijah daughter of
Zechariah. 2He did what was right in the eyes of the LORD, just as his father David[n]
had done.
3In the first month of the first year of his reign, he opened the doors of the tem-

28:9 [q] 2Ch 25:15; Isa 10:6; 47:6; Zec 1:15 [r] Ezr 9:6; Rev 18:5
28:10 [s] Lev 25:39-46
28:11 [t] 2Ch 11:4; Jas 2:13
28:15 [u] 2Ki 6:22; Pr 25:21-22 [v] Dt 34:3; Jdg 1:16
28:16 [w] 2Ki 16:7
28:17 [x] Ps 137:7; Isa 34:5 [y] 2Ch 29:9
28:18 [z] Eze 16:27,57 [a] Jos 10:12
28:19 [b] 2Ch 21:2
28:20 [c] 2Ki 15:29; 1Ch 5:6 [d] 2Ki 16:7
28:22 [e] Jer 5:3
28:23 [f] 2Ch 25:14 [g] Jer 44:17-18
28:24 [h] 2Ki 16:18 [i] 2Ch 29:7 [j] 2Ch 30:14
28:27 [k] Isa 14:28-32 [l] 2Ch 21:20; 24:25
29:1 [m] 1Ch 3:13
29:2 [n] 2Ch 28:1; 34:2

[a] *16* One Hebrew manuscript, Septuagint and Vulgate (see also 2 Kings 16:7); most Hebrew manuscripts *kings* [b] *19* That is, Judah, as frequently in 2 Chronicles [c] *20* Hebrew *Tilgath-Pilneser*, a variant of *Tiglath-Pileser* [d] *24* Or *and cut them up*

Western democracies today take for granted the separation of church and state, yet in practice their laws and high court rulings often "institutionalize" agnosticism or atheism. A recent news release reported that a particular U.S. city had voted to eliminate opening prayers at its council meetings—after having opened the meeting with prayer. Yet Americans are quick to solicit God's help in times of war or other crisis. Linking Christianity with nationalism is a dangerous road, but so is leaving God out of our public affairs. A nation whose currency expressly states "In God we trust" had better take this declaration seriously.

29:3
o 2Ch 28:24

29:5
p 2Ch 35:6
29:6
q Ps 106:6-47;
Jer 2:27 r 1Ch 5:25;
Eze 8:16

29:8
s Dt 28:25;
2Ch 24:18
t Jer 18:16; 19:8;
25:9,18
29:9
u 2Ch 28:5-8,17
29:10
v 2Ch 15:12; 23:16
29:11
w Nu 3:6; 8:6,14
x 1Ch 15:2
29:12
y Nu 3:17-20
z 2Ch 31:15

29:13
a 1Ch 6:39

29:15
b ver 5; 1Ch 23:28;
2Ch 30:12

29:16
c 2Sa 15:23

29:19
d 2Ch 28:24

29:21
e Lev 4:13-14

ple of the LORD and repaired^o them. ⁴He brought in the priests and the Levites, assembled them in the square on the east side ⁵and said: "Listen to me, Levites! Consecrate^p yourselves now and consecrate the temple of the LORD, the God of your fathers. Remove all defilement from the sanctuary. ⁶Our fathers^q were unfaithful;^r they did evil in the eyes of the LORD our God and forsook him. They turned their faces away from the LORD's dwelling place and turned their backs on him. ⁷They also shut the doors of the portico and put out the lamps. They did not burn incense or present any burnt offerings at the sanctuary to the God of Israel. ⁸Therefore, the anger of the LORD has fallen on Judah and Jerusalem; he has made them an object of dread and horror^s and scorn,^t as you can see with your own eyes. ⁹This is why our fathers have fallen by the sword and why our sons and daughters and our wives are in captivity.^u ¹⁰Now I intend to make a covenant^v with the LORD, the God of Israel, so that his fierce anger will turn away from us. ¹¹My sons, do not be negligent now, for the LORD has chosen you to stand before him and serve him,^w to minister^x before him and to burn incense."

¹²Then these Levites^y set to work:

from the Kohathites,
    Mahath son of Amasai and Joel son of Azariah;
from the Merarites,
    Kish son of Abdi and Azariah son of Jehallelel;
from the Gershonites,
    Joah son of Zimmah and Eden^z son of Joah;
¹³from the descendants of Elizaphan,
    Shimri and Jeiel;
from the descendants of Asaph,^a
    Zechariah and Mattaniah;
¹⁴from the descendants of Heman,
    Jehiel and Shimei;
from the descendants of Jeduthun,
    Shemaiah and Uzziel.

¹⁵When they had assembled their brothers and consecrated themselves, they went in to purify^b the temple of the LORD, as the king had ordered, following the word of the LORD. ¹⁶The priests went into the sanctuary of the LORD to purify it. They brought out to the courtyard of the LORD's temple everything unclean that they found in the temple of the LORD. The Levites took it and carried it out to the Kidron Valley.^c ¹⁷They began the consecration on the first day of the first month, and by the eighth day of the month they reached the portico of the LORD. For eight more days they consecrated the temple of the LORD itself, finishing on the sixteenth day of the first month.

¹⁸Then they went in to King Hezekiah and reported: "We have purified the entire temple of the LORD, the altar of burnt offering with all its utensils, and the table for setting out the consecrated bread, with all its articles. ¹⁹We have prepared and consecrated all the articles^d that King Ahaz removed in his unfaithfulness while he was king. They are now in front of the LORD's altar."

²⁰Early the next morning King Hezekiah gathered the city officials together and went up to the temple of the LORD. ²¹They brought seven bulls, seven rams, seven male lambs and seven male goats as a sin offering^e for the kingdom, for the sanctu-

---

2 Chronicles 29:1–36

The proper worship of God was an immediate priority for Hezekiah as he initiated the cleansing of the temple in his first month of rule (v. 3) and celebrated the religious festivals in his second (30:2). The acts of reopening the temple doors shut up by King Ahaz (28:24) and repairing them were symbolic, indicating that the temple was once again serviceable for worship. Hezekiah humbly identified with the past sins of his people. In advocating covenant renewal, he was almost a Moses-

type figure, acting as intercessor for the nation (v. 10; cf. Ex. 32:9–14,30–32).

The rejoicing reported upon the reestablishment of the temple celebrated the rescue of the people of Judah by God, since they realized they had come perilously close to sharing the fate of the northern kingdom, which had been destroyed by the Assyrians seven years earlier. That the restoration of temple worship was truly an act of God was seen in the fact that it was accomplished so quickly (v. 36).

ary and for Judah. The king commanded the priests, the descendants of Aaron, to offer these on the altar of the Lord. ²²So they slaughtered the bulls, and the priests took the blood and sprinkled it on the altar; next they slaughtered the rams and sprinkled their blood on the altar; then they slaughtered the lambs and sprinkled their blood[f] on the altar. ²³The goats for the sin offering were brought before the king and the assembly, and they laid their hands[g] on them. ²⁴The priests then slaughtered the goats and presented their blood on the altar for a sin offering to atone[h] for all Israel, because the king had ordered the burnt offering and the sin offering for all Israel.

²⁵He stationed the Levites in the temple of the Lord with cymbals, harps and lyres in the way prescribed by David[i] and Gad[j] the king's seer and Nathan the prophet; this was commanded by the Lord through his prophets. ²⁶So the Levites stood ready with David's instruments,[k] and the priests with their trumpets.[l]

²⁷Hezekiah gave the order to sacrifice the burnt offering on the altar. As the offering began, singing to the Lord began also, accompanied by trumpets and the instruments[m] of David king of Israel. ²⁸The whole assembly bowed in worship, while the singers sang and the trumpeters played. All this continued until the sacrifice of the burnt offering was completed.

²⁹When the offerings were finished, the king and everyone present with him knelt down and worshiped.[n] ³⁰King Hezekiah and his officials ordered the Levites to praise the Lord with the words of David and of Asaph the seer. So they sang praises with gladness and bowed their heads and worshiped.

³¹Then Hezekiah said, "You have now dedicated yourselves to the Lord. Come and bring sacrifices[o] and thank offerings to the temple of the Lord." So the assembly brought sacrifices and thank offerings, and all whose hearts were willing[p] brought burnt offerings.

³²The number of burnt offerings the assembly brought was seventy bulls, a hundred rams and two hundred male lambs—all of them for burnt offerings to the Lord. ³³The animals consecrated as sacrifices amounted to six hundred bulls and three thousand sheep and goats. ³⁴The priests, however, were too few to skin all the burnt offerings;[q] so their kinsmen the Levites helped them until the task was finished and until other priests had been consecrated,[r] for the Levites had been more conscientious in consecrating themselves than the priests had been. ³⁵There were burnt offerings in abundance, together with the fat[s] of the fellowship offerings[a][t] and the drink offerings[u] that accompanied the burnt offerings.

So the service of the temple of the Lord was reestablished. ³⁶Hezekiah and all the people rejoiced at what God had brought about for his people, because it was done so quickly.

Hezekiah Celebrates the Passover

30 Hezekiah sent word to all Israel and Judah and also wrote letters to Ephraim and Manasseh,[v] inviting them to come to the temple of the Lord in Jerusalem and celebrate the Passover[w] to the Lord, the God of Israel. ²The king and his officials and the whole assembly in Jerusalem decided to celebrate[x] the Passover in the second month. ³They had not been able to celebrate it at the regular time be-

---

^a 35 Traditionally *peace offerings*

Cross references (margin):

29:22
f Lev 4:18

29:23
g Lev 4:15
29:24
h Ex 29:36;
Lev 4:26

29:25
i 1Ch 25:6;
2Ch 8:14
j 1Sa 22:5;
2Sa 24:11
29:26
k 1Ch 15:16
l 1Ch 15:24; 23:5;
2Ch 5:12
29:27
m 2Ch 23:18

29:29
n 2Ch 20:18

29:31
o Heb 13:15-16
p Ex 25:2; 35:22

29:34
q 2Ch 35:11
r 2Ch 30:3, 15

29:35
s Ex 29:13; Lev 3:16
t Lev 7:11-21
u Nu 15:5-10

30:1
v Ge 41:52
w Ex 12:11;
Nu 28:16
30:2
x Nu 9:10

Like Hezekiah, the leaders of Christ's church are called to identify with and intercede for God's people. But this need and calling can't be limited to leaders. God's words in 2 Chronicles 7:14 apply to us all: "If my *people* [emphasis added], who are called by my name, will humble themselves and pray and seek my face and turn from their wicked ways, then will I hear from heaven and will forgive their sin and will heal their land." Is such prayer included in your devotional life?

2 Chronicles 30:1—31:1

The Chronicler emphasized Hezekiah's role in the initiative to reunite Israel and Judah through worship at God's chosen and consecrated site. Hezekiah's letters were sent throughout Israel, from Beersheba in the south to Dan in the north (v. 5), signifying the king's desire to rejoin the tribes (i.e., Judah and those Israelites who had survived the Assyrian invasion) after the collapse of the northern kingdom. Many in Israel spurned the invitation, but the overwhelming response of the Judahites was a remarkable demonstration of solidarity which the Chronicler attributed to the "hand of God" on the people (v. 12).

30:3
y 2Ch 29:34

30:5
z Jdg 20:1

cause not enough priests had consecrated[y] themselves and the people had not assembled in Jerusalem. [4]The plan seemed right both to the king and to the whole assembly. [5]They decided to send a proclamation throughout Israel, from Beersheba to Dan,[z] calling the people to come to Jerusalem and celebrate the Passover to the LORD, the God of Israel. It had not been celebrated in large numbers according to what was written.

[6]At the king's command, couriers went throughout Israel and Judah with letters from the king and from his officials, which read:

30:7
a Ps 78:8,57; 106:6;
Eze 20:18
b 2Ch 29:8
30:8
c Ex 32:9
d Nu 25:4;
2Ch 29:10

30:9
e Dt 30:2-5;
Isa 1:16; 55:7
f 1Ki 8:50;
Ps 106:46
g Ex 34:6-7;
Dt 4:31; Mic 7:18

"People of Israel, return to the LORD, the God of Abraham, Isaac and Israel, that he may return to you who are left, who have escaped from the hand of the kings of Assyria. [7]Do not be like your fathers[a] and brothers, who were unfaithful to the LORD, the God of their fathers, so that he made them an object of horror,[b] as you see. [8]Do not be stiff-necked,[c] as your fathers were; submit to the LORD. Come to the sanctuary, which he has consecrated forever. Serve the LORD your God, so that his fierce anger[d] will turn away from you. [9]If you return[e] to the LORD, then your brothers and your children will be shown compassion[f] by their captors and will come back to this land, for the LORD your God is gracious and compassionate.[g] He will not turn his face from you if you return to him."

30:10
h 2Ch 36:16
30:11
i ver 25
30:12
j Jer 32:39;
Eze 11:19;
Php 2:13

[10]The couriers went from town to town in Ephraim and Manasseh, as far as Zebulun, but the people scorned and ridiculed[h] them. [11]Nevertheless, some men of Asher, Manasseh and Zebulun humbled themselves and went to Jerusalem.[i] [12]Also in Judah the hand of God was on the people to give them unity[j] of mind to carry out what the king and his officials had ordered, following the word of the LORD.

30:13
k Nu 28:16
30:14
l 2Ch 28:24
m 2Sa 15:23
30:15
n 2Ch 29:34

[13]A very large crowd of people assembled in Jerusalem to celebrate the Feast of Unleavened Bread[k] in the second month. [14]They removed the altars[l] in Jerusalem and cleared away the incense altars and threw them into the Kidron Valley.[m]

30:16
o 2Ch 35:10

30:17
p 2Ch 29:34

[15]They slaughtered the Passover lamb on the fourteenth day of the second month. The priests and the Levites were ashamed and consecrated[n] themselves and brought burnt offerings to the temple of the LORD. [16]Then they took up their regular positions[o] as prescribed in the Law of Moses the man of God. The priests sprinkled the blood handed to them by the Levites. [17]Since many in the crowd had not consecrated themselves, the Levites had to kill[p] the Passover lambs for all those who were not ceremonially clean and could not consecrate ⌊their lambs⌋ to the LORD. [18]Although most of the many people who came from Ephraim, Manasseh, Issachar and Zebulun had not purified themselves,[q] yet they ate the Passover, contrary to what was written. But Hezekiah prayed for them, saying, "May the LORD, who is good, pardon everyone [19]who sets his heart on seeking God—the LORD, the God of his fathers—even if he is not clean according to the rules of the sanctuary." [20]And the LORD heard[r] Hezekiah and healed[s] the people.[t]

30:18
q Ex 12:43-49;
Nu 9:6-10

30:20
r 2Ch 6:20
s 2Ch 7:14; Mal 4:2
t Jas 5:16
30:21
u Ex 12:15,17; 13:6

[21]The Israelites who were present in Jerusalem celebrated the Feast of Unleavened Bread[u] for seven days with great rejoicing, while the Levites and priests sang to the LORD every day, accompanied by the LORD's instruments of praise.[a]

[22]Hezekiah spoke encouragingly to all the Levites, who showed good understanding of the service of the LORD. For the seven days they ate their assigned portion and offered fellowship offerings[b] and praised the LORD, the God of their fathers.

30:23
v 1Ki 8:65; 2Ch 7:9

[23]The whole assembly then agreed to celebrate[v] the festival seven more days; so for another seven days they celebrated joyfully. [24]Hezekiah king of Judah provid-

---

[a] 21 Or *priests praised the LORD every day with resounding instruments belonging to the LORD*
[b] 22 Traditionally *peace offerings*

The Chronicler portrayed Hezekiah as an encourager (cf. 29:5,11,31; 30:6,22; 31:8; 32:6–8). The New Testament values encouragement as a Christian virtue because it serves to buoy up the timid in Christ's service (1 Thess. 5:14; 2 Tim. 1:3–7). An encourager also contributes to the spiritual health of fellow believers in that consistent mutual encouragement motivates discipleship and prevents the heart from being hardened by sin's deceitfulness (Heb. 3:12–13; 10:24–25). Who has built you up in your Christian life? Who can you encourage today?

ed[w] a thousand bulls and seven thousand sheep and goats for the assembly, and the officials provided them with a thousand bulls and ten thousand sheep and goats. A great number of priests consecrated themselves. 25The entire assembly of Judah rejoiced, along with the priests and Levites and all who had assembled from Israel[x], including the aliens who had come from Israel and those who lived in Judah. 26There was great joy in Jerusalem, for since the days of Solomon[y] son of David king of Israel there had been nothing like this in Jerusalem. 27The priests and the Levites stood to bless[z] the people, and God heard them, for their prayer reached heaven, his holy dwelling place.

31 When all this had ended, the Israelites who were there went out to the towns of Judah, smashed the sacred stones and cut down[a] the Asherah poles. They destroyed the high places and the altars throughout Judah and Benjamin and in Ephraim and Manasseh. After they had destroyed all of them, the Israelites returned to their own towns and to their own property.

Contributions for Worship

2Hezekiah[b] assigned the priests and Levites to divisions[c]—each of them according to their duties as priests or Levites—to offer burnt offerings and fellowship offerings,[a] to minister,[d] to give thanks and to sing praises[e] at the gates of the LORD's dwelling.[f] 3The king contributed[g] from his own possessions for the morning and evening burnt offerings and for the burnt offerings on the Sabbaths, New Moons and appointed feasts as written in the Law of the LORD.[h] 4He ordered the people living in Jerusalem to give the portion[i] due the priests and Levites so they could devote themselves to the Law of the LORD. 5As soon as the order went out, the Israelites generously gave the firstfruits[j] of their grain, new wine,[k] oil and honey and all that the fields produced. They brought a great amount, a tithe of everything. 6The men of Israel and Judah who lived in the towns of Judah also brought a tithe[l] of their herds and flocks and a tithe of the holy things dedicated to the LORD their God, and they piled them in heaps.[m] 7They began doing this in the third month and finished in the seventh month.[n] 8When Hezekiah and his officials came and saw the heaps, they praised the LORD and blessed[o] his people Israel.

9Hezekiah asked the priests and Levites about the heaps; 10and Azariah the chief priest, from the family of Zadok,[p] answered, "Since the people began to bring their contributions to the temple of the LORD, we have had enough to eat and plenty to spare, because the LORD has blessed his people, and this great amount is left over."[q]

11Hezekiah gave orders to prepare storerooms in the temple of the LORD, and this was done. 12Then they faithfully brought in the contributions, tithes and dedicated gifts. Conaniah,[r] a Levite, was in charge of these things, and his brother Shimei was next in rank. 13Jehiel, Azaziah, Nahath, Asahel, Jerimoth, Jozabad,[s] Eliel, Ismakiah, Mahath and Benaiah were supervisors under Conaniah and Shimei his

---

[a] 2 Traditionally *peace offerings*

30:24
w 1Ki 8:5;
2Ch 29:34; 35:7;
Ezr 6:17; 8:35

30:25
x ver 11
30:26
y 2Ch 7:8

30:27
z Ex 39:43;
Nu 6:23; Dt 26:15;
2Ch 23:18; Ps 68:5

31:1
a 2Ki 18:4;
2Ch 32:12; Isa 36:7

31:2
b 2Ch 29:9
c 1Ch 24:1
d 1Ch 15:2
e Ps 7:17; 9:2; 47:6;
71:22 f
31:3
g 1Ch 29:3;
2Ch 35:7;
Eze 45:17
h Nu 28:1-29:40
31:4
i Nu 18:8; Dt 18:8;
Ne 13:10; Mal 2:7
31:5
j Nu 18:12,24;
Ne 13:12;
Eze 44:30
k Dt 12:17
31:6
l Lev 27:30;
Ne 13:10-12
m Dt 14:28; Ru 3:7
31:7
n Ex 23:16
31:8
o Ps 144:13-15
31:10
p 2Sa 8:17
q Eze 36:5;
Eze 44:30;
Mal 3:10-12

31:12
r 2Ch 35:9
31:13
s 2Ch 35:9

---

2 Chronicles 31:2–21

Hezekiah reinstated the system of tithes and offerings designed both to worship God and to financially underwrite the ministry of the priests and Levites (cf. Lev. 6:14—7:36; Num. 18:8–32; Deut. 14:27–29). These reforms were necessary because presumably the priestly orders devoted to the sacrificial liturgy and the Levitical divisions assigned to various ministries had been abolished when Ahaz had closed the temple (2 Chron. 28:24).

The Chronicler associated Hezekiah's blessing of the people in verse 10 with those of David and Solomon (cf. 1 Chron. 16:2; 2 Chron. 6:3); compared the people's generous giving with the overflow of contributions collected for the building of the tabernacle and the temple

(cf. Ex. 36:2–7; 1 Chron. 29:6–9); and reported that the bounty of goods received was inventoried, stored, maintained, and distributed with equity among the families of the priests and Levites.

How often have you met individuals who have left the pastorate for some other line of employment? If you have felt comfortable drilling down a bit further, you may have learned that lack of financial remuneration and consequent family hardship had made their situations as parish pastors untenable. Many others are forced into part- or full-time employment over and above their ministry positions. God's provisions for the livelihoods of the Old Testament priests and Levites says something about our care for ministers in our churches today.

brother, by appointment of King Hezekiah and Azariah the official in charge of the temple of God.

¹⁴Kore son of Imnah the Levite, keeper of the East Gate, was in charge of the freewill offerings given to God, distributing the contributions made to the LORD and also the consecrated gifts. ¹⁵Eden,^t Miniamin, Jeshua, Shemaiah, Amariah and Shecaniah assisted him faithfully in the towns^u of the priests, distributing to their fellow priests according to their divisions, old and young alike.

¹⁶In addition, they distributed to the males three years old or more whose names were in the genealogical records^v—all who would enter the temple of the LORD to perform the daily duties of their various tasks, according to their responsibilities and their divisions. ¹⁷And they distributed to the priests enrolled by their families in the genealogical records and likewise to the Levites twenty years old or more, according to their responsibilities and their divisions. ¹⁸They included all the little ones, the wives, and the sons and daughters of the whole community listed in these genealogical records. For they were faithful in consecrating themselves.

¹⁹As for the priests, the descendants of Aaron, who lived on the farm lands around their towns or in any other towns,^w men were designated by name to distribute portions to every male among them and to all who were recorded in the genealogies of the Levites.

²⁰This is what Hezekiah did throughout Judah, doing what was good and right and faithful^x before the LORD his God. ²¹In everything that he undertook in the service of God's temple and in obedience to the law and the commands, he sought his God and worked wholeheartedly. And so he prospered.^y

Sennacherib Threatens Jerusalem

32 After all that Hezekiah had so faithfully done, Sennacherib^z king of Assyria came and invaded Judah. He laid siege to the fortified cities, thinking to conquer them for himself. ²When Hezekiah saw that Sennacherib had come and that he intended to make war on Jerusalem,^a ³he consulted with his officials and military staff about blocking off the water from the springs outside the city, and they helped him. ⁴A large force of men assembled, and they blocked all the springs^b and the stream that flowed through the land. "Why should the kings^a of Assyria come and find plenty of water?" they said. ⁵Then he worked hard repairing all the broken sections of the wall^c and building towers on it. He built another wall outside that one and reinforced the supporting terraces^{b d} of the City of David. He also made large numbers of weapons^e and shields.

⁶He appointed military officers over the people and assembled them before him in the square at the city gate and encouraged them with these words: ⁷"Be strong and courageous.^f Do not be afraid or discouraged^g because of the king of Assyria and the vast army with him, for there is a greater power with us than with him.^h ⁸With him is only the arm of flesh,ⁱ but with us^j is the LORD our God to help us and to fight our battles."^k And the people gained confidence from what Hezekiah the king of Judah said.

⁹Later, when Sennacherib king of Assyria and all his forces were laying siege to Lachish,^l he sent his officers to Jerusalem with this message for Hezekiah king of Judah and for all the people of Judah who were there:

^a 4 Hebrew; Septuagint and Syriac *king*   ^b 5 Or *the Millo*

Cross references

31:15
t 2Ch 29:12
u Jos 21:9-19

31:16
v 1Ch 23:3; Ezr 3:4

31:19
w ver 12-15;
Lev 25:34;
Nu 35:2-5

31:20
x 2Ki 20:3; 22:2

31:21
y Dt 29:9

32:1
z 2Ki 18:13-19;
Isa 36:1; 37:9,17,37

32:2
a Isa 22:7; Jer 1:15

32:4
b 2Ki 18:17; 20:20;
Isa 22:9,11;
Na 3:14

32:5
c 2Ch 25:23;
Isa 22:10
d 1Ki 9:24;
1Ch 11:8 e Isa 22:8

32:7
f Dt 31:6;
1Ch 22:13
g 2Ch 20:15
h Nu 14:9; 2Ki 6:16
32:8
i Job 40:9;
Isa 52:10; Jer 17:5;
32:21 j Dt 3:22;
1Sa 17:45;
2Ch 13:12
k 1Ch 5:22;
2Ch 20:17; Ps 20:7;
Isa 28:6
32:9
l Jos 10:3,31

---

2 Chronicles 32:1–23

Sennacherib's invasion of Judah was one of the most critical events in the history of the southern kingdom. The Chronicler assumed a thorough knowledge on the part of his audience of the earlier parallel accounts in 2 Kings 18–19 and Isaiah 36–37. The Assyrian campaign occurred in 701 B.C., during the 14th year of Hezekiah's reign (2 Kings 18:13). The Chronicler's summary of the invasion largely consisted of two speeches,

one by Hezekiah (vv. 7–8) and one by an officer of Sennacherib's army (vv. 10–15). This was followed by the report of a joint prayer by Hezekiah and Isaiah (v. 20).

Hezekiah's words proved true: God's power was greater than that of the Assyrians, and he had indeed fought the battle for Judah. The expression in verse 22, "He took care of them on every side" (lit., "He gave them rest round about"), is shorthand in Chronicles for blessing as a reward for faithfulness (cf. 15:15; 20:30).

10 "This is what Sennacherib king of Assyria says: On what are you basing your confidence,[m] that you remain in Jerusalem under siege? 11 When Hezekiah says, 'The LORD our God will save us from the hand of the king of Assyria,' he is misleading[n] you, to let you die of hunger and thirst. 12 Did not Hezekiah himself remove this god's high places and altars, saying to Judah and Jerusalem, 'You must worship before one altar[o] and burn sacrifices on it'?

13 "Do you not know what I and my fathers have done to all the peoples of the other lands? Were the gods of those nations ever able to deliver their land from my hand?[p] 14 Who of all the gods of these nations that my fathers destroyed has been able to save his people from me? How then can your god deliver you from my hand? 15 Now do not let Hezekiah deceive[q] you and mislead you like this. Do not believe him, for no god of any nation or kingdom has been able to deliver[r] his people from my hand or the hand of my fathers.[s] How much less will your god deliver you from my hand!"

16 Sennacherib's officers spoke further against the LORD God and against his servant Hezekiah. 17 The king also wrote letters[t] insulting[u] the LORD, the God of Israel, and saying this against him: "Just as the gods[v] of the peoples of the other lands did not rescue their people from my hand, so the god of Hezekiah will not rescue his people from my hand." 18 Then they called out in Hebrew to the people of Jerusalem who were on the wall, to terrify them and make them afraid in order to capture the city. 19 They spoke about the God of Jerusalem as they did about the gods of the other peoples of the world—the work of men's hands.[w]

20 King Hezekiah and the prophet Isaiah son of Amoz cried out in prayer to heaven about this. 21 And the LORD sent an angel,[x] who annihilated all the fighting men and the leaders and officers in the camp of the Assyrian king. So he withdrew to his own land in disgrace. And when he went into the temple of his god, some of his sons cut him down with the sword.[y]

22 So the LORD saved Hezekiah and the people of Jerusalem from the hand of Sennacherib king of Assyria and from the hand of all others. He took care of them[a] on every side. 23 Many brought offerings to Jerusalem for the LORD and valuable gifts[z] for Hezekiah king of Judah. From then on he was highly regarded by all the nations.

Hezekiah's Pride, Success and Death

24 In those days Hezekiah became ill and was at the point of death. He prayed to the LORD, who answered him and gave him a miraculous sign. 25 But Hezekiah's heart was proud[a] and he did not respond to the kindness shown him; therefore the LORD's wrath[b] was on him and on Judah and Jerusalem. 26 Then Hezekiah repented[c] of the pride of his heart, as did the people of Jerusalem; therefore the LORD's wrath did not come upon them during the days of Hezekiah.[d]

[a] 22 Hebrew; Septuagint and Vulgate *He gave them rest*

Cross references
32:10 [m] Eze 29:16
32:11 [n] Isa 37:10
32:12 [o] 2Ch 31:1
32:13 [p] ver 15
32:15 [q] Isa 37:10 [r] Da 3:15 [s] Ex 5:2
32:17 [t] Isa 37:14 [u] Ps 74:22; Isa 37:4,17 [v] 2Ki 19:12
32:19 [w] 2Ki 19:18; Ps 115:4-8; Isa 2:8; 17:8
32:21 [x] Ge 19:13 [y] 2Ki 19:7
32:23 [z] 2Ch 9:24; 17:5; Isa 45:14; Zec 14:16-17
32:25 [a] 2Ki 14:10; 2Ch 26:16 [b] 2Ch 19:2; 24:18
32:26 [c] Jer 26:18-19 [d] 2Ch 34:27,28; Isa 39:8

What comfort does it afford you to think of God taking care of you "on every side"? Of your not having to look back over your shoulder for the aftermath of troubles from the past, "both ways" as you enter the daily traffic of life for unforeseen threats, or into the murky distance for unpleasant surprises lurking there? Problems and tragedies will, of course, come your way—they are an inevitable component of human life—but God is greater than any of them. So relax, and allow him today to give you "rest round about."

2 Chronicles 32:24–33

Hezekiah's "success" (v. 30) may have included God's reward for overcoming the circumstances of God's testing in his life (v. 31; see 2 Kings 20 and notes there for additional background information). Divine testing is a recurrent Old Testament theme, but not because God

needs to know the intents of the human heart. Rather, he tests the hearts of his servants so that they may respond to him in complete faith as a result of the discernment emerging from this kind of self-knowledge (cf. Deut. 8:2–3).

How would I respond in a similar situation? we sometimes ask when misfortune, temptation, or tragedy enters someone else's life. If we have never been under similar circumstances, we might doubt the degree of our faith or our ability to withstand such pressure. There are times when a crisis situation—a job loss, the necessity of a frightening risk or difficult decision—forces us out of our comfort zone. The results, including our gain in self-knowledge, are often pleasantly surprising. We might not be able with certainty to identify the situation as God's testing, but this is one possible reason for our suffering.

32:27
e 1Ch 29:12

32:29
f 1Ch 29:12
32:30
g 2Ki 18:17
h 1Ki 1:33
32:31
i Isa 39:1 j ver 24;
Isa 38:7 k Ge 22:1;
Dt 8:16

27 Hezekiah had very great riches and honor,[e] and he made treasuries for his silver and gold and for his precious stones, spices, shields and all kinds of valuables. 28 He also made buildings to store the harvest of grain, new wine and oil; and he made stalls for various kinds of cattle, and pens for the flocks. 29 He built villages and acquired great numbers of flocks and herds, for God had given him very great riches.[f]

30 It was Hezekiah who blocked[g] the upper outlet of the Gihon[h] spring and channeled the water down to the west side of the City of David. He succeeded in everything he undertook. 31 But when envoys were sent by the rulers of Babylon[i] to ask him about the miraculous sign[j] that had occurred in the land, God left him to test[k] him and to know everything that was in his heart.

32 The other events of Hezekiah's reign and his acts of devotion are written in the vision of the prophet Isaiah son of Amoz in the book of the kings of Judah and Israel. 33 Hezekiah rested with his fathers and was buried on the hill where the tombs of David's descendants are. All Judah and the people of Jerusalem honored him when he died. And Manasseh his son succeeded him as king.

Manasseh King of Judah

33:1
l 1Ch 3:13
33:2
m Jer 15:4
n Dt 18:9; 2Ch 28:3

33:3
o Dt 16:21-22
p Dt 17:3; 2Ch 31:1

33:4
q 2Ch 7:16
33:5
r 2Ch 4:9
33:6
s Lev 18:21;
Dt 18:10; 2Ch 28:3
t Lev 19:31
u 1Sa 28:13
33:7
v 2Ch 7:16

33:8
w 2Sa 7:10

33:9
x Jer 15:4

33:11
y Dt 28:36
z Ps 149:8

33:12
a 2Ch 6:37; 32:26;
1Pe 5:6

33 Manasseh[l] was twelve years old when he became king, and he reigned in Jerusalem fifty-five years. 2 He did evil in the eyes of the LORD,[m] following the detestable[n] practices of the nations the LORD had driven out before the Israelites. 3 He rebuilt the high places his father Hezekiah had demolished; he also erected altars to the Baals and made Asherah poles.[o] He bowed down[p] to all the starry hosts and worshiped them. 4 He built altars in the temple of the LORD, of which the LORD had said, "My Name[q] will remain in Jerusalem forever." 5 In both courts of the temple of the LORD,[r] he built altars to all the starry hosts. 6 He sacrificed his sons[s] in[a] the fire in the Valley of Ben Hinnom, practiced sorcery, divination and witchcraft, and consulted mediums[t] and spiritists.[u] He did much evil in the eyes of the LORD, provoking him to anger.

7 He took the carved image he had made and put it in God's temple,[v] of which God had said to David and to his son Solomon, "In this temple and in Jerusalem, which I have chosen out of all the tribes of Israel, I will put my Name forever. 8 I will not again make the feet of the Israelites leave the land[w] I assigned to your forefathers, if only they will be careful to do everything I commanded them concerning all the laws, decrees and ordinances given through Moses." 9 But Manasseh led Judah and the people of Jerusalem astray, so that they did more evil than the nations the LORD had destroyed before the Israelites.[x]

10 The LORD spoke to Manasseh and his people, but they paid no attention. 11 So the LORD brought against them the army commanders of the king of Assyria, who took Manasseh prisoner,[y] put a hook in his nose, bound him with bronze shackles[z] and took him to Babylon. 12 In his distress he sought the favor of the LORD his God and humbled[a] himself greatly before the God of his fathers. 13 And when he prayed to him, the LORD was moved by his entreaty and listened to his plea; so he brought him back to Jerusalem and to his kingdom. Then Manasseh knew that the LORD is God.

___

a 6 Or *He made his sons pass through*

___

2 Chronicles 33:1–20

Trouble frequently came upon God's Old Testament people to punish and/or purify them. Unlike Ahaz, Manasseh turned to God in his distress (v. 12; cf. 28:22). The expression "seek the favor" (lit., "soften the face") is found in the intercessory prayers of Moses, Hezekiah, and Daniel (cf. Ex. 32:11; Jer. 26:19; Dan. 9:13). The report of Manasseh's genuine repentance and prayer of forgiveness reminds us of the language of God's promise to Solomon to restore those who "humble themselves and pray" (2 Chron. 7:14).

The story of Manasseh's repentance foreshadowed that of the believing thief on the cross (Luke 23:40–43). Both illustrate that the God of the Bible forgives sin and that his door of salvation and restoration is always open. Both Testaments portray God as gracious, merciful, compassionate, and slow to anger—not desiring that anyone should perish (Ex. 34:6–7; Ezek. 18:32; John 3:16; 2 Peter 3:9). This knowledge can be both an encouragement and a motivator for those involved in ministry/mission endeavors.

14Afterward he rebuilt the outer wall of the City of David, west of the Gihon[b] spring in the valley, as far as the entrance of the Fish Gate[c] and encircling the hill of Ophel;[d] he also made it much higher. He stationed military commanders in all the fortified cities in Judah.

15He got rid of the foreign gods and removed[e] the image from the temple of the LORD, as well as all the altars he had built on the temple hill and in Jerusalem; and he threw them out of the city. 16Then he restored the altar of the LORD and sacrificed fellowship offerings[a] and thank offerings[f] on it, and told Judah to serve the LORD, the God of Israel. 17The people, however, continued to sacrifice at the high places, but only to the LORD their God.

18The other events of Manasseh's reign, including his prayer to his God and the words the seers spoke to him in the name of the LORD, the God of Israel, are written in the annals of the kings of Israel.[b] 19His prayer and how God was moved by his entreaty, as well as all his sins and unfaithfulness, and the sites where he built high places and set up Asherah poles and idols before he humbled[g] himself—all are written in the records of the seers.[c][h] 20Manasseh rested with his fathers and was buried[i] in his palace. And Amon his son succeeded him as king.

Amon King of Judah

21Amon[j] was twenty-two years old when he became king, and he reigned in Jerusalem two years. 22He did evil in the eyes of the LORD, as his father Manasseh had done. Amon worshiped and offered sacrifices to all the idols Manasseh had made. 23But unlike his father Manasseh, he did not humble[k] himself before the LORD; Amon increased his guilt.

24Amon's officials conspired against him and assassinated him in his palace. 25Then the people[l] of the land killed all who had plotted against King Amon, and they made Josiah his son king in his place.

Josiah's Reforms

34 Josiah[m] was eight years old when he became king,[n] and he reigned in Jerusalem thirty-one years. 2He did what was right in the eyes of the LORD and walked in the ways of his father David,[o] not turning aside to the right or to the left.

3In the eighth year of his reign, while he was still young, he began to seek the God[p] of his father David. In his twelfth year he began to purge Judah and Jerusalem of high places, Asherah poles, carved idols and cast images. 4Under his direction the altars of the Baals were torn down; he cut to pieces the incense altars that were above them, and smashed the Asherah poles,[q] the idols and the images. These

33:14
b 1Ki 1:33 c Ne 3:3; 12:39; Zep 1:10
d 2Ch 27:3; Ne 3:26

33:15
e ver 3-7; 2Ki 23:12

33:16
f Lev 7:11-18

33:19
g 2Ch 6:37
h 2Ki 21:17
33:20
i 2Ki 21:18; 2Ch 21:20

33:21
j 1Ch 3:14

33:23
k ver 12; Ex 10:3; 2Ch 7:14; Ps 18:27; 147:6; Pr 3:34

33:25
l 2Ch 22:1

34:1
m 1Ch 3:14
n Zep 1:1
34:2
o 2Ch 29:2

34:3
p 1Ki 13:2; 1Ch 16:11; 2Ch 15:2; 33:17,22

34:4
q Ex 34:13

---

a 16 Traditionally *peace offerings*   b 18 That is, Judah, as frequently in 2 Chronicles
c 19 One Hebrew manuscript and Septuagint; most Hebrew manuscripts *of Hozai*

---

2 Chronicles 33:21–25

Unlike his father, Manasseh, Amon refused to humble himself and repent. As a result, he increased his guilt before God (v. 23). The Old Testament prophets promised restoration to those who would turn to God in repentance (cf. Isa. 59:20; Jer. 36:3; Hos. 14:1–4), while those who spurned God's mercy and rejected his forgiveness would experience judgment (Jer. 5:3–6; Ezek. 3:4–7). There is a foreshadowing of later New Testament teaching here when we consider the judgment Jesus would pronounce on Korazin, Bethsaida, and Capernaum for their failure to turn to God in repentance despite the miracles they had witnessed (Matt. 11:20–24).

Jesus declared in Matthew 11:20–24 that those cities that had witnessed most of his miracles but failed to believe and repent would be judged more harshly than others, like Sodom and Gomorrah (cf. Gen. 18:16—19:29), that could plead on the day of judgment a de-

gree of legitimate ignorance of God's will. Those of us who have grown up in "Christian" cultures do well to consider the many opportunities we (both personally and nationally) have been given for repentance and obedience. How will God judge us in comparison to, say, a remote people group with whom no one has ever shared the Good News?

2 Chronicles 34:1–13

The need for carpenters and builders indicates that the temple was in a serious state of disrepair. Blame for its "ruin" was placed on the kings of Judah (v. 11), perhaps going as far back as Ahaz. The Chronicler connected the success of the temple repairs to the faithfulness of the workers and the effective supervision of the Levites. The various roles filled by the Levites in the renovation project were in keeping with the wide-ranging duties David had assigned them (1 Chron. 25–26).

34:4
r Ex 32:20;
Lev 26:30;
2Ki 23:11; Mic 1:5
34:5
s 1Ki 13:2
34:7
t Ex 32:20;
2Ch 31:1

he broke to pieces and scattered over the graves of those who had sacrificed to them.[r] [5]He burned[s] the bones of the priests on their altars, and so he purged Judah and Jerusalem. [6]In the towns of Manasseh, Ephraim and Simeon, as far as Naphtali, and in the ruins around them, [7]he tore down the altars and the Asherah poles and crushed the idols to powder[t] and cut to pieces all the incense altars throughout Israel. Then he went back to Jerusalem.

[8]In the eighteenth year of Josiah's reign, to purify the land and the temple, he sent Shaphan son of Azaliah and Maaseiah the ruler of the city, with Joah son of Joahaz, the recorder, to repair the temple of the LORD his God.

34:9
u 1Ch 6:13;
2Ch 35:8

[9]They went to Hilkiah[u] the high priest and gave him the money that had been brought into the temple of God, which the Levites who were the doorkeepers had collected from the people of Manasseh, Ephraim and the entire remnant of Israel and from all the people of Judah and Benjamin and the inhabitants of Jerusalem. [10]Then they entrusted it to the men appointed to supervise the work on the LORD's temple. These men paid the workers who repaired and restored the temple. [11]They also gave money[v] to the carpenters and builders to purchase dressed stone, and timber for joists and beams for the buildings that the kings of Judah had allowed to fall into ruin.[w]

34:11
v 2Ch 24:12
w 2Ch 33:4-7

34:12
x 2Ki 12:15
y 1Ch 25:1

[12]The men did the work faithfully.[x] Over them to direct them were Jahath and Obadiah, Levites descended from Merari, and Zechariah and Meshullam, descended from Kohath. The Levites—all who were skilled in playing musical instruments—[y] [13]had charge of the laborers[z] and supervised all the workers from job to job. Some of the Levites were secretaries, scribes and doorkeepers.

34:13
z 1Ch 23:4

Comparing our own church buildings to the temple is an "apples to oranges" assessment, since God's special presence is no longer limited to a specific place. Yet the upkeep of our sanctuaries says something about our priorities and our degree of reverence for and appreciation of our Lord. Whether we worship in a clapboard building or a cathedral, we can do our part to ensure that our own "house of God" adequately reflects his honor and glory. How much more does our kindness and care for others signify respect for the God who has given his Spirit to live in us!

Snapshots

34:3

Aleksandr Men

Aleksandr Vladimirovich Men (1935–1990), a Russian Orthodox priest, writer, and preacher, served for two decades as the main link between the Soviet intelligentsia and the Christian church. Born into a Jewish Christian family in Moscow during Stalin's reign of terror and baptized as an infant in the underground "Catacomb Church," Men adopted the priest of his childhood as a spiritual father, acquiring from him his orthodoxy and nonconformist courage.

Men brought hundreds into the church and influenced thousands by his books.

Expelled for his religious views two weeks before his university graduation in 1958, Men became a deacon and, in 1960, a priest. After serving several country parishes until 1970, he was appointed to a church near Moscow, which became a meeting place for Soviet intellectuals (many of them Jews) and a stronghold of Christianity. Men brought hundreds into the church and influenced thousands by his books, published outside Russia and circulated in secret from the early 70s.

During the years of *perestroika*, Gorbachev's program of economic, political, and social *restructuring begun in 1986*, Men preached to large audiences, drawing opposition in anti-ecumenical and anti-Semitic circles. His murder, on his way to church on September 9, 1990, remains unsolved.

(See "Here and Now" for 2 Chron. 36:11–14.)

The Book of the Law Found

¹⁴While they were bringing out the money that had been taken into the temple of the LORD, Hilkiah the priest found the Book of the Law of the LORD that had been given through Moses. ¹⁵Hilkiah said to Shaphan the secretary, "I have found the Book of the Law *a* in the temple of the LORD." He gave it to Shaphan.

¹⁶Then Shaphan took the book to the king and reported to him: "Your officials are doing everything that has been committed to them. ¹⁷They have paid out the money that was in the temple of the LORD and have entrusted it to the supervisors and workers." ¹⁸Then Shaphan the secretary informed the king, "Hilkiah the priest has given me a book." And Shaphan read from it in the presence of the king.

¹⁹When the king heard the words of the Law, *b* he tore *c* his robes. ²⁰He gave these orders to Hilkiah, Ahikam son of Shaphan *d*, Abdon son of Micah, *a* Shaphan the secretary and Asaiah the king's attendant: ²¹"Go and inquire of the LORD for me and for the remnant in Israel and Judah about what is written in this book that has been found. Great is the LORD's anger that is poured out *e* on us because our fathers have not kept the word of the LORD; they have not acted in accordance with all that is written in this book."

²²Hilkiah and those the king had sent with him *b* went to speak to the prophetess *f* Huldah, who was the wife of Shallum son of Tokhath, *c* the son of Hasrah, *d* keeper of the wardrobe. She lived in Jerusalem, in the Second District.

²³She said to them, "This is what the LORD, the God of Israel, says: Tell the man who sent you to me, ²⁴'This is what the LORD says: I am going to bring disaster *g* on this place and its people *h*—all the curses *i* written in the book that has been read in the presence of the king of Judah. ²⁵Because they have forsaken me *j* and burned incense to other gods and provoked me to anger by all that their hands have made, *e* my anger will be poured out on this place and will not be quenched.' ²⁶Tell the king of Judah, who sent you to inquire of the LORD, 'This is what the LORD, the God of Israel, says concerning the words you heard: ²⁷Because your heart was responsive *k* and you humbled *l* yourself before God when you heard what he spoke against this place and its people, and because you humbled yourself before me and tore your robes and wept in my presence, I have heard you, declares the LORD. ²⁸Now I will gather you to your fathers, *m* and you will be buried in peace. Your eyes will not see all the disaster I am going to bring on this place and on those who live here.' " *n*

So they took her answer back to the king.

²⁹Then the king called together all the elders of Judah and Jerusalem. ³⁰He went up to the temple of the LORD *o* with the men of Judah, the people of Jerusalem, the priests and the Levites—all the people from the least to the greatest. He read in their hearing all the words of the Book of the Covenant, which had been found in the temple of the LORD. ³¹The king stood by his pillar *p* and renewed the covenant *q* in the presence of the LORD—to follow *r* the LORD and keep his commands, regulations

34:15
a 2Ki 22:8; Ezr 7:6; Ne 8:1

34:19
b Dt 28:3-68
c Jos 7:6; Isa 36:22; 37:1
34:20
d 2Ki 22:3

34:21
e 2Ch 29:8; La 2:4; 4:11; Eze 36:18

34:22
f Ex 15:20; Ne 6:14

34:24
g Pr 16:4; Isa 3:9; Jer 40:2; 42:10; 44:2, 11
h 2Ch 36:14-20
i Dt 28:15-68
34:25
j 2Ch 33:3-6; Jer 22:9

34:27
k 2Ch 12:7; 32:26
l Ex 10:3; 2Ch 6:37

34:28
m 2Ch 35:20-25
n 2Ch 32:26

34:30
o 2Ki 23:2; Ne 8:1-3

34:31
p 1Ki 7:15; 2Ki 11:14
q 2Ki 11:17; 2Ch 23:16; 29:10
r Dt 13:4

---

a 20 Also called *Acbor son of Micaiah*   *b* 22 One Hebrew manuscript, Vulgate and Syriac; most Hebrew manuscripts do not have *had sent with him.*   *c* 22 Also called *Tikvah*   *d* 22 Also called *Harhas*   *e* 25 Or *by everything they have done*

---

2 Chronicles 34:14–33

The idea of God's grace extended to his disobedient people wasn't lost on the Chronicler. What God did in Israel through the covenant-renewal ceremonies of Asa, Hezekiah, and Josiah was "repeatable" history for the Jews in postexilic Judah—if they would humble themselves and pray and pledge covenant loyalty to God.

The "Book of the Law" (vv. 14,15), or "Book of the Covenant" (v. 30), was probably either the entire Pentateuch (first five books of the OT) or all or part of the book of Deuteronomy. It didn't in and of itself create change in Israel's corporate religious life. Spiritual re-

newal and true transformation, then and now, begins at the individual level, through the Spirit's power.

How easily do you take for granted the Bible's availability? You are reading one right now—most likely one of several in your possession. Chances are that particular passages at particular times move you as though you have never heard them before. But for the most part many of us find it difficult to lift our devotional life above the routine. Josiah was truly awed, amazed, and convicted upon hearing the words of Scripture. Why not ask God today to reach you as never before through his Word and Spirit, and to motivate you to share your treasure with those who have never heard?

and decrees with all his heart and all his soul, and to obey the words of the covenant written in this book. ³²Then he had everyone in Jerusalem and Benjamin pledge themselves to it; the people of Jerusalem did this in accordance with the covenant of God, the God of their fathers.

34:33
ˢ ver 3-7; Dt 18:9

³³Josiah removed all the detestable ˢ idols from all the territory belonging to the Israelites, and he had all who were present in Israel serve the LORD their God. As long as he lived, they did not fail to follow the LORD, the God of their fathers.

Josiah Celebrates the Passover

35:1
ᵗ Ex 12:1-30;
Nu 9:3; 28:16

35:3
ᵘ Dt 33:10;
1Ch 23:26;
2Ch 5:7; 17:7

35:4
ᵛ ver 10;
1Ch 9:10-13; 24:1;
2Ch 8:14; Ezr 6:18

35:6
ʷ Lev 11:44;
2Ch 29:5,15

35:7
ˣ 2Ch 30:24
ʸ 2Ch 31:3
35:8
ᶻ 1Ch 29:3;
2Ch 29:31-36
ᵃ 1Ch 6:13

35 Josiah celebrated the Passover ᵗ to the LORD in Jerusalem, and the Passover lamb was slaughtered on the fourteenth day of the first month. ²He appointed the priests to their duties and encouraged them in the service of the LORD's temple. ³He said to the Levites, who instructed ᵘ all Israel and who had been consecrated to the LORD: "Put the sacred ark in the temple that Solomon son of David king of Israel built. It is not to be carried about on your shoulders. Now serve the LORD your God and his people Israel. ⁴Prepare yourselves by families in your divisions, ᵛ according to the directions written by David king of Israel and by his son Solomon.

⁵"Stand in the holy place with a group of Levites for each subdivision of the families of your fellow countrymen, the lay people. ⁶Slaughter the Passover lambs, consecrate yourselves ʷ and prepare ⌞the lambs⌟ for your fellow countrymen, doing what the LORD commanded through Moses."

⁷Josiah provided for all the lay people who were there a total of thirty thousand sheep and goats for the Passover offerings, ˣ and also three thousand cattle—all from the king's own possessions. ʸ

⁸His officials also contributed ᶻ voluntarily to the people and the priests and Levites. Hilkiah, ᵃ Zechariah and Jehiel, the administrators of God's temple, gave the priests twenty-six hundred Passover offerings and three hundred cattle. ⁹Also Con-

---

2 Chronicles 35:1–19

The Passover was the most important religious festival for postexilic Judah and the high point of temple worship for the Chronicler. The reason for the prominence of this feast in the restoration community stemmed from the Passover observed after completion of the second temple in 516 B.C. (cf. Ezra 6:19–22) and the understanding that the return from Babylonian captivity was in a sense a "second exodus." The Passover celebration drew the Israelites back to their roots by reminding them that, as former slaves in Egypt, their life as

the people of God was grounded in God's redemptive act in the exodus.

The priests were responsible for slaughtering the lambs, sprinkling the blood on the altar, and sacrificing the burnt offerings. The Levites, meanwhile, were skinning and roasting the animals and serving the Passover meal to the people. The Levites not only served the people "quickly" (v. 13), as a reminder of the hasty meal eaten at the first Passover, but modeled eager servanthood by providing food for the priests, musicians, and gatekeepers, who remained on duty the entire day.

35:2

Encourage Others In the Lord's Service

Encouragement is a complex Christian virtue. It has elements of emotion and intellect, but it also must lead to action in order to move beyond simple compliments or cheerleading.

As Christians, we are to:

- encourage one another through exhortation (strong urging; motivating to meaningful action), inspiring others to follow God (Col. 1:28).

- feel good about helping others (2 Cor. 4:16–18).
- give others good reasons for hope (Josh. 1:8–9; 1 Peter 3:15).

- inspire others to do good, not evil (2 Chron. 22:2–3).
- do good things for those we wish to motivate (Isa. 35:3–4).

- determine to be encouraging, think about what will be heartening in a particular situation, and be willing to back up our words with helpful actions (Col. 4:7–8).

Some people, like Barnabas, are natural encouragers, people innately gifted in this area (Acts 4:36; cf. Rom. 12:8). But this doesn't let the rest of us off the hook. Encouragement is, after all, a byproduct of love, the cardinal Christian virtue. In Paul's words, "Love . . . always hopes, always perseveres" (1 Cor. 13:7). What can you do today to instill renewed hope and vision in another believer's heart, to inspire a disillusioned disciple to press on?

aniah[b] along with Shemaiah and Nethanel, his brothers, and Hashabiah, Jeiel and Jozabad,[c] the leaders of the Levites, provided five thousand Passover offerings and five hundred head of cattle for the Levites.

[10]The service was arranged and the priests stood in their places with the Levites in their divisions[d] as the king had ordered.[e] [11]The Passover lambs were slaughtered,[f] and the priests sprinkled the blood handed to them, while the Levites skinned the animals. [12]They set aside the burnt offerings to give them to the subdivisions of the families of the people to offer to the LORD, as is written in the Book of Moses. They did the same with the cattle. [13]They roasted the Passover animals over the fire as prescribed,[g] and boiled the holy offerings in pots, caldrons and pans and served them quickly to all the people. [14]After this, they made preparations for themselves and for the priests, because the priests, the descendants of Aaron, were sacrificing the burnt offerings and the fat portions[h] until nightfall. So the Levites made preparations for themselves and for the Aaronic priests.

[15]The musicians,[i] the descendants of Asaph, were in the places prescribed by David, Asaph, Heman and Jeduthun the king's seer. The gatekeepers at each gate did not need to leave their posts, because their fellow Levites made the preparations for them.

[16]So at that time the entire service of the LORD was carried out for the celebration of the Passover and the offering of burnt offerings on the altar of the LORD, as King Josiah had ordered. [17]The Israelites who were present celebrated the Passover at that time and observed the Feast of Unleavened Bread for seven days. [18]The Passover had not been observed like this in Israel since the days of the prophet Samuel; and none of the kings of Israel had ever celebrated such a Passover as did Josiah, with the priests, the Levites and all Judah and Israel who were there with the people of Jerusalem. [19]This Passover was celebrated in the eighteenth year of Josiah's reign.

The Death of Josiah

[20]After all this, when Josiah had set the temple in order, Neco king of Egypt went up to fight at Carchemish[j] on the Euphrates,[k] and Josiah marched out to meet him in battle. [21]But Neco sent messengers to him, saying, "What quarrel is there between you and me, O king of Judah? It is not you I am attacking at this time, but the house with which I am at war. God has told[l] me to hurry; so stop opposing God, who is with me, or he will destroy you."

[22]Josiah, however, would not turn away from him, but disguised[m] himself to engage him in battle. He would not listen to what Neco had said at God's command but went to fight him on the plain of Megiddo.

[23]Archers[n] shot King Josiah, and he told his officers, "Take me away; I am badly wounded." [24]So they took him out of his chariot, put him in the other chariot he had and brought him to Jerusalem, where he died. He was buried in the tombs of his fathers, and all Judah and Jerusalem mourned for him.

35:9
b 2Ch 31:12
c 2Ch 31:13

35:10
d ver 4; Ezr 6:18
e 2Ch 30:16
35:11
f 2Ch 29:22, 34; 30:17

35:13
g Ex 12:2-11; Lev 6:25; 1Sa 2:13-15

35:14
h Ex 29:13

35:15
i 1Ch 25:1; 26:12-19; 2Ch 29:30; Ne 12:46; Ps 68:25

35:20
j Isa 10:9; Jer 46:2
k Ge 2:14

35:21
l 1Ki 13:18; 2Ki 18:25
35:22
m Jdg 5:19; 1Sa 28:8; 2Ch 18:29

35:23
n 1Ki 22:34

📖 The Levites went above and beyond the call of duty during Josiah's Passover celebration, thereby causing the massive operation to run smoothly with no "casualties" in terms of the endurance of those directly involved. The church appreciates members who are willing to see work and jump in and help wherever needed. How many members of your church toil regularly behind the scenes to allow your worship and fellowship to move forward seamlessly? Which people are most likely to notice and fill in for unanticipated gaps? An encouraging word or a helping hand might be an appreciated morale boost for such willing servants.

2 Chronicles 35:20—36:1

📖 Key to the Chronicler's rendition of Josiah's death was the statement that Josiah "would not listen to what Neco had said at God's command" (v. 22). Previously, Josiah had been commended by Huldah the

prophetess for his responsiveness to God (34:27). Now he stood in opposition to God's word—to his own destruction. But how was Josiah to discern that the Egyptian king was delivering a message from God? We can only assume that, through the ministry of God's Spirit, Josiah could recognize the divine origin of the truth and authority of Neco's speech.

📖 Particularly when we face difficult decisions—whether or not to involve ourselves in a missions venture or leave a lucrative business position for a Christian service opportunity, for example—we strive sincerely to identify and follow God's leading. Assurance of God's will often eludes us, and well-intentioned advice may be conflicting or unhelpful. The best we can do at such times is to immerse ourselves in the Word and open our hearts to the Spirit's voice. Whether the decision is minor or momentous, God won't leave us clueless.

35:25
o Jer 22:10,15-16

25 Jeremiah composed laments for Josiah, and to this day all the men and women singers commemorate Josiah in the laments. *o* These became a tradition in Israel and are written in the Laments.

26 The other events of Josiah's reign and his acts of devotion, according to what is written in the Law of the LORD— 27 all the events, from beginning to end, are

36

written in the book of the kings of Israel and Judah. 1 And the people of the land took Jehoahaz son of Josiah and made him king in Jerusalem in place of his father.

Jehoahaz King of Judah

2 Jehoahaz *a* was twenty-three years old when he became king, and he reigned in Jerusalem three months. 3 The king of Egypt dethroned him in Jerusalem and imposed on Judah a levy of a hundred talents *b* of silver and a talent *c* of gold. 4 The king of Egypt made Eliakim, a brother of Jehoahaz, king over Judah and Jerusalem and changed Eliakim's name to Jehoiakim. But Neco *p* took Eliakim's brother Jehoahaz and carried him off to Egypt.

36:4
p Jer 22:10-12

Jehoiakim King of Judah

36:5
q Jer 22:18; 26:1; 35:1
36:6
r Jer 25:9; 27:6; Eze 29:18
s 2Ch 33:11; Eze 19:9; Da 1:1
36:7
t 2Ki 24:13; Ezr 1:7; Da 1:2

5 Jehoiakim *q* was twenty-five years old when he became king, and he reigned in Jerusalem eleven years. He did evil in the eyes of the LORD his God. 6 Nebuchadnezzar *r* king of Babylon attacked him and bound him with bronze shackles to take him to Babylon. *s* 7 Nebuchadnezzar also took to Babylon articles from the temple of the LORD and put them in his temple *d* there. *t*

8 The other events of Jehoiakim's reign, the detestable things he did and all that was found against him, are written in the book of the kings of Israel and Judah. And Jehoiachin his son succeeded him as king.

Jehoiachin King of Judah

36:9
u Jer 22:24-28; 52:31

9 Jehoiachin *u* was eighteen *e* years old when he became king, and he reigned in Jerusalem three months and ten days. He did evil in the eyes of the LORD. 10 In the

---

a 2 Hebrew *Joahaz*, a variant of *Jehoahaz*; also in verse 4   *b 3* That is, about 3 3/4 tons (about 3.4 metric tons)   *c 3* That is, about 75 pounds (about 34 kilograms)   *d 7* Or *palace*
e 9 One Hebrew manuscript, some Septuagint manuscripts and Syriac (see also 2 Kings 24:8); most Hebrew manuscripts *eight*

---

2 Chronicles 36:2–4

An alliance between Egypt and Assyria failed to save the disintegrating Assyrian Empire, but Pharaoh Neco's campaign (cf. 35:20–21) did result in Egyptian control of the area only much later known as Palestine. It's unclear whether Josiah had been obligated to oppose Neco as a vassal of Babylon or whether he had acted independently. Either way, his death marked the end of Judah's autonomy. Josiah's successor, his son Jehoahaz, was dethroned by Neco and deported to Egypt. Neco placed Eliakim (Jehoiakim) on the throne, and Judah became a vassal state to Egypt.

Has it ever struck you how often in the Old Testament a devout and effective leader was succeeded by a spineless, uncommitted, and evil son? The scenario repeats itself over and over again; in the case of Judah's monarchy, good and bad kings seem to have alternated without explanation. We wonder at the good kings arising from corrupt fathers and attribute this to God's inner *working*. But what about the corrupt leaders issuing from godly fathers? An explanation that makes us squirm is the possibility that these fathers were so caught up in their careers/ministries that child-rearing took second place.

2 Chronicles 36:5–8

When Babylon emerged as a new superpower in the region, Jehoiakim shifted his allegiance from Egypt and Judah became a vassal of Babylon. A subsequent stalemate between Babylon and Egypt afforded Jehoiakim the opportunity to throw off the yoke of vassalage and rebel against Nebuchadnezzar (see 2 Kings 24:1). Nebuchadnezzar retaliated and captured Jehoiakim, but it's uncertain whether he was actually able to take him to Babylon before Jehoiakim died (2 Chron. 36:6; cf. 2 Kings 24:6).

Jehoiakim played the odds in his allegiances with the superpowers of the day, but his lack of loyalty to God proved his undoing. If you are an American, do you find yourself relying on your nation's military power and feeling anxious about increasing reports of the lack of U.S. "popularity" among dubious allies? Equating God's "backing" with nationalistic zeal isn't justifiable, but we are mistaken if we assume that he no longer opposes the proud and evil. Whether or not you are involved politically, you can do your part to counter national sin by living a life of personal righteousness. And you can make certain that your primary allegiance is focused not on your country but on your faithful God.

spring, King Nebuchadnezzar sent for him and brought him to Babylon,^{v} together with articles of value from the temple of the LORD, and he made Jehoiachin's uncle,^{a} Zedekiah, king over Judah and Jerusalem.

Zedekiah King of Judah

¹¹Zedekiah^w was twenty-one years old when he became king, and he reigned in Jerusalem eleven years. ¹²He did evil in the eyes of the LORD^x his God and did not humble^y himself before Jeremiah the prophet, who spoke the word of the LORD. ¹³He also rebelled against King Nebuchadnezzar, who had made him take an oath^z in God's name. He became stiff-necked^a and hardened his heart and would not turn to the LORD, the God of Israel. ¹⁴Furthermore, all the leaders of the priests and the people became more and more unfaithful,^{b} following all the detestable practices of the nations and defiling the temple of the LORD, which he had consecrated in Jerusalem.

The Fall of Jerusalem

¹⁵The LORD, the God of their fathers, sent word to them through his messengers^c again and again,^{d} because he had pity on his people and on his dwelling place. ¹⁶But they mocked God's messengers, despised his words and scoffed^e at his prophets until the wrath^f of the LORD was aroused against his people and there was no remedy.^{g} ¹⁷He brought up against them the king of the Babylonians,^{b} who killed their young men with the sword in the sanctuary, and spared neither young man^h nor young woman, old man or aged. God handed all of them over to Nebuchadnezzar.^{i} ¹⁸He carried to Babylon all the articles^j from the temple of God, both large

---

^{a} 10 Hebrew *brother*, that is, relative (see 2 Kings 24:17) ^{b} 17 Or *Chaldeans*

36:10
^{v} ver 18; 2Ki 20:17; Ezr 1:7; Jer 22:25; 24:1; 29:1; 37:1; Eze 17:12

36:11
^{w} 2Ki 24:17; Jer 27:1; 28:1
36:12
^{x} Jer 37:1-39:18
^{y} Dt 8:3; 2Ch 7:14; 33:23; Jer 21:3-7
36:13
^{z} Eze 17:13
^{a} 2Ki 17:14; 2Ch 30:8
36:14
^{b} 1Ch 5:25

36:15
^{c} Isa 5:4; 44:26; Jer 7:25; Hag 1:13; Zec 1:4; Mal 2:7; 3:1 ^{d} Jer 7:13,25; 25:3-4; 35:14,15; 44:4-6
36:16
^{e} 2Ki 2:23; Pr 1:25; Jer 5:13 ^{f} Ezr 5:12; Pr 1:30-31
^{g} 2Ch 30:10; Pr 29:1; Zec 1:2
36:17
^{h} Jer 6:11
^{i} Ezr 5:12; Jer 32:28
36:18
^{j} ver 7,10

---

2 Chronicles 36:9–10

Jehoiachin succeeded his father, Jehoiakim, as king of Judah, but in 597 B.C. he surrendered to Nebuchadnezzar's siege after reigning for only three months (v. 9; cf. 2 Kings 24:10–12). Jehoiachin was deported to Babylon along with the queen mother, other high-ranking officials, and numerous soldiers, craftsmen, and artisans (cf. 2 Kings 24:14–16). Nebuchadnezzar installed Jehoiachin's uncle, Mattaniah (changing his name to Zedekiah), as a puppet king (v. 10; cf. 2 Kings 24:17).

The Chronicler wasted little time on Jehoiachin's brief and ineffective reign. Judah was in a free fall, with no more good kings appearing to mitigate the situation. Looking back on world history, we can't help but note a pattern in the rise and fall of empires, with increases in decadence and sin inversely related to decreases in glory and influence. Many today feel that the United States, despite its relatively brief history, is "over the hill" and sliding in terms of its morality and Christian values. We can be grateful for those leaders at whatever level who do express and live out their faith, and we can do the same in whatever circumstances we find ourselves.

2 Chronicles 36:11–14

We know from the book of Jeremiah that Zedekiah was a weak king, unable to control the resurgent nationalism in Judah and apparently easily manipulated by the nobles and advisers around him (cf. Jer. 37–38). After a series of political missteps, Zedekiah finally rebelled against the king of Babylon (2 Chron. 36:13). The response was swift and thorough. King Nebuchadnezzar laid siege to Jerusalem early in 588 B.C. The end came in July of 586 B.C., with the carnage so appalling and the devastation so sweeping that survivors could only sit aghast in silence as they mourned "the Daughter of Zion" (see the book of Lam.).

The Chronicler's four brief accounts of the reigns of Jehoahaz, Jehoiakim, Jehoiachin, and Zedekiah summarize the deadly game of "musical thrones" that saw the end of the kingdom of Judah. These four reports, totaling only 13 verses, are much less detailed than the parallel narrative in 2 Kings 23:31—24:20. A fifth report (vv. 15–20) provides an abbreviated account of Jerusalem's fall (cf. 2 Kings 25:1–21; Jer. 39:1–10; 52:4–27).

Given the Chronicler's aim of encouraging and fortifying his community, he seems to have fast-forwarded through his account of Judah's demise. We too live in evil days, and it's easy for us to become discouraged. Too often our "heroes" are sports or entertainment figures. God has ensured that there is no shortage of true heroes in our day, but we need to work a little harder at being aware of and finding encouragement and motivation from their influence.

2 Chronicles 36:15–23

The Chronicler understood the exile as God's work. God himself handed his people over to Nebuchadnezzar—and eventually brought them back to the promised land—in fulfillment of Jeremiah's words (vv. 17,21; cf. Jer. 25:8–11; 29:10). It was vital that the Chronicler affirm God's faithfulness to his word. The restoration period witnessed a shift away from prophetic revelation to priestly instruction based on previous revelation from God. The postexilic generation needed assurance that God keeps his word, whether of blessing or of judgment (cf. Ps. 33:4–5).

and small, and the treasures of the LORD's temple and the treasures of the king and his officials. ¹⁹They set fire^k to God's temple^l and broke down the wall^m of Jerusalem; they burned all the palaces and destroyed^n everything of value there. ^{o}

²⁰He carried into exile^p to Babylon the remnant, who escaped from the sword, and they became servants^q to him and his sons until the kingdom of Persia came to power. ²¹The land enjoyed its sabbath rests;^{r} all the time of its desolation it rested,^{s} until the seventy years^t were completed in fulfillment of the word of the LORD spoken by Jeremiah.

²²In the first year of Cyrus^u king of Persia, in order to fulfill the word of the LORD spoken by Jeremiah, the LORD moved the heart of Cyrus king of Persia to make a proclamation throughout his realm and to put it in writing:

²³"This is what Cyrus king of Persia says:

" 'The LORD, the God of heaven, has given me all the kingdoms of the earth and he has appointed^v me to build a temple for him at Jerusalem in Judah. Anyone of his people among you—may the LORD his God be with him, and let him go up.' "

The last two verses splice together separate documents (Chron. and Ezra-Neh.), permitting the later reader to make the transition historically to the accounts of the aftermath of Cyrus's edict (cf. Ezra 1:1–3). The Chronicler's closing paragraph became a directive to his own audience to "go up" to the newly reconstructed temple and offer up appropriate worship to God, in this way rebuilding Judah and Jerusalem spiritually.

Repentance doesn't necessarily suspend sin's consequences. Judah was destroyed and the people exiled despite Josiah's national revival (cf. 34:1—35:19). God's forgiveness may not be mistaken for indulgence or complacency. Nor are we to be seduced by the notion of "cheap grace." We can't tame God and fashion him after our own image. It's important for us to remember that, though he's loving and faithful, he's also just and holy.

INTRODUCTION TO

Ezra

AUTHOR
The books of Ezra and Nehemiah were originally one book. Ezra has traditionally been considered the primary author of Ezra-Nehemiah, but his authorship is uncertain.

DATE WRITTEN
Ezra was probably written around 440 B.C., during the period of restoration in and around
Jerusalem.

ORIGINAL READERS
Ezra was written to the Jews who were returning from exile to encourage them to continue
the work of restoring Jerusalem, the temple, and the community.

TIMELINE

	1400BC	1300	1200	1100	1000	900	800	700	600	500	400

Fall of Jerusalem (586 B.C.)

Persia's conquest of Babylon (539 B.C.)

First return of exiles to Jerusalem (538 B.C.)

Ministries of Haggai and Zechariah (c. 520-480 B.C.)

Completion of temple (516 B.C.)

Second return to Jerusalem under Ezra (458 B.C.)

Third return to Jerusalem under Nehemiah (445 B.C.)

Book of Ezra written (c. 440 B.C.)

THEMES
Ezra describes God's faithfulness in keeping his promise to return his people to Jerusalem to
rebuild the temple. It includes the following themes:

1. *God's sovereignty.* Ezra demonstrates that God is sovereign over all peoples and rulers, even
pagan kings (1:1; 6:22; 7:6,27). He controls history and orchestrates events for his purposes.
Despite opposition, God will fulfill his promises and protect his people.

2. *Restoration.* Ezra describes not only the restoration of the temple (3:1—6:22) but also the
renewal of the spiritual, moral, and social fabric of the community (9:1—10:44) for the returnees. While the overt goals were temple reconstruction and worship renewal, the restoration of the Jews' sense of community and heritage was equally important. It was essential that
they reclaim the separateness that distinguished them from the peoples around them and
marked them as God's people. Organizing the community around the law (7:10; Neh. 8:1–8)
and renouncing the compromises they had made with the nations around them (9:1—10:16;
Neh. 9:1–3) were crucial steps toward that restoration.

3. *Action.* Ezra clearly teaches that faith leads to action (10:4–5). It's not enough to sit back and say that we believe (10:3). We're to "rise up" (10:4) and make whatever change God requires—whether that be an act of service (6:14–15) or repentance (10:2–3,16–17). Ezra also demonstrates that service requires unity and obedience (10:4); each of us will certainly meet opposition as we put our faith in action.

FAITH IN ACTION

The pages of Ezra contain life lessons and role models of faith—people who challenge believers to put their faith in action.

Role Models

- KINGS CYRUS AND DARIUS (1:1–11; 6:1–12; 8:22–23), acknowledging that governing authority comes from God, issued proclamations, granted protection, and released resources that would allow the Jews to return and rebuild Jerusalem and the temple. Do you live in a way that encourages nonbelievers to honor and acknowledge God? Where and how can you or your church partner with established governmental authority to see God's kingdom flourish? How can Christian ministries make better use of secular resources for building the kingdom? When is it appropriate to seek the Lord instead of the government for help?

- GOD'S PEOPLE (1:5) responded to his call to return and rebuild. Are you responsive to his call to kingdom service? Are you willing to set aside your comfort and well-being to do so?

- ZERUBBABEL (4:1–5) used spiritual discernment to recognize the deception of those offering to help rebuild the temple, choosing instead to trust God to supply the builders' needs. What can you learn from Zerubbabel about accepting help from others?

- HAGGAI AND ZECHARIAH (6:14–15) taught the people God's ways, paving the way for their success in the rebuilding project. Are you gifted in the areas of encouragement or teaching? Can you help others understand God's ways so that they too can prosper in them?

- EZRA (9:1—10:5) boldly faced those involved in spiritual compromise and challenged them to turn their hearts back to God. What spiritual concessions do you see being made around you? What might be a wise course of action?

Challenges

- Pray for powerful leaders, whether or not they are Christians. Ask God to move their hearts to accomplish his purposes (1:1–2; 6:1–12).

- Great tasks require great resources and many workers. Do your part, regardless of the function(s) you are asked to fulfill (1:3–4).

- Ask God to move your heart (1:5) so that inner transformation may lead to faithful action (1:6) and participation in some aspect of God's work in the world.

- Give generously, according to your ability (2:68–69) and from your heart (2 Cor. 8:12).

- Use your gifts to help other people walk in God's ways (6:14).

- Guard against societal pressures that threaten to compromise your faith (9:1–2).

- Ask God to grant you discernment in every situation you face (4:1–5; 8:22–23).

OUTLINE

   I. First Exiles Return to Judah (1–2)
  II. Rebuilding of the Temple (3–6)
 III. Ezra's Return (7–8)
 IV. Ezra's Ministry (9–10)

Cyrus Helps the Exiles to Return

1 In the first year of Cyrus king of Persia, in order to fulfill the word of the LORD spoken by Jeremiah,[a] the LORD moved the heart[b] of Cyrus king of Persia to make a proclamation throughout his realm and to put it in writing:

1:1
a Jer 25:11-12; 29:10-14
b 2Ch 36:22,23

2 "This is what Cyrus king of Persia says:

" 'The LORD, the God of heaven, has given me all the kingdoms of the earth and he has appointed[c] me to build[d] a temple for him at Jerusalem in Judah. 3 Anyone of his people among you—may his God be with him, and let him go up to Jerusalem in Judah and build the temple of the LORD, the God of Israel, the God who is in Jerusalem. 4 And the people of any place where survivors[e] may now be living are to provide him with silver and gold, with goods and livestock, and with freewill offerings[f] for the temple of God in Jerusalem.' " [g]

1:2
c Isa 44:28; 45:13
d Ezr 5:13

1:4
e Isa 10:20-22
f Nu 15:3; Ps 50:14; 54:6; 116:17
g Ezr 4:3; 5:13; 6:3, 14

5 Then the family heads of Judah and Benjamin,[h] and the priests and Levites—everyone whose heart God had moved[i]—prepared to go up and build the house[j] of the LORD in Jerusalem. 6 All their neighbors assisted them with articles of silver and gold, with goods and livestock, and with valuable gifts, in addition to all the freewill offerings. 7 Moreover, King Cyrus brought out the articles belonging to the temple of the LORD, which Nebuchadnezzar had carried away from Jerusalem and had placed in the temple of his god.[a][k] 8 Cyrus king of Persia had them brought by Mithredath the treasurer, who counted them out to Sheshbazzar[l] the prince of Judah.

1:5
h Ezr 4:1; Ne 11:4
i ver 1; Ex 35:20-22; 2Ch 36:22; Hag 1:14; Php 2:13
j Ps 127:1

1:7
k 2Ki 24:13; 2Ch 36:7,10; Ezr 5:14; 6:5
1:8
l Ezr 5:14

9 This was the inventory:

gold dishes	30
silver dishes	1,000
silver pans[b]	29
10 gold bowls	30

Return From Exile (1:3)

Then: Cyrus, king of Persia, stood to benefit from a strong Israel acting as a buffer state between his kingdom and Egypt. This may have been one motive for sending the captives home, but God's direct intervention provides the ultimate explanation.

Now: Cyrus's policies anticipated the balance of power theories of modern nations.

---

a 7 Or gods   b 9 The meaning of the Hebrew for this word is uncertain.

Ezra 1:1–11

Cyrus, the founder of the Persian Empire, ruled the Persians from 559–530 B.C. The reference in verse 1 to the "first year" of his reign is connected to Cyrus's expanded rule following his capture of Babylon in 539. Cyrus instituted an enlightened policy of appeasing the gods of his subject peoples, rather than destroying their temples and carrying off their representative idols as the Babylonians had done. Ultimately, though, it was God who moved his heart.

It had been nearly 70 years since the first deportation of Jews by the Babylonians in 605 B.C. Though the initial years must have been difficult, the second and third generations of Jews born in exile had adjusted to their surroundings. The "people of any place" in verse 4 and "neighbors" in verse 6 undoubtedly included the many Jews, especially of the subsequent generation(s), who didn't want to leave Babylon. Others, sustained by the examples and teachings of leaders like Daniel and Ezekiel, retained their faith in God's promises and their allegiance to their homeland.

It's easy for us to criticize the Jews who declined to return to Judah when given the opportunity. But it might not have been so easy a proposition. Most of them had never seen the "promised land." They had not only adapted to life in Babylon but in many cases had even prospered. How much motivation would *you* have had to leave the only home you knew to take a dangerous, expensive, four-month, thousand-mile journey to rebuild from scratch in a war-torched land with hostile new residents?

How great a hold do physical and material comfort and security have on you (cf. Luke 8:14)? Do they keep you from fully following God's call on your life—or do you maintain a loose grip on the things of this world, as someone who is just "passing through" (cf. Ps. 39:12; Heb. 13:14; 1 Peter 2:11)?

matching silver bowls	410
other articles	1,000

[11] In all, there were 5,400 articles of gold and of silver. Sheshbazzar brought all these along when the exiles came up from Babylon to Jerusalem.

The List of the Exiles Who Returned

2 Now these are the people of the province who came up from the captivity of the exiles,[m] whom Nebuchadnezzar king of Babylon[n] had taken captive to Babylon (they returned to Jerusalem and Judah, each to his own town,[o] [2] in company with Zerubbabel,[p] Jeshua, [q] Nehemiah, Seraiah,[r] Reelaiah, Mordecai, Bilshan, Mispar, Bigvai, Rehum and Baanah):

The list of the men of the people of Israel:

[3] the descendants of Parosh[s]	2,172
[4] of Shephatiah	372
[5] of Arah	775
[6] of Pahath-Moab (through the line of Jeshua and Joab)	2,812
[7] of Elam	1,254
[8] of Zattu	945
[9] of Zaccai	760
[10] of Bani	642
[11] of Bebai	623
[12] of Azgad	1,222
[13] of Adonikam[t]	666
[14] of Bigvai	2,056
[15] of Adin	454
[16] of Ater (through Hezekiah)	98
[17] of Bezai	323
[18] of Jorah	112
[19] of Hashum	223
[20] of Gibbar	95
[21] the men of Bethlehem[u]	123
[22] of Netophah	56
[23] of Anathoth	128
[24] of Azmaveth	42
[25] of Kiriath Jearim,[a] Kephirah and Beeroth	743

Marginal cross-references:
- 2:1 — [m] 2Ch 36:20; Ne 7:6 [n] 2Ki 24:16; 25:12 [o] Ne 7:73
- 2:2 — [p] 1Ch 3:19 [q] Ezr 3:2 [r] Ne 10:2
- 2:3 — [s] Ezr 8:3
- 2:13 — [t] Ezr 8:13
- 2:21 — [u] Mic 5:2

[a] 25 See Septuagint (see also Neh. 7:29); Hebrew *Kiriath Arim*.

Ezra 2:1–70

This listing of returning exiles follows these categories: leaders (v. 2); Israelites distinguished by family lineage (vv. 3–20); Israelites distinguished by cities and villages of origin (vv. 21–35); priests (vv. 36–39); Levites, including singers and gatekeepers (vv. 40–42); temple servants and descendants of the servants of Solomon—probably non-Israelites whom Solomon had forced into temple duty (vv. 43–58); individuals, including some priests, who had emigrated from Mesopotamia but couldn't prove Jewish ancestry (vv. 59–63).

The caravan probably followed the Euphrates River up to a point east of Aleppo and crossed west to the Orontes River Valley, then south. It would have passed either through the Beqa'a Valley in Lebanon or through Damascus en route to the promised land.

Since the people were already exhausting much of their savings to fund the trip, their giving (v. 69) demonstrated a true spirit of dedication to God's service. A parallel passage in Nehemiah 7:70–72 offers a more systematic account. A mina (1.26 pounds of silver) equated to five years' wages. The Greek term *drachma* may have been substituted for the Persian *daric*—a gold coin famed for its purity and named either after Darius I or the Old Persian word *dari*, for gold. A daric (8.42 grams of gold) equaled the price of an ox or of a month's wages for a soldier.

Genealogies provided important credentials for the Jewish people (e.g., in relation to property inheritance and eligibility to serve as priests or Levites). The knowledge of family relationships is still important in many societies. A.S. Kirkbride recounted "that on one occasion, while he was in an Arab encampment, an Arab got up and related the history of his forebears back to forty generations, and that there were others in the assembly who obviously could have done the same" (cited in *The Biblical Archaeologist Reader*, 1961).

26 of Ramah[v] and Geba   621
27 of Micmash   122
28 of Bethel and Ai[w]   223
29 of Nebo   52
30 of Magbish   156
31 of the other Elam   1,254
32 of Harim   320
33 of Lod, Hadid and Ono   725
34 of Jericho[x]   345
35 of Senaah   3,630

36 The priests:

the descendants of Jedaiah[y] (through the family
of Jeshua)   973
37 of Immer[z]   1,052
38 of Pashhur[a]   1,247
39 of Harim[b]   1,017

40 The Levites:[c]

the descendants of Jeshua[d] and Kadmiel (through
the line of Hodaviah)   74

41 The singers:[e]

the descendants of Asaph   128

42 The gatekeepers[f] of the temple:

the descendants of
Shallum, Ater, Talmon,
Akkub, Hatita and Shobai   139

43 The temple servants:[g]

the descendants of
Ziha, Hasupha, Tabbaoth,
44 Keros, Siaha, Padon,
45 Lebanah, Hagabah, Akkub,
46 Hagab, Shalmai, Hanan,
47 Giddel, Gahar, Reaiah,
48 Rezin, Nekoda, Gazzam,
49 Uzza, Paseah, Besai,
50 Asnah, Meunim, Nephusim,
51 Bakbuk, Hakupha, Harhur,
52 Bazluth, Mehida, Harsha,
53 Barkos, Sisera, Temah,
54 Neziah and Hatipha

55 The descendants of the servants of Solomon:

the descendants of
Sotai, Hassophereth, Peruda,
56 Jaala, Darkon, Giddel,
57 Shephatiah, Hattil,
Pokereth-Hazzebaim and Ami

2:26
v Jos 18:25

2:28
w Ge 12:8

2:34
x 1Ki 16:34;
2Ch 28:15

2:36
y 1Ch 24:7
2:37
z 1Ch 24:14
2:38
a 1Ch 9:12
2:39
b 1Ch 24:8
2:40
c Ge 29:34; Nu 3:9;
Dt 18:6-7;
1Ch 16:4; Ezr 7:7;
8:15; Ne 12:24
d Ezr 3:9
2:41
e 1Ch 15:16

2:42
f 1Sa 3:15;
1Ch 9:17

2:43
g 1Ch 9:2;
Ne 11:21

What does your ancestry mean to you? Regardless of how much you know and appreciate about your family tree, you can rejoice in your shared legacy of faith with other people of God (cf. Rom. 4:16; Gal. 3:6–9).While the amount of a gift is immaterial in and of itself, we can't ignore the sacrificial nature of the giving in this passage. Families gave according to their ability. Do you endeavor to make giving a family matter in your household? If not, what activities could you introduce to engage everyone in the process? Have you considered foregoing one latte, a meal out, or one trip to the mall each week or month in order to donate those resources to a special church project or service ministry? What is your daily wage or monthly salary? How does that calculate into your giving?

2:58
h 1Ki 9:21; 1Ch 9:2

2:59
i Nu 1:18

2:61
j 2Sa 17:27
2:62
k Nu 3:10; 16:39-40
2:63
l Lev 2:3,10
m Ex 28:30;
Nu 27:21

2:65
n 2Sa 19:35
2:66
o Isa 66:20

2:68
p Ex 25:2

2:70
q ver 1; 1Ch 9:2;
Ne 11:3-4

3:1
r Ne 7:73; 8:1
s Lev 23:24
3:2
t Ezr 2:2;
Ne 12:1,8; Hag 2:2
u Hag 1:1; Zec 6:11
v 1Ch 3:17
w Ex 20:24;
Dt 12:5-6
3:3
x Ezr 4:4; Da 9:25
y Ex 29:39;
Nu 28:1-8
3:4
z Ex 23:16;
Nu 29:12-38;
Ne 8:14-18;
Zec 14:16-19
3:5
a Nu 28:3,11,14;
Col 2:16
b Lev 23:1-44;
Nu 29:39

58 The temple servants [h] and the descendants
of the servants of Solomon   392

59 The following came up from the towns of Tel Melah, Tel Harsha, Kerub, Addon and Immer, but they could not show that their families were descended [i] from Israel:

60 The descendants of
Delaiah, Tobiah and Nekoda   652

61 And from among the priests:

The descendants of
Hobaiah, Hakkoz and Barzillai (a man who had married a daughter of Barzillai the Gileadite [j] and was called by that name).
62 These searched for their family records, but they could not find them and so were excluded from the priesthood [k] as unclean. 63 The governor ordered them not to eat any of the most sacred food [l] until there was a priest ministering with the Urim and Thummim. [m]

64 The whole company numbered 42,360, 65 besides their 7,337 menservants and maidservants; and they also had 200 men and women singers. [n] 66 They had 736 horses, [o] 245 mules, 67 435 camels and 6,720 donkeys.

68 When they arrived at the house of the LORD in Jerusalem, some of the heads of the families [p] gave freewill offerings toward the rebuilding of the house of God on its site. 69 According to their ability they gave to the treasury for this work 61,000 drachmas [a] of gold, 5,000 minas [b] of silver and 100 priestly garments.
70 The priests, the Levites, the singers, the gatekeepers and the temple servants settled in their own towns, along with some of the other people, and the rest of the Israelites settled in their towns. [q]

Rebuilding the Altar

3 When the seventh month came and the Israelites had settled in their towns, [r] the people assembled [s] as one man in Jerusalem. 2 Then Jeshua [t] son of Jozadak [u] and his fellow priests and Zerubbabel son of Shealtiel [v] and his associates began to build the altar of the God of Israel to sacrifice burnt offerings on it, in accordance with what is written in the Law of Moses [w] the man of God. 3 Despite their fear [x] of the peoples around them, they built the altar on its foundation and sacrificed burnt offerings on it to the LORD, both the morning and evening sacrifices. [y] 4 Then in accordance with what is written, they celebrated the Feast of Tabernacles [z] with the required number of burnt offerings prescribed for each day. 5 After that, they presented the regular burnt offerings, the New Moon [a] sacrifices and the sacrifices for all the appointed sacred feasts of the LORD, [b] as well as those brought as freewill offerings to the LORD. 6 On the first day of the seventh month they be-

---

a 69 That is, about 1,100 pounds (about 500 kilograms)   b 69 That is, about 3 tons (about 2.9 metric tons)

Ezra 3:1–6

📖 "The seventh month," Tishri (Sept.–Oct.), fell about three months after the exiles' return. Tishri was one of the most sacred months of the Jewish year. Its first day was the New Year's Day (Rosh Hashanah) of the civil calendar, proclaimed with the blowing of trumpets and a holy convocation (Lev. 23:24). Ten days later the Day of Atonement (Yom Kippur) was observed (Lev. 23:27). From the fifteenth to the twenty-second day, the Feast of Tabernacles (Succoth) was celebrated (Lev. 23:34–36).

It's significant to note that in their zeal to renew their worship through sacrifices the returnees rebuilt the altar and made sacrifices on it before rebuilding the temple itself.

📖 During their long stay in Babylon, the Jews had been unable to offer sacrifices, as this could only be done in Jerusalem. Instead they had been surrounded by pagan temples and open-air shrines. Take a moment to read Psalm 137, especially verses 5–6. Then try to imagine succeeding generations keeping alive this passion for God. Consider the recent resurgence of interest in Christianity in China and the former Soviet Union. Excluding the many recent converts, how much of this do you suppose can be attributed to parents in these countries passing down a faith legacy? How does this challenge you?

gan to offer burnt offerings to the LORD, though the foundation of the LORD's temple had not yet been laid.

Rebuilding the Temple

[7]Then they gave money to the masons and carpenters, and gave food and drink and oil to the people of Sidon and Tyre, so that they would bring cedar logs[c] by sea from Lebanon[d] to Joppa, as authorized by Cyrus[e] king of Persia.

[8]In the second month of the second year after their arrival at the house of God in Jerusalem, Zerubbabel[f] son of Shealtiel, Jeshua son of Jozadak and the rest of their brothers (the priests and the Levites and all who had returned from the captivity to Jerusalem) began the work, appointing Levites twenty[g] years of age and older to supervise the building of the house of the LORD. [9]Jeshua[h] and his sons and brothers and Kadmiel and his sons (descendants of Hodaviah[a]) and the sons of Henadad and their sons and brothers—all Levites—joined together in supervising those working on the house of God.

[10]When the builders laid[i] the foundation of the temple of the LORD, the priests in their vestments and with trumpets,[j] and the Levites (the sons of Asaph) with cymbals, took their places to praise[k] the LORD, as prescribed by David[l] king of Israel.[m] [11]With praise and thanksgiving they sang to the LORD:

> "He is good;
>   his love to Israel endures forever."[n]

And all the people gave a great shout[o] of praise to the LORD, because the foundation of the house of the LORD was laid. [12]But many of the older priests and Levites and family heads, who had seen the former temple,[p] wept aloud when they saw the foundation of this temple being laid, while many others shouted for joy. [13]No one could distinguish the sound of the shouts of joy[q] from the sound of weeping, because the people made so much noise. And the sound was heard far away.

Opposition to the Rebuilding

4 When the enemies of Judah and Benjamin heard that the exiles were building a temple for the LORD, the God of Israel, [2]they came to Zerubbabel and to the heads of the families and said, "Let us help you build because, like you, we seek

[a] 9 Hebrew *Yehudah*, probably a variant of *Hodaviah*

3:7
[c] 1Ch 14:1
[d] Isa 35:2
[e] Ezr 1:2-4; 6:3

3:8
[f] Zec 4:9
[g] 1Ch 23:24

3:9
[h] Ezr 2:40

3:10
[i] Ezr 5:16 / Nu 10:2; 1Ch 16:6
[k] 1Ch 25:1
[l] 1Ch 6:31
[m] Zec 6:12

3:11
[n] 1Ch 16:34,41; 2Ch 7:3; Ps 107:1; 118:1 [o] Ne 12:24

3:12
[p] Hag 2:3,9

3:13
[q] Job 8:21; Ps 27:6; Isa 16:9

Ezra 3:7–13

🔲 Loud shouting expresses great jubilation or intense purpose (cf. 10:12; Josh. 6:5,20; 1 Sam. 4:5; Ps. 95:1–2). Traditionally, Israelites showed their emotions by weeping aloud (cf. 10:1; Neh. 1:4; 8:9). (The Israelis reacted similarly when they reached the Wailing Wall in their war against the Arabs in 1967.)

The elders were overcome with memories of the splendors of Solomon's temple, while the younger returnees shouted with exuberance at the prospect of a new temple. The God who had permitted judgment also was the God who had brought his people back and would enable them to complete this project. A Babylonian cornerstone reads, "I started the work weeping, I finished it rejoicing" (cf. Ps. 126:5: "Those who sow in tears will reap with songs of joy").

🔲 When have you, individually or as part of a larger group working for the Lord's cause, sown in tears but reaped with songs of joy? If this hasn't been your experience yet, one day it will be. Don't allow lack of resources or hostile neighbors (as we will see next in the book of Ezra) to get you down. God is vitally interested in pro-

jects undertaken in his name—and he will help us see them through to completion as we rely on him.

Ezra 4:1–5

🔲 The people offering "help" to the returnees were evidently from Samaria, the area of the former northern kingdom of Israel. After the northern kingdom's fall in 722 B.C., Assyrian kings had imported new inhabitants from Mesopotamia and Aram, who continued to worship their own gods but also tried to worship the Lord as the god of the land (2 Kings 17:24–41). The newcomers' influence no doubt diluted further the faith of the remaining Israelites, who had already apostasized from sole worship of the Lord in the 10th century B.C.

🔲 To "discourage" (v. 4) means literally "to weaken the hands," a Hebrew idiom (cf. Neh. 6:9; Jer. 38:4). Its opposite is "to strengthen the hands" (Isa. 35:3; Jer. 23:14). When have adverse circumstances "weakened your hands"? Can you think of some English sayings that convey the same idea? What were the practical outcomes of your discouragement? What did it take for you to regain your strength and resolve?

4:2
r 2Ki 17:24; 19:37
s 2Ki 17:41

your God and have been sacrificing to him since the time of Esarhaddon[r] king of Assyria, who brought us here." [s]

³But Zerubbabel, Jeshua and the rest of the heads of the families of Israel answered, "You have no part with us in building a temple to our God. We alone will build it for the LORD, the God of Israel, as King Cyrus, the king of Persia, commanded us." [t]

4:3
t Ezr 1:1-4; Ne 2:20

4:4
u Ezr 3:3

⁴Then the peoples around them set out to discourage the people of Judah and make them afraid to go on building. [a][u] ⁵They hired counselors to work against them and frustrate their plans during the entire reign of Cyrus king of Persia and down to the reign of Darius king of Persia.

Later Opposition Under Xerxes and Artaxerxes

4:6
v Est 1:1; Da 9:1
w Est 3:13; 9:5
4:7
x Ezr 7:1; Ne 2:1
y 2Ki 18:26;
Isa 36:11; Da 2:4

⁶At the beginning of the reign of Xerxes, [b][v] they lodged an accusation against the people of Judah and Jerusalem. [w]

⁷And in the days of Artaxerxes[x] king of Persia, Bishlam, Mithredath, Tabeel and the rest of his associates wrote a letter to Artaxerxes. The letter was written in Aramaic script and in the Aramaic[y] language. [c,d]

⁸Rehum the commanding officer and Shimshai the secretary wrote a letter against Jerusalem to Artaxerxes the king as follows:

4:9
z Ezr 5:6; 6:6, 13

⁹Rehum the commanding officer and Shimshai the secretary, together with the rest of their associates[z]—the judges and officials over the men from Tripolis, Persia, [e] Erech and Babylon, the Elamites of Susa, ¹⁰and the other people whom the great and honorable Ashurbanipal[f] deported and settled in the city of Samaria and elsewhere in Trans-Euphrates. [a]

4:10
a ver 17; Ne 4:2

¹¹(This is a copy of the letter they sent him.)

To King Artaxerxes,

From your servants, the men of Trans-Euphrates:

4:12
b Ezr 5:3, 9

¹²The king should know that the Jews who came up to us from you have gone to Jerusalem and are rebuilding that rebellious and wicked city. They are restoring the walls and repairing the foundations. [b]

4:13
c Ezr 7:24; Ne 5:4

¹³Furthermore, the king should know that if this city is built and its walls are restored, no more taxes, tribute or duty[c] will be paid, and the royal revenues will suffer. ¹⁴Now since we are under obligation to the palace and it is not proper for us to see the king dishonored, we are sending this message to inform the king, ¹⁵so that a search may be made in the archives[d] of your predecessors. In these records you will find that this city is a rebellious city, troublesome to kings and provinces, a place of rebellion from ancient times. That is why this city was destroyed. [e] ¹⁶We inform the king that if this city is built and its walls are restored, you will be left with nothing in Trans-Euphrates.

4:15
d Ezr 5:17; 6:1
e Est 3:8

---

[a] 4 Or *and troubled them as they built*   [b] 6 Hebrew *Ahasuerus,* a variant of Xerxes' Persian name
[c] 7 Or *written in Aramaic and translated*   [d] 7 The text of Ezra 4:8—6:18 is in Aramaic.
[e] 9 Or *officials, magistrates and governors over the men from*   [f] 10 Aramaic *Osnappar,* a variant of Ashurbanipal

---

Ezra 4:6–24

Chapter 4 summarizes various attempts to thwart the Jews' efforts. In verses 1–5 the author continued to describe events under Cyrus (c. 536–530 B.C.). But in verse 6 he fast-forwarded to events under Xerxes (485–465) and in verses 7–23 to occurrences under Artaxerxes I (464–424). The situation involving Artaxerxes, which took place many years after the completion of the temple rebuilding project in 516, pertained to the rebuilding of the walls of Jerusalem—a primary setting for the book of Nehemiah. The author then reverted in

verse 24 to the second year of Darius (520), when work on the temple was renewed.

This chapter illustrates the reality of persistent opposition to God's people. We are reminded of Paul's words in 2 Timothy 3:12: "Everyone who wants to live a godly life in Christ Jesus will be persecuted." You probably won't see that "promise" as the verse-for-the-month on a scenic calendar or the theme of an inspirational e-mail forward! But the ancient Israelites' experience and Paul's sobering words prepare those who are faithful to God for tough times. Are you ready?

4:4–5

Planning and constructing a church building can be a divisive process. When was the last time any congregation voted 100 percent in favor of a building project? The church I presently serve sits on our city's main north-south artery, Meridian Street. Our local fire department simply refers to us as "the rock pile on Meridian." But many of our congregants think it's next to heaven itself. Change it? Why?

Ezra 4 reflects all the intrigue of a church building campaign run amuck in controversy. The Hebrew people return to Jerusalem following years of exile and set out in jubilation to rebuild the temple. The establishment—what sociologists call the old class, the people of the land living in and around Jerusalem (not necessarily Jews)—take issue. The exiles represent for them the new class known as the *Golah*. These up-and-comers, on the other hand, see themselves as the true community of faith. A culture war ensues.

As the situation deteriorates, the scene turns ugly. First the old class expresses a desire to partner with the returnees (4:2). The newcomers decline for both political and religious reasons. They understand the tenuous political situation. As exiles they had managed to turn disaster into deliverance. In the end they had been given the right by Cyrus to return home and rebuild the temple. They don't wish to jeopardize the decree Cyrus has given to them alone. Religiously, they view the old class as somewhat less than real Jews—because they have combined Judaism with the surrounding religions.

> God's kingdom comes hard and slow because his people sometimes behave more like curmudgeons than saints.

Shunned by the settlers, the entrenched do what the old guard usually does so well: They begin to play politics with gleeful vengeance. They sabotage the rebuilding project via withdrawn building permits, stop-work orders, and labor union hassles (vv. 4–5). They mount a letter-writing campaign, going public with threats and charges (vv. 6ff.). They feed the economic fears of government officials by suggesting that reconstruction will lead to a loss of tax revenue. Their campaign succeeds! Work on the temple is temporarily halted (vv. 24ff.).

In his book *Leadership Without Easy Answers*, Ronald Heifetz observes that the first thing savvy leaders do when a situation turns against them is to "get on the balcony"—where they can talk about living above the fray while observing what's happening on the dance floor below.

From the balcony we can see what can't be observed from ground level: the bigger picture. The patterns forming on the dance floor. Who is dancing with whom, in what groups, in what locations? Who is sitting it out? As we observe the swirl of motion below, we ask ourselves penetrating questions like Why are things as they are? What's causing the distress? Who is upset and why? What are we (or am I) doing that is so threatening? The balcony allows us to depersonalize the conflict, to avoid losing focus and misdiagnosing. The balcony experience puts things in perspective.

The balcony also is a sanctuary providing us with spiritual and psychological space to listen. Opposition is part of life in God's world and in his church. God's kingdom comes hard and slow because his people sometimes behave more like curmudgeons than saints. What then may Christian leaders do? Get on the balcony. Go to their knees. Trust God to be God!

So it was in Ezra's story. In time the stop-work order was lifted. The opposition quieted. As construction began again God's glory stood tall in the land.

William Enright, pastor of Central Presbyterian Church in Indianapolis, Indiana

17The king sent this reply:

4:17
f ver 10

To Rehum the commanding officer, Shimshai the secretary and the rest of their associates living in Samaria and elsewhere in Trans-Euphrates:[f]

Greetings.

18The letter you sent us has been read and translated in my presence. **19**I issued an order and a search was made, and it was found that this city has a long history of revolt[g] against kings and has been a place of rebellion and sedition. **20**Jerusalem has had powerful kings ruling over the whole of Trans-Euphrates,[h] and taxes, tribute and duty were paid to them. **21**Now issue an order to these men to stop work, so that this city will not be rebuilt until I so order. **22**Be careful not to neglect this matter. Why let this threat grow, to the detriment of the royal interests?[i]

4:19
g 2Ki 18:7
4:20
h Ge 15:18-21;
Ex 23:31; Jos 1:4;
1Ki 4:21; 1Ch 18:3;
Ps 72:8-11

4:22
i Da 6:2

4:23
j ver 9

23As soon as the copy of the letter of King Artaxerxes was read to Rehum and Shimshai the secretary and their associates,[j] they went immediately to the Jews in Jerusalem and compelled them by force to stop.

4:24
k Ne 2:1-8;
Da 9:25;
Hag 1:1,15; Zec 1:1

24Thus the work on the house of God in Jerusalem came to a standstill until the second year of the reign of Darius[k] king of Persia.

Tattenai's Letter to Darius

5:1
l Ezr 6:14;
Hag 1:1,3,12;
2:1,10,20
m Zec 1:1; 7:1
n Hag 1:14-2:9;
Zec 4:9-10; 8:9
5:2
o 1Ch 3:19;
Hag 1:14; 2:21;
Zec 4:6-10
p Ezr 2:2; 3:2
q ver 8; Hag 2:2-5
5:3
r Ezr 6:6 s Ezr 6:6
t ver 9; Ezr 1:3;
4:12
5:5
u 2Ki 25:28;
Ezr 7:6,9,28; 8:18,
22,31; Ne 2:8,18;
Ps 33:18; Isa 66:14

5 Now Haggai[l] the prophet and Zechariah[m] the prophet, a descendant of Iddo, prophesied[n] to the Jews in Judah and Jerusalem in the name of the God of Israel, who was over them. **2**Then Zerubbabel[o] son of Shealtiel and Jeshua[p] son of Jozadak set to work[q] to rebuild the house of God in Jerusalem. And the prophets of God were with them, helping them.

3At that time Tattenai,[r] governor of Trans-Euphrates, and Shethar-Bozenai[s] and their associates went to them and asked, "Who authorized you to rebuild this temple and restore this structure?"[t] **4**They also asked, "What are the names of the men constructing this building?"[a] **5**But the eye of their God[u] was watching over the elders of the Jews, and they were not stopped until a report could go to Darius and his written reply be received.

6This is a copy of the letter that Tattenai, governor of Trans-Euphrates, and Shethar-Bozenai and their associates, the officials of Trans-Euphrates, sent to King Darius. **7**The report they sent him read as follows:

To King Darius:

Cordial greetings.

8The king should know that we went to the district of Judah, to the temple

---

[a] *4* See Septuagint; Aramaic *We told them the names of the men constructing this building.*

Ezra 5:1–17

Beginning on August 29, 520 B.C. (Hag. 1:1) and continuing until December 18 (Hag. 2:1,10,20), the prophet Haggai delivered a series of speeches to stir up the people to resume work on the temple. Two months after Haggai's first message, Zechariah joined him (Zech. 1:1). "Zerubbabel" was a Babylonian name meaning "offspring of Babylon," referring to his birth in exile. He was the son of Shealtiel and the grandson of Jehoiachin (1 Chron. 3:17), the next-to-last king of Judah. Zerubbabel was the last of the Davidic line to be entrusted with political authority by the occupying powers. He was also an ancestor of Jesus (Matt. 1:12). Jeshua (*Joshua* in Hag. 1:1) was the current high priest.

Tattenai and his associates were part of the elaborate system of informers and spies used by Near Eastern kings. Egyptian sources refer to the "ears and eyes" of the pharaoh. Two officials who reported to the Persian monarch were known as "the king's eye" and "the king's ear." But "the eye of their God" was watching over the Jews (v. 5).

Both Sheshbazzar and Zerubbabel were "governors" (v. 14; Hag. 2:2). Sheshbazzar may have been the official Persian "governor," whereas Zerubbabel was the popular leader—a possible reason the Jews mentioned Sheshbazzar in official documents like this letter. Though Sheshbazzar presided over laying the temple foundation in 536 B.C., so little was accomplished that Zerubbabel evidently had to preside over the laying of a second foundation some 16 years later (v. 16; Hag. 2:2–4).

of the great God. The people are building it with large stones and placing the timbers in the walls. The work[v] is being carried on with diligence and is making rapid progress under their direction.

[9] We questioned the elders and asked them, "Who authorized you to rebuild this temple and restore this structure?"[w] [10] We also asked them their names, so that we could write down the names of their leaders for your information.

[11] This is the answer they gave us:

"We are the servants of the God of heaven and earth, and we are rebuilding the temple[x] that was built many years ago, one that a great king of Israel built and finished. [12] But because our fathers angered[y] the God of heaven, he handed them over to Nebuchadnezzar the Chaldean, king of Babylon, who destroyed this temple and deported the people to Babylon.[z]

[13] "However, in the first year of Cyrus king of Babylon, King Cyrus issued a decree[g] to rebuild this house of God. [14] He even removed from the temple[a] of Babylon the gold and silver articles of the house of God, which Nebuchadnezzar had taken from the temple in Jerusalem and brought to the temple[a] in Babylon.[b]

"Then King Cyrus gave them to a man named Sheshbazzar,[c] whom he had appointed governor, [15] and he told him, 'Take these articles and go and deposit them in the temple in Jerusalem. And rebuild the house of God on its site.' [16] So this Sheshbazzar came and laid the foundations of the house of God[d] in Jerusalem. From that day to the present it has been under construction but is not yet finished."

[17] Now if it pleases the king, let a search be made in the royal archives[e] of Babylon to see if King Cyrus did in fact issue a decree to rebuild this house of God in Jerusalem. Then let the king send us his decision in this matter.

The Decree of Darius

6 King Darius then issued an order, and they searched in the archives[f] stored in the treasury at Babylon. [2] A scroll was found in the citadel of Ecbatana in the province of Media, and this was written on it:

Memorandum:

[3] In the first year of King Cyrus, the king issued a decree concerning the temple of God in Jerusalem:

Let the temple be rebuilt as a place to present sacrifices, and let its founda-

---

a 14 Or palace

5:8
v ver 2

5:9
w Ezr 4:12

5:11
x 1Ki 6:1; 2Ch 3:1-2
5:12
y 2Ch 36:16
z Dt 21:10; 28:36;
2Ki 24:1; 25:8,9,11;
Jer 1:3

5:13
a Ezr 1:1

5:14
b Ezr 1:7; 6:5;
Da 5:2 c 1Ch 3:18

5:16
d Ezr 3:10; 6:15

5:17
e Ezr 4:15; 6:1,2

6:1
f Ezr 4:15; 5:17

📖 How little has changed over the ages! Red tape and tattletales remain factors in life. The office rumor mill and school grapevine remain the eyes and ears of corporate bosses, schoolteachers, and administrators. Building projects require various permits and sometimes zoning hearings or environmental impact studies. How do you handle a particularly intrusive fellow employee or student? How do you respond to behind-your-back accusations? What do you do when officials attempt to block a church, office, or home building project? Have encouragers like Haggai and Zechariah made a difference to you?

Ezra 6:1–12

🔗 When Darius complied with the Jews' request to search the archives for Cyrus's earlier decree, the Jews were vindicated and their opponents silenced. Since the accounts in Haggai and Zechariah don't speak of support from the Persian treasury, some have questioned the

promises made in verse 8. Extrabiblical evidence, though, makes it clear that Persian kings consistently helped restore sanctuaries in their empire. For example, Cyrus's successor Cambyses contributed funds for the temple at Sais in Egypt. The words of Darius, who would have believed in a multitude of deities, in verse 10 reveal something of an ulterior motive: A temple in Jerusalem could have led to additional prayer for his own benefit.

📖 Can you identify situations in recent history in which government policies in various parts of the world have tolerated or supported activities promoting the well-being of God's children and/or the spread of the gospel? Which of these represent radical breaks from previous strategy? What have been the results?

Take a moment to pray for the "well-being" (v. 10) of governments in a way that results in the advancement of the work of Christ's church and the silencing of its enemies (cf. 1 Tim. 2:1–3).

6:3
g Ezr 3:10; Hag 2:3
6:4
h 1Ki 6:36 *i* ver 8;
Ezr 7:20
6:5
j 1Ch 29:2
k Ezr 1:7; 5:14

6:6
l Ezr 5:3 *m* Ezr 5:3

6:8
n ver 4 *o* 1Sa 9:20
6:9
p Lev 1:3, 10

6:10
q Ezr 7:23;
1Ti 2:1-2
6:11
r Dt 21:22-23;
Est 2:23; 5:14; 9:14
s Ezr 7:26; Da 2:5;
3:29
6:12
t Ex 20:24; Dt 12:5;
1Ki 9:3; 2Ch 6:2
u ver 14

6:13
v Ezr 4:9
6:14
w Ezr 5:1
x Ezr 1:1-4 *y* ver 12
z Ezr 7:1; Ne 2:1

6:15
a Zec 1:1; 4:9

6:16
b 1Ki 8:63; 2Ch 7:5
6:17
c 2Sa 6:13;
2Ch 29:21; 30:24;
Ezr 8:35

tions be laid. *g* It is to be ninety feet[a] high and ninety feet wide, [4]with three courses[h] of large stones and one of timbers. The costs are to be paid by the royal treasury.[i] [5]Also, the gold[j] and silver articles of the house of God, which Nebuchadnezzar took from the temple in Jerusalem and brought to Babylon, are to be returned to their places in the temple in Jerusalem; they are to be deposited in the house of God.[k]

[6]Now then, Tattenai,[l] governor of Trans-Euphrates, and Shethar-Bozenai[m] and you, their fellow officials of that province, stay away from there. [7]Do not interfere with the work on this temple of God. Let the governor of the Jews and the Jewish elders rebuild this house of God on its site.

[8]Moreover, I hereby decree what you are to do for these elders of the Jews in the construction of this house of God:

The expenses of these men are to be fully paid out of the royal treasury,[n] from the revenues[o] of Trans-Euphrates, so that the work will not stop. [9]Whatever is needed—young bulls, rams, male lambs for burnt offerings[p] to the God of heaven, and wheat, salt, wine and oil, as requested by the priests in Jerusalem—must be given them daily without fail, [10]so that they may offer sacrifices pleasing to the God of heaven and pray for the well-being of the king and his sons.[q]

[11]Furthermore, I decree that if anyone changes this edict, a beam is to be pulled from his house and he is to be lifted up and impaled[r] on it. And for this crime his house is to be made a pile of rubble.[s] [12]May God, who has caused his Name to dwell there,[t] overthrow any king or people who lifts a hand to change this decree or to destroy this temple in Jerusalem.

I Darius[u] have decreed it. Let it be carried out with diligence.

Completion and Dedication of the Temple

[13]Then, because of the decree King Darius had sent, Tattenai, governor of Trans-Euphrates, and Shethar-Bozenai and their associates[v] carried it out with diligence. [14]So the elders of the Jews continued to build and prosper under the preaching[w] of Haggai the prophet and Zechariah, a descendant of Iddo. They finished building the temple according to the command of the God of Israel and the decrees of Cyrus,[x] Darius[y] and Artaxerxes,[z] kings of Persia. [15]The temple was completed on the third day of the month Adar, in the sixth year of the reign of King Darius.[a]

[16]Then the people of Israel—the priests, the Levites and the rest of the exiles—celebrated the dedication[b] of the house of God with joy. [17]For the dedication of this house of God they offered[c] a hundred bulls, two hundred rams, four hundred male

---

[a] 3 Aramaic *sixty cubits* (about 27 meters)

Ezra 6:13–18

Work on the temple had made little progress, not only because of opposition but also because of the preoccupation of the returnees with building their own homes (Hag. 1:2–3). Because they had placed their own interests first, God had sent famine as judgment (Hag. 1:5–6, 10–11). Spurred by the preaching of Haggai and Zechariah, and under the leadership of Zerubbabel and Jeshua, a new effort was begun (Ezra 5:1–2; Hag. 1:12–15).

The reference to Artaxerxes seems out of place because this king didn't contribute to the rebuilding process. His name may have been inserted here because he contributed to the work of the temple at a later date under Ezra (7:21–24).

The temple was finished on March 12, 516 B.C., almost 70 years after its destruction. The renewed work had begun on September 21, 520 (Hag. 1:15), and sustained effort had continued for about three and a half years. The second temple, though not as grand as Solomon's, lasted much longer. The general plan of the second resembled that of the first. But the Most Holy Place was left empty; the ark of the covenant had been lost through the Babylonian conquest.

The number of animals sacrificed at the temple dedication was small compared to the thousands in similar situations under Solomon (1 Kings 8:5, 63), Hezekiah (2 Chron. 30:24), and Josiah (2 Chron. 35:7). But it represented a real sacrifice under the prevailing conditions. We have no need to offer animal sacrifices to atone for our sins, since Jesus Christ has done this vicariously on our behalf. But Romans 12:1 advises us that believers are to be living sacrifices, and Hebrews 13:15–16 instructs us to offer two sacrifices to God: verbal praise and doing good and sharing with others. Are you being faithful on all counts?

lambs and, as a sin offering for all Israel, twelve male goats, one for each of the tribes of Israel. [18]And they installed the priests in their divisions[d] and the Levites in their groups[e] for the service of God at Jerusalem, according to what is written in the Book of Moses.[f]

The Passover

[19]On the fourteenth day of the first month, the exiles celebrated the Passover.[g] [20]The priests and Levites had purified themselves and were all ceremonially clean. The Levites slaughtered[h] the Passover lamb for all the exiles, for their brothers the priests and for themselves. [21]So the Israelites who had returned from the exile ate it, together with all who had separated themselves[i] from the unclean practices[j] of their Gentile neighbors in order to seek the LORD,[k] the God of Israel. [22]For seven days they celebrated with joy the Feast of Unleavened Bread,[l] because the LORD had filled them with joy by changing the attitude[m] of the king of Assyria, so that he assisted them in the work on the house of God, the God of Israel.

Ezra Comes to Jerusalem

7 After these things, during the reign of Artaxerxes[n] king of Persia, Ezra son of Seraiah, the son of Azariah, the son of Hilkiah,[o] [2]the son of Shallum, the son of Zadok,[p] the son of Ahitub,[q] [3]the son of Amariah, the son of Azariah, the son of Meraioth, [4]the son of Zerahiah, the son of Uzzi, the son of Bukki, [5]the son of Abishua, the son of Phinehas, the son of Eleazar, the son of Aaron the chief priest— [6]this Ezra[r] came up from Babylon. He was a teacher well versed in the Law of Moses, which the LORD, the God of Israel, had given. The king had granted him everything he asked, for the hand of the LORD his God was on him.[s] [7]Some of the Israelites, including priests, Levites, singers, gatekeepers and temple servants, also came up to Jerusalem in the seventh year of King Artaxerxes.[t]

[8]Ezra arrived in Jerusalem in the fifth month of the seventh year of the king. [9]He had begun his journey from Babylon on the first day of the first month, and he arrived in Jerusalem on the first day of the fifth month, for the gracious hand of his

6:18
d 1Ch 23:6; 2Ch 35:4; Lk 1:5
e 1Ch 24:1
f Nu 3:6-9; 8:9-11; 18:1-32

6:19
g Ex 12:11; Nu 28:16

6:20
h 2Ch 30:15,17; 35:11
6:21
i Ne 9:1; Ne 9:2
j Dt 18:9; Ezr 9:11; Eze 36:25
k 1Ch 22:19; Ps 14:2
6:22
l Ex 12:17 m Ezr 1:1

7:1
n Ezr 4:7; 6:14; Ne 2:1 o 2Ki 22:4

7:2
p 1Ki 1:8; 1Ch 6:8
q Ne 11:11

7:6
r Ne 12:36
s Ezr 5:5; Isa 41:20

7:7
t Ezr 8:1

Ezra 6:19–22

🔲 The returning exiles began celebrating Passover and the Feast of Unleavened Bread on April 21, 516 B.C. They weren't uncompromising separatists but were willing to accept any who would disconnect themselves from the paganism of the foreigners introduced into the area by the Assyrians (see "There and Then" for 4:1–5). This likely refers to Gentile converts but could also mean Israelites from the former northern kingdom or Judahites who had remained in Judah rather than being taken into exile.

"The king of Assyria" is a surprising description of Darius, the Persian monarch. But even after the fall of Assyria in 612 B.C. the term "Assyria" was used for territories formerly occupied by the Assyrians. Persian kings adopted a variety of titles (much as they accumulated gods; see notes for 6:1–12), including "king of Babylon" (cf. 5:13; Neh. 13:6).

🔲 The Persians assimilated the "best" ideas (gods and titles) from the cultures under their domination, adopting what seemed to fit and discarding what didn't. Many people today take a similar approach. They will dabble in a bit of astrology, sprinkling in pinches of humanism, Christianity, Buddhism, yoga, and/or meditation. But our God isn't an accessory to be added onto our "package" or more RAM to boost our computing

power. He's the "King of kings" and "Lord of lords" from eternity past and forever. His absolute holiness places him above all other powers and all created beings. He's utterly worthy of our complete devotion and worship.

Ezra 7:1–10

🔲 With chapter 7 comes a major shift in the book of Ezra. "After these things" refers to the completion and dedication of the temple (in 516 B.C.), recounted in chapter 6. Now, almost 60 years later, in 458, Ezra led a group of exiles to Jerusalem. In addition to being a priest who could trace his ancestry back to Israel's first priest, Aaron, Ezra was a committed student and teacher (lit., "scribe," as in Neh. 8:1,4,9,13) of the Law of Moses. We are not told why Ezra hadn't joined the post-exilic community in Judah sooner, but his activities in Babylon were obviously esteemed even by King Artaxerxes and others in the Persian government.

🔲 Some form of the striking phrase "the gracious hand of his God was on [him]" occurs in verses 6 and 9, as well as in 7:28, 8:18, 8:22, 8:31, Nehemiah 2:8, and Nehemiah 2:18. The phrase denotes God's permanent help and grace that rest on a person or group. What more beautiful sign of God's approval and blessing would be possible? What indications do you or your fellowship have of God's gracious hand being on you as you endeavor to further his kingdom?

God was on him. *u* 10For Ezra had devoted himself to the study and observance of the Law of the LORD, and to teaching *v* its decrees and laws in Israel.

King Artaxerxes' Letter to Ezra

11This is a copy of the letter King Artaxerxes had given to Ezra the priest and teacher, a man learned in matters concerning the commands and decrees of the LORD for Israel:

12 *a* Artaxerxes, king of kings, *w*

To Ezra the priest, a teacher of the Law of the God of heaven:

Greetings.

13Now I decree that any of the Israelites in my kingdom, including priests and Levites, who wish to go to Jerusalem with you, may go. 14You are sent by the king and his seven advisers *x* to inquire about Judah and Jerusalem with regard to the Law of your God, which is in your hand. 15Moreover, you are to

7:15
y 1Ch 29:6
z 1Ch 29:6,9;
2Ch 6:2
7:16
a Ezr 8:25
b Zec 6:10
7:17
c 2Ki 3:4
d Nu 15:5-12
e Dt 12:5-11

take with you the silver and gold that the king and his advisers have freely given *y* to the God of Israel, whose dwelling *z* is in Jerusalem, 16together with all the silver and gold *a* you may obtain from the province of Babylon, as well as the freewill offerings of the people and priests for the temple of their God in Jerusalem. *b* 17With this money be sure to buy bulls, rams and male lambs, *c* together with their grain offerings and drink offerings, *d* and sacrifice *e* them on the altar of the temple of your God in Jerusalem.

18You and your brother Jews may then do whatever seems best with the rest of the silver and gold, in accordance with the will of your God. 19Deliver *f* to the God of Jerusalem all the articles entrusted to you for worship in the temple of your God. 20And anything else needed for the temple of your God that

you may have occasion to supply, you may provide from the royal treasury. *g*

21Now I, King Artaxerxes, order all the treasurers of Trans-Euphrates to provide with diligence whatever Ezra the priest, a teacher of the Law of the God of heaven, may ask of you— 22up to a hundred talents *b* of silver, a hundred cors *c* of wheat, a hundred baths *d* of wine, a hundred baths *d* of olive oil, and salt without limit. 23Whatever the God of heaven has prescribed, let it be done with diligence for the temple of the God of heaven. Why should there be

wrath against the realm of the king and of his sons? *h* 24You are also to know that you have no authority to impose taxes, tribute or duty *i* on any of the priests, Levites, singers, gatekeepers, temple servants or other workers at this house of God. *j*

25And you, Ezra, in accordance with the wisdom of your God, which you possess, appoint *k* magistrates and judges to administer justice to all the people of Trans-Euphrates—all who know the laws of your God. And you are to teach *l* any who do not know them. 26Whoever does not obey the law of your God and the law of the king must surely be punished by death, banishment, confiscation of property, or imprisonment. *m*

a 12 The text of Ezra 7:12-26 is in Aramaic.   *b* 22 That is, about 3 3/4 tons (about 3.4 metric tons)   *c* 22 That is, probably about 600 bushels (about 22 kiloliters)   *d* 22 That is, probably about 600 gallons (about 2.2 kiloliters)

Ezra 7:11–28

The extensive powers given to Ezra by King Artaxerxes are striking. He received an enormous "blank check" (vv. 18–22; see NIV text note for v. 22 regarding the amount of silver), and his authority extended to secular fields—with grave consequences for disobedience (vv. 25–26).

Verse 27 begins a section, continuing through chapter 9, written in the first person. This portion of the book was evidently taken from Ezra's personal memoirs.

Later passages from the book of Nehemiah show that Ezra was primarily a priest and teacher, not an administrator and visionary leader. That role fell to Nehemiah, as governor of Judah. Yet the assurance that God had called him and opened the doors gave Ezra the courage and strength to undertake his great task (v. 28). When has God called you to do something in his name outside your normal sphere of influence, comfort zone, training, vocation, or experience? How faithfully did he work to see you through?

[27] Praise be to the LORD, the God of our fathers, who has put it into the king's heart[n] to bring honor[o] to the house of the LORD in Jerusalem in this way [28] and who has extended his good favor[p] to me before the king and his advisers and all the king's powerful officials. Because the hand of the LORD my God was on me,[q] I took courage and gathered leading men from Israel to go up with me.

List of the Family Heads Returning With Ezra

8 These are the family heads and those registered with them who came up with me from Babylon during the reign of King Artaxerxes:[r]

[2] of the descendants of Phinehas, Gershom;
of the descendants of Ithamar, Daniel;
of the descendants of David, Hattush [3] of the descendants of Shecaniah;[s]

of the descendants of Parosh,[t] Zechariah, and with him were registered 150 men;
[4] of the descendants of Pahath-Moab,[u] Eliehoenai son of Zerahiah, and with him 200 men;

7:27
n Ezr 1:1; 6:22
o 1Ch 29:12
7:28
p 2Ki 25:28
q Ezr 5:5; 9:9

8:1
r Ezr 7:7

8:3
s 1Ch 3:22 t Ezr 2:3

8:4
u Ezr 2:6

Ezra 8:1–14

 Verses 1–14 list those who accompanied Ezra from Mesopotamia, including the descendants of 15 individuals. The figures of the men listed total 1,496, in addition to the individuals named. There were also a considerable number of women and children (v. 21). An additional group of about 40 Levites (vv. 18–19) and 220 "temple servants" (v. 20) also is indicated.

Humanly speaking, the devotion of the temple servants was remarkable. Socially, they were a group with mixed origins, inferior to the Levites in status. But God's Spirit had motivated them to respond in larger numbers than the Levites—as had also been the case in the earlier return (cf. 2:40–42; 2:43–58). When in your experience have less prominent or low-profile individuals played a significant role in furthering God's kingdom cause (cf. 1 Cor. 1:26–31)? Are you quick to accept a challenge when the Spirit calls you, or do you mentally tick off the names of others who are more "obviously" qualified? Can you cite similar Biblical examples?

Snapshots

8:2–3

The Girl Preacher

Thirteen-year-old Mary—the "girl preacher"—lives in Malawi. A childcare facilitator takes me to her home. Her sponsors' photographs on the wall remind me of an incredible bond spanning the distance.

Mary appears in the doorway. Reserved and shy, she's also very polite.
"I have heard a very interesting story that you love reading the Bible," I encourage.
"I love it so much!"
"Would you like to read to me your favorite verse?"
"Why not?" (with surging confidence).
Mary dashes to her room, returning with a Tumbuka Bible. "All the good things you people have done for me have culminated into the joy of having my own Bible," she offers. Mary deftly flips pages.
"I have found the verse," she announces. "It is Mark 13:33. I will read for you: 'Be on guard! Be alert! You do not know when that time will come.'" She reads with an amazing accuracy, precise intonation, rhythmically, and with an accent typical of her vernacular.
"Why do you like this verse, Mary?"
"You know, Sir, these are the last days when those who believe must believe more, and those who do not believe in Jesus must repent and believe before this warning takes them over," she responds, looking at the floor and playing with the pages.
"Amen!" I agree, chuckling—but also impressed and touched.

> "All the good things you people have done for me have culminated into the joy of having my own Bible."

8:6
v Ezr 2:15; Ne 7:20;
10:16

5 of the descendants of Zattu,ᵃ Shecaniah son of Jahaziel, and with him 300 men;

6 of the descendants of Adin,ᵛ Ebed son of Jonathan, and with him 50 men;

7 of the descendants of Elam, Jeshaiah son of Athaliah, and with him 70 men;

8 of the descendants of Shephatiah, Zebadiah son of Michael, and with him 80 men;

9 of the descendants of Joab, Obadiah son of Jehiel, and with him 218 men;

10 of the descendants of Bani,ᵇ Shelomith son of Josiphiah, and with him 160 men;

11 of the descendants of Bebai, Zechariah son of Bebai, and with him 28 men;

12 of the descendants of Azgad, Johanan son of Hakkatan, and with him 110 men;

8:13
w Ezr 2:13

13 of the descendants of Adonikam,ʷ the last ones, whose names were Eliphelet, Jeuel and Shemaiah, and with them 60 men;

14 of the descendants of Bigvai, Uthai and Zaccur, and with them 70 men.

The Return to Jerusalem

8:15
x ver 21,31
y Ezr 2:40; 7:7

15 I assembled them at the canal that flows toward Ahava,ˣ and we camped there three days. When I checked among the people and the priests, I found no Levitesʸ there. 16 So I summoned Eliezer, Ariel, Shemaiah, Elnathan, Jarib, Elnathan, Nathan, Zechariah and Meshullam, who were leaders, and Joiarib and Elnathan, who were men of learning, 17 and I sent them to Iddo, the leader in Casiphia. I told them what

8:17
z Ezr 2:43

to say to Iddo and his kinsmen, the temple servantsᶻ in Casiphia, so that they might bring attendants to us for the house of our God. 18 Because the gracious hand of our

8:18
a Ezr 5:5

God was on us,ᵃ they brought us Sherebiah, a capable man, from the descendants of Mahli son of Levi, the son of Israel, and Sherebiah's sons and brothers, 18 men; 19 and Hashabiah, together with Jeshaiah from the descendants of Merari, and his

8:20
b 1Ch 9:2; Ezr 2:43

brothers and nephews, 20 men. 20 They also brought 220 of the temple servantsᵇ— a body that David and the officials had established to assist the Levites. All were registered by name.

8:21
c ver 15; 2Ch 20:3
d Ps 5:8; 107:7

21 There, by the Ahava Canal,ᶜ I proclaimed a fast, so that we might humble ourselves before our God and ask him for a safe journeyᵈ for us and our children, with

8:22
e Ne 2:9;
Ezr 7:6,9,28
f Ezr 5:5
g Dt 31:17;
2Ch 15:2
8:23
h 2Ch 20:3; 33:13

all our possessions. 22 I was ashamed to ask the king for soldiersᵉ and horsemen to protect us from enemies on the road, because we had told the king, "The gracious hand of our God is on everyoneᶠ who looks to him, but his great anger is against all who forsake him.ᵍ" 23 So we fastedʰ and petitioned our God about this, and he answered our prayer.

8:24
i ver 18
8:25
j ver 33;
Ezr 7:15,16

24 Then I set apart twelve of the leading priests, together with Sherebiah,ⁱ Hashabiah and ten of their brothers, 25 and I weighed outʲ to them the offering of silver and gold and the articles that the king, his advisers, his officials and all Israel present there had donated for the house of our God. 26 I weighed out to them 650 talentsᶜ of silver, silver articles weighing 100 talents,ᵈ 100 talentsᵈ of gold, 27 20 bowls of gold valued at 1,000 darics,ᵉ and two fine articles of polished bronze, as precious as gold.

ᵃ 5 Some Septuagint manuscripts (also 1 Esdras 8:32); Hebrew does not have *Zattu*.   ᵇ 10 Some Septuagint manuscripts (also 1 Esdras 8:36); Hebrew does not have *Bani*.   ᶜ 26 That is, about 25 tons (about 22 metric tons)   ᵈ 26 That is, about 3 3/4 tons (about 3.4 metric tons)   ᵉ 27 That is, about 19 pounds (about 8.5 kilograms)

Ezra 8:15–36

📖 Scripture speaks often of unholy shame (Jer. 48:13; Mic. 3:7) and sometimes, as here in verse 22 (cf. 9:6), of a sense of holy shame. Having proclaimed his faith in God's ability to protect the caravan, Ezra was embarrassed to ask for human protection. Grave dangers faced those traveling the great distance from Babylon to Judah. The vast treasures they were carrying—the amounts of silver and gold described in verse 26 would be worth millions of dollars today—offered a tempting bait for thieves.

🔲 "Children" (v. 21) designated those younger than twenty, with a stress on the younger ages. Such "little ones" (as the Hebrew word is translated in Deut. 1:39) are most vulnerable in times of war or danger. Still today, the most tragic victims of conflict are too often those least able to care for themselves. What can you do to help when such situations arise around the globe? Though some are called to respond more directly (e.g., on site), prayer and fasting and monetary giving are effective responses available to most of us.

28I said to them, "You as well as these articles are consecrated to the LORD.*k* The silver and gold are a freewill offering to the LORD, the God of your fathers. 29Guard them carefully until you weigh them out in the chambers of the house of the LORD in Jerusalem before the leading priests and the Levites and the family heads of Israel." 30Then the priests and Levites received the silver and gold and sacred articles that had been weighed out to be taken to the house of our God in Jerusalem.

31On the twelfth day of the first month we set out from the Ahava Canal*l* to go to Jerusalem. The hand of our God was on us, and he protected us from enemies and bandits along the way. 32So we arrived in Jerusalem, where we rested three days.*m*

33On the fourth day, in the house of our God, we weighed out the silver and gold and the sacred articles into the hands of Meremoth*n* son of Uriah, the priest. Eleazar son of Phinehas was with him, and so were the Levites Jozabad son of Jeshua and Noadiah son of Binnui.*o* 34Everything was accounted for by number and weight, and the entire weight was recorded at that time.

35Then the exiles who had returned from captivity sacrificed burnt offerings to the God of Israel: twelve bulls for all Israel, ninety-six rams, seventy-seven male lambs and, as a sin offering, twelve male goats.*p* All this was a burnt offering to the LORD. 36They also delivered the king's orders*q* to the royal satraps and to the governors of Trans-Euphrates, who then gave assistance to the people and to the house of God.*r*

Ezra's Prayer About Intermarriage

9 After these things had been done, the leaders came to me and said, "The people of Israel, including the priests and the Levites, have not kept themselves separate*s* from the neighboring peoples with their detestable practices, like those of the Canaanites, Hittites, Perizzites, Jebusites, Ammonites,*t* Moabites, Egyptians and Amorites.*u* 2They have taken some of their daughters*v* as wives for themselves and their sons, and have mingled the holy race*w* with the peoples around them. And the leaders and officials have led the way in this unfaithfulness."*x*

3When I heard this, I tore my tunic and cloak, pulled hair from my head and beard and sat down appalled. 4Then everyone who trembled*y* at the words of the God of Israel gathered around me because of this unfaithfulness of the exiles. And I sat there appalled until the evening sacrifice.

5Then, at the evening sacrifice,*z* I rose from my self-abasement, with my tunic and cloak torn, and fell on my knees with my hands spread out to the LORD my God 6and prayed:

"O my God, I am too ashamed and disgraced to lift up my face to you, my God, because our sins are higher than our heads and our guilt has reached to the heavens.*a* 7From the days of our forefathers*b* until now, our guilt has been great. Because of our sins, we and our kings and our priests have been subjected to the sword*c* and captivity,*d* to pillage and humiliation*e* at the hand of foreign kings, as it is today.

8:28
k Lev 21:6; 22:2-3

8:31
l ver 15

8:32
m Ge 40:13; Ne 2:11

8:33
n Ne 3:4,21
o Ne 3:24

8:35
p 2Ch 29:21; Ezr 6:17
8:36
q Ezr 7:21-24
r Est 9:3

9:1
s Ezr 6:21; Ne 9:2
t Ge 19:38
u Ex 13:5
9:2
v Ex 34:16
w Ex 22:31
x Ezr 10:2

9:4
y Ezr 10:3

9:5
z Ex 29:41

9:6
a 2Ch 28:9; Job 42:6; Ps 38:4; Rev 18:5
9:7
b 2Ch 29:6
9:7
c Eze 21:1-32
d Dt 28:64
e Dt 28:37

Ezra 9:1–15

Ezra's act of pulling out his hair from his head and beard (v. 3) is unique in the Bible. Nehemiah demonstrated a different response: When confronted with the same problem of intermarriage, he pulled out the hair of the offenders (Neh. 13:25)!

Ezra's prayer (vv. 6–15) may be compared to those of Nehemiah (Neh. 9:5–37) and Daniel (Dan. 9:4–19). It included a general confession (v. 6), an acknowledgement of sins of former times (v. 7), a recital of God's mercy and goodness (vv. 8–9), a further confession of Israel's sins (vv. 10–12), and a final admission of guilt and an appeal for mercy (vv. 13–15).

Judah's leaders "led the way" (v. 2) in disobey-

ing God's commandment against intermarriage with the pagan nations (Deut. 7:1–4). When those in positions of responsibility fall, they often lead others astray. Humanly speaking, there may have been reasons for such intermarriages, such as a shortage of available Jewish women. But human reasoning and excuses never justify disobedience. When has this difficult lesson been driven home for you?

The word "appalled" (vv. 3,4) means to be stunned by the horror of something (cf. Dan. 4:19, "greatly perplexed"; Dan. 8:27). How often are Christians today truly appalled by sin? What factors contribute to our indifference? How can we (with the Spirit's help) be moved, like Ezra, to confess our own sins and those of God's people?

9:8
f Ps 25:16; Isa 33:2
g Ge 45:7
h Ecc 12:11;
Isa 22:23 / Ps 13:3
9:9
i Ex 1:14; Ne 9:36
k Ezr 7:28
l Ps 69:35; Isa 43:1;
Jer 32:44

9:10
m Dt 11:8;
Isa 1:19-20
9:11
n Lev 18:25-28
o Dt 9:4

9:12
p Ex 34:15; Dt 7:3;
23:6

9:13
q Job 11:6;
Ps 103:10

9:14
r Ne 13:27 *s* Dt 9:8
t Dt 9:14
9:15
u Ge 18:25;
Ps 51:4; Jer 12:1;
Da 9:7 *v* Ne 9:33;
Ps 130:3; Mal 3:2
w 1Ki 8:47

10:1
x 2Ch 20:9; Da 9:20

10:2
y Ezr 9:2; Ne 13:27
z Dt 30:8-10

10:3
a 2Ch 34:31
b Ex 34:16;
Dt 7:2-3; Ezr 9:4

10:5
c Ne 5:12; 13:25

10:6
d Ex 34:28; Dt 9:18

8 "But now, for a brief moment, the LORD our God has been gracious *f* in leaving us a remnant *g* and giving us a firm place *h* in his sanctuary, and so our God gives light to our eyes *i* and a little relief in our bondage. 9 Though we are slaves, *i* our God has not deserted us in our bondage. He has shown us kindness *k* in the sight of the kings of Persia: He has granted us new life to rebuild the house of our God and repair its ruins, *l* and he has given us a wall of protection in Judah and Jerusalem.

10 "But now, O our God, what can we say after this? For we have disregarded the commands *m* 11 you gave through your servants the prophets when you said: 'The land you are entering to possess is a land polluted *n* by the corruption of its peoples. By their detestable practices *o* they have filled it with their impurity from one end to the other. 12 Therefore, do not give your daughters in marriage to their sons or take their daughters for your sons. Do not seek a treaty of friendship with them *p* at any time, that you may be strong and eat the good things of the land and leave it to your children as an everlasting inheritance.'

13 "What has happened to us is a result of our evil deeds and our great guilt, and yet, our God, you have punished us less than our sins have deserved *q* and have given us a remnant like this. 14 Shall we again break your commands and intermarry *r* with the peoples who commit such detestable practices? Would you not be angry enough with us to destroy us, *s* leaving us no remnant *t* or survivor? 15 O LORD, God of Israel, you are righteous! *u* We are left this day as a remnant. Here we are before you in our guilt, though because of it not one of us can stand *v* in your presence. *w*"

The People's Confession of Sin

10 While Ezra was praying and confessing, *x* weeping and throwing himself down before the house of God, a large crowd of Israelites—men, women and children—gathered around him. They too wept bitterly. 2 Then Shecaniah son of Jehiel, one of the descendants of Elam, said to Ezra, "We have been unfaithful *y* to our God by marrying foreign women from the peoples around us. But in spite of this, there is still hope for Israel. *z* 3 Now let us make a covenant *a* before our God to send away *b* all these women and their children, in accordance with the counsel of my lord and of those who fear the commands of our God. Let it be done according to the Law. 4 Rise up; this matter is in your hands. We will support you, so take courage and do it."

5 So Ezra rose up and put the leading priests and Levites and all Israel under oath *c* to do what had been suggested. And they took the oath. 6 Then Ezra withdrew from before the house of God and went to the room of Jehohanan son of Eliashib. While he was there, he ate no food and drank no water, *d* because he continued to mourn over the unfaithfulness of the exiles.

7 A proclamation was then issued throughout Judah and Jerusalem for all the exiles to assemble in Jerusalem. 8 Anyone who failed to appear within three days

---

Ezra 10:1–17

Verse 3 reflects the fact that in ancient societies, as often in ours, mothers were given custody of their children when marriages were dissolved (cf. Gen. 21:14). In Babylon divorced women were granted their children and had to wait for them to grow up before remarrying. In Greece, though, the children remained with their fathers.

According to verse 9, this assembly occurred in the "ninth month" (Kislev, Nov.–Dec.), in the middle of the "rainy season" (v. 13). The Hebrew word for "rain" in verse 9 indicates heavy, torrential downpours. December is a relatively cold month in Jerusalem, with temperatures in the fifties or even forties (Fahrenheit). The

people shivered, not only because they were drenched, but probably also because they sensed a sign of divine displeasure in the abnormally heavy rains (cf. 1 Sam. 12:16–18; Ezek. 13:10–13).

The words in verses 2–4 were a clarion call to action. Weeping wasn't enough. Courageous and painful decisions had to be made—by the people, not just their leadership. Compare verse 4 and David's exhortation: "Arise and be doing! The LORD be with you!" (1 Chron. 22:16, lit. tr.). When has God called your nation, your church—or you yourself—to get busy and right a wrong, rather than just confessing it and feeling bad? What were the results?

would forfeit all his property, in accordance with the decision of the officials and
elders, and would himself be expelled from the assembly of the exiles.

9 Within the three days, all the men of Judah and Benjamin[e] had gathered in Jerusalem. And on the twentieth day of the ninth month, all the people were sitting
in the square before the house of God, greatly distressed by the occasion and because of the rain. 10 Then Ezra the priest stood up and said to them, "You have been
unfaithful; you have married foreign women, adding to Israel's guilt. 11 Now make
confession to the LORD, the God of your fathers, and do his will. Separate yourselves
from the peoples around you and from your foreign wives."[f]
12 The whole assembly responded with a loud voice:[g] "You are right! We must do
as you say. 13 But there are many people here and it is the rainy season; so we cannot
stand outside. Besides, this matter cannot be taken care of in a day or two, because
we have sinned greatly in this thing. 14 Let our officials act for the whole assembly.
Then let everyone in our towns who has married a foreign woman come at a set time,
along with the elders and judges[h] of each town, until the fierce anger[i] of our God in
this matter is turned away from us." 15 Only Jonathan son of Asahel and Jahzeiah son
of Tikvah, supported by Meshullam and Shabbethai[j] the Levite, opposed this.
16 So the exiles did as was proposed. Ezra the priest selected men who were family heads, one from each family division, and all of them designated by name. On
the first day of the tenth month they sat down to investigate the cases, 17 and by the
first day of the first month they finished dealing with all the men who had married
foreign women.

Those Guilty of Intermarriage

18 Among the descendants of the priests, the following had married foreign
women:[k]

From the descendants of Jeshua[l] son of Jozadak, and his brothers: Maaseiah,
Eliezer, Jarib and Gedaliah. 19 (They all gave their hands[m] in pledge to put
away their wives, and for their guilt they each presented a ram from the flock
as a guilt offering.)[n]
20 From the descendants of Immer:[o]
Hanani and Zebadiah.
21 From the descendants of Harim:[p]
Maaseiah, Elijah, Shemaiah, Jehiel and Uzziah.
22 From the descendants of Pashhur:[q]
Elioenai, Maaseiah, Ishmael, Nethanel, Jozabad and Elasah.

23 Among the Levites:[r]

Jozabad, Shimei, Kelaiah (that is, Kelita), Pethahiah, Judah and Eliezer.
24 From the singers:
Eliashib.[s]

10:9 [e] Ezr 1:5
10:11 [f] ver 3; Dt 24:1; Ne 9:2; Mal 2:10-16
10:12 [g] Jos 6:5
10:14 [h] Dt 16:18 [i] Nu 25:4; 2Ch 29:10; 30:8
10:15 [j] Ne 11:16
10:18 [k] Jdg 3:6 [l] Ezr 2:2
10:19 [m] 2Ki 10:15 [n] Lev 5:15; 6:6
10:20 [o] 1Ch 24:14
10:21 [p] 1Ch 24:8
10:22 [q] 1Ch 9:12
10:23 [r] Ne 8:7; 9:4
10:24 [s] Ne 3:1; 12:10; 13:7,28

Ezra 10:18–44

The committee of investigating elders and judges finished its work in three months (vv. 14–17). A ram (v. 19) was the prescribed guilt offering for a sin committed either unintentionally (Lev. 5:14–19) or intentionally (Lev. 6:1–7). Though the guilty may not have fully realized the gravity of their offense, they had no excuse. The Scriptures plainly set forth God's standards on marriage. Some of the marriages had produced children (Ezra 10:44), but this wasn't accepted as a reason for halting the proceedings.

What happened to a Jewish community that was lax concerning intermarriage can be seen in the example of the Elephantine settlement in Egypt, which was contemporary with Ezra and Nehemiah. There the Jews who had married pagan spouses expressed their devotion to pagan gods in addition to the Lord. The Elephantine community was gradually assimilated into the broader Egyptian culture and disappeared.

A total of about 110 men out of the thousands of returnees mentioned in chapters 2 and 8 had married pagan women. A drop in the bucket, we might say. Surely nothing to warrant such radical actions! But drastic times can indeed call for drastic measures. Ezra's zero tolerance policy no doubt quashed a trend that would have devastated the already vulnerable returnees. As a parent or church member, for which issues have you drawn a line in the sand? What are the non-negotiables for you personally? How do you hold firmly to your values without acting judgmentally toward others?

From the gatekeepers:
Shallum, Telem and Uri.

²⁵And among the other Israelites:

10:25
t Ezr 2:3

From the descendants of Parosh:^{*t*}
Ramiah, Izziah, Malkijah, Mijamin, Eleazar, Malkijah and Benaiah.

10:26
u ver 2

²⁶From the descendants of Elam:^{*u*}
Mattaniah, Zechariah, Jehiel, Abdi, Jeremoth and Elijah.
²⁷From the descendants of Zattu:
Elioenai, Eliashib, Mattaniah, Jeremoth, Zabad and Aziza.
²⁸From the descendants of Bebai:
Jehohanan, Hananiah, Zabbai and Athlai.
²⁹From the descendants of Bani:
Meshullam, Malluch, Adaiah, Jashub, Sheal and Jeremoth.
³⁰From the descendants of Pahath-Moab:
Adna, Kelal, Benaiah, Maaseiah, Mattaniah, Bezalel, Binnui and Manasseh.
³¹From the descendants of Harim:
Eliezer, Ishijah, Malkijah, Shemaiah, Shimeon, ³²Benjamin, Malluch and Shemariah.
³³From the descendants of Hashum:
Mattenai, Mattattah, Zabad, Eliphelet, Jeremai, Manasseh and Shimei.
³⁴From the descendants of Bani:
Maadai, Amram, Uel, ³⁵Benaiah, Bedeiah, Keluhi, ³⁶Vaniah, Meremoth, Eliashib, ³⁷Mattaniah, Mattenai and Jaasu.
³⁸From the descendants of Binnui:^{*a*}
Shimei, ³⁹Shelemiah, Nathan, Adaiah, ⁴⁰Macnadebai, Shashai, Sharai, ⁴¹Azarel, Shelemiah, Shemariah, ⁴²Shallum, Amariah and Joseph.
⁴³From the descendants of Nebo:
Jeiel, Mattithiah, Zabad, Zebina, Jaddai, Joel and Benaiah.

⁴⁴All these had married foreign women, and some of them had children by these wives.^{*b*}

---

^{*a*} 37,38 See Septuagint (also 1 Esdras 9:34); Hebrew *Jaasu* ³⁸*and Bani and Binnui,*   ^{*b*} 44 Or *and they sent them away with their children*

INTRODUCTION TO
Nehemiah

AUTHOR
The books of Ezra and Nehemiah were originally one book. Ezra has traditionally been considered the primary author of Ezra-Nehemiah, but his authorship is uncertain. If Ezra was the author of Nehemiah, he apparently was quoting directly from the writings of Nehemiah, because the content is described as "the words of Nehemiah" (1:1) and the book is written in the first person.

DATE WRITTEN
Nehemiah was probably written around 430 B.C., during the period of restoration in and around Jerusalem.

ORIGINAL READERS
Nehemiah was written to the Jews who were returning from exile to encourage them to continue the work of restoring Jerusalem, the temple, and the community.

TIMELINE

	1400BC	1300	1200	1100	1000	900	800	700	600	500	400
Fall of Jerusalem (586 B.C.)											
Persia's conquest of Babylon (539 B.C.)											
First return of exiles to Jerusalem (538 B.C.)											
Ministries of Haggai and Zechariah (c. 520–480 B.C.)											
Temple restoration completed (516 B.C.)											
Second return to Jerusalem under Ezra (458 B.C.)											
Third return to Jerusalem under Nehemiah (445 B.C.)											
Jerusalem's wall rebuilt (445 B.C.)											
Book of Nehemiah written (c. 430 B.C.)											

THEMES
Nehemiah describes the rebuilding of the walls of Jerusalem and the restoration of God's people. It contains the following themes:

1. *Renewal.* While rebuilding the walls of Jerusalem was the obvious material challenge facing Nehemiah, reestablishing the Jews' commitment to God and to the Mosaic Law was his primary spiritual concern. Nehemiah 9:1—12:47 captures the people's dramatic response to the reading of the law by Ezra (8:1–18): They confessed their sins (9:1–37) and voluntarily recommitted themselves to God's covenant (9:38—10:39). Later, during a second visit from Nehemiah, they agreed to support the temple (13:4–14), keep the Sabbath (13:15–22), and divorce their foreign wives (13:23–31). Commitment to God requires more than words; it necessitates action.

2. *Prayer.* Prayer is essential to any work of God, and Nehemiah was a model leader who initiated his plans only after consultation with God. A man of prayer (1:4; 2:4; 4:4; 5:19; 6:9,14; 13:14,22,29,31), his efforts were richly blessed by God. God uses people, especially godly lead-

ers, to care for his people, and a leader's dependence on God through prayer is an essential ingredient for success.

3. *Opposition.* Any time we undertake a task for God, the possibility is quite real that we will encounter opposition. Nehemiah's task of rebuilding the walls of Jerusalem was met with strong resistance, which was overcome with God's help (2:19–20; 4:1–15; 5:1–19; 6:1–14). Despite opposition, God always fulfills his promises.

FAITH IN ACTION

The pages of Nehemiah contain life lessons and role models of faith—people who challenge believers to put their faith in action.

Role Models

- NEHEMIAH (4:14–16) encouraged the people to work, prepared to fight and trusting God to help them. Is there someone you can encourage today to stand up and actively resist God's enemies?

- SHALLUM AND HIS DAUGHTERS (3:12) represent one of many families united in their effort to rebuild the walls of Jerusalem. How can your family be strengthened by working together to accomplish a task for God? Do you join with your brothers and sisters in Christ to participate in God's work in the world?

- EZRA (8:5–6) openly praised God, modeling worship to the people. Do you need courage to drop your façade and express publicly your worship of, and love for, God? How can Ezra and the people's response encourage you?

- EZRA AND NEHEMIAH (8:1–9) partnered in leading God's people. What do you learn from this example? How were their strikingly different individual gifts complementary? How can working with a partner or within a team make your service to the Lord more effective?

Challenges

- Pray for your nation, identifying yourself with its people as you confess national sin and seek God's direction (1:5–11).

- Seek out service opportunities that can involve your entire family (3:3–32).

- Don't think you are too important to perform menial labor (3:5), especially when the task has a divine purpose.

- Determine to "work with all [your] heart" (4:6) to accomplish the tasks to which God has called you.

- When you feel your physical or emotional strength "giving out" (4:10), take courage by focusing on God's power and purposes through prayer (4:14), depending on him to fight for you (4:20).

- Resolve to confront injustice and work to help the poor and powerless (5:1–12).

- Serve others with humility, working alongside them and supplying their needs—even when it means having less for yourself (5:14–18).

- Expect personal attacks—lies, rumors, deceit, treachery, intimidation—from those who oppose God's work (6:2–14). Stand firm (6:11), trust God to protect you and your reputation (6:14), and focus on completing the work (6:15).

- If you don't work with a partner or as a team member in your kingdom endeavors, resolve to explore this as a possibility. Find news ways to collaborate with others in God's work.

- Review your life and God's interventions on your behalf. Can you conclude your review with *Nehemiah's statement to God:* "In all that has happened to [me], you have been just; you have acted faithfully, while [I] did wrong" (9:33)? Thank God for his mercy and faithfulness to you.

OUTLINE

I. Nehemiah Leads in the Rebuilding of the Wall (1:1—7:3)
II. Changes Under Ezra (7:4—10:39)
III. Jerusalem Repopulated and Wall Dedicated (11–12)
IV. Nehemiah's Return to Jerusalem and Leadership Role (13)

Nehemiah's Prayer

1 The words of Nehemiah son of Hacaliah:

In the month of Kislev[a] in the twentieth year, while I was in the citadel of Susa, 2Hanani,[b] one of my brothers, came from Judah with some other men, and I questioned them about the Jewish remnant[c] that survived the exile, and also about Jerusalem.

3They said to me, "Those who survived the exile and are back in the province are in great trouble and disgrace. The wall of Jerusalem is broken down, and its gates have been burned with fire.[d]"

4When I heard these things, I sat down and wept.[e] For some days I mourned and fasted[f] and prayed before the God of heaven. 5Then I said:

"O LORD, God of heaven, the great and awesome God,[g] who keeps his covenant of love[h] with those who love him and obey his commands, 6let your ear be attentive and your eyes open to hear[i] the prayer[j] your servant is praying before you day and night for your servants, the people of Israel. I confess the sins we Israelites, including myself and my father's house, have committed against you. 7We have acted very wickedly[k] toward you. We have not obeyed the commands, decrees and laws you gave your servant Moses.

8"Remember[l] the instruction you gave your servant Moses, saying, 'If you are unfaithful, I will scatter[m] you among the nations, 9but if you return to me and obey my commands, then even if your exiled people are at the farthest horizon, I will gather[n] them from there and bring them to the place I have chosen as a dwelling for my Name.'[o]

10"They are your servants and your people, whom you redeemed by your great strength and your mighty hand.[p] 11O Lord, let your ear be attentive[q] to the prayer of this your servant and to the prayer of your servants who delight in revering your name. Give your servant success today by granting him favor in the presence of this man."

I was cupbearer[r] to the king.

1:1
a Ne 10:1; Zec 7:1
1:2
b Ne 7:2
c Jer 52:28

1:3
d 2Ki 25:10; Ne 2:3,13,17
1:4
e Ps 137:1 f Ezr 9:4

1:5
g Dt 7:21; Ne 4:14
h Ex 20:6; Da 9:4
1:6
i 1Ki 8:29 j Da 9:17

1:7
k Dt 28:14-15; Ps 106:6
1:8
l 2Ki 20:3
m Lev 26:33

1:9
n Dt 30:4
o 1Ki 8:48; Jer 29:14

1:10
p Ex 32:11; Dt 9:29
1:11
q ver 6 r Ge 40:1

Nehemiah 1:1–11

The "twentieth year" (v. 1) referred to the twentieth year of the reign of the Persian king Artaxerxes I (cf. 2:1)—445 B.C. Jerusalem's walls that had been destroyed by the Babylonians in 586, despite abortive attempts to rebuild them (Ezra 4:7–23), remained in ruins. Without protective walls, Jerusalem was vulnerable to her numerous enemies. Yet, from a mixture of apathy and fear, the Jews failed to correct this glaring deficiency. They needed the dynamic catalyst of an inspired leader—a man named Nehemiah.

One of the cupbearer's duties was to choose and taste the king's wine to make sure it wasn't poisoned (see 2:1). Thus Nehemiah was undoubtedly a man who enjoyed the king's unreserved confidence. The need for trustworthy court attendants is underscored by the intrigues that characterized the Persian court. Xerxes, the father of Artaxerxes I, was killed in his own bedchamber by a courtier.

How easy it would have been for Nehemiah, serving in the Persian court at Susa, to separate himself from the guilt of the returnees in his intercessory prayer. Yet he made it a point not to exclude either himself or his family members (whether in Judah or Persia) in his confession of national sins (v. 6). A true sense of God's awesomeness inevitably reveals the depths of our own sinfulness (see Isa. 6:1–5; Luke 5:8). When you petition God on behalf of your nation, do you implicate yourself along with those others "out there"?

People of wealth and position typically have many "hangers on"—those who stay around them for what they can get—but very few they can really trust. Nehemiah's integrity was a testimony to this pagan king. Do you have a reputation for trustworthiness in your relationships with nonbelievers? Can people trust you not to take advantage of them?

Artaxerxes Sends Nehemiah to Jerusalem

2:1
s Ezr 7:1

2 In the month of Nisan in the twentieth year of King Artaxerxes, *s* when wine was brought for him, I took the wine and gave it to the king. I had not been sad in his presence before; ²so the king asked me, "Why does your face look so sad when you are not ill? This can be nothing but sadness of heart."

2:3
t 1Ki 1:31; Da 2:4;
5:10; 6:6,21
u Ps 137:6 v Ne 1:3

I was very much afraid, ³but I said to the king, "May the king live forever! *t* Why should my face not look sad when the city *u* where my fathers are buried lies in ruins, and its gates have been destroyed by fire? *v*"

⁴The king said to me, "What is it you want?"

Then I prayed to the God of heaven, ⁵and I answered the king, "If it pleases the king and if your servant has found favor in his sight, let him send me to the city in Judah where my fathers are buried so that I can rebuild it."

2:6
w Ne 5:14; 13:6

⁶Then the king *w*, with the queen sitting beside him, asked me, "How long will your journey take, and when will you get back?" It pleased the king to send me; so I set a time.

2:7
x Ezr 8:36

⁷I also said to him, "If it pleases the king, may I have letters to the governors of Trans-Euphrates, *x* so that they will provide me safe-conduct until I arrive in Judah?

2:8
y Ne 7:2 z ver 18;
Ezr 5:5; 7:6

⁸And may I have a letter to Asaph, keeper of the king's forest, so he will give me timber to make beams for the gates of the citadel *y* by the temple and for the city wall and for the residence I will occupy?" And because the gracious hand of my God was upon me, *z* the king granted my requests. ⁹So I went to the governors of Trans-Euphrates and gave them the king's letters. The king had also sent army officers and cavalry *a* with me.

2:9
a Ezr 8:22
2:10
b ver 19; Ne 4:1,7
c Ne 4:3; 13:4-7

¹⁰When Sanballat *b* the Horonite and Tobiah *c* the Ammonite official heard about

---

Nehemiah 2:1–10

🔖 There was a delay of about four months from the time Nehemiah first heard the news about Jerusalem's condition (1:1–3) until he broached the subject to the king. Even though Nehemiah was a royal favorite, he carefully bided his time, constantly praying for the right opportunity.

The king's servants were expected to keep their feelings to themselves and to display a cheerful disposition at all times before him. Yet anxiety gripped Nehemiah,

---

Snapshots

2:10

Friend of Family

Joseph is an experienced paraprofessional in monitoring, mobilizing, and teaching families in rural communities in Ghana. He has worked with a Christian relief organization there for almost 12 years. Joseph came to the job as an experienced farmer.

> "It is my wish that the school facilities and the homes of these families would be improved."

"I have to take care of about 350 families," he reports, summarizing his job description as a Friend of Family. During a typical working day, Joseph visits five to ten families. He mounts his bicycle every morning to visit distant communities to check on his clients' welfare. Joseph advises them on agricultural methods and encourages them to enroll their children, particularly the girls, in school.

"It is my wish that the school facilities and the homes of these families would be improved. I believe this would prevent the frequent migration of school children to the urban areas so in the future they could help develop their communities," he states.

Joseph faces daily challenges. Due to bad roads, some communities are cut off. And on account of the frequent movement of children it's difficult to trace all of them. But the advocacy role he plays for these deprived people gives him a sense of fulfillment. "It's not easy being away from my family, but I am coping," he concludes.

this, they were very much disturbed that someone had come to promote the welfare of the Israelites. [d]

Nehemiah Inspects Jerusalem's Walls

[11]I went to Jerusalem, and after staying there three days [e] [12]I set out during the night with a few men. I had not told anyone what my God had put in my heart to do for Jerusalem. There were no mounts with me except the one I was riding on. [13]By night I went out through the Valley Gate [f] toward the Jackal [a] Well and the Dung Gate, [g] examining the walls [h] of Jerusalem, which had been broken down, and its gates, which had been destroyed by fire. [14]Then I moved on toward the Fountain Gate [i] and the King's Pool, [j] but there was not enough room for my mount to get through; [15]so I went up the valley by night, examining the wall. Finally, I turned back and reentered through the Valley Gate. [16]The officials did not know where I had gone or what I was doing, because as yet I had said nothing to the Jews or the priests or nobles or officials or any others who would be doing the work.

[17]Then I said to them, "You see the trouble we are in: Jerusalem lies in ruins, and its gates have been burned with fire. [k] Come, let us rebuild the wall [l] of Jerusalem, and we will no longer be in disgrace. [m] [18]I also told them about the gracious hand of my God upon me [n] and what the king had said to me.

They replied, "Let us start rebuilding." So they began this good work.

[19]But when Sanballat the Horonite, Tobiah the Ammonite official and Geshem [o] the Arab heard about it, they mocked and ridiculed us. [p] "What is this you are doing?" they asked. "Are you rebelling against the king?"

[20]I answered them by saying, "The God of heaven will give us success. We his servants will start rebuilding, but as for you, you have no share [q] in Jerusalem or any claim or historic right to it."

Builders of the Wall

3 Eliashib [r] the high priest and his fellow priests went to work and rebuilt [s] the Sheep Gate. [t] They dedicated it and set its doors in place, building as far as the Tower of the Hundred, which they dedicated, and as far as the Tower of Hananel. [u]

[a] 13 Or *Serpent* or *Fig*

Side references

2:10
[d] Est 10:3

2:11
[e] Ge 40:13

2:13
[f] 2Ch 26:9 [g] Ne 3:13 [h] Ne 1:3

2:14
[i] Ne 3:15 [j] 2Ki 18:17

2:17
[k] Ne 1:3 [l] Ps 102:16; Isa 30:13; 58:12 [m] Eze 5:14

2:18
[n] 2Sa 2:7

2:19
[o] Ne 6:1,2,6 [p] Ps 44:13-16

2:20
[q] Ezr 4:3

3:1
[r] Ezr 10:24 [s] Isa 58:12 [t] ver 32; Ne 12:39 [u] Ne 12:39; Jer 31:38; Zec 14:10

---

likely not so much because of the king's question but in anticipation of the request he was to make. Nehemiah knew full well that Artaxerxes himself had stopped the Jewish efforts at rebuilding the wall (Ezra 4:17–23).

In addition to safe-conduct letters, Nehemiah probably asked for a brief leave of absence, which was later extended. Nehemiah 5:14 implies that he devoted 12 years to his first term as governor of Judah. Nehemiah then returned to report to the king before going back to Jerusalem for a second term (13:6–7).

This scene contains a beautiful example of spontaneous prayer. Before turning to answer the king, Nehemiah "prayed to the God of heaven" (v. 4). Despite his fear, he knew that he stood not only in the presence of an earthly monarch but before his God—the King of heaven. One of the most striking characteristics of Nehemiah was his ready recourse to prayer (cf. 1:4; 4:4,9; 5:19; 6:9,14; 13:14,22,29,31). Those who are boldest for God have a great need for prayer. How can you attest to this truth from your own life experience?

Nehemiah 2:11–20

Nehemiah didn't make a complete circuit of the walls, but only of the southern area. Jerusalem had always been attacked where she was most vulnerable,

from the north. So he likely assumed that the walls in that direction were totally destroyed. Jerusalem's walls and gates had lain in ruins since their destruction by Nebuchadnezzar some 140 years earlier, despite aborted attempts to rebuild them. The leaders and people had evidently become reconciled to this sad state of affairs. It took an outsider to assess the situation and rally them to renewed efforts.

Nehemiah appealed to historical claims to reject the interference of the opposing leaders (vv. 19–20; see "There and Then" for 4:1–23 regarding their identities). By his great confidence and dependence upon God for success, Nehemiah inspired the Jewish leaders and people to a task they had considered beyond their abilities. What part does morale play when God's people face a difficult or discouraging job? How can godly leaders and inspired laypersons encourage the workers? Who are the "Barnabases" in your Christian circles (see Acts 4:36 and "Barnabas" article at Acts 11:22, p. 1813)? Is this a role for which you might be gifted?

Nehemiah 3:1–32

This record of builders begins at the Sheep Gate, in the northeast corner of Jerusalem, and moves in a counterclockwise direction as it describes the recon-

3:2
v Ne 7:36

²The men of Jericho ^{v} built the adjoining section, and Zaccur son of Imri built next to them.

3:3
w 2Ch 33:14;
Ne 12:39

³The Fish Gate ^{w} was rebuilt by the sons of Hassenaah. They laid its beams and put its doors and bolts and bars in place. ⁴Meremoth son of Uriah, the son of Hakkoz, repaired the next section. Next to him Meshullam son of Berekiah, the son of Meshezabel, made repairs, and next to him Zadok son of Baana also made repairs.

3:5
x 2Sa 14:2

⁵The next section was repaired by the men of Tekoa, ^{x} but their nobles would not put their shoulders to the work under their supervisors. ^{a}

3:6
y Ne 12:39

⁶The Jeshanah ^{b} Gate ^{y} was repaired by Joiada son of Paseah and Meshullam son of Besodeiah. They laid its beams and put its doors and bolts and bars in place.

3:7
z Jos 9:3; Ne 2:7

⁷Next to them, repairs were made by men from Gibeon ^{z} and Mizpah—Melatiah of Gibeon and Jadon of Meronoth—places under the authority of the governor of Trans-Euphrates. ⁸Uzziel son of Harhaiah, one of the goldsmiths, repaired the next

3:8
a Ne 12:38

section; and Hananiah, one of the perfume-makers, made repairs next to that. They restored ^{c} Jerusalem as far as the Broad Wall. ^{a} ⁹Rephaiah son of Hur, ruler of a half-district of Jerusalem, repaired the next section. ¹⁰Adjoining this, Jedaiah son of Harumaph made repairs opposite his house, and Hattush son of Hashabneiah

3:11
b Ne 12:38

made repairs next to him. ¹¹Malkijah son of Harim and Hasshub son of Pahath-Moab repaired another section and the Tower of the Ovens. ^{b} ¹²Shallum son of Hallohesh, ruler of a half-district of Jerusalem, repaired the next section with the help of his daughters.

3:13
c 2Ch 26:9
d Jos 15:34
e Ne 2:13

¹³The Valley Gate ^{c} was repaired by Hanun and the residents of Zanoah. ^{d} They rebuilt it and put its doors and bolts and bars in place. They also repaired five hundred yards ^{d} of the wall as far as the Dung Gate. ^{e}

3:14
f Jer 6:1

¹⁴The Dung Gate was repaired by Malkijah son of Recab, ruler of the district of Beth Hakkerem. ^{f} He rebuilt it and put its doors and bolts and bars in place.

3:15
g Isa 8:6; Jn 9:7

¹⁵The Fountain Gate was repaired by Shallun son of Col-Hozeh, ruler of the district of Mizpah. He rebuilt it, roofing it over and putting its doors and bolts and bars in place. He also repaired the wall of the Pool of Siloam, ^{eg} by the King's Garden, as far as the steps going down from the City of David. ¹⁶Beyond him, Nehemiah

3:16
h Jos 15:58
i Ac 2:29

son of Azbuk, ruler of a half-district of Beth Zur, ^{h} made repairs up to a point opposite the tombs ^{fi} of David, as far as the artificial pool and the House of the Heroes.

3:17
j Jos 15:44

¹⁷Next to him, the repairs were made by the Levites under Rehum son of Bani. Beside him, Hashabiah, ruler of half the district of Keilah, ^{j} carried out repairs for his district. ¹⁸Next to him, the repairs were made by their countrymen under Binnui ^{g} son of Henadad, ruler of the other half-district of Keilah. ¹⁹Next to him, Ezer son of Jeshua, ruler of Mizpah, repaired another section, from a point facing the ascent to the armory as far as the angle. ²⁰Next to him, Baruch son of Zabbai zealously repaired another section, from the angle to the entrance of the house of Eliashib

---

^{a} 5 Or *their Lord* or *the governor* ^{b} 6 Or *Old* ^{c} 8 Or *They left out part of* ^{d} 13 Hebrew *a thousand cubits* (about 450 meters) ^{e} 15 Hebrew *Shelah,* a variant of *Shiloah,* that is, Siloam ^{f} 16 Hebrew; Septuagint, some Vulgate manuscripts and Syriac *tomb* ^{g} 18 Two Hebrew manuscripts and Syriac (see also Septuagint and verse 24); most Hebrew manuscripts *Bavvai*

---

struction of about 45 sections of wall. The account suggests that most of the rebuilding was concerned with the gates, as enemy assaults would focus on those structures. The towns listed as the builders' homes seem to have represented the administrative centers of the Judean province.

It was fitting that the high priest should set the example (v. 1). Conversely, the nobles from Tekoa, 11 miles south of Jerusalem, refused to do manual labor—while the common people of that town did double duty (vv. 5,27).

Viggo Olsen, who helped rebuild 10,000 houses in war-ravaged Bangladesh in 1972, derived unexpected inspiration from reading this chapter: "I was struck . . . that no expert builders were listed in the 'Holy Land brigade.' There were priests, priests' helpers, goldsmiths, perfume makers, and women, but no expert builders or carpenters were named." Have you volunteered your time and muscle on a short term mission trip or for an organization like Habitat for Humanity? You don't have to be a professional or a skilled laborer to serve.

the high priest. [21] Next to him, Meremoth[k] son of Uriah, the son of Hakkoz, repaired another section, from the entrance of Eliashib's house to the end of it.

[22] The repairs next to him were made by the priests from the surrounding region. [23] Beyond them, Benjamin and Hasshub made repairs in front of their house; and next to them, Azariah son of Maaseiah, the son of Ananiah, made repairs beside his house. [24] Next to him, Binnui[l] son of Henadad repaired another section, from Azariah's house to the angle and the corner, [25] and Palal son of Uzai worked opposite the angle and the tower projecting from the upper palace near the court of the guard.[m] Next to him, Pedaiah son of Parosh[n] [26] and the temple servants[o] living on the hill of Ophel[p] made repairs up to a point opposite the Water Gate[q] toward the east and the projecting tower. [27] Next to them, the men of Tekoa[r] repaired another section, from the great projecting tower[s] to the wall of Ophel.

[28] Above the Horse Gate,[t] the priests made repairs, each in front of his own house. [29] Next to them, Zadok son of Immer made repairs opposite his house. Next to him, Shemaiah son of Shecaniah, the guard at the East Gate, made repairs. [30] Next to him, Hananiah son of Shelemiah, and Hanun, the sixth son of Zalaph, repaired another section. Next to them, Meshullam son of Berekiah made repairs opposite his living quarters. [31] Next to him, Malkijah, one of the goldsmiths, made repairs as far as the house of the temple servants and the merchants, opposite the Inspection Gate, and as far as the room above the corner; [32] and between the room above the corner and the Sheep Gate[u] the goldsmiths and merchants made repairs.

Opposition to the Rebuilding

4 When Sanballat[v] heard that we were rebuilding the wall, he became angry and was greatly incensed. He ridiculed the Jews, [2] and in the presence of his associates[w] and the army of Samaria, he said, "What are those feeble Jews doing? Will they restore their wall? Will they offer sacrifices? Will they finish in a day? Can they bring the stones back to life from those heaps of rubble[x]—burned as they are?"

[3] Tobiah[y] the Ammonite, who was at his side, said, "What they are building—if even a fox climbed up on it, he would break down their wall of stones!"[z]

[4] Hear us, O our God, for we are despised.[a] Turn their insults back on their own heads. Give them over as plunder in a land of captivity. [5] Do not cover up their guilt[b]

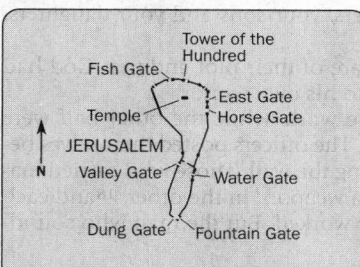

Fish Gate
Tower of the Hundred
Temple
East Gate
Horse Gate
JERUSALEM
N
Valley Gate
Water Gate
Dung Gate
Fountain Gate

Rebuilding the Wall (4:1–3)

Then: Nehemiah's building project drew criticism from non-Jews, political neighbors, and others because it threatened their personal interests.

Now: Many building projects today—even good, God ordained ones—draw criticism from special interest groups.

3:21
k Ezr 8:33

3:24
l Ezr 8:33

3:25
m Jer 32:2; 37:21; 39:14 n Ezr 2:3
3:26
o Ne 7:46; 11:21
p 2Ch 33:14
q Ne 8:1,3,16; 12:37
3:27
r ver 5 s Ps 48:12
3:28
t 2Ki 11:16; 2Ch 23:15; Jer 31:40

3:32
u ver 1; Jn 5:2

4:1
v Ne 2:10

4:2
w Ezr 4:9-10
x Ps 79:1; Jer 26:18

4:3
y Ne 2:10
z Job 13:12; 15:3

4:4
a Ps 44:13; 79:12; 123:3-4; Jer 33:24
4:5
b Isa 2:9; La 1:22

Nehemiah 4:1–23

Other ancient sources specify that Sanballat was the governor of Samaria, the area north of Judah (another name for the former northern kingdom of Israel). Tobiah, though an Ammonite, probably saw himself as a worshiper of the Lord—as indicated by his name ("The Lord is good") and that of his son Jehohanan (6:17–18), which means "The Lord is gracious." Tobiah was likely the governor of Ammon, or Transjordan.

The reasons Sanballat and Tobiah opposed Nehemiah weren't basically religious but political. The authority of the Samaritan governor in particular was threatened by the arrival of Nehemiah—the new governor of Judah (cf. 5:14). The Arabs (4:7), led by Geshem (2:19), were probably afraid that Judah's strengthening under Nehemiah would cut into their lucrative trade enterprise.

Verse 10 pictures a worker tottering under the weight of his load, ready to fall at any step. Nehemiah assured his discouraged comrades that the best way to dispel fear was to remember the Lord, who alone is to be feared (v. 14; cf. Deut. 3:22; 31:6). Throughout this inspiring and suspenseful passage we see the combination of faith and action (cf. James 2:22–26), as expressed in verse 9: "We prayed to our God and posted a guard day and night." Which side of the equation is more stretching for you—the divine side of faith and prayer or the human side of assertive action?

4:5
c 2Ki 14:27;
Ps 51:1; 69:27-28;
109:14; Jer 18:23

or blot out their sins from your sight, c for they have thrown insults in the face of a the builders.

6So we rebuilt the wall till all of it reached half its height, for the people worked with all their heart.

4:7
d Ne 2:10

4:8
e Ps 2:2; 83:1-18

7But when Sanballat, Tobiah, d the Arabs, the Ammonites and the men of Ashdod heard that the repairs to Jerusalem's walls had gone ahead and that the gaps were being closed, they were very angry. 8They all plotted together e to come and fight against Jerusalem and stir up trouble against it. 9But we prayed to our God and posted a guard day and night to meet this threat.

4:10
f 1Ch 23:4

10Meanwhile, the people in Judah said, "The strength of the laborers f is giving out, and there is so much rubble that we cannot rebuild the wall."

11Also our enemies said, "Before they know it or see us, we will be right there among them and will kill them and put an end to the work."

12Then the Jews who lived near them came and told us ten times over, "Wherever you turn, they will attack us."

13Therefore I stationed some of the people behind the lowest points of the wall at the exposed places, posting them by families, with their swords, spears and bows.

4:14
g Ge 28:15;
Nu 14:9; Dt 1:29
h Ne 1:8 i Ne 1:5
j 2Sa 10:12

14After I looked things over, I stood up and said to the nobles, the officials and the rest of the people, "Don't be afraid g of them. Remember h the Lord, who is great and awesome, i and fight j for your brothers, your sons and your daughters, your wives and your homes."

4:15
k 2Sa 17:14;
Job 5:12

15When our enemies heard that we were aware of their plot and that God had frustrated it, k we all returned to the wall, each to his own work.

16From that day on, half of my men did the work, while the other half were equipped with spears, shields, bows and armor. The officers posted themselves behind all the people of Judah 17who were building the wall. Those who carried materials did their work with one hand and held a weapon l in the other, 18and each of the builders wore his sword at his side as he worked. But the man who sounded the trumpet m stayed with me.

4:17
l Ps 149:6

4:18
m Nu 10:2

19Then I said to the nobles, the officials and the rest of the people, "The work is extensive and spread out, and we are widely separated from each other along the wall. 20Wherever you hear the sound of the trumpet, n join us there. Our God will fight o for us!"

4:20
n Eze 33:3
o Ex 14:14; Dt 1:30;
20:4; Jos 10:14

21So we continued the work with half the men holding spears, from the first light of dawn till the stars came out. 22At that time I also said to the people, "Have every man and his helper stay inside Jerusalem at night, so they can serve us as guards by night and workmen by day." 23Neither I nor my brothers nor my men nor the guards with me took off our clothes; each had his weapon, even when he went for water. b

Nehemiah Helps the Poor

5 Now the men and their wives raised a great outcry against their Jewish brothers. 2Some were saying, "We and our sons and daughters are numerous; in order for us to eat and stay alive, we must get grain."

5:3
p Ps 109:11
q Ge 47:23

3Others were saying, "We are mortgaging our fields, p our vineyards and our homes to get grain during the famine." q

---

a 5 Or *have provoked you to anger before*   b 23 The meaning of the Hebrew for this clause is uncertain.

Nehemiah 5:1–19

During his intense effort to rebuild the walls of Jerusalem, Nehemiah faced a socioeconomic crisis. Since the building of the wall took only 52 days (6:15), it *may seem surprising that he called a "large meeting"* (5:7) in the middle of the project. The financial pressures created by the rebuilding program brought to a head problems that had long simmered and now had to be resolved before work could continue.

If the former governors were extortionate (v. 15), their assistants were more oppressive. Among the classes affected by the economic crisis were (1) the landless, who were short of food (v. 2); (2) landowners compelled to mortgage their properties (v. 3); and (3) those forced to borrow money at exorbitant rates and sell their children into slavery (vv. 4–5). The gravity of the situation was underscored by the wives' participation in the protest (v. 1). The people's complaints weren't lodged

4 Still others were saying, "We have had to borrow money to pay the king's tax[r] on our fields and vineyards. 5 Although we are of the same flesh and blood[s] as our countrymen and though our sons are as good as theirs, yet we have to subject our sons and daughters to slavery.[t] Some of our daughters have already been enslaved, but we are powerless, because our fields and our vineyards belong to others."[u]

6 When I heard their outcry and these charges, I was very angry. 7 I pondered them in my mind and then accused the nobles and officials. I told them, "You are exacting usury[v] from your own countrymen!" So I called together a large meeting to deal with them 8 and said: "As far as possible, we have bought[w] back our Jewish brothers who were sold to the Gentiles. Now you are selling your brothers, only for them to be sold back to us!" They kept quiet, because they could find nothing to say.[x]

9 So I continued, "What you are doing is not right. Shouldn't you walk in the fear of our God to avoid the reproach[y] of our Gentile enemies? 10 I and my brothers and my men are also lending the people money and grain. But let the exacting of usury stop![z] 11 Give back to them immediately their fields, vineyards, olive groves and houses, and also the usury[a] you are charging them—the hundredth part of the money, grain, new wine and oil."

12 "We will give it back," they said. "And we will not demand anything more from them. We will do as you say."

Then I summoned the priests and made the nobles and officials take an oath[b] to do what they had promised. 13 I also shook[c] out the folds of my robe and said, "In this way may God shake out of his house and possessions every man who does not keep this promise. So may such a man be shaken out and emptied!"

At this the whole assembly said, "Amen,"[d] and praised the LORD. And the people did as they had promised.

14 Moreover, from the twentieth year of King Artaxerxes,[e] when I was appointed to be their governor[f] in the land of Judah, until his thirty-second year—twelve years—neither I nor my brothers ate the food allotted to the governor. 15 But the earlier governors—those preceding me—placed a heavy burden on the people and took forty shekels[a] of silver from them in addition to food and wine. Their assistants also lorded it over the people. But out of reverence for God[g] I did not act like that. 16 Instead,[h] I devoted myself to the work on this wall. All my men were assembled there for the work; we[b] did not acquire any land.

17 Furthermore, a hundred and fifty Jews and officials ate at my table, as well as those who came to us from the surrounding nations. 18 Each day one ox, six choice sheep and some poultry[i] were prepared for me, and every ten days an abundant supply of wine of all kinds. In spite of all this, I never demanded the food allotted to the governor, because the demands were heavy on these people.

19 Remember[j] me with favor, O my God, for all I have done for these people.

Further Opposition to the Rebuilding

6 When word came to Sanballat, Tobiah,[k] Geshem[l] the Arab and the rest of our enemies that I had rebuilt the wall and not a gap was left in it—though up to

---

a 15 That is, about 1 pound (about 0.5 kilogram)   b 16 Most Hebrew manuscripts; some Hebrew manuscripts, Septuagint, Vulgate and Syriac I

5:4
r Ezr 4:13
5:5
s Ge 29:14
t Lev 25:39-43,47;
2Ki 4:1; Isa 50:1
u Dt 15:7-11;
2Ki 4:1

5:7
v Ex 22:25-27;
Lev 25:35-37;
Dt 23:19-20;
24:10-13
5:8
w Lev 25:47
x Jer 34:8
5:9
y Isa 52:5

5:10
z Ex 22:25
5:11
a Isa 58:6

5:12
b Ezr 10:5
5:13
c Mt 10:14; Ac 18:6
d Dt 27:15-26

5:14
e Ne 2:6; 13:6
f Ge 42:6; Ezr 6:7;
Jer 40:7; Hag 1:1

5:15
g Ge 20:11
5:16
h 2Th 3:7-10

5:18
i 1Ki 4:23

5:19
j Ge 8:1; 2Ki 20:3;
Ne 1:8;
13:14,22,31

6:1
k Ne 2:10 l Ne 2:19

---

against foreign authorities but against fellow countrymen exploiting their poorer brothers and sisters at a time when all were needed to defend the country.

📖 This chapter provides a practical lesson on how to help right a wrong: (1) Listen to the cries for help (vv. 1–6). (2) Allow the unjust practice to produce in you righteous anger over people's suffering (v. 6). (3) Think about possible solutions (v. 7). (4) Confront and dialogue with those who are doing wrong (vv. 7–10). (5) Propose a solution (v. 11). And (6) help the parties reconcile and come to an agreement (vv. 12–13).

Nehemiah could have taxed the people to help provide meals for officials at his table, which was considered his social responsibility. But he opted not to, knowing the burden this would have created. Like Paul, he bent over backward and sacrificed even what was normally his due to serve as an example to the people (cf. 1 Cor. 9; 2 Thess. 3:6–10). Nehemiah's behavior as governor was guided by principles of service, not opportunism and greed (v. 16). What principles guide your behavior? Is this an issue you have to think about, or does a service mentality seem to come naturally for you?

6:2
m 1Ch 8:12
that time I had not set the doors in the gates— ²Sanballat and Geshem sent me this message: "Come, let us meet together in one of the villages ᵃ on the plain of Ono. ᵐ"

But they were scheming to harm me; ³so I sent messengers to them with this reply: "I am carrying on a great project and cannot go down. Why should the work stop while I leave it and go down to you?" ⁴Four times they sent me the same message, and each time I gave them the same answer.

6:5
n Ne 2:10
⁵Then, the fifth time, Sanballat ⁿ sent his aide to me with the same message, and in his hand was an unsealed letter ⁶in which was written:

6:6
o Ne 2:19
"It is reported among the nations—and Geshem ᵇ ᵒ says it is true—that you and the Jews are plotting to revolt, and therefore you are building the wall. Moreover, according to these reports you are about to become their king ⁷and have even appointed prophets to make this proclamation about you in Jerusalem: 'There is a king in Judah!' Now this report will get back to the king; so come, let us confer together."

⁸I sent him this reply: "Nothing like what you are saying is happening; you are just making it up out of your head."

⁹They were all trying to frighten us, thinking, "Their hands will get too weak for the work, and it will not be completed."

But I prayed, "Now strengthen my hands."

6:10
p Nu 18:7
¹⁰One day I went to the house of Shemaiah son of Delaiah, the son of Mehetabel, who was shut in at his home. He said, "Let us meet in the house of God, inside the temple ᵖ, and let us close the temple doors, because men are coming to kill you—by night they are coming to kill you."

¹¹But I said, "Should a man like me run away? Or should one like me go into the temple to save his life? I will not go!" ¹²I realized that God had not sent him, but that he had prophesied against me �q because Tobiah and Sanballat ʳ had hired him.
6:12
q Eze 13:22-23
r Ne 2:10
6:13
s Jer 20:10
¹³He had been hired to intimidate me so that I would commit a sin by doing this, and then they would give me a bad name to discredit me. ˢ

6:14
t Ne 1:8 u Ne 2:10
v Ex 15:20;
Eze 13:17-23;
Ac 21:9; Rev 2:20
w Ne 13:29;
Jer 23:9-40;
Zec 13:2-3
¹⁴Remember ᵗ Tobiah and Sanballat, ᵘ O my God, because of what they have done; remember also the prophetess ᵛ Noadiah and the rest of the prophets ʷ who have been trying to intimidate me.

The Completion of the Wall

¹⁵So the wall was completed on the twenty-fifth of Elul, in fifty-two days. ¹⁶When all our enemies heard about this, all the surrounding nations were afraid and lost

---

ᵃ 2 Or *in Kephirim*   ᵇ 6 Hebrew *Gashmu*, a variant of *Geshem*

Nehemiah 6:1–14

📖 Chapter 6 records further attempts on the part of hostile neighbors to frustrate Nehemiah's efforts. His enemies resorted to intrigue (vv. 1–4), innuendo (vv. 5–9), and intimidation (vv. 10–14). Regarding Sanballat, Tobiah, and Geshem, see "There and Then" for 4:1–23.

Since Shemaiah had access to the temple, he was probably a priest. He could have legitimately proposed that Nehemiah take refuge in the temple area at the altar of asylum (cf. Ex. 21:13–14; 1 Kings 1:50–53), but not in "the house of God" (Neh. 6:10), the temple building itself. Even if Nehemiah's life was genuinely threatened, he wasn't a coward who would run into hiding. Nor would he transgress the law to save his life, since as a layman he wasn't permitted to enter the sanctuary (Num. 18:7).

📖 Had Nehemiah wavered in the face of the threat against him, his leadership would have been discredited (v. 13) and morale among the people would have plummeted. When have you found yourself in a situation in which

the confidence of others depended upon your attitude or action? Did you, like Nehemiah, withstand the test?

Nehemiah 6:15—7:3

📖 Remarkably, the walls neglected for nearly a century and a half were rebuilt in less than two months. How? For one thing, the people were galvanized into action by the catalyst of Nehemiah's leadership. More importantly, though, "this work had been done with the help of . . . God" (v. 16). This knowledge made Nehemiah's enemies thoroughly ill at ease (cf. 1 Chron. 14:17).

Tobiah was related to influential families in Judah both through his wife and his daughter-in-law. His friends and relatives attempted to propagandize on his behalf as well as to act as an intelligence system for him, as he continued trying to intimidate Nehemiah.

Normally a city's gates would be opened each day at dawn, but Nehemiah delayed unlocking the gates to prevent an enemy attack before Jerusalem's residents were awake and alert.

their self-confidence, because they realized that this work had been done with the help of our God.

17Also, in those days the nobles of Judah were sending many letters to Tobiah, and replies from Tobiah kept coming to them. 18For many in Judah were under oath to him, since he was son-in-law to Shecaniah son of Arah, and his son Jehohanan had married the daughter of Meshullam son of Berekiah. 19Moreover, they kept reporting to me his good deeds and then telling him what I said. And Tobiah sent letters to intimidate me.

7 After the wall had been rebuilt and I had set the doors in place, the gatekeepers[x] and the singers[y] and the Levites[z] were appointed. 2I put in charge of Jerusalem my brother Hanani,[a] along with[a] Hananiah[b] the commander of the citadel,[c] because he was a man of integrity and feared[d] God more than most men do. 3I said to them, "The gates of Jerusalem are not to be opened until the sun is hot. While the gatekeepers are still on duty, have them shut the doors and bar them. Also appoint residents of Jerusalem as guards, some at their posts and some near their own houses."

The List of the Exiles Who Returned

4Now the city was large and spacious, but there were few people in it,[e] and the houses had not yet been rebuilt. 5So my God put it into my heart to assemble the nobles, the officials and the common people for registration by families. I found the genealogical record of those who had been the first to return. This is what I found written there:

6These are the people of the province who came up from the captivity of the exiles[f] whom Nebuchadnezzar king of Babylon had taken captive (they returned to Jerusalem and Judah, each to his own town, 7in company with Zerubbabel,[g] Jeshua, Nehemiah, Azariah, Raamiah, Nahamani, Mordecai, Bilshan, Mispereth, Bigvai, Nehum and Baanah):

The list of the men of Israel:

8 the descendants of Parosh	2,172
9 of Shephatiah	372
10 of Arah	652
11 of Pahath-Moab (through the line of Jeshua and Joab)	2,818
12 of Elam	1,254
13 of Zattu	845
14 of Zaccai	760
15 of Binnui	648
16 of Bebai	628

a 2 Or Hanani, that is,

7:1
x 1Ch 9:27; 26:12-19; Ne 6:1,15
y Ps 68:25 z Ne 8:9
7:2
a Ne 1:2
b Ne 10:23
c Ne 2:8 d 1Ki 18:3

7:4
e Ne 11:1

7:6
f 2Ch 36:20; Ezr 2:1-70; Ne 1:2

7:7
g 1Ch 3:19; Ezr 2:2

When have you been part of a great group accomplishment? To what big task might God be calling your church, or another group you are part of, in the near future? How will you help? In a sense, when the wall was finished the work had just begun. Now the people needed to guard the wall and its gates. Do you have a hard time following through and moving into active maintenance after finishing a major project? Is that a current issue for you, your church, or another group with which you are involved?

This passage points to the complexity of relationships and political/social realities each of us faces in daily life. Notice Nehemiah's determination to keep doing what God had called him to do. What is your response when political/social influences are working against you?

Nehemiah 7:4–73a

This record that Nehemiah found is essentially the same as that of Ezra 2, with some variations in names and numbers. The fact that only 74 Levites returned (7:43; Ezra 2:40) is striking. Later, when Ezra was about to leave Babylon, he found not one Levite in the company and delayed his departure until he could recruit some (Ezra 8:15–20). Since the Levites had been entrusted with the everyday tasks of temple service, many of them may have found a more comfortable way of life in exile.

Many returning exiles may not have been from Jerusalem, whose population had no doubt suffered the greatest number of casualties in the Babylonian attacks. The returnees naturally gravitated to their own ancestral hometowns, leaving Jerusalem underpopulated (Neh. 7:4,73; cf. 11:1–2).

	17 of Azgad	2,322
	18 of Adonikam	667
	19 of Bigvai	2,067
7:20	20 of Adin [h]	655
h Ezr 8:6	21 of Ater (through Hezekiah)	98
	22 of Hashum	328
	23 of Bezai	324
	24 of Hariph	112
	25 of Gibeon	95
7:26	26 the men of Bethlehem and Netophah [i]	188
i 2Sa 23:28;	27 of Anathoth [j]	128
1Ch 2:54	28 of Beth Azmaveth	42
7:27	29 of Kiriath Jearim, Kephirah [k] and Beeroth [l]	743
j Jos 21:18	30 of Ramah and Geba	621
7:29	31 of Micmash	122
k Jos 18:26	32 of Bethel and Ai [m]	123
l Jos 18:25	33 of the other Nebo	52
7:32	34 of the other Elam	1,254
m Ge 12:8	35 of Harim	320
	36 of Jericho [n]	345
7:36	37 of Lod, Hadid and Ono [o]	721
n Ne 3:2	38 of Senaah	3,930
7:37		
o 1Ch 8:12		

39 The priests:

the descendants of Jedaiah (through the family of Jeshua)	973
40 of Immer	1,052
41 of Pashhur	1,247
42 of Harim	1,017

43 The Levites:

7:44	the descendants of Jeshua (through Kadmiel through the line of Hodaviah)
p Ne 11:23	

| | 74 |

44 The singers: [p]

7:45	the descendants of Asaph	148
q 1Ch 9:17		

45 The gatekeepers: [q]

the descendants of
Shallum, Ater, Talmon, Akkub, Hatita and Shobai   138

7:46
r Ne 3:26   46 The temple servants: [r]

the descendants of
Ziha, Hasupha, Tabbaoth,
47 Keros, Sia, Padon,
48 Lebana, Hagaba, Shalmai,
49 Hanan, Giddel, Gahar,
50 Reaiah, Rezin, Nekoda,
51 Gazzam, Uzza, Paseah,
52 Besai, Meunim, Nephusim,
53 Bakbuk, Hakupha, Harhur,
54 Bazluth, Mehida, Harsha,

📖 If you were a second- or third-generation descendant of displaced persons and were now living in relative comfort, having assimilated into a "new" culture without experiential knowledge of your parents' or grandparents' cultural heritage, how quick would you be to pick up stakes and knowingly face depravation, danger, and uncertainty? What if a long-term, unchangeable promise from God were added to the equation? Would you be likely to trust him so much that this knowledge would tilt your decision in favor of the unknown?

⁵⁵Barkos, Sisera, Temah,
⁵⁶Neziah and Hatipha

⁵⁷The descendants of the servants of Solomon:

the descendants of
  Sotai, Sophereth, Perida,
⁵⁸Jaala, Darkon, Giddel,
⁵⁹Shephatiah, Hattil,
  Pokereth-Hazzebaim and Amon

⁶⁰The temple servants and the descendants
  of the servants of Solomonˢ   392

⁶¹The following came up from the towns of Tel Melah, Tel Harsha, Kerub, Addon and Immer, but they could not show that their families were descended from Israel:

⁶²the descendants of
  Delaiah, Tobiah and Nekoda   642

⁶³And from among the priests:

the descendants of
  Hobaiah, Hakkoz and Barzillai (a man who had married a daughter of
  Barzillai the Gileadite and was called by that name).
⁶⁴These searched for their family records, but they could not find them and so were excluded from the priesthood as unclean. ⁶⁵The governor, therefore, ordered them not to eat any of the most sacred food until there should be a priest ministering with the Urim and Thummim.ᵗ

⁶⁶The whole company numbered 42,360, ⁶⁷besides their 7,337 menservants and maidservants; and they also had 245 men and women singers. ⁶⁸There were 736 horses, 245 mules,ᵃ ⁶⁹435 camels and 6,720 donkeys.

⁷⁰Some of the heads of the families contributed to the work. The governor gave to the treasury 1,000 drachmasᵇ of gold, 50 bowls and 530 garments for priests. ⁷¹Some of the heads of the familiesᵘ gave to the treasury for the work 20,000 drachmasᶜ of gold and 2,200 minasᵈ of silver. ⁷²The total given by the rest of the people was 20,000 drachmas of gold, 2,000 minasᵉ of silver and 67 garments for priests.ᵛ

⁷³The priests, the Levites, the gatekeepers, the singers and the temple servants,ʷ along with certain of the people and the rest of the Israelites, settled in their own towns.ˣ

Ezra Reads the Law

When the seventh month came and the Israelites had settled in their towns,ʸ
8 ¹all the people assembled as one man in the square before the Water Gate.ᶻ They told Ezra the scribe to bring out the Book of the Law of Moses,ᵃ which the LORD had commanded for Israel.

²So on the first day of the seventh monthᵇ Ezra the priest brought the Lawᶜ be-

---

ᵃ 68 Some Hebrew manuscripts (see also Ezra 2:66); most Hebrew manuscripts do not have this verse.   ᵇ 70 That is, about 19 pounds (about 8.5 kilograms)   ᶜ 71 That is, about 375 pounds (about 170 kilograms); also in verse 72   ᵈ 71 That is, about 1 1/3 tons (about 1.2 metric tons)   ᵉ 72 That is, about 1 1/4 tons (about 1.1 metric tons)

7:60
ˢ 1Ch 9:2

7:65
ᵗ Ex 28:30; Ne 8:9

7:71
ᵘ 1Ch 29:7

7:72
ᵛ Ex 25:2

7:73
ʷ Ne 1:10;
Ps 34:22; 103:21;
113:1; 135:1
ˣ Ezr 3:1; Ne 11:1
ʸ Ezr 3:1

8:1
ᶻ Ne 3:26
ᵃ Dt 28:61;
2Ch 34:15; Ezr 7:6

8:2
ᵇ Lev 23:23-25;
Nu 29:1-6
ᶜ Dt 31:11

Nehemiah 7:73b—8:18

📖 Ezra the priest and scribe (or teacher) is mentioned here for the first time in the book of Nehemiah. The last reference to him, in Ezra 10, was 13 years earlier. "The first day of the seventh month" (Neh. 8:2), October 8, 444 B.C., was the New Year's Day of the civil calendar—celebrated also as the Feast of Trumpets, with a solemn assembly and rest from work (cf. Lev. 23:23–25; Num. 29:1–6). Women didn't participate in ordinary meetings but were included, together with children, on such sacred occasions (cf. Deut. 31:12–13; Josh. 8:35; Neh. 10:28; 12:43).

8:3
d Ne 3:26

8:4
e 2Ch 6:13

8:5
f Jdg 3:20

8:6
g Ex 4:31; Ezr 9:5;
1Ti 2:8

8:7
h Ezr 10:23
i Lev 10:11;
2Ch 17:7

8:9
j Ne 7:1,65,70
k Dt 12:7,12;
16:14-15

8:10
l 1Sa 25:8;
Lk 14:12-14
m Lev 23:40;
Dt 12:18;
16:11,14-15

fore the assembly, which was made up of men and women and all who were able to understand. ³He read it aloud from daybreak till noon as he faced the square before the Water Gate[d] in the presence of the men, women and others who could understand. And all the people listened attentively to the Book of the Law.

⁴Ezra the scribe stood on a high wooden platform[e] built for the occasion. Beside him on his right stood Mattithiah, Shema, Anaiah, Uriah, Hilkiah and Maaseiah; and on his left were Pedaiah, Mishael, Malkijah, Hashum, Hashbaddanah, Zechariah and Meshullam.

⁵Ezra opened the book. All the people could see him because he was standing[f] above them; and as he opened it, the people all stood up. ⁶Ezra praised the LORD, the great God; and all the people lifted their hands[g] and responded, "Amen! Amen!" Then they bowed down and worshiped the LORD with their faces to the ground.

⁷The Levites[h]—Jeshua, Bani, Sherebiah, Jamin, Akkub, Shabbethai, Hodiah, Maaseiah, Kelita, Azariah, Jozabad, Hanan and Pelaiah—instructed[i] the people in the Law while the people were standing there. ⁸They read from the Book of the Law of God, making it clear[a] and giving the meaning so that the people could understand what was being read.

⁹Then Nehemiah the governor, Ezra the priest and scribe, and the Levites[j] who were instructing the people said to them all, "This day is sacred to the LORD your God. Do not mourn or weep."[k] For all the people had been weeping as they listened to the words of the Law.

¹⁰Nehemiah said, "Go and enjoy choice food and sweet drinks, and send some to those who have nothing[l] prepared. This day is sacred to our Lord. Do not grieve, for the joy[m] of the LORD is your strength."

¹¹The Levites calmed all the people, saying, "Be still, for this is a sacred day. Do not grieve."

¹²Then all the people went away to eat and drink, to send portions of food and

---

[a] 8 Or God, translating it

As the people came to understand God's Word, they wept in remorse for their own failures and those of their ancestors. But the leaders instructed them to accept the joy of God's forgiveness on this day of celebration, and also challenged them to remember the less fortunate. The assembly's attention and obedience to the Law of Moses led next to the observance of the Feast of Tabernacles, or Booths (cf. Lev. 23:33–43). From the time of Joshua, this feast hadn't been celebrated with such joy (Neh. 8:17).

What are the limits of your attention span when it comes to listening to a sermon? For many of us, the mind starts wandering after the first 20 minutes or so. These people evidently stood for five or six hours attentively listening to the reading and explanation of the Scriptures. Does the reading and explication of the Bible affect you as it did the Jews in this story—with earnest worship, conviction of sin, repentance, "the joy of the LORD," sharing with those in need, and fresh obedience? As part of your celebrations of God's goodness, do you remember to share with people in need?

8:1–3

Four Questions to Ask of a Biblical Text

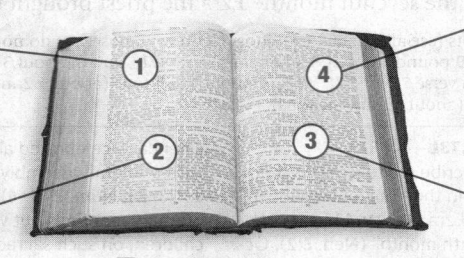

How does this text help me distinguish truth from error, good from bad?
Discernment develops through study, both individual and group, and by prayer for the Holy Spirit's guidance.

What goals does this text ask me to pursue?
This question reveals God's purpose in this text.

Based on what I have read, who should I be?
This is the question of character. Sound Bible study develops sound character.

What should I, personally, do as a result of this text?
God gives every one duties, revealed on a daily basis through Scripture study.

Source: Doriani (2001:97–121)

to celebrate with great joy, [n] because they now understood the words that had been made known to them.

13 On the second day of the month, the heads of all the families, along with the priests and the Levites, gathered around Ezra the scribe to give attention to the words of the Law. 14 They found written in the Law, which the LORD had commanded through Moses, that the Israelites were to live in booths during the feast of the seventh month 15 and that they should proclaim this word and spread it throughout their towns and in Jerusalem: "Go out into the hill country and bring back branches from olive and wild olive trees, and from myrtles, palms and shade trees, to make booths"—as it is written. [a]

16 So the people went out and brought back branches and built themselves booths on their own roofs, in their courtyards, in the courts of the house of God and in the square by the Water Gate and the one by the Gate of Ephraim. [o] 17 The whole company that had returned from exile built booths and lived in them. From the days of Joshua son of Nun until that day, the Israelites had not celebrated[p] it like this. And their joy was very great.

18 Day after day, from the first day to the last, Ezra read[q] from the Book of the Law of God. They celebrated the feast for seven days, and on the eighth day, in accordance with the regulation, [r] there was an assembly.

The Israelites Confess Their Sins

9 On the twenty-fourth day of the same month, the Israelites gathered together, fasting and wearing sackcloth and having dust on their heads. [s] 2 Those of Israelite descent had separated themselves from all foreigners. [t] They stood in their places and confessed their sins and the wickedness of their fathers. [u] 3 They stood where they were and read from the Book of the Law of the LORD their God for a quarter of the day, and spent another quarter in confession and in worshiping the LORD their God. 4 Standing on the stairs were the Levites [v]—Jeshua, Bani, Kadmiel, Shebaniah, Bunni, Sherebiah, Bani and Kenani—who called with loud voices to the LORD their God. 5 And the Levites—Jeshua, Kadmiel, Bani, Hashabneiah, Sherebiah, Hodiah, Shebaniah and Pethahiah—said: "Stand up and praise the LORD your God, [w] who is from everlasting to everlasting. [b]"

"Blessed be your glorious name, and may it be exalted above all blessing and praise. 6 You alone are the LORD. [x] You made the heavens, [y] even the highest heavens, and all their starry host, the earth [z] and all that is on it, the seas [a] and all that is in them. [b] You give life to everything, and the multitudes of heaven worship you.

7 "You are the LORD God, who chose Abram and brought him out of Ur of the Chaldeans [c] and named him Abraham. [d] 8 You found his heart faithful to you, and you made a covenant with him to give to his descendants the land of the Canaanites, Hittites, Amorites, Perizzites, Jebusites and Girgashites. [e] You have kept your promise[f] because you are righteous. [g]

9 "You saw the suffering of our forefathers in Egypt; [h] you heard their cry at

a 15 See Lev. 23:37-40.   b 5 Or God for ever and ever

8:12
n Est 9:22

8:16
o 2Ki 14:13;
Ne 12:39

8:17
p 2Ch 7:8; 8:13;
30:21

8:18
q Dt 31:11
r Lev 23:36,40;
Nu 29:35

9:1
s Jos 7:6; 1Sa 4:12
9:2
t Ne 13:3,30
u Ezr 10:11;
Ps 106:6

9:4
v Ezr 10:23

9:5
w Ps 78:4

9:6
x Dt 6:4 y 2Ki 19:15
z Ge 1:1; Isa 37:16
a Ps 95:5
b Dt 10:14

9:7
c Ge 11:31
d Ge 17:5
9:8
e Ge 15:18-21
f Jos 21:45
g Ge 15:6; Ezr 9:15
9:9
h Ex 3:7

Nehemiah 9:1–37

Now the people set aside a day of penance in the spirit of the Day of Atonement, normally held on the tenth day of the seventh month (cf. Lev. 16:29–31). The congregation spent about three hours studying the Scripture and another three worshiping the Lord (Neh. 9:3). The result was a beautiful prayer, a mosaic of Scriptures. It reviewed God's grace and power in creation (v. 6), in the Abrahamic covenant (vv. 7–8), in Egypt and at the Red Sea (vv. 9–11), in the desert and at Sinai (vv. 12–21), at the conquest of Canaan (vv. 22–25), through the judges (vv. 26–28), through the prophets (vv. 29–31),

and in the current situation (vv. 32–37).

Verses 32–37 are gripping in their honesty. The present great distress was in no way the fault of Israel's faithful God. He had upheld his side of the covenant bargain impeccably, having been indisputably and unwaveringly just. While the people acknowledged total responsibility for the accumulated disasters, they still felt comfortable asking God to intervene in their dire situation. Have you had the courage to approach him for help under similar circumstances, without offering excuses or rationalizing whatever behavior had gotten you into trouble?

9:9
i Ex 14:10-30
9:10
j Ex 10:1
k Jer 32:20;
Da 9:15
9:11
l Ex 14:21; Ps 78:13
m Ex 15:4-5, 10;
Heb 11:29
9:12
n Ex 15:13
o Ex 13:21
9:13
p Ex 19:11
q Ex 19:19
r Ps 119:137
s Ex 20:1
9:14
t Ge 2:3; Ex 20:8-11
9:15
u Ex 16:4; Jn 6:31
v Ex 17:6;
Nu 20:7-13
w Dt 1:8,21

9:16
x Dt 1:26-33; 31:29
9:17
y Ps 78:42
z Nu 14:1-4
a Ex 34:6
b Nu 14:17-19
c Ps 78:11
9:18
d Ex 32:4

9:20
e Nu 11:17;
Isa 63:11,14
f Ex 16:15 *g* Ex 17:6
9:21
h Dt 2:7 *i* Dt 8:4

9:22
j Nu 21:21
k Nu 21:33

9:24
l Jos 11:23

the Red Sea.[a][i] [10]You sent miraculous signs[j] and wonders against Pharaoh, against all his officials and all the people of his land, for you knew how arrogantly the Egyptians treated them. You made a name[k] for yourself, which remains to this day. [11]You divided the sea before them,[l] so that they passed through it on dry ground, but you hurled their pursuers into the depths, like a stone into mighty waters.[m] [12]By day you led[n] them with a pillar of cloud,[o] and by night with a pillar of fire to give them light on the way they were to take.

[13]"You came down on Mount Sinai;[p] you spoke[q] to them from heaven. You gave them regulations and laws that are just[r] and right, and decrees and commands that are good.[s] [14]You made known to them your holy Sabbath[t] and gave them commands, decrees and laws through your servant Moses. [15]In their hunger you gave them bread from heaven[u] and in their thirst you brought them water from the rock;[v] you told them to go in and take possession of the land you had sworn with uplifted hand to give them.[w]

[16]"But they, our forefathers, became arrogant and stiff-necked, and did not obey your commands.[x] [17]They refused to listen and failed to remember[y] the miracles you performed among them. They became stiff-necked and in their rebellion appointed a leader in order to return to their slavery.[z] But you are a forgiving God, gracious and compassionate, slow to anger[a] and abounding in love.[b] Therefore you did not desert them,[c] [18]even when they cast for themselves an image of a calf[d] and said, 'This is your god, who brought you up out of Egypt,' or when they committed awful blasphemies.

[19]"Because of your great compassion you did not abandon them in the desert. By day the pillar of cloud did not cease to guide them on their path, nor the pillar of fire by night to shine on the way they were to take. [20]You gave your good Spirit[e] to instruct them. You did not withhold your manna[f] from their mouths, and you gave them water[g] for their thirst. [21]For forty years you sustained them in the desert; they lacked nothing,[h] their clothes did not wear out nor did their feet become swollen.[i]

[22]"You gave them kingdoms and nations, allotting to them even the remotest frontiers. They took over the country of Sihon[b][j] king of Heshbon and the country of Og king of Bashan.[k] [23]You made their sons as numerous as the stars in the sky, and you brought them into the land that you told their fathers to enter and possess. [24]Their sons went in and took possession of the land.[l] You subdued before them the Canaanites, who lived in the land; you handed the Canaanites over to them, along with their kings and the peoples of the land, to deal with them as they pleased. [25]They captured fortified cities and fertile

---

[a] 9 Hebrew *Yam Suph*; that is, Sea of Reeds   [b] 22 One Hebrew manuscript and Septuagint; most Hebrew manuscripts *Sihon, that is, the country of the*

9:15

Costs of Clean Water

God satisfies all our thirsts, but it's becoming more and more difficult to quench physical thirst:

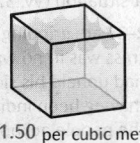

$1.50 per cubic meter is the typical cost to desalinize seawater.

$42 billion is spent each year on bottled water worldwide.

28 percent of people worldwide lack access to clean, safe drinking water.

FIVE MILLION PEOPLE

5 million people die each year because of polluted water.

Source: United Nations Development Programme, *World Resources 2000–2001* (2000:12)

$1.4 billion is spent by U.S. consumers annually on home water filtration systems.

90 percent of urban sewage in the developing world is discharged, untreated, into rivers, lakes, and coastal areas.

land; they took possession of houses filled with all kinds of good things, wells already dug, vineyards, olive groves and fruit trees in abundance. They ate to the full and were well-nourished;[m] they reveled in your great goodness.[n]

26 "But they were disobedient and rebelled against you; they put your law behind their backs.[o] They killed your prophets,[p] who had admonished them in order to turn them back to you; they committed awful blasphemies.[q] 27 So you handed them over to their enemies,[r] who oppressed them. But when they were oppressed they cried out to you. From heaven you heard them, and in your great compassion[s] you gave them deliverers, who rescued them from the hand of their enemies.

28 "But as soon as they were at rest, they again did what was evil in your sight. Then you abandoned them to the hand of their enemies so that they ruled over them. And when they cried out to you again, you heard from heaven, and in your compassion you delivered them[t] time after time.

29 "You warned them to return to your law, but they became arrogant[u] and disobeyed your commands. They sinned against your ordinances, by which a man will live if he obeys them.[v] Stubbornly they turned their backs on you, became stiff-necked and refused to listen.[w] 30 For many years you were patient with them. By your Spirit you admonished them through your prophets.[x] Yet they paid no attention, so you handed them over to the neighboring peoples. 31 But in your great mercy you did not put an end[y] to them or abandon them, for you are a gracious and merciful God.

32 "Now therefore, O our God, the great, mighty[z] and awesome God, who keeps his covenant of love,[a] do not let all this hardship seem trifling in your eyes—the hardship that has come upon us, upon our kings and leaders, upon our priests and prophets, upon our fathers and all your people, from the days of the kings of Assyria until today. 33 In all that has happened to us, you have been just;[b] you have acted faithfully, while we did wrong.[c] 34 Our kings,[d] our leaders, our priests and our fathers[e] did not follow your law; they did not pay attention to your commands or the warnings you gave them. 35 Even while they were in their kingdom, enjoying your great goodness[f] to them in the spacious and fertile land you gave them, they did not serve you[g] or turn from their evil ways.

36 "But see, we are slaves[h] today, slaves in the land you gave our forefathers so they could eat its fruit and the other good things it produces. 37 Because of our sins, its abundant harvest goes to the kings you have placed over us. They rule over our bodies and our cattle as they please. We are in great distress.[i]

The Agreement of the People

38 "In view of all this, we are making a binding agreement,[j] putting it in writing,[k] and our leaders, our Levites and our priests are affixing their seals to it."

Cross references

9:25
m Dt 6:10-12
n Nu 13:27; Dt 32:12-15
9:26
o 1Ki 14:9
p Mt 21:35-36
q Jdg 2:12-13
9:27
r Jdg 2:14
s Ps 106:45

9:28
t Ps 106:43
9:29
u Ps 5:5; Isa 2:11; Jer 43:2 v Dt 30:16
w Zec 7:11-12

9:30
x 2Ki 17:13-18; 2Ch 36:16
9:31
y Isa 48:9; Jer 4:27

9:32
z Ps 24:8 a Dt 7:9

9:33
b Ge 18:25
c Jer 44:3; Da 9:7-8,14
9:34
d 2Ki 23:11
e Jer 44:17
9:35
f Isa 63:7
g Dt 28:45-48
9:36
h Dt 28:48; Ezr 9:9

9:37
i Dt 28:33; La 5:5

9:38
j 2Ch 23:16
k Isa 44:5

9:26-31

Signs of a Stagnant Congregation

Most of us haven't experienced anything close to the problems Nehemiah endured in rebuilding the walls of Jerusalem. But there are warning signs that point to stagnant—or stagnating—church groups:

- Dwelling on past "glory" days
- Lack of intentional plan for growth
- Uninformed membership
- Criticism of leadership and staff
- Decision-makers all from "old guard"
- Overemphasis on resource conservation
- High dependence on paid staff
- Perpetual anxiety over finances
- Neglect of physical plant
- Generational gaps in membership (young or old)

Source: Galindo (2002:103)

If your congregation is exhibiting some of these symptoms, take a few minutes to read and reflect upon Jesus' message to the church in Sardis in Revelation 3:1–4. What strategies come to mind for turning things around? Make a list, and begin the implementation this week.

10 Those who sealed it were:

Nehemiah the governor, the son of Hacaliah.

10:2
l Ezr 2:2
10:3
m 1Ch 9:12

Zedekiah, 2Seraiah,*l* Azariah, Jeremiah,
3Pashhur,*m* Amariah, Malkijah,
4Hattush, Shebaniah, Malluch,

10:5
n 1Ch 24:8

5Harim,*n* Meremoth, Obadiah,
6Daniel, Ginnethon, Baruch,
7Meshullam, Abijah, Mijamin,
8Maaziah, Bilgai and Shemaiah.
These were the priests.

10:9
o Ne 12:1

9The Levites:*o*

Jeshua son of Azaniah, Binnui of the sons of Henadad, Kadmiel,
10and their associates: Shebaniah,
Hodiah, Kelita, Pelaiah, Hanan,
11Mica, Rehob, Hashabiah,
12Zaccur, Sherebiah, Shebaniah,
13Hodiah, Bani and Beninu.

14The leaders of the people:

Parosh, Pahath-Moab, Elam, Zattu, Bani,
15Bunni, Azgad, Bebai,

10:16
p Ezr 8:6

16Adonijah, Bigvai, Adin,*p*
17Ater, Hezekiah, Azzur,
18Hodiah, Hashum, Bezai,
19Hariph, Anathoth, Nebai,

10:20
q 1Ch 24:15

20Magpiash, Meshullam, Hezir,*q*
21Meshezabel, Zadok, Jaddua,
22Pelatiah, Hanan, Anaiah,

10:23
r Ne 7:2

23Hoshea, Hananiah,*r* Hasshub,
24Hallohesh, Pilha, Shobek,
25Rehum, Hashabnah, Maaseiah,
26Ahiah, Hanan, Anan,
27Malluch, Harim and Baanah.

10:28
s Ps 135:1
t 2Ch 6:26; Ne 9:2

28"The rest of the people—priests, Levites, gatekeepers, singers, temple servants*s* and all who separated themselves from the neighboring peoples*t* for the sake of the Law of God, together with their wives and all their sons and daughters who are able to understand— 29all these now join their brothers the nobles, and bind themselves with a curse and an oath*u* to follow the Law of God given through Moses the servant of God and to obey carefully all the commands, regulations and decrees of the LORD our Lord.

10:29
u Nu 5:21;
Ps 119:106

Nehemiah 9:38—10:39

Nehemiah 10:1–27 constitutes a legal list, bearing the official seal and containing a roster of 84 names, arranged according to the following categories: Nehemiah the governor, priests, Levites, and leaders. "The rest of the people" (10:28) didn't affix their seals to the agreement (cf. 9:38—10:1).

The practice of giving a tenth (10:37) was ancient (see Gen. 14:20; 28:22). The Law of Moses decreed that a *tenth portion of plant crops* was holy to the Lord (Lev. 27:30), but there is no reference here to a tithe of cattle (cf. Lev. 27:32–33). Tithes were meant for the support of the Levites (Neh. 10:37; cf. Num. 18:21–24; Neh. 13:10–12), who in turn were to give "a tenth of the

tithes" (Neh. 10:38; cf. Num. 18:25–32). Chambers in the outer temple courts were used as "storerooms" for silver, gold, and other objects (Neh. 10:38–39; 12:44; 13:4–5,9).

Through the prophet Malachi, likely a contemporary of Nehemiah, the Lord accused the Israelites of robbing him by withholding tithes and offerings (Mal. 3:8). We are no longer held to a strict expectation of tithing, but God does expect us to give freely and generously, as we are able. Paul advised the church in Corinth to "excel in this grace of giving" (2 Cor. 8:7). Each Christian is called to personally address the possibility that he or she may be withholding from God. Are you comfortable—as opposed to complacent—about your "standard of giving"?

30 "We promise not to give our daughters in marriage to the peoples around us or take their daughters for our sons. [v]

31 "When the neighboring peoples bring merchandise or grain to sell on the Sabbath, [w] we will not buy from them on the Sabbath or on any holy day. Every seventh year we will forgo working the land [x] and will cancel all debts. [y]

32 "We assume the responsibility for carrying out the commands to give a third of a shekel [a] each year for the service of the house of our God: **33** for the bread set out on the table; [z] for the regular grain offerings and burnt offerings; for the offerings on the Sabbaths, New Moon [a] festivals and appointed feasts; for the holy offerings; for sin offerings to make atonement for Israel; and for all the duties of the house of our God. [b]

34 "We—the priests, the Levites and the people—have cast lots [c] to determine when each of our families is to bring to the house of our God at set times each year a contribution of wood [d] to burn on the altar of the LORD our God, as it is written in the Law.

35 "We also assume responsibility for bringing to the house of the LORD each year the firstfruits [e] of our crops and of every fruit tree. [f]

36 "As it is also written in the Law, we will bring the firstborn [g] of our sons and of our cattle, of our herds and of our flocks to the house of our God, to the priests ministering there. [h]

37 "Moreover, we will bring to the storerooms of the house of our God, to the priests, the first of our ground meal, of our ⌊grain⌋ offerings, of the fruit of all our trees and of our new wine and oil. [i] And we will bring a tithe [j] of our crops to the Levites, [k] for it is the Levites who collect the tithes in all the towns where we work. [l] **38** A priest descended from Aaron is to accompany the Levites when they receive the tithes, and the Levites are to bring a tenth of the tithes [m] up to the house of our God, to the storerooms of the treasury. **39** The people of Israel, including the Levites, are to bring their contributions of grain, new wine and oil to the storerooms where the articles for the sanctuary are kept and where the ministering priests, the gatekeepers and the singers stay.

"We will not neglect the house of our God." [n]

The New Residents of Jerusalem

11 Now the leaders of the people settled in Jerusalem, and the rest of the people cast lots to bring one out of every ten to live in Jerusalem, [o] the holy city, [p] while the remaining nine were to stay in their own towns. [q] **2** The people commended all the men who volunteered to live in Jerusalem.

3 These are the provincial leaders who settled in Jerusalem (now some Israelites, priests, Levites, temple servants and descendants of Solomon's servants lived in the towns of Judah, each on his own property in the various towns, [r] **4** while other people from both Judah and Benjamin [s] lived in Jerusalem): [t]

From the descendants of Judah:

Athaiah son of Uzziah, the son of Zechariah, the son of Amariah, the son of Shephatiah, the son of Mahalalel, a descendant of Perez; **5** and Maaseiah son of Baruch, the son of Col-Hozeh, the son of Hazaiah, the son of Adaiah, the son of Joiarib, the son of Zechariah, a descendant of Shelah. **6** The descendants of Perez who lived in Jerusalem totaled 468 able men.

7 From the descendants of Benjamin:

[a] 32 That is, about 1/8 ounce (about 4 grams)

10:30 v Ex 34:16; Dt 7:3; Ne 13:23
10:31 w Ne 13:16,18; Jer 17:27; Eze 23:38; Am 8:5 x Ex 23:11; Lev 25:1-7 y Dt 15:1
10:33 z Lev 24:6 a Nu 10:10; Ps 81:3; Isa 1:14 b 2Ch 24:5
10:34 c Lev 16:8 d Ne 13:31
10:35 e Ex 22:29; 23:19; Nu 18:12 f Dt 26:1-11
10:36 g Ex 13:2; Nu 18:14-16 h Ne 13:31
10:37 i Lev 23:17; Nu 18:12 j Lev 27:30; Nu 18:21 k Dt 14:22-29 l Eze 44:30
10:38 m Nu 18:26
10:39 n Dt 12:6; Ne 13:11,12
11:1 o Ne 7:4 p ver 18; Isa 48:2; 52:1; 64:10; Zec 14:20-21 q Ne 7:73
11:3 r 1Ch 9:2-3; Ezr 2:1
11:4 s Ezr 1:5 t Ezr 2:70

Nehemiah 11:1–36

The practice of redistributing populations was also used to establish Greek and Hellenistic cities. Known as *synoikismos*, it involved forcible transfer from rural settlements to urban centers. In addition to those chosen by lot (v. 1), some volunteered to live in Jerusalem (v. 2). But evidently most chose to stay in their hometowns. The 1st-century Jewish historian Josephus asserted: "Nehemiah, seeing that the city had a small population, urged the priests and Levites to leave the countryside and move to the city and remain there, for he had prepared houses for them at his own expense."

Sallu son of Meshullam, the son of Joed, the son of Pedaiah, the son of Kolaiah, the son of Maaseiah, the son of Ithiel, the son of Jeshaiah, [8]and his followers, Gabbai and Sallai—928 men. [9]Joel son of Zicri was their chief officer, and Judah son of Hassenuah was over the Second District of the city.

[10]From the priests:

Jedaiah; the son of Joiarib; Jakin; [11]Seraiah[u] son of Hilkiah, the son of Meshullam, the son of Zadok, the son of Meraioth, the son of Ahitub,[v] supervisor in the house of God, [12]and their associates, who carried on work for the temple—822 men; Adaiah son of Jeroham, the son of Pelaliah, the son of Amzi, the son of Zechariah, the son of Pashhur, the son of Malkijah, [13]and his associates, who were heads of families—242 men; Amashsai son of Azarel, the son of Ahzai, the son of Meshillemoth, the son of Immer, [14]and his[a] associates, who were able men—128. Their chief officer was Zabdiel son of Haggedolim.

[15]From the Levites:

Shemaiah son of Hasshub, the son of Azrikam, the son of Hashabiah, the son of Bunni; [16]Shabbethai[w] and Jozabad,[x] two of the heads of the Levites, who had charge of the outside work of the house of God; [17]Mattaniah[y] son of Mica, the son of Zabdi, the son of Asaph,[z] the director who led in thanksgiving and prayer; Bakbukiah, second among his associates; and Abda son of Shammua, the son of Galal, the son of Jeduthun.[a] [18]The Levites in the holy city[b] totaled 284.

[19]The gatekeepers:

Akkub, Talmon and their associates, who kept watch at the gates—172 men.

[20]The rest of the Israelites, with the priests and Levites, were in all the towns of Judah, each on his ancestral property.

[21]The temple servants[c] lived on the hill of Ophel, and Ziha and Gishpa were in charge of them.

[22]The chief officer of the Levites in Jerusalem was Uzzi son of Bani, the son of Hashabiah, the son of Mattaniah,[d] the son of Mica. Uzzi was one of Asaph's descendants, who were the singers responsible for the service of the house of God. [23]The singers[e] were under the king's orders, which regulated their daily activity.

[24]Pethahiah son of Meshezabel, one of the descendants of Zerah[f] son of Judah, was the king's agent in all affairs relating to the people.

[25]As for the villages with their fields, some of the people of Judah lived in Kiriath Arba[g] and its surrounding settlements, in Dibon[h] and its settlements, in Jekabzeel and its villages, [26]in Jeshua, in Moladah, in Beth Pelet,[i] [27]in Hazar Shual, in Beersheba[j] and its settlements, [28]in Ziklag,[k] in Meconah and its settlements, [29]in En Rimmon, in Zorah,[l] in Jarmuth,[m] [30]Zanoah, Adullam[n] and their villages, in Lachish[o] and its fields, and in Azekah[p] and its settlements. So they were living all the way from Beersheba[q] to the Valley of Hinnom.

[31]The descendants of the Benjamites from Geba[r] lived in Micmash,[s] Aija, Bethel and its settlements, [32]in Anathoth,[t] Nob[u] and Ananiah, [33]in Hazor,[v] Ramah and Gittaim,[w] [34]in Hadid, Zeboim[x] and Neballat, [35]in Lod and Ono,[y] and in the Valley of the Craftsmen.

[36]Some of the divisions of the Levites of Judah settled in Benjamin.

---

a 14 Most Septuagint manuscripts; Hebrew *their*

11:11
u 2Ki 25:18; Ezr 2:2
v Ezr 7:2

11:16
w Ezr 10:15
x Ezr 8:33
11:17
y 1Ch 9:15; Ne 12:8
z 2Ch 5:12
a 1Ch 25:1
11:18
b Rev 21:2

11:21
c Ezr 2:43; Ne 3:26
11:22
d 1Ch 9:15
11:23
e Ne 7:44
11:24
f Ge 38:30
11:25
g Ge 35:27;
Jos 14:15
h Nu 21:30
11:26
i Jos 15:27
11:27
j Ge 21:14
11:28
k 1Sa 27:6
11:29
l Jos 15:33
m Jos 10:3
11:30
n Jos 15:35
o Jos 10:3
p Jos 10:10
q Jos 15:28
11:31
r Jos 21:17;
Isa 10:29 *s* 1Sa 13:2
11:32
t Jos 21:18;
Isa 10:30 *u* 1Sa 21:1
11:33
v Jos 11:1
w 2Sa 4:3
11:34
x 1Sa 13:18
11:35
y 1Ch 8:12

Verses 3–4a preview the specifics of 4b–36. Verses 3–19 constitute a census roster, comparable to the list in 1 Chronicles 9:2–21 of the first residents of Jerusalem after the return from Babylon. About half the names in the two lists are identical.

📖 How well would you have taken to a forced move based on a lottery system? Jerusalem, despite its defenses, was still a vulnerable place, and its survival (not to downgrade God's intervention and protection on behalf of his own) depended on the strength of its numbers to resist enemy incursions. Have you ever placed your family in relative danger because of your faith? Have you chosen to live or attend church in a troubled neighborhood in order to infiltrate it in the name of Christ? Whether or not you are still there, in what ways did God bless your efforts?

Priests and Levites

12 These were the priests[z] and Levites who returned with Zerubbabel[a] son of Shealtiel and with Jeshua:[b]

Seraiah,[c] Jeremiah, Ezra,
2 Amariah, Malluch, Hattush,
3 Shecaniah, Rehum, Meremoth,
4 Iddo,[d] Ginnethon,[a] Abijah,[e]
5 Mijamin,[b] Moadiah, Bilgah,
6 Shemaiah, Joiarib, Jedaiah,[f]
7 Sallu, Amok, Hilkiah and Jedaiah.

These were the leaders of the priests and their associates in the days of Jeshua.

8 The Levites were Jeshua, Binnui, Kadmiel, Sherebiah, Judah, and also Mattaniah,[g] who, together with his associates, was in charge of the songs of thanksgiving. 9 Bakbukiah and Unni, their associates, stood opposite them in the services.

10 Jeshua was the father of Joiakim, Joiakim the father of Eliashib,[h] Eliashib the father of Joiada, 11 Joiada the father of Jonathan, and Jonathan the father of Jaddua.

12 In the days of Joiakim, these were the heads of the priestly families:

of Seraiah's family, Meraiah;
of Jeremiah's, Hananiah;
13 of Ezra's, Meshullam;
of Amariah's, Jehohanan;
14 of Malluch's, Jonathan;
of Shecaniah's,[c] Joseph;
15 of Harim's, Adna;
of Meremoth's,[d] Helkai;
16 of Iddo's,[i] Zechariah;
of Ginnethon's, Meshullam;
17 of Abijah's, Zicri;
of Miniamin's and of Moadiah's, Piltai;
18 of Bilgah's, Shammua;
of Shemaiah's, Jehonathan;
19 of Joiarib's, Mattenai;
of Jedaiah's, Uzzi;
20 of Sallu's, Kallai;
of Amok's, Eber;
21 of Hilkiah's, Hashabiah;
of Jedaiah's, Nethanel.

22 The family heads of the Levites in the days of Eliashib, Joiada, Johanan and Jaddua, as well as those of the priests, were recorded in the reign of Darius the Persian.

[a] 4 Many Hebrew manuscripts and Vulgate (see also Neh. 12:16); most Hebrew manuscripts *Ginnethoi*   [b] 5 A variant of *Miniamin*   [c] 14 Very many Hebrew manuscripts, some Septuagint manuscripts and Syriac (see also Neh. 12:3); most Hebrew manuscripts *Shebaniah's*   [d] 15 Some Septuagint manuscripts (see also Neh. 12:3); Hebrew *Meraioth's*

Cross-references
12:1 z Ne 10:1-8 a 1Ch 3:19 b Ezr 2:2 c Ezr 2:2
12:4 d Zec 1:1 e Lk 1:5
12:6 f 1Ch 24:7
12:8 g Ne 11:17
12:10 h Ezr 10:24
12:16 i ver 4

Nehemiah 12:1–26

A rotation of 24 priestly divisions had been established under David's leadership (1 Chron. 24:3,7–19). Twenty-two heads of priestly families are mentioned (vv. 1–7) as part of those who had returned from exile in 538/537 B.C. (The Ezra included in verse 1 isn't the well-known Ezra who led a group of returnees 80 years later.) In verses 12–21—a listing that dates to the time of Joiakim, high priest around 500 B.C.—all but one (Hattush, v. 2) of the 22 priestly families listed in verses 1–7 are repeated (Rehum, v. 3, is a variant of Harim, v. 15; Mijamin, v. 5, is a variant of Miniamin, v. 17).

Names, names, names. Such lists appear over and over in Ezra and Nehemiah, making tedious reading material for us. But God was using Ezra and Nehemiah to restore the Jewish people both physically and spiritually. This list of priests and Levites reminded the beleaguered "remnant" of their direct and ongoing connection to God and to each other.

Have you ever visited a war memorial and seen the names of those who have given their lives inscribed on the marble or stone slabs? It's moving to read name after name, realizing the sacrifice made on behalf of others. The list in this passage acknowledges people who sacrificed a great deal to follow the Lord. Thank him today for those who have blazed a trail of faith before you, so that you might follow. Allow their commitment and sacrifice to inform and inspire your actions today.

12:24
i Ezr 2:40

23The family heads among the descendants of Levi up to the time of Johanan son of Eliashib were recorded in the book of the annals. 24And the leaders of the Levites*j* were Hashabiah, Sherebiah, Jeshua son of Kadmiel, and their associates, who stood opposite them to give praise and thanksgiving, one section responding to the other, as prescribed by David the man of God.

25Mattaniah, Bakbukiah, Obadiah, Meshullam, Talmon and Akkub were gatekeepers who guarded the storerooms at the gates. 26They served in the days of Joiakim son of Jeshua, the son of Jozadak, and in the days of Nehemiah the governor and of Ezra the priest and scribe.

Dedication of the Wall of Jerusalem

12:27
k Dt 20:5 *l* 2Sa 6:5
m 1Ch 15:16,28;
25:6; Ps 92:3

27At the dedication*k* of the wall of Jerusalem, the Levites were sought out from where they lived and were brought to Jerusalem to celebrate joyfully the dedication with songs of thanksgiving and with the music of cymbals,*l* harps and lyres.*m*

12:28
n 1Ch 2:54; 9:16

28The singers also were brought together from the region around Jerusalem—from the villages of the Netophathites,*n* 29from Beth Gilgal, and from the area of Geba and Azmaveth, for the singers had built villages for themselves around Jerusalem.

12:30
o Ex 19:10; Job 1:5

30When the priests and Levites had purified themselves ceremonially, they purified the people,*o* the gates and the wall.

12:31
p Ne 2:13
12:34
q Ezr 1:5
12:35
r Ezr 3:10

31I had the leaders of Judah go up on top[a] of the wall. I also assigned two large choirs to give thanks. One was to proceed on top[b] of the wall to the right, toward the Dung Gate.*p* 32Hoshaiah and half the leaders of Judah followed them, 33along with Azariah, Ezra, Meshullam, 34Judah, Benjamin,*q* Shemaiah, Jeremiah, 35as well as some priests with trumpets,*r* and also Zechariah son of Jonathan, the son of Shemaiah, the son of Mattaniah, the son of Micaiah, the son of Zaccur, the son of Asaph, 36and his associates—Shemaiah, Azarel, Milalai, Gilalai, Maai, Nethan-

12:36
s 1Ch 15:16
t 2Ch 8:14 *u* Ezr 7:6
12:37
v Ne 2:14; 3:15
w Ne 3:26

el, Judah and Hanani—with musical instruments[s] ⌊prescribed by⌋ David the man of God.[t] Ezra[u] the scribe led the procession. 37At the Fountain Gate[v] they continued directly up the steps of the City of David on the ascent to the wall and passed above the house of David to the Water Gate[w] on the east.

12:38
x Ne 3:11 *y* Ne 3:8
12:39
z 2Ki 14:13;
Ne 8:16 *a* Ne 3:6
b 2Ch 33:14;
Ne 3:3
c Ne 3:1 *d* Ne 3:1
e Ne 3:1

38The second choir proceeded in the opposite direction. I followed them on top[c] of the wall, together with half the people—past the Tower of the Ovens[x] to the Broad Wall,[y] 39over the Gate of Ephraim,[z] the Jeshanah[d] Gate,[a] the Fish Gate,[b] the Tower of Hananel[c] and the Tower of the Hundred,[d] as far as the Sheep Gate.[e] At the Gate of the Guard they stopped.

40The two choirs that gave thanks then took their places in the house of God; so did I, together with half the officials, 41as well as the priests—Eliakim, Maaseiah, Miniamin, Micaiah, Elioenai, Zechariah and Hananiah with their trumpets— 42and also Maaseiah, Shemaiah, Eleazar, Uzzi, Jehohanan, Malkijah, Elam and Ezer. The choirs sang under the direction of Jezrahiah. 43And on that day they offered great

---

[a] 31 Or *go alongside*   [b] 31 Or *proceed alongside*   [c] 38 Or *them alongside*   [d] 39 Or *Old*

Nehemiah 12:27–47

The dedication of the wall culminated the efforts of the people under Nehemiah's inspired leadership. Celebration and dedication are important ingredients of any endeavor undertaken by God's people. The word "dedication" (v. 27) translates the Aramaic word *hanukkah*. The Jewish holiday in December that celebrates the recapture of the temple from the Seleucids and its rededication (165 B.C.) is formally known as Hanukkah.

The two great processions probably started from the area of the Valley Gate (2:13,15; 3:13) near the center of the western section of the wall. The first procession, led by Ezra (v. 36), moved in a counterclockwise direction

on the wall; the second, under Nehemiah (v. 38), marched clockwise. They met between the Water Gate and the Gate of the Guard, then together entered the temple area (cf. Ps. 48:12–13).

Following the account of the exuberant dedication celebration, with rejoicing that "could be heard far away" (v. 43), the final paragraph of this passage is striking in its quiet optimism—leaving a peaceful sense that all was as it should be. Not only was the religious system operating properly, but appropriate motivations seemed to assure its maintenance. Is all well on your front? Are "all systems go" in your church community—and is this smooth mechanism fueled by healthy attitudes and heartfelt devotion?

sacrifices, rejoicing because God had given them great joy. The women and children also rejoiced. The sound of rejoicing in Jerusalem could be heard far away.

[44]At that time men were appointed to be in charge of the storerooms[f] for the contributions, firstfruits and tithes. [g] From the fields around the towns they were to bring into the storerooms the portions required by the Law for the priests and the Levites, for Judah was pleased with the ministering priests and Levites. [h] [45]They performed the service of their God and the service of purification, as did also the singers and gatekeepers, according to the commands of David[i] and his son Solomon. [j] [46]For long ago, in the days of David and Asaph, [k] there had been directors for the singers and for the songs of praise[l] and thanksgiving to God. [47]So in the days of Zerubbabel and of Nehemiah, all Israel contributed the daily portions for the singers and gatekeepers. They also set aside the portion for the other Levites, and the Levites set aside the portion for the descendants of Aaron. [m]

Nehemiah's Final Reforms

13 On that day the Book of Moses was read aloud in the hearing of the people and there it was found written that no Ammonite or Moabite should ever be admitted into the assembly of God, [n] [2]because they had not met the Israelites with food and water but had hired Balaam[o] to call a curse down on them. [p] (Our God, however, turned the curse into a blessing.) [q] [3]When the people heard this law, they excluded from Israel all who were of foreign descent. [r]

[4]Before this, Eliashib the priest had been put in charge of the storerooms[s] of the house of our God. He was closely associated with Tobiah, [t] [5]and he had provided him with a large room formerly used to store the grain offerings and incense and temple articles, and also the tithes[u] of grain, new wine and oil prescribed for the Levites, singers and gatekeepers, as well as the contributions for the priests.

[6]But while all this was going on, I was not in Jerusalem, for in the thirty-second year of Artaxerxes[v] king of Babylon I had returned to the king. Some time later I asked his permission [7]and came back to Jerusalem. Here I learned about the evil thing Eliashib[w] had done in providing Tobiah a room in the courts of the house of God. [8]I was greatly displeased and threw all Tobiah's household goods out of the room. [x] [9]I gave orders to purify the rooms, [y] and then I put back into them the equipment of the house of God, with the grain offerings and the incense.

[10]I also learned that the portions assigned to the Levites had not been given to them, [z] and that all the Levites and singers responsible for the service had gone back to their own fields. [11]So I rebuked the officials and asked them, "Why is the house of God neglected?" [a] Then I called them together and stationed them at their posts. [12]All Judah brought the tithes[b] of grain, new wine and oil into the storerooms. [c] [13]I put Shelemiah the priest, Zadok the scribe, and a Levite named Pedaiah in charge of the storerooms and made Hanan son of Zaccur, the son of Mattaniah,

Cross references

12:44
f Ne 13:4, 13
g Lev 27:30
h Dt 18:8

12:45
i 1Ch 25:1; 2Ch 8:14
j 1Ch 6:31; 23:5

12:46
k 2Ch 35:15
l 2Ch 29:27; Ps 137:4

12:47
m Nu 18:21; Dt 18:8

13:1
n ver 23; Dt 23:3
13:2
o Nu 22:3-11
p Nu 23:7; Dt 23:3
q Nu 23:11; Dt 23:4-5
13:3
r ver 23; Ne 9:2
13:4
s Ne 12:44
t Ne 2:10

13:5
u Lev 27:30; Nu 18:21

13:6
v Ne 2:6; 5:14

13:7
w Ezr 10:24

13:8
x Mt 21:12-13; Jn 2:13-16
13:9
y 1Ch 23:28; 2Ch 29:5
13:10
z Dt 12:19
13:11
a Ne 10:37-39; Hag 1:1-9
13:12
b 2Ch 31:6
c 1Ki 7:51; Ne 10:37-39; Mal 3:10

Nehemiah 13:1–31

Deuteronomy 23:3–6 prohibited Ammonites and Moabites from joining with the assembly of the Lord to the tenth generation. Ruth the Moabitess had not only been fully accepted into Israel but had become the great-grandmother of King David. But at this later point these people of "foreign descent" (Neh. 13:3) weren't permitted to worship the Lord. During Nehemiah's absence to return to the Persian king's court, Tobiah, who was both an Ammonite and one of Nehemiah's archenemies, had used his influence with Eliashib to gain illicit residence inside the temple.

Unlike Ezra, Nehemiah was a man of a volcanic temperament, who quickly expressed his indignation by taking action (see vv. 8, 21, 25–28; cf. 5:6–13). Compare Jesus' expulsion of the money changers from the temple

area (Matt. 21:12–13). Some 25 years earlier a distraught Ezra had pulled out his own hair over the identical issue of intermarriage (Ezra 9:3). Here Nehemiah beat some of the men and pulled out *their* hair (Neh. 13:25)! Nehemiah acted to prevent future intermarriages, in contrast to Ezra, who had dissolved existing unions.

How tragic that the situation in Judah had deteriorated so badly in Nehemiah's absence (see previous "Here and Now"). When has a strong leader like Nehemiah made a difference in your experience? On a related note, 25 years can make a tremendous difference in the attitudes of people. What differences (both positive and negative) do you see in your own congregation or Christian circles? What new areas of danger or temptation concern you?

Frederick Douglass

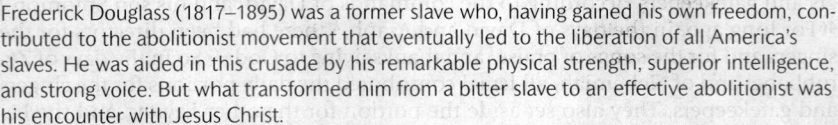

13:14

Frederick Douglass (1817–1895) was a former slave who, having gained his own freedom, contributed to the abolitionist movement that eventually led to the liberation of all America's slaves. He was aided in this crusade by his remarkable physical strength, superior intelligence, and strong voice. But what transformed him from a bitter slave to an effective abolitionist was his encounter with Jesus Christ.

From then on this powerful man worked tirelessly to promote the cause of his people. He started a newspaper that promoted antislavery issues, traveled and spoke at meetings around the country and in Great Britain, lobbied elected officials to vote their consciences on the emancipation issue, and challenged elements of the church still supporting slavery.

Douglass succeeded. His lifelong battle wasn't without setbacks. But he persevered and lived to see the official end of American slavery. After legal freedom for slaves was realized at the end of the Civil War, Frederick Douglass tackled the formidable task of working to make legal freedom an everyday reality.

> **Like Ezra and Nehemiah, Frederick Douglass spent the rest of his life working to transform freedom of spirit and law into freedom of life.**

The work done at this point by Douglass and the other abolitionists wasn't unlike that accomplished by Ezra and Nehemiah. These two Biblical heroes were faced with the seemingly insurmountable challenge of making the official freedom King Cyrus had granted God's people real in the form of a return to Jerusalem and the rebuilding of the temple and city walls. They had to overcome not only the negative expectations of former captors and slave owners but also the negative inertia of captives who had spent their lifetimes developing habits enabling them to cope with bondage. Like Ezra and Nehemiah, Frederick Douglass spent the rest of his life working to transform freedom of spirit and law into freedom of life.

In the process, Douglass learned and then taught many lessons. One was that although religion in general and Christianity in particular should have been allies in the freedom struggle, not all Christians supported the abolitionist movement. Lesson: *There are good and bad manifestations of religion. Religion that is truly of Christ is good religion.*

In a time when it was almost unheard of for black men to travel internationally, Frederick Douglass did. His experiences in England with British abolitionists gave him a global perspective on events that helped him perceive people's myopia when it came to evaluating their own cultures. Lesson: *Seeing injustice "over there" is far easier than identifying it "here."*

Finally, Douglass found himself courted by two strategic camps in the American abolitionist movement. On the one side were those who argued that the way to change America was to repeal the laws supporting slavery. On the other were proponents of working from the inside to change America's views on slavery through a spiritual process that changed hearts and minds through the power and love of God. The political camp viewed the spiritual group as a collection of dreamers and theorists, while the spiritual camp saw the political group as a bunch of secular pragmatists unguided by any principle of enduring worth and willing to sacrifice principle for political compromise.

In many ways Frederick Douglass supported both viewpoints. Recognizing that true freedom begins with a free spirit, he was fond of quoting John 8:36: "If the Son sets you free, you will be free indeed." Yet he also recognized the value of political support. He became a good friend of Abraham Lincoln, who consulted him regularly in the process of emancipating the slaves. Lesson: *In any fight for justice, the spiritual and temporal sides of the issue must be attacked simultaneously.*

their assistant, because these men were considered trustworthy. They were made responsible for distributing the supplies to their brothers. *d*

[14] Remember*e* me for this, O my God, and do not blot out what I have so faithfully done for the house of my God and its services.

[15] In those days I saw men in Judah treading winepresses on the Sabbath and bringing in grain and loading it on donkeys, together with wine, grapes, figs and all other kinds of loads. And they were bringing all this into Jerusalem on the Sabbath. *f* Therefore I warned them against selling food on that day. [16] Men from Tyre who lived in Jerusalem were bringing in fish and all kinds of merchandise and selling them in Jerusalem on the Sabbath *g* to the people of Judah. [17] I rebuked the nobles of Judah and said to them, "What is this wicked thing you are doing—desecrating the Sabbath day? [18] Didn't your forefathers do the same things, so that our God brought all this calamity upon us and upon this city? Now you are stirring up more wrath against Israel by desecrating the Sabbath." *h*

[19] When evening shadows fell on the gates of Jerusalem before the Sabbath, *i* I ordered the doors to be shut and not opened until the Sabbath was over. I stationed some of my own men at the gates so that no load could be brought in on the Sabbath day. [20] Once or twice the merchants and sellers of all kinds of goods spent the night outside Jerusalem. [21] But I warned them and said, "Why do you spend the night by the wall? If you do this again, I will lay hands on you." From that time on they no longer came on the Sabbath. [22] Then I commanded the Levites to purify themselves and go and guard the gates in order to keep the Sabbath day holy.

Remember*j* me for this also, O my God, and show mercy to me according to your great love.

[23] Moreover, in those days I saw men of Judah who had married *k* women from Ashdod, Ammon and Moab. *l* [24] Half of their children spoke the language of Ashdod or the language of one of the other peoples, and did not know how to speak the language of Judah. [25] I rebuked them and called curses down on them. I beat some of the men and pulled out their hair. I made them take an oath *m* in God's name and said: "You are not to give your daughters in marriage to their sons, nor are you to take their daughters in marriage for your sons or for yourselves. [26] Was it not because of marriages like these that Solomon king of Israel sinned? Among the many nations there was no king like him. *n* He was loved by his God, *o* and God made him king over all Israel, but even he was led into sin by foreign women. *p* [27] Must we hear now that you too are doing all this terrible wickedness and are being unfaithful to our God by marrying *q* foreign women?"

[28] One of the sons of Joiada son of Eliashib*r* the high priest was son-in-law to Sanballat*s* the Horonite. And I drove him away from me.

[29] Remember*t* them, O my God, because they defiled the priestly office and the covenant of the priesthood and of the Levites.

[30] So I purified the priests and the Levites of everything foreign, *u* and assigned them duties, each to his own task. [31] I also made provision for contributions of wood*v* at designated times, and for the firstfruits.

Remember*w* me with favor, O my God.

13:13
d Ne 12:44;
Ac 6:1-5
13:14
e Ge 8:1

13:15
f Ex 20:8-11; 34:21;
Dt 5:12-15;
Ne 10:31

13:16
g Ne 10:31

13:18
h Ne 10:31;
Jer 17:21-23
13:19
i Lev 23:32

13:22
j Ge 8:1; Ne 12:30

13:23
k Ezr 9:1-2;
Mal 2:11 *l* ver 1;
Ne 10:30

13:25
m Ezr 10:5

13:26
n 1Ki 3:13;
2Ch 1:12
o 2Sa 12:25
p 1Ki 11:3
13:27
q Ezr 9:14; 10:2
13:28
r Ezr 10:24
s Ne 2:10

13:29
t Ne 6:14

13:30
u Ne 10:30

13:31
v Ne 10:34
w ver 14,22; Ge 8:1

The last recorded words of Nehemiah—"Remember me with favor, O my God" (v. 31)—capture a theme running throughout this final chapter (vv. 14,22), as well as in Nehemiah's life in general (see "Here and Now" for 2:1–10). Nehemiah demonstrated his devotion by serving God and others. Jesus also modeled service and instructed his disciples to serve others (cf. John 13:14–17). Would you characterize your relationship to God and others this way? Do you willingly and easily lay aside your priorities/agenda/rights for the welfare of others as a service to God? How has Nehemiah's example challenged you to participate more fully in God's kingdom?

4:14 "WHO KNOWS BUT THAT YOU [ESTHER] HAVE COME TO
ROYAL POSITION FOR SUCH A TIME AS THIS?"

INTRODUCTION TO
Esther

AUTHOR
The author of Esther is unknown, but the writer was certainly a Jew and, given the description of Persian life, probably lived in Persia during this period (Esther became queen in 479 B.C.).

DATE WRITTEN
Esther was probably written between 460 and 350 B.C.

ORIGINAL READERS
This brief account was written to record the events that led to the establishment of the celebration of Purim (9:24–32) as a commemoration of the deliverance of the Jews during the Persian period. It was likely also written to demonstrate God's sovereignty and care for his people.

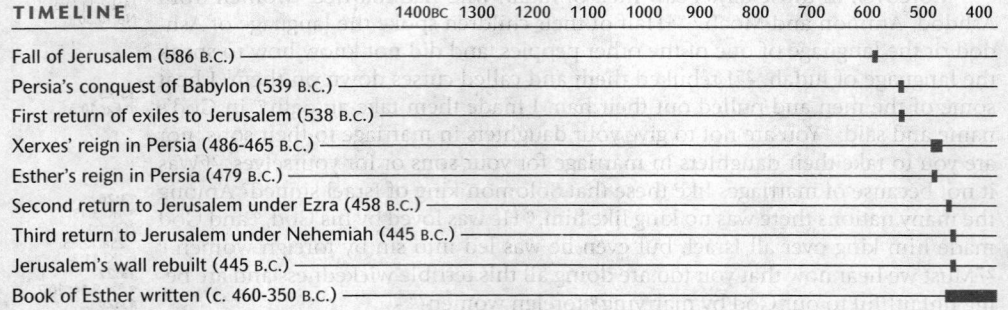

TIMELINE	1400BC	1300	1200	1100	1000	900	800	700	600	500	400
Fall of Jerusalem (586 B.C.)											
Persia's conquest of Babylon (539 B.C.)											
First return of exiles to Jerusalem (538 B.C.)											
Xerxes' reign in Persia (486-465 B.C.)											
Esther's reign in Persia (479 B.C.)											
Second return to Jerusalem under Ezra (458 B.C.)											
Third return to Jerusalem under Nehemiah (445 B.C.)											
Jerusalem's wall rebuilt (445 B.C.)											
Book of Esther written (c. 460-350 B.C.)											

THEMES
Esther describes the events leading to the establishment of the feast of Purim, which commemorates the deliverance of the Jews during the Persian period. It includes the following themes:

1. *God's sovereignty.* Who is the real hero in Esther? While both Mordecai and Esther performed admirable, self-sacrificing acts of courage, the book clearly implies that there is an unnamed force behind the scenes, orchestrating history. The "coincidences" are just too perfect to be ascribed to chance. The book of Esther demonstrates that God is in control of history and that he is the hero who saves and protects his own, often using ordinary people and events.

2. *Racism.* Throughout the story, racial hatred is shown to be a powerful force for evil (3:8–9). Esther demonstrates that racial animosity and ethnic prejudice are sins that aren't to be condoned.

3. *Service.* Esther and Mordecai were ordinary people God used at a particular time and place to accomplish his purposes (4:14). Courage, wisdom, and self-sacrificing action are sometimes required when God calls us to serve him. Confidence in God's providential care and ability to work behind the scenes is essential for anyone called to accomplish his work and purposes.

4. *Obedience.* Conflicting demands for obedience and contrary loyalties sometimes force believers to make difficult choices. Esther opted to obey Mordecai (2:10,20; 4:8–16), but in so doing she stood up against Persian law (4:11,16; 5:1–2). Mordecai refused to obey the king's command (3:2–8) but carried out Esther's instructions (4:17). Obeying God always takes precedence over obeying humans (Acts 4:19–20; 5:29).

5. *Pride.* Haman is a prototype of the arrogant individual (3:5; 5:9–14; 7:8–10), illustrating Proverbs 16:18: "Pride goes before destruction, a haughty spirit before a fall." He is contrasted with Mordecai, who didn't seek status but allowed the Lord to elevate him in the king's eyes (6:1–13; 8:9–15; cf. James 4:10).

FAITH IN ACTION

The pages of Esther contain life lessons and role models of faith—people who challenge believers to put their faith in action.

Role Models

- VASHTI (1:10–12), a pagan queen, refused to honor her husband's drunken and debasing request. Has an unbeliever's moral stand ever served as an example to you or taught you a significant lesson?

- MORDECAI (2:10–11,19–20; 4:12–14; 8:9) exhibited wisdom and trust in God's providence in a dangerous situation. Is there currently an opportunity for you to demonstrate your trust in God? Do you ask for God's wisdom (cf. James 1:2–5) when facing trying circumstances?

- ESTHER (4:16) intervened for God's people despite the risk to her own life, trusting God to protect her. What is God calling you to do today? Given your present position, what do you believe to be his purpose for you?

Challenges

- Despite your situation—perhaps because of it—God wants to use you. Be obedient when he calls you.

- Determine to watch for the good lessons you can learn from unbelievers.

- Refuse to compromise your faith (3:2), even if the result means death (3:5–6). Your devotion to God means more than your life.

- Confess racism and refuse to condone prejudicial hatred (3:6).

- Realize that if you fail to answer God's call to service, he will turn to someone else who will faithfully obey him (4:14). Determine to pass the test of faith.

- Trust God to "work in the details" of your life and in the lives of those around you. Even a sleepless night (6:1) can be part of his plan.

- Ask for God's wisdom when facing difficult situations.

- Don't succumb to the sin of pride but humble yourself before God and wait for his timing.

OUTLINE

   I. The Feasts of Xerxes (1:1—2:18)
  II. The Feasts of Esther (2:19—7:10)
 III. The Feasts of Purim (8–10)

Queen Vashti Deposed

1:1
a Ezr 4:6; Da 9:1
b Est 9:30; Da 3:2;
6:1 *c* Est 8:9

1 This is what happened during the time of Xerxes, [a][a] the Xerxes who ruled over 127 provinces[b] stretching from India to Cush[b: c] ²At that time King Xerxes reigned from his royal throne in the citadel of Susa,[d] ³and in the third year of his reign he gave a banquet[e] for all his nobles and officials. The military leaders of Persia and Media, the princes, and the nobles of the provinces were present.

1:2
d Ezr 4:9; Ne 1:1;
Est 2:8
1:3
e 1Ki 3:15; Est 2:18

⁴For a full 180 days he displayed the vast wealth of his kingdom and the splendor and glory of his majesty. ⁵When these days were over, the king gave a banquet, lasting seven days,[f] in the enclosed garden[g] of the king's palace, for all the people from the least to the greatest, who were in the citadel of Susa. ⁶The garden had hangings of white and blue linen, fastened with cords of white linen and purple material to silver rings on marble pillars. There were couches[h] of gold and silver on a mosaic pavement of porphyry, marble, mother-of-pearl and other costly stones. ⁷Wine was served in goblets of gold, each one different from the other, and the royal wine was abundant, in keeping with the king's liberality.[i] ⁸By the king's command each guest was allowed to drink in his own way, for the king instructed all the wine stewards to serve each man what he wished.

1:5
f Jdg 14:17
g 2Ki 21:18;
Est 7:7-8

1:6
h Est 7:8;
Eze 23:41;
Am 3:12; 6:4

1:7
i Est 2:18; Da 5:2

⁹Queen Vashti also gave a banquet[j] for the women in the royal palace of King Xerxes.

1:9
j 1Ki 3:15

¹⁰On the seventh day, when King Xerxes was in high spirits[k] from wine,[l] he commanded the seven eunuchs who served him—Mehuman, Biztha, Harbona,[m] Bigtha, Abagtha, Zethar and Carcas— ¹¹to bring[n] before him Queen Vashti, wearing her royal crown, in order to display her beauty[o] to the people and nobles, for she was lovely to look at. ¹²But when the attendants delivered the king's command, Queen Vashti refused to come. Then the king became furious and burned with anger.[p]

1:10
k Jdg 16:25; Ru 3:7
l Ge 14:18;
Est 3:15; 5:6; 7:2;
Pr 31:4-7; Da 5:1-4
m Est 7:9
1:11
n SS 2:4 *o* Ps 45:11;
Eze 16:14
1:12
p Ge 39:19;
Est 2:21; 7:7;
Pr 19:12

¹³Since it was customary for the king to consult experts in matters of law and justice, he spoke with the wise men who understood the times[q] ¹⁴and were closest to the king—Carshena, Shethar, Admatha, Tarshish, Meres, Marsena and Memucan, the seven nobles[r] of Persia and Media who had special access to the king and were highest in the kingdom.

1:13
q 1Ch 12:32;
Jer 10:7; Da 2:12
1:14
r 2Ki 25:19;
Ezr 7:14

---

a 1 Hebrew *Ahasuerus*, a variant of Xerxes' Persian name; here and throughout Esther   *b 1* That is, the upper Nile region

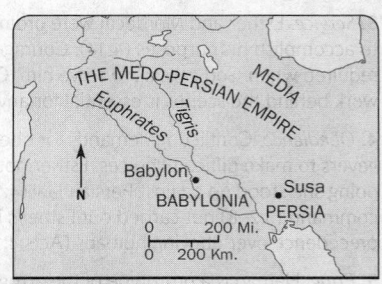

Setting of Esther (1:1)

Then: Persia, under King Xerxes, was the dominant political, military, and cultural power of its time.

Now: Biblical Persia is modern Iran, still a political, military, and cultural power in the Middle East, though not as dominant as it was in Biblical times.

Esther 1:1–22

The beautiful Vashti was a trophy of Xerxes' power and glory. He desired her dramatic entrance before the men being asked to go to war for the empire. Perhaps the sight of the queen was intended to inspire patriotism, but Xerxes' drunken state may have been a factor as well. The Greek historian Herodotus explained that the Persians drank as they deliberated matters of state (cf. Est. 3:15), believing that intoxication put them in closer touch with the spiritual world.

The author revealed the workings of human power and showed its inability to determine the destiny of God's people. In a world ruled by men, he highlighted an incident involving gender and ethnic interaction: In this story powerful Persian men are outwitted by a Jewish woman. Esther had to overcome two levels of conflict—as a woman and as a Jew.

Do you want to do something great for God but feel plagued by a monotonous life? Redemptive history involves a series of miracles—linked together by a chain of faithful obedience in seemingly "insignificant" events. Through them all God is moving history forward to fulfill his purposes of creation in preparation for Christ's return.

The stewardship of power is a major Biblical theme. Every era has been marked by those who have risen to power and exposed their personal flaws, often leading to reigns of terror. Businesses sometimes lack the checks and balances of government structure that, in principle, limit the power of any one individual. Even the church isn't immune to the misuse of power by spiritual leaders. What can you do to influence the situation in your country, church, or community?

15 "According to law, what must be done to Queen Vashti?" he asked. "She has not obeyed the command of King Xerxes that the eunuchs have taken to her."

16 Then Memucan replied in the presence of the king and the nobles, "Queen Vashti has done wrong, not only against the king but also against all the nobles and the peoples of all the provinces of King Xerxes. 17 For the queen's conduct will become known to all the women, and so they will despise their husbands and say, 'King Xerxes commanded Queen Vashti to be brought before him, but she would not come.' 18 This very day the Persian and Median women of the nobility who have heard about the queen's conduct will respond to all the king's nobles in the same way. There will be no end of disrespect and discord. *s*

19 "Therefore, if it pleases the king, *t* let him issue a royal decree and let it be written in the laws of Persia and Media, which cannot be repealed, *u* that Vashti is never again to enter the presence of King Xerxes. Also let the king give her royal position to someone else who is better than she. 20 Then when the king's edict is proclaimed throughout all his vast realm, all the women will respect their husbands, from the least to the greatest."

21 The king and his nobles were pleased with this advice, so the king did as Memucan proposed. 22 He sent dispatches to all parts of the kingdom, to each province in its own script and to each people in its own language, *v* proclaiming in each people's tongue that every man should be ruler over his own household.

Esther Made Queen

2 Later when the anger of King Xerxes had subsided, *w* he remembered Vashti and what she had done and what he had decreed about her. 2 Then the king's personal attendants proposed, "Let a search be made for beautiful young virgins for the king. 3 Let the king appoint commissioners in every province of his realm to bring all these beautiful girls into the harem at the citadel of Susa. Let them be placed under the care of Hegai, the king's eunuch, who is in charge of the women; and let beauty treatments be given to them. 4 Then let the girl who pleases the king be queen instead of Vashti." This advice appealed to the king, and he followed it.

5 Now there was in the citadel of Susa a Jew of the tribe of Benjamin, named Mordecai son of Jair, the son of Shimei, the son of Kish, *x* 6 who had been carried into exile from Jerusalem by Nebuchadnezzar king of Babylon, among those taken captive with Jehoiachin *a* *y* king of Judah. *z* 7 Mordecai had a cousin named Hadassah, whom he had brought up because she had neither father nor mother. This girl, who was also known as Esther, *a* was lovely *b* in form and features, and Mordecai had taken her as his own daughter when her father and mother died.

8 When the king's order and edict had been proclaimed, many girls were brought to the citadel of Susa *c* and put under the care of Hegai. Esther also was taken to the king's palace and entrusted to Hegai, who had charge of the harem. 9 The girl pleased him and won his favor. *d* Immediately he provided her with her beauty treat-

a 6 Hebrew *Jeconiah*, a variant of *Jehoiachin*

1:18
s Pr 19:13; 27:15
1:19
t Ecc 8:4 *u* Est 8:8;
Da 6:8, 12

1:22
v Ne 13:24; Est 8:9;
Eph 5:22-24;
1Ti 2:12

2:1
w Est 1:19-20; 7:10

2:5
x 1Sa 9:1; Est 3:2

2:6
y 2Ki 24:6, 15;
2Ch 36:10, 20
z Da 1:1-5; 5:13
2:7
a Ge 41:45
b Ge 39:6

2:8
c ver 3, 15; Ne 1:1;
Est 1:2; Da 8:2

2:9
d Ge 39:21

Esther 2:1–18

During the four years between Vashti's demotion and Esther's becoming queen, Xerxes was off fighting a disastrous war with Greece. His humiliating defeat depleted the empire's treasuries and discredited him in the eyes of his subjects. The historian Herodotus described the king's life afterward as one of sensual overindulgence. He dallied with the wives of his officers, sowing the anger that led to his eventual assassination.

After spending one night in the king's bed, each woman prior to Esther was returned to the harem of concubines, where she was to remain permanently. Xerxes' violation of people didn't stop with the abuse of women. Herodotus reported that 500 young boys were gathered each year and castrated to serve as eunuchs in the Persian court. No one was exempt from the king's abusive whims.

Esther wasn't only a captive but also an orphan. She epitomized a vulnerable person. Yet God used her to change a nation and save her people. When we think of working with the poor and powerless, we often focus on the resources we bring to help them. But God's strength is made perfect through weakness, and it's often the powerless of the world—orphans, children, and the poor—through whom God works most powerfully. Can you think of someone in our present era who, though socially powerless, was able to accomplish wonderful things? How might God be positioning you to defend other vulnerable people?

2:9
e ver 3,12; Ge 37:3;
1Sa 9:22-24;
2Ki 25:30;
Eze 16:9-13; Da 1:5
2:10
f ver 20

ments and special food. e He assigned to her seven maids selected from the king's palace and moved her and her maids into the best place in the harem.

¹⁰Esther had not revealed her nationality and family background, because Mordecai had forbidden her to do so. f ¹¹Every day he walked back and forth near the courtyard of the harem to find out how Esther was and what was happening to her.

2:12
g Pr 27:9; SS 1:3;
Isa 3:24

¹²Before a girl's turn came to go in to King Xerxes, she had to complete twelve months of beauty treatments prescribed for the women, six months with oil of myrrh and six with perfumes g and cosmetics. ¹³And this is how she would go to the king: Anything she wanted was given her to take with her from the harem to the king's palace. ¹⁴In the evening she would go there and in the morning return to another part of the harem to the care of Shaashgaz, the king's eunuch who was in charge of the concubines. h She would not return to the king unless he was pleased with her and summoned her by name. i

2:14
h 1Ki 11:3; SS 6:8;
Da 5:2 i Est 4:11

2:15
j Est 9:29 k Ps 45:14
l Ge 18:3; 30:27;
Est 5:8

¹⁵When the turn came for Esther (the girl Mordecai had adopted, the daughter of his uncle Abihail j) to go to the king, k she asked for nothing other than what Hegai, the king's eunuch who was in charge of the harem, suggested. And Esther won the favor l of everyone who saw her. ¹⁶She was taken to King Xerxes in the royal residence in the tenth month, the month of Tebeth, in the seventh year of his reign.

2:17
m Est 1:11;
Eze 16:9-13
2:18
n 1Ki 3:15; Est 1:3
o Ge 40:20
p Est 1:7

¹⁷Now the king was attracted to Esther more than to any of the other women, and she won his favor and approval more than any of the other virgins. So he set a royal crown on her head and made her queen m instead of Vashti. ¹⁸And the king gave a great banquet, n Esther's banquet, for all his nobles and officials. o He proclaimed a holiday throughout the provinces and distributed gifts with royal liberality. p

Mordecai Uncovers a Conspiracy

2:19
q ver 21; Est 3:2;
4:2; 5:13

¹⁹When the virgins were assembled a second time, Mordecai was sitting at the king's gate. q ²⁰But Esther had kept secret her family background and nationality just as Mordecai had told her to do, for she continued to follow Mordecai's instructions as she had done when he was bringing her up. r

2:20
r ver 10

2:21
s Ge 40:2; Est 6:2
t Est 1:12; 3:5; 5:9;
7:7

²¹During the time Mordecai was sitting at the king's gate, Bigthana a and Teresh, two of the king's officers s who guarded the doorway, became angry t and conspired to assassinate King Xerxes. ²²But Mordecai found out about the plot and told Queen Esther, who in turn reported it to the king, giving credit to Mordecai. ²³And when the report was investigated and found to be true, the two officials were hanged u on a gallows. b All this was recorded in the book of the annals v in the presence of the king.

2:23
u Ge 40:19;
Ps 7:14-16;
Pr 26:27 v Est 6:1;
10:2

Haman's Plot to Destroy the Jews

3:1
w ver 10;
Ex 17:8-16;
Nu 24:7;
Dt 25:17-19;
1Sa 14:48; Est 5:11

3 After these events, King Xerxes honored Haman son of Hammedatha, the Agagite, w elevating him and giving him a seat of honor higher than that of all the other nobles. ²All the royal officials at the king's gate knelt down and paid honor

---

a 21 Hebrew *Bigthan*, a variant of *Bigthana*   b 23 Or *were hung* (or *impaled*) *on poles*; similarly elsewhere in Esther

---

Esther 2:19–23

Herodotus referred to an official list of the king's "benefactors," recorded in the Persian archives. Acts of loyalty were usually rewarded immediately and generously by Persian kings, but Mordecai's reward was initially overlooked, even though his action had been noted.

Have you ever been overlooked? It's frustrating to have your actions ignored when they should have been rewarded. We can speculate as to why Mordecai's loyalty *was passed over, but the reason isn't important.* As a believer, whose approval and reward do you look to receive (cf. Matt. 6:1–4,18,33)? God is invisibly at work, making even life's greatest disappointments a link in a chain of good things yet to come (cf. Gen. 50:20).

Esther 3:1–15

In chapter 1, Memucan's fear of losing respect drove him to escalate an incident between Xerxes and Vashti. A similar pattern is seen in this episode, where the disobedience of one Jew brought an edict against all Jews in the empire. When such maniacal need for honor and respect is coupled with absolute power, the result is oppression and injustice.

The *pur* or "lot" introduces the element of destiny into the story (cf. Prov. 16:33; Acts 1:26). Haman cast the lot (rolled the dice) to determine the date of death for the Jews. The edict was sent out on the thirteenth day of the first month—ironically, the eve of Passover. But God determined how the dice fell.

to Haman, for the king had commanded this concerning him. But Mordecai would not kneel down or pay him honor.

3Then the royal officials at the king's gate asked Mordecai, "Why do you disobey the king's command?" x 4Day after day they spoke to him but he refused to comply. y Therefore they told Haman about it to see whether Mordecai's behavior would be tolerated, for he had told them he was a Jew.

5When Haman saw that Mordecai would not kneel down or pay him honor, he was enraged. z 6Yet having learned who Mordecai's people were, he scorned the idea of killing only Mordecai. Instead Haman looked for a way a to destroy b all Mordecai's people, the Jews, c throughout the whole kingdom of Xerxes.

7In the twelfth year of King Xerxes, in the first month, the month of Nisan, they cast the pur d (that is, the lot e) in the presence of Haman to select a day and month. And the lot fell on a the twelfth month, the month of Adar. f

8Then Haman said to King Xerxes, "There is a certain people dispersed and scattered among the peoples in all the provinces of your kingdom whose customs g are different from those of all other people and who do not obey h the king's laws; it is not in the king's best interest to tolerate them. i 9If it pleases the king, let a decree be issued to destroy them, and I will put ten thousand talents b of silver into the royal treasury for the men who carry out this business." j

10So the king took his signet ring k from his finger and gave it to Haman son of Hammedatha, the Agagite, the enemy of the Jews. 11"Keep the money," the king said to Haman, "and do with the people as you please."

12Then on the thirteenth day of the first month the royal secretaries were summoned. They wrote out in the script of each province and in the language l of each people all Haman's orders to the king's satraps, the governors of the various provinces and the nobles of the various peoples. These were written in the name of King Xerxes himself and sealed m with his own ring. 13Dispatches were sent by couriers to all the king's provinces with the order to destroy, kill and annihilate all the Jews n—young and old, women and little children—on a single day, the thirteenth day of the twelfth month, the month of Adar, o and to plunder p their goods. 14A copy of the text of the edict was to be issued as law in every province and made known to the people of every nationality so they would be ready for that day. q

15Spurred on by the king's command, the couriers went out, and the edict was issued in the citadel of Susa. r The king and Haman sat down to drink, s but the city of Susa was bewildered. t

Mordecai Persuades Esther to Help

4 When Mordecai learned of all that had been done, he tore his clothes, u put on sackcloth and ashes, v and went out into the city, wailing w loudly and bitterly. 2But he went only as far as the king's gate, x because no one clothed in sackcloth was allowed to enter it. 3In every province to which the edict and order of the king came, there was great mourning among the Jews, with fasting, weeping and wailing. Many lay in sackcloth and ashes.

a 7 Septuagint; Hebrew does not have And the lot fell on.   b 9 That is, about 375 tons (about 345 metric tons)

3:3 x Est 5:9; Da 3:12
3:4 y Ge 39:10
3:5 z Est 2:21; 5:9
3:6 a Pr 16:25 b Ps 74:8; 83:4 c Est 9:24
3:7 d Est 9:24,26 e Lev 16:8; 1Sa 10:21 f ver 13; Ezr 6:15; Est 9:19
3:8 g Ac 16:20-21 h Jer 29:7; Da 6:13 i Ezr 4:15
3:9 j Est 7:4
3:10 k Ge 41:42; Est 7:6; 8:2
3:12 l Ne 13:24 m Ge 38:18; 1Ki 21:8; Est 8:8-10
3:13 n 1Sa 15:3; Ezr 4:6; Est 8:10-14 o ver 7 p Est 8:11; 9:10
3:14 q Est 8:8; 9:1
3:15 r Est 8:14 s Est 1:10 t Est 8:15
4:1 u Nu 14:6 v 2Sa 13:19; Eze 27:30-31; Jnh 3:5-6 w Ex 11:6; Ps 30:11
4:2 x Est 2:19

The final book of the New Testament, Revelation, was written to encourage Christians who, like the Jews of Persia, found their existence threatened when their government turned beastly. The religious tolerance enjoyed in the West today hasn't been the experience of Christians in many other parts of the world. One source reports that, at least for part of the 20th century, approximately 300,000 Christians were martyred each year.

Though most of us aren't threatened with death, we are continually tempted to compromise our convictions in order to fit in and get along with others. Are there some areas in your life in which you are tempted to "bow down or do obeisance" to others' expectations and deny your fundamental beliefs?

Esther 4:1–17

Because of her beauty and grace, the orphaned exile Esther had been made queen of the kingdom. Yet her position wasn't simply for her own power and prestige. She had been prepared and positioned by God to save her people. Challenging a tyrant king, even as his queen, involved great risk, but God gave Esther a choice in the matter. She turned to her community, asking her fellow Jews to pray and fast on her behalf.

4When Esther's maids and eunuchs came and told her about Mordecai, she was in great distress. She sent clothes for him to put on instead of his sackcloth, but he would not accept them. 5Then Esther summoned Hathach, one of the king's eunuchs assigned to attend her, and ordered him to find out what was troubling Mordecai and why.

6So Hathach went out to Mordecai in the open square of the city in front of the king's gate. 7Mordecai told him everything that had happened to him, including the exact amount of money Haman had promised to pay into the royal treasury for the destruction of the Jews.*y* 8He also gave him a copy of the text of the edict for their annihilation, which had been published in Susa, to show to Esther and explain it to her, and he told him to urge her to go into the king's presence to beg for mercy and plead with him for her people.

9Hathach went back and reported to Esther what Mordecai had said. 10Then she instructed him to say to Mordecai, 11 "All the king's officials and the people of the royal provinces know that for any man or woman who approaches the king in the inner court without being summoned*z* the king has but one law:*a* that he be put to death. The only exception to this is for the king to extend the gold scepter*b* to him and spare his life. But thirty days have passed since I was called to go to the king."

12When Esther's words were reported to Mordecai, 13he sent back this answer: "Do not think that because you are in the king's house you alone of all the Jews will escape. 14For if you remain silent*c* at this time, relief*d* and deliverance*e* for the Jews will arise from another place, but you and your father's family will perish. And who knows but that you have come to royal position for such a time as this?"*f*

15Then Esther sent this reply to Mordecai: 16 "Go, gather together all the Jews who are in Susa, and fast*g* for me. Do not eat or drink for three days, night or day. I and my maids will fast as you do. When this is done, I will go to the king, even though it is against the law. And if I perish, I perish."*h*

17So Mordecai went away and carried out all of Esther's instructions.

Esther's Request to the King

5 On the third day Esther put on her royal robes*i* and stood in the inner court of the palace, in front of the king's*j* hall. The king was sitting on his royal throne in the hall, facing the entrance. 2When he saw Queen Esther standing in the court, he was pleased with her and held out to her the gold scepter that was in his hand. So Esther approached and touched the tip of the scepter.*k*

3Then the king asked, "What is it, Queen Esther? What is your request? Even up to half the kingdom,*l* it will be given you."

Marginal references

4:7
y Est 3:9; 7:4

4:11
z Est 2:14 *a* Da 2:9
b Est 5:1,2; 8:4

4:14
c Ecc 3:7; Isa 62:1;
Am 5:13
d Est 9:16,22
e Ge 45:7; Dt 28:29
f Ge 50:20

4:16
g 2Ch 20:3;
Est 9:31 *h* Ge 43:14

5:1
i Est 4:16;
Eze 16:13 *j* Est 6:4;
Pr 21:1

5:2
k Est 4:11; 8:4;
Pr 21:1

5:3
l Est 7:2; Da 5:16;
Mk 6:23

God has prepared good works for each of us to live out (Eph. 2:10). But doing so involves risk and choice. We are tempted on every side to protect our security, prestige, and position and to compromise what we know to be right. To walk the way of God, especially when such a course is threatening and unpopular, requires the support of others. To whom would you turn to pray and fast for you if you knew you had to do something that threatened your security? Around the world Christians are being called to speak God's truth to powerful people in government and business, to stand up on behalf of the right. How can you support them?

Esther 5:1–8

Vashti had risked her life by refusing to appear before Xerxes when summoned (1:12). Now Esther jeopardized hers by appearing before the same king uninvited. Archaeological evidence shows that her fear was

well founded. Two images excavated from Persepolis show a Persian king seated on his throne with a scepter in his right hand. A soldier standing behind the throne holds a large ax. The threat of death and the hope of life were equally present as Esther approached the king. Rather than merely blurting out her story, Esther acted with guarded wisdom, setting a context for the king to hear the truth.

In our decision-making, we become the people God has created us to be by participating, through the help of the Holy Spirit, with his covenant in Christ. Like Esther, we need a character transformation so that we no longer live as pagans. Obeying laws can't bring about true change, because law can't alter our character. Without the Spirit's work, we can't attain fully to the purpose of our lives as agents of God's redemptive work in history. How aware and responsive are you to the Spirit's promptings in your heart?

Can We Learn Lessons From Esther?

 4:12–14

Some people attempting to make ethical decisions about controversial contemporary issues approach the Bible looking for a commanding word. For such individuals, if the Scripture clearly addresses the matter at hand, the Biblical word is either to be accepted or rejected. Other people consult the Bible expecting it to offer an informative word that can contribute to the process of decision-making. Still others anticipate that God's Word can at best only offer an irrelevant word. They see the Bible as a relic from an immaterial past, of purely antiquarian interest but with no real significance for today's world and problems. In light of these differences of opinion, how are we to hear, assimilate, and apply what the Bible has to say?

Only persons with a will to listen for a Biblical word will find that Scripture has something to say. If we approach God's Word assuming irrelevance, whatever we find will be irrelevant. Listening to Scripture requires careful, comprehensive, consistent attention to all pertinent Biblical texts, precisely because—as honest exploration of the Bible shows—not all passages speak in the same manner. A conscious awareness of the potential range of ways the Bible conveys meaning in relation to various topics clarifies not only how it speaks but also how we are to listen for and hear what it's saying.

In various places the Bible addresses ethical matters directly, indirectly—or not at all. Direct and indirect statements in Scripture invite readers to grasp and comprehend what the text articulates. At times the sense of either kind of statement (direct or indirect) may be plain—with virtually all readers in agreement about the substance of the Biblical commentary. Equipped with a secure understanding of the plain sense of a text, individual readers are free to accept, reject, or challenge (and then accept or reject) what it says.

At other times both direct and indirect Biblical statements may be opaque—with readers interpreting the sense of the statements in different ways. Having arrived at a personal understanding of a Biblical text that is recognized to be debatable (no matter how convinced a particular reader may be that one specific understanding is correct and others wrong), once again that reader may accept, reject, or challenge (and then accept or reject) what he or she believes and understands the material to say.

Because of these diverse ways of reading and responding to the Bible, anyone attempting to make ethical decisions while engaging Biblical materials is obliged to: (a) articulate an understanding of the statement, (b) recognize the relative degree of certainty he or she may have about the basic sense of the text—are there other opinions and, if so, what are they?—and (c) articulate an understanding that the Biblical material either does or doesn't impact the process of ethical reflection.

The book of Esther never mentions God once, but interpretations vary as to whether the story has direct relevance, indirect application, or none at all. What does this intriguing narrative say to you? How sure can you be? Are you convinced that God allowed this book to be incorporated into the canon of Scripture because its words carry divine significance?

> **A**re you convinced that God allowed this book to be incorporated into the canon of Scripture because its words carry divine significance?

Marion L. Soards, professor of New Testament at Louisville Presbyterian Theological Seminary in Louisville, Kentucky

4 "If it pleases the king," replied Esther, "let the king, together with Haman, come today to a banquet I have prepared for him."

5 "Bring Haman at once," the king said, "so that we may do what Esther asks."

So the king and Haman went to the banquet Esther had prepared. 6As they were drinking wine, *m* the king again asked Esther, "Now what is your petition? It will be given you. And what is your request? Even up to half the kingdom, *n* it will be granted." *o*

7 Esther replied, "My petition and my request is this: 8If the king regards me with favor *p* and if it pleases the king to grant my petition and fulfill my request, let the king and Haman come tomorrow to the banquet *q* I will prepare for them. Then I will answer the king's question."

Haman's Rage Against Mordecai

9 Haman went out that day happy and in high spirits. But when he saw Mordecai at the king's gate and observed that he neither rose nor showed fear in his presence, he was filled with rage *r* against Mordecai. *s* 10 Nevertheless, Haman restrained himself and went home.

Calling together his friends and Zeresh, *t* his wife, 11 Haman boasted *u* to them about his vast wealth, his many sons, *v* and all the ways the king had honored him and how he had elevated him above the other nobles and officials. 12 "And that's not all," Haman added. "I'm the only person *w* Queen Esther invited to accompany the king to the banquet she gave. And she has invited me along with the king tomorrow. 13 But all this gives me no satisfaction as long as I see that Jew Mordecai sitting at the king's gate. *x* "

14 His wife Zeresh and all his friends said to him, "Have a gallows built, seventy-five feet *a* high, *y* and ask the king in the morning to have Mordecai hanged *z* on it. Then go with the king to the dinner and be happy." This suggestion delighted Haman, and he had the gallows built.

Mordecai Honored

6 That night the king could not sleep; *a* so he ordered the book of the chronicles, *b* the record of his reign, to be brought in and read to him. 2It was found recorded there that Mordecai had exposed Bigthana and Teresh, two of the king's officers who guarded the doorway, who had conspired to assassinate King Xerxes.

3 "What honor and recognition has Mordecai received for this?" the king asked.

"Nothing has been done for him," *c* his attendants answered.

4 The king said, "Who is in the court?" Now Haman had just entered the outer

---

Cross references (margin):

5:6
m Est 1:10
n Mk 6:23 *o* Est 7:2; 9:12

5:8
p Est 2:15; 7:3; 8:5
q 1Ki 3:15; Est 6:14

5:9
r Est 2:21; Pr 14:17
s Est 3:3,5
5:10
t Est 6:13
5:11
u Pr 13:16
v Est 9:7-10,13
5:12
w Job 22:29; Pr 16:18; 29:23
5:13
x Est 2:19
5:14
y Est 7:9 *z* Ezr 6:11; Est 6:4

6:1
a Da 2:1; 6:18
b Est 2:23; 10:2

6:3
c Ecc 9:13-16

---

a 14 Hebrew *fifty cubits* (about 23 meters)

Esther 5:9–14

Zeresh counseled Haman simply to kill Mordecai. In the pagan world of ancient Persia and often today, the satisfaction of human pride in its demand for honor and respect outweighs the value of human life. Yet history shows that those who use power to enforce their positions will eventually fall by force and power.

Mordecai kept his dignity and respect before the terror of Haman's power and pride. Rather than cowering in fear, he remained confident and at peace. The Spirit God has given us isn't of fear but of power, love, and self-control (2 Tim. 1:7). How has God delivered you from fear before the threats of others? Pray for children, women, and ethnic minorities around the world who are being intimidated by others into destructive submission. May God give them the spirit of power, love, and self-control.

Esther 6:1–14

This is one of the Bible's most "comic" scenes. While Haman plotted Mordecai's death, the king planned to honor Mordecai's faithful service. Scripture speaks of God instructing us while we sleep (Ps. 16:7). It could be that in response to people's prayers, God brought Mordecai to the king's mind. An unsuspecting Haman entered the court, where he magnificently tripped over his own ego. If there was ever a picture of pride going before a fall, Haman was it. His humiliation resulted from a series of apparent coincidences, each believable in itself but completely beyond his control.

Three pairs of feasts mark the beginning, climax, and conclusion of the story of Esther. Two banquets were given by Xerxes in chapter 1, and the Jews celebrated two consecutive feast days in chapter 9. In the middle of the story, Esther hosted two banquets for the king and Haman.

court of the palace to speak to the king about hanging Mordecai on the gallows he had erected for him.

⁵His attendants answered, "Haman is standing in the court."

"Bring him in," the king ordered.

⁶When Haman entered, the king asked him, "What should be done for the man the king delights to honor?"

Now Haman thought to himself, "Who is there that the king would rather honor than me?" ⁷So he answered the king, "For the man the king delights to honor, ⁸have them bring a royal robe^d the king has worn and a horse^e the king has ridden, one with a royal crest placed on its head. ⁹Then let the robe and horse be entrusted to one of the king's most noble princes. Let them robe the man the king delights to honor, and lead him on the horse through the city streets, proclaiming before him, 'This is what is done for the man the king delights to honor!^f '"

¹⁰"Go at once," the king commanded Haman. "Get the robe and the horse and do just as you have suggested for Mordecai the Jew, who sits at the king's gate. Do not neglect anything you have recommended."

¹¹So Haman got^g the robe and the horse. He robed Mordecai, and led him on horseback through the city streets, proclaiming before him, "This is what is done for the man the king delights to honor!"

¹²Afterward Mordecai returned to the king's gate. But Haman rushed home, with his head covered^h in grief, ¹³and told Zereshⁱ his wife and all his friends everything that had happened to him.

His advisers and his wife Zeresh said to him, "Since Mordecai, before whom your downfall^j has started, is of Jewish origin, you cannot stand against him—you will surely come to ruin!" ¹⁴While they were still talking with him, the king's eunuchs arrived and hurried Haman away to the banquet^k Esther had prepared.

Haman Hanged

7 So the king and Haman went to dine^l with Queen Esther, ²and as they were drinking wine^m on that second day, the king again asked, "Queen Esther, what is your petition? It will be given you. What is your request? Even up to half the kingdom,ⁿ it will be granted.^o"

³Then Queen Esther answered, "If I have found favor^p with you, O king, and if it pleases your majesty, grant me my life—this is my petition. And spare my people—this is my request. ⁴For I and my people have been sold for destruction and slaughter and annihilation.^q If we had merely been sold as male and female slaves, I would have kept quiet, because no such distress would justify disturbing the king.^a"

^a 4 Or *quiet, but the compensation our adversary offers cannot be compared with the loss the king would suffer*

6:8 ^d Ge 41:42; Isa 52:1 ^e 1Ki 1:33
6:9 ^f Ge 41:43
6:11 ^g Ge 41:42
6:12 ^h 2Sa 15:30; Jer 14:3,4; Mic 3:7
6:13 ⁱ Est 5:10 ^j Ps 57:6; Pr 26:27; 28:18
6:14 ^k 1Ki 3:15; Est 5:8
7:1 ^l Ge 40:20-22; Mt 22:1-14
7:2 ^m Est 1:10 ⁿ Est 5:3 ^o Est 9:12
7:3 ^p Est 2:15
7:4 ^q Est 3:9

God is so powerful that he can work without miracles through the ordinary events of billions of lives through millennia of time. He delivered an entire race of people because a woman found herself in the bedroom of a ruthless man, a man refused to bow to his superior, and a king had a sleepless night. How did you come to meet your spouse or obtain the job you now hold? Consider how "tiny" miracles of God's providence have directed your everyday steps (see Ps. 37:23; Prov. 16:9).

Esther 7:1–10

Esther had to incite the king against his friend and closest advisor without bringing down the king's wrath on herself. Protocol dictated that no one but the king could be left alone with a woman of the harem. Once the king had exited, Haman should have left Esther's presence. That he moved onto her couch was unthinkable! Once set in motion, the scene moves with

breathtaking speed toward Haman's destruction.

From chapter 5 onward, Esther is portrayed as queen of the world's mightiest empire. She came into her own only after deciding to align herself with God's covenant people. She was no longer a trophy wife. By donning her royal robes in defense of her people she took up the power of her position.

The author of Esther shows us that evil is personal. In order to deliver his people from annihilation as he had promised in his covenant, God had to destroy the evil that threatened them. Haman's death illustrates that the divinely appointed path to destruction proceeds step-by-step from the will of the wicked person. Theologian John Calvin observed, "Man falls according as God's providence ordains, but he falls by his own fault." Think of some other Biblical/historical examples that support this statement.

Judgment

7:3–4

From the 1960s to the present in the United States, one of the most biting accusations you can make is to say to someone, "You're judging me." Yet "judging" meant something quite different in Esther's time. Today the word makes us think of someone deciding cases in a court of law, but back then it brought to mind a person helping to deliver others from enemies and encouraging them to stay on a morally straight path. An Old Testament judge was a leader who helped rescue people from both external and internal enemies. After a whole book telling stories of such judges (the book of Judges), the story of Esther depicts an unofficial "judge" helping to deliver her people from their enemies.

Is there anything in this Biblical understanding of "judging" that can help us cope with our modern discomfort with moral judgment?

The core issue in both Judges and Esther isn't whether or not judging was going on, but who was functioning as God's servant in doing the judging. The Bible anticipated the current discomfort with individual judges. Though the prominent judges in the books of Judges and Esther are often held up as models of ethical integrity—Deborah, Gideon, and Samson come to mind—closer examination often fails to warrant that "judgment." These flawed men and women were deliverers of Israel only because they were doing the work of the True Judge. We truly understand these books only when we place the focus on the necessity of righteous living, not on the personal ethics of the "heroes" of the stories.

> **L**eadership abuses can be overcome (or overshadowed) by the overall strengths and commitments of the group.

Here's where the contribution of these books becomes especially helpful today. The most important issue for us is to recognize that judgment gets done by God one way or another. The implementation of that recognition for us as God's people is to figure out how that judgment is best communicated to the church, and indeed to the whole world. At different times in Biblical history leaders of various sorts have served as God's primary vehicles of communication: judges, kings, prophets, apostles, etc. The judgment has remained the same; only the messengers have varied.

What's the proper vehicle for us today? The problem is, of course, that individual human judges are fallible. Perhaps the most appropriate model for us isn't one of the Biblical judges, but Esther. Why is it that when the Bible's great leaders are listed, Esther rarely makes the cut? Not that she's ignored. Almost anyone who reads her story agrees that she was an extraordinary person. But "leader" or "judge" isn't a label we would typically affix to her name. We more often see Esther as the model of a good citizen, ready to help any and all so that the "family" could remain strong, faithful, and effective.

Perhaps this good citizen role is precisely where the functions of protecting the community from external enemies and keeping us all aware of the righteousness demanded by God should lie today. In communities of people dedicated to living out the moral vision God sets before us, the moral failure of one individual in such a context doesn't have the same disastrous consequences as the fall of a leader. Leadership abuses can be overcome (or overshadowed) by the overall strengths and commitments of the group. God's judgment—or rather, his righteousness—will reign intact as his flawed creation moves on together toward reconciliation.

5King Xerxes asked Queen Esther, "Who is he? Where is the man who has dared to do such a thing?"

6Esther said, "The adversary and enemy is this vile Haman."

Then Haman was terrified before the king and queen. 7The king got up in a rage,[r] left his wine and went out into the palace garden.[s] But Haman, realizing that the king had already decided his fate,[t] stayed behind to beg Queen Esther for his life.

8Just as the king returned from the palace garden to the banquet hall, Haman was falling on the couch[u] where Esther was reclining.[v]

The king exclaimed, "Will he even molest the queen while she is with me in the house?"[w]

As soon as the word left the king's mouth, they covered Haman's face.[x] 9Then Harbona,[y] one of the eunuchs attending the king, said, "A gallows seventy-five feet[a] high[z] stands by Haman's house. He had it made for Mordecai, who spoke up to help the king."

The king said, "Hang him on it!"[a] 10So they hanged Haman[b] on the gallows[c] he had prepared for Mordecai.[d] Then the king's fury subsided.[e]

The King's Edict in Behalf of the Jews

8 That same day King Xerxes gave Queen Esther the estate of Haman,[f] the enemy of the Jews. And Mordecai came into the presence of the king, for Esther had told how he was related to her. 2The king took off his signet ring,[g] which he had reclaimed from Haman, and presented it to Mordecai. And Esther appointed him over Haman's estate.[h]

3Esther again pleaded with the king, falling at his feet and weeping. She begged him to put an end to the evil plan of Haman the Agagite, which he had devised against the Jews. 4Then the king extended the gold scepter[i] to Esther and she arose and stood before him.

5"If it pleases the king," she said, "and if he regards me with favor and thinks it the right thing to do, and if he is pleased with me, let an order be written overruling the dispatches that Haman son of Hammedatha, the Agagite, devised and wrote to destroy the Jews in all the king's provinces. 6For how can I bear to see disaster fall on my people? How can I bear to see the destruction of my family?"[j]

7King Xerxes replied to Queen Esther and to Mordecai the Jew, "Because Haman attacked the Jews, I have given his estate to Esther, and they have hanged him on the gallows. 8Now write another decree[k] in the king's name in behalf of the Jews as seems best to you, and seal it with the king's signet ring[l]—for no document written in the king's name and sealed with his ring can be revoked."[m]

9At once the royal secretaries were summoned—on the twenty-third day of the third month, the month of Sivan. They wrote out all Mordecai's orders to the Jews, and to the satraps, governors and nobles of the 127 provinces stretching from India to Cush.[b][n] These orders were written in the script of each province and the language of each people and also to the Jews in their own script and language.[o] 10Mor-

---

a 9 Hebrew fifty cubits (about 23 meters)   b 9 That is, the upper Nile region

---

7:7 r Ge 34:7; Est 1:12; Pr 19:12; 20:1-2 s 2Ki 21:18 t Est 6:13

7:8 u Est 1:6 v Ge 39:14 w Ge 34:7 x Est 6:12

7:9 y Est 1:10 z Est 5:14 a Ps 7:14-16; 9:16; Pr 11:5-6; 26:27; Mt 7:2

7:10 b Pr 10:28 c Est 9:25 d Da 6:24 e Est 2:1

8:1 f Est 2:7; 7:6; Pr 22:22-23

8:2 g Ge 41:42; Est 3:10 h Pr 13:22; Da 2:48

8:4 i Est 4:11; 5:2

8:6 j Est 7:4; 9:1

8:8 k Est 3:12-14 l Ge 41:42 m Est 1:19; Da 6:15

8:9 n Est 1:1 o Est 1:22

Esther 8:1–17

Esther pleaded with Xerxes to override Haman's decree, but Persian laws were irrevocable (cf. v. 8; 1:19; Dan. 6:8,12). Now, though, Esther and Mordecai had power and authority equal to what had been Haman's. The only solution to their dilemma was to write another decree to counteract the first with equal force.

Why is retributive violence found throughout the Old Testament, while Jesus teaches us to love our enemies as ourselves (Matt. 5:44; Luke 6:27,35)? Jesus' death provides the only basis for the termination of holy war and hostility. Holy war ceased because Jesus fought its last episode on the cross. And the Holy Spirit within

us provides the only power by which we may love our enemies. It's no accident that modern nations that endorse the notion of holy war also reject the gospel of Christ.

We often want God to destroy sin but leave people alone. But sin and evil don't exist apart from beings who do evil, whether angelic or human. Sin entered the world because Adam and Eve aligned themselves against God (Gen. 3). Because we are all sinners, the resulting death decree applies to us as well. But God chose to issue a counter-decree to redeem us as his people (cf. 2 Cor. 5:17–21). How have you responded? Why not take the time right now to thank him once again?

decai wrote in the name of King Xerxes, sealed the dispatches with the king's signet ring, and sent them by mounted couriers, who rode fast horses especially bred for the king.

8:11
p Est 9:10,15,16

[11]The king's edict granted the Jews in every city the right to assemble and protect themselves; to destroy, kill and annihilate any armed force of any nationality or province that might attack them and their women and children; and to plunder[p] the property of their enemies. [12]The day appointed for the Jews to do this in all the provinces of King Xerxes was the thirteenth day of the twelfth month, the month of Adar.[q] [13]A copy of the text of the edict was to be issued as law in every province and made known to the people of every nationality so that the Jews would be ready on that day[r] to avenge themselves on their enemies.

8:12
q Est 3:13; 9:1
8:13
r Est 3:14

[14]The couriers, riding the royal horses, raced out, spurred on by the king's command. And the edict was also issued in the citadel of Susa.

8:15
s Est 9:4 t Ge 41:42
u Est 3:15

[15]Mordecai[s] left the king's presence wearing royal garments of blue and white, a large crown of gold and a purple robe of fine linen.[t] And the city of Susa held a joyous celebration.[u] [16]For the Jews it was a time of happiness and joy,[v] gladness and honor.[w] [17]In every province and in every city, wherever the edict of the king went, there was joy[x] and gladness among the Jews, with feasting and celebrating. And many people of other nationalities became Jews because fear[y] of the Jews had seized them.[z]

8:16
v Ps 97:10-12
w Ps 112:4
8:17
x Est 9:19,27;
Ps 35:27; Pr 11:10
y Ex 15:14,16;
Dt 11:25 z Est 9:3

Triumph of the Jews

9:1
a Est 8:12
b Jer 29:4-7
c Est 3:12-14;
Pr 22:22-23
9:2
d ver 15-18
e Est 8:11,17;
Ps 71:13,24

9 On the thirteenth day of the twelfth month, the month of Adar,[a] the edict commanded by the king was to be carried out. On this day the enemies of the Jews had hoped to overpower them, but now the tables were turned and the Jews got the upper hand[b] over those who hated them.[c] [2]The Jews assembled in their cities[d] in all the provinces of King Xerxes to attack those seeking their destruction. No one could stand against them,[e] because the people of all the other nationalities were afraid of them. [3]And all the nobles of the provinces, the satraps, the governors and the king's administrators helped the Jews,[f] because fear of Mordecai had seized them. [4]Mordecai was prominent[g] in the palace; his reputation spread throughout the provinces, and he became more and more powerful.[h]

9:3
f Ezr 8:36
9:4
g Ex 11:3 h 2Sa 3:1;
1Ch 11:9

[5]The Jews struck down all their enemies with the sword, killing and destroying them,[i] and they did what they pleased to those who hated them. [6]In the citadel of Susa, the Jews killed and destroyed five hundred men. [7]They also killed Parshandatha, Dalphon, Aspatha, [8]Poratha, Adalia, Aridatha, [9]Parmashta, Arisai, Aridai and Vaizatha, [10]the ten sons[j] of Haman son of Hammedatha, the enemy of the Jews. But they did not lay their hands on the plunder.[k]

9:5
i Ezr 4:6

9:10
j Est 5:11
k Ge 14:23;
1Sa 14:32; Est 3:13;
8:11

[11]The number of those slain in the citadel of Susa was reported to the king that same day. [12]The king said to Queen Esther, "The Jews have killed and destroyed five hundred men and the ten sons of Haman in the citadel of Susa. What have they done in the rest of the king's provinces? Now what is your petition? It will be given you. What is your request? It will also be granted."[l]

9:12
l Est 5:6; 7:2

[13]"If it pleases the king," Esther answered, "give the Jews in Susa permission to carry out this day's edict tomorrow also, and let Haman's ten sons[m] be hanged[n] on gallows."

9:13
m Est 5:11
n Dt 21:22-23

[14]So the king commanded that this be done. An edict was issued in Susa, and they

---

Esther 9:1–17

The author repeated three times that the Jews "did not lay their hands on the plunder," even though Mordecai's decree would have allowed it (8:11). Mordecai included this permission because he was reversing the exact terms of Haman's decree (3:13). But a rule of ancient holy war was that plunder wasn't to be taken. Abram (Gen. 14) wouldn't accept any material reward from the king of Sodom, not wanting that wicked city to be the source of his prosperity.

This set the precedent for God's people.

Events in this book invite us to ponder the nature of faith in a world in which God is unseen. The definition of faith (see Heb. 11:1) calls us to be certain of the reality lying behind or beyond what we experience through our five senses. Awareness of God's power and presence should encourage us to pray with anticipation. The answers are already on their way, set in motion through a chain of events that might appear insignificant even if we were to become aware of them.

hanged[o] the ten sons of Haman. [15]The Jews in Susa came together on the four-teenth day of the month of Adar, and they put to death in Susa three hundred men, but they did not lay their hands on the plunder.[p]

[16]Meanwhile, the remainder of the Jews who were in the king's provinces also as-sembled to protect themselves and get relief[q] from their enemies.[r] They killed sev-enty-five thousand of them[s] but did not lay their hands on the plunder. [17]This hap-pened on the thirteenth day of the month of Adar, and on the fourteenth they rested and made it a day of feasting[t] and joy.

Purim Celebrated

[18]The Jews in Susa, however, had assembled on the thirteenth and fourteenth, and then on the fifteenth they rested and made it a day of feasting and joy.

[19]That is why rural Jews—those living in villages—observe the fourteenth of the month of Adar[u] as a day of joy and feasting, a day for giving presents to each other.[v]

[20]Mordecai recorded these events, and he sent letters to all the Jews throughout the provinces of King Xerxes, near and far, [21]to have them celebrate annually the fourteenth and fifteenth days of the month of Adar [22]as the time when the Jews got relief[w] from their enemies, and as the month when their sorrow was turned into joy and their mourning into a day of celebration.[x] He wrote them to observe the days as days of feasting and joy and giving presents of food[y] to one another and gifts to the poor.

[23]So the Jews agreed to continue the celebration they had begun, doing what Mordecai had written to them. [24]For Haman son of Hammedatha, the Agagite,[z] the enemy of all the Jews, had plotted against the Jews to destroy them and had cast the pur[a] (that is, the lot[b]) for their ruin and destruction. [25]But when the plot came to the king's attention,[a] he issued written orders that the evil scheme Haman had de-vised against the Jews should come back onto his own head,[c] and that he and his sons should be hanged[d] on the gallows.[e] [26](Therefore these days were called Pu-rim, from the word pur.[f]) Because of everything written in this letter and because of what they had seen and what had happened to them, [27]the Jews took it upon themselves to establish the custom that they and their descendants and all who join them should without fail observe these two days every year, in the way prescribed and at the time appointed. [28]These days should be remembered and observed in every generation by every family, and in every province and in every city. And these days of Purim should never cease to be celebrated by the Jews, nor should the mem-ory of them die out among their descendants.

[29]So Queen Esther, daughter of Abihail,[g] along with Mordecai the Jew, wrote with full authority to confirm this second letter concerning Purim. [30]And Mordecai sent letters to all the Jews in the 127 provinces[h] of the kingdom of Xerxes—words of goodwill and assurance— [31]to establish these days of Purim at their designated times, as Mordecai the Jew and Queen Esther had decreed for them, and as they had established for themselves and their descendants in regard to their times of fasting[i] and lamentation.[j] [32]Esther's decree confirmed these regulations about Purim, and it was written down in the records.

[a] 25 Or *when Esther came before the king*

Reference column

9:14
[o] Ezr 6:11

9:15
[p] Ge 14:23;
Est 8:11

9:16
[q] Est 4:14
[r] Dt 25:19
[s] 1Ch 4:43

9:17
[t] 1Ki 3:15

9:19
[u] Est 3:7 [v] ver 22;
Dt 16:11, 14;
Ne 8:10,12; Est 2:9;
Rev 11:10

9:22
[w] Est 4:14
[x] Ne 8:12;
Ps 30:11-12
[y] 2Ki 25:30

9:24
[z] Ex 17:8-16
[a] Est 3:7 [b] Lev 16:8

9:25
[c] Ps 7:16
[d] Dt 21:22-23
[e] Est 7:10
9:26
[f] ver 20; Est 3:7

9:29
[g] Est 2:15

9:30
[h] Est 1:1

9:31
[i] Est 4:16 [j] Est 4:1-3

Esther 9:18–32

Purim joined the existing five Jewish feasts that were commanded by Moses in the Torah. Rather than being prescribed by God's command, this celebration began as a spontaneous response to his covenant faith-fulness. Purim is still celebrated today. The entire book of Esther is read in the synagogue on the holiday, during which noisemakers are used. People cheer at the sound of Mordecai's name and boo and hiss at the mention of Haman.

Today we read Esther in the dark shadow of the Holocaust, deeply grieved that one-third of the world's Jews were murdered during the 20th century. We needn't be Jewish to feel terror when such immense evil grasps the reins of a government. We as Christians feel the same horror at the threat of genocide against races in other parts of the world today. After all Jesus, the Jewish Messiah, is now Jesus, the Christ of all na-tions. Do you regularly include such tragic world events and their victims in your intercessory prayers?

10:1
k Ps 72:10; 97:1;
Isa 24:15
10:2
l Est 8:15; 9:4
m Ge 41:44
n Est 2:23
10:3
o Da 5:7
p Ge 41:43
q Ge 41:40
r Ne 2:10;
Jer 29:4-7; Da 6:3

The Greatness of Mordecai

10 King Xerxes imposed tribute throughout the empire, to its distant shores. *k* ²And all his acts of power and might, together with a full account of the greatness of Mordecai *l* to which the king had raised him, *m* are they not written in the book of the annals *n* of the kings of Media and Persia? ³Mordecai the Jew was second *o* in rank *p* to King Xerxes, *q* preeminent among the Jews, and held in high esteem by his many fellow Jews, because he worked for the good of his people and spoke up for the welfare of all the Jews. *r*

Esther 10:1–3

Both Esther and Mordecai were indispensable to God's work. Esther wasn't a religious leader (and because of her gender couldn't have been). But neither was Mordecai. It was only as they acted in concert that they were able to lead God's people through near-death into deliverance. Neither aspired to the role, nor perhaps deserved it. Nevertheless, their unlikely partnership accomplished God's ancient promise. The Jewish race was preserved until, in the fullness of time, God entered history through this people as the Messiah.

Since the time of Christ, believing men and women have a responsibility beyond the confines of the home. At least in Western society, both receive the same education, fill similar positions in the workplace, and worship side by side in the church. Scripture affirms that both bear the image of God (Gen. 1:27) and share equal standing in Christ (Gal. 3:28). The relationship of men and women in community outside the family can work for the glory of God and the fulfillment of his redemptive purposes.

INTRODUCTION TO

Job

AUTHOR

The author of Job is unknown, but this individual was obviously a well-educated, profound thinker familiar with foreign cultures.

DATE WRITTEN

Although the events of Job most likely took place during the second millennium B.C., the story was probably put into written form much later, perhaps sometime between the reign of Solomon (970 B.C.) and the exile (586 B.C.).

ORIGINAL READERS

Job was written to address the question of suffering, a subject that is pondered as much today as it was 3,000 years ago.

TIMELINE

	2200BC	2100	2000	1900	1800	1700	1600	1500	1400
Creation, Fall, Flood									
Abraham's life (c. 2166-1991 B.C.)									
Isaac's life (c. 2066-1886 B.C.)									
Jacob's life (c. 2006-1859 B.C.)									
Job written (c. 2000-1000 B.C.)									
Joseph's life (c. 1915-1805 B.C.)									
Historical setting of Job (c. 1900-1700 B.C.)									
Moses' life (c. 1526-1406 B.C.)									

THEMES

Job describes the suffering of a "blameless and upright" man (1:1). It contains the following themes:

1. *God's sovereignty.* God is in control of everything (37:14–24; 42:2), even Satan (1:12; 2:6). His ways are beyond human comprehension (28:1–28), and our ability to understand wisdom is limited to fearing God and obeying his commands (28:28). We might never understand our suffering while on Earth, and God might never explain himself. Yet he does offer us himself—his presence, comfort, and love.

2. *God's goodness and justice.* How can God be good and just if he allows the innocent to suffer while the godless enjoy prosperity (12:6)? Job affirms God's goodness (1:1—2:13; 42:7–17) while conceding that sometimes bad things happen to good people and good things to bad people. The book of Job reminds us that not all suffering is the direct result of specific sins, a reality Jesus confirmed (cf. John 9:1–3).

3. *Satan.* Satan is the adversary of God and, thus, of God's people. As the accuser (Zech. 3:1; Rev. 12:9–10), his goal is to alienate people from God and generate unbelief (Gen. 3; Matt. 4:1; 2 Cor. 4:4). While we are usually unaware of what goes on in the spiritual realm, it affects us nonetheless.

4. *A proper response to suffering.* As we struggle with our own suffering and that of others, it's important for us to balance our honest questions with humility and reverence for God (28:28; 42:1–6; Deut. 4:5–6; Prov. 8:4–9; 9:10; Eccl. 12:13). The temptations to justify ourselves at God's expense or blame him are to be resisted. We may not know why we suffer, but we may be assured that God is in charge and trust in his love for us. God expects us to be faithful and trust him despite our suffering.

FAITH IN ACTION
The pages of Job contain life lessons and role models of faith—people who challenge believers to put their faith in action.

Role Models

- JOB (24:1–25; 29:12–17) correctly observed how the world and the wicked oppress people, yet he himself had rescued the poor, assisted the fatherless, helped the disabled, and advocated for the disenfranchised. How can you actively serve those in need?

- ELIHU (32:2) defended God's righteousness and justice and respectfully rebuked Job for being more concerned with justifying himself than with justifying God. It took courage to confront Job, an older, highly respected man. Is there a situation that requires special boldness on your part? What will be your approach and tone?

- GOD (38:1—40:34) answered Job by asking him to understand God's character and power. That the Lord engaged Job demonstrates his desire to be known by his people. Do you seek to help others encounter God?

- JOB (42:6) was quick to repent in response to God's questioning. Do you examine yourself for erroneous thinking or misconceptions about God's character? Do you repent readily and learn from your mistakes?

Challenges

- Look beyond the surface, realizing that spiritual warfare may be involved in someone's suffering (1:6–12; 2:1–7).

- Resist the influence of others who may try to make you doubt God's goodness in times of trouble or pain (2:9–10).

- Guard against being this kind of a hindrance to someone else who is hurting. Your silent presence (not your inadequate condolences or clichés) can be comforting (2:11–13). Compassion (16:1–5), not misguided advice (15:17–18; 21:34), demonstrates godly wisdom at such times.

- Withhold your judgment of those undergoing suffering (4:7–8; 8:1–22; 11:1–20; 22:4–5); only God knows its root cause (28:20–28).

- Be patient with hurting individuals who express anger at God (6:1—7:21) or with those who despair at God's seeming lack of love for them (16:7—17:16). God is able to handle people's honesty and frustration, and your judgments aren't helpful.

- Understand the general nature of suffering in the world. Much of it results from people taking advantage of the weak or unprotected (24:2–4,9,13–14,21).

- You can't help everyone, but do what you can to ease others' pain and not contribute to it (29:12–17).

- Take comfort in knowing that the all-powerful Creator of the universe (26:7–14; 38:1—41:34) loves you and is in full control of all that happens (42:1–6).

OUTLINE

   I. Prologue: Job's Happiness; Job's Testing (1–2)
  II. Dialogue-Dispute: Job and His Friends (3–27)
      A. Job's Opening Lament (3)
      B. Round 1: Eliphaz, Bildad, Zophar Speak; Job Answers (4–14)
      C. Round 2: Three Friends Speak; Job Answers (15–21)
      D. Round 3: Two Friends Speak; Job Answers (22–26)
      E. Job's Closing Speech (27)
 III. Interlude on Wisdom (28)
 IV. Monologues (29:1—42:6)
      A. Job (29–31)
      B. Elihu (32–37)
      C. God (38:1—42:6)
  V. Epilogue: God Judges Three Friends; Job Restored (42:7–17)

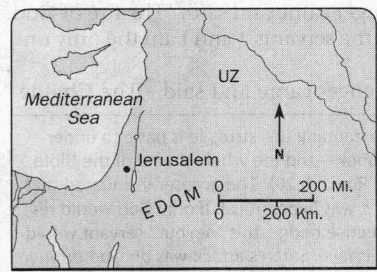

Location of Uz (1:1)
Then: Uz was a region east of Canaan.
Now: The site of Biblical Uz is in the modern nation of Syria.

Prologue

1 In the land of Uz[a] there lived a man whose name was Job.[b] This man was blameless[c] and upright; he feared God[d] and shunned evil. [2]He had seven sons and three daughters,[e] [3]and he owned seven thousand sheep, three thousand camels, five hundred yoke of oxen and five hundred donkeys, and had a large number of servants. He was the greatest man[f] among all the people of the East.

[4]His sons used to take turns holding feasts in their homes, and they would invite their three sisters to eat and drink with them. [5]When a period of feasting had run its course, Job would send and have them purified. Early in the morning he would sacrifice a burnt offering[g] for each of them, thinking, "Perhaps my children have sinned[h] and cursed God[i] in their hearts." This was Job's regular custom.

Job's First Test

[6]One day the angels[aj] came to present themselves before the LORD, and Satan[b] also came with them.[k] [7]The LORD said to Satan, "Where have you come from?"

1:1
a Jer 25:20
b Eze 14:14,20;
Jas 5:11 *c* Ge 6:9;
17:1 *d* Ge 22:12;
Ex 18:21

1:2
e Job 42:13

1:3
f Job 29:25

1:5
g Ge 8:20; Job 42:8
h Job 8:4
i 1Ki 21:10,13

1:6
j Job 38:7 *k* Job 2:1

---

a 6 Hebrew *the sons of God*   *b* 6 *Satan* means *accuser.*

Job 1:1–5

Job lived in Uz, a land somewhere east of Canaan on the edge of the desert (vv. 1,19). He's presented as a man who worshiped ("feared") God and shunned evil—and whose life was crowned with prosperity. Fearing the Lord and shunning evil were considered the controlling principles of wisdom (28:28) in the Old Testament wisdom literature, of which Job is a part. And wisdom is the essence of true religion in this Old Testament literary genre.

Verse 5 reveals that Job, like the patriarchs Abraham, Isaac, and Jacob, functioned as a priest for his family. He took his sacrificial obligation seriously, making atonement even for sins of the heart. The matter of cursing or not cursing God is key in the development of this ancient drama.

The fact that Job was "blameless" and "upright" (v. 1) didn't mean he was sinless (cf. 13:26; 14:16–17). "Blameless" referred to a person's spiritual maturity and the integrity (purity) of his or her inner being. "Upright," literally meaning "straight" or "level," dealt with human behavior in line with God's ways. When Jesus instructed the crowd in his Sermon on the Mount, "Be perfect . . . as your heavenly Father is perfect" (Matt. 5:48), he was getting at the same point. Certainly, you are a sinner (Isa. 53:6). But is the direction or trajectory of your life generally moving in a line toward God and his ways? How can you tell?

1:7
l 1Pe 5:8
1:8
m Jos 1:7;
Job 42:7-8
n ver 1

1:9
o 1Ti 6:5
1:10
p Ps 34:7 q ver 3;
Job 29:6; 31:25;
Ps 128:1-2
1:11
r Job 19:21
s Job 2:5

Satan answered the LORD, "From roaming through the earth and going back and forth in it."[l]

[8]Then the LORD said to Satan, "Have you considered my servant Job?[m] There is no one on earth like him; he is blameless and upright, a man who fears God and shuns evil."[n]

[9]"Does Job fear God for nothing?"[o] Satan replied. [10]"Have you not put a hedge around him and his household and everything he has?[p] You have blessed the work of his hands, so that his flocks and herds are spread throughout the land.[q] [11]But stretch out your hand and strike everything he has,[r] and he will surely curse you to your face."[s]

[12]The LORD said to Satan, "Very well, then, everything he has is in your hands, but on the man himself do not lay a finger."

Then Satan went out from the presence of the LORD.

[13]One day when Job's sons and daughters were feasting and drinking wine at the oldest brother's house, [14]a messenger came to Job and said, "The oxen were plowing and the donkeys were grazing nearby, [15]and the Sabeans[t] attacked and carried them off. They put the servants to the sword, and I am the only one who has escaped to tell you!"

1:15
t Ge 10:7; Job 6:19

[16]While he was still speaking, another messenger came and said, "The fire of God fell from the sky[u] and burned up the sheep and the servants,[v] and I am the only one who has escaped to tell you!"

1:16
u Ge 19:24
v Lev 10:2;
Nu 11:1-3

[17]While he was still speaking, another messenger came and said, "The Chalde-

---

Job 1:6–22

God's statement that Job was his servant (v. 8) implied more than mere servitude; it meant that God and Job were in a covenant relationship based on mutual allegiance. The Lord, not Satan (lit., "the accuser"; see NIV text note on v. 6), initiated the conversation that led to Job's testing. God saw fit to use a secondary means to accomplish his purpose. That purpose wasn't to test Job as an end in itself but to give him the opportunity to honor his Lord, to whom he had pledged his loyalty. That allegiance would become a significant part of the cosmic struggle between Job's (and our) adversary and the Lord. Would Job curse (reject) God or not?

Understanding this struggle is basic to understanding this book—and the whole drama of the Bible (cf. Gen. 3:15; Rom. 16:20). The accuser insinuated that Job's allegiance was hypocritical: If only God would remove his protective hedge, this "devout" servant would curse him to his face. Satan's attack was *on God through* Job. God gradually allowed the devil increasing access to Job—his possessions, his family, his physical well-being. Would Job come through as "Exhibit A" for the defense or for the prosecution? What about you? Satan still loves the strategy of focusing his assaults on a believer.

What's your first response to trouble or suffering? Job's initial response (v. 21) was one of supreme faith

1:5

United States Children at Risk

Children are often blamed for failures over which they have no control or influence. In truth, it's more often the children who are abused:

Children Abused

One million U.S. children—
15 of every 1000—
were abused in 1997.

Of those abused:

54% Neglect   22% Physical abuse   16% Emotional abuse   8% Sexual abuse

Children at Risk

Factors that increase the likelihood that a child will be abused or oppressed:

- Low family income
- Low family savings
- Low amount of parental time and attention
- Limited access to health care
- Ethnicity
- Locale

HIGH RISK U.S. CHILDREN

13%

Children living in homes with four or more of these factors (13 percent of all U.S. children) are considered high risk.

Source: Wurman (2000:64)

ans^w formed three raiding parties and swept down on your camels and carried them off. They put the servants to the sword, and I am the only one who has escaped to tell you!"

¹⁸While he was still speaking, yet another messenger came and said, "Your sons and daughters were feasting and drinking wine at the oldest brother's house, ¹⁹when suddenly a mighty wind^x swept in from the desert and struck the four corners of the house. It collapsed on them and they are dead, and I am the only one who has escaped to tell you!"

²⁰At this, Job got up and tore his robe^y and shaved his head. Then he fell to the ground in worship^z ²¹and said:

> "Naked I came from my mother's womb,
>   and naked I will depart.^{a a}
> The LORD gave and the LORD has taken away;^b
>   may the name of the LORD be praised."^c

²²In all this, Job did not sin by charging God with wrongdoing.^d

Job's Second Test

2 On another day the angels^b came to present themselves before the LORD, and Satan also came with them^e to present himself before him. ²And the LORD said to Satan, "Where have you come from?"

Satan answered the LORD, "From roaming through the earth and going back and forth in it."

³Then the LORD said to Satan, "Have you considered my servant Job? There is no one on earth like him; he is blameless and upright, a man who fears God and shuns evil.^f And he still maintains his integrity,^g though you incited me against him to ruin him without any reason."^h

⁴"Skin for skin!" Satan replied. "A man will give all he has for his own life. ⁵But stretch out your hand and strike his flesh and bones,ⁱ and he will surely curse you to your face."^j

⁶The LORD said to Satan, "Very well, then, he is in your hands; but you must spare his life."^k

⁷So Satan went out from the presence of the LORD and afflicted Job with painful sores from the soles of his feet to the top of his head.^l ⁸Then Job took a piece of broken pottery and scraped himself with it as he sat among the ashes.^m

⁹His wife said to him, "Are you still holding on to your integrity? Curse God and die!"

^a 21 Or *will return there*   ^b 1 Hebrew *the sons of God*

1:17
w Ge 11:28,31

1:19
x Jer 4:11; 13:24

1:20
y Ge 37:29
z 1Pe 5:6

1:21
a Ecc 5:15; 1Ti 6:7
b 1Sa 2:7
c Job 2:10;
Eph 5:20; 1Th 5:18

1:22
d Job 2:10

2:1
e Job 1:6

2:3
f Job 1:1,8
g Job 27:6
h Job 9:17

2:5
i Job 19:20
j Job 1:11

2:6
k Job 1:12

2:7
l Dt 28:35; Job 7:5
2:8
m Job 42:6;
Jer 6:26; Eze 27:30;
Mt 11:21

---

and total submission to God's sovereign will. He didn't understand why but believed that his trouble had come from God. God's use of a secondary means didn't, and still doesn't, solve the problem of evil—nor was it the purpose of this book to do so. In a very real sense, Job's statement of trust in God went as far as he or any other human can go in solving this mystery. One day our understanding will be complete—but only on the opposite side of Christ's return.

Job 2:1–10

The Lord's words to Satan, "You incited me against [Job] to ruin him without any reason" (v. 3), use human language to try to explain supernatural realities. They don't imply that God can be stirred up to act against his will. On the contrary, the Lord himself had suggested and was again suggesting Job *to* the accuser (1:8; 2:3a) as an example of godliness. All Job's suffering was part of the divine purpose, as God would say in 38:2: "Who is this that darkens my counsel with words

without knowledge?" But when God uses a secondary cause to affect a human life, even Satan can be said to stir him up.

Not knowing the limitation God had put on Satan, Job's wife diagnosed his disease as incurable and recommended that he curse God and die. Chrysostom (347?–407), an early church father, suggested that Satan didn't destroy Job's wife along with the rest of the family because he wanted to use her as his tool. Job's mental anguish was certainly intensified by her advice.

Job's reply to his wife is remarkable in its compassion and in its total acceptance of God's will for his life (v. 10). He might have accused her of blasphemy but chose instead to accept her statement as evidence of desperation. Job conceded only that his wife was *talking* like a blasphemer. He was willing to receive with meekness whatever prosperity or disaster God might send. Think about the worst crisis you have endured. How did your attitude and response compare with Job's or his wife's?

2:10
n Job 1:21
o Job 1:22; Ps 39:1;
Jas 1:12; 5:11

[10]He replied, "You are talking like a foolish[a] woman. Shall we accept good from God, and not trouble?"[n]

In all this, Job did not sin in what he said.[o]

Job's Three Friends

2:11
p Ge 36:11;
Jer 49:7 q Ge 25:2
r Job 42:11;
Ro 12:15

[11]When Job's three friends, Eliphaz the Temanite,[p] Bildad the Shuhite[q] and Zophar the Naamathite, heard about all the troubles that had come upon him, they set out from their homes and met together by agreement to go and sympathize with him and comfort him.[r] [12]When they saw him from a distance, they could hardly recognize him; they began to weep aloud, and they tore their robes and sprinkled dust on their heads.[s] [13]Then they sat on the ground with him for seven days and seven nights.[t] No one said a word to him, because they saw how great his suffering was.

2:12
s Jos 7:6; Ne 9:1;
La 2:10; Eze 27:30
2:13
t Ge 50:10;
Eze 3:15

Job Speaks

3 After this, Job opened his mouth and cursed the day of his birth. [2]He said:

3:3
u Job 10:18-19;
Jer 20:14-18

[3]"May the day of my birth perish,
　　and the night it was said, 'A boy is born!'[u]
[4]That day—may it turn to darkness;
　　may God above not care about it;
　　may no light shine upon it.

3:5
v Job 10:21,22;
Ps 23:4; Jer 2:6;
13:16

[5]May darkness and deep shadow[b][v] claim it once more;
　　may a cloud settle over it;
　　may blackness overwhelm its light.

3:6
w Job 23:17

[6]That night—may thick darkness[w] seize it;
　　may it not be included among the days of the year
　　nor be entered in any of the months.
[7]May that night be barren;
　　may no shout of joy be heard in it.

3:8
x Job 41:1,8,10,25

[8]May those who curse days[c] curse that day,
　　those who are ready to rouse Leviathan.[x]
[9]May its morning stars become dark;
　　may it wait for daylight in vain

3:9
y Job 41:18

　　and not see the first rays of dawn,[y]
[10]for it did not shut the doors of the womb on me
　　to hide trouble from my eyes.

---

[a] 10 The Hebrew word rendered *foolish* denotes moral deficiency.　[b] 5 Or *and the shadow of death*
[c] 8 Or *the sea*

Job 2:11–13

In light of Job's words in 7:3, months evidently passed before news of his troubles had passed by word of mouth and the three friends of Job arrived. Stunned by Job's appearance, they went into a drastic form of mourning, usually reserved for death or total disaster. They tore their robes of nobility, wailed, and threw dust into the air—then sat in silence before Job for seven days and nights (cf. Gen. 50:10; Josh. 7:6; 2 Sam. 13:19; Ezek. 3:15). To speak prior to the sufferer would have been considered bad taste. And as it turned out, their silence was a wiser response than their subsequent speeches (cf. 16:1–5).

How comfortable are you when facing a friend, acquaintance, or relative suffering excruciating pain or loss? Do you prefer condolences to awkward silence? Still today, people in deep need often want the comfort of our presence, not necessarily our inadequate words

or attempts at answers. The implications of words spoken too soon may in fact be guilt inducing—clichés like "This too shall pass," "Count your blessings," "Maybe what you wanted wasn't his will," or "Try to put the situation behind you and move on with life." Don't shy away from a respectful silence, unless the sufferer prompts you to speak.

Job 3:1–26

Job's tone changed dramatically here. The man of patience and faith sank into a state of despondency and spiritual depression, so frequently a problem for those enduring severe physical illness or impairment. In chapter 3 Job established an attitude that would largely color all he would say from then on. Nowhere would he come closer to cursing God to his face (see 2:5) than here in chapter 3. By cursing the day of his birth, Job questioned the Creator's sovereign wisdom. The accuser, who we won't see again, seems to have triumphed.

11 "Why did I not perish at birth,
    and die as I came from the womb?ᶻ
12 Why were there knees to receive meᵃ
    and breasts that I might be nursed?
13 For now I would be lying downᵇ in peace;
    I would be asleep and at restᶜ
14 with kings and counselors of the earth,ᵈ
    who built for themselves places now lying in ruins,ᵉ
15 with rulersᶠ who had gold,
    who filled their houses with silver.ᵍ
16 Or why was I not hidden in the ground like a stillborn child,ʰ
    like an infant who never saw the light of day?
17 There the wicked cease from turmoil,
    and there the weary are at rest.ⁱ
18 Captives also enjoy their ease;
    they no longer hear the slave driver's shout.ʲ
19 The small and the great are there,
    and the slave is freed from his master.

20 "Why is light given to those in misery,
    and life to the bitter of soul,ᵏ
21 to those who long for death that does not come,ˡ
    who search for it more than for hidden treasure,ᵐ
22 who are filled with gladness
    and rejoice when they reach the grave?
23 Why is life given to a man
    whose way is hidden,
    whom God has hedged in?ⁿ
24 For sighing comes to me instead of food;ᵒ
    my groans pour out like water.ᵖ
25 What I feared has come upon me;
    what I dreadedᵠ has happened to me.
26 I have no peace, no quietness;
    I have no rest,ʳ but only turmoil."

3:11
z Job 10:18
3:12
a Ge 30:3; Isa 66:12
3:13
b Job 17:13
c Job 7:8-10,21;
10:22; 14:10-12;
19:27; 21:13,23
3:14
d Job 12:17
e Job 15:28
3:15
f Job 12:21
g Job 27:17
3:16
h Ps 58:8; Ecc 6:3
3:17
i Job 17:16
3:18
j Job 39:7
3:20
k 1Sa 1:10;
Jer 20:18;
Eze 27:30-31
3:21
l Rev 9:6 m Pr 2:4
3:23
n Job 19:6,8,12;
Ps 88:8; La 3:7
3:24
o Job 6:7; 33:20
p Ps 42:3,4
3:25
q Job 30:15
3:26
r Job 7:4,14

History is full of examples of people of great faith falling into depression and desolation. The fact that someone as godly as Job should have experienced such a struggle of faith can be a source of support to those similarly afflicted. God prefers that we speak with him honestly, even in our moments of deepest gloom, rather than mouth clichés far removed from reality. How honest have you dared to be with God? If you haven't dared verbalize your true feelings, try it next time you are in a difficult situation. You might be surprised at his response.

3:1–16

Godly Emotions?

God gave humans emotions. Channeled properly toward godly ends, they become constructions in his kingdom enterprise. There are many categorical schemes of human emotions. One model recognizes discrete emotions, arranged on the right as continuations from the weaker to the stronger form:

Weaker	Stronger
Interest	EXCITEMENT
Anger	RAGE
Contempt	SCORN
Fear	TERROR
Distress	ANGUISH
Like	LOVE
Surprise	STARTLE
Enjoyment	JOY
Shyness	HUMILIATION
Disgust	REVULSION
Guilt	REMORSE
Sadness	SORROW

How, if at all, does each of these varied emotions, in its stronger or weaker form, come into play in your Christian life? Do you recognize those typically labeled "negative" as gifts from God, or do you try to suppress them at all costs, ultimately to your own detriment or that of others? Think of some Biblical examples of God's people honestly displaying one or another of these less-desirable emotions, perhaps in some way that turned out positively.

Source: Izard (1991:112–114)

Eliphaz

4

Then Eliphaz the Temanite replied:

2 "If someone ventures a word with you, will you be impatient?
 But who can keep from speaking? [s]
3 Think how you have instructed many,
 how you have strengthened feeble hands. [t]
4 Your words have supported those who stumbled;
 you have strengthened faltering knees. [u]
5 But now trouble comes to you, and you are discouraged;
 it strikes [v] you, and you are dismayed. [w]
6 Should not your piety be your confidence [x]
 and your blameless [y] ways your hope?

7 "Consider now: Who, being innocent, has ever perished? [z]
 Where were the upright ever destroyed? [a]
8 As I have observed, those who plow evil [b]
 and those who sow trouble reap it. [c]
9 At the breath of God [d] they are destroyed;
 at the blast of his anger they perish. [e]
10 The lions may roar and growl,
 yet the teeth of the great lions are broken. [f]
11 The lion perishes for lack of prey, [g]
 and the cubs of the lioness are scattered.

12 "A word was secretly brought to me,
 my ears caught a whisper [h] of it. [i]
13 Amid disquieting dreams in the night,
 when deep sleep falls on men, [j]
14 fear and trembling seized me
 and made all my bones shake. [k]
15 A spirit glided past my face,
 and the hair on my body stood on end.
16 It stopped,
 but I could not tell what it was.

 A form stood before my eyes,
 and I heard a hushed voice:
17 'Can a mortal be more righteous than God? [l]
 Can a man be more pure than his Maker? [m]
18 If God places no trust in his servants,
 if he charges his angels with error, [n]
19 how much more those who live in houses of clay, [o]
 whose foundations [p] are in the dust, [q]
 who are crushed more readily than a moth!
20 Between dawn and dusk they are broken to pieces;
 unnoticed, they perish forever. [r]
21 Are not the cords of their tent pulled up, [s]
 so that they die without wisdom?' [a] [t]

---

[a] 21 Some interpreters end the quotation after verse 17.

4:2
s Job 32:20
4:3
t Isa 35:3;
Heb 12:12
4:4
u Isa 35:3;
Heb 12:12
4:5
v Job 19:21
w Job 6:14
4:6
x Pr 3:26 y Job 1:1
4:7
z Job 36:7
a Job 8:20;
Ps 37:25
4:8
b Job 15:35
c Pr 22:8;
Hos 10:13;
Gal 6:7-8
4:9
d Job 15:30;
Isa 30:33; 2Th 2:8
e Job 40:13
4:10
f Job 5:15; Ps 58:6
4:11
g Job 27:14;
Ps 34:10
4:12
h Job 26:14
i Job 33:14
4:13
j Job 33:15
4:14
k Jer 23:9;
Hab 3:16
4:17
l Job 9:2
m Job 35:10
4:18
n Job 15:15
4:19
o Job 10:9
p Job 22:16
q Ge 2:7
4:20
r Job 14:2,20; 20:7;
Ps 90:5-6
4:21
s Job 8:22
t Job 18:21; 36:12

Job 4:1—5:27

📖 With artistic flare, Eliphaz sounded the keynote for all else that he and his companions would say. Job in chapter 3 was so obviously wrong that it wasn't hard for Eliphaz to appear to be right. His words were so good that the apostle Paul would quote 5:13a in 1 Corinthians 3:19. But we are wise to keep in mind that the overall purpose of the book of Job includes the concept that the counselors were fundamentally wrong (see 42:7–8), even though their words were often right. Subtle flaws in logic can easily be missed by a casual reading.

5

"Call if you will, but who will answer you?
   To which of the holy ones^u will you turn?
2 Resentment kills a fool,
   and envy slays the simple.^v
3 I myself have seen a fool taking root,^w
   but suddenly his house was cursed.^x
4 His children are far from safety,^y
   crushed in court^z without a defender.
5 The hungry consume his harvest,^a
   taking it even from among thorns,
   and the thirsty pant after his wealth.
6 For hardship does not spring from the soil,
   nor does trouble sprout from the ground.
7 Yet man is born to trouble^b
   as surely as sparks fly upward.

8 "But if it were I, I would appeal to God;
   I would lay my cause before him.^c
9 He performs wonders that cannot be fathomed,^d
   miracles that cannot be counted.
10 He bestows rain on the earth;
   he sends water upon the countryside.^e
11 The lowly he sets on high,^f
   and those who mourn are lifted to safety.
12 He thwarts the plans^g of the crafty,
   so that their hands achieve no success.
13 He catches the wise in their craftiness,^h
   and the schemes of the wily are swept away.
14 Darkness^i comes upon them in the daytime;
   at noon they grope as in the night.^j
15 He saves the needy^k from the sword in their mouth;

5:1
u Job 15:15
5:2
v Pr 12:16
5:3
w Ps 37:35;
Jer 12:2
x Job 24:18
5:4
y Job 4:11
z Am 5:12
5:5
a Job 18:8-10

5:7
b Job 14:1

5:8
c Ps 35:23; 50:15
5:9
d Job 42:3; Ps 40:5

5:10
e Job 36:28
5:11
f Ps 113:7-8

5:12
g Ne 4:15; Ps 33:10

5:13
h 1Co 3:19*

5:14
i Job 12:25
j Dt 28:29
5:15
k Ps 35:10

What Eliphaz didn't know—God's hidden purpose—made all his beautiful poetry and grand truth only a snare for Job. While things he said were good even for a sufferer to contemplate—like the disciplining aspect of suffering—these words didn't apply to the case at hand. Eliphaz's patronizing attitude revealed in his closing sentence (5:27) must have been galling to Job, his peer. How careful we need to be in counseling those in pain! Do you seek the Spirit's guidance when discussing the spiritual aspects of suffering with the wounded? Or do you seek to point out the "chink in their armor" that (you feel) caused the circumstance?

5:8

Modern Attempts to Prove God's Existence

Job wondered about God's ways, but never about God's reality. Under the modern mindset many people turn this around: They struggle to prove God's existence before grappling to understand his ways. Following are conclusions that have historically satisfied some people. What clinches the argument for God's existence in your mind? What role does your faith play?

Ontological Argument: God is that, the greater than which can't be conceived.

Unmoved Mover Argument: If everything has a cause, an original cause must exist.

Cosmological Argument: The world exists, therefore someone must have made it.

Degrees of Qualities Argument: Qualities like goodness, truth, etc., must have perfect forms.

Teleological Argument: There must be an intelligent designer behind the orderliness of the universe.

Moral Argument: Without a God, everything would be permitted.

Final Benefits Argument: If God is true, the benefits far outweigh any alternative.

Immediate Benefits Argument: Belief in God, however conceived, produces better effects than disbelief.

5:15
l Job 4:10

5:16
m Ps 107:42

5:17
n Jas 1:12
o Ps 94:12; Pr 3:11
p Heb 12:5-11

5:18
q Isa 30:26
r 1Sa 2:6

5:19
s Ps 34:19; 91:10

5:20
t Ps 33:19
u Ps 144:10

5:21
v Ps 31:20
w Ps 91:5

5:22
x Ps 91:13;
Eze 34:25

5:23
y Ps 91:12
z Isa 11:6-9

5:24
a Job 8:6

5:25
b Ps 112:2
c Ps 72:16;
Isa 44:3-4

5:26
d Ge 15:15

he saves them from the clutches of the powerful. *l*

16 So the poor have hope,
    and injustice shuts its mouth. *m*

17 "Blessed is the man whom God corrects; *n*
    so do not despise the discipline *o* of the Almighty. *a p*
18 For he wounds, but he also binds up; *q*
    he injures, but his hands also heal. *r*
19 From six calamities he will rescue you;
    in seven no harm will befall you. *s*
20 In famine *t* he will ransom you from death,
    and in battle from the stroke of the sword. *u*
21 You will be protected from the lash of the tongue, *v*
    and need not fear *w* when destruction comes.
22 You will laugh at destruction and famine,
    and need not fear the beasts of the earth. *x*
23 For you will have a covenant with the stones *y* of the field,
    and the wild animals will be at peace with you. *z*
24 You will know that your tent is secure;
    you will take stock of your property and find nothing missing. *a*
25 You will know that your children will be many, *b*
    and your descendants like the grass of the earth. *c*
26 You will come to the grave in full vigor, *d*
    like sheaves gathered in season.

27 "We have examined this, and it is true.
    So hear it and apply it to yourself."

Job

6

Then Job replied:

6:2
e Job 31:6

6:3
f Pr 27:3 *g* Job 23:2

6:4
h Ps 38:2
i Job 16:12,13
j Job 21:20
k Job 30:15
l Ps 88:15-18

2 "If only my anguish could be weighed
    and all my misery be placed on the scales! *e*
3 It would surely outweigh the sand *f* of the seas—
    no wonder my words have been impetuous. *g*
4 The arrows *h* of the Almighty are in me, *i*
    my spirit drinks *j* in their poison;
    God's terrors *k* are marshaled against me. *l*
5 Does a wild donkey bray when it has grass,
    or an ox bellow when it has fodder?
6 Is tasteless food eaten without salt,
    or is there flavor in the white of an egg *b*?

6:7
m Job 3:24

7 I refuse to touch it;
    such food makes me ill. *m*

6:8
n Job 14:13

8 "Oh, that I might have my request,
    that God would grant what I hope for, *n*
9 that God would be willing to crush me,

---

a 17 Hebrew *Shaddai*; here and throughout Job   *b* 6 The meaning of the Hebrew for this phrase is
uncertain.

Job 6:1—7:21

Job attacked his counselors (ch. 6) and God (ch. 7), offering as an excuse for his rage the depth of his misery (6:2–3; 7:11). His words, disturbing as they are, arose from his limited knowledge (38:2) and determination to speak only the truth as he saw it. Job viewed God as the author of his misery and opened (6:4) and closed (7:20) his speech with images of God shooting arrows at

him. Job's suffering was so intense that death would have come as a welcome release (6:8–10).

Job argued persuasively against his counselors (though only Eliphaz has been quoted so far). They had been no help. Their words were bad medicine, or, as Job put it, bad food (6:6–7). They were undependable and cruel. Job challenged them to prove him wrong (6:24) and pleaded with them for the courtesy of human kindness.

to let loose his hand and cut me off! [o]
10 Then I would still have this consolation—
my joy in unrelenting pain—
that I had not denied the words [p] of the Holy One. [q]

11 "What strength do I have, that I should still hope?
What prospects, that I should be patient? [r]
12 Do I have the strength of stone?
Is my flesh bronze?
13 Do I have any power to help myself, [s]
now that success has been driven from me?

14 "A despairing man [t] should have the devotion [u] of his friends,
even though he forsakes the fear of the Almighty.
15 But my brothers are as undependable as intermittent streams, [v]
as the streams that overflow
16 when darkened by thawing ice
and swollen with melting snow,
17 but that cease to flow in the dry season,
and in the heat [w] vanish from their channels.
18 Caravans turn aside from their routes;
they go up into the wasteland and perish.
19 The caravans of Tema [x] look for water,
the traveling merchants of Sheba look in hope.
20 They are distressed, because they had been confident;
they arrive there, only to be disappointed. [y]
21 Now you too have proved to be of no help;
you see something dreadful and are afraid. [z]
22 Have I ever said, 'Give something on my behalf,
pay a ransom for me from your wealth,
23 deliver me from the hand of the enemy,
ransom me from the clutches of the ruthless'?

24 "Teach me, and I will be quiet; [a]
show me where I have been wrong.
25 How painful are honest words! [b]
But what do your arguments prove?
26 Do you mean to correct what I say,
and treat the words of a despairing man as wind? [c]
27 You would even cast lots [d] for the fatherless
and barter away your friend.

28 "But now be so kind as to look at me.
Would I lie to your face? [e]
29 Relent, do not be unjust;
reconsider, for my integrity is at stake. [a][f]
30 Is there any wickedness on my lips? [g]
Can my mouth not discern [h] malice?

7 "Does not man have hard service [i] on earth? [j]
Are not his days like those of a hired man? [k]
2 Like a slave longing for the evening shadows,
or a hired man waiting eagerly for his wages, [l]

a 29 Or *my righteousness still stands*

Cross References
6:9
o Nu 11:15; 1Ki 19:4
6:10
p Job 22:22; 23:12
q Lev 19:2; Isa 57:15
6:11
r Job 21:4
6:13
s Job 26:2
6:14
t Job 4:5 *u* Job 15:4
6:15
v Ps 38:11; Jer 15:18
6:17
w Job 24:19
6:19
x Ge 25:15; Isa 21:14
6:20
y Jer 14:3
6:21
z Ps 38:11
6:24
a Ps 39:1
6:25
b Ecc 12:11
6:26
c Job 8:2; 15:3
6:27
d Joel 3:3; Na 3:10; 2Pe 2:3
6:28
e Job 27:4; 33:1,3; 36:3,4
6:29
f Job 23:7,10; 34:5,36; 42:6
6:30
g Job 27:4 *h* Job 12:11
7:1
i Job 14:14; Isa 40:2 *j* Job 5:7 *k* Job 14:6
7:2
l Lev 19:13

Few suffer as intensely as Job, so it's difficult for us to identify fully with his rage (6:27). But for those who do endure devastating circumstances, his words can bring immense comfort. Why? For the simple reason that many hurting people have felt rage but been too ashamed to express it. That a man who had experienced such faith could speak from the depth of his being such words of anguish can only strengthen those enduring torment.

Shared Suffering

A young pastor observed to me recently: "The biggest difference between my present church and my former church is in how they deal with pain. My former church assumed that pain was temporary and removable. Virtually all prayer requests were to escape or eliminate some form of suffering. Prayer was primarily a tool for pain removal.

"The church where I am now is trying to learn the language of the Biblical prayers of lament—not just praying to escape pain, but to learn to dwell in the land of pain and uncertainty, because that is where people live today." The pastor's current church was sinking its roots into the depths of Job's story.

Job had been blessed by God with health, wealth, and family. And Job was grateful and obedient. But when those blessings are removed, the plot thickens. Job loses his health, possessions, and children, and the rest of the book explores the mysteries of undeserved suffering (suffering that comes not as direct punishment for specific sins).

A common phrase refers to "the patience of Job," but in this book you will see precious little quiet endurance. Job dared to confront God. He disdained his friends' clichéd comfort and passionately argued with those who suggested that he needed to get right with God to stop the suffering.

In the end, these "comforters" receive God's sternest treatment. God rebukes them for their assumptions and for their confident preaching to Job of his need to repent.

The book of Job is a warning to those who work with the broken, sick, and suffering. Beware of technically correct answers that lack soul.

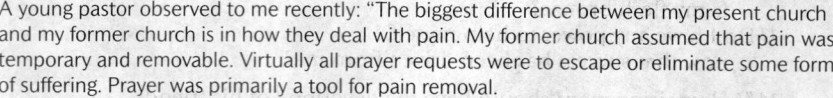

"**P**ity can be near-sighted and condescending; shared suffering can be dignifying and life changing."

"We don't like to see people suffer," writes Eugene Peterson in *The Message.* "And so our instincts are aimed at preventing and alleviating suffering. No doubt that is a good impulse. But if we really want to reach out to others who are suffering, we should be careful not to be like Job's friends, not to do our 'helping' with the presumption that we can fix things, get rid of them, or make them 'better.'"

In our efforts to help the hurting, we do well to admit that no matter how insightful we pretend to be, we don't understand the whole story. Job's friends assumed that his suffering was due to some correctable flaw in Job's life. More contemporary comforters tend to assume that suffering people are victims of their environment or of some imposed injustice. At times, they are absolutely right. But at least for Job's comforters, the idea that God was at work *in* the suffering was an enormous blind spot.

So what's a comforter to do?

Instead of concentrating only on its prevention or removal, comforters can *enter* the suffering, identifying with it as much as they are able and looking for God in the midst of it all.

In Peterson's words, "We need to quit feeling sorry for people who suffer and instead look up to them, learn from them, and—if they will let us—join them in protest and prayer. Pity can be near-sighted and condescending; shared suffering can be dignifying and life changing."

Do you remember the classical distinction between virtue and innocence? Virtue, unlike innocence, has successfully passed a point of temptation.

Perhaps a similar distinction applies to faith: Innocent faith trusts God because it hasn't seen the abyss; virtuous faith has known the terror and chooses to trust. True comforters are willing to set aside pre-packaged answers and enter into the terror of shared suffering.

As Abraham Heschel observed, "Job's faith was unshakable because it was the result of being shaken."

Marshall Shelley, vice president of Christianity Today International in Carol Stream, Illinois

3 so I have been allotted months of futility,
   and nights of misery have been assigned to me. [m]
4 When I lie down I think, 'How long before I get up?' [n]
   The night drags on, and I toss till dawn.
5 My body is clothed with worms [o] and scabs,
   my skin is broken and festering.

6 "My days are swifter than a weaver's shuttle, [p]
   and they come to an end without hope. [q]
7 Remember, O God, that my life is but a breath; [r]
   my eyes will never see happiness again. [s]
8 The eye that now sees me will see me no longer;
   you will look for me, but I will be no more. [t]
9 As a cloud vanishes and is gone,
   so he who goes down to the grave [a] [u] does not return. [v]
10 He will never come to his house again;
   his place [w] will know him no more. [x]

11 "Therefore I will not keep silent; [y]
   I will speak out in the anguish of my spirit,
   I will complain in the bitterness of my soul. [z]
12 Am I the sea, or the monster of the deep, [a]
   that you put me under guard?
13 When I think my bed will comfort me
   and my couch will ease my complaint, [b]
14 even then you frighten me with dreams
   and terrify [c] me with visions,
15 so that I prefer strangling and death, [d]
   rather than this body of mine.
16 I despise my life; [e] I would not live forever.
   Let me alone; my days have no meaning.

17 "What is man that you make so much of him,
   that you give him so much attention, [f]
18 that you examine him every morning
   and test him every moment? [g]
19 Will you never look away from me,
   or let me alone even for an instant? [h]
20 If I have sinned, what have I done to you, [i]
   O watcher of men?
   Why have you made me your target? [j]
   Have I become a burden to you? [b]
21 Why do you not pardon my offenses
   and forgive my sins? [k]
   For I will soon lie down in the dust; [l]
   you will search for me, but I will be no more."

Bildad

8 Then Bildad the Shuhite replied:

2 "How long will you say such things?
   Your words are a blustering wind. [m]

---

[a] 9 Hebrew *Sheol*   [b] 20 A few manuscripts of the Masoretic Text, an ancient Hebrew scribal tradition and Septuagint; most manuscripts of the Masoretic Text *I have become a burden to myself.*

Job 8:1–22
Bildad heard Job's words with his ears, but his heart heard nothing. Repeatedly in chapter 6 Job had called himself a helpless, despairing man in need of his friends' compassion and devotion. It seems incredible that Bildad would have replied so callously. This "friend" demonstrated not only steely indifference to Job's plight but an arrogant certainty that Job's children had gotten

Cross references (right margin)

7:3 [m] Job 16:7; Ps 6:6
7:4 [n] Dt 28:67
7:5 [o] Job 17:14; Isa 14:11
7:6 [p] Job 9:25 [q] Job 13:15; 17:11,15
7:7 [r] Ps 78:39; Jas 4:14 [s] Job 9:25
7:8 [t] Job 20:7,9,21
7:9 [u] Job 11:8 [v] 2Sa 12:23; Job 30:15
7:10 [w] Job 27:21,23 [x] Job 8:18
7:11 [y] Ps 40:9 [z] 1Sa 1:10
7:12 [a] Eze 32:2-3
7:13 [b] Job 9:27
7:14 [c] Job 9:34
7:15 [d] 1Ki 19:4
7:16 [e] Job 9:21; 10:1
7:17 [f] Ps 8:4; 144:3; Heb 2:6
7:18 [g] Job 14:3
7:19 [h] Job 9:18
7:20 [i] Job 35:6 [j] Job 16:12
7:21 [k] Job 10:14 [l] Job 10:9; Ps 104:29
8:2 [m] Job 6:26

8:3
n Dt 32:4;
2Ch 19:7; Ro 3:5
o Ge 18:25

8:4
p Job 1:19

8:5
q Job 11:13

8:6
r Ps 7:6 s Job 5:24

8:7
t Job 42:12

8:8
u Dt 4:32; 32:7;
Job 15:18
8:9
v Ge 47:9
w 1Ch 29:15;
Job 7:6

3 Does God pervert justice? n
    Does the Almighty pervert what is right? o
4 When your children sinned against him,
    he gave them over to the penalty of their sin. p
5 But if you will look to God
    and plead q with the Almighty,
6 if you are pure and upright,
    even now he will rouse himself on your behalf r
    and restore you to your rightful place. s
7 Your beginnings will seem humble,
    so prosperous t will your future be.

8 "Ask the former generations u
    and find out what their fathers learned,
9 for we were born only yesterday and know nothing, v
    and our days on earth are but a shadow. w
10 Will they not instruct you and tell you?
    Will they not bring forth words from their understanding?
11 Can papyrus grow tall where there is no marsh?
    Can reeds thrive without water?

8:12
x Ps 129:6; Jer 17:6
8:13
y Ps 9:17
z Job 11:20; 13:16;
15:34; Pr 10:28

8:14
a Isa 59:5
8:15
b Job 27:18
c Ps 49:11

8:16
d Ps 80:11
e Ps 37:35;
Jer 11:16

12 While still growing and uncut,
    they wither more quickly than grass. x
13 Such is the destiny of all who forget God; y
    so perishes the hope of the godless. z
14 What he trusts in is fragile a;
    what he relies on is a spider's web. a
15 He leans on his web, b but it gives way;
    he clings to it, but it does not hold. c
16 He is like a well-watered plant in the sunshine,
    spreading its shoots d over the garden; e
17 it entwines its roots around a pile of rocks
    and looks for a place among the stones.
18 But when it is torn from its spot,
    that place disowns it and says, 'I never saw you.' f

8:18
f Job 7:8; Ps 37:36
8:19
g Job 20:5
h Ecc 1:4

8:20
i Job 1:1
j Job 21:30
8:21
k Job 5:22
l Ps 126:2; 132:16

8:22
m Ps 35:26; 109:29;
132:18
n Job 18:6,14,21

19 Surely its life withers g away,
    and b from the soil other plants grow. h

20 "Surely God does not reject a blameless i man
    or strengthen the hands of evildoers. j
21 He will yet fill your mouth with laughter k
    and your lips with shouts of joy. l
22 Your enemies will be clothed in shame, m
    and the tents of the wicked will be no more." n

Job

9

Then Job replied:

2 "Indeed, I know that this is true.
    But how can a mortal be righteous before God? o

9:2
o Job 4:17;
Ps 143:2; Ro 3:20

a 14 The meaning of the Hebrew for this word is uncertain.   b 19 Or Surely all the joy it has / is that

---

what they deserved and that Job was well on his way to the same fate.

📖 Have you encountered Christians who have done heartless disservice to others under the guise of being God's representatives? What damage have they done to you or to other sufferers? On the other hand, have you ever felt an inward glee in concluding that

someone had gotten what they deserved? All of us as humans are capable of great cruelty—at times expressed in deceptively civilized ways.

Christians do well to remember that because of Christ, we who are believers won't "get" what we deserve. The Scriptures teach that "all have sinned" and that the "wages of sin is death but the gift of God is eter-

3 Though one wished to dispute with him,
he could not answer him one time out of a thousand. p

4 His wisdom q is profound, his power is vast. r
Who has resisted him and come out unscathed? s

5 He moves mountains without their knowing it
and overturns them in his anger. t

6 He shakes the earth u from its place
and makes its pillars tremble. v

7 He speaks to the sun and it does not shine;
he seals off the light of the stars. w

8 He alone stretches out the heavens x
and treads on the waves of the sea. y

9 He is the Maker of the Bear and Orion,
the Pleiades and the constellations of the south. z

10 He performs wonders a that cannot be fathomed,
miracles that cannot be counted. b

11 When he passes me, I cannot see him;
when he goes by, I cannot perceive him. c

12 If he snatches away, who can stop him? d
Who can say to him, 'What are you doing?' e

13 God does not restrain his anger;
even the cohorts of Rahab f cowered at his feet.

14 "How then can I dispute with him?
How can I find words to argue with him?

15 Though I were innocent, I could not answer him; g
I could only plead h with my Judge for mercy.

16 Even if I summoned him and he responded,
I do not believe he would give me a hearing.

17 He would crush me i with a storm j
and multiply k my wounds for no reason. l

18 He would not let me regain my breath
but would overwhelm me with misery. m

19 If it is a matter of strength, he is mighty!
And if it is a matter of justice, who will summon him a?

20 Even if I were innocent, my mouth would condemn me;
if I were blameless, it would pronounce me guilty.

21 "Although I am blameless, n
I have no concern for myself;
I despise my own life. o

22 It is all the same; that is why I say,
'He destroys both the blameless and the wicked.' p

23 When a scourge q brings sudden death,
he mocks the despair of the innocent. r

24 When a land falls into the hands of the wicked, s
he blindfolds its judges. t
If it is not he, then who is it?

25 "My days are swifter than a runner; u

a 19 See Septuagint; Hebrew me.

9:3 p Job 10:2; 40:2
9:4 q Job 11:6; r Job 36:5; s 2Ch 13:12
9:5 t Mic 1:4
9:6 u Isa 2:21; Hag 2:6; Heb 12:26; v Job 26:11
9:7 w Isa 13:10; Eze 32:8
9:8 x Ge 1:6; Ps 104:2-3; y Job 38:16; Ps 77:19
9:9 z Ge 1:16; Job 38:31; Am 5:8
9:10 a Ps 71:15; b Job 5:9
9:11 c Job 23:8-9; 35:14
9:12 d Job 11:10; e Isa 45:9; Ro 9:20
9:13 f Job 26:12; Ps 89:10; Isa 30:7; 51:9
9:15 g Job 10:15; h Job 8:5
9:17 i Job 16:12; j Job 30:22; k Job 16:14; l Job 2:3
9:18 m Job 7:19; 27:2
9:21 n Job 1:1; o Job 7:16
9:22 p Job 10:8; Ecc 9:2,3; Eze 21:3
9:23 q Heb 11:36; r Job 24:1,12
9:24 s Job 10:3; 16:11; t Job 12:6
9:25 u Job 7:6

nal life in Christ Jesus our Lord" (cf. Rom. 3:23; 6:23). Allow this reality to penetrate your heart and inform your response to those who suffer.

Job 9:1—10:22

In his reply, Job moved from praising God (9:1–13) to blaming him (9:14—10:22). Would God ever treat him justly? He doubted it. The God of Job's imagination destroyed the blameless, mocked the innocent, and blocked the administration of justice (9:22–24). These were hard words, but Job's use of a question instead of a statement—"If it is not he, then who is it?" (9:24)—implied that he wasn't sure.

9:26
v Isa 18:2
w Hab 1:8
9:27
x Job 7:11

9:28
y Job 3:25;
Ps 119:120
z Job 7:21

9:29
a Ps 37:33

9:30
b Job 31:7
c Jer 2:22

9:32
d Ro 9:20
e Ps 143:2; Ecc 6:10
9:33
f 1Sa 2:25

9:34
g Job 13:21;
Ps 39:10

9:35
h Job 13:21

10:1
i 1Ki 19:4 j Job 7:11

10:2
k Job 9:29
10:3
l Job 9:22
m Job 14:15;
Ps 138:8; Isa 64:8
n Job 21:16; 22:18

10:4
o 1Sa 16:7

10:5
p Ps 90:2,4; 2Pe 3:8

10:6
q Job 14:16

10:8
r Ps 119:73

10:9
s Isa 64:8 t Ge 2:7

10:11
u Ps 139:13,15

they fly away without a glimpse of joy.
26 They skim past like boats of papyrus, [v]
    like eagles swooping down on their prey. [w]
27 If I say, 'I will forget my complaint, [x]
    I will change my expression, and smile,'
28 I still dread [y] all my sufferings,
    for I know you will not hold me innocent. [z]
29 Since I am already found guilty,
    why should I struggle in vain? [a]
30 Even if I washed myself with soap [a]
    and my hands [b] with washing soda, [c]
31 you would plunge me into a slime pit
    so that even my clothes would detest me.

32 "He is not a man like me that I might answer him, [d]
    that we might confront each other in court. [e]
33 If only there were someone to arbitrate between us, [f]
    to lay his hand upon us both,
34 someone to remove God's rod from me, [g]
    so that his terror would frighten me no more.
35 Then I would speak up without fear of him,
    but as it now stands with me, I cannot. [h]

10 "I loathe my very life; [i]
    therefore I will give free rein to my complaint
    and speak out in the bitterness of my soul. [j]
2 I will say to God: Do not condemn me,
    but tell me what charges [k] you have against me.
3 Does it please you to oppress me, [l]
    to spurn the work of your hands, [m]
    while you smile on the schemes of the wicked? [n]
4 Do you have eyes of flesh?
    Do you see as a mortal sees? [o]
5 Are your days like those of a mortal
    or your years like those of a man, [p]
6 that you must search out my faults
    and probe after my sin [q]—
7 though you know that I am not guilty
    and that no one can rescue me from your hand?

8 "Your hands shaped [r] me and made me.
    Will you now turn and destroy me?
9 Remember that you molded me like clay. [s]
    Will you now turn me to dust again? [t]
10 Did you not pour me out like milk
    and curdle me like cheese,
11 clothe me with skin and flesh
    and knit me together [u] with bones and sinews?

---

a 30 Or *snow*

Job expressed in 9:32–35 a yearning for someone strong enough to take up his cause with God. But in chapter 10 he decided to plead his own case. How could God, who had created him, want to destroy him—and *that without any formal charges?*

📖 Job's words were those of a sick and desperate man. They stand for us as a forceful reminder that people who face deep trials often say irresponsible things in

their struggle to understand their suffering in the light of God's compassion and ability to change circumstances. Not all Job's words were wrong, but it's a mistake to try to make them all represent valid theology rather than the half-truths of a man struggling to understand. They deal with the mystery at the very heart of this book: the problems of evil and pain for which no human being has a logical explanation.

12 You gave me life[v] and showed me kindness,
    and in your providence watched over my spirit.

13 "But this is what you concealed in your heart,
    and I know that this was in your mind:[w]
14 If I sinned, you would be watching me
    and would not let my offense go unpunished.[x]
15 If I am guilty—woe to me![y]
    Even if I am innocent, I cannot lift my head,[z]
    for I am full of shame
    and drowned in[a] my affliction.
16 If I hold my head high, you stalk me like a lion[a]
    and again display your awesome power against me.[b]
17 You bring new witnesses against me[c]
    and increase your anger toward me;[d]
    your forces come against me wave upon wave.

18 "Why then did you bring me out of the womb?[e]
    I wish I had died before any eye saw me.
19 If only I had never come into being,
    or had been carried straight from the womb to the grave!
20 Are not my few days[f] almost over?[g]
    Turn away from me[h] so I can have a moment's joy
21 before I go to the place of no return,[i]
    to the land of gloom and deep shadow,[b][j]
22 to the land of deepest night,
    of deep shadow and disorder,
    where even the light is like darkness."

Zophar

11 Then Zophar the Naamathite replied:

2 "Are all these words to go unanswered?[k]
    Is this talker to be vindicated?
3 Will your idle talk reduce men to silence?
    Will no one rebuke you when you mock?[l]
4 You say to God, 'My beliefs are flawless[m]
    and I am pure[n] in your sight.'
5 Oh, how I wish that God would speak,
    that he would open his lips against you
6 and disclose to you the secrets of wisdom,[o]
    for true wisdom has two sides.
    Know this: God has even forgotten some of your sin.[p]

7 "Can you fathom[q] the mysteries of God?

---

a 15 Or and aware of   b 21 Or and the shadow of death; also in verse 22

Side references

10:12
v Job 33:4

10:13
w Job 23:13

10:14
x Job 7:21
10:15
y Job 9:13; Isa 3:11
z Job 9:15

10:16
a Isa 38:13; La 3:10
b Job 5:9

10:17
c Job 16:8
d Ru 1:21

10:18
e Job 3:11

10:20
f Job 14:1
g Job 7:19
h Job 7:16
10:21
i 2Sa 12:23;
Job 3:13; 16:22
j Ps 23:4; 88:12

11:2
k Job 8:2

11:3
l Job 17:2; 21:3
11:4
m Job 6:10
n Job 10:7

11:6
o Job 9:4
p Ezr 9:13; Job 15:5

11:7
q Ecc 3:11;
Ro 11:33

Job 11:1–20

Zophar lacked compassion and was ruthlessly judgmental. He contended that Job had mocked God and claimed sinless perfection. Though Job complained bitterly about the treatment God appeared to be giving him, he hadn't mocked God. And though he had steadfastly maintained his innocence or blamelessness in contrast with wickedness (9:22), he didn't claim to be perfectly pure (7:21). Zophar's harsh words were designed to humble Job, but he apparently doubted that they would. In verses 11–12 Zophar insinuated that it would take a miracle to change Job.

It was arrogant of Zophar to assume that he knew why Job was suffering. He had reduced the solution to this complex human problem to a simplistic formula: Every pain has a sin behind it. Zophar suggested that if a person repents and gets right with God, he or she is guaranteed that the struggles and troubles of life will dissolve—that "life will be brighter than noonday" (v. 17). Where else have you heard this logic/language? What disservice does it do to vulnerable seekers or new believers tentatively submerging their big toes in the waters of faith?

When you consider that by this time Job had been

Can you probe the limits of the Almighty?
8 They are higher than the heavens *r*—what can you do?
They are deeper than the depths of the grave *a*—what can you know?
9 Their measure is longer than the earth
and wider than the sea.

10 "If he comes along and confines you in prison
and convenes a court, who can oppose him? *s*
11 Surely he recognizes deceitful men;
and when he sees evil, does he not take note? *t*
12 But a witless man can no more become wise
than a wild donkey's colt can be born a man. *b*

13 "Yet if you devote your heart *u* to him
and stretch out your hands to him, *v*
14 if you put away the sin that is in your hand
and allow no evil *w* to dwell in your tent, *x*
15 then you will lift up your face *y* without shame;
you will stand firm and without fear.
16 You will surely forget your trouble, *z*
recalling it only as waters gone by. *a*
17 Life will be brighter than noonday, *b*
and darkness will become like morning.
18 You will be secure, because there is hope;
you will look about you and take your rest *c* in safety. *d*
19 You will lie down, with no one to make you afraid, *e*
and many will court your favor. *f*
20 But the eyes of the wicked will fail, *g*
and escape will elude them; *h*
their hope will become a dying gasp." *i*

Job

12 Then Job replied:

2 "Doubtless you are the people,
and wisdom will die with you! *j*
3 But I have a mind as well as you;
I am not inferior to you.
Who does not know all these things? *k*

4 "I have become a laughingstock *l* to my friends,
though I called upon God and he answered *m*—

a 8 Hebrew *than Sheol*   *b 12* Or *wild donkey can be born tame*

Side notes:
11:8 *r* Job 22:12
11:10 *s* Job 9:12; Rev 3:7
11:11 *t* Job 34:21-25; Ps 10:14
11:13 *u* 1Sa 7:3; Ps 78:8 *v* Ps 88:9
11:14 *w* Ps 101:4 *x* Job 22:23
11:15 *y* Job 22:26; 1Jn 3:21
11:16 *z* Isa 65:16 *a* Job 22:11
11:17 *b* Job 22:28; Ps 37:6; Isa 58:8,10
11:18 *c* Ps 3:5 *d* Lev 26:6; Pr 3:24
11:19 *e* Lev 26:6 *f* Isa 45:14
11:20 *g* Dt 28:65; Job 17:5 *h* Job 27:22; 34:22 *i* Job 8:13
12:2 *j* Job 17:10
12:3 *k* Job 13:2
12:4 *l* Job 21:3 *m* Ps 91:15

reduced to poverty, the arrogance of Bildad, Zophar, and Eliphaz takes on another dimension. How many of us accuse the poor of bringing on their own circumstances or contributing to their condition? The reality is that the world's poor often are victims of injustice, bad politics, wars, natural disasters, or inconducive weather conditions. To gain perspective, how many families in your neighborhood are one job loss or catastrophic illness away from bankruptcy or homelessness? What if all their safety nets (other family members, social programs, and faith-based care groups) were to fail as well? This is the position of billions in our world today.

Job 12:1—14:22

Job answered his condescending "friends" (12:1—13:19) and then addressed God (13:20—14:22).

His patience running out, he chose to match Zophar's harshness with sarcasm (12:2). Job was sure he knew as much as his counselors did and begged to differ with their view of suffering. Being comfortable themselves, they could afford to be contemptuous toward him.

In chapter 14 Job mused on the misery of human beings in their pathetically brief life. He turned again to death as the only way out of his impasse. People are like a flower that lives its short life and is gone (14:2), not like a tree that revives even after it's been cut down (14:7–12). But in 14:13–17 Job's spirit appeared to rise above the despair generated by his decaying body. Though resurrection in the fullest sense isn't taught here, Job was saying that if God so desired he could hide Job in the grave until his anger had passed and then raise him back to life.

a mere laughingstock, though righteous and blameless![n]
5 Men at ease have contempt for misfortune
as the fate of those whose feet are slipping.
6 The tents of marauders are undisturbed,[o]
and those who provoke God are secure[p]—
those who carry their god in their hands.[a]

7 "But ask the animals, and they will teach you,
or the birds of the air, and they will tell you;
8 or speak to the earth, and it will teach you,
or let the fish of the sea inform you.
9 Which of all these does not know
that the hand of the LORD has done this?[q]
10 In his hand is the life of every creature
and the breath of all mankind.[r]
11 Does not the ear test words
as the tongue tastes food?[s]
12 Is not wisdom found among the aged?[t]
Does not long life bring understanding?[u]

13 "To God belong wisdom[v] and power;[w]
counsel and understanding are his.[x]
14 What he tears down[y] cannot be rebuilt;[z]
the man he imprisons cannot be released.
15 If he holds back the waters,[a] there is drought;[b]
if he lets them loose, they devastate the land.[c]
16 To him belong strength and victory;
both deceived and deceiver are his.[d]
17 He leads counselors away stripped[e]
and makes fools of judges.[f]
18 He takes off the shackles[g] put on by kings
and ties a loincloth[b] around their waist.
19 He leads priests away stripped
and overthrows men long established.[h]
20 He silences the lips of trusted advisers
and takes away the discernment of elders.[i]
21 He pours contempt on nobles
and disarms the mighty.
22 He reveals the deep things of darkness[j]
and brings deep shadows[k] into the light.[l]
23 He makes nations great, and destroys them;[m]
he enlarges nations,[n] and disperses them.
24 He deprives the leaders of the earth of their reason;
he sends them wandering through a trackless waste.[o]
25 They grope in darkness with no light;[p]
he makes them stagger like drunkards.[q]

13 "My eyes have seen all this,
my ears have heard and understood it.
2 What you know, I also know;
I am not inferior to you.[r]

[a] 6 Or secure / in what God's hand brings them   [b] 18 Or shackles of kings / and ties a belt

---

Job had faith in God's power over death but was convinced that God wouldn't even allow him that blessed release. The waters of suffering continued to erode his former hope until it was only a dim memory (14:19). Nothing mattered anymore except the pain wracking his body and the despair poisoning his soul (14:22). Have you had occasion to discuss eternal matters with someone whose perspective was clouded in this way? Were you able to accept his or her exaggerations and distortions as natural outgrowths of extreme pain? Have you experienced such bitter thoughts yourself?

12:4
[n] Job 6:29
12:6
[o] Job 22:18
[p] Job 9:24; 21:9

12:9
[q] Isa 41:20
12:10
[r] Job 27:3; 33:4; Ac 17:28
12:11
[s] Job 34:3
12:12
[t] Job 15:10
[u] Job 32:7,9
12:13
[v] Job 11:6
[w] Job 9:4
[x] Job 32:8; 38:36
12:14
[y] Job 19:10
[z] Job 37:7; Isa 25:2
12:15
[a] 1Ki 8:35
[b] 1Ki 17:1
[c] Ge 7:11
12:16
[d] Job 13:7,9
12:17
[e] Job 19:9
[f] Job 3:14
12:18
[g] Ps 116:16
12:19
[h] Job 24:12,22; 34:20,28; 35:9
12:20
[i] Job 32:9
12:22
[j] 1Co 4:5 [k] Job 3:5
[l] Da 2:22
12:23
[m] Jer 25:9
[n] Ps 107:38; Isa 9:3; 26:15
12:24
[o] Ps 107:40
12:25
[p] Job 5:14
[q] Ps 107:27; Isa 24:20

13:2
[r] Job 12:3

3 But I desire to speak to the Almighty
  and to argue my case with God. [s]
4 You, however, smear me with lies; [t]
  you are worthless physicians, all of you!
5 If only you would be altogether silent!
  For you, that would be wisdom. [u]
6 Hear now my argument;
  listen to the plea of my lips.
7 Will you speak wickedly on God's behalf?
  Will you speak deceitfully for him? [v]
8 Will you show him partiality? [w]
  Will you argue the case for God?
9 Would it turn out well if he examined you?
  Could you deceive him as you might deceive men? [x]
10 He would surely rebuke you
  if you secretly showed partiality.
11 Would not his splendor [y] terrify you?
  Would not the dread of him fall on you?
12 Your maxims are proverbs of ashes;
  your defenses are defenses of clay.

13 "Keep silent and let me speak;
  then let come to me what may.
14 Why do I put myself in jeopardy
  and take my life in my hands?
15 Though he slay me, yet will I hope [z] in him; [a]
  I will surely [a] defend my ways to his face. [b]
16 Indeed, this will turn out for my deliverance, [c]
  for no godless man would dare come before him!
17 Listen carefully to my words; [d]
  let your ears take in what I say.
18 Now that I have prepared my case, [e]
  I know I will be vindicated.
19 Can anyone bring charges against me? [f]
  If so, I will be silent and die. [g]

20 "Only grant me these two things, O God,
  and then I will not hide from you:
21 Withdraw your hand [h] far from me,
  and stop frightening me with your terrors.
22 Then summon me and I will answer, [i]
  or let me speak, and you reply. [j]
23 How many wrongs and sins have I committed? [k]
  Show me my offense and my sin.
24 Why do you hide your face [l]
  and consider me your enemy? [m]
25 Will you torment a windblown leaf? [n]
  Will you chase after dry chaff? [o]
26 For you write down bitter things against me
  and make me inherit the sins of my youth. [p]
27 You fasten my feet in shackles; [q]
  you keep close watch on all my paths
  by putting marks on the soles of my feet.

28 "So man wastes away like something rotten,
  like a garment eaten by moths. [r]

---

a 15 Or *He will surely slay me; I have no hope — / yet I will*

Cross references (left margin):

13:3
s Job 23:3-4
13:4
t Ps 119:69;
Jer 23:32

13:5
u Pr 17:28

13:7
v Job 36:4
13:8
w Lev 19:15

13:9
x Job 12:16; Gal 6:7

13:11
y Job 31:23

13:15
z Job 7:6 a Ps 23:4;
Pr 14:32 b Job 27:5

13:16
c Isa 12:1

13:17
d Job 21:2

13:18
e Job 23:4

13:19
f Job 40:4; Isa 50:8
g Job 10:8

13:21
h Ps 39:10

13:22
i Job 14:15
j Job 9:16

13:23
k 1Sa 26:18

13:24
l Dt 32:20; Ps 13:1;
Isa 8:17
m Job 19:11; La 2:5
13:25
n Lev 26:36
o Job 21:18;
Isa 42:3

13:26
p Ps 25:7
13:27
q Job 33:11

13:28
r Isa 50:9; Jas 5:2

14

¹ "Man born of woman
   is of few days and full of trouble. ˢ
² He springs up like a flower ᵗ and withers away; ᵘ
   like a fleeting shadow, ᵛ he does not endure.
³ Do you fix your eye on such a one? ʷ
   Will you bring him ᵃ before you for judgment? ˣ
⁴ Who can bring what is pure ʸ from the impure? ᶻ
   No one! ᵃ
⁵ Man's days are determined;
   you have decreed the number of his months ᵇ
   and have set limits he cannot exceed.
⁶ So look away from him and let him alone, ᶜ
   till he has put in his time like a hired man. ᵈ

⁷ "At least there is hope for a tree:
   If it is cut down, it will sprout again,
   and its new shoots will not fail.
⁸ Its roots may grow old in the ground
   and its stump die in the soil,
⁹ yet at the scent of water it will bud
   and put forth shoots like a plant.
¹⁰ But man dies and is laid low;
   he breathes his last and is no more. ᵉ
¹¹ As water disappears from the sea
   or a riverbed becomes parched and dry, ᶠ
¹² so man lies down and does not rise;
   till the heavens are no more, ᵍ men will not awake
   or be roused from their sleep. ʰ

¹³ "If only you would hide me in the grave ᵇ
   and conceal me till your anger has passed! ⁱ
   If only you would set me a time
   and then remember me!
¹⁴ If a man dies, will he live again?
   All the days of my hard service
   I will wait for my renewal ᶜ to come.
¹⁵ You will call and I will answer you; ʲ
   you will long for the creature your hands have made.
¹⁶ Surely then you will count my steps ᵏ
   but not keep track of my sin. ˡ
¹⁷ My offenses will be sealed up in a bag; ᵐ
   you will cover over my sin. ⁿ

¹⁸ "But as a mountain erodes and crumbles
   and as a rock is moved from its place,
¹⁹ as water wears away stones
   and torrents wash away the soil,
   so you destroy man's hope. ᵒ
²⁰ You overpower him once for all, and he is gone;
   you change his countenance and send him away.
²¹ If his sons are honored, he does not know it;
   if they are brought low, he does not see it. ᵖ
²² He feels but the pain of his own body
   and mourns only for himself."

14:1
ˢ Job 5:7; Ecc 2:23
14:2
ᵗ Jas 1:10
ᵘ Ps 90:5-6
ᵛ Job 8:9
14:3
ʷ Ps 8:4; 144:3
ˣ Ps 143:2
14:4
ʸ Ps 51:10
ᶻ Eph 2:1-3
ᵃ Jn 3:6; Ro 5:12
14:5
ᵇ Job 21:21
14:6
ᶜ Job 7:19
ᵈ Job 7:1,2; Ps 39:13
14:10
ᵉ Job 13:19
14:11
ᶠ Isa 19:5
14:12
ᵍ Rev 20:11; 21:1
ʰ Ac 3:21
14:13
ⁱ Isa 26:20
14:15
ʲ Job 13:22
14:16
ᵏ Ps 139:1-3; Pr 5:21; Jer 32:19
ˡ Job 10:6
14:17
ᵐ Dt 32:34
ⁿ Hos 13:12
14:19
ᵒ Job 7:6
14:21
ᵖ Ecc 9:5; Isa 63:16

ᵃ 3 Septuagint, Vulgate and Syriac; Hebrew *me*   ᵇ 13 Hebrew *Sheol*   ᶜ 14 Or *release*

Eliphaz

15

Then Eliphaz the Temanite replied:

15:2
a Job 6:26

2 "Would a wise man answer with empty notions
　or fill his belly with the hot east wind? [a]
3 Would he argue with useless words,
　with speeches that have no value?
4 But you even undermine piety
　and hinder devotion to God.

15:5
r Job 5:13

5 Your sin prompts your mouth;
　you adopt the tongue of the crafty. [r]

15:6
s Lk 19:22

6 Your own mouth condemns you, not mine;
　your own lips testify against you. [s]

15:7
t Job 38:21
u Ps 90:2; Pr 8:25
15:8
v Ro 11:34;
1Co 2:11

7 "Are you the first man ever born? [t]
　Were you brought forth before the hills? [u]
8 Do you listen in on God's council? [v]
　Do you limit wisdom to yourself?

15:9
w Job 13:2
15:10
x Job 32:6-7

9 What do you know that we do not know?
　What insights do you have that we do not have? [w]
10 The gray-haired and the aged [x] are on our side,
　men even older than your father.

15:11
y 2Co 1:3-4
z Zec 1:13
a Job 36:16
15:12
b Job 11:13

11 Are God's consolations [y] not enough for you,
　words [z] spoken gently to you? [a]
12 Why has your heart [b] carried you away,
　and why do your eyes flash,
13 so that you vent your rage against God
　and pour out such words from your mouth?

15:14
c Job 14:4; 25:4
d Pr 20:9; Ecc 7:20

14 "What is man, that he could be pure,
　or one born of woman, [c] that he could be righteous? [d]

15:15
e Job 4:18; 25:5
15:16
f Ps 14:1
g Job 34:7;
Pr 19:28

15 If God places no trust in his holy ones,
　if even the heavens are not pure in his eyes, [e]
16 how much less man, who is vile and corrupt, [f]
　who drinks up evil like water! [g]

17 "Listen to me and I will explain to you;
　let me tell you what I have seen,

15:18
h Job 8:8

18 what wise men have declared,
　hiding nothing received from their fathers [h]
19 (to whom alone the land was given
　when no alien passed among them):

15:20
i Job 24:1; 27:13-23
15:21
j Job 18:11; 20:25
k Job 27:20;
1Th 5:3

20 All his days the wicked man suffers torment,
　the ruthless through all the years stored up for him. [i]
21 Terrifying sounds fill his ears; [j]
　when all seems well, marauders attack him. [k]

15:22
l Job 19:29; 27:14

22 He despairs of escaping the darkness;
　he is marked for the sword. [l]

Job 15:1–35

Eliphaz had been the most sympathetic of the three friends, but he too had lost patience with Job and now denounced him severely. For the first 13 verses of this chapter, Eliphaz plied Job with questions designed *to shame him into silence. Verses 14–16 are the crux* of the chapter, repeating Eliphaz's thesis from 4:17–19: God's holiness versus humanity's corruption. The remaining half of the chapter is a dramatic description of the dreadful fate of the wicked.

Eliphaz's words in verses 14–16, beginning with the question "What is man, that he could be pure?" clearly state his view of humanity. Nothing in his comments supports a conclusion that God has any love for sinful human beings. The deity Eliphaz worshiped was mechanical, behaving like the laws of nature. Sinners in his view could expect no mercy. The sinner always gets paid in full—trouble and darkness, terror and distress, the flame and the sword. Is this viewpoint still alive today?

23 He wanders about[m]—food for vultures[a];
  he knows the day of darkness is at hand.[n]
24 Distress and anguish fill him with terror;
  they overwhelm him, like a king poised to attack,
25 because he shakes his fist at God
  and vaunts himself against the Almighty,[o]
26 defiantly charging against him
  with a thick, strong shield.

27 "Though his face is covered with fat
  and his waist bulges with flesh,[p]
28 he will inhabit ruined towns
  and houses where no one lives,[q]
  houses crumbling to rubble.[r]
29 He will no longer be rich and his wealth will not endure,[s]
  nor will his possessions spread over the land.
30 He will not escape the darkness;[t]
  a flame[u] will wither his shoots,
  and the breath of God's mouth[v] will carry him away.
31 Let him not deceive himself by trusting what is worthless,[w]
  for he will get nothing in return.
32 Before his time[x] he will be paid in full,[y]
  and his branches will not flourish.[z]
33 He will be like a vine stripped of its unripe grapes,[a]
  like an olive tree shedding its blossoms.
34 For the company of the godless will be barren,
  and fire will consume the tents of those who love bribes.[b]
35 They conceive trouble and give birth to evil;[c]
  their womb fashions deceit."

Job

16

Then Job replied:

2 "I have heard many things like these;
  miserable comforters are you all![d]
3 Will your long-winded speeches never end?
  What ails you that you keep on arguing?[e]
4 I also could speak like you,
  if you were in my place;
  I could make fine speeches against you
  and shake my head[f] at you.
5 But my mouth would encourage you;
  comfort from my lips would bring you relief.

6 "Yet if I speak, my pain is not relieved;
  and if I refrain, it does not go away.
7 Surely, O God, you have worn me out;[g]
  you have devastated my entire household.
8 You have bound me—and it has become a witness;

Reference column

15:23
m Ps 59:15; 109:10
n Job 18:12

15:25
o Job 36:9

15:27
p Ps 17:10

15:28
q Isa 5:9 r Job 3:14

15:29
s Job 27:16-17

15:30
t Job 5:14
u Job 22:20
v Job 4:9

15:31
w Isa 59:4

15:32
x Ecc 7:17
y Job 22:16;
Ps 55:23
z Job 18:16

15:33
a Hab 3:17

15:34
b Job 8:22

15:35
c Ps 7:14; Isa 59:4;
Hos 10:13

16:2
d Job 13:4

16:3
e Job 6:26

16:4
f Ps 22:7; 109:25;
La 2:15; Zep 2:15;
Mt 27:39

16:7
g Job 7:3

---

a 23 Or about, looking for food

Job 16:1—17:16

Job's thoughts countered those of Eliphaz in chapter 15, though his opening words answered the introductory statements of all three of his counselors (cf. 8:2; 11:2–3; 15:2–6). Eliphaz accused Job of attacking God, but Job claimed that the reverse was true: God was assaulting him (16:6–14). Eliphaz saw humanity as corrupt in God's eyes. Job believed he had been upright and would be vindicated (16:15–21). Eliphaz thought the words of the wise supported him. Job was convinced that there wasn't a word of wisdom in what Eliphaz had to say (17:10–12). Because God had closed his friends' minds to understanding (17:4), they were incapable of doing anything but scolding him (16:4–5; 17:2).

my gauntness[h] rises up and testifies against me.[i]

9 God assails me and tears[j] me in his anger
  and gnashes his teeth at me;[k]
  my opponent fastens on me his piercing eyes.[l]

10 Men open their mouths[m] to jeer at me;
  they strike my cheek[n] in scorn
  and unite together against me.[o]

11 God has turned me over to evil men
  and thrown me into the clutches of the wicked.[p]

12 All was well with me, but he shattered me;
  he seized me by the neck and crushed me.[q]
  He has made me his target;[r]

13   his archers surround me.
  Without pity, he pierces[s] my kidneys
  and spills my gall on the ground.

14 Again and again[t] he bursts upon me;
  he rushes at me like a warrior.[u]

15 "I have sewed sackcloth[v] over my skin
  and buried my brow in the dust.

16 My face is red with weeping,
  deep shadows ring my eyes;

17 yet my hands have been free of violence[w]
  and my prayer is pure.

18 "O earth, do not cover my blood;[x]
  may my cry never be laid to rest![y]

19 Even now my witness[z] is in heaven;
  my advocate is on high.

20 My intercessor is my friend[a]
  as my eyes pour out[a] tears to God;

21 on behalf of a man he pleads[b] with God
  as a man pleads for his friend.

22 "Only a few years will pass
  before I go on the journey of no return.[c]

17

1 My spirit is broken,
  my days are cut short,
  the grave awaits me.[d]

2 Surely mockers[e] surround me;
  my eyes must dwell on their hostility.

3 "Give me, O God, the pledge you demand.[f]
  Who else will put up security[g] for me?[h]

4 You have closed their minds to understanding;
  therefore you will not let them triumph.

5 If a man denounces his friends for reward,
  the eyes of his children will fail.[i]

6 "God has made me a byword[j] to everyone,

Cross references

16:8
h Job 19:20
i Job 10:17
16:9
j Hos 6:1
k Ps 35:16; La 2:16;
Ac 7:54 l Job 13:24
16:10
m Ps 22:13
n Isa 50:6; La 3:30;
Mic 5:1; Ac 23:2
o Ps 35:15

16:11
p Job 1:15,17

16:12
q Job 9:17 r La 3:12

16:13
s Job 20:24

16:14
t Job 9:17
u Joel 2:7

16:15
v Ge 37:34

16:17
w Isa 59:6; Jnh 3:8

16:18
x Isa 26:21
y Ps 66:18-19
16:19
z Ge 31:50; Ro 1:9;
1Th 2:5

16:20
a La 2:19
16:21
b Ps 9:4

16:22
c Ecc 12:5

17:1
d Ps 88:3-4
17:2
e 1Sa 1:6-7

17:3
f Ps 119:122
g Pr 6:1 h Isa 38:14

17:5
i Job 11:20

17:6
j Job 30:9

a 20 Or My friends treat me with scorn

Job thought that he would die before he could be vindicated before his peers, so he was concerned that the injustice done to him should never be forgotten (16:18—17:2). He firmly believed that he had a witness, an advocate, an intercessor, a friend who would plead his cause. Job envisioned someone other than God, since this one would plead with God (16:21)—but greater than a human being, since he was in heaven (16:19).

God gave Job hope in the midst of his darkest hours by giving him a shadowy glimpse of what would become crystal clear in the New Testament: Jesus Christ came to graciously advocate and intercede on our behalf. What comfort does it give you to know that he "is at the right hand of God and is also interceding for us" (Rom. 8:34; cf. Heb. 7:25; 1 Jn. 2:1)?

a man in whose face people spit.
7 My eyes have grown dim with grief; [k]
  my whole frame is but a shadow.
8 Upright men are appalled at this;
  the innocent are aroused [l] against the ungodly.
9 Nevertheless, the righteous [m] will hold to their ways,
  and those with clean hands [n] will grow stronger.

10 "But come on, all of you, try again!
  I will not find a wise man among you. [o]
11 My days have passed, my plans are shattered,
  and so are the desires of my heart. [p]
12 These men turn night into day;
  in the face of darkness they say, 'Light is near.'
13 If the only home I hope for is the grave, [a][q]
  if I spread out my bed in darkness,
14 if I say to corruption, [r] 'You are my father,'
  and to the worm, [s] 'My mother' or 'My sister,'
15 where then is my hope? [t]
  Who can see any hope for me?
16 Will it go down to the gates of death [b]? [u]
  Will we descend together into the dust?"

Bildad

18 Then Bildad the Shuhite replied:

2 "When will you end these speeches?
  Be sensible, and then we can talk.
3 Why are we regarded as cattle
  and considered stupid in your sight? [v]
4 You who tear yourself [w] to pieces in your anger,
  is the earth to be abandoned for your sake?
  Or must the rocks be moved from their place?

5 "The lamp of the wicked is snuffed out; [x]
  the flame of his fire stops burning.
6 The light in his tent becomes dark;
  the lamp beside him goes out.
7 The vigor of his step is weakened; [y]
  his own schemes [z] throw him down. [a]
8 His feet thrust him into a net [b]
  and he wanders into its mesh.
9 A trap seizes him by the heel;
  a snare holds him fast.
10 A noose is hidden for him on the ground;
  a trap lies in his path.
11 Terrors startle him on every side [c]
  and dog [d] his every step.
12 Calamity is hungry [e] for him;
  disaster is ready for him when he falls.
13 It eats away parts of his skin;

17:7	k Job 16:8
17:8	l Job 22:19
17:9	m Pr 4:18
	n Job 22:30
17:10	o Job 12:2
17:11	p Job 7:6
17:13	q Job 3:13
17:14	r Job 13:28; 30:28,30; Ps 16:10
	s Job 21:26
17:15	t Job 7:6
17:16	u Job 3:17-19; Jnh 2:6
18:3	v Ps 73:22
18:4	w Job 13:14
18:5	x Job 21:17; Pr 13:9; 20:20; 24:20
18:7	y Pr 4:12 z Job 5:13 a Job 15:6
18:8	b Job 22:10; Ps 9:15; 35:7
18:11	c Job 15:21; Jer 6:25; 20:3 d Job 20:8
18:12	e Isa 8:21

---

[a] 13 Hebrew *Sheol* [b] 16 Hebrew *Sheol*

Job 18:1–21

📖 Bildad wanted to convince Job that wicked people get paid back in full, in this life, for their deeds. He said nothing of a final judgment but was sure the lamp of the wicked would be snuffed out. Death in Bildad's view was part of the punishment, not a dividing line after which punishment would come. The only after-death payback Bildad envisioned was having one's memory (name) cut off, leaving him no offspring or survivors.

18:13
f Zec 14:12
18:14
g Job 8:22

18:15
h Ps 11:6
18:16
i Isa 5:24; Hos 9:1-
16;
Am 2:9 j Job 15:30;
Mal 4:1

18:17
k Ps 34:16; Pr 2:22;
10:7
18:18
l Job 5:14
18:19
m Jer 22:30
n Isa 14:22
o Job 27:14-15
18:20
p Ps 37:13;
Jer 50:27,31
18:21
q Job 21:28
r Jer 9:3; 1Th 4:5

death's firstborn devours his limbs. f

14 He is torn from the security of his tent g
    and marched off to the king of terrors.

15 Fire resides a in his tent;
    burning sulfur h is scattered over his dwelling.

16 His roots dry up below i
    and his branches wither above. j

17 The memory of him perishes from the earth;
    he has no name in the land. k

18 He is driven from light into darkness l
    and is banished from the world.

19 He has no offspring m or descendants n among his people,
    no survivor where once he lived. o

20 Men of the west are appalled at his fate; p
    men of the east are seized with horror.

21 Surely such is the dwelling q of an evil man;
    such is the place of one who knows not God." r

Job
19

Then Job replied:

2 "How long will you torment me
    and crush me with words?

3 Ten times now you have reproached me;
    shamelessly you attack me.

4 If it is true that I have gone astray,
    my error s remains my concern alone.

5 If indeed you would exalt yourselves above me t
    and use my humiliation against me,

6 then know that God has wronged me u
    and drawn his net v around me.

7 "Though I cry, 'I've been wronged!' I get no response; w
    though I call for help, there is no justice. x

8 He has blocked my way so I cannot pass; y
    he has shrouded my paths in darkness. z

9 He has stripped a me of my honor
    and removed the crown from my head. b

10 He tears me down c on every side till I am gone;
    he uproots my hope d like a tree. e

11 His anger f burns against me;
    he counts me among his enemies. g

12 His troops advance in force; h
    they build a siege ramp i against me
    and encamp around my tent.

19:4
s Job 6:24
19:5
t Ps 35:26; 38:16;
55:12
19:6
u Job 27:2
v Job 18:8

19:7
w Job 30:20
x Job 9:24;
Hab 1:2-4
19:8
y Job 3:23; La 3:7
z Job 30:26
19:9
a Job 12:17
b Ps 89:39,44;
La 5:16
19:10
c Job 12:14
d Job 7:6
e Job 24:20
19:11
f Job 16:9
g Job 13:24
19:12
h Job 16:13
i Job 30:12

a 15 Or Nothing he had remains

Bildad personified death in verses 13–14. This "king of terrors" was reminiscent of the Canaanite deity Mot (Death), whose devouring throat supposedly reached from earth to sky. The prophet Isaiah would reverse the figure, picturing God swallowing up death forever (Isa. 25:8; cf. 1 Cor. 15:54). What are the predominant views of death today? How does our message of the kingdom bring hope to people in fear of death?

Job 19:1–29

Job showed increasing irritation over his counselors' shameless attacks and superior claims (vv. 2–5),

then expressed his feelings of abandonment by God and perception that God's attack on him was unfounded (vv. 6–12). He blamed God for alienating his family and friends, including his wife (vv. 13–20). In verses 23–27 Job ended his lament, to our amazement, with a triumphant expression of faith in the One who would finally champion his cause and vindicate him. This stanza is bracketed by words to his friends whom Job didn't believe would ever have pity (v. 21) and by his warning of the dire consequences of their false accusations (vv. 28–29).

13 "He has alienated my brothers^j from me;
   my acquaintances are completely estranged from me. ^k
14 My kinsmen have gone away;
   my friends have forgotten me.
15 My guests and my maidservants count me a stranger;
   they look upon me as an alien.
16 I summon my servant, but he does not answer,
   though I beg him with my own mouth.
17 My breath is offensive to my wife;
   I am loathsome to my own brothers.
18 Even the little boys^l scorn me;
   when I appear, they ridicule me.
19 All my intimate friends^m detest me; ⁿ
   those I love have turned against me.
20 I am nothing but skin and bones; ^o
   I have escaped with only the skin of my teeth. ^a

21 "Have pity on me, my friends, have pity,
   for the hand of God has struck me.
22 Why do you pursue^p me as God does?
   Will you never get enough of my flesh? ^q

23 "Oh, that my words were recorded,
   that they were written on a scroll, ^r
24 that they were inscribed with an iron tool on^b lead,
   or engraved in rock forever!
25 I know that my Redeemer^c ^s lives, ^t
   and that in the end he will stand upon the earth. ^d
26 And after my skin has been destroyed,
   yet^e in^f my flesh I will see God; ^u
27 I myself will see him
   with my own eyes—I, and not another.
   How my heart yearns^v within me!

28 "If you say, 'How we will hound him,
   since the root of the trouble lies in him,'^g
29 you should fear the sword yourselves;
   for wrath will bring punishment by the sword, ^w
   and then you will know that there is judgment. ^h" ^x

Zophar

20

Then Zophar the Naamathite replied:

2 "My troubled thoughts prompt me to answer
   because I am greatly disturbed.

---

^a 20 Or *only my gums*   ^b 24 Or *and*   ^c 25 Or *defender*   ^d 25 Or *upon my grave*   ^e 26 Or *And after I awake, / though this ⌊body⌋ has been destroyed, / then*   ^f 26 Or */ apart from*   ^g 28 Many Hebrew manuscripts, Septuagint and Vulgate; most Hebrew manuscripts *me*   ^h 29 Or */ that you may come to know the Almighty*

Cross-references (margin):

19:13 / Ps 69:8 / k Job 16:7; Ps 88:8
19:18 / l 2Ki 2:23
19:19 / m Ps 55:12-13 / n Ps 38:11
19:20 / o Job 33:21; Ps 102:5
19:22 / p Job 13:25; 16:11 / q Ps 69:26
19:23 / r Isa 30:8
19:25 / s Ps 78:35; Pr 23:11; Isa 43:14; Jer 50:34 / t Job 16:19
19:26 / u Ps 17:15; Mt 5:8; 1Co 13:12; 1Jn 3:2
19:27 / v Ps 73:26
19:29 / w Job 15:22 / x Job 22:4; Ps 1:5; 9:7

One of the enduring themes of the book of Job is that suffering doesn't prove that God has deserted us. Job's feelings of abandonment and his friends' condemnation made him crave a redeemer—every human's basic need before a holy God (cf. 1 Tim. 2:5–6). Job realized that *God himself* would appear to him, that in spite of death he would see God with his own eyes (Job 19:26–27; cf. Job 42:5; Matt. 5:8; 1 Jn. 3:2). Ultimately Job would learn that God was neither separated from him nor unconcerned.

On the contrary, God himself was both his Redeemer and his Friend. Have you made the same discovery?

Job 20:1–29

Zophar took Job's words, especially his closing remarks in 19:28–29, as a personal insult (20:2–3). The most emotional of the three friends, Zophar wasn't about to let Job's rebuke go unanswered. His response was another poem on the terrible fate of the wicked as understood by the theology of the three counselors.

20:3
y Job 19:3

20:5
z Job 8:12;
Ps 37:35-36; 73:19
20:6
a Isa 14:13-14;
Ob 1:3-4
20:7
b Job 4:20
c Job 7:10; 8:18
20:8
d Ps 73:20
e Job 27:21-23
f Job 18:18
g Ps 90:5
20:9
h Job 7:8
20:10
i Job 5:4
j Job 27:16-17
20:11
k Job 13:26
l Job 21:26

20:13
m Nu 11:18-20

20:16
n Dt 32:32
o Dt 32:24

20:17
p Dt 32:13
q Job 29:6

20:19
r Job 24:4,14; 35:9

20:20
s Ecc 5:12-14

20:21
t Job 15:29

20:23
u Ps 78:30-31
20:24
v Isa 24:18;
Am 5:19

3 I hear a rebuke[y] that dishonors me,
    and my understanding inspires me to reply.

4 "Surely you know how it has been from of old,
    ever since man[a] was placed on the earth,
5 that the mirth of the wicked is brief,
    the joy of the godless lasts but a moment.[z]
6 Though his pride reaches to the heavens
    and his head touches the clouds,[a]
7 he will perish forever,[b] like his own dung;
    those who have seen him will say, 'Where is he?'[c]
8 Like a dream[d] he flies away,[e] no more to be found,
    banished[f] like a vision of the night.[g]
9 The eye that saw him will not see him again;
    his place will look on him no more.[h]
10 His children[i] must make amends to the poor;
    his own hands must give back his wealth.[j]
11 The youthful vigor[k] that fills his bones
    will lie with him in the dust.[l]

12 "Though evil is sweet in his mouth
    and he hides it under his tongue,
13 though he cannot bear to let it go
    and keeps it in his mouth,[m]
14 yet his food will turn sour in his stomach;
    it will become the venom of serpents within him.
15 He will spit out the riches he swallowed;
    God will make his stomach vomit them up.
16 He will suck the poison[n] of serpents;
    the fangs of an adder will kill him.[o]
17 He will not enjoy the streams,
    the rivers flowing with honey[p] and cream.[q]
18 What he toiled for he must give back uneaten;
    he will not enjoy the profit from his trading.
19 For he has oppressed the poor and left them destitute;[r]
    he has seized houses he did not build.

20 "Surely he will have no respite from his craving;[s]
    he cannot save himself by his treasure.
21 Nothing is left for him to devour;
    his prosperity will not endure.[t]
22 In the midst of his plenty, distress will overtake him;
    the full force of misery will come upon him.
23 When he has filled his belly,
    God will vent his burning anger against him
    and rain down his blows upon him.[u]
24 Though he flees[v] from an iron weapon,
    a bronze-tipped arrow pierces him.
25 He pulls it out of his back,
    the gleaming point out of his liver.

a 4 Or *Adam*

Despite the error of Zophar's assumptions, his words can be appreciated as a masterful piece of literature containing elements of genuine truth.

Zophar had eloquence and sincerity, but no compassion. He left no room for repentance and put all his stress on material things. Job, on the other hand, was concerned at this point about his relationship with God, no matter what happened to his body or possessions (19:23–27). Take a few moments to review Paul's love passage of 1 Corinthians 13. Did either Zophar or Job gain anything by Zophar's lecture? Which of the two had a better handle on love?

Terrors[w] will come over him;[x]
26   total darkness[y] lies in wait for his treasures.
A fire unfanned will consume him[z]
and devour what is left in his tent.
27 The heavens will expose his guilt;
the earth will rise up against him.[a]
28 A flood will carry off his house,[b]
rushing waters[a] on the day of God's wrath.[c]
29 Such is the fate God allots the wicked,
the heritage appointed for them by God."[d]

Job 21

Then Job replied:

2 "Listen carefully to my words;
let this be the consolation you give me.
3 Bear with me while I speak,
and after I have spoken, mock on.[e]

4 "Is my complaint directed to man?
Why should I not be impatient?[f]
5 Look at me and be astonished;
clap your hand over your mouth.[g]
6 When I think about this, I am terrified;
trembling seizes my body.
7 Why do the wicked live on,
growing old and increasing in power?[h]
8 They see their children established around them,
their offspring before their eyes.[i]
9 Their homes are safe and free from fear;[j]
the rod of God is not upon them.
10 Their bulls never fail to breed;
their cows calve and do not miscarry.[k]
11 They send forth their children as a flock;
their little ones dance about.
12 They sing to the music of tambourine and harp;
they make merry to the sound of the flute.[l]
13 They spend their years in prosperity[m]
and go down to the grave[b] in peace.[c]
14 Yet they say to God, 'Leave us alone![n]
We have no desire to know your ways.[o]
15 Who is the Almighty, that we should serve him?
What would we gain by praying to him?'[p]

	20:25
	w Job 18:11
	x Job 16:13
	20:26
	y Job 18:18
	z Ps 21:9
	20:27
	a Dt 31:28
	20:28
	b Dt 28:31
	c Job 21:17,20,30
	20:29
	d Job 27:13
	21:3
	e Job 16:10
	21:4
	f Job 6:11
	21:5
	g Jdg 18:19; Job 29:9; 40:4
	21:7
	h Job 12:6; Ps 73:3; Jer 12:1; Hab 1:13
	21:8
	i Ps 17:14
	21:9
	j Ps 73:5
	21:10
	k Ex 23:26
	21:12
	l Ps 81:2
	21:13
	m Job 36:11
	21:14
	n Job 22:17
	o Pr 1:29
	21:15
	p Ex 5:2; Job 34:9; Mal 3:14

a 28 Or The possessions in his house will be carried off, / washed away   b 13 Hebrew Sheol
c 13 Or in an instant

Job 21:1–34

📖 Job was determined to prove that he had listened to what his counselors had said. So he quoted or alluded to their words and then refuted them. They had elaborated on the fate of the wicked (8:11–19; 15:20–35; 18:5–21; ch. 20), but Job insisted that experience shows just the reverse. The wicked, who don't want to know anything of God's ways and even consider prayer a useless exercise (vv. 14–15), often flourish in all they do. Far from dying prematurely, as Zophar assumed (20:11), they often live long and increase in power (v. 7). Job flatly denied (vv. 8,11) Bildad's claim that

the wicked have no offspring or descendants (18:19).

🖥 In verse 22 Job admitted that his knowledge of God's ways was deficient, but it was precisely this high view of God that had created a dilemma. Those who don't believe in an absolutely sovereign God can't possibly appreciate the depth of the problem Job presented in verses 23–26. The answer still eludes us. Even with our additional revelation (Rom. 8:28), how often don't we stand in anguish over the apparent injustice and seeming cruelty of God's providence? Is this apparent contradiction a problem for you? Are you willing to wait for heaven to understand fully?

21:17
q Job 18:5

21:18
r Job 13:25; Ps 1:4
21:19
s Ex 20:5;
Jer 31:29; Eze 18:2

21:20
t Ps 75:8; Isa 51:17
u Jer 25:15;
Rev 14:10
21:21
v Job 14:5
21:22
w Job 35:11; 36:22;
Isa 40:13-14;
Ro 11:34 x Ps 82:1

21:24
y Pr 3:8

21:26
z Job 24:20;
Ecc 9:2-3; Isa 14:11

21:28
a Job 1:3; 12:21;
31:37 b Job 8:22

21:30
c Pr 16:4
d Job 20:22,28;
2Pe 2:9

21:33
e Job 3:22; 17:16;
24:24 f Job 3:19

21:34
g Job 16:2

22:2
h Lk 17:10

16 But their prosperity is not in their own hands,
    so I stand aloof from the counsel of the wicked.

17 "Yet how often is the lamp of the wicked snuffed out? q
    How often does calamity come upon them,
    the fate God allots in his anger?

18 How often are they like straw before the wind,
    like chaff r swept away by a gale?

19 ⌞It is said,⌟ 'God stores up a man's punishment for his sons.' s
    Let him repay the man himself, so that he will know it!

20 Let his own eyes see his destruction;
    let him drink t of the wrath of the Almighty. a u

21 For what does he care about the family he leaves behind
    when his allotted months v come to an end?

22 "Can anyone teach knowledge to God, w
    since he judges even the highest? x

23 One man dies in full vigor,
    completely secure and at ease,

24 his body b well nourished,
    his bones rich with marrow. y

25 Another man dies in bitterness of soul,
    never having enjoyed anything good.

26 Side by side they lie in the dust,
    and worms cover them both. z

27 "I know full well what you are thinking,
    the schemes by which you would wrong me.

28 You say, 'Where now is the great man's a house,
    the tents where wicked men lived?' b

29 Have you never questioned those who travel?
    Have you paid no regard to their accounts—

30 that the evil man is spared from the day of calamity, c
    that he is delivered from c the day of wrath? d

31 Who denounces his conduct to his face?
    Who repays him for what he has done?

32 He is carried to the grave,
    and watch is kept over his tomb.

33 The soil in the valley is sweet to him; e
    all men follow after him,
    and a countless throng goes d before him. f

34 "So how can you console me g with your nonsense?
    Nothing is left of your answers but falsehood!"

Eliphaz

22

Then Eliphaz the Temanite replied:

2 "Can a man be of benefit to God? h
    Can even a wise man benefit him?

---

a 17-20 Verses 17 and 18 may be taken as exclamations and 19 and 20 as declarations.
b 24 The meaning of the Hebrew for this word is uncertain.   c 30 Or *man is reserved for the day of calamity, / that he is brought forth to*   d 33 Or */ as a countless throng went*

Job 22:1-30

Eliphaz, the least spiteful of the three, felt compelled to agree with Bildad and Zophar that Job was a wicked man. He accused Job of terrible social evils (vv. 6–9)—based solely on Job's suffering (vv. 10–11). Eliphaz made one last attempt to reach Job through a plea for

repentance (vv. 21–30). He was no doubt sincere, and in many ways his challenge was commendable. But his advice assumed that Job was an evil man whose primary desire was a return to health and prosperity (v. 21). In reality, Job wasn't ungodly and had made it clear that he yearned to see God and to be his friend (19:25–27).

3 What pleasure would it give the Almighty if you were righteous?
What would he gain if your ways were blameless?

4 "Is it for your piety that he rebukes you
and brings charges against you?[i]
5 Is not your wickedness great?
Are not your sins[j] endless?
6 You demanded security[k] from your brothers for no reason;
you stripped men of their clothing, leaving them naked.
7 You gave no water to the weary
and you withheld food from the hungry,[l]
8 though you were a powerful man, owning land—
an honored man,[m] living on it.
9 And you sent widows away empty-handed[n]
and broke the strength of the fatherless.
10 That is why snares are all around you,
why sudden peril terrifies you,
11 why it is so dark[o] you cannot see,
and why a flood of water covers you.[p]

12 "Is not God in the heights of heaven?[q]
And see how lofty are the highest stars!
13 Yet you say, 'What does God know?[r]
Does he judge through such darkness?[s]
14 Thick clouds[t] veil him, so he does not see us
as he goes about in the vaulted heavens.'
15 Will you keep to the old path
that evil men have trod?
16 They were carried off before their time,[u]
their foundations washed away by a flood.[v]
17 They said to God, 'Leave us alone!
What can the Almighty do to us?'[w]

22:4 [i] Job 14:3; 19:29; Ps 143:2
22:5 [j] Job 11:6; 15:5
22:6 [k] Ex 22:26; Dt 24:6,17; Eze 18:12,16
22:7 [l] Job 31:17,21,31
22:8 [m] Isa 3:3; 9:15
22:9 [n] Job 24:3,21
22:11 [o] Job 5:14 [p] Ps 69:1-2; 124:4-5; La 3:54
22:12 [q] Job 11:8
22:13 [r] Ps 10:11; Isa 29:15 [s] Eze 8:12
22:14 [t] Job 26:9
22:16 [u] Job 15:32 [v] Job 14:19; Mt 7:26-27
22:17 [w] Job 21:15

Eliphaz didn't "get" Job's wrestling with God. Job was expressing his deepest feelings of fear and bewilderment over what appeared to be an unjust and cruel providence, and Eliphaz was scandalized. To Eliphaz's black-and-white mentality, Job's words (backed by his troubles) were sad proof of his need to "get right" with God.

Do you use the comfort you have received to comfort others who suffer (2 Cor. 1:3–5)? Or do you use it as a hammer? Offering Christian counsel to a hurting person is serious business. Suffering can be a result of sin (cf. James 5:16), but Jesus was clear that this isn't always the case (John 9:1–3). We aren't to shy away from bringing comfort or Biblical reproof—but neither are we to heap false guilt or condemnation on a vulnerable brother or sister. Think on your own experience. Who has helped you the most in times of trouble? How were they of help to you? What spiritual counsel proved most beneficial? What part did compassion play?

22:12–14

Modern Arguments Against God's Existence

If anyone had a right to question God's power over evil, it was Job. Yet to their credit, neither Job nor his friends thought to question God's existence—though his interest and availability were at times sticking points for them. What do you think of the following modern arguments against God's existence? How would you refute them?

Problem of Evil: The coexistence of (1) an all-powerful God, (2) a perfectly good God, and (3) evil is logically impossible.

Absurdity: It's unreasonable to suggest that a single, all powerful, personal being is behind all of life.

Observation: Since we can't find empirical, scientific evidence of God, he must not exist.

Delusional: God is the childish longing for a perfect father.

Social: God is created by those in power to control the masses.

Projection: God is the projected image of a human being's essential nature.

22:18
x Job 12:6
y Job 21:16

22:19
z Ps 58:10; 107:42
a Ps 52:6

22:20
b Job 15:30

22:21
c Ps 34:8-10

22:23
d Job 8:5; Isa 31:6;
Zec 1:3 e Isa 19:22;
Ac 20:32
f Job 11:14
22:24
g Job 31:25

22:25
h Isa 33:6
22:26
i Job 27:10;
Isa 58:14
22:27
j Job 33:26; 34:28;
Isa 58:9

22:29
k Mt 23:12; 1Pe 5:5

22:30
l Job 42:7-8

18 Yet it was he who filled their houses with good things, x
    so I stand aloof from the counsel of the wicked. y

19 "The righteous see their ruin and rejoice; z
    the innocent mock a them, saying,
20 'Surely our foes are destroyed,
    and fire b devours their wealth.'

21 "Submit to God and be at peace with him;
    in this way prosperity will come to you. c
22 Accept instruction from his mouth
    and lay up his words in your heart.
23 If you return d to the Almighty, you will be restored: e
    If you remove wickedness far from your tent f
24 and assign your nuggets to the dust,
    your gold of Ophir to the rocks in the ravines, g
25 then the Almighty will be your gold,
    the choicest silver for you. h
26 Surely then you will find delight in the Almighty i
    and will lift up your face to God.
27 You will pray to him, j and he will hear you,
    and you will fulfill your vows.
28 What you decide on will be done,
    and light will shine on your ways.
29 When men are brought low and you say, 'Lift them up!'
    then he will save the downcast. k
30 He will deliver even one who is not innocent,
    who will be delivered through the cleanness of your hands." l

Job 23

Then Job replied:

23:2
m Job 7:11
n Job 6:3

23:4
o Job 13:18

23:6
p Job 9:4

2 "Even today my complaint m is bitter; n
    his hand a is heavy in spite of b my groaning.
3 If only I knew where to find him;
    if only I could go to his dwelling!
4 I would state my case o before him
    and fill my mouth with arguments.
5 I would find out what he would answer me,
    and consider what he would say.
6 Would he oppose me with great power? p
    No, he would not press charges against me.

---

a 2 Septuagint and Syriac; Hebrew / the hand on me   b 2 Or heavy on me in

---

Job 23:1—24:25

🔲 Chapter 23 finds Job again wanting a fair trial, in which case he was confident that he would be acquitted (cf. 13:13–19). Job was still frustrated over his apparent inability to have an audience with God, who knew he was an upright man.

In 24:1–12 Job described the terrible injustice that often exists in the world. The scene he depicted is heart-rending. Job couldn't understand why God is silent and indifferent (vv. 1,12) in the face of such misery, but the fact that God waits disproved his friends' theory of suffering. Job was no more out of God's favor as one of the victims than the criminal in verses 13–17 was in God's favor because of God's inaction.

In 24:18–24 Job seemed to agree with his counselors that suffering is God's punishment for sin. But he was agreeing only that eventually the wicked are punished. He still didn't accept that his suffering offered proof of his guilt. There had to be some other explanation, though he didn't know at the time what it was.

🔲 In the final verses of chapter 23, Job offered a rationale for his emotional language, which his friends had misunderstood. He was terrified by what he had come to accept as God's plan for his life (vv. 13–16). But the mystery was still there. Job didn't understand what God was doing. In verse 17 he cried out for removal of the thick darkness clouding the issues.

7 There an upright man could present his case before him, *q*
    and I would be delivered forever from my judge.

8 "But if I go to the east, he is not there;
    if I go to the west, I do not find him.
9 When he is at work in the north, I do not see him;
    when he turns to the south, I catch no glimpse of him. *r*
10 But he knows the way that I take;
    when he has tested me, *s* I will come forth as gold. *t*
11 My feet have closely followed his steps; *u*
    I have kept to his way without turning aside. *v*
12 I have not departed from the commands of his lips; *w*
    I have treasured the words of his mouth more than my daily bread. *x*

13 "But he stands alone, and who can oppose him?
    He does whatever he pleases. *y*
14 He carries out his decree against me,
    and many such plans he still has in store. *z*
15 That is why I am terrified before him;
    when I think of all this, I fear him.
16 God has made my heart faint; *a*
    the Almighty *b* has terrified me.
17 Yet I am not silenced by the darkness, *c*
    by the thick darkness that covers my face.

24 "Why does the Almighty not set times for judgment? *d*
        Why must those who know him look in vain for such days? *e*
2 Men move boundary stones; *f*
    they pasture flocks they have stolen.
3 They drive away the orphan's donkey
    and take the widow's ox in pledge. *g*
4 They thrust the needy from the path
    and force all the poor *h* of the land into hiding. *i*
5 Like wild donkeys in the desert,
    the poor go about their labor *j* of foraging food;
    the wasteland provides food for their children.
6 They gather fodder in the fields
    and glean in the vineyards of the wicked.
7 Lacking clothes, they spend the night naked;
    they have nothing to cover themselves in the cold. *k*
8 They are drenched by mountain rains
    and hug *l* the rocks for lack of shelter.
9 The fatherless *m* child is snatched from the breast;
    the infant of the poor is seized for a debt.
10 Lacking clothes, they go about naked;
    they carry the sheaves, but still go hungry.
11 They crush olives among the terraces *a*;
    they tread the winepresses, yet suffer thirst.
12 The groans of the dying rise from the city,

---

a 11 Or *olives between the millstones*; the meaning of the Hebrew for this word is uncertain.

23:7
q Job 13:3

23:9
r Job 9:11

23:10
s Ps 66:10; 139:1-3
t 1Pe 1:7

23:11
u Ps 17:5 *v* Ps 44:18

23:12
w Job 6:10
x Jn 4:32,34

23:13
y Ps 115:3

23:14
z 1Th 3:3

23:16
a Dt 20:3; Ps 22:14; Jer 51:46
b Job 27:2

23:17
c Job 19:8

24:1
d Jer 46:10 *e* Ac 1:7

24:2
f Dt 19:14; 27:17; Pr 23:10

24:3
g Dt 24:6,10,12,17; Job 22:6

24:4
h Job 29:12; 30:25; Ps 41:1 *i* Pr 28:28

24:5
j Ps 104:23

24:7
k Ex 22:27; Job 22:6

24:8
l La 4:5

24:9
m Dt 24:17

Chapter 24 deals with realities that are no less applicable today. Particularly wrenching is the description of children who are sold/seized to pay a debt and then forced into dangerous/oppressive labor (vv. 9–11). Have you heard the "souls of the wounded" crying for help? What are you doing about it?

Can you recall a time when you were so confused by the course your life was taking that you too begged God to drive away the fog and clue you in to his reasoning? The apostle Paul addressed this with words that still can give us tremendous hope: "Now we see but a poor reflection as in a mirror; then we shall see face to face. Now I know in part; then I shall know fully, even as I am fully known" (1 Cor. 13:12). Do you look forward to the "aha" of that day when everything falls into place?

24:12
n Eze 26:15
o Job 9:23
24:13
p Jn 3:19-20
q Isa 5:20

and the souls of the wounded cry out for help. [n]
But God charges no one with wrongdoing. [o]

13 "There are those who rebel against the light, [p]
who do not know its ways
or stay in its paths. [q]
14 When daylight is gone, the murderer rises up
and kills the poor and needy;
in the night he steals forth like a thief. [r]

24:14
r Ps 10:9
24:15
s Pr 7:8-9 t Ps 10:11

15 The eye of the adulterer watches for dusk; [s]
he thinks, 'No eye will see me,' [t]
and he keeps his face concealed.

24:16
u Ex 22:2; Mt 6:19
v Jn 3:20

16 In the dark, men break into houses, [u]
but by day they shut themselves in;
they want nothing to do with the light. [v]
17 For all of them, deep darkness is their morning[a];
they make friends with the terrors of darkness. [b]

24:18
w Job 9:26
x Job 22:16

18 "Yet they are foam [w] on the surface of the water; [x]
their portion of the land is cursed,
so that no one goes to the vineyards.

24:19
y Job 6:17
z Job 21:13

19 As heat and drought snatch away the melted snow, [y]
so the grave[c][z] snatches away those who have sinned.
20 The womb forgets them,
the worm feasts on them;
evil men are no longer remembered[a]
but are broken like a tree. [b]

24:20
a Job 18:17;
Pr 10:7 b Ps 31:12;
Da 4:14

21 They prey on the barren and childless woman,
and to the widow show no kindness. [c]
22 But God drags away the mighty by his power;

24:21
c Job 22:9

a 17 Or *them, their morning is like the shadow of death*   b 17 Or *of the shadow of death*
c 19 Hebrew *Sheol*

Snapshots

24:1–11

A Stolen Car and a Changed Life

One day in 1986, Charles Mully, a Kenyan businessman, arrived in Nairobi and began searching for a parking space. Some street children offered to help, but Mully ignored them. Returning from his errand, he was shocked to find his car missing. The boy he questioned was uncooperative, and the vehicle was never recovered.

Ironically, its loss irrevocably changed Mully's heart. The street children reminded him of his own disadvantaged early life. He was moved by their suffering but uncertain how to respond. The Mullys turned to God for answers.

> "I was convinced that God was calling me to start a street children ministry."

"After more than two years of prayer, I was convinced that God was calling me to start a street children ministry," explains Mully. He and his wife and their eight children determined to open their home to street children. He elected further to sell his several lucrative businesses. "Some people called me a fool and others even spread word . . . that I had gone crazy," recalls Mully. But his resolve was unstoppable.

Mully's ministry began humbly in 1989, when he convinced three children to live with his family—and help persuade others to abandon life on the streets. Today 450 children reside in two locations of Mully's Children's Home.

though they become established, they have no assurance of life. *d*

23 He may let them rest in a feeling of security, *e*
  but his eyes are on their ways. *f*
24 For a little while they are exalted, and then they are gone; *g*
  they are brought low and gathered up like all others;
  they are cut off like heads of grain. *h*

25 "If this is not so, who can prove me false
  and reduce my words to nothing?" *i*

Bildad

25 Then Bildad the Shuhite replied:

2 "Dominion and awe belong to God; *j*
  he establishes order in the heights of heaven.
3 Can his forces be numbered?
  Upon whom does his light not rise? *k*
4 How then can a man be righteous before God?
  How can one born of woman be pure? *l*
5 If even the moon *m* is not bright
  and the stars are not pure in his eyes, *n*
6 how much less man, who is but a maggot—
  a son of man, *o* who is only a worm!" *p*

Job

26 Then Job replied:

2 "How you have helped the powerless! *q*
  How you have saved the arm that is feeble! *r*
3 What advice you have offered to one without wisdom!
  And what great insight you have displayed!
4 Who has helped you utter these words?
  And whose spirit spoke from your mouth?

5 "The dead are in deep anguish, *s*
  those beneath the waters and all that live in them.
6 Death *a* *t* is naked before God;

a 6 Hebrew *Sheol*

24:22
d Dt 28:66
24:23
e Job 12:6
f Job 11:11
24:24
g Job 14:21;
Ps 37:10 *h* Isa 17:5

24:25
i Job 6:28; 27:4

25:2
j Job 9:4; Rev 1:6

25:3
k Jas 1:17

25:4
l Job 4:17; 14:4
25:5
m Job 31:26
n Job 15:15

25:6
o Job 7:17
p Ps 22:6

26:2
q Job 6:12 *r* Ps 71:9

26:5
s Ps 88:10

26:6
t Ps 139:8

Job 25:1–6

This speech is the last we hear of Job's three counselors. Bildad didn't bother to answer Job's recent challenge. In essence, he repeated what Eliphaz had already said about human depravity (4:17–21; 15:14–16). Bildad first attempted to show how God's power established order in the heavenly realm and that his dominion extends to all created beings. Then, in verse 4, he repeated the critical question Job had asked in 9:2, "How can a mortal man be righteous before God?" Bildad's answer: God is inaccessible because he's too pure. Every human being, like Job, is a hopeless worm.

Aren't you glad that even if Bildad had the last word in the three counselors' attempts to "straighten out" Job, he didn't have the last word from God's perspective?! Beyond the rebuke Bildad and his friends would receive from the Lord in 42:7–8, God had said, "Let us make man in our image" (Gen. 1:26). And God inspired David, in his reflections about life, to declare: "You made [man] a little lower than the heavenly beings

and crowned him with glory and honor" (Ps. 8:5).

God's Word asserts the reality of our fallen nature but also announces the remedy of God's grace (e.g., Paul's argument in Rom. 8). Thanks be to God that we don't have to come crawling to him like a worm and that we *can* "be righteous before God" (Job 25:4) by appropriating Christ's righteousness as our own (2 Cor. 5:21)!

Job 26:1—31:40

Chapter 26 breaks into two parts: Job's sarcastic reaction to Bildad (vv. 1–4) and a poem celebrating God's unlimited power (vv. 5–14), which was also the theme of Bildad's final speech. Job wanted to know who had "written Bildad's material" (v. 4). He scoffed at the argument that God's very majesty and power made it impossible for people to be righteous before him (25:4–6). If Job was a sinful worm whose case was hopeless, his "friends" were equally hopeless as counselors. Job left humans standing before the mystery of God's power with unanswered questions (26:14)—but not as maggots (25:6).

Destruction[a] lies uncovered. [u]

26:6
u Job 41:11;
Pr 15:11; Heb 4:13
26:7
v Job 9:8
26:8
w Pr 30:4
x Job 37:11

7 He spreads out the northern ˌskies [v] over empty space;
    he suspends the earth over nothing.
8 He wraps up the waters [w] in his clouds, [x]
    yet the clouds do not burst under their weight.

26:9
y Job 22:14;
Ps 97:2
26:10
z Pr 8:27,29
a Job 38:8-11

9 He covers the face of the full moon,
    spreading his clouds [y] over it.
10 He marks out the horizon on the face of the waters [z]
    for a boundary between light and darkness. [a]
11 The pillars of the heavens quake,
    aghast at his rebuke.

26:12
b Ex 14:21;
Isa 51:15; Jer 31:35
c Job 12:13

12 By his power he churned up the sea; [b]
    by his wisdom [c] he cut Rahab to pieces.

26:13
d Isa 27:1

13 By his breath the skies became fair;
    his hand pierced the gliding serpent. [d]

26:14
e Job 36:29

14 And these are but the outer fringe of his works;
    how faint the whisper we hear of him!
    Who then can understand the thunder of his power?" [e]

27:1
f Job 29:1

27 And Job continued his discourse: [f]

27:2
g Job 34:5
h Job 9:18

2 "As surely as God lives, who has denied me justice, [g]
    the Almighty, who has made me taste bitterness of soul, [h]

27:3
i Job 32:8; 33:4

3 as long as I have life within me,
    the breath of God [i] in my nostrils,

27:4
j Job 6:28

4 my lips will not speak wickedness,
    and my tongue will utter no deceit. [j]

27:5
k Job 2:9; 13:15

5 I will never admit you are in the right;
    till I die, I will not deny my integrity. [k]

27:6
l Job 2:3

6 I will maintain my righteousness and never let go of it;
    my conscience will not reproach me as long as I live. [l]

7 "May my enemies be like the wicked,
    my adversaries like the unjust!

27:8
m Job 8:13
n Job 11:20;
Lk 12:20

8 For what hope has the godless [m] when he is cut off,
    when God takes away his life? [n]

27:9
o Job 35:12;
Pr 1:28; Isa 1:15;
Jer 14:12; Mic 3:4
27:10
p Job 22:26

9 Does God listen to his cry
    when distress comes upon him? [o]
10 Will he find delight in the Almighty? [p]
    Will he call upon God at all times?

11 "I will teach you about the power of God;
    the ways of the Almighty I will not conceal.
12 You have all seen this yourselves.
    Why then this meaningless talk?

27:13
q Job 15:20; 20:29
27:14
r Dt 28:41;
Job 15:22;
Hos 9:13

13 "Here is the fate God allots to the wicked,
    the heritage a ruthless man receives from the Almighty: [q]
14 However many his children, their fate is the sword; [r]

a 6 Hebrew *Abaddon*

Chapter 27 also divides into two parts: Job spoke directly to his friends with words a falsely accused victim might utter before a tribunal (vv. 1–12), followed by a poem describing the ultimate fate of the wicked (vv. 13–23). Chapter 28 is comprised of a striking poem that answers the question "Where can wisdom be found?" (vv. 12,20). The ultimate answer is that wisdom is found only in God and in fearing him (vv. 21–28).

Like a lawyer's summation, Job presented a three-part closing argument. He began with an emotional memory of his former happiness, wealth, and honor (ch. 29); proceeded to lament his loss of everything—especially his dignity, even in relation to God (ch. 30); and concluded with a final protest of innocence (ch. 31). There was no more Job could say. The case rested in God's hands.

his offspring will never have enough to eat. [s]

15 The plague will bury those who survive him,
   and their widows will not weep for them. [t]

16 Though he heaps up silver like dust
   and clothes like piles of clay, [u]

17 what he lays up the righteous will wear, [v]
   and the innocent will divide his silver.

18 The house he builds is like a moth's cocoon, [w]
   like a hut [x] made by a watchman.

19 He lies down wealthy, but will do so no more; [y]
   when he opens his eyes, all is gone.

20 Terrors overtake him like a flood; [z]
   a tempest snatches him away in the night. [a]

21 The east wind carries him off, and he is gone;
   it sweeps him out of his place. [b]

22 It hurls itself against him without mercy [c]
   as he flees headlong from its power. [d]

23 It claps its hands in derision
   and hisses him out of his place. [e]

28

"There is a mine for silver
   and a place where gold is refined.

2 Iron is taken from the earth,
   and copper is smelted from ore. [f]

3 Man puts an end to the darkness; [g]
   he searches the farthest recesses
   for ore in the blackest darkness.

4 Far from where people dwell he cuts a shaft,
   in places forgotten by the foot of man;
   far from men he dangles and sways.

5 The earth, from which food comes, [h]
   is transformed below as by fire;

6 sapphires [a] come from its rocks,
   and its dust contains nuggets of gold.

7 No bird of prey knows that hidden path,
   no falcon's eye has seen it.

8 Proud beasts do not set foot on it,
   and no lion prowls there.

9 Man's hand assaults the flinty rock
   and lays bare the roots of the mountains.

10 He tunnels through the rock;
   his eyes see all its treasures.

11 He searches [b] the sources of the rivers
   and brings hidden things to light.

12 "But where can wisdom be found? [i]

a 6 Or *lapis lazuli*; also in verse 16   b 11 Septuagint, Aquila and Vulgate; Hebrew *He dams up*

27:14
s Job 20:10
27:15
t Ps 78:64
27:16
u Zec 9:3
27:17
v Pr 28:8; Ecc 2:26
27:18
w Job 8:14 x Isa 1:8
27:19
y Job 7:8
27:20
z Job 15:21
a Job 20:8

27:21
b Job 7:10; 21:18
27:22
c Jer 13:14;
Eze 5:11; 24:14
d Job 11:20
27:23
e Job 18:18

28:2
f Dt 8:9
28:3
g Ecc 1:13

28:5
h Ps 104:14

28:12
i Ecc 7:24

As do ours! And the endless problems confronting our world. God wants to hear from us, and that burning desire for our communication and feedback goes beyond his longing for praise and worship. But in the final analysis we can rest in the certain knowledge that the whole world/cosmos is indeed "in his hands."

One fundamental "plank" in Job's summation was his treatment of the poor (29:12–17). Job refuted Eliphaz's claim that he must have harmed the needy and defenseless (22:5–9). He insisted that his righteousness

had been demonstrated by the good deeds he had done: rescuing the destitute and fatherless, caring for widows, upholding justice, helping the disabled, siding with the just cause of strangers, and snatching vulnerable victims from those who intended them harm. Could you make the same claims before God and the community of faith? Others need to know that we are people of faith. What acts of kindness/compassion demonstrate your faith in the living God?

Where does understanding dwell?
13 Man does not comprehend its worth; *j*
   it cannot be found in the land of the living.
14 The deep says, 'It is not in me';
   the sea says, 'It is not with me.'
15 It cannot be bought with the finest gold,
   nor can its price be weighed in silver. *k*
16 It cannot be bought with the gold of Ophir,
   with precious onyx or sapphires.
17 Neither gold nor crystal can compare with it,
   nor can it be had for jewels of gold. *l*
18 Coral and jasper are not worthy of mention;
   the price of wisdom is beyond rubies. *m*
19 The topaz of Cush cannot compare with it;
   it cannot be bought with pure gold. *n*

20 "Where then does wisdom come from?
   Where does understanding dwell? *o*
21 It is hidden from the eyes of every living thing,
   concealed even from the birds of the air.
22 Destruction *a p* and Death say,
   'Only a rumor of it has reached our ears.'
23 God understands the way to it
   and he alone knows where it dwells, *q*
24 for he views the ends of the earth *r*
   and sees everything under the heavens. *s*
25 When he established the force of the wind
   and measured out the waters, *t*
26 when he made a decree for the rain
   and a path for the thunderstorm, *u*
27 then he looked at wisdom and appraised it;
   he confirmed it and tested it.
28 And he said to man,
   'The fear of the Lord—that is wisdom,
   and to shun evil is understanding.' *v* "

29

Job continued his discourse: *w*

2 "How I long for the months gone by,
   for the days when God watched over me, *x*
3 when his lamp shone upon my head
   and by his light I walked through darkness! *y*
4 Oh, for the days when I was in my prime,
   when God's intimate friendship blessed my house, *z*
5 when the Almighty was still with me
   and my children were around me,
6 when my path was drenched with cream *a*
   and the rock *b* poured out for me streams of olive oil. *c*

7 "When I went to the gate *d* of the city
   and took my seat in the public square,
8 the young men saw me and stepped aside
   and the old men rose to their feet;
9 the chief men refrained from speaking
   and covered their mouths with their hands; *e*
10 the voices of the nobles were hushed,
   and their tongues stuck to the roof of their mouths. *f*

a 22 Hebrew *Abaddon*

Cross references (left margin):

28:13 *j* Pr 3:15; Mt 13:44-46

28:15 *k* Pr 3:13-14; 8:10-11; 16:16

28:17 *l* Pr 16:16

28:18 *m* Pr 3:15

28:19 *n* Pr 8:19

28:20 *o* ver 23,28

28:22 *p* Job 26:6

28:23 *q* Pr 8:22-31
28:24 *r* Ps 33:13-14; *s* Pr 15:3

28:25 *t* Job 12:15; Ps 135:7

28:26 *u* Job 37:3,8,11; 38:25,27

28:28 *v* Dt 4:6; Ps 111:10; Pr 1:7; 9:10
29:1 *w* Job 13:12; 27:1

29:2 *x* Jer 31:28

29:3 *y* Job 11:17

29:4 *z* Ps 25:14; Pr 3:32

29:6 *a* Job 20:17 *b* Ps 81:16 *c* Dt 32:13

29:7 *d* Job 31:21

29:9 *e* Job 21:5

29:10 *f* Ps 137:6

11 Whoever heard me spoke well of me,
  and those who saw me commended me,
12 because I rescued the poor *g* who cried for help,
  and the fatherless *h* who had none to assist him. *i*
13 The man who was dying blessed me; *j*
  I made the widow's *k* heart sing.
14 I put on righteousness *l* as my clothing;
  justice was my robe and my turban.
15 I was eyes *m* to the blind
  and feet to the lame.
16 I was a father to the needy; *n*
  I took up the case of the stranger.
17 I broke the fangs of the wicked
  and snatched the victims from their teeth. *o*
18 "I thought, 'I will die in my own house,
  my days as numerous as the grains of sand. *p*
19 My roots will reach to the water, *q*
  and the dew will lie all night on my branches.
20 My glory will remain fresh in me,
  the bow *r* ever new in my hand.' *s*
21 "Men listened to me expectantly,
  waiting in silence for my counsel.
22 After I had spoken, they spoke no more;
  my words fell gently on their ears. *t*
23 They waited for me as for showers
  and drank in my words as the spring rain.
24 When I smiled at them, they scarcely believed it;

29:12
g Job 24:4
h Job 31:17,21
i Ps 72:12; Pr 21:13
29:13
j Job 31:20
k Job 22:9
29:14
l Job 27:6;
Ps 132:9; Isa 59:17;
61:10; Eph 6:14
29:15
m Nu 10:31

29:16
n Job 24:4; Pr 29:7

29:17
o Ps 3:7

29:18
p Ps 30:6

29:19
q Job 18:16;
Jer 17:8

29:20
r Ps 18:34
s Ge 49:24

29:22
t Dt 32:2

Snapshots

29:12–13

A Place for Children

In the late 1980s, Angela Miyanda found herself caught up in change. Her husband had helped form a political party to challenge Zambia's one-party system. Only a few years later the family was thrust into the second most powerful position in the land.

While Mr. Miyanda was occupied with affairs of state, Mrs. Miyanda also was busy. Five kilometers from Government House is a shanty compound called Kalikiliki—a place lacking social infrastructure, a primary school, a clinic, or safe running water. Mrs. Miyanda worked to empower the women there.

Mrs. Miyanda focused her attention on children. Kabwata Orphanage and Transit Home was registered in 1997. What had been conceived out of a vision, compassion, and challenging Biblical messages finally gave birth to a haven for abused children. Babies born in the Lusaka's two prisons also are taken there. And it has been recognized by international organizations as a place for refugee children separated from their families.

With Zambia reeling from the effects of HIV/AIDS and the traditional extended family system collapsing, Mrs. Miyanda foresees a day when the number of orphans will be overwhelming.

> **W**hat had been conceived out of a vision, compassion, and challenging Biblical messages finally gave birth to a haven for abused children.

the light of my face was precious to them. [a]

29:25
u Job 1:3; 31:37
v Job 4:4

25 I chose the way for them and sat as their chief;
    I dwelt as a king [u] among his troops;
    I was like one who comforts mourners. [v]

30:1
w Job 12:4

30

"But now they mock me, [w]
    men younger than I,
whose fathers I would have disdained
    to put with my sheep dogs.
2 Of what use was the strength of their hands to me,
    since their vigor had gone from them?
3 Haggard from want and hunger,
    they roamed [b] the parched land
    in desolate wastelands at night.
4 In the brush they gathered salt herbs,
    and their food [c] was the root of the broom tree.
5 They were banished from their fellow men,
    shouted at as if they were thieves.
6 They were forced to live in the dry stream beds,
    among the rocks and in holes in the ground.
7 They brayed among the bushes
    and huddled in the undergrowth.
8 A base and nameless brood,
    they were driven out of the land.

30:9
x Ps 69:11
y Job 12:4;
La 3:14,63
z Job 17:6
30:10
a Nu 12:14;
Dt 25:9; Isa 50:6;
Mt 26:67
30:11
b Ru 1:21 e Ps 32:9
30:12
d Ps 140:4-5
e Job 19:12
30:13
f Isa 3:12

9 "And now their sons mock me [x] in song; [y]
    I have become a byword [z] among them.
10 They detest me and keep their distance;
    they do not hesitate to spit in my face. [a]
11 Now that God has unstrung my bow and afflicted me, [b]
    they throw off restraint [c] in my presence.
12 On my right the tribe [d] attacks;
    they lay snares for my feet, [d]
    they build their siege ramps against me. [e]
13 They break up my road; [f]
    they succeed in destroying me—
    without anyone's helping them. [e]
14 They advance as through a gaping breach;
    amid the ruins they come rolling in.

30:15
g Job 31:23;
Ps 55:4-5
h Job 3:25;
Hos 13:3
30:16
i Job 3:24;
Ps 22:14; 42:4

15 Terrors overwhelm me; [g]
    my dignity is driven away as by the wind,
    my safety vanishes like a cloud. [h]
16 "And now my life ebbs away; [i]
    days of suffering grip me.
17 Night pierces my bones;
    my gnawing pains never rest.
18 In his great power ⌊God⌋ becomes like clothing to me [f];
    he binds me like the neck of my garment.

30:19
j Ps 69:2,14

19 He throws me into the mud, [j]
    and I am reduced to dust and ashes.

30:20
k Job 19:7

20 "I cry out to you, O God, but you do not answer; [k]
    I stand up, but you merely look at me.

30:21
l Job 19:6,22
m Job 16:9,14
n Job 10:3

21 You turn on me ruthlessly; [l]
    with the might of your hand [m] you attack me. [n]

---

[a] 24 The meaning of the Hebrew for this clause is uncertain.   [b] 3 Or gnawed   [c] 4 Or fuel
[d] 12 The meaning of the Hebrew for this word is uncertain.   [e] 13 Or me. / 'No one can help him,'
⌊they say⌋.   [f] 18 Hebrew; Septuagint ⌊God⌋ grasps my clothing

22 You snatch me up and drive me before the wind;[o]
    you toss me about in the storm.[p]
23 I know you will bring me down to death,[q]
    to the place appointed for all the living.[r]

24 "Surely no one lays a hand on a broken man
    when he cries for help in his distress.[s]
25 Have I not wept for those in trouble?
    Has not my soul grieved for the poor?[t]
26 Yet when I hoped for good, evil came;
    when I looked for light, then came darkness.[u]
27 The churning inside me never stops;[v]
    days of suffering confront me.
28 I go about blackened,[w] but not by the sun;
    I stand up in the assembly and cry for help.[x]
29 I have become a brother of jackals,[y]
    a companion of owls.[z]
30 My skin grows black and peels;[a]
    my body burns with fever.[b]
31 My harp is tuned to mourning,[c]
    and my flute to the sound of wailing.

31

"I made a covenant with my eyes
    not to look lustfully at a girl.[d]
2 For what is man's lot from God above,
    his heritage from the Almighty on high?[e]
3 Is it not ruin[f] for the wicked,
    disaster for those who do wrong?[g]
4 Does he not see my ways[h]
    and count my every step?[i]

5 "If I have walked in falsehood
    or my foot has hurried after deceit[j]—
6 let God weigh me in honest scales[k]
    and he will know that I am blameless—
7 if my steps have turned from the path,[l]
    if my heart has been led by my eyes,
    or if my hands[m] have been defiled,
8 then may others eat what I have sown,[n]
    and may my crops be uprooted.[o]

9 "If my heart has been enticed[p] by a woman,
    or if I have lurked at my neighbor's door,
10 then may my wife grind another man's grain,
    and may other men sleep with her.[q]
11 For that would have been shameful,
    a sin to be judged.[r]
12 It is a fire[s] that burns to Destruction[a];[t]
    it would have uprooted my harvest.[u]

13 "If I have denied justice to my menservants and maidservants
    when they had a grievance against me,[v]
14 what will I do when God confronts me?
    What will I answer when called to account?
15 Did not he who made me in the womb make them?
    Did not the same one form us both within our mothers?[w]

16 "If I have denied the desires of the poor[x]
    or let the eyes of the widow[y] grow weary,

a 12 Hebrew Abaddon

Cross references

30:22
o Job 27:21
p Job 9:17
30:23
q Job 9:22; 10:8
r Job 3:19

30:24
s Job 19:7

30:25
t Job 24:4;
Ps 35:13-14;
Ro 12:15
30:26
u Job 3:25-26; 19:8;
Jer 8:15
30:27
v La 2:11
30:28
w Ps 38:6; 42:9;
43:2 x Job 19:7
30:29
y Ps 44:19
z Ps 102:6; Mic 1:8

30:30
a La 4:8 b Ps 102:3

30:31
c Isa 24:8

31:1
d Mt 5:28

31:2
e Job 20:29
31:3
f Job 21:30
g Job 34:22
31:4
h 2Ch 16:9 i Pr 5:21

31:5
j Mic 2:11
31:6
k Job 6:2; 27:5-6

31:7
l Job 23:11
m Job 9:30

31:8
n Lev 26:16;
Job 20:18
o Mic 6:15
31:9
p Job 24:15

31:10
q Dt 28:30; Jer 8:10

31:11
r Ge 38:24;
Lev 20:10;
Dt 22:22-24
31:12
s Job 15:30
t Job 26:6
u Job 20:28
31:13
v Dt 24:14-15

31:15
w Job 10:3
31:16
x Job 5:16; 20:19
y Job 22:9

17 if I have kept my bread to myself,
    not sharing it with the fatherless ^z—
18 but from my youth I reared him as would a father,
    and from my birth I guided the widow—
19 if I have seen anyone perishing for lack of clothing, ^a
    or a needy ^b man without a garment,
20 and his heart did not bless me
    for warming him with the fleece from my sheep,
21 if I have raised my hand against the fatherless, ^c
    knowing that I had influence in court,
22 then let my arm fall from the shoulder,
    let it be broken off at the joint. ^d
23 For I dreaded destruction from God,
    and for fear of his splendor ^e I could not do such things.

24 "If I have put my trust in gold ^f
    or said to pure gold, 'You are my security,' ^g
25 if I have rejoiced over my great wealth, ^h
    the fortune my hands had gained,
26 if I have regarded the sun ⁱ in its radiance
    or the moon moving in splendor,
27 so that my heart was secretly enticed
    and my hand offered them a kiss of homage,
28 then these also would be sins to be judged, ^j
    for I would have been unfaithful to God on high.

29 "If I have rejoiced at my enemy's misfortune ^k
    or gloated over the trouble that came to him ^l—
30 I have not allowed my mouth to sin
    by invoking a curse against his life—
31 if the men of my household have never said,
    'Who has not had his fill of Job's meat?' ^m—
32 but no stranger had to spend the night in the street,
    for my door was always open to the traveler ⁿ—
33 if I have concealed ^o my sin as men do, ^a
    by hiding ^p my guilt in my heart
34 because I so feared the crowd ^q
    and so dreaded the contempt of the clans
    that I kept silent and would not go outside—

35 ("Oh, that I had someone to hear me! ^r
    I sign now my defense—let the Almighty answer me;
    let my accuser ^s put his indictment in writing.
36 Surely I would wear it on my shoulder,
    I would put it on like a crown.
37 I would give him an account of my every step;
    like a prince ^t I would approach him.)—

38 "if my land cries out against me ^u
    and all its furrows are wet with tears,
39 if I have devoured its yield without payment ^v
    or broken the spirit of its tenants, ^w
40 then let briers ^x come up instead of wheat
    and weeds instead of barley."

The words of Job are ended.

^a 33 Or *as Adam did*

Elihu

32 So these three men stopped answering Job, because he was righteous in his own eyes. [y] 2 But Elihu son of Barakel the Buzite, [z] of the family of Ram, became very angry with Job for justifying himself rather than God. [a] 3 He was also angry with the three friends, because they had found no way to refute Job, and yet had condemned him. [a] 4 Now Elihu had waited before speaking to Job because they were older than he. 5 But when he saw that the three men had nothing more to say, his anger was aroused.

6 So Elihu son of Barakel the Buzite said:

> "I am young in years,
>   and you are old; [b]
> that is why I was fearful,
>   not daring to tell you what I know.
> 7 I thought, 'Age should speak;
>   advanced years should teach wisdom.'
> 8 But it is the spirit [b] in a man,
>   the breath of the Almighty, [c] that gives him understanding. [d]
> 9 It is not only the old [c] who are wise, [e]
>   not only the aged who understand what is right.

> 10 "Therefore I say: Listen to me;
>   I too will tell you what I know.
> 11 I waited while you spoke,
>   I listened to your reasoning;
> while you were searching for words,
> 12   I gave you my full attention.
> But not one of you has proved Job wrong;
>   none of you has answered his arguments.
> 13 Do not say, 'We have found wisdom; [f]
>   let God refute him, not man.'
> 14 But Job has not marshaled his words against me,
>   and I will not answer him with your arguments.

> 15 "They are dismayed and have no more to say;
>   words have failed them.
> 16 Must I wait, now that they are silent,
>   now that they stand there with no reply?
> 17 I too will have my say;
>   I too will tell what I know.
> 18 For I am full of words,
>   and the spirit within me compels me;
> 19 inside I am like bottled-up wine,
>   like new wineskins ready to burst.
> 20 I must speak and find relief;
>   I must open my lips and reply.
> 21 I will show partiality [g] to no one, [h]

---

[a] 3 Masoretic Text; an ancient Hebrew scribal tradition *Job, and so had condemned God*
[b] 8 Or *Spirit*; also in verse 18   [c] 9 Or *many*; or *great*

Cross references (margin):
32:1 [y] Job 10:7; 33:9
32:2 [z] Ge 22:21   [a] Job 27:5; 30:21
32:6 [b] Job 15:10
32:8 [c] Job 27:3; 33:4   [d] Pr 2:6
32:9 [e] 1Co 1:26
32:13 [f] Jer 9:23
32:21 [g] Lev 19:15; Job 13:10   [h] Mt 22:16

Job 32:1—37:24

Enter Elihu, a young man who in deference to age had waited with increasing impatience for the opportunity to speak. Three times in 32:2–4 we are told that he was angry: once at Job, for vindicating himself rather than God, then twice at the friends because of their inability to prove Job wrong—which he felt, in effect, also condemned God (see NIV text note on v. 3).

In chapter 33 Elihu turned and spoke directly to Job.

Unlike the three friends, he addressed Job by name (vv. 1,31; cf. 37:14). Elihu's refutation of Job beginning in verse 8 reveals his style: quotations (or paraphrases) of Job's words (vv. 9–11), followed by explanation of how he was "wrong." Elihu, a self-proclaimed teacher of wisdom, claimed that he wanted Job cleared. Yet he believed this would only happen if Job would "speak up"—in repentance (vv. 31–33).

Again in chapter 34, Elihu's method was to quote Job

nor will I flatter any man;
22 for if I were skilled in flattery,
my Maker would soon take me away.

33 "But now, Job, listen to my words;
pay attention to everything I say.[i]
2 I am about to open my mouth;
my words are on the tip of my tongue.
3 My words come from an upright heart;
my lips sincerely speak what I know.[j]
4 The Spirit of God has made me;[k]
the breath of the Almighty[l] gives me life.
5 Answer me[m] then, if you can;
prepare[n] yourself and confront me.
6 I am just like you before God;
I too have been taken from clay.[o]
7 No fear of me should alarm you,
nor should my hand be heavy upon you.[p]

8 "But you have said in my hearing—
I heard the very words—
9 'I am pure[q] and without sin;[r]
I am clean and free from guilt.
10 Yet God has found fault with me;
he considers me his enemy.[s]
11 He fastens my feet in shackles;[t]
he keeps close watch on all my paths.'[u]

12 "But I tell you, in this you are not right,
for God is greater than man.[v]
13 Why do you complain to him[w]
that he answers none of man's words[a]?
14 For God does speak[x]—now one way, now another—
though man may not perceive it.
15 In a dream,[y] in a vision of the night,
when deep sleep falls on men
as they slumber in their beds,
16 he may speak[z] in their ears
and terrify them with warnings,
17 to turn man from wrongdoing
and keep him from pride,
18 to preserve his soul from the pit,[b][a]
his life from perishing by the sword.[c][b]
19 Or a man may be chastened on a bed of pain
with constant distress in his bones,[c]
20 so that his very being finds food[d] repulsive
and his soul loathes the choicest meal.[e]
21 His flesh wastes away to nothing,
and his bones, once hidden, now stick out.[f]
22 His soul draws near to the pit,[d]
and his life to the messengers of death.[e][g]

33:1 [i] Job 13:6
33:3 [j] Job 6:28; 27:4; 36:4
33:4 [k] Ge 2:7; Job 10:3 [l] Job 27:3
33:5 [m] ver 32 [n] Job 13:18
33:6 [o] Job 4:19
33:7 [p] Job 9:34; 13:21; 2Co 2:4
33:9 [q] Job 10:7 [r] Job 13:23; 16:17
33:10 [s] Job 13:24
33:11 [t] Job 13:27 [u] Job 14:16
33:12 [v] Ecc 7:20
33:13 [w] Job 40:2; Isa 45:9
33:14 [x] Ps 62:11
33:15 [y] Job 4:13
33:16 [z] Job 36:10,15
33:18 [a] ver 22,24,28,30 [b] Job 15:22
33:19 [c] Job 30:17
33:20 [d] Ps 107:18 [e] Job 3:24; 6:6
33:21 [f] Job 16:8; 19:20
33:22 [g] Ps 88:3

[a] 13 Or *that he does not answer for any of his actions* [b] 18 Or *preserve him from the grave* [c] 18 Or *from crossing the River* [d] 22 Or *He draws near to the grave* [e] 22 Or *to the dead*

(vv. 5–6)—with the purpose of showing that his words were theologically unsound. Like the counselors, Elihu picked out only those words of Job he needed to prove his point. But, unlike them, he didn't totally condemn Job. Elihu thought that Job, through association with the wicked, had picked up some of their views (vv. 8–9). He was zealous to counter Job's complaint that God treats the wicked and the righteous alike, for this would mean that God does evil (vv. 10–30). Elihu was convinced Job needed to repent of such a rebellious notion (vv. 31–37).

23 "Yet if there is an angel on his side
    as a mediator, one out of a thousand,
    to tell a man what is right for him, [h]
24 to be gracious to him and say,
    'Spare him from going down to the pit [a]; [i]
    I have found a ransom for him'—
25 then his flesh is renewed like a child's;
    it is restored as in the days of his youth. [j]
26 He prays to God and finds favor with him, [k]
    he sees God's face and shouts for joy; [l]
    he is restored by God to his righteous state. [m]
27 Then he comes to men and says,
    'I sinned, [n] and perverted what was right, [o]
    but I did not get what I deserved. [p]
28 He redeemed my soul from going down to the pit, [b]
    and I will live to enjoy the light.' [q]

29 "God does all these things to a man [r]—
    twice, even three times—
30 to turn back his soul from the pit, [c]
    that the light of life [s] may shine on him.

31 "Pay attention, Job, and listen to me;
    be silent, and I will speak.
32 If you have anything to say, answer me;
    speak up, for I want you to be cleared.
33 But if not, then listen to me;
    be silent, and I will teach you wisdom. [t]"

34

Then Elihu said:

2 "Hear my words, you wise men;
    listen to me, you men of learning.
3 For the ear tests words
    as the tongue tastes food. [u]
4 Let us discern for ourselves what is right;
    let us learn together what is good. [v]

5 "Job says, 'I am innocent, [w]
    but God denies me justice. [x]
6 Although I am right,
    I am considered a liar;
    although I am guiltless,
    his arrow inflicts an incurable wound.' [y]
7 What man is like Job,
    who drinks scorn like water? [z]
8 He keeps company with evildoers;
    he associates with wicked men. [a]
9 For he says, 'It profits a man nothing
    when he tries to please God.' [b]

10 "So listen to me, you men of understanding.
    Far be it from God to do evil, [c]
    from the Almighty to do wrong. [d]
11 He repays a man for what he has done; [e]
    he brings upon him what his conduct deserves. [f]
12 It is unthinkable that God would do wrong,

---

[a] 24 Or grave   [b] 28 Or redeemed me from going down to the grave   [c] 30 Or turn him back from the grave

---

33:23
[h] Mic 6:8

33:24
[i] Isa 38:17

33:25
[j] 2Ki 5:14
33:26
[k] Job 34:28
[l] Job 22:26
[m] Ps 50:15; 51:12

33:27
[n] 2Sa 12:13
[o] Lk 15:21
[p] Ro 6:21
33:28
[q] Job 22:28
33:29
[r] 1Co 12:6;
Eph 1:11; Php 2:13

33:30
[s] Ps 56:13

33:33
[t] Ps 34:11

34:3
[u] Job 12:11

34:4
[v] 1Th 5:21
34:5
[w] Job 33:9
[x] Job 27:2

34:6
[y] Job 6:4

34:7
[z] Job 15:16

34:8
[a] Job 22:15;
Ps 50:18
34:9
[b] Job 21:15; 35:3

34:10
[c] Ge 18:25
[d] Dt 32:4; Job 8:3;
Ro 9:14
34:11
[e] Ps 62:12;
Mt 16:27; Ro 2:6;
2Co 5:10
[f] Jer 32:19;
Eze 33:20

34:12
g Job 8:3

that the Almighty would pervert justice. *g*

34:13
h Job 38:4,6

13 Who appointed him over the earth?
Who put him in charge of the whole world? *h*

34:14
i Ps 104:29

14 If it were his intention
and he withdrew his spirit *a* and breath, *i*

34:15
j Ge 3:19; Job 9:22

15 all mankind would perish together
and man would return to the dust. *j*

16 "If you have understanding, hear this;
listen to what I say.

34:17
k 2Sa 23:3-4
l Job 40:8

17 Can he who hates justice govern? *k*
Will you condemn the just and mighty One? *l*

34:18
m Ex 22:28
34:19
n Dt 10:17;
Ac 10:34
o Lev 19:15
p Job 10:3

18 Is he not the One who says to kings, 'You are worthless,'
and to nobles, 'You are wicked,' *m*
19 who shows no partiality *n* to princes
and does not favor the rich over the poor, *o*
for they are all the work of his hands? *p*

34:20
q Ex 12:29
r Job 12:19

20 They die in an instant, in the middle of the night; *q*
the people are shaken and they pass away;
the mighty are removed without human hand. *r*

34:21
s Job 31:4; Pr 15:3
34:22
t Ps 139:12
u Am 9:2-3

21 "His eyes are on the ways of men;
he sees their every step. *s*
22 There is no dark place, *t* no deep shadow, *u*
where evildoers can hide.

34:23
v Job 11:11
34:24
w Job 12:19
x Da 2:21

23 God has no need to examine men further,
that they should come before him for judgment. *v*
24 Without inquiry he shatters the mighty *w*
and sets up others in their place. *x*
25 Because he takes note of their deeds,
he overthrows them in the night and they are crushed.
26 He punishes them for their wickedness
where everyone can see them,

34:27
y Ps 28:5; Isa 5:12
z 1Sa 15:11

27 because they turned from following him *y*
and had no regard for any of his ways. *z*

34:28
a Ex 22:23;
Job 35:9; Jas 5:4

28 They caused the cry of the poor to come before him,
so that he heard the cry of the needy. *a*
29 But if he remains silent, who can condemn him?
If he hides his face, who can see him?
Yet he is over man and nation alike,

34:30
b Pr 29:2-12

30 to keep a godless man from ruling,
from laying snares for the people. *b*

31 "Suppose a man says to God,
'I am guilty but will offend no more.

34:32
c Job 35:11; Ps 25:4
d Job 33:27

32 Teach me what I cannot see; *c*
if I have done wrong, I will not do so again.' *d*

34:33
e Job 41:11

33 Should God then reward you on your terms,
when you refuse to repent? *e*
You must decide, not I;
so tell me what you know.

34 "Men of understanding declare,
wise men who hear me say to me,

34:35
f Job 35:16; 38:2

35 'Job speaks without knowledge; *f*
his words lack insight.'

34:36
g Job 22:15

36 Oh, that Job might be tested to the utmost
for answering like a wicked man! *g*

a 14 Or *Spirit*

37 To his sin he adds rebellion;
  scornfully he claps his hands[h] among us
  and multiplies his words against God."[i]

35 Then Elihu said:

2 "Do you think this is just?
  You say, 'I will be cleared by God.[a]
3 Yet you ask him, 'What profit is it to me,[b]
  and what do I gain by not sinning?'[j]

4 "I would like to reply to you
  and to your friends with you.
5 Look up at the heavens[k] and see;
  gaze at the clouds so high above you.[l]
6 If you sin, how does that affect him?
  If your sins are many, what does that do to him?[m]
7 If you are righteous, what do you give to him,[n]
  or what does he receive[o] from your hand?[p]
8 Your wickedness affects only a man like yourself,
  and your righteousness only the sons of men.

9 "Men cry out[q] under a load of oppression;
  they plead for relief from the arm of the powerful.[r]
10 But no one says, 'Where is God my Maker,[s]
  who gives songs in the night,[t]
11 who teaches[u] more to us than to[c] the beasts of the earth
  and makes us wiser than[d] the birds of the air?'
12 He does not answer[v] when men cry out
  because of the arrogance of the wicked.
13 Indeed, God does not listen to their empty plea;
  the Almighty pays no attention to it.[w]
14 How much less, then, will he listen
  when you say that you do not see him,[x]
that your case[y] is before him
  and you must wait for him,
15 and further, that his anger never punishes
  and he does not take the least notice of wickedness.[e]
16 So Job opens his mouth with empty talk;
  without knowledge he multiplies words."[z]

36 Elihu continued:

2 "Bear with me a little longer and I will show you
  that there is more to be said in God's behalf.

[a] 2 Or My righteousness is more than God's   [b] 3 Or you   [c] 11 Or teaches us by   [d] 11 Or us wise by
[e] 15 Symmachus, Theodotion and Vulgate; the meaning of the Hebrew for this word is uncertain.

34:37 [h] Job 27:23 [i] Job 23:2

35:3 [j] Job 9:29-31; 34:9

35:5 [k] Ge 15:5 [l] Job 22:12

35:6 [m] Pr 8:36 **35:7** [n] Ro 11:35 [o] Pr 9:12 [p] Job 22:2-3; Lk 17:10

35:9 [q] Ex 2:23 [r] Job 12:19

35:10 [s] Job 27:10; Isa 51:13 [t] Ps 42:8; 149:5; Ac 16:25 **35:11** [u] Ps 94:12

35:12 [v] Pr 1:28

35:13 [w] Job 27:9; Pr 15:29; Isa 1:15; Jer 11:11 **35:14** [x] Job 9:11 [y] Ps 37:6

35:16 [z] Job 34:35,37

In chapter 35 Elihu expressed questions and claims based on Job's problem with God's justice: (1) If God is so unjust, why did Job want to be vindicated by him (vv. 1–3)? But Elihu had missed Job's point that he wanted to be vindicated *because* God is just. (2) God received no benefit from Job, whether Job did right or wrong (vv. 4–8). (3) God isn't indifferent to people, but people are to God (vv. 9–16). Human arrogance keeps God from responding to people's empty cries for help.

Chapters 36–37 close Elihu's monologue. Some key points from chapter 36: (1) No matter what life may bring, God never takes his eyes off the righteous but uses their troubles for disciplinary instruction and to call them to repentance (vv. 7–10). (2) Responding to his call determines the course of people's lives (vv. 11–14). (3) God uses affliction to amplify his voice and catch people's attention (vv. 15–17). (4) God is accountable to no one, makes no mistakes, and does no wrong (vv. 22–24). Chapter 37 is a continuation of Elihu's poetic description of God's marvels exhibited in the earth's atmosphere (begun in 36:27). Elihu challenged Job to ponder God's power over the elements.

36:3
a Job 8:3; 37:23
36:4
b Job 33:3
c Job 37:5, 16, 23

36:5
d Ps 22:24
e Job 12:13

36:6
f Job 8:22
g Job 5:15
36:7
h Ps 33:18
i Ps 113:8

36:8
j Ps 107:10, 14

36:9
k Job 15:25
36:10
l Job 33:16
m 2Ki 17:13
36:11
n Isa 1:19

36:12
o Job 15:22
p Job 4:21

36:13
q Ro 2:5

36:14
r Dt 23:17

3 I get my knowledge from afar;
   I will ascribe justice to my Maker. [a]

4 Be assured that my words are not false; [b]
   one perfect in knowledge [c] is with you.

5 "God is mighty, but does not despise men; [d]
   he is mighty, and firm in his purpose. [e]

6 He does not keep the wicked alive [f]
   but gives the afflicted their rights. [g]

7 He does not take his eyes off the righteous; [h]
   he enthrones them with kings [i]
   and exalts them forever.

8 But if men are bound in chains, [j]
   held fast by cords of affliction,

9 he tells them what they have done—
   that they have sinned arrogantly. [k]

10 He makes them listen [l] to correction
   and commands them to repent of their evil. [m]

11 If they obey and serve him, [n]
   they will spend the rest of their days in prosperity
   and their years in contentment.

12 But if they do not listen,
   they will perish by the sword [a][o]
   and die without knowledge. [p]

13 "The godless in heart [q] harbor resentment;
   even when he fetters them, they do not cry for help.

14 They die in their youth,
   among male prostitutes of the shrines. [r]

15 But those who suffer he delivers in their suffering;
   he speaks to them in their affliction.

a 12 Or *will cross the River*

No doubt Elihu's motives were sincere, but he was presumptuous in assuming he had Job's life figured out. Unfortunately, like so many well-meaning messengers of grace, Elihu was so fully convinced of his good intentions that he became insufferably overbearing. Does that hit home with you (on either side of a relationship)?

36:11

Obey God and Serve Him

According to Elihu, if we obey and serve God we will spend the days of our lives in prosperity and contentment. Obviously, the statement is simplistic, an over-generalization. But, like the many general truths in the Old Testament's wisdom literature, Elihu's observation has some merit. In light of the big picture, encompassing all of global Christianity, contentment applies more often than prosperity. Contentment is, after all, a matter of attitude and choice (Phil. 4:12).

Elihu went on, though, in verse 12, to state the reverse: If we don't listen and obey, we will perish. Eternally. Elihu had it exactly right this time.

So what precisely can service to God entail? Consider these aspects:

• Worshiping God	Rom. 12:1
• Providing for our immediate families	1 Tim. 5:8
• Loving our neighbors	Rom. 13:8–10; Gal. 5:13–15
• Witnessing to others about Jesus Christ	Acts 1:8
• Using our gifts to serve the body of Christ	1 Cor. 12:27–31
• Providing material assistance to the poor, widowed, orphaned, sick, homeless—anyone in need	Matt. 25:36-40; James 1:27
• Living holy lives as models for others	Matt. 5:16
• Tending God's creation with care	Ps. 104:14; Prov. 12:10
• Creating beauty in our own lives, the lives of those around us, and our "corner" of the world	Matt. 26:10

16 "He is wooing[s] you from the jaws of distress
  to a spacious place free from restriction,
  to the comfort of your table[t] laden with choice food.
17 But now you are laden with the judgment due the wicked;
  judgment and justice have taken hold of you.[u]
18 Be careful that no one entices you by riches;
  do not let a large bribe turn you aside.[v]
19 Would your wealth
  or even all your mighty efforts
  sustain you so you would not be in distress?
20 Do not long for the night,[w]
  to drag people away from their homes.[a]
21 Beware of turning to evil,[x]
  which you seem to prefer to affliction.[y]

22 "God is exalted in his power.
  Who is a teacher like him?[z]
23 Who has prescribed his ways for him,[a]
  or said to him, 'You have done wrong'?[b]
24 Remember to extol his work,[c]
  which men have praised in song.[d]
25 All mankind has seen it;
  men gaze on it from afar.
26 How great is God—beyond our understanding![e]
  The number of his years is past finding out.[f]

27 "He draws up the drops of water,
  which distill as rain to the streams[b];[g]
28 the clouds pour down their moisture
  and abundant showers fall on mankind.[h]
29 Who can understand how he spreads out the clouds,
  how he thunders from his pavilion?[i]
30 See how he scatters his lightning about him,
  bathing the depths of the sea.
31 This is the way he governs[c] the nations[j]
  and provides food in abundance.[k]
32 He fills his hands with lightning
  and commands it to strike its mark.[l]
33 His thunder announces the coming storm;
  even the cattle make known its approach.[d]

37

  "At this my heart pounds
  and leaps from its place.
2 Listen! Listen to the roar of his voice,
  to the rumbling that comes from his mouth.[m]
3 He unleashes his lightning beneath the whole heaven
  and sends it to the ends of the earth.
4 After that comes the sound of his roar;
  he thunders with his majestic voice.
  When his voice resounds,
  he holds nothing back.
5 God's voice thunders in marvelous ways;
  he does great things beyond our understanding.[n]
6 He says to the snow,[o] 'Fall on the earth,'
  and to the rain shower, 'Be a mighty downpour.'[p]
7 So that all men he has made may know his work,

36:16
s Hos 2:14 t Ps 23:5

36:17
u Job 22:11

36:18
v Job 34:33

36:20
w Job 34:20,25

36:21
x Ps 66:18
y Heb 11:25

36:22
z Isa 40:13;
1Co 2:16
36:23
a Job 34:13
b Job 8:3
36:24
c Ps 92:5; 138:5
d Ps 59:16;
Rev 15:3

36:26
e 1Co 13:12
f Job 10:5; Ps 90:2;
102:24; Heb 1:12

36:27
g Job 38:28;
Ps 147:8

36:28
h Job 5:10

36:29
i Job 26:14; 37:16

36:31
j Job 37:13
k Ps 136:25;
Ac 14:17

36:32
l Job 37:12,15

37:2
m Ps 29:3-9

37:5
n Job 5:9

37:6
o Job 38:22
p Job 36:27

---

a 20 The meaning of the Hebrew for verses 18-20 is uncertain.   b 27 Or *distill from the mist as rain*
c 31 Or *nourishes*   d 33 Or *announces his coming— / the One zealous against evil*

37:7
q Job 12:14

37:8
r Job 38:40;
Ps 104:22

37:10
s Job 38:29-30;
Ps 147:17
37:11
t Job 36:27,29

37:12
u Ps 148:8
37:13
v 1Sa 12:17
w Ex 9:18;
1Ki 18:45;
Job 38:27

37:16
x Job 36:4

37:18
y Job 9:8; Ps 104:2;
Isa 44:24

37:23
z Job 9:4; 36:4;
1Ti 6:16 *a* Job 8:3
b Isa 63:9;
Eze 18:23,32
37:24
c Mt 10:28
d Mt 11:25

38:1
e Job 40:6

38:2
f Job 35:16; 42:3;
1Ti 1:7

38:3
g Job 40:7

he stops every man from his labor. *a q*

8 The animals take cover;
   they remain in their dens. *r*
9 The tempest comes out from its chamber,
   the cold from the driving winds.
10 The breath of God produces ice,
   and the broad waters become frozen. *s*
11 He loads the clouds with moisture;
   he scatters his lightning through them. *t*
12 At his direction they swirl around
   over the face of the whole earth
   to do whatever he commands them. *u*
13 He brings the clouds to punish men, *v*
   or to water his earth *b* and show his love. *w*

14 "Listen to this, Job;
   stop and consider God's wonders.
15 Do you know how God controls the clouds
   and makes his lightning flash?
16 Do you know how the clouds hang poised,
   those wonders of him who is perfect in knowledge? *x*
17 You who swelter in your clothes
   when the land lies hushed under the south wind,
18 can you join him in spreading out the skies, *y*
   hard as a mirror of cast bronze?

19 "Tell us what we should say to him;
   we cannot draw up our case because of our darkness.
20 Should he be told that I want to speak?
   Would any man ask to be swallowed up?
21 Now no one can look at the sun,
   bright as it is in the skies
   after the wind has swept them clean.
22 Out of the north he comes in golden splendor;
   God comes in awesome majesty.
23 The Almighty is beyond our reach and exalted in power; *z*
   in his justice *a* and great righteousness, he does not oppress. *b*
24 Therefore, men revere him, *c*
   for does he not have regard for all the wise *d* in heart? *c*"

The LORD Speaks

38 Then the LORD answered Job out of the storm. *e* He said:

2 "Who is this that darkens my counsel
   with words without knowledge? *f*
3 Brace yourself like a man;
   I will question you,
   and you shall answer me. *g*

a 7 Or | he fills all men with fear by his power   *b 13 Or to favor them*   *c 24 Or for he does not have regard for any who think they are wise.*

Job 38:1—41:34
Job had requested, "Let the Almighty answer me" (31:35). He got his wish. But God didn't vindicate Job in the way Job had demanded. Rather, out of the windstorm he informed Job that the wisdom that directs God's ways is beyond the reach of human intellect. In the first of God's two speeches, his works in creation were in view—first the inanimate (38:4–38), then the animate creation (38:39—39:30). The second speech consisted of God's assertion of his ability and determination to administer justice (40:6–14), illustrated by two poems (40:15–24 and 41:1–34) related to powerful beasts (see NIV text notes on 40:15 and 41:1), repeating the theme of the animal kingdom in 38:39—39:30.

4 "Where were you when I laid the earth's foundation?[h]
  Tell me, if you understand.

5 Who marked off its dimensions?[i] Surely you know!
  Who stretched a measuring line across it?

6 On what were its footings set,
  or who laid its cornerstone[j]—

7 while the morning stars sang together
  and all the angels[a] shouted for joy?

8 "Who shut up the sea behind doors[k]
  when it burst forth from the womb,[l]

9 when I made the clouds its garment
  and wrapped it in thick darkness,

10 when I fixed limits for it[m]
  and set its doors and bars in place,[n]

11 when I said, 'This far you may come and no farther;
  here is where your proud waves halt'?[o]

12 "Have you ever given orders to the morning,
  or shown the dawn its place,

13 that it might take the earth by the edges
  and shake the wicked[p] out of it?

14 The earth takes shape like clay under a seal;
  its features stand out like those of a garment.

15 The wicked are denied their light,[q]
  and their upraised arm is broken.[r]

16 "Have you journeyed to the springs of the sea
  or walked in the recesses of the deep?[s]

17 Have the gates of death[t] been shown to you?
  Have you seen the gates of the shadow of death[b]?

18 Have you comprehended the vast expanses of the earth?[u]
  Tell me, if you know all this.

19 "What is the way to the abode of light?
  And where does darkness reside?

20 Can you take them to their places?
  Do you know the paths[v] to their dwellings?

21 Surely you know, for you were already born![w]
  You have lived so many years!

22 "Have you entered the storehouses of the snow[x]
  or seen the storehouses of the hail,

23 which I reserve for times of trouble,[y]
  for days of war and battle?[z]

24 What is the way to the place where the lightning is dispersed,
  or the place where the east winds are scattered over the earth?

25 Who cuts a channel for the torrents of rain,
  and a path for the thunderstorm,[a]

26 to water[b] a land where no man lives,
  a desert with no one in it,

27 to satisfy a desolate wasteland
  and make it sprout with grass?[c]

28 Does the rain have a father?[d]
  Who fathers the drops of dew?

29 From whose womb comes the ice?
  Who gives birth to the frost from the heavens[e]

a 7 Hebrew *the sons of God*   b 17 Or *gates of deep shadows*

38:4
h Ps 104:5; Pr 8:29

38:5
i Pr 8:29; Isa 40:12

38:6
j Job 26:7

38:8
k Jer 5:22
l Ge 1:9-10

38:10
m Ps 33:7; 104:9
n Job 26:10

38:11
o Ps 89:9

38:13
p Ps 104:35

38:15
q Job 18:5
r Ps 10:15

38:16
s Ps 77:19
38:17
t Ps 9:13

38:18
u Job 28:24

38:20
v Job 26:10
38:21
w Job 15:7

38:22
x Job 37:6

38:23
y Isa 30:30;
Eze 13:11
z Ex 9:18;
Jos 10:11;
Rev 16:21

38:25
a Job 28:26
38:26
b Job 36:27

38:27
c Ps 104:14; 107:35
38:28
d Ps 147:8;
Jer 14:22

38:29
e Ps 147:16-17

38:30
f Job 37:10

38:31
g Job 9:9; Am 5:8

38:33
h Ps 148:6;
Jer 31:36

38:34
i Job 22:11;
36:27-28
38:35
j Job 36:32; 37:3
38:36
k Job 9:4
l Job 32:8; Ps 51:6;
Ecc 2:26

38:39
m Ps 104:21
38:40
n Job 37:8

38:41
o Lk 12:24
p Ps 147:9; Mt 6:26

39:1
q Dt 14:5

39:5
r Job 6:5; 11:12;
24:5

39:6
s Job 24:5;
Ps 107:34; Jer 2:24
t Hos 8:9

39:7
u Job 3:18

39:9
v Nu 23:22;
Dt 33:17

30 when the waters become hard as stone,
  when the surface of the deep is frozen?[f]

31 "Can you bind the beautiful[a] Pleiades?
  Can you loose the cords of Orion?[g]
32 Can you bring forth the constellations in their seasons[b]
  or lead out the Bear[c] with its cubs?
33 Do you know the laws[h] of the heavens?
  Can you set up ⌜God's[d]⌝ dominion over the earth?

34 "Can you raise your voice to the clouds
  and cover yourself with a flood of water?[i]
35 Do you send the lightning bolts on their way?[j]
  Do they report to you, 'Here we are'?
36 Who endowed the heart[e] with wisdom[k]
  or gave understanding[l] to the mind[e]?
37 Who has the wisdom to count the clouds?
  Who can tip over the water jars of the heavens
38 when the dust becomes hard
  and the clods of earth stick together?

39 "Do you hunt the prey for the lioness
  and satisfy the hunger of the lions[m]
40 when they crouch in their dens[n]
  or lie in wait in a thicket?
41 Who provides food for the raven[o]
  when its young cry out to God
  and wander about for lack of food?[p]

39 "Do you know when the mountain goats[q] give birth?
  Do you watch when the doe bears her fawn?
2 Do you count the months till they bear?
  Do you know the time they give birth?
3 They crouch down and bring forth their young;
  their labor pains are ended.
4 Their young thrive and grow strong in the wilds;
  they leave and do not return.

5 "Who let the wild donkey[r] go free?
  Who untied his ropes?
6 I gave him the wasteland[s] as his home,
  the salt flats as his habitat.[t]
7 He laughs at the commotion in the town;
  he does not hear a driver's shout.[u]
8 He ranges the hills for his pasture
  and searches for any green thing.

9 "Will the wild ox[v] consent to serve you?
  Will he stay by your manger at night?
10 Can you hold him to the furrow with a harness?
  Will he till the valleys behind you?
11 Will you rely on him for his great strength?
  Will you leave your heavy work to him?

a 31 Or the twinkling; or the chains of the b 32 Or the morning star in its season c 32 Or out Leo
d 33 Or his; or their e 36 The meaning of the Hebrew for this word is uncertain.

God's format for responding to Job was to ply him with rhetorical questions, to which Job obviously had to plead ignorance. God didn't say anything about Job's suffering or answer his questions about divine justice.

Job got neither a verdict of guilt nor of innocence. But neither did God humiliate or condemn him, as the counselors had. So by implication Job was vindicated, and later his vindication would be clearly affirmed (42:7-8).

12 Can you trust him to bring in your grain
　　and gather it to your threshing floor?

13 "The wings of the ostrich flap joyfully,
　　but they cannot compare with the pinions and feathers of the stork.
14 She lays her eggs on the ground
　　and lets them warm in the sand,
15 unmindful that a foot may crush them,
　　that some wild animal may trample them.
16 She treats her young harshly, *w* as if they were not hers;
　　she cares not that her labor was in vain,
17 for God did not endow her with wisdom
　　or give her a share of good sense. *x*
18 Yet when she spreads her feathers to run,
　　she laughs at horse and rider.

19 "Do you give the horse his strength
　　or clothe his neck with a flowing mane?
20 Do you make him leap like a locust, *y*
　　striking terror with his proud snorting? *z*
21 He paws fiercely, rejoicing in his strength,
　　and charges into the fray. *a*
22 He laughs at fear, afraid of nothing;
　　he does not shy away from the sword.
23 The quiver rattles against his side,
　　along with the flashing spear and lance.
24 In frenzied excitement he eats up the ground;
　　he cannot stand still when the trumpet sounds. *b*
25 At the blast of the trumpet *c* he snorts, 'Aha!'
　　He catches the scent of battle from afar,
　　the shout of commanders and the battle cry. *d*

26 "Does the hawk take flight by your wisdom
　　and spread his wings toward the south?
27 Does the eagle soar at your command
　　and build his nest on high? *e*
28 He dwells on a cliff and stays there at night;
　　a rocky crag is his stronghold.
29 From there he seeks out his food; *f*
　　his eyes detect it from afar.
30 His young ones feast on blood,
　　and where the slain are, there is he." *g*

40

The Lord said to Job: *h*

2 "Will the one who contends with the Almighty correct him?
　　Let him who accuses God answer him!"

3 Then Job answered the Lord:

4 "I am unworthy *i*—how can I reply to you?
　　I put my hand over my mouth. *j*
5 I spoke once, but I have no answer *k*—
　　twice, but I will say no more." *l*

6 Then the Lord spoke to Job out of the storm: *m*

7 "Brace yourself like a man;
　　I will question you,
　　and you shall answer me. *n*

39:16
w La 4:3

39:17
x Job 35:11

39:20
y Joel 2:4-5
z Jer 8:16

39:21
a Jer 8:6

39:24
b Jer 4:5,19;
Eze 7:14; Am 3:6
39:25
c Jos 6:5
d Am 1:14; 2:2

39:27
e Jer 49:16; Ob 1:4

39:29
f Job 9:26

39:30
g Mt 24:28;
Lk 17:37
40:1
h Job 10:2; 13:3;
23:4; 31:35; 33:13

40:4
i Job 42:6
j Job 29:9
40:5
k Job 9:3 l Job 9:15

40:6
m Job 38:1

40:7
n Job 38:3; 42:4

40:8
o Job 27:2; Ro 3:3

40:9
p 2Ch 32:8
q Job 37:5;
Ps 29:3-4

40:10
r Ps 93:1; 104:1
40:11
s Isa 42:25; Na 1:6
t Isa 2:11,12,17;
Da 4:37
40:12
u 1Sa 2:7
v Isa 13:11; 63:2-
3,6

40:14
w Ps 20:6; 60:5;
108:6

40:19
x Job 41:33

40:20
y Ps 104:14
z Ps 104:26

40:22
a Isa 44:4

40:24
b Job 41:2,7,26
41:1
c Job 3:8;
Ps 104:26; Isa 27:1

41:2
d Isa 37:29

41:4
e Ex 21:6

8 "Would you discredit my justice? [o]
  Would you condemn me to justify yourself?
9 Do you have an arm like God's, [p]
  and can your voice thunder like his? [q]
10 Then adorn yourself with glory and splendor,
  and clothe yourself in honor and majesty. [r]
11 Unleash the fury of your wrath, [s]
  look at every proud man and bring him low, [t]
12 look at every proud man and humble him, [u]
  crush [v] the wicked where they stand.
13 Bury them all in the dust together;
  shroud their faces in the grave.
14 Then I myself will admit to you
  that your own right hand can save you. [w]

15 "Look at the behemoth, [a]
  which I made along with you
  and which feeds on grass like an ox.
16 What strength he has in his loins,
  what power in the muscles of his belly!
17 His tail [b] sways like a cedar;
  the sinews of his thighs are close-knit.
18 His bones are tubes of bronze,
  his limbs like rods of iron.
19 He ranks first among the works of God, [x]
  yet his Maker can approach him with his sword.
20 The hills bring him their produce, [y]
  and all the wild animals play [z] nearby.
21 Under the lotus plants he lies,
  hidden among the reeds in the marsh.
22 The lotuses conceal him in their shadow;
  the poplars by the stream [a] surround him.
23 When the river rages, he is not alarmed;
  he is secure, though the Jordan should surge against his mouth.
24 Can anyone capture him by the eyes, [c]
  or trap him and pierce his nose? [b]

41

"Can you pull in the leviathan [d] [c] with a fishhook
  or tie down his tongue with a rope?
2 Can you put a cord through his nose
  or pierce his jaw with a hook? [d]
3 Will he keep begging you for mercy?
  Will he speak to you with gentle words?
4 Will he make an agreement with you
  for you to take him as your slave for life? [e]
5 Can you make a pet of him like a bird
  or put him on a leash for your girls?
6 Will traders barter for him?
  Will they divide him up among the merchants?
7 Can you fill his hide with harpoons

a 15 Possibly the hippopotamus or the elephant   b 17 Possibly trunk   c 24 Or by a water hole
d 1 Possibly the crocodile

Job knew little of God's world. We moderns have learned much more—only to discover how much lies tantalizingly beyond us. Contemporary scientific study, for all its apparent sophistication, has barely scratched the surface of understanding, whether its arena be chemistry or medicine or astronomy or physics. Does humanity's lack of understanding leave you restless and anxious, or do you take comfort in the knowledge that the all-knowing, all-loving Creator remains actively in charge of the events of the cosmos?

or his head with fishing spears?
⁸ If you lay a hand on him,
    you will remember the struggle and never do it again!
⁹ Any hope of subduing him is false;
    the mere sight of him is overpowering.
¹⁰ No one is fierce enough to rouse him.[f]
    Who then is able to stand against me?[g]
¹¹ Who has a claim against me that I must pay?[h]
    Everything under heaven belongs to me.[i]

¹² "I will not fail to speak of his limbs,
    his strength and his graceful form.
¹³ Who can strip off his outer coat?
    Who would approach him with a bridle?
¹⁴ Who dares open the doors of his mouth,
    ringed about with his fearsome teeth?
¹⁵ His back has[a] rows of shields
    tightly sealed together;
¹⁶ each is so close to the next
    that no air can pass between.
¹⁷ They are joined fast to one another;
    they cling together and cannot be parted.
¹⁸ His snorting throws out flashes of light;
    his eyes are like the rays of dawn.[j]
¹⁹ Firebrands stream from his mouth;
    sparks of fire shoot out.
²⁰ Smoke pours from his nostrils
    as from a boiling pot over a fire of reeds.
²¹ His breath[k] sets coals ablaze,
    and flames dart from his mouth.[l]
²² Strength resides in his neck;
    dismay goes before him.
²³ The folds of his flesh are tightly joined;
    they are firm and immovable.
²⁴ His chest is hard as rock,
    hard as a lower millstone.
²⁵ When he rises up, the mighty are terrified;
    they retreat before his thrashing.
²⁶ The sword that reaches him has no effect,
    nor does the spear or the dart or the javelin.
²⁷ Iron he treats like straw
    and bronze like rotten wood.
²⁸ Arrows do not make him flee;
    slingstones are like chaff to him.
²⁹ A club seems to him but a piece of straw;
    he laughs at the rattling of the lance.
³⁰ His undersides are jagged potsherds,
    leaving a trail in the mud like a threshing sledge.[m]
³¹ He makes the depths churn like a boiling caldron
    and stirs up the sea like a pot of ointment.
³² Behind him he leaves a glistening wake;
    one would think the deep had white hair.
³³ Nothing on earth is his equal[n]—
    a creature without fear.
³⁴ He looks down on all that are haughty;
    he is king over all that are proud.[o]

a 15 Or His pride is his

41:10
f Job 3:8
g Jer 50:44
41:11
h Ro 11:35
i Ex 19:5; Dt 10:14;
Ps 24:1; 50:12;
1Co 10:26

41:18
j Job 3:9

41:21
k Isa 40:7 l Ps 18:8

41:30
m Isa 41:15

41:33
n Job 40:19

41:34
o Job 28:8

Job

42

Then Job replied to the Lord:

2 "I know that you can do all things;*p*
  no plan of yours can be thwarted. *q*
3 ᴸYou asked,ᴶ 'Who is this that obscures my counsel without
    knowledge?' *r*
  Surely I spoke of things I did not understand,
    things too wonderful for me to know. *s*

4 ᴸ"You said,ᴶ 'Listen now, and I will speak;
  I will question you,
    and you shall answer me.' *t*
5 My ears had heard of you *u*
  but now my eyes have seen you. *v*
6 Therefore I despise myself *w*
  and repent in dust and ashes." *x*

Epilogue

7 After the Lord had said these things to Job, he said to Eliphaz the Temanite, "I am angry with you and your two friends, *y* because you have not spoken of me what is right, as my servant Job has. 8 So now take seven bulls and seven rams *z* and go to my servant Job and sacrifice a burnt offering *a* for yourselves. My servant Job will pray for you, and I will accept his prayer *b* and not deal with you according to your folly. *c* You have not spoken of me what is right, as my servant Job has." 9 So Eliphaz the Temanite, Bildad the Shuhite and Zophar the Naamathite did what the Lord told them; and the Lord accepted Job's prayer.

10 After Job had prayed for his friends, the Lord made him prosperous again *d* and gave him twice as much as he had before. *e* 11 All his brothers and sisters and everyone who had known him before *f* came and ate with him in his house. They comforted and consoled him over all the trouble the Lord had brought upon him, and each one gave him a piece of silver *a* and a gold ring.

12 The Lord blessed the latter part of Job's life more than the first. He had fourteen thousand sheep, six thousand camels, a thousand yoke of oxen and a thousand donkeys. 13 And he also had seven sons and three daughters. 14 The first daughter he

---

a 11 Hebrew him a kesitah; *a* kesitah *was a unit of money of unknown weight and value.*

Job 42:1–6

📖 Job responded to God's first speech by humbly committing himself to silence (40:3–5). Now, after God's second speech, Job opened his mouth to tell him he had gotten the message: God's purpose is all that counts, and since he's God, he's able to bring that purpose to pass (42:2). Job submitted himself to the Lord, quoting God's own words in verses 3 (38:2) and 4 (38:3; 40:7).

Now that Job had seen God, he "despised" himself (vv. 5–6). But "I despise myself" could be translated "I reject what I said." Job didn't need to repent for sins that had brought on his suffering—it wasn't the result of sin. But he humbly repented of the presumptuous words he had spoken about God since then.

📖 With his newly opened eyes of spiritual understanding, Job could accept God's ways in his life—which at this point still included suffering. As you face a volatile world, and possibly an explosive or unstable personal situation, can you do the same? In this same vein, God had instructed Job to leave "justice," including

his own vindication, in God's hands (40:8–14). How hard is that for you to do?

Job 42:7–17

📖 Job had spoken without understanding (by his own admission; 42:3) and had been full of rage (cf. 15:12–13; 18:4). His opinions were often misguided, but his facts were right: He wasn't being punished for sins he had committed. And he was determined to speak honestly before God. But his friends, claiming certainty of things they didn't know, had falsely accused him while mouthing beautiful words about God. Job had rightly accused them of lying about him and trying to flatter God (13:4,7–11).

God created humans so that he might bless them, not curse them. The lavish restoration—the same number of sons and daughters and exactly twice as many animals (cf. 1:2–3)—wasn't based on Job's righteousness but on God's love for him as one who had suffered the loss of all things for God's sake. This book has taken us along on Job's journey of faith. How did it change him? How has your faith journey changed you?

named Jemimah, the second Keziah and the third Keren-Happuch. [15]Nowhere in all the land were there found women as beautiful as Job's daughters, and their father granted them an inheritance along with their brothers.

[16]After this, Job lived a hundred and forty years; he saw his children and their children to the fourth generation. [17]And so he died, old and full of years. *g*

42:17
g Ge 15:15; 25:8

The cosmic contest with Satan, the accuser, was over, and Job had been spiritually restored to friendship with God. In the context of Job's story, there was no longer a reason for him to experience physical and material suffering—unless he was sinful and deserved it, which wasn't the case. God doesn't allow us to suffer for no reason either, even though that reason may be hidden in the mystery of his divine purpose (see Isa. 55:8–9). Whether or not we can understand in this life the purposes of our own suffering or that of others, we can—no, *must*—trust in him as the God who does only what's right. And we can help ease the burden of hurting people by our words and deeds of compassion—not by condescension or condemnation.

82:3–4 "DEFEND THE CAUSE OF THE WEAK AND FATHERLESS;
MAINTAIN THE RIGHTS OF THE POOR AND OPPRESSED. RESCUE
THE WEAK AND NEEDY."

INTRODUCTION TO
Psalms

AUTHORS
Psalms is a collection of poems and songs written by David, Asaph, the sons of Korah, Solomon, Moses, Ethan the Ezrahite, and various other unknown authors.

DATE WRITTEN
The psalms were written over a period of almost 1,000 years, dating from about the time of Moses (c. 1400 B.C.) to the time of the Babylonian captivity (586 B.C.) and beyond.

ORIGINAL READERS
The psalms were originally individual poems meant to be sung. In the course of time, they were collected to form small books that were used for worship. Psalms is a collection of five of these books.

TIMELINE

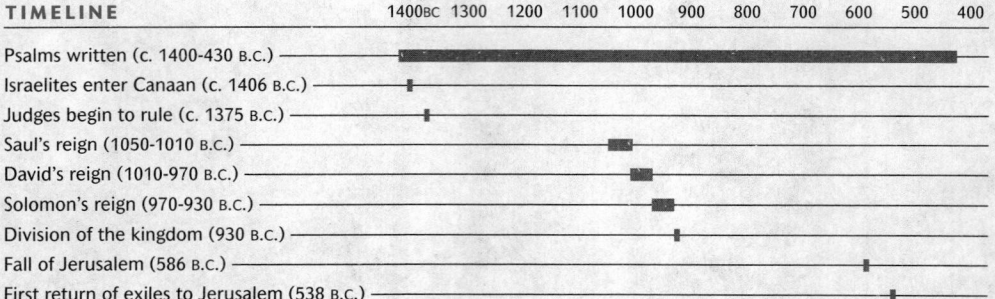

	1400BC	1300	1200	1100	1000	900	800	700	600	500	400
Psalms written (c. 1400-430 B.C.)											
Israelites enter Canaan (c. 1406 B.C.)											
Judges begin to rule (c. 1375 B.C.)											
Saul's reign (1050-1010 B.C.)											
David's reign (1010-970 B.C.)											
Solomon's reign (970-930 B.C.)											
Division of the kingdom (930 B.C.)											
Fall of Jerusalem (586 B.C.)											
First return of exiles to Jerusalem (538 B.C.)											

THEMES
Psalms is a compilation of 150 poems that model a personal relationship with God. Because the book covers nearly every area of life and doctrine, it's impossible to summarize its many themes and teachings. Psalms is perhaps most easily described as:

1. *A portrait of God.* The psalms portray God as our shepherd (Ps. 23; 95; 100) and the warrior who saves us from our oppressors (Ps. 18). He's our King (Ps. 45; 47; 97), our refuge (Ps. 46; 91), and our judge (Ps. 50; 52; 75–76). He's great (Ps. 48; 135), eternal (Ps. 90), perfect (Ps. 92), powerful (Ps. 76; 104; 145; 147), patient (Ps. 78), just (82; 101), forgiving (Ps. 103), loving (Ps. 136; 145), and good (Ps. 86; 104; 116). He's the champion of the poor and downtrodden (Ps. 72; 113) and the One who gives hope to the struggling righteous by giving them a glimpse of their glorious future (Ps. 37; 73). These portraits of God impact our relationship with him as we come to know him better.

2. *A model of a personal relationship with God.* The psalms openly express the range of emotions experienced in life—for example, fear (Ps. 56), love (Ps. 91; 116), distress (Ps. 31; 42; 120; 142), dismay (Ps. 10), joy (Ps. 98; 100; 117), impatience (Ps. 13), gratitude (Ps. 107; 118;

136), shame (Ps. 25; 38; 44; 69), guilt (Ps. 32; 38; 51), joy of forgiveness (Ps. 32; 103), and depression that turns to hope (Ps. 31; 42–43; 130). This openness inspires us to authentic communication with our loving, compassionate, and understanding God. Enjoyment of a dynamic, personal relationship with God requires intimacy with him. As we disclose our true feelings and selves, our relationship with him, our trust, and our faith in him continue to grow.

3. *A contrast of the ways of the righteous with those of the wicked.* Psalm 1 sets the stage: The righteous are blessed and watched over by God, but the way of the wicked will perish. The wicked are those who selfishly use and abuse others and don't think about God (Ps. 26; 37). The righteous walk before God with integrity of heart, helping their neighbors and those in need (Ps. 15; 28). See also Psalms 9, 10, 40, 68, 84, 112, and 128.

FAITH IN ACTION
The pages of Psalms contain life lessons and role models of faith—people who challenge believers to put their faith in action.

Role Models

- DAVID (3:3–4) confidently cried to God for help, believing in faith that God would answer and rescue him. Who do you call upon for assistance?

- SOLOMON (72:12–14) understood that a good leader cares for the weak, needy, and oppressed, just as God does. What are you doing to help those in need?

- ASAPH (73:1–3,18–28) questioned the prosperity of the wicked until he realized that true riches and hope are found in God's presence and guidance. Have you ever envied the wicked? How can this psalm of Asaph encourage you?

- THE SONS OF KORAH (84:1–2,10–12) experienced the joy of God's radiant presence and praised God for his care. Have you or someone you know wandered from God's presence? His promise stands secure: Return to him, and he will return to you (Zech. 1:3).

- MOSES (90:14–18) testified of God's unfailing love, which brings joy even in times of affliction. How does his love encourage you in your struggles?

- AN AFFLICTED MAN (102:17,19–20) cried to the Lord for help, affirming that God answers the prayers of the destitute. Are you in need? God will respond to your prayers.

Challenges

- Read one psalm each day at the beginning of your prayer time.

- Praise God for who he is (29:1–11; 48:1; 113:1–9), for what he's done (111:1–9; 145:1–21), for his Word (1:2; 19:7–11; 119:1–176), and for his unchanging love (36:5–10).

- Allow your worship and praise to be richly varied and unencumbered (46:10; 105; 149; 150).

- Cultivate characteristics of the righteous: love, generosity, kindness, compassion, patience, etc. Find ways each day to demonstrate that you belong to God's family.

- Seek God's deliverance when you are in need or surrounded by evil, putting your faith and hope in him (31:1–24; 46:1–11; 52:8–9; 102:17).

- Establish God's Word as central in your life (119:1–176).

- Care for those God is concerned about (10:17–18; 41:1–3; 68:5–6,10; 72:2–4,12–14; 82:3–4; 112; 146:5–9).

- Confess your sins to your forgiving, loving God (19:12–13; 32:1–11; 51:1–19).

- Thank God for his blessings (112:1–9; 115:12–15), faithfulness (40:10; 57:3–10; 89), and love (33:1–22; 107:1–43; 115:1; 118:1–29; 136:1–26).

OUTLINE

I. Book One: Psalms 1–41
II. Book Two: Psalms 42–72
III. Book Three: Psalms 73–89
IV. Book Four: Psalms 90–106
V. Book Five: Psalms 107–150

BOOK I

Psalms 1–41

Psalm 1

1:1
a Pr 4:14 *b* Ps 26:4;
Jer 15:17

1 Blessed is the man
  who does not walk*a* in the counsel of the wicked
or stand in the way of sinners
  or sit*b* in the seat of mockers.

1:2
c Ps 119:16,35
d Ps 119:1 *e* Jos 1:8
1:3
f Ps 128:3
g Jer 17:8
h Eze 47:12
i Ge 39:3

2 But his delight*c* is in the law of the LORD, *d*
  and on his law he meditates*e* day and night.
3 He is like a tree*f* planted by streams of water, *g*
  which yields its fruit*h* in season
and whose leaf does not wither.
  Whatever he does prospers. *i*

1:4
j Job 21:18;
Isa 17:13

4 Not so the wicked!
  They are like chaff*j*
  that the wind blows away.

1:5
k Ps 5:5
l Ps 9:7-8,16

5 Therefore the wicked will not stand*k* in the judgment, *l*
  nor sinners in the assembly of the righteous.

1:6
m Ps 37:18;
2Ti 2:19 *n* Ps 9:6

6 For the LORD watches over*m* the way of the righteous,
  but the way of the wicked will perish. *n*

Psalm 2

2:1
o Ps 21:11
2:2
p Ps 48:4

1 Why do the nations conspire*a*
  and the peoples plot*o* in vain?
2 The kings*p* of the earth take their stand
  and the rulers gather together

a 1 Hebrew; Septuagint *rage*

Psalm 1

🔲 Psalm 1 overlaps categories as both a wisdom and a Torah psalm. Wisdom psalms typically recognize "two ways" of living—righteousness and wickedness, and often begin with "Blessed"—the happy condition of those who honor and obey God. Torah psalms acknowledge the Torah (NIV "law") of God as central to life. Psalm 1 is arranged into a series of two-verse comparisons between the "ways" of the righteous and those of the wicked.

In medieval times, Psalm 1 was treated as an introduction to the entire Psalter and wasn't numbered. The final editors may have chosen it as the gateway to the book because it encourages people to consider the songs that follow as a source of divine guidance.

🔲 The psalms can and should be a part of our constant practice of the presence of God. Regularly read from beginning to end, they lead us again and again to consider aspects of life and of God's will that we might not otherwise choose to remember or confront—let alone embody in our living. As exemplified in Psalm 1, psalms are more than worship songs or heartfelt prayers: They are God's Word speaking to us in all parts of our being: body, soul, mind, and spirit.

Psalm 2

🔲 Psalm 2 is the first of a category known as "royal psalms"—concerned with the kings of Judah, who understood themselves to be uniquely authorized and empowered as God's adopted sons. This psalm was

against the LORD
and against his Anointed[q] One.[a][r]

3 "Let us break their chains," they say,
"and throw off their fetters."[s]

4 The One enthroned in heaven laughs;[t]
the Lord scoffs at them.

5 Then he rebukes them in his anger
and terrifies them in his wrath,[u] saying,

6 "I have installed my King[b]
on Zion, my holy hill."

7 I will proclaim the decree of the LORD:

He said to me, "You are my Son[c];
today I have become your Father.[d][v]

8 Ask of me,
and I will make the nations your inheritance,
the ends of the earth[w] your possession.

9 You will rule them with an iron scepter[e][x];
you will dash them to pieces[y] like pottery.[z]"

10 Therefore, you kings, be wise;
be warned, you rulers of the earth.

11 Serve the LORD with fear
and rejoice[a] with trembling.[b]

12 Kiss the Son,[c] lest he be angry
and you be destroyed in your way,
for his wrath[d] can flare up in a moment.
Blessed are all who take refuge[e] in him.

Psalm 3

A psalm of David. When he fled from his son Absalom.[f]

1 O LORD, how many are my foes!
How many rise up against me!

2 Many are saying of me,
"God will not deliver him.[g]"   Selah[f]

3 But you are a shield[h] around me, O LORD;
you bestow glory on me and lift[g] up my head.[i]

a 2 Or *anointed one*   b 6 Or *king*   c 7 Or *son; also in verse 12*   d 7 Or *have begotten you*
e 9 Or *will break them with a rod of iron*   f 2 A word of uncertain meaning, occurring frequently in
the Psalms; possibly a musical term   g 3 Or LORD, / *my Glorious One, who lifts*

Cross references

2:2
q Jn 1:41
r Ps 74:18,23;
Ac 4:25-26*
2:3
s Jer 5:5
2:4
t Ps 37:13; 59:8;
Pr 1:26
2:5
u Ps 21:9; 78:49-50
2:7
v Ac 13:33*;
Heb 1:5*
2:8
w Ps 22:27
2:9
x Rev 12:5
y Ps 89:23
z Rev 2:27*
2:11
a Heb 12:28
b Ps 119:119-120
2:12
c Jn 5:23
d Rev 6:16
e Ps 34:8; Ro 9:33
3:1
f 2Sa 15:14
3:2
g Ps 71:11
3:3
h Ge 15:1; Ps 28:7
i Ps 27:6

---

likely written for the coronation of a Davidic king, and it offers us insight into how the kings understood themselves—their authority, roles, and hopes. In the aftermath of the fall of Jerusalem (586 B.C.) and the exile, such psalms took on a new life of Messianic hope and expectation.

The nations in this psalm wanted to throw off the "fetters" and "chains" of God, thinking of them as heavy shackles weighing them down and preventing them from becoming what they wanted to be. In reality, though, when we submit our lives to God we discover instead the "bonds" of relationship—family "ties" that bind us closely in loyal love. As in marriage, the bonds of commitment some consider a "ball and chain" represent for others the boundless freedom of love.

Psalm 3

This psalm presents us with a number of "firsts" in the Psalter. It's the first psalm attributed to David and the first of 13 psalms with a heading related to an episode in his life (see 2 Sam. 15:13—17:22 with regard to this one). It includes the first occurrence of the term *Selah*—probably some type of musical or liturgical notation. Finally, it represents the first lament, a category dominating the first two-thirds of the Psalter (covering Ps. 1–89).

We live in a world in which verbal, psychological, and physical abuse are commonplace. Having our spirits violated by those we trust undermines our sense of value. Experiences like this can help us tap into this psalm's vision—a picture of human honor and dignity, proceeding from God and made real in our hearts because God lifts up our heads when we are under attack.

3:4
i Ps 2:6
3:5
k Lev 26:6; Pr 3:24

3:6
l Ps 27:3

3:7
m Ps 7:6 *n* Ps 6:4
o Job 16:10
p Ps 58:6

3:8
q Isa 43:3,11

[4]To the LORD I cry aloud,
   and he answers me from his holy hill.[i]   *Selah*

[5]I lie down and sleep;[k]
   I wake again, because the LORD sustains me.
[6]I will not fear[l] the tens of thousands
   drawn up against me on every side.

[7]Arise,[m] O LORD!
   Deliver me,[n] O my God!
Strike[o] all my enemies on the jaw;
   break the teeth[p] of the wicked.

[8]From the LORD comes deliverance.[q]
   May your blessing be on your people.   *Selah*

Psalm 4

For the director of music. With stringed instruments. A psalm of David.

4:1
r Ps 25:16 *s* Ps 17:6

[1]Answer me when I call to you,
   O my righteous God.
Give me relief from my distress;
   be merciful[r] to me and hear my prayer.[s]

4:2
t Ps 31:6
4:3
u Ps 31:23 *v* Ps 6:8

4:4
w Eph 4:26*
x Ps 77:6

[2]How long, O men, will you turn my glory into shame[a]?
   How long will you love delusions and seek false gods[b]?[t]   *Selah*
[3]Know that the LORD has set apart the godly[u] for himself;
   the LORD will hear[v] when I call to him.

[4]In your anger do not sin;[w]
   when you are on your beds,[x]
   search your hearts and be silent.   *Selah*

4:5
y Dt 33:19; Ps 37:3

[5]Offer right sacrifices
   and trust in the LORD.[y]

4:6
z Nu 6:25
4:7
a Ac 14:17 *b* Isa 9:3
4:8
c Ps 3:5 *d* Lev 25:18

[6]Many are asking, "Who can show us any good?"
   Let the light of your face shine upon us,[z] O LORD.
[7]You have filled my heart[a] with greater joy[b]
   than when their grain and new wine abound.
[8]I will lie down and sleep[c] in peace,
   for you alone, O LORD,
   make me dwell in safety.[d]

Psalm 5

For the director of music. For flutes. A psalm of David.

5:2
e Ps 3:4

[1]Give ear to my words, O LORD,
   consider my sighing.
[2]Listen to my cry for help,[e]

---

[a] 2 Or *you dishonor my Glorious One*   [b] 2 Or *seek lies*

Psalm 4

Psalm 4 is an individual lament, based apparently on a crop failure resulting from some natural calamity, like a drought. Such distress, not uncommon in Israel, raised questions about God's ability to provide agriculturally for his people and drove many to worship foreign fertility gods. In this psalm David rejected these false gods, counseled the people to remain confident in the Lord, and appealed to God to demonstrate his good intent for his people by providing for their needs.

Think about the modern equivalent of the question in verse 6—"What works for me?" Making it our aim to know God as he deserves to be known rewrites the equation of our relationship with him so that our personal benefit is no longer central. With God at the center, we sense a *rightness* that can't be wiped out by suffering or pain, instilling within us the kind of confident faith Job experienced: "Though he slay me, yet will I hope in him" (Job 13:15).

my King and my God, *f*
  for to you I pray.
³In the morning, *g* O LORD, you hear my voice;
  in the morning I lay my requests before you
  and wait in expectation.

⁴You are not a God who takes pleasure in evil;
  with you the wicked *h* cannot dwell.
⁵The arrogant *i* cannot stand *j* in your presence;
  you hate *k* all who do wrong.
⁶You destroy those who tell lies; *l*
  bloodthirsty and deceitful men
  the LORD abhors.

⁷But I, by your great mercy,
  will come into your house;
in reverence will I bow down *m*
  toward your holy temple.
⁸Lead me, O LORD, in your righteousness *n*
  because of my enemies—
  make straight your way *o* before me.

⁹Not a word from their mouth can be trusted;
  their heart is filled with destruction.
Their throat is an open grave; *p*
  with their tongue they speak deceit. *q*
¹⁰Declare them guilty, O God!
  Let their intrigues be their downfall.
Banish them for their many sins, *r*
  for they have rebelled *s* against you.

¹¹But let all who take refuge in you be glad;
  let them ever sing for joy. *t*
Spread your protection over them,
  that those who love your name *u* may rejoice in you. *v*

¹²For surely, O LORD, you bless the righteous;
  you surround them *w* with your favor as with a shield.

Psalm 6

For the director of music. With stringed instruments. According to *sheminith*. *a*
A psalm of David.

¹O LORD, do not rebuke me in your anger *x*
  or discipline me in your wrath.
²Be merciful to me, LORD, for I am faint;

a Title: Probably a musical term

5:2 *f* Ps 84:3
5:3 *g* Ps 88:13
5:4 *h* Ps 11:5; 92:15
5:5 *i* Ps 73:3 / Ps 1:5 *k* Ps 11:5
5:6 *l* Ps 55:23; Rev 21:8
5:7 *m* Ps 138:2
5:8 *n* Ps 31:1 *o* Ps 27:11
5:9 *p* Lk 11:44 *q* Ro 3:13*
5:10 *r* Ps 9:16 *s* Ps 107:11
5:11 *t* Ps 2:12 *u* Ps 69:36 *v* Isa 65:13
5:12 *w* Ps 32:7
6:1 *x* Ps 38:1

Psalm 5

This psalm is a plea for deliverance, grounded in the psalmist's unshakable confidence in God's nature and characterized by a series of contrasts between those who take refuge in the Lord and those who opposed the psalmist and God. Following the opening plea (vv. 1–4), the psalm divides into four two-verse stanzas alternating in focus between the rebellious wicked and the hopeful righteous (vv. 5–12)—and concluding with confident hope for blessing and protection.

Sometimes the "enemies" in the Psalter were those outside God's people who opposed the foundations of Israel's faith. At other times they were part of the community of faith; they participated in Israel's social institutions, trying to use them to harm the psalmists and others.

We hope in God because, despite the evil around and within us, his character remains holy and constant. The faithful can call confidently on him to right life's wrongs. As a Christian, are you bothered by the so-called curses the psalmists heaped on their enemies, such as in verse 10 of Psalm 5? It may help to know that these were appeals to God to redress wrongs in a way commensurate with the harm done. Jesus was never afraid to identify evil for what it was and to condemn it in all its forms (cf. Matt. 12:34; 23:13–35). See also the notes on Psalm 109.

6:2
y Hos 6:1
z Ps 22:14; 31:10
6:3
a Jn 12:27
b Ps 90:13
6:4
c Ps 17:13
6:5
d Ps 30:9; 88:10-12;
Ecc 9:10; Isa 38:18
6:6
e Ps 69:3 f Ps 42:3
6:7
g Ps 31:9
6:8
h Ps 119:115
i Mt 7:23; Lk 13:27
6:9
j Ps 116:1
6:10
k Ps 71:24; 73:19
7:1
l Ps 31:15
7:2
m Isa 38:13
n Ps 50:22
7:3
o 1Sa 24:11;
Isa 59:3

O Lord, heal me, [y] for my bones are in agony. [z]
3 My soul is in anguish. [a]
How long, [b] O Lord, how long?

4 Turn, O Lord, and deliver me;
    save me because of your unfailing love. [c]
5 No one remembers you when he is dead.
    Who praises you from the grave [a]? [d]
6 I am worn out [e] from groaning;
    all night long I flood my bed with weeping
    and drench my couch with tears. [f]
7 My eyes grow weak [g] with sorrow;
    they fail because of all my foes.

8 Away from me, [h] all you who do evil, [i]
    for the Lord has heard my weeping.
9 The Lord has heard my cry for mercy; [j]
    the Lord accepts my prayer.
10 All my enemies will be ashamed and dismayed;
    they will turn back in sudden disgrace. [k]

Psalm 7

A *shiggaion* [b] of David, which he sang to the Lord concerning Cush, a Benjamite.

1 O Lord my God, I take refuge in you;
    save and deliver me from all who pursue me, [l]
2 or they will tear me like a lion [m]
    and rip me to pieces with no one to rescue [n] me.

3 O Lord my God, if I have done this
    and there is guilt on my hands [o]—
4 if I have done evil to him who is at peace with me
    or without cause have robbed my foe—
5 then let my enemy pursue and overtake me;

---

[a] 5 Hebrew *Sheol*   [b] Title: Probably a literary or musical term

---

Psalm 6

📖 A plea for deliverance, Psalm 6 dramatically describes physical pain and anguish and the resulting emotional distress. David didn't see the wrongness encountered in the world as something to be glossed over. He and the other psalmists didn't try to explain away suffering and oppression or find ways to interpret them positively. They appealed to God to restore order in all of life. Suffering and oppression invite us to depend on God as did the psalmists, but they remain evil just the same.

📖 Instead of seeing in psalms like this one a mirror of our own experience or allowing them to challenge our worldview, we can end up avoiding them as we might a negative friend who threatens to drag us down. But before hopping and skipping through the Psalter in search of more positive content, remember that these psalms are much more than the collected comments of negative people. They are God's words *to* his people. No matter what uncomfortable feelings they may stir, they remain an essential part of the "whole counsel of God."

Psalm 7

📖 This psalm was an appeal for deliverance from David's enemies, who were attacking him like ferocious

beasts. Using legal language, David appealed to God to base his judgment on righteousness alone—to acquit the innocent and judge the wicked.

The "Cush" named in the heading is otherwise unknown. Being from the same tribe as King Saul, though, he was probably one of his supporters. If so, the heading associates Psalm 7 with Saul's determined efforts to take David's life.

David's assertion of innocence wasn't a brash claim to spiritual excellence or perfection. It was a clear recognition that taking refuge in God's presence isn't a condition to be entered into lightly.

📖 Do you ever confuse righteousness with self-righteousness (a negative term for self-assured people you want to avoid)? God's righteousness is the living out of his character of holiness. Because God is holy and righteous, the psalmist could depend on him to uphold the godly and protect them from attack. As such, this divine quality takes on a softer dimension, defined by mercy and blessing. The twin consequences of divine holiness and righteousness—judgment and mercy—can never be separated but coexist in perfect balance.

    let him trample my life to the ground
    and make me sleep in the dust.   *Selah*

6 Arise,[p] O LORD, in your anger;
    rise up against the rage of my enemies.[q]
    Awake,[r] my God; decree justice.
7 Let the assembled peoples gather around you.
    Rule over them from on high;
8   let the LORD judge the peoples.
  Judge me, O LORD, according to my righteousness,[s]
    according to my integrity, O Most High.
9 O righteous God,[t]
    who searches minds and hearts,[u]
  bring to an end the violence of the wicked
    and make the righteous secure.[v]

10 My shield[a] is God Most High,
    who saves the upright in heart.[w]
11 God is a righteous judge,[x]
    a God who expresses his wrath every day.
12 If he does not relent,
    he[b] will sharpen his sword;[y]
    he will bend and string his bow.
13 He has prepared his deadly weapons;
    he makes ready his flaming arrows.
14 He who is pregnant with evil
    and conceives trouble gives birth[z] to disillusionment.
15 He who digs a hole and scoops it out
    falls into the pit he has made.[a]
16 The trouble he causes recoils on himself;
    his violence comes down on his own head.

17 I will give thanks to the LORD because of his righteousness[b]
    and will sing praise[c] to the name of the LORD Most High.

Psalm 8

For the director of music. According to *gittith*.[c] A psalm of David.

1 O LORD, our Lord,
    how majestic is your name in all the earth!

  You have set your glory
    above the heavens.[d]
2 From the lips of children and infants
    you have ordained praise[d][e]
  because of your enemies,
    to silence the foe[f] and the avenger.

---

[a] 10 Or *sovereign*   [b] 12 Or *If a man does not repent, / God*   [c] Title: Probably a musical term
[d] 2 Or *strength*

Cross references (right margin):

7:6
[p] Ps 94:2
[q] Ps 138:7
[r] Ps 44:23

7:8
[s] Ps 18:20; 96:13

7:9
[t] Jer 11:20
[u] 1Ch 28:9;
Ps 26:2; Rev 2:23
[v] Ps 37:23

7:10
[w] Ps 125:4
7:11
[x] Ps 50:6

7:12
[y] Dt 32:41

7:14
[z] Job 15:35;
Isa 59:4; Jas 1:15

7:15
[a] Job 4:8

7:17
[b] Ps 71:15-16
[c] Ps 9:2

8:1
[d] Ps 57:5; 113:4;
148:13
8:2
[e] Mt 21:16*
[f] Ps 44:16;
1Co 1:27

Psalm 8

After the dark valleys of lament and pleas for deliverance in the five previous psalms, we hear the strains of a joyous melody rising from the hilltop. Psalm 8 is our first experience in the Psalter of joyful praise and adoration. Darkness and suffering are driven away, at least temporarily, by this commanding vision of the sovereign God of the created universe and his immeasurable care for humanity.

Does the distance between who you would like to be and how you see yourself sometimes leave you in guilt and despair? This psalm holds up a new mirror on who we are. We see our flaws and weaknesses, but God bestows us with royal "glory and honor" (v. 5). Even though we are rebellious sinners, God in Christ has provided a way for us to change. We are no longer his enemies. Christ has prepared the way for sinners to be known as "children of God" (cf. John 1:12).

8:3
g Ps 89:11
h Ps 136:9

3 When I consider your heavens, [g]
   the work of your fingers,
the moon and the stars, [h]
   which you have set in place,

8:4
i Job 7:17;
Ps 144:3; Heb 2:6
8:5
j Ps 21:5; 103:4

4 what is man that you are mindful of him,
   the son of man that you care for him? [i]
5 You made him a little lower than the heavenly beings [a]
   and crowned him with glory and honor. [j]

8:6
k Ge 1:28
l Heb 2:6-8*
m 1Co 15:25,27*;
Eph 1:22

6 You made him ruler [k] over the works of your hands;
   you put everything under his feet: [l][m]
7 all flocks and herds,
   and the beasts of the field,
8 the birds of the air,
   and the fish of the sea,
   all that swim the paths of the seas.

8:9
n ver 1

9 O LORD, our Lord,
   how majestic is your name in all the earth! [n]

Psalm 9 [b]

For the director of music. To the tune of "The Death of the Son." A psalm of David.

9:1
o Ps 86:12
p Ps 26:7

1 I will praise you, O LORD, with all my heart; [o]
   I will tell of all your wonders. [p]

9:2
q Ps 5:11 r Ps 92:1;
83:18

2 I will be glad and rejoice [q] in you;
   I will sing praise to your name, [r] O Most High.

3 My enemies turn back;
   they stumble and perish before you.

9:4
s Ps 140:12
t 1Pe 2:23

4 For you have upheld my right and my cause; [s]
   you have sat on your throne, judging righteously. [t]

9:5
u Pr 10:7

5 You have rebuked the nations and destroyed the wicked;
   you have blotted out their name [u] for ever and ever.

9:6
v Ps 34:16

6 Endless ruin has overtaken the enemy,
   you have uprooted their cities;
   even the memory of them [v] has perished.

9:7
w Ps 89:14
9:8
x Ps 96:13

7 The LORD reigns forever;
   he has established his throne [w] for judgment.
8 He will judge the world in righteousness; [x]
   he will govern the peoples with justice.

9:9
y Ps 32:7
9:10
z Ps 91:14
a Ps 37:28

9 The LORD is a refuge for the oppressed,
   a stronghold in times of trouble. [y]
10 Those who know your name [z] will trust in you,
   for you, LORD, have never forsaken [a] those who seek you.

9:11
b Ps 76:2
c Ps 107:22
d Ps 105:1

11 Sing praises to the LORD, enthroned in Zion; [b]
   proclaim among the nations [c] what he has done. [d]

a 5 Or *than God*   b Psalms 9 and 10 may have been originally a single acrostic poem, the stanzas of which begin with the successive letters of the Hebrew alphabet. In the Septuagint they constitute one psalm.

Psalm 9

Psalms 9 and 10 may originally have been one *composition. If so, they probably came to be separated for purposes of liturgical use.* It's impossible to date this psalm to a certain period in David's personal life or Israel's national history.

The psalm gives the needy child of God a sense of confidence in his just rule. God isn't just Lord of individual lives, or of Israel, but Lord and Judge of the nations. The problems nations face are of their own making. But God looks out for the helpless. He defends the oppressed, remembers the needy, and brings hope to the poor (vv. 9,18).

The Antidote for Meaninglessness

 8:3–9

According to Emile Durkheim, in his classic study of suicide, the greatest number of suicides are caused by *anomie*, which could be rendered "normlessness" or "meaninglessness." An "anomic" suicide takes place when somebody either has no goal in life or pursues an unattainable goal, whether power, success or prestige. "No human being can be happy or even exist unless his needs are sufficiently proportioned to his means."

Now I venture to claim that Jesus Christ can fulfill this basic human aspiration. He gives us a sense of personal significance because he tells us who we are. To begin with, he took over from the Old Testament that great affirmation . . . : "God created man in his own image, in the image of God he created him; male and female he created them" (Gen. 1:27).

That is to say . . . the Creator endowed us with a cluster of rational, moral, social and spiritual faculties that make us like God and unlike the animals. Human beings are godlike beings, and the divine image in us, although it has been marked, has not been destroyed. Hence Jesus spoke of our value. He said that we were of much more value than a sheep (Matt. 12:12) or than many sparrows (Matt. 10:31; Luke 12:24).

He not only taught it; he exhibited it. His whole mission demonstrated the value he placed on people. He treated everybody with respect—women and men, children and adults, the sinner and the righteous. For he was the good shepherd, he said, who missed only one lost sheep and risked danger and death to find it. So he went to the cross, deliberately and voluntarily, to lay down his life for his sheep. Nothing can convince us of our personal significance like the cross of Christ. As Archbishop William Temple put it, "My worth is what I am worth to God, and that is a marvelous great deal, for Christ died for me."

Christian teaching on the dignity and worth of human beings is of the utmost importance today, not only for our own self-image and self-respect but also for the welfare of society. When human beings are devalued, everything in society tends to turn sour. There is no freedom, no dignity, no carefree joy. Human life seems not worth living because it is scarcely human any longer. But when human beings are valued as persons, because of their intrinsic worth, everything changes. Why? Because people matter. Because every man, woman, and child has worth and significance as a human being made in God's image and likeness.

> **He** treated everybody with respect—women and men, children and adults, the sinner and the righteous.

John Stott, preacher, evangelist, and principal framer of the landmark Lausanne Covenant (1974)
Source: John Stott, *Why I Am a Christian* (Downers Grove, Ill.: InterVarsity, 2003), 106–107

9:12
e Ge 9:5

9:13
f Ps 38:19

9:14
g Ps 106:2
h Ps 13:5; 51:12

9:15
i Ps 7:15-16
j Ps 35:8; 57:6

9:17
k Ps 49:14
l Job 8:13; Ps 50:22

9:18
m Ps 71:5; Pr 23:18
n Ps 12:5

9:20
o Ps 62:9; Isa 31:3

10:1
p Ps 22:1,11
q Ps 13:1

10:3
r Ps 94:4

10:4
s Ps 14:1; 36:1

10:6
t Rev 18:7

12 For he who avenges blood[e] remembers;
  he does not ignore the cry of the afflicted.

13 O Lord, see how my enemies[f] persecute me!
  Have mercy and lift me up from the gates of death,
14 that I may declare your praises[g]
  in the gates of the Daughter of Zion
  and there rejoice in your salvation.[h]
15 The nations have fallen into the pit they have dug;[i]
  their feet are caught in the net they have hidden.[j]
16 The Lord is known by his justice;
  the wicked are ensnared by the work of their hands.   *Higgaion.*[a] *Selah*
17 The wicked return to the grave,[b][k]
  all the nations that forget God.[l]
18 But the needy will not always be forgotten,
  nor the hope[m] of the afflicted[n] ever perish.

19 Arise, O Lord, let not man triumph;
  let the nations be judged in your presence.
20 Strike them with terror, O Lord;
  let the nations know they are but men.[o]   *Selah*

Psalm 10[c]

1 Why, O Lord, do you stand far off?[p]
  Why do you hide yourself[q] in times of trouble?

2 In his arrogance the wicked man hunts down the weak,
  who are caught in the schemes he devises.
3 He boasts[r] of the cravings of his heart;
  he blesses the greedy and reviles the Lord.
4 In his pride the wicked does not seek him;
  in all his thoughts there is no room for God.[s]
5 His ways are always prosperous;
  he is haughty and your laws are far from him;
  he sneers at all his enemies.
6 He says to himself, "Nothing will shake me;
  I'll always be happy[t] and never have trouble."

a 16 Or *Meditation;* possibly a musical notation   b 17 Hebrew *Sheol*   c Psalms 9 and 10 may have
been originally a single acrostic poem, the stanzas of which begin with the successive letters of the
Hebrew alphabet. In the Septuagint they constitute one psalm.

Jerusalem (Zion) was the seat of God's earthly throne for the ancient Israelites, but we also see glimpses in the Old Testament of God's praise "among the nations" (v. 11; cf. Ps. 96:1–3; Isa. 66:18–19). In Christ, we see this psalm's perspective regarding the nations fulfilled: (1) God will rule them with complete justice (Rev. 12:5; 19:11–16; cf. Ps. 2:7–9). (2) He will be worshiped among all nations (Acts 10:34–35; Rom. 16:26; Rev. 7:9–10). In the face of international turmoil, tyrants, and the deep suffering of the poor, what helps you remember that "the nations are only human" (v. 20) and that God is the hope of the poor (v. 18)?

Psalm 10

Psalm 10 is predominantly a prayer against the greed of individuals within Israel—as arrogant and evil in their dealings with the "weak" (v. 2) as the nations were in their attacks on Israel in Psalm 9 (see "There and Then" for Ps. 9). An unusual number of terms for defense-less people groups are found in Psalms 9 and 10. Thus one major concern of the Psalter is revealed: the oppression of powerless people by the wicked, who deny God and forsake their divinely given role of extending his care to the world. God will rule righteously, taking the side of society's weak, defenseless, and oppressed against the wicked, so that they may "terrify no more" (10:18).

Psalms 9 and 10 challenge those of us with resources or authority to use our influence to seek justice, in particular defending those lacking access to power and representation: widows, children in general and orphans in particular, the needy, the weak, the disabled, the otherwise vulnerable. Each individual Christian and church can ask: "What activities can I/we develop that will allow the building of relationships, two-way sharing of resources, and a real witness to Christ's power to tear down barriers of race, class, wealth, age, and ability in my/our community and the world?"

7 His mouth is full of curses[u] and lies and threats;[v]
  trouble and evil are under his tongue.[w]
8 He lies in wait near the villages;
  from ambush he murders the innocent,[x]
  watching in secret for his victims.
9 He lies in wait like a lion in cover;
  he lies in wait to catch the helpless;[y]
  he catches the helpless and drags them off in his net.
10 His victims are crushed, they collapse;
  they fall under his strength.
11 He says to himself, "God has forgotten;[z]
  he covers his face and never sees."

12 Arise, LORD! Lift up your hand,[a] O God.
  Do not forget the helpless.[b]
13 Why does the wicked man revile God?
  Why does he say to himself,
  "He won't call me to account"?
14 But you, O God, do see trouble[c] and grief;
  you consider it to take it in hand.
  The victim commits himself to you;[d]
  you are the helper[e] of the fatherless.
15 Break the arm of the wicked and evil man;[f]
  call him to account for his wickedness
  that would not be found out.

16 The LORD is King for ever and ever;[g]
  the nations[h] will perish from his land.
17 You hear, O LORD, the desire of the afflicted;[i]
  you encourage them, and you listen to their cry,
18 defending the fatherless[j] and the oppressed,[k]
  in order that man, who is of the earth, may terrify no more.

Psalm 11

For the director of music. Of David.

1 In the LORD I take refuge.[l]
  How then can you say to me:
  "Flee like a bird to your mountain.
2 For look, the wicked bend their bows;
  they set their arrows[m] against the strings
  to shoot from the shadows
  at the upright in heart.[n]
3 When the foundations[o] are being destroyed,
  what can the righteous do[a]?"

a 3 Or what is the Righteous One doing

10:7
u Ro 3:14*
v Ps 73:8
w Ps 140:3
10:8
x Ps 94:6
10:9
y Ps 17:12; 59:3; 140:5
10:11
z Job 22:13
10:12
a Ps 17:7; Mic 5:9
b Ps 9:12
10:14
c Ps 22:11 d Ps 37:5
e Ps 68:5
10:15
f Ps 37:17
10:16
g Ps 29:10
h Dt 8:20
10:17
i 1Ch 29:18; Ps 34:15
10:18
j Ps 82:3 k Ps 9:9
11:1
l Ps 56:11
11:2
m Ps 7:13
n Ps 64:3-4
11:3
o Ps 82:5

Psalm 11

Verse 3 asks the psalm's central question: "When the foundations are being destroyed, what can the righteous do?" In David's mind there were only two choices: flee to the mountains, as his counselors were suggesting, or take refuge in God. By acknowledging God's steady provision even within a horrific situation, by surrendering to his will, or by assuming the role of suffering servant for others, believers can come into God's presence and know true refuge.

How are Christians to respond to loss that destroys life's hopes and dreams? In foundation-shaking circumstances (like a layoff or serious health problem), Scripture lays out two basic choices: Look for an escape hatch or take refuge in God. Escape symptoms can include gambling, alcoholism, withdrawal, and other self-focused or abusive behaviors. Taking refuge in God may appear to non-believers to be escapism. But as Jesus demonstrated, it's not a way to avoid suffering or persecution. The refuge God offers calls us to give ourselves away (cf. Luke 9:24).

God's Rescue Plan

"Why, O LORD, do you stand far off?" (Ps. 10:1). I was asking the same question as I stood amidst thousands of rotting corpses in Rwanda in 1994. As the lawyer assigned to direct the United Nations' genocide investigation, I spent long days sorting through the remains of some of the 800,000 victims of eight weeks of genocide. One of the qualities I appreciate most deeply about the psalmists is their willingness to ask hard questions. In a world full of unspeakably brutal injustice, this psalmist's urgent question begs for an answer: Where is God?

From years of service as president of the International Justice Mission, I can testify that there is nothing exaggerated or antiquated about the psalmists' descriptions of oppression and injustice. I see a world where at least a million children are taken into forced prostitution each year, where more than ten million children are held illegally in bonded slavery, where thousands of prisoners languish under illegal detention and torture, where widows are forced off their land by ruthless neighbors, where street children are subjected to brutal police abuse.

> The ultimate question that emerges from Psalm 10 isn't "Where is God?" for we know where he is. It's "Where are God's people?"

Unfortunately, in many circles, the word *injustice* has been trivialized beyond recognition, describing anything vaguely unfair. But in Scripture, the Hebrew term refers to a specific kind of sin and a profound source of suffering. Injustice is the abuse of power to pry from others the good things God has given them—life, liberty, dignity, and the fruits of their love and labor. This was David's sin when he abused his power to steal another man's wife—and eventually his life (2 Sam. 11–12). This was the sin for which God brought judgment against Jerusalem's rulers (Ezek. 22:27). This was the sin John the Baptist confronted in Luke 3:13–14.

And this is precisely the sin that torments millions of victims today. They are suffering under an oppressor, a bully (whether personal, institutional, or national) who abuses power to rip from them, the weak, the good things God has given them.

How does God respond to such suffering? As the psalmist affirmed: God sees it, condemns it, and yearns to bring rescue. He's a God of compassion who "see[s] trouble and grief . . . to take it in hand" (v. 14), a God of holy judgment who has the power to "break the arm of the wicked and evil man" and "call him to account for his wickedness" (v. 15). And he's a God of rescue (vv. 17–18).

This is good news. But it raises a question: What is God's plan, his modus operandi, for rescuing victims of injustice? According to Scripture, *we are* his plan. Jesus has called us—his disciples—to love these neighbors suffering from injustice, to bring them the rescue we would yearn for if we were oppressed (Luke 10:25–37). Like everything else God wants to accomplish on Earth—proclaiming the gospel, feeding the hungry, healing the sick—he could perform these miracles on his own. But he has given to *us* the privilege of being his hands of love and justice (Mic. 6:8) in this world. And we can take him at his word that he doesn't give us a ministry without empowering us (Acts 1:8).

Not only have I seen in my work with the International Justice Mission that the God of justice is faithful to bring rescue when his people obey his call, but history testifies that if God's people had lifted their voices for Rwanda, hundreds of thousands of lives could have been spared. The ultimate question that emerges from Psalm 10 isn't "Where is God?" for we know where he is. It begs the question "Where are God's people?"

Gary A. Haugen, president of the International Justice Mission in Washington D.C.

4 The LORD is in his holy temple; [p]
    the LORD is on his heavenly throne. [q]
He observes the sons of men; [r]
    his eyes examine [s] them.
5 The LORD examines the righteous, [t]
    but the wicked [a] and those who love violence
    his soul hates. [u]
6 On the wicked he will rain
    fiery coals and burning sulfur; [v]
    a scorching wind [w] will be their lot.

7 For the LORD is righteous, [x]
    he loves justice; [y]
    upright men will see his face. [z]

Psalm 12

For the director of music. According to *sheminith*. [b] A psalm of David.

1 Help, LORD, for the godly are no more; [a]
    the faithful have vanished from among men.
2 Everyone lies to his neighbor;
    their flattering lips speak with deception. [b]

3 May the LORD cut off all flattering lips
    and every boastful tongue [c]
4 that says, "We will triumph with our tongues;
    we own our lips [c]—who is our master?"

5 "Because of the oppression of the weak
    and the groaning of the needy,
I will now arise," says the LORD.
    "I will protect them [d] from those who malign them."
6 And the words of the LORD are flawless, [e]
    like silver refined in a furnace of clay,
    purified seven times.

7 O LORD, you will keep us safe
    and protect us from such people forever. [f]
8 The wicked freely strut [g] about
    when what is vile is honored among men.

Psalm 13

For the director of music. A psalm of David.

1 How long, O LORD? Will you forget me forever?
    How long will you hide your face [h] from me?
2 How long must I wrestle with my thoughts [i]

a 5 Or *The LORD, the Righteous One, examines the wicked,* /
c 4 Or / *our lips are our plowshares*
b Title: Probably a musical term

Side references

11:4
p Ps 18:6
q Ps 103:19
r Ps 33:13
s Ps 34:15-16

11:5
t Ge 22:1; Jas 1:12
u Ps 5:5

11:6
v Eze 38:22
w Jer 4:11-12

11:7
x Ps 7:9,11; 45:7
y Ps 33:5 z Ps 17:15

12:1
a Isa 57:1

12:2
b Ps 10:7; 41:6;
55:21; Ro 16:18
12:3
c Da 7:8; Rev 13:5

12:5
d Ps 10:18; 34:6
12:6
e 2Sa 22:31;
Ps 18:30; Pr 30:5

12:7
f Ps 37:28
12:8
g Ps 55:10-11

13:1
h Job 13:24;
Ps 44:24
13:2
i Ps 42:4

Psalm 12

Psalm 12 is another plea for deliverance, but here David's primary complaint had to do with the lies and deceptively flattering speech the enemy was using to put down the weak and needy. Human words have an effect, but they are not eternally effective. They can help or hinder, wound or heal, but they can't counter the creative, sustaining word of God. In the conversation between humans and God, the Lord always has the last word (cf. Job 9:3,14).

God not only has the last word, but the "flawless" character of his words, like refined silver (v. 6), illumines a certain transparency in him. What he says reveals who he is. Likewise, the Lord wants to know us intimately; but exposing our inner selves is difficult, steeped as we are in society's expectation of a good front. He already knows, of course, all there is to know about us. But he wants a relationship with us in which we open up our lives fully to him, as he has opened himself to us. And God wants us to know ourselves and each

13:2
j Ps 42:9

13:3
k Ps 5:1 l Ezr 9:8
m Jer 51:39

13:4
n Ps 25:2

13:5
o Ps 52:8 p Ps 9:14

13:6
q Ps 116:7

and every day have sorrow in my heart?
How long will my enemy triumph over me?[j]

3 Look on me and answer,[k] O LORD my God.
  Give light to my eyes,[l] or I will sleep in death;[m]
4 my enemy will say, "I have overcome him,"[n]
  and my foes will rejoice when I fall.

5 But I trust in your unfailing love;[o]
  my heart rejoices in your salvation.[p]
6 I will sing[q] to the LORD,
  for he has been good to me.

Psalm 14

For the director of music. Of David.

14:1
r Ps 10:4

1 The fool[a] says in his heart,
  "There is no God."[r]
They are corrupt, their deeds are vile;
  there is no one who does good.

14:2
s Ps 33:13 t Ps 92:6

2 The LORD looks down from heaven[s]
  on the sons of men
to see if there are any who understand,[t]
  any who seek God.

14:3
u Ps 58:3 v Ps 143:2
w Ro 3:10-12*

3 All have turned aside,
  they have together become corrupt;[u]
there is no one who does good,[v]
  not even one.[w]

14:4
x Ps 82:5 y Ps 27:2
z Ps 79:6; Isa 64:7

4 Will evildoers never learn—[x]
  those who devour my people[y] as men eat bread
  and who do not call on the LORD?[z]
5 There they are, overwhelmed with dread,
  for God is present in the company of the righteous.

a 1 The Hebrew words rendered *fool* in Psalms denote one who is morally deficient.

other with the same vulnerability and transparency that led Christ to the cross on our behalf. How open are you when it comes to relating to God?

Psalm 13

📖 The six verses of this lament plumb the depths of near despair before concluding with an unexpected confession of trust and confidence. Questioning God was an ancient tradition in Israel. At issue were human misgivings about his character and activity and their effect on people's circumstances. These questions sought divine presence and action on the petitioner's behalf and revealed a faith that groped for understanding in the midst of life's painful experiences.

📖 Many in our world live with a sense of abandonment. Some assume that God has withdrawn himself because *he doesn't want to associate with me*. Others deny his existence altogether, relying on personal power and *self-control. The response of Psalm 13 is to trust in God as an acknowledgement of our own powerlessness and dependence.

How can we regain a lost sense of God's presence?

Helpful actions from Psalm 13 include voicing our complaint honestly and openly, seeking the testimony of his presence in the community of faith, and singing of God's goodness with other believers.

Psalm 14

📖 Psalm 14 is a meditation on the folly of the wicked, who deny God's existence and expend their energies on corrupt lives dedicated to personal gain through exploitation of the poor. Divine scrutiny of the situation becomes God's opportunity to display both sides of his character: his incompatibility with evil and his relentless goodness toward those who fear him. Psalm 14 is duplicated with variations as Psalm 53.

In any conflict between oppressed and oppressor, God has always sided with the righteous poor. Delayed action on his part is never due to lack of justice, equity, or compassion. The oppression of the righteous is a sign that God's intended creation order has been corrupted. That the poor can turn to the Lord for refuge is a source of comfort. That they *must* do so for protection is no joyful event, but it serves as the basis of divine judgment on the oppressors.

⁶ You evildoers frustrate the plans of the poor,
  but the LORD is their refuge. *a*

⁷ Oh, that salvation for Israel would come out of Zion!
  When the LORD restores the fortunes *b* of his people,
  let Jacob rejoice and Israel be glad!

14:6
a Ps 9:9; 40:17

14:7
b Ps 53:6

Psalm 15

A psalm of David.

¹ LORD, who may dwell in your sanctuary? *c*
  Who may live on your holy hill? *d*

² He whose walk is blameless
  and who does what is righteous,
  who speaks the truth *e* from his heart

³   and has no slander *f* on his tongue,
  who does his neighbor no wrong
  and casts no slur on his fellowman,

⁴ who despises a vile man
  but honors *g* those who fear the LORD,
  who keeps his oath *h*
  even when it hurts,

⁵ who lends his money without usury *i*
  and does not accept a bribe *j* against the innocent.

He who does these things
  will never be shaken. *k*

15:1
c Ps 27:5-6
d Ps 24:3-5

15:2
e Ps 24:4;
Zec 8:3,16;
Eph 4:25
15:3
f Ex 23:1

15:4
g Ac 28:10
h Jdg 11:35

15:5
i Ex 22:25 *j* Ex 23:8;
Dt 16:19 *k* 2Pe 1:10

Psalm 16

A *miktam* *a* of David.

¹ Keep me safe, *l* O God,
  for in you I take refuge. *m*

² I said to the LORD, "You are my Lord;
  apart from you I have no good thing." *n*

³ As for the saints who are in the land, *o*
  they are the glorious ones in whom is all my delight. *b*

16:1
l Ps 17:8 *m* Ps 7:1

16:2
n Ps 73:25
16:3
o Ps 101:6

a Title: Probably a literary or musical term   *b* 3 Or *As for the pagan priests who are in the land / and the nobles in whom all delight, I said:*

📖 When we—particularly those of us who find ourselves blessed by birth or circumstance to be part of the "first world"—hurry to classify ourselves with the righteous poor, we fail to acknowledge the many ways our comparatively abundant lifestyle is founded on the exploitation of people in the "two-thirds" world who truly have so little. The psalmist's words challenge *us*, not just those foolish evildoers "out there."

Psalm 15

📖 This brief poem instructs those who want to enter God's presence in his sanctuary. It may represent a type of priestly teaching presented to those approaching the temple mount in Jerusalem, encouraging them to prepare physically and spiritually for their access to the "Holy Place" for worship.

📖 How do you prepare for a worship service? Psalm 15 emphasizes personal integrity and appropriate relationship to others. The person ready to enter God's presence isn't necessarily the one who has taken the prescribed ritual precautions or who knows how to adopt the expected outer attitudes of worship. When we live lives of transparency—when our hearts are accessible to God drawing us to repentance and our inner thoughts are reflected in our speech and actions—we are ready to meet God.

Psalm 16

📖 Psalm 16 is about confident resting in God. Its central imagery is drawn from the allotment of land following the conquest of Canaan (cf. Josh. 12–24). The Lord who apportioned the land also provided security for those who received it as their inheritance.

Thanks to the security God gives, David declared that he wouldn't "be shaken" (v. 8)—a verb describing the kind of insecurity experienced when a person's feet are on rough, untrustworthy ground (Ps. 38:16; 66:9; 121:3) or the earth is shaken by an earthquake or landslide (46:1–3).

16:4
p Ps 32:10
q Ps 106:37-38
r Ex 23:13

4 The sorrows[p] of those will increase
  who run after other gods.[q]
I will not pour out their libations of blood
  or take up their names[r] on my lips.

16:5
s Ps 73:26 t Ps 23:5

5 LORD, you have assigned me my portion[s] and my cup;[t]
  you have made my lot secure.
6 The boundary lines have fallen for me in pleasant places;
  surely I have a delightful inheritance.[u]

16:6
u Ps 78:55; Jer 3:19

16:7
v Ps 73:24
w Ps 77:6

7 I will praise the LORD, who counsels me;[v]
  even at night[w] my heart instructs me.
8 I have set the LORD always before me.
  Because he is at my right hand,[x]
  I will not be shaken.

16:8
x Ps 73:23

16:9
y Ps 4:7; 30:11
z Ps 4:8

9 Therefore my heart is glad[y] and my tongue rejoices;
  my body also will rest secure,[z]
10 because you will not abandon me to the grave,[a]
  nor will you let your Holy One[b] see decay.[a]
11 You have made[c] known to me the path of life;[b]
  you will fill me with joy in your presence,[c]
  with eternal pleasures[d] at your right hand.

16:10
a Ac 13:35*
16:11
b Mt 7:14
c Ac 2:25-28*
d Ps 36:7-8

Psalm 17

A prayer of David.

17:1
e Ps 61:1 f Isa 29:13

1 Hear, O LORD, my righteous plea;
  listen to my cry.[e]
Give ear to my prayer—
  it does not rise from deceitful lips.[f]
2 May my vindication come from you;
  may your eyes see what is right.

17:3
g Ps 26:2; 66:10
h Job 23:10;
Jer 50:20 i Ps 39:1

3 Though you probe my heart and examine me at night,
  though you test me,[g] you will find nothing;[h]
  I have resolved that my mouth will not sin.[i]
4 As for the deeds of men—
  by the word of your lips
I have kept myself
  from the ways of the violent.
5 My steps have held to your paths;[j]
  my feet have not slipped.[k]

17:5
j Ps 44:18; 119:133
k Ps 18:36

a 10 Hebrew *Sheol*   b 10 Or *your faithful one*   c 11 Or *You will make*

📖 Earthquakes, drought, hunger, war, civil violence, and poverty are common in much of our world. Even our relatively secure society can experience the destabilizing effects of natural and man-made disasters. How can we respond? God's presence doesn't make life's insecurities disappear, but it empowers us in him to find the path of life *within* and *through* painful times.

Psalm 17

📖 Psalm 17 pleads for deliverance from enemy attacks. Various phrases and themes link it to Psalms 15 and 16. All three seek the protection of the divine presence and use the Hebrew verb translated "be shaken" or "slip"

(15:5; 16:8; 17:5; see also "There and Then" for Ps. 16).
    Key to Psalm 17 is David's anticipation of seeing God's "face" (v. 15). To "seek" or "see" God's face was viewed in the Old Testament as the appropriate goal of the righteous (2 Chron. 7:14; Ps. 105:4), but numerous other passages point to fearful consequences (e.g., Gen. 32:30; Ex. 33:20–23; Isa. 6:5). The solution is perhaps found in Numbers 12:8, where God said of Moses, "With him I speak face to face . . . he sees the form of the LORD." Moses was in God's presence but physically saw the "form" of God rather than his very person. Likewise, David would be satisfied being in God's presence and seeing his "likeness."

6 I call on you, O God, for you will answer me;[l]
give ear to me[m] and hear my prayer.[n]
7 Show the wonder of your great love,[o]
you who save by your right hand[p]
those who take refuge in you from their foes.
8 Keep me as the apple of your eye;[q]
hide me in the shadow of your wings
9 from the wicked who assail me,
from my mortal enemies who surround me.[r]

10 They close up their callous hearts,[s]
and their mouths speak with arrogance.[t]
11 They have tracked me down, they now surround me,[u]
with eyes alert, to throw me to the ground.
12 They are like a lion[v] hungry for prey,
like a great lion crouching in cover.

13 Rise up, O LORD, confront them, bring them down;[w]
rescue me from the wicked by your sword.
14 O LORD, by your hand save me from such men,
from men of this world[x] whose reward is in this life.

You still the hunger of those you cherish;
their sons have plenty,
and they store up wealth[y] for their children.
15 And I—in righteousness I will see your face;
when I awake, I will be satisfied with seeing your likeness.[z]

17:6 [l] Ps 86:7 [m] Ps 116:2 [n] Ps 88:2 **17:7** [o] Ps 31:21 [p] Ps 20:6 **17:8** [q] Dt 32:10 **17:9** [r] Ps 31:20; 109:3 **17:10** [s] Ps 73:7 [t] 1Sa 2:3 **17:11** [u] Ps 37:14; 88:17 **17:12** [v] Ps 7:2; 10:9 **17:13** [w] Ps 7:12; 22:20; 73:18 **17:14** [x] Lk 16:8 [y] Ps 73:3-7 **17:15** [z] Nu 12:8; Ps 4:6-7; 16:11; 1Jn 3:2

When we look to this world for satisfaction, we are doomed to frustration and disillusionment. Earthly rewards are short-lived. But Job and David agreed on the only source of continuing satisfaction. Job laid down his defenses and demands when confronted by the undeniable presence of the Almighty: "My ears had heard of you but now my eyes have seen you" (Job 42:5). His response affirmed David's hope that the righteous will

---

Snapshots

17:7–9

Josefa Andrianaivoravelona

Josefa Andrianaivoravelona (1835–1897) was one of the first Malagasy ministers of the Reformed Church in Madagascar. Born into a non-Christian, noble family but converted and baptized in 1857, he dropped his original name, Andriantseheno, and adopted Andrianaivoravelona as more in keeping with his Christian faith.

Andrianaivoravelona, unrelenting in his efforts to convert his people, had to hide from religious persecution spurred by the queen, Ranavalona I, who was antagonistic both to Christianity and to foreign influence. Andrianaivoravelona founded his first church in Fianarantsoa but later returned to Antananarivo, the capital, where he worked as a self-educated preacher until the persecution ended in 1861, thanks to secret protection of Christians by the queen's son and the prime minister.

Andrianaivoravelona, unrelenting in his efforts to convert his people, had to hide from religious persecution.

Andrianaivoravelona became pastor of the congregation of Ampamarinana—the first native minister of the church in Madagascar. The new queen, Ranavalona II, became a Christian, and in 1869 Josefa became a pastor in the palace church (shepherding both congregations until 1897). Andrianaivoravelona was a prolific hymn writer, popular preacher, and member of the committee for revision of the Bible from 1873 to 1887.

Psalm 18

For the director of music. Of David the servant of the LORD. He sang to the LORD the words of this song when the LORD delivered him from the hand of all his enemies and from the hand of Saul. He said:

1 I love you, O LORD, my strength.

2 The LORD is my rock, [a] my fortress and my deliverer;
  my God is my rock, in whom I take refuge.
  He is my shield [b] and the horn [a] of my salvation, [c] my stronghold.

3 I call to the LORD, who is worthy of praise, [d]
  and I am saved from my enemies.

4 The cords of death [e] entangled me;
  the torrents [f] of destruction overwhelmed me.

5 The cords of the grave [b] coiled around me;
  the snares of death [g] confronted me.

6 In my distress I called to the LORD;
  I cried to my God for help.
  From his temple he heard my voice; [h]
  my cry came before him, into his ears.

7 The earth trembled and quaked, [i]
  and the foundations of the mountains shook;
  they trembled because he was angry. [j]

8 Smoke rose from his nostrils;
  consuming fire [k] came from his mouth,
  burning coals blazed out of it.

9 He parted the heavens and came down; [l]
  dark clouds were under his feet.

10 He mounted the cherubim [m] and flew;
  he soared on the wings of the wind. [n]

11 He made darkness his covering, [o] his canopy around him—
  the dark rain clouds of the sky.

12 Out of the brightness of his presence [p] clouds advanced,
  with hailstones and bolts of lightning. [q]

13 The LORD thundered [r] from heaven;
  the voice of the Most High resounded. [c]

14 He shot his arrows and scattered ⌊the enemies⌋,
  great bolts of lightning and routed them. [s]

a 2 Horn here symbolizes strength.   b 5 Hebrew Sheol   c 13 Some Hebrew manuscripts and Septuagint (see also 2 Samuel 22:14); most Hebrew manuscripts resounded, / amid hailstones and bolts of lightning

18:2
a Ps 19:14
b Ps 59:11
c Ps 75:10
18:3
d Ps 48:1
18:4
e Ps 116:3
f Ps 124:4
18:5
g Ps 116:3
18:6
h Ps 34:15
18:7
i Jdg 5:4 j Ps 68:7-8
18:8
k Ps 50:3
18:9
l Ps 144:5
18:10
m Ps 80:1
n Ps 103:3
18:11
o Dt 4:11; Ps 97:2
18:12
p Ps 104:2
q Ps 97:3
18:13
r Ps 29:3; 104:7
18:14
s Ps 144:6

see God's face and find satisfaction. Where does your search for contentment begin—and end?

Psalm 18

🕮 Psalm 18 also is found, with slight variation, in 2 Samuel 22. According to the psalm's heading and 2 Samuel 22:1, this hymn was David's response to divine deliverance from "the hand of all his enemies," including Saul. The descriptions of God as strength, rock, fortress, deliverer, refuge, shield, horn, and stronghold are arrayed throughout in a complex literary structure that illustrates the poet's artistry.

When the psalmists used fearsome imagery to capture the radical "otherness" that marks God's approach to humans, they often emphasized the chaotic effects of his presence on the physical world. These descriptions communicate significant truths: (1) Like the humans who reside within it, the created world is corrupted by evil and can be threatened by God's approach and presence (cf. Rom. 8:19–22). (2) By undoing creation's stability, God undermines false reliance on a seemingly secure environment.

🕮 God, asserted David, "makes my way perfect" (v. 32). David didn't claim sinless perfection but relied on God's gracious provision. For those who trust in his equipping power to confront and defeat opposing powers, God makes their path a "blameless" way that mirrors his own (v. 25). This is the gospel in Old Testament language! What we can't do for ourselves—make our way perfect—God can and will do for us. Faith, trust, commitment, and reliance on Christ can turn our fumbling steps into a "way" that fulfills his purposes for us.

15 The valleys of the sea were exposed
    and the foundations of the earth laid bare
at your rebuke, [t] O LORD,
    at the blast of breath from your nostrils.

16 He reached down from on high and took hold of me;
    he drew me out of deep waters. [u]
17 He rescued me from my powerful enemy,
    from my foes, who were too strong for me. [v]
18 They confronted me in the day of my disaster,
    but the LORD was my support. [w]
19 He brought me out into a spacious place; [x]
    he rescued me because he delighted in me. [y]

20 The LORD has dealt with me according to my righteousness;
    according to the cleanness of my hands [z] he has rewarded me.
21 For I have kept the ways of the LORD; [a]
    I have not done evil by turning [b] from my God.
22 All his laws are before me; [c]
    I have not turned away from his decrees.
23 I have been blameless before him
    and have kept myself from sin.
24 The LORD has rewarded me according to my righteousness, [d]
    according to the cleanness of my hands in his sight.

25 To the faithful [e] you show yourself faithful,
    to the blameless you show yourself blameless,
26 to the pure you show yourself pure,
    but to the crooked you show yourself shrewd. [f]
27 You save the humble
    but bring low those whose eyes are haughty. [g]
28 You, O LORD, keep my lamp burning;
    my God turns my darkness into light. [h]
29 With your help [i] I can advance against a troop [a];
    with my God I can scale a wall.

30 As for God, his way is perfect; [j]
    the word of the LORD is flawless. [k]

[a] 29 Or *can run through a barricade*

18:15 [t] Ps 76:6; 106:9
18:16 [u] Ps 144:7
18:17 [v] Ps 35:10
18:18 [w] Ps 59:16
18:19 [x] Ps 31:8 [y] Ps 118:5
18:20 [z] Ps 24:4
18:21 [a] 2Ch 34:33 [b] Ps 119:102
18:22 [c] Ps 119:30
18:24 [d] 1Sa 26:23
18:25 [e] 1Ki 8:32; Ps 62:12; Mt 5:7
18:26 [f] Pr 3:34
18:27 [g] Pr 6:17
18:28 [h] Job 18:6; 29:3
18:29 [i] Heb 11:34
18:30 [j] Dt 32:4; Rev 15:3 [k] Ps 12:6

Profile of World Christianity

You are only one person, and at times you no doubt feel pretty powerless in the face of the world's urgent and ongoing problems. But think of the God who is lifting you up. Imagine yourself easily scaling a ten-foot brick wall with only a gentle heft of his hand. Take a moment to dwell on the ramifications of the tremendous resources listed above. With God's help you can indeed advance against a troop, scale a wall . . . whatever it is he might be asking you to do (cf. Ps. 18:29).

Source: Barrett and Johnson (2001:40)

18:29

Category	Number worldwide
• Number of Christians	2 billion
• Total income of Christians	$16,590 billion
• Giving to Christian causes	$330 billion
• Computers in Christian use	430 million
• Books about Christianity	5.5 million
• Christian periodicals	41,000
• Bibles owned	1.5 billion
• Number of churches	3.7 million
• Number of denominations	37,000
• Average number of Christian martyrs/year	167,000

He is a shield
    for all who take refuge[l] in him.
31 For who is God besides the LORD?[m]
    And who is the Rock[n] except our God?
32 It is God who arms me with strength[o]
    and makes my way perfect.
33 He makes my feet like the feet of a deer;[p]
    he enables me to stand on the heights.[q]
34 He trains my hands for battle;[r]
    my arms can bend a bow of bronze.
35 You give me your shield of victory,
    and your right hand sustains[s] me;
    you stoop down to make me great.
36 You broaden the path beneath me,
    so that my ankles do not turn.

37 I pursued my enemies[t] and overtook them;
    I did not turn back till they were destroyed.
38 I crushed them so that they could not rise;[u]
    they fell beneath my feet.[v]
39 You armed me with strength for battle;
    you made my adversaries bow at my feet.
40 You made my enemies turn their backs[w] in flight,
    and I destroyed[x] my foes.
41 They cried for help, but there was no one to save them[y]—
    to the LORD, but he did not answer.[z]
42 I beat them as fine as dust borne on the wind;
    I poured them out like mud in the streets.

43 You have delivered me from the attacks of the people;
    you have made me the head of nations;[a]
    people I did not know[b] are subject to me.
44 As soon as they hear me, they obey me;
    foreigners[c] cringe before me.
45 They all lose heart;
    they come trembling from their strongholds.[d]

46 The LORD lives! Praise be to my Rock!
    Exalted be God my Savior![e]
47 He is the God who avenges me,
    who subdues nations[f] under me,
48   who saves[g] me from my enemies.
You exalted me above my foes;
    from violent men you rescued me.
49 Therefore I will praise you among the nations, O LORD;
    I will sing[h] praises to your name.[i]
50 He gives his king great victories;
    he shows unfailing kindness to his anointed,
    to David[j] and his descendants forever.[k]

Psalm 19

For the director of music. A psalm of David.

1 The heavens[l] declare[m] the glory of God;
    the skies proclaim the work of his hands.

Psalm 19

📖 Psalm 19 is an awed description of God's self-revelation through his creative acts (particularly the heavens) and gracious instruction in the law. Rather than a heavy burden, God's law was for Old Testament believers the guide to continued life and restoration of

Cross references (margin)

18:30
l Ps 17:7
18:31
m Dt 32:39; 86:8;
Isa 45:5,6,14,18,21
n Dt 32:31; 1Sa 2:2
18:32
o Isa 45:5
18:33
p Hab 3:19
q Dt 32:13
18:34
r Ps 144:1
18:35
s Ps 119:116
18:37
t Ps 37:20; 44:5
18:38
u Ps 36:12 v Ps 47:3
18:40
w Ps 21:12
x Ps 94:23
18:41
y Ps 50:22
z Job 27:9; Pr 1:28
18:43
a 2Sa 8:1-14
b Isa 52:15; 55:5
18:44
c Ps 66:3
18:45
d Mic 7:17
18:46
e Ps 51:14
18:47
f Ps 47:3
18:48
g Ps 59:1
18:49
h Ps 108:1
i Ro 15:9*
18:50
j Ps 144:10
k Ps 89:4
19:1
l Isa 40:22
m Ps 50:6; Ro 1:19

² Day after day they pour forth speech;
　　night after night they display knowledge. *n*

³ There is no speech or language
　　where their voice is not heard. *a*

⁴ Their voice *b* goes out into all the earth,
　　their words to the ends of the world. *o*

　In the heavens he has pitched a tent *p* for the sun,
⁵　which is like a bridegroom coming forth from his pavilion,
　　like a champion rejoicing to run his course.

⁶ It rises at one end of the heavens
　　and makes its circuit to the other; *q*
　　nothing is hidden from its heat.

⁷ The law of the LORD is perfect,
　　reviving the soul. *r*
　The statutes of the LORD are trustworthy, *s*
　　making wise the simple. *t*

⁸ The precepts of the LORD are right, *u*
　　giving joy to the heart.
　The commands of the LORD are radiant,
　　giving light to the eyes.

⁹ The fear of the LORD is pure,
　　enduring forever.
　The ordinances of the LORD are sure
　　and altogether righteous. *v*

¹⁰ They are more precious than gold, *w*
　　than much pure gold;
　they are sweeter than honey,
　　than honey from the comb.

¹¹ By them is your servant warned;
　　in keeping them there is great reward.

¹² Who can discern his errors?
　　Forgive my hidden faults. *x*

¹³ Keep your servant also from willful sins;
　　may they not rule over me.
　Then will I be blameless,
　　innocent of great transgression.

¹⁴ May the words of my mouth and the meditation of my heart
　　be pleasing *y* in your sight,
　　O LORD, my Rock *z* and my Redeemer. *a*

a 3 Or *They have no speech, there are no words; / no sound is heard from them*　*b* 4 Septuagint, Jerome and Syriac; Hebrew *line*

19:2
n Ps 74:16

19:4
o Ro 10:18*
p Ps 104:2

19:6
q Ps 113:3; Ecc 1:5

19:7
r Ps 23:3 *s* Ps 93:5; 111:7
t Ps 119:98-100

19:8
u Ps 12:6; 119:128

19:9
v Ps 119:138,142
19:10
w Pr 8:10

19:12
x Ps 51:2; 90:8; 139:6

19:14
y Ps 104:34
z Ps 18:2 *a* Isa 47:4

communion with himself. Though Jesus came not "to abolish the Law or the Prophets . . . but to fulfill them" (Matt. 5:17), he responded to misinterpretation and abuse of God's law when he criticized the teachers of the law and the Pharisees for piling up burdens on those seeking to approach God (Matt. 23:1–4; cf. Matt. 11:28–30).

When Jesus charged his disciples to have a righteousness "surpass[ing] that of the Pharisees and the teachers of the law" (Matt. 5:20), his point wasn't that the law was about sinless perfectionism. It was and is about acknowledging sin and committing our way wholly to God. Psalm 19 puts legalism in its place. God's law drives those who know they are sinners to rely on his gracious mercy. That is the gospel according to the Old Testament (and it's still valid today!): not that humans can keep God's demands perfectly but that God graciously provides a way for us to be restored to a right relationship with himself.

Forgiving—and Forgiven

Last week, while at prayer, I suddenly discovered—or felt as if I did—that I had really forgiven someone I have been trying to forgive for over thirty years. Trying, and praying that I might. When the thing actually happened—sudden as the longed-for cessation of one's neighbour's radio—my feeling was "But it's so easy. Why didn't you do it ages ago?" So many things are done easily the moment you can do them at all. But until then, sheerly impossible, like learning to swim. There are months during which no efforts will keep you up; then comes the day and hour and minute after which, and ever after, it becomes almost impossible to sink. It also

> **No** evil habit is so ingrained nor so long prayed against (as it seemed) in vain, that it cannot, even in dry old age, be whisked away.

seemed to me that forgiving (that man's cruelty) and being forgiven (my resentment) were the very same thing. "Forgive and you shall be forgiven" sounds like a bargain. But perhaps it is something much more. By heavenly standards, that is, for pure intelligence, it is perhaps a tautology—forgiving and being forgiven are two names for the same thing. The important thing is that a discord has been resolved, and it is certainly the great Resolver who has done it. Finally, and perhaps best of all, I believed anew what is taught us in the parable of the Unjust Judge [Luke 18:1–8]. No evil habit is so ingrained nor so long prayed against (as it seemed) in vain, that it cannot, even in dry old age, be whisked away.

I wonder, do the long dead know it when we at last, after countless failures, succeed in forgiving them? It would be a pity if they don't. A pardon given but not received would be frustrated.

C.S. Lewis, writer, novelist and critic, and former chair of Medieval and Renaissance studies at Cambridge University in Cambridge, United Kingdom
Source: C.S. Lewis, *Letters to Malcolm: Chiefly on Prayer* (New York: Harcourt, Brace & World, 1963), 106–107.

Psalm 20

For the director of music. A psalm of David.

1 May the LORD answer you when you are in distress;
  may the name of the God of Jacob[b] protect you.[c]
2 May he send you help from the sanctuary[d]
  and grant you support from Zion.
3 May he remember[e] all your sacrifices
  and accept your burnt offerings.[f]   *Selah*
4 May he give you the desire of your heart[g]
  and make all your plans succeed.
5 We will shout for joy when you are victorious
  and will lift up our banners[h] in the name of our God.
  May the LORD grant all your requests.[i]

6 Now I know that the LORD saves his anointed;[j]
  he answers him from his holy heaven
  with the saving power of his right hand.
7 Some trust in chariots and some in horses,[k]
  but we trust in the name of the LORD our God.[l]
8 They are brought to their knees and fall,
  but we rise up[m] and stand firm.[n]

9 O LORD, save the king!
  Answer[a] us[o] when we call!

Psalm 21

For the director of music. A psalm of David.

1 O LORD, the king rejoices in your strength.
  How great is his joy in the victories you give![p]
2 You have granted him the desire of his heart[q]
  and have not withheld the request of his lips.   *Selah*
3 You welcomed him with rich blessings
  and placed a crown of pure gold[r] on his head.
4 He asked you for life, and you gave it to him—
  length of days, for ever and ever.[s]
5 Through the victories[t] you gave, his glory is great;
  you have bestowed on him splendor and majesty.

a 9 Or *save! / O King, answer*

20:1 b Ps 46:7,11 c Ps 91:14
20:2 d Ps 3:4
20:3 e Ac 10:4 f Ps 51:19
20:4 g Ps 21:2; 145:16, 19
20:5 h Ps 9:14; 60:4 i 1Sa 1:17
20:6 j Ps 28:8; 41:11; Isa 58:9
20:7 k Ps 33:17; Isa 31:1 l 2Ch 32:8
20:8 m Mic 7:8 n Ps 37:23
20:9 o Ps 3:7; 17:6
21:1 p Ps 59:16-17
21:2 q Ps 37:4
21:3 r 2Sa 12:30
21:4 s Ps 61:5-6; 91:16; 133:3
21:5 t Ps 18:50

Psalm 20

Like Psalms 18 and 21, Psalm 20 is a "royal psalm," concerned with the king's military activities. The people (or army) spoke to the king, expressing their desire for divine assistance and victory. Bible commentators have noted the similarity of setting to the events described in 2 Chronicles 20. The psalm most likely functioned as a pledge of loyalty by the army to its ruler before a military campaign.

The Hebrew in verse 4 doesn't contain the word "desire"; a literal translation would be, "May he give to you according to your heart." God's gifts to us depend in part on the condition of our hearts. To the degree to which they are aligned with or against God's will and purpose, we can expect to receive blessing or judgment.

In this psalm we may see ourselves both as intercessors for others who suffer and as sufferers in need

of intercession. In the final cry on behalf of the king, we can find hope for our own deliverance: "Answer us when we call!"

What's in your heart? Rather than an invitation to license, this is a wake-up call to bring our hearts into alignment with God's. Psalm 20 offers two guidelines for how this might be accomplished: Pay close attention to matters of restoration and communion with God (v. 3), and put your trust in him alone (vv. 7–8).

Psalm 21

Psalm 21 responds to the promise of divine intervention and victory in Psalm 20. It still anticipates victory (vv. 8–12) and praises God for his promised support and strength (vv. 1,13). A number of emphases and themes link these psalms: (1) divine promise of victory, (2) "the king," (3) God's "right hand" effecting the king's deliverance, (4) the Lord's "strength," and (5) trusting in the Lord.

21:6
u Ps 43:4
v 1Ch 17:27

6 Surely you have granted him eternal blessings
　　and made him glad with the joy[u] of your presence.[v]
7 For the king trusts in the LORD;
　　through the unfailing love of the Most High
　　he will not be shaken.

21:8
w Isa 10:10

8 Your hand will lay hold[w] on all your enemies;
　　your right hand will seize your foes.
9 At the time of your appearing
　　you will make them like a fiery furnace.
　In his wrath the LORD will swallow them up,
　　and his fire will consume them.[x]

21:9
x Ps 50:3; La 2:2;
Mal 4:1
21:10
y Dt 28:18;
Ps 37:28
21:11
z Ps 2:1 a Ps 10:2

10 You will destroy their descendants from the earth,
　　their posterity from mankind.[y]
11 Though they plot evil[z] against you
　　and devise wicked schemes,[a] they cannot succeed;

21:12
b Ps 7:12-13; 18:40

12 for you will make them turn their backs[b]
　　when you aim at them with drawn bow.

13 Be exalted, O LORD, in your strength;
　　we will sing and praise your might.

Psalm 22

For the director of music. To ⌊the tune of⌋ "The Doe of the Morning." A psalm
of David.

22:1
c Mt 27:46*;
Mk 15:34*
d Ps 10:1

1 My God, my God, why have you forsaken me?[c]
　　Why are you so far[d] from saving me,
　　so far from the words of my groaning?

22:2
e Ps 42:3

2 O my God, I cry out by day, but you do not answer,
　　by night,[e] and am not silent.

22:3
f Ps 99:9 g Dt 10:21

3 Yet you are enthroned as the Holy One;[f]
　　you are the praise[g] of Israel.[a]
4 In you our fathers put their trust;
　　they trusted and you delivered them.

22:5
h Isa 49:23

5 They cried to you and were saved;
　　in you they trusted and were not disappointed.[h]

22:6
i Job 25:6;
Isa 41:14 j Ps 31:11
k Isa 49:7; 53:3

6 But I am a worm[i] and not a man,
　　scorned by men[j] and despised[k] by the people.

22:7
l Mt 27:39,44
m Mk 15:29

7 All who see me mock me;
　　they hurl insults,[l] shaking their heads:[m]
8 "He trusts in the LORD;

---

a 3 Or Yet you are holy, / enthroned on the praises of Israel

---

　Do you understand your victories as God's deliverance? Or do you see your own power and ability in your accomplishments? Ask most recovering addicts how they resist addictive compulsions, and you will hear: "I can't. God can, if I let him!" This psalm mirrors just such recognition of personal powerlessness and a turning to the power of God. When we surrender to his strength, we experience not only salvation but eternal blessings as well.

Psalm 22

　A powerful psalm of deep lament, Psalm 22 shares a number of connections with Psalms 69, 70, and 71. No other psalm is quoted more frequently in the New Testament. It was used on a number of occasions to interpret Jesus' suffering and death, and Jesus himself quoted portions of it from the cross. It reflects a model of response to abandonment and divine delay with which Jesus could identify and by which he could open windows for others into his spiritual conflict.

　Psalm 22 offers insight into how oppression dehumanizes both oppressed and oppressor. In our relationships, we are often tempted to view others as less than human. In lust we can make them objects to satisfy our desires. As we pursue our upward ambitions, our competitors can too easily become rungs to be stepped on. When we use others in this way, we give up our exalted status as image-bearers of God and take our place among the beasts.

let the L<small>ORD</small> rescue him. [n]
Let him deliver him,
   since he delights [o] in him."

9 Yet you brought me out of the womb; [p]
   you made me trust in you
   even at my mother's breast.
10 From birth [q] I was cast upon you;
   from my mother's womb you have been my God.
11 Do not be far from me,
   for trouble is near
   and there is no one to help. [r]

12 Many bulls [s] surround me;
   strong bulls of Bashan [t] encircle me.
13 Roaring lions [u] tearing their prey
   open their mouths wide [v] against me.
14 I am poured out like water,
   and all my bones are out of joint. [w]
My heart has turned to wax;
   it has melted away [x] within me.
15 My strength is dried up like a potsherd,
   and my tongue sticks to the roof of my mouth; [y]
   you lay me [a] in the dust [z] of death.
16 Dogs [a] have surrounded me;
   a band of evil men has encircled me,
   they have pierced [bb] my hands and my feet.
17 I can count all my bones;
   people stare [c] and gloat over me. [d]
18 They divide my garments among them
   and cast lots [e] for my clothing.

19 But you, O L<small>ORD</small>, be not far off;
   O my Strength, come quickly [f] to help me.
20 Deliver my life from the sword,
   my precious life [g] from the power of the dogs.
21 Rescue me from the mouth of the lions;
   save [c] me from the horns of the wild oxen.

22 I will declare your name to my brothers;
   in the congregation I will praise you. [h]
23 You who fear the L<small>ORD</small>, praise him! [i]
   All you descendants of Jacob, honor him!
   Revere him, [j] all you descendants of Israel!
24 For he has not despised or disdained
   the suffering of the afflicted one;
he has not hidden his face [k] from him
   but has listened to his cry for help. [l]
25 From you comes the theme of my praise in the great assembly; [m]
   before those who fear you [d] will I fulfill my vows. [n]
26 The poor will eat [o] and be satisfied;
   they who seek the L<small>ORD</small> will praise him— [p]
   may your hearts live forever!
27 All the ends of the earth [q]
   will remember and turn to the L<small>ORD</small>,
   and all the families of the nations

22:8
n Ps 91:14
o Mt 27:43

22:9
p Ps 71:6

22:10
q Isa 46:3

22:11
r Ps 72:12

22:12
s Ps 68:30
t Dt 32:14
22:13
u Ps 17:12
v Ps 35:21

22:14
w Ps 31:10
x Job 30:16; Da 5:6

22:15
y Ps 38:10; Jn 19:28
z Ps 104:29
22:16
a Ps 59:6 b Isa 53:5;
Zec 12:10; Jn 19:34

22:17
c Lk 23:35
d Lk 23:27
22:18
e Mt 27:35*;
Lk 23:34; Jn 19:24*

22:19
f Ps 70:5

22:20
g Ps 35:17

22:22
h Heb 2:12*
22:23
i Ps 86:12; 135:19
j Ps 33:8

22:24
k Ps 69:17
l Heb 5:7

22:25
m Ps 35:18
n Ecc 5:4
22:26
o Ps 107:9
p Ps 40:16

22:27
q Ps 2:8

---

[a] 15 Or / I am laid   [b] 16 Some Hebrew manuscripts, Septuagint and Syriac; most Hebrew
manuscripts / like the lion,   [c] 21 Or / you have heard   [d] 25 Hebrew him

22:27
r Ps 86:9
22:28
s Ps 47:7-8

22:29
t Ps 45:12
u Isa 26:19

22:30
v Ps 102:28

22:31
w Ps 78:6

23:1
x Isa 40:11;
Jn 10:11; 1Pe 2:25
y Php 4:19
23:2
z Eze 34:14;
Rev 7:17
23:3
a Ps 19:7 b Ps 5:8;
85:13

23:4
c Job 10:21-22
d Ps 3:6; 27:1
e Isa 43:2

will bow down before him, [r]

28 for dominion belongs to the LORD [s]
   and he rules over the nations.

29 All the rich [t] of the earth will feast and worship;
   all who go down to the dust [u] will kneel before him—
   those who cannot keep themselves alive.

30 Posterity [v] will serve him;
   future generations will be told about the Lord.

31 They will proclaim his righteousness
   to a people yet unborn [w]—
   for he has done it.

Psalm 23

A psalm of David.

1 The LORD is my shepherd, [x] I shall not be in want. [y]

2   He makes me lie down in green pastures,
   he leads me beside quiet waters, [z]

3   he restores my soul. [a]
   He guides me in paths of righteousness [b]
   for his name's sake.

4 Even though I walk
   through the valley of the shadow of death, [a][c]
   I will fear no evil, [d]
   for you are with me; [e]

a 4 Or through the darkest valley

Psalm 23

Psalm 23 is one of the most familiar and best loved poems in the Psalter, but such familiarity can make it difficult to read with fresh eyes. At its heart Psalm 23 is an expression of confidence in the protective care of God, upon whom the psalmist David expressed

---

Snapshots

23:4–6

Agness: A Positive Outlook

Agness, the development facilitator for a Christian organization in Zambia, had to cope, without explanation, with the loss of a daughter, son, and two husbands within ten years. She finally reached resolution of the ominous puzzle by insisting on HIV/AIDS testing for herself—testing she and her last spouse had incredibly been denied.

"My experience has helped me to understand what the people I work with pass through."

Agness, despite her HIV-positive status, hasn't given up on life and intends to pursue her long-standing dreams of acquiring higher qualifications in human resource management and owning a farm. She faces an uncertain future by clinging to hope in Jesus Christ. "At first I felt frustrated, cheated, used, and betrayed by everyone around, including God. But my experience has helped me to understand what the people I work with pass through."

"Do not feel too comfortable now," she counsels her colleagues, "because you might not even know your status . . . . As for organizations, your employee who is [HIV] positive is still very useful to you as before; do not neglect them now [when] they need you more than ever. Show them you care not only for the fruit they produce but also for who they are."

your rod and your staff,
    they comfort me.
5 You prepare a table before me
    in the presence of my enemies.
You anoint my head with oil;^f
    my cup^g overflows.
6 Surely goodness and love will follow me
    all the days of my life,
and I will dwell in the house of the Lord
    forever.

23:5
f Ps 92:10 g Ps 16:5

Psalm 24

Of David. A psalm.

1 The earth is the Lord's, ^h and everything in it,
    the world, and all who live in it;ⁱ
2 for he founded it upon the seas
    and established it upon the waters.

24:1
h Ex 9:29;
Job 41:11; Ps 89:11
i 1Co 10:26*

3 Who may ascend the hill^j of the Lord?
    Who may stand in his holy place?^k
4 He who has clean hands^l and a pure heart,^m
    who does not lift up his soul to an idol
    or swear by what is false.^a
5 He will receive blessing from the Lord
    and vindication from God his Savior.
6 Such is the generation of those who seek him,
    who seek your face,ⁿ O God of Jacob.^b

24:3
j Ps 2:6 k Ps 15:1;
65:4

24:4
l Job 17:9 m Mt 5:8

Selah

24:6
n Ps 27:8
24:7
o Isa 26:2 p Ps 97:6;
1Co 2:8

7 Lift up your heads, O you gates;^o
    be lifted up, you ancient doors,
    that the King of glory^p may come in.
8 Who is this King of glory?
    The Lord strong and mighty,
    the Lord mighty in battle.^q
9 Lift up your heads, O you gates;

24:8
q Ps 76:3-6

^a 4 Or *swear falsely*   ^b 6 Two Hebrew manuscripts and Syriac (see also Septuagint); most Hebrew manuscripts *face, Jacob*

---

absolute dependence. The idea of a pilgrimage through dangerous territory to "the house of the Lord" (v. 6) is subtly interwoven with images of shepherd and flock.

📖 Our desire to dwell in God's house is more than a hope of escape from our enemies. It involves coming into and remaining in the presence of God's glory. Being in God's presence implies our ability to gain his guidance, as well as to experience the blessings of divine hospitality: abundant provision, steadfast love, forgiveness, light, and life. Dwelling with God is to experience what Paul spoke of as the mature Christian's goal: to see God face-to-face and to know him fully, as we are fully known by him (1 Cor. 13:12).

Psalm 24

🔖 After affirming God's creative power and continuing authority over the whole world (vv. 1–2), Psalm 24 focuses on the creature who wants to enter the presence of this creator God. A person whose internal world (a "pure heart") and external world ("clean hands") are

integrated in loyalty to God "will receive blessing from the Lord" (vv. 4–5).

With its series of questions and answers, many commentators picture this psalm being sung by a throng of pilgrim worshipers approaching the temple mount in Jerusalem. Having gained admission to the temple precincts, the worshipers anticipate the arrival of the Lord himself (vv. 7–10).

📖 The entire world, not just Israel, belongs to the Lord (v. 1). This means that God's concern for the well-being of his creation extends far beyond the borders of the covenant people to include the Gentiles, the animals, and the physical creation. As God's agents (see Gen. 1:28; 2:15), we are called to view the world with his eyes—not to exert our own power to control, exploit, or use the earth to benefit ourselves. When we realize that our lives are in God's hands (see Matt. 6:25–34), we are emboldened to make decisions about our finances, relationships, and the environment that are based on something far greater than personal concern.

lift them up, you ancient doors,
   that the King of glory may come in.
10 Who is he, this King of glory?
   The LORD Almighty—
   he is the King of glory.

Selah

Psalm 25 [a]

Of David.

25:1
r Ps 86:4
25:2
s Ps 41:11

1 To you, O LORD, I lift up my soul; [r]
2   in you I trust, [s] O my God.
   Do not let me be put to shame,
      nor let my enemies triumph over me.

25:3
t Isa 49:23

3 No one whose hope is in you
      will ever be put to shame, [t]
   but they will be put to shame
      who are treacherous without excuse.

25:4
u Ex 33:13

4 Show me your ways, O LORD,
      teach me your paths; [u]
5 guide me in your truth and teach me,
      for you are God my Savior,
      and my hope is in you all day long.

25:6
v Ps 103:17;
Isa 63:7,15
25:7
w Job 13:26;
Jer 3:25 x Ps 51:1

6 Remember, O LORD, your great mercy and love, [v]
      for they are from of old.
7 Remember not the sins of my youth [w]
      and my rebellious ways;
   according to your love [x] remember me,
      for you are good, O LORD.

25:8
y Ps 92:15 z Ps 32:8

8 Good and upright [y] is the LORD;
      therefore he instructs [z] sinners in his ways.

25:9
a Ps 23:3
b Ps 27:11

9 He guides [a] the humble in what is right
      and teaches them [b] his way.

25:10
c Ps 40:11
d Ps 103:18
25:11
e Ps 31:3; 79:9

10 All the ways of the LORD are loving and faithful [c]
      for those who keep the demands of his covenant. [d]
11 For the sake of your name, [e] O LORD,
      forgive my iniquity, though it is great.

25:12
f Ps 37:23
25:13
g Pr 19:23
h Ps 37:11

12 Who, then, is the man that fears the LORD?
      He will instruct him in the way [f] chosen for him.
13 He will spend his days in prosperity, [g]
      and his descendants will inherit the land. [h]

25:14
i Pr 3:32

14 The LORD confides [i] in those who fear him;

a This psalm is an acrostic poem, the verses of which begin with the successive letters of the Hebrew alphabet.

Psalm 25

The 22 verses of this psalm form, with a few irregularities, an alphabetic acrostic poem (one that begins each verse with a successive letter of the Hebrew alphabet). The theme is finding the "way" or "ways" of God. This involves experiencing deliverance, prosperity, and divine grace. Closely related is the idea of "covenant," by which the "way" and its demands are made clear (vv. 10,14).

This psalm chips away at our traditional view of an Old Testament covenant of law and sharpens our vision of a covenant of grace offered to sinners in *both* Testaments. The law is the guidebook by which sinners are led to grace, acknowledging their sinfulness and relying wholly on God's mercy for salvation.

The covenant for sinners that Psalm 25 describes is a divine gift for which each of us may be personally grateful. How easily we identify with those personalities from both Testaments who struggled honestly with doubts, fears, and other inner conflicts. How thankful we can be that God calls sinners into relationship with himself, forgives our sin, and releases us from our guilt, as well as from the traps that would bind and hinder us. Thank the Lord today, the One who alone will free us from the snares of life (v. 15).

he makes his covenant known[j] to them.
15 My eyes are ever on the LORD,[k]
    for only he will release my feet from the snare.

16 Turn to me[l] and be gracious to me,
    for I am lonely and afflicted.
17 The troubles of my heart have multiplied;
    free me from my anguish.[m]
18 Look upon my affliction and my distress[n]
    and take away all my sins.
19 See how my enemies[o] have increased
    and how fiercely they hate me!
20 Guard my life[p] and rescue me;
    let me not be put to shame,
    for I take refuge in you.
21 May integrity[q] and uprightness protect me,
    because my hope is in you.

22 Redeem Israel,[r] O God,
    from all their troubles!

Psalm 26

Of David.

1 Vindicate me, O LORD,
    for I have led a blameless life;[s]
  I have trusted[t] in the LORD
    without wavering.[u]
2 Test me,[v] O LORD, and try me,
    examine my heart and my mind;[w]
3 for your love is ever before me,
    and I walk continually[x] in your truth.
4 I do not sit[y] with deceitful men,
    nor do I consort with hypocrites;
5 I abhor[z] the assembly of evildoers
    and refuse to sit with the wicked.
6 I wash my hands in innocence,[a]
    and go about your altar, O LORD,
7 proclaiming aloud your praise
    and telling of all your wonderful deeds.[b]
8 I love[c] the house where you live, O LORD,
    the place where your glory dwells.

9 Do not take away my soul along with sinners,
    my life with bloodthirsty men,[d]
10 in whose hands are wicked schemes,
    whose right hands are full of bribes.[e]
11 But I lead a blameless life;
    redeem me[f] and be merciful to me.

25:14
j Jn 7:17
25:15
k Ps 141:8

25:16
l Ps 69:16
25:17
m Ps 107:6
25:18
n 2Sa 16:12
25:19
o Ps 3:1
25:20
p Ps 86:2
25:21
q Ps 41:12
25:22
r Ps 130:8

26:1
s Ps 7:8; Pr 20:7
t Ps 28:7
u 2Ki 20:3;
Heb 10:23
26:2
v Ps 17:3 w Ps 7:9
26:3
x 2Ki 20:3
26:4
y Ps 1:1
26:5
z Ps 31:6; 139:21
26:6
a Ps 73:13
26:7
b Ps 9:1
26:8
c Ps 27:4
26:9
d Ps 28:3
26:10
e 1Sa 8:3
26:11
f Ps 69:18

Psalm 26

Psalm 26 is a prayer of redemption founded on a claim of personal innocence, which David invited God's penetrating gaze to confirm and honor. Psalm 26 shares with Psalm 25 a concern for vindication and is linked with Psalms 23–30 through a common focus on God's "house" or "dwelling." Psalm 26 lays out David's case for having lived the humble, innocent, trusting life Psalm 25 describes.

Have you ever wondered how you could gain confidence like David's in terms of your acceptability to God? Our trust is in what Paul calls "the righteousness from God" (Rom. 3:21–24)—the righteousness God confers on those who accept salvation through Christ. In the Bible's legal terms, we are declared "not guilty" by God and thus "justified." As Romans 5:1–5 makes clear, this righteousness gives us confidence to stand in the presence of our holy God without fear and to anticipate with great joy "the hope of the glory of God."

26:12
g Ps 27:11; 40:2
h Ps 22:22

12 My feet stand on level ground;*g*
  in the great assembly*h* I will praise the LORD.

Psalm 27

Of David.

27:1
i Isa 60:19 / Ex 15:2
k Ps 118:6

1 The LORD is my light*i* and my salvation*j*—
  whom shall I fear?
The LORD is the stronghold of my life—
  of whom shall I be afraid?*k*

27:2
l Ps 9:3; 14:4

2 When evil men advance against me
  to devour my flesh,*a*
when my enemies and my foes attack me,
  they will stumble and fall.*l*

27:3
m Ps 3:6 *n* Job 4:6

3 Though an army besiege me,
  my heart will not fear;*m*
though war break out against me,
  even then will I be confident.*n*

27:4
o Ps 90:17
p Ps 23:6; 26:8

4 One thing*o* I ask of the LORD,
  this is what I seek:
that I may dwell in the house of the LORD
  all the days of my life,*p*
to gaze upon the beauty of the LORD
  and to seek him in his temple.

27:5
q Ps 17:8; 31:20
r Ps 40:2
27:6
s Ps 3:3 *t* Ps 107:22

5 For in the day of trouble
  he will keep me safe in his dwelling;
he will hide me*q* in the shelter of his tabernacle
  and set me high upon a rock.*r*
6 Then my head will be exalted*s*
  above the enemies who surround me;
at his tabernacle will I sacrifice*t* with shouts of joy;
  I will sing and make music to the LORD.

27:7
u Ps 13:3

7 Hear my voice when I call, O LORD;
  be merciful to me and answer me.*u*
8 My heart says of you, "Seek his*b* face!"
  Your face, LORD, I will seek.

27:9
v Ps 69:17

9 Do not hide your face*v* from me,
  do not turn your servant away in anger;
  you have been my helper.
Do not reject me or forsake me,
  O God my Savior.
10 Though my father and mother forsake me,
  the LORD will receive me.
11 Teach me your way, O LORD;

---

a 2 Or *to slander me*   *b* 8 Or *To you, O my heart, he has said, "Seek my*

Psalm 27

Psalm 27 exudes confidence, though at its core it's a desperate plea for divine presence while under attack. The psalm is bracketed by declarations of David's trust in the Lord (vv. 1–6,13–14), which surround his prayer for God's presence and deliverance (vv. 7–12). In his repeated concluding instruction to "wait for the LORD," David leads the reader to embrace the same pattern of faithful endurance he modeled: In the face of suffering and attack, the faithful continue to trust in the Lord.

How hard has it been for you to wait on the Lord? Yet such patient assurance is perhaps the best way of demonstrating God's strength in our weakness. Whenever we frantically rush about, trying to make it on our own, we become functional atheists—denying by our actions God's activity in our lives. To admit that we are powerless is the first step toward acknowledging God's strength unleashed in our circumstances. Acceptance isn't resignation or despair but a step of trust and commitment—acknowledgment of our need to rely on God alone.

lead me in a straight path [w]
    because of my oppressors.
12 Do not turn me over to the desire of my foes,
    for false witnesses [x] rise up against me,
    breathing out violence.

13 I am still confident of this:
    I will see the goodness of the LORD [y]
    in the land of the living. [z]
14 Wait [a] for the LORD;
    be strong and take heart
    and wait for the LORD.

Psalm 28

Of David.

1 To you I call, O LORD my Rock;
    do not turn a deaf ear to me.
For if you remain silent, [b]
    I will be like those who have gone down to the pit. [c]
2 Hear my cry for mercy [d]
    as I call to you for help,
as I lift up my hands
    toward your Most Holy Place. [e]

3 Do not drag me away with the wicked,
    with those who do evil,
who speak cordially with their neighbors
    but harbor malice in their hearts. [f]
4 Repay them for their deeds
    and for their evil work;
repay them for what their hands have done [g]
    and bring back upon them what they deserve. [h]
5 Since they show no regard for the works of the LORD
    and what his hands have done, [i]
he will tear them down
    and never build them up again.

6 Praise be to the LORD,
    for he has heard my cry for mercy.
7 The LORD is my strength [j] and my shield;
    my heart trusts [k] in him, and I am helped.
My heart leaps for joy
    and I will give thanks to him in song. [l]

8 The LORD is the strength of his people,
    a fortress of salvation for his anointed one. [m]
9 Save your people and bless your inheritance; [n]
    be their shepherd [o] and carry them [p] forever.

27:11
w Ps 5:8; 25:4; 86:11

27:12
x Mt 26:60; Ac 9:1

27:13
y Ps 31:19
z Jer 11:19; Eze 26:20
27:14
a Ps 40:1

28:1
b Ps 83:1 c Ps 88:4

28:2
d Ps 138:2; 140:6
e Ps 5:7

28:3
f Ps 12:2; Ps 26:9; Jer 9:8

28:4
g 2Ti 4:14; Rev 22:12
h Rev 18:6

28:5
i Isa 5:12

28:7
j Ps 18:1 k Ps 13:5
l Ps 40:3; 69:30

28:8
m Ps 20:6
28:9
n Dt 9:29; Ezr 1:4
o Isa 40:11
p Dt 1:31; 32:11

Psalm 28

This brief psalm is a plea for deliverance. The psalmist felt close to death (v. 1) and sought retribution from God on his attackers (vv. 3–5). Using an economic term, "repay," he called for divine judgment on evildoers. Wages are tied to performance; we already know the quality of these evildoers' works. Certain that God had heard his appeal, the psalmist broke into praise (vv. 6–7). The psalm concludes with a plea for God to be Israel's "shepherd"—an appeal that forms a thematic parenthesis around Psalms 23–28 (see Ps. 23:1).

In the closing verse of this psalm, the psalmist first called on God to act in the two primary ways by which he brings about the well-being of his people: God "saves" us from time to time as circumstances require, and he "blesses" us day by day to make our lives and labors fruitful. The last, full answer to the psalmist's final prayer has come in the ministry of the "good shepherd," Jesus Christ. Read Psalm 28, aloud if you feel so moved. Then turn to John 10:7–18 and do the same.

Psalm 29

A psalm of David.

29:1
q 1Ch 16:28
r Ps 96:7-9

1 Ascribe to the LORD, *q* O mighty ones,
   ascribe to the LORD glory *r* and strength.

29:2
s 2Ch 20:21

2 Ascribe to the LORD the glory due his name;
   worship the LORD in the splendor of his *a* holiness. *s*

29:3
t Job 37:5
u Ps 18:13

3 The voice *t* of the LORD is over the waters;
   the God of glory thunders, *u*
   the LORD thunders over the mighty waters.

29:4
v Ps 68:33

4 The voice of the LORD is powerful; *v*
   the voice of the LORD is majestic.

29:5
w Jdg 9:15
29:6
x Ps 114:4 *y* Dt 3:9

5 The voice of the LORD breaks the cedars;
   the LORD breaks in pieces the cedars of Lebanon. *w*
6 He makes Lebanon skip *x* like a calf,
   Sirion *b y* like a young wild ox.
7 The voice of the LORD strikes
   with flashes of lightning.

29:8
z Nu 13:26

8 The voice of the LORD shakes the desert;
   the LORD shakes the Desert of Kadesh. *z*

29:9
a Ps 26:8

9 The voice of the LORD twists the oaks *c*
   and strips the forests bare.
   And in his temple all cry, "Glory!" *a*

29:10
b Ge 6:17
c Ps 10:16

10 The LORD sits *d* enthroned over the flood; *b*
   the LORD is enthroned as King forever. *c*

29:11
d Ps 28:8 *e* Ps 37:11

11 The LORD gives strength to his people; *d*
   the LORD blesses his people with peace. *e*

Psalm 30

*A psalm. A song. For the dedication of the temple. *e* Of David.*

1 I will exalt you, O LORD,
   for you lifted me out of the depths
   and did not let my enemies gloat over me. *f*

30:1
f Ps 25:2; 28:9
30:2
g Ps 88:13 *h* Ps 6:2

2 O LORD my God, I called to you for help *g*
   and you healed me. *h*

30:3
i Ps 28:1; 86:13

3 O LORD, you brought me up from the grave *f*;
   you spared me from going down into the pit. *i*

a 2 Or LORD *with the splendor of*   *b* 6 That is, Mount Hermon   *c* 9 Or LORD *makes the deer give birth*   *d* 10 Or *sat*   *e* Title: Or *palace*   *f* 3 Hebrew *Sheol*

Psalm 29

Psalm 29 presents a powerful description of God's appearance in the devastating power of a storm. Its poetry is characterized by repetition and expansion of words and ideas. This repetition builds excitement and intensity as the reader, with the poet, is caught in the midst of the riveting display of a rattling thunderstorm. Central to the psalm is the "voice" of God, who makes his glorious kingship known through the exhibition.

The cedars of Lebanon were the largest, most spectacular stands of trees in the region. They supplied *building materials for structures throughout the Mediterranean and were considered sacred by locals. Solomon imported these trees for use in building his palace and the temple (1 Kings 5:6–10; 7:1–12). God's power was displayed in his ability to break these symbols of strength and majesty.

When was the last time you were overwhelmed by a sense of God's powerful presence? When we really see him as he is, our only appropriate response is to kneel in acknowledgement of how far our lives, even at their best, are utterly removed from his righteousness. Then we catch a glimpse of how undeserved is the gracious love and salvation he pours out on us day by day.

Psalm 30

If "Of David" in the heading indicates authorship, the most probable occasion for Psalm 30 is recorded in 1 Chronicles 21:1—22:6. If this is the case, verses 2–3 refer to the psalmist's predicament as described in 1 Chronicles 21:17–30. Later, the psalm came to be

⁴Sing to the LORD, you saints ʲ of his;
    praise his holy name. ᵏ
⁵For his anger ˡ lasts only a moment,
    but his favor lasts a lifetime;
weeping may remain for a night,
    but rejoicing comes in the morning. ᵐ

⁶When I felt secure, I said,
    "I will never be shaken."
⁷O LORD, when you favored me,
    you made my mountain ᵃ stand firm;
but when you hid your face, ⁿ
    I was dismayed.

⁸To you, O LORD, I called;
    to the Lord I cried for mercy:
⁹"What gain is there in my destruction, ᵇ
    in my going down into the pit?
Will the dust praise you?
    Will it proclaim your faithfulness? ᵒ
¹⁰Hear, O LORD, and be merciful to me;
    O LORD, be my help."

¹¹You turned my wailing into dancing;

ᵃ 7 Or *hill country*   ᵇ 9 Or *there if I am silenced*

30:4	
ʲ Ps 149:1	
ᵏ Ps 97:12	
30:5	
ˡ Ps 103:9	
ᵐ 2Co 4:17	
30:7	
ⁿ Dt 31:17;	
Ps 104:29	
30:9	
ᵒ Ps 6:5	

applied to Israel's exilic experience. In such communal use, the "I" of the psalm became the corporate "person" of Israel—a common Old Testament mode of speaking.

Our perceptions of God's presence and involvement in our lives aren't always the best judges of reality. God is there even when we doubt his presence or fail to see him. Nevertheless, as Psalm 30 indicates, our ability to perceive him at work in the midst of a troubled time makes all the difference in the world. When we place our complete trust in God, our wailing can turn into a dance of joy, and rich "party clothes" can replace our sense of sorrow or dismay.

Snapshots

 30:4–7

Temka School

Around 900 children attend Temka School in Georgia (part of the former Soviet Union). Most come from poor families of a range of ethnicities. The opportunity for a free education was one thing they could count on—until the earthquake in April, 2001, nearly took that away.

During the Soviet period, when the train maintenance factory had been in operation and many parents were employed, the school achieved good results. But socioeconomic distress has contributed to a decline, and families now focus on survival.

On the day after the earthquake, families were informed that the school would remain closed until further notice. Happily, due to the rapid response and financial support of a Christian relief agency, the school was saved. Not only was it reopened in the fall, but children and teachers enjoy a safer and better insulated building, with improved sanitation facilities and a refurbished sports hall.

A letter from Giorgi, a fourth grader, represents the students' overwhelming response: "My kind friends, I was very worried when I thought about ruined walls . . . I could not see help anywhere, but finally you appeared and now I am afraid of nothing. Thank you very much."

> "I could not see help anywhere, but finally you appeared and now I am afraid of nothing."

30:11
p Ps 4:7;
Jer 31:4,13
30:12
q Ps 16:9 *r* Ps 44:8

you removed my sackcloth and clothed me with joy,*p*
12 that my heart may sing to you and not be silent.
O Lord my God, I will give you thanks*q* forever.*r*

Psalm 31

For the director of music. A psalm of David.

1 In you, O Lord, I have taken refuge;
   let me never be put to shame;
   deliver me in your righteousness.

31:2
s Ps 18:2

2 Turn your ear to me,
   come quickly to my rescue;
   be my rock of refuge,*s*
   a strong fortress to save me.

31:3
t Ps 18:2 *u* Ps 23:3

3 Since you are my rock and my fortress,*t*
   for the sake of your name*u* lead and guide me.

31:4
v Ps 25:15
31:5
w Lk 23:46; Ac 7:59

4 Free me from the trap that is set for me,
   for you are my refuge.*v*
5 Into your hands I commit my spirit;*w*
   redeem me, O Lord, the God of truth.

31:6
x Jnh 2:8

6 I hate those who cling to worthless idols;
   I trust in the Lord.*x*

31:7
y Ps 90:14
z Ps 10:14; Jn 10:27

7 I will be glad and rejoice in your love,
   for you saw my affliction*y*
   and knew the anguish*z* of my soul.

31:8
a Dt 32:30

8 You have not handed me over*a* to the enemy
   but have set my feet in a spacious place.

31:9
b Ps 6:7

9 Be merciful to me, O Lord, for I am in distress;
   my eyes grow weak with sorrow,*b*
   my soul and my body with grief.

31:10
c Ps 13:2 *d* Ps 38:3;
39:11

10 My life is consumed by anguish
   and my years by groaning;*c*
   my strength fails because of my affliction,*a*
   and my bones grow weak.*d*

31:11
e Job 19:13;
Ps 38:11; 64:8;
Isa 53:4

11 Because of all my enemies,
   I am the utter contempt of my neighbors;*e*
   I am a dread to my friends—
   those who see me on the street flee from me.

31:12
f Ps 88:4

12 I am forgotten by them as though I were dead;*f*

a 10 Or *guilt*

Psalm 31

This psalm is a plea for deliverance from the intrigues, plots, and conspiracies of an enemy. David appealed to the "God of truth" (v. 5) for protection from the "lying lips," arrogant speech, and "accusing tongues" of his opponents (vv. 18,20). He pictured God once again as the "strong fortress" and "refuge" (vv. 1–4) by which the beleaguered psalmist was protected from attack and preserved from the personal shame resulting from public slander (vv. 13,17). Luke's Gospel (23:46) records some of the words from verse 5 as Jesus' last utterance from the cross.

The testimony of this psalm refutes the common misperception, frequently implied in Proverbs and elsewhere in the Old Testament, that obedience leads unquestionably to benefit and prosperity. David (like Job)

knew the inward reality of innocence and yet experienced suffering and public ridicule. The lesson is twofold: The righteous can and often do suffer, and the blessing of righteousness is to be understood as different from the physical benefit and prosperity commonly anticipated.

David had learned to dwell in the shelter of the divine presence even when his personal life was in disarray and his situation offered no reasonable hope for escape. He was able to experience peace because of two discoveries—discoveries that can transform the outlooks of God's people in all generations in times of disgrace, public disapproval, or ridicule: (1) a personal identity, value, and hope found in God, independent of context or circumstance; and (2) the lesson of surrender, made possible by this newfound identity.

I have become like broken pottery.
13 For I hear the slander of many;
　　there is terror on every side;[g]
　they conspire against me
　　and plot to take my life.[h]

14 But I trust[i] in you, O LORD;
　　I say, "You are my God."
15 My times[j] are in your hands;
　　deliver me from my enemies
　　and from those who pursue me.
16 Let your face shine[k] on your servant;
　　save me in your unfailing love.
17 Let me not be put to shame,[l] O LORD,
　　for I have cried out to you;
　but let the wicked be put to shame
　　and lie silent[m] in the grave.[a]
18 Let their lying lips[n] be silenced,
　　for with pride and contempt
　　they speak arrogantly[o] against the righteous.

19 How great is your goodness,[p]
　　which you have stored up for those who fear you,
　which you bestow in the sight of men[q]
　　on those who take refuge in you.
20 In the shelter of your presence you hide[r] them
　　from the intrigues of men;[s]
　in your dwelling you keep them safe
　　from accusing tongues.

21 Praise be to the LORD,
　　for he showed his wonderful love[t] to me
　　when I was in a besieged city.[u]
22 In my alarm[v] I said,
　　"I am cut off from your sight!"
　Yet you heard my cry[w] for mercy
　　when I called to you for help.

23 Love the LORD, all his saints![x]
　　The LORD preserves the faithful,[y]
　but the proud he pays back[z] in full.
24 Be strong and take heart,[a]
　　all you who hope in the LORD.

Psalm 32

Of David. A *maskil*.[b]

1 Blessed is he
　　whose transgressions are forgiven,
　　whose sins are covered.[b]
2 Blessed is the man

---

[a] 17 Hebrew *Sheol*　　[b] Title: Probably a literary or musical term

---

31:13
[g] Jer 20:3, 10;
La 2:22 [h] Mt 27:1

31:14
[i] Ps 140:6

31:15
[j] Job 24:1; Ps 143:9

31:16
[k] Nu 6:25; Ps 4:6

31:17
[l] Ps 25:2-3
[m] Ps 115:17

31:18
[n] Ps 120:2
[o] Ps 94:4

31:19
[p] Ro 11:22
[q] Isa 64:4

31:20
[r] Ps 27:5 [s] Job 5:21

31:21
[t] Ps 17:7 [u] 1Sa 23:7

31:22
[v] Ps 116:11
[w] La 3:54

31:23
[x] Ps 34:9
[y] Ps 145:20
[z] Ps 94:2

31:24
[a] Ps 27:14

32:1
[b] Ps 85:2

Psalm 32

Psalm 32 couples thanksgiving with instruction encouraging the reader not to resist God's guidance but to trust fully in him. The affirmation in verse 5 that God "forgave" David's guilt is expressed in Hebrew as the lifting away or bearing of that guilt. This term is used re-peatedly in the Old Testament in relation to God (e.g., Ex. 34:7; Num. 14:18; Mic. 7:18). Isaiah (Isa. 33:24) said that the sins of those who dwelt in Jerusalem would be forgiven (lit., "lifted up") by God. Ultimately, God's "lifting up" or bearing our sin and guilt was accomplished by Jesus on the cross.

The Eternal Now and the Temporal Now

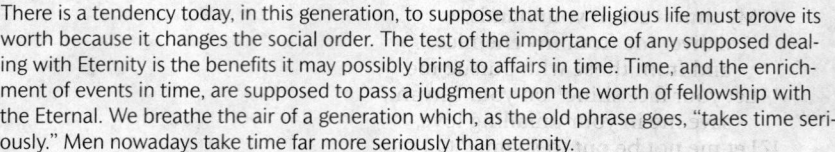

31:14–16

There is a tendency today, in this generation, to suppose that the religious life must prove its worth because it changes the social order. The test of the importance of any supposed dealing with Eternity is the benefits it may possibly bring to affairs in time. Time, and the enrichment of events in time, are supposed to pass a judgment upon the worth of fellowship with the Eternal. We breathe the air of a generation which, as the old phrase goes, "takes time seriously." Men nowadays take time far more seriously than eternity.

German theology of a century ago emphasized a useful distinction between This-sidedness and Other-sidedness, or Here and Yonder. The church used to be chiefly concerned with Yonder, it was oriented toward the world beyond, and was little concerned with this world and its sorrows and hungers. Because the sincere workingman, who suffered under economic privations, called out for bread, for whole-wheat-flour bread, the church of that day replied,

> **Time is no judge of Eternity. It is the Eternal who is the judge and tester of time.**

"You are worldly-minded, you are crass, you are materialistic, you are oriented toward the Here. You ought to seek the heavenly, the eternal, the Yonder." But the workingman wasn't materialistic, he was hungry; and Marxian socialism promised him just the temporal bread he needed, whereas the church had rebuked him for not hungering for the eternal Bread.

All this is now changed. We are in an era of This-sidedness, with a passionate anxiety about economics and political organization. And the church itself has largely gone "this-sided," and large areas of the Society of Friends seem to be predominantly concerned with this world, with time, and with the temporal order. And the test of the worthwhileness of any experience of Eternity has become: "Does it change things in time? If so, let us keep it, if not, let us discard it."

I submit that this is a lamentable reversal of the true order of dependence. Time is no judge of Eternity. It is the Eternal who is the judge and tester of time.

But in saying this I am not proposing that we leave the one-sidedness of the Here and of time-preoccupation for the equal one-sidedness of the Yonder, nor advocate a lofty scorn of this maimed and bleeding world while we bask serenely upon the sunny shores of the Eternal. But I am persuaded that in the Quaker experience of Divine Presence there is a serious retention of both time and the timeless, with the final value and significance located in the Eternal, who is the creative root of time itself. For "I saw also that there was an ocean of darkness and death, but an infinite ocean of light and love which flowed over the ocean of darkness."

Thomas R. Kelly, devotional author
Source: Thomas R. Kelly, *A Testament of Devotion* (New York: Harper & Row, 1941), 89–90

whose sin the LORD does not count against him[c]
and in whose spirit is no deceit.[d]

[3] When I kept silent,
    my bones wasted away[e]
    through my groaning all day long.
[4] For day and night
    your hand was heavy[f] upon me;
  my strength was sapped
    as in the heat of summer.   *Selah*
[5] Then I acknowledged my sin to you
    and did not cover up my iniquity.
I said, "I will confess[g]
    my transgressions[h] to the LORD"—
and you forgave
    the guilt of my sin.[i]   *Selah*

[6] Therefore let everyone who is godly pray to you
    while you may be found;[j]
surely when the mighty waters rise,
    they will not reach him.[k]
[7] You are my hiding place;
    you will protect me from trouble[l]
    and surround me with songs of deliverance.[m]   *Selah*

[8] I will instruct[n] you and teach you in the way you should go;
    I will counsel you and watch over[o] you.
[9] Do not be like the horse or the mule,
    which have no understanding
but must be controlled by bit and bridle[p]
    or they will not come to you.
[10] Many are the woes of the wicked,[q]
    but the LORD's unfailing love
    surrounds the man who trusts[r] in him.
[11] Rejoice in the LORD[s] and be glad, you righteous;
    sing, all you who are upright in heart!

Psalm 33

[1] Sing joyfully to the LORD, you righteous;
    it is fitting[t] for the upright[u] to praise him.
[2] Praise the LORD with the harp;
    make music to him on the ten-stringed lyre.[v]
[3] Sing to him a new song;[w]
    play skillfully, and shout for joy.

[4] For the word of the LORD is right[x] and true;
    he is faithful in all he does.
[5] The LORD loves righteousness and justice;[y]
    the earth is full of his unfailing love.[z]

32:2
[c] Ro 4:7-8*;
2Co 5:19 [d] Jn 1:47

32:3
[e] Ps 31:10

32:4
[f] Job 33:7

32:5
[g] Pr 28:13
[h] Ps 103:12
[i] Lev 26:40

32:6
[j] Ps 69:13; Isa 55:6
[k] Isa 43:2

32:7
[l] Ps 9:9 [m] Ex 15:1

32:8
[n] Ps 25:8
[o] Ps 33:18

32:9
[p] Pr 26:3

32:10
[q] Ro 2:9 [r] Pr 16:20

32:11
[s] Ps 64:10

33:1
[t] Ps 147:1
[u] Ps 32:11

33:2
[v] Ps 92:3
33:3
[w] Ps 96:1

33:4
[x] Ps 19:8

33:5
[y] Ps 11:7
[z] Ps 119:64

How comfortable are you with public confession of sin, either personally or from others? Particularly in North America, two factors inhibit our willingness to admit faults even among fellow Christians. (1) A fierce independent streak characterizes our society. The desire—even demand—for personal privacy is linked to a sense of conditional tolerance (what's "good" for you is okay with me as long as you treat me the same way). (2) A sense of perfectionism pervades much of the church, making it even less likely for us to admit to our mistakes and sins.

Psalm 33

Psalm 33 is a hymn of praise to God, celebrating his righteous character, creative power, and sovereignty—qualities that make him the only reliable foundation for trust and hope. The original occasion of the psalm is un-

33:6
a Heb 11:3

33:8
b Ps 67:7; 96:9

33:9
c Ge 1:3; Ps 148:5
33:10
d Isa 8:10

33:11
e Job 23:13

33:12
f Ps 144:15
g Ex 19:5; Dt 7:6

33:13
h Job 28:24;
Ps 11:4
33:14
i 1Ki 8:39
33:15
j Job 10:8
k Jer 32:19

33:16
l Ps 44:6

33:17
m Ps 20:7; Pr 21:31

33:18
n Job 36:7;
Ps 34:15
o Ps 147:11

33:19
p Job 5:20

33:20
q Ps 130:6

33:21
r Zec 10:7; Jn 16:22

34:1
s Ps 71:6; Eph 5:20

6 By the word *a* of the LORD were the heavens made,
their starry host by the breath of his mouth.
7 He gathers the waters of the sea into jars*a*;
he puts the deep into storehouses.
8 Let all the earth fear the LORD;
let all the people of the world revere him. *b*
9 For he spoke, and it came to be;
he commanded, *c* and it stood firm.
10 The LORD foils the plans of the nations; *d*
he thwarts the purposes of the peoples.
11 But the plans of the LORD stand firm forever,
the purposes *e* of his heart through all generations.

12 Blessed is the nation whose God is the LORD, *f*
the people he chose *g* for his inheritance.
13 From heaven the LORD looks down
and sees all mankind; *h*
14 from his dwelling place *i* he watches
all who live on earth—
15 he who forms *j* the hearts of all,
who considers everything they do. *k*
16 No king is saved by the size of his army; *l*
no warrior escapes by his great strength.
17 A horse *m* is a vain hope for deliverance;
despite all its great strength it cannot save.
18 But the eyes *n* of the LORD are on those who fear him,
on those whose hope is in his unfailing love, *o*
19 to deliver them from death
and keep them alive in famine. *p*

20 We wait *q* in hope for the LORD;
he is our help and our shield.
21 In him our hearts rejoice, *r*
for we trust in his holy name.
22 May your unfailing love rest upon us, O LORD,
even as we put our hope in you.

Psalm 34 *b*

Of David. When he pretended to be insane before Abimelech, who drove him away,
and he left.

1 I will extol the LORD at all times; *s*
his praise will always be on my lips.

a 7 Or *sea as into a heap*   *b* This psalm is an acrostic poem, the verses of which begin with the
successive letters of the Hebrew alphabet.

---

known, but a time of national deliverance is suggested—
perhaps following a famine (v. 19). The scene is a joyous
occasion with the community joining in exuberant praise.

📖 Have you ever been delivered from near disaster
or had an unusually miraculous recovery from a difficult
situation? If so, you understand the emotions expressed
here. Praise to God is the appropriate ("fitting") response for his intervention and deliverance. Moreover,
God's essential character is grounded in justice and
righteousness. It's who he is at his core. He's trustworthy
because of the daily evidence of his faithful care over
the world he has made.

Psalm 34

📖 The heading assigns this psalm to the occasion
in David's life recorded in 1 Samuel 21:10–15. Not all
agree with this tradition, though. Some feel it's more
likely that early Hebrew editors of the Psalms linked
1 Samuel 21 with Psalm 34 on the basis of word association. The psalm is an acrostic (each verse beginning with
a successive letter of the Hebrew alphabet) that starts
with praising God for deliverance in answer to prayer (vv.
1–7) and then shifts to a collection of proverbial sayings.

The psalmist had an intense desire to "extol the LORD
at all times" (v. 1). He made it clear that those who are
called to praise God aren't beyond suffering and pain.

²My soul will boast^t in the LORD;
   let the afflicted hear and rejoice. ^u

³Glorify the LORD with me;
   let us exalt^v his name together.

⁴I sought the LORD, ^w and he answered me;
   he delivered me from all my fears.

⁵Those who look to him are radiant; ^x
   their faces are never covered with shame. ^y

⁶This poor man called, and the LORD heard him;
   he saved him out of all his troubles.

⁷The angel of the LORD^z encamps around those who fear him,
   and he delivers them.

⁸Taste and see that the LORD is good; ^a
   blessed is the man who takes refuge^b in him.

⁹Fear the LORD, you his saints,
   for those who fear him lack nothing. ^c

¹⁰The lions may grow weak and hungry,
   but those who seek the LORD lack no good thing. ^d

¹¹Come, my children, listen to me;
   I will teach you^e the fear of the LORD.

¹²Whoever of you loves life^f
   and desires to see many good days,

¹³keep your tongue from evil
   and your lips from speaking lies. ^g

¹⁴Turn from evil and do good;^h
   seek peaceⁱ and pursue it.

¹⁵The eyes of the LORD^j are on the righteous^k
   and his ears are attentive to their cry;

¹⁶the face of the LORD is against^l those who do evil, ^m
   to cut off the memoryⁿ of them from the earth.

¹⁷The righteous cry out, and the LORD hears^o them;
   he delivers them from all their troubles.

¹⁸The LORD is close^p to the brokenhearted^q
   and saves those who are crushed in spirit.

¹⁹A righteous man may have many troubles, ^r
   but the LORD delivers him from them all; ^s

²⁰he protects all his bones,
   not one of them will be broken. ^t

²¹Evil will slay the wicked; ^u
   the foes of the righteous will be condemned.

²²The LORD redeems^v his servants;
   no one will be condemned who takes refuge in him.

34:2
t Jer 9:24; 1Co 1:31
u Ps 119:74

34:3
v Lk 1:46

34:4
w Mt 7:7

34:5
x Ps 36:9 y Ps 25:3

34:7
z 2Ki 6:17; Da 6:22

34:8
a 1Pe 2:3 b Ps 2:12

34:9
c Ps 23:1

34:10
d Ps 84:11

34:11
e Ps 32:8
34:12
f 1Pe 3:10

34:13
g 1Pe 2:22
34:14
h Ps 37:27
i Heb 12:14

34:15
j Ps 33:18
k Job 36:7

34:16
l Lev 17:10;
Jer 44:11
m 1Pe 3:10-12*
n Pr 10:7
34:17
o Ps 145:19

34:18
p Ps 145:18
q Isa 57:15

34:19
r ver 17 s ver 4,6;
Pr 24:16

34:20
t Jn 19:36*
34:21
u Ps 94:23

34:22
v 1Ki 1:29; Ps 71:23

Jesus' Beatitudes (Matt. 5:3–12) bear striking similarities to this psalm. God's nearness to the "broken-hearted" and "crushed in spirit" (v. 18) parallels Jesus' comments about the "poor in spirit." Compare "those who seek the LORD lack no good thing" (v. 10) with "those who hunger and thirst for righteousness . . . will be filled." The psalmist called the reader to "seek peace" (v. 14); Matthew 5:9 speaks of blessing for "peacemakers." Still today, God's kingdom comes to those who reject the world's power tactics and rely wholly on him as a refuge.

We often identify divine blessing with "getting the goods" in one way or another. We thank God for health, a comfortable lifestyle, a good reputation, a relatively trouble-free family life, and national security. And in so doing we rightly acknowledge our dependence on him. But this may lead us to associate God's blessing exclusively with such external evidence. This is to miss Jesus' point in the Beatitudes: The righteous suffer undeservedly, but in their suffering they glorify God and receive his blessing.

Psalm 35

Of David.

35:1
w Ps 43:1

¹ Contend, O LORD, with those who contend with me;
    fight ^w against those who fight against me.

35:2
x Ps 62:2

² Take up shield and buckler;
    arise ^x and come to my aid.
³ Brandish spear and javelin ^a
    against those who pursue me.
  Say to my soul,
    "I am your salvation."

35:4
y Ps 70:2

⁴ May those who seek my life
    be disgraced ^y and put to shame;
  may those who plot my ruin
    be turned back in dismay.

35:5
z Job 21:18; Ps 1:4;
Isa 29:5

⁵ May they be like chaff ^z before the wind,
    with the angel of the LORD driving them away;
⁶ may their path be dark and slippery,
    with the angel of the LORD pursuing them.
⁷ Since they hid their net for me without cause
    and without cause dug a pit for me,

35:8
a 1Th 5:3 b Ps 9:15

⁸ may ruin overtake them by surprise— ^a
  may the net they hid entangle them,
  may they fall into the pit, ^b to their ruin.

35:9
c Lk 1:47
d Isa 61:10

⁹ Then my soul will rejoice ^c in the LORD
    and delight in his salvation. ^d

35:10
e Ex 15:11
f Ps 18:17
g Ps 37:14

¹⁰ My whole being will exclaim,
    "Who is like you, ^e O LORD?
  You rescue the poor from those too strong ^f for them,
    the poor and needy ^g from those who rob them."

35:11
h Ps 27:12

¹¹ Ruthless witnesses ^h come forward;
    they question me on things I know nothing about.

35:12
i Jn 10:32

¹² They repay me evil for good ⁱ
    and leave my soul forlorn.

35:13
j Job 30:25;
Ps 69:10

¹³ Yet when they were ill, I put on sackcloth
    and humbled myself with fasting. ^j
  When my prayers returned to me unanswered,
¹⁴   I went about mourning
    as though for my friend or brother.
  I bowed my head in grief
    as though weeping for my mother.
¹⁵ But when I stumbled, they gathered in glee;
    attackers gathered against me when I was unaware.

35:15
k Job 30:1,8

  They slandered ^k me without ceasing.
¹⁶ Like the ungodly they maliciously mocked ^b;

---

^a 3 Or *and block the way*   ^b 16 Septuagint; Hebrew may mean *ungodly circle of mockers*.

Psalm 35

📖 Psalm 35 falls into the category of prayers for deliverance. It couches the incomparable nature of God not only in terms of power and might but also in light of his care for, and rescue of, the needy (v. 10). God is so superior in all things that he has no need to use power for self-interest. He's free to fight for the oppressed. This was the enduring hope Israel could cling to.

💻 This psalm cautions us to be clear about our motives when we seek public vindication or desire the downfall of our detractors. The psalmist's desire for public shame for his accusers (vv. 4,26) might leave you uncomfortable, especially in light of Jesus' admonition to "love your enemies" (Matt. 5:44; Luke 6:27,35). But the text emphasizes not so much wishing an enemy ill as desiring that God's justice prevail, with its necessary consequences. When we pray that God will set all things right, our plea also places *us* in need of mercy and forgiveness.

they gnashed their teeth[l] at me.

17 O Lord, how long[m] will you look on?
   Rescue my life from their ravages,
   my precious life[n] from these lions.
18 I will give you thanks in the great assembly;[o]
   among throngs of people I will praise you.[p]

19 Let not those gloat over me
   who are my enemies without cause;
   let not those who hate me without reason[q]
   maliciously wink the eye.[r]
20 They do not speak peaceably,
   but devise false accusations
   against those who live quietly in the land.
21 They gape[s] at me and say, "Aha! Aha![t]
   With our own eyes we have seen it."

22 O Lord, you have seen[u] this; be not silent.
   Do not be far[v] from me, O Lord.
23 Awake,[w] and rise to my defense!
   Contend for me, my God and Lord.
24 Vindicate me in your righteousness, O Lord my God;
   do not let them gloat over me.
25 Do not let them think, "Aha, just what we wanted!"
   or say, "We have swallowed him up."[x]

26 May all who gloat over my distress
   be put to shame[y] and confusion;
   may all who exalt themselves over me[z]
   be clothed with shame and disgrace.
27 May those who delight in my vindication[a]
   shout for joy[b] and gladness;
   may they always say, "The Lord be exalted,
   who delights[c] in the well-being of his servant."
28 My tongue will speak of your righteousness[d]
   and of your praises all day long.

Psalm 36

For the director of music. Of David the servant of the Lord.

1 An oracle is within my heart
   concerning the sinfulness of the wicked:[a]
   There is no fear of God
   before his eyes.[e]
2 For in his own eyes he flatters himself
   too much to detect or hate his sin.
3 The words of his mouth[f] are wicked and deceitful;
   he has ceased to be wise[g] and to do good.[h]
4 Even on his bed he plots evil;[i]
   he commits himself to a sinful course[j]
   and does not reject what is wrong.[k]

[a] 1 Or heart: / Sin proceeds from the wicked.

35:16 [l] Job 16:9; La 2:16
35:17 [m] Hab 1:13 [n] Ps 22:20
35:18 [o] Ps 22:25 [p] Ps 22:22
35:19 [q] Ps 38:19; 69:4; Jn 15:25* [r] Ps 13:4; Pr 6:13
35:21 [s] Ps 22:13 [t] Ps 40:15
35:22 [u] Ex 3:7 [v] Ps 10:1; 28:1
35:23 [w] Ps 44:23
35:25 [x] La 2:16
35:26 [y] Ps 40:14; 109:29 [z] Ps 38:16
35:27 [a] Ps 9:4 [b] Ps 32:11 [c] Ps 40:16; 147:11
35:28 [d] Ps 51:14
36:1 [e] Ro 3:18*
36:3 [f] Ps 10:7 [g] Ps 94:8 [h] Jer 4:22
36:4 [i] Pr 4:16; Mic 2:1 [j] Isa 65:2 [k] Ps 52:3; Ro 12:9

Psalm 36

Psalm 36 offers us the confidence to withstand the arrogant evil of the wicked because of a divine revelation of the all-encompassing love of God for those who know him. Its central theme concerning the downfall of evildoers, as well as its concluding declaration ("See how the evildoers lie fallen"), prepares the way for the extended description of the destruction of the wicked that occupies much of Psalm 37.

Rather than focusing only on evildoers and on diffi-

36:6
l Job 11:8;
Ps 77:19; Ro 11:33

36:7
m Ru 2:12; Ps 17:8
36:8
n Ps 65:4
o Job 20:17;
Rev 22:1
36:9
p Jer 2:13 *q* 1Pe 2:9

36:12
r Ps 140:10

37:1
s Pr 23:17-18
t Ps 73:3
37:2
u Ps 90:6

37:3
v Dt 30:20
w Isa 40:11; Jn 10:9
37:4
x Isa 58:14

37:5
y Ps 4:5; Ps 55:22;
Pr 16:3; 1Pe 5:7
37:6
z Mic 7:9
a Job 11:17
37:7
b Ps 62:5; La 3:26
c Ps 40:1

5 Your love, O LORD, reaches to the heavens,
   your faithfulness to the skies.
6 Your righteousness is like the mighty mountains,
   your justice like the great deep. *l*
   O LORD, you preserve both man and beast.
7   How priceless is your unfailing love!
   Both high and low among men
      find *a* refuge in the shadow of your wings. *m*
8 They feast on the abundance of your house; *n*
   you give them drink from your river *o* of delights.
9 For with you is the fountain of life; *p*
   in your light *q* we see light.

10 Continue your love to those who know you,
   your righteousness to the upright in heart.
11 May the foot of the proud not come against me,
   nor the hand of the wicked drive me away.
12 See how the evildoers lie fallen—
   thrown down, not able to rise! *r*

Psalm 37 *b*

Of David.

1 Do not fret because of evil men
   or be envious *s* of those who do wrong; *t*
2 for like the grass they will soon wither,
   like green plants they will soon die away. *u*

3 Trust in the LORD and do good;
   dwell in the land *v* and enjoy safe pasture. *w*
4 Delight *x* yourself in the LORD
   and he will give you the desires of your heart.

5 Commit your way to the LORD;
   trust in him *y* and he will do this:
6 He will make your righteousness *z* shine like the dawn, *a*
   the justice of your cause like the noonday sun.

7 Be still *b* before the LORD and wait patiently *c* for him;
   do not fret when men succeed in their ways,
   when they carry out their wicked schemes.

a 7 Or *love, O God! / Men find; or love! / Both heavenly beings and men / find*   *b* This psalm is an acrostic poem, the stanzas of which begin with the successive letters of the Hebrew alphabet.

cult circumstances, David entrusted himself to the God of steadfast love. God is so faithful that he saves animals as well as humans (v. 6)!

Are you bothered by the fact that the wicked often prosper while the righteous suffer? The apparent contradiction between what is and what ought to be tempts some to give up on God, his world, and even life. But the psalmist chose to focus on God's character. Grumbling and complaining destroy life and faith, while praise and thanksgiving embolden us to trust God despite our circumstances.

Psalm 37

This is an acrostic psalm (each verse begins with a successive letter of the Hebrew alphabet). It contains numerous proverbial sayings in a loose framework that explores two major themes: the problem of the apparent prosperity of the wicked and the need for the faithful to trust the Lord and find refuge in him. The pledge that the wicked "will be cut off" is repeatedly coupled with the promise that the faithful "will inherit the land."

Observation and experience uncovered exceptions to the psalmist's concept of justice for evil. He responded in two ways: (1) by refusing to allow the success of the wicked to undermine his confidence in God's justice and goodness; and (2) by acknowledging that, in spite of the faithful endurance of God's people, the score isn't always evened out in this life. This understanding opens a window on a new value system that finds a relationship with God supported by righteous living far superior to wealth, power, or health.

8 Refrain from anger[d] and turn from wrath;
do not fret—it leads only to evil.
9 For evil men will be cut off,
but those who hope in the LORD will inherit the land.[e]

10 A little while, and the wicked will be no more;[f]
though you look for them, they will not be found.
11 But the meek will inherit the land[g]
and enjoy great peace.

12 The wicked plot against the righteous
and gnash their teeth[h] at them;
13 but the Lord laughs at the wicked,
for he knows their day is coming.[i]

14 The wicked draw the sword
and bend the bow[j]
to bring down the poor and needy,[k]
to slay those whose ways are upright.
15 But their swords will pierce their own hearts,[l]
and their bows will be broken.

16 Better the little that the righteous have
than the wealth[m] of many wicked;
17 for the power of the wicked will be broken,[n]
but the LORD upholds the righteous.

18 The days of the blameless are known to the LORD,[o]
and their inheritance will endure forever.
19 In times of disaster they will not wither;
in days of famine they will enjoy plenty.

20 But the wicked will perish:
The LORD's enemies will be like the beauty of the fields,
they will vanish—vanish like smoke.[p]

21 The wicked borrow and do not repay,
but the righteous give generously;[q]
22 those the LORD blesses will inherit the land,
but those he curses[r] will be cut off.

23 If the LORD delights[s] in a man's way,
he makes his steps firm;[t]
24 though he stumble, he will not fall,[u]
for the LORD upholds[v] him with his hand.

25 I was young and now I am old,
yet I have never seen the righteous forsaken[w]
or their children begging bread.
26 They are always generous and lend freely;
their children will be blessed.[x]

27 Turn from evil and do good;[y]
then you will dwell in the land forever.
28 For the LORD loves the just
and will not forsake his faithful ones.

37:8 [d] Eph 4:31; Col 3:8
37:9 [e] Isa 57:13; 60:21
37:10 [f] Job 7:10; 24:24
37:11 [g] Mt 5:5
37:12 [h] Ps 35:16
37:13 [i] 1Sa 26:10; Ps 2:4
37:14 [j] Ps 11:2 [k] Ps 35:10
37:15 [l] Ps 9:16
37:16 [m] Pr 15:16
37:17 [n] Job 38:15; Ps 10:15
37:18 [o] Ps 1:6
37:20 [p] Ps 102:3
37:21 [q] Ps 112:5
37:22 [r] Job 5:3; Pr 3:33
37:23 [s] Ps 147:11 [t] 1Sa 2:9
37:24 [u] Pr 24:16 [v] Ps 145:14; 147:6
37:25 [w] Heb 13:5
37:26 [x] Ps 147:13
37:27 [y] Ps 34:14

Fretting about the characteristics of a fallen world can dull us to the richness of our relationship with God and diminish our determination to confront and eliminate suffering and injustice: To struggle against evil is to remain faithful to the vision of a holy God, who calls us to be holy too. It may be that in our world righteous people seem forsaken and their children beg for food (v. 25) because God has been waiting to act through us to provide for them. We can't by our own efforts eradicate evil or put ourselves in God's place, but at times God does wait to work out his purposes through us.

37:28
z Ps 21:10;
Isa 14:20
37:29
a ver 9; Pr 2:21

They will be protected forever,
but the offspring of the wicked will be cut off;[z]
29 the righteous will inherit the land[a]
and dwell in it forever.

30 The mouth of the righteous man utters wisdom,
and his tongue speaks what is just.

37:31
b Dt 6:6; Ps 40:8;
Isa 51:7 c ver 23

31 The law of his God is in his heart;[b]
his feet do not slip.[c]

37:32
d Ps 10:8

32 The wicked lie in wait[d] for the righteous,
seeking their very lives;

37:33
e Ps 109:31;
2Pe 2:9
37:34
f Ps 27:14 g Ps 52:6

33 but the LORD will not leave them in their power
or let them be condemned when brought to trial.[e]

34 Wait for the LORD[f]
and keep his way.
He will exalt you to inherit the land;
when the wicked are cut off, you will see[g] it.

37:35
h Job 5:3

35 I have seen a wicked and ruthless man
flourishing[h] like a green tree in its native soil,

37:36
i Job 20:5

36 but he soon passed away and was no more;
though I looked for him, he could not be found.[i]

37:37
j Isa 57:1-2

37 Consider the blameless, observe the upright;
there is a future[a] for the man of peace.[j]

37:38
k Ps 1:4

38 But all sinners will be destroyed;
the future[b] of the wicked will be cut off.[k]

37:39
l Ps 3:8 m Ps 9:9
37:40
n 1Ch 5:20
o Isa 31:5

39 The salvation[l] of the righteous comes from the LORD;
he is their stronghold in time of trouble.[m]
40 The LORD helps[n] them and delivers[o] them;
he delivers them from the wicked and saves them,
because they take refuge in him.

Psalm 38

A psalm of David. A petition.

38:1
p Ps 6:1
38:2
q Job 6:4; Ps 32:4

1 O LORD, do not rebuke me in your anger
or discipline me in your wrath.[p]
2 For your arrows[q] have pierced me,
and your hand has come down upon me.

38:3
r Ps 6:2; Isa 1:6

3 Because of your wrath there is no health in my body;
my bones[r] have no soundness because of my sin.

38:4
s Ezr 9:6

4 My guilt has overwhelmed me
like a burden too heavy to bear.[s]

38:5
t Ps 69:5

5 My wounds fester and are loathsome
because of my sinful folly.[t]
6 I am bowed down and brought very low;

a 37 Or there will be posterity   b 38 Or posterity

Psalm 38

Psalm 38 is a lament, a plea for deliverance from trouble—in this case, from severe anguish as a result of personal sin. Verses 5–10 count the physical consequences of sin. Verses 11–20 relay the disruptive effects of sin on David's relationships: with friends, companions, and neighbors who distanced themselves because of his wounds, and with opponents who considered David's sickness an opportunity to take advantage of him.

David's final cry (vv. 21–22) was directed to God within the hearing of the community of faith. It was a plea for divine response and a testimony of faithful reliance. David was both calling for divine deliverance and acknowledging God as the one source of hope for those who fail.

all day long I go about mourning.[u]

7 My back is filled with searing pain;[v]
  there is no health in my body.
8 I am feeble and utterly crushed;
  I groan[w] in anguish of heart.

9 All my longings lie open before you, O Lord;
  my sighing[x] is not hidden from you.
10 My heart pounds, my strength fails[y] me;
  even the light has gone from my eyes.[z]
11 My friends and companions avoid me because of my wounds;[a]
  my neighbors stay far away.
12 Those who seek my life set their traps,[b]
  those who would harm me talk of my ruin;[c]
  all day long they plot deception.[d]

13 I am like a deaf man, who cannot hear,
  like a mute, who cannot open his mouth;
14 I have become like a man who does not hear,
  whose mouth can offer no reply.
15 I wait[e] for you, O Lord;
  you will answer,[f] O Lord my God.
16 For I said, "Do not let them gloat[g]
  or exalt themselves over me when my foot slips."[h]

17 For I am about to fall,
  and my pain is ever with me.
18 I confess my iniquity;[i]
  I am troubled by my sin.
19 Many are those who are my vigorous enemies;[j]
  those who hate me without reason[k] are numerous.
20 Those who repay my good with evil[l]
  slander me when I pursue what is good.

21 O Lord, do not forsake me;
  be not far[m] from me, O my God.
22 Come quickly to help me,[n]
  O Lord my Savior.[o]

Psalm 39

For the director of music. For Jeduthun. A psalm of David.

1 I said, "I will watch my ways[p]
  and keep my tongue from sin;[q]
I will put a muzzle on my mouth
  as long as the wicked are in my presence."
2 But when I was silent[r] and still,
  not even saying anything good,
  my anguish increased.
3 My heart grew hot within me,

38:6
u Job 30:28;
Ps 35:14; 42:9
38:7
v Ps 102:3
38:8
w Ps 22:1
38:9
x Job 3:24; Ps 6:6;
10:17
38:10
y Ps 31:10 z Ps 6:7
38:11
a Ps 31:11
38:12
b Ps 140:5
c Ps 35:4; 54:3
d Ps 35:20
38:15
e Ps 39:7 f Ps 17:6
38:16
g Ps 35:26
h Ps 13:4
38:18
i Ps 32:5
38:19
j Ps 18:17
k Ps 35:19
38:20
l Ps 35:12; 1Jn 3:12
38:21
m Ps 35:22
38:22
n Ps 40:13
o Ps 27:1
39:1
p 1Ki 2:4
q Job 2:10; Jas 3:2
39:2
r Ps 38:13

The public today seems fascinated with the fall of heroes or with good men or women gone wrong. Psalm 38 helps us see that individual acknowledgment of sin is the only way out of its fear and destruction. The text also calls us in the community of faith to lend a caring hand and listening ear to the fallen. In this way we demonstrate the wholeness of God, who desires all to recognize their sin and experience his forgiveness and restoration (cf. Ezek. 33:10–12).

Psalm 39

Psalms 38 and 39 both speak of divine "rebuke" and "discipline" for sin (38:1; 39:11) as "blows" or "wounds" (38:11; 39:10) from the "hand" of God (38:2; 39:10). In both psalms David acknowledged personal sin as the cause of divine judgment and adopted an attitude of silent waiting in the presence of attackers. Both psalms stress—though in different ways—the fragile nature of human life.

and as I meditated, the fire burned;
    then I spoke with my tongue:

4 "Show me, O LORD, my life's end
    and the number of my days;[s]
    let me know how fleeting is my life.[t]
5 You have made my days[u] a mere handbreadth;
    the span of my years is as nothing before you.
    Each man's life is but a breath.[v]   Selah
6 Man is a mere phantom[w] as he goes to and fro:
    He bustles about, but only in vain;[x]
    he heaps up wealth, not knowing who will get it.[y]

7 "But now, Lord, what do I look for?
    My hope is in you.[z]
8 Save me[a] from all my transgressions;[b]
    do not make me the scorn of fools.[c]
9 I was silent; I would not open my mouth,[c]
    for you are the one who has done this.
10 Remove your scourge from me;
    I am overcome by the blow of your hand.[d]
11 You rebuke[e] and discipline men for their sin;
    you consume their wealth like a moth[f]—
    each man is but a breath.   Selah

12 "Hear my prayer, O LORD,
    listen to my cry for help;
    be not deaf to my weeping.
  For I dwell with you as an alien,[g]
    a stranger,[h] as all my fathers were.
13 Look away from me, that I may rejoice again
    before I depart and am no more."[i]

Psalm 40

For the director of music. Of David. A psalm.

1 I waited patiently[j] for the LORD;
    he turned to me and heard my cry.[k]
2 He lifted me out of the slimy pit,
    out of the mud and mire;[l]
  he set my feet on a rock[m]
    and gave me a firm place to stand.
3 He put a new song[n] in my mouth,
    a hymn of praise to our God.
  Many will see and fear
    and put their trust in the LORD.

Cross references

39:4
s Ps 90:12
t Ps 103:14

39:5
u Ps 89:45 v Ps 62:9

39:6
w 1Pe 1:24
x Ps 127:2
y Lk 12:20

39:7
z Ps 38:15
39:8
a Ps 51:9
b Ps 44:13
39:9
c Job 2:10

39:10
d Job 9:34; Ps 32:4
39:11
e 2Pe 2:16
f Job 13:28

39:12
g 1Pe 2:11
h Heb 11:13

39:13
i Job 10:21; 14:10

40:1
j Ps 27:14
k Ps 34:15

40:2
l Ps 69:14
m Ps 27:5

40:3
n Ps 33:3

The terms "alien" and "stranger" (v. 12) indicate a class of non-Israelites who were permitted to reside among God's people within the promised land but who had no "inheritance" there. These resident aliens could experience a degree of social interaction with the native inhabitants but enjoyed few rights. David drew on their experience as an analogy to the kind of painful barriers sin had erected between himself and God.

Sin is the great separator. Life moves quickly (v. 6), and sometimes we fail to take full measure of how our sin affects us physically, mentally, and spiritually. Have you, like David, thought of the ways in which sin

has alienated you from God? His initial response—silence—can be helpful to us as well. This period of stillness motivated David to meditate or reflect on God's actions, helping him turn wholly to God, understand and accept his discipline, and search for a renewed relationship with God in prayer.

Psalm 40

Like Psalms 37–39, Psalm 40 is a plea for deliverance from suffering as the consequence of personal sin. The theme of waiting for God in the midst of trouble, seen in these psalms, reaches a resolution in verse 1. Whereas in the former psalms God's response was antic-

4 Blessed is the man[o]
  who makes the LORD his trust,[p]
who does not look to the proud,
  to those who turn aside to false gods.[a]
5 Many, O LORD my God,
  are the wonders[q] you have done.
The things you planned for us
  no one can recount[r] to you;
were I to speak and tell of them,
  they would be too many to declare.

6 Sacrifice and offering you did not desire,[s]
  but my ears you have pierced[b,c];
burnt offerings[t] and sin offerings
  you did not require.
7 Then I said, "Here I am, I have come—
  it is written about me in the scroll.[d]
8 I desire to do your will,[u] O my God;
  your law is within my heart."[v]

9 I proclaim righteousness in the great assembly;[w]
  I do not seal my lips,
  as you know,[x] O LORD.
10 I do not hide your righteousness in my heart;
  I speak of your faithfulness[y] and salvation.
I do not conceal your love and your truth
  from the great assembly.[z]

11 Do not withhold your mercy from me, O LORD;
  may your love[a] and your truth[b] always protect me.
12 For troubles[c] without number surround me;
  my sins have overtaken me, and I cannot see.[d]
They are more than the hairs of my head,[e]
  and my heart fails[f] within me.

13 Be pleased, O LORD, to save me;
  O LORD, come quickly to help me.[g]
14 May all who seek to take my life
  be put to shame and confusion;
may all who desire my ruin[h]
  be turned back in disgrace.
15 May those who say to me, "Aha! Aha!"
  be appalled at their own shame.
16 But may all who seek you
  rejoice and be glad in you;

40:4
[o] Ps 34:8
[p] Ps 84:12

40:5
[q] Ps 136:4
[r] Ps 139:18; Isa 55:8

40:6
[s] 1Sa 15:22; Am 5:22 [t] Isa 1:11

40:8
[u] Jn 4:34 [v] Ps 37:31

40:9
[w] Ps 22:25
[x] Jos 22:22; Ps 119:13

40:10
[y] Ps 89:1
[z] Ac 20:20

40:11
[a] Pr 20:28 [b] Ps 43:3
40:12
[c] Ps 116:3 [d] Ps 38:4
[e] Ps 69:4 [f] Ps 73:26

40:13
[g] Ps 70:1

40:14
[h] Ps 35:4

---

[a] 4 Or *to falsehood*   [b] 6 Hebrew; Septuagint *but a body you have prepared for me* (see also Symmachus and Theodotion)   [c] 6 Or *opened*   [d] 7 Or *come / with the scroll written for me*

---

ipated and hoped for, here it's an experienced reality: "He turned to me and heard my cry."

One way to understand the harsh words in verse 6 about the sacrificial system is to take them as a reference to David's specific experience. He testified that, rather than demanding gifts and sacrifices as payment for his sin, God wanted his ears to be "pierced" (or "open"; see NIV text note)—attentive to God's instruction—and his heart to be willing to allow God's law for guidance. The result was plain: a desire within David to do God's will.

📖 At the heart of Psalm 40 stands David's self-description as one who, rather than "sealing [his] lips,"

proclaimed God's righteousness, love, and truth "in the great assembly" (vv. 9–10). As Christians we are encouraged in 1 John 1:9 to confess our sins, and James 5:14–16 asserts that such confession can be part of physical healing. While neither John nor James specified how we are to carry out the confession—privately or publicly—Psalm 40 leaves no doubt that the proclamation of God's righteousness is part of corporate (communal) worship. How has worshiping within the body of Christ helped you through a period of personal failure? How is confession of sin encouraged or facilitated in your fellowship of believers?

40:16
i Ps 35:27

may those who love your salvation always say,
    "The LORD be exalted!" *i*

17 Yet I am poor and needy;
    may the Lord think of me.
You are my help and my deliverer;
    O my God, do not delay. *j*

40:17
j Ps 70:5

Psalm 41

For the director of music. A psalm of David.

41:1
k Ps 82:3-4;
Pr 14:21

1 Blessed is he who has regard for the weak; *k*
    the LORD delivers him in times of trouble.

41:2
l Ps 37:22
m Ps 27:12

2 The LORD will protect him and preserve his life;
    he will bless him in the land *l*
    and not surrender him to the desire of his foes. *m*

3 The LORD will sustain him on his sickbed
    and restore him from his bed of illness.

41:4
n Ps 6:2 *o* Ps 51:4

4 I said, "O LORD, have mercy *n* on me;
    heal me, for I have sinned *o* against you."

41:5
p Ps 38:12

5 My enemies say of me in malice,
    "When will he die and his name perish? *p*"

41:6
q Ps 12:2 *r* Pr 26:24

6 Whenever one comes to see me,
    he speaks falsely, *q* while his heart gathers slander; *r*
    then he goes out and spreads it abroad.

41:7
s Ps 56:5; 71:10-11

7 All my enemies whisper together *s* against me;
    they imagine the worst for me, saying,

8 "A vile disease has beset him;
    he will never get up from the place where he lies."

41:9
t 2Sa 15:12;
Ps 55:12
u Job 19:19;
Ps 55:20; Mt 26:23;
Jn 13:18*

9 Even my close friend, *t* whom I trusted,
    he who shared my bread,
    has lifted up his heel against me. *u*

41:10
v Ps 3:3
41:11
w Ps 147:11
x Ps 25:2
41:12
y Ps 37:17
z Job 36:7

10 But you, O LORD, have mercy on me;
    raise me up, *v* that I may repay them.
11 I know that you are pleased with me, *w*
    for my enemy does not triumph over me. *x*
12 In my integrity you uphold me *y*
    and set me in your presence forever. *z*

41:13
a Ps 72:18
b Ps 89:52; 106:48

13 Praise be to the LORD, the God of Israel, *a*
    from everlasting to everlasting.
        Amen and Amen. *b*

Psalm 41

Psalm 41 closes Book I of the Psalter, with verse 13 serving as its doxology. The psalm is a lament in response to the malicious plotting of David's enemies during a debilitating sickness that had reduced his capacity to respond effectively to hostile insinuations and had raised his enemies' hopes for his coming downfall.

The person who has regard for the "weak" (v. 1) experiences God's blessing. But who are the *dallim* the NIV here calls the "weak"? Most Biblical occurrences of this Hebrew word have more to do with a lack of financial resources than with physical weakness. It was the king's responsibility to ensure the rights of the *dallim* and to provide equity for them. "If a king judges the poor with

fairness, his throne will always be secure," claims Proverbs 29:14 (cf. Ps. 72:1–4,12–14; Prov. 28:3; Jer. 22:16).

How can we respond effectively to or "regard" the needy today? We can (1) move beyond compassionate concern by taking the time to get to know and understand those we seek to serve; (2) acknowledge our essential unity with them; and (3) build listening relationships that allow us to relate as individuals. When we acknowledge that our own needs and desires are essentially the same as theirs, we realize they have much to offer us.

The concluding verses (vv. 10–12) promise that the person of integrity will experience God's upholding hand. This pictures those of us willing to take a stand in the power of God to confront, resist, and counter wrong

BOOK II

Psalms 42–72

Psalm 42 [a]

For the director of music. A *maskil* [b] of the Sons of Korah.

[1] As the deer pants for streams of water,
  so my soul pants [c] for you, O God.
[2] My soul thirsts [d] for God, for the living God. [e]
  When can I go [f] and meet with God?
[3] My tears [g] have been my food
    day and night,
  while men say to me all day long,
    "Where is your God?" [h]
[4] These things I remember
    as I pour out my soul:
  how I used to go with the multitude,
    leading the procession to the house of God, [i]
  with shouts of joy and thanksgiving [j]
    among the festive throng.

[5] Why are you downcast, [k] O my soul?
    Why so disturbed within me?
  Put your hope in God, [l]
    for I will yet praise him,
    my Savior [m] and [6] my God.

My [c] soul is downcast within me;
    therefore I will remember you
  from the land of the Jordan,
    the heights of Hermon—from Mount Mizar.
[7] Deep calls to deep
    in the roar of your waterfalls;
  all your waves and breakers
    have swept over me. [n]

[8] By day the LORD directs his love, [o]
    at night [p] his song [q] is with me—
  a prayer to the God of my life.

	42:1 [c] Ps 119:131
	42:2 [d] Ps 63:1 [e] Jer 10:10 [f] Ps 43:4
	42:3 [g] Ps 80:5 [h] Ps 79:10
	42:4 [i] Isa 30:29 [j] Ps 100:4
	42:5 [k] Ps 38:6; 77:3 [l] La 3:24 [m] Ps 44:3
	42:7 [n] Ps 88:7; Jnh 2:3
	42:8 [o] Ps 57:3 [p] Job 35:10 [q] Ps 63:6; 149:5

[a] In many Hebrew manuscripts Psalms 42 and 43 constitute one psalm.   [b] Title: Probably a literary or musical term   [c] 5,6 A few Hebrew manuscripts, Septuagint and Syriac; most Hebrew manuscripts *praise him for his saving help.* / [6]*O my God, my*

---

and injustice. Out of this kind of integrated life true regard for the weak is possible.

Psalm 42

Several factors suggest that Psalms 42 and 43 should be read as a unified composition. Structurally, the three stanzas of this psalm are symmetrical (each contains four verses), and each is followed by the same chorus (42:5,11; 43:5). The middle stanza, though, has at its center an additional verse (42:8) that interrupts the developing thought and injects a note of confidence. The "Sons of Korah" mentioned in the heading is a reference to the choir made up of Levites descended from Korah. David appointed them to serve in the temple and facilitate worship.

Hebrew Scripture reflects the need to preserve (remember) the works of God and so to proclaim his faithfulness to future generations. Forgetting God in the Hebrew mind was a willful act of "unlearning," whereby rebellious humans rejected what they had known and sought instead to create a world in which God didn't act or exist. Such people might cry (as did the enemies in vv. 3,10) "Where is your God?"

How do you counter the defeating sense of having been abandoned by God (vv. 3,9–10)? The psalmist held out one effective suggestion: to remember when God has been present—those times when you came joyfully into his presence in the company of the faithful (v. 4). Worship is a place for testimony, celebration, confession, and forgiveness. It's a context in which we remember the past, receive power to face the present, and embrace hope for tomorrow.

42:9
r Ps 38:6

9 I say to God my Rock,
 "Why have you forgotten me?
Why must I go about mourning, ʳ
 oppressed by the enemy?"
10 My bones suffer mortal agony
 as my foes taunt me,
saying to me all day long,
 "Where is your God?"

11 Why are you downcast, O my soul?
 Why so disturbed within me?
Put your hope in God,
 for I will yet praise him,
 my Savior and my God. ˢ

42:11
s Ps 43:5

Psalm 43 ᵃ

1 Vindicate me, O God,
 and plead my cause ᵗ against an ungodly nation;
 rescue me from deceitful and wicked men. ᵘ
2 You are God my stronghold.
 Why have you rejected ᵛ me?
Why must I go about mourning,
 oppressed by the enemy? ʷ
3 Send forth your light ˣ and your truth,
 let them guide me;
let them bring me to your holy mountain, ʸ
 to the place where you dwell. ᶻ
4 Then will I go to the altar ᵃ of God,
 to God, my joy and my delight.
I will praise you with the harp, ᵇ
 O God, my God.

5 Why are you downcast, O my soul?
 Why so disturbed within me?
Put your hope in God,
 for I will yet praise him,
 my Savior and my God. ᶜ

43:1
t 1Sa 24:15;
Ps 26:1; 35:1
u Ps 5:6

43:2
v Ps 44:9 w Ps 42:9

43:3
x Ps 36:9 y Ps 42:4
z Ps 84:1

43:4
a Ps 26:6 b Ps 33:2

43:5
c Ps 42:6

Psalm 44

For the director of music. Of the Sons of Korah. A *maskil*. ᵇ

1 We have heard with our ears, O God;
 our fathers have told us ᵈ
what you did in their days,

44:1
d Ex 12:26; Ps 78:3

ᵃ In many Hebrew manuscripts Psalms 42 and 43 constitute one psalm.   ᵇ Title: Probably a literary or musical term

---

Psalm 43

The goal and purpose of this combined psalm (see previous "There and Then") now becomes clear. At the beginning of Psalm 42 the psalmist, like a deer panting for water, longed to come into God's presence and remembered wonderful moments of worship in the temple. After crying out to God for vindication and deliverance (43:1–2), he concluded with joyful anticipation of being led once more into the temple, up to the altar, to God himself.

Another way to remember God's faithfulness

(see previous "Here and Now") is to long for and take advantage of opportunities to stand together with others in worship. Even if we feel distant or abandoned, the celebration will renew our certainty and hope. One role of the congregation is to worship when we can't—for instance, to celebrate Christ's resurrection when we are mourning a death or struggling with our own sin. The congregation declares the wonderful works of God even when we no longer sense his presence. Because we are part of the same body, their experience becomes ours and lifts us to renewed hope.

in days long ago.
2 With your hand you drove out[e] the nations
   and planted[f] our fathers;
 you crushed the peoples
   and made our fathers flourish.[g]
3 It was not by their sword[h] that they won the land,
   nor did their arm bring them victory;
 it was your right hand, your arm,[i]
   and the light of your face, for you loved[j] them.

4 You are my King[k] and my God,
   who decrees[a] victories for Jacob.
5 Through you we push back our enemies;
   through your name we trample[l] our foes.
6 I do not trust in my bow,[m]
   my sword does not bring me victory;
7 but you give us victory[n] over our enemies,
   you put our adversaries to shame.[o]
8 In God we make our boast[p] all day long,
   and we will praise your name forever.[q]   Selah

9 But now you have rejected[r] and humbled us;
   you no longer go out with our armies.[s]
10 You made us retreat[t] before the enemy,
   and our adversaries have plundered us.
11 You gave us up to be devoured like sheep[u]
   and have scattered us among the nations.[v]
12 You sold your people for a pittance,[w]
   gaining nothing from their sale.

13 You have made us a reproach to our neighbors,[x]
   the scorn[y] and derision of those around us.
14 You have made us a byword among the nations;
   the peoples shake their heads[z] at us.
15 My disgrace is before me all day long,
   and my face is covered with shame
16 at the taunts of those who reproach and revile[a] me,
   because of the enemy, who is bent on revenge.

17 All this happened to us,
   though we had not forgotten[b] you
   or been false to your covenant.
18 Our hearts had not turned[c] back;
   our feet had not strayed from your path.

[a] 4 Septuagint, Aquila and Syriac; Hebrew King, O God; / command

44:2
e Ps 78:55
f Ex 15:17 g Ps 80:9

44:3
h Dt 8:17;
Jos 24:12 i Ps 77:15
j Dt 4:37; 7:7-8

44:4
k Ps 74:12

44:5
l Ps 108:13
44:6
m Ps 33:16
44:7
n Ps 136:24
o Ps 53:5
44:8
p Ps 34:2
q Ps 30:12

44:9
r Ps 74:1
s Ps 60:1,10
44:10
t Lev 26:17; Jos 7:8; Ps 89:41
44:11
u Ro 8:36 v Dt 4:27; 28:64; Ps 106:27
44:12
w Isa 52:3; Jer 15:13

44:13
x Ps 79:4; 80:6
y Dt 28:37

44:14
z Ps 109:25; Jer 24:9

44:16
a Ps 74:10

44:17
b Ps 78:7,57; Da 9:13

44:18
c Job 23:11

Psalm 44

It's no accident that the first corporate (community) prayer for help in the Psalter follows the combined Psalms 42/43, with their description of an individual in crisis upheld by the memory and reality of God's presence in Israel's communal worship. Psalm 44 reflects the same sense of bewilderment at the absence of God in a time of extreme need.

In the context of feeling abandoned by God for no apparent reason or fault of their own, members of the faith community made an amazing leap of understanding—understanding that shaped their will to commit themselves in a new and painful way: "Yet for your sake we face death all day long" (v. 22). The "yet" reminds us

of Job's assertion, "Though he slay me, yet will I hope in him" (Job 13:15). Regardless of the pain that accompanied its faith, the community remained firmly committed to God—for his sake.

Pain and loss are significant opportunities for the glory of God and his Son to be revealed (cf. John 9:3; 11:4). We may be tempted to vent our rage, seek revenge, or play the victim (and Ps. 44 encourages us to speak honestly to God). But in verse 22 we understand that the appropriate response can become a "kingdom moment," one that doesn't reflect this world's values. This is part of what it means to "share in [Christ's] sufferings" (Rom. 8:17–18; Phil. 3:10–11; 1 Peter 4:13).

44:19
d Ps 51:8 *e* Job 3:5

19 But you crushed *d* us and made us a haunt for jackals
　　and covered us over with deep darkness. *e*

44:20
f Ps 78:11
g Dt 6:14; Ps 81:9

20 If we had forgotten *f* the name of our God
　　or spread out our hands to a foreign god, *g*

21 would not God have discovered it,

44:21
h Ps 139:1-2;
Jer 17:10
44:22
i Isa 53:7; Ro 8:36*

　　since he knows the secrets of the heart? *h*
22 Yet for your sake we face death all day long;
　　we are considered as sheep to be slaughtered. *i*

44:23
j Ps 7:6 *k* Ps 78:65
l Ps 77:7
44:24
m Job 13:24
n Ps 42:9

23 Awake, *j* O Lord! Why do you sleep? *k*
　　Rouse yourself! Do not reject us forever. *l*
24 Why do you hide your face *m*
　　and forget our misery and oppression? *n*

44:25
o Ps 119:25

25 We are brought down to the dust; *o*
　　our bodies cling to the ground.

44:26
p Ps 35:2
q Ps 25:22

26 Rise up *p* and help us;
　　redeem *q* us because of your unfailing love.

Psalm 45

For the director of music. To ⌊the tune of⌋ "Lilies." Of the Sons of Korah. A *maskil*. *a*
A wedding song.

1 My heart is stirred by a noble theme
　　as I recite my verses for the king;
　　my tongue is the pen of a skillful writer.

a Title: Probably a literary or musical term

Psalm 45

📖 Psalm 45 is a hymn in celebration of the Is-raelite king. As the heading indicates, it seems to have been written originally for a royal wedding. The psalm praises the "royal bride" (v. 9) as well as the king and concludes with hopes for the succession of Davidic kings. After the exile, this psalm was applied to the Messiah, the promised son of David who would sit on David's throne (for the application of vv. 6–7 to Christ, see Heb. 1:8–9).

Snapshots

44:22

Do Not Fear: Johanna Veenstra

In 1919, at the age of twenty-five, Johanna Veenstra, a young woman of Dutch Reformed descent who had grown up among the bright lights and social whirl of New York City, left her exciting life to live in an ant-infested mud hut in Nigeria. God had called her, and she had joyfully accepted. "There has been no sacrifice," she wrote," because the Lord Jesus himself is my constant companion."

> "There has been no sacrifice, because the Lord Jesus himself is my constant companion."

Despite the hardships and frustrations of living in primitive surroundings, Johanna established an effective medical and educational ministry. Her work was successful and rewarding.

In a letter home, Johanna told about a particular African Christian who had died. "He went from a mud hut to a mansion," she wrote. But before her letter had reached home, Johanna herself had passed away, suddenly and unexpectedly, at the age of thirty-nine. The words she had written of her African friend rang true for her as well.

Johanna Veenstra, one of the first foreign missionaries of the Christian Reformed Church, was a major influence in the early formation of a still thriving sister denomination in Nigeria.

2 You are the most excellent of men
    and your lips have been anointed with grace, [r]
    since God has blessed you forever.
3 Gird your sword [s] upon your side, O mighty one; [t]
    clothe yourself with splendor and majesty.
4 In your majesty ride forth victoriously [u]
    in behalf of truth, humility and righteousness;
    let your right hand display awesome deeds.
5 Let your sharp arrows pierce the hearts of the king's enemies;
    let the nations fall beneath your feet.
6 Your throne, O God, will last for ever and ever; [v]
    a scepter of justice will be the scepter of your kingdom.
7 You love righteousness [w] and hate wickedness;
    therefore God, your God, has set you above your companions
    by anointing [x] you with the oil of joy. [y]
8 All your robes are fragrant [z] with myrrh and aloes and cassia;
    from palaces adorned with ivory
    the music of the strings makes you glad.
9 Daughters of kings [a] are among your honored women;
    at your right hand [b] is the royal bride in gold of Ophir.

10 Listen, O daughter, consider and give ear:
    Forget your people [c] and your father's house.
11 The king is enthralled by your beauty;
    honor [d] him, for he is your lord. [e]
12 The Daughter of Tyre will come with a gift, [a][f]
    men of wealth will seek your favor.
13 All glorious [g] is the princess within ⌊her chamber⌋;
    her gown is interwoven with gold.
14 In embroidered garments she is led to the king; [h]
    her virgin companions follow her
    and are brought to you.
15 They are led in with joy and gladness;
    they enter the palace of the king.

16 Your sons will take the place of your fathers;
    you will make them princes throughout the land.
17 I will perpetuate your memory through all generations; [i]
    therefore the nations will praise you [j] for ever and ever.

Psalm 46

For the director of music. Of the Sons of Korah. According to *alamoth*. [b] A song.

1 God is our refuge [k] and strength,
    an ever-present [l] help in trouble.
2 Therefore we will not fear, [m] though the earth give way [n]

a 12 Or *A Tyrian robe is among the gifts*   b Title: Probably a musical term

45:2
r Lk 4:22

45:3
s Heb 4:12;
Rev 1:16 t Isa 9:6
45:4
u Rev 6:2

45:6
v Ps 93:2; 98:9

45:7
w Ps 33:5 x Isa 61:1
y Ps 21:6; Heb 1:8-
9*

45:8
z SS 1:3

45:9
a SS 6:8 b 1Ki 2:19

45:10
c Dt 21:13

45:11
d Ps 95:6 e Isa 54:5
45:12
f Ps 22:29; Isa 49:23

45:13
g Isa 61:10

45:14
h SS 1:4

45:17
i Mal 1:11
j Ps 138:4

46:1
k Ps 9:9; 14:6
l Dt 4:7
46:2
m Ps 23:4 n Ps 82:5

Rich garments, luxurious surroundings, festive music, and prestigious company characterized the wedding ceremony of an ancient Near Eastern king. Gold of Ophir (v. 9) was a rare commodity (Isa. 13:12), imported into Israel by ships that sailed from Ezion Geber (1 Kings 9:26–28; 22:48) to a destination conjectured to be India, Africa, the Arabian peninsula, or even South America. It came to be the standard for gold of purity and quality.

    📖 This poem contains expectations of, and appeals for, justice and equality. The marriage presented an op-portunity for the couple to commit themselves to the important aspects of royal rule: justice, equity, truth, humility, and righteousness. How wonderful for everyone if nations were to adopt these as standards of good government. As Christians we have the opportunity to live out these principles as representatives of God's kingdom here on Earth.

Psalm 46

    📖 Psalm 46 is a psalm of radical trust in the face of overwhelming threat. The specific danger isn't spelled

46:2
o Ps 18:7
46:3
p Ps 93:3
46:4
q Ps 48:1,8;
Isa 60:14
46:5
r Isa 12:6; Eze 43:7
s Ps 37:40
46:6
t Ps 2:1 u Ps 68:32
v Mic 1:4
46:7
w 2Ch 13:12
x Ps 9:9
46:8
y Ps 66:5 z Isa 61:4
46:9
a Isa 2:4 b Ps 76:3
c Eze 39:9
46:10
d Ps 100:3
e Isa 2:11

and the mountains fall[o] into the heart of the sea,

3 though its waters roar[p] and foam
  and the mountains quake with their surging.   *Selah*

4 There is a river whose streams make glad the city of God,[q]
  the holy place where the Most High dwells.

5 God is within her,[r] she will not fall;
  God will help[s] her at break of day.

6 Nations[t] are in uproar, kingdoms[u] fall;
  he lifts his voice, the earth melts.[v]

7 The LORD Almighty is with us;[w]
  the God of Jacob is our fortress.[x]   *Selah*

8 Come and see the works of the LORD,[y]
  the desolations[z] he has brought on the earth.

9 He makes wars[a] cease to the ends of the earth;
  he breaks the bow[b] and shatters the spear,
  he burns the shields[a] with fire.[c]

10 "Be still, and know that I am God;[d]
  I will be exalted[e] among the nations,
  I will be exalted in the earth."

11 The LORD Almighty is with us;
  the God of Jacob is our fortress.   *Selah*

Psalm 47

For the director of music. Of the Sons of Korah. A psalm.

47:1
f Ps 98:8; Isa 55:12
g Ps 106:47
47:2
h Dt 7:21 i Mal 1:14
47:3
j Ps 18:39,47
47:4
k 1Pe 1:4

1 Clap your hands,[f] all you nations;
  shout to God with cries of joy.[g]

2 How awesome[h] is the LORD Most High,
  the great King[i] over all the earth!

3 He subdued[j] nations under us,
  peoples under our feet.

4 He chose our inheritance[k] for us,
  the pride of Jacob, whom he loved.   *Selah*

47:5
l Ps 68:33; 98:6
47:6
m Ps 68:4; 89:18

5 God has ascended amid shouts of joy,
  the LORD amid the sounding of trumpets.[l]

6 Sing praises[m] to God, sing praises;
  sing praises to our King, sing praises.

---

a 9 Or *chariots*

out, but it had to do with the uproar of pagan nations. The psalm has a universal tone, beginning with the cosmic turmoil of chaotic waters before creation and continuing to God's ending of wars "to the ends of the earth." Throughout all the menace and upheaval, God remains "our refuge and strength, an ever-present help in trouble."

In Christianity, the hope for the restored "city of God" (v. 4) is viewed through the lens of Christ's death and resurrection to become an experience of God outside time and space. Revelation takes up this theme: "He carried me away in the Spirit . . . and showed me the Holy City, Jerusalem, coming down out of heaven from God" (Rev. 21:10).

Can we live faithfully in the face of threats? Life with God transcends our need to live here and now at

any cost. Life lived in the power of his refuge and strength becomes eternal life—not just life that hopes to be restored in some perfect existence, but life that isn't threatened by the imperfections of our world or even by the loss of all we know. Because we exist in that heavenly realm (Eph. 1:3), we can hear and apply these ancient words: "Be still, and know that I am God" (v. 10).

Psalm 47

Psalm 47 celebrates God's worldwide kingship. The pagan nations, defeated in Psalm 46, were called to submit to his rule and join in his praise, clapping their hands and raising their voices in song along with all "the kings of the earth" (v. 9). God's ultimate purpose is to restore his original intention for creation by redeeming the human race and re-creating the harmony and unity with which the world began. Psalm 47 anticipates a day when

7 For God is the King of all the earth;[n]
  sing to him a psalm[a][o] of praise.
8 God reigns[p] over the nations;
  God is seated on his holy throne.
9 The nobles of the nations assemble
  as the people of the God of Abraham,
  for the kings[b] of the earth belong to God;[q]
  he is greatly exalted.[r]

Psalm 48

A song. A psalm of the Sons of Korah.

1 Great is the LORD,[s] and most worthy of praise,
  in the city of our God,[t] his holy mountain.[u]
2 It is beautiful[v] in its loftiness,
  the joy of the whole earth.
  Like the utmost heights of Zaphon[c] is Mount Zion,
  the[d] city of the Great King.[w]
3 God is in her citadels;
  he has shown himself to be her fortress.[x]

4 When the kings joined forces,
  when they advanced together,[y]
5 they saw ⌊her⌋ and were astounded;
  they fled in terror.[z]
6 Trembling seized them there,
  pain like that of a woman in labor.
7 You destroyed them like ships of Tarshish
  shattered by an east wind.[a]

8 As we have heard,
  so have we seen
  in the city of the LORD Almighty,
  in the city of our God:
  God makes her secure forever.[b]   Selah

9 Within your temple, O God,
  we meditate on your unfailing love.[c]
10 Like your name,[d] O God,
  your praise reaches to the ends of the earth;[e]

Marginal references:
47:7 [n] Zec 14:9 [o] Col 3:16
47:8 [p] 1Ch 16:31
47:9 [q] Ps 72:11; 89:18 [r] Ps 97:9
48:1 [s] Ps 96:4 [t] Ps 46:4 [u] Isa 2:2-3; Mic 4:1; Zec 8:3
48:2 [v] Ps 50:2; La 2:15 [w] Mt 5:35
48:3 [x] Ps 46:7
48:4 [y] 2Sa 10:1-19
48:5 [z] Ex 15:16
48:7 [a] Jer 18:17; Eze 27:26
48:8 [b] Ps 87:5
48:9 [c] Ps 26:3
48:10 [d] Dt 28:58; Jos 7:9 [e] Isa 41:10

[a] 7 Or a maskil (probably a literary or musical term) [b] 9 Or shields [c] 2 Zaphon can refer to a sacred mountain or the direction north. [d] 2 Or earth, / Mount Zion, on the northern side / of the

all people everywhere will join with Israel as God's people to praise the Lord.

When humans with all their fears and prejudices begin to declare with Paul, "There is neither Jew nor Greek, slave nor free, male nor female, for you are all one in Christ Jesus" (Gal. 3:28), then the redeeming grace of God has broken in among us and begun setting things right. We won't see the completion of that restoration until the last day. But isn't the infiltration of God's kingdom into our daily lives reason enough for us to join the chorus of unity and praise this psalm invites?

Psalm 48
Psalm 48 falls into the category often called "Zion Songs" because they celebrate the glory of Mount Zion, the hill on which Jerusalem and the temple stood. Several psalms honor Zion. According to these psalms,

Mount Zion had been chosen by God (76:2; 132:13) as the place where he would be particularly present with Israel (46:4–5; 48:3). Zion was protected (46:5; 48:8) and her inhabitants blessed (84:4); it was an honor to be a citizen of Jerusalem (87:5–6). The choice of Zion as God's eternal throne was connected with his promise to David of a continuing dynasty (132:11–18).

What are the Jerusalems of your life? Where has God erected fortifications for your protection? When have your enemies been turned back by his power? How can you step into the light to see God at work in your life—caring, protecting, and saving? The psalms provide us with examples of people experiencing God's extraordinary presence. Drawing on these examples, we are encouraged to see God at work in our lives and to praise him for these mighty acts.

your right hand is filled with righteousness.

11 Mount Zion rejoices,
   the villages of Judah are glad
   because of your judgments. ^{f}

48:11
f Ps 97:8

12 Walk about Zion, go around her,
   count her towers,
13 consider well her ramparts,
   view her citadels, ^{g}
   that you may tell of them to the next generation. ^{h}

48:13
g ver 3; Ps 122:7
h Ps 78:6

14 For this God is our God for ever and ever;
   he will be our guide ^{i} even to the end.

48:14
i Ps 23:4

Psalm 49

For the director of music. Of the Sons of Korah. A psalm.

49:1
j Ps 78:1 k Ps 33:8

1 Hear this, all you peoples; ^{j}
   listen, all who live in this world, ^{k}
2 both low and high,
   rich and poor alike:

49:3
l Ps 37:30
m Ps 119:130

3 My mouth will speak words of wisdom; ^{l}
   the utterance from my heart will give understanding. ^{m}

49:4
n Ps 78:2 o Nu 12:8

4 I will turn my ear to a proverb; ^{n}
   with the harp I will expound my riddle: ^{o}

49:5
p Ps 23:4

5 Why should I fear ^{p} when evil days come,
   when wicked deceivers surround me—

49:6
q Job 31:24

6 those who trust in their wealth ^{q}
   and boast of their great riches?
7 No man can redeem the life of another
   or give to God a ransom for him—

49:8
r Mt 16:26
49:9
s Ps 22:29; 89:48

8 the ransom for a life is costly,
   no payment is ever enough— ^{r}
9 that he should live on ^{s} forever
   and not see decay.

49:10
t Ecc 2:16
u Ecc 2:18,21

10 For all can see that wise men die; ^{t}
   the foolish and the senseless alike perish
   and leave their wealth to others. ^{u}
11 Their tombs will remain their houses ^{a} forever,
   their dwellings for endless generations,
   though they had ^{b} named ^{v} lands after themselves.

49:11
v Ge 4:17; Dt 3:14

12 But man, despite his riches, does not endure;
   he is ^{c} like the beasts that perish.

49:13
w Lk 12:20

13 This is the fate of those who trust in themselves, ^{w}

---

^{a} 11 Septuagint and Syriac; Hebrew *In their thoughts their houses will remain* ^{b} 11 Or / *for they have*
^{c} 12 Hebrew; Septuagint and Syriac read verse 12 the same as verse 20.

Psalm 49

Psalm 49 is a "wisdom psalm." Its primary concern or "riddle" (v. 4) is the apparent injustice of a world in which wicked fools may prosper while the righteous wise may live in poverty. This psalm shares with Job and *Ecclesiastes* a hard-won, *enduring faith in God* that rejects any naïve assumption in which prosperity and ease of life can be associated only with divine blessing for righteous living, while poverty is always considered the consequence of sin.

Christians today tend to spiritualize the psalmists' complaints. But this Psalm has a real and practical application. Listen to it speak for those who are truly suffering want, pain, abuse, and exploitation. Recognize and acknowledge how your society's consumerism and materialism feed the cycle of abuse in which the relatively few rich live well off the misery of the many poor. Hear the psalm as God's words—challenging and confronting us with our cooperation in the exploitation of others through what we buy, sell, and use.

and of their followers, who approve their sayings.   *Selah*

14 Like sheep they are destined for the grave, [a][x]
    and death will feed on them.
The upright will rule[y] over them in the morning;
    their forms will decay in the grave, [a]
    far from their princely mansions.
15 But God will redeem my life[b] from the grave; [z]
    he will surely take me to himself. [a]   *Selah*

16 Do not be overawed when a man grows rich,

49:14
x Job 24:19;
Ps 9:17 y Da 7:18;
Mal 4:3; 1Co 6:2;
Rev 2:26

49:15
z Ps 56:13;
Hos 13:14
a Ps 73:24

a 14 Hebrew *Sheol*; also in verse 15   b 15 Or *soul*

49:1–2

Biblical Instruction to the Rich

Psalm 49 teaches that the rich and poor stand equal before God. Yet the Bible contains instructions and cautionary advice to those who have greater resources. The following are key points:

Instruction	Reference
• If you lend to the poor, don't charge interest.	Ex. 22:25
• Allow the poor to retain basic necessities for living.	Ex. 22:26–27
• Don't deny the underprivileged justice in court.	Ex. 23:6
• Make provisions so that the poor won't go hungry.	Ex. 23:11
• Don't turn a needy individual into a slave.	Lev. 25:39
• Treat the lower-income worker with respect, not ruthlessness.	Lev. 25:40–43
• God alone grants the ability to become wealthy.	Deut. 8:17–18
• Don't be tightfisted or hardhearted toward the poor, but be generous.	Deut. 15:7–11
• Pay just wages.	Deut. 24:14–15
• Rich and poor stand equal before God.	Ps. 49:1–2
• Wealth is a blessing from the Lord.	Prov. 10:22
• God is the Creator of *all* people.	Prov. 22:2
• Don't wear yourself out to become wealthy.	Prov. 23:4
• Whoever loves wealth is never satisfied.	Eccl. 5:10–11
• Don't boast in your affluence.	Jer. 9:23–24
• It's harder for the rich to enter the kingdom of God.	Mark 10:17–31
• Be rich toward God.	Luke 12:13–21
• Give according to your ability.	2 Cor. 9:7–11
• The love of money is a root of evil and a hindrance to faith.	1 Tim. 6:9–10
• Don't be arrogant in wealth or place your ultimate hope in it.	1 Tim. 6:17
• Be rich in good deeds.	1 Tim. 6:18
• God has chosen the poor to be rich in faith.	James 2:5
• Riches can be corrosive.	James 5:1–5
• Wealth can mask spiritual poverty.	Rev. 3:17–18

when the splendor of his house increases;

17 for he will take nothing with him when he dies,
  his splendor will not descend with him. *b*

18 Though while he lived he counted himself blessed— *c*
  and men praise you when you prosper—

19 he will join the generation of his fathers, *d*
  who will never see the light *e* ⌊of life⌋.

20 A man who has riches without understanding
  is like the beasts that perish. *f*

Psalm 50

A psalm of Asaph.

1 The Mighty One, God, the LORD, *g*
  speaks and summons the earth
  from the rising of the sun to the place where it sets. *h*

2 From Zion, perfect in beauty, *i*
  God shines forth. *j*

3 Our God comes *k* and will not be silent;
  a fire devours before him, *l*
  and around him a tempest rages.

4 He summons the heavens above,
  and the earth, *m* that he may judge his people:

5 "Gather to me my consecrated ones, *n*
  who made a covenant *o* with me by sacrifice."

6 And the heavens proclaim *p* his righteousness,
  for God himself is judge. *q*   *Selah*

7 "Hear, O my people, and I will speak,
  O Israel, and I will testify *r* against you:
  I am God, your God. *s*

8 I do not rebuke you for your sacrifices
  or your burnt offerings, *t* which are ever before me.

9 I have no need of a bull *u* from your stall
  or of goats from your pens,

10 for every animal of the forest is mine,
  and the cattle on a thousand hills. *v*

11 I know every bird in the mountains,
  and the creatures of the field are mine.

12 If I were hungry I would not tell you,
  for the world *w* is mine, and all that is in it.

13 Do I eat the flesh of bulls
  or drink the blood of goats?

14 Sacrifice thank offerings *x* to God,
  fulfill your vows *y* to the Most High,

15 and call *z* upon me in the day of trouble;
  I will deliver you, and you will honor *a* me."

16 But to the wicked, God says:

  "What right have you to recite my laws

49:17
b Ps 17:14; 1Ti 6:7
49:18
c Dt 29:19;
Lk 12:19
49:19
d Ge 15:15
e Job 33:30

49:20
f Ecc 3:19

50:1
g Jos 22:22
h Ps 113:3

50:2
i Ps 48:2 *j* Dt 33:2;
Ps 80:1

50:3
k Ps 96:13 *l* Ps 97:3;
Da 7:10

50:4
m Dt 4:26; Isa 1:2
50:5
n Ps 30:4 *o* Ex 24:7
50:6
p Ps 89:5 *q* Ps 75:7

50:7
r Ps 81:8 *s* Ex 20:2

50:8
t Ps 40:6; Hos 6:6
50:9
u Ps 69:31

50:10
v Ps 104:24

50:12
w Ex 19:5

50:14
x Heb 13:15
y Dt 23:21

50:15
z Ps 81:7 *a* Ps 22:23

Psalm 50

📖 The first psalm in the Psalter attributed to
Asaph, Psalm 50 breaks the string of psalms credited
to the Sons of Korah (see "There and Then" for Ps. 42).
Asaph was one of the chief Levite temple musicians appointed by David (cf. 1 Chron. 6:31–32,39; 16:1–6).

Psalm 50 is a "covenant lawsuit" brought by God

against his "consecrated ones, who made a covenant with
[him] by sacrifice" (v. 5). This sort of legal proceeding was
common in the Old Testament as a means by which God
aired Israel's failures and justified his judgment on the nation. Psalm 50 admonished the covenant people to "consider" (v. 22) their failings in worship and conduct—in
their relationships with God and their fellow humans.

or take my covenant on your lips? [b]

¹⁷ You hate my instruction
 and cast my words behind [c] you.
¹⁸ When you see a thief, you join [d] with him;
 you throw in your lot with adulterers.
¹⁹ You use your mouth for evil
 and harness your tongue to deceit. [e]
²⁰ You speak continually against your brother [f]
 and slander your own mother's son.
²¹ These things you have done and I kept silent; [g]
 you thought I was altogether [a] like you.
 But I will rebuke you
 and accuse [h] you to your face.

²² "Consider this, you who forget God, [i]
 or I will tear you to pieces, with none to rescue: [j]
²³ He who sacrifices thank offerings honors me,
 and he prepares the way [k]
 so that I may show him [b] the salvation of God. [l]"

Psalm 51

For the director of music. A psalm of David. When the prophet Nathan came to him after David had committed adultery with Bathsheba.

¹ Have mercy on me, O God,
 according to your unfailing love;
 according to your great compassion
 blot out [m] my transgressions. [n]
² Wash away [o] all my iniquity
 and cleanse [p] me from my sin.

³ For I know my transgressions,
 and my sin is always before me. [q]
⁴ Against you, you only, have I sinned
 and done what is evil in your sight, [r]
 so that you are proved right when you speak
 and justified when you judge. [s]
⁵ Surely I was sinful [t] at birth,
 sinful from the time my mother conceived me.
⁶ Surely you desire truth in the inner parts [c];
 you teach [d] me wisdom [u] in the inmost place. [v]

⁷ Cleanse me with hyssop, [w] and I will be clean;
 wash me, and I will be whiter than snow. [x]

50:16
b Isa 29:13
50:17
c Ne 9:26;
Ro 2:21-22
50:18
d Ro 1:32; 1Ti 5:22

50:19
e Ps 10:7; 52:2
50:20
f Mt 10:21

50:21
g Ecc 8:11;
Isa 42:14 h Ps 90:8

50:22
i Job 8:13; Ps 9:17
j Ps 7:2

50:23
k Ps 85:13
l Ps 91:16

51:1
m Ac 3:19
n Isa 43:25;
Col 2:14
51:2
o 1Jn 1:9
p Heb 9:14

51:3
q Isa 59:12
51:4
r Ge 20:6; Lk 15:21
s Ro 3:4*

51:5
t Job 14:4

51:6
u Pr 2:6 v Ps 15:2
51:7
w Lev 14:4;
Heb 9:19 x Isa 1:18

---

[a] 21 Or *thought the 'I* ᴀᴍ*' was*   [b] 23 Or *and to him who considers his way / I will show*
[c] 6 The meaning of the Hebrew for this phrase is uncertain.   [d] 6 Or *you desired . . . ; / you taught*

📖 Praise and thanksgiving are vital parts of worship, but only parts. True worship requires the fear of God, acknowledgement of sin, and petition for forgiveness. It involves opening our eyes to see the hurts of the world outside—and acting on what we see. Then our praises have meaning beyond our own well-being and sound with new sweetness in God's ears.

Psalm 51

📖 Psalm 51 is the fourth of seven "penitential psalms" (Ps. 6; 32; 38; 51; 102; 130; 143), focusing on confession and repentance from personal sin. Regarding the events mentioned in the heading, see 2 Samuel 11:1—

12:25. David's claim that his sin was against God "only" (v. 4) may seem to downplay his wrongs against Bathsheba, Uriah, or society as a whole. But David was acknowledging that covenant violations are ultimately offenses against God—judged by him rather than by society alone. The real measure of sin is "what is evil in [God's] sight."

The forgiveness David sought is described with three verbs: "blot out," "wash away," and "cleanse" (vv. 1–2). David also used three words for sin: "transgressions," "iniquity," and "sin." He apparently intended this list of violations to be comprehensive; his confession was far-reaching and seemingly complete.

51:8
y Isa 35:10

8 Let me hear joy and gladness; y
  let the bones you have crushed rejoice.

51:9
z Jer 16:17

9 Hide your face from my sins z
  and blot out all my iniquity.

51:10
a Ps 78:37; Ac 15:9
b Eze 18:31

10 Create in me a pure heart, a O God,
   and renew a steadfast spirit within me. b

51:11
c Eph 4:30
51:12
d Ps 13:5

11 Do not cast me from your presence
   or take your Holy Spirit c from me.
12 Restore to me the joy of your salvation d
   and grant me a willing spirit, to sustain me.

51:13
e Ac 9:21-22
f Ps 22:27

13 Then I will teach transgressors your ways, e
   and sinners will turn back to you. f

51:14
g 2Sa 12:9
h Ps 25:5 i Ps 35:28

14 Save me from bloodguilt, g O God,
   the God who saves me, h
   and my tongue will sing of your righteousness. i

51:15
j Ps 9:14

15 O Lord, open my lips, j
   and my mouth will declare your praise.

51:16
k 1Sa 15:22;
Ps 40:6

16 You do not delight in sacrifice, k or I would bring it;
   you do not take pleasure in burnt offerings.

51:17
l Ps 34:18

17 The sacrifices of God are a a broken spirit;
   a broken and contrite heart, l
   O God, you will not despise.

51:18
m Ps 102:16;
Isa 51:3
51:19
n Ps 4:5 o Ps 66:13
p Ps 66:15

18 In your good pleasure make Zion m prosper;
   build up the walls of Jerusalem.
19 Then there will be righteous sacrifices, n
   whole burnt offerings o to delight you;
   then bulls p will be offered on your altar.

Psalm 52

52:1
q 1Sa 22:9 r Ps 94:4

For the director of music. A *maskil* b of David. When Doeg the Edomite q had gone to
Saul and told him: "David has gone to the house of Ahimelech."

1 Why do you boast of evil, you mighty man?
  Why do you boast r all day long,
  you who are a disgrace in the eyes of God?

a 17 Or *My sacrifice, O God, is*   b Title: Probably a literary or musical term

God wants transparency in the lives of his people. When we hide our failings, we deny others the benefit of our experience, since our struggles can encourage them to acknowledge and confess their own sin. Our experience of salvation, forgiveness, and restoration can convince others that they, too, can know the "joy of salvation" (vv. 12–13). The value of our forgiven sin is the possibility of testifying to God's gracious mercy—our proper response to his re-creation of our inward selves.

Psalm 52
The heading of Psalm 52 indicates that this psalm represents David's response to the events of 1 Samuel 22:9–19, where Doeg informed Saul that David had received assistance from the priestly family of Ahimelech of Nob. Saul, who feared David's growing popularity, condemned Ahimelech and his family for this supposed treason. When none of Saul's men would carry out the execution, Doeg accepted the commission and killed 85 priests and everyone else in Nob—men, women, and children. The fall of the deceitful wicked,

like Doeg, provides an object lesson the righteous can take to heart.

Though there is evidence that ancient Israel was far more forested than it is today, the presence of flourishing trees was still a sign of divine blessing for former nomads, living on the fringes of a settled, agricultural society. The Old Testament presents a thriving tree as symbolic of the blessing of the righteous (see Ps. 1:3; Isa. 61:3; Jer. 17:8). This blessing is frequently contrasted with the sad state of the wicked, depicted in terms of nonproductive dryness.

The key to a life of blessing is trust in God. A tree can't get up and move closer to a water source; it must depend on the gardener or nearby water to provide for its needs. When planted in the right spot, the tree sends its roots deep into the life-giving resources of the stream. If we are to be olive trees "flourishing in the house of God," we can become lively and fruitful only by sending down our roots into the revitalizing source God provides in his unfailing love.

2 Your tongue plots destruction;
   it is like a sharpened razor, ^s
   you who practice deceit. ^t
3 You love evil rather than good,
   falsehood ^u rather than speaking the truth.   *Selah*
4 You love every harmful word,
   O you deceitful tongue! ^v

5 Surely God will bring you down to everlasting ruin:
   He will snatch you up and tear ^w you from your tent;
   he will uproot ^x you from the land of the living. ^y   *Selah*
6 The righteous will see and fear;
   they will laugh ^z at him, saying,
7 "Here now is the man
   who did not make God his stronghold
   but trusted in his great wealth ^a
   and grew strong by destroying others!"

8 But I am like an olive tree ^b
   flourishing in the house of God;
   I trust ^c in God's unfailing love
   for ever and ever.
9 I will praise you forever ^d for what you have done;
   in your name I will hope, for your name is good. ^e
   I will praise you in the presence of your saints.

Psalm 53

For the director of music. According to *mahalath.* ^a A *maskil* ^b of David.

1 The fool ^f says in his heart,
   "There is no God." ^g
They are corrupt, and their ways are vile;
   there is no one who does good.

2 God looks down from heaven ^h
   on the sons of men
to see if there are any who understand,
   any who seek God. ⁱ
3 Everyone has turned away,
   they have together become corrupt;
there is no one who does good,
   not even one. ^j

4 Will the evildoers never learn—
   those who devour my people as men eat bread
   and who do not call on God?

^a Title: Probably a musical term   ^b Title: Probably a literary or musical term

52:2
^s Ps 57:4 ^t Ps 50:19

52:3
^u Jer 9:5

52:4
^v Ps 120:2,3

52:5
^w Isa 22:19
^x Pr 2:22 ^y Ps 27:13

52:6
^z Job 22:19;
Ps 37:34; 40:3

52:7
^a Ps 49:6

52:8
^b Jer 11:16
^c Ps 13:5

52:9
^d Ps 30:12 ^e Ps 54:6

53:1
^f Ps 14:1-7; Ro 3:10
^g Ps 10:4

53:2
^h Ps 33:13
ⁱ 2Ch 15:2

53:3
^j Ro 3:10-12*

Psalm 53

Psalm 53 is a near duplicate of Psalm 14, a wisdom meditation on the folly of the wicked, who deny God's existence and oppress the poor.

Psalm 53 lends itself to the suggestion of the horror of cannibalism with its reference to evildoers who "devour my people as men eat bread" (v. 4). This savagery as a metaphor for exploitation of the poor and powerless also is found in 14:4, 27:2, and Micah 3:1–3. It's as though people try to gain power by consuming the very lives of others, an apt image for the vicious attacks by the powerful on the poor, whom they feel they can manipulate and overtake at will.

Like it or not, our consumption in the West often comes at the price of exploiting others, "eating" them as though they were bread. We are challenged by this psalm to reflect deeply and carefully on how our lives participate directly or indirectly in the oppression of those the world considers expendable because they are, for the most part, invisible to us. But there are no disposable people to God! If we claim to be *his* people, how can we allow others to be used for our own comfort or pleasure?

53:5
k Lev 26:17
l Eze 6:5

5 There they were, overwhelmed with dread,
  where there was nothing to dread. *k*
God scattered the bones *l* of those who attacked you;
  you put them to shame, for God despised them.

6 Oh, that salvation for Israel would come out of Zion!
  When God restores the fortunes of his people,
  let Jacob rejoice and Israel be glad!

Psalm 54

For the director of music. With stringed instruments. A *maskil* [a] of David. When the Ziphites had gone to Saul and said, "Is not David hiding among us?"

54:1
m Ps 20:1
n 2Ch 20:6

54:2
o Ps 5:1; 55:1

54:3
p Ps 86:14
q Ps 40:14 r Ps 36:1

54:4
s Ps 118:7
t Ps 41:12

54:5
u Ps 94:23
v Ps 89:49; 143:12

54:6
w Ps 50:14
x Ps 52:9

54:7
y Ps 34:6 z Ps 59:10

1 Save me, O God, by your name; *m*
  vindicate me by your might. *n*
2 Hear my prayer, O God; *o*
  listen to the words of my mouth.

3 Strangers are attacking me; *p*
  ruthless men seek my life *q*—
  men without regard for God. *r*   *Selah*

4 Surely God is my help; *s*
  the Lord is the one who sustains me. *t*

5 Let evil recoil *u* on those who slander me;
  in your faithfulness *v* destroy them.

6 I will sacrifice a freewill offering *w* to you;
  I will praise your name, O LORD,
  for it is good. *x*
7 For he has delivered me *y* from all my troubles,
  and my eyes have looked in triumph on my foes. *z*

Psalm 55

For the director of music. With stringed instruments. A *maskil* [a] of David.

55:1
a Ps 27:9; 61:1
55:2
b Ps 66:19
c Ps 77:3; Isa 38:14

1 Listen to my prayer, O God,
  do not ignore my plea; *a*
2   hear me and answer me. *b*
  My thoughts trouble me and I am distraught *c*
3   at the voice of the enemy,

[a] Title: Probably a literary or musical term

Psalm 54

Psalm 54 is a plea for deliverance. Verse 4 voices its major theme: "Surely God is my help; the Lord is the one who sustains me." References to God's "name" as the basis of David's hope for deliverance bracket the psalm (vv. 1,6). Concern with the divine name also links it to 52:9, which expresses similar confidence.

David's enemies failed because they were "without regard for God" (v. 3). This phrase in the Hebrew means something like "they didn't set God before them." In verse 4 God is called David's "help," or "helper." He's our helper too, if only we will "set him before us."

How do we "set God before us"? It means that we keep our eyes fastened on him. Think of lovers in a restaurant—hands clasped across the table, eyes locked as though no one else is in the room. Placing our gaze fully on God changes the way in which we see the world.

We find that he's just and equitable, taking no pleasure in evil—the Creator who cares for the whole creation. We can no longer ignore the call to participate in the restoration of his creation, to seek its interests rather than our own. And even if the people closest to us betray us, God is there to hold us up and sustain us (v. 4).

Psalm 55

Psalm 55 was David's prayer for God's help when he was threatened by a powerful conspiracy in Jerusalem under the leadership of a former friend. The situation described was like that of Absalom's conspiracy against the king (see 2 Sam. 15–17): The city was in turmoil; danger was everywhere; there was uncertainty as to who could be trusted; rumors, false reports, and slander circulated freely. Under such circumstances David longed for a quiet retreat to escape it all. That being out of the question, he cast his cares on the Lord, whom he knew he could trust.

at the stares of the wicked;
for they bring down suffering upon me [d]
    and revile me in their anger. [e]

4 My heart is in anguish within me;
    the terrors [f] of death assail me.
5 Fear and trembling [g] have beset me;
    horror has overwhelmed me.
6 I said, "Oh, that I had the wings of a dove!
    I would fly away and be at rest—
7 I would flee far away
    and stay in the desert;
8 I would hurry to my place of shelter,
    far from the tempest and storm. [h]"

9 Confuse the wicked, O Lord, confound their speech,
    for I see violence and strife [i] in the city.
10 Day and night they prowl about on its walls;
    malice and abuse are within it.
11 Destructive forces [j] are at work in the city;
    threats and lies [k] never leave its streets.

12 If an enemy were insulting me,
    I could endure it;
if a foe were raising himself against me,
    I could hide from him.
13 But it is you, a man like myself,
    my companion, my close friend, [l]
14 with whom I once enjoyed sweet fellowship
    as we walked with the throng at the house of God. [m]

15 Let death take my enemies by surprise; [n]
    let them go down alive to the grave, [a][o]
    for evil finds lodging among them.

16 But I call to God,
    and the LORD saves me.
17 Evening, [p] morning [q] and noon
    I cry out in distress,
    and he hears my voice.
18 He ransoms me unharmed
    from the battle waged against me,
    even though many oppose me.
19 God, who is enthroned forever, [r]
    will hear [s] them and afflict them—
men who never change their ways
    and have no fear of God.

20 My companion attacks his friends; [t]
    he violates his covenant. [u]
21 His speech is smooth as butter,
    yet war is in his heart;
his words are more soothing than oil, [v]
    yet they are drawn swords. [w]

a 15 Hebrew Sheol

Selah

Selah

55:3
d 2Sa 16:6-8;
Ps 17:9 e Ps 71:11

55:4
f Ps 116:3
55:5
g Job 21:6;
Ps 119:120

55:8
h Isa 4:6

55:9
i Jer 6:7

55:11
j Ps 5:9 k Ps 10:7

55:13
l 2Sa 15:12; Ps 41:9

55:14
m Ps 42:4

55:15
n Ps 64:7
o Nu 16:30,33

55:17
p Ps 141:2; Ac 3:1
q Ps 5:3

55:19
r Dt 33:27
s Ps 78:59

55:20
t Ps 7:4 u Ps 89:34

55:21
v Pr 5:3 w Ps 28:3;
57:4; 59:7

Jesus serves as a model for us when we face false accusation. Paraded before a jeering public to the place of execution, he didn't strike back, even though he could have called an angelic army to his defense (cf. Matt. 26:53). To give up the rights of vindication, to for-give the unforgivable, and to seek the restoration of our attackers seem impossible tasks. Yet that is what we, by the power of God's grace, are called to do—to allow Christ to live in and through us and to change how we relate to a hostile world.

55:22
x Ps 37:5; Mt 6:25-
34; 1Pe 5:7
y Ps 37:24

55:23
z Ps 73:18 a Ps 5:6
b Job 15:32;
Pr 10:27 c Ps 25:2

22 Cast your cares on the Lord
    and he will sustain you; [x]
    he will never let the righteous fall. [y]
23 But you, O God, will bring down the wicked
    into the pit [z] of corruption;
    bloodthirsty and deceitful men [a]
    will not live out half their days. [b]

But as for me, I trust in you. [c]

Psalm 56

For the director of music. To the tune of, "A Dove on Distant Oaks." Of David.
A *miktam.* [a] When the Philistines had seized him in Gath.

56:1
d Ps 57:1-3

56:2
e Ps 57:3 f Ps 35:1

56:3
g Ps 55:4-5

56:4
h Ps 118:6;
Heb 13:6
56:5
i Ps 41:7

56:6
j Ps 59:3 k Ps 71:10

56:7
l Ps 36:12; 55:23

56:8
m Mal 3:16
56:9
n Ps 9:3 o Ps 102:2
p Ro 8:31

56:12
q Ps 50:14

56:13
r Ps 116:8

1 Be merciful to me, O God, for men hotly pursue me; [d]
    all day long they press their attack.
2 My slanderers pursue me all day long; [e]
    many are attacking me in their pride. [f]
3 When I am afraid, [g]
    I will trust in you.
4 In God, whose word I praise,
    in God I trust; I will not be afraid.
    What can mortal man do to me? [h]

5 All day long they twist my words; [i]
    they are always plotting to harm me.
6 They conspire, [j] they lurk,
    they watch my steps,
    eager to take my life. [k]

7 On no account let them escape;
    in your anger, O God, bring down the nations. [l]
8 Record my lament;
    list my tears on your scroll [b]—
    are they not in your record? [m]

9 Then my enemies will turn back [n]
    when I call for help. [o]
    By this I will know that God is for me. [p]
10 In God, whose word I praise,
    in the Lord, whose word I praise—
11 in God I trust; I will not be afraid.
    What can man do to me?

12 I am under vows [q] to you, O God;
    I will present my thank offerings to you.
13 For you have delivered me [c] from death [r]
    and my feet from stumbling,

---

a Title: Probably a literary or musical term   b 8 Or / *put my tears in your wineskin*   c 13 Or *my soul*

Psalm 56

"Scroll" in verse 8 interpretively translates a Hebrew word ordinarily meaning "wineskin." The literal meaning of the Hebrew clause is "put my tears in your wineskin" (see NIV text note). This image seems to reflect the practice in the arid climate of Israel of preserving precious liquids in a leak-proof leather bag. The image of saving tears is powerful: David's tears of lament were precious to God. Regardless of the terminology, verse 8 stresses the recording of David's pain and sorrow in God's record book.

In their confident reliance on God's care and deliverance, the psalmists often painted a picture in which they seemed to be untouchable by the woes and evils of this life (e.g., vv. 4,11). Yet their poems continue to give abundant testimony to the vicious realities of a fallen world. Still, when God is on our side, we can find refuge in the midst of any storm.

that I may walk before God
    in the light of life.[a][s]

56:13
[s] Job 33:30

Psalm 57

For the director of music. ⌐To the tune of⌐ "Do Not Destroy." Of David. A *miktam*.[b]
When he had fled from Saul into the cave.

[1] Have mercy on me, O God, have mercy on me,
    for in you my soul takes refuge.[t]
I will take refuge in the shadow of your wings[u]
    until the disaster has passed.[v]

57:1
[t] Ps 2:12 [u] Ps 17:8
[v] Isa 26:20

[2] I cry out to God Most High,
    to God, who fulfills ⌐his purpose⌐ for me.[w]
[3] He sends from heaven and saves me,[x]
    rebuking those who hotly pursue me;[y]   *Selah*
God sends his love and his faithfulness.[z]

57:2
[w] Ps 138:8
57:3
[x] Ps 18:9,16
[y] Ps 56:1 [z] Ps 40:11

[4] I am in the midst of lions;[a]
    I lie among ravenous beasts—
men whose teeth are spears and arrows,
    whose tongues are sharp swords.[b]

57:4
[a] Ps 35:17
[b] Ps 55:21;
Pr 30:14

[5] Be exalted, O God, above the heavens;
    let your glory be over all the earth.[c]

57:5
[c] Ps 108:5

[6] They spread a net for my feet—
    I was bowed down[d] in distress.
They dug a pit[e] in my path—
    but they have fallen into it themselves.[f]   *Selah*

57:6
[d] Ps 145:14
[e] Ps 35:7 [f] Ps 7:15;
Pr 28:10

[7] My heart is steadfast, O God,
    my heart is steadfast;[g]
I will sing and make music.

57:7
[g] Ps 108:1

[8] Awake, my soul!
    Awake, harp and lyre![h]
    I will awaken the dawn.

57:8
[h] Ps 16:9; 30:12;
150:3

[9] I will praise you, O Lord, among the nations;
    I will sing of you among the peoples.
[10] For great is your love, reaching to the heavens;
    your faithfulness reaches to the skies.[i]

57:10
[i] Ps 36:5; 103:11

[11] Be exalted, O God, above the heavens;
    let your glory be over all the earth.[j]

57:11
[j] ver 5

[a] 13 Or *the land of the living*   [b] Title: Probably a literary or musical term

Psalm 57

📖 Psalm 57 is once again, like the three previous psalms, a prayer for deliverance from vicious and slanderous enemy attacks. For the event referred to in the heading, see 1 Samuel 24:1–3. The image of hiding under the protective spread of God's "wings" (v. 1) is used several times in the Psalter (cf. Ps. 17:8; 36:7; 63:7) and may draw on the image of a protective hen gathering her brood under her wings (cf. Isa. 34:15; Matt. 23:37). In verse 3, God's love and faithfulness are personified as his messengers from heaven sent to save his servant.

📖 In considering God's plan for our lives, we may easily conclude that unless we discern and follow his will rightly in all instances, we will never be able to fulfill that purpose. Psalm 57 offers a fresh perspective: *He will fulfill it for us!* (v. 2). Life offers an unlimited number of pathways. From any point we can decide to turn toward God and proceed along a path to reunion. And along the way, as we seek the track that leads home, God sends out his love and faithfulness to guide us.

Psalm 58

For the director of music. ⌊To the tune of⌋ "Do Not Destroy." Of David. A *miktam*. [a]

58:1
k Ps 82:2

1 Do you rulers indeed speak justly? [k]
   Do you judge uprightly among men?

58:2
l Ps 94:20; Mal 3:15

2 No, in your heart you devise injustice,
   and your hands mete out violence on the earth. [l]

3 Even from birth the wicked go astray;
   from the womb they are wayward and speak lies.

58:4
m Ps 140:3;
Ecc 10:11

4 Their venom is like the venom of a snake, [m]
   like that of a cobra that has stopped its ears,

5 that will not heed the tune of the charmer,
   however skillful the enchanter may be.

58:6
n Ps 3:7 o Job 4:10

6 Break the teeth in their mouths, O God; [n]
   tear out, O LORD, the fangs of the lions! [o]

58:7
p Jos 7:5; Ps 112:10
q Ps 64:3

7 Let them vanish like water that flows away; [p]
   when they draw the bow, let their arrows be blunted. [q]

58:8
r Job 3:16

8 Like a slug melting away as it moves along,
   like a stillborn child, [r] may they not see the sun.

58:9
s Ps 118:12
t Pr 10:25
58:10
u Ps 64:10; 91:8
v Ps 68:23

9 Before your pots can feel ⌊the heat of⌋ the thorns [s]—
   whether they be green or dry—the wicked will be swept away. [b] [t]

10 The righteous will be glad when they are avenged, [u]
   when they bathe their feet in the blood of the wicked. [v]

58:11
w Ps 9:8; 18:20

11 Then men will say,
   "Surely the righteous still are rewarded;
   surely there is a God who judges the earth." [w]

Psalm 59

For the director of music. ⌊To the tune of⌋ "Do Not Destroy." Of David. A *miktam*. [a]
When Saul had sent men to watch David's house in order to kill him.

59:1
x Ps 143:9

1 Deliver me from my enemies, O God; [x]
   protect me from those who rise up against me.

59:2
y Ps 139:19

2 Deliver me from evildoers
   and save me from bloodthirsty men. [y]

---

[a] Title: Probably a literary or musical term uncertain.   [b] 9 The meaning of the Hebrew for this verse is

---

Psalm 58

Does it matter that God is a deity of moral consistency, compassionate justice, and equity? Without these characteristics, he would have been no different from the 400-plus ancient Near Eastern pagan gods that made life among humans a painful experience at best, and God's power couldn't have been relied upon to match that of an opponent. However, Psalm 58 declares him to be the One "who judges the earth" with uprightness (vv. 1,11). Wickedness doesn't dwell in him; he's absolutely and thoroughly good.

We have a hard time squaring the activity of splashing joyfully about in our enemies' blood (v. 10) with an appropriate Christian response to the world. Yet this is a traditional Biblical image, borrowed from ancient *Near Eastern literature, for victory over an enemy* (see 68:21–23; Isa. 63:2–3; Ezek. 28:23; Rev. 14:19–20)—especially the national variety when threaten a whole people or the universal defeat of Satan and his demons. The images are extreme, but the joy in response to the restora-

tion of God's true order is real and not to be downplayed.

The destruction of God's enemies is part of bringing a fallen and distorted creation back under his sovereignty. It's part of transforming the world by removing evil once and for all in order to restore God's original purpose and intention. We long for restoration, when evil will be destroyed and creation harmony will reign at last among human beings, among humans and animals, and between all of us and the physical world (cf. Rom. 8:19–23).

Psalm 59

Psalm 59 continues the string of laments going back to Psalm 54. If originally composed by David under the circumstances noted in the heading (see 1 Sam. 19:11), the psalm must have been revised for use by one of David's successors when Jerusalem was under siege by a hostile force made up of troops from many nations (see vv. 5,8). Some, however, ascribe it to Nehemiah (cf. Neh. 4).

³See how they lie in wait for me!
    Fierce men conspire ᶻ against me
    for no offense or sin of mine, O LORD.
⁴I have done no wrong, yet they are ready to attack me. ᵃ
    Arise to help me; look on my plight!
⁵O LORD God Almighty, the God of Israel,
    rouse yourself to punish all the nations;
    show no mercy to wicked traitors. ᵇ   *Selah*

⁶They return at evening,
    snarling like dogs, ᶜ
    and prowl about the city.
⁷See what they spew from their mouths—
    they spew out swords ᵈ from their lips,
    and they say, "Who can hear us?" ᵉ
⁸But you, O LORD, laugh at them; ᶠ
    you scoff at all those nations. ᵍ

⁹O my Strength, I watch for you;
    you, O God, are my fortress, ʰ ¹⁰my loving God.

God will go before me
    and will let me gloat over those who slander me.
¹¹But do not kill them, O Lord our shield, ᵃⁱ
    or my people will forget. ʲ
In your might make them wander about,
    and bring them down. ᵏ
¹²For the sins of their mouths, ˡ
    for the words of their lips, ᵐ
    let them be caught in their pride. ⁿ
For the curses and lies they utter,
¹³   consume them in wrath,
    consume them till they are no more. ᵒ
Then it will be known to the ends of the earth
    that God rules over Jacob. ᵖ   *Selah*

¹⁴They return at evening,
    snarling like dogs,
    and prowl about the city.
¹⁵They wander about for food ᑫ
    and howl if not satisfied.
¹⁶But I will sing of your strength, ʳ
    in the morning ˢ I will sing of your love; ᵗ
for you are my fortress,
    my refuge in times of trouble. ᵘ

¹⁷O my Strength, I sing praise to you;
    you, O God, are my fortress, my loving God.

ᵃ 11 Or *sovereign*

59:3
z Ps 56:6

59:4
a Ps 35:19,23

59:5
b Jer 18:23

59:6
c ver 14

59:7
d Ps 57:4 e Ps 10:11

59:8
f Ps 37:13; Pr 1:26
g Ps 2:4

59:9
h Ps 9:9; 62:2

59:11
i Ps 84:9 j Dt 4:9
k Ps 106:27

59:12
l Ps 10:7 m Pr 12:13
n Zep 3:11

59:13
o Ps 104:35
p Ps 83:18

59:15
q Job 15:23

59:16
r Ps 21:13
s Ps 88:13
t Ps 101:1 u Ps 46:1

Once again the primary theme is the verbal attack of the enemy—twice described as a snarling pack of dogs—through slander and curses. The besieged psalmist remained confident, though; God is a refuge and fortress in times of trouble.

The "dogs" of life still snarl, bare their fangs, and nip at our heels, threatening to undo us. What hope do we have? Psalm 59 offers us the picture of a laughing God (v. 8). He laughs because the dogs' pretension to ultimate power over life is ridiculous. Yet he not only laughs, but loves (vv. 9,16,17)! His love for us is grounded in a commitment to relationship. This kind of love is what marriage should convey—not emotion or feeling alone or even benefit, but commitment.

Psalm 60

For the director of music. To ˌthe tune ofˌ "The Lily of the Covenant." A *miktam*[a] of David. For teaching. When he fought Aram Naharaim[b] and Aram Zobah,[c] and when Joab returned and struck down twelve thousand Edomites in the Valley of Salt.

60:1
v 2Sa 5:20; Ps 44:9
w Ps 79:5 x Ps 80:3

1 You have rejected us,[v] O God, and burst forth upon us;
  you have been angry[w]—now restore us![x]

60:2
y Ps 18:7
z 2Ch 7:14

2 You have shaken the land[y] and torn it open;
  mend its fractures,[z] for it is quaking.

60:3
a Ps 71:20
b Isa 51:17;
Jer 25:16

3 You have shown your people desperate times;[a]
  you have given us wine that makes us stagger.[b]

4 But for those who fear you, you have raised a banner
  to be unfurled against the bow.   *Selah*

60:5
c Ps 17:7; 108:6
d Ps 127:2

5 Save us and help us with your right hand,[c]
  that those you love[d] may be delivered.

60:6
e Ge 12:6

6 God has spoken from his sanctuary:
  "In triumph I will parcel out Shechem[e]
  and measure off the Valley of Succoth.

60:7
f Jos 13:31
g Dt 33:17
h Ge 49:10

7 Gilead[f] is mine, and Manasseh is mine;
  Ephraim is my helmet,
  Judah[g] my scepter.[h]

60:8
i 2Sa 8:1

8 Moab is my washbasin,
  upon Edom I toss my sandal;
  over Philistia I shout in triumph.[i]"

9 Who will bring me to the fortified city?
  Who will lead me to Edom?

60:10
j Jos 7:12; Ps 44:9;
108:11

10 Is it not you, O God, you who have rejected us
  and no longer go out with our armies?[j]

60:11
k Ps 146:3

11 Give us aid against the enemy,
  for the help of man is worthless.[k]

60:12
l Nu 24:18; Ps 44:5

12 With God we will gain the victory,
  and he will trample down our enemies.[l]

Psalm 61

For the director of music. With stringed instruments. Of David.

61:1
m Ps 64:1 n Ps 86:6

1 Hear my cry, O God;[m]
  listen to my prayer.[n]

61:2
o Ps 77:3

2 From the ends of the earth I call to you,
  I call as my heart grows faint;[o]

[a] Title: Probably a literary or musical term   [b] Title: That is, Arameans of Northwest Mesopotamia
[c] Title: That is, Arameans of central Syria

Psalm 60

📖 Psalm 60 is a national lament and plea for deliverance following a painful defeat by a foreign enemy, presumably Edom (see v. 9). The defeat is viewed as divine rejection and punishment, and the plea is for restoration of divine love and favor. Confronted by the people's helplessness, the psalmist was forced to approach the only stronghold and hope he had: the apparently absent God (see vv. 5,10–11).

The Old Testament is full of descriptions of divine abandonment. Often these experiences were seen as the result of human failure; at other times no explanation was offered. In these cases Israel pleaded with God to explain his distance, remember his covenant, and respond in renewed relationship and deliverance. Such accounts remind us that true victory is possible only through God's power.

📖 When our plans fail, we are wise to consider the possibility that God wasn't in them. But not all failure implies sin and divine punishment. Psalm 60 offers guidelines to help us assess such situations. (1) Relying on human strength alone is worthless. (2) Our failures don't undermine God's plans and purposes. (3) Broken relationships can be repaired—when we are tempted to label ourselves or others as unredeemable, God steps firmly into the breach with an offer of salvation and restoration.

lead me to the rock[p] that is higher than I.
3 For you have been my refuge,[q]
a strong tower against the foe.[r]

4 I long to dwell[s] in your tent forever
and take refuge in the shelter of your wings.[t] *Selah*
5 For you have heard my vows,[u] O God;
you have given me the heritage of those who fear your name.[v]

6 Increase the days of the king's life,
his years for many generations.[w]
7 May he be enthroned in God's presence forever;[x]
appoint your love and faithfulness to protect him.[y]

8 Then will I ever sing praise to your name[z]
and fulfill my vows day after day.

Psalm 62

For the director of music. For Jeduthun. A psalm of David.

1 My soul finds rest[a] in God alone;
my salvation comes from him.
2 He alone is my rock[b] and my salvation;
he is my fortress, I will never be shaken.

3 How long will you assault a man?
Would all of you throw him down—
this leaning wall,[c] this tottering fence?
4 They fully intend to topple him
from his lofty place;
they take delight in lies.
With their mouths they bless,
but in their hearts they curse.[d] *Selah*

5 Find rest, O my soul, in God alone;
my hope comes from him.
6 He alone is my rock and my salvation;
he is my fortress, I will not be shaken.
7 My salvation and my honor depend on God[a];
he is my mighty rock, my refuge.[e]
8 Trust in him at all times, O people;

[a] 7 Or / *God Most High is my salvation and my honor*

61:2
[p] Ps 18:2
61:3
[q] Ps 62:7 [r] Pr 18:10
61:4
[s] Ps 23:6 [t] Ps 91:4
61:5
[u] Ps 56:12
[v] Ps 86:11
61:6
[w] Ps 21:4
61:7
[x] Ps 41:12
[y] Ps 40:11
61:8
[z] Ps 65:1; 71:22

62:1
[a] Ps 33:20
62:2
[b] Ps 89:26

62:3
[c] Isa 30:13

62:4
[d] Ps 28:3

62:7
[e] Ps 46:1; 85:9;
Jer 3:23

Psalm 61

📖 Psalm 61 is a plea for restoration to God's presence. If David wrote this psalm, he may have composed it when he fled during Absalom's conspiracy (see 2 Sam. 17:21–29). Isolated and distant from sources of support and hope, the psalmist's heart grew "faint" (v. 2), here taking on the meaning of "losing heart" or "becoming discouraged." He drew on past experiences of rescue by God as grounds for renewed hope (v. 3).

📖 How do you keep your eyes on your Refuge and your pathway clear so that you will be unhindered in times of trouble? Psalm 61 advises that: (1) Trouble will indeed come. If we assume the righteous will never experience hardship, we will be unprepared for it. (2) It's important for us to bind ourselves to God in longing and desire (v. 4). (3) It's imperative that we remain committed to the relationship (v. 5). We become people shaped

by God's qualities of loyalty and faithfulness as we remain close to him—in storms and in periods of calm.

Psalm 62

📖 Psalm 62 reflects a situation of trouble for the psalmist but doesn't follow the usual pattern of the laments or pleas for deliverance. It has more in common with speeches both to the wicked (who are chastised in vv. 3–4) and to the reader, for whom the psalm encouraged faithful endurance. The last section (vv. 9–12) is a series of wise sayings similar to those found in Proverbs 30:7–31.

The psalmist committed himself to God when threatened by the assaults of conspirators who wished to "topple him from his lofty place" (v. 4). The author may have been a king, possibly David. Verse 3 suggests a time of weakness and may indicate advanced age.

62:8
f 1Sa 1:15; Ps 42:4;
La 2:19
62:9
g Ps 39:5,11
h Isa 40:15

pour out your hearts to him, [f]
for God is our refuge.   *Selah*

9 Lowborn men are but a breath, [g]
   the highborn are but a lie;
if weighed on a balance, [h] they are nothing;
   together they are only a breath.

62:10
i Isa 61:8
j Job 31:25; 1Ti 6:6-
10

10 Do not trust in extortion
    or take pride in stolen goods; [i]
though your riches increase,
    do not set your heart on them. [j]

11 One thing God has spoken,
    two things have I heard:
that you, O God, are strong,
12   and that you, O Lord, are loving.
Surely you will reward each person
    according to what he has done. [k]

62:12
k Job 34:11;
Mt 16:27

Psalm 63

A psalm of David. When he was in the Desert of Judah.

1 O God, you are my God,
   earnestly I seek you;
my soul thirsts for you, [l]
   my body longs for you,
in a dry and weary land
   where there is no water.

63:1
l Ps 42:2; 84:2

2 I have seen you in the sanctuary [m]
   and beheld your power and your glory.
3 Because your love is better than life, [n]
   my lips will glorify you.
4 I will praise you as long as I live, [o]
   and in your name I will lift up my hands. [p]
5 My soul will be satisfied as with the richest of foods; [q]
   with singing lips my mouth will praise you.

63:2
m Ps 27:4
63:3
n Ps 69:16
63:4
o Ps 104:33
p Ps 28:2
63:5
q Ps 36:8

6 On my bed I remember you;
   I think of you through the watches of the night. [r]
7 Because you are my help, [s]
   I sing in the shadow of your wings.
8 My soul clings to you;
   your right hand upholds me. [t]

63:6
r Ps 42:8
63:7
s Ps 27:9

63:8
t Ps 18:35

📖 Can you identify a time when you felt particularly vulnerable? Even though the eerie and unnatural calm experienced during the eye of a hurricane isn't an entirely accurate metaphor for the serenity we need to face life's storms, it does provide a helpful image of a moment of calm when all around us is swirling out of control. Only when we are able to focus on God alone does the power of the storm recede in response to his command, "Quiet! Be still!" (Mark 4:39). In what situations have you experienced your utter lack of power being swallowed up in his complete adequacy?

Psalm 63

📖 Psalm 63 pleads for God's presence. The psalmist spoke about an experience of isolation from God, characterized as an earnest search for water in a

"dry and weary land" (v. 1) This imagery allows God to be seen both as the "water of life" (cf. v. 5; John 4:7–15; Rev. 22:17) that satisfies completely and as the God who saves from life-threatening circumstances—whether the hostile desert environment or the enemies surrounding the psalmist (vv. 9–10).

📖 When is God's love "better than life" (v. 3)? Martyrs from Scriptural times forward have asked this question when confronted with the choice of recanting their faith in God or facing torturous forms of death. Is there some way here and now that the love of God makes this kind of difference in your life? Is your tie to God so important that you would sacrifice all your future hopes and dreams to remain in relationship with him?

9 They who seek my life will be destroyed;[u]
  they will go down to the depths of the earth.[v]
10 They will be given over to the sword
  and become food for jackals.

11 But the king will rejoice in God;
  all who swear by God's name will praise him,[w]
  while the mouths of liars will be silenced.

Psalm 64

For the director of music. A psalm of David.

1 Hear me, O God, as I voice my complaint;[x]
  protect my life from the threat of the enemy.[y]
2 Hide me from the conspiracy of the wicked,[z]
  from that noisy crowd of evildoers.

3 They sharpen their tongues like swords
  and aim their words like deadly arrows.[a]
4 They shoot from ambush at the innocent man;[b]
  they shoot at him suddenly, without fear.[c]

5 They encourage each other in evil plans,
  they talk about hiding their snares;
  they say, "Who will see them[a]?"[d]
6 They plot injustice and say,
  "We have devised a perfect plan!"
  Surely the mind and heart of man are cunning.

7 But God will shoot them with arrows;
  suddenly they will be struck down.
8 He will turn their own tongues against them[e]
  and bring them to ruin;
  all who see them will shake their heads[f] in scorn.

9 All mankind will fear;
  they will proclaim the works of God
  and ponder what he has done.[g]
10 Let the righteous rejoice in the LORD
  and take refuge in him;[h]
  let all the upright in heart praise him![i]

a 5 Or us

63:9 u Ps 40:14 v Ps 55:15
63:11 w Dt 6:13; Ps 21:1; Isa 45:23
64:1 x Ps 55:2 y Ps 140:1
64:2 z Ps 56:6; 59:2
64:3 a Ps 58:7
64:4 b Ps 11:2 c Ps 55:19
64:5 d Ps 10:11
64:8 e Ps 9:3; Pr 18:7 f Ps 22:7
64:9 g Jer 51:10
64:10 h Ps 25:20 i Ps 32:11

Psalm 64

Psalm 64 is part of a group of psalms (56–68) in which God's mighty acts demonstrate his power over all the earth so that an increasingly wide-ranging group joins in praising him. This crescendo of praise ultimately includes the whole earth (66:1,4,8; 67:3–5; 68) as the nations are subdued (66:7), acknowledge God's power, and join in praise (67:3–7).

An unruly lynch mob is an example of a negative form of mutual encouragement and solidarity. We see in this psalm the result of such a "conspiracy of the wicked" (v. 2). In such an environment it's easy to deny personal responsibility. Psalm 64 applies a different stan-dard in the judgment of human arrogance: God judges right and wrong. Yet the psalm ends with a renewed call to harmony. The destruction of the wicked will bring together all of humankind to reverently reflect on God's works and praise him for his power.

How much pity would you have if a terrorist bomb-maker were to blow himself or herself up while creating a bomb? "They got what they had coming," you might smugly observe. But these kinds of scenarios in the psalms always carry a hidden price tag. When we rejoice in the destruction of the wicked, we might want to be cautious. What if we were to receive what we deserve?

Psalm 65

For the director of music. A psalm of David. A song.

65:1
j Ps 116:18

1 Praise awaits[a] you, O God, in Zion;
 to you our vows will be fulfilled.[j]

65:2
k Isa 66:23
65:3
l Ps 38:4
m Heb 9:14
65:4
n Ps 4:3; 33:12
o Ps 36:8

2 O you who hear prayer,
 to you all men will come.[k]
3 When we were overwhelmed by sins,[l]
 you forgave[b] our transgressions.[m]
4 Blessed are those you choose[n]
 and bring near to live in your courts!
We are filled with the good things of your house,[o]
 of your holy temple.

65:5
p Ps 85:4
q Ps 107:23

5 You answer us with awesome deeds of righteousness,
 O God our Savior,[p]
 the hope of all the ends of the earth
 and of the farthest seas,[q]

65:6
r Ps 93:1
65:7
s Mt 8:26
t Isa 17:12-13

6 who formed the mountains by your power,
 having armed yourself with strength,[r]
7 who stilled the roaring of the seas,[s]
 the roaring of their waves,
 and the turmoil of the nations.[t]
8 Those living far away fear your wonders;
 where morning dawns and evening fades
 you call forth songs of joy.

65:9
u Ps 68:9-10
v Ps 46:4; 104:14

9 You care for the land and water it;[u]
 you enrich it abundantly.
The streams of God are filled with water
 to provide the people with grain,[v]
 for so you have ordained it.[c]
10 You drench its furrows
 and level its ridges;
you soften it with showers
 and bless its crops.
11 You crown the year with your bounty,
 and your carts overflow with abundance.

65:12
w Job 28:26

12 The grasslands of the desert overflow;[w]
 the hills are clothed with gladness.

65:13
x Ps 144:13
y Ps 72:16
z Ps 98:8; Isa 55:12

13 The meadows are covered with flocks[x]
 and the valleys are mantled with grain;[y]
 they shout for joy and sing.[z]

---

[a] 1 Or *befits*; the meaning of the Hebrew for this word is uncertain.   [b] 3 Or *made atonement for*
[c] 9 Or *for that is how you prepare the land*

Psalm 65

📖 Psalm 65 continues the outpouring of praise begun in Psalm 56 (see "There and Then" for Ps. 55) and exhibits a number of themes and phrases in common with the earlier psalms in the grouping. It begins with a promise to fulfill "our vows" and speaks of the universal recognition of Israel's God. In addition, it expresses concern for the temple and its blessings. The psalmist gave thanks for forgiveness of sin, for God's provision of security and stability in the midst of turmoil, and for his abundant provision of life's necessities for people and animals.

📖 The Christian mission movement developed out of a desire to fulfill Christ's call, laid out in the Great Commission of Matthew 28:19–20. But in the last 50 years or so more and more persons of diverse ethnic and national origins have been congregating in world cities. This influx of peoples represents a tremendous opportunity for the church (and individual Christians) to work at a local level to fulfill the vision of Psalm 65.

Psalm 66

For the director of music. A song. A psalm.

1 Shout with joy to God, all the earth! [a]
2   Sing the glory of his name; [b]
     make his praise glorious!
3 Say to God, "How awesome are your deeds! [c]
     So great is your power
     that your enemies cringe [d] before you.
4 All the earth bows down [e] to you;
     they sing praise [f] to you,
     they sing praise to your name."   *Selah*

5 Come and see what God has done,
     how awesome his works [g] in man's behalf!
6 He turned the sea into dry land, [h]
     they passed through the waters on foot—
     come, let us rejoice in him.
7 He rules forever [i] by his power,
     his eyes watch [j] the nations—
     let not the rebellious [k] rise up against him.   *Selah*

8 Praise [l] our God, O peoples,
     let the sound of his praise be heard;
9 he has preserved our lives
     and kept our feet from slipping. [m]
10 For you, O God, tested us;
     you refined us like silver. [n]
11 You brought us into prison
     and laid burdens [o] on our backs.
12 You let men ride over our heads; [p]
     we went through fire and water,
     but you brought us to a place of abundance. [q]

13 I will come to your temple with burnt offerings
     and fulfill my vows [r] to you—
14 vows my lips promised and my mouth spoke
     when I was in trouble.
15 I will sacrifice fat animals to you
     and an offering of rams;
     I will offer bulls and goats. [s]   *Selah*

16 Come and listen, [t] all you who fear God;
     let me tell [u] you what he has done for me.
17 I cried out to him with my mouth;
     his praise was on my tongue.
18 If I had cherished sin in my heart,
     the Lord would not have listened; [v]

66:1
[a] Ps 100:1
66:2
[b] Ps 79:9
66:3
[c] Ps 65:5 [d] Ps 18:44
66:4
[e] Ps 22:27 [f] Ps 67:3
66:5
[g] Ps 106:22
66:6
[h] Ex 14:22
66:7
[i] Ps 145:13
[j] Ps 11:4 [k] Ps 140:8
66:8
[l] Ps 98:4
66:9
[m] Ps 121:3
66:10
[n] Ps 17:3;
Isa 48:10; Zec 13:9;
1Pe 1:6-7
66:11
[o] La 1:13
66:12
[p] Isa 51:23
[q] Isa 43:2
66:13
[r] Ecc 5:4
66:15
[s] Nu 6:14; Ps 51:19
66:16
[t] Ps 34:11
[u] Ps 71:15,24
66:18
[v] Job 36:21;
Isa 1:15; Jas 4:3

Psalm 66

Psalm 66 is a song of praise for God's "awesome deeds" that demonstrate his universal rule over all humanity. According to the Westminster Shorter Catechism, the chief end or goal of a human being is "to glorify God, and to enjoy him forever." Psalm 66 takes a nearly identical position when it calls "all the earth" to "sing the glory of his name; make his praise glorious!" (vv. 1–2). In deeds, words, thoughts, and relationships believers are to make God's glory known. That is what being in God's image and likeness (Gen. 1:26) is all about: communicating the divine likeness to his creation.

How can a loving God allow pain and suffering in the world? Some people think that God's power can only be displayed when believers live charmed, painless lives of abundant goodness. Such a perspective can alienate people whose experience is quite opposite and prevent us from talking honestly and openly about life's failures, struggles, hurts, and attacks. This psalm acknowledged human struggle and suffering as real, but not as barriers to the experience of God's love and care.

66:19
w Ps 116:1-2

66:20
x Ps 22:24; 68:35

19 but God has surely listened
    and heard my voice[w] in prayer.
20 Praise be to God,
    who has not rejected[x] my prayer
    or withheld his love from me!

Psalm 67

For the director of music. With stringed instruments. A psalm. A song.

67:1
y Nu 6:24-26;
Ps 4:6

1 May God be gracious to us and bless us
    and make his face shine upon us,[y]   *Selah*

67:2
z Isa 52:10
a Tit 2:11

2 that your ways may be known on earth,
    your salvation[z] among all nations.[a]

3 May the peoples praise you, O God;
    may all the peoples praise you.

67:4
b Ps 96:10-13

4 May the nations be glad and sing for joy,
    for you rule the peoples justly[b]
    and guide the nations of the earth.   *Selah*

5 May the peoples praise you, O God;
    may all the peoples praise you.

67:6
c Lev 26:4;
Ps 85:12; Eze 34:27

6 Then the land will yield its harvest,[c]
    and God, our God, will bless us.

67:7
d Ps 33:8

7 God will bless us,
    and all the ends of the earth will fear him.[d]

Psalm 68

For the director of music. Of David. A psalm. A song.

68:1
e Nu 10:35; Isa 33:3
68:2
f Hos 13:3
g Isa 9:18; Mic 1:4

1 May God arise, may his enemies be scattered;
    may his foes flee[e] before him.
2 As smoke[f] is blown away by the wind,
    may you blow them away;
  as wax melts[g] before the fire,
    may the wicked perish before God.

68:3
h Ps 32:11

3 But may the righteous be glad
    and rejoice[h] before God;
    may they be happy and joyful.

68:4
i Ps 66:2

4 Sing to God, sing praise to his name,[i]

Psalm 67

Psalm 67 is absorbed with the concern that all humanity should know, acknowledge, and respond in praise for the blessing of God's salvation. Its non-adversarial attitude toward pagan nations is striking. The basis of the psalmist's thought appears to be God's covenant with Abraham (Gen. 12:1–3), in which the blessing of Abraham is linked with God's intention to bless "all peoples on earth."

The covenant name *Yahweh*, with its exclusive ties to Israel (in a sense, "God of his people"), is almost completely omitted from Psalms 60–67, which use instead the more inclusive name *Elohim*—God of the universe. Is it possible that this section of the Psalter may be, in a loose sense, a kind of "evangelistic pamphlet" preparing all the peoples of the earth for their inclusion in God's saving purposes for his whole creation?

It's especially meaningful for non-Israelite, non-Jewish readers from the "ends of the earth" (67:7) to hear the words of special relationship pronounced over us and all our brothers and sisters in Christ. We have much to be thankful for in that we have been "grafted into" God's family through Jesus' work to establish God's salvation among all the nations (see Rom. 11:17–24). "May the peoples praise you, O God; may *all the peoples* praise you" (67:3, emphasis added).

Psalm 68

Clearly evident in this psalm are God's demonstration of his universal power and authority, the acknowledgment of that authority by the nations and their submission to it, and joyful praise for his righteous kingship by the whole earth. Psalm 68 is a praise hymn celebrating God's power to save.

extol him who rides on the clouds[a][j]—
his name is the LORD[k]—
and rejoice before him.
5 A father to the fatherless,[l] a defender of widows,[m]
is God in his holy dwelling.[n]
6 God sets the lonely in families,[b][o]
he leads forth the prisoners[p] with singing;
but the rebellious live in a sun-scorched land.[q]

7 When you went out[r] before your people, O God,
when you marched through the wasteland,   *Selah*
8 the earth shook,
the heavens poured down rain,[s]
before God, the One of Sinai,[t]
before God, the God of Israel.
9 You gave abundant showers,[u] O God;
you refreshed your weary inheritance.
10 Your people settled in it,
and from your bounty, O God, you provided[v] for the poor.

11 The Lord announced the word,
and great was the company of those who proclaimed it:
12 "Kings and armies flee[w] in haste;
in the camps men divide the plunder.

68:4	[j] Dt 33:26 [k] Ex 6:3; Ps 83:18
68:5	[l] Ps 10:14 [m] Dt 10:18 [n] Dt 26:15
68:6	[o] Ps 113:9 [p] Ac 12:6 [q] Ps 107:34
68:7	[r] Ex 13:21; Jdg 4:14
68:8	[s] Jdg 5:4 [t] Ex 19:16,18
68:9	[u] Dt 11:11
68:10	[v] Ps 74:19
68:12	[w] Jos 10:16

[a] 4 Or *I prepare the way for him who rides through the deserts*   [b] 6 Or *the desolate in a homeland*

God, whose power is unmistakable in the storm, is also compassionate, concerned with the welfare of those lacking status or power (vv. 5–6). In ancient times adult males represented the family and provided access to the resources society provided. Widows and orphans, then and now in developing nations, were at an extreme disadvantage, having no one to secure their rights or basic needs. They were dependent on their own abilities to scratch out a meager existence or on acts of charity by compassionate individuals.

Snapshots

 68:5–6a

Jacquiline

From a winding road eked out of steep hills in northeastern Rwanda, community worker Jacquiline steps from her jeep and cautiously climbs down, knowing that a false step could end in a bad fall. Cheerily, she greets her clients: teenagers tilling the wet earth. With speed calculated not to look hurried, Jacquiline checks what they have accomplished this week, determines their needs, and offers assistance in any area to this child-headed household.

Next she visits another village. Greeting sixteen-year-old Janet and her younger sister Mkandaisenga, she falls to her knees to chat with baby Urayeneza. Jacquiline determines that none of the siblings has a major problem this week. Two others are in school: brother Mujarugamba and sister Uwajeneza.

Jacquiline moves on to visit a brick-making group of young people from child-headed households. The community, which began making bricks with the assistance of a Christian nongovernment organization (NGO), has recently set up a grocery kiosk for alternative income during the wet season.

> Jacquiline . . . offers assistance in any area to this child-headed household.

Jacquiline talks to group leader Anastase, who assures her that business is picking up. Other members inform her that they are grateful for the school supplies obtained at subsidized prices from the kiosk. Without them, younger siblings would have been barred from attending classes.

68:13
x Ge 49:14

68:14
y Jos 10:10

68:16
z Dt 12:5

68:17
a Dt 33:2; Da 7:10

68:18
b Jdg 5:12
c Eph 4:8*

68:19
d Ps 65:5 e Ps 55:22

68:20
f Ps 56:13
68:21
g Ps 110:5;
Hab 3:13

68:22
h Nu 21:33
68:23
i Ps 58:10
j 1Ki 21:19

68:24
k Ps 63:2

68:25
l Jdg 11:34;
1Ch 13:8
68:26
m Ps 26:12; Isa 48:1
68:27
n 1Sa 9:21

68:29
o Ps 72:10

68:30
p Ps 22:12
q Ps 89:10

68:31
r Isa 19:19; 45:14

13 Even while you sleep among the campfires, [a] [x]
  the wings of ⌊my⌋ dove are sheathed with silver,
  its feathers with shining gold."
14 When the Almighty [b] scattered [y] the kings in the land,
  it was like snow fallen on Zalmon.

15 The mountains of Bashan are majestic mountains;
  rugged are the mountains of Bashan.
16 Why gaze in envy, O rugged mountains,
  at the mountain where God chooses [z] to reign,
  where the Lord himself will dwell forever?
17 The chariots of God are tens of thousands
  and thousands of thousands; [a]
  the Lord ⌊has come⌋ from Sinai into his sanctuary.
18 When you ascended on high,
  you led captives [b] in your train;
  you received gifts from men, [c]
 even from [c] the rebellious—
  that you, [d] O Lord God, might dwell there.

19 Praise be to the Lord, to God our Savior, [d]
  who daily bears our burdens. [e]   *Selah*
20 Our God is a God who saves;
  from the Sovereign Lord comes escape from death. [f]

21 Surely God will crush the heads [g] of his enemies,
  the hairy crowns of those who go on in their sins.
22 The Lord says, "I will bring them from Bashan;
  I will bring them from the depths of the sea, [h]
23 that you may plunge your feet in the blood of your foes, [i]
  while the tongues of your dogs [j] have their share."

24 Your procession has come into view, O God,
  the procession of my God and King into the sanctuary. [k]
25 In front are the singers, after them the musicians;
  with them are the maidens playing tambourines. [l]
26 Praise God in the great congregation;
  praise the Lord in the assembly of Israel. [m]
27 There is the little tribe [n] of Benjamin, leading them,
  there the great throng of Judah's princes,
  and there the princes of Zebulun and of Naphtali.

28 Summon your power, O God [e];
  show us your strength, O God, as you have done before.
29 Because of your temple at Jerusalem
  kings will bring you gifts. [o]
30 Rebuke the beast among the reeds,
  the herd of bulls [p] among the calves of the nations.
 Humbled, may it bring bars of silver.
  Scatter the nations [q] who delight in war.
31 Envoys will come from Egypt; [r]
  Cush [f] will submit herself to God.

a 13 Or *saddlebags* b 14 Hebrew *Shaddai* c 18 Or *gifts for men, / even* d 18 Or *they*
e 28 Many Hebrew manuscripts, Septuagint and Syriac; most Hebrew manuscripts *Your God has summoned power for you* f 31 That is, the upper Nile region

---

God mandated helping defenseless persons by encouraging compassion toward them and laying down commands regarding their care and treatment by society at large (cf. Deut 14:29; 16:11,14; 24:17–21; 26:12–13; 27:19). In ancient times, many were left destitute because of war and disease. Those causes today also include HIV/AIDS in the developing world and divorce and mental illness in the West. Regardless of the cause, shouldn't we as Christians today be involved in demonstrating Christ's love and care for the people society ignores?

³²Sing to God, O kingdoms of the earth,
　　sing praise to the Lord,　　　　　　*Selah*
³³to him who rides ˢ the ancient skies above,
　　who thunders with mighty voice. ᵗ
³⁴Proclaim the power ᵘ of God,
　　whose majesty is over Israel,
　　whose power is in the skies.
³⁵You are awesome, O God, in your sanctuary;
　　the God of Israel gives power and strength to his people. ᵛ

　　Praise be to God! ʷ

68:33
ˢ Ps 18:10 ᵗ Ps 29:4

68:34
ᵘ Ps 29:1

68:35
ᵛ Ps 29:11
ʷ Ps 66:20

Psalm 69

For the director of music. To the tune of "Lilies." Of David.

¹Save me, O God,
　　for the waters have come up to my neck. ˣ
²I sink in the miry depths, ʸ
　　where there is no foothold.
　I have come into the deep waters;
　　the floods engulf me.
³I am worn out calling for help; ᶻ
　　my throat is parched.
　My eyes fail, ᵃ
　　looking for my God.
⁴Those who hate me without reason ᵇ
　　outnumber the hairs of my head;
　many are my enemies without cause, ᶜ
　　those who seek to destroy me.
　I am forced to restore
　　what I did not steal.

⁵You know my folly, ᵈ O God;
　　my guilt is not hidden from you. ᵉ

⁶May those who hope in you
　　not be disgraced because of me,
　　O Lord, the Lᴏʀᴅ Almighty;
　may those who seek you
　　not be put to shame because of me,
　　O God of Israel.
⁷For I endure scorn for your sake, ᶠ
　　and shame covers my face. ᵍ
⁸I am a stranger to my brothers,
　　an alien to my own mother's sons; ʰ

69:1
ˣ Jnh 2:5
69:2
ʸ Ps 40:2

69:3
ᶻ Ps 6:6
ᵃ Ps 119:82;
Isa 38:14

69:4
ᵇ Jn 15:25*
ᶜ Ps 35:19; 38:19

69:5
ᵈ Ps 38:5 ᵉ Ps 44:21

69:7
ᶠ Jer 15:15
ᵍ Ps 44:15

69:8
ʰ Ps 31:11; Isa 53:3

Psalm 69

Psalm 69 introduces a new grouping (Ps. 69–71) that returns to earlier themes of lament and pleas for deliverance from mocking and threatening enemies. The hoped-for divine rule over the nations gives way to the reality of something far less—isolation, oppression, and ridicule by the enemy. The psalmist—who acknowledged sin and accepted divine discipline (vv. 5,26)—experienced an environment of scorn and rejection that seemed out of proportion to his real guilt. If, as tradition claims, David authored the original psalm (see the heading), the occasion is unknown. In its present (possibly adapted) form, the prayer suggests a later son of David who ruled over the southern kingdom of Judah (see v. 35).

Even if we have no experience with the kind of anger and hatred pictured in this psalm, others do, and they need assurance that honest expression of their emotions doesn't deny them a relationship with a loving God. Verbalizing their feelings to God is both good theology and good therapy. People who suffer abuse, torture, and otherwise undeserved pain need our compassion and empathy, not our judgment. God knows their anguish and, in Jesus, experienced similar suffering and pain unto death. If God went so far as to stand in solidarity with people's suffering, how can we do less?

69:9
i Jn 2:17*
j Ps 89:50-51;
Ro 15:3*
69:10
k Ps 35:13
69:11
l Ps 35:13

[9] for zeal for your house consumes me,[i]
and the insults of those who insult you fall on me.[j]
[10] When I weep and fast,[k]
I must endure scorn;
[11] when I put on sackcloth,[l]
people make sport of me.

69:12
m Job 30:9

[12] Those who sit at the gate mock me,
and I am the song of the drunkards.[m]

69:13
n Isa 49:8; 2Co 6:2
o Ps 51:1

[13] But I pray to you, O LORD,
in the time of your favor;[n]
in your great love,[o] O God,
answer me with your sure salvation.
[14] Rescue me from the mire,
do not let me sink;
deliver me from those who hate me,
from the deep waters.[p]

69:14
p ver 2; Ps 144:7
69:15
q Ps 124:4-5
r Nu 16:33

[15] Do not let the floodwaters[q] engulf me
or the depths swallow me up[r]
or the pit close its mouth over me.

69:16
s Ps 63:3

[16] Answer me, O LORD, out of the goodness of your love;[s]
in your great mercy turn to me.

69:17
t Ps 27:9 *u* Ps 66:14

[17] Do not hide your face[t] from your servant;
answer me quickly, for I am in trouble.[u]

69:18
v Ps 49:15
69:19
w Ps 22:6

[18] Come near and rescue me;
redeem[v] me because of my foes.

[19] You know how I am scorned,[w] disgraced and shamed;
all my enemies are before you.

69:20
x Job 16:2
y Isa 63:5
69:21
z Mt 27:34;
Mk 15:23;
Jn 19:28-30

[20] Scorn has broken my heart
and has left me helpless;
I looked for sympathy, but there was none,
for comforters,[x] but I found none.[y]
[21] They put gall in my food
and gave me vinegar for my thirst.[z]

[22] May the table set before them become a snare;
may it become retribution and[a] a trap.

69:23
a Isa 6:9-10;
Ro 11:9-10*
69:24
b Ps 79:6

[23] May their eyes be darkened so they cannot see,
and their backs be bent forever.[a]
[24] Pour out your wrath[b] on them;
let your fierce anger overtake them.

69:25
c Mt 23:38
d Ac 1:20*

[25] May their place be deserted;[c]
let there be no one to dwell in their tents.[d]

69:26
e Isa 53:4; Zec 1:15
69:27
f Ne 4:5
g Ps 109:14;
Isa 26:10
69:28
h Ex 32:32-33;
Lk 10:20; Php 4:3
i Eze 13:9

[26] For they persecute those you wound
and talk about the pain of those you hurt.[e]
[27] Charge them with crime upon crime;[f]
do not let them share in your salvation.[g]
[28] May they be blotted out of the book of life[h]
and not be listed with the righteous.[i]

69:29
j Ps 59:1; 70:5

[29] I am in pain and distress;
may your salvation, O God, protect me.[j]

69:30
k Ps 28:7 *l* Ps 34:3

[30] I will praise God's name in song[k]
and glorify him[l] with thanksgiving.
[31] This will please the LORD more than an ox,
more than a bull with its horns and hoofs.[m]

69:31
m Ps 50:9-13

[a] 22 Or *snare / and their fellowship become*

32 The poor will see and be glad [n]—
    you who seek God, may your hearts live! [o]
33 The LORD hears the needy [p]
    and does not despise his captive people.

34 Let heaven and earth praise him,
    the seas and all that move in them, [q]
35 for God will save Zion [r]
    and rebuild the cities of Judah. [s]
Then people will settle there and possess it;
36   the children of his servants will inherit it,
    and those who love his name will dwell there. [t]

Psalm 70

For the director of music. Of David. A petition.

1 Hasten, O God, to save me;
    O LORD, come quickly to help me. [u]
2 May those who seek my life [v]
    be put to shame and confusion;
may all who desire my ruin
    be turned back in disgrace. [w]
3 May those who say to me, "Aha! Aha!"
    turn back because of their shame.
4 But may all who seek you
    rejoice and be glad in you;
may those who love your salvation always say,
    "Let God be exalted!"

5 Yet I am poor and needy; [x]
    come quickly to me, [y] O God.
You are my help and my deliverer;
    O LORD, do not delay.

Psalm 71

1 In you, O LORD, I have taken refuge;
    let me never be put to shame. [z]
2 Rescue me and deliver me in your righteousness;
    turn your ear [a] to me and save me.

69:32
[n] Ps 34:2
[o] Ps 22:26
69:33
[p] Ps 12:5; 68:6

69:34
[q] Ps 96:11; 148:1;
Isa 44:23; 49:13;
55:12
69:35
[r] Ob 17
[s] Ps 51:18;
Isa 44:26
69:36
[t] Ps 37:29; 102:28

70:1
[u] Ps 40:13
70:2
[v] Ps 35:4
[w] Ps 35:26

70:5
[x] Ps 40:17
[y] Ps 141:1

71:1
[z] Ps 25:2-3; 31:1

71:2
[a] Ps 17:6

Psalm 70

Like Psalms 9/10, 32/33, and 42/43, Psalms 70 and 71 are combined in many ancient manuscripts, indicating that they were at some point read as a single psalm. A slightly altered form of Psalm 70 appears in 40:13–17. The psalm functions here as an introduction to the combined composition. The two psalms are considered together in the notes to follow, though they apply more specifically to Psalm 71.

The unique voice in this lament is that of advanced age. Although the aged in Old Testament society were respected and honored, they experienced a similar diminishment of capacity, independence, and freedom as the elderly do today, along with the realization of approaching death. In this light we understand the psalmist's fear of shame and desire for refuge in God. Experience had taught him that age makes no difference in the need for the faithful to rely on God.

The psalmist's fears expressed in the combined composition reflect concerns today. It's appropriate here to examine how modern society increasingly discards its older generations, extolling the supposed "virtues" of youth and beauty. Throughout the Scripture, however, respect between older and younger, men and women, rich and poor, is the standard. How are these Biblical values reflected in your own attitudes and practices?

Psalm 71

Regardless of any diminished capacity due to age, the psalmist remained able to declare the righteous acts of God to all who would listen (v. 18). There is a significant shift from "Preserve my life" to "Allow me to leave a legacy of hope and faithfulness." The psalmist couldn't stave off death forever, but he wanted to live long enough to transmit his faithful message to those who would come after. His repeated requests for restoration of life and honor reflect his desire that his message of praise be heard and received with respect (vv. 20–23).

71:3
b Ps 18:2; 31:2-3;
44:4
71:4
c Ps 140:4

71:5
d Job 4:6; Jer 17:7
71:6
e Ps 22:10
f Ps 22:9; Isa 46:3
g Ps 9:1; 34:1; 52:9;
119:164; 145:2
71:7
h Isa 8:18; 1Co 4:9
i 2Sa 22:3; Ps 61:3

71:8
j Ps 51:15; 63:5
k Ps 35:28; 96:6;
104:1
71:9
l Ps 51:11 m ver 18;
Ps 92:14; Isa 46:4

71:10
n Ps 10:8; 59:3;
Pr 1:18 o Ps 31:13;
56:6; Mt 12:14

71:11
p Ps 7:2
71:12
q Ps 35:22; 38:21
r Ps 38:22; 70:1

71:13
s ver 24

71:14
t Ps 130:7

71:15
u Ps 35:28; 40:5

71:16
v Ps 106:2

71:17
w Dt 4:5 x Ps 26:7

71:18
y ver 9
z Ps 22:30,31;
78:4

71:19
a Ps 36:5; 57:10
b Ps 126:2; Lk 1:49
c Ps 35:10

71:20
d Ps 60:3 e Hos 6:2

71:21
f Ps 18:35
g Ps 23:4; 86:17;
Isa 12:1; 49:13

3 Be my rock of refuge,
    to which I can always go;
  give the command to save me,
    for you are my rock and my fortress. b
4 Deliver me, O my God, from the hand of the wicked, c
    from the grasp of evil and cruel men.

5 For you have been my hope, O Sovereign LORD,
    my confidence d since my youth.
6 From birth e I have relied on you;
    you brought me forth from my mother's womb. f
  I will ever praise g you.
7 I have become like a portent h to many,
    but you are my strong refuge. i
8 My mouth j is filled with your praise,
    declaring your splendor k all day long.

9 Do not cast l me away when I am old; m
    do not forsake me when my strength is gone.
10 For my enemies speak against me;
    those who wait to kill n me conspire o together.
11 They say, "God has forsaken him;
    pursue him and seize him,
    for no one will rescue p him."
12 Be not far q from me, O God;
    come quickly, O my God, to help r me.
13 May my accusers perish in shame;
    may those who want to harm me
    be covered with scorn and disgrace. s

14 But as for me, I will always have hope; t
    I will praise you more and more.
15 My mouth will tell u of your righteousness,
    of your salvation all day long,
    though I know not its measure.
16 I will come and proclaim your mighty acts, v O Sovereign LORD;
    I will proclaim your righteousness, yours alone.
17 Since my youth, O God, you have taught w me,
    and to this day I declare your marvelous deeds. x
18 Even when I am old and gray, y
    do not forsake me, O God,
  till I declare your power to the next generation,
    your might to all who are to come. z

19 Your righteousness reaches to the skies, a O God,
    you who have done great things. b
    Who, O God, is like you? c
20 Though you have made me see troubles, d many and bitter,
    you will restore e my life again;
  from the depths of the earth
    you will again bring me up.
21 You will increase my honor f
    and comfort g me once again.

📖 The psalmist cited four reasons for hope for the aging: (1) His active recall of a life faithfully spent allowed him to accept God's evaluation and proclaim it confidently—in the words of Matthew 25:21, "Well done, good and faithful servant!" (2) The ability to enter God's waiting refuge in time of trouble can be a matter of lifelong practice. (3) The psalmist's words in verse 9 recall for us Paul's realization, via a revelation from Christ, that "when I am weak, then I am strong" (2 Cor. 12:7–10). (4) Age provides a natural opportunity to testify to God's strength.

22 I will praise you with the harp[h]
for your faithfulness, O my God;
I will sing praise to you with the lyre,[i]
O Holy One of Israel.[j]
23 My lips will shout for joy
when I sing praise to you—
I, whom you have redeemed.[k]
24 My tongue will tell of your righteous acts
all day long,[l]
for those who wanted to harm me[m]
have been put to shame and confusion.

71:22 [h] Ps 33:2 [i] Ps 92:3; 144:9 [j] 2Ki 19:22
71:23 [k] Ps 103:4
71:24 [l] Ps 35:28 [m] ver 13

Psalm 72

Of Solomon.

1 Endow the king with your justice, O God,
the royal son with your righteousness.
2 He will[a] judge your people in righteousness,[n]
your afflicted ones with justice.
3 The mountains will bring prosperity to the people,
the hills the fruit of righteousness.
4 He will defend the afflicted among the people
and save the children of the needy;[o]
he will crush the oppressor.

5 He will endure[b] as long as the sun,
as long as the moon, through all generations.
6 He will be like rain[p] falling on a mown field,
like showers watering the earth.
7 In his days the righteous will flourish;[q]
prosperity will abound till the moon is no more.

8 He will rule from sea to sea
and from the River[c][r] to the ends of the earth.[d][s]
9 The desert tribes will bow before him
and his enemies will lick the dust.
10 The kings of Tarshish and of distant shores
will bring tribute to him;
the kings of Sheba[t] and Seba
will present him gifts.[u]
11 All kings will bow down to him
and all nations will serve him.

72:2 [n] Isa 9:7; 11:4-5; 32:1
72:4 [o] Isa 11:4
72:6 [p] Dt 32:2; Hos 6:3
72:7 [q] Ps 92:12; Isa 2:4
72:8 [r] Ex 23:31 [s] Zec 9:10
72:10 [t] Ge 10:7 [u] 2Ch 9:24

[a] 2 Or *May he;* similarly in verses 3-11 and 17 [b] 5 Septuagint; Hebrew *You will be feared*
[c] 8 That is, the Euphrates [d] 8 Or *the end of the land*

Psalm 72

Psalm 72 is the last psalm of Book II (Ps. 42–72), which is marked by the doxology in verses 18–19. The addition of verse 20, the only postscript in the Psalter, suggests that the first two books were at some point combined into a unified "Davidic" collection. The heading "Of Solomon" indicates that the psalm was written by or for Solomon. It also was likely used with regard to later kings of Judah.

The text is clear about the king's responsibility—to rule rightly over God's people by defending the poor and needy in a special way. The God-ordained responsibility of government is to defend those who can't defend themselves, by protecting and providing for the vulnerable and underprivileged.

Can we hold modern nations and leaders to the standard of righteousness defined in verses 1–4 and 12–14? The description of just rule here is God's standard for leaders, still acknowledged by the global community as "good rule" goals. God the Creator holds every person to his standard; no one is excused on the basis of ignorance (cf. Rom 1:18–20,32). He calls us through this psalm to pray not only for the well-being of our leaders (v. 15) but also for their wisdom to see that all justice is ultimately God's justice—for which they will be held accountable.

¹² For he will deliver the needy who cry out,
 the afflicted who have no one to help.
¹³ He will take pity on the weak and the needy
 and save the needy from death.
¹⁴ He will rescue^v them from oppression and violence,
 for precious^w is their blood in his sight.

¹⁵ Long may he live!
 May gold from Sheba^x be given him.
May people ever pray for him
 and bless him all day long.
¹⁶ Let grain abound throughout the land;
 on the tops of the hills may it sway.
Let its fruit flourish like Lebanon;^y
 let it thrive like the grass of the field.
¹⁷ May his name endure forever;^z
 may it continue as long as the sun.^a

All nations will be blessed through him,
 and they will call him blessed.^b

¹⁸ Praise be to the LORD God, the God of Israel,^c
 who alone does marvelous deeds.^d
¹⁹ Praise be to his glorious name forever;
 may the whole earth be filled with his glory.^e
 Amen and Amen.^f

²⁰ This concludes the prayers of David son of Jesse.

BOOK III
Psalms 73–89

Psalm 73
A psalm of Asaph.

¹ Surely God is good to Israel,
 to those who are pure in heart.^g

² But as for me, my feet had almost slipped;
 I had nearly lost my foothold.
³ For I envied^h the arrogant
 when I saw the prosperity of the wicked.ⁱ

⁴ They have no struggles;
 their bodies are healthy and strong.^a
⁵ They are free^j from the burdens common to man;

---

^a 4 With a different word division of the Hebrew; Masoretic Text *struggles at their death; / their bodies are healthy*

Cross references (margin)

72:14
v Ps 69:18
w 1Sa 26:21;
 Ps 116:15

72:15
x Isa 60:6

72:16
y Ps 104:16

72:17
z Ex 3:15 a Ps 89:36
b Ge 12:3; Lk 1:48

72:18
c 1Ch 29:10;
 Ps 41:13; 106:48
d Job 5:9

72:19
e Nu 14:21; Ne 9:5
f Ps 41:13

73:1
g Mt 5:8

73:3
h Ps 37:1; Pr 23:17
i Job 21:7; Jer 12:1

73:5
j Job 21:9

Psalm 73

Book III of the Psalter begins with this psalm ascribed to Asaph, the leader of one of the Levitical choirs appointed by David (cf. 1 Chron. 6:31–32,39; 16:1–6). It begins a collection of 11 Asaphite psalms (Ps. 73–83). Since these psalms were obviously written during various historical periods, we can conclude either that some were written by descendants of Asaph or that they were penned as tributes to him or reflect his style or spirit. The "psalms of Asaph" are character-

ized by a theme of God's rule over his people and the nations.

Psalm 73 is best categorized as a wisdom psalm. The psalmist struggled within himself as to the appropriate response to the evil and injustice that characterized his (and our) world. His accurate description of the prosperity of the wicked moved him to greater despair—until he reflected on God. Then he again claimed the promises of God's presence and protection and sought his glory, reserved for him in this life and in the life to come.

they are not plagued by human ills.
[6] Therefore pride is their necklace; [k]
  they clothe themselves with violence. [l]
[7] From their callous hearts [m] comes iniquity [a];
  the evil conceits of their minds know no limits.
[8] They scoff, and speak with malice;
  in their arrogance [n] they threaten oppression.
[9] Their mouths lay claim to heaven,
  and their tongues take possession of the earth.
[10] Therefore their people turn to them
  and drink up waters in abundance. [b]
[11] They say, "How can God know?
  Does the Most High have knowledge?"

[12] This is what the wicked are like—
  always carefree, they increase in wealth. [o]

[13] Surely in vain [p] have I kept my heart pure;
  in vain have I washed my hands in innocence. [q]
[14] All day long I have been plagued;
  I have been punished every morning.

[15] If I had said, "I will speak thus,"
  I would have betrayed your children.
[16] When I tried to understand [r] all this,
  it was oppressive to me
[17] till I entered the sanctuary [s] of God;
  then I understood their final destiny. [t]

[18] Surely you place them on slippery ground; [u]
  you cast them down to ruin.
[19] How suddenly [v] are they destroyed,
  completely swept away by terrors!
[20] As a dream [w] when one awakes, [x]
  so when you arise, O Lord,
  you will despise them as fantasies.

[21] When my heart was grieved
  and my spirit embittered,
[22] I was senseless [y] and ignorant;
  I was a brute beast [z] before you.

[23] Yet I am always with you;
  you hold me by my right hand.
[24] You guide [a] me with your counsel, [b]
  and afterward you will take me into glory.
[25] Whom have I in heaven but you?
  And earth has nothing I desire besides you. [c]
[26] My flesh and my heart [d] may fail, [e]
  but God is the strength of my heart
  and my portion forever.

[27] Those who are far from you will perish; [f]

---

[a] 7 Syriac (see also Septuagint); Hebrew *Their eyes bulge with fat*   [b] 10 The meaning of the Hebrew for this verse is uncertain.

An acknowledgement of God's justice (vv. 18–20) marks the turning point in Psalm 73. Jesus asked his followers to pray for God's kingdom to come "on earth as it is in heaven" (Matt. 6:10), a kingdom characterized by righteousness and goodness. The problem of the suffering of the righteous still has no clear resolution, but our pain and that of others worldwide can and will be relieved as we experience God's living presence together. Where and how might you bring kingdom characteristics to bear in our world today?

Cross references

73:6   [k] Ge 41:42   [l] Ps 109:18
73:7   [m] Ps 17:10
73:8   [n] Ps 17:10; Jude 16
73:12   [o] Ps 49:6
73:13   [p] Job 21:15; 34:9   [q] Ps 26:6
73:16   [r] Ecc 8:17
73:17   [s] Ps 77:13   [t] Ps 37:38
73:18   [u] Ps 35:6
73:19   [v] Isa 47:11
73:20   [w] Job 20:8   [x] Ps 78:65
73:22   [y] Ps 49:10; 92:6   [z] Ecc 3:18
73:24   [a] Ps 48:14   [b] Ps 32:8
73:25   [c] Php 3:8
73:26   [d] Ps 84:2   [e] Ps 40:12
73:27   [f] Ps 119:155

73:28
g Heb 10:22;
Jas 4:8 h Ps 40:5

you destroy all who are unfaithful to you.
28 But as for me, it is good to be near God. ^g
I have made the Sovereign LORD my refuge;
I will tell of all your deeds. ^h

Psalm 74

A *maskil*^a of Asaph.

74:1
i Dt 29:20; Ps 44:23
j Ps 79:13; 95:7;
100:3
74:2
k Ex 15:16 l Dt 32:7
m Ex 15:13
n Ps 68:16

1 Why have you rejected us forever, ⁱ O God?
   Why does your anger smolder against the sheep of your pasture?^j
2 Remember the people you purchased^k of old, ^l
   the tribe of your inheritance, whom you redeemed^m—
   Mount Zion, where you dwelt. ⁿ
3 Turn your steps toward these everlasting ruins,
   all this destruction the enemy has brought on the sanctuary.

74:4
o La 2:7 p Nu 2:2

4 Your foes roared^o in the place where you met with us;
   they set up their standards^p as signs.
5 They behaved like men wielding axes
   to cut through a thicket of trees.^q

74:5
q Jer 46:22
74:6
r 1Ki 6:18

6 They smashed all the carved^r paneling
   with their axes and hatchets.
7 They burned your sanctuary to the ground;
   they defiled the dwelling place of your Name.

74:8
s Ps 83:4

8 They said in their hearts, "We will crush^s them completely!"
   They burned every place where God was worshiped in the land.
9 We are given no miraculous signs;
   no prophets^t are left,
   and none of us knows how long this will be.

74:9
t 1Sa 3:1

74:10
u Ps 44:16
74:11
v La 2:3

10 How long will the enemy mock you, O God?
    Will the foe revile^u your name forever?
11 Why do you hold back your hand, your right hand?^v
    Take it from the folds of your garment and destroy them!

74:12
w Ps 44:4

12 But you, O God, are my king^w from of old;
    you bring salvation upon the earth.

74:13
x Ex 14:21
y Isa 51:9; Eze 29:3

13 It was you who split open the sea^x by your power;
    you broke the heads of the monster^y in the waters.
14 It was you who crushed the heads of Leviathan
    and gave him as food to the creatures of the desert.

74:15
z Ex 17:6; Nu 20:11
a Jos 2:10; 3:13

15 It was you who opened up springs^z and streams;
    you dried up^a the ever flowing rivers.
16 The day is yours, and yours also the night;
    you established the sun and moon. ^b

74:16
b Ge 1:16;
Ps 136:7-9
74:17
c Dt 32:8; Ac 17:26
d Ge 8:22

17 It was you who set all the boundaries^c of the earth;
    you made both summer and winter. ^d

^a Title: Probably a literary or musical term

Psalm 74

The community in exile wept over the destruction of the temple in Jerusalem (in 586 B.C.), as well as the mocking of their enemies since then. The temple had symbolized God's presence and protection, but the Lord had permitted the Babylonians to ravage the land and destroy his own sanctuary. Through these acts God had demonstrated his judgment of his people. In this community lament, they still affirmed the creative and redemptive power of their covenant God as grounds for their appeal for redemption.

Though the punishment of the exile was deserved, the people felt as though God had abandoned them forever. This lament began with a searching question, the same one believers still ask when they feel crushed by life's unexpected twists and turns: *"Why?"* The exiles weren't questioning the rightness of God's judgment but appealing to his fatherly heart. Some of our own suffering may represent punishment, though much of it does not. Either way, what a comfort to know that God takes seriously our anguished expressions of bewilderment and frustration.

18 Remember how the enemy has mocked you, O LORD,
   how foolish people [e] have reviled your name.
19 Do not hand over the life of your dove to wild beasts;
   do not forget the lives of your afflicted [f] people forever.
20 Have regard for your covenant, [g]
   because haunts of violence fill the dark places of the land.
21 Do not let the oppressed [h] retreat in disgrace;
   may the poor and needy [i] praise your name.

22 Rise up, O God, and defend your cause;
   remember how fools [j] mock you all day long.
23 Do not ignore the clamor of your adversaries, [k]
   the uproar of your enemies, which rises continually.

74:18
e Dt 32:6; Ps 39:8
74:19
f Ps 9:18
74:20
g Ge 17:7;
Ps 106:45
74:21
h Ps 103:6
i Ps 35:10
74:22
j Ps 53:1
74:23
k Ps 65:7

Psalm 75

For the director of music. To the tune of "Do Not Destroy." A psalm of Asaph.
A song.

1 We give thanks to you, O God,
   we give thanks, for your Name is near; [l]
   men tell of your wonderful deeds. [m]

2 You say, "I choose the appointed time;
   it is I who judge uprightly.
3 When the earth and all its people quake, [n]
   it is I who hold its pillars [o] firm.   Selah
4 To the arrogant I say, 'Boast no more,'
   and to the wicked, 'Do not lift up your horns. [p]
5 Do not lift your horns against heaven;
   do not speak with outstretched neck.' "

6 No one from the east or the west
   or from the desert can exalt a man.
7 But it is God who judges: [q]
   He brings one down, he exalts another. [r]
8 In the hand of the LORD is a cup
   full of foaming wine mixed [s] with spices;
he pours it out, and all the wicked of the earth
   drink it down to its very dregs. [t]

9 As for me, I will declare [u] this forever;
   I will sing praise to the God of Jacob.
10 I will cut off the horns of all the wicked,
   but the horns of the righteous will be lifted up. [v]

75:1
l Ps 145:18
m Ps 44:1; 71:16
75:3
n Isa 24:19
o 1Sa 2:8
75:4
p Zec 1:21
75:7
q Ps 50:6 r 1Sa 2:7;
Ps 147:6; Da 2:21
75:8
s Pr 23:30
t Job 21:20;
Jer 25:15
75:9
u Ps 40:10
75:10
v Ps 89:17; 92:10;
148:14

Psalm 75

The setting of Psalm 75 appears to have been a time when Israel's security was threatened, as, for example, when Assyria was on the verge of invading Judah in Hezekiah's day (2 Kings 18:13—19:37). In view of the strong opposition of the arrogant, the godly community looked to God for deliverance. In theme the psalm is similar both to Hannah's song (1 Sam. 2:1–10) and Mary's Magnificat (Luke 1:46–55). It has characteristics of a community thanksgiving hymn, possibly sung when the people gathered to worship.

God is in control, even when it seems as though everything is falling to pieces. The great Judge-Ruler won't permit wickedness, evil powers, or the arrogant to undermine the foundations of his kingdom, to rock the earth's stability, or to threaten society's survival. In our own experiences of wicked arrogance, reminiscent of Sennacherib's Assyria or Nebuchadnezzar's Babylon, God still proclaims that he graciously upholds his creation. His "pillars" (see v. 3) still shore up the moral order, preventing his creation from collapsing.

Psalm 76

For the director of music. With stringed instruments. A psalm of Asaph. A song.

1 In Judah God is known;
  his name is great in Israel.
2 His tent is in Salem, [w]
  his dwelling place in Zion.
3 There he broke the flashing arrows,
  the shields and the swords, the weapons of war. [x]   Selah

4 You are resplendent with light,
  more majestic than mountains rich with game.
5 Valiant men lie plundered,
  they sleep their last sleep; [y]
  not one of the warriors
  can lift his hands.
6 At your rebuke, O God of Jacob,
  both horse and chariot [z] lie still.
7 You alone are to be feared. [a]
  Who can stand [b] before you when you are angry? [c]
8 From heaven you pronounced judgment,
  and the land feared [d] and was quiet—
9 when you, O God, rose up to judge, [e]
  to save all the afflicted of the land.   Selah
10 Surely your wrath against men brings you praise, [f]
  and the survivors of your wrath are restrained. [a]

11 Make vows to the LORD your God and fulfill them; [g]
  let all the neighboring lands
  bring gifts [h] to the One to be feared.
12 He breaks the spirit of rulers;
  he is feared by the kings of the earth.

Psalm 77

For the director of music. For Jeduthun. Of Asaph. A psalm.

1 I cried out to God [i] for help;
  I cried out to God to hear me.
2 When I was in distress, [j] I sought the Lord;
  at night I stretched out untiring hands [k]
  and my soul refused to be comforted. [l]

3 I remembered you, O God, and I groaned;
  I mused, and my spirit grew faint. [m]   Selah

[a] 10 Or *Surely the wrath of men brings you praise, / and with the remainder of wrath you arm yourself*

Marginal references

76:2 w Ge 14:18
76:3 x Ps 46:9
76:5 y Ps 13:3
76:6 z Ex 15:1
76:7 a 1Ch 16:25; b Ezr 9:15; Rev 6:17 c Ps 2:5; Na 1:6
76:8 d 1Ch 16:30; 2Ch 20:29-30
76:9 e Ps 9:8
76:10 f Ex 9:16; Ro 9:17
76:11 g Ps 50:14; Ecc 5:4-5 h 2Ch 32:23; Ps 68:29
77:1 i Ps 3:4
77:2 j Ps 50:15; Isa 26:9, 16 k Job 11:13 l Ge 37:35
77:3 m Ps 143:4

Psalm 76

Psalm 76 is in the form of a victory hymn. According to an ancient tradition, it was written after God had destroyed Sennacherib's army when the Assyrians threatened Jerusalem (see 2 Kings 19:35). God, the Divine Warrior who dwelt in Zion, was to be praised among his own and feared by the nations. The adoration of the Divine Warrior by his own people includes both a reflection on past victories and hope for a full establishment of his kingdom on Earth. When all kings and nations submit to him, the earth will be quiet.

Are you sobered by the question in verse 7, "Who can stand?" In the presence of the Judge of the universe, all nations and kingdoms fall silent. And no individual can stand before God in his anger (cf. 1:5; 130:3; Nah. 1:6). But the psalmist couldn't see what we as Christians know today: The God of judgment has, through the death and resurrection of his Son, delivered us *from his own judgment* (cf. Rom. 5:15–7; 8:31–34).

Psalm 77

Psalm 77 may be categorized as an individual lament (cry of desperation to God), though the mood of the psalm changes from lament (vv. 1–9) to reflection (vv. 10–12) to a joyful hymn celebrating God's greatness (vv. 13–20). The original context isn't clear, but the distress seems to have been personal, not national.

4 You kept my eyes from closing;
   I was too troubled to speak.
5 I thought about the former days, *n*
   the years of long ago;
6 I remembered my songs in the night.
   My heart mused and my spirit inquired:

7 "Will the Lord reject forever?
   Will he never show his favor *o* again?
8 Has his unfailing love vanished forever?
   Has his promise *p* failed for all time?
9 Has God forgotten to be merciful? *q*
   Has he in anger withheld his compassion? *r*"   Selah

10 Then I thought, "To this I will appeal:
   the years of the right hand *s* of the Most High."
11 I will remember the deeds of the LORD;
   yes, I will remember your miracles *t* of long ago.
12 I will meditate on all your works
   and consider all your mighty deeds.

13 Your ways, O God, are holy.
   What god is so great as our God? *u*
14 You are the God who performs miracles;
   you display your power among the peoples.
15 With your mighty arm you redeemed your people, *v*
   the descendants of Jacob and Joseph.   Selah

16 The waters *w* saw you, O God,
   the waters saw you and writhed; *x*
   the very depths were convulsed.
17 The clouds poured down water, *y*
   the skies resounded with thunder;
   your arrows flashed back and forth.
18 Your thunder was heard in the whirlwind,
   your lightning lit up the world;
   the earth trembled and quaked. *z*
19 Your path led through the sea, *a*
   your way through the mighty waters,
   though your footprints were not seen.

20 You led your people *b* like a flock *c*
   by the hand of Moses and Aaron.

Psalm 78

A *maskil* *a* of Asaph.

1 O my people, hear my teaching; *d*
   listen to the words of my mouth.

a Title: Probably a literary or musical term

Cross references:
77:5 *n* Dt 32:7; Ps 44:1; 143:5; Isa 51:9
77:7 *o* Ps 85:1
77:8 *p* 2Pe 3:9
77:9 *q* Ps 25:6; 40:11; 51:1 *r* Isa 49:15
77:10 *s* Ps 31:22
77:11 *t* Ps 143:5
77:13 *u* Ex 15:11; Ps 71:19; 86:8
77:15 *v* Ex 6:6; Dt 9:29
77:16 *w* Ex 14:21,28; Hab 3:8 *x* Ps 114:4; Hab 3:10
77:17 *y* Jdg 5:4
77:18 *z* Jdg 5:4
77:19 *a* Hab 3:15
77:20 *b* Ex 13:21 *c* Ps 78:52; Isa 63:11
78:1 *d* Isa 51:4; 55:3

Agonizing doubts and questions, as in verses 7–9, were expressed by Old Testament saints and by Jesus himself on the cross: "My God, my God, why have you forsaken me?" (Matt. 27:46, quoting Ps. 22:1). While we tend to personalize the psalms, imagine the faithful around the globe down through history uttering these same cries for help. People worldwide suffer unimaginable difficulties, even horrors. For them, God may seem absent as well. Yet we have a message of hope to deliver.

How much better if that message were to come packaged with practical help to ease their suffering?

Psalm 78

This psalm, probably composed during the time of the divided kingdom, is a teaching psalm. Contrasting Israel's faithlessness against God's faithfulness—either in the history of redemption or in forms of discipline—the psalmist warned the people not to repeat the sins of the past but rather to remember God's saving acts.

78:2
e Ps 49:4;
Mt 13:35*

78:3
f Ps 44:1
78:4
g Dt 11:19
h Ps 26:7; 71:17

78:5
i Ps 19:7; 81:5
j Ps 147:19

78:6
k Ps 22:31; 102:18

78:7
l Dt 6:12 m Dt 5:29

78:8
n 2Ch 30:7
o Ex 32:9 p ver 37;
Isa 30:9

78:9
q ver 57; 1Ch 12:2
r Jdg 20:39
78:10
s 2Ki 17:15

78:11
t Ps 106:13

78:12
u Ps 106:22
v Ex 7-12
w Nu 13:22
78:13
x Ex 14:21;
Ps 136:13 y Ex 15:8

78:14
z Ex 13:21;
Ps 105:39
78:15
a Nu 20:11;
1Co 10:4

78:17
b Dt 9:22;
Isa 63:10; Heb 3:16

78:18
c 1Co 10:9
d Ex 16:2; Nu 11:4
78:19
e Nu 21:5

78:20
f Nu 20:11
g Nu 11:18

78:21
h Nu 11:1

2 I will open my mouth in parables, [e]
  I will utter hidden things, things from of old—
3 what we have heard and known,
  what our fathers have told us. [f]
4 We will not hide them from their children; [g]
  we will tell the next generation
  the praiseworthy deeds [h] of the LORD,
  his power, and the wonders he has done.
5 He decreed statutes [i] for Jacob [j]
  and established the law in Israel,
  which he commanded our forefathers
  to teach their children,
6 so the next generation would know them,
  even the children yet to be born, [k]
  and they in turn would tell their children.
7 Then they would put their trust in God
  and would not forget [l] his deeds
  but would keep his commands. [m]
8 They would not be like their forefathers [n]—
  a stubborn [o] and rebellious [p] generation,
  whose hearts were not loyal to God,
  whose spirits were not faithful to him.

9 The men of Ephraim, though armed with bows, [q]
  turned back on the day of battle; [r]
10 they did not keep God's covenant [s]
  and refused to live by his law.
11 They forgot what he had done, [t]
  the wonders he had shown them.
12 He did miracles [u] in the sight of their fathers
  in the land of Egypt, [v] in the region of Zoan. [w]
13 He divided the sea [x] and led them through;
  he made the water stand firm like a wall. [y]
14 He guided them with the cloud by day
  and with light from the fire all night. [z]
15 He split the rocks [a] in the desert
  and gave them water as abundant as the seas;
16 he brought streams out of a rocky crag
  and made water flow down like rivers.

17 But they continued to sin [b] against him,
  rebelling in the desert against the Most High.
18 They willfully put God to the test [c]
  by demanding the food they craved. [d]
19 They spoke against God, [e] saying,
  "Can God spread a table in the desert?
20 When he struck the rock, water gushed out, [f]
  and streams flowed abundantly.
  But can he also give us food?
  Can he supply meat [g] for his people?"
21 When the LORD heard them, he was very angry;
  his fire broke out [h] against Jacob,
  and his wrath rose against Israel,

Psalm 78 focuses on this back-and-forth interplay during the journey between Egypt and the promised land, as well as on God's early patience with the nation versus his utter rejection of the northern kingdom of Israel (also known as Ephraim) in favor of the southern kingdom of Judah (vv. 59,67–68). David and Jerusalem were chosen out of all the tribes (vv. 70–72). Why? Because God is free to choose as he pleases.

22 for they did not believe in God
    or trust[i] in his deliverance.
23 Yet he gave a command to the skies above
    and opened the doors of the heavens;[j]
24 he rained down manna[k] for the people to eat,
    he gave them the grain of heaven.
25 Men ate the bread of angels;
    he sent them all the food they could eat.
26 He let loose the east wind[l] from the heavens
    and led forth the south wind by his power.
27 He rained meat down on them like dust,
    flying birds like sand on the seashore.
28 He made them come down inside their camp,
    all around their tents.
29 They ate till they had more than enough,[m]
    for he had given them what they craved.
30 But before they turned from the food they craved,
    even while it was still in their mouths,[n]
31 God's anger rose against them;
    he put to death the sturdiest[o] among them,
    cutting down the young men of Israel.

32 In spite of all this, they kept on sinning;
    in spite of his wonders,[p] they did not believe.[q]
33 So he ended their days in futility[r]
    and their years in terror.
34 Whenever God slew them, they would seek[s] him;
    they eagerly turned to him again.
35 They remembered that God was their Rock,[t]
    that God Most High was their Redeemer.[u]
36 But then they would flatter him with their mouths,[v]
    lying to him with their tongues;
37 their hearts were not loyal[w] to him,
    they were not faithful to his covenant.
38 Yet he was merciful;[x]
    he forgave[y] their iniquities[z]
    and did not destroy them.
    Time after time he restrained his anger
    and did not stir up his full wrath.
39 He remembered that they were but flesh,[a]
    a passing breeze[b] that does not return.

40 How often they rebelled[c] against him in the desert[d]
    and grieved him[e] in the wasteland!
41 Again and again they put God to the test;[f]
    they vexed the Holy One of Israel.[g]
42 They did not remember his power—
    the day he redeemed them from the oppressor,
43 the day he displayed his miraculous signs in Egypt,
    his wonders in the region of Zoan.

78:22
[i] Dt 1:32; Heb 3:19
78:23
[j] Ge 7:11; Mal 3:10
78:24
[k] Ex 16:4; Jn 6:31*
78:26
[l] Nu 11:31
78:29
[m] Nu 11:20
78:30
[n] Nu 11:33
78:31
[o] Isa 10:16
78:32
[p] ver 11 [q] ver 22
78:33
[r] Nu 14:29,35
78:34
[s] Hos 5:15
78:35
[t] Dt 32:4 [u] Dt 9:26
78:36
[v] Eze 33:31
78:37
[w] ver 8; Ac 8:21
78:38
[x] Ex 34:6
[y] Isa 48:10
[z] Nu 14:18,20
78:39
[a] Ge 6:3; Ps 103:14
[b] Job 7:7; Jas 4:14
78:40
[c] Heb 3:16
[d] Ps 95:8; 106:14
[e] Eph 4:30
78:41
[f] Nu 14:22
[g] 2Ki 19:22; Ps 89:18

God's people failed to enjoy his blessings because of their flagrant disobedience and disregard for his covenant. They were no longer affected by the amazing history of their redemption. To what degree are you moved when you hear the familiar gospel story? In the words of a classic African-American spiritual, does the memory of the cross cause you to "tremble?" What memories of God's deliverance from personal tight spots still hold powerful meaning for you?

In 1 Corinthians 10:1–13, Paul reminded believers that the disobedience of God's people in the Old Testament was to be an example and warning to us. We are not to presume on his grace, freely given to us through the gift of Jesus Christ. What behavior or lifestyle changes does Psalm 78 prompt for you?

78:44
h Ex 7:20-21;
Ps 105:29
78:45
i Ex 8:24; Ps 105:31
j Ex 8:2,6

78:46
k Ex 10:13
78:47
l Ex 9:23; Ps 105:32

78:48
m Ex 9:25
78:49
n Ex 15:7

78:51
o Ex 12:29;
Ps 135:8
p Ps 105:23; 106:22
78:52
q Ps 77:20

78:53
r Ex 14:28
s Ps 106:10

78:54
t Ex 15:17; Ps 44:3
78:55
u Ps 44:2 v Jos 13:7

78:57
w Eze 20:27
x Hos 7:16

78:58
y Jdg 2:12
z Lev 26:30
a Ex 20:4; Dt 32:21

78:59
b Dt 32:19
78:60
c Jos 18:1

78:61
d Ps 132:8
e 1Sa 4:17

78:63
f Nu 11:1
g Jer 7:34; 16:9
78:64
h 1Sa 4:17; 22:18

78:65
i Ps 44:23

78:66
j 1Sa 5:6

78:68
k Ps 87:2

44 He turned their rivers to blood; [h]
   they could not drink from their streams.
45 He sent swarms of flies [i] that devoured them,
   and frogs [j] that devastated them.
46 He gave their crops to the grasshopper,
   their produce to the locust. [k]
47 He destroyed their vines with hail [l]
   and their sycamore-figs with sleet.
48 He gave over their cattle to the hail,
   their livestock [m] to bolts of lightning.
49 He unleashed against them his hot anger, [n]
   his wrath, indignation and hostility—
   a band of destroying angels.
50 He prepared a path for his anger;
   he did not spare them from death
   but gave them over to the plague.
51 He struck down all the firstborn of Egypt, [o]
   the firstfruits of manhood in the tents of Ham. [p]
52 But he brought his people out like a flock; [q]
   he led them like sheep through the desert.
53 He guided them safely, so they were unafraid;
   but the sea engulfed [r] their enemies. [s]
54 Thus he brought them to the border of his holy land,
   to the hill country his right hand [t] had taken.
55 He drove out nations [u] before them
   and allotted their lands to them as an inheritance; [v]
   he settled the tribes of Israel in their homes.

56 But they put God to the test
   and rebelled against the Most High;
   they did not keep his statutes.
57 Like their fathers [w] they were disloyal and faithless,
   as unreliable as a faulty bow. [x]
58 They angered him [y] with their high places; [z]
   they aroused his jealousy with their idols. [a]
59 When God heard them, he was very angry;
   he rejected Israel [b] completely.
60 He abandoned the tabernacle of Shiloh, [c]
   the tent he had set up among men.
61 He sent ⌊the ark of⌋ his might [d] into captivity, [e]
   his splendor into the hands of the enemy.
62 He gave his people over to the sword;
   he was very angry with his inheritance.
63 Fire consumed [f] their young men,
   and their maidens had no wedding songs; [g]
64 their priests were put to the sword, [h]
   and their widows could not weep.
65 Then the Lord awoke as from sleep, [i]
   as a man wakes from the stupor of wine.
66 He beat back his enemies;
   he put them to everlasting shame. [j]
67 Then he rejected the tents of Joseph,
   he did not choose the tribe of Ephraim;
68 but he chose the tribe of Judah,
   Mount Zion, [k] which he loved.
69 He built his sanctuary like the heights,
   like the earth that he established forever.

70 He chose David *l* his servant
    and took him from the sheep pens;
71 from tending the sheep he brought him
    to be the shepherd *m* of his people Jacob,
    of Israel his inheritance.
72 And David shepherded them with integrity of heart; *n*
    with skillful hands he led them.

Psalm 79

A psalm of Asaph.

1 O God, the nations have invaded your inheritance; *o*
    they have defiled your holy temple,
    they have reduced Jerusalem to rubble. *p*
2 They have given the dead bodies of your servants
    as food to the birds of the air,
    the flesh of your saints to the beasts of the earth. *q*
3 They have poured out blood like water
    all around Jerusalem,
    and there is no one to bury the dead. *r*
4 We are objects of reproach to our neighbors,
    of scorn and derision to those around us. *s*

5 How long, *t* O LORD? Will you be angry *u* forever?
    How long will your jealousy burn like fire? *v*
6 Pour out your wrath *w* on the nations
    that do not acknowledge *x* you,
  on the kingdoms
    that do not call on your name; *y*
7 for they have devoured Jacob
    and destroyed his homeland.
8 Do not hold against us the sins of the fathers; *z*
    may your mercy come quickly to meet us,
    for we are in desperate need. *a*

9 Help us, *b* O God our Savior,
    for the glory of your name;
  deliver us and forgive our sins
    for your name's sake. *c*
10 Why should the nations say,
    "Where is their God?" *d*
  Before our eyes, make known among the nations
    that you avenge *e* the outpoured blood of your servants.
11 May the groans of the prisoners come before you;
    by the strength of your arm
    preserve those condemned to die.

12 Pay back into the laps *f* of our neighbors seven times *g*
    the reproach they have hurled at you, O Lord.
13 Then we your people, the sheep of your pasture, *h*

Cross references

78:70 *l* 1Sa 16:1
78:71 *m* 2Sa 5:2; Ps 28:9
78:72 *n* 1Ki 9:4

79:1 *o* Ps 74:2 *p* 2Ki 25:9
79:2 *q* Dt 28:26; Jer 7:33
79:3 *r* Jer 16:4
79:4 *s* Ps 44:13; 80:6
79:5 *t* Ps 74:10 *u* Ps 74:1; 85:5 *v* Dt 29:20; Ps 89:46; Zep 3:8
79:6 *w* Ps 69:24; Rev 16:1 *x* Jer 10:25; 2Th 1:8 *y* Ps 14:4
79:8 *z* Isa 64:9 *a* Ps 116:6; 142:6
79:9 *b* 2Ch 14:11 *c* Ps 25:11; 31:3; Jer 14:7
79:10 *d* Ps 42:10 *e* Ps 94:1
79:12 *f* Ps 65:6; Jer 32:18 *g* Ge 4:15
79:13 *h* Ps 74:1; 95:7

Psalm 79

This lament was probably written on the occasion of Jerusalem's fall and Judah's subsequent exile (586 B.C.). Its concerns resemble those of Psalms 44 and 74. Central to the psalmist's prayer was the question of how long the Lord would remain angry with his people. The structure of the psalm reflects the characteristic elements of the national lament: questions, prayer, and hope.

The psalm concludes on a note of hope, as God's people looked for the day of redemption (cf. 2 Thess. 1:5–10). They remained the sheep of his pasture, even though they had been forcibly removed from the land. They looked forward to praising God for their redemption from their oppressors and for his forgiveness. Still today, how sweet is the hope of the children of God, even in our hour of deepest distress!

79:13
i Ps 44:8

will praise you forever; *i*
from generation to generation
   we will recount your praise.

Psalm 80

For the director of music. To ⌊the tune of⌋ "The Lilies of the Covenant." Of Asaph.
A psalm.

80:1
j Ps 77:20
k Ex 25:22

1 Hear us, O Shepherd of Israel,
   you who lead Joseph like a flock; *j*
you who sit enthroned between the cherubim, *k* shine forth

80:2
l Nu 2:18-24
m Ps 35:23

2   before Ephraim, Benjamin and Manasseh. *l*
Awaken *m* your might;
   come and save us.

80:3
n Ps 85:4; La 5:21
o Nu 6:25

3 Restore *n* us, *o* O God;
   make your face shine upon us,
   that we may be saved.

4 O Lord God Almighty,
   how long will your anger smolder
   against the prayers of your people?

80:5
p Ps 42:3; Isa 30:20

5 You have fed them with the bread of tears;
   you have made them drink tears by the bowlful. *p*

80:6
q Ps 79:4

6 You have made us a source of contention to our neighbors,
   and our enemies mock us. *q*

7 Restore us, O God Almighty;
   make your face shine upon us,
   that we may be saved.

80:8
r Isa 5:1-2; Jer 2:21
s Jos 13:6; Ac 7:45

8 You brought a vine *r* out of Egypt;
   you drove out *s* the nations and planted it.
9 You cleared the ground for it,
   and it took root and filled the land.
10 The mountains were covered with its shade,
   the mighty cedars with its branches.

80:11
t Ps 72:8
80:12
u Ps 89:40; Isa 5:5

11 It sent out its boughs to the Sea, *a*
   its shoots as far as the River. *b t*

12 Why have you broken down its walls *u*
   so that all who pass by pick its grapes?

80:13
v Jer 5:6

13 Boars from the forest ravage *v* it
   and the creatures of the field feed on it.

80:14
w Isa 63:15

14 Return to us, O God Almighty!
   Look down from heaven and see! *w*

---

a 11 Probably the Mediterranean   *b 11* That is, the Euphrates

---

Psalm 80

This psalm is a community lament and prayer for restoration following a time of defeat. Like Psalm 79, it likely reflects the occasion of the fall of the northern kingdom of Israel, and its capital of Samaria, at the hands of Assyria in 722 B.C. (see 2 Kings 17:1–6). Survivors of the northern tribes ("Ephraim, Benjamin and Manasseh"; v. 2) may have sought asylum in Judah. This would explain their presence at the temple (v. 1) and set the psalmist's prayer in the context of pleading with God that the same lot not overtake the southern kingdom.

The ground for the people's hope of restoration

lay in "the man at your right hand"—"the son of man" (v. 17). This may simply have been an expression for Israel collectively (see v. 15) or a reference to the Lord's anointed king, seated in the place of honor (cf. 110:1). Such allusions to the Davidic dynasty focused the hope of the godly on the continuity of God's redemptive purposes. Regardless of what had happened at Samaria or what might happen to Jerusalem, God would be true to his promises to David. His kingdom would be established by the Messiah of David (see Ps. 2). From our vantage point in history, we can look back and praise God for the glorious fulfillment of these ancient hopes.

Watch over this vine,

15   the root your right hand has planted,
     the son[a] you have raised up for yourself.

16 Your vine is cut down, it is burned with fire;
     at your rebuke[x] your people perish.

17 Let your hand rest on the man at your right hand,
     the son of man you have raised up for yourself.

18 Then we will not turn away from you;
     revive us, and we will call on your name.

19 Restore us, O LORD God Almighty;
     make your face shine upon us,
     that we may be saved.

80:16
x Ps 39:11; 76:6

Psalm 81

For the director of music. According to *gittith*.[b] Of Asaph.

1 Sing for joy to God our strength;
     shout aloud to the God of Jacob![y]

2 Begin the music, strike the tambourine,[z]
     play the melodious harp[a] and lyre.

3 Sound the ram's horn at the New Moon,
     and when the moon is full, on the day of our Feast;

4 this is a decree for Israel,
     an ordinance of the God of Jacob.

5 He established it as a statute for Joseph
     when he went out against Egypt,[b]
     where we heard a language we did not understand.[cc]

6 He says, "I removed the burden from their shoulders;[d]
     their hands were set free from the basket.

7 In your distress you called[e] and I rescued you,
     I answered[f] you out of a thundercloud;
     I tested you at the waters of Meribah.[g]   Selah

8 "Hear, O my people,[h] and I will warn you—
     if you would but listen to me, O Israel!

9 You shall have no foreign god[i] among you;
     you shall not bow down to an alien god.

10 I am the LORD your God,
     who brought you up out of Egypt.[j]
     Open wide your mouth and I will fill[k] it.

11 "But my people would not listen to me;
     Israel would not submit to me.[l]

12 So I gave them over[m] to their stubborn hearts
     to follow their own devices.

81:1
y Ps 66:1
81:2
z Ex 15:20 a Ps 92:3

81:5
b Ex 11:4 c Ps 114:1

81:6
d Isa 9:4

81:7
e Ex 2:23; Ps 50:15
f Ex 19:19 g Ex 17:7

81:8
h Ps 50:7

81:9
i Ex 20:3; Dt 32:12;
Isa 43:12

81:10
j Ex 20:2 k Ps 107:9

81:11
l Ex 32:1-6
81:12
m Ac 7:42; Ro 1:24

a 15 Or *branch*   b Title: Probably a musical term   c 5 Or / *and we heard a voice we had not known*

Psalm 81

Psalm 81 was a festival song, to be sung during one or possibly all the following feasts: Passover/Unleavened Bread, the Jewish New Year, or the Feast of Tabernacles. As memorials of God's saving acts, these feasts called Israel to celebration, remembrance, and recommitment. This psalm was an appropriate "invitation" to covenant renewal during the feast, when God's people reflected on his past acts. As their hearts longed for the redemption to come, they heard anew God's promises but were also reminded of their responsibility of loyalty.

The Lord offers a new day of deliverance, if only his people will respond in faith (v. 13). The progress of redemption unveils the constancy of the Father's repeated call to return, repent, and live by faith (cf. Heb. 4:6–11). There is a constant "now"ness to redemption: It's continually made available, whenever people hear God's word, respond in faith and repentance, and live according to his will.

81:13
n Dt 5:29; Isa 48:18
81:14
o Ps 47:3 p Am 1:8

81:16
q Dt 32:14

13 "If my people would but listen to me, [n]
    if Israel would follow my ways,
14 how quickly would I subdue [o] their enemies
    and turn my hand against [p] their foes!
15 Those who hate the LORD would cringe before him,
    and their punishment would last forever.
16 But you would be fed with the finest of wheat; [q]
    with honey from the rock I would satisfy you."

Psalm 82

A psalm of Asaph.

82:1
r Ps 58:11; Isa 3:13

1 God presides in the great assembly;
    he gives judgment [r] among the "gods":

82:2
s Dt 1:17
t Ps 58:1-2; Pr 18:5
82:3
u Dt 24:17
v Jer 22:16

2 "How long will you [a] defend the unjust
    and show partiality [s] to the wicked? [t]   *Selah*
3 Defend the cause of the weak and fatherless; [u]
    maintain the rights of the poor [v] and oppressed.
4 Rescue the weak and needy;
    deliver them from the hand of the wicked.

82:5
w Ps 14:4; Mic 3:1
x Isa 59:9 y Ps 11:3

5 "They know nothing, they understand nothing. [w]
    They walk about in darkness; [x]
    all the foundations [y] of the earth are shaken.

82:6
z Jn 10:34*

6 "I said, 'You are "gods"; [z]
    you are all sons of the Most High.'

82:7
a Ps 49:12;
Eze 31:14

7 But you will die [a] like mere men;
    you will fall like every other ruler."

82:8
b Ps 12:5 c Ps 2:8;
Rev 11:15

8 Rise up, [b] O God, judge the earth,
    for all the nations are your inheritance. [c]

Psalm 83

A song. A psalm of Asaph.

83:1
d Ps 28:1; 35:22

1 O God, do not keep silent; [d]
    be not quiet, O God, be not still.

83:2
e Ps 2:1; Isa 17:12
f Jdg 8:28; Ps 81:15
83:3
g Ps 31:13

2 See how your enemies are astir, [e]
    how your foes rear their heads. [f]
3 With cunning they conspire [g] against your people;
    they plot against those you cherish.

83:4
h Est 3:6 i Jer 11:19

4 "Come," they say, "let us destroy [h] them as a nation,
    that the name of Israel be remembered [i] no more."

---

a 2 The Hebrew is plural.

Psalm 82

Psalm 82 pictures God presiding over his heavenly court. As the Great King and Judge of the earth, he calls to account those responsible for defending the weak and oppressed. Early Rabbinic tradition saw the "gods" (vv. 1,6) as unjust rulers and judges in Israel. Today many identify them as kings of surrounding nations, who ruled in lofty disregard for justice. Others view them as the *supposedly divine beings in whose names these kings claimed to rule.* At any rate, the psalm confronted rulers and judges with their King and Judge (see Ps. 58).

This psalm concludes with a timely prayer for God's justice to appear on Earth. "Your kingdom come"

(Matt. 6:10) remains for us an appropriate response to injustice. Sometimes Christians think that to talk of justice is to seem too "political" in their faith. Yet this prayer for justice and deliverance for the weak, orphaned, lowly, destitute, and needy is repeated continually throughout the psalms (and the entire Bible). An appropriate central act of faith for us as believers is to ask God to restore justice and to offer ourselves as his servants in the reconciliation/redemption of brokenness.

Psalm 83

In this national lament the psalmist prayed for God's intervention against Israel's many enemies. It may be that the psalm arose in a particular historical context

5 With one mind they plot together;[j]
  they form an alliance against you—
6 the tents of Edom[k] and the Ishmaelites,
  of Moab[l] and the Hagrites,[m]
7 Gebal,[a][n] Ammon and Amalek,
  Philistia, with the people of Tyre.[o]
8 Even Assyria has joined them
  to lend strength to the descendants of Lot.[p]   Selah

9 Do to them as you did to Midian,[q]
  as you did to Sisera and Jabin at the river Kishon,[r]
10 who perished at Endor
  and became like refuse[s] on the ground.
11 Make their nobles like Oreb and Zeeb,[t]
  all their princes like Zebah and Zalmunna,[u]
12 who said, "Let us take possession[v]
  of the pasturelands of God."

13 Make them like tumbleweed, O my God,
  like chaff[w] before the wind.
14 As fire consumes the forest
  or a flame sets the mountains ablaze,[x]
15 so pursue them with your tempest
  and terrify them with your storm.[y]
16 Cover their faces with shame[z]
  so that men will seek your name, O LORD.

17 May they ever be ashamed and dismayed;
  may they perish in disgrace.[a]
18 Let them know that you, whose name is the LORD—
  that you alone are the Most High over all the earth.[b]

Psalm 84

For the director of music. According to *gittith*.[b] Of the Sons of Korah. A psalm.

1 How lovely is your dwelling place,[c]
  O LORD Almighty!
2 My soul yearns,[d] even faints,
  for the courts of the LORD;
my heart and my flesh cry out
  for the living God.

[a] 7 That is, Byblos   [b] Title: Probably a musical term

83:5
[j] Ps 2:2

83:6
[k] Ps 137:7
[l] 2Ch 20:1
[m] Ge 25:16
83:7
[n] Jos 13:5
[o] Eze 27:3

83:8
[p] Dt 2:9

83:9
[q] Jdg 7:1-23
[r] Jdg 4:23-24

83:10
[s] Zep 1:17
83:11
[t] Jdg 7:25
[u] Jdg 8:12,21
83:12
[v] 2Ch 20:11

83:13
[w] Ps 35:5; Isa 17:13

83:14
[x] Dt 32:22; Isa 9:18

83:15
[y] Job 9:17
83:16
[z] Ps 109:29; 132:18

83:17
[a] Ps 35:4

83:18
[b] Ps 59:13

84:1
[c] Ps 27:4; 43:3; 132:5

84:2
[d] Ps 42:1-2

(cf. 2 Chron. 20:1–30) or that the ten nations mentioned are symbolic of the enemies of God's people. Regardless, the psalmist affirmed that God is the Lord of all nations. He pled that these enemies might be shamed and instead seek the name of the Lord (v. 16).

This is the last in the collection of psalms attributed to Asaph (50; 73–83). See "There and Then" for Psalm 73.

Evil still seeks to erase God from the picture by eliminating God's people. Tyrants and evil governments throughout history have maintained a particular vengeance against God's will and his ways. But the psalmist showed a deep awareness of God's gracious nature as he opened a door to those among the nations willing to seek the Lord. God's mighty acts of judgment still today confirm the undeniable reality that he alone is God (v. 18)! Where do you see such a door of opportunity opening today for the gospel message?

Psalm 84

The "Sons of Korah" in the heading was a reference to the Levitical choir made up of the descendants of Korah, appointed by David to serve in the temple liturgy. Like the author of Psalm 42, the psalmist longed for the house of the Lord. He was evidently a Levite who had been barred from access to the temple, possibly at the time of the exile. Reference to God and his temple and to the "blessedness" of those having free access to both dominated his prayer.

A beautiful image in the psalms is the joyous hope of "living" or "dwelling" in the house of God (see 65:4; 15:1). To experience God's hospitality is the ultimate in luxury, honor, and security (23:5–6; 36:8; 52:8; 65:4; 92:12–15). The metaphor expresses the longing of the passionate worshiper for God's nearness and the sustaining practice of worship itself, perhaps best seen in

84:3
e Ps 43:4 f Ps 5:2

3 Even the sparrow has found a home,
  and the swallow a nest for herself,
    where she may have her young—
a place near your altar, e
  O LORD Almighty, my King and my God. f

4 Blessed are those who dwell in your house;
  they are ever praising you.   Selah

84:5
g Ps 81:1 h Jer 31:6

5 Blessed are those whose strength g is in you,
  who have set their hearts on pilgrimage. h

84:6
i Joel 2:23
84:7
j Pr 4:18 k Dt 16:16

6 As they pass through the Valley of Baca,
  they make it a place of springs;
    the autumn i rains also cover it with pools. a
7 They go from strength to strength, j
  till each appears k before God in Zion.

8 Hear my prayer, O LORD God Almighty;
  listen to me, O God of Jacob.   Selah

84:9
l Ps 59:11
m 1Sa 16:6; Ps 2:2;
132:17

9 Look upon our shield, b l O God;
  look with favor on your anointed one. m

84:10
n 1Ch 23:5

10 Better is one day in your courts
   than a thousand elsewhere;
 I would rather be a doorkeeper n in the house of my God
   than dwell in the tents of the wicked.

84:11
o Isa 60:19;
Rev 21:23
p Ge 15:1
q Ps 34:10

11 For the LORD God is a sun o and shield; p
   the LORD bestows favor and honor;
 no good thing does he withhold q
   from those whose walk is blameless.

84:12
r Ps 2:12

12 O LORD Almighty,
   blessed r is the man who trusts in you.

Psalm 85

For the director of music. Of the Sons of Korah. A psalm.

85:1
s Ps 14:7; Jer 30:18;
Eze 39:25
85:2
t Nu 14:19
u Ps 78:38
85:3
v Ps 106:23
w Ex 32:12;
Dt 13:17; Ps 78:38;
Jnh 3:9
85:4
x Ps 80:3,7

1 You showed favor to your land, O LORD;
  you restored the fortunes s of Jacob.
2 You forgave t the iniquity u of your people
  and covered all their sins.   Selah
3 You set aside all your wrath v
  and turned from your fierce anger. w

4 Restore x us again, O God our Savior,

a 6 Or blessings   b 9 Or sovereign

---

verse 10, where the psalmist is willing to take up the menial status of doorkeeper to remain at the center of God's presence.

Verse 2 pictures the psalmist yearning for the experience of God's presence with his whole being. In *Reflections on the Psalms*, C.S. Lewis described this longing as an "appetite for God." To what degree is your desire for God's presence and fellowship a good, healthy appetite? Do you experience hunger pangs when you feel separated from him? Does your time spent with him in his Word or in prayer feed your soul to the point of satisfaction? What might you do to ensure that your soul benefits from the nutrients Christ offers as the "bread of life" (John 6:35)?

Psalm 85

In a time of national catastrophe, God's people cried out for deliverance. They had already experienced his wrath and forgiveness, so the psalm was probably written after the return from exile. This national lament has four parts: proclamation of God's past acts (vv. 1–3), lament and prayer for restoration (vv. 4–7), anticipation of salvation (vv. 8–9), and words of hope (vv. 10–13).

God's blessings to us confirm his rule. "Righteousness," pictured in verses 11 and 13 as a messenger, tells of his victory and salvation. Those who worship him even now enjoy the benefits of his kingdom: forgiveness, reconciliation, covenant status, and restoration. As we await Christ's return, we as Christians already experi-

and put away your displeasure toward us.
5 Will you be angry with us forever?[y]
  Will you prolong your anger through all generations?
6 Will you not revive[z] us again,
  that your people may rejoice in you?
7 Show us your unfailing love, O LORD,
  and grant us your salvation.

8 I will listen to what God the LORD will say;
  he promises peace[a] to his people, his saints—
  but let them not return to folly.
9 Surely his salvation[b] is near those who fear him,
  that his glory[c] may dwell in our land.

10 Love and faithfulness[d] meet together;
  righteousness[e] and peace kiss each other.
11 Faithfulness springs forth from the earth,
  and righteousness[f] looks down from heaven.
12 The LORD will indeed give what is good,[g]
  and our land will yield[h] its harvest.
13 Righteousness goes before him
  and prepares the way for his steps.

Psalm 86

A prayer of David.

1 Hear, O LORD, and answer[i] me,
  for I am poor and needy.
2 Guard my life, for I am devoted to you.
  You are my God; save your servant
  who trusts in you.[j]
3 Have mercy[k] on me, O Lord,
  for I call[l] to you all day long.
4 Bring joy to your servant,
  for to you, O Lord,
  I lift[m] up my soul.

5 You are forgiving and good, O Lord,
  abounding in love[n] to all who call to you.
6 Hear my prayer, O LORD;
  listen to my cry for mercy.
7 In the day of my trouble[o] I will call to you,
  for you will answer me.

8 Among the gods there is none like you,[p] O Lord;
  no deeds can compare with yours.
9 All the nations you have made
  will come and worship[q] before you, O Lord;
  they will bring glory[r] to your name.
10 For you are great and do marvelous deeds;[s]
  you alone[t] are God.

Cross references (right margin)

85:5
[y] Ps 79:5

85:6
[z] Ps 80:18; Hab 3:2

85:8
[a] Zec 9:10

85:9
[b] Isa 46:13
[c] Zec 2:5

85:10
[d] Ps 89:14; Pr 3:3
[e] Ps 72:2-3;
Isa 32:17

85:11
[f] Isa 45:8
85:12
[g] Ps 84:11; Jas 1:17
[h] Lev 26:4; Ps 67:6;
Zec 8:12

86:1
[i] Ps 17:6

86:2
[j] Ps 25:2; 31:14
86:3
[k] Ps 4:1; 57:1
[l] Ps 88:9

86:4
[m] Ps 25:1; 143:8

86:5
[n] Ex 34:6; Ne 9:17;
Ps 103:8; 145:8;
Joel 2:13; Jnh 4:2

86:7
[o] Ps 50:15

86:8
[p] Ex 15:11; Dt 3:24;
Ps 89:6

86:9
[q] Ps 66:4; Rev 15:4
[r] Isa 43:7
86:10
[s] Ps 72:18
[t] Dt 6:4; Mk 12:29;
1Co 8:4

---

ence the firstfruits (early evidences) of righteousness—a righteousness that characterizes the new age of hope in which we are privileged to live (Gal. 5:5; 2 Peter 3:13).

Psalm 86

📖 This is the only psalm associated with David in Book III (Ps. 73–89). It's an individual lament, with thoughts and expressions common to many other psalms. David's need is only generally stated; references to his af-

fliction and enemies may stand for adversity in general, unlike others psalms that reference specific situations. His concluding section (vv. 14–17) expressed hope, focusing on God's love for him and his confidence in God.

📖 The psalmist confided in the Lord because he knew the nature of his God. What characteristics of God do you see in this passage? How do they encourage your trust in him?

Transfer of Use

The task of applying Scripture to modern life means more than just "translating words" from ancient to modern languages or "transposing meanings" from Bible times to 21st-century cultures. It also implies finding appropriate ways to use the Biblical text, ways that may be different from how they were used in their original settings. Let's call it "transfer of use."

For example, the Psalms were originally used in public Jewish worship. Only centuries after they were first composed and sung did they become meaningful in private devotional settings, one of their most common uses today. Is this "transfer of use" legitimate? Sometimes. But sometimes not. Many of us cringe, for example, when the words of Scripture are mouthed for demonic ends by Satanists or misquoted by cultists. Satan himself used/uses Scripture with the "best" (and worst) of them. What makes "transfer of use" faithful?

Two rules of thumb, one negative and one positive, can guide us. First, in question form, the negative: Does the use we make of the Psalms contradict their intrinsic message? Though the Psalms contain many "messages" of a historical, theological, and practical nature, their primary gist is that God is great and good. A corollary of this overriding message is God's call for us to base all our thinking, feeling, and acting on an acknowledgement of his primacy.

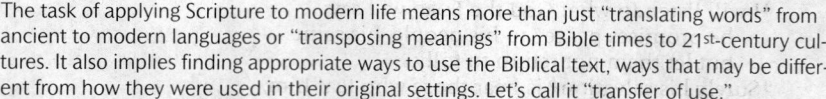

Biblical texts aren't infinitely elastic in either their definition or their use.

More than anything else, the Psalms tell us that God is great. Psalm 29 begins: "Ascribe to the LORD, O mighty ones, ascribe to the LORD glory and strength. Ascribe to the LORD the glory due his name; worship the LORD in the splendor of his holiness" (vv. 1–2). But the Psalms also emphasize God's goodness, as in: "Praise the LORD, for the LORD is good; sing praise to his name, for that is pleasant" (135:3). The psalmists put God first in all things. Psalm 86 demonstrates the proper sequence of thinking—God's greatness first, our needs second: "You are forgiving and good, O Lord, abounding in love to all who call to you. Hear my prayer, O LORD; listen to my cry for mercy" (vv. 5–6).

The second rule is more positive. Expressed again as a question: Are we using the Psalms in ways that will glorify God—or glorify us? A popular use of individual psalms is as personal devotionals. Although this use, on the face of it, is legitimate, it can become self-centered. The psalms aren't mantras designed to transport us into alternate states of consciousness. They are not psychological recipes for healthier living. They are opportunities for us to get right, one more time, the proper relationship between us, God's created beings, and God, the Creator and Ruler of the universe.

Contrast these therapeutic uses of individual psalms with Eugene Peterson's brilliant translation of the Psalms in *Praying With the Psalms* (HarperCollins, 1993). Peterson insists that we see in the Psalms the ultimate textual guide to acknowledging our Maker and the proper way for us to make requests to God.

One of the reasons we properly understand Scripture to be God's final and complete revelation to us is the extraordinary versatility of its texts. They do indeed address all of life's needs, in ways that more than keep pace with the developments of modern culture. But the Biblical texts aren't infinitely elastic in either their definition or their use. The surest way to keep a rein on the boundaries is to fully absorb the main lessons of the Psalms: God reigns. God is great, and God is good.

11 Teach me your way,ᵘ O Lᴏʀᴅ,
    and I will walk in your truth;
  give me an undivided ᵛ heart,
    that I may fear your name.
12 I will praise you, O Lord my God, with all my heart;
    I will glorify your name forever.
13 For great is your love toward me;
    you have delivered me from the depths of the grave.ᵃ

14 The arrogant are attacking me, O God;
    a band of ruthless men seeks my life—
  men without regard for you.ʷ
15 But you, O Lord, are a compassionate and graciousˣ God,
    slow to anger, abounding in love and faithfulness.ʸ
16 Turn to me and have mercy on me;
    grant your strength to your servant
    and save the son of your maidservant.ᵇ ᶻ
17 Give me a sign of your goodness,
    that my enemies may see it and be put to shame,
    for you, O Lᴏʀᴅ, have helped me and comforted me.

Psalm 87

Of the Sons of Korah. A psalm. A song.

1 He has set his foundation on the holy mountain;
2   the Lᴏʀᴅ loves the gates of Zionᵃ
    more than all the dwellings of Jacob.
3 Glorious things are said of you,
    O city of God:ᵇ   Selah
4 "I will record Rahabᶜ ᶜ and Babylon
    among those who acknowledge me—
  Philistia too, and Tyreᵈ, along with Cushᵈ—
    and will say, 'Thisᵉ one was born in Zion.ᵉ' "

5 Indeed, of Zion it will be said,
    "This one and that one were born in her,
    and the Most High himself will establish her."
6 The Lᴏʀᴅ will write in the registerᶠ of the peoples:
    "This one was born in Zion."   Selah
7 As they make musicᵍ they will sing,
    "All my fountainsʰ are in you."

ᵃ 13 Hebrew *Sheol*   ᵇ 16 Or *save your faithful son*   ᶜ 4 A poetic name for Egypt   ᵈ 4 That is, the upper Nile region   ᵉ 4 Or *"O Rahab and Babylon, / Philistia, Tyre and Cush, / I will record concerning those who acknowledge me: / 'This*

Psalm 87

Psalm 87, along with Psalms 46, 48, 76, 125, 129, and 137, is a Zion song. It's difficult to determine whether it was written before, during, or after the exile.

Key to interpreting this psalm is deciding how to translate verse 4 (see NIV text note). The nations listed ("Rahab" in this case is a reference to Egypt) represent all Gentile peoples. As translated by the NIV, the psalmist foresaw a widespread conversion to the Lord from the peoples who from time immemorial had been hostile to him and his kingdom. Psalm 87 predicted the ingathering of the nations into Zion as fellow citizens with Israel in the kingdom of God—after the manner of prophetic visions like Isaiah 2:2–4, 19:19–25, 45:14, 22–24, Micah 4:1–3, and Zechariah 8:23 and 14:16.

Our God isn't exclusivistic! Regardless of how the nations had related to God's people in the past, individuals hailing from any of them still could participate in God's "city." Those who would acknowledge him as the living God would have their names recorded as having been "born in Zion." Try to imagine a greater privilege than participating with people from every nation in the worship of your mutual God!

Psalm 88

A song. A psalm of the Sons of Korah. For the director of music. According to *mahalath leannoth.* [a] A *maskil* [b] of Heman the Ezrahite.

88:1
i Ps 51:14 *j* Ps 22:2;
27:9; Lk 18:7

1 O LORD, the God who saves me,[i]
  day and night I cry out[j] before you.
2 May my prayer come before you;
  turn your ear to my cry.

88:3
k Ps 107:18,26
88:4
l Ps 28:1

3 For my soul is full of trouble
  and my life draws near the grave.[c][k]
4 I am counted among those who go down to the pit;[l]
  I am like a man without strength.
5 I am set apart with the dead,
  like the slain who lie in the grave,

88:5
m Ps 31:22; Isa 53:8

  whom you remember no more,
  who are cut off[m] from your care.

88:6
n Ps 69:15; La 3:55

6 You have put me in the lowest pit,
  in the darkest depths.[n]

88:7
o Ps 42:7
88:8
p Job 19:13;
Ps 31:11 *q* Jer 32:2

7 Your wrath lies heavily upon me;
  you have overwhelmed me with all your waves.[o]   *Selah*
8 You have taken from me my closest friends[p]
  and have made me repulsive to them.
  I am confined[q] and cannot escape;

88:9
r Ps 38:10 *s* Ps 86:3
t Job 11:13;
Ps 143:6

9   my eyes[r] are dim with grief.

  I call[s] to you, O LORD, every day;
  I spread out my hands[t] to you.

88:10
u Ps 6:5

10 Do you show your wonders to the dead?
  Do those who are dead rise up and praise you?[u]   *Selah*

88:11
v Ps 30:9

11 Is your love declared in the grave,
  your faithfulness[v] in Destruction[d]?
12 Are your wonders known in the place of darkness,
  or your righteous deeds in the land of oblivion?

88:13
w Ps 30:2 *x* Ps 5:3
y Ps 119:147
88:14
z Ps 43:2
a Job 13:24;
Ps 13:1

13 But I cry to you for help,[w] O LORD;
  in the morning[x] my prayer comes before you.[y]
14 Why, O LORD, do you reject[z] me
  and hide your face[a] from me?

88:15
b Job 6:4

15 From my youth I have been afflicted and close to death;
  I have suffered your terrors[b] and am in despair.
16 Your wrath has swept over me;
  your terrors have destroyed me.

88:17
c Ps 22:16; 124:4

17 All day long they surround me like a flood;[c]
  they have completely engulfed me.

[a] Title: Possibly a tune, "The Suffering of Affliction"   [b] Title: Probably a literary or musical term
[c] 3 Hebrew *Sheol*   [d] 11 Hebrew *Abaddon*

Psalm 88

In this individual lament the psalmist expressed knowing nothing but sorrow. Yet even in grief he turned to God for help. The dialogue can only be understood from the perspective of faith, in which the godly are free to share their frustrations with their heavenly Father. We don't know the circumstances of the author's distress, only that he had suffered a long time, was shunned by family and friends, and had looked to God regularly for deliverance.

The term "cry" (v. 1) is a deeply piercing shout. The same word may denote a shout of joy in other contexts (cf. 47:1; 105:43), but here it's a loud wail for divine help.

Psalm 88 is close in spirit to Psalm 22. The two are often linked in Good Friday readings. Like Christ, our example, the person of faith calls with the confidence of experience on "the God who saves me" (v. 1). Even in despair faith holds doggedly to the One who has promised to deliver. Like Jesus in Gethsemane, do you call to God in life's crises? Do you have a sufficient history of prayer to approach God in unrelenting faith?

¹⁸ You have taken my companions ^d and loved ones from me;
the darkness is my closest friend.

88:18
d ver 8; Job 19:13;
Ps 38:11

Psalm 89

A *maskil* ^a of Ethan the Ezrahite.

¹ I will sing ^e of the LORD's great love forever;
with my mouth I will make your faithfulness known ^f through all
generations.
² I will declare that your love stands firm forever,
that you established your faithfulness in heaven itself. ^g

89:1
e Ps 59:16; Ps 101:1
f Ps 36:5; 40:10
89:2
g Ps 36:5

³ You said, "I have made a covenant with my chosen one,
I have sworn to David my servant,
⁴ 'I will establish your line forever
and make your throne firm through all generations.' " ^h   *Selah*

89:4
h 2Sa 7:12-16;
1Ki 8:16;
Ps 132:11-12;
Isa 9:7; Lk 1:33

⁵ The heavens ⁱ praise your wonders, O LORD,
your faithfulness too, in the assembly of the holy ones.
⁶ For who in the skies above can compare with the LORD?
Who is like the LORD among the heavenly beings? ^j
⁷ In the council of the holy ones God is greatly feared;
he is more awesome than all who surround him. ^k
⁸ O LORD God Almighty, who is like you? ^l
You are mighty, O LORD, and your faithfulness surrounds you.

89:5
i Ps 19:1
89:6
j Ps 113:5
89:7
k Ps 47:2
89:8
l Ps 71:19

⁹ You rule over the surging sea;
when its waves mount up, you still them. ^m
¹⁰ You crushed Rahab ⁿ like one of the slain;
with your strong arm you scattered ^o your enemies.
¹¹ The heavens are yours, and yours also the earth; ^p
you founded the world and all that is in it. ^q
¹² You created the north and the south;
Tabor ^r and Hermon ^s sing for joy ^t at your name.
¹³ Your arm is endued with power;
your hand is strong, your right hand exalted.

89:9
m Ps 65:7
89:10
n Ps 87:4 o Ps 68:1
89:11
p 1Ch 29:11;
Ps 24:1 q Ge 1:1
89:12
r Jos 19:22 s Dt 3:8;
Jos 12:1 t Ps 98:8

¹⁴ Righteousness and justice are the foundation of your throne; ^u
love and faithfulness go before you.
¹⁵ Blessed are those who have learned to acclaim you,
who walk in the light ^v of your presence, O LORD.
¹⁶ They rejoice in your name ^w all day long;
they exult in your righteousness.
¹⁷ For you are their glory and strength,
and by your favor you exalt our horn. ^{b x}

89:14
u Ps 97:2
89:15
v Ps 44:3
89:16
w Ps 105:3
89:17
x Ps 75:10; 92:10;
148:14

^a Title: Probably a literary or musical term   ^b 17 *Horn* here symbolizes strong one.

Psalm 89

Psalm 89 is a prayer mourning the downfall of the Davidic dynasty and pleading for its restoration. The historical context may have been the attack on Jerusalem by Nebuchadnezzar and the exile of King Jehoiachin in 597 B.C. (2 Kings 24:8–17).

A massive foundation is laid for the prayer with which the psalm concludes. An introduction sings of God's love and faithfulness (vv. 1–2) and his covenant with David (vv. 3–4). These two themes are then jubilantly expanded through verses 5–18. Suddenly jubilation turned to sorrow, as the psalmist recounted in detail how God had rejected his anointed (vv. 38–45). Thus he

came to his prayer, impatient and urgent, that God would remember once again his covenant with David (vv. 46–51).

The bitter shock of the loss of Davidic kings (reflected in the sudden transition of v. 38) was almost unbearable for the psalmist, evoking in him a lament bordering on reproach of God. Once again we see in the Psalter the total honesty of a person who genuinely trusts in the Lord. The psalmist knew that the reality he saw wasn't how things had to be! Are you able to follow his example by praising God for his love and faithfulness *and* appealing to him to apply his mercy and justice to the world's great needs?

89:18
y Ps 47:9

89:20
z Ac 13:22
a Ps 78:70
b 1Sa 16:1,12

89:21
c Ps 18:35

89:22
d 2Sa 7:10
89:23
e Ps 18:40 f 2Sa 7:9

89:24
g 2Sa 7:15

89:25
h Ps 72:8
89:26
i 2Sa 7:14
j 2Sa 22:47

89:27
k Col 1:18 l Nu 24:7
m Rev 1:5; 19:16

89:28
n ver 33-34;
Isa 55:3
89:29
o ver 4,36;
Dt 11:21; Jer 33:17

89:32
p 2Sa 7:14
89:33
q 2Sa 7:15

89:34
r Nu 23:19

89:38
s Dt 32:19;
1Ch 28:9; Ps 44:9

89:39
t La 5:16
89:40
u Ps 80:12 v La 2:2

89:41
w Ps 44:13

89:42
x Ps 13:2; 80:6

89:43
y Ps 44:10

18 Indeed, our shield[a] belongs to the LORD,
    our king[y] to the Holy One of Israel.

19 Once you spoke in a vision,
    to your faithful people you said:
  "I have bestowed strength on a warrior;
    I have exalted a young man from among the people.
20 I have found David[z] my servant;[a]
    with my sacred oil I have anointed[b] him.
21 My hand will sustain him;
    surely my arm will strengthen him.[c]
22 No enemy will subject him to tribute;
    no wicked man will oppress[d] him.
23 I will crush his foes before him[e]
    and strike down his adversaries.[f]
24 My faithful love will be with him,[g]
    and through my name his horn[b] will be exalted.
25 I will set his hand over the sea,
    his right hand over the rivers.[h]
26 He will call out to me, 'You are my Father,[i]
    my God, the Rock my Savior.'[j]
27 I will also appoint him my firstborn,[k]
    the most exalted[l] of the kings[m] of the earth.
28 I will maintain my love to him forever,
    and my covenant with him will never fail.[n]
29 I will establish his line forever,
    his throne as long as the heavens endure.[o]

30 "If his sons forsake my law
    and do not follow my statutes,
31 if they violate my decrees
    and fail to keep my commands,
32 I will punish their sin with the rod,
    their iniquity with flogging;[p]
33 but I will not take my love from him,[q]
    nor will I ever betray my faithfulness.
34 I will not violate my covenant
    or alter what my lips have uttered.[r]
35 Once for all, I have sworn by my holiness—
    and I will not lie to David—
36 that his line will continue forever
    and his throne endure before me like the sun;
37 it will be established forever like the moon,
    the faithful witness in the sky."
                                        Selah

38 But you have rejected,[s] you have spurned,
    you have been very angry with your anointed one.
39 You have renounced the covenant with your servant
    and have defiled his crown in the dust.[t]
40 You have broken through all his walls[u]
    and reduced his strongholds[v] to ruins.
41 All who pass by have plundered him;
    he has become the scorn of his neighbors.[w]
42 You have exalted the right hand of his foes;
    you have made all his enemies rejoice.[x]
43 You have turned back the edge of his sword
    and have not supported him in battle.[y]

a 18 Or *sovereign*   b 24 *Horn* here symbolizes strength.

910

44 You have put an end to his splendor
  and cast his throne to the ground.
45 You have cut short the days of his youth;
  you have covered him with a mantle of shame. *z*   *Selah*   **89:45**
                                                                                      z Ps 44:15; 109:29

46 How long, O Lord? Will you hide yourself forever?
  How long will your wrath burn like fire? *a*   **89:46**
                                                                                      a Ps 79:5
47 Remember how fleeting is my life. *b*   **89:47**
  For what futility you have created all men!   *b* Job 7:7; Ps 39:5
48 What man can live and not see death,
  or save himself from the power of the grave *a*? *c*   *Selah*   **89:48**
                                                                                      c Ps 22:29; 49:9
49 O Lord, where is your former great love,
  which in your faithfulness you swore to David?
50 Remember, Lord, how your servant has *b* been mocked, *d*   **89:50**
  how I bear in my heart the taunts of all the nations,   *d* Ps 69:19
51 the taunts with which your enemies have mocked, O Lord,
  with which they have mocked every step of your anointed one. *e*   **89:51**
                                                                                      e Ps 74:10

52 Praise be to the Lord forever!
  Amen and Amen. *f*   **89:52**
                                                                                      f Ps 41:13; 72:19

BOOK IV

Psalms 90–106

Psalm 90

A prayer of Moses the man of God.

1 Lord, you have been our dwelling place *g*   **90:1**
  throughout all generations.   *g* Dt 33:27;
2 Before the mountains were born *h*   Eze 11:16
  or you brought forth the earth and the world,   **90:2**
  from everlasting to everlasting you are God. *i*   *h* Job 15:7; Pr 8:25
                                                                                      i Ps 102:24-27

3 You turn men back to dust,   **90:3**
  saying, "Return to dust, O sons of men." *j*   *j* Ge 3:19;
                                                                                      Job 34:15
4 For a thousand years in your sight
  are like a day that has just gone by,
  or like a watch in the night. *k*   **90:4**
                                                                                      k 2Pe 3:8
5 You sweep men away *l* in the sleep of death;   **90:5**
  they are like the new grass of the morning—   *l* Ps 73:20; Isa 40:6
6 though in the morning it springs up new,
  by evening it is dry and withered. *m*   **90:6**
                                                                                      m Mt 6:30; Jas 1:10

7 We are consumed by your anger
  and terrified by your indignation.
8 You have set our iniquities before you,

---

a 48 Hebrew *Sheol*   *b 50* Or *your servants have*

Psalm 90

As indicated in its heading, tradition has ascribed Psalm 90 to Moses. Whether or not Moses wrote it, his spirit is evident in its deep sense of life's stealthy passing; the connection between sin, suffering, and God's anger; and the submissive attitude of prayer for God's blessing. The psalmist reflected on life in light of God's just wrath and affirmed the necessity of living rightly in his presence. The psalm has three parts: a hymn of praise (vv. 1–2), a lament on the brevity of life (vv. 3–12), and a prayer for restoration of God's favor (vv. 13–17).

Have you ever thought of asking God, like the psalmist did in verse 17, to "establish" your work—to give it lasting value? God's very acceptance of us as his own gives our work a quality of permanence. People under his judgment can accomplish no ultimate good, but the godly and wise can pray that God will accept their efforts and use them for his glory. Who knows what influence our words or gestures may have on someone else's life? What better can we do than to keep this in mind as we go about the business of each day?

90:8
n Ps 19:12
90:9
o Ps 78:33

90:10
p Job 20:8

90:11
q Ps 76:7
90:12
r Ps 39:4 s Dt 32:29

90:13
t Ps 6:3 u Dt 32:36;
Ps 135:14

90:14
v Ps 103:5
w Ps 85:6 x Ps 31:7

90:16
y Ps 44:1; Hab 3:2

90:17
z Isa 26:12

91:1
a Ps 31:20
b Ps 17:8

91:2
c Ps 142:5

91:3
d Ps 124:7; Pr 6:5
e 1Ki 8:37

91:4
f Ps 17:8 g Ps 35:2

91:5
h Job 5:21

91:8
i Ps 37:34; 58:10;
Mal 1:5

our secret sins[n] in the light of your presence.
9 All our days pass away under your wrath;
  we finish our years with a moan.[o]
10 The length of our days is seventy years—
  or eighty, if we have the strength;
  yet their span[a] is but trouble and sorrow,
  for they quickly pass, and we fly away.[p]

11 Who knows the power of your anger?
  For your wrath is as great as the fear that is due you.[q]
12 Teach us to number our days[r] aright,
  that we may gain a heart of wisdom.[s]

13 Relent, O Lord! How long[t] will it be?
  Have compassion on your servants.[u]
14 Satisfy[v] us in the morning with your unfailing love,
  that we may sing for joy[w] and be glad all our days.[x]
15 Make us glad for as many days as you have afflicted us,
  for as many years as we have seen trouble.
16 May your deeds be shown to your servants,
  your splendor to their children.[y]

17 May the favor[b] of the Lord our God rest upon us;
  establish the work of our hands for us—
  yes, establish the work of our hands.[z]

Psalm 91

1 He who dwells in the shelter[a] of the Most High
  will rest in the shadow[b] of the Almighty.[c]
2 I will say[d] of the Lord, "He is my refuge[c] and my fortress,
  my God, in whom I trust."

3 Surely he will save you from the fowler's snare[d]
  and from the deadly pestilence.[e]
4 He will cover you with his feathers,
  and under his wings you will find refuge;[f]
  his faithfulness will be your shield[g] and rampart.
5 You will not fear[h] the terror of night,
  nor the arrow that flies by day,
6 nor the pestilence that stalks in the darkness,
  nor the plague that destroys at midday.
7 A thousand may fall at your side,
  ten thousand at your right hand,
  but it will not come near you.
8 You will only observe with your eyes
  and see the punishment of the wicked.[i]

a 10 Or yet the best of them   b 17 Or beauty   c 1 Hebrew Shaddai   d 2 Or He says

Psalm 91

Psalm 91 is a glowing testimony to the security of those who trust in God—likely placed after Psalm 90 as a counterpoint to the negative depiction of the human condition found there.

Two Hebrew words, translated respectively as "shadow" and "shelter," compete in the Old Testament to provide the image of baby birds under the wings of their mother (cf. 61:4). Both are used in Psalm 91:1 to describe the psalmist's confident hope: "He who dwells in the shelter of the Most High will rest in the shadow of the Almighty." The use of the image as a metaphor for divine protection is perhaps clearest in Ruth 2:12: "May you be richly rewarded by the Lord, the God of Israel, under whose wings you have come to take refuge."

Who may dwell in God's presence and enjoy his protection? Unlike Psalms 15 and 24, this psalm gives the answer in a personal, experiential manner: "I will say of the Lord, 'He is my refuge and my fortress, my God, in whom I trust'" (v. 2). All who take on their lips this confession walk in wisdom and confidence. The Lord assures us that we will enjoy the privilege of being his children, not only in this life, but also in the life to come.

⁹ If you make the Most High your dwelling—
    even the Lord, who is my refuge—
¹⁰ then no harm^j will befall you,
    no disaster will come near your tent.
¹¹ For he will command his angels^k concerning you
    to guard you in all your ways;^l
¹² they will lift you up in their hands,
    so that you will not strike your foot against a stone.^m
¹³ You will tread upon the lion and the cobra;
    you will trample the great lion and the serpent.^n

¹⁴ "Because he loves me," says the Lord, "I will rescue him;
    I will protect him, for he acknowledges my name.
¹⁵ He will call upon me, and I will answer him;
    I will be with him in trouble,
    I will deliver him and honor him.^o
¹⁶ With long life^p will I satisfy him
    and show him my salvation.^q"

Psalm 92

A psalm. A song. For the Sabbath day.

¹ It is good to praise the Lord
    and make music to your name,^r O Most High,^s
² to proclaim your love in the morning^t
    and your faithfulness at night,
³ to the music of the ten-stringed lyre
    and the melody of the harp.^u

⁴ For you make me glad by your deeds, O Lord;
    I sing for joy at the works of your hands.^v
⁵ How great are your works,^w O Lord,
    how profound your thoughts!^x
⁶ The senseless man^y does not know,
    fools do not understand,
⁷ that though the wicked spring up like grass
    and all evildoers flourish,
they will be forever destroyed.

⁸ But you, O Lord, are exalted forever.

⁹ For surely your enemies, O Lord,
    surely your enemies will perish;
    all evildoers will be scattered.^z

¹⁰ You have exalted my horn^a^a like that of a wild ox;
    fine oils^b have been poured upon me.

---

^a 10 *Horn* here symbolizes strength.

91:10
j Pr 12:21
91:11
k Heb 1:14
l Ps 34:7
91:12
m Mt 4:6*; Lk 4:10-11*
91:13
n Da 6:22; Lk 10:19

91:15
o 1Sa 2:30; Ps 50:15; Jn 12:26
91:16
p Dt 6:2; Ps 21:4
q Ps 50:23

92:1
r Ps 147:1
s Ps 135:3
92:2
t Ps 89:1

92:3
u 1Sa 10:5; Ne 12:27; Ps 33:2

92:4
v Ps 8:6; 143:5
92:5
w Rev 15:3
x Ps 40:5; 139:17; Isa 28:29; Ro 11:33
92:6
y Ps 73:22

92:9
z Ps 68:1; 89:10
92:10
a Ps 89:17
b Ps 23:5

Psalm 92

📖 Psalm 92 is a celebration of God's righteous rule. Verses 10–11 suggest that the psalmist may have been one of Israel's kings. Regarding the notation in the heading, in the liturgy of the temple after the exile this psalm came to be sung at the time of the morning sacrifice on the Sabbath.

Following the introduction on praise (vv. 1–3), verses 4–5 offer the motivation for the praise, which is picked up again in verses 10–11. Verses 6–9 present the folly and destiny of evildoers, while verses 12–15 describe the prosperity of the righteous.

🗨 Praising means more than verbally pronouncing praise! For us to live in ways consistent with God's character implies that we live up to his name and thus praise it. Israel blasphemed God's name not only when she used it profanely, but when she took that name as her defining characteristic and then lived in ways that violated God's very nature. To rely on our worship, the "house of the Lord" (v. 13), for protection while exploiting others through deceit, injustice, or abusive power is to reject God (Jer. 7:4–11). "It is good to praise the Lord" (Ps. 92:1)—both with our lips and with our lives.

92:11
c Ps 54:7; 91:8

92:12
d Ps 1:3; 52:8;
Jer 17:8; Hos 14:6

92:13
e Ps 100:4
92:14
f Jn 15:2

92:15
g Job 34:10

93:1
h Ps 97:1 i Ps 104:1
j Ps 65:6 k Ps 96:10

93:2
l Ps 45:6

93:3
m Ps 96:11

93:4
n Ps 65:7

93:5
o Ps 29:2

94:1
p Na 1:2; Ro 12:19
q Ps 80:1

94:2
r Ge 18:25
s Ps 31:23

94:4
t Ps 31:18 u Ps 52:1

11 My eyes have seen the defeat of my adversaries;
   my ears have heard the rout of my wicked foes. c

12 The righteous will flourish like a palm tree,
   they will grow like a cedar of Lebanon; d
13 planted in the house of the LORD,
   they will flourish in the courts of our God. e
14 They will still bear fruit f in old age,
   they will stay fresh and green,
15 proclaiming, "The LORD is upright;
   he is my Rock, and there is no wickedness in him. g"

Psalm 93

1 The LORD reigns, h he is robed in majesty; i
   the LORD is robed in majesty
   and is armed with strength. j
 The world is firmly established;
   it cannot be moved. k
2 Your throne was established long ago;
   you are from all eternity. l

3 The seas m have lifted up, O LORD,
   the seas have lifted up their voice;
   the seas have lifted up their pounding waves.
4 Mightier than the thunder n of the great waters,
   mightier than the breakers of the sea—
   the LORD on high is mighty.

5 Your statutes stand firm;
   holiness o adorns your house
   for endless days, O LORD.

Psalm 94

1 O LORD, the God who avenges, p
   O God who avenges, shine forth. q
2 Rise up, O Judge r of the earth;
   pay back s to the proud what they deserve.
3 How long will the wicked, O LORD,
   how long will the wicked be jubilant?

4 They pour out arrogant t words;
   all the evildoers are full of boasting. u

Psalm 93

Psalm 93 belongs to a group of psalms (47; 93–100) that affirm God's rule over the earth. These hymns were probably composed for use in a high religious festival in which the Lord's kingship was annually celebrated.

The assertion of God as universal Creator stands in stark contrast to pagan teachings of chaos, primordial forces, and random happenings. God's reign is evident in his creation and acts of redemption. The rule of God is visible, as his glorious mantle spreads out all over his kingdom.

Paul linked a failure to recognize and worship God with humanity's downward spiral into depravity (cf. Rom. 1:18–32). Today the full force of rejecting God as Creator is seen in our society's headlong rush into vio-

lence, sexual sin, and other evils. How does our care for creation affect others' perception of the Creator? How can we, as bearers of the kingdom, help people encounter the God who loves what he has so carefully made (Ps. 145:17)?

Psalm 94

This psalm is a prayer for God's kingdom to shine forth so that oppressed and downtrodden saints may experience the light of his rule. Its two parts, a national lament (vv. 1–15) and an individual lament (vv. 16–23), bring together the community and the individual in their common concern for justice. Psalm 94 represents the voice of the oppressed within Israel, who sought redress at God's throne for injustices done to them by the "fools" smugly established in the nation's power structures.

5 They crush your people,[v] O LORD;
they oppress your inheritance.
6 They slay the widow and the alien;
they murder the fatherless.
7 They say, "The LORD does not see;[w]
the God of Jacob pays no heed."

8 Take heed, you senseless ones[x] among the people;
you fools, when will you become wise?
9 Does he who implanted the ear not hear?
Does he who formed the eye not see?[y]
10 Does he who disciplines nations not punish?
Does he who teaches[z] man lack knowledge?
11 The LORD knows the thoughts of man;
he knows that they are futile.[a]

12 Blessed is the man you discipline,[b] O LORD,
the man you teach[c] from your law;
13 you grant him relief from days of trouble,
till a pit[d] is dug for the wicked.
14 For the LORD will not reject his people;[e]
he will never forsake his inheritance.
15 Judgment will again be founded on righteousness,[f]
and all the upright in heart will follow it.

16 Who will rise up[g] for me against the wicked?
Who will take a stand for me against evildoers?[h]
17 Unless the LORD had given me help,[i]
I would soon have dwelt in the silence of death.
18 When I said, "My foot is slipping,[j]"
your love, O LORD, supported me.
19 When anxiety was great within me,
your consolation brought joy to my soul.

20 Can a corrupt throne be allied with you—
one that brings on misery by its decrees?[k]
21 They band together[l] against the righteous
and condemn the innocent[m] to death.
22 But the LORD has become my fortress,
and my God the rock in whom I take refuge.[n]
23 He will repay[o] them for their sins
and destroy them for their wickedness;
the LORD our God will destroy them.

Psalm 95

1 Come, let us sing for joy to the LORD;
let us shout aloud[p] to the Rock[q] of our salvation.
2 Let us come before him[r] with thanksgiving
and extol him with music[s] and song.

94:5 [v] Isa 3:15
94:7 [w] Job 22:14; Ps 10:11
94:8 [x] Ps 92:6
94:9 [y] Ex 4:11; Pr 20:12
94:10 [z] Job 35:11; Isa 28:26
94:11 [a] 1Co 3:20*
94:12 [b] Job 5:17; Heb 12:5 [c] Dt 8:3
94:13 [d] Ps 55:23
94:14 [e] 1Sa 12:22; Ps 37:28; Ro 11:2
94:15 [f] Ps 97:2
94:16 [g] Nu 10:35; Ps 17:13 [h] Ps 59:2
94:17 [i] Ps 124:2
94:18 [j] Ps 38:16
94:20 [k] Ps 58:2
94:21 [l] Ps 56:6 [m] Ps 106:38; Pr 17:15,26
94:22 [n] Ps 18:2; 59:9
94:23 [o] Ps 7:16
95:1 [p] Ps 81:1 [q] 2Sa 22:47
95:2 [r] Mic 6:6 [s] Ps 81:2; Eph 5:19

When the ungodly harass God's children, they shamelessly sin against the Lord himself. The language of verses 5–6 ("crush . . . oppress . . . slay . . . murder") may be exaggerated. But any prejudice or injustice, any trampling on the rights of God's people, is an assault on God—who has promised to care for them, particularly the widows, aliens, and fatherless (Ex. 22:21–22; Deut. 10:18; 24:19; James 1:27). What obligation does this place on individual Christians as God's representatives on Earth?

Psalm 95

Psalm 95 is a call to worship the Lord, spoken by a priest or Levite to the assembled Israelites at the temple. It contains a sharp reminder that their sense of security under God's rule—from which sprang both their prayers and their praise—was warranted only if they

95:3
t Ps 48:1; 145:3
u Ps 96:4; 97:9

³For the LORD is the great God,*t*
  the great King above all gods.*u*

⁴In his hand are the depths of the earth,
  and the mountain peaks belong to him.

95:5
v Ge 1:9; Ps 146:6

⁵The sea is his, for he made it,
  and his hands formed the dry land.*v*

95:6
w Php 2:10
x 2Ch 6:13
y Ps 100:3; 149:2;
Isa 17:7;
Da 6:10-11;
Hos 8:14
95:7
z Ps 74:1; 79:13

⁶Come, let us bow down*w* in worship,
  let us kneel*x* before the LORD our Maker;*y*

⁷for he is our God
  and we are the people of his pasture,*z*
  the flock under his care.

Today, if you hear his voice,

95:8
a Ex 17:7

⁸ do not harden your hearts as you did at Meribah,ᵃ*a*
  as you did that day at Massah*b* in the desert,

95:9
b Nu 14:22;
Ps 78:18; 1Co 10:9

⁹where your fathers tested*b* and tried me,
  though they had seen what I did.

95:10
c Ac 7:36; Heb 3:17

¹⁰For forty years*c* I was angry with that generation;
  I said, "They are a people whose hearts go astray,
  and they have not known my ways."

95:11
d Nu 14:23
e Dt 1:35; Heb 4:3*

¹¹So I declared on oath*d* in my anger,
  "They shall never enter my rest."*e*

Psalm 96

96:1
f 1Ch 16:23

¹Sing to the LORD*f* a new song;
  sing to the LORD, all the earth.

96:2
g Ps 71:15

²Sing to the LORD, praise his name;
  proclaim his salvation*g* day after day.

³Declare his glory among the nations,
  his marvelous deeds among all peoples.

96:4
h Ps 18:3; 145:3
i Ps 89:7 *j* Ps 95:3

⁴For great is the LORD and most worthy of praise;*h*
  he is to be feared*i* above all gods.*j*

96:5
k Ps 115:15

⁵For all the gods of the nations are idols,
  but the LORD made the heavens.*k*

96:6
l Ps 29:1

⁶Splendor and majesty are before him;
  strength and glory*l* are in his sanctuary.

96:7
m Ps 29:1
n Ps 22:27

⁷Ascribe to the LORD,*m* O families of nations,*n*
  ascribe to the LORD glory and strength.

⁸Ascribe to the LORD the glory due his name;
  bring an offering*o* and come into his courts.

96:8
o Ps 45:12; 72:10

ᵃ 8 *Meribah* means *quarreling.*   ᵇ 8 *Massah* means *testing.*

showed themselves to be his loyal and obedient servants. The psalm is composed of two parts: calls to praise the Lord of all the earth (vv. 1–5) and to acknowledge by submissive attitude and obedient heart his kingship over his people (vv. 6–11).

The objects of God's wrath at the end of this psalm were the rebellious Israelites ("that generation") during their forty-year desert standstill. They couldn't and didn't enter the promised land ("my rest" in v. 11; cf. Deut. 12:9; Ps. 132:8,14). Joshua and David didn't succeed in providing "rest" for God's people either, but in Jesus, the Messiah, that rest was, and is still, being offered (Heb. 4:1–11). This is the "today" of the gospel message (cf. Ps. 95:7–8 with Heb. 4:7).

Psalm 96

Psalm 96 belongs to a grouping of psalms (93–100) affirming God's rule over the earth. By being incorporated into a larger unit in 1 Chronicles 16 (Ps. 96 is nearly duplicated there in vv. 23–33), the psalm became associated with the glorious entry of the ark of the covenant into Jerusalem. There also are marked similarities between this psalm and material in Isaiah 40–66. Like these passages in Isaiah, Psalm 96 represents the Old Testament's anticipation of the New Testament's worldwide mission (see Matt. 28:16–20).

9 Worship the LORD in the splendor of his[a] holiness;[p]
   tremble[q] before him, all the earth.[r]
10 Say among the nations, "The LORD reigns.[s]"
   The world is firmly established, it cannot be moved;[t]
   he will judge the peoples with equity.[u]
11 Let the heavens rejoice, let the earth be glad;[v]
   let the sea resound, and all that is in it;
12   let the fields be jubilant, and everything in them.
   Then all the trees of the forest[w] will sing for joy;[x]
13   they will sing before the LORD, for he comes,
   he comes to judge[y] the earth.
   He will judge the world in righteousness
   and the peoples in his truth.

Psalm 97

1 The LORD reigns,[z] let the earth be glad;[a]
   let the distant shores rejoice.

2 Clouds and thick darkness[b] surround him;
   righteousness and justice are the foundation of his throne.[c]
3 Fire[d] goes before[e] him
   and consumes[f] his foes on every side.
4 His lightning lights up the world;
   the earth sees and trembles.[g]
5 The mountains melt[h] like wax before the LORD,
   before the Lord of all the earth.[i]
6 The heavens proclaim his righteousness,[j]
   and all the peoples see his glory.[k]

7 All who worship images[l] are put to shame,[m]
   those who boast in idols—
   worship him,[n] all you gods!

8 Zion hears and rejoices
   and the villages of Judah are glad
   because of your judgments,[o] O LORD.
9 For you, O LORD, are the Most High over all the earth;[p]
   you are exalted[q] far above all gods.

10 Let those who love the LORD hate evil,[r]
   for he guards the lives of his faithful ones[s]
   and delivers[t] them from the hand of the wicked.[u]
11 Light is shed[v] upon the righteous
   and joy on the upright in heart.

a 9 Or LORD with the splendor of

Cross references

96:9
p Ps 29:2
q Ps 114:7 r Ps 33:8
96:10
s Ps 97:1 t Ps 93:1
u Ps 67:4

96:11
v Ps 97:1; 98:7;
Isa 49:13

96:12
w Isa 44:23
x Ps 65:13

96:13
y Rev 19:11

97:1
z Ps 96:10
a Ps 96:11

97:2
b Ex 19:9; Ps 18:11
c Ps 89:14

97:3
d Da 7:10
e Hab 3:5 f Ps 18:8

97:4
g Ps 104:32
97:5
h Ps 46:2,6; Mic 1:4
i Jos 3:11
97:6
j Ps 50:6 k Ps 19:1

97:7
l Lev 26:1
m Jer 10:14
n Heb 1:6

97:8
o Ps 48:11
97:9
p Ps 83:18; 95:3
q Ex 18:11

97:10
r Ps 34:14;
Am 5:15; Ro 12:9
s Pr 2:8 t Da 3:28
u Ps 37:40;
Jer 15:21
97:11
v Job 22:28

📖 All the nations (v. 7) are invited to participate in praising God for his rule, sovereignty, and majesty. All may worship, but our motivation is important: The Lord expects reverence, submission, holiness, and awe. Is this the message we as Christians consistently convey to those around us? It's a tall order, coming as it does to a world too often short on respect.

Psalm 97

📖 This psalm belongs to a group of psalms (93–100) united by type and theme. See "There and Then" for Psalm 96. Psalm 97 gives particular focus to the benefits of God's reign enjoyed by his people. The godly receive the gifts of God's light and joy (v. 11). Light here symbolizes life and well-being (cf. Prov. 13:9; Lam. 3:1–2). The psalm contains many allusions to other parts of the Old Testament, all of which have here been shaped into a magnificent hymn.

📖 Psalm 97 calls us to a "love/hate" relationship: "Let those who love the LORD hate evil" (v. 10). The world expects us not to rock the boat but instead to compromise—or better yet, capitulate. But only those who both love God and hate evil have cause to rejoice in his righteous rule and expect the benefits of his reign. How intense is your love for the Lord—and for what he loves? How intense is your hatred for evil—for everything God hates?

97:12
w Ps 30:4

12 Rejoice in the LORD, you who are righteous,
  and praise his holy name. [w]

Psalm 98

A psalm.

98:1
x Ps 96:1 y Ps 96:3
z Ex 15:6
a Isa 52:10

1 Sing to the LORD a new song, [x]
  for he has done marvelous things; [y]
his right hand [z] and his holy arm [a]
  have worked salvation for him.

98:2
b Isa 52:10

2 The LORD has made his salvation known [b]
  and revealed his righteousness to the nations.

98:3
c Lk 1:54

3 He has remembered [c] his love
  and his faithfulness to the house of Israel;
all the ends of the earth have seen
  the salvation of our God.

98:4
d Isa 44:23

4 Shout for joy [d] to the LORD, all the earth,
  burst into jubilant song with music;

98:5
e Ps 92:3 f Isa 51:3

5 make music to the LORD with the harp, [e]
  with the harp and the sound of singing, [f]

98:6
g Nu 10:10
h Ps 47:7

6 with trumpets [g] and the blast of the ram's horn—
  shout for joy before the LORD, the King. [h]

98:7
i Ps 24:1

7 Let the sea resound, and everything in it,
  the world, and all who live in it. [i]

98:8
j Isa 55:12

8 Let the rivers clap their hands,
  let the mountains [j] sing together for joy;

9 let them sing before the LORD,
  for he comes to judge the earth.
He will judge the world in righteousness

98:9
k Ps 96:10

  and the peoples with equity. [k]

Psalm 99

99:1
l Ps 97:1
m Ex 25:22

1 The LORD reigns, [l]
  let the nations tremble;
he sits enthroned between the cherubim, [m]
  let the earth shake.

99:2
n Ps 48:1 o Ps 97:9;
113:4

2 Great is the LORD [n] in Zion;
  he is exalted [o] over all the nations.

99:3
p Ps 76:1

3 Let them praise your great and awesome name [p]—
  he is holy.

Psalm 98

📖 Like Psalm 96, this psalm reflects on the reasons God deserves universal praise. The themes are so similar that some scholars have assumed a common authorship, but it's more likely that the two psalms share a common literary heritage. Psalm 98 progressively extended the call to celebrate God's righteous rule: from the worshiping congregation of Israel to all the peoples of the earth to the whole creation. Likewise, the psalm moves from reflection on the revelation of God's righteousness in the past through Israel to a joyful anticipation of the restoration of all things, when God's kingdom will be established on Earth.

🔲 Our restoration helps us anticipate the final restoration of all creation. Nature is God's stage; it echoes and reverberates our joy as we look forward to his coming

(cf. Isa. 55:12)—to nature's "groaning" giving way to rejoicing (Rom. 8:19–23). When have you witnessed creation in such a breathtaking way that you could almost picture images like singing mountains or clapping rivers (Ps. 98:8)? When have you witnessed nature groaning? Do you get a picture of urban blight? Polluted streams? How can you help redeem a piece of creation?

Psalm 99

📖 Again, this psalm belongs to a group of psalms (93–100) united by type and theme. They are sometimes called enthronement psalms or designated as psalms celebrating God's kingship. Psalm 99 emphasizes the benefits of the Lord's reign for Israel, an emphasis it shares with Psalm 97. God's acts in Israel reveal his nature and confirm his universal rule, of which all people are beneficiaries.

4 The King is mighty, he loves justice q—
    you have established equity; r
  in Jacob you have done
    what is just and right.
5 Exalt s the LORD our God
    and worship at his footstool;
  he is holy.

6 Moses t and Aaron were among his priests,
    Samuel u was among those who called on his name;
  they called on the LORD
    and he answered v them.
7 He spoke to them from the pillar of cloud; w
    they kept his statutes and the decrees he gave them.

8 O LORD our God,
    you answered them;
  you were to Israel a a forgiving God, x
    though you punished their misdeeds. b
9 Exalt the LORD our God
    and worship at his holy mountain,
  for the LORD our God is holy.

Psalm 100

A psalm. For giving thanks.

1 Shout for joy y to the LORD, all the earth.
2   Worship the LORD with gladness;
    come before him z with joyful songs.
3 Know that the LORD is God. a
    It is he who made us, b and we are his c;
    we are his people, the sheep of his pasture. c

4 Enter his gates with thanksgiving
    and his courts with praise;
    give thanks to him and praise his name. d
5 For the LORD is good e and his love endures forever; f
    his faithfulness g continues through all generations.

Psalm 101

Of David. A psalm.

1 I will sing of your love h and justice;
    to you, O LORD, I will sing praise.

a 8 Hebrew them   b 8 Or / an avenger of the wrongs done to them   c 3 Or and not we ourselves

99:4
q Ps 11:7 r Ps 98:9

99:5
s Ps 132:7

99:6
t Ex 24:6 u Jer 15:1
v 1Sa 7:9

99:7
w Ex 33:9

99:8
x Nu 14:20

100:1
y Ps 98:4

100:2
z Ps 95:2
100:3
a Ps 46:10
b Job 10:3
c Ps 74:1; Eze 34:31

100:4
d Ps 116:17
100:5
e 1Ch 16:34;
Ps 25:8 f Ezr 3:11;
Ps 106:1
g Ps 119:90

101:1
h Ps 51:14; 89:1;
145:7

Because God is "exalted" over all the nations and "holy" in his awe-inspiring presence, his people are called to lead the nations in praising him. They do this by submitting themselves to his sovereignty and responding properly to his holy presence. Many would say that Christians on continents other than North America and Europe are currently leading the nations in God's praise. What factors do you think may have caused this shift in the focal point of Christian activity?

Psalm 100

Psalm 100 probably functions as a conclusion to the collection of kingship psalms (93–100) of which it's a part. The notation in the heading, "For giving thanks," may indicate that the psalm was intended to accompany a thank offering (see Lev. 7:12). Its structure is straightforward: a call to give thanks (vv. 1–2), a rationale for giving thanks (v. 3), a second call to offer thanks (v. 4), and an additional rationale for doing so (v. 5). Stated simply, the Lord is God, and the Lord is good.

Why does Scripture commonly compare God's people to sheep? Probably because we are so dependent upon him, as sheep are upon their shepherd. After all, the Lord created us; and only he can save us and guide us into "green pastures" (23:1–2; 65:6–7; John 10:9–11). In spite of their helplessness and weaknesses, sheep were the wealth of Israel, and shepherds dedicated a lifetime to their care. Take a moment to do as Psalm 100 invites: Enter his presence with thanksgiving, thank him, and praise his name.

2 I will be careful to lead a blameless life—
    when will you come to me?

I will walk in my house
    with blameless heart.
3 I will set before my eyes
    no vile thing. *i*

The deeds of faithless men I hate; *j*
    they will not cling to me.
4 Men of perverse heart *k* shall be far from me;
    I will have nothing to do with evil.

5 Whoever slanders his neighbor *l* in secret,
    him will I put to silence;
whoever has haughty eyes *m* and a proud heart,
    him will I not endure.

6 My eyes will be on the faithful in the land,
    that they may dwell with me;
he whose walk is blameless *n*
    will minister to me.

7 No one who practices deceit
    will dwell in my house;
no one who speaks falsely
    will stand in my presence.

8 Every morning *o* I will put to silence
    all the wicked *p* in the land;
I will cut off every evildoer *q*
    from the city of the LORD. *r*

Psalm 102

A prayer of an afflicted man. When he is faint and pours out his lament
before the LORD.

1 Hear my prayer, O LORD;
    let my cry for help *s* come to you.
2 Do not hide your face *t* from me

101:3
i Dt 15:9 *j* Ps 40:4

101:4
k Pr 11:20

101:5
l Ps 50:20
m Ps 10:5; Pr 6:17

101:6
n Ps 119:1

101:8
o Jer 21:12
p Ps 75:10
q Ps 118:10-12
r Ps 46:4

102:1
s Ex 2:23
102:2
t Ps 69:17

Psalm 101

🔖 This psalm was written by one of Israel's kings, either David or one of his descendants (see heading). It's similar in form to ancient treaties. The king solemnly vowed to administer justice and live up to the theocratic (God-governed) ideal in Israel. In Deuteronomy 17:14–20 God had instructed the king to prepare a personal copy of the law so that he would learn to live rightly and manage well the affairs of state as Israel's chief executive. The king was God's servant, appointed to carry out the wishes of his master or overlord.

📖 The qualities of Jesus, the Messiah, spelled out in Isaiah 11:1–5 and in this psalm, fulfill the theocratic ideals of integrity, justice, and devotion. His followers are to conform to the same high standards (cf. 1 Tim. 3:1–16; 2 Tim. 2:14–26; Titus 1:6–9). Paul was writing in these passages to pastors and church office holders, but his words apply to all believers. Why not take the time to read and reflect on these verses? Do they begin to describe your Christian standards? Your lifestyle?

Psalm 102

🔖 This psalm is classified as one of the seven penitential psalms (Ps. 6; 32; 38; 51; 102; 130; 143). Some of them are so designated because of their confessional nature, others because of their use within the Christian community. Psalm 102 is an example of the latter. Rather than an explicit confession of sin, it emphasizes the suffering and discipline often associated with sin. Though no specifics are given regarding the historical setting, this lament most likely tied into the situation of the exile.

📖 This psalm gives us the "insider's view" of someone who has sinned. This individual experiences personal anguish (vv. 3–7) demonstrated in feverish anxiety (v. 3), adversity (vv. 4,11), and the loneliness of suffering (vv. 5–7). His words denote deep despair and articulate the questions that arise about one's existence in view of life's transitory nature (vv. 3,11). From the text we understand not only people's need for God, but their own perceptions of their standing before him. But we have Good News! We can affirm that God doesn't reject any

when I am in distress.
Turn your ear to me;
when I call, answer me quickly.

3 For my days vanish like smoke; [u]
my bones burn like glowing embers.
4 My heart is blighted and withered like grass; [v]
I forget to eat my food.
5 Because of my loud groaning
I am reduced to skin and bones.
6 I am like a desert owl, [w]
like an owl among the ruins.
7 I lie awake; [x] I have become
like a bird alone [y] on a roof.
8 All day long my enemies taunt me;
those who rail against me use my name as a curse.
9 For I eat ashes as my food
and mingle my drink with tears [z]
10 because of your great wrath, [a]
for you have taken me up and thrown me aside.
11 My days are like the evening shadow; [b]
I wither away like grass.

12 But you, O LORD, sit enthroned forever; [c]
your renown endures [d] through all generations.
13 You will arise and have compassion [e] on Zion,
for it is time to show favor to her;
the appointed time has come.
14 For her stones are dear to your servants;
her very dust moves them to pity.
15 The nations will fear [f] the name of the LORD,
all the kings [g] of the earth will revere your glory.
16 For the LORD will rebuild Zion
and appear in his glory. [h]
17 He will respond to the prayer [i] of the destitute;
he will not despise their plea.

18 Let this be written [j] for a future generation,
that a people not yet created [k] may praise the LORD:
19 "The LORD looked down [l] from his sanctuary on high,
from heaven he viewed the earth,
20 to hear the groans of the prisoners [m]
and release those condemned to death."
21 So the name of the LORD will be declared [n] in Zion
and his praise in Jerusalem
22 when the peoples and the kingdoms
assemble to worship the LORD.

23 In the course of my life [a] he broke my strength;
he cut short my days.
24 So I said:
"Do not take me away, O my God, in the midst of my days;
your years go on [o] through all generations.
25 In the beginning [p] you laid the foundations of the earth,
and the heavens are the work of your hands.

[a] 23 Or By his power

102:3
[u] Jas 4:14
102:4
[v] Ps 37:2
102:6
[w] Job 30:29;
Isa 34:11
102:7
[x] Ps 77:4 [y] Ps 38:11
102:9
[z] Ps 42:3
102:10
[a] Ps 38:3
102:11
[b] Job 14:2
102:12
[c] Ps 9:7 [d] Ps 135:13
102:13
[e] Isa 60:10
102:15
[f] 1Ki 8:43
[g] Ps 138:4
102:16
[h] Isa 60:1-2
102:17
[i] Ne 1:6
102:18
[j] Ro 15:4 [k] Ps 22:31
102:19
[l] Dt 26:15
102:20
[m] Ps 79:11
102:21
[n] Ps 22:22
102:24
[o] Ps 90:2; Isa 38:10
102:25
[p] Ge 1:1;
Heb 1:10-12*

of us because of our sin but hears those who turn to him (v. 17), that he wants to free people from sin's terrible bondage (v. 20). This is cause for all nations to praise the Lord (vv. 21–22).

102:26
q Isa 34:4;
Mt 24:35;
2Pe 3:7-10;
Rev 20:11

102:27
r Mal 3:6;
Heb 13:8; Jas 1:17
102:28
s Ps 69:36 t Ps 89:4

26 They will perish, *q* but you remain;
  they will all wear out like a garment.
 Like clothing you will change them
  and they will be discarded.
27 But you remain the same, *r*
  and your years will never end.
28 The children of your servants *s* will live in your presence;
  their descendants *t* will be established before you."

Psalm 103

Of David.

103:1
u Ps 104:1

1 Praise the LORD, O my soul; *u*
  all my inmost being, praise his holy name.
2 Praise the LORD, O my soul,
  and forget not all his benefits—

103:3
v Ps 130:8
w Ex 15:26

3 who forgives all your sins *v*
  and heals *w* all your diseases,
4 who redeems your life from the pit
  and crowns you with love and compassion,

103:5
x Isa 40:31

5 who satisfies your desires with good things
  so that your youth is renewed like the eagle's. *x*

6 The LORD works righteousness
  and justice for all the oppressed.

103:7
y Ps 99:7; 147:19
z Ex 33:13
a Ps 106:22
103:8
b Ex 34:6; Ps 86:15;
Jas 5:11

7 He made known *y* his ways *z* to Moses,
  his deeds *a* to the people of Israel:
8 The LORD is compassionate and gracious, *b*
  slow to anger, abounding in love.

103:9
c Ps 30:5; Isa 57:16;
Jer 3:5, 12;
Mic 7:18
103:10
d Ezr 9:13

9 He will not always accuse,
  nor will he harbor his anger forever; *c*
10 he does not treat us as our sins deserve *d*
  or repay us according to our iniquities.

103:11
e Ps 57:10

11 For as high as the heavens are above the earth,
  so great is his love *e* for those who fear him;

103:12
f 2Sa 12:13
103:13
g Mal 3:17

12 as far as the east is from the west,
  so far has he removed our transgressions *f* from us.
13 As a father has compassion *g* on his children,
  so the LORD has compassion on those who fear him;

103:14
h Isa 29:16

14 for he knows how we are formed, *h*
  he remembers that we are dust.

103:15
i Ps 90:5 j Job 14:2;
Jas 1:10; 1Pe 1:24

15 As for man, his days are like grass, *i*
  he flourishes like a flower *j* of the field;

103:16
k Isa 40:7 l Job 7:10

16 the wind blows *k* over it and it is gone,
  and its place *l* remembers it no more.

Psalm 103

This memorable psalm is a hymn of individual thanksgiving. Praise of God begins with the self; as the psalmist exhorted himself to praise the Lord with his "soul" and "inmost being" (v. 1), he envisioned a full commitment to the act of giving thanks.

The name of the Lord calls to remembrance all his perfections and acts of deliverance ("all his benefits," v. 2). The psalmist recited many of the Lord's blessings to the covenant community (vv. 3–19). The opposite of praise is forgetfulness; to "forget" (v. 2) God's benefits is to disregard his covenantal lordship (Deut. 4:9,23; 8:11).

Forgiveness is a gift. We humans can never take it for granted, precisely because we are human. Over against the weakness of our existence is the greatness of God's love for those of us who fear him.

Wise living, then, in the presence of the Great King requires responsiveness from the heart. Keeping God's covenant means obeying his "precepts" or laws (v. 18; cf. Ex. 20:6; Deut. 7:9). Jesus restated this principle to his disciples in the Upper Room: "If you love me, you will obey what I command" (John 14:15). In the final analysis, our love for God is expressed by what we do.

17 But from everlasting to everlasting
  the LORD's love is with those who fear him,
  and his righteousness with their children's children—
18 with those who keep his covenant
  and remember to obey his precepts. *m*

19 The LORD has established his throne in heaven,
  and his kingdom rules *n* over all.

20 Praise the LORD, you his angels, *o*
  you mighty ones *p* who do his bidding,
  who obey his word.
21 Praise the LORD, all his heavenly hosts, *q*
  you his servants who do his will.
22 Praise the LORD, all his works *r*
  everywhere in his dominion.

  Praise the LORD, O my soul.

Psalm 104

1 Praise the LORD, O my soul. *s*

O LORD my God, you are very great;
  you are clothed with splendor and majesty.
2 He wraps *t* himself in light as with a garment;
  he stretches out the heavens *u* like a tent
3   and lays the beams *v* of his upper chambers on their waters.
He makes the clouds *w* his chariot
  and rides on the wings of the wind. *x*
4 He makes winds his messengers, *a y*
  flames of fire *z* his servants.

5 He set the earth *a* on its foundations;
  it can never be moved.
6 You covered it *b* with the deep *c* as with a garment;
  the waters stood above the mountains.
7 But at your rebuke *d* the waters fled,
  at the sound of your thunder they took to flight;
8 they flowed over the mountains,
  they went down into the valleys,
  to the place you assigned *e* for them.
9 You set a boundary they cannot cross;
  never again will they cover the earth.

10 He makes springs *f* pour water into the ravines;
  it flows between the mountains.
11 They give water to all the beasts of the field;
  the wild donkeys quench their thirst.
12 The birds of the air *g* nest by the waters;
  they sing among the branches.
13 He waters the mountains *h* from his upper chambers;

a 4 Or *angels*

Cross references

103:18 *m* Dt 7:9
103:19 *n* Ps 47:2
103:20 *o* Ps 148:2; Heb 1:14 *p* Ps 29:1
103:21 *q* 1Ki 22:19
103:22 *r* Ps 145:10
104:1 *s* Ps 103:22
104:2 *t* Da 7:9 *u* Isa 40:22
104:3 *v* Am 9:6 *w* Isa 19:1 *x* Ps 18:10
104:4 *y* Ps 148:8; Heb 1:7* *z* 2Ki 2:11
104:5 *a* Job 26:7; Ps 24:1-2
104:6 *b* Ge 7:19 *c* Ge 1:2
104:7 *d* Ps 18:15
104:8 *e* Ps 33:7
104:10 *f* Ps 107:33; Isa 41:18
104:12 *g* Mt 8:20
104:13 *h* Ps 147:8; Jer 10:13

Psalm 104

The theme of Psalm 104, a descriptive and beautiful psalm of praise, is God's greatness in ruling and sustaining his vast creation. While Psalm 103 praises the Redeemer-King, Psalm 104 extols the Creator-King. In a sense, this psalm is the poetic version of the creation story, complementing the historical account in Genesis 1. God's involvement with creation is expressed in the psalm's vivid imagery. He alone controls the elements, and he's surrounded by his servants, whether they are created beings or powers in the created order, like winds and lightning. God's care for creation, especially in the provision of water and food, dominate the text.

the earth is satisfied by the fruit of his work.

104:14
i Job 38:27;
Ps 147:8 j Ge 1:30;
Job 28:5

14 He makes grass grow[i] for the cattle,
  and plants for man to cultivate—
  bringing forth food[j] from the earth:

104:15
k Jdg 9:13 l Ps 23:5;
92:10; Lk 7:46

15 wine[k] that gladdens the heart of man,
  oil[l] to make his face shine,
  and bread that sustains his heart.
16 The trees of the LORD are well watered,
  the cedars of Lebanon that he planted.

104:17
m ver 12

17 There the birds[m] make their nests;
  the stork has its home in the pine trees.

104:18
n Pr 30:26

18 The high mountains belong to the wild goats;
  the crags are a refuge for the coneys.[a][n]

104:19
o Ge 1:14 p Ps 19:6

19 The moon marks off the seasons,[o]
  and the sun[p] knows when to go down.

104:20
q Isa 45:7
r Ps 74:16
s Ps 50:10

20 You bring darkness,[q] it becomes night,[r]
  and all the beasts of the forest[s] prowl.

104:21
t Job 38:39;
Ps 145:15;
Joel 1:20
104:22
u Job 37:8
104:23
v Ge 3:19

21 The lions roar for their prey
  and seek their food from God.[t]
22 The sun rises, and they steal away;
  they return and lie down in their dens.[u]
23 Then man goes out to his work,[v]
  to his labor until evening.

104:24
w Ps 40:5 x Pr 3:19

24 How many are your works,[w] O LORD!
  In wisdom you made[x] them all;
  the earth is full of your creatures.

104:25
y Ps 69:34

25 There is the sea,[y] vast and spacious,
  teeming with creatures beyond number—
  living things both large and small.

104:26
z Ps 107:23;
Eze 27:9 a Job 41:1

26 There the ships[z] go to and fro,
  and the leviathan,[a] which you formed to frolic there.

27 These all look to you
  to give them their food[b] at the proper time.

104:27
b Job 36:31;
Ps 136:25; 145:15;
147:9

28 When you give it to them,
  they gather it up;
  when you open your hand,
  they are satisfied[c] with good things.

104:28
c Ps 145:16
104:29
d Dt 31:17
e Job 34:14;
Ecc 12:7

29 When you hide your face,[d]
  they are terrified;
  when you take away their breath,
  they die and return to the dust.[e]
30 When you send your Spirit,
  they are created,
  and you renew the face of the earth.

104:31
f Ge 1:31
104:32
g Ps 97:4
h Ex 19:18
i Ps 144:5

31 May the glory of the LORD endure forever;
  may the LORD rejoice in his works[f]—
32 he who looks at the earth, and it trembles,[g]
  who touches the mountains,[h] and they smoke.[i]

a 18 That is, the hyrax or rock badger

The sheer abundance in our grocery stores and ease of access to clean water in our homes can dull our senses to God's marvelous provision and to the needs that exist for a majority of our world's inhabitants. You can express your thanks for God's provision in praise and service, such as giving canned goods to food banks/shelters or donating to an organization that provides food for the hungry or drills wells to help people access clean water. In this way you become one of God's servants, helping show his care for his creation.

33 I will sing[j] to the LORD all my life;
  I will sing praise to my God as long as I live.
34 May my meditation be pleasing to him,
  as I rejoice[k] in the LORD.
35 But may sinners vanish[l] from the earth
  and the wicked be no more.

Praise the LORD, O my soul.

Praise the LORD. [a][m]

Psalm 105

1 Give thanks to the LORD,[n] call on his name;[o]
  make known among the nations what he has done.
2 Sing to him,[p] sing praise to him;
  tell of all his wonderful acts.
3 Glory in his holy name;
  let the hearts of those who seek the LORD rejoice.
4 Look to the LORD and his strength;
  seek his face[q] always.
5 Remember the wonders[r] he has done,
  his miracles, and the judgments he pronounced,[s]
6 O descendants of Abraham his servant,[t]
  O sons of Jacob, his chosen[u] ones.
7 He is the LORD our God;
  his judgments are in all the earth.

8 He remembers his covenant[v] forever,
  the word he commanded, for a thousand generations,
9 the covenant he made with Abraham,[w]
  the oath he swore to Isaac.
10 He confirmed it[x] to Jacob as a decree,
  to Israel as an everlasting covenant:
11 "To you I will give the land of Canaan[y]
  as the portion you will inherit."

12 When they were but few in number,[z]
  few indeed, and strangers in it,[a]
13 they wandered from nation to nation,
  from one kingdom to another.
14 He allowed no one to oppress[b] them;
  for their sake he rebuked kings:[c]
15 "Do not touch[d] my anointed ones;
  do my prophets no harm."

16 He called down famine[e] on the land

a 35 Hebrew *Hallelu Yah*; in the Septuagint this line stands at the beginning of Psalm 105.

104:33
j Ps 63:4

104:34
k Ps 9:2
104:35
l Ps 37:38
m Ps 105:45;
106:48

105:1
n 1Ch 16:34
o Ps 99:6

105:2
p Ps 96:1

105:4
q Ps 27:8

105:5
r Ps 40:5 s Ps 77:11

105:6
t ver 42 u Ps 106:5

105:8
v Ps 106:45; Lk 1:72

105:9
w Ge 12:7; 17:2;
22:16-18;
Gal 3:15-18
105:10
x Ge 28:13-15

105:11
y Ge 13:15; 15:18

105:12
z Ge 34:30; Dt 7:7
a Ge 23:4;
Heb 11:9

105:14
b Ge 35:5
c Ge 12:17-20
105:15
d Ge 26:11

105:16
e Ge 41:54;
Lev 26:26; Isa 3:1;
Eze 4:16

Psalm 105

In the form of a hymn, Psalm 105 celebrates the history of redemption from Israel's stay in Egypt to the conquest of Canaan. Psalm 105 complements the creation hymn of Psalm 104, as well as the hymn of God's faithfulness in Psalm 106. These three psalms share the theme of God's faithfulness as Creator-Ruler and Redeemer of his people. Psalm 105 (vv. 1–15) was used in association with David's returning the ark of the covenant to Jerusalem (1 Chron. 16:8–22).

God is the *object* of our worship; his acts reveal for us who he is. The *subjects* of worship are us: the people for whose benefit he performed these acts. Through praise, public rejoicing, and remembering his deeds in redemptive history, we express our covenant unity. Our *goal* in worship is threefold: Praise (1) magnifies God ("enlarges" his reputation and esteem); (2) intensifies our appreciation of what he has done, is doing, and will do; and (3) witnesses to those outside the faith. What part does worship play in your life? Does *giving to* God rank for you above *getting from* him?

105:17
f Ge 37:28; 45:5;
Ac 7:9
105:18
g Ge 40:15

105:19
h Ge 40:20-22

105:20
i Ge 41:14

105:22
j Ge 41:43-44

105:23
k Ge 46:6; Ac 13:17

105:24
l Ex 1:7,9
105:25
m Ex 4:21
n Ex 1:6-10;
Ac 7:19
105:26
o Ex 3:10
p Nu 16:5; 17:5-8
105:27
q Ex 7:8-12:51

105:28
r Ex 10:22

105:29
s Ps 78:44 t Ex 7:21

105:30
u Ex 8:2,6

105:31
v Ex 8:21-24
w Ex 8:16-18
105:32
x Ex 9:22-25

105:33
y Ps 78:47

105:34
z Ex 10:4,12-15

105:36
a Ex 12:29

105:37
b Ex 12:35

105:38
c Ex 12:33; 15:16
105:39
d Ex 13:21
e Ne 9:12; Ps 78:14
105:40
f Ps 78:18,24
g Ex 16:13
h Jn 6:31
105:41
i Ex 17:6; Nu 20:11;
Ps 78:15-16;
1Co 10:4
105:42
j Ge 15:13-16

105:43
k Ex 15:1-18;
Ps 106:12

and destroyed all their supplies of food;
17 and he sent a man before them—
   Joseph, sold as a slave. f
18 They bruised his feet with shackles, g
   his neck was put in irons,
19 till what he foretold h came to pass,
   till the word of the LORD proved him true.
20 The king sent and released him,
   the ruler of peoples set him free. i
21 He made him master of his household,
   ruler over all he possessed,
22 to instruct his princes j as he pleased
   and teach his elders wisdom.

23 Then Israel entered Egypt; k
   Jacob lived as an alien in the land of Ham.
24 The LORD made his people very fruitful;
   he made them too numerous l for their foes,
25 whose hearts he turned m to hate his people,
   to conspire n against his servants.
26 He sent Moses o his servant,
   and Aaron, whom he had chosen. p
27 They performed q his miraculous signs among them,
   his wonders in the land of Ham.
28 He sent darkness r and made the land dark—
   for had they not rebelled against his words?
29 He turned their waters into blood, s
   causing their fish to die. t
30 Their land teemed with frogs, u
   which went up into the bedrooms of their rulers.
31 He spoke, and there came swarms of flies, v
   and gnats w throughout their country.
32 He turned their rain into hail, x
   with lightning throughout their land;
33 he struck down their vines y and fig trees
   and shattered the trees of their country.
34 He spoke, and the locusts came, z
   grasshoppers without number;
35 they ate up every green thing in their land,
   ate up the produce of their soil.
36 Then he struck down all the firstborn a in their land,
   the firstfruits of all their manhood.

37 He brought out Israel, laden with silver and gold, b
   and from among their tribes no one faltered.
38 Egypt was glad when they left,
   because dread of Israel c had fallen on them.
39 He spread out a cloud d as a covering,
   and a fire to give light at night. e
40 They asked, f and he brought them quail g
   and satisfied them with the bread of heaven. h
41 He opened the rock, i and water gushed out;
   like a river it flowed in the desert.
42 For he remembered his holy promise j
   given to his servant Abraham.
43 He brought out his people with rejoicing, k
   his chosen ones with shouts of joy;

44 he gave them the lands of the nations, l
  and they fell heir to what others had toiled for—
45 that they might keep his precepts
  and observe his laws. m

Praise the LORD. a

Psalm 106

1 Praise the LORD. b

Give thanks to the LORD, for he is good; n
  his love endures forever.
2 Who can proclaim the mighty acts o of the LORD
  or fully declare his praise?
3 Blessed are they who maintain justice,
  who constantly do what is right. p
4 Remember me, q O LORD, when you show favor to your people,
  come to my aid when you save them,
5 that I may enjoy the prosperity r of your chosen ones,
  that I may share in the joy s of your nation
  and join your inheritance in giving praise.

6 We have sinned, t even as our fathers did;
  we have done wrong and acted wickedly.
7 When our fathers were in Egypt,
  they gave no thought to your miracles;
they did not remember u your many kindnesses,
  and they rebelled by the sea, v the Red Sea. c
8 Yet he saved them for his name's sake, w
  to make his mighty power known.
9 He rebuked x the Red Sea, and it dried up; y
  he led them through z the depths as through a desert.
10 He saved them a from the hand of the foe;
  from the hand of the enemy he redeemed them. b
11 The waters covered c their adversaries;
  not one of them survived.
12 Then they believed his promises
  and sang his praise. d

13 But they soon forgot e what he had done
  and did not wait for his counsel.
14 In the desert they gave in to their craving;
  in the wasteland they put God to the test. f
15 So he gave them g what they asked for,
  but sent a wasting disease h upon them.

16 In the camp they grew envious i of Moses
  and of Aaron, who was consecrated to the LORD.

a 45 Hebrew *Hallelu Yah*   b 1 Hebrew *Hallelu Yah*; also in verse 48   c 7 Hebrew *Yam Suph*; that is,
Sea of Reeds; also in verses 9 and 22

105:44
l Jos 13:6-7

105:45
m Dt 4:40; 6:21-24

106:1
n Ps 100:5; 105:1

106:2
o Ps 145:4,12

106:3
p Ps 15:2
106:4
q Ps 119:132
106:5
r Ps 1:3 s Ps 118:15

106:6
t Da 9:5

106:7
u Ps 78:11,42
v Ex 14:11-12

106:8
w Ex 9:16

106:9
x Ps 18:15
y Ex 14:21; Na 1:4
z Isa 63:11-14
106:10
a Ex 14:30
b Ps 107:2
106:11
c Ex 14:28; 15:5

106:12
d Ex 15:1-21

106:13
e Ex 15:24

106:14
f 1Co 10:9
106:15
g Nu 11:31
h Isa 10:16

106:16
i Nu 16:1-3

Psalm 106

Psalm 106, which fluctuates between hymn and lament, complements Psalm 78 in its thematic approach to Israel's history. It reveals Israel's lack of response to God's mighty and good acts. In its stress on Israel's failure, it contrasts with Psalm 105, where the psalmist recorded God's faithfulness in his presence, protection, and providence. The psalm was probably composed in Jerusalem after the return of some of the exiles.

We who enjoy God's benefits are "blessed" (v. 3). As in Psalm 1, though, this blessing is conditional: We are to please the Lord. The psalmist singled out two qualities of a life of integrity: "justice" and "right." God expects our actions to conform to his standards. Why? Because by so doing we *establish his kingdom* (cf. Ps. 15; Isa. 11:3–5; 33:15–17). Take a moment to reflect on your activities over the past day or week. What specific things have you done that were just and right? Unfair or wrong?

106:17
j Dt 11:6

106:18
k Nu 16:35

106:19
l Ex 32:4

106:20
m Jer 2:11; Ro 1:23

106:21
n Ps 78:11
o Dt 10:21
106:22
p Ps 105:27

106:23
q Ex 32:10
r Ex 32:11-14

106:24
s Dt 8:7; Eze 20:6
t Heb 3:18-19

106:25
u Nu 14:2

106:26
v Eze 20:15;
Heb 3:11
w Nu 14:28-35

106:27
x Lev 26:33;
Ps 44:11
106:28
y Nu 25:2-3;
Hos 9:10

106:30
z Nu 25:8
106:31
a Nu 25:11-13

106:32
b Nu 20:2-13;
Ps 81:7

106:33
c Nu 20:8-12

106:34
d Jdg 1:21
e Dt 7:16
106:35
f Jdg 3:5-6

106:36
g Jdg 2:12

106:37
h 2Ki 16:3; 17:17

106:38
i Nu 35:33

106:39
j Eze 20:18
k Lev 17:7;
Nu 15:39
106:40
l Jdg 2:14; Ps 78:59
m Dt 9:29

106:41
n Jdg 2:14; Ne 9:27

17 The earth opened[j] up and swallowed Dathan;
    it buried the company of Abiram.
18 Fire blazed[k] among their followers;
    a flame consumed the wicked.
19 At Horeb they made a calf[l]
    and worshiped an idol cast from metal.
20 They exchanged their Glory[m]
    for an image of a bull, which eats grass.
21 They forgot the God[n] who saved them,
    who had done great things[o] in Egypt,
22 miracles in the land of Ham[p]
    and awesome deeds by the Red Sea.
23 So he said he would destroy[q] them—
    had not Moses, his chosen one,
    stood in the breach[r] before him
    to keep his wrath from destroying them.

24 Then they despised the pleasant land;[s]
    they did not believe[t] his promise.
25 They grumbled[u] in their tents
    and did not obey the LORD.
26 So he swore[v] to them with uplifted hand
    that he would make them fall in the desert,[w]
27 make their descendants fall among the nations
    and scatter[x] them throughout the lands.

28 They yoked themselves to the Baal of Peor[y]
    and ate sacrifices offered to lifeless gods;
29 they provoked the LORD to anger by their wicked deeds,
    and a plague broke out among them.
30 But Phinehas stood up and intervened,
    and the plague was checked.[z]
31 This was credited to him[a] as righteousness
    for endless generations to come.

32 By the waters of Meribah[b] they angered the LORD,
    and trouble came to Moses because of them;
33 for they rebelled against the Spirit of God,
    and rash words came from Moses' lips. [a][c]

34 They did not destroy[d] the peoples
    as the LORD had commanded[e] them,
35 but they mingled[f] with the nations
    and adopted their customs.
36 They worshiped their idols, [g]
    which became a snare to them.
37 They sacrificed their sons[h]
    and their daughters to demons.
38 They shed innocent blood,
    the blood of their sons[i] and daughters,
    whom they sacrificed to the idols of Canaan,
    and the land was desecrated by their blood.
39 They defiled themselves[j] by what they did;
    by their deeds they prostituted[k] themselves.

40 Therefore the LORD was angry[l] with his people
    and abhorred his inheritance. [m]
41 He handed them over[n] to the nations,

---

a 33 Or against his spirit, / and rash words came from his lips

and their foes ruled over them.
42 Their enemies oppressed them
   and subjected them to their power.
43 Many times he delivered them,
   but they were bent on rebellion[o]
   and they wasted away in their sin.

44 But he took note of their distress
   when he heard their cry;[p]
45 for their sake he remembered his covenant[q]
   and out of his great love[r] he relented.
46 He caused them to be pitied[s]
   by all who held them captive.

47 Save us, O LORD our God,
   and gather us[t] from the nations,
that we may give thanks to your holy name
   and glory in your praise.

48 Praise be to the LORD, the God of Israel,
   from everlasting to everlasting.
Let all the people say, "Amen!"[u]

Praise the LORD.

BOOK V

Psalms 107–150

Psalm 107

1 Give thanks to the LORD,[v] for he is good;
   his love endures forever.
2 Let the redeemed[w] of the LORD say this—
   those he redeemed from the hand of the foe,
3 those he gathered[x] from the lands,
   from east and west, from north and south.[a]

4 Some wandered in desert[y] wastelands,
   finding no way to a city where they could settle.
5 They were hungry and thirsty,
   and their lives ebbed away.
6 Then they cried out[z] to the LORD in their trouble,
   and he delivered them from their distress.
7 He led them by a straight way[a]
   to a city where they could settle.
8 Let them give thanks to the LORD for his unfailing love

---

a 3 Hebrew *north and the sea*

106:43
o Jdg 2:16-19

106:44
p Jdg 3:9; 10:10
106:45
q Lev 26:42;
Ps 105:8 r Jdg 2:18
106:46
s Ezr 9:9; Jer 42:12

106:47
t Ps 147:2

106:48
u Ps 41:13

107:1
v Ps 106:1
107:2
w Ps 106:10
107:3
x Ps 106:47;
Isa 43:5-6

107:4
y Nu 14:33; 32:13

107:6
z Ps 50:15

107:7
a Ezr 8:21

Psalm 107

📖 This is the first psalm in the fifth and last book of the Psalter. Psalm 107 begins like 106, but there the similarity ends. It's a thanksgiving-wisdom psalm, complementing the confession of sin and prayer for divine favor and restoration in Psalm 106. The psalmist presented case studies of God delivering people in need and encouraged the godly to observe God's great love for his creation and especially his people.

Psalm 107 was probably written after the exile (see vv. 2–3). Psalm 106:47 prayed for God to re-gather his people after the exile. Psalm 107 appears to express thanks and praise for his answer.

💭 God can change things; his authority to do so is limitless! This psalm's permanent significance lies in the variety of ways in which and from which God redeems his people. He delivers us from all kinds of afflictions, and he isn't limited by space or time restrictions. All who have experienced his love may join together with his ancient covenant people to give thanks for their own deliverance, whether spiritual, psychological, or material. Beyond the freedom offered through faith in Christ, from what specific problems has God rescued you? How have you expressed your thanks?

107:9
b Ps 22:26; Lk 1:53
c Ps 34:10

107:10
d Lk 1:79 e Job 36:8

107:11
f Ps 106:7; La 3:42
g 2Ch 36:16

107:12
h Ps 22:11

107:14
i Ps 116:16;
Lk 13:16; Ac 12:7

107:17
j Isa 65:6-7; La 3:39
107:18
k Job 33:20
l Job 33:22;
Ps 9:13; 88:3

107:20
m Mt 8:8 n Ps 103:3
o Job 33:28
p Ps 30:3; 49:15

107:22
q Lev 7:12;
Ps 50:14; 116:17
r Ps 9:11; 73:28;
118:17

107:25
s Ps 105:31
t Jnh 1:4 u Ps 93:3

107:26
v Ps 22:14

107:29
w Mt 8:26 x Ps 89:9

107:32
y Ps 22:22,25;
35:18

107:33
z 1Ki 17:1; Ps 74:15

107:34
a Ge 13:10; 14:3;
19:25
107:35
b Ps 114:8;
Isa 41:18

and his wonderful deeds for men,
9 for he satisfies [b] the thirsty
and fills the hungry with good things. [c]

10 Some sat in darkness [d] and the deepest gloom,
prisoners suffering in iron chains, [e]
11 for they had rebelled [f] against the words of God
and despised the counsel [g] of the Most High.
12 So he subjected them to bitter labor;
they stumbled, and there was no one to help. [h]
13 Then they cried to the LORD in their trouble,
and he saved them from their distress.
14 He brought them out of darkness and the deepest gloom
and broke away their chains. [i]
15 Let them give thanks to the LORD for his unfailing love
and his wonderful deeds for men,
16 for he breaks down gates of bronze
and cuts through bars of iron.

17 Some became fools through their rebellious ways
and suffered affliction [j] because of their iniquities.
18 They loathed all food [k]
and drew near the gates of death. [l]
19 Then they cried to the LORD in their trouble,
and he saved them from their distress.
20 He sent forth his word [m] and healed them; [n]
he rescued [o] them from the grave. [p]
21 Let them give thanks to the LORD for his unfailing love
and his wonderful deeds for men.
22 Let them sacrifice thank offerings [q]
and tell of his works [r] with songs of joy.

23 Others went out on the sea in ships;
they were merchants on the mighty waters.
24 They saw the works of the LORD,
his wonderful deeds in the deep.
25 For he spoke [s] and stirred up a tempest [t]
that lifted high the waves. [u]
26 They mounted up to the heavens and went down to the depths;
in their peril their courage melted [v] away.
27 They reeled and staggered like drunken men;
they were at their wits' end.
28 Then they cried out to the LORD in their trouble,
and he brought them out of their distress.
29 He stilled the storm [w] to a whisper;
the waves [x] of the sea were hushed.
30 They were glad when it grew calm,
and he guided them to their desired haven.
31 Let them give thanks to the LORD for his unfailing love
and his wonderful deeds for men.
32 Let them exalt him in the assembly [y] of the people
and praise him in the council of the elders.

33 He turned rivers into a desert, [z]
flowing springs into thirsty ground,
34 and fruitful land into a salt waste, [a]
because of the wickedness of those who lived there.
35 He turned the desert into pools of water [b]
and the parched ground into flowing springs;

36 there he brought the hungry to live,
and they founded a city where they could settle.
37 They sowed fields and planted vineyards c
that yielded a fruitful harvest;
38 he blessed them, and their numbers greatly increased, d
and he did not let their herds diminish.

39 Then their numbers decreased, e and they were humbled
by oppression, calamity and sorrow;
40 he who pours contempt on nobles f
made them wander in a trackless waste. g
41 But he lifted the needy h out of their affliction
and increased their families like flocks.
42 The upright see and rejoice, i
but all the wicked shut their mouths. j

43 Whoever is wise, k let him heed these things
and consider the great love l of the LORD.

Psalm 108

A song. A psalm of David.

1 My heart is steadfast, O God;
I will sing and make music with all my soul.
2 Awake, harp and lyre!
I will awaken the dawn.
3 I will praise you, O LORD, among the nations;
I will sing of you among the peoples.
4 For great is your love, higher than the heavens;
your faithfulness reaches to the skies.
5 Be exalted, O God, above the heavens,
and let your glory be over all the earth. m

6 Save us and help us with your right hand,
that those you love may be delivered.
7 God has spoken from his sanctuary:
"In triumph I will parcel out Shechem
and measure off the Valley of Succoth.
8 Gilead is mine, Manasseh is mine;
Ephraim is my helmet,
Judah n my scepter.
9 Moab is my washbasin,
upon Edom I toss my sandal;
over Philistia I shout in triumph."

10 Who will bring me to the fortified city?
Who will lead me to Edom?
11 Is it not you, O God, you who have rejected us
and no longer go out with our armies? o

107:37
c Isa 65:21

107:38
d Ge 12:2;
17:16,20; Ex 1:7

107:39
e 2Ki 10:32;
Eze 5:12

107:40
f Job 12:21
g Job 12:24

107:41
h 1Sa 2:8;
Ps 113:7-9

107:42
i Job 22:19
j Job 5:16;
Ps 63:11; Ro 3:19

107:43
k Jer 9:12; Hos 14:9
l Ps 64:9

108:5
m Ps 57:5

108:8
n Ge 49:10

108:11
o Ps 44:9

Psalm 108

This psalm consists of two parts (vv. 1–5 and 6–13), each of which duplicates another psalm. Verses 1–5 repeat Psalm 57:7–11, and verses 6–13 repeat Psalm 60:5–12. Here verses 1–5 praise God for his love—perhaps as a confession of trust in God, to whom appeal is to be made. Verses 6–13 make that appeal, asking for deliverance from Israel's enemies (see "There and Then" for Ps. 60).

Notice that the first section of this prayer psalm offers unqualified praise, while the second asks for help in a time of trouble. Is this a reversal of your usual pattern, or do you approach God in much the same way? Are you able in the tough times to make the claim that your "heart is steadfast" (firm, unwavering, committed)? If you haven't tried praising God before petitioning him, you might be surprised at how centering praise can be. Acknowledging his control at the outset can make all the difference.

12 Give us aid against the enemy,
　　for the help of man is worthless.
13 With God we will gain the victory,
　　and he will trample down our enemies.

Psalm 109

For the director of music. Of David. A psalm.

1 O God, whom I praise,
　　do not remain silent, [p]
2 for wicked and deceitful men
　　have opened their mouths against me;
　　they have spoken against me with lying tongues. [q]

3 With words of hatred [r] they surround me;
　　they attack me without cause. [s]
4 In return for my friendship they accuse me,
　　but I am a man of prayer. [t]

5 They repay me evil for good, [u]
　　and hatred for my friendship.

6 Appoint [a] an evil man [b] to oppose him;
　　let an accuser [c][v] stand at his right hand.
7 When he is tried, let him be found guilty,
　　and may his prayers condemn [w] him.

8 May his days be few;
　　may another take his place [x] of leadership.
9 May his children be fatherless
　　and his wife a widow. [y]

10 May his children be wandering beggars;
　　may they be driven [d] from their ruined homes.

11 May a creditor seize all he has;
　　may strangers plunder the fruits of his labor. [z]

12 May no one extend kindness to him
　　or take pity [a] on his fatherless children.
13 May his descendants be cut off, [b]
　　their names blotted out [c] from the next generation.
14 May the iniquity of his fathers [d] be remembered before the LORD;
　　may the sin of his mother never be blotted out.

15 May their sins always remain before the LORD,
　　that he may cut off the memory [e] of them from the earth.

16 For he never thought of doing a kindness,
　　but hounded to death the poor
　　and the needy [f] and the brokenhearted. [g]

17 He loved to pronounce a curse—
　　may it [e] come on him; [h]
　　he found no pleasure in blessing—
　　may it be [f] far from him.

18 He wore cursing [i] as his garment;
　　it entered into his body like water, [i]

---

[a] 6 Or They say: "Appoint (with quotation marks at the end of verse 19)　　[b] 6 Or the Evil One
[c] 6 Or let Satan　　[d] 10 Septuagint; Hebrew sought　　[e] 17 Or curse, / and it has　　[f] 17 Or blessing, /
and it is

Psalm 109

Psalm 109 is David's prayer for deliverance from false accusers. He asked God, who had responded in the past, to act again on behalf of his covenant child by not remaining silent (cf. 35:22; 39:12; 83:1). The wicked had upset the moral order by their deceptions and their exchange of evil for good and hatred for friendliness. Would the Judge of the universe notice and respond? David prayed that God would punish them in accordance with their crime.

into his bones like oil.
¹⁹ May it be like a cloak wrapped about him,
like a belt tied forever around him.
²⁰ May this be the LORD's payment *k* to my accusers,
to those who speak evil *l* of me.

²¹ But you, O Sovereign LORD,
deal well with me for your name's sake; *m*
out of the goodness of your love, *n* deliver me.
²² For I am poor and needy,
and my heart is wounded within me.
²³ I fade away like an evening shadow; *o*
I am shaken off like a locust.
²⁴ My knees give *p* way from fasting;
my body is thin and gaunt.
²⁵ I am an object of scorn *q* to my accusers;
when they see me, they shake their heads. *r*

²⁶ Help me, *s* O LORD my God;
save me in accordance with your love.
²⁷ Let them know *t* that it is your hand,
that you, O LORD, have done it.
²⁸ They may curse, *u* but you will bless;
when they attack they will be put to shame,
but your servant will rejoice. *v*
²⁹ My accusers will be clothed with disgrace
and wrapped in shame *w* as in a cloak.

³⁰ With my mouth I will greatly extol the LORD;
in the great throng *x* I will praise him.
³¹ For he stands at the right hand *y* of the needy one,
to save his life from those who condemn him.

Psalm 110

Of David. A psalm.

¹ The LORD says *z* to my Lord:
"Sit at my right hand
until I make your enemies
a footstool for your feet." *a*

² The LORD will extend your mighty scepter *b* from Zion;

Cross references (margin)

109:20
k Ps 94:23; 2Ti 4:14
l Ps 71:10

109:21
m Ps 79:9
n Ps 69:16

109:23
o Ps 102:11

109:24
p Heb 12:12

109:25
q Ps 22:6
r Mt 27:39; Mk 15:29

109:26
s Ps 119:86

109:27
t Job 37:7

109:28
u 2Sa 16:12
v Isa 65:14

109:29
w Ps 35:26; 132:18

109:30
x Ps 35:18; 111:1
109:31
y Ps 16:8; 73:23; 121:5

110:1
z Mt 22:44*; Mk 12:36*; Lk 20:42*; Ac 2:34*
a 1Co 15:25

110:2
b Ps 45:6

Hatred is so opposite Jesus' emphasis on love, how can we as Christians pray a prayer like the one in verses 6–15? Since the evil David had observed contrasts so completely with God's nature and plan, he prayed—under divine inspiration—for God's intervention. If we as Christians fail to uproot from our hearts selfish passions, judgmentalism, and personal desire for revenge, we will be judged ourselves (Gal. 5:14–15; James 3:13–16). But psalms like this can help us pray through our anger, frustration, and spite to arrive on the other side at submission to God's will. Only then can we pray with sincere conviction for the eradication of evil and the full establishment of God's kingdom.

Psalm 110

Psalm 110 (specifically its two brief oracles; vv. 1,4) is frequently referred to in the New Testament testimony to Christ. Like Psalm 2, this psalm has the marks of a coronation psalm, composed for use at the enthronement of a new Davidic king. Before the Christian era Jews already viewed it as Messianic.

Because of the way it's been interpreted in the New Testament—especially by Jesus (see Luke 20:42–44) but also by Peter (see Acts 2:34–36) and the author of Hebrews (see "Here and Now" to follow), Christians have generally held that this is the most directly "prophetic" of the psalms. If so, David, speaking prophetically, composed a coronation psalm for his great future son, of whom the prophets wouldn't speak until later. It may be, though, that David composed the psalm for the coronation of his son Solomon, calling him "my Lord" (v. 1) in view of his new status, which placed him above the aged David. If so, David spoke a word that had far larger meaning than he knew.

you will rule in the midst of your enemies.
3 Your troops will be willing
on your day of battle.
Arrayed in holy majesty,[c]
from the womb of the dawn
you will receive the dew of your youth.[a]

4 The LORD has sworn
and will not change his mind:[d]
"You are a priest forever,[e]
in the order of Melchizedek.[f]"

5 The Lord is at your right hand;[g]
he will crush kings[h] on the day of his wrath.[i]
6 He will judge the nations,[j] heaping up the dead[k]
and crushing the rulers[l] of the whole earth.
7 He will drink from a brook beside the way[b];
therefore he will lift up his head.[m]

110:3 [c] Jdg 5:2; Ps 96:9
110:4 [d] Nu 23:19 [e] Heb 5:6*; 7:21* [f] Heb 7:15-17*
110:5 [g] Ps 16:8 [h] Ps 2:12 [i] Ps 2:5; Ro 2:5
110:6 [j] Isa 2:4 [k] Isa 66:24 [l] Ps 68:21
110:7 [m] Ps 27:6

Psalm 111[c]

1 Praise the LORD.[d]

I will extol the LORD with all my heart
in the council of the upright and in the assembly.

2 Great are the works[n] of the LORD;
they are pondered by all who delight in them.
3 Glorious and majestic are his deeds,
and his righteousness endures forever.
4 He has caused his wonders to be remembered;
the LORD is gracious and compassionate.[o]
5 He provides food[p] for those who fear him;
he remembers his covenant forever.
6 He has shown his people the power of his works,
giving them the lands of other nations.
7 The works of his hands are faithful and just;
all his precepts are trustworthy.[q]
8 They are steadfast for ever[r] and ever,
done in faithfulness and uprightness.
9 He provided redemption[s] for his people;

111:2 [n] Ps 92:5; 143:5
111:4 [o] Ps 103:8
111:5 [p] Mt 6:26,31-33
111:7 [q] Ps 19:7; Rev 15:3
111:8 [r] Isa 40:8; Mt 5:18
111:9 [s] Lk 1:68

[a] *3* Or / *your young men will come to you like the dew* [b] *7* Or / *The One who grants succession will set him in authority* [c] This psalm is an acrostic poem, the lines of which begin with the successive letters of the Hebrew alphabet. [d] *1* Hebrew *Hallelu Yah*

David and his royal sons performed many worship-focused activities, like overseeing the temple and its worship liturgy. But they couldn't engage in those specifically priestly functions that had been assigned to the priests (cf. 2 Chron. 26:16–18). In Psalm 110:4 the Davidic king was installed by God as king-priest in Zion after the manner of Melchizedek, the king-priest of God Most High at Jerusalem in the days of Abraham (Gen. 14:18). The author of Hebrews quoted this psalm to show that Jesus would be a priest forever (Heb. 5:6; 7:17–21). What are the implications for you that Jesus is *both your Priest and King for all time?*

Psalm 111

Psalms 111 and 112 form a unit and were probably written by the same author in the period after the exile. Psalm 111 is a hymn of praise for God's involvement in history and revelation, combined with wisdom instruction. It uses an acrostic format, with each line beginning with a successive letter of the Hebrew alphabet. The psalm may have been used in an educational setting, like a school or synagogue.

God's faithfulness to his promises means that he's our God for all seasons—a God who backs up his words by his power to establish justice (v. 7). "He has shown his people the power of his works" (v. 6). He has confirmed his covenant in Jesus, and his faithfulness and justice are as active today as ever. Paul assured believers that no hardship can separate us from God's love in Christ, as he continues to work out his purposes on Earth (Rom. 8:28–39).

he ordained his covenant forever—
holy and awesome[t] is his name.

[10] The fear of the LORD is the beginning of wisdom;[u]
all who follow his precepts have good understanding.[v]
To him belongs eternal praise.[w]

Psalm 112[a]

[1] Praise the LORD.[b]

Blessed is the man who fears the LORD,[x]
who finds great delight[y] in his commands.

[2] His children will be mighty in the land;
the generation of the upright will be blessed.
[3] Wealth and riches are in his house,
and his righteousness endures forever.
[4] Even in darkness light dawns[z] for the upright,
for the gracious and compassionate and righteous[a] man.[c]
[5] Good will come to him who is generous and lends freely,[b]
who conducts his affairs with justice.
[6] Surely he will never be shaken;
a righteous man will be remembered[c] forever.
[7] He will have no fear of bad news;
his heart is steadfast,[d] trusting in the LORD.
[8] His heart is secure, he will have no fear;
in the end he will look in triumph on his foes.[e]
[9] He has scattered abroad his gifts to the poor,[f]
his righteousness endures forever;
his horn[d] will be lifted[g] high in honor.
[10] The wicked man will see[h] and be vexed,
he will gnash his teeth[i] and waste away;[j]
the longings of the wicked will come to nothing.[k]

Psalm 113

[1] Praise the LORD.[e]

Praise, O servants of the LORD,[l]
praise the name of the LORD.
[2] Let the name of the LORD be praised,
both now and forevermore.[m]
[3] From the rising of the sun[n] to the place where it sets,
the name of the LORD is to be praised.

[a] This psalm is an acrostic poem, the lines of which begin with the successive letters of the Hebrew alphabet.   [b] 1 Hebrew *Hallelu Yah*   [c] 4 Or / *for the LORD, is gracious and compassionate and righteous*   [d] 9 *Horn* here symbolizes dignity.   [e] 1 Hebrew *Hallelu Yah*; also in verse 9

Margin refs: 111:9 t Ps 99:3; Lk 1:49 | 111:10 u Pr 9:10 v Ecc 12:13 w Ps 145:2 | 112:1 x Ps 128:1 y Ps 119:14,16,47,92 | 112:4 z Job 11:17 a Ps 97:11 | 112:5 b Ps 37:21,26 | 112:6 c Pr 10:7 | 112:7 d Ps 57:7; Pr 1:33 | 112:8 e Ps 59:10 | 112:9 f 2Co 9:9* g Ps 75:10 | 112:10 h Ps 86:17 i Ps 37:12 j Ps 58:7-8 k Pr 11:7 | 113:1 l Ps 135:1 | 113:2 m Da 2:20 | 113:3 n Isa 59:19; Mal 1:11

Psalm 112

Psalm 112 is patterned after Psalm 111 (see previous "There and Then"), even sharing the same number of Hebrew syllables. A wisdom song, it again uses an acrostic form. The psalm employs common "wisdom" vocabulary (like "blessed is the man") and concerns, contrasts the righteous and the wicked, and points out the blessings of wisdom. Three times the psalmist brought out the great advantage of godly wisdom, even in adversity. His concern wasn't about *getting* God's blessings so much as about living God's ways. The psalmist assumed that a normal and natural way of life for the righteous was to give freely to the poor (v. 9).

Righteous, or upright, people care about the needy and generously lend to them (vv. 4–5; cf. 37:21,26). They don't necessarily donate their money but "invest" it in people with the expectation of repayment—without interest. Many Christian groups today provide micro-loans to the poor so they can get a small business going or make improvements to one they have already started.

On other occasions, the upright give to the poor outright—"scattering abroad" their gifts (v. 9). Paul quoted this verse when writing to the Corinthians about being "cheerful givers" (2 Cor. 9:6–9)—people whose expressions of self, in words or deeds, reflect their heartfelt sense of "justice" (Ps. 112:5).

113:4
o Ps 99:2 p Ps 8:1;
97:9
113:5
q Ps 89:6
r Ps 103:19
113:6
s Ps 11:4; 138:6;
Isa 57:15
113:7
t 1Sa 2:8
u Ps 107:41
113:8
v Job 36:7
113:9
w 1Sa 2:5; Ps 68:6;
Isa 54:1

4 The LORD is exalted o over all the nations,
   his glory above the heavens. p
5 Who is like the LORD our God, q
   the One who sits enthroned r on high,
6 who stoops down to look s
   on the heavens and the earth?

7 He raises the poor t from the dust
   and lifts the needy u from the ash heap;
8 he seats them v with princes,
   with the princes of their people.
9 He settles the barren w woman in her home
   as a happy mother of children.

   Praise the LORD.

Psalm 114

114:1
x Ex 13:3

1 When Israel came out of Egypt, x
   the house of Jacob from a people of foreign tongue,
2 Judah became God's sanctuary,
   Israel his dominion.

114:3
y Ex 14:21;
Ps 77:16 z Jos 3:16

3 The sea looked and fled, y
   the Jordan turned back; z
4 the mountains skipped like rams,
   the hills like lambs.

5 Why was it, O sea, that you fled,
   O Jordan, that you turned back,
6 you mountains, that you skipped like rams,
   you hills, like lambs?

114:7
a Ps 96:9

7 Tremble, O earth, a at the presence of the Lord,
   at the presence of the God of Jacob,

114:8
b Ex 17:6;
Nu 20:11;
Ps 107:35

8 who turned the rock into a pool,
   the hard rock into springs of water. b

Psalm 113

The "Hallel Psalms" (*hallel* is Hebrew for "praise") appear in three collections: the "Egyptian Hallel" (113–118), the "Great Hallel" (120–136), and the concluding Hallel psalms (146–150). The Egyptian and Great Hallel (mostly pilgrimage songs: 120–134) came to be sung during the annual feasts (Lev. 23; Num 10:10). The Egyptian Hallel was part of the Passover liturgy; Psalms 113–114 were recited or sung before and 115–118 after the festive meal (cf. Matt. 26:30; Mark 14:26). And the concluding Hallel psalms were incorporated into the daily prayers in the synagogue after the temple's destruction in A.D. 70.

Psalms 113 and 114 are both descriptive praise psalms. The repetition at the beginning (v. 1) and conclusion (v. 9) of Psalm 113—"Praise the LORD"—serves as a magnificent opening to the Hallel collection.

Grand hymns of the church such as Wesley's *O For A Thousand Tongues to Sing* have inspired generations of believers. Do you have a favorite hymn? Do you sing certain hymns, gospel songs, or Scripture/worship choruses at certain times of the year or for special occasions? If so, you are following the tradition of God's people throughout history—singing of and to our great God. Paul reminded the church of the potential for renewal and teaching through song (cf. Col. 3:16). Lyrics and melodies combine in such a way as to lift our spirits, helping us reflect on the goodness of the Lord.

Psalm 114

The theme of Psalm 114 is God's great deliverance of Israel in the exodus. He redeemed the Israelites from Egypt, consecrated his people to be his royal nation, and brought them across the Jordan into the promised land. This theme made the psalm an appropriate hymn for the annual Passover ceremony.

The powerful and marvelous "way" of Israel's God hasn't ceased. The exodus and conquest of the promised land have long since receded into the annals of ancient history, but God still provides streams of blessing for us, his people. In what way(s) has God turned hard granite into springs of water for *you*?

Psalm 115

[1] Not to us, O LORD, not to us
 but to your name be the glory, [c]
 because of your love and faithfulness.

[2] Why do the nations say,
 "Where is their God?" [d]
[3] Our God is in heaven; [e]
 he does whatever pleases him. [f]
[4] But their idols are silver and gold,
 made by the hands of men. [g]
[5] They have mouths, but cannot speak, [h]
 eyes, but they cannot see;
[6] they have ears, but cannot hear,
 noses, but they cannot smell;
[7] they have hands, but cannot feel,
 feet, but they cannot walk;
 nor can they utter a sound with their throats.
[8] Those who make them will be like them,
 and so will all who trust in them.

[9] O house of Israel, trust in the LORD—
 he is their help and shield.
[10] O house of Aaron, [i] trust in the LORD—
 he is their help and shield.
[11] You who fear him, trust in the LORD—
 he is their help and shield.

[12] The LORD remembers us and will bless us:
 He will bless the house of Israel,
 he will bless the house of Aaron,
[13] he will bless those who fear [j] the LORD—
 small and great alike.

[14] May the LORD make you increase, [k]
 both you and your children.
[15] May you be blessed by the LORD,
 the Maker of heaven [l] and earth.

[16] The highest heavens belong to the LORD, [m]
 but the earth he has given [n] to man.
[17] It is not the dead [o] who praise the LORD,
 those who go down to silence;
[18] it is we who extol the LORD,
 both now and forevermore. [p]

 Praise the LORD. [a]

[a] 18 Hebrew *Hallelu Yah*

Margin references

115:1 [c] Ps 96:8; Isa 48:11; Eze 36:32
115:2 [d] Ps 42:3; 79:10
115:3 [e] Ps 103:19 [f] Ps 135:6; Da 4:35
115:4 [g] Dt 4:28; Jer 10:3-5
115:5 [h] Jer 10:5
115:10 [i] Ps 118:3
115:13 [j] Ps 128:1,4
115:14 [k] Dt 1:11
115:15 [l] Ge 1:1; 14:19; Ps 96:5
115:16 [m] Ps 89:11 [n] Ps 8:6-8
115:17 [o] Ps 6:5; 88:10-12; Isa 38:18
115:18 [p] Ps 113:2; Da 2:20

Psalm 115

Psalm 115 is a psalm of *communal* (community or public) *confidence*. The three psalms in this category (115; 125; 129) are closely related to communal thanksgiving songs and communal laments. They convey a sense of need—and a deep trust in God's ability to care for his people.

Structurally, the song advances in five movements, involving a liturgical exchange between the people and the temple worship leaders: (1) verses 1–8: the people; (2) verses 9–11: Levitical choir leader (the refrain perhaps spoken by the Levitical choir); (3) verses 12–13: the people; (4) verses 14–15: the priests; and (5) verses 16–18: the people.

God has delegated dominion over this world to humans (v. 16), not to make us more important or give us personal power, but to give us opportunity to serve him. People rule over Earth by divine right (cf. Gen. 1:28), but we are deputized to be responsible to and called to obey God alone. Part of our submission involves praising him as the true and only God (v. 18).

Psalm 116

116:1
q Ps 18:1 r Ps 66:19

1 I love the LORD, q for he heard my voice;
  he heard my cry r for mercy.

116:2
s Ps 40:1

2 Because he turned his ear s to me,
  I will call on him as long as I live.

116:3
t Ps 18:4-5

3 The cords of death t entangled me,
  the anguish of the grave a came upon me;
  I was overcome by trouble and sorrow.

116:4
u Ps 118:5
v Ps 22:20

4 Then I called on the name u of the LORD:
  "O LORD, save me! v"

116:5
w Ezr 9:15; Ne 9:8;
Ps 103:8; 145:17

5 The LORD is gracious and righteous; w
  our God is full of compassion.

116:6
x Ps 19:7; 79:8

6 The LORD protects the simplehearted;
  when I was in great need, x he saved me.

116:7
y Jer 6:16;
Mt 11:29 z Ps 13:6

7 Be at rest y once more, O my soul,
  for the LORD has been good z to you.

116:8
a Ps 56:13

8 For you, O LORD, have delivered my soul a from death,
  my eyes from tears,
  my feet from stumbling,

116:9
b Ps 27:13
116:10
c 2Co 4:13*

9 that I may walk before the LORD
  in the land of the living. b

10 I believed; c therefore b I said,
  "I am greatly afflicted."

116:11
d Ro 3:4

11 And in my dismay I said,
  "All men are liars." d

12 How can I repay the LORD
  for all his goodness to me?

116:13
e Ps 16:5; 80:18
116:14
f Ps 22:25; Jnh 2:9

13 I will lift up the cup of salvation
  and call on the name e of the LORD.

14 I will fulfill my vows f to the LORD
  in the presence of all his people.

116:15
g Ps 72:14

15 Precious in the sight g of the LORD
  is the death of his saints.

116:16
h Ps 119:125;
143:12 i Ps 86:16

16 O LORD, truly I am your servant; h
  I am your servant, the son of your maidservant c; i
  you have freed me from my chains.

16:17
j Lev 7:12; Ps 50:14

17 I will sacrifice a thank offering j to you
  and call on the name of the LORD.

18 I will fulfill my vows to the LORD
  in the presence of all his people,

116:19
k Ps 96:8; 135:2

19 in the courts k of the house of the LORD—
  in your midst, O Jerusalem.

Praise the LORD. d

---

a 3 Hebrew *Sheol*   b 10 Or *believed even when*   c 16 Or *servant, your faithful son*   d 19 Hebrew *Hallelu Yah*

Psalm 116

One of the Egyptian Hallel psalms (see "There and Then" for Ps. 113), Psalm 116 is an individual hymn of thanksgiving, also containing prayer, lament, confidence, and vows. The psalmist thanked God for delivering him from some great trouble, alternating in focus between the experience of deliverance and outbursts of thanksgiving.

In his need the psalmist clung stubbornly to God's promises, asking in response to his faithfulness, "How can I repay the LORD for all his goodness to me?" (v. 12). The answer is implied: There is no way we can "pay" or "repay" God. But the psalmist still brought a thank offering, calling again on God's name (v. 17; cf. v. 2)—this time in praise of his promise keeping. The public presentation of the offering (v. 14) wasn't for show

Psalm 117

[1] Praise the LORD, all you nations;[l]
extol him, all you peoples.
[2] For great is his love toward us,
and the faithfulness of the LORD[m] endures forever.

Praise the LORD.[a]

Psalm 118

[1] Give thanks to the LORD,[n] for he is good;
his love endures forever.[o]

[2] Let Israel say:[p]
"His love endures forever."
[3] Let the house of Aaron say:
"His love endures forever."
[4] Let those who fear the LORD say:
"His love endures forever."

[5] In my anguish[q] I cried to the LORD,
and he answered[r] by setting me free.
[6] The LORD is with me;[s] I will not be afraid.
What can man do to me?[t]
[7] The LORD is with me; he is my helper.[u]
I will look in triumph on my enemies.[v]

[8] It is better to take refuge in the LORD[w]
than to trust in man.[x]
[9] It is better to take refuge in the LORD
than to trust in princes.[y]

[10] All the nations surrounded me,
but in the name of the LORD I cut them off.[z]
[11] They surrounded me[a] on every side,[b]
but in the name of the LORD I cut them off.
[12] They swarmed around me like bees,[c]

[a] 2 Hebrew *Hallelu Yah*

Side references

117:1 *l* Ro 15:11*
117:2 *m* Ps 100:5
118:1 *n* 1Ch 16:8
o Ps 106:1; 136:1
118:2 *p* Ps 115:9
118:5 *q* Ps 120:1
r Ps 18:19
118:6 *s* Heb 13:6*
t Ps 27:1; 56:4
118:7 *u* Ps 54:4 *v* Ps 59:10
118:8 *w* Ps 40:4 *x* Jer 17:5
118:9 *y* Ps 146:3
118:10 *z* Ps 18:40
118:11 *a* Ps 88:17 *b* Ps 3:6
118:12 *c* Dt 1:44

---

but for encouraging the godly. How do you encourage other Christians to trust in—and then to thank and praise—the Lord?

Psalm 117

Psalm 117 has the distinction of being the shortest psalm in the Psalter and the shortest chapter in the Bible. Its theme of praise concerns God's love, and its universal appeal makes it a jewel. Paul quoted verse 1 in Romans 15:11—revealing that God's love and plan has always included Gentiles, a promise made early on to the patriarchs (Gen. 12:3; Gal. 3:8).

"Praise the LORD" in the Egyptian Hallel psalms (see "There and Then" for Ps. 113) was a call and invitation usually directed to the covenant community. This time the psalmist called on the "nations" and "peoples" to praise God. The reason for the appeal for universal praise lay, though, in God's loving, faithful dealings with his covenant people. His love is deep, high, and long (Rom. 8:39; Eph. 3:18). In Christ that love has been powerfully demonstrated to both Jews and Gentiles, so that all may praise him (Rom. 15:8–9). Praise the Lord!

Psalm 118

Psalm 118 is the last of the collection known as the Egyptian Hallel Psalms (see "There and Then" for Ps. 113). It was used during the Passover Seder (ceremonial meal) and the Feast of Tabernacles. The psalm has features of both individual and communal (collective, public) thanksgiving, and it also may have been a thanksgiving liturgy used in religious processions. The suggestion has been made that this is an old psalm that received a new interpretation after the exile. If so, with Christ's coming its significance has been enhanced even more.

When life's foundations seem shaky, what holds things together for you? Verses 22–23, referring to the king, also apply to Jesus' suffering and glory (cf. Matt. 21:42; Mark 12:10–11; Luke 20:17; Acts 4:11; Eph. 2:20; 1 Peter 2:7). Jesus was rejected by people, but the Father demonstrated his acceptance of the Son by making him the "chief cornerstone" (an important stone holding together two rows of stones in a corner; Eph. 2:20). If the cornerstone of our life is intact, our "building" may groan and sway, but it won't topple.

118:12
d Ps 58:9

118:13
e Ps 86:17; 140:4
118:14
f Ex 15:2 g Isa 12:2

118:15
h Ps 68:3 i Ps 89:13

118:17
j Ps 6:5; Hab 1:12
k Ex 15:6; Ps 73:28

118:18
l 2Co 6:9
118:19
m Isa 26:2

118:20
n Ps 24:7; Isa 35:8;
Rev 22:14
118:21
o Ps 116:1

118:22
p Mt 21:42;
Mk 12:10;
Lk 20:17*;
Ac 4:11*; 1Pe 2:7*

118:26
q Mt 21:9*;
Mk 11:9*;
Lk 13:35*; 19:38*;
Jn 12:13*

118:27
r 1Pe 2:9

118:28
s Isa 25:1 t Ex 15:2

119:1
u Ps 128:1

119:2
v Dt 6:5

but they died out as quickly as burning thorns; [d]
in the name of the LORD I cut them off.

13 I was pushed back and about to fall,
but the LORD helped me. [e]
14 The LORD is my strength [f] and my song;
he has become my salvation. [g]

15 Shouts of joy [h] and victory
resound in the tents of the righteous:
"The LORD's right hand [i] has done mighty things!
16 The LORD's right hand is lifted high;
the LORD's right hand has done mighty things!"

17 I will not die [j] but live,
and will proclaim [k] what the LORD has done.
18 The LORD has chastened me severely,
but he has not given me over to death. [l]

19 Open for me the gates [m] of righteousness;
I will enter and give thanks to the LORD.
20 This is the gate of the LORD
through which the righteous may enter. [n]
21 I will give you thanks, for you answered me; [o]
you have become my salvation.

22 The stone the builders rejected
has become the capstone; [p]
23 the LORD has done this,
and it is marvelous in our eyes.
24 This is the day the LORD has made;
let us rejoice and be glad in it.

25 O LORD, save us;
O LORD, grant us success.
26 Blessed is he who comes [q] in the name of the LORD.
From the house of the LORD we bless you. [a]
27 The LORD is God,
and he has made his light shine [r] upon us.
With boughs in hand, join in the festal procession
up [b] to the horns of the altar.

28 You are my God, and I will give you thanks;
you are my God, [s] and I will exalt [t] you.

29 Give thanks to the LORD, for he is good;
his love endures forever.

Psalm 119 [c]

א Aleph

1 Blessed are they whose ways are blameless,
who walk [u] according to the law of the LORD.
2 Blessed are they who keep his statutes
and seek him with all their heart. [v]

---

a 26 The Hebrew is plural.   b 27 Or Bind the festal sacrifice with ropes / and take it   c This psalm is
an acrostic poem; the verses of each stanza begin with the same letter of the Hebrew alphabet.

Psalm 119

〰 The longest psalm in the Psalter, Psalm 119 is
well known for its teaching on God's law. But its beauty

lies not only in the psalmist's devotion to the law but in
his absolute commitment to God. Most likely writing in
the postexilic era, he knew oppression firsthand. He had

³They do nothing wrong;ʷ
  they walk in his ways.
⁴You have laid down precepts
  that are to be fully obeyed.
⁵Oh, that my ways were steadfast
  in obeying your decrees!
⁶Then I would not be put to shame
  when I consider all your commands.
⁷I will praise you with an upright heart
  as I learn your righteous laws.
⁸I will obey your decrees;
  do not utterly forsake me.

119:3
ʷ 1Jn 3:9; 5:18

been surrounded by wickedness, pursued by the arrogant, and humbled by sorrow and disgrace. Still, his refuge was in God. This is a psalm, not just of law, but of love.

📖 The psalmist used eight synonyms for God's law, all with different nuances of meaning. One or them, "word" (or "promise") refers to *anything* God has spo-ken, commanded, or promised (e.g., v. 140). In Matthew 4:4 Jesus, quoting from Deuteronomy 8:3, reminded Satan: "Man does not live on bread alone, but on every word that comes from the mouth of God." Do you "hang on to" Jesus' words? Is Scripture as essential to you each day as your meals?

119:1–8

Eight Terms for God's Law in Psalm 119

Psalm 119 is an alphabetic acrostic psalm (as are 111 and 112), consisting of 22 stanzas of eight verses each. Bible scholars have described it as "a monotonous repetition, which is, nevertheless, impressive even in its repetitiveness" and "a massive intellectual achievement." In it the psalmist uses eight words for God's law:

Word	Hebrew	Occurs	Meaning
• law	*Torah*	25 times	Can be interpreted in a broad or narrow sense. Broadly, it refers to any "instruction" flowing from the revelation of God as the basis for life and action, including both Mosaic and prophetic messages. Narrowly, it denotes the Torah of Moses, whether the Pentateuch (first five books of the Bible), the priestly law, or the Deuteronomic law.
• word	*Dabar*	24 times	Any word that proceeds from the mouth of the Lord is *dabar*, whether it pertains to the Ten Commandments, the Law of Moses, or the word revealed through the prophets.
• laws	*Mispatim*	23 times	In general, the term refers to cases or legal decisions pertaining to particular legal issues. Here the word denotes the revelation given by the supreme Judge, God himself. The verdicts he renders are authoritative and liberating (cf. "righteous laws," vv. 7,62,106,164).
• statute(s)	*Edut/Edot*	23 times	Derived from a term for "witness" or "testify" (cf. Ex. 31:18; 25:22). The tablets and the ark were symbols of the covenant relationship. Therefore, *testimony* is often synonymous with *covenant*. Observance of the *statutes* signifies loyalty to the terms of the covenant made between the Lord and Israel.
• command(s)	*Miswah/ Miswot*	22 times	A frequent designation for anything that the Lord, the covenant God, has ordered.
• decrees	*Huqqim*	21 times	Derived from a word meaning "engrave" or "inscribe." God, being the Author of his decrees, reveals his royal sovereignty by establishing his divine will in nature and in the covenant community.
• precepts	*Piqqudim*	21 times	This word only occurs in the psalms and appears to be synonymous with *covenant* and with God's revelation. The root connotes the authority to determine the relationship between the speaker and the object. So the Lord commands *precepts*, and our response is to guard, love, choose out, long for, respond positively to, seek, meditate on, and gain understanding from them, so as never to forget, forsake, or stray.
• word *or* promise	*Imrah*	19 times	Anything God has spoken, commanded, or promised.

Source: Expositor's Bible Commentary, Psalms (1990:737–738)

‫ב‬ Beth

119:9
x 2Ch 6:16
119:10
y 2Ch 15:15
z ver 21,118

9 How can a young man keep his way pure?
    By living according to your word. x
10 I seek you with all my heart; y
    do not let me stray from your commands. z

119:11
a Ps 37:31;
Lk 2:19,51

11 I have hidden your word in my heart a
    that I might not sin against you.

119:12
b ver 26

12 Praise be to you, O Lord;
    teach me your decrees. b

119:13
c Ps 40:9

13 With my lips I recount
    all the laws that come from your mouth. c
14 I rejoice in following your statutes
    as one rejoices in great riches.

119:15
d Ps 1:2

15 I meditate on your precepts d
    and consider your ways.

119:16
e Ps 1:2

16 I delight e in your decrees;
    I will not neglect your word.

‫ג‬ Gimel

119:17
f Ps 13:6; 116:7

17 Do good to your servant, f and I will live;
    I will obey your word.
18 Open my eyes that I may see
    wonderful things in your law.

119:19
g 1Ch 29:15;
Ps 39:12; 2Co 5:6;
Heb 11:13
119:20
h Ps 42:2; 84:2
i Ps 63:1

19 I am a stranger on earth; g
    do not hide your commands from me.
20 My soul is consumed h with longing
    for your laws i at all times.

119:21
j ver 10
119:22
k Ps 39:8

21 You rebuke the arrogant, who are cursed
    and who stray j from your commands.
22 Remove from me scorn k and contempt,
    for I keep your statutes.
23 Though rulers sit together and slander me,
    your servant will meditate on your decrees.
24 Your statutes are my delight;
    they are my counselors.

‫ד‬ Daleth

119:25
l Ps 44:25
m Ps 143:11

25 I am laid low in the dust; l
    preserve my life m according to your word.

119:26
n Ps 25:4; 27:11;
86:11
119:27
o Ps 145:5
119:28
p Ps 107:26
q Ps 20:2; 1Pe 5:10

26 I recounted my ways and you answered me;
    teach me your decrees. n
27 Let me understand the teaching of your precepts;
    then I will meditate on your wonders. o
28 My soul is weary with sorrow; p
    strengthen me q according to your word.
29 Keep me from deceitful ways;
    be gracious to me through your law.
30 I have chosen the way of truth;
    I have set my heart on your laws.

119:31
r Dt 11:22

31 I hold fast r to your statutes, O Lord;
    do not let me be put to shame.
32 I run in the path of your commands,
    for you have set my heart free.

‫ה‬ He

119:33
s ver 12

33 Teach me, s O Lord, to follow your decrees;
    then I will keep them to the end.

34 Give me understanding, and I will keep your law
    and obey it with all my heart.
35 Direct me in the path of your commands,
    for there I find delight.
36 Turn my heart *t* toward your statutes
    and not toward selfish gain. *u*
37 Turn my eyes away from worthless things;
    preserve my life *v* according to your word. *a*
38 Fulfill your promise *w* to your servant,
    so that you may be feared.
39 Take away the disgrace I dread,
    for your laws are good.
40 How I long *x* for your precepts!
    Preserve my life in your righteousness.

ו Waw

41 May your unfailing love come to me, O LORD,
    your salvation according to your promise;
42 then I will answer *y* the one who taunts me,
    for I trust in your word.
43 Do not snatch the word of truth from my mouth,
    for I have put my hope in your laws.
44 I will always obey your law,
    for ever and ever.
45 I will walk about in freedom,
    for I have sought out your precepts.
46 I will speak of your statutes before kings *z*
    and will not be put to shame,
47 for I delight in your commands
    because I love them.
48 I lift up my hands to *b* your commands, which I love,
    and I meditate on your decrees.

ז Zayin

49 Remember your word to your servant,
    for you have given me hope.
50 My comfort in my suffering is this:
    Your promise preserves my life. *a*
51 The arrogant mock me *b* without restraint,
    but I do not turn *c* from your law.
52 I remember *d* your ancient laws, O LORD,
    and I find comfort in them.
53 Indignation grips me *e* because of the wicked,
    who have forsaken your law. *f*
54 Your decrees are the theme of my song
    wherever I lodge.
55 In the night I remember *g* your name, O LORD,
    and I will keep your law.
56 This has been my practice:
    I obey your precepts.

ח Heth

57 You are my portion, *h* O LORD;
    I have promised to obey your words.
58 I have sought your face with all my heart;

---

a 37 Two manuscripts of the Masoretic Text and Dead Sea Scrolls; most manuscripts of the Masoretic Text *life in your way*   *b 48* Or *for*

119:36
t 1Ki 8:58
u Eze 33:31;
Mk 7:21-22;
Lk 12:15; Heb 13:5

119:37
v Ps 71:20;
Isa 33:15
119:38
w 2Sa 7:25

119:40
x ver 20

119:42
y Pr 27:11

119:46
z Mt 10:18;
Ac 26:1-2

119:50
a Ro 15:4
119:51
b Jer 20:7
c ver 157;
Job 23:11; Ps 44:18
119:52
d Ps 103:18

119:53
e Ezr 9:3 *f* Ps 89:30

119:55
g Ps 63:6

119:57
h Ps 16:5; La 3:24

119:58
i 1Ki 13:6
j ver 41
119:59
k Lk 15:17-18

be gracious to me[i] according to your promise.[j]
59 I have considered my ways[k]
    and have turned my steps to your statutes.
60 I will hasten and not delay
    to obey your commands.

119:61
l Ps 140:5
119:62
m Ac 16:25

61 Though the wicked bind me with ropes,
    I will not forget[l] your law.
62 At midnight[m] I rise to give you thanks
    for your righteous laws.

119:63
n Ps 101:6-7

63 I am a friend to all who fear you,[n]
    to all who follow your precepts.

119:64
o Ps 33:5

64 The earth is filled with your love,[o] O Lord;
    teach me your decrees.

ת Teth

65 Do good to your servant
    according to your word, O Lord.
66 Teach me knowledge and good judgment,
    for I believe in your commands.

119:67
p Jer 31:18-19;
Heb 12:11

67 Before I was afflicted I went astray,[p]
    but now I obey your word.

119:68
q Ps 106:1; 107:1;
Mt 19:17 *r* ver 12
119:69
s Job 13:4; Ps 109:2

68 You are good,[q] and what you do is good;
    teach me your decrees.[r]
69 Though the arrogant have smeared me with lies,[s]
    I keep your precepts with all my heart.

119:70
t Ps 17:10; Isa 6:10;
Ac 28:27

70 Their hearts are callous[t] and unfeeling,
    but I delight in your law.
71 It was good for me to be afflicted
    so that I might learn your decrees.

119:72
u Ps 19:10;
Pr 8:10-11, 19

72 The law from your mouth is more precious to me
    than thousands of pieces of silver and gold.[u]

י Yodh

119:73
v Job 10:8;
Ps 100:3; 138:8;
139:13-16
119:74
w Ps 34:2

73 Your hands made me[v] and formed me;
    give me understanding to learn your commands.
74 May those who fear you rejoice[w] when they see me,
    for I have put my hope in your word.

119:75
x Heb 12:5-11

75 I know, O Lord, that your laws are righteous,
    and in faithfulness[x] you have afflicted me.
76 May your unfailing love be my comfort,
    according to your promise to your servant.

119:77
y ver 41

77 Let your compassion[y] come to me that I may live,
    for your law is my delight.

119:78
z Jer 50:32
a ver 86,161

78 May the arrogant[z] be put to shame for wronging me without cause;[a]
    but I will meditate on your precepts.
79 May those who fear you turn to me,
    those who understand your statutes.
80 May my heart be blameless toward your decrees,
    that I may not be put to shame.

כ Kaph

119:81
b Ps 84:2

81 My soul faints[b] with longing for your salvation,
    but I have put my hope in your word.

119:82
c Ps 69:3; La 2:11

82 My eyes fail,[c] looking for your promise;
    I say, "When will you comfort me?"
83 Though I am like a wineskin in the smoke,
    I do not forget your decrees.

84 How long *d* must your servant wait?
  When will you punish my persecutors?
85 The arrogant dig pitfalls *e* for me,
  contrary to your law.
86 All your commands are trustworthy; *f*
  help me, *g* for men persecute me without cause. *h*
87 They almost wiped me from the earth,
  but I have not forsaken *i* your precepts.
88 Preserve my life according to your love,
  and I will obey the statutes of your mouth.

ל *Lamedh*

89 Your word, O LORD, is eternal; *j*
  it stands firm in the heavens.
90 Your faithfulness *k* continues through all generations;
  you established the earth, and it endures. *l*
91 Your laws endure *m* to this day,
  for all things serve you.
92 If your law had not been my delight,
  I would have perished in my affliction.
93 I will never forget your precepts,
  for by them you have preserved my life.
94 Save me, for I am yours;
  I have sought out your precepts.
95 The wicked are waiting to destroy me,
  but I will ponder your statutes.
96 To all perfection I see a limit;
  but your commands are boundless.

מ *Mem*

97 Oh, how I love your law!
  I meditate *n* on it all day long.
98 Your commands make me wiser *o* than my enemies,
  for they are ever with me.
99 I have more insight than all my teachers,
  for I meditate on your statutes.
100 I have more understanding than the elders,
  for I obey your precepts. *p*
101 I have kept my feet *q* from every evil path
  so that I might obey your word.
102 I have not departed from your laws,
  for you yourself have taught me.
103 How sweet are your words to my taste,
  sweeter than honey *r* to my mouth! *s*
104 I gain understanding from your precepts;
  therefore I hate every wrong path. *t*

נ *Nun*

105 Your word is a lamp to my feet
  and a light *u* for my path.
106 I have taken an oath *v* and confirmed it,
  that I will follow your righteous laws.
107 I have suffered much;
  preserve my life, O LORD, according to your word.
108 Accept, O LORD, the willing praise of my mouth, *w*
  and teach me your laws.
109 Though I constantly take my life in my hands, *x*
  I will not forget your law.

119:84
d Ps 39:4; Rev 6:10
119:85
e Ps 35:7; Jer 18:20,22
119:86
f Ps 35:19
g Ps 109:26
h ver 78
119:87
i Isa 58:2

119:89
j Mt 24:34-35; 1Pe 1:25
119:90
k Ps 36:5 *l* Ps 148:6; Ecc 1:4
119:91
m Jer 33:25

119:97
n Ps 1:2
119:98
o Dt 4:6

119:100
p Job 32:7-9
119:101
q Pr 1:15

119:103
r Ps 19:10; Pr 8:11
s Pr 24:13-14
119:104
t ver 128

119:105
u Pr 6:23
119:106
v Ne 10:29

119:108
w Hos 14:2; Heb 13:15
119:109
x Jdg 12:3; Job 13:14

119:110
y Ps 140:5; 141:9
z ver 10

119:112
a ver 33

119:113
b Jas 1:8

119:114
c Ps 32:7; 91:1
d ver 74
119:115
e Ps 6:8; 139:19;
Mt 7:23

119:116
f Ps 54:4 g Ps 25:2;
Ro 5:5; 9:33

119:119
h Eze 22:18,19

119:120
i Hab 3:16

119:122
j Job 17:3

119:123
k ver 82

119:124
l ver 12
119:125
m Ps 116:16

119:127
n Ps 19:10

119:128
o ver 104,163

119:130
p Pr 6:23 q Ps 19:7

119:131
r Ps 42:1 s ver 20

119:132
t Ps 25:16; 106:4

119:133
u Ps 17:5
v Ps 19:13; Ro 6:12
119:134
w Ps 142:6; Lk 1:74

119:135
x Nu 6:25; Ps 4:6

110 The wicked have set a snare[y] for me,
   but I have not strayed[z] from your precepts.
111 Your statutes are my heritage forever;
   they are the joy of my heart.
112 My heart is set on keeping your decrees
   to the very end.[a]

ס Samekh

113 I hate double-minded men,[b]
   but I love your law.
114 You are my refuge and my shield;[c]
   I have put my hope[d] in your word.
115 Away from me,[e] you evildoers,
   that I may keep the commands of my God!
116 Sustain me[f] according to your promise, and I will live;
   do not let my hopes be dashed.[g]
117 Uphold me, and I will be delivered;
   I will always have regard for your decrees.
118 You reject all who stray from your decrees,
   for their deceitfulness is in vain.
119 All the wicked of the earth you discard like dross;[h]
   therefore I love your statutes.
120 My flesh trembles[i] in fear of you;
   I stand in awe of your laws.

ע Ayin

121 I have done what is righteous and just;
   do not leave me to my oppressors.
122 Ensure your servant's well-being;[j]
   let not the arrogant oppress me.
123 My eyes fail, looking for your salvation,
   looking for your righteous promise.[k]
124 Deal with your servant according to your love
   and teach me your decrees.[l]
125 I am your servant;[m] give me discernment
   that I may understand your statutes.
126 It is time for you to act, O LORD;
   your law is being broken.
127 Because I love your commands
   more than gold,[n] more than pure gold,
128 and because I consider all your precepts right,
   I hate every wrong path.[o]

פ Pe

129 Your statutes are wonderful;
   therefore I obey them.
130 The unfolding of your words gives light;[p]
   it gives understanding to the simple.[q]
131 I open my mouth and pant,[r]
   longing for your commands.[s]
132 Turn to me and have mercy[t] on me,
   as you always do to those who love your name.
133 Direct my footsteps according to your word;[u]
   let no sin rule[v] over me.
134 Redeem me from the oppression of men,[w]
   that I may obey your precepts.
135 Make your face shine[x] upon your servant
   and teach me your decrees.

136 Streams of tears[y] flow from my eyes,
  for your law is not obeyed.[z]

צ *Tsadhe*

137 Righteous are you,[a] O LORD,
  and your laws are right.[b]
138 The statutes you have laid down are righteous;[c]
  they are fully trustworthy.
139 My zeal wears me out,[d]
  for my enemies ignore your words.
140 Your promises have been thoroughly tested,[e]
  and your servant loves them.
141 Though I am lowly and despised,[f]
  I do not forget your precepts.
142 Your righteousness is everlasting
  and your law is true.[g]
143 Trouble and distress have come upon me,
  but your commands are my delight.
144 Your statutes are forever right;
  give me understanding[h] that I may live.

ק *Qoph*

145 I call with all my heart; answer me, O LORD,
  and I will obey your decrees.
146 I call out to you; save me
  and I will keep your statutes.
147 I rise before dawn[i] and cry for help;
  I have put my hope in your word.
148 My eyes stay open through the watches of the night,[j]
  that I may meditate on your promises.
149 Hear my voice in accordance with your love;
  preserve my life, O LORD, according to your laws.
150 Those who devise wicked schemes are near,
  but they are far from your law.
151 Yet you are near,[k] O LORD,
  and all your commands are true.[l]
152 Long ago I learned from your statutes
  that you established them to last forever.[m]

ר *Resh*

153 Look upon my suffering[n] and deliver me,
  for I have not forgotten[o] your law.
154 Defend my cause[p] and redeem me;[q]
  preserve my life according to your promise.
155 Salvation is far from the wicked,
  for they do not seek out[r] your decrees.
156 Your compassion is great, O LORD;
  preserve my life[s] according to your laws.
157 Many are the foes who persecute me,[t]
  but I have not turned from your statutes.
158 I look on the faithless with loathing,[u]
  for they do not obey your word.
159 See how I love your precepts;
  preserve my life, O LORD, according to your love.
160 All your words are true;
  all your righteous laws are eternal.

שׂ *Sin and Shin*

161 Rulers persecute me[v] without cause,

119:136 y Jer 9:1,18 z Eze 9:4
119:137 a Ezr 9:15; Jer 12:1 b Ne 9:13
119:138 c Ps 19:7
119:139 d Ps 69:9; Jn 2:17
119:140 e Ps 12:6
119:141 f Ps 22:6
119:142 g Ps 19:7
119:144 h Ps 19:9
119:147 i Ps 5:3; 57:8; 108:2
119:148 j Ps 63:6
119:151 k Ps 34:18; 145:18 l ver 142
119:152 m Lk 21:33
119:153 n La 5:1 o Pr 3:1
119:154 p Mic 7:9 q 1Sa 24:15
119:155 r Job 5:4
119:156 s 2Sa 24:14
119:157 t Ps 7:1
119:158 u Ps 139:21
119:161 v 1Sa 24:11

but my heart trembles at your word.

119:162
w 1Sa 30:16

162 I rejoice in your promise
   like one who finds great spoil. *w*

163 I hate and abhor falsehood
   but I love your law.

164 Seven times a day I praise you
   for your righteous laws.

119:165
x Pr 3:2;
Isa 26:3,12; 32:17

165 Great peace *x* have they who love your law,
   and nothing can make them stumble.

119:166
y Ge 49:18

166 I wait for your salvation, *y* O LORD,
   and I follow your commands.

167 I obey your statutes,
   for I love them greatly.

119:168
z Pr 5:21

168 I obey your precepts and your statutes,
   for all my ways are known *z* to you.

119:169
a Ps 18:6

ת *Taw*

169 May my cry come *a* before you, O LORD;
   give me understanding according to your word.

119:170
b Ps 28:2 c Ps 31:2

170 May my supplication come *b* before you;
   deliver me *c* according to your promise.

119:171
d Ps 51:15
e Ps 94:12

171 May my lips overflow with praise, *d*
   for you teach me *e* your decrees.

172 May my tongue sing of your word,
   for all your commands are righteous.

119:173
f Ps 37:24
g Jos 24:22

173 May your hand be ready to help *f* me,
   for I have chosen *g* your precepts.

119:174
h ver 166

174 I long for your salvation, *h* O LORD,
   and your law is my delight.

119:175
i Isa 55:3

175 Let me live *i* that I may praise you,
   and may your laws sustain me.

119:176
j Isa 53:6

176 I have strayed like a lost sheep. *j*
   Seek your servant,
   for I have not forgotten your commands.

Psalm 120

A song of ascents.

120:1
k Ps 102:2; Jnh 2:2

1 I call on the LORD in my distress, *k*
   and he answers me.

120:2
l Pr 12:22 m Ps 52:4

2 Save me, O LORD, from lying lips *l*
   and from deceitful tongues. *m*

3 What will he do to you,
   and what more besides, O deceitful tongue?

120:4
n Ps 45:5

4 He will punish you with a warrior's sharp arrows, *n*
   with burning coals of the broom tree.

Psalm 120

Psalms 120–134 form a collection called the "Songs of Ascents." They are also the major portion of the "Great Hallel" psalms (120–136; see "There and Then" for Ps. 113). The meaning of "A song of ascents" in these psalms' headings isn't clear. Some link this collection of 15 songs with the 15 steps of the temple, suggesting that worshipers sang them as they ascended the stairs. More likely, though, the psalms were sung in the three annual festival processions, as the pilgrims jour-

neyed upward toward Jerusalem.

The psalmist reminded the Lord that he had long suffered in his situation of living "among those who hate peace" (v. 6). As "a man of peace" (v. 7), he longed for the establishment of God's peace (cf. 119:165; Matt. 5:9; Rom. 12:18; James 3:17–18). The godly speak words of peace, but the ungodly stir up strife and discord (cf. Gal. 5:19–21; James 4:1–2). What does it mean to be a man or woman of peace during a time of war or conflict? How can you become a "peacemaker" (Matt. 5:9)?

5 Woe to me that I dwell in Meshech,
that I live among the tents of Kedar![o]
6 Too long have I lived
among those who hate peace.
7 I am a man of peace;
but when I speak, they are for war.

120:5
[o] Ge 25:13; Jer 49:28

Psalm 121

A song of ascents.

1 I lift up my eyes to the hills—
where does my help come from?
2 My help comes from the LORD,
the Maker of heaven and earth.[p]

3 He will not let your foot slip—
he who watches over you will not slumber;
4 indeed, he who watches over Israel
will neither slumber nor sleep.

5 The LORD watches over[q] you—
the LORD is your shade at your right hand;
6 the sun[r] will not harm you by day,
nor the moon by night.

7 The LORD will keep you from all harm[s]—
he will watch over your life;
8 the LORD will watch over your coming and going
both now and forevermore.[t]

121:2
[p] Ps 115:15; 124:8

121:5
[q] Isa 25:4

121:6
[r] Ps 91:5; Isa 49:10; Rev 7:16

121:7
[s] Ps 41:2; 91:10-12

121:8
[t] Dt 28:6

Psalm 122

A song of ascents. Of David.

1 I rejoiced with those who said to me,
"Let us go to the house of the LORD."
2 Our feet are standing
in your gates, O Jerusalem.

3 Jerusalem is built like a city
that is closely compacted together.
4 That is where the tribes go up,
the tribes of the LORD,
to praise the name of the LORD

Psalm 121

This beautiful and encouraging psalm reads like a dialogue, a two-way conversation between two parties or between the psalmist and his inner self. In structure, it represents a "stairlike" parallelism (God is the Creator, the Guardian of Israel, as well as *your* Guardian), followed by a blessing.

Pagans "permitted" their gods to sleep, but the God of Israel isn't like any other god—he doesn't need to recreate, rest, or eat. Regardless of life's happenings, whether we are at work or at home, asleep or awake, God is "there" for us.

Psalm 122

In addition to being one of the "Songs of Ascents" (see "There and Then" for Ps. 120), Psalm 122 is also a song of Zion. Songs of Zion have much in common with royal psalms. Both celebrated the glories associated with Jerusalem: temple and kingship. But the songs of Zion proclaimed the city's glories in universal language: Zion (Jerusalem) was the center of God's judgment and peace (vv. 5–9). Psalm 122 expresses the joy of Zion from the perspective of a pilgrim who had traveled there to worship.

Pilgrimages were held three times annually, during the feasts of Passover, Firstfruits, and Tabernacles. As the psalmist looked at Jerusalem and stood within her gates, he rejoiced. His joy spilled over into praise, which instigated hope, which in turn led him to pray for God's kingship on Earth. Think about this progression from joy to praise to hope to prayer. Have you experienced the same chain reaction/response?

according to the statute given to Israel.
5 There the thrones for judgment stand,
　the thrones of the house of David.

122:6
u Ps 51:18

6 Pray for the peace of Jerusalem:
　"May those who love u you be secure.
7 May there be peace within your walls
　and security within your citadels."
8 For the sake of my brothers and friends,
　I will say, "Peace be within you."
9 For the sake of the house of the LORD our God,
　I will seek your prosperity. v

122:9
v Ne 2:10

Psalm 123

A song of ascents.

123:1
w Ps 11:4; 121:1;
141:8

1 I lift up my eyes to you,
　to you whose throne w is in heaven.
2 As the eyes of slaves look to the hand of their master,
　as the eyes of a maid look to the hand of her mistress,
so our eyes look to the LORD x our God,
　till he shows us his mercy.

123:2
x Ps 25:15

3 Have mercy on us, O LORD, have mercy on us,
　for we have endured much contempt.
4 We have endured much ridicule from the proud,
　much contempt from the arrogant.

Psalm 124

A song of ascents. Of David.

124:1
y Ps 129:1

1 If the LORD had not been on our side—
　let Israel say y —
2 if the LORD had not been on our side
　when men attacked us,
3 when their anger flared against us,
　they would have swallowed us alive;
4 the flood would have engulfed us,
　the torrent would have swept over us,
5 the raging waters
　would have swept us away.

Psalm 123

🕮 The life situation and date of composition are uncertain, but Psalm 123 reflects a time of persecution and/or oppression. The psalm is the humble prayer of God's people for relief and deliverance. In the opening statement the psalmist spoke as a representative of his community, as demonstrated by the first-person plurals used in the remainder of the psalm.

📖 Still today, we as God's children often find ourselves ridiculed by the self-important. The psalmist pictured the godly as slaves—but not to their critics. The beseeching eyes of verse 2 are a haunting simile, but these eyes are also expectant, fixed on the open hand of a good, kind master or mistress. Ours is a voluntary, hopeful servitude, because we know and trust our Lord. If he's for us, who can be against us (cf. Rom. 8:31)? And even if the arrogant *are* against us, what can they do to really harm us?

Psalm 124

🕮 Besides being one of the "Songs of Ascents" (see "There and Then" for Ps. 120), Psalm 124 is a communal thanksgiving psalm. The community of God's people reflected on the possible and real disasters from which the Lord had delivered them (vv. 1–5) as their ground for giving thanks (vv. 6–8).

📖 Is your Christian life characterized by hope? The psalmist repeated "If the LORD had not been on our side" for emphasis (cf. 129:1–2). The implication was that, because God *had* been with his people, they could hope (cf. Neh. 4:20). Old Testament believers were gratefully aware of God's presence, even though they hadn't yet seen the Messiah. In fact, the phrase "had been on our side" is the past tense of the Hebrew *Immanuel* ("God is with us")—one of Jesus' names!

⁶Praise be to the LORD,
who has not let us be torn by their teeth.
⁷We have escaped like a bird
out of the fowler's snare; ᶻ
the snare has been broken,
and we have escaped.
⁸Our help is in the name of the LORD,
the Maker of heaven ᵃ and earth.

Psalm 125

A song of ascents.

¹Those who trust in the LORD are like Mount Zion,
which cannot be shaken ᵇ but endures forever.
²As the mountains surround Jerusalem,
so the LORD surrounds ᶜ his people
both now and forevermore.

³The scepter of the wicked will not remain ᵈ
over the land allotted to the righteous,
for then the righteous might use
their hands to do evil. ᵉ

⁴Do good, O LORD, ᶠ to those who are good,
to those who are upright in heart. ᵍ
⁵But those who turn ʰ to crooked ways ⁱ
the LORD will banish with the evildoers.

Peace be upon Israel. ʲ

Psalm 126

A song of ascents.

¹When the LORD brought back ᵏ the captives to ᵃ Zion,
we were like men who dreamed. ᵇ
²Our mouths were filled with laughter,
our tongues with songs of joy. ˡ
Then it was said among the nations,
"The LORD has done great things ᵐ for them."
³The LORD has done great things for us,
and we are filled with joy. ⁿ

⁴Restore our fortunes, ᶜ O LORD,

ᵃ 1 Or LORD *restored the fortunes of*   ᵇ 1 Or *men restored to health*   ᶜ 4 Or *Bring back our captives*

Side notes:
124:7 ᶻ Ps 91:3; Pr 6:5
124:8 ᵃ Ge 1:1; Ps 121:2; 134:3
125:1 ᵇ Ps 46:5
125:2 ᶜ Ps 121:8; Zec 2:4-5
125:3 ᵈ Ps 89:22; Pr 22:8; Isa 14:5 ᵉ 1Sa 24:10; Ps 55:20
125:4 ᶠ Ps 119:68 ᵍ Ps 7:10; 36:10; 94:15
125:5 ʰ Job 23:11 ⁱ Pr 2:15; Isa 59:8 ʲ Ps 128:6
126:1 ᵏ Ps 85:1; Hos 6:11
126:2 ˡ Job 8:21; Ps 51:14 ᵐ Ps 71:19
126:3 ⁿ Isa 25:9

Psalm 125

Psalm 125 speaks of unshakable confidence in the Lord, by whose judgment the power of the wicked over the righteous will be removed. As a psalm of *communal confidence*, it conveys a deep trust in God's ability to care for his people's need (cf. Ps. 115; 129).

Mount Zion isn't the highest peak in the mountain range around Jerusalem. In fact, surrounded by mountains, the city is secure from ground attack on the basis of its natural defensibility. The psalmist compared God to the hills around Jerusalem and his people to Mount Zion.

Mountains suggest endurance, assurance, and protection. The highest peaks evoke awe and wonder. God was and is "around" his people (cf. 34:7; Zech.

2:3–5). What a beautiful picture of his encircling presence! What other word pictures, from the Bible or otherwise, make you feel secure in God? What is there about God that inspires you to worship him?

Psalm 126

In this psalm the community reflected with thanksgiving on God's gracious acts in the past, while praying for his continued goodness. The situation appears related to the return of the small exilic community to the land after 538 B.C. The returnees' joy was tempered by their harsh life in Canaan. They prayed that their restoration would be "like streams in the Negev" (v. 4). The wadis, or gullies, in this area are usually bone-dry; but when it rains the water gushes down with great force, a sudden and powerful unleashing of blessing.

951

126:4
o Isa 35:6; 43:19
126:5
p Isa 35:10

like streams in the Negev. *o*
⁵ Those who sow in tears
will reap with songs of joy. *p*
⁶ He who goes out weeping,
carrying seed to sow,
will return with songs of joy,
carrying sheaves with him.

Psalm 127

A song of ascents. Of Solomon.

127:1
q Ps 78:69
r Ps 121:4

¹ Unless the LORD builds *q* the house,
its builders labor in vain.
Unless the LORD watches *r* over the city,
the watchmen stand guard in vain.

127:2
s Ge 3:17
t Job 11:18

² In vain you rise early
and stay up late,
toiling for food *s* to eat—
for he grants sleep *t* to *a* those he loves.

127:3
u Ge 33:5

³ Sons are a heritage from the LORD,
children a reward *u* from him.
⁴ Like arrows in the hands of a warrior
are sons born in one's youth.
⁵ Blessed is the man
whose quiver is full of them.

127:5
v Pr 27:11

They will not be put to shame
when they contend with their enemies *v* in the gate.

Psalm 128

A song of ascents.

128:1
w Ps 112:1
x Ps 119:1-3
128:2
y Isa 3:10
z Ecc 8:12
128:3
a Eze 19:10

¹ Blessed are all who fear the LORD, *w*
who walk in his ways. *x*
² You will eat the fruit of your labor; *y*
blessings and prosperity *z* will be yours.
³ Your wife will be like a fruitful vine *a*

a 2 Or *eat— / for while they sleep he provides for*

📖 Have you become weary in doing what's right, or do you know someone else who has (2 Thess. 3:13)? This kind of burnout isn't uncommon for people in helping professions, like missionaries, pastors, or those who serve in Christian organizations that minister to the needy (cf. 2 Cor. 11:27–28). Pray today that God will unleash a sudden blessing for those who may be feeling worn out or overwhelmed while participating in God's work in the world. E-mail or call a struggling worker with a word of encouragement from this psalm.

Psalm 127

📖 Life's pointlessness and God's blessing contrast in this wisdom psalm. The psalmist declared the anxiety of life without God, while at the same time encouraging the godly to trust him in all areas of life. Psalm 127 is closely connected to Psalm 128. In Jewish practice, it's recited as part of a thanksgiving service after the birth of a child.

As a "song of ascents" (see "There and Then" for Ps. 120), this psalm reminded the pilgrims on their way to Jerusalem that all of life's securities and blessings are gifts from God (cf. Deut. 28:1–14). The heading also attributes Psalm 127 to Solomon. If Solomon wasn't the author (not all witnesses ascribe it to him), it's easy to see why some have thought him so.

📖 In the wake of 9/11, American (and international) airports, factories, government offices, arenas, and other venues expend considerable energy ensuring security from possible assault. The psalmist, familiar with the anxiety of a nervous population, encouraged people with the knowledge that God himself guarded the city (cf. 121:3–8). Does the knowledge of God's care affect the quality of your night's sleep? Or does worry rob you of this blessing? Remember, Jesus instructed his disciples to place their worries squarely on God's capable shoulders (cf. Matt. 6:25–34).

Psalm 128

📖 Like Psalm 127, this is a wisdom psalm. It describes the godly individual who is blessed by the Lord.

within your house;
your sons will be like olive shoots[b]
around your table.
4 Thus is the man blessed
who fears the LORD.

5 May the LORD bless you from Zion[c]
all the days of your life;
may you see the prosperity of Jerusalem,
6   and may you live to see your children's children. [d]

Peace be upon Israel. [e]

Psalm 129

A song of ascents.

1 They have greatly oppressed me from my youth[f]—
let Israel say[g]—
2 they have greatly oppressed me from my youth,
but they have not gained the victory[h] over me.
3 Plowmen have plowed my back
and made their furrows long.
4 But the LORD is righteous;[i]
he has cut me free from the cords of the wicked.

5 May all who hate Zion[j]
be turned back in shame.[k]
6 May they be like grass on the roof,
which withers[l] before it can grow;
7 with it the reaper cannot fill his hands,
nor the one who gathers fill his arms.
8 May those who pass by not say,
"The blessing of the LORD be upon you;
we bless you[m] in the name of the LORD."

Psalm 130

A song of ascents.

1 Out of the depths[n] I cry to you, O LORD;
2   O Lord, hear my voice. [o]
Let your ears be attentive[p]
to my cry for mercy.

128:3
b Ps 52:8; 144:12

128:5
c Ps 20:2; 134:3

128:6
d Ge 50:23; Job 42:16
e Ps 125:5

129:1
f Ps 88:15; Hos 2:15 g Ps 124:1

129:2
h Mt 16:18

129:4
i Ps 119:137

129:5
j Mic 4:11 k Ps 71:13

129:6
l Ps 37:2

129:8
m Ru 2:4; Ps 118:26

130:1
n Ps 42:7; 69:2; La 3:55
130:2
o Ps 28:2
p 2Ch 6:40; Ps 64:1

The concluding benediction suggests that Psalm 128 originally served as a Levitical (priestly) word of instruction to those assembled for worship in Jerusalem. All Israelite men were required to attend the three great yearly festivals (Ex. 23:17; Deut. 16:16), though they normally were accompanied by their families (e.g., 1 Sam. 1; Luke 2:41–42).

An olive tree might not bear fruit for 40 years, but it's a symbol of long life and productivity. So are children in a household of faith. They are not like grass— here today, gone tomorrow. In the same manner as many of the proverbs, the psalmist expressed a "rule" that is generally true: The blessedness of the godly parent will extend to upcoming generations. What a privilege God gives us in this life to already taste the firstfruits of our heritage! If you are a Christian parent, how does this encourage you? Where do you need to improve?

Psalm 129

The writer's words pique our interest: "They have greatly oppressed me from my youth." Then in a disturbing but unforgettable metaphor, he likened his enemies to a farmer plowing fields with long rows. The "plowmen" were the warriors, the long furrows Israel's wounds and adversities, and the field Israel's "back" (v. 3). Yet God had intervened, snapping the yoke of the wicked. The "cords" (v. 4) picture the yoke as a whole, fastened to an animal's neck (cf. Jer. 27:2; 30:8).

An application to Jesus is easily drawn, especially in the wounds to the back of this young person (cf. 2 Peter 2:24). What others come to mind? Have you ever observed a group of Christians or a young church in such a position? How about an individual serving the Lord? Pray today for the delivery of a person or group who is being oppressed by the enemy.

130:3 [q] Ps 76:7; 143:2
130:4 [r] Ex 34:7; Isa 55:7; Jer 33:8 [s] 1Ki 8:40
130:5 [t] Ps 27:14; 33:20; Isa 8:17 [u] Ps 119:81
130:6 [v] Ps 63:6 [w] Ps 119:147
130:7 [x] Ps 131:3
130:8 [y] Lk 1:68

3 If you, O LORD, kept a record of sins,
O Lord, who could stand?[q]
4 But with you there is forgiveness;[r]
therefore you are feared.[s]

5 I wait for the LORD,[t] my soul waits,
and in his word[u] I put my hope.
6 My soul waits for the Lord
more than watchmen[v] wait for the morning,
more than watchmen wait for the morning.[w]

7 O Israel, put your hope[x] in the LORD,
for with the LORD is unfailing love
and with him is full redemption.
8 He himself will redeem[y] Israel
from all their sins.

Psalm 131

A song of ascents. Of David.

131:1 [z] Ps 101:5; Ro 12:16
131:2 [a] Mt 18:3; 1Co 14:20
131:3 [b] Ps 130:7

1 My heart is not proud,[z] O LORD,
my eyes are not haughty;
I do not concern myself with great matters
or things too wonderful for me.
2 But I have stilled and quieted my soul;
like a weaned child with its mother,
like a weaned child is my soul[a] within me.

3 O Israel, put your hope[b] in the LORD
both now and forevermore.

Psalm 132

A song of ascents.

132:2 [c] Ge 49:24

1 O LORD, remember David
and all the hardships he endured.

2 He swore an oath to the LORD
and made a vow to the Mighty One of Jacob:[c]

Psalm 130

This psalm is considered one of the seven penitential psalms (6; 32; 38; 51; 102; 130; 143). It's a testimony of trust in the Lord—by one who knew that even though he was a sinner, God heard his cry from the depths. The description of the weight of sin, confession of guilt, and expression of confidence in God form an individual expression on behalf of others.

Experiencing sin, guilt, and God's discipline can feel like being cast into "the depths" of the sea (cf. 69:1–2,14–15; Ezek. 27:34). Jonah's prayer from the belly of the fish expressed his anguish: "The engulfing waters threatened me, the deep surrounded me; seaweed was wrapped around my head" (Jonah 2:5). Do you get a panicky feeling reading this, not just of claustrophobia or drowning, but of complete alienation from God? When have you felt yourself sinking into a vast ocean of despair? How do Scriptures like this help you out of the pit?

Psalm 131

The writer (not all ancient sources ascribe the piece to David) of this psalm of confidence had experienced the wonder of complete submission to God. Submission implies humility—the opposite of "haughty eyes" and a preoccupation with "great matters." The proud person looks, compares, competes, and is never content. Such people scheme in their hearts ways to outdo and outperform. But the psalmist knew and shared an often well-kept secret: True godliness begins in the "heart" that isn't proud (cf. Prov. 18:12).

When have you last rested in God, so completely content that you felt, at least for the moment, that you lacked for nothing? The word for "weaned" in verse 2 can also mean "contented." A weaned child is no longer restless when it's with its mother because it no longer frets for milk. But a baby satisfied with its mother's milk also can lie contented on its mother's breast. The essential picture is of satisfaction, regardless of age. The psalmist felt a deep sense of peace and tranquility with his God.

3 "I will not enter my house
   or go to my bed—
4 I will allow no sleep to my eyes,
   no slumber to my eyelids,
5 till I find a place ^{d} for the LORD,
   a dwelling for the Mighty One of Jacob."

6 We heard it in Ephrathah, ^{e}
   we came upon it in the fields of Jaar: $^{a;\,b\,f}$
7 "Let us go to his dwelling place; ^{g}
   let us worship at his footstool ^{h}—
8 arise, O LORD, ^{i} and come to your resting place,
   you and the ark of your might.
9 May your priests be clothed with righteousness; ^{j}
   may your saints sing for joy."

10 For the sake of David your servant,
   do not reject your anointed one.
11 The LORD swore an oath to David, ^{k}
   a sure oath that he will not revoke:
"One of your own descendants ^{l}
   I will place on your throne—
12 if your sons keep my covenant
   and the statutes I teach them,
   then their sons will sit
   on your throne ^{m} for ever and ever."

13 For the LORD has chosen Zion, ^{n}
   he has desired it for his dwelling:
14 "This is my resting place for ever and ever; ^{o}
   here I will sit enthroned, for I have desired it—
15 I will bless her with abundant provisions;
   her poor will I satisfy with food. ^{p}
16 I will clothe her priests ^{q} with salvation,
   and her saints will ever sing for joy.
17 "Here I will make a horn ^{c} grow ^{r} for David
   and set up a lamp ^{s} for my anointed one.
18 I will clothe his enemies with shame, ^{t}
   but the crown on his head will be resplendent."

Psalm 133

A song of ascents. Of David.

1 How good and pleasant it is
   when brothers live together ^{u} in unity!

a 6 That is, Kiriath Jearim   b 6 Or heard of it in Ephrathah, / we found it in the fields of Jaar. (And no
quotes around verses 7-9)   c 17 Horn here symbolizes strong one, that is, king.

Sidenotes
132:5 d Ac 7:46
132:6 e 1Sa 17:12 f 1Sa 7:2
132:7 g Ps 5:7 h Ps 99:5
132:8 i Nu 10:35; Ps 78:61
132:9 j Job 29:14; Isa 61:3,10
132:11 k Ps 89:3-4,35 l 2Sa 7:12
132:12 m Lk 1:32; Ac 2:30
132:13 n Ps 48:1-2
132:14 o Ps 68:16
132:15 p Ps 107:9; 147:14
132:16 q 2Ch 6:41
132:17 r Eze 29:21; Lk 1:69 s 1Ki 11:36; 2Ch 21:7
132:18 t Ps 35:26; 109:29
133:1 u Ge 13:8; Heb 13:1

Psalm 132
Psalm 132, a prayer for God's favor on David's dynasty (see vv. 1,10), can be classified as a Song of Zion or a royal psalm. Three suggestions have been made regarding its historical context: (1) It celebrated David's bringing the ark of the covenant into Jerusalem (vv. 6–8; cf. 2 Sam. 6:12–19). (2) It was composed for the dedication of the temple (2 Chron. 6:41–42 incorporates vv. 8–10 into Solomon's prayer of dedication). (3) It was used in the coronation ceremony for Davidic kings (cf. Ps. 2; 110).

Have you noted the number of times in the Psalms that the king's rule is expressed in terms of care for the poor (v. 15)? Such concern is a kingdom priority. Isaiah 61:1–2 carries the theme in poetry expressing how the Messiah will come. Jesus read from this Isaiah passage (cf. Luke 4:18–19) at the inauguration of his earthly ministry. God's kingdom is a matter of the heart, and one primary sign of a changed heart is how that individual cares for and about the world's most vulnerable people.

133:2
v Ex 30:25

2 It is like precious oil poured on the head, [v]
 running down on the beard,
running down on Aaron's beard,
 down upon the collar of his robes.

133:3
w Dt 4:48
x Lev 25:21;
Dt 28:8 y Ps 42:8

3 It is as if the dew of Hermon [w]
 were falling on Mount Zion.
For there the LORD bestows his blessing, [x]
 even life forevermore. [y]

Psalm 134

A song of ascents.

134:1
z Ps 135:1-2
a 1Ch 9:33
134:2
b Ps 28:2; 1Ti 2:8

1 Praise the LORD, all you servants [z] of the LORD
 who minister by night [a] in the house of the LORD.
2 Lift up your hands [b] in the sanctuary
 and praise the LORD.

134:3
c Ps 124:8
d Ps 128:5

3 May the LORD, the Maker of heaven [c] and earth,
 bless you from Zion. [d]

Psalm 135

1 Praise the LORD. [a]

135:1
e Ps 113:1; 134:1
135:2
f Lk 2:37
g Ps 116:19

Praise the name of the LORD;
 praise him, you servants [e] of the LORD,
2 you who minister in the house [f] of the LORD,
 in the courts [g] of the house of our God.

135:3
h Ps 119:68
i Ps 147:1
135:4
j Dt 10:15; 1Pe 2:9
k Ex 19:5; Dt 7:6

3 Praise the LORD, for the LORD is good; [h]
 sing praise to his name, for that is pleasant. [i]
4 For the LORD has chosen Jacob [j] to be his own,
 Israel to be his treasured possession. [k]

a 1 Hebrew Hallelu Yah; also in verses 3 and 21

Psalm 133

As one of the "Song of Ascents," the Israelites likely sang Psalm 133 as they made their pilgrimages to Jerusalem for the three annual festivals (see "There and Then" for Ps. 120). They came from many different walks of life, regions, and tribes but assembled for one purpose: to worship the Lord together in Jerusalem.

Though the heading attributes the psalm to David, not all ancient sources agree. If David was the author, he may have been inspired to compose the psalm when, after years of conflict, all Israel came to Hebron to make him king (2 Sam. 5:1–3).

With its high altitude, regular precipitation, and heavy dew, Mount Hermon is known for its lush greenery even during the summer. The experience of the pilgrims was like Hermon's refreshing dew. From May to October virtually no rain—or even dew—falls on Jerusalem. During these months at least two pilgrimages were held. Regardless of the harsh conditions of life in general, or of the pilgrimage in particular, the unity of God's people was refreshing—and remains so today. In what ways are you revived and invigorated by the gift of fellowship?

Psalm 134

This liturgical hymn forms a magnificent conclusion to the collection of psalms known as the Songs of Ascents (see "There and Then" for Ps. 120). It consists of a brief exchange between the worshipers, as they were about to leave the temple after the evening service (vv. 1–2), and the Levites, who kept the temple watch through the night (v. 3).

Through what medium (song, prayer, other?) do you offer God your best praise? The Israelites offered prayers with hands lifted up (28:2; 63:4; 141:2; cf. 1 Tim. 2:8). Today God dwells within believers through his Spirit, but we also, at least symbolically, think of him as living in heaven—a "place" thought to be above us. Whether you are comfortable lifting your hands or prefer to lift your heart (cf. 25:1), do you find this a fitting picture of your praise posture?

Psalm 135

Psalm 135 is a call to praise the Lord—the one true God. It's a hymn of descriptive praise of God the Creator, Israel's Redeemer and the Lord of history. Likely postexilic, the psalm echoes many lines found elsewhere in the Old Testament. It was clearly composed for the temple liturgy.

5 I know that the LORD is great,[l]
  that our Lord is greater than all gods.[m]
6 The LORD does whatever pleases him,[n]
  in the heavens and on the earth,
  in the seas and all their depths.
7 He makes clouds rise from the ends of the earth;
  he sends lightning with the rain[o]
  and brings out the wind[p] from his storehouses.[q]
8 He struck down the firstborn[r] of Egypt,
  the firstborn of men and animals.
9 He sent his signs[s] and wonders into your midst, O Egypt,
  against Pharaoh and all his servants.[t]
10 He struck down many[u] nations
  and killed mighty kings—
11 Sihon[v] king of the Amorites,
  Og king of Bashan
  and all the kings of Canaan[w]—
12 and he gave their land as an inheritance,[x]
  an inheritance to his people Israel.

13 Your name, O LORD, endures forever,[y]
  your renown,[z] O LORD, through all generations.
14 For the LORD will vindicate his people
  and have compassion on his servants.[a]

15 The idols of the nations are silver and gold,
  made by the hands of men.
16 They have mouths, but cannot speak,
  eyes, but they cannot see;
17 they have ears, but cannot hear,
  nor is there breath in their mouths.
18 Those who make them will be like them,
  and so will all who trust in them.

19 O house of Israel, praise the LORD;
  O house of Aaron, praise the LORD;
20 O house of Levi, praise the LORD;
  you who fear him, praise the LORD.
21 Praise be to the LORD from Zion,[b]
  to him who dwells in Jerusalem.

  Praise the LORD.

Psalm 136

1 Give thanks to the LORD, for he is good.[c]
  His love endures forever.[d]
2 Give thanks to the God of gods.[e]
  His love endures forever.

Cross-references

135:5
l Ps 48:1 m Ps 97:9
135:6
n Ps 115:3
135:7
o Jer 10:13;
Zec 10:1
p Job 28:25
q Job 38:22
135:8
r Ex 12:12; Ps 78:51
135:9
s Dt 6:22
t Ps 136:10-15
135:10
u Nu 21:21-25;
Ps 136:17-21
135:11
v Nu 21:21
w Jos 12:7-24
135:12
x Ps 78:55
135:13
y Ex 3:15
z Ps 102:12
135:14
a Dt 32:36
135:21
b Ps 134:3
136:1
c Ps 106:1
d 1Ch 16:34;
2Ch 20:21
136:2
e Dt 10:17

Verses 10–21 lift up God as the Redeemer of his people. Even if Israel suffered, the history of redemption continued. This is a good reminder for those of us who are locked in time. Paul assured us that "he who began a good work in you will carry it on to completion until the day of Christ Jesus" (Phil. 1:6). Kingdoms rise and fall. People come and go in our lives. Yet God remains completely faithful to his people, and our redemption is indeed nearer now than when we first believed (Rom. 13:11).

Psalm 136

Psalm 136 is the last of the Great Hallel psalms (see "There and Then" for Ps. 113). It's a liturgy of praise to the Lord as Creator and as Israel's Redeemer. Its theme and many of its verses parallel much of Psalm 135. Psalm 136 is an antiphonal hymn. A leader sang each verse, after which the people responded with the repeated refrain. This echoing response ("His love endures forever") occurs 26 times, the numerical value of the divine name Yahweh (when the Hebrew letters were used as numbers).

³ Give thanks to the Lord of lords:

His love endures forever.

136:4
f Ps 72:18

⁴ to him who alone does great wonders, ^f

His love endures forever.

136:5
g Pr 3:19; Jer 51:15
h Ge 1:1
136:6
i Ge 1:9; Jer 10:12
j Ps 24:2
136:7
k Ge 1:14,16

⁵ who by his understanding ^g made the heavens, ^h

His love endures forever.

⁶ who spread out the earth ⁱ upon the waters, ^j

His love endures forever.

⁷ who made the great lights ^k—

His love endures forever.

136:8
l Ge 1:16

⁸ the sun to govern ^l the day,

His love endures forever.

⁹ the moon and stars to govern the night;

His love endures forever.

136:10
m Ex 12:29;
Ps 135:8

¹⁰ to him who struck down the firstborn ^m of Egypt

His love endures forever.

136:11
n Ex 6:6; 12:51

¹¹ and brought Israel out ⁿ from among them

His love endures forever.

136:12
o Dt 4:34; Ps 44:3

¹² with a mighty hand and outstretched arm; ^o

His love endures forever.

136:13
p Ex 14:21;
Ps 78:13
136:14
q Ex 14:22

¹³ to him who divided the Red Sea ^a ^p asunder

His love endures forever.

¹⁴ and brought Israel through ^q the midst of it,

His love endures forever.

136:15
r Ex 14:27; Ps 135:9

¹⁵ but swept Pharaoh and his army into the Red Sea; ^r

His love endures forever.

136:16
s Ex 13:18

¹⁶ to him who led his people through the desert, ^s

His love endures forever.

136:17
t Ps 135:9-12

¹⁷ who struck down great kings, ^t

His love endures forever.

136:18
u Dt 29:7

¹⁸ and killed mighty kings ^u—

His love endures forever.

136:19
v Nu 21:21-25

¹⁹ Sihon king of the Amorites ^v

His love endures forever.

²⁰ and Og king of Bashan—

His love endures forever.

136:21
w Jos 12:1

²¹ and gave their land ^w as an inheritance,

His love endures forever.

²² an inheritance to his servant Israel;

His love endures forever.

²³ to the One who remembered us ^x in our low estate

His love endures forever.

136:23
x Ps 113:7

²⁴ and freed us from our enemies, ^y

His love endures forever.

136:24
y Ps 107:2

²⁵ and who gives food ^z to every creature.

His love endures forever.

136:25
z Ps 104:27; 145:15

²⁶ Give thanks to the God of heaven.

His love endures forever.

^a 13 Hebrew *Yam Suph*; that is, Sea of Reeds; also in verse 15

The psalmist focused in verses 7–9 on God's handiwork in space (cf. Gen. 1:14–18; Ps. 8:1,3; 19:1–6). The sun and moon affect life on Earth and evidence God's goodness to all creatures (v. 25), especially his people (vv. 10–24). Which impresses you more: thinking about the macro (unimaginably vast) outreaches of space or the micro (unbelievably tiny) aspects of God's perfect creation? Do you ever reflect on the reality that *you* represent the crowning achievement of his creation (see Gen. 1:26; Ps. 8:5–8)? How does this perspective

Psalm 137

[1] By the rivers of Babylon[a] we sat and wept[b]
  when we remembered Zion.
[2] There on the poplars
  we hung our harps,
[3] for there our captors asked us for songs,
  our tormentors demanded[c] songs of joy;
  they said, "Sing us one of the songs of Zion!"

[4] How can we sing the songs of the LORD
  while in a foreign land?
[5] If I forget you, O Jerusalem,
  may my right hand forget its skill.
[6] May my tongue cling to the roof[d] of my mouth
  if I do not remember you,
if I do not consider Jerusalem
  my highest joy.

[7] Remember, O LORD, what the Edomites[e] did
  on the day Jerusalem fell.[f]
"Tear it down," they cried,
  "tear it down to its foundations!"

[8] O Daughter of Babylon, doomed to destruction,[g]
  happy is he who repays you
  for what you have done to us—
[9] he who seizes your infants
  and dashes them[h] against the rocks.

Psalm 138

Of David.

[1] I will praise you, O LORD, with all my heart;
  before the "gods"[i] I will sing your praise.
[2] I will bow down toward your holy temple[j]
  and will praise your name
  for your love and your faithfulness,
for you have exalted above all things

137:1
a Eze 1:1,3
b Ne 1:4

137:3
c Ps 80:6

137:6
d Eze 3:26

137:7
e Jer 49:7;
La 4:21-22;
Eze 25:12
f Ob 1:11

137:8
g Isa 13:1,19;
Jer 25:12,26;
Jer 50:15; Rev 18:6

137:9
h 2Ki 8:12;
Isa 13:16

138:1
i Ps 95:3; 96:4
138:2
j 1Ki 8:29; Ps 5:7;
28:2

---

affect the value you place, not just on yourself, but also on other people, no matter what their status?

Psalm 137

Psalm 137 is the plaintive song of an exile—of one who had recently returned from Babylon but in whose soul lingered the bitter memory of years in a foreign land and perhaps even of cruel events leading up to that enforced stay. The editors of the Psalter attached this song to the Great Hallel (see "There and Then" for Ps. 113) as a closing expression of supreme devotion to the city at the center of Israel's worship of God.

Those who would want to see an enemy's infants dashed against rocks (v. 9) might well have witnessed their own little ones suffering war's atrocities. We don't have to defend the psalmist's feelings in order to feel compassion. Today, as then, wars kill and maim the innocent, displace families, and ruthlessly starve refugees to death.

It's still difficult for us as Christians to understand how sentiments like this could be contained in the Bible. But those who wrote what are often called "imprecatory" or "cursing" psalms were concerned about something far more significant than revenge. They were focused on God's holiness—and recognized that he is offended by violence against people. They also were concerned about justice, recognizing that right will triumph only when evil has been overthrown and punished.

Psalm 138

Psalm 138 begins a final collection of psalms "of David" (see headings of Ps. 138–145). While much in some of these psalms points to a later, even postexilic, date, they clearly stand in the tradition of psalm composition of which David was the reputed father. They echo the language and concerns of earlier Davidic psalms.

Psalm 138 is a song of praise, understood by many to have originated on the lips of a king, for God's saving help against threatening foes. If David was in fact the author, the reference in verse 2 to the temple was to the tent he had set up for the ark (2 Sam. 6:17).

your name and your word. [k]

³ When I called, you answered me;
you made me bold and stouthearted. [l]

⁴ May all the kings of the earth [m] praise you, O LORD,
when they hear the words of your mouth.
⁵ May they sing of the ways of the LORD,
for the glory of the LORD is great.

⁶ Though the LORD is on high, he looks upon the lowly, [n]
but the proud [o] he knows from afar.
⁷ Though I walk [p] in the midst of trouble,
you preserve my life;
you stretch out your hand against the anger of my foes, [q]
with your right hand [r] you save me. [s]
⁸ The LORD will fulfill his purpose [t] for me;
your love, O LORD, endures forever—
do not abandon the works of your hands. [u]

Psalm 139

For the director of music. Of David. A psalm.

¹ O LORD, you have searched me [v]
and you know [w] me.

138:2
k Isa 42:21

138:3
l Ps 28:7
138:4
m Ps 102:15

138:6
n Ps 113:6;
Isa 57:15 o Pr 3:34;
Jas 4:6
138:7
p Ps 23:4
q Jer 51:25
r Ps 20:6 s Ps 71:20

138:8
t Ps 57:2; Php 1:6
u Job 10:3,8; 14:15

139:1
v Ps 17:3 w Jer 12:3

Confidence comes from recognizing that God has a purpose—one that includes each of us individually (v. 8; cf. 57:2; Rom. 8:28). Such confidence isn't misplaced; God has shown an interest in his creation and his people ("the works of [his] hands"; cf. 90:16; 92:5; 143:5, Isa. 60:21; 64:8). His concern is of the most profound and lasting kind: nothing less than his enduring love! How has God revealed his purposes for your life? How is he continuing to do so?

Psalm 139

Psalm 139 is a prayer for God to examine the heart and see its true devotion. Since the Lord knows and loves his people, they, in turn, need not fear his scrutiny. The various components of this psalm—hymn,

---

Snapshots

138:6–7

A Long Trek to Nowhere?

Eight-year-old Armida had to trudge 187 kilometers with her family to flee the Angolan government's systematic shelling of the town of Jamba. Armida's father, Rufin, a double amputee after having stepped on a landmine, also had to endure the grueling journey to safety.

The long tramp to Zambia exhausted the family. Armida's mother, with the help of her two young daughters, carried a smaller child, two worn blankets, some food, and a can of water. They left Angola in January of 2000, finally managing to cross the Zambezi River in February. Besides torrential rains and the threat of wild animals, the family had to be alert for landmines—still less terrifying than the guns and mortars behind them.

> Besides torrential rains and the threat of wild animals, the family had to be alert for landmines.

Upon reaching Zambia, they were driven to a refugee camp, then home to 8,000 people (14,100 by July of 2001). The family was provided with a tent, two blankets, a basin, two pots, a small bucket, five spoons, and five cups. That was almost two years ago.

"If I was okay," bemoans Rufin, "I could have built a better structure a long time ago. As a refugee, it's like a taboo, or like we have committed a crime and have to wait to be given whatever is made available to us by the authorities."

2 You know when I sit and when I rise;^x
  you perceive my thoughts^y from afar.
3 You discern my going out and my lying down;
  you are familiar with all my ways.^z
4 Before a word is on my tongue
  you know it completely,^a O LORD.

5 You hem me in^b—behind and before;
  you have laid your hand upon me.
6 Such knowledge is too wonderful for me,
  too lofty^c for me to attain.

7 Where can I go from your Spirit?
  Where can I flee^d from your presence?
8 If I go up to the heavens,^e you are there;
  if I make my bed^f in the depths,^a you are there.
9 If I rise on the wings of the dawn,
  if I settle on the far side of the sea,
10 even there your hand will guide me,^g
  your right hand will hold me fast.

11 If I say, "Surely the darkness will hide me
  and the light become night around me,"
12 even the darkness will not be dark^h to you;
  the night will shine like the day,
  for darkness is as light to you.

13 For you created my inmost being;ⁱ
  you knit me together^j in my mother's womb.
14 I praise you because I am fearfully and wonderfully made;

^a 8 Hebrew *Sheol*

139:2
^x 2Ki 19:27
^y Mt 9:4; Jn 2:24
139:3
^z Job 31:4
139:4
^a Heb 4:13
139:5
^b Ps 34:7
139:6
^c Job 42:3;
Ro 11:33
139:7
^d Jer 23:24; Jnh 1:3
139:8
^e Am 9:2-3
^f Pr 15:11
139:10
^g Ps 23:3
139:12
^h Job 34:22;
Da 2:22
139:13
ⁱ Ps 119:73
^j Job 10:11

thanksgiving, lament—expose us to the intensely personal relationship between the psalmist and his God.

God's presence is everywhere; hence he perceives all things in all places. The psalmist wasn't trying to evade God (vv. 7–12) but further amplified that God's knowledge is beyond human ability to grasp. God's knowledge or discernment can never be limited, because his sovereignty extends to the whole created universe.

All creatures owe their existence and praise to the Creator-God. How much more those of us who walk with him daily! This beloved psalm expresses for many their confidence in the Lord who has formed us with a specific purpose in mind. We stand in wonder and amazement at God's design for each life. The psalmist revealed a unique awareness of God's grace toward him and responded with a hymn of thanksgiving. Whether you adapt the words here or create your own song of praise, exalt him today for his loving concern for the details of your life.

139:13–14

Fearfully and Wonderfully Made

The world as created by God is extraordinarily diverse. Scientists estimate that there are 1.75 million described species in the world, with another 12 million or more as yet unknown. The most fully understood are the vertebrates and the plants. The least known are bacteria, viruses, and fungi:

Species	Number Known	Estimated Percent of Known
VERTEBRATES	52,000	95
PLANTS	270,000	84
INSECTS (PLUS SPIDERS)	1,400,000	11
FUNGI	72,000	5
BACTERIA	4,000	5
VIRUSES	4,000	1

Source: America Association for the Advancement of Science (2002:164)   0   50   100%

your works are wonderful,[k]
I know that full well.
15 My frame was not hidden from you
when I was made in the secret place.
When I was woven together[l] in the depths of the earth,[m]
16 your eyes saw my unformed body.
All the days ordained for me
were written in your book
before one of them came to be.

17 How precious to[a] me are your thoughts, O God![n]
How vast is the sum of them!
18 Were I to count them,
they would outnumber the grains of sand.
When I awake,
I am still with you.

19 If only you would slay the wicked,[o] O God!
Away from me,[p] you bloodthirsty men!
20 They speak of you with evil intent;
your adversaries misuse your name.[q]
21 Do I not hate those[r] who hate you, O LORD,
and abhor those who rise up against you?
22 I have nothing but hatred for them;
I count them my enemies.

23 Search me,[s] O God, and know my heart;[t]
test me and know my anxious thoughts.
24 See if there is any offensive way in me,
and lead me[u] in the way everlasting.

Psalm 140

For the director of music. A psalm of David.

1 Rescue me,[v] O LORD, from evil men;
protect me from men of violence,[w]
2 who devise evil plans[x] in their hearts
and stir up war every day.
3 They make their tongues as sharp as[y] a serpent's;
the poison of vipers[z] is on their lips.   *Selah*

4 Keep me,[a] O LORD, from the hands of the wicked;[b]
protect me from men of violence
who plan to trip my feet.
5 Proud men have hidden a snare for me;
they have spread out the cords of their net
and have set traps[c] for me along my path.   *Selah*

---

a 17 Or *concerning*

Sidenotes (left column):

139:14
k Ps 40:5

139:15
l Job 10:11
m Ps 63:9

139:17
n Ps 40:5

139:19
o Isa 11:4
p Ps 119:115

139:20
q Jude 15
139:21
r 2Ch 19:2; Ps 31:6;
119:113; 119:158

139:23
s Job 31:6; Ps 26:2
t Jer 11:20

139:24
u Ps 5:8; 143:10;
Pr 15:9

140:1
v Ps 17:13
w Ps 18:48

140:2
x Ps 36:4; 56:6

140:3
y Ps 57:4 z Ps 58:4;
Jas 3:8

140:4
a Ps 141:9
b Ps 71:4

140:5
c Ps 31:4; 35:7

Psalm 140

In this individual lament, the psalmist expressed that he had been falsely accused and that he turned to the Lord, the righteous Judge, for deliverance. He resisted complaining against God for having permitted evil men to cause him so much pain. Instead, he committed his future to the Lord, who "secures justice" for the poor and needy (v. 12). Prayer, in the psalmist's view, is a privilege; the pray-er may bring his or her individual concerns before God, confident that he will respond.

The psalmist's prayer in verses 9–11 wasn't a personal vendetta but an expression of his concern for God's just rule (see notes for Ps. 139). He pleaded that the Lord would boomerang on the heads of the wicked the evil they had spoken. The "burning coals," "fire," and "miry pits" (v. 10) are metaphors for divine judgment.

Does the idea of leaving justice to God (via prayer) comfort you? How do you feel about the "reverse psychology," of sorts, espoused by Proverbs 25:21 and 22 (and quoted in Rom. 12:20): doing acts of kindness for your enemies as a way of "heaping burning coals" on

6 O LORD, I say to you, "You are my God."[d]
Hear, O LORD, my cry for mercy.[e]
7 O Sovereign LORD,[f] my strong deliverer,
who shields my head in the day of battle—
8 do not grant the wicked[g] their desires, O LORD;
do not let their plans succeed,
or they will become proud. *Selah*

9 Let the heads of those who surround me
be covered with the trouble their lips have caused.[h]
10 Let burning coals fall upon them;
may they be thrown into the fire,[i]
into miry pits, never to rise.
11 Let slanderers not be established in the land;
may disaster hunt down men of violence.[j]

12 I know that the LORD secures justice for the poor
and upholds the cause[k] of the needy.[l]
13 Surely the righteous will praise your name[m]
and the upright will live[n] before you.

Psalm 141

A psalm of David.

1 O LORD, I call to you; come quickly[o] to me.
Hear my voice[p] when I call to you.
2 May my prayer be set before you like incense;[q]
may the lifting up of my hands[r] be like the evening sacrifice.[s]

3 Set a guard over my mouth, O LORD;
keep watch over the door of my lips.
4 Let not my heart be drawn to what is evil,
to take part in wicked deeds
with men who are evildoers;
let me not eat of their delicacies.[t]

5 Let a righteous man[a] strike me—it is a kindness;
let him rebuke me[u]—it is oil on my head.[v]
My head will not refuse it.

Yet my prayer is ever against the deeds of evildoers;
6 their rulers will be thrown down from the cliffs,
and the wicked will learn that my words were well spoken.
7 ⌞They will say,⌟ "As one plows and breaks up the earth,
so our bones have been scattered at the mouth[w] of the grave.[b]"

8 But my eyes are fixed[x] on you, O Sovereign LORD;

140:6 [d] Ps 16:2 [e] Ps 116:1; 143:1
140:7 [f] Ps 28:8
140:8 [g] Ps 10:2-3
140:9 [h] Ps 7:16
140:10 [i] Ps 11:6; 21:9
140:11 [j] Ps 34:21
140:12 [k] Ps 9:4 [l] Ps 35:10
140:13 [m] Ps 97:12 [n] Ps 11:7
141:1 [o] Ps 22:19; 70:5 [p] Ps 143:1
141:2 [q] Rev 5:8; 8:3 [r] 1Ti 2:8 [s] Ex 29:39, 41
141:4 [t] Pr 23:6
141:5 [u] Pr 9:8 [v] Ps 23:5
141:7 [w] Ps 53:5
141:8 [x] Ps 25:15

[a] 5 Or *Let the Righteous One* [b] 7 Hebrew *Sheol*

their heads? Have you tried out the advice of either method? What were the results?

Psalm 141

This psalm, like Psalm 140, is an individual lament. It includes, in addition to lament, an expression of confidence in the Lord and a prayer against the wicked. Reflecting a concern for wisdom, the poet prayed for guidance in his speech and relations and for instruction by the righteous. He then cited a proverb (v. 7) and contrasted the wicked and the righteous. In second-temple Judaism (after 516 B.C.), the psalm was used with the evening sacrifice (see v. 2); this also may have been true when it was first written.

Though the psalmist was in a precarious situation, his prayer was like a pleasing offering to the Lord. Gradually incense and prayer had become associated. The sweet smoke of incense arose as a pleasing offering to God (cf. Ex. 30:1–8; Rev. 5:8). Have you ever pictured your prayer wafting upward to God like the soft, curling, fragrant smoke of incense? God takes delight in communing with us—and he wants the pleasure of the relationship to be mutual.

141:8
y Ps 2:12
141:9
z Ps 140:4
a Ps 38:12
141:10
b Ps 35:8

in you I take refuge[y]—do not give me over to death.
9 Keep me[z] from the snares they have laid for me,
from the traps set[a] by evildoers.
10 Let the wicked fall[b] into their own nets,
while I pass by in safety.

Psalm 142

A *maskil*[a] of David. When he was in the cave. A prayer.

142:1
c Ps 30:8
142:2
d Isa 26:16

142:3
e Ps 140:5; 143:4,7

1 I cry aloud to the LORD;
I lift up my voice to the LORD for mercy.[c]
2 I pour out my complaint[d] before him;
before him I tell my trouble.

3 When my spirit grows faint[e] within me,
it is you who know my way.
In the path where I walk
men have hidden a snare for me.

142:4
f Ps 31:11;
Jer 30:17

142:5
g Ps 46:1 h Ps 16:5
i Ps 27:13

142:6
j Ps 17:1 k Ps 79:8;
116:6

4 Look to my right and see;
no one is concerned for me.
I have no refuge;
no one cares[f] for my life.

5 I cry to you, O LORD;
I say, "You are my refuge,[g]
my portion[h] in the land of the living."[i]
6 Listen to my cry,[j]
for I am in desperate need;[k]
rescue me from those who pursue me,
for they are too strong for me.

142:7
l Ps 146:7
m Ps 13:6

7 Set me free from my prison,[l]
that I may praise your name.
Then the righteous will gather about me
because of your goodness to me.[m]

Psalm 143

A psalm of David.

143:1
n Ps 140:6
o Ps 89:1-2
p Ps 71:2

1 O LORD, hear my prayer,
listen to my cry for mercy;[n]
in your faithfulness[o] and righteousness[p]
come to my relief.

a Title: Probably a literary or musical term

Psalm 142

In this individual lament, the psalmist spoke of his great distress. The "prison" of verse 7 is likely a metaphor for oppression or affliction. If David was the author of the psalm, as indicated by its heading (but see "There and Then" for Ps. 138), the "prison" may refer to his hiding in a cave while being pursued by Saul, possibly at Adullam (1 Sam. 22:1) or En Gedi (1 Sam. 24:1–3).

The psalmist's praise for the resolution of his *problem would have encouraged his faith community* (v. 7) and heartens us today as well. He envisioned the godly crowding around him, listening to his words of thanks for God's deliverance. Have loved ones or acquaintances ever stood or sat around you as you recalled God's re-

sponse to your prayers in a tough situation? Can you remember conversing with a fellow believer who was rejoicing over what God had done for him or her? If so, how did you feel when you walked away?

Psalm 143

This individual lament is also the last of the seven penitential psalms (with 6; 32; 38; 51; 102; 130). Part of the reason for the designation lies in their confessional nature and part in the way they were later used in the Christian community. Because of its emphasis on God's grace and favor, the Reformer Martin Luther referred to Psalm 143 as a "Pauline Psalm" (reminding him of the writings of the apostle Paul), along with Psalms 32, 51, and 130.

2 Do not bring your servant into judgment,
    for no one living is righteous ^q before you.

3 The enemy pursues me,
    he crushes me to the ground;
  he makes me dwell in darkness
    like those long dead.

4 So my spirit grows faint within me;
    my heart within me is dismayed. ^r

5 I remember ^s the days of long ago;
    I meditate on all your works
    and consider what your hands have done.

6 I spread out my hands ^t to you;
    my soul thirsts for you like a parched land.   *Selah*

7 Answer me quickly, ^u O LORD;
    my spirit fails.
  Do not hide your face ^v from me
    or I will be like those who go down to the pit.

8 Let the morning bring me word of your unfailing love, ^w
    for I have put my trust in you.
  Show me the way ^x I should go,
    for to you I lift up my soul. ^y

9 Rescue me from my enemies, ^z O LORD,
    for I hide myself in you.

10 Teach me to do your will,
    for you are my God;
  may your good Spirit
    lead ^a me on level ground.

11 For your name's sake, O LORD, preserve my life; ^b
    in your righteousness, ^c bring me out of trouble.

12 In your unfailing love, silence my enemies;
    destroy all my foes, ^d
  for I am your servant. ^e

Psalm 144

Of David.

1 Praise be to the LORD my Rock, ^f
    who trains my hands for war,
    my fingers for battle.

2 He is my loving God and my fortress, ^g
    my stronghold and my deliverer,
  my shield, ^h in whom I take refuge,
    who subdues peoples ^a under me.

---

^a 2 Many manuscripts of the Masoretic Text, Dead Sea Scrolls, Aquila, Jerome and Syriac; most manuscripts of the Masoretic Text *subdues my people*

143:2
q Ps 14:3; Ecc 7:20; Ro 3:20

143:4
r Ps 142:3

143:5
s Ps 77:6

143:6
t Ps 63:1; 88:9

143:7
u Ps 69:17
v Ps 27:9; 28:1

143:8
w Ps 46:5; 90:14
x Ps 27:11
y Ps 25:1-2

143:9
z Ps 31:15

143:10
a Ne 9:20; Ps 23:3; 25:4-5
143:11
b Ps 119:25
c Ps 31:1

143:12
d Ps 52:5; 54:5
e Ps 116:16

144:1
f Ps 18:2,34

144:2
g Ps 59:9; 91:2
h Ps 84:9

📖 The psalmist, aware of his sin, appealed to God's faithfulness and righteousness. How different in spirit from the statements of innocence found in several other psalms (e.g., 7:3–5)! Both approaches are valid, depending on the situation. The confession of innocence is appropriate when we are insulted for Christ's sake—and the confession of guilt when we are confronted with our failings. Both also have potential hazards: Confidence can lead to spiritual pride and independence, but feel-ings of worthlessness can result in spiritual depression. Which snag is more typically a problem for you?

Psalm 144

🕮 David was clearly the author of this psalm (see "There and Then" for Ps. 138), as seen in verse 10. A shift takes place in verse 12, making the psalm in a sense two separate units. It has an essential unity, though: a need for God to act (a royal lament, vv. 1–11) and the resulting blessings of his actions (a psalm of blessing, vv. 12–15).

Blessing the Children

Psalm 144:12 is a blessing—yet far from a reality for an estimated 600 million children, according to UNICEF, the United Nations International Children's Emergency Fund. Poverty, war, HIV/AIDS, natural disasters, and resulting orphanhood force children to fend for themselves in unwholesome conditions. The situation is especially acute in Africa, Asia, Latin and Central America, and Eastern Europe. Children are being sold or kidnapped into slavery and pressed into military service, prostitution, and growth-inhibiting work. Illiteracy and non-hygienic conditions rob them of the chance to realize the blessing the psalmist envisioned.

Following widespread famine in the pre-industrialized world, industrialized nations responded to the plight of the world's children in the 1980s with child survival and development programs of unprecedented scope. In 1989 the UN General Assembly adopted the Convention on the Rights of the Child. And 71 heads of state and governmental representatives drafted goals for the improvement of child and adolescent heath and welfare at the 1990 World Summit for Children.

We have seen much progress in child health initiatives since then: polio immunizations, iodizing of salt, and provision of vitamin A supplements to reduce micro-nutrient deficiencies. International relief and development agencies have promoted breastfeeding standards and improved access to safe water. The next hurdle in the war against malnutrition is the reduction of anemia through iron supplements.

Evidence suggests, though, that good will and financial commitments are insufficient to address these global problems. The nations in which they abound must cooperate with relief efforts. Political and cultural impediments severely hamper efforts to enable children to grow into the psalmist's vision of fully grown plants that can become the corner pillars of thriving societies.

> Political and cultural impediments severely hamper efforts to enable children to grow into the psalmist's vision of fully grown plants that can become the corner pillars of thriving societies.

Thousands of children under age five die daily from preventable diseases like measles, diphtheria, tetanus, and diarrhea, as well as tragedies like exposure. Mothers die in childbirth from lack of adequate medical care and the absence of sanitary conditions. Preventable illnesses, neglect, accidents, and assaults continue to reflect a lack of understanding and respect for children worldwide. Girls are especially vulnerable in large parts of the world where they are undervalued, uneducated, and/or mistreated. Illiterate and uneducated women are vulnerable to illness, sepsis, and death in childbirth, perpetuating the cycle of orphanhood and poverty for their daughters.

Economic exploitation of children also endangers their chances for healthy adulthood. Poverty forces thousands to be sold and trafficked for debt bondage, serfdom, forced or compulsory labor or armed conflict, prostitution, pornography, or drug production and trafficking.

Ongoing international efforts support an Optional Protocol to the Convention on the Rights of the Child that would raise the minimum age for children's recruitment into armed forces and conflict participation from fifteen to eighteen years. And in 1998 the International Criminal Court was given authority to prosecute as war criminals those conscripting and using children under age eighteen in hostilities.

While industrialized nations are often cast in the role of helper, problems are negatively impacting their children as well. Family disintegration and consumer exploitation breed stresses on children and adolescents that are more subtle and difficult to alleviate than nutritional deficiencies. Recognizing that children and adolescents can be psychologically and spiritually stunted and debilitated in wealth as well as in poverty deepens our insight into the delicacy of these tender plants, wherever God has planted them.

Ellen Charry, professor of theology at Princeton Theological Seminary in Princeton, New Jersey

3 O Lᴏʀᴅ, what is man[i] that you care for him,
  the son of man that you think of him?
4 Man is like a breath;
  his days are like a fleeting shadow.[j]

5 Part your heavens,[k] O Lᴏʀᴅ, and come down;
  touch the mountains, so that they smoke.[l]
6 Send forth lightning and scatter ᴸthe enemiesᴶ;
  shoot your arrows[m] and rout them.
7 Reach down your hand from on high;
  deliver me and rescue me
from the mighty waters,[n]
from the hands of foreigners[o]
8 whose mouths are full of lies,[p]
  whose right hands are deceitful.

9 I will sing a new song to you, O God;
  on the ten-stringed lyre[q] I will make music to you,
10 to the One who gives victory to kings,
  who delivers his servant David[r] from the deadly sword.

11 Deliver me and rescue me
  from the hands of foreigners
whose mouths are full of lies,
  whose right hands are deceitful.[s]

12 Then our sons in their youth
  will be like well-nurtured plants,[t]
and our daughters will be like pillars
  carved to adorn a palace.
13 Our barns will be filled
  with every kind of provision.
Our sheep will increase by thousands,
  by tens of thousands in our fields;
14   our oxen will draw heavy loads.[a]
There will be no breaching of walls,
  no going into captivity,
  no cry of distress in our streets.

15 Blessed are the people[u] of whom this is true;
  blessed are the people whose God is the Lᴏʀᴅ.

Psalm 145[b]

A psalm of praise. Of David.

1 I will exalt you,[v] my God the King;[w]
  I will praise your name for ever and ever.
2 Every day I will praise[x] you
  and extol your name for ever and ever.

144:3 [i] Ps 8:4; Heb 2:6
144:4 [j] Ps 39:11; 102:11
144:5 [k] Ps 18:9; Isa 64:1 [l] Ps 104:32
144:6 [m] Ps 7:12-13; 18:14
144:7 [n] Ps 69:2 [o] Ps 18:44
144:8 [p] Ps 12:2
144:9 [q] Ps 33:2-3
144:10 [r] Ps 18:50
144:11 [s] Ps 12:2; Isa 44:20
144:12 [t] Ps 128:3
144:15 [u] Ps 33:12
145:1 [v] Ps 30:1; 34:1 [w] Ps 5:2
145:2 [x] Ps 71:6

---

[a] 14 Or *our chieftains will be firmly established*   [b] This psalm is an acrostic poem, the verses of which (including verse 13b) begin with the successive letters of the Hebrew alphabet.

David's burst of praise in verses 1–2 encouraged him, a humble human being, to rouse the Divine Warrior to action! He didn't present his petition timidly but with boldness. Why? Because he knew his God. He was convinced that, despite human shortcomings, the Lord did "care for him" and "think of him" (v. 3). How well do you know your God? Well enough to feel confident reminding him of his promises in times of particular need?

Psalm 145

This beautiful psalm is an acrostic, in which each verse begins with a successive letter of the Hebrew alphabet. The theme of this moving hymn is praise of the Great King for his attributes, or characteristics, and acts. In fulfillment of verses 1–2 ("for ever and ever . . . Every day . . . for ever and ever"), in Jewish practice this psalm was recited twice each morning and once each evening.

145:3
y Job 5:9; Ps 147:5;
Ro 11:33
145:4
z Isa 38:19

145:5
a Ps 119:27
145:6
b Ps 66:3 c Dt 32:3

145:7
d Isa 63:7
e Ps 51:14

145:8
f Ps 86:15
g Ex 34:6; Nu 14:18

145:9
h Ps 100:5

145:10
i Ps 19:1 i Ps 68:26

145:12
k Ps 105:1

145:13
l 1Ti 1:17; 2Pe 1:11

145:14
m Ps 37:24
n Ps 146:8

145:15
o Ps 104:27; 136:25

145:16
p Ps 104:28

145:18
q Dt 4:7 r Jn 4:24
145:19
s Ps 37:4 t Pr 15:29

145:20
u Ps 31:23; 97:10
v Ps 9:5

145:21
w Ps 71:8 x Ps 65:2

146:1
y Ps 103:1
146:2
z Ps 104:33

3 Great is the LORD and most worthy of praise;
 his greatness no one can fathom. *y*
4 One generation *z* will commend your works to another;
 they will tell of your mighty acts.
5 They will speak of the glorious splendor of your majesty,
 and I will meditate on your wonderful works. *a a*
6 They will tell of the power of your awesome works, *b*
 and I will proclaim *c* your great deeds.
7 They will celebrate your abundant goodness *d*
 and joyfully sing of your righteousness. *e*

8 The LORD is gracious and compassionate, *f*
 slow to anger and rich in love. *g*
9 The LORD is good *h* to all;
 he has compassion on all he has made. *j*
10 All you have made will praise you, *i* O LORD;
 your saints will extol you. *j*
11 They will tell of the glory of your kingdom
 and speak of your might,
12 so that all men may know of your mighty acts *k*
 and the glorious splendor of your kingdom.
13 Your kingdom is an everlasting kingdom, *l*
 and your dominion endures through all generations.

 The LORD is faithful to all his promises
 and loving toward all he has made. *b*
14 The LORD upholds *m* all those who fall
 and lifts up all *n* who are bowed down.
15 The eyes of all look to you,
 and you give them their food *o* at the proper time.
16 You open your hand
 and satisfy the desires *p* of every living thing.
17 The LORD is righteous in all his ways
 and loving toward all he has made.
18 The LORD is near *q* to all who call on him, *r*
 to all who call on him in truth.
19 He fulfills the desires *s* of those who fear him;
 he hears their cry *t* and saves them.
20 The LORD watches over all who love him, *u*
 but all the wicked he will destroy. *v*

21 My mouth will speak *w* in praise of the LORD.
 Let every creature *x* praise his holy name
 for ever and ever.

Psalm 146

1 Praise the LORD. *c*

 Praise the LORD, *y* O my soul.
2 I will praise the LORD all my life; *z*
 I will sing praise to my God as long as I live.

---

a 5 Dead Sea Scrolls and Syriac (see also Septuagint); Masoretic Text *On the glorious splendor of your majesty / and on your wonderful works I will meditate* b 13 One manuscript of the Masoretic Text, Dead Sea Scrolls and Syriac (see also Septuagint); most manuscripts of the Masoretic Text do not have the last two lines of verse 13. c 1 Hebrew *Hallelu Yah*; also in verse 10

God's acts of love and compassion extend to his whole creation—to "all he has made"; the phrase is repeated three times (vv. 9,13b,17). If God's love for all creatures is evident, Christians, as his ambassadors on Earth, are responsible to convey the same message (2 Cor. 5:20). Do we make God's loving, compassionate message clear? If someone was watching you yesterday (and they were!), what message about God did they learn?

3 Do not put your trust in princes,[a]
in mortal men,[b] who cannot save.
4 When their spirit departs, they return to the ground;[c]
on that very day their plans come to nothing.[d]

5 Blessed is he[e] whose help[f] is the God of Jacob,
whose hope is in the LORD his God,
6 the Maker of heaven[g] and earth,
the sea, and everything in them—
the LORD, who remains faithful[h] forever.
7 He upholds the cause of the oppressed[i]
and gives food to the hungry.[j]
The LORD sets prisoners free,[k]
8 the LORD gives sight to the blind,[l]
the LORD lifts up those who are bowed down,
the LORD loves the righteous.
9 The LORD watches over the alien
and sustains the fatherless and the widow,[m]
but he frustrates the ways of the wicked.

10 The LORD reigns[n] forever,
your God, O Zion, for all generations.

Praise the LORD.

146:3 [a] Ps 118:9 [b] Isa 2:22
146:4 [c] Ps 104:29; Ecc 12:7 [d] Ps 33:10; 1Co 2:6
146:5 [e] Ps 144:15; Jer 17:7 [f] Ps 71:5
146:6 [g] Ps 115:15; Ac 14:15; Rev 14:7 [h] Ps 117:2
146:7 [i] Ps 103:6 [j] Ps 107:9 [k] Ps 68:6
146:8 [l] Mt 9:30
146:9 [m] Ex 22:22; Dt 10:18; Ps 68:5
146:10 [n] Ex 15:18; Ps 10:16

Psalm 147

1 Praise the LORD.[a]

How good it is to sing praises to our God,
how pleasant[o] and fitting to praise him![p]

2 The LORD builds up Jerusalem;[q]
he gathers the exiles[r] of Israel.
3 He heals the brokenhearted
and binds up their wounds.

4 He determines the number of the stars[s]
and calls them each by name.
5 Great is our Lord[t] and mighty in power;
his understanding has no limit.[u]
6 The LORD sustains the humble[v]
but casts the wicked to the ground.

147:1 [o] Ps 135:3 [p] Ps 33:1
147:2 [q] Ps 102:16 [r] Dt 30:3
147:4 [s] Isa 40:26
147:5 [t] Ps 48:1 [u] Isa 40:28
147:6 [v] Ps 146:8-9

[a] *1* Hebrew *Hallelu Yah*; also in verse 20

Psalm 146

Psalms 146–150 constitute the last Hallel (praise) collection (see "There and Then" for Ps. 113). These hymns were probably composed after the exile. All five are bracketed by shouts of *Hallelujah!* (Hebrew for "Praise the LORD"; see NIV text note for v. 1)—which may have been added by the final editors of the Psalter.

In hymnic style, Psalm 146 describes the many ways in which God, the Maker of heaven and Earth (v. 6), sustains those who put their faith in him—with particular emphasis on the needy. The psalmist expressed that God "upholds . . . gives . . . sets free . . . gives sight . . . lifts up . . . loves . . . [and] watches" (vv. 7–9).

The great wonder and privilege of being a Christian is that the Lord allows us to participate in his work! In practical (physical) and spiritual ways we can help uphold the cause of the oppressed, set people free from bondage, bring healing, and feed the hungry. We can help him watch over and care for the widow and fatherless (orphaned, displaced, or abandoned). Ultimately, it's the Lord who heals, fills, releases, and lifts people up. Can you think of anything more exciting and rewarding than to share in such a project with God?

Psalm 147

Psalm 147 is a hymn of praise to God, the Creator, for his special mercies to Israel. It may have been composed for the Levitical choirs on the joyous occasion of the dedication of the rebuilt walls of Jerusalem (see v. 2; Neh. 12:27–43). Psalm 147 is similar in language to other sections of Scripture (Deut. 4; Job 37–39; Ps. 33; 104; Isa. 40–66).

147:7
w Ps 33:3

147:8
x Job 38:26
y Ps 104:14

147:9
z Ps 104:27-28;
Mt 6:26
a Job 38:41

147:10
b 1Sa 16:7
c Ps 33:16-17

147:14
d Isa 60:17-18
e Ps 132:15

147:15
f Job 37:12

147:16
g Job 37:6
h Job 38:29

147:18
i Ps 33:9

147:19
j Dt 33:4; Mal 4:4
147:20
k Dt 4:7-8,32-34

148:2
l Ps 103:20

148:4
m Ge 1:7; 1Ki 8:27

148:5
n Ge 1:1,6;
Ps 33:6,9

7 Sing to the LORD [w] with thanksgiving;
  make music to our God on the harp.
8 He covers the sky with clouds;
  he supplies the earth with rain [x]
  and makes grass grow [y] on the hills.
9 He provides food [z] for the cattle
  and for the young ravens [a] when they call.

10 His pleasure is not in the strength [b] of the horse, [c]
  nor his delight in the legs of a man;
11 the LORD delights in those who fear him,
  who put their hope in his unfailing love.

12 Extol the LORD, O Jerusalem;
  praise your God, O Zion,
13 for he strengthens the bars of your gates
  and blesses your people within you.
14 He grants peace [d] to your borders
  and satisfies you [e] with the finest of wheat.

15 He sends his command [f] to the earth;
  his word runs swiftly.
16 He spreads the snow [g] like wool
  and scatters the frost [h] like ashes.
17 He hurls down his hail like pebbles.
  Who can withstand his icy blast?
18 He sends his word [i] and melts them;
  he stirs up his breezes, and the waters flow.

19 He has revealed his word to Jacob,
  his laws and decrees [j] to Israel.
20 He has done this for no other nation; [k]
  they do not know his laws.

Praise the LORD.

Psalm 148

1 Praise the LORD. [a]

Praise the LORD from the heavens,
  praise him in the heights above.
2 Praise him, all his angels, [l]
  praise him, all his heavenly hosts.
3 Praise him, sun and moon,
  praise him, all you shining stars.
4 Praise him, you highest heavens
  and you waters above the skies. [m]
5 Let them praise the name of the LORD,
  for he commanded [n] and they were created.

a 1 Hebrew *Hallelu Yah*; also in verse 14

We are moved to praise by reflecting on God's power in nature (vv. 15–18). The same God who controls natural seasons and cycles also regulates the seasons and cycles of human life (the exodus; the settling of the promised land; the exile and restoration of the Israelites; life's ups and downs; ages and stages; past, present, and future for his children in all generations). We as humans know to "expect the unexpected," yet there remains a predictability to life that no upheaval can shake. How does your certain knowledge of the final outcome affect your ability to cope with life's unpleasant surprises?

Psalm 148

Each of the two major sections of this hymn begins with a call to worship (vv. 1,7), and the whole song is framed between calls to "Praise the LORD" (see "There and Then" for Ps. 146). The psalmist developed God's praise in relation to worship in heaven (vv. 1–6), on Earth (vv. 7–12), and by his people (vv. 13–14).

⁶ He set them in place for ever and ever;
  he gave a decree^o that will never pass away.

148:6
o Job 38:33;
Ps 89:37; Jer 33:25

⁷ Praise the LORD from the earth,
  you great sea creatures^p and all ocean depths,
⁸ lightning and hail, snow and clouds,
  stormy winds that do his bidding, ^q

148:7
p Ps 74:13-14
148:8
q Ps 147:15-18

⁹ you mountains and all hills, ^r
  fruit trees and all cedars,
¹⁰ wild animals and all cattle,
  small creatures and flying birds,
¹¹ kings of the earth and all nations,
  you princes and all rulers on earth,
¹² young men and maidens,
  old men and children.

148:9
r Isa 44:23; 49:13;
55:12

¹³ Let them praise the name of the LORD, ^s
  for his name alone is exalted;
  his splendor is above the earth and the heavens. ^t
¹⁴ He has raised up for his people a horn, ^{a u}
  the praise of all his saints,
  of Israel, the people close to his heart.

148:13
s Isa 12:4 t Ps 8:1;
113:4

148:14
u Ps 75:10

Praise the LORD.

Psalm 149

¹ Praise the LORD. ^{b v}

Sing to the LORD a new song,
  his praise in the assembly^w of the saints.

149:1
v Ps 33:2
w Ps 35:18

² Let Israel rejoice in their Maker; ^x
  let the people of Zion be glad in their King. ^y
³ Let them praise his name with dancing
  and make music to him with tambourine and harp. ^z
⁴ For the LORD takes delight^a in his people;
  he crowns the humble with salvation. ^b
⁵ Let the saints rejoice^c in this honor
  and sing for joy on their beds. ^d

149:2
x Ps 95:6 y Ps 47:6;
Zec 9:9

149:3
z Ps 81:2; 150:4
149:4
a Ps 35:27
b Ps 132:16
149:5
c Ps 132:16
d Job 35:10

^a 14 *Horn* here symbolizes strong one, that is, king.   ^b 1 Hebrew *Hallelu Yah*; also in verse 9

Psalm 148 develops extensively heaven's partici-pation in the worship of God. The "heights above," where God rules, together with outer space and Earth's atmosphere, are called to join in Israel's praise. When have you experienced an irresistible call to praise God in some awesome natural setting (e.g., a star-filled sky, breathtaking sunset, the aurora australis or borealis, or a spectacular full moon)? In the unforgettable words of Psalm 19, "The heavens declare the glory of God . . . There is no speech or language where their voice is not heard" (vv. 1,3).

Psalm 149

Psalm 149 celebrates a victory. Since it shares much of the language and hope of Isaiah 40–66, it can be viewed as an eschatological (end times) hymn. Verses 1–5 celebrate the present joy of the saints and verses 6–9 their continuing hope.

In addition to the praise in their mouths, God's people wield the sword of God's judgment in their hands—his just retribution on those who have attacked his kingdom. The Old Testament speaks often of this divine retribution (e.g., Num. 31:2; 2 Kings 9:7; Ps. 58:10; 79:10; Isa. 59:17; 61:2). In the New Testament age, God's people are armed with the "sword of the Spirit" for overcoming the powers arrayed against his kingdom (2 Cor. 6:7; 10:4; Eph. 6:12, 17; Heb. 4:12). But our participation in God's retribution on the world awaits the final judgment (1 Cor. 6:2–3).

The psalmist called on the people to sing "a new song" about Israel's restoration and the expectation of God's coming, full victory over evil (cf. Rev. 14:3). Verses 1–5 describe specific, triumphant attitudes and actions of praise: rejoicing, dancing, making music—even singing in bed! Is praise your companion, whether that involves tapping your toes, writing a poem, listening to a praise recording, or kicking autumn leaves? Do the lyrics or music of a song or hymn, new or old, sometimes over-whelm your soul? It so, you are in the company of those who for generations have sung "a new song" to the Lord.

The Mission of Prayer

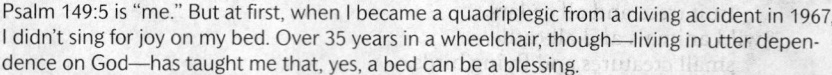

149:4–5

Psalm 149:5 is "me." But at first, when I became a quadriplegic from a diving accident in 1967, I didn't sing for joy on my bed. Over 35 years in a wheelchair, though—living in utter dependence on God—has taught me that, yes, a bed can be a blessing.

Why? My bed is where I pray best. Because my paralysis forces me to lie down early in the evening, I sometimes invite a friend to pray with me. While my husband is in the TV room, she and I will prop ourselves up, make a prayer list, and intercede for the world.

Last week she sprang a surprise—a small shortwave radio. A window to the world, she called it. She flicked it on and tuned in to Trans World Radio from the Caribbean. Another jiggle of the knob and we picked up a Bible study over station HCJB in Ecuador. A little more fiddling and we pulled in the BBC from Hong Kong. Together we tuned in to the world.

Within the walls of my room were voices from around the globe. We covered the planet, yet didn't budge beyond my four-poster. So many conversations from across the globe inspired us to pray. We interceded for mothers of spina bifida children in Mozambique and for men in the Philippine jungles who had become paralyzed from a fall from a palm tree. We prayed for mentally handicapped people in dismal institutions in closed-access countries like North Korea. And we lifted up the needs of families in western China, Bulgaria, and beyond.

Halfway through our prayers, it struck me that I rarely feel trapped or confined in my bed. Because of energetic times of praying, I know I'm a living testimony of Psalm 149:4–5. In fact, that night as we tuned in to Voice of America and Armed Forces Radio, and as we began praying for our men and women in uniform, we could sense the Lord taking delight in us. We could rejoice in that honor and *sing for joy in bed.*

> ***All*** of us can serve in a foreign mission field. We can be missionaries through prayer.

With his blood, Jesus has purchased men and women for God from every tribe, language, people, and nation (Rev. 5:9). No matter how limited you are, you *can* partner with him to reach these people worldwide. How? You can *pray.* And there is no better place than on a "bed of affliction." This bed can become an altar of praise to reach people around the world.

How so? Listen to the way my friend and I prayed that night. We prayed that people would ask, "Who can I trust in life?" or "What is life's meaning?" We prayed that people from Peru to Poland might look up into the blanket of stars and ask, "Where will I go when I die?" We asked the Lord to reveal himself supernaturally to those who had no access to the written Word.

I purchased my own shortwave radio not long after my friend's visit. I placed it by my bedside as a reminder that the people for whom we had prayed that night were just beyond my bedroom walls. And you know what? They were. Just as their voices had reached us via shortwave, my prayers, immediate and instant, could touch them in return. Every second as I prayed, godly grace was being applied. I didn't even have to leave my room.

The Lord takes delight in his people when they pray, and we can rejoice in this honor. *All of us can serve in a foreign mission field. We can be missionaries through prayer.*

Joni Eareckson Tada, president of Joni and Friends in Agura Hills, California

⁶May the praise of God be in their mouths *e*
  and a double-edged *f* sword in their hands,
⁷to inflict vengeance on the nations
  and punishment on the peoples,
⁸to bind their kings with fetters,
  their nobles with shackles of iron,
⁹to carry out the sentence written against them. *g*
  This is the glory of all his saints. *h*

Praise the LORD.

Psalm 150

¹Praise the LORD. *a*

Praise God in his sanctuary; *i*
  praise him in his mighty heavens. *j*
²Praise him for his acts of power; *k*
  praise him for his surpassing greatness. *l*
³Praise him with the sounding of the trumpet,
  praise him with the harp and lyre, *m*
⁴praise him with tambourine and dancing, *n*
  praise him with the strings *o* and flute,
⁵praise him with the clash of cymbals, *p*
  praise him with resounding cymbals.

⁶Let everything *q* that has breath praise the LORD.

Praise the LORD.

a 1 Hebrew *Hallelu Yah*; also in verse 6

149:6
e Ps 66:17
f Heb 4:12;
Rev 1:16

149:9
g Dt 7:1; Eze 28:26
h Ps 148:14

150:1
i Ps 102:19
j Ps 19:1
150:2
k Dt 3:24
l Ps 145:5-6

150:3
m Ps 149:3
150:4
n Ex 15:20
o Isa 38:20

150:5
p 1Ch 13:8; 15:16

150:6
q Ps 145:21

Psalm 150

🕮🕮 If Psalm 1 is an intentional introduction to the Psalter, Psalm 150 is its appropriate conclusion, functioning as a final doxology and bringing the collection to a solemn, yet joyful end. Psalm 150 is also the final Hallel psalm (see "There and Then" for Ps. 113 and 146).

Psalm 150 moves from *where* God is to be praised (v. 1) to *why* he's to be praised (v. 2) to *how* he's to be praised (vv. 3–5) to *who* is to praise him (v. 6).

📖 All God's creation that "has breath" (v. 6; cf. Gen. 2:7; 7:21–22)—particularly humanity—is called to praise the Lord (cf. 148:7–12). The Hebrew word used here applies to all living creatures, endowed with life by the Creator, but always in distinction from him. Why not take the time as you close the Psalter to thank God for those basic gifts you might easily take for granted: life, breath, love, God's Word, salvation, home, family, food . . . ? How might you fill out the list?

INTRODUCTION TO
Proverbs

AUTHORS
Solomon wrote most of the sayings that comprise the book of Proverbs, but other authors include Agur (30:1) and King Lemuel (31:1). The scribes of King Hezekiah copied additional proverbs of Solomon to form chapters 25–29 (see 25:1).

DATE WRITTEN
Solomon's proverbs were written between 970 and 930 B.C. Hezekiah's scribes compiled the additional proverbs of Solomon between 729 and 686 B.C. Nothing is known of Agur and King Lemuel, so the dates of composition of their proverbs are unknown.

ORIGINAL READERS
These proverbs were written to the people of Israel to show them how wisdom can be practically applied to everyday life.

TIMELINE

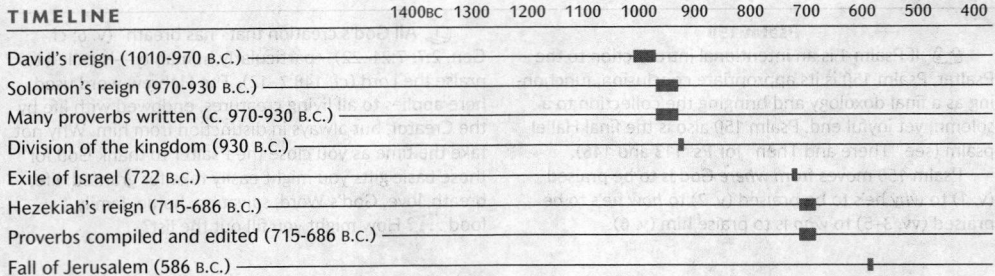

| | 1400BC | 1300 | 1200 | 1100 | 1000 | 900 | 800 | 700 | 600 | 500 | 400 |

David's reign (1010-970 B.C.)
Solomon's reign (970-930 B.C.)
Many proverbs written (c. 970-930 B.C.)
Division of the kingdom (930 B.C.)
Exile of Israel (722 B.C.)
Hezekiah's reign (715-686 B.C.)
Proverbs compiled and edited (715-686 B.C.)
Fall of Jerusalem (586 B.C.)

THEMES
A proverb is a general truth condensed into a short, catchy statement or story giving practical insights applicable to everyday life. The book of Proverbs gives instructions for practical living that include the following themes:

1. *Wisdom.* The predominant theme of the extended discourse in 1:1—9:18 is that of two women: Wisdom and Folly. Wisdom is a personification of God's attribute of wisdom and ultimately stands for God himself, while Folly stands for idols and the false gods vying for Israel's devotion. The truth expressed is that there is no real wisdom apart from God. To fear God is to begin on the path of wisdom (1:7).

2. *Practical living.* Proverbs presents principles for godly living. Therefore it has much to say about wealth, work, giving, and matters of the heart. It teaches that the rich are to use their resources wisely, showing generosity toward those in need (11:24–25; 28:27). Wealth gained by unjust means, like the exploitation of others (22:16), is seen as temporary and harmful to those who accumulate it (10:2). Individuals, especially political leaders, are to act with justice and generosity (29:4,7,14; 31:4–9). Business owners aren't to cheat their customers (11:1), and courts of law are to exercise justice toward all (17:15), not allowing themselves to be swayed

by bribes (17:23). Parents are vital to a child's spiritual development (1:8; 22:15), and trusting God is the key to understanding and godly living (3:5–6).

FAITH IN ACTION

The pages of Proverbs contain life lessons and role models of faith—people who challenge believers to put their faith in action.

Role Models

- A TRUSTWORTHY MAN (10:9; 11:3) keeps a secret, proving his loyalty and integrity. How do your relationships display your faith?

- THE RIGHTEOUS (10:3,6–7,11,16,20–21,24–25,28–32) are blessed, surviving life's storms and finding joy by following the way of the Lord; their words nourish many. How have you weathered life's storms? Do you have joy? Are your conversations nourishing?

- A KINDHEARTED WOMAN (11:16) is respected. What kindness can you show today?

- A GENEROUS MAN (11:24–25; 22:9) prospers. Are you open-hearted and open-handed in light of the needs all around you?

- A WIFE OF NOBLE CHARACTER (12:4; 31:10–31) is loved by her family and respected by all. Have you engaged lately in a personal character check-up?

- PEOPLE WHO ACCEPT DISCIPLINE AND CORRECTION (10:17; 12:1; 13:1,13,18; 15:31) learn wisdom, knowledge, understanding, and discernment. How do you receive correction? Is it hard for you to acknowledge when you are wrong?

- THOSE WHO ARE KIND TO THE NEEDY (14:21,31; 19:17; 28:8; 31:20) honor God. Is your respect for God demonstrated in your treatment of the poor?

- A WISE WOMAN (14:1; 24:3–4) builds her house. In what ways do you build up or edify your own and God's extended families?

Challenges

- Seek wisdom and accept instruction (9:9–10).

- Read a chapter from Proverbs every day. In one year you will cycle through this thought-provoking book 12 times.

- Resolve to live a life of integrity (10:9) that includes hard work (6:6–11; 10:4; 31:17–19) and compassion for the disadvantaged and needy (14:21; 31:20).

- Choose to turn from immorality (2:16–18; 22:14; 23:27; 30:20).

- Refrain from gossip (11:13; 17:9; 18:8; 26:22), revenge (20:22), quarreling (19:13; 21:9,19; 26:21), and anger (14:17,29; 29:11,22).

- Accept correction and discipline as instruments of learning (10:17).

- Understand that there are severe consequences for harming the defenseless and depriving them of justice (22:16,22–23; 23:10–11; 24:23–25; 28:8).

- Defend the rights of society's defenseless and vulnerable (29:7; 31:8–9).

OUTLINE

  I. Prologue: Purpose and Theme (1:1–7)
 II. Superiority of the Way of Wisdom (1:8—9:18)
III. Proverbs of Solomon (10:1—22:16)
 IV. Sayings of the Wise (22:17—24:34)
  V. More Proverbs of Solomon (25–29)
 VI. The Words of Agur and Lemuel (30:1—31:9)
VII. Epilogue: The Excellent Wife (31:10–31)

Prologue: Purpose and Theme

1:1
a 1Ki 4:29-34
b Pr 10:1; 25:1;
Ecc 1:1

1 The proverbs of Solomon *a* son of David, king of Israel: *b*

2 for attaining wisdom and discipline;
for understanding words of insight;
3 for acquiring a disciplined and prudent life,
doing what is right and just and fair;

1:4
c Pr 8:5 *d* Pr 2:10-
11; 8:12

4 for giving prudence to the simple, *c*
knowledge and discretion *d* to the young—

1:5
e Pr 9:9

5 let the wise listen and add to their learning, *e*
and let the discerning get guidance—

1:6
f Ps 49:4; 78:2
g Nu 12:8

6 for understanding proverbs and parables, *f*
the sayings and riddles *g* of the wise.

1:7
h Job 28:28;
Ps 111:10; Pr 9:10;
15:33; Ecc 12:13

7 The fear of the LORD *h* is the beginning of knowledge,
but fools *a* despise wisdom and discipline.

Exhortations to Embrace Wisdom

Warning Against Enticement

1:8
i Pr 4:1 *j* Pr 6:20

8 Listen, my son, *i* to your father's instruction
and do not forsake your mother's teaching. *j*

1:9
k Pr 4:1-9

9 They will be a garland to grace your head
and a chain to adorn your neck. *k*

1:10
l Ge 39:7 *m* Dt 13:8
n Pr 16:29;
Eph 5:11

10 My son, if sinners entice *l* you,
do not give in *m* to them. *n*

1:11
o Ps 10:8

11 If they say, "Come along with us;
let's lie in wait *o* for someone's blood,
let's waylay some harmless soul;

1:12
p Ps 28:1

12 let's swallow them alive, like the grave, *b*
and whole, like those who go down to the pit; *p*

---

a 7 The Hebrew words rendered *fool* in Proverbs, and often elsewhere in the Old Testament, denote one who is morally deficient.   *b* 12 Hebrew *Sheol*

Proverbs 1:1–7

The prologue connects the book of Proverbs with Solomon, who was renowned for his wisdom in general and for his prolific composition of proverbs in particular (cf. 1 Kings 4:29–34). Though some compiling and editing were involved, it's likely that Solomon was the source of most of Proverbs. The prologue also states the book's purpose—in a word, to pass along wisdom. Such an introductory statement wasn't unusual in the ancient world. Egyptian instructions in wisdom often named the speaker and recipient as part of their purpose statement: to pass on wisdom for successful living from one generation to the next.

The "fear of the LORD" is a critical concept in Proverbs. A form of the expression frames the book by appearing both at the beginning (v. 7) and the ending (31:30). The phrase recurs throughout Proverbs and guides our reading. As God is the source of every beginning, so our fear of him (worship and faithfulness) is the beginning of the study of wisdom and its primary goal.

Proverbs describes three basic qualities the wise are to display: the humility of the learner, love for our neighbor, and the fear of the Lord, of which the latter is paramount. Fear of the Lord is about turning from rebel-

lion to teachability before God. The life of wisdom isn't just good sense or a list of principles for a happy life (though they help); it's an attitude toward God that influences our decisions and actions.

Proverbs 1:8–19

The setting for chapters 1–9 is the home schooling of a young man. In Proverbs 1 he's told to pay attention to his parents' teachings and to the correction of Woman Wisdom but to ignore the offer to join violent gangs. The motif of competing voices, calls, and seductions runs throughout Proverbs 1–9, and the repetition urges the reader to consider the consequences of crucial life decisions. Lesson one is learning how, and to whom, to listen.

Few of us are enticed by violence or ill-gotten gain. Yet we can miss the passage's caution against the underlying issue: greed. If we listen to the media barrage with this in mind, we may be surprised at the level of desire, if not outright greed, underlying not only the commercials but also the programming itself. Americans are still keeping up with the Joneses, but the Joneses no longer live next door. The "reference groups" we form at work and play tell us what we need to acquire to show we are successful.

The Wise Man According to Proverbs: An Outline

I. His Character

A. He is teachable, not intractable.
1. He receives and loves instruction (18:15; 19:20).
2. He grows in wisdom (1:5; 9:9; 10:14).

B. He is righteous, not wicked.
1. He fears the Lord (1:7; 14:16; see below under relationship to the Lord).
2. He hates what is false (13:5).
3. He shuns evil (3:7; 14:16; 16:6).
4. He does what is righteous (2:20).
5. He speaks the truth (22:21).

C. He is humble, not proud (15:33).

D. He is self-controlled, not rash.
1. His temperament
   a. He is self-controlled (29:11).
   b. He has a calm spirit (17:27).
   c. He is slow to become angry (29:8,11).
2. His actions
   a. He is cautious, not hasty (19:2).
   b. He thinks before he acts (13:16; 14:8).
   c. He thinks before he speaks (12:23; 15:2).

E. He is forgiving, not vindictive.
1. He is patient (19:11).
2. He is concerned about goodwill/peace (14:9).
3. He forgives those who wrong him (10:12; 17:9).
4. He is not vindictive (20:22; 24:29).

II. His Relationships

A. To the Lord
1. He fears the Lord (9:10; 14:16; 15:33).
2. He trusts in the Lord (3:5; 16:3,20).
3. He is ever mindful of the Lord (3:6).
4. He chooses the Lord's way/wisdom (8:10–11; 17:24).
5. He submits to the Lord's discipline (1:2–3; 3:11).
6. He confesses his sin (28:13).

B. To his family
1. To his parents
   a. He respects them (17:6; cf. 30:17).
   b. He listens to them (23:22; cf. 1:8; 4:1).
   c. He seeks to bring them honor and joy.
      1) By being wise (10:1; 15:20; 29:3).
      2) By being righteous (23:24).
      3) By being diligent (10:5).
2. To his wife
   a. He appreciates her
      1) As a gift from the Lord (18:22; 19:14).
      2) As his crowning glory (12:4; 31:10–31).
   b. He praises her (31:28).
   c. He trusts her (31:11).
   d. He is faithful to her (5:15–20).
3. To his children
   a. He loves them (3:12; 13:24).
   b. He is concerned about them (1:8—9:18).
   c. He trains them (22:6).
      1) Reasons for training them

         a) His peace of mind and joy (29:17)
         b) Their honor and well-being (1:8–9; 4:9; 19:18; 23:13–14)
      2) By teaching/instructing them (1:10; chs. 5–7; 28:7; cf. 4:1–9)
      3) By disciplining them
         a) Through verbal correction (13:1)
         b) Through physical discipline (13:24; 23:13–14)
   d. He provides for their
      1) Physical needs (21:20; cf. 27:23–27).
      2) Spiritual heritage (14:26; 20:7).

C. To his friends and neighbors
1. To his friends
   a. He values them (27:10).
   b. He is constant to them (17:17; 18:24).
   c. He gives them counsel (27:9,17; cf. 27:6; 28:23).
2. To his neighbors
   a. He fulfills his obligations (3:27–28).
   b. He strives for peace (3:29–30).
   c. He does not outstay his welcome (25:17).
   d. He does not deceive or mislead them (16:29; 26:18–19).

III. His Words

A. He realizes the power of words.
1. Their power
   a. Of life and death (12:6; 13:14; 15:4; 18:21)
   b. To heal or to wound (11:9,11; 12:18; 15:4,30; 16:24)
2. Their limitation
   a. No substitute for deeds (14:23)
   b. Cannot alter the facts (26:23–26)
   c. Cannot compel response (29:19)

B. The character of his words
1. They are honest, not false (12:22; 16:13).
2. They are few, not many (10:19).
   a. Not boastful (27:2)
   b. Not argumentative (17:14)
   c. Not contentious (29:9)
   d. He is not a gossip
      1) Doesn't reveal secrets (11:13; 20:19)
      2) Doesn't spread slander (10:18; 26:20–22)
3. They are calm, not emotional.
   a. Rational (15:28; 17:27)
   b. Gentle and peaceable (15:1,18)
   c. Yet persuasive (25:15)
4. They are apt, not untimely (15:23; 25:11).

C. The source of his words
1. His heart/character (cf. 4:23 with Matt. 12:33–35)
   a. Positively, he is righteous (cf. 10:11;13:14).
   b. Negatively, he is not
      1) Proud (13:10; cf. 6:16–19).
      2) Hateful (26:24,28).
2. His companions (13:20; 27:17)
3. Reflections (15:28)

Wisdom

The book of Proverbs teaches applied knowledge—that is, wisdom.

This makes Proverbs an extremely important book. Wisdom is in short supply these days. Look around, and you will find plenty of knowledgeable people. Look in other places, and you will find no lack of good-hearted individuals. But chances are you will have to look hard to find many people exhibiting both qualities, people who have learned how to integrate their hard-won knowledge with their grace-imparted goodness.

Western culture suffers from having separated knowledge from ethics. Because of the importance and influence of science and technology in our world, we live with the notion that a person can know things without necessarily knowing how those same things are to be used. Scientists working on an atomic bomb, for example, could delude themselves into thinking they were simply extending the frontiers of knowledge, when in fact they were creating knowledge that could be used for horrific human ends.

What makes wisdom so difficult to achieve? At least five factors:

(1) Wisdom often seems *cryptic*—not easy to understand. This isn't necessarily because its content is so difficult but because it's typically radical and subversive. It often goes against established cultural norms that are geared toward economic success or political power. It takes ears specially trained in the ways of the gospel to hear the wisdom of many proverbs. "Ears to hear," Jesus called them (Mark 4:9). Otherwise, how could you hear someone say "A trustworthy man keeps a secret" (Prov. 11:13) without thinking of Enron, concealment, and corporate greed? Without thinking of the writer of that proverb as more than a little out of touch?

> **Western culture suffers from having separated knowledge from ethics.**

(2) And wisdom often seems *ambiguous*. Ambiguity is the very thing you would think wisdom was designed to do away with. But Proverbs teaches the opposite. Wisdom is sometimes found in the interaction between two proverbs rather than in the statement of just one: "Do not answer a fool according to his folly, or you will be like him yourself. Answer a fool according to his folly, or he will be wise in his own eyes" (26:4–5).

You have to read both parts, understand both, and then read and understand them together before wisdom emerges.

(3) Wisdom, like everything else human, is *culture specific*. Wisdom in one culture isn't necessarily wise in another. When you read Proverbs 7, all about the seductive charm of a wayward woman, a natural question is What about a good man? Proverbs is the product of a culture that didn't think to warn its daughters about men to avoid. So Alice Ogden Bellis transposed for her daughter: "Do not be misled by handsome faces, by beautiful bodies, by the right clothes, or the correct manners. Especially do not be deluded by flatterers who tell you that you are beautiful (of course you are!) and then ask you to give them your body and soul . . . Rather, spend your time with men of substance and worth. A good man is hard to find, but he is more precious than jewels."

(4) Wisdom takes *courage* to implement. It's not enough to be wise, to see what action is required by the knowledge you attain. You have to do more than recognize and acknowledge the action wisdom requires; you have to take it.

(5) Finally, wisdom is *broadminded*. Not just any actions implied by our knowledge will do. They are to be measured by the extent to which they contribute to God's plan: the building up of God's kingdom, the flourishing of people, and the well-being of creation.

13 we will get all sorts of valuable things
  and fill our houses with plunder;
14 throw in your lot with us,
  and we will share a common purse"—
15 my son, do not go along with them,
  do not set foot *q* on their paths; *r*
16 for their feet rush into sin,
  they are swift to shed blood. *s*
17 How useless to spread a net
  in full view of all the birds!
18 These men lie in wait for their own blood;
  they waylay only themselves!
19 Such is the end of all who go after ill-gotten gain;
  it takes away the lives of those who get it. *t*

Warning Against Rejecting Wisdom

20 Wisdom calls aloud *u* in the street,
  she raises her voice in the public squares;
21 at the head of the noisy streets *a* she cries out,
  in the gateways of the city she makes her speech:

22 "How long will you simple ones *b v* love your simple ways?
  How long will mockers delight in mockery
  and fools hate knowledge?
23 If you had responded to my rebuke,
  I would have poured out my heart to you
  and made my thoughts known to you.
24 But since you rejected me when I called *w*
  and no one gave heed when I stretched out my hand,
25 since you ignored all my advice
  and would not accept my rebuke,
26 I in turn will laugh *x* at your disaster;
  I will mock when calamity overtakes you *y*—
27 when calamity overtakes you like a storm,
  when disaster sweeps over you like a whirlwind,
  when distress and trouble overwhelm you.

28 "Then they will call to me but I will not answer; *z*
  they will look for me but will not find me. *a*
29 Since they hated knowledge
  and did not choose to fear the LORD, *b*
30 since they would not accept my advice
  and spurned my rebuke, *c*
31 they will eat the fruit of their ways
  and be filled with the fruit of their schemes. *d*
32 For the waywardness of the simple will kill them,

a 21 Hebrew; Septuagint / *on the tops of the walls*   *b 22* The Hebrew word rendered *simple* in Proverbs generally denotes one without moral direction and inclined to evil.

1:15
q Ps 119:101
r Ps 1:1; Pr 4:14
1:16
s Pr 6:18; Isa 59:7

1:19
t Pr 15:27

1:20
u Pr 8:1;
9:1-3,13-15

1:22
v Pr 8:5; 9:4,16

1:24
w Isa 65:12; 66:4;
Jer 7:13; Zec 7:11

1:26
x Ps 2:4 *y* Pr 6:15;
10:24

1:28
z 1Sa 8:18; Isa 1:15;
Jer 11:11; Mic 3:4
a Job 27:9; Pr 8:17;
Eze 8:18; Zec 7:13
1:29
b Job 21:14

1:30
c ver 25; Ps 81:11

1:31
d Job 4:8; Pr 14:14;
Isa 3:11; Jer 6:19

Proverbs 1:20–33
Wisdom speaks like a teacher and prophet but identifies herself with the Lord by using words and describing actions that normally come from God alone. Yet the identification is incomplete; she calls her hearers to "fear the LORD," not herself. Like God, she threatens to be unreachable when the day of trouble comes, but she doesn't say she will bring the trouble. She's a personification, not a deity, and her calls are made to offer guidance, not to solicit obedience and worship.

Without the negativity of Proverbs 1, we might get the notion that the goal of wisdom teaching is to prepare Christians for a successful and happy life. Not so. Professor Tony Campolo tells college students not to worry about self-fulfillment but to seek a sense of mission. Wisdom offers success and happiness as rewards and by-products but won't set us on a course of irresponsible self-fulfillment. Her warnings prevent us from thinking too highly of ourselves and too little of God and others.

1:32
e Jer 2:19
1:33
f Ps 25:12; Pr 3:23
g Ps 112:8

and the complacency of fools will destroy them; ^e

33 but whoever listens to me will live in safety ^f
    and be at ease, without fear of harm." ^g

Moral Benefits of Wisdom

2 My son, if you accept my words
    and store up my commands within you,

2:2
h Pr 22:17

2 turning your ear to wisdom
    and applying your heart to understanding, ^h
3 and if you call out for insight
    and cry aloud for understanding,
4 and if you look for it as for silver

2:4
i Job 3:21; Pr 3:14;
Mt 13:44
2:5
j Pr 1:7
2:6
k 1Ki 3:9,12;
Jas 1:5

    and search for it as for hidden treasure, ⁱ
5 then you will understand the fear of the LORD
    and find the knowledge of God. ^j
6 For the LORD gives wisdom, ^k
    and from his mouth come knowledge and understanding.

2:7
l Pr 30:5-6
m Ps 84:11

7 He holds victory in store for the upright,
    he is a shield ^l to those whose walk is blameless, ^m
8 for he guards the course of the just

2:8
n 1Sa 2:9; Ps 66:9

    and protects the way of his faithful ones. ⁿ

9 Then you will understand what is right and just
    and fair—every good path.

2:10
o Pr 14:33

10 For wisdom will enter your heart, ^o
    and knowledge will be pleasant to your soul.

2:11
p Pr 4:6; 6:22

11 Discretion will protect you,
    and understanding will guard you. ^p

12 Wisdom will save you from the ways of wicked men,
    from men whose words are perverse,

2:13
q Pr 4:19; Jn 3:19

13 who leave the straight paths
    to walk in dark ways, ^q

2:14
r Pr 10:23;
Jer 11:15
2:15
s Ps 125:5 t Pr 21:8

14 who delight in doing wrong
    and rejoice in the perverseness of evil, ^r
15 whose paths are crooked ^s
    and who are devious in their ways. ^t

2:16
u Pr 5:1-6; 6:20-29;
7:5-27

16 It will save you also from the adulteress, ^u
    from the wayward wife with her seductive words,

2:17
v Mal 2:14

17 who has left the partner of her youth
    and ignored the covenant she made before God. ^{a v}

2:18
w Pr 7:27

18 For her house leads down to death
    and her paths to the spirits of the dead. ^w

2:19
x Ecc 7:26

19 None who go to her return
    or attain the paths of life. ^x

a 17 Or *covenant of her God*

Proverbs 2:1–22

Whereas chapter 1 opens with the invitation to study and adds warnings to those who refuse, chapter 2 calls the "son" to begin the study, followed by promises of finding wisdom and enjoying its protection. As was common in the ancient Near East, each section of teaching follows a predictable pattern or form. An address ("My son") is followed by a charge or condition ("if you accept my words"), which is followed in turn by a series of motivations or rewards ("then you will understand the fear of the LORD").

Directions about behavior are part of the teaching of these "proverbial" parents. But rather than nagging their son, they hold out the goal of his becoming wise and free, able to decide right for himself. Knowing that God through wisdom protects their son, these parents learn to let go in trust and confidence that inspires us to do the same. (If you are a parent, how hard is that for you to do?) Parents also learn in the process. The matters of desire, understanding, and protection are just as central to the life of wisdom for us as adults—perhaps more so, because the seductions have become more subtle.

²⁰Thus you will walk in the ways of good men
    and keep to the paths of the righteous.
²¹For the upright will live in the land,^y
    and the blameless will remain in it;
²²but the wicked will be cut off from the land,^z
    and the unfaithful will be torn from it. ^a

Further Benefits of Wisdom

3 My son, do not forget my teaching,^b
    but keep my commands in your heart,
²for they will prolong your life many years^c
    and bring you prosperity.

³Let love and faithfulness never leave you;
    bind them around your neck,
    write them on the tablet of your heart. ^d
⁴Then you will win favor and a good name
    in the sight of God and man. ^e

⁵Trust in the Lord^f with all your heart
    and lean not on your own understanding;
⁶in all your ways acknowledge him,
    and he will make your paths^g straight. ^{a h}

⁷Do not be wise in your own eyes;ⁱ
    fear the Lord and shun evil.^j
⁸This will bring health to your body^k
    and nourishment to your bones. ^l

⁹Honor the Lord with your wealth,
    with the firstfruits^m of all your crops;
¹⁰then your barns will be filledⁿ to overflowing,
    and your vats will brim over with new wine. ^o

¹¹My son, do not despise the Lord's discipline^p
    and do not resent his rebuke,
¹²because the Lord disciplines those he loves,^q
    as a father^b the son he delights in. ^r

¹³Blessed is the man who finds wisdom,
    the man who gains understanding,
¹⁴for she is more profitable than silver
    and yields better returns than gold. ^s
¹⁵She is more precious than rubies;^t
    nothing you desire can compare with her. ^u

---

^a 6 Or *will direct your paths*   ^b 12 Hebrew; Septuagint / *and he punishes*

2:21	y Ps 37:29
2:22	z Job 18:17; Ps 37:38 a Dt 28:63; Pr 10:30
3:1	b Pr 4:5
3:2	c Pr 4:10
3:3	d Ex 13:9; Pr 6:21; 7:3; 2Co 3:3
3:4	e 1Sa 2:26; Lk 2:52
3:5	f Ps 37:3,5
3:6	g 1Ch 28:9 h Pr 16:3; Isa 45:13
3:7	i Ro 12:16 j Job 1:1; Pr 16:6
3:8	k Pr 4:22 l Job 21:24
3:9	m Ex 22:29; 23:19; Dt 26:1-15
3:10	n Dt 28:8 o Joel 2:24
3:11	p Job 5:17
3:12	q Pr 13:24; Rev 3:19 r Dt 8:5; Heb 12:5-6*
3:14	s Job 28:15; Pr 8:19; 16:16
3:15	t Job 28:18 u Pr 8:11

Proverbs 3:1–35

📖 This chapter challenges its readers to give up their fantasies of self-determination and self-sufficiency and turn to wisdom, a guide and protector from the real danger of self-destruction. This theme, introduced in chapter 2, is repeated and developed, adding the benefits of long life, wealth, and honor. The name of the Lord is prominent: He is to be trusted, feared, and honored (vv. 1–10). He disciplines and creates (vv. 11–20) and looks after those who walk in his way, while opposing the wicked (vv. 21–35).

📖 The principles in Proverbs aren't ironclad promises of success or formulas that will give us mastery over our future. Instead, they describe how life generally turns out for those who understand the principles. They offer no guarantees against suffering but recommend ways by which we can avoid bringing it on ourselves.

Chapter 3 urges us to honor God, find wisdom, and do good to our neighbors. Though the chapter contains some directives regarding behavior, the primary strategy it promotes is making attitudinal changes that will lead to changes in action. An attitude is, after all, an action waiting to happen. C.S. Lewis stated that only two things last forever: God and human beings. How easy it is to try to use God and people in our love of things, instead of the other way around. Proverbs 3 advocates that this deadly reversal of priorities can itself be turned around.

3:16
v Pr 8:18

3:17
w Pr 16:7;
Mt 11:28-30
3:18
x Ge 2:9; Pr 11:30;
Rev 2:7

3:19
y Ps 104:24
z Pr 8:27-29

3:21
a Pr 4:20-22

3:22
b Pr 1:8-9

3:23
c Ps 37:24; Pr 4:12
3:24
d Lev 26:6; Ps 3:5
e Job 11:18

3:26
f 1Sa 2:9

3:28
g Lev 19:13;
Dt 24:15

3:31
h Ps 37:1; Pr 24:1-2

3:32
i Pr 11:20
j Job 29:4; Ps 25:14

3:33
k Dt 11:28; Mal 2:2
l Zec 5:4 m Ps 1:3

3:34
n Jas 4:6*; 1Pe 5:5*

4:1
o Pr 1:8

16 Long life is in her right hand;
    in her left hand are riches and honor. v

17 Her ways are pleasant ways,
    and all her paths are peace. w

18 She is a tree of life x to those who embrace her;
    those who lay hold of her will be blessed.

19 By wisdom the LORD laid the earth's foundations, y
    by understanding he set the heavens z in place;

20 by his knowledge the deeps were divided,
    and the clouds let drop the dew.

21 My son, preserve sound judgment and discernment,
    do not let them out of your sight; a

22 they will be life for you,
    an ornament to grace your neck. b

23 Then you will go on your way in safety,
    and your foot will not stumble; c

24 when you lie down, d you will not be afraid;
    when you lie down, your sleep e will be sweet.

25 Have no fear of sudden disaster
    or of the ruin that overtakes the wicked,

26 for the LORD will be your confidence
    and will keep your foot f from being snared.

27 Do not withhold good from those who deserve it,
    when it is in your power to act.

28 Do not say to your neighbor,
    "Come back later; I'll give it tomorrow"—
    when you now have it with you. g

29 Do not plot harm against your neighbor,
    who lives trustfully near you.

30 Do not accuse a man for no reason—
    when he has done you no harm.

31 Do not envy h a violent man
    or choose any of his ways,

32 for the LORD detests a perverse man i
    but takes the upright into his confidence. j

33 The LORD's curse k is on the house of the wicked, l
    but he blesses the home of the righteous. m

34 He mocks proud mockers
    but gives grace to the humble. n

35 The wise inherit honor,
    but fools he holds up to shame.

Wisdom Is Supreme

4 Listen, my sons, o to a father's instruction;
    pay attention and gain understanding.

2 I give you sound learning,
    so do not forsake my teaching.

3 When I was a boy in my father's house,
    still tender, and an only child of my mother,

Proverbs 4:1–27

Chapter 4 doesn't mention the Lord, who took center stage in chapter 3. Chapter 3 gives the view from above and chapter 4 the view from below, in which fa-

thers teach sons to observe the ways of both the righteous and the wicked. It would be a mistake to separate the wisdom instruction of the home from the wisdom teaching of God. Parents pass on what they have

⁴he taught me and said,
    "Lay hold of my words with all your heart;
    keep my commands and you will live. ᵖ
⁵Get wisdom, ᑫ get understanding;
    do not forget my words or swerve from them.
⁶Do not forsake wisdom, and she will protect you; ʳ
    love her, and she will watch over you.
⁷Wisdom is supreme; therefore get wisdom.
    Though it cost allˢ you have, ᵃ get understanding. ᵗ
⁸Esteem her, and she will exalt you;
    embrace her, and she will honor you. ᵘ
⁹She will set a garland of grace on your head
    and present you with a crown of splendor. ᵛ"

¹⁰Listen, my son, accept what I say,
    and the years of your life will be many. ʷ
¹¹I guideˣ you in the way of wisdom
    and lead you along straight paths.
¹²When you walk, your steps will not be hampered;
    when you run, you will not stumble. ʸ
¹³Hold on to instruction, do not let it go;
    guard it well, for it is your life. ᶻ
¹⁴Do not set foot on the path of the wicked
    or walk in the way of evil men. ᵃ
¹⁵Avoid it, do not travel on it;
    turn from it and go on your way.
¹⁶For they cannot sleep till they do evil; ᵇ
    they are robbed of slumber till they make someone fall.
¹⁷They eat the bread of wickedness
    and drink the wine of violence.

¹⁸The path of the righteousᶜ is like the first gleam of dawn,
    shining ever brighter till the full light of day. ᵈ
¹⁹But the way of the wicked is like deep darkness; ᵉ
    they do not know what makes them stumble.

²⁰My son, pay attention to what I say;
    listen closely to my words. ᶠ
²¹Do not let them out of your sight, ᵍ
    keep them within your heart;
²²for they are life to those who find them
    and health to a man's whole body. ʰ
²³Above all else, guard your heart,
    for it is the wellspring of life. ⁱ
²⁴Put away perversity from your mouth;
    keep corrupt talk far from your lips.
²⁵Let your eyes look straight ahead,
    fix your gaze directly before you.
²⁶Make levelᵇ paths for your feetʲ
    and take only ways that are firm.

ᵃ 7 Or *Whatever else you get*   ᵇ 26 Or *Consider the*

4:4 p Pr 7:2
4:5 q Pr 16:16
4:6 r 2Th 2:10
4:7 s Mt 13:44-46 | t Pr 23:23
4:8 u 1Sa 2:30; Pr 3:18
4:9 v Pr 1:8-9
4:10 w Pr 3:2
4:11 x 1Sa 12:23
4:12 y Job 18:7; Pr 3:23
4:13 z Pr 3:22
4:14 a Ps 1:1; Pr 1:15
4:16 b Ps 36:4; Mic 2:1
4:18 c Isa 26:7 | d 2Sa 23:4; Da 12:3; Mt 5:14; Php 2:15
4:19 e Job 18:5; Pr 2:13; Isa 59:9-10; Jn 12:35
4:20 f Pr 5:1
4:21 g Pr 3:21; 7:1-2
4:22 h Pr 3:8; 12:18
4:23 i Mt 12:34; Lk 6:45
4:26 j Heb 12:13*

---

received from the Lord (cf. 3:12), the source and beginning of wisdom teaching. The emphasis in chapter 4 is on the transmission and legacy of wisdom.

The chapter's invitation to watch a tradition of parents teaching their children can encourage today's parents to share openly about how the tradition has been good for them, a source of protection and honor,

something that has become more valuable over time. The emphasis on testimony may encourage parents to share their own mistakes and failings when appropriate. It can be a sign that wisdom doesn't arrive in a single, neat package. If you are a parent/grandparent, how do you incorporate passing along your faith into life's fleeting moments?

4:27
k Dt 5:32; 28:14

27 Do not swerve to the right or the left;[k]
    keep your foot from evil.

Warning Against Adultery

5:1
l Pr 4:20; 22:17

5 My son, pay attention to my wisdom,
    listen well to my words[l] of insight,
2 that you may maintain discretion
    and your lips may preserve knowledge.

5:3
m Ps 55:21;
Pr 2:16; 7:5
5:4
n Ecc 7:26

3 For the lips of an adulteress drip honey,
    and her speech is smoother than oil;[m]
4 but in the end she is bitter as gall,[n]
    sharp as a double-edged sword.

5:5
o Pr 7:26-27

5 Her feet go down to death;
    her steps lead straight to the grave.[a][o]

5:6
p Pr 30:20

6 She gives no thought to the way of life;
    her paths are crooked, but she knows it not.[p]

5:7
q Pr 7:24

7 Now then, my sons, listen[q] to me;
    do not turn aside from what I say.

5:8
r Pr 7:1-27

8 Keep to a path far from her,[r]
    do not go near the door of her house,
9 lest you give your best strength to others
    and your years to one who is cruel,
10 lest strangers feast on your wealth
    and your toil enrich another man's house.
11 At the end of your life you will groan,
    when your flesh and body are spent.

5:12
s Pr 1:29; 12:1

12 You will say, "How I hated discipline!
    How my heart spurned correction![s]
13 I would not obey my teachers
    or listen to my instructors.
14 I have come to the brink of utter ruin
    in the midst of the whole assembly."

15 Drink water from your own cistern,
    running water from your own well.
16 Should your springs overflow in the streets,
    your streams of water in the public squares?
17 Let them be yours alone,
    never to be shared with strangers.

5:18
t SS 4:12-15
u Ecc 9:9; Mal 2:14

18 May your fountain[t] be blessed,
    and may you rejoice in the wife of your youth.[u]

---

[a] 5 Hebrew *Sheol*

Proverbs 5:1–23

Chapter 5 develops the idea of "guarding your heart" (4:23) by urging the son to preserve knowledge, to keep hold of wisdom in the face of temptations to lose or reject it. In the economy of the sages, to lose or forsake wisdom is to lose everything else as well. The example in this chapter is the marriage relationship. To offer our intimacy to strangers is to risk losing all to them, but to "drink from our own well" is to keep all that is our own, including our life.

The teaching of this chapter may be summed up as: Guard your heart to live well; live well to guard your heart. Good practice shapes good character, which in turn leads to more good practice. A person becomes good by doing good. Good people do good deeds, and good deeds shape good people. This practice of faithfulness dispels the illusions and deceptions of folly.

The call to an exclusive marital relationship is a call to joy. Ironically, the *discipline* brings pleasure. Love may begin as a feeling, but it must be continued as a conscious choice if it's to continue at all. Yet the choice, surprisingly, keeps the feeling alive. Certainly a relationship of commitment brings with it its own joys. The word isn't used here, but we can speak of a marriage *covenant*—something more solid than a breakable contract. If you are married, what are you doing to "guard your heart" from unfaithfulness and "rejoice" in the gift of your spouse (5:18)?

¹⁹ A loving doe, a graceful deer^v—
 may her breasts satisfy you always,
 may you ever be captivated by her love.
²⁰ Why be captivated, my son, by an adulteress?
 Why embrace the bosom of another man's wife?

²¹ For a man's ways are in full view^w of the LORD,
 and he examines all his paths.^x
²² The evil deeds of a wicked man ensnare him;^y
 the cords of his sin hold him fast.^z
²³ He will die for lack of discipline,^a
 led astray by his own great folly.

Warnings Against Folly

6 My son, if you have put up security for your neighbor,^b
 if you have struck hands in pledge^c for another,
² if you have been trapped by what you said,
 ensnared by the words of your mouth,
³ then do this, my son, to free yourself,
 since you have fallen into your neighbor's hands:
Go and humble yourself;
 press your plea with your neighbor!
⁴ Allow no sleep to your eyes,
 no slumber to your eyelids.^d
⁵ Free yourself, like a gazelle from the hand of the hunter,
 like a bird from the snare of the fowler.^e

⁶ Go to the ant, you sluggard;^f
 consider its ways and be wise!
⁷ It has no commander,
 no overseer or ruler,
⁸ yet it stores its provisions in summer
 and gathers its food at harvest.^g

⁹ How long will you lie there, you sluggard?^h
 When will you get up from your sleep?
¹⁰ A little sleep, a little slumber,
 a little folding of the hands to restⁱ—
¹¹ and poverty^j will come on you like a bandit
 and scarcity like an armed man.^a

¹² A scoundrel and villain,
 who goes about with a corrupt mouth,
¹³ who winks with his eye,^k

---

^a 11 Or *like a vagrant / and scarcity like a beggar*

5:19
v SS 2:9; 4:5

5:21
w Ps 119:168;
Hos 7:2
x Job 14:16;
Job 31:4; 34:21;
Pr 15:3; Jer 16:17;
32:19; Heb 4:13
5:22
y Ps 9:16
z Nu 32:23;
Ps 7:15-16;
Pr 1:31-32
5:23
a Job 4:21; 36:12
6:1
b Pr 17:18
c Pr 11:15;
22:26-27

6:4
d Ps 132:4

6:5
e Ps 91:3

6:6
f Pr 20:4

6:8
g Pr 10:4
6:9
h Pr 24:30-34

6:10
i Pr 24:33
6:11
j Pr 24:30-34

6:13
k Ps 35:19

Proverbs 6:1–19

Three sections in this passage (vv. 1–5, 6–11, and 12–15) work together to create a portrait of folly in various forms. Each section concludes with a negative outcome: The person who pledges is caught in a trap; the lazy individual will be ambushed by poverty and the scoundrel overtaken by disaster. Verses 16–19 expand on verses 12–15, showing why disaster will fall on the rascal described here.

The term translated "sluggard" occurs 14 times in Proverbs and nowhere else in the Old Testament. The sluggard exemplifies folly (19:15; 21:24–26; 26:12–16), particularly in matters of food production. Hands folded when they should be working is the ultimate sign of sloth (laziness or "sluggishness").

The irony of contemporary life is that we are lazy about a great number of things in the middle of frenetic activity. We can test our commitments by asking whether they give us an excuse to neglect what is most important in life. The principle of avoiding bad commitments will lead us to take stock of how we have apportioned our time, money, and other resources, so we can make and keep good ones. We know we have made bad choices when someone else loses because we have chosen poorly. These verses certainly advise diligence in financial matters but ultimately warn us against all forms of "sluggardliness."

signals with his feet
and motions with his fingers,

14 who plots evil *l* with deceit in his heart—
he always stirs up dissension. *m*

15 Therefore disaster will overtake him in an instant;
he will suddenly be destroyed—without remedy. *n*

16 There are six things the LORD hates,
seven that are detestable to him:

17 haughty eyes,
a lying tongue, *o*
hands that shed innocent blood, *p*

18 a heart that devises wicked schemes,
feet that are quick to rush into evil, *q*

19 a false witness *r* who pours out lies
and a man who stirs up dissension among brothers. *s*

Warning Against Adultery

20 My son, keep your father's commands
and do not forsake your mother's teaching. *t*

21 Bind them upon your heart forever;
fasten them around your neck. *u*

22 When you walk, they will guide you;
when you sleep, they will watch over you;
when you awake, they will speak to you.

23 For these commands are a lamp,
this teaching is a light, *v*
and the corrections of discipline
are the way to life,

24 keeping you from the immoral woman,
from the smooth tongue of the wayward wife. *w*

25 Do not lust in your heart after her beauty
or let her captivate you with her eyes,

26 for the prostitute reduces you to a loaf of bread,
and the adulteress preys upon your very life. *x*

27 Can a man scoop fire into his lap
without his clothes being burned?

28 Can a man walk on hot coals
without his feet being scorched?

29 So is he who sleeps *y* with another man's wife; *z*
no one who touches her will go unpunished.

30 Men do not despise a thief if he steals
to satisfy his hunger when he is starving.

31 Yet if he is caught, he must pay sevenfold, *a*
though it costs him all the wealth of his house.

Proverbs 6:20–35

Serious warnings continue as the teacher once again reminds the son that no one who touches another man's wife will go unpunished. This third teaching on adultery (cf. 2:16–19; 5:1–20) continues into chapter 7. Three analogies drive home the parents' point: (1) the toll taken by the prostitute and the adulteress (v. 26); (2) adultery as "playing with fire" (vv. 27–29); and (3) the fates of the hungry thief and the adulterer (vv. 30–31). Three consequences are named, respectively: loss of life, punishment like burning, and the combination of public disgrace and a husband's angry vengeance.

Adultery destroys not only the one who practices it but also the wronged partner(s), both families, and their communities. Saying no to its seductions demonstrates commitment and contentment: commitment, because the person who says no is careful to consider costs and maintain vows and promises; contentment, because the decision to say no not only respects our neighbor but refuses to look somewhere else for a "better deal." The wise person takes the long view, looking to the end of the road, visualizing positive and negative outcomes, and choosing what's truly best for ourselves and those around us.

³²But a man who commits adultery[b] lacks judgment;[c]
    whoever does so destroys himself.
³³Blows and disgrace are his lot,
    and his shame will never[d] be wiped away;
³⁴for jealousy[e] arouses a husband's fury,[f]
    and he will show no mercy when he takes revenge.
³⁵He will not accept any compensation;
    he will refuse the bribe, however great it is.[g]

Warning Against the Adulteress

7 My son,[h] keep my words
    and store up my commands within you.
²Keep my commands and you will live;[i]
    guard my teachings as the apple of your eye.
³Bind them on your fingers;
    write them on the tablet of your heart.[j]
⁴Say to wisdom, "You are my sister,"
    and call understanding your kinsman;
⁵they will keep you from the adulteress,
    from the wayward wife with her seductive words.[k]

6:32
b Ex 20:14 c Pr 7:7; 9:4,16
6:33
d Pr 5:9-14
6:34
e Nu 5:14 f Ge 34:7
6:35
g Job 31:9-11; SS 8:7
7:1
h Pr 1:8; 2:1
7:2
i Pr 4:4
7:3
j Dt 6:8; Pr 3:3
7:5
k ver 21; Job 31:9; Pr 2:16; 6:24

Proverbs 7:1–27

The parental teachers have saved their most vivid images and warnings about the adulteress for last. The fourth appearance of this woman is the longest, most descriptive, and most important—a narrative in which the smooth speech mentioned in every appearance is finally heard (vv. 14–21; cf. 2:16; 5:3; 6:24). Only when it's too late does this young man realize that these words have made him prey and taken his life. The fault is his. Had he followed his parents' instruction and called to wisdom, he would have been protected.

We are wise to find ways to talk about the goodness of sex *and* of boundaries in a culture that makes too much of sex and too little of boundaries. Our culture has made sex an idol. We have not only worshiped it with our attention and dollars, but many of us expect it to serve and fulfill our most basic physical and emotional needs for esteem and intimacy. Ironically, such a view of sex trivializes it, isolating it from the essential dimensions of commitment and transparency that mark honest, committed relationships. What boundaries have you erected to protect yourself from failing in this area? What part do your family and church fellowship play in these strategies?

Snapshots

6:23

Betsey Stockton

Betsey Stockton (1798–1865) was born a slave in Princeton, New Jersey, but given as a child by her owner to his daughter, Elizabeth, and her husband, Ashbel Green, a Presbyterian minister and president of the College of New Jersey (later Princeton University). Betsey was raised as a family member. A single, black American woman, she was appointed as a young adult to a missionary post under the American Board of Commissioners for Foreign Missions. In 1822 she sailed to the Sandwich Island mission along with the Charles Stewart family.

A pioneer missionary at Lahaina, Maui, Hawaii, Stockton opened a school for the lower classes there. After returning to America with the Stewarts four years later, she taught at an "infant school" in Philadelphia, going on for a brief period to help some Canadian missionaries in an educational program for Native American children.

Betsey returned to Princeton, where she served for many years as principal of a school for black children. The humble "Aunt Betsey" was loved and respected by many.

> **A** single, black American woman, she was appointed as a young adult to a missionary post.

⁶At the window of my house
   I looked out through the lattice.
⁷I saw among the simple,
   I noticed among the young men,
   a youth who lacked judgment.^l
⁸He was going down the street near her corner,
   walking along in the direction of her house
⁹at twilight,^m as the day was fading,
   as the dark of night set in.

¹⁰Then out came a woman to meet him,
   dressed like a prostitute and with crafty intent.
¹¹(She is loudⁿ and defiant,
   her feet never stay at home;
¹²now in the street, now in the squares,
   at every corner she lurks.)^o
¹³She took hold of him^p and kissed him
   and with a brazen face she said:^q

¹⁴"I have fellowship offerings^a^r at home;
   today I fulfilled my vows.
¹⁵So I came out to meet you;
   I looked for you and have found you!
¹⁶I have covered my bed
   with colored linens from Egypt.
¹⁷I have perfumed my bed^s
   with myrrh,^t aloes and cinnamon.
¹⁸Come, let's drink deep of love till morning;
   let's enjoy ourselves with love!^u
¹⁹My husband is not at home;
   he has gone on a long journey.
²⁰He took his purse filled with money
   and will not be home till full moon."

²¹With persuasive words she led him astray;
   she seduced him with her smooth talk.^v
²²All at once he followed her
   like an ox going to the slaughter,
   like a deer^b stepping into a noose^c^w
²³   till an arrow pierces^x his liver,
   like a bird darting into a snare,
   little knowing it will cost him his life.^y

²⁴Now then, my sons, listen^z to me;
   pay attention to what I say.
²⁵Do not let your heart turn to her ways
   or stray into her paths.^a
²⁶Many are the victims she has brought down;
   her slain are a mighty throng.
²⁷Her house is a highway to the grave,^d
   leading down to the chambers of death.^b

Wisdom's Call

8   Does not wisdom call out?^c
   Does not understanding raise her voice?
   ²On the heights along the way,
   where the paths meet, she takes her stand;

Cross references (margin)

7:7 l Pr 1:22; 6:32
7:9 m Job 24:15
7:11 n Pr 9:13; 1Ti 5:13
7:12 o Pr 8:1-36; 23:26-28
7:13 p Ge 39:12 q Pr 1:20
7:14 r Lev 7:11-18
7:17 s Est 1:6; Isa 57:7; Eze 23:41; Am 6:4 t Ge 37:25
7:18 u Ge 39:7
7:21 v Pr 5:3
7:22 w Job 18:10
7:23 x Job 15:22; 16:13 y Pr 6:26; Ecc 7:26; 9:12
7:24 z Pr 1:8-9; 5:7; 8:32
7:25 a Pr 5:7-8
7:27 b Pr 2:18; 5:5; 9:18; Rev 22:15
8:1 c Pr 1:20; 9:3

---

^a 14 Traditionally *peace offerings*   ^b 22 Syriac (see also Septuagint); Hebrew *fool*
^c 22 The meaning of the Hebrew for this line is uncertain.   ^d 27 Hebrew *Sheol*

³beside the gates leading into the city,
  at the entrances, she cries aloud: *d*

⁴"To you, O men, I call out;
  I raise my voice to all mankind.

⁵You who are simple, *e* gain prudence; *f*
  you who are foolish, gain understanding.

⁶Listen, for I have worthy things to say;
  I open my lips to speak what is right.

⁷My mouth speaks what is true, *g*
  for my lips detest wickedness.

⁸All the words of my mouth are just;
  none of them is crooked or perverse.

⁹To the discerning all of them are right;
  they are faultless to those who have knowledge.

¹⁰Choose my instruction instead of silver,
  knowledge rather than choice gold, *h*

¹¹for wisdom is more precious *i* than rubies,
  and nothing you desire can compare with her. *j*

¹²"I, wisdom, dwell together with prudence;
  I possess knowledge and discretion. *k*

¹³To fear the LORD is to hate evil; *l*
  I hate *m* pride and arrogance,
  evil behavior and perverse speech.

¹⁴Counsel and sound judgment are mine;
  I have understanding and power. *n*

¹⁵By me kings reign
  and rulers *o* make laws that are just;

¹⁶by me princes govern,
  and all nobles who rule on earth. *a*

¹⁷I love those who love me, *p*
  and those who seek me find me. *q*

¹⁸With me are riches and honor, *r*
  enduring wealth and prosperity. *s*

¹⁹My fruit is better than fine gold;
  what I yield surpasses choice silver. *t*

²⁰I walk in the way of righteousness,
  along the paths of justice,

²¹bestowing wealth on those who love me
  and making their treasuries full. *u*

8:3
d Job 29:7

8:5
e Pr 1:22 *f* Pr 1:4

8:7
g Ps 37:30; Jn 8:14

8:10
h Pr 3:14-15
8:11
i Job 28:17-19
j Pr 3:13-15

8:12
k Pr 1:4
8:13
l Pr 16:6 *m* Jer 44:4

8:14
n Pr 21:22; Ecc 7:19

8:15
o Da 2:21; Ro 13:1

8:17
p 1Sa 2:30;
Ps 91:14;
Jn 14:21-24
q Pr 1:28; Jas 1:5
8:18
r Pr 3:16 *s* Dt 8:18;
Mt 6:33
8:19
t Pr 3:13-14; 10:20

8:21
u Pr 24:4

a 16 Many Hebrew manuscripts and Septuagint; most Hebrew manuscripts *and nobles—all righteous rulers*

Proverbs 8:1–36

📖 Along with the ode to the woman of strength in chapter 31, this speech of Woman Wisdom is one of the best-known portions of Proverbs. Here for the second time personified Wisdom calls out like a street preacher (cf. 1:20–33). She describes herself, her qualities, and her gifts and speaks of her existence at the dawn of creation. Her words contribute to our understanding not only of that creation but also of the Word, who was with God from the beginning (John 1:1).

The content of Proverbs isn't simply shared bits of life's lessons but instruction in the workings of the world from one who watched it come into being. In essence, the speech in chapter 8 says to the reader, "Seek Wisdom, and find wealth and life as well. Seek wealth or life apart from her, and you will miss Wisdom and find death." In many ways the message resembles Jesus' teaching in Mark 8:35–38 (cf. Matt. 10:39; Luke 17:33; John 12:25).

📖 Wisdom's offer of enduring wealth encourages Christians to assess their attitudes toward material goods (cf. 3:1–18). Recalling Jesus' teaching on the priceless kingdom pearl (Matt. 13:45–46), believers hear in these words a call to make comparisons, to reflect on the relative values of wealth and wisdom. Wisdom has something to say about the way wealth is gained and distributed. But she speaks against unreflective rejection of wealth. It's not the refusal to acquire or spend that marks the righteous person, but the desire to do right by self, neighbor, and God.

8:24
v Ge 7:11

8:25
w Job 15:7

8:26
x Ps 90:2
8:27
y Pr 3:19

8:29
z Ge 1:9;
Job 38:10; Ps 16:6
a Ps 104:9
b Job 38:5
8:30
c Jn 1:1-3

8:31
d Ps 16:3; 104:1-30

8:32
e Lk 11:28
f Ps 119:1-2

8:34
g Pr 3:13,18

22 "The LORD brought me forth as the first of his works, [a, b]
    before his deeds of old;
23 I was appointed [c] from eternity,
    from the beginning, before the world began.
24 When there were no oceans, I was given birth,
    when there were no springs abounding with water; [v]
25 before the mountains were settled in place,
    before the hills, I was given birth, [w]
26 before he made the earth or its fields
    or any of the dust of the world. [x]
27 I was there when he set the heavens in place, [y]
    when he marked out the horizon on the face of the deep,
28 when he established the clouds above
    and fixed securely the fountains of the deep,
29 when he gave the sea its boundary [z]
    so the waters would not overstep his command, [a]
    and when he marked out the foundations of the earth. [b]
30 Then I was the craftsman at his side. [c]
    I was filled with delight day after day,
    rejoicing always in his presence,
31 rejoicing in his whole world
    and delighting in mankind. [d]

32 "Now then, my sons, listen to me;
    blessed are [e] those who keep my ways. [f]
33 Listen to my instruction and be wise;
    do not ignore it.
34 Blessed is the man who listens [g] to me,
    watching daily at my doors,

[a] 22 Or *way*; or *dominion*   [b] 22 Or *The LORD possessed me at the beginning of his work*; or *The LORD brought me forth at the beginning of his work*   [c] 23 Or *fashioned*

If Wisdom rejoices in the order and beauty of creation, we may conclude that creation is worth preserving. Christians differ over how best to manage the physical resources placed in our care. Some advocate use and development, while others think of preservation and limits on development. Proponents of preservation argue the need for untouched places where Earth and heaven can sing forth God's glory. What are your views on this complex issue?

8:32

Sobering Stats on Children

In order for children to keep their parents' ways, they need to live and thrive, free from hunger and secure in their homes. Yet:

85 percent of all children live in the two-thirds world.[1]

70 percent of the world's children are growing up in non-Christian settings.[2]

20 MILLION

20 million children worldwide die each year from hunger-related diseases.[3]

15 MILLION

15 million children die each year from preventable causes other than hunger.[4]

More than 100 million children live and work on the streets of our world's megacities.[5]

Over one million children become involved in the sex trade each year.[6]

One third of the world's population is under the age of 15.[7]

More than 200,000 children under the age of 15 are currently fighting in wars.[8]

Sources: [1] Myers (2003:31) [2] Myers (2003:67) [3] Smith (1999:30) [4] Myers (2003:31) [5] Myers (2003:72) [6] "Sickness or Symptom?" *The Economist* (February 7, 2004): 69 [7] Bellamy (2001:68) [8] Smith (1999:57)

waiting at my doorway.
35 For whoever finds me^h finds life
  and receives favor from the LORD.ⁱ
36 But whoever fails to find me harms himself;^j
  all who hate me love death."

Invitations of Wisdom and of Folly

9 Wisdom has built^k her house;
  she has hewn out its seven pillars.
2 She has prepared her meat and mixed her wine;
  she has also set her table.^l
3 She has sent out her maids, and she calls^m
  from the highest point of the city.ⁿ
4 "Let all who are simple come in here!"
  she says to those who lack judgment.^o
5 "Come, eat my food
  and drink the wine I have mixed.^p
6 Leave your simple ways and you will live;^q
  walk in the way of understanding.

7 "Whoever corrects a mocker invites insult;
  whoever rebukes a wicked man incurs abuse.^r
8 Do not rebuke a mocker^s or he will hate you;
  rebuke a wise man and he will love you.^t
9 Instruct a wise man and he will be wiser still;
  teach a righteous man and he will add to his learning.^u
10 "The fear of the LORD^v is the beginning of wisdom,
  and knowledge of the Holy One is understanding.
11 For through me your days will be many,
  and years will be added to your life.^w
12 If you are wise, your wisdom will reward you;
  if you are a mocker, you alone will suffer."

13 The woman Folly is loud;^x
  she is undisciplined and without knowledge.^y
14 She sits at the door of her house,
  on a seat at the highest point of the city,^z
15 calling out to those who pass by,
  who go straight on their way.
16 "Let all who are simple come in here!"
  she says to those who lack judgment.
17 "Stolen water is sweet;

8:35
h Pr 3:13-18
i Pr 12:2

8:36
j Pr 15:32

9:1
k Eph 2:20-22;
1Pe 2:5

9:2
l Lk 14:16-23
9:3
m Pr 8:1-3 n ver 14

9:4
o Pr 6:32

9:5
p Isa 55:1
9:6
q Pr 8:35

9:7
r Pr 23:9
9:8
s Pr 15:12
t Ps 141:5

9:9
u Pr 1:5,7

9:10
v Job 28:28; Pr 1:7

9:11
w Pr 3:16; 10:27

9:13
x Pr 7:11 y Pr 5:6

9:14
z ver 3

Proverbs 9:1–18

Chapter 9 concludes the first major section of the book of Proverbs with a final appeal to study and embrace wisdom, here depicted as an able and generous host. The outstanding feature of this finale is the juxtaposition of messages from Wisdom and her nemesis, Folly. Both call out from a house situated in the highest place (vv. 1,3,14). They begin with the same invitation: "Let all who are simple come in here!" (vv. 4,16), adding an invitation to a meal. Both use proverbs—Wisdom a series of proverbs (vv. 7–12) and Folly one revealing proverb (v. 17).

But the similarities only point out glaring differences. Wisdom works at preparing a sumptuous banquet for her guests (v. 2), while Folly sits at her door, loud, undisciplined, and without knowledge (vv. 13–14). Wisdom of-

fers meat and wine (v. 2), Folly only generic food (literally, "bread") and [stolen] water (v. 17). Wisdom offers a future, a call to maturity—in a word, life. Folly holds out only the immediate pleasure of good things enjoyed outside their intended boundaries, hiding the fact that such pleasure brings death.

Knowing God is our only basis for knowing how to live and to choose wisely. Wisdom isn't concerned with the day-to-day choices we make, at least at the start, because it's more important for us to get this one, *big* decision right. The way of living right begins with the knowledge of God. This advice is echoed in Paul's prayer for believers (Eph. 1:17–23): "I keep asking God . . . that you might know him better" (v. 17). How is your knowledge of God increasing every day?

9:17
a Pr 20:17

9:18
b Pr 2:18; 7:26-27

10:1
c Pr 1:1
d Pr 15:20; 29:3

10:2
e Pr 21:6 *f* Pr 11:4, 19

10:3
g Mt 6:25-34

10:4
h Pr 19:15
i Pr 12:24; 13:4; 21:5

food eaten in secret is delicious! *a"*

18 But little do they know that the dead are there,
   that her guests are in the depths of the grave. *a b*

Proverbs of Solomon

10 The proverbs of Solomon: *c*

A wise son brings joy to his father, *d*
   but a foolish son grief to his mother.

2 Ill-gotten treasures are of no value, *e*
   but righteousness delivers from death. *f*

3 The LORD does not let the righteous go hungry *g*
   but he thwarts the craving of the wicked.

4 Lazy hands make a man poor, *h*
   but diligent hands bring wealth. *i*

5 He who gathers crops in summer is a wise son,
   but he who sleeps during harvest is a disgraceful son.

a 18 Hebrew *Sheol*

There are no sectional divisions in the "Proverbs of Solomon" section. Study notes are separated by chapters.

Proverbs 10:1–32

As a major new section (10:1—22:16) begins, a connection with King Solomon is repeated (see "There and Then" for 1:1–7). The themes of Proverbs 1–9 are extended by placing them in a new setting. Relation to parents has been the primary focus. Now the emphasis turns to relation to the community. Personified Wisdom has become a teacher as well. Having made her initial appeals about the worth of her teaching in chapters 1–9, she now makes her instruction known through the collective wisdom of the sayings.

A call for relationship with God, one of the main emphases of the parents' instructions (along with learning and character), is sounded three times in the last part of chapter 10—focusing on the *blessing*, *fear*, and *way* "of the LORD" (vv. 22,27,29). This chapter shares themes, images, and vocabulary from Psalm 37, marking a common intention to affirm God's righteous role of the world's moral order.

Snapshots

10:1

Isaac

Eight-year-old Isaac, one of eight children in a Ghanian family, carries the physical and emotional burden of someone much older. His mother, Afua, though blind and virtually deserted by her husband, is highly motivated on behalf of her family. Afua used to crack palm nuts to make money to feed her children but has abandoned that work because of the meager 1000 cedis (U.S. $.09) she received for a two-kilogram tin of nuts.

> **"M**y mother is special to me! I will build a house for her in future."

"Despite my mother's blindness, she sells produce from her farm to pay my school fees. I know a lot of children who loiter about the community and do not go to school because their mothers won't pay their fees," Isaac notes, adding, "I'm not shy of my mother's blindness, and my friends don't mock me."

Isaac leads his mother to the washroom, fetches water for her, walks to the family farm to bring foodstuffs, and runs errands. "I go to the farm very early to hunt for mushrooms and gather plantain, which she sells to provide food for us," Isaac confides, tears welling up in his eyes.

"My mother is special to me! I will build a house for her in future." That is Isaac's dream for his disabled mom—and he will probably do just that!

⁶ Blessings crown the head of the righteous,
　but violence overwhelms the mouth of the wicked. ᵃʲ

10:6
j ver 8,11,14

⁷ The memory of the righteous ᵏ will be a blessing,
　but the name of the wicked ˡ will rot. ᵐ

10:7
k Ps 112:6
l Ps 109:13
m Ps 9:6

⁸ The wise in heart accept commands,
　but a chattering fool comes to ruin. ⁿ

10:8
n Mt 7:24-27

⁹ The man of integrity ᵒ walks securely, ᵖ
　but he who takes crooked paths will be found out. �q

10:9
o Isa 33:15
p Ps 23:4 q Pr 28:18

¹⁰ He who winks maliciously ʳ causes grief,
　and a chattering fool comes to ruin.

10:10
r Ps 35:19

¹¹ The mouth of the righteous is a fountain of life, ˢ
　but violence overwhelms the mouth of the wicked. ᵗ

10:11
s Ps 37:30;
Pr 13:12,14,19
t ver 6

¹² Hatred stirs up dissension,
　but love covers over all wrongs. ᵘ

10:12
u Pr 17:9;
1Co 13:4-7; 1Pe 4:8

¹³ Wisdom is found on the lips of the discerning, ᵛ
　but a rod is for the back of him who lacks judgment. ʷ

10:13
v ver 31 w Pr 26:3

¹⁴ Wise men store up knowledge,
　but the mouth of a fool invites ruin. ˣ

10:14
x Pr 18:6,7

¹⁵ The wealth of the rich is their fortified city, ʸ
　but poverty is the ruin of the poor. ᶻ

10:15
y Pr 18:11 z Pr 19:7

¹⁶ The wages of the righteous bring them life,
　but the income of the wicked brings them punishment. ᵃ

10:16
a Pr 11:18-19

¹⁷ He who heeds discipline shows the way to life, ᵇ
　but whoever ignores correction leads others astray.

10:17
b Pr 6:23

¹⁸ He who conceals his hatred has lying lips,
　and whoever spreads slander is a fool.

¹⁹ When words are many, sin is not absent,
　but he who holds his tongue is wise. ᶜ

10:19
c Pr 17:28; Ecc 5:3;
Jas 1:19; 3:2-12

²⁰ The tongue of the righteous is choice silver,
　but the heart of the wicked is of little value.

²¹ The lips of the righteous nourish many,
　but fools die for lack of judgment. ᵈ

10:21
d Pr 5:22-23;
Hos 4:1,6,14
10:22
e Ge 24:35;
Ps 37:22

²² The blessing of the LORD brings wealth, ᵉ
　and he adds no trouble to it.

²³ A fool finds pleasure in evil conduct, ᶠ
　but a man of understanding delights in wisdom.

10:23
f Pr 2:14; 15:21

ᵃ 6 Or *but the mouth of the wicked conceals violence*; also in verse 11

📖 In chapters 1–9 the parents urged their son to *get* wisdom, but here the collected wisdom of the community adds a call to *give* wisdom in speech that nourishes others (10:21). As we, along with the son, grow to take our place in the community as responsible adults, we are to learn that care for others involves stewardship of our gifts of material resources and verbal communications. Followers of Jesus practice wise speaking and living when they resist the temptations to profit from and gain power over others, instead speaking and doing only that which uplifts and restores.

The focus on God in verses 22–32 inspires Christian readers to praise and hope, for he is the source of wisdom's benefits. Hope comes from our taking the long view, assuming that God is present and watching, even at those times when he seems absent. These proverbs inspire our faith, giving us permission to voice our doubts and questions, while refusing to walk away from God in times of trouble.

10:24
g Isa 66:4
h Ps 145:17-19;
Mt 5:6; 1Jn 5:14-15

24 What the wicked dreads *g* will overtake him;
what the righteous desire will be granted. *h*

10:25
i Ps 15:5 / Pr 12:3,
7; Mt 7:24-27

25 When the storm has swept by, the wicked are gone,
but the righteous stand firm *i* forever. *j*

10:26
k Pr 26:6

26 As vinegar to the teeth and smoke to the eyes,
so is a sluggard to those who send him. *k*

10:27
l Pr 9:10-11
m Job 15:32

27 The fear of the LORD adds length to life, *l*
but the years of the wicked are cut short. *m*

10:28
n Job 8:13; Pr 11:7

28 The prospect of the righteous is joy,
but the hopes of the wicked come to nothing. *n*

10:29
o Pr 21:15

29 The way of the LORD is a refuge for the righteous,
but it is the ruin of those who do evil. *o*

10:30
p Ps 37:9, 28-29;
Pr 2:20-22
10:31
q Ps 37:30

30 The righteous will never be uprooted,
but the wicked will not remain in the land. *p*

31 The mouth of the righteous brings forth wisdom, *q*
but a perverse tongue will be cut out.

10:32
r Ecc 10:12
11:1
s Lev 19:36;
Dt 25:13-16;
Pr 20:10,23
t Pr 16:11
11:2
u Pr 16:18
v Pr 18:12; 29:23

32 The lips of the righteous know what is fitting, *r*
but the mouth of the wicked only what is perverse.

11 The LORD abhors dishonest scales, *s*
but accurate weights are his delight. *t*

2 When pride comes, then comes disgrace, *u*
but with humility comes wisdom. *v*

11:3
w Pr 13:6

3 The integrity of the upright guides them,
but the unfaithful are destroyed by their duplicity. *w*

11:4
x Eze 7:19;
Zep 1:18 y Ge 7:1;
Pr 10:2

4 Wealth is worthless in the day of wrath, *x*
but righteousness delivers from death. *y*

11:5
z Pr 5:21-23

5 The righteousness of the blameless makes a straight way for them,
but the wicked are brought down by their own wickedness. *z*

6 The righteousness of the upright delivers them,
but the unfaithful are trapped by evil desires.

11:7
a Pr 10:28

7 When a wicked man dies, his hope perishes;
all he expected from his power comes to nothing. *a*

Proverbs 11:1–31

The picture of persons who bring harm and ruin wherever they go is filled in with details on the harm that comes back on them: They lose the wealth they have so eagerly grasped, their honor in the eyes of the community, and their hopes and expectations. The last four verses alternate images of fruit-bearing trees and failed inheritances. Both the righteous and the wicked are surprised: the righteous because in seeking the good of others they find themselves blessed, the wicked because what they grasp so tenaciously slips from their hands.

Generous giving, scattered like seed, yields a great crop, like a drink offered to others that will be returned (v. 25). Business practices are included in such generosity. For example, it may be more profitable to withhold grain from sale until the price goes up, but the one who

sells food at a fair price during a time of need finds that blessing returned (v. 26).

Perhaps the difference between stealing and hoarding isn't as great as we might think. One action takes what doesn't belong to us; the other keeps what could belong to others. This chapter reminds us that "it is in giving that we receive." One way to counteract wealth's power and seductiveness is to practice liberal, lavish giving, giving when it doesn't make sense, when it doesn't fit our budget. Such generosity demonstrates our trust in the One who holds the future, a trust that answers our fears and worries.

Wealth in Proverbs seems only to be a problem when it becomes a primary goal that replaces neighbor love. Wisdom teaches us to develop a holy freedom, one that allows us to keep a loose grip on our belongings and a generous embrace around others.

8 The righteous man is rescued from trouble,
  and it comes on the wicked instead. *b*

9 With his mouth the godless destroys his neighbor,
  but through knowledge the righteous escape.

10 When the righteous prosper, the city rejoices; *c*
   when the wicked perish, there are shouts of joy.

11 Through the blessing of the upright a city is exalted,
   but by the mouth of the wicked it is destroyed. *d*

12 A man who lacks judgment derides his neighbor, *e*
   but a man of understanding holds his tongue.

13 A gossip betrays a confidence, *f*
   but a trustworthy man keeps a secret.

14 For lack of guidance a nation falls, *g*
   but many advisers make victory sure. *h*

15 He who puts up security *i* for another will surely suffer,
   but whoever refuses to strike hands in pledge is safe.

16 A kindhearted woman gains respect, *j*
   but ruthless men gain only wealth.

17 A kind man benefits himself,
   but a cruel man brings trouble on himself.

18 The wicked man earns deceptive wages,
   but he who sows righteousness reaps a sure reward. *k*

19 The truly righteous man attains life,
   but he who pursues evil goes to his death.

20 The LORD detests men of perverse heart
   but he delights in those whose ways are blameless. *l*

21 Be sure of this: The wicked will not go unpunished,
   but those who are righteous will go free. *m*

22 Like a gold ring in a pig's snout
   is a beautiful woman who shows no discretion.

23 The desire of the righteous ends only in good,
   but the hope of the wicked only in wrath.

24 One man gives freely, yet gains even more;
   another withholds unduly, but comes to poverty.

25 A generous man will prosper;
   he who refreshes others will himself be refreshed. *n*

26 People curse the man who hoards grain,
   but blessing crowns him who is willing to sell.

27 He who seeks good finds goodwill,
   but evil comes to him who searches for it. *o*

28 Whoever trusts in his riches will fall, *p*
   but the righteous will thrive like a green leaf. *q*

29 He who brings trouble on his family will inherit only wind,
   and the fool will be servant to the wise. *r*

30 The fruit of the righteous is a tree of life, *s*
   and he who wins souls is wise.

11:8
b Pr 21:18

11:10
c Pr 28:12

11:11
d Pr 29:8

11:12
e Pr 14:21

11:13
f Lev 19:16;
Pr 20:19; 1Ti 5:13

11:14
g Pr 20:18
h Pr 15:22; 24:6

11:15
i Pr 6:1

11:16
j Pr 31:31

11:18
k Hos 10:12-13

11:20
l 1Ch 29:17;
Ps 119:1;
Pr 12:2,22
11:21
m Pr 16:5

11:25
n Mt 5:7; 2Co 9:6-9

11:27
o Est 7:10;
Ps 7:15-16
11:28
p Job 31:24-28;
Ps 49:6; 52:7;
Mk 10:25; 1Ti 6:17
q Ps 1:3; 92:12-14;
Jer 17:8
11:29
r Pr 14:19

11:30
s Jas 5:20

11:31
t Pr 13:21;
Jer 25:29; 1Pe 4:18

31 If the righteous receive their due[t] on earth,
how much more the ungodly and the sinner!

12:1
u Pr 9:7-9;
15:5,10,12,32

12 Whoever loves discipline loves knowledge,
but he who hates correction is stupid.[u]

2 A good man obtains favor from the LORD,
but the LORD condemns a crafty man.

12:3
v Pr 10:25

3 A man cannot be established through wickedness,
but the righteous cannot be uprooted.[v]

12:4
w Pr 14:30

4 A wife of noble character is her husband's crown,
but a disgraceful wife is like decay in his bones.[w]

5 The plans of the righteous are just,
but the advice of the wicked is deceitful.

12:6
x Pr 14:3

6 The words of the wicked lie in wait for blood,
but the speech of the upright rescues them.[x]

12:7
y Ps 37:36
z Pr 10:25

7 Wicked men are overthrown and are no more,[y]
but the house of the righteous stands firm.[z]

8 A man is praised according to his wisdom,
but men with warped minds are despised.

9 Better to be a nobody and yet have a servant
than pretend to be somebody and have no food.

10 A righteous man cares for the needs of his animal,
but the kindest acts of the wicked are cruel.

12:11
a Pr 28:19

11 He who works his land will have abundant food,
but he who chases fantasies lacks judgment.[a]

12 The wicked desire the plunder of evil men,
but the root of the righteous flourishes.

12:13
b Pr 18:7
c Pr 21:23; 2Pe 2:9

13 An evil man is trapped by his sinful talk,[b]
but a righteous man escapes trouble.[c]

12:14
d Pr 13:2; 15:23;
18:20 e Isa 3:10-11

14 From the fruit of his lips a man is filled with good things[d]
as surely as the work of his hands rewards him.[e]

12:15
f Pr 14:12; 16:2,25;
Lk 18:11

15 The way of a fool seems right to him,[f]
but a wise man listens to advice.

12:16
g Pr 29:11

16 A fool shows his annoyance at once,
but a prudent man overlooks an insult.[g]

12:17
h Pr 14:5,25

17 A truthful witness gives honest testimony,
but a false witness tells lies.[h]

Proverbs 12:1–28

In chapter 12, the contrast between the ways of the righteous and those of the wicked extends and develops the theme of outcomes and rewards. Heart and lips are actors, every bit as much as hands and feet. The interlocking sayings create a series of pictures on the self-disciplines of speaking, the nature of public honor and shame, and God's reaction to these character choices. We are reminded that we need the teaching, correction, and counsel of others but also their encouragement and approval. Most of all, we need communities where truthfulness is prized.

No one is either all good or all bad. But our daily choices assemble themselves into a character that weighs in on one side or the other. All of us face daily opportunities to speak truth, deal fairly, and receive correction when necessary. Choices made in favor of the uplifting or truthful word can become the "way" of our lives. We may think without speaking or speak without thinking. But the ideal is to know when to speak and when to keep silent. Good speech is a combination of thinking and speaking. To speak is to act, so we are wise to consider the effects of our words.

Of Works Done in Charity

 11:24–25

Not for anything in the world or for the love of any created thing is evil to be done. But sometimes, for the need and comfort of our neighbor, a good deed may be deferred or turned into another good deed. Thereby the good deed is not destroyed, but is changed for the better.

The outward deed without charity is little to be praised, but whatever is done from charity, even if it be ever so little and worthless in the sight of the world, is very profitable before God, who judges all things according to the intent of the doer, not according to the greatness or worthiness of the deed. He does much who loves God much, and he does much who does his deed well, and he does his deed well who does it rather for the common good than for his own will. A deed sometimes seems to be done in charity and from a love of God, when it is really done out of worldly and fleshly love, rather than out of a love of charity. Commonly, some worldly inclination toward our friends, some inordinate love of ourselves, or some hope of a temporal reward or desire of some other gain moves us to do the deed, and not the pure love of charity.

> Charity will not joy in itself, but desires above all things to be blessed in God.

Charity does not seek itself in what it does, but it desires to do only what will honor and praise God. Charity envies no man, for it loves no personal love. Charity will not joy in itself, but desires above all things to be blessed in God. Charity knows well that no goodness begins originally from man, and therefore charity refers all goodness to God, from whom all things proceed, and in whom all the blessed saints rest in everlasting fruition. Oh, he who has a little spark of this perfect charity should feel in his soul with certain truth that all earthly things are full of vanity.

Thomas à Kempis, German mystic and religious author
Source: Thomas à Kempis, *The Imitation of Christ* (New York: Doubleday, 1989), 48–49

12:18
i Ps 57:4 j Pr 15:4

18 Reckless words pierce like a sword, [i]
    but the tongue of the wise brings healing. [j]

19 Truthful lips endure forever,
    but a lying tongue lasts only a moment.

20 There is deceit in the hearts of those who plot evil,
    but joy for those who promote peace.

12:21
k Ps 91:10

21 No harm befalls the righteous, [k]
    but the wicked have their fill of trouble.

12:22
l Pr 6:17; Rev 22:15
m Pr 11:20

22 The LORD detests lying lips, [l]
    but he delights in men who are truthful. [m]

12:23
n Pr 10:14; 13:16

23 A prudent man keeps his knowledge to himself, [n]
    but the heart of fools blurts out folly.

12:24
o Pr 10:4
12:25
p Pr 15:13; Isa 50:4

24 Diligent hands will rule,
    but laziness ends in slave labor. [o]

25 An anxious heart weighs a man down, [p]
    but a kind word cheers him up.

26 A righteous man is cautious in friendship, [a]
    but the way of the wicked leads them astray.

27 The lazy man does not roast [b] his game,
    but the diligent man prizes his possessions.

12:28
q Dt 30:15

28 In the way of righteousness there is life; [q]
    along that path is immortality.

13:1
r Pr 10:1

13

A wise son heeds his father's instruction,
    but a mocker does not listen to rebuke. [r]

13:2
s Pr 12:14

2 From the fruit of his lips a man enjoys good things, [s]
    but the unfaithful have a craving for violence.

13:3
t Jas 3:2 u Pr 21:23
v Pr 18:7,20-21

3 He who guards his lips [t] guards his life, [u]
    but he who speaks rashly will come to ruin. [v]

4 The sluggard craves and gets nothing,
    but the desires of the diligent are fully satisfied.

5 The righteous hate what is false,
    but the wicked bring shame and disgrace.

13:6
w Pr 11:3,5

6 Righteousness guards the man of integrity,
    but wickedness overthrows the sinner. [w]

13:7
x 2Co 6:10

7 One man pretends to be rich, yet has nothing;
    another pretends to be poor, yet has great wealth. [x]

a 26 Or *man is a guide to his neighbor*   b 27 The meaning of the Hebrew for this word is uncertain.

Proverbs 13:1–25

The blessings of God may favor the poor, but the astute observer also will note that their gain can be taken over by injustice. The pessimism of verse 23 stands out from its context and provides a realistic counterbalance to the optimism of verses 21–22. Proverbs describe what *usually* happens, not what *must* happen. We often encounter situations worldwide that resemble verse 23, though the unseen resolution of verse 22 is the one to look for. Wise learners are challenged to practice foresight, patience, and faith, while maintaining a strong sense of justice.

The sayings about the rich and poor challenge us to try to see life through the eyes of those who have less than we do and encourage us to "walk a mile in another's shoes." They prod us with truths held in tension. While holding up the virtues of work and its rewards of wealth, they warn us away from a one-sided view that equates wealth and virtue. We are equally misguided if we regard the wealthy as ineligible to be counted among the righteous or view the poor as the cause of their own circumstances.

⁸A man's riches may ransom his life,
    but a poor man hears no threat.

⁹The light of the righteous shines brightly,
    but the lamp of the wicked is snuffed out. *y*

13:9
y Job 18:5;
Pr 4:18-19; 24:20

¹⁰Pride only breeds quarrels,
    but wisdom is found in those who take advice.

¹¹Dishonest money dwindles away, *z*
    but he who gathers money little by little makes it grow.

13:11
z Pr 10:2

¹²Hope deferred makes the heart sick,
    but a longing fulfilled is a tree of life.

¹³He who scorns instruction will pay for it, *a*
    but he who respects a command is rewarded.

13:13
a Nu 15:31;
2Ch 36:16

¹⁴The teaching of the wise is a fountain of life, *b*
    turning a man from the snares of death. *c*

13:14
b Pr 10:11
c Pr 14:27

¹⁵Good understanding wins favor,
    but the way of the unfaithful is hard. *a*

¹⁶Every prudent man acts out of knowledge,
    but a fool exposes his folly. *d*

13:16
d Pr 12:23

¹⁷A wicked messenger falls into trouble,
    but a trustworthy envoy brings healing. *e*

13:17
e Pr 25:13

¹⁸He who ignores discipline comes to poverty and shame,
    but whoever heeds correction is honored. *f*

13:18
f Pr 15:5,31-32

¹⁹A longing fulfilled is sweet to the soul,
    but fools detest turning from evil.

²⁰He who walks with the wise grows wise,
    but a companion of fools suffers harm. *g*

13:20
g Pr 15:31

²¹Misfortune pursues the sinner,
    but prosperity is the reward of the righteous. *h*

13:21
h Ps 32:10

²²A good man leaves an inheritance for his children's children,
    but a sinner's wealth is stored up for the righteous. *i*

13:22
i Job 27:17;
Ecc 2:26

²³A poor man's field may produce abundant food,
    but injustice sweeps it away.

²⁴He who spares the rod hates his son,
    but he who loves him is careful to discipline him. *j*

13:24
j Pr 19:18; 22:15;
23:13-14; 29:15,17;
Heb 12:7

²⁵The righteous eat to their hearts' content,
    but the stomach of the wicked goes hungry. *k*

13:25
k Ps 34:10; Pr 10:3

14 The wise woman builds her house, *l*
    but with her own hands the foolish one tears hers down.

14:1
l Pr 24:3

²He whose walk is upright fears the LORD,
    but he whose ways are devious despises him.

---

a 15 Or *unfaithful does not endure*

The way we live reveals whether or not we have placed our futures in God's hands. A life spent focused on accumulation shows that we trust in our own powers to build a hedge against whatever may come. It's fully as foolish to think we can leave that kind of legacy to our children if we name them in our wills but fail to pass on wisdom. Are you leaving your children an enduring legacy or relying on a trust fund? Only the combination of wealth and wisdom endures.

14:3
m Pr 12:6

3 A fool's talk brings a rod to his back,
   but the lips of the wise protect them. *m*

4 Where there are no oxen, the manger is empty,
   but from the strength of an ox comes an abundant harvest.

14:5
n Pr 6:19; 12:17

5 A truthful witness does not deceive,
   but a false witness pours out lies. *n*

6 The mocker seeks wisdom and finds none,
   but knowledge comes easily to the discerning.

7 Stay away from a foolish man,
   for you will not find knowledge on his lips.

14:8
o ver 24

8 The wisdom of the prudent is to give thought to their ways,
   but the folly of fools is deception. *o*

9 Fools mock at making amends for sin,
   but goodwill is found among the upright.

10 Each heart knows its own bitterness,
   and no one else can share its joy.

14:11
p Pr 3:33; 12:7

11 The house of the wicked will be destroyed,
   but the tent of the upright will flourish. *p*

14:12
q Pr 12:15
r Pr 16:25

12 There is a way that seems right to a man, *q*
   but in the end it leads to death. *r*

14:13
s Ecc 2:2

13 Even in laughter *s* the heart may ache,
   and joy may end in grief.

14:14
t Pr 1:31 *u* Pr 12:14

14 The faithless will be fully repaid for their ways, *t*
   and the good man rewarded for his. *u*

15 A simple man believes anything,
   but a prudent man gives thought to his steps.

14:16
v Pr 22:3

16 A wise man fears the LORD and shuns evil, *v*
   but a fool is hotheaded and reckless.

14:17
w ver 29

17 A quick-tempered man does foolish things, *w*
   and a crafty man is hated.

18 The simple inherit folly,
   but the prudent are crowned with knowledge.

14:19
x Pr 11:29

19 Evil men will bow down in the presence of the good,
   and the wicked at the gates of the righteous. *x*

14:20
y Pr 19:4,7

20 The poor are shunned even by their neighbors,
   but the rich have many friends. *y*

Proverbs 14:1–35

The personal always intersects with the political. What's good for the individual is good for the people, and the house that wisdom builds and inhabits is both the heart and the nation (vv. 30,33–34). To talk about kings and politics is to talk about a nation's moral health, measured in Biblical terms by its treatment of the poor.

The just society will always be under attack from without and within. The only refuge to be had is found in "the fear of the LORD"—right living that results in safety and trust (vv. 26–27). This fear is more than emotion.

It's also reverence and obedience that lead us to walk rightly before God. If we forsake this fear that brings us safety, we will be afraid of everything else and in danger of slipping.

In ancient days people could use the legal system to cheat the poor. Do we face similar temptations today? Whether such cheating takes the form of negligent landlords or corporate restructuring that benefits stockholders at the cost of jobs, kindness to the needy requires justice and charity. Whoever "oppresses the poor shows contempt for their Maker, but whoever is kind to the needy honors God" (v. 31; cf. v. 21).

21 He who despises his neighbor sins,*z*
  but blessed is he who is kind to the needy.*a*

22 Do not those who plot evil go astray?
  But those who plan what is good find*a* love and faithfulness.

23 All hard work brings a profit,
  but mere talk leads only to poverty.

24 The wealth of the wise is their crown,
  but the folly of fools yields folly.

25 A truthful witness saves lives,
  but a false witness is deceitful.*b*

26 He who fears the LORD has a secure fortress,*c*
  and for his children it will be a refuge.

27 The fear of the LORD is a fountain of life,
  turning a man from the snares of death.*d*

28 A large population is a king's glory,
  but without subjects a prince is ruined.

29 A patient man has great understanding,
  but a quick-tempered man displays folly.*e*

30 A heart at peace gives life to the body,
  but envy rots the bones.*f*

31 He who oppresses the poor shows contempt for their Maker,*g*
  but whoever is kind to the needy honors God.

32 When calamity comes, the wicked are brought down,*h*
  but even in death the righteous have a refuge.*i*

33 Wisdom reposes in the heart of the discerning*i*
  and even among fools she lets herself be known.*b*

34 Righteousness exalts a nation,*k*
  but sin is a disgrace to any people.

35 A king delights in a wise servant,
  but a shameful servant incurs his wrath.*l*

15 A gentle answer turns away wrath,*m*
  but a harsh word stirs up anger.

2 The tongue of the wise commends knowledge,
  but the mouth of the fool gushes folly.*n*

3 The eyes*o* of the LORD are everywhere,*p*
  keeping watch on the wicked and the good.*q*

4 The tongue that brings healing is a tree of life,
  but a deceitful tongue crushes the spirit.

5 A fool spurns his father's discipline,
  but whoever heeds correction shows prudence.*r*

a 22 Or *show*   *b* 33 Hebrew; Septuagint and Syriac / *but in the heart of fools she is not known*

Cross references (right margin):

14:21
z Pr 11:12
a Ps 41:1; Pr 19:17

14:25
b ver 5
14:26
c Pr 18:10; 19:23; Isa 33:6

14:27
d Pr 13:14

14:29
e Ecc 7:8-9; Jas 1:19

14:30
f Pr 12:4
14:31
g Pr 17:5

14:32
h Pr 6:15
i Job 13:15; 2Ti 4:18
14:33
j Pr 2:6-10

14:34
k Pr 11:11

14:35
l Mt 24:45-51; 25:14-30
15:1
m Pr 25:15

15:2
n Pr 12:23

15:3
o 2Ch 16:9
p Job 31:4; Heb 4:13
q Job 34:21; Jer 16:17

15:5
r Pr 13:1

Proverbs 15:1–33

Three themes draw these proverbs together and bring the collection of contrasts in chapters 10–15 to a crescendo: (1) new insights into speaking and listening as functions of the heart; (2) repeated statements that God sees and understands all those heart functions; and (3) multiple images of life lived in fear of the Lord, a life of "cheerfulness" and "joy." The contrasts we see again and again between the righteous and the wicked show us what true goodness looks like—goodness of life to be sure, but even more important the goodness of God, who won't allow his intentions to be thwarted forever.

6 The house of the righteous contains great treasure, [s]
  but the income of the wicked brings them trouble.

7 The lips of the wise spread knowledge;
  not so the hearts of fools.

8 The LORD detests the sacrifice of the wicked, [t]
  but the prayer of the upright pleases him. [u]

9 The LORD detests the way of the wicked
  but he loves those who pursue righteousness. [v]

10 Stern discipline awaits him who leaves the path;
  he who hates correction will die. [w]

11 Death and Destruction [a] lie open before the LORD [x]—
  how much more the hearts of men! [y]

12 A mocker resents correction; [z]
  he will not consult the wise.

13 A happy heart makes the face cheerful,
  but heartache crushes the spirit. [a]

14 The discerning heart seeks knowledge, [b]
  but the mouth of a fool feeds on folly.

15 All the days of the oppressed are wretched,
  but the cheerful heart has a continual feast. [c]

16 Better a little with the fear of the LORD
  than great wealth with turmoil. [d]

17 Better a meal of vegetables where there is love
  than a fattened calf with hatred. [e]

18 A hot-tempered man stirs up dissension, [f]
  but a patient man calms a quarrel. [g]

19 The way of the sluggard is blocked with thorns, [h]
  but the path of the upright is a highway.

20 A wise son brings joy to his father, [i]
  but a foolish man despises his mother.

21 Folly delights a man who lacks judgment, [j]
  but a man of understanding keeps a straight course.

22 Plans fail for lack of counsel,
  but with many advisers they succeed. [k]

23 A man finds joy in giving an apt reply [l]—
  and how good is a timely word! [m]

24 The path of life leads upward for the wise
  to keep him from going down to the grave. [b]

25 The LORD tears down the proud man's house [n]
  but he keeps the widow's boundaries intact. [o]

Cross references:

15:6 [s] Pr 8:21
15:8 [t] Pr 21:27; Isa 1:11; Jer 6:20 [u] ver 29
15:9 [v] Pr 21:21; 1Ti 6:11
15:10 [w] Pr 1:31-32; 5:12
15:11 [x] Job 26:6; Ps 139:8 [y] 2Ch 6:30; Ps 44:21
15:12 [z] Am 5:10
15:13 [a] Pr 12:25; 17:22; 18:14
15:14 [b] Pr 18:15
15:15 [c] ver 13
15:16 [d] Ps 37:16-17; Pr 16:8; 1Ti 6:6
15:17 [e] Pr 17:1
15:18 [f] Pr 26:21 [g] Ge 13:8
15:19 [h] Pr 22:5
15:20 [i] Pr 10:1
15:21 [j] Pr 10:23
15:22 [k] Pr 11:14
15:23 [l] Pr 12:14 [m] Pr 25:11
15:25 [n] Pr 12:7 [o] Dt 19:14; Ps 68:5-6; Pr 23:10-11

[a] 11 Hebrew *Sheol and Abaddon*   [b] 24 Hebrew *Sheol*

The contentment we enjoy when we surrender our self-determined lives of achievement and acquisition for lives that offer good work and good rewards is better than any hoard of selfish riches. The connections between instruction and God's oversight of human affairs sound very much like the instruction of chapters 1–9. But here the Lord's presence is more strongly felt. As the proverbs tell you more about God and his intentions and desires, do you find yourself more and more wanting the same?

26 The LORD detests the thoughts of the wicked,^p
but those of the pure are pleasing to him.

15:26
p Pr 6:16

27 A greedy man brings trouble to his family,
but he who hates bribes will live.^q

15:27
q Ex 23:8; Isa 33:15

28 The heart of the righteous weighs its answers,^r
but the mouth of the wicked gushes evil.

15:28
r 1Pe 3:15

29 The LORD is far from the wicked
but he hears the prayer of the righteous.^s

15:29
s Ps 145:18-19

30 A cheerful look brings joy to the heart,
and good news gives health to the bones.

31 He who listens to a life-giving rebuke
will be at home among the wise.^t

15:31
t ver 5

32 He who ignores discipline despises himself,^u
but whoever heeds correction gains understanding.

15:32
u Pr 1:7

33 The fear of the LORD^v teaches a man wisdom,^a
and humility comes before honor.^w

15:33
v Pr 1:7 w Pr 18:12

16 To man belong the plans of the heart,
but from the LORD comes the reply of the tongue.^x

16:1
x Pr 19:21

2 All a man's ways seem innocent to him,
but motives are weighed by the LORD.^y

16:2
y Pr 21:2

3 Commit to the LORD whatever you do,
and your plans will succeed.^z

16:3
z Ps 37:5-6;
Pr 3:5-6

4 The LORD works out everything for his own ends^a—
even the wicked for a day of disaster.^b

16:4
a Isa 43:7 b Ro 9:22

5 The LORD detests all the proud of heart.^c
Be sure of this: They will not go unpunished.^d

16:5
c Pr 6:16
d Pr 11:20-21

6 Through love and faithfulness sin is atoned for;
through the fear of the LORD a man avoids evil.^e

16:6
e Pr 14:16

7 When a man's ways are pleasing to the LORD,
he makes even his enemies live at peace with him.

8 Better a little with righteousness
than much gain^f with injustice.

16:8
f Ps 37:16

9 In his heart a man plans his course,
but the LORD determines his steps.^g

16:9
g Jer 10:23

10 The lips of a king speak as an oracle,
and his mouth should not betray justice.

11 Honest scales and balances are from the LORD;
all the weights in the bag are of his making.^h

16:11
h Pr 11:1

^a 33 Or Wisdom teaches the fear of the LORD

Proverbs 16:1–33

📖 Coming at the midpoint of the book, the proverbs of chapter 16 draw portraits of scoundrels and fools but also of those who recognize God's strong presence in everyday affairs. These figures are set against each other like pictures in a hinged frame: the Lord and the king in verses 1–15, the wise person and the foolish/proud individual in verses 16–30.

Wisdom and its accompanying humility are "better

than" any form of wealth (vv. 16–19). The echo of "better a little than" (v. 8) indicates the importance of a theme repeated throughout the book. Between these two contrasts a pair of proverbs about traveling draws a contrast between the one whose way avoids evil and the one who stumbles into pride.

📖 The temptations described in this chapter may hit a little too close to home for many of us. They por-

16:12
i Pr 25:5

16:13
j Pr 14:35
16:14
k Pr 19:12

16:15
l Job 29:24

16:16
m Pr 8:10,19

16:18
n Pr 11:2; 18:12

16:20
o Ps 2:12; 34:8;
Pr 19:8; Jer 17:7

16:21
p ver 23

16:22
q Pr 13:14

16:24
r Pr 24:13-14
16:25
s Pr 12:15
t Pr 14:12

16:27
u Jas 3:6

16:28
v Pr 15:18
w Pr 17:9

16:29
x Pr 1:10; 12:26

12 Kings detest wrongdoing,
  for a throne is established through righteousness. *i*

13 Kings take pleasure in honest lips;
  they value a man who speaks the truth. *j*

14 A king's wrath is a messenger of death, *k*
  but a wise man will appease it.

15 When a king's face brightens, it means life; *l*
  his favor is like a rain cloud in spring.

16 How much better to get wisdom than gold,
  to choose understanding rather than silver! *m*

17 The highway of the upright avoids evil;
  he who guards his way guards his life.

18 Pride goes before destruction,
  a haughty spirit before a fall. *n*

19 Better to be lowly in spirit and among the oppressed
  than to share plunder with the proud.

20 Whoever gives heed to instruction prospers,
  and blessed is he who trusts in the LORD. *o*

21 The wise in heart are called discerning,
  and pleasant words promote instruction. *a p*

22 Understanding is a fountain of life to those who have it, *q*
  but folly brings punishment to fools.

23 A wise man's heart guides his mouth,
  and his lips promote instruction. *b*

24 Pleasant words are a honeycomb,
  sweet to the soul and healing to the bones. *r*

25 There is a way that seems right to a man, *s*
  but in the end it leads to death. *t*

26 The laborer's appetite works for him;
  his hunger drives him on.

27 A scoundrel plots evil,
  and his speech is like a scorching fire. *u*

28 A perverse man stirs up dissension, *v*
  and a gossip separates close friends. *w*

29 A violent man entices his neighbor
  and leads him down a path that is not good. *x*

30 He who winks with his eye is plotting perversity;
  he who purses his lips is bent on evil.

---

a 21 Or *words make a man persuasive*   *b* 23 Or *mouth / and makes his lips persuasive*

---

tray financial gain as a source of pride. That pride can be seen as arrogance that leaves God out of the picture, a trust in our own capabilities to make our way and a reliance on our power over others to get what we want. As you read further in Proverbs, take note of other problems associated with the illegitimate use of wealth.

Every age has had its status symbols, those accoutrements to affluence that signify success, strength, and intelligence. People of every age are tempted to choose the power of gold over wisdom and its responsibilities. So also the pride that comes with it can move us to plunder others—to take what they have as our own—even if this is done via corporate means and the language of commerce. The associations of money, arrogance, and evil help us as Christians to draw the right conclusions, making humble identification with the oppressed all the more attractive. Is this your frequent choice?

31 Gray hair is a crown of splendor;^y
  it is attained by a righteous life.

32 Better a patient man than a warrior,
  a man who controls his temper than one who takes a city.

33 The lot is cast into the lap,
  but its every decision is from the LORD. ^z

17 Better a dry crust with peace and quiet
  than a house full of feasting,^a with strife. ^a

2 A wise servant will rule over a disgraceful son,
  and will share the inheritance as one of the brothers.

3 The crucible for silver and the furnace for gold, ^b
  but the LORD tests the heart. ^c

4 A wicked man listens to evil lips;
  a liar pays attention to a malicious tongue.

5 He who mocks the poor shows contempt for their Maker; ^d
  whoever gloats over disaster ^e will not go unpunished. ^f

6 Children's children ^g are a crown to the aged,
  and parents are the pride of their children.

7 Arrogant ^b lips are unsuited to a fool—
  how much worse lying lips to a ruler!

---

^a 1 Hebrew *sacrifices*   ^b 7 Or *Eloquent*

16:31
y Pr 20:29

16:33
z Pr 18:18; 29:26

17:1
a Pr 15:16,17

17:3
b Pr 27:21
c 1Ch 29:17;
Ps 26:2; Jer 17:10

17:5
d Pr 14:31
e Job 31:29
f Ob 1:12

17:6
g Pr 13:22

Proverbs 17:1–28

Implicit throughout this chapter is an emphasis on the twin virtues of love and justice. Just as the Creator is insulted when the poor he created are mocked (v. 5), so he's disgusted when legal verdicts are perverted for personal gain (vv. 8,15,23). God tests hearts to see whether intentions are pure; he's looking for love that rejoices in righteousness (v. 3). The God of justice looks to see that righteousness isn't rewarded with evil (vv. 13,26), nor evil with good (v. 20). If love looks out for a neighbor in need, justice makes sure that no one falls into want because of someone else's greed.

17:6

Gifted Children of the Bible

In some prosperous cultures today, a fairly high percentage of children are provided with every reasonable opportunity for growth and success. Yet giftedness is no respecter of circumstances. Consider the following precocious children of the Bible, stopping to take their unique life situations into account:

 Moses: "No prophet has risen in Israel like Moses, whom the LORD knew face to face" (Deut. 34:10). Moses' birth and subsequent adoption constitute an incredible story of God's care for his anointed (Ex. 2:1–10).

 Isaac: Called after the second of the three fathers of Israel, "the house of Isaac" (Amos 7:16) became synonymous with the people of God. Isaac's perceptiveness, even as a child, was evident when his father took him to the top of a mountain as a sacrifice to God (Gen. 22:6–8).

 Joseph: Genesis 47–50 recounts the inspiring story of a young man who always seemed able to figure out, and then do, God's will. What events in Joseph's childhood helped shape his character? How might things have gone differently?

 Samuel: After having been given to the temple as a priest-in-training, the young Samuel heard and responded to God's voice often and early (1 Sam. 1–3).

 David: David's slaying of Goliath while David was still a boy is the model of the weak becoming strong in God's service (1 Sam. 17).

 Jesus: He stunned the religious teachers in the temple with his knowledge and wisdom—while still a boy. (Luke 2:41–52).

⁸ A bribe is a charm to the one who gives it;
 wherever he turns, he succeeds.

17:9
h Pr 10:12
i Pr 16:28

⁹ He who covers over an offense promotes love, ^h
 but whoever repeats the matter separates close friends. ⁱ

¹⁰ A rebuke impresses a man of discernment
 more than a hundred lashes a fool.

¹¹ An evil man is bent only on rebellion;
 a merciless official will be sent against him.

¹² Better to meet a bear robbed of her cubs
 than a fool in his folly.

17:13
j Ps 109:4-5;
Jer 18:20

¹³ If a man pays back evil^j for good,
 evil will never leave his house.

17:14
k Pr 20:3

¹⁴ Starting a quarrel is like breaching a dam;
 so drop the matter before a dispute breaks out. ^k

17:15
l Pr 18:5
m Ex 23:6-7;
Isa 5:23

¹⁵ Acquitting the guilty and condemning the innocent^l—
 the LORD detests them both. ^m

17:16
n Pr 23:23

¹⁶ Of what use is money in the hand of a fool,
 since he has no desire to get wisdom?ⁿ

¹⁷ A friend loves at all times,
 and a brother is born for adversity.

17:18
o Pr 6:1-5; 11:15;
22:26-27

¹⁸ A man lacking in judgment strikes hands in pledge
 and puts up security for his neighbor. ^o

¹⁹ He who loves a quarrel loves sin;
 he who builds a high gate invites destruction.

²⁰ A man of perverse heart does not prosper;
 he whose tongue is deceitful falls into trouble.

17:21
p Pr 10:1

²¹ To have a fool for a son brings grief;
 there is no joy for the father of a fool. ^p

17:22
q Ps 22:15;
Pr 15:13

²² A cheerful heart is good medicine,
 but a crushed spirit dries up the bones. ^q

17:23
r Ex 23:8

²³ A wicked man accepts a bribe^r in secret
 to pervert the course of justice.

17:24
s Ecc 2:14

²⁴ A discerning man keeps wisdom in view,
 but a fool's eyes^s wander to the ends of the earth.

17:25
t Pr 10:1

²⁵ A foolish son brings grief to his father
 and bitterness to the one who bore him. ^t

17:26
u Pr 18:5

²⁶ It is not good to punish an innocent man, ^u
 or to flog officials for their integrity.

17:27
v Pr 14:29; Jas 1:19

²⁷ A man of knowledge uses words with restraint,
 and a man of understanding is even-tempered. ^v

Are you generous? Wisdom's blend of generosity and restraint in this chapter teaches us how to be a friend at all times—one born for adversity, certainly helping those in need but also weathering disappointments in our relationships. We may require more help with the latter because so many today are wounded due to unmet expectations or because love and justice have failed them.

Proverbs 17 teaches us what is best, most valuable, and deeply satisfying—giving appropriate gifts or loans and canceling debts at the right time. We also need God's help in learning to give generously of our understanding, kindness, and forgiveness, as well as in knowing when to hold back words that will tear apart relationships.

28 Even a fool is thought wise if he keeps silent,
   and discerning if he holds his tongue. *w*

18 An unfriendly man pursues selfish ends;
   he defies all sound judgment.

2 A fool finds no pleasure in understanding
   but delights in airing his own opinions. *x*

3 When wickedness comes, so does contempt,
   and with shame comes disgrace.

4 The words of a man's mouth are deep waters,
   but the fountain of wisdom is a bubbling brook.

5 It is not good to be partial to the wicked *y*
   or to deprive the innocent of justice. *z*

6 A fool's lips bring him strife,
   and his mouth invites a beating.

7 A fool's mouth is his undoing,
   and his lips are a snare *a* to his soul. *b*

8 The words of a gossip are like choice morsels;
   they go down to a man's inmost parts. *c*

9 One who is slack in his work
   is brother to one who destroys. *d*

10 The name of the LORD is a strong tower; *e*
   the righteous run to it and are safe.

11 The wealth of the rich is their fortified city; *f*
   they imagine it an unscalable wall.

12 Before his downfall a man's heart is proud,
   but humility comes before honor. *g*

13 He who answers before listening—
   that is his folly and his shame. *h*

14 A man's spirit sustains him in sickness,
   but a crushed spirit who can bear? *i*

15 The heart of the discerning acquires knowledge;
   the ears of the wise seek it out.

16 A gift *k* opens the way for the giver
   and ushers him into the presence of the great.

17 The first to present his case seems right,
   till another comes forward and questions him.

17:28
w Job 13:5

18:2
x Pr 12:23

18:5
y Lev 19:15;
Pr 24:23-25; 28:21
z Ps 82:2; Pr 17:15

18:7
a Ps 140:9
b Ps 64:8; Pr 10:14;
12:13; 13:3;
Ecc 10:12
18:8
c Pr 26:22

18:9
d Pr 28:24
18:10
e 2Sa 22:3; Ps 61:3

18:11
f Pr 10:15

18:12
g Pr 11:2; 15:33;
16:18

18:13
h Pr 20:25; Jn 7:51

18:14
i Pr 15:13; 17:22
18:15
j Pr 15:14

18:16
k Ge 32:20

Proverbs 18:1–24

This chapter begins with a proverb about selfish isolation and ends with one about friendship so close it resembles family intimacy. Between these reflections on social life are a myriad of images, most commonly focusing on the use of words. The negative pictures of foolish speech with its resulting strife are answered with the possibility of finding a friend like a brother or a good wife—and with her "favor from the LORD" (v. 22; cf. 8:35, where finding wisdom brings the same benefit). Each theme explores the many ways we humans act to draw near to each other in love or separate ourselves into lonely worlds of our own making.

How can you combat the age-old vices of self-centered pride (see v. 12) and inappropriate speech? For one thing, you can be on the lookout for ways to practice the kingdom principle of moving downward instead of climbing upward (cf. John 3:27–30).

Yet the upward mobility of pride is different from legitimate recognitions of excellence that come with promotions and awards. The latter serve the community, while the former concerns the self, especially when scrambling up requires stepping on or over others. The problem of pride is its isolation and lack of concern for others, not the lift that comes with genuine success and accomplishment.

18:18
l Pr 16:33

18 Casting the lot settles disputes[l]
and keeps strong opponents apart.

19 An offended brother is more unyielding than a fortified city,
and disputes are like the barred gates of a citadel.

18:20
m Pr 12:14

20 From the fruit of his mouth a man's stomach is filled;
with the harvest from his lips he is satisfied. [m]

18:21
n Pr 13:2-3;
Mt 12:37
18:22
o Pr 12:4
p Pr 19:14; 31:10

21 The tongue has the power of life and death,
and those who love it will eat its fruit. [n]

22 He who finds a wife finds what is good[o]
and receives favor from the LORD. [p]

23 A poor man pleads for mercy,
but a rich man answers harshly.

18:24
q Pr 17:17;
Jn 15:13-15

24 A man of many companions may come to ruin,
but there is a friend who sticks closer than a brother. [q]

19:1
r Pr 28:6

19 Better a poor man whose walk is blameless
than a fool whose lips are perverse. [r]

19:2
s Pr 29:20

2 It is not good to have zeal without knowledge,
nor to be hasty and miss the way. [s]

3 A man's own folly ruins his life,
yet his heart rages against the LORD.

19:4
t Pr 14:20

4 Wealth brings many friends,
but a poor man's friend deserts him. [t]

19:5
u Ex 23:1
v Dt 19:19;
Pr 21:28
19:6
w Pr 29:26
x Pr 17:8; 18:16

5 A false witness[u] will not go unpunished,
and he who pours out lies will not go free. [v]

6 Many curry favor with a ruler, [w]
and everyone is the friend of a man who gives gifts. [x]

19:7
y ver 4; Ps 38:11

7 A poor man is shunned by all his relatives—
how much more do his friends avoid him!
Though he pursues them with pleading,
they are nowhere to be found. [a][y]

19:8
z Pr 16:20

8 He who gets wisdom loves his own soul;
he who cherishes understanding prospers. [z]

19:9
a ver 5

9 A false witness will not go unpunished,
and he who pours out lies will perish. [a]

19:10
b Pr 26:1
c Pr 30:21-23;
Ecc 10:5-7

10 It is not fitting for a fool[b] to live in luxury—
how much worse for a slave to rule over princes! [c]

[a] 7 The meaning of the Hebrew for this sentence is uncertain.

Proverbs 19:1–29

Of the varied scenes presented in this collection, a number of repeated words and themes stand out. The repeated emphasis on discipline and instruction sounds like the parental teaching of Proverbs 1–9, the sayings about the rich and poor speak about integrity and friendship, and the five references to "the LORD" keep him at center stage. The teachings of these proverbs on integrity and truthfulness speak to our dealings with wealth and our neighbors, all in the sight of God, who loves justice and establishes his counsel.

It won't do for us to simply observe the lives and hear the stories of people who live in devastating poverty. They need friends (vv. 4–7), others who visibly and personally care about their welfare. Some of us show our support through works of compassion, others by working and calling for justice. Whatever form it takes, a commitment to those who feel they have no advocate can be the greatest contribution the church and individual Christians can make. To be present among them is to acknowledge that these people exist. To stay away or ignore them is to propagate the lie that they don't matter, perhaps itself a form of false witness.

¹¹ A man's wisdom gives him patience;^d
  it is to his glory to overlook an offense.

¹² A king's rage is like the roar of a lion,
  but his favor is like dew^e on the grass.^f

¹³ A foolish son is his father's ruin,^g
  and a quarrelsome wife is like a constant dripping.^h

¹⁴ Houses and wealth are inherited from parents,ⁱ
  but a prudent wife is from the LORD.^j

¹⁵ Laziness brings on deep sleep,
  and the shiftless man goes hungry.^k

¹⁶ He who obeys instructions guards his life,
  but he who is contemptuous of his ways will die.^l

¹⁷ He who is kind to the poor lends to the LORD,
  and he will reward him for what he has done.^m

¹⁸ Discipline your son, for in that there is hope;
  do not be a willing party to his death.ⁿ

¹⁹ A hot-tempered man must pay the penalty;
  if you rescue him, you will have to do it again.

²⁰ Listen to advice and accept instruction,^o
  and in the end you will be wise.^p

²¹ Many are the plans in a man's heart,
  but it is the LORD's purpose that prevails.^q

²² What a man desires is unfailing love^a;
  better to be poor than a liar.

²³ The fear of the LORD leads to life:
  Then one rests content, untouched by trouble.^r

²⁴ The sluggard buries his hand in the dish;
  he will not even bring it back to his mouth!^s

²⁵ Flog a mocker, and the simple will learn prudence;
  rebuke a discerning man, and he will gain knowledge.^t

²⁶ He who robs his father and drives out his mother^u
  is a son who brings shame and disgrace.

²⁷ Stop listening to instruction, my son,
  and you will stray from the words of knowledge.

²⁸ A corrupt witness mocks at justice,
  and the mouth of the wicked gulps down evil.^v

²⁹ Penalties are prepared for mockers,
  and beatings for the backs of fools.^w

20 Wine is a mocker and beer a brawler;
  whoever is led astray by them is not wise.^x

² A king's wrath is like the roar of a lion;^y
  he who angers him forfeits his life.^z

^a 22 Or *A man's greed is his shame*

Proverbs 20:1–30
Themes of discerning intentions and reading others' behaviors weave throughout this collection of proverbs that includes four sayings about kings (vv. 2,8,26,28) and two versions of a maxim about differing weights and measures (vv. 10,23). These reflections go

20:3
a Pr 17:14

20:6
b Ps 12:1

20:7
c Ps 37:25-26;
112:2

20:8
d ver 26; Pr 25:4-5

20:9
e 1Ki 8:46;
Ecc 7:20; 1Jn 1:8

20:10
f ver 23; Pr 11:1

20:11
g Mt 7:16

20:12
h Ps 94:9

20:13
i Pr 6:11; 19:15

20:16
j Ex 22:26
k Pr 27:13
20:17
l Pr 9:17

20:18
m Pr 11:14; 24:6

20:19
n Pr 11:13

20:20
o Pr 30:11
p Ex 21:17;
Job 18:5

3 It is to a man's honor to avoid strife,
but every fool is quick to quarrel. a

4 A sluggard does not plow in season;
so at harvest time he looks but finds nothing.

5 The purposes of a man's heart are deep waters,
but a man of understanding draws them out.

6 Many a man claims to have unfailing love,
but a faithful man who can find? b

7 The righteous man leads a blameless life;
blessed are his children after him. c

8 When a king sits on his throne to judge,
he winnows out all evil with his eyes. d

9 Who can say, "I have kept my heart pure;
I am clean and without sin"? e

10 Differing weights and differing measures—
the LORD detests them both. f

11 Even a child is known by his actions,
by whether his conduct is pure g and right.

12 Ears that hear and eyes that see—
the LORD has made them both. h

13 Do not love sleep or you will grow poor;
stay awake and you will have food to spare.

14 "It's no good, it's no good!" says the buyer;
then off he goes and boasts about his purchase.

15 Gold there is, and rubies in abundance,
but lips that speak knowledge are a rare jewel.

16 Take the garment of one who puts up security for a stranger;
hold it in pledge j if he does it for a wayward woman. k

17 Food gained by fraud tastes sweet to a man, l
but he ends up with a mouth full of gravel.

18 Make plans by seeking advice;
if you wage war, obtain guidance. m

19 A gossip betrays a confidence; n
so avoid a man who talks too much.

20 If a man curses his father or mother, o
his lamp will be snuffed out in pitch darkness. p

beyond the practical skills of life to pondering its mysteries. Many of these proverbs read like riddles—teasing, provoking, and stimulating thought. The many doubled adages and images suggest that a clue for understanding can be found by watching for repetition.

Do you "understand [your] own way" (v. 24)? One practice of wise speaking is to speak truth to ourselves, praying for eyes that see and awareness of the darkness in our own hearts. This may be what Jesus had in mind when he called the eye the "lamp of the body," reminding us to be sure that our eye is good so that our bodies will be full of light (Matt. 6:22–23). Daily prayer

for self-understanding doesn't have to be a sign of self-hatred; it can be a mark of growth in grace. In the words of the hymn Amazing Grace, "I once was lost but now am found, was blind, but now I see."

The proverbs of this chapter are, like the purposes of our hearts, deep waters, difficult to fathom. These reflections go beyond teaching the practical skills of life to pondering its mysteries, optimistic that what's dark can become a little more light, that the unknown can become known, if only in part. As they urge their readers to meditate on the wonders of God's work within human society and in the human heart, they also make us a little less mysterious to ourselves.

21 An inheritance quickly gained at the beginning
　　will not be blessed at the end.

22 Do not say, "I'll pay you back for this wrong!" *q*
　　Wait for the LORD, and he will deliver you. *r*

23 The LORD detests differing weights,
　　and dishonest scales do not please him. *s*

24 A man's steps are directed by the LORD.
　　How then can anyone understand his own way? *t*

25 It is a trap for a man to dedicate something rashly
　　and only later to consider his vows. *u*

26 A wise king winnows out the wicked;
　　he drives the threshing wheel over them. *v*

27 The lamp of the LORD searches the spirit of a man *a*;
　　it searches out his inmost being.

28 Love and faithfulness keep a king safe;
　　through love his throne is made secure. *w*

29 The glory of young men is their strength,
　　gray hair the splendor of the old. *x*

30 Blows and wounds cleanse *y* away evil,
　　and beatings purge the inmost being.

21
The king's heart is in the hand of the LORD;
　　he directs it like a watercourse wherever he pleases.

2 All a man's ways seem right to him,
　　but the LORD weighs the heart. *z*

3 To do what is right and just
　　is more acceptable to the LORD than sacrifice. *a*

4 Haughty eyes *b* and a proud heart,
　　the lamp of the wicked, are sin!

5 The plans of the diligent lead to profit *c*
　　as surely as haste leads to poverty.

6 A fortune made by a lying tongue
　　is a fleeting vapor and a deadly snare. *b d*

7 The violence of the wicked will drag them away,
　　for they refuse to do what is right.

8 The way of the guilty is devious, *e*
　　but the conduct of the innocent is upright.

9 Better to live on a corner of the roof
　　than share a house with a quarrelsome wife. *f*

10 The wicked man craves evil;
　　his neighbor gets no mercy from him.

20:22	*q* Pr 24:29
	r Ro 12:19
20:23	*s* ver 10
20:24	*t* Jer 10:23
20:25	*u* Ecc 5:2,4-5
20:26	*v* ver 8
20:28	*w* Pr 29:14
20:29	*x* Pr 16:31
20:30	*y* Pr 22:15
21:2	*z* Pr 16:2; 24:12; Lk 16:15
21:3	*a* 1Sa 15:22; Pr 15:8; Isa 1:11; Hos 6:6; Mic 6:6-8
21:4	*b* Pr 6:17
21:5	*c* Pr 10:4; 28:22
21:6	*d* 2Pe 2:3
21:8	*e* Pr 2:15
21:9	*f* Pr 25:24

a 27 Or *The spirit of man is the LORD's lamp*　　*b 6* Some Hebrew manuscripts, Septuagint and Vulgate; most Hebrew manuscripts *vapor for those who seek death*

Proverbs 21:1–31
Both the wicked and the lazy person reject love for neighbor. Some are vulnerable to temptations that do their neighbors active harm, but most are prone to careless negligence of their need and failure to give and to care. In seeking to appropriate the principles of these proverbs for their day, representatives of each generation are called to ask whether they are primarily tuned in to the cry of their own desires or to those of others, especially the poor (v. 13).

21:11
g Pr 19:25

21:12
h Pr 14:11

21:13
i Mt 18:30-34;
Jas 2:13

21:14
j Pr 18:16; 19:6

21:15
k Pr 10:29

21:16
l Ps 49:14

21:17
m Pr 23:20-21,
29-35
21:18
n Pr 11:8; Isa 43:3

21:19
o ver 9

21:21
p Mt 5:6

21:22
q Ecc 9:15-16

21:23
r Jas 3:2 s Pr 12:13;
13:3

21:24
t Ps 1:1; Pr 1:22;
Isa 16:6; Jer 48:29

21:25
u Pr 13:4

21:26
v Ps 37:26; Mt 5:42;
Eph 4:28

21:27
w Isa 66:3; Jer 6:20;
Am 5:22 x Pr 15:8

21:28
y Pr 19:5

11 When a mocker is punished, the simple gain wisdom;
  when a wise man is instructed, he gets knowledge. g

12 The Righteous One a takes note of the house of the wicked
  and brings the wicked to ruin. h

13 If a man shuts his ears to the cry of the poor,
  he too will cry out and not be answered. i

14 A gift given in secret soothes anger,
  and a bribe concealed in the cloak pacifies great wrath. j

15 When justice is done, it brings joy to the righteous
  but terror to evildoers. k

16 A man who strays from the path of understanding
  comes to rest in the company of the dead. l

17 He who loves pleasure will become poor;
  whoever loves wine and oil will never be rich. m

18 The wicked become a ransom n for the righteous,
  and the unfaithful for the upright.

19 Better to live in a desert
  than with a quarrelsome and ill-tempered wife. o

20 In the house of the wise are stores of choice food and oil,
  but a foolish man devours all he has.

21 He who pursues righteousness and love
  finds life, prosperity b and honor. p

22 A wise man attacks the city of the mighty q
  and pulls down the stronghold in which they trust.

23 He who guards his mouth r and his tongue
  keeps himself from calamity. s

24 The proud and arrogant t man—"Mocker" is his name;
  he behaves with overweening pride.

25 The sluggard's craving will be the death of him, u
  because his hands refuse to work.

26 All day long he craves for more,
  but the righteous give without sparing. v

27 The sacrifice of the wicked is detestable w—
  how much more so when brought with evil intent! x

28 A false witness will perish, y
  and whoever listens to him will be destroyed forever. c

29 A wicked man puts up a bold front,
  but an upright man gives thought to his ways.

a 12 Or *The righteous man*   b 21 Or *righteousness*   c 28 Or */ but the words of an obedient man will live on*

📖 Don't we feel the most anger and resentment when we ourselves have suffered a wrong? Yet how often have you found yourself silently standing by when injustice has been dealt to another? As an antidote to acts of evil that fail to love our neighbors (or actively harm them), many of these proverbs hold out a love for justice. The triumph of justice stands out in verses 11–15, but that cluster is framed with the consequences that come to those who harm others (vv. 5–7,16–18). If we reverse that picture of evil, we can look for ways to love and pursue justice. Cultivating a habit of giving and a love for fairness does more than reject the path of evil; it seeks to "overcome evil with good" (Rom. 12:21).

30 There is no wisdom, ^{z} no insight, no plan
that can succeed against the LORD. ^{a}

31 The horse is made ready for the day of battle,
but victory rests with the LORD. ^{b}

22 A good name is more desirable than great riches;
to be esteemed is better than silver or gold. ^{c}

2 Rich and poor have this in common:
The LORD is the Maker of them all. ^{d}

3 A prudent man sees danger and takes refuge, ^{e}
but the simple keep going and suffer for it. ^{f}

4 Humility and the fear of the LORD
bring wealth and honor and life.

5 In the paths of the wicked lie thorns and snares, ^{g}
but he who guards his soul stays far from them.

6 Train ^{a} a child in the way he should go, ^{h}
and when he is old he will not turn from it.

7 The rich rule over the poor,
and the borrower is servant to the lender.

^{a} 6 Or Start

21:30	
	^{z} Jer 9:23
	^{a} Isa 8:10; Ac 5:39
21:31	
	^{b} Ps 3:8; 33:12-19; Isa 31:1
22:1	
	^{c} Ecc 7:1
22:2	
	^{d} Job 31:15
22:3	
	^{e} Pr 14:16
	^{f} Pr 27:12
22:5	
	^{g} Pr 15:19
22:6	
	^{h} Eph 6:4

Proverbs 22:1–16

📖 The conclusion of this major section (10:1—22:16) repeats its primary themes. Here proverbs about responsible adulthood stand side by side with those about teaching and discipline. Verses 10 and 15 suggest that one can forgive a young person's folly, but if it isn't driven out it can turn to evil. When that happens, it's not only the young who suffer but also the family and community, especially its poor. Together, these proverbs present their closing argument: One can either become a student of wisdom and a gracious member of society or an example of folly and a curse to the community.

Snapshots

22:6

Anna

Anna has a quiet demeanor, but she can talk at length when it comes to training people for the Lord's work. As a Christian witness program officer and Child Evangelism Fellowship resource person, she's been able to train 25 Bible club volunteers, who in turn have established 22 Bible clubs in Ghana.

Anna's vision for her ministry is that families in the communities for which she's responsible would come to know the salvation Christ offers. "After receiving Christ into their lives, I want to see these families mature as Christians, thereby bringing about transformation," she states earnestly. And she shares the joys of her work: "Children responding positively to their teachers fills me with great satisfaction."

Though she enjoys her work, Anna's main challenge is the frequently inaccessible roads leading to various isolated communities. Her inability to visit these areas is a source of worry, as it adversely affects her capacity to achieve her objectives. Her prayer is that the government would intervene and construct good roads to these remote villages.

> "**After receiving Christ into their lives, I want to see these families mature as Christians, thereby bringing about transformation.**"

22:8
i Job 4:8 / Ps 125:3

22:9
k 2Co 9:6 / Pr 19:17

22:10
m Pr 18:6; 26:20

22:11
n Pr 16:13; Mt 5:8

22:13
o Pr 26:13

22:14
p Pr 2:16; 5:3-5;
7:5; 23:27
q Ecc 7:26

22:15
r Pr 13:24; 23:14

22:17
s Pr 5:1

8 He who sows wickedness reaps trouble, *i*
  and the rod of his fury will be destroyed. *j*

9 A generous man will himself be blessed, *k*
  for he shares his food with the poor. *l*

10 Drive out the mocker, and out goes strife;
  quarrels and insults are ended. *m*

11 He who loves a pure heart and whose speech is gracious
  will have the king for his friend. *n*

12 The eyes of the LORD keep watch over knowledge,
  but he frustrates the words of the unfaithful.

13 The sluggard says, "There is a lion outside!" *o*
  or, "I will be murdered in the streets!"

14 The mouth of an adulteress is a deep pit; *p*
  he who is under the LORD's wrath will fall into it. *q*

15 Folly is bound up in the heart of a child,
  but the rod of discipline will drive it far from him. *r*

16 He who oppresses the poor to increase his wealth
  and he who gives gifts to the rich—both come to poverty.

Sayings of the Wise

17 Pay attention and listen to the sayings of the wise; *s*
  apply your heart to what I teach,

This passage begins with a proverb about honor and ends with one about shame, both calling for a proper attitude toward wealth (vv. 1,16). Two pairs of proverbs juxtapose the process of teaching and relations between rich and poor (vv. 6–7,15–16). The frequent mention of "haves" and "have-nots" throughout implies that a primary objective of this teaching is an understanding of money and its power, a knowledge that leads to fair and generous treatment of the poor.

📖 Our choices about money say much about our decisions, as individuals and groups of people, for or against wisdom. The many proverbs about the poor remind us that people (and groups) with resources have—and sometimes abuse—power (vv. 7,16).

Gaining and distributing worldly goods contrary to the ways of wisdom can't occur without a system—a network of relationships in which oppression goes unchecked. While the presence of institutional or systemic sin isn't directly addressed in these proverbs, it's everywhere implied. Corporate sin is a perversion of the Biblical sense of community and of Proverbs' emphasis on relationships. The contrast between a king who loves integrity and a person who oppresses the poor (vv. 11,16) suggests that personal sin, like spilled wine, often seeps into social structures, staining everything it touches.

Proverbs 22:17—24:22
🔖 The shift from individual sayings to an address by a particular teacher in 22:17 alerts us that we have entered a new section, spanning 22:17—24:22 (with an appendix: 24:23–34). These "thirty sayings" (see 22:20) are similar to the thirty units of the Egyptian "Wisdom of Amenemope," written prior to Solomon's time. The

22:17

Groups Wisdom was vitally important to the writers of Proverbs. This elusive entity is often discovered in groups of Christians engaged in Bible study, prayer, and discussion. When have you experienced an "aha!" moment while participating in a small group or fellowshiping with God's people? Some hints on the most productive settings for discussion:

Optimal number of people in a group for discussion:
3

Optimal number of people in a group for case studies:
4-5

Optimal number of people in a group for problem solving:
9

Maximum number of people for an effective sharing group:
15

Source: Galindo (2002:98)

¹⁸for it is pleasing when you keep them in your heart
   and have all of them ready on your lips.
¹⁹So that your trust may be in the LORD,
   I teach you today, even you.
²⁰Have I not written thirty ᵃ sayings for you,
   sayings of counsel and knowledge,
²¹teaching you true and reliable words, ᵗ
   so that you can give sound answers
   to him who sent you?

²²Do not exploit the poor ᵘ because they are poor
   and do not crush the needy in court, ᵛ
²³for the LORD will take up their case ʷ
   and will plunder those who plunder them. ˣ

²⁴Do not make friends with a hot-tempered man,
   do not associate with one easily angered,
²⁵or you may learn his ways
   and get yourself ensnared. ʸ
²⁶Do not be a man who strikes hands in pledge ᶻ
   or puts up security for debts;
²⁷if you lack the means to pay,
   your very bed will be snatched from under you. ᵃ

²⁸Do not move an ancient boundary stone ᵇ
   set up by your forefathers.

22:21
ᵗ Lk 1:3-4; 1Pe 3:15

22:22
ᵘ Zec 7:10
ᵛ Ex 23:6; Mal 3:5

22:23
ʷ Ps 12:5
ˣ 1Sa 25:39;
   Pr 23:10-11

22:25
ʸ 1Co 15:33
22:26
ᶻ Pr 11:15

22:27
ᵃ Pr 17:18

22:28
ᵇ Dt 19:14;
   Pr 23:10

ᵃ 20 Or *not formerly written;* or *not written excellent*

---

primary point of comparison is the purpose each was to serve. If "Amenemope" was written as an instructional guide for those preparing for public service, we can look for a similar purpose here in Proverbs.

The sayings at the beginning and end of the first portion urge the learner to "pay attention," either by listening (22:17) or by looking (v. 29). In either case, the goal is to learn attitudes and practices in preparation for effective service to the one who sends (v. 21), perhaps the king himself (v. 29). A series of snapshots in chapter 23 presents the king's would-be servant with warnings to resist temptation by exercising discipline over desire.

If this section was written to teach those heading for public service, the symbols of the legal system ("court" in 22:22 and "gate" in 24:7) and the accompanying emphasis on speaking (22:21; 24:7) call for personal integrity and for using power to speak for the powerless (24:5–12).

 The Biblical writer James reminded his readers how easy it is to fall into the trap of favoring the rich over the poor (James 2:1–9). Whatever our venue of service/ministry or employment, we are called to serve the neediest and weakest persons, not only by refusing to abuse them but by doing all we can to protect them

22:22–23

Biblical Attitudes Toward the Poor

Attention:
"If there is a poor man among your brothers in any of the towns of the land that the LORD your God is giving you, do not be hardhearted or tightfisted toward your poor brother. Rather be openhanded and freely lend him whatever he needs" (Deut. 15:7–8).

Care:
"The man with two tunics should share with him who has none, and the one who has food should do the same" (Luke 3:11).

Compassion:
"Do not exploit the poor because they are poor and do not crush the needy in court, for the LORD will take up their case and will plunder those who plunder them" (Prov. 22:22–23).

Humble Generosity:
"When you give to the needy, do not announce it with trumpets, as the hypocrites do in the synagogues and on the streets, to be honored by men" (Matt. 6:2).

Justice:
"Do not deny justice to your poor people in their lawsuits. Have nothing to do with a false charge and do not put an innocent or honest person to death" (Ex. 23:6–7).

Special Rights:
"When you reap the harvest of your land, do not reap to the very edges of your field or gather the gleanings of your harvest. Do not go over your vineyard a second time or pick up the grapes that have fallen. Leave them for the poor" (Lev. 19:9–10).

22:29
c Ge 41:46

29 Do you see a man skilled in his work?
   He will serve ^c before kings;
   he will not serve before obscure men.

23 When you sit to dine with a ruler,
   note well what ^a is before you,
² and put a knife to your throat
   if you are given to gluttony.

23:3
d ver 6-8

³ Do not crave his delicacies, ^d
   for that food is deceptive.

⁴ Do not wear yourself out to get rich;
   have the wisdom to show restraint.

23:5
e Pr 27:24

⁵ Cast but a glance at riches, and they are gone,
   for they will surely sprout wings
   and fly off to the sky like an eagle. ^e

23:6
f Ps 141:4

⁶ Do not eat the food of a stingy man,
   do not crave his delicacies; ^f
⁷ for he is the kind of man
   who is always thinking about the cost. ^b
   "Eat and drink," he says to you,
   but his heart is not with you.
⁸ You will vomit up the little you have eaten
   and will have wasted your compliments.

23:9
g Pr 1:7; 9:7; Mt 7:6

⁹ Do not speak to a fool,
   for he will scorn the wisdom of your words. ^g

23:10
h Dt 19:14;
Pr 22:28

10 Do not move an ancient boundary stone ^h
   or encroach on the fields of the fatherless,

23:11
i Job 19:25
j Pr 22:22-23

11 for their Defender ⁱ is strong;
   he will take up their case against you. ^j

12 Apply your heart to instruction
   and your ears to words of knowledge.

13 Do not withhold discipline from a child;
   if you punish him with the rod, he will not die.
14 Punish him with the rod
   and save his soul from death. ^c

15 My son, if your heart is wise,
   then my heart will be glad;
16 my inmost being will rejoice

23:16
k ver 24; Pr 27:11

   when your lips speak what is right. ^k

^a 1 Or *who*   ^b 7 Or *for as he thinks within himself, / so he is;* or *for as he puts on a feast, / so he is*
^c 14 Hebrew *Sheol*

---

from those who would. In our world of larger and larger circles of business and professional relationships, it isn't always easy to spot abuse, but even the commitment to be aware of such issues is a step forward.

Chapter 23 reminds us that reflecting on our pursuits, recognizing and dealing with addictions, and setting a mission statement to guide us are three ways of putting the teaching of the sages to work. This much is clear: Given that the quality of life is so poor for many in our world and that our efforts to achieve satisfaction by having plenty have failed miserably, the directive in 23:2 to put a (figurative) knife to our own throats (desires)

doesn't sound like all that bad an idea! How can you implement it?

The goal of this brief manual on public and political service was to serve both those in power and those in need, and to do so by speaking honestly. We serve when we tell the truth about ourselves, insist that truth be told about others, refuse dishonest testimony, and insist on right judgments. Service to those in power is never to be at the expense of the powerless. The purpose of this set of writings was stated at the outset: to teach true and reliable words so that sound answers might be returned (22:21).

17 Do not let your heart envy[l] sinners,
    but always be zealous for the fear of the LORD.
18 There is surely a future hope for you,
    and your hope will not be cut off.[m]

19 Listen, my son, and be wise,
    and keep your heart on the right path.
20 Do not join those who drink too much wine[n]
    or gorge themselves on meat,
21 for drunkards and gluttons become poor,[o]
    and drowsiness clothes them in rags.

22 Listen to your father, who gave you life,
    and do not despise your mother when she is old.[p]
23 Buy the truth and do not sell it;
    get wisdom, discipline and understanding.[q]
24 The father of a righteous man has great joy;
    he who has a wise son delights in him.[r]
25 May your father and mother be glad;
    may she who gave you birth rejoice!

26 My son,[s] give me your heart
    and let your eyes keep to my ways,[t]
27 for a prostitute is a deep pit[u]
    and a wayward wife is a narrow well.
28 Like a bandit she lies in wait,[v]
    and multiplies the unfaithful among men.

29 Who has woe? Who has sorrow?
    Who has strife? Who has complaints?
    Who has needless bruises? Who has bloodshot eyes?
30 Those who linger over wine,[w]
    who go to sample bowls of mixed wine.
31 Do not gaze at wine when it is red,
    when it sparkles in the cup,
    when it goes down smoothly!
32 In the end it bites like a snake
    and poisons like a viper.
33 Your eyes will see strange sights
    and your mind imagine confusing things.
34 You will be like one sleeping on the high seas,
    lying on top of the rigging.
35 "They hit me," you will say, "but I'm not hurt!
    They beat me, but I don't feel it!
    When will I wake up
    so I can find another drink?"

24

1 Do not envy[x] wicked men,
    do not desire their company;
2 for their hearts plot violence,
    and their lips talk about making trouble.[y]

3 By wisdom a house is built,[z]
    and through understanding it is established;
4 through knowledge its rooms are filled
    with rare and beautiful treasures.[a]

5 A wise man has great power,
    and a man of knowledge increases strength;
6 for waging war you need guidance,
    and for victory many advisers.[b]

Cross-references

23:17 [l] Ps 37:1; Pr 28:14

23:18 [m] Ps 9:18; Pr 24:14,19-20

23:20 [n] Isa 5:11,22; Ro 13:13; Eph 5:18

23:21 [o] Pr 21:17

23:22 [p] Lev 19:32; Pr 1:8; 30:17; Eph 6:1-2
23:23 [q] Pr 4:7

23:24 [r] ver 15-16; Pr 10:1; 15:20

23:26 [s] Pr 3:1; 5:1-6
[t] Ps 18:21; Pr 4:4
23:27 [u] Pr 22:14

23:28 [v] Pr 7:11-12; Ecc 7:26

23:30 [w] Ps 75:8; Isa 5:11; Eph 5:18

24:1 [x] Ps 37:1; 73:3; Pr 3:31-32; 23:17-18

24:2 [y] Ps 10:7

24:3 [z] Pr 14:1

24:4 [a] Pr 8:21

24:6 [b] Pr 11:14; 20:18; Lk 14:31

7 Wisdom is too high for a fool;
  in the assembly at the gate he has nothing to say.

8 He who plots evil
  will be known as a schemer.
9 The schemes of folly are sin,
  and men detest a mocker.

24:10
c Job 4:5;
Jer 51:46; Heb 12:3

10 If you falter in times of trouble,
  how small is your strength! [c]

24:11
d Ps 82:4;
Isa 58:6-7
24:12
e Pr 21:2
f Job 34:11;
Ps 62:12; Ro 2:6*

11 Rescue those being led away to death;
  hold back those staggering toward slaughter. [d]
12 If you say, "But we knew nothing about this,"
  does not he who weighs [e] the heart perceive it?
Does not he who guards your life know it?
  Will he not repay each person according to what he has done? [f]

13 Eat honey, my son, for it is good;
  honey from the comb is sweet to your taste.
14 Know also that wisdom is sweet to your soul;
  if you find it, there is a future hope for you,
  and your hope will not be cut off. [g][h]

24:14
g Ps 119:103;
Pr 16:24 h Pr 23:18

15 Do not lie in wait like an outlaw against a righteous man's house,
  do not raid his dwelling place;
16 for though a righteous man falls seven times, he rises again,
  but the wicked are brought down by calamity. [i]

24:16
i Job 5:19;
Ps 34:19; Mic 7:8
24:17
j Ob 1:12
k Job 31:29

17 Do not gloat[j] when your enemy falls;
  when he stumbles, do not let your heart rejoice, [k]
18 or the LORD will see and disapprove
  and turn his wrath away from him.

24:19
l Ps 37:1

19 Do not fret[l] because of evil men
  or be envious of the wicked,
20 for the evil man has no future hope,
  and the lamp of the wicked will be snuffed out. [m]

24:20
m Job 18:5;
Pr 13:9; 23:17-18
24:21
n Ro 13:1-5;
1Pe 2:17

21 Fear the LORD and the king, [n] my son,
  and do not join with the rebellious,
22 for those two will send sudden destruction upon them,
  and who knows what calamities they can bring?

Further Sayings of the Wise

24:23
o Pr 1:6 p Lev 19:15
q Pr 28:21

23 These also are sayings of the wise: [o]

To show partiality[p] in judging is not good: [q]

24:24
r Pr 17:15

24 Whoever says to the guilty, "You are innocent" [r]—

Proverbs 24:23–34

📖 This appendix to the "sayings of the wise" (22:17—24:22) combines direct teaching on jurisprudence with indirect teaching on laziness through the metaphor of the overgrown field. It's not good to show partiality in judging, to declare the guilty innocent, to bear false witness against a neighbor, or to plot revenge. It may seem strange to interweave this teaching with advice about fields and houses, but the phrase "build your house" directs the reader to wisdom. If the house is a symbol for acquiring wisdom in heart, mind, and practice, then right speaking in the community is like preparing fields or putting the most important tasks first.

📖 If the "sayings of the wise" and its appendix have anything to teach us, it's that serving honestly and faithfully is hard work, that snares and temptations are always before us, and that they are often hidden under the camouflage of seeking what appears to be good. It's natural for us as human beings to act out of greed, envy, or a desire for vengeance, even when it appears that we only want what's good. But we do well to learn that faithful service is the path toward the good—and that it's only in giving that we receive.

There are no sectional divisions in Proverbs 25–29. Study notes are separated by chapters.

peoples will curse him and nations denounce him.
25 But it will go well with those who convict the guilty,
    and rich blessing will come upon them.

26 An honest answer
    is like a kiss on the lips.

27 Finish your outdoor work
    and get your fields ready;
    after that, build your house.

28 Do not testify against your neighbor without cause, *s*
    or use your lips to deceive.

29 Do not say, "I'll do to him as he has done to me;
    I'll pay that man back for what he did." *t*

30 I went past the field of the sluggard, *u*
    past the vineyard of the man who lacks judgment;
31 thorns had come up everywhere,
    the ground was covered with weeds,
    and the stone wall was in ruins.
32 I applied my heart to what I observed
    and learned a lesson from what I saw:
33 A little sleep, a little slumber,
    a little folding of the hands to rest *v*—
34 and poverty will come on you like a bandit
    and scarcity like an armed man. *a w*

More Proverbs of Solomon

25 These are more proverbs *x* of Solomon, copied by the men of Hezekiah king of Judah: *y*

2 It is the glory of God to conceal a matter;
    to search out a matter is the glory of kings. *z*

3 As the heavens are high and the earth is deep,
    so the hearts of kings are unsearchable.

4 Remove the dross from the silver,
    and out comes material for *b* the silversmith;
5 remove the wicked from the king's presence, *a*
    and his throne will be established *b* through righteousness. *c*

6 Do not exalt yourself in the king's presence,
    and do not claim a place among great men;
7 it is better for him to say to you, "Come up here," *d*
    than for him to humiliate you before a nobleman.

What you have seen with your eyes

---

a 34 Or like a vagrant / and scarcity like a beggar   *b 4 Or comes a vessel from*

24:28
s Ps 7:4; Pr 25:18;
Eph 4:25

24:29
t Pr 20:22;
Mt 5:38-41;
Ro 12:17
24:30
u Pr 6:6-11;
26:13-16

24:33
v Pr 6:10

24:34
w Pr 10:4;
Ecc 10:18

25:1
x 1Ki 4:32 *y* Pr 1:1

25:2
z Pr 16:10-15

25:5
a Pr 20:8 *b* 2Sa 7:13
c Pr 16:12; 29:14

25:7
d Lk 14:7-10

Proverbs 25:1–28

📖 The composition of the book of Proverbs returns to the proverbs of Solomon (see "There and Then" for 1:1–7), also noting that these were "copied by the men of Hezekiah king of Judah." Hezekiah's reign, more than 200 years after Solomon's, saw a great revival—which explains his interest in a compilation of Solomon's proverbs. Many of the sayings in this section (25:1—29:27) were meant to be read and interpreted as pairs, one shedding more light on the other.

The proverbs in chapter 25 are like riddles. Each pair or cluster asks: How is *x* like (or opposite) *y*? Metaphors of general experience are applied to particular situations, as, for example, "too much of a good thing" is first compared to eating honey (v. 16), then to visiting (v. 17), and finally to self-promotion (v. 27). There are no exclusive sets of ethics for kings, courtiers, and subjects, and the ethical principles laid out here still find a place in our culture of consumption.

25:8
e Mt 5:25-26

8   do not bring[a] hastily to court,
  for what will you do in the end
    if your neighbor puts you to shame?[e]

9 If you argue your case with a neighbor,
  do not betray another man's confidence,
10 or he who hears it may shame you
  and you will never lose your bad reputation.

25:11
f ver 12; Pr 15:23

11 A word aptly spoken
  is like apples of gold in settings of silver.[f]

25:12
g ver 11; Ps 141:5;
Pr 13:18; 15:31

12 Like an earring of gold or an ornament of fine gold
  is a wise man's rebuke to a listening ear.[g]

25:13
h Pr 10:26; 13:17

13 Like the coolness of snow at harvest time
  is a trustworthy messenger to those who send him;
  he refreshes the spirit of his masters.[h]

14 Like clouds and wind without rain
  is a man who boasts of gifts he does not give.

25:15
i Ecc 10:4 j Pr 15:1

15 Through patience a ruler can be persuaded,[i]
  and a gentle tongue can break a bone.[j]

25:16
k ver 27

16 If you find honey, eat just enough—
  too much of it, and you will vomit.[k]
17 Seldom set foot in your neighbor's house—
  too much of you, and he will hate you.

25:18
l Ps 57:4; Pr 12:18

18 Like a club or a sword or a sharp arrow
  is the man who gives false testimony against his neighbor.[l]

19 Like a bad tooth or a lame foot
  is reliance on the unfaithful in times of trouble.

20 Like one who takes away a garment on a cold day,
  or like vinegar poured on soda,
  is one who sings songs to a heavy heart.

21 If your enemy is hungry, give him food to eat;
  if he is thirsty, give him water to drink.

25:22
m Ps 18:8
n 2Sa 16:12;
2Ch 28:15; Mt 5:44;
Ro 12:20*

22 In doing this, you will heap burning coals[m] on his head,
  and the LORD will reward you.[n]

23 As a north wind brings rain,
  so a sly tongue brings angry looks.

25:24
o Pr 21:9

24 Better to live on a corner of the roof
  than share a house with a quarrelsome wife.[o]

25:25
p Pr 15:30

25 Like cold water to a weary soul
  is good news from a distant land.[p]

26 Like a muddied spring or a polluted well
  is a righteous man who gives way to the wicked.

25:27
q ver 16 r Pr 27:2;
Mt 23:12

27 It is not good to eat too much honey,[q]
  nor is it honorable to seek one's own honor.[r]

a 7,8 Or *nobleman* / *on whom you had set your eyes.* / [8]Do not go

---

📖 Proverbs' remedies for self-centered and unwise living are restraint and reflection. On a personal level, we do well to cultivate the habit of stopping and waiting to ask whose interests are being served by a particular decision or action. When have you found that actions you thought were loving weren't seen that way through another's eyes? So also our communities, governments, and churches can act in self-deceiving ways—all the more reason to consult those outside our circles for "a word aptly spoken" (v. 11).

28 Like a city whose walls are broken down
   is a man who lacks self-control.

26

Like snow in summer or rain[s] in harvest,
   honor is not fitting for a fool.[t]

2 Like a fluttering sparrow or a darting swallow,
   an undeserved curse does not come to rest.[u]

3 A whip for the horse, a halter for the donkey,[v]
   and a rod for the backs of fools![w]

4 Do not answer a fool according to his folly,
   or you will be like him yourself.[x]

5 Answer a fool according to his folly,
   or he will be wise in his own eyes.[y]

6 Like cutting off one's feet or drinking violence
   is the sending of a message by the hand of a fool.[z]

7 Like a lame man's legs that hang limp
   is a proverb in the mouth of a fool.[a]

8 Like tying a stone in a sling
   is the giving of honor to a fool.[b]

9 Like a thornbush in a drunkard's hand
   is a proverb in the mouth of a fool.[c]

10 Like an archer who wounds at random
   is he who hires a fool or any passer-by.

11 As a dog returns to its vomit,[d]
   so a fool repeats his folly.[e]

12 Do you see a man wise in his own eyes?[f]
   There is more hope for a fool than for him.[g]

13 The sluggard says,[h] "There is a lion in the road,
   a fierce lion roaming the streets!"[i]

14 As a door turns on its hinges,
   so a sluggard turns on his bed.[j]

15 The sluggard buries his hand in the dish;
   he is too lazy to bring it back to his mouth.[k]

16 The sluggard is wiser in his own eyes
   than seven men who answer discreetly.

17 Like one who seizes a dog by the ears
   is a passer-by who meddles in a quarrel not his own.

18 Like a madman shooting
   firebrands or deadly arrows

26:1
s 1Sa 12:17 t ver 8;
Pr 19:10

26:2
u Nu 23:8; Dt 23:5

26:3
v Ps 32:9
w Pr 10:13

26:4
x ver 5; Isa 36:21

26:5
y ver 4; Pr 3:7

26:6
z Pr 10:26

26:7
a ver 9

26:8
b ver 1

26:9
c ver 7

26:11
d 2Pe 2:22*
e Ex 8:15; Ps 85:8

26:12
f Pr 3:7 g Pr 29:20

26:13
h Pr 6:6-11;
24:30-34
i Pr 22:13

26:14
j Pr 6:9

26:15
k Pr 19:24

Proverbs 26:1–28

The second chapter of these proverbs of Solomon "copied by the men of Hezekiah" (25:1) helps readers "search out matters" (cf. 25:2) by commenting on fools (26:1–16) and troublemakers (vv. 17–28). The chapter begins with proverbs about what is and isn't "fitting" and closes with maxims about just rewards, identifying appropriate consequences. Those who learn wisdom observe wisdom's laws of nature and social life and learn to make decisions that fit the situation.

We may as well admit that we have all played the fool or troublemaker. Who hasn't sought honors by dropping a name or an accomplishment in the hope of fishing some word of praise from a conversation? Who of us hasn't said an unkind word, either to another in a quarrel or about another in gossip, hoping to prove that we are right or better than someone else? We too often speak to lift ourselves up or to stand on top of somebody else. If honor won't come to us, our subconscious seems to assert, let dishonor fall on another.

¹⁹ is a man who deceives his neighbor
  and says, "I was only joking!"

²⁰ Without wood a fire goes out;
  without gossip a quarrel dies down. *l*

²¹ As charcoal to embers and as wood to fire,
  so is a quarrelsome man for kindling strife. *m*

²² The words of a gossip are like choice morsels;
  they go down to a man's inmost parts. *n*

²³ Like a coating of glaze ª over earthenware
  are fervent lips with an evil heart.

²⁴ A malicious man disguises himself with his lips, *o*
  but in his heart he harbors deceit. *p*

²⁵ Though his speech is charming, *q* do not believe him,
  for seven abominations fill his heart. *r*

²⁶ His malice may be concealed by deception,
  but his wickedness will be exposed in the assembly.

²⁷ If a man digs a pit, *s* he will fall into it; *t*
  if a man rolls a stone, it will roll back on him. *u*

²⁸ A lying tongue hates those it hurts,
  and a flattering mouth *v* works ruin.

27

¹ Do not boast *w* about tomorrow,
  for you do not know what a day may bring forth. *x*

² Let another praise you, and not your own mouth;
  someone else, and not your own lips. *y*

³ Stone is heavy and sand *z* a burden,
  but provocation by a fool is heavier than both.

⁴ Anger is cruel and fury overwhelming,
  but who can stand before jealousy? *a*

⁵ Better is open rebuke
  than hidden love.

⁶ Wounds from a friend can be trusted,
  but an enemy multiplies kisses. *b*

⁷ He who is full loathes honey,
  but to the hungry even what is bitter tastes sweet.

⁸ Like a bird that strays from its nest *c*
  is a man who strays from his home.

ª 23 With a different word division of the Hebrew; Masoretic Text *of silver dross*

Cross references (margin)

- 26:20 / Pr 22:10
- 26:21 *m* Pr 14:17; 15:18
- 26:22 *n* Pr 18:8
- 26:24 *o* Ps 31:18 *p* Ps 41:6; Pr 10:18; 12:20
- 26:25 *q* Ps 28:3 *r* Jer 9:4-8
- 26:27 *s* Ps 7:15 *t* Est 6:13 *u* Est 2:23; 7:9; Ps 35:8; 141:10; Pr 28:10; 29:6; Isa 50:11
- 26:28 *v* Ps 12:3; Pr 29:5
- 27:1 *w* 1Ki 20:11 *x* Mt 6:34; Lk 12:19-20; Jas 4:13-16
- 27:2 *y* Pr 25:27
- 27:3 *z* Job 6:3
- 27:4 *a* Nu 5:14
- 27:6 *b* Ps 141:5; Pr 28:23
- 27:8 *c* Isa 16:2

Proverbs 27:1–27

This collection of proverbs explores the themes of friendship and trusting relationships. The first 22 verses gather into clusters of two, though the relationship between some pairs is clearer than others. The last five verses form a longer poem that uses shepherding/farming imagery to describe the rewards of care and diligence. This poem challenges our superficial assumptions about human self-sufficiency, skills, accomplishments, or anything else that might displace our need to love and depend on family, neighbors, and even the plants and animals of God's good Earth.

The media makes it seem as though we either live for self, like greedy capitalists, or for others, like Mother Teresa. Yet most of us live and work in the daily grind of earning a living, caring for our families, and trying to be good neighbors. We want "enough," not excess, but still wish there were a little more to take the edge off our financial worries. The proverbs and poems of this chapter show us an approach to life and possessions that sets them in proper perspective, helping us to realize our need for one another, not just for things we can own.

Some forms of work exploit others, either by their product, as in the case of pornography or tobacco, or by

9 Perfume[d] and incense bring joy to the heart,
    and the pleasantness of one's friend springs from his earnest
        counsel.

10 Do not forsake your friend and the friend of your father,
    and do not go to your brother's house when disaster[e] strikes you—
    better a neighbor nearby than a brother far away.

11 Be wise, my son, and bring joy to my heart;[f]
    then I can answer anyone who treats me with contempt.[g]

12 The prudent see danger and take refuge,
    but the simple keep going and suffer for it.[h]

13 Take the garment of one who puts up security for a stranger;
    hold it in pledge if he does it for a wayward woman.[i]

14 If a man loudly blesses his neighbor early in the morning,
    it will be taken as a curse.

15 A quarrelsome wife is like
    a constant dripping[j] on a rainy day;
16 restraining her is like restraining the wind
    or grasping oil with the hand.

17 As iron sharpens iron,
    so one man sharpens another.

18 He who tends a fig tree will eat its fruit,[k]
    and he who looks after his master will be honored.[l]

19 As water reflects a face,
    so a man's heart reflects the man.

20 Death and Destruction[a] are never satisfied,[m]
    and neither are the eyes of man.[n]

21 The crucible for silver and the furnace for gold,[o]
    but man is tested by the praise he receives.

22 Though you grind a fool in a mortar,
    grinding him like grain with a pestle,
    you will not remove his folly from him.

23 Be sure you know the condition of your flocks,[p]
    give careful attention to your herds;
24 for riches do not endure forever,[q]
    and a crown is not secure for all generations.
25 When the hay is removed and new growth appears
    and the grass from the hills is gathered in,
26 the lambs will provide you with clothing,
    and the goats with the price of a field.
27 You will have plenty of goats' milk
    to feed you and your family
    and to nourish your servant girls.

28 The wicked man flees[r] though no one pursues,[s]
    but the righteous are as bold as a lion.[t]

a 20 Hebrew *Sheol and Abaddon*

27:9
d Est 2:12; Ps 45:8

27:10
e Pr 17:17; 18:24

27:11
f Pr 10:1; 23:15-16
g Ge 24:60

27:12
h Pr 22:3

27:13
i Pr 20:16

27:15
j Est 1:18; Pr 19:13

27:18
k 1Co 9:7
l Lk 19:12-27

27:20
m Pr 30:15-16;
Hab 2:5 n Ecc 1:8;
6:7

27:21
o Pr 17:3

27:23
p Pr 12:10

27:24
q Pr 23:5

28:1
r 2Ki 7:7
s Lev 26:17; Ps 53:5
t Ps 138:3

unfair treatment of workers. Yet many occupations make some contribution to the well-being of others and therefore reflect the work of God in the world. Providing for our own needs is only part of our motivation to work. Provision and service need not be mutually exclusive. In what ways does your daily work benefit others?

2 When a country is rebellious, it has many rulers,
　but a man of understanding and knowledge maintains order.

3 A ruler[a] who oppresses the poor
　is like a driving rain that leaves no crops.

4 Those who forsake the law praise the wicked,
　but those who keep the law resist them.

5 Evil men do not understand justice,
　but those who seek the LORD understand it fully.

6 Better a poor man whose walk is blameless
　than a rich man whose ways are perverse.[u]

7 He who keeps the law is a discerning son,
　but a companion of gluttons disgraces his father.[v]

8 He who increases his wealth by exorbitant interest[w]
　amasses it for another,[x] who will be kind to the poor.[y]

9 If anyone turns a deaf ear to the law,
　even his prayers are detestable.[z]

10 He who leads the upright along an evil path
　will fall into his own trap,[a]
　but the blameless will receive a good inheritance.

11 A rich man may be wise in his own eyes,
　but a poor man who has discernment sees through him.

a 3 Or A poor man

28:6
u Pr 19:1

28:7
v Pr 23:19-21

28:8
w Ex 18:21
x Job 27:17;
Pr 13:22 y Ps 112:9;
Pr 14:31; Lk 14:12-
14
28:9
z Ps 66:18; 109:7;
Pr 15:8; Isa 1:13

28:10
a Pr 26:27

Proverbs 28:1–28

Chapters 28 and 29, the last two preserved by "the men of Hezekiah" (chs. 25–29), combine proverbs on rule and government with wise sayings about good relations with family and neighbors. These proverbs of righteous character and righteous rule lie side by side, suggesting that the concern for fairness and compassion are sure guides for both. Central to chapter 28 is the appearance of the Hebrew word *torah* ("law"). Each occurrence is preceded by a reference to the poor (vv. 3–4, 6–7,8–9), reinforcing that "neighbor" includes everyone.

Snapshots

 27:26–27

A Struggle and a Dream

Valentin had hit rock bottom. A Romanian farmer with a family, a small herd of goats, two cows, and big plans, he was tapped out by a hard winter.

Valentin applied for and received from a relief organization a rural credit loan of $600. With that he leveraged a smaller bank loan and purchased 20 goats, which he added to his existing herd of 20. He has since doubled his herd through breeding and dreams of qualifying for a contract with a dairy firm specializing in natural products.

Once Valentin has 100 goats, he will sign that contract and double his profit for each liter of goat milk—a dream about two years off.

The family is close, as evidenced in the affection freely shared among this couple and their two sons. Strong Christians, they love the countryside. Theirs is a world of animals and unfenced hills.

Yet Valentin and Luminita worry about their boys' futures. "Chances are poor for our sons to continue school after fourth grade," Valentin explains. Adds Luminita: "One school offering the next grades is a 90-minute walk one way. While another is closer, an hour, the way is dangerous . . . It's hard to be a boy in the country."

> "It's hard to be a boy in the country."

12 When the righteous triumph, there is great elation;[b]
   but when the wicked rise to power, men go into hiding.[c]

13 He who conceals his sins[d] does not prosper,
   but whoever confesses and renounces them finds mercy.[e]

14 Blessed is the man who always fears the LORD,
   but he who hardens his heart falls into trouble.

15 Like a roaring lion or a charging bear
   is a wicked man ruling over a helpless people.

16 A tyrannical ruler lacks judgment,
   but he who hates ill-gotten gain will enjoy a long life.

17 A man tormented by the guilt of murder
   will be a fugitive[f] till death;
   let no one support him.

18 He whose walk is blameless is kept safe,
   but he whose ways are perverse will suddenly fall.[g]

19 He who works his land will have abundant food,
   but the one who chases fantasies will have his fill of poverty.[h]

20 A faithful man will be richly blessed,
   but one eager to get rich will not go unpunished.[i]

21 To show partiality is not good[j]—
   yet a man will do wrong for a piece of bread.[k]

22 A stingy man is eager to get rich
   and is unaware that poverty awaits him.[l]

23 He who rebukes a man will in the end gain more favor
   than he who has a flattering tongue.[m]

24 He who robs his father or mother[n]
   and says, "It's not wrong"—
   he is partner to him who destroys.[o]

25 A greedy man stirs up dissension,
   but he who trusts in the LORD[p] will prosper.

26 He who trusts in himself is a fool,[q]
   but he who walks in wisdom is kept safe.

27 He who gives to the poor will lack nothing,[r]
   but he who closes his eyes to them receives many curses.

28 When the wicked rise to power, people go into hiding;[s]
   but when the wicked perish, the righteous thrive.

29 A man who remains stiff-necked after many rebukes
   will suddenly be destroyed—without remedy.[t]

2 When the righteous thrive, the people rejoice;[u]
   when the wicked rule, the people groan.[v]

28:12	b 2Ki 11:20
	c Pr 11:10; 29:2
28:13	d Job 31:33
	e Ps 32:1-5; 1Jn 1:9
28:17	f Ge 9:6
28:18	g Pr 10:9
28:19	h Pr 12:11
28:20	i ver 22; Pr 10:6; 1Ti 6:9
28:21	j Pr 18:5
	k Eze 13:19
28:22	l ver 20; Pr 23:6
28:23	m Pr 27:5-6
28:24	n Pr 19:26 o Pr 18:9
28:25	p Pr 29:25
28:26	q Ps 4:5; Pr 3:5
28:27	r Dt 15:7; 24:19; Pr 19:17; 22:9
28:28	s ver 12
29:1	t 2Ch 36:16; Pr 6:15
29:2	u Est 8:15
	v Pr 28:12

This chapter in general, and verse 27 in particular, calls us to give to the poor rather than close our eyes to their needs. Where did we get the idea that life is about getting all we can and maybe giving some away? Reversing those priorities can be as simple as learning to give generously to those in need. But it's clear that giving alone won't keep some from taking unfair advantage of the poor. Another way Christians can open their eyes to the poor is by becoming aware of policies that impact people of low income—supporting those that help and voting against those that would hinder them.

Proverbs 29:1–27

The final chapter of proverbs collected by "the men of Hezekiah," like the others in the collection (25:1—

29:3
w Pr 10:1
x Pr 5:8-10;
Lk 15:11-32
29:4
y Pr 8:15-16

³A man who loves wisdom brings joy to his father, ^w
  but a companion of prostitutes squanders his wealth. ^x

⁴By justice a king gives a country stability, ^y
  but one who is greedy for bribes tears it down.

⁵Whoever flatters his neighbor
  is spreading a net for his feet.

29:6
z Ecc 9:12

⁶An evil man is snared by his own sin, ^z
  but a righteous one can sing and be glad.

29:7
a Job 29:16;
Ps 41:1; Pr 31:8-9

⁷The righteous care about justice for the poor, ^a
  but the wicked have no such concern.

29:8
b Pr 11:11; 16:14

⁸Mockers stir up a city,
  but wise men turn away anger. ^b

⁹If a wise man goes to court with a fool,
  the fool rages and scoffs, and there is no peace.

29:10
c 1Jn 3:12

¹⁰Bloodthirsty men hate a man of integrity
  and seek to kill the upright. ^c

29:11
d Pr 12:16; 19:11

¹¹A fool gives full vent to his anger,
  but a wise man keeps himself under control. ^d

¹²If a ruler listens to lies,
  all his officials become wicked.

29:13
e Pr 22:2; Mt 5:45

¹³The poor man and the oppressor have this in common:
  The LORD gives sight to the eyes of both. ^e

29:14
f Ps 72:1-5;
Pr 16:12

¹⁴If a king judges the poor with fairness,
  his throne will always be secure. ^f

29:15
g Pr 10:1; 13:24;
17:21,25

¹⁵The rod of correction imparts wisdom,
  but a child left to himself disgraces his mother. ^g

29:16
h Ps 37:35-36;
58:10; 91:8; 92:11

¹⁶When the wicked thrive, so does sin,
  but the righteous will see their downfall. ^h

29:17
i ver 15; Pr 10:1

¹⁷Discipline your son, and he will give you peace;
  he will bring delight to your soul. ⁱ

29:18
j Ps 1:1-2; 119:1-2;
Jn 13:17

¹⁸Where there is no revelation, the people cast off restraint;
  but blessed is he who keeps the law. ^j

¹⁹A servant cannot be corrected by mere words;
  though he understands, he will not respond.

29:27), intertwines reflections on rule and public character with general sayings about the moral life. These concluding proverbs demonstrate wisdom at work at every level of social interaction. Nations, like sons and servants, need discipline. Each needs teaching, correction, and even the threat of punishment or restraint when the first two aren't heeded. The effects of wisdom and folly vibrate throughout the social network the way an entire spider web shakes when one strand is disturbed.

We may have grown cynical about our expectations of our leaders, believing that a certain amount of savvy requires some level of moral compromise. True, the choices facing governments are complex, and decisions sometimes hurt one group over another or require mak-

ing a call from among multiple distasteful options. But the Christian leader is to acknowledge that the human tendency toward self-serving behavior worms its way into our actions, individual and collective. These proverbs place a large share of the burden on leaders to bring the guiding rule of wisdom to bear for the people's sake.

Moreover, there is accountability in these verses. Do our leaders appeal to standards of fairness and compassion or only of our own (and their) interests? Sayings in this chapter about king and God sit side by side, reminding us that the shaping of personal and national character is never removed from the One who gives light to the eyes of rich and poor (v. 13), sets those who trust on high (v. 25), and brings justice to those who seek it (v. 26).

²⁰ Do you see a man who speaks in haste?
　There is more hope for a fool than for him.^k

²¹ If a man pampers his servant from youth,
　he will bring grief^a in the end.

²² An angry man stirs up dissension,
　and a hot-tempered one commits many sins.^l

²³ A man's pride brings him low,
　but a man of lowly spirit gains honor.^m

²⁴ The accomplice of a thief is his own enemy;
　he is put under oath and dare not testify.ⁿ

²⁵ Fear of man will prove to be a snare,
　but whoever trusts in the LORD^o is kept safe.

²⁶ Many seek an audience with a ruler,^p
　but it is from the LORD that man gets justice.

²⁷ The righteous detest the dishonest;
　the wicked detest the upright.^q

Sayings of Agur

30

The sayings of Agur son of Jakeh—an oracle^b:

This man declared to Ithiel,
　to Ithiel and to Ucal:^c

² "I am the most ignorant of men;
　I do not have a man's understanding.
³ I have not learned wisdom,
　nor have I knowledge of the Holy One.^r
⁴ Who has gone up^s to heaven and come down?
　Who has gathered up the wind in the hollow^t of his hands?
Who has wrapped up the waters^u in his cloak?^v
　Who has established all the ends of the earth?
What is his name,^w and the name of his son?
　Tell me if you know!

⁵ "Every word of God is flawless;^x
　he is a shield^y to those who take refuge in him.
⁶ Do not add^z to his words,
　or he will rebuke you and prove you a liar.

⁷ "Two things I ask of you, O LORD;
　do not refuse me before I die:
⁸ Keep falsehood and lies far from me;

29:20
k Pr 26:12; Jas 1:19

29:22
l Pr 14:17; 15:18;
26:21

29:23
m Pr 11:2; 15:33;
16:18; Isa 66:2;
Mt 23:12

29:24
n Lev 5:1

29:25
o Pr 28:25

29:26
p Pr 19:6

29:27
q ver 10

30:3
r Pr 9:10
30:4
s Ps 24:1-2; Jn 3:13;
Eph 4:7-10
t Ps 104:3;
Isa 40:12
u Job 26:8; 38:8-9
v Ge 1:2
w Rev 19:12

30:5
x Ps 12:6; 18:30
y Ge 15:1; Ps 84:11
30:6
z Dt 4:2; 12:32;
Rev 22:18

---

^a 21 The meaning of the Hebrew for this word is uncertain.　^b 1 Or *Jakeh of Massa*　^c 1 Masoretic Text; with a different word division of the Hebrew *declared, "I am weary, O God; / I am weary, O God, and faint.*

Proverbs 30:1–33

Chapter 30 is the first of two chapters serving as the conclusion to Proverbs. Agur was likely a non-Israelite wise man like Job and his friends. The first section of his sayings (vv. 1–14) begins with a series of rhetorical questions and is in essence a prayer in two parts—first for knowledge of God and second for a life lived before him in wisdom. The importance of proper speaking runs throughout this section.

The second part of the chapter's teaching (vv. 15–33) comes in numerical sayings, drawing together observations on life and nature to illustrate various aspects of wisdom. Agur observed two, three, and four things that either cry "Give!" or never know when to say "Enough!" The hungers of the leech, the grave, the barren womb, dry land, and blazing fire show the dangers of unrestrained appetite. Even if they have never learned to say "enough," we who claim to serve a God who provides certainly can.

30:8
a Mt 6:11
30:9
b Jos 24:27; Isa 1:4;
59:13 c Dt 6:12;
8:10-14; Hos 13:6
d Dt 8:12

give me neither poverty nor riches,
but give me only my daily bread. a
9 Otherwise, I may have too much and disown b you
and say, 'Who is the LORD?' c
Or I may become poor and steal,
and so dishonor the name of my God. d

10 "Do not slander a servant to his master,
or he will curse you, and you will pay for it.

30:11
e Pr 20:20
30:12
f Pr 16:2; Lk 18:11
g Jer 2:23,35

11 "There are those who curse their fathers
and do not bless their mothers; e
12 those who are pure in their own eyes f
and yet are not cleansed of their filth; g

30:13
h 2Sa 22:28;
Job 41:34;
Ps 131:1; Pr 6:17
30:14
i Job 4:11; 29:17;
Ps 3:7 j Ps 57:4
k Job 24:9; Ps 14:4
l Am 8:4; Mic 2:2
m Job 19:22

13 those whose eyes are ever so haughty, h
whose glances are so disdainful;
14 those whose teeth i are swords
and whose jaws are set with knives j
to devour k the poor l from the earth,
the needy from among mankind. m

15 "The leech has two daughters.
'Give! Give!' they cry.

30:15
n Pr 27:20

"There are three things that are never satisfied, n
four that never say, 'Enough!':

30:16
o Pr 27:20; Isa 5:14;
14:9,11; Hab 2:5

16 the grave, a o the barren womb,
land, which is never satisfied with water,
and fire, which never says, 'Enough!'

30:17
p Dt 21:18-21;
Pr 23:22
q Job 15:23

17 "The eye that mocks p a father,
that scorns obedience to a mother,
will be pecked out by the ravens of the valley,
will be eaten by the vultures. q

18 "There are three things that are too amazing for me,
four that I do not understand:
19 the way of an eagle in the sky,
the way of a snake on a rock,
the way of a ship on the high seas,
and the way of a man with a maiden.

30:20
r Pr 5:6

20 "This is the way of an adulteress:
She eats and wipes her mouth
and says, 'I've done nothing wrong.' r

21 "Under three things the earth trembles,
under four it cannot bear up:

30:22
s Pr 19:10; 29:2

22 a servant who becomes king, s
a fool who is full of food,
23 an unloved woman who is married,
and a maidservant who displaces her mistress.

---

a 16 Hebrew Sheol

Christians in the West, and perhaps particularly in America, do well to watch for the connection between pride and insatiability, remembering that haughtiness and unrestrained desire often travel together (v. 20). When we see a mountainous SUV with a vanity plate that says "I Want Gaz" and then hear a news report that we are using up Earth's resources of ozone and forests faster than it can replace them, we have witnessed a manifestation of inappropriate pride and appetite.

The numerical sayings illustrate for us the various forms of pride in its images of grasping and strutting. Insatiable hunger is symbolized by individuals who devour the poor or gulp down illicit sexual experience. This same pride inspires evil speaking, falsehood, cursing, and boasts. Believers avoid these behaviors and follow the way of wisdom.

24 "Four things on earth are small,
    yet they are extremely wise:
25 Ants are creatures of little strength,
    yet they store up their food in the summer; [t]
26 coneys[a][u] are creatures of little power,
    yet they make their home in the crags;
27 locusts[v] have no king,
    yet they advance together in ranks;
28 a lizard can be caught with the hand,
    yet it is found in kings' palaces.

29 "There are three things that are stately in their stride,
    four that move with stately bearing:
30 a lion, mighty among beasts,
    who retreats before nothing;
31 a strutting rooster, a he-goat,
    and a king with his army around him. [b]

32 "If you have played the fool and exalted yourself,
    or if you have planned evil,
    clap your hand over your mouth! [w]
33 For as churning the milk produces butter,
    and as twisting the nose produces blood,
    so stirring up anger produces strife."

Sayings of King Lemuel

31 The sayings[x] of King Lemuel—an oracle[c] his mother taught him:

2 "O my son, O son of my womb,
    O son of my vows, [d][y]
3 do not spend your strength on women,
    your vigor on those who ruin kings. [z]

4 "It is not for kings, O Lemuel—

[a] 26 That is, the hyrax or rock badger   [b] 31 Or *king secure against revolt*   [c] 1 Of *Lemuel king of Massa, which*   [d] 2 Or / *the answer to my prayers*

30:25	[t] Pr 6:6-8
30:26	[u] Ps 104:18
30:27	[v] Ex 10:4
30:32	[w] Job 21:5; 29:9
31:1	[x] Pr 22:17
31:2	[y] Jdg 11:30; Isa 49:15
31:3	[z] Dt 17:17; 1Ki 11:3; Ne 13:26; Pr 5:1-14

Proverbs 31:1–9

Like chapter 30, this passage consists of the "sayings" of a foreigner. King Lemuel, like Agur, is unknown outside of Proverbs. We may be troubled to hear a suggestion of drinking alcohol to escape trouble, but we also can note that in verse 5 "drink and forget" describes the actions of an irresponsible king who, having no particular misery to forget, drinks anyway. Total abstinence from alcohol was rare in the ancient world, even while the problems of addiction to drink were recognized. Also, behind the recommendation to offer alcohol is a concern for the least powerful members of the kingdom. The king was to offer wine (instead of storing it) to comfort those who hurt.

31:1–9

Learner Retention

You may wonder how and why King Lemuel learned his lessons so well from his mother's lips. It's likely that multiple approaches were used to impress upon him the importance of her counsel:

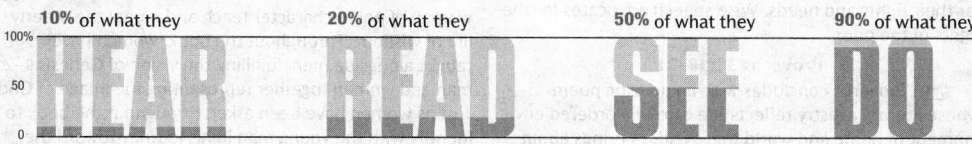

Typical Learners Retain:
10% of what they HEAR   20% of what they READ   50% of what they SEE   90% of what they DO

How refreshing for a Christian parent to observe godly behavior in a child or young adult.
If you are a parent, remember to practice as well as teach.

Source: Galindo (2002:99)

31:4
a Pr 20:1;
Ecc 10:16-17;
Isa 5:22
31:5
b 1Ki 16:9
c Pr 16:12;
Hos 4:11
31:6
d Ge 14:18
31:7
e Est 1:10

31:8
f 1Sa 19:4;
Job 29:12-17

31:9
g Lev 19:15;
Dt 1:16; Pr 24:23;
29:7; Isa 1:17;
Jer 22:16
31:10
h Ru 3:11; Pr 12:4;
18:22 *i* Pr 8:35;
19:14
31:11
j Ge 2:18 *k* Pr 12:4

31:13
l 1Ti 2:9-10

31:20
m Dt 15:11;
Eph 4:28;
Heb 13:16

not for kings to drink wine, *a*
  not for rulers to crave beer,
⁵ lest they drink *b* and forget what the law decrees, *c*
  and deprive all the oppressed of their rights.
⁶ Give beer to those who are perishing,
  wine *d* to those who are in anguish;
⁷ let them drink *e* and forget their poverty
  and remember their misery no more.

⁸ "Speak *f* up for those who cannot speak for themselves,
  for the rights of all who are destitute.
⁹ Speak up and judge fairly;
  defend the rights of the poor and needy." *g*

Epilogue: The Wife of Noble Character

¹⁰ *a* A wife of noble character *h* who can find? *i*
  She is worth far more than rubies.
¹¹ Her husband *j* has full confidence in her
  and lacks nothing of value. *k*
¹² She brings him good, not harm,
  all the days of her life.
¹³ She selects wool and flax
  and works with eager hands. *l*
¹⁴ She is like the merchant ships,
  bringing her food from afar.
¹⁵ She gets up while it is still dark;
  she provides food for her family
  and portions for her servant girls.
¹⁶ She considers a field and buys it;
  out of her earnings she plants a vineyard.
¹⁷ She sets about her work vigorously;
  her arms are strong for her tasks.
¹⁸ She sees that her trading is profitable,
  and her lamp does not go out at night.
¹⁹ In her hand she holds the distaff
  and grasps the spindle with her fingers.
²⁰ She opens her arms to the poor
  and extends her hands to the needy. *m*
²¹ When it snows, she has no fear for her household;
  for all of them are clothed in scarlet.

a 10 Verses 10-31 are an acrostic, each verse beginning with a successive letter of the Hebrew alphabet.

The queen mother instructs Lemuel to set aside wine, women, and song for the responsibilities of leadership. The injustice of Naboth's vineyard, stolen for the king's wine (1 Kings 21), reminds modern readers of large-scale indifference to fair trade between nations, unequal opportunity in hiring and housing, and robber-baron CEOs. The conclusion of Proverbs recognizes that the poor will be forgotten unless someone speaks out for their rights and needs. Wise speech advocates for the rights of the poor.

Proverbs 31:10–31

Proverbs concludes with an acrostic poem whose literary artistry reflects the carefully ordered environment of home and world that Wisdom brings about (cf. 3:13–20; 8:1–36). Over the centuries the poem has taken on a life of its own. In Jewish tradition it's recited by husband to wife on Sabbath evenings, and many Christians read it on Mother's Day. Certainly it was designed to persuade young men to seek good wives, but we also see in this woman another embodiment of wisdom, similar to the personifications of Wisdom throughout the book.

Perhaps the most important aspect of the final chapter of Proverbs is that both Lemuel's mother and the woman of noble character teach and model the orderly life of wisdom. Throughout the book, women have taught alongside men, fulfilling the vision of Genesis 1–2: man and woman together representing the image of God. Just as women have been asked throughout the book to identify with the young man in his journey toward the wise life, so now men of all generations are asked to identify with the core values of these wise women.

22 She makes coverings for her bed;
    she is clothed in fine linen and purple.
23 Her husband is respected at the city gate,
    where he takes his seat among the elders[n] of the land.
24 She makes linen garments and sells them,
    and supplies the merchants with sashes.
25 She is clothed with strength and dignity;
    she can laugh at the days to come.
26 She speaks with wisdom,
    and faithful instruction is on her tongue.[o]
27 She watches over the affairs of her household
    and does not eat the bread of idleness.
28 Her children arise and call her blessed;
    her husband also, and he praises her:
29 "Many women do noble things,
    but you surpass them all."
30 Charm is deceptive, and beauty is fleeting;
    but a woman who fears the LORD is to be praised.
31 Give her the reward she has earned,
    and let her works bring her praise[p] at the city gate.

31:23
[n] Ex 3:16;
Ru 4:1,11;
Pr 12:4

31:26
[o] Pr 10:31

31:31
[p] Pr 11:16

Snapshots

31:29–30

K'ang Ch'eng, Gertrude Howe, and Shih Mei-yü

K'ang Ch'eng (Ida Kahn; 1873–1930), a Chinese medical doctor and church leader, was adopted by an American Methodist missionary, Gertrude Howe. In 1896 K'ang and her friend Shih Mei-yü graduated from the medical school of the University of Michigan. Sent back to China as a medical missionary, she and Shih Mei-yü together established the Elizabeth Skelton Danforth Hospital. K'ang involved herself in welfare and relief work, medical education, evangelistic work, social welfare, and women's issues.

Gertrude Howe (1847–1928) was a pioneer missionary of the Woman's Foreign Missionary Society of the Methodist Episcopal Church. In 1873 she founded the Rulison Girls' High School, which insisted on unbound feet for admittance. Howe adopted four Chinese girls, transferring in 1883 to Chungking, where a new girls' school was destroyed by riots two years later. Howe preached throughout the countryside, training "Bible women." In 1892 she brought five Chinese pupils to the University of Michigan, supporting them through their studies.

Shih Mei-yü (Mary Stone; 1873–1954) worked for some 20 years at the Elizabeth Skelton Danforth Hospital, caring for patients, training nurses, and promoting public hygiene. In the 1920s she moved to Shanghai, where she established a hospital and mission with Jennie V. Hughes.

> **K'ang involved herself in welfare and relief work, medical education, evangelistic work, social welfare, and women's issues.**

INTRODUCTION TO
Ecclesiastes

AUTHOR

Though the author refers to himself only as "the Teacher," Solomon has traditionally been credited with the writing of Ecclesiastes. While Solomon fits the description of the Teacher as "a son of David, king in Jerusalem" (1:1), his authorship has been questioned. Some suggest that a wise man collected these perspectives as a tool for his son's instruction (12:11–12). Others suggest Ezra as a possible author.

DATE WRITTEN

If Solomon was the author of Ecclesiastes, the book may have been written during his period of apostasy (see 1 Kings 11) or shortly afterward (c. 935 B.C.). Those who suggest Ezra as the author place its composition in the exilic or postexilic period (c. 450 B.C.).

ORIGINAL READERS

Ecclesiastes was written to the people of Israel to demonstrate the meaninglessness of a life without God.

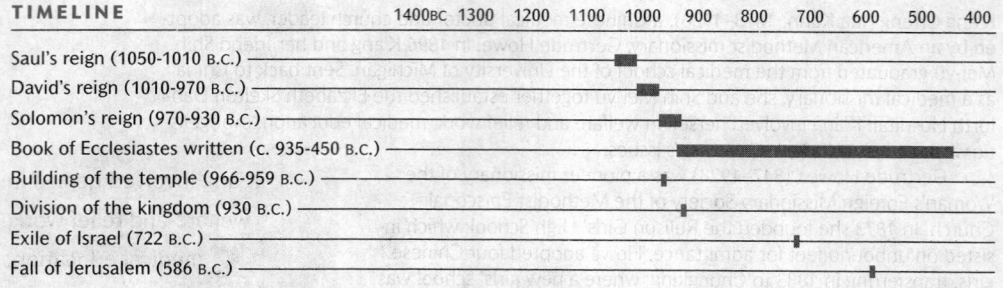

TIMELINE	1400BC	1300	1200	1100	1000	900	800	700	600	500	400
Saul's reign (1050-1010 B.C.)											
David's reign (1010-970 B.C.)											
Solomon's reign (970-930 B.C.)											
Book of Ecclesiastes written (c. 935-450 B.C.)											
Building of the temple (966-959 B.C.)											
Division of the kingdom (930 B.C.)											
Exile of Israel (722 B.C.)											
Fall of Jerusalem (586 B.C.)											

THEMES

Ecclesiastes describes the struggle to find significance in a life that seems meaningless (12:8,13). The book includes the following themes:

1. *Wisdom and pleasure alone are worthless.* Ecclesiastes points out the truth that work, pleasure, status, wealth, and even wisdom have no lasting significance (1:12—2:16) because death renders all earthly achievements futile.

2. *God gives meaning to work.* Ecclesiastes describes the pointlessness of human toil (2:17—3:8), comparing it with God's enduring work (3:9—6:7). It concludes that people should enjoy their labor (3:22), trusting that God has a purpose for it (3:1).

3. *The injustice of oppression.* The Teacher displayed concern for the oppression of the weak by the powerful (4:1–3) and expressed dismay that, from his viewpoint, the wicked often thrive and the godly suffer (7:15–18). The perspective that little, if anything, can be done about injustice is later refuted by an authoritative reminder that God will one day bring justice to all (12:14).

4. *Human wisdom versus God's wisdom.* Ecclesiastes demonstrates the futility of humans contending with God (6:10). His ways are mysterious—far beyond human understanding (6:8—12:7).

5. *God gives meaning to life.* The ultimate conclusion is that life is meaningless without God. Because humans can't fathom God's purposes or understand his ways, submission to him is our best course of action (12:1–14), especially in view of God's final judgment of every "hidden thing" (12:14).

FAITH IN ACTION

The pages of Ecclesiastes contain life lessons and role models of faith—people who challenge believers to put their faith in action.

Role Models

- THE TEACHER (1:12) studied wisdom and shared the insights he learned. What wisdom can you share with others? Have the lessons you have learned benefited someone else in similar circumstances?

- A WISE INDIVIDUAL (10:12) speaks gracious words. What adjectives would you use to describe words you have spoken this week?

- A HAPPY MAN (5:19) accepts his lot in life and enjoys the gifts God has given him. Are you basically content with your life?

- THE PERSON WHO FEARS GOD (12:13) fulfills his or her duty by obeying him. Are you daily submitting yourself to God?

- A POOR, WISE PERSON (9:13–18) deserves an audience, but his or her words too often go unrecognized and unremembered. Can you accept advice or a lesson from someone with limited material resources?

Challenges

- Reflect back on your life and the various avenues of success you have pursued (wealth, pleasure, relationships, career, etc.). Have they brought you happiness, peace, and meaning?

- Rest in God's timing for your life (3:1–8).

- Be happy and do good (3:12). Be content and enjoy your life and work, recognizing and appreciating them as gifts from God (3:13; 5:18–19).

- Choose to "fear God" (12:13) by acknowledging him and putting him first in your life (12:1–7).

- Determine to maintain a right relationship with God through faith and obedience (12:13–14).

- Live your life guided by the knowledge that "God will bring every deed into judgment" (12:14).

- If you are still young, don't leave God out of your life and decision making (12:1–7).

- Understand that people living in poverty are often unable to control the circumstances surrounding their condition (4:1; 5:8–9). Too many are taken advantage of and oppressed.

OUTLINE

I. Author (1:1)
II. Theme: The Efforts of People Are Meaningless Apart From God (1:2)
III. Introduction: Accumulating Things Will Fail to Bring Happiness (1:3–11)
IV. Life Is to Be Enjoyed As a Gift From God (1:12—11:6)
V. Begin Enjoying Life in Your Youth Because God Will Judge (11:7—12:8)
VI. Conclusion: Reverently Trust In and Obey God (12:9–14)

Everything Is Meaningless

1:1
a ver 12; Ecc 7:27;
12:10 b Pr 1:1

1 The words of the Teacher, [a]a son of David, king in Jerusalem: [b]

2 "Meaningless! Meaningless!"
  says the Teacher.
"Utterly meaningless!
  Everything is meaningless." [c]

1:2
c Ps 39:5-6; 62:9;
144:4; Ecc 12:8;
Ro 8:20-21
1:3
d Ecc 2:11,22; 3:9;
5:15-16

3 What does man gain from all his labor
  at which he toils under the sun? [d]
4 Generations come and generations go,
  but the earth remains forever. [e]

1:4
e Ps 104:5; 119:90

5 The sun rises and the sun sets,
  and hurries back to where it rises. [f]

1:5
f Ps 19:5-6

6 The wind blows to the south
  and turns to the north;
round and round it goes,
  ever returning on its course.
7 All streams flow into the sea,
  yet the sea is never full.
To the place the streams come from,
  there they return again. [g]

1:7
g Job 36:28

8 All things are wearisome,
  more than one can say.
The eye never has enough of seeing, [h]
  nor the ear its fill of hearing.

1:8
h Pr 27:20

9 What has been will be again,
  what has been done will be done again; [i]
  there is nothing new under the sun.

1:9
i Ecc 2:12; 3:15

10 Is there anything of which one can say,
  "Look! This is something new"?
It was here already, long ago;
  it was here before our time.
11 There is no remembrance of men of old,
  and even those who are yet to come
  will not be remembered
  by those who follow. [j]

1:11
j Ecc 2:16

Wisdom Is Meaningless

1:12
k ver 1

12 I, the Teacher, [k] was king over Israel in Jerusalem. 13 I devoted myself to study and to explore by wisdom all that is done under heaven. What a heavy burden God

a 1 Or leader of the assembly; also in verses 2 and 12

Ecclesiastes 1:1–11

The leading question of this book is "What does man gain from all his labor at which he toils under the sun?" We are reminded of the nature of the universe as an ongoing, solid reality on which it's impossible to make a lasting impression. Human activity is short-lived and insignificant. Creation—to be reckoned with but not owned or manipulated—is a reality that escapes our grasp (cf. Job 28:12–28; Ps. 90:3–6; Isa. 40:6–8). No "gain" can be realized from striving and struggling in pursuit of our own interests.

The New Testament version of the introductory question is "What good will it be for a man if he gains the whole world, yet forfeits his soul?" (Matt. 16:26). How relevant is this question for you? God calls us to love him and our neighbor and to tend the "garden" he's entrusted to us (Gen. 2:15). Western culture would like reality to be different. It tries to dethrone God, worships self-declared "gods" and heroes, and exploits the earth for its own ends. These tendencies sound so evil that we rightly want to distance ourselves from them in disgust. But a moment of soul searching convinces us that we are, at least in part, products of our culture.

Ecclesiastes 1:12–18

From 1:12—2:26 the Teacher pursues in several ways the issue of "gain[ing] from . . . labor" (1:3). The report isn't encouraging. Wisdom is useful for understanding the world, but it mainly helps people in all ages to comprehend how impossible it is to ultimately control and profit from it.

has laid on men!*l* **14**I have seen all the things that are done under the sun; all of them are meaningless, a chasing after the wind.*m*

15What is twisted cannot be straightened;*n*
    what is lacking cannot be counted.

16I thought to myself, "Look, I have grown and increased in wisdom more than anyone who has ruled over Jerusalem before me;*o* I have experienced much of wisdom and knowledge." **17**Then I applied myself to the understanding of wisdom,*p* and also of madness and folly,*q* but I learned that this, too, is a chasing after the wind.

18For with much wisdom comes much sorrow;
    the more knowledge, the more grief.*r*

Pleasures Are Meaningless

2 I thought in my heart, "Come now, I will test you with pleasure*s* to find out what is good." But that also proved to be meaningless. **2**"Laughter,"*t* I said, "is foolish. And what does pleasure accomplish?" **3**I tried cheering myself with wine,*u* and embracing folly*v*—my mind still guiding me with wisdom. I wanted to see what was worthwhile for men to do under heaven during the few days of their lives.

4I undertook great projects: I built houses for myself*w* and planted vineyards.*x* **5**I made gardens and parks and planted all kinds of fruit trees in them. **6**I made reservoirs to water groves of flourishing trees. **7**I bought male and female slaves and had other slaves who were born in my house. I also owned more herds and flocks than anyone in Jerusalem before me. **8**I amassed silver and gold*y* for myself, and the treasure of kings and provinces. I acquired men and women singers,*z* and a harem*a* as well—the delights of the heart of man. **9**I became greater by far than anyone in Jerusalem before me.*a* In all this my wisdom stayed with me.

10I denied myself nothing my eyes desired;
    I refused my heart no pleasure.
My heart took delight in all my work,
    and this was the reward for all my labor.
11Yet when I surveyed all that my hands had done
    and what I had toiled to achieve,
everything was meaningless, a chasing after the wind;*b*
    nothing was gained under the sun.*c*

---

a 8 The meaning of the Hebrew for this phrase is uncertain.

1:13
l Ge 3:17; Ecc 3:10
1:14
m Ecc 2:11,17
1:15
n Ecc 7:13
1:16
o 1Ki 3:12; 4:30; Ecc 2:9
1:17
p Ecc 7:23
q Ecc 2:3,12; 7:25
1:18
r Ecc 2:23; 12:12
2:1
s Ecc 7:4; 8:15; Lk 12:19
2:2
t Pr 14:13; Ecc 7:6
2:3
u ver 24-25; Ecc 3:12-13
v Ecc 1:17
2:4
w 1Ki 7:1-12
x SS 8:11
2:8
y 1Ki 9:28; 10:10,14,21
z 2Sa 19:35
2:9
a 1Ch 29:25; Ecc 1:16
2:11
b Ecc 1:14 *c* Ecc 1:3

The Teacher saw the fundamental human problem as a lack of harmony between human desires, including the search for wisdom, and the nature of reality. The pointlessness of verse 14 is about human refusal to accept things as they are. People have always insisted that the impossible can be achieved by human effort. This thinking was and remains futile: God is God, and the world is the way it is. Refusing to accept reality can only result in disillusionment and weariness.

We moderns presume to understand better than any previous generation how to make the world work for us. We stand on the edge of a revolution in genetics that will, we believe, give us control over human life itself. We have looked scientifically into the nature of things, and this has bred enormous self-confidence in our ability to govern ourselves and, in due course, to usher in a perfect world. The irony is that those who have pursued this wisdom most relentlessly often understand best the limitations of our understanding.

Ecclesiastes 2:1–11

The king tried pleasure. Would a determined effort at enjoyment bring a return on his investment? His reward proved inadequate when measured against the hopes that had driven the experiment. He concluded that, if one's resources are exhausted in finding it, pleasure has no reward beyond momentary enjoyment. Life is a gift from God. Manipulating it to arrive at "gain" is useless.

Ancient kings—like many world and industry leaders today—tended to grasp after god-likeness, attempting to burst through the confines of human life and achieve some real "gain." Biblical examples include Sennacherib (2 Kings 18–19) and Nebuchadnezzar (Dan. 1–4). Such individuals had resources at their disposal to make what they saw as a credible attempt at equivalence with "the gods."

The perspective of this section (1:12—2:26) is specifically male. But this passage speaks to all who are

Wisdom and Folly Are Meaningless

12 Then I turned my thoughts to consider wisdom,
   and also madness and folly. *d*
What more can the king's successor do
   than what has already been done? *e*
13 I saw that wisdom *f* is better than folly, *g*
   just as light is better than darkness.
14 The wise man has eyes in his head,
   while the fool walks in the darkness;
but I came to realize
   that the same fate overtakes them both. *h*

15 Then I thought in my heart,

"The fate of the fool will overtake me also.
   What then do I gain by being wise?" *i*
I said in my heart,
   "This too is meaningless."
16 For the wise man, like the fool, will not be long remembered;
   in days to come both will be forgotten. *j*
Like the fool, the wise man too must die!

Toil Is Meaningless

17 So I hated life, because the work that is done under the sun was grievous to me. All of it is meaningless, a chasing after the wind. *k* 18 I hated all the things I had toiled for under the sun, because I must leave them to the one who comes after me. *l* 19 And who knows whether he will be a wise man or a fool? Yet he will have control over all the work into which I have poured my effort and skill under the sun. This too is meaningless. 20 So my heart began to despair over all my toilsome labor under the sun. 21 For a man may do his work with wisdom, knowledge and skill, and then he must leave all he owns to someone who has not worked for it. This too is meaningless and a great misfortune. 22 What does a man get for all the toil and anx-

2:12
d Ecc 1:17
e Ecc 1:9; 7:25

2:13
f Ecc 7:19; 9:18
g Ecc 7:11-12

2:14
h Ps 49:10;
Pr 17:24; Ecc 3:19;
6:6; 7:2; 9:3, 11-12

2:15
i Ecc 6:8

2:16
j Ecc 1:11; 9:5

2:17
k Ecc 4:2
2:18
l Ps 39:6; 49:10

---

tempted to indulge a lust for divinity. It's just as possible today for a woman who loves herself more than she loves God to use, abuse, and misuse others as it is for a man. Idolatry always has enormous social consequences. To what degree are you guilty of stepping on, around, or over other people to elevate yourself?

Ecclesiastes 2:12–16

The question here (v. 13) once again concerns ultimate gain. What's the point of surplus wisdom if it doesn't result in surplus profit? In the end, death makes fools of all people, whether or not they have been wise in life. From a material standpoint, there is nothing left after life has ended. Not only does wisdom fail to offer release from the vain business of living, but it can't solve the problem of death.

From the beginning human beings have chosen to transgress God's boundaries in search of something "more," turning the life that comes to them as a gift into capital to fund exploitation and expansion. The Teacher is only one Biblical voice seeking to persuade us that the "more" doesn't exist—and that, in pursuing it, we lose our selves.

If we are honest, we will have to admit that our culture bears out the lack of fulfillment and gain in the pursuit of wisdom, wealth, and their elusive partner, joy.

Great projects, personal monuments, power, entertainment, wealth, and the pursuit of sexual adventure all add up to "a chasing after wind," accompanied by stress, insomnia, and eventual death—the ultimate auditor's report. What can you do to extricate yourself from one or another of these subtle traps?

Ecclesiastes 2:17–26

The Teacher made clear that chasing the wind isn't only pointless but wrong. The "sinner" gathers and stores up wealth—only to lose it to another. Such a life is "meaningless," the sorry business of 1:13–14. The ultimate beneficiary of this loss is the person who pleases God, who has given up the striving after gain, but who gains an inheritance anyway.

Why do people pursue "gain" through meaningless and unsuccessful ventures? The answer is found in sin's irrationality. Life is designed to be lived in humility and obedience before God—the best kept secret around. This entails accepting our limitations and finding satisfaction in ordinary things. All around us people are desperately seeking to simplify their lives, but without Christ they overlook the *why* of their instinctive search for a better way. What can you do, today, to point someone to God's way?

ious striving with which he labors under the sun?[m] 23All his days his work is pain and grief;[n] even at night his mind does not rest. This too is meaningless.

24A man can do nothing better than to eat and drink[o] and find satisfaction in his work.[p] This too, I see, is from the hand of God,[q] 25for without him, who can eat or find enjoyment? 26To the man who pleases him, God gives wisdom, knowledge and happiness, but to the sinner he gives the task of gathering and storing up wealth[r] to hand it over to the one who pleases God.[s] This too is meaningless, a chasing after the wind.

A Time for Everything

3 There is a time[t] for everything,
and a season for every activity under heaven:

2 a time to be born and a time to die,
a time to plant and a time to uproot,
3 a time to kill and a time to heal,
a time to tear down and a time to build,
4 a time to weep and a time to laugh,
a time to mourn and a time to dance,
5 a time to scatter stones and a time to gather them,
a time to embrace and a time to refrain,
6 a time to search and a time to give up,
a time to keep and a time to throw away,
7 a time to tear and a time to mend,
a time to be silent[u] and a time to speak,
8 a time to love and a time to hate,
a time for war and a time for peace.

9What does the worker gain from his toil?[v] 10I have seen the burden God has laid on men.[w] 11He has made everything beautiful in its time.[x] He has also set eternity in the hearts of men; yet they cannot fathom[y] what God has done from beginning to end.[z] 12I know that there is nothing better for men than to be happy and do good while they live. 13That everyone may eat and drink,[a] and find satisfaction[b] in all his toil—this is the gift of God.[c] 14I know that everything God does will endure forever; nothing can be added to it and nothing taken from it. God does it so that men will revere him.[d]

15Whatever is has already been,[e]
and what will be has been before;[f]
and God will call the past to account.[a]

---

[a] 15 Or God calls back the past

Marginal references

2:22 [m] Ecc 1:3; 3:9
2:23 [n] Job 5:7; 14:1; Ecc 1:18
2:24 [o] Ecc 8:15; 1Co 15:32 [p] Ecc 3:22 [q] Ecc 3:12-13; 5:17-19; 9:7-10
2:26 [r] Job 27:17 [s] Pr 13:22
3:1 [t] ver 11,17; Ecc 8:6
3:7 [u] Am 5:13
3:9 [v] Ecc 1:3
3:10 [w] Ecc 1:13
3:11 [x] ver 1 [y] Job 11:7; Ecc 8:17 [z] Job 28:23; Ro 11:33
3:13 [a] Ecc 2:3 [b] Ps 34:12 [c] Dt 12:7,18; Ecc 2:24; 5:19
3:14 [d] Job 23:15; Ecc 5:7; 7:18; 8:12-13; Jas 1:17
3:15 [e] Ecc 6:10 [f] Ecc 1:9

Ecclesiastes 3:1–22

The Teacher captured life's totality in verses 1–8 by using a series of extreme opposites, with the assumption that everything in between was included. Aside from the placement of the first pair, there is no apparent purpose to the order. The examples represent various aspects of human life between birth and death, as well as the flow and regularity of the universe—all beyond human control.

The Creator has "made everything beautiful in its time" in the sense of all things fitting skillfully and delightfully together. There is an elegance about how life works, as "time" follows "time." Yet humans can't discover the almanac that will allow them to predict and control the times to realize their desired gains. Happily, there is an alternative: to give up the quest for profit and reorient life toward God.

Prominent in verses 16–17 is an oft-repeated prophetic theme: God will make all things right in the end. The wealthy and powerful may well escape human justice, since they typically control it, and those with fewer resources and less power will fail to attain it. Yet God himself is the ultimate Guarantor of justice. He will bring it to everyone at the final judgment (cf. Isa. 10:1–4; Amos 5:7–17). What comfort does this truth afford you? How does it affect your daily life?

Biblical religion reveals a God who made the world beautiful and fruitful, to be enjoyed by his creatures in fellowship with himself. The writer of Ecclesiastes promoted a seize-the-day philosophy, not a greedy consumption of experiences and pleasures before oblivion consumes us. He encouraged the patient and joyful embrace of daily life as it comes to us as a gift from God. And he advocated a worshipful response to the God of

16And I saw something else under the sun:

In the place of judgment—wickedness was there,
in the place of justice—wickedness was there.

17I thought in my heart,

"God will bring to judgmentg
both the righteous and the wicked,
for there will be a time for every activity,
a time for every deed."h

18I also thought, "As for men, God tests them so that they may see that they are like the animals.i 19Man's fatej is like that of the animals; the same fate awaits them both: As one dies, so dies the other. All have the same breatha; man has no advantage over the animal. Everything is meaningless. 20All go to the same place; all come from dust, and to dust all return.k 21Who knows if the spirit of man rises upwardl and if the spirit of the animalb goes down into the earth?"

22So I saw that there is nothing better for a man than to enjoy his work,m because that is his lot.n For who can bring him to see what will happen after him?

Oppression, Toil, Friendlessness

4 Again I looked and saw all the oppressiono that was taking place under the sun:

I saw the tears of the oppressed—

a 19 Or spirit   b 21 Or Who knows the spirit of man, which rises upward, or the spirit of the animal, which

---

creation—who also is the God of the new creation and the resurrection. To what extent does this philosophy describe your lifestyle?

Ecclesiastes 4:1–12

The Ten Commandments link love for God with love for neighbor (cf. also Matt. 22:37–40), just as idolatry

3:11

Beauty

Beauty is that pleasing aesthetic quality present in many facets of life:

1. The Beauty of Creation	"God saw all that he had made, and it was very good" (Gen. 1:31).
	The exquisite loveliness and magnificent splendor of our world make us grateful to God and inspire us to care for his creation.
2. The Beauty of a Holy Life	"Be imitators of God, therefore, as dearly loved children and live a life of love, just as Christ loved us and gave himself up for us as a fragrant offering and sacrifice to God" (Eph. 5:1–2).
	The pleasing example of a holy life attracts us to live in the same way in obedience to God.
3. The Beauty of Human Beings	"I praise you because I am fearfully and wonderfully made; your works are wonderful" (Ps. 139:14).
	The intrinsic beauty in human beings encourages us to express our love for others.
4. The Beauty of Relationships	"Therefore, my brothers, you whom I love and long for, my joy and crown, that is how you should stand firm in the Lord" (Phil. 4:1).
	The beauty of relationships urges us on to work for the reconciliation of all in God's name.
5. The Beauty of God Himself	". . . that I may dwell in the house of the LORD all the days of my life, to gaze upon the beauty of the LORD" (Ps. 27:4).
	All true beauty leads us to the worship of God, the Creator of all.

The Bible teaches that the physical beauty to be found in this world is passing (cf. Prov. 31:30), but beauty of character and spirit last (1 Peter 3:3). And God's beauty isn't only eternal but complete. Our challenge is to look at others through the lens of the Spirit, penetrating beneath their surface appearances (1 Sam. 16:7).

and they have no comforter;
power was on the side of their oppressors—
and they have no comforter. [p]

4:1 [p] La 1:16

[2] And I declared that the dead, [q]
who had already died,
are happier than the living,
who are still alive. [r]

4:2 [q] Jer 20:17-18; 22:10 [r] Job 3:17; 10:18

[3] But better than both
is he who has not yet been, [s]
who has not seen the evil
that is done under the sun. [t]

4:3 [s] Job 3:16; Ecc 6:3 [t] Job 3:22

[4] And I saw that all labor and all achievement spring from man's envy of his neighbor. This too is meaningless, a chasing after the wind. [u]

4:4 [u] Ecc 1:14
4:5

[5] The fool folds his hands [v]
and ruins himself.

[v] Pr 6:10

[6] Better one handful with tranquillity
than two handfuls with toil [w]
and chasing after the wind.

4:6 [w] Pr 15:16-17; 16:8

[7] Again I saw something meaningless under the sun:

[8] There was a man all alone;
he had neither son nor brother.
There was no end to his toil,
yet his eyes were not content [x] with his wealth.
"For whom am I toiling," he asked,
"and why am I depriving myself of enjoyment?"
This too is meaningless—
a miserable business!

4:8 [x] Pr 27:20

[9] Two are better than one,
because they have a good return for their work:
[10] If one falls down,
his friend can help him up.
But pity the man who falls
and has no one to help him up!
[11] Also, if two lie down together, they will keep warm.
But how can one keep warm alone?
[12] Though one may be overpowered,
two can defend themselves.
A cord of three strands is not quickly broken.

Advancement Is Meaningless

[13] Better a poor but wise youth than an old but foolish king who no longer knows how to take warning. [14] The youth may have come from prison to the kingship, or he may have been born in poverty within his kingdom. [15] I saw that all who

---

is linked with social injustice and oppression (cf. 1 Kings 21:1–26). This passage, related to 3:16–17, makes it clear that the life of striving is fundamentally anti-neighbor. It's not surprising that 4:7–12 first focuses on the loneliness of the striving individual and then moves on to offer a stirring commendation of community.

As believers, our proper goal is a right relationship with God, neighbor, and God's world. We as Christians are to root out from our hearts the sinful thoughts that lead us to pursue a selfish and individualistic path through life, as well as any inclination to deny that *all*

humans have a stake in the world. Our family or nation has no more right to the world's resources than others do. What can you do, personally, to contribute to your community, locally and globally?

Ecclesiastes 4:13–16

The king was the one person in Israel who might have been expected to "gain from all his labor" (1:3). He also might have been a major source of oppression (cf. 1 Sam. 8:10–18). Either way, he represented the pinnacle of human success and the lifestyle to which many aspired. But the Teacher appears to have had in

1039

lived and walked under the sun followed the youth, the king's successor. ¹⁶There was no end to all the people who were before them. But those who came later were not pleased with the successor. This too is meaningless, a chasing after the wind.

Stand in Awe of God

5 Guard your steps when you go to the house of God. Go near to listen rather than to offer the sacrifice of fools, who do not know that they do wrong.

² Do not be quick with your mouth,
    do not be hasty in your heart
        to utter anything before God.ʸ
God is in heaven
    and you are on earth,
        so let your words be few.ᶻ
³ As a dreamᵃ comes when there are many cares,
    so the speech of a fool when there are many words.ᵇ

⁴When you make a vow to God, do not delay in fulfilling it.ᶜ He has no pleasure in fools; fulfill your vow.ᵈ ⁵It is better not to vow than to make a vow and not ful-

5:2
y Jdg 11:35
z Job 6:24;
Pr 10:19; 20:25
5:3
a Job 20:8
b Ecc 10:14
5:4
c Dt 23:21;
Jdg 11:35;
Ps 119:60
d Nu 30:2;
Ps 66:13-14; 76:11

---

mind human advancement and achievement in general. Poverty with wisdom, he pointed out, trumps wealth with folly. Advancement too often brings with it loss of self, as people lose touch with their roots (4:13–14). It brings increased toil—but no greater thanks (vv. 15–16).

Individuals are precious to God. Ironically, modern individualism arose in part from this truth. But secular individualism, which has everything to do with self-sufficiency and self-fulfillment and little with the worship of God and social responsibility, is unbiblical at its core. Even the religious individualism that lays greater emphasis on a person's relationship with God than on his or her social, economic, political, and religious relationships

with other people misses the Biblical mark. How Biblical is your view of people?

Ecclesiastes 5:1–7

In the middle of observations on the worship of wealth and advancement, we find this reflection on the worship of God. The worshiper's first task is to "go near to listen," with a view to obeying the divine voice. The contrasting activity is offering "the sacrifice of fools"— the careless observance of religion based on custom, peer pressure, or habit. This is the brand of religion frequently attacked by the prophets, who associated it with oppression of one's neighbor (e.g., Isa. 1:10–20).

Snapshots

 4:10–12

Reflections of a Sponsored Child

Edwin, a Kenyan aid worker, reflects on his own past:

"In 1981, when I was six years old, my father was disabled when he was attacked by thugs while working as a waiter . . . He has since died. My father's condition affected everything in our family. My mom could not give us food or shelter. We were thrown out of our house in Nairobi. So we moved in with my two sisters back in the rural area we had originally come from . . .

"I became a sponsored child. From that moment on, my life changed dramatically. Sponsorship acted as security for me and my family. I knew I was bright, but lack of funds had hampered me from going to school. Now I could return to school feeling secure.

"It did not take my family long to change its views of Christianity. They saw Christianity as something which was practical and helped people. They became Christians, like me.

"**I wanted an education which would help the marginalized.**"

"I wanted an education which would help the marginalized, I chose environmental studies because this program was a social science. It influenced people threatened by poverty, people who were the same as me."

fill it. *e* ⁶Do not let your mouth lead you into sin. And do not protest to the ˪temple˩ messenger, "My vow was a mistake." Why should God be angry at what you say and destroy the work of your hands? ⁷Much dreaming and many words are meaningless. Therefore stand in awe of God. *f*

Riches Are Meaningless

⁸If you see the poor oppressed *g* in a district, and justice and rights denied, do not be surprised at such things; for one official is eyed by a higher one, and over them both are others higher still. ⁹The increase from the land is taken by all; the king himself profits from the fields.

¹⁰Whoever loves money never has money enough;
> whoever loves wealth is never satisfied with his income.
> This too is meaningless.

¹¹As goods increase,
> so do those who consume them.
And what benefit are they to the owner
> except to feast his eyes on them?

¹²The sleep of a laborer is sweet,
> whether he eats little or much,
but the abundance of a rich man
> permits him no sleep. *h*

¹³I have seen a grievous evil under the sun: *i*

> wealth hoarded to the harm of its owner,
¹⁴ or wealth lost through some misfortune,
so that when he has a son
> there is nothing left for him.
¹⁵Naked a man comes from his mother's womb,
> and as he comes, so he departs. *j*
He takes nothing from his labor *k*
> that he can carry in his hand. *l*

¹⁶This too is a grievous evil:

> As a man comes, so he departs,
> and what does he gain,
> since he toils for the wind? *m*
¹⁷All his days he eats in darkness,
> with great frustration, affliction and anger.

¹⁸Then I realized that it is good and proper for a man to eat and drink, *n* and to

5:5
e Nu 30:2-4;
Pr 20:25; Jnh 2:9;
Ac 5:4
5:7
f Ecc 3:14; 12:13

5:8
g Ps 12:5; Ecc 4:1

5:12
h Job 20:20

5:13
i Ecc 6:1-2

5:15
j Job 1:21
k Ps 49:17; 1Ti 6:7
l Ecc 1:3

5:16
m Pr 11:29; Ecc 1:3

5:18
n Ecc 2:3

📖 Silence is undervalued in our noisy, intrusive world. We have made it hard for ourselves in our technological sophistication to "be still, and know that I am God" (Ps. 46:10). Silence gives us time to think, and thinking raises awkward questions in our minds. Deliberate reflection and inactivity are necessary if we are to regain perspective. We need to hear God's words in Exodus 3:5: "Do not come any closer. Take off your sandals, for the place where you are standing is holy ground." But to hear them, we need to stop talking!

Ecclesiastes 5:8—6:12

🔁 The Teacher had seen a "grievous evil" (lit., "sick evil") in the world: wealth hoarded to the harm of its owner (5:13). The rich man had kept his wealth when he ought to have been "keeping" his neighbor. His goods had increased (v. 11), but his bottom line had only been

"harm" (lit., "evil," playing on the question of whether "goods" are really *good* for a person). Consumers, then as well as now, lusted after the good things of life but ended up consuming their neighbors—and eventually themselves. This sin is structural—rooted in institutions and customs—as well as personal.

🔁 "Mammon" is a word used in some Bible translations for the idolatrous elevation of money and material things to the status of divinity (Matt. 6:24). Belief in capitalism and in endless progress, facilitated by scientific and technological control and sound management principles, are typically thought of in our culture as Christian. But we often display only a lightly Christianized version of the world's prejudices about the nature of reality. Many believers come to value (worship) the world's idols. Where do you stand in this regard?

5:18
o Ecc 2:10, 24

5:19
p 1Ch 29:12;
2Ch 1:12 q Ecc 6:2
r Job 31:2
s Ecc 2:24; 3:13

5:20
t Dt 12:7, 18

6:2
u Ps 17:14;
Ecc 5:19 v Ecc 5:13

6:3
w Job 3:16; Ecc 4:3
x Job 3:3

6:7
y Pr 16:26; 27:20

6:8
z Ecc 2:15

6:9
a Ecc 1:14

6:12
b Job 10:20
c Job 14:2; Ps 39:6;
Jas 4:14

7:1
d Pr 22:1; SS 1:3

7:2
e Pr 11:19
f Ps 90:12

7:3
g Pr 14:13

7:4
h Ecc 2:1; Jer 16:8

7:5
i Ps 141:5;
Pr 13:18; 15:31-32

7:6
j Ps 58:9; 118:12
k Ecc 2:2

7:7
l Ex 18:21; 23:8;
Dt 16:19

find satisfaction in his toilsome labor[o] under the sun during the few days of life God has given him—for this is his lot. [19]Moreover, when God gives any man wealth and possessions,[p] and enables him to enjoy them,[q] to accept his lot[r] and be happy in his work—this is a gift of God.[s] [20]He seldom reflects on the days of his life, because God keeps him occupied with gladness of heart.[t]

6 I have seen another evil under the sun, and it weighs heavily on men: [2]God gives a man wealth, possessions and honor, so that he lacks nothing his heart desires, but God does not enable him to enjoy them,[u] and a stranger enjoys them instead. This is meaningless, a grievous evil.[v]

[3]A man may have a hundred children and live many years; yet no matter how long he lives, if he cannot enjoy his prosperity and does not receive proper burial, I say that a stillborn[w] child is better off than he.[x] [4]It comes without meaning, it departs in darkness, and in darkness its name is shrouded. [5]Though it never saw the sun or knew anything, it has more rest than does that man— [6]even if he lives a thousand years twice over but fails to enjoy his prosperity. Do not all go to the same place?

[7]All man's efforts are for his mouth,
    yet his appetite is never satisfied.[y]
[8]What advantage has a wise man
    over a fool?[z]
What does a poor man gain
    by knowing how to conduct himself before others?
[9]Better what the eye sees
    than the roving of the appetite.
This too is meaningless,
    a chasing after the wind.[a]

[10]Whatever exists has already been named,
    and what man is has been known;
no man can contend
    with one who is stronger than he.
[11]The more the words,
    the less the meaning,
    and how does that profit anyone?

[12]For who knows what is good for a man in life, during the few and meaningless days[b] he passes through like a shadow?[c] Who can tell him what will happen under the sun after he is gone?

Wisdom

7 A good name is better than fine perfume,[d]
    and the day of death better than the day of birth.
[2]It is better to go to a house of mourning
    than to go to a house of feasting,
for death[e] is the destiny[f] of every man;
    the living should take this to heart.
[3]Sorrow is better than laughter,[g]
    because a sad face is good for the heart.
[4]The heart of the wise is in the house of mourning,
    but the heart of fools is in the house of pleasure.[h]
[5]It is better to heed a wise man's rebuke[i]
    than to listen to the song of fools.
[6]Like the crackling of thorns[j] under the pot,
    so is the laughter[k] of fools.
    This too is meaningless.
[7]Extortion turns a wise man into a fool,
    and a bribe[l] corrupts the heart.

Right Use of God's Gifts

 5:18–19

Earthly things are gifts of God.

1. The first principle we should consider is that the use of gifts of God cannot be wrong, if they are directed to the same purpose for which the Creator himself has created and destined them.

For he has made the earthly blessings for our benefit, and not for our harm . . .

2. If we study, for instance, why he has created the various kinds of food, we shall find that it was his intention not only to provide for our needs, but likewise for our pleasure, and for our delight.

In clothing he did not only keep in mind our needs, but also propriety and decency.

In herbs, trees, and fruit, besides being useful in various ways, he planned to please us by their gracious lines and pleasant odors.

For, if this were not true, the Psalmist would not enumerate among the divine blessings "the wine that makes glad the heart of man, and the oil that makes his face to shine."

And the Scriptures would not declare everywhere that he has given all these things to mankind that they might praise his goodness.

3. Even the natural properties of things sufficiently point out to what purpose and to what extent we are allowed to use them.

Should the Lord have attracted our eyes to the beauty of the flowers, and our sense of smell to pleasant odors, and should it then be sin to drink them in?

Has he not even made the colors so that the one is more wonderful than the other?

. . . In one word, has he not made many things worthy of our attention that go far beyond our needs (Ps. 104:15)?

Let us live with moderation

1. . . . . There is no surer and shorter way (to gratitude) than to turn our eyes away from the present life, and to meditate on the immortality of heaven.

From this flow two general principles:

The first is, "that they that have wives be as though they had none; and they that buy as though they possessed not; and they that use this world as not abusing it," according to the precept of Paul.

The second is that we should learn to bear poverty quietly and patiently, and to enjoy abundance with moderation.

2. He who commands us to use this world as though we used it not, forbids not only all intemperance in eating and drinking, and excessive pleasure, ambition, pride, and fastidiousness in our furniture, home, and apparel, but every care and affection which would drag down our spiritual level, or destroy our devotion . . .

3. Therefore, though the liberty of believers in external things cannot be restricted by hard and fast rules, yet it is surely subject to this law, that they should indulge as little as possible.

On the contrary, we should continually and resolutely exert ourselves to shun all that is superfluous, and avoid all vain display of luxury.

We should zealously beware that anything the Lord gave us to enrich life become a stumbling block (1 Cor. 7:29–31).

> The use of gifts of God cannot be wrong, if they are directed to the same purpose for which the Creator himself has created and destined them.

John Calvin, French theologian, church reformer, humanist, and pastor
Source: John Calvin, trans. by Henry J. Van Andel, *Golden Booklet of the True Christian Life* (Grand Rapids, Mich.: Baker, 1952), 87–88

7:8
m Pr 14:29;
Gal 5:22; Eph 4:2
7:9
n Mt 5:22; Pr 14:17;
Jas 1:19

8 The end of a matter is better than its beginning,
  and patience[m] is better than pride.
9 Do not be quickly provoked[n] in your spirit,
  for anger resides in the lap of fools.

10 Do not say, "Why were the old days better than these?"
  For it is not wise to ask such questions.

7:11
o Pr 8:10-11;
Ecc 2:13 p Ecc 11:7

11 Wisdom, like an inheritance, is a good thing[o]
  and benefits those who see the sun.[p]
12 Wisdom is a shelter
  as money is a shelter,
  but the advantage of knowledge is this:
  that wisdom preserves the life of its possessor.

7:13
q Ecc 2:24
r Ecc 1:15

13 Consider what God has done:[q]

Who can straighten
  what he has made crooked?[r]
14 When times are good, be happy;
  but when times are bad, consider:
God has made the one
  as well as the other.
Therefore, a man cannot discover
  anything about his future.

7:15
s Job 7:7
t Ecc 8:12-14;
Jer 12:1

15 In this meaningless life[s] of mine I have seen both of these:

a righteous man perishing in his righteousness,
  and a wicked man living long in his wickedness.[t]
16 Do not be overrighteous,
  neither be overwise—
  why destroy yourself?
17 Do not be overwicked,
  and do not be a fool—
  why die before your time?[u]

7:17
u Job 15:32;
Ps 55:23

18 It is good to grasp the one
  and not let go of the other.
  The man who fears God[v] will avoid all ⌊extremes⌋.[a]

7:18
v Ecc 3:14

19 Wisdom[w] makes one wise man more powerful[x]
  than ten rulers in a city.

7:19
w Ecc 2:13
x Ecc 9:13-18

20 There is not a righteous man[y] on earth
  who does what is right and never sins.[z]

7:20
y Ps 14:3
z 1Ki 8:46;
2Ch 6:36; Pr 20:9;
Ro 3:23

a 18 Or *will follow them both*

Ecclesiastes 7:1—8:1

The "wise" person who joins the insane race after possessions, compromising integrity in the process (7:7), becomes just as much a fool as the one who joins with fools in empty laughter. The pursuit of God integrates laughter and wealth into the abundant life and makes them wholesome. Money is something of a shelter against the winds of misfortune that so often blow through life, but it can't match the comprehensive protection provided by God's wisdom (v. 12).

Biblical faith isn't escapist. The healing of our pain comes by confronting realities. One of these is death, considered by Paul an enemy to be conquered (1 Cor. 15:54–57). Those who have met and understood death truly understand who God is and what our Christian faith means. The path to resurrection passes through death; this is the mystery and reality of Christianity. How has your experience with the death of friends and loved ones helped you to better understand your faith?

The only safe wisdom is rooted in God and centered in Christ, thus knowing its limitations and boundaries. The nature and character of God as revealed in Jesus and the Bible are the reference points Christians need when confronted by counter claims about reality and the human plans that arise from these claims. How safe is the wisdom you value? Do you sift new ideas through the standard of God's Word?

21 Do not pay attention to every word people say,
   or you[a] may hear your servant cursing you—
22 for you know in your heart
   that many times you yourself have cursed others.

23 All this I tested by wisdom and I said,

   "I am determined to be wise"[b]—
      but this was beyond me.
24 Whatever wisdom may be,
   it is far off and most profound—
      who can discover it?[c]
25 So I turned my mind to understand,
   to investigate and to search out wisdom and the scheme of things[d]
and to understand the stupidity of wickedness
   and the madness of folly.[e]

26 I find more bitter than death
   the woman who is a snare,[f]
whose heart is a trap
   and whose hands are chains.
The man who pleases God will escape her,
   but the sinner she will ensnare.[g]

27 "Look," says the Teacher,[a][h] "this is what I have discovered:

   "Adding one thing to another to discover the scheme of things—
28   while I was still searching
      but not finding—
   I found one ⌐upright⌐ man among a thousand,
      but not one ⌐upright⌐ woman[i] among them all.
29 This only have I found:
      God made mankind upright,
      but men have gone in search of many schemes."

8 Who is like the wise man?
   Who knows the explanation of things?
   Wisdom brightens a man's face
      and changes its hard appearance.

Obey the King

2 Obey the king's command, I say, because you took an oath before God. 3 Do not be in a hurry to leave the king's presence.[j] Do not stand up for a bad cause, for he

---

[a] 27 Or *leader of the assembly*

Cross-references

7:21 a Pr 30:10
7:23 b Ecc 1:17; Ro 1:22
7:24 c Job 28:12
7:25 d Job 28:3 e Ecc 1:17
7:26 f Ex 10:7; Jdg 14:15 g Pr 2:16-19; 5:3-5; 7:23; 22:14
7:27 h Ecc 1:1
7:28 i 1Ki 11:3
8:3 j Ecc 10:4

7:24

Famous Theological Wisdom Bytes

Augustine: "Anger is a weed, hate is the tree."

Aquinas: "Three things are necessary for salvation: To know what to believe, to know what to desire, to know what to do."

Luther: "Here I stand, I cannot do otherwise."

Calvin: "The chief end of man is to glorify God and enjoy him forever."

Wesley: "I look on the whole world as my parish."

Edwards: "Resolved: Never do anything which I should be afraid to do if it were the last hour of my life."

Barth: "Jesus loves me, this I know, for the Bible tells me so."

will do whatever he pleases. 4Since a king's word is supreme, who can say to him, "What are you doing?"[k]

8:4
k Job 9:12;
Est 1:19; Da 4:35

5Whoever obeys his command will come to no harm,
   and the wise heart will know the proper time and procedure.
6For there is a proper time and procedure for every matter,[l]
   though a man's misery weighs heavily upon him.

8:6
l Ecc 3:1

7Since no man knows the future,
   who can tell him what is to come?
8No man has power over the wind to contain it[a];
   so no one has power over the day of his death.
As no one is discharged in time of war,
   so wickedness will not release those who practice it.

9All this I saw, as I applied my mind to everything done under the sun. There is a time when a man lords it over others to his own[b] hurt. 10Then too, I saw the wicked buried[m]—those who used to come and go from the holy place and receive praise[c] in the city where they did this. This too is meaningless.

8:10
m Ecc 1:11

11When the sentence for a crime is not quickly carried out, the hearts of the people are filled with schemes to do wrong. 12Although a wicked man commits a hundred crimes and still lives a long time, I know that it will go better[n] with God-fearing men,[o] who are reverent before God.[p] 13Yet because the wicked do not fear God,[q] it will not go well with them, and their days[r] will not lengthen like a shadow.

8:12
n Dt 12:28;
Ps 37:11,18-19;
Pr 1:32-33;
Isa 3:10-11
o Ex 1:20
p Ecc 3:14
8:13
q Ecc 3:14; Isa 3:11
r Dt 4:40; Job 5:26;
Ps 34:12; Isa 65:20

14There is something else meaningless that occurs on earth: righteous men who get what the wicked deserve, and wicked men who get what the righteous deserve.[s] This too, I say, is meaningless.[t] 15So I commend the enjoyment of life[u], because nothing is better for a man under the sun than to eat and drink[v] and be glad.[w] Then joy will accompany him in his work all the days of the life God has given him under the sun.

8:14
s Job 21:7;
Ps 73:14; Mal 3:15
t Ecc 7:15
8:15
u Ps 42:8 v Ex 32:6;
Ecc 2:3 w Ecc 2:24;
3:12-13; 5:18; 9:7

16When I applied my mind to know wisdom[x] and to observe man's labor on earth[y]—his eyes not seeing sleep day or night— 17then I saw all that God has done.[z] No one can comprehend what goes on under the sun. Despite all his efforts to search it out, man cannot discover its meaning. Even if a wise man claims he knows, he cannot really comprehend it.[a]

8:16
x Ecc 1:17
y Ecc 1:13
8:17
z Job 28:3
a Job 5:9; 28:23;
Ecc 3:11; Ro 11:33

A Common Destiny for All

9 So I reflected on all this and concluded that the righteous and the wise and what they do are in God's hands, but no man knows whether love or hate awaits him.[b] 2All share a common destiny—the righteous and the wicked, the

9:1
b Dt 33:3;
Job 12:10;
Ecc 10:14

---

a 8 Or over his spirit to retain it   b 9 Or to their   c 10 Some Hebrew manuscripts and Septuagint (Aquila); most Hebrew manuscripts and are forgotten

---

Ecclesiastes 8:2–17

Wicked people may live a long life. Still, sin doesn't pay. It will go better over the long haul for the person who fears God (vv. 12–13). As seen in the closing remarks of this chapter, the Teacher didn't doubt God's ultimate justice but only his own limited ability to understand how that justice works out in practice.

The broader Biblical context in which Ecclesiastes 8 is to be understood is provided by the volumes of Scriptural material that speak of foolish and oppressive rulers, under whose power God's people must live for a time. *Much human government is wicked. Still, government in general is instituted by God for human good and isn't to be opposed lightly* (Rom. 13:1–2). The Teacher's advice—shrewd caution, patient faith, and courageous integrity—is on display in Bible stories about God's people

living under evil rulers (e.g., Gen. 37–50; Ex. 1–14; the books of Est. and Dan.; Acts 6–7).

God is the only God there is. We as Christians are called to "worship the Lord [our] God, and serve him only" (Matt. 4:10). The Bible counsels respect for authority, but it also assumes that sooner or later conflict will arise. At such times worshipers of the living God are obligated to expose as idols those others think of as gods (cf. Dan. 3)—often to their peril. Are you willing to exchange temporary risk or ridicule for the long-term security of knowing God?

Ecclesiastes 9:1–12

Life's outcomes (other than death) are unpredictable; good and bad come to all. The things humans desire and seek to develop aren't necessarily bad in

good and the bad,[a] the clean and the unclean, those who offer sacrifices and those who do not.

> As it is with the good man,
> so with the sinner;
> as it is with those who take oaths,
> so with those who are afraid to take them.[c]

³This is the evil in everything that happens under the sun: The same destiny overtakes all.[d] The hearts of men, moreover, are full of evil and there is madness in their hearts while they live,[e] and afterward they join the dead.[f] ⁴Anyone who is among the living has hope[b]—even a live dog is better off than a dead lion!

> ⁵For the living know that they will die,
> but the dead know nothing;[g]
> they have no further reward,
> and even the memory of them[h] is forgotten.[i]
> ⁶Their love, their hate
> and their jealousy have long since vanished;
> never again will they have a part
> in anything that happens under the sun.[j]

⁷Go, eat your food with gladness, and drink your wine[k] with a joyful heart,[l] for it is now that God favors what you do. ⁸Always be clothed in white,[m] and always anoint your head with oil. ⁹Enjoy life with your wife,[n] whom you love, all the days of this meaningless life that God has given you under the sun—all your meaningless days. For this is your lot[o] in life and in your toilsome labor under the sun. ¹⁰Whatever[p] your hand finds to do, do it with all your might,[q] for in the grave,[c] where you are going, there is neither working nor planning nor knowledge nor wisdom.[s]

¹¹I have seen something else under the sun:

> The race is not to the swift
> or the battle to the strong,[t]
> nor does food come to the wise[u]
> or wealth to the brilliant
> or favor to the learned;
> but time and chance[v] happen to them all.[w]

¹²Moreover, no man knows when his hour will come:

> As fish are caught in a cruel net,
> or birds are taken in a snare,
> so men are trapped by evil times[x]
> that fall unexpectedly upon them.[y]

Wisdom Better Than Folly

¹³I also saw under the sun this example of wisdom[z] that greatly impressed me:

---

[a] 2 Septuagint (Aquila), Vulgate and Syriac; Hebrew does not have *and the bad*.   [b] 4 Or *What then is to be chosen? With all who live, there is hope*   [c] 10 Hebrew *Sheol*

9:2
c Job 9:22;
Ecc 2:14; 6:6; 7:2

9:3
d Job 9:22;
Ecc 2:14 e Jer 11:8;
13:10; 16:12; 17:9
f Job 21:26

9:5
g Job 14:21
h Ps 9:6 i Ecc 1:11;
2:16; Isa 26:14

9:6
j Job 21:21

9:7
k Nu 6:20
l Ecc 2:24; 8:15
9:8
m Ps 23:5; Rev 3:4
9:9
n Pr 5:18
o Job 31:2
9:10
p 1Sa 10:7
q Ecc 11:6;
Ro 12:11; Col 3:23
r Nu 16:33
s Ecc 2:24

9:11
t Am 2:14-15
u Job 32:13;
Isa 47:10; Jer 9:23
v Ecc 2:14
w Dt 8:18

9:12
x Pr 29:6
y Ps 73:22;
Ecc 2:14; 8:7

9:13
z 2Sa 20:22

---

themselves, but they don't control the "times" (vv. 11–12; cf. 3:1–11). Events often happen that are unforeseen and beyond human control.

The Bible doesn't promise that we will experience only good health, financial prosperity, and happiness, and it doesn't tie faith and righteousness to the attainment of these things in any simplistic way. The path of faith and obedience to God is the blessed way, but the faithful and obedient person can't avoid life's unpleasant realities simply by mustering enough religious devotion. Biblical faith isn't about controlling or manipulating God so that he will

do as we wish—that's the definition of idolatry.

The universe is an ordered place, and cause-and-effect are built-in features. But it's not a machine. The cosmos is a personally created and governed space, whose Originator and Sustainer is the living God. Our calling is to love God and our neighbor and to look after the earth—not to take advantage of the order in the universe to engage in self-centered and manipulative living. The God of order sometimes allows sin's chaos (our own and others' sin) into our lives to remind us that we are not gods. How effective have these reminders been for you?

14There was once a small city with only a few people in it. And a powerful king came against it, surrounded it and built huge siegeworks against it. 15Now there lived in that city a man poor but wise, and he saved the city by his wisdom. But nobody remembered that poor man. *a* 16So I said, "Wisdom is better than strength." But the poor man's wisdom is despised, and his words are no longer heeded. *b*

17The quiet words of the wise are more to be heeded
    than the shouts of a ruler of fools.
18Wisdom*c* is better than weapons of war,
    but one sinner destroys much good.

10 As dead flies give perfume a bad smell,
    so a little folly*d* outweighs wisdom and honor.
2The heart of the wise inclines to the right,
    but the heart of the fool to the left.
3Even as he walks along the road,
    the fool lacks sense
    and shows everyone*e* how stupid he is.
4If a ruler's anger rises against you,
    do not leave your post;*f*
    calmness can lay great errors to rest.*g*

9:15
a Ge 40:14;
Ecc 1:11; 2:16; 4:13
9:16
b Pr 21:22; Ecc 7:19

9:18
c ver 16

10:1
d Pr 13:16; 18:2

10:3
e Pr 13:16; 18:2

10:4
f Ecc 8:3 *g* Pr 16:14;
25:15

Ecclesiastes 9:13—10:20

The Teacher was interested in the consequences of undervaluing wisdom. At the heart of human existence is a "madness" (10:13) that leads people to value what they shouldn't and despise what's truly important. Left to their own devices, human beings are incapable even of enlightened self-interest, much less of selfless love of God or neighbor. Does that sound wrong to you? Think about how children act when left without parental or adult guidance for almost any length of time.

9:11

Intelligence

The Bible cautions us not to overrate human intelligence. Instead, wisdom, a spiritual and moral concept, is praised. The Bible also warns us not to belittle others because they lack our particular kind or degree of intelligence. Still, we are to use our God-given human intelligence to his glory as these Biblical people did:

	Verbal/Linguistic: Paul, a master presenter of the gospel in verbal (and written) form
	Visual/Spatial: John, whose images in Revelation create fantastic pictures in our minds of God's world
	Musical: David, the gifted harpist and author of many psalms (songs) of praise to God
	Logical/Mathematical: Gamaliel, whose gifts of reason, conciliation, and common sense were profound (Acts 5:34)
	Bodily/Kinesthetic: Noah, who constructed an impressive boat, presumably with only crude tools
	Interpersonal: Esther, whose interpersonal skills saved the Jewish people from annihilation in Persia
	Scientific: Luke, a doctor (Col. 4:14)
	Artistic: Bezalel, a master craftsman/artisan with gold, silver, bronze, and precious stones (Ex. 31:1–5)

What special kinds of intelligence do you possess? Through what methods do you learn best? Who do you know who, despite a disability of some sort, excels in some other area? Though we are called to use our intelligence(s) to serve in the kingdom, godly wisdom trumps intelligence. Psalm 19:7 affirms, "The law of the LORD is perfect, reviving the soul. The statutes of the LORD are trustworthy, making wise the simple." Anyone can ask God for wisdom, and he promises to supply the need liberally (James 1:5).

Source: Gardner (1985:24)

5 There is an evil I have seen under the sun,
  the sort of error that arises from a ruler:
6 Fools are put in many high positions,[h]
  while the rich occupy the low ones.
7 I have seen slaves on horseback,
  while princes go on foot like slaves.[i]
8 Whoever digs a pit may fall into it;[j]
  whoever breaks through a wall may be bitten by a snake.[k]
9 Whoever quarries stones may be injured by them;
  whoever splits logs may be endangered by them.[l]

10 If the ax is dull
  and its edge unsharpened,
 more strength is needed
  but skill will bring success.

11 If a snake bites before it is charmed,
  there is no profit for the charmer.[m]

12 Words from a wise man's mouth are gracious,[n]
  but a fool is consumed by his own lips.[o]
13 At the beginning his words are folly;
  at the end they are wicked madness—
14 and the fool multiplies words.[p]

  No one knows what is coming—
  who can tell him what will happen after him?[q]

15 A fool's work wearies him;
  he does not know the way to town.

16 Woe to you, O land whose king was a servant[a][r]
  and whose princes feast in the morning.
17 Blessed are you, O land whose king is of noble birth
  and whose princes eat at a proper time—
  for strength and not for drunkenness.[s]

18 If a man is lazy, the rafters sag;
  if his hands are idle, the house leaks.[t]

19 A feast is made for laughter,
  and wine[u] makes life merry,
  but money is the answer for everything.

20 Do not revile the king[v] even in your thoughts,
  or curse the rich in your bedroom,
 because a bird of the air may carry your words,
  and a bird on the wing may report what you say.

Bread Upon the Waters

11 Cast[w] your bread upon the waters,
   for after many days you will find it again.[x]
  2 Give portions to seven, yes to eight,
   for you do not know what disaster may come upon the land.

---

[a] 16 Or *king is a child*

10:6
h Pr 29:2

10:7
i Pr 19:10
10:8
j Ps 7:15; 57:6;
Pr 26:27 k Est 2:23;
Ps 9:16; Am 5:19

10:9
l Pr 26:27

10:11
m Ps 58:5; Isa 3:3
10:12
n Pr 10:32
o Pr 10:14; 14:3;
15:2; 18:7

10:14
p Pr 15:2; Ecc 5:3;
6:12; 8:7 q Ecc 9:1

10:16
r Isa 3:4-5, 12

10:17
s Dt 14:26;
1Sa 25:36; Pr 31:4

10:18
t Pr 20:4; 24:30-34

10:19
u Ge 14:18;
Jdg 9:13

10:20
v Ex 22:28

11:1
w ver 6; Isa 32:20;
Hos 10:12
x Dt 24:19;
Pr 19:17; Mt 10:42

We live in a world where wisdom (especially that associated with authority and tradition) is suspected, mocked, and despised. Truth has become a personal matter—changing even with the circumstances of the person proclaiming it. We all need wisdom from above to know who we are, what life is about, and where we are going. If we are to sort out truth from fiction, we need to know God's Truth as a constant. We can find it only in his revelation of Jesus Christ, the touchstone of all reality and the focus of all wisdom (cf. John 14:6). Are you willing to share the truth about the Truth?

³ If clouds are full of water,
　　they pour rain upon the earth.
Whether a tree falls to the south or to the north,
　　in the place where it falls, there will it lie.
⁴ Whoever watches the wind will not plant;
　　whoever looks at the clouds will not reap.

⁵ As you do not know the path of the wind,ʸ
　　or how the body is formedᵃ in a mother's womb,ᶻ
so you cannot understand the work of God,
　　the Maker of all things.

⁶ Sow your seed in the morning,
　　and at evening let not your hands be idle,ᵃ
for you do not know which will succeed,
　　whether this or that,
　　or whether both will do equally well.

ᵃ 5 Or *know how life* (or *the spirit*) / *enters the body being formed*

Ecclesiastes 11:1–6

Again the Teacher reminded those in his audience of their inability to control "the times," emphasizing human ignorance of what is and will be happening in the world: (1) No one knows "what disaster may come upon the land." (2) God's creative work is as mysterious as the movements of the wind or the development of the fetus in the womb. (3) People can't predict which projects and activities will succeed.

The Teacher's consistent advice about holding loosely to life and possessions and living life to the full is paralleled in the New Testament. Jesus counseled his followers not to store up temporary treasures on Earth but to think long-term and invest in heaven (Matt. 6:19–21). He illustrated the foolishness of hoarding possessions in the parable of the rich fool (Luke 12:16–21), going on to advocate a carefree attitude toward life in the context of faith in God and generosity toward the poor (Luke 12:22–34).

The Bible replaces the myth that people keep rising toward divinity with the harsh reality of our fallenness—our sin nature. It teaches us to be content with the life God has given us, rather than pursuing one we might have preferred, and to learn to live each moment well and generously. Christians can give the impression

---

Snapshots

11:1–6

Unexpected Disaster

In April 2004, a tornado ripped through a bicycle repair shop in Bangladesh, sending its owner, Mohammad, rolling across the floor. Mohammad barely managed to rescue his elderly father, Lal Mohammad, who had been sitting beside him. After seeing the family's mud house totally flattened, Mohammad collapsed.

> "We are all alive. God has saved us."

Upon regaining consciousness, his first concern was the well-being of his children. His wife, Moimuna, reassured him: "We are all alive. God has saved us." Due to his fragile condition, she hesitated revealing that two of their three children had been injured.

The family received emergency medical treatment from a mobile medical team set up by a Christian relief organization. Though they have recovered physically, the trauma is still evident in their eyes.

The children lost their precious school books. "We have no clothes apart from what we are wearing," explained one of them. With despair in his voice, Mohammad added: "We have absolutely nothing—no house, no business, no capital, no shop, except the empty homestead."

The family is temporarily sharing a neighbor's house and receiving relief supplies, for which they are grateful. Their immediate needs are food, housing, clothes, bedding, and utensils. "The monsoon season is approaching. We cannot live under the open sky," sighs Moimuna.

Remember Your Creator While Young

7 Light is sweet,
  and it pleases the eyes to see the sun. [b]
8 However many years a man may live,
  let him enjoy them all.
But let him remember [c] the days of darkness,
  for they will be many.
  Everything to come is meaningless.

9 Be happy, young man, while you are young,
  and let your heart give you joy in the days of your youth.
Follow the ways of your heart
  and whatever your eyes see,
but know that for all these things
  God will bring you to judgment. [d]
10 So then, banish anxiety [e] from your heart
  and cast off the troubles of your body,
  for youth and vigor are meaningless. [f]

12 Remember [g] your Creator
    in the days of your youth,
  before the days of trouble [h] come
    and the years approach when you will say,
    "I find no pleasure in them"—
2 before the sun and the light
    and the moon and the stars grow dark,
    and the clouds return after the rain;
3 when the keepers of the house tremble,
    and the strong men stoop,
  when the grinders cease because they are few,
    and those looking through the windows grow dim;
4 when the doors to the street are closed
    and the sound of grinding fades;
  when men rise up at the sound of birds,
    but all their songs grow faint; [i]
5 when men are afraid of heights
    and of dangers in the streets;
  when the almond tree blossoms
    and the grasshopper drags himself along
    and desire no longer is stirred.
Then man goes to his eternal home [j]
    and mourners [k] go about the streets.

6 Remember him—before the silver cord is severed,

11:7	*b* Ecc 7:11
11:8	*c* Ecc 12:1
11:9	*d* Job 19:29; Ecc 2:24; 3:17; 12:14; Ro 14:10
11:10	*e* Ps 94:19 *f* Ecc 2:24
12:1	*g* Ecc 11:8 *h* 2Sa 19:35
12:4	*i* Jer 25:10
12:5	*j* Job 17:13; 10:21 *k* Jer 9:17; Am 5:16

that faith is about refusal to live today to the full for fear of losing heaven. The truth is that we're not called to suspend earthly life in the hope of eternal life. We're to live out eternal life as a present reality already here on Earth, demonstrating the love, joy, peace, and freedom of the gospel. Are you enjoying your eternal life *now*?

Ecclesiastes 11:7—12:8

The Teacher's description of old age recalls the language in Ezekiel 32:7–8. Every person in the end is in a sense "unmade." The writer wanted young people to confront this unavoidable decay and to realize that it's never too early to acknowledge their Creator.

The description of the "unmaking" in 12:2–8 has often been seen as an allegory, using powerful imagery to refer to the multiple aspects of aging. Others see parallels between the aging process and the end times. The last days of human life are pictured, in this view, in terms of the end of the world: darkness, terror, suspension of normal activity, and ecological chaos (see Isa. 24:1–23).

Adult role models are wise not to hold back from proclaiming God's life-affirming goodness or to refuse to enjoy God's world. They can be prepared to say along with Nobel Peace Prize-winner Dag Hammarskjöld (1905–1961), "Do not seek death. Death will find you. But seek the road that makes death a fulfillment." How are you an example to younger people of acknowledging God in your everyday activities?

Fine Hammered Steel of Woe

Herman Melville, in *Moby Dick,* noted that, "The truest of all books is Solomon's, and Ecclesiastes is the fine hammered steel of woe."

Yet Ecclesiastes is a difficult book. The language is difficult; the book is filled with word plays; the argumentation is complex; and the book doesn't mention other major Biblical figures, like Abraham, Isaac, and Jacob, or any of God's dealings with Israel. Ecclesiastes is an unusual piece of writing.

Consider: Tradition tells us that Solomon was the author of Ecclesiastes. Although evidence points to his authorship (Eccl. 1:1), we really don't know the author's identity for sure. The book effectively veils the information so that we are forced to focus on the content. This pattern was typical of Near Eastern literature, where it was commonplace to write anonymously. Perhaps we do well to learn the lesson that some things are effectively revealed by the veiling of others. That is, ideas don't always need to be associated with personality.

> We don't seem to understand the basic nature of our existence any better than our ancestors understood the far fewer facts at their fingertips.

Consider another example: The text of Ecclesiastes is filled with apparent contradictions. In one place pleasure is condemned ("What does pleasure accomplish?"; 2:2) and in another endorsed ("I commend the enjoyment of life"; 8:15). Two theories have regularly been put forth in an attempt to explain away these discrepancies. The first is called the *quotation theory*—the idea that the author of Ecclesiastes quoted people with whom he disagreed in order to contrast and thereby highlight his own views. The second is labeled the *addition theory*—the suggestion that a later editor or editors added material in order to "correct" the author's misconceptions. Perhaps a better explanation is that by juxtaposing simple truths the author revealed a still deeper, separate truth on his primary subject. This explanation advocates revelation through comparison.

Or consider a third example: The tone of Ecclesiastes is often gloomy. Perhaps the best-known and most-quoted verse in the whole text is 1:2—"Everything is meaningless." Another pessimistic observation in 12:7—"The dust returns to the ground it came from"—wins no happy-face awards. Death is a frequent topic in Ecclesiastes. Yet we don't come away from reading this book viewing death as a victor. On the contrary, it's obvious that life is the theme—or, more specifically, the life we have in God. Such life, the author seems to have been saying, can only be understood in the context of human death and futility.

We live in a paradoxical age, a time of unparalleled discovery and knowledge. Science has made it possible for us to orbit distant planets and focus in on the microscopic atom. We know more than our ancestors could ever have dreamed. Yet we don't seem to understand the basic nature of our existence any better than our ancestors understood the far fewer facts at their fingertips. Beneath all the uncovered facts we discover only additional, vast knowledge-frontiers and ever-increasing fields of mystery.

The writer of Ecclesiastes declared life to be meaningless. Perhaps he meant that we as human beings too quickly exhaust our capacity to "make" meaning and find ourselves falling at the feet of God, asking for the meaning we can't seem to discern. God obliges, of course, as the writer later explains (12:14). If we listen, that is!

or the golden bowl is broken;
before the pitcher is shattered at the spring,
or the wheel broken at the well,
[7] and the dust returns [l] to the ground it came from,
and the spirit returns to God [m] who gave it. [n]

[8] "Meaningless! Meaningless!" says the Teacher. [a]
"Everything is meaningless! [o]"

The Conclusion of the Matter

[9] Not only was the Teacher wise, but also he imparted knowledge to the people. He pondered and searched out and set in order many proverbs. [p] [10] The Teacher searched to find just the right words, and what he wrote was upright and true. [q]

[11] The words of the wise are like goads, their collected sayings like firmly embedded nails [r]—given by one Shepherd. [12] Be warned, my son, of anything in addition to them.

Of making many books there is no end, and much study wearies the body. [s]

[13] Now all has been heard;
here is the conclusion of the matter:
Fear God and keep his commandments, [t]
for this is the whole ⌞duty⌟ of man. [u]
[14] For God will bring every deed into judgment, [v]
including every hidden thing, [w]
whether it is good or evil.

[a] 8 Or *the leader of the assembly*; also in verses 9 and 10

12:7
[l] Ge 3:19;
Job 34:15; Ps 146:4
[m] Ecc 3:21
[n] Job 20:8;
Zec 12:1
12:8
[o] Ecc 1:2

12:9
[p] 1Ki 4:32
12:10
[q] Pr 22:20-21

12:11
[r] Ezr 9:8

12:12
[s] Ecc 1:18

12:13
[t] Dt 4:2; 10:12
[u] Mic 6:8
12:14
[v] Ecc 3:17
[w] Mt 10:26;
1Co 4:5

Ecclesiastes 12:9–14

The Teacher's words here weren't about pursuing literary or intellectual ends. They were designed to help people live well before God, reverencing him and bearing always in mind that the universe is a moral place of accountability.

Quoting the Bible doesn't necessarily communicate God's Word. The history of its misuse in supporting human agendas and institutions is long. Paul requested that Timothy be one who "correctly handles the word of truth" (2 Tim. 2:15). Can you think of a time when someone "spouting" a verse only complicated your problem or hurt your feelings? Conversely, how would you have responded if that individual had spent time with you and explained Biblical wisdom for your situation, sharing from the whole counsel of God?

The Bible is a vast ocean of material that requires steady and patient exploration, under the guidance of the Holy Spirit and other more learned students, if we are to begin to comprehend how it fits together and speaks to us with God's voice. We need to learn how to "set things in order," because we can understand what one part means only in relation to every other. Scripture must interpret Scripture, each part helping form our view of the whole.

INTRODUCTION TO
Song of Songs

AUTHOR

Solomon has traditionally been named the author of Song of Songs, primarily based on the phrase "Solomon's Song of Songs" (1:1), but his authorship isn't certain. Some have suggested that the Song of Songs is a collection (like Psalms and Proverbs) of love poems written by various authors and compiled by a single editor. The study notes for this book assume Solomon's authorship.

DATE WRITTEN

Evidence suggests a date of composition during the 10th century B.C., which would place its composition during or slightly after Solomon's reign (970–930 B.C.).

ORIGINAL READERS

Song of Songs is a love poem or compilation of love poems written to God's people to honor and celebrate his gift of romantic, sexual love. Because of the book's highly sensual nature, some scholars have interpreted it as an allegory of God's love for his people. Others have set aside these interpretive explanations.

TIMELINE

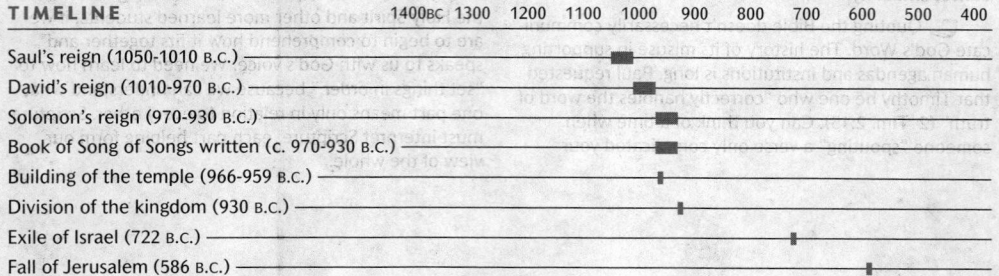

	1400BC	1300	1200	1100	1000	900	800	700	600	500	400
Saul's reign (1050-1010 B.C.)											
David's reign (1010-970 B.C.)											
Solomon's reign (970-930 B.C.)											
Book of Song of Songs written (c. 970-930 B.C.)											
Building of the temple (966-959 B.C.)											
Division of the kingdom (930 B.C.)											
Exile of Israel (722 B.C.)											
Fall of Jerusalem (586 B.C.)											

THEMES

Song of Songs describes God's gift of romantic love. It includes the following themes:

1. *Love is a beautiful gift from God.* Song of Songs is love poetry that articulates a beautiful relationship between a man and a woman. Its lyrics remind God's people that the intimate sexual relationship in marriage is a divine gift to be valued and enjoyed. Love is portrayed as precious (8:7b), spontaneous (2:7), and powerful (8:6–7a).

2. *Marital contentment.* Song of Songs demonstrates that contentment and fulfillment are found in the exclusivity (2:16) of the marriage relationship. The erotic love expressed in the *Song* is tender, delightful, and natural—not shameful or debasing. The lovers are equals, praising each other and sharing the role of initiator.

3. *Love is both pleasurable and painful.* Joy is the dominant note of the Song of Songs, but the reader also is warned that love is a powerful emotion that may bring disappointments (5:2—6:3). The Song's young woman repeatedly warned her female friends not to hurry love (2:7; 3:5; 8:4). Love has a dangerous side (8:6) and deserves to be treated with caution.

FAITH IN ACTION

The pages of Song of Songs contain life lessons and role models of faith—people who challenge believers to put their faith in action.

Role Models

• THE BELOVED (1:2–4a) expressed her love for, and delight in, her husband. If you are married, have you spoken words of love to your spouse today?

• THE FRIENDS (1:4b) rejoiced in the love of the married couple. Do you express joy at your friends' happiness? Do you encourage and support them in maintaining their faithful relationships?

• THE LOVER (4:1) openly proclaimed his love for his wife. Do you regularly communicate your love and admiration to your spouse?

• THE COUPLE (8:6–7) understood the wonder and longevity of their love. Have you protected your marital relationship, treating it with respect?

Challenges

• Evaluate your marriage or, if you are single, contemplate what an ideal marriage would be like. How can a spouse bring fulfillment and contentment in a way no one else can?

• Encourage and support the marriage relationships of others.

• View your spouse as a gift from God. See in him or her a special partner and friend—never an adversary.

• Verbalize and demonstrate your love to your spouse each day, expressing admiration for his or her traits. How might this improve your relationship?

• Accept the reality that love relationships may at times be painful due to separation, misunderstanding, or inappropriate family involvement.

• Cherish your spouse. Respect your marital relationship, doing all you can to protect and promote it.

OUTLINE

   I. First Meeting (1:1—2:7)
  II. Second Meeting (2:8—3:5)
 III. Third Meeting (3:6—5:1)
 IV. Fourth Meeting (5:2—6:3)
  V. Fifth Meeting (6:4—8:4)
 VI. Literary Climax (8:5—7)
VII. Conclusion (8:8—14)

1

1:1
a 1Ki 4:32

Solomon's Song of Songs. *a*

Beloved *a*

1:2
b SS 4:10
1:3
c SS 4:10 *d* Ecc 7:1
e Ps 45:14

2 Let him kiss me with the kisses of his mouth—
    for your love *b* is more delightful than wine.
3 Pleasing is the fragrance of your perfumes; *c*
    your name *d* is like perfume poured out.
    No wonder the maidens *e* love you!

1:4
f Ps 45:15

4 Take me away with you—let us hurry!
    Let the king bring me into his chambers. *f*

Friends

We rejoice and delight in you *b*;
    we will praise your love more than wine.

Beloved

How right they are to adore you!

1:5
g SS 2:14; 4:3
h SS 2:7; 5:8; 5:16

5 Dark am I, yet lovely, *g*
    O daughters of Jerusalem, *h*
    dark like the tents of Kedar,
    like the tent curtains of Solomon. *c*
6 Do not stare at me because I am dark,
    because I am darkened by the sun.
    My mother's sons were angry with me

1:6
i Ps 69:8; SS 8:12

    and made me take care of the vineyards; *i*
    my own vineyard I have neglected.
7 Tell me, you whom I love, where you graze your flock

a Primarily on the basis of the gender of the Hebrew pronouns used, male and female speakers are
indicated in the margins by the captions *Lover* and *Beloved* respectively. The words of others are
marked *Friends.* In some instances the divisions and their captions are debatable.   *b* 4 The Hebrew
is masculine singular.   *c* 5 Or *Salma*

The Song of Songs study notes differ from those in other
books, in that they are grouped logically, rather than
corresponding to the exact headings in the NIV text,
some of which comprise only one verse of the dialogue.

Song of Songs 1:1–4a

The title of the book comes from the opening
line of the Hebrew text. "Solomon's Song of Songs"
means that the song was written by, for, or about
Solomon. "Song of songs" literally means "the greatest
of all songs." In the author's mind, this song (or poem)
was the ultimate—the epitome of all love songs.

The Song opens with the words of the woman, who
expressed a passionate desire for her lover, first in the
third person and then in the second. The simplest interpretation of the story line is to assume that the "lover"
(who speaks throughout the Song) and the "king" (v. 4,
as well as 1:12 and 7:5) refer to Solomon—in light of the
book's clear connection to him (1:1; cf. 1:5; 3:7–11;
8:11–12). But some interpreters think that the two lovers
were common people (see "There and Then" to follow)
who used royal language to embellish their affection. In
that case, in verse 4 the maiden was referring to her
lover as *her* "king."

The woman speaks first, apparently seeing herself
as of equal status with the man. There is a sense in which

she's the major character. Song of Songs challenges all
worldviews that insist that women aren't fully persons in
their own right, that they aren't to take initiative or communicate sexual desire. Male-female relationships, when
lived out in fulfillment of God's creative purposes, are
about mutuality—not domination/subjection. What is
your view of male/female relationships under God?

Song of Songs 1:4b–8

The "Friends," who speak for the first time in
verse 4 and repeatedly again throughout the Song, were
probably the "maidens" of verse 3 and the "daughters of
Jerusalem" of verse 5. Though they called the beloved
the "most beautiful of women" (v. 8), she was self-con-
scious about her dark skin—considered unattractive by
privileged women of the time. Kedar was a territory
southeast of Damascus where the Bedouin roamed.
Their tents were made of the skins of black goats. The
woman was obviously from a family where the females
had to work. She was compelled to care for her brothers'
concerns at the expense of her own body ("vineyard").

The lover is portrayed as a shepherd in verse 7 and
the beloved as a shepherdess in verse 8. The maiden
wanted to know where her lover was grazing his flock so
she could be near him. Yet she didn't want to look for
him among the shepherds, appearing as though she were
a "veiled woman"—a prostitute (cf. Gen. 38:13–15).

and where you rest your sheep^j at midday.
    Why should I be like a veiled woman
        beside the flocks of your friends?

Friends

    ^{8} If you do not know, most beautiful of women, ^{k}
        follow the tracks of the sheep
    and graze your young goats
        by the tents of the shepherds.

Lover

    ^{9} I liken you, my darling, to a mare
        harnessed to one of the chariots^l of Pharaoh.
    ^{10} Your cheeks^m are beautiful with earrings,
        your neck with strings of jewels. ^{n}
    ^{11} We will make you earrings of gold,
        studded with silver.

Beloved

    ^{12} While the king was at his table,
        my perfume spread its fragrance. ^{o}
    ^{13} My lover is to me a sachet of myrrh
        resting between my breasts.
    ^{14} My lover is to me a cluster of henna^p blossoms
        from the vineyards of En Gedi. ^{q}

Lover

    ^{15} How beautiful^r you are, my darling!
        Oh, how beautiful!
        Your eyes are doves. ^{s}

1:7
j SS 3:1-4; Isa 13:20

1:8
k SS 5:9; 6:1

1:9
l 2Ch 1:17
1:10
m SS 5:13
n Isa 61:10

1:12
o SS 4:11-14

1:14
p SS 4:13
q 1Sa 23:29

1:15
r SS 4:7 s SS 2:14; 4:1; 5:2,12; 6:9

Human beauty is a prioritized value in Western culture. Attempts to achieve and prolong it are widespread, artificial, and near neurotic. To the extent that it becomes an idol, it causes damage—to those who have, want, or lack it. To the degree that it's received as a gift of God and set in the context of all that is good in creation, it enhances our lives and points to God, whose Person it reflects. Only as the church integrates a proper view of beauty into its thinking will we be able to act as salt and light in a culture obsessed with physical appearance but lacking perspective about it.

Song of Songs 1:9–11

The lover now speaks for the first time. Modern readers understand "darling," but the next concept is unexpected by us. The lover compared his beloved to "a mare harnessed to one of the chariots of Pharaoh." Since Egypt's royal chariots were typically drawn by stallions hitched in pairs, the presence of a mare among them would have been the ultimate distraction. Thus the lover paid his beloved a teasing compliment about her sexual attractiveness. And he would provide her with the costly jewelry to match her natural charms.

It's clear that the lover relished his thoughts about his beloved. Do you invest the time and energy necessary to playfully compliment your spouse? Do you

consistently and creatively affirm others who are close to you? How does the giving/receiving of gifts enhance your marital, family, and friendship relationships?

Song of Songs 1:12–17

The setting of the Song moves to the king's table. The beloved pondered her impact on her lover. It was as though his table was surrounded by the most delightful fragrance—herself. And his impact on her was just as great. Thinking of him brought sensations as real and pleasurable as the smell of myrrh and henna blossoms.

At chapter close the lovers are lying together on lush foliage. They had found a bedroom in a private forest "palace." This hints of a return to Eden (Gen. 2:8–25) with its simplicity, naïveté, equality, and purity. It's as though this were the original, guilt-free couple.

The Old Testament is best understood in the context of God's plan for the world in creation and redemption. Song of Songs presents a male-female relationship that recalls the innocence of Genesis 1–2, not the fallen condition of Genesis 3. Similarly, the redeemed community of the church (cf. Gal. 3:28) is no longer to yield to gender or societal divisions. It's to emphasize the importance of all persons finding their identity in a love relationship with God and neighbors. How close has your congregation come to realizing this ideal?

Beloved

16 How handsome you are, my lover!
    Oh, how charming!
    And our bed is verdant.

Lover

1:17
t 1Ki 6:9

17 The beams of our house are cedars; [t]
    our rafters are firs.

Beloved [a]

2:1
u Isa 35:1
v 1Ch 27:29
w SS 5:13; Hos 14:5

2 I am a rose [b] [u] of Sharon, [v]
    a lily [w] of the valleys.

Lover

2 Like a lily among thorns
    is my darling among the maidens.

Beloved

2:3
x SS 1:14 y SS 1:4
z SS 4:16

3 Like an apple tree among the trees of the forest
    is my lover [x] among the young men.
  I delight [y] to sit in his shade,
    and his fruit is sweet to my taste. [z]

2:4
a Est 1:11
b Nu 1:52

4 He has taken me to the banquet hall, [a]
    and his banner [b] over me is love.

2:5
c SS 7:8 d SS 5:8

5 Strengthen me with raisins,
    refresh me with apples, [c]
  for I am faint with love. [d]

2:6
e SS 8:3
2:7
f SS 5:8 g SS 3:5;
8:4

6 His left arm is under my head,
    and his right arm embraces me. [e]
7 Daughters of Jerusalem, I charge you [f]
    by the gazelles and by the does of the field:
  Do not arouse or awaken love
    until it so desires. [g]

2:8
h ver 17; SS 8:14
2:9
i 2Sa 2:18 j ver 17;
SS 8:14

8 Listen! My lover!
  Look! Here he comes,
  leaping across the mountains,
    bounding over the hills. [h]
9 My lover is like a gazelle [i] or a young stag. [j]
  Look! There he stands behind our wall,
  gazing through the windows,
    peering through the lattice.
10 My lover spoke and said to me,

---

[a] Or *Lover*   [b] 1 Possibly a member of the crocus family

---

Song of Songs 2:1–13

📖 The couple was becoming more direct in their expressions of love, and their desire for each other was intense. The beloved was "faint with love" (v. 5). Is the Song here describing scenes from the courtship (likely the case if the book follows a chronological story line as opposed to being a series of individual poems)? Is it describing their romanticized memories of their courtship (or a dream about it)? Or is it expressing the passion of their marital relationship? We can't tell for sure. But we can be certain that a book describing sexual intimacy outside of marriage would hardly stand a chance of being included in the Scriptures.

📖 Just as the lovers were about to surrender themselves to each other and forget the world, attention was turned to the larger world—hence the addresses to the "daughters of Jerusalem" in verse 7 and twice again later (3:5; 8:4). The beloved adjured them not to encourage love beyond its right and proper place. Do you find it difficult to ignore the possibility or suggestion of premarital sex as you approach Song of Songs? Where do you draw the line between "making out" and "having sex"? We can look to other Scriptures, which explicitly qualify sex as a pleasure to be enjoyed only within the context of a marital relationship. Use the concordance at the back of this Bible to locate some of them.

"Arise, my darling,
my beautiful one, and come with me.
[11] See! The winter is past;
the rains are over and gone.
[12] Flowers appear on the earth;
the season of singing has come,
the cooing of doves
is heard in our land.
[13] The fig tree forms its early fruit;[k]
the blossoming[l] vines spread their fragrance.
Arise, come, my darling;
my beautiful one, come with me."

Lover

[14] My dove[m] in the clefts of the rock,
in the hiding places on the mountainside,
show me your face,
let me hear your voice;
for your voice is sweet,
and your face is lovely.[n]
[15] Catch for us the foxes,[o]
the little foxes
that ruin the vineyards,[p]
our vineyards that are in bloom.[q]

Beloved

[16] My lover is mine and I am his;[r]
he browses among the lilies.[s]
[17] Until the day breaks
and the shadows flee,[t]
turn, my lover,[u]
and be like a gazelle
or like a young stag[v]
on the rugged hills.[a][w]

[a] 17 Or the hills of Bether

2:13
[k] Isa 28:4; Jer 24:2; Hos 9:10; Mic 7:1; Na 3:12 [l] SS 7:12

2:14
[m] Ge 8:8; SS 1:15 [n] SS 1:5; 8:13

2:15
[o] Jdg 15:4 [p] SS 1:6 [q] SS 7:12

2:16
[r] SS 7:10 [s] SS 4:5; 6:3

2:17
[t] SS 4:6 [u] SS 1:14 [v] ver 9 [w] ver 8

Song of Songs 2:14–15

🔲 Small foxes were evidently known to dig around and destroy blossoming vines. The lovers were appealing to outsiders, in verse 15, to help prevent those forces that could destroy the purity of their love—wanting nothing to spoil it.

📖 If you are married, what "little foxes" might threaten the purity of your love? How have you linked up with others to help protect your relationship (e.g., a small group or accountability partner)? Do you and your spouse consistently pray together, asking for God's protection and direction for your marriage?

Song of Songs 2:16—3:11

🔲 The first part of chapter 3 seems to revolve around a dream. The woman may have been recounting a dream during their courtship, in which she longed to

---

2:3–13

Six Biblical Sources for Application

The Bible is a book made up of many kinds of literature. Each style has value, of course, but each communicates God's truth in a slightly different way. At least six different styles offer guidance:

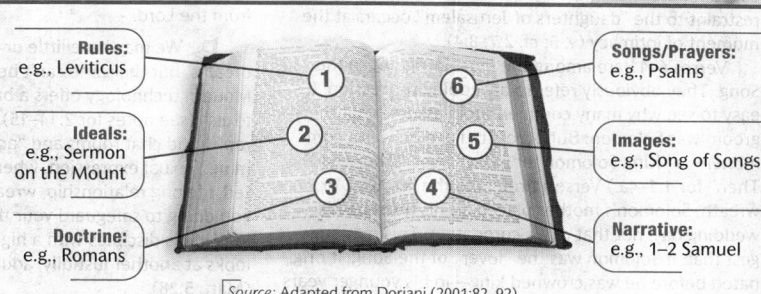

Rules: e.g., Leviticus — 1
Ideals: e.g., Sermon on the Mount — 2
Doctrine: e.g., Romans — 3
4 — Narrative: e.g., 1–2 Samuel
5 — Images: e.g., Song of Songs
6 — Songs/Prayers: e.g., Psalms

Source: Adapted from Doriani (2001:82–92)

3:1
x SS 5:6; Isa 26:9

3 All night long on my bed
    I looked[x] for the one my heart loves;
    I looked for him but did not find him.
[2] I will get up now and go about the city,
    through its streets and squares;
    I will search for the one my heart loves.
    So I looked for him but did not find him.

3:3
y SS 5:7

[3] The watchmen found me
    as they made their rounds in the city.[y]
    "Have you seen the one my heart loves?"
[4] Scarcely had I passed them
    when I found the one my heart loves.
    I held him and would not let him go

3:4
z SS 8:2 a SS 6:9

    till I had brought him to my mother's house,[z]
    to the room of the one who conceived me.[a]

3:5
b SS 2:7 c SS 8:4

[5] Daughters of Jerusalem, I charge you[b]
    by the gazelles and by the does of the field:
    Do not arouse or awaken love
    until it so desires.[c]

3:6
d SS 8:5 e SS 1:13; 4:6,14 f Ex 30:34

[6] Who is this coming up from the desert[d]
    like a column of smoke,
    perfumed with myrrh[e] and incense
    made from all the spices[f] of the merchant?

3:7
g 1Sa 8:11

[7] Look! It is Solomon's carriage,
    escorted by sixty warriors,[g]
    the noblest of Israel,
[8] all of them wearing the sword,
    all experienced in battle,
    each with his sword at his side,

3:8
h Job 15:22; Ps 91:5

    prepared for the terrors of the night.[h]
[9] King Solomon made for himself the carriage;
    he made it of wood from Lebanon.
[10] Its posts he made of silver,
    its base of gold.
    Its seat was upholstered with purple,
    its interior lovingly inlaid

3:11
i Isa 4:4 j Isa 62:5

    by[a] the daughters of Jerusalem.
[11] Come out, you daughters of Zion,[i]
    and look at King Solomon wearing the crown,
    the crown with which his mother crowned him
    on the day of his wedding,
    the day his heart rejoiced.[j]

---

[a] 10 Or *its inlaid interior a gift of love / from*

---

consummate their marriage. Once again, the charge to restraint to the "daughters of Jerusalem" occurs at the moment of intimacy (v. 5; cf. 2:7; 8:4).

Verses 6–11 are among the most intriguing in the Song. They obviously refer to a wedding procession. It's easy to see why many commentators assume that the groom was Solomon. But others believe he was a commoner—a "King Solomon for a day." (See "There and Then" for 1:1–4a.) Verse 11 refers to the "crown," or wreath, Solomon's mother placed on his head on his wedding day, not that of his coronation. This may suggest that, if Solomon was the "lover" of the Song, it originated before he was crowned king—in his younger years

before he married numerous wives and his heart strayed from the Lord.

We may have little or no control over our dreams, but the same can't be said about our fantasies. Modern technology offers a barrage of dangerous "little foxes" (see notes for 2:14–15), such as Internet pornography and chat rooms and "adult" cable TV programming. Sexual expression, when not rooted in a committed, lifelong relationship, wreaks destruction. What are you doing to safeguard your thought life? Jesus challenged his disciples with a higher standard: If one person looks at another lustfully, adultery has been committed (Matt. 5:28).

Lover

4

How beautiful you are, my darling!
  Oh, how beautiful!
  Your eyes behind your veil are doves. *k*
Your hair is like a flock of goats
  descending from Mount Gilead. *l*
² Your teeth are like a flock of sheep just shorn,
  coming up from the washing.
Each has its twin;
  not one of them is alone. *m*
³ Your lips are like a scarlet ribbon;
  your mouth *n* is lovely.
Your temples behind your veil
  are like the halves of a pomegranate. *o*
⁴ Your neck is like the tower *p* of David,
  built with elegance ª;
on it hang a thousand shields, *q*
  all of them shields of warriors.
⁵ Your two breasts *r* are like two fawns,
  like twin fawns of a gazelle *s*
  that browse among the lilies. *t*
⁶ Until the day breaks
  and the shadows flee, *u*
I will go to the mountain of myrrh *v*
  and to the hill of incense.
⁷ All beautiful *w* you are, my darling;
  there is no flaw in you.

⁸ Come with me from Lebanon, my bride, *x*
  come with me from Lebanon.
Descend from the crest of Amana,
  from the top of Senir, *y* the summit of Hermon, *z*
from the lions' dens
  and the mountain haunts of the leopards.
⁹ You have stolen my heart, my sister, my bride;
  you have stolen my heart
with one glance of your eyes,
  with one jewel of your necklace. *a*
¹⁰ How delightful *b* is your love *c*, my sister, my bride!
  How much more pleasing is your love than wine,
  and the fragrance of your perfume than any spice!
¹¹ Your lips drop sweetness as the honeycomb, my bride;
  milk and honey are under your tongue. *d*
  The fragrance of your garments is like that of Lebanon. *e*
¹² You are a garden locked up, my sister, my bride;

ª 4 The meaning of the Hebrew for this word is uncertain.

4:1
k SS 1:15; 5:12
l SS 6:5; Mic 7:14

4:2
m SS 6:6

4:3
n SS 5:16 *o* SS 6:7

4:4
p SS 7:4
q Eze 27:10

4:5
r SS 7:3 *s* Pr 5:19
t SS 2:16; 6:2-3

4:6
u SS 2:17 *v* ver 14

4:7
w SS 1:15

4:8
x SS 5:1 *y* Dt 3:9
z 1Ch 5:23

4:9
a Ge 41:42
4:10
b SS 7:6 *c* SS 1:2

4:11
d Ps 19:10; SS 5:1
e Hos 14:6

Song of Songs 4:1–15

With the wedding, the time for consummation of the relationship had arrived. With exhilarated anticipation, the bridegroom described his beloved's beauty through the use of metaphors that may seem strange to us. But even so, the power of this love poetry is moving. The man began calling the woman his "bride" for the first time in the Song. He also called her his "sister," a common term of endearment in the love poetry of the ancient Near East. In verse 12, the lover was likely describing his bride and her virginity on their wedding night.

Virginity has gotten a bad reputation in our time, even being perceived as a "disgrace" in some youthful circles. Song of Songs helps us see virginity as a sacred gift—a "garden locked up" or a "sealed fountain." These images convey both the value of chastity that "waits" and its power when unleashed at the proper time. Is your church (and you, if you are a parent) doing a good job of holding up and affirming virginity before your children and young people? If you are not married, how has the perception of friends affected your view of this sacred gift?

1061

4:12
f Pr 5:15-18
4:13
g SS 6:11; 7:12
h SS 1:14

4:14
i Ex 30:23 / SS 3:6
k SS 1:12

4:16
l SS 2:3; 5:1

5:1
m SS 4:8 n SS 4:11;
Isa 55:1

5:2
o SS 4:7 p SS 6:9

you are a spring enclosed, a sealed fountain. f

13 Your plants are an orchard of pomegranates g
   with choice fruits,
   with henna h and nard,
14   nard and saffron,
   calamus and cinnamon, i
   with every kind of incense tree,
   with myrrh j and aloes
   and all the finest spices. k
15 You are a a garden fountain,
   a well of flowing water
   streaming down from Lebanon.

Beloved

16 Awake, north wind,
   and come, south wind!
Blow on my garden,
   that its fragrance may spread abroad.
Let my lover come into his garden
   and taste its choice fruits. l

Lover

5 I have come into my garden, my sister, my bride; m
   I have gathered my myrrh with my spice.
I have eaten my honeycomb and my honey;
   I have drunk my wine and my milk. n

Friends

Eat, O friends, and drink;
   drink your fill, O lovers.

Beloved

2 I slept but my heart was awake.
   Listen! My lover is knocking:
"Open to me, my sister, my darling,
   my dove, my flawless o one. p
My head is drenched with dew,
   my hair with the dampness of the night."
3 I have taken off my robe—

a 15 Or *I am* (spoken by the *Beloved*)

Song of Songs 4:16—5:1

The consummation of the marriage is wonderfully portrayed here. The new wife showed no hesitancy or fear but welcomed her husband's approach—hoping the wind would blow on her garden and send its fragrance to draw him. He entered the garden and consumed its delights. Meanwhile, the "Friends" encouraged the couple to "eat" and "drink" to their hearts' content. During the weeklong wedding feasts, the guests celebrated the consummated union.

When a man and woman give themselves to each other as these two did, the relationship of each changes toward all the rest of the human race. That is why traditionally in our culture a wedding can't be performed without witnesses who represent the broader society. The woman now belongs to the man and the man to the woman. This changes all other personal

relationships. Self-giving love between a man and a woman is of social significance. How else can marriage be a witness and testimony to the relationship between Christ and the church (Eph. 5:31–32)?

Song of Songs 5:2–8

Chapter 4 is bracketed between two dreams about loss and desire (3:1–5; 5:2–8). The ecstasy of the preceding section is replaced by deep apprehension. The beloved dreamed that her lover came for her. But she was slow to acknowledge his overture. Her hesitancy reflects a paralysis we often experience both in dreams and in real life. She finally rose to open the door to him, but he had misunderstood and left. Sick now with longing for him, she urged her friends to tell him, should they see him, that she was lovesick. Absence, not presence, was the reality. Longing, not fulfillment, is the theme.

must I put it on again?
I have washed my feet—
    must I soil them again?
4 My lover thrust his hand through the latch-opening;
    my heart began to pound for him.
5 I arose to open for my lover,
    and my hands dripped with myrrh, q
my fingers with flowing myrrh,
    on the handles of the lock.
6 I opened for my lover, r
    but my lover had left; he was gone. s
My heart sank at his departure. a
I looked t for him but did not find him.
    I called him but he did not answer.
7 The watchmen found me
    as they made their rounds in the city. u
They beat me, they bruised me;
    they took away my cloak,
    those watchmen of the walls!
8 O daughters of Jerusalem, I charge you v—
    if you find my lover,
what will you tell him?
    Tell him I am faint with love. w

Friends

9 How is your beloved better than others,
    most beautiful of women? x
How is your beloved better than others,
    that you charge us so?

Beloved

10 My lover is radiant and ruddy,
    outstanding among ten thousand. y
11 His head is purest gold;
    his hair is wavy
    and black as a raven.
12 His eyes are like doves z
    by the water streams,
washed in milk, a
    mounted like jewels.

a 6 Or *heart had gone out to him when he spoke*

5:5
q ver 13

5:6
r SS 6:1 s SS 6:2
t SS 3:1

5:7
u SS 3:3

5:8
v SS 2:7; 3:5
w SS 2:5

5:9
x SS 1:8; 6:1

5:10
y Ps 45:2

5:12
z SS 1:15; 4:1
a Ge 49:12

📖 We can all relate at one level or another to the frustration and anxiety in this passage. It's no different in our relationship with God. He invites us, his creatures, to move beyond mere acquaintance to *know* him. Like the lover who stands at his beloved's door, Christ stands and knocks (Rev. 3:20). But there is no guarantee of a happy outcome. We are responsible to hear and open the door to the relationship. Do you see this as a one-time commitment or as a repeated welcoming? Can you recall a time when you rebuffed the Lord's call? What was his response?

Song of Songs 5:9–16

👫 This is one of only a few poems that have come down to us from the ancient world in which the female gives an inventory of the male's features. It appears to have been her response to his description of her in 4:1–7. Her description witnesses to the uniqueness of this little book in its world: It illustrates in its own way the equality of position and freedom she enjoyed. You might want to take a moment to reread Genesis 2:18–25. How is the perspective similar?

📖 The Song is unabashedly sensual. Yet it's never content with the physical alone. A normal person finds the erotic ultimately meaningful only if there is also trust and commitment, delight in the other's person as well as body. The writer of the Song understood this. Our hero is the woman's lover, but he's more: He's her "friend" (v. 16) and "brother" (see 4:9,10,12). If you are married, how important a role does friendship play in your relationship? How about your mutual commitment to God as members of his family? Is God in a real way a party to your marital intimacy?

5:13
b SS 1:10 c SS 6:2
d SS 2:1

13 His cheeks [b] are like beds of spice [c]
  yielding perfume.
His lips are like lilies [d]
  dripping with myrrh.
14 His arms are rods of gold
  set with chrysolite.

5:14
e Job 28:6

His body is like polished ivory
  decorated with sapphires. [a][e]
15 His legs are pillars of marble
  set on bases of pure gold.

5:15
f 1Ki 4:33; SS 7:4

His appearance is like Lebanon, [f]
  choice as its cedars.

5:16
g SS 4:3 h SS 7:9
i SS 1:5

16 His mouth [g] is sweetness itself;
  he is altogether lovely.
This is my lover, [h] this my friend,
  O daughters of Jerusalem. [i]

Friends

6:1
j SS 5:6 k SS 1:8

6

Where has your lover [j] gone,
  most beautiful of women? [k]
Which way did your lover turn,
  that we may look for him with you?

Beloved

6:2
l SS 5:6 m SS 4:12
n SS 5:13

2 My lover has gone [l] down to his garden, [m]
  to the beds of spices, [n]
to browse in the gardens
  and to gather lilies.

6:3
o SS 7:10 p SS 2:16

3 I am my lover's and my lover is mine; [o]
  he browses among the lilies. [p]

Lover

6:4
q Jos 12:24
r Ps 48:2; 50:2
s ver 10

4 You are beautiful, my darling, as Tirzah, [q]
  lovely as Jerusalem, [r]
  majestic as troops with banners. [s]
5 Turn your eyes from me;
  they overwhelm me.

6:5
t SS 4:1

Your hair is like a flock of goats
  descending from Gilead. [t]
6 Your teeth are like a flock of sheep
  coming up from the washing.

a 14 Or lapis lazuli

Song of Songs 6:1–10

The young wife's fears, expressed in 5:2–8, had been groundless. She now knew exactly where her lover was—in his own garden, that "place" where he had become accustomed to spending his time. First the lover, and then the "friends," praised her beauty and charm. Tirzah was chosen by Jeroboam I as the first capital of the northern kingdom. Its name, which means "pleasure" or "beauty," suggests that—like Jerusalem—it was a beautiful city. Comparing the beloved's beauty to that of a city wasn't surprising, since cities were regularly depicted as women.

If Solomon wrote this poem, verse 8 may indicate that he did so when he was relatively young—before he acquired 700 wives and 300 concubines (1 Kings 11:3). But if the "lover" was a commoner, he was simply boasting that his bride was more impressive than a royal harem and virgins without number. (See "There and Then" for 2:16—3:11.)

Physical love expressed with integrity calls us to acceptance, respect, intimacy, and constant recognition of the other—the one who honors us not because he or she has no choice but out of self-giving, committed love. It calls us to make courtship an ongoing feature of our marriages, not just a prelude to them. This kind of love constantly pushes beyond the legal institution of marriage to its heart, recognizing that divine love is revealed in the reality of human love.

Each has its twin,
not one of them is alone. ^u
⁷ Your temples behind your veil ^v
are like the halves of a pomegranate. ^w
⁸ Sixty queens ^x there may be,
and eighty concubines, ^y
and virgins beyond number;
⁹ but my dove, ^z my perfect one, ^a is unique,
the only daughter of her mother,
the favorite of the one who bore her. ^b
The maidens saw her and called her blessed;
the queens and concubines praised her.

Friends

¹⁰ Who is this that appears like the dawn,
fair as the moon, bright as the sun,
majestic as the stars in procession?

Lover

¹¹ I went down to the grove of nut trees
to look at the new growth in the valley,
to see if the vines had budded
or the pomegranates were in bloom. ^c
¹² Before I realized it,
my desire set me among the royal chariots of my people. ^a

Friends

¹³ Come back, come back, O Shulammite;
come back, come back, that we may gaze on you!

Lover

Why would you gaze on the Shulammite
as on the dance ^d of Mahanaim?

7 How beautiful your sandaled feet,
O prince's ^e daughter!
Your graceful legs are like jewels,
the work of a craftsman's hands.
² Your navel is a rounded goblet
that never lacks blended wine.
Your waist is a mound of wheat
encircled by lilies.
³ Your breasts ^f are like two fawns,
twins of a gazelle.

6:6
u SS 4:2
6:7
v Ge 24:65 w SS 4:3
6:8
x Ps 45:9
y Ge 22:24
6:9
z SS 1:15 a SS 5:2
b SS 3:4

6:11
c SS 7:12

6:13
d Ex 15:20

7:1
e Ps 45:13

7:3
f SS 4:5

---

^a 12 Or *among the chariots of Amminadab; or among the chariots of the people of the prince*

Song of Songs 6:11—7:9a

📖 The last part of chapter 6 is quite difficult to interpret—in terms of translation, vocabulary, and identifying the speaker. "Shulammite" is probably either a variant of "Shunammite" (cf. 1 Kings 1:3)—that is, a young woman from Shunem (cf. Josh. 19:18)—or a feminine form of "Solomon," meaning "Solomon's girl."

The groom's description of his bride moves up from the feet rather than down from the head (cf. 4:1–7; 5:10–16). This is the fullest detailing of her physical features in the Song, reflecting the perpetual charm of the female form to the male. Even the beloved's feet were considered beautiful!

💻 We shouldn't miss the element of near-adoration in the lover's depiction of his beloved nor be unmindful of the high value placed on the human body in Scripture. Our bodies aren't unworthy shells to be shucked in death. Rather, they are destined for resurrection (1 Cor. 15). The physical body may be the vehicle for sin, but it can also be the very clothing of deity, as in the incarnation of our Lord Jesus Christ. Take a moment to thank God for the gift of your body—and, if you are married, for that of your spouse.

7:4
g Ps 144:12; SS 4:4
h Nu 21:26
i SS 5:15

4 Your neck is like an ivory tower. [g]
   Your eyes are the pools of Heshbon [h]
      by the gate of Bath Rabbim.
   Your nose is like the tower of Lebanon [i]
      looking toward Damascus.

7:5
j Isa 35:2

5 Your head crowns you like Mount Carmel. [j]
   Your hair is like royal tapestry;
      the king is held captive by its tresses.

7:6
k SS 1:15 l SS 4:10

6 How beautiful [k] you are and how pleasing,
   O love, with your delights! [l]

7:7
m SS 4:5

7 Your stature is like that of the palm,
   and your breasts [m] like clusters of fruit.
8 I said, "I will climb the palm tree;
   I will take hold of its fruit."

7:8
n SS 2:5

May your breasts be like the clusters of the vine,
   the fragrance of your breath like apples, [n]
9   and your mouth like the best wine.

7:9
o SS 5:16

Beloved

May the wine go straight to my lover, [o]
   flowing gently over lips and teeth. [a]

7:10
p Ps 45:11
q SS 2:16; 6:3

10 I belong to my lover,
   and his desire [p] is for me. [q]
11 Come, my lover, let us go to the countryside,
   let us spend the night in the villages. [b]

7:12
r SS 1:6 s SS 2:15
t SS 2:13 u SS 4:13
v SS 6:11

12 Let us go early to the vineyards [r]
   to see if the vines have budded, [s]
if their blossoms [t] have opened,
   and if the pomegranates [u] are in bloom [v]—
      there I will give you my love.

7:13
w Ge 30:14
x SS 4:16

13 The mandrakes [w] send out their fragrance,
   and at our door is every delicacy,
both new and old,
   that I have stored up for you, my lover. [x]

8 If only you were to me like a brother,
   who was nursed at my mother's breasts!
Then, if I found you outside,
   I would kiss you,
   and no one would despise me.

8:2
y SS 3:4

2 I would lead you
   and bring you to my mother's house [y]—
      she who has taught me.
I would give you spiced wine to drink,

---

a 9 Septuagint, Aquila, Vulgate and Syriac; Hebrew *lips of sleepers*   b 11 Or *henna bushes*

Song of Songs 7:9b—8:4

The bride responded to her husband's romantic words. There was no holding back: She belonged to him and freely gave him the wine of her love. She was anxious to go and offer herself to him in the countryside. The mandrake plant, with its pungent blossoms and forked roots resembling the lower part of a human body, was associated with the ability to arouse sexual desire and *increase fertility* (cf. Gen. 30:9–18).

The beloved was frustrated by the cultural standard that allowed family members to show public affection but forbade married couples from doing so. That thought evidently led her to envision taking her lover to the place of her own conception and giving herself to him there.

Our fallen world and fallen nature emphasize receiving over giving, especially when it comes to sexual pleasure and fulfillment. That doesn't have to be the case. Just in this one section of Song of Songs, we hear the beloved repeatedly voicing her longing to give herself to her partner. Of course the enjoyment is mutual, but what percentage of your motivation in a relationship (and if you are married, especially in your sex life) is to *give* rather than to *receive*?

the nectar of my pomegranates.
3 His left arm is under my head
  and his right arm embraces me. z

8:3
z SS 2:6

4 Daughters of Jerusalem, I charge you:
  Do not arouse or awaken love
    until it so desires. a

8:4
a SS 2:7; 3:5

Friends

5 Who is this coming up from the desert b
  leaning on her lover?

8:5
b SS 3:6 c SS 3:4

Beloved

Under the apple tree I roused you;
  there your mother conceived c you,
  there she who was in labor gave you birth.
6 Place me like a seal over your heart,
  like a seal on your arm;
  for love d is as strong as death,
    its jealousy a e unyielding as the grave. b
  It burns like blazing fire,
    like a mighty flame. c

8:6
d SS 1:2 e Nu 5:14

7 Many waters cannot quench love;
  rivers cannot wash it away.
  If one were to give
    all the wealth of his house for love,
    it d would be utterly scorned. f

8:7
f Pr 6:35

Friends

8 We have a young sister,
  and her breasts are not yet grown.
  What shall we do for our sister
    for the day she is spoken for?
9 If she is a wall,
  we will build towers of silver on her.
  If she is a door,
  we will enclose her with panels of cedar.

Beloved

10 I am a wall,
  and my breasts are like towers.
  Thus I have become in his eyes

a 6 Or *ardor*   b 6 Hebrew *Sheol*   c 6 Or / *like the very flame of the* LORD   d 7 Or *he*

Song of Songs 8:5–7

Rather than the beloved taking her husband to her mother's home where she was conceived (3:4; 8:2), he apparently took her to the site of *his* conception. There they sealed more deeply their love, and in verses 6–7 she spoke of the depth of that sealing. With these powerful statements the Song reaches its literary climax. Marital love is characterized as the strongest, most invincible, and most valuable force in human experience.

The Biblical story, as it moves from creation through human rebellion and death (Gen. 1–3; see especially 2:17) on toward redemption and renewal, makes sense of the "hopelessly optimistic" statement in verse 6 that "love is as strong as death." It even helps us see that

this statement isn't quite optimistic enough. The power of God's love is vastly greater than that of death—outlasting it by the distance of eternity. Have you truly experienced that power?

Song of Songs 8:8–14

Verses 8–9 were evidently spoken by the beloved's brothers. As brothers were often guardians of their sisters, especially in matters pertaining to marriage, they probably were recalling their determination to defend her until the proper time for love and marriage had come. In verse 10 she seemed to be looking back with joy that she had come to marriage as a virgin (a "wall"), as well as rejoicing in her maturity (symbolized by her developed breasts; cf. v. 8) that was now pleasing her husband.

like one bringing contentment.

8:11
g Ecc 2:4 h Isa 7:23

11 Solomon had a vineyard[g] in Baal Hamon;
he let out his vineyard to tenants.
Each was to bring for its fruit
a thousand shekels[a][h] of silver.

8:12
i SS 1:6

12 But my own vineyard[i] is mine to give;
the thousand shekels are for you, O Solomon,
and two hundred[b] are for those who tend its fruit.

Lover

13 You who dwell in the gardens
with friends in attendance,
let me hear your voice!

Beloved

8:14
j Pr 5:19 k SS 2:9
l SS 2:8,17

14 Come away, my lover,
and be like a gazelle[j]
or like a young stag[k]
on the spice-laden mountains.[l]

---

[a] 11 That is, about 25 pounds (about 11.5 kilograms); also in verse 12   [b] 12 That is, about 5 pounds (about 2.3 kilograms)

Assuming that Solomon was the "lover" of the Song (see "There and Then" for 1:1–4a), his bride was saying in verses 11–12 that as he was master of his (literal) vineyard, so she was mistress of her (symbolic) vineyard—and could share her charms as she chose. In her typical self-giving fashion (see notes for 7:9b—8:4), she offered Solomon the standard owner's portion (1,000 out of 1,200 shekels, or five sixths) of her "vineyard."

💻 The final two verses of the Song illustrate that while the lover and beloved couldn't be expected to always be in each other's presence (see also "There and Then" for 5:2–8), the love they shared hadn't diminished. Intimate union, in actuality, isn't the constant experience of men and women committed to each other in love and marriage. Nor is it the continuous experience of men and women committed to God, even though he's steadfastly faithful to them. The complete union of Christ and his church—as well as of Christ and individual believers—is a reality for the future (cf. Rev. 19:6–8). All human unions, in their mixture of intimacy and alienation, point toward and help us long for that glorious future.

The Relevance of Old Testament Prophets

What makes the Old Testament prophets relevant? How can their messages, spoken to ancient Israel more than 25 centuries ago, apply to contemporary culture? The remarkable freshness of these messages springs from several distinct characteristics:

- Their power to penetrate past the maze of appearances to identify the essential, underlying human or theological facts of a given circumstance or historical situation
- Their ability to define essential justice and essential religion amid moral confusion, secular influence, and human waywardness
- Their shrewd understanding of human nature and the human predicament as a result of their own suffering
- Their sensitivity to the urgent meaning of history as the sphere of humanity's moral decisions and of God's sovereign intervention
- Their knowledge of God as the fountainhead of ultimate meaning and purpose in the context of everyday life
- Their intuitive comprehension of the reality of God's presence in the inner world of their own hearts and spirits
- Their capacity to communicate concretely, in universal terms, and with both passion and conviction—to speak with divine authority by the power of God's Spirit as choice servants commissioned by God—unlike their rivals, who told "fortunes for money" (Mic. 3:8,11; cf. Amos 3:8)

How can the prophetic messages be applied?

Category	Issues	Scripture
• History	Sovereignty of God as the One who "sets up kings and deposes them"	Dan. 2:21
	God's redemptive purpose in history	Isa. 52:7; Jer. 51:29
• Social Order	Individual behavior matters—people are accountable for their deeds.	Jer. 11:4–5
	Social justice is rooted in the Mosaic covenant.	Amos 4:1; 5:11
• Religion	Essential religion is personal, communal, and covenantal.	Jer. 31:31–33
	Emphasis on knowing God and personal holiness	Isa. 29:23; 35:8
	Demanded a whole-person response of love and obedience in worship and in actions that promote social justice	Isa. 1:10–20; Amos 5:23–24; Mic. 6:6–8
• Theology	Knowledge of God as:	
	• an imminent and transcendent diety	Hos. 6:3; Isa. 57:15; 66:2
	• a consuming fire of holiness	Isa. 30:27
	• a refuge in his goodness	Nah. 1:7
	His revelation of himself:	
	• was rooted in historical reality.	Isa. 6:1
	• called people to spiritual warfare.	1 Kings 18
	• was a divine punishment for sin and mercy as a means of grace.	Isa. 54:7
• Preaching	Authority to preach	Jer. 2:5
	Message of repentance	Joel 2:12–13
	Medium of both word and images or example of a "living parable"	Jer. 13:1–11; Hos. 1–3
• Culture	"Contextualized" God's message by living and ministering to people within their cultural settings	1 Kings 17–18
• Politics	Sometimes called to "iconoclastic" ministry, focused on opposition to existing religious and political offices and institutions	Ezek. 2:5–8; Dan. 4:24–27; Hag. 2:1–3
	The "conscience" of the high priest and the king as they spoke against the exercise of social power without responsibility. Their message: Religion and government must serve the common good.	1 Sam. 12:1–14; Ezek. 22:6–12; Mic. 3:1–12

Taken from *NIV Application Commentary, 1 & 2 Chronicles* (2003:502–504), adapted by author from R.B.Y. Scott, *The Relevance of the Prophets* (New York: Macmillan, 1953)

INTRODUCTION TO

Isaiah

AUTHOR

The prophet Isaiah is identified as the book's author (1:1), and other Scripture passages concur (Matt. 12:17–21; John 12:38–41; Rom. 10:16,20–21).

DATE WRITTEN

The book of Isaiah was probably written between 700 and 680 B.C.

ORIGINAL READERS

Isaiah's primary ministry was to the people of Judah, who weren't living according to God's law. But he prophesied judgment upon Judah, Israel, and the surrounding nations. He also preached a message of repentance and salvation for those who would turn to God.

TIMELINE

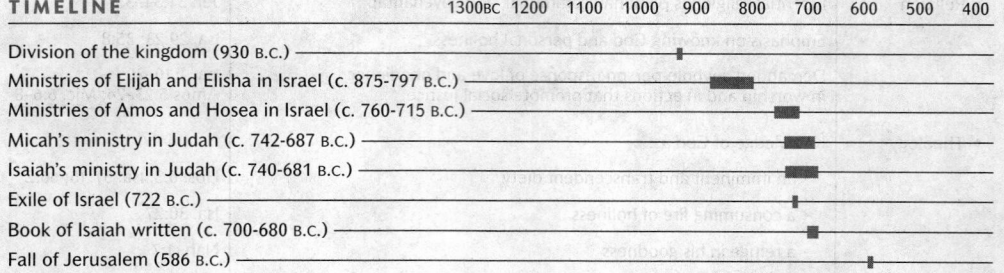

	1300BC	1200	1100	1000	900	800	700	600	500	400
Division of the kingdom (930 B.C.)										
Ministries of Elijah and Elisha in Israel (c. 875-797 B.C.)										
Ministries of Amos and Hosea in Israel (c. 760-715 B.C.)										
Micah's ministry in Judah (c. 742-687 B.C.)										
Isaiah's ministry in Judah (c. 740-681 B.C.)										
Exile of Israel (722 B.C.)										
Book of Isaiah written (c. 700-680 B.C.)										
Fall of Jerusalem (586 B.C.)										

THEMES

Isaiah describes God's judgment of sin as well as his forgiveness, comfort, and hope. Other than the Psalms, Isaiah contains the most Messianic prophecies of any Old Testament book. It includes the following themes:

1. *Judgment and salvation.* God is "the Holy One of Israel" (1:4), who is obligated by his very nature to punish his rebellious (1:2) and sinful (1:4) people. But after judgment, he will have compassion on them (14:1–2) and redeem them (41:14; 43:3; 49:8). His rescue of his own is compared to the exodus (43:2,16–19; 52:10–12). The theme of a highway for the returning exiles also is prominent (11:16; 40:3).

2. *God as King.* Isaiah pictures God as the sovereign King. This divine ruler is characterized by justice, righteousness, and holiness (5:16). He calls his people to do right and seek justice (1:17) and stands against those who take advantage of the poor (5:8–10) and undermine justice (1:21).

3. *The suffering servant.* Isaiah contains four "servant songs" (42:1–9; 49:1–7; 50:4–9; 52:13—53:12) that describe the coming King. This Messianic King is called "my servant" in chapters 42–53, a term also applied to Cyrus (45:1–4), God's prophets (44:26), and Israel as a nation (41:8–9; 42:19; 44:1–2,21; 45:4; 48:20). The suffering servant would bring justice (42:1–4; 51:4)

and salvation—not just for Israel (42:1–17; 43:1–7,14–21; 44:21–23), but for the Gentiles as well (42:6; 55:4–5; 53:5–12; 61:1–2). The New Testament identifies this servant as Jesus Christ (Matt. 12:18–21; Luke 4:20–21).

FAITH IN ACTION

The pages of Isaiah contain life lessons and role models of faith—people who challenge believers to put their faith in action.

Role Models

• ISAIAH (6:1–8) humbly accepted God's call to serve him. Have you discovered, acceded to, and complied with God's call on and purposes for your life?

• HEZEKIAH (37:14–20) turned to God during a crisis, trusting God to direct him and rescue his people. To whom do you turn when you are in crisis mode?

• URIAH THE PRIEST AND ZECHARIAH (8:2) were reliable witnesses concerning one of Isaiah's prophecies. Are you a witness of God's work in the world (cf. Acts 1:8)?

• A PROPHETESS (8:3) was married to Isaiah. Do you acknowledge and openly recognize the gifted women in your life?

Challenges

• Accept God's call to be his ambassador in the world, understanding that not everyone who hears the Good News will accept it (6:9–10).

• Don't ignore God's direction when it's given (7:11–12).

• Take a stand against injustice of all kinds, oppression of the poor, and exploitation of the vulnerable (10:1–2; 58:6; 59:8–14). Share what you have with the needy and demoralized (58:7,10).

• Let the truth of God's judgment on sin (14:26–27; 24:1–3) inspire you to spread the Good News of Christ to everyone with whom you come in contact—before it's too late.

• Remember God (17:10–11), acknowledging that all your plans and successes will come to nothing without him (19:3–15).

• Examine your life and worship for evidences of hypocrisy (29:13). Does your life reflect your faith? Does your worship of God come from the heart?

• As one who represents the interests of God, be sure to care for the lambs (children) and protect those who are carrying young (40:11).

• Wait on the Lord for strength (40:29–31). In times of fear, rely on him to see you through (41:10–13); he will never leave you undefended (43:1–2).

• Acknowledge and even list the "idols" you have adopted or made (44:6–23). Repent and return to the Lord.

• Become a messenger of peace (52:7) by proclaiming salvation and freedom in Christ (57:15–19; 61:1–3).

OUTLINE

   I. Messages of Rebuke and Promise (1–6)
  II. Immanuel and His Kingdom (7–12)
 III. God's Judgment Against the Nations (13–23)
 IV. Judgment and Promise (24–27)
  V. Five Woes on Unfaithful Israel and One on Assyria (28–33)
 VI. More Judgment and Promise (34–35)
VII. Transition From Assyrian Threat to Babylonian Exile (36–39)
VIII. Deliverance and Restoration of Israel (40–48)
 IX. The Servant's Ministry and Israel's Restoration (49–57)
  X. Everlasting Deliverance and Judgment (58–66)

1:1
a Nu 12:6
b Isa 40:9 c Isa 2:1
d 2Ch 26:22
e 2Ki 16:1

1 The vision[a] concerning Judah and Jerusalem[b] that Isaiah son of Amoz saw[c] during the reigns of Uzziah,[d] Jotham, Ahaz[e] and Hezekiah, kings of Judah.

A Rebellious Nation

1:2
f Mic 1:2
g Isa 30:1,9; 65:2

2 Hear, O heavens! Listen, O earth!
    For the LORD has spoken:[f]
"I reared children and brought them up,
    but they have rebelled[g] against me.

1:3
h Jer 8:7; 9:3,6

3 The ox knows his master,
    the donkey his owner's manger,
but Israel does not know,[h]
    my people do not understand."

1:4
i Isa 14:20
j Isa 5:19,24

4 Ah, sinful nation,
    a people loaded with guilt,
a brood of evildoers,[i]
    children given to corruption!
They have forsaken the LORD;
    they have spurned the Holy One[j] of Israel
    and turned their backs on him.

1:5
k Isa 31:6
l Isa 33:6,24

5 Why should you be beaten anymore?
    Why do you persist in rebellion?[k]
Your whole head is injured,
    your whole heart afflicted.[l]

1:6
m Ps 38:3
n Isa 30:26;
Jer 8:22 o Lk 10:34

6 From the sole of your foot to the top of your head
    there is no soundness[m]—
only wounds and welts
    and open sores,
not cleansed or bandaged[n]
    or soothed with oil.[o]

1:7
p Lev 26:34

7 Your country is desolate,[p]
    your cities burned with fire;
your fields are being stripped by foreigners
    right before you,
    laid waste as when overthrown by strangers.
8 The Daughter of Zion is left
    like a shelter in a vineyard,

Isaiah 1:1

The dates of the four kings mentioned extend from approximately 790 to 690 B.C., but chapter 6 makes it plain that Isaiah's ministry began in the last year of King Uzziah, about 740 B.C. Isaiah mentioned only the kings of the southern kingdom of Judah because he ministered primarily to Judah.

Over the years Isaiah has come to be known as "the prince of the prophets." There is majesty in the book, with its theological sweep, towering vision, and powerful language, that sets it off from almost any other in the Bible. In many ways the book of Isaiah represents the Bible in miniature: All its main themes can be found here. Like the Bible as a whole, it has two major divisions: the first part about judgment (chs. 1–39) and the second about hope (chs. 40–66).

In our busy world, we like to get to the point quickly. While it will give you the big picture from God's perspective, Isaiah isn't an abridged classic. It's so complete that the prophet described the suffering of

the coming Messiah with stunning clarity (cf. 52:13—53:12), a point the disciples and religious leaders in Jesus' time missed entirely. So, before you grab the headlines and move on, remember that there is rich material here for those who apply themselves to study the text carefully.

Isaiah 1:2–31

Rebellion and corruption, Isaiah charged, had resulted in desolation in Judah. It was only because of God's mercy that the land continued to exist at all. Just as a critically wounded body will die if left untended, so rebellion against the Creator of the universe will result in spiritual corruption and death.

The covenant in which the sacrificial laws appear also requires ethical treatment of neighbors. God's people can't persist in evil deeds and expect ritual to deliver them from the consequences. God wants right and just behavior, especially toward those who are helpless to demand it on their own behalf, such as the oppressed, the fatherless, and widows (vv. 17,23).

like a hut[q] in a field of melons,
   like a city under siege.
⁹Unless the LORD Almighty
   had left us some survivors,[r]
we would have become like Sodom,
   we would have been like Gomorrah.[s]

¹⁰Hear the word of the LORD,[t]
   you rulers of Sodom;[u]
listen to the law[v] of our God,
   you people of Gomorrah!
¹¹"The multitude of your sacrifices—
   what are they to me?" says the LORD.
"I have more than enough of burnt offerings,
   of rams and the fat of fattened animals;[w]
I have no pleasure
   in the blood of bulls[x] and lambs and goats.[y]
¹²When you come to appear before me,
   who has asked this of you,[z]
   this trampling of my courts?
¹³Stop bringing meaningless offerings![a]
   Your incense[b] is detestable to me.
New Moons, Sabbaths and convocations[c]—
   I cannot bear your evil assemblies.
¹⁴Your New Moon festivals and your appointed feasts[d]
   my soul hates.
They have become a burden to me;
   I am weary[e] of bearing them.
¹⁵When you spread out your hands in prayer,
   I will hide[f] my eyes from you;
even if you offer many prayers,
   I will not listen.
Your hands are full of blood;[g]

¹⁶   wash and make yourselves clean.
Take your evil deeds
   out of my sight![h]
Stop doing wrong,[i]
¹⁷   learn to do right!
Seek justice,[j]

1:8
q Job 27:18

1:9
r Isa 10:20-22;
37:4,31-32
s Ge 19:24;
Ro 9:29*

1:10
t Isa 28:14 u Isa 3:9;
Eze 16:49; Ro 9:29;
Rev 11:8 v Isa 8:20

1:11
w Ps 50:8 x Jer 6:20
y 1Sa 15:22;
Mal 1:10

1:12
z Ex 23:17

1:13
a Isa 66:3 b Jer 7:9
c 1Ch 23:31

1:14
d Lev 23:1-44;
Nu 28:11-29:39;
Isa 29:1 e Isa 7:13;
43:22,24

1:15
f Isa 8:17; 59:2;
Mic 3:4 g Isa 59:3

1:16
h Isa 52:11
i Isa 55:7; Jer 25:5

1:17
j Zep 2:3

1:16-17

The Geneva Conventions

The Geneva Conventions are four international treaties governing the protection of civilians in time of war (1949), the treatment of prisoners of war (1929; amended 1949), and the care of the wounded and sick in the armed forces (1864; amended 1906). The fourth convention (1949) codified general principles of international law governing the treatment of civilians in wartime.

	1860	1880	1900	1920	1940	1960
1 PROTECTION OF CIVILIANS						• 1949
2 TREATMENT OF POWS				• 1929		• 1949 (amended)
3 CARE OF WOUNDED SOLDIERS	• 1864		• 1906 (amended)			
4 SAFEGUARDS FOR CIVILIANS						• 1949

The 1949 convention for civilians provided special safeguards for wounded persons, children under fifteen, pregnant women, and the elderly. Discrimination is forbidden on racial, religious, national, or political grounds. Torture, collective punishment, unwarranted destruction of property, and forcible use of civilians for military purposes are forbidden. The following points are pertinent:

• Most countries have signed the conventions.
• A nation isn't free to withdraw from the conventions in wartime.
• There is no permanent machinery in place to apprehend, try, or punish violators.

Source: World Almanac and Book of Facts 2003 (2003:864)

Isaiah, Which Will It Be?

The first chapter of Isaiah is like a preamble. In one short chapter Isaiah painted the problem God had with Israel. But it's a confusing preamble, interspersing worship with social justice. What's the bottom line? Right worship or just behavior?

In verses two through four, God clarified his problem with Israel, announcing to the heavens that his children had rebelled against him. They had forsaken their Lord, spurned him, and turned their backs on him. Israel had forgotten who she was and to whom she belonged. And the evidence of her identity crisis was in her worship, which God declared to be empty and meaningless (v. 13).

God's confirmation of this assessment? Their rulers "do not defend the cause of the fatherless; the widow's case does not come before them" (v. 23). Interesting. The test of right worship seems to have been the way the least among them were treated.

Chapter 2 varies the theme against the nation as a whole: "They are full of superstitions from the East; they practice divination like the Philistines and clasp hands with pagans" (2:6). And "Their land is full of idols" (v. 8). So we are back on the theme of right worship. God's reaction to this illegitimate worship would be judgment.

Yet when God brought judgment, his verdict never mentioned worship or idols: "What do you mean by crushing my people and grinding the faces of the poor?" (3:15). Once again, God justified his judgment for unfaithful worship on the basis of lack of justice and its impact on the poor.

> Isaiah wasn't the only prophet to move seamlessly and effortlessly from right worship to social justice and vice versa.

This apparent contradiction continues throughout Isaiah. Isaiah 58 addresses the issue of fasting: "Is not this the kind of fasting I have chosen: to loose the chains of injustice and untie the cords of the yoke, to set the oppressed free and break every yoke? Is it not to share your food with the hungry and to provide the poor wanderer with shelter—when you see the naked, to clothe him, and not to turn away from your own flesh and blood?" (58:6–7).

Isaiah wasn't the only prophet to move seamlessly and effortlessly from right worship to social justice and vice versa. Ezekiel echoed the theme: "Men accept bribes to shed blood; you take usury and excessive interest and make unjust gain from your neighbors by extortion. And you have forgotten me, declares the Sovereign LORD" (Ezek. 22:12).

So which is it? True worship or just social practice? Were God's prophets confused? Or might we be the ones who fail to get it? Jesus gave the answer, and it's really pretty simple. When asked about the requirements for inheriting eternal life, he replied with "the greatest commandment": "Love the Lord your God" and "your neighbor as yourself" (Luke 10:27).

This is one mandate, not two. It's a directive about our relationships, about who we are to love, not just what we are to believe or even do. Loving God and loving other people are inseparable sides of the same coin. When we attempt to do one and avoid the other, we fall into the same error Israel did. Our worship becomes empty. At the end of the day, how we treat the poor is a measure of who we truly worship.

Bryant L. Myers, vice president of World Vision International in Monrovia, California

    encourage the oppressed. [a]
Defend the cause of the fatherless, [k]
    plead the case of the widow.

18 "Come now, let us reason together," [l]
    says the LORD.
"Though your sins are like scarlet,
    they shall be as white as snow; [m]
though they are red as crimson,
    they shall be like wool.
19 If you are willing and obedient,
    you will eat the best from the land; [n]
20 but if you resist and rebel,
    you will be devoured by the sword." [o]
        For the mouth of the LORD has spoken. [p]

21 See how the faithful city
    has become a harlot! [q]
She once was full of justice;
    righteousness used to dwell in her—
    but now murderers!

[a] 17 Or / rebuke the oppressor

1:17
[k] Ps 82:3
1:18
[l] Isa 41:1; 43:9,26
[m] Ps 51:7; Rev 7:14

1:19
[n] Dt 30:15-16;
Isa 55:2
1:20
[o] Isa 3:25; 65:12
[p] Isa 34:16; 40:5;
58:14; Mic 4:4

1:21
[q] Isa 57:3-9;
Jer 2:20

 We live in a society with deep-seated, pervasive, and vocal hostility to spiritual norms. A good reminder is that the same Holy One who created the law of justice also ordained the law of gravity. Both describe the way he designed our world to function, and ignoring either puts us in peril. Our religious activities are intended to symbolize deeper realities. Like Isaiah's audience, we can do all the right "religious" things, yet live in self-centered rebellion.

With few exceptions, the last decades haven't seen the church adequately addressing the great issues of today—like the HIV/AIDS crisis. What should our attitude be? Isaiah would counsel us to look inward at our own lives and outward at a lost and broken world. Once we have allowed the Holy Spirit to purify us, we can gain life by losing ourselves in service to others.

Snapshots

1:17

Varsenik

"Is this all for me?" Eighty-two-year-old Varsenik opens a plastic bag filled with clothing. Varsenik is one of 800 people in Armenia's Tavush region who have become involved in an elderly care project. Some have no one to look after them, while others care for disabled children or orphaned grandchildren. They survive on a small government pension—sometimes insufficient for bills or firewood.

It's been a long time since "Grandma Varsenik" has received a present. Unable to curb her emotions, she cries and laughs simultaneously, endlessly thanking the caregiver.

Last year Varsenik's daughter, Lusine, brought her to Ijevan to live with herself and her own daughter, Naira. Lusine can offer only her love and a bed in an old container perched on a hillside. Also widowed, she's unemployed. She keeps a few hens and chickens and grows vegetables on a tiny plot. The container boasts neither water nor bathroom; the old metal basin in the yard serves as a sink.

"When my husband passed away, I felt so lonely and insecure," muses Grandma Varsenik. "Now I am happy, I know that there are people who care about me. May I sing a song for you?" Her voice tremulous, she croons an old Armenian folk song about love and happiness.

> "**N**ow I am happy, I know that there are people who care about me."

1:23
r Ex 23:8 s Isa 10:2;
Jer 5:28;
Eze 22:6-7;
Zec 7:10

22 Your silver has become dross,
  your choice wine is diluted with water.
23 Your rulers are rebels,
  companions of thieves;
 they all love bribes [r]
  and chase after gifts.
 They do not defend the cause of the fatherless;
  the widow's case does not come before them. [s]

1:24
t Isa 35:4; 59:17;
61:2; 63:4

24 Therefore the Lord, the LORD Almighty,
  the Mighty One of Israel, declares:
 "Ah, I will get relief from my foes
  and avenge [t] myself on my enemies.

1:25
u Eze 22:22;
Mal 3:3
1:26
v Jer 33:7,11
w Isa 33:5; 62:1;
Zec 8:3 x Isa 60:14;
62:2

25 I will turn my hand against you;
  I will thoroughly purge away your dross
  and remove all your impurities. [u]
26 I will restore your judges as in days of old, [v]
  your counselors as at the beginning.
 Afterward you will be called
  the City of Righteousness, [w]
  the Faithful City. [x]"

1:27
y Isa 35:10; 62:12;
63:4
1:28
z Ps 9:5; Isa 24:20;
66:24; 2Th 1:8-9
1:29
a Isa 57:5
b Isa 65:3; 66:17

27 Zion will be redeemed with justice,
  her penitent ones with righteousness. [y]
28 But rebels and sinners will both be broken,
  and those who forsake the LORD will perish. [z]

29 "You will be ashamed because of the sacred oaks [a]
  in which you have delighted;
 you will be disgraced because of the gardens [b]
  that you have chosen.
30 You will be like an oak with fading leaves,
  like a garden without water.
31 The mighty man will become tinder
  and his work a spark;
 both will burn together,
  with no one to quench the fire. [c]"

1:31
c Isa 5:24; 9:18-19;
26:11; 33:14;
66:15-16,24

2:1
d Isa 1:1

The Mountain of the LORD

2 This is what Isaiah son of Amoz saw concerning Judah and Jerusalem: [d]

2 In the last days

2:2
e Isa 27:13; 56:7;
66:20; Mic 4:7

 the mountain [e] of the LORD's temple will be established
  as chief among the mountains;
 it will be raised above the hills,
  and all nations will stream to it.

3 Many peoples will come and say,

 "Come, let us go up to the mountain of the LORD,

Isaiah 2:1–5

The Biblical writers believed that the Lord is God of the whole world. Both Isaiah and Micah (cf. Mic. 4:1–3) emphasized that God's "ways" are for all people. The ethical standards of the covenant are for everyone, because God, the Creator of heaven and Earth, built his character into them. Living by these standards produces physical and relational health. If all peoples were to follow them publicly and privately, wars would cease.

Christ is the only way to God, and he expects everyone to live by his standards (cf. John 14:6,21). But the "exclusivity" of the gospel message is no longer considered politically correct. The gospel is intended, though, to promote an inclusive kingdom—for all peoples and nations. Part of our challenge is to communicate the truth without diluting it or becoming belligerent messengers. Jesus' advice about being "as shrewd as snakes and as innocent as doves" applies here. Every

to the house of the God of Jacob.
He will teach us his ways,
    so that we may walk in his paths."
The law[f] will go out from Zion,
    the word of the LORD from Jerusalem.[g]
⁴He will judge between the nations
    and will settle disputes for many peoples.
They will beat their swords into plowshares
    and their spears into pruning hooks.[h]
Nation will not take up sword against nation,[i]
    nor will they train for war anymore.

⁵Come, O house of Jacob,[j]
    let us walk in the light[k] of the LORD.

The Day of the LORD

⁶You have abandoned[l] your people,
    the house of Jacob.
They are full of superstitions from the East;
    they practice divination like the Philistines[m]
    and clasp hands[n] with pagans.[o]
⁷Their land is full of silver and gold;
    there is no end to their treasures.
Their land is full of horses;[p]
    there is no end to their chariots.[q]
⁸Their land is full of idols;[r]
    they bow down to the work of their hands,
    to what their fingers[s] have made.
⁹So man will be brought low[t]
    and mankind humbled[u]—
    do not forgive them.[a][v]

¹⁰Go into the rocks,
    hide in the ground
from dread of the LORD
    and the splendor of his majesty![w]
¹¹The eyes of the arrogant man will be humbled
    and the pride[x] of men brought low;
    the LORD alone will be exalted in that day.

¹²The LORD Almighty has a day in store
    for all the proud and lofty,
    for all that is exalted[y]
    (and they will be humbled),[z]
¹³for all the cedars of Lebanon, tall and lofty,

a 9 Or not raise them up

2:3
f Isa 51:4,7
g Lk 24:47

2:4
h Joel 3:10
i Ps 46:9; Isa 9:5;
11:6-9; 32:18;
Hos 2:18; Zec 9:10

2:5
j Isa 58:1
k Isa 60:1,19-20;
1Jn 1:5,7
2:6
l Dt 31:17
m 2Ki 1:2 n Pr 6:1
o 2Ki 16:7

2:7
p Dt 17:16
q Isa 31:1; Mic 5:10
2:8
r Isa 10:9-11
s Isa 17:8

2:9
t Ps 62:9 u Isa 5:15
v Ne 4:5

2:10
w 2Th 1:9;
Rev 6:15-16
2:11
x Isa 5:15; 37:23

2:12
y Isa 24:4,21;
Mal 4:1 z Job 40:11

time we share the gospel we need to depend absolutely on the Spirit's leading (Matt. 10:16–20).

Isaiah 2:6–22

These verses shift radically from the hopeful note of verses 1–5. The Israelites had focused on the world's ways and values: idolatry, wealth, and power. So whatever good the future might have held, the present was dark indeed. At the center of that ominous present was human arrogance. Yet the theme isn't arrogance per se but the humiliation arrogance brings upon itself. Because Judah had been seduced by human power and glory and had abandoned the Creator, her people were doomed to terrible shame.

We humans have often grabbed for ourselves the place of God in the universe—a fundamental mistake. In reality, the divine Christ, by taking human form, has given humanity its true worth. The essence of humility isn't feeling bad about yourself but forgetting about yourself. It's the ability to go about the tasks God has given us, secure in his love and valuing, without wondering whether others appreciate us. To paraphrase a popular saying, "Humility is knowing that only God is God—and that you are not him!"

2:13
a Zec 11:2

2:14
b Isa 30:25; 40:4

2:15
c Isa 25:2, 12
2:16
d 1Ki 10:22

2:17
e ver 11
2:18
f Isa 21:9

2:19
g Heb 12:26

2:20
h Lev 11:19

2:21
i ver 19

2:22
j Ps 146:3; Jer 17:5
k Ps 8:4; 144:3;
Isa 40:15; Jas 4:14

3:1
l Lev 26:26
m Isa 5:13; Eze 4:16
3:2
n Eze 17:13
o 2Ki 24:14;
Isa 9:14-15

3:4
p Ecc 10:16 fn

3:5
q Isa 9:19; Jer 9:8;
Mic 7:2,6

and all the oaks of Bashan, [a]
14 for all the towering mountains
    and all the high hills, [b]
15 for every lofty tower
    and every fortified wall, [c]
16 for every trading ship [a] [d]
    and every stately vessel.
17 The arrogance of man will be brought low
    and the pride of men humbled;
    the LORD alone will be exalted in that day, [e]
18   and the idols will totally disappear. [f]

19 Men will flee to caves in the rocks
    and to holes in the ground
    from dread of the LORD
    and the splendor of his majesty,
    when he rises to shake the earth. [g]
20 In that day men will throw away
    to the rodents and bats [h]
    their idols of silver and idols of gold,
    which they made to worship.
21 They will flee to caverns in the rocks
    and to the overhanging crags
    from dread of the LORD
    and the splendor of his majesty,
    when he rises to shake the earth. [i]

22 Stop trusting in man, [j]
    who has but a breath in his nostrils.
    Of what account is he? [k]

Judgment on Jerusalem and Judah

3 See now, the Lord,
    the LORD Almighty,
is about to take from Jerusalem and Judah
    both supply and support:
all supplies of food [l] and all supplies of water, [m]
2   the hero and warrior, [n]
    the judge and prophet,
    the soothsayer and elder, [o]
3 the captain of fifty and man of rank,
    the counselor, skilled craftsman and clever enchanter.

4 I will make boys their officials;
    mere children will govern them. [p]
5 People will oppress each other—
    man against man, neighbor against neighbor. [q]

a 16 Hebrew *every ship of Tarshish*

Isaiah 3:1—4:1

📖 Continuing the previous passage's theme of arrogance producing humiliation, Isaiah 3:1–15 illustrates the theme by looking at Judah's leadership. The people had trusted in humans and would now be deprived of such leadership. This wasn't merely because such trust was wrong, but because the leaders had failed in their responsibilities. The result would be anarchy, with violence undermining the last vestiges of order.

The section on human arrogance (3:16—4:1) is the most graphic. The haughty women of Jerusalem, whose undivided attention was given to appearance and image, represented the nation as a whole. But their arrogant heads would be bowed in shame—their lavish hair shaved off to reveal sores seeping puss. Isaiah foresaw a day when so many men would die that there wouldn't be enough fathers and husbands to go around. In utter humiliation, seven women would beg one man for his name with no obligation on his part.

The young will rise up against the old,
the base against the honorable.

6 A man will seize one of his brothers
at his father's home, and say,
"You have a cloak, you be our leader;
take charge of this heap of ruins!"
7 But in that day he will cry out,
"I have no remedy.ʳ
I have no food or clothing in my house;
do not make me the leader of the people."

8 Jerusalem staggers,
Judah is falling;ˢ
their wordsᵗ and deeds are against the Lᴏʀᴅ,
defyingᵘ his glorious presence.
9 The look on their faces testifies against them;
they parade their sin like Sodom;ᵛ
they do not hide it.
Woe to them!
They have brought disasterʷ upon themselves.

10 Tell the righteous it will be wellˣ with them,
for they will enjoy the fruit of their deeds.ʸ
11 Woe to the wicked! Disasterᶻ is upon them!
They will be paid back for what their hands have done.

12 Youthsᵃ oppress my people,
women rule over them.
O my people, your guides lead you astray;ᵇ
they turn you from the path.

13 The Lᴏʀᴅ takes his place in court;
he rises to judgeᶜ the people.
14 The Lᴏʀᴅ enters into judgmentᵈ
against the elders and leaders of his people:
"It is you who have ruined my vineyard;
the plunderᵉ from the poor is in your houses.
15 What do you mean by crushing my peopleᶠ
and grinding the faces of the poor?"
declares the Lord, the Lᴏʀᴅ Almighty.

16 The Lᴏʀᴅ says,
"The women of Zionᵍ are haughty,
walking along with outstretched necks,
flirting with their eyes,
tripping along with mincing steps,
with ornaments jingling on their ankles.
17 Therefore the Lord will bring sores on the heads of the women of Zion;
the Lᴏʀᴅ will make their scalps bald."

18 In that day the Lord will snatch away their finery: the bangles and headbands and crescent necklaces,ʰ 19 the earrings and bracelets and veils, 20 the headdressesⁱ and ankle chains and sashes, the perfume bottles and charms, 21 the signet rings and

---

3:7
ʳ Eze 34:4;
Hos 5:13

3:8
ˢ Isa 1:7
ᵗ Isa 9:15,17
ᵘ Ps 73:9,11

3:9
ᵛ Ge 13:13
ʷ Pr 8:36; Ro 6:23

3:10
ˣ Dt 28:1-14
ʸ Ps 128:2

3:11
ᶻ Dt 28:15-68

3:12
ᵃ ver 4 ᵇ Isa 9:16

3:13
ᶜ Mic 6:2
3:14
ᵈ Job 22:4
ᵉ Job 24:9; Jas 2:6

3:15
ᶠ Ps 94:5

3:16
ᵍ SS 3:11

3:18
ʰ Jdg 8:21
3:20
ⁱ Ex 39:28

Humiliation and humility are contrasted in this passage. "Humiliation" carries the idea of being disgraced, while "humility" describes an individual who chooses an attitude of meekness. God values what the world doesn't. He won't work with people who have all the answers, want to control their own destinies, and think life revolves around their desires—those who lack humility. According to the prophet, such people will suffer humiliation despite their best efforts to avoid it. Obviously, not all humiliation is brought upon us by our own doing. Which is more predominant in your experience—humiliation or humility?

nose rings, 22the fine robes and the capes and cloaks, the purses 23and mirrors, and the linen garments and tiaras and shawls.

3:24
i Est 2:12 k Pr 31:24
l Isa 22:12
m La 2:10;
Eze 27:30-31
n 1Pe 3:3

24Instead of fragrance*i* there will be a stench;
    instead of a sash,*k* a rope;
instead of well-dressed hair, baldness;*l*
    instead of fine clothing, sackcloth;*m*
    instead of beauty,*n* branding.

3:25
o Isa 1:20

25Your men will fall by the sword,*o*
    your warriors in battle.

3:26
p Jer 14:2 q La 2:10

26The gates of Zion will lament and mourn;*p*
    destitute, she will sit on the ground.*q*

4:1
r Isa 13:12
s 2Th 3:12
t Ge 30:23

4 In that day seven women
    will take hold of one man*r*
and say, "We will eat our own food*s*
    and provide our own clothes;
only let us be called by your name.
    Take away our disgrace!"*t*

The Branch of the LORD

4:2
u Isa 11:1-5; 53:2;
Jer 23:5-6; Zec 3:8;
6:12 v Ps 72:16
4:3
w Ro 11:5
x Isa 52:1; 60:21
y Lk 10:20
4:4
z Isa 3:24 a Isa 1:15
b Isa 28:6
c Isa 1:31; Mt 3:11
4:5
d Ex 13:21
e Isa 60:1
4:6
f Ps 27:5 g Isa 25:4

2In that day the Branch of the LORD *u* will be beautiful and glorious, and the fruit*v* of the land will be the pride and glory of the survivors in Israel. 3Those who are left in Zion, who remain*w* in Jerusalem, will be called holy,*x* all who are recorded*y* among the living in Jerusalem. 4The Lord will wash away the filth*z* of the women of Zion; he will cleanse the bloodstains*a* from Jerusalem by a spirit*a* of judgment*b* and a spirit*a* of fire.*c* 5Then the LORD will create over all of Mount Zion and over those who assemble there a cloud of smoke by day and a glow of flaming fire by night;*d* over all the glory*e* will be a canopy. 6It will be a shelter*f* and shade from the heat of the day, and a refuge*g* and hiding place from the storm and rain.

The Song of the Vineyard

5:1
h Ps 80:8-9

5 I will sing for the one I love
    a song about his vineyard:*h*
My loved one had a vineyard
    on a fertile hillside.

5:2
i Jer 2:21

2He dug it up and cleared it of stones
    and planted it with the choicest vines.*i*
He built a watchtower in it
    and cut out a winepress as well.

---

a 4 Or *the Spirit*

Isaiah 4:2–6

These promises weren't in place of judgment but through it. The survivors would be the remnant left after the fire of judgment had done its work. There would be three results of the firestorm: The people would be holy (belong to God and reflect his character), be cleansed, and experience God's presence not as a threat but as a blessing. By that presence ("the glory"), he would provide the security for which they had mistakenly turned to idols.

When we face difficulties, it's easy for us to think that God has abandoned us. It helps to recognize that comfort, pleasure, and security are by-products (Matt. 6:33). If we make them primary, we become idolaters. But if we focus on God's presence and character, then comfort, pleasure, and security will fall on us unawares. They will come when and where God chooses, and that will be enough because we will know he's all we need. He has no desire to deprive us but seeks our good, even in the fire.

Isaiah 5:1–7

Tending a vineyard required preparation and care. The first year was dedicated to clearing the land of its foliage and abundant rocks. The second year the farmer purchased and carefully planted the finest vines he could afford, then built the cleared rocks into fences and watchtowers to keep out intruders. Finally, in the third year, the fruit of all that labor was ready.

It's easy to imagine Isaiah's listeners' outrage when they heard that the outcome was only bitter grapes—and their hearty agreement that the vineyard should be destroyed. But like the religious leaders to whom Jesus told the story of the wicked tenants (Luke 20:9–19), the hearers suddenly realized that Isaiah was talking about them: "The vineyard of the LORD Almighty is the house of Israel" (v. 7).

Then he looked for a crop of good grapes,
    but it yielded only bad fruit. *j*

³ "Now you dwellers in Jerusalem and men of Judah,
    judge between me and my vineyard. *k*
⁴ What more could have been done for my vineyard
    than I have done for it? *l*
When I looked for good grapes,
    why did it yield only bad?
⁵ Now I will tell you
    what I am going to do to my vineyard:
I will take away its hedge,
    and it will be destroyed;
I will break down its wall, *m*
    and it will be trampled. *n*
⁶ I will make it a wasteland,
    neither pruned nor cultivated,
    and briers and thorns *o* will grow there.
I will command the clouds
    not to rain on it."

⁷ The vineyard *p* of the LORD Almighty
    is the house of Israel,
and the men of Judah
    are the garden of his delight.
And he looked for justice, *q* but saw bloodshed;
    for righteousness, but heard cries of distress.

Woes and Judgments

⁸ Woe *r* to you who add house to house
    and join field to field *s*
till no space is left
    and you live alone in the land.

⁹ The LORD Almighty has declared in my hearing: *t*

"Surely the great houses will become desolate, *u*
    the fine mansions left without occupants.
¹⁰ A ten-acre *a* vineyard will produce only a bath *b* of wine,
    a homer *c* of seed only an ephah *d* of grain." *v*

¹¹ Woe to those who rise early in the morning
    to run after their drinks,
who stay up late at night
    till they are inflamed with wine. *w*

a 10 Hebrew *ten-yoke*, that is, the land plowed by 10 yoke of oxen in one day   *b 10* That is, probably about 6 gallons (about 22 liters)   *c 10* That is, probably about 6 bushels (about 220 liters)   *d 10* That is, probably about 3/5 bushel (about 22 liters)

5:2
j Mt 21:19;
Mk 11:13; Lk 13:6

5:3
k Mt 21:40

5:4
l 2Ch 36:15;
Jer 2:5-7; Mic 6:3-
4; Mt 23:37

5:5
m Ps 80:12
n Isa 28:3,18;
La 1:15; Lk 21:24

5:6
o Isa 7:23,24;
Heb 6:8

5:7
p Ps 80:8
q Isa 59:15

5:8
r Jer 22:13
s Mic 2:2;
Hab 2:9-12

5:9
t Isa 22:14
u Isa 6:11-12;
Mt 23:38

5:10
v Lev 26:26

5:11
w Pr 23:29-30

📖 Like both Isaiah's and Jesus' audience, we do well to sit up and take notice of this alarming parable and the subsequent applications in the rest of chapter 5. Of course Christ's church will survive; that is a given. But will the church *in the West* survive? Not if we allow the Bible's authority to be stripped away. It's our only reason for existing. Why are greed and self-indulgence wrong? Why is it wrong to make up our own moral code or to deprive the poor of justice? Because the Creator of the universe says so. Because that is not the way he acts or wants us to behave.

Isaiah 5:8–30

🔖 In this passage, Isaiah identified the "bad fruit" from the symbolic song of verses 1–6, condemning six specific behaviors ("woes") and their consequences: greed (vv. 8–10), self-indulgence (vv. 11–17), cynicism (vv. 18–19), moral perversion (v. 20), pride (v. 21), and social injustice (vv. 22–25). There was nothing left but to tear down the vineyard walls and call in the animals (i.e., the "distant nations"; v. 26) to trample the useless vines and strip off their leaves. God's people needed to come to terms, not with the strength of their enemies (who

5:12
x Job 34:27
y Ps 28:5; Am 6:5-6

5:13
z Hos 4:6 a Isa 1:3;
Hos 4:6

5:14
b Pr 30:16
c Nu 16:30

5:15
d Isa 10:33 e Isa 2:9
f Isa 2:11

5:16
g Isa 28:17; 30:18;
33:5; 61:8
h Isa 29:23
5:17
i Isa 7:25;
Zep 2:6,14

5:18
j Isa 59:4-8;
Jer 23:14

5:19
k Jer 17:15;
Eze 12:22; 2Pe 3:4

5:20
l Mt 6:22-23;
Lk 11:34-35
m Am 5:7

5:21
n Pr 3:7; Ro 12:16;
1Co 3:18-20

5:22
o Pr 23:20

5:23
p Ex 23:8 q Isa 10:2
r Ps 94:21; Jas 5:6

5:24
s Job 18:16
t Isa 8:6; 30:9,12

5:25
u 2Ki 22:13

12 They have harps and lyres at their banquets,
  tambourines and flutes and wine,
 but they have no regard[x] for the deeds of the LORD,
  no respect for the work of his hands.[y]
13 Therefore my people will go into exile[z]
  for lack of understanding;[a]
 their men of rank will die of hunger
  and their masses will be parched with thirst.
14 Therefore the grave[a][b] enlarges its appetite
  and opens its mouth[c] without limit;
 into it will descend their nobles and masses
  with all their brawlers and revelers.
15 So man will be brought low[d]
  and mankind humbled,[e]
  the eyes of the arrogant[f] humbled.
16 But the LORD Almighty will be exalted by his justice,[g]
  and the holy God will show himself holy[h] by his righteousness.
17 Then sheep will graze as in their own pasture;[i]
  lambs will feed[b] among the ruins of the rich.

18 Woe to those who draw sin along with cords of deceit,
  and wickedness[j] as with cart ropes,
19 to those who say, "Let God hurry,
  let him hasten his work
  so we may see it.
 Let it approach,
  let the plan of the Holy One of Israel come,
  so we may know it."[k]

20 Woe to those who call evil good
  and good evil,
 who put darkness for light
  and light for darkness,[l]
 who put bitter for sweet
  and sweet for bitter.[m]

21 Woe to those who are wise in their own eyes[n]
  and clever in their own sight.

22 Woe to those who are heroes at drinking wine[o]
  and champions at mixing drinks,
23 who acquit the guilty for a bribe,[p]
  but deny justice[q] to the innocent.[r]
24 Therefore, as tongues of fire lick up straw
  and as dry grass sinks down in the flames,
 so their roots will decay[s]
  and their flowers blow away like dust;
 for they have rejected the law of the LORD Almighty
  and spurned the word[t] of the Holy One of Israel.
25 Therefore the LORD's anger[u] burns against his people;
  his hand is raised and he strikes them down.

---

a 14 Hebrew *Sheol*   *b 17* Septuagint; Hebrew / *strangers will eat*

---

were merely God's instruments), but with God's moral *character.*

📖 Following his song of the vineyard, the behaviors Isaiah highlighted begin and end with injustice (vv. 7,22–23). In fact, how we treat each other is probably the most significant indicator of our own relationship to God. If we are to be in fellowship with him, we need to agree to treat one another fairly and with fundamental respect, recognizing that each person's life, possessions, reputation, and marriage are inviolable. What's the quality of this "fruit" in your life?

The mountains shake,
and the dead bodies are like refuse[v] in the streets.

Yet for all this, his anger is not turned away,[w]
his hand is still upraised.[x]

26 He lifts up a banner for the distant nations,
he whistles[y] for those at the ends of the earth.[z]
Here they come,
swiftly and speedily!

27 Not one of them grows tired or stumbles,
not one slumbers or sleeps;
not a belt is loosened at the waist,[a]
not a sandal thong is broken.[b]

28 Their arrows are sharp,[c]
all their bows[d] are strung;
their horses' hoofs seem like flint,
their chariot wheels like a whirlwind.

29 Their roar is like that of the lion,[e]
they roar like young lions;
they growl as they seize[f] their prey
and carry it off with no one to rescue.[g]

30 In that day they will roar over it
like the roaring of the sea.[h]
And if one looks at the land,
he will see darkness and distress;[i]
even the light will be darkened[j] by the clouds.

Isaiah's Commission

6 In the year that King Uzziah[k] died,[l] I saw the Lord[m] seated on a throne,[n] high and exalted, and the train of his robe filled the temple. 2Above him were seraphs,[o] each with six wings: With two wings they covered their faces, with two they covered their feet,[p] and with two they were flying. 3And they were calling to one another:

"Holy, holy, holy is the LORD Almighty;
the whole earth is full of his glory."[q]

4At the sound of their voices the doorposts and thresholds shook and the temple was filled with smoke.

5"Woe to me!" I cried. "I am ruined! For I am a man of unclean lips, and I live

---

Isaiah 6:1–13

Isaiah's commission likely came before he began preaching. But he evidently placed his account of it here as a climax to the dilemma expressed in the opening prophecies of his book: How could the present corrupt, rebellious Israel that defied God's instruction ever become the promised clean, obedient Israel from whom all nations would learn God's instruction?

If the "people of unclean lips" would have the same kind of experience as Isaiah, the "man of unclean lips" (v. 5), the dilemma would be solved. But Isaiah was called upon to preach a message that, given the hardened hearts of his own generation and those to follow, would only push them farther from God. Yet some would respond to God and preserve Isaiah's words until a century and a half later when the cauterizing fire (cf. vv. 6–7) of the exile would fall. Only then would there be a generation willing to listen—"and turn and be healed" (v. 10).

We are not "basically nice folks with an unfortunate tendency to mess up." We are proud, arrogant, self-centered, perverse, cruel, violent rebels in whom the stain of sin and sinfulness goes down to the last atom. At every turn we consciously and unconsciously miss the targets God has set up for us, his creatures. Is there a part of you that bristles at so blatant and unqualified a statement? The fact is that there is a strong likelihood that until we come to understand ourselves in this way, as Isaiah did, we will treat the grace of God—his unfailing, undeserved love—as a throwaway.

But when we do come to that place of recognizing and receiving the incredible grace of God that cleanses us, we are ready to glimpse his heart and holiness and to offer ourselves to him in service. Of course, that experience of grace isn't for the purpose of winning human praise or fulfilling our own dreams. Like Isaiah, our calling isn't to succeed as the world counts success, but to faithfulness.

5:25
v 2Ki 9:37
w Jer 4:8; Da 9:16
x Isa 9:12,17,21;
10:4

5:26
y Isa 7:18; Zec 10:8
z Dt 28:49;
Isa 13:5; 18:3

5:27
a Job 12:18
b Joel 2:7-8

5:28
c Ps 45:5 d Ps 7:12

5:29
e Jer 51:38;
Zep 3:3; Zec 11:3
f Isa 10:6; 49:24-25
g Isa 42:22; Mic 5:8

5:30
h Lk 21:25
i Isa 8:22;
Jer 4:23-28
j Joel 2:10

6:1
k 2Ch 26:22,23
l 2Ki 15:7
m Jn 12:41
n Rev 4:2
6:2
o Rev 4:8
p Eze 1:11

6:3
q Ps 72:19; Rev 4:8

among a people of unclean lips, [r] and my eyes have seen the King, [s] the LORD Almighty."

⁶Then one of the seraphs flew to me with a live coal in his hand, which he had taken with tongs from the altar. ⁷With it he touched my mouth and said, "See, this has touched your lips; [t] your guilt is taken away and your sin atoned for. [u]"

⁸Then I heard the voice [v] of the Lord saying, "Whom shall I send? And who will go for us?"

And I said, "Here am I. Send me!"

⁹He said, "Go [w] and tell this people:

" 'Be ever hearing, but never understanding;
    be ever seeing, but never perceiving.' [x]

6:10
y Dt 32:15;
Ps 119:70
z Jer 5:21
a Mt 13:13-15;
Mk 4:12*;
Ac 28:26-27*
¹⁰Make the heart of this people calloused; [y]
    make their ears dull
    and close their eyes. [a]
Otherwise they might see with their eyes,
    hear with their ears, [z]
    understand with their hearts,
and turn and be healed." [a]

¹¹Then I said, "For how long, O Lord?" [b]
And he answered:

"Until the cities lie ruined [c]
    and without inhabitant,
until the houses are left deserted
    and the fields ruined and ravaged,

¹²until the LORD has sent everyone far away [d]
    and the land is utterly forsaken. [e]

¹³And though a tenth remains [f] in the land,
    it will again be laid waste.
But as the terebinth and oak
    leave stumps when they are cut down,
    so the holy seed will be the stump in the land." [g]

The Sign of Immanuel

7 When Ahaz son of Jotham, the son of Uzziah, was king of Judah, King Rezin [h] of Aram [i] and Pekah [j] son of Remaliah king of Israel marched up to fight against Jerusalem, but they could not overpower it.

²Now the house of David [k] was told, "Aram has allied itself with [b] Ephraim [l]"; so the hearts of Ahaz and his people were shaken, as the trees of the forest are shaken by the wind.

³Then the LORD said to Isaiah, "Go out, you and your son Shear-Jashub, [c] to meet Ahaz at the end of the aqueduct of the Upper Pool, on the road to the Washerman's

---

[a] 9,10 Hebrew; Septuagint *'You will be ever hearing, but never understanding; / you will be ever seeing, but never perceiving.' /* [10]*This people's heart has become calloused; / they hardly hear with their ears, / and they have closed their eyes*   [b] 2 Or *has set up camp in*   [c] 3 *Shear-Jashub* means *a remnant will return.*

Isaiah 7:1–25

📖 The predicted rejection of Isaiah's message (6:9–10) was immediate. King Ahaz preferred to trust his ultimate enemy, Assyria, for deliverance from Aram and Israel (also called Ephraim) rather than to risk trusting God. To this, Isaiah replied with the sign of Immanuel—"God with us" (see "There and Then" for 8:1–10). *Whether or not Ahaz admitted it, God was with Judah*—not good news if Judah were to reject him. In 7:16—8:22 the prophet talked about the tragic consequences of trusting one's worst enemy while trying to leave God out of his or her life's equation.

📖 It's essential that we avoid what Ahaz did—deciding what we want and then asking God to bless our choices. Are you instead in the habit of coming to him at the beginning and asking his will with the blankest possible page? When we have the confidence of his word, we can go forward with a clean conscience, courageous heart, and confident step. If we live in trust, we can have the watchful quietness Isaiah urged upon Ahaz: "Be careful, keep calm and don't be afraid" (v. 4). Only then can we make decisions that are thoughtful and reasoned responses, not emotional reactions.

Field.[m] [4]Say to him, 'Be careful, keep calm[n] and don't be afraid.[o] Do not lose heart[p] because of these two smoldering stubs[q] of firewood—because of the fierce anger[r] of Rezin and Aram and of the son of Remaliah. [5]Aram, Ephraim and Remaliah's son have plotted your ruin, saying, [6]"Let us invade Judah; let us tear it apart and divide it among ourselves, and make the son of Tabeel king over it." [7]Yet this is what the Sovereign LORD says:

> " 'It will not take place,
>   it will not happen,[s]
> [8]for the head of Aram is Damascus,[t]
>   and the head of Damascus is only Rezin.
> Within sixty-five years
>   Ephraim will be too shattered[u] to be a people.
> [9]The head of Ephraim is Samaria,
>   and the head of Samaria is only Remaliah's son.
> If you do not stand firm in your faith,[v]
>   you will not stand at all.' "[w]

[10]Again the LORD spoke to Ahaz, [11]"Ask the LORD your God for a sign, whether in the deepest depths or in the highest heights."

[12]But Ahaz said, "I will not ask; I will not put the LORD to the test."

[13]Then Isaiah said, "Hear now, you house of David! Is it not enough to try the patience of men? Will you try the patience of my God[x] also? [14]Therefore the Lord himself will give you[a] a sign: The virgin will be with child and will give birth to a son,[y] and[b] will call him Immanuel.[cz] [15]He will eat curds and honey[a] when he knows enough to reject the wrong and choose the right. [16]But before the boy knows[b] enough to reject the wrong and choose the right, the land of the two kings you dread will be laid waste.[c] [17]The LORD will bring on you and on your people and on the house of your father a time unlike any since Ephraim broke away[d] from Judah—he will bring the king of Assyria.[e]"

[18]In that day the LORD will whistle[f] for flies from the distant streams of Egypt and for bees from the land of Assyria.[g] [19]They will all come and settle in the steep ravines and in the crevices[h] in the rocks, on all the thornbushes and at all the water holes. [20]In that day the Lord will use[i] a razor hired from beyond the River[d]—the king of Assyria[j]—to shave your head and the hair of your legs, and to take off your beards also. [21]In that day, a man will keep alive a young cow and two goats. [22]And because of the abundance of the milk they give, he will have curds to eat. All who remain in the land will eat curds and honey. [23]In that day, in every place where there were a thousand vines worth a thousand silver shekels,[e] there will be only briers and thorns.[k] [24]Men will go there with bow and arrow, for the land will be cov-

Cross references

7:3 [m] 2Ki 18:17; Isa 36:2
7:4 [n] Isa 30:15 [o] Isa 35:4 [p] Dt 20:3 [q] Zec 3:2 [r] Isa 10:24
7:7 [s] Isa 8:10; Ac 4:25
7:8 [t] Ge 14:15 [u] Isa 17:1-3
7:9 [v] 2Ch 20:20 [w] Isa 8:6-8; 30:12-14
7:13 [x] Isa 25:1
7:14 [y] Lk 1:31 [z] Isa 8:8, 10; Mt 1:23*
7:15 [a] ver 22
7:16 [b] Isa 8:4 [c] Isa 17:3; Hos 5:9,13; Am 1:3-5
7:17 [d] 1Ki 12:16 [e] 2Ch 28:20
7:18 [f] Isa 5:26 [g] Isa 13:5
7:19 [h] Isa 2:19
7:20 [i] Isa 10:15 [j] Isa 8:7; 10:5
7:23 [k] Isa 5:6

---

[a] 14 The Hebrew is plural. [b] 14 Masoretic Text; Dead Sea Scrolls *and he* or *and they*
[c] 14 *Immanuel* means *God with us.* [d] 20 That is, the Euphrates [e] 23 That is, about 25 pounds (about 11.5 kilograms)

7:18

Malaria

Similar to the situation today, insects in Bible times were seen as general nuisances, but some as harbingers of destruction and disease. A modern scourge—malaria—is spread by the mosquito.

Cases per year worldwide: 300–500 million

Symptoms: High fever, chills, sweating, anemia

TWO MILLION deaths per year

90 percent of deaths occur in Sub-Saharan Africa.

Nearly all deaths occur in children under five years of age.

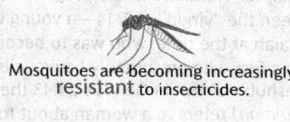

Mosquitoes are becoming increasingly resistant to insecticides.

Childhood cases (and deaths) can be dramatically reduced (over 30 percent) by people sleeping under bednets.

Source: World Health Organization (2002:82)

ered with briers and thorns. 25As for all the hills once cultivated by the hoe, you will no longer go there for fear of the briers and thorns; they will become places where cattle are turned loose and where sheep run. [l]

Assyria, the LORD's Instrument

8 The LORD said to me, "Take a large scroll [m] and write on it with an ordinary pen: Maher-Shalal-Hash-Baz. [a] [n] 2And I will call in Uriah [o] the priest and Zechariah son of Jeberekiah as reliable witnesses for me."

3Then I went to the prophetess, and she conceived and gave birth to a son. And the LORD said to me, "Name him Maher-Shalal-Hash-Baz. 4Before the boy knows [p] how to say 'My father' or 'My mother,' the wealth of Damascus and the plunder of Samaria will be carried off by the king of Assyria. [q]"

5The LORD spoke to me again:

6 "Because this people has rejected [r]
  the gently flowing waters of Shiloah [s]
and rejoices over Rezin
  and the son of Remaliah, [t]
7therefore the Lord is about to bring against them
  the mighty floodwaters [u] of the River [b]—
  the king of Assyria [v] with all his pomp.
It will overflow all its channels,
  run over all its banks
8and sweep on into Judah, swirling over it,
  passing through it and reaching up to the neck.
Its outspread wings will cover the breadth of your land,
  O Immanuel [c] [w]!"

9Raise the war cry, [d] [x] you nations, and be shattered!
  Listen, all you distant lands.
Prepare [y] for battle, and be shattered!
  Prepare for battle, and be shattered!
10Devise your strategy, but it will be thwarted; [z]
  propose your plan, but it will not stand, [a]
for God is with us. [e] [b]

Fear God

11The LORD spoke to me with his strong hand upon me, [c] warning me not to follow [d] the way of this people. He said:

7:25
[l] Isa 5:17

8:1
[m] Isa 30:8; Hab 2:2
[n] ver 3; Hab 2:2
8:2
[o] 2Ki 16:10

8:4
[p] Isa 7:16 [q] Isa 7:8

8:6
[r] Isa 5:24 [s] Jn 9:7
[t] Isa 7:1

8:7
[u] Isa 17:12-13
[v] Isa 7:20

8:8
[w] Isa 7:14

8:9
[x] Isa 17:12-13
[y] Joel 3:9

8:10
[z] Job 5:12 [a] Isa 7:7
[b] Isa 7:14; Ro 8:31

8:11
[c] Eze 3:14 [d] Eze 2:8

---

[a] 1 *Maher-Shalal-Hash-Baz* means *quick to the plunder, swift to the spoil*; also in verse 3.   [b] 7 That is, the Euphrates   [c] 8 *Immanuel* means *God with us.*   [d] 9 Or *Do your worst*   [e] 10 Hebrew *Immanuel*

Isaiah 8:1–10

There is good reason to believe that Isaiah's son was to be the first fulfillment of the Immanuel sign of chapter 7. Isaiah's wife ("prophetess") of 8:3 may have been the "virgin" of 7:14—a young woman, betrothed to Isaiah at the time, who was to become his second wife (his first wife presumably having died after Shear-Jashub's birth). In Genesis 24:43 the same Hebrew word ('*almah*) refers to a woman about to be married (cf. Prov. 30:19). Matthew understood the woman mentioned here to be a type, or foreshadowing, of the Virgin Mary (Matt. 1:22–23).

The child's symbolic name, Maher-Shalal-Hash-Baz (see NIV text note on 8:1), meant that Judah's immediate enemies would be plundered but also that Judah would suffer. The boy wouldn't be old enough to speak clearly before Damascus (Aram) and Samaria (Israel) would be plundered by Assyria (with whom Ahaz of Judah presently had an ill-advised alliance). Judah would nearly be swept away by the conquering Assyrians also, but would be spared because of the Immanuel promise.

Many Christians today believe that, since God's love is unconditional and since he will never forsake us, our behavior is fundamentally unimportant. How far this thinking is from Isaiah's perspective!

God told his people of Judah to stop worrying about what the Arameans, the Israelites, and the Assyrians were going to do and to start worrying about what *he* was going to do! Are you anxious about the volatility of the world situation? Or personal circumstances facing you? If so, are you following Isaiah's advice?

12 "Do not call conspiracy*e*
    everything that these people call conspiracy^a;
do not fear what they fear,
    and do not dread it.*f*
13 The LORD Almighty is the one you are to regard as holy,*g*
    he is the one you are to fear,
    he is the one you are to dread,*h*
14 and he will be a sanctuary;*i*
    but for both houses of Israel he will be
a stone that causes men to stumble
    and a rock that makes them fall.*j*
And for the people of Jerusalem he will be
    a trap and a snare.*k*
15 Many of them will stumble;*l*
    they will fall and be broken,
    they will be snared and captured."

16 Bind up the testimony
    and seal*m* up the law among my disciples.
17 I will wait*n* for the LORD,
    who is hiding*o* his face from the house of Jacob.
I will put my trust in him.

18 Here am I, and the children the LORD has given me.*p* We are signs*q* and symbols in Israel from the LORD Almighty, who dwells on Mount Zion.*r*

19 When men tell you to consult*s* mediums and spiritists, who whisper and mutter,*t* should not a people inquire of their God? Why consult the dead on behalf of the living? 20 To the law*u* and to the testimony! If they do not speak according to this word, they have no light*v* of dawn. 21 Distressed and hungry, they will roam through the land; when they are famished, they will become enraged and, looking upward, will curse*w* their king and their God. 22 Then they will look toward the earth and see only distress and darkness and fearful gloom, and they will be thrust into utter darkness.*x*

To Us a Child Is Born

9 Nevertheless, there will be no more gloom for those who were in distress. In the past he humbled the land of Zebulun and the land of Naphtali,*y* but in the future he will honor Galilee of the Gentiles, by the way of the sea, along the Jordan—

2 The people walking in darkness
    have seen a great light;*z*
on those living in the land of the shadow of death*b a*
    a light has dawned.*b*

---

a 12 Or *Do not call for a treaty / every time these people call for a treaty*   *b 2* Or *land of darkness*

8:12
e Isa 7:2; 30:1
f 1Pe 3:14*

8:13
g Nu 20:12
h Isa 29:23

8:14
i Isa 4:6; Eze 11:16
j Lk 2:34; Ro 9:33*; 1Pe 2:8*
k Isa 24:17-18
8:15
l Isa 28:13; 59:10; Lk 20:18; Ro 9:32

8:16
m Isa 29:11-12
8:17
n Hab 2:3
o Dt 31:17; Isa 54:8

8:18
p Heb 2:13*
q Lk 2:34 *r* Ps 9:11

8:19
s 1Sa 28:8 *t* Isa 29:4

8:20
u Isa 1:10; Lk 16:29
v Mic 3:6

8:21
w Rev 16:11

8:22
x ver 20; Isa 5:30

9:1
y 2Ki 15:29

9:2
z Eph 5:8 *a* Lk 1:79
b Mt 4:15-16*

Isaiah 8:11–22

God's presence is the one inescapable fact of life. People of every generation, like Ahaz and Judah, *will* encounter him one way or another. Those of every era who make a place for him find him to be the glue that holds everything together, while those who ignore him find their lives unaccountably out of kilter. Both Israel and Judah had chosen the latter. Preferring to pay only ritual attention to God, they fell prey to every new fear that came along. And being prey to their fears, they made all the wrong decisions.

Our culture has discovered that material wealth hasn't made us happier. But instead of turning back to the Biblical God of our ancestors, we have looked to op-

tions more "modern" and "scientific." Thinking ourselves too educated to believe in miracles, we moderns willingly swallow the most amazing hodge-podge of superstition, science, technology, and paganism. Then we are surprised at the rapid increase of spiritual darkness around us. God has become the stumbling block (v. 14; cf. Rom. 9:33; 1 Peter 2:6–8)—and we are falling all over him. Have you observed this truth in people around you? Commit to present the Biblical truth to people who are searching for answers.

Isaiah 9:1–7

The Assyrian conquests began in the tribal territory of Zebulun and Naphtali, in the northern part of Israel. But God is greater than Assyria, and he promised that

³You have enlarged the nation
and increased their joy;
they rejoice before you
as people rejoice at the harvest,
as men rejoice
when dividing the plunder.

9:4
c Jdg 7:25
d Isa 14:25
e Isa 10:27
f Isa 14:4; 49:26;
51:13; 54:14

⁴For as in the day of Midian's defeat,^c
you have shattered
the yoke^d that burdens them,
the bar across their shoulders,^e
the rod of their oppressor.^f

9:5
g Isa 2:4

⁵Every warrior's boot used in battle
and every garment rolled in blood
will be destined for burning,^g
will be fuel for the fire.

9:6
h Isa 53:2; Lk 2:11
i Jn 3:16 j Mt 28:18
k Isa 28:29
l Isa 10:21; 11:2
m Isa 26:3,12;
66:12

⁶For to us a child is born,^h
to us a son is given,ⁱ
and the government^j will be on his shoulders.
And he will be called
Wonderful Counselor,^a^k Mighty God,^l
Everlasting Father, Prince of Peace.^m

9:7
n Da 2:44; Lk 1:33
o Isa 11:4; 16:5;
32:1,16 p Isa 37:32;
59:17

⁷Of the increase of his government and peace
there will be no end.ⁿ
He will reign on David's throne
and over his kingdom,
establishing and upholding it
with justice^o and righteousness
from that time on and forever.
The zeal^p of the LORD Almighty
will accomplish this.

The LORD's Anger Against Israel

⁸The Lord has sent a message against Jacob;
it will fall on Israel.

9:9
q Isa 7:9

⁹All the people will know it—
Ephraim and the inhabitants of Samaria^q—

---

^a 6 Or Wonderful, Counselor

just as his people had experienced the despair of conquest, they would see the triumph of victory. How would God accomplish this feat? Through the birth of a child!

For the third time in as many chapters, a birth is imbued with great significance. In chapter 7 the birth was a sign that it was unnecessary for Judah to trust in Assyria for deliverance from Aram and Israel. In chapter 8 it signified additionally that misplaced trust was going to result in disaster for Judah. Now this birth carried the message one step further: Out of the disaster God would bring victory. Isaiah's son was the immediate fulfillment of the sign of Immanuel. The "son of David" would bring it to ultimate realization.

If God is transcendent, morally perfect, infinite, and eternal, how can he be "with us" who are created, sinful, finite, and mortal? Aren't the barriers just too great to be crossed? This passage sets the stage for the most astounding event in history: The child born of the virgin is the son of David—but also the Son of God (cf. 7:14; Matt. 1:23).

The contemporary significance of this passage comes down to this: Have we allowed the Child-King to take over the government of our lives? Only then can we know the benefits of "God with us." We can't receive the light, honor, joy, abundance, or integration he offers in any other way.

Isaiah 9:8—10:4

Though Isaiah's ministry was primarily directed to Judah, on occasion he also proclaimed the word of the Lord to Israel (also referred to in v. 9 as Ephraim and Samaria). This passage consists of four stanzas, each closing with the refrain first encountered in 5:25: "Yet for all this, his anger is not turned away, his hand is still upraised." It wasn't Assyria's anger but God's that had to be dealt with. Through these four stanzas God lodged four charges against Israel, each dealing with ethical behavior: (1) arrogance; (2) exaltation of men instead of God; (3) lack of love for one another; and (4) social injustice (inescapable in a society with everyone looking out for "number one").

who say with pride
and arrogance[r] of heart,

10 "The bricks have fallen down,
but we will rebuild with dressed stone;
the fig trees have been felled,
but we will replace them with cedars."

11 But the LORD has strengthened Rezin's[s] foes against them
and has spurred their enemies on.

12 Arameans[t] from the east and Philistines[u] from the west
have devoured[v] Israel with open mouth.

Yet for all this, his anger is not turned away,
his hand is still upraised.[w]

13 But the people have not returned to him who struck[x] them,
nor have they sought[y] the LORD Almighty.

14 So the LORD will cut off from Israel both head and tail,
both palm branch and reed[z] in a single day;[a]

15 the elders[b] and prominent men are the head,
the prophets who teach lies are the tail.

16 Those who guide[c] this people mislead them,
and those who are guided are led astray.[d]

17 Therefore the Lord will take no pleasure in the young men,[e]
nor will he pity[f] the fatherless and widows,
for everyone is ungodly[g] and wicked,[h]
every mouth speaks vileness.[i]

Yet for all this, his anger is not turned away,
his hand is still upraised.[j]

18 Surely wickedness burns like a fire;[k]
it consumes briers and thorns,
it sets the forest thickets ablaze,[l]
so that it rolls upward in a column of smoke.

19 By the wrath[m] of the LORD Almighty
the land will be scorched
and the people will be fuel for the fire;[n]
no one will spare his brother.[o]

20 On the right they will devour,
but still be hungry;[p]
on the left they will eat,[q]
but not be satisfied.
Each will feed on the flesh of his own offspring[a]:

21   Manasseh will feed on Ephraim, and Ephraim on Manasseh;
together they will turn against Judah.[r]

Yet for all this, his anger is not turned away,
his hand is still upraised.[s]

a 20 Or arm

Cross references

9:9 r Isa 46:12

9:11 s Isa 7:8

9:12 t 2Ki 16:6
u 2Ch 28:18
v Ps 79:7 w Isa 5:25

9:13 x Jer 5:3 y Isa 31:1;
Hos 7:7,10

9:14 z Isa 19:15
a Rev 18:8
9:15 b Isa 3:2-3

9:16 c Mt 15:14; 23:16,
24 d Isa 3:12

9:17 e Jer 18:21
f Isa 27:11
g Isa 10:6 h Isa 1:4
i Mt 12:34 j Isa 5:25

9:18 k Mal 4:1 l Ps 83:14

9:19 m Isa 13:9,13
n Isa 1:31
o Mic 7:2,6

9:20 p Lev 26:26
q Isa 49:26

9:21 r 2Ch 28:6
s Isa 5:25

God *is* love, and he *gets* angry. But his isn't the selfish anger of a fallen human or the temper tantrum of an overbearing monarch who won't permit his lowly subjects to do what they want. It's the heartbroken response of an Artist who watches his creation doing things that are a violation not only of his original dream but of their very natures.

One of the problems we face when confronted with social injustice is failing to feel directly involved. But it might be time for a reality check. Ask yourself: Am I gouging those who work for me on the lawn, in cleaning, or in childcare? What about those I supervise in the office? Do they feel taken advantage of by me? Am I involved in institutions that profit from oppression? When is the minimum wage the wrong wage? What can I do to address injustice(s) where I live?

10:1
t Ps 58:2
10:2
u Isa 3:14 v Isa 5:23

10:3
w Job 31:14;
Hos 9:7 x Lk 19:44
y Isa 20:6

10:4
z Isa 24:22
a Isa 22:2; 34:3;
66:16 b Isa 5:25

10:5
c Isa 14:25;
Zep 2:13
d Jer 51:20
e Isa 13:3,5,13;
30:30; 66:14
10:6
f Isa 9:17 g Isa 9:19
h Isa 5:29

10:7
i Ge 50:20;
Ac 4:23-28

10:8
j 2Ki 18:24
10:9
k Ge 10:10
l 2Ch 35:20
m 2Ki 17:6
n 2Ki 16:9
10:10
o 2Ki 19:18

10:12
p Isa 28:21-22; 65:7
q 2Ki 19:31
r Jer 50:18

10:13
s Isa 37:24; Da 4:30
t Eze 28:4

10 Woe to those who make unjust laws,
    to those who issue oppressive decrees,[t]
2 to deprive[u] the poor of their rights
    and withhold justice from the oppressed of my people,[v]
making widows their prey
    and robbing the fatherless.
3 What will you do on the day of reckoning,[w]
    when disaster[x] comes from afar?
To whom will you run for help?[y]
    Where will you leave your riches?
4 Nothing will remain but to cringe among the captives[z]
    or fall among the slain.[a]

Yet for all this, his anger is not turned away,[b]
    his hand is still upraised.

God's Judgment on Assyria

5 "Woe to the Assyrian,[c] the rod of my anger,
    in whose hand is the club[d] of my wrath![e]
6 I send him against a godless[f] nation,
    I dispatch him against a people who anger me,[g]
to seize loot and snatch plunder,[h]
    and to trample them down like mud in the streets.
7 But this is not what he intends,[i]
    this is not what he has in mind;
his purpose is to destroy,
    to put an end to many nations.
8 'Are not my commanders[j] all kings?' he says.
9   'Has not Calno[k] fared like Carchemish?[l]
Is not Hamath like Arpad,
    and Samaria[m] like Damascus?[n]
10 As my hand seized the kingdoms of the idols,[o]
    kingdoms whose images excelled those of Jerusalem and Samaria—
11 shall I not deal with Jerusalem and her images
    as I dealt with Samaria and her idols?' "

12 When the Lord has finished all his work[p] against Mount Zion[q] and Jerusalem, he will say, "I will punish the king of Assyria[r] for the willful pride of his heart and the haughty look in his eyes. 13 For he says:

" 'By the strength of my hand I have done this,[s]
    and by my wisdom, because I have understanding.
I removed the boundaries of nations,
    I plundered their treasures;[t]
    like a mighty one I subdued[a] their kings.

a 13 Or / I subdued the mighty,

Isaiah 10:5–19

The Assyrian king's boastful rhetoric (vv. 8–11) must have seemed irrefutable to the people of his day. By the time of this prophecy, Israel (Samaria) hadn't withstood the might of his armies any more than the pagan states, and Jerusalem ruled over an even smaller kingdom. Sadly, neither the northern nor the southern kingdom was free of idolatry (cf. 2:8,20). But the Assyrians hadn't counted on God's special purpose for his people, especially his determination to deliver Jerusalem.

However great the Assyrian power, it operated only by God's permission. In carrying out God's purposes, Assyria would be subject to the same moral scrutiny as any

other nation. The Assyrians denied accountability to their Creator, insisting that they were the product of their own hands—one more expression of the creaturely pride that has such deadly effect on God's creatures.

Will any nation every truly learn Assyria's lesson? If a state does discover its divine purpose, will it carry it out humbly, recognizing the terrible risks of pride? History isn't encouraging. Many nations have come to power proclaiming dependence upon God, but one after another they have exited the scene in disgrace, having come to believe in their absolute self-sufficiency. How would you rate your own nation, both in terms of its government and its citizenry?

14 As one reaches into a nest,[u]
  so my hand reached for the wealth[v] of the nations;
as men gather abandoned eggs,
  so I gathered all the countries;
not one flapped a wing,
  or opened its mouth to chirp.' "

15 Does the ax raise itself above him who swings it,
  or the saw boast against him who uses it?[w]
As if a rod were to wield him who lifts it up,
  or a club[x] brandish him who is not wood!

16 Therefore, the Lord, the LORD Almighty,
  will send a wasting disease[y] upon his sturdy warriors;
under his pomp[z] a fire will be kindled
  like a blazing flame.

17 The Light of Israel will become a fire,[a]
  their Holy One[b] a flame;
in a single day it will burn and consume
  his thorns[c] and his briers.[d]

18 The splendor of his forests[e] and fertile fields
  it will completely destroy,
  as when a sick man wastes away.

19 And the remaining trees of his forests will be so few[f]
  that a child could write them down.

The Remnant of Israel

20 In that day[g] the remnant of Israel,
  the survivors of the house of Jacob,
will no longer rely[h] on him
  who struck them down[i]
but will truly rely[j] on the LORD,
  the Holy One of Israel.

21 A remnant[k] will return,[a] a remnant of Jacob
  will return to the Mighty God.[l]

22 Though your people, O Israel, be like the sand by the sea,
  only a remnant will return.[m]
Destruction has been decreed,[n]
  overwhelming and righteous.

23 The Lord, the LORD Almighty, will carry out
  the destruction decreed upon the whole land.[o]

24 Therefore, this is what the Lord, the LORD Almighty, says:

"O my people who live in Zion,[p]
  do not be afraid of the Assyrians,

a 21 Hebrew *shear-jashub*; also in verse 22

10:14 u Jer 49:16; Ob 1:4 v Job 31:25
10:15 w Isa 45:9; Ro 9:20-21 x ver 5
10:16 y ver 18; Isa 17:4 z Isa 8:7
10:17 a Isa 31:9 b Isa 37:23 c Nu 11:1-3 d Isa 9:18
10:18 e 2Ki 19:23
10:19 f Isa 21:17
10:20 g Isa 11:10,11 h 2Ki 16:7 i 2Ch 28:20 j Isa 17:7
10:21 k Isa 6:13 l Isa 9:6
10:22 m Ro 9:27-28 n Isa 28:22; Da 9:27
10:23 o Isa 28:22; Ro 9:27-28*
10:24 p Ps 87:5-6

Isaiah 10:20-34

Isaiah prophesied that a remnant would survive—as happened when Judah under Hezekiah endured the Assyrian invasion of 701 B.C.—and that a remnant would return—as happened many years later when the first band of exiles trekked back from Babylon. Since Assyria would be judged, why did the people of Judah still live in fear of the enemy? Their foreign policy and spiritual outlook shouldn't have been shaped by either the offers or the threats of that great power. When God's purposes for Assyria were complete, that nation would drop out of the picture. The Judahites would have been wise to make their plans with that in mind.

Do you find yourself tempted to give in to a spiritual Alzheimer's disease, forgetting the ways in which God has intervened in, provided for, guided, and sustained your life? Have you discovered that, when your spiritual memory is intact, so is your spiritual identity? Only then can we confidently face the "Assyrias" in our lives, ready to learn whatever lessons God has for us, but also able to see their future doom. That is precisely how Christians in former Soviet bloc nations survived until the God of history intervened on their behalf.

10:24
q Ex 5:14

10:25
r Isa 17:14 *s* ver 5;
Da 11:36

10:26
t Isa 37:36-38
u Isa 9:4 *v* Ex 14:16

10:27
w Isa 9:4
x Isa 14:25

10:28
y 1Sa 14:2
z 1Sa 13:2

10:29
a Jos 18:25

10:30
b 1Sa 25:44
c Ne 11:32

10:32
d 1Sa 21:1
e Jer 6:23

10:33
f Am 2:9

11:1
g ver 10; Isa 9:7;
Rev 5:5 *h* Isa 4:2

11:2
i Isa 42:1; 48:16;
61:1; Mt 3:16;
Jn 1:32-33
j Eph 1:17 *k* 2Ti 1:7

11:3
l Jn 7:24 *m* Jn 2:25

11:4
n Ps 72:2

who beat *q* you with a rod
  and lift up a club against you, as Egypt did.
25 Very soon *r* my anger against you will end
  and my wrath *s* will be directed to their destruction."

26 The LORD Almighty will lash *t* them with a whip,
  as when he struck down Midian *u* at the rock of Oreb;
and he will raise his staff over the waters, *v*
  as he did in Egypt.
27 In that day their burden will be lifted from your shoulders,
  their yoke *w* from your neck; *x*
the yoke will be broken
  because you have grown so fat. *a*

28 They enter Aiath;
  they pass through Migron; *y*
  they store supplies at Micmash. *z*
29 They go over the pass, and say,
  "We will camp overnight at Geba."
Ramah *a* trembles;
  Gibeah of Saul flees.
30 Cry out, O Daughter of Gallim! *b*
  Listen, O Laishah!
  Poor Anathoth! *c*
31 Madmenah is in flight;
  the people of Gebim take cover.
32 This day they will halt at Nob; *d*
  they will shake their fist
at the mount of the Daughter of Zion, *e*
  at the hill of Jerusalem.

33 See, the Lord, the LORD Almighty,
  will lop off the boughs with great power.
The lofty trees will be felled,
  the tall *f* ones will be brought low.
34 He will cut down the forest thickets with an ax;
  Lebanon will fall before the Mighty One.

The Branch From Jesse

11 A shoot will come up from the stump of Jesse; *g*
  from his roots a Branch *h* will bear fruit.
2 The Spirit *i* of the LORD will rest on him—
  the Spirit of wisdom *j* and of understanding,
  the Spirit of counsel and of power, *k*
  the Spirit of knowledge and of the fear of the LORD—
3 and he will delight in the fear of the LORD.

He will not judge by what he sees with his eyes, *l*
  or decide by what he hears with his ears; *m*
4 but with righteousness *n* he will judge the needy,

a 27 Hebrew; Septuagint broken / from your shoulders

Isaiah 11:1–16

Though the house of David in the person of Ahaz had failed to trust the Lord and had thus brought disaster on Judah (ch. 7), God wouldn't allow calamity to be his final word. Instead, as promised also in 9:1–7, he would one day bring a righteous descendant of Jesse (David's father) to rule over the entire earth. Filled with the Spirit of God, this Messianic King would rule with fairness and justice. The poor and meek would finally receive justice. The images in verses 6–9, depicting the aggressive and helpless living in harmony, describe the future culmination of the Messianic kingdom—and portray the dramatic change in human nature God desires now.

with justice° he will give decisions for the poor^p of the earth.
He will strike^q the earth with the rod of his mouth;
    with the breath^r of his lips he will slay the wicked.
5 Righteousness will be his belt
    and faithfulness^s the sash around his waist. ^t

6 The wolf will live with the lamb, ^u
    the leopard will lie down with the goat,
    the calf and the lion and the yearling^a together;
    and a little child will lead them.
7 The cow will feed with the bear,
    their young will lie down together,
    and the lion will eat straw like the ox.
8 The infant will play near the hole of the cobra,
    and the young child put his hand into the viper's nest.
9 They will neither harm nor destroy^v
    on all my holy mountain,
    for the earth^w will be full of the knowledge^x of the Lord
    as the waters cover the sea.

10 In that day the Root of Jesse will stand as a banner^y for the peoples; the nations^z will rally to him, ^a and his place of rest^b will be glorious. 11 In that day^c the Lord will reach out his hand a second time to reclaim the remnant that is left of his people from Assyria, ^d from Lower Egypt, from Upper Egypt, ^b from Cush, ^c from Elam, ^e from Babylonia, ^d from Hamath and from the islands^f of the sea.

12 He will raise a banner for the nations
    and gather the exiles of Israel;
    he will assemble the scattered people^g of Judah
    from the four quarters of the earth.

^a 6 Hebrew; Septuagint *lion will feed*   ^b 11 Hebrew *from Pathros*   ^c 11 That is, the upper Nile region   ^d 11 Hebrew *Shinar*

11:4
o Isa 9:7 p Isa 3:14
q Mal 4:6 r Job 4:9;
2Th 2:8
11:5
s Isa 25:1
t Eph 6:14
11:6
u Isa 65:25

11:9
v Job 5:23
w Ps 98:2-3;
Isa 52:10 x Isa 45:6,
14; Hab 2:14

11:10
y Jn 12:32
z Isa 49:23; Lk 2:32
a Ro 15:12*
b Isa 14:3; 28:12;
32:17-18
11:11
c Isa 10:20
d Isa 19:24;
Hos 11:11;
Mic 7:12; Zec 10:10
e Ge 10:22
f Isa 42:4,10,12;
66:19
11:12
g Zep 3:10

How often have aggression and oppression been justified in Biblical terms? We look to a coming day when there will be no harm or destruction, because "the earth will be full of the knowledge of the Lord" (v. 9). We are to live today in light of this coming future because God's kingdom is both now and future. The Holy Spirit dwells within every believer. He enables us to know God in a way that changes our behavior, empowering us to live faithful, faith-filled lives. To what degree is this already true for you?

11:1–3

Education

Christians believe that study of the Word shapes the Christian life. Thus, education and literacy are vitally important. Some challenges and hopeful signs:

Challenges

Primary School Attendance:
An estimated
120 million
primary-school-age
children across the globe
are not in school,
a number expected
to grow.[1]

Drop-outs:
School children
dropping out of school
after grade five range
in percentages from

● 36 percent in South Asia to

● 7 percent in Arab countries.[2]

Hope

Literacy: Worldwide literacy is increasing, from 72 percent in 1985 to 77 percent in 1995 to an expected 81 percent in 2005.[3]

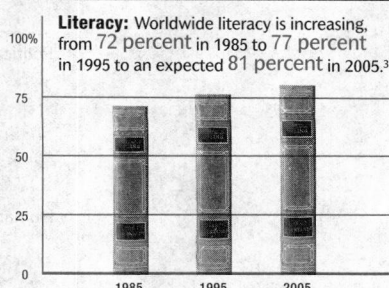

Sources: [1] "Primary School Attendance" *The Economist* (December 14, 2002): 98 [2] Smith (1999:71)
[3] United Nations Educational, Scientific and Cultural Organization (1998)

Quality of Life

Isaiah 11 presents a scenario of fullness of life. Later, in chapter 58, the prophet claimed that some of these issues were being ignored by God's people. He called them in chapter 59 to repent for perverting or denying justice.

The measurements listed on the right define how a nation today is rated in terms of the health and well-being of its citizenry. Many are priority concerns for mission, Christian relief, and development organizations as well:

For us as Christians, the quality of our life is directly related to the quality of our relationship with Jesus Christ. Yet how many of these items are basic to our standard of living? How would you manage without food, housing, a livable income, or clean water? How might you feel if you had no way to provide an education for your children? Where could you turn for help?

Similarly, how do these concerns affect Christian populations or mission/ministry efforts around the globe? Certainly the gospel can be ministered despite the poorest conditions. Yet Isaiah 58 contends that God would have his people help those who suffer rather than participate in unrelated religious activities while ignoring those in need.

Index	Measurements
• Quality of Life Index	Life expectancy Infant mortality rate Female illiteracy rate
• Education Index	School enrollment ratio Pupil teacher ratio Percent of adult illiteracy Percent of GNP used for education
• Health Status Index	Infant mortality rate Population per physician Male life expectancy
• Women's Status Index	Percentage of girls in primary education Percentage of children in primary education Percentage of adult female illiteracy Years since women's suffrage in nation Years since women's suffrage equal to men
• Economic Index	Economic growth rate Per capita income Rate of inflation Per capita food production
• Human Suffering Index	Income levels Inflation rate Demand for new jobs Urban population pressures Infant mortality rate Nutrition Clean water Energy use Adult literacy Personal freedom
• Demography Index	Total population Birth rate Death rate Rate of population increase Percentage of population under 15
• Geography Index	Percentage of arable land Number of major natural disasters Lives lost in natural disasters
• Political Stability Index	Number of political protests Number of political riots Number of political strikes Number of armed attacks Number of deaths from domestic violence
• Political Participation Index	Years since independence Years since constitution Presence of parliamentary system Presence of political party system Degree of influence of military Number of popular elections
• Human Development Index	Life expectancy Adult literacy rate School enrollment ratio Per capita income

Source: See publications of the United Nations Development Programme (*www.undp.org*)

13 Ephraim's jealousy will vanish,
and Judah's enemies[a] will be cut off;
Ephraim will not be jealous of Judah,
nor Judah hostile toward Ephraim.[h]
14 They will swoop down on the slopes of Philistia to the west;
together they will plunder the people to the east.
They will lay hands on Edom[i] and Moab,[j]
and the Ammonites will be subject to them.
15 The LORD will dry up
the gulf of the Egyptian sea;
with a scorching wind he will sweep his hand[k]
over the Euphrates River.[b][l]
He will break it up into seven streams
so that men can cross over in sandals.
16 There will be a highway[m] for the remnant of his people
that is left from Assyria,
as there was for Israel
when they came up from Egypt.[n]

Songs of Praise

12 In that day you will say:

"I will praise[o] you, O LORD.
Although you were angry with me,
your anger has turned away
and you have comforted me.
2 Surely God is my salvation;
I will trust[p] and not be afraid.
The LORD, the LORD, is my strength and my song;
he has become my salvation.[q]"
3 With joy you will draw water[r]
from the wells of salvation.

4 In that day you will say:

"Give thanks to the LORD, call on his name;[s]
make known among the nations what he has done,
and proclaim that his name is exalted.
5 Sing[t] to the LORD, for he has done glorious things;[u]
let this be known to all the world.
6 Shout aloud and sing for joy, people of Zion,
for great is the Holy One of Israel[v] among you.[w]"

A Prophecy Against Babylon

13 An oracle concerning Babylon that Isaiah son of Amoz saw:

2 Raise a banner[x] on a bare hilltop,

---

a 13 Or *hostility*   b 15 Hebrew *the River*

11:13 h Jer 3:18; Eze 37:16-17,22; Hos 1:11
11:14 i Da 11:41; Joel 3:19 j Isa 16:14; 25:10
11:15 k Isa 19:16 l Isa 7:20
11:16 m Isa 19:23; 62:10 n Ex 14:26-31
12:1 o Isa 25:1
12:2 p Isa 26:3 q Ex 15:2; Ps 118:14
12:3 r Jn 4:10,14
12:4 s Ps 105:1; Isa 24:15
12:5 t Ex 15:1 u Ps 98:1
12:6 v Isa 49:26 w Zep 3:14-17
13:2 x Jer 50:2; 51:27

Isaiah 12:1–6

This beautiful song of praise forms a fitting climax to chapters 7–11. Once Judah faced the fact that the Lord and not Assyria controlled her destiny, God would demonstrate that truth by destroying arrogant Assyria and bringing about a Messianic kingdom of peace made up not only of his own people but of representatives of all the nations. Through this hymn, consisting of two brief psalms (vv. 1–3,4–6), Isaiah represented Judah in praising God for his deliverance.

God alone initiates salvation. Judah did nothing to earn his grace. If there was to be reconciliation, it would have to come from God. This song of praise draws us as Christians to reflect on what Christ has accomplished for us. God restored us to harmony with himself through Christ's work on the cross. Reconciliation is usually a two-way street, but not in this case. We had nothing to bring to the negotiating table. But God satisfied his own justice—Christ died in our place. Now that is something to sing about!

shout to them;
beckon to them
    to enter the gates of the nobles.
3 I have commanded my holy ones;
    I have summoned my warriors[y] to carry out my wrath—
    those who rejoice[z] in my triumph.

4 Listen, a noise on the mountains,
    like that of a great multitude![a]
Listen, an uproar among the kingdoms,
    like nations massing together!
The LORD Almighty is mustering
    an army for war.
5 They come from faraway lands,
    from the ends of the heavens[b]—
the LORD and the weapons of his wrath—
    to destroy[c] the whole country.

6 Wail,[d] for the day[e] of the LORD is near;
    it will come like destruction from the Almighty.[a]
7 Because of this, all hands will go limp,
    every man's heart will melt.[f]
8 Terror[g] will seize them,
    pain and anguish will grip them;
    they will writhe like a woman in labor.
They will look aghast at each other,
    their faces aflame.[h]

9 See, the day of the LORD is coming
    —a cruel day, with wrath and fierce anger—
to make the land desolate
    and destroy the sinners within it.
10 The stars of heaven and their constellations
    will not show their light.
The rising sun[i] will be darkened[j]
    and the moon will not give its light.[k]
11 I will punish[l] the world for its evil,
    the wicked for their sins.
I will put an end to the arrogance of the haughty
    and will humble the pride of the ruthless.
12 I will make man[m] scarcer than pure gold,
    more rare than the gold of Ophir.
13 Therefore I will make the heavens tremble;[n]
    and the earth will shake from its place
at the wrath of the LORD Almighty,
    in the day of his burning anger.

13:3
y Joel 3:11
z Ps 149:2

13:4
a Joel 3:14

13:5
b Isa 5:26 c Isa 24:1

13:6
d Eze 30:2
e Isa 2:12; Joel 1:15

13:7
f Eze 21:7
13:8
g Isa 21:4 h Na 2:10

13:10
i Isa 24:23
j Isa 5:30; Rev 8:12
k Eze 32:7;
Mt 24:29*;
Mk 13:24*
13:11
l Isa 3:11; 11:4;
26:21

13:12
m Isa 4:1

13:13
n Isa 34:4; 51:6;
Hag 2:6

[a] 6 Hebrew *Shaddai*

Isaiah 13:1—14:23

Chapters 13–23 fall into a category found in several of the prophets: oracles (messages from God) against the nations. Just because God used the nations as his tool to judge disobedient Israel and Judah didn't mean these other nations would get off scot-free. Israel *would be restored after disciplinary punishment*, but some of these nations would disappear from the earth.

Concerning the identity of "Babylon," see "There and Then" for 14:24–27. The poem in 14:4b–21 is one of the finest in the Hebrew language. The four stanzas form a lament, a song mourning a death. The first stanza considers Earth's reaction to the death (vv. 4b–8); the second, the underworld's response (vv. 9–11); the third, heaven's perspective (vv. 12–15); the fourth, a return to contemplate the dead person's tragic fate on Earth (vv. 16–21). Yet this wasn't a typical lament but a biting parody of one—a "taunt," as Isaiah called it (v. 4a). Instead of expressing grief, it communicated delight and satisfaction. Death was welcomed as the leveler of the tyrant's proud, oppressive ambition.

¹⁴Like a hunted gazelle,
    like sheep without a shepherd, ⁰
each will return to his own people,
    each will flee to his native land. ᵖ
¹⁵Whoever is captured will be thrust through;
    all who are caught will fall �q by the sword. ʳ
¹⁶Their infants ˢ will be dashed to pieces before their eyes;
    their houses will be looted and their wives ravished.
¹⁷See, I will stir up ᵗ against them the Medes,
    who do not care for silver
    and have no delight in gold. ᵘ
¹⁸Their bows will strike down the young men;
    they will have no mercy on infants
    nor will they look with compassion on children.
¹⁹Babylon, the jewel of kingdoms,
    the glory ᵛ of the Babylonians' ᵃ pride,
will be overthrown ʷ by God
    like Sodom and Gomorrah. ˣ
²⁰She will never be inhabited ʸ
    or lived in through all generations;

ᵃ 19 Or *Chaldeans'*

13:14
⁰ 1Ki 22:17
ᵖ Jer 50:16

13:15
q Jer 51:4
ʳ Isa 14:19;
Jer 50:25
13:16
ˢ Ps 137:9
13:17
ᵗ Jer 51:1
ᵘ Pr 6:34-35

13:19
ᵛ Da 4:30
ʷ Rev 14:8
ˣ Ge 19:24
13:20
ʸ Isa 14:23;
34:10-15

📖 We humans are neither self-originating nor self-authenticating, so we are foolish to trust in humanity. We may love our country and grieve over signs of its demise. But hope in its permanent success is vain. God may give us a revival, but he alone determines our nation's final outcome.

We have been created to reflect the glory of the only God. If a mirror says "No, I will reflect only myself," pulls down the shades, and turns off the lights, it shouldn't be surprised that there is nothing to reflect. It has violated the terms of its creation. Likewise, when humans say "I will live only for myself," it should come as no surprise that there is no real life to be lived.

Snapshots

13:14

Tension in Macedonia

Imagine 50,000 weary, traumatized people turning up on your doorstep, all wanting food, drink, and a warm bed. An unsettling prospect, but the kind of dilemma faced by Judy, a New Zealand-born aid worker.

As ethnic tensions simmer in Macedonia, Judy watches from neighboring Albania, fearing that as many as 200,000 Albanians might flee to their homeland in circumstances mirroring those following bloody conflicts elsewhere in the Balkans.

Judy presides over an office bubbling with activity. There are supplies to be procured—mattresses, blankets, hygiene kits, and baby needs. Sites earmarked for temporary accommodation—old barracks, sports stadiums, schools—need to be checked.

"There is an adventurous streak in me," admits Judy with a mischievous smile when she manages to tear herself away from the melee. "I'm not the regular grandmother that sits at home and knits."

> "**P**eople don't realize that what happens in the Balkans could potentially happen to them."

"People don't realize that what happens in the Balkans could potentially happen to them. Someone starts playing with guns, and sons are killed and husbands are killed and houses are burnt down . . . You are left only with . . . horrific memories."

In times like this Judy—a born-again Christian—relies on the inner strength God alone gives her.

no Arab[z] will pitch his tent there,
no shepherd will rest his flocks there.

21 But desert creatures[a] will lie there,
jackals will fill her houses;
there the owls will dwell,
and there the wild goats will leap about.

22 Hyenas will howl in her strongholds,[b]
jackals[c] in her luxurious palaces.
Her time is at hand,[d]
and her days will not be prolonged.

14 The LORD will have compassion[e] on Jacob;
once again he will choose[f] Israel
and will settle them in their own land.
Aliens[g] will join them
and unite with the house of Jacob.
2 Nations will take them
and bring[h] them to their own place.
And the house of Israel will possess the nations[i]
as menservants and maidservants in the LORD's land.
They will make captives of their captors
and rule over their oppressors.[j]

3 On the day the LORD gives you relief[k] from suffering and turmoil and cruel bondage, 4 you will take up this taunt[l] against the king of Babylon:

How the oppressor[m] has come to an end!
How his fury[a] has ended!
5 The LORD has broken the rod of the wicked,[n]
the scepter of the rulers,
6 which in anger struck down peoples[o]
with unceasing blows,
and in fury subdued nations
with relentless aggression.[p]
7 All the lands are at rest and at peace;
they break into singing.[q]
8 Even the pine trees[r] and the cedars of Lebanon
exult over you and say,
"Now that you have been laid low,
no woodsman comes to cut us down."
9 The grave[b][s] below is all astir

---

a 4 Dead Sea Scrolls, Septuagint and Syriac; the meaning of the word in the Masoretic Text is uncertain.   b 9 Hebrew *Sheol*; also in verses 11 and 15

Cross references

13:20
z 2Ch 17:11

13:21
a Rev 18:2

13:22
b Isa 25:2
c Isa 34:13
d Jer 51:33

14:1
e Ps 102:13; Isa 49:10,13; 54:7-8,10
f Isa 41:8; 44:1; 49:7; Zec 1:17; 2:12
g Eph 2:12-19

14:2
h Isa 60:9 i Isa 49:7, 23 j Isa 60:14; 61:5

14:3
k Isa 11:10

14:4
l Hab 2:6 m Isa 9:4

14:5
n Ps 125:3

14:6
o Isa 10:14
p Isa 47:6

14:7
q Ps 98:1; 126:1-3

14:8
r Eze 31:16

14:9
s Eze 32:21

13:18

Look With Compassion on Children

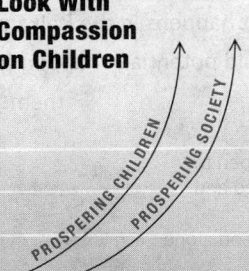

PROSPERING CHILDREN
PROSPERING SOCIETY

Isaiah cited as an example of extreme depravity and evil the refusal to look with compassion on children. As a society's children prosper, the society prospers. If its children suffer, it will suffer. Signs of care for children include:

• Sufficient, fairly distributed, nutritious food
• Access to clean water
• Adequate and appropriate health care
• Safe, clean shelter
• Equal and excellent educational opportunity
• Plenty of love and positive attention
• Emotional support
• Spiritual nurture—opportunity to grow in the things of God

How are the children—*all* the children—in your community faring according to these criteria?

to meet you at your coming;
  it rouses the spirits of the departed to greet you—
  all those who were leaders in the world;
  it makes them rise from their thrones—
  all those who were kings over the nations.
¹⁰They will all respond,
  they will say to you,
  "You also have become weak, as we are;
  you have become like us." ᵗ

¹¹ All your pomp has been brought down to the grave,
  along with the noise of your harps;
  maggots are spread out beneath you
  and worms ᵘ cover you.

¹² How you have fallen ᵛ from heaven,
  O morning star, ʷ son of the dawn!
  You have been cast down to the earth,
  you who once laid low the nations!
¹³ You said in your heart,
  "I will ascend ˣ to heaven;
  I will raise my throne ʸ
  above the stars of God;
  I will sit enthroned on the mount of assembly,
  on the utmost heights of the sacred mountain. ᵃ
¹⁴ I will ascend above the tops of the clouds;
  I will make myself like the Most High." ᶻ
¹⁵ But you are brought down to the grave,
  to the depths ᵃ of the pit.

¹⁶ Those who see you stare at you,
  they ponder your fate: ᵇ
  "Is this the man who shook the earth
  and made kingdoms tremble,
¹⁷ the man who made the world a desert, ᶜ
  who overthrew its cities
  and would not let his captives go home?"

¹⁸ All the kings of the nations lie in state,
  each in his own tomb.
¹⁹ But you are cast out ᵈ of your tomb
  like a rejected branch;
  you are covered with the slain,
  with those pierced by the sword,
  those who descend to the stones of the pit. ᵉ
  Like a corpse trampled underfoot,
²⁰   you will not join them in burial,
  for you have destroyed your land
  and killed your people.

  The offspring ᶠ of the wicked ᵍ
  will never be mentioned ʰ again.
²¹ Prepare a place to slaughter his sons
  for the sins of their forefathers; ⁱ
  they are not to rise to inherit the land
  and cover the earth with their cities.

²² "I will rise up against them,"
  declares the LORD Almighty.

ᵃ 13 Or *the north;* Hebrew *Zaphon*

14:10
ᵗ Eze 32:21

14:11
ᵘ Isa 51:8
14:12
ᵛ Isa 34:4; Lk 10:18
ʷ 2Pe 1:19;
Rev 2:28; 8:10; 9:1

14:13
ˣ Da 5:23; 8:10;
Mt 11:23
ʸ Eze 28:2; 2Th 2:4

14:14
ᶻ Isa 47:8; 2Th 2:4

14:15
ᵃ Mt 11:23;
Lk 10:15

14:16
ᵇ Jer 50:23

14:17
ᶜ Joel 2:3

14:19
ᵈ Isa 22:16-18
ᵉ Jer 41:7-9

14:20
ᶠ Job 18:19
ᵍ Isa 1:4 h Ps 21:10

14:21
ⁱ Ex 20:5; Lev 26:39

14:22
j 1Ki 14:10;
Job 18:19
14:23
k Isa 34:11-15;
Zep 2:14

"I will cut off from Babylon her name and survivors,
  her offspring and descendants, *j* "

                                        declares the LORD.

23 "I will turn her into a place for owls *k*
  and into swampland;
I will sweep her with the broom of destruction,"
  declares the LORD Almighty.

14:24
l Isa 45:23
m Ac 4:28

A Prophecy Against Assyria

24 The LORD Almighty has sworn, *l*

"Surely, as I have planned, so it will be,
  and as I have purposed, so it will stand. *m*

14:25
n Isa 10:5,12
o. Isa 9:4 p Isa 10:27

25 I will crush the Assyrian *n* in my land;
  on my mountains I will trample him down.
His yoke *o* will be taken from my people,
  and his burden removed from their shoulders. *p* "

14:26
q Isa 23:9
r Ex 15:12

26 This is the plan *q* determined for the whole world;
  this is the hand *r* stretched out over all nations.

14:27
s 2Ch 20:6;
Isa 43:13; Da 4:35

27 For the LORD Almighty has purposed, and who can thwart him?
  His hand is stretched out, and who can turn it back? *s*

14:28
t Isa 13:1
u 2Ki 16:20
14:29
v 2Ch 26:6
w Isa 11:8

A Prophecy Against the Philistines

28 This oracle *t* came in the year King Ahaz *u* died:

29 Do not rejoice, all you Philistines, *v*
  that the rod that struck you is broken;
from the root of that snake will spring up a viper, *w*
  its fruit will be a darting, venomous serpent.

14:30
x Isa 3:15
y Isa 7:21-22
z Isa 8:21; 9:20;
51:19 a Jer 25:16

30 The poorest of the poor will find pasture,
  and the needy *x* will lie down in safety. *y*
But your root I will destroy by famine; *z*
  it will slay *a* your survivors.

14:31
b Isa 3:26 c Jer 1:14

31 Wail, O gate! *b* Howl, O city!
  Melt away, all you Philistines!
A cloud of smoke comes from the north, *c*
  and there is not a straggler in its ranks.

Isaiah 14:24–27

The lack of an introductory "oracle" formula here (cf. 13:1; 14:28; 15:1) clues us that this wasn't a separate oracle against Assyria but a conclusion to the "Babylon" oracle. Assyria likely represented all the Mesopotamian powers included in the term "Babylon," who had exalted themselves to the heights but were consigned to go down to the pit (14:11–15). Isaiah asserted that any person or nation lifting itself up against God's plan and purpose marked itself for destruction.

A little self-respect is a good thing. But much of the modern "self-esteem" movement is a failed attempt to counteract the effects of Western society's increasing self-centeredness. Our only hope for rediscovering our individual worth is to discover our worth to God. He was willing to die in our place. He not only loves us; he likes us! The sense of value that springs from that knowledge is the furthest thing from the proud, lonely self-love that shouts to a deaf universe, "I'm somebody!"

Isaiah 14:28–32

It would appear that the Philistines were inviting Judah to join them in revolt against Assyria (cf. v. 32). Isaiah answered that God would take care of Judah without Philistine help. Would Judah trust the nations or the Lord? God's people didn't need to ally themselves with the Philistines; they themselves were the flock of God, and he could tend them (v. 30). In fact, the Philistines would be consumed by "a cloud of smoke from the north" (v. 31).

The issue here is the folly of turning away from the secure to depend on the failing. Do the material and physical at times feel so real that God's help seems illusory and intangible? Often in the church and in our personal lives we are attracted to ideas based on the subtle assumption that "God helps those who help themselves." Count Bismarck is reported to have stated that "God is on the side of the big battalions." That is the world talking. The Bible says, "Trust in the LORD with all your heart and lean not on your own understanding" (Prov. 3:5). That is just what Isaiah was saying.

32 What answer shall be given
  to the envoys[d] of that nation?
"The LORD has established Zion,[e]
  and in her his afflicted people will find refuge.[f]"

A Prophecy Against Moab

15 An oracle concerning Moab:[g]

Ar in Moab is ruined,[h]
  destroyed in a night!
Kir in Moab is ruined,
  destroyed in a night!
2 Dibon goes up to its temple,
  to its high places[i] to weep;
Moab wails over Nebo and Medeba.
Every head is shaved[j]
  and every beard cut off.
3 In the streets they wear sackcloth;
  on the roofs and in the public squares[k]
they all wail,
  prostrate with weeping.[l]
4 Heshbon and Elealeh[m] cry out,
  their voices are heard all the way to Jahaz.
Therefore the armed men of Moab cry out,
  and their hearts are faint.

5 My heart cries out over Moab;[n]
  her fugitives flee as far as Zoar,
  as far as Eglath Shelishiyah.
They go up the way to Luhith,
  weeping as they go;
on the road to Horonaim[o]
  they lament their destruction.[p]
6 The waters of Nimrim are dried up[q]
  and the grass is withered;[r]
the vegetation is gone
  and nothing green is left.
7 So the wealth they have acquired[s] and stored up
  they carry away over the Ravine of the Poplars.
8 Their outcry echoes along the border of Moab;
  their wailing reaches as far as Eglaim,
  their lamentation as far as Beer Elim.
9 Dimon's[a] waters are full of blood,
  but I will bring still more upon Dimon[a]—
a lion[t] upon the fugitives of Moab
  and upon those who remain in the land.

Cross references:
14:32 [d] Isa 37:9; [e] Ps 87:2,5; Isa 44:28; 54:11; [f] Isa 4:6; Jas 2:5
15:1 [g] Isa 11:14; [h] Jer 48:24,41
15:2 [i] Jer 48:35; [j] Lev 21:5
15:3 [k] Jer 48:38; [l] Isa 22:4
15:4 [m] Nu 32:3
15:5 [n] Jer 48:31; [o] Jer 48:3,34; [p] Jer 4:20; 48:5
15:6 [q] Isa 19:5-7; Jer 48:34; [r] Joel 1:12
15:7 [s] Isa 30:6; Jer 48:36
15:9 [t] 2Ki 17:25

[a] 9 Masoretic Text; Dead Sea Scrolls, some Septuagint manuscripts and Vulgate *Dibon*

Isaiah 15:1—16:13

Though several of the sites mentioned in chapter 15 are uncertain, there seems to be a north-to-south progression in the listing, which would have been characteristic of the flight of the Moabites southward before a marauding army heading south along the King's Highway. The Ravine of the Poplars (15:7) was probably at Moab's southern border with Edom. It would have been natural for the fugitives to seek refuge in Edom. But that wasn't the case. Instead, they begged permission for refuge in Judah (16:1–4a).

In 16:4b–5 Isaiah took an opportunity to speak about ultimate trust not only for the Moabites but for the whole world. This short statement is reminiscent not only of 11:1–16 but also of 9:1–7. A new Davidic king would replace oppression, destruction, and aggression with love, justice, and righteousness. Neither the people of Moab nor those of Judah would live to see him, but members of both nations could, in their own day, put their trust in the God who had made such a promise.

16:1
u 2Ki 3:4 v 2Ki 14:7
w Isa 10:32

16

Send lambs[u] as tribute
  to the ruler of the land,
from Sela,[v] across the desert,
  to the mount of the Daughter of Zion.[w]

16:2
x Pr 27:8
y Nu 21:13-14;
Jer 48:20

2 Like fluttering birds
  pushed from the nest,[x]
so are the women of Moab
  at the fords of the Arnon.[y]

16:3
z 1Ki 18:4

3 "Give us counsel,
  render a decision.
Make your shadow like night—
  at high noon.
Hide the fugitives,[z]
  do not betray the refugees.

16:4
a Isa 9:4

4 Let the Moabite fugitives stay with you;
  be their shelter from the destroyer."

The oppressor[a] will come to an end,
  and destruction will cease;
the aggressor will vanish from the land.

16:5
b Da 7:14; Mic 4:7
c Lk 1:32 d Isa 9:7

5 In love a throne[b] will be established;
  in faithfulness a man will sit on it—
one from the house[a] of David[c]—
  one who in judging seeks justice[d]
  and speeds the cause of righteousness.

16:6
e Am 2:1; Zep 2:8
f Ob 1:3; Zep 2:10

6 We have heard of Moab's[e] pride[f]—
  her overweening pride and conceit,
her pride and her insolence—
  but her boasts are empty.

16:7
g Jer 48:20
h 1Ch 16:3
i 2Ki 3:25

7 Therefore the Moabites wail,[g]
  they wail together for Moab.
Lament and grieve
  for the men[b][h] of Kir Hareseth.[i]

8 The fields of Heshbon wither,
  the vines of Sibmah also.
The rulers of the nations
  have trampled down the choicest vines,
which once reached Jazer
  and spread toward the desert.
Their shoots spread out
  and went as far as the sea.

16:9
j Isa 15:3
k Jer 40:12

9 So I weep,[j] as Jazer weeps,
  for the vines of Sibmah.
O Heshbon, O Elealeh,
  I drench you with tears!
The shouts of joy over your ripened fruit
  and over your harvests[k] have been stilled.

16:10
l Isa 24:7-8

10 Joy and gladness are taken away from the orchards;[l]

---

a 5 Hebrew *tent* b 7 Or *"raisin cakes,"* a wordplay

The Moabites made one right move: They turned for help to Judah instead of Edom. Did they recognize that *Judah's God was different than their gods* and had the power and grace to deliver his people and those who allied themselves with them? In view of the rest of chapter 16, it doesn't appear that their understanding was nearly that deep. Similarly, many hurting people today turn to the church for reasons they themselves may not fully understand, or for practical reasons, like a children's program or food pantry. Yet the church has one ultimate, unfailing Word to offer these "refugees"—*Jesus* (16:5). How does your congregation help such lost souls encounter the One they are really looking for?

no one sings or shouts in the vineyards;
no one treads[m] out wine at the presses,[n]
    for I have put an end to the shouting.
11 My heart laments for Moab[o] like a harp,
    my inmost being[p] for Kir Hareseth.
12 When Moab appears at her high place,
    she only wears herself out;
when she goes to her shrine[q] to pray,
    it is to no avail.[r]

13 This is the word the LORD has already spoken concerning Moab. 14 But now the LORD says: "Within three years, as a servant bound by contract would count them, Moab's splendor and all her many people will be despised,[s] and her survivors will be very few and feeble."[t]

An Oracle Against Damascus

17 An oracle concerning Damascus:[u]

"See, Damascus will no longer be a city
    but will become a heap of ruins.[v]
2 The cities of Aroer will be deserted
    and left to flocks,[w] which will lie down,
    with no one to make them afraid.[x]
3 The fortified city will disappear from Ephraim,
    and royal power from Damascus;
the remnant of Aram will be
    like the glory[y] of the Israelites,"[z]
                    declares the LORD Almighty.

4 "In that day the glory of Jacob will fade;
    the fat of his body will waste[a] away.
5 It will be as when a reaper gathers the standing grain
    and harvests[b] the grain with his arm—
as when a man gleans heads of grain
    in the Valley of Rephaim.
6 Yet some gleanings will remain,[c]
    as when an olive tree is beaten,[d]
leaving two or three olives on the topmost branches,
    four or five on the fruitful boughs,"
                    declares the LORD, the God of Israel.

7 In that day men will look[e] to their Maker
    and turn their eyes to the Holy One[f] of Israel.

16:10
m Jdg 9:27
n Job 24:11
16:11
o Isa 15:5
p Isa 63:15;
Hos 11:8; Php 2:1
16:12
q Isa 15:2
r 1Ki 18:29
16:14
s Isa 25:10;
Jer 48:42
t Isa 21:17
17:1
u Ge 14:15;
Jer 49:23; Ac 9:2
v Isa 25:2; Am 1:3;
Zec 9:1
17:2
w Isa 7:21; Eze 25:5
x Jer 7:33; Mic 4:4
17:3
y ver 4; Hos 9:11
z Isa 7:8,16; 8:4
17:4
a Isa 10:16
17:5
b ver 11; Jer 51:33;
Joel 3:13; Mt 13:30
17:6
c Dt 4:27; Isa 24:13
d Isa 27:12
17:7
e Isa 10:20 f Mic 7:7

Isaiah 17:1–14

Isaiah 17:1–3 speaks of the fall of Aram, northeast of the Sea of Galilee (modern Syria). The nation was represented by its capital city, Damascus, and by Aroer, located east of the Dead Sea at the farthest southern point of Aram's control. Verse 3 leads to the change of subject from Aram to Israel (probably the northern kingdom, specifically) for the rest of the passage. Chapter 7 reflects this same connection of judgment on Damascus and Israel.

Asherah poles (v. 8) were sacred trees or wooden poles dedicated to the worship of the fertility goddess Asherah, the "consort" (husband or companion) of El, the chief Canaanite god. Recent archaeological discoveries confirm that some Israelites worshiped Asherah as the Lord's consort. Isaiah's emphasis is on their worshiping "their Maker" instead of what "their fingers have made" (vv. 7–8). The prophet's hope was that the people would abandon their idolatry, but the present held out only the reality of judgment.

Why does religion based on human effort so often degenerate into sexual fascination? Once we have abandoned the worship of the Maker, we need an outlet for worshiping something we have made. So we turn to the creative powers within ourselves. But since mere creativity as a concept is far too abstract and bland— and we who were created to worship God can't live without mystery—the mystery of sexuality comes to rule our lives. The sad harvest of this false worship is disease, degeneration, and perversion.

17:8
g Isa 2:18,20; 30:22

8 They will not look to the altars,
　　the work of their hands, [g]
and they will have no regard for the Asherah poles [a]
and the incense altars their fingers have made.

9 In that day their strong cities, which they left because of the Israelites, will be like places abandoned to thickets and undergrowth. And all will be desolation.

17:10
h Isa 51:13
i Ps 68:19; Isa 12:2

10 You have forgotten [h] God your Savior; [i]
　　you have not remembered the Rock, your fortress.
Therefore, though you set out the finest plants
　　and plant imported vines,

17:11
j Ps 90:6 k Hos 8:7
l Job 4:8

11 though on the day you set them out, you make them grow,
　　and on the morning [j] when you plant them, you bring them to bud,
yet the harvest will be as nothing [k]
　　in the day of disease and incurable pain. [l]

17:12
m Ps 18:4; Jer 6:23;
Lk 21:25

12 Oh, the raging of many nations—
　　they rage like the raging sea! [m]
Oh, the uproar of the peoples—
　　they roar like the roaring of great waters!

17:13
n Ps 9:5 o Isa 13:14
p Isa 41:2,15-16
q Job 21:18

13 Although the peoples roar like the roar of surging waters,
　　when he rebukes [n] them they flee [o] far away,
driven before the wind like chaff [p] on the hills,
　　like tumbleweed before a gale. [q]

17:14
r 2Ki 19:35

14 In the evening, sudden terror!
　　Before the morning, they are gone! [r]
This is the portion of those who loot us,
　　the lot of those who plunder us.

A Prophecy Against Cush

18:1
s Isa 20:3-5;
Eze 30:4-5,9;
Zep 2:12; 3:10
18:2
t Ex 2:3
u Ge 10:8-9;
2Ch 12:3
v ver 7

18 Woe to the land of whirring wings [b]
　　along the rivers of Cush, [c] [s]
2 which sends envoys by sea
　　in papyrus [t] boats over the water.

Go, swift messengers,
to a people tall and smooth-skinned,
　　to a people feared far and wide,
an aggressive [u] nation of strange speech,
　　whose land is divided by rivers. [v]

18:3
w Isa 5:26

3 All you people of the world,
　　you who live on the earth,
when a banner [w] is raised on the mountains,
　　you will see it,
and when a trumpet sounds,
　　you will hear it.

---

a 8 That is, symbols of the goddess Asherah   b 1 Or of locusts   c 1 That is, the upper Nile region

---

Isaiah 18:1–7

Cush, located south of Egypt, was also known as Ethiopia (not to be confused with modern Ethiopia, farther to the south). In about 740 B.C. the Cushite Piankhy took over Egypt. He and his successor, Shabako, brought new energy to Egyptian affairs. Most likely both attempted to cement alliances with various surrounding countries in order to counter the Assyrian threat. Imagine the stir in Jerusalem from the tall, regal-looking Cushite messengers. But Isaiah insisted that the envoys should go home and tell their people to beware of the world's true Ruler.

Nations take drastic steps to elevate themselves to positions of absolute power. But God has reserved that power for himself, and their efforts are about as useful as a two-year-old's struggling against the restraints in a car-seat. To the child this is a matter of serious rebellion. To the adults looking on, it's laughable. Psalm 46:6 makes a similar point: "Nations are in uproar, kingdoms fall; he lifts his voice, the earth melts."

⁴This is what the LORD says to me:
  "I will remain quiet and will look on from my dwelling place, ˣ
like shimmering heat in the sunshine,
  like a cloud of dewʸ in the heat of harvest."
⁵For, before the harvest, when the blossom is gone
  and the flower becomes a ripening grape,
he will cut off the shoots with pruning knives,
  and cut down and take away the spreading branches. ᶻ
⁶They will all be left to the mountain birds of prey
  and to the wild animals;ᵃ
the birds will feed on them all summer,
  the wild animals all winter.

⁷At that time gifts will be brought to the LORD Almighty

  from a people tall and smooth-skinned,
    from a people feared far and wide,
  an aggressive nation of strange speech,
    whose land is divided by rivers—

the gifts will be brought to Mount Zion, the place of the Name of the LORD Almighty. ᵇ

A Prophecy About Egypt

19 An oracleᶜ concerning Egypt: ᵈ ᵉ

  See, the LORD rides on a swift cloudᶠ
    and is coming to Egypt.
  The idols of Egypt tremble before him,
    and the hearts of the Egyptians meltᵍ within them.

²"I will stir up Egyptian against Egyptian—
  brother will fight against brother, ʰ
  neighbor against neighbor,
  city against city,
  kingdom against kingdom. ⁱ
³The Egyptians will lose heart,
  and I will bring their plans to nothing;
they will consult the idols and the spirits of the dead,
  the mediums and the spiritists. ʲ
⁴I will hand the Egyptians over
  to the power of a cruel master,
and a fierce kingᵏ will rule over them,"
  declares the Lord, the LORD Almighty.

⁵The waters of the river will dry up, ˡ
  and the riverbed will be parched and dry.
⁶The canals will stink; ᵐ
  the streams of Egypt will dwindle and dry up. ⁿ

18:4
x Isa 26:21;
Hos 5:15
y Isa 26:19;
Hos 14:5

18:5
z Isa 17:10-11;
Eze 17:6

18:6
a Isa 56:9; Jer 7:33;
Eze 32:4; 39:17

18:7
b Ps 68:31

19:1
c Isa 13:1; Jer 43:12
d Joel 3:19
e Ex 12:12
f Ps 18:10; 104:3;
Rev 1:7 g Jos 2:11

19:2
h Jdg 7:22;
Mt 10:21,36
i 2Ch 20:23

19:3
j Isa 8:19; 47:13;
Da 2:2,10

19:4
k Isa 20:4;
Jer 46:26;
Eze 29:19

19:5
l Jer 51:36
19:6
m Ex 7:18
n Isa 37:25;
Eze 30:12

Isaiah 19:1–25

📖 The oracle (message) about Egypt divides into three parts. The first (vv. 1–15) predicted Egypt's fall; none of the gifts this nation had historically relied upon could save her from judgment. The second (vv. 16–25) spoke of Egypt's eventual turning to Israel's God. The third (20:1–6; see note to follow) reverted back to Isaiah's time and the certainty of Egypt's judgment. Why trust Egypt? She couldn't save herself and would one day turn to worship the very God Israel now feared to trust.

Non-believers are tempted to trust in three things (idols) to make sense of life: human wisdom, the natural environment, and the spirit world. Each of these is rooted in creation and therefore unworthy of worship. This passage teaches three truths: the inadequacy of the things of Earth to give meaning to life, God's intention to save people from every nation on Earth, and the inevitable failure of all false hopes. Our challenge today is to find the right means to effectively communicate these truths.

19:6
o Isa 15:6

19:7
p Isa 23:3

19:8
q Eze 47:10
r Hab 1:15

19:9
s Pr 7:16; Eze 27:7

19:11
t Nu 13:22
u 1Ki 4:30; Ac 7:22

19:12
v 1Co 1:20
w Isa 14:24;
Ro 9:17

19:13
x Jer 2:16;
Eze 30:13,16

19:14
y Mt 17:17

19:15
z Isa 9:14

19:16
a Jer 51:30;
Na 3:13
b Heb 10:31
c Isa 11:15
19:17
d Isa 14:24

19:18
e Zep 3:9
19:19
f Jos 22:10
g Ge 28:18

19:20
h Isa 49:24-26

19:21
i Isa 11:9 j Isa 56:7;
Mal 1:11
19:22
k Heb 12:11
l Isa 45:14;
Hos 14:1
m Dt 32:39
19:23
n Isa 11:16
o Isa 27:13

19:25
p Ps 100:3
q Isa 29:23; 45:11;
60:21; 64:8;
Eph 2:10 r Hos 2:23

The reeds and rushes will wither,[o]
7   also the plants along the Nile,
    at the mouth of the river.
Every sown field[p] along the Nile
    will become parched, will blow away and be no more.
8 The fishermen[q] will groan and lament,
    all who cast hooks[r] into the Nile;
those who throw nets on the water
    will pine away.
9 Those who work with combed flax will despair,
    the weavers of fine linen[s] will lose hope.
10 The workers in cloth will be dejected,
    and all the wage earners will be sick at heart.

11 The officials of Zoan[t] are nothing but fools;
    the wise counselors of Pharaoh give senseless advice.
How can you say to Pharaoh,
    "I am one of the wise men,[u]
    a disciple of the ancient kings"?

12 Where are your wise men[v] now?
    Let them show you and make known
what the LORD Almighty
    has planned[w] against Egypt.
13 The officials of Zoan have become fools,
    the leaders of Memphis[a][x] are deceived;
the cornerstones of her peoples
    have led Egypt astray.
14 The LORD has poured into them
    a spirit of dizziness;[y]
they make Egypt stagger in all that she does,
    as a drunkard staggers around in his vomit.
15 There is nothing Egypt can do—
    head or tail, palm branch or reed.[z]

16 In that day the Egyptians will be like women.[a] They will shudder with fear[b] at the uplifted hand[c] that the LORD Almighty raises against them. 17 And the land of Judah will bring terror to the Egyptians; everyone to whom Judah is mentioned will be terrified, because of what the LORD Almighty is planning[d] against them.

18 In that day five cities in Egypt will speak the language of Canaan and swear allegiance[e] to the LORD Almighty. One of them will be called the City of Destruction.[b]

19 In that day there will be an altar[f] to the LORD in the heart of Egypt, and a monument[g] to the LORD at its border. 20 It will be a sign and witness to the LORD Almighty in the land of Egypt. When they cry out to the LORD because of their oppressors, he will send them a savior and defender, and he will rescue[h] them. 21 So the LORD will make himself known to the Egyptians, and in that day they will acknowledge[i] the LORD. They will worship[j] with sacrifices and grain offerings; they will make vows to the LORD and keep them. 22 The LORD will strike[k] Egypt with a plague; he will strike them and heal them. They will turn[l] to the LORD, and he will respond to their pleas and heal[m] them.

23 In that day there will be a highway[n] from Egypt to Assyria. The Assyrians will go to Egypt and the Egyptians to Assyria. The Egyptians and Assyrians will worship[o] together. 24 In that day Israel will be the third, along with Egypt and Assyria, a blessing on the earth. 25 The LORD Almighty will bless them, saying, "Blessed be Egypt my people,[p] Assyria my handiwork,[q] and Israel my inheritance.[r]"

---

[a] 13 Hebrew *Noph*   [b] 18 Most manuscripts of the Masoretic Text; some manuscripts of the Masoretic Text, Dead Sea Scrolls and Vulgate *City of the Sun* (that is, Heliopolis)

A Prophecy Against Egypt and Cush

20 In the year that the supreme commander, *s* sent by Sargon king of Assyria, came to Ashdod and attacked and captured it— ²at that time the LORD spoke through Isaiah son of Amoz. *t* He said to him, "Take off the sackcloth *u* from your body and the sandals *v* from your feet." And he did so, going around stripped *w* and barefoot. *x*

³Then the LORD said, "Just as my servant Isaiah has gone stripped and barefoot for three years, as a sign *y* and portent against Egypt and Cush, *a z* ⁴so the king *a* of Assyria will lead away stripped and barefoot the Egyptian captives and Cushite exiles, young and old, with buttocks bared—to Egypt's shame. *b* ⁵Those who trusted in Cush and boasted in Egypt *c* will be afraid and put to shame. ⁶In that day the people who live on this coast will say, 'See what has happened to those we relied on, those we fled to for help *d* and deliverance from the king of Assyria! How then can we escape? *e* '"

A Prophecy Against Babylon

21 An oracle concerning the Desert *f* by the Sea:

Like whirlwinds sweeping through the southland, *g*
    an invader comes from the desert,
    from a land of terror.

²A dire *h* vision has been shown to me:
    The traitor betrays, *i* the looter takes loot.
Elam, *j* attack! Media, lay siege!
    I will bring to an end all the groaning she caused.

³At this my body is racked with pain,
    pangs seize me, like those of a woman in labor; *k*
I am staggered by what I hear,
    I am bewildered by what I see.
⁴My heart falters,
    fear makes me tremble;
the twilight I longed for
    has become a horror to me.

⁵They set the tables,
    they spread the rugs,
    they eat, they drink! *l*

---

a 3 That is, the upper Nile region; also in verse 5

20:1
s 2Ki 18:17

20:2
t Isa 13:1
u Zec 13:4; Mt 3:4
v Eze 24:17,23
w 1Sa 19:24
x Mic 1:8

20:3
y Isa 8:18
z Isa 37:9; 43:3
20:4
a Isa 19:4
b Isa 47:3;
Jer 13:22,26
20:5
c 2Ki 18:21;
Isa 30:5
20:6
d Isa 10:3
e Jer 30:15-17;
Mt 23:33; 1Th 5:3;
Heb 2:3
21:1
f Isa 13:21;
Jer 51:43
g Zec 9:14

21:2
h Ps 60:3; Isa 33:1
i Isa 22:6; Jer 49:34

21:3
k Ps 48:6; Isa 26:17

21:5
l Jer 51:39,57;
Da 5:2

Isaiah 20:1–6

This is the only recorded example of Isaiah's performing symbolic actions—more typical of other prophets, like Ezekiel. It's uncertain whether Isaiah was fully nude during this three-year period. The Hebrew word for "stripped" could connote either full or partial nudity, such as wearing only a loincloth. In any case, Isaiah was called by God to act out Egypt's coming defeat and exile by the Assyrians. Why would Judah want to trust a nation that would soon fall to the enemy from whom it was promising to protect Judah (cf. 30:1–2; 31:1)? It's quite possible that because of Isaiah's faithfulness Hezekiah trusted God instead of Egypt and Judah gained another 115 years before judgment fell.

How important was it that the people of Judah, and particularly Hezekiah, learn to trust God rather than Egypt? More important than Isaiah's dignity? Or just a matter of personal preference whether or not to obey

God? Closer to home, how seriously are we to take the spiritual condition of those around us? Seriously enough to be thought a fool if that will reach them? Each of us is called to make the claims of the gospel visible in the most powerful way possible (cf. 1 Cor. 9:19–23).

Isaiah 21:1–10

Verse 9 makes clear that the subject of this oracle (message) concerning "the Desert by the Sea" (v. 1) was Babylon. But what destruction was in view? The mention of Media (v. 2) suggests the conquest by the Medes and Persians in 539 B.C., because prior to that time the Medes were allies of Babylon. Yet the general time frame of chapters 13–23 seems to relate to events closer to Isaiah's time (i.e., Babylon's fall to the Assyrians in 689 B.C.). Isaiah may have been telescoping together more than one destruction in order to argue the folly of trusting Babylon.

The grief that wracked Isaiah in verses 3–4 likely per-

Get up, you officers,
　　oil the shields!

[6]This is what the Lord says to me:

"Go, post a lookout
　　and have him report what he sees.
[7]When he sees chariots[m]
　　with teams of horses,
riders on donkeys
　　or riders on camels,
let him be alert,
　　fully alert."

[8]And the lookout[a][n] shouted,

"Day after day, my lord, I stand on the watchtower;
　　every night I stay at my post.
[9]Look, here comes a man in a chariot
　　with a team of horses.
And he gives back the answer:
'Babylon[o] has fallen,[p] has fallen!
All the images of its gods[q]
　　lie shattered on the ground!' "

[10]O my people, crushed on the threshing floor,[r]
　　I tell you what I have heard
from the LORD Almighty,
　　from the God of Israel.

A Prophecy Against Edom

[11]An oracle concerning Dumah[b][s]

Someone calls to me from Seir,[t]
　　"Watchman, what is left of the night?
　　Watchman, what is left of the night?"
[12]The watchman replies,
　　"Morning is coming, but also the night.
If you would ask, then ask;
　　and come back yet again."

Side notes

21:7
m ver 9

21:8
n Hab 2:1

21:9
o Rev 14:8
p Jer 51:8; Rev 18:2
q Isa 46:1; Jer 50:2;
51:44

21:10
r Jer 51:33

21:11
s Ge 25:14
t Ge 32:3

---

a 8 Dead Sea Scrolls and Syriac; Masoretic Text *A lion*　　b 11 *Dumah* means *silence* or *stillness*, a wordplay on *Edom*.

---

tained to those who put their trust in Babylon and would be destroyed when that trust would fail. The prophet also may have foreseen that the Babylon Judah was trusting for deliverance from Assyria would eventually become Judah's oppressor (before being destroyed herself).

Isaiah addressed God's sovereignty, the foolishness of trusting human power, and the fickleness of human promises. We can constantly remind ourselves of these truths and think about these issues as they affect us personally. Are people depending on us? Have we, like Babylon, made promises to get people involved in "our agenda"? Do we use others to our advantage? Have we made promises we can't or don't intend to keep?

Isaiah 21:11–12

Dumah means "silence" or "stillness" and is a wordplay on Edom (see NIV text note), also known as Seir. Perhaps the meaning of this short oracle is found in this pun. God gave revelation to his people in the midst of perplexing historical circumstances; Isaiah's very ministry evidenced this. But that wasn't the case with Judah's pagan neighbors. This dialogue with the watchman is so vague and mysterious that we're not sure what it means. Isaiah seemed to be saying that dawn would give way swiftly to night—perhaps meaning that Assyrian oppression was nearly over, only to be replaced by Babylonian rule.

We who know the Lord can be thankful for the light he gives and praise him for this specific promise: "His anger lasts only a moment, but his favor lasts a lifetime; weeping may remain for a night, but rejoicing comes in the morning" (Ps. 30:4–5). Rather than seeing nothing but darkness and sorrow before us, we can bank on joy coming in the "morning"—if not literally tomorrow, then at the dawning of God's new heaven and earth (Rev. 21:1–4; cf. Isa. 25:8).

A Prophecy Against Arabia

¹³An oracle^u concerning Arabia:

You caravans of Dedanites,
who camp in the thickets of Arabia,
¹⁴ bring water for the thirsty;
you who live in Tema,^v
bring food for the fugitives.
¹⁵They flee^w from the sword,
from the drawn sword,
from the bent bow
and from the heat of battle.

¹⁶This is what the Lord says to me: "Within one year, as a servant bound by contract^x would count it, all the pomp^y of Kedar^z will come to an end. ¹⁷The survivors of the bowmen, the warriors of Kedar, will be few.^a" The LORD, the God of Israel, has spoken.

A Prophecy About Jerusalem

22 An oracle^b concerning the Valley^c of Vision:

What troubles you now,
that you have all gone up on the roofs,
²O town full of commotion,
O city of tumult and revelry?^d
Your slain were not killed by the sword,
nor did they die in battle.
³All your leaders have fled together;
they have been captured without using the bow.
All you who were caught were taken prisoner together,
having fled while the enemy was still far away.
⁴Therefore I said, "Turn away from me;
let me weep^e bitterly.
Do not try to console me
over the destruction of my people."^f

⁵The Lord, the LORD Almighty, has a day
of tumult and trampling and terror^g
in the Valley of Vision,
a day of battering down walls

21:13
u Isa 13:1

21:14
v Ge 25:15

21:15
w Isa 13:14

21:16
x Isa 16:14
y Isa 17:3
z Ps 120:5; Isa 60:7
21:17
a Isa 10:19

22:1
b Isa 13:1
c Ps 125:2;
Jer 21:13;
Joel 3:2, 12, 14

22:2
d Isa 32:13

22:4
e Isa 15:3; Lk 19:41
f Jer 9:1

22:5
g La 1:5

Isaiah 21:13–17

📖 This message was addressed to Arabian tribes who lived in the desert between Babylon and Judah. Both Dedan and Tema were located in an area of northwest Arabia known as Kedar. War would overtake proud Kedar "within one year," and her armies would be destroyed.

📖 The prophecies against Arabia—and the other nations—were certain because "the LORD, the God of Israel, [had] spoken" (v. 17). If there is a sovereign God who can reveal himself and his will to human beings, then there is a divine resource we can turn to in the midst of trouble and uncertainty. We do well to listen to the message Isaiah wanted his compatriots to hear: People fail, and they will fail you, but God is faithful, and you can abandon yourself to his care.

Isaiah 22:1–25

📖 Chapter 22 divides into two scenes: the Valley of Vision (vv. 1–14) and a picture of two men (vv.

15–25). Ironically, a valley isn't typically where one goes to get vision. Perhaps Isaiah was condemning the Judahites for their *lack* of vision. They definitely couldn't see the prophet's long-range view—of the events just before the fall of Jerusalem, when King Zedekiah would flee from the city with his bodyguard, only to be captured near Jericho (v. 3). The people were rejoicing over a short-term lifting of the Assyrian threat, while Isaiah wept over the final outcome more than a century later (v. 4).

Shebna held a position comparable to that of prime minister, with sweeping spiritual and material responsibilities. Instead of giving himself to bring life to the nation, he was trying to make sure he would be remembered in death! Eliakim would be concerned about the people and act as a "father" to them. The danger was that he would become like a "peg" in the wall: Everything would hang on him, and he would be unable to endure the pressure.

and of crying out to the mountains.
6 Elam[h] takes up the quiver,[i]
  with her charioteers and horses;
  Kir[j] uncovers the shield.
7 Your choicest valleys are full of chariots,
  and horsemen are posted at the city gates;[k]
8   the defenses of Judah are stripped away.

And you looked in that day
  to the weapons[l] in the Palace of the Forest;[m]
9 you saw that the City of David
  had many breaches in its defenses;
you stored up water
  in the Lower Pool.[n]
10 You counted the buildings in Jerusalem
  and tore down houses to strengthen the wall.
11 You built a reservoir between the two walls[o]
  for the water of the Old Pool,[p]
but you did not look to the One who made it,
  or have regard for the One who planned it long ago.

12 The Lord, the LORD Almighty,
  called you on that day
to weep[q] and to wail,
  to tear out your hair[r] and put on sackcloth.[s]
13 But see, there is joy and revelry,
  slaughtering of cattle and killing of sheep,
  eating of meat and drinking of wine!t
"Let us eat and drink," you say,
  "for tomorrow we die!"[u]

14 The LORD Almighty has revealed this in my hearing:[v] "Till your dying day this sin will not be atoned[w] for," says the Lord, the LORD Almighty.

15 This is what the Lord, the LORD Almighty, says:

"Go, say to this steward,
  to Shebna,[x] who is in charge of the palace:
16 What are you doing here and who gave you permission
  to cut out a grave[y] for yourself here,
hewing your grave on the height
  and chiseling your resting place in the rock?

17 "Beware, the LORD is about to take firm hold of you
  and hurl you away, O you mighty man.
18 He will roll you up tightly like a ball
  and throw[z] you into a large country.
There you will die
  and there your splendid chariots will remain—
  you disgrace to your master's house!
19 I will depose you from your office,
  and you will be ousted from your position.

20 "In that day I will summon my servant, Eliakim[a] son of Hilkiah. 21 I will clothe him with your robe and fasten your sash around him and hand your authority over

---

22:6
h Isa 21:2
i Jer 49:35
j 2Ki 16:9

22:7
k 2Ch 32:1-2

22:8
l 2Ch 32:5
m 1Ki 7:2

22:9
n 2Ch 32:4

22:11
o 2Ki 25:4; Jer 39:4
p 2Ch 32:4

22:12
q Joel 2:17
r Mic 1:16
s Joel 1:13

22:13
t Isa 5:22; 28:7-8;
56:12; Lk 17:26-29
u 1Co 15:32*

22:14
v Isa 5:9
w Isa 13:11; 26:21;
30:13-14; Eze 24:13

22:15
x 2Ki 18:18;
Isa 36:3

22:16
y Mt 27:60

22:18
z Isa 17:13

22:20
a 2Ki 18:18;
Isa 36:3

In Isaiah's day Judah's leaders were worried about walls, water supplies (vv. 9–10), and building memorials to themselves (v. 16), when they should have been concerned about sin in the camp. Consider whether it's easier for church members today to plan for bigger facilities or a new sound system or to deal with spiritual deadness or speak out against greed. Eliakim exemplified selfless service that countered the trend of his day and ours. If we remain yoked with Christ in our ministry to others, we can avoid being broken by stress as Eliakim was (cf. Matt. 11:28–30).

to him. He will be a father to those who live in Jerusalem and to the house of Judah. [22]I will place on his shoulder the key[b] to the house of David;[c] what he opens no one can shut, and what he shuts no one can open.[d] [23]I will drive him like a peg[e] into a firm place;[f] he will be a seat[a] of honor[g] for the house of his father. [24]All the glory of his family will hang on him: its offspring and offshoots—all its lesser vessels, from the bowls to all the jars.

[25]"In that day," declares the LORD Almighty, "the peg[h] driven into the firm place will give way; it will be sheared off and will fall, and the load hanging on it will be cut down." The LORD has spoken.[i]

A Prophecy About Tyre

23

An oracle concerning Tyre:[j]

Wail, O ships[k] of Tarshish![l]
    For Tyre is destroyed
    and left without house or harbor.
From the land of Cyprus[b]
    word has come to them.

[2]Be silent, you people of the island
    and you merchants of Sidon,
    whom the seafarers have enriched.
[3]On the great waters
    came the grain of the Shihor;
the harvest of the Nile[c][m] was the revenue of Tyre,[n]
    and she became the marketplace of the nations.

[4]Be ashamed, O Sidon,[o] and you, O fortress of the sea,
    for the sea has spoken:
"I have neither been in labor nor given birth;
    I have neither reared sons nor brought up daughters."
[5]When word comes to Egypt,
    they will be in anguish at the report from Tyre.

[6]Cross over to Tarshish;
    wail, you people of the island.
[7]Is this your city of revelry,[p]
    the old, old city,
whose feet have taken her
    to settle in far-off lands?
[8]Who planned this against Tyre,
    the bestower of crowns,
    whose merchants are princes,

Cross references (margin)

22:22
b Rev 3:7 c Isa 7:2
d Job 12:14
22:23
e Zec 10:4 f Ezr 9:8
g 1Sa 2:7-8;
Job 36:7

22:25
h ver 23 i Isa 46:11;
Mic 4:4

23:1
j Jos 19:29; 1Ki 5:1;
Jer 47:4; Eze 26,27,
28; Joel 3:4-8;
Am 1:9-10;
Zec 9:2-4
k 1Ki 10:22
l Ge 10:4;
Isa 2:16 fn

23:3
m Isa 19:7
n Eze 27:3

23:4
o Ge 10:15,19

23:7
p Isa 22:2; 32:13

Isaiah 23:1–18

The last of Isaiah's oracles against the nations (chs. 13–23) was addressed to Tyre, the great Phoenician seaport on the east coast of the Mediterranean Sea. As Babylon was the commercial power at the eastern end of the ancient Near Eastern world, Tyre held that position in the west. It was a proud, old city. But a terrible disaster was coming. Tyre would fall—not by reason of the superior might of the Assyrians, Babylonians, or Greeks (each of which would inflict destruction, until Tyre was devastated by Alexander the Great in 332 B.C.)—but according to the eternal purposes of the Holy One of Israel.

Babylon's love was glory and military power, but Tyre's passion was for money and the luxury and influence it could buy. Few Christians would admit to loving money for itself. But British preacher John Wesley (1703–1791) had it right: All of a Christian's money is God's; the only issue is how much of God's money we are to spend on ourselves. Would you have to agree that we Western Christians tend to gain all we can and then spend the bulk of it on ourselves in ways that can't help but anger a holy God whose heart bleeds for a lost and hurting world? If we learn the lesson of Tyre, we will hold loosely to our money and tightly to our relationship with the living God.

whose traders are renowned in the earth?
⁹The LORD Almighty planned it,
　to bring low*q* the pride of all glory
　and to humble*r* all who are renowned*s* on the earth.

23:9
q Job 40:11
r Isa 13:11
s Isa 5:13; 9:15

¹⁰Till*a* your land as along the Nile,
　O Daughter of Tarshish,
　for you no longer have a harbor.
¹¹The LORD has stretched out his hand*t* over the sea
　and made its kingdoms tremble.
He has given an order concerning Phoenicia*b*
　that her fortresses be destroyed.*u*
¹²He said, "No more of your reveling,*v*
　O Virgin Daughter*w* of Sidon, now crushed!

23:11
t Ex 14:21
u Isa 25:2;
Zec 9:3-4

23:12
v Rev 18:22
w Isa 47:1

"Up, cross over to Cyprus*c*;
　even there you will find no rest."
¹³Look at the land of the Babylonians,*d*
　this people that is now of no account!
The Assyrians*x* have made it
　a place for desert creatures;
they raised up their siege towers,
　they stripped its fortresses bare
　and turned it into a ruin.*y*

23:13
x Isa 10:5 y Isa 10:7

¹⁴Wail, you ships of Tarshish;*z*
　your fortress is destroyed!

23:14
z Isa 2:16 fn

¹⁵At that time Tyre*a* will be forgotten for seventy years, the span of a king's life. But at the end of these seventy years, it will happen to Tyre as in the song of the prostitute:

23:15
a Jer 25:22

¹⁶"Take up a harp, walk through the city,
　O prostitute forgotten;
play the harp well, sing many a song,
　so that you will be remembered."

¹⁷At the end of seventy years, the LORD will deal with Tyre. She will return to her hire as a prostitute*b* and will ply her trade with all the kingdoms on the face of the earth. ¹⁸Yet her profit and her earnings will be set apart for the LORD;*c* they will not be stored up or hoarded. Her profits will go to those who live before the LORD,*d* for abundant food and fine clothes.

23:17
b Eze 16:26;
Na 3:4; Rev 17:1
23:18
c Ex 28:36;
Ps 72:10
d Isa 60:5-9;
Mic 4:13

The LORD's Devastation of the Earth

24:1
e ver 20;
Isa 2:19-21; 33:9

24 See, the LORD is going to lay waste the earth*e*
　and devastate it;
he will ruin its face
　and scatter its inhabitants—
²it will be the same
　for priest as for people,*f*

24:2
f Hos 4:9

a 10 Dead Sea Scrolls and some Septuagint manuscripts; Masoretic Text *Go through Canaan*　　*b 11* Hebrew　　*c 12* Hebrew *Kittim*　　*d 13* Or *Chaldeans*

Isaiah 24:1–23

Chapters 24–27 serve as a conclusion to the prophecies against the nations in chapters 13–23. In chapter 24, Isaiah stated that the entire earth is under God's judgment. God himself will bring about the world's destruction. The disaster will come as the direct result of the choices Earth's inhabitants have made. The "everlasting covenant" (v. 6) may refer to God's covenant with Noah (Gen. 9:8–17), with its ban on bloodshed. If Christians of any era violate God's standards of appropriate behavior, they do so to their own destruction. This understanding between creature and Creator has been passed down through the ages as our common human heritage.

for master as for servant,
for mistress as for maid,
for seller as for buyer, *g*
for borrower as for lender,
for debtor as for creditor. *h*

³ The earth will be completely laid waste
and totally plundered. *i*

The LORD has spoken this word.

⁴ The earth dries up and withers,
the world languishes and withers,
the exalted *j* of the earth languish.
⁵ The earth is defiled *k* by its people;
they have disobeyed *l* the laws,
violated the statutes
and broken the everlasting covenant.
⁶ Therefore a curse consumes the earth;
its people must bear their guilt.
Therefore earth's inhabitants are burned up, *m*
and very few are left.
⁷ The new wine dries up and the vine withers; *n*
all the merrymakers groan. *o*
⁸ The gaiety of the tambourines *p* is stilled,
the noise *q* of the revelers has stopped,
the joyful harp *r* is silent. *s*
⁹ No longer do they drink wine *t* with a song;
the beer is bitter *u* to its drinkers.
¹⁰ The ruined city lies desolate;
the entrance to every house is barred.
¹¹ In the streets they cry out for wine;
all joy turns to gloom, *v*
all gaiety is banished from the earth.
¹² The city is left in ruins,
its gate is battered to pieces.
¹³ So will it be on the earth
and among the nations,
as when an olive tree is beaten, *w*
or as when gleanings are left after the grape harvest.
¹⁴ They raise their voices, they shout for joy; *x*
from the west they acclaim the LORD's majesty.
¹⁵ Therefore in the east give glory *y* to the LORD;
exalt *z* the name of the LORD, the God of Israel,
in the islands of the sea.
¹⁶ From the ends of the earth we hear singing:
"Glory *a* to the Righteous One."

But I said, "I waste away, I waste away!
Woe to me!
The treacherous betray!
With treachery the treacherous betray! *b*"
¹⁷ Terror and pit and snare *c* await you,
O people of the earth.

24:2
g Eze 7:12
h Lev 25:35-37;
Dt 23:19-20

24:3
i Isa 6:11-12

24:4
j Isa 2:12
24:5
k Ge 3:17;
Nu 35:33 *l* Isa 10:6;
59:12

24:6
m Isa 1:31

24:7
n Joel 1:10-12
o Isa 16:8-10
24:8
p Isa 5:12
q Jer 7:34; 16:9;
25:10; Hos 2:11
r Rev 18:22
s Eze 26:13
24:9
t Isa 5:11,22
u Isa 5:20

24:11
v Isa 16:10; 32:13;
Jer 14:3

24:13
w Isa 17:6

24:14
x Isa 12:6
24:15
y Isa 66:19
z Isa 25:3; Mal 1:11

24:16
a Isa 28:5
b Isa 21:2; Jer 5:11

24:17
c Jer 48:43

📖 What is God to do with a creation gone badly astray from its original purpose? He could destroy the earth and start over. But God won't do so until the full harvest of both sin and righteousness has been reached (v. 13). We may question with a shudder what the sins of the future will be like if those of our recent past weren't the "full measure" (see Gen. 15:16). But until the end comes, we are to continually relearn the lessons of Isaiah 24. We are wise to guard against acting as if this world is our true home and that it defines who God is.

1113

18 Whoever flees at the sound of terror
  will fall into a pit;
whoever climbs out of the pit
  will be caught in a snare.

The floodgates of the heavens [d] are opened,
  the foundations of the earth shake. [e]
19 The earth is broken up,
  the earth is split asunder, [f]
  the earth is thoroughly shaken.
20 The earth reels like a drunkard, [g]
  it sways like a hut in the wind;
so heavy upon it is the guilt of its rebellion [h]
  that it falls—never to rise again.

21 In that day the LORD will punish [i]
  the powers in the heavens above
  and the kings on the earth below.
22 They will be herded together
  like prisoners [j] bound in a dungeon; [k]
they will be shut up in prison
  and be punished [a] after many days. [l]
23 The moon will be abashed, the sun [m] ashamed;
  for the LORD Almighty will reign [n]
on Mount Zion [o] and in Jerusalem,
  and before its elders, gloriously. [p]

Praise to the LORD

25 O LORD, you are my God;
  I will exalt you and praise your name,
for in perfect faithfulness
  you have done marvelous things, [q]
  things planned [r] long ago.
2 You have made the city a heap of rubble, [s]
  the fortified [t] town a ruin,
the foreigners' stronghold [u] a city no more;
  it will never be rebuilt.
3 Therefore strong peoples will honor you;
  cities of ruthless [v] nations will revere you.
4 You have been a refuge [w] for the poor,
  a refuge for the needy in his distress,
a shelter from the storm
  and a shade from the heat.
For the breath of the ruthless [x]
  is like a storm driving against a wall
5   and like the heat of the desert.
You silence [y] the uproar of foreigners;

24:18
d Ge 7:11 e Ps 18:7

24:19
f Dt 11:6

24:20
g Isa 19:14
h Isa 1:2,28; 43:27

24:21
i Isa 10:12

24:22
j Isa 10:4
k Isa 42:7,22
l Eze 38:8

24:23
m Isa 13:10
n Rev 22:5
o Heb 12:22
p Isa 60:19

25:1
q Ps 98:1
r Nu 23:19

25:2
s Isa 17:1 t Isa 17:3
u Isa 13:22

25:3
v Isa 13:11
25:4
w Isa 4:6; 17:10;
  27:5; 33:16
x Isa 29:5; 49:25

25:5
y Jer 51:55

a 22 Or released

Isaiah 25:1–12

This chapter is a song of praise sung at the coronation feast of the Messianic King and echoed in Revelation 21. The guests at the coronation feast (vv. 4–8), the poor, needy, and aliens—all who call on the Lord—are a surprise. Redemption and deliverance are for all people everywhere who turn to God in faith and humility. Death will be destroyed, tears wiped away, and disgrace removed. The holy One of Israel is the God of all the nations. When he finally declares the rule of death to be at an end, his sole lordship will become crystal clear.

Isaiah 25 and its New Testament fulfillment portray the foundation of our hope. The world isn't out of control, and the future isn't in our hands. Sorrow, injustice, and death itself will one day end. The future is portrayed as a holy feast, with people from all the nations gathered at the banquet of the Lamb of God.

as heat is reduced by the shadow of a cloud,
so the song of the ruthless is stilled.

6 On this mountain[z] the LORD Almighty will prepare
a feast[a] of rich food for all peoples,
a banquet of aged wine—
the best of meats and the finest of wines.[b]
7 On this mountain he will destroy
the shroud[c] that enfolds all peoples,
the sheet that covers all nations;
8 he will swallow up death[d] forever.
The Sovereign LORD will wipe away the tears[e]
from all faces;
he will remove the disgrace[f] of his people
from all the earth.

The LORD has spoken.

9 In that day they will say,

"Surely this is our God;[g]
we trusted in him, and he saved[h] us.
This is the LORD, we trusted in him;
let us rejoice[i] and be glad in his salvation."

10 The hand of the LORD will rest on this mountain;
but Moab[j] will be trampled under him
as straw is trampled down in the manure.
11 They will spread out their hands in it,
as a swimmer spreads out his hands to swim.
God will bring down[k] their pride[l]
despite the cleverness[a] of their hands.
12 He will bring down your high fortified walls
and lay them low;[m]
he will bring them down to the ground,
to the very dust.

A Song of Praise

26 In that day this song will be sung in the land of Judah:

We have a strong city;[n]
God makes salvation
its walls[o] and ramparts.
2 Open the gates
that the righteous[p] nation may enter,
the nation that keeps faith.
3 You will keep in perfect peace
him whose mind is steadfast,
because he trusts in you.
4 Trust[q] in the LORD forever,
for the LORD, the LORD, is the Rock eternal.
5 He humbles those who dwell on high,
he lays the lofty city low;

---

a 11 The meaning of the Hebrew for this word is uncertain.

25:6
z Isa 2:2 a Isa 1:19;
Mt 8:11; 22:4
b Pr 9:2

25:7
c 2Co 3:15-16;
Eph 4:18

25:8
d Hos 13:14;
1Co 15:54-55*
e Isa 30:19; 35:10;
51:11; 65:19;
Rev 7:17; 21:4
f Mt 5:11; 1Pe 4:14

25:9
g Isa 40:9 h Ps 20:5;
Isa 33:22; 35:4;
49:25-26; 60:16
i Isa 35:2,10

25:10
j Am 2:1-3

25:11
k Isa 5:25; 14:26;
16:14 l Job 40:12

25:12
m Isa 15:1

26:1
n Isa 14:32
o Isa 60:18

26:2
p Isa 54:14; 58:8;
62:2

26:4
q Isa 12:2; 50:10

Isaiah 26:1–21

Chapter 26 begins with a tale of two cities. In contrast to the silent, ruined city of the world (v. 5) is the city of God, inhabited by the faithful who sing his praises. This city has God's salvation for its "walls," mak-ing it plain that it's more than a geographical place. The Lord is its eternal Rock, while the city that symbolizes earthly power will be crushed into dust. The poor and needy will finally live in peace.

26:5
r Isa 25:12

26:6
s Isa 3:15

26:7
t Isa 42:16
26:8
u Isa 56:1 v Isa 12:4

26:9
w Ps 63:1; 78:34;
Isa 55:6 x Mt 6:33

26:10
y Isa 32:6
z Isa 22:12-13;
Hos 11:7;
Jn 5:37-38; Ro 2:4

26:11
a Isa 44:9,18
b Heb 10:27

26:13
c Isa 2:8; 10:5,11
d Isa 63:7
26:14
e Dt 4:28 f Isa 10:3

26:15
g Isa 33:17

26:16
h Hos 5:15

26:17
i Jn 16:21

26:18
j Isa 33:11; 59:4
k Ps 17:14

26:19
l Isa 25:8; Eph 5:14

he levels it to the ground[r]
  and casts it down to the dust.
6 Feet trample it down—
  the feet of the oppressed,
  the footsteps of the poor.[s]

7 The path of the righteous is level;
  O upright One, you make the way of the righteous smooth.[t]
8 Yes, LORD, walking in the way of your laws,[a][u]
  we wait for you;
  your name[v] and renown
  are the desire of our hearts.
9 My soul yearns for you in the night;
  in the morning my spirit longs[w] for you.
  When your judgments come upon the earth,
  the people of the world learn righteousness.[x]
10 Though grace is shown to the wicked,
  they do not learn righteousness;
  even in a land of uprightness they go on doing evil[y]
  and regard[z] not the majesty of the LORD.
11 O LORD, your hand is lifted high,
  but they do not see[a] it.
  Let them see your zeal for your people and be put to shame;
  let the fire[b] reserved for your enemies consume them.

12 LORD, you establish peace for us;
  all that we have accomplished you have done for us.
13 O LORD, our God, other lords[c] besides you have ruled over us,
  but your name alone do we honor.[d]
14 They are now dead,[e] they live no more;
  those departed spirits do not rise.
  You punished them and brought them to ruin;[f]
  you wiped out all memory of them.
15 You have enlarged the nation, O LORD;
  you have enlarged the nation.
  You have gained glory for yourself;
  you have extended all the borders[g] of the land.

16 LORD, they came to you in their distress;[h]
  when you disciplined them,
  they could barely whisper a prayer.[b]
17 As a woman with child and about to give birth[i]
  writhes and cries out in her pain,
  so were we in your presence, O LORD.
18 We were with child, we writhed in pain,
  but we gave birth[j] to wind.
  We have not brought salvation[k] to the earth;
  we have not given birth to people of the world.

19 But your dead[l] will live;
  their bodies will rise.
  You who dwell in the dust,

---

[a] 8 Or judgments   [b] 16 The meaning of the Hebrew for this clause is uncertain.

How do you demonstrate your allegiance to that future city to be built by God (cf. Heb. 11:8–10)? One way to honor God's name is to express his righteousness and justice for the poor and needy (vv. 6–7). Another is to acknowledge that only God is Lord, regardless of whomever else may seek to rule over us (vv. 12–13). This frees us to trust God in whatever may come our way—even discipline (vv. 16–18)! Even death itself isn't something to fear, for one day the dead themselves will sing for joy (v. 19).

wake up and shout for joy.
Your dew is like the dew of the morning;
  the earth will give birth to her dead. [m]

20 Go, my people, enter your rooms
  and shut the doors [n] behind you;
hide [o] yourselves for a little while
  until his wrath has passed by. [p]
21 See, the LORD is coming [q] out of his dwelling [r]
  to punish [s] the people of the earth for their sins.
The earth will disclose the blood [t] shed upon her;
  she will conceal her slain no longer.

Deliverance of Israel

27 In that day,

the LORD will punish with his sword, [u]
  his fierce, great and powerful sword,
Leviathan [v] the gliding serpent,
Leviathan the coiling serpent;
  he will slay the monster [w] of the sea.

2 In that day—

"Sing about a fruitful vineyard: [x]
3   I, the LORD, watch over it;
  I water [y] it continually.
I guard it day and night
  so that no one may harm it.
4   I am not angry.
If only there were briers and thorns confronting me!
  I would march against them in battle;
  I would set them all on fire. [z]
5 Or else let them come to me for refuge; [a]
  let them make peace [b] with me,
  yes, let them make peace with me. "

6 In days to come Jacob will take root,
  Israel will bud and blossom [c]
  and fill all the world with fruit. [d]

7 Has ˌthe LORDˌ struck her
  as he struck [e] down those who struck her?
Has she been killed
  as those were killed who killed her?
8 By warfare [a] and exile [f] you contend with her—
  with his fierce blast he drives her out,

---

a 8 See Septuagint; the meaning of the Hebrew for this word is uncertain.

Cross References

26:19
m Eze 37:1-14;
Da 12:2

26:20
n Ex 12:23
o Ps 91:1,4
p Ps 30:5;
Isa 54:7-8
26:21
q Jude 1:14
r Mic 1:3
s Isa 13:9,11;
30:12-14
t Job 16:18;
Lk 11:50-51

27:1
u Isa 34:6; 66:16
v Job 3:8
w Ps 74:13

27:2
x Jer 2:21
27:3
y Isa 58:11

27:4
z Isa 10:17;
Mt 3:12; Heb 6:8
27:5
a Isa 25:4
b Job 22:21; Ro 5:1;
2Co 5:20

27:6
c Hos 14:5-6
d Isa 37:31

27:7
e Isa 37:36-38

27:8
f Isa 50:1; 54:7

Isaiah 27:1–13

This picture is opposite that in chapter 5. There God called in wild animals (5:26–29) to destroy his vineyard of bitter grapes, his nation. He tore down the walls and left the vineyard to "briers and thorns" (5:6). Here he stated that he was "not angry" and wished there were "briers and thorns" for him to contend with so he could chop them down and burn them (27:4). God *was* angry enough with his people to destroy them. But he brought destruction on Israel not to annihilate his vineyard but to cleanse his people. The fruit of the removal of Israel's (Ja-cob's) sin would be the destruction of idol worship (v. 9).

God's actions in our lives are still for the purpose of refinement, not destruction. If we think of him as passionately loving "the old house" that we are, the ripping of the saw and crashing of the hammer will be easier for us to bear. But if we think of him as the hardhearted judge determined to wring the last ounce of retribution out of us, the blows will seem unbearable. If our suffering isn't for discipline, it may be for a testimony of God's grace in the conflict with evil (cf. the book of Job; Heb. 12: 7-11; 1 Peter 5:8–10).

27:9
g Ro 11:27*
h Ex 34:13

27:10
i Isa 32:14; Jer 26:6
j Isa 17:2

27:11
k Dt 32:28; Isa 1:3;
Jer 8:7 l Dt 32:18;
Isa 43:1,7,15; 44:1-
2,21,24
m Isa 9:17

27:12
n Ge 15:18
o Dt 30:4;
Isa 11:12; 17:6
27:13
p Lev 25:9;
Mt 24:31
q Isa 19:21,25

28:1
r ver 3; Isa 9:9
s ver 4 t Hos 7:5
28:2
u Isa 40:10
v Isa 30:30;
Eze 13:11
w Isa 29:6 x Isa 8:7

28:3
y ver 1

28:4
z ver 1 a Hos 9:10;
Na 3:12

28:5
b Isa 62:3

28:6
c Isa 11:2-4;
32:1,16
d Jn 5:30
e 2Ch 32:8

as on a day the east wind blows.
⁹ By this, then, will Jacob's guilt be atoned for,
and this will be the full fruitage of the removal of his sin: ᵍ
When he makes all the altar stones
to be like chalk stones crushed to pieces,
no Asherah poles ᵃ ʰ or incense altars
will be left standing.
¹⁰ The fortified city stands desolate, ⁱ
an abandoned settlement, forsaken like the desert;
there the calves graze,
there they lie down; ʲ
they strip its branches bare.
¹¹ When its twigs are dry, they are broken off
and women come and make fires with them.
For this is a people without understanding; ᵏ
so their Maker has no compassion on them,
and their Creator ˡ shows them no favor. ᵐ

¹² In that day the LORD will thresh from the flowing Euphrates ᵇ to the Wadi of Egypt, ⁿ and you, O Israelites, will be gathered ᵒ up one by one. ¹³ And in that day a great trumpet ᵖ will sound. Those who were perishing in Assyria and those who were exiled in Egypt ᑫ will come and worship the LORD on the holy mountain in Jerusalem.

Woe to Ephraim

28 Woe to that wreath, the pride of Ephraim's ʳ drunkards,
to the fading flower, his glorious beauty,
set on the head of a fertile valley ˢ—
to that city, the pride of those laid low by wine! ᵗ
² See, the Lord has one who is powerful ᵘ and strong.
Like a hailstorm ᵛ and a destructive wind, ʷ
like a driving rain and a flooding ˣ downpour,
he will throw it forcefully to the ground.
³ That wreath, the pride of Ephraim's ʸ drunkards,
will be trampled underfoot.
⁴ That fading flower, his glorious beauty,
set on the head of a fertile valley, ᶻ
will be like a fig ᵃ ripe before harvest—
as soon as someone sees it and takes it in his hand,
he swallows it.

⁵ In that day the LORD Almighty
will be a glorious crown, ᵇ
a beautiful wreath
for the remnant of his people.
⁶ He will be a spirit of justice ᶜ
to him who sits in judgment, ᵈ
a source of strength
to those who turn back the battle ᵉ at the gate.

ᵃ 9 That is, symbols of the goddess Asherah   ᵇ 12 Hebrew *River*

Isaiah 28:1–29

Chapters 28–33 contain a series of messages beginning with the funeral word "woe" (28:1; 29:1; 29:15; 30:1; 31:1; 33:1). Most of these are focused on Judah, but chapter 28 begins with a "woe" on Ephraim (Israel). By verse 14 the focus shifts to Jerusalem in Judah.

Political leaders, nobility, priests, and prophets were all guilty not only of alcohol abuse but of an unwilling-

ness to surrender their needs and desires to the Lord (cf. Mal. 2:1–9). Those who should have been giving guidance were staggering around in a stupor. "Who does he think he is," they asked of the true prophet, "treating us like children?" The Assyrians would teach them that Isaiah's words were valid. If the people wouldn't learn the easy way of faith, there was always the hard way of experience (Isa. 28:9–13).

7 And these also stagger from wine[f]
   and reel[g] from beer:
Priests[h] and prophets[i] stagger from beer
   and are befuddled with wine;
they reel from beer,
   they stagger when seeing visions,[j]
   they stumble when rendering decisions.
8 All the tables are covered with vomit[k]
   and there is not a spot without filth.

9 "Who is it he is trying to teach?[l]
   To whom is he explaining his message?
To children weaned[m] from their milk,[n]
   to those just taken from the breast?
10 For it is:
   Do and do, do and do,
   rule on rule, rule on rule[a];
   a little here, a little there."

11 Very well then, with foreign lips and strange tongues[o]
   God will speak to this people,[p]
12 to whom he said,
   "This is the resting place, let the weary rest";[q]
and, "This is the place of repose"—
   but they would not listen.
13 So then, the word of the LORD to them will become:
   Do and do, do and do,
   rule on rule, rule on rule;
   a little here, a little there—
so that they will go and fall backward,
   be injured[r] and snared and captured.[s]

14 Therefore hear the word of the LORD,[t] you scoffers
   who rule this people in Jerusalem.
15 You boast, "We have entered into a covenant with death,
   with the grave[b] we have made an agreement.
When an overwhelming scourge sweeps by,[u]
   it cannot touch us,
for we have made a lie[v] our refuge
   and falsehood[c] our hiding place.[w]"

16 So this is what the Sovereign LORD says:

   "See, I lay a stone in Zion,
      a tested stone,[x]
   a precious cornerstone for a sure foundation;
      the one who trusts will never be dismayed.[y]
17 I will make justice[z] the measuring line
   and righteousness the plumb line;[a]
hail will sweep away your refuge, the lie,
   and water will overflow your hiding place.

---

a 10 Hebrew / *sav lasav sav lasav* / *kav lakav kav lakav* (possibly meaningless sounds; perhaps a mimicking of the prophet's words); also in verse 13   b 15 Hebrew *Sheol*; also in verse 18
c 15 Or *false gods*

28:7
f Isa 22:13
g Isa 56:10-12
h Isa 24:2 / Isa 9:15
i Isa 29:11;
Hos 4:11

28:8
k Jer 48:26

28:9
l ver 26; Isa 30:20;
48:17; 50:4; 54:13
m Ps 131:2
n Heb 5:12-13

28:11
o Isa 33:19
p 1Co 14:21*

28:12
q Isa 11:10;
Mt 11:28-29

28:13
r Mt 21:44
s Isa 8:15
28:14
t Isa 1:10

28:15
u ver 2,18;
Isa 8:7-8; 30:28;
Da 11:22
v Isa 9:15
w Isa 29:15

28:16
x Ps 118:22;
Isa 8:14-15;
Mt 21:42; Ac 4:11;
Eph 2:20
y Ro 9:33*; 10:11*;
1Pe 2:6*
28:17
z Isa 5:16
a 2Ki 21:13

In the ancient Near East (and in many places today), difficulty finding clean water made it necessary to drink wine and beer. Yet despite the abundance of clean water in the West, alcohol addiction is a serious problem. An impression is successfully promoted by the media and alcohol industry that drinking is sophisticated—even that binge drinking is fun and funny. We have an opportunity to demonstrate to our culture—and our children—that it's possible to have a good time without indulging in a substance that lowers our God-given inhibitions.

28:18
b Isa 7:7 *c* ver 15
d Da 8:13

28:19
e 2Ki 24:2
f Job 18:11

28:20
g Isa 59:6
28:21
h 1Ch 14:11
i Jos 10:10,12;
1Ch 14:16
j Isa 10:12;
Lk 19:41-44

28:22
k Isa 10:22
l Isa 10:23

28:25
m Mt 23:23
n Ex 9:32

28:29
o Isa 9:6 *p* Ro 11:33

29:1
q Isa 22:12-13
r 2Sa 5:9 *s* Isa 1:14

29:2
t Isa 3:26; La 2:5

18 Your covenant with death will be annulled;
　　your agreement with the grave will not stand. *b*
When the overwhelming scourge sweeps by, *c*
　　you will be beaten down *d* by it.
19 As often as it comes it will carry you away; *e*
　　morning after morning, by day and by night,
　　it will sweep through."

The understanding of this message
　　will bring sheer terror. *f*
20 The bed is too short to stretch out on,
　　the blanket too narrow to wrap around you. *g*
21 The LORD will rise up as he did at Mount Perazim, *h*
　　he will rouse himself as in the Valley of Gibeon *i*—
to do his work, *j* his strange work,
　　and perform his task, his alien task.
22 Now stop your mocking,
　　or your chains will become heavier;
the Lord, the LORD Almighty, has told me
　　of the destruction decreed *k* against the whole land. *l*

23 Listen and hear my voice;
　　pay attention and hear what I say.
24 When a farmer plows for planting, does he plow continually?
　　Does he keep on breaking up and harrowing the soil?
25 When he has leveled the surface,
　　does he not sow caraway and scatter cummin? *m*
Does he not plant wheat in its place, *a*
　　barley in its plot, *a*
　　and spelt *n* in its field?
26 His God instructs him
　　and teaches him the right way.

27 Caraway is not threshed with a sledge,
　　nor is a cartwheel rolled over cummin;
caraway is beaten out with a rod,
　　and cummin with a stick.
28 Grain must be ground to make bread;
　　so one does not go on threshing it forever.
Though he drives the wheels of his threshing cart over it,
　　his horses do not grind it.
29 All this also comes from the LORD Almighty,
　　wonderful in counsel *o* and magnificent in wisdom. *p*

Woe to David's City

29 Woe *q* to you, Ariel, Ariel, *r*
　　the city where David settled!
Add year to year
　　and let your cycle of festivals *s* go on.
2 Yet I will besiege Ariel;
　　she will mourn and lament, *t*

a 25 The meaning of the Hebrew for this word is uncertain.

Isaiah 29:1–24

The second "woe" in this series (vv. 1–14) was addressed to Jerusalem, the city of David. Isaiah likely used "Ariel" because it sounded like the Hebrew word for "altar hearth"; bloodshed would turn the city into a virtual altar hearth (see NIV text note on v. 2). Jeru- salem's religion had become a performance, with no real connection between the worshipers and God. They had lost their sense of wonder. God said that he *would* en- counter them with wonders—meaning that the wonder of the God they thought they had under control would burst forth to become their enemy.

she will be to me like an altar hearth. [a]

3 I will encamp against you all around;
  I will encircle [u] you with towers
  and set up my siege works against you.
4 Brought low, you will speak from the ground;
  your speech will mumble [v] out of the dust.
  Your voice will come ghostlike from the earth;
  out of the dust your speech will whisper.

5 But your many enemies will become like fine dust,
  the ruthless hordes like blown chaff. [w]
  Suddenly, [x] in an instant,
6   the LORD Almighty will come
  with thunder and earthquake [y] and great noise,
  with windstorm and tempest and flames of a devouring fire.
7 Then the hordes of all the nations [z] that fight against Ariel,
  that attack her and her fortress and besiege her,
  will be as it is with a dream, [a]
  with a vision in the night—
8 as when a hungry man dreams that he is eating,
  but he awakens, [b] and his hunger remains;
  as when a thirsty man dreams that he is drinking,
  but he awakens faint, with his thirst unquenched.
  So will it be with the hordes of all the nations
  that fight against Mount Zion.

9 Be stunned and amazed,
  blind yourselves and be sightless;
  be drunk, [c] but not from wine, [d]
  stagger, but not from beer.
10 The LORD has brought over you a deep sleep:
  He has sealed your eyes [e] (the prophets); [f]
  he has covered your heads (the seers). [g]

11 For you this whole vision is nothing but words sealed [h] in a scroll. And if you give the scroll to someone who can read, and say to him, "Read this, please," he will answer, "I can't; it is sealed." 12 Or if you give the scroll to someone who cannot read, and say, "Read this, please," he will answer, "I don't know how to read."

13 The Lord says:

"These people come near to me with their mouth
  and honor me with their lips,
  but their hearts are far from me. [i]

[a] 2 The Hebrew for *altar hearth* sounds like the Hebrew for *Ariel*.

29:3	[u] Lk 19:43-44
29:4	[v] Isa 8:19
29:5	[w] Isa 17:13 [x] Isa 17:14; 1Th 5:3
29:6	[y] Mt 24:7; Mk 13:8; Lk 21:11; Rev 11:19
29:7	[z] Mic 4:11-12; Zec 12:9 [a] Job 20:8
29:8	[b] Ps 73:20
29:9	[c] Isa 51:17 [d] Isa 51:21-22
29:10	[e] Ps 69:23; Isa 6:9-10; Ro 11:8* [f] Mic 3:6 [g] 1Sa 9:9
29:11	[h] Isa 8:16; Mt 13:11; Rev 5:1-2
29:13	[i] Eze 33:31

In the third "woe" (vv. 15–24), Isaiah warned the Judahites not to "hide their plans from the LORD"—probably a reference to their alliance with Egypt (cf. 30:1–2). But along with a warning, Isaiah offered hope. The promises made in verses 17–24 were more far-reaching than mere physical restoration. They dealt primarily with the nation's spiritual needs, promising a day when the kinds of attitudes and behaviors that had brought them to this dark day would be radically changed. Gracious redemption would result in holy living.

Some of us try to manipulate God. We don't necessarily want him meddling in our lives but do desire what he can do for us. But God has already done many times more than we could ever deserve. He wants to bless us even more, but too often our attempts to use him, while still maintaining control of our lives, block the very blessing he longs to give.

The Old Testament is the story of Israel's failure to be a holy people. Here God promised a day when his people could fulfill the covenant demands. The Holy Spirit is available to us today to do what the old covenant couldn't—*enable* the Israelites (and us) to live holy lives. Through what Christ has done for us in forgiving the sin of the broken covenant and giving us his Spirit, we can now fulfill the "righteous requirements of the law" (Rom. 8:3–4). We can "acknowledge the holiness of the Holy One" (Isa. 29:23) by demonstrating his holiness in our lives.

29:13
j Mt 15:8-9*;
Mk 7:6-7*; Col 2:22
29:14
k Hab 1:5 *l* Jer 8:9;
49:7 *m* Isa 6:9-10;
1Co 1:19*

Their worship of me
 is made up only of rules taught by men. [a][j]
14 Therefore once more I will astound these people
 with wonder upon wonder;[k]
the wisdom of the wise[l] will perish,
 the intelligence of the intelligent will vanish.[m]"
15 Woe to those who go to great depths
 to hide their plans from the LORD,
who do their work in darkness and think,
 "Who sees us?[n] Who will know?"[o]

29:15
n Ps 10:11-13; 94:7;
Isa 57:12
o Job 22:13

16 You turn things upside down,
 as if the potter were thought to be like the clay!
Shall what is formed say to him who formed it,
 "He did not make me"?
Can the pot say of the potter,[p]
 "He knows nothing"?

29:16
p Isa 45:9; 64:8;
Ro 9:20-21*

17 In a very short time, will not Lebanon be turned into a fertile field[q]
 and the fertile field seem like a forest?[r]
18 In that day the deaf[s] will hear the words of the scroll,
 and out of gloom and darkness
 the eyes of the blind will see.[t]
19 Once more the humble[u] will rejoice in the LORD;
 the needy[v] will rejoice in the Holy One of Israel.
20 The ruthless will vanish,
 the mockers[w] will disappear,
 and all who have an eye for evil[x] will be cut down—
21 those who with a word make a man out to be guilty,
 who ensnare the defender in court[y]
 and with false testimony deprive the innocent of justice.[z]

29:17
q Ps 84:6
r Isa 32:15
29:18
s Mk 7:37
t Isa 32:3; 35:5;
Mt 11:5
29:19
u Isa 61:1; Mt 5:5;
11:29 *v* Isa 14:30;
Mt 11:5; Jas 1:9;
2:5
29:20
w Isa 28:22
x Isa 59:4; Mic 2:1
29:21
y Am 5:10,15
z Isa 5:23; 32:7

22 Therefore this is what the LORD, who redeemed Abraham,[a] says to the house of Jacob:

"No longer will Jacob be ashamed;[b]
 no longer will their faces grow pale.
23 When they see among them their children,[c]
 the work of my hands,[d]
 they will keep my name holy;
 they will acknowledge the holiness of the Holy One of Jacob,
 and will stand in awe of the God of Israel.
24 Those who are wayward[e] in spirit will gain understanding;[f]
 those who complain will accept instruction."[g]

29:22
a Isa 41:8; 63:16
b Isa 49:23
29:23
c Isa 49:20-26
d Isa 19:25
29:24
e Isa 28:7; Heb 5:2
f Isa 41:20; 60:16
g Isa 30:21

Woe to the Obstinate Nation

30:1
h Isa 29:15 *i* Isa 1:2
j Isa 8:12

30 "Woe[h] to the obstinate children,"[i]
 declares the LORD,
"to those who carry out plans that are not mine,
 forming an alliance,[j] but not by my Spirit,
 heaping sin upon sin;
2 who go down to Egypt[k]

30:2
k Isa 31:1

a 13 Hebrew; Septuagint *They worship me in vain; / their teachings are but rules taught by men*

Isaiah 30:1-33

This chapter, consisting of the fourth in a series of "woes," deals with Judah's apparent alliance with Egypt. Isaiah spoke pointedly of the foolishness of such a course, for Egypt couldn't offer any real help (vv. 1–7). Because Judah had rejected the true help offered by God, her people would be devastated, as though a high wall had suddenly collapsed. Yet God would wait for them to come to their senses (vv. 8–18). When they did, he promised redemption and restoration for his people (vv. 19–26) and defeat for all their enemies (vv. 27–33).

without consulting[l] me;
who look for help to Pharaoh's protection, [m]
to Egypt's shade for refuge.
3 But Pharaoh's protection will be to your shame,
Egypt's shade will bring you disgrace. [n]
4 Though they have officials in Zoan [o]
and their envoys have arrived in Hanes,
5 everyone will be put to shame
because of a people[p] useless to them,
who bring neither help nor advantage,
but only shame and disgrace."

6 An oracle concerning the animals of the Negev:

Through a land of hardship and distress, [q]
of lions and lionesses,
of adders and darting snakes, [r]
the envoys carry their riches on donkeys' backs,
their treasures[s] on the humps of camels,
to that unprofitable nation,
7   to Egypt, whose help is utterly useless.
Therefore I call her
Rahab the Do-Nothing.

8 Go now, write it on a tablet for them,
inscribe it on a scroll, [t]
that for the days to come
it may be an everlasting witness.
9 These are rebellious people, deceitful[u] children,
children unwilling to listen to the LORD's instruction. [v]
10 They say to the seers,
"See no more visions[w]!"
and to the prophets,
"Give us no more visions of what is right!
Tell us pleasant things, [x]
prophesy illusions. [y]
11 Leave this way,
get off this path,
and stop confronting[z] us
with the Holy One of Israel!"

12 Therefore, this is what the Holy One of Israel says:

"Because you have rejected this message, [a]
relied on oppression[b]
and depended on deceit,
13 this sin will become for you
like a high wall, [c] cracked and bulging,
that collapses[d] suddenly, [e] in an instant.
14 It will break in pieces like pottery, [f]

Cross references (right margin):

30:2
[l] Nu 27:21
[m] Isa 36:9

30:3
[n] Isa 20:4-5; 36:6
30:4
[o] Isa 19:11

30:5
[p] ver 7

30:6
[q] Ex 5:10,21;
Isa 8:22; Jer 11:4
[r] Dt 8:15 [s] Isa 15:7

30:8
[t] Isa 8:1; Hab 2:2

30:9
[u] Isa 28:15; 59:3-4
[v] Isa 1:10

30:10
[w] Jer 11:21;
Am 7:13 [x] 1Ki 22:8
[y] Eze 13:7;
Ro 16:18

30:11
[z] Job 21:14

30:12
[a] Isa 5:24 [b] Isa 5:7

30:13
[c] Ps 62:3
[d] 1Ki 20:30
[e] Isa 29:5
30:14
[f] Ps 2:9;
Jer 19:10-11

In verses 19–26, Isaiah emphasized the principles of divine blessing. These principles are important for our day. The key point is that blessings are inseparably *both* spiritual and material. Jesus' teachings make it clear that we are not to serve God in order to become rich. As Isaiah stated in verses 19–22, blessing is a matter of a transformed heart that can take adversity and affliction and see God's hand in them. Is this a familiar attitude for you?

But to say that all the Old Testament promises are only symbolic misses the fact that God the Father wants to give good things to his children. When we repent of trying to supply our own needs, commit them to him, and delight to serve him in love, we will experience the good things he wants to give us. For those who seek only physical blessing, there will never be enough. But for those who seek God, everything from his hand is an undeserved blessing—enough, because *he's* enough (cf. Matt. 6:33).

shattered so mercilessly
that among its pieces not a fragment will be found
for taking coals from a hearth
or scooping water out of a cistern."

15 This is what the Sovereign LORD, the Holy One of Israel, says:

"In repentance and rest is your salvation,
in quietness and trust[g] is your strength,
but you would have none of it.
16 You said, 'No, we will flee on horses.'[h]
Therefore you will flee!
You said, 'We will ride off on swift horses.'
Therefore your pursuers will be swift!
17 A thousand will flee
at the threat of one;
at the threat of five[i]
you will all flee[j] away,
till you are left
like a flagstaff on a mountaintop,
like a banner on a hill."

18 Yet the LORD longs[k] to be gracious to you;
he rises to show you compassion.
For the LORD is a God of justice.[l]
Blessed are all who wait for him![m]

19 O people of Zion, who live in Jerusalem, you will weep no more.[n] How gracious he will be when you cry for help! As soon as he hears, he will answer[o] you. 20 Although the Lord gives you the bread[p] of adversity and the water of affliction, your teachers will be hidden[q] no more; with your own eyes you will see them. 21 Whether you turn to the right or to the left, your ears will hear a voice[r] behind you, saying, "This is the way; walk in it." 22 Then you will defile your idols[s] overlaid with silver and your images covered with gold; you will throw them away like a menstrual cloth and say to them, "Away with you!"

23 He will also send you rain[t] for the seed you sow in the ground, and the food that comes from the land will be rich and plentiful. In that day your cattle will graze in broad meadows.[u] 24 The oxen and donkeys that work the soil will eat fodder and mash, spread out with fork[v] and shovel. 25 In the day of great slaughter, when the towers[w] fall, streams of water will flow[x] on every high mountain and every lofty hill. 26 The moon will shine like the sun,[y] and the sunlight will be seven times brighter, like the light of seven full days, when the LORD binds up the bruises of his people and heals[z] the wounds he inflicted.

27 See, the Name[a] of the LORD comes from afar,
with burning anger[b] and dense clouds of smoke;
his lips are full of wrath,[c]
and his tongue is a consuming fire.
28 His breath[d] is like a rushing torrent,
rising up to the neck.[e]
He shakes the nations in the sieve[f] of destruction;
he places in the jaws of the peoples
a bit[g] that leads them astray.
29 And you will sing
as on the night you celebrate a holy festival;
your hearts will rejoice
as when people go up with flutes
to the mountain[h] of the LORD,
to the Rock of Israel.
30 The LORD will cause men to hear his majestic voice
and will make them see his arm coming down

30:15
g Isa 32:17

30:16
h Isa 31:1,3

30:17
i Lev 26:8;
Jos 23:10
j Lev 26:36;
Dt 28:25

30:18
k Isa 42:14;
2Pe 3:9,15
l Isa 5:16 m Isa 25:9

30:19
n Isa 60:20; 61:3
o Ps 50:15; Isa 58:9;
65:24; Mt 7:7-11
30:20
p 1Ki 22:27
q Ps 74:9; Am 8:11
30:21
r Isa 29:24
30:22
s Ex 32:4

30:23
t Isa 65:21-22
u Ps 65:13

30:24
v Mt 3:12; Lk 3:17
30:25
w Isa 2:15
x Isa 41:18
30:26
y Isa 24:23;
60:19-20;
Rev 21:23; 22:5
z Dt 32:39; Isa 1:5
30:27
a Isa 59:19
b Isa 66:14
c Isa 10:5

30:28
d Isa 11:4 e Isa 8:8
f Am 9:9
g 2Ki 19:28;
Isa 37:29

30:29
h Ps 42:4

with raging anger and consuming fire,
  with cloudburst, thunderstorm and hail.
31 The voice of the LORD will shatter Assyria;[i]
  with his scepter he will strike[j] them down.
32 Every stroke the LORD lays on them
  with his punishing rod
will be to the music of tambourines and harps,
  as he fights them in battle with the blows of his arm.[k]
33 Topheth[l] has long been prepared;
  it has been made ready for the king.
Its fire pit has been made deep and wide,
  with an abundance of fire and wood;
the breath of the LORD,
  like a stream of burning sulfur,[m]
  sets it ablaze.

Woe to Those Who Rely on Egypt

31 Woe to those who go down to Egypt[n] for help,
  who rely on horses,
who trust in the multitude of their chariots[o]
  and in the great strength of their horsemen,
but do not look to the Holy One of Israel,
  or seek help from the LORD.[p]
2 Yet he too is wise[q] and can bring disaster;[r]
  he does not take back his words.[s]
He will rise up against the house of the wicked,[t]
  against those who help evildoers.
3 But the Egyptians[u] are men and not God;[v]
  their horses are flesh and not spirit.
When the LORD stretches out his hand,[w]
  he who helps will stumble,
  he who is helped[x] will fall;
  both will perish together.

4 This is what the LORD says to me:

"As a lion[y] growls,
  a great lion over his prey—
and though a whole band of shepherds
  is called together against him,
he is not frightened by their shouts
  or disturbed by their clamor—
so the LORD Almighty will come down[z]
  to do battle on Mount Zion and on its heights.
5 Like birds hovering overhead,
  the LORD Almighty will shield[a] Jerusalem;
he will shield it and deliver[b] it,
  he will 'pass over' it and will rescue it."

30:31
i Isa 10:5,12
j Isa 11:4

30:32
k Isa 11:15;
Eze 32:10
30:33
l 2Ki 23:10
m Ge 19:24

31:1
n Dt 17:16;
Isa 30:2,5 o Isa 2:7
p Ps 20:7; Da 9:13

31:2
q Ro 16:27
r Isa 45:7
s Nu 23:19
t Isa 32:6

31:3
u Isa 36:9
v Eze 28:9; 2Th 2:4
w Isa 9:17,21
x Isa 30:5-7

31:4
y Nu 24:9;
Hos 11:10; Am 3:8
z Isa 42:13

31:5
a Ps 91:4
b Isa 37:35; 38:6

Isaiah 31:1–9

The "woe" of chapter 31 says many of the same things stated at greater length in chapter 30. Up to verse 4, Isaiah had been counseling the Judahites not to trust Egypt because Egypt couldn't deliver. In verses 4–9 he flipped the argument: Trust the Lord because he is the only One who *can* deliver you. His major points: God would defend Jerusalem, his people should turn back to him and away from idols, and Assyria was no match for the Lord. It was much wiser to trust God than Egypt in a battle against Assyria. The Assyrians would put Egypt to flight, but God would put Assyria to flight.

Nations in a fallen world use weapons of defense, but should they be a believer's source of confidence? Does sleeping with a pistol under your pillow mean that you don't have to trust God for your life? There are no easy answers to these questions, but it's important that we ask them. Who, or what, are you ultimately trusting in?

31:7
c Isa 2:20; 30:22

31:8
d Isa 10:12
e Isa 14:25; 37:7
f Ge 49:15

31:9
g Dt 32:31,37
h Isa 10:17

[6] Return to him you have so greatly revolted against, O Israelites. [7] For in that day every one of you will reject the idols of silver and gold[c] your sinful hands have made.

[8] "Assyria[d] will fall by a sword that is not of man;
a sword, not of mortals, will devour[e] them.
They will flee before the sword
and their young men will be put to forced labor.[f]
[9] Their stronghold[g] will fall because of terror;
at sight of the battle standard their commanders will panic,"
declares the LORD,
whose fire[h] is in Zion,
whose furnace is in Jerusalem.

The Kingdom of Righteousness

32:1
i Eze 37:24
j Ps 72:1-4; Isa 9:7

32:2
k Isa 4:6

32 See, a king[i] will reign in righteousness
and rulers will rule with justice.[j]
[2] Each man will be like a shelter[k] from the wind
and a refuge from the storm,
like streams of water in the desert
and the shadow of a great rock in a thirsty land.

32:3
l Isa 29:18

[3] Then the eyes of those who see will no longer be closed,[l]
and the ears of those who hear will listen.

32:4
m Isa 29:24

[4] The mind of the rash will know and understand,[m]
and the stammering tongue will be fluent and clear.

32:5
n 1Sa 25:25

[5] No longer will the fool[n] be called noble
nor the scoundrel be highly respected.

32:6
o Pr 19:3 p Isa 9:17
q Isa 9:16 r Isa 3:15

[6] For the fool speaks folly,[o]
his mind is busy with evil:
He practices ungodliness[p]
and spreads error[q] concerning the LORD;
the hungry he leaves empty[r]
and from the thirsty he withholds water.

32:7
s Jer 5:26-28
t Mic 7:3 u Isa 61:1

[7] The scoundrel's methods are wicked,[s]
he makes up evil schemes[t]
to destroy the poor with lies,
even when the plea of the needy[u] is just.

32:8
v Pr 11:25

[8] But the noble man makes noble plans,
and by noble deeds[v] he stands.

The Women of Jerusalem

32:9
w Isa 28:23

[9] You women who are so complacent,
rise up and listen[w] to me;

Isaiah 32:1–8

The King God promised would reign in righteousness and justice. The standard by which God judges human rulers is their treatment of the poor and hungry (vv. 6–7). Rather than nobles looking out only for other nobles, they are to have regard for the marginalized.

Throughout history and now, throughout our world, rulers have shown special favor to the influential. By securing their favor they can preserve their own power. Promises are made to the poor to pacify them, but threat and force are used to keep them in their "place." This pattern of oppression drove Francis of Assisi (1182?–1226) to minister to the poor. Similarly, the resistance of the rich and the powerful in England to John

Wesley's (1703–1791) message sent him out the doors of the established church to care for the poor. In what situations do churches today cater to the affluent, ignoring Jesus' call to bring the good news of God's justice to the needy (cf. Luke 4:18)?

Isaiah 32:9–20

Isaiah condemned women who were self-satisfied and secure, apparently because of a good harvest. Their complacency was terribly misplaced, for in only one year—perhaps with the Assyrian invasion of 701 B.C.—everything would change. The land would become barren and deserted, matching the people's spiritual condition.

But again, the prediction of tragedy and defeat was

you daughters who feel secure,[x]
    hear what I have to say!
10 In little more than a year
    you who feel secure will tremble;
the grape harvest will fail,[y]
    and the harvest of fruit will not come.
11 Tremble, you complacent women;
    shudder, you daughters who feel secure!
Strip off your clothes,[z]
    put sackcloth around your waists.
12 Beat your breasts[a] for the pleasant fields,
    for the fruitful vines
13 and for the land of my people,
    a land overgrown with thorns and briers[b]—
yes, mourn for all houses of merriment
    and for this city of revelry.[c]
14 The fortress[d] will be abandoned,
    the noisy city deserted;[e]
citadel and watchtower[f] will become a wasteland forever,
    the delight of donkeys,[g] a pasture for flocks,
15 till the Spirit[h] is poured upon us from on high,
    and the desert becomes a fertile field,[i]

32:9
[x] Isa 47:8; Am 6:1; Zep 2:15

32:10
[y] Isa 5:5-6; 24:7

32:11
[z] Isa 47:2

32:12
[a] Na 2:7

32:13
[b] Isa 5:6 [c] Isa 22:2

32:14
[d] Isa 13:22
[e] Isa 6:11; 27:10
[f] Isa 34:13
[g] Ps 104:11

32:15
[h] Isa 11:2; Joel 2:28
[i] Ps 107:35; Isa 35:1-2

immediately followed with God's promise of hope. Just as rain falls and the barren land springs back to life, so God's Spirit would fall on barren hearts, causing the qualities the covenant required but couldn't produce—justice and righteousness—to spring up. The fruit of righteousness and justice are peace and trust.

We pursue peace and tranquility in vain if we don't also seek righteousness and justice. We try to provide peace through weapons and pleasurable circumstances, but unless we pursue justice for the oppressed our self-made tranquility will be fragile. The Messiah, through the Holy Spirit, makes it possible for us as Christians to live lives of true nobility—of generosity, justice, righteousness, and an assurance that uncertainties can't disrupt. Living in the kingdom of God endows us with inner resources with which to meet and triumph over every circumstance that may come our way.

32:17–18

The Nobel Peace Prize

The promise of and hope for peace is a beautiful strand running throughout Isaiah. According to Isaiah 32:17, one of the qualities that brings peace is "righteousness."

The Nobel Peace Prize is an annual award given to the person(s) who have "done the most or the best work for fraternity between nations, for the abolition or reduction of standing armies and for the holding and promotion of peace congresses." Since its beginning in 1901, just over 100 Nobel Peace prizes have been awarded, 10 of them to persons working in a specifically religious capacity:

Source: Wright (2003:851–853)

1930	Nathan Soderblom (Sweden), Lutheran archbishop, leader in the ecumenical movement
1946	John R. Mott (United States), leader of the Christian ecumenical movement
1947	The Friends Service Council and the American Friends Service Committee (the Quakers)
1952	Albert Schweitzer (France), missionary surgeon/founder of Lambarene Hospital in Africa
1958	George Pire (Belgium), Dominican priest who led a relief organization for refugees
1964	Martin Luther King (United States), leader of the American civil rights movement
1979	Mother Teresa (India), worker for the poor in Calcutta
1984	Desmond Tutu (South Africa), Bishop of Johannesburg, leader in anti-apartheid movement
1986	Elie Wiesel (United States), writer on the Holocaust
1989	Dalai Lama (Tibet), exiled religious and political leader working for Tibetan independence

32:15
j Isa 29:17

32:17
k Ps 119:165;
Ro 14:17; Jas 3:18
l Isa 30:15

32:18
m Hos 2:18-23
32:19
n Isa 28:17; 30:30
o Isa 10:19;
Zec 11:2
p Isa 24:10; 27:10

32:20
q Ecc 11:1
r Isa 30:24

33:1
s Hab 2:8; Mt 7:2
t Isa 21:2

33:2
u Isa 40:10; 51:9;
59:16 v Isa 25:9

33:3
w Isa 59:16-18

33:5
x Ps 97:9 y Isa 28:6
z Isa 1:26

33:6
a Isa 51:6
b Isa 11:2-3;
Mt 6:33

33:7
c 2Ki 18:37

33:8
d Jdg 5:6; Isa 35:8

33:9
e Isa 3:26 f Isa 2:13;
35:2 g Isa 24:4

and the fertile field seems like a forest.*j*

16 Justice will dwell in the desert
and righteousness live in the fertile field.
17 The fruit of righteousness will be peace;*k*
the effect of righteousness will be quietness and confidence*l* forever.
18 My people will live in peaceful dwelling places,
in secure homes,
in undisturbed places of rest.*m*
19 Though hail*n* flattens the forest*o*
and the city is leveled*p* completely,
20 how blessed you will be,
sowing*q* your seed by every stream,
and letting your cattle and donkeys range free.*r*

Distress and Help

33 Woe to you, O destroyer,
you who have not been destroyed!
Woe to you, O traitor,
you who have not been betrayed!
When you stop destroying,
you will be destroyed;*s*
when you stop betraying,
you will be betrayed.*t*

2 O LORD, be gracious to us;
we long for you.
Be our strength*u* every morning,
our salvation*v* in time of distress.
3 At the thunder of your voice, the peoples flee;
when you rise up,*w* the nations scatter.
4 Your plunder, O nations, is harvested as by young locusts;
like a swarm of locusts men pounce on it.

5 The LORD is exalted,*x* for he dwells on high;
he will fill Zion with justice*y* and righteousness.*z*
6 He will be the sure foundation for your times,
a rich store of salvation*a* and wisdom and knowledge;
the fear*b* of the LORD is the key to this treasure.*a*

7 Look, their brave men cry aloud in the streets;
the envoys*c* of peace weep bitterly.
8 The highways are deserted,
no travelers are on the roads.*d*
The treaty is broken,
its witnesses*b* are despised,
no one is respected.
9 The land mourns*c**e* and wastes away,
Lebanon*f* is ashamed and withers;*g*
Sharon is like the Arabah,
and Bashan and Carmel drop their leaves.

a 6 Or *is a treasure from him*   *b* 8 Dead Sea Scrolls; Masoretic Text / *the cities*   *c* 9 Or *dries up*

Isaiah 33:1–24

Chapter 33 is introduced by the sixth and final "woe" in the series begun in chapter 28. The "destroyer" was almost certainly Assyria. Verses 2–9 represent Judah's prayer for deliverance. With verse 10, God promised to take action—by disciplining his people. Verse 17 introduces the divinely provided leader who would be for Judah what their drunken, confused leaders had never been (cf. 28:7; 29:9–10). In this context, there can be little question that the "king" referred to here is the Lord (see v. 22). This prophecy would be realized when God revealed his Messiah, Jesus Christ. And it will finally and fully become reality in the last days, when Christ rules the earth.

10 "Now will I arise,[h]" says the LORD.
   "Now will I be exalted;
   now will I be lifted up.
11 You conceive[i] chaff,
   you give birth[j] to straw;
   your breath is a fire[k] that consumes you.
12 The peoples will be burned as if to lime;
   like cut thornbushes they will be set ablaze.[l]"
13 You who are far away,[m] hear[n] what I have done;
   you who are near, acknowledge my power!
14 The sinners in Zion are terrified;
   trembling[o] grips the godless:
   "Who of us can dwell with the consuming fire?[p]
   Who of us can dwell with everlasting burning?"
15 He who walks righteously[q]
   and speaks what is right,[r]
who rejects gain from extortion
   and keeps his hand from accepting bribes,
who stops his ears against plots of murder
   and shuts his eyes[s] against contemplating evil—
16 this is the man who will dwell on the heights,
   whose refuge[t] will be the mountain fortress.[u]
His bread will be supplied,
   and water will not fail[v] him.

17 Your eyes will see the king[w] in his beauty
   and view a land that stretches afar.[x]
18 In your thoughts you will ponder the former terror:[y]
   "Where is that chief officer?
   Where is the one who took the revenue?
   Where is the officer in charge of the towers?"
19 You will see those arrogant people no more,
   those people of an obscure speech,
   with their strange, incomprehensible tongue.[z]

20 Look upon Zion, the city of our festivals;
   your eyes will see Jerusalem,
   a peaceful abode,[a] a tent that will not be moved;[b]
its stakes will never be pulled up,
   nor any of its ropes broken.
21 There the LORD will be our Mighty One.
   It will be like a place of broad rivers and streams.[c]
No galley with oars will ride them,
   no mighty ship will sail them.
22 For the LORD is our judge,[d]
   the LORD is our lawgiver,[e]
the LORD is our king;[f]
   it is he who will save[g] us.
23 Your rigging hangs loose:
   The mast is not held secure,

33:10
[h] Ps 12:5; Isa 2:21

33:11
[i] Ps 7:14; Isa 59:4;
Jas 1:15 [j] Isa 26:18
[k] Isa 1:31

33:12
[l] Isa 10:17

33:13
[m] Ps 48:10; 49:1
[n] Isa 49:1

33:14
[o] Isa 32:11
[p] Isa 30:30;
Heb 12:29

33:15
[q] Isa 58:8 [r] Ps 15:2;
24:4 [s] Ps 119:37

33:16
[t] Isa 25:4 [u] Isa 26:1
[v] Isa 49:10

33:17
[w] Isa 6:5
[x] Isa 26:15
33:18
[y] Isa 17:14

33:19
[z] Isa 28:11; Jer 5:15

33:20
[a] Isa 32:18
[b] Ps 46:5; 125:1-2

33:21
[c] Isa 41:18; 48:18;
66:12

33:22
[d] Isa 11:4 [e] Isa 2:3;
Jas 4:12 [f] Ps 89:18
[g] Isa 25:9

Isaiah was clear in verses 14–16 that the mark of membership in God's kingdom is behaving as the King does. We are reminded of Psalm 15, which says that the person who is fit to "dwell in [God's] sanctuary" is the one "whose walk is blameless and who does what is righteous" (Ps. 15:1–2). Passages like Romans 6 confirm that God expects us as Christians to share his character, as "slaves to righteousness" rather than "slaves to sin." The New Testament will never, though, let us believe that we can *earn* a place in God's house because we live like him. Rather, we are *given* that place because Jesus Christ has died for us.

33:23
h 2Ki 7:8 i 2Ki 7:16
33:24
j Isa 30:26
k Jer 50:20;
1Jn 1:7-9

the sail is not spread.
Then an abundance of spoils will be divided
and even the lame[h] will carry off plunder.[i]
24 No one living in Zion will say, "I am ill";[j]
and the sins of those who dwell there will be forgiven.[k]

Judgment Against the Nations

34:1
l Isa 41:1; 43:9
m Ps 49:1 n Dt 32:1

34 Come near, you nations, and listen;
pay attention, you peoples![l]
Let the earth[m] hear, and all that is in it,
the world, and all that comes out of it![n]

34:2
o Isa 13:5
p Isa 30:25

2 The LORD is angry with all nations;
his wrath is upon all their armies.
He will totally destroy[a][o] them,
he will give them over to slaughter.[p]

34:3
q Joel 2:20;
Am 4:10 r ver 7;
Eze 14:19; 35:6;
38:22
34:4
s Isa 13:13;
2Pe 3:10
t Eze 32:7-8
u Joel 2:31;
Mt 24:29*;
Rev 6:13

3 Their slain will be thrown out,
their dead bodies will send up a stench;[q]
the mountains will be soaked with their blood.[r]
4 All the stars of the heavens will be dissolved[s]
and the sky rolled up[t] like a scroll;
all the starry host will fall[u]
like withered leaves from the vine,
like shriveled figs from the fig tree.

34:5
v Dt 32:41-42;
Jer 46:10; Eze 21:5
w Am 1:11-12
x Isa 24:6; Mal 1:4

5 My sword[v] has drunk its fill in the heavens;
see, it descends in judgment on Edom,[w]
the people I have totally destroyed.[x]
6 The sword of the LORD is bathed in blood,
it is covered with fat—
the blood of lambs and goats,
fat from the kidneys of rams.
For the LORD has a sacrifice in Bozrah
and a great slaughter in Edom.

34:7
y Ps 68:30

7 And the wild oxen will fall with them,
the bull calves and the great bulls.[y]
Their land will be drenched with blood,
and the dust will be soaked with fat.

34:8
z Isa 63:4

8 For the LORD has a day of vengeance,[z]
a year of retribution, to uphold Zion's cause.

---

a 2 The Hebrew term refers to the irrevocable giving over of things or persons to the LORD, often by totally destroying them; also in verse 5.

Isaiah 34:1–17

Chapters 34–35 offer a conclusion not only to chapters 28–33, but to the whole of chapters 13–33. God, through Isaiah, had been showing his people why they should trust him and not the nations. Now in chapters 34–35 the alternatives were depicted in glaring contrast. Chapter 34 begins with a general announcement of judgment on the nations (vv. 1–4), then applies it by way of example to Edom (vv. 5–17)—which, like Moab in 25:10–12, represented all the enemies of God and his people.

The general announcement uses court language. God called the defendants, the "nations" and the "peoples," to hear the decree pronounced against them. But the judgment didn't merely affect the earth; it involved the entire cosmos, with the stars being "dissolved" and the sky "rolled up."

Most of us eat meat, but how often do we think about the butchering process? Ironically, the language we may find offensive in this passage was probably comforting to the early hearers. Blood and gore were part of their lives—from the slaughter of animals for food and worship to brutal warfare. This "street language" confirmed to Judah that a day would come when God would even the scales for the oppressed. There was going to be justice in the world after all.

The apostle Paul built on this concept when he wrote, "Do not take revenge, my friends, but leave room for God's wrath, for it is written: 'It is mine to avenge; I will repay,' says the Lord" (Rom. 12:19). How freeing this is. It frees us from carrying around a heavy load of anger and resentment. When we are treated unjustly, we can trust God to do the right thing for us.

9 Edom's streams will be turned into pitch,
her dust into burning sulfur;
her land will become blazing pitch!
10 It will not be quenched night and day;
its smoke will rise forever.[a]
From generation to generation it will lie desolate;[b]
no one will ever pass through it again.
11 The desert owl[a][c] and screech owl[a] will possess it;
the great owl[a] and the raven will nest there.
God will stretch out over Edom
the measuring line of chaos
and the plumb line[d] of desolation.
12 Her nobles will have nothing there to be called a kingdom,
all her princes[e] will vanish[f] away.
13 Thorns will overrun her citadels,
nettles and brambles her strongholds.[g]
She will become a haunt for jackals,[h]
a home for owls.
14 Desert creatures will meet with hyenas,[i]
and wild goats will bleat to each other;
there the night creatures will also repose
and find for themselves places of rest.
15 The owl will nest there and lay eggs,
she will hatch them, and care for her young under the shadow of her wings;
there also the falcons[j] will gather,
each with its mate.

16 Look in the scroll[k] of the LORD and read:

None of these will be missing,
not one will lack her mate.
For it is his mouth[l] that has given the order,
and his Spirit will gather them together.
17 He allots their portions;[m]
his hand distributes them by measure.
They will possess it forever
and dwell there from generation to generation.[n]

Joy of the Redeemed

35 The desert[o] and the parched land will be glad;
the wilderness will rejoice and blossom.[p]
Like the crocus, 2 it will burst into bloom;
it will rejoice greatly and shout for joy.[q]
The glory of Lebanon[r] will be given to it,
the splendor of Carmel[s] and Sharon;
they will see the glory of the LORD,
the splendor of our God.[t]

34:10 [a] Rev 14:10-11; 19:3 [b] Isa 13:20; 24:1; Eze 29:12; Mal 1:3
34:11 [c] Zep 2:14; Rev 18:2 [d] 2Ki 21:13; La 2:8
34:12 [e] Jer 27:20; 39:6 [f] Isa 41:11-12
34:13 [g] Isa 13:22; 32:13 [h] Ps 44:19; Jer 9:11; 10:22
34:14 [i] Isa 13:22
34:15 [j] Dt 14:13
34:16 [k] Isa 30:8 [l] Isa 1:20; 58:14
34:17 [m] Isa 17:14; Jer 13:25 [n] ver 10
35:1 [o] Isa 27:10; 41:18-19 [p] Isa 51:3
35:2 [q] Isa 25:9; 55:12 [r] Isa 32:15 [s] SS 7:5 [t] Isa 25:9

[a] 11 The precise identification of these birds is uncertain.

Isaiah 35:1–10

This chapter is a mirror image of the last. Isaiah 34 spoke of the fate of the arrogant nations and of all who trusted in them. This one discusses the destiny of those who turn from that path to unwavering trust in God. These chapters don't mention trust as such, but it's the underlying issue. What happens when God's people trust in him instead of the nations? The answer is beautifully represented here.

God hasn't delivered us from our sins so that we can sit and contemplate our saved condition until the day we die. He has delivered us so that we can participate in his life and character in a progressive, ongoing way. He makes it possible for us to walk with him in greater and greater likeness to him, until that last day when we arrive in the heavenly city where gladness will displace sorrow forever.

35:3 [u] Job 4:4; Heb 12:12
35:4 [v] Isa 1:24; 34:8
35:5 [w] Mt 11:5; Jn 9:6-7 [x] Isa 29:18; 50:4
35:6 [y] Mt 15:30; Jn 5:8-9; Ac 3:8 [z] Isa 32:4; Mt 9:32-33; 12:22; Lk 11:14 [a] Isa 41:18; Jn 7:38
35:7 [b] Isa 49:10 [c] Isa 13:22
35:8 [d] Isa 11:16; 33:8; Mt 7:13-14 [e] Isa 4:3; 1Pe 1:15 [f] Isa 52:1
35:9 [g] Isa 30:6 [h] Isa 34:14 [i] Isa 51:11; 62:12; 63:4
35:10 [j] Isa 25:9 [k] Isa 30:19; 51:11; Rev 7:17; 21:4

3 Strengthen the feeble hands,
steady the knees[u] that give way;
4 say to those with fearful hearts,
"Be strong, do not fear;
your God will come,
he will come with vengeance;[v]
with divine retribution
he will come to save you."

5 Then will the eyes of the blind be opened[w]
and the ears of the deaf[x] unstopped.
6 Then will the lame[y] leap like a deer,
and the mute tongue[z] shout for joy.
Water will gush forth in the wilderness
and streams[a] in the desert.
7 The burning sand will become a pool,
the thirsty ground bubbling springs.[b]
In the haunts where jackals[c] once lay,
grass and reeds and papyrus will grow.

8 And a highway[d] will be there;
it will be called the Way of Holiness.[e]
The unclean[f] will not journey on it;
it will be for those who walk in that Way;
wicked fools will not go about on it.[a]
9 No lion[g] will be there,
nor will any ferocious beast[h] get up on it;
they will not be found there.
But only the redeemed[i] will walk there,
10 and the ransomed of the LORD will return.
They will enter Zion with singing;
everlasting joy[j] will crown their heads.
Gladness and joy will overtake them,
and sorrow and sighing will flee away.[k]

Sennacherib Threatens Jerusalem

36:1 [l] 2Ch 32:1
36:2 [m] Isa 7:3
36:3 [n] Isa 22:20-21 [o] 2Ki 18:18

36 In the fourteenth year of King Hezekiah's reign, Sennacherib[l] king of Assyria attacked all the fortified cities of Judah and captured them. 2 Then the
king of Assyria sent his field commander with a large army from Lachish to King
Hezekiah at Jerusalem. When the commander stopped at the aqueduct of the Upper Pool, on the road to the Washerman's Field,[m] 3 Eliakim[n] son of Hilkiah the palace administrator, Shebna[o] the secretary, and Joah son of Asaph the recorder went
out to him.
4 The field commander said to them, "Tell Hezekiah,

36:5 [p] 2Ki 18:7
36:6 [q] Isa 30:2,5

" 'This is what the great king, the king of Assyria, says: On what are you basing this confidence of yours? 5 You say you have strategy and military strength—
but you speak only empty words. On whom are you depending, that you rebel[p] against me? 6 Look now, you are depending on Egypt,[q] that splintered

[a] 8 Or / *the simple will not stray from it*

Isaiah 36:1–22

Though Isaiah 36–39 may appear to be a historical appendix (cf. 2 Kings 18:13–20:19), in reality these *chapters climax the book's whole argument to this point.* The prophet had asserted over and over that God can be trusted. Now the test of whether to trust in God or the nations was administered to King Hezekiah and Judah as they were threatened by the Assyrians in 701 B.C.

The Assyrian field commander's argument had a fatal flaw: He assumed that the Lord was just one of many gods. But as Isaiah had been saying all along, God is a different sort of being altogether. Hezekiah's representatives made no attempt to answer the man's arguments. That was just as well; they weren't meant to be answered. This was psychological warfare, an attempt to break Judah's will to resist.

reed[r] of a staff, which pierces a man's hand and wounds him if he leans on it! Such is Pharaoh king of Egypt to all who depend on him. 7And if you say to me, "We are depending on the LORD our God"—isn't he the one whose high places and altars Hezekiah removed,[s] saying to Judah and Jerusalem, "You must worship before this altar"?[t]

8" 'Come now, make a bargain with my master, the king of Assyria: I will give you two thousand horses—if you can put riders on them! 9How then can you repulse one officer of the least of my master's officials, even though you are depending on Egypt[u] for chariots and horsemen?[v] 10Furthermore, have I come to attack and destroy this land without the LORD? The LORD himself told[w] me to march against this country and destroy it.' "

11Then Eliakim, Shebna and Joah said to the field commander, "Please speak to your servants in Aramaic,[x] since we understand it. Don't speak to us in Hebrew in the hearing of the people on the wall."

12But the commander replied, "Was it only to your master and you that my master sent me to say these things, and not to the men sitting on the wall—who, like you, will have to eat their own filth and drink their own urine?"

13Then the commander stood and called out in Hebrew,[y] "Hear the words of the great king, the king of Assyria! 14This is what the king says: Do not let Hezekiah deceive you. He cannot deliver you! 15Do not let Hezekiah persuade you to trust in the LORD when he says, 'The LORD will surely deliver us; this city will not be given into the hand of the king of Assyria.'[z]

16"Do not listen to Hezekiah. This is what the king of Assyria says: Make peace with me and come out to me. Then every one of you will eat from his own vine and fig tree[a] and drink water from his own cistern,[b] 17until I come and take you to a land like your own—a land of grain and new wine, a land of bread and vineyards.

18"Do not let Hezekiah mislead you when he says, 'The LORD will deliver us.' Has the god of any nation ever delivered his land from the hand of the king of Assyria? 19Where are the gods of Hamath and Arpad? Where are the gods of Sepharvaim? Have they rescued Samaria from my hand? 20Who of all the gods[c] of these countries has been able to save his land from me? How then can the LORD deliver Jerusalem from my hand?"

21But the people remained silent and said nothing in reply, because the king had commanded, "Do not answer him."[d]

22Then Eliakim son of Hilkiah the palace administrator, Shebna the secretary, and Joah son of Asaph the recorder went to Hezekiah, with their clothes torn, and told him what the field commander had said.

Jerusalem's Deliverance Foretold

37 When King Hezekiah heard this, he tore his clothes and put on sackcloth and went into the temple of the LORD. 2He sent Eliakim the palace administrator, Shebna the secretary, and the leading priests, all wearing sackcloth, to the prophet Isaiah son of Amoz.[e] 3They told him, "This is what Hezekiah says: This day is a day of distress and rebuke and disgrace, as when children come to the point of birth[f] and there is no strength to deliver them. 4It may be that the LORD your God

36:6 r Eze 29:6-7
36:7 s 2Ki 18:4 t Dt 12:2-5
36:9 u Isa 31:3 v Isa 30:2-5
36:10 w 1Ki 13:18
36:11 x Ezr 4:7
36:13 y 2Ch 32:18
36:15 z Isa 37:10
36:16 a 1Ki 4:25; Zec 3:10 b Pr 5:15
36:20 c 1Ki 20:23
36:21 d Pr 9:7-8; 26:4
37:2 e Isa 1:1
37:3 f Isa 26:18; 66:9; Hos 13:13

Sometimes we give our opponents ammunition to use against us because we have betrayed our faith in God by trusting the world instead. If practices or relationships in our lives give others a chance to say that we talk a good show but are really no different from the world in our lifestyle, we might want to consider getting rid of them now. These decisions are personal, but the issue is this: Do I really trust the Lord, or does my behavior say I lie?

The enemy of our souls still uses psychological tactics against God's people today. That is why Paul encouraged believers to put on the armor of God to withstand

such spiritual attacks (Eph. 6:11–18). What issue(s) seems to trip you up? How can Paul's instruction and this passage in Isaiah help you in the particular battle you are facing right now?

Isaiah 37:1–13
Hezekiah's response to his advisors' report is instructive. He didn't closet himself with them to consider what "spin" to put on the events. We needn't make Hezekiah look better than he was: We know from 2 Kings 18:13–16 that he had already tried to buy himself out of the situation by giving Sennacherib a large

will hear the words of the field commander, whom his master, the king of Assyria, has sent to ridicule the living God, and that he will rebuke him for the words the LORD your God has heard.[g] Therefore pray for the remnant[h] that still survives."

37:4
g Isa 36:13,18-20
h Isa 1:9

[5]When King Hezekiah's officials came to Isaiah, [6]Isaiah said to them, "Tell your master, 'This is what the LORD says: Do not be afraid[i] of what you have heard—those words with which the underlings of the king of Assyria have blasphemed me. [7]Listen! I am going to put a spirit in him so that when he hears a certain report,[j] he will return to his own country, and there I will have him cut down with the sword.' "

37:6
i Isa 7:4
37:7
j ver 9

[8]When the field commander heard that the king of Assyria had left Lachish, he withdrew and found the king fighting against Libnah.[k]

37:8
k Nu 33:20
37:9
l ver 7

[9]Now Sennacherib received a report[l] that Tirhakah, the Cushite[a] king ⌊of Egypt⌋, was marching out to fight against him. When he heard it, he sent messengers to Hezekiah with this word: [10]"Say to Hezekiah king of Judah: Do not let the god you depend on deceive you when he says, 'Jerusalem will not be handed over to the king of Assyria.'[m] [11]Surely you have heard what the kings of Assyria have done to all the countries, destroying them completely. And will you be delivered?[n] [12]Did the gods of the nations that were destroyed by my forefathers[o] deliver them—the gods of Gozan, Haran,[p] Rezeph and the people of Eden who were in Tel Assar? [13]Where is the king of Hamath, the king of Arpad, the king of the city of Sepharvaim, or of Hena or Ivvah?"

37:10
m Isa 36:15
37:11
n Isa 36:18-20
37:12
o 2Ki 18:11
p Ge 11:31; 12:1-4;
Ac 7:2

Hezekiah's Prayer

[14]Hezekiah received the letter from the messengers and read it. Then he went up to the temple of the LORD and spread it out before the LORD. [15]And Hezekiah prayed to the LORD: [16]"O LORD Almighty, God of Israel, enthroned between the cherubim, you alone are God[q] over all the kingdoms of the earth. You have made heaven and earth. [17]Give ear, O LORD, and hear;[r] open your eyes, O LORD, and see;[s] listen to all the words Sennacherib has sent to insult the living God.

37:16
q Dt 10:17;
Ps 86:10; 136:2-3
37:17
r 2Ch 6:40
s Da 9:18

[18]"It is true, O LORD, that the Assyrian kings have laid waste all these peoples and their lands.[t] [19]They have thrown their gods into the fire and destroyed them,[u] for they were not gods[v] but only wood and stone, fashioned by human hands. [20]Now, O LORD our God, deliver us from his hand, so that all kingdoms on earth may know that you alone, O LORD, are God.[b][w]"

37:18
t 2Ki 15:29;
Na 2:11-12
37:19
u Isa 26:14
v Isa 41:24,29
37:20
w Ps 46:10

Sennacherib's Fall

37:21
x ver 2

[21]Then Isaiah son of Amoz[x] sent a message to Hezekiah: "This is what the LORD,

---

[a] 9 That is, from the upper Nile region   [b] 20 Dead Sea Scrolls (see also 2 Kings 19:19); Masoretic Text *alone are the LORD*

---

sum of money. But, in contrast, it would be hard to imagine Judah's kings in the Babylonian crisis 100 years later turning to God this openly at any point in the process (cf. 2 Kings 23:31—24:20).

📖 The reason the Biblical prophets concentrated on the folly of idolatry is that this was the Achilles heel of pagan belief. Rather than getting into complex arguments, they simply asked how a piece of stone or block of wood could save people (v. 19). Many intelligent people today insist on the eternity of matter, believing that life came from nowhere and goes nowhere. We still face Hezekiah's conflict: whether the God we worship is different from, or superior to, what this world calls "gods." Christians with concrete faith in God through Jesus Christ can answer the question, "How can a natural system save us from a natural system?": It can't; only our sovereign, transcendent God can.

Isaiah 37:14–20

🔑 Hezekiah called on the Lord to observe the way that Sennacherib had insulted God. The crucial issue wasn't whether Jerusalem would be taken but whether Sennacherib's claim would stand that the Lord was just one more god created by humans—which other humans could destroy at will. Later on Jerusalem would fall, but God's identity and character wouldn't be on the line at that time (cf. Jer. 37:6–10).

🔑 Refusing to play the game of one-upmanship, Hezekiah put his reputation into God's hands. A person who responds to God's love knows a number of things, according to 1 John 5. We know how much we are worth: the life of God's Son. We know that pulsating in us is eternal life and that we have instant access to the Father's throne room. We know we are in a life-and-death struggle with the powers presently ruling this world—and that Jesus has given us power to understand the issues and remain true. What more do we need to know?

the God of Israel, says: Because you have prayed to me concerning Sennacherib king of Assyria, 22this is the word the LORD has spoken against him:

> "The Virgin Daughter of Zion
>   despises and mocks you.
> The Daughter of Jerusalem
>   tosses her head[y] as you flee.
> 23Who is it you have insulted and blasphemed?[z]
>   Against whom have you raised your voice
> and lifted your eyes in pride?[a]
>   Against the Holy One of Israel!
> 24By your messengers
>   you have heaped insults on the Lord.
> And you have said,
>   'With my many chariots
> I have ascended the heights of the mountains,
>   the utmost heights of Lebanon.[b]
> I have cut down its tallest cedars,
>   the choicest of its pines.
> I have reached its remotest heights,
>   the finest of its forests.
> 25I have dug wells in foreign lands[a]
>   and drunk the water there.
> With the soles of my feet
>   I have dried up all the streams of Egypt.[c]
>
> 26"Have you not heard?
>   Long ago I ordained[d] it.
> In days of old I planned[e] it;
>   now I have brought it to pass,
> that you have turned fortified cities
>   into piles of stone.[f]
> 27Their people, drained of power,
>   are dismayed and put to shame.
> They are like plants in the field,
>   like tender green shoots,
> like grass sprouting on the roof,[g]
>   scorched[b] before it grows up.
>
> 28"But I know where you stay
>   and when you come and go[h]
>   and how you rage[i] against me.
> 29Because you rage against me
>   and because your insolence[j] has reached my ears,
> I will put my hook in your nose[k]

37:22 [y] Job 16:4
37:23 [z] ver 4 [a] Isa 2:11
37:24 [b] Isa 14:8
37:25 [c] Dt 11:10
37:26 [d] Ac 2:23; 4:27-28; 1Pe 2:8 [e] Isa 10:6; 25:1 [f] Isa 25:2
37:27 [g] Ps 129:6
37:28 [h] Ps 139:1-3 [i] Ps 2:1
37:29 [j] Isa 10:12 [k] Isa 30:28; Eze 38:4

[a] 25 Dead Sea Scrolls (see also 2 Kings 19:24); Masoretic Text does not have *in foreign lands.*
[b] 27 Some manuscripts of the Masoretic Text, Dead Sea Scrolls and some Septuagint manuscripts (see also 2 Kings 19:26); most manuscripts of the Masoretic Text *roof / and terraced fields*

Isaiah 37:21–38

God's response to Hezekiah's prayer came through Isaiah. Assyria was nothing more than a puppet being moved by Israel's God. God had "brought it to pass" that this nation had conquered fortified cities and reduced their inhabitants to "scorched plants" (vv. 26–27). Just as God had brought Sennacherib on the stage, he could and would remove him. To God, the mighty Assyrian monarch was no more than a bull with a ring in its nose or a horse with a bit in its mouth (v. 29).

Verses 36–38 are an understated, matter-of-fact report of God's answer to Hezekiah's prayer. The same is true of the account of Peter's release from jail in Acts 12:1–19—almost humorous but for its profound implications. Such examples can unfortunately encourage our natural tendency to use prayer as a device to pry the maximum out of God with a minimum of personal investment. But prayer isn't so much about answers. It's about our relationship with God—at its best, an intimate conversation between a trusting child and a loving Father.

and my bit in your mouth,
> and I will make you return
>> by the way you came. [l]

37:29
[l] ver 34

30 "This will be the sign for you, O Hezekiah:

> "This year you will eat what grows by itself,
>> and the second year what springs from that.
> But in the third year sow and reap,
>> plant vineyards and eat their fruit.
> 31 Once more a remnant of the house of Judah
>> will take root below and bear fruit [m] above.
> 32 For out of Jerusalem will come a remnant,
>> and out of Mount Zion a band of survivors.
> The zeal [n] of the LORD Almighty
>> will accomplish this.

37:31
[m] Isa 27:6

37:32
[n] Isa 9:7

33 "Therefore this is what the LORD says concerning the king of Assyria:

> "He will not enter this city
>> or shoot an arrow here.
> He will not come before it with shield
>> or build a siege ramp against it.
> 34 By the way that he came he will return; [o]
>> he will not enter this city,"

> declares the LORD.

37:34
[o] ver 29

35 "I will defend [p] this city and save it,
> for my sake [q] and for the sake of David [r] my servant!"

37:35
[p] Isa 31:5; 38:6
[q] Isa 43:25; 48:9,11
[r] 2Ki 20:6

36 Then the angel of the LORD went out and put to death a hundred and eighty-five thousand men in the Assyrian [s] camp. When the people got up the next morning—there were all the dead bodies! 37 So Sennacherib king of Assyria broke camp and withdrew. He returned to Nineveh [t] and stayed there.

37:36
[s] Isa 10:12

37:37
[t] Ge 10:11

38 One day, while he was worshiping in the temple of his god Nisroch, his sons Adrammelech and Sharezer cut him down with the sword, and they escaped to the land of Ararat. [u] And Esarhaddon his son succeeded him as king.

37:38
[u] Ge 8:4; Jer 51:27

Hezekiah's Illness

38 In those days Hezekiah became ill and was at the point of death. The prophet Isaiah son of Amoz [v] went to him and said, "This is what the LORD says: Put your house in order, [w] because you are going to die; you will not recover."

38:1
[v] Isa 37:2
[w] 2Sa 17:23

2 Hezekiah turned his face to the wall and prayed to the LORD, 3 "Remember, O LORD, how I have walked [x] before you faithfully and with wholehearted devotion [y] and have done what is good in your eyes. [z]" And Hezekiah wept [a] bitterly.

38:3
[x] Ne 13:14; Ps 26:3
[y] 1Ch 29:19
[z] Dt 6:18 [a] Ps 6:8

4 Then the word of the LORD came to Isaiah: 5 "Go and tell Hezekiah, 'This is what the LORD, the God of your father David, says: I have heard your prayer and seen your tears; I will add fifteen years [b] to your life. 6 And I will deliver you and this city from the hand of the king of Assyria. I will defend [c] this city.

38:5
[b] 2Ki 18:2
38:6
[c] Isa 31:5; 37:35
38:7
[d] Isa 7:11,14

7 " 'This is the LORD's sign [d] to you that the LORD will do what he has promised: 8 I will make the shadow cast by the sun go back the ten steps it has gone down on the stairway of Ahaz.' " So the sunlight went back the ten steps it had gone down. [e]

38:8
[e] Jos 10:13

9 A writing of Hezekiah king of Judah after his illness and recovery:

10 I said, "In the prime of my life [f]

38:10
[f] Ps 102:24

Isaiah 38:1–22

Like his father, Ahaz (ch. 7), Hezekiah was offered a sign to confirm God's gracious promise of deliverance. Ahaz had refused the sign: He had already made arrangements to take care of himself. But Hezekiah was happy to receive whatever evidence God cared to give. Perhaps this particular sign—the sun's shadow moving back up the steps—was chosen to signify that just as God can move time backward, he can add days to our lives.

must I go through the gates of death[a][g]
and be robbed of the rest of my years?[h]"

[11] I said, "I will not again see the LORD,
the LORD, in the land of the living;[i]
no longer will I look on mankind,
or be with those who now dwell in this world.[b]

[12] Like a shepherd's tent[j] my house
has been pulled down[k] and taken from me.
Like a weaver I have rolled[l] up my life,
and he has cut me off from the loom;[m]
day and night[n] you made an end of me.

[13] I waited patiently till dawn,
but like a lion he broke[o] all my bones;[p]
day and night you made an end of me.

[14] I cried like a swift or thrush,
I moaned like a mourning dove.[q]
My eyes grew weak as I looked to the heavens.
I am troubled; O Lord, come to my aid!"[r]

[15] But what can I say?
He has spoken to me, and he himself has done this.[s]
I will walk humbly[t] all my years
because of this anguish of my soul.[u]

[16] Lord, by such things men live;
and my spirit finds life in them too.
You restored me to health
and let me live.[v]

[17] Surely it was for my benefit
that I suffered such anguish.
In your love you kept me
from the pit[w] of destruction;
you have put all my sins[x]
behind your back.[y]

[18] For the grave[c][z] cannot praise you,
death cannot sing your praise;[a]
those who go down to the pit[b]
cannot hope for your faithfulness.

[19] The living, the living—they praise[c] you,
as I am doing today;
fathers tell their children[d]
about your faithfulness.

[20] The LORD will save me,
and we will sing[e] with stringed instruments[f]
all the days of our lives[g]
in the temple[h] of the LORD.

[21] Isaiah had said, "Prepare a poultice of figs and apply it to the boil, and he will recover."

---

[a] 10 Hebrew *Sheol*   [b] 11 A few Hebrew manuscripts; most Hebrew manuscripts *in the place of cessation*   [c] 18 Hebrew *Sheol*

38:10
g Ps 107:18;
2Co 1:9
h Job 17:11

38:11
i Ps 27:13; 116:9

38:12
j 2Co 5:1,4;
2Pe 1:13-14
k Job 4:21
l Heb 1:12
m Job 7:6
n Ps 73:14

38:13
o Ps 51:8
p Job 10:16;
Da 6:24

38:14
q Isa 59:11
r Job 17:3

38:15
s Ps 39:9
t 1Ki 21:27
u Job 7:11

38:16
v Ps 119:25

38:17
w Ps 30:3
x Jer 31:34
y Isa 43:25;
Mic 7:19
38:18
z Ecc 9:10 *a* Ps 6:5;
88:10-11; 115:17
b Ps 30:9

38:19
c Dt 6:7; Ps 118:17;
119:175 *d* Dt 11:19

38:20
e Ps 68:25 *f* Ps 33:2
g Ps 116:2
h Ps 116:17-19

God doesn't change his mind about the basic nature of things or his purposes with humanity. But his commitment to do good to people means that he will gladly change what he has said if greater blessing will result. The Bible teaches both that God is sovereign and that humans can make real choices. Any attempt on our part to reduce these teachings to simple logic will do harm to one or the other element. We can bring our petitions to God with intensity and conviction, confident that he will remain consistent with his own nature and work things out for our good (cf. Rom. 8:28).

22Hezekiah had asked, "What will be the sign that I will go up to the temple of the LORD?"

Envoys From Babylon

39 At that time Merodach-Baladan son of Baladan king of Babylon*i* sent Hezekiah letters and a gift, because he had heard of his illness and recovery. 2Hezekiah received the envoys*j* gladly and showed them what was in his storehouses—the silver, the gold,*k* the spices, the fine oil, his entire armory and everything found among his treasures. There was nothing in his palace or in all his kingdom that Hezekiah did not show them.

3Then Isaiah the prophet went to King Hezekiah and asked, "What did those men say, and where did they come from?"

"From a distant land,*l*" Hezekiah replied. "They came to me from Babylon."

4The prophet asked, "What did they see in your palace?"

"They saw everything in my palace," Hezekiah said. "There is nothing among my treasures that I did not show them."

5Then Isaiah said to Hezekiah, "Hear the word of the LORD Almighty: 6The time will surely come when everything in your palace, and all that your fathers have stored up until this day, will be carried off to Babylon.*m* Nothing will be left, says the LORD. 7And some of your descendants, your own flesh and blood who will be born to you, will be taken away, and they will become eunuchs in the palace of the king of Babylon.*n*

8"The word of the LORD you have spoken is good," Hezekiah replied. For he thought, "There will be peace and security in my lifetime.*o*

Comfort for God's People

40 Comfort, comfort*p* my people,
    says your God.
2Speak tenderly*q* to Jerusalem,
    and proclaim to her
that her hard service has been completed,*r*
    that her sin has been paid for,
that she has received from the LORD's hand
    double*s* for all her sins.

3A voice of one calling:
"In the desert prepare
    the way*t* for the LORD*a*;

a 3 Or A voice of one calling in the desert: / "Prepare the way for the LORD

Isaiah 39:1–8

It's easy to understand why Hezekiah would be glad to receive the envoys from the king of Babylon: A great world leader was paying attention to little Judah. Likewise, each of us is flattered when someone we consider important pays attention to us. But there is something dangerous here as well: that we, like Hezekiah, will fall prey to the temptation to convince the individual that such attention is justified. Here was a wonderful opportunity for the king to declare God's glory to the nations. But instead of making God look good, Hezekiah took the opportunity to make himself look good.

Have you seen the bumper sticker "He who has the most toys wins"? We humans easily confuse ends with means. This is even more likely if we evaluate our success in life, as Hezekiah seems to have done, in terms of our possessions. The intended end of our lives is abundant life, the life in which God pours his fullness into us

and we share that fullness with others and enable them to access it. A by-product—and *only* a by-product—is physical and material blessing. When we make it an end and display it as evidence of our success, manipulation of God in order to secure that end is almost inescapable. But manipulation and trust are incompatible.

Isaiah 40:1–31

With chapter 40 comes the most significant transition in the book of Isaiah. The question of God's trustworthiness had been answered. But other questions remained: What would motivate God's people to trust him and be the servants they were called to be? How could the sinful Israelites become God's servants at all? For the remainder of the book, God would project Isaiah 100 years into Judah's coming Babylonian exile, where these questions would be seen in their full poignancy. He would address the questions he knew the exiles would be prompted to ask by that crisis.

make straight in the wilderness
a highway for our God. [a][u]

[4] Every valley shall be raised up,
every mountain and hill made low;
the rough ground shall become level, [v]
the rugged places a plain.

[5] And the glory of the LORD will be revealed,
and all mankind together will see it. [w]

For the mouth of the LORD has spoken." [x]

[6] A voice says, "Cry out."
And I said, "What shall I cry?"

"All men are like grass, [y]
and all their glory is like the flowers of the field.

[7] The grass withers and the flowers fall,
because the breath [z] of the LORD blows on them.
Surely the people are grass.

[8] The grass withers and the flowers fall,
but the word [a] of our God stands forever. [b]"

[9] You who bring good tidings [c] to Zion,
go up on a high mountain.
You who bring good tidings to Jerusalem, [b]

40:3
u Mt 3:3*; Mk 1:3*;
Jn 1:23*

40:4
v Isa 45:2,13

40:5
w Isa 52:10;
Lk 3:4-6*
x Isa 1:20; 58:14

40:6
y Job 14:2

40:7
z Job 41:21

40:8
a Isa 55:11; 59:21
b Mt 5:18;
1Pe 1:24-25*
40:9
c Isa 52:7-10; 61:1;
Ro 10:15

a 3 Hebrew; Septuagint *make straight the paths of our God*   b 9 Or *O Zion, bringer of good tidings, / go up on a high mountain. / O Jerusalem, bringer of good tidings*

40:8

English Bible Major Translation Timeline
(Literally hundreds of lesser known translations have been completed over the years.)

1382	Wycliffe Bible
1525	Tyndale Bible
1535	Coverdale Bible
1536	Matthew's Bible
1539	Archbishop Cranmer's Great Bible
1560	Geneva Bible
1568	Bishop's Bible
1582	Douay Bible
1609	Roman Catholic Authorized Version
1611	King James Version
1881	Revised Version
1901	American Standard Version
1946	Revised Standard Version
1961	New English Bible
1963	New American Standard Bible
1964	Amplified Bible
1966	Jerusalem Bible
1970	New American Bible
1971	Living Bible
1976	Good News Translation
1978	New International Version
1982	New King James Version
1982	Reader's Digest Bible
1985	New Jerusalem Bible
1987	Updated Amplified Bible
1990	New Revised Standard Version
1994	New International Reader's Version
1995	Contemporary English Version
1995	Updated New American Standard Bible
1996	New Living Translation
2000	Holman Christian Standard Bible
2001	English Standard Version
2002	The Message
2005	Today's New International Version

Timeline markers: 1400 1500 1600 1700 1800 1900 2000

lift up your voice with a shout,
lift it up, do not be afraid;
say to the towns of Judah,
"Here is your God!" [d]

40:9
d Isa 25:9
40:10
e Rev 22:7
f Isa 59:16
g Isa 9:6-7
h Isa 62:11;
Rev 22:12

10 See, the Sovereign LORD comes [e] with power,
and his arm [f] rules [g] for him.
See, his reward [h] is with him,
and his recompense accompanies him.

40:11
i Eze 34:23;
Mic 5:4; Jn 10:11

11 He tends his flock like a shepherd: [i]
He gathers the lambs in his arms
and carries them close to his heart;
he gently leads those that have young.

40:12
j Job 38:10
k Pr 30:4
l Heb 1:10-12

12 Who has measured the waters [j] in the hollow of his hand, [k]
or with the breadth of his hand marked off the heavens? [l]
Who has held the dust of the earth in a basket,
or weighed the mountains on the scales
and the hills in a balance?

40:13
m Ro 11:34*;
1Co 2:16*

13 Who has understood the mind [a] of the LORD,
or instructed him as his counselor? [m]

40:14
n Job 21:22;
Col 2:3

14 Whom did the LORD consult to enlighten him,
and who taught him the right way?
Who was it that taught him knowledge [n]
or showed him the path of understanding?

15 Surely the nations are like a drop in a bucket;
they are regarded as dust on the scales;
he weighs the islands as though they were fine dust.

40:16
o Ps 50:9-11;
Mic 6:7; Heb 10:5-9
40:17
p Isa 30:28
q Isa 29:7 r Da 4:35

16 Lebanon is not sufficient for altar fires,
nor its animals [o] enough for burnt offerings.
17 Before him all the nations [p] are as nothing; [q]
they are regarded by him as worthless
and less than nothing. [r]

40:18
s Ex 8:10; 1Sa 2:2;
Isa 46:5 t Ac 17:29
40:19
u Ps 115:4
v Isa 41:7; Jer 10:3
w Isa 2:20

18 To whom, then, will you compare God? [s]
What image [t] will you compare him to?
19 As for an idol, [u] a craftsman casts it,
and a goldsmith [v] overlays it with gold [w]
and fashions silver chains for it.

40:20
x 1Sa 5:3

20 A man too poor to present such an offering
selects wood that will not rot.
He looks for a skilled craftsman
to set up an idol that will not topple. [x]

21 Do you not know?
Have you not heard?

40:21
y Ps 19:1; 50:6;
Ac 14:17 z Ro 1:19
a Isa 48:13; 51:13

Has it not been told [y] you from the beginning?
Have you not understood [z] since the earth was founded? [a]

---

a 13 Or *Spirit;* or *spirit*

In chapter 40 God is introduced as outside the systems of time and space—not conditioned or restricted by them. He can intervene at will and change them to suit his grand design. God is aware of his people's distress and captivity, their joys and accomplishments, and able to come to them. He's great enough to be able to help—and near enough to want to.

The concept of trust as waiting has already been seen three times in this book (8:17; 25:9: 33:2). It appears here in verse 31 and will show up again in 49:23 and 64:4. To "wait" on God isn't simply to mark time; rather, it's to live in confident expectation of his action on our behalf.

📖 Isaiah spoke by inspiration to people who had lost hope: There is nothing beyond God's compassion or power—"Do you not know? Have you not heard?" There is nothing our caring Creator can't change. We can't dictate the terms or means of those changes, but we can hold onto him with confident hope.

22 He sits enthroned above the circle of the earth,
　　and its people are like grasshoppers. [b]
He stretches out the heavens like a canopy, [c]
　　and spreads them out like a tent [d] to live in.
23 He brings princes [e] to naught
　　and reduces the rulers of this world to nothing. [f]
24 No sooner are they planted,
　　no sooner are they sown,
　　no sooner do they take root in the ground,
than he blows [g] on them and they wither,
　　and a whirlwind sweeps them away like chaff.

25 "To whom will you compare me? [h]
　　Or who is my equal?" says the Holy One.
26 Lift your eyes and look to the heavens: [i]
　　Who created [j] all these?
He who brings out the starry host [k] one by one,
　　and calls them each by name.
Because of his great power and mighty strength,
　　not one of them is missing. [l]

27 Why do you say, O Jacob,
　　and complain, O Israel,
"My way is hidden from the LORD;
　　my cause is disregarded by my God"? [m]
28 Do you not know?
　　Have you not heard? [n]
The LORD is the everlasting [o] God,
　　the Creator of the ends of the earth.
He will not grow tired or weary,
　　and his understanding no one can fathom. [p]
29 He gives strength to the weary [q]
　　and increases the power of the weak.
30 Even youths grow tired and weary,
　　and young men [r] stumble and fall;
31 but those who hope [s] in the LORD
　　will renew their strength. [t]
They will soar on wings like eagles; [u]
　　they will run and not grow weary,
　　they will walk and not be faint. [v]

The Helper of Israel

41 "Be silent [w] before me, you islands! [x]
　　Let the nations renew their strength!
Let them come forward [y] and speak;
　　let us meet together [z] at the place of judgment.

2 "Who has stirred [a] up one from the east, [b]
　　calling him in righteousness to his service [a]?

[a] 2 Or / whom victory meets at every step

40:22
[b] Nu 13:33;
Ps 104:2; Isa 42:5
[c] Job 22:14
[d] Job 36:29
40:23
[e] Isa 34:12
[f] Job 12:21;
Ps 107:40

40:24
[g] Isa 41:16

40:25
[h] ver 18
40:26
[i] Isa 51:6
[j] Ps 89:11-13;
Isa 42:5 [k] Ps 147:4
[l] Isa 34:16

40:27
[m] Job 27:2;
Lk 18:7-8
40:28
[n] ver 21 [o] Ps 90:2
[p] Ps 147:5;
Ro 11:33

40:29
[q] Isa 50:4;
Jer 31:25

40:30
[r] Isa 9:17; Jer 6:11;
9:21
40:31
[s] Lk 18:1 [t] 2Co 4:16
[u] Ex 19:4; Ps 103:5
[v] 2Co 4:1;
Heb 12:1-3

41:1
[w] Hab 2:20;
Zec 2:13
[x] Isa 11:11
[y] Isa 48:16
[z] Isa 1:18; 34:1;
50:8
41:2
[a] Ezr 1:2 [b] ver 25;
Isa 45:1,13

We need lives of faith shaped by God's Word, its view of reality, and the principles that emerge from it. If we can't believe and hope in God in the sense of surrendering ourselves to him in a lifestyle we know pleases him, then his power can't transform us. But if we actively believe his word, there is no limit to what he can do for us, our families, and our society. What wonderful things has he done already for you and yours?

Isaiah called on his generation, the future exiles, and ourselves to trust God to solve our problems. If we are worn out and weary, hardly daring to believe there is any future for us, the God of all strength can give us exactly what we need—to "soar," "run," or "walk." Wait on him today for your particular need.

Isaiah 41:1–29

God would call "one from the east" (v. 2), Cyrus the Great, king of Persia (cf. 45:1), to bring down the Babylonian Empire. Cyrus would conquer Babylon in 539

He hands nations over to him
and subdues kings before him.
He turns them to dust [c] with his sword,
to windblown chaff [d] with his bow.
[3] He pursues them and moves on unscathed,
by a path his feet have not traveled before.
[4] Who has done this and carried it through,
calling forth the generations from the beginning? [e]
I, the LORD—with the first of them
and with the last [f]—I am he."

[5] The islands [g] have seen it and fear;
the ends of the earth tremble.
They approach and come forward;
[6]   each helps the other
and says to his brother, "Be strong!"
[7] The craftsman encourages the goldsmith, [h]
and he who smooths with the hammer
spurs on him who strikes the anvil.
He says of the welding, "It is good."
He nails down the idol so it will not topple.

[8] "But you, O Israel, my servant,
Jacob, whom I have chosen,
you descendants of Abraham [i] my friend, [j]
[9] I took you from the ends of the earth, [k]
from its farthest corners I called you.
I said, 'You are my servant';
I have chosen [l] you and have not rejected you.
[10] So do not fear, for I am with you; [m]
do not be dismayed, for I am your God.
I will strengthen you and help [n] you;
I will uphold you with my righteous right hand.

[11] "All who rage [o] against you
will surely be ashamed and disgraced; [p]
those who oppose [q] you
will be as nothing and perish. [r]
[12] Though you search for your enemies,
you will not find them. [s]
Those who wage war against you
will be as nothing [t] at all.
[13] For I am the LORD, your God,
who takes hold of your right hand [u]
and says to you, Do not fear;
I will help [v] you.

Cross references (left margin)

41:2
c 2Sa 22:43
d Isa 40:24

41:4
e ver 26; Isa 46:10
f Isa 44:6; 48:12;
Rev 1:8, 17; 22:13

41:5
g Eze 26:17-18

41:7
h Isa 40:19

41:8
i Isa 29:22; 51:2;
63:16 / 2Ch 20:7;
Jas 2:23
41:9
k Isa 11:12 / Dt 7:6

41:10
m Jos 1:9; Isa 43:2,
5; Ro 8:31
n ver 13-14;
Isa 44:2; 49:8

41:11
o Isa 17:12
p Isa 45:24
q Ex 23:22
r Isa 29:8

41:12
s Ps 37:35-36
t Isa 17:14

41:13
u Isa 42:6; 45:1
v ver 10

B.C. and then issue a decree permitting the Jews to re-turn to Jerusalem. The Lord would give the nations into Cyrus's hand. God wasn't just a part of the process. He stands outside of time, calling it into existence, directing its path, and bringing it to an end. "I am he" (v. 4) is a statement of self-existence and self-identity (cf. Ex. 3:14). Every other life form on the planet is an offshoot.

God asserted that, unlike the powerful nations around them, the captives of Judah had nothing to fear. Their God was no idol they had made. He had both the power and the desire to deliver Israel, his "servant" (vv. 8–10). This term is critical in chapters 41–53, referring in some instances to the nation of Israel and in others to an individual.

📖 Only a Being outside the "system" could have brought it into existence and directed it. The system can give us information about him, but he can't ultimately be discovered through creation alone. We need the Scripture's evidence (God's self-revelation)—evidence of a God outside the system, who can both predict what it will do and redirect it as necessary to achieve his goals. Our challenge is to demonstrate to the world that there is a faithful, consistent, true God—One who has broken in upon us and "done this" (v. 20).

14 Do not be afraid, O worm Jacob,
   O little Israel,
   for I myself will help you," declares the LORD,
   your Redeemer, the Holy One of Israel.
15 "See, I will make you into a threshing sledge,ʷ
   new and sharp, with many teeth.
   You will thresh the mountains and crush them,
   and reduce the hills to chaff.
16 You will winnowˣ them, the wind will pick them up,
   and a gale will blow them away.
   But you will rejoice in the LORD
   and gloryʸ in the Holy One of Israel.

17 "The poor and needy search for water,ᶻ
   but there is none;
   their tongues are parched with thirst.
   But I the LORD will answerᵃ them;
   I, the God of Israel, will not forsake them.
18 I will make rivers flowᵇ on barren heights,
   and springs within the valleys.
   I will turn the desertᶜ into pools of water,
   and the parched ground into springs.ᵈ
19 I will put in the desert
   the cedar and the acacia, the myrtle and the olive.
   I will set pines in the wasteland,
   the fir and the cypress together,ᵉ
20 so that people may see and know,
   may consider and understand,
   that the hand of the LORD has done this,
   that the Holy One of Israel has createdᶠ it.

21 "Present your case," says the LORD.
   "Set forth your arguments," says Jacob's King.ᵍ
22 "Bring in ₗyour idolsₗ to tell us
   what is going to happen.ʰ
   Tell us what the former things were,
   so that we may consider them
   and know their final outcome.
   Or declare to us the things to come,ⁱ
23   tell us what the future holds,
   so we may knowʲ that you are gods.
   Do something, whether good or bad,ᵏ
   so that we will be dismayed and filled with fear.
24 But you are less than nothingˡ
   and your works are utterly worthless;
   he who chooses you is detestable.ᵐ

25 "I have stirred up one from the north,ⁿ and he comes—
   one from the rising sun who calls on my name.
   He treadsᵒ on rulers as if they were mortar,
   as if he were a potter treading the clay.
26 Who told of this from the beginning, so we could know,
   or beforehand, so we could say, 'He was right'?
   No one told of this,
   no one foretold it,
   no one heard any wordsᵖ from you.
27 I was the first to tellᑫ Zion, 'Look, here they are!'
   I gave to Jerusalem a messenger of good tidings.ʳ

41:15
w Mic 4:13

41:16
x Jer 51:2
y Isa 45:25

41:17
z Isa 43:20
a Isa 30:19

41:18
b Isa 30:25
c Isa 43:19
d Isa 35:7

41:19
e Isa 60:13

41:20
f Job 12:9

41:21
g Isa 43:15

41:22
h Isa 43:9; 45:21
i Isa 46:10

41:23
j Isa 42:9; 44:7-8;
45:3 k Jer 10:5

41:24
l Isa 37:19; 44:9;
1Co 8:4 m Ps 115:8

41:25
n ver 2 o 2Sa 22:43

41:26
p Hab 2:18-19
41:27
q Isa 48:3,16
r Isa 40:9

41:28
s Isa 50:2; 59:16;
63:5 t Isa 40:13-14

28 I look but there is no one[s]—
  no one among them to give counsel,[t]
  no one to give answer when I ask them.

41:29
u ver 24 v Jer 5:13

29 See, they are all false!
  Their deeds amount to nothing;[u]
  their images are but wind[v] and confusion.

The Servant of the LORD

42:1
w Isa 43:10;
Lk 9:35; 1Pe 2:4,6
x Isa 11:2;
Mt 3:16-17; Jn 3:34

42 "Here is my servant, whom I uphold,
  my chosen one[w] in whom I delight;
I will put my Spirit[x] on him
  and he will bring justice to the nations.
2 He will not shout or cry out,
  or raise his voice in the streets.

42:3
y Ps 72:2

3 A bruised reed he will not break,
  and a smoldering wick he will not snuff out.
In faithfulness he will bring forth justice;[y]
4   he will not falter or be discouraged

42:4
z Ge 49:10;
Mt 12:18-21*

till he establishes justice on earth.
  In his law the islands will put their hope."[z]

42:5
a Ps 24:2
b Ac 17:25

5 This is what God the LORD says—
he who created the heavens and stretched them out,
  who spread out the earth and all that comes out of it,[a]
who gives breath[b] to its people,
  and life to those who walk on it:

42:6
c Isa 43:1 d Jer 23:6
e Isa 26:3 f Isa 49:8
g Lk 2:32; Ac 13:47

6 "I, the LORD, have called[c] you in righteousness;[d]
  I will take hold of your hand.
I will keep[e] you and will make you
  to be a covenant[f] for the people
  and a light for the Gentiles,[g]

42:7
h Isa 35:5 i Isa 49:9;
61:1 j Lk 4:19;
2Ti 2:26;
Heb 2:14-15

7 to open eyes that are blind,[h]
  to free[i] captives from prison[j]
  and to release from the dungeon those who sit in darkness.

42:8
k Ex 3:15 l Isa 48:11

8 "I am the LORD; that is my name![k]
  I will not give my glory to another[l]
  or my praise to idols.
9 See, the former things have taken place,
  and new things I declare;
before they spring into being
  I announce them to you."

Song of Praise to the LORD

42:10
m Ps 33:3; 40:3;
98:1 n Isa 49:6
o 1Ch 16:32;
Ps 96:11

10 Sing to the LORD a new song,[m]
  his praise from the ends of the earth,[n]
  you who go down to the sea, and all that is in it,[o]

Isaiah 42:1–9

The repeated statements that the Lord's "servant" would bring justice on the earth, that God's Spirit would be on him, and that his accomplishment wouldn't be through oppression remind us of the Messianic prophecies in Isaiah 9, 11, and 32. There we see the servant as King; here we see the king as Servant. The idea that the "islands," which couldn't defend the deity of their gods (41:1), would "put their hope in his law" (42:4) further indicates that this figure was Messianic.

These verses shed light on the dimensions and nature of Christ's ministry. (1) Its purpose is to restore God's right order to the world. The cross is about dealing with all sin's effects, about restoring God's work on all levels of society. (2) Its scope is worldwide. The covenant is for all nations, a light for all people. (3) Ancient kings boasted about the ferocious means they used to bring about "justice," but the Servant wouldn't break an already-bent reed or snuff out a flickering candle. Christ disarmed his enemies with love, grace, and gentleness. Are you doing the same?

you islands, and all who live in them.
11 Let the desert[p] and its towns raise their voices;
　　let the settlements where Kedar[q] lives rejoice.
　Let the people of Sela sing for joy;
　　let them shout from the mountaintops.[r]
12 Let them give glory[s] to the LORD
　　and proclaim his praise in the islands.
13 The LORD will march out like a mighty[t] man,
　　like a warrior he will stir up his zeal;[u]
　with a shout[v] he will raise the battle cry
　　and will triumph over his enemies.[w]

14 "For a long time I have kept silent,
　　I have been quiet and held myself back.
　But now, like a woman in childbirth,
　　I cry out, I gasp and pant.
15 I will lay waste[x] the mountains and hills
　　and dry up all their vegetation;
　I will turn rivers into islands
　　and dry up[y] the pools.
16 I will lead[z] the blind[a] by ways they have not known,
　　along unfamiliar paths I will guide them;
　I will turn the darkness into light before them
　　and make the rough places smooth.[b]
　These are the things I will do;
　　I will not forsake[c] them.
17 But those who trust in idols,
　　who say to images, 'You are our gods,'
　　will be turned back in utter shame.[d]

Israel Blind and Deaf

18 "Hear, you deaf;[e]
　　look, you blind, and see!
19 Who is blind[f] but my servant,[g]
　　and deaf like the messenger[h] I send?
　Who is blind like the one committed[i] to me,
　　blind like the servant of the LORD?
20 You have seen many things, but have paid no attention;
　　your ears are open, but you hear nothing."[j]
21 It pleased the LORD
　　for the sake of his righteousness

42:11
p Isa 32:16
q Isa 60:7 r Isa 52:7;
Na 1:15

42:12
s Isa 24:15

42:13
t Isa 9:6 u Isa 26:11
v Hos 11:10
w Isa 66:14

42:15
x Eze 38:20
y Isa 50:2; Na 1:4-6

42:16
z Lk 1:78-79
a Isa 32:3 b Lk 3:5
c Heb 13:5

42:17
d Ps 97:7; Isa 1:29;
44:11; 45:16

42:18
e Isa 35:5

42:19
f Isa 43:8; Eze 12:2
g Isa 41:8-9
h Isa 44:26
i Isa 26:3

42:20
j Jer 6:10

Isaiah 42:10–17

Isaiah called on the whole world to praise the Lord. God was more than simply the God of Judah, and what he was going to do for his exiled people had joyous, worldwide implications. If he could deliver Judah from captivity, there was no one whose distress or difficulty lay beyond his delivering power.

The evidence of both Testaments convinces us that history is still under God's rule. The coming of Christ and the growth of the church are evidences of that control, as is the survival of the Jewish people. God's Word gives enough guidance for us to recognize the outlines of his hand at work around the world today.

Isaiah 42:18–25

God called on people to recognize that what would befall them in the exile wouldn't result from his failure to deliver them but from their own failure to walk in his ways and keep his law. The Babylonians weren't taking God's people into captivity against God's will. Because of their failure to live God's way, they already were "blind," "deaf," and "imprisoned."

Failing to live God's way blinds us and plunders our lives of his goodness. We become trapped and imprisoned in patterns of behavior and ways of living that deafen us to God's will and ways. God made a cause-and-effect world but doesn't directly *cause* everything that happens. Just as in the physical world there are consequences for defying God's law, if we find ourselves in adverse circumstances, we are wise to ask ourselves whether we have been failing to live God's way. On the other hand, our circumstances may have nothing to do with any particular sin (cf. Job 2:3; John 9:2–3).

42:21
k ver 4

42:22
l Isa 24:18
m Isa 24:22

to make his law[k] great and glorious.

22 But this is a people plundered and looted,
    all of them trapped in pits[l]
    or hidden away in prisons.[m]
They have become plunder,
    with no one to rescue them;
they have been made loot,
    with no one to say, "Send them back."

42:23
n Isa 48:18

23 Which of you will listen to this
    or pay close attention[n] in time to come?
24 Who handed Jacob over to become loot,
    and Israel to the plunderers?
Was it not the LORD,
    against whom we have sinned?

42:24
o Isa 30:15

For they would not follow[o] his ways;
    they did not obey his law.
25 So he poured out on them his burning anger,
    the violence of war.

42:25
p 2Ki 25:9
q Isa 29:13; 47:7;
57:1,11; Hos 7:9

It enveloped them in flames,[p] yet they did not understand;
    it consumed them, but they did not take it to heart.[q]

Israel's Only Savior

43 But now, this is what the LORD says—
    he who created you, O Jacob,
    he who formed[r] you, O Israel:[s]
"Fear not, for I have redeemed[t] you;
    I have summoned you by name;[u] you are mine.

43:1
r ver 7 s Ge 32:28;
Isa 44:21 t Isa 44:2,
6 u Isa 42:6; 45:3-4

2 When you pass through the waters,[v]
    I will be with you;[w]
and when you pass through the rivers,
    they will not sweep over you.
When you walk through the fire,[x]
    you will not be burned;
    the flames will not set you ablaze.[y]

43:2
v Isa 8:7 w Dt 31:6,
8 x Isa 29:6; 30:27
y Ps 66:12;
Da 3:25-27

3 For I am the LORD, your God,[z]
    the Holy One of Israel, your Savior;
I give Egypt for your ransom,
    Cush[aa] and Seba in your stead.[b]

43:3
z Ex 20:2 a Isa 20:3
b Pr 21:18

4 Since you are precious and honored in my sight,
    and because I love[c] you,
I will give men in exchange for you,
    and people in exchange for your life.

43:4
c Isa 63:9

5 Do not be afraid,[d] for I am with you;[e]

43:5
d Isa 44:2
e Jer 30:10-11

---

a 3 That is, the upper Nile region

Isaiah 43:1–13

The shift in tone from the end of chapter 42 to the beginning of chapter 43 is breathtaking. What God would now do was grace. There was nothing the Judahites needed to do in advance for this grace to become available to them. The key was God's personal relationship with his people. The Creator would give himself to them as their personal possession because they were "precious" to him (v. 4). Why would the One who is beyond the stars pay attention to rebel beings on this small planet? He simply does, and though this particular people had broken their covenant with him time

and again, God's love would ensure that he would keep his side of the bargain.

Because God values us, he acts out of concern for our well-being. For too many Christians, the personal relationship side of faith is more theory than fact. God's passion for us seems more an idea than a reality. Our faith functions as a system of beliefs or a set of religious habits more or less to be followed. But to personally relate to God on a day-to-day basis is foreign to many of us. That is not the way God wants it to be. We are his treasure, and if we are to become all he's created us for, we are to live in that reality.

I will bring your children[f] from the east
   and gather you from the west.
6 I will say to the north, 'Give them up!'
   and to the south,[g] 'Do not hold them back.'
Bring my sons from afar
   and my daughters[h] from the ends of the earth—
7 everyone who is called by my name,[i]
   whom I created for my glory,
   whom I formed and made.[j]"

8 Lead out those who have eyes but are blind,[k]
   who have ears but are deaf.[l]
9 All the nations gather together[m]
   and the peoples assemble.
Which of them foretold[n] this
   and proclaimed to us the former things?
Let them bring in their witnesses to prove they were right,
   so that others may hear and say, "It is true."
10 "You are my witnesses," declares the LORD,
   "and my servant[o] whom I have chosen,
so that you may know and believe me
   and understand that I am he.
Before me no god[p] was formed,
   nor will there be one after me.
11 I, even I, am the LORD,
   and apart from me there is no savior.[q]
12 I have revealed and saved and proclaimed—
   I, and not some foreign god[r] among you.
You are my witnesses,[s] declares the LORD, "that I am God.
13   Yes, and from ancient days[t] I am he.
No one can deliver out of my hand.
   When I act, who can reverse it?"[u]

God's Mercy and Israel's Unfaithfulness

14 This is what the LORD says—
   your Redeemer, the Holy One of Israel:
"For your sake I will send to Babylon
   and bring down as fugitives[v] all the Babylonians,[a][w]
   in the ships in which they took pride.
15 I am the LORD, your Holy One,
   Israel's Creator, your King."

a 14 Or Chaldeans

43:5
f Isa 41:8

43:6
g Ps 107:3
h 2Co 6:18

43:7
i Isa 56:5; 63:19;
Jas 2:7 j ver 1,21;
Ps 100:3; Eph 2:10

43:8
k Isa 6:9-10
l Isa 42:20; Eze 12:2
43:9
m Isa 41:1
n Isa 41:26

43:10
o Isa 41:8-9
p Isa 44:6,8

43:11
q Isa 45:21

43:12
r Dt 32:12; Ps 81:9
s Isa 44:8

43:13
t Ps 90:2
u Job 9:12;
Isa 14:27

43:14
v Isa 13:14-15
w Isa 23:13

Isaiah 43:14–28

In verses 14–21 God told his people once again that he was going to deliver them from Babylon. He reminded them of what he had done in the exodus in making a way for Israel through the Red Sea. But then he instructed them to "forget" the past. God isn't predictable like false gods; he's the Creator, and he loves doing things in new ways.

Beginning with verse 22, God moved from the past and the future to talk about the present reality. He couldn't be manipulated into forgiving his people. He had already done so, and they had only to receive his gift. Their sacrifices were to be symbols of changed hearts and lives. God didn't want their offerings; he wanted *them*, as symbolized by the sacrifices. All the offerings they kept bringing, which they considered to be a burden imposed by God, added to the mountain of unconfessed sins they kept piling on God's back.

A danger of maturation is calcification. We have finally figured things out. We know what we want and how to get it. The result can be that we think we don't need faith anymore—or any more faith. We know the questions and the answers, so God, who seems to enjoy disturbing the comfortable, should keep his distance. This is the point at which God comes to us and dares us to believe him for a "new thing" (cf. vv. 18–19) in our lives, something that will force us to let go of the hard-won strings of control, daring us to let him stretch our vision. Where is your predetermined view of God and life being challenged? What new thing might God want to do in you?

¹⁶This is what the LORD says—
 he who made a way through the sea,
 a path through the mighty waters,^x
¹⁷who drew out^y the chariots and horses,
 the army and reinforcements together,^z
and they lay there, never to rise again,
 extinguished, snuffed out like a wick:
¹⁸"Forget the former things;
 do not dwell on the past.
¹⁹See, I am doing a new thing!^a
 Now it springs up; do you not perceive it?
I am making a way in the desert^b
 and streams in the wasteland.
²⁰The wild animals honor me,
 the jackals^c and the owls,
because I provide water^d in the desert
 and streams in the wasteland,
to give drink to my people, my chosen,
²¹ the people I formed for myself
 that they may proclaim my praise.^e

²²"Yet you have not called upon me, O Jacob,
 you have not wearied yourselves for me, O Israel.^f
²³You have not brought me sheep for burnt offerings,
 nor honored^g me with your sacrifices.^h
I have not burdened you with grain offerings
 nor wearied you with demandsⁱ for incense.^j
²⁴You have not bought any fragrant calamus^k for me,
 or lavished on me the fat of your sacrifices.
But you have burdened me with your sins
 and wearied^l me with your offenses.^m

43:16
x Ps 77:19;
Isa 11:15; 51:10
43:17
y Ps 118:12;
Isa 1:31 z Ex 14:9

43:19
a 2Co 5:17;
Rev 21:5 b Ex 17:6;
Nu 20:11

43:20
c Isa 13:22
d Isa 48:21

43:21
e Ps 102:18;
1Pe 2:9

43:22
f Isa 30:11

43:23
g Zec 7:5-6;
Mal 1:6-8
h Am 5:25
i Jer 7:22
j Ex 30:35; Lev 2:1
43:24
k Ex 30:23
l Isa 1:14; 7:13
m Mal 2:17

Snapshots

43:18–19

Joining in God's Program

Mike spends his days studying a bank of computer screens to monitor fluctuations in the global oil market. But after his return from a ten-day "vision trip" to West Africa in 1998 with Eric and other American donors, all he saw were images of malnourished African children.

He picked up the phone. "Eric, I'm thinking about quitting my job and going to seminary."

"What about the gifts God has given you?" cautioned Eric. "Let's take a close look at the burden God has placed in your heart." The two spent hours together reading Scripture and praying. They discovered that Mike's burden was for helping American youth see their ability to help less fortunate children around the world.

> "Figure out what God is doing and try to become a part of it."

Today, Mike still trades oil. He's also the national spokesperson for World Vision's 30 Hour Famine and has personally adopted a program that cares for 2,000 Rwandan orphans.

"Eric helped me to not blindly react to the overwhelming feelings I had but to be patient and seek God's direction," says Mike.

Eric often uses the advice World Vision's founder, Bob Pierce, gave to people on their way to minister overseas: "I can't tell you what to do. But when you get there, figure out what God is doing and try to become a part of it."

25 "I, even I, am he who blots out
   your transgressions, [n] for my own sake, [o]
   and remembers your sins no more. [p]
26 Review the past for me,
   let us argue the matter together; [q]
   state the case [r] for your innocence.
27 Your first father sinned;
   your spokesmen [s] rebelled against me.
28 So I will disgrace the dignitaries of your temple,
   and I will consign Jacob to destruction [a]
   and Israel to scorn. [t]

Israel the Chosen

44 "But now listen, O Jacob, my servant, [u]
   Israel, whom I have chosen.
2 This is what the LORD says—
   he who made you, who formed you in the womb,
   and who will help [v] you:
   Do not be afraid, O Jacob, my servant,
   Jeshurun, [w] whom I have chosen.
3 For I will pour water [x] on the thirsty land,
   and streams on the dry ground;
   I will pour out my Spirit [y] on your offspring,
   and my blessing on your descendants. [z]
4 They will spring up like grass in a meadow,
   like poplar trees [a] by flowing streams. [b]
5 One will say, 'I belong to the LORD';
   another will call himself by the name of Jacob;
   still another will write on his hand, [c] 'The LORD's,' [d]
   and will take the name Israel.

The LORD, Not Idols

6 "This is what the LORD says—
   Israel's King [e] and Redeemer, [f] the LORD Almighty:
   I am the first and I am the last; [g]
   apart from me there is no God.
7 Who then is like me? Let him proclaim it.
   Let him declare and lay out before me
   what has happened since I established my ancient people,
   and what is yet to come—
   yes, let him foretell [h] what will come.
8 Do not tremble, do not be afraid.
   Did I not proclaim this and foretell it long ago?

---

a 28 The Hebrew term refers to the irrevocable giving over of things or persons to the LORD, often by totally destroying them.

Cross references

43:25
n Ac 3:19
o Isa 37:35;
Eze 36:22
p Isa 38:17;
Jer 31:34
43:26
q Isa 1:18 r Isa 41:1;
50:8
43:27
s Isa 9:15; 28:7;
Jer 5:31
43:28
t Jer 24:9; Eze 5:15

44:1
u ver 21; Jer 30:10;
46:27-28

44:2
v Isa 41:10
w Dt 32:15

44:3
x Joel 3:18
y Joel 2:28; Ac 2:17
z Isa 61:9; 65:23

44:4
a Lev 23:40
b Job 40:22

44:5
c Ex 13:9
d Zec 8:20-22

44:6
e Isa 41:21
f Isa 43:1 g Isa 41:4;
Rev 1:8,17; 22:13

44:7
h Isa 41:22,26

Isaiah 44:1–5

Just as God was strong enough to do something about his people's physical captivity, he was great enough to deal with their persistent sinning. Not only had he found a way to forgive their sin without destroying the justice upon which the world rests; he had also found a way to transform a proud, self-centered people, who seemed incapable of giving themselves away, into people who would gladly find their central identity in surrendering to their Father. The means of transformation would be his Spirit.

God has made his Spirit available to each of us through his Son, the Messiah. What will the Spirit do for us when we allow him to fill us? For one thing, he will enable us to identify with our Lord and his people without reservation, to state clearly and confidently, "I belong to the LORD" (v. 5). Allow the Spirit to move you today to a new place of surrender to God and to his work in your life. Then follow his call to serve others.

Isaiah 44:6–23

God hates idolatry because it reduces human beings—the crown of his creation—to nothing and de-

44:8
i Isa 43:10
j Dt 4:35; 1Sa 2:2

44:9
k Isa 41:24

44:10
l Isa 41:29;
Jer 10:5; Ac 19:26
44:11
m Isa 1:29
n Isa 42:17

44:12
o Isa 40:19; 41:6-7
p Jer 10:3-5;
Ac 17:29

44:13
q Isa 41:7
r Ps 115:4-7
s Jdg 17:4-5

44:15
t ver 19
u 2Ch 25:14

44:17
v 1Ki 18:26
w Isa 45:20

44:18
x Isa 1:3
y Isa 6:9-10

You are my witnesses. Is there any God[i] besides me?
No, there is no other Rock;[j] I know not one."

9 All who make idols are nothing,
and the things they treasure are worthless.[k]
Those who would speak up for them are blind;
they are ignorant, to their own shame.
10 Who shapes a god and casts an idol,
which can profit him nothing?[l]
11 He and his kind will be put to shame;[m]
craftsmen are nothing but men.
Let them all come together and take their stand;
they will be brought down to terror and infamy.[n]

12 The blacksmith[o] takes a tool
and works with it in the coals;
he shapes an idol with hammers,
he forges it with the might of his arm.[p]
He gets hungry and loses his strength;
he drinks no water and grows faint.
13 The carpenter[q] measures with a line
and makes an outline with a marker;
he roughs it out with chisels
and marks it with compasses.
He shapes it in the form of man,[r]
of man in all his glory,
that it may dwell in a shrine.[s]
14 He cut down cedars,
or perhaps took a cypress or oak.
He let it grow among the trees of the forest,
or planted a pine, and the rain made it grow.
15 It is man's fuel[t] for burning;
some of it he takes and warms himself,
he kindles a fire and bakes bread.
But he also fashions a god and worships it;
he makes an idol and bows[u] down to it.
16 Half of the wood he burns in the fire;
over it he prepares his meal,
he roasts his meat and eats his fill.
He also warms himself and says,
"Ah! I am warm; I see the fire."
17 From the rest he makes a god, his idol;
he bows down to it and worships.
He prays[v] to it and says,
"Save[w] me; you are my god."
18 They know nothing, they understand[x] nothing;
their eyes[y] are plastered over so they cannot see,
and their minds closed so they cannot understand.

---

stroys their power to think logically. Idolatry is using a created thing in a way that violates its character. God gave all of nature to humans to care for in a way that would produce blessing (Gen. 1:28–30). For people to elevate nature to the place of God and bow down to what he has made for them is a violation. Spiritually speaking, it's to "feed on ashes" (v. 20).

We must refuse to bow to the false gods of this world just as believers did in Babylon 2,600 years ago.

The meaninglessness of life in a world where God has been shut out is vividly portrayed in today's media. We are reaping the bitter fruit of the view that this world is all there is. Can things made with human hands save us from ourselves today any more now than in Isaiah's day? The gods and goddesses of beauty, youth, power through wealth or position, technology, and science are all to be rejected by Christians as we seek the face of the one God. He alone can redeem us from the "deluded heart" (v. 20) these idols produce in us.

19 No one stops to think,
no one has the knowledge or understanding[z] to say,
"Half of it I used for fuel;
I even baked bread over its coals,
I roasted meat and I ate.
Shall I make a detestable[a] thing from what is left?
Shall I bow down to a block of wood?"
20 He feeds on ashes,[b] a deluded[c] heart misleads him;
he cannot save himself, or say,
"Is not this thing in my right hand a lie?[d]"

21 "Remember[e] these things, O Jacob,
for you are my servant, O Israel.
I have made you, you are my servant;[f]
O Israel, I will not forget you.[g]
22 I have swept away[h] your offenses like a cloud,
your sins like the morning mist.
Return[i] to me,
for I have redeemed[j] you."

23 Sing for joy,[k] O heavens, for the LORD has done this;
shout aloud, O earth[l] beneath.
Burst into song, you mountains,[m]
you forests and all your trees,
for the LORD has redeemed Jacob,
he displays his glory[n] in Israel.

Jerusalem to Be Inhabited

24 "This is what the LORD says—
your Redeemer,[o] who formed you in the womb:

I am the LORD,
who has made all things,
who alone stretched out the heavens,[p]
who spread out the earth by myself,

25 who foils[q] the signs of false prophets
and makes fools of diviners,[r]
who overthrows the learning of the wise[s]
and turns it into nonsense,[t]
26 who carries out the words[u] of his servants
and fulfills[v] the predictions of his messengers,

who says of Jerusalem, 'It shall be inhabited,'
of the towns of Judah, 'They shall be built,'
and of their ruins, 'I will restore them,'[w]
27 who says to the watery deep, 'Be dry,
and I will dry up your streams,'
28 who says of Cyrus,[x] 'He is my shepherd
and will accomplish all that I please;
he will say of Jerusalem, [y] "Let it be rebuilt,"
and of the temple,[z] "Let its foundations be laid." '

44:19	z Isa 5:13; 27:11; 45:20 a Dt 27:15
44:20	b Ps 102:9 c Job 15:31; Ro 1:21-23, 28; 2Th 2:11; 2Ti 3:13 d Isa 59:3, 4, 13; Ro 1:25
44:21	e Isa 46:8; Zec 10:9 f ver 1-2 g Isa 49:15
44:22	h Isa 43:25; Ac 3:19 i Isa 55:7 j 1Co 6:20
44:23	k Isa 42:10 l Ps 148:7 m Ps 98:8 n Isa 61:3
44:24	o Isa 43:14 p Isa 42:5
44:25	q Ps 33:10 r Isa 47:13 s 1Co 1:27 t 2Sa 15:31; 1Co 1:19-20
44:26	u Zec 1:6 v Isa 55:11; Mt 5:18 w Isa 49:8-21
44:28	x 2Ch 36:22 y Isa 14:32 z Ezr 1:2-4

Isaiah 44:24—45:25
God identified and commissioned his "anointed," Cyrus, who would deliver the people of Judah from Babylonian exile. In response to an apparent challenge to the appropriateness of using a pagan in this way, God asserted his right to do as he chooses. Isaiah 45:14–25 contrasts God's ability to save with that of idols. First-person pronouns and verbs in this passage are prominent. Although the naming of Cyrus is the dramatic center, the passage is about God, not Cyrus.

1151

45

"This is what the LORD says to his anointed,
  to Cyrus, whose right hand I take hold *a* of
to subdue nations *b* before him
  and to strip kings of their armor,
to open doors before him
  so that gates will not be shut:
² I will go before you
  and will level *c* the mountains*ᵃ*;
I will break down gates of bronze
  and cut through bars of iron. *d*
³ I will give you the treasures *e* of darkness,
  riches stored in secret places, *f*
so that you may know *g* that I am the LORD,
  the God of Israel, who summons you by name. *h*
⁴ For the sake of Jacob my servant, *i*
  of Israel my chosen,
I summon you by name
  and bestow on you a title of honor,
  though you do not acknowledge *j* me.
⁵ I am the LORD, and there is no other; *k*
  apart from me there is no God. *l*
I will strengthen you, *m*
  though you have not acknowledged me,
⁶ so that from the rising of the sun
  to the place of its setting*ⁿ*
men may know there is none besides me. *o*
  I am the LORD, and there is no other.
⁷ I form the light and create darkness,
  I bring prosperity and create disaster; *p*
  I, the LORD, do all these things.

⁸ "You heavens above, rain *q* down righteousness; *r*
  let the clouds shower it down.
Let the earth open wide,
  let salvation *s* spring up,
let righteousness grow with it;
  I, the LORD, have created it.

⁹ "Woe to him who quarrels *t* with his Maker,
  to him who is but a potsherd among the potsherds on the ground.
Does the clay say to the potter, *u*
  'What are you making?'
Does your work say,
  'He has no hands'?
¹⁰ Woe to him who says to his father,
  'What have you begotten?'
or to his mother,
  'What have you brought to birth?'

¹¹ "This is what the LORD says—

Cross refs: 45:1 a Ps 73:23; Isa 41:13; 42:6 b Jer 50:35 | 45:2 c Isa 40:4 d Ps 107:16; Jer 51:30 | 45:3 e Jer 50:37 f Jer 41:8 g Isa 41:23 h Ex 33:12; Isa 43:1 | 45:4 i Isa 41:8-9 j Ac 17:23 | 45:5 k Isa 44:8 l Ps 18:31 m Ps 18:39 | 45:6 n Isa 43:5; Mal 1:11 o ver 5,18 | 45:7 p Isa 31:2; Am 3:6 | 45:8 q Ps 72:6; Joel 3:18 r Ps 85:11; Isa 60:21; 61:10,11; Hos 10:12 s Isa 12:3 | 45:9 t Job 15:25 u Isa 29:16; Ro 9:20-21

ᵃ 2 Dead Sea Scrolls and Septuagint; the meaning of the word in the Masoretic Text is uncertain.

Reflecting on God's sharp challenges to those who question his ways in 45:9–13, we are reminded of Jesus' challenges to the Pharisees. They were passionate students of Scripture, who wanted to please God but didn't accept Jesus as the Messiah and friend of sinners or approve of his delivering the oppressed in ways they thought violated the way God was "supposed" to act.

How many of us are to some degree "Christian Pharisees"? Have we become eager students of the Word, with our theology all sewn up—but relative failures at loving people into the kingdom or acknowledging that God is God and that he can choose people we wouldn't choose or act in ways we might not understand?

the Holy One of Israel, and its Maker:
Concerning things to come,
  do you question me about my children,
  or give me orders about the work of my hands? [v]

45:11
v Isa 19:25

12 It is I who made the earth
  and created mankind upon it.
My own hands stretched out the heavens; [w]
  I marshaled their starry hosts. [x]

45:12
w Ge 2:1; Isa 42:5
x Ne 9:6

13 I will raise up Cyrus [a][y] in my righteousness:
  I will make all his ways straight.
He will rebuild my city
  and set my exiles free,
but not for a price or reward, [z]
  says the Lord Almighty."

45:13
y 2Ch 36:22;
Isa 41:2 z Isa 52:3

14 This is what the Lord says:

"The products of Egypt and the merchandise of Cush, [b]
  and those tall Sabeans—
they will come over to you
  and will be yours;
they will trudge behind you,
  coming over to you in chains. [a]
They will bow down before you
  and plead [b] with you, saying,
'Surely God is with you, [c] and there is no other;
  there is no other god.' "

45:14
a Isa 14:1-2
b Jer 16:19;
Zec 8:20-23
c 1Co 14:25

15 Truly you are a God who hides [d] himself,
  O God and Savior of Israel.

45:15
d Ps 44:24

16 All the makers of idols will be put to shame and disgraced; [e]
  they will go off into disgrace together.

45:16
e Isa 44:9,11

17 But Israel will be saved [f] by the Lord
  with an everlasting salvation; [g]
you will never be put to shame or disgraced,
  to ages everlasting.

45:17
f Ro 11:26
g Isa 26:4

18 For this is what the Lord says—
he who created the heavens,
  he is God;
he who fashioned and made the earth,
  he founded it;
he did not create it to be empty, [h]
  but formed it to be inhabited [i]—
he says:
"I am the Lord,
  and there is no other. [j]

45:18
h Ge 1:2 i Ge 1:26;
Isa 42:5 j ver 5

19 I have not spoken in secret, [k]
  from somewhere in a land of darkness;
I have not said to Jacob's descendants, [l]
  'Seek me in vain.'
I, the Lord, speak the truth;
  I declare what is right. [m]

45:19
k Isa 48:16
l Isa 41:8
m Dt 30:11

20 "Gather together [n] and come;
  assemble, you fugitives from the nations.
Ignorant [o] are those who carry [p] about idols of wood,
  who pray to gods that cannot save. [q]

45:20
n Isa 43:9
o Isa 44:19
p Isa 46:1; Jer 10:5
q Isa 44:17; 46:6-7

---

a 13 Hebrew *him*   b 14 That is, the upper Nile region

45:21
r Isa 41:22 s ver 5

21 Declare what is to be, present it—
    let them take counsel together.
Who foretold[r] this long ago,
    who declared it from the distant past?
Was it not I, the LORD?
    And there is no God apart from me,[s]
a righteous God and a Savior;
    there is none but me.

45:22
t Zec 12:10
u Nu 21:8-9;
2Ch 20:12
v Isa 49:6,12
45:23
w Ge 22:16
x Heb 6:13
y Isa 55:11
z Ps 63:11;
Isa 19:18;
Ro 14:11*;
Php 2:10-11

22 "Turn[t] to me and be saved,[u]
    all you ends of the earth;[v]
    for I am God, and there is no other.
23 By myself I have sworn,[w]
    my mouth has uttered in all integrity[x]
    a word that will not be revoked:[y]
Before me every knee will bow;
    by me every tongue will swear.[z]

45:24
a Jer 33:16
b Isa 41:11

24 They will say of me, 'In the LORD alone
    are righteousness[a] and strength.' "
All who have raged against him
    will come to him and be put to shame.[b]

45:25
c Isa 41:16

25 But in the LORD all the descendants of Israel
    will be found righteous and will exult.[c]

Gods of Babylon

46:1
d Isa 21:9; Jer 50:2;
51:44 e Isa 45:20

46 Bel[d] bows down, Nebo stoops low;
    their idols are borne by beasts of burden.[a]
The images that are carried[e] about are burdensome,
    a burden for the weary.
2 They stoop and bow down together;
    unable to rescue the burden,
    they themselves go off into captivity.[f]

46:2
f Jdg 18:17-18;
2Sa 5:21
46:3
g ver 12

3 "Listen[g] to me, O house of Jacob,
    all you who remain of the house of Israel,
you whom I have upheld since you were conceived,
    and have carried since your birth.

46:4
h Ps 71:18
i Isa 43:13

4 Even to your old age and gray hairs[h]
    I am he,[i] I am he who will sustain you.
I have made you and I will carry you;
    I will sustain you and I will rescue you.

46:5
j Isa 40:18,25

5 "To whom will you compare me or count me equal?
    To whom will you liken me that we may be compared?[j]
6 Some pour out gold from their bags
    and weigh out silver on the scales;
they hire a goldsmith[k] to make it into a god,

46:6
k Isa 40:19

a 1 Or are but beasts and cattle

Isaiah 46:1–13

Verses 1–7 continue the contrast between God and idols—using much more concrete imagery. The theme of "carrying" is prominent. Those who had depended on the Babylonian gods Bel and Nebo loaded their idols onto oxcarts to be carried into captivity. Instead of being saved by their gods, they had to save the gods! In emotional language God reminded his people that he had carried them since their conception, and he promised to continue to carry them through to old age. In verses 8–13 Isaiah called on his hearers to take all this to heart and not give up hope that God would deliver them.

Only God can provide meaning, purpose, identity, and fulfillment. We truly begin to experience his loving act of carrying us when we let go of "our" things. But we are afraid—afraid that God will do a worse job of directing our lives than we can. Until we are willing to relinquish our tightly held will to control, we will continue to allow our fears to keep us from fully experiencing his care and deliverance.

and they bow down and worship it. *[l]*

[7] They lift it to their shoulders and carry *[m]* it;
  they set it up in its place, and there it stands.
  From that spot it cannot move.
Though one cries out to it, it does not answer;
  it cannot save *[n]* him from his troubles.

[8] "Remember *[o]* this, fix it in mind,
  take it to heart, you rebels.
[9] Remember the former things, those of long ago; *[p]*
  I am God, and there is no other;
  I am God, and there is none like me. *[q]*
[10] I make known the end from the beginning,
  from ancient times, *[r]* what is still to come.
I say: My purpose will stand, *[s]*
  and I will do all that I please.
[11] From the east I summon a bird of prey;
  from a far-off land, a man to fulfill my purpose.
What I have said, that will I bring about;
  what I have planned, that will I do.
[12] Listen *[t]* to me, you stubborn-hearted,
  you who are far from righteousness. *[u]*
[13] I am bringing my righteousness near,
  it is not far away;
  and my salvation will not be delayed.
I will grant salvation to Zion,
  my splendor *[v]* to Israel.

The Fall of Babylon

47 "Go down, sit in the dust,
  Virgin Daughter *[w]* of Babylon;
sit on the ground without a throne,
  Daughter of the Babylonians. *[a][x]*
No more will you be called
  tender or delicate. *[y]*
[2] Take millstones *[z]* and grind *[a]* flour;
  take off your veil. *[b]*
Lift up your skirts, *[c]* bare your legs,
  and wade through the streams.
[3] Your nakedness *[d]* will be exposed
  and your shame *[e]* uncovered.
I will take vengeance; *[f]*
  I will spare no one."

[4] Our Redeemer—the LORD Almighty is his name *[g]*—
  is the Holy One of Israel.

[5] "Sit in silence, go into darkness, *[h]*

---

[a] 1 Or *Chaldeans;* also in verse 5

46:6
l Isa 44:17
46:7
m ver 1 *n* Isa 44:17;
Isa 45:20

46:8
o Isa 44:21
46:9
p Dt 32:7
q Isa 45:5,21

46:10
r Isa 45:21
s Pr 19:21; Ac 5:39

46:12
t ver 3
u Ps 119:150;
Isa 48:1; Jer 2:5

46:13
v Isa 44:23

47:1
w Isa 23:12
x Ps 137:8;
Jer 50:42; 51:33;
Zec 2:7 *y* Dt 28:56

47:2
z Ex 11:5; Mt 24:41
a Jdg 16:21
b Ge 24:65
c Isa 32:11

47:3
d Eze 16:37; Na 3:5
e Isa 20:4 *f* Isa 34:8

47:4
g Jer 50:34

47:5
h Isa 13:10

Isaiah 47:1–15

This chapter is a poem that relentlessly declares the fall of Babylon. It makes its point in three stanzas, focused on Babylon's humiliation (vv. 1–4), false pride (vv. 5–11), and helplessness (vv. 12–15). The ultimate issue is pride, the same concern dealt with in regard to the nations earlier in the book. Could any of the nations compare to Israel's Holy One? The answer was and continues to be a resounding no.

The Babylonians thought they could do whatever they wanted to captive nations (v. 6); in their eyes there was no one greater. They made the fatal errors of believing they were self-existent and self-perpetuating. It never occurred to them that Someone greater would hold them accountable. Part of that wickedness included attempting to control the spirit world through magic, astrology, and divination (v. 9).

Daughter of the Babylonians;
no more will you be called
    queen of kingdoms. [i]

6 I was angry [j] with my people
    and desecrated my inheritance;
I gave them into your hand, [k]
    and you showed them no mercy.
Even on the aged
    you laid a very heavy yoke.
7 You said, 'I will continue forever—
    the eternal queen!' [l]
But you did not consider these things
    or reflect [m] on what might happen. [n]

8 "Now then, listen, you wanton creature,
    lounging in your security [o]
and saying to yourself,
    'I am, and there is none besides me. [p]
I will never be a widow [q]
    or suffer the loss of children.'
9 Both of these will overtake you
    in a moment, [r] on a single day:
loss of children [s] and widowhood.
They will come upon you in full measure,
    in spite of your many sorceries [t]
    and all your potent spells. [u]
10 You have trusted [v] in your wickedness
    and have said, 'No one sees me.' [w]
Your wisdom [x] and knowledge mislead [y] you
    when you say to yourself,
    'I am, and there is none besides me.'
11 Disaster will come upon you,
    and you will not know how to conjure it away.
A calamity will fall upon you
    that you cannot ward off with a ransom;
a catastrophe you cannot foresee
    will suddenly [z] come upon you.

12 "Keep on, then, with your magic spells
    and with your many sorceries, [a]
which you have labored at since childhood.
Perhaps you will succeed,
    perhaps you will cause terror.
13 All the counsel you have received has only worn you out! [b]
    Let your astrologers [c] come forward,
those stargazers who make predictions month by month,
    let them save [d] you from what is coming upon you.
14 Surely they are like stubble; [e]
    the fire will burn them up.

47:5
[i] Isa 13:19
47:6
[j] 2Ch 28:9
[k] Isa 10:13

47:7
[l] ver 5; Rev 18:7
[m] Isa 42:23,25
[n] Dt 32:29

47:8
[o] Isa 32:9
[p] Isa 45:6; Zep 2:15
[q] Rev 18:7

47:9
[r] Ps 73:19; 1Th 5:3; Rev 18:8-10
[s] Isa 13:18 [t] Na 3:4
[u] Rev 18:23

47:10
[v] Ps 52:7; 62:10
[w] Isa 29:15
[x] Isa 5:21
[y] Isa 44:20

47:11
[z] 1Th 5:3

47:12
[a] ver 9

47:13
[b] Isa 57:10; Jer 51:58
[c] Isa 44:25 [d] ver 15

47:14
[e] Isa 5:24; Na 1:10

Many moderns who deny that Jesus ever did a miracle consult their horoscopes daily. But this is nothing more than a continuation of failed Babylonian wisdom (see v. 10). The astrologic organization of the sky is Babylonian, and the names of the zodiac signs are Greek versions of the Babylonian names. So what's the attraction? The same as it's been for five thousand years: the illusion of gaining control of life by glimpsing what's "fated" to occur. God asks us to surrender our futures into his hands. Are you sometimes tempted to apply your intelligence or resources to controlling "your" world? How do you resist this temptation?

Does how we treat others matter? Is it *really* that big of a deal? Christians are to resist the world's errors and claims that it doesn't matter. Christ reinforced God's requirements: Love God, and love your neighbor as yourself (cf. Luke 10:27–28).

They cannot even save themselves
   from the power of the flame.[f]
Here are no coals to warm anyone;
   here is no fire to sit by.
15 That is all they can do for you—
   these you have labored with
   and trafficked[g] with since childhood.
Each of them goes on in his error;
   there is not one that can save you.

Stubborn Israel

48 "Listen to this, O house of Jacob,
   you who are called by the name of Israel
   and come from the line of Judah,
you who take oaths in the name of the LORD
   and invoke[h] the God of Israel—
   but not in truth[i] or righteousness—
2 you who call yourselves citizens of the holy city[j]
   and rely[k] on the God of Israel—
   the LORD Almighty is his name:
3 I foretold the former things[l] long ago,
   my mouth announced[m] them and I made them known;
   then suddenly I acted, and they came to pass.
4 For I knew how stubborn[n] you were;
   the sinews of your neck[o] were iron,
   your forehead[p] was bronze.
5 Therefore I told you these things long ago;
   before they happened I announced them to you
so that you could not say,
   'My idols did them;[q]
   my wooden image and metal god ordained them.'
6 You have heard these things; look at them all.
   Will you not admit them?

"From now on I will tell you of new things,
   of hidden things unknown to you.
7 They are created now, and not long ago;
   you have not heard of them before today.
So you cannot say,
   'Yes, I knew of them.'
8 You have neither heard nor understood;
   from of old your ear has not been open.
Well do I know how treacherous you are;
   you were called a rebel[r] from birth.
9 For my own name's sake I delay my wrath;[s]
   for the sake of my praise I hold it back from you,
   so as not to cut you off.[t]
10 See, I have refined you, though not as silver;

47:14
f Isa 10:17;
Jer 51:30,32,58

47:15
g Rev 18:11

48:1
h Isa 58:2 i Jer 4:2
48:2
j Isa 52:1
k Isa 10:20;
Mic 3:11; Ro 2:17

48:3
l Isa 41:22
m Isa 45:21

48:4
n Dt 31:27
o Ex 32:9; Ac 7:51
p Eze 3:9

48:5
q Jer 44:15-18

48:8
r Dt 9:7,24; Ps 58:3
48:9
s Ps 78:38;
Isa 30:18 t Ne 9:31

Isaiah 48:1–11

God summed up his claim to be an entirely different order of being from the nations' gods. The people had heard his past predictions and knew they would come true. Now he would predict new things that hadn't been heard of before. The nature of these events weren't specified here. The point was that God the Creator, as opposed to idols, can say and do new things. No one can "defame" him by comparing him to an idol, and

no idol can possibly share his glory (v. 11).

If ever there was a new thing, Christ's coming was it. Can the immortal God become mortal? If we believe that the Creator of the universe isn't limited by his creation, the answer is yes. God can do the impossible and bring about change. He has nailed our death certificate to Christ's cross (Col. 2:14), reconciling us to himself (2 Cor. 5:19). Have you thanked the Creator today for transforming you into "a new creation" (2 Cor. 5:17)?

48:10
u 1Ki 8:51
48:11
v 1Sa 12:22;
Isa 37:35
w Dt 32:27;
Jer 14:7,21;
Eze 20:9,14,22,44
x Isa 42:8
48:12
y Isa 46:3
z Isa 41:4;
Rev 1:17; 22:13

48:13
a Heb 1:10-12
b Ex 20:11
c Isa 40:26

48:14
d Isa 43:9
e Isa 46:10-11

48:15
f Isa 45:1

48:16
g Isa 41:1
h Isa 45:19
i Zec 2:9,11

48:17
j Isa 49:7
k Isa 43:14
l Isa 49:10
m Ps 32:8

48:18
n Dt 32:29
o Ps 119:165;
Isa 66:12 p Isa 45:8

48:19
q Ge 22:17
r Isa 56:5; 66:22

I have tested you in the furnace[u] of affliction.
11 For my own sake,[v] for my own sake, I do this.
How can I let myself be defamed?[w]
I will not yield my glory to another.[x]

Israel Freed

12 "Listen[y] to me, O Jacob,
Israel, whom I have called:
I am he;
I am the first and I am the last.[z]
13 My own hand laid the foundations of the earth,[a]
and my right hand spread out the heavens;[b]
when I summon them,
they all stand up together.[c]

14 "Come together,[d] all of you, and listen:
Which of the idols has foretold these things?
The LORD's chosen ally
will carry out his purpose[e] against Babylon;
his arm will be against the Babylonians.[a]
15 I, even I, have spoken;
yes, I have called[f] him.
I will bring him,
and he will succeed in his mission.

16 "Come near[g] me and listen to this:

"From the first announcement I have not spoken in secret;[h]
at the time it happens, I am there."

And now the Sovereign LORD has sent[i] me,
with his Spirit.

17 This is what the LORD says—
your Redeemer,[j] the Holy One[k] of Israel:
"I am the LORD your God,
who teaches you what is best for you,
who directs[l] you in the way[m] you should go.
18 If only you had paid attention[n] to my commands,
your peace[o] would have been like a river,
your righteousness[p] like the waves of the sea.
19 Your descendants would have been like the sand,
your children like its numberless grains;[q]
their name would never be cut off[r]
nor destroyed from before me."

20 Leave Babylon,

a 14 Or *Chaldeans*; also in verse 20

Isaiah 48:12–22

Three times God's people were commanded to "listen" (vv. 12,14,16). The Hebrew word doesn't permit a separation between understanding and action. If people truly "heard" an admonition, they would obey it. If they didn't, they had evidently failed to hear it. If God's people listened to what God said, they would believe his words and act accordingly. They would retain their faith in him despite adverse circumstances, be ready when the time came to leave the known in Babylon, and take the risk of the unknown in returning to Judah.

Hearing God and doing what he required were inseparable for the Hebrews. Why do we try to make an artifical separation between them? Salvation offers the possibility of real change in our lives as God does new things for us, but that change is available only to those who are willing to "listen." "The man who looks intently into the perfect law that gives freedom, and continues to do this, not forgetting what he has heard, but doing it— he will be blessed in what he does" (James 1:25). As Jesus put it, "everyone who hears these words of mine and puts them into practice is like a wise man who built his house on the rock" (Matt. 7:24).

flee[s] from the Babylonians!
Announce this with shouts of joy[t]
    and proclaim it.
Send it out to the ends of the earth;
    say, "The LORD has redeemed[u] his servant Jacob."
21 They did not thirst[v] when he led them through the deserts;
    he made water flow[w] for them from the rock;
he split the rock
    and water gushed out.[x]

22 "There is no peace," says the LORD, "for the wicked."[y]

The Servant of the LORD

49 Listen to me, you islands;
    hear this, you distant nations:
Before I was born[z] the LORD called[a] me;
    from my birth he has made mention of my name.
2 He made my mouth like a sharpened sword,[b]
    in the shadow of his hand he hid me;
he made me into a polished arrow
    and concealed me in his quiver.
3 He said to me, "You are my servant,[c]
    Israel, in whom I will display my splendor.[d]"
4 But I said, "I have labored to no purpose;
    I have spent my strength in vain[e] and for nothing.
Yet what is due me is in the LORD's hand,
    and my reward[f] is with my God."

5 And now the LORD says—
    he who formed me in the womb to be his servant
to bring Jacob back to him
    and gather Israel[g] to himself,
for I am honored[h] in the eyes of the LORD
    and my God has been my strength—
6 he says:
"It is too small a thing for you to be my servant
    to restore the tribes of Jacob
    and bring back those of Israel I have kept.
I will also make you a light for the Gentiles,[i]
    that you may bring my salvation to the ends of the earth."[j]

7 This is what the LORD says—

Cross references

48:20
s Jer 50:8; 51:6,45;
Zec 2:6-7; Rev 18:4
t Isa 49:13
u Isa 52:9; 63:9

48:21
v Isa 41:17
w Isa 30:25
x Ex 17:6;
Nu 20:11;
Ps 105:41; Isa 35:6

48:22
y Isa 57:21

49:1
z Isa 44:24; 46:3;
Mt 1:20 a Isa 7:14;
9:6; 44:2; Jer 1:5;
Gal 1:15
49:2
b Isa 11:4; Rev 1:16

49:3
c Zec 3:8
d Isa 44:23

49:4
e Isa 65:23
f Isa 35:4

49:5
g Isa 11:12
h Isa 43:4

49:6
i Lk 2:32
j Ac 13:47*

Isaiah 49:1–7

The coming Babylonian captivity had been dealt with in chapters 40–48. God had a plan of physical deliverance and restoration for his people, even before the tragedy had occurred. But what of the sin that had gotten God's people into this dilemma in the first place? The answer is given in chapters 49–55. Beginning here, a different kind of captivity is addressed. The deliverer would be the Servant of the Lord, first introduced in 42:1–9. His servanthood would make possible their salvation—and ours. As he became the means of the Israelites' restoration to God, he would make them the model for the restoration of the world.

The contrast between the Messianic Servant and God's servant Israel (cf. 41:8–9) is obvious here. Why then is the Servant specifically named "Israel" in verse 3? The term can't refer to literal, national Israel, since we are told in verses 5–6 that the Servant had a mission to Israel. Rather, the Messiah would be the ideal Israel— "Israel" as Israel was meant to be. This Servant would succeed where national Israel had failed.

As we participate in the life of the Servant, we too are enabled by God to "display [his] splendor" (v. 3) as an obedient Israel might have done. Each of us can be a "sharpened sword" or "polished arrow" in the Lord's hand (v. 2). This doesn't necessarily mean we are doing something earthshaking, as the Servant, Jesus Christ, did. But the simple tasks we perform may have more significance than we will ever know on this side of the grave. Do you at certain moments experience a sense of being divinely fitted for just what you are doing? If not, have you talked to your Creator about the disconnect?

49:7
k Isa 48:17
l Ps 22:6; 69:7-9
m Isa 52:15

the Redeemer and Holy One of Israel[k]—
to him who was despised[l] and abhorred by the nation,
    to the servant of rulers:
"Kings[m] will see you and rise up,
    princes will see and bow down,
because of the LORD, who is faithful,
    the Holy One of Israel, who has chosen you."

Restoration of Israel

[8]This is what the LORD says:

49:8
n Ps 69:13
o 2Co 6:2*
p Isa 26:3 q Isa 42:6
r Isa 44:26

"In the time of my favor[n] I will answer you,
    and in the day of salvation I will help you;[o]
I will keep[p] you and will make you
    to be a covenant for the people,[q]
to restore the land[r]
    and to reassign its desolate inheritances,
[9]to say to the captives,[s] 'Come out,'
    and to those in darkness, 'Be free!'

49:9
s Isa 42:7; 61:1;
Lk 4:19 t Isa 41:18

"They will feed beside the roads
    and find pasture on every barren hill.[t]
[10]They will neither hunger nor thirst,[u]
    nor will the desert heat or the sun beat upon them.[v]
He who has compassion[w] on them will guide them
    and lead them beside springs[x] of water.
[11]I will turn all my mountains into roads,
    and my highways[y] will be raised up.[z]
[12]See, they will come from afar[a]—
    some from the north, some from the west,
    some from the region of Aswan.[a]"

49:10
u Isa 33:16
v Ps 121:6;
Rev 7:16 w Isa 14:1
x Isa 35:7

49:11
y Isa 11:16
z Isa 40:4
49:12
a Isa 43:5-6

[13]Shout for joy, O heavens;
    rejoice, O earth;
    burst into song, O mountains![b]
For the LORD comforts[c] his people
    and will have compassion on his afflicted ones.

49:13
b Isa 44:23
c Isa 40:1

[14]But Zion said, "The LORD has forsaken me,
    the Lord has forgotten me."

a 12 Dead Sea Scrolls; Masoretic Text *Sinim*

Isaiah 49:8–26

📖 The Servant would represent God's covenant to his people. Like a new Joshua he would settle the people in a land of freedom and abundance, where the God of compassion would tend them as a shepherd tends his flock. But the people declared that the great promises about the Servant's redemptive ministry were in vain; God had clearly forsaken and forgotten his own (v. 14; cf. 40:27).

God refuted that charge: He wouldn't forget them, and the proof of his love would be seen both in Zion's restoration to the land and in the abundance of descendants born to her when she thought herself barren (vv. 15–21). In addition, God would cause the nations to bring home Israel's lost children (vv. 22–23). But these promises elicited another pessimistic response: Who could break the grip of the captors (v. 24)? Again God responded: He could do that very thing (vv. 25–26).

📖 Most likely some of the exiles lost hope because they couldn't really believe in God's love for them. The same kind of reasoning exists today. (1) Some claim that God has treated them unfairly: "If God really loved me, he wouldn't have allowed me to be born into this abusive family, to have this disease, etc." (2) Others admit that God has been fair—and therefore can't imagine he could love failures like themselves. (3) Still others take a despairing stance. Fair or unfair, their situation seems hopeless: "It doesn't matter whether God loves me or not. He can't change my circumstances."

God responds the same way today: He can no more forget us than a mother her nursing baby (v. 17). And we have even more evidence of that truth than Isaiah did. When he spoke of God's people being "engraved . . . on the palms of [God's] hands" (v. 16), he couldn't have forseen the nail scars in the palms of God's Son (cf. John 20:24–27). How could such a Savior possibly forget his own?

15 "Can a mother forget the baby at her breast
   and have no compassion on the child she has borne?
   Though she may forget,
   I will not forget you! [d]
16 See, I have engraved [e] you on the palms of my hands;
   your walls [f] are ever before me.
17 Your sons hasten back,
   and those who laid you waste [g] depart from you.
18 Lift up your eyes and look around;
   all your sons gather [h] and come to you.
   As surely as I live," declares the LORD,
   "you will wear [j] them all as ornaments;
   you will put them on, like a bride.

19 "Though you were ruined and made desolate [k]
   and your land laid waste, [l]
   now you will be too small for your people, [m]
   and those who devoured you will be far away.
20 The children born during your bereavement
   will yet say in your hearing,
   'This place is too small for us;
   give us more space to live in.' [n]
21 Then you will say in your heart,
   'Who bore me these?
   I was bereaved and barren;
   I was exiled and rejected. [o]
   Who brought these up?
   I was left [p] all alone,
   but these—where have they come from?' "

22 This is what the Sovereign LORD says:

   "See, I will beckon to the Gentiles,
   I will lift up my banner [q] to the peoples;
   they will bring your sons in their arms
   and carry your daughters on their shoulders. [r]
23 Kings [s] will be your foster fathers,
   and their queens your nursing mothers. [t]
   They will bow down before you with their faces to the ground;
   they will lick the dust [u] at your feet.
   Then you will know that I am the LORD; [v]
   those who hope in me will not be disappointed."

24 Can plunder be taken from warriors, [w]
   or captives rescued from the fierce [a]?

25 But this is what the LORD says:

   "Yes, captives [x] will be taken from warriors, [y]
   and plunder retrieved from the fierce;
   I will contend with those who contend with you,
   and your children I will save. [z]
26 I will make your oppressors [a] eat [b] their own flesh;
   they will be drunk on their own blood, [c] as with wine.
   Then all mankind will know [d]
   that I, the LORD, am your Savior,
   your Redeemer, the Mighty One of Jacob."

___

[a] 24 Dead Sea Scrolls, Vulgate and Syriac (see also Septuagint and verse 25); Masoretic Text *righteous*

49:15
d Isa 44:21
49:16
e SS 8:6
f Ps 48:12-13;
Isa 62:6
49:17
g Isa 10:6
49:18
h Isa 43:5; 54:7;
Isa 60:4 i Isa 45:23
j Isa 52:1
49:19
k Isa 54:1,3 l Isa 5:6
m Zec 10:10
49:20
n Isa 54:1-3
49:21
o Isa 5:13 p Isa 1:8
49:22
q Isa 11:10
r Isa 60:4
49:23
s Isa 60:3,10-11
t Isa 60:16
u Ps 72:9
v Mic 7:17
49:24
w Mt 12:29;
Lk 11:21
49:25
x Isa 14:2
y Jer 50:33-34
z Isa 25:9; 35:4
49:26
a Isa 9:4 b Isa 9:20
c Rev 16:6
d Eze 39:7

Israel's Sin and the Servant's Obedience

50 This is what the LORD says:

"Where is your mother's certificate of divorce[e]
  with which I sent her away?
Or to which of my creditors
  did I sell[f] you?
Because of your sins you were sold;[g]
  because of your transgressions your mother was sent away.
[2] When I came, why was there no one?
  When I called, why was there no one to answer?[h]
Was my arm too short[i] to ransom you?
  Do I lack the strength[j] to rescue you?
By a mere rebuke I dry up the sea,[k]
  I turn rivers into a desert;
their fish rot for lack of water
  and die of thirst.
[3] I clothe the sky with darkness
  and make sackcloth[l] its covering."

[4] The Sovereign LORD has given me an instructed tongue,[m]
  to know the word that sustains the weary.[n]
He wakens me morning by morning,[o]
  wakens my ear to listen like one being taught.
[5] The Sovereign LORD has opened my ears,[p]
  and I have not been rebellious;[q]
  I have not drawn back.
[6] I offered my back to those who beat[r] me,
  my cheeks to those who pulled out my beard;
I did not hide my face
  from mocking and spitting.[s]
[7] Because the Sovereign LORD helps[t] me,
  I will not be disgraced.
Therefore have I set my face like flint,[u]
  and I know I will not be put to shame.
[8] He who vindicates me is near.
  Who then will bring charges against me?[v]
  Let us face each other![w]
Who is my accuser?
  Let him confront me!
[9] It is the Sovereign LORD who helps[x] me.
  Who is he that will condemn me?

50:1
e Dt 24:1; Jer 3:8;
Hos 2:2 / Ne 5:5;
Mt 18:25
g Dt 32:30; Isa 52:3

50:2
h Isa 41:28
i Nu 11:23; Isa 59:1
j Ge 18:14
k Ex 14:22; Jos 3:16

50:3
l Rev 6:12

50:4
m Ex 4:12
n Mt 11:28
o Ps 5:3; 119:147;
143:8

50:5
p Isa 35:5
q Mt 26:39;
Jn 8:29; 14:31;
15:10; Ac 26:19;
Heb 5:8
50:6
r Isa 53:5;
Mt 27:30;
Mk 14:65; 15:19;
Lk 22:63 s La 3:30;
Mt 26:67
50:7
t Isa 42:1
u Eze 3:8-9

50:8
v Isa 43:26;
Ro 8:32-34
w Isa 41:1

50:9
x Isa 41:10

Isaiah 50:1–11

It would be no historical accident that Judah would eventually experience exile; it would be the natural and inevitable result of her sins. But had God "divorced" his people? If so, where was the certificate? It didn't exist. Judah, not the Lord, had initiated the breakup. The exile would be only a temporary "separation."

In verse 4, the Messianic Servant was once again introduced. His obedience to God would result in suffering. This "servant" clearly wasn't Israel, since her people suffered because of rebellion—not obedience. An individual's response to God's word through the Servant is the watershed issue. Those who have "no light" can walk safely if they entrust themselves to God in the way he's revealed. But those who reject that way and try to manufacture their own light will find that the way they have chosen leads to "torment" (vv. 10–11).

To live for God, and especially to speak for him, is to invite abuse. North American Christians hardly think of persecution as a sign of blessing (see Matt. 5:10–12). In fact, we tend to think we are blessed when everyone speaks well of us. But that is not the message of Isaiah—or of Christ—and it's not the experience of Jesus or of millions of Christians around the world today. We are called to faithful obedience, recognizing that we may not as a result be as comfortable, wealthy, or prominent as we might otherwise have been. We are called to "set our faces like flint" (Isa. 50:7), following in the footsteps of our Servant-Master (cf. 1 Peter 2:21–23).

They will all wear out like a garment;
    the moths[y] will eat them up.

[10]Who among you fears the LORD
    and obeys the word of his servant?[z]
Let him who walks in the dark,
    who has no light,
trust[a] in the name of the LORD
    and rely on his God.
[11]But now, all you who light fires
    and provide yourselves with flaming torches,[b]
go, walk in the light of your fires[c]
    and of the torches you have set ablaze.
This is what you shall receive from my hand:
    You will lie down in torment.[d]

Everlasting Salvation for Zion

51 "Listen[e] to me, you who pursue righteousness[f]
    and who seek the LORD:
Look to the rock from which you were cut
    and to the quarry from which you were hewn;
[2]look to Abraham,[g] your father,
    and to Sarah, who gave you birth.
When I called him he was but one,
    and I blessed him and made him many.[h]
[3]The LORD will surely comfort[i] Zion
    and will look with compassion on all her ruins;[j]
he will make her deserts like Eden,[k]
    her wastelands like the garden of the LORD.
Joy and gladness[l] will be found in her,
    thanksgiving and the sound of singing.

[4]"Listen to me, my people;[m]
    hear me, my nation:
The law will go out from me;
    my justice[n] will become a light to the nations.[o]
[5]My righteousness draws near speedily,
    my salvation is on the way,[p]
and my arm[q] will bring justice to the nations.
The islands will look to me
    and wait in hope for my arm.
[6]Lift up your eyes to the heavens,
    look at the earth beneath;
the heavens will vanish like smoke,[r]
    the earth will wear out like a garment[s]
    and its inhabitants die like flies.

50:9
y Job 13:28;
Isa 51:8

50:10
z Isa 49:3 a Isa 26:4

50:11
b Pr 26:18 c Jas 3:6
d Isa 65:13-15

51:1
e Isa 46:3 f ver 7;
Ps 94:15;
Ro 9:30-31

51:2
g Isa 29:22;
Ro 4:16; Heb 11:11
h Ge 12:2

51:3
i Isa 40:1 j Isa 52:9
k Ge 2:8 l Isa 25:9;
66:10

51:4
m Ps 50:7 n Isa 2:4
o Isa 42:4,6

51:5
p Isa 46:13
q Isa 40:10; 63:1,5

51:6
r Mt 24:35;
2Pe 3:10
s Ps 102:25-26

Isaiah 51:1–16

Israel's number one problem wasn't captivity in a foreign land. It was the same problem faced by the whole human race—alienation from God—and the needed deliverance required more than sincere obedience and well-motivated living. If those qualities could have alleviated the problem, there would have been no need for divine intervention. Still, persons who demonstrate these characteristics were and are in a position of being able to receive deliverance. Their heartfelt commitment to God's law places them in a unique position to accept his liberation.

The eternal salvation brought by the Lord's Messiah is ours as Christians. We who have experienced the down payment of God's universal, timeless salvation accomplished through Christ's death and resurrection can look ahead with greater confidence than the exiles in Babylon. With the humble assurance of the redeemed—not the arrogance of conquerors—we ought to be able to face any persecution or hatred to come with the same quiet endurance our brothers and sisters in other parts of the world have manifested and continue to demonstrate.

But my salvation will last forever,
    my righteousness will never fail.

7 "Hear me, you who know what is right,[t]
    you people who have my law in your hearts:[u]
Do not fear the reproach of men
    or be terrified by their insults.[v]
8 For the moth will eat them up like a garment;[w]
    the worm will devour them like wool.
But my righteousness will last forever,[x]
    my salvation through all generations."

9 Awake, awake! Clothe yourself with strength,[y]
    O arm of the LORD;
awake, as in days gone by,
    as in generations of old.[z]
Was it not you who cut Rahab to pieces,
    who pierced that monster[a] through?
10 Was it not you who dried up the sea,[b]
    the waters of the great deep,
who made a road in the depths of the sea
    so that the redeemed might cross over?
11 The ransomed[c] of the LORD will return.
    They will enter Zion with singing;
everlasting joy will crown their heads.
    Gladness and joy[d] will overtake them,
    and sorrow and sighing will flee away.[e]

12 "I, even I, am he who comforts[f] you.
    Who are you that you fear mortal men,[g]
    the sons of men, who are but grass,[h]
13 that you forget[i] the LORD your Maker,[j]
    who stretched out the heavens[k]
    and laid the foundations of the earth,
that you live in constant terror[l] every day
    because of the wrath of the oppressor,
    who is bent on destruction?
For where is the wrath of the oppressor?
14   The cowering prisoners will soon be set free;
they will not die in their dungeon,
    nor will they lack bread.[m]
15 For I am the LORD your God,
    who churns up the sea[n] so that its waves roar—
    the LORD Almighty is his name.
16 I have put my words in your mouth[o]
    and covered you with the shadow of my hand[p]—
I who set the heavens in place,
    who laid the foundations of the earth,
    and who say to Zion, 'You are my people.' "

The Cup of the LORD's Wrath

17 Awake, awake![q]
    Rise up, O Jerusalem,
    you who have drunk from the hand of the LORD

51:7
t ver 1 u Ps 37:31
v Mt 5:11; Ac 5:41

51:8
w Isa 50:9 x ver 6

51:9
y Isa 52:1 z Dt 4:34
a Ps 74:13

51:10
b Ex 14:22

51:11
c Isa 35:9
d Jer 33:11
e Rev 7:17

51:12
f 2Co 1:4
g Ps 118:6; Isa 2:22
h Isa 40:6-7;
1Pe 1:24
51:13
i Isa 17:10
j Isa 45:11
k Ps 104:2;
Isa 48:13 l Isa 7:4

51:14
m Isa 49:10

51:15
n Jer 31:35

51:16
o Dt 18:18;
Isa 59:21 p Ex 33:22

51:17
q Isa 52:1

Isaiah 51:17—52:12

In 51:17–23 God declared that Zion's punishment was ended. In fact, the atrocities the Babylonians had visited on her would now befall them. In 52:1–2 God called Jerusalem to do the opposite of what he had required of Babylon in 47:1: Babylon was called to step down from the throne and sit in the dust, while Jerusalem was to put on "garments of splendor," "shake off [her]

the cup of his wrath,[r]
you who have drained to its dregs
   the goblet that makes men stagger.[s]
18 Of all the sons[t] she bore
   there was none to guide her;[u]
of all the sons she reared
   there was none to take her by the hand.
19 These double calamities[v] have come upon you—
   who can comfort you?—
ruin and destruction, famine[w] and sword—
   who can[a] console you?
20 Your sons have fainted;
   they lie at the head of every street,[x]
   like antelope caught in a net.
They are filled with the wrath of the LORD
   and the rebuke of your God.

21 Therefore hear this, you afflicted one,
   made drunk,[y] but not with wine.
22 This is what your Sovereign LORD says,
   your God, who defends[z] his people:
"See, I have taken out of your hand
   the cup[a] that made you stagger;
from that cup, the goblet of my wrath,
   you will never drink again.
23 I will put it into the hands of your tormentors,[b]
   who said to you,
   'Fall prostrate[c] that we may walk[d] over you.'
And you made your back like the ground,
   like a street to be walked over."

52 Awake, awake,[e] O Zion,
   clothe yourself with strength.[f]
Put on your garments of splendor,[g]
   O Jerusalem, the holy city.[h]
The uncircumcised and defiled
   will not enter you again.[i]
2 Shake off your dust;[j]
   rise up, sit enthroned, O Jerusalem.
Free yourself from the chains on your neck,
   O captive Daughter of Zion.

3 For this is what the LORD says:

"You were sold for nothing,[k]
   and without money[l] you will be redeemed."

---

a 19 Dead Sea Scrolls, Septuagint, Vulgate and Syriac; Masoretic Text / how can I

51:17
r Job 21:20;
Rev 14:10; 16:19
s Ps 60:3
51:18
t Ps 88:18
u Isa 49:21

51:19
v Isa 47:9
w Isa 14:30

51:20
x Isa 5:25; Jer 14:16

51:21
y ver 17; Isa 29:9
51:22
z Isa 49:25 a ver 17

51:23
b Isa 49:26;
Jer 25:15-17,26,28;
49:12 c Zec 12:2
d Jos 10:24

52:1
e Isa 51:17
f Isa 51:9 g Ex 28:2,
40; Ps 110:3;
Zec 3:4 h Ne 11:1;
Mt 4:5; Rev 21:2
i Na 1:15;
Rev 21:27

52:2
j Isa 29:4

52:3
k Ps 44:12
l Isa 45:13

---

dust," and "sit enthroned." God's honor was at stake because of the nations' claim that he couldn't deliver his people (52:5–6). Therefore, he would deliver them in the sight of "all the ends of the earth" (52:10). In a climactic conclusion, God called on his people to depart with deliberate speed. He would go both before and behind them.

This passage speaks of those who are powerless to defend themselves. The picture in 51:17–23 is of a widow who hopes to depend on her children's help as the contents of the cup she's forced to drink leaves her staggering. But no children come to her aid. In reality,

though, she isn't helpless. God, "who defends his people," will take action.

Contrary to the maxim "God helps those who help themselves," the Bible asserts that God helps precisely those who can't help themselves. How often have you experienced that it's only when you come to the end of your resources that you are able to turn to him in faith and receive what he wants to do for you? But why does God wait until we're helpless, or at least aware of our helplessness, before acting? One of the big reasons is that we too often are unwilling to give up control until we come to that extreme condition.

52:4
m Ge 46:6

4For this is what the Sovereign LORD says:

"At first my people went down to Egypt m to live;
  lately, Assyria has oppressed them.

5 "And now what do I have here?" declares the LORD.

"For my people have been taken away for nothing,
  and those who rule them mock, a"

declares the LORD.

52:5
n Eze 36:20;
Ro 2:24*
52:6
o Isa 49:23

"And all day long
  my name is constantly blasphemed. n
6 Therefore my people will know o my name;
  therefore in that day they will know
that it is I who foretold it.
  Yes, it is I."

52:7
p Isa 40:9;
Ro 10:15*
q Na 1:15; Eph 6:15
r Ps 93:1

7 How beautiful on the mountains
  are the feet of those who bring good news, p
who proclaim peace, q
  who bring good tidings,
  who proclaim salvation,
who say to Zion,
  "Your God reigns!" r

52:8
s Isa 62:6

8 Listen! Your watchmen s lift up their voices;
  together they shout for joy.
When the LORD returns to Zion,
  they will see it with their own eyes.

52:9
t Ps 98:4 u Isa 51:3
v Isa 48:20

9 Burst into songs of joy t together,
  you ruins u of Jerusalem,
for the LORD has comforted his people,
  he has redeemed Jerusalem. v
10 The LORD will lay bare his holy arm

a 5 Dead Sea Scrolls and Vulgate; Masoretic Text *wail*

Snapshots

52:7

Salomey

Salomey ("Salo") loves her job as manager of a Christian humanitarian organization's family sponsorship program. A wife and mother of two, she's left her family in Accra, Ghana, to work in isolated rural communities.

Her vision "is to allow Christ to use me as an instrument to help others see and know him in their lives."

The ever-smiling Salo joined the program in June, 2000. Before that time she had worked with a well-drilling project, animating, sensitizing, and organizing community people on health, hygiene, and proper sanitation before drilling took place in their areas.

A typical day finds Salo up early, biking to communities inaccessible by car or walking long distances to ensure that families within her jurisdiction are well cared for. Due to the poor condition of the roads—and the 15 riverbeds she has to cross—Salo at times has to travel 184 kilometers to cover a distance of only 60 kilometers.

Her vision "is to allow Christ to use me as an instrument to help others see and know him in their lives." Of particular importance to Salo, "I believe I could be a challenge to the girls in the community, so they can be up and doing things."

in the sight of all the nations, [w]
and all the ends of the earth will see
the salvation [x] of our God.

[11] Depart, [y] depart, go out from there!
Touch no unclean thing! [z]
Come out from it and be pure, [a]
you who carry the vessels of the LORD.
[12] But you will not leave in haste [b]
or go in flight;
for the LORD will go before you, [c]
the God of Israel will be your rear guard. [d]

The Suffering and Glory of the Servant

[13] See, my servant [e] will act wisely [a];
he will be raised and lifted up and highly exalted. [f]
[14] Just as there were many who were appalled at him [b]—
his appearance was so disfigured beyond that of any man
and his form marred beyond human likeness—
[15] so will he sprinkle many nations, [c]
and kings will shut their mouths because of him.
For what they were not told, they will see,
and what they have not heard, they will understand. [g]

53
Who has believed our message [h]
and to whom has the arm of the LORD been revealed? [i]
[2] He grew up before him like a tender shoot,
and like a root out of dry ground.
He had no beauty or majesty to attract us to him,
nothing in his appearance [j] that we should desire him.
[3] He was despised and rejected by men,
a man of sorrows, and familiar with suffering. [k]
Like one from whom men hide their faces
he was despised, [l] and we esteemed him not.

[4] Surely he took up our infirmities
and carried our sorrows, [m]
yet we considered him stricken by God, [n]
smitten by him, and afflicted.
[5] But he was pierced for our transgressions, [o]
he was crushed for our iniquities;
the punishment that brought us peace was upon him,

52:10
w Isa 66:18
x Ps 98:2-3; Lk 3:6

52:11
y Isa 48:20
z Isa 1:16;
2Co 6:17*
a 2Ti 2:19

52:12
b Ex 12:11
c Mic 2:13
d Ex 14:19

52:13
e Isa 42:1
f Isa 57:15; Php 2:9

52:15
g Ro 15:21*;
Eph 3:4-5
53:1
h Ro 10:16*
i Jn 12:38*

53:2
j Isa 52:14

53:3
k ver 4,10;
Lk 18:31-33
l Ps 22:6;
Jn 1:10-11

53:4
m Mt 8:17*
n Jn 19:7

53:5
o Ro 4:25;
1Co 15:3; Heb 9:28

---

[a] 13 Or *will prosper*   [b] 14 Hebrew *you*   [c] 15 Hebrew; Septuagint *so will many nations marvel at him*

Isaiah 52:13—53:12

Isaiah 52:13—53:12 is the central and most important passage in this major section (chs. 40–66). It's quoted more often in the New Testament than any other Old Testament passage and is commonly called the "gospel in the Old Testament."

This poem is divided into five stanzas of three verses each. It moves from an introductory note of ironic triumph (52:13–15) to the Servant's rejection (53:1–3) to his carrying of "our" sins and sorrows (53:4–6) to the results of that carrying (53:7–9) to a revelation of the atoning nature of the carrying (53:10–12). This careful structuring demonstrates the care with which the prophet approached his statement and the importance he attached to it.

At least as early as Philip's encounter with the Ethiopian eunuch (Acts 8:26–40), Christians have understood Jesus Christ to be the Servant Isaiah had in mind. Christ appeared on Earth under humble circumstances (Luke 2:4–7), was horribly disfigured in his crucifixion, and went to his death without protest or defense (Mark 14:53–65; 15:1–39).

It's likely that the inspiration for Paul's famous hymn in Philippians 2:5–11 was this passage. Which brings us to the present. Paul called believers to imitate the attitude Christ demonstrated—self-denial for the sake of others. One of the many ironies of the Christian faith is that we truly live only when we put others' needs ahead of our own. Is this the attitude you adopt daily?

53:5
p 1Pe 2:24-25

and by his wounds we are healed.[p]

6 We all, like sheep, have gone astray,
  each of us has turned to his own way;
and the Lord has laid on him
  the iniquity of us all.

53:7
q Mk 14:61

7 He was oppressed and afflicted,
  yet he did not open his mouth;[q]
he was led like a lamb to the slaughter,
  and as a sheep before her shearers is silent,
  so he did not open his mouth.
8 By oppression[a] and judgment he was taken away.
  And who can speak of his descendants?
For he was cut off from the land of the living;[r]
  for the transgression[s] of my people he was stricken.[b]

53:8
r Da 9:26; Ac 8:32-
33* s ver 12

9 He was assigned a grave with the wicked,
  and with the rich[t] in his death,
though he had done no violence,[u]
  nor was any deceit in his mouth.[v]

53:9
t Mt 27:57-60
u Isa 42:1-3
v 1Pe 2:22*

10 Yet it was the Lord's will[w] to crush[x] him and cause him to suffer,[y]
  and though the Lord makes[c] his life a guilt offering,
he will see his offspring[z] and prolong his days,
  and the will of the Lord will prosper in his hand.

53:10
w Isa 46:10 x ver 5
y ver 3 z Ps 22:30

11 After the suffering[a] of his soul,
  he will see the light ˌof lifeˌ[d] and be satisfied[e];
by his knowledge[f] my righteous servant will justify[b] many,
  and he will bear their iniquities.

53:11
a Jn 10:14-18
b Ro 5:18-19

12 Therefore I will give him a portion among the great,[g][c]
  and he will divide the spoils with the strong,[h]
because he poured out his life unto death,[d]
  and was numbered with the transgressors.[e]
For he bore the sin of many,
  and made intercession for the transgressors.

53:12
c Php 2:9
d Mt 26:28,38,39,
42 e Mk 15:27*;
Lk 22:37*; 23:32

The Future Glory of Zion

54 "Sing, O barren woman,
  you who never bore a child;
burst into song, shout for joy,
  you who were never in labor;
because more are the children[f] of the desolate woman
  than of her who has a husband,[g]"

says the Lord.

54:1
f Isa 49:20
g 1Sa 2:5; Gal 4:27*

2 "Enlarge the place of your tent,[h]

54:2
h Isa 49:19-20

a 8 Or From arrest   b 8 Or away. / Yet who of his generation considered / that he was cut off from the land of the living / for the transgression of my people, / to whom the blow was due?   c 10 Hebrew though you make   d 11 Dead Sea Scrolls (see also Septuagint); Masoretic Text does not have the light ˌof lifeˌ.   e 11 Or (with Masoretic Text) ᵘHe will see the result of the suffering of his soul / and be satisfied   f 11 Or by knowledge of him   g 12 Or many   h 12 Or numerous

Isaiah 54:1–17

The declaration of salvation through the Lord's Messianic Servant gives way to invitation and celebration. The coming of God's Son to make this reconciliation possible wouldn't take place for nearly 700 years. But the revelation was complete, and those who would accept the promise could enjoy a foretaste of that reconciliation.

Chapter 54 is a love song from God to Zion (Jeru-salem), his separated bride, informing her of his plans to restore her. In the ancient Near East (and still in many parts of the world), a terrible fate for a woman was infertility. Widowhood also was a disgrace, for a woman could contribute to society only through her husband. There was still one worse humiliation: divorce—the assumption being that the woman was in some way deficient. To each of these images of Israel and Jerusalem, God spoke promises of hope and restoration.

stretch your tent curtains wide,
　do not hold back;
lengthen your cords,
　strengthen your stakes.*i*

3 For you will spread out to the right and to the left;
　your descendants will dispossess nations
　and settle in their desolate*j* cities.

4 "Do not be afraid; you will not suffer shame.
　Do not fear disgrace; you will not be humiliated.
You will forget the shame of your youth
　and remember no more the reproach*k* of your widowhood.
5 For your Maker is your husband*l*—
　the LORD Almighty is his name—
the Holy One of Israel is your Redeemer;*m*
　he is called the God of all the earth.*n*
6 The LORD will call you back*o*
　as if you were a wife deserted*p* and distressed in spirit—
a wife who married young,
　only to be rejected," says your God.
7 "For a brief moment*q* I abandoned you,
　but with deep compassion I will bring you back.*r*
8 In a surge of anger*s*
　I hid my face from you for a moment,
but with everlasting kindness*t*
　I will have compassion on you,"
　says the LORD your Redeemer.

9 "To me this is like the days of Noah,
　when I swore that the waters of Noah would never again cover the
　　earth.*u*
So now I have sworn not to be angry*v* with you,
　never to rebuke you again.
10 Though the mountains be shaken*w*
　and the hills be removed,
yet my unfailing love for you will not be shaken*x*
　nor my covenant*y* of peace be removed,"
　says the LORD, who has compassion*z* on you.

11 "O afflicted*a* city, lashed by storms*b* and not comforted,*c*
　I will build you with stones of turquoise,*a* *d*
　your foundations*e* with sapphires.*b*
12 I will make your battlements of rubies,
　your gates of sparkling jewels,
　and all your walls of precious stones.
13 All your sons will be taught by the LORD,*f*
　and great will be your children's peace.*g*
14 In righteousness you will be established:
Tyranny*h* will be far from you;
　you will have nothing to fear.
Terror will be far removed;
　it will not come near you.

---

a 11 The meaning of the Hebrew for this word is uncertain.　　　*b* 11 Or *lapis lazuli*

Cross-references

54:2 *i* Ex 35:18; 39:40
54:3 *j* Isa 49:19
54:4 *k* Isa 51:7
54:5 *l* Jer 3:14 *m* Isa 48:17 *n* Isa 6:3
54:6 *o* Isa 49:14-21 *p* Isa 50:1-2; 62:4,12
54:7 *q* Isa 26:20 *r* Isa 49:18
54:8 *s* Isa 60:10 *t* ver 10
54:9 *u* Ge 8:21 *v* Isa 12:1
54:10 *w* Ps 46:2 *x* Isa 51:6 *y* Ps 89:34 *z* ver 8
54:11 *a* Isa 14:32 *b* Isa 28:2; 29:6 *c* Isa 51:19 *d* 1Ch 29:2; Rev 21:18 *e* Isa 28:16; Rev 21:19-20
54:13 *f* Jn 6:45* *g* Isa 48:18
54:14 *h* Isa 9:4

This is the true face of God—not that of the cold-hearted judge rehearsing the endless list of our crimes and grimly meting out exactly what we deserve—but the tender countenance of our compassionate Lord, who will go to any lengths to see that we *don't* get what we deserve.

Our punishment has been taken by the Judge himself, who now proclaims that there is no more judgment outstanding against us. This is from God's side. But there is one thing we are to do if we are to experience his covenant forever: continually choose to live under its terms.

1169

54:15
i Isa 41:11-16

15 If anyone does attack you, it will not be my doing;
  whoever attacks you will surrender*i* to you.

16 "See, it is I who created the blacksmith
  who fans the coals into flame
  and forges a weapon fit for its work.
And it is I who have created the destroyer to work havoc;

54:17
j Isa 29:8
k Isa 45:24-25

17 no weapon forged against you will prevail,*j*
  and you will refute*k* every tongue that accuses you.
This is the heritage of the servants of the LORD,
  and this is their vindication from me,"

declares the LORD.

Invitation to the Thirsty

55:1
l Jn 4:14; 7:37
m La 5:4; Mt 13:44;
Rev 3:18 *n* SS 5:1
o Hos 14:4;
Mt 10:8; Rev 21:6

55 "Come, all you who are thirsty,*l*
  come to the waters;
and you who have no money,
  come, buy*m* and eat!
Come, buy wine and milk*n*
  without money and without cost.*o*

55:2
p Ps 22:26; Ecc 6:2;
Hos 8:7 *q* Isa 1:19

2 Why spend money on what is not bread,
  and your labor on what does not satisfy?*p*
Listen, listen to me, and eat what is good,*q*
  and your soul will delight in the richest of fare.

55:3
r Lev 18:5; Ro 10:5
s Isa 61:8 *t* Isa 54:8
u Ac 13:34*

3 Give ear and come to me;
  hear me, that your soul may live.*r*
I will make an everlasting covenant*s* with you,
  my faithful love*t* promised to David.*u*

55:4
v Jer 30:9;
Eze 34:23-24
55:5
w Isa 49:6
x Isa 60:9

4 See, I have made him a witness to the peoples,
  a leader and commander*v* of the peoples.
5 Surely you will summon nations*w* you know not,
  and nations that do not know you will hasten to you,
because of the LORD your God,
  the Holy One of Israel,
  for he has endowed you with splendor."*x*

55:6
y Ps 32:6; Isa 49:8;
2Co 6:1-2
z Isa 65:24

6 Seek the LORD while he may be found;*y*
  call*z* on him while he is near.
7 Let the wicked forsake his way

55:7
a Isa 32:7; 59:7
b Isa 44:22
c Isa 54:10
d Isa 1:18; 40:2

  and the evil man his thoughts.*a*
Let him turn*b* to the LORD, and he will have mercy*c* on him,
  and to our God, for he will freely pardon.*d*

Isaiah 55:1–13

Together with chapter 54, this passage is one of the Bible's most beautiful pieces of literature. We turn from the announcement of forgiveness to the invitation to experience that forgiveness. The tone is one of earnest appeal. All is ready. How tragic if the invited guests should fail to come! Once again, we sense the significance of the prophecy in 52:13—53:12. Something has been revealed there that changes the tone of all that follows. The bride *is* restored (54:1–10) and the city *is* rebuilt (54:11–17). Those on the guest list *have to* come.

Those in Isaiah's audience couldn't deny the reality of the choice before them: to stay where they were in unbelief or to move forward in uncertainty. Surely for people in the prophet's own day, but no less for those who later read these words in the exile, the message of the Messianic Servant was largely a mystery (cf. 55:8–9). But God promised that his word was indeed reliable and that forgiveness and abundance were theirs, if only they would seek him sincerely and unreservedly.

One of the problems of life on Earth is that the longer we live here, the more its ways can become ours. A child has no difficulty believing that God can do the impossible, but adults feel the need to rein in "youthful enthusiasm." Yet God holds out an urgent invitation for us to leave striving and self-made ways and come to God, receiving the pleasures and comforts for which we vainly struggle. When we seek the Lord and live in his abundant blessings, the nations will come running to us, desiring to live the same way. All of creation will exult in joy, experiencing the harmony God intends.

As Poor as the Poor

 55:1–3

Two Kinds of Poverty

We receive everything free and give everything freely, purely for the love of God.

Our people, the poor people, are very great people. They give us much more, much joy in accepting us and the little things that we do for them.

Our life of poverty is as necessary as the work itself.

God always provides. He will always provide. Though we have no income, no salary, no grants, no church maintenance, yet we have never had to send anybody away because we didn't have.

I have never been in need, but I accept what people give me for the poor.

I need nothing for myself. I never refuse what people give. I accept whatever.

There must be a reason why some people can afford to live well. They must have worked for it. I only feel angry when I see waste, when I see people throwing away things that we could use.

There are two kinds of poverty.

We have the poverty of material things. (For example, in some places like India and Ethiopia, and in other places where people are hungry, not only for bread: real hunger!)

But there is also a much deeper, much greater hunger. That is the hunger for love and that terrible loneliness of being unwanted, unloved, being abandoned by everybody. Such are some people that you find, people that are sleeping in the streets of London, Rome, or Madrid, even people who are found in their homes (they are often called shut-ins). Maybe there is that kind of unwantedness, that unloved feeling even in our homes! We may know somebody who is handicapped like that and nobody takes notice!

> **T**he biggest disease today is not leprosy or cancer or tuberculosis, but rather the feeling of being unwanted, uncared for, deserted by everybody.

Today's Biggest Disease

The biggest disease today is not leprosy or cancer or tuberculosis, but rather the feeling of being unwanted, uncared for, deserted by everybody. The greatest evil is the lack of love and charity, the terrible indifference toward one's neighbor who lives at the roadside, the victim of exploitation, corruption, poverty, and disease.

It is easy to think of the poverty far away and forget very quickly. Today a great disease is that feeling of terrible loneliness, the feeling of being unwanted, having forgotten what human joy is, what the human feeling is of being wanted or loved. I think this is found in very well-to-do families also.

We may not have people hungry for a plate of rice or for a piece of bread in New York City, but there is a tremendous hunger and a tremendous feeling of unwantedness everywhere. And that is really a very great poverty.

To Share With a Pure Heart

I find the poverty in the West much more difficult, much greater than the poverty I meet in India, in Ethiopia and in the Middle East, which is a material poverty. For example, when a few months ago, before coming to Europe and America, I picked up a woman from the streets of Calcutta, dying of hunger, I had only to give her a plate of rice and I satisfied her hunger. But the lonely and the unwanted and the homeless, the shut-ins who are spending their lives in such terrible loneliness, who are known by the number of their room and not by their name! I think this is the greatest poverty that a human being cannot bear and accept and go through.

Mother Teresa, Roman Catholic nun and founder of the Sisters of Charity in Calcutta, India
Source: Mother Teresa, *My Life for the Poor* (Ballantine, 1985), 53–55,57

55:8
e Isa 53:6

55:9
f Ps 103:11

55:10
g Isa 30:23
h 2Co 9:10

55:11
i Isa 45:23
j Isa 44:26

55:12
k Isa 54:10,13
l 1Ch 16:33
m Ps 98:8

55:13
n Isa 5:6 o Isa 41:19
p Isa 63:12

56:1
q Isa 1:17 r Ps 85:9

56:2
s Ps 119:2
t Ex 20:8,10;
Isa 58:13

8 "For my thoughts are not your thoughts,
　　neither are your ways my ways," e

　　　　　　　　　　　　　　　　　　　　　　　declares the LORD.

9 "As the heavens are higher than the earth, f
　　so are my ways higher than your ways
　　and my thoughts than your thoughts.
10 As the rain g and the snow
　　come down from heaven,
　and do not return to it
　　without watering the earth
　and making it bud and flourish,
　　so that it yields seed for the sower and bread for the eater, h
11 so is my word that goes out from my mouth:
　　It will not return to me empty, i
　but will accomplish what I desire
　　and achieve the purpose j for which I sent it.
12 You will go out in joy
　　and be led forth in peace; k
　the mountains and hills
　　will burst into song before you,
　and all the trees l of the field
　　will clap their hands. m
13 Instead of the thornbush will grow the pine tree,
　　and instead of briers n the myrtle o will grow.
　This will be for the LORD's renown, p
　　for an everlasting sign,
　　which will not be destroyed."

Salvation for Others

56 This is what the LORD says:

　"Maintain justice q
　　and do what is right,
　for my salvation r is close at hand
　　and my righteousness will soon be revealed.
2 Blessed s is the man who does this,
　　the man who holds it fast,
　who keeps the Sabbath t without desecrating it,
　　and keeps his hand from doing any evil."

3 Let no foreigner who has bound himself to the LORD say,
　　"The LORD will surely exclude me from his people."

Isaiah 56:1–8

A superficial reading of chapters 40–55 might have led Isaiah's readers to believe that since they were unable to do right and God had delivered them from the effects of that failure by a righteous act of grace, right living wasn't really incumbent on them except as an unrealistic ideal. No, insisted Isaiah, they were to "maintain justice and do what is right" (56:1) as a necessary expression of God's salvation.

Yet the person pleasing to God wasn't the purebred Israelite simply doing his or her part to continue Abraham's physical line. If the foreigner, who wasn't part of that line, and the eunuch, who couldn't pass it along, chose to live in obedience to God's covenant, they would receive an everlasting name and the joy of living in God's presence. Such righteousness is more than legalistic lawkeeping. Verse 6 speaks in relational terms of binding oneself to God as an act of love, service, and worship.

It's imperative that we recover the understanding that while we are saved by grace through faith, not by works (Eph. 2:8–9), we are saved for good works (Eph. 2:10). Our righteousness earns us no favor with God, but it's proof positive that we have been transferred from the kingdom of darkness into the kingdom of light (Col. 1:12–13). Those who are regarded as unworthy and as outsiders are welcomed. When Jesus cleansed the temple, he cleansed the "Court of the Gentiles," which was to be the place where people from all nations would gather to pray to the Lord.

And let not any eunuch [u] complain,
"I am only a dry tree."

[4] For this is what the LORD says:

"To the eunuchs who keep my Sabbaths,
who choose what pleases me
and hold fast to my covenant—
[5] to them I will give within my temple and its walls [v]
a memorial and a name
better than sons and daughters;
I will give them an everlasting name
that will not be cut off. [w]
[6] And foreigners who bind themselves to the LORD
to serve [x] him,
to love the name of the LORD,
and to worship him,
all who keep the Sabbath [y] without desecrating it
and who hold fast to my covenant—
[7] these I will bring to my holy mountain [z]
and give them joy in my house of prayer.
Their burnt offerings and sacrifices [a]
will be accepted on my altar;
for my house will be called
a house of prayer for all nations. [b" c]
[8] The Sovereign LORD declares—
he who gathers the exiles of Israel:
"I will gather [d] still others to them
besides those already gathered."

God's Accusation Against the Wicked

[9] Come, all you beasts of the field, [e]
come and devour, all you beasts of the forest!
[10] Israel's watchmen [f] are blind,
they all lack knowledge;
they are all mute dogs,
they cannot bark;
they lie around and dream,
they love to sleep. [g]
[11] They are dogs with mighty appetites;
they never have enough.
They are shepherds [h] who lack understanding; [i]
they all turn to their own way,
each seeks his own gain. [j]
[12] "Come," each one cries, "let me get wine!
Let us drink our fill of beer!
And tomorrow will be like today,
or even far better." [k]

56:3
u Jer 38:7 fn;
Ac 8:27

56:5
v Isa 26:1; 60:18
w Isa 48:19; 55:13

56:6
x Isa 60:7,10; 61:5
y ver 2,4

56:7
z Isa 2:2 a Ro 12:1;
Heb 13:15
b Mt 21:13*;
Lk 19:46*
c Mk 11:17*

56:8
d Isa 11:12;
60:3-11; Jn 10:16

56:9
e Isa 18:6; Jer 12:9

56:10
f Eze 3:17
g Na 3:18

56:11
h Eze 34:2 i Isa 1:3
j Isa 57:17;
Eze 13:19; Mic 3:11

56:12
k Ps 10:6;
Lk 12:18-19

Isaiah 56:9—57:13

This passage was an indictment against Judah in general and her "watchmen/shepherds"—the spiritual leaders, especially the prophets—in particular. A return from captivity wouldn't guarantee new behavior for the people unless it was accompanied by a radical change in the attitudes and behavior of the leaders from what Isaiah had experienced in his day (chs. 27–28). If they continued to be self-centered and power-hungry, the flock entrusted to them would remain susceptible to enemies (56:9). There would be so little spiritual perception that the passing away of the "righteous" among them would go unnoticed (57:1–2). With 57:3, Isaiah turned directly to the people. Using strong language, he described their behavior and pronounced God's judgment.

57:1
l Ps 12:1
m Isa 42:25
n 2Ki 22:20

57

The righteous perish,[l]
  and no one ponders it in his heart;[m]
devout men are taken away,
  and no one understands
that the righteous are taken away
  to be spared from evil.[n]

57:2
o Isa 26:7

2 Those who walk uprightly[o]
  enter into peace;
  they find rest as they lie in death.

57:3
p Mt 16:4 *q* Isa 1:21

3 "But you—come here, you sons of a sorceress,
  you offspring of adulterers[p] and prostitutes![q]
4 Whom are you mocking?
  At whom do you sneer
  and stick out your tongue?
Are you not a brood of rebels,
  the offspring of liars?

57:5
r 2Ki 16:4
s Lev 18:21;
Ps 106:37-38;
Eze 16:20
57:6
t Jer 3:9 *u* Jer 7:18
v Jer 5:9,29; 9:9

5 You burn with lust among the oaks
  and under every spreading tree;[r]
you sacrifice your children[s] in the ravines
  and under the overhanging crags.
6 The idols[t] among the smooth stones of the ravines are your portion;
  they, they are your lot.
Yes, to them you have poured out drink offerings[u]
  and offered grain offerings.
  In the light of these things, should I relent?[v]

57:7
w Jer 3:6;
Eze 16:16

7 You have made your bed on a high and lofty hill;[w]
  there you went up to offer your sacrifices.
8 Behind your doors and your doorposts
  you have put your pagan symbols.
Forsaking me, you uncovered your bed,
  you climbed into it and opened it wide;

57:8
x Eze 16:26; 23:7
y Eze 23:18

you made a pact with those whose beds you love,[x]
  and you looked on their nakedness.[y]
9 You went to Molech[a] with olive oil
  and increased your perfumes.

57:9
z Eze 23:16,40

You sent your ambassadors[b][z] far away;
  you descended to the grave[c] itself!

57:10
a Jer 2:25; 18:12

10 You were wearied by all your ways,
  but you would not say, 'It is hopeless.'[a]
You found renewal of your strength,
  and so you did not faint.

57:11
b Pr 29:25
c Jer 2:32; 3:21
d Ps 50:21

11 "Whom have you so dreaded and feared[b]
  that you have been false to me,
and have neither remembered[c] me
  nor pondered this in your hearts?
Is it not because I have long been silent[d]
  that you do not fear me?

57:12
e Isa 29:15;
Mic 3:2-4,8

12 I will expose your righteousness and your works,[e]
  and they will not benefit you.

[a] 9 Or *to the king*   [b] 9 Or *idols*   [c] 9 Hebrew *Sheol*

Both leaders and people in Isaiah's day were focused primarily on the satisfaction of their desires and appetites—the identical driving force of so many today. God made our needs and desires, and they are basically good. The key is in self-surrender, in "dying to [ourselves]" (Rom. 6:11; Gal. 2:20; Col. 3:3–5). We are to surrender our needs and wants to him, determined to be faithful to him and his ways and leaving their fulfillment in his hands. Here there is freedom and satisfaction without excess, because we know that in the end *God* is what we want.

13 When you cry out[f] for help,
  let your collection ⌊of idols⌋ save you!
The wind will carry all of them off,
  a mere breath will blow them away.
But the man who makes me his refuge
  will inherit the land[g]
  and possess my holy mountain."[h]

Comfort for the Contrite

14 And it will be said:

"Build up, build up, prepare the road!
  Remove the obstacles out of the way of my people."[i]
15 For this is what the high and lofty[j] One says—
  he who lives forever,[k] whose name is holy:
"I live in a high and holy place,
  but also with him who is contrite[l] and lowly in spirit,[m]
to revive the spirit of the lowly
  and to revive the heart of the contrite.[n]
16 I will not accuse forever,
  nor will I always be angry,[o]
for then the spirit of man would grow faint before me—
  the breath of man that I have created.
17 I was enraged by his sinful greed;[p]
  I punished him, and hid my face in anger,
  yet he kept on in his willful ways.[q]
18 I have seen his ways, but I will heal[r] him;
  I will guide him and restore comfort[s] to him,
19   creating praise on the lips[t] of the mourners in Israel.
Peace, peace,[u] to those far and near,"[v]
  says the LORD. "And I will heal them."
20 But the wicked[w] are like the tossing sea,
  which cannot rest,
  whose waves cast up mire and mud.
21 "There is no peace,"[x] says my God, "for the wicked."[y]

True Fasting

58 "Shout it aloud,[z] do not hold back.
  Raise your voice like a trumpet.
Declare to my people their rebellion[a]
  and to the house of Jacob their sins.
2 For day after day they seek[b] me out;
  they seem eager to know my ways,
  as if they were a nation that does what is right

57:13
f Jer 22:20; 30:15
g Ps 37:9
h Isa 65:9-11

57:14
i Isa 62:10; Jer 18:15
57:15
j Isa 52:13
k Dt 33:27
l Ps 147:3
m Ps 34:18; 51:17; Isa 66:2 n Isa 61:1

57:16
o Ps 85:5; 103:9; Mic 7:18
57:17
p Isa 56:11 q Isa 1:4

57:18
r Isa 30:26
s Isa 61:1-3
57:19
t Isa 6:7; Heb 13:15
u Eph 2:17
v Ac 2:39
57:20
w Job 18:5-21

57:21
x Isa 59:8
y Isa 48:22

58:1
z Isa 40:6 a Isa 48:8

58:2
b Isa 48:1; Tit 1:16; Jas 4:8

Isaiah 57:14–21

This passage stands in sharp contrast to the previous one. There the focus was on human inability to live the righteous lives to which redemption calls God's people; here it's on God's activity to revive and heal them. There the focus was on "your" failings; here it's on what "I" [God] will do. He will do for people in every age what they can't do for themselves—heal their greedy, self-centered hearts. God will revive the humble and contrite, leading them in the paths of peace.

Jesus' parable of the Pharisee and the tax collector (Luke 18:10–14) is an illustration of the principles in this passage. The issue? Pride and self-reliance versus reliance on God—even in spiritual matters. Whenever righteousessness becomes an end in itself, it becomes an idol to us. God's Spirit will replicate his behavior, attitudes, and passions in the lives of those of us who say that we know God.

Isaiah 58:1–14

Isaiah returned again to the people's apparent inability—or unwillingness—to "maintain justice and do what is right," as they had been commanded in 56:1. They were going through the motions of religion—specifically fasting—for the same reason as the pagans: to manipulate God to act in their favor (58:3).

Fasting and other religious observances are insuffi-

and has not forsaken the commands of its God.
They ask me for just decisions
    and seem eager for God to come near[c] them.
3 'Why have we fasted,'[d] they say,
    'and you have not seen it?
Why have we humbled ourselves,
    and you have not noticed?'[e]

"Yet on the day of your fasting, you do as you please[f]
    and exploit all your workers.
4 Your fasting ends in quarreling and strife,[g]
    and in striking each other with wicked fists.
You cannot fast as you do today
    and expect your voice to be heard[h] on high.
5 Is this the kind of fast[i] I have chosen,
    only a day for a man to humble[j] himself?
Is it only for bowing one's head like a reed
    and for lying on sackcloth and ashes?[k]
Is that what you call a fast,
    a day acceptable to the LORD?

58:2
c Isa 29:13
58:3
d Lev 16:29
e Mal 3:14
f Isa 22:13;
Zec 7:5-6

58:4
g 1Ki 21:9-13;
Isa 59:6 h Isa 59:2

58:5
i Zec 7:5
j 1Ki 21:27
k Job 2:8

---

cient expressions of faith. Those who serve God will overcome injustice, feed the hungry, and care for the homeless (vv. 6–10). Experiencing the fullness of God's blessing hinges on caring for the oppressed, not just on the quality of worship.

 We want to live in the light, have God answer our prayers, and receive his blessing. This blessing isn't found simply in outward expressions of devotion or in dramatic worship services. We may not be experiencing answers to prayer or intimacy with God because

58:6–7

Easing the Hunger Equation

When it comes to hunger in our world, there are signs of hope, but also some disturbing trends:

Positive	Negative:
Between 1960 and 2000:	
Food prices decreased by 50 percent.[1]	
Food production increased by 150 percent.[2]	World population increased by 100 percent.[2]
The gross world product (in 1987 dollars) increased by 500 percent.[3]	
Average available daily calories per person rose by 23 percent (to 2,790 calories/day).[4]	The number of people without enough to eat rose by 150 percent.[4]
Between 1990 and 1995:	
19 countries reduced their overall number of hungry people by over 80 million.[5]	The number of hungry people in 26 other countries increased by 60 million.[5]

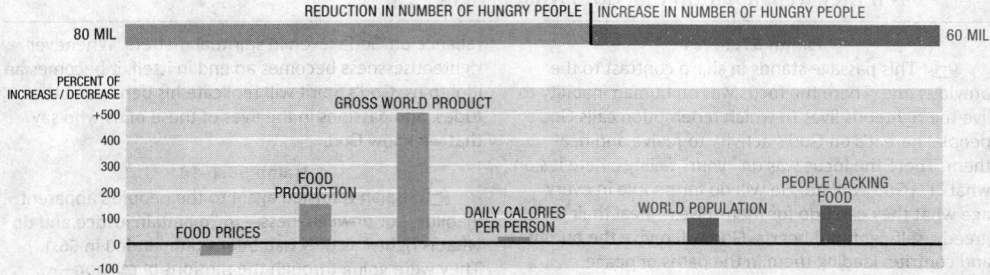

REDUCTION IN NUMBER OF HUNGRY PEOPLE | INCREASE IN NUMBER OF HUNGRY PEOPLE
80 MIL — 60 MIL

PERCENT OF INCREASE / DECREASE
+500, 400, 300, 200, 100, 0, -100
GROSS WORLD PRODUCT
FOOD PRODUCTION
DAILY CALORIES PER PERSON
WORLD POPULATION
PEOPLE LACKING FOOD
FOOD PRICES

Sources: [1] Worldwatch Institute, *State of the World 2002* (2002:54) [2] World Bank, *World Development Indicators 2002* (2002:145) [3] Worldwatch Institute, *Vital Signs 2002* (2002:75) [4] World Bank, *World Development Indicators 2002* (2002:55) [5] Food and Agriculture Organization of the United Nations (www.fao.org)

6 "Is not this the kind of fasting I have chosen:
　　to loose the chains of injustice[l]
　　　　and untie the cords of the yoke,
　　to set the oppressed[m] free
　　　　and break every yoke?
7 Is it not to share your food with the hungry[n]
　　and to provide the poor wanderer with shelter[o]—
　when you see the naked, to clothe[p] him,
　　and not to turn away from your own flesh and blood?[q]
8 Then your light will break forth like the dawn,[r]
　　and your healing[s] will quickly appear;
　then your righteousness[a] will go before you,
　　and the glory of the LORD will be your rear guard.[t]
9 Then you will call,[u] and the LORD will answer;
　　you will cry for help, and he will say: Here am I.

　"If you do away with the yoke of oppression,
　　with the pointing finger[v] and malicious talk,[w]
10 and if you spend yourselves in behalf of the hungry
　　and satisfy the needs of the oppressed,[x]
　then your light[y] will rise in the darkness,
　　and your night will become like the noonday.[z]
11 The LORD will guide you always;
　　he will satisfy your needs[a] in a sun-scorched land
　　and will strengthen your frame.
　You will be like a well-watered garden,[b]
　　like a spring[c] whose waters never fail.
12 Your people will rebuild the ancient ruins[d]
　　and will raise up the age-old foundations;[e]
　you will be called Repairer of Broken Walls,
　　Restorer of Streets with Dwellings.

13 "If you keep your feet from breaking the Sabbath[f]
　　and from doing as you please on my holy day,
　if you call the Sabbath a delight[g]
　　and the LORD's holy day honorable,
　and if you honor it by not going your own way
　　and not doing as you please or speaking idle words,
14 then you will find your joy[h] in the LORD,
　　and I will cause you to ride on the heights[i] of the land
　　and to feast on the inheritance of your father Jacob."
　　　　　　　The mouth of the LORD has spoken.[j]

a 8 Or *your righteous One*

58:6
l Ne 5:10-11
m Jer 34:9
58:7
n Eze 18:16;
Lk 3:11 o Isa 16:4;
Heb 13:2
p Job 31:19-20;
Mt 25:36
q Ge 29:14;
Lk 10:31-32
58:8
r Job 11:17
s Isa 30:26
t Ex 14:19
58:9
u Ps 50:15 v Pr 6:13
w Ps 12:2; Isa 59:13
58:10
x Dt 15:7-8
y Isa 42:16
z Job 11:17
58:11
a Ps 107:9
b SS 4:15 c Jn 4:14
58:12
d Isa 49:8
e Isa 44:28
58:13
f Isa 56:2
g Ps 84:2,10
58:14
h Job 22:26
i Dt 32:13 j Isa 1:20

---

we aren't participating in his work of caring for the suffering and enabling justice. Service to the poor is a necessary and expected expression of our worship and devotion.

58:6–10

Why Should We Be Compassionate?

Imitation:
Because God is compassionate (Joel 2:13), and while on Earth Jesus modeled compassion (Matt. 9:36)

Obedience:
Because the Bible instructs us to be compassionate (1 Peter 3:8)

Empathy:
Because we are all human: "There but for the grace of God go I" (Josh. 1:14b; 1 Thess. 4:9)

Knowledge:
Who of us can look into the eyes of a hungry child and not know compassion is right (1 Kings 3:26)?

Sin, Confession and Redemption

59:1
k Nu 11:23; Isa 50:2
l Isa 58:9; 65:24

59 Surely the arm of the LORD is not too short *k* to save,
　　nor his ear too dull to hear. *l*
² But your iniquities have separated
　　you from your God;

59:2
m Isa 1:15; 58:4
59:3
n Isa 1:15

your sins have hidden his face from you,
　　so that he will not hear. *m*
³ For your hands are stained with blood, *n*
　　your fingers with guilt.
Your lips have spoken lies,
　　and your tongue mutters wicked things.

59:4
o Job 15:35;
Ps 7:14

⁴ No one calls for justice;
　　no one pleads his case with integrity.
They rely on empty arguments and speak lies;
　　they conceive trouble and give birth to evil. *o*

59:5
p Job 8:14

⁵ They hatch the eggs of vipers
　　and spin a spider's web. *p*
Whoever eats their eggs will die,
　　and when one is broken, an adder is hatched.

59:6
q Isa 28:20
r Isa 58:4

⁶ Their cobwebs are useless for clothing;
　　they cannot cover themselves with what they make. *q*
Their deeds are evil deeds,
　　and acts of violence *r* are in their hands.

59:7
s Pr 6:17
t Mk 7:21-22
u Ro 3:15-17*

⁷ Their feet rush into sin;
　　they are swift to shed innocent blood. *s*
Their thoughts are evil thoughts; *t*
　　ruin and destruction mark their ways. *u*

59:8
v Isa 57:21; Lk 1:79

⁸ The way of peace they do not know;
　　there is no justice in their paths.
They have turned them into crooked roads;
　　no one who walks in them will know peace. *v*

59:9
w Isa 5:30; 8:20

⁹ So justice is far from us,
　　and righteousness does not reach us.
We look for light, but all is darkness; *w*
　　for brightness, but we walk in deep shadows.

59:10
x Dt 28:29
y Isa 8:15 *z* La 3:6

¹⁰ Like the blind *x* we grope along the wall,
　　feeling our way like men without eyes.
At midday we stumble *y* as if it were twilight;
　　among the strong, we are like the dead. *z*

59:11
a Isa 38:14;
Eze 7:16

¹¹ We all growl like bears;
　　we moan mournfully like doves. *a*
We look for justice, but find none;
　　for deliverance, but it is far away.

59:12
b Ezr 9:6 *c* Isa 3:9

¹² For our offenses *b* are many in your sight,
　　and our sins testify *c* against us.
Our offenses are ever with us,
　　and we acknowledge our iniquities:

Isaiah 59:1–21

This chapter constitutes one of the more poignant statements of human sinfulness in the Bible. The people's sins had separated them from God and from one another. Spiritual and social brokenness result in distance from God and in violence and injustice.

But the rest of the chapter shows God coming and doing for his people what neither they nor anyone else could do. The same "arm" that had made possible restoration to fellowship with God (53:1) would defeat the sin that reigned in them (59:1,16). Whereas in 52:13—53:12 the suffering Servant was submissive, now the Lord was revealed as a conquering warrior. Verse 21 concludes that the goal is the Spirit of God filling the lives and relationships of people.

13 rebellion and treachery against the LORD,
    turning our backs[d] on our God,
  fomenting oppression[e] and revolt,
    uttering lies[f] our hearts have conceived.
14 So justice is driven back,
    and righteousness[g] stands at a distance;
  truth[h] has stumbled in the streets,
    honesty cannot enter.
15 Truth is nowhere to be found,
    and whoever shuns evil becomes a prey.

The LORD looked and was displeased
    that there was no justice.
16 He saw that there was no one,[i]
  he was appalled that there was no one to intervene;
so his own arm worked salvation[j] for him,
  and his own righteousness sustained him.
17 He put on righteousness as his breastplate,[k]
  and the helmet[l] of salvation on his head;
he put on the garments[m] of vengeance
  and wrapped himself in zeal[n] as in a cloak.
18 According to what they have done,
  so will he repay
wrath to his enemies
  and retribution to his foes;
he will repay the islands their due.
19 From the west,[o] men will fear the name of the LORD,
  and from the rising of the sun,[p] they will revere his glory.
For he will come like a pent-up flood
  that the breath of the LORD drives along.[a]

20 "The Redeemer will come to Zion,
  to those in Jacob who repent of their sins,"[q]
               declares the LORD.

21 "As for me, this is my covenant with them," says the LORD. "My Spirit,[r] who is on you, and my words that I have put in your mouth will not depart from your mouth, or from the mouths of your children, or from the mouths of their descendants from this time on and forever," says the LORD.

The Glory of Zion

60   "Arise,[s] shine, for your light[t] has come,
    and the glory of the LORD rises upon you.
2 See, darkness covers the earth
    and thick darkness[u] is over the peoples,
  but the LORD rises upon you

---

[a] 19 Or *When the enemy comes in like a flood, / the Spirit of the LORD will put him to flight*

59:13
[d] Pr 30:9; Mt 10:33; Tit 1:16 [e] Isa 5:7 [f] Mk 7:21-22

59:14
[g] Isa 1:21 [h] Isa 48:1

59:16
[i] Isa 41:28 / Ps 98:1; Isa 63:5

59:17
[k] Eph 6:14 [l] Eph 6:17; 1Th 5:8 [m] Isa 63:3 [n] Isa 9:7

59:19
[o] Isa 49:12 [p] Ps 113:3

59:20
[q] Ac 2:38-39; Ro 11:26-27*

59:21
[r] Isa 11:2; 44:3

60:1
[s] Isa 52:2 [t] Eph 5:14

60:2
[u] Jer 13:16; Col 1:13

📖 Too many people in the church have come to believe that Romans 7 is the end of the matter—that God has forgiven our sins but is helpless to deliver us from sinning. But that chapter is the lead-in to Romans 8, much as Isaiah 59:1–15 is the prelude to verses 16–21. Sin, as a way of behaving and relating, *can* be defeated in our lives because of what God has done for us in the Divine Warrior, Jesus Christ. Intimacy can be restored in our relationship with God, truth can be returned to the public square (v. 14), and righteousness can fill our relationships with one another.

Isaiah 60:1–22

📖 Chapter 60 may be divided into four stanzas. (1) Verses 1–3 constitute a vividly poetic introduction, announcing the light emanating from God's glory (cf. 59:9–10). (2) Verses 4–9 focus on the return of Zion's dispersed sons and daughters, accompanied by the wealth of the world. (3) In verses 10–14 the kings of the oppressor nations submit to Zion. (4) Verses 15–22 demonstrate that God wouldn't cast off Israel forever but would fully restore her to himself.

Isaiah didn't foresee a day when Israel would "get it

and his glory appears over you.
3 Nations[v] will come to your light,
and kings[w] to the brightness of your dawn.

4 "Lift up your eyes and look about you:
All assemble[x] and come to you;
your sons come from afar,
and your daughters[y] are carried on the arm.[z]
5 Then you will look and be radiant,
your heart will throb and swell with joy;
the wealth on the seas will be brought to you,
to you the riches of the nations will come.
6 Herds of camels will cover your land,
young camels of Midian[a] and Ephah.[b]
And all from Sheba[c] will come,
bearing gold and incense[d]
and proclaiming the praise[e] of the LORD.
7 All Kedar's[f] flocks will be gathered to you,
the rams of Nebaioth will serve you;
they will be accepted as offerings on my altar,
and I will adorn my glorious temple.[g]

8 "Who are these[h] that fly along like clouds,
like doves to their nests?
9 Surely the islands[i] look to me;
in the lead are the ships of Tarshish,[a][j]
bringing[k] your sons from afar,
with their silver and gold,
to the honor of the LORD your God,
the Holy One of Israel,
for he has endowed you with splendor.[l]

10 "Foreigners[m] will rebuild your walls,
and their kings[n] will serve you.
Though in anger I struck you,
in favor I will show you compassion.[o]
11 Your gates[p] will always stand open,
they will never be shut, day or night,
so that men may bring you the wealth of the nations[q]—
their kings[r] led in triumphal procession.
12 For the nation or kingdom that will not serve[s] you will perish;
it will be utterly ruined.
13 "The glory of Lebanon[t] will come to you,
the pine, the fir and the cypress together,[u]
to adorn the place of my sanctuary;
and I will glorify the place of my feet.[v]

[a] 9 Or *the trading ships*

Cross references (left margin):

60:3
v Isa 45:14;
Rev 21:24
w Isa 49:23

60:4
x Isa 11:12
y Isa 43:6
z Isa 49:20-22

60:6
a Ge 25:2 b Ge 25:4
c Ps 72:10
d Isa 43:23; Mt 2:11
e Isa 42:10

60:7
f Ge 25:13 g ver 13;
Hag 2:3,7,9

60:8
h Isa 49:21

60:9
i Isa 11:11
j Isa 2:16 fn
k Isa 14:2; 43:6
l Isa 55:5

60:10
m Isa 14:1-2
n Isa 49:23;
Rev 21:24
o Isa 54:8

60:11
p ver 18; Isa 62:10;
Rev 21:25 q ver 5;
Rev 21:26
r Ps 149:8

60:12
s Isa 14:2

60:13
t Isa 35:2
u Isa 41:19
v 1Ch 28:2;
Ps 132:7

---

all together" and bring in God's kingdom. Rather, he anticipated that Israel would finally allow God to do his work in and through his people. The ultimate transformation the Savior produces isn't changing bronze into gold (v. 17) but changing people helpless in sin into righteous individuals who reflect their Creator's glory. What higher place than to be "the work of my hands, for the display of my splendor"? (v. 21). Thus, Israel would truly be a servant of the Lord.

There can be no question about Jesus' commission to us—to draw all nations to him, making them his disciples (Matt. 28:16–20). Isaiah stated that the nations will come to God when they see him "shining" in us. How does he do so? Chapters 56–59 are clear: God "shines" through us when his ethical life is reproduced in us by his grace—when we lay down our pride in submission to him, put the good of others ahead of our own religious accomplishments, and live lives that embody truth and justice. Are you truly letting your—or rather *his*—light shine?

14 The sons of your oppressors[w] will come bowing before you;
    all who despise you will bow down[x] at your feet
and will call you the City of the LORD,
    Zion[y] of the Holy One of Israel.

60:14
w Isa 14:2
x Isa 49:23; Rev 3:9
y Heb 12:22

15 "Although you have been forsaken[z] and hated,
    with no one traveling[a] through,
I will make you the everlasting pride[b]
    and the joy[c] of all generations.

60:15
z Isa 1:7-9; 6:12
a Isa 33:8 b Isa 4:2
c Isa 65:18

16 You will drink the milk of nations
    and be nursed[d] at royal breasts.
Then you will know that I, the LORD, am your Savior,
    your Redeemer,[e] the Mighty One of Jacob.

60:16
d Isa 49:23;
66:11,12
e Isa 59:20

17 Instead of bronze I will bring you gold,
    and silver in place of iron.
Instead of wood I will bring you bronze,
    and iron in place of stones.
I will make peace your governor
    and righteousness your ruler.
18 No longer will violence be heard in your land,
    nor ruin or destruction within your borders,
but you will call your walls Salvation[f]
    and your gates Praise.

60:18
f Isa 26:1

19 The sun will no more be your light by day,
    nor will the brightness of the moon shine on you,
for the LORD will be your everlasting light,[g]
    and your God will be your glory.[h]
20 Your sun[i] will never set again,
    and your moon will wane no more;
the LORD will be your everlasting light,
    and your days of sorrow[j] will end.

60:19
g Rev 22:5
h Zec 2:5;
Rev 21:23
60:20
i Isa 30:26
j Isa 35:10

21 Then will all your people be righteous[k]
    and they will possess[l] the land forever.
They are the shoot I have planted,[m]
    the work of my hands,[n]
    for the display of my splendor.[o]
22 The least of you will become a thousand,
    the smallest a mighty nation.
I am the LORD;
    in its time I will do this swiftly."

60:21
k Rev 21:27
l Ps 37:11,22;
Isa 57:13; 61:7
m Mt 15:13
n Isa 19:25; 29:23;
Eph 2:10 o Isa 52:1

The Year of the LORD's Favor

61 The Spirit[p] of the Sovereign LORD is on me,
    because the LORD has anointed[q] me
    to preach good news to the poor.[r]
He has sent me to bind up[s] the brokenhearted,
    to proclaim freedom for the captives[t]
    and release from darkness for the prisoners,[a]
2 to proclaim the year of the LORD's favor[u]
    and the day of vengeance[v] of our God,

61:1
p Isa 11:2 q Ps 45:7
r Mt 11:5; Lk 7:22
s Isa 57:15
t Isa 42:7; 49:9

61:2
u Isa 49:8;
Lk 4:18-19*
v Isa 34:8

a 1 Hebrew; Septuagint *the blind*

Isaiah 61:1–11

📖 This chapter introduces us again to the means by which God's people will be enabled to live righteous lives, which will in turn draw the nations to God: through the Anointed One, the Messiah. Verses 1–7 present the benefits the Messiah's people will receive. In verses 8–9 God speaks, making it explicit that he desires covenant righteousness and that he alone makes that righteousness possible. Finally, the servant people break into a psalm of praise to God, who makes them a righteous people in the sight of the nations (vv. 10–11).

The 13 Shackles

61:1–3a

Poverty has more to do with *relationships* than *resources*, with *power* than *possessions*. The fall resulted in alienation from God and distorted relationships, out of which arise oppression, conflict, apathy, isolation, prejudice, moral confusion, and the deprivations and hardships we call poverty. Poverty occurs in three dimensions—relationships with God (spiritual), humanity (social), and the environment (physical).

The gospel alone addresses the relationship issues that keep people shackled in poverty. At least 13 specific shackles bind the poor:

> **The gospel alone addresses the relationship issues that keep people shackled in poverty.**

1. *Power elites limit their options.* People with "god-complexes" exist in every sphere of human activity. They owe their status to the contrast between their condition and that of those at the opposite end of the spectrum.
2. *Society's mainstream views the poor as non-factors*—a self-fulfilling prophecy: "Non-factors" can't influence societal change.
3. *The community of the poor isolates them from the rest of society.* It not only fails to act like a community but prevents the poor from seeking community elsewhere.
4. When traditional networks of caring break down, the poor turn to outsiders. But *professional caregivers fail to genuinely love those* they are hired to serve. True compassion is lost on the way to good intentions.
5. *The poor live in physical isolation from the rest of society.* They can't compete economically for the choice locations, and the non-poor have no reason to seek them out.
6. *The poor live in areas vulnerable to natural disasters.* And in virtually every disaster, they take the longest to recover—at best a position of vulnerability.
7. *The poor live in increasing dependence on an environment in decline.* They are more dependent on the physical environment for their livelihood and thus more subject to negative changes in that environment.
8. *The poor are rendered physically weak by their living conditions.* They live at the edge of survival, with no safety margin.
9. *The poor are fed distorted interpretations of history by the powerful.* Often illiterate and nonanalytic, they allow the telling and retelling of ancient and modern myths to govern their views of past and future. They become pawns in the hands of the history-spinners, with little hope of becoming history-makers.
10. *The poor falsely believe there is no hope for meaningful change.* Hope is more than a feeling or state of mind. It's an attitude or frame of reference that enormously influences the choices, directions, and destinies of individuals, communities, and nations.
11. *The poor develop the habit of equating their identity with their poverty.* Poverty becomes the only legacy left behind for ensuing generations.
12. *The poor tolerate abuse because they think it's normal.* The powerful learn to divide them against each other, while the poor learn to keep a safe distance from the powerful instead of confronting them or collaborating with them for change.
13. *The poor are in bondage to rebellious spiritual forces* whose aim is to control their actions and attitudes, defame God, and keep humans alienated from him.

The Good News is that Jesus came to proclaim freedom and health to *all* people. When we understand the gospel in its full breadth and all its dimensions, we see that God has a plan to reverse the effects of the fall. When put into practice by men and women of faith, it brings justice for the oppressed, healing for the weak, compassion for the needy, and reconciliation for the alienated.

Jayakumar Christian, country director of World Vision India

to comfort[w] all who mourn,
3   and provide for those who grieve in Zion—
to bestow on them a crown of beauty
    instead of ashes,
the oil of gladness
    instead of mourning,
and a garment of praise
    instead of a spirit of despair.
They will be called oaks of righteousness,
    a planting of the LORD
    for the display of his splendor.[x]

4 They will rebuild the ancient ruins[y]
    and restore the places long devastated;
they will renew the ruined cities
    that have been devastated for generations.
5 Aliens[z] will shepherd your flocks;
    foreigners will work your fields and vineyards.
6 And you will be called priests[a] of the LORD,
    you will be named ministers of our God.
You will feed on the wealth[b] of nations,
    and in their riches you will boast.

7 Instead of their shame
    my people will receive a double[c] portion,
and instead of disgrace

61:2
w Isa 57:18; Mt 5:4

61:3
x Isa 60:20-21

61:4
y Isa 49:8;
Eze 36:33; Am 9:14

61:5
z Isa 14:1-2

61:6
a Ex 19:6; 1Pe 2:5
b Isa 60:11

61:7
c Isa 40:2; Zec 9:12

This text was quoted by Jesus in his first sermon (Luke 4), declaring that he was the fulfillment of its Messianic hope. The Good News of the gospel isn't only that our sins are forgiven but also that our lives and relationships can be transformed. The captives are freed, the broken-hearted are comforted, and the poor receive provision. Faith in Christ, the Messiah, is for the purpose of changing us into Christ's (and thus God's) likeness. Forgiveness is only the means. The end is that we will live out the righteousness of God *by putting our faith in action*.

Snapshots

   61:1–3

Bob Pierce

Robert Willard (Bob) Pierce (1914–1978) was the founder of both World Vision and Samaritan's Purse. As a youth evangelist in Los Angeles and Seattle, the young Pierce became known through his involvement in the burgeoning Youth for Christ movement, after which he was ordained by the Church of the Nazarene.

Sent overseas on preaching assignments in China and Korea, Pierce was deeply touched by the needs he observed there. He founded World Vision in 1950 as a result of his personal global vision. The new organization sponsored orphans, helped train indigenous church leaders, constructed hospitals, provided aid to refugees and war and disaster victims, and ultimately became the world's largest Christian relief and development agency. World Vision now works in nearly 100 countries, serving millions of needy children and their families annually.

> "**Let** my heart be broken with the things that break the heart of God."

Pierce's memorable words, "Let my heart be broken with the things that break the heart of God," demonstrated his compassion for hurting people everywhere. For Pierce, need was equivalent to mandate. Having resigned from World Vision in 1967, Pierce established Samaritan's Pursue, which he headed until his death in 1978 of leukemia.

they will rejoice in their inheritance;
and so they will inherit a double portion in their land,
and everlasting joy will be theirs.

61:8
d Ps 11:7; Isa 5:16
e Isa 55:3

8 "For I, the LORD, love justice; [d]
I hate robbery and iniquity.
In my faithfulness I will reward them
and make an everlasting covenant [e] with them.
9 Their descendants will be known among the nations
and their offspring among the peoples.
All who see them will acknowledge
that they are a people the LORD has blessed."

61:10
f Isa 25:9; Hab 3:18
g Ps 132:9; Isa 52:1
h Isa 49:18;
Rev 21:2

10 I delight greatly in the LORD;
my soul rejoices [f] in my God.
For he has clothed me with garments of salvation
and arrayed me in a robe of righteousness, [g]
as a bridegroom adorns his head like a priest,
and as a bride [h] adorns herself with her jewels.

61:11
i Ps 85:11

11 For as the soil makes the sprout come up
and a garden causes seeds to grow,
so the Sovereign LORD will make righteousness [i] and praise
spring up before all nations.

Zion's New Name

62:1
j Isa 1:26

62 For Zion's sake I will not keep silent,
for Jerusalem's sake I will not remain quiet,
till her righteousness [j] shines out like the dawn,
her salvation like a blazing torch.

62:2
k Isa 52:10; 60:3
l ver 4,12

2 The nations [k] will see your righteousness,
and all kings your glory;
you will be called by a new name [l]
that the mouth of the LORD will bestow.

62:3
m Isa 28:5;
Zec 9:16; 1Th 2:19

3 You will be a crown [m] of splendor in the LORD's hand,
a royal diadem in the hand of your God.

62:4
n Isa 54:6
o Jer 32:41;
Zep 3:17
p Jer 3:14;
Hos 2:19

4 No longer will they call you Deserted, [n]
or name your land Desolate.
But you will be called Hephzibah, [a]
and your land Beulah [b];
for the LORD will take delight [o] in you,
and your land will be married. [p]
5 As a young man marries a maiden,
so will your sons [c] marry you;

62:5
q Isa 65:19

as a bridegroom rejoices over his bride,
so will your God rejoice [q] over you.

---

[a] 4 *Hephzibah* means *my delight is in her.*   [b] 4 *Beulah* means *married.*   [c] 5 Or *Builder*

Isaiah 62:1–12

In this statement of God's joy in his people, the idea of the display of his handiwork before the nations is never far from the surface. Just as Israel had been a butt of Gentile jokes, she had become the object of Gentile praise and wonder. The ends of the earth would hear God's proclamation that a Savior had come to Zion. People everywhere have a choice: They can come to the city that is now "sought after" to share in its salvation, or they can continue to set themselves against it and be reduced to becoming its servants.

As we become a part of God's people, we discover our true value. When the church is functioning as it should, each of us playing our part in the complex dance, we find ourselves. We don't have to be told that we have worth. We know it. Like the people of Israel contributing to the building of the tabernacle, we each, moved by the Spirit, have something to contribute (Ex. 35:20–29). Those on the outside look in with wonder and longing, just as God says the nations will look in upon his redeemed people.

⁶ I have posted watchmen[r] on your walls, O Jerusalem;
   they will never be silent day or night.
You who call on the LORD,
   give yourselves no rest,
⁷ and give him no rest[s] till he establishes Jerusalem
   and makes her the praise of the earth.

⁸ The LORD has sworn by his right hand
   and by his mighty arm:
"Never again will I give your grain[t]
   as food for your enemies,
and never again will foreigners drink the new wine
   for which you have toiled;
⁹ but those who harvest it will eat it
   and praise the LORD,
and those who gather the grapes will drink it
   in the courts of my sanctuary."

¹⁰ Pass through, pass through the gates![u]
   Prepare the way for the people.
Build up, build up the highway![v][w]
   Remove the stones.
Raise a banner[x] for the nations.

¹¹ The LORD has made proclamation
   to the ends of the earth:
"Say to the Daughter of Zion,[y]
   'See, your Savior comes![z]
See, his reward is with him,
   and his recompense accompanies him.'"[a]
¹² They will be called[b] the Holy People,[c]
   the Redeemed[d] of the LORD;
and you will be called Sought After,
   the City No Longer Deserted.[e]

God's Day of Vengeance and Redemption

63 Who is this coming from Edom,
   from Bozrah,[f] with his garments stained crimson?
Who is this, robed in splendor,
   striding forward in the greatness of his strength?

"It is I, speaking in righteousness,
   mighty to save."[g]

² Why are your garments red,
   like those of one treading the winepress?

³ "I have trodden the winepress[h] alone;
   from the nations no one was with me.
I trampled them in my anger
   and trod them down in my wrath;[i]
their blood spattered my garments,[j]
   and I stained all my clothing.
⁴ For the day of vengeance was in my heart,

62:6 r Isa 52:8; Eze 3:17
62:7 s Mt 15:21-28; Lk 18:1-8
62:8 t Dt 28:30-33; Isa 1:7; Jer 5:17
62:10 u Isa 60:11 v Isa 57:14 w Isa 11:16 x Isa 11:10
62:11 y Zec 9:9; Mt 21:5 z Rev 22:12 a Isa 40:10
62:12 b ver 4 c 1Pe 2:9 d Isa 35:9 e Isa 42:16
63:1 f Am 1:12 g Zep 3:17
63:3 h Rev 14:20; 19:15 i Isa 22:5 j Rev 19:13

Isaiah 63:1–6

The nation of Edom, and one of its leading cities, Bozrah, represented a world that hated God's people (cf. 34:6–7,9–15). Why couldn't anyone assist the Lord in bringing judgment against the wicked (63:3,5)? Because he alone didn't have to die for his own sins (cf. 53:4–10); no one else could make a similar claim. He alone is the righteous Judge, the only sinless One. But this isn't destruction for its own sake. It's for the purpose of making "redemption" and "salvation" (63:4–5) available.

and the year of my redemption has come.

5 I looked, but there was no one[k] to help,
    I was appalled that no one gave support;
so my own arm[l] worked salvation for me,
    and my own wrath sustained me.[m]

6 I trampled the nations in my anger;
    in my wrath I made them drunk[n]
    and poured their blood[o] on the ground."

Praise and Prayer

7 I will tell of the kindnesses[p] of the LORD,
    the deeds for which he is to be praised,
    according to all the LORD has done for us—
yes, the many good things he has done
    for the house of Israel,
according to his compassion[q] and many kindnesses.

8 He said, "Surely they are my people,[r]
    sons who will not be false to me";
    and so he became their Savior.

9 In all their distress he too was distressed,
    and the angel of his presence[s] saved them.
In his love and mercy he redeemed[t] them;
    he lifted them up and carried[u] them
    all the days of old.

10 Yet they rebelled[v]
    and grieved his Holy Spirit.[w]
So he turned and became their enemy[x]
    and he himself fought against them.

11 Then his people recalled[a] the days of old,
    the days of Moses and his people—
where is he who brought them through the sea,[y]
    with the shepherd of his flock?
Where is he who set
    his Holy Spirit[z] among them,
12 who sent his glorious arm of power
    to be at Moses' right hand,
who divided the waters[a] before them,
    to gain for himself everlasting renown,

Cross references (left margin):

63:5
k Isa 41:28
l Ps 44:3; 98:1
m Isa 59:16

63:6
n Isa 29:9 o Isa 34:3

63:7
p Isa 54:8 q Ps 51:1;
Eph 2:4

63:8
r Isa 51:4

63:9
s Ex 33:14
t Dt 7:7-8
u Dt 1:31

63:10
v Ps 78:40
w Ps 51:11;
Ac 7:51; Eph 4:30
x Ps 106:40

63:11
y Ex 14:22,30
z Nu 11:17

63:12
a Ex 14:21-22;
Isa 11:15

---

a 11 Or *But may he recall*

As Christians, we look forward to the day when sin will be completely defeated (cf. Rev. 19:11–16). How can we make a place in our lives for what we know must be destroyed in the end if Christ is to reign? How can we act as though our personal sin is unimportant while corporate sin is a terrible evil? How can we condemn promiscuity while winking an eye at those who gouge the poor? How can I excuse my sins while condemning yours? If Christ is the Divine Warrior, who will eventually triumph over sin in the world at large, the time is now to let him defeat sin in our own lives and help us hate it in all its forms.

Isaiah 63:7—64:12

In this passage, Isaiah lamented the human failure to do what's right and questioned why God would allow this condition to persist. The prophet complained that God was far from his people, isolated in holiness

and glory, and petitioned him to come to their aid. But while God is able to break down time and space barriers to make his people righteous, their unrighteousness in this case prevented him from hearing the petition. Surely, Isaiah pleaded, God could break the cycle, stop the punishment, and restore them to himself.

Much like the ancient Israelites, we tend to see ourselves as victims of fate. "This is just the way I am," we sigh. "If God would break in and make me different, things would be better." If we think that redemption means having our personalities "zapped," we misunderstand God's creative role. We need to be cleansed and purified. With our cooperation, he wants to free us from the blights in our personalities that hinder our uniqueness. God's power is unleashed in us when we step toward him in faith and do what we need to do to crucify our self-will—his enemy.

¹³who led[b] them through the depths?
  Like a horse in open country,
    they did not stumble;[c]
¹⁴like cattle that go down to the plain,
    they were given rest by the Spirit of the Lord.
  This is how you guided your people
    to make for yourself a glorious name.

¹⁵Look down from heaven[d] and see
    from your lofty throne,[e] holy and glorious.
  Where are your zeal[f] and your might?
    Your tenderness and compassion[g] are withheld from us.
¹⁶But you are our Father,
    though Abraham does not know us
    or Israel acknowledge[h] us;
  you, O Lord, are our Father,
    our Redeemer[i] from of old is your name.
¹⁷Why, O Lord, do you make us wander from your ways
    and harden our hearts so we do not revere[j] you?
  Return[k] for the sake of your servants,
    the tribes that are your inheritance.
¹⁸For a little while your people possessed your holy place,
    but now our enemies have trampled down your sanctuary.[l]
¹⁹We are yours from of old;
    but you have not ruled over them,
    they have not been called by your name.[a]

64

Oh, that you would rend the heavens[m] and come down,[n]
    that the mountains[o] would tremble before you!
²As when fire sets twigs ablaze
    and causes water to boil,
  come down to make your name known to your enemies
    and cause the nations to quake[p] before you!
³For when you did awesome[q] things that we did not expect,
    you came down, and the mountains trembled before you.
⁴Since ancient times no one has heard,
    no ear has perceived,
  no eye has seen any God besides you,
    who acts on behalf of those who wait for him.[r]
⁵You come to the help of those who gladly do right,[s]
    who remember your ways.
  But when we continued to sin against them,
    you were angry.
    How then can we be saved?
⁶All of us have become like one who is unclean,
    and all our righteous[t] acts are like filthy rags;
  we all shrivel up like a leaf,[u]
    and like the wind our sins sweep us away.
⁷No one[v] calls on your name
    or strives to lay hold of you;
  for you have hidden[w] your face from us
    and made us waste away[x] because of our sins.

⁸Yet, O Lord, you are our Father.[y]
    We are the clay, you are the potter;[z]
    we are all the work of your hand.
⁹Do not be angry[a] beyond measure, O Lord;

---

[a] 19 Or *We are like those you have never ruled, / like those never called by your name*

Reference column:

63:13
[b] Dt 32:12
[c] Jer 31:9

63:15
[d] Dt 26:15;
Ps 80:14 [e] Ps 123:1
[f] Isa 9:7; 26:11
[g] Jer 31:20;
Hos 11:8

63:16
[h] Job 14:21
[i] Isa 41:14; 44:6

63:17
[j] Isa 29:13
[k] Nu 10:36

63:18
[l] Ps 74:3-8

64:1
[m] Ps 18:9; 144:5
[n] Mic 1:3
[o] Ex 19:18

64:2
[p] Ps 99:1; Jer 5:22;
33:9
64:3
[q] Ps 65:5

64:4
[r] Isa 30:18;
1Co 2:9*
64:5
[s] Isa 26:8

64:6
[t] Isa 46:12; 48:1
[u] Ps 90:5-6

64:7
[v] Isa 59:4
[w] Dt 31:18;
Isa 1:15; 54:8
[x] Isa 9:18

64:8
[y] Isa 63:16
[z] Isa 29:16

64:9
[a] Isa 57:17; 60:10

64:9
b Isa 43:25

do not remember our sins [b] forever.
Oh, look upon us, we pray,
    for we are all your people.
10 Your sacred cities have become a desert;
    even Zion is a desert, Jerusalem a desolation.

64:11
c Ps 74:3-7 d La 1:7,
10

11 Our holy and glorious temple, [c] where our fathers praised you,
    has been burned with fire,
    and all that we treasured [d] lies in ruins.

64:12
e Ps 74:10-11;
Isa 42:14 f Ps 83:1

12 After all this, O LORD, will you hold yourself back? [e]
    Will you keep silent [f] and punish us beyond measure?

Judgment and Salvation

65:1
g Hos 1:10;
Ro 9:24-26; 10:20*
h Eph 2:12

65 "I revealed myself to those who did not ask for me;
    I was found by those who did not seek me. [g]
To a nation [h] that did not call on my name,
    I said, 'Here am I, here am I.'

65:2
i Isa 1:2,23;
Ro 10:21*
j Ps 81:11-12;
Isa 66:18

2 All day long I have held out my hands
    to an obstinate people, [i]
who walk in ways not good,
    pursuing their own imaginations [j]—

65:3
k Job 1:11 l Isa 1:29

3 a people who continually provoke me
    to my very face, [k]
offering sacrifices in gardens [l]
    and burning incense on altars of brick;

65:4
m Lev 11:7

4 who sit among the graves
    and spend their nights keeping secret vigil;
who eat the flesh of pigs, [m]
    and whose pots hold broth of unclean meat;

65:5
n Mt 9:11; Lk 7:39;
18:9-12

5 who say, 'Keep away; don't come near me,
    for I am too sacred [n] for you!'
Such people are smoke in my nostrils,
    a fire that keeps burning all day.

65:6
o Ps 50:3
p Jer 16:18
q Ps 79:12
65:7
r Isa 22:14 s Ex 20:5
t Isa 57:7

6 "See, it stands written before me:
    I will not keep silent [o] but will pay back [p] in full;
    I will pay it back into their laps [q]—
7 both your sins [r] and the sins of your fathers," [s]
    says the LORD.
"Because they burned sacrifices on the mountains
    and defied me on the hills, [t]
I will measure into their laps
    the full payment for their former deeds."

8 This is what the LORD says:

"As when juice is still found in a cluster of grapes
    and men say, 'Don't destroy it,
    there is yet some good in it,'

Isaiah 65:1-16

These verses constitute God's answer to the preceding lament. He responded to the real issue: the people's continuing rebellion. They not only sought to please him with insincere worship but even flaunted their unfaithful idolatry. They relied on their status as God's elect while continuing to live in self-willed, self-serving sin. They called themselves his servants—but they definitely were not.

If we really have a loving relationship with God, we will want to express that love in every way, from meeting together with Christian brothers and sisters, to worshiping him in the most profound ways possible, to telling others about him, to reaching out to the exploited and vulnerable for him, to working for justice in the world. If external behaviors are offered in place of a loving, servant heart, they are worthless. But if a loving, servant heart doesn't express itself in external behaviors, we are deceiving ourselves.

so will I do in behalf of my servants;
  I will not destroy them all.
⁹ I will bring forth descendants *u* from Jacob,
  and from Judah those who will possess *v* my mountains;
my chosen people will inherit them,
  and there will my servants live. *w*
¹⁰ Sharon *x* will become a pasture for flocks,
  and the Valley of Achor *y* a resting place for herds,
for my people who seek *z* me.

¹¹ "But as for you who forsake *a* the LORD
  and forget my holy mountain,
who spread a table for Fortune
  and fill bowls of mixed wine for Destiny,
¹² I will destine you for the sword, *b*
  and you will all bend down for the slaughter;
for I called but you did not answer, *c*
  I spoke but you did not listen. *d*
You did evil in my sight
  and chose what displeases me."

¹³ Therefore this is what the Sovereign LORD says:

"My servants will eat, *e*
  but you will go hungry;
my servants will drink,
  but you will go thirsty; *f*
my servants will rejoice,
  but you will be put to shame. *g*
¹⁴ My servants will sing
  out of the joy of their hearts,
but you will cry out *h*
  from anguish of heart
  and wail in brokenness of spirit.
¹⁵ You will leave your name
  to my chosen ones as a curse; *i*
the Sovereign LORD will put you to death,
  but to his servants he will give another name.
¹⁶ Whoever invokes a blessing in the land
  will do so by the God of truth; *j*
he who takes an oath in the land
  will swear *k* by the God of truth.
For the past troubles will be forgotten
  and hidden from my eyes.

65:9 *u* Isa 45:19 *v* Am 9:11-15 *w* Isa 32:18
65:10 *x* Isa 35:2 *y* Jos 7:26 *z* Isa 51:1
65:11 *a* Dt 29:24-25; Isa 1:28
65:12 *b* Isa 27:1 *c* Pr 1:24-25; Isa 41:28; 66:4 *d* 2Ch 36:15-16; Jer 7:13
65:13 *e* Isa 1:19 *f* Isa 41:17 *g* Isa 44:9
65:14 *h* Mt 8:12; Lk 13:28
65:15 *i* Zec 8:13
65:16 *j* Ps 31:5 *k* Isa 19:18

Isaiah 65:17–25

The "new heavens and . . . new earth," while remaining in continuity with what has been, will be a completely new expression of that reality. The tragedies of this world need not be repeated. God's people can experience the reality of joy without that of weeping, the delight of birth without the despair of death, the satisfaction of building without the fear of destruction. Isaiah's words weren't just a poetic expression of the certainty of future justice but a prediction of actual events in a still coming age.

This passage pictures a "perfect world" from God's viewpoint. It's one of community, harmony, tranquility, rejoicing, abundance, long life, productivity, and blessing. Rather than merely an utopian ideal, it portrays God's inevitable future for his creation.

Because the new heaven and the new earth are coming, we can be bold in our obedience today. All acts of service to the poor, of justice, and of compassion are expressions of the coming future. This certain hope floods our lives with meaning and purpose.

Jesus pointed out that "the kingdom of heaven is within [us]" (Luke 17:21). This is one way the people of the "nations" will come to understand the love of their Creator and ultimately accept his Messiah.

New Heavens and a New Earth

65:17
l Isa 66:22;
2Pe 3:13
m Isa 43:18;
Jer 3:16
65:18
n Ps 98:1-9;
Isa 25:9

17 "Behold, I will create
new heavens and a new earth.[l]
The former things will not be remembered,[m]
nor will they come to mind.

18 But be glad and rejoice[n] forever
in what I will create,
for I will create Jerusalem to be a delight
and its people a joy.

65:19
o Isa 35:10; 62:5
p Isa 25:8; Rev 7:17

19 I will rejoice[o] over Jerusalem
and take delight in my people;
the sound of weeping and of crying[p]
will be heard in it no more.

65:20
q Ecc 8:13

20 "Never again will there be in it
an infant who lives but a few days,
or an old man who does not live out his years;[q]
he who dies at a hundred
will be thought a mere youth;
he who fails to reach[a] a hundred
will be considered accursed.

65:21
r Isa 32:18
s Isa 37:30;
Am 9:14

21 They will build houses[r] and dwell in them;
they will plant vineyards and eat their fruit.[s]

22 No longer will they build houses and others live in them,
or plant and others eat.

65:22
t Ps 92:12-14
u Ps 21:4; 91:16

For as the days of a tree,[t]
so will be the days[u] of my people;
my chosen ones will long enjoy
the works of their hands.

23 They will not toil in vain
or bear children doomed to misfortune;

65:23
v Dt 28:3-12;
Isa 61:9 *w* Ac 2:39

for they will be a people blessed[v] by the Lord,
they and their descendants[w] with them.

65:24
x Isa 55:6
y Da 9:20-23; 10:12
65:25
z Isa 11:6
a Ge 3:14; Mic 7:17

24 Before they call[x] I will answer;
while they are still speaking[y] I will hear.

25 The wolf and the lamb[z] will feed together,
and the lion will eat straw like the ox,
but dust will be the serpent's[a] food.
They will neither harm nor destroy
on all my holy mountain,"
says the Lord.

Judgment and Hope

66:1
b Mt 23:22
c 1Ki 8:27;
Mt 5:34-35
d 2Sa 7:7;
Jn 4:20-21;
Ac 7:49*; 17:24

66 This is what the Lord says:

"Heaven is my throne,[b]
and the earth is my footstool.[c]
Where is the house[d] you will build for me?
Where will my resting place be?

---

a 20 Or / *the sinner who reaches*

Isaiah 66:1–24

Isaiah concluded his book in characteristic fashion, with an interplay of the twin themes of judgment and hope. Instead of ending with the previous passage's vision of the new heaven and new earth, the book brings a grim note of judgment directly to the fore in its closing words. But judgment isn't what God wants, and that is equally clear. The response of the nations to Israel's mission will be to restore the last remnants of the Israelites to Israel in a final, great ingathering. Yet verse 21 represents Isaiah's strongest statement that the election of Israel won't be for Israel alone but for the world: Some individuals from the Gentile nations will become "priests and Levites."

65:17–25

God's will is for everyone to have decent housing and a good paying job. When the kingdom of God comes on Earth as it is in heaven, there will be an end to infant mortality, and the elderly will live out their long lives in health and well-being. In the world God envisions for us, mothers won't worry about what will become of their sons and daughters when they come of age. Environmental irresponsibility won't scar the land, and there will be a restoration of the peaceable kingdom God created for us.

This new world the prophet envisioned is a world God is even now initiating through those who are willing to follow the Spirit's leading in transforming the world that is. Christians are increasingly catching this vision and promoting God's holistic salvation that not only provides eternal life but also challenges all God's people to love the oppressed and look for justice in this present age.

Millard Fuller is one such visionary. More than 25 years ago his life was in shambles. He was a millionaire without meaning, with a marriage on the rocks. In desperation, he and his wife Linda sought a new lifestyle. They recommitted themselves to Jesus and to each other and determined to make their lives count. Eventually the Fullers founded Habitat for Humanity, a Christian organization that calls on volunteers to build houses for the poor. These houses are then purchased by people who provide no down payment and obtain long-term mortgages without interest. The Fullers contend that the "no interest principle" is mandated by Scripture for loans to the poor (Ex. 22:25). After 25 years, Habitat has completed over 100,000 homes worldwide and expects to construct as many more in less than ten years.

When a hurricane tore through Homestead, Florida, most of the homes were destroyed—except for the houses built by Habitat volunteers. When reporters asked Millard to explain this anomaly, he replied, with tongue in cheek, "It's because Habitat builds its houses on The Rock!" In reality, it was because the volunteers had "overbuilt" them. If a particular beam needed ten nails to be held in place, the uncertain builders had used fifteen. They had put extra cement in the foundations. In short, they had built stronger houses than knowledgeable builders would have deemed necessary.

Another venture that works toward realizing Isaiah's vision of God's kingdom is Opportunity International, a faith-based program that creates jobs for the poor in third world countries. In Philippine slums, impoverished Latin American barrios, and desolate African villages, Opportunity International gathers groups of potential entrepreneurs and, in the context of prayer and Bible study, helps them design and create micro businesses and cottage industries they can own and run themselves. Promoters of Opportunity International believe that fairly compensated employment enables the poor to escape permanently from poverty. During the past ten years, Opportunity International has created over two and a half million jobs!

> The Jesus who will complete his kingdom on the day of his coming is already at work through his people in the here and now.

Eastern College, an Evangelical school located in St. Davids, Pennsylvania, has recently established an urban campus in downtown Philadelphia with the express purpose of replicating the work of Opportunity International in urban America. Offering a specialized course of study, Eastern is training urban missionary entrepreneurs to create micro enterprises in "at risk" neighborhoods. Young people who might have earned money selling drugs are now gainfully employed in ventures that offer them dignity.

All the programs cited above are evidence that the Jesus who will complete his kingdom on the day of his coming is already at work through his people in the here and now (Phil. 1:6).

Tony Campolo, professor emeritus of sociology at Eastern College in St. Davids, Pennsylvania

66:2
e Isa 40:26;
Ac 7:50*
f Isa 57:15; Mt 5:3-
4; Lk 18:13-14
g Ezr 9:4

2 Has not my hand made all these things, e
and so they came into being?"

declares the LORD.

"This is the one I esteem:
he who is humble and contrite in spirit, f
and trembles at my word. g

66:3
h Isa 1:11 i Lev 2:2
j Isa 57:17

3 But whoever sacrifices a bull h
is like one who kills a man,
and whoever offers a lamb,
like one who breaks a dog's neck;
whoever makes a grain offering
is like one who presents pig's blood,
and whoever burns memorial incense, i
like one who worships an idol.
They have chosen their own ways, j
and their souls delight in their abominations;

66:4
k Pr 10:24 l Pr 1:24;
Jer 7:13 m 2Ki 21:2,
4,6 n Isa 65:12

4 so I also will choose harsh treatment for them
and will bring upon them what they dread. k
For when I called, no one answered, l
when I spoke, no one listened.
They did evil m in my sight
and chose what displeases me." n

66:5
o Ps 38:20;
Isa 60:15 p Lk 13:17

5 Hear the word of the LORD,
you who tremble at his word:
"Your brothers who hate o you,
and exclude you because of my name, have said,
'Let the LORD be glorified,
that we may see your joy!'
Yet they will be put to shame. p

66:6
q Isa 65:6; Joel 3:7

6 Hear that uproar from the city,
hear that noise from the temple!
It is the sound of the LORD
repaying q his enemies all they deserve.

66:7
r Isa 54:1
s Rev 12:5

7 "Before she goes into labor, r
she gives birth;
before the pains come upon her,
she delivers a son. s

66:8
t Isa 64:4

8 Who has ever heard of such a thing?
Who has ever seen t such things?
Can a country be born in a day
or a nation be brought forth in a moment?
Yet no sooner is Zion in labor
than she gives birth to her children.

66:9
u Isa 37:3

9 Do I bring to the moment of birth u
and not give delivery?" says the LORD.
"Do I close up the womb
when I bring to delivery?" says your God.

There *will* be a new heaven and a new earth (v. 22), and those who worship the one true God *will* participate in it. Whether or not we involve ourselves in those promises will be strictly up to us—a reality Isaiah wanted his *audience never to forget.*

The person who truly knows God humbly and joyously reflects God's life in his or her behavior. That

will never be possible as a result of human effort or performance but only as a consequence of complete reliance on him. God calls us today to showcase his righteous life in all our relationships. That can happen only as we live in so submissive a relationship to God that our will is utterly surrendered to the Holy Spirit, enabling his life to be lived through us. That is what heaven will be— and it begins now.

10 "Rejoice[v] with Jerusalem and be glad for her,
    all you who love[w] her;
rejoice greatly with her,
    all you who mourn over her.
11 For you will nurse[x] and be satisfied
    at her comforting breasts;
you will drink deeply
    and delight in her overflowing abundance."

12 For this is what the LORD says:

"I will extend peace to her like a river,[y]
    and the wealth[z] of nations like a flooding stream;
you will nurse and be carried[a] on her arm
    and dandled on her knees.
13 As a mother comforts her child,
    so will I comfort[b] you;
and you will be comforted over Jerusalem."

14 When you see this, your heart will rejoice
    and you will flourish like grass;
the hand of the LORD will be made known to his servants,
    but his fury[c] will be shown to his foes.
15 See, the LORD is coming with fire,
    and his chariots[d] are like a whirlwind;
he will bring down his anger with fury,
    and his rebuke[e] with flames of fire.
16 For with fire[f] and with his sword[g]
    the LORD will execute judgment upon all men,
    and many will be those slain by the LORD.

17 "Those who consecrate and purify themselves to go into the gardens,[h] following the one in the midst of[a] those who eat the flesh of pigs[i] and rats and other abominable things—they will meet their end[j] together," declares the LORD.

18 "And I, because of their actions and their imaginations, am about to come[b] and gather all nations and tongues, and they will come and see my glory.

19 "I will set a sign[k] among them, and I will send some of those who survive to the nations—to Tarshish,[l] to the Libyans[c] and Lydians[m] (famous as archers), to Tubal[n] and Greece, and to the distant islands[o] that have not heard of my fame or seen my glory.[p] They will proclaim my glory among the nations. 20 And they will bring all your brothers, from all the nations, to my holy mountain in Jerusalem as an offering to the LORD—on horses, in chariots and wagons, and on mules and camels," says the LORD. "They will bring them, as the Israelites bring their grain offerings, to the temple of the LORD in ceremonially clean vessels.[q] 21 And I will select some of them also to be priests[r] and Levites," says the LORD.

22 "As the new heavens and the new earth[s] that I make will endure before me," declares the LORD, "so will your name and descendants endure.[t] 23 From one New Moon to another and from one Sabbath[u] to another, all mankind will come and bow down[v] before me," says the LORD. 24 "And they will go out and look upon the dead bodies of those who rebelled against me; their worm[w] will not die, nor will their fire be quenched,[x] and they will be loathsome to all mankind."

---

a 17 Or *gardens behind one of your temples, and*   b 18 The meaning of the Hebrew for this clause is uncertain.   c 19 Some Septuagint manuscripts *Put* (Libyans); Hebrew *Pul*

66:10 v Dt 32:43; Ro 15:10 w Ps 26:8
66:11 x Isa 60:16
66:12 y Isa 48:18 z Ps 72:3; Isa 60:5; 61:6 a Isa 60:4
66:13 b Isa 40:1; 2Co 1:4
66:14 c Isa 10:5
66:15 d Ps 68:17 e Ps 9:5
66:16 f Isa 30:30 g Isa 27:1
66:17 h Isa 1:29 i Lev 11:7 j Ps 37:20; Isa 1:28
66:19 k Isa 11:10; 49:22 l Isa 2:16 m Eze 27:10 n Ge 10:2 o Isa 11:11 p 1Ch 16:24; Isa 24:15
66:20 q Isa 52:11
66:21 r Ex 19:6; Isa 61:6; 1Pe 2:5,9
66:22 s Isa 65:17; Heb 12:26-27; 2Pe 3:13; Rev 21:1 t Jn 10:27-29; 1Pe 1:4-5
66:23 u Eze 46:1-3 v Isa 19:21
66:24 w Isa 14:11 x Isa 1:31; Mk 9:48*

INTRODUCTION TO

Jeremiah

AUTHOR
The book itself states that its contents are "the words of Jeremiah son of Hilkiah" (1:1). The prophet Jeremiah dictated most of his prophecies to his secretary, Baruch, who wrote them down word for word (36:4). Chapter 52, an addendum (see 51:64) that is almost identical to 2 Kings 24:18—25:30, may have been added by a later editor.

DATE WRITTEN
Jeremiah wrote these words over the course of his ministry (626–585 B.C.). Chapter 52 was added sometime after Jehoiachin's release from captivity (c. 560 B.C.).

ORIGINAL READERS
Jeremiah was written to the people of Judah in the southern kingdom and to Jerusalem, its capital city.

TIMELINE

	1300BC	1200	1100	1000	900	800	700	600	500	400
Division of the kingdom (930 B.C.)										
Ministries of Elijah and Elisha in Israel (c. 875-797 B.C.)										
Ministries of Amos and Hosea in Israel (c. 760-715 B.C.)										
Ministries of Micah and Isaiah in Judah (c. 742-681 B.C.)										
Exile of Israel (722 B.C.)										
Jeremiah's ministry in Judah (c. 626-585 B.C.)										
Fall of Jerusalem (586 B.C.)										
Book of Jeremiah written (c. 626-585 B.C.)										

THEMES
Jeremiah describes God's just judgment on the people of Judah for their continuing sin. It includes the following themes:

1. *Repentance.* Jeremiah called God's people to repent and return to God in order to avoid divine judgment (e.g., 7:1–15). The people responded negatively (5:20–25; 8:4–7). As a consequence, some of the oracles assert that the coming judgment was certain, with no possibility of repentance (6:16–21).

2. *Judgment.* Jeremiah announced that Israel's covenant rebellion would bring judgment (11:1—13:27). The prophet pointed out that the people had broken the covenant by their idolatry (2:11; 7:30; 9:13–14; 10:1–16; 16:10–13; 22:9; 29:10; 44:2–3,8,17–19,25), their attempts to save themselves through military alliances (2:36), and their injustice and ethical violations (7:5–11; 9:3–11; 17:19–27; 21:11—22:30). Their sin would be punished (5:20–29).

3. *Restoration.* Jeremiah's prophetic vision extended beyond judgment to restoration. Jeremiah 30:1—33:26 (called the "book of consolation") describes a new covenant (31:31–33)—better than those that had preceded it. While these salvation oracles would come to preliminary fulfillment with the defeat of Babylon and the return of the people in 538 B.C., Jesus himself ultimately fulfilled the new covenant (1 Cor. 11:25; 2 Cor. 3:6; Heb. 9:15; 12:24). Jeremiah reminds us that faith demands action. Covenant living requires a faithful response to God in the form of proper worship and of helping, not exploiting, the vulnerable.

FAITH IN ACTION

The pages of Jeremiah contain life lessons and role models of faith—people who challenge believers to put their faith in action.

Role Models

- JEREMIAH (1:6–8) recognized his weaknesses and his youth but obeyed God's call, trusting God to rescue him. What does this suggest about God's ability to use you?

- AHIKAM (26:24) supported Jeremiah and prevented the priests and officials from putting Jeremiah to death. Do you selflessly stand up for what's right?

- ELASAH AND GEMARIAH (29:3) were entrusted with Jeremiah's letter to the exiles who had been carried away by Nebuchadnezzar. Are you trustworthy?

- BARUCH (36:1–8) did "everything" (36:8) Jeremiah instructed. He was faithful, even when his loyalty meant danger. How far are you willing to go in your service to others in Christ's body?

- THE RECABITES (35:12–19) were an example to the other Israelites of obedience and faithfulness to God through the generations. What kind of track record does your family have? How are you preparing the coming generations to follow God?

- EBED-MELECH (38:6–13), a Cushite (Ethiopian), feared God more than his peers among Judah's palace officials. He intervened with the king and rescued Jeremiah from certain death. What's your response to injustice? Do you use whatever position you may hold as a platform for doing good? Can you resist peer pressure and take an unpopular stand for what's right?

- SHAPHAN (40:6), instrumental in bringing the lost Word of God to King Josiah (2 Chron. 34:15–21), evidently instilled godly values in his family. His sons Ahikam and Elasah helped Jeremiah, as did his grandson, Gedaliah. Do you lead your family to respect and assist God's servants?

Challenges

- Don't make excuses as to why God can't use you (1:6). God made you (1:5) and will give you the resources you need to serve him (1:7–9).

- As a "bearer of his name," do you consistently represent God well (14:9; 15:16)?

- Evaluate how you personally and your country as a whole have rebelled against God (5:23) in your treatment of people. Have you grown deceptive, greedy, complacent? Have you ignored the defenseless and poor (5:27–29; 22:3,16–7)?

- Be honest with God, revealing to him your fears and complaints (12:1–4; 15:15–18; 18:19–20; 20:7–18). But when he directs you, trust and obey him (17:16; 20:9–12).

- Obey God and his standards rather than adopting society's standards as your own (35:15–19).

- Use any position you might hold to do good (23:10; 26:24; 38:6–13).

- Resolve to do all within your power to prevent children from being sacrificed in any way or for any reason (32:33–35).

- Leave a rich legacy within your family of respect and care for God's servants (40:6).

1195

OUTLINE

I. Jeremiah's Call (1)
II. Warnings and Exhortations to Judah (2–29)
III. Promises of Restoration (30–33)
IV. Historical Insertion (34–35)
V. The Sufferings of Jeremiah (36–38)
VI. Fall of Jerusalem and Following Events (39–45)
VII. Judgment Against the Nations (46–51)
VIII. Historical Appendix (52)

1:1
a Jos 21:18;
1Ch 6:60;
Jer 32:7-9
1:3
b 2Ki 23:34
c 2Ki 24:17;
Jer 39:2 d Jer 52:15

1 The words of Jeremiah son of Hilkiah, one of the priests at Anathoth [a] in the territory of Benjamin. [2] The word of the LORD came to him in the thirteenth year of the reign of Josiah son of Amon king of Judah, [3] and through the reign of Jehoiakim [b] son of Josiah king of Judah, down to the fifth month of the eleventh year of Zedekiah [c] son of Josiah king of Judah, when the people of Jerusalem went into exile. [d]

The Call of Jeremiah

[4] The word of the LORD came to me, saying,

1:5
e Ps 139:16
f Isa 49:1 g ver 10;
Jer 25:15-26

[5] "Before I formed you in the womb I knew [a][e] you,
    before you were born [f] I set you apart;
    I appointed you as a prophet to the nations. [g]"

1:6
h Ex 4:10; 6:12
i 1Ki 3:7
1:8
j Eze 2:6 k Jos 1:5;
Jer 15:20
1:9
l Isa 6:7 m Ex 4:12

[6] "Ah, Sovereign LORD," I said, "I do not know how to speak; [h] I am only a child." [i] [7] But the LORD said to me, "Do not say, 'I am only a child.' You must go to everyone I send you to and say whatever I command you. [8] Do not be afraid [j] of them, for I am with you [k] and will rescue you," declares the LORD.

[9] Then the LORD reached out his hand and touched [l] my mouth and said to me, "Now, I have put my words in your mouth. [m] [10] See, today I appoint you over nations and kingdoms to uproot and tear down, to destroy and overthrow, to build and to plant." [n]

1:10
n Jer 18:7-10; 24:6;
31:4,28

[a] 5 Or *chose*

Jeremiah 1:1–3

🔾 The 40-plus years of Jeremiah's ministry (c. 627–584 B.C.) covered some of the most tumultuous and tragic events of Judah's history. Included among them were rebellions against foreign control, the death of Judahite kings at the hands of foreign powers, the downfall and virtual destruction of the nation itself, and the forced displacement of the prophet to Egypt in its aftermath.

Jeremiah's prophecy did more than interpret historical events. It offered judgment on shared failures and promises that God would see his people through the consequences of their sin to a point of healing. This pattern of judgment and redemption was meaningful for later generations, who saw themselves addressed as God's people of their day.

🔾 For the people of God today, the timely nature of Jeremiah's ministry can be viewed as a corporate (community) address, inviting the church to consider God's judging and redeeming activities. For us individually, Jeremiah's words provide testimony that God uses people and events to advance his purposes and to instruct us as his followers. Who has God used in a special way in your life? How is he using you?

Jeremiah 1:4–19

🔾 Jeremiah's call to prophetic ministry is similar to other Old Testament accounts. God prevailed upon Moses in spite of his objections (Ex. 3:1–15). Ezekiel swallowed a scroll given to him through divine revelation (Ezek. 2:1—3:11), signifying that his words would have a divine origin. In this passage God touched Jeremiah's mouth, declaring, "I have put my words in your mouth" (v. 9; cf. Isa. 6:1–8). Human weakness is no excuse before God's expressed will to grant a person the words to say and the opportunities to speak.

🔾 Jeremiah's call is relevant to contemporary debates over abortion, euthanasia, assisted suicide, and the value of human life. Life as God's gift is subject to his decisions; the womb is the home of a *person* he knows and values. Jeremiah's bitterness over mistreatment by his contemporaries (and, in his mind, even by God) would eventually lead him to curse the day of his birth (20:14–18; cf. 15:10). God would disagree with Jeremiah's verdict that his life was worthless. Have you ever felt as though yours had no value? How has God used you since?

Righteous Kings

1:1–3

The theme of righteous kings, aided by powerful religious figures, reforming wayward people groups is common in Middle Eastern and Asian history. Examples are Asoka in Buddhist India, Constantine in Christian Rome, and Saladin in Islamic Palestine.

Typically, these righteous kings didn't attempt to become religious leaders themselves by usurping power from bhikkhus, priests, or imams. Instead, they attempted the reform of declining and/or wayward religious institutions. They rebuilt dilapidated religious buildings—or constructed new ones. They replaced immoral religious leaders with moral successors. They convened councils of religious leaders to more fully articulate doctrine in the face of new challenges. Often, they reemphasized religion's privileged place in the life of their cultures. In general, they acted as the consciences of religiously drifting people.

The beginning of the book of Jeremiah is set in the context of such a king, Josiah. With the help of a prophet, Jeremiah, Josiah attempted to restore Judah's political and spiritual life. Ultimately, though, Josiah's reforms failed. Their temporary successes were brought into sharp relief by the growing failures of his successors to maintain the people's fidelity to their agreement with God.

How are we to understand this series of events? Should we pray for a modern "king/prophet" pairing to rise up and cleanse us? What would make them successful?

Biblical stories of king-prophet alliances attempting to keep their societies on the straight and narrow shared a common theme: Spiritual faithfulness is more important than political good fortune. Though prophets frequently labeled political meltdowns as God's judgment and political successes as evidence of his blessings, they managed to elevate the importance of the spiritual over the political. Thus, a powerful king was brought low by Nathan's spiritual judgment (2 Sam. 12:1–14). And even though Josiah's political strategies ultimately failed at the hands of his Egyptian killers, his attempts at moral reform earned him recognition as a ruler without equal (2 Kings 23:25).

> **T**he Bible is clear that "politics" by any name is temporal and that a relationship with God ushers us into eternity.

But to read the prophets is to note again and again that spiritual faithfulness and political good fortune went hand-in-hand in a cause-and-effect relationship. The spiritual task of faithfully upholding the human end of the covenant led to God's protection from political enemies and economic ruin. And vice versa. But the common wisdom that spirituality was more important than political expertise didn't quite correlate with God's judgments. We are left feeling that a broader understanding is needed.

It's important for us to recognize that the identification between spiritual faithfulness and political success was much greater in Jeremiah's day than in ours. Uniquely in all of history, Israel was, at least ideally, to function as a true theocracy—rulership by God himself, with management by priests. Even after the institution of the monarchy, it was clear that Israel's kings ruled by God's choice and at his discretion. No political ruler today comes close to having such a mandate.

Even after we recognize this difference, we need to clearly prioritize the two factors: spirituality first, politics second. Or better, politics as a fruit of spirituality, not its root or synonym. The Bible is clear that "politics" by any name is temporal and that a relationship with God ushers us into eternity. Blessings along the way are nice, and to some extent needed for the journey. But they are just rest stops. Great "kings" were like hotel managers, making life more comfortable and faithful, but always ready to move people on—and eventually to move on themselves.

Frances Elizabeth Caroline Willard

Frances Willard (1839–1898), corresponding secretary and president of the Women's Christian Temperance Union, combined religious and secular forces to lead the first mass women's movement. The WCTU was founded in 1874 in Cleveland, Ohio, with the aim of educating people, especially young people, on the harmful effects of alcohol, narcotic drugs, and tobacco. It became known chiefly for its crusade against alcohol, a fight that resulted in the 18th Amendment to the Constitution of the United States, passed in 1919, which prohibited the manufacture, import, export, and sale of alcoholic beverages. This amendment remained in force from 1920 to 1933, when the 21st Amendment repealed it.

Willard organized the temperance movement and lectured tirelessly on its behalf. She traveled to all 48 states, many of them more than once.

Willard was a hero of the faith in spite of the fact that the war on alcohol was as much a secular campaign as a religious one. One of her great contributions, in fact, was in organizing a model social movement that harmonized religious and secular energies in a positive campaign. These same energies had threatened to tear apart the abolitionist movement, and Willard learned from its mistakes. *Lesson: Secular and religious institutions can form effective partnerships when the goal is clearly defined and clearly in the best interest of society at large.*

> "**W**oman will bless and brighten every place she enters, and will enter every place."

For Willard, alcohol was both a religious (moral) problem and a societal one. She came from Methodist abstainer roots. But she lived in a culture in which alcohol abuse was rampant. According to the United States Bureau of the Census, Americans spent $1.8 billion on alcoholic beverages in 1909, in contrast to $2 billion on all other products, including non-alcoholic beverages, combined.

Willard and the WCTU, however, didn't limit their activities to this massive social problem. They also took on women's suffrage, education, child welfare, and world peace. By 1896, for example, 25 of the 39 departments into which the national WCTU was organized were dealing with non-temperance issues. Clearly the WCTU lived (and lives) by its motto, "Woman will bless and brighten every place she enters, and will enter every place." *Lesson: No problems are just "religious" or just secular, and all are potential ministry opportunities for would-be heroes of the faith.*

This reality of Willard's ministry has created something of a dilemma for those of us who would like to learn from the way she expressed her faith. Should she be seen as a religious worker or as a social reformer? This is a little like asking whether Jeremiah, in attempting to bring God's message to Judah, was a prophet or a political irritant. Surely he was both. Jeremiah was called by God to perform a ministry that was motivated by kingdom values but also had enormous social implications. His call was to tear down evil social structures and build up good ones. "I appoint you over nations and kingdoms to uproot and tear down, to destroy and overthrow, to build and plant" (Jer. 1:10).

Frances Willard as an early feminist? Perhaps.

Frances Willard as an organizer of social movements to tear down the bad and build up the good? Yes.

Frances Willard as a social revivalist in her own right? Definitely.

11The word of the LORD came to me: "What do you see, Jeremiah?" *o*
"I see the branch of an almond tree," I replied.
12The LORD said to me, "You have seen correctly, for I am watching*a* to see that my word is fulfilled."
13The word of the LORD came to me again: "What do you see?" *p*
"I see a boiling pot, tilting away from the north," I answered.
14The LORD said to me, "From the north disaster will be poured out on all who live in the land. 15I am about to summon all the peoples of the northern kingdoms," declares the LORD.

> "Their kings will come and set up their thrones
>   in the entrance of the gates of Jerusalem;
> they will come against all her surrounding walls
>   and against all the towns of Judah. *q*
> 16I will pronounce my judgments on my people
>   because of their wickedness*r* in forsaking me,*s*
> in burning incense to other gods*t*
>   and in worshiping what their hands have made.

17"Get yourself ready! Stand up and say to them whatever I command you. Do not be terrified*u* by them, or I will terrify you before them. 18Today I have made you*v* a fortified city, an iron pillar and a bronze wall to stand against the whole land—against the kings of Judah, its officials, its priests and the people of the land. 19They will fight against you but will not overcome you, for I am with you*w* and will rescue*x* you," declares the LORD.

Israel Forsakes God

2 The word of the LORD came to me: 2"Go and proclaim in the hearing of Jerusalem:

> " 'I remember the devotion of your youth,*y*
>   how as a bride you loved me
> and followed me through the desert,*z*
>   through a land not sown.
> 3Israel was holy*a* to the LORD, *b*
>   the firstfruits*c* of his harvest;
> all who devoured*d* her were held guilty,*e*
>   and disaster overtook them,' "

declares the LORD.

> 4Hear the word of the LORD, O house of Jacob,
>   all you clans of the house of Israel.

5This is what the LORD says:

> "What fault did your fathers find in me,
>   that they strayed so far from me?
> They followed worthless idols
>   and became worthless*f* themselves.
> 6They did not ask, 'Where is the LORD,
>   who brought us up out of Egypt*g*
> and led us through the barren wilderness,

a 12 The Hebrew for *watching* sounds like the Hebrew for *almond tree.*

Reference column:
1:11 *o* Jer 24:3; Am 7:8
1:13 *p* Zec 4:2
1:15 *q* Jer 4:16; 9:11
1:16 *r* Dt 28:20 *s* Jer 17:13 *t* Jer 7:9; 19:4
1:17 *u* Eze 2:6
1:18 *v* Isa 50:7
1:19 *w* Jer 20:11 *x* ver 8
2:2 *y* Eze 16:8-14,60; Hos 2:15 *z* Dt 2:7
2:3 *a* Dt 7:6 *b* Ex 19:6 *c* Jas 1:18; Rev 14:4 *d* Isa 41:11; Jer 30:16 *e* Jer 50:7
2:5 *f* 2Ki 17:15
2:6 *g* Hos 13:4

Jeremiah 2:1—3:5 This passage is like a "sampler" whose topics will appear again and again. Its primary themes are Judah's defection from following the Lord and the importance of obeying his revealed will. Judah's personification as a prostitute or adulteress involved more than an issue of worship. Mention of the blood of the innocent poor whose lives had been consumed by others' sinful activities (2:34) introduces an element of social criticism. Injustice and unrighteousness flow from a wrong understanding of who God is and what he desires from his covenant people.

2:6
h Dt 8:15 i Dt 32:10

2:7
j Nu 13:27;
Dt 8:7-9; 11:10-12
k Ps 106:34-39;
Jer 16:18

2:8
l Jer 4:22
m Jer 23:13
n Jer 16:19

2:9
o Eze 20:35-36;
Mic 6:2

2:11
p Isa 37:19;
Jer 16:20
q Ps 106:20;
Ro 1:23

2:13
r Ps 36:9; Jn 4:14

2:14
s Ex 4:22

2:15
t Jer 4:7; 50:17
u Isa 1:7

2:16
v Isa 19:13
w Jer 43:7-9

2:17
x Jer 4:18

2:18
y Isa 30:2 z Jos 13:3

through a land of deserts[h] and rifts,[i]
a land of drought and darkness,[a]
a land where no one travels and no one lives?'

[7] I brought you into a fertile land
to eat its fruit and rich produce.[j]
But you came and defiled my land
and made my inheritance detestable.[k]

[8] The priests did not ask,
'Where is the LORD?'
Those who deal with the law did not know me;[l]
the leaders rebelled against me.
The prophets prophesied by Baal,[m]
following worthless idols.[n]

[9] "Therefore I bring charges[o] against you again,"

declares the LORD.

"And I will bring charges against your children's children.

[10] Cross over to the coasts of Kittim[b] and look,
send to Kedar[c] and observe closely;
see if there has ever been anything like this:

[11] Has a nation ever changed its gods?
(Yet they are not gods[p] at all.)
But my people have exchanged their[d] Glory[q]
for worthless idols.

[12] Be appalled at this, O heavens,
and shudder with great horror,"

declares the LORD.

[13] "My people have committed two sins:
They have forsaken me,
the spring of living water,[r]
and have dug their own cisterns,
broken cisterns that cannot hold water.

[14] Is Israel a servant, a slave[s] by birth?
Why then has he become plunder?

[15] Lions[t] have roared;
they have growled at him.
They have laid waste[u] his land;
his towns are burned and deserted.

[16] Also, the men of Memphis[e][v] and Tahpanhes[w]
have shaved the crown of your head.[f]

[17] Have you not brought this on yourselves[x]
by forsaking the LORD your God
when he led you in the way?

[18] Now why go to Egypt[y]
to drink water from the Shihor[g]?[z]
And why go to Assyria
to drink water from the River[h]?

[19] Your wickedness will punish you;

---

a 6 Or *and the shadow of death*   b 10 That is, Cyprus and western coastlands   c 10 The home of
Bedouin tribes in the Syro-Arabian desert   d 11 Masoretic Text; an ancient Hebrew scribal tradition
my   e 16 Hebrew *Noph*   f 16 Or *have cracked your skull*   g 18 That is, a branch of the Nile
h 18 That is, the Euphrates

📖 Judah's situation doesn't have to be reproduced in every detail for the prophet's message to be
relevant. God's people today can read the criticisms
and expectations of ancient Judah and determine
where they still apply. These messages from God question Judah's fitness to serve as God's covenant partner—the validity of her identity as his beloved bride. A
congregation can approach this text as a guide to evaluate its own spiritual fitness. So can you.

your backsliding[a] will rebuke[b] you.
Consider then and realize
    how evil and bitter[c] it is for you
when you forsake the LORD your God
    and have no awe[d] of me,"
                        declares the Lord, the LORD Almighty.

20 "Long ago you broke off your yoke[e]
    and tore off your bonds;
    you said, 'I will not serve you!'
Indeed, on every high hill[f]
    and under every spreading tree[g]
    you lay down as a prostitute.
21 I had planted[h] you like a choice vine[i]
    of sound and reliable stock.
How then did you turn against me
    into a corrupt,[j] wild vine?
22 Although you wash yourself with soda
    and use an abundance of soap,
    the stain of your guilt is still before me,"
                        declares the Sovereign LORD.

23 "How can you say, 'I am not defiled;[k]
    I have not run after the Baals'?[l]
See how you behaved in the valley;[m]
    consider what you have done.
You are a swift she-camel
    running[n] here and there,
24 a wild donkey[o] accustomed to the desert,
    sniffing the wind in her craving—
    in her heat who can restrain her?
Any males that pursue her need not tire themselves;
    at mating time they will find her.
25 Do not run until your feet are bare
    and your throat is dry.
But you said, 'It's no use!
    I love foreign gods,[p]
    and I must go after them.'

26 "As a thief is disgraced[q] when he is caught,
    so the house of Israel is disgraced—
they, their kings and their officials,
    their priests and their prophets.
27 They say to wood, 'You are my father,'
    and to stone,[r] 'You gave me birth.'
They have turned their backs to me
    and not their faces;[s]
yet when they are in trouble,[t] they say,
    'Come and save us!'
28 Where then are the gods[u] you made for yourselves?
    Let them come if they can save you
    when you are in trouble![v]
For you have as many gods
    as you have towns,[w] O Judah.

29 "Why do you bring charges against me?
    You have all[x] rebelled against me,"
                        declares the LORD.

30 "In vain I punished your people;
    they did not respond to correction.

2:19
a Jer 3:11,22
b Isa 3:9; Hos 5:5
c Job 20:14;
Am 8:10 d Ps 36:1

2:20
e Lev 26:13
f Isa 57:7; Jer 17:2
g Dt 12:2

2:21
h Ex 15:17 i Ps 80:8
j Isa 5:4

2:23
k Pr 30:12 l Jer 9:14
m Jer 7:31 n ver 33;
Jer 31:22

2:24
o Jer 14:6

2:25
p Dt 32:16;
Jer 3:13; 14:10

2:26
q Jer 48:27

2:27
r Jer 3:9
s Jer 18:17; 32:33
t Jdg 10:10;
Isa 26:16

2:28
u Isa 45:20
v Dt 32:37
w 2Ki 17:29;
Jer 11:13

2:29
x Jer 5:1; 6:13;
Da 9:11

2:30
y Ne 9:26; Ac 7:52;
1Th 2:15

Your sword has devoured your prophets[y]
    like a ravening lion.

31 "You of this generation, consider the word of the LORD:

2:31
z Isa 45:19

"Have I been a desert to Israel
    or a land of great darkness?[z]
Why do my people say, 'We are free to roam;
    we will come to you no more'?
32 Does a maiden forget her jewelry,
    a bride her wedding ornaments?
Yet my people have forgotten me,
    days without number.
33 How skilled you are at pursuing love!
    Even the worst of women can learn from your ways.

2:34
a 2Ki 21:16
b Ex 22:2

34 On your clothes men find
    the lifeblood[a] of the innocent poor,
    though you did not catch them breaking in. [b]
Yet in spite of all this

2:35
c Jer 25:31
d 1Jn 1:8,10

35   you say, 'I am innocent;
    he is not angry with me.'
But I will pass judgment[c] on you
    because you say, 'I have not sinned.'[d]

2:36
e Jer 31:22
f Isa 30:2,3,7

36 Why do you go about so much,
    changing[e] your ways?
You will be disappointed by Egypt[f]
    as you were by Assyria.

2:37
g 2Sa 13:19
h Jer 37:7

37 You will also leave that place
    with your hands on your head, [g]
for the LORD has rejected those you trust;
    you will not be helped[h] by them.

3:1
i Dt 24:1-4
j Jer 2:20,25;
Eze 16:26,29

3 "If a man divorces[i] his wife
    and she leaves him and marries another man,
should he return to her again?
    Would not the land be completely defiled?
But you have lived as a prostitute with many lovers[j]—
    would you now return to me?"

                                declares the LORD.

3:2
k Ge 38:14;
Eze 16:25 l Jer 2:7

2 "Look up to the barren heights and see.
    Is there any place where you have not been ravished?
By the roadside[k] you sat waiting for lovers,
    sat like a nomad[a] in the desert.
You have defiled the land[l]
    with your prostitution and wickedness.

3:3
m Lev 26:19
n Jer 14:4
o Jer 6:15; 8:12;
Zep 3:5

3 Therefore the showers have been withheld, [m]
    and no spring rains[n] have fallen.
Yet you have the brazen look of a prostitute;
    you refuse to blush with shame.[o]

3:4
p ver 19 q Jer 2:2
3:5
r Ps 103:9;
Isa 57:16

4 Have you not just called to me:
    'My Father, [p] my friend from my youth, [q]
5 will you always be angry?[r]
    Will your wrath continue forever?'
This is how you talk,
    but you do all the evil you can."

a 2 Or an Arab

Unfaithful Israel

⁶During the reign of King Josiah, the LORD said to me, "Have you seen what faithless Israel has done? She has gone up on every high hill and under every spreading tree ˢ and has committed adultery ᵗ there. ⁷I thought that after she had done all this she would return to me but she did not, and her unfaithful sister ᵘ Judah saw it. ⁸I gave faithless Israel her certificate of divorce and sent her away because of all her adulteries. Yet I saw that her unfaithful sister Judah had no fear; ᵛ she also went out and committed adultery. ⁹Because Israel's immorality mattered so little to her, she defiled the land ʷ and committed adultery with stone ˣ and wood. ʸ ¹⁰In spite of all this, her unfaithful sister Judah did not return to me with all her heart, but only in pretense, ᶻ" declares the LORD.

¹¹The LORD said to me, "Faithless Israel is more righteous ᵃ than unfaithful ᵇ Judah. ¹²Go, proclaim this message toward the north: ᶜ

" 'Return, ᵈ faithless Israel,' declares the LORD,
    'I will frown on you no longer,
for I am merciful,' declares the LORD,
    'I will not be angry ᵉ forever.
¹³ Only acknowledge ᶠ your guilt—
    you have rebelled against the LORD your God,
you have scattered your favors to foreign gods ᵍ
    under every spreading tree, ʰ
    and have not obeyed ⁱ me,' "

declares the LORD.

¹⁴"Return, ʲ faithless people," declares the LORD, "for I am your husband. I will choose you—one from a town and two from a clan—and bring you to Zion. ¹⁵Then I will give you shepherds ᵏ after my own heart, who will lead you with knowledge and understanding. ¹⁶In those days, when your numbers have increased greatly in the land," declares the LORD, "men will no longer say, 'The ark of the covenant of the LORD.' It will never enter their minds or be remembered; ˡ it will not be missed, nor will another one be made. ¹⁷At that time they will call Jerusalem The Throne ᵐ of the LORD, and all nations will gather in Jerusalem to honor ⁿ the name of the LORD. No longer will they follow the stubbornness of their evil hearts. ᵒ ¹⁸In those days the house of Judah will join the house of Israel, ᵖ and together ᑫ they will come from a northern ʳ land to the land ˢ I gave your forefathers as an inheritance.

¹⁹"I myself said,

" 'How gladly would I treat you like sons
    and give you a desirable land,
    the most beautiful inheritance of any nation.'
I thought you would call me 'Father' ᵗ
    and not turn away from following me.
²⁰But like a woman unfaithful to her husband,
    so you have been unfaithful to me, O house of Israel,"

declares the LORD.

²¹A cry is heard on the barren heights, ᵘ

3:6	ˢ Jer 17:2 ᵗ Jer 2:20
3:7	ᵘ Eze 16:46
3:8	ᵛ Eze 16:47; 23:11
3:9	ʷ ver 2 ˣ Isa 57:6 ʸ Jer 2:27
3:10	ᶻ Jer 12:2
3:11	ᵃ Eze 16:52; 23:11 ᵇ ver 7
3:12	ᶜ 2Ki 17:3-6 ᵈ ver 14; Jer 31:21,22; Eze 33:11 ᵉ Ps 86:15
3:13	ᶠ Dt 30:1-3; Jer 14:20; 1Jn 1:9 ᵍ Jer 2:25 ʰ Dt 12:2 ⁱ ver 25
3:14	ʲ Hos 2:19
3:15	ᵏ Ac 20:28
3:16	ˡ Isa 65:17
3:17	ᵐ Jer 17:12; Eze 43:7 ⁿ Isa 60:9 ᵒ Jer 11:8
3:18	ᵖ Hos 1:11 ᑫ Isa 11:13; Jer 50:4 ʳ Jer 16:15; 31:8 ˢ Am 9:15
3:19	ᵗ ver 4; Isa 63:16
3:21	ᵘ ver 2

Jeremiah 3:6—4:4

This section contains messages from God concerned with the faithless acts of Israel and Judah, their foolishness in rejecting the Lord, and calls to repentance. Israel and Judah are described as sisters who have both committed adultery against their spouse (cf. Ezek. 23). Sadly, Judah had learned nothing from Israel's fall to the Assyrians (cf. 2 Kings 17). Josiah was a godly, reforming king, but Judah's covenant renewal was short-lived and evidently superficial. Judah failed to return to the Lord "with all her heart" (3:10).

Christ's disciples are bound to him through his resurrection, and the working of the Holy Spirit is present within them and the church. Sin isn't just failure to observe a behavioral norm, but the breaking of a bond and an insult to our Lord. Spiritual adultery is a crime against grace—unfaithfulness against God who in Christ has called us into intimate fellowship and has formed the church as Christ's holy bride. How does this understanding impact your reading of this passage in Jeremiah?

the weeping and pleading of the people of Israel,
because they have perverted their ways
and have forgotten the LORD their God.

22 "Return, ᵛ faithless people;
I will cure ʷ you of backsliding."

"Yes, we will come to you,
for you are the LORD our God.
23 Surely the ⌞idolatrous⌟ commotion on the hills
and mountains is a deception;
surely in the LORD our God
is the salvation ˣ of Israel.

24 From our youth shameful ʸ gods have consumed
the fruits of our fathers' labor—
their flocks and herds,
their sons and daughters.

25 Let us lie down in our shame, ᶻ
and let our disgrace cover us.
We have sinned against the LORD our God,
both we and our fathers;
from our youth ᵃ till this day
we have not obeyed the LORD our God."

4 "If you will return ᵇ, O Israel,
return to me,"

declares the LORD.

"If you put your detestable idols ᶜ out of my sight
and no longer go astray,

2 and if in a truthful, just and righteous way
you swear, ᵈ 'As surely as the LORD lives,' ᵉ
then the nations will be blessed ᶠ by him
and in him they will glory."

3 This is what the LORD says to the men of Judah and to Jerusalem:

"Break up your unplowed ground ᵍ
and do not sow among thorns. ʰ

4 Circumcise yourselves to the LORD,
circumcise your hearts, ⁱ
you men of Judah and people of Jerusalem,
or my wrath ʲ will break out and burn like fire
because of the evil you have done—
burn with no one to quench ᵏ it.

Disaster From the North

5 "Announce in Judah and proclaim in Jerusalem and say:
'Sound the trumpet throughout the land!'
Cry aloud and say:
'Gather together!

Let us flee to the fortified cities!' ˡ
6 Raise the signal to go to Zion!
Flee for safety without delay!

Jeremiah 4:5–31

The prophet called Judah and Jerusalem to lament the approach of a foe from the north. This enemy was really the Lord, who came against his own people like a lion and whose blast of anger was like a searing wind. From Jeremiah's visionary perspective, the land-scape was transformed into something "formless and empty" (v. 23), as though judgment on Judah would undo creation's goodness and order (cf. Gen. 1:1,31). God would speak and judgment would come, just as surely as in the creation account God had spoken order out of chaos.

For I am bringing disaster from the north,[m]
    even terrible destruction."

⁷A lion[n] has come out of his lair;
    a destroyer of nations has set out.
He has left his place
    to lay waste[o] your land.
Your towns will lie in ruins[p]
    without inhabitant.
⁸So put on sackcloth,[q]
    lament and wail,
for the fierce anger[r] of the LORD
    has not turned away from us.

⁹"In that day," declares the LORD,
    "the king and the officials will lose heart,
the priests will be horrified,
    and the prophets will be appalled."[s]

¹⁰Then I said, "Ah, Sovereign LORD, how completely you have deceived[t] this people and Jerusalem by saying, 'You will have peace,'[u] when the sword is at our throats."

¹¹At that time this people and Jerusalem will be told, "A scorching wind[v] from the barren heights in the desert blows toward my people, but not to winnow or cleanse; ¹²a wind too strong for that comes from me.[a] Now I pronounce my judgments[w] against them."

¹³Look! He advances like the clouds,[x]
    his chariots[y] come like a whirlwind,[z]
his horses are swifter than eagles.[a]
    Woe to us! We are ruined!
¹⁴O Jerusalem, wash[b] the evil from your heart and be saved.
    How long will you harbor wicked thoughts?
¹⁵A voice is announcing from Dan,[c]
    proclaiming disaster from the hills of Ephraim.
¹⁶"Tell this to the nations,
    proclaim it to Jerusalem:
'A besieging army is coming from a distant land,
    raising a war cry[d] against the cities of Judah.
¹⁷They surround[e] her like men guarding a field,
    because she has rebelled[f] against me,'"

declares the LORD.

¹⁸"Your own conduct and actions[g]
    have brought this upon you.[h]
This is your punishment.
    How bitter[i] it is!
    How it pierces to the heart!"

¹⁹Oh, my anguish, my anguish![j]
    I writhe in pain.

---

[a] 12 Or comes at my command

Cross-references

4:6 [m] Jer 1:13-15; 50:3
4:7 [n] 2Ki 24:1; Jer 2:15 [o] Isa 1:7 [p] Jer 25:9
4:8 [q] Isa 22:12; Jer 6:26 [r] Jer 30:24
4:9 [s] Isa 29:9
4:10 [t] 2Th 2:11 [u] Jer 14:13
4:11 [v] Eze 17:10; Hos 13:15
4:12 [w] Jer 1:16
4:13 [x] Isa 19:1 [y] Isa 66:15 [z] Isa 5:28 [a] Dt 28:49; Hab 1:8
4:14 [b] Jas 4:8
4:15 [c] Jer 8:16
4:16 [d] Eze 21:22
4:17 [e] 2Ki 25:1,4 [f] Jer 5:23
4:18 [g] Ps 107:17; Isa 50:1 [h] Jer 2:17 [i] Jer 2:19
4:19 [j] Isa 16:11; 22:4; Jer 9:10

Jeremiah's message was in sync with that of fellow prophets like Isaiah, Amos, Hosea, Micah, and Ezekiel. Judgment begins with the "family of God" (cf. 1 Peter 4:17). No generation is guaranteed security when it stands in bold violation of God-given standards. This prophetic call for loyalty and obedience to the Lord has a flip side of judgment on a faithless and rebellious people.

There is great concern today about the decline of order and civility in society. Among many churches there is corresponding concern over the diminished morality and declining spiritual vitality of members. Does Jeremiah's vision of coming chaos point out where these trends will lead? His image of chaos stemmed spiritually from his deep involvement with a people who refused to obey divine standards and were skeptical that God would actually judge them. Does this scenario apply today?

Oh, the agony of my heart!
  My heart pounds within me,
  I cannot keep silent. [k]
For I have heard the sound of the trumpet;
  I have heard the battle cry. [l]

20 Disaster follows disaster; [m]
  the whole land lies in ruins.
In an instant my tents [n] are destroyed,
  my shelter in a moment.

21 How long must I see the battle standard
  and hear the sound of the trumpet?

22 "My people are fools; [o]
  they do not know me. [p]
They are senseless children;
  they have no understanding.
They are skilled in doing evil; [q]
  they know not how to do good." [r]

23 I looked at the earth,
  and it was formless and empty; [s]
and at the heavens,
  and their light was gone.

24 I looked at the mountains,
  and they were quaking; [t]
  all the hills were swaying.

25 I looked, and there were no people;
  every bird in the sky had flown away. [u]

26 I looked, and the fruitful land was a desert;
  all its towns lay in ruins
  before the LORD, before his fierce anger.

27 This is what the LORD says:

4:27
v Jer 5:10, 18;
12:12; 30:11; 46:28
4:28
w Jer 12:4, 11; 14:2;
Hos 4:3 x Isa 5:30;
50:3 y Nu 23:19
z Jer 23:20; 30:24

"The whole land will be ruined,
  though I will not destroy [v] it completely.
28 Therefore the earth will mourn [w]
  and the heavens above grow dark, [x]
because I have spoken and will not relent, [y]
  I have decided and will not turn back. [z]"

29 At the sound of horsemen and archers [a]
  every town takes to flight. [b]
Some go into the thickets;
  some climb up among the rocks.
All the towns are deserted; [c]
  no one lives in them.

30 What are you doing, [d] O devastated one?
  Why dress yourself in scarlet
  and put on jewels [e] of gold?
Why shade your eyes with paint? [f]
  You adorn yourself in vain.
Your lovers [g] despise you;
  they seek your life.

31 I hear a cry as of a woman in labor, [h]
  a groan as of one bearing her first child—
the cry of the Daughter of Zion gasping for breath, [i]
  stretching out her hands [j] and saying,

"Alas! I am fainting;
my life is given over to murderers."

Not One Is Upright

5 "Go up and down[k] the streets of Jerusalem,
look around and consider,
search through her squares.
If you can find but one person[l]
who deals honestly and seeks the truth,
I will forgive[m] this city.
[2] Although they say, 'As surely as the LORD lives,'[n]
still they are swearing falsely."

[3] O LORD, do not your eyes[o] look for truth?
You struck[p] them, but they felt no pain;
you crushed them, but they refused correction.[q]
They made their faces harder than stone[r]
and refused to repent.
[4] I thought, "These are only the poor;
they are foolish,
for they do not know[s] the way of the LORD,
the requirements of their God.
[5] So I will go to the leaders[t]
and speak to them;
surely they know the way of the LORD,
the requirements of their God."
But with one accord they too had broken off the yoke
and torn off the bonds.[u]
[6] Therefore a lion from the forest will attack them,
a wolf from the desert will ravage them,
a leopard[v] will lie in wait near their towns
to tear to pieces any who venture out,
for their rebellion is great
and their backslidings many.[w]

[7] "Why should I forgive you?
Your children have forsaken me
and sworn[x] by gods that are not gods.[y]
I supplied all their needs,
yet they committed adultery[z]
and thronged to the houses of prostitutes.
[8] They are well-fed, lusty stallions,
each neighing for another man's wife.[a]
[9] Should I not punish them for this?"[b]
declares the LORD.
"Should I not avenge myself
on such a nation as this?

5:1
[k] 2Ch 16:9;
Eze 22:30
[l] Ge 18:32
[m] Ge 18:24

5:2
[n] Jer 4:2

5:3
[o] 2Ch 16:9
[p] Isa 9:13
[q] Jer 2:30; Zep 3:2
[r] Jer 7:26; 19:15;
Eze 3:8-9

5:4
[s] Jer 8:7

5:5
[t] Mic 3:1,9
[u] Ps 2:3; Jer 2:20

5:6
[v] Hos 13:7
[w] Jer 30:14

5:7
[x] Jos 23:7; Zep 1:5
[y] Dt 32:21;
Jer 2:11; Gal 4:8
[z] Nu 25:1

5:8
[a] Jer 29:23;
Eze 22:11

5:9
[b] ver 29; Jer 9:9

Jeremiah 5:1–31

The prophet challenged the people to search Jerusalem for anyone who "deals honestly and seeks the truth" (v. 1). Compare this to Abraham's conversation with God about Sodom (Gen. 18:16–33). Apparently in this case no one fit the requirements. Jeremiah joined with other prophets in calling for social justice among a greedy, callous, and violent people.

Jeremiah's painful prophecies aren't at odds with the gospel but are part of its foundation, begin-

ning with the convictions that no one is righteous and that the wages of sin is death (Rom. 3:10; 6:23). Renewal can't begin until people recognize that corruption infects all human institutions. These prophecies of judgment insist that the hearers think seriously about human affairs. To paraphrase the prophet, the way a culture treats its poor, vulnerable, and suffering matters to God and should be a priority for his people. Is it one for you?

5:10
c Jer 4:27

10 "Go through her vineyards and ravage them,
   but do not destroy them completely. c
Strip off her branches,
   for these people do not belong to the LORD.

5:11
d Jer 3:20

11 The house of Israel and the house of Judah
   have been utterly unfaithful d to me,"

declares the LORD.

12 They have lied about the LORD;
   they said, "He will do nothing!
No harm will come to us; e
   we will never see sword or famine. f

5:12
e Jer 23:17
f 2Ch 36:16;
Jer 14:13
5:13
g Jer 14:15

13 The prophets g are but wind
   and the word is not in them;
   so let what they say be done to them."

14 Therefore this is what the LORD God Almighty says:

5:14
h Jer 1:9; Hos 6:5
i Jer 23:29

"Because the people have spoken these words,
   I will make my words in your mouth h a fire i
   and these people the wood it consumes.

5:15
j Dt 28:49; Isa 5:26;
Jer 4:16 k Isa 28:11

15 O house of Israel," declares the LORD,
   "I am bringing a distant nation j against you—
an ancient and enduring nation,
   a people whose language k you do not know,
   whose speech you do not understand.

16 Their quivers are like an open grave;
   all of them are mighty warriors.

5:17
l Jer 8:16
m Lev 26:16
n Jer 50:7,17
o Dt 28:32
p Dt 28:31
q Dt 28:33

17 They will devour l m your harvests and food,
   devour n o your sons and daughters;
they will devour p your flocks and herds,
   devour your vines and fig trees.
With the sword they will destroy
   the fortified cities in which you trust. q

5:18
r Jer 4:27
5:19
s Dt 29:24-26;
1Ki 9:9 t Jer 16:13
u Dt 28:48

18 "Yet even in those days," declares the LORD, "I will not destroy r you completely. 19 And when the people ask, s 'Why has the LORD our God done all this to us?' you
will tell them, 'As you have forsaken me and served foreign gods t in your own land,
so now you will serve foreigners u in a land not your own.'

20 "Announce this to the house of Jacob
   and proclaim it in Judah:
21 Hear this, you foolish and senseless people,
   who have eyes v but do not see,
   who have ears but do not hear: w

5:21
v Isa 6:10; Eze 12:2
w Mt 13:15;
Mk 8:18
5:22
x Dt 28:58

22 Should you not fear x me?" declares the LORD.
   "Should you not tremble in my presence?
I made the sand a boundary for the sea,
   an everlasting barrier it cannot cross.
The waves may roll, but they cannot prevail;
   they may roar, but they cannot cross it.

5:23
y Dt 21:18

23 But these people have stubborn and rebellious y hearts;
   they have turned aside and gone away.
24 They do not say to themselves,
   'Let us fear the LORD our God,

5:24
z Ps 147:8;
Joel 2:23
a Ge 8:22; Ac 14:17

who gives autumn and spring rains z in season,
   who assures us of the regular weeks of harvest.' a
25 Your wrongdoings have kept these away;
   your sins have deprived you of good.

26 "Among my people are wicked men
　who lie in wait[b] like men who snare birds
　and like those who set traps to catch men.
27 Like cages full of birds,
　their houses are full of deceit;[c]
　they have become rich[d] and powerful
28 　and have grown fat[e] and sleek.
　Their evil deeds have no limit;
　　they do not plead the case of the fatherless[f] to win it,
　　they do not defend the rights of the poor.[g]
29 Should I not punish them for this?"
　declares the LORD.
　"Should I not avenge myself
　　on such a nation as this?

30 "A horrible[h] and shocking thing
　has happened in the land:
31 The prophets prophesy lies,[i]
　the priests rule by their own authority,
and my people love it this way.
But what will you do in the end?

Jerusalem Under Siege

6 "Flee for safety, people of Benjamin!
　Flee from Jerusalem!
Sound the trumpet in Tekoa![j]
　Raise the signal over Beth Hakkerem![k]
For disaster looms out of the north,[l]
　even terrible destruction.
2 I will destroy the Daughter of Zion,
　so beautiful and delicate.
3 Shepherds[m] with their flocks will come against her;
　they will pitch their tents around[n] her,
　each tending his own portion."

4 "Prepare for battle against her!
　Arise, let us attack at noon![o]
But, alas, the daylight is fading,
　and the shadows of evening grow long.
5 So arise, let us attack at night
　and destroy her fortresses!"

6 This is what the LORD Almighty says:

"Cut down the trees[p]
　and build siege ramps[q] against Jerusalem.
This city must be punished;
　it is filled with oppression.
7 As a well pours out its water,

Side references

5:26
b Ps 10:8; Pr 1:11

5:27
c Jer 9:6 d Jer 12:1

5:28
e Dt 32:15
f Zec 7:10
g Isa 1:23; Jer 7:6

5:30
h Jer 23:14;
Hos 6:10
5:31
i Eze 13:6; Mic 2:11

6:1
j 2Ch 11:6
k Ne 3:14 l Jer 4:6

6:3
m Jer 12:10
n 2Ki 25:4; Lk 19:43

6:4
o Jer 15:8

6:6
p Dt 20:19-20
q Jer 32:24

Jeremiah 6:1–30

Jeremiah called the people to flee from the enemy (v. 1) and mourn for Jerusalem (v. 26). The effect of these calls was to remind future readers that Jeremiah had announced in advance the siege and fall of the city at the hands of the Babylonians.

Through Jeremiah, God asked the people to (re)consider the "good way," the "ancient paths," that lead to security (v. 16). The prophet, as mediator, represented both God and the people in conversation. While they rudely rejected divine guidance, God rejected their sacrifices in light of their moral and spiritual disobedience.

Jeremiah criticized his temple-going peers as representatives of an immoral society, specifically mentioning oppression, violence, destruction, greed, and deceit. His audience found God's message offensive. The same can be true today when a minister preaches about social sin, injustice, and the church's individual and communal responsibility to help right wrongs and minister to the suffering in Jesus' name. Are you open to such messages?

6:7
r Ps 55:9; Eze 7:11, 23 s Jer 20:8

so she pours out her wickedness.
Violence[r] and destruction[s] resound in her;
her sickness and wounds are ever before me.

6:8
t Eze 23:18; Hos 9:12

[8]Take warning, O Jerusalem,
or I will turn away[t] from you
and make your land desolate
so no one can live in it."

[9]This is what the LORD Almighty says:

"Let them glean the remnant of Israel
as thoroughly as a vine;
pass your hand over the branches again,
like one gathering grapes."

6:10
u Ac 7:51 v Jer 20:8

[10]To whom can I speak and give warning?
Who will listen to me?
Their ears are closed[a][u]
so they cannot hear.
The word[v] of the LORD is offensive to them;
they find no pleasure in it.

6:11
w Jer 7:20
x Job 32:20; Jer 20:9 y Jer 9:21

[11]But I am full of the wrath[w] of the LORD,
and I cannot hold it in.[x]

"Pour it out on the children in the street
and on the young men[y] gathered together;
both husband and wife will be caught in it,
and the old, those weighed down with years.

6:12
z Dt 28:30
a Jer 8:10; 38:22
b Isa 5:25

[12]Their houses will be turned over to others,[z]
together with their fields and their wives,[a]
when I stretch out my hand[b]
against those who live in the land,"

declares the LORD.

6:13
c Isa 56:11
d Jer 8:10

[13]"From the least to the greatest,
all are greedy for gain;[c]
prophets and priests alike,
all practice deceit.[d]

6:14
e Jer 4:10; 8:11; Eze 13:10

[14]They dress the wound of my people
as though it were not serious.
'Peace, peace,' they say,
when there is no peace.[e]

[15]Are they ashamed of their loathsome conduct?
No, they have no shame at all;
they do not even know how to blush.[f]

6:15
f Jer 3:3; 8:10-12

So they will fall among the fallen;
they will be brought down when I punish them,"

says the LORD.

[16]This is what the LORD says:

6:16
g Jer 18:15
h Ps 119:3
i Mt 11:29

"Stand at the crossroads and look;
ask for the ancient paths,[g]
ask where the good way[h] is, and walk in it,
and you will find rest[i] for your souls.
But you said, 'We will not walk in it.'

a 10 Hebrew uncircumcised

God evaluates cultures, nations, denominations, congregations, families, and individuals. We participate in society and help determine its character. We personally may be doing what's right, but groups to which we belong may need corrective measures to better reflect Christ in the world. What is your impact on society for good?

¹⁷I appointed watchmen^j over you and said,
    'Listen to the sound of the trumpet!'
But you said, 'We will not listen.'^k

¹⁸Therefore hear, O nations;
    observe, O witnesses,
    what will happen to them.
¹⁹Hear, O earth:^l
I am bringing disaster on this people,
    the fruit of their schemes,^m
because they have not listened to my words
    and have rejected my law.ⁿ
²⁰What do I care about incense from Sheba
    or sweet calamus^o from a distant land?
Your burnt offerings are not acceptable;^p
    your sacrifices^q do not please me."^r

²¹Therefore this is what the LORD says:

"I will put obstacles before this people.
    Fathers and sons alike will stumble^s over them;
    neighbors and friends will perish."

²²This is what the LORD says:

"Look, an army is coming
    from the land of the north;^t
a great nation is being stirred up
    from the ends of the earth.
²³They are armed with bow and spear;
    they are cruel and show no mercy.^u
They sound like the roaring sea
    as they ride on their horses;^v
they come like men in battle formation
    to attack you, O Daughter of Zion."

²⁴We have heard reports about them,
    and our hands hang limp.
Anguish^w has gripped us,
    pain like that of a woman in labor.^x
²⁵Do not go out to the fields
    or walk on the roads,
for the enemy has a sword,
    and there is terror on every side.^y
²⁶O my people, put on sackcloth^z
    and roll in ashes;^a
mourn with bitter wailing
    as for an only son,^b
for suddenly the destroyer
    will come upon us.

²⁷"I have made you a tester^c of metals
    and my people the ore,
that you may observe
    and test their ways.
²⁸They are all hardened rebels,^d
    going about to slander.^e
They are bronze and iron;^f
    they all act corruptly.
²⁹The bellows blow fiercely
    to burn away the lead with fire,

6:17
j Eze 3:17
k Jer 11:7-8; 25:4

6:19
l Isa 1:2; Jer 22:29
m Pr 1:31 n Jer 8:9

6:20
o Ex 30:23
p Am 5:22
q Ps 50:8-10;
Jer 7:21; Mic 6:7-8
r Isa 1:11

6:21
s Isa 8:14

6:22
t Jer 1:15; 10:22

6:23
u Isa 13:18
v Jer 4:29

6:24
w Jer 4:19
x Jer 4:31; 50:41-43

6:25
y Jer 49:29
6:26
z Jer 4:8
a Jer 25:34;
Mic 1:10
b Zec 12:10

6:27
c Jer 9:7

6:28
d Jer 5:23 e Jer 9:4
f Eze 22:18

but the refining goes on in vain;
the wicked are not purged out.
³⁰They are called rejected silver,
because the LORD has rejected them." *g*

False Religion Worthless

7 This is the word that came to Jeremiah from the LORD: ²"Stand*h* at the gate of the LORD's house and there proclaim this message:

" 'Hear the word of the LORD, all you people of Judah who come through these gates to worship the LORD. ³This is what the LORD Almighty, the God of Israel, says: Reform your ways*i* and your actions, and I will let you live in this place. ⁴Do not trust in deceptive*j* words and say, "This is the temple of the LORD, the temple of the LORD, the temple of the LORD!" ⁵If you really change your ways and your actions and deal with each other justly,*k* ⁶if you do not oppress the alien, the fatherless or the widow and do not shed innocent blood*l* in this place, and if you do not follow other gods*m* to your own harm, ⁷then I will let you live in this place, in the land*n* I gave your forefathers for ever and ever. ⁸But look, you are trusting in deceptive words that are worthless.

⁹" 'Will you steal and murder, commit adultery and perjury,*a* burn incense to Baal*o* and follow other gods*p* you have not known, ¹⁰and then come and stand before me in this house,*q* which bears my Name, and say, "We are safe"—safe to do all these detestable things? ¹¹Has this house,*r* which bears my Name, become a den of robbers*s* to you? But I have been watching!*t* declares the LORD.

¹²" 'Go now to the place in Shiloh*u* where I first made a dwelling for my Name, and see what I did*v* to it because of the wickedness of my people Israel. ¹³While you were doing all these things, declares the LORD, I spoke to you again and again,*w* but you did not listen;*x* I called you, but you did not answer.*y* ¹⁴Therefore, what I did to Shiloh I will now do to the house that bears my Name,*z* the temple you trust in, the place I gave to you and your fathers. ¹⁵I will thrust you from my presence, just as I did all your brothers, the people of Ephraim.'*a*

¹⁶"So do not pray for this people nor offer any plea*b* or petition for them; do not plead with me, for I will not listen to you. ¹⁷Do you not see what they are doing in the towns of Judah and in the streets of Jerusalem? ¹⁸The children gather wood, the fathers light the fire, and the women knead the dough and make cakes of bread for the Queen of Heaven.*c* They pour out drink offerings*d* to other gods to provoke*e* me to anger. ¹⁹But am I the one they are provoking? declares the LORD. Are they not rather harming themselves, to their own shame?*f*

²⁰" 'Therefore this is what the Sovereign LORD says: My anger*g* and my wrath will be poured out on this place, on man and beast, on the trees of the field and on the fruit of the ground, and it will burn and not be quenched.

²¹" 'This is what the LORD Almighty, the God of Israel, says: Go ahead, add your burnt offerings to your other sacrifices*h* and eat*i* the meat yourselves! ²²For when I brought your forefathers out of Egypt and spoke to them, I did not just give them

a 9 Or and swear by false gods

commands about burnt offerings and sacrifices,^{j} 23but I gave them this command: Obey^k me, and I will be your God and you will be my people.^{l} Walk in all the ways I command you, that it may go well^m with you. 24But they did not listen or pay attention;^{n} instead, they followed the stubborn inclinations of their evil hearts. They went backward and not forward. 25From the time your forefathers left Egypt until now, day after day, again and again I sent you my servants the prophets.^{o} 26But they did not listen to me or pay attention. They were stiff-necked and did more evil than their forefathers.'^{p}

27"When you tell^q them all this, they will not listen^r to you; when you call to them, they will not answer. 28Therefore say to them, 'This is the nation that has not obeyed the LORD its God or responded to correction. Truth has perished; it has vanished from their lips. 29Cut off^s your hair and throw it away; take up a lament on the barren heights, for the LORD has rejected and abandoned^t this generation that is under his wrath.

The Valley of Slaughter

30" 'The people of Judah have done evil in my eyes, declares the LORD. They have set up their detestable idols^u in the house that bears my Name and have defiled^v it. 31They have built the high places of Topheth^w in the Valley of Ben Hinnom to burn their sons and daughters^x in the fire—something I did not command, nor did it enter my mind.^{y} 32So beware, the days are coming, declares the LORD, when people will no longer call it Topheth or the Valley of Ben Hinnom, but the Valley of Slaughter,^{z} for they will bury^a the dead in Topheth until there is no more room. 33Then the carcasses of this people will become food^b for the birds of the air and the beasts of the earth, and there will be no one to frighten them away. 34I will bring an end to the sounds^c of joy and gladness and to the voices of bride and bridegroom^d in the towns of Judah and the streets of Jerusalem, for the land will become desolate.^{e}

8 " 'At that time, declares the LORD, the bones of the kings and officials of Judah, the bones of the priests and prophets, and the bones of the people of Jerusalem will be removed from their graves. 2They will be exposed to the sun and the moon and all the stars of the heavens, which they have loved and served^f and which they have followed and consulted and worshiped. They will not be gathered up or buried, but will be like refuse lying on the ground. 3Wherever I banish them, all the survivors of this evil nation will prefer death to life,^{g} declares the LORD Almighty.'

Sin and Punishment

4"Say to them, 'This is what the LORD says:

" 'When men fall down, do they not get up?^{h}
    When a man turns away, does he not return?
5Why then have these people turned away?
    Why does Jerusalem always turn away?
They cling to deceit;^{i}

Cross-references (margin):

7:22 j 1Sa 15:22; Ps 51:16; Hos 6:6
7:23 k Ex 19:5 l Lev 26:12 m Ex 15:26
7:24 n Ps 81:11-12; Jer 11:8
7:25 o Jer 25:4
7:26 p Jer 16:12
7:27 q Eze 2:7 r Eze 3:7
7:29 s Job 1:20; Isa 15:2; Mic 1:16 t Jer 6:30
7:30 u Eze 7:20-22 v Jer 32:34
7:31 w 2Ki 23:10 x Ps 106:38 y Jer 19:5
7:32 z Jer 19:6 a Jer 19:11
7:33 b Dt 28:26
7:34 c Isa 24:8; Eze 26:13 d Rev 18:23 e Lev 26:34
8:2 f 2Ki 23:5; Ac 7:42
8:3 g Job 3:22; Rev 9:6
8:4 h Pr 24:16
8:5 i Jer 5:27

Jeremiah 7:30—8:3

In a valley near Jerusalem, the people of Judah participated in the horrifying practice of child sacrifice (cf. 19:1–15). The ancient world considered this a supremely religious act, since it gave the god what was most precious to the worshiper. Some Judahites must have believed they had appeased the Lord by these rituals, but God had prohibited such sacrifice (Lev. 18:21; Deut. 18:9–12). Jerusalem itself would become a "Valley of Slaughter" because of this wickedness.

Children around the world are still sacrificed to humanity's greed, lust, anger, and religious ignorance. Some countries allow them to live on the streets, to be

sold into sexual slavery or bonded labor, or to be exploited as soldiers or instruments of terrorist acts. Others fail to protect the young from violence, abuse, or abortion. As Christ's representatives on Earth, we are love- and duty-bound to advocate for change and to act to protect these helpless ones from harm. Might the violence in our societies be to some degree a result and reflection of the harm inflicted on children today?

Jeremiah 8:4—9:26

God's people seemed clueless, woefully and willfully ignorant of his laws. In 8:18—9:11 we encounter a merging of Jeremiah's and God's voices. Jeremiah's tears represented God's sorrow (cf. 9:7) over the judg-

they refuse to return.[i]

8:5
[i] Jer 7:24; 9:6

6 I have listened attentively,
   but they do not say what is right.
No one repents[k] of his wickedness,
   saying, "What have I done?"
Each pursues his own course[l]
   like a horse charging into battle.

8:6
[k] Rev 9:20
[l] Ps 14:1-3

7 Even the stork in the sky
   knows her appointed seasons,
and the dove, the swift and the thrush
   observe the time of their migration.
But my people do not know[m]
   the requirements of the LORD.

8:7
[m] Isa 1:3; Jer 5:4-5

8 " 'How can you say, "We are wise,
   for we have the law[n] of the LORD,"
when actually the lying pen of the scribes
   has handled it falsely?

8:8
[n] Ro 2:17

9 The wise[o] will be put to shame;
   they will be dismayed and trapped.
Since they have rejected the word[p] of the LORD,
   what kind of wisdom do they have?

8:9
[o] Jer 6:15
[p] Jer 6:19

10 Therefore I will give their wives to other men
   and their fields to new owners.[q]
From the least to the greatest,
   all are greedy for gain;[r]
prophets and priests alike,
   all practice deceit.

8:10
[q] Jer 6:12
[r] Isa 56:11

11 They dress the wound of my people
   as though it were not serious.
"Peace, peace," they say,
   when there is no peace.[s]

8:11
[s] Jer 6:14

12 Are they ashamed of their loathsome conduct?
   No, they have no shame[t] at all;
   they do not even know how to blush.
So they will fall among the fallen;
   they will be brought down when they are punished,[u]

8:12
[t] Jer 3:3
[u] Ps 52:5-7; Isa 3:9
[v] Jer 6:15

says the LORD.[v]

---

ment he had to execute. The shared pain of God and the prophet is paralleled in Hosea 11:1–9 and above all in the agony of God's Son, who later wept over the same city that killed prophets and would be the site of his own crucifixion (cf. Luke 13:34–35; 19:41–44; 23:26–33).

The charge that people no longer blushed over shameful circumstances (8:12) strikes a chord with Chris-

tians confronted daily with our culture's pleasure-centered values. How can we assume that all is well? Do our churches mirror cultural values or encourage believers to live Scripturally (cf. Eph. 5:3–5)? A sad commentary on Western Christianity is that some nations reject our missionaries because they don't want our immorality and lax standards to infect their societies.

8:11

Number of Wars in the World by Year

Perhaps no other Bible verse captures the feelings of many in the 21st century more than Jeremiah 8:11: " 'Peace peace,' they say, 'when there is no peace.' " If statistics from the last decade of the 20th century are any indication, we are a long way from Biblical peace:

Source: Smith (1999:58)

Year	Value
1990	54
1991	65
1992	66
1993	57
1994	60
1995	55
1996	50
1997	52

13 " 'I will take away their harvest,

There will be no grapes on the vine. ^w
There will be no figs ^x on the tree,
and their leaves will wither. ^y
What I have given them
will be taken ^z from them. ^{a'} "

declares the LORD.

14 "Why are we sitting here?
Gather together!
Let us flee to the fortified cities ^a
and perish there!
For the LORD our God has doomed us to perish
and given us poisoned water ^b to drink,
because we have sinned ^c against him.

15 We hoped for peace ^d
but no good has come,
for a time of healing
but there was only terror. ^e

16 The snorting of the enemy's horses
is heard from Dan; ^f
at the neighing of their stallions
the whole land trembles.
They have come to devour
the land and everything in it,
the city and all who live there."

17 "See, I will send venomous snakes ^g among you,
vipers that cannot be charmed, ^h
and they will bite you,"

declares the LORD.

18 O my Comforter ^b in sorrow,
my heart is faint ⁱ within me.

19 Listen to the cry of my people
from a land far away: ^j
"Is the LORD not in Zion?
Is her King no longer there?"

"Why have they provoked me to anger with their images,
with their worthless foreign idols?" ^k

20 "The harvest is past,
the summer has ended,
and we are not saved."

21 Since my people are crushed, I am crushed;
I mourn, ^l and horror grips me.

22 Is there no balm in Gilead? ^m
Is there no physician there?
Why then is there no healing ⁿ
for the wound of my people?

9 1 Oh, that my head were a spring of water
and my eyes a fountain of tears!
I would weep ^o day and night
for the slain of my people. ^p

2 Oh, that I had in the desert
a lodging place for travelers,

8:13
^w Joel 1:7 ^x Lk 13:6
^y Mt 21:19
^z Jer 5:17

8:14
^a Jer 4:5; 35:11
^b Dt 29:18;
Jer 9:15; 23:15
^c Jer 14:7,20

8:15
^d ver 11 ^e Jer 14:19

8:16
^f Jer 4:15

8:17
^g Nu 21:6; Dt 32:24
^h Ps 58:5

8:18
ⁱ La 5:17
8:19
^j Jer 9:16
^k Dt 32:21

8:21
^l Jer 14:17
8:22
^m Ge 37:25
ⁿ Jer 30:12

9:1
^o Jer 13:17;
La 2:11,18
^p Isa 22:4

---

^a 13 The meaning of the Hebrew for this sentence is uncertain.   ^b 18 The meaning of the Hebrew
for this word is uncertain.

so that I might leave my people
    and go away from them;
for they are all adulterers, *q*
    a crowd of unfaithful people.

3 "They make ready their tongue
    like a bow, to shoot lies; *r*
it is not by truth
    that they triumph*a* in the land.
They go from one sin to another;
    they do not acknowledge me,"

                  declares the LORD.

4 "Beware of your friends;
    do not trust your brothers. *s*
For every brother is a deceiver, *b t*
    and every friend a slanderer.
5 Friend deceives friend,
    and no one speaks the truth.
They have taught their tongues to lie;
    they weary themselves with sinning.

6 You*c* live in the midst of deception; *u*
    in their deceit they refuse to acknowledge me,"

                  declares the LORD.

7 Therefore this is what the LORD Almighty says:

"See, I will refine*v* and test*w* them,
    for what else can I do
    because of the sin of my people?

8 Their tongue*x* is a deadly arrow;
    it speaks with deceit.
With his mouth each speaks cordially to his neighbor,
    but in his heart he sets a trap*y* for him.
9 Should I not punish them for this?"
    declares the LORD.

"Should I not avenge*z* myself
    on such a nation as this?"

10 I will weep and wail for the mountains
    and take up a lament concerning the desert pastures.
They are desolate and untraveled,
    and the lowing of cattle is not heard.

The birds of the air*a* have fled
    and the animals are gone.

11 "I will make Jerusalem a heap of ruins,
    a haunt of jackals; *b*
and I will lay waste the towns of Judah
    so no one can live there." *c*

12 What man is wise*d* enough to understand this? Who has been instructed by the LORD and can explain it? Why has the land been ruined and laid waste like a desert that no one can cross?

9:13
e 2Ch 7:19;
Ps 89:30-32
9:14
f Jer 2:8,23
g Jer 7:24
9:15
h La 3:15 *i* Jer 8:14

13 The LORD said, "It is because they have forsaken my law, which I set before them; they have not obeyed me or followed my law. *e* 14 Instead, they have followed*f* the stubbornness of their hearts; *g* they have followed the Baals, as their fathers taught them." 15 Therefore, this is what the LORD Almighty, the God of Israel, says: "See, I will make this people eat bitter food*h* and drink poisoned water. *i* 16 I will

---

a 3 Or *lies; / they are not valiant for truth*   *b* 4 Or *a deceiving Jacob*   *c* 6 That is, Jeremiah (the Hebrew is singular)

scatter them among nations[j] that neither they nor their fathers have known,[k] and I will pursue them with the sword[l] until I have destroyed them."[m]

[17]This is what the LORD Almighty says:

"Consider now! Call for the wailing women[n] to come;
  send for the most skillful of them.
  [18]Let them come quickly
    and wail over us
  till our eyes overflow with tears
    and water streams from our eyelids.[o]
[19]The sound of wailing is heard from Zion:
  'How ruined[p] we are!
  How great is our shame!
  We must leave our land
    because our houses are in ruins.' "

[20]Now, O women, hear the word of the LORD;
  open your ears to the words of his mouth.
  Teach your daughters how to wail;
    teach one another a lament.[q]
[21]Death has climbed in through our windows
    and has entered our fortresses;
  it has cut off the children from the streets
    and the young men[r] from the public squares.

[22]Say, "This is what the LORD declares:

" 'The dead bodies of men will lie
  like refuse[s] on the open field,
like cut grain behind the reaper,
  with no one to gather them.' "

[23]This is what the LORD says:

"Let not the wise man boast of his wisdom[t]
  or the strong man boast of his strength[u]
  or the rich man boast of his riches,[v]
[24]but let him who boasts boast[w] about this:
  that he understands and knows me,
that I am the LORD,[x] who exercises kindness,[y]
  justice and righteousness[z] on earth,
  for in these I delight,"

declares the LORD.

[25]"The days are coming," declares the LORD, "when I will punish all who are circumcised only in the flesh[a]— [26]Egypt, Judah, Edom, Ammon, Moab and all who live in the desert in distant places.[a b] For all these nations are really uncircumcised, and even the whole house of Israel is uncircumcised in heart.[c]"

God and Idols

10 Hear what the LORD says to you, O house of Israel. [2]This is what the LORD says:

"Do not learn the ways of the nations[d]
  or be terrified by signs in the sky,

[a] 26 Or *desert and who clip the hair by their foreheads*

Cross references

9:16
[j] Lev 26:33
[k] Dt 28:64 / Eze 5:2
[m] Jer 44:27;
Eze 5:12

9:17
[n] 2Ch 35:25;
Ecc 12:5; Am 5:16

9:18
[o] Jer 14:17

9:19
[p] Jer 4:13

9:20
[q] Isa 32:9-13

9:21
[r] 2Ch 36:17

9:22
[s] Jer 8:2

9:23
[t] Ecc 9:11
[u] 1Ki 20:11
[v] Eze 28:4-5

9:24
[w] 1Co 1:31*;
Gal 6:14
[x] 2Co 10:17*
[y] Ps 51:1; Mic 7:18
[z] Ps 36:6

9:25
[a] Ro 2:8-9
9:26
[b] Jer 25:23
[c] Lev 26:41;
Ac 7:51; Ro 2:28

10:2
[d] Lev 20:23

Jeremiah 10:1–16

Much of this section was intended to instruct Israel and Judah during the time of the exile. Not that it was irrelevant to the circumstances of Judah before the Babylonian onslaught, but the house of Israel was called to avoid "the ways of the nations" (v. 2). Assimilation

though the nations are terrified by them.

3 For the customs of the peoples are worthless;
they cut a tree out of the forest,
and a craftsman[e] shapes it with his chisel.

10:3
e Isa 40:19

4 They adorn it with silver and gold;
they fasten it with hammer and nails
so it will not totter.[f]

10:4
f Isa 41:7

5 Like a scarecrow in a melon patch,
their idols cannot speak;[g]
they must be carried
because they cannot walk.[h]
Do not fear them;
they can do no harm
nor can they do any good." [i]

10:5
g 1Co 12:2
h Ps 115:5,7
i Isa 41:24; 46:7

6 No one is like you, O LORD;
you are great,[j]
and your name is mighty in power.

10:6
j Ps 48:1

7 Who should not revere you,
O King of the nations?[k]
This is your due.
Among all the wise men of the nations
and in all their kingdoms,
there is no one like you.

10:7
k Ps 22:28;
Rev 15:4

8 They are all senseless and foolish;[l]
they are taught by worthless wooden idols.

10:8
l Isa 40:19; Jer 4:22

9 Hammered silver is brought from Tarshish
and gold from Uphaz.
What the craftsman and goldsmith have made[m]
is then dressed in blue and purple—
all made by skilled workers.

10:9
m Ps 115:4;
Isa 40:19

10 But the LORD is the true God;
he is the living God, the eternal King.
When he is angry, the earth trembles;
the nations cannot endure his wrath.[n]

10:10
n Ps 76:7

11 "Tell them this: 'These gods, who did not make the heavens and the earth, will perish[o] from the earth and from under the heavens.' " [a]

10:11
o Ps 96:5; Isa 2:18

12 But God made the earth by his power;
he founded the world by his wisdom
and stretched out the heavens[p] by his understanding.

13 When he thunders,[q] the waters in the heavens roar;
he makes clouds rise from the ends of the earth.
He sends lightning with the rain[r]
and brings out the wind from his storehouses.

10:12
p Ge 1:1,8; Job 9:8;
Isa 40:22
10:13
q Job 36:29
r Ps 135:7

14 Everyone is senseless and without knowledge;
every goldsmith is shamed by his idols.
His images are a fraud;

---

a 11 The text of this verse is in Aramaic.

---

into a dominant culture would have been a real issue for Jews dispersed from their homeland. Idolatry is folly. When other nations talk about creation, God's people are reminded that the real Creator of heaven and Earth is none other than the God of Israel.

📖 Idolatry, often in sophisticated and subtle forms, is alive and well on Planet Earth. The human tendency to deify and worship something or someone of our own making is as ingrained in us as it was in the minds and hearts of the ancients. It's easy to brush off a passage like this, shake our heads at the ignorance and superstition of our predecessors, and move on to the next chapter in search of relevant material. But pause here and reflect: To what do I "bow the knee"?

they have no breath in them.
15 They are worthless,^{s} the objects of mockery;
  when their judgment comes, they will perish.
16 He who is the Portion^t of Jacob is not like these,
  for he is the Maker of all things,^{u}
including Israel, the tribe of his inheritance^v—
  the LORD Almighty is his name.^{w}

Coming Destruction

17 Gather up your belongings^x to leave the land,
  you who live under siege.
18 For this is what the LORD says:
  "At this time I will hurl^y out
  those who live in this land;
I will bring distress on them
  so that they may be captured."

19 Woe to me because of my injury!
  My wound^z is incurable!
Yet I said to myself,
  "This is my sickness, and I must endure^a it."
20 My tent^b is destroyed;
  all its ropes are snapped.
My sons are gone from me and are no more;^{c}
  no one is left now to pitch my tent
  or to set up my shelter.
21 The shepherds are senseless
  and do not inquire of the LORD;
so they do not prosper
  and all their flock is scattered.^{d}
22 Listen! The report is coming—
  a great commotion from the land of the north!
It will make the towns of Judah desolate,
  a haunt of jackals.^{e}

Jeremiah's Prayer

23 I know, O LORD, that a man's life is not his own;
  it is not for man to direct his steps.^{f}
24 Correct me, LORD, but only with justice—
  not in your anger,^{g}
  lest you reduce me to nothing.^{h}

10:15
^{s} Isa 41:24;
Jer 14:22
10:16
^{t} Dt 32:9; Ps 119:57
^{u} ver 12 ^{v} Ps 74:2
^{w} Jer 31:35; 32:18
10:17
^{x} Eze 12:3-12
10:18
^{y} 1Sa 25:29
10:19
^{z} Jer 14:17
^{a} Mic 7:9
10:20
^{b} Jer 4:20
^{c} Jer 31:15; La 1:5
10:21
^{d} Jer 23:2
10:22
^{e} Jer 9:11
10:23
^{f} Pr 20:24
10:24
^{g} Ps 6:1; 38:1
^{h} Jer 30:11

Jeremiah 10:17–22

The topic and setting change from the previous section. Jerusalem was addressed as a city under siege, forced to recognize that her predicament had no cure. This was an almost unbearable burden for Jeremiah, who grieved on behalf of the people. Jerusalem was seen as a tent-dwelling mother, bereft of her children and home. No one was left to rebuild the destroyed nation. Responsibility fell on the leaders ("shepherds") of Israel. Doom was near—word had it that the enemy army was approaching.

The "pack your bags" language in verse 17 warns of a disaster. But disastrous events often take place without warning or possibility of escape. Earthquakes, crop failures, floods, and other natural and manmade disasters put people on the edge of survival. Most

emergency situations are the results of living in a fallen world—not judgmental "acts of God" like the one in this passage. Such events give Christians a unique window of opportunity to share Christ's love in tangible ways that can open hearts to his grace. Have you been involved personally in a disaster relief effort? If so, how did the experience change you?

Jeremiah 10:23–25

The poetry of 8:4—10:25 concludes with the prayer of a chastened individual. Jeremiah spoke as a member of a wounded and judged people. In his prayer he frankly admitted that human resources aren't enough to keep a person on the pathway marked out by God. An individual doesn't ultimately direct his or her own life course; it's in the hands of God. Recognizing this is a first step toward wisdom.

10:25
i Zep 3:8
j Job 18:21; Ps 14:4
k Ps 79:7; Jer 8:16
l Ps 79:6-7

25 Pour out your wrath on the nations[i]
    that do not acknowledge you,
    on the peoples who do not call on your name.[j]
For they have devoured[k] Jacob;
    they have devoured him completely
    and destroyed his homeland.[l]

The Covenant Is Broken

11:3
m Dt 27:26;
Gal 3:10

11 This is the word that came to Jeremiah from the LORD: 2 "Listen to the terms of this covenant and tell them to the people of Judah and to those who live in Jerusalem. 3 Tell them that this is what the LORD, the God of Israel, says: 'Cursed[m] is the man who does not obey the terms of this covenant— 4 the terms I command-

11:4
n Dt 4:20; 1Ki 8:51
o Ex 24:8
p Jer 7:23; 31:33
11:5
q Ex 13:5; Dt 7:12;
Ps 105:8-11

ed your forefathers when I brought them out of Egypt, out of the iron-smelting furnace.[n] I said, 'Obey[o] me and do everything I command you, and you will be my people,[p] and I will be your God. 5 Then I will fulfill the oath I swore[q] to your forefathers, to give them a land flowing with milk and honey'—the land you possess today."

I answered, "Amen, LORD."

11:6
r Dt 15:5; Ro 2:13;
Jas 1:22
11:7
s 2Ch 36:15
11:8
t Jer 7:26
u Lev 26:14-43
11:9
v Eze 22:25
11:10
w Dt 9:7
x Jdg 2:12-13

6 The LORD said to me, "Proclaim all these words in the towns of Judah and in the streets of Jerusalem: 'Listen to the terms of this covenant and follow[r] them. 7 From the time I brought your forefathers up from Egypt until today, I warned them again and again,[s] saying, "Obey me." 8 But they did not listen or pay attention;[t] instead, they followed the stubbornness of their evil hearts. So I brought on them all the curses[u] of the covenant I had commanded them to follow but that they did not keep.' "

9 Then the LORD said to me, "There is a conspiracy[v] among the people of Judah and those who live in Jerusalem. 10 They have returned to the sins of their forefathers,[w] who refused to listen to my words. They have followed other gods[x] to serve them. Both the house of Israel and the house of Judah have broken the covenant I made

11:11
y 2Ki 22:16
z Jer 14:12;
Eze 8:18 *a* ver 14;
Pr 1:28; Isa 1:15;
Zec 7:13
11:12
b Jer 44:17
c Dt 32:37
11:13
d Jer 7:9 *e* Jer 3:24
11:14
f Ex 32:10 *g* ver 11

with their forefathers. 11 Therefore this is what the LORD says: 'I will bring on them a disaster[y] they cannot escape. Although they cry[z] out to me, I will not listen[a] to them. 12 The towns of Judah and the people of Jerusalem will go and cry out to the gods to whom they burn incense,[b] but they will not help them at all when disaster[c] strikes. 13 You have as many gods as you have towns, O Judah; and the altars you have set up to burn incense[d] to that shameful[e] god Baal are as many as the streets of Jerusalem.'

14 "Do not pray[f] for this people nor offer any plea or petition for them, because I will not listen[g] when they call to me in the time of their distress.

15 "What is my beloved doing in my temple
    as she works out her evil schemes with many?

📖 The book of Jeremiah is a prophetic reminder of the deep sorrow that should affect all Christians when we reflect on the circumstances of those who don't know God (Eph. 2:1–3). Jesus, after all, wept and died for them. As Paul reminded the church, it's only because of God's great kindness, mercy, and love that we have received his gracious gift of salvation in Christ (Eph. 2:4–10). When have you "wept" in prayer for someone who was resisting Christ's gracious offer? Or for a larger group of unnamed individuals you didn't personally know?

Jeremiah 11:1–17

👥 We may compare the basic marriage formulation ("I will be your husband and you will be my wife") with the covenant between God and Israel ("You will be *my people, and I will be your God*"; v. 4). They are similar in form, and both assume an exclusive, intimate relationship as the basis on which a broader community is to be built. The covenant was based on God's gifts of deliverance and instruction. It was extended by him to the

people and spelled out consequences for disobedience.

📖 It's helpful to view Jeremiah's judgment speech in light of his later prophecy of the coming new covenant (31:31–34) Christ would initiate through his death and resurrection (cf. 1 Cor. 11:23–26). What God demands in terms of faithfulness (cf. Heb. 10:26–39) are the very things he has given as gifts through his Son's obedience. Christ is God's self-binding promise, gaining for his people what they can't obtain for themselves. We grasp the radical nature of grace and forgiveness only when we recognize that judgment for failure is what we deserve—but not what we have received.

Our fragile commitments in modern society are constantly under threat as marriages break up, friendships fail, churches turn their backs on neighborhood needs, and faithfulness to God takes a back seat to other life issues. In a swift-paced, mobile society, the place of enduring promises is easily crowded out. How do such pressures influence you and your commitments?

Can consecrated meat avert ⌊your punishment⌋?
When you engage in your wickedness,
then you rejoice.[a]"

16 The LORD called you a thriving olive tree
with fruit beautiful in form.
But with the roar of a mighty storm
he will set it on fire,[h]
and its branches will be broken.[i]

17 The LORD Almighty, who planted[j] you, has decreed disaster for you, because the
house of Israel and the house of Judah have done evil and provoked me to anger
by burning incense to Baal.[k]

Plot Against Jeremiah

18 Because the LORD revealed their plot to me, I knew it, for at that time he showed
me what they were doing. 19 I had been like a gentle lamb led to the slaughter; I did
not realize that they had plotted[l] against me, saying,

"Let us destroy the tree and its fruit;
let us cut him off from the land of the living,[m]
that his name be remembered[n] no more."
20 But, O LORD Almighty, you who judge righteously
and test the heart and mind,[o]
let me see your vengeance upon them,
for to you I have committed my cause.

21 "Therefore this is what the LORD says about the men of Anathoth who are seeking your life[p] and saying, 'Do not prophesy in the name of the LORD or you will die[q]
by our hands'— 22 therefore this is what the LORD Almighty says: 'I will punish them.
Their young men[r] will die by the sword, their sons and daughters by famine. 23 Not
even a remnant[s] will be left to them, because I will bring disaster on the men of Anathoth in the year of their punishment.[t]' "

Jeremiah's Complaint

12 You are always righteous,[u] O LORD,
when I bring a case before you.
Yet I would speak with you about your justice:
Why does the way of the wicked prosper?[v]
Why do all the faithless live at ease?
2 You have planted[w] them, and they have taken root;
they grow and bear fruit.
You are always on their lips

11:16 [h] Jer 21:14 [i] Isa 27:11; Ro 11:17-24
11:17 [j] Isa 5:2; Jer 12:2 [k] Jer 7:9
11:19 [l] Jer 18:18; 20:10 [m] Job 28:13; Isa 53:8 [n] Ps 83:4
11:20 [o] Ps 7:9
11:21 [p] Jer 12:6 [q] Jer 26:8,11; 38:4
11:22 [r] Jer 18:21
11:23 [s] Jer 6:9 [t] Jer 23:12
12:1 [u] Ezr 9:15 [v] Jer 5:27-28
12:2 [w] Jer 11:17

[a] 15 Or *Could consecrated meat avert your punishment? / Then you would rejoice*

Jeremiah 11:18–23

God revealed to Jeremiah the true intentions of those from his hometown of Anathoth (just north of Jerusalem). They wanted to humiliate—and murder—the prophet. Jeremiah described himself as a lamb led to slaughter, implying his innocence.

Christians are reminded of John the Baptist's description of Jesus as "the Lamb of God, who takes away the sin of the world" (John 1:29). Scripture is rich with imagery of the lamb or sheep for slaughter (e.g., Gen. 22; Ex. 12–13; Isa. 53:7). Christ's redemptive self-offering includes forgiveness of his persecutors (Luke 23:34)—a miracle of grace that moves beyond Jeremiah's words but not beyond the reach of the God who inspired them.

Jeremiah's opposition and despair resulted from the exercise of his faith in responding to God's call. Likewise, Christians in Indonesia, India, the Philippines, and Sudan have recently been attacked for their belief in Christ. We also can cite the despicable treatment of Jews in Iran, where many were put on trial in 2000 and charged, without evidence, of being agents for Israel. Their only crime seems to have been that they held to their faith in the God of Israel despite overwhelming pressure to do otherwise. In a similar position, would you have been found "guilty" as charged?

Jeremiah 12:1–4

Jeremiah asked why a righteous God would allow the wicked to prosper. If God is so opposed to their evil activity, why doesn't he judge them and be done with it? Jeremiah prayed for their destruction because of

but far from their hearts. *x*

12:2
x Isa 29:13;
Jer 3:10; Mt 15:8;
Tit 1:16
12:3
y Ps 7:9; 11:5;
139:1-4; Jer 11:20
z Jer 17:18
12:4
a Jer 4:28
b Joel 1:10-12
c Jer 4:25; 9:10

3 Yet you know me, O LORD;
    you see me and test *y* my thoughts about you.
Drag them off like sheep to be butchered!
    Set them apart for the day of slaughter! *z*
4 How long will the land lie parched *a a*
    and the grass in every field be withered? *b*
Because those who live in it are wicked,
    the animals and birds have perished. *c*
Moreover, the people are saying,
    "He will not see what happens to us."

God's Answer

5 "If you have raced with men on foot
    and they have worn you out,
    how can you compete with horses?
If you stumble in safe country, *b*
    how will you manage in the thickets *d* by *c* the Jordan?

12:5
d Jer 49:19; 50:44

6 Your brothers, your own family—
    even they have betrayed you;
    they have raised a loud cry against you. *e*
Do not trust them,
    though they speak well of you. *f*

12:6
e Pr 26:24-25;
Jer 9:4 *f* Ps 12:2

7 "I will forsake my house,
    abandon *g* my inheritance;
I will give the one I love
    into the hands of her enemies.
8 My inheritance has become to me
    like a lion in the forest.
She roars at me;
    therefore I hate her. *h*
9 Has not my inheritance become to me
    like a speckled bird of prey
    that other birds of prey surround and attack?
Go and gather all the wild beasts;

12:7
g Jer 7:29
12:8
h Hos 9:15; Am 6:8

a 4 Or *land mourn*   *b* 5 Or *If you put your trust in a land of safety*   *c* 5 Or *the flooding of*

the harm they had brought to the land, asking that *they* be taken like sheep to slaughter. His prayer reminds us of the language of the psalms (cf. Ps. 73). The many individual and communal laments or complaints of the Psalter reflect the personal crises of people of faith.

When we pray for our enemies and persecutors, we ask that God will help them recognize their errors and find the forgiveness that is ultimately his to give. Their sins deserve his judgment (as do ours), but by his grace that judgment has already been borne by Christ. Does this reality make Jeremiah's prayer for vindication and judgment wrong for Christians? No. But we are wise to pray for vindication *of the gospel* and the frustration of the devil's plans and schemes.

Jeremiah 12:5–17

God responded that though the prophet was weary now, more hardship lay ahead. There was no way around persecution or the strain of prophetic work—but there is always a way *through* it. God's reply didn't reflect indifference to Jeremiah's circumstances but recognized

the advanced state of decay in Judah and Jerusalem, the consequences of which were unavoidable.

God was concerned about the salvation of Israel's neighbors and intended to judge them with righteousness. He spoke of temporary judgment but held out the possibility that they would be restored in their homeland and related to the Lord. It remained for the New Testament to spell out the glorious inheritance available to the nations in God's Son.

At most points along the journey of faith, we can't see beyond the twists and turns ahead. Do we really need to know more than that our life is hidden in Christ (cf. Col. 3:3) and our ultimate vindication rests with him? Our relationship with God isn't a cure-all for life's problems but our basis for facing those problems. If we try to run the race based on our resources, we will fail. If we run in dependence on God, we are guaranteed not victory according to worldly standards but the assurance that we belong to God (2 Tim. 4:7–8; Heb. 12:1). Under what circumstances has this realization been a comfort to you?

bring them to devour.[i]
10 Many shepherds[j] will ruin my vineyard
  and trample down my field;
they will turn my pleasant field
  into a desolate wasteland.[k]
11 It will be made a wasteland,
  parched and desolate before me;[l]
the whole land will be laid waste
  because there is no one who cares.
12 Over all the barren heights in the desert
  destroyers will swarm,
for the sword of the LORD[m] will devour
  from one end of the land to the other;[n]
  no one will be safe.
13 They will sow wheat but reap thorns;
  they will wear themselves out but gain nothing.[o]
So bear the shame of your harvest
  because of the LORD's fierce anger."[p]

14 This is what the LORD says: "As for all my wicked neighbors who seize the inheritance I gave my people Israel, I will uproot[q] them from their lands and I will uproot the house of Judah from among them. 15 But after I uproot them, I will again have compassion and will bring[r] each of them back to his own inheritance and his own country. 16 And if they learn well the ways of my people and swear by my name, saying, 'As surely as the LORD lives'[s]—even as they once taught my people to swear by Baal[t]—then they will be established among my people.[u] 17 But if any nation does not listen, I will completely uproot and destroy[v] it," declares the LORD.

A Linen Belt

13 This is what the LORD said to me: "Go and buy a linen belt and put it around your waist, but do not let it touch water." 2 So I bought a belt, as the LORD directed, and put it around my waist.

3 Then the word of the LORD came to me a second time: 4 "Take the belt you bought and are wearing around your waist, and go now to Perath[a] and hide it there in a crevice in the rocks." 5 So I went and hid it at Perath, as the LORD told me.[w]

6 Many days later the LORD said to me, "Go now to Perath and get the belt I told you to hide there." 7 So I went to Perath and dug up the belt and took it from the place where I had hidden it, but now it was ruined and completely useless.

8 Then the word of the LORD came to me: 9 "This is what the LORD says: 'In the same way I will ruin the pride of Judah and the great pride[x] of Jerusalem. 10 These wicked people, who refuse to listen to my words, who follow the stubbornness of their hearts[y] and go after other gods[z] to serve and worship them, will be like this belt—completely useless! 11 For as a belt is bound around a man's waist, so I bound the whole house of Israel and the whole house of Judah to me,' declares the LORD,

[a] 4 Or possibly the Euphrates; also in verses 5-7

Jeremiah 13:1–11

The Hebrew verb meaning "to be bound," used twice in verse 11, also appears in Genesis 2:24 to describe the man who leaves his parents to "be united" to his wife and become one flesh with her. Israel was called to be united or to "hold fast" to the Lord (Deut. 10:20; 11:22; 13:4; 30:20). Israel and Judah—whose separation from God was caused by their faithlessness—were like the ruined belt.

This is the first example of Jeremiah performing a symbolic act as part of his prophetic ministry. We are not told directly, but perhaps he wore the fouled waistcloth as a sign to the people—offering oral commentary when opportunity presented itself. At any rate, Jeremiah's action was a physical demonstration to the Israelites of the divine message.

God's purpose for Israel and Judah was for their inhabitants to be bound to him as Lord. Though their behavior is a negative example for us, their fundamental identity resided in their selection by God as his people (cf. 1 Cor. 10:1–14). This made them the spiritual ancestors of Christians today. Consider the cords of love that bind you to Christ and to your fellow believers. They are gifts of great value.

13:11
a Jer 32:20; 33:9
b Ex 19:5-6
c Jer 7:26

'to be my people for my renown *a* and praise and honor. *b* But they have not listened.' *c*

Wineskins

12 "Say to them: 'This is what the LORD, the God of Israel, says: Every wineskin should be filled with wine.' And if they say to you, 'Don't we know that every wineskin should be filled with wine?' 13 then tell them, 'This is what the LORD says: I am going to fill with drunkenness *d* all who live in this land, including the kings who sit on David's throne, the priests, the prophets and all those living in Jerusalem. 14 I will smash them one against the other, fathers and sons alike, declares the LORD. I will allow no pity or mercy or compassion *e* to keep me from destroying *f* them.' "

13:13
d Ps 60:3; 75:8;
Isa 51:17; 63:6;
Jer 51:57

13:14
e Jer 16:5
f Dt 29:20; Eze 5:10

Threat of Captivity

15 Hear and pay attention,
    do not be arrogant,
    for the LORD has spoken.
16 Give glory *g* to the LORD your God
    before he brings the darkness,
    before your feet stumble *h*
    on the darkening hills.
You hope for light,
    but he will turn it to thick darkness
    and change it to deep gloom. *i*
17 But if you do not listen, *j*
    I will weep in secret
    because of your pride;
my eyes will weep bitterly,
    overflowing with tears, *k*
    because the LORD's flock *l* will be taken captive. *m*

13:16
g Jos 7:19
h Jer 23:12
i Isa 59:9

13:17
j Mal 2:2 k Jer 9:1
l Ps 80:1; Jer 23:1
m Jer 14:18

18 Say to the king and to the queen mother,
    "Come down from your thrones,
for your glorious crowns
    will fall from your heads."
19 The cities in the Negev will be shut up,
    and there will be no one to open them.
All Judah *n* will be carried into exile,
    carried completely away.

13:19
n Jer 20:4; 52:30

20 Lift up your eyes and see
    those who are coming from the north. *o*
Where is the flock *p* that was entrusted to you,
    the sheep of which you boasted?
21 What will you say when ⌊the LORD⌋ sets over you

13:20
o Jer 6:22; Hab 1:6
p Jer 23:2

Jeremiah 13:12–14

🔁 God commanded Jeremiah to repeat a proverbial saying: "Every wineskin should be filled with wine." Of course, this was the expectation for wineskins. The punch line was that God would fill the land's inhabitants with drunkenness so that they would crash into one another. Neither the belt in the previous prophecy nor the wineskins here had fulfilled their intended functions. Both were failures.

📖 Are you living up to your full potential? Every generation of God's people is called to examine themselves for evidence that they may have lost their first love, squandered their inheritance, or spurned the Lord (Isa. 1:4; Luke 15:11–16; Rev. 2:4). After such reflection

some people live in guilt. But the Good News is that in Christ we don't have to be condemned by yesterday (cf. Rom. 8:1-2). We have the opportunity to live today and tomorrow in the Spirit, fulfilling God's will for us.

Jeremiah 13:15–27

🔁 Jeremiah pronounced judgment against pride that leads to a fall (cf. Prov. 16:18). He would weep over the folly of the people whose pride made them heedless of their dire circumstances. Verse 18 points to a particular source of pride, the king and the queen mother. Their crowns would fall from their heads as a sign of the fall of the people. These two royal figures aren't specifically named but were likely Jehoiachin and his mother, Nehushta (cf. 2 Kings 24:8–15).

those you cultivated as your special allies? [q]
Will not pain grip you
  like that of a woman in labor? [r]

22 And if you ask yourself,
  "Why has this happened to me?"—
it is because of your many sins [s]
  that your skirts have been torn off
  and your body mistreated. [t]

23 Can the Ethiopian [a] change his skin
  or the leopard its spots?
Neither can you do good
  who are accustomed to doing evil.

24 "I will scatter you like chaff [u]
  driven by the desert wind. [v]

25 This is your lot,
  the portion [w] I have decreed for you,"

declares the LORD,

"because you have forgotten me
  and trusted in false gods.

26 I will pull up your skirts over your face
  that your shame may be seen [x]—

27 your adulteries and lustful neighings,
  your shameless prostitution! [y]
I have seen your detestable acts
  on the hills and in the fields. [z]
Woe to you, O Jerusalem!
  How long will you be unclean?" [a]

Drought, Famine, Sword

14 This is the word of the LORD to Jeremiah concerning the drought:

2 "Judah mourns, [b]
  her cities languish;
they wail for the land,
  and a cry goes up from Jerusalem.

3 The nobles send their servants for water;
  they go to the cisterns
  but find no water. [c]
They return with their jars unfilled;
  dismayed and despairing,
  they cover their heads. [d]

[a] 23 Hebrew *Cushite* (probably a person from the upper Nile region)

13:21
q Jer 38:22
r Jer 4:31

13:22
s Jer 9:2-6;
16:10-12
t Eze 16:37;
Na 3:5-6

13:24
u Ps 1:4 v Lev 26:33

13:25
w Job 20:29;
Mt 24:51

13:26
x La 1:8; Eze 16:37;
Hos 2:10
13:27
y Jer 2:20
z Eze 6:13
a Hos 8:5

14:2
b Isa 3:26; Jer 8:21

14:3
c 2Ki 18:31;
Job 6:19-20
d 2Sa 15:30

Listed as one of the sins God hates (cf. Prov. 6:16–19; 8:13), pride prevents people from receiving God's grace (James 4:6). Unfortunately for many of us, it's also a blind spot: We can't see how it robs us of our relationship with God and others. James 4:10 calls us to humble ourselves before God, confessing our inability to love him and our neighbors as he has commanded. This humble posture allows God to work in us in ways we could never have imagined.

Jeremiah 14:1—15:21

In chapter 14 Judah and Jerusalem mourn over the devastating effects of a drought, linked to the people's sinfulness. It's difficult to determine whether the prayers in 14:7–9 and 19–22 are Jeremiah's on behalf of the people (and advice to them in light of God's judgment)—or the people's. If the latter, they express appropriate words of confession and repentance—that are totally insincere. Both prayers are followed by God's emphatic rejection of his unrepentant people.

In lamenting the day of his birth (15:10), Jeremiah evaluated his own life and ministry (cf. Job 3:1–26). The prophet noted that his enemies were God's enemies; he suffered reproach because he represented God's word to the people (15:15). Yet he wasn't given permission to carry out personal retribution. God would deliver Jeremiah for a "good purpose" and bring his enemies to a place where they would plead with him (15:11).

14:4
e Jer 3:3

4The ground is cracked
　　because there is no rain in the land; e
the farmers are dismayed
　　and cover their heads.

14:5
f Isa 15:6
14:6
g Job 39:5-6;
Jer 2:24

5Even the doe in the field
　　deserts her newborn fawn
　　because there is no grass. f
6Wild donkeys stand on the barren heights g
　　and pant like jackals;
their eyesight fails
　　for lack of pasture."

14:7
h Hos 5:5 i Jer 5:6
j Jer 8:14

7Although our sins testify h against us,
　　O LORD, do something for the sake of your name.
For our backsliding i is great;
　　we have sinned j against you.

14:8
k Jer 17:13

8O Hope k of Israel,
　　its Savior in times of distress,
why are you like a stranger in the land,
　　like a traveler who stays only a night?

14:9
l Isa 50:2
m Jer 8:19
n Isa 63:19;
Jer 15:16

9Why are you like a man taken by surprise,
　　like a warrior powerless to save? l
You are among m us, O LORD,
　　and we bear your name; n
do not forsake us!

10This is what the LORD says about this people:

14:10
o Ps 119:101;
Jer 2:25 p Jer 6:20;
Am 5:22 q Hos 9:9
r Jer 44:21-23;
Hos 8:13

"They greatly love to wander;
　　they do not restrain their feet. o
So the LORD does not accept p them;
　　he will now remember q their wickedness
　　and punish them for their sins." r

14:11
s Ex 32:10
14:12
t Isa 1:15; Jer 11:11
u Jer 7:21
v Jer 6:20

11Then the LORD said to me, "Do not pray s for the well-being of this people. 12Although they fast, I will not listen to their cry; t though they offer burnt offerings u and grain offerings, I will not accept v them. Instead, I will destroy them with the sword, famine and plague."

14:13
w Jer 5:12
14:14
x Jer 27:14
y Jer 23:21,32
z Jer 23:16
a Eze 12:24

13But I said, "Ah, Sovereign LORD, the prophets keep telling them, 'You will not see the sword or suffer famine. w Indeed, I will give you lasting peace in this place.' "

14Then the LORD said to me, "The prophets are prophesying lies x in my name. I have not sent y them or appointed them or spoken to them. They are prophesying to you false visions, z divinations, a idolatries a and the delusions of their own minds.

14:15
b Eze 14:9
c Jer 5:12-13

14:16
d Ps 79:3 e Jer 7:33
f Pr 1:31

15Therefore, this is what the LORD says about the prophets who are prophesying in my name: I did not send them, yet they are saying, 'No sword or famine will touch this land.' Those same prophets will perish b by sword and famine. c 16And the people they are prophesying to will be thrown out into the streets of Jerusalem because of the famine and sword. There will be no one to bury d them or their wives, their sons or their daughters. e I will pour out on them the calamity they deserve. f

a 14 Or visions, worthless divinations

Drought, water rights, and water distribution are still major issues today in the Middle East and elsewhere around the globe. When drought occurs, prayers for rain are frequent, even from the lips of those who don't typically acknowledge God. When the rain comes, though, God's deliverance is often forgotten.

Jeremiah's lament was an understandably human response to mistreatment. It was therapeutic for him to cry out. But God didn't directly answer his appeals for vengeance—at least not on Jeremiah's scale of justice—any more than he will answer our pleas for judgment based on our opinions. As Christ's followers, we are to pray for our enemies and "do good" to them when the opportunity arises (Rom. 12:14–21). In what particular situation have you done just that? What were the results, both short- and long-term?

17 "Speak this word to them:

" 'Let my eyes overflow with tears ^g
night and day without ceasing;
for my virgin daughter—my people—
has suffered a grievous wound,
a crushing blow. ^h
18 If I go into the country,
I see those slain by the sword;
if I go into the city,
I see the ravages of famine. ⁱ
Both prophet and priest
have gone to a land they know not.' "

19 Have you rejected Judah completely? ^j
Do you despise Zion?
Why have you afflicted us
so that we cannot be healed? ^k
We hoped for peace
but no good has come,
for a time of healing
but there is only terror. ^l
20 O LORD, we acknowledge our wickedness
and the guilt of our fathers;
we have indeed sinned ^m against you.
21 For the sake of your name ⁿ do not despise us;
do not dishonor your glorious throne. ^o
Remember your covenant with us
and do not break it.
22 Do any of the worthless idols of the nations bring rain? ^p
Do the skies themselves send down showers?
No, it is you, O LORD our God.
Therefore our hope is in you,
for you are the one who does all this.

15 Then the LORD said to me: "Even if Moses ^q and Samuel ^r were to stand before me, my heart would not go out to this people. ^s Send them away from my presence! ^t Let them go! 2 And if they ask you, 'Where shall we go?' tell them, 'This is what the LORD says:

" 'Those destined for death, to death;
those for the sword, to the sword; ^u
those for starvation, to starvation; ^v
those for captivity, to captivity.' ^w

3 "I will send four kinds of destroyers ^x against them," declares the LORD, "the sword to kill and the dogs to drag away and the birds ^y of the air and the beasts of the earth to devour and destroy. ^z 4 I will make them abhorrent ^a to all the kingdoms of the earth ^b because of what Manasseh ^c son of Hezekiah king of Judah did in Jerusalem.

5 "Who will have pity ^d on you, O Jerusalem?
Who will mourn for you?
Who will stop to ask how you are?
6 You have rejected ^e me," declares the LORD.
"You keep on backsliding.
So I will lay hands ^f on you and destroy you;
I can no longer show compassion.
7 I will winnow them with a winnowing fork
at the city gates of the land.

14:17
g Jer 9:1 h Jer 8:21

14:18
i Eze 7:15

14:19
j Jer 7:29
k Jer 30:12-13
l Jer 8:15

14:20
m Da 9:7-8
14:21
n ver 7 o Jer 3:17

14:22
p Ps 135:7

15:1
q Ex 32:11;
Nu 14:13-20
r 1Sa 7:9 s Jer 7:16;
Eze 14:14,20
t 2Ki 17:20

15:2
u Jer 43:11
v Jer 14:12
w Rev 13:10

15:3
x Lev 26:16
y Dt 28:26
z Lev 26:22;
Eze 14:21
15:4
a Jer 24:9; 29:18
b Dt 28:25
c 2Ki 21:2; 23:26-27
15:5
d Isa 51:19;
Jer 13:14; 21:7;
Na 3:7

15:6
e Jer 6:19; 7:24
f Zep 1:4

I will bring bereavement and destruction on my people,[g]
    for they have not changed their ways.
[8] I will make their widows more numerous
    than the sand of the sea.
At midday I will bring a destroyer[h]
    against the mothers of their young men;
suddenly I will bring down on them
    anguish and terror.
[9] The mother of seven will grow faint[i]
    and breathe her last.
Her sun will set while it is still day;
    she will be disgraced and humiliated.
I will put the survivors to the sword[j]
    before their enemies,"

                declares the LORD.

[10] Alas, my mother, that you gave me birth,[k]
    a man with whom the whole land strives and contends![l]
I have neither lent[m] nor borrowed,
    yet everyone curses me.

[11] The LORD said,

"Surely I will deliver you[n] for a good purpose;
    surely I will make your enemies plead[o] with you
    in times of disaster and times of distress.

[12] "Can a man break iron—
    iron from the north[p]—or bronze?
[13] Your wealth and your treasures
    I will give as plunder, without charge,[q]
because of all your sins
    throughout your country.[r]
[14] I will enslave you to your enemies
    in[a] a land you do not know,[s]
for my anger will kindle a fire[t]
    that will burn against you."

[15] You understand, O LORD;
    remember me and care for me.
    Avenge me on my persecutors.[u]
You are long-suffering—do not take me away;
    think of how I suffer reproach for your sake.[v]
[16] When your words came, I ate[w] them;
    they were my joy and my heart's delight,[x]
for I bear your name,[y]
    O LORD God Almighty.
[17] I never sat[z] in the company of revelers,
    never made merry with them;
I sat alone because your hand was on me
    and you had filled me with indignation.
[18] Why is my pain unending
    and my wound grievous and incurable?[a]
Will you be to me like a deceptive brook,
    like a spring that fails?[b]

[19] Therefore this is what the LORD says:

---

[a] 14 Some Hebrew manuscripts, Septuagint and Syriac (see also Jer. 17:4); most Hebrew manuscripts *I will cause your enemies to bring you / into*

15:7
g Jer 18:21

15:8
h Jer 6:4

15:9
i 1Sa 2:5 / Jer 21:7

15:10
k Job 3:1 l Jer 1:19
m Lev 25:36

15:11
n Jer 40:4
o Jer 21:1-2; 37:3;
  42:1-3

15:12
p Jer 28:14

15:13
q Ps 44:12
r Jer 17:3

15:14
s Dt 28:36;
  Jer 16:13
t Dt 32:22; Ps 21:9

15:15
u Jer 12:3
v Ps 69:7-9

15:16
w Eze 3:3;
  Rev 10:10
x Ps 119:72,103
y Jer 14:9

15:17
z Ps 1:1; 26:4-5;
  Jer 16:8

15:18
a Jer 30:15; Mic 1:9
b Job 6:15

"If you repent, I will restore you
    that you may serve[c] me;
if you utter worthy, not worthless, words,
    you will be my spokesman.
Let this people turn to you,
    but you must not turn to them.
20 I will make you a wall to this people,
    a fortified wall of bronze;
they will fight against you
    but will not overcome you,
for I am with you
    to rescue and save you,"[d]

                                    declares the LORD.

21 "I will save you from the hands of the wicked
    and redeem[e] you from the grasp of the cruel."[f]

Day of Disaster

16 Then the word of the LORD came to me: 2 "You must not marry[g] and have sons or daughters in this place." 3 For this is what the LORD says about the sons and daughters born in this land and about the women who are their mothers and the men who are their fathers: [h] 4 "They will die of deadly diseases. They will not be mourned or buried[i] but will be like refuse lying on the ground.[j] They will perish by sword and famine, and their dead bodies will become food for the birds of the air and the beasts of the earth."[k]

5 For this is what the LORD says: "Do not enter a house where there is a funeral meal; do not go to mourn or show sympathy, because I have withdrawn my blessing, my love and my pity from this people," declares the LORD. 6 "Both high and low will die in this land.[l] They will not be buried or mourned, and no one will cut[m] himself or shave[n] his head for them. 7 No one will offer food to comfort those who mourn[o] for the dead—not even for a father or a mother—nor will anyone give them a drink to console them.

8 "And do not enter a house where there is feasting and sit down to eat and drink.[p] 9 For this is what the LORD Almighty, the God of Israel, says: Before your eyes and in your days I will bring an end to the sounds[q] of joy and gladness and to the voices of bride and bridegroom in this place.[r]

10 "When you tell these people all this and they ask you, 'Why has the LORD decreed such a great disaster against us? What wrong have we done? What sin have we committed against the LORD our God?'[s] 11 then say to them, 'It is because your fathers forsook me,' declares the LORD, 'and followed other gods and served and worshiped them. They forsook me and did not keep my law.[t] 12 But you have behaved more wickedly than your fathers.[u] See how each of you is following the stubbornness of his evil heart[v] instead of obeying me. 13 So I will throw you out of this land into a land neither you nor your fathers have known,[w] and there you will serve other gods[x] day and night, for I will show you no favor.'[y]

14 "However, the days are coming," declares the LORD, "when men will no longer say, 'As surely as the LORD lives, who brought the Israelites up out of Egypt,'[z] 15 but they will say, 'As surely as the LORD lives, who brought the Israelites up out of the

Cross references (margin)

15:19
c Zec 3:7

15:20
d Jer 20:11; Eze 3:8

15:21
e Jer 50:34
f Ge 48:16

16:2
g 1Co 7:26-27

16:3
h Jer 6:21
16:4
i Jer 25:33
j Ps 83:10; Jer 9:22
k Ps 79:1-3;
Jer 15:3; 34:20

16:6
l Eze 9:5-6
m Lev 19:28
n Jer 41:5; 47:5
16:7
o Eze 24:17;
Hos 9:4

16:8
p Ecc 7:2-4;
Jer 15:17
16:9
q Isa 24:8;
Eze 26:13;
Hos 2:11
r Rev 18:23

16:10
s Dt 29:24; Jer 5:19

16:11
t Dt 29:25-26;
1Ki 9:9;
Ps 106:35-43;
Jer 22:9
16:12
u Jer 7:26
v Ecc 9:3; Jer 13:10
16:13
w Dt 28:36;
Jer 5:19 x Dt 4:28
y Jer 15:5
16:14
z Dt 15:15;
Jer 23:7-8

Jeremiah 16:1—17:18

Jeremiah's celibacy represented his message, like Hosea's marriage to a prostitute (Hos. 1:2–3) or God's ban against Ezekiel's publicly mourning his wife's death (Ezek. 24:15–27). The prophet delivered God's message in part by restricting his social life. Judgment was at hand. But in 16:14–15 God announced an abrupt change: The judgment of the exile would be matched by another saving exodus from foreign territory back to the promised land.

Jeremiah's portrayal of human fallibility has links with other Biblical writers, who also saw sinfulness not just as a harmful deed or process but as a condition of human existence. In contemporary Western culture, where guilt is seldom discussed apart from the decisions of law courts, recovering a Biblical understanding of the universal nature of sin and its devastating effects—both individually and corporately—will aid us in proclaiming that God has spoken decisively to the world in Jesus Christ.

16:15
a Isa 11:11;
Jer 23:8 b Jer 24:6

16:16
c Am 4:2;
Hab 1:14-15
d Am 9:3; Mic 7:2
e 1Sa 26:20
16:17
f 1Co 4:5; Heb 4:13
g Pr 15:3
16:18
h Isa 40:2; Rev 18:6
i Nu 35:34; Jer 2:7

16:19
j Isa 2:2; Jer 3:17
k Ps 4:2

16:20
l Ps 115:4-7;
Isa 37:19; Jer 2:11

17:1
m Job 19:24
n Pr 3:3; 2Co 3:3

17:2
o 2Ch 24:18
p Jer 2:20

17:3
q 2Ki 24:13
r Jer 26:18;
Mic 3:12
s Jer 15:13

17:4
t La 5:2 u Dt 28:48;
Jer 12:7 v Jer 16:13
w Jer 7:20; 15:14

17:5
x Isa 2:22; 30:1-3

17:6
y Dt 29:23;
Job 39:6
17:7
z Ps 34:8; 40:4;
Pr 16:20

land of the north and out of all the countries where he had banished them.' [a] For I will restore [b] them to the land I gave their forefathers.

16 "But now I will send for many fishermen," declares the LORD, "and they will catch them. [c] After that I will send for many hunters, and they will hunt [d] them down on every mountain and hill and from the crevices of the rocks. [e] 17 My eyes are on all their ways; they are not hidden [f] from me, nor is their sin concealed from my eyes. [g] 18 I will repay them double [h] for their wickedness and their sin, because they have defiled my land [i] with the lifeless forms of their vile images and have filled my inheritance with their detestable idols."

19 O LORD, my strength and my fortress,
　　my refuge in time of distress,
to you the nations will come [j]
　　from the ends of the earth and say,
"Our fathers possessed nothing but false gods, [k]
　　worthless idols that did them no good.
20 Do men make their own gods?
　　Yes, but they are not gods!" [l]

21 "Therefore I will teach them—
　　this time I will teach them
　　my power and might.
Then they will know
　　that my name is the LORD.

17 "Judah's sin is engraved with an iron tool, [m]
　　inscribed with a flint point,
on the tablets of their hearts [n]
　　and on the horns of their altars.
2 Even their children remember
　　their altars and Asherah poles [a] [o]
beside the spreading trees
　　and on the high hills. [p]
3 My mountain in the land
　　and your [b] wealth and all your treasures
I will give away as plunder, [q]
　　together with your high places, [r]
　　because of sin throughout your country. [s]
4 Through your own fault you will lose
　　the inheritance [t] I gave you.
I will enslave you to your enemies [u]
　　in a land [v] you do not know,
for you have kindled my anger,
　　and it will burn [w] forever."

5 This is what the LORD says:

"Cursed is the one who trusts in man, [x]
　　who depends on flesh for his strength
　　and whose heart turns away from the LORD.
6 He will be like a bush in the wastelands;
　　he will not see prosperity when it comes.
He will dwell in the parched places of the desert,
　　in a salt [y] land where no one lives.

7 "But blessed is the man who trusts [z] in the LORD,
　　whose confidence is in him.
8 He will be like a tree planted by the water
　　that sends out its roots by the stream.

a 2　That is, symbols of the goddess Asherah　　b 2,3　Or hills / 3and the mountains of the land. / Your

It does not fear when heat comes;
  its leaves are always green.
It has no worries in a year of drought[a]
  and never fails to bear fruit."[b]

[9] The heart[c] is deceitful above all things
  and beyond cure.
  Who can understand it?

[10] "I the LORD search the heart[d]
  and examine the mind,[e]
to reward[f] a man according to his conduct,
  according to what his deeds deserve."[g]

[11] Like a partridge that hatches eggs it did not lay
  is the man who gains riches by unjust means.
When his life is half gone, they will desert him,
  and in the end he will prove to be a fool.[h]

[12] A glorious throne,[i] exalted from the beginning,
  is the place of our sanctuary.
[13] O LORD, the hope[j] of Israel,
  all who forsake[k] you will be put to shame.
Those who turn away from you will be written in the dust
  because they have forsaken the LORD,
  the spring of living water.

[14] Heal me, O LORD, and I will be healed;
  save me and I will be saved,
  for you are the one I praise.[l]
[15] They keep saying to me,
  "Where is the word of the LORD?
  Let it now be fulfilled!"[m]
[16] I have not run away from being your shepherd;
  you know I have not desired the day of despair.
  What passes my lips is open before you.
[17] Do not be a terror[n] to me;
  you are my refuge[o] in the day of disaster.
[18] Let my persecutors be put to shame,
  but keep me from shame;
let them be terrified,
  but keep me from terror.
Bring on them the day of disaster;
  destroy them with double destruction.[p]

Keeping the Sabbath Holy

[19] This is what the LORD said to me: "Go and stand at the gate of the people, through which the kings of Judah go in and out; stand also at all the other gates of Jerusalem.[q] [20] Say to them, 'Hear the word of the LORD, O kings of Judah and all people of Judah and everyone living in Jerusalem[r] who come through these gates.[s] [21] This is what the LORD says: Be careful not to carry a load on the Sabbath[t] day or bring it through the gates of Jerusalem. [22] Do not bring a load out of your houses or do any work on the Sabbath, but keep the Sabbath day holy, as I commanded your forefathers.[u] [23] Yet they did not listen or pay attention;[v] they were stiff-necked[w]

Jeremiah 17:19–27

This section is Jeremiah's mini-sermon on the Sabbath. Honoring the Sabbath is the bridge commandment in the Ten Commandments (Ex. 20:1–17), coming between those about relating to God and those about relating to family and neighbor. Sabbath-keeping is a pattern instituted by God (Gen. 2:1–3) and an activity blessed by him. Jesus would offer severe criticism of a legalistic interpretation of the Sabbath (e.g., Mark 2:23—3:6), while acknowledging its divine origin and purpose.

17:8 a Jer 14:1-6 b Ps 1:3; 92:12-14
17:9 c Ecc 9:3; Mt 13:15; Mk 7:21-22
17:10 d 1Sa 16:7; Rev 2:23 e Ps 17:3; 139:23; Jer 11:20; 20:12; Ro 8:27 f Ps 62:12; Jer 32:19 g Ro 2:6
17:11 h Lk 12:20
17:12 i Jer 3:17
17:13 j Jer 14:8 k Isa 1:28; Jer 2:17
17:14 l Ps 109:1
17:15 m Isa 5:19; 2Pe 3:4
17:17 n Ps 88:15-16 o Jer 16:19; Na 1:7
17:18 p Ps 35:1-8
17:19 q Jer 7:2; 26:2
17:20 r Jer 19:3 s Jer 22:2
17:21 t Nu 15:32-36; Ne 13:15-21; Jn 5:10
17:22 u Ex 20:8; 31:13; Isa 56:2-6; Eze 20:12
17:23 v Jer 7:26 w Jer 19:15

17:23
x Jer 7:28

and would not listen or respond to discipline.[x] 24But if you are careful to obey me, declares the LORD, and bring no load through the gates of this city on the Sabbath, but keep the Sabbath day holy by not doing any work on it, 25then kings who sit on David's throne[y] will come through the gates of this city with their officials. They and their officials will come riding in chariots and on horses, accompanied by the men of Judah and those living in Jerusalem, and this city will be inhabited forever. 26People will come from the towns of Judah and the villages around Jerusalem, from the territory of Benjamin and the western foothills, from the hill country and the Negev,[z] bringing burnt offerings and sacrifices, grain offerings, incense and thank offerings to the house of the LORD. 27But if you do not obey[a] me to keep the Sabbath day holy by not carrying any load as you come through the gates of Jerusalem on the Sabbath day, then I will kindle an unquenchable fire[b] in the gates of Jerusalem that will consume her fortresses.' "[c]

17:25
y 2Sa 7:13; Isa 9:7;
Jer 22:2,4; Lk 1:32

17:26
z Jer 32:44; 33:13;
Zec 7:7
17:27
a Jer 22:5
b Jer 7:20
c 2Ki 25:9; Am 2:5

At the Potter's House

18 This is the word that came to Jeremiah from the LORD: 2"Go down to the potter's house, and there I will give you my message." 3So I went down to the potter's house, and I saw him working at the wheel. 4But the pot he was shaping from the clay was marred in his hands; so the potter formed it into another pot, shaping it as seemed best to him.

18:6
d Isa 45:9;
Ro 9:20-21

5Then the word of the LORD came to me: 6"O house of Israel, can I not do with you as this potter does?" declares the LORD. "Like clay[d] in the hand of the potter, so are you in my hand, O house of Israel. 7If at any time I announce that a nation or kingdom is to be uprooted,[e] torn down and destroyed, 8and if that nation I warned repents of its evil, then I will relent[f] and not inflict on it the disaster[g] I had planned. 9And if at another time I announce that a nation or kingdom is to be built[h] up and planted, 10and if it does evil[i] in my sight and does not obey me, then I will reconsider[j] the good I had intended to do for it.

18:7
e Jer 1:10
18:8
f Jer 26:13;
Jnh 3:8-10
g Eze 18:21;
Hos 11:8-9
18:9
h Jer 1:10; 31:28
18:10
i Eze 33:18
j 1Sa 2:29-30
18:11
k Jer 4:6
l 2Ki 17:13;
Isa 1:16-19
m Jer 7:3
18:12
n Isa 57:10;
Jer 2:25

11"Now therefore say to the people of Judah and those living in Jerusalem, 'This is what the LORD says: Look! I am preparing a disaster[k] for you and devising a plan against you. So turn[l] from your evil ways,[m] each one of you, and reform your ways and your actions.' 12But they will reply, 'It's no use.[n] We will continue with our own plans; each of us will follow the stubbornness of his evil heart.' "

13Therefore this is what the LORD says:

18:13
o Isa 66:8; Jer 2:10
p Jer 5:30

"Inquire among the nations:
   Who has ever heard anything like this?[o]
A most horrible[p] thing has been done
   by Virgin Israel.
14Does the snow of Lebanon
   ever vanish from its rocky slopes?
Do its cool waters from distant sources
   ever cease to flow?[a]
15Yet my people have forgotten me;

[a] 14 The meaning of the Hebrew for this sentence is uncertain.

Jeremiah focused on the importance of not working on the Sabbath. Interestingly, there is nothing explicit in his mini-sermon and little in the rest of Scripture about *worshiping* on the Sabbath. Perhaps a Christian Sabbath can become a sign in a tension-packed world that we don't live by work alone but by the rest and renewal that come from God. Our setting apart a day for rest can *illustrate* to the world our growth in the process of loving God and enjoying him forever. What besides worship (certainly a vital element of your Sabbath) characterizes this one day in seven for you?

Jeremiah 18:1—19:15

Just as a potter may form and re-form the same blob of clay until he or she is satisfied or decides to discard it, so God could form and reform Israel or any other nation. God judges nations and not just individuals, based on (1) their faithfulness to him and his ways, (2) their protection of the innocent, and (3) their regard for children (19:4–5). If God announced judgment on a nation and that nation repented, he would "relent" from inflicting disaster (18:7–8). But if he announced goodness for a kingdom and it acted faithlessly, he would "reconsider"; blessing wouldn't be forthcoming (18:9–10).

they burn incense to worthless idols,[q]
which made them stumble in their ways
    and in the ancient paths.[r]
They made them walk in bypaths
    and on roads not built up.[s]
16 Their land will be laid waste,[t]
    an object of lasting scorn;[u]
all who pass by will be appalled
    and will shake their heads.[v]
17 Like a wind[w] from the east,
    I will scatter them before their enemies;
I will show them my back and not my face[x]
    in the day of their disaster."

18 They said, "Come, let's make plans[y] against Jeremiah; for the teaching of the law by the priest[z] will not be lost, nor will counsel from the wise, nor the word from the prophets.[a] So come, let's attack him with our tongues[b] and pay no attention to anything he says."

19 Listen to me, O LORD;
    hear what my accusers are saying!
20 Should good be repaid with evil?
    Yet they have dug a pit[c] for me.
Remember that I stood before you
    and spoke in their behalf[d]
to turn your wrath away from them.
21 So give their children over to famine;[e]
    hand them over to the power of the sword.
Let their wives be made childless and widows;[f]
    let their men be put to death,
    their young men slain by the sword in battle.
22 Let a cry[g] be heard from their houses
    when you suddenly bring invaders against them,
for they have dug a pit to capture me
    and have hidden snares[h] for my feet.
23 But you know, O LORD,
    all their plots to kill[i] me.
Do not forgive[j] their crimes
    or blot out their sins from your sight.
Let them be overthrown before you;
    deal with them in the time of your anger.

19 This is what the LORD says: "Go and buy a clay jar from a potter.[k] Take along some of the elders[l] of the people and of the priests 2 and go out to the Valley of Ben Hinnom,[m] near the entrance of the Potsherd Gate. There proclaim the words I tell you, 3 and say, 'Hear the word of the LORD, O kings[n] of Judah and people of Jerusalem. This is what the LORD Almighty, the God of Israel, says: Listen! I am going to bring a disaster[o] on this place that will make the ears of everyone who hears of it tingle.[p] 4 For they have forsaken[q] me and made this a place of foreign gods; they have burned sacrifices[r] in it to gods that neither they nor their fathers nor the kings of Judah ever knew, and they have filled this place with the blood of the innocent.[s]

18:15
q Jer 10:15
r Jer 6:16
s Isa 57:14; 62:10

18:16
t Jer 25:9 u Jer 19:8
v Ps 22:7

18:17
w Jer 13:24
x Jer 2:27

18:18
y Jer 11:19
z Mal 2:7 a Jer 5:13
b Ps 52:2

18:20
c Ps 35:7; 57:6
d Ps 106:23

18:21
e Jer 11:22
f Ps 109:9

18:22
g Jer 6:26
h Ps 140:5

18:23
i Jer 11:21
j Ps 109:14

19:1
k Jer 18:2
l Nu 11:17

19:2
m Jos 15:8
19:3
n Jer 17:20
o Jer 6:19
p 1Sa 3:11
19:4
q Dt 28:20;
Isa 65:11
r Lev 18:21
s 2Ki 21:16;
Jer 2:34

The wonder of Jeremiah's announcement that God can "relent" and "reconsider" isn't that God changes his approach. Rather, he opens up ways of transformation and change in the midst of sinful and painful circumstances.

Our confidence in the Potter rests in developing a relationship with him—something Jeremiah's audience refused to do. The Potter calls us to flee from giving our devotion to other gods and to serve only God, reject the shedding of innocent blood, and protect our children. We may not worship Baals in our world today, but what are some other "gods" to whom many seem to offer their devotion? In what ways are innocent blood shed or children sacrificed to people's own ambitions and pleasures?

19:5
t Lev 18:21;
Ps 106:37-38
u Jer 7:31; 32:35
19:6
v Jos 15:8
w Jer 7:32
19:7
x Lev 26:17;
Dt 28:25 y Jer 16:4;
34:20 z Ps 79:2
19:8
a Jer 18:16
19:9
b Lev 26:29;
Dt 28:49-57;
La 4:10 c Isa 9:20
19:10
d ver 1
19:11
e Ps 2:9; Isa 30:14
f Jer 7:32
19:13
g Jer 32:29; 52:13
h Dt 4:19; Ac 7:42
i Jer 7:18;
Eze 20:28
19:14
j 2Ch 20:5; Jer 26:2
19:15
k Ne 9:16; Jer 7:26;
17:23
20:1
l 1Ch 24:14
m 2Ki 25:18
20:2
n Jer 1:19
o Job 13:27
p Jer 37:13; 38:7;
Zec 14:10
20:3
q ver 10
20:4
r Jer 29:21
s Jer 21:10
t Jer 52:27
20:5
u Jer 17:3
v 2Ki 20:17
20:6
w Jer 14:15;
La 2:14

5 They have built the high places of Baal to burn their sons[t] in the fire as offerings to Baal—something I did not command or mention, nor did it enter my mind.[u] 6 So beware, the days are coming, declares the LORD, when people will no longer call this place Topheth or the Valley of Ben Hinnom,[v] but the Valley of Slaughter.[w]

7 " 'In this place I will ruin[a] the plans of Judah and Jerusalem. I will make them fall by the sword before their enemies,[x] at the hands of those who seek their lives, and I will give their carcasses[y] as food[z] to the birds of the air and the beasts of the earth. 8 I will devastate this city and make it an object of scorn;[a] all who pass by will be appalled and will scoff because of all its wounds. 9 I will make them eat[b] the flesh of their sons and daughters, and they will eat one another's flesh during the stress of the siege imposed on them by the enemies[c] who seek their lives.'

10 "Then break the jar[d] while those who go with you are watching, 11 and say to them, 'This is what the LORD Almighty says: I will smash[e] this nation and this city just as this potter's jar is smashed and cannot be repaired. They will bury[f] the dead in Topheth until there is no more room. 12 This is what I will do to this place and to those who live here, declares the LORD. I will make this city like Topheth. 13 The houses[g] in Jerusalem and those of the kings of Judah will be defiled like this place, Topheth—all the houses where they burned incense on the roofs to all the starry hosts[h] and poured out drink offerings[i] to other gods.' "

14 Jeremiah then returned from Topheth, where the LORD had sent him to prophesy, and stood in the court[j] of the LORD's temple and said to all the people, 15 "This is what the LORD Almighty, the God of Israel, says: 'Listen! I am going to bring on this city and the villages around it every disaster I pronounced against them, because they were stiff-necked[k] and would not listen to my words.' "

Jeremiah and Pashhur

20 When the priest Pashhur son of Immer,[l] the chief officer[m] in the temple of the LORD, heard Jeremiah prophesying these things, 2 he had Jeremiah the prophet beaten[n] and put in the stocks[o] at the Upper Gate of Benjamin[p] at the LORD's temple. 3 The next day, when Pashhur released him from the stocks, Jeremiah said to him, "The LORD's name for you is not Pashhur, but Magor-Missabib.[b][q] 4 For this is what the LORD says: 'I will make you a terror to yourself and to all your friends; with your own eyes[r] you will see them fall by the sword of their enemies. I will hand[s] all Judah over to the king of Babylon, who will carry[t] them away to Babylon or put them to the sword. 5 I will hand over to their enemies all the wealth[u] of this city—all its products, all its valuables and all the treasures of the kings of Judah. They will take it away[v] as plunder and carry it off to Babylon. 6 And you, Pashhur, and all who live in your house will go into exile to Babylon. There you will die and be buried, you and all your friends to whom you have prophesied[w] lies.' "

Jeremiah's Complaint

7 O LORD, you deceived[c] me, and I was deceived[c];
you overpowered me and prevailed.

a 7 The Hebrew for *ruin* sounds like the Hebrew for *jar* (see verses 1 and 10).   b 3 *Magor-Missabib* means *terror on every side*.   c 7 Or *persuaded*

Jeremiah 20:1–6

Pashhur's position as "chief officer" in the temple was second only to that of the chief priest. Among other things, he headed the security detail for the large complex. The humiliation of being beaten and placed in stocks by the religious establishment must have been especially galling for Jeremiah, since he too was from a priestly family.

Rather than being intimidated by his suffering, Jeremiah emerged from it with boldness, speaking the truth of God's judgment against the priests and Judah. It

doesn't take much imagination to see the parallels between Jeremiah's and Jesus' humiliation and suffering. Jeremiah's experience was prophetic in the sense that it points us to Christ, the perfect Mediator, whose suffering is representative of guilty and innocent suffering alike.

Jeremiah 20:7–18

Jeremiah's persecutors lay in wait to ambush and ridicule him with his own phrase, "terror on every side." It was as though they were calling him a deluded madman who had spoken incessantly about horrific

I am ridiculed all day long;
    everyone mocks me.
[8]Whenever I speak, I cry out
    proclaiming violence and destruction.[x]
So the word of the LORD has brought me
    insult and reproach[y] all day long.
[9]But if I say, "I will not mention him
    or speak any more in his name,"
his word is in my heart like a fire,[z]
    a fire shut up in my bones.
I am weary of holding it in;[a]
    indeed, I cannot.
[10]I hear many whispering,
    "Terror[b] on every side!
    Report[c] him! Let's report him!"
All my friends[d]
    are waiting for me to slip,[e] saying,
"Perhaps he will be deceived;
    then we will prevail[f] over him
    and take our revenge on him."

[11]But the LORD[g] is with me like a mighty warrior;
    so my persecutors[h] will stumble and not prevail.[i]
They will fail and be thoroughly disgraced;[j]
    their dishonor will never be forgotten.
[12]O LORD Almighty, you who examine the righteous
    and probe the heart and mind,[k]
let me see your vengeance[l] upon them,
    for to you I have committed[m] my cause.

[13]Sing to the LORD!
    Give praise to the LORD!
He rescues[n] the life of the needy
    from the hands of the wicked.

[14]Cursed be the day I was born![o]
    May the day my mother bore me not be blessed!
[15]Cursed be the man who brought my father the news,
    who made him very glad, saying,
    "A child is born to you—a son!"
[16]May that man be like the towns[p]
    the LORD overthrew without pity.
May he hear wailing in the morning,
    a battle cry at noon.
[17]For he did not kill me in the womb,[q]
    with my mother as my grave,
    her womb enlarged forever.
[18]Why did I ever come out of the womb
    to see trouble and sorrow
    and to end my days in shame?[r]

20:8 x Jer 6:7; y 2Ch 36:16; Jer 6:10
20:9 z Ps 39:3; a Job 32:18-20; Ac 4:20
20:10 b Ps 31:13; Jer 6:25; c Isa 29:21; d Ps 41:9; e Lk 11:53-54; f 1Ki 19:2
20:11 g Jer 1:8; Ro 8:31; h Jer 17:18; i Jer 15:20; j Jer 23:40
20:12 k Jer 17:10; l Ps 54:7; 59:10; m Ps 62:8; Jer 11:20
20:13 n Ps 35:10
20:14 o Job 3:3; Jer 15:10
20:16 p Ge 19:25
20:17 q Job 10:18-19
20:18 r Ps 90:9

---

events to come. In his frustration and bitterness Jeremiah accused God of "deceiving" him, a strong term that could also refer to seduction. The prophet had reached his wits' end and had lost confidence that God would rescue him.

It's no failure on our part if we feel crushed by the burdens that come to us even when we are being faithful to God's call. The best response when that occurs is for us to bring our frustrations and complaints to God, for in doing this we still affirm our faith and deepen our relationship with him. Have you been tempted to feel that God wasn't interested or present in your pain? Jeremiah's suffering instructs us about the cost of discipleship and testifies that God is faithful—beyond our limited understanding and in spite of our complaints.

God Rejects Zedekiah's Request

21 The word came to Jeremiah from the LORD when King Zedekiah^s sent to him Pashhur^t son of Malkijah and the priest Zephaniah^u son of Maaseiah. They said: [2] "Inquire^v now of the LORD for us because Nebuchadnezzar^{a w} king of Babylon is attacking us. Perhaps the LORD will perform wonders^x for us as in times past so that he will withdraw from us."

[3] But Jeremiah answered them, "Tell Zedekiah, [4] 'This is what the LORD, the God of Israel, says: I am about to turn^y against you the weapons of war that are in your hands, which you are using to fight the king of Babylon and the Babylonians^b who are outside the wall besieging^z you. And I will gather them inside this city. [5] I myself will fight against you with an outstretched hand^a and a mighty arm in anger and fury and great wrath. [6] I will strike down those who live in this city—both men and animals—and they will die of a terrible plague.^b [7] After that, declares the LORD, I will hand over Zedekiah^c king of Judah, his officials and the people in this city who survive the plague, sword and famine, to Nebuchadnezzar king of Babylon^d and to their enemies who seek their lives. He will put them to the sword; he will show them no mercy or pity or compassion.'^e

[8] "Furthermore, tell the people, 'This is what the LORD says: See, I am setting before you the way of life and the way of death. [9] Whoever stays in this city will die by the sword, famine or plague.^f But whoever goes out and surrenders to the Babylonians who are besieging you will live; he will escape with his life.^g [10] I have determined to do this city harm^h and not good, declares the LORD. It will be given into the handsⁱ of the king of Babylon, and he will destroy it with fire.'^j

[11] "Moreover, say to the royal house^k of Judah, 'Hear the word of the LORD; [12] O house of David, this is what the LORD says:

" 'Administer justice^l every morning;
    rescue from the hand of his oppressor
    the one who has been robbed,
or my wrath will break out and burn like fire
    because of the evil you have done—
    burn with no one to quench^m it.
[13] I am againstⁿ you, ⌐Jerusalem,⌐
    you who live above this valley^o
    on the rocky plateau,

                declares the LORD—

you who say, "Who can come against us?
    Who can enter our refuge?"^p
[14] I will punish you as your deeds^q deserve,

                declares the LORD.

I will kindle a fire^r in your forests^s
    that will consume everything around you.' "

---

^a 2 Hebrew *Nebuchadrezzar*, of which *Nebuchadnezzar* is a variant; here and often in Jeremiah and Ezekiel   ^b 4 Or *Chaldeans*; also in verse 9

Cross-references (margin)

21:1 ^s 2Ki 24:18; Jer 52:1 ^t Jer 38:1 ^u 2Ki 25:18; Jer 29:25; 37:3
21:2 ^v Jer 37:3,7 ^w 2Ki 25:1 ^x Ps 44:1-4; Jer 32:17
21:4 ^y Jer 32:5 ^z Jer 37:8-10
21:5 ^a Jer 6:12
21:6 ^b Jer 14:12
21:7 ^c 2Ki 25:7; Jer 52:9 ^d Jer 37:17; 39:5 ^e 2Ch 36:17; Eze 7:9; Hab 1:6
21:9 ^f Jer 14:12 ^g Jer 38:2,17; 39:18; 45:5
21:10 ^h Jer 44:11,27; Am 9:4 ⁱ Jer 32:28; 38:2-3 ^j Jer 52:13
21:11 ^k Jer 13:18
21:12 ^l Jer 22:3 ^m Isa 1:31
21:13 ⁿ Eze 13:8 ^o Ps 125:2 ^p Jer 49:4; Ob 1:3-4
21:14 ^q Isa 3:10-11 ^r 2Ch 36:19; Jer 52:13 ^s Eze 20:47

Jeremiah 21:1–14

The name of one of the officials (Pashur) is the same as that of the priest in chapter 20, though they were two different people. This passage provides one of the few "dates" (inferred from Zedekiah's reign) in the first half of the book.

According to the divine message, God wouldn't wage war against the Babylonian army but against Judah. Jerusalem's fall was certain. The Hebrew for the word translated "determined" in verse 10 is an idiom meaning "the setting of the face," indicating God's single-minded resolve to judge his people. Ominously, there was no call for repentance. The best the Judahites could do was surrender to the Babylonians.

The allusion in verse 8 to God's covenant proclamation through Moses in Deuteronomy 30:19—"I have set before you life and death"—sets the announcement of Jerusalem's doom within a broader Biblical context. Even though both alternatives (death or surrender) were grim, the inhabitants of Jerusalem had a choice of "ways." Jesus' warning about the ways of life and destruction (Matt. 7:13–14) follows the same pattern. To every generation comes the call to obey and choose life over death.

Judgment Against Evil Kings

22 This is what the LORD says: "Go down to the palace of the king of Judah and proclaim this message there: 2'Hear the word of the LORD, O king of Judah, you who sit on David's throne[t]—you, your officials and your people who come through these gates.[u] 3This is what the LORD says: Do what is just[v] and right. Rescue from the hand of his oppressor[w] the one who has been robbed. Do no wrong or violence to the alien, the fatherless or the widow,[x] and do not shed innocent blood in this place. 4For if you are careful to carry out these commands, then kings[y] who sit on David's throne will come through the gates of this palace, riding in chariots and on horses, accompanied by their officials and their people. 5But if you do not obey[z] these commands, declares the LORD, I swear[a] by myself that this palace will become a ruin.' "

6For this is what the LORD says about the palace of the king of Judah:

"Though you are like Gilead to me,
  like the summit of Lebanon,
I will surely make you like a desert,[b]
  like towns not inhabited.

22:2
t Jer 17:25; Lk 1:32
u Jer 17:20
22:3
v Mic 6:8; Zec 7:9
w Ps 72:4;
Jer 21:12
x Ex 22:22
22:4
y Jer 17:25
22:5
z Jer 17:27
a Heb 6:13
22:6
b Mic 3:12

Jeremiah 22:1–30

Jeremiah recognized the intimate connection between the people's faithfulness to God and their social, economic, and political relations. Love for God and neighbor are interwoven. Thus the prophet announced God's judgment based on how the Judahites treated strangers and foreigners, orphans and widows, and the innocent (v. 3). God has a special concern for the poor and needy (v. 16), and his people are called to express the same.

22:1–5

Uneven Distribution of Wealth in the United States

Poverty isn't just a problem "over there." Jeremiah teaches us that the poor aren't to be neglected no matter where they are. For example:

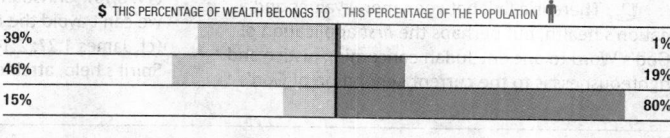

In the United States:

$ THIS PERCENTAGE OF WEALTH BELONGS TO	THIS PERCENTAGE OF THE POPULATION
39%	1%
46%	19%
15%	80%

In the United States:

16.5 million WHITES ARE POOR	**8.6%** OF THE WHITE POPULATION
9.1 million BLACKS ARE POOR	**26.5%** OF THE BLACK POPULATION
8.3 million HISPANICS ARE POOR	**27.1%** OF THE HISPANIC POPULATION

In the United States the median income is $37,005:

THE WHITE MEDIAN INCOME IS	$40,577
THE BLACK MEDIAN INCOME IS $20,050	
THE HISPANIC MEDIAN INCOME IS $26,628	
THE ASIAN MEDIAN INCOME IS	$45,249

In the United States:

13 percent of all Americans (35.6 million) live below the poverty line.

6 million are severely poor, with income less than half the poverty threshold.

Children make up 26 percent of the total population but 40 percent of the poor.

Source: Wurman (2000)

The poverty threshold is determined by household size. For example:

THE POVERTY THRESHOLD FOR A HOUSEHOLD OF ONE IS
$8,183

THE POVERTY THRESHOLD FOR A HOUSEHOLD OF FOUR IS
$16,400

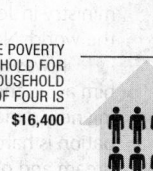

THE POVERTY THRESHOLD FOR A HOUSEHOLD OF EIGHT IS
$27,593

22:7
c Jer 4:7 *d* Isa 10:34

7 I will send destroyers *c* against you,
    each man with his weapons,
    and they will cut *d* up your fine cedar beams
    and throw them into the fire.

22:8
e Dt 29:25-26;
1Ki 9:8-9;
Jer 16:10-11
22:9
f 2Ki 22:17;
2Ch 34:25
22:10
g Ecc 4:2 *h* ver 18

8 "People from many nations will pass by this city and will ask one another, 'Why has the LORD done such a thing to this great city?'*e* 9 And the answer will be: 'Because they have forsaken the covenant of the LORD their God and have worshiped and served other gods.*f* ' "

10 Do not weep for the dead *g* ⌊king⌋ or mourn *h* his loss;
    rather, weep bitterly for him who is exiled,
  because he will never return
    nor see his native land again.

22:11
i 2Ki 23:31

11 For this is what the LORD says about Shallum *a* *i* son of Josiah, who succeeded his father as king of Judah but has gone from this place: "He will never return. 12 He will die *j* in the place where they have led him captive; he will not see this land again."

22:12
j 2Ki 23:34

22:13
k Mic 3:10; Hab 2:9

13 "Woe to him who builds *k* his palace by unrighteousness,
    his upper rooms by injustice,

---

a 11 Also called *Jehoahaz*

The criticisms of three kings and the list of social crimes were part of a larger Biblical concern for righteousness. God's prophets were universal in announcing judgment based on oppression and injustice (cf. Amos 5:7,12–15,21–24; 6:12; Mic. 2:1–2; 3:1).

📖 There is a link between moral values and a nation's health, but perhaps the *first* application of God's Word to ancient Judah concerning justice and righteousness is to the current generation of God's people—the body of Christ.

The test of knowing God is the commitment of an individual to doing the things of God—including advocating and acting for justice on behalf of the poor, widowed, orphaned, foreigners, and other oppressed groups (vv. 3,16). Christians can try to ignore this message, but we can't avoid the truth that faith without action is dead (cf. James 1:27; 2:14–26). Do you feel you have, with the Spirit's help, attained a healthy balance in this regard?

Snapshots

22:2–3

Hamedi

To my anonymous friend in another country:
How are you? If you would like to know how I have been feeling lately, let me tell you that I have been very sad as the situation in Palestine is devastating. Despite everything, I was able to participate in a camp here in the Old City of Jerusalem. With the camp, I go to many nice places and sometimes this helps me forget the sad life that we live.
Thank you,
Hamedi, 13

> **"No one should be superior to anyone else."**

Hamedi is a Palestinian boy who regularly attends a children's club sponsored by a Christian ministry in Jerusalem. His dreams: "There should neither be poor people nor rich people in the world. No one should be superior to anyone else."

It was a great relief to Hamedi's family to have access to this program, because it helps him avoid the streets and encourages him to invest his time cultivating his talents and exploring new dimensions of life. The club's activities are considered a privilege, as life under occupation is hard. Yet the children here taste a bit of childhood and have the opportunity to dream and plan for their future.

making his countrymen work for nothing,
  not paying[l] them for their labor.
14 He says, 'I will build myself a great palace[m]
    with spacious upper rooms.'
  So he makes large windows in it,
    panels it with cedar[n]
    and decorates it in red.

15 "Does it make you a king
    to have more and more cedar?
  Did not your father have food and drink?
    He did what was right and just,[o]
    so all went well[p] with him.
16 He defended the cause of the poor and needy,[q]
    and so all went well.
  Is that not what it means to know me?"
    declares the LORD.
17 "But your eyes and your heart
    are set only on dishonest gain,
  on shedding innocent blood[r]
    and on oppression and extortion."

18 Therefore this is what the LORD says about Jehoiakim son of Josiah king of Judah:

  "They will not mourn for him:
    'Alas, my brother! Alas, my sister!'
  They will not mourn for him:
    'Alas, my master! Alas, his splendor!'
19 He will have the burial of a donkey—
    dragged away and thrown[s]
    outside the gates of Jerusalem."

20 "Go up to Lebanon and cry out,
    let your voice be heard in Bashan,
  cry out from Abarim,[t]
    for all your allies are crushed.
21 I warned you when you felt secure,
    but you said, 'I will not listen!'
  This has been your way from your youth;[u]
    you have not obeyed[v] me.
22 The wind will drive all your shepherds away,
    and your allies will go into exile.
  Then you will be ashamed and disgraced
    because of all your wickedness.
23 You who live in 'Lebanon,[a]
    who are nestled in cedar buildings,
  how you will groan when pangs come upon you,
    pain[w] like that of a woman in labor!

24 "As surely as I live," declares the LORD, "even if you, Jehoiachin[b][x] son of Jehoiakim king of Judah, were a signet ring on my right hand, I would still pull you off. 25 I will hand you over[y] to those who seek your life, those you fear—to Nebuchadnezzar king of Babylon and to the Babylonians.[c] 26 I will hurl[z] you and the mother who gave you birth into another country, where neither of you was born, and there you both will die. 27 You will never come back to the land you long to return to."

28 Is this man Jehoiachin a despised, broken pot,[a]
    an object no one wants?

---

[a] 23 That is, the palace in Jerusalem (see 1 Kings 7:2) [b] 24 Hebrew *Coniah*, a variant of *Jehoiachin*; also in verse 28 [c] 25 Or *Chaldeans*

22:13
[l] Lev 19:13; Jas 5:4
22:14
[m] Isa 5:8-9
[n] 2Sa 7:2

22:15
[o] 2Ki 23:25
[p] Ps 128:2; Isa 3:10
22:16
[q] Ps 72:1-4, 12-13

22:17
[r] 2Ki 24:4

22:19
[s] Jer 36:30

22:20
[t] Nu 27:12

22:21
[u] Jer 3:25; 32:30
[v] Jer 7:23-28

22:23
[w] Jer 4:31

22:24
[x] 2Ki 24:6,8; Jer 37:1

22:25
[y] 2Ki 24:16; Jer 34:20
22:26
[z] 2Ki 24:8; 2Ch 36:10

22:28
[a] Ps 31:12; Jer 48:38; Hos 8:8

22:28
b Jer 15:1
c Jer 17:4
22:29
d Jer 6:19; Mic 1:2

22:30
e 1Ch 3:18; Mt 1:12
f Jer 10:21
g Ps 94:20

Why will he and his children be hurled[b] out,
    cast into a land[c] they do not know?
29 O land,[d] land, land,
    hear the word of the LORD!
30 This is what the LORD says:
    "Record this man as if childless,[e]
        a man who will not prosper[f] in his lifetime,
    for none of his offspring will prosper,
        none will sit on the throne[g] of David
        or rule anymore in Judah."

The Righteous Branch

23:1
h Jer 10:21;
Eze 34:1-10;
Zec 11:15-17
i Isa 56:11
j Eze 34:31

23:2
k Jer 21:12
23:3
l Isa 11:10-12;
Jer 32:37;
Eze 34:11-16
23:4
m Jer 3:15; 31:10;
Eze 34:23
n Jer 30:10;
46:27-28
o Jn 6:39
23:5
p Isa 4:2 q Isa 9:7
r Isa 11:1; Zec 6:12

23 "Woe to the shepherds[h] who are destroying and scattering[i] the sheep of my pasture!"[j] declares the LORD. 2 Therefore this is what the LORD, the God of Israel, says to the shepherds who tend my people: "Because you have scattered my flock and driven them away and have not bestowed care on them, I will bestow punishment on you for the evil[k] you have done," declares the LORD. 3 "I myself will gather the remnant[l] of my flock out of all the countries where I have driven them and will bring them back to their pasture, where they will be fruitful and increase in number. 4 I will place shepherds[m] over them who will tend them, and they will no longer be afraid[n] or terrified, nor will any be missing,[o]" declares the LORD.

5 "The days are coming," declares the LORD,
    "when I will raise up to David[a] a righteous Branch,[p]
    a King who will reign[q] wisely
        and do what is just and right[r] in the land.
6 In his days Judah will be saved
        and Israel will live in safety.
    This is the name[s] by which he will be called:
        The LORD Our Righteousness.[t]

23:6
s Jer 33:16;
Mt 1:21-23
t Ro 3:21-22;
1Co 1:30

23:7
u Jer 16:14

23:8
v Isa 43:5-6;
Am 9:14-15

7 "So then, the days are coming," declares the LORD, "when people will no longer say, 'As surely as the LORD lives, who brought the Israelites up out of Egypt,'[u] 8 but they will say, 'As surely as the LORD lives, who brought the descendants of Israel up out of the land of the north and out of all the countries where he had banished them.' Then they will live in their own land."[v]

Lying Prophets

9 Concerning the prophets:

My heart is broken within me;
    all my bones tremble.
I am like a drunken man,
    like a man overcome by wine,

a 5 Or *up from David's line*

Jeremiah 23:1-8

Jeremiah 23 contains a number of harsh sayings against the leaders who opposed Jeremiah. Included among the "shepherds" mentioned at the beginning of the chapter were almost certainly kings—perhaps the three kings mentioned in the previous two chapters. But God intended to restore his scattered people, to raise up a shepherd in whom Judah and Israel would find security. His name—"The LORD Our Righteousness"—is a play on the name Zedekiah ("The LORD is my righteousness"), who was Judah's final, unfaithful king.

Old Testament saints heard the Messianic promise in this passage as God's faithfulness to the Davidic line and his grace in saving a remnant of his people. In Christ God has both demonstrated his own righteousness and accepted his Son's righteousness on behalf of those who trust in his saving work. Christ, the culmination of the hopes of the royal office, faithfully fulfilled the Davidic hopes and represents them in a grander way than could possibly have been anticipated in Jeremiah's day (cf. 2 Cor. 5:21).

Jeremiah 23:9-32

Jeremiah related a repulsive fact about the earlier prophets of Samaria (capital of the already exiled northern kingdom): They had prophesied by Baal and led Israel astray. He then reported something equally

because of the LORD
and his holy words. *w*

10 The land is full of adulterers; *x*
because of the curse *a* the land lies parched *b*
and the pastures *y* in the desert are withered. *z*
The ⌊prophets⌋ follow an evil course
and use their power unjustly.

11 "Both prophet and priest are godless; *a*
even in my temple *b* I find their wickedness,"

declares the LORD.

12 "Therefore their path will become slippery; *c*
they will be banished to darkness
and there they will fall.
I will bring disaster on them
in the year they are punished, *d*"

declares the LORD.

13 "Among the prophets of Samaria
I saw this repulsive thing:
They prophesied by Baal *e*
and led my people Israel astray.
14 And among the prophets of Jerusalem
I have seen something horrible: *f*
They commit adultery and live a lie. *g*
They strengthen the hands of evildoers, *h*
so that no one turns from his wickedness.
They are all like Sodom *i* to me;
the people of Jerusalem are like Gomorrah." *j*

15 Therefore, this is what the LORD Almighty says concerning the prophets:

"I will make them eat bitter food
and drink poisoned water, *k*
because from the prophets of Jerusalem
ungodliness has spread throughout the land."

16 This is what the LORD Almighty says:

"Do not listen *l* to what the prophets are prophesying to you;
they fill you with false hopes.
They speak visions *m* from their own minds,
not from the mouth *n* of the LORD.
17 They keep saying to those who despise me,
'The LORD says: You will have peace.' *o*
And to all who follow the stubbornness *p* of their hearts
they say, 'No harm *q* will come to you.'
18 But which of them has stood in the council of the LORD
to see or to hear his word?

23:9
w Jer 20:8-9
23:10
x Jer 9:2
y Ps 107:34;
Jer 9:10
z Hos 4:2-3

23:11
a Jer 6:13; 8:10;
Zep 3:4 *b* Jer 7:10

23:12
c Ps 35:6; Jer 13:16
d Jer 11:23

23:13
e Jer 2:8

23:14
f Jer 5:30
g Jer 29:23
h Eze 13:22
i Ge 18:20
j Isa 1:9-10;
Jer 20:16

23:15
k Jer 8:14; 9:15

23:16
l Jer 27:9-10,14;
Mt 7:15
m Jer 14:14
n Jer 9:20

23:17
o Jer 8:11
p Jer 13:10
q Jer 5:12;
Am 9:10; Mic 3:11

---

a 10 Or *because of these things*   *b 10* Or *land mourns*

---

shocking about the prophets in Jerusalem (capital of the southern kingdom): They were adulterers and living a lie (cf. 29:21–23).

Deuteronomy 13 and 18 warn against prophets promoting the worship of other deities. The penalty for such prophetic activity was death. Similarly, Jesus judged false prophets harshly because of the damage they did (Matt. 7:15–23).

Jeremiah's stinging criticisms in this chapter touch on a sensitive but central Biblical theme: the spiritual and moral character of the leaders of God's people. It's a sobering exercise for Christians to ask who among the church's leadership downplay issues of moral character or soft-pedal important spiritual characteristics needed to shepherd God's flock. How can any of us (leaders or not), as spokespersons for the faith, say one thing but represent another in our personal lives?

Who has listened and heard his word?
19 See, the storm [r] of the LORD
will burst out in wrath,
a whirlwind swirling down
on the heads of the wicked.
20 The anger [s] of the LORD will not turn back [t]
until he fully accomplishes
the purposes of his heart.
In days to come
you will understand it clearly.
21 I did not send [u] these prophets,
yet they have run with their message;
I did not speak to them,
yet they have prophesied.
22 But if they had stood in my council,
they would have proclaimed my words to my people
and would have turned [v] them from their evil ways
and from their evil deeds.

23 "Am I only a God nearby, [w]"

declares the LORD,

"and not a God far away?
24 Can anyone hide [x] in secret places
so that I cannot see him?"

declares the LORD.

"Do not I fill heaven and earth?" [y]

declares the LORD.

25 "I have heard what the prophets say who prophesy lies [z] in my name. They say, 'I had a dream! [a] I had a dream!' 26 How long will this continue in the hearts of these lying prophets, who prophesy the delusions [b] of their own minds? 27 They think the dreams they tell one another will make my people forget [c] my name, just as their fathers forgot [d] my name through Baal worship. 28 Let the prophet who has a dream tell his dream, but let the one who has my word speak it faithfully. For what has straw to do with grain?" declares the LORD. 29 "Is not my word like fire," [e] declares the LORD, "and like a hammer that breaks a rock in pieces?

30 "Therefore," declares the LORD, "I am against [f] the prophets [g] who steal from one another words supposedly from me. 31 Yes," declares the LORD, "I am against the prophets who wag their own tongues and yet declare, 'The LORD declares.' [h] 32 Indeed, I am against those who prophesy false dreams, [i]" declares the LORD. "They tell them and lead my people astray with their reckless lies, yet I did not send or appoint them. They do not benefit [j] these people in the least," declares the LORD.

False Oracles and False Prophets

33 "When these people, or a prophet or a priest, ask you, 'What is the oracle [a] [k] of the LORD?' say to them, 'What oracle? [b] I will forsake [l] you, declares the LORD.' 34 If a

a 33 Or *burden* (see Septuagint and Vulgate)   b 33 Hebrew; Septuagint and Vulgate *'You are the burden.* (The Hebrew for *oracle* and *burden* is the same.)

Jeremiah 23:33–40

Jeremiah announced that Judah had to change, or judgment would come. Eventually he understood that any repentance would be too little and too late. Those prophets who disagreed with him were simply wrong. *Their denial of judgment was in effect a denial of God's redemptive work through judgment.* Their words diverted the people's attention from seeking the Lord through repentance to a false assurance that he would protect them.

In an age when false "christs" and counterfeit teachers can sit in church pews (cf. Matt. 24:23–25; 2 Peter 2:1), it's important for believers to be sure that their leaders are thoroughly Biblical in their teaching and practice. As the Bereans did with Paul's message, it's our responsibility to know God's Word well enough to ensure that we are being discipled in authentic Christian truth (Acts 17:11). Is your church blessed with Biblically accountable leadership? Why not take the time to thank God for these godly servant shepherds?

Cross-references (margin)

23:19
r Jer 25:32; 30:23

23:20
s 2Ki 23:26
t Jer 30:24

23:21
u Jer 14:14; 27:15

23:22
v Jer 25:5; Zec 1:4

23:23
w Ps 139:1-10

23:24
x Job 22:12-14
y 1Ki 8:27

23:25
z Jer 14:14
a ver 28,32;
Jer 29:8
23:26
b 1Ti 4:1-2
23:27
c Dt 13:1-3;
Jer 29:8 d Jdg 3:7;
8:33-34

23:29
e Jer 5:14

23:30
f Ps 34:16
g Dt 18:20;
Jer 14:15
23:31
h ver 17
23:32
i ver 25 j Jer 7:8;
La 2:14

23:33
k Mal 1:1 l ver 39

prophet or a priest or anyone else claims, 'This is the oracle[m] of the LORD,' I will punish[n] that man and his household. [35]This is what each of you keeps on saying to his friend or relative: 'What is the LORD's answer?'[o] or 'What has the LORD spoken?' [36]But you must not mention 'the oracle of the LORD' again, because every man's own word becomes his oracle and so you distort[p] the words of the living God, the LORD Almighty, our God. [37]This is what you keep saying to a prophet: 'What is the LORD's answer to you?' or 'What has the LORD spoken?' [38]Although you claim, 'This is the oracle of the LORD,' this is what the LORD says: You used the words, 'This is the oracle of the LORD,' even though I told you that you must not claim, 'This is the oracle of the LORD.' [39]Therefore, I will surely forget you and cast[q] you out of my presence along with the city I gave to you and your fathers. [40]I will bring upon you everlasting disgrace[r]—everlasting shame that will not be forgotten."

Two Baskets of Figs

24 After Jehoiachin[a,s] son of Jehoiakim king of Judah and the officials, the craftsmen and the artisans of Judah were carried into exile from Jerusalem to Babylon by Nebuchadnezzar king of Babylon, the LORD showed me two baskets of figs[t] placed in front of the temple of the LORD. [2]One basket had very good figs, like those that ripen early; the other basket had very poor[u] figs, so bad they could not be eaten.

[3]Then the LORD asked me, "What do you see,[v] Jeremiah?"

"Figs," I answered. "The good ones are very good, but the poor ones are so bad they cannot be eaten."

[4]Then the word of the LORD came to me: [5]"This is what the LORD, the God of Israel, says: 'Like these good figs, I regard as good the exiles from Judah, whom I sent away from this place to the land of the Babylonians.[b] [6]My eyes will watch over them for their good, and I will bring them back[w] to this land. I will build[x] them up and not tear them down; I will plant them and not uproot them. [7]I will give them a heart to know me, that I am the LORD. They will be my people,[y] and I will be their God, for they will return[z] to me with all their heart.[a]

[8]"'But like the poor[b] figs, which are so bad they cannot be eaten,' says the LORD, 'so will I deal with Zedekiah king of Judah, his officials[c] and the survivors[d] from Jerusalem, whether they remain in this land or live in Egypt.[e] [9]I will make them abhorrent[f] and an offense to all the kingdoms of the earth, a reproach and a byword,[g] an object of ridicule and cursing,[h] wherever I banish[i] them. [10]I will send the sword,[j] famine and plague[k] against them until they are destroyed from the land I gave to them and their fathers.'"

Seventy Years of Captivity

25 The word came to Jeremiah concerning all the people of Judah in the fourth year of Jehoiakim[l] son of Josiah king of Judah, which was the first year of Nebuchadnezzar[m] king of Babylon. [2]So Jeremiah the prophet said to all the people of Judah[n] and to all those living in Jerusalem: [3]For twenty-three years—from the thirteenth year of Josiah[o] son of Amon king of Judah until this very day—the word of the LORD has come to me and I have spoken to you again and again,[p] but you have not listened.[q]

[a] 1 Hebrew *Jeconiah*, a variant of *Jehoiachin*   [b] 5 Or *Chaldeans*

Jeremiah 24:1–10

The setting is in Zedekiah's reign—sometime between 597 B.C., when Nebuchadnezzar took Jehoiachin and a group of Judah's leading citizens into exile, and 587/586, when the Babylonians besieged and destroyed Jerusalem. This report is a shorthand version of the book's message. God announced his intention to "build . . . up" the exiles and "plant" them again in the promised land. Their eventual physical return would be a sign of something more fundamental: a wholehearted return to the Lord (v. 7).

The divided fate of the two communities in Jeremiah's day illustrates God's use of the historical process for judgment and restoration. God is just in judgment and yet justifies (accepts as righteous) those who trust him for their salvation (cf. Rom. 3:26). He brings judgment on those who reject him and his covenant. But he also seeks to save the lost and give a new heart to those who respond to his invitation to fellowship.

25:4
r Jer 7:25

25:6
s Dt 8:19

25:7
t Dt 32:21
u 2Ki 21:15

25:9
v Isa 13:3-5
w Jer 1:15
x Jer 27:6
y Jer 18:16

25:10
z Isa 24:8;
Eze 26:13
a Jer 7:34
b Ecc 12:3-4
c Rev 18:22-23
25:11
d Jer 4:26-27;
12:11-12
e 2Ch 36:21
25:12
f Jer 29:10
g Isa 13:19-22;
14:22-23
25:14
h Jer 27:7
i Jer 50:9; 51:27-28
j Jer 51:6

25:15
k Isa 51:17; Ps 75:8;
Rev 14:10
25:16
l Na 3:11
m Jer 51:7
25:17
n Jer 1:10
25:18
o Jer 24:9
p Jer 44:22
25:20
q Job 1:1 r Jer 47:5
25:21
s Jer 49:1
25:22
t Jer 47:4
u Jer 31:10
25:23
v Jer 9:26; 49:32
25:24
w 2Ch 9:14
25:25
x Ge 10:22
25:26
y Jer 50:3,9

⁴And though the LORD has sent all his servants the prophets^r to you again and again, you have not listened or paid any attention. ⁵They said, "Turn now, each of you, from your evil ways and your evil practices, and you can stay in the land the LORD gave to you and your fathers for ever and ever. ⁶Do not follow other gods^s to serve and worship them; do not provoke me to anger with what your hands have made. Then I will not harm you."

⁷"But you did not listen to me," declares the LORD, "and you have provoked me with what your hands have made,^t and you have brought harm^u to yourselves."

⁸Therefore the LORD Almighty says this: "Because you have not listened to my words, ⁹I will summon^v all the peoples of the north^w and my servant^x Nebuchadnezzar king of Babylon," declares the LORD, "and I will bring them against this land and its inhabitants and against all the surrounding nations. I will completely destroy^a them and make them an object of horror and scorn,^y and an everlasting ruin. ¹⁰I will banish from them the sounds^z of joy and gladness, the voices of bride and bridegroom,^a the sound of millstones^b and the light of the lamp.^c ¹¹This whole country will become a desolate wasteland,^d and these nations will serve the king of Babylon seventy years.^e

¹²"But when the seventy years^f are fulfilled, I will punish the king of Babylon and his nation, the land of the Babylonians,^b for their guilt," declares the LORD, "and will make it desolate^g forever. ¹³I will bring upon that land all the things I have spoken against it, all that are written in this book and prophesied by Jeremiah against all the nations. ¹⁴They themselves will be enslaved^h by many nationsⁱ and great kings; I will repay^j them according to their deeds and the work of their hands."

The Cup of God's Wrath

¹⁵This is what the LORD, the God of Israel, said to me: "Take from my hand this cup^k filled with the wine of my wrath and make all the nations to whom I send you drink it. ¹⁶When they drink it, they will stagger^l and go mad^m because of the sword I will send among them."

¹⁷So I took the cup from the LORD's hand and made all the nations to whom he sentⁿ me drink it: ¹⁸Jerusalem and the towns of Judah, its kings and officials, to make them a ruin and an object of horror and scorn and cursing,^o as they are today;^p ¹⁹Pharaoh king of Egypt, his attendants, his officials and all his people, ²⁰and all the foreign people there; all the kings of Uz;^q all the kings of the Philistines (those of Ashkelon,^r Gaza, Ekron, and the people left at Ashdod); ²¹Edom, Moab and Ammon;^s ²²all the kings of Tyre and Sidon;^t the kings of the coastlands^u across the sea; ²³Dedan, Tema, Buz and all who are in distant places^{c; v} ²⁴all the kings of Arabia^w and all the kings of the foreign people who live in the desert; ²⁵all the kings of Zimri, Elam^x and Media; ²⁶and all the kings of the north,^y near and

---

^a 9 The Hebrew term refers to the irrevocable giving over of things or persons to the LORD, often by totally destroying them.   ^b 12 Or *Chaldeans*   ^c 23 Or *who clip the hair by their foreheads*

Jeremiah 25:1–14

📖 The description of Nebuchadnezzar as God's "servant," though shocking at first, was consistent with Jeremiah's message. Nebuchadnezzar wasn't a "loose cannon" but an agent in God's employ. In the book of Daniel this king would bear witness, through his own humiliation, that God is sovereign (Dan. 4:1–37). Sadly, the king's servanthood didn't make him morally superior or grant him a saving knowledge of God (cf. Isa. 45:1–7 concerning Cyrus, the king of Persia).

📖 The pattern in chapter 25 repeats itself throughout history. The injustice and faithlessness of God's people lead to judgment. Yet how things change when seen in the light of God's plan to use whatever means may be necessary to carry out his judgment amid his larger redemptive purposes! Nebuchadnezzar's spiritual heirs (cf. Babylon, Rev. 17:5) still struggle against God, but the heirs of Jeremiah's words are open to receiving God's grace.

Jeremiah 25:15–38

📖 It wasn't Judah alone who would bear judgment. The other nations would drink from God's "cup" of wrath as well. This cup (picturing the staggering that results from intoxication) stood for the turmoil to come when God's sword of judgment would be unleashed. As a prophetic symbol of judgment, God's cup of wrath is widespread. In 51:7 Babylon herself is described as the intoxicating cup, but it's more often related directly to God and his judgment (cf. Isa. 51:17–23). In verse 26 Babylon is referred to as Sheshach, a cryptogram or symbolic name. Babylon too would drink the cup of wrath.

far, one after the other—all the kingdoms on the face of the earth. And after all of them, the king of Sheshach[a][z] will drink it too.

27 "Then tell them, 'This is what the LORD Almighty, the God of Israel, says: Drink, get drunk[a] and vomit, and fall to rise no more because of the sword[b] I will send among you.' 28 But if they refuse to take the cup from your hand and drink, tell them, 'This is what the LORD Almighty says: You must drink it! 29 See, I am beginning to bring disaster[c] on the city that bears my Name,[d] and will you indeed go unpunished?[e] You will not go unpunished, for I am calling down a sword upon all[f] who live on the earth, declares the LORD Almighty.'

30 "Now prophesy all these words against them and say to them:

" 'The LORD will roar[g] from on high;
    he will thunder[h] from his holy dwelling
    and roar mightily against his land.
He will shout like those who tread the grapes,
    shout against all who live on the earth.
31 The tumult will resound to the ends of the earth,
    for the LORD will bring charges[i] against the nations;
he will bring judgment on all mankind
    and put the wicked to the sword,' "
                                                  declares the LORD.

32 This is what the LORD Almighty says:

"Look! Disaster is spreading
    from nation to nation;[j]
a mighty storm[k] is rising
    from the ends of the earth."

33 At that time those slain[l] by the LORD will be everywhere—from one end of the earth to the other. They will not be mourned or gathered[m] up or buried,[n] but will be like refuse lying on the ground.

34 Weep and wail, you shepherds;
    roll[o] in the dust, you leaders of the flock.
For your time to be slaughtered[p] has come;
    you will fall and be shattered like fine pottery.
35 The shepherds will have nowhere to flee,
    the leaders of the flock no place to escape.[q]
36 Hear the cry of the shepherds,
    the wailing of the leaders of the flock,
    for the LORD is destroying their pasture.
37 The peaceful meadows will be laid waste
    because of the fierce anger of the LORD.
38 Like a lion[r] he will leave his lair,
    and their land will become desolate
because of the sword[b] of the oppressor
    and because of the LORD's fierce anger.

Jeremiah Threatened With Death

26 Early in the reign of Jehoiakim[s] son of Josiah king of Judah, this word came from the LORD: 2 "This is what the LORD says: Stand in the courtyard[t]

---

[a] 26 Sheshach is a cryptogram for Babylon.   [b] 38 Some Hebrew manuscripts and Septuagint (see also Jer. 46:16 and 50:16); most Hebrew manuscripts anger

---

Cross references
25:26 z Jer 51:41
25:27 a ver 16,28; Hab 2:16 b Eze 21:4
25:29 c Jer 13:12-14 d 1Pe 4:17 e Pr 11:31 f ver 30-31
25:30 g Isa 16:10; 42:13 h Joel 3:16; Am 1:2
25:31 i Hos 4:1; Joel 3:2; Mic 6:2
25:32 j Isa 34:2 k Jer 23:19
25:33 l Isa 66:16; Eze 39:17-20 m Jer 16:4 n Ps 79:3
25:34 o Isa 6:26 p Isa 34:6; Jer 50:27
25:35 q Job 11:20
25:38 r Jer 4:7
26:1 s 2Ki 23:36
26:2 t Jer 19:14

One way modern Christians can read the judgments against the nations is as signs of what the future will hold for oppressive regimes. Think about the surprising changes of the late 20th century. Who would have predicted the disbanding of the USSR, the changes in Eastern Europe, or the overthrow of apartheid in South Africa? Only time will tell their full impact, but even now God is at work in the aftermath of those events and through the church in these regions to bring healing and restoration.

26:2
u Jer 1:17;
Mt 28:20; Ac 20:27
v Dt 4:2
26:3
w Jer 36:7
x Jer 18:8
26:4
y Lev 26:14
z 1Ki 9:6
26:5
a Jer 25:4
26:6
b Jos 18:1
c 2Ki 22:19

26:9
d Jer 9:11

26:11
e Dt 18:20;
Jer 18:23; 38:4;
Mt 26:66; Ac 6:11
26:12
f Jer 1:18
g Am 7:15;
Ac 4:18-20; 5:29
h ver 2, 15
26:13
i Jer 7:5;
Joel 2:12-14
26:14
j Jer 38:5

26:16
k Ac 23:9
l Ac 5:34-39; 23:29

26:18
m Mic 1:1 n Isa 2:3
o Ne 4:2; Jer 9:11
p Mic 4:1; Zec 8:3
q Jer 17:3

26:19
r 2Ch 32:24-26;
Isa 37:14-20
s Ex 32:14;
2Sa 24:16 t Jer 44:7
u Hab 2:10
26:20
v Jos 9:17

of the LORD's house and speak to all the people of the towns of Judah who come to worship in the house of the LORD. Tell[u] them everything I command you; do not omit[v] a word. [3]Perhaps they will listen and each will turn[w] from his evil way. Then I will relent[x] and not bring on them the disaster I was planning because of the evil they have done. [4]Say to them, 'This is what the LORD says: If you do not listen[y] to me and follow my law,[z] which I have set before you, [5]and if you do not listen to the words of my servants the prophets, whom I have sent to you again and again (though you have not listened[a]), [6]then I will make this house like Shiloh[b] and this city an object of cursing[c] among all the nations of the earth.' "

[7]The priests, the prophets and all the people heard Jeremiah speak these words in the house of the LORD. [8]But as soon as Jeremiah finished telling all the people everything the LORD had commanded him to say, the priests, the prophets and all the people seized him and said, "You must die! [9]Why do you prophesy in the LORD's name that this house will be like Shiloh and this city will be desolate and deserted?"[d] And all the people crowded around Jeremiah in the house of the LORD.

[10]When the officials of Judah heard about these things, they went up from the royal palace to the house of the LORD and took their places at the entrance of the New Gate of the LORD's house. [11]Then the priests and the prophets said to the officials and all the people, "This man should be sentenced to death[e] because he has prophesied against this city. You have heard it with your own ears!"

[12]Then Jeremiah said to all the officials[f] and all the people: "The LORD sent me to prophesy[g] against this house and this city all the things you have heard.[h] [13]Now reform[i] your ways and your actions and obey the LORD your God. Then the LORD will relent and not bring the disaster he has pronounced against you. [14]As for me, I am in your hands;[j] do with me whatever you think is good and right. [15]Be assured, however, that if you put me to death, you will bring the guilt of innocent blood on yourselves and on this city and on those who live in it, for in truth the LORD has sent me to you to speak all these words in your hearing."

[16]Then the officials[k] and all the people said to the priests and the prophets, "This man should not be sentenced to death![l] He has spoken to us in the name of the LORD our God."

[17]Some of the elders of the land stepped forward and said to the entire assembly of people, [18]"Micah[m] of Moresheth prophesied in the days of Hezekiah king of Judah. He told all the people of Judah, 'This is what the LORD Almighty says:

" 'Zion[n] will be plowed like a field,
    Jerusalem will become a heap of rubble,[o]
    the temple hill[p] a mound overgrown with thickets.'[a][q]

[19]"Did Hezekiah king of Judah or anyone else in Judah put him to death? Did not Hezekiah[r] fear the LORD and seek his favor? And did not the LORD relent,[s] so that he did not bring the disaster[t] he pronounced against them? We are about to bring a terrible disaster[u] on ourselves!"

[20](Now Uriah son of Shemaiah from Kiriath Jearim[v] was another man who prophesied in the name of the LORD; he prophesied the same things against this city

a 18 Micah 3:12

Jeremiah 26:1–24

Chapter 26 begins a historical section. Jeremiah's words, summarized in verses 1–6, are a shortened version of the message in Jeremiah 7. Opposition to his "temple sermon," with its prediction that Jerusalem and the temple would be destroyed, was widespread and intense. Priests, prophets, and people proposed the death sentence for what appeared to them to be blasphemy and treason. After hearing his defense, the officials ruled in Jeremiah's favor. Still, Jeremiah might have been executed like his fellow faithful prophet Uriah, had it not been for

an important official, Ahikam, standing by his side.

Ahikam was a believer, one of those effective witnesses in any age whose work has great influence at a crucial time but whose name is remembered by few. He stood as an example of the truth that God's Word doesn't return to him void or empty (Isa. 55:11)—nor in the end does the life of God's servants become void. By God's grace there will always be people like Ahikam who have the spiritual ears to hear and the nerve to support a true prophet even when the majority believes a lie. Who do you know, or know of, who falls into this category?

and this land as Jeremiah did. [21]When King Jehoiakim[w] and all his officers and officials heard his words, the king sought to put him to death. But Uriah heard of it and fled[x] in fear to Egypt. [22]King Jehoiakim, however, sent Elnathan[y] son of Acbor to Egypt, along with some other men. [23]They brought Uriah out of Egypt and took him to King Jehoiakim, who had him struck down with a sword and his body thrown into the burial place of the common people.)

[24]Furthermore, Ahikam[z] son of Shaphan supported Jeremiah, and so he was not handed over to the people to be put to death.

Judah to Serve Nebuchadnezzar

27 Early in the reign of Zedekiah[a][a] son of Josiah king of Judah, this word came to Jeremiah from the LORD: [2]This is what the LORD said to me: "Make a yoke[b] out of straps and crossbars and put it on your neck. [3]Then send word to the kings of Edom, Moab, Ammon,[c] Tyre and Sidon through the envoys who have come to Jerusalem to Zedekiah king of Judah. [4]Give them a message for their masters and say, 'This is what the LORD Almighty, the God of Israel, says: "Tell this to your masters: [5]With my great power and outstretched arm[d] I made the earth and its people and the animals that are on it, and I give[e] it to anyone I please. [6]Now I will hand all your countries over to my servant[f] Nebuchadnezzar[g] king of Babylon; I will make even the wild animals subject to him.[h] [7]All nations will serve[i] him and his son and his grandson until the time[j] for his land comes; then many nations and great kings will subjugate[k] him.

[8]"'If, however, any nation or kingdom will not serve Nebuchadnezzar king of Babylon or bow its neck under his yoke, I will punish that nation with the sword, famine and plague, declares the LORD, until I destroy it by his hand. [9]So do not listen to your prophets, your diviners, your interpreters of dreams, your mediums[l] or your sorcerers who tell you, 'You will not serve the king of Babylon.' [10]They prophesy lies[m] to you that will only serve to remove you far from your lands; I will banish you and you will perish. [11]But if any nation will bow its neck under the yoke[n] of the king of Babylon and serve him, I will let that nation remain in its own land to till it and to live there, declares the LORD.'"'

[12]I gave the same message to Zedekiah king of Judah. I said, "Bow your neck under the yoke of the king of Babylon; serve him and his people, and you will live. [13]Why will you and your people die[o] by the sword, famine and plague with which the LORD has threatened any nation that will not serve the king of Babylon? [14]Do not listen to the words of the prophets who say to you, 'You will not serve the king of Babylon,' for they are prophesying lies[p] to you. [15]'I have not sent[q] them,' declares the LORD. 'They are prophesying lies in my name. Therefore, I will banish you and you will perish,[s] both you and the prophets who prophesy to you.'"

[16]Then I said to the priests and all these people, "This is what the LORD says: Do not listen to the prophets who say, 'Very soon now the articles[t] from the LORD's

a 1 A few Hebrew manuscripts and Syriac (see also Jer. 27:3, 12 and 28:1); most Hebrew manuscripts *Jehoiakim* (Most Septuagint manuscripts do not have this verse.)

Cross references

26:21
w 1Ki 19:2
x Mt 10:23
26:22
y Jer 36:12,25

26:24
z 2Ki 22:12

27:1
a 2Ch 36:11

27:2
b Jer 28:10,13
27:3
c Jer 25:21

27:5
d Dt 9:29
e Ps 115:16
27:6
f Jer 25:9
g Jer 21:7; Eze 29:18-20
h Jer 28:14; Da 2:37-38
27:7
i 2Ch 36:20
j Jer 25:12
k Jer 25:14; Da 5:28

27:9
l Dt 18:11

27:10
m Jer 23:25
27:11
n Jer 21:9

27:13
o Eze 18:31

27:14
p Jer 14:14
27:15
q Jer 23:21
r Jer 29:9 s Jer 6:15

27:16
t 2Ki 24:13; 2Ch 36:7,10; Jer 28:3; Da 1:2

Jeremiah 27:1–22

The Lord had commanded Jeremiah to make and wear a yoke as a sign that God had given Nebuchadnezzar a limited historical sovereignty over nations. To oppose Babylon at this time was to oppose God's will as Creator and Lord. Through his obedience, Jeremiah showed himself to be a prophet to the nations.

We aren't to assume that all peoples who languish under oppressive regimes or all individuals who suffer emotionally or physically are bound in these circumstances by God's judgment. Scripture gives no blanket warrant for such a claim. But neither does it back the assumption that oppression can *never* be an instrument

of God's refining judgment today. The Israelites had yet to see the error of their ways. Until God had dealt with them there would be no successful liberation from political oppression—or anything else.

Word and deed go together in prophetic ministry. Consistency in these areas doesn't guarantee the authenticity of a message, but it's a valuable indicator of commitment. Jesus' message was effective precisely because it included both (Acts 1:1). As his disciples and witnesses, we are to follow his example. James put it like this: "Suppose a brother or sister is without clothes and daily food. If one of you says to him 'Go, I wish you well: keep warm and well fed,' but does nothing about his physical needs, what good is it?" (James 2:15–16).

house will be brought back from Babylon.' They are prophesying lies to you. [17]Do not listen to them. Serve the king of Babylon, and you will live. Why should this city become a ruin? [18]If they are prophets and have the word of the LORD, let them plead[u] with the LORD Almighty that the furnishings remaining in the house of the LORD and in the palace of the king of Judah and in Jerusalem not be taken to Babylon. [19]For this is what the LORD Almighty says about the pillars, the Sea,[v] the movable stands and the other furnishings[w] that are left in this city, [20]which Nebuchadnezzar king of Babylon did not take away when he carried[x] Jehoiachin[a][y] son of Jehoiakim king of Judah into exile from Jerusalem to Babylon, along with all the nobles of Judah and Jerusalem— [21]yes, this is what the LORD Almighty, the God of Israel, says about the things that are left in the house of the LORD and in the palace of the king of Judah and in Jerusalem: [22]'They will be taken[z] to Babylon and there they will remain until the day[a] I come for them,' declares the LORD. 'Then I will bring[b] them back and restore them to this place.' "

The False Prophet Hananiah

28 In the fifth month of that same year, the fourth year, early in the reign of Zedekiah[c] king of Judah, the prophet Hananiah son of Azzur, who was from Gibeon,[d] said to me in the house of the LORD in the presence of the priests and all the people: [2]"This is what the LORD Almighty, the God of Israel, says: 'I will break the yoke[e] of the king of Babylon. [3]Within two years I will bring back to this place all the articles[f] of the LORD's house that Nebuchadnezzar king of Babylon removed from here and took to Babylon. [4]I will also bring back to this place Jehoiachin[a][g] son of Jehoiakim king of Judah and all the other exiles from Judah who went to Babylon,' declares the LORD, 'for I will break the yoke of the king of Babylon.' "

[5]Then the prophet Jeremiah replied to the prophet Hananiah before the priests and all the people who were standing in the house of the LORD. [6]He said, "Amen! May the LORD do so! May the LORD fulfill the words you have prophesied by bringing the articles of the LORD's house and all the exiles back to this place from Babylon. [7]Nevertheless, listen to what I have to say in your hearing and in the hearing of all the people: [8]From early times the prophets who preceded you and me have prophesied war, disaster and plague[h] against many countries and great kingdoms. [9]But the prophet who prophesies peace will be recognized as one truly sent by the LORD only if his prediction comes true.[i]"

[10]Then the prophet Hananiah took the yoke[j] off the neck of the prophet Jeremiah and broke it, [11]and he said[k] before all the people, "This is what the LORD says: 'In the same way will I break the yoke of Nebuchadnezzar king of Babylon off the neck of all the nations within two years.' " At this, the prophet Jeremiah went on his way.

[12]Shortly after the prophet Hananiah had broken the yoke off the neck of the prophet Jeremiah, the word of the LORD came to Jeremiah: [13]"Go and tell Hananiah, 'This is what the LORD says: You have broken a wooden yoke, but in its place you will get a yoke of iron. [14]This is what the LORD Almighty, the God of Israel, says: I will put an iron yoke[l] on the necks of all these nations to make them serve[m] Neb-

---

Cross references (left margin):

27:18
u 1Sa 7:8

27:19
v 2Ki 25:13
w Jer 52:17-23

27:20
x 2Ch 36:10;
Jer 24:1 y Jer 22:24

27:22
z 2Ki 25:13
a 2Ch 36:21
b Ezr 1:7; 7:19

28:1
c Jer 27:1,3
d Jos 9:3

28:2
e Jer 27:12
28:3
f 2Ki 24:13
28:4
g Jer 22:24-27

28:8
h Lev 26:14-17;
Isa 5:5-7

28:9
i Dt 18:22
28:10
j Jer 27:2
28:11
k Jer 14:14; 27:10

28:14
l Dt 28:48
m Jer 25:11

---

[a] 20,4 Hebrew *Jeconiah*, a variant of *Jehoiachin*

Jeremiah 28:1–17

Jeremiah's first response ("Amen!") seems to indicate that Hananiah's message had impressed him— even though it went against Jeremiah's own words. Jeremiah was open to hearing God speak through Hananiah. But he reminded his fellow prophet and their temple audience that prophets had regularly announced disaster and judgment. The prophet who predicted peace would be proven right only when that word came to pass.

When Hananiah broke the yoke Jeremiah wore, Jeremiah didn't reply immediately. Subsequently the word of the Lord came to Jeremiah: Hananiah was preaching falsehoods in the name of the Lord—for which death was the prescribed penalty (Deut. 18:20–22).

Hananiah was right to believe that God desired his people's return, but his timing was wrong. In Christian terms, Hananiah wanted to proclaim a resurrection without acknowledging the necessity of a cross. What about the church in the modern West, which is declining in many ways? Should we proclaim that renewal is just around the corner—or that God will give the church over to its failures until disaster has prepared us to faithfully respond? Remember that God may work judgment and renewal simultaneously in his flock.

uchadnezzar king of Babylon, and they will serve him. I will even give him control over the wild animals. *n'* "

[15] Then the prophet Jeremiah said to Hananiah the prophet, "Listen, Hananiah! The LORD has not sent[o] you, yet you have persuaded this nation to trust in lies.[p] [16] Therefore, this is what the LORD says: 'I am about to remove you from the face of the earth.[q] This very year you are going to die, because you have preached rebellion[r] against the LORD.' "

[17] In the seventh month of that same year, Hananiah the prophet died.

A Letter to the Exiles

29 This is the text of the letter that the prophet Jeremiah sent from Jerusalem to the surviving elders among the exiles and to the priests, the prophets and all the other people Nebuchadnezzar had carried into exile from Jerusalem to Babylon.[s] [2] (This was after King Jehoiachin[a][t] and the queen mother, the court officials and the leaders of Judah and Jerusalem, the craftsmen and the artisans had gone into exile from Jerusalem.) [3] He entrusted the letter to Elasah son of Shaphan and to Gemariah son of Hilkiah, whom Zedekiah king of Judah sent to King Nebuchadnezzar in Babylon. It said:

[4] This is what the LORD Almighty, the God of Israel, says to all those I carried[u] into exile from Jerusalem to Babylon: [5] "Build[v] houses and settle down; plant gardens and eat what they produce. [6] Marry and have sons and daughters; find wives for your sons and give your daughters in marriage, so that they too may have sons and daughters. Increase in number there; do not decrease. [7] Also, seek the peace and prosperity of the city to which I have carried you into exile. Pray[w] to the LORD for it, because if it prospers, you too will prosper." [8] Yes, this is what the LORD Almighty, the God of Israel, says: "Do not let the prophets and diviners among you deceive[x] you. Do not listen to the dreams you encourage them to have.[y] [9] They are prophesying lies[z] to you in my name. I have not sent them," declares the LORD.

[10] This is what the LORD says: "When seventy years[a] are completed for Babylon, I will come to you and fulfill my gracious promise to bring you back[b] to this place. [11] For I know the plans[c] I have for you," declares the LORD, "plans to prosper you and not to harm you, plans to give you hope and a future. [12] Then you will call upon me and come and pray to me, and I will listen[d] to you. [13] You will seek[e] me and find me when you seek me with all your heart.[f] [14] I will be found by you," declares the LORD, "and will bring you back[g] from captivity.[b] I will gather you from all the nations and places where I have banished you," declares the LORD, "and will bring you back to the place from which I carried you into exile."[h]

[15] You may say, "The LORD has raised up prophets for us in Babylon," [16] but this is what the LORD says about the king who sits on David's throne and all

---

[a] 2 Hebrew *Jeconiah*, a variant of *Jehoiachin*   [b] 14 Or *will restore your fortunes*

Jeremiah 29:1–23

This letter was written by Jeremiah to those taken into exile in 597 B.C., a decade before the destruction of Jerusalem and the mass deportation of Jews. These exiles could have adopted a victim mentality. If so, they would have avoided needed self-examination while blaming the Babylonians for their failures. Instead, Jeremiah asked them to pray for Babylon. It was their home now, and its future would affect them as well. God would continue to use this enemy to instruct his people. Perhaps they in turn would offer some witness leading to another aspect of God's instruction—to be a light to the nations (Isa. 42:6; 49:6; 51:4).

Verses 10–14 prepared readers for the hopeful section known as Jeremiah's "Book of Consolation" (chs. 30–33). The exiles' future rested on God's "gracious promise"—his plans to give his people "prosperity" and "hope." Future restoration depended on their willingness to seek God wholeheartedly.

Recent tremendous changes in relations between East and West—the end of the so-called "Cold War"—illustrate the phrase "if it prospers, you too will prosper" (v. 7). Christians on both sides can see that God has done more than instruct us about our enemies. Praying for "them" has changed both them and *us*. How many more tensions could be alleviated if Christians would pray for the welfare of opponents in other countries, as well as against ethnic conflict?

Cross references: 28:14 n Jer 27:6; 28:15 o Jer 29:31 p Jer 20:6; 29:21; La 2:14; Eze 13:6; 28:16 q Ge 7:4 r Dt 13:5; Jer 29:32; 29:1 s 2Ch 36:10; 29:2 t 2Ki 24:12; Jer 22:24-28; 29:4 u Jer 24:5; 29:5 v ver 28; 29:7 w Ezr 6:10; 1Ti 2:1-2; 29:8 x Jer 37:9 y Jer 23:27; 29:9 z Jer 14:14; 27:15; 29:10 a 2Ch 36:21; Jer 25:12; Da 9:2 b Jer 21:22; 29:11 c Ps 40:5; 29:12 d Ps 145:19; 29:13 e Mt 7:7 f Dt 4:29; Jer 24:7; 29:14 g Dt 30:3; Jer 30:3 h Jer 23:3-4

29:17
i Jer 27:8
j Jer 24:8-10

29:18
k Jer 15:4
l Dt 28:25;
Jer 42:18
29:19
m Jer 6:19
n Jer 25:4

29:20
o Jer 24:5

29:21
p ver 9; Jer 14:14

29:22
q Da 3:6
29:23
r Jer 23:14
s Heb 4:13

29:25
t 2Ki 25:18;
Jer 21:1

29:26
u 2Ki 9:11; Hos 9:7;
Jn 10:20 *v* Jer 20:2

29:28
w ver 1 *x* ver 10
y ver 5

29:31
z ver 24
a Jer 14:14; 28:15

29:32
b 1Sa 2:30-33
c ver 10 *d* Jer 28:16

30:2
e Isa 30:8
30:3
f Jer 29:14
g Jer 16:15

the people who remain in this city, your countrymen who did not go with you into exile— [17]yes, this is what the LORD Almighty says: "I will send the sword, famine and plague[i] against them and I will make them like poor figs[j] that are so bad they cannot be eaten. [18]I will pursue them with the sword, famine and plague and will make them abhorrent[k] to all the kingdoms of the earth and an object of cursing and horror,[l] of scorn and reproach, among all the nations where I drive them. [19]For they have not listened to my words,"[m] declares the LORD, "words that I sent to them again and again by my servants the prophets.[n] And you exiles have not listened either," declares the LORD.

[20]Therefore, hear the word of the LORD, all you exiles whom I have sent[o] away from Jerusalem to Babylon. [21]This is what the LORD Almighty, the God of Israel, says about Ahab son of Kolaiah and Zedekiah son of Maaseiah, who are prophesying lies[p] to you in my name: "I will hand them over to Nebuchadnezzar king of Babylon, and he will put them to death before your very eyes. [22]Because of them, all the exiles from Judah who are in Babylon will use this curse: 'The LORD treat you like Zedekiah and Ahab, whom the king of Babylon burned[q] in the fire.' [23]For they have done outrageous things in Israel; they have committed adultery[r] with their neighbors' wives and in my name have spoken lies, which I did not tell them to do. I know[s] it and am a witness to it," declares the LORD.

Message to Shemaiah

[24]Tell Shemaiah the Nehelamite, [25]"This is what the LORD Almighty, the God of Israel, says: You sent letters in your own name to all the people in Jerusalem, to Zephaniah[t] son of Maaseiah the priest, and to all the other priests. You said to Zephaniah, [26]'The LORD has appointed you priest in place of Jehoiada to be in charge of the house of the LORD; you should put any madman[u] who acts like a prophet into the stocks[v] and neck-irons. [27]So why have you not reprimanded Jeremiah from Anathoth, who poses as a prophet among you? [28]He has sent this message[w] to us in Babylon: It will be a long time.[x] Therefore build[y] houses and settle down; plant gardens and eat what they produce.'"

[29]Zephaniah the priest, however, read the letter to Jeremiah the prophet. [30]Then the word of the LORD came to Jeremiah: [31]"Send this message to all the exiles: 'This is what the LORD says about Shemaiah[z] the Nehelamite: Because Shemaiah has prophesied to you, even though I did not send[a] him, and has led you to believe a lie, [32]this is what the LORD says: I will surely punish Shemaiah the Nehelamite and his descendants.[b] He will have no one left among this people, nor will he see the good[c] things I will do for my people, declares the LORD, because he has preached rebellion[d] against me.'"

Restoration of Israel

30 This is the word that came to Jeremiah from the LORD: [2]"This is what the LORD, the God of Israel, says: 'Write[e] in a book all the words I have spoken to you. [3]The days are coming,' declares the LORD, 'when I will bring[f] my people Israel and Judah back from captivity[a] and restore[g] them to the land I gave their forefathers to possess,' says the LORD."

---

[a] 3 Or *will restore the fortunes of my people Israel and Judah*

Jeremiah 29:24–32

One opponent of Jeremiah, Shemaiah, was singled out for criticism and judgment. Like Ahab and Zedekiah, who were indicted in the previous passage (not the infamous kings of those names, but false prophets), Shemaiah was a prophet who had proclaimed lies to the exiles. He wouldn't see the "good things" God would do for the people because he had "preached rebellion" against God. This last element was the same charge leveled against Hananiah in 28:16.

Jeremiah 29 includes pronouncements of judgment on individuals. Jeremiah didn't take judgment into his own hands or urge others to do so. He simply noted that the work of people like Ahab, Zedekiah, and Shemaiah was opposed to God's purposes and that God would deal with them. It's important for us as Christians to remember that judgment is God's affair. The apostle Paul didn't personally punish false apostles but noted that they would receive what their actions deserved (2 Cor. 11:13–15; cf. Rom. 12:17–21).

4These are the words the LORD spoke concerning Israel and Judah: 5 "This is what the LORD says:

" 'Cries of fear[h] are heard—
    terror, not peace.
6 Ask and see:
    Can a man bear children?
Then why do I see every strong man
    with his hands on his stomach like a woman in labor,[i]
    every face turned deathly pale?
7 How awful that day[j] will be!
    None will be like it.
It will be a time of trouble[k] for Jacob,
    but he will be saved[l] out of it.

8 " 'In that day,' declares the LORD Almighty,
    'I will break the yoke[m] off their necks
and will tear off their bonds;
    no longer will foreigners enslave them.[n]
9 Instead, they will serve the LORD their God
    and David[o] their king,[p]
    whom I will raise up for them.

10 " 'So do not fear,[q] O Jacob my servant;[r]
    do not be dismayed, O Israel,'

declares the LORD.

'I will surely save[s] you out of a distant place,
    your descendants from the land of their exile.
Jacob will again have peace and security,[t]
    and no one will make him afraid.
11 I am with you and will save you,'
    declares the LORD.
'Though I completely destroy all the nations
    among which I scatter you,
    I will not completely destroy[u] you.
I will discipline[v] you but only with justice;
    I will not let you go entirely unpunished.'[w]

12 "This is what the LORD says:

" 'Your wound is incurable,
    your injury beyond healing.[x]
13 There is no one to plead your cause,
    no remedy for your sore,
    no healing[y] for you.
14 All your allies[z] have forgotten you;
    they care nothing for you.
I have struck you as an enemy[a] would
    and punished you as would the cruel,[b]

30:5
h Jer 6:25

30:6
i Jer 4:31

30:7
j Isa 2:12; Joel 2:11
k Zep 1:15 l ver 10

30:8
m Isa 9:4
n Eze 34:27

30:9
o Isa 55:3-4;
Lk 1:69; Ac 2:30;
13:23
p Eze 34:23-24;
37:24; Hos 3:5
30:10
q Isa 43:5;
Jer 46:27-28
r Isa 44:2
s Jer 29:14
t Isa 35:9

30:11
u Jer 4:27; 46:28
v Jer 10:24
w Am 9:8

30:12
x Jer 15:18

30:13
y Jer 8:22; 14:19;
46:11
30:14
z Jer 22:20; La 1:2
a Job 13:24
b Job 30:21

Jeremiah 30:1—31:40

Jeremiah's prophecies in this lengthy passage pertained to the near future but would be fully realized only in the distant future. His words would be preserved as a witness from the past and as an inspired prediction of a future in which God would judge all sin. The passage makes clear that God intended a transformed future for his people. The quality of this future stands out here. The poetic presentation and variety of claims are best understood as indications of the multiple ways in which God will bring (even in our own future) these words to fulfillment.

Jeremiah 31:31–34, the well-known passage promising a "new covenant," summarizes Jeremiah's message. The striking claim that God would "write [his law] on their hearts" harks back to his writing the Ten Commandments on tablets of stone. Knowledge of God must be internalized (become "heart knowledge," not just "head knowledge").

30:14
c Jer 5:6

because your guilt is so great
and your sins ^{c} so many.
15 Why do you cry out over your wound,
your pain that has no cure?
Because of your great guilt and many sins
I have done these things to you.

30:16
d Isa 33:1; Jer 2:3;
10:25 e Isa 14:2;
Joel 3:4-8
f Jer 50:10

16 " 'But all who devour ^{d} you will be devoured;
all your enemies will go into exile. ^{e}
Those who plunder ^{f} you will be plundered;
all who make spoil of you I will despoil.
17 But I will restore you to health
and heal your wounds,'

declares the LORD,

30:17
g Jer 33:24

'because you are called an outcast, ^{g}
Zion for whom no one cares.'

18 "This is what the LORD says:

30:18
h ver 3; Jer 31:23
i Ps 102:13
j Jer 31:4,24,38

" 'I will restore the fortunes ^{h} of Jacob's tents
and have compassion ^{i} on his dwellings;
the city will be rebuilt ^{j} on her ruins,
and the palace will stand in its proper place.

30:19
k Isa 35:10; 51:11
l Isa 51:3
m Ps 126:1-2;
Jer 31:4 n Jer 33:22
o Isa 60:9

19 From them will come songs ^{k} of thanksgiving ^{l}
and the sound of rejoicing. ^{m}
I will add to their numbers, ^{n}
and they will not be decreased;
I will bring them honor, ^{o}
and they will not be disdained.

30:20
p Isa 54:13;
Jer 31:17
q Isa 54:14

20 Their children ^{p} will be as in days of old,
and their community will be established ^{q} before me;
I will punish all who oppress them.

Snapshots

30:17

Paulina

Prior to Paulina's work with a Christian humanitarian aid organization, she had been employed in a Presbyterian hospital and served as district organizer with the Red Cross. Her love for community work has made this affable woman well loved by her clients.

Her current work involves visiting families and improving their welfare. With her background, she can handle minor health problems, referring more serious cases to hospitals.

"My challenge now is the increasing nature of Buruli ulcer cases in my zone. There is no known cause for this disease," Paulina reports. These ulcers are debilitating sores caused by parasites that eat the skin, sometimes affecting a victim's bones. To Paulina, the high incidence of this disease, contracted from unsanitary environments and dirty water, presents a real challenge. Another is the bad roads she has to travel.

"I really want to see the transformation of these families and share the gospel with them."

Paulina is married and a mother of six (one child is adopted). Sometimes she worries because her ailing husband and children live 15 kilometers from her work place.

"I have never regretted coming [here] despite these challenges," Paulina asserts. "I really want to see the transformation of these families and share the gospel with them."

21 Their leader[r] will be one of their own;
    their ruler will arise from among them.
I will bring him near[s] and he will come close to me,
    for who is he who will devote himself
    to be close to me?'
                                    declares the LORD.

22 " 'So you will be my people,
    and I will be your God.' "

23 See, the storm[t] of the LORD
    will burst out in wrath,
a driving wind swirling down
    on the heads of the wicked.
24 The fierce anger[u] of the LORD will not turn back[v]
    until he fully accomplishes
    the purposes of his heart.
In days to come
    you will understand[w] this.

31

"At that time," declares the LORD, "I will be the God[x] of all the clans of Israel, and they will be my people."
2 This is what the LORD says:

"The people who survive the sword
    will find favor[y] in the desert;
    I will come to give rest[z] to Israel."

3 The LORD appeared to us in the past,[a] saying:

"I have loved[a] you with an everlasting love;
    I have drawn[b] you with loving-kindness.
4 I will build you up again
    and you will be rebuilt, O Virgin Israel.
Again you will take up your tambourines
    and go out to dance with the joyful.[c]
5 Again you will plant vineyards
    on the hills of Samaria;[d]
the farmers will plant them
    and enjoy their fruit.[e]
6 There will be a day when watchmen cry out
    on the hills of Ephraim,
'Come, let us go up to Zion,
    to the LORD our God.' "[f]

7 This is what the LORD says:

"Sing with joy for Jacob;
    shout for the foremost[g] of the nations.
Make your praises heard, and say,

---

[a] 3 Or LORD has appeared to us from afar

30:21
[r] ver 9 [s] Nu 16:5

30:23
[t] Jer 23:19

30:24
[u] Jer 4:8 [v] Jer 4:28
[w] Jer 23:19-20

31:1
[x] Jer 30:22

31:2
[y] Nu 14:20
[z] Ex 33:14

31:3
[a] Dt 4:37
[b] Hos 11:4

31:4
[c] Jer 30:19

31:5
[d] Jer 50:19
[e] Isa 65:21;
Am 9:14

31:6
[f] Isa 2:3; Jer 50:4-5;
Mic 4:2

31:7
[g] Dt 28:13; Isa 61:9

New Testament references to the new covenant indicate that the future redemption promised by God through Jeremiah dawned in the ministry of Christ and will come to final fulfillment in his second coming. Jeremiah's promise to Israel and Judah (31:31) applies to the church, consisting of both Jewish and Gentile Christians. Because of Christ's coming and through the Spirit's ministry, the church has tasted of the future Jeremiah foresaw. Still, there remains a future culmination of God's marvelous plan.

If the church has inherited by faith the promises made to Israel, does that mean that God has turned his back on the Jews? Certainly not! (Cf. Rom. 11:11–12,25–27.) Christians have the responsibility to proclaim the gospel to Jews, just as to any others who don't know Christ as Savior and Lord. We can do so with confidence that God has made promises to Israel—promises that will find ultimate fulfillment in the New Jerusalem (Rev. 21:2–4).

31:7
h Ps 14:7; 28:9
i Isa 37:31
31:8
j Jer 3:18; 23:8
k Dt 30:4;
Eze 34:12-14
l Isa 42:16
m Eze 34:16;
Mic 4:6

31:9
n Ps 126:5
o Isa 63:13
p Isa 49:11
q Ex 4:22; Jer 3:4

31:10
r Isa 66:19;
Jer 25:22
s Jer 50:19
t Isa 40:11;
Eze 34:12

31:11
u Isa 44:23; 48:20
v Ps 142:6
31:12
w Eze 17:23;
Mic 4:1 x Joel 3:18
y Hos 2:21-22
z Isa 58:11
a Isa 65:19;
Jn 16:22; Rev 7:17

31:13
b Isa 61:3
c Ps 30:11;
Isa 51:11
31:14
d ver 25

31:15
e Jos 18:25
f Ge 37:35
g Jer 10:20;
Mt 2:17-18*

31:16
h Isa 25:8; 30:19
i Ru 2:12 j Jer 30:3;
Eze 11:17

31:18
k Job 5:17
l Hos 4:16
m Ps 80:3

31:19
n Eze 36:31

'O LORD, save[h] your people,
the remnant[i] of Israel.'

8 See, I will bring them from the land of the north[j]
and gather[k] them from the ends of the earth.
Among them will be the blind[l] and the lame,[m]
expectant mothers and women in labor;
a great throng will return.
9 They will come with weeping;[n]
they will pray as I bring them back.
I will lead[o] them beside streams of water
on a level[p] path where they will not stumble,
because I am Israel's father,[q]
and Ephraim is my firstborn son.

10 "Hear the word of the LORD, O nations;
proclaim it in distant coastlands:[r]
'He who scattered Israel will gather[s] them
and will watch over his flock like a shepherd.'[t]
11 For the LORD will ransom Jacob
and redeem[u] them from the hand of those stronger[v] than they.
12 They will come and shout for joy on the heights[w] of Zion;
they will rejoice in the bounty[x] of the LORD—
the grain, the new wine and the oil,[y]
the young of the flocks and herds.
They will be like a well-watered garden,[z]
and they will sorrow[a] no more.
13 Then maidens will dance and be glad,
young men and old as well.
I will turn their mourning[b] into gladness;
I will give them comfort and joy[c] instead of sorrow.
14 I will satisfy[d] the priests with abundance,
and my people will be filled with my bounty,"

declares the LORD.

15 This is what the LORD says:

"A voice is heard in Ramah,[e]
mourning and great weeping,
Rachel weeping for her children
and refusing to be comforted,[f]
because her children are no more."[g]

16 This is what the LORD says:

"Restrain your voice from weeping
and your eyes from tears,[h]
for your work will be rewarded,[i]"

declares the LORD.

"They will return[j] from the land of the enemy.
17 So there is hope for your future,"

declares the LORD.

"Your children will return to their own land.

18 "I have surely heard Ephraim's moaning:
'You disciplined[k] me like an unruly calf,[l]
and I have been disciplined.
Restore[m] me, and I will return,
because you are the LORD my God.
19 After I strayed,[n]
I repented;

after I came to understand,
I beat*o* my breast.
I was ashamed and humiliated
because I bore the disgrace of my youth.'
²⁰ Is not Ephraim my dear son,
the child in whom I delight?
Though I often speak against him,
I still remember*p* him.
Therefore my heart yearns for him;
I have great compassion*q* for him,"

declares the LORD.

²¹ "Set up road signs;
put up guideposts.
Take note of the highway,*r*
the road that you take.
Return,*s* O Virgin*t* Israel,
return to your towns.
²² How long will you wander,*u*
O unfaithful*v* daughter?
The LORD will create a new thing on earth—
a woman will surround*a* a man."

²³This is what the LORD Almighty, the God of Israel, says: "When I bring them back from captivity,*b w* the people in the land of Judah and in its towns will once again use these words: 'The LORD bless you, O righteous dwelling,*x* O sacred mountain.'*y* ²⁴People will live*z* together in Judah and all its towns—farmers and those who move about with their flocks. ²⁵I will refresh the weary and satisfy the faint."*a* ²⁶At this I awoke*b* and looked around. My sleep had been pleasant to me.

²⁷"The days are coming," declares the LORD, "when I will plant*c* the house of Israel and the house of Judah with the offspring of men and of animals. ²⁸Just as I watched over them to uproot and tear down, and to overthrow, destroy and bring disaster,*d* so I will watch over them to build and to plant,"*e* declares the LORD. ²⁹"In those days people will no longer say,

'The fathers*f* have eaten sour grapes,
and the children's teeth are set on edge.'*g*

³⁰Instead, everyone will die for his own sin;*h* whoever eats sour grapes—his own teeth will be set on edge.

³¹ "The time is coming," declares the LORD,
"when I will make a new covenant*i*
with the house of Israel
and with the house of Judah.
³² It will not be like the covenant*j*
I made with their forefathers*k*
when I took them by the hand
to lead them out of Egypt,
because they broke my covenant,
though I was a husband to*c* them,*d*"

declares the LORD.

³³ "This is the covenant I will make with the house of Israel
after that time," declares the LORD.
"I will put my law in their minds
and write it on their hearts.*l*
I will be their God,
and they will be my people.*m*

a 22 Or *will go about seeking*; or *will protect*   *b 23* Or *I restore their fortunes*   *c 32* Hebrew;
Septuagint and Syriac / *and I turned away from*   *d 32* Or *was their master*

31:19
o Eze 21:12;
Lk 18:13

31:20
p Hos 4:4; 11:8
q Isa 55:7; 63:15;
Mic 7:18

31:21
r Jer 50:5
s Isa 52:11 *t* ver 4

31:22
u Jer 2:23 *v* Jer 3:6

31:23
w Jer 30:18
x Isa 1:26 *y* Ps 48:1;
Zec 8:3
31:24
z Zec 8:4-8
31:25
a Jn 4:14
31:26
b Zec 4:1
31:27
c Eze 36:9-11;
Hos 2:23
31:28
d Jer 18:8; 44:27
e Jer 1:10

31:29
f La 5:7 *g* Eze 18:2

31:30
h Isa 3:11; Gal 6:7

31:31
i Jer 32:40;
Eze 37:26;
Lk 22:20;
Heb 8:8-12*;
10:16-17
31:32
j Ex 24:8 *k* Dt 5:3

31:33
l 2Co 3:3
m Jer 24:7;
Heb 10:16

31:34
n 1Jn 2:27
o Jn 6:45
p Isa 54:13;
Jer 33:8; 50:20
q Mic 7:19;
Ro 11:27;
Heb 10:17*

34 No longer will a man teach[n] his neighbor,
    or a man his brother, saying, 'Know the LORD,'
because they will all know[o] me,
    from the least of them to the greatest,"

declares the LORD.

"For I will forgive[p] their wickedness
    and will remember their sins[q] no more."

35 This is what the LORD says,

31:35
r Ps 136:7-9
s Ge 1:16
t Jer 10:16

he who appoints[r] the sun
    to shine by day,
who decrees the moon and stars
    to shine by night,[s]
who stirs up the sea
    so that its waves roar—
the LORD Almighty is his name:[t]

31:36
u Isa 54:9-10;
Jer 33:20-26
v Ps 89:36-37

36 "Only if these decrees[u] vanish from my sight,"
    declares the LORD,
"will the descendants[v] of Israel ever cease
    to be a nation before me."

37 This is what the LORD says:

31:37
w Jer 33:22
x Jer 33:24-26;
Ro 11:1-5

"Only if the heavens above can be measured[w]
    and the foundations of the earth below be searched out
will I reject[x] all the descendants of Israel
    because of all they have done,"

declares the LORD.

31:38
y Jer 30:18 z Ne 3:1
a 2Ki 14:13;
Zec 14:10

38 "The days are coming," declares the LORD, "when this city will be rebuilt[y] for me from the Tower of Hananel[z] to the Corner Gate.[a] 39 The measuring line will stretch from there straight to the hill of Gareb and then turn to Goah. 40 The whole

31:40
b Jer 7:31-32
c Jer 8:2
d 2Sa 15:23;
Jn 18:1 e 2Ki 11:16
f Joel 3:17;
Zec 14:21

valley[b] where dead bodies[c] and ashes are thrown, and all the terraces out to the Kidron Valley[d] on the east as far as the corner of the Horse Gate,[e] will be holy[f] to the LORD. The city will never again be uprooted or demolished."

Jeremiah Buys a Field

32:1
g 2Ki 25:1
h Jer 25:1; 39:1

32 This is the word that came to Jeremiah from the LORD in the tenth[g] year of Zedekiah king of Judah, which was the eighteenth[h] year of Nebuchadnezzar. 2 The army of the king of Babylon was then besieging Jerusalem, and Jeremiah the prophet was confined in the courtyard of the guard[i] in the royal palace of Judah.

32:2
i Ne 3:25; Jer 37:21

32:3
j Jer 26:8-9
k ver 28; Jer 34:2-3
32:4
l Jer 38:18,23;
39:5-7; 52:9

3 Now Zedekiah king of Judah had imprisoned him there, saying, "Why do you prophesy[j] as you do? You say, 'This is what the LORD says: I am about to hand this city over to the king of Babylon, and he will capture[k] it. 4 Zedekiah king of Judah will not escape[l] out of the hands of the Babylonians[a] but will certainly be handed over to the king of Babylon, and will speak with him face to face and see him with his own eyes. 5 He will take[m] Zedekiah to Babylon, where he will remain until I deal with him, declares the LORD. If you fight against the Babylonians, you will not succeed.' "[n]

32:5
m Jer 39:7;
Eze 12:13
n Jer 21:4

6 Jeremiah said, "The word of the LORD came to me: 7 Hanamel son of Shallum your uncle is going to come to you and say, 'Buy my field at Anathoth, because as nearest relative it is your right and duty[o] to buy it.'

32:7
o Lev 25:24-25;
Ru 4:3-4; Mt 27:10*

a 4 Or *Chaldeans*; also in verses 5, 24, 25, 28, 29 and 43

Jeremiah 32:1–44

The year was 587 B.C., just prior to Jerusalem's fall. Babylon had besieged the city a second time, and Jeremiah was confined in it by a royal guard. Jeremiah's purchase of Hanamel's property was symbolic. At one of the darkest moments in Judah's history, he went ahead with the purchase because "houses, fields and vineyards will again be bought in this land" (v. 15). This wasn't a "good" business deal, but Jeremiah's obedience to the Lord illustrated that God would indeed redeem his people.

8 "Then, just as the LORD had said, my cousin Hanamel came to me in the court-yard of the guard and said, 'Buy my field at Anathoth in the territory of Benjamin. Since it is your right to redeem it and possess it, buy it for yourself.'

"I knew that this was the word of the LORD; 9so I bought the field at Anathoth from my cousin Hanamel and weighed out for him seventeen shekels a of silver. P 10I signed and sealed the deed, had it witnessed, q and weighed out the silver on the scales. 11I took the deed of purchase—the sealed copy containing the terms and conditions, as well as the unsealed copy— 12and I gave this deed to Baruch r son of Neriah, s the son of Mahseiah, in the presence of my cousin Hanamel and of the witnesses who had signed the deed and of all the Jews sitting in the courtyard of the guard.

13 "In their presence I gave Baruch these instructions: 14'This is what the LORD Almighty, the God of Israel, says: Take these documents, both the sealed and unsealed copies of the deed of purchase, and put them in a clay jar so they will last a long time. 15For this is what the LORD Almighty, the God of Israel, says: Houses, fields and vineyards will again be bought in this land.' t

16 "After I had given the deed of purchase to Baruch son of Neriah, I prayed to the LORD:

17 "Ah, Sovereign LORD, u you have made the heavens and the earth by your great power and outstretched arm. v Nothing is too hard w for you. 18You show love x to thousands but bring the punishment for the fathers' sins into the laps of their children y after them. O great and powerful God, whose name is the LORD Almighty, z 19great are your purposes and mighty are your deeds. a Your eyes are open to all the ways of men; b you reward everyone according to his conduct and as his deeds deserve. c 20You performed miraculous signs and wonders in Egypt d and have continued them to this day, both in Israel and among all mankind, and have gained the renown that is still yours. 21You brought your people Israel out of Egypt with signs and wonders, by a mighty hand e and an outstretched arm and with great terror. f 22You gave them this land you had sworn to give their forefathers, a land flowing with milk and honey. g 23They came in and took possession h of it, but they did not obey you or follow your law; i they did not do what you commanded them to do. So you brought all this disaster j upon them.

24 "See how the siege ramps are built up to take the city. Because of the sword, famine and plague, k the city will be handed over to the Babylonians who are attacking it. What you said l has happened, as you now see. 25And though the city will be handed over to the Babylonians, you, O Sovereign LORD, say to me, 'Buy the field with silver and have the transaction witnessed.' "

26Then the word of the LORD came to Jeremiah: 27"I am the LORD, the God of all mankind. m Is anything too hard for me? 28Therefore, this is what the LORD says: I am about to hand this city over to the Babylonians and to Nebuchadnezzar n king of Babylon, who will capture it. o 29The Babylonians who are attacking this city will come in and set it on fire; they will burn it down, p along with the houses q where the people provoked me to anger by burning incense on the roofs to Baal and by pouring out drink offerings r to other gods.

30 "The people of Israel and Judah have done nothing but evil in my sight from their youth; s indeed, the people of Israel have done nothing but provoke t me with what their hands have made, u declares the LORD. 31From the day it was built until now, this city has so aroused my anger and wrath that I must remove v it from my

a 9 That is, about 7 ounces (about 200 grams)

📖 Not only did Jeremiah buy a field, he prayed. To praise God as Creator, Judge, and Redeemer—as Jeremiah did—is to focus not on our own resources but on God, who calls us to obedience. Prayer is an acknowledgment that God is at work in the world and not aloof from the circumstances of his people. Trusting God in difficult circumstances and asking for guidance and deliverance become for us both a privilege and a responsibility. In what ways are both true for you?

Cross references (margin):

32:9 p Ge 23:16
32:10 q Ru 4:9
32:12 r ver 16; Jer 36:4; 43:3,6; 45:1 s Jer 51:59
32:15 t ver 43-44; Jer 30:18; Am 9:14-15
32:17 u Jer 1:6 v 2Ki 19:15; Ps 102:25 w Mt 19:26
32:18 x Dt 5:10 y Ex 20:5 z Jer 10:16
32:19 a Isa 28:29 b Pr 5:21; Jer 16:17 c Jer 17:10; Mt 16:27
32:20 d Ex 9:16
32:21 e Ex 6:6; 1Ch 17:21; Da 9:15 f Dt 26:8
32:22 g Ex 3:8; Jer 11:5
32:23 h Ps 44:2; 78:54-55 i Ne 9:26; Jer 11:8 j Da 9:14
32:24 k Jer 14:12 l Dt 4:25-26; Jos 23:15-16
32:27 m Nu 16:22
32:28 n 2Ch 36:17 o ver 3
32:29 p 2Ch 36:19; Jer 21:10; 37:8,10; 52:13 q Jer 19:13 r Jer 44:18
32:30 s Jer 22:21 t Jer 8:19 u Jer 25:7
32:31 v 2Ki 23:27; 24:3

32:32
w Isa 1:4-6; Da 9:8

32:33
x Jer 2:27; Eze 8:16
y Jer 7:13

32:34
z Jer 7:30
32:35
a Lev 18:21
b Jer 7:31; 19:5
32:36
c ver 24

32:37
d Jer 23:3,6
e Dt 30:3;
Eze 34:28
32:38
f Jer 24:7;
2Co 6:16*
32:39
g Eze 11:19
32:40
h Isa 55:3 i Jer 24:7
32:41
j Dt 30:9 k Jer 24:6;
31:28; Am 9:15

32:42
l Jer 31:28
32:43
m ver 15

32:44
n ver 10 o Jer 17:26
p Jer 33:7,11,26

sight. [32]The people of Israel and Judah have provoked me by all the evil[w] they have done—they, their kings and officials, their priests and prophets, the men of Judah and the people of Jerusalem. [33]They turned their backs[x] to me and not their faces; though I taught[y] them again and again, they would not listen or respond to discipline. [34]They set up their abominable idols in the house that bears my Name and defiled[z] it. [35]They built high places for Baal in the Valley of Ben Hinnom to sacrifice their sons and daughters[a] to Molech,[a] though I never commanded, nor did it enter my mind,[b] that they should do such a detestable thing and so make Judah sin.

[36]"You are saying about this city, 'By the sword, famine and plague[c] it will be handed over to the king of Babylon'; but this is what the LORD, the God of Israel, says: [37]I will surely gather[d] them from all the lands where I banish them in my furious anger and great wrath; I will bring them back to this place and let them live in safety.[e] [38]They will be my people,[f] and I will be their God. [39]I will give them singleness[g] of heart and action, so that they will always fear me for their own good and the good of their children after them. [40]I will make an everlasting covenant[h] with them: I will never stop doing good to them, and I will inspire them to fear me, so that they will never turn away from me.[i] [41]I will rejoice in doing them good[j] and will assuredly plant[k] them in this land with all my heart and soul.

[42]"This is what the LORD says: As I have brought all this great calamity on this people, so I will give them all the prosperity I have promised[l] them. [43]Once more fields will be bought[m] in this land of which you say, 'It is a desolate waste, without men or animals, for it has been handed over to the Babylonians.' [44]Fields will be bought for silver, and deeds[n] will be signed, sealed and witnessed in the territory of Benjamin, in the villages around Jerusalem, in the towns of Judah and in the towns of the hill country, of the western foothills and of the Negev,[o] because I will restore[p] their fortunes,[b] declares the LORD."

Promise of Restoration

33:1
q Jer 32:2-3; 37:21;
38:28

33:2
r Jer 10:16
s Ex 3:15; 15:3
33:3
t Isa 55:6; Jer 29:12

33:4
u Eze 4:2
v Jer 32:24;
Hab 1:10
33:5
w Jer 21:4-7
x Isa 8:17
33:7
y Jer 32:44
z Jer 30:3; Am 9:14
a Isa 1:26
33:8
b Heb 9:13-14
c Jer 31:34;
Mic 7:18; Zec 13:1
33:9
d Jer 13:11
e Isa 62:7; Jer 3:17

33 While Jeremiah was still confined in the courtyard[q] of the guard, the word of the LORD came to him a second time: [2]"This is what the LORD says, he who made the earth,[r] the LORD who formed it and established it—the LORD is his name:[s] [3]'Call[t] to me and I will answer you and tell you great and unsearchable things you do not know.' [4]For this is what the LORD, the God of Israel, says about the houses in this city and the royal palaces of Judah that have been torn down to be used against the siege[u] ramps[v] and the sword [5]in the fight with the Babylonians[c]: 'They will be filled with the dead bodies of the men I will slay in my anger and wrath.[w] I will hide my face[x] from this city because of all its wickedness.

[6]"'Nevertheless, I will bring health and healing to it; I will heal my people and will let them enjoy abundant peace and security. [7]I will bring Judah[y] and Israel back from captivity[d][z] and will rebuild them as they were before.[a] [8]I will cleanse[b] them from all the sin they have committed against me and will forgive[c] all their sins of rebellion against me. [9]Then this city will bring me renown, joy, praise[d] and honor[e] before all nations on earth that hear of all the good things I do for it; and they will be in awe and will tremble at the abundant prosperity and peace I provide for it.'

[10]"This is what the LORD says: 'You say about this place, "It is a desolate waste,

---

a 35 Or to make their sons and daughters pass through the fire;   b 44 Or will bring them back from captivity   c 5 Or Chaldeans   d 7 Or will restore the fortunes of Judah and Israel

---

Jeremiah 33:1–26

This chapter concludes the "Book of Consolation" (chs. 30–33). The emphasis has been on God speaking (vv. 2,10,12,17,19,23), but Jeremiah's readers and hearers did well to note that God's communication to Jeremiah was ultimately meant for them. Even as a "listener," Jeremiah was in the prophetic mode of passing on the Lord's message by repeating what he had heard.

In addition to the restoration of the people, Jeremiah announced that "a righteous Branch . . . from David's line" would arise and bring about justice and righteousness (see also 23:5–6). This promise was Messianic, dependent upon God's promises to David. Jerusalem would even receive a new, symbolic name: "The LORD Our Righteousness" (33:15–16).

without men or animals."[f] Yet in the towns of Judah and the streets of Jerusalem that are deserted, inhabited by neither men nor animals, there will be heard once more [11]the sounds of joy and gladness,[g] the voices of bride and bridegroom, and the voices of those who bring thank offerings[h] to the house of the LORD, saying,

> "Give thanks to the LORD Almighty,
>   for the LORD is good;[i]
>   his love endures forever."[j]

For I will restore the fortunes of the land as they were before,' says the LORD.

[12]"This is what the LORD Almighty says: 'In this place, desolate[k] and without men or animals—in all its towns there will again be pastures for shepherds to rest their flocks.[l] [13]In the towns of the hill country, of the western foothills and of the Negev,[m] in the territory of Benjamin, in the villages around Jerusalem and in the towns of Judah, flocks will again pass under the hand[n] of the one who counts them,' says the LORD.

[14]"'The days are coming,' declares the LORD, 'when I will fulfill the gracious promise[o] I made to the house of Israel and to the house of Judah.

[15]"'In those days and at that time
    I will make a righteous[p] Branch[q] sprout from David's line;
    he will do what is just and right in the land.
[16]In those days Judah will be saved[r]
    and Jerusalem will live in safety.
This is the name by which it[a] will be called:
    The LORD Our Righteousness.'[s]

[17]For this is what the LORD says: 'David will never fail[t] to have a man to sit on the throne of the house of Israel, [18]nor will the priests, who are Levites,[u] ever fail to have a man to stand before me continually to offer burnt offerings, to burn grain offerings and to present sacrifices.'[v]"

[19]The word of the LORD came to Jeremiah: [20]"This is what the LORD says: 'If you can break my covenant with the day[w] and my covenant with the night, so that day and night no longer come at their appointed time, [21]then my covenant[x] with David my servant—and my covenant with the Levites who are priests ministering before me—can be broken and David will no longer have a descendant to reign on his throne.[y] [22]I will make the descendants of David my servant and the Levites who minister before me as countless[z] as the stars of the sky and as measureless as the sand on the seashore.'"

[23]The word of the LORD came to Jeremiah: [24]"Have you not noticed that these people are saying, 'The LORD has rejected the two kingdoms[b][a] he chose'? So they despise[b] my people and no longer regard them as a nation.[c] [25]This is what the LORD says: 'If I have not established my covenant with day and night[d] and the fixed laws of heaven and earth,[e] [26]then I will reject[f] the descendants of Jacob[g] and David my servant and will not choose one of his sons to rule over the descendants of Abraham, Isaac and Jacob. For I will restore their fortunes[c][h] and have compassion on them.'"

---

[a] 16 Or *he*   [b] 24 Or *families*   [c] 26 Or *will bring them back from captivity*

33:10
[f] Jer 32:43
33:11
[g] Isa 51:3
[h] Lev 7:12
[i] 1Ch 16:8; Ps 136:1
[j] 1Ch 16:34; 2Ch 5:13; Ps 100:4-5
33:12
[k] Jer 32:43
[l] Isa 65:10; Eze 34:11-15
33:13
[m] Jer 17:26
[n] Lev 27:32
33:14
[o] Jer 29:10
33:15
[p] Ps 72:2 [q] Isa 4:2; 11:1; Jer 23:5
33:16
[r] Isa 45:17
[s] 1Co 1:30
33:17
[t] 2Sa 7:13; 1Ki 2:4; Ps 89:29-37; Lk 1:33
33:18
[u] Dt 18:1
[v] Heb 13:15
33:20
[w] Ps 89:36
33:21
[x] Ps 89:34
[y] 2Ch 7:18
33:22
[z] Ge 15:5
33:24
[a] Eze 37:22
[b] Ne 4:4
[c] Jer 30:17
33:25
[d] Jer 31:35-36
[e] Ps 74:16-17
33:26
[f] Jer 31:37
[g] Isa 14:1 [h] ver 7

📖 Christian hope is like Old Testament prophetic hope: It has a present and a future tense. The restoration Jeremiah predicted is still today "in process." Who could have foreseen the events of 1948 and the Jewish people being gathered to Israel yet again? Contemporary Christians can be prepared for surprise and wonder when God brings in his future kingdom in all its fullness.

What is there about prison life that gives rise to such deep reflections as those recorded in the Bible from prisoners? In addition to Jeremiah, Joseph, Paul, and John come to mind. Modern examples include Corrie ten Boom (see page 558), Aleksandr Solzhenitsyn, Charles Colson, and Nelson Mandela. Non-believers may find this dynamic odd: Lose your freedom and gain a new level of relationship with God. God's promised future (29:11) can change the perspective of people in any circumstances as they yield to the Spirit's leading.

Warning to Zedekiah

34:1
i Jer 27:7
j 2Ki 25:1; Jer 39:1

34 While Nebuchadnezzar king of Babylon and all his army and all the kingdoms and peoples*i* in the empire he ruled were fighting against Jerusalem*j* and all its surrounding towns, this word came to Jeremiah from the LORD: 2 "This

34:2
k 2Ch 36:11
l ver 22; Jer 32:29;
37:8

is what the LORD, the God of Israel, says: Go to Zedekiah*k* king of Judah and tell him, 'This is what the LORD says: I am about to hand this city over to the king of Babylon, and he will burn it down.*l* 3You will not escape from his grasp but will

34:3
m 2Ki 25:7;
Jer 21:7; 32:4

surely be captured and handed over*m* to him. You will see the king of Babylon with your own eyes, and he will speak with you face to face. And you will go to Babylon.

4 " 'Yet hear the promise of the LORD, O Zedekiah king of Judah. This is what the LORD says concerning you: You will not die by the sword; 5you will die peacefully.

34:5
n 2Ch 16:14; 21:19
o Jer 22:18

As people made a funeral fire*n* in honor of your fathers, the former kings who preceded you, so they will make a fire in your honor and lament, "Alas,*o* O master!" I myself make this promise, declares the LORD.' "

6Then Jeremiah the prophet told all this to Zedekiah king of Judah, in Jerusalem,

34:7
p Jos 10:3
q Jos 10:10;
2Ch 11:9

7while the army of the king of Babylon was fighting against Jerusalem and the other cities of Judah that were still holding out—Lachish*p* and Azekah.*q* These were the only fortified cities left in Judah.

Freedom for Slaves

34:8
r 2Ki 11:17
s Ex 21:2;
Lev 25:10,39-41;
Ne 5:5-8
34:9
t Lev 25:39-46

8The word came to Jeremiah from the LORD after King Zedekiah had made a covenant with all the people*r* in Jerusalem to proclaim freedom*s* for the slaves. 9Everyone was to free his Hebrew slaves, both male and female; no one was to hold a fellow Jew in bondage.*t* 10So all the officials and people who entered into this covenant agreed that they would free their male and female slaves and no longer hold them in bondage. They agreed, and set them free. 11But afterward they changed their minds and took back the slaves they had freed and enslaved them again.

34:13
u Ex 24:8

12Then the word of the LORD came to Jeremiah: 13 "This is what the LORD, the God of Israel, says: I made a covenant with your forefathers*u* when I brought them out of Egypt, out of the land of slavery. I said, 14'Every seventh year each of you must

34:14
v Ex 21:2
w Dt 15:12;
2Ki 17:14
34:15
x ver 8 *y* Jer 7:10-
11; 32:34
34:16
z Eze 3:20; 18:24
a Ex 20:7;
Lev 19:12

free any fellow Hebrew who has sold himself to you. After he has served you six years, you must let him go free.'*a v* Your fathers, however, did not listen to me or pay attention*w* to me. 15Recently you repented and did what is right in my sight: Each of you proclaimed freedom to his countrymen.*x* You even made a covenant before me in the house that bears my Name.*y* 16But now you have turned around*z* and profaned*a* my name; each of you has taken back the male and female slaves you had set free to go where they wished. You have forced them to become your slaves again.

a 14 Deut. 15:12

Jeremiah 34:1–7

This passage is best read in the context of 38:17–18, 39:7, 52:8–11, and 2 Kings 25:1–7. The fate of Zedekiah and of the city and nation were bound together. The statements about the future were announcements contingent on the reactions of the king and people to the Babylonian siege.

Sometime after this prophecy, Zedekiah was captured while fleeing the city. His last days were spent in darkness because the Babylonians had blinded him—a cruel act that came after he had witnessed the execution of his family members (39:5–7). Chapter 34:21 updates the prophecy in verses 1–5, perhaps anticipating the king's continuing defiance and its sorry conclusion. Zedekiah's actions would condemn him to the same fate as that of Jerusalem.

Christians see in the hard words of the book of Jeremiah the "razor's edge" of Biblical truth. God fights against the powers of evil and corruption—and as with any battle, the results aren't pretty. Positively, God will combat the powers of evil when they oppress his people. But he's not an indulgent parent, indifferent to our own sins. If we are doing the oppressing, as the next passage in this chapter demonstrates once again, God can use the powers of evil in this world to correct us.

Jeremiah 34:8–22

The ceremonial freeing of slaves was likely a last-ditch attempt to convince God that the people had changed. There was no conversion or repentance—only desperate people scrambling to get God on their side. After the former owners had reclaimed the slaves, Jeremiah alluded to the debt-slavery laws of Deuteronomy 15:12–18, accusing them of breaking the covenant God had made with his people after freeing them from Egyptian slavery. God hadn't gone back on his promise—and neither should they.

[17]"Therefore, this is what the LORD says: You have not obeyed me; you have not proclaimed freedom for your fellow countrymen. So I now proclaim 'freedom' for you, [b] declares the LORD—'freedom' to fall by the sword, plague and famine. I will make you abhorrent to all the kingdoms of the earth. [c] [18]The men who have violated my covenant and have not fulfilled the terms of the covenant they made before me, I will treat like the calf they cut in two and then walked between its pieces. [d] [19]The leaders of Judah and Jerusalem, the court officials, [e] the priests and all the people of the land who walked between the pieces of the calf, [20]I will hand over[f] to their enemies who seek their lives. [g] Their dead bodies will become food for the birds of the air and the beasts of the earth. [h]

[21]"I will hand Zedekiah [i] king of Judah and his officials[j] over to their enemies who seek their lives, to the army of the king of Babylon, which has withdrawn[k] from you. [22]I am going to give the order, declares the LORD, and I will bring them back to this city. They will fight against it, take[l] it and burn[m] it down. And I will lay waste the towns of Judah so no one can live there."

The Recabites

35 This is the word that came to Jeremiah from the LORD during the reign of Jehoiakim[n] son of Josiah king of Judah: [2]"Go to the Recabite[o] family and invite them to come to one of the side rooms[p] of the house of the LORD and give them wine to drink."

[3]So I went to get Jaazaniah son of Jeremiah, the son of Habazziniah, and his brothers and all his sons—the whole family of the Recabites. [4]I brought them into the house of the LORD, into the room of the sons of Hanan son of Igdaliah the man of God. [q] It was next to the room of the officials, which was over that of Maaseiah son of Shallum[r] the doorkeeper. [s] [5]Then I set bowls full of wine and some cups before the men of the Recabite family and said to them, "Drink some wine."

[6]But they replied, "We do not drink wine, because our forefather Jonadab[t] son of Recab gave us this command: 'Neither you nor your descendants must ever drink wine. [u] [7]Also you must never build houses, sow seed or plant vineyards; you must never have any of these things, but must always live in tents. [v] Then you will live a long time in the land[w] where you are nomads.' [8]We have obeyed everything our forefather[x] Jonadab son of Recab commanded us. Neither we nor our wives nor our sons and daughters have ever drunk wine [9]or built houses to live in or had vineyards, fields or crops. [y] [10]We have lived in tents and have fully obeyed everything our forefather Jonadab commanded us. [11]But when Nebuchadnezzar king of Babylon invaded[z] this land, we said, 'Come, we must go to Jerusalem[a] to escape the Babylonian[a] and Aramean armies.' So we have remained in Jerusalem."

---

[a] 11 Or *Chaldean*

Cross-references

34:17
[b] Mt 7:2; Gal 6:7
[c] Dt 28:25,64; Jer 29:18

34:18
[d] Ge 15:10
34:19
[e] Zep 3:3-4
34:20
[f] Jer 21:7
[g] Jer 11:21
[h] Dt 28:26; Jer 7:33; 19:7
34:21
[i] Jer 32:4 [j] Jer 39:6; 52:24-27 [k] Jer 37:5
34:22
[l] Jer 39:1-2
[m] Jer 39:8

35:1
[n] 2Ch 36:5
35:2
[o] 2Ki 10:15; 1Ch 2:55 [p] 1Ki 6:5

35:4
[q] Dt 33:1
[r] 1Ch 9:19
[s] 2Ki 12:9

35:6
[t] 2Ki 10:15
[u] Lev 10:9; Nu 6:2-4; Lk 1:15

35:7
[v] Heb 11:9
[w] Ex 20:12; Eph 6:2-3
35:8
[x] Pr 1:8; Col 3:20

35:9
[y] 1Ti 6:6

35:11
[z] 2Ki 24:1
[a] Jer 8:14

What will historians say about the tumultuous social changes of the 20th and early 21st centuries? Change spurs many people to keep their options open, to make no commitments without an easy "out." But God has called his people to be people of their (and his) word. Christians with the courage to point out—and live out—those promises, both divine and human, are the rock on which all relationships stand. They can be an active witness of God's truth to their families, friends, neighbors, coworkers, and acquaintances.

Jeremiah 35:1-19
The Recabites were related to Moses' father-in-law, Jethro the Kenite (Judg. 1:16; 1 Chron. 2:55). Though not ethnic Jews, this nomadic tribe lived among or near the Israelites and zealously attempted to be faithful to the Lord. They got their name from their forefather Jonadab (or Jehonadab), son of Recab, who had helped remove Baal worship temporarily from Israel 250

years earlier (2 Kings 10:15–28). He commanded his clan to take a permanent vow not to drink wine (cf. the Nazirites' ordinarily temporary vow; Num. 6:2–3,20).

The Recabites had obeyed Jonadab's instructions, including living in tents rather than in houses and towns—until the Babylonian invasion forced them to take refuge in Jerusalem. Their faithfulness to their community's values contrasted starkly with the lack of integrity in Judah and Jerusalem regarding the people's covenant with God.

Do you follow the crowd, or the Lord? The Recabites lived by the standards of their founder. We are to do the same. Jesus Christ, the risen Lord, is the foundation of the community of faith we call the church. Its life provides a witness to the larger society. The promise of the risen Lord is even grander than God's to the Recabites: The gates of hell won't triumph over the community that confesses Christ and lives as he has commanded (Matt. 16:18).

35:13
b Jer 6:10; 32:33

35:14
c Jer 7:13; 25:3
d Isa 30:9
35:15
e Jer 7:25 f Jer 26:3
g Isa 1:16-17;
Jer 4:1; 18:11;
Eze 18:30
h Jer 25:5 i Jer 7:26

35:16
i Mal 1:6

35:17
k Jos 23:15;
Jer 21:4-7 l Pr 1:24;
Ro 10:21
m Isa 65:12; 66:4;
Jer 7:13

35:19
n Jer 33:17
o Jer 15:19

36:1
p 2Ch 36:5
36:2
q Ex 17:14;
Jer 30:2; Hab 2:2
r Jer 1:2; 25:3
36:3
s ver 7; Eze 12:3
t Mk 4:12
u Jer 26:3; Jnh 3:8;
Ac 3:19 v Jer 18:8
36:4
w Jer 32:12
x ver 18 y Eze 2:9

36:6
z ver 9

36:7
a Jer 26:3
b Dt 31:17

36:9
c ver 22 d 2Ch 20:3

36:10
e Jer 52:25
f Jer 26:10

36:12
g Jer 26:22

12Then the word of the LORD came to Jeremiah, saying: 13"This is what the LORD Almighty, the God of Israel, says: Go and tell the men of Judah and the people of Jerusalem, 'Will you not learn a lesson[b] and obey my words?' declares the LORD. 14'Jonadab son of Recab ordered his sons not to drink wine and this command has been kept. To this day they do not drink wine, because they obey their forefather's command. But I have spoken to you again and again,[c] yet you have not obeyed[d] me. 15Again and again I sent all my servants the prophets[e] to you. They said, "Each of you must turn[f] from your wicked ways and reform[g] your actions; do not follow other gods to serve them. Then you will live in the land[h] I have given to you and your fathers." But you have not paid attention or listened[i] to me. 16The descendants of Jonadab son of Recab have carried out the command their forefather[j] gave them, but these people have not obeyed me.'

17"Therefore, this is what the LORD God Almighty, the God of Israel, says: 'Listen! I am going to bring on Judah and on everyone living in Jerusalem every disaster[k] I pronounced against them. I spoke to them, but they did not listen;[l] I called to them, but they did not answer.'"[m]

18Then Jeremiah said to the family of the Recabites, "This is what the LORD Almighty, the God of Israel, says: 'You have obeyed the command of your forefather Jonadab and have followed all his instructions and have done everything he ordered.' 19Therefore, this is what the LORD Almighty, the God of Israel, says: 'Jonadab son of Recab will never fail[n] to have a man to serve[o] me.'"

Jehoiakim Burns Jeremiah's Scroll

36 In the fourth year of Jehoiakim[p] son of Josiah king of Judah, this word came to Jeremiah from the LORD: 2"Take a scroll[q] and write on it all the words I have spoken to you concerning Israel, Judah and all the other nations from the time I began speaking to you in the reign of Josiah[r] till now. 3Perhaps[s] when the people of Judah hear[t] about every disaster I plan to inflict on them, each of them will turn[u] from his wicked way; then I will forgive[v] their wickedness and their sin."

4So Jeremiah called Baruch[w] son of Neriah, and while Jeremiah dictated[x] all the words the LORD had spoken to him, Baruch wrote them on the scroll.[y] 5Then Jeremiah told Baruch, "I am restricted; I cannot go to the LORD's temple. 6So you go to the house of the LORD on a day of fasting[z] and read to the people from the scroll the words of the LORD that you wrote as I dictated. Read them to all the people of Judah who come in from their towns. 7Perhaps they will bring their petition before the LORD, and each will turn[a] from his wicked ways, for the anger[b] and wrath pronounced against this people by the LORD are great."

8Baruch son of Neriah did everything Jeremiah the prophet told him to do; at the LORD's temple he read the words of the LORD from the scroll. 9In the ninth month[c] of the fifth year of Jehoiakim son of Josiah king of Judah, a time of fasting[d] before the LORD was proclaimed for all the people in Jerusalem and those who had come from the towns of Judah. 10From the room of Gemariah son of Shaphan the secretary,[e] which was in the upper courtyard at the entrance of the New Gate[f] of the temple, Baruch read to all the people at the LORD's temple the words of Jeremiah from the scroll.

11When Micaiah son of Gemariah, the son of Shaphan, heard all the words of the LORD from the scroll, 12he went down to the secretary's room in the royal palace, where all the officials were sitting: Elishama the secretary, Delaiah son of Shemaiah, Elnathan[g] son of Acbor, Gemariah son of Shaphan, Zedekiah son of Hanani-

---

Jeremiah 36:1–32

During the time frame of this chapter Nebuchadnezzar's army was poised to attack Jerusalem. Most likely that was the reason why a solemn fast was declared and many people in Judah streamed to the temple to pray (v. 9). This fast became the occasion for Baruch to deliver the prophetic message of Jeremiah's scroll—the very word they needed to hear. But with the exception of Micaiah, there is no mention of audience reaction. We can assume that the words were familiar and that the people didn't repent.

Jehoiakim's coldhearted rejection of Jeremiah's words contrasts the king with his godly father, Josiah. When Josiah had heard the words of the Book of the Law, discovered during temple repairs, he had torn his garments in recognition of the authority of the prophetic scroll (2 Kings 22).

ah, and all the other officials. ¹³After Micaiah told them everything he had heard Baruch read to the people from the scroll, ¹⁴all the officials sent Jehudi[h] son of Nethaniah, the son of Shelemiah, the son of Cushi, to say to Baruch, "Bring the scroll from which you have read to the people and come." So Baruch son of Neriah went to them with the scroll in his hand. ¹⁵They said to him, "Sit down, please, and read it to us."

So Baruch read it to them. ¹⁶When they heard all these words, they looked at each other in fear and said to Baruch, "We must report all these words to the king." ¹⁷Then they asked Baruch, "Tell us, how did you come to write all this? Did Jeremiah dictate it?"

¹⁸"Yes," Baruch replied, "he dictated[i] all these words to me, and I wrote them in ink on the scroll."

¹⁹Then the officials said to Baruch, "You and Jeremiah, go and hide.[j] Don't let anyone know where you are."

²⁰After they put the scroll in the room of Elishama the secretary, they went to the king in the courtyard and reported everything to him. ²¹The king sent Jehudi[k] to get the scroll, and Jehudi brought it from the room of Elishama the secretary and read it to the king[l] and all the officials standing beside him. ²²It was the ninth month and the king was sitting in the winter apartment,[m] with a fire burning in the firepot in front of him. ²³Whenever Jehudi had read three or four columns of the scroll, the king cut them off with a scribe's knife and threw them into the firepot, until the entire scroll was burned in the fire.[n] ²⁴The king and all his attendants who heard all these words showed no fear,[o] nor did they tear their clothes.[p] ²⁵Even though Elnathan, Delaiah and Gemariah urged the king not to burn the scroll, he would not listen to them. ²⁶Instead, the king commanded Jerahmeel, a son of the king, Seraiah son of Azriel and Shelemiah son of Abdeel to arrest[q] Baruch the scribe and Jeremiah the prophet. But the LORD had hidden[r] them.

²⁷After the king burned the scroll containing the words that Baruch had written at Jeremiah's dictation,[s] the word of the LORD came to Jeremiah: ²⁸"Take another scroll and write on it all the words that were on the first scroll, which Jehoiakim king of Judah burned up. ²⁹Also tell Jehoiakim king of Judah, 'This is what the LORD says: You burned that scroll and said, "Why did you write on it that the king of Babylon would certainly come and destroy this land and cut off both men and animals from it?"[t] ³⁰Therefore, this is what the LORD says about Jehoiakim king of Judah: He will have no one to sit on the throne of David; his body will be thrown out[u] and exposed to the heat by day and the frost by night. ³¹I will punish him and his children and his attendants for their wickedness; I will bring on them and those living in Jerusalem and the people of Judah every disaster[v] I pronounced against them, because they have not listened.' "

³²So Jeremiah took another scroll and gave it to the scribe Baruch son of Neriah, and as Jeremiah dictated,[w] Baruch wrote[x] on it all the words of the scroll that Jehoiakim king of Judah had burned[y] in the fire. And many similar words were added to them.

Jeremiah in Prison

37 Zedekiah[z] son of Josiah was made king[a] of Judah by Nebuchadnezzar king of Babylon; he reigned in place of Jehoiachin[a][b] son of Jehoiakim. ²Neither

---

[a] 1 Hebrew *Coniah*, a variant of *Jehoiachin*

Cross-references (margin)

36:14 [h] ver 21
36:18 [i] ver 4
36:19 [j] 1Ki 17:3
36:21 [k] ver 14 [l] 2Ki 22:10
36:22 [m] Am 3:15
36:23 [n] 1Ki 22:8
36:24 [o] Ps 36:1 [p] Ge 37:29; 2Ki 22:11; Isa 37:1
36:26 [q] Mt 23:34 [r] Jer 15:21
36:27 [s] ver 4
36:29 [t] Isa 30:10
36:30 [u] Jer 22:19
36:31 [v] Pr 29:1
36:32 [w] ver 4 [x] Ex 34:1 [y] ver 23
37:1 [z] 2Ki 24:17 [a] Eze 17:13 [b] 2Ki 24:8,12; 2Ch 36:10; Jer 22:24

📖 During an interview Mother Teresa was asked about her "success." Her answer was simple: She spent an hour each day in prayer and didn't do anything she knew to be wrong. The paradox of Jeremiah 36 was a people at worship who didn't hear or respond to the word of instruction and change God was providing them. Unless worshipers seek to honor God through word *and* deed, participation in worship or spiritual disciplines alone is a poor witness that he exists or that his Word is reliable.

Jeremiah 37:1–21

🔖 Zedekiah appears to have been a classic case of a divided mind under pressure. On the one hand, he desperately sought guidance for Judah's difficulties, in-

37:2
c 2Ki 24:19;
2Ch 36:12,14

37:3
d Jer 29:25; 52:24
e 1Ki 13:6;
Jer 21:1-2; 42:2

37:4
f ver 15; Jer 32:2
37:5
g Eze 17:15
h Jer 34:21
i 2Ki 24:7

37:7
j 2Ki 22:18
k Jer 2:36; La 4:17

37:8
l Jer 34:22; 39:8
37:9
m Jer 29:8

37:11
n ver 5

37:12
o Jer 32:9

37:14
p Jer 40:4
37:15
q Jer 20:2
r Jer 38:26

37:17
s Jer 15:11
t Jer 38:16
u Jer 21:7

37:18
v 1Sa 26:18;
Jn 10:32; Ac 25:8

37:21
w Isa 33:16;
Jer 38:9 *x* 2Ki 25:3;
Jer 52:6 *y* Jer 32:2;
38:6,13,28

38:1
z Jer 37:3

he nor his attendants nor the people of the land paid any attention[c] to the words the LORD had spoken through Jeremiah the prophet.

[3] King Zedekiah, however, sent Jehucal son of Shelemiah with the priest Zephaniah[d] son of Maaseiah to Jeremiah the prophet with this message: "Please pray[e] to the LORD our God for us."

[4] Now Jeremiah was free to come and go among the people, for he had not yet been put in prison.[f] [5] Pharaoh's army had marched out of Egypt,[g] and when the Babylonians[a] who were besieging Jerusalem heard the report about them, they withdrew[h] from Jerusalem.[i]

[6] Then the word of the LORD came to Jeremiah the prophet: [7] "This is what the LORD, the God of Israel, says: Tell the king of Judah, who sent you to inquire[j] of me, 'Pharaoh's army, which has marched out to support you, will go back to its own land, to Egypt.[k] [8] Then the Babylonians will return and attack this city; they will capture it and burn[l] it down.'

[9] "This is what the LORD says: Do not deceive[m] yourselves, thinking, 'The Babylonians will surely leave us.' They will not! [10] Even if you were to defeat the entire Babylonian[b] army that is attacking you and only wounded men were left in their tents, they would come out and burn this city down."

[11] After the Babylonian army had withdrawn[n] from Jerusalem because of Pharaoh's army, [12] Jeremiah started to leave the city to go to the territory of Benjamin to get his share of the property[o] among the people there. [13] But when he reached the Benjamin Gate, the captain of the guard, whose name was Irijah son of Shelemiah, the son of Hananiah, arrested him and said, "You are deserting to the Babylonians!"

[14] "That's not true!" Jeremiah said. "I am not deserting to the Babylonians." But Irijah would not listen to him; instead, he arrested[p] Jeremiah and brought him to the officials. [15] They were angry with Jeremiah and had him beaten[q] and imprisoned in the house[r] of Jonathan the secretary, which they had made into a prison.

[16] Jeremiah was put into a vaulted cell in a dungeon, where he remained a long time. [17] Then King Zedekiah sent for him and had him brought to the palace, where he asked[s] him privately,[t] "Is there any word from the LORD?"

"Yes," Jeremiah replied, "you will be handed over[u] to the king of Babylon."

[18] Then Jeremiah said to King Zedekiah, "What crime[v] have I committed against you or your officials or this people, that you have put me in prison? [19] Where are your prophets who prophesied to you, 'The king of Babylon will not attack you or this land'? [20] But now, my lord the king, please listen. Let me bring my petition before you: Do not send me back to the house of Jonathan the secretary, or I will die there."

[21] King Zedekiah then gave orders for Jeremiah to be placed in the courtyard of the guard and given bread from the street of the bakers each day until all the bread[w] in the city was gone.[x] So Jeremiah remained in the courtyard of the guard.[y]

Jeremiah Thrown Into a Cistern

38 Shephatiah son of Mattan, Gedaliah son of Pashhur, Jehucal[c][z] son of Shelemiah, and Pashhur son of Malkijah heard what Jeremiah was telling all the people when he said, [2] "This is what the LORD says: 'Whoever stays in this city will

---

[a] 5 Or *Chaldeans*; also in verses 8, 9, 13 and 14   [b] 10 Or *Chaldean*; also in verse 11   [c] 1 Hebrew *Jucal*, a variant of *Jehucal*

---

cluding a request that Jeremiah pray (v. 3) and communicate God's will to him (v. 17; cf. ch. 21). On the other hand, the word of the Lord put demands on him that his self-serving, vacillating nature wouldn't allow. God had previously informed Zedekiah that his actions and those of the people were unacceptable (v. 2), but nothing had changed. God hadn't changed his assessment, and Zedekiah seemed oblivious to the message.

Jesus' disciples can't blatantly disregard his Word and then assume that a prayer for deliverance will be effective, any more than Zedekiah could presume that his rejection of God's word would somehow persuade him to send a different word. Do you think there are circumstances in which prayer isn't what God really wants? Prayer is a staple of the Christian life, but we have no business hiding behind it to shirk responsibility or excuse disobedience.

die by the sword, famine or plague, [a] but whoever goes over to the Babylonians[a] will live. He will escape with his life; he will live.' [b] 3And this is what the LORD says: 'This city will certainly be handed over to the army of the king of Babylon, who will capture it.' " [c]

4Then the officials[d] said to the king, "This man should be put to death.[e] He is discouraging the soldiers who are left in this city, as well as all the people, by the things he is saying to them. This man is not seeking the good of these people but their ruin."

5"He is in your hands," King Zedekiah answered. "The king can do nothing to oppose you."

6So they took Jeremiah and put him into the cistern of Malkijah, the king's son, which was in the courtyard of the guard.[f] They lowered Jeremiah by ropes into the cistern; it had no water in it, only mud, and Jeremiah sank down into the mud.

7But Ebed-Melech,[g] a Cushite,[b] an official[c][h] in the royal palace, heard that they had put Jeremiah into the cistern. While the king was sitting in the Benjamin Gate,[i] 8Ebed-Melech went out of the palace and said to him, 9"My lord the king, these men have acted wickedly in all they have done to Jeremiah the prophet. They have thrown him into a cistern, where he will starve to death when there is no longer any bread[j] in the city."

10Then the king commanded Ebed-Melech the Cushite, "Take thirty men from here with you and lift Jeremiah the prophet out of the cistern before he dies."

11So Ebed-Melech took the men with him and went to a room under the treasury in the palace. He took some old rags and worn-out clothes from there and let them down with ropes to Jeremiah in the cistern. 12Ebed-Melech the Cushite said to Jeremiah, "Put these old rags and worn-out clothes under your arms to pad the ropes." Jeremiah did so, 13and they pulled him up with the ropes and lifted him out of the cistern. And Jeremiah remained in the courtyard of the guard.[k]

Zedekiah Questions Jeremiah Again

14Then King Zedekiah sent for Jeremiah the prophet and had him brought to the third entrance to the temple of the LORD. "I am going to ask you something," the king said to Jeremiah. "Do not hide[l] anything from me."

15Jeremiah said to Zedekiah, "If I give you an answer, will you not kill me? Even if I did give you counsel, you would not listen to me."

16But King Zedekiah swore this oath secretly[m] to Jeremiah: "As surely as the LORD lives, who has given us breath,[n] I will neither kill you nor hand you over to those who are seeking your life."[o]

17Then Jeremiah said to Zedekiah, "This is what the LORD God Almighty, the God of Israel, says: 'If you surrender to the officers of the king of Babylon, your life will

---

[a] 2 Or *Chaldeans*; also in verses 18, 19 and 23   [b] 7 Probably from the upper Nile region
[c] 7 Or *a eunuch*

38:2
a Jer 34:17
b Jer 21:9; 39:18; 45:5
38:3
c Jer 21:4,10; 32:3
38:4
d Jer 36:12
e Jer 26:11

38:6
f Jer 37:21

38:7
g Jer 39:16
h Ac 8:27 *i* Job 29:7

38:9
j Jer 37:21

38:13
k Jer 37:21

38:14
l 1Sa 3:17

38:16
m Jer 37:17
n Isa 42:5; 57:16
o ver 4

Jeremiah 38:1–13

It's instructive to note how various people reacted during this time of siege and the awful predicament in which the inhabitants of Jerusalem found themselves. Some officials heard Jeremiah's prophetic word as a threat, undermining the resolve necessary for continued survival. Zedekiah heard the message repeatedly but was unable to face up to its demands.

Ebed-Melech also heard the debate and acted on his convictions. In spite of great risk and no doubt personal fear, Ebed-Melech (though he didn't even have a Jewish background) stood with the prophet. As a result, God stood with him (39:15–18). We recognize in this man spiritual discernment, as well as the courage to act on his convictions—examples any generation can follow.

Tests of faith, like ocean storms, can come without warning. We can ask God for wisdom (James 1:2–5),

but courage is often developed along the path of discipleship. (Consider the contrast in the apostle Peter's life before his denial of Christ and afterward.) If we haven't spent time in the practice of discerning God's will and being open to the Spirit's leading, the pressure of the moment may cause us to lose courage and doubt or abandon our Christian convictions. Has this happened to you? With the Spirit's help, have you been able to get back on track?

Jeremiah 38:14–28

Both Jeremiah and Zedekiah were the subjects of rumor and conspiracy, and Zedekiah evidently had precious few people he could trust. He seemed more worried about his personal safety and future than about the city and nation. Zedekiah asked Jeremiah not to reveal their conversation. Jeremiah consented, feeling no obligation to reveal information shared in confidence.

38:17
p 2Ki 24:12;
Jer 21:9
38:18
q ver 3; Jer 34:3
r Jer 37:8
s Jer 24:8; 32:4
38:19
t Isa 51:12;
Jn 12:42 u Jer 39:9

38:20
v Jer 11:4
w Isa 55:3

38:22
x Jer 6:12

38:23
y 2Ki 25:6
z Jer 41:10

38:26
a Jer 37:15

38:28
b Jer 37:21; 39:14

39:1
c 2Ki 25:1; Jer 52:4;
Eze 24:2

39:3
d Jer 21:4

be spared and this city will not be burned down; you and your family will live.[p] [18]But if you will not surrender to the officers of the king of Babylon, this city will be handed over[q] to the Babylonians and they will burn[r] it down; you yourself will not escape[s] from their hands.' "

[19]King Zedekiah said to Jeremiah, "I am afraid[t] of the Jews who have gone over[u] to the Babylonians, for the Babylonians may hand me over to them and they will mistreat me."

[20]"They will not hand you over," Jeremiah replied. "Obey[v] the LORD by doing what I tell you. Then it will go well with you, and your life[w] will be spared. [21]But if you refuse to surrender, this is what the LORD has revealed to me: [22]All the women[x] left in the palace of the king of Judah will be brought out to the officials of the king of Babylon. Those women will say to you:

" 'They misled you and overcame you—
    those trusted friends of yours.
Your feet are sunk in the mud;
    your friends have deserted you.'

[23]"All your wives and children[y] will be brought out to the Babylonians. You yourself will not escape from their hands but will be captured[z] by the king of Babylon; and this city will[a] be burned down."

[24]Then Zedekiah said to Jeremiah, "Do not let anyone know about this conversation, or you may die. [25]If the officials hear that I talked with you, and they come to you and say, 'Tell us what you said to the king and what the king said to you; do not hide it from us or we will kill you,' [26]then tell them, 'I was pleading with the king not to send me back to Jonathan's house[a] to die there.' "

[27]All the officials did come to Jeremiah and question him, and he told them everything the king had ordered him to say. So they said no more to him, for no one had heard his conversation with the king.

[28]And Jeremiah remained in the courtyard of the guard[b] until the day Jerusalem was captured.

The Fall of Jerusalem

39 This is how Jerusalem was taken: [1]In the ninth year of Zedekiah king of Judah, in the tenth month, Nebuchadnezzar king of Babylon marched against Jerusalem with his whole army and laid siege[c] to it. [2]And on the ninth day of the fourth month of Zedekiah's eleventh year, the city wall was broken through. [3]Then all the officials[d] of the king of Babylon came and took seats in the Middle Gate: Nergal-Sharezer of Samgar, Nebo-Sarsekim[b] a chief officer, Nergal-Sharezer a high

---

[a] 23 Or and you will cause this city to   [b] 3 Or Nergal-Sharezer, Samgar-Nebo, Sarsekim

---

📖 Have you ever been paralyzed by fear? Not to decide on a course of action—or staying a familiar course—may at times be wise, but this option isn't satisfactory when God has called his people to accountability and action. In Zedekiah's case, not acting decisively and obediently to Jeremiah's prophetic word meant continuing the old policies of failure and rebellion. In his case, as sometimes in our own, not to decide is actually to make a fateful and tragic decision.

Jeremiah 39:1–18

📖 Nebuchadnezzar may have heard that a prophet in Judah had proclaimed the Babylonian monarch's supremacy. He turned Jeremiah over to Gedaliah, who came from a family that had supported Jeremiah. Nebuchadnezzar appointed Gedaliah governor of Judah, which hadn't been totally depopulated. The foreign conquerors showed more kindness to poor

Judahites than their own government had: They gave them vineyards and fields (v. 10).

Zedekiah's chosen path ultimately failed him; act and consequence were tragically bound together. In contrast, Ebed-Melech opted for the difficult path and found that God was with him (see "There and Then" for 38:1–13). He acted responsibly on his spiritual and moral convictions—and was granted life.

📖 Is there such a thing as an expected tragedy? The very concept of tragedy suggests that an event or process doesn't have to turn out disastrously. As with the fall of Jerusalem, God may have preferred another outcome (cf. 42:10; Ezek. 18:31–32). Yet there can be a personal word from God in the midst of tragedy or judgment (e.g., the unexpected gift of life to Ebed-Melech). Grace happens, but we can't presume upon it. God is the God of new beginnings, but he's also the sovereign King of kings.

official and all the other officials of the king of Babylon. 4When Zedekiah king of
Judah and all the soldiers saw them, they fled; they left the city at night by way of
the king's garden, through the gate between the two walls, and headed toward the
Arabah.[a]
5But the Babylonian[b] army pursued them and overtook Zedekiah[e] in the plains
of Jericho. They captured him and took him to Nebuchadnezzar king of Babylon
at Riblah[f] in the land of Hamath, where he pronounced sentence on him. 6There
at Riblah the king of Babylon slaughtered the sons of Zedekiah before his eyes and
also killed all the nobles of Judah. 7Then he put out Zedekiah's eyes[g] and bound
him with bronze shackles to take him to Babylon.[h]
8The Babylonians[c] set fire[i] to the royal palace and the houses of the people and
broke down the walls[j] of Jerusalem. 9Nebuzaradan commander of the imperial
guard carried into exile to Babylon the people who remained in the city, along with
those who had gone over to him, and the rest of the people.[k] 10But Nebuzaradan
the commander of the guard left behind in the land of Judah some of the poor people, who owned nothing; and at that time he gave them vineyards and fields.
11Now Nebuchadnezzar king of Babylon had given these orders about Jeremiah
through Nebuzaradan commander of the imperial guard: 12"Take him and look after him; don't harm[l] him but do for him whatever he asks." 13So Nebuzaradan the
commander of the guard, Nebushazban a chief officer, Nergal-Sharezer a high official and all the other officers of the king of Babylon 14sent and had Jeremiah tak-
en out of the courtyard of the guard.[m] They turned him over to Gedaliah son of Ahikam,[n] the son of Shaphan, to take him back to his home. So he remained among
his own people.[o]
15While Jeremiah had been confined in the courtyard of the guard, the word of
the LORD came to him: 16"Go and tell Ebed-Melech[p] the Cushite, 'This is what the
LORD Almighty, the God of Israel, says: I am about to fulfill my words against this
city through disaster,[q] not prosperity. At that time they will be fulfilled before your
eyes. 17But I will rescue[r] you on that day, declares the LORD; you will not be handed over to those you fear. 18I will save you; you will not fall by the sword[s] but will
escape with your life,[t] because you trust[u] in me, declares the LORD.' "

Jeremiah Freed

40 The word came to Jeremiah from the LORD after Nebuzaradan commander
of the imperial guard had released him at Ramah. He had found Jeremiah
bound in chains among all the captives from Jerusalem and Judah who were being
carried into exile to Babylon. 2When the commander of the guard found Jeremiah,
he said to him, "The LORD your God decreed this disaster for this place.[v] 3And now
the LORD has brought it about; he has done just as he said he would. All this happened because you people sinned[w] against the LORD and did not obey[x] him. 4But
today I am freeing you from the chains on your wrists. Come with me to Babylon,
if you like, and I will look after you; but if you do not want to, then don't come.
Look, the whole country lies before you; go wherever you please."[y] 5However, before Jeremiah turned to go,[d] Nebuzaradan added, "Go back to Gedaliah[z] son of
Ahikam, the son of Shaphan, whom the king of Babylon has appointed over the

39:5 [e] Jer 32:4 [f] 2Ki 23:33
39:7 [g] Eze 12:13 [h] Jer 32:5
39:8 [i] Jer 38:18 [j] Ne 1:3
39:9 [k] Jer 40:1
39:12 [l] Pr 16:7; 1Pe 3:13
39:14 [m] Jer 38:28 [n] 2Ki 22:12 [o] Jer 40:5
39:16 [p] Jer 38:7 [q] Jer 21:10; Da 9:12
39:17 [r] Ps 41:1-2
39:18 [s] Jer 45:5 [t] Jer 21:9; 38:2 [u] Jer 17:7
40:2 [v] Jer 50:7
40:3 [w] Da 9:11 [x] Dt 29:24-28; Ro 2:5-9
40:4 [y] Ge 13:9; Jer 39:11-12
40:5 [z] 2Ki 25:22

[a] 4 Or *the Jordan Valley* [b] 5 Or *Chaldean* [c] 8 Or *Chaldeans* [d] 5 Or *Jeremiah answered*

Jeremiah 40:1–6

Jeremiah was given a choice to go to Babylon with the exiles or to remain in Judah. In terms of personal security, it probably would have been better for him to go with Nebuzaradan to Babylon. But his choice signaled his commitment to the land and its renewal, just as his symbolic purchase of property during the Babylonian siege had done (32:1–15). So Jeremiah became a member of the remnant community associated with Gedaliah.

A church may find itself, due to urban blight or other circumstances, an isolated fortress in the middle of increasingly hostile surroundings. The option to flee to the safer territory of the suburbs may seem sensible and appealing. But God may be calling that church to a new mission, to be a beacon of light in a darkening world. In such circumstances individual believers and churches are wise to prayerfully seek the Spirit's guidance. The world says "flight or fight." The Lord offers another option: "Stand" (cf. Eph 6:10–12).

towns of Judah, and live with him among the people, or go anywhere else you please." *a*

Then the commander gave him provisions and a present and let him go. 6 So Jeremiah went to Gedaliah son of Ahikam at Mizpah *b* and stayed with him among the people who were left behind in the land.

Gedaliah Assassinated

7 When all the army officers and their men who were still in the open country heard that the king of Babylon had appointed Gedaliah son of Ahikam as governor over the land and had put him in charge of the men, women and children who were the poorest *c* in the land and who had not been carried into exile to Babylon, 8 they came to Gedaliah at Mizpah *d*—Ishmael *e* son of Nethaniah, Johanan and Jonathan the sons of Kareah, Seraiah son of Tanhumeth, the sons of Ephai the Netophathite, *f* and Jaazaniah *a* the son of the Maacathite, *g* and their men. 9 Gedaliah son of Ahikam, the son of Shaphan, took an oath to reassure them and their men. "Do not be afraid to serve *h* the Babylonians, *b*" he said. "Settle down in the land and serve the king of Babylon, and it will go well with you. *i* 10 I myself will stay at Mizpah *j* to represent you before the Babylonians who come to us, but you are to harvest the wine, summer fruit and oil, and put them in your storage jars, and live in the towns you have taken over." *k*

11 When all the Jews in Moab, *l* Ammon, Edom and all the other countries heard that the king of Babylon had left a remnant in Judah and had appointed Gedaliah son of Ahikam, the son of Shaphan, as governor over them, 12 they all came back to the land of Judah, to Gedaliah at Mizpah, from all the countries where they had been scattered. *m* And they harvested an abundance of wine and summer fruit.

13 Johanan son of Kareah and all the army officers still in the open country came to Gedaliah at Mizpah *n* 14 and said to him, "Don't you know that Baalis king of the Ammonites *o* has sent Ishmael son of Nethaniah to take your life?" But Gedaliah son of Ahikam did not believe them.

15 Then Johanan son of Kareah said privately to Gedaliah in Mizpah, "Let me go and kill Ishmael son of Nethaniah, and no one will know it. Why should he take your life and cause all the Jews who are gathered around you to be scattered and the remnant of Judah to perish?"

16 But Gedaliah son of Ahikam said to Johanan son of Kareah, "Don't do such a thing! What you are saying about Ishmael is not true."

41 In the seventh month Ishmael *p* son of Nethaniah, the son of Elishama, who was of royal blood and had been one of the king's officers, came with ten men to Gedaliah son of Ahikam at Mizpah. While they were eating together there, 2 Ishmael *q* son of Nethaniah and the ten men who were with him got up and struck down Gedaliah son of Ahikam, the son of Shaphan, with the sword, killing the one whom the king of Babylon had appointed *r* as governor over the land. *s* 3 Ishmael also killed all the Jews who were with Gedaliah at Mizpah, as well as the Babylonian *c* soldiers who were there.

4 The day after Gedaliah's assassination, before anyone knew about it, 5 eighty

a 8 Hebrew *Jezaniah*, a variant of *Jaazaniah*   *b* 9 Or *Chaldeans*; also in verse 10   *c* 3 Or *Chaldean*

Jeremiah 40:7—41:15

It was a precarious time for those who remained in the land. The tasks of bringing community life back to a more even keel were daunting. Gedaliah may well have been able to represent the interests of the remnant to the Babylonian provincial administration. Unfortunately, this couldn't happen because of his tragic and untimely demise at the hand of Ishmael.

Life in the land after Jerusalem's fall clearly illustrates human community gone bad, with no mechanism to help it repair itself. Reading these chapters, we reflect on the human tendency toward self-destruction. Only the larger context of God's grace, shown in his resolve to stay with such a people, provides hope beyond tragedy.

If God uses tragedy to instruct his people and spur them on to repentance, it serves a larger purpose. When has a failure on your part led you in a new and positive direction? In the midst of national humiliation, Gedaliah encouraged his contemporaries not to fear. Jeremiah chose the more difficult road rather than setting off to Babylon. Do those of us who have tasted new life in the crucified and risen Lord have eyes to see and ears to hear what the Spirit is saying?

men who had shaved off their beards,[t] torn their clothes and cut themselves came from Shechem,[u] Shiloh[v] and Samaria,[w] bringing grain offerings and incense with them to the house of the LORD.[x] 6Ishmael son of Nethaniah went out from Mizpah to meet them, weeping[y] as he went. When he met them, he said, "Come to Gedaliah son of Ahikam." 7When they went into the city, Ishmael son of Nethaniah and the men who were with him slaughtered them and threw them into a cistern. 8But ten of them said to Ishmael, "Don't kill us! We have wheat and barley, oil and honey, hidden in a field."[z] So he let them alone and did not kill them with the others. 9Now the cistern where he threw all the bodies of the men he had killed along with Gedaliah was the one King Asa[a] had made as part of his defense[b] against Baasha[c] king of Israel. Ishmael son of Nethaniah filled it with the dead.

10Ishmael made captives of all the rest of the people[d] who were in Mizpah—the king's daughters along with all the others who were left there, over whom Nebuzaradan commander of the imperial guard had appointed Gedaliah son of Ahikam. Ishmael son of Nethaniah took them captive and set out to cross over to the Ammonites.[e]

11When Johanan[f] son of Kareah and all the army officers who were with him heard about all the crimes Ishmael son of Nethaniah had committed, 12they took all their men and went to fight Ishmael son of Nethaniah. They caught up with him near the great pool[g] in Gibeon. 13When all the people[h] Ishmael had with him saw Johanan son of Kareah and the army officers who were with him, they were glad. 14All the people Ishmael had taken captive at Mizpah turned and went over to Johanan son of Kareah. 15But Ishmael son of Nethaniah and eight of his men escaped[i] from Johanan and fled to the Ammonites.

Flight to Egypt

16Then Johanan son of Kareah and all the army officers who were with him led away all the survivors[j] from Mizpah whom he had recovered from Ishmael son of Nethaniah after he had assassinated Gedaliah son of Ahikam: the soldiers, women, children and court officials he had brought from Gibeon. 17And they went on, stopping at Geruth Kimham[k] near Bethlehem on their way to Egypt[l] 18to escape the Babylonians.[a] They were afraid[m] of them because Ishmael son of Nethaniah had killed Gedaliah[n] son of Ahikam, whom the king of Babylon had appointed as governor over the land.

42 Then all the army officers, including Johanan[o] son of Kareah and Jezaniah[b] son of Hoshaiah, and all the people from the least to the greatest[p] approached 2Jeremiah the prophet and said to him, "Please hear our petition and pray[q] to the LORD your God for this entire remnant.[r] For as you now see, though we were once many, now only a few[s] are left. 3Pray that the LORD your God will tell us where we should go and what we should do."[t]

4"I have heard you," replied Jeremiah the prophet. "I will certainly pray[u] to the LORD your God as you have requested; I will tell you everything the LORD says and will keep nothing back from you."[v]

5Then they said to Jeremiah, "May the LORD be a true and faithful witness[w] against us if we do not act in accordance with everything the LORD your God sends

---

a 18 Or *Chaldeans*   b 1 Hebrew; Septuagint (see also 43:2) *Azariah*

41:5
t Lev 19:27
u Ge 33:18;
Jdg 9:1-57;
1Ki 12:1 v Jos 18:1
w 1Ki 16:24
x 2Ki 25:9
41:6
y 2Sa 3:16
41:8
z Isa 45:3
41:9
a 1Ki 15:22;
2Ch 16:6 b Jdg 6:2
c 2Ch 16:1
41:10
d Jer 40:7,12
e Jer 40:14
41:11
f Jer 40:8
41:12
g 2Sa 2:13
41:13
h ver 10
41:15
i Job 21:30;
Pr 28:17
41:16
j Jer 43:4
41:17
k 2Sa 19:37
l Jer 42:14
41:18
m Isa 51:12;
Jer 42:16; Lk 12:4-5
n Jer 40:5
42:1
o Jer 40:13; 41:11
p Jer 6:13; 44:12
42:2
q Jer 36:7; Ac 8:24;
Jas 5:16 r Isa 1:9
s Lev 26:22; La 1:1
42:3
t Ps 86:11; Pr 3:6
42:4
u Ex 8:29;
1Sa 12:23
v 1Ki 22:14;
1Sa 3:17
42:5
w Ge 31:50

Jeremiah 41:16—43:13

Johanan and company, worried about Babylonian reprisals for Gedaliah's death, considered escaping to Egypt. Jeremiah offered both a prophetic message from God (42:9–18) and a personal warning (vv. 19–22) against such a flight. Members of Johanan's group accused Jeremiah of lying and conspiring with Baruch, casting blame on someone they considered less spiritual than Jeremiah. In the end the people went to Egypt, accompanied—no doubt unwillingly—by Jeremiah and Baruch.

The exchange between this group and the prophet is one of the clearest examples in Jeremiah of outright disobedience to God's revealed will. Readers are invited not just to note the "why" of the continuing tragedy but to understand the call to choose the path of obedience. Jeremiah wasn't ignorant of the circumstances and risks. But he placed concern for the group's safety in the larger context of listening to God's guidance and having the courage to follow it.

42:6
x Dt 5:29; 6:3;
Jer 7:23 y Ex 24:7;
Jos 24:24
42:8
z ver 1
42:9
a 2Ki 22:15
42:10
b Jer 24:6
c Jer 31:28
d Eze 36:36
e Jer 18:8
42:11
f Jer 27:11
g Nu 14:9
h Isa 43:5 i Jer 1:8;
Ro 8:31
42:12
j Ps 106:44-46
42:13
k Jer 44:16
42:14
l Nu 11:4-5
42:16
m Eze 11:8
42:17
n ver 22; Jer 44:13
42:18
o Dt 29:18-20;
Jer 7:20
p 2Ch 36:19;
Jer 39:1-9
q Jer 29:18
r Jer 22:10
42:19
s Dt 17:16; Isa 30:7
42:20
t ver 2
42:21
u Eze 2:7;
Zec 7:11-12
42:22
v ver 17; Eze 6:11
w Hos 9:6
43:1
x Jer 26:8; 42:9-22
43:2
y Jer 42:1
43:3
z Jer 38:4
43:4
a Jer 42:5-6
b Jer 42:10

you to tell us. 6Whether it is favorable or unfavorable, we will obey the LORD our God, to whom we are sending you, so that it will go well x with us, for we will obey y the LORD our God."

7Ten days later the word of the LORD came to Jeremiah. 8So he called together Johanan son of Kareah and all the army officers z who were with him and all the people from the least to the greatest. 9He said to them, "This is what the LORD, the God of Israel, to whom you sent me to present your petition, says: a 10'If you stay in this land, I will build b you up and not tear you down; I will plant c you and not uproot you, d for I am grieved over the disaster I have inflicted on you. e 11Do not be afraid of the king of Babylon, f whom you now fear. g Do not be afraid of him, declares the LORD, for I am with you and will save h you and deliver you from his hands. i 12I will show you compassion so that he will have compassion on you and restore you to your land.' j

13"However, if you say, 'We will not stay in this land,' and so disobey k the LORD your God, 14and if you say, 'No, we will go and live in Egypt, l where we will not see war or hear the trumpet or be hungry for bread,' 15then hear the word of the LORD, O remnant of Judah. This is what the LORD Almighty, the God of Israel, says: 'If you are determined to go to Egypt and you do go to settle there, 16then the sword m you fear will overtake you there, and the famine you dread will follow you into Egypt, and there you will die. 17Indeed, all who are determined to go to Egypt to settle there will die by the sword, famine and plague; n not one of them will survive or escape the disaster I will bring on them.' 18This is what the LORD Almighty, the God of Israel, says: 'As my anger and wrath o have been poured out on those who lived in Jerusalem, p so will my wrath be poured out on you when you go to Egypt. You will be an object of cursing and horror, q of condemnation and reproach; you will never see this place again.' r

19"O remnant of Judah, the LORD has told you, 'Do not go to Egypt.' s Be sure of this: I warn you today 20that you made a fatal mistake a when you sent me to the LORD your God and said, 'Pray to the LORD our God for us; tell us everything he says and we will do it.' t 21I have told you today, but you still have not obeyed the LORD your God in all he sent me to tell you. u 22So now, be sure of this: You will die by the sword, famine and plague v in the place where you want to go to settle." w

43 When Jeremiah finished telling the people all the words of the LORD their God—everything the LORD had sent him to tell them x— 2Azariah son of Hoshaiah and Johanan y son of Kareah and all the arrogant men said to Jeremiah, "You are lying! The LORD our God has not sent you to say, 'You must not go to Egypt to settle there.' 3But Baruch son of Neriah is inciting you against us to hand us over to the Babylonians, b so they may kill us or carry us into exile to Babylon." z

4So Johanan son of Kareah and all the army officers and all the people disobeyed the LORD's command a to stay in the land of Judah. b 5Instead, Johanan son of Kareah and all the army officers led away all the remnant of Judah who had come back to live in the land of Judah from all the nations where they had

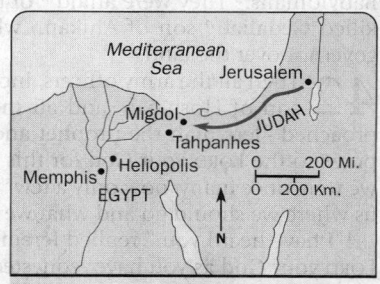

Flight to Egypt (43:5)
Then: Escape from physical forces and human powers is possible; flight from God is not.
Now: Modern people often leave their native countries for safety (refugees) and/or economic gain (immigrants).

a 20 Or *you erred in your hearts*   b 3 Or *Chaldeans*

How's your OQ: your obedience quotient? Today's culture elevates freedom of choice and avoids lasting commitments, also placing a premium on personal "happiness." But Christians aren't to understand obedience to God as an irrelevant burden or needless requirement. Obedience is the proper response to our relationship of love with Christ. How do John 15:9–10 and Hebrews 5:8–9 contribute to your understanding of Biblical obedience?

been scattered.[c] [6]They also led away all the men, women and children and the king's daughters whom Nebuzaradan commander of the imperial guard had left with Gedaliah son of Ahikam, the son of Shaphan, and Jeremiah the prophet and Baruch son of Neriah. [7]So they entered Egypt in disobedience to the LORD and went as far as Tahpanhes.[d]

[8]In Tahpanhes[e] the word of the LORD came to Jeremiah: [9]"While the Jews are watching, take some large stones with you and bury them in clay in the brick pavement at the entrance to Pharaoh's palace in Tahpanhes. [10]Then say to them, 'This is what the LORD Almighty, the God of Israel, says: I will send for my servant[f] Nebuchadnezzar king of Babylon, and I will set his throne over these stones I have buried here; he will spread his royal canopy above them. [11]He will come and attack Egypt,[g] bringing death to those destined for death, captivity to those destined for captivity, and the sword to those destined for the sword.[h] [12]He[a] will set fire to the temples of the gods[i] of Egypt; he will burn their temples and take their gods captive. As a shepherd wraps[j] his garment around him, so will he wrap Egypt around himself and depart from there unscathed. [13]There in the temple of the sun[b] in Egypt he will demolish the sacred pillars and will burn down the temples of the gods of Egypt.' "

Disaster Because of Idolatry

44 This word came to Jeremiah concerning all the Jews living in Lower Egypt—in Migdol,[k] Tahpanhes[l] and Memphis[c][m]—and in Upper Egypt[d]:[n] [2]"This is what the LORD Almighty, the God of Israel, says: You saw the great disaster I brought on Jerusalem and on all the towns of Judah. Today they lie deserted and in ruins[o] [3]because of the evil they have done. They provoked me to anger by burning incense and by worshiping other gods[p] that neither they nor you nor your fathers[q] ever knew. [4]Again and again[r] I sent my servants the prophets,[s] who said, 'Do not do this detestable thing that I hate!' [5]But they did not listen or pay attention; they did not turn from their wickedness or stop burning incense to other gods.[t] [6]Therefore, my fierce anger was poured out; it raged against the towns of Judah and the streets of Jerusalem and made them the desolate ruins they are today.

[7]"Now this is what the LORD God Almighty, the God of Israel, says: Why bring such great disaster[u] on yourselves by cutting off from Judah the men and women,[v] the children and infants, and so leave yourselves without a remnant? [8]Why provoke me to anger with what your hands have made,[w] burning incense to other gods in Egypt, where you have come to live?[x] You will destroy yourselves and make yourselves an object of cursing and reproach[y] among all the nations on earth. [9]Have you forgotten the wickedness committed by your fathers and by the kings and queens of Judah and the wickedness committed by you and your wives in the land of Judah and the streets of Jerusalem?[z] [10]To this day they have not humbled themselves or shown reverence, nor have they followed my law[a] and the decrees I set before you and your fathers.[b]

[11]"Therefore, this is what the LORD Almighty, the God of Israel, says: I am determined to bring disaster[c] on you and to destroy all Judah. [12]I will take away the remnant[d] of Judah who were determined to go to Egypt to settle there. They will all per-

[a]12 Or I   [b]13 Or in Heliopolis   [c]1 Hebrew Noph   [d]1 Hebrew in Pathros

43:5 / c Jer 40:12

43:7 / d Jer 2:16; 44:1
43:8 / e Jer 2:16

43:10 / f Isa 44:28; Jer 25:9; 27:6
43:11 / g Jer 46:13-26; Eze 29:19-20 / h Jer 15:2; 44:13; Zec 11:9
43:12 / i Jer 46:25; Eze 30:13 / j Ps 104:2; 109:18-19

44:1 / k Ex 14:2 / l Jer 43:7, 8 / m Isa 19:13 / n Isa 11:11; Jer 46:14
44:2 / o Isa 6:11; Jer 9:11; 34:22
44:3 / p ver 8; Dt 13:6-11; 29:26 / q Dt 32:17; Jer 19:4
44:4 / r Jer 7:13 / s Jer 7:25; 25:4; 26:5
44:5 / t Jer 11:8-10

44:7 / u Jer 26:19 / v Jer 51:22
44:8 / w Jer 25:6-7 / x 1Co 10:22 / y Jer 42:18

44:9 / z ver 17,21
44:10 / a Jos 1:7 / b 1Ki 9:6-9

44:11 / c Jer 21:10; Am 9:4
44:12 / d ver 7

Jeremiah 44:1–30

The bitter exchange between prophet and people highlighted the deep cultural and religious divisions within the Jewish community. This chapter concentrates on idolatry (particularly devotion to a pagan goddess, the "Queen of Heaven") and worship of multiple gods, if not outright apostasy against the ancestral faith. The people's testy reply to the prophet's speech—"We *will* burn incense to the Queen of Heaven"—reflected two significant assumptions about their religion: (1) Its primary function was securing health and safety, and (2) they would worship whichever deity promised a better fortune.

Modern movements toward worship of other gods may be motivated by spiritual hunger. This kind of hunger is real, but so is the spiritual blindness that keeps people from seeing the truth in Jesus. The pathway to life begins by acknowledging that every road except the one charted by God leads to death (cf. Matt. 7:13–14). Some people add belief in Christ to their backpack of religious values, but by his own word Jesus is "the [only] way and the truth and the life" (John 14:6; cf. John 10:9). Once we've found true faith in Christ, we'll find it impossible to follow other beliefs.

44:12
e Isa 1:28
f Jer 29:18;
42:15-18
44:13
g Jer 42:17

44:14
h ver 28;
Jer 22:24-27;
Ro 9:27

44:16
i Jer 11:8-10

44:17
j Dt 23:23 k ver 25;
Jer 7:18
l Hos 2:5-13

44:18
m Mal 3:13-15
44:19
n Jer 7:18

44:21
o Isa 64:9;
Jer 14:10
p Jer 11:13 q ver 9
r Ps 79:8

44:22
s Jer 25:18
t Ge 19:13;
Ps 107:33-34
44:23
u Jer 40:2 v 1Ki 9:9;
Jer 7:13-15;
Da 9:11-12
44:24
w ver 15 x Jer 43:7

44:25
y ver 17
z Eze 20:39
44:26
a Ge 22:16;
Isa 48:1;
Heb 6:13-17
b Dt 32:40;
Ps 50:16
44:27
c Jer 31:28

44:28
d ver 13-14;
Isa 10:19 e ver 17,
25-26

44:29
f Pr 19:21
44:30
g Jer 46:26;
Eze 30:21
h 2Ki 25:1-7
i Jer 39:5

45:1
j Jer 32:12;
36:4,18,32
k 2Ch 36:5

ish in Egypt; they will fall by the sword or die from famine. From the least to the greatest, they will die by sword or famine. [e] They will become an object of cursing and horror, of condemnation and reproach. [f] 13I will punish those who live in Egypt with the sword, famine and plague, [g] as I punished Jerusalem. 14None of the remnant of Judah who have gone to live in Egypt will escape or survive to return to the land of Judah, to which they long to return and live; none will return except a few fugitives." [h]

15Then all the men who knew that their wives were burning incense to other gods, along with all the women who were present—a large assembly—and all the people living in Lower and Upper Egypt, [a] said to Jeremiah, 16"We will not listen [i] to the message you have spoken to us in the name of the LORD! 17We will certainly do everything we said we would: [j] We will burn incense to the Queen of Heaven [k] and will pour out drink offerings to her just as we and our fathers, our kings and our officials did in the towns of Judah and in the streets of Jerusalem. At that time we had plenty of food and were well off and suffered no harm. [l] 18But ever since we stopped burning incense to the Queen of Heaven and pouring out drink offerings to her, we have had nothing and have been perishing by sword and famine. [m]"

19The women added, "When we burned incense to the Queen of Heaven [n] and poured out drink offerings to her, did not our husbands know that we were making cakes like her image and pouring out drink offerings to her?"

20Then Jeremiah said to all the people, both men and women, who were answering him, 21 "Did not the LORD remember [o] and think about the incense [p] burned in the towns of Judah and the streets of Jerusalem [q] by you and your fathers, [r] your kings and your officials and the people of the land? 22When the LORD could no longer endure your wicked actions and the detestable things you did, your land became an object of cursing [s] and a desolate waste without inhabitants, as it is today. [t] 23Because you have burned incense and have sinned against the LORD and have not obeyed him or followed his law or his decrees or his stipulations, this disaster [u] has come upon you, as you now see." [v]

24Then Jeremiah said to all the people, including the women, [w] "Hear the word of the LORD, all you people of Judah in Egypt. [x] 25This is what the LORD Almighty, the God of Israel, says: You and your wives have shown by your actions what you promised when you said, 'We will certainly carry out the vows we made to burn incense and pour out drink offerings to the Queen of Heaven.' [y]

"Go ahead then, do what you promised! Keep your vows! [z] 26But hear the word of the LORD, all Jews living in Egypt: 'I swear [a] by my great name,' says the LORD, 'that no one from Judah living anywhere in Egypt will ever again invoke my name or swear, "As surely as the Sovereign LORD lives." [b] 27For I am watching over them for harm, [c] not for good; the Jews in Egypt will perish by sword and famine until they are all destroyed. 28Those who escape the sword and return to the land of Judah from Egypt will be very few. [d] Then the whole remnant of Judah who came to live in Egypt will know whose word will stand—mine or theirs. [e]

29" 'This will be the sign to you that I will punish you in this place,' declares the LORD, 'so that you will know that my threats of harm against you will surely stand.' [f] 30This is what the LORD says: 'I am going to hand Pharaoh [g] Hophra king of Egypt over to his enemies who seek his life, just as I handed Zedekiah [h] king of Judah over to Nebuchadnezzar king of Babylon, the enemy who was seeking his life.' " [i]

A Message to Baruch

45 This is what Jeremiah the prophet told Baruch [j] son of Neriah in the fourth year of Jehoiakim [k] son of Josiah king of Judah, after Baruch had written on a scroll the words Jeremiah was then dictating: 2"This is what the LORD, the God of

---

a 15 Hebrew *in Egypt and Pathros*

Jeremiah 45:1–5

⌘ This prophecy doesn't fit the timeline of chapters 37–44. Yet verse 1 provides a date in the fourth year

of Jehoiakim's reign (605 B.C.), coinciding with God's command in 36:1 for Jeremiah to prepare a scroll of his prophecies. The fallout over Baruch's reading from the

Israel, says to you, Baruch: ³You said, 'Woe to me! The LORD has added sorrow to my pain; I am worn out with groaning*ˡ* and find no rest.' "

⁴ₗThe LORD said,ₗ "Say this to him: 'This is what the LORD says: I will overthrow what I have built and uproot what I have planted,*ᵐ* throughout the land.*ⁿ* ⁵Should you then seek great things for yourself? Seek them not.*ᵒ* For I will bring disaster on all people, declares the LORD, but wherever you go I will let you escape with your life.' "*ᵖ*

A Message About Egypt

46 This is the word of the LORD that came to Jeremiah the prophet concerning the nations:*q*

²Concerning Egypt:

This is the message against the army of Pharaoh Neco*ʳ* king of Egypt, which was defeated at Carchemish*ˢ* on the Euphrates River by Nebuchadnezzar king of Babylon in the fourth year of Jehoiakim*ᵗ* son of Josiah king of Judah:

³ "Prepare your shields,*ᵘ* both large and small,
    and march out for battle!
⁴ Harness the horses,
    mount the steeds!
Take your positions
    with helmets on!
Polish*ᵛ* your spears,
    put on your armor!*ʷ*
⁵ What do I see?
    They are terrified,
they are retreating,
    their warriors are defeated.
They flee*ˣ* in haste
    without looking back,
    and there is terror*ʸ* on every side,"
                                    declares the LORD.

⁶ "The swift cannot flee*ᶻ*
    nor the strong escape.
In the north by the River Euphrates
    they stumble and fall.*ᵃ*

⁷ "Who is this that rises like the Nile,
    like rivers of surging waters?*ᵇ*
⁸ Egypt rises like the Nile,
    like rivers of surging waters.
She says, 'I will rise and cover the earth;
    I will destroy cities and their people.'

45:3	*l* Ps 69:3
45:4	*m* Jer 11:17
	n Isa 5:5-7;
	Jer 18:7-10
45:5	*o* Mt 6:25-27,33
	p Jer 21:9; 38:2;
	39:18
46:1	*q* Jer 1:10; 25:15-38
46:2	*r* 2Ki 23:29
	s 2Ch 35:20
	t Jer 45:1
46:3	*u* Isa 21:5;
	Jer 51:11-12
46:4	*v* Eze 21:9-11
	w 1Sa 17:5,38;
	2Ch 26:14; Ne 4:16
46:5	*x* ver 21 *y* Jer 49:29
46:6	*z* Isa 30:16
	a ver 12,16;
	Da 11:19
46:7	*b* Jer 47:2

---

scroll may have included public persecution of Jeremiah's secretary. Baruch's "woe" corresponded to Jeremiah's laments: There is a cost to serving the Lord in troubled times. God's response to Baruch—as well as its placement here in the book of Jeremiah—confirms that God takes care of his own.

At a time when you have felt isolated or depressed, or when you have been forced into unfamiliar territory or caught up in overwhelming and destructive forces, has it occurred to you to measure your life against those of faith heroes like Joseph, Moses, John the Baptist, Stephen, Paul, the apostle John, Jeremiah, and Baruch—all of whom faced struggles as a result of God's call? None lacked the attention of their faithful

God. Their lives were gifts in service to God, and through their difficulties he formed them as his faithful followers.

Jeremiah 46:1–28

The fact that the oracles (divine messages) against the nations (chs. 46–51) were collected at the end of Jeremiah suggests that they were preserved as witnesses to God's sovereign justice. They adopted classical forms of Hebrew poetry used for prophecy against nations since at least the time of Amos (c. 750 B.C.). The oracles announced divine judgment, often using sarcasm to reveal a particular nation's arrogance and cruelty. They witnessed against human injustice and called for the administration of God's justice.

46:9
c Jer 47:3
d Isa 66:19

9 Charge, O horses!
    Drive furiously, O charioteers! c
March on, O warriors—
    men of Cush a and Put who carry shields,
    men of Lydia d who draw the bow.

46:10
e Joel 1:15
f Dt 32:42
g Zep 1:7

10 But that day e belongs to the Lord, the LORD Almighty—
    a day of vengeance, for vengeance on his foes.
The sword will devour f till it is satisfied,
    till it has quenched its thirst with blood.
For the Lord, the LORD Almighty, will offer sacrifice g
    in the land of the north by the River Euphrates.

46:11
h Jer 8:22 i Isa 47:1
j Jer 30:13; Mic 1:9

11 "Go up to Gilead and get balm, h
    O Virgin i Daughter of Egypt.
But you multiply remedies in vain;
    there is no healing j for you.

12 The nations will hear of your shame;
    your cries will fill the earth.
One warrior will stumble over another;
    both will fall k down together."

46:12
k Isa 19:4;
Na 3:8-10

46:13
l Isa 19:1

13 This is the message the LORD spoke to Jeremiah the prophet about the coming of Nebuchadnezzar king of Babylon to attack Egypt: l

46:14
m Jer 43:8

14 "Announce this in Egypt, and proclaim it in Migdol;
    proclaim it also in Memphis b and Tahpanhes: m
'Take your positions and get ready,
    for the sword devours those around you.'

46:15
n Isa 66:15-16
46:16
o Lev 26:37 p ver 6

15 Why will your warriors be laid low?
    They cannot stand, for the LORD will push them down. n
16 They will stumble o repeatedly;
    they will fall p over each other.
They will say, 'Get up, let us go back
    to our own people and our native lands,
    away from the sword of the oppressor.'

46:17
q Isa 19:11-16

17 There they will exclaim,
    'Pharaoh king of Egypt is only a loud noise;
    he has missed his opportunity. q'

46:18
r Jer 48:15
s Jos 19:22
t 1Ki 18:42

18 "As surely as I live," declares the King, r
    whose name is the LORD Almighty,
"one will come who is like Tabor s among the mountains,
    like Carmel t by the sea.

46:19
u Isa 20:4

19 Pack your belongings for exile, u
    you who live in Egypt,
for Memphis will be laid waste
    and lie in ruins without inhabitant.

20 "Egypt is a beautiful heifer,

---

a 9 That is, the upper Nile region   b 14 Hebrew *Noph*; also in verse 19

Verses 2–12, dated in 605 B.C. during Jehoiakim's reign, were directed against Pharaoh Neco. This was the year of the fateful battle at Carchemish between the forces of Neco and Nebuchadnezzar, in which the Egyptians were routed. The language of the oracle pictures the Egyptian army preparing to fight but resorting to flight. The prophecy in verses 13–26 is undated. Essentially it announced that Babylon would work God's judgment on Egypt.

The long tradition in the Old Testament of oracles against nations reminds us that God can't be mocked—people *will* reap what they sow (Gal. 6:7). The wheels of justice may grind slowly and leave much unanswered from the limited vantage point of any generation (2 Peter 3:8–9). But a glance at the long histories of Egypt or Rome testifies that political power doesn't guarantee right or continuing might.

but a gadfly is coming
against her from the north. *v*
21 The mercenaries *w* in her ranks
are like fattened calves.
They too will turn and flee *x* together,
they will not stand their ground,
for the day *y* of disaster is coming upon them,
the time for them to be punished.
22 Egypt will hiss like a fleeing serpent
as the enemy advances in force;
they will come against her with axes,
like men who cut down trees.
23 They will chop down her forest,"

declares the LORD,

"dense though it be.
They are more numerous than locusts, *z*
they cannot be counted.
24 The Daughter of Egypt will be put to shame,
handed over to the people of the north. *a*"

25 The LORD Almighty, the God of Israel, says: "I am about to bring punishment on Amon god of Thebes, *a* *b* on Pharaoh, on Egypt and her gods *c* and her kings, and on those who rely *d* on Pharaoh. 26 I will hand them over *e* to those who seek their lives, to Nebuchadnezzar king *f* of Babylon and his officers. Later, however, Egypt will be inhabited *g* as in times past," declares the LORD.

27 "Do not fear, *h* O Jacob my servant;
do not be dismayed, O Israel.
I will surely save you out of a distant place,
your descendants from the land of their exile. *i*
Jacob will again have peace and security,
and no one will make him afraid.
28 Do not fear, O Jacob my servant,
for I am with you," *j* declares the LORD.
"Though I completely destroy *k* all the nations
among which I scatter you,
I will not completely destroy you.
I will discipline you but only with justice;
I will not let you go entirely unpunished."

A Message About the Philistines

47 This is the word of the LORD that came to Jeremiah the prophet concerning the Philistines before Pharaoh attacked Gaza: *l*

2 This is what the LORD says:

"See how the waters are rising in the north; *m*
they will become an overflowing torrent.
They will overflow the land and everything in it,
the towns and those who live in them.
The people will cry out;
all who dwell in the land will wail

a 25 Hebrew *No*

Cross references

46:20
v ver 24; Jer 47:2
46:21
w 2Ki 7:6 *x* ver 5
y Ps 37:13

46:23
z Jdg 7:12

46:24
a Jer 1:15

46:25
b Eze 30:14; Na 3:8
c Jer 43:12
d Isa 20:6
46:26
e Jer 44:30
f Eze 32:11
g Eze 29:11-16
46:27
h Isa 41:13; 43:5
i Isa 11:11;
Jer 50:19

46:28
j Isa 8:9-10
k Jer 4:27

47:1
l Ge 10:19; Am 1:6;
Zec 9:5-7

47:2
m Isa 8:7; 14:31

Jeremiah 47:1–7

The Philistines, neighbors and often enemies of Judah since the days of Israel's judges, lived along the Mediterranean coast. Two Philistine cities are named here: Gaza and Ashkelon. It's difficult to place this prophecy in a specific historical context, but there are several plausible options because of frequent military actions in the region. This oracle is similar to the previous one against Egypt. The Philistines would be defeated on some future day.

³ at the sound of the hoofs of galloping steeds,
   at the noise of enemy chariots
   and the rumble of their wheels.
Fathers will not turn to help their children;
   their hands will hang limp.
⁴ For the day has come
   to destroy all the Philistines
and to cut off all survivors
   who could help Tyre[n] and Sidon.[o]
The LORD is about to destroy the Philistines,[p]
   the remnant from the coasts of Caphtor.[a][q]
⁵ Gaza will shave[r] her head in mourning;
   Ashkelon[s] will be silenced.
O remnant on the plain,
   how long will you cut yourselves?

⁶ " 'Ah, sword[t] of the LORD,' ⌊you cry,⌋
   'how long till you rest?
Return to your scabbard;
   cease and be still.'
⁷ But how can it rest
   when the LORD has commanded it,
when he has ordered it
   to attack Ashkelon and the coast?"

A Message About Moab

48

Concerning Moab:

This is what the LORD Almighty, the God of Israel, says:

"Woe to Nebo,[u] for it will be ruined.
   Kiriathaim[v] will be disgraced and captured;
   the stronghold[b] will be disgraced and shattered.
² Moab will be praised[w] no more;
   in Heshbon[c][x] men will plot her downfall:
   'Come, let us put an end to that nation.'
You too, O Madmen,[d] will be silenced;
   the sword will pursue you.
³ Listen to the cries from Horonaim,[y]
   cries of great havoc and destruction.
⁴ Moab will be broken;
   her little ones will cry out.[e]
⁵ They go up the way to Luhith,[z]
   weeping bitterly as they go;
on the road down to Horonaim

Cross references (margin)

47:4
n Am 1:9-10;
Zec 9:2-4
o Jer 25:22
p Ge 10:14;
Joel 3:4 q Dt 2:23
47:5
r Jer 41:5; Mic 1:16
s Jer 25:20

47:6
t Jer 12:12

48:1
u Nu 32:38
v Nu 32:37

48:2
w Isa 16:14
x Nu 21:25

48:3
y Isa 15:5

48:5
z Isa 15:5

---

a 4 That is, Crete   b 1 Or / Misgab   c 2 The Hebrew for Heshbon sounds like the Hebrew for plot.
d 2 The name of the Moabite town Madmen sounds like the Hebrew for be silenced.   e 4 Hebrew;
Septuagint / proclaim it to Zoar

The oracles against the nations are a catalyst for the kinds of discussions Christians need to engage in concerning the place of public values. The prophecies put the emphasis on God, who evaluates people and their values rather than seeking consensus on values. In our society we can't expect agreement. But this shouldn't stop us as Christians from claiming that normative values do exist and play an important role in the moral evaluation that history (and ultimately God) provides of nations. What are some Christian values our culture generally espouses or rejects?

Jeremiah 48:1–47

According to Genesis 19:30–38, Abraham's drunken nephew Lot slept with his two daughters. They bore him two sons, one of whom was Moab. Thus the Israelites were distantly related to the Moabites, their neighbors to the east of Judah and the Dead Sea. Later, David's family was related to the Moabites through Ruth, his great-grandmother (Ruth 4:13–22).

The repetition of a concluding formula ("declares the

anguished cries over the destruction are heard.
⁶ Flee! Run for your lives;
  become like a bush^a in the desert. ^a
⁷ Since you trust in your deeds and riches,
  you too will be taken captive,
and Chemosh^b will go into exile, ^c
  together with his priests and officials.
⁸ The destroyer will come against every town,
  and not a town will escape.
The valley will be ruined
  and the plateau destroyed,
because the LORD has spoken.
⁹ Put salt on Moab,
  for she will be laid waste^b;
her towns will become desolate,
  with no one to live in them.

¹⁰ "A curse on him who is lax in doing the LORD's work!
  A curse on him who keeps his sword^d from bloodshed!^e

¹¹ "Moab has been at rest^f from youth,
  like wine left on its dregs, ^g
not poured from one jar to another—
  she has not gone into exile.
So she tastes as she did,
  and her aroma is unchanged.
¹² But days are coming,"
  declares the LORD,
"when I will send men who pour from jars,
  and they will pour her out;
they will empty her jars
  and smash her jugs.
¹³ Then Moab will be ashamed^h of Chemosh,
  as the house of Israel was ashamed
when they trusted in Bethel.

¹⁴ "How can you say, 'We are warriors,ⁱ
  men valiant in battle'?
¹⁵ Moab will be destroyed and her towns invaded;
  her finest young men will go down in the slaughter,^j"
declares the King, ^k whose name is the LORD Almighty. ^l
¹⁶ "The fall of Moab is at hand;^m
  her calamity will come quickly.
¹⁷ Mourn for her, all who live around her,
  all who know her fame;
say, 'How broken is the mighty scepter,
  how broken the glorious staff!'

¹⁸ "Come down from your glory
  and sit on the parched ground,ⁿ

---

^a 6 Or *like Aroer*   ^b 9 Or *Give wings to Moab, / for she will fly away*

LORD") in verses 25, 30, 35, 38, 43, 44, and 47 suggests that several prophetic announcements were collected in chapter 48. Jeremiah was so moved by the intensity of depicting Moab's downfall that he portrayed himself in mourning (vv. 31–32).

Jeremiah's oracles against the nations continue to bear witness to the outworking of God's Word. They also expose the corporate character traits God disdains. These prophecies are valuable as more than just a checklist to determine how and when, or if, judgment befell the nations addressed. They go beyond simply predicting what would inevitably come to pass. Hopefully every generation in every nation will pay attention to God's standards and warnings—before it's too late.

48:6	^a Jer 17:6
48:7	^b Nu 21:29
	^c Isa 46:1-2; Jer 49:3
48:10	^d Jer 47:6
	^e 1Ki 20:42; 2Ki 13:15-19
48:11	^f Zec 1:15
	^g Zep 1:12
48:13	^h Hos 10:6
48:14	ⁱ Ps 33:16
48:15	^j Jer 50:27
	^k Jer 46:18
	^l Jer 51:57
48:16	^m Isa 13:22
48:18	ⁿ Isa 47:1

48:18
o Nu 21:30;
Jos 13:9 *p* ver 8

O inhabitants of the Daughter of Dibon, *o*
for he who destroys Moab
   will come up against you
   and ruin your fortified cities. *p*

48:19
q Dt 2:36

19 Stand by the road and watch,
   you who live in Aroer. *q*
Ask the man fleeing and the woman escaping,
   ask them, 'What has happened?'

48:20
r Isa 16:7
s Nu 21:13

20 Moab is disgraced, for she is shattered.
   Wail *r* and cry out!
Announce by the Arnon *s*
   that Moab is destroyed.

48:21
t Nu 21:23; Isa 15:4
u Jos 13:18
48:22
v Jos 13:9,17
48:23
w Jos 13:17
48:24
x Am 2:2
48:25
y Ps 75:10
z Ps 10:15;
Eze 30:21

21 Judgment has come to the plateau—
   to Holon, Jahzah *t* and Mephaath, *u*
22   to Dibon, *v* Nebo and Beth Diblathaim,
23   to Kiriathaim, Beth Gamul and Beth Meon, *w*
24   to Kerioth *x* and Bozrah—
   to all the towns of Moab, far and near.
25 Moab's horn *a y* is cut off;
   her arm *z* is broken,"

                                        declares the LORD.

48:26
a Jer 25:16,27

26 "Make her drunk, *a*
   for she has defied the LORD.
Let Moab wallow in her vomit;
   let her be an object of ridicule.

48:27
b Jer 2:26
c Job 16:4;
Jer 18:16
d Mic 7:8-10

27 Was not Israel the object of your ridicule? *b*
   Was she caught among thieves,
that you shake your head *c* in scorn *d*
   whenever you speak of her?

48:28
e Ps 55:6-7
f Jdg 6:2

28 Abandon your towns and dwell among the rocks,
   you who live in Moab.
Be like a dove *e* that makes its nest
   at the mouth of a cave. *f*

48:29
g Job 40:12;
Isa 16:6

29 "We have heard of Moab's pride *g*—
   her overweening pride and conceit,
her pride and arrogance
   and the haughtiness of her heart.
30 I know her insolence but it is futile,"

                                        declares the LORD,

   "and her boasts accomplish nothing.

48:31
h Isa 15:5-8
i 2Ki 3:25

31 Therefore I wail *h* over Moab,
   for all Moab I cry out,
   I moan for the men of Kir Hareseth. *i*

48:32
j Isa 16:8-9

32 I weep for you, as Jazer weeps,
   O vines of Sibmah. *j*
Your branches spread as far as the sea;
   they reached as far as the sea of Jazer.
The destroyer has fallen
   on your ripened fruit and grapes.

33 Joy and gladness are gone
   from the orchards and fields of Moab.

48:33
k Isa 16:10
l Joel 1:12

I have stopped the flow of wine *k* from the presses;
   no one treads them with shouts of joy. *l*
Although there are shouts,
   they are not shouts of joy.

---

a 25 *Horn* here symbolizes strength.

34 "The sound of their cry rises
from Heshbon to Elealeh[m] and Jahaz,[n]
from Zoar[o] as far as Horonaim[p] and Eglath Shelishiyah,
for even the waters of Nimrim are dried up.[q]
35 In Moab I will put an end
to those who make offerings on the high places[r]
and burn incense[s] to their gods,"

declares the LORD.

36 "So my heart laments[t] for Moab like a flute;
it laments like a flute for the men of Kir Hareseth.
The wealth they acquired[u] is gone.
37 Every head is shaved[v]
and every beard cut off;
every hand is slashed
and every waist is covered with sackcloth.[w]
38 On all the roofs in Moab
and in the public squares
there is nothing but mourning,
for I have broken Moab
like a jar[x] that no one wants,"

declares the LORD.

39 "How shattered she is! How they wail!
How Moab turns her back in shame!
Moab has become an object of ridicule,
an object of horror to all those around her."

40 This is what the LORD says:

"Look! An eagle is swooping[y] down,
spreading its wings[z] over Moab.
41 Kerioth[a] will be captured
and the strongholds taken.
In that day the hearts of Moab's warriors
will be like the heart of a woman in labor.[a]
42 Moab will be destroyed[b] as a nation[c]
because she defied[d] the LORD.
43 Terror and pit and snare[e] await you,
O people of Moab,"

declares the LORD.

44 "Whoever flees[f] from the terror
will fall into a pit,
whoever climbs out of the pit
will be caught in a snare;
for I will bring upon Moab
the year[g] of her punishment,"

declares the LORD.

45 "In the shadow of Heshbon
the fugitives stand helpless,
for a fire has gone out from Heshbon,
a blaze from the midst of Sihon;[h]
it burns the foreheads of Moab,
the skulls[i] of the noisy boasters.
46 Woe to you, O Moab![j]
The people of Chemosh are destroyed;
your sons are taken into exile
and your daughters into captivity.

a 41 Or *The cities*

48:34
m Nu 32:3
n Isa 15:4
o Ge 13:10
p Isa 15:5 q Isa 15:6

48:35
r Isa 15:2; 16:12
s Jer 11:13

48:36
t Isa 16:11
u Isa 15:7

48:37
v Isa 15:2; Jer 41:5
w Ge 37:34

48:38
x Jer 22:28

48:40
y Dt 28:49; Hab 1:8
z Isa 8:8

48:41
a Isa 21:3
48:42
b Ps 83:4; Isa 16:14
c ver 2 d ver 26
48:43
e Isa 24:17

48:44
f 1Ki 19:17;
Isa 24:18
g Jer 11:23

48:45
h Nu 21:21,26-28
i Nu 24:17

48:46
j Nu 21:29

48:47
k Jer 12:15; 49:6,39

47 "Yet I will restore[k] the fortunes of Moab
  in days to come,"

declares the LORD.

Here ends the judgment on Moab.

A Message About Ammon

49:1
l Am 1:13;
Zep 2:8-9

49 Concerning the Ammonites:[l]

This is what the LORD says:

"Has Israel no sons?
  Has she no heirs?
Why then has Molech[a] taken possession of Gad?
  Why do his people live in its towns?
2 But the days are coming,"
  declares the LORD,

49:2
m Jer 4:19
n Dt 3:11
o Isa 14:2;
Eze 21:28-32;
25:2-11

"when I will sound the battle cry[m]
  against Rabbah[n] of the Ammonites;
it will become a mound of ruins,
  and its surrounding villages will be set on fire.
Then Israel will drive out
  those who drove her out,[o]"

says the LORD.

49:3
p Jos 8:28
q Jer 48:7

3 "Wail, O Heshbon, for Ai[p] is destroyed!
  Cry out, O inhabitants of Rabbah!
Put on sackcloth and mourn;
  rush here and there inside the walls,
for Molech will go into exile,[q]
  together with his priests and officials.
4 Why do you boast of your valleys,
  boast of your valleys so fruitful?

49:4
r Jer 9:23; 1Ti 6:17
s Jer 21:13

O unfaithful daughter,
  you trust in your riches[r] and say,
  'Who will attack me?'[s]
5 I will bring terror on you
  from all those around you,"

declares the Lord, the LORD Almighty.

"Every one of you will be driven away,
  and no one will gather the fugitives.

49:6
t ver 39; Jer 48:47

6 "Yet afterward, I will restore[t] the fortunes of the Ammonites,"

declares the LORD.

49:7
u Ge 25:30;
Eze 25:12
v Ge 36:11,15,34

A Message About Edom

7 Concerning Edom:[u]

This is what the LORD Almighty says:

"Is there no longer wisdom in Teman?[v]

a 1 Or their king; Hebrew malcam; also in verse 3

Jeremiah 49:1–6

Ben-Ammi, ancestor of the Ammonites, was Lot's other incestuous son (see previous "There and Then"). Ammon was located north of Moab and east of the Jordan River. Molech was the chief deity of the Ammonites (1 Kings 11:5,7,33) and the god to whom child sacrifices were tragically offered in Judah (Jer. 32:35; cf. Lev. 20:2–5; 2 Kings 23:10). Rabbah was Ammon's capital.

Its remains form part of the impressive citadel at the heart of modern Amman, Jordan. The judgment to come on Ammon was depicted in the prophecy as defeat and exile.

Mysterious affirmations come at the end of the oracles against Egypt, Moab, Ammon, and Elam; they proclaim restoration after judgment (46:26; 48:47; 49:6,39). The good news is that God's judgment often serves a wider, saving purpose. His church will be com-

Has counsel perished from the prudent?
Has their wisdom decayed?
⁸Turn and flee, hide in deep caves,
you who live in Dedan,ʷ
for I will bring disaster on Esau
at the time I punish him.
⁹If grape pickers came to you,
would they not leave a few grapes?
If thieves came during the night,
would they not steal only as much as they wanted?
¹⁰But I will strip Esau bare;
I will uncover his hiding places,
so that he cannot conceal himself.
His children, relatives and neighbors will perish,
and he will be no more.ˣ
¹¹Leave your orphans;ʸ I will protect their lives.
Your widows too can trust in me."

¹²This is what the LORD says: "If those who do not deserve to drink the cupᶻ must drink it, why should you go unpunished?ᵃ You will not go unpunished, but must drink it. ¹³I swearᵇ by myself," declares the LORD, "that Bozrahᶜ will become a ruin and an object of horror, of reproach and of cursing; and all its towns will be in ruins forever."

¹⁴I have heard a message from the LORD:
An envoy was sent to the nations to say,
"Assemble yourselves to attack it!
Rise up for battle!"

¹⁵"Now I will make you small among the nations,
despised among men.
¹⁶The terror you inspire
and the pride of your heart have deceived you,
you who live in the clefts of the rocks,
who occupy the heights of the hill.
Though you build your nestᵈ as high as the eagle's,
from there I will bring you down,"
declares the LORD.

¹⁷"Edom will become an object of horror;ᵉ
all who pass by will be appalled and will scoff
because of all its wounds.ᶠ
¹⁸As Sodom and Gomorrahᵍ were overthrown,
along with their neighboring towns,"
says the LORD,

"so no one will live there;
no man will dwellʰ in it.

49:8 w Jer 25:23
49:10 x Mal 1:2-5
49:11 y Hos 14:3
49:12 z Jer 25:15 a Jer 25:28-29
49:13 b Ge 22:16 c Ge 36:33; Isa 34:6
49:16 d Job 39:27; Am 9:2
49:17 e ver 13 f Jer 50:13; Eze 35:7
49:18 g Ge 19:24; Dt 29:23 h ver 33

prised of people from every nation. In heaven this joyful fact is part of a song sung by the redeemed (Rev. 5:9–10). Shouldn't this also be a song of the church on Earth and a cause for our rejoicing?

Jeremiah 49:7–22

Edom was in a remote region south of Moab and the Dead Sea. Like Ammon and Moab, the Edomites were related to God's people—through Esau, whose name became synonymous with Edom (vv. 8,10; cf. Gen. 36:1). The bitterness in the relationship between Jacob and Esau was reflected through the centuries in that between Israel and Edom. Edom's strongholds on mountains and cliffs wouldn't save her people from God's judg-

ment. Unlike the prophecies to Moab and Ammon, Jeremiah made no reference to Edom's future restoration.

The oracles against the nations in Jeremiah reveal humanity's fallen condition. As we read these prophetic messages, we are reminded that injustice and cruelty are historical companions. But so, often, are words of grace and future hope. While such words are glaringly absent from this oracle to Edom, they have been offered unconditionally through Jesus' atoning death until the end of the age to all nations—to all who will believe. Have you taken time to reflect on how blessed you are to live under the new covenant of grace?

49:19
i Jer 12:5
j Jer 50:44

19 "Like a lion coming up from Jordan's thickets[i]
    to a rich pastureland,
I will chase Edom from its land in an instant.
    Who is the chosen one I will appoint for this?
    Who is like me and who can challenge me?[j]
    And what shepherd can stand against me?"

49:20
k Isa 14:27
l Jer 50:45
m Mal 1:3-4

20 Therefore, hear what the LORD has planned against Edom,
    what he has purposed[k] against those who live in Teman:
The young of the flock[l] will be dragged away;
    he will completely destroy[m] their pasture because of them.

49:21
n Eze 26:15
o Jer 50:46;
Eze 26:18
49:22
p Hos 8:1
q Isa 13:8;
Jer 48:40-41

21 At the sound of their fall the earth will tremble;[n]
    their cry[o] will resound to the Red Sea.[a]
22 Look! An eagle will soar and swoop[p] down,
    spreading its wings over Bozrah.
In that day the hearts of Edom's warriors
    will be like the heart of a woman in labor.[q]

A Message About Damascus

49:23
r Ge 14:15;
2Ch 16:2; Ac 9:2
s Isa 10:9; Am 6:2;
Zec 9:2 *t* 2Ki 18:34
u Ge 49:4; Isa 57:20

23 Concerning Damascus:[r]

"Hamath[s] and Arpad[t] are dismayed,
    for they have heard bad news.
They are disheartened,
    troubled like[b] the restless sea.[u]
24 Damascus has become feeble,
    she has turned to flee
    and panic has gripped her;
anguish and pain have seized her,
    pain like that of a woman in labor.
25 Why has the city of renown not been abandoned,
    the town in which I delight?

49:26
v Jer 50:30

26 Surely, her young men will fall in the streets;
    all her soldiers will be silenced[v] in that day,"
                                declares the LORD Almighty.

49:27
w Jer 43:12;
Am 1:4 × 1Ki 15:18

27 "I will set fire[w] to the walls of Damascus;
    it will consume the fortresses of Ben-Hadad.[x]"

A Message About Kedar and Hazor

49:28
y Ge 25:13

28 Concerning Kedar[y] and the kingdoms of Hazor, which Nebuchadnezzar king
of Babylon attacked:

---

a 21 Hebrew *Yam Suph*; that is, Sea of Reeds   *b* 23 Hebrew *on* or *by*

Jeremiah 49:23–27

📖 Damascus, the capital of Aram (today's southern Syria), was located northeast of the Sea of Galilee. The Arameans of Damascus had been Israel's frequent enemies since the time of David (e.g., 2 Sam. 8:5; 1 Kings 22:31; 2 Kings 24:2). Hamath and Arpad, in northern Syria, were named in the oracle as cities that would be dismayed by the news of judgment to fall on the region through the Babylonian invasion.

The reference to Ben-Hadad comes as an "update" of Amos's earlier prophecy (Amos 1:3–5) against Damascus. Hadad was a well-known Aramaen deity, and the name Ben-Hadad designated a king as the adopted "son" (*ben* means "son") of this god. Comparable to the term *pharaoh* in Egypt, several kings from Damascus used this title/name (e.g., 2 Kings 6:24).

💻 Though the royal line in Damascus identified him as their "father," the god Hadad's "heyday" was brief—and his power, of course, nonexistent. Yet each of us as Christians can rejoice eternally in the reality of our adoption as sons and daughters—eternal heirs—of the One transcendent, everlasting, almighty King (Eph. 1:4–5).

Jeremiah 49:28–33

📖 Kedar was a region of northern Arabia, to the east of Judah. Kedar is also negatively referred to in Psalm 120:5 and Isaiah 21:16–17. Hazor is something of a mystery, since no location with that name is known in northern Arabia. It's not the city north of the Sea of Galilee frequently mentioned in the Old Testament. Both Kedar and Hazor likely refer to groups of Arab tribesmen who were attacked by the Babylonians under Nebuchadnezzar in 599 B.C.

This is what the LORD says:

> "Arise, and attack Kedar
> and destroy the people of the East. z

29 Their tents and their flocks will be taken;
> their shelters will be carried off
> with all their goods and camels.
> Men will shout to them,
> 'Terror^a on every side!'

30 "Flee quickly away!
> Stay in deep caves, you who live in Hazor,"

> declares the LORD.

> "Nebuchadnezzar king of Babylon has plotted against you;
> he has devised a plan against you.

31 "Arise and attack a nation at ease,
> which lives in confidence,"

> declares the LORD,

> "a nation that has neither gates nor bars;^b
> its people live alone.

32 Their camels will become plunder,
> and their large herds will be booty.
> I will scatter to the winds those who are in distant places^{a c}
> and will bring disaster on them from every side,"

> declares the LORD.

33 "Hazor will become a haunt of jackals,
> a desolate^d place forever.
> No one will live there;
> no man will dwell^e in it."

A Message About Elam

34 This is the word of the LORD that came to Jeremiah the prophet concerning Elam,^f early in the reign of Zedekiah^g king of Judah:

35 This is what the LORD Almighty says:

> "See, I will break the bow^h of Elam,
> the mainstay of their might.
36 I will bring against Elam the four windsⁱ
> from the four quarters of the heavens;
> I will scatter them to the four winds,
> and there will not be a nation
> where Elam's exiles do not go.

---

a 32 Or *who clip the hair by their foreheads*

49:28	z Jdg 6:3
49:29	a Jer 6:25; 46:5
49:31	b Eze 38:11
49:32	c Jer 9:26
49:33	d Jer 10:22 e ver 18; Jer 51:37
49:34	f Ge 10:22 g 2Ki 24:18
49:35	h Isa 22:6
49:36	i ver 32

📖 A mysterious "time warp" has kept nomadic Arab herders for more than two millennia from the encroachment (good or bad) of modern civilization. While Kedar and Hazor may no longer exist, many places like them still dot the desert regions of the Middle East and northern Africa. Jeremiah's oracle offered no restoration language. But such peoples today have the opportunity to receive, like all others who inhabit the globe, the wonderful gift of God's grace. It's the church's task to reach them and others with Christ's message of reconciliation and hope.

Jeremiah 49:34–39

📖 Elam was in the southern part of modern-day Iran. The Elamites were perpetual enemies of Assyria and Babylon. They became part of the Persian army that conquered Babylon under Cyrus in 539 B.C. The judg-

ment oracle against Elam—which mentions no specific violation—followed by the promise of restoration, leaves us with more questions than answers. One takeaway from this brief passage is the realization that God is sovereign. Judgment and deliverance both belong to him.

📖 No mention is made of sins by Elam against Judah. God has always been deeply concerned about all peoples—and not only as they relate to Israel. Think of Jonah's reluctance to preach to the Ninevites, for fear that they would repent and escape the judgment the prophet wished on them. These prophecies remind us that God is an active player in *all* national and international affairs. We are mistaken if we think he sits disinterestedly on the sidelines. What does this reality say to Christians who believe their country enjoys God's particular favor?

37 I will shatter Elam before their foes,
    before those who seek their lives;
I will bring disaster upon them,
    even my fierce anger," [j]

declares the LORD.

"I will pursue them with the sword [k]
    until I have made an end of them.
38 I will set my throne in Elam
    and destroy her king and officials,"

declares the LORD.

39 "Yet I will restore [l] the fortunes of Elam
    in days to come,"

declares the LORD.

A Message About Babylon

50 This is the word the LORD spoke through Jeremiah the prophet concerning Babylon [m] and the land of the Babylonians [a]:

2 "Announce and proclaim [n] among the nations,
    lift up a banner and proclaim it;
    keep nothing back, but say,
'Babylon will be captured; [o]
    Bel [p] will be put to shame,
    Marduk [q] filled with terror.
Her images will be put to shame
    and her idols filled with terror.'
3 A nation from the north will attack her
    and lay waste her land.
No one will live [r] in it;
    both men and animals [s] will flee away.

4 "In those days, at that time,"
    declares the LORD,
"the people of Israel and the people of Judah together [t]
    will go in tears [u] to seek [v] the LORD their God.
5 They will ask the way to Zion
    and turn their faces toward it.
They will come [w] and bind themselves to the LORD
    in an everlasting covenant [x]
    that will not be forgotten.

6 "My people have been lost sheep; [y]
    their shepherds have led them astray
    and caused them to roam on the mountains.
They wandered over mountain and hill [z]
    and forgot their own resting place. [a]
7 Whoever found them devoured them;

Side references:

49:37
j Jer 30:24
k Jer 9:16

49:39
l Jer 48:47

50:1
m Ge 10:10;
Isa 13:1
50:2
n Jer 4:16
o Jer 51:31
p Isa 46:1
q Jer 51:47

50:3
r ver 13;
Isa 14:22-23
s Zep 1:3

50:4
t Jer 3:18; Hos 1:11
u Ezr 3:12; Jer 31:9
v Hos 3:5

50:5
w Jer 33:7
x Isa 55:3;
Jer 32:40;
Heb 8:6-10

50:6
y Isa 53:6; Mt 9:36;
10:6 z Jer 3:6;
Eze 34:6 a ver 19

---

[a] 1 Or *Chaldeans*; also in verses 8, 25, 35 and 45

Jeremiah 50:1—51:64

These two chapters concern Babylon and God's just judgment on that nation for its arrogance and oppression of others. The prophecy was a testimony to the *role Babylon had played and would play in God's plan*. The gods of Babylon were discredited and judged along with her. Bel (equivalent to the Canaanite "Baal"), also known as Marduk, was the chief deity of Babylon (50:2; 51:44; cf. Isa. 46:1–2).

These chapters complete the collection of divine messages against the nations begun in chapter 46. The last line of chapter 51 states that "the words of Jeremiah end here." Readers may want to recall the way Jeremiah's work began. He was called to be "a prophet to the nations" (1:5). His words conclude with an extended prophecy against Babylon, the great imperial power of the day. Note that those words have lasted thousands of years longer than that great political and military entity.

their enemies said, 'We are not guilty,[b]
for they sinned against the LORD, their true pasture,
  the LORD, the hope[c] of their fathers.'

8 "Flee[d] out of Babylon;
  leave the land of the Babylonians,
  and be like the goats that lead the flock.
9 For I will stir up and bring against Babylon
  an alliance of great nations from the land of the north.
They will take up their positions against her,
  and from the north she will be captured.
Their arrows will be like skilled warriors
  who do not return empty-handed.
10 So Babylonia[a] will be plundered;
  all who plunder her will have their fill,"

declares the LORD.

11 "Because you rejoice and are glad,
  you who pillage my inheritance,[e]
because you frolic like a heifer threshing grain
  and neigh like stallions,
12 your mother will be greatly ashamed;
  she who gave you birth will be disgraced.
She will be the least of the nations—
  a wilderness, a dry land, a desert.
13 Because of the LORD's anger she will not be inhabited
  but will be completely desolate.
All who pass Babylon will be horrified and scoff[f]
  because of all her wounds.[g]

14 "Take up your positions around Babylon,
  all you who draw the bow.[h]
Shoot at her! Spare no arrows,
  for she has sinned against the LORD.
15 Shout[i] against her on every side!
  She surrenders, her towers fall,
  her walls[j] are torn down.
Since this is the vengeance[k] of the LORD,
  take vengeance on her;
  do to her[l] as she has done to others.
16 Cut off from Babylon the sower,
  and the reaper with his sickle at harvest.
Because of the sword[m] of the oppressor
  let everyone return to his own people,[n]
  let everyone flee to his own land.[o]

17 "Israel is a scattered flock
  that lions[p] have chased away.
The first to devour him
  was the king[q] of Assyria;

---

[a] 10 Or *Chaldea*

50:7
[b] Jer 2:3 [c] Jer 14:8

50:8
[d] Isa 48:20;
Jer 51:6; Rev 18:4

50:11
[e] Isa 47:6

50:13
[f] Jer 18:16
[g] Jer 49:17

50:14
[h] ver 29,42

50:15
[i] Jer 51:14
[j] Jer 51:44,58
[k] Jer 51:6
[l] Ps 137:8; Rev 18:6

50:16
[m] Jer 25:38
[n] Isa 13:14
[o] Jer 51:9

50:17
[p] Jer 2:15
[q] 2Ki 17:6

No group emerges unscathed in Jeremiah. There is plenty of failure to go around, whether in Judah, Egypt, Edom, or Babylon. So it is in our world. God's promise to rescue his people comes not because they are morally perfect but because of his grace toward them. His standards of judgment remind us of how much grace is needed for the salvation of people in any generation.

How sad that at the beginning of a new century Christians are still being persecuted for their faith in many places around the world. The believer's weapon is prayer—both for the persecuted church and for its oppressors. How regularly do your petitions include both groups?

1285

the last to crush his bones
  was Nebuchadnezzar[r] king[s] of Babylon."

50:17
r 2Ki 24:10,14
s 2Ki 25:7

18 Therefore this is what the LORD Almighty, the God of Israel, says:

"I will punish the king of Babylon and his land
  as I punished the king[t] of Assyria.[u]
19 But I will bring[v] Israel back to his own pasture
  and he will graze on Carmel and Bashan;
his appetite will be satisfied
  on the hills[w] of Ephraim and Gilead.
20 In those days, at that time,"
  declares the LORD,
"search will be made for Israel's guilt,
  but there will be none,
and for the sins[x] of Judah,
  but none will be found,
  for I will forgive[y] the remnant[z] I spare.

50:18
t Isa 10:12
u Eze 31:3
50:19
v Jer 31:10;
Eze 34:13
w Jer 31:5; 33:12

50:20
x Mic 7:18,19
y Jer 31:34 z Isa 1:9

21 "Attack the land of Merathaim
  and those who live in Pekod.[a]
Pursue, kill and completely destroy[a] them,"
  declares the LORD.

50:21
a Eze 23:23

"Do everything I have commanded you.
22 The noise[b] of battle is in the land,
  the noise of great destruction!
23 How broken and shattered
  is the hammer of the whole earth!
How desolate[c] is Babylon
  among the nations!
24 I set a trap[d] for you, O Babylon,
  and you were caught before you knew it;
you were found and captured[e]
  because you opposed[f] the LORD.
25 The LORD has opened his arsenal
  and brought out the weapons[g] of his wrath,
for the Sovereign LORD Almighty has work to do
  in the land of the Babylonians.[h]
26 Come against her from afar.
  Break open her granaries;
  pile her up like heaps of grain.
Completely destroy[i] her
  and leave her no remnant.
27 Kill all her young bulls;
  let them go down to the slaughter!
Woe to them! For their day has come,
  the time for them to be punished.
28 Listen to the fugitives and refugees from Babylon
  declaring in Zion[j]
how the LORD our God has taken vengeance,[k]
  vengeance for his temple.

50:22
b Jer 4:19-21; 51:54

50:23
c Isa 14:16

50:24
d Da 5:30-31
e Jer 51:31
f Job 9:4

50:25
g Isa 13:5
h Jer 51:25,55

50:26
i Isa 14:22-23

50:28
j Isa 48:20;
Jer 51:10 k ver 15

29 "Summon archers against Babylon,
  all those who draw the bow.[l]
Encamp all around her;
  let no one escape.
Repay[m] her for her deeds;[n]

50:29
l ver 14 m Rev 18:6
n Jer 51:56

a 21 The Hebrew term refers to the irrevocable giving over of things or persons to the LORD, often by totally destroying them; also in verse 26.

do to her as she has done.
For she has defied[o] the LORD,
the Holy One of Israel.

30 Therefore, her young men[p] will fall in the streets;
all her soldiers will be silenced in that day,"

declares the LORD.

31 "See, I am against[q] you, O arrogant one,"
declares the Lord, the LORD Almighty,
"for your day has come,
the time for you to be punished.
32 The arrogant one will stumble and fall
and no one will help her up;
I will kindle a fire[r] in her towns
that will consume all who are around her."

33 This is what the LORD Almighty says:

"The people of Israel are oppressed,[s]
and the people of Judah as well.
All their captors hold them fast,
refusing to let them go.[t]
34 Yet their Redeemer is strong;
the LORD Almighty[u] is his name.
He will vigorously defend their cause[v]
so that he may bring rest[w] to their land,
but unrest to those who live in Babylon.

35 "A sword[x] against the Babylonians!"
declares the LORD—
"against those who live in Babylon
and against her officials and wise[y] men!
36 A sword against her false prophets!
They will become fools.
A sword against her warriors![z]
They will be filled with terror.
37 A sword against her horses and chariots[a]
and all the foreigners in her ranks!
They will become women.[b]
A sword against her treasures!
They will be plundered.
38 A drought on[a] her waters!
They will dry[c] up.
For it is a land of idols,[d]
idols that will go mad with terror.

39 "So desert creatures and hyenas will live there,
and there the owl will dwell.
It will never again be inhabited
or lived in from generation to generation.[e]
40 As God overthrew Sodom and Gomorrah[f]
along with their neighboring towns,"

declares the LORD,

"so no one will live there;
no man will dwell in it.

41 "Look! An army is coming from the north;[g]
a great nation and many kings
are being stirred up from the ends of the earth.[h]

---

[a] 38 Or A sword against

50:29
o Isa 47:10

50:30
p Isa 13:18;
Jer 49:26

50:31
q Jer 21:13

50:32
r Jer 21:14; 49:27

50:33
s Isa 58:6
t Isa 14:17

50:34
u Jer 51:19
v Jer 15:21; 51:36
w Isa 14:7

50:35
x Jer 47:6 y Da 5:7

50:36
z Jer 49:22

50:37
a Jer 51:21
b Jer 51:30;
Na 3:13

50:38
c Jer 51:36 d ver 2

50:39
e Isa 13:19-22;
34:13-15; Jer 51:37;
Rev 18:2
50:40
f Ge 19:24

50:41
g Jer 6:22
h Isa 13:4;
Jer 51:22-28

50:42
i ver 14 / Isa 13:18
k Isa 5:30 / Jer 6:23

42 They are armed with bows[i] and spears;
　　they are cruel and without mercy.[j]
They sound like the roaring sea[k]
　　as they ride on their horses;
they come like men in battle formation
　　to attack you, O Daughter of Babylon.[l]
43 The king of Babylon has heard reports about them,
　　and his hands hang limp.
Anguish has gripped him,
　　pain like that of a woman in labor.
44 Like a lion coming up from Jordan's thickets
　　to a rich pastureland,
I will chase Babylon from its land in an instant.
　　Who is the chosen[m] one I will appoint for this?
Who is like me and who can challenge me?[n]
　　And what shepherd can stand against me?"

50:44
m Nu 16:5
n Job 41:10;
Isa 46:9; Jer 49:19

45 Therefore, hear what the LORD has planned against Babylon,
　　what he has purposed[o] against the land of the Babylonians:
The young of the flock will be dragged away;
　　he will completely destroy their pasture because of them.

50:45
o Ps 33:11;
Isa 14:24; Jer 51:11

46 At the sound of Babylon's capture the earth will tremble;
　　its cry[p] will resound among the nations.

50:46
p Rev 18:9-10

51

This is what the LORD says:

"See, I will stir up the spirit of a destroyer
　　against Babylon and the people of Leb Kamai.[a]
2 I will send foreigners to Babylon
　　to winnow[q] her and to devastate her land;
they will oppose her on every side
　　in the day of her disaster.

51:2
q Isa 41:16;
Jer 15:7; Mt 3:12

3 Let not the archer string his bow,[r]
　　nor let him put on his armor.[s]
Do not spare her young men;
　　completely destroy[b] her army.

51:3
r Jer 50:29
s Jer 46:4

4 They will fall[t] down slain in Babylon,[c]
　　fatally wounded in her streets.[u]

51:4
t Isa 13:15
u Jer 49:26; 50:30

5 For Israel and Judah have not been forsaken[v]
　　by their God, the LORD Almighty,
though their land[d] is full of guilt[w]
　　before the Holy One of Israel.

51:5
v Isa 54:6-8
w Hos 4:1

6 "Flee[x] from Babylon!
　　Run for your lives!
Do not be destroyed because of her sins.[y]
It is time for the LORD's vengeance;[z]
　　he will pay[a] her what she deserves.

51:6
x Jer 50:8
y Nu 16:26;
Rev 18:4
z Jer 50:15
a Jer 25:14

7 Babylon was a gold cup[b] in the LORD's hand;
　　she made the whole earth drunk.
The nations drank her wine;
　　therefore they have now gone mad.

51:7
b Jer 25:15-16;
Rev 14:8-10; 17:4

8 Babylon will suddenly fall[c] and be broken.
　　Wail over her!
Get balm[d] for her pain;
　　perhaps she can be healed.

51:8
c Isa 21:9; Rev 14:8
d Jer 46:11

---

[a] 1 *Leb Kamai* is a cryptogram for Chaldea, that is, Babylonia.　　[b] 3 The Hebrew term refers to the irrevocable giving over of things or persons to the LORD, often by totally destroying them.
[c] 4 Or *Chaldea*　　[d] 5 Or / *and the land of the Babylonians*

9 " 'We would have healed Babylon,
    but she cannot be healed;
  let us leave[e] her and each go to his own land,
    for her judgment[f] reaches to the skies,
    it rises as high as the clouds.'

10 " 'The LORD has vindicated[g] us;
    come, let us tell in Zion
    what the LORD our God has done.'[h]

11 "Sharpen the arrows,[i]
    take up the shields![j]
  The LORD has stirred up the kings of the Medes,[k]
    because his purpose[l] is to destroy Babylon.
  The LORD will take vengeance,
    vengeance for his temple.[m]

12 Lift up a banner against the walls of Babylon!
  Reinforce the guard,
    station the watchmen,
    prepare an ambush!
  The LORD will carry out his purpose,
    his decree against the people of Babylon.

13 You who live by many waters[n]
    and are rich in treasures,[o]
  your end has come,
    the time for you to be cut off.

14 The LORD Almighty has sworn by himself:[p]
    I will surely fill you with men, as with a swarm of locusts,[q]
    and they will shout[r] in triumph over you.

15 "He made the earth by his power;
    he founded the world by his wisdom
    and stretched[s] out the heavens by his understanding.

16 When he thunders,[t] the waters in the heavens roar;
    he makes clouds rise from the ends of the earth.
  He sends lightning with the rain
    and brings out the wind from his storehouses.[u]

17 "Every man is senseless and without knowledge;
    every goldsmith is shamed by his idols.
  His images are a fraud;[v]
    they have no breath in them.

18 They are worthless,[w] the objects of mockery;
    when their judgment comes, they will perish.

19 He who is the Portion of Jacob is not like these,
    for he is the Maker of all things,
  including the tribe of his inheritance—
    the LORD Almighty is his name.

20 "You are my war club,[x]
    my weapon for battle—
  with you I shatter[y] nations,
    with you I destroy kingdoms,

21 with you I shatter horse and rider,[z]
    with you I shatter chariot and driver,

22 with you I shatter man and woman,
    with you I shatter old man and youth,
    with you I shatter young man and maiden,[a]

23 with you I shatter shepherd and flock,

51:9
e Isa 13:14;
Jer 50:16
f Rev 18:4-5

51:10
g Mic 7:9
h Jer 50:28

51:11
i Jer 50:9 j Jer 46:4
k ver 28 l Jer 50:45
m Jer 50:28

51:13
n Rev 17:1,15
o Isa 45:3; Hab 2:9

51:14
p Am 6:8 q ver 27;
Na 3:15 r Jer 50:15

51:15
s Ge 1:1; Job 9:8;
Ps 104:2
51:16
t Ps 18:11-13
u Ps 135:7; Jnh 1:4

51:17
v Isa 44:20;
Hab 2:18-19
51:18
w Jer 18:15

51:20
x Isa 10:5
y Mic 4:13

51:21
z Ex 15:1

51:22
a 2Ch 36:17;
Isa 13:17-18

with you I shatter farmer and oxen,
with you I shatter governors and officials. *b*

24 "Before your eyes I will repay*c* Babylon and all who live in Babylonia*a* for all the wrong they have done in Zion," declares the LORD.

25 "I am against you, O destroying mountain,
you who destroy the whole earth,"

declares the LORD.

"I will stretch out my hand against you,
roll you off the cliffs,
and make you a burned-out mountain. *d*
26 No rock will be taken from you for a cornerstone,
nor any stone for a foundation,
for you will be desolate*e* forever,"

declares the LORD.

27 "Lift up a banner*f* in the land!
Blow the trumpet among the nations!
Prepare the nations for battle against her;
summon against her these kingdoms:*g*
Ararat, *h* Minni and Ashkenaz. *i*
Appoint a commander against her;
send up horses like a swarm of locusts.
28 Prepare the nations for battle against her—
the kings of the Medes,*j*
their governors and all their officials,
and all the countries they rule.
29 The land trembles and writhes,
for the LORD's purposes against Babylon stand—
to lay waste the land of Babylon
so that no one will live there. *k*
30 Babylon's warriors*l* have stopped fighting;
they remain in their strongholds.
Their strength is exhausted;
they have become like women. *m*
Her dwellings are set on fire;
the bars*n* of her gates are broken.
31 One courier*o* follows another
and messenger follows messenger
to announce to the king of Babylon
that his entire city is captured,
32 the river crossings seized,
the marshes set on fire,
and the soldiers terrified. *p*"

33 This is what the LORD Almighty, the God of Israel, says:

"The Daughter of Babylon is like a threshing floor*q*
at the time it is trampled;
the time to harvest*r* her will soon come."

34 "Nebuchadnezzar*s* king of Babylon has devoured us,
he has thrown us into confusion,
he has made us an empty jar.
Like a serpent he has swallowed us
and filled his stomach with our delicacies,
and then has spewed us out.
35 May the violence done to our flesh*b* be upon Babylon,"

a 24 Or *Chaldea*; also in verse 35   *b* 35 Or *done to us and to our children*

say the inhabitants of Zion.
"May our blood be on those who live in Babylonia,"
says Jerusalem. [t]

51:35
[t] ver 24; Ps 137:8

36 Therefore, this is what the LORD says:

"See, I will defend your cause [u]
and avenge [v] you;
I will dry up [w] her sea
and make her springs dry.
37 Babylon will be a heap of ruins,
a haunt [x] of jackals,
an object of horror and scorn,
a place where no one lives. [y]
38 Her people all roar like young lions,
they growl like lion cubs.
39 But while they are aroused,
I will set out a feast for them
and make them drunk,
so that they shout with laughter—
then sleep forever and not awake,"

51:36
[u] Ps 140:12;
Jer 50:34; La 3:58
[v] ver 6; Ro 12:19
[w] Jer 50:38

51:37
[x] Isa 13:22;
Rev 18:2
[y] Jer 50:13,39

declares the LORD. [z]

51:39
[z] ver 57

40 "I will bring them down
like lambs to the slaughter,
like rams and goats.

41 "How Sheshach [a][a] will be captured, [b]
the boast of the whole earth seized!
What a horror Babylon will be
among the nations!
42 The sea will rise over Babylon;
its roaring waves [c] will cover her.
43 Her towns will be desolate,
a dry and desert land,
a land where no one lives,
through which no man travels. [d]
44 I will punish Bel [e] in Babylon
and make him spew out [f] what he has swallowed.
The nations will no longer stream to him.
And the wall [g] of Babylon will fall.

51:41
[a] Jer 25:26
[b] Isa 13:19

51:42
[c] Isa 8:7

51:43
[d] ver 29,62;
Isa 13:20; Jer 2:6
51:44
[e] Isa 46:1 [f] ver 34
[g] ver 58; Jer 50:15

45 "Come out [h] of her, my people!
Run [i] for your lives!
Run from the fierce anger of the LORD.
46 Do not lose heart or be afraid [j]
when rumors [k] are heard in the land;
one rumor comes this year, another the next,
rumors of violence in the land
and of ruler against ruler.
47 For the time will surely come
when I will punish the idols [l] of Babylon;
her whole land will be disgraced [m]
and her slain will all lie fallen within her.
48 Then heaven and earth and all that is in them
will shout [n] for joy over Babylon,
for out of the north [o]
destroyers will attack her,"

51:45
[h] Rev 18:4 [i] ver 6;
Isa 48:20; Jer 50:8

51:46
[j] Jer 46:27
[k] 2Ki 19:7

51:47
[l] ver 52; Isa 46:1-2;
Jer 50:2
[m] Jer 50:12

51:48
[n] Isa 44:23;
Rev 18:20 [o] ver 11

declares the LORD.

[a] 41 Sheshach is a cryptogram for Babylon.

51:49
p Ps 137:8;
Jer 50:29

51:50
q ver 45 r Ps 137:6

51:51
s Ps 44:13-16; 79:4
t La 1:10

51:52
u ver 47

51:53
v Ge 11:4;
Isa 14:13-14
w Jer 49:16

51:54
x Jer 50:22

51:55
y Ps 18:4

51:56
z ver 48 a Ps 46:9
b ver 6; Ps 94:1-2;
Hab 2:8

51:57
c Ps 76:5; Jer 25:27
d Jer 46:18; 48:15

51:58
e ver 44 f ver 64
g Hab 2:13

51:59
h Jer 36:4 i Jer 52:1
j Jer 28:1

51:60
k Jer 30:2; 36:2

51:62
l Isa 13:20;
Jer 50:13,39

51:64
m ver 58
n Job 31:40

49 "Babylon must fall because of Israel's slain,
  just as the slain in all the earth
  have fallen because of Babylon. p
50 You who have escaped the sword,
  leave q and do not linger!
Remember r the LORD in a distant land,
  and think on Jerusalem."

51 "We are disgraced, s
  for we have been insulted
  and shame covers our faces,
because foreigners have entered
  the holy places of the LORD's house." t

52 "But days are coming," declares the LORD,
  "when I will punish her idols, u
and throughout her land
  the wounded will groan.
53 Even if Babylon reaches the sky v
  and fortifies her lofty stronghold,
  I will send destroyers w against her,"

  declares the LORD.

54 "The sound of a cry comes from Babylon,
  the sound of great destruction x
  from the land of the Babylonians. a
55 The LORD will destroy Babylon;
  he will silence her noisy din.
Waves y of enemies will rage like great waters;
  the roar of their voices will resound.
56 A destroyer z will come against Babylon;
  her warriors will be captured,
  and their bows will be broken. a
For the LORD is a God of retribution;
  he will repay b in full.
57 I will make her officials and wise men drunk,
  her governors, officers and warriors as well;
they will sleep c forever and not awake,"
  declares the King, d whose name is the LORD Almighty.

58 This is what the LORD Almighty says:

"Babylon's thick wall e will be leveled
  and her high gates set on fire;
the peoples f exhaust themselves for nothing,
  the nations' labor is only fuel for the flames." g

59 This is the message Jeremiah gave to the staff officer Seraiah son of Neriah, h the son of Mahseiah, when he went to Babylon with Zedekiah i king of Judah in the fourth j year of his reign. 60 Jeremiah had written on a scroll k about all the disasters that would come upon Babylon—all that had been recorded concerning Babylon. 61 He said to Seraiah, "When you get to Babylon, see that you read all these words aloud. 62 Then say, 'O LORD, you have said you will destroy this place, so that neither man nor animal will live in it; it will be desolate l forever.' 63 When you finish reading this scroll, tie a stone to it and throw it into the Euphrates. 64 Then say, 'So will Babylon sink to rise no more because of the disaster I will bring upon her. And her people m will fall.' "

The words of Jeremiah end n here.

a 54 Or *Chaldeans*

The Fall of Jerusalem

52 Zedekiah[o] was twenty-one years old when he became king, and he reigned in Jerusalem eleven years. His mother's name was Hamutal daughter of Jeremiah; she was from Libnah.[p] ²He did evil in the eyes of the LORD, just as Jehoiakim[q] had done. ³It was because of the LORD's anger that all this happened to Jerusalem and Judah,[r] and in the end he thrust them from his presence.

Now Zedekiah rebelled[s] against the king of Babylon.

⁴So in the ninth year of Zedekiah's reign, on the tenth[t] day of the tenth month, Nebuchadnezzar king of Babylon marched against Jerusalem[u] with his whole army. They camped outside the city and built siege works all around it.[v] ⁵The city was kept under siege until the eleventh year of King Zedekiah.

⁶By the ninth day of the fourth month the famine in the city had become so severe that there was no food for the people to eat.[w] ⁷Then the city wall was broken through, and the whole army fled. They left the city at night through the gate between the two walls near the king's garden, though the Babylonians[a] were surrounding the city. They fled toward the Arabah,[b] ⁸but the Babylonian[c] army pursued King Zedekiah and overtook him in the plains of Jericho. All his soldiers were separated from him and scattered, ⁹and he was captured.[x]

He was taken to the king of Babylon at Riblah[y] in the land of Hamath,[z] where he pronounced sentence on him. ¹⁰There at Riblah the king of Babylon slaughtered the sons[a] of Zedekiah before his eyes; he also killed all the officials of Judah. ¹¹Then he put out Zedekiah's eyes, bound him with bronze shackles and took him to Babylon, where he put him in prison till the day of his death.[b]

¹²On the tenth day of the fifth[c] month, in the nineteenth year of Nebuchadnezzar king of Babylon, Nebuzaradan[d] commander of the imperial guard, who served the king of Babylon, came to Jerusalem. ¹³He set fire[e] to the temple[f] of the LORD, the royal palace and all the houses of Jerusalem. Every important building he burned down. ¹⁴The whole Babylonian army under the commander of the imperial guard broke down all the walls[g] around Jerusalem. ¹⁵Nebuzaradan the commander of the guard carried into exile some of the poorest people and those who remained in the city, along with the rest of the craftsmen[d] and those who had gone over to the king of Babylon. ¹⁶But Nebuzaradan left behind[h] the rest of the poorest people of the land to work the vineyards and fields.

¹⁷The Babylonians broke up the bronze pillars,[i] the movable stands[j] and the bronze Sea[k] that were at the temple of the LORD and they carried all the bronze to Babylon.[l] ¹⁸They also took away the pots, shovels, wick trimmers, sprinkling bowls, dishes and all the bronze articles used in the temple service.[m] ¹⁹The commander of the imperial guard took away the basins, censers,[n] sprinkling bowls, pots, lampstands, dishes and bowls used for drink offerings—all that were made of pure gold or silver.

²⁰The bronze from the two pillars, the Sea and the twelve bronze bulls under it,

---

52:1 o 2Ki 24:17 p Jos 10:29; 2Ki 8:22
52:2 q Jer 36:30
52:3 r Isa 3:1 s Eze 17:12-16
52:4 t Zec 8:19 u 2Ki 25:1-7; Jer 39:1 v Eze 24:1-2
52:6 w Isa 3:1
52:9 x Jer 32:4 y Nu 34:11 z Nu 13:21
52:10 a Jer 22:30
52:11 b Eze 12:13
52:12 c Zec 7:5; 8:19 d Jer 39:9
52:13 e 2Ch 36:19; Ps 74:8; La 2:6 f Ps 79:1; Mic 3:12
52:14 g Ne 1:3
52:16 h Jer 40:6
52:17 i 1Ki 7:15 j 1Ki 7:27-37 k 1Ki 7:23 l Jer 27:19-22
52:18 m Ex 27:3; 1Ki 7:45
52:19 n 1Ki 7:50

---

a 7 Or *Chaldeans*; also in verse 17   b 7 Or *the Jordan Valley*   c 8 Or *Chaldean*; also in verse 14
d 15 Or *populace*

Jeremiah 52:1-30

Jeremiah 52, an appendix to the book, was written by someone other than Jeremiah—perhaps Baruch. (Note also that the Jeremiah mentioned in verse 1 wasn't the prophet Jeremiah.) The chapter closely parallels the conclusion of 2 Kings. Rather than one copying the other, it's likely that the two writers used the same sources.

The book of Jeremiah has already provided details of the fall of Jerusalem and its aftermath (cf. 39:1–10 with 52:4–16). In addition, 52:28–30 records three waves of exiles during Nebuchadnezzar's reign: (1) those taken in 597 B.C. (this number probably only included adult males, since the figures in 2 Kings 24 are significantly higher);

(2) those deported rather than killed when Jerusalem fell in 586 B.C.; and (3) those exiled in 581 B.C.—perhaps as punishment for Gedaliah's assassination (41:1–3).

Since retelling the past is typically done to help understand the present, we may ask why the account of Jerusalem's fall was rehearsed again. One reason is reflected in the maxim, "Those who don't remember the past are doomed to repeat it." We are to live and learn from others' mistakes (cf. 1 Cor. 10:11). Such a reading can be instructive on the personal or corporate level. It may point us toward introspection regarding our personal histories ("unfinished business"), as well as those of our nation and church.

52:20
o 1Ki 7:47
52:21
p 1Ki 7:15
52:22
q 1Ki 7:16

52:23
r 1Ki 7:20
52:24
s 2Ki 25:18
t Jer 21:1; 37:3

52:26
u ver 12

52:27
v Jer 20:4
52:28
w 2Ki 24:14-16;
2Ch 36:20

and the movable stands, which King Solomon had made for the temple of the LORD, was more than could be weighed. o 21 Each of the pillars was eighteen cubits high and twelve cubits in circumference a; each was four fingers thick, and hollow. p 22 The bronze capital q on top of the one pillar was five cubits b high and was decorated with a network and pomegranates of bronze all around. The other pillar, with its pomegranates, was similar. 23 There were ninety-six pomegranates on the sides; the total number of pomegranates r above the surrounding network was a hundred.

24 The commander of the guard took as prisoners Seraiah s the chief priest, Zephaniah t the priest next in rank and the three doorkeepers. 25 Of those still in the city, he took the officer in charge of the fighting men, and seven royal advisers. He also took the secretary who was chief officer in charge of conscripting the people of the land and sixty of his men who were found in the city. 26 Nebuzaradan u the commander took them all and brought them to the king of Babylon at Riblah. 27 There at Riblah, in the land of Hamath, the king had them executed.

So Judah went into captivity, away v from her land. 28 This is the number of the people Nebuchadnezzar carried into exile: w

in the seventh year, 3,023 Jews;

29 in Nebuchadnezzar's eighteenth year,
832 people from Jerusalem;

30 in his twenty-third year,
745 Jews taken into exile by Nebuzaradan the commander of the imperial guard.
There were 4,600 people in all.

Jehoiachin Released

31 In the thirty-seventh year of the exile of Jehoiachin king of Judah, in the year Evil-Merodach c became king of Babylon, he released Jehoiachin king of Judah and freed him from prison on the twenty-fifth day of the twelfth month. 32 He spoke kindly to him and gave him a seat of honor higher than those of the other kings who were with him in Babylon. 33 So Jehoiachin put aside his prison clothes and for the rest of his life ate regularly at the king's table. x 34 Day by day the king of Babylon gave Jehoiachin a regular allowance y as long as he lived, till the day of his death.

52:33
x 2Sa 9:7
52:34
y 2Sa 9:10

a 21 That is, about 27 feet (about 8.1 meters) high and 18 feet (about 5.4 meters) in circumference
b 22 That is, about 7 1/2 feet (about 2.3 meters)   c 31 Also called Amel-Marduk

Jeremiah 52:31–34

The account of Jehoiachin's release comes like the hand-sized cloud of Elijah's ministry during a time of drought (1 Kings 18:41–46). There was a possibility of change and deliverance to come. The shape of that change was indicated by the person released—the king from the line of David. Though Jehoiachin would die in Babylon, he remained the agent of continuity in God's covenant with David (cf. 2 Sam. 7:14–16) and in the history of the Messiah, which would reach its culmination in the birth of Jesus Christ.

The last chapter of Jeremiah stands between the promise that judgment isn't the end and the fulfill-

ment of the promises of a better future. We too live "between the times," in the "already" of Christ's first coming and the "not yet" preceding his second. In the short term we are vulnerable to failure and weakness, but God's promised deliverance is sure—as certain and indestructible as Christ's resurrection from the dead.

Jehoiachin's greater son, Jesus Christ, arrived in the fullness of time only to die at the hands of another imperial power. The story of which the book of Jeremiah is a part is still unfolding because Christ is alive, inviting the current generation of God's people to discipleship and faithful living.

INTRODUCTION TO
Lamentations

AUTHOR

This book has traditionally been attributed to the prophet Jeremiah from as early as the third
century B.C., but its authorship is uncertain. Some scholars believe it was compiled from various sources rather than written by a single author.

DATE WRITTEN

Lamentations was written after the fall of Jerusalem to the Babylonians (586 B.C.) but before
the temple was rebuilt (c. 516 B.C.).

ORIGINAL READERS

Lamentations was written to express the Jewish people's pain, grief, and horror at the destruction of Jerusalem and the temple.

TIMELINE

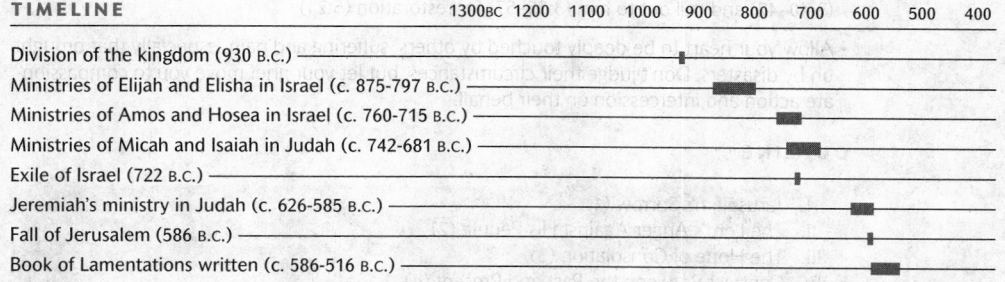

	1300BC	1200	1100	1000	900	800	700	600	500	400

Division of the kingdom (930 B.C.)

Ministries of Elijah and Elisha in Israel (c. 875-797 B.C.)

Ministries of Amos and Hosea in Israel (c. 760-715 B.C.)

Ministries of Micah and Isaiah in Judah (c. 742-681 B.C.)

Exile of Israel (722 B.C.)

Jeremiah's ministry in Judah (c. 626-585 B.C.)

Fall of Jerusalem (586 B.C.)

Book of Lamentations written (c. 586-516 B.C.)

THEMES

Lamentations describes the overwhelming grief, anger, fear, loneliness, and hopelessness that
accompanied the destruction of Jerusalem and the temple. It contains the following themes:

1. *Judgment.* There are consequences for sin. Lamentations demonstrates that God often uses
human agents to execute his judgment (1:14–15; 2:1–8,17,22; 4:11).

2. *Appropriate response to judgment.* The fitting response to judgment is repentance (3:40–42)
and a cry for forgiveness and restoration (5:21–22). God doesn't abandon those who turn to
him for help. The Israelites had sinned (1:8,14,18; 2:14; 4:13) but appealed to God for help, expecting him to forgive and restore.

3. *God's character.* God is just, but he also is the God of hope (3:21,24–25), love (3:22), compassion (3:22), faithfulness (3:23), and salvation (3:26). Lamentations expresses the assurance
that God doesn't abandon those who turn to him for help (3:22–33).

FAITH IN ACTION

The pages of Lamentations contain life lessons and role models of faith—people who challenge believers to put their faith in action.

Role Models

- THE PEOPLE OF JERUSALEM (2:18) cried out to God for mercy. Their sin had brought judgment, but in their sorrow they turned to him for forgiveness. Do you respond in this way, or are you more likely to run from him in an attempt to hide your sin?

- THOSE WHO HOPE IN THE LORD (3:22–25) have strength to wait patiently for God to deliver them. They recall his past care and trust in his faithfulness and mercy. Are you despairing today? Find hope in God and wait patiently for his deliverance.

- THE WRITER (2:11–12; 3:48–51; 4:9–10) was moved to tears and grief over the devastation of Judah's people, especially of women and children as a result of the city's destruction. He demonstrated a depth of understanding for those caught by disaster. Regardless of the cause, does people's suffering stir your grief and compassion, moving you to action? Are you concerned about the plight of women and children who have experienced the devastations of war or some other disaster?

Challenges

- Search your heart for signs of rebellion. Repent before it's too late; rebellion brings only distress, torment, and trouble (1:18–20).

- Pour out your heart (2:19) in confession and repentance to God. Depend on his love and compassion (3:22) to save you, for he is faithful (3:23).

- Think about the reality of God's compassions being new each morning (3:23). How does this truth bring you comfort and move your heart to express gratitude to him?

- When you find yourself in a position of having to endure the consequences of your sin, remember to receive God's discipline with humility (3:28–29), trusting in his faithful, unfailing love (3:31–32). Don't blame God for your affliction (3:33) but learn from his correction (3:40–42) and call out to him (3:55–57) for restoration (5:21).

- Allow your heart to be deeply touched by others' suffering and pain, especially that brought on by disasters. Don't judge their circumstances, but let your grief move you to compassionate action and intercession on their behalf.

OUTLINE

I. Jerusalem's Sorrow (1)
II. The Lord's Anger Against His People (2)
III. The Hope of Consolation (3)
IV. Contrast Between the Past and Present (4)
V. Judah's Appeal for God's Forgiveness (5)

1 ᵃ

How deserted lies the city,
 once so full of people!
How like a widow ᵃ is she,
 who once was great ᵇ among the nations!
She who was queen among the provinces
 has now become a slave. ᶜ

² Bitterly she weeps ᵈ at night,
 tears are upon her cheeks.
Among all her lovers ᵉ
 there is none to comfort her.
All her friends have betrayed ᶠ her;
 they have become her enemies. ᵍ

³ After affliction and harsh labor,
 Judah has gone into exile. ʰ
She dwells among the nations;
 she finds no resting place. ⁱ
All who pursue her have overtaken her
 in the midst of her distress.

⁴ The roads to Zion mourn,
 for no one comes to her appointed feasts.
All her gateways are desolate, ʲ
 her priests groan,
her maidens grieve,
 and she is in bitter anguish. ᵏ

⁵ Her foes have become her masters;
 her enemies are at ease.
The LORD has brought her grief ˡ
 because of her many sins.
Her children have gone into exile, ᵐ
 captive before the foe.

⁶ All the splendor has departed
 from the Daughter of Zion. ⁿ
Her princes are like deer
 that find no pasture;
in weakness they have fled
 before the pursuer.

⁷ In the days of her affliction and wandering

ᵃ This chapter is an acrostic poem, the verses of which begin with the successive letters of the Hebrew alphabet.

1:1
ᵃ Isa 47:8
ᵇ 1Ki 4:21
ᶜ Isa 3:26; Jer 40:9

1:2
ᵈ Ps 6:6 ᵉ Jer 3:1
ᶠ Jer 4:30; Mic 7:5
ᵍ ver 16

1:3
ʰ Jer 13:19
ⁱ Dt 28:65

1:4
ʲ Jer 9:11
ᵏ Joel 1:8-13

1:5
ˡ Jer 30:15
ᵐ Jer 39:9;
52:28-30

1:6
ⁿ Jer 13:18

The study notes for this book are separated by chapters, since the book contains no sectional headings.

Lamentations 1:1–22

Chapter 1 is an acrostic poem, with each verse beginning with a word whose initial letter follows the 22-letter sequence of the Hebrew alphabet. The poet began, and his voice was followed by that of Jerusalem—pictured as a wounded, desolate female. The back-and-forth interplay of the two voices (with the woman's in quotes) reinforced Jerusalem's tragic dilemma.

How this text makes its point clues us to its meaning. (1) Jerusalem was a part representing a whole. As the royal "daughter," her failures were challenges to family identity and responsibility. (2) The city's mourning sounded like a funeral lament. Daughter Zion had lost her status as a virgin princess and even as a family member. At certain levels of relationship, she had died. (3) Zion brought her lament directly to God. Her humiliation implied his loss, too. Only God could fully comprehend and resolve her desperate need.

Failure is a hard pill to swallow, especially if it had been within our power to change course before the full consequences came crashing down. But Christ bore Jerusalem's, the world's, and our own personal failures on the cross. The poetry of Lamentations is one of the Bible's most articulate expressions of confession and sorrow over sinful failure. Most importantly, its words are directed to the only One who can respond with healing grace and mercy for the person or nation who repents.

Jerusalem remembers all the treasures
    that were hers in days of old.
When her people fell into enemy hands,
    there was no one to help her. *o*
Her enemies looked at her
    and laughed at her destruction.

⁸ Jerusalem has sinned *p* greatly
    and so has become unclean.
All who honored her despise her,
    for they have seen her nakedness; *q*
she herself groans *r*
    and turns away.

⁹ Her filthiness clung to her skirts;
    she did not consider her future. *s*
Her fall *t* was astounding;
    there was none to comfort *u* her.
"Look, O LORD, on my affliction, *v*
    for the enemy has triumphed."

¹⁰ The enemy laid hands
    on all her treasures; *w*
she saw pagan nations
    enter her sanctuary *x*—
those you had forbidden *y*
    to enter your assembly.

¹¹ All her people groan *z*
    as they search for bread; *a*
they barter their treasures for food
    to keep themselves alive.
"Look, O LORD, and consider,
    for I am despised."

¹² "Is it nothing to you, all you who pass by? *b*
    Look around and see.
Is any suffering like my suffering *c*
    that was inflicted on me,
that the LORD brought on me
    in the day of his fierce anger? *d*

¹³ "From on high he sent fire,
    sent it down into my bones. *e*
He spread a net for my feet
    and turned me back.
He made me desolate, *f*
    faint *g* all the day long.

¹⁴ "My sins have been bound into a yoke *a; h*
    by his hands they were woven together.
They have come upon my neck
    and the Lord has sapped my strength.
He has handed me over *i*
    to those I cannot withstand.

¹⁵ "The Lord has rejected
    all the warriors in my midst; *j*
he has summoned an army *k* against me
    to *b* crush my young men. *l*

1:7
o Jer 37:7; La 4:17

1:8
p ver 20;
Isa 59:2-13
q Jer 13:22,26
r ver 21,22

1:9
s Dt 32:28-29;
Isa 47:7; Eze 24:13
t Jer 13:18
u Ecc 4:1; Jer 16:7
v Ps 25:18

1:10
w Isa 64:11
x Ps 74:7-8;
Jer 51:51 *y* Dt 23:3

1:11
z Ps 38:8 *a* Jer 52:6

1:12
b Jer 18:16 *c* ver 18
d Isa 13:13;
Jer 30:24

1:13
e Job 30:30
f Jer 44:6
g Hab 3:16

1:14
h Dt 28:48; Isa 47:6
i Jer 32:5

1:15
j Jer 37:10
k Isa 41:2
l Isa 28:18;
Jer 18:21

---

a 14 Most Hebrew manuscripts; Septuagint *He kept watch over my sins*   *b* 15 Or *has set a time for me / when he will*

In his winepress the Lord has trampled
the Virgin Daughter of Judah.

16 "This is why I weep
and my eyes overflow with tears. *m*
No one is near to comfort *n* me,
no one to restore my spirit.
My children are destitute
because the enemy has prevailed." *o*

17 Zion stretches out her hands, *p*
but there is no one to comfort her.
The LORD has decreed for Jacob
that his neighbors become his foes;
Jerusalem has become
an unclean thing among them.

18 "The LORD is righteous,
yet I rebelled *q* against his command.
Listen, all you peoples;
look upon my suffering. *r*
My young men and maidens
have gone into exile. *s*

19 "I called to my allies
but they betrayed me.
My priests and my elders
perished *t* in the city
while they searched for food
to keep themselves alive.

20 "See, O LORD, how distressed *u* I am!
I am in torment *v* within,
and in my heart I am disturbed,
for I have been most rebellious.
Outside, the sword bereaves;
inside, there is only death. *w*

21 "People have heard my groaning, *x*
but there is no one to comfort me. *y*
All my enemies have heard of my distress;
they rejoice *z* at what you have done.
May you bring the day *a* you have announced
so they may become like me.

22 "Let all their wickedness come before you;
deal with them
as you have dealt with me
because of all my sins. *b*
My groans are many
and my heart is faint."

2 *a* How the Lord has covered the Daughter of Zion
with the cloud of his anger *b*! *c*
He has hurled down the splendor of Israel

---

a This chapter is an acrostic poem, the verses of which begin with the successive letters of the Hebrew
alphabet.   *b* 1 Or *How the Lord in his anger / has treated the Daughter of Zion with contempt*

1:16
m La 2:11,18;
3:48-49 *n* Ps 69:20;
Ecc 4:1 *o* ver 2;
Jer 13:17; 14:17

1:17
p Jer 4:31

1:18
q 1Sa 12:14 *r* ver 12
s Dt 28:32,41

1:19
t Jer 14:15; La 2:20

1:20
u Jer 4:19 *v* La 2:11
w Dt 32:25;
Eze 7:15

1:21
x ver 8 *y* ver 4
z La 2:15
a Isa 47:11;
Jer 30:16

1:22
b Ne 4:5

2:1
c La 3:44

Lamentations 2:1–22

Chapter 2 also uses an acrostic pattern with multiple voices. God used an enemy to judge his people and his city. In pointed, anguished language, the poet asked God whether he had ever before treated anyone like this. It's as though God had become the enemy by

1299

2:1
d Ps 99:5; 132:7

2:2
e La 3:43 f Ps 21:9
g Ps 89:39-40;
Mic 5:11
h Isa 25:12

2:3
i Ps 75:5,10
j Ps 74:11
k Isa 42:25;
Jer 21:4-5,14

2:4
l Job 16:13;
La 3:12-13
m Eze 24:16,25
n Isa 42:25;
Jer 7:20

2:5
o Jer 30:14 p ver 2
q Jer 9:17-20

2:6
r Jer 52:13 s La 1:4;
Zep 3:18 t La 4:16

2:7
u Ps 74:7-8;
Isa 64:11;
Jer 33:4-5

from heaven to earth;
he has not remembered his footstool[d]
in the day of his anger.

2 Without pity[e] the Lord has swallowed[f] up
all the dwellings of Jacob;
in his wrath he has torn down
the strongholds[g] of the Daughter of Judah.
He has brought her kingdom and its princes
down to the ground[h] in dishonor.

3 In fierce anger he has cut off
every horn[a][i] of Israel.
He has withdrawn his right hand[j]
at the approach of the enemy.
He has burned in Jacob like a flaming fire
that consumes everything around it.[k]

4 Like an enemy he has strung his bow;[l]
his right hand is ready.
Like a foe he has slain
all who were pleasing to the eye;[m]
he has poured out his wrath like fire[n]
on the tent of the Daughter of Zion.

5 The Lord is like an enemy;[o]
he has swallowed up Israel.
He has swallowed up all her palaces
and destroyed her strongholds.[p]
He has multiplied mourning and lamentation
for the Daughter of Judah.[q]

6 He has laid waste his dwelling like a garden;
he has destroyed his place of meeting.[r]
The LORD has made Zion forget
her appointed feasts and her Sabbaths;[s]
in his fierce anger he has spurned
both king and priest.[t]

7 The Lord has rejected his altar
and abandoned his sanctuary.
He has handed over to the enemy
the walls of her palaces;[u]
they have raised a shout in the house of the LORD
as on the day of an appointed feast.

8 The LORD determined to tear down
the wall around the Daughter of Zion.

a 3 Or / all the strength; or every king; horn here symbolizes strength.

using his people's enemy against them. The effect of the chapter is to give a personal portrait of those judged and bereaved and to question God about the rightness of the devastation.

The language of judgment and destruction in Lamentations is a tragic reversal of that of the Zion psalms, like Psalms 46 and 48. They celebrate the greatness of Jerusalem as the secure home of God's faithful people. The function of this opposite image in Lamentations was to underscore the necessity of responsibility. His people may never assume that God will protect his

own at any cost, no matter what they do.

The poet's frank language assures us that God is open to our real feelings and honest reactions to tragedy. There is often no "answer" in the face of overwhelming sorrow, and our prayers can reflect that. Yet in all circumstances God works for our good, with a goal of making us more and more like his Son (Rom. 8:28–29). Not every experience is good in and of itself, but every event in our lives does work toward the good purpose of our Christian maturity. What trials have enhanced your spiritual growth?

He stretched out a measuring line[v]
 and did not withhold his hand from destroying.
He made ramparts and walls lament;
 together they wasted away.[w]

9 Her gates[x] have sunk into the ground;
 their bars he has broken and destroyed.
Her king and her princes are exiled[y] among the nations,
 the law[z] is no more,
and her prophets no longer find
 visions[a] from the LORD.

10 The elders of the Daughter of Zion
 sit on the ground in silence;
they have sprinkled dust on their heads[b]
 and put on sackcloth.[c]
The young women of Jerusalem
 have bowed their heads to the ground.[d]

11 My eyes fail from weeping,[e]
 I am in torment within,[f]
my heart is poured out[g] on the ground
 because my people are destroyed,
because children and infants faint[h]
 in the streets of the city.

12 They say to their mothers,
 "Where is bread and wine?"
as they faint like wounded men
 in the streets of the city,
as their lives ebb away
 in their mothers' arms.[i]

13 What can I say for you?
 With what can I compare you,
 O Daughter of Jerusalem?
To what can I liken you,
 that I may comfort you,
 O Virgin Daughter of Zion?[j]
Your wound is as deep as the sea.[k]
 Who can heal you?

14 The visions of your prophets
 were false and worthless;
they did not expose your sin
 to ward off your captivity.[l]
The oracles they gave you
 were false and misleading.[m]

15 All who pass your way
 clap their hands at you;[n]
they scoff[o] and shake their heads
 at the Daughter of Jerusalem:
"Is this the city that was called
 the perfection of beauty,[p]
 the joy of the whole earth?"[q]

16 All your enemies open their mouths
 wide against you;[r]
they scoff and gnash their teeth[s]
 and say, "We have swallowed her up.[t]

2:8
v 2Ki 21:13;
Isa 34:11 w Isa 3:26

2:9
x Ne 1:3
y Dt 28:36;
2Ki 24:15
z 2Ch 15:3
a Jer 14:14

2:10
b Job 2:12
c Isa 15:3
d Job 2:13; Isa 3:26

2:11
e La 1:16; 3:48-51
f La 1:20 g ver 19;
Ps 22:14 h La 4:4

12:12
i La 4:4

2:13
j Isa 37:22
k Jer 14:17; La 1:12

2:14
l Isa 58:1 m Jer 2:8;
23:25-32,33-40;
29:9; Eze 13:3;
22:28

2:15
n Eze 25:6
o Jer 19:8 p Ps 50:2
q Ps 48:2

2:16
r Ps 56:2; La 3:46
s Job 16:9
t Ps 35:25

This is the day we have waited for;
  we have lived to see it."

17 The LORD has done what he planned;
  he has fulfilled his word,
  which he decreed long ago. *u*
He has overthrown you without pity, *v*
  he has let the enemy gloat over you,
  he has exalted the horn*a* of your foes. *w*

2:17
u Dt 28:15-45
v ver 2; Eze 5:11
w Ps 89:42

18 The hearts of the people
  cry out to the Lord. *x*
O wall of the Daughter of Zion,
  let your tears*y* flow like a river
  day and night; *z*
give yourself no relief,
  your eyes no rest. *a*

2:18
x Ps 119:145
y La 1:16 *z* Jer 9:1
a La 3:49

19 Arise, cry out in the night,
  as the watches of the night begin;
pour out your heart*b* like water
  in the presence of the Lord. *c*
Lift up your hands to him
  for the lives of your children,
who faint*d* from hunger
  at the head of every street.

2:19
b 1Sa 1:15; Ps 62:8
c Isa 26:9
d Isa 51:20

20 "Look, O LORD, and consider:
  Whom have you ever treated like this?
Should women eat their offspring, *e*
  the children they have cared for? *f*
Should priest and prophet be killed*g*
  in the sanctuary of the Lord?

2:20
e Dt 28:53; Jer 19:9
f La 4:10
g Ps 78:64;
Jer 14:15

21 "Young and old lie together
  in the dust of the streets;
my young men and maidens
  have fallen by the sword. *h*
You have slain them in the day of your anger;
  you have slaughtered them without pity. *i*

2:21
h 2Ch 36:17;
Ps 78:62-63;
Jer 6:11 *i* Jer 13:14;
La 3:43; Zec 11:6

22 "As you summon to a feast day,
  so you summoned against me terrors*j* on every side.

2:22
j Ps 31:13; Jer 6:25

a 17 Horn here symbolizes strength.

2:19

Child Starvation

Is there anything more lamentable than the plight of starving children? We can do many things to keep our world's children from going without food. Some indicators that affect nutrition, positively or negatively:

 Household Factors

 Community

 National

Household Factors	Community	National
Amount of and nutritional mix of food available, breastfeeding, access to health care, livable family income	Agricultural training, well-functioning and accessible food markets, access to clean water, available health care, nutritional education, support for microenterprise programs	Women's health care, girls' education, immunizations, wages/employment rates, violence and conflict, poverty levels, justice in court/legal systems

In what way(s) might you become involved in alleviating one or more problems related to any of these factors?

Source: World Bank, *World Development Indicators 2002* (2002:47)

> In the day of the LORD's anger
>   no one escaped or survived;
> those I cared for and reared, [k]
>   my enemy has destroyed."

2:22
k Hos 9:13

3 [a]

> I am the man who has seen affliction
>   by the rod of his wrath. [l]

3:1
l Job 19:21; Ps 88:7

> 2 He has driven me away and made me walk
>   in darkness [m] rather than light;
> 3 indeed, he has turned his hand against me [n]
>   again and again, all day long.

3:2
m Jer 4:23
3:3
n Isa 5:25

> 4 He has made my skin and my flesh grow old
>   and has broken my bones. [o]
> 5 He has besieged me and surrounded me
>   with bitterness [p] and hardship. [q]
> 6 He has made me dwell in darkness
>   like those long dead. [r]

3:4
o Ps 51:8; Isa 38:13; Jer 50:17
3:5
p ver 19 q Jer 23:15
3:6
r Ps 88:5-6

> 7 He has walled me in so I cannot escape; [s]
>   he has weighed me down with chains. [t]
> 8 Even when I call out or cry for help,
>   he shuts out my prayer. [u]
> 9 He has barred my way with blocks of stone;
>   he has made my paths crooked. [v]

3:7
s Job 3:23
t Jer 40:4
3:8
u Job 30:20; Ps 22:2
3:9
v Isa 63:17; Hos 2:6

> 10 Like a bear lying in wait,
>   like a lion in hiding,
> 11 he dragged me from the path and mangled [w] me
>   and left me without help.
> 12 He drew his bow [x]
>   and made me the target [y] for his arrows. [z]

3:11
w Hos 6:1
3:12
x La 2:4 y Job 7:20
z Ps 7:12-13; 38:2

> 13 He pierced my heart
>   with arrows from his quiver. [a]
> 14 I became the laughingstock [b] of all my people;
>   they mock me in song [c] all day long.
> 15 He has filled me with bitter herbs
>   and sated me with gall. [d]

3:13
a Job 6:4
3:14
b Jer 20:7
c Job 30:9
3:15
d Jer 9:15

> 16 He has broken my teeth with gravel; [e]
>   he has trampled me in the dust.
> 17 I have been deprived of peace;
>   I have forgotten what prosperity is.
> 18 So I say, "My splendor is gone
>   and all that I had hoped from the LORD." [f]

3:16
e Pr 20:17
3:18
f Job 17:15

> 19 I remember my affliction and my wandering,
>   the bitterness and the gall.
> 20 I well remember them,
>   and my soul is downcast [g] within me. [h]

3:20
g Ps 42:5
h Ps 42:11

[a] This chapter is an acrostic poem; the verses of each stanza begin with the successive letters of the Hebrew alphabet, and the verses within each stanza begin with the same letter.

Lamentations 3:1–66

Chapter 3 expands on the acrostic pattern. This chapter has 66 verses, compiled into 22 stanzas. Each stanza has three verses, and the initial word of each verse in a stanza begins with the same letter of the Hebrew alphabet.

While Jerusalem's tragic fate is still in the background, front and center in this chapter is the anguish of an individual. Some scholars have suggested the prophet Jeremiah as the author, while others feel that Lamentations and Jeremiah reflect different tones and styles (see Introduction). In either case, the poet's "I" extends beyond himself to represent his readers and those who pray the Lamentations. This author gives a voice to all who suffer.

3:22
i Ps 78:38; Mal 3:6
3:23
j Zep 3:5
3:24
k Ps 16:5

3:25
l Isa 25:9; 30:18

3:26
m Ps 37:7; 40:1

3:28
n Jer 15:17

3:29
o Jer 31:17
3:30
p Job 16:10;
Isa 50:6

3:31
q Ps 94:14; Isa 54:7

3:32
r Ps 78:38;
Hos 11:8
3:33
s Eze 33:11

3:36
t Jer 22:3; Hab 1:13

3:37
u Ps 33:9-11

3:38
v Job 2:10; Isa 45:7;
Jer 32:42
3:39
w Jer 30:15;
Mic 7:9
3:40
x 2Co 13:5
y Ps 119:59;
139:23-24

3:41
z Ps 25:1; 28:2
3:42
a Da 9:5
b Jer 5:7-9

21 Yet this I call to mind
 and therefore I have hope:

22 Because of the LORD's great love we are not consumed,
 for his compassions never fail. *i*

23 They are new every morning;
 great is your faithfulness. *j*

24 I say to myself, "The LORD is my portion; *k*
 therefore I will wait for him."

25 The LORD is good to those whose hope is in him,
 to the one who seeks him; *l*

26 it is good to wait quietly
 for the salvation of the LORD. *m*

27 It is good for a man to bear the yoke
 while he is young.

28 Let him sit alone in silence, *n*
 for the LORD has laid it on him.

29 Let him bury his face in the dust—
 there may yet be hope. *o*

30 Let him offer his cheek to one who would strike him, *p*
 and let him be filled with disgrace.

31 For men are not cast off
 by the Lord forever. *q*

32 Though he brings grief, he will show compassion,
 so great is his unfailing love. *r*

33 For he does not willingly bring affliction
 or grief to the children of men. *s*

34 To crush underfoot
 all prisoners in the land,

35 to deny a man his rights
 before the Most High,

36 to deprive a man of justice—
 would not the Lord see such things? *t*

37 Who can speak and have it happen
 if the Lord has not decreed it? *u*

38 Is it not from the mouth of the Most High
 that both calamities and good things come? *v*

39 Why should any living man complain
 when punished for his sins? *w*

40 Let us examine our ways and test them, *x*
 and let us return to the LORD. *y*

41 Let us lift up our hearts and our hands
 to God in heaven, *z* and say:

42 "We have sinned and rebelled *a*
 and you have not forgiven. *b*

The text reminds us of the individual laments in the book of Psalms and of the complaints of Job. These parallels help us apply the passage to a modern setting. Both Job and Lamentations are oriented toward two issues: God's character, and the human response to God *in the context of suffering*. Three principles emerge: (1) God isn't absent from our affliction and tragedy. (2) He loves us in spite of our sinfulness (see the well-known stanza of vv. 22–24). (3) An open door invites us to return to him.

The poet learned a measure of obedience from his sufferings (cf. Heb. 5:8). Christian spirituality has a goal: conformity to Christ's image. Suffering can be a means to that end, but not in a masochistic or pain-denying way. Just as the poet's experience was meant to be shared, Paul reminded us that we are to use the comfort we receive from God to comfort others going through similar, difficult experiences (cf. 2 Cor. 1:3–11). When have you been able to empathize with and minister to another's pain based on the memory of your own?

43 "You have covered yourself with anger and pursued us;
   you have slain without pity. c
44 You have covered yourself with a cloud d
   so that no prayer e can get through.
45 You have made us scum f and refuse
   among the nations.

46 "All our enemies have opened their mouths
   wide against us. g
47 We have suffered terror and pitfalls, h
   ruin and destruction. i "
48 Streams of tears flow from my eyes j
   because my people are destroyed. k

49 My eyes will flow unceasingly,
   without relief, l
50 until the LORD looks down
   from heaven and sees. m
51 What I see brings grief to my soul
   because of all the women of my city.

52 Those who were my enemies without cause
   hunted me like a bird. n
53 They tried to end my life in a pit o
   and threw stones at me;
54 the waters closed over my head, p
   and I thought I was about to be cut off.

55 I called on your name, O LORD,
   from the depths of the pit. q
56 You heard my plea: r "Do not close your ears
   to my cry for relief."

3:43 c La 2:2,17,21
3:44 d Ps 97:2 e ver 8
3:45 f 1Co 4:13
3:46 g La 2:16
3:47 h Jer 48:43 i Isa 24:17-18; 51:19
3:48 j La 1:16 k La 2:11
3:49 l Jer 14:17
3:50 m Isa 63:15
3:52 n Ps 35:7
3:53 o Jer 37:16
3:54 p Ps 69:2; Jnh 2:3-5
3:55 q Ps 130:1; Jnh 2:2
3:56 r Ps 55:1

Snapshots

 3:31–36

Another Dangerous Day

Nearly every day the Palestinian staff of a Christian humanitarian office in Jerusalem is confronted with violence. One employee reported that Bethlehem was under siege. This didn't stop him and two colleagues from making their way home there.

On the previous Friday afternoon the three had used the dangerous Jewish settler road, built to link settlements to each other and to Israel. They had been held at a checkpoint with some Jewish settlers for 45 minutes.

Today the same staffer's wife was waiting at his parents' home, so he went there. They heard shooting at a nearby refugee camp, and minutes later explosions and gun shots reverberated around them. Fearful of trauma to their infant, the couple left. Clutching their baby, they picked their way home, careful to avoid bullets and explosions.

> Nearly every day the Palestinian staff of a Christian humanitarian office in Jerusalem is confronted with violence.

There was no electricity in their neighborhood, but they heard gunfire across the valley. That night, ambulances were hauling injured Palestinians from the refugee camp there. The Israeli army had plowed into the camp, demolishing the thin walls of residences on their approach. The troops eventually retreated. Another dangerous day had passed in the life of one employee, his family, and many others in the Holy Land.

3:57
s Isa 41:10
3:58
t Jer 51:36
u Ps 34:22;
Jer 50:34
3:59
v Jer 18:19-20

3:60
w Jer 11:20; 18:18

3:62
x Eze 36:3

3:64
y Ps 28:4
3:65
z Isa 6:10

4:1
a Eze 7:19

4:3
b Job 39:16

4:4
c Ps 22:15
d La 2:11,12

4:5
e Jer 6:2 f Am 6:3-7

4:6
g Ge 19:25

57 You came near when I called you,
   and you said, "Do not fear." [s]

58 O Lord, you took up my case; [t]
   you redeemed my life. [u]

59 You have seen, O Lᴏʀᴅ, the wrong done to me. [v]
   Uphold my cause!

60 You have seen the depth of their vengeance,
   all their plots against me. [w]

61 O Lᴏʀᴅ, you have heard their insults,
   all their plots against me—

62 what my enemies whisper and mutter
   against me all day long. [x]

63 Look at them! Sitting or standing,
   they mock me in their songs.

64 Pay them back what they deserve, O Lᴏʀᴅ,
   for what their hands have done. [y]

65 Put a veil over their hearts, [z]
   and may your curse be on them!

66 Pursue them in anger and destroy them
   from under the heavens of the Lᴏʀᴅ.

4 [a] How the gold has lost its luster,
   the fine gold become dull!
The sacred gems are scattered
   at the head of every street. [a]

2 How the precious sons of Zion,
   once worth their weight in gold,
are now considered as pots of clay,
   the work of a potter's hands!

3 Even jackals offer their breasts
   to nurse their young,
but my people have become heartless
   like ostriches in the desert. [b]

4 Because of thirst the infant's tongue
   sticks to the roof of its mouth; [c]
the children beg for bread,
   but no one gives it to them. [d]

5 Those who once ate delicacies
   are destitute in the streets.
Those nurtured in purple [e]
   now lie on ash heaps. [f]

6 The punishment of my people
   is greater than that of Sodom, [g]
which was overthrown in a moment
   without a hand turned to help her.

[a] This chapter is an acrostic poem, the verses of which begin with the successive letters of the Hebrew alphabet.

Lamentations 4:1–22

📖 **Chapter 4**, like chapters 1 and 2, is a 22-verse *acrostic. It presents Jerusalem's fall from a different per-spective. The poet contrasted the former splendor of the city and its inhabitants with the pitiful conditions of his own day.*

One shocking effect of the Babylonian siege was its horrendous effect on families. With nothing to eat, chil-dren were forced to beg. Some mothers were even com-pelled to cook their own children. The emotional impact of this cannibalism can't be overestimated. The poet un-derscored the pain and despair of his generation by not-ing how drawn-out and painful it is to starve, as opposed to dying by the sword.

7 Their princes were brighter than snow
    and whiter than milk,
  their bodies more ruddy than rubies,
    their appearance like sapphires. [a]

8 But now they are blacker[h] than soot;
    they are not recognized in the streets.
  Their skin has shriveled on their bones;[i]
    it has become as dry as a stick.

9 Those killed by the sword are better off
    than those who die of famine;
  racked with hunger, they waste away
    for lack of food from the field.[j]

10 With their own hands compassionate women
    have cooked their own children,[k]
  who became their food
    when my people were destroyed.

11 The LORD has given full vent to his wrath;
    he has poured out his fierce anger.
  He kindled a fire[l] in Zion
    that consumed her foundations.[m]

12 The kings of the earth did not believe,
    nor did any of the world's people,
  that enemies and foes could enter
    the gates of Jerusalem.[n]

13 But it happened because of the sins of her prophets
    and the iniquities of her priests,[o]
  who shed within her
    the blood of the righteous.

14 Now they grope through the streets
    like men who are blind.[p]
  They are so defiled with blood[q]
    that no one dares to touch their garments.

15 "Go away! You are unclean!" men cry to them.
    "Away! Away! Don't touch us!"
  When they flee and wander about,
    people among the nations say,
    "They can stay here no longer."[r]

16 The LORD himself has scattered them;
    he no longer watches over them.[s]
  The priests are shown no honor,
    the elders[t] no favor.

17 Moreover, our eyes failed,
    looking in vain[u] for help;[v]
  from our towers we watched
    for a nation[w] that could not save us.

a 7 Or lapis lazuli

4:8
h Job 30:28
i Ps 102:3-5

4:9
j Jer 15:2; 16:4

4:10
k Lev 26:29;
Dt 28:53-57;
Jer 19:9; La 2:20;
Eze 5:10

4:11
l Jer 17:27
m Dt 32:22;
Jer 7:20; Eze 22:31

4:12
n 1Ki 9:9; Jer 21:13

4:13
o Jer 5:31; 6:13;
Eze 22:28; Mic 3:11

4:14
p Isa 59:10
q Jer 2:34; 19:4

4:15
r Lev 13:46

4:16
s Isa 9:14-16
t La 5:12

4:17
u Isa 20:5;
Eze 29:16 v La 1:7
w Jer 37:7

We would like to think that situations like this no longer exist. Yet the choices countless people are still forced to make daily to avoid hunger are vile. Further, the young still bear the brunt of hunger as they did in this ancient time. Children today bear the consequences of malnutrition—early death or lasting sickness—in their bodies. Most chronically hungry children never reach their full intellectual potential, let alone their spiritual potential as people created by God to know and love him forever. Yet individuals can and do make a difference by their involvement. How is the Spirit leading you to respond?

18 Men stalked us at every step,
   so we could not walk in our streets.
Our end was near, our days were numbered,
   for our end had come. x

19 Our pursuers were swifter
   than eagles y in the sky;
they chased us z over the mountains
   and lay in wait for us in the desert.

20 The LORD's anointed, a our very life breath,
   was caught in their traps. b
We thought that under his shadow
   we would live among the nations.

21 Rejoice and be glad, O Daughter of Edom,
   you who live in the land of Uz.
But to you also the cup c will be passed;
   you will be drunk and stripped naked. d

22 O Daughter of Zion, your punishment will end; e
   he will not prolong your exile.
But, O Daughter of Edom, he will punish your sin
   and expose your wickedness. f

5 Remember, O LORD, what has happened to us;
   look, and see our disgrace. g
2 Our inheritance h has been turned over to aliens,
   our homes i to foreigners.
3 We have become orphans and fatherless,
   our mothers like widows. j
4 We must buy the water we drink;
   our wood can be had only at a price. k
5 Those who pursue us are at our heels;
   we are weary l and find no rest.
6 We submitted to Egypt and Assyria m
   to get enough bread.
7 Our fathers sinned and are no more,
   and we bear their punishment. n
8 Slaves o rule over us,
   and there is none to free us from their hands. p
9 We get our bread at the risk of our lives
   because of the sword in the desert.
10 Our skin is hot as an oven,
   feverish from hunger. q

Lamentations 5:1–22

Chapter 5 is a mournful corporate address to God, seeking his recognition of his people's suffering and reminding him of its continuing effects on them. The text isn't arranged as an acrostic, but there are 22 verses, corresponding to the number of letters in the Hebrew alphabet.

Verse 1 calls on God to remember what had happened to his people, and verse 20 comes back to the issue by asking, "Why do you always forget us?" In between, only verse 19 doesn't describe their circumstances. There is little new content here but continued heartrending language about Jerusalem's fall and its effects on Judah.

The abiding value of chapter 5, which is essentially a concluding prayer, may be found when a believing community finds itself feeling weary and outcast. The language of Biblical lamentation can provide needed resources to verbalize pain and the spiritual discernment to push beyond hopelessness to renewal.

Lamentations encourages all who read its despairing poetry to reflect on the meaning and purpose of their own lives. Within its anguish are indications that God speaks a renewing, redeeming Word—a Living Word that was made flesh, crucified, and resurrected. God isn't aloof to our despair or absent in our suffering. He has, in Christ, taken that suffering upon himself, canceling its curse and bringing healing and immortality to those who believe.

11 Women have been ravished[r] in Zion,
 and virgins in the towns of Judah.
12 Princes have been hung up by their hands;
 elders are shown no respect. [s]
13 Young men toil at the millstones;
 boys stagger under loads of wood.
14 The elders are gone from the city gate;
 the young men have stopped their music. [t]
15 Joy is gone from our hearts;
 our dancing has turned to mourning. [u]
16 The crown[v] has fallen from our head.
 Woe to us, for we have sinned! [w]
17 Because of this our hearts[x] are faint,
 because of these things our eyes[y] grow dim
18 for Mount Zion, which lies desolate, [z]
 with jackals prowling over it.

19 You, O LORD, reign forever;
 your throne endures[a] from generation to generation.
20 Why do you always forget us?[b]
 Why do you forsake us so long?
21 Restore[c] us to yourself, O LORD, that we may return;
 renew our days as of old
22 unless you have utterly rejected us
 and are angry with us beyond measure. [d]

5:11
r Zec 14:2

5:12
s La 4:16

5:14
t Isa 24:8; Jer 7:34

5:15
u Jer 25:10

5:16
v Ps 89:39
w Isa 3:11
5:17
x Isa 1:5 y Ps 6:7

5:18
z Mic 3:12

5:19
a Ps 45:6;
102:12,24-27
5:20
b Ps 13:1; 44:24

5:21
c Ps 80:3

5:22
d Isa 64:9

INTRODUCTION TO
Ezekiel

AUTHOR

The book identifies its author as Ezekiel (1:3), a priest exiled to Babylon by Nebuchadnezzar in 597 B.C., before the fall of Jerusalem (586 B.C.).

DATE WRITTEN

Ezekiel probably wrote this book over the course of his ministry, between 593 and 571 B.C.

ORIGINAL READERS

Ezekiel addressed his words to the Israelites living in exile. Initially he wrote to warn them of coming judgment; later, to encourage them with promises of the coming restoration and of God's mercy.

TIMELINE

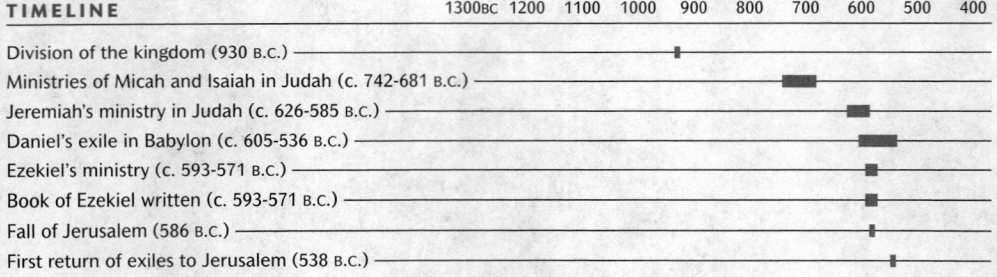

	1300BC	1200	1100	1000	900	800	700	600	500	400
Division of the kingdom (930 B.C.)					▪					
Ministries of Micah and Isaiah in Judah (c. 742-681 B.C.)							▬			
Jeremiah's ministry in Judah (c. 626-585 B.C.)								▬		
Daniel's exile in Babylon (c. 605-536 B.C.)								▬		
Ezekiel's ministry (c. 593-571 B.C.)								▪		
Book of Ezekiel written (c. 593-571 B.C.)								▪		
Fall of Jerusalem (586 B.C.)								▪		
First return of exiles to Jerusalem (538 B.C.)									▪	

THEMES

Ezekiel warned of the coming judgment on Israel and other nations and promised the future salvation of God's people. The book contains the following themes:

1. *Judgment.* The prophet Ezekiel used unusual means to prophesy God's coming judgment. He baked food using human excrement for fuel (4:9–17); shaved his head and beard, burning a third of the hair (5:1–4); dug a hole in the wall and went through it (12:1–6); and lay down without moving for extended periods of time (3:24–27; 4:4–8). These visible acts were matched by prophetic visions and images (1:1–28; 8:1—11:25; 40:1—48:35). Ezekiel teaches that God will judge both his people (1:1—24:27) and foreign nations (25:1—32:32) for sinful behavior.

2. *God's sovereignty.* God is sovereign over all creation, including the course of history. His judgments often are a means of making himself known (as seen in the repeated phrase "then they will know"). He is absolutely free either to judge or to be gracious and merciful.

3. *Future hope.* There is hope after judgment (33:1—39:29). Ezekiel demonstrated that God would restore the temple, city, and land (40:1—48:35) so that his holy presence might once again dwell among his people (48:35).

FAITH IN ACTION

The pages of Ezekiel contain life lessons and role models of faith—people who challenge believers to put their faith in action.

Role Models

• EZEKIEL (3:7–9) was shaped by God into the exact person God needed to deliver his message to his people. God prepared Ezekiel for his mission. How is God shaping you for yours?

• THE WATCHMAN (3:17–19), a type of security guard, was to give warning of coming judgment. While all people are individually responsible for their own sin (18:4–32), Christians have a special responsibility to warn all people of God's coming judgment. Are you fulfilling your role as a watchman to those around you? Do you protect people from judgment to come by sharing with them the Good News available through Christ?

Challenges

• You are God's ambassador to the world (2 Cor. 5:20), and your mission is to proclaim the gospel. Fulfill that mission, regardless of how other people respond (2:3–7).

• Evaluate your lifestyle. What "idols" are you worshiping? Do you that assume God doesn't see (8:12)? Be warned: Your actions aren't a "trivial matter" (8:17). What you believe and practice is important.

• God's presence can leave a church, just as it abandoned the temple because of the people's sin. Note that the departure of God's glory was gradual (9:3; 10:4,18; 11:22–23).

• Determine to obey God and not to be "conformed to the standards of the nations around you" (11:12).

• Don't play the "blame game." Accept responsibility for your own sin (18:4–32).

• Don't rank or prioritize one sin as worse than another; all sin offends God. As well as committing individual sins, such as adultery, theft, immorality, and idol worship, the Israelites were condemned as a group for shedding innocent blood, abusing power, mistreating widows and orphans, charging excessive interest, and other social wrongs (22:1–12).

• All people will one day "tremble at [God's] presence" (38:20). They will experience either his grace (because they have accepted him) or his judgment (because they have rejected him). What will characterize your experience of God?

OUTLINE

   I. Ezekiel's Call and Commission (1–3)
   II. Judgment Against Judah and Jerusalem (4–24)
     A. The Siege of Jerusalem Symbolized (4–5)
     B. Prophecy of God's Judgment on His People (6–7)
     C. Prophecy of the Temple Corrupted by Idolatry (8–11)
     D. The Coming Exile Acted Out and Prophesied (12)
     E. Prophecies of Judgment on Sin (13–24)
   III. Judgment on the Nations (25–32)
   IV. The Hope of Consolation and Preparation for Restoration (33–39)
     A. The Prophet as a Watchman (33:1–20)
     B. The Reasons for Jerusalem's Fall (33:21–33)
     C. Unfaithful Shepherds and the Good Shepherd (34)
     D. God's Judgment on Edom (35)
     E. Hope for the Mountains of Israel (36:1–15)
     F. Recap of the Prophet's Message (36:16–38)
     G. New Life for the Valley of Dry Bones (37)
     H. The Battle With Gog (38–39)
   V. Renewed Worship (40–48)

The Living Creatures and the Glory of the LORD

1:1
a Eze 11:24-25
b Mt 3:16; Ac 7:56
c Ex 24:10

1 In the[a] thirtieth year, in the fourth month on the fifth day, while I was among the exiles[a] by the Kebar River, the heavens were opened[b] and I saw visions[c] of God.

1:2
d 2Ki 24:15

2On the fifth of the month—it was the fifth year of the exile of King Jehoiachin[d]— 3the word of the LORD came to Ezekiel the priest, the son of Buzi,[b] by the Kebar River in the land of the Babylonians.[c] There the hand of the LORD was upon him.[e]

1:3
e 2Ki 3:15;
Eze 3:14,22

1:4
f Jer 1:14 *g* Eze 8:2

4I looked, and I saw a windstorm coming out of the north[f]—an immense cloud with flashing lightning and surrounded by brilliant light. The center of the fire looked like glowing metal,[g] 5and in the fire was what looked like four living creatures.[h] In appearance their form was that of a man,[i] 6but each of them had

1:5
h Rev 4:6 *i* ver 26

Ezekiel in Babylon (1:1)

Then: Visions and visionary language were often the only ways to communicate truth in dangerous settings such as exile.

Now: Ezekiel's general warnings about judgment and hope still communicate to us today, even though the conditions of exile have changed.

---

[a] 1 Or [my]   [b] 3 Or *Ezekiel son of Buzi the priest*   [c] 3 Or *Chaldeans*

Ezekiel 1:1–28

We are not sure what "the thirtieth year" in verse 1 refers to, but the NIV footnote suggests that Ezekiel's age may have been in view ("*my* thirtieth year"). Verses 2–3, the only third-person story portion in the book, pinpoint the year as 593 B.C. Ezekiel was one of about 10,000 Jews who had been exiled to Babylon along with King Jehoiachin in 597 B.C. (2 Kings 24:14). They

1:1

Dates in Ezekiel

Scripture	Year	Month	Day	Modern Reckoning	Event
1:1	30	4	5	July 31, 593 B.C.	Inaugural vision
1:2	5	—	5		
3:16	"At the end of seven days"				
8:1	6	6	5	Sept. 17, 592	Transport to Jerusalem
20:1–2	7	5	10	Aug. 14, 591	Negative view of Israel's history
24:1	9	10	10	Jan. 15, 588	Beginning of siege (see also 2 Kings 25:1)
26:1	11	—	1	Apr. 23, 587 to Apr. 13, 586	Oracle against Tyre
29:1	10	10	12	Jan. 7, 587	Oracle against Egypt
29:17	27	1	1	Apr. 26, 571	Egypt in exchange for Tyre
30:20	11	1	7	Apr. 29, 587	Oracle against Pharaoh
31:1	11	3	1	June 21, 587	Oracle against Pharaoh
32:1	12	12	1	Mar. 3, 585	Lament over Pharaoh
32:17	12	—	15	Apr. 13, 586 to Apr. 1, 585	Egypt dead
33:21	12	10	5	Jan. 8, 585	Arrival of first fugitive
40:1	25	1	10	Apr. 28, 573	Vision of the future
40:1	"fourteenth year after the fall of the city"				

Visions of Truth

Some people think Ezekiel is difficult to interpret because of the visions. By their nature, they say, such books aren't meant to communicate truth in a literal manner. These truths, they have decided, don't lend themselves to scientific language. They are heavy with a surplus of meaning beyond the scientific.

True, the book is challenging. The church fathers called it difficult, early rabbis considered it dangerous, and most of us at one time or another have despaired of deciphering the word of the Lord we seek in its pages.

Ezekiel's difficulty, though, emerged not just from the visions. His book was produced over a number of years spanning a chaotic time. Ezekiel spoke to people in three different phases of crisis: when they were (1) about to be overrun by a desperately cruel foreign political power, (2) overrun and deported to an alien land, and (3) in the process of being restored to their lost land. Each phase elicited a distinct prophetic message.

As any parent knows, the content and tone of messages delivered before and after disaster are likely to be very different. When my son David was ten, I presented him with a Swiss army knife. Along with the knife, I gifted him with a speech: "You are a responsible young man now," I explained, "capable of handling a valuable tool that at its worst can also be used as a weapon. I fully expect you never to misuse it in that way."

Two days later I arrived home to a house filled with tension. David had threatened the seven-year-old boy next door with his knife. I found him in his room and delivered another speech: "You have misused your trust. You will have to apologize. And you must give me back the knife." Several days later, I made a third speech: "I love you still and always will. I believe now that you can handle a Swiss army knife in the way it was meant to be used. Together we will discover the time and place for you to be a knife owner again." Three very different speeches about the same subject: the first ritualistic, the second disciplinary, the third pastoral. The first aimed at celebration of life, the second at rule-keeping and correction, the third at restoration. I didn't change in my understanding of the identity and intended use of a Swiss army knife. But the circumstances of David's and my relationship and life—and the nature of the speeches—did change.

A key ingredient in the Ezekiel enigma is still missing. Where did the story come from, the story that holds all the changing pieces together? It didn't come from the Assyrians, the Egyptians, or even from the changing fortunes of Judah, Israel, or Jerusalem. To fully understand Ezekiel we have to fast forward 600 years to the life of Jesus. There we discover an account so inspiring, so unifying, so redemptive that the difficulties, dangers, and despairs of life begin to take on a slightly unrealistic cast, like the horrors of a bad movie. In their place what becomes increasingly, overwhelmingly real is the fact of our restoration in the hands of a loving God.

> To fully understand Ezekiel we have to fast forward 600 years to the life of Jesus.

The last event of our lives—God's third speech—is so filled with his love that everything that precedes it takes on additional meaning. In our darkest hours, the cupped hands of God are there to catch us. God is—and always has been—in control.

1:6
j Eze 10:14
1:7
k Da 10:6; Rev 1:15
1:8
l Eze 10:8
1:9
m Eze 10:22

1:10
n Eze 10:14; Rev 4:7
1:11
o Isa 6:2

1:13
p Rev 4:5
1:14
q Ps 29:7

1:16
r Eze 10:9-11; Da 10:6
1:17
s ver 9
1:18
t Eze 10:12; Rev 4:6

1:20
u ver 12

1:21
v Eze 10:17

1:22
w Eze 10:1

1:24
x Eze 10:5; 43:2; Da 10:6; Rev 1:15; 19:6 y 2Ki 7:6

1:26
z Ex 24:10; Eze 10:1 a Rev 1:13

1:27
b Eze 8:2
1:28
c Ge 9:13; Rev 10:1 d Rev 4:2 e Eze 8:4 f Eze 3:23; Da 8:17; Rev 1:17

four faces[j] and four wings. [7]Their legs were straight; their feet were like those of a calf and gleamed like burnished bronze. [k] [8]Under their wings on their four sides they had the hands of a man. [l] All four of them had faces and wings, [9]and their wings touched one another. Each one went straight ahead; they did not turn as they moved. [m]

[10]Their faces looked like this: Each of the four had the face of a man, and on the right side each had the face of a lion, and on the left the face of an ox; each also had the face of an eagle. [n] [11]Such were their faces. Their wings[o] were spread out upward; each had two wings, one touching the wing of another creature on either side, and two wings covering its body. [12]Each one went straight ahead. Wherever the spirit would go, they would go, without turning as they went. [13]The appearance of the living creatures was like burning coals of fire or like torches. Fire moved back and forth among the creatures; it was bright, and lightning[p] flashed out of it. [14]The creatures sped back and forth like flashes of lightning. [q]

[15]As I looked at the living creatures, I saw a wheel on the ground beside each creature with its four faces. [16]This was the appearance and structure of the wheels: They sparkled like chrysolite, [r] and all four looked alike. Each appeared to be made like a wheel intersecting a wheel. [17]As they moved, they would go in any one of the four directions the creatures faced; the wheels did not turn[s] about[a] as the creatures went. [18]Their rims were high and awesome, and all four rims were full of eyes[t] all around.

[19]When the living creatures moved, the wheels beside them moved; and when the living creatures rose from the ground, the wheels also rose. [20]Wherever the spirit would go, they would go, [u] and the wheels would rise along with them, because the spirit of the living creatures was in the wheels. [21]When the creatures moved, they also moved; when the creatures stood still, they also stood still; and when the creatures rose from the ground, the wheels rose along with them, because the spirit of the living creatures was in the wheels. [v]

[22]Spread out above the heads of the living creatures was what looked like an expanse, [w] sparkling like ice, and awesome. [23]Under the expanse their wings were stretched out one toward the other, and each had two wings covering its body. [24]When the creatures moved, I heard the sound of their wings, like the roar of rushing waters, like the voice[x] of the Almighty, [b] like the tumult of an army. [y] When they stood still, they lowered their wings.

[25]Then there came a voice from above the expanse over their heads as they stood with lowered wings. [26]Above the expanse over their heads was what looked like a throne of sapphire, [c][z] and high above on the throne was a figure like that of a man. [a] [27]I saw that from what appeared to be his waist up he looked like glowing metal, as if full of fire, and that from there down he looked like fire; and brilliant light surrounded him. [b] [28]Like the appearance of a rainbow[c] in the clouds on a rainy day, so was the radiance around him. [d]

This was the appearance of the likeness of the glory[e] of the LORD. When I saw it, I fell facedown, [f] and I heard the voice of one speaking.

---

[a] 17 Or *aside*   [b] 24 Hebrew *Shaddai*   [c] 26 Or *lapis lazuli*

---

joined those already exiled in 605 B.C. (cf. Dan. 1:1).

Ezekiel's inauguration into prophetic mission came with an overwhelming vision of God's glory. He saw the Lord in the midst of a windstorm in the land of exile. God wasn't dead or sleeping but on the move. Normally this would have been encouraging. But God's activity didn't bode well for his people. It's only a short step from chapter 1, where God's glory was in motion, to chapter 10, where his glory abandoned the temple— leaving it defenseless against the Babylonians, who would destroy it and the rest of Jerusalem in 586 B.C.

Ezekiel's vision initiated God's two-pronged message of judgment and hope. Trying to run from God's judgment is useless. His throne-chariot can proceed easily to any point on the compass: In fact, he is everywhere present. And, as pictured by the wheels covered with eyes, he's all-knowing. The revelation of God's glory and certain judgment was terrifying to behold. No wonder Ezekiel fell on his face (cf. Rev. 1:17). Have you ever tried to hide from God? How successful were you?

But at the same time God's coming in judgment was *good* news. Though God had left his temple in Jerusalem, he was appearing to people in exile. This book brings a message of comfort to people today who find themselves displaced or without a home—many through no direct fault or sin of their own. No matter how black the gathering storm clouds may appear, those who trust in God still live in the light of his faithfulness and in the hope of deliverance.

Ezekiel's Call

2 He said to me, "Son of man, stand*g* up on your feet and I will speak to you." ²As he spoke, the Spirit came into me and raised me*h* to my feet, and I heard him speaking to me.

³He said: "Son of man, I am sending you to the Israelites, to a rebellious nation that has rebelled against me; they and their fathers have been in revolt against me to this very day.*i* ⁴The people to whom I am sending you are obstinate and stubborn.*j* Say to them, 'This is what the Sovereign LORD says.' ⁵And whether they listen or fail to listen*k*—for they are a rebellious house*l*—they will know that a prophet has been among them.*m* ⁶And you, son of man, do not be afraid*n* of them or their words. Do not be afraid, though briers and thorns*o* are all around you and you live among scorpions. Do not be afraid of what they say or terrified by them, though they are a rebellious house.*p* ⁷You must speak my words to them, whether they listen or fail to listen, for they are rebellious.*q* ⁸But you, son of man, listen to what I say to you. Do not rebel like that rebellious house;*r* open your mouth and eat*s* what I give you."

⁹Then I looked, and I saw a hand*t* stretched out to me. In it was a scroll, ¹⁰which he unrolled before me. On both sides of it were written words of lament and mourning and woe.*u*

3 And he said to me, "Son of man, eat what is before you, eat this scroll; then go and speak to the house of Israel." ²So I opened my mouth, and he gave me the scroll to eat.

³Then he said to me, "Son of man, eat this scroll I am giving you and fill your stomach with it." So I ate*v* it, and it tasted as sweet as honey*w* in my mouth.

⁴He then said to me: "Son of man, go now to the house of Israel and speak my words to them. ⁵You are not being sent to a people of obscure speech and difficult language,*x* but to the house of Israel— ⁶not to many peoples of obscure speech and difficult language, whose words you cannot understand. Surely if I had sent you to them, they would have listened to you.*y* ⁷But the house of Israel is not willing to listen to you because they are not willing to listen to me, for the whole house of Israel is hardened and obstinate.*z* ⁸But I will make you as unyielding and hardened as they are.*a* ⁹I will make your forehead like the hardest stone, harder than flint. Do not be afraid of them or terrified by them, though they are a rebellious house.*b*"

¹⁰And he said to me, "Son of man, listen carefully and take to heart all the words I speak to you. ¹¹Go now to your countrymen in exile and speak to them. Say to them, 'This is what the Sovereign LORD says,' whether they listen or fail to listen.*c*"

¹²Then the Spirit lifted me up,*d* and I heard behind me a loud rumbling sound— May the glory of the LORD be praised in his dwelling place!— ¹³the sound of the wings of the living creatures brushing against each other and the sound of the wheels beside them, a loud rumbling sound.*e* ¹⁴The Spirit then lifted me up and took me away, and I went in bitterness and in the anger of my spirit, with the strong hand of the LORD upon me. ¹⁵I came to the exiles who lived at Tel Abib near the Kebar River.*f* And there, where they were living, I sat among them for seven days*g*— overwhelmed.

2:1 *g* Da 10:11
2:2 *h* Eze 3:24; Da 8:18
2:3 *i* Jer 3:25; Eze 20:8-24
2:4 *j* Eze 3:7
2:5 *k* Eze 3:11 *l* Eze 3:27 *m* Eze 33:33
2:6 *n* Jer 1:8,17 *o* Isa 9:18; Mic 7:4 *p* Eze 3:9
2:7 *q* Jer 1:7; Eze 3:10-11
2:8 *r* Isa 50:5 *s* Jer 15:16; Rev 10:9
2:9 *t* Eze 8:3
2:10 *u* Rev 8:13
3:3 *v* Jer 15:16 *w* Ps 19:10; Ps 119:103; Rev 10:9-10
3:5 *x* Isa 28:11; Jnh 1:2
3:6 *y* Mt 11:21-23
3:7 *z* Eze 2:4; Jn 15:20-23
3:8 *a* Jer 1:18
3:9 *b* Isa 50:7; Eze 2:6; Mic 3:8
3:11 *c* Eze 2:4-5,7
3:12 *d* Eze 8:3; Ac 8:39
3:13 *e* Eze 1:24; 10:5,16-17
3:15 *f* Ps 137:1 *g* Job 2:13

Ezekiel 2:1—3:15

God entrusted Ezekiel with a critical message. If openness on the part of his listeners was any measure of his success, his mission failed before it began: They turned deaf ears to Ezekiel because they had no intention of listening to the One who had sent him. The Spirit-empowered prophet was called to provide an alternative model of behavior—listening to God without rebelling.

The term "Son of man" (lit., "son of Adam") occurs more than 90 times in Ezekiel. The expression suggests that the prophet was first in a line of people enabled by the Spirit to live in radical obedience. By calling himself Son of Man (e.g., Matt. 11:19; Luke 18:8; John 12:34), Jesus later identified the human aspect of his ministry

and hinted at the glory to be revealed (Rev. 1:12–18).

We all, as Christians, follow the Son of Man, who came to his own but wasn't on the whole well received (John 1:11; cf. Matt. 10:16). Yet to those who did receive him—and to those who do so today through our word and example—he gives the right to become children of God (John 1:12). Eugene Peterson in his book *Reversed Thunder* put it this way: "This Son of Man has dinner with a prostitute, stops off for lunch with a tax collector, wastes time blessing children when there were Roman legions to be chased from the land, heals unimportant losers and ignores high-achieving Pharisees and influential Sadducees." This is a revolutionary ministry model. What are its implications for today?

3:16
h Jer 42:7
3:17
i Isa 52:8; Jer 6:17;
Eze 33:7-9

3:18
j ver 20; Eze 33:6

3:19
k 2Ki 17:13;
Eze 14:14,20;
Ac 18:6; 20:26;
1Ti 4:14-16

3:20
l Ps 125:5;
Eze 18:24; 33:12,18

3:21
m Ac 20:31
3:22
n Eze 1:3 o Ac 9:6
p Eze 8:4

3:23
q Eze 1:1 r Eze 1:28
3:24
s Eze 2:2

3:25
t Eze 4:8

3:26
u Eze 2:5; 24:27;
33:22

3:27
v ver 11
w Eze 12:3; 24:27;
33:22

4:2
x Jer 6:6
y Eze 21:22

4:3
z Isa 8:18; 20:3;
Eze 12:3-6;
24:24,27
a Jer 39:1

Warning to Israel

16At the end of seven days the word of the LORD came to me:[h] 17"Son of man, I have made you a watchman[i] for the house of Israel; so hear the word I speak and give them warning from me. 18When I say to a wicked man, 'You will surely die,' and you do not warn him or speak out to dissuade him from his evil ways in order to save his life, that wicked man will die for[a] his sin, and I will hold you accountable for his blood.[j] 19But if you do warn the wicked man and he does not turn from his wickedness or from his evil ways, he will die for his sin; but you will have saved yourself.[k]

20"Again, when a righteous man turns from his righteousness and does evil, and I put a stumbling block before him, he will die. Since you did not warn him, he will die for his sin. The righteous things he did will not be remembered, and I will hold you accountable for his blood.[l] 21But if you do warn the righteous man not to sin and he does not sin, he will surely live because he took warning, and you will have saved yourself.[m]

22The hand of the LORD[n] was upon me there, and he said to me, "Get up and go[o] out to the plain,[p] and there I will speak to you." 23So I got up and went out to the plain. And the glory of the LORD was standing there, like the glory I had seen by the Kebar River,[q] and I fell facedown.[r]

24Then the Spirit came into me and raised me[s] to my feet. He spoke to me and said: "Go, shut yourself inside your house. 25And you, son of man, they will tie with ropes; you will be bound so that you cannot go out among the people.[t] 26I will make your tongue stick to the roof of your mouth so that you will be silent and unable to rebuke them, though they are a rebellious house.[u] 27But when I speak to you, I will open your mouth and you shall say to them, 'This is what the Sovereign LORD says.'[v] Whoever will listen let him listen, and whoever will refuse let him refuse; for they are a rebellious house.[w]

Siege of Jerusalem Symbolized

4 "Now, son of man, take a clay tablet, put it in front of you and draw the city of Jerusalem on it. 2Then lay siege to it: Erect siege works against it, build a ramp[x] up to it, set up camps against it and put battering rams around it.[y] 3Then take an iron pan, place it as an iron wall between you and the city and turn your face toward it. It will be under siege, and you shall besiege it. This will be a sign[z] to the house of Israel.[a]

4"Then lie on your left side and put the sin of the house of Israel upon yourself.[b]

a 18 Or in; also in verses 19 and 20   b 4 Or your side

Ezekiel 3:16–27

Ezekiel was responsible to warn his fellow Israelites, regardless of their response. The two classes of people ("wicked" and "righteous") cover everybody. Verses 17–21 didn't expand the scope of his ministry beyond what God had already required of him in 2:7. But they spelled out the consequences of failure to fulfill his responsibilities.

Ezekiel's restraints bound him more closely to the exiles but restricted his ability to proclaim God's message. He couldn't go wherever or say whatever he desired. There was no room in his life for a spirit of independence or for involvement with lesser tasks. He was entirely controlled by his calling as God's mouthpiece, to proclaim as a watchman the warning of impending judgment—even though he was unable in any way to prevent the disaster.

We, too, are God's ambassadors to the world (2 Cor. 5:20)—presenting his dual message of "bad" and "Good News." How balanced a perspective do you present when you talk to others about the things of God?

Are you tempted to skirt the issue of judgment, assuming that a new convert will deal with that reality at a more mature spiritual level?

The Spirit who inspired the prophets now lives in us. But instead of swallowing a scroll (Ezek. 3:3), we are called to digest a book—the Bible, through whose pages God continues to address the world (2 Peter 1:19–21). This is the message we have been given to communicate and to which we are confined. We may be creative in communication techniques but never in the content of what we, through the Spirit, have to say.

Ezekiel 4:1—5:17

Ezekiel portrayed the imminent judgment to come upon Jerusalem through a series of symbolic actions, or "sign-acts." He likely acted out the symbols in silence until he was given God's interpretive message to proclaim to his fellow exiles in 5:5–17 (cf. 3:24–27). The thoroughness of the coming devastation was clear from the signs. Now the reason became clearer: Israel had broken her covenant with God.

You are to bear their sin for the number of days you lie on your side. ⁵I have assigned you the same number of days as the years of their sin. So for 390 days you will bear the sin of the house of Israel.

⁶"After you have finished this, lie down again, this time on your right side, and bear the sin of the house of Judah. I have assigned you 40 days, a day for each year.ᵇ ⁷Turn your face toward the siege of Jerusalem and with bared arm prophesy against her. ⁸I will tie you up with ropes so that you cannot turn from one side to the other until you have finished the days of your siege.ᶜ

⁹"Take wheat and barley, beans and lentils, millet and spelt;ᵈ put them in a storage jar and use them to make bread for yourself. You are to eat it during the 390 days you lie on your side. ¹⁰Weigh out twenty shekelsᵃ of food to eat each day and eat it at set times. ¹¹Also measure out a sixth of a hinᵇ of water and drink it at set times. ¹²Eat the food as you would a barley cake; bake it in the sight of the people, using human excrementᵉ for fuel." ¹³The LORD said, "In this way the people of Israel will eat defiled food among the nations where I will drive them."ᶠ

¹⁴Then I said, "Not so, Sovereign LORD!ᵍ I have never defiled myself. From my youth until now I have never eaten anything found deadʰ or torn by wild animals. No unclean meat has ever entered my mouth.ⁱ"

¹⁵"Very well," he said, "I will let you bake your bread over cow manure instead of human excrement."

¹⁶He then said to me: "Son of man, I will cut offʲ the supply of food in Jerusalem. The people will eat rationed food in anxiety and drink rationed water in despair,ᵏ ¹⁷for food and water will be scarce. They will be appalled at the sight of each other and will waste away because ofᶜ their sin.ˡ

5 "Now, son of man, take a sharp sword and use it as a barber's razorᵐ to shaveⁿ your head and your beard.ᵒ Then take a set of scales and divide up the hair. ²When the days of your siege come to an end, burn a third of the hair with fire inside the city. Take a third and strike it with the sword all around the city. And scatter a third to the wind. For I will pursue them with drawn sword.ᵖ ³But take a few strands of hair and tuck them away in the folds of your garment.�q ⁴Again, take a few of these and throw them into the fire and burn them up. A fire will spread from there to the whole house of Israel.

⁵"This is what the Sovereign LORD says: This is Jerusalem, which I have set in the center of the nations, with countries all around her. ⁶Yet in her wickedness she has rebelled against my laws and decrees more than the nations and countries around her. She has rejected my laws and has not followed my decrees.ʳ

⁷"Therefore this is what the Sovereign LORD says: You have been more unruly than the nations around you and have not followed my decrees or kept my laws. You have not evenᵈ conformed to the standards of the nations around you.ˢ

⁸"Therefore this is what the Sovereign LORD says: I myself am against you, Jerusalem, and I will inflict punishment on you in the sight of the nations.ᵗ ⁹Because of all your detestable idols, I will do to you what I have never done before and will never do again.ᵘ ¹⁰Therefore in your midst fathers will eat their children, and children will eat their fathers.ᵛ I will inflict punishment on you and will scatter all your survivors to the winds.ʷ ¹¹Therefore as surely as I live, declares the Sovereign LORD, because you have defiled my sanctuary with all your vile imagesˣ and detestable

---

ᵃ 10 That is, about 8 ounces (about 0.2 kilogram)   ᵇ 11 That is, about 2/3 quart (about 0.6 liter)
ᶜ 17 Or away in   ᵈ 7 Most Hebrew manuscripts; some Hebrew manuscripts and Syriac You have

---

4:6
ᵇ Nu 14:34;
Da 9:24-26;
12:11-12
4:8
ᶜ Eze 3:25
4:9
ᵈ Isa 28:25

4:12
ᵉ Isa 36:12
4:13
ᶠ Hos 9:3
4:14
ᵍ Jer 1:6; Eze 9:8;
20:49 ʰ Lev 11:39
ⁱ Ex 22:31; Dt 14:3;
Ac 10:14

4:16
ʲ Ps 105:16;
Eze 5:16
ᵏ ver 10-11;
Lev 26:26; Isa 3:1;
Eze 12:19
4:17
ˡ Lev 26:39;
Eze 24:23; 33:10
5:1
ᵐ Isa 7:20
ⁿ Eze 44:20
ᵒ Lev 21:5

5:2
ᵖ ver 12; Lev 26:33
5:3
q Jer 39:10

5:6
ʳ Jer 11:10;
Eze 16:47-51;
Zec 7:11

5:7
ˢ 2Ch 33:9;
Jer 2:10-11;
Eze 16:47
5:8
ᵗ Eze 15:7

5:9
ᵘ Da 9:12;
Mt 24:21
5:10
ᵛ Lev 26:29; La 2:20
ʷ Lev 26:33;
Ps 44:11;
Eze 12:14; Zec 2:6
5:11
ˣ Eze 7:20

The language in 5:5–17 reflects Leviticus 26, which laid out the blessings and curses connected to that covenant. The coming judgment would be neither arbitrary nor unfair. Israel hadn't only failed to live up to God's standards; she hadn't even managed those of neighboring nations!

📖 God communicated his anger and love through the ultimate sign-act—the Word becoming flesh and dwelling among us (John 1:14). And the climax of Jesus' earthly ministry was the sign-act of the cross, where God's wrath and mercy met. God demonstrated his fury against sin when he temporarily abandoned his sinless Son (Matt. 27:46), opening the way for us to receive God's mercy (Matt. 27:51; Eph. 2:5–7). Jesus took upon himself the curse we deserved as covenant breakers, so that we might be redeemed by his blood (Eph. 1:7).

5:11
y 2Ch 36:14;
Eze 8:6 *z* Jer 7:4,9
5:12
a ver 2,17;
Jer 15:2; 21:9;
Eze 6:11-12; 29:14
5:13
b Eze 21:17; 36:6
c Isa 1:24

5:14
d Lev 26:32;
Ne 2:17;
Ps 74:3-10; 79:1-4
5:15
e 1Ki 9:7;
Jer 22:8-9; 24:9
f Eze 25:17
5:16
g Dt 32:24
5:17
h Eze 38:22
i Eze 14:21

practices, *y* I myself will withdraw my favor; I will not look on you with pity or spare you. *z* 12A third of your people will die of the plague or perish by famine inside you; a third will fall by the sword outside your walls; and a third I will scatter to the winds and pursue with drawn sword. *a*

13"Then my anger will cease and my wrath *b* against them will subside, and I will be avenged. *c* And when I have spent my wrath upon them, they will know that I the LORD have spoken in my zeal.

14"I will make you a ruin and a reproach among the nations around you, in the sight of all who pass by. *d* 15You will be a reproach and a taunt, a warning and an object of horror to the nations around you when I inflict punishment on you in anger and in wrath and with stinging rebuke. *e* I the LORD have spoken. *f* 16When I shoot at you with my deadly and destructive arrows of famine, I will shoot to destroy you. I will bring more and more famine upon you and cut off your supply of food. *g* 17I will send famine and wild beasts against you, and they will leave you childless. Plague and bloodshed *h* will sweep through you, and I will bring the sword against you. I the LORD have spoken. *i*"

A Prophecy Against the Mountains of Israel

6:2
j Eze 36:1

6 The word of the LORD came to me: 2"Son of man, set your face against the mountains*j* of Israel; prophesy against them 3and say: 'O mountains of Israel, hear the word of the Sovereign LORD. This is what the Sovereign LORD says to the

6:3
k Eze 36:4
l Lev 26:30
6:4
m 2Ch 14:5

mountains and hills, to the ravines and valleys:*k* I am about to bring a sword against you, and I will destroy your high places.*l* 4Your altars will be demolished and your incense altars*m* will be smashed; and I will slay your people in front of your idols. 5I will lay the dead bodies of the Israelites in front of their idols, and I

6:5
n Jer 8:1-2

will scatter your bones*n* around your altars. 6Wherever you live, the towns will be laid waste and the high places demolished, so that your altars will be laid waste and

6:6
o Mic 1:7; Zec 13:2
p Lev 26:30
q Isa 6:11; Eze 5:14

devastated, your idols*o* smashed and ruined, your incense altars*p* broken down, and what you have made wiped out. *q* 7Your people will fall slain among you, and you will know that I am the LORD.

6:8
r Jer 44:28
s Isa 6:13;
Jer 44:14;
Eze 12:16; 14:22
6:9
t Ps 78:40; Isa 7:13
u Eze 20:7,24
v Eze 20:43; 36:31

8" 'But I will spare some, for some of you will escape*r* the sword when you are scattered among the lands and nations. *s* 9Then in the nations where they have been carried captive, those who escape will remember me—how I have been grieved*t* by their adulterous hearts, which have turned away from me, and by their eyes, which have lusted after their idols. *u* They will loathe themselves for the evil they have done and for all their detestable practices. *v* 10And they will know that I am the LORD; I did not threaten in vain to bring this calamity on them.

11" 'This is what the Sovereign LORD says: Strike your hands together and stamp your feet and cry out "Alas!" because of all the wicked and detestable practices of

6:11
w Eze 5:12;
21:14,17; 25:6
6:12
x Eze 5:12
6:13
y Isa 57:5
z 1Ki 14:23;
Jer 2:20; Eze 20:28;
Hos 4:13
6:14
a Isa 5:25

the house of Israel, for they will fall by the sword, famine and plague. *w* 12He that is far away will die of the plague, and he that is near will fall by the sword, and he that survives and is spared will die of famine. So will I spend my wrath upon them. *x* 13And they will know that I am the LORD, when their people lie slain among their idols around their altars, on every high hill and on all the mountaintops, under every spreading tree and every leafy oak*y*—places where they offered fragrant incense to all their idols. *z* 14And I will stretch out my hand*a* against them and make

---

Ezekiel 6:1–14

Ezekiel had just addressed the city of Jerusalem. Now he was told to prophesy against the mountains of Israel. Israel's borders had changed during its history, but the central highlands were always the nation's pride. They were the Lord's "home turf"—yet it was precisely into this territory that idolatry had penetrated. Here "high places," raised stone platforms, had been erected to worship the Canaanite deities Baal and Asherah.

We too live in a world of idolatry. Our "high place" may be an office, where we sacrifice relationships to win the blessing of the god "career"; a family room, where we consecrate our "prime time" to entertainment; or a kitchen, where we devote ourselves to meeting our family's physical wants perfectly. Even church can function as an idol, the place from which we seek approval and affirmation or a base to exercise personal power. How do you know when a legitimate blessing in your life may have crossed the line in your affections to become your god?

the land a desolate waste from the desert to Diblah [a]—wherever they live. Then they will know that I am the LORD. [b'] "

6:14
b Eze 14:13

The End Has Come

7 The word of the LORD came to me: [2] "Son of man, this is what the Sovereign LORD says to the land of Israel: The end! [c] The end has come upon the four corners [d] of the land. [3] The end is now upon you and I will unleash my anger against you. I will judge you according to your conduct and repay you for all your detestable practices. [4] I will not look on you with pity [e] or spare you; I will surely repay you for your conduct and the detestable practices among you. Then you will know that I am the LORD.

[5] "This is what the Sovereign LORD says: Disaster! [f] An unheard-of [b] disaster is coming. [6] The end has come! The end has come! It has roused itself against you. It has come! [7] Doom has come upon you—you who dwell in the land. The time has come, the day is near; [g] there is panic, not joy, upon the mountains. [8] I am about to pour out my wrath [h] on you and spend my anger against you; I will judge you according to your conduct and repay you for all your detestable practices. [i] [9] I will not look on you with pity or spare you; I will repay you in accordance with your conduct and the detestable practices among you. Then you will know that it is I the LORD who strikes the blow.

[10] "The day is here! It has come! Doom has burst forth, the rod [j] has budded, arrogance has blossomed! [11] Violence has grown into [c] a rod to punish wickedness; none of the people will be left, none of that crowd—no wealth, nothing of value. [k] [12] The time has come, the day has arrived. Let not the buyer rejoice nor the seller grieve, for wrath is upon the whole crowd. [l] [13] The seller will not recover the land he has sold as long as both of them live, for the vision concerning the whole crowd will not be reversed. Because of their sins, not one of them will preserve his life. [m] [14] Though they blow the trumpet and get everything ready, no one will go into battle, for my wrath is upon the whole crowd.

[15] "Outside is the sword, inside are plague and famine; those in the country will die by the sword, and those in the city will be devoured by famine and plague. [n] [16] All who survive and escape will be in the mountains, moaning like doves [o] of the valleys, each because of his sins. [p] [17] Every hand will go limp, [q] and every knee will become as weak as water. [18] They will put on sackcloth and be clothed with terror. [r] Their faces will be covered with shame and their heads will be shaved. [s] [19] They will throw their silver into the streets, and their gold will be an unclean thing. Their silver and gold will not be able to save them in the day of the LORD's wrath. [t] They will not satisfy their hunger or fill their stomachs with it, for it has made them stumble [u] into sin. [v] [20] They were proud of their beautiful jewelry and used it to make their detestable idols and vile images. [w] Therefore I will turn these into an unclean thing for them. [21] I will hand it all over as plunder to foreigners and as loot to the wicked of the earth, and they will defile it. [x] [22] I will turn my face [y] away from them, and they will desecrate my treasured place; robbers will enter it and desecrate it.

[23] "Prepare chains, because the land is full of bloodshed [z] and the city is full of violence. [24] I will bring the most wicked of the nations to take possession of their

7:2
c Am 8:2,10
d Rev 7:1; 20:8

7:4
e Eze 5:11

7:5
f 2Ki 21:12

7:7
g Eze 12:23;
Zep 1:14
7:8
h Isa 42:25;
Eze 9:8; 14:19;
Na 1:6
i Eze 20:8,21; 36:19

7:10
j Ps 89:32; Isa 10:5

7:11
k Jer 16:6;
Zep 1:18

7:12
l ver 7; Isa 5:13-14;
Eze 30:3
7:13
m Lev 25:24-28
7:15
n Dt 32:25;
Jer 14:18; La 1:20;
Eze 5:12

7:16
o Isa 59:11
p Ezr 9:15; Eze 6:8
7:17
q Isa 13:7;
Eze 21:7; 22:14
7:18
r Ps 55:5
s Isa 15:2-3;
Eze 27:31; Am 8:10
7:19
t Eze 13:5;
Zep 1:7,18
u Eze 14:3
v Pr 11:4
7:20
w Jer 7:30

7:21
x 2Ki 24:13
7:22
y Eze 39:23-24
7:23
z 2Ki 21:16

a 14 Most Hebrew manuscripts; a few Hebrew manuscripts Riblah   b 5 Most Hebrew manuscripts; some Hebrew manuscripts and Syriac Disaster after   c 11 Or The violent one has become

Ezekiel 7:1–27

In Ezekiel 7 the scope of the judgment is expanded in two ways: geography and time frame. Ezekiel began with Jerusalem (ch. 5) and moved to the heartland of Judah, the mountains of Israel (ch. 6). Now he focused on all of Israel. Many people think of the message of the prophets as "Repent—the end is near!" But Ezekiel's point in this chapter was: "It's too late to repent—the end has come!" Sadly, this passage contains no glimmer of light or mention of a remnant of survivors to be saved.

Does the situation in Ezekial's time seem unrelated to our own? We live in a world where immediate, comprehensive justice often isn't poured out in obvious ways on nations or individuals who break God's laws. But judgment delayed isn't justice denied. It may not be immediate, but the coming day of reckoning will be all-inclusive and entirely fair.

7:24
a Eze 24:21
b 2Ch 7:20;
Eze 28:7
7:25
c Eze 13:10,16
7:26
d Jer 4:20
e Isa 47:11;
Eze 20:1-3; Mic 3:6
7:27
f Ps 109:19;
Eze 26:16
g Eze 18:20 h ver 4

houses; I will put an end to the pride of the mighty, and their sanctuaries ^a will be desecrated. ^b 25When terror comes, they will seek peace, but there will be none. ^c 26Calamity upon calamity ^d will come, and rumor upon rumor. They will try to get a vision from the prophet; the teaching of the law by the priest will be lost, as will the counsel of the elders. ^e 27The king will mourn, the prince will be clothed with despair, ^f and the hands of the people of the land will tremble. I will deal with them according to their conduct, ^g and by their own standards I will judge them. Then they will know that I am the LORD. ^h"

Idolatry in the Temple

8:1
i Eze 14:1
j Eze 33:31
k Eze 1:1-3

8 In the sixth year, in the sixth month on the fifth day, while I was sitting in my house and the elders ⁱ of Judah were sitting before ^j me, the hand of the Sovereign LORD came upon me there. ^k 2I looked, and I saw a figure like that of a man. ^a From what appeared to be his waist down he was like fire, and from there up his appearance was as bright as glowing metal. ^l 3He stretched out what looked like a hand and took me by the hair of my head. The Spirit lifted me up ^m between earth and heaven and in visions of God he took me to Jerusalem, to the entrance to the north gate of the inner court, where the idol that provokes to jealousy ⁿ stood. 4And there before me was the glory ^o of the God of Israel, as in the vision I had seen in the plain. ^p

8:2
l Eze 1:4,26-27
8:3
m Eze 3:12; 11:1
n Ex 20:5; Dt 32:16

8:4
o Eze 1:28
p Eze 3:22
8:5
q Ps 78:58;
Jer 32:34

5Then he said to me, "Son of man, look toward the north." So I looked, and in the entrance north of the gate of the altar I saw this idol ^q of jealousy.

8:6
r Eze 5:11

6And he said to me, "Son of man, do you see what they are doing—the utterly detestable ^r things the house of Israel is doing here, things that will drive me far from my sanctuary? But you will see things that are even more detestable."

7Then he brought me to the entrance to the court. I looked, and I saw a hole in the wall. 8He said to me, "Son of man, now dig into the wall." So I dug into the wall and saw a doorway there.

8:10
s Ex 20:4

9And he said to me, "Go in and see the wicked and detestable things they are doing here." 10So I went in and looked, and I saw portrayed all over the walls all kinds of crawling things and detestable animals and all the idols of the house of Israel. ^s

8:11
t Nu 16:17
u Nu 16:35

11In front of them stood seventy elders of the house of Israel, and Jaazaniah son of Shaphan was standing among them. Each had a censer ^t in his hand, and a fragrant cloud of incense ^u was rising.

8:12
v Ps 10:11;
Isa 29:15; Eze 9:9

12He said to me, "Son of man, have you seen what the elders of the house of Israel are doing in the darkness, each at the shrine of his own idol? They say, 'The LORD does not see ^v us; the LORD has forsaken the land.' " 13Again, he said, "You will see them doing things that are even more detestable."

14Then he brought me to the entrance to the north gate of the house of the LORD, and I saw women sitting there, mourning for Tammuz. 15He said to me, "Do you see this, son of man? You will see things that are even more detestable than this."

8:16
w Joel 2:17

16He then brought me into the inner court of the house of the LORD, and there at the entrance to the temple, between the portico and the altar, ^w were about twen-

---

a 2 Or saw a fiery figure

Ezekiel 8:1–18

📖 Ezekiel was shown a vision of four scenes of idolatrous worship in Jerusalem, each moving nearer to the temple: (1) an "idol of jealousy," possibly the Canaanite fertility goddess Asherah (cf. 2 Kings 21:7); (2) the worship of "crawling things and detestable animals," likely of Egyptian origin; (3) "mourning for Tammuz," an annual ritual in the worship of this Babylonian fertility god; and (4) "bowing down to the sun," while *turning their backs on the Lord and his temple.*

The people had abandoned God and run after every available alternative. If the temple—the stronghold of true religion—had become so infected, did pure worship survive anywhere in Israel?

💭 Our culture would tell us differently, but the choice we face isn't between equally valid methods of expressing our spirituality—it's between truth and lies. Idolatry isn't so much denying God's *reality* as it is his *relevance* (see Ezek. 8:12). Why otherwise would an overwhelming number of Americans believe in God's existence and in the Bible as his Word, yet never attend church or read the Bible and follow its principles? Such individuals are practical idol worshipers, people who have created a religion to fit their own preferences. Is God a relevant presence in your daily activities?

ty-five men. With their backs toward the temple of the LORD and their faces toward the east, they were bowing down to the sun in the east.[x]

[17]He said to me, "Have you seen this, son of man? Is it a trivial matter for the house of Judah to do the detestable things they are doing here? Must they also fill the land with violence[y] and continually provoke me to anger?[z] Look at them putting the branch to their nose! [18]Therefore I will deal with them in anger; I will not look on them with pity[a] or spare them. Although they shout in my ears, I will not listen[b] to them."

Idolaters Killed

9 Then I heard him call out in a loud voice, "Bring the guards of the city here, each with a weapon in his hand." [2]And I saw six men coming from the direction of the upper gate, which faces north, each with a deadly weapon in his hand. With them was a man clothed in linen[c] who had a writing kit at his side. They came in and stood beside the bronze altar.

[3]Now the glory[d] of the God of Israel went up from above the cherubim,[e] where it had been, and moved to the threshold of the temple. Then the LORD called to the man clothed in linen who had the writing kit at his side [4]and said to him, "Go throughout the city of Jerusalem and put a mark[f] on the foreheads of those who grieve and lament[g] over all the detestable things that are done in it.[h]"

[5]As I listened, he said to the others, "Follow him through the city and kill, without showing pity[i] or compassion. [6]Slaughter old men, young men and maidens, women and children, but do not touch anyone who has the mark. Begin at my sanctuary." So they began with the elders[j] who were in front of the temple.[k]

[7]Then he said to them, "Defile the temple and fill the courts with the slain. Go!" So they went out and began killing throughout the city. [8]While they were killing and I was left alone, I fell facedown,[l] crying out, "Ah, Sovereign LORD! Are you going to destroy the entire remnant of Israel in this outpouring of your wrath on Jerusalem?[m]"

[9]He answered me, "The sin of the house of Israel and Judah is exceedingly great; the land is full of bloodshed and the city is full of injustice.[n] They say, 'The LORD has forsaken the land; the LORD does not see.'[o] [10]So I will not look on them with pity[p] or spare them, but I will bring down on their own heads what they have done.[q]"

[11]Then the man in linen with the writing kit at his side brought back word, saying, "I have done as you commanded."

The Glory Departs From the Temple

10 I looked, and I saw the likeness of a throne[r] of sapphire[a][s] above the expanse[t] that was over the heads of the cherubim. [2]The LORD said to the man clothed in linen,[u] "Go in among the wheels[v] beneath the cherubim. Fill[w] your hands with

[a] *1* Or *lapis lazuli*

Cross references

8:16 [x] Dt 4:19; 17:3; Job 31:28; Jer 2:27; Eze 11:1,12

8:17 [y] Eze 9:9 [z] Eze 16:26

8:18 [a] Eze 9:10; 24:14 [b] Isa 1:15; Jer 11:11; Mic 3:4; Zec 7:13

9:2 [c] Lev 16:4; Eze 10:2; Rev 15:6

9:3 [d] Eze 10:4 [e] Eze 11:22

9:4 [f] Ex 12:7; 2Co 1:22; Rev 7:3; 9:4 [g] Ps 119:136; Jer 13:17; Eze 21:6 [h] Ps 119:53

9:5 [i] Eze 5:11

9:6 [j] Eze 8:11-13,16 [k] 2Ch 36:17; Jer 25:29; 1Pe 4:17

9:8 [l] Jos 7:6 [m] Eze 11:13; Am 7:1-6

9:9 [n] Eze 22:29 [o] Job 22:13; Eze 8:12

9:10 [p] Eze 7:4; 8:18 [q] Isa 65:6; Eze 11:21

10:1 [r] Rev 4:2 [s] Ex 24:10 [t] Eze 1:22

10:2 [u] Eze 9:2 [v] Eze 1:15 [w] Rev 8:5

Ezekiel 9:1–11

This vision reminds us of the Passover of Exodus 12, except that Judah, not Egypt, was the scene of devastation. In the midst of the carnage, Ezekiel began to fear he would be left totally alone—a remnant of *one*—and cried out in intercession. Just when hope seemed lost, the seventh angel reappeared, announcing that he had done his job. We're not told how many people the angel had marked, but his presence eased slightly the awful severity of the judgment. As in the Passover, there was shelter from God's destruction for those willing to take refuge in the appointed sign. But this time, it seemed that precious few would be saved.

The concept of divine judgment is unpalatable to the modern mind. Yet in periods when the church has been comfortable proclaiming God's judgment, Christians have sometimes been quick to set themselves up as agents of divine vengeance (cf. Luke 9: 51–56). Jesus called us to win over hostile unbelievers with tolerance and kindness (cf. Matt. 5:39–42; Rom. 12:17–21). On the other end of the spectrum, we are not to fall for the contemporary myth that "it doesn't matter what people believe as long as they are sincere." Judgment is coming, beginning "with the family of God." What will the outcome be for those who don't obey the gospel requirements (1 Peter 4:17)?

Ezekiel 10:1–22

Chapter 10 continues the judgment scene of the previous chapter. As the angel began to carry out God's judgment by fire, Ezekiel experienced a renewed

burning coals from among the cherubim and scatter them over the city." And as I watched, he went in.

10:4
x Eze 1:28; 9:3

³Now the cherubim were standing on the south side of the temple when the man went in, and a cloud filled the inner court. ⁴Then the glory of the LORD ˣ rose from above the cherubim and moved to the threshold of the temple. The cloud filled the temple, and the court was full of the radiance of the glory of the LORD. ⁵The sound of the wings of the cherubim could be heard as far away as the outer court, like the voice ʸ of God Almighty ᵃ when he speaks.

10:5
y Job 40:9;
Eze 1:24

⁶When the LORD commanded the man in linen, "Take fire from among the wheels, from among the cherubim," the man went in and stood beside a wheel. ⁷Then one of the cherubim reached out his hand to the fire that was among them. He took up some of it and put it into the hands of the man in linen, who took it and went out. ⁸(Under the wings of the cherubim could be seen what looked like the hands of a man.) ᶻ

10:8
z Eze 1:8

⁹I looked, and I saw beside the cherubim four wheels, one beside each of the cherubim; the wheels sparkled like chrysolite. ᵃ ¹⁰As for their appearance, the four of them looked alike; each was like a wheel intersecting a wheel. ¹¹As they moved, they would go in any one of the four directions the cherubim faced; the wheels did not turn about ᵇ as the cherubim went. The cherubim went in whatever direction the head faced, without turning as they went. ¹²Their entire bodies, including their backs, their hands and their wings, were completely full of eyes, ᵇ as were their four wheels. ᶜ ¹³I heard the wheels being called "the whirling wheels." ¹⁴Each of the cherubim ᵈ had four faces: ᵉ One face was that of a cherub, the second the face of a man, the third the face of a lion, and the fourth the face of an eagle. ᶠ

10:9
a Eze 1:15-16;
Rev 21:20

10:12
b Rev 4:6-8
c Eze 1:15-21
10:14
d 1Ki 7:36 e Eze 1:6
f Eze 1:10; Rev 4:7

¹⁵Then the cherubim rose upward. These were the living creatures ᵍ I had seen by the Kebar River. ¹⁶When the cherubim moved, the wheels beside them moved; and when the cherubim spread their wings to rise from the ground, the wheels did not leave their side. ¹⁷When the cherubim stood still, they also stood still; and when the cherubim rose, they rose with them, because the spirit of the living creatures was in them. ʰ

10:15
g Eze 1:3,5

10:17
h Eze 1:20-21

¹⁸Then the glory of the LORD departed from over the threshold of the temple and stopped above the cherubim. ⁱ ¹⁹While I watched, the cherubim spread their wings and rose from the ground, and as they went, the wheels went with them. ʲ They stopped at the entrance to the east gate of the LORD's house, and the glory of the God of Israel was above them.

10:18
i Ps 18:10
10:19
j Eze 11:1,22

²⁰These were the living creatures I had seen beneath the God of Israel by the Kebar River, ᵏ and I realized that they were cherubim. ²¹Each had four faces ˡ and four wings, ᵐ and under their wings was what looked like the hands of a man. ²²Their faces had the same appearance as those I had seen by the Kebar River. Each one went straight ahead.

10:20
k Eze 1:1
10:21
l Eze 41:18
m Eze 1:6

Judgment on Israel's Leaders

11 Then the Spirit lifted me up and brought me to the gate of the house of the LORD that faces east. There at the entrance to the gate were twenty-five men,

---

ᵃ 5 Hebrew *El-Shaddai*   ᵇ 11 Or *aside*

---

vision of the first chapter's divine chariot with its supernatural attendants. But now the location was Jerusalem, not Babylon.

Ezekiel saw a cloud filling the inner court and the glory of God on the move once more, just as it had been in the days of the desert wanderings (cf. Ex. 40:34–37). It departed slowly, haltingly, as if reluctant to leave. Gradually it passed from above the cherubim in the Most Holy Place to the east gate of the temple courtyard. Soon it would move on to the Mount of Olives east of Jerusalem, outside the city limits (11:23). The city itself

would be effectively doomed.

God's presence in the midst of his people isn't to be taken lightly or presumed upon. The risen Christ issued stern warnings to the churches in the province of Asia (Rev. 2:5; 2:16; 3:3; 3:16). God's presence can be removed from a church, just as it abandoned the temple—leaving that church a hollow shell. Outwardly everything may seem intact, but without the internal reality of God's presence it's merely a matter of time before the edifice collapses. What can you and others in your fellowship do to ensure your congregation's spiritual health?

and I saw among them Jaazaniah son of Azzur and Pelatiah son of Benaiah, leaders of the people.[n] 2The LORD said to me, "Son of man, these are the men who are plotting evil and giving wicked advice in this city. 3They say, 'Will it not soon be time to build houses?[a] This city is a cooking pot,[o] and we are the meat.'[p] 4Therefore prophesy[q] against them; prophesy, son of man."

5Then the Spirit of the LORD came upon me, and he told me to say: "This is what the LORD says: That is what you are saying, O house of Israel, but I know what is going through your mind.[r] 6You have killed many people in this city and filled its streets with the dead.[s]

7"Therefore this is what the Sovereign LORD says: The bodies you have thrown there are the meat and this city is the pot, but I will drive you out of it.[t] 8You fear the sword, and the sword is what I will bring against you, declares the Sovereign LORD.[u] 9I will drive you out of the city and hand you over[v] to foreigners and inflict punishment on you.[w] 10You will fall by the sword, and I will execute judgment on you at the borders of Israel.[x] Then you will know that I am the LORD. 11This city will not be a pot[y] for you, nor will you be the meat in it; I will execute judgment on you at the borders of Israel. 12And you will know that I am the LORD, for you have not followed my decrees[z] or kept my laws but have conformed to the standards of the nations around you.[a]"

13Now as I was prophesying, Pelatiah[b] son of Benaiah died. Then I fell facedown and cried out in a loud voice, "Ah, Sovereign LORD! Will you completely destroy the remnant of Israel?[c]"

14The word of the LORD came to me: 15"Son of man, your brothers—your brothers who are your blood relatives[b] and the whole house of Israel—are those of whom the people of Jerusalem have said, 'They are[c] far away from the LORD; this land was given to us as our possession.'[d]

Promised Return of Israel

16"Therefore say: 'This is what the Sovereign LORD says: Although I sent them far away among the nations and scattered them among the countries, yet for a little while I have been a sanctuary[e] for them in the countries where they have gone.'

17"Therefore say: 'This is what the Sovereign LORD says: I will gather you from the nations and bring you back from the countries where you have been scattered, and I will give you back the land of Israel again.'[f]

18"They will return to it and remove all its vile images[g] and detestable idols.[h] 19I will give them an undivided heart[i] and put a new spirit in them; I will remove from them their heart of stone[j] and give them a heart of flesh.[k] 20Then they will follow my decrees and be careful to keep my laws.[l] They will be my people, and I will be their God.[m] 21But as for those whose hearts are devoted to their vile images and de-

---

a 3 Or This is not the time to build houses.   b 15 Or are in exile with you (see Septuagint and Syriac)
c 15 Or those to whom the people of Jerusalem have said, 'Stay

---

11:1
n Eze 8:16; 10:19; 43:4-5
11:3
o Jer 1:13; Eze 24:3
p ver 7,11
11:4
q Eze 3:4,17
11:5
r Jer 17:10
11:6
s Eze 7:23; 22:6
11:7
t Eze 24:3-13; Mic 3:2-3
11:8
u Pr 10:24
11:9
v Ps 106:41
w Dt 28:36; Eze 5:8
11:10
x 2Ki 14:25
11:11
y ver 3
11:12
z Lev 18:4; Eze 18:9
a Eze 8:10
11:13
b ver 1 c Eze 9:8
11:15
d Eze 33:24
11:16
e Ps 90:1; 91:9; Isa 8:14
11:17
f Jer 3:18; 24:5-6; Eze 28:25; 34:13
11:18
g Eze 5:11
h Eze 37:23
11:19
i Jer 32:39
j Zec 7:12
k Eze 18:31; 36:26; 2Co 3:3
11:20
l Ps 105:45
m Eze 14:11; 36:26-28

Ezekiel 11:1–15

The "leaders of the people" (v. 1) were a small council of high officials who wielded significant power in Judah and had been able to remain in Jerusalem when many Jews were exiled by the Babylonians in 597 B.C. They arrogantly boasted that they were the "meat," the best portion—implying that the exiles were the refuse.

Through Ezekiel the Lord declared that the "meat" wasn't the elite in Jerusalem but the innocent people they had killed. Now the leaders themselves would be destroyed. Furthermore, Israel's future lay with the exiles. Though labeled "far away from the LORD" (v. 15), the exiles, not the "left behinds," constituted the privileged remnant after all.

God always preserves for himself a people. That he deliberately chose refugees here for preservation speaks to his care for groups our world defines as "throwaways." Those of us who profess Jesus as Lord are to be particularly alert to the danger of thinking of ourselves "more highly" than we ought (Rom. 12:3)—the error of the religious in Ezekiel's time. God often accomplishes his work through the small, despised, neglected, and insignificant (Luke 5:27–32; 1 Cor. 1:26–29), another mystery of his kingdom.

Ezekiel 11:16–25

This is one of the most significant passages in Ezekiel, the first substantive indication of a solid hope for the future for God's people in exile. The exiles had been thrust from Jerusalem and its temple/sanctuary, but God himself had become their sanctuary. Besides, the exile represented only a temporary state of affairs. There would be a new exodus as God's true people

11:21
n Eze 9:10; 16:43

11:22
o Eze 10:19
11:23
p Eze 8:4; 10:4
q Zec 14:4
11:24
r Eze 8:3
s 2Co 12:2-4
11:25
t Eze 3:4,11

12:2
u Isa 6:10;
Eze 2:6-8; Mt 13:15

12:3
v Jer 36:3
w Jer 26:3
x 2Ti 2:25-26

12:4
y ver 12; Jer 39:4

12:6
z ver 12; Isa 8:18;
20:3; Eze 4:3; 24:24
12:7
a Eze 24:18; 37:10

12:9
b Eze 17:12; 20:49;
24:19

12:11
c 2Ki 25:7; Jer 15:2;
52:15
12:12
d Jer 39:4
e Jer 52:7
12:13
f Eze 17:20; 19:8;
Hos 7:12
g Isa 24:17-18
h Jer 39:7
i Jer 52:11;
Eze 17:16
12:14
j 2Ki 25:5;
Eze 5:10,12

testable idols, I will bring down on their own heads what they have done, declares the Sovereign LORD. [n]"

22Then the cherubim, with the wheels beside them, spread their wings, and the glory of the God of Israel was above them. [o] 23The glory [p] of the LORD went up from within the city and stopped above the mountain [q] east of it. 24The Spirit [r] lifted me up and brought me to the exiles in Babylonia [a] in the vision [s] given by the Spirit of God.

Then the vision I had seen went up from me, 25and I told the exiles everything the LORD had shown me. [t]

The Exile Symbolized

12 The word of the LORD came to me: 2"Son of man, you are living among a rebellious people. They have eyes to see but do not see and ears to hear but do not hear, for they are a rebellious people. [u]

3"Therefore, son of man, pack your belongings for exile and in the daytime, as they watch, set out and go from where you are to another place. Perhaps [v] they will understand, [w] though they are a rebellious house. [x] 4During the daytime, while they watch, bring out your belongings packed for exile. Then in the evening, while they are watching, go out like those who go into exile. [y] 5While they watch, dig through the wall and take your belongings out through it. 6Put them on your shoulder as they are watching and carry them out at dusk. Cover your face so that you cannot see the land, for I have made you a sign [z] to the house of Israel."

7So I did as I was commanded. [a] During the day I brought out my things packed for exile. Then in the evening I dug through the wall with my hands. I took my belongings out at dusk, carrying them on my shoulders while they watched.

8In the morning the word of the LORD came to me: 9"Son of man, did not that rebellious house of Israel ask you, 'What are you doing?' [b]

10"Say to them, 'This is what the Sovereign LORD says: This oracle concerns the prince in Jerusalem and the whole house of Israel who are there.' 11Say to them, 'I am a sign to you.'

"As I have done, so it will be done to them. They will go into exile as captives. [c]

12"The prince among them will put his things on his shoulder at dusk [d] and leave, and a hole will be dug in the wall for him to go through. He will cover his face so that he cannot see the land. [e] 13I will spread my net [f] for him, and he will be caught in my snare; [g] I will bring him to Babylonia, the land of the Chaldeans, but he will not see [h] it, and there he will die. [i] 14I will scatter to the winds all those around him— his staff and all his troops—and I will pursue them with drawn sword. [j]

15"They will know that I am the LORD, when I disperse them among the nations and scatter them through the countries. 16But I will spare a few of them from the

a 24 Or Chaldea

returned and rid the land of idolatry. The impetus for this change of behavior would be a change of heart. God would create in his new people "an undivided heart," not so much in the sense of mutual agreement among themselves but of undivided loyalty to himself. The result of such renewal would be nothing less than fulfillment of the goal of the first exodus: "They will be my people, and I will be their God" (v. 20; cf. Ex. 6:7).

A "heart of stone," unresponsive to God, isn't natural to us. We were created to have a heart that responds joyfully and obediently to him. Yet since Adam and Eve's fall into sin our humanity has been warped so that we have become "by nature objects of [God's] wrath" (Eph. 2:3). We don't need simply to keep New Year's resolutions or turn over a new leaf. We need radical heart surgery—nothing less than a new birth from above (John 3:3). Thanks be to God for the gift of Christ,

in whom we as Christians are a new creation, reconciled to God (2 Cor. 5:17–18)!

Ezekiel 12: 1–28

If Ezekiel cherished hopes of revolutionary change in the exiles based on his visions in chapters 8–11 (see 11:24–25), he was in for a reality check. His fellow exiles were rebellious and hard-hearted. In the two "sign-acts" (see notes for 4:1—5:17) of verses 3–16 and 17–20, the prophet's point was the people's looking but failing to see: They watched him perform the symbolic acts but didn't "get it."

Ezekiel argued against two popular slogans. (1) "The days go by and every vision comes to nothing." The people had grown so used to visions of future disaster that they concluded they were empty threats. But when the judgment took place and the false prophets were cut off, God assured them, they would recognize the true

sword, famine and plague, so that in the nations where they go they may acknowledge all their detestable practices. Then they will know that I am the LORD. *k* "

[17] The word of the LORD came to me: [18] "Son of man, tremble as you eat your food, *l* and shudder in fear as you drink your water. [19] Say to the people of the land: 'This is what the Sovereign LORD says about those living in Jerusalem and in the land of Israel: They will eat their food in anxiety and drink their water in despair, for their land will be stripped of everything *m* in it because of the violence of all who live there. *n* [20] The inhabited towns will be laid waste and the land will be desolate. Then you will know that I am the LORD. *o* '"

[21] The word of the LORD came to me: [22] "Son of man, what is this proverb you have in the land of Israel: 'The days go by and every vision comes to nothing'? *p* [23] Say to them, 'This is what the Sovereign LORD says: I am going to put an end to this proverb, and they will no longer quote it in Israel.' Say to them, 'The days are near when every vision will be fulfilled. *q* [24] For there will be no more false visions or flattering divinations *r* among the people of Israel. [25] But I the LORD will speak what I will, and it shall be fulfilled without delay. For in your days, you rebellious house, I will fulfill whatever I say, declares the Sovereign LORD. *s* '"

[26] The word of the LORD came to me: [27] "Son of man, the house of Israel is saying, 'The vision he sees is for many years from now, and he prophesies about the distant future.' *t*

[28] "Therefore say to them, 'This is what the Sovereign LORD says: None of my words will be delayed any longer; whatever I say will be fulfilled, declares the Sovereign LORD.' "

False Prophets Condemned

13 The word of the LORD came to me: [2] "Son of man, prophesy against the prophets of Israel who are now prophesying. Say to those who prophesy out of their own imagination: 'Hear the word of the LORD! *u* [3] This is what the Sovereign LORD says: Woe to the foolish*a* prophets *v* who follow their own spirit and have seen nothing! *w* [4] Your prophets, O Israel, are like jackals among ruins. [5] You have not gone up to the breaks in the wall to repair *x* it for the house of Israel so that it will stand firm in the battle on the day of the LORD. *y* [6] Their visions are false and their divinations a lie. They say, "The LORD declares," when the LORD has not sent them; yet they expect their words to be fulfilled. *z* [7] Have you not seen false visions and uttered lying divinations when you say, "The LORD declares," though I have not spoken?

[8] "Therefore this is what the Sovereign LORD says: Because of your false words and lying visions, I am against you, declares the Sovereign LORD. [9] My hand will be

a 3 Or wicked

12:16 *k* Jer 22:8-9; Eze 6:8-10; 14:22
12:18 *l* La 5:9; Eze 4:16
12:19 *m* Eze 6:6-14; Mic 7:13; Zec 7:14 *n* Eze 4:16; 23:33
12:20 *o* Isa 7:23-24; Jer 4:7
12:22 *p* Eze 11:3; Am 6:3; 2Pe 3:4
12:23 *q* Ps 37:13; Joel 2:1; Zep 1:14
12:24 *r* Jer 14:14; Eze 13:23; Zec 13:2-4
12:25 *s* Isa 14:24; Hab 1:5
12:27 *t* Da 10:14

13:2 *u* ver 17; Jer 23:16; 37:19
13:3 *v* La 2:14 *w* Jer 23:25-32
13:5 *x* Isa 58:12; Eze 22:30 *y* Eze 7:19
13:6 *z* Jer 28:15; Eze 22:28

prophets (cf. Ezek. 2:5). (2) "The vision [Ezekiel] sees is for many years from now." This group received a "red alert" response from God.

We as God's people are signs and witnesses before a watching world (Acts 1:8). Our testimony is to be both verbal and visual, particularly in cultures and locations that are inhospitable to our message. We are to speak clearly of the tragic and dangerous state of men and women without Christ, but also demonstrate, in word and deed, the love of God manifested in Christ's death for sinners (Rom. 5:8).

How does God's Word take on flesh through us? Some Christians have been accused of turning the Word who became flesh back into words again. We can talk a good talk but don't always have the walk to match. A world with ears tightly closed against truth is looking to see the reality of our faith written in actions. It needs to see our costly witness, whereby our deeds underline the

reality of our words, while our words explain the meaning of our deeds.

Ezekiel 13:1–23

The implications of verse 9 for the false prophets were far-reaching: (1) To be excluded from "the council of [God's] people" was to be cut off from the true Israel. (2) To be left off the records of the people was to be banned from the community (see Neh. 7). (3) They wouldn't participate in the return from exile.

Because the false prophets' message originated in their own hearts, Ezekiel criticized its content—or lack of it. It was as though they had been whitewashing a poorly constructed wall, giving it a misleadingly solid appearance. Its true nature would be exposed by the coming storm. The source of the prophetesses' predictions was also their own imaginations, expressed in forms of magic. They weren't concerned with the nation's fate but viewed their clients and communities as disposable objects, to be exploited for profit.

13:9
a Jer 17:13
b Eze 20:38

13:10
c Jer 50:6
d Eze 7:25; 22:28

13:11
e Eze 38:22

13:13
f Rev 11:19; 16:21
g Ex 9:25; Isa 30:30

13:14
h Mic 1:6 *i* Jer 6:15

13:16
j Isa 57:21; Jer 6:14
13:17
k Rev 2:20 *l* ver 2

13:19
m Eze 20:39; 22:26
n Pr 28:21

13:21
o Ps 91:3

13:22
p Jer 23:14;
Eze 33:14-16
13:23
q ver 6; Eze 12:24
r Mic 3:6

14:1
s Eze 8:1; 20:1

14:3
t ver 7; Eze 7:19
u Isa 1:15;
Eze 20:31

against the prophets who see false visions and utter lying divinations. They will not belong to the council of my people or be listed in the records *a* of the house of Israel, nor will they enter the land of Israel. Then you will know that I am the Sovereign LORD. *b*

10 " 'Because they lead my people astray, *c* saying, "Peace," when there is no peace, and because, when a flimsy wall is built, they cover it with whitewash, *d* 11 therefore tell those who cover it with whitewash that it is going to fall. Rain will come in torrents, and I will send hailstones hurtling down, and violent winds will burst forth. *e* 12 When the wall collapses, will people not ask you, "Where is the whitewash you covered it with?"

13 " 'Therefore this is what the Sovereign LORD says: In my wrath I will unleash a violent wind, and in my anger hailstones *f* and torrents of rain will fall with destructive fury. *g* 14 I will tear down the wall you have covered with whitewash and will level it to the ground so that its foundation *h* will be laid bare. When it *a* falls, *i* you will be destroyed in it; and you will know that I am the LORD. 15 So I will spend my wrath against the wall and against those who covered it with whitewash. I will say to you, "The wall is gone and so are those who whitewashed it, 16 those prophets of Israel who prophesied to Jerusalem and saw visions of peace for her when there was no peace, declares the Sovereign LORD. *j* "

17 "Now, son of man, set your face against the daughters *k* of your people who prophesy out of their own imagination. Prophesy against them *l* 18 and say, 'This is what the Sovereign LORD says: Woe to the women who sew magic charms on all their wrists and make veils of various lengths for their heads in order to ensnare people. Will you ensnare the lives of my people but preserve your own? 19 You have profaned *m* me among my people for a few handfuls of barley and scraps of bread. By lying to my people, who listen to lies, you have killed those who should not have died and have spared those who should not live. *n*

20 " 'Therefore this is what the Sovereign LORD says: I am against your magic charms with which you ensnare people like birds and I will tear them from your arms; I will set free the people that you ensnare like birds. 21 I will tear off your veils and save my people from your hands, and they will no longer fall prey to your power. Then you will know that I am the LORD. *o* 22 Because you disheartened the righteous with your lies, when I had brought them no grief, and because you encouraged the wicked not to turn from their evil ways and so save their lives, *p* 23 therefore you will no longer see false visions or practice divination. *q* I will save my people from your hands. And then you will know that I am the LORD. *r* "

Idolaters Condemned

14 Some of the elders of Israel came to me and sat down in front of me. *s* 2 Then the word of the LORD came to me: 3 "Son of man, these men have set up idols in their hearts and put wicked stumbling blocks *t* before their faces. Should I let them inquire of me at all? *u* 4 Therefore speak to them and tell them, 'This is what

a 14 Or *the city*

We who possess the completed Scriptures have an advantage: Our fellow church members can test our words against a fail-safe measuring rod. We are to test all claims by the standard of God's Word, but our interpretation isn't perfect (Acts 17:11). We are wise to exercise cautious humility when it comes to identifying "false prophets," to be willing to enter into patient dialogue, seeking to grow in mutual understanding of how the Word applies.

Contrary to the prophetesses' actions here, Scripture specifies that the godly aren't to pursue "dishonest gain" (1 Tim. 3:8). Yet how often do Christians engage in or support businesses that devalue people? What is your

stance, for example, on playing the lottery, buying items manufactured with off-shore child labor, or investing in corporations that produce offensive entertainment?

Ezekiel 14:1–11

The "elders," the heads of exiled families, came to Ezekiel seeking an encouraging word from the Lord. They were met instead with a stinging accusation. These leaders, along with the rest of the exiles, were tainted with the same fundamental sin as those left behind in Judah: idolatry. They may not have given in to the flagrant idolatry going on in Jerusalem, but their hearts were divided. And as idolaters, they were destined to be cut off from God's covenant people.

the Sovereign LORD says: When any Israelite sets up idols in his heart and puts a wicked stumbling block before his face and then goes to a prophet, I the LORD will answer him myself in keeping with his great idolatry. ⁵I will do this to recapture the hearts of the people of Israel, who have all deserted ᵛ me for their idols.' ʷ

⁶"Therefore say to the house of Israel, 'This is what the Sovereign LORD says: Repent! Turn from your idols and renounce all your detestable practices! ˣ

⁷"'When any Israelite or any alien ʸ living in Israel separates himself from me and sets up idols in his heart and puts a wicked stumbling block before his face and then goes to a prophet to inquire of me, I the LORD will answer him myself. ⁸I will set my face against ᶻ that man and make him an example and a byword. ᵃ I will cut him off from my people. Then you will know that I am the LORD.

⁹"'And if the prophet ᵇ is enticed ᶜ to utter a prophecy, I the LORD have enticed that prophet, and I will stretch out my hand against him and destroy him from among my people Israel. ᵈ ¹⁰They will bear their guilt—the prophet will be as guilty as the one who consults him. ¹¹Then the people of Israel will no longer stray ᵉ from me, nor will they defile themselves anymore with all their sins. They will be my people, and I will be their God, declares the Sovereign LORD.' ᶠ "

Judgment Inescapable

¹²The word of the LORD came to me: ¹³"Son of man, if a country sins against me by being unfaithful and I stretch out my hand against it to cut off its food supply ᵍ and send famine upon it and kill its men and their animals, ʰ ¹⁴even if these three men—Noah, ⁱ Daniel ᵃʲ and Job ᵏ—were in it, they could save only themselves by their righteousness, ˡ declares the Sovereign LORD.

¹⁵"Or if I send wild beasts ᵐ through that country and they leave it childless and it becomes desolate so that no one can pass through it because of the beasts, ⁿ ¹⁶as surely as I live, declares the Sovereign LORD, even if these three men were in it, they could not save their own sons or daughters. They alone would be saved, but the land would be desolate. ᵒ

¹⁷"Or if I bring a sword ᵖ against that country and say, 'Let the sword pass throughout the land,' and I kill its men and their animals, ᵠ ¹⁸as surely as I live, declares the Sovereign LORD, even if these three men were in it, they could not save their own sons or daughters. They alone would be saved.

¹⁹"Or if I send a plague into that land and pour out my wrath ʳ upon it through bloodshed, killing its men and their animals, ˢ ²⁰as surely as I live, declares the Sovereign LORD, even if Noah, Daniel and Job were in it, they could save neither son nor daughter. They would save only themselves by their righteousness. ᵗ

ᵃ 14 Or *Danel*; the Hebrew spelling may suggest a person other than the prophet Daniel; also in verse 20.

14:5
v Zec 11:8
w Jer 2:11

14:6
x Isa 2:20; 30:22
14:7
y Ex 12:48; 20:10

14:8
z Eze 15:7
a Eze 5:15
14:9
b Jer 14:15
c Jer 4:10
d 1Ki 22:23

14:11
e Eze 48:11
f Eze 11:19-20; 37:23

14:13
g Lev 26:26
h Eze 5:16; 6:14; 15:8
14:14
i Ge 6:8 j ver 20; Eze 28:3; Da 1:6; 6:13 k Job 1:1
l Job 42:9; Jer 15:1; Eze 18:20
14:15
m Eze 5:17
n Lev 26:22
14:16
o Eze 18:20
14:17
p Lev 26:25; Eze 5:12; 21:3-4
q Eze 25:13; Zep 1:3

14:19
r Eze 7:8
s Eze 38:22

14:20
t ver 14

Yet this prophecy ended on a positive note. The result of God's purifying judgment would be a faithful and undefiled people. The goal of the covenant—God dwelling in the midst of his people—wouldn't be thwarted, not even by Israel's sin.

📖 Due to our sinful natures, we all have deep-seated idolatries—desires for something other than God as the motivating force and source of meaning in our lives. This is the sin behind every sin, the life-lie that drives so many of our choices and values. The only way to deal with our idols is to come to God in repentance, finding refuge in him alone. Do you, with Ezekiel, look forward to the day when your idols will be forever smashed, to the moment when you can worship and serve God with an undivided heart (cf. 11:18–20; Rev. 21:3–4)?

Ezekiel 14:12–23

📖 This prophecy focused on the inevitability and

justice of God's decision to destroy Jerusalem. Some people would survive the catastrophe—although they would be "brought out" of the city as prisoners of war. Their survival wouldn't be due to their own righteousness or to that of godly relatives. God's purpose in sparing this group would be to "console" those already in exile by allowing them to see the extent of Jerusalem's corruption. When they saw their recently exiled fellow Israelites' sinful behavior, they would realize God hadn't acted without cause.

📖 People often start from the assumption that we are basically good and wonder how bad things can happen to us. The Bible is clear, though, that we are all sinners (Rom. 3:23). When we experience genuine guilt over our actions, our eyes are opened to our real standing in God's sight. Are you more astonished by the bad things that happen to good people or by the good things that happen to bad people? God's kindness to sinners is the mysterious side of his providence.

14:21
u Jer 15:3;
Eze 5:17; 33:27;
Am 4:6-10; Rev 6:8
14:22
v Eze 12:16
w Eze 20:43
14:23
x Jer 22:8-9

21 "For this is what the Sovereign LORD says: How much worse will it be when I send against Jerusalem my four dreadful judgments—sword and famine and wild beasts and plague—to kill its men and their animals! *u* 22Yet there will be some survivors—sons and daughters who will be brought out of it. *v* They will come to you, and when you see their conduct *w* and their actions, you will be consoled regarding the disaster I have brought upon Jerusalem—every disaster I have brought upon it. 23You will be consoled when you see their conduct and their actions, for you will know that I have done nothing in it without cause, declares the Sovereign LORD. *x*"

Jerusalem, A Useless Vine

15:2
y Isa 5:1-7;
Jer 2:21; Hos 10:1

15:4
z Eze 19:14; Jn 15:6

15 The word of the LORD came to me: 2"Son of man, how is the wood of a vine *y* better than that of a branch on any of the trees in the forest? 3Is wood ever taken from it to make anything useful? Do they make pegs from it to hang things on? 4And after it is thrown on the fire as fuel and the fire burns both ends and chars the middle, is it then useful for anything? *z* 5If it was not useful for anything when it was whole, how much less can it be made into something useful when the fire has burned it and it is charred?

15:7
a Ps 34:16;
Eze 14:8
b Isa 24:18;
Am 9:1-4
15:8
c Eze 14:13
d Eze 17:20

6"Therefore this is what the Sovereign LORD says: As I have given the wood of the vine among the trees of the forest as fuel for the fire, so will I treat the people living in Jerusalem. 7I will set my face against *a* them. Although they have come out of the fire, the fire will yet consume them. And when I set my face against them, you will know that I am the LORD. *b* 8I will make the land desolate *c* because they have been unfaithful, *d* declares the Sovereign LORD."

An Allegory of Unfaithful Jerusalem

16:2
e Eze 20:4; 22:2
16:3
f Eze 21:30 *g* ver 45
16:4
h Hos 2:3

16 The word of the LORD came to me: 2"Son of man, confront Jerusalem with her detestable practices *e* 3and say, 'This is what the Sovereign LORD says to Jerusalem: Your ancestry *f* and birth were in the land of the Canaanites; your father was an Amorite and your mother a Hittite. *g* 4On the day you were born *h* your cord was not cut, nor were you washed with water to make you clean, nor were you rubbed with salt or wrapped in cloths. 5No one looked on you with pity or had compassion enough to do any of these things for you. Rather, you were thrown out into the open field, for on the day you were born you were despised.

16:6
i Ex 19:4
16:7
j Dt 1:10

6" 'Then I passed by and saw you kicking about in your blood, and as you lay there in your blood I said to you, "Live!" *a* *i* 7I made you grow *j* like a plant of the

---

a 6 A few Hebrew manuscripts, Septuagint and Syriac; most Hebrew manuscripts *"Live!" And as you lay there in your blood I said to you, "Live!"*

Ezekiel 15:1–8

Jerusalem was like a pruning cut from a vine—thrown into the fire as useless. Sadly, the first "burning," the initial defeat of Judah in 597 B.C. and the first exile, hadn't achieved for God's people a redemptive purpose. Back into the fire they would go, because they were fit for nothing else—and this time the destruction would be complete.

Ezekiel's message invited the question, If those remaining in the land were the prunings, was there still a true vine, a real Israel, somewhere else? This fits with his insistence in chapter 11 that God's presence was no longer in Jerusalem. Those people left in the land were the part destined for burning (11:7–12). God's chosen remnant existed among the exiles (11:16).

Why is suffering redemptive for one person while for another it merely foreshadows the judgment to come? Jesus is the true vine that God tends—the true Israel (John 15:1). To be "in [him]" is to be part of the true, fruit-bearing Israel (v. 4). To be apart from him, on the other hand, is

to be worthless, fit only to be burned (vv. 5–6). Freedom from suffering *isn't* the expected result of remaining on the vine: Fruitful branches are "pruned," while fruitless ones are thrown into the fire (vv. 2,6). Suffering is part of every life, but for the Christian it's a "fruitful" part of life, producing "a harvest of righteousness and peace" (Heb. 12:11).

Ezekiel 16:1–63

This graphic allegory about Jerusalem starts by depicting the city's dubious origins. Long before the Israelites had entered Canaan, Jerusalem had been founded by Amorites and Hittites. God had seen and cared for her when she was weak. Later he had "married" her, when David had captured Jerusalem and it had become Israel's capital city. But though God had provided for her richly, she had turned to false gods to meet her needs and allied herself with other nations for security.

Jerusalem's behavior descended to still deeper depths. A typical prostitute was motivated by financial need, but in this case *she* was doing the paying. The consequence of Jerusalem's adulterous lifestyle would be an

field. You grew up and developed and became the most beautiful of jewels.[a] Your
breasts were formed and your hair grew, you who were naked and bare.[k]
8 " 'Later I passed by, and when I looked at you and saw that you were old enough
for love, I spread the corner of my garment[l] over you and covered your nakedness.
I gave you my solemn oath and entered into a covenant with you, declares the Sovereign LORD, and you became mine.[m]
9 " 'I bathed[b] you with water and washed[n] the blood from you and put ointments
on you. 10 I clothed you with an embroidered[o] dress and put leather sandals on you.
I dressed you in fine linen[p] and covered you with costly garments.[q] 11 I adorned you
with jewelry:[r] I put bracelets[s] on your arms and a necklace[t] around your neck,
12 and I put a ring on your nose,[u] earrings on your ears and a beautiful crown[v] on
your head. 13 So you were adorned with gold and silver; your clothes were of fine
linen and costly fabric and embroidered cloth. Your food was fine flour, honey and
olive oil.[w] You became very beautiful and rose to be a queen.[x] 14 And your fame[y]
spread among the nations on account of your beauty,[z] because the splendor I had
given you made your beauty perfect, declares the Sovereign LORD.
15 " 'But you trusted in your beauty and used your fame to become a prostitute.
You lavished your favors on anyone who passed by[a] and your beauty became his.[c][b]
16 You took some of your garments to make gaudy high places, where you carried
on your prostitution.[c] Such things should not happen, nor should they ever occur.
17 You also took the fine jewelry I gave you, the jewelry made of my gold and silver,
and you made for yourself male idols and engaged in prostitution with them.[d]
18 And you took your embroidered clothes to put on them, and you offered my oil
and incense before them. 19 Also the food I provided for you—the fine flour, olive
oil and honey I gave you to eat—you offered as fragrant incense before them. That
is what happened, declares the Sovereign LORD.[e]
20 " 'And you took your sons and daughters[f] whom you bore to me[g] and sacrificed
them as food to the idols. Was your prostitution not enough?[h] 21 You slaughtered
my children and sacrificed them[d] to the idols.[i] 22 In all your detestable practices and
your prostitution you did not remember the days of your youth,[j] when you were
naked and bare, kicking about in your blood.[k]
23 " 'Woe! Woe to you, declares the Sovereign LORD. In addition to all your other
wickedness, 24 you built a mound for yourself and made a lofty shrine[l] in every public square.[m] 25 At the head of every street you built your lofty shrines and degraded your
beauty, offering your body with increasing promiscuity to anyone who passed by.[n]
26 You engaged in prostitution with the Egyptians, your lustful neighbors, and provoked[o] me to anger with your increasing promiscuity.[p] 27 So I stretched out my hand[q]
against you and reduced your territory; I gave you over to the greed of your enemies,
the daughters of the Philistines,[r] who were shocked by your lewd conduct. 28 You engaged in prostitution with the Assyrians[s] too, because you were insatiable; and even
after that, you still were not satisfied. 29 Then you increased your promiscuity to include
Babylonia,[e][t] a land of merchants, but even with this you were not satisfied.

16:7 [k] Ex 1:7
16:8 [l] Ru 3:9 [m] Jer 2:2; Hos 2:7,19-20
16:9 [n] Ru 3:3
16:10 [o] Ex 26:36 [p] Eze 27:16 [q] ver 18
16:11 [r] Eze 23:40 [s] Isa 3:19; Eze 23:42 [t] Ge 41:42
16:12 [u] Isa 3:21 [v] Isa 28:5; Jer 13:18
16:13 [w] 1Sa 10:1 [x] Dt 32:13-14; 1Ki 4:21
16:14 [y] 1Ki 10:24 [z] La 2:15
16:15 [a] ver 25 [b] Isa 57:8; Jer 2:20; Eze 23:3; 27:3
16:16 [c] 2Ki 23:7
16:17 [d] Eze 7:20
16:19 [e] Hos 2:8
16:20 [f] Jer 7:31 [g] Ex 13:2 [h] Ps 106:37-38; Isa 57:5; Eze 23:37
16:21 [i] 2Ki 17:17; Jer 19:5
16:22 [j] Jer 2:2; Hos 11:1 [k] ver 6
16:24 [l] ver 31; Isa 57:7 [m] Ps 78:58; Jer 2:20; 3:2; Eze 20:28
16:25 [n] ver 15; Pr 9:14
16:26 [o] Eze 8:17 [p] Eze 20:8; 23:19-21
16:27 [q] Eze 20:33 [r] 2Ch 28:18
16:28 [s] 2Ki 16:7
16:29 [t] Eze 23:14-17

[a] 7 Or *became mature* [b] 9 Or *I had bathed* [c] 15 Most Hebrew manuscripts; one Hebrew manuscript (see some Septuagint manuscripts) *by. Such a thing should not happen* [d] 21 Or *and made them pass through* ⌊*the fire*⌋ [e] 29 Or *Chaldea*

adulteress's death. Yet judgment wouldn't be God's last word: He would renew his covenant with her. In doing so, he would create in her the two qualities so lacking at present: memory and shame.

When did you last hear a sermon on this chapter? Ezekiel 16 calls us, like it or not, to face sin in all its ugliness. Fire and brimstone sermons that focus on hell and God's wrath can seriously misrepresent the true God, but so does a constant diet of polite sermons that mention only heaven and God's love. Sin—like the cross—is ugly and offensive, and people need to hear that side of the Christian message too.

The realization of the price of restoration stirs in our hearts remembrance and shame (see v. 63). Perhaps we, like the Corinthians, were once sexually immoral, idolaters, thieves, greedy, drunkards, slanderers, or swindlers (1 Cor. 6:9–10). Or we were none of the above and proud of it, like the Pharisee who congratulated himself on being better than the tax collector (Luke 18:11). No matter what our specific sins (and sin is sin!), let's never forget what we once were (1 Cor. 6:11)—because that is the true measure of the greatness of God's work in our lives.

16:30
u Jer 3:3
16:31
v ver 24

16:33
w Isa 30:6; 57:9
x Hos 8:9-10

16:36
y Jer 19:5;
Eze 23:10

16:37
z Jer 13:22
16:38
a Eze 23:45
b Lev 20:10;
Eze 23:25

16:39
c Eze 23:26;
Hos 2:3
16:40
d Jn 8:5,7
16:41
e Dt 13:16
f Eze 23:10
g Eze 23:27,48
16:42
h Isa 54:9;
Eze 5:13; 39:29
16:43
i Ps 78:42
j Eze 22:31
k ver 22; Eze 11:21

16:45
l Eze 23:2

16:46
m Ge 13:10-13;
Eze 23:4
16:47
n 2Ki 21:9; Eze 5:7
16:48
o Mt 10:15;
11:23-24
16:49
p Ge 13:13
q Ps 138:6
r Eze 18:7,12,16;
Lk 12:16-20
16:50
s Ge 18:20-21; 19:5

16:51
t Jer 3:8-11

16:53
u Isa 19:24-25

16:54
v Jer 2:26;
Eze 14:22

16:55
w Mal 3:4

30 " 'How weak-willed you are, declares the Sovereign LORD, when you do all these things, acting like a brazen prostitute! *u* 31 When you built your mounds at the head of every street and made your lofty shrines *v* in every public square, you were unlike a prostitute, because you scorned payment.

32 " 'You adulterous wife! You prefer strangers to your own husband! 33 Every prostitute receives a fee, but you give gifts *w* to all your lovers, bribing them to come to you from everywhere for your illicit favors. *x* 34 So in your prostitution you are the opposite of others; no one runs after you for your favors. You are the very opposite, for you give payment and none is given to you.

35 " 'Therefore, you prostitute, hear the word of the LORD! 36 This is what the Sovereign LORD says: Because you poured out your wealth *a* and exposed your nakedness in your promiscuity with your lovers, and because of all your detestable idols, and because you gave them your children's blood, *y* 37 therefore I am going to gather all your lovers, with whom you found pleasure, those you loved as well as those you hated. I will gather them against you from all around and will strip you in front of them, and they will see all your nakedness. *z* 38 I will sentence you to the punishment of women who commit adultery and who shed blood; *a* I will bring upon you the blood vengeance of my wrath and jealous anger. *b* 39 Then I will hand you over to your lovers, and they will tear down your mounds and destroy your lofty shrines. They will strip you of your clothes and take your fine jewelry and leave you naked and bare. *c* 40 They will bring a mob against you, who will stone *d* you and hack you to pieces with their swords. 41 They will burn down *e* your houses and inflict punishment on you in the sight of many women. *f* I will put a stop *g* to your prostitution, and you will no longer pay your lovers. 42 Then my wrath against you will subside and my jealous anger will turn away from you; I will be calm and no longer angry. *h*

43 " 'Because you did not remember *i* the days of your youth but enraged me with all these things, I will surely bring down *j* on your head what you have done, declares the Sovereign LORD. Did you not add lewdness to all your other detestable practices? *k*

44 " 'Everyone who quotes proverbs will quote this proverb about you: "Like mother, like daughter." 45 You are a true daughter of your mother, who despised her husband and her children; and you are a true sister of your sisters, who despised their husbands and their children. Your mother was a Hittite and your father an Amorite. *l* 46 Your older sister was Samaria, who lived to the north of you with her daughters; and your younger sister, who lived to the south of you with her daughters, was Sodom. *m* 47 You not only walked in their ways and copied their detestable practices, but in all your ways you soon became more depraved than they. *n* 48 As surely as I live, declares the Sovereign LORD, your sister Sodom and her daughters never did what you and your daughters have done. *o*

49 " 'Now this was the sin of your sister Sodom: *p* She and her daughters were arrogant, *q* overfed and unconcerned; they did not help the poor and needy. *r* 50 They were haughty and did detestable things before me. Therefore I did away with them as you have seen. *s* 51 Samaria did not commit half the sins you did. You have done more detestable things than they, and have made your sisters seem righteous by all these things you have done. *t* 52 Bear your disgrace, for you have furnished some justification for your sisters. Because your sins were more vile than theirs, they appear more righteous than you. So then, be ashamed and bear your disgrace, for you have made your sisters appear righteous.

53 " 'However, I will restore *u* the fortunes of Sodom and her daughters and of Samaria and her daughters, and your fortunes along with them, 54 so that you may bear your disgrace *v* and be ashamed of all you have done in giving them comfort. 55 And your sisters, Sodom with her daughters and Samaria with her daughters, will return to what they were before; and you and your daughters will return to what you were before. *w* 56 You would not even mention your sister Sodom in the day of your pride, 57 before your wickedness was uncovered. Even so, you are now scorned by

a 36 Or *lust*

the daughters of Edom [a][x] and all her neighbors and the daughters of the Philistines—all those around you who despise you. [58] You will bear the consequences of your lewdness and your detestable practices, declares the LORD. [y]

[59] "'This is what the Sovereign LORD says: I will deal with you as you deserve, because you have despised my oath by breaking the covenant. [z] [60] Yet I will remember the covenant I made with you in the days of your youth, and I will establish an everlasting covenant [a] with you. [61] Then you will remember your ways and be ashamed [b] when you receive your sisters, both those who are older than you and those who are younger. I will give them to you as daughters, but not on the basis of my covenant with you. [62] So I will establish my covenant with you, and you will know that I am the LORD. [c] [63] Then, when I make atonement [d] for you for all you have done, you will remember and be ashamed and never again open your mouth [e] because of your humiliation, declares the Sovereign LORD. [f] '"

Two Eagles and a Vine

17 The word of the LORD came to me: [2] "Son of man, set forth an allegory and tell the house of Israel a parable. [g] [3] Say to them, 'This is what the Sovereign LORD says: A great eagle [h] with powerful wings, long feathers and full plumage of varied colors came to Lebanon. [i] Taking hold of the top of a cedar, [4] he broke off its topmost shoot and carried it away to a land of merchants, where he planted it in a city of traders.

[5] "'He took some of the seed of your land and put it in fertile soil. He planted it like a willow by abundant water, [j] [6] and it sprouted and became a low, spreading vine. Its branches turned toward him, but its roots remained under it. So it became a vine and produced branches and put out leafy boughs.

[7] "'But there was another great eagle with powerful wings and full plumage. The vine now sent out its roots toward him from the plot where it was planted and stretched out its branches to him for water. [k] [8] It had been planted in good soil by abundant water so that it would produce branches, bear fruit and become a splendid vine.'

[9] "Say to them, 'This is what the Sovereign LORD says: Will it thrive? Will it not be uprooted and stripped of its fruit so that it withers? All its new growth will wither. It will not take a strong arm or many people to pull it up by the roots. [10] Even if it [l] is transplanted, will it thrive? Will it not wither completely when the east wind strikes it—wither away in the plot where it grew?' "

[11] Then the word of the LORD came to me: [12] "Say to this rebellious house, 'Do you not know what these things mean? [m] ' Say to them: 'The king of Babylon went to Jerusalem and carried off her king and her nobles, [n] bringing them back with him to Babylon. [o] [13] Then he took a member of the royal family and made a treaty with him, putting him under oath. [p] He also carried away the leading men of the land, [14] so that the kingdom would be brought low, [q] unable to rise again, surviving only

---

[a] 57 Many Hebrew manuscripts and Syriac; most Hebrew manuscripts, Septuagint and Vulgate *Aram*

Cross references (margin)

16:57 [x] 2Ki 16:6
16:58 [y] Eze 23:49
16:59 [z] Eze 17:19
16:60 [a] Jer 32:40; Eze 37:26
16:61 [b] Eze 20:43
16:62 [c] Jer 24:7; Eze 20:37,43-44; Hos 2:19-20
16:63 [d] Ps 65:3; 79:9 [e] Ro 3:19 [f] Ps 39:9; Da 9:7-8
17:2 [g] Eze 20:49
17:3 [h] Hos 8:1 [i] Jer 22:23
17:5 [j] Dt 8:7-9; Isa 44:4
17:7 [k] Eze 31:4
17:10 [l] Hos 13:15
17:12 [m] Eze 12:9 [n] 2Ki 24:15 [o] Eze 24:19
17:13 [p] 2Ch 36:13
17:14 [q] Eze 29:14

Ezekiel 17:1–24

God gave Ezekiel a detailed parable followed by an interpretation. The first eagle was Nebuchadnezzar, king of Babylon. He came to "Lebanon" (Jerusalem) and carried off King Jehoiachin, along with the exiles that included Ezekiel. Nebuchadnezzar replaced Jehoiachin with Zedekiah, the "seed" of verse 5. The second eagle was Egypt's pharaoh. Zedekiah foolishly sought help from a lesser power against the dominant superpower.

Not only did Zedekiah break the oath of loyalty he had made to Nebuchadnezzar in God's name, his rebellion against his covenant overlord represented Israel's rebellion against God himself. The end of the chapter reworks the symbols in an unexpected but exciting way. A new shoot (a Davidic king) would grow into a lofty tree,

and all the trees of the field (the nations) would recognize God's sovereignty. The fulfillment of this prophecy is found in Jesus Christ and his kingdom (cf. Mark 4:30–32).

Like Zedekiah, we tend to think the problems in our world are essentially political. We pour our energy into campaigns and boycotts or, on a personal level, into gathering information necessary for informed decision making. Yet we can be so busy doing these good things that we miss out on the one essential: maintaining our spiritual life with God (Matt. 16:26). How many people have planned for every unforeseen event, yet ignored their coming great encounter with God (Rev. 20:11–12)? How "long-range" is your planning?

Side notes (cross-references):

17:15
r Jer 52:3
s Dt 17:16
t Jer 34:3; 38:18
17:16
u Jer 52:11;
Eze 12:13
v 2Ki 24:17
17:17
w Jer 37:7 × Eze 4:2
y Isa 36:6; Jer 37:5;
Eze 29:6-7
17:18
z 1Ch 29:24
17:19
a Eze 16:59
17:20
b Eze 12:13; 32:3
c Jer 2:35;
Eze 20:36
17:21
d Eze 12:14
e 2Ki 25:11
f 2Ki 25:5
17:22
g Jer 23:5;
Eze 20:40; 36:1,36;
37:22
17:23
h Ps 92:12; Isa 2:2;
Eze 31:6; Da 4:12;
Hos 14:5-7;
Mt 13:32
17:24
i Ps 96:12
j Eze 19:12; 21:26;
22:14; Am 9:11
18:2
k Isa 3:15;
Jer 31:29; La 5:7
18:4
l ver 20; Isa 42:5;
Ro 6:23
18:6
m Eze 22:9
n Dt 4:19; Eze 6:13;
20:24
18:7
o Ex 22:21
p Ex 22:26;
Dt 24:12
q Dt 15:11;
Mt 25:36

---

by keeping his treaty. 15But the king rebelled r against him by sending his envoys to Egypt to get horses and a large army. s Will he succeed? Will he who does such things escape? Will he break the treaty and yet escape? t

16 " 'As surely as I live, declares the Sovereign LORD, he shall die u in Babylon, in the land of the king who put him on the throne, whose oath he despised and whose treaty he broke. v 17Pharaoh w with his mighty army and great horde will be of no help to him in war, when ramps x are built and siege works erected to destroy many lives. y 18He despised the oath by breaking the covenant. Because he had given his hand in pledge z and yet did all these things, he shall not escape.

19 " 'Therefore this is what the Sovereign LORD says: As surely as I live, I will bring down on his head my oath that he despised and my covenant that he broke. a 20I will spread my net b for him, and he will be caught in my snare. I will bring him to Babylon and execute judgment c upon him there because he was unfaithful to me. 21All his fleeing troops will fall by the sword, d and the survivors e will be scattered to the winds. f Then you will know that I the LORD have spoken.

22 " 'This is what the Sovereign LORD says: I myself will take a shoot from the very top of a cedar and plant it; I will break off a tender sprig from its topmost shoots and plant it on a high and lofty mountain. g 23On the mountain heights of Israel I will plant it; it will produce branches and bear fruit and become a splendid cedar. Birds of every kind will nest in it; they will find shelter in the shade of its branches. h 24All the trees of the field i will know that I the LORD bring down the tall tree and make the low tree grow tall. I dry up the green tree and make the dry tree flourish.

" 'I the LORD have spoken, and I will do it.' "

The Soul Who Sins Will Die

18 The word of the LORD came to me: 2"What do you people mean by quoting this proverb about the land of Israel:

" 'The fathers eat sour grapes,
and the children's teeth are set on edge'? k

3"As surely as I live, declares the Sovereign LORD, you will no longer quote this proverb in Israel. 4For every living soul belongs to me, the father as well as the son—both alike belong to me. The soul who sins is the one who will die. l

5"Suppose there is a righteous man
who does what is just and right.
6He does not eat at the mountain m shrines
or look to the idols n of the house of Israel.
He does not defile his neighbor's wife
or lie with a woman during her period.
7He does not oppress o anyone,
but returns what he took in pledge p for a loan.
He does not commit robbery
but gives his food to the hungry
and provides clothing for the naked. q
8He does not lend at usury

Ezekiel 18:1–32

The word of the Lord responded to the people's own proverb (cf. Jer. 31:29–30). Sometimes children do suffer because of their parents' actions. But the Israelites of Ezekiel's day misapplied the proverb to mean "Our fathers sinned, but we are paying the price; that is the way it is, and nothing can be done about it." God categorically denied this application—countering with "The soul who sins is the one who will die."

God wanted, through Ezekiel, to do more than demonstrate that he was just in condemning his people to death. In spite of everything we do, God remains "pro-life." Even when the lives in question are those of rebels, God wants them to turn and live (v. 23). Ezekiel pressed on relentlessly from the abstract "Where does suffering come from?" to the intensely personal "What is your relationship to God?" Isn't this still the question of the hour? Have you grappled with it and come away grounded, centered, and secure?

or take excessive interest. [a][r]
He withholds his hand from doing wrong
and judges fairly[s] between man and man.
⁹ He follows my decrees
and faithfully keeps my laws.
That man is righteous;[t]
he will surely live,[u]

declares the Sovereign LORD.

18:8
r Ex 22:25;
Lev 25:35-37;
Dt 23:19-20
s Zec 8:16

18:9
t Hab 2:4
u Lev 18:5;
Eze 20:11; Am 5:4

¹⁰ "Suppose he has a violent son, who sheds blood[v] or does any of these other things[b] ¹¹ (though the father has done none of them):

"He eats at the mountain shrines.
He defiles his neighbor's wife.
¹² He oppresses the poor[w] and needy.
He commits robbery.
He does not return what he took in pledge.
He looks to the idols.
He does detestable things.[x]
¹³ He lends at usury and takes excessive interest.[y]

18:10
v Ex 21:12

18:12
w Am 4:1
x 2Ki 21:11;
Isa 59:6-7;
Jer 22:17;
Eze 8:6,17

18:13
y Ex 22:25
z Eze 33:4-5

Will such a man live? He will not! Because he has done all these detestable things, he will surely be put to death and his blood will be on his own head.[z]

¹⁴ "But suppose this son has a son who sees all the sins his father commits, and though he sees them, he does not do such things:[a]

18:14
a 2Ch 34:21;
Pr 23:24

¹⁵ "He does not eat at the mountain shrines
or look to the idols of the house of Israel.
He does not defile his neighbor's wife.
¹⁶ He does not oppress anyone
or require a pledge for a loan.
He does not commit robbery
but gives his food to the hungry
and provides clothing for the naked.[b]
¹⁷ He withholds his hand from sin[c]
and takes no usury or excessive interest.
He keeps my laws and follows my decrees.

18:16
b Ps 41:1; Isa 58:10

He will not die for his father's sin; he will surely live. ¹⁸ But his father will die for his own sin, because he practiced extortion, robbed his brother and did what was wrong among his people.

¹⁹ "Yet you ask, 'Why does the son not share the guilt of his father?' Since the son has done what is just and right and has been careful to keep all my decrees, he will surely live.[c] ²⁰ The soul who sins is the one who will die. The son will not share the guilt of the father, nor will the father share the guilt of the son. The righteousness of the righteous man will be credited to him, and the wickedness of the wicked will be charged against him.[d]

²¹ "But if a wicked man turns away from all the sins he has committed and keeps all my decrees and does what is just and right, he will surely live; he will not die.[e] ²² None of the offenses he has committed will be remembered against him. Because of the righteous things he has done, he will live.[f] ²³ Do I take any pleasure in the death of the wicked? declares the Sovereign LORD. Rather, am I not pleased[g] when they turn from their ways and live?[h]

²⁴ "But if a righteous man turns from his righteousness and commits sin and does the same detestable things the wicked man does, will he live? None of the righteous things he has done will be remembered. Because of the unfaithfulness he is guilty of and because of the sins he has committed, he will die.[i]

18:19
c Ex 20:5; Dt 5:9;
Jer 15:4; Zec 1:3-6

18:20
d Dt 24:16;
1Ki 8:32; 2Ki 14:6;
Isa 3:11; Mt 16:27;
Ro 2:9
18:21
e Eze 33:12,19
18:22
f Ps 18:20-24;
Isa 43:25; Mic 7:19
18:23
g Ps 147:11
h Eze 33:11; 1Ti 2:4

18:24
i 1Sa 15:11;
2Ch 24:17-20;
Eze 3:20; 20:27;
2Pe 2:20-22

---

[a] 8 Or take interest; similarly in verses 13 and 17   [b] 10 Or things to a brother   [c] 17 Septuagint (see also verse 8); Hebrew from the poor

The Poor and the Lost

In God's world . . .
- A very large proportion of those who haven't heard the gospel are also poor.
- Eighty-five percent of the world's poorest countries lie within the unevangelized world.
- "With the demise of Marxism and communism, there is no global ideology which places the poor at the center of its vision for a better human future."

LESS NEED FOR THE GOSPEL ◀ | ▶ **MORE NEED FOR THE GOSPEL**

(Vertical axis: POORER at top → RICHER at bottom)

		Chad		Guinea / Burkina Faso / Afghanistan / Sierra Leone/Niger/Mali / Gambia / Somalia / Guinea-Bissau / Bhutan / Mauritania
	CAR / Malawi	Ethiopia / Eritrea	Mozambique / Benin	Sudan	Nepal / Cambodia
Angola / Uganda / Rwanda / Burundi		Tanzania	Togo / Liberia		Bangladesh / Yemen / Senegal
	Zaire / Zambia	Nigeria	Haiti		
				Cote d'Ivoire	India
					Laos
		Ghana / Madagascar			Pakistan
Papua New Guinea	Namibia / Kenya				Myanmar
	Lesotho	Cameroon / Congo / Zimbabwe			
		Swaziland / Gabon / El Salvador	Honduras	Bolivia / Egypt	Vietnam / Morocco / Algeria
		Guatemala			
			Guyana / Nicaragua / Lebanon	Indonesia	West Bank / Mongolia/North Korea / Iraq
				Philippines	Jordan/Tadzhikstan
				Dominican Republic	China / Oman
	South Africa		Peru		
		Paraguay / Belize / Botswana	Suriname	Cuba / Uzbekistan	Sri Lanka / Iran
					Kyrgystan/Tunisia / Turkmenistan
		Moldavia	Ecuador	Albania	Azerbaijan / Syria / Saudi Arabia
	Romania / Jamaica		Georgia / Brazil	Kazakhstan / Mauritius	UAE
		Fiji			Malaysia / Thailand / Kuwait
		Armenia		Mexico / Venezuela	
Poland		Colombia / Ukraine	Bulgaria / Panama	Slovakia	Singapore
		Belarus / Chile	Portugal / Costa Rica		
	Lithuania	Trinidad & Tobago / Estonia	Russia / South Korea	Argentina	
Ireland				Uruguay	
	New Zealand		Latvia / Spain	Hungary / Cyprus	Greece/Hong Kong / Taiwan / Israel
		Austria / USA		Italy / Finland / Iceland / Belgium / Czech Republic / Germany / Netherlands / France / Norway / Canada	Denmark / UK / Australia / Sweden/Japan / Switzerland

Source: Myers (1996:17)

25 "Yet you say, 'The way of the Lord is not just.' Hear, O house of Israel: Is my way unjust?[j] Is it not your ways that are unjust? 26 If a righteous man turns from his righteousness and commits sin, he will die for it; because of the sin he has committed he will die. 27 But if a wicked man turns away from the wickedness he has committed and does what is just and right, he will save his life.[k] 28 Because he considers all the offenses he has committed and turns away from them, he will surely live; he will not die. 29 Yet the house of Israel says, 'The way of the Lord is not just.' Are my ways unjust, O house of Israel? Is it not your ways that are unjust?

30 "Therefore, O house of Israel, I will judge you, each one according to his ways, declares the Sovereign LORD. Repent![l] Turn away from all your offenses; then sin will not be your downfall.[m] 31 Rid yourselves of all the offenses you have committed, and get a new heart[n] and a new spirit. Why will you die, O house of Israel?[o] 32 For I take no pleasure in the death of anyone, declares the Sovereign LORD. Repent and live![p]

A Lament for Israel's Princes

19 "Take up a lament[q] concerning the princes[r] of Israel 2 and say:

" 'What a lioness was your mother
    among the lions!
She lay down among the young lions
    and reared her cubs.
3 She brought up one of her cubs,
    and he became a strong lion.
He learned to tear the prey
    and he devoured men.
4 The nations heard about him,
    and he was trapped in their pit.
They led him with hooks
    to the land of Egypt.[s]

5 " 'When she saw her hope unfulfilled,
    her expectation gone,
she took another of her cubs
    and made him a strong lion.[t]
6 He prowled among the lions,
    for he was now a strong lion.
He learned to tear the prey
    and he devoured men.[u]
7 He broke down[a] their strongholds
    and devastated[v] their towns.
The land and all who were in it
    were terrified by his roaring.
8 Then the nations[w] came against him,
    those from regions round about.

---

[a] 7 Targum (see Septuagint); Hebrew *He knew*

Reference column

18:25
j Ge 18:25;
Jer 12:1; Eze 33:17;
Zep 3:5; Mal 2:17;
3:13-15
18:27
k Isa 1:18

18:30
l Eze 7:3;
33:20; Hos 12:6
18:31
n Ps 51:10
o Isa 1:16-17;
Eze 11:19; 36:26
18:32
p Eze 33:11

19:1
q Eze 26:17;
27:2,32 *r* 2Ki 24:6

19:4
s 2Ki 23:33-34;
2Ch 36:4

19:5
t 2Ki 23:34

19:6
u 2Ki 24:9;
2Ch 36:9
19:7
v Eze 30:12

19:8
w 2Ki 24:2

Ezekiel 19:1–14

A funeral lament eulogized the virtues of the departed while grieving the tragic circumstances surrounding the death (cf. 2 Sam. 1:17–27). The prophets replaced the catalog of virtues with a list of faults and projected the tragic circumstances ahead to the future.

The fate of Judah's princes, ending with Zedekiah (see Ezek. 19:14), was sealed. The lions would be trapped, the vine chopped down from its lofty position and replanted in a desert land. The ruler's scepter was gone. Even though there was ultimate hope, as 17:22–24 makes clear, the present situation was one of unmitigated doom.

The genre of lament is unfamiliar to contemporary readers, especially in an American context. We like to believe in surprising comebacks, victory snatched from the jaws of defeat, and happy endings. If we have been sold a bill of goods that life is always wonderful, we may live in denial of its unpleasantness or blame ourselves for failing to measure up (if we were "*really* spiritual" life wouldn't be this way). The truth is that our present existence is frequently less than wonderful—and we as Christians shouldn't be surprised (see John 16:33; 2 Tim. 3:12).

They spread their net for him,
  and he was trapped in their pit. x
9 With hooks they pulled him into a cage
  and brought him to the king of Babylon. y
They put him in prison,
  so his roar was heard no longer
  on the mountains of Israel. z

10 " 'Your mother was like a vine in your vineyard a
  planted by the water;
it was fruitful and full of branches
  because of abundant water. a
11 Its branches were strong,
  fit for a ruler's scepter.
It towered high
  above the thick foliage,
conspicuous for its height
  and for its many branches. b
12 But it was uprooted c in fury
  and thrown to the ground.
The east wind made it shrivel,
  it was stripped of its fruit;
its strong branches withered
  and fire consumed them. d
13 Now it is planted in the desert, e
  in a dry and thirsty land. f
14 Fire spread from one of its main b branches
  and consumed g its fruit.
No strong branch is left on it
  fit for a ruler's scepter.' h

This is a lament and is to be used as a lament."

Rebellious Israel

20 In the seventh year, in the fifth month on the tenth day, some of the elders of Israel came to inquire of the LORD, and they sat down in front of me. i

2 Then the word of the LORD came to me: 3 "Son of man, speak to the elders of Israel and say to them, 'This is what the Sovereign LORD says: Have you come to inquire j of me? As surely as I live, I will not let you inquire of me, declares the Sovereign LORD. k'

4 "Will you judge them? Will you judge them, son of man? Then confront them with the detestable practices of their fathers l 5 and say to them: 'This is what the Sovereign LORD says: On the day I chose m Israel, I swore with uplifted hand to the descendants of the house of Jacob and revealed myself to them in Egypt. With uplifted hand I said to them, "I am the LORD your God. n" 6 On that day I swore to them

a 10 Two Hebrew manuscripts; most Hebrew manuscripts your blood   b 14 Or from under its

---

Ezekiel 20:1–29

The elders (see "There and Then" for 14:1–11) came to Ezekiel to "inquire of the LORD." Normally that would have been commendable. But seeking the Lord is, by definition, exclusive (the only way to seek God is to seek God only). Because the elders were involved in idolatrous practices, God wouldn't answer them. In fact, they may not have reached the point of making their request before being cut off.

Yet the interaction didn't end there. God had a message for the elders: He presented to them a history of Israel from his perspective—a history that focused not on cultural or political achievements but on their track record of idolatry.

People today often choose their religion based on what "works" for them. But "attending the church or synagogue of their choice" had led Ezekiel's original audience into idol worship. What matters isn't what we think of God but what he thinks of us. This flies in the face of our "enlightened" day and age, in which everything is tolerated except intolerance. Ezekiel had a word for this attitude, and it wasn't broad-mindedness: It was rebellion against the one true and living God.

that I would bring them out of Egypt into a land I had searched out for them, a land flowing with milk and honey, *o* the most beautiful of all lands. *p* 7And I said to them, "Each of you, get rid of the vile images *q* you have set your eyes on, and do not defile yourselves with the idols of Egypt. I am the LORD your God. *r*"

8" 'But they rebelled against me and would not listen to me; they did not get rid of the vile images they had set their eyes on, nor did they forsake the idols of Egypt. *s* So I said I would pour out my wrath on them and spend my anger against them in Egypt. *t* 9But for the sake of my name I did what would keep it from being profaned in the eyes of the nations they lived among and in whose sight I had revealed myself to the Israelites by bringing them out of Egypt. *u* 10Therefore I led them out of Egypt and brought them into the desert. *v* 11I gave them my decrees and made known to them my laws, for the man who obeys them will live by them. *w* 12Also I gave them my Sabbaths as a sign *x* between us, so they would know that I the LORD made them holy.

13" 'Yet the people of Israel rebelled *y* against me in the desert. They did not follow my decrees but rejected my laws—although the man who obeys them will live by them—and they utterly desecrated my Sabbaths. So I said I would pour out my wrath *z* on them and destroy them in the desert. *a* 14But for the sake of my name I did what would keep it from being profaned in the eyes of the nations in whose sight I had brought them out. *b* 15Also with uplifted hand I swore to them in the desert that I would not bring them into the land I had given them—a land flowing with milk and honey, most beautiful of all lands *c*— 16because they rejected my laws and did not follow my decrees and desecrated my Sabbaths. For their hearts *d* were devoted to their idols. *e* 17Yet I looked on them with pity and did not destroy them or put an end to them in the desert. 18I said to their children in the desert, "Do not follow the statutes of your fathers *f* or keep their laws or defile yourselves with their idols. 19I am the LORD your God; *g* follow my decrees and be careful to keep my laws. *h* 20Keep my Sabbaths holy, that they may be a sign between us. Then you will know that I am the LORD your God. *i*"

21" 'But the children rebelled against me: They did not follow my decrees, they were not careful to keep my laws—although the man who obeys them will live by them—and they desecrated my Sabbaths. So I said I would pour out my wrath on them and spend my anger against them in the desert. 22But I withheld *j* my hand, and for the sake of my name I did what would keep it from being profaned in the eyes of the nations in whose sight I had brought them out. 23Also with uplifted hand I swore to them in the desert that I would disperse them among the nations and scatter *k* them through the countries, 24because they had not obeyed my laws but had rejected my decrees and desecrated my Sabbaths, *l* and their eyes lusted after *m* their fathers' idols. *n* 25I also gave them over *o* to statutes that were not good and laws they could not live by; *p* 26I let them become defiled through their gifts—the sacrifice of every firstborn *a*—that I might fill them with horror so they would know that I am the LORD. *q*

27"Therefore, son of man, speak to the people of Israel and say to them, 'This is what the Sovereign LORD says: In this also your fathers blasphemed *r* me by forsaking me: *s* 28When I brought them into the land *t* I had sworn to give them and they saw any high hill or any leafy tree, there they offered their sacrifices, made offerings

---

a 26 Or —*making every firstborn pass through the fire*

20:6
o Ex 3:8; Jer 32:22
p Dt 8:7; Ps 48:2; Da 8:9
20:7
q Ex 20:4 *r* Ex 20:2; Lev 18:3; Dt 29:18
20:8
s Eze 7:8 *t* Isa 63:10

20:9
u Eze 36:22; 39:7
20:10
v Ex 13:18
20:11
w Lev 18:5; Dt 4:7-8; Ro 10:5
20:12
x Ex 31:13
20:13
y Ps 78:40 *z* Dt 9:8 *a* Nu 14:29; Ps 95:8-10; Isa 56:6

20:14
b Eze 36:23

20:15
c Ps 95:11; 106:26
20:16
d Nu 15:39
e Am 5:26

20:18
f Zec 1:4
20:19
g Ex 20:2
h Dt 5:32-33; 6:1-2; 8:1; 11:1; 12:1
20:20
i Jer 17:22

20:22
j Ps 78:38

20:23
k Lev 26:33; Dt 28:64
20:24
l ver 13 *m* Eze 6:9
n ver 16
20:25
o Ps 81:12
p 2Th 2:11
20:26
q 2Ki 17:17

20:27
r Ro 2:24
s Eze 18:24
20:28
t Ps 78:55,58

Ezekiel 20:30–44

If the people chose to be like the other nations, they would pay the price. In that case, a new exodus would bring them nothing but judgment, just as the first exodus had led to judgment for a whole generation (cf. Heb. 3:16–17). But God's salvation purposes remain unshakable: He will establish his chosen ones not in the "church or synagogue of their choice" (see previous "Here and Now") but in the holy mountain of his choosing, the new city of God.

Jesus proclaimed to the woman of Samaria a new era of worship (John 4:21–24). We no longer worship on Mount Gerizim, in Jerusalem, or on Ezekiel's high mountain, but in spirit and in truth. Since the coming of Jesus, the initiator of the new covenant, the redeemed community worships in the presence of God himself (Heb. 12:22–24). What does this astounding privilege mean to you?

20:28
u Eze 6:13

20:30
v ver 43
w Jer 16:12
20:31
x Eze 16:20
y Ps 106:37-39;
Jer 7:31

20:33
z Jer 21:5
20:34
a 2Co 6:17*
b Isa 27:12-13;
Jer 44:6; La 2:4
20:35
c Jer 2:35

20:36
d Nu 11:1-35;
1Co 10:5-10
20:37
e Lev 27:32;
Jer 33:13
f Eze 16:62
20:38
g Eze 34:17-22;
Am 9:9-10
h Ps 95:11;
Jer 44:14; Eze 13:9;
Mal 3:3; Heb 4:3
20:39
i Jer 44:25
j Isa 1:13; Eze 43:7;
Am 4:4
20:40
k Isa 60:7 l Isa 56:7;
Mal 3:4

20:41
m Eze 28:25; 36:23
n Eze 11:17
20:42
o Eze 38:23
p Eze 34:13; 36:24

20:43
q Eze 6:9; 16:61;
Hos 5:15
20:44
r Eze 36:22
s Eze 24:24

that provoked me to anger, presented their fragrant incense and poured out their drink offerings. [u] 29Then I said to them: What is this high place you go to?' " (It is called Bamah[a] to this day.)

Judgment and Restoration

30 "Therefore say to the house of Israel: 'This is what the Sovereign LORD says: Will you defile yourselves[v] the way your fathers did and lust after their vile images?[w] 31When you offer your gifts—the sacrifice of your sons[x] in[b] the fire—you continue to defile yourselves with all your idols to this day. Am I to let you inquire of me, O house of Israel? As surely as I live, declares the Sovereign LORD, I will not let you inquire of me.[y]

32 " 'You say, "We want to be like the nations, like the peoples of the world, who serve wood and stone." But what you have in mind will never happen. 33As surely as I live, declares the Sovereign LORD, I will rule over you with a mighty hand and an outstretched arm and with outpoured wrath.[z] 34I will bring you from the nations[a] and gather you from the countries where you have been scattered—with a mighty hand and an outstretched arm and with outpoured wrath.[b] 35I will bring you into the desert of the nations and there, face to face, I will execute judgment[c] upon you. 36As I judged your fathers in the desert of the land of Egypt, so I will judge you, declares the Sovereign LORD.[d] 37I will take note of you as you pass under my rod,[e] and I will bring you into the bond of the covenant.[f] 38I will purge[g] you of those who revolt and rebel against me. Although I will bring them out of the land where they are living, yet they will not enter the land of Israel. Then you will know that I am the LORD.[h]

39 " 'As for you, O house of Israel, this is what the Sovereign LORD says: Go and serve your idols,[i] every one of you! But afterward you will surely listen to me and no longer profane my holy name with your gifts and idols.[j] 40For on my holy mountain, the high mountain of Israel, declares the Sovereign LORD, there in the land the entire house of Israel will serve me, and there I will accept them. There I will require your offerings[k] and your choice gifts,[c] along with all your holy sacrifices.[l] 41I will accept you as fragrant incense when I bring you out from the nations and gather you from the countries where you have been scattered, and I will show myself holy[m] among you in the sight of the nations.[n] 42Then you will know that I am the LORD,[o] when I bring you into the land of Israel,[p] the land I had sworn with uplifted hand to give to your fathers. 43There you will remember your conduct and all the actions by which you have defiled yourselves, and you will loathe yourselves for all the evil you have done.[q] 44You will know that I am the LORD, when I deal with you for my name's sake[r] and not according to your evil ways and your corrupt practices, O house of Israel, declares the Sovereign LORD.[s] "

Prophecy Against the South

45The word of the LORD came to me: 46"Son of man, set your face toward the

---

[a] 29 Bamah means high place.   [b] 31 Or —making your sons pass through   [c] 40 Or and the gifts of your firstfruits

---

Ezekiel 20:45–49

This prophecy, in the form of a parable, both reveals and conceals. The fiery judgment would be all-consuming in three ways: (1) the *what* (both green and dry tree), (2) the *where* (from the south northwards), (3) and the *when* (it was about to be lit and wouldn't be extinguished). But what exactly did this "southern forest" represent? Without this information byte the parable remained a riddle, as seen in the people's reaction (v. 49).

How can the fire of God's wrath pass over us without consuming us? Because it has already passed over Jesus and poured its heat on him. His death in our place allows us to come close to the avenging God without being destroyed. Through Jesus, a safe way has been made for us to approach God. The fire of his wrath is transformed into a refiner's fire; it purifies and tests but doesn't destroy (cf. 1 Peter 1:6–7).

Lack of fear of the still coming fire for us as Christians doesn't mean that we can relax. Our works will be tested by fire—and they are far from fireproof (cf. 1 Cor. 3:11–15). How often do we fill our lives with the trivial, passing time instead of spending it, living alongside people instead of with them? Instead of burning out for God, how often do we heap up empty actions for his bonfire? From eternity's perspective, how wasted will much of our lives seem to have been?

south; preach against the south and prophesy against[t] the forest of the southland. [u] ⁴⁷Say to the southern forest: 'Hear the word of the LORD. This is what the Sovereign LORD says: I am about to set fire to you, and it will consume all your trees, both green and dry. The blazing flame will not be quenched, and every face from south to north will be scorched by it. [v] ⁴⁸Everyone will see that I the LORD have kindled it; it will not be quenched. [w] '"

⁴⁹Then I said, "Ah, Sovereign LORD! They are saying of me, 'Isn't he just telling parables?[x] '"

Babylon, God's Sword of Judgment

21 The word of the LORD came to me: ²"Son of man, set your face against Jerusalem and preach against the sanctuary. Prophesy against[y] the land of Israel ³and say to her: 'This is what the LORD says: I am against you.[z] I will draw my sword from its scabbard and cut off from you both the righteous and the wicked. [a] ⁴Because I am going to cut off the righteous and the wicked, my sword will be unsheathed against everyone from south to north. [b] ⁵Then all people will know that I the LORD have drawn my sword from its scabbard; it will not return[c] again.' [d]

⁶"Therefore groan, son of man! Groan before them with broken heart and bitter grief. [e] ⁷And when they ask you, 'Why are you groaning?' you shall say, 'Because of the news that is coming. Every heart will melt and every hand go limp;[f] every spirit will become faint and every knee become as weak as water.' It is coming! It will surely take place, declares the Sovereign LORD."

⁸The word of the LORD came to me: ⁹"Son of man, prophesy and say, 'This is what the Lord says:

" 'A sword, a sword,
    sharpened and polished—
¹⁰sharpened for the slaughter, [g]
    polished to flash like lightning!

" 'Shall we rejoice in the scepter of my son ˪Judah˻? The sword despises every such stick.

¹¹ " 'The sword is appointed to be polished, [h]
    to be grasped with the hand;
it is sharpened and polished,
    made ready for the hand of the slayer.
¹²Cry out and wail, son of man,
    for it is against my people;
it is against all the princes of Israel.
They are thrown to the sword
    along with my people.
Therefore beat your breast. [i]

¹³" 'Testing will surely come. And what if the scepter ˪of Judah˻, which the sword despises, does not continue? declares the Sovereign LORD.'

20:46
t Eze 21:2; Am 7:16
u Isa 30:6;
Jer 13:19

20:47
v Isa 9:18-19; 13:8;
Jer 21:14
20:48
w Jer 7:20
20:49
x Mt 13:13;
Jn 16:25

21:2
y Eze 20:46
21:3
z Jer 21:13
a ver 9-11; Job 9:22

21:4
b Eze 20:47
21:5
c ver 30 d Na 1:9

21:6
e Isa 22:4
21:7
f Eze 22:14; 7:17

21:10
g Ps 110:5-6;
Isa 34:5-6

21:11
h Jer 46:4

21:12
i Jer 31:19

Ezekiel 21:1–32

The answers to the parable became clear in this interpretation. The three Hebrew terms for "south" in the parable are matched by three objects of judgment: Jerusalem, the sanctuary, and the land of Israel. The fire image from the previous prophecy is linked with that of the sword of the Lord.

Ezekiel was to strike his hands together in a threatening gesture, not once or twice but three times, symbolizing the totality of the coming judgment. Verse 19 introduces the human agent who would carry out God's will, the king of Babylon. The Babylonian invasion would come from north to south, but also from "south to north"

(20:47; 21:4)—from border to border, a comprehensive destruction. God's judgment would fall both on the righteous (the green tree) and the wicked (the dry tree).

Are you acquainted with people who hesitate to believe that the Bible's teaching on eternal punishment should be taken literally? The destruction of Jerusalem in 586 B.C., when God handed over judgment to the sword of Babylon, was total. Yet it pales in comparison to the comprehensive judgment coming in the end times (cf. Rev. 14:6–20). Like the Jerusalemites in Ezekiel's day, many today are convinced that the Judge will choose another road and the unrighteous will be spared. But the Bible minces no words, and its content doesn't mislead us.

14 "So then, son of man, prophesy
  and strike your hands*j* together.
Let the sword strike twice,
  even three times.
It is a sword for slaughter—
  a sword for great slaughter,
  closing in on them from every side.*k*
15 So that hearts may melt*l*
  and the fallen be many,
I have stationed the sword for slaughter*a*
  at all their gates.
Oh! It is made to flash like lightning,
  it is grasped for slaughter.*m*
16 O sword, slash to the right,
  then to the left,
  wherever your blade is turned.
17 I too will strike my hands*n* together,
  and my wrath*o* will subside.
I the LORD have spoken."

18 The word of the LORD came to me: 19 "Son of man, mark out two roads for the sword of the king of Babylon to take, both starting from the same country. Make a signpost where the road branches off to the city. 20 Mark out one road for the sword to come against Rabbah of the Ammonites*p* and another against Judah and fortified Jerusalem. 21 For the king of Babylon will stop at the fork in the road, at the junction of the two roads, to seek an omen: He will cast lots*q* with arrows, he will consult his idols, he will examine the liver.*r* 22 Into his right hand will come the lot for Jerusalem, where he is to set up battering rams, to give the command to slaughter, to sound the battle cry, to set battering rams against the gates, to build a ramp and to erect siege works.*s* 23 It will seem like a false omen to those who have sworn allegiance to him, but he will remind*t* them of their guilt and take them captive.

24 "Therefore this is what the Sovereign LORD says: 'Because you people have brought to mind your guilt by your open rebellion, revealing your sins in all that you do—because you have done this, you will be taken captive.

25 " 'O profane and wicked prince of Israel, whose day has come, whose time of punishment has reached its climax,*u* 26 this is what the Sovereign LORD says: Take off the turban, remove the crown.*v* It will not be as it was: The lowly will be exalted and the exalted will be brought low.*w* 27 A ruin! A ruin! I will make it a ruin! It will not be restored until he comes to whom it rightfully belongs; to him I will give it.'*x*

28 "And you, son of man, prophesy and say, 'This is what the Sovereign LORD says about the Ammonites*y* and their insults:

" 'A sword,*z* a sword,
  drawn for the slaughter,
polished to consume
  and to flash like lightning!
29 Despite false visions concerning you
  and lying divinations about you,
it will be laid on the necks
  of the wicked who are to be slain,
whose day has come,
  whose time of punishment has reached its climax.*a*
30 Return the sword to its scabbard.*b*
  In the place where you were created,
in the land of your ancestry,*c*
  I will judge you.
31 I will pour out my wrath upon you

a 15 Septuagint; the meaning of the Hebrew for this word is uncertain.

and breathe out my fiery anger[d] against you;
    I will hand you over to brutal men,
        men skilled in destruction.[e]
32 You will be fuel for the fire,[f]
    your blood will be shed in your land,
    you will be remembered[g] no more;
        for I the LORD have spoken.' "

Jerusalem's Sins

22 The word of the LORD came to me: 2 "Son of man, will you judge her? Will you judge this city of bloodshed?[h] Then confront her with all her detestable practices[i] 3 and say: 'This is what the Sovereign LORD says: O city that brings on herself doom by shedding blood[j] in her midst and defiles herself by making idols, 4 you have become guilty because of the blood you have shed[k] and have become defiled by the idols you have made. You have brought your days to a close, and the end of your years has come.[l] Therefore I will make you an object of scorn to the nations and a laughingstock to all the countries.[m] 5 Those who are near and those who are far away will mock you, O infamous city, full of turmoil.

6 " 'See how each of the princes of Israel who are in you uses his power to shed blood.[n] 7 In you they have treated father and mother with contempt;[o] in you they have oppressed the alien and mistreated the fatherless and the widow.[p] 8 You have despised my holy things and desecrated my Sabbaths.[q] 9 In you are slanderous men[r] bent on shedding blood; in you are those who eat at the mountain shrines[s] and commit lewd acts.[t] 10 In you are those who dishonor their fathers' bed; in you are those who violate women during their period, when they are ceremonially unclean.[u] 11 In you one man commits a detestable offense with his neighbor's wife, another shamefully defiles his daughter-in-law,[v] and another violates his sister,[w] his own father's daughter. 12 In you men accept bribes[x] to shed blood; you take usury and excessive interest[a] and make unjust gain from your neighbors[y] by extortion. And you have forgotten me, declares the Sovereign LORD.

13 " 'I will surely strike my hands[z] together at the unjust gain[a] you have made and at the blood[b] you have shed in your midst. 14 Will your courage endure or your hands be strong in the day I deal with you? I the LORD have spoken,[c] and I will do it.[d] 15 I will disperse you among the nations and scatter[e] you through the countries; and I will put an end to your uncleanness.[f] 16 When you have been defiled[b] in the eyes of the nations, you will know that I am the LORD.' "

17 Then the word of the LORD came to me: 18 "Son of man, the house of Israel has become dross[g] to me; all of them are the copper, tin, iron and lead left inside a furnace. They are but the dross of silver.[h] 19 Therefore this is what the Sovereign LORD says: 'Because you have all become dross, I will gather you into Jerusalem. 20 As men

---

a 12 Or *usury and interest*   b 16 Or *When I have allotted you your inheritance*

21:31
d Eze 22:20-21
e Jer 51:20-23

21:32
f Mal 4:1
g Eze 25:10

22:2
h Eze 24:6,9;
Na 3:1 i Eze 16:2
22:3
j ver 6,13,27;
Eze 23:37,45
22:4
k 2Ki 21:16
l Eze 21:25
m Eze 5:14

22:6
n Isa 1:23
22:7
o Dt 5:16; 27:16
p Ex 22:21-22
22:8
q Eze 23:38-39
22:9
r Lev 19:16
s Eze 18:11
t Hos 4:10,14
22:10
u Lev 18:8,19
22:11
v Lev 18:15
w Lev 18:9;
2Sa 13:14
22:12
x Dt 27:25; Mic 7:3
y Lev 19:13
22:13
z Eze 21:17
a Isa 33:15 b ver 3
22:14
c Eze 24:14
d Eze 17:24; 21:7
22:15
e Dt 4:27; Zec 7:14
f Eze 23:27

22:18
g Ps 119:119;
Isa 1:22
h Jer 6:28-30

Ezekiel 22:1–31

God required Jerusalem, as a consequence of its unique spiritual significance, to be a place of radical holiness (cf. Ps. 15; 24:3–4). But the "holy city" had become the entirely "unholy city." Ezekiel denounced two categories of sin: social injustices and idol worship.

At the end of this chapter we read that the Lord looked for someone who would "build up the wall and stand before [him] in the gap on behalf of the land" (v. 30). In other words, he sought a true prophet (cf. 13:1–5)—who would take on the difficult and dangerous task of interceding for the people, just as Moses had done after the incident of the golden calf (Ps. 106:23). But this time no one was found to deflect God's wrath, and an all-consuming judgment would fall (Ezek. 22:31).

God desires social justice. Sexual sins are listed here alongside charging interest, abusing neighbors, and forgetting God (vv. 11–12). False teaching is mentioned alongside robbery, oppressing the poor, and taking advantage of foreigners. In how many of our churches do we tend to focus on sexual sins and on the correctness of our teaching—while ignoring issues related to our finances or treatment of the poor? Do you have a similar passion about these issues as your heavenly Father? Does that passion translate into action on your part?

We are called to share in the prophetic ministry of "standing in the gap." How do we go about this critical calling? By interceding in prayer for the lost, risking ridicule or rejection to share the gospel, and living transparent lives so that nothing may hinder the message of life we proclaim.

gather silver, copper, iron, lead and tin into a furnace to melt it with a fiery blast, so will I gather you in my anger and my wrath and put you inside the city and melt you. [i] 21 I will gather you and I will blow on you with my fiery wrath, and you will be melted inside her. 22 As silver is melted[j] in a furnace, so you will be melted inside her, and you will know that I the LORD have poured out my wrath upon you.' " [k]

23 Again the word of the LORD came to me: 24 "Son of man, say to the land, 'You are a land that has had no rain or showers[a] in the day of wrath.'[l] 25 There is a conspiracy[m] of her princes[b] within her like a roaring lion tearing its prey; they devour people,[n] take treasures and precious things and make many widows[o] within her. 26 Her priests do violence to my law[p] and profane my holy things; they do not distinguish between the holy and the common;[q] they teach that there is no difference between the unclean and the clean;[r] and they shut their eyes to the keeping of my Sabbaths, so that I am profaned among them. [s] 27 Her officials within her are like wolves tearing their prey; they shed blood and kill people to make unjust gain. [t] 28 Her prophets whitewash[u] these deeds for them by false visions and lying divinations. They say, 'This is what the Sovereign LORD says'—when the LORD has not spoken. [v] 29 The people of the land practice extortion and commit robbery; they oppress the poor and needy and mistreat the alien,[w] denying them justice. [x]

30 "I looked for a man among them who would build up the wall[y] and stand before me in the gap on behalf of the land so I would not have to destroy it, but I found none. [z] 31 So I will pour out my wrath on them and consume them with my fiery anger, bringing down[a] on their own heads all they have done, declares the Sovereign LORD. [b]"

Two Adulterous Sisters

23 The word of the LORD came to me: 2 "Son of man, there were two women, daughters of the same mother. [c] 3 They became prostitutes in Egypt, [d] engaging in prostitution[e] from their youth. In that land their breasts were fondled and their virgin bosoms caressed. 4 The older was named Oholah, and her sister was Oholibah. They were mine and gave birth to sons and daughters. Oholah is Samaria, and Oholibah is Jerusalem.

5 "Oholah engaged in prostitution while she was still mine; and she lusted after her lovers, the Assyrians[f]—warriors[g] 6 clothed in blue, governors and commanders, all of them handsome young men, and mounted horsemen. 7 She gave herself as a prostitute to all the elite of the Assyrians and defiled herself with all the idols of everyone she lusted after. [h] 8 She did not give up the prostitution she began in Egypt,[i] when during her youth men slept with her, caressed her virgin bosom and poured out their lust upon her.[j]

9 "Therefore I handed her over[k] to her lovers, the Assyrians, for whom she lusted.[l] 10 They stripped[m] her naked, took away her sons and daughters and killed her with the sword. She became a byword among women,[n] and punishment was inflicted on her. [o]

11 "Her sister Oholibah saw this, yet in her lust and prostitution she was more depraved than her sister. [p] 12 She too lusted after the Assyrians—governors and commanders, warriors in full dress, mounted horsemen, all handsome young men. [q] 13 I saw that she too defiled herself; both of them went the same way.

14 "But she carried her prostitution still further. She saw men portrayed on a

---

[a] 24 Septuagint; Hebrew *has not been cleansed or rained on*   [b] 25 Septuagint; Hebrew *prophets*

Cross-reference column

22:20
[i] Mal 3:2
22:22
[j] Isa 1:25
[k] Eze 20:8,33

22:24
[l] Eze 24:13
22:25
[m] Jer 11:9
[n] Hos 6:9
[o] Jer 15:8
22:26
[p] Mal 2:7-8
[q] Eze 44:23
[r] Lev 10:10
[s] 1Sa 2:12-17; Jer 2:8,26; Hag 2:11-14
22:27
[t] Isa 1:23
22:28
[u] Eze 13:10
[v] Eze 13:2,6-7
22:29
[w] Ex 22:21; 23:9
[x] Isa 5:7
22:30
[y] Eze 13:5
[z] Ps 106:23; Jer 5:1

22:31
[a] Eze 16:43
[b] Eze 7:8-9; 9:10; Ro 2:8

23:2
[c] Jer 3:7; Eze 16:45
23:3
[d] Jos 24:14
[e] Lev 17:7

23:5
[f] 2Ki 16:7; Hos 5:13
[g] Hos 8:9

23:7
[h] Hos 5:3; 6:10

23:8
[i] Ex 32:4
[j] Eze 16:15
23:9
[k] 2Ki 18:11
[l] Hos 11:5
23:10
[m] Hos 2:10
[n] Eze 16:41
[o] Eze 16:36

23:11
[p] Jer 3:8-11; Eze 16:51
23:12
[q] 2Ki 16:7-15; 2Ch 28:16

Ezekiel 23:1–49

Ohⓛ Oholah means "her tent," probably an allusion to the fact that Samaria, the capital of the northern kingdom of Israel, had its own unauthorized worship sanctuary. The similar sounding *Oholibah* means "My tent is in her," likely a reference to the Lord's sanctuary in Jerusalem.

Oholah traded her trust in God for an alliance with Assyria, with the disastrous result of being destroyed by the Assyrians in 722 B.C. But rather than learning her lesson, Oholibah became even worse than her sister. With all the emotional impact of a detailed portrayal of sexual perversion, Ezekiel drove home the point that Jerusalem's coming destruction was deserved and inevitable.

wall,[r] figures of Chaldeans[a] portrayed in red,[s] [15]with belts around their waists and flowing turbans on their heads; all of them looked like Babylonian chariot officers, natives of Chaldea.[b] [16]As soon as she saw them, she lusted after them and sent messengers to them in Chaldea. [17]Then the Babylonians came to her, to the bed of love, and in their lust they defiled her. After she had been defiled by them, she turned away from them in disgust. [18]When she carried on her prostitution openly and exposed her nakedness, I turned away[t] from her in disgust, just as I had turned away from her sister. [u] [19]Yet she became more and more promiscuous as she recalled the days of her youth, when she was a prostitute in Egypt. [20]There she lusted after her lovers, whose genitals were like those of donkeys and whose emission was like that of horses. [21]So you longed for the lewdness of your youth, when in Egypt your bosom was caressed and your young breasts fondled.[c][v]

[22]"Therefore, Oholibah, this is what the Sovereign LORD says: I will stir up your lovers against you, those you turned away from in disgust, and I will bring them against you from every side[w]— [23]the Babylonians[x] and all the Chaldeans, the men of Pekod[y] and Shoa and Koa, and all the Assyrians with them, handsome young men, all of them governors and commanders, chariot officers and men of high rank, all mounted on horses.[z] [24]They will come against you with weapons,[d] chariots and wagons[a] and with a throng of people; they will take up positions against you on every side with large and small shields and with helmets. I will turn you over to them for punishment,[b] and they will punish you according to their standards. [25]I will direct my jealous anger against you, and they will deal with you in fury. They will cut off your noses and your ears, and those of you who are left will fall by the sword. They will take away your sons and daughters,[c] and those of you who are left will be consumed by fire.[d] [26]They will also strip[e] you of your clothes and take your fine jewelry.[f] [27]So I will put a stop[g] to the lewdness and prostitution you began in Egypt. You will not look on these things with longing or remember Egypt anymore.

[28]"For this is what the Sovereign LORD says: I am about to hand you over[h] to those you hate, to those you turned away from in disgust. [29]They will deal with you in hatred and take away everything you have worked for. They will leave you naked and bare, and the shame of your prostitution will be exposed. Your lewdness and promiscuity[i] [30]have brought this upon you, because you lusted after the nations and defiled yourself with their idols.[j] [31]You have gone the way of your sister; so I will put her cup[k] into your hand.[l]

[32]"This is what the Sovereign LORD says:

"You will drink your sister's cup,
    a cup large and deep;
it will bring scorn and derision,
    for it holds so much.[m]
[33]You will be filled with drunkenness and sorrow,
    the cup of ruin and desolation,
    the cup of your sister Samaria.[n]
[34]You will drink it[o] and drain it dry;
    you will dash it to pieces
    and tear your breasts.

I have spoken, declares the Sovereign LORD.

---

[a] 14 Or *Babylonians*   [b] 15 Or *Babylonia; also in verse 16*   [c] 21 Syriac (see also verse 3); Hebrew *caressed because of your young breasts*   [d] 24 The meaning of the Hebrew for this word is uncertain.

📖 Ezekiel 23 isn't just a spicy fantasy about sex and violence. Yes, it shocks us, as did chapter 16, the other "R-rated" section of Ezekiel's prophecy. But this shock jolts the comfortable into recognizing God's abhorrence of our compromising with our surrounding society and failing to live his way. Ignoring God's call for us to worship only him, idolizing money or possessions, and refusing to care for the poor are graphically likened here to prostitution—to being whores to the world's values. This forces us to face the utter folly of trusting in anything—or anyone—other than the living God. It strips away any pretensions and exposes the naked truth: We all deserve the full force of God's fury over our sin.

23:14
[r] Eze 8:10
[s] Jer 22:14

23:18
[t] Ps 78:59; 106:40; Jer 6:8 [u] Jer 12:8; Am 5:21

23:21
[v] Eze 16:26

23:22
[w] Eze 16:37
23:23
[x] 2Ki 20:14-18
[y] Jer 50:21
[z] 2Ki 24:2

23:24
[a] Jer 47:3; Eze 26:7,10; Na 2:4
[b] Jer 39:5-6

23:25
[c] ver 47
[d] Eze 20:47-48
23:26
[e] Jer 13:22
[f] Isa 3:18-23; Eze 16:39
23:27
[g] Eze 16:41
23:28
[h] Jer 34:20

23:29
[i] Dt 28:48
23:30
[j] Eze 6:9
23:31
[k] Jer 25:15
[l] 2Ki 21:13

23:32
[m] Ps 60:3; Isa 51:17; Jer 25:15

23:33
[n] Jer 25:15-16
23:34
[o] Ps 75:8; Isa 51:17

23:35
p Isa 17:10;
Jer 3:21 q 1Ki 14:9

23:36
r Eze 16:2
s Isa 58:1; Eze 22:2;
Mic 3:8
23:37
t Eze 16:36

23:39
u 2Ki 21:4
v Jer 7:10
23:40
w Isa 57:9
x 2Ki 9:30
y Jer 4:30;
Eze 16:13-19
23:41
z Est 1:6; Pr 7:17;
Am 6:4 a Isa 65:11;
Eze 44:16
23:42
b Ge 24:30
c Eze 16:11-12
23:43
d ver 3

23:45
e Lev 20:10;
Eze 16:38; Hos 6:5
23:46
f Eze 16:40

23:47
g 2Ch 36:19
h 2Ch 36:17;
Eze 16:40-41
23:48
i 2Pe 2:6
23:49
j Eze 7:4; 9:10;
20:38

24:1
k Eze 8:1
24:2
l 2Ki 25:1; Jer 39:1;
52:4
24:3
m Isa 1:2; Eze 2:3,6
n Eze 17:2; 20:49
o Jer 1:13; Eze 11:3

24:5
p Jer 52:10
q Jer 52:24-27

35 "Therefore this is what the Sovereign LORD says: Since you have forgotten[p] me and thrust me behind your back,[q] you must bear the consequences of your lewdness and prostitution."

36 The LORD said to me: "Son of man, will you judge Oholah and Oholibah? Then confront[r] them with their detestable practices.[s] 37 for they have committed adultery and blood is on their hands. They committed adultery with their idols; they even sacrificed their children, whom they bore to me,[a] as food for them.[t] 38 They have also done this to me: At that same time they defiled my sanctuary and desecrated my Sabbaths. 39 On the very day they sacrificed their children to their idols, they entered my sanctuary and desecrated[u] it. That is what they did in my house.[v]

40 "They even sent messengers for men who came from far away,[w] and when they arrived you bathed yourself for them, painted your eyes[x] and put on your jewelry.[y] 41 You sat on an elegant couch,[z] with a table[a] spread before it on which you had placed the incense and oil that belonged to me.

42 "The noise of a carefree crowd was around her; Sabeans[b] were brought from the desert along with men from the rabble, and they put bracelets[b] on the arms of the woman and her sister and beautiful crowns on their heads.[c] 43 Then I said about the one worn out by adultery, 'Now let them use her as a prostitute,[d] for that is all she is.' 44 And they slept with her. As men sleep with a prostitute, so they slept with those lewd women, Oholah and Oholibah. 45 But righteous men will sentence them to the punishment of women who commit adultery and shed blood, because they are adulterous and blood is on their hands.[e]

46 "This is what the Sovereign LORD says: Bring a mob[f] against them and give them over to terror and plunder. 47 The mob will stone them and cut them down with their swords; they will kill their sons and daughters and burn[g] down their houses.[h]

48 "So I will put an end to lewdness in the land, that all women may take warning and not imitate you.[i] 49 You will suffer the penalty for your lewdness and bear the consequences of your sins of idolatry. Then you will know that I am the Sovereign LORD.[j]"

The Cooking Pot

24 In the ninth year, in the tenth month on the tenth day, the word of the LORD came to me:[k] 2 "Son of man, record this date, this very date, because the king of Babylon has laid siege to Jerusalem this very day.[l] 3 Tell this rebellious house[m] a parable[n] and say to them: 'This is what the Sovereign LORD says:

" 'Put on the cooking pot;[o] put it on
      and pour water into it.
4 Put into it the pieces of meat,
      all the choice pieces—the leg and the shoulder.
   Fill it with the best of these bones;
5   take the pick of the flock.[p]
   Pile wood beneath it for the bones;
      bring it to a boil
      and cook the bones in it.[q]

a 37 Or *even made the children they bore to me pass through the fire*   b 42 Or *drunkards*

Ezekiel 24:1–14

On the very day Nebuchadnezzar began his siege of Jerusalem, God gave Ezekiel this parable. The siege of Jerusalem is portrayed as her people boiling in the pot of God's wrath, with the Babylonians' siege works providing "wood" for the fire. The "choice pieces" were the residents of Jerusalem who wrongly thought they had been spared from the exile of 597 B.C. (cf. 11:3 and "There and Then" for 11:1–15).

After the contents had been removed (through deportation), the empty pot was transformed into a kind of refiner's furnace in a final attempt to melt away the impurities. But again, all efforts to purify Judah proved to be ineffective. The time for words had ended (v. 14).

What does this ancient history have to do with us? The fall of Jerusalem in 586 B.C. portends the ultimate destruction of the world, as described in 2 Peter 3. Scoffers may view the merciful delay on God's part as evidence that such a day will never occur (vv. 3–4), but God's judgment will come in due season. He wants every person to repent rather than perish (v. 9). But his patience will ultimately be exhausted, and his wrath *will* be poured out on the world. Bad news? Yes. But take an opportunity to share the Good News you know!

6 " 'For this is what the Sovereign Lord says:

" 'Woe to the city of bloodshed,[r]
to the pot now encrusted,
whose deposit will not go away!
Empty it piece by piece
without casting lots[s] for them.

7 " 'For the blood she shed is in her midst:
She poured it on the bare rock;
she did not pour it on the ground,
where the dust would cover it.[t]
8 To stir up wrath and take revenge
I put her blood on the bare rock,
so that it would not be covered.

9 " 'Therefore this is what the Sovereign Lord says:

" 'Woe to the city of bloodshed!
I, too, will pile the wood high.
10 So heap on the wood
and kindle the fire.
Cook the meat well,
mixing in the spices;
and let the bones be charred.
11 Then set the empty pot on the coals
till it becomes hot and its copper glows
so its impurities may be melted
and its deposit burned away.[u]
12 It has frustrated all efforts;
its heavy deposit has not been removed,
not even by fire.

13 " 'Now your impurity is lewdness. Because I tried to cleanse you but you would not be cleansed from your impurity, you will not be clean again until my wrath against you has subsided.[v]

14 " 'I the Lord have spoken. The time has come for me to act. I will not hold back; I will not have pity, nor will I relent. You will be judged according to your conduct and your actions,[w] declares the Sovereign Lord.[x]' "

Ezekiel's Wife Dies

15 The word of the Lord came to me: 16 "Son of man, with one blow I am about to take away from you the delight of your eyes. Yet do not lament or weep or shed

24:6
[r] Eze 22:2
[s] Ob 1:11; Na 3:10

24:7
[t] Lev 17:13

24:11
[u] Jer 21:10; Eze 22:15

24:13
[v] Jer 6:28-30; Eze 16:42; 22:24

24:14
[w] Eze 36:19
[x] Eze 18:30

Ezekiel 24:15–27

Ezekiel was asked to undertake the most painful and personal of his prophetic sign-acts. His wife, "the delight of [his] eyes," would be taken from him, and he wouldn't be permitted to mourn publicly. Instead of the normal expressions of grief, he would only be able to groan inwardly. The "delight" of the exiles' eyes—the temple in Jerusalem—also was to be destroyed, along with the children they had left there. Far from Jerusalem, they too would experience overwhelming remorse but be incapable of normal grief.

Yet from the deepest gloom hope arose. On the very day the exiles received the news of Jerusalem's fall, the silence God had imposed on Ezekiel at the outset of his ministry would be lifted (3:26–27; 33:21–22). Ezekiel would be able to intercede for the people and offer

them words of encouragement and hope.

The day will come when "time" will be called on mercy, and God's wrath will be loosed. In the meantime we live like Ezekiel, as men and women under orders. We have been commissioned for battle, and even the most precious things we possess on Earth we hold as trustees. We don't own our spouses, our children, even our bodies. Bearing God's message to the world can be costly for us, as it was for Ezekiel. This level of commitment is something the world finds hard to understand. What has your mission cost you?

God was willing to give up into the hands of sinful people the delight of his eyes, his only Son—to be beaten, tortured, mocked, and crucified. Yet the blackness of Good Friday causes the light of Easter Sunday to break forth with fresh power for us as Jesus' disciples.

24:16
y Jer 13:17; 16:5;
22:10
24:17
z Jer 16:7

24:19
a Eze 12:9; 37:18

24:21
b Ps 27:4
c Eze 23:25
d Jer 7:14,15;
Eze 23:47
24:22
e Jer 16:7
24:23
f Job 27:15
g Ps 78:64
24:24
h Isa 20:3; Eze 4:3;
12:11

24:25
i Jer 11:22
24:26
j 1Sa 4:12;
Job 1:15-19
24:27
k Eze 3:26; 33:22

any tears. y 17Groan quietly; do not mourn for the dead. Keep your turban fastened and your sandals on your feet; do not cover the lower part of your face or eat the customary food ⌊of mourners⌋. z"

18So I spoke to the people in the morning, and in the evening my wife died. The next morning I did as I had been commanded.

19Then the people asked me, "Won't you tell us what these things have to do with us? a"

20So I said to them, "The word of the LORD came to me: 21Say to the house of Israel, 'This is what the Sovereign LORD says: I am about to desecrate my sanctuary— the stronghold in which you take pride, the delight of your eyes, b the object of your affection. The sons and daughters c you left behind will fall by the sword. d 22And you will do as I have done. You will not cover the lower part of your face or eat the customary food ⌊of mourners⌋. e 23You will keep your turbans on your heads and your sandals on your feet. You will not mourn f or weep but will waste away because of a your sins and groan among yourselves. g 24Ezekiel will be a sign h to you; you will do just as he has done. When this happens, you will know that I am the Sovereign LORD.'

25"And you, son of man, on the day I take away their stronghold, their joy and glory, the delight of their eyes, their heart's desire, and their sons and daughters i as well— 26on that day a fugitive will come to tell you j the news. 27At that time your mouth will be opened; you will speak with him and will no longer be silent. So you will be a sign to them, and they will know that I am the LORD. k"

A Prophecy Against Ammon

25:2
l Eze 21:28;
Zep 2:8-9
m Jer 49:1-6
25:3
n Eze 26:2; 36:2
o Pr 17:5
25:4
p Jdg 6:3
q Dt 28:33,51;
Jdg 6:33
25:5
r Dt 3:11; Eze 21:20
s Isa 17:2

25:6
t Ob 1:12; Zep 2:8
25:7
u Zep 1:4
v Eze 21:31
w Am 1:14-15

25 The word of the LORD came to me: 2"Son of man, set your face against the Ammonites l and prophesy against them. m 3Say to them, 'Hear the word of the Sovereign LORD. This is what the Sovereign LORD says: Because you said "Aha! n" over my sanctuary when it was desecrated and over the land of Israel when it was laid waste and over the people of Judah when they went into exile, o 4therefore I am going to give you to the people of the East p as a possession. They will set up their camps and pitch their tents among you; they will eat your fruit and drink your milk. q 5I will turn Rabbah r into a pasture for camels and Ammon into a resting place for sheep. s Then you will know that I am the LORD. 6For this is what the Sovereign LORD says: Because you have clapped your hands and stamped your feet, rejoicing with all the malice of your heart against the land of Israel, t 7therefore I will stretch out my hand u against you and give you as plunder to the nations. I will cut you off from the nations and exterminate you from the countries. I will destroy v you, and you will know that I am the LORD. w' "

A Prophecy Against Moab

25:8
x Jer 48:1; Am 2:1

8"This is what the Sovereign LORD says: 'Because Moab x and Seir said, "Look, the

---

a 23 Or away in

Ezekiel 25:1–7

🔎 Chapter 25 begins a series of oracles (prophetic messages) against the surrounding nations. Six are addressed to Judah's immediate neighbors (chs. 25–28, the first four in ch. 25) and a seventh to her traditional enemy, Egypt (chs. 29–32). There is no evidence that these oracles were ever actually delivered to the nations. So what message did they have for their intended audience, the Jews? Assurance that (1) God doesn't operate on a double standard, (2) they were still his precious people, and (3) God's consistent designs are behind all of history.

Oracles against foreign nations are common in the Prophets. Ezekiel's typical pattern was: (1) charges of evildoing; (2) a prediction of the nation's doom; and

(3) forced recognition of God's sovereignty ("You will know that I am the LORD"). All of these elements are found in classic form in the prophecy against Ammon and its capital, Rabbah.

📖 A common theme in God's accusation against the nations was that they had rejoiced at the judgment falling on others (25:3; 26:2). We may at times act like these neighbors of Israel rather than God's suffering people. When have you been pleased at the opposition's apparent comeuppance? With reverent fear we are to (1) remember that the measure we use to judge others will be used against us (Luke 6:37–38) and (2) seek to persuade all people (enemies or not) to be prepared for the judgment to come (2 Cor. 5:10–11).

house of Judah has become like all the other nations," ⁹therefore I will expose the flank of Moab, beginning at its frontier towns—Beth Jeshimoth ⁿ, Baal Meon ᶻ and Kiriathaim ᵃ—the glory of that land. ¹⁰I will give Moab along with the Ammonites to the people of the East as a possession, so that the Ammonites will not be remembered ᵇ among the nations; ¹¹and I will inflict punishment on Moab. Then they will know that I am the LORD.' "

A Prophecy Against Edom

¹²"This is what the Sovereign LORD says: 'Because Edom ᶜ took revenge on the house of Judah and became very guilty by doing so, ¹³therefore this is what the Sovereign LORD says: I will stretch out my hand against Edom and kill its men and their animals. ᵈ I will lay it waste, and from Teman to Dedan ᵉ they will fall by the sword. ¹⁴I will take vengeance on Edom by the hand of my people Israel, and they will deal with Edom in accordance with my anger ᶠ and my wrath; they will know my vengeance, declares the Sovereign LORD.' "

A Prophecy Against Philistia

¹⁵"This is what the Sovereign LORD says: 'Because the Philistines ᵍ acted in vengeance and took revenge with malice in their hearts, and with ancient hostility sought to destroy Judah, ¹⁶therefore this is what the Sovereign LORD says: I am about to stretch out my hand against the Philistines, ʰ and I will cut off the Kerethites ⁱ and destroy those remaining along the coast. ¹⁷I will carry out great vengeance on them and punish them in my wrath. Then they will know that I am the LORD, when I take vengeance on them.' "

25:9
ⁿ Nu 33:49
ᶻ Nu 32:3;
Jos 13:17
ᵃ Nu 32:37;
Jos 13:19
25:10
ᵇ Eze 21:32

25:12
ᶜ 2Ch 28:17

25:13
ᵈ Eze 29:8
ᵉ Jer 25:23

25:14
ᶠ Eze 35:11

25:15
ᵍ 2Ch 28:18

25:16
ʰ Jer 47:1-7
ⁱ 1Sa 30:14;
Zep 2:4-5

Ezekiel 25:8–11

The nations around Judah were addressed in clockwise order, starting with Ammon east of the Jordan River and moving south, then west and north. Moab and Seir (another name for Edom, the nation addressed in the next prophecy) claimed that Judah had "become like all the other nations." There was truth in that statement, especially in Judah's giving herself over to idolatry. But it could never be true in the intended sense (that Judah's fall showed her claim to elect status by God to be worthless—that she was a reject nation, thrown onto the scrap heap of history along with her God). So God responded to the statement as blasphemy.

Satan's assaults on the church boil down to three basic strategies: persecution (1 Peter 5:8), seduction (Rev. 18), and deception (2 Cor. 11:14). All three were at work in Satan's assault on Judah through the surrounding nations. Taking advantage of God's judgment on his people, they rejoiced at her downfall and added their own abuse. The message to the church or believer experiencing persecution or mistreatment today is that God sees and in due season will act. The blood of the martyrs cries out for justice—and justice it will receive (cf. Rev. 16:5–6).

Ezekiel 25:12–14

The Edomites hadn't just gloated over Judah's downfall; they had participated in it. The statement that "Edom took revenge on the house of Judah" is fleshed out in Obadiah 10–14, where Edom is accused of aiding Babylon, seizing Judah's wealth, cutting down the fugitives, and handing over the survivors. Even though the Edomites, as descendants of Esau, were related to the Israelites, their history demonstrated a lack of compassion

for their brothers (cf. Num. 20:14–21). God would use his own people to execute judgment on Edom.

If God will ultimately take vengeance on the wicked, why does he often wait so long? One factor is that he wants to show mercy even to them. Peter answered those who accused God of tardiness in keeping his promises of justice that "[God] is patient with you, not wanting anyone to perish, but everyone to come to repentance" (2 Peter 3:9). God, after all, delayed the coming of judgment so that Saul the persecutor could be transformed into Paul the apostle (1 Tim. 1:12–13). For whose transformation are you praying today?

Ezekiel 25:15–17

Like the Edomites, the Philistines were charged with trying to settle old scores. As longtime enemies of Israel, with malice in their hearts they sought to work out their "ancient hostility" by taking vengeance on God's chosen people. They, in turn, would experience God's vengeance and recognize his sovereign power. The Kerethites, related or perhaps identical to the Philistines, would be cut off (Kereth sounds like the Hebrew word for "cut off") and the Philistines destroyed.

God's merciful patience toward the wicked isn't the only reason for his delay in judgment (see previous "Here and Now"). Whether persecution in a particular situation strengthens the church or seems to stamp it out, it testifies to Christ's lordship. That testimony may be accepted or rejected by the persecutors, but ultimately God will be known as the God of those who have suffered for him. The knowledge of his universal lordship will be recognized, even by those who have sought to eliminate it (Phil. 2:9–11).

A Prophecy Against Tyre

26:2
i 2Sa 5:11; Isa 23
k Eze 25:3

26:3
l Isa 5:30;
Jer 50:42; 51:42
26:4
m Isa 23:1,11
n Am 1:10
26:5
o Eze 27:32
p Eze 29:19

26:7
q Jer 27:6
r Ezr 7:12; Da 2:37
s Isa 23:24;
Na 2:3-4
26:8
t Jer 6:6
u Eze 21:22

26:10
v Jer 4:13
26:11
w Isa 5:28
x Jer 43:13
y Isa 26:5

26:12
z Isa 23:8;
Eze 27:3-27; 28:8
26:13
a Jer 7:34
b Isa 14:11
c Jer 25:10;
Rev 18:22
26:14
d Job 12:14;
Mal 1:4
26:15
e Eze 27:35
f Jer 49:21
26:16
g Job 8:22
h Hos 11:10
i Eze 32:10
26:17
j Eze 19:1; 27:32
k Isa 14:12

26 In the eleventh year, on the first day of the month, the word of the LORD came to me: 2 "Son of man, because Tyre[j] has said of Jerusalem, 'Aha![k] The gate to the nations is broken, and its doors have swung open to me; now that she lies in ruins I will prosper,' 3 therefore this is what the Sovereign LORD says: I am against you, O Tyre, and I will bring many nations against you, like the sea[l] casting up its waves. 4 They will destroy[m] the walls of Tyre[n] and pull down her towers; I will scrape away her rubble and make her a bare rock. 5 Out in the sea[o] she will become a place to spread fishnets, for I have spoken, declares the Sovereign LORD. She will become plunder[p] for the nations, 6 and her settlements on the mainland will be ravaged by the sword. Then they will know that I am the LORD.

7 "For this is what the Sovereign LORD says: From the north I am going to bring against Tyre Nebuchadnezzar[a][q] king of Babylon, king of kings,[r] with horses and chariots,[s] with horsemen and a great army. 8 He will ravage your settlements on the mainland with the sword; he will set up siege works[t] against you, build a ramp[u] up to your walls and raise his shields against you. 9 He will direct the blows of his battering rams against your walls and demolish your towers with his weapons. 10 His horses will be so many that they will cover you with dust. Your walls will tremble at the noise of the war horses, wagons and chariots[v] when he enters your gates as men enter a city whose walls have been broken through. 11 The hoofs[w] of his horses will trample all your streets; he will kill your people with the sword, and your strong pillars[x] will fall to the ground.[y] 12 They will plunder your wealth and loot your merchandise; they will break down your walls and demolish your fine houses and throw your stones, timber and rubble into the sea.[z] 13 I will put an end[a] to your noisy songs, and the music of your harps[b] will be heard no more.[c] 14 I will make you a bare rock, and you will become a place to spread fishnets. You will never be rebuilt,[d] for I the LORD have spoken, declares the Sovereign LORD.

15 "This is what the Sovereign LORD says to Tyre: Will not the coastlands[e] tremble[f] at the sound of your fall, when the wounded groan and the slaughter takes place in you? 16 Then all the princes of the coast will step down from their thrones and lay aside their robes and take off their embroidered garments. Clothed[g] with terror, they will sit on the ground, trembling[h] every moment, appalled[i] at you. 17 Then they will take up a lament[j] concerning you and say to you:

" 'How you are destroyed, O city of renown,
	peopled by men of the sea!
You were a power on the seas,
	you and your citizens;
you put your terror
	on all who lived there.[k]
18 Now the coastlands tremble

---

[a] 7 Hebrew *Nebuchadrezzar*, of which *Nebuchadnezzar* is a variant; here and often in Ezekiel and Jeremiah

---

Ezekiel 26:1–21

The oracle against Tyre covers almost three chapters (26:1—28:19). Tyre rejoiced when Jerusalem fell, seeing an opportunity for gain. A potential rival for her trading empire had been eliminated, opening up new avenues to prosperity. Ezekiel was quick to point out the flaw in Tyre's thinking. The God who brought judgment on Jerusalem was also against Tyre and would judge her in almost exactly the same manner.

The assault of the nations on Tyre would be "like the sea casting up its waves" (26:3), a fitting image for this city. It was built on an island about a mile long and half a mile wide, just off the Mediterranean coast. Tyre would be reduced to a bare rock, the haunt of local fishermen,

not the destination of long-distance trading partners. The city whose strength came from her location in the heart of the seas would be drowned in the depths of those seas.

With the destruction of Jerusalem, the "good life" enjoyed in Tyre must have become even more attractive to the downtrodden Jews. It's one thing to proclaim to people who are comfortably off that God is greater than money, but quite another to say the same thing to people who feel abandoned by God. To those tempted to be seduced by Tyre's prosperity, Ezekiel proclaimed Tyre's ultimate doom. Money's allure is defused by showing its ultimate insecurity and final end.

on the day of your fall;
the islands in the sea
are terrified at your collapse.'[l]

19 "This is what the Sovereign LORD says: When I make you a desolate city, like cities no longer inhabited, and when I bring the ocean depths over you and its vast waters cover you,[m] 20then I will bring you down with those who go down to the pit,[n] to the people of long ago. I will make you dwell in the earth below, as in ancient ruins, with those who go down to the pit, and you will not return or take your place[a] in the land of the living.[o] 21I will bring you to a horrible end and you will be no more. You will be sought, but you will never again be found, declares the Sovereign LORD."[p]

A Lament for Tyre

27 The word of the LORD came to me: 2"Son of man, take up a lament concerning Tyre. 3Say to Tyre, situated at the gateway to the sea,[q] merchant of peoples on many coasts, 'This is what the Sovereign LORD says:

" 'You say, O Tyre,
    "I am perfect in beauty."[r]
4Your domain was on the high seas;
    your builders brought your beauty to perfection.
5They made all your timbers
    of pine trees from Senir;[b][s]
they took a cedar from Lebanon
    to make a mast for you.
6Of oaks[t] from Bashan
    they made your oars;
of cypress wood[c] from the coasts of Cyprus[d][u]
    they made your deck, inlaid with ivory.
7Fine embroidered linen from Egypt was your sail
    and served as your banner;
your awnings were of blue and purple[v]
    from the coasts of Elishah.
8Men of Sidon and Arvad[w] were your oarsmen;
    your skilled men, O Tyre, were aboard as your seamen.[x]
9Veteran craftsmen of Gebal[e][y] were on board
    as shipwrights to caulk your seams.
All the ships of the sea and their sailors
    came alongside to trade for your wares.

10" 'Men of Persia,[z] Lydia and Put[a]
    served as soldiers in your army.
They hung their shields and helmets on your walls,
    bringing you splendor.
11Men of Arvad and Helech

26:18
l Isa 23:5; 41:5;
Eze 27:35

26:19
m Isa 8:7-8
26:20
n Eze 32:18;
Am 9:2; Jnh 2:2,6
o Eze 32:24,30

26:21
p Eze 27:36; 28:19;
Rev 18:21

27:3
q ver 33 r Eze 28:2

27:5
s Dt 3:9

27:6
t Nu 21:33;
Jer 22:20; Zec 11:2
u Ge 10:4; Isa 23:12

27:7
v Ex 25:4; Jer 10:9

27:8
w Ge 10:18
x 1Ki 9:27
27:9
y Jos 13:5; 1Ki 5:18

27:10
z Eze 38:5
a Eze 30:5

---

a 20 Septuagint; Hebrew return, and I will give glory   b 5 That is, Hermon   c 6 Targum; the Masoretic Text has a different division of the consonants.   d 6 Hebrew Kittim   e 9 That is, Byblos

---

Ezekiel 27:1–36

Ezekiel described Tyre's glory as that of a majestic ship. But his praise only heightened the tragedy of her coming downfall, represented as a lament. Like the *Titanic*, Tyre would fall victim to her own self-propaganda. A crashing east wind (from Babylon) would blow, the mighty vessel would sink, and all hands would be lost (vv. 26–27). Beauty and security would count for exactly nothing when the storm struck.

The "great prostitute" of Revelation 17–18, "Babylon" (seen by many as an allusion to Rome), was modeled in many respects after Ezekiel's description of Tyre. Rather than Tyre, Babylon, or Rome, today the "great prostitute" lives in Hollywood and along Madison Avenue. Her seductive voice draws people away from God toward materialistic excess. Her power is seen in the fact that the "good news" of designer jeans and fast food is more widely proclaimed than the Good News of Jesus Christ. Ask for the Holy Spirit's help as you seek to convince people that a life devoted to things is really a ticket for the *Titanic*.

> manned your walls on every side;
>> men of Gammad
>>> were in your towers.
>> They hung their shields around your walls;
>>> they brought your beauty to perfection.

27:12
b Ge 10:4
c ver 18,33

12 " 'Tarshish *b* did business with you because of your great wealth of goods; *c* they exchanged silver, iron, tin and lead for your merchandise.

27:13
d Ge 10:2;
Isa 66:19; Eze 38:2
e Rev 18:13

13 " 'Greece, Tubal and Meshech *d* traded with you; they exchanged slaves *e* and articles of bronze for your wares.

27:14
f Ge 10:3; Eze 38:6

14 " 'Men of Beth Togarmah *f* exchanged work horses, war horses and mules for your merchandise.

27:15
g Ge 10:7
h Jer 25:22
i 1Ki 10:22;
Rev 18:12

15 " 'The men of Rhodes *a g* traded with you, and many coastlands *h* were your customers; they paid you with ivory *i* tusks and ebony.

27:16
j Jdg 10:6; Isa 7:1-8
k Eze 28:13
27:17
l Jdg 11:33

16 " 'Aram *b j* did business with you because of your many products; they exchanged turquoise, *k* purple fabric, embroidered work, fine linen, coral and rubies for your merchandise.

17 " 'Judah and Israel traded with you; they exchanged wheat from Minnith *l* and confections, *c* honey, oil and balm for your wares.

27:18
m Ge 14:15;
Eze 47:16-18

18 " 'Damascus, *m* because of your many products and great wealth of goods, did business with you in wine from Helbon and wool from Zahar.

19 " 'Danites and Greeks from Uzal bought your merchandise; they exchanged wrought iron, cassia and calamus for your wares.

20 " 'Dedan traded in saddle blankets with you.

27:21
n Ge 25:13; Isa 60:7

21 " 'Arabia and all the princes of Kedar *n* were your customers; they did business with you in lambs, rams and goats.

27:22
o Ge 10:7,28;
1Ki 10:1-2; Isa 60:6
p Ge 43:11
27:23
q 2Ki 19:12
r Isa 37:12

22 " 'The merchants of Sheba *o* and Raamah traded with you; for your merchandise they exchanged the finest of all kinds of spices *p* and precious stones, and gold.

23 " 'Haran, *q* Canneh and Eden *r* and merchants of Sheba, Asshur and Kilmad traded with you. 24 In your marketplace they traded with you beautiful garments, blue fabric, embroidered work and multicolored rugs with cords twisted and tightly knotted.

27:25
s Isa 2:16 *fn*

> 25 " 'The ships of Tarshish *s* serve
>> as carriers for your wares.
> You are filled with heavy cargo
>> in the heart of the sea.

27:26
t Ps 48:7; Jer 18:17

> 26 Your oarsmen take you
>> out to the high seas.
> But the east wind *t* will break you to pieces
>> in the heart of the sea.

27:27
u Pr 11:4

> 27 Your wealth, *u* merchandise and wares,
>> your mariners, seamen and shipwrights,
> your merchants and all your soldiers,
>> and everyone else on board
> will sink into the heart of the sea
>> on the day of your shipwreck.

27:28
v Eze 26:15

> 28 The shorelands will quake *v*
>> when your seamen cry out.
> 29 All who handle the oars
>> will abandon their ships;
> the mariners and all the seamen
>> will stand on the shore.

27:30
w 2Sa 1:2 *x* Jer 6:26
y Rev 18:18-19

> 30 They will raise their voice
>> and cry bitterly over you;
> they will sprinkle dust *w* on their heads
>> and roll *x* in ashes. *y*

---

a 15 Septuagint; Hebrew *Dedan*   *b 16* Most Hebrew manuscripts; some Hebrew manuscripts and Syriac *Edom*   *c 17* The meaning of the Hebrew for this word is uncertain.

31 They will shave their heads because of you
and will put on sackcloth.
They will weep[z] over you with anguish of soul
and with bitter mourning.[a]
32 As they wail and mourn over you,
they will take up a lament[b] concerning you:
"Who was ever silenced like Tyre,
surrounded by the sea?"
33 When your merchandise went out on the seas,
you satisfied many nations;
with your great wealth[c] and your wares
you enriched the kings of the earth.
34 Now you are shattered by the sea
in the depths of the waters;
your wares and all your company
have gone down with you.[d]
35 All who live in the coastlands[e]
are appalled at you;
their kings shudder with horror
and their faces are distorted with fear.
36 The merchants among the nations hiss at you;[f]
you have come to a horrible end
and will be no more.[g]' "

A Prophecy Against the King of Tyre

28 The word of the LORD came to me: 2 "Son of man, say to the ruler of Tyre, 'This is what the Sovereign LORD says:

" 'In the pride of your heart
you say, "I am a god;
I sit on the throne[h] of a god
in the heart of the seas."
But you are a man and not a god,
though you think you are as wise as a god.[i]
3 Are you wiser than Daniel[a]?[j]
Is no secret hidden from you?
4 By your wisdom and understanding
you have gained wealth for yourself
and amassed gold and silver
in your treasuries.[k]
5 By your great skill in trading
you have increased your wealth,
and because of your wealth
your heart has grown proud.[l]

6 " 'Therefore this is what the Sovereign LORD says:

[a] 3 Or Danel; the Hebrew spelling may suggest a person other than the prophet Daniel.

27:31 z Isa 16:9; a Isa 22:12; Eze 7:18
27:32 b Eze 26:17
27:33 c ver 12; Eze 28:4-5
27:34 d Zec 9:4
27:35 e Eze 26:15
27:36 f Jer 18:16; 19:8; 49:17; 50:13; Zep 2:15; g Ps 37:10,36; Eze 26:21
28:2 h Isa 14:13; i Ps 9:20; 82:6-7; Isa 31:3; 2Th 2:4
28:3 j Da 1:20; 5:11-12
28:4 k Zec 9:3
28:5 l Job 31:25; Ps 52:7; 62:10; Hos 12:8; 13:6

Ezekiel 28:1–19

This portion of the oracle against Tyre combined prophecy with lament, this time directed at the ruler of Tyre, who in his character and fate personified the city. He was accused of arrogance, of saying in his heart, "I am a god; I sit on the throne of a god in the heart of the seas" (v. 2). The numerous and sometimes veiled references to the Genesis creation account set up the picture of Tyre's king as the first and foremost of all men, greater even than Adam. This "superman" persona simply underlined the greatness of his coming, Humpty-Dumpty fall.

The king of Tyre prided himself that his god-like "wisdom" was the source of his material prosperity. Today that same worldly brand of wisdom purports to offer us a God-like ability to succeed in everything we try, while living pain-free lives. We can also be seduced by the world's power—intellectual, political, or economic. But these are foolishness to God (1 Cor. 1:20). For us as Christians, wisdom consists not in consulting "experts" or in seeking "inner enlightenment," but in seeking God and living according to his Word. Jesus Christ embodies for us God's power and wisdom (1 Cor. 1:24).

" 'Because you think you are wise,
    as wise as a god,
[7] I am going to bring foreigners against you,
    the most ruthless of nations; [m]
they will draw their swords against your beauty and wisdom
    and pierce your shining splendor.
[8] They will bring you down to the pit, [n]
    and you will die a violent death
    in the heart of the seas. [o]
[9] Will you then say, "I am a god,"
    in the presence of those who kill you?
You will be but a man, not a god,
    in the hands of those who slay you.
[10] You will die the death of the uncircumcised [p]
    at the hands of foreigners.

I have spoken, declares the Sovereign LORD.' "

[11] The word of the LORD came to me: [12] "Son of man, take up a lament [q] concerning the king of Tyre and say to him: 'This is what the Sovereign LORD says:

" 'You were the model of perfection,
    full of wisdom and perfect in beauty. [r]
[13] You were in Eden, [s]
    the garden of God; [t]
every precious stone adorned you:
    ruby, topaz and emerald,
    chrysolite, onyx and jasper,
    sapphire, [a] turquoise [u] and beryl. [b]
Your settings and mountings [c] were made of gold;
    on the day you were created they were prepared.
[14] You were anointed [v] as a guardian cherub, [w]
    for so I ordained you.
You were on the holy mount of God;
    you walked among the fiery stones.
[15] You were blameless in your ways
    from the day you were created
    till wickedness was found in you.
[16] Through your widespread trade
    you were filled with violence, [x]
    and you sinned.
So I drove you in disgrace from the mount of God,

[a] 13 Or lapis lazuli   [b] 13 The precise identification of some of these precious stones is uncertain.
[c] 13 The meaning of the Hebrew for this phrase is uncertain.

Ezekiel 28:20–26

Sidon was a harbor city 25 miles north of Tyre. This is the only Old Testament reference to Sidon apart from Tyre. There was no particular charge leveled against her; presumably she too rejoiced in and profited from Jerusalem's downfall.

As Ezekiel concluded the circular tour of judgment on Israel's immediate neighbors, he was instructed to address God's people so they could understand what they saw happening. God would demonstrate his holiness not only by judging the nations but by once again gathering his people to the promised land. Both they and the other nations would see that Israel was God's people and he their God—the goal of his covenant relationship with them all along (Gen. 12:1–3; Ex. 6:7–8).

World powers may act as Satan's agents, opposed to God's people in any age. The modern nation may arrogate to itself semi-divine status, claiming and receiving the allegiance of all citizens, just as Herod received the worship of the people of Tyre and Sidon in Acts 12:22. What have you observed about those nations today that follow such a course?

God loves the people he created (John 3:16). His invitation is open to all, restricted to none, including the nations of the world (Rev. 21:24–27). The goal: "The dwelling of God [will be] with men, and he will live with them. They will be his people, and God himself will be with them and be their God" (Rev. 21:3). This is a beautiful picture of people living in complete fellowship with God and each other.

and I expelled you, O guardian cherub,[y]
  from among the fiery stones.
[17] Your heart became proud[z]
    on account of your beauty,
  and you corrupted your wisdom
    because of your splendor.
  So I threw you to the earth;
    I made a spectacle of you before kings.
[18] By your many sins and dishonest trade
    you have desecrated your sanctuaries.
  So I made a fire come out from you,
    and it consumed you,
  and I reduced you to ashes[a] on the ground
    in the sight of all who were watching.
[19] All the nations who knew you
    are appalled at you;
  you have come to a horrible end
    and will be no more.[b'] "

A Prophecy Against Sidon

[20] The word of the LORD came to me: [21] "Son of man, set your face against[c] Sidon;[d] prophesy against her [22] and say: 'This is what the Sovereign LORD says:

  " 'I am against you, O Sidon,
    and I will gain glory[e] within you.
  They will know that I am the LORD,
    when I inflict punishment[f] on her
    and show myself holy within her.
  [23] I will send a plague upon her
    and make blood flow in her streets.
  The slain will fall within her,
    with the sword against her on every side.
  Then they will know that I am the LORD.[g]

[24] " 'No longer will the people of Israel have malicious neighbors who are painful briers and sharp thorns.[h] Then they will know that I am the Sovereign LORD.

[25] " 'This is what the Sovereign LORD says: When I gather[i] the people of Israel from the nations where they have been scattered,[j] I will show myself holy[k] among them in the sight of the nations. Then they will live in their own land, which I gave to my servant Jacob.[l] [26] They will live there in safety[m] and will build houses and plant vineyards; they will live in safety when I inflict punishment on all their neighbors who maligned them. Then they will know that I am the LORD their God.[n'] '"

A Prophecy Against Egypt

29 In the tenth year, in the tenth month on the twelfth day, the word of the LORD came to me:[o] [2] "Son of man, set your face against Pharaoh king of Egypt[p] and prophesy against him and against all Egypt.[q] [3] Speak to him and say: 'This is what the Sovereign LORD says:

  " 'I am against you, Pharaoh[r] king of Egypt,
    you great monster[s] lying among your streams.
  You say, "The Nile is mine;

Cross references

28:16
[y] Ge 3:24
28:17
[z] Eze 31:10

28:18
[a] Mal 4:3

28:19
[b] Jer 51:64;
Eze 26:21; 27:36

28:21
[c] Eze 6:2
[d] Ge 10:15;
Jer 25:22

28:22
[e] Eze 39:13
[f] Eze 30:19

28:23
[g] Eze 38:22

28:24
[h] Nu 33:55;
Jos 23:13; Eze 2:6
28:25
[i] Ps 106:47;
Jer 32:37
[j] Isa 11:12
[k] Eze 20:41
[l] Jer 23:8;
Eze 11:17; 34:27;
37:25
28:26
[m] Jer 23:6
[n] Isa 65:21;
Jer 32:15; Eze 38:8;
Am 9:14-15

29:1
[o] ver 17; Eze 26:1
29:2
[p] Jer 25:19
[q] Isa 19:1-17;
Jer 46:2;
Eze 30:1-26; 31:1-
18; 32:1-32
29:3
[r] Jer 44:30
[s] Ps 74:13; Isa 27:1;
Eze 32:2

Ezekiel 29:1–21

Ezekiel 29–32 records a series of seven oracles against Egypt. In the first (29:1–16), for all Pharaoh's boasts of divinity, he would be trapped with hooks like a crocodile, brought into the desert, and executed along with his allies—"all the fish of [his] streams." The reason for this act of judgment becomes clear in verses 6–7. Egypt had been to Judah a "staff of reed"—a ridiculous contradiction, since a staff needs to be strong, while a reed is by definition fragile. Egypt would encourage Judah's rebellion against Babylon but then fail to come to her defense.

I made it for myself."

29:4
t 2Ki 19:28
u Eze 38:4

⁴But I will put hooks ᵗ in your jaws
and make the fish of your streams stick to your scales.
I will pull you out from among your streams,
with all the fish sticking to your scales. ᵘ
⁵I will leave you in the desert,
you and all the fish of your streams.
You will fall on the open field
and not be gathered or picked up.

29:5
v Jer 7:33; 34:20;
Eze 32:4-6; 39:4

I will give you as food
to the beasts of the earth and the birds of the air. ᵛ

⁶Then all who live in Egypt will know that I am the LORD.

29:6
w 2Ki 18:21;
Isa 36:6
29:7
x Isa 36:6
y Eze 17:15-17

" 'You have been a staff of reed ʷ for the house of Israel. ⁷When they grasped you with their hands, you splintered ˣ and you tore open their shoulders; when they leaned on you, you broke and their backs were wrenched. ᵃ ʸ

29:8
z Eze 14:17;
32:11-13

⁸" 'Therefore this is what the Sovereign LORD says: I will bring a sword against you and kill your men and their animals. ᶻ ⁹Egypt will become a desolate wasteland. Then they will know that I am the LORD.

29:9
a Eze 30:7-8,13-19

" 'Because you said, "The Nile is mine; I made it, ᵃ" ¹⁰therefore I am against you and against your streams, and I will make the land of Egypt a ruin and a desolate waste from Migdol to Aswan, ᵇ as far as the border of Cush. ᵇ ¹¹No foot of man or animal will pass through it; no one will live there for forty years. ᶜ ¹²I will make the land of Egypt desolate among devastated lands, and her cities will lie desolate forty years among ruined cities. And I will disperse the Egyptians among the nations and scatter them through the countries. ᵈ

29:10
b Eze 30:6
29:11
c Eze 32:13

29:12
d Jer 46:19;
Eze 30:7,23,26

¹³" 'Yet this is what the Sovereign LORD says: At the end of forty years I will gather the Egyptians from the nations where they were scattered. ¹⁴I will bring them back from captivity and return them to Upper Egypt, ᶜ ᵉ the land of their ancestry. There they will be a lowly ᶠ kingdom. ¹⁵It will be the lowliest of kingdoms and will never again exalt itself above the other nations. ᵍ I will make it so weak that it will never again rule over the nations. ¹⁶Egypt will no longer be a source of confidence ʰ for the people of Israel but will be a reminder of their sin in turning to her for help. Then they will know that I am the Sovereign LORD. ⁱ' "

29:14
e Eze 30:14
f Eze 17:14

29:15
g Zec 10:11

29:16
h Isa 36:4,6
i Isa 30:2; Hos 8:13

¹⁷In the twenty-seventh year, in the first month on the first day, the word of the LORD came to me: ʲ ¹⁸"Son of man, Nebuchadnezzar ᵏ king of Babylon drove his army in a hard campaign against Tyre; every head was rubbed bare ˡ and every shoulder made raw. Yet he and his army got no reward from the campaign he led against Tyre. ¹⁹Therefore this is what the Sovereign LORD says: I am going to give Egypt to Nebuchadnezzar king of Babylon, and he will carry off its wealth. He will loot and plunder the land as pay for his army. ᵐ ²⁰I have given him Egypt as a reward for his efforts because he and his army did it for me, declares the Sovereign LORD. ⁿ

29:17
j Eze 24:1
29:18
k Jer 27:6;
Eze 26:7-8
l Jer 48:37

29:19
m Jer 43:10-13;
Eze 30:4,10,24-25

29:20
n Isa 10:6-7; 45:1;
Jer 25:9

²¹"On that day I will make a horn ᵈ ᵒ grow for the house of Israel, and I will open your mouth ᵖ among them. Then they will know that I am the LORD. ᑫ"

29:21
o Ps 132:17
p Eze 33:22
q Eze 24:27

ᵃ 7 Syriac (see also Septuagint and Vulgate); Hebrew *and you caused their backs to stand*   ᵇ 10 That is, the upper Nile region   ᶜ 14 Hebrew *to Pathros*   ᵈ 21 *Horn* here symbolizes strength.

The second oracle (29:17–21) bears the latest date in Ezekiel (April 26, 571 B.C.). Nebuchadnezzar's campaign against Tyre had been successful but the booty gained by the end of the campaign minimal. God would give Egypt's wealth as plunder to Nebuchadnezzar's army; even an unrighteous laborer is worthy of pay.

📖 Egypt was always, from an Israelite perspective, attractive. The exodus generation nostalgically remembered it as a place of tasty food—while somehow forgetting the whips of its slave masters (Num. 11:4–6). Our world, too, has many powerful attractions, idolatries that offer easy routes to security and success. What are some of these for you? If we place our trust in any of them, though, they will prove to be broken reeds. For all their claims of godlike strength and ability to create and sustain a prosperous universe, the reality can never match the promise.

A Lament for Egypt

30 The word of the LORD came to me: ²"Son of man, prophesy and say: 'This is what the Sovereign LORD says:

" 'Wail[r] and say,
"Alas for that day!"
³For the day is near,[s]
the day of the LORD[t] is near—
a day of clouds,
a time of doom for the nations.
⁴A sword will come against Egypt,
and anguish will come upon Cush.[a]
When the slain fall in Egypt,
her wealth will be carried away
and her foundations torn down.[u]

⁵Cush and Put,[v] Lydia and all Arabia, Libya[b] and the people[w] of the covenant land will fall by the sword along with Egypt.

⁶" 'This is what the LORD says:

" 'The allies of Egypt will fall
and her proud strength will fail.
From Migdol to Aswan[x]
they will fall by the sword within her,

declares the Sovereign LORD.

⁷" 'They will be desolate
among desolate lands,
and their cities will lie
among ruined cities.[y]
⁸Then they will know that I am the LORD,
when I set fire to Egypt
and all her helpers are crushed.

⁹" 'On that day messengers will go out from me in ships to frighten Cush[z] out of her complacency. Anguish[a] will take hold of them on the day of Egypt's doom, for it is sure to come.[b]

¹⁰" 'This is what the Sovereign LORD says:

" 'I will put an end to the hordes of Egypt
by the hand of Nebuchadnezzar king of Babylon.[c]
¹¹He and his army—the most ruthless of nations[d]—
will be brought in to destroy the land.
They will draw their swords against Egypt

30:2 r Isa 13:6

30:3 s Eze 7:7; Joel 2:1,11; Ob 15; t ver 18; Eze 7:12,19

30:4 u Eze 29:19

30:5 v Eze 27:10; w Jer 25:20

30:6 x Eze 29:10

30:7 y Eze 29:12

30:9 z Isa 18:1-2; a Isa 23:5; b Eze 32:9-10

30:10 c Eze 29:19

30:11 d Eze 28:7

ᵃ 4 That is, the upper Nile region; also in verses 5 and 9   ᵇ 5 Hebrew *Cub*

Ezekiel 30:1–26

In the third prophetic revelation against Egypt (vv. 1–19), the content of the first (29:1–16) was replayed as a lament. Ezekiel was instructed to wail and mourn the coming day of God's judgment on Egypt. Her allies ("the fish of your streams" in 29:4) snapped into focus as distinct nations, all of which would fall (30:4–12) along with Egypt's cities (vv. 13–19).

The fourth oracle (vv. 20–26) declared that God had begun to act, breaking Pharaoh's arm. The prophecy came shortly before Jerusalem's fall and ruled out the possibility of relief from Egypt. The arm in the Old Testament was the body part through which a person acted—a symbol of strength. In the background of the struggle between the "arms" of Egypt and Babylon was the "arm" that acted most frequently and powerfully in the Old Testament: that of the Lord of Hosts.

Egypt had given false hope to God's people, and she, with them, would experience the weight of his wrath. We feel the pain of life's sharp edges and are tempted to find relief in whatever form it's offered. Yet all too often "relief" involves compromise in the arms of the world. We have conveniently forgotten that sin never ultimately delivers what it promises, that those who make a compact with it will see the source of their hopes turned to ashes. Under what circumstances have you experienced this? What did you learn?

and fill the land with the slain.

30:12
e Isa 19:6 f Eze 29:9

12 I will dry up^e the streams of the Nile^f
   and sell the land to evil men;
by the hand of foreigners
   I will lay waste the land and everything in it.

I the LORD have spoken.

13 " 'This is what the Sovereign LORD says:

30:13
g Jer 43:12
h Isa 19:13
i Zec 10:11

   " 'I will destroy the idols^g
      and put an end to the images in Memphis.^{a h}
   No longer will there be a prince in Egypt,ⁱ
      and I will spread fear throughout the land.

30:14
j Eze 29:14
k Ps 78:12,43
l Jer 46:25

14 I will lay^j waste Upper Egypt,^b
      set fire to Zoan^k
      and inflict punishment on Thebes.^{c l}
15 I will pour out my wrath on Pelusium,^d
      the stronghold of Egypt,
   and cut off the hordes of Thebes.
16 I will set fire to Egypt;
      Pelusium will writhe in agony.
   Thebes will be taken by storm;
      Memphis will be in constant distress.

30:17
m Ge 41:45

17 The young men of Heliopolis^{e m} and Bubastis^f
      will fall by the sword,
   and the cities themselves will go into captivity.

30:18
n Lev 26:13 o ver 3

18 Dark will be the day at Tahpanhes
      when I break the yoke of Egypt;ⁿ
   there her proud strength will come to an end.
   She will be covered with clouds,
      and her villages will go into captivity.^o
19 So I will inflict punishment on Egypt,
      and they will know that I am the LORD.' "

30:20
p Eze 26:1; 29:17;
31:1
30:21
q Jer 48:25
r Jer 30:13; 46:11
30:22
s Jer 46:25
t Ps 37:17
30:23
u Eze 29:12
30:24
v Zec 10:6,12
w Eze 21:14;
Zep 2:12

20 In the eleventh year, in the first month on the seventh day, the word of the LORD came to me:^p 21 "Son of man, I have broken the arm^q of Pharaoh king of Egypt. It has not been bound up for healing^r or put in a splint so as to become strong enough to hold a sword. 22 Therefore this is what the Sovereign LORD says: I am against Pharaoh king of Egypt.^s I will break both his arms, the good arm as well as the broken one, and make the sword fall from his hand.^t 23 I will disperse the Egyptians among the nations and scatter them through the countries.^u 24 I will strengthen^v the arms of the king of Babylon and put my sword^w in his hand, but I will break the arms of Pharaoh, and he will groan before him like a mortally wounded man. 25 I will strengthen the arms of the king of Babylon, but the arms of Pharaoh will fall limp. Then they will know that I am the LORD, when I put my sword into the hand of the king of Babylon and he brandishes it against Egypt. 26 I will disperse the Egyptians among the nations and scatter them through the countries. Then they will know that I am the LORD.^x"

30:26
x Eze 29:12

31:1
y Jer 52:5
z Eze 30:20

A Cedar in Lebanon

31 In the eleventh year,^y in the third month on the first day, the word of the LORD came to me:^z 2 "Son of man, say to Pharaoh king of Egypt and to his hordes:

   " 'Who can be compared with you in majesty?
3 Consider Assyria, once a cedar in Lebanon,
      with beautiful branches overshadowing the forest;

^a 13 Hebrew *Noph;* also in verse 16   ^b 14 Hebrew *waste Pathros*   ^c 14 Hebrew *No;* also in verses 15 and 16   ^d 15 Hebrew *Sin;* also in verse 16   ^e 17 Hebrew *Awen* (or *On*)   ^f 17 Hebrew *Pi Beseth*

it towered on high,
  its top above the thick foliage. *a*
⁴The waters nourished it,
  deep springs made it grow tall;
their streams flowed
  all around its base
and sent their channels
  to all the trees of the field.
⁵So it towered higher
  than all the trees of the field;
its boughs increased
  and its branches grew long,
  spreading because of abundant waters. *b*
⁶All the birds of the air
  nested in its boughs,
all the beasts of the field
  gave birth under its branches;
all the great nations
  lived in its shade. *c*
⁷It was majestic in beauty,
  with its spreading boughs,
for its roots went down
  to abundant waters.
⁸The cedars *d* in the garden of God
  could not rival it,
nor could the pine trees
  equal its boughs,
nor could the plane trees
  compare with its branches—
no tree in the garden of God
  could match its beauty. *e*
⁹I made it beautiful
  with abundant branches,
the envy of all the trees of Eden *f*
  in the garden of God. *g*

¹⁰" 'Therefore this is what the Sovereign LORD says: Because it towered on high, lifting its top above the thick foliage, and because it was proud *h* of its height, ¹¹I handed it over to the ruler of the nations, for him to deal with according to its wickedness. I cast it aside, *i* ¹²and the most ruthless of foreign nations *j* cut it down and left it. Its boughs fell on the mountains and in all the valleys; *k* its branches lay broken in all the ravines of the land. All the nations of the earth came out from under its

31:3
a Isa 10:34

31:5
b Eze 17:5

31:6
c Eze 17:23;
Mt 13:32

31:8
d Ps 80:10
e Ge 2:8-9

31:9
f Ge 2:8
g Ge 13:10;
Eze 28:13

31:10
h Isa 14:13-14;
Eze 28:17
31:11
i Da 5:20
31:12
j Eze 28:7
k Eze 32:5; 35:8

Ezekiel 31:1–18

The fifth oracle against Egypt pictured a great cedar of Lebanon, the tallest of known trees, to represent Assyria. This majestic cedar was well-watered, a reference to the Tigris and Euphrates rivers. Egypt equally prided herself in her unending supply of Nile water. Assyria, like Egypt, had provided security for—and domination over—other nations (the "birds of the air" and "beasts of the field"). But proud Assyria would be handed over to the Babylonians to treat her as she had treated others—ruthlessly. If Egypt thought she had greater splendor, God reminded her that she too would "be brought down" (v. 18).

As with the preceding oracles against Egypt, this message was to be understood in light of what Egypt represented to Israel. This nation frequently figured in Judah's fantasies as a substitute for God, providing chariots and horses to prop up her efforts to secure independence from the great world powers of the East. These fantasies had to be shattered before the people could be restored.

The same basic temptations (see final paragraph of "There and Then," above) assail us. The declaration on U.S. bank notes is explicit: "In God we trust." Unfortunately, this reflects a single-mindedness few Americans, even Christians, live out in practice. Our temptation is to trust in the paper on which the slogan is written, or on the nation backing the currency, not in the God of whom it speaks. But the security of money or nations is shaky indeed.

31:12
l Eze 32:11-12;
Da 4:14
31:13
m Isa 18:6;
Eze 29:5; 32:4
31:14
n Ps 82:7 *o* Ps 63:9;
Eze 26:20; 32:24

31:16
p Eze 26:15
q Isa 14:8
r Eze 14:22; 32:31
s Isa 14:15;
Eze 32:18

31:17
t Ps 9:17

31:18
u Jer 9:26;
Eze 32:19,21

shade and left it. [l] 13All the birds of the air settled on the fallen tree, and all the beasts of the field were among its branches. [m] 14Therefore no other trees by the waters are ever to tower proudly on high, lifting their tops above the thick foliage. No other trees so well-watered are ever to reach such a height; they are all destined for death, [n] for the earth below, among mortal men, with those who go down to the pit. [o]

15 " 'This is what the Sovereign LORD says: On the day it was brought down to the grave [a] I covered the deep springs with mourning for it; I held back its streams, and its abundant waters were restrained. Because of it I clothed Lebanon with gloom, and all the trees of the field withered away. 16I made the nations tremble [p] at the sound of its fall when I brought it down to the grave with those who go down to the pit. Then all the trees [q] of Eden, the choicest and best of Lebanon, all the trees that were well-watered, were consoled [r] in the earth below. [s] 17Those who lived in its shade, its allies among the nations, had also gone down to the grave with it, joining those killed by the sword. [t]

18 " 'Which of the trees of Eden can be compared with you in splendor and majesty? Yet you, too, will be brought down with the trees of Eden to the earth below; you will lie among the uncircumcised, [u] with those killed by the sword.

" 'This is Pharaoh and all his hordes, declares the Sovereign LORD.' "

A Lament for Pharaoh

32:1
v Eze 31:1; 33:21
32:2
w Eze 19:1; 27:2
x Eze 19:3,6;
Na 2:11-13
y Eze 29:3; 34:18

32 In the twelfth year, in the twelfth month on the first day, the word of the LORD came to me: [v] 2"Son of man, take up a lament [w] concerning Pharaoh king of Egypt and say to him:

" 'You are like a lion [x] among the nations;
    you are like a monster in the seas
thrashing about in your streams,
    churning the water with your feet
    and muddying the streams. [y]

3 " 'This is what the Sovereign LORD says:

" 'With a great throng of people
    I will cast my net over you,
    and they will haul you up in my net. [z]

32:3
z Eze 12:13

4I will throw you on the land
    and hurl you on the open field.
I will let all the birds of the air settle on you
    and all the beasts of the earth gorge themselves on you. [a]

32:4
a Isa 18:6;
Eze 31:12-13

5I will spread your flesh on the mountains
    and fill the valleys [b] with your remains.

32:5
b Eze 31:12
32:6
c Isa 34:3

6I will drench the land with your flowing blood [c]
    all the way to the mountains,
    and the ravines will be filled with your flesh.

---

[a] 15 Hebrew *Sheol*; also in verses 16 and 17

Ezekiel 32:1-32

In the sixth oracle against Egypt (vv. 1–16), Ezekiel returned to the image of Pharaoh as a crocodile (cf. 29:3), combining it with that of another mighty beast—the lion. God would cast his net over Pharaoh, a hunting method suitable to crocodiles or lions. The scale of Pharaoh's demise takes on near-mythical proportions: His dead body would be big enough to spread on the *mountains and fill the valleys,* his blood enough to water the land and fill the ravines.

The final oracle (vv. 17–32) takes us on a tour of the underworld, where Egypt would join the nations already there. Her future home would be among the unquiet

dead—those outside the covenant ("the uncircumcised") and those who had fallen by the sword. Though all of these other, once-mighty nations had administered reigns of terror, a place of punishment—"the pit"—was now prepared for them. Pharaoh certainly qualified to join the club.

Death remains the great leveler of society. As a grim Spanish proverb puts it, "there are no pockets in the shroud." On the day of death, the inability of wealth to deliver lasting blessings becomes thoroughly evident, as deceased millionaires rub shoulders with paupers. Read Jesus' parable in Luke 16:19–31 about the deaths of rich and poor men. What conclusions can you draw?

7 When I snuff you out, I will cover the heavens
    and darken their stars;
I will cover the sun with a cloud,
    and the moon will not give its light. *d*
8 All the shining lights in the heavens
    I will darken over you;
I will bring darkness over your land,
                    declares the Sovereign LORD.
9 I will trouble the hearts of many peoples
    when I bring about your destruction among the nations,
    among*a* lands you have not known.
10 I will cause many peoples to be appalled at you,
    and their kings will shudder with horror because of you
    when I brandish my sword before them.
On the day*e* of your downfall
    each of them will tremble
    every moment for his life. *f*

11 " 'For this is what the Sovereign LORD says:

" 'The sword of the king of Babylon*g*
    will come against you.
12 I will cause your hordes to fall
    by the swords of mighty men—
    the most ruthless of all nations. *h*
They will shatter the pride of Egypt,
    and all her hordes will be overthrown. *i*
13 I will destroy all her cattle
    from beside abundant waters
no longer to be stirred by the foot of man
    or muddied by the hoofs of cattle.*j*
14 Then I will let her waters settle
    and make her streams flow like oil,
                    declares the Sovereign LORD.
15 When I make Egypt desolate
    and strip the land of everything in it,
when I strike down all who live there,
    then they will know that I am the LORD. *k'*

16 "This is the lament*l* they will chant for her. The daughters of the nations will chant it; for Egypt and all her hordes they will chant it, declares the Sovereign LORD."

17 In the twelfth year, on the fifteenth day of the month, the word of the LORD came to me:*m* 18 "Son of man, wail for the hordes of Egypt and consign*n* to the earth below both her and the daughters of mighty nations, with those who go down to the pit.*o* 19 Say to them, 'Are you more favored than others? Go down and be laid among the uncircumcised.'*p* 20 They will fall among those killed by the sword. The sword is drawn; let her be dragged*q* off with all her hordes. 21 From within the grave*br* the mighty leaders will say of Egypt and her allies, 'They have come down and they lie with the uncircumcised, with those killed by the sword.'*r*

a 9 Hebrew; Septuagint *bring you into captivity among the nations, / to*   *b* 21 Hebrew *Sheol*; also in verse 27

32:7
d Isa 13:10; 34:4;
Eze 30:3; Joel 2:2,
31; 3:15; Mt 24:29;
Rev 8:12

32:10
e Jer 46:10
f Eze 26:16; 27:35

32:11
g Jer 46:26

32:12
h Eze 28:7
i Eze 31:11-12

32:13
j Eze 29:8,11

32:15
k Ex 7:5; 14:4,18;
Ps 107:33-34;
Eze 6:7
32:16
l 2Sa 1:17;
2Ch 35:25;
Eze 26:17
32:17
m ver 1
32:18
n Jer 1:10
o Eze 31:14,16;
Mic 1:8
32:19
p ver 29-30;
Eze 28:10; 31:18
32:20
q Ps 28:3
32:21
r Isa 14:9

Ezekiel 33:1–20

The turning point in Ezekiel is chapter 33, which pictures the news of Jerusalem's fall reaching the exiles (v. 21). Though Ezekiel would continue offering words of warning and judgment, the tenor of his ministry would shift to hope and restoration. Chapter 33 opens with a picture of the prophet as a "watchman," just as

his prophecies of destruction had in 3:16–21.

The exiles' words in verse 10 show that despair was a real danger, now that Jerusalem was on the brink of destruction. God's answer was that he took no pleasure in the death of the wicked but sought their repentance. The problem the people faced wasn't God's justice, of which they complained, but their own lack of righteous-

32:23
s Isa 14:15

32:24
t Ge 10:22
u Jer 49:37
v Job 28:13
w Eze 26:20

32:26
x Ge 10:2;
Eze 27:13

22 "Assyria is there with her whole army; she is surrounded by the graves of all her slain, all who have fallen by the sword. 23Their graves are in the depths of the pit[s] and her army lies around her grave. All who had spread terror in the land of the living are slain, fallen by the sword.

24 "Elam[t] is there, with all her hordes around her grave. All of them are slain, fallen by the sword.[u] All who had spread terror in the land of the living[v] went down uncircumcised to the earth below. They bear their shame with those who go down to the pit.[w] 25A bed is made for her among the slain, with all her hordes around her grave. All of them are uncircumcised, killed by the sword. Because their terror had spread in the land of the living, they bear their shame with those who go down to the pit; they are laid among the slain.

26 "Meshech and Tubal[x] are there, with all their hordes around their graves. All of them are uncircumcised, killed by the sword because they spread their terror in the land of the living. 27Do they not lie with the other uncircumcised warriors who have fallen, who went down to the grave with their weapons of war, whose swords were placed under their heads? The punishment for their sins rested on their bones, though the terror of these warriors had stalked through the land of the living.

28 "You too, O Pharaoh, will be broken and will lie among the uncircumcised, with those killed by the sword.

32:29
y Isa 34:5-15;
Jer 49:7; Eze 35:15;
Ob 1 z Eze 25:12-
14
32:30
a Jer 25:26;
Eze 38:6; 39:2
b Jer 25:22;
Eze 28:21

32:31
c Eze 14:22; 31:16

29 "Edom[y] is there, her kings and all her princes; despite their power, they are laid with those killed by the sword. They lie with the uncircumcised, with those who go down to the pit.[z]

30 "All the princes of the north[a] and all the Sidonians[b] are there; they went down with the slain in disgrace despite the terror caused by their power. They lie uncircumcised with those killed by the sword and bear their shame with those who go down to the pit.

31 "Pharaoh—he and all his army—will see them and he will be consoled[c] for all his hordes that were killed by the sword, declares the Sovereign LORD. 32Although I had him spread terror in the land of the living, Pharaoh and all his hordes will be laid among the uncircumcised, with those killed by the sword, declares the Sovereign LORD."

Ezekiel a Watchman

33:2
d Jer 12:12
e Eze 3:11

33:3
f Hos 8:1
33:4
g 2Ch 25:16
h Jer 6:17;
Eze 18:13; Zec 1:4;
Ac 18:6

33:6
i Eze 3:18

33:7
j Jer 26:2; Eze 3:17
33:8
k ver 14 l Eze 18:4

33:9
m Eze 3:17-19

33 The word of the LORD came to me: 2 "Son of man, speak to your countrymen and say to them: 'When I bring the sword[d] against a land, and the people of the land choose one of their men and make him their watchman,[e] 3and he sees the sword coming against the land and blows the trumpet[f] to warn the people, 4then if anyone hears the trumpet but does not take warning[g] and the sword comes and takes his life, his blood will be on his own head.[h] 5Since he heard the sound of the trumpet but did not take warning, his blood will be on his own head. If he had taken warning, he would have saved himself. 6But if the watchman sees the sword coming and does not blow the trumpet to warn the people and the sword comes and takes the life of one of them, that man will be taken away because of his sin, but I will hold the watchman accountable for his blood.'[i]

7 "Son of man, I have made you a watchman for the house of Israel; so hear the word I speak and give them warning from me.[j] 8When I say to the wicked, 'O wicked man, you will surely die,[k'] and you do not speak out to dissuade him from his ways, that wicked man will die for[a] his sin, and I will hold you accountable for his blood.[l] 9But if you do warn the wicked man to turn from his ways and he does not do so, he will die for his sin, but you will have saved yourself.[m]

---

a 8 Or in; also in verse 9

---

ness (v. 17). They had consistently chosen the path to death over life.

📖 In times of crisis, have you caught yourself asking, "Why is this happening to me? What did I do to deserve this?" Sometimes, but not always, the devastating things that happen result from our own sin. Either way, our responsibility is the same: to turn wholeheartedly to God. It's not God's design to annihilate us through painful experiences. It's to redeem us and cover over our despair with hope.

10 "Son of man, say to the house of Israel, 'This is what you are saying: "Our offenses and sins weigh us down, and we are wasting away[n] because of[a] them. How then can we live?[o] ' 11 Say to them, 'As surely as I live, declares the Sovereign LORD, I take no pleasure in the death of the wicked, but rather that they turn from their ways and live.[p] Turn! Turn from your evil ways! Why will you die, O house of Israel?'[q]

12 "Therefore, son of man, say to your countrymen, 'The righteousness of the righteous man will not save him when he disobeys, and the wickedness of the wicked man will not cause him to fall when he turns from it. The righteous man, if he sins, will not be allowed to live because of his former righteousness.'[r] 13 If I tell the righteous man that he will surely live, but then he trusts in his righteousness and does evil, none of the righteous things he has done will be remembered; he will die for the evil he has done.[s] 14 And if I say to the wicked man, 'You will surely die,' but he then turns away from his sin and does what is just[t] and right— 15 if he gives back what he took in pledge for a loan, returns what he has stolen,[u] follows the decrees that give life, and does no evil, he will surely live; he will not die.[v] 16 None of the sins he has committed will be remembered against him. He has done what is just and right; he will surely live.[w]

17 "Yet your countrymen say, 'The way of the Lord is not just.' But it is their way that is not just. 18 If a righteous man turns from his righteousness and does evil, he will die for it.[x] 19 And if a wicked man turns away from his wickedness and does what is just and right, he will live by doing so. 20 Yet, O house of Israel, you say, 'The way of the Lord is not just.' But I will judge each of you according to his own ways."

Jerusalem's Fall Explained

21 In the twelfth year of our exile, in the tenth month on the fifth day, a man who had escaped[y] from Jerusalem came to me and said, "The city has fallen![z] 22 Now the evening before the man arrived, the hand of the LORD was upon me,[a] and he opened my mouth[b] before the man came to me in the morning. So my mouth was opened and I was no longer silent.[c]

23 Then the word of the LORD came to me: 24 "Son of man, the people living in those ruins[d] in the land of Israel are saying, 'Abraham was only one man, yet he possessed the land. But we are many; surely the land has been given to us as our possession.'[e] 25 Therefore say to them, 'This is what the Sovereign LORD says: Since you eat meat with the blood[f] still in it and look to your idols and shed blood, should you then possess the land?[g] 26 You rely on your sword, you do detestable things, and each of you defiles his neighbor's wife.[h] Should you then possess the land?'

27 "Say this to them: 'This is what the Sovereign LORD says: As surely as I live, those who are left in the ruins will fall by the sword, those out in the country I will give to the wild animals to be devoured, and those in strongholds and caves will die of a plague.[i] 28 I will make the land a desolate waste, and her proud strength will come to an end, and the mountains of Israel will become desolate so that no one will

[a] 10 Or away in

33:10 n Eze 24:23; o Lev 26:39; Eze 4:17
33:11 p Eze 18:32; 2Pe 3:9 q Eze 18:23
33:12 r 2Ch 7:14; Eze 3:20
33:13 s Eze 18:24; Heb 10:38; 2Pe 2:20-21
33:14 t Eze 18:27
33:15 u Ex 22:1-4; Lev 6:2-5 v Eze 20:11; Lk 19:8
33:16 w Isa 43:25; Eze 18:22
33:18 x Eze 3:20; Eze 18:26
33:21 y Eze 24:26 z 2Ki 25:4,10; Jer 39:1-2; Eze 32:1
33:22 a Eze 1:3 b Lk 1:64 c Eze 3:26-27; 24:27
33:24 d Eze 36:4 e Isa 51:2; Jer 40:7; Eze 11:15; Ac 7:5
33:25 f Ge 9:4; Dt 12:16 g Jer 7:9-10; Eze 22:6,27
33:26 h Eze 22:11
33:27 i 1Sa 13:6; Isa 2:19; Jer 42:22; Eze 39:4

Ezekiel 33:21–33

A survivor's testimony of Jerusalem's fall brought with it a radical turning point in the fortunes of God's people and in Ezekiel's own life. The prophet's muteness was removed, as had been promised in 24:25–27.

But those remaining in Judah saw the situation as an opportunity for economic gain, not repentance. Claiming to be Abraham's children, they interpreted God's covenant promise of the land to Abraham as an inalienable right. Meanwhile, Ezekiel's fellow exiles hummed along to his tune—paying no attention to his lyrics.

Have you ever been tempted to appeal, even subconsciously, to the fact that you may have grown up in the church and/or in America as your basis for being named a Christian? Even though God promises to deal faithfully with his people's children (Gen. 17:8; Acts 2:39), that promise doesn't work *apart* from our faith but *through* it. The blessings of a relationship with God come to those who live in obedience to the Word.

Some respond in a superficial way to the preaching and teaching of God's Word. They listen, yet never learn or *do* (cf. Matt. 7:26–27). How long does a sermon, even a "good" one, typically stick with you? When did God's word, expressed through his spokesperson, grab you at the heart and change you from the inside out?

cross them. 29Then they will know that I am the LORD, when I have made the land a desolate waste because of all the detestable things they have done.'

30 "As for you, son of man, your countrymen are talking together about you by the walls and at the doors of the houses, saying to each other, 'Come and hear the message that has come from the LORD.' 31My people come to you, as they usually do, and sit before[j] you to listen to your words, but they do not put them into practice. With their mouths they express devotion, but their hearts are greedy for unjust gain.[k] 32Indeed, to them you are nothing more than one who sings love songs with a beautiful voice and plays an instrument well, for they hear your words but do not put them into practice.[l]

33 "When all this comes true—and it surely will—then they will know that a prophet has been among them.[m]"

Shepherds and Sheep

34 The word of the LORD came to me: 2 "Son of man, prophesy against the shepherds of Israel; prophesy and say to them: 'This is what the Sovereign LORD says: Woe to the shepherds of Israel who only take care of themselves! Should not shepherds take care of the flock?[n] 3You eat the curds, clothe yourselves with the wool and slaughter the choice animals, but you do not take care of the flock.[o] 4You have not strengthened the weak or healed the sick or bound up the injured. You have not brought back the strays or searched for the lost. You have ruled them harshly and brutally.[p] 5So they were scattered because there was no shepherd,[q] and when they were scattered they became food for all the wild animals.[r] 6My sheep wandered over all the mountains and on every high hill. They were scattered over the whole earth, and no one searched or looked for them.[s]

7 " 'Therefore, you shepherds, hear the word of the LORD: 8As surely as I live, declares the Sovereign LORD, because my flock lacks a shepherd and so has been plundered and has become food for all the wild animals, and because my shepherds did not search for my flock but cared for themselves rather than for my flock, 9therefore, O shepherds, hear the word of the LORD: 10This is what the Sovereign LORD says: I am against[t] the shepherds and will hold them accountable for my flock. I will remove them from tending the flock so that the shepherds can no longer feed themselves. I will rescue[u] my flock from their mouths, and it will no longer be food for them.[v]

11 " 'For this is what the Sovereign LORD says: I myself will search for my sheep and look after them. 12As a shepherd[w] looks after his scattered flock when he is with them, so will I look after my sheep. I will rescue them from all the places where they were scattered on a day of clouds and darkness.[x] 13I will bring them out from the nations and gather them from the countries, and I will bring them into their own land. I will pasture them on the mountains of Israel, in the ravines and in all the settlements in the land.[y] 14I will tend them in a good pasture, and the mountain heights of Israel[z] will be their grazing land. There they will lie down in good graz-

---

Ezekiel 34:1–31

The "shepherds of Israel" included her kings and officials, as well as the priests and prophets. God was against his shepherds because, instead of caring for the flock, they viewed their position as an opportunity for personal gain. The exiles could look forward to a return to the promised land, where they would experience the full blessing of God's shepherding: He would feed them on rich pasture; cause them to lie down in safety; search for the lost; bind up the injured; and establish justice, punishing the oppressors and strengthening the weak.

God's solution to a history of bad shepherds wasn't to replace shepherding with a better system but to replace the bad shepherds with a good One. This future ruler would be like David, the king after God's own heart

(1 Sam. 13:14). In addition, God would make "a covenant of peace" with his flock (cf. Jer. 31:31–34), pointing to the final peace later initiated by Christ.

Just as in the Old Testament the notion of God as Chief Shepherd was combined with that of the king as shepherd, so Christ rules today through church leaders, his undershepherds (1 Peter 5:2–4). This position combines authority with service: They are to "oversee" the flock but not "lord it" over them. Like the Chief Shepherd, they are to be on the lookout for prowling wolves, while watching tenderly over the flock committed to their care (Acts 20:28–29). The image of the shepherd uniquely conveys this special combination of toughness and tenderness.

Margin refs: 33:31 j Eze 8:1; k Ps 78:36-37; Isa 29:13; Eze 22:27; Mt 13:22; 1Jn 3:18. 33:32 l Mk 6:20. 33:33 m 1Sa 3:20; Jer 28:9; Eze 2:5. 34:2 n Ps 78:70-72; Isa 40:11; Jer 3:15; 23:1; Mic 3:11; Jn 10:11; 21:15-17. 34:3 o Isa 56:11; Eze 22:27; Zec 11:16. 34:4 p Zec 11:15-17. 34:5 q Nu 27:17; r ver 28; Isa 56:9. 34:6 s Ps 142:4; 1Pe 2:25. 34:10 t Jer 21:13; u Ps 72:14; v 1Sa 2:29-30; Zec 10:3. 34:12 w Isa 40:11; Jer 31:10; Lk 19:10; x Eze 30:3. 34:13 y Jer 23:3. 34:14 z Eze 20:40.

ing land, and there they will feed in a rich pasture^a on the mountains of Israel.^b ¹⁵I myself will tend my sheep and have them lie down, declares the Sovereign LORD.^c ¹⁶I will search for the lost and bring back the strays. I will bind up the injured and strengthen the weak,^d but the sleek and the strong I will destroy. I will shepherd the flock with justice.^e

¹⁷ "'As for you, my flock, this is what the Sovereign LORD says: I will judge between one sheep and another, and between rams and goats.^f ¹⁸Is it not enough for you to feed on the good pasture? Must you also trample the rest of your pasture with your feet? Is it not enough for you to drink clear water? Must you also muddy the rest with your feet? ¹⁹Must my flock feed on what you have trampled and drink what you have muddied with your feet?

²⁰ "'Therefore this is what the Sovereign LORD says to them: See, I myself will judge between the fat sheep and the lean sheep. ²¹Because you shove with flank and shoulder, butting all the weak sheep with your horns^g until you have driven them away, ²²I will save my flock, and they will no longer be plundered. I will judge between one sheep and another.^h ²³I will place over them one shepherd, my servant David, and he will tendⁱ them; he will tend them and be their shepherd. ²⁴I the LORD will be their God,^j and my servant David will be prince among them. I the LORD have spoken.^k

²⁵ "'I will make a covenant of peace with them and rid the land of wild beasts^l so that they may live in the desert and sleep in the forests in safety.^m ²⁶I will blessⁿ them and the places surrounding my hill.^a I will send down showers in season;^o there will be showers of blessing.^p ²⁷The trees of the field will yield their fruit and the ground will yield its crops; the people will be secure in their land. They will know that I am the LORD, when I break the bars of their yoke^q and rescue them from the hands of those who enslaved them.^r ²⁸They will no longer be plundered by the nations, nor will wild animals devour them. They will live in safety, and no one will make them afraid.^s ²⁹I will provide for them a land renowned^t for its crops, and they will no longer be victims of famine^u in the land or bear the scorn^v of the na-

^a 26 Or I will make them and the places surrounding my hill a blessing

34:14
^a Ps 23:2
^b Eze 36:29-30
34:15
^c Ps 23:1-2
34:16
^d Mic 4:6
^e Isa 10:16; Lk 5:32
34:17
^f Mt 25:32-33

34:21
^g Dt 33:17
34:22
^h Ps 72:12-14; Jer 23:2-3
34:23
ⁱ Isa 40:11
34:24
^j Eze 36:28
^k Jer 30:9
34:25
^l Lev 26:6
^m Isa 11:6-9; Hos 2:18
34:26
ⁿ Ge 12:2 ^o Ps 68:9
^p Dt 11:13-15; Isa 44:3
34:27
^q Lev 26:13
^r Jer 30:8
34:28
^s Jer 30:10; Eze 39:26
34:29
^t Isa 4:2
^u Eze 36:29
^v Eze 36:6

Snapshots

 34:26–27

Martha

Martha, age seventeen, lives in one of the world's poorest countries, Ethiopia, which is often ravaged by drought and relies heavily on international aid. Nearly half its 67 million residents are chronically malnourished, with many families eking out a living on less than $5.00 per month. Children frequently forego education to scrounge for daily food, which may consist of roots or bark.

But Martha, a sponsored child, has reason to rejoice. "The long drought, followed by months of severe famine that claimed the lives of many of our relatives, is always remembered with anguish," she concedes. But prompt action by a humanitarian organization prevented further deaths.

> "Now we are living life in all its fullness. Praise the Lord!"

One of the benefits of its development program has been access to schooling. Martha, a ninth grader, has aspirations of becoming a pilot. Improved roads and water supply, as well as a health clinic, have drastically altered her quality of life.

"My village, Ambowuha, is saturated with different kinds of fresh fruit and vegetables that were introduced by the [aid group]," she enthuses. "My father often tells me that the area was referred to as a bowl of dust . . . I would say now we are living life in all its fullness. Praise the Lord!"

34:29
w Eze 36:15
34:30
x Eze 14:11; 37:27
34:31
y Ps 100:3; Jer 23:1

tions. [w] 30Then they will know that I, the LORD their God, am with them and that they, the house of Israel, are my people, declares the Sovereign LORD. [x] 31You my sheep, the sheep of my pasture, [y] are people, and I am your God, declares the Sovereign LORD.' "

A Prophecy Against Edom

35:3
z Jer 6:12
a Eze 25:12-14
35:4
b ver 9

35 The word of the LORD came to me: 2"Son of man, set your face against Mount Seir; prophesy against it 3and say: 'This is what the Sovereign LORD says: I am against you, Mount Seir, and I will stretch out my hand [z] against you and make you a desolate waste. [a] 4I will turn your towns into ruins and you will be desolate. Then you will know that I am the LORD. [b]

35:5
c Ps 137:7;
Eze 21:29
35:6
d Isa 63:2-6

5 " 'Because you harbored an ancient hostility and delivered the Israelites over to the sword at the time of their calamity, the time their punishment reached its climax, [c] 6therefore as surely as I live, declares the Sovereign LORD, I will give you over to bloodshed and it will pursue you. [d] Since you did not hate bloodshed, bloodshed will pursue you. 7I will make Mount Seir a desolate waste and cut off from it all who come and go. 8I will fill your mountains with the slain; those killed by the sword will fall on your hills and in your valleys and in all your ravines. [e] 9I will make you desolate forever; your towns will not be inhabited. Then you will know that I am the LORD. [f]

35:8
e Eze 31:12

35:9
f Jer 49:13

35:10
g Ps 83:12;
Eze 36:2,5

35:11
h Eze 25:14
i Ps 9:16; Mt 7:2

10 " 'Because you have said, "These two nations and countries will be ours and we will take possession [g] of them," even though I the LORD was there, 11therefore as surely as I live, declares the Sovereign LORD, I will treat you in accordance with the anger [h] and jealousy you showed in your hatred of them and I will make myself known among them when I judge you. [i] 12Then you will know that I the LORD have heard all the contemptible things you have said against the mountains of Israel. You said, "They have been laid waste and have been given over to us to devour." [j] 13You boasted against me and spoke against me without restraint, and I heard it. [k] 14This is what the Sovereign LORD says: While the whole earth rejoices, I will make you desolate. [l] 15Because you rejoiced [m] when the inheritance of the house of Israel became desolate, that is how I will treat you. You will be desolate, O Mount Seir, [n] you and all of Edom. [o] Then they will know that I am the LORD.' "

35:12
j Jer 50:7
35:13
k Da 11:36

35:14
l Jer 51:48
35:15
m Ob 1:12 n ver 3
o Isa 34:5-6,11;
Jer 50:11-13;
La 4:21

A Prophecy to the Mountains of Israel

36:2
p Eze 25:3
q Dt 32:13
r Eze 35:10

36 "Son of man, prophesy to the mountains of Israel and say, 'O mountains of Israel, hear the word of the LORD. 2This is what the Sovereign LORD says: The enemy said of you, "Aha! [p] The ancient heights [q] have become our possession.'" ' [r] 3Therefore prophesy and say, 'This is what the Sovereign LORD says: Because they ravaged and hounded you from every side so that you became the possession of the rest of the nations and the object of people's malicious talk and slander, [s] 4therefore, O mountains of Israel, hear the word of the Sovereign LORD: This is what the Sovereign LORD says to the mountains and hills, to the ravines and valleys, [t] to the desolate ruins and the deserted towns that have been plundered and ridiculed by the rest of the nations around you [u]— 5this is what the Sovereign LORD says: In my

36:3
s Ps 44:13-14

36:4
t Eze 6:3
u Dt 11:11; Ps 79:4;
Eze 34:28

Ezekiel 35:1–15

Ezekiel 35 is a prophesy against Edom, symbolized by its central mountain, Mount Seir. It might seem out of place among the surrounding chapters that speak of Israel's restoration, especially since Ezekiel had already delivered a brief prophecy against Edom (see 25:12–14). But the Edomites, descendants of Esau, wanted to reclaim by force their stolen birthright—the lands of Israel and Judah (v. 10; cf. Gen. 25:21–34). This ambition would be thwarted by God's judgment of Edom, a necessary prerequisite for Judah's restoration.

Lasting possession of the land wasn't achieved by Edom's power, nor by Israel's tricky strategies, but by

sovereign, divine action (cf. Rom. 9:10–16). God had determined from eternity to save a people for himself. That purpose stands despite all the forces arrayed against it. Similarly, our salvation assurance can't rest on our own merits or spiritual heredity. We were grafted into Christ the vine because he chose us to bear lasting fruit for him (John 15:16). All is of grace—even our fruitfulness. What does this truth mean, practically, to you today?

Ezekiel 36:1–38

If Ezekiel 35 pictures the future's dark side (Edom's destruction), chapter 36 presents its opposite: the return of God's people to the land of promise. The address to the "mountains of Israel" parallels the one to

burning zeal I have spoken against the rest of the nations, and against all Edom, for with glee and with malice in their hearts they made my land their own possession so that they might plunder its pastureland.' ^v 6Therefore prophesy concerning the land of Israel and say to the mountains and hills, to the ravines and valleys: "This is what the Sovereign LORD says: I speak in my jealous wrath because you have suffered the scorn of the nations. ^w 7Therefore this is what the Sovereign LORD says: I swear with uplifted hand that the nations around you will also suffer scorn.

8 " 'But you, O mountains of Israel, will produce branches and fruit^x for my people Israel, for they will soon come home. 9I am concerned for you and will look on you with favor; you will be plowed and sown, 10and I will multiply the number of people upon you, even the whole house of Israel. The towns will be inhabited and the ruins rebuilt.^y 11I will increase the number of men and animals upon you, and they will be fruitful and become numerous. I will settle people on you as in the past^z and will make you prosper more than before.^a Then you will know that I am the LORD. 12I will cause people, my people Israel, to walk upon you. They will possess you, and you will be their inheritance;^b you will never again deprive them of their children.

13 " 'This is what the Sovereign LORD says: Because people say to you, "You devour men^c and deprive your nation of its children," 14therefore you will no longer devour men or make your nation childless, declares the Sovereign LORD. 15No longer will I make you hear the taunts of the nations, and no longer will you suffer the scorn of the peoples or cause your nation to fall, declares the Sovereign LORD.^d ' "

16Again the word of the LORD came to me: 17"Son of man, when the people of Israel were living in their own land, they defiled it by their conduct and their actions. Their conduct was like a woman's monthly uncleanness in my sight.^e 18So I poured out^f my wrath on them because they had shed blood in the land and because they had defiled it with their idols. 19I dispersed them among the nations, and they were scattered^g through the countries; I judged them according to their conduct and their actions.^h 20And wherever they went among the nations they profanedⁱ my holy name, for it was said of them, 'These are the LORD's people, and yet they had to leave his land.'^j 21I had concern for my holy name, which the house of Israel profaned among the nations where they had gone.^k

22"Therefore say to the house of Israel, 'This is what the Sovereign LORD says: It is not for your sake, O house of Israel, that I am going to do these things, but for the sake of my holy name, which you have profaned^l among the nations where you have gone.^m 23I will show the holiness of my great name, which has been profaned among the nations, the name you have profaned among them. Then the nations will know that I am the LORD, declares the Sovereign LORD, when I show myself holyⁿ through you before their eyes.^o

24 " 'For I will take you out of the nations; I will gather you from all the countries and bring you back into your own land.^p 25I will sprinkle^q clean water on you, and you will be clean; I will cleanse^r you from all your impurities and from all your idols.^s 26I will give you a new heart^t and put a new spirit in you; I will remove from you your heart of stone and give you a heart of flesh.^u 27And I will put my Spirit^v

36:5 v Jer 50:11; Eze 25:12-14; 35:10,15
36:6 w Ps 123:3-4; Eze 34:29
36:8 x Isa 27:6
36:10 y ver 33; Isa 49:17-23
36:11 z Mic 7:14 a Jer 31:28; Eze 16:55
36:12 b Eze 47:14,22
36:13 c Nu 13:32
36:15 d Ps 89:50-51; Eze 34:29
36:17 e Jer 2:7
36:18 f 2Ch 34:21
36:19 g Dt 28:64 h Eze 39:24
36:20 i Ro 2:24 j Isa 52:5; Jer 33:24; Eze 12:16
36:21 k Ps 74:18; Isa 48:9
36:22 l Ro 2:24* m Ps 106:8
36:23 n Eze 20:41 o Ps 126:2; Isa 5:16
36:24 p Eze 34:13; 37:21
36:25 q Heb 9:13; 10:22 r Ps 51:2,7 s Zec 13:2
36:26 t Jer 24:7 u Ps 51:10; Eze 11:19
36:27 v Eze 37:14

Mount Seir in chapter 35, as well as the earlier oracle of destruction to those same mountains in chapter 6. Edom had sought to possess the mountains of Israel, but the Israelites would return to repossess their land, now in the hands of many nations.

The honor of God's name would be vindicated by a show of power among the nations when he brought Israel back home. But it wouldn't be enough for God to give Israel a new shepherd-leader (34:23-24) and a renewed land. A total transformation would be required. The root of God's restoration of his people would be his holiness. Their resettlement in the land would also involve a change in their nature. The life-giving Spirit of

God would create in them the will and ability to follow God's decrees (see also the notes on 11:16-25).

We can be confident that God's people will not only be saved but also made holy. Like Israel, the church must be purified from her sins and perfected in righteousness. God's Spirit has been given to us in full measure, so that by him we might put to death the misdeeds of our bodies (Rom. 8:13). We are saved not *by our* works but *through his* work. To what end? *For* good works (Eph. 2:8-10). How readily do you connect your salvation with God's eternal purpose for you to accomplish good in his name?

36:28
w Jer 30:22
x Eze 14:11;
37:14,27
36:29
y Eze 34:29

36:30
z Lev 26:4-5;
Eze 34:27;
Hos 2:21-22
36:31
a Eze 6:9; 20:43
36:32
b Dt 9:5

36:35
c Joel 2:3 d Isa 51:3

36:36
e Eze 17:22; 22:14;
37:14; 39:27-28

36:38
f 1Ki 8:63;
2Ch 35:7-9

37:1
g Eze 1:3; 8:3
h Eze 11:24; Lk 4:1;
Ac 8:39 i Jer 7:32
j Jer 8:2; Eze 40:1

in you and move you to follow my decrees and be careful to keep my laws. [28]You will live in the land I gave your forefathers; you will be my people,[w] and I will be your God.[x] [29]I will save you from all your uncleanness. I will call for the grain and make it plentiful and will not bring famine[y] upon you. [30]I will increase the fruit of the trees and the crops of the field, so that you will no longer suffer disgrace among the nations because of famine.[z] [31]Then you will remember your evil ways and wicked deeds, and you will loathe yourselves for your sins and detestable practices.[a] [32]I want you to know that I am not doing this for your sake, declares the Sovereign LORD. Be ashamed and disgraced for your conduct, O house of Israel![b]

[33]"'This is what the Sovereign LORD says: On the day I cleanse you from all your sins, I will resettle your towns, and the ruins will be rebuilt. [34]The desolate land will be cultivated instead of lying desolate in the sight of all who pass through it. [35]They will say, "This land that was laid waste has become like the garden of Eden;[c] the cities that were lying in ruins, desolate and destroyed, are now fortified and inhabited.[d]" [36]Then the nations around you that remain will know that I the LORD have rebuilt what was destroyed and have replanted what was desolate. I the LORD have spoken, and I will do it.'[e]

[37]"This is what the Sovereign LORD says: Once again I will yield to the plea of the house of Israel and do this for them: I will make their people as numerous as sheep, [38]as numerous as the flocks for offerings[f] at Jerusalem during her appointed feasts. So will the ruined cities be filled with flocks of people. Then they will know that I am the LORD.'"

The Valley of Dry Bones

37 The hand of the LORD was upon me,[g] and he brought me out by the Spirit[h] of the LORD and set me in the middle of a valley;[i] it was full of bones.[j]

Ezekiel 37:1–14

From flourishing garden-cities full of vibrantly alive people (36:33–38), Ezekiel was now transported to the valley of the shadow of death. But even the "Death Valley" of exile had to be swallowed up in victory. The prophet saw God fulfill in visionary form his promise of

---

Snapshots

36:23

David Z. T. Yui (aka Yu Jih-Chang; Yu Rizhang)

David Z.T. Yui (1882–1936), a longtime leader of the Chinese YMCA and the National Christian Counsel, studied at St. John's University in Shanghai and received an M.S. in education from Harvard in 1910. Back home in China, this vigorous young man held a variety of posts in education, journalism, and government, affiliating with the Chinese YMCA in 1913 and becoming its secretary-general from 1916 until 1932.

> Yui believed in nation building through individual Christian character.

The YMCA grew rapidly until the mid-20s, when it drew the rancor of nationalistic critics. Yui struggled through the crisis, despite serious personal health problems. During this time he also led a fund-raising movement to redeem Chinese railroads from Japanese control; chaired the National Christian Council, a position requiring tact and mediation; founded the Institute of Pacific Relations, an important scholarly forum; and played a prominent role at the 1928 Jerusalem meeting of the International Missionary Council.

In the United States in 1933 to rally support following Japan's invasion of Mongolia, Yui suffered a cerebral hemorrhage, from which he never fully recovered. Yui believed in nation building through individual Christian character and saw the YMCA as an instrument of China's national and individual development.

2He led me back and forth among them, and I saw a great many bones on the floor
of the valley, bones that were very dry. 3He asked me, "Son of man, can these
bones live?"
I said, "O Sovereign LORD, you alone know.[k]"
4Then he said to me, "Prophesy to these bones and say to them, 'Dry bones, hear
the word of the LORD![l] 5This is what the Sovereign LORD says to these bones: I will
make breath[a] enter you, and you will come to life.[m] 6I will attach tendons to you
and make flesh come upon you and cover you with skin; I will put breath in you,
and you will come to life. Then you will know that I am the LORD.[n]' "
7So I prophesied as I was commanded. And as I was prophesying, there was a
noise, a rattling sound, and the bones came together, bone to bone. 8I looked, and
tendons and flesh appeared on them and skin covered them, but there was no
breath in them.
9Then he said to me, "Prophesy to the breath;[o] prophesy, son of man, and say to
it, 'This is what the Sovereign LORD says: Come from the four winds, O breath, and
breathe into these slain, that they may live.' " 10So I prophesied as he commanded me,
and breath entered them; they came to life and stood up on their feet—a vast army.[p]
11Then he said to me: "Son of man, these bones are the whole house of Israel.
They say, 'Our bones are dried up and our hope is gone; we are cut off.'[q] 12There-
fore prophesy and say to them: 'This is what the Sovereign LORD says: O my people, I am going to open your graves and bring you up from them; I will bring you
back to the land of Israel.[r] 13Then you, my people, will know that I am the LORD,
when I open your graves and bring you up from them. 14I will put my Spirit[s] in you
and you will live, and I will settle you in your own land. Then you will know that
I the LORD have spoken, and I have done it, declares the LORD.[t]' "

One Nation Under One King

15The word of the LORD came to me: 16"Son of man, take a stick of wood and
write on it, 'Belonging to Judah and the Israelites[u] associated with him.[v]' Then take
another stick of wood, and write on it, 'Ephraim's stick, belonging to Joseph and
all the house of Israel associated with him.' 17Join them together into one stick so
that they will become one in your hand.[w]
18"When your countrymen ask you, 'Won't you tell us what you mean by this?'[x]
19say to them, 'This is what the Sovereign LORD says: I am going to take the stick of
Joseph—which is in Ephraim's hand—and of the Israelite tribes associated with
him, and join it to Judah's stick, making them a single stick of wood, and they will

37:3 [k] Dt 32:39; 1Sa 2:6; Isa 26:19
37:4 [l] Jer 22:29
37:5 [m] Ge 2:7; Ps 104:29-30
37:6 [n] Eze 38:23; Joel 2:27; 3:17
37:9 [o] Ps 104:30
37:10 [p] Rev 11:11
37:11 [q] La 3:54
37:12 [r] Dt 32:39; 1Sa 2:6; Isa 26:19; Hos 13:14; Am 9:14-15
37:14 [s] Joel 2:28-29 [t] Eze 36:27-28,36
37:16 [u] 1Ki 12:20; 2Ch 10:17-19 [v] Nu 17:2-3; 2Ch 15:9
37:17 [w] ver 24; Isa 11:13; Jer 50:4; Hos 1:11
37:18 [x] Eze 24:19

[a] 5 The Hebrew for this word can also mean *wind* or *spirit* (see verses 6-14).

36:27 to put his life-giving Spirit within his people. Like the creation of Adam in Genesis 2:7, the re-creation of God's people occurred in two stages: forming and then filling with the breath of life. The prophecy following the vision (37:11–14) made clear that God wasn't speaking of physical resurrection but of Israel's restoration in the promised land.

The Israelites, "dead" though physically alive, lamented, "Our bones are dried up and our hope is gone; we are cut off" (v. 11). They were indeed cut off—from the life-giving presence of the living God—and therefore without hope. We all share by nature that spiritual condition (cf. Eph. 2:1–2). Can such dead people live? Thanks be to God, the answer for us is a resounding yes—as it was for Israel. "Because of his great love for us, God, who is rich in mercy, made us alive with Christ even when we were dead in transgressions" (Eph. 2:4–5).

Ezekiel 37:15–28

This passage contains Ezekiel's final sign-act and a related prophecy concerning the future reunification of God's people. God would duplicate Ezekiel's symbolic act by uniting the northern and southern kingdoms, separated since the death of David's son Solomon. Just as David had earlier welded the disparate tribes into a united kingdom, so the new David—the future Messianic ruler—would unite the one nation under one King. And just as the former division had resulted in separate centers of worship (1 Kings 12:25–33), the reunion would bring a return to a single, divinely approved sanctuary in their midst.

What's the basis for the Christian unity we so desire? This passage gives the key: Christian unity is grounded in Jesus Christ, our true king (Eph. 1:18–23; Rev. 19:16) and true temple (John 2:19–22; Eph. 2:14–22). If there is ever hope of peace and reconciliation for any situation on Earth, it's available through us as his agents (peacemakers). But remember, peacemaking isn't for the fainthearted. Jesus directly followed up the Beatitude on peacemaking with one on persecution (Matt. 5:9–12).

New Identities

37:11–14

Devastated by war, a conquered and pitiable people were driven from the lands of their ancestors into the despair of captivity and exile. They were wraiths of their former selves, lacking in social form and community substance, a once proud race reduced to dead people walking. This is the opening portrait of God's people in Ezekiel 37.

Were it not for their unique role in God's plan for the nations, countless millions in the developing world today could take the place of the Israelites of Ezekiel's day. They are the people whose faces flash across our television screens as social or geographic exiles of war. They are the statistics of refugee camps and HIV/AIDS hospices. They are the unnamed thousands who are political prisoners and prisoners of conscience. All reduced to a skeleton of their former selves. All with the same soulless look of despair.

Transformational development works primarily to better economic circumstances, political stability, social parity, and educational advancement for the world's poor and socially deprived. But too often these programs miss the central requirement of any group of human beings to engage in sustainable, transformational development: a clear, satisfying, and healthy sense of who they are and what they have—a valued identity.

> "Without individuals deciding to pursue their own healing, there is nothing that can be done to heal them or assist them in their healing."

A valued identity and its attendant sense of well-being and belonging are perhaps the most significant developmental needs in all of humanity. In fact, the apostle Paul named identity fulfillment as the uppermost achievement of our relationship with Christ (Col. 2:9–10). And when Nehemiah stirred his people to work on the wall and begin to establish their collective identity once again, he began to transform them. The king's money alone wouldn't have built the wall, sustained the project, or renewed the people. A Native American Mohawk social worker noted that, "without individuals deciding to pursue their own healing, there is nothing that can be done to heal them or assist them in their healing." Strong words. Cutting words to those who need a hand-up and those who feel compelled from a sense of obligation or compassion to provide it.

If any single loss can be said to contribute most profoundly to the certainty of an unrealized life, it's loss of identity. Many in aboriginal and other damaged "developing" societies wander life's road with no clear destination. This lack traces to an inability to see in themselves value, significance, and the potential to control their own lives and futures.

Through God's prophetic words, people are transformed and healed—not just physically or materially but spiritually and, perhaps as significantly, in terms of their uniqueness and distinctiveness as a nation. Ultimately, they are renewed to the identity he himself fashions for them. Change occurs as his Spirit breathes life into them once again and they are restored to their identity as his chosen ones, the people of the promise.

Development is about more than food or money. It calls us to be agents of the wind of God's Spirit blowing through his people, raising them from the depths of despair and hopelessness—the living dead—and instilling in them a sense of value and purpose, meaning and expectation.

Without a clear sense of one's identity, place, and role, all the rest is just bones and lifeless flesh.

Terry LeBlanc, director of aboriginal programs at World Vision Canada in Mississauga, Ontario

become one in my hand.'[y] 20 Hold before their eyes the sticks you have written on
21 and say to them, 'This is what the Sovereign LORD says: I will take the Israelites out
of the nations where they have gone. I will gather them from all around and bring
them back into their own land.[z] 22 I will make them one nation in the land, on the
mountains of Israel. There will be one king over all of them and they will never
again be two nations or be divided into two kingdoms.[a] 23 They will no longer defile[b] themselves with their idols and vile images or with any of their offenses, for I
will save them from all their sinful backsliding,[a] and I will cleanse them. They will
be my people, and I will be their God.[c]

24 " 'My servant David[d] will be king over them, and they will all have one shepherd.[e] They will follow my laws and be careful to keep my decrees.[f] 25 They will live
in the land I gave to my servant Jacob, the land where your fathers lived.[g] They and
their children and their children's children will live there forever,[h] and David my
servant will be their prince forever.[i] 26 I will make a covenant of peace[j] with them;
it will be an everlasting covenant. I will establish them and increase their numbers,[k] and I will put my sanctuary among them forever.[l] 27 My dwelling place[m] will
be with them; I will be their God, and they will be my people.[n] 28 Then the nations
will know that I the LORD make Israel holy,[o] when my sanctuary is among them
forever.' "

A Prophecy Against Gog

38 The word of the LORD came to me: 2 "Son of man, set your face against Gog,
of the land of Magog,[p] the chief prince of[b] Meshech and Tubal;[q] prophesy
against him 3 and say: 'This is what the Sovereign LORD says: I am against you,
O Gog, chief prince of[c] Meshech and Tubal.[r] 4 I will turn you around, put hooks[s]
in your jaws and bring you out with your whole army—your horses, your horsemen
fully armed, and a great horde with large and small shields, all of them brandish-
ing their swords.[t] 5 Persia, Cush[d][u] and Put[v] will be with them, all with shields and
helmets, 6 also Gomer[w] with all its troops, and Beth Togarmah[x] from the far north
with all its troops—the many nations with you.

7 " 'Get ready; be prepared,[y] you and all the hordes gathered about you, and take
command of them. 8 After many days[z] you will be called to arms. In future years you
will invade a land that has recovered from war, whose people were gathered from
many nations[a] to the mountains of Israel, which had long been desolate. They had
been brought out from the nations, and now all of them live in safety.[b] 9 You and
all your troops and the many nations with you will go up, advancing like a storm;[c]
you will be like a cloud[d] covering the land.

10 " 'This is what the Sovereign LORD says: On that day thoughts will come into
your mind and you will devise an evil scheme.[e] 11 You will say, "I will invade a land
of unwalled villages; I will attack a peaceful and unsuspecting people—all of them
living without walls and without gates and bars.[f] 12 I will plunder and loot and turn
my hand against the resettled ruins and the people gathered from the nations, rich
in livestock and goods, living at the center of the land." 13 Sheba[g] and Dedan and
the merchants of Tarshish and all her villages[e] will say to you, "Have you come to

37:19 [y] Zec 10:6
37:21 [z] Isa 43:5-6; Eze 36:24; 39:27
37:22 [a] Isa 11:13; Jer 3:18; Hos 1:11
37:23 [b] Eze 36:25; 43:7 [c] Eze 11:18; 36:28
37:24 [d] Hos 3:5 [e] Isa 40:11; Eze 34:23 [f] Ps 78:70-71
37:25 [g] Eze 28:25 [h] Am 9:15 [i] Isa 11:1
37:26 [j] Isa 55:3 [k] Jer 30:19 [l] Eze 16:62
37:27 [m] Lev 26:11; Jn 1:14 [n] 2Co 6:16*
37:28 [o] Ex 31:13; Eze 20:12
38:2 [p] Ge 10:2 [q] Rev 20:8
38:3 [r] Eze 39:1
38:4 [s] 2Ki 19:28 [t] Eze 29:4; Da 11:40
38:5 [u] Ge 10:6 [v] Eze 27:10
38:6 [w] Ge 10:2 [x] Eze 27:14
38:7 [y] Isa 8:9
38:8 [z] Isa 24:22 [a] Isa 11:11 [b] Jer 23:6
38:9 [c] Isa 28:2 [d] Jer 4:13; Joel 2:2
38:10 [e] Ps 36:4; Mic 2:1
38:11 [f] Jer 49:31; Zec 2:4
38:13 [g] Eze 27:22

[a] *23* Many Hebrew manuscripts (see also Septuagint); most Hebrew manuscripts *all their dwelling places where they sinned* [b] *2* Or *the prince of Rosh,* [c] *3* Or *Gog, prince of Rosh,* [d] *5* That is, the upper Nile region [e] *13* Or *her strong lions*

Ezekiel 38:1—39:29

Few Old Testament passages have seen as many attempts at interpretation in light of current events as have Ezekiel 38–39. Over the centuries, "Gog" and "Magog" have been identified with any number of people and places. It's no coincidence that Gog was commander-in-chief of a coalition of seven nations gathered from the farthest reaches of the then-known world (38:2–6). The point of the prophecy wasn't that these *particular* nations would oppose Israel. They represented a supreme attempt by the united forces of evil to crush the peace of God's people after their restoration to the promised land.

This fits the interpretation given to "Gog and Magog" in Revelation 20. There they represent "the nations in the four corners of the earth" whom Satan will gather for the final battle against "God's people, the city he loves" (Rev. 20:8–9). Their defeat will make way for the new Jerusalem (Rev. 21), which has much in common with Ezekiel's visionary temple in chapters 40–48.

38:13
h Isa 10:6;
Jer 15:13
38:14
i ver 8; Zec 2:5

38:15
j Eze 39:2
38:16
k ver 9 / Isa 29:23;
Eze 39:21

38:19
m Ps 18:7;
Eze 5:13;
Hag 2:6,21
38:20
n Hos 4:3; Na 1:5
38:21
o Eze 14:17
p 1Sa 14:20;
2Ch 20:23;
Hag 2:22
38:22
q Isa 66:16;
Jer 25:31
r Ps 18:12;
Rev 16:21
38:23
s Eze 36:23
39:1
t Eze 38:2,3
39:3
u Hos 1:5 v Ps 76:3

39:4
w ver 17-20;
Eze 29:5; 33:27
39:6
x Eze 30:8; Am 1:4
y Jer 25:22

39:7
z Ex 20:7 a Isa 12:6;
Eze 36:16,23

39:9
b Ps 46:9

39:10
c Isa 14:2; 33:1;
Hab 2:8

39:11
d Eze 38:2

39:12
e Dt 21:23
39:13
f Eze 28:22

plunder? Have you gathered your hordes to loot, to carry off silver and gold, to take away livestock and goods and to seize much plunder?ʰ" '

14 "Therefore, son of man, prophesy and say to Gog: 'This is what the Sovereign LORD says: In that day, when my people Israel are living in safety,ⁱ will you not take notice of it? 15 You will come from your place in the far north, you and many nations with you, all of them riding on horses, a great horde, a mighty army.ʲ 16 You will advance against my people Israel like a cloudᵏ that covers the land. In days to come, O Gog, I will bring you against my land, so that the nations may know me when I show myself holy through you before their eyes.ˡ

17 " 'This is what the Sovereign LORD says: Are you not the one I spoke of in former days by my servants the prophets of Israel? At that time they prophesied for years that I would bring you against them. 18 This is what will happen in that day: When Gog attacks the land of Israel, my hot anger will be aroused, declares the Sovereign LORD. 19 In my zeal and fiery wrath I declare that at that time there shall be a great earthquake in the land of Israel.ᵐ 20 The fish of the sea, the birds of the air, the beasts of the field, every creature that moves along the ground, and all the people on the face of the earth will tremble at my presence. The mountains will be overturned, the cliffs will crumble and every wall will fall to the ground.ⁿ 21 I will summon a swordᵒ against Gog on all my mountains, declares the Sovereign LORD. Every man's sword will be against his brother.ᵖ 22 I will execute judgmentᵠ upon him with plague and bloodshed; I will pour down torrents of rain, hailstonesʳ and burning sulfur on him and on his troops and on the many nations with him. 23 And so I will show my greatness and my holiness, and I will make myself known in the sight of many nations. Then they will know that I am the LORD.ˢ

39 "Son of man, prophesy against Gog and say: 'This is what the Sovereign LORD says: I am against you, O Gog, chief prince ofᵃ Meshech and Tubal.ᵗ 2 I will turn you around and drag you along. I will bring you from the far north and send you against the mountains of Israel. 3 Then I will strike your bowᵘ from your left hand and make your arrowsᵛ drop from your right hand. 4 On the mountains of Israel you will fall, you and all your troops and the nations with you. I will give you as food to all kinds of carrion birds and to the wild animals.ʷ 5 You will fall in the open field, for I have spoken, declares the Sovereign LORD. 6 I will send fireˣ on Magog and on those who live in safety in the coastlands,ʸ and they will know that I am the LORD.

7 " 'I will make known my holy name among my people Israel. I will no longer let my holy name be profaned,ᶻ and the nations will know that I the LORD am the Holy One in Israel.ᵃ 8 It is coming! It will surely take place, declares the Sovereign LORD. This is the day I have spoken of.

9 " 'Then those who live in the towns of Israel will go out and use the weapons for fuel and burn them up—the small and large shields, the bows and arrows, the war clubs and spears. For seven years they will use them for fuel.ᵇ 10 They will not need to gather wood from the fields or cut it from the forests, because they will use the weapons for fuel. And they will plunder those who plundered them and loot those who looted them, declares the Sovereign LORD.ᶜ

11 " 'On that day I will give Gog a burial place in Israel, in the valley of those who travel east towardᵇ the Sea.ᶜ It will block the way of travelers, because Gog and all his hordes will be buried there. So it will be called the Valley of Hamon Gog.ᵈ ᵈ

12 " 'For seven months the house of Israel will be burying them in order to cleanse the land.ᵉ 13 All the people of the land will bury them, and the day I am glorifiedᶠ will be a memorable day for them, declares the Sovereign LORD.

ᵃ 1 Or Gog, prince of Rosh,   ᵇ 11 Or of   ᶜ 11 That is, the Dead Sea   ᵈ 11 Hamon Gog means hordes of Gog.

📖 *Ezekiel 38–39 is a word of encouragement to all saints in all times and places: No matter what the forces of evil may do, God's purpose and victory will stand secure. If God can defeat the combined forces of Gog and his allies and turn them into fodder for scavengers, how much more can he care for us—whatever historical manifestation of Satan's hostility we may face? As Paul so eloquently wrote, no power exists that can "separate us from the love of God that is in Christ Jesus our Lord" (Rom. 8:35–39).*

14 " 'Men will be regularly employed to cleanse the land. Some will go throughout the land and, in addition to them, others will bury those that remain on the ground. At the end of the seven months they will begin their search. 15As they go through the land and one of them sees a human bone, he will set up a marker beside it until the gravediggers have buried it in the Valley of Hamon Gog. 16(Also a town called Hamonah*a* will be there.) And so they will cleanse the land.'

17"Son of man, this is what the Sovereign LORD says: Call out to every kind of bird*g* and all the wild animals: 'Assemble and come together from all around to the sacrifice I am preparing for you, the great sacrifice on the mountains of Israel. There you will eat flesh and drink blood. 18You will eat the flesh of mighty men and drink the blood of the princes of the earth as if they were rams and lambs, goats and bulls—all of them fattened animals from Bashan.*h* 19At the sacrifice I am preparing for you, you will eat fat till you are glutted and drink blood till you are drunk. 20At my table you will eat your fill of horses and riders, mighty men and soldiers of every kind,' declares the Sovereign LORD.*i*

21"I will display my glory among the nations, and all the nations will see the punishment I inflict and the hand I lay upon them.*j* 22From that day forward the house of Israel will know that I am the LORD their God. 23And the nations will know that the people of Israel went into exile for their sin, because they were unfaithful to me. So I hid my face from them and handed them over to their enemies, and they all fell by the sword.*k* 24I dealt with them according to their uncleanness and their offenses, and I hid my face from them.*l*

25"Therefore this is what the Sovereign LORD says: I will now bring Jacob back from captivity*b m* and will have compassion*n* on all the people of Israel, and I will be zealous for my holy name.*o* 26They will forget their shame and all the unfaithfulness they showed toward me when they lived in safety*p* in their land with no one to make them afraid.*q* 27When I have brought them back from the nations and have gathered them from the countries of their enemies, I will show myself holy through them in the sight of many nations.*r* 28Then they will know that I am the LORD their God, for though I sent them into exile among the nations, I will gather them to their own land, not leaving any behind. 29I will no longer hide my face from them, for I will pour out my Spirit*s* on the house of Israel, declares the Sovereign LORD."

The New Temple Area

40 In the twenty-fifth year of our exile, at the beginning of the year, on the tenth of the month, in the fourteenth year after the fall of the city*t*—on that very day the hand of the LORD was upon me*u* and he took me there. 2In visions*v* of God he took me to the land of Israel and set me on a very high mountain,*w* on whose south side were some buildings that looked like a city. 3He took me there, and I saw a man whose appearance was like bronze;*x* he was standing in the gateway with a linen cord and a measuring rod*y* in his hand. 4The man said to me, "Son of man, look with your eyes and hear with your ears and pay attention to everything I am

a 16 Hamonah means horde.   b 25 Or now restore the fortunes of Jacob

39:17 g Rev 19:17
39:18 h Ps 22:12; Jer 51:40
39:20 i Rev 19:17-18
39:21 j Ex 9:16; Isa 37:20; Eze 38:16
39:23 k Isa 1:15; 59:2; Jer 22:8-9; 44:23
39:24 l Jer 2:17,19; 4:18; Eze 36:19
39:25 m Jer 33:7; Eze 34:13 n Jer 30:18 o Isa 27:12-13
39:26 p 1Ki 4:25 q Isa 17:2; Eze 34:28; Mic 4:4
39:27 r Eze 36:23-24; 37:21; 38:16
39:29 s Joel 2:28; Ac 2:17
40:1 t 2Ki 25:7; Jer 39:1-10; 52:4-11; Eze 33:21 u Eze 1:3
40:2 v Da 7:1,7 w Eze 17:22; Rev 21:10
40:3 x Eze 1:7; Da 10:6; y Eze 47:3; Zec 2:1-2; Rev 11:1; 21:15

Ezekiel 40:1–4

Ezekiel's vision came on the Day of Atonement. Every fiftieth year on this day, trumpets were to announce a holy year called Jubilee, a year of proclaiming liberty throughout the land (Lev. 25:8–13). Coming 25 years after the exile of 597 B.C., this vision marked the halfway point to the next Jubilee—a natural time of looking forward to the release announced in chapters 34–37. It wasn't hard for the exiles to connect their landless, enslaved state with the condition of those who had in earlier times lived between Jubilees.

Just what is this temple described in Ezekiel?

Some see it as the plans for a temple Ezekiel intended the exiles to build after returning to Jerusalem. Others view it as the plan for a future millennial temple in Jerusalem following Christ's return. But some see in chapters 40–48 a visionary reordering of an entire new world, following the creation of the new people of God in chapters 36–37 and the birth pangs of chapters 38–39. It's a view of heaven from halfway there, as the semi-Jubilee date indicates, showing people living with God's "absence" a glimpse of his presence. It was an encouragement to God's people in Ezekiel's day. How does it encourage you today?

40:4
z Jer 26:2
a Eze 44:5
going to show you, for that is why you have been brought here. Tell[z] the house of Israel everything you see.[a]"

The East Gate to the Outer Court

40:5
b Eze 42:20
40:6
c Eze 8:16
40:7
d ver 36
[5]I saw a wall completely surrounding the temple area. The length of the measuring rod in the man's hand was six long cubits, each of which was a cubit[a] and a handbreadth.[b] He measured[b] the wall; it was one measuring rod thick and one rod high. [6]Then he went to the gate facing east.[c] He climbed its steps and measured the threshold of the gate; it was one rod deep.[c] [7]The alcoves[d] for the guards were one rod long and one rod wide, and the projecting walls between the alcoves were five cubits thick. And the threshold of the gate next to the portico facing the temple was one rod deep.

[8]Then he measured the portico of the gateway; [9]it[d] was eight cubits deep and its jambs were two cubits thick. The portico of the gateway faced the temple.

[10]Inside the east gate were three alcoves on each side; the three had the same measurements, and the faces of the projecting walls on each side had the same measurements. [11]Then he measured the width of the entrance to the gateway; it was ten cubits and its length was thirteen cubits. [12]In front of each alcove was a wall one cubit high, and the alcoves were six cubits square. [13]Then he measured the gateway from the top of the rear wall of one alcove to the top of the opposite one; the distance was twenty-five cubits from one parapet opening to the opposite one. [14]He measured along the faces of the projecting walls all around the inside of the gateway—

40:14
e Ex 27:9
sixty cubits. The measurement was up to the portico[e] facing the courtyard.[f e] [15]The distance from the entrance of the gateway to the far end of its portico was fifty cubits. [16]The alcoves and the projecting walls inside the gateway were surmounted by narrow parapet openings all around, as was the portico; the openings all around faced inward. The faces of the projecting walls were decorated with palm trees.[f]

40:16
f ver 21-22;
2Ch 3:5; Eze 41:26

The Outer Court

40:17
g Rev 11:2
h Eze 41:6
i Eze 42:1
[17]Then he brought me into the outer court.[g] There I saw some rooms and a pavement that had been constructed all around the court; there were thirty rooms[h] along the pavement.[i] [18]It abutted the sides of the gateways and was as wide as they were long; this was the lower pavement. [19]Then he measured the distance from the

a 5 The common cubit was about 1 1/2 feet (about 0.5 meter). b 5 That is, about 3 inches (about 8 centimeters) c 6 Septuagint; Hebrew *deep, the first threshold, one rod deep* d 8,9 Many Hebrew manuscripts, Septuagint, Vulgate and Syriac; most Hebrew manuscripts *gateway facing the temple; it was one rod deep. 9Then he measured the portico of the gateway; it* e 14 Septuagint; Hebrew *projecting wall* f 14 The meaning of the Hebrew for this verse is uncertain.

Ezekiel 40:5–16

The first thing Ezekiel saw in his vision was a wall surrounding the temple area. This wall was no minor obstacle: Its height and thickness (both over ten feet) solidly divided the holy space inside from the "profane" area outside. The massive gateways with their guardhouses added to the impression of a mighty fortress clearly separating the sacred from the secular.

The New Testament reveals that Christ himself is the new temple (see John 2:19). "The Word became flesh and made his dwelling [lit., *tabernacled*] among us" (John 1:14). Just as Ezekiel's temple was in the midst of the people, yet was no longer able to be corrupted by them, so also the Son of God lived in the midst of a sinful world, yet remained undefiled (Heb. 4:15). And since the church is Christ's body, it's also part of the new temple.

Ezekiel 40:17–19

The outer courtyard was of little interest to the prophet or his angelic guide. It's passed over with a brief reference to a paved area containing 30 rooms of unspecified purpose. The key measurement of the outer court is its breadth: Over 170 feet separated the outer from the inner wall. This substantial area wasn't intended to provide space for a throng of worshipers but to serve as a buffer zone around the holy things in the inner courtyard.

Ezekiel's vision came at a time when God seemed absent. It lifts the veil, providing us a glimpse of the heavenly order behind the disorder we see daily. In this realm there is a place for everything—and everything (and everyone) has its place. Most significantly, this applies to God. Chapters 40–42 lead up to the climactic reentry of God's glory into the temple in chapter 43, following its tragic departure in chapters 8–11. How does this revelation lift your view of God the Father and his Son Jesus Christ (Eph. 1:20–21)?

inside of the lower gateway to the outside of the inner court;[i] it was a hundred cubits[k] on the east side as well as on the north.

The North Gate

20Then he measured the length and width of the gate facing north, leading into the outer court. 21Its alcoves[l]—three on each side—its projecting walls and its portico had the same measurements as those of the first gateway. It was fifty cubits long and twenty-five cubits wide. 22Its openings, its portico[m] and its palm tree decorations had the same measurements as those of the gate facing east. Seven steps led up to it, with its portico opposite them. 23There was a gate to the inner court facing the north gate, just as there was on the east. He measured from one gate to the opposite one; it was a hundred cubits.[n]

The South Gate

24Then he led me to the south side and I saw a gate facing south. He measured its jambs and its portico, and they had the same measurements as the others. 25The gateway and its portico had narrow openings all around, like the openings of the others. It was fifty cubits long and twenty-five cubits wide.[o] 26Seven steps led up to it, with its portico opposite them; it had palm tree decorations on the faces of the projecting walls on each side.[p] 27The inner court[q] also had a gate facing south, and he measured from this gate to the outer gate on the south side; it was a hundred cubits.

Gates to the Inner Court

28Then he brought me into the inner court through the south gate, and he measured the south gate; it had the same measurements[r] as the others. 29Its alcoves, its projecting walls and its portico had the same measurements as the others. The gateway and its portico had openings all around. It was fifty cubits long and twenty-five cubits wide. 30(The porticoes[s] of the gateways around the inner court were twenty-five cubits wide and five cubits deep.) 31Its portico[t] faced the outer court; palm trees decorated its jambs, and eight steps led up to it.

32Then he brought me to the inner court on the east side, and he measured the gateway; it had the same measurements as the others. 33Its alcoves, its projecting walls and its portico had the same measurements as the others. The gateway and its portico had openings all around. It was fifty cubits long and twenty-five cubits

---

40:19
i Eze 46:1
k ver 23,27

40:21
l ver 7

40:22
m ver 49

40:23
n ver 19

40:25
o ver 33

40:26
p ver 22
40:27
q ver 32

40:28
r ver 35

40:30
s ver 21
40:31
t ver 22

Ezekiel 40:20–23

The north and south gates (vv. 20–27) were identical to the east gate (vv. 6–16), and these three outer-court gates were similar to the three in the inner court (vv. 28,32,35). Comparable gates have been discovered at Megiddo, Gezer, and Hazor, all dating from the time of Solomon (see 1 Kings 9:15). The guards excluded anyone who might defile the temple.

What does it mean for God not to be "in his place" (see previous "Here and Now")? For the exiles, the world had fallen apart. God had packed his bags and left. The sky had fallen, and they walked in thick darkness. It's hard for us, living under the New Testament covenant of grace, to imagine this kind of desperation or feeling of abandonment. As Christians we live with the Holy Spirit *in* our lives and hearts (John 14:15–20) and the promise that God is always with us (Heb. 13:5).

Ezekiel 40:24–27

Like the east and north gates into the outer court, the south gate had seven steps. The gate to the inner court had eight steps (v. 31), and the last gate to the temple proper had ten (see v. 49 and its textual note; the specific number isn't found in the Hebrew text but appears later in the Septuagint—the early Greek translation of the Hebrew OT). The rising numbers may indicate increasing degrees of sacredness.

Ezekiel's vision pictures a paradise with walls—think of a new Eden—and guarded gates to prevent the new humanity from being driven from God's presence (as in Gen. 3) or from driving God from their midst (as in Ezek. 8–11). Thank God today that you belong to his people. Thank him for sending Jesus to win you back. Pray that the Spirit will enable you to live in a manner that honors such a sacred relationship.

Ezekiel 40:28–37

The inner courtyard was securely separated from the outer. It was defended by gates identical to those of the outer courtyard, except that each portico, or porch, faced outward rather than inward. There is no mention of a wall, but it most likely may be assumed. A fortress of gates and walls between God and sinners wasn't good news—except in comparison to the unthinkable alternative: that God would no longer be present in the midst of his people *at all*.

40:34
u ver 22
40:35
v Eze 44:4; 47:2
40:36
w ver 7

wide. ³⁴Its portico^u faced the outer court; palm trees decorated the jambs on either side, and eight steps led up to it.

³⁵Then he brought me to the north gate^v and measured it. It had the same measurements as the others, ³⁶as did its alcoves, ^w its projecting walls and its portico, and it had openings all around. It was fifty cubits long and twenty-five cubits wide. ³⁷Its portico^a faced the outer court; palm trees decorated the jambs on either side, and eight steps led up to it.

The Rooms for Preparing Sacrifices

³⁸A room with a doorway was by the portico in each of the inner gateways, where the burnt offerings^x were washed. ³⁹In the portico of the gateway were two tables on each side, on which the burnt offerings, ^y sin offerings^z and guilt offerings^a were slaughtered. ⁴⁰By the outside wall of the portico of the gateway, near the steps at the entrance to the north gateway were two tables, and on the other side of the steps were two tables. ⁴¹So there were four tables on one side of the gateway and four on the other—eight tables in all—on which the sacrifices were slaughtered. ⁴²There were also four tables of dressed stone^b for the burnt offerings, each a cubit and a half long, a cubit and a half wide and a cubit high. On them were placed the utensils for slaughtering the burnt offerings and the other sacrifices. ^c ⁴³And double-pronged hooks, each a handbreadth long, were attached to the wall all around. The tables were for the flesh of the offerings.

Rooms for the Priests

⁴⁴Outside the inner gate, within the inner court, were two rooms, one^b at the side of the north gate and facing south, and another at the side of the south^c gate and facing north. ⁴⁵He said to me, "The room facing south is for the priests who have charge of the temple, ^d ⁴⁶and the room facing north^e is for the priests who have charge of the altar. ^f These are the sons of Zadok, ^g who are the only Levites who may draw near to the LORD to minister before him. ^h"

40:38
x 2Ch 4:6;
Eze 42:13
40:39
y Eze 46:2
z Lev 4:3,28
a Lev 7:1

40:42
b Ex 20:25 c ver 39

40:45
d 1Ch 9:23
40:46
e Eze 42:13
f Nu 18:5
g 1Ki 2:35
h Nu 16:5;
Eze 43:19; 44:15;
45:4; 48:11

^a 37 Septuagint (see also verses 31 and 34); Hebrew *jambs*   ^b 44 Septuagint; Hebrew *were rooms for singers, which were*   ^c 44 Septuagint; Hebrew *east*

📖 We who are in Christ have direct access to the very throne of grace, where Jesus himself intercedes for us with the Father (Heb. 4:16; 7:25; 8:1). No walls bar us from God's presence—not because we are more deserving than Ezekiel and his audience, but because we have been credited with Christ's perfect righteousness. Shouldn't we, as privileged "insiders," rejoice at the greatness of our salvation and strive to be pure, as our Lord Jesus was pure?

Ezekiel 40:38–43

🕊 There were rooms beside the portico of each gate in the inner courtyard for washing sacrifices; the porticoes themselves were for slaughtering animals. The temple's main function was sacrifice—the people needed atonement for their sins so they could stand in God's presence. This passage mentions three of the five major categories of sacrifice (see Lev. 1–7): burnt offerings, sin offerings, and guilt offerings. Notably absent are the more festive fellowship and grain offerings.

📖 In this new world order, God's holiness wasn't—and couldn't be—compromised in any way. Sacrifices *were offered to maintain the renewed covenant relationship* between God and his people. But Jesus' once-for-all sacrifice on the cross has effected the transition that turned us from "aliens and strangers, without hope and without God in the world" (Eph. 2:12), to those who ap-

proach God's presence with confidence (Heb. 4:16). Why not do so right now? You don't need an appointment, and the invitation has already been issued.

Ezekiel 40:44–47

🕊 Ezekiel saw two rooms for the Zadokite priests. Since they were the only persons able to minister before God (see "There and Then" for 44:1–31), the function of these rooms served the overall thrust of the vision: limiting access to a restricted space so that proper sacrifices could be offered. The ideas of holiness and sacrifice appear in the summary statement of verse 47. (1) The inner courtyard was a perfect square—the "shape" of the holy. (2) At the inner court's geometric center was the altar, the place of sacrifice.

📖 One barrier is still intact, as countless souls remain outsiders to God's grace. Some live beyond the sound of gospel proclamation, while others have repeatedly rejected the message. Even the most moral person, without belief in Christ, is on the outside and will perish eternally (John 3:16–18). Our calling as priests of the new temple is to teach others the one way to holiness (through faith in Christ), to draw them into the new world, where Paradise again stands open and the tree of life is accessible to all. Do you resonate with the urgency of this priestly calling (1 Peter 2:9)?

⁴⁷Then he measured the court: It was square—a hundred cubits long and a hundred cubits wide. And the altar was in front of the temple.

The Temple

⁴⁸He brought me to the portico of the temple[i] and measured the jambs of the portico; they were five cubits wide on either side. The width of the entrance was fourteen cubits and its projecting walls were[a] three cubits wide on either side. ⁴⁹The portico[j] was twenty cubits wide, and twelve[b] cubits from front to back. It was reached by a flight of stairs,[c] and there were pillars[k] on each side of the jambs.

41 Then the man brought me to the outer sanctuary[l] and measured the jambs; the width of the jambs was six cubits[d] on each side.[e] ²The entrance was ten cubits wide, and the projecting walls on each side of it were five cubits wide. He also measured the outer sanctuary; it was forty cubits long and twenty cubits wide.[m]

³Then he went into the inner sanctuary and measured the jambs of the entrance; each was two cubits wide. The entrance was six cubits wide, and the projecting walls on each side of it were seven cubits wide. ⁴And he measured the length of the inner sanctuary; it was twenty cubits, and its width was twenty cubits across the end of the outer sanctuary.[n] He said to me, "This is the Most Holy Place.[o]"

⁵Then he measured the wall of the temple; it was six cubits thick, and each side room around the temple was four cubits wide. ⁶The side rooms were on three levels, one above another, thirty[p] on each level. There were ledges all around the wall of the temple to serve as supports for the side rooms, so that the supports were not inserted into the wall of the temple.[q] ⁷The side rooms all around the temple were wider at each successive level. The structure surrounding the temple was built in ascending stages, so that the rooms widened as one went upward. A stairway[r] went up from the lowest floor to the top floor through the middle floor.

⁸I saw that the temple had a raised base all around it, forming the foundation of the side rooms. It was the length of the rod, six long cubits. ⁹The outer wall of the side rooms was five cubits thick. The open area between the side rooms of the temple ¹⁰and the ˪priests'˩ rooms was twenty cubits wide all around the temple. ¹¹There were entrances to the side rooms from the open area, one on the north and another on the south; and the base adjoining the open area was five cubits wide all around.

¹²The building facing the temple courtyard on the west side was seventy cubits wide. The wall of the building was five cubits thick all around, and its length was ninety cubits.

¹³Then he measured the temple; it was a hundred cubits long, and the temple courtyard and the building with its walls were also a hundred cubits long. ¹⁴The width of the temple courtyard on the east, including the front of the temple, was a hundred cubits.[s]

¹⁵Then he measured the length of the building facing the courtyard at the rear of the temple, including its galleries[t] on each side; it was a hundred cubits.

The outer sanctuary, the inner sanctuary and the portico facing the court, ¹⁶as well

40:48 i 1Ki 6:2

40:49 j ver 22; 1Ki 6:3 k 1Ki 7:15

41:1 l ver 23

41:2 m 2Ch 3:3

41:4 n 1Ki 6:20 o Ex 26:33; Heb 9:3-8

41:6 p Eze 40:17 q 1Ki 6:5

41:7 r 1Ki 6:8

41:14 s Eze 40:47

41:15 t Eze 42:3

---

a 48 Septuagint; Hebrew *entrance was*   b 49 Septuagint; Hebrew *eleven*   c 49 Hebrew; Septuagint *Ten steps led up to it*   d 1 The common cubit was about 1 1/2 feet (about 0.5 meter).   e 1 One Hebrew manuscript and Septuagint; most Hebrew manuscripts *side, the width of the tent*

Ezekiel 40:48—41:26

Ezekiel moved from the outer and inner courts to the temple itself. Its importance was marked in three ways: (1) It was located at the protected center of the complex. (2) It was conspicuous in its elevation, the highest point in this structure atop a high mountain. (3) The descriptions are detailed and precise.

The inner sanctuary, the only square space within the temple building itself, was reached by passing through three openings of increasing narrowness. This underlines its sanctity—so great that Ezekiel himself wasn't permitted to enter.

If each of us is "a temple of the Holy Spirit" (1 Cor. 6:19), do we reflect the features of the temple in Ezekiel's vision? The holy and inviolable part of us is lodged in the protected center of our being, in our hearts. But this doesn't conceal our temples from onlookers. If we truly reflect God's glory in our lives, our temples will be magnificent edifices, drawing the eyes of those around us toward the holy and the wholesome. As Christ's ambassadors, we are to be knowledgeable and clear about our message and careful not to mislead.

41:16
u 1Ki 6:4
v ver 25-26;
1Ki 6:15; Eze 42:3

41:18
w 1Ki 6:18
x Ex 37:7; 2Ch 3:7
y 1Ki 6:29; 7:36
z Eze 10:21

41:19
a Eze 10:14

41:21
b ver 1
41:22
c Ex 30:1
d Ex 25:23;
Eze 23:41; 44:16;
Mal 1:7,12
41:23
e ver 1 f 1Ki 6:32
41:24
g 1Ki 6:34

41:26
h ver 15-16;
Eze 40:16

42:1
i ver 13
j Eze 41:12-14
k Eze 40:17

42:3
l Eze 41:15
m Eze 41:16

42:4
n Eze 46:19

42:9
o Eze 44:5; 46:19

42:10
p ver 1

as the thresholds and the narrow windows[u] and galleries around the three of them—everything beyond and including the threshold was covered with wood. The floor, the wall up to the windows, and the windows were covered.[v] 17In the space above the outside of the entrance to the inner sanctuary and on the walls at regular intervals all around the inner and outer sanctuary 18were carved[w] cherubim[x] and palm trees.[y] Palm trees alternated with cherubim. Each cherub had two faces:[z] 19the face of a man toward the palm tree on one side and the face of a lion toward the palm tree on the other. They were carved all around the whole temple.[a] 20From the floor to the area above the entrance, cherubim and palm trees were carved on the wall of the outer sanctuary.

21The outer sanctuary[b] had a rectangular doorframe, and the one at the front of the Most Holy Place was similar. 22There was a wooden altar[c] three cubits high and two cubits square[a]; its corners, its base[b] and its sides were of wood. The man said to me, "This is the table[d] that is before the Lord." 23Both the outer sanctuary[e] and the Most Holy Place had double doors.[f] 24Each door had two leaves—two hinged leaves[g] for each door. 25And on the doors of the outer sanctuary were carved cherubim and palm trees like those carved on the walls, and there was a wooden overhang on the front of the portico. 26On the sidewalls of the portico were narrow windows with palm trees carved on each side. The side rooms of the temple also had overhangs.[h]

Rooms for the Priests

42 Then the man led me northward into the outer court and brought me to the rooms[i] opposite the temple courtyard[j] and opposite the outer wall on the north side.[k] 2The building whose door faced north was a hundred cubits[c] long and fifty cubits wide. 3Both in the section twenty cubits from the inner court and in the section opposite the pavement of the outer court, gallery[l] faced gallery at the three levels.[m] 4In front of the rooms was an inner passageway ten cubits wide and a hundred cubits[d] long. Their doors were on the north.[n] 5Now the upper rooms were narrower, for the galleries took more space from them than from the rooms on the lower and middle floors of the building. 6The rooms on the third floor had no pillars, as the courts had; so they were smaller in floor space than those on the lower and middle floors. 7There was an outer wall parallel to the rooms and the outer court; it extended in front of the rooms for fifty cubits. 8While the row of rooms on the side next to the outer court was fifty cubits long, the row on the side nearest the sanctuary was a hundred cubits long. 9The lower rooms had an entrance[o] on the east side as one enters them from the outer court.

10On the south side[e] along the length of the wall of the outer court, adjoining the temple courtyard and opposite the outer wall, were rooms[p] 11with a passageway in front of them. These were like the rooms on the north; they had the same length and width, with similar exits and dimensions. Similar to the doorways on the

---

a 22 Septuagint; Hebrew *long*   b 22 Septuagint; Hebrew *length*   c 2 The common cubit was about 1 1/2 feet (about 0.5 meter).   d 4 Septuagint and Syriac; Hebrew *and one cubit*
e 10 Septuagint; Hebrew *Eastward*

Ezekiel 42:1–20

🔲 Having described the temple building, Ezekiel was headed outward again when his attention was drawn to a series of rooms for the priests. They were to eat the sacred offerings and leave their sacred clothes in these designated rooms. Both restrictions emphasized the distinction between priest and non-priest.

Ezekiel was led back out to survey the temple from *the outside*. Unlike Moses' tabernacle and Solomon's temple, the idealized temple's total area was a perfect square. Lastly, Ezekiel repeated the function of the wall—"to separate the holy from the common." Never again would the profane intrude upon the holy. The sep-

aration had to be clearly established so that God could return to his place at the center of his people.

🔲 Paul's words in Ephesians 2:14–18 contrast with the measures Ezekiel spelled out to separate the sacred from the secular: "[Christ] himself is our peace, who has made the two one and has destroyed the barrier, the dividing wall of hostility, by abolishing in his flesh the law with its commandments and regulations . . . He came and preached peace to you who were far away and peace to those who were near. For through him we both have access to the Father by one Spirit." This is the age in which we are privileged to live.

north [12] were the doorways of the rooms on the south. There was a doorway at the beginning of the passageway that was parallel to the corresponding wall extending eastward, by which one enters the rooms.

[13] Then he said to me, "The north[q] and south rooms facing the temple courtyard are the priests' rooms, where the priests who approach the LORD will eat the most holy offerings. There they will put the most holy offerings—the grain offerings, the sin offerings[r] and the guilt offerings[s]—for the place is holy.[t] [14] Once the priests enter the holy precincts, they are not to go into the outer court until they leave behind the garments[u] in which they minister, for these are holy. They are to put on other clothes before they go near the places that are for the people.[v]"

[15] When he had finished measuring what was inside the temple area, he led me out by the east gate[w] and measured the area all around: [16] He measured the east side with the measuring rod; it was five hundred cubits.[a] [17] He measured the north side; it was five hundred cubits[b] by the measuring rod. [18] He measured the south side; it was five hundred cubits by the measuring rod. [19] Then he turned to the west side and measured; it was five hundred cubits by the measuring rod. [20] So he measured[x] the area on all four sides. It had a wall around it,[y] five hundred cubits long and five hundred cubits wide,[z] to separate the holy from the common.[a]

The Glory Returns to the Temple

43 Then the man brought me to the gate facing east,[b] [2] and I saw the glory of the God of Israel coming from the east. His voice was like the roar of rushing waters,[c] and the land was radiant with his glory.[d] [3] The vision I saw was like the vision I had seen when he[c] came to destroy the city and like the visions I had seen by the Kebar River, and I fell facedown. [4] The glory[e] of the LORD entered the temple through the gate facing east.[f] [5] Then the Spirit[g] lifted me up[h] and brought me into the inner court, and the glory of the LORD filled the temple.

[6] While the man was standing beside me, I heard someone speaking to me from inside the temple. [7] He said: "Son of man, this is the place of my throne and the place for the soles of my feet. This is where I will live among the Israelites forever. The house of Israel will never again defile my holy name—neither they nor their kings—by their prostitution[d] and the lifeless idols[e] of their kings at their high places.[i] [8] When they placed their threshold next to my threshold and their doorposts beside my doorposts, with only a wall between me and them, they defiled my holy name by their detestable practices. So I destroyed them in my anger. [9] Now let them put away from me their prostitution and the lifeless idols of their kings, and I will live among them forever.[j]

[10] "Son of man, describe the temple to the people of Israel, that they may be ashamed[k] of their sins. Let them consider the plan, [11] and if they are ashamed of all they have done, make known to them the design of the temple—its arrangement, its exits and entrances—its whole design and all its regulations[f] and laws. Write

---

42:13
q Eze 40:46
r Lev 10:17; 6:25
s Lev 14:13
t Ex 29:31;
Lev 6:29; 7:6;
10:12-13;
Nu 18:9-10

42:14
u Eze 44:19
v Ex 29:9; Lev 8:7-9

42:15
w Eze 43:1

42:20
x Eze 40:5
y Zec 2:5
z Eze 45:2;
Rev 21:16
a Eze 22:26

43:1
b Eze 10:19; 42:15;
44:1; 46:1
43:2
c Rev 1:15 d Isa 6:3;
Eze 11:23; Rev 18:1

43:4
e Eze 1:28
f Eze 10:19
43:5
g Eze 11:24
h Eze 3:12; 8:3

43:7
i Lev 26:30

43:9
j Eze 37:26-28

43:10
k Eze 16:61

---

a 16 See Septuagint of verse 17; Hebrew *rods*; also in verses 18 and 19.   b 17 Septuagint; Hebrew *rods*   c 3 Some Hebrew manuscripts and Vulgate; most Hebrew manuscripts *I*   d 7 Or *their spiritual adultery*; also in verse 9   e 7 Or *the corpses*; also in verse 9   f 11 Some Hebrew manuscripts and Septuagint; most Hebrew manuscripts *regulations and its whole design*

Ezekiel 43:1–12

The return of God's glory to the new temple is the high point of chapters 40–48. It reversed God's abandonment of the temple and its destruction described in visionary form in chapters 8–11 and fulfilled the promise of restoration: God dwelling in the midst of his people forever (37:26–28). The glory returned through the east gate, from the same direction from which it had gone (10:18–19). Its departure had been slow and halting, but its return was rapid and direct.

God's glory is an intangible concept, difficult for people to understand. But in the Old Testament it was a substantial, even concrete, presence, the visible manifestation of his presence among his people. Still, this awesome reality wasn't necessarily good news for sinners: Isaiah was afraid that his vision of God's glory would destroy him (Isa. 6:5–7). The danger that concerned Ezekiel wasn't so much God's presence as his absence. Today, unfortunately, just as God's tangible presence is foreign to many people, so also is the idea that he could be absent because of their sin.

43:11
l Eze 44:5
43:12
m Eze 40:2

these down before them so that they may be faithful to its design and follow all its regulations.*l*

12 "This is the law of the temple: All the surrounding area*m* on top of the mountain will be most holy. Such is the law of the temple.

The Altar

43:13
n 2Ch 4:1

13 "These are the measurements of the altar*n* in long cubits, that cubit being a cubit*a* and a handbreadth*b*: Its gutter is a cubit deep and a cubit wide, with a rim of one span*c* around the edge. And this is the height of the altar: 14From the gutter on the ground up to the lower ledge it is two cubits high and a cubit wide, and from the smaller ledge up to the larger ledge it is four cubits high and a cubit wide. 15The

43:15
o Ex 27:2

altar hearth is four cubits high, and four horns*o* project upward from the hearth. 16The altar hearth is square, twelve cubits long and twelve cubits wide. 17The up-

43:17
p Ex 20:26

per ledge also is square, fourteen cubits long and fourteen cubits wide, with a rim of half a cubit and a gutter of a cubit all around. The steps*p* of the altar face east."

43:18
q Ex 40:29
r Lev 1:5,11;
Heb 9:21-22
43:19
s Lev 4:3;
Eze 45:18-19
t Eze 44:15
u Nu 16:40;
Eze 40:46
43:20
v ver 17
w Lev 16:19
43:21
x Ex 29:14;
Heb 13:11

18Then he said to me, "Son of man, this is what the Sovereign LORD says: These will be the regulations for sacrificing burnt offerings*q* and sprinkling blood*r* upon the altar when it is built: 19You are to give a young bull*s* as a sin offering to the priests, who are Levites, of the family of Zadok,*t* who come near*u* to minister before me, declares the Sovereign LORD. 20You are to take some of its blood and put it on the four horns of the altar and on the four corners of the upper ledge*v* and all around the rim, and so purify the altar*w* and make atonement for it. 21You are to take the bull for the sin offering and burn it in the designated part of the temple area outside the sanctuary.*x*

22 "On the second day you are to offer a male goat without defect for a sin offering, and the altar is to be purified as it was purified with the bull. 23When you have finished purifying it, you are to offer a young bull and a ram from the flock, both

43:23
y Ex 29:1
43:24
z Lev 2:13;
Mk 9:49-50
43:25
a Lev 8:33
b Ex 29:37
43:27
c Lev 9:1 *d* Lev 17:5

without defect.*y* 24You are to offer them before the LORD, and the priests are to sprinkle salt*z* on them and sacrifice them as a burnt offering to the LORD.

25 "For seven days*a* you are to provide a male goat daily for a sin offering; you are also to provide a young bull and a ram from the flock, both without defect.*b* 26For seven days they are to make atonement for the altar and cleanse it; thus they will dedicate it. 27At the end of these days, from the eighth day*c* on, the priests are to present your burnt offerings and fellowship offerings*d**d* on the altar. Then I will accept you, declares the Sovereign LORD."

The Prince, the Levites, the Priests

44:1
e Eze 43:1

44 Then the man brought me back to the outer gate of the sanctuary, the one facing east,*e* and it was shut. 2The LORD said to me, "This gate is to remain

---

a 13 The common cubit was about 1 1/2 feet (about 0.5 meter).   *b 13* That is, about 3 inches (about 8 centimeters)   *c 13* That is, about 9 inches (about 22 centimeters)   *d 27* Traditionally *peace offerings*

Ezekiel 43:13–27

📖 Ezekiel's attention was drawn once more to the altar in the inner court, the central piece of furniture mentioned in the earlier tour (40:47). The importance of the altar was evident from its detailed description and its place at the geometric center of the temple complex. Ezekiel was then given instructions for the eight-day purification process that would make the altar fit for use. The heavenly altar had been defiled by the people's sins and needed to be ritually purified before true worship could resume.

📖 Jesus fulfilled Ezekiel's actions in purifying the heavenly altar, but he did his work with his own blood (Heb. 9:12). That sacrifice didn't cleanse the sanctuary so the endless round of animal sacrifices could begin

again; it was a once-for-all sacrifice. Yet it brought about exactly what Ezekiel had envisioned: our confidence of God's presence with us forever (Heb. 9:25–28).

Ezekiel 44:1–31

📖 In contrast to the Israelites in general and the other Levites in particular, whose access was restricted, the "descendants of Zadok" received the privileges of sole access to the inner court and the ability to offer sacrifices inside the sanctuary itself. Zadok, a descendant of Aaron, had served as priest (along with Abiathar) in David's time. God had chosen Zadok and his descendants to minister in the temple when Abiathar was removed for supporting Adonijah rather than Solomon as David's successor (1 Kings 2:35).

The key issue was the Zadokites' loyalty. They

shut. It must not be opened; no one may enter through it.[f] It is to remain shut because the LORD, the God of Israel, has entered through it. [3]The prince himself is the only one who may sit inside the gateway to eat in the presence[g] of the LORD. He is to enter by way of the portico of the gateway and go out the same way.[h]"

[4]Then the man brought me by way of the north gate to the front of the temple. I looked and saw the glory of the LORD filling the temple[i] of the LORD, and I fell face-down.[j]

[5]The LORD said to me, "Son of man, look carefully, listen closely and give attention to everything I tell you concerning all the regulations regarding the temple of the LORD. Give attention to the entrance of the temple and all the exits of the sanctuary.[k] [6]Say to the rebellious house[l] of Israel, 'This is what the Sovereign LORD says: Enough of your detestable practices, O house of Israel! [7]In addition to all your other detestable practices, you brought foreigners uncircumcised in heart[m] and flesh into my sanctuary, desecrating my temple while you offered me food, fat and blood, and you broke my covenant.[n] [8]Instead of carrying out your duty in regard to my holy things, you put others in charge of my sanctuary.[o] [9]This is what the Sovereign LORD says: No foreigner uncircumcised in heart and flesh is to enter my sanctuary, not even the foreigners who live among the Israelites.[p]

[10]" 'The Levites who went far from me when Israel went astray[q] and who wandered from me after their idols must bear the consequences of their sin.[r] [11]They may serve in my sanctuary, having charge of the gates of the temple and serving in it; they may slaughter the burnt offerings[s] and sacrifices for the people and stand before the people and serve them.[t] [12]But because they served them in the presence of their idols and made the house of Israel fall into sin, therefore I have sworn with uplifted hand[u] that they must bear the consequences of their sin, declares the Sovereign LORD.[v] [13]They are not to come near to serve me as priests or come near any of my holy things or my most holy offerings; they must bear the shame[w] of their detestable practices.[x] [14]Yet I will put them in charge of the duties of the temple and all the work that is to be done in it.[y]

[15]" 'But the priests, who are Levites and descendants of Zadok and who faithfully carried out the duties of my sanctuary when the Israelites went astray from me, are to come near to minister before me; they are to stand before me to offer sacrifices of fat and blood, declares the Sovereign LORD.[z] [16]They alone are to enter my sanctuary; they alone are to come near my table[a] to minister before me and perform my service.[b]

[17]" 'When they enter the gates of the inner court, they are to wear linen clothes;[c] they must not wear any woolen garment while ministering at the gates of the inner court or inside the temple. [18]They are to wear linen turbans[d] on their heads and linen undergarments[e] around their waists. They must not wear anything that makes them perspire.[f] [19]When they go out into the outer court where the people are, they are to take off the clothes they have been ministering in and are to leave them in the sacred rooms, and put on other clothes, so that they do not consecrate[g] the people by means of their garments.[h]

[20]" 'They must not shave their heads or let their hair grow long, but they are to keep the hair of their heads trimmed.[i] [21]No priest is to drink wine when he enters the inner court.[j] [22]They must not marry widows or divorced women; they may marry only virgins of Israelite descent or widows of priests.[k] [23]They are to teach my peo-

44:2
f Eze 43:4-5
44:3
g Ex 24:9-11
h Eze 46:2,8
44:4
i Isa 6:4; Rev 15:8
j Eze 1:28; 3:23
44:5
k Eze 40:4;
43:10-11
44:6
l Eze 3:9
44:7
m Lev 26:41
n Ge 17:14;
Ex 12:48; Lev 22:25
44:8
o Lev 22:2; Nu 18:7
44:9
p Joel 3:17;
Zec 14:21
44:10
q 2Ki 23:8
r Nu 18:23
44:11
s 2Ch 29:34
t Nu 3:5-37; 16:9;
1Ch 26:12-19
44:12
u Ps 106:26
v 2Ki 16:10-16
44:13
w Eze 16:61
x Nu 18:3
44:14
y Nu 18:4;
1Ch 23:28-32
44:15
z Jer 33:18;
Eze 40:46; Zec 3:7
44:16
a Eze 41:22
b Nu 18:5
44:17
c Ex 39:27-28;
Rev 19:8
44:18
d Ex 28:39; Isa 3:20
e Ex 28:42
f Lev 16:4
44:19
g Lev 6:27;
Eze 46:20
h Lev 6:10-11;
Eze 42:14
44:20
i Lev 21:5; Nu 6:5
44:21
j Lev 10:9
44:22
k Lev 21:7

weren't without moral blemish, but their reward for loyalty to God in a day of small things was a place of responsible service in his kingdom.

For the Zadokites, access to God's presence meant heavy lifestyle restrictions. If they were to minister in the presence of the all-holy God, there were things they couldn't touch, places they couldn't go, food they couldn't eat, and clothes they couldn't wear. The same applies to us: If we expect to experience the blessing of

God's presence, then our lifestyle will be (from the world's perspective) restricted. What are some ways in which this is true for you?

People around us may see us as strange and "narrow" because we don't do many of the things they do (1 Peter 4:4). But we are accountable to God, and our scale of values is centered on the glory of communion with him now and eternal life in his presence in the days to come—both of which motivate us to lives of purity (1 Jn. 3:1–3).

44:23
l Eze 22:26
m Mal 2:7
44:24
n Dt 17:8-9;
1Ch 23:4
o 2Ch 19:8
44:25
p Lev 21:1-4

44:26
q Nu 19:14

44:28
r Nu 18:20;
Dt 10:9; 18:1-2;
Jos 13:33
44:29
s Lev 27:21
t Nu 18:9,14
44:30
u Nu 18:12-13
v Nu 15:18-21
w Mal 3:10
x Ne 10:35-37
44:31
y Ex 22:31;
Lev 22:8

45:1
z Eze 47:21-22
a Eze 48:8-9,29
45:2
b Eze 42:20

45:4
c Eze 40:46
d Eze 48:10-11

45:5
e Eze 48:13

45:6
f Eze 48:15-18

45:7
g Eze 48:21
45:8
h Nu 26:53;
Eze 46:18
45:9
i Jer 22:3;
Zec 7:9-10; 8:16
45:10
j Dt 25:15; Pr 11:1;
Am 8:4-6;
Mic 6:10-11
k Lev 19:36
45:11
l Isa 5:10

ple the difference between the holy and the common[l] and show them how to distinguish between the unclean and the clean.[m]

24 " 'In any dispute, the priests are to serve as judges[n] and decide it according to my ordinances. They are to keep my laws and my decrees for all my appointed feasts, and they are to keep my Sabbaths holy.[o]

25 " 'A priest must not defile himself by going near a dead person; however, if the dead person was his father or mother, son or daughter, brother or unmarried sister, then he may defile himself.[p] 26 After he is cleansed, he must wait seven days.[q] 27 On the day he goes into the inner court of the sanctuary to minister in the sanctuary, he is to offer a sin offering for himself, declares the Sovereign LORD.

28 " 'I am to be the only inheritance[r] the priests have. You are to give them no possession in Israel; I will be their possession. 29 They will eat the grain offerings, the sin offerings and the guilt offerings; and everything in Israel devoted[a] to the LORD[s] will belong to them.[t] 30 The best of all the firstfruits[u] and of all your special gifts will belong to the priests. You are to give them the first portion of your ground meal[v] so that a blessing[w] may rest on your household.[x] 31 The priests must not eat anything, bird or animal, found dead or torn by wild animals.[y]

Division of the Land

45 " 'When you allot the land as an inheritance,[z] you are to present to the LORD a portion of the land as a sacred district, 25,000 cubits long and 20,000[b] cubits wide; the entire area will be holy.[a] 2 Of this, a section 500 cubits square[b] is to be for the sanctuary, with 50 cubits around it for open land. 3 In the sacred district, measure off a section 25,000 cubits[c] long and 10,000 cubits[d] wide. In it will be the sanctuary, the Most Holy Place. 4 It will be the sacred portion of the land for the priests,[c] who minister in the sanctuary and who draw near to minister before the LORD. It will be a place for their houses as well as a holy place for the sanctuary.[d] 5 An area 25,000 cubits long and 10,000 cubits wide will belong to the Levites, who serve in the temple, as their possession for towns to live in.[e][e]

6 " 'You are to give the city as its property an area 5,000 cubits wide and 25,000 cubits long, adjoining the sacred portion; it will belong to the whole house of Israel.[f]

7 " 'The prince will have the land bordering each side of the area formed by the sacred district and the property of the city. It will extend westward from the west side and eastward from the east side, running lengthwise from the western to the eastern border parallel to one of the tribal portions.[g] 8 This land will be his possession in Israel. And my princes will no longer oppress my people but will allow the house of Israel to possess the land according to their tribes.[h]

9 " 'This is what the Sovereign LORD says: You have gone far enough, O princes of Israel! Give up your violence and oppression and do what is just and right.[i] Stop dispossessing my people, declares the Sovereign LORD. 10 You are to use accurate scales,[j] an accurate ephah[f][k] and an accurate bath.[g] 11 The ephah[l] and the bath are

---

[a] 29 The Hebrew term refers to the irrevocable giving over of things or persons to the LORD.   [b] 1 Septuagint (see also verses 3 and 5 and 48:9); Hebrew *10,000*   [c] 3 That is, about 7 miles (about 12 kilometers)   [d] 3 That is, about 3 miles (about 5 kilometers)   [e] 5 Septuagint; Hebrew *temple; they will have as their possession 20 rooms*   [f] 10 An ephah was a dry measure.   [g] 10 A bath was a liquid measure.

Ezekiel 45:1–12

The final chapters of Ezekiel point to a new division of the promised land, beginning here with a sacred strip running from the Mediterranean Sea in the west to the eastern edge of the land. The primary purpose of this sacred district was to provide a zone of progressive holiness outside the temple, analogous to that inside.

Commentators have struggled with the identity of the prince in Ezekiel 44–48. Is he a Messianic figure, as the prince of Ezekiel 34:24 and 37:25 appears to have been?

Ezekiel underlined the message that the temple was at the center of time and space in the new world of his vision. The prince's position, tasks, and responsibilities were all subordinated to the central vision of God's temple in the midst of his people. If *Jesus* is represented by the new temple, then that temple is the primary "Messianic" figure in Ezekiel 44–48. Then the temple, not the prince, points to Jesus. As the temple was central to Ezekiel's vision, so Jesus is the Head of the church today. The prince may represent us—the body of people who make up the church—made royal by our relationship to Jesus (1 Peter 2:9).

to be the same size, the bath containing a tenth of a homer[a] and the ephah a tenth of a homer; the homer is to be the standard measure for both. [12]The shekel[b] is to consist of twenty gerahs.[m] Twenty shekels plus twenty-five shekels plus fifteen shekels equal one mina.[c]

45:12
m Ex 30:13;
Lev 27:25; Nu 3:47

Offerings and Holy Days

[13] " 'This is the special gift you are to offer: a sixth of an ephah from each homer of wheat and a sixth of an ephah from each homer of barley. [14]The prescribed portion of oil, measured by the bath, is a tenth of a bath from each cor (which consists of ten baths or one homer, for ten baths are equivalent to a homer). [15]Also one sheep is to be taken from every flock of two hundred from the well-watered pastures of Israel. These will be used for the grain offerings, burnt offerings[n] and fellowship offerings[d] to make atonement[o] for the people, declares the Sovereign LORD. [16]All the people of the land will participate in this special gift for the use of the prince in Israel. [17]It will be the duty of the prince to provide the burnt offerings, grain offerings and drink offerings at the festivals, the New Moons and the Sabbaths[p]—at all the appointed feasts of the house of Israel. He will provide the sin offerings, grain offerings, burnt offerings and fellowship offerings to make atonement for the house of Israel. [q]

[18] " 'This is what the Sovereign LORD says: In the first month[r] on the first day you are to take a young bull without defect[s] and purify the sanctuary. [t] [19]The priest is to take some of the blood of the sin offering and put it on the doorposts of the temple, on the four corners of the upper ledge[u] of the altar[v] and on the gateposts of the inner court. [20]You are to do the same on the seventh day of the month for anyone who sins unintentionally[w] or through ignorance; so you are to make atonement for the temple.

[21] " 'In the first month on the fourteenth day you are to observe the Passover,[x] a feast lasting seven days, during which you shall eat bread made without yeast. [22]On that day the prince is to provide a bull as a sin offering for himself and for all the people of the land. [y] [23]Every day during the seven days of the Feast he is to provide seven bulls and seven rams[z] without defect as a burnt offering to the LORD, and a male goat for a sin offering. [a] [24]He is to provide as a grain offering[b] an ephah for each bull and an ephah for each ram, along with a hin[e] of oil for each ephah. [c]

[25] " 'During the seven days of the Feast, [d] which begins in the seventh month on the fifteenth day, he is to make the same provision for sin offerings, burnt offerings, grain offerings and oil. [e]

45:15
n Lev 1:4 o Lev 6:30

45:17
p Lev 23:38;
Isa 66:23
q 1Ki 8:62;
2Ch 31:3;
Eze 46:4-12
45:18
r Ex 12:2
s Lev 22:20;
Heb 9:14
t Lev 16:16,33
45:19
u Eze 43:17
v Lev 16:18-19;
Eze 43:20
45:20
w Lev 4:27

45:21
x Ex 12:11;
Lev 23:5-6

45:22
y Lev 4:14
45:23
z Job 42:8
a Nu 28:16-25
45:24
b Nu 28:12-13
c Eze 46:5-7
45:25
d Dt 16:13
e Lev 23:34-43;
Nu 29:12-38
46:1
f Eze 40:19
g 1Ch 9:18 h ver 6;
Isa 66:23

46:2
i ver 8

46

" 'This is what the Sovereign LORD says: The gate of the inner court[f] facing east[g] is to be shut on the six working days, but on the Sabbath day and on the day of the New Moon[h] it is to be opened. [2]The prince is to enter from the outside through the portico[i] of the gateway and stand by the gatepost. The priests are to sacrifice his burnt offering and his fellowship offerings.[f] He is to worship at the

---

a 11 A homer was a dry measure.   b 12 A shekel weighed about 2/5 ounce (about 11.5 grams).
c 12 That is, 60 shekels; the common mina was 50 shekels.   d 15 Traditionally peace offerings; also
in verse 17   e 24 That is, probably about 4 quarts (about 4 liters)   f 2 Traditionally peace
offerings; also in verse 12

Ezekiel 45:13—46:24

This section varies so much from the Pentateuch (first five OT books) that Jewish rabbis have exerted great effort to reconcile them. In fact, the difficulty of harmonizing the two put the book of Ezekiel in danger of exclusion from the canon of Jewish Scriptures. The rabbis forgot that Ezekiel was representing a vision, not legislation.

If God's intent through this vision was to supplement or supersede the Law of Moses, it was a failure. The returning Jews made no apparent effort to implement these changes. But a vision doesn't need to be carried out to achieve its purpose. Ezekiel's was intended to bring the exiles to repentance, faithful endurance, and hope through a vision of reordered worship.

This passage reminds us that the heavenly order is different from the appearances of our mundane world. In our worship, we function within an alternative view of reality, a perspective that challenges the worldview of the majority. We come apart from our everyday existence and experience a place where we "exiles" can find a home. Ezekiel's temple provides a four-dimensional map of that sacred space, inviting us along with his first hearers to repent and leave behind our earthbound focus (1 Peter 2:11–12).

46:2
i ver 12; Eze 44:3
46:3
k Lk 1:10

threshold of the gateway and then go out, but the gate will not be shut until evening.[i] [3]On the Sabbaths and New Moons the people of the land are to worship in the presence of the LORD at the entrance to that gateway.[k] [4]The burnt offering the prince brings to the LORD on the Sabbath day is to be six male lambs and a ram, all without defect. [5]The grain offering given with the ram is to be an ephah,[a] and the grain offering with the lambs is to be as much as he pleases, along with a hin[b] of oil for each ephah.[l] [6]On the day of the New Moon[m] he is to offer a young bull, six lambs and a ram, all without defect. [7]He is to provide as a grain offering one ephah with the bull, one ephah with the ram, and with the lambs as much as he wants to give, along with a hin of oil with each ephah.[n] [8]When the prince enters, he is to go in through the portico[o] of the gateway, and he is to come out the same way.[p]

46:5
l ver 11; Eze 45:24
46:6
m ver 1; Nu 10:10

46:7
n Eze 45:24
46:8
o ver 2 *p* Eze 44:3
46:9
q Ex 23:14; 34:20

[9]" 'When the people of the land come before the LORD at the appointed feasts,[q] whoever enters by the north gate to worship is to go out the south gate; and whoever enters by the south gate is to go out the north gate. No one is to return through the gate by which he entered, but each is to go out the opposite gate. [10]The prince is to be among them, going in when they go in and going out when they go out.[r]

46:10
r 2Sa 6:14-15;
Ps 42:4

[11]" 'At the festivals and the appointed feasts, the grain offering is to be an ephah with a bull, an ephah with a ram, and with the lambs as much as one pleases, along with a hin of oil for each ephah.[s] [12]When the prince provides[t] a freewill offering[u] to the LORD—whether a burnt offering or fellowship offerings—the gate facing east is to be opened for him. He shall offer his burnt offering or his fellowship offerings as he does on the Sabbath day. Then he shall go out, and after he has gone out, the gate will be shut.[v]

46:11
s ver 5
46:12
t Eze 45:17
u Lev 7:16 *v* ver 2

[13]" 'Every day you are to provide a year-old lamb without defect for a burnt offering to the LORD; morning by morning you shall provide it.[w] [14]You are also to provide with it morning by morning a grain offering, consisting of a sixth of an ephah with a third of a hin of oil to moisten the flour. The presenting of this grain offering to the LORD is a lasting ordinance.[x] [15]So the lamb and the grain offering and the oil shall be provided morning by morning for a regular[y] burnt offering.[z]

46:13
w Ex 29:38;
Nu 28:3

46:14
x Da 8:11
46:15
y Ex 29:42
z Ex 29:38;
Nu 28:5-6

[16]" 'This is what the Sovereign LORD says: If the prince makes a gift from his inheritance to one of his sons, it will also belong to his descendants; it is to be their property by inheritance.[a] [17]If, however, he makes a gift from his inheritance to one of his servants, the servant may keep it until the year of freedom;[b] then it will revert to the prince. His inheritance belongs to his sons only; it is theirs. [18]The prince must not take any of the inheritance[c] of the people, driving them off their property. He is to give his sons their inheritance out of his own property, so that none of my people will be separated from his property.' "

46:16
a 2Ch 21:3
46:17
b Lev 25:10

46:18
c Lev 25:23;
Eze 45:8; Mic 2:1-2

[19]Then the man brought me through the entrance[d] at the side of the gate to the sacred rooms facing north, which belonged to the priests, and showed me a place at the western end. [20]He said to me, "This is the place where the priests will cook the guilt offering and the sin offering and bake the grain offering, to avoid bringing them into the outer court and consecrating[e] the people."[f]

46:19
d Eze 42:9

[21]He then brought me to the outer court and led me around to its four corners, and I saw in each corner another court. [22]In the four corners of the outer court were enclosed[c] courts, forty cubits long and thirty cubits wide; each of the courts in the four corners was the same size. [23]Around the inside of each of the four courts was a ledge of stone, with places for fire built all around under the ledge. [24]He said to me, "These are the kitchens where those who minister at the temple will cook the sacrifices of the people."

46:20
e Lev 6:27
f Zec 14:20

The River From the Temple

47:1
g Isa 55:1 *h* Ps 46:4;
Joel 3:18; Rev 22:1

47 The man brought me back to the entrance of the temple, and I saw water[g] coming out from under the threshold of the temple toward the east (for the temple faced east). The water was coming down from under the south side of the temple, south of the altar.[h] [2]He then brought me out through the north gate and

---

[a] 5 That is, probably about 3/5 bushel (about 22 liters)   [b] 5 That is, probably about 4 quarts (about 4 liters)   [c] 22 The meaning of the Hebrew for this word is uncertain.

led me around the outside to the outer gate facing east, and the water was flowing from the south side.

[3]As the man went eastward with a measuring line[i] in his hand, he measured off a thousand cubits[a] and then led me through water that was ankle-deep. [4]He measured off another thousand cubits and led me through water that was knee-deep. He measured off another thousand and led me through water that was up to the waist. [5]He measured off another thousand, but now it was a river that I could not cross, because the water had risen and was deep enough to swim in—a river that no one could cross.[j] [6]He asked me, "Son of man, do you see this?"

Then he led me back to the bank of the river. [7]When I arrived there, I saw a great number of trees on each side of the river.[k] [8]He said to me, "This water flows toward the eastern region and goes down into the Arabah,[b][l] where it enters the Sea.[c] When it empties into the Sea,[c] the water there becomes fresh.[m] [9]Swarms of living creatures will live wherever the river flows. There will be large numbers of fish, because this water flows there and makes the salt water fresh; so where the river flows everything will live.[n] [10]Fishermen[o] will stand along the shore; from En Gedi[p] to En Eglaim there will be places for spreading nets.[q] The fish will be of many kinds[r]—like the fish of the Great Sea.[d][s] [11]But the swamps and marshes will not become fresh; they will be left for salt.[t] [12]Fruit trees of all kinds will grow on both banks of the river.[u] Their leaves will not wither, nor will their fruit[v] fail. Every month they will bear, because the water from the sanctuary flows to them. Their fruit will serve for food and their leaves for healing.[w]"

The Boundaries of the Land

[13]This is what the Sovereign LORD says: "These are the boundaries[x] by which you are to divide the land for an inheritance among the twelve tribes of Israel, with two portions for Joseph.[y] [14]You are to divide it equally among them. Because I swore with uplifted hand to give it to your forefathers, this land will become your inheritance.[z]

[15]"This is to be the boundary of the land:

"On the north side it will run from the Great Sea by the Hethlon road[a] past Lebo[e] Hamath to Zedad, [16]Berothah[f][b] and Sibraim (which lies on the border between Damascus and Hamath),[c] as far as Hazer Hatticon, which is on the border of Hauran. [17]The boundary will extend from the sea to Hazar Enan,[g]

---

[a] 3 That is, about 1,500 feet (about 450 meters)   [b] 8 Or *the Jordan Valley*   [c] 8 That is, the Dead Sea   [d] 10 That is, the Mediterranean; also in verses 15, 19 and 20   [e] 15 Or *past the entrance to*   [f] 15,16 See Septuagint and Ezekiel 48:1; Hebrew *road to go into Zedad,* [16]*Hamath, Berothah*   [g] 17 Hebrew *Enon*, a variant of *Enan*

Cross-references

47:3 [i] Eze 40:3
47:5 [j] Isa 11:9; Hab 2:14
47:7 [k] ver 12; Rev 22:2
47:8 [l] Dt 3:17; Jos 3:16 [m] Isa 41:18
47:9 [n] Isa 12:3; 55:1; Jn 4:14; 7:37-38
47:10 [o] Mt 4:19 [p] Jos 15:62 [q] Eze 26:5 [r] Ps 104:25; Mt 13:47 [s] Nu 34:6
47:11 [t] Dt 29:23
47:12 [u] ver 7; Rev 22:2 [v] Ps 1:3 [w] Ge 2:9; Jer 17:8
47:13 [x] Nu 34:2-12 [y] Ge 48:5
47:14 [z] Ge 12:7; Dt 1:8; Eze 20:5-6
47:15 [a] Eze 48:1
47:16 [b] 2Sa 8:8 [c] Nu 13:21; Eze 48:1

Ezekiel 47:1–12

Ezekiel's vision turned outward to the land and to the influence of the restored temple, expressed as a life-giving river flowing from within it. After flowing east and then south through the Arabah, the region of the Jordan Valley, this visionary river transformed the Dead Sea—the saltiest, most hostile-to-life body of water in the world. The Hebrew in verse 8 for "the water there becomes fresh" means literally "the water there becomes healed."

Images of a life-giving stream act as bookends to the Bible; they are also found in the opening scenes of Genesis (2:8–14) and the closing chapter of Revelation. Revelation 22 features a river similar in many respects to that of Ezekiel 47. A striking uniqueness about Ezekiel's river is that it started as a trickle but grew from this insignificant beginning (cf. Zech. 4:10; Matt. 13:31–32).

God's people still experience life in all its fullness through his transforming presence in their midst. A temple-centered—God-centered—life is the way to true freedom. The river flowing from that center has the power to take a dead life and resurrect it with health. This freedom is contagiously life-giving. Our lives as believers are to have an infectious attractiveness to people observing us. The Holy Spirit lives in us, making us miniature temples, centers from which life-giving water flows out to the nations (John 7:38–39; Rev. 22:2).

Ezekiel 47:13–23

Ezekiel's final section records the distribution of the renewed land. The boundaries were similar to the original area God had promised the Israelites through Moses in Numbers 34:1–12—stretching from Lebo Hamath in the north to the Wadi of Egypt and Meribah Kadesh in the south, from the Mediterranean in the west roughly to the Jordan River and the Dead Sea in the east. Strikingly absent is the area east of the Jordan River, which though occupied by Israel for much of its history wasn't part of God's original promise.

47:17
d Eze 48:1

47:19
e Dt 32:51
f Isa 27:12
g Eze 48:28

47:20
h Eze 48:1
i Nu 34:6

47:22
j Isa 14:1
k Nu 26:55-56;
Isa 56:6-7;
Ro 10:12; Eph 2:12-
16; 3:6; Col 3:11

along the northern border of Damascus, with the border of Hamath to the north. This will be the north boundary. [d]

18 "On the east side the boundary will run between Hauran and Damascus, along the Jordan between Gilead and the land of Israel, to the eastern sea and as far as Tamar. [a] This will be the east boundary.

19 "On the south side it will run from Tamar as far as the waters of Meribah Kadesh, [e] then along the Wadi ⌐of Egypt⌐ [f] to the Great Sea. [g] This will be the south boundary.

20 "On the west side, the Great Sea will be the boundary to a point opposite Lebo [b] Hamath. [h] This will be the west boundary. [i]

21 "You are to distribute this land among yourselves according to the tribes of Israel. 22 You are to allot it as an inheritance for yourselves and for the aliens [j] who have settled among you and who have children. You are to consider them as native-born Israelites; along with you they are to be allotted an inheritance among the tribes of Israel. [k] 23 In whatever tribe the alien settles, there you are to give him his inheritance," declares the Sovereign LORD.

The Division of the Land

48:1
l Ge 30:6
m Eze 47:15-17
n Eze 47:20

48 "These are the tribes, listed by name: At the northern frontier, Dan [l] will have one portion; it will follow the Hethlon road [m] to Lebo [c] Hamath; [n] Hazar Enan and the northern border of Damascus next to Hamath will be part of its border from the east side to the west side.

48:2
o Jos 19:24-31

2 "Asher [o] will have one portion; it will border the territory of Dan from east to west.

48:3
p Jos 19:32-39

3 "Naphtali [p] will have one portion; it will border the territory of Asher from east to west.

48:4
q Jos 17:1-11

4 "Manasseh [q] will have one portion; it will border the territory of Naphtali from east to west.

48:5
r Jos 16:5-9
s Jos 17:7-10
t Jos 17:17

5 "Ephraim [r] will have one portion; it will border the territory of Manasseh [s] from east to west. [t]

48:6
u Jos 13:15-21

6 "Reuben [u] will have one portion; it will border the territory of Ephraim from east to west.

48:7
v Jos 15:1-63

7 "Judah [v] will have one portion; it will border the territory of Reuben from east to west.

8 "Bordering the territory of Judah from east to west will be the portion you are to present as a special gift. It will be 25,000 cubits [d] wide, and its length from east to west will equal one of the tribal portions; the sanctuary will be in the center of it. [w]

48:8
w ver 21

9 "The special portion you are to offer to the LORD will be 25,000 cubits long and

---

a 18 Septuagint and Syriac; Hebrew *Israel. You will measure to the eastern sea*   b 20 Or *opposite the entrance to*   c 1 Or *to the entrance to*   d 8 That is, about 7 miles (about 12 kilometers)

There would be a land inheritance not just for native Israelites but also for resident aliens. In earlier Old Testament legislation aliens were protected as a powerless class. Because they couldn't own land, they lacked full citizenship rights. But they could participate fully in religious life, and some had relocated for this reason. God recognized these proselytes/converts by giving them a hereditary portion of the renewed land.

It was a high privilege for aliens to receive the right to inherit land. Paul described in Ephesians 2:12 the plight of Gentile nonbelievers as those who were "separate from Christ, excluded from citizenship in Israel and foreigners to the covenants of the promise, without hope and without God in the world." He went on to say in verses 13–22 that through Christ's blood we have

been granted access to God's very presence, along with full membership in the holy temple of Christ's one, united body. This is high privilege indeed!

Ezekiel 48:1–29

The tribes were assigned equal portions of land, running in strips from east to west. This was a fair way to divide a country whose major topographic features ran from north to south. But more significantly it oriented the land along the sacred east-west axis of the temple. The tribal strips themselves were undefined, with the borders between tribes unmarked by geographic indicators. This contrasted with the historical division of the land in Joshua 14–21, in which tribal boundaries were clearly defined.

Verses 8–22 expand upon the description of the

10,000 cubits ^a wide. ^x ¹⁰This will be the sacred portion for the priests. It will be 25,000 cubits long on the north side, 10,000 cubits wide on the west side, 10,000 cubits wide on the east side and 25,000 cubits long on the south side. In the center of it will be the sanctuary of the LORD. ^y ¹¹This will be for the consecrated priests, the Zadokites, ^z who were faithful in serving me ^a and did not go astray as the Levites did when the Israelites went astray. ^b ¹²It will be a special gift to them from the sacred portion of the land, a most holy portion, bordering the territory of the Levites.

¹³ "Alongside the territory of the priests, the Levites will have an allotment 25,000 cubits long and 10,000 cubits wide. Its total length will be 25,000 cubits and its width 10,000 cubits. ^c ¹⁴They must not sell or exchange any of it. This is the best of the land and must not pass into other hands, because it is holy to the LORD. ^d

¹⁵ "The remaining area, 5,000 cubits wide and 25,000 cubits long, will be for the common use of the city, for houses and for pastureland. The city will be in the center of it ¹⁶and will have these measurements: the north side 4,500 cubits, the south side 4,500 cubits, the east side 4,500 cubits, and the west side 4,500 cubits. ^e ¹⁷The pastureland for the city will be 250 cubits on the north, 250 cubits on the south, 250 cubits on the east, and 250 cubits on the west. ¹⁸What remains of the area, bordering on the sacred portion and running the length of it, will be 10,000 cubits on the east side and 10,000 cubits on the west side. Its produce will supply food for the workers of the city. ^f ¹⁹The workers from the city who farm it will come from all the tribes of Israel. ²⁰The entire portion will be a square, 25,000 cubits on each side. As a special gift you will set aside the sacred portion, along with the property of the city.

²¹ "What remains on both sides of the area formed by the sacred portion and the city property will belong to the prince. It will extend eastward from the 25,000 cubits of the sacred portion to the eastern border, and westward from the 25,000 cubits to the western border. Both these areas running the length of the tribal portions will belong to the prince, and the sacred portion with the temple sanctuary will be in the center of them. ^g ²²So the property of the Levites and the property of the city will lie in the center of the area that belongs to the prince. The area belonging to the prince will lie between the border of Judah and the border of Benjamin.

²³ "As for the rest of the tribes: Benjamin ^h will have one portion; it will extend from the east side to the west side.

²⁴ "Simeon ⁱ will have one portion; it will border the territory of Benjamin from east to west.

²⁵ "Issachar ^j will have one portion; it will border the territory of Simeon from east to west.

²⁶ "Zebulun ^k will have one portion; it will border the territory of Issachar from east to west.

²⁷ "Gad ^l will have one portion; it will border the territory of Zebulun from east to west.

²⁸ "The southern boundary of Gad will run south from Tamar ^m to the waters of Meribah Kadesh, then along the Wadi ⌊of Egypt⌋ to the Great Sea. ^b ⁿ

^a 9 That is, about 3 miles (about 5 kilometers)   ^b 28 That is, the Mediterranean

48:9
x Eze 45:1

48:10
y ver 21; Eze 45:3-4
48:11
z 2Sa 8:17
a Lev 8:35
b Eze 14:11; 44:15

48:13
c Eze 45:5
48:14
d Lev 25:34; 27:10,28

48:16
e Rev 21:16

48:18
f Eze 45:6

48:21
g ver 8,10; Eze 45:7

48:23
h Jos 18:11-28

48:24
i Ge 29:33; Jos 19:1-9
48:25
j Jos 19:17-23

48:26
k Jos 19:10-16

48:27
l Jos 13:24-28

48:28
m Ge 14:7
n Eze 47:19

sacred district introduced in 45:8. Its importance is indicated not only by its central location and detailed dimensions but by the amount of attention devoted to it.

The theme of 47:13—48:35 is inheritance. Through Ezekiel, God made a commitment to landless exiles that his promise to Abraham, Isaac, and Moses would be fulfilled. His people would possess the land as an inheritance for themselves, their descendants, and the resident aliens God had called out from the nations to join them.

What significance could God's ancient promise of land have had for a refugee people who felt abandoned by him? Their probable reasoning: Let's assimilate into the local culture and live to accumulate things. Many people today are driven to own a significant slice of this world's action. To what extent is this a natural response to the lack of a relationship with the living God?

Have you ever been involved in a dispute over an inheritance? There is much fighting today in our courts over wills and estates. But this view in Ezekiel is assuring. All receive a fair and equitable portion of the inheritance, even the alien and the stranger. No one is left out, except by his or her own choice.

29 "This is the land you are to allot as an inheritance to the tribes of Israel, and these will be their portions," declares the Sovereign LORD.

The Gates of the City

30 "These will be the exits of the city: Beginning on the north side, which is 4,500 cubits long, 31 the gates of the city will be named after the tribes of Israel. The three gates on the north side will be the gate of Reuben, the gate of Judah and the gate of Levi.

32 "On the east side, which is 4,500 cubits long, will be three gates: the gate of Joseph, the gate of Benjamin and the gate of Dan.

33 "On the south side, which measures 4,500 cubits, will be three gates: the gate of Simeon, the gate of Issachar and the gate of Zebulun.

34 "On the west side, which is 4,500 cubits long, will be three gates: the gate of Gad, the gate of Asher and the gate of Naphtali.

35 "The distance all around will be 18,000 cubits.

"And the name of the city from that time on will be:

THE LORD IS THERE. *o*

48:35
o Isa 12:6; 24:23;
Jer 3:17; 14:9;
33:16; Joel 3:21;
Zec 2:10; Rev 21:3

Ezekiel 48:30–35

These closing verses call us back to contemplate the new city. Like the temple, it's pictured as a perfect square. With its 12 gates, named after the 12 tribes of Israel, it functioned as a visible focus on the unity of the restored people.

The twin themes of God's transcendence (holiness; separateness) and immanence (closeness) are developed in Ezekiel 40–48. The high temple walls remind us of God's transcendent presence—in the midst of his people but separate from them—while the river of life speaks of his immanent presence for blessing. God's transcendence is emphasized in the separation of the temple from the city, but his immanence is represented by that city's sacred shape and new name, "THE LORD IS THERE."

As we await Christ's return, we are to live lives completely centered on the new covenant temple, Jesus himself (Heb. 12:22–28). Such lives revolve around worship of our awe-inspiring God, Jesus' living presence in our hearts, and the Spirit's life-giving activity. So nourished, we are empowered to take the gospel to all nations. They will be brought from all directions to feast together with us in the heavenly city, with the Lord of hosts and the Lamb in our midst. Then and only then will the new Jerusalem fittingly bear the name Ezekiel gave it: "THE LORD IS THERE."

INTRODUCTION TO
Daniel

AUTHOR
The book identifies its author as Daniel (9:2; 10:2; 12:4), and Jesus attributed it to Daniel as
well (Matt. 24:15). Daniel was among the first Jews carried off to Babylon in 605 B.C. (Jewish
captives were taken to Babylon in three stages: first in 605 B.C., again in 597 B.C., and finally in
586 B.C., when Jerusalem was destroyed.)

DATE WRITTEN
Daniel was probably written between 536 and 530 B.C., shortly after Cyrus had captured Babylon (539 B.C.).

ORIGINAL READERS
Daniel wrote to his fellow Jewish exiles in Babylon to remind them of God's sovereign control
over world history and to encourage them with God's promises of restoration.

TIMELINE

	1400BC	1300	1200	1100	1000	900	800	700	600	500	400
Jeremiah's ministry in Judah (c. 626-585 B.C.)											
Daniel's exile in Babylon (c. 605-536 B.C.)											
Fall of Jerusalem (586 B.C.)											
Persia's conquest of Babylon (539 B.C.)											
Daniel in the lions' den (c. 539 B.C.)											
First return of exiles to Jerusalem (538 B.C.)											
Book of Daniel written (c. 536-530 B.C.)											
End of Daniel's ministry (c. 536 B.C.)											

THEMES
Daniel describes six historical narratives (1:1—6:28) and four visions (7:1—12:13). It contains
the following themes:

1. *God's sovereignty.* The narratives in Daniel emphasize God's faithfulness and his absolute
sovereignty over world history (2:47; 3:17–18; 4:28–37; 5:18–31). Despite appearances, God is
in control over global events, kingdoms, and governments (5:21).

2. *Faithfulness to God.* God rewards those who are sincerely devoted to him and acknowledge
him (cf. 1:8 with 1:15–20; 2:17–18 with 2:19; 2:27–28 with 2:48–49; 3:12,16–18 with 3:26–30;
5:16–18 with 5:29; 6:7–12 with 6:19–24). Daniel demonstrates that our witness to the world
makes an impact on those around us (4:34–35,37; 6:26–27). It also reveals that it's possible,
though not guaranteed, that God's oppressed people may survive and even thrive in a culture
hostile to their faith.

3. *Prophecies of future events.* Daniel's four visions contain predictions of future times of persecution and the return of the triumphant Christ (7:11,26–27; 8:25; 9:27; 11:45; 12:13). Daniel's visions encourage God's faithful people who are living under oppression and persecution. They give a divine perspective on reality that differs from what's visible: God will ultimately win the victory, so live life with the expectation of final triumph (2:44; 7:27; Rev. 11:15).

FAITH IN ACTION
The pages of Daniel contain life lessons and role models of faith—people who challenge believers to put their faith in action.

Role Models

- DANIEL (1:8; 2:20–27; 5:11–12; 6:4,10–13; 9:1–21; 10:11,19) was a man of convictions and prayer, obeying God at any cost. Do you engage in daily prayer? Do you have integrity? What is your reputation among your friends, family, and coworkers?

- SHADRACH, MESHACH, AND ABEDNEGO (3:4–23) were targeted by prejudiced and envious colleagues and thrown into a fiery furnace because they refused to worship an idol at the king's command. God delivered and rewarded them—and received praise from the pagan king and all the people (3:24–30). Are you willing to stand up for God, even if your actions mean discomfort or even death?

Challenges

- If you achieve success from the world's standpoint, hold firmly to your integrity and godly principles (1:8).

- In times of crisis, seek God's direction through prayer (2:20–23; 9:1–21).

- When God gives you a gift or ability, remember to give him the credit (2:26–28) and humbly complete your service (2:30).

- Ask God to build your faith so that you, too, can respond with quiet confidence that your God is able to save you in any circumstance (3:16–18). Are you willing, if necessary, to commit an act of civil disobedience and face the consequences—whether or not God rescues you?

- Take to heart the truth that "those who walk in pride [God] is able to humble" (4:37).

- When God seems not to hear your prayers, remember that a spiritual battle may be raging (10:12–13). Be patient and trust him.

OUTLINE

I. The Captivity, Faithfulness, and Elevation of Daniel and His Three Friends (1)
II. The Destinies of the Nations (2–7)
   A. Nebuchadnezzar's Dream of a Statue (2)
   B. Nebuchadnezzar's Golden Image and Its Worship (3)
   C. Nebuchadnezzar's Vision of a Large Tree (4)
   D. Belshazzar's and Babylon's Downfall (5)
   E. Daniel's Deliverance From the Lions' Den (6)
   F. Daniel's Dream of Four Beasts (7)
III. Israel's Destiny (8–12)
   A. Daniel's Vision of a Ram and a Goat (8)
   B. Daniel's Prayer and His Vision of the 70 "Sevens" (9)
   C. Daniel's Vision of Israel's Future (10–12)

Daniel's Training in Babylon

1 In the third year of the reign of Jehoiakim king of Judah, Nebuchadnezzar[a] king of Babylon came to Jerusalem and besieged it.[b] 2And the Lord delivered Jehoiakim king of Judah into his hand, along with some of the articles from the temple of God. These he carried off to the temple of his god in Babylonia[a] and put in the treasure house of his god.[c]

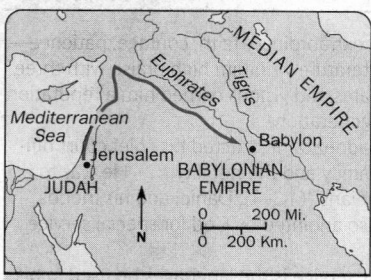

Daniel in Babylon (1:6)

Then: Daniel personified God's complex character, committed to punishing evil (hence the exile) but also to the hope of his everlasting presence and protection (Daniel's empowerment).

Now: God still hates sin but loves sinners—and offers them redemption.

3Then the king ordered Ashpenaz, chief of his court officials, to bring in some of the Israelites from the royal family and the nobility[d]— 4young men without any physical defect, handsome, showing aptitude for every kind of learning, well informed, quick to understand, and qualified to serve in the king's palace. He was to teach them the language and literature of the Babylonians.[b] 5The king assigned them a daily amount of food and wine[e] from the king's table. They were to be trained for three years, and after that they were to enter the king's service.[f]

6Among these were some from Judah: Daniel,[g] Hananiah, Mishael and Azariah. 7The chief official gave them new names: to Daniel, the name Belteshazzar;[h] to Hananiah, Shadrach; to Mishael, Meshach; and to Azariah, Abednego.[i]

8But Daniel resolved not to defile[j] himself with the royal food and wine, and he asked the chief official for permission not to defile himself this way. 9Now God had caused the official to show favor[k] and sympathy[l] to Daniel, 10but the official told Daniel, "I am afraid of my lord the king, who has assigned your[c] food and drink. Why should he see you looking worse than the other young men your age? The king would then have my head because of you."

11Daniel then said to the guard whom the chief official had appointed over Daniel, Hananiah, Mishael and Azariah, 12"Please test your servants for ten days: Give us nothing but vegetables to eat and water to drink. 13Then compare our appearance with that of the young men who eat the royal food, and treat your servants in accordance with what you see." 14So he agreed to this and tested them for ten days.

15At the end of the ten days they looked healthier and better nourished than any of the young men who ate the royal food.[m] 16So the guard took away their choice food and the wine they were to drink and gave them vegetables instead.[n]

1:1 a 2Ki 24:1 b 2Ch 36:6

1:2 c 2Ch 36:7; Jer 27:19-20; Zec 5:5-11

1:3 d 2Ki 20:18; 24:15; Isa 39:7

1:5 e ver 8,10 f ver 19

1:6 g Eze 14:14

1:7 h Da 4:8; 5:12 i Da 2:49; 3:12

1:8 j Eze 4:13-14

1:9 k Ge 39:21; Pr 16:7 l 1Ki 8:50; Ps 106:46

1:15 m Ex 23:25
1:16 n ver 12-13

---

a 2 Hebrew *Shinar*   b 4 Or *Chaldeans*   c 10 The Hebrew for *your* and *you* in this verse is plural.

Daniel 1:1–21

The first chapter of the book of Daniel begins and ends with chronological markers that allow us to date Daniel's career. Though Jerusalem was destroyed by the Babylonians in 586 B.C., Daniel was carried off to Babylon as part of an earlier deportation in 605. Verse 21 tells us that he was still there in 539. Since Daniel mentions in 10:1 that he received a vision in the third year of Cyrus, we know that he was still alive when the first exiles returned to Jerusalem.

Chapter 1 introduces us to the book's theme: In spite of appearances, God is in control. Three times God drove home this reality by giving something to someone (vv. 2,9,17). For the time being his control was understood only in private by Daniel and his three friends. But the effect was there for all to see. And the episode from

the experience of Daniel and his friends in this first chapter demonstrates another important lesson: Even though they were in exile, God gave his people the ability to prosper and be faithful.

Do you know where and when to draw the line? The church today finds itself in a situation like Daniel's. We too live in a strange land, in a "toxic" culture at odds with our faith. Daniel tolerated much cultural assimilation but knew where he had to draw the line to be true to his faith. God rewarded his stance and, as we will see in the following chapters, gave him wonderful opportunities to make even bolder statements of his faith. The book of Daniel communicates the liberating, yet potentially unsettling, news that God gives believers both flexibility *and* mandates in our interaction with our unbelieving culture.

Literacy: An Open Door

1:3–4,17

Daniel's adventures led him through events requiring extraordinary faith, courage, patience— and learning. His natural ability with languages and literature won him high praise with three different kings, while his supernatural ability with dreams and visions earned him a reputation as the wisest, most able representative of God to his generation.

After conquering Jerusalem in 605 B.C., Nebuchadnezzar instructed his chief court official to "bring in some of the Israelites from the royal family and the nobility . . . He was to teach them the language and literature of the Babylonians" (1:3–4). Daniel and his friends were singled out for special training. But they were also anointed by God for special service (v. 17).

An early clue to Daniel's unusual preparation for service is the languages he used in his book: About half is written in his native Hebrew (1:1—2:4,8–12) and the other half in Aramaic (2:4—7:28), the common language of Babylon. In addition, Daniel studied two unusually difficult languages, Chaldean and Akkadian, Babylon's official, literary language. And he probably knew Sumerian, from which Akkadian borrowed its writing system and many religious terms.

> "**W**henever I would see girls much younger than me read the Bible in the local language at church, I would feel such pain in my heart."

The word "language" is used in Daniel more than in any other Old Testament book. Of the eight appearances in the book, seven times the word is used in the phrase "men [or 'people'] of every language" (3:4,7,29; 4:1; 5:19; 6:25; 7:14). Daniel understood that language is an important cultural classification. Further, the word "literature" is mentioned in the Old Testament only in Daniel (1:4,17). Clearly God used Daniel's ability to read and understand in interpreting the king's dreams (Dan. 2; 4) and the handwriting on the wall (Dan. 5).

Relatively few believers today are called to learn multiple languages and the literature of diverse cultures, but the ability to read and write is no less central to the understanding and spreading of God's Good News. This is true of a young woman in a small community in Zambia, a continent away from Daniel's home in exile. There Fredah Chipemba, now in her mid-twenties, had always desired to read Scripture for herself. "Whenever I would see girls much younger than me read the Bible in the local language at church, I would feel such pain in my heart," she reflected.

Fredah wished she had continued school to master reading. But she had dropped out in the sixth grade because she felt she was "too dull in class to pick out anything." There was no use pretending: Fredah and school weren't friends. It wasn't long before she regretted her decision: "Each time I picked up a book or piece of paper, I couldn't make out anything."

Finally one day Fredah registered for an adult literacy class in her village. But she soon dropped out because she couldn't endure having people laugh at her. Months later she tried again, this time successfully. Beaming with confidence, Fredah confesses: "I felt so good when I learned to read. I kept asking myself, *Is it really me?*"

Like Daniel, Fredah recognized that God's message is understood best when people read and study it for themselves. Many years after Daniel's day and before Fredah's, Paul wrote that "faith comes from hearing the message, and the message is heard through the word of Christ" (Rom. 10:17). Reading and writing open the door to knowing and doing. How could you help the Fredahs in your community to learn more, or perhaps learn for the first time, that God's message is a personal invitation to them?

Timothy J. Beals, publisher of World Vision Press in Federal Way, Washington

17To these four young men God gave knowledge and understanding[o] of all kinds of literature and learning.[p] And Daniel could understand visions and dreams of all kinds.[q]

18At the end of the time[r] set by the king to bring them in, the chief official presented them to Nebuchadnezzar. 19The king talked with them, and he found none equal to Daniel, Hananiah, Mishael and Azariah; so they entered the king's service.[s] 20In every matter of wisdom and understanding about which the king questioned them, he found them ten times better than all the magicians and enchanters in his whole kingdom.[t]

21And Daniel remained there until the first year of King Cyrus.[u]

Nebuchadnezzar's Dream

2 In the second year of his reign, Nebuchadnezzar had dreams;[v] his mind was troubled[w] and he could not sleep.[x] 2So the king summoned the magicians,[y] enchanters, sorcerers[z] and astrologers[aa] to tell him what he had dreamed.[b] When they came in and stood before the king, 3he said to them, "I have had a dream that troubles[c] me and I want to know what it means.[b]"

4Then the astrologers answered the king in Aramaic,[cd] "O king, live forever![e] Tell your servants the dream, and we will interpret it."

5The king replied to the astrologers, "This is what I have firmly decided: If you do not tell me what my dream was and interpret it, I will have you cut into pieces[f] and your houses turned into piles of rubble.[g] 6But if you tell me the dream and explain it, you will receive from me gifts and rewards and great honor.[h] So tell me the dream and interpret it for me."

7Once more they replied, "Let the king tell his servants the dream, and we will interpret it."

8Then the king answered, "I am certain that you are trying to gain time, because you realize that this is what I have firmly decided: 9If you do not tell me the dream, there is just one penalty[i] for you. You have conspired to tell me misleading and wicked things, hoping the situation will change. So then, tell me the dream, and I will know that you can interpret it for me."[j]

10The astrologers answered the king, "There is not a man on earth who can do what the king asks! No king, however great and mighty, has ever asked such a thing of any magician or enchanter or astrologer.[k] 11What the king asks is too difficult. No one can reveal it to the king except the gods,[l] and they do not live among men."

12This made the king so angry and furious[m] that he ordered the execution[n] of all the wise men of Babylon. 13So the decree was issued to put the wise men to death, and men were sent to look for Daniel and his friends to put them to death.[o]

14When Arioch, the commander of the king's guard, had gone out to put to death the wise men of Babylon, Daniel spoke to him with wisdom and tact. 15He asked the king's officer, "Why did the king issue such a harsh decree?" Arioch then

---

a 2 Or *Chaldeans;* also in verses 4, 5 and 10   b 3 Or *was*   c 4 The text from here through chapter 7 is in Aramaic.

1:17
o 1Ki 3:12
p Da 2:23; Jas 1:5
q Da 2:19,30; 7:1; 8:1
1:18
r ver 5
1:19
s Ge 41:46
1:20
t 1Ki 4:30; Da 2:13,28
1:21
u Da 6:28; 10:1

2:1
v Job 33:15,18; Da 4:5 w Ge 41:8 x Est 6:1; Da 6:18
2:2
y Ge 41:8 z Ex 7:11 a ver 10; Da 5:7 b Da 4:6
2:3
c Da 4:5
2:4
d Ezr 4:7 e Da 3:9; 5:10
2:5
f ver 12 g Ezr 6:11; Da 3:29
2:6
h ver 48; Da 5:7,16

2:9
i Est 4:11
j Isa 41:22-24

2:10
k ver 27
2:11
l Da 5:11
2:12
m Da 3:13,19 n ver 5
2:13
o Da 1:20

Daniel 2:1–23

In his prayer, Daniel highlighted two aspects of God's character pivotal to this chapter and the book as a whole: (1) God is powerful. Nebuchadnezzar was king because God "sets up kings and deposes them" (v. 21). (2) God is wise. Daniel understood that his own wisdom came from God. The "wisdom and tact" (v. 14) Daniel displayed might be confused with the common sense available to any sensitive human being, but the ability to describe someone else's dream could only have come from a divine source.

Daniel's wisdom in chapter 1 is similar to the kind of wisdom we see in the book of Proverbs: "street smarts," knowing how to navigate life in the midst of its

troubles and obstacles. But the kind of divinely inspired wisdom he displayed in chapter 2 is more striking from a human perspective. Today Christians debate whether such wisdom is available to God's followers. Some believe that God still speaks directly, revealing his will and ways to his people. Others think such communication came to a conclusion with Jesus' death and resurrection and the record and interpretation of that climactic act. God speaks to us, they argue, only through his completed revelation, the Bible.

We can all agree that wisdom comes from God. If you want greater wisdom, why not begin by seeking to enrich your relationship with Christ, "in whom are hidden all the treasures of wisdom and knowledge" (Col. 2:3)?

explained the matter to Daniel. [16]At this, Daniel went in to the king and asked for time, so that he might interpret the dream for him.

[17]Then Daniel returned to his house and explained the matter to his friends Hananiah, Mishael and Azariah. [p] [18]He urged them to plead for mercy [q] from the God of heaven concerning this mystery, [r] so that he and his friends might not be executed with the rest of the wise men of Babylon. [19]During the night the mystery [s] was revealed to Daniel in a vision. [t] Then Daniel praised the God of heaven [20]and said:

> "Praise be to the name of God for ever and ever; [u]
> wisdom and power [v] are his.
> [21] He changes times and seasons; [w]
> he sets up kings and deposes [x] them.
> He gives wisdom [y] to the wise
> and knowledge to the discerning.
> [22] He reveals deep and hidden things; [z]
> he knows what lies in darkness, [a]
> and light [b] dwells with him.
> [23] I thank and praise you, O God of my fathers: [c]
> You have given me wisdom [d] and power,
> you have made known to me what we asked of you,
> you have made known to us the dream of the king."

Daniel Interprets the Dream

[24]Then Daniel went to Arioch, [e] whom the king had appointed to execute the wise men of Babylon, and said to him, "Do not execute the wise men of Babylon. Take me to the king, and I will interpret his dream for him."

[25]Arioch took Daniel to the king at once and said, "I have found a man among the exiles from Judah [f] who can tell the king what his dream means."

[26]The king asked Daniel (also called Belteshazzar), [g] "Are you able to tell me what I saw in my dream and interpret it?"

[27]Daniel replied, "No wise man, enchanter, magician or diviner can explain to the king the mystery he has asked about, [h] [28]but there is a God in heaven who reveals mysteries. [i] He has shown King Nebuchadnezzar what will happen in days to come. [j] Your dream and the visions that passed through your mind [k] as you lay on your bed are these:

[29]"As you were lying there, O king, your mind turned to things to come, and the revealer of mysteries showed you what is going to happen. [30]As for me, this mystery has been revealed [l] to me, not because I have greater wisdom than other living men, but so that you, O king, may know the interpretation and that you may understand what went through your mind.

[31]"You looked, O king, and there before you stood a large statue—an enormous, dazzling statue, [m] awesome in appearance. [32]The head of the statue was made of pure

Cross references (margin)

2:17
p Da 1:6
2:18
q Isa 37:4 r Jer 33:3
2:19
s ver 28
t Job 33:15;
Da 1:17
2:20
u Ps 113:2; 145:1-2
v Jer 32:19
2:21
w Da 7:25
x Job 12:19;
Ps 75:6-7 y Jas 1:5
2:22
z Job 12:22;
Ps 25:14; Da 5:11
a Ps 139:11-12;
Jer 23:24; Heb 4:13
b Isa 45:7; Jas 1:17
2:23
c Ex 3:15 d Da 1:17
2:24
e ver 14
2:25
f Da 1:6; 5:13; 6:13
2:26
g Da 1:7
2:27
h ver 10
2:28
i Ge 40:8; Am 4:13
j Ge 49:1; Da 10:14
k Da 4:5
2:30
l Isa 45:3; Da 1:17;
Am 4:13
2:31
m Hab 1:7

Daniel 2:24–49

The traditional interpretation of the statue is that the gold head represented Nebuchadnezzar and the Babylonian empire; the silver chest and arms, the Medo-Persian empire established by Cyrus following his conquest of Babylon; the bronze belly and thighs, the Greek empire established by Alexander the Great; and the iron legs and feet, the Roman empire.

Regardless of what kingdoms the statue represented, most important here are two principles: (1) The statue, an object made with human hands and ingenuity, is contrasted with the object of its demise, the rock— God's kingdom that will obliterate all human kingdoms. (2) Only Daniel's God knows the future, reminding us once again of the overall theme of the book: In spite of present appearances, God is in control.

In Nebuchadnezzar's dream, the rock cut out of a mountain without human hands wouldn't only crush the statue but would grow to incredible proportions (vv. 34–35). Believers look to Jesus Christ as the Rock who establishes God's kingdom by crushing godless nations (v. 44; cf. Ps. 118:22; Isa. 8:14; 28:16; Matt. 7: 24–27; 21:42–44; Mark 12:10; Luke 20:17–18; Rom. 9:33; 1 Peter 2:6–8).

Those who reject Jesus the Messiah will be doomed. But those who turn to Christ become part of God's eternal kingdom, of which the Bible's concluding book says: "The kingdom of the world has become the kingdom of our Lord and of his Christ, and he will reign for ever and ever" (Rev. 11:15).

gold, its chest and arms of silver, its belly and thighs of bronze, [33]its legs of iron, its feet partly of iron and partly of baked clay. [34]While you were watching, a rock was cut out, but not by human hands.[n] It struck the statue on its feet of iron and clay and smashed them.[o] [35]Then the iron, the clay, the bronze, the silver and the gold were broken to pieces at the same time and became like chaff on a threshing floor in the summer. The wind swept them away[p] without leaving a trace. But the rock that struck the statue became a huge mountain[q] and filled the whole earth.

[36]"This was the dream, and now we will interpret it to the king. [37]You, O king, are the king of kings.[r] The God of heaven has given you dominion[s] and power and might and glory; [38]in your hands he has placed mankind and the beasts of the field and the birds of the air. Wherever they live, he has made you ruler over them all.[t] You are that head of gold.

[39]"After you, another kingdom will rise, inferior to yours. Next, a third kingdom, one of bronze, will rule over the whole earth. [40]Finally, there will be a fourth kingdom, strong as iron—for iron breaks and smashes everything—and as iron breaks things to pieces, so it will crush and break all the others.[u] [41]Just as you saw that the feet and toes were partly of baked clay and partly of iron, so this will be a divided kingdom; yet it will have some of the strength of iron in it, even as you saw iron mixed with clay. [42]As the toes were partly iron and partly clay, so this kingdom will be partly strong and partly brittle. [43]And just as you saw the iron mixed with baked clay, so the people will be a mixture and will not remain united, any more than iron mixes with clay.

[44]"In the time of those kings, the God of heaven will set up a kingdom that will never be destroyed, nor will it be left to another people. It will crush[v] all those kingdoms[w] and bring them to an end, but it will itself endure forever.[x] [45]This is the meaning of the vision of the rock[y] cut out of a mountain, but not by human hands[z]—a rock that broke the iron, the bronze, the clay, the silver and the gold to pieces.

"The great God has shown the king what will take place in the future. The dream is true and the interpretation is trustworthy."

[46]Then King Nebuchadnezzar fell prostrate[a] before Daniel and paid him honor and ordered that an offering[b] and incense be presented to him. [47]The king said to Daniel, "Surely your God is the God of gods[c] and the Lord of kings[d] and a revealer of mysteries,[e] for you were able to reveal this mystery."

[48]Then the king placed Daniel in a high position and lavished many gifts on him. He made him ruler over the entire province of Babylon and placed him in charge of all its wise men.[f] [49]Moreover, at Daniel's request the king appointed Shadrach, Meshach and Abednego administrators over the province of Babylon,[g] while Daniel himself remained at the royal court.

The Image of Gold and the Fiery Furnace

3 King Nebuchadnezzar made an image[h] of gold, ninety feet high and nine feet[a] wide, and set it up on the plain of Dura in the province of Babylon. [2]He then summoned the satraps, prefects, governors, advisers, treasurers, judges, magistrates and all the other provincial officials[i] to come to the dedication of the image he had set up. [3]So the satraps, prefects, governors, advisers, treasurers, judges, magistrates and all the other provincial officials assembled for the dedication of the image that King Nebuchadnezzar had set up, and they stood before it.

[4]Then the herald loudly proclaimed, "This is what you are commanded to do,

[a] 1 Aramaic *sixty cubits high and six cubits wide* (about 27 meters high and 2.7 meters wide)

Cross references

2:34
[n] Zec 4:6
[o] ver 44-45; Ps 2:9; Isa 60:12; Da 8:25

2:35
[p] Ps 1:4; 37:10; Isa 17:13 [q] Isa 2:3; Mic 4:1

2:37
[r] Eze 26:7
[s] Jer 27:7
2:38
[t] Jer 27:6; Da 4:21-22

2:40
[u] Da 7:7,23

2:44
[v] Ps 2:9; 1Co 15:24
[w] Isa 60:12
[x] Ps 145:13; Isa 9:7; Da 4:34; 6:26; 7:14,27; Mic 4:7,13; Lk 1:33
2:45
[y] Isa 28:16
[z] Da 8:25

2:46
[a] Da 8:17; Ac 10:25
[b] Ac 14:13
2:47
[c] Da 11:36
[d] Da 4:25
[e] ver 22,28

2:48
[f] ver 6; Da 4:9; 5:11
2:49
[g] Da 1:7

3:1
[h] Isa 46:6; Jer 16:20; Hab 2:19

3:2
[i] ver 27; Da 6:7

Daniel 3:1–30

In chapter 2 God had made known his great wisdom. Here he revealed his power (see "There and Then" for 2:1–23). This story once again supports the book's theme: Despite appearances, God is in control. Only the true God, a proven liberator, could have pro-

claimed that "no one can deliver out of my hand" (Deut. 32:39). When God had rescued his people from Egypt centuries earlier, Moses had told the Israelites that God had "brought [them] out of the iron-smelting furnace, out of Egypt, to be the people of his inheritance" (Deut. 4:20). God's power transcends even death.

3:4
j Da 4:1; 6:25
3:5
k ver 10,15
3:6
l ver 11,15,21;
Jer 29:22; Da 6:7;
Mt 13:42,50;
Rev 13:15
3:7
m ver 5
3:8
n Da 2:10
3:9
o Ne 2:3; Da 5:10;
6:6
3:10
p Da 6:12 q ver 4-6

3:12
r Da 2:49 s Da 6:13
t Est 3:3
3:13
u Da 2:12

3:14
v Isa 46:1; Jer 50:2
w ver 1

3:15
x Isa 36:18-20
y Ex 5:2; 2Ch 32:15
3:16
z Da 1:7

3:17
a Ps 27:1-2
b Job 5:19; Jer 1:8
3:18
c ver 28; Jos 24:15

3:19
d Lev 26:18-28

3:22
e Da 1:7

3:26
f Da 4:2,34

O peoples, nations and men of every language:[j] [5]As soon as you hear the sound of the horn, flute, zither, lyre, harp, pipes and all kinds of music, you must fall down and worship the image of gold that King Nebuchadnezzar has set up.[k] [6]Whoever does not fall down and worship will immediately be thrown into a blazing furnace."[l]

[7]Therefore, as soon as they heard the sound of the horn, flute, zither, lyre, harp and all kinds of music, all the peoples, nations and men of every language fell down and worshiped the image of gold that King Nebuchadnezzar had set up.[m]

[8]At this time some astrologers[a][n] came forward and denounced the Jews. [9]They said to King Nebuchadnezzar, "O king, live forever![o] [10]You have issued a decree,[p] O king, that everyone who hears the sound of the horn, flute, zither, lyre, harp, pipes and all kinds of music must fall down and worship the image of gold,[q] [11]and that whoever does not fall down and worship will be thrown into a blazing furnace. [12]But there are some Jews whom you have set over the affairs of the province of Babylon—Shadrach, Meshach and Abednego[r]—who pay no attention[s] to you, O king. They neither serve your gods nor worship the image of gold you have set up."[t]

[13]Furious[u] with rage, Nebuchadnezzar summoned Shadrach, Meshach and Abednego. So these men were brought before the king, [14]and Nebuchadnezzar said to them, "Is it true, Shadrach, Meshach and Abednego, that you do not serve my gods[v] or worship the image[w] of gold I have set up? [15]Now when you hear the sound of the horn, flute, zither, lyre, harp, pipes and all kinds of music, if you are ready to fall down and worship the image I made, very good. But if you do not worship it, you will be thrown immediately into a blazing furnace. Then what god[x] will be able to rescue[y] you from my hand?"

[16]Shadrach, Meshach and Abednego[z] replied to the king, "O Nebuchadnezzar, we do not need to defend ourselves before you in this matter. [17]If we are thrown into the blazing furnace, the God we serve is able to save[a] us from it, and he will rescue[b] us from your hand, O king. [18]But even if he does not, we want you to know, O king, that we will not serve your gods or worship the image of gold you have set up.[c]"

[19]Then Nebuchadnezzar was furious with Shadrach, Meshach and Abednego, and his attitude toward them changed. He ordered the furnace heated seven[d] times hotter than usual [20]and commanded some of the strongest soldiers in his army to tie up Shadrach, Meshach and Abednego and throw them into the blazing furnace. [21]So these men, wearing their robes, trousers, turbans and other clothes, were bound and thrown into the blazing furnace. [22]The king's command was so urgent and the furnace so hot that the flames of the fire killed the soldiers who took up Shadrach, Meshach and Abednego,[e] [23]and these three men, firmly tied, fell into the blazing furnace.

[24]Then King Nebuchadnezzar leaped to his feet in amazement and asked his advisers, "Weren't there three men that we tied up and threw into the fire?"

They replied, "Certainly, O king."

[25]He said, "Look! I see four men walking around in the fire, unbound and unharmed, and the fourth looks like a son of the gods."

[26]Nebuchadnezzar then approached the opening of the blazing furnace and shouted, "Shadrach, Meshach and Abednego, servants of the Most High God,[f] come out! Come here!"

So Shadrach, Meshach and Abednego came out of the fire, [27]and the satraps, pre-

---

[a] 8 Or *Chaldeans*

The friends' courage is amazing when we reflect on what they might have thought about life after death. Earlier Scriptures say little about resurrection, eternal life, or heaven. These young men stood firm simply because they trusted God—no matter what.

📖 We all struggle with the temptation to worship the idols of contemporary culture: Material possessions, addictions, relationships, higher education, success, entertainment, and much more can engage our hearts and minds with subtle seduction. But our only worship is to be directed to the One who is the true and full image of God—Jesus Christ (cf. Col. 1:15).

Like the three Hebrews, we are called to do more than resist idolatry. We are to be prepared to do so to the point of death. American Christians are rarely confronted with that kind of decision. This isn't true of Christians in many other parts of the world, where faith and witness can realistically lead to a prison term or death penalty.

fects, governors and royal advisers *g* crowded around them. *h* They saw that the fire *i* had not harmed their bodies, nor was a hair of their heads singed; their robes were not scorched, and there was no smell of fire on them.

28Then Nebuchadnezzar said, "Praise be to the God of Shadrach, Meshach and Abednego, who has sent his angel *j* and rescued his servants! They trusted *k* in him and defied the king's command and were willing to give up their lives rather than serve or worship any god except their own God. *l* 29Therefore I decree *m* that the people of any nation or language who say anything against the God of Shadrach, Meshach and Abednego be cut into pieces and their houses be turned into piles of rubble, *n* for no other god can save *o* in this way."

30Then the king promoted Shadrach, Meshach and Abednego in the province of Babylon. *p*

Nebuchadnezzar's Dream of a Tree

4 King Nebuchadnezzar,

To the peoples, nations and men of every language, *q* who live in all the world:

May you prosper greatly! *r*

2It is my pleasure to tell you about the miraculous signs *s* and wonders that the Most High God *t* has performed for me.

3 How great are his signs,
   how mighty his wonders! *u*
His kingdom is an eternal kingdom;
   his dominion endures *v* from generation to generation.

4I, Nebuchadnezzar, was at home in my palace, contented *w* and prosperous. 5I had a dream *x* that made me afraid. As I was lying in my bed, the images and visions that passed through my mind *y* terrified me. 6So I commanded that all the wise men of Babylon be brought before me to interpret *z* the dream for me. 7When the magicians, *a* enchanters, astrologers *a* and diviners *b* came, I told them the dream, but they could not interpret it for me. *c* 8Finally, Daniel came into my presence and I told him the dream. (He is called Belteshazzar, *d* after the name of my god, and the spirit of the holy gods *e* is in him.)

9I said, "Belteshazzar, chief *f* of the magicians, I know that the spirit of the holy gods *g* is in you, and no mystery is too difficult for you. Here is my dream; interpret it for me. 10These are the visions I saw while lying in my bed: *h* I looked, and there before me stood a tree in the middle of the land. Its height was enormous. *i* 11The tree grew large and strong and its top touched the sky;

---

a 7 Or *Chaldeans*

3:27
g ver 2 *h* Isa 43:2;
Heb 11:32-34
i Da 6:23

3:28
j Ps 34:7; Da 6:22;
Ac 5:19
k Job 13:15;
Ps 26:1; 84:12;
Jer 17:7 *l* ver 18
3:29
m Da 6:26
n Ezr 6:11
o Da 6:27

3:30
p Da 2:49

4:1
q Da 3:4 *r* Da 6:25

4:2
s Ps 74:9 *t* Da 3:26

4:3
u Ps 105:27;
Da 6:27 *v* Da 2:44

4:4
w Ps 30:6
4:5
x Da 2:1 *y* Da 2:28
4:6
z Da 2:2
4:7
a Ge 41:8
b Isa 44:25; Da 2:2
c Da 2:10
4:8
d Da 1:7
e Da 5:11,14
4:9
f Da 2:48
g Da 5:11-12
4:10
h ver 5 *i* Eze 31:3-4

Daniel 4:1–18

This chapter is in the form of a letter or written decree of King Nebuchadnezzar himself. It was written largely in the first person, though verses 19–33 revert to the third person. As in chapter 2, a dream forms the center of the action. Nebuchadnezzar was again the recipient of a dream he couldn't understand. This time he made no threats but summoned Daniel immediately after the failure of his local corps of wise men.

The fact that Nebuchadnezzar still hadn't really "gotten it" was indicated by his calling the Babylonian wise men first (v. 6), his use of Daniel's Babylonian name Belteshazzar—which connected him to the king's native god (vv. 8,9,18), and his polytheistic reference to Daniel as the one in whom "the spirit of the holy gods" resided (vv. 9,18).

All that was to be left of the cosmic tree in Nebuchadnezzar's dream was the stump and its roots (v. 15), indicating that it would later be revived. The dream's metaphors were mixed: The tree became a beast wandering the earth for "seven times," usually understood to be seven years (see NIV text note for v. 16).

Nebuchadnezzar reached the convictions expressed in verses 2–3 after his experiences in the rest of the chapter. As we will see, his praise of "the Most High God" followed his severe humbling. If the king had humbled himself sooner, he would have saved himself a lot of grief. Can you relate? We can all take a lesson: How much better it is to humbly worship and submit to God in the first place!

it was visible to the ends of the earth. [12]Its leaves were beautiful, its fruit abundant, and on it was food for all. Under it the beasts of the field found shelter, and the birds of the air lived in its branches;[j] from it every creature was fed.

[13]"In the visions I saw while lying in my bed,[k] I looked, and there before me was a messenger,[a] a holy one,[l] coming down from heaven. [14]He called in a loud voice: 'Cut down the tree and trim off its branches; strip off its leaves and scatter its fruit. Let the animals flee from under it and the birds from its branches.[m] [15]But let the stump and its roots, bound with iron and bronze, remain in the ground, in the grass of the field.

" 'Let him be drenched with the dew of heaven, and let him live with the animals among the plants of the earth. [16]Let his mind be changed from that of a man and let him be given the mind of an animal, till seven times[b] pass by for him.[n]

[17]" 'The decision is announced by messengers, the holy ones declare the verdict, so that the living may know that the Most High[o] is sovereign[p] over the kingdoms of men and gives them to anyone he wishes and sets over them the lowliest[q] of men.'

[18]"This is the dream that I, King Nebuchadnezzar, had. Now, Belteshazzar, tell me what it means, for none of the wise men in my kingdom can interpret it for me.[r] But you can,[s] because the spirit of the holy gods is in you."[t]

Daniel Interprets the Dream

[19]Then Daniel (also called Belteshazzar) was greatly perplexed for a time, and his thoughts terrified[u] him. So the king said, "Belteshazzar, do not let the dream or its meaning alarm you."

Belteshazzar answered, "My lord, if only the dream applied to your enemies and its meaning to your adversaries! [20]The tree you saw, which grew large and strong, with its top touching the sky, visible to the whole earth, [21]with beautiful leaves and abundant fruit, providing food for all, giving shelter to the beasts of the field, and having nesting places in its branches for the birds of the air— [22]you, O king, are that tree![v] You have become great and strong; your greatness has grown until it reaches the sky, and your dominion extends to distant parts of the earth.[w]

[23]"You, O king, saw a messenger, a holy one,[x] coming down from heaven and saying, 'Cut down the tree and destroy it, but leave the stump, bound with iron and bronze, in the grass of the field, while its roots remain in the ground. Let him be drenched with the dew of heaven; let him live like the wild animals, until seven times pass by for him.'[y]

[24]"This is the interpretation, O king, and this is the decree[z] the Most High has issued against my lord the king: [25]You will be driven away from people and will live with the wild animals; you will eat grass like cattle and be drenched with the dew of heaven. Seven times will pass by for you until you acknowledge that the Most High[a] is sovereign over the kingdoms of men and gives

---

Cross references (margin)

4:12
j Eze 17:23;
Mt 13:32
4:13
k Da 7:1 / ver 23;
Dt 33:2; Da 8:13

4:14
m Eze 31:12;
Mt 3:10

4:16
n ver 23,32

4:17
o ver 2,25; Ps 83:18
p Jer 27:5-7;
Da 2:21; 5:18-21
q Da 11:21

4:18
r Ge 41:8;
Da 5:8,15
s Ge 41:15
t ver 7-9

4:19
u Da 7:15,28; 8:27;
10:16-17

4:22
v 2Sa 12:7
w Jer 27:7;
Da 2:37-38; 5:18-19

4:23
x ver 13 y Da 5:21

4:24
z Job 40:12;
Ps 107:40

4:25
a ver 17; Ps 83:18

---

[a] 13 Or *watchman*; also in verses 17 and 23   [b] 16 Or *years*; also in verses 23, 25 and 32

Daniel 4:19–27

The relationship between Daniel and Nebuchadnezzar was remarkable, considering that this king had destroyed Jerusalem. God's prophet showed concern for Nebuchadnezzar's well-being, not a desire for revenge. A message of judgment confronted Nebuchadnezzar, but it was a conditional message. Daniel's advice was to avoid sin and be kind to others. In other words, the king wasn't to fall prey to the temptation to think of himself as a god. In spite of being the head of the largest and most powerful empire in that part of the world up to that time, he was to acknowledge the one true God and exhibit humility.

Are your relationships with unbelievers exceptional? Do you demonstrate sincere care for those outside the family of faith? Can you boldly communicate the gospel of the kingdom to others without transmitting a judgmental attitude? Believers who desire to be effective in their witness can follow Daniel's example, showing respect for individuals and their beliefs, regardless of a person's demeanor or personal power. Yet Daniel didn't back away from clearly communicating God's message to this decidedly ungodly ruler. What other principles of relating to and communicating with unbelievers do you find in this passage?

them to anyone he wishes. *b* 26The command to leave the stump of the tree with its roots *c* means that your kingdom will be restored to you when you acknowledge that Heaven rules. *d* 27Therefore, O king, be pleased to accept my advice: Renounce your sins by doing what is right, and your wickedness by being kind to the oppressed. *e* It may be that then your prosperity will continue. *f*"

The Dream Is Fulfilled

28All this happened *g* to King Nebuchadnezzar. 29Twelve months later, as the king was walking on the roof of the royal palace of Babylon, 30he said, "Is not this the great Babylon I have built as the royal residence, by my mighty power and for the glory of my majesty?" *h*

31The words were still on his lips when a voice came from heaven, "This is what is decreed for you, King Nebuchadnezzar: Your royal authority has been taken from you. 32You will be driven away from people and will live with the wild animals; you will eat grass like cattle. Seven times will pass by for you until you acknowledge that the Most High is sovereign over the kingdoms of men and gives them to anyone he wishes."

33Immediately what had been said about Nebuchadnezzar was fulfilled. He was driven away from people and ate grass like cattle. His body was drenched with the dew of heaven until his hair grew like the feathers of an eagle and his nails like the claws of a bird. *i*

34At the end of that time, I, Nebuchadnezzar, raised my eyes toward heaven, and my sanity was restored. Then I praised the Most High; I honored and glorified him who lives forever. *j*

His dominion is an eternal dominion;
  his kingdom endures from generation to generation. *k*
35All the peoples of the earth
  are regarded as nothing. *l*
He does as he pleases *m*
  with the powers of heaven
  and the peoples of the earth.
No one can hold back his hand
  or say to him: "What have you done?" *n*

36At the same time that my sanity was restored, my honor and splendor were returned to me for the glory of my kingdom. *o* My advisers and nobles sought me out, and I was restored to my throne and became even greater than before. 37Now I, Nebuchadnezzar, praise and exalt and glorify the King of heaven, be-

4:25
b Jer 27:5; Da 5:21
4:26
c ver 15 *d* Da 2:37
4:27
e Isa 55:6-7
f 1Ki 21:29;
Ps 41:3; Eze 18:22
4:28
g Nu 23:19
4:30
h Isa 37:24-25;
Da 5:20; Hab 2:4
4:33
i Da 5:20-21
4:34
j Da 12:7; Rev 4:10
k Ps 145:13;
Da 2:44; 5:21; 6:26;
Lk 1:33
4:35
l Isa 40:17
m Ps 115:3; 135:6
n Isa 45:9; Ro 9:20
4:36
o Pr 22:4

Daniel 4:28–37

Babylon, containing two of the seven wonders of the ancient world, was grand indeed, and Nebuchadnezzar had much to do with its greatness. He asked rhetorically, "Is not this the great Babylon *I* have built as the royal residence, by *my* mighty power and for the glory of *my* majesty?" (v. 30; emphasis added). Immediately the king lost his sanity and was "driven away," possibly into the palace gardens, while his aides administered the kingdom, perhaps led by Daniel (cf. 2:48–49).

The divine prescription worked. At the appointed time the king "raised [his] eyes toward heaven, and [his] sanity was restored" (v. 34; cf. v. 25). Nebuchadnezzar at least temporarily understood his place in the scheme of things: Whatever power he enjoyed was a gift from God. If it's foolish to ask a human king "What are you doing?" (Eccl. 8:4), how much less prudent for

a human ruler to ask the divine King, "What have you done?" (Dan. 4:35).

New Testament believers naturally contrast Christ's humility with Nebuchadnezzar's pride. Nebuchadnezzar, a mere man, glorified himself as a virtual god. Notice the extreme contrast in Paul's words of praise concerning Jesus in Philippians 2:6–11. What can we make of the glorious One, who voluntarily humbled himself to take on human flesh, in the context of a mortal who took on divine airs?

Like Nebuchadnezzar, Jesus felt shame, but he underwent the experience to free us from shame and invite us to the glory of the resurrection. "Let us fix our eyes on Jesus, the author and perfecter of our faith, who for the joy set before him endured the cross, scorning its shame, and sat down at the right hand of the throne of God" (Heb. 12:2).

4:37
p Dt 32:4; Ps 33:4-5
q Ex 18:11;
Job 40:11-12;
Da 5:20,23

5:1
r Est 1:3

5:2
s 2Ki 24:13;
Jer 52:19 t Est 1:7;
Da 1:2

5:4
u Ps 135:15-18;
Hab 2:19; Rev 9:20

5:6
v Da 4:5 w Eze 7:17

5:7
x Isa 44:25
y Da 4:6-7
z Ge 41:42
a Da 2:5-6,48; 6:2-3

5:8
b Da 2:10,27
5:9
c Isa 21:4

5:10
d Da 3:9
5:11
e Da 4:8-9,19
f ver 14; Da 1:17
g Da 2:47-48

5:12
h Da 1:7
i ver 14-16; Da 6:3

5:13
j Da 6:13

5:17
k 2Ki 5:16

cause everything he does is right and all his ways are just. *p* And those who walk in pride he is able to humble. *q*

The Writing on the Wall

5 King Belshazzar gave a great banquet *r* for a thousand of his nobles and drank wine with them. ²While Belshazzar was drinking his wine, he gave orders to bring in the gold and silver goblets *s* that Nebuchadnezzar his father *a* had taken from the temple in Jerusalem, so that the king and his nobles, his wives and his concubines might drink from them. *t* ³So they brought in the gold goblets that had been taken from the temple of God in Jerusalem, and the king and his nobles, his wives and his concubines drank from them. ⁴As they drank the wine, they praised the gods of gold and silver, of bronze, iron, wood and stone. *u*

⁵Suddenly the fingers of a human hand appeared and wrote on the plaster of the wall, near the lampstand in the royal palace. The king watched the hand as it wrote. ⁶His face turned pale and he was so frightened *v* that his knees knocked together and his legs gave way. *w*

⁷The king called out for the enchanters, astrologers *b* and diviners *x* to be brought and said to these wise *y* men of Babylon, "Whoever reads this writing and tells me what it means will be clothed in purple and have a gold chain placed around his neck, *z* and he will be made the third highest ruler in the kingdom." *a*

⁸Then all the king's wise men came in, but they could not read the writing or tell the king what it meant. *b* ⁹So King Belshazzar became even more terrified *c* and his face grew more pale. His nobles were baffled.

¹⁰The queen, *c* hearing the voices of the king and his nobles, came into the banquet hall. "O king, live forever! *d* she said. "Don't be alarmed! Don't look so pale! ¹¹There is a man in your kingdom who has the spirit of the holy gods *e* in him. In the time of your father he was found to have insight and intelligence and wisdom *f* like that of the gods. King Nebuchadnezzar your father—your father the king, I say—appointed him chief of the magicians, enchanters, astrologers and diviners. *g* ¹²This man Daniel, whom the king called Belteshazzar, *h* was found to have a keen mind and knowledge and understanding, and also the ability to interpret dreams, explain riddles and solve difficult problems. *i* Call for Daniel, and he will tell you what the writing means."

¹³So Daniel was brought before the king, and the king said to him, "Are you Daniel, one of the exiles my father the king brought from Judah? *j* ¹⁴I have heard that the spirit of the gods is in you and that you have insight, intelligence and outstanding wisdom. ¹⁵The wise men and enchanters were brought before me to read this writing and tell me what it means, but they could not explain it. ¹⁶Now I have heard that you are able to give interpretations and to solve difficult problems. If you can read this writing and tell me what it means, you will be clothed in purple and have a gold chain placed around your neck, and you will be made the third highest ruler in the kingdom."

¹⁷Then Daniel answered the king, "You may keep your gifts for yourself and give your rewards to someone else. *k* Nevertheless, I will read the writing for the king and tell him what it means.

---

a 2 Or *ancestor*; or *predecessor*; also in verses 11, 13 and 18   b 7 Or *Chaldeans*; also in verse 11
c 10 Or *queen mother*

Daniel 5:1–31

The year was now 539 B.C. Nebuchadnezzar had died in 562, and his son Nabonidus had become king of Babylon in 556. Belshazzar was Nabonidus's son (see NIV text notes for vv. 2,22). As co-regent with his father, Belshazzar ruled Babylon during Nabonidus's ten-year absence from the capital city. This arrangement explains Belshazzar's offered reward of becoming "the third highest ruler in the kingdom" (vv. 7,16).

The focus of this chapter quickly shifts from Belshaz-

zar to the implements that had been taken from the Lord's temple and were now being used at the king's rowdy party. Praising his gods while drinking from these holy objects was like spitting in God's eye. Belshazzar combined blasphemy with idolatry; his actions were more profane than Nebuchadnezzar's prideful boasting. That Belshazzar ruled at all was by God's sovereign permission. But as the handwriting indicated, neither he nor the Babylonians had measured up.

18 "O king, the Most High God gave your father Nebuchadnezzar sovereignty and greatness and glory and splendor. *l* 19 Because of the high position he gave him, all the peoples and nations and men of every language dreaded and feared him. Those the king wanted to put to death, he put to death; *m* those he wanted to spare, he spared; those he wanted to promote, he promoted; and those he wanted to humble, he humbled. 20 But when his heart became arrogant and hardened with pride, *n* he was deposed from his royal throne and stripped *o* of his glory. *p* 21 He was driven away from people and given the mind of an animal; he lived with the wild donkeys and ate grass like cattle; and his body was drenched with the dew of heaven, until he acknowledged that the Most High God is sovereign *q* over the kingdoms of men and sets over them anyone he wishes. *r*

22 "But you his son, *a* O Belshazzar, have not humbled *s* yourself, though you knew all this. 23 Instead, you have set yourself up against *t* the Lord of heaven. You had the goblets from his temple brought to you, and you and your nobles, your wives and your concubines drank wine from them. You praised the gods of silver and gold, of bronze, iron, wood and stone, which cannot see or hear or understand. *u* But you did not honor the God who holds in his hand your life *v* and all your ways. *w* 24 Therefore he sent the hand that wrote the inscription.

25 "This is the inscription that was written:

MENE, MENE, TEKEL, PARSIN *b*

26 "This is what these words mean:

Mene *c*: God has numbered the days *x* of your reign and brought it to an end. *y*
27 *Tekel* *d*: You have been weighed on the scales and found wanting. *z*
28 *Peres* *e*: Your kingdom is divided and given to the Medes *a* and Persians." *b*

29 Then at Belshazzar's command, Daniel was clothed in purple, a gold chain was placed around his neck, and he was proclaimed the third highest ruler in the kingdom.

30 That very night Belshazzar, *c* king of the Babylonians, *f* was slain, *d* 31 and Darius *e* the Mede took over the kingdom, at the age of sixty-two.

Daniel in the Den of Lions

6 It pleased Darius *f* to appoint 120 satraps *g* to rule throughout the kingdom, 2 with three administrators over them, one of whom was Daniel. *h* The satraps were made accountable *i* to them so that the king might not suffer loss. 3 Now Daniel so distinguished himself among the administrators and the satraps by his exceptional qualities that the king planned to set him over the whole kingdom. *j* 4 At this, the administrators and the satraps tried to find grounds for charges against Daniel in his conduct of government affairs, but they were unable to do so. They could find

---

a 22 Or *descendant;* or *successor*   *b* 25 Aramaic *UPARSIN* (that is, *AND PARSIN*)   *c* 26 *Mene* can mean *numbered* or *mina* (a unit of money).   *d* 27 *Tekel* can mean *weighed* or *shekel.*   *e* 28 *Peres* (the singular of *Parsin*) can mean *divided* or *Persia* or *a half mina* or *a half shekel.*   *f* 30 Or *Chaldeans*

Jesus' death and resurrection moved us into a new era (cf. Matt. 27:51; Heb. 10:19–22). The temple and its contents had symbolized the great gulf between a holy God and sinful humanity, but now *everything*— not just temple articles—is holy (cf. Zech. 14:20–21). Such an understanding intensifies the concept of blasphemy. Blasphemy goes beyond defacing a church or cross to abusing any part of God's creation. An assault against a fellow human being is an act of blasphemy since people are created in God's image (Gen. 1:27; James 3:9). The destruction of the environment for selfish reasons is blasphemy; land, air, and seas are the creation of our holy God (Gen. 2:4–6). Such an understanding has staggering implications for our lives.

Daniel 6:1–28

This chapter concludes the stories of Daniel's activities in Babylon. He hadn't changed location, but the Medes and Persians had taken control of the empire. The identity of "King Darius" ("Darius the Mede" in 5:31) is puzzling. Cyrus was the king of Persia when Babylon fell. Darius was a well-known Persian royal name (Darius I ruled from 522 to 486 B.C. and Darius II from 423 to 404)—but not until after the deaths of Cyrus and his son Cambyses. In this instance, "Darius" was evidently a throne name for someone ruling on orders from Cyrus or else Cyrus's throne name in Babylon (see NIV text note on 6:28).

Daniel 6 parallels Daniel 3. While the story of

Cross references (margin):

5:18 *l* Jer 27:7; Da 2:37-38
5:19 *m* Da 2:12-13; 3:6
5:20 *n* Da 4:30 *o* Jer 13:18 *p* Job 40:12; Isa 14:13-15
5:21 *q* Eze 17:24 *r* Da 4:16-17,35
5:22 *s* Ex 10:3; 2Ch 33:23
5:23 *t* Jer 50:29 *u* Ps 115:4-8; Hab 2:19 *v* Job 12:10 *w* Job 31:4; Jer 10:23
5:26 *x* Jer 27:7 *y* Isa 13:6
5:27 *z* Ps 62:9
5:28 *a* Isa 13:17 *b* Da 6:28
5:30 *c* ver 1 *d* Isa 21:9; Jer 51:31
5:31 *e* Da 6:1; 9:1
6:1 *f* Da 5:31 *g* Est 1:1
6:2 *h* Da 2:48-49 *i* Ezr 4:22
6:3 *j* Ge 41:41; Est 10:3; Da 5:12-14

no corruption in him, because he was trustworthy and neither corrupt nor negligent. [5]Finally these men said, "We will never find any basis for charges against this man Daniel unless it has something to do with the law of his God."[k]

[6]So the administrators and the satraps went as a group to the king and said: "O King Darius, live forever! [l] [7]The royal administrators, prefects, satraps, advisers and governors[m] have all agreed that the king should issue an edict and enforce the decree that anyone who prays to any god or man during the next thirty days, except to you, O king, shall be thrown into the lions' den.[n] [8]Now, O king, issue the decree and put it in writing so that it cannot be altered—in accordance with the laws of the Medes and Persians, which cannot be repealed."[o] [9]So King Darius put the decree in writing.

[10]Now when Daniel learned that the decree had been published, he went home to his upstairs room where the windows opened toward[p] Jerusalem. Three times a day he got down on his knees[q] and prayed, giving thanks to his God, just as he had done before.[r] [11]Then these men went as a group and found Daniel praying and asking God for help. [12]So they went to the king and spoke to him about his royal decree: "Did you not publish a decree that during the next thirty days anyone who prays to any god or man except to you, O king, would be thrown into the lions' den?"

The king answered, "The decree stands—in accordance with the laws of the Medes and Persians, which cannot be repealed."[s]

[13]Then they said to the king, "Daniel, who is one of the exiles from Judah,[t] pays no attention[u] to you, O king, or to the decree you put in writing. He still prays three times a day." [14]When the king heard this, he was greatly distressed;[v] he was determined to rescue Daniel and made every effort until sundown to save him.

Marginal references

6:5 k Ac 24:13-16
6:6 l Ne 2:3; Da 2:4
6:7 m Da 3:2 n Ps 59:3; 64:2-6; Da 3:6
6:8 o Est 1:19
6:10 p 1Ki 8:48-49 q Ps 95:6 r Ac 5:29
6:12 s Est 1:19; Da 3:8-12
6:13 t Da 2:25; 5:13 u Est 3:8; Da 3:12
6:14 v Mk 6:26

Daniel's three friends in the furnace pictured the faithful refusing to participate in idolatrous practices, this chapter describes Daniel's refusal to refrain from proper worship of God. Daniel obeyed God's eternal law, not the unchangeable law of the Medes and Persians. Darius reacted with dismay, wanting to save the aged Jewish counselor, in contrast to Nebuchadnezzar's anger at the three friends' refusal to participate in the pagan rite.

Darius wasn't above his own law. What about God? In one sense we want to say yes: God is above everything and can do whatever he pleases. But going down that road is misleading and wrong. God's law is always the perfect expression of his character. He knows himself and the consequences of his acts and pronouncements perfectly. This is why the psalmist in Psalm 19:7–11 and Psalm 119 could speak of God's law in a way that couldn't apply to any human law.

Daniel not only survived his ordeal but prospered in the foreign court (v. 28). Hebrews 11:33 cites this episode as an example of faith and its results. The power of Daniel's quiet but courageous faithfulness was clearly expressed in Darius's testimony (Dan. 6:26–27). Our willingness to take risks for God will turn the heads of the secular culture around us as well.

6:10–11

Regular Prayer

Practicing regular, daily prayer has numerous benefits. Prayer was no less important in the New Testament than in the Old Testament for maintaining a right relationship with God (cf. Acts 12:24; 3:1).

The chart at 2 Kings 23:30, page 580, mentions the daily "office" of prayer. The *Book of Common Prayer* is a vestige of the morning/evening cycles of the daily office. Here are some reasons for practicing daily prayer or participating in the daily office:

- It permits believers and churches to learn the ancient rhythm of prayer.
- It points back to the temple as the house of prayer (2 Chron. 6:40).
- It helps us discover one way to recover God's order out of chaos.
- It's helpful as a "countercultural" discipline for Christians in a society where people are affected by hours of weekly immersion in television and other means of entertainment.
- It encourages us to pray more frequently and with greater organization.

- It helps us reconnect with the rich tradition of prayer in the church.
- It deepens our faith and instills a sense of awe and wonder at the mystery of Christ and the gospel.
- Whether observed individually or corporately, it fosters a communal aspect of prayer because we stand in solidarity with others worldwide who are praying at the same time(s).
- It teaches us Scripture, since use of psalms in prayer is a common practice and many believers have adopted the practice of "praying God's Word"—using Scripture as a basis for prayer.

Source: NIV Application Commentary, 1 & 2 Chronicles (2003:428)

Can you think of other reasons to pray regularly throughout the day?
How has customary, routine, habitual prayer helped your development as a believer?

15Then the men went as a group to the king and said to him, "Remember, O king,
that according to the law of the Medes and Persians no decree or edict that the king
issues can be changed."[w]
16So the king gave the order, and they brought Daniel and threw him into the lions' den.[x] The king said to Daniel, "May your God, whom you serve continually,
rescue[y] you!"
17A stone was brought and placed over the mouth of the den, and the king
sealed[z] it with his own signet ring and with the rings of his nobles, so that Daniel's
situation might not be changed. 18Then the king returned to his palace and spent
the night without eating[a] and without any entertainment being brought to him.
And he could not sleep.[b]
19At the first light of dawn, the king got up and hurried to the lions' den. 20When
he came near the den, he called to Daniel in an anguished voice, "Daniel, servant
of the living God, has your God, whom you serve continually, been able to rescue
you from the lions?"[c]
21Daniel answered, "O king, live forever![d] 22My God sent his angel,[e] and he shut
the mouths of the lions.[f] They have not hurt me, because I was found innocent in
his sight.[g] Nor have I ever done any wrong before you, O king."
23The king was overjoyed and gave orders to lift Daniel out of the den. And
when Daniel was lifted from the den, no wound[h] was found on him, because he
had trusted[i] in his God.
24At the king's command, the men who had falsely accused Daniel were brought
in and thrown into the lions' den,[j] along with their wives and children.[k] And before they reached the floor of the den, the lions overpowered them and crushed all
their bones.[l]
25Then King Darius wrote to all the peoples, nations and men of every language
throughout the land:

"May you prosper greatly![m]

26"I issue a decree that in every part of my kingdom people must fear and
reverence the God of Daniel.[n]

"For he is the living God
    and he endures forever;
his kingdom will not be destroyed,
    his dominion will never end.[o]
27He rescues and he saves;
    he performs signs and wonders[p]
    in the heavens and on the earth.
He has rescued Daniel
    from the power of the lions."[q]

28So Daniel prospered during the reign of Darius and the reign of Cyrus[a][r] the Persian.

Daniel's Dream of Four Beasts

7 In the first year of Belshazzar[s] king of Babylon, Daniel had a dream, and visions
passed through his mind[t] as he was lying on his bed. He wrote[u] down the substance of his dream.
2Daniel said: "In my vision at night I looked, and there before me were the four

6:15 [w] Est 8:8
6:16 [x] ver 7 [y] Job 5:19; Ps 37:39-40
6:17 [z] Mt 27:66
6:18 [a] 2Sa 12:17 [b] Est 6:1; Da 2:1
6:20 [c] Da 3:17
6:21 [d] Da 2:4
6:22 [e] Da 3:28 [f] Ps 91:11-13; Heb 11:33 [g] Ac 12:11; 2Ti 4:17
6:23 [h] Da 3:27 [i] 1Ch 5:20
6:24 [j] Dt 19:18-19; Est 7:9-10; Ps 54:5 [k] Dt 24:16; 2Ki 14:6 [l] Isa 38:13
6:25 [m] Da 4:1
6:26 [n] Ps 99:1-3; Da 3:29 [o] Da 2:44; 4:34
6:27 [p] Da 4:3 [q] ver 22
6:28 [r] 2Ch 36:22; Da 1:21
7:1 [s] Da 5:1 [t] Da 1:17 [u] Jer 36:4

[a] 28 Or *Darius, that is, the reign of Cyrus*

Daniel 7:1–14

The book of Daniel makes a radical shift between chapters 6 and 7. While children resonate with the lessons of Daniel 1–6, seasoned Bible scholars scratch their heads over Daniel 7–12—with its move from simple stories to obscure apocalyptic visions, using larger than life images and symbols to teach by analogy. The word *apocalyptic* as it's used today carries a sense of impending doom. But the Biblical books of Daniel and Revelation radiate with optimism as they celebrate victory over God's enemies.

Daniel's dream of chapter 7 occurred before the

7:2
v Rev 7:1
7:3
w Rev 13:1
7:4
x Jer 4:7 y Eze 17:3

winds of heaven[v] churning up the great sea. [3]Four great beasts,[w] each different from the others, came up out of the sea.

[4]"The first was like a lion,[x] and it had the wings of an eagle.[y] I watched until its wings were torn off and it was lifted from the ground so that it stood on two feet like a man, and the heart of a man was given to it.

7:5
z Da 2:39

[5]"And there before me was a second beast, which looked like a bear. It was raised up on one of its sides, and it had three ribs in its mouth between its teeth. It was told, 'Get up and eat your fill of flesh!'[z]

7:6
a Rev 13:2

[6]"After that, I looked, and there before me was another beast, one that looked like a leopard.[a] And on its back it had four wings like those of a bird. This beast had four heads, and it was given authority to rule.

7:7
b Da 2:40
c Rev 12:3

[7]"After that, in my vision at night I looked, and there before me was a fourth beast—terrifying and frightening and very powerful. It had large iron[b] teeth; it crushed and devoured its victims and trampled underfoot whatever was left. It was different from all the former beasts, and it had ten horns.[c]

7:8
d Da 8:9 e Rev 9:7
f Ps 12:3;
Rev 13:5-6

[8]"While I was thinking about the horns, there before me was another horn, a little[d] one, which came up among them; and three of the first horns were uprooted before it. This horn had eyes like the eyes of a man[e] and a mouth that spoke boastfully.[f]

[9]"As I looked,

> "thrones were set in place,
>   and the Ancient of Days took his seat.

7:9
g Rev 1:14
h Eze 1:15; 10:6

> His clothing was as white as snow;
>   the hair of his head was white like wool.[g]
> His throne was flaming with fire,
>   and its wheels[h] were all ablaze.

7:10
i Ps 50:3; 97:3;
Isa 30:27 j Dt 33:2;
Ps 68:17; Rev 5:11
k Rev 20:11-15

> [10]A river of fire[i] was flowing,
>   coming out from before him.[j]
> Thousands upon thousands attended him;
>   ten thousand times ten thousand stood before him.
> The court was seated,
>   and the books[k] were opened.

7:11
l Rev 19:20

[11]"Then I continued to watch because of the boastful words the horn was speaking. I kept looking until the beast was slain and its body destroyed and thrown into the blazing fire.[l] [12](The other beasts had been stripped of their authority, but were allowed to live for a period of time.)

7:13
m Mt 8:20*;
Rev 1:13*
n Mt 24:30; Rev 1:7
7:14
o Mt 28:18
p Ps 72:11; 102:22;
1Co 15:27;
Eph 1:22 q Da 2:44;
Heb 12:28;
Rev 11:15

[13]"In my vision at night I looked, and there before me was one like a son of man,[m] coming with the clouds of heaven.[n] He approached the Ancient of Days and was led into his presence. [14]He was given authority,[o] glory and sovereign power; all peoples, nations and men of every language worshiped him.[p] His dominion is an everlasting dominion that will not pass away, and his kingdom is one that will never be destroyed.[q]

---

events of chapter 5. He had this dream "in the first year of Belshazzar" (v. 1), probably 553 B.C. The four beasts that "came up out of the sea" (v. 3) are generally interpreted as synonymous with the four kingdoms (see v. 17) of chapter 2 (see "There and Then" for 2:24–49).

Verse 9 is an abrupt transition from the scene by the sea to a courtroom. While it's uncertain whether this takes place in heaven or on Earth, the imagery makes clear that the two main participants are divine and that the attendants are celestial rather than human. The first figure is called the "Ancient of Days." This is God, specifically in his role as judge. With the second figure comes the first reference in Scripture to the Messiah as the "son of man," a title Jesus later applied to himself. He

would be enthroned as ruler over the whole world, previously misruled by the four kingdoms opposing God's rule, and his kingdom would never be destroyed.

This vision is descriptive of the two realms of human evil and divine judgment. Beyond that, it narrates a conflict between the two, with a specific and certain conclusion. The "beast," presumably the boastful horn, was destroyed, while the "one like a son of man" was exalted and given an eternal kingdom. In a word, though human evil thrives in the present, God is in control and will have the final victory. The implicit message to God's people—then and now—is: "Remain faithful in spite of appearances."

The Interpretation of the Dream

15 "I, Daniel, was troubled in spirit, and the visions that passed through my mind disturbed me.ʳ 16I approached one of those standing there and asked him the true meaning of all this.

"So he told me and gave me the interpretationˢ of these things: 17'The four great beasts are four kingdoms that will rise from the earth. 18But the saints of the Most High will receive the kingdom and will possess it forever—yes, for ever and ever.'ᵗ

19 "Then I wanted to know the true meaning of the fourth beast, which was different from all the others and most terrifying, with its iron teeth and bronze claws—the beast that crushed and devoured its victims and trampled underfoot whatever was left. 20I also wanted to know about the ten horns on its head and about the other horn that came up, before which three of them fell—the horn that looked more imposing than the others and that had eyes and a mouth that spoke boastfully. 21As I watched, this horn was waging war against the saints and defeating them,ᵘ 22until the Ancient of Days came and pronounced judgment in favor of the saints of the Most High, and the time came when they possessed the kingdom.

23 "He gave me this explanation: 'The fourth beast is a fourth kingdom that will appear on earth. It will be different from all the other kingdoms and will devour the whole earth, trampling it down and crushing it.ᵛ 24The ten hornsʷ are ten kings who will come from this kingdom. After them another king will arise, different from the earlier ones; he will subdue three kings. 25He will speak against the Mostᵡ High and oppress his saints and try to change the set timesʸ and the laws. The saints will be handed over to him for a time, times and half a time.ᵃᶻ

26 "But the court will sit, and his power will be taken away and completely destroyed forever. 27Then the sovereignty, power and greatness of the kingdoms under the whole heaven will be handed over to the saints, the people of the Most High. His kingdom will be an everlastingᵃ kingdom, and all rulers will worshipᵇ and obey him.'

28 "This is the end of the matter. I, Daniel, was deeply troubledᶜ by my thoughts, and my face turned pale, but I kept the matter to myself."

Daniel's Vision of a Ram and a Goat

8 In the third year of King Belshazzar's reign, I, Daniel, had a vision, after the one that had already appeared to me. 2In my vision I saw myself in the citadel of Susaᵈ in the province of Elam;ᵉ in the vision I was beside the Ulai Canal. 3I looked up,ᶠ and there before me was a ram with two horns, standing beside the canal, and the horns were long. One of the horns was longer than the other but grew up later. 4I watched the ram as he charged toward the west and the north and the south. No animal could stand against him, and none could rescue from his power. He did as he pleasedᵍ and became great.

ᵃ 25 Or for a year, two years and half a year

Daniel 7:15–28

Daniel reacted to the vision with fear and confusion, signaling the overwhelming force of the revelation. He was looking into the abyss of evil and into the very throne room of God. Daniel's confusion drove him to an angel ("one of those standing there") to assist him with the interpretation. He learned that the "saints," the Messiah's followers, would receive the kingdom and its privileges (vv. 18,22,27).

Daniel's confusion and fear hadn't fully subsided, so he asked about the nature of the fourth beast. The significance of this beast is its climactic place in the future. It intensified the evil of its predecessors and produced eleven deadly horns, the eleventh being the most rebellious.

Daniel 7 depicts a great cosmic battle—a battle God will win. The New Testament rips away the curtain,

letting us see to the heart of this conflict (see Eph. 6:12) that will rage until Earth's final day. In Revelation 13 we encounter a beast emerging from the sea, an image drawn from Daniel (see Dan. 7:3). In Daniel 7:13–14, a "son of man" rides a cloud to rescue those oppressed by the beastly human kingdoms. In Revelation 1:7 (cf. Matt. 24:30), Jesus himself rides the cloud chariot into the final battle. He alone is the Warrior who will defeat the beast and his forces of evil at the end of time.

Daniel 8:1–14

The historical identification of the figures in this vision, which occurred two years after the one in chapter 7, is amazingly clear and specific. The ram symbolized the Medo-Persian empire (see v. 20). The longer horn (v. 3) was a reference to Persia's dominant position over Media. The goat represented Greece and the

⁵As I was thinking about this, suddenly a goat with a prominent horn between his eyes came from the west, crossing the whole earth without touching the ground. ⁶He came toward the two-horned ram I had seen standing beside the canal and charged at him in great rage. ⁷I saw him attack the ram furiously, striking the ram and shattering his two horns. The ram was powerless to stand against him; the goat knocked him to the ground and trampled on him, ʰ and none could rescue the ram from his power. ⁸The goat became very great, but at the height of his power his large horn was broken off, ⁱ and in its place four prominent horns grew up toward the four winds of heaven. ʲ

⁹Out of one of them came another horn, which started small but grew in power to the south and to the east and toward the Beautiful Land. ᵏ ¹⁰It grew until it reached ˡ the host of the heavens, and it threw some of the starry host down to the earth ᵐ and trampled ⁿ on them. ¹¹It set itself up to be as great as the Prince of the host; ᵒ it took away the daily sacrifice ᵖ from him, and the place of his sanctuary was brought low. �q ¹²Because of rebellion, the host ∟of the saints⌐ ᵃ and the daily sacrifice were given over to it. It prospered in everything it did, and truth was thrown to the ground.

¹³Then I heard a holy one ʳ speaking, and another holy one said to him, "How long will it take for the vision to be fulfilled ˢ—the vision concerning the daily sacrifice, the rebellion that causes desolation, and the surrender of the sanctuary and of the host that will be trampled ᵗ underfoot?"

¹⁴He said to me, "It will take 2,300 evenings and mornings; then the sanctuary will be reconsecrated." ᵘ

The Interpretation of the Vision

¹⁵While I, Daniel, was watching the vision ᵛ and trying to understand it, there before me stood one who looked like a man. ʷ ¹⁶And I heard a man's voice from the Ulai calling, "Gabriel, ˣ tell this man the meaning of the vision."

¹⁷As he came near the place where I was standing, I was terrified and fell prostrate. ʸ "Son of man," he said to me, "understand that the vision concerns the time of the end." ᶻ

ᵃ 12 Or rebellion, the armies

Cross references (margin)

8:7 ʰ Da 7:7

8:8 ⁱ 2Ch 26:16-21; Da 5:20 ʲ Da 7:2; Rev 7:1

8:9 ᵏ Da 11:16
8:10 ˡ Isa 14:13 ᵐ Rev 12:4 ⁿ Da 7:7
8:11 ᵒ Da 11:36-37 ᵖ Eze 46:13-14 q Da 11:31; 12:11

8:13 ʳ Da 4:23 ˢ Da 12:6 ᵗ Lk 21:24; Rev 11:2

8:14 ᵘ Da 12:11-12

8:15 ᵛ ver 1 ʷ Da 10:16-18

8:16 ˣ Da 9:21; Lk 1:19

8:17 ʸ Eze 1:28; Da 2:46; Rev 1:17 ᶻ Hab 2:3

"prominent horn" Alexander the Great—"the first king" (v. 21). Verse 8 referred to Alexander's sudden death in 323 B.C., followed by his empire's dissolution into four divisions (v. 22; cf. the "four heads" of 7:6).

"Another horn" (v. 9) emerged not from the ten horns belonging to the fourth kingdom (as in 7:7–8) but from one of the four horns belonging to the third kingdom of 7:6. This horn would be Antiochus IV, who during the last years of his reign would make a determined effort to obliterate the Jewish faith. Antiochus would extend his power over Israel, "the Beautiful Land," killing many faithful Jews. Then he would set himself up to be the equal of God ("the Prince of the host") and replace the daily sacrifices to the Lord with pagan sacrifices. Eventually the army of Judas Maccabeus would recapture Jerusalem and rededicate the temple to the Lord (v. 14)—the origin of the Feast of Hanukkah, still celebrated by Jews today.

📖 Verse 14 could refer to 2,300 full days. But as there were morning and evening sacrifices offered at the temple each day (9:21; Ex. 29:38–39), "2,300 evenings and mornings" quite possibly referred to the number of *sacrifices consecutively offered on 1,150 days*—the interval between the desecration of the altar by Antiochus and its reconsecration by Judas Maccabeus in December of 165 B.C. The number 2,300 was evidently given not so

much so that those who read Daniel's 6th-century (B.C.) predictions in the 2nd century would be able to compute when their suffering would stop as to assure them that God had events under control.

The symbolic numbers in Daniel, Revelation, and elsewhere in the Bible remind us that God is sovereign and has set a limit on how long the present evil world will oppress us. Attempts to set dates for God's future timetable result in disruption in the church and in our own lives and in disregard for present realities (Matt. 24:36,42). God calls us to live in the present, while awaiting the future with hope.

Daniel 8:15–27

🕮 While Daniel was struggling to understand the vision, Gabriel—a leading angel in God's heavenly army (cf. Luke 1:19,26)—appeared. God himself instructed Gabriel to explain the vision to Daniel, referred to here as "Son of man" (not to be confused with "one like a son of man" in 7:13). Verses 23–25 describe Antiochus IV and his rise to power by political manipulation. The fact that he would "consider himself superior" would be proved by his naming himself "Epiphanes" ("God manifest"). The final sentence of verse 25 would be fulfilled when Antiochus died in 164 B.C. through an accident or illness. God "destroyed" him.

[18]While he was speaking to me, I was in a deep sleep, with my face to the ground.[a] Then he touched me and raised me to my feet.[b]

[19]He said: "I am going to tell you what will happen later in the time of wrath, because the vision concerns the appointed time of the end.[a c] [20]The two-horned ram that you saw represents the kings of Media and Persia. [21]The shaggy goat is the king of Greece,[d] and the large horn between his eyes is the first king.[e] [22]The four horns that replaced the one that was broken off represent four kingdoms that will emerge from his nation but will not have the same power.

[23]"In the latter part of their reign, when rebels have become completely wicked, a stern-faced king, a master of intrigue, will arise. [24]He will become very strong, but not by his own power. He will cause astounding devastation and will succeed in whatever he does. He will destroy the mighty men and the holy people.[f] [25]He will cause deceit to prosper, and he will consider himself superior. When they feel secure, he will destroy many and take his stand against the Prince of princes.[g] Yet he will be destroyed, but not by human power.[h]

[26]"The vision of the evenings and mornings that has been given you is true,[i] but seal[j] up the vision, for it concerns the distant future."[k]

[27]I, Daniel, was exhausted and lay ill for several days. Then I got up and went about the king's business.[l] I was appalled[m] by the vision; it was beyond understanding.

Daniel's Prayer

9 In the first year of Darius[n] son of Xerxes[b] (a Mede by descent), who was made ruler over the Babylonian[c] kingdom— [2]in the first year of his reign, I, Daniel, understood from the Scriptures, according to the word of the LORD given to Jeremiah the prophet, that the desolation of Jerusalem would last seventy[o] years. [3]So I turned to the Lord God and pleaded with him in prayer and petition, in fasting, and in sackcloth and ashes.[p]

[4]I prayed to the LORD my God and confessed:

"O Lord, the great and awesome God,[q] who keeps his covenant of love[r] with all who love him and obey his commands, [5]we have sinned and done wrong.[s] We have been wicked and have rebelled; we have turned away[t] from your commands and laws.[u] [6]We have not listened to your servants the prophets,[v] who spoke in your name to our kings, our princes and our fathers, and to all the people of the land.

[7]"Lord, you are righteous, but this day we are covered with shame[w]—the men of Judah and people of Jerusalem and all Israel, both near and far, in all the countries where you have scattered[x] us because of our unfaithfulness to you.[y] [8]O LORD, we and our kings, our princes and our fathers are covered with shame

---

8:18
a Da 10:9
b Eze 2:2;
Da 10:16-18
8:19
c Hab 2:3
8:21
d Da 10:20
e Da 11:3
8:24
f Da 7:25; 11:36
8:25
g Da 11:36
h Da 2:34; 11:21
8:26
i Da 10:1
j Rev 22:10
k Da 10:14
8:27
l Da 2:48
m Da 7:28
9:1
n Da 5:31
9:2
o 2Ch 36:21;
Jer 29:10; Zec 7:5
9:3
p Ne 1:4; Jer 29:12
9:4
q Dt 7:21 r Dt 7:9
9:5
s Ps 106:6 t Isa 53:6
u ver 11; La 1:20
9:6
v 2Ch 36:16;
Jer 44:5
9:7
w Ps 44:15
x Dt 4:27; Am 9:9
y Jer 3:25

---

a 19 Or because the end will be at the appointed time   b 1 Hebrew Ahasuerus   c 1 Or Chaldean

---

Antiochus took a stand against the "Prince of princes" (v. 25)—God. He served as a type of the even more ruthless beast of the last days (the antichrist), who is also referred to in 7:8 as the little horn. With his godlike airs, Antiochus represented all who seek to replace God on the throne of the universe. Satan was the first to attempt such rebellion against the Creator. As Christians we know that an antichrist is still coming who will activate the events leading to God's final, redemptive intervention in human affairs (cf. 2 Thess. 1:1–12; Rev. 13:1–10).

Daniel 9:1–19

"The first year of Darius" (see "There and Then" for 6:1–28) was 539 B.C., the year Cyrus decreed that some Jews could return home. Daniel appears to have prayed in anticipation of this decree. His witness to the fall of Babylon may have helped him read Jeremiah's

prophecies—which Daniel viewed as part of "the Scriptures"—with new eyes. Daniel surely had passages like Jeremiah 25:11–12 and 29:10 in mind. The round number of 70 years (cf. Ps. 90:10; Isa. 23:15) represented the period from 605 B.C., with the first deportation of exiles (see "There and Then" for Dan. 1:1–21), to the fulfillment of Jeremiah's predictions, with the return of the first exiles in 538/537 B.C.

Daniel understood Israel's situation to be the result of the breaking of God's law and the consequent curses spelled out in his covenant (see, e.g., Deut. 28:64–68). And he realized that the road to recovery was through repentance. There is no evidence that Daniel had personally participated in the sins that had led to this state of affairs, but he identified with the people by including himself in his confession. (See the notes for Ezra 9 and Neh. 9, which contain similar prayers.)

9:9
z Ps 130:4
a Ne 9:17; Jer 14:7
9:10
b 2Ki 17:13-15;
18:12

9:11
c Isa 1:4-6;
Jer 8:5-10
9:12
d Isa 44:26; Zec 1:6
e Jer 44:2-6;
Eze 5:9

9:13
f Isa 9:13; Jer 2:30
9:14
g Jer 44:27
h Ne 9:33
9:15
i Jer 32:21
j Ne 9:10

9:16
k Ps 31:1
l Jer 32:32
m Zec 8:3
n Eze 5:14

9:17
o Nu 6:24-26;
Ps 80:19
9:18
p Ps 80:14
q Isa 37:17;
Jer 7:10-12; 25:29
9:19
r Ps 44:23

9:20
s ver 3; Ps 145:18;
Isa 58:9
9:21
t Da 8:16; Lk 1:19
u Ex 29:39

9:23
v Da 10:19; Lk 1:28
w Da 10:11-12;
Mt 24:15
9:24
x Isa 53:10
y Isa 56:1

because we have sinned against you. [9]The Lord our God is merciful and forgiving, z even though we have rebelled against him; a [10]we have not obeyed the LORD our God or kept the laws he gave us through his servants the prophets. b [11]All Israel has transgressed your law and turned away, refusing to obey you.

"Therefore the curses and sworn judgments written in the Law of Moses, the servant of God, have been poured out on us, because we have sinned c against you. [12]You have fulfilled d the words spoken against us and against our rulers by bringing upon us great disaster. Under the whole heaven nothing has ever been done like what has been done to Jerusalem. e [13]Just as it is written in the Law of Moses, all this disaster has come upon us, yet we have not sought the favor of the LORD our God by turning from our sins and giving attention to your truth. f [14]The LORD did not hesitate to bring the disaster g upon us, for the LORD our God is righteous in everything he does; yet we have not obeyed him. h

[15]"Now, O Lord our God, who brought your people out of Egypt with a mighty hand i and who made for yourself a name j that endures to this day, we have sinned, we have done wrong. [16]O Lord, in keeping with all your righteous acts, k turn away your anger and your wrath from Jerusalem, l your city, your holy hill. m Our sins and the iniquities of our fathers have made Jerusalem and your people an object of scorn n to all those around us.

[17]"Now, our God, hear the prayers and petitions of your servant. For your sake, O Lord, look with favor o on your desolate sanctuary. [18]Give ear, O God, and hear; open your eyes and see p the desolation of the city that bears your Name. q We do not make requests of you because we are righteous, but because of your great mercy. [19]O Lord, listen! O Lord, forgive! r O Lord, hear and act! For your sake, O my God, do not delay, because your city and your people bear your Name."

The Seventy "Sevens"

[20]While I was speaking and praying, confessing my sin and the sin of my people Israel and making my request to the LORD my God for his holy hill s— [21]while I was still in prayer, Gabriel, t the man I had seen in the earlier vision, came to me in swift flight about the time of the evening sacrifice. u [22]He instructed me and said to me, "Daniel, I have now come to give you insight and understanding. [23]As soon as you began to pray, an answer was given, which I have come to tell you, for you are highly esteemed. v Therefore, consider the message and understand the vision: w

[24]"Seventy 'sevens' a are decreed for your people and your holy city to finish b transgression, to put an end to sin, to atone x for wickedness, to bring in everlasting righteousness, y to seal up vision and prophecy and to anoint the most holy. c

---

a 24 Or 'weeks'; also in verses 25 and 26   b 24 Or restrain   c 24 Or Most Holy Place; or most holy One

---

Repentance stands at the heart of Christian belief. It's not that our faith results from repentance, but repentance flows from faith in a forgiving God. God doesn't just "forgive and forget" without confession. Yes, he initiates the movement toward repentance in our hearts, but our relationship with God, once broken, is restored through repentance: "The time has come . . . The kingdom of God is near. Repent and believe the good news!" (Mark 1:15).

Daniel 9:20–27

Daniel's prayer for forgiveness and restoration was motivated by his reading of Jeremiah's prophecy that the exile would last 70 years (9:2). The angel Gabriel seemed to suggest that the end of the exile began a process that would last for 70 "sevens," or weeks of years—usually understood as 490 years—ending with the coming of the Messiah, the "Anointed One."

Some interpreters believe that the six actions in

verse 24 were accomplished through Jesus' earthly ministry, which took place about 490 years after the decree authorizing the rebuilding of Jerusalem (see v. 25). Others expect that the last three actions won't be completely fulfilled until the seventieth seven-year period, just prior to Christ's return (see vv. 26–27).

Daniel set a good example for us as he turned to "the Scriptures" (9:2) to know God's will. But unlike Daniel, we have the complete Bible to reveal God to us. We see the pattern of his progressive revelation of the redemption story, with Jesus as its centerpiece (see Heb. 1:1–2). That is why we insist on reading the Old Testament in light of the New. It's essential, though, that we first consider Old Testament teaching on its own grounds—asking what it meant to the original audience. Otherwise, we risk the danger of reading into it what isn't there or of missing important points.

25 "Know and understand this: From the issuing of the decree[a] to restore and re-build[z] Jerusalem until the Anointed One,[b][a] the ruler, comes, there will be seven 'sevens,' and sixty-two 'sevens.' It will be rebuilt with streets and a trench, but in times of trouble. 26After the sixty-two 'sevens,' the Anointed One will be cut off[b] and will have nothing.[c] The people of the ruler who will come will destroy the city and the sanctuary. The end will come like a flood:[c] War will continue until the end, and desolations have been decreed. 27He will confirm a covenant with many for one 'seven.'[d] In the middle of the 'seven'[d] he will put an end to sacrifice and offering. And on a wing ˌof the templeˌ he will set up an abomination that causes desolation, until the end that is decreed[d] is poured out on him.[e]"[f]

Daniel's Vision of a Man

10 In the third year of Cyrus[e] king of Persia, a revelation was given to Daniel (who was called Belteshazzar).[f] Its message was true[g] and it concerned a great war.[g] The understanding of the message came to him in a vision.

2At that time I, Daniel, mourned[h] for three weeks. 3I ate no choice food; no meat or wine touched my lips; and I used no lotions at all until the three weeks were over.

4On the twenty-fourth day of the first month, as I was standing on the bank of the great river, the Tigris,[i] 5I looked up and there before me was a man dressed in linen,[j] with a belt of the finest gold[k] around his waist. 6His body was like chrysolite, his face like lightning,[l] his eyes like flaming torches,[m] his arms and legs like the gleam of burnished bronze,[n] and his voice like the sound of a multitude.

7I, Daniel, was the only one who saw the vision; the men with me did not see it,[o] but such terror overwhelmed them that they fled and hid themselves. 8So I was left alone,[p] gazing at this great vision; I had no strength left,[q] my face turned deathly pale and I was helpless.[r] 9Then I heard him speaking, and as I listened to him, I fell into a deep sleep, my face to the ground.[s]

10A hand touched me[t] and set me trembling on my hands and knees.[u] 11He said, "Daniel, you who are highly esteemed,[v] consider carefully the words I am about to speak to you, and stand up,[w] for I have now been sent to you." And when he said this to me, I stood up trembling.

12Then he continued, "Do not be afraid, Daniel. Since the first day that you set your mind to gain understanding and to humble[x] yourself before your God, your words were heard, and I have come in response to them.[y] 13But the prince of the Persian kingdom resisted me twenty-one days. Then Michael,[z] one of the chief princes, came to help me, because I was detained there with the king of Persia. 14Now I have come to explain[a] to you what will happen to your people in the future, for the vision concerns a time yet to come.[b]"

15While he was saying this to me, I bowed with my face toward the ground and

---

9:25
z Ezr 4:24 a Jn 4:25

9:26
b Isa 53:8 c Na 1:8

9:27
d Isa 10:22

10:1
e Da 1:21 f Da 1:7
g Da 8:26

10:2
h Ezr 9:4

10:4
i Ge 2:14
10:5
j Eze 9:2; Rev 15:6
k Jer 10:9
10:6
l Mt 17:2
m Rev 19:12
n Rev 1:15
10:7
o 2Ki 6:17-20;
Ac 9:7
10:8
p Ge 32:24
q Da 8:27
r Hab 3:16
10:9
s Da 8:18
10:10
t Jer 1:9 u Rev 1:17
10:11
v Da 9:23 w Eze 2:1

10:12
x Da 9:3 y Da 9:20

10:13
z ver 21; Da 12:1;
Jude 1:9

10:14
a Da 9:22
b Da 2:28; 8:26;
Hab 2:3

---

[a] 25 Or *word*   [b] 25 Or *an anointed one; also in verse 26*   [c] 26 Or *off and will have no one; or off, but not for himself*   [d] 27 Or *'week'*   [e] 27 Or *it*   [f] 27 Or *And one who causes desolation will come upon the pinnacle of the abominable ˌtempleˌ, until the end that is decreed is poured out on the desolated ˌcityˌ*   [g] 1 Or *true and burdensome*

Daniel 10:1—11:1

During the year 537/536 B.C. Daniel's troubled state of mind led him to intense prayer (vv. 2–3), in response to which God sent a messenger with some striking revelations (v. 12). This angelic messenger, though unnamed, was probably Gabriel. He had been battling "the prince of the Persian kingdom," evidently a demon who exerted influence on the Persian state (cf. "the prince of Greece" in v. 20). The evil spirit was finally overcome with the help of Michael, the "chief prince" or archangel (cf. v. 21; 12:1; Jude 9; Rev. 12:7). After describing the conflict that led to the delayed answer to Daniel's prayer, the heavenly messenger announced in verse 14 the substance of his message,

which would be delivered in chapters 11–12.

The visions at the end of the book of Daniel pertain to a coming "great war" (10:1). Jesus has won the cosmic conflict about which we read throughout the Old Testament, the battle begun in Genesis 3:15 and provocatively described here in Daniel 10. He has "disarmed the powers and authorities" (Col. 2:15). But the victory is an already/not yet affair: It has been secured on the cross but awaits completion. The New Testament continues to use military language to communicate two important truths: (1) We are still in the midst of a tremendous battle against the forces of evil, and (2) the final victory is in sight.

10:15
c Eze 24:27; Lk 1:20
10:16
d Isa 6:7; Jer 1:9;
Da 8:15-18
e Isa 21:3
10:17
f Da 4:19
10:18
g ver 16
10:19
h Jdg 6:23; Isa 35:4
i Jos 1:9 j Isa 6:1-8

was speechless. [c] 16Then one who looked like a man[a] touched my lips, and I opened my mouth and began to speak. [d] I said to the one standing before me, "I am overcome with anguish[e] because of the vision, my lord, and I am helpless. 17How can I, your servant, talk with you, my lord? My strength is gone and I can hardly breathe."[f]

18Again the one who looked like a man touched[g] me and gave me strength. 19"Do not be afraid, O man highly esteemed," he said. "Peace![h] Be strong now; be strong."[i]

When he spoke to me, I was strengthened and said, "Speak, my lord, since you have given me strength."[j]

10:20
k Da 8:21; 11:2
10:21
l Da 11:2 m ver 13;
Jude 1:9
11:1
n Da 5:31

20So he said, "Do you know why I have come to you? Soon I will return to fight against the prince of Persia, and when I go, the prince of Greece[k] will come; 21but first I will tell you what is written in the Book of Truth.[l] (No one supports me against them except Michael,[m] your prince. 1And in the first year of Darius[n]

11 the Mede, I took my stand to support and protect him.)

11:2
o Da 10:21
p Da 10:20

The Kings of the South and the North

2"Now then, I tell you the truth:[o] Three more kings will appear in Persia, and then a fourth, who will be far richer than all the others. When he has gained power by his wealth, he will stir up everyone against the kingdom of Greece.[p] 3Then a mighty

11:3
q Da 8:4,21

king will appear, who will rule with great power and do as he pleases.[q] 4After he has appeared, his empire will be broken up and parceled out toward the four

11:4
r Da 7:2; 8:22

winds of heaven.[r] It will not go to his descendants, nor will it have the power he exercised, because his empire will be uprooted and given to others.

5"The king of the South will become strong, but one of his commanders will become even stronger than he and will rule his own kingdom with great power. 6After some years, they will become allies. The daughter of the king of the South will go to the king of the North to make an alliance, but she will not retain her power, and he and his power[b] will not last. In those days she will be handed over, together with her royal escort and her father[c] and the one who supported her.

11:7
s ver 6
11:8
t Isa 37:19; 46:1-2
u Jer 43:12

7"One from her family line will arise to take her place. He will attack the forces of the king of the North[s] and enter his fortress; he will fight against them and be victorious. 8He will also seize their gods,[t] their metal images and their valuable articles of silver and gold and carry them off to Egypt.[u] For some years he will leave the king of the North alone. 9Then the king of the North will invade the realm of the king of the South but will retreat to his own country. 10His sons will prepare for

11:10
v Isa 8:8; Jer 46:8;
Da 9:26

war and assemble a great army, which will sweep on like an irresistible flood[v] and carry the battle as far as his fortress.

11"Then the king of the South will march out in a rage and fight against the king

---

a 16 Most manuscripts of the Masoretic Text; one manuscript of the Masoretic Text, Dead Sea Scrolls and Septuagint *Then something that looked like a man's hand*   b 6 Or *offspring*   c 6 Or *child* (see Vulgate and Syriac)

In this chapter Daniel also provided an excellent example for the fight: He fasted, prayed, sought to gain spiritual understanding, allowed God to cleanse him, and received God's peace and strength. How do these activities inform your spiritual battles? How does this passage complement Paul's message to believers in Ephesians 6:10–20?

Daniel 11:2–35

The prophecies of this section began with the kings of Persia, who were ruling their great empire at the time of Daniel's vision. The fourth Persian king (v. 2) would be Xerxes I, who unsuccessfully attempted to conquer Greece in 480 B.C. The "mighty king" of verses 3–4 would be Alexander the Great, whose Greek empire was eventually divided into four parts by his four gener-

als (cf. 7:6; 8:21–22). Two of those parts would be under the rule of the Ptolemies of Egypt ("the kings of the South") and the Seleucids of Syria ("the kings of the North"), respectively. Daniel predicted their conflicts, alliances, and intrigues with the accuracy of a historian.

In verse 21 Daniel's prophecies returned to Antiochus IV Epiphanes (see "There and Then" for 8:1–14), a most contemptible "king of the North." In 169 B.C. Antiochus would take action "against the holy covenant" (v. 28)—plundering the temple in Jerusalem, setting up a garrison there, and massacring many Jews (cf. v. 33). Antiochus's ultimate indignity would be "the abomination that causes desolation" (v. 31): He would profane the temple by setting up an altar to the god Zeus, to which he would sacrifice an "unclean" animal, a pig.

of the North, who will raise a large army, but it will be defeated. [w] 12When the army is carried off, the king of the South will be filled with pride and will slaughter many thousands, yet he will not remain triumphant. 13For the king of the North will muster another army, larger than the first; and after several years, he will advance with a huge army fully equipped.

14"In those times many will rise against the king of the South. The violent men among your own people will rebel in fulfillment of the vision, but without success. 15Then the king of the North will come and build up siege ramps [x] and will capture a fortified city. The forces of the South will be powerless to resist; even their best troops will not have the strength to stand. 16The invader will do as he pleases; [y] no one will be able to stand against him. [z] He will establish himself in the Beautiful Land and will have the power to destroy it. [a] 17He will determine to come with the might of his entire kingdom and will make an alliance with the king of the South. And he will give him a daughter in marriage in order to overthrow the kingdom, but his plans [a] will not succeed [b] or help him. 18Then he will turn his attention to the coastlands [c] and will take many of them, but a commander will put an end to his insolence and will turn his insolence back upon him. [d] 19After this, he will turn back toward the fortresses of his own country but will stumble and fall, [e] to be seen no more. [f]

20"His successor will send out a tax collector to maintain the royal splendor. [g] In a few years, however, he will be destroyed, yet not in anger or in battle.

21"He will be succeeded by a contemptible [h] person who has not been given the honor of royalty. [i] He will invade the kingdom when its people feel secure, and he will seize it through intrigue. 22Then an overwhelming army will be swept away before him; both it and a prince of the covenant will be destroyed. [j] 23After coming to an agreement with him, he will act deceitfully, [k] and with only a few people he will rise to power. 24When the richest provinces feel secure, he will invade them and will achieve what neither his fathers nor his forefathers did. He will distribute plunder, loot and wealth among his followers. [l] He will plot the overthrow of fortresses—but only for a time.

25"With a large army he will stir up his strength and courage against the king of the South. The king of the South will wage war with a large and very powerful army, but he will not be able to stand because of the plots devised against him. 26Those who eat from the king's provisions will try to destroy him; his army will be swept away, and many will fall in battle. 27The two kings, with their hearts bent on evil, [m] will sit at the same table and lie [n] to each other, but to no avail, because an end will still come at the appointed time. [o] 28The king of the North will return to his own country with great wealth, but his heart will be set against the holy covenant. He will take action against it and then return to his own country.

29"At the appointed time he will invade the South again, but this time the outcome will be different from what it was before. 30Ships of the western coastlands [b] [p] will oppose him, and he will lose heart. Then he will turn back and vent his fury against the holy covenant. He will return and show favor to those who forsake the holy covenant.

31"His armed forces will rise up to desecrate the temple fortress and will abolish the daily sacrifice. Then they will set up the abomination that causes desolation. [q] 32With flattery he will corrupt those who have violated the covenant, but the people who know their God will firmly resist [r] him.

a 17 Or *but she*   b 30 Hebrew *of Kittim*

11:11
w Da 8:7-8

11:15
x Eze 4:2

11:16
y Da 8:4 z Jos 1:5;
Da 8:7 a Da 8:9

11:17
b Ps 20:4
11:18
c Isa 66:19;
Jer 25:22
d Hos 12:14
11:19
e Ps 27:2
f Ps 37:36;
Eze 26:21
11:20
g Isa 60:17
11:21
h Da 4:17 i Da 8:25
11:22
j Da 8:10-11

11:23
k Da 8:25

11:24
l Ne 9:25

11:27
m Ps 64:6
n Ps 12:2; Jer 9:5
o Hab 2:3

11:30
p Ge 10:4

11:31
q Da 8:11-13; 9:27;
Mt 24:15*;
Mk 13:14*
11:32
r Mic 5:7-9

Perhaps in no other chapter is God's sovereignty displayed so profoundly as in Daniel 11, replete with predictive detail. God remains in control in spite of any circumstance. In 6th-century (B.C.) Babylon, it looked to the godly as though Babylon and then Persia were in control. But these nations weren't. In the 2nd century (B.C.) Holy Land it appeared that Antiochus Epiphanes was in charge—but he wasn't. In the 1st century (A.D.) of Jesus and Paul, it seemed that Rome held the reins—but it didn't. To Christians living 2,000 years after Jesus, it may look as though Satan is in control—but he isn't. God is, and because of that we can have boundless joy and optimism even in our struggles.

11:33
s Mal 2:7 t Mt 24:9;
Jn 16:2; Heb 11:32-
38
11:34
u Mt 7:15; Ro 16:18
11:35
v Ps 78:38;
Da 12:10; Zec 13:9;
Jn 15:2

11:36
w Rev 13:5-6
x Dt 10:17;
Isa 14:13-14;
Da 7:25; 8:11-12,
25; 2Th 2:4
y Isa 10:25; 26:20

11:40
z Isa 21:1 a Isa 5:28
b Eze 38:4

11:41
c Isa 11:14
d Jer 48:47

11:43
e Eze 30:4
f 2Ch 12:3; Na 3:9

12:1
g Da 10:13
h Da 9:12;
Mt 24:21;
Mk 13:19;
Rev 16:18
i Ex 32:32; Ps 56:8
j Jer 30:7
12:2
k Isa 26:19;
Mt 25:46;
Jn 5:28-29
12:3
l Da 11:33
m Mt 13:43; Jn 5:35
n 1Co 15:42

33 "Those who are wise will instruct[s] many, though for a time they will fall by the sword or be burned or captured or plundered.[t] 34When they fall, they will receive a little help, and many who are not sincere[u] will join them. 35Some of the wise will stumble, so that they may be refined,[v] purified and made spotless until the time of the end, for it will still come at the appointed time.

The King Who Exalts Himself

36 "The king will do as he pleases. He will exalt and magnify himself above every god and will say unheard-of things[w] against the God of gods.[x] He will be successful until the time of wrath[y] is completed, for what has been determined must take place. 37He will show no regard for the gods of his fathers or for the one desired by women, nor will he regard any god, but will exalt himself above them all. 38Instead of them, he will honor a god of fortresses; a god unknown to his fathers he will honor with gold and silver, with precious stones and costly gifts. 39He will attack the mightiest fortresses with the help of a foreign god and will greatly honor those who acknowledge him. He will make them rulers over many people and will distribute the land at a price.[a]

40 "At the time of the end the king of the South[z] will engage him in battle, and the king of the North will storm[a] out against him with chariots and cavalry and a great fleet of ships. He will invade many countries and sweep through them like a flood.[b] 41He will also invade the Beautiful Land. Many countries will fall, but Edom,[c] Moab[d] and the leaders of Ammon will be delivered from his hand. 42He will extend his power over many countries; Egypt will not escape. 43He will gain control of the treasures of gold and silver and all the riches of Egypt,[e] with the Libyans[f] and Nubians in submission. 44But reports from the east and the north will alarm him, and he will set out in a great rage to destroy and annihilate many. 45He will pitch his royal tents between the seas at[b] the beautiful holy mountain. Yet he will come to his end, and no one will help him.

The End Times

12 "At that time Michael,[g] the great prince who protects your people, will arise. There will be a time of distress[h] such as has not happened from the beginning of nations until then. But at that time your people—everyone whose name is found written in the book[i]—will be delivered.[j] 2Multitudes who sleep in the dust of the earth will awake: some to everlasting life, others to shame and everlasting contempt.[k] 3Those who are wise[c][l] will shine[m] like the brightness of the heavens, and those who lead many to righteousness, like the stars for ever and ever.[n]

a 39 Or land for a reward   b 45 Or the sea and   c 3 Or who impart wisdom

---

Daniel 11:36–45

In this passage Daniel evidently shifted his attention from Antiochus Epiphanes to the antichrist (see notes for 8:15–27). His language seems larger than life and doesn't fit what's known from history about Antiochus. Plus, this prophecy referred to the "time of the end" (v. 40; cf. v. 35). At the conclusion of the conflict between the antichrist and his political enemies, he will meet his end at the "beautiful holy mountain" (v. 45), the temple mount of Jerusalem—perhaps in connection with the battle of Armageddon (Rev. 16:13–16).

What does the Bible teach about the interplay between divine sovereignty and human responsibility? It shows that God is in control but also stresses our need to make responsible decisions. God saves us, but we play a vital part in the process (see Phil. 2:12). He controls history, but our actions can and do affect its direction in large and small ways. Daniel may have emphasized the former reality because God's people at the time were relatively helpless. The truth of God's sovereignty was for them much needed good news.

We all experience struggles. They may be political, cultural, emotional, psychological, or relational in nature. But God never gives up control. In spite of appearances, he will bring victory over evil and honor to those who remain faithful to him. The book of Daniel is a call to God's people to remain steadfast in their love and obedience to him—no matter what.

Daniel 12:1–13

This final chapter begins with the clearest reference to a resurrection of both the righteous and the wicked in the entire Old Testament. The book of Daniel in general, and 12:2–3 in particular, make it clear that the wicked will ultimately get what they deserve—destruction and shame—while the godly will receive their portion—honor and life.

God Is in Control

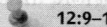

12:9–10

In spite of present appearances, God is in control. This is the core message of Daniel. How appropriate for Daniel's original hearers/readers. Helpless exiles in Babylon, they must have assumed that the world's great powers—the Babylonians, Medes, and Persians—were in control. But by recounting his experiences as a captive Israelite who had gained power in Babylon, Daniel assured his fellow detainees that God, not a human king, was ultimately in control.

When we look at our own society and see overwhelming evidences of what some call cultural decay or the loss of a moral center, it's tempting to question who is really is charge. Maybe we are sophisticated enough to know intellectually that human kingdoms aren't. The failure of Maoist China, the breakup of the Soviet Union, and the steep decline in the fortunes of the United States all impress upon us daily that nations and states rise and fall. Still, we tend to see behind all this misfortune powers that are anything but godlike—impersonal forces of fate; theories of deterministic science; and Satan, the master of evil.

Since God's control is the universal message of Daniel, the one that bridges 6th century B.C. and 21st century A.D. contexts, it's worth our while to see how Daniel went about convincing suffering readers of this hope-full truth. Daniel used a two pronged approach, telling six gripping stories of God's providence and relating five visions that together blast our senses with impressions of God's limitless power. Why this combination of literal, historical stories and mystical visions?

Recently I sat alongside Long Lake in Mercer, Wisconsin, observing a loon feeding in the bay. At least I assume the loon was feeding. The bird would bob and float on top of the water for some seconds, then suddenly dive, stay under water for two or three minutes, and then resurface, sometimes hundreds of feet from the diving point. My observation of the loon was of a series of lake-top appearances. But to fully comprehend their meaning, I had to infer what the bird was doing during the intervals between those appearances. Both observation and assumption were required.

> In order to fully understand, we need to know what's happening beneath the surface.

Daniel was doing something similar. The historical stories of how God cared for him as he navigated the tricky waters of Babylonian court politics were necessary to demonstrate that God really does provide for his own.

Yet such stories have limitations. God's providence doesn't always show itself in "success" stories. Sometimes, as the book of Job attests, his children suffer terribly. "Success" stories are necessary to give us hope, but alone they tend to concretize abstract and transitory elements of the stories. As in, Daniel succeeded because he was a vegetarian; if we all become vegetarians, we will succeed too. Or even the more plausible, Daniel succeeded because he prayed in an upper room in full view of the people of Babylon. If we all pray like that we will succeed too. Not really. These stories aren't irrelevant. But they are like the lake-top appearances of the loon. In order to fully understand, we need to know what's happening beneath the surface.

Enter the apocalyptic visions. The last six chapters of Daniel attempt to fill us in on what was happening "underwater." Such stories tell us the rest of the story. They describe the unseen things of God in language and images designed to move us beyond the natural realm to see the work of God.

12:4
o Isa 8:16
p ver 9,13;
Rev 22:10

4But you, Daniel, close up and seal o the words of the scroll until the time of the end. p Many will go here and there to increase knowledge."

12:5
q Da 10:4
12:6
r Eze 9:2 s Da 8:13

5Then I, Daniel, looked, and there before me stood two others, one on this bank of the river and one on the opposite bank. q 6One of them said to the man clothed in linen, r who was above the waters of the river, "How long will it be before these astonishing things are fulfilled?" s

12:7
t Rev 10:5-6
u Da 7:25 v Da 8:24
w Lk 21:24;
Rev 10:7

7The man clothed in linen, who was above the waters of the river, lifted his right hand and his left hand toward heaven, and I heard him swear by him who lives forever, t saying, "It will be for a time, times and half a time. a u When the power of the holy people v has been finally broken, all these things will be completed. w"

8I heard, but I did not understand. So I asked, "My lord, what will the outcome of all this be?"

12:9
x ver 4
12:10
y Da 11:35
z Isa 32:7;
Rev 22:11
a Hos 14:9
12:11
b Da 8:11; 9:27;
Mt 24:15*;
Mk 13:14*
12:12
c Isa 30:18
d Da 8:14
12:13
e Isa 57:2 f Ps 16:5;
Rev 14:13

9He replied, "Go your way, Daniel, because the words are closed up and sealed until the time of the end. x 10Many will be purified, made spotless and refined, y but the wicked will continue to be wicked. z None of the wicked will understand, but those who are wise will understand. a

11"From the time that the daily sacrifice is abolished and the abomination that causes desolation b is set up, there will be 1,290 days. 12Blessed is the one who waits c for and reaches the end of the 1,335 days. d

13"As for you, go your way till the end. You will rest, e and then at the end of the days you will rise to receive your allotted inheritance. f"

a 7 Or *a year, two years and half a year*

In verses 5–13, we return to the scene of 10:4–21—at the bank of the Tigris River, where Daniel overheard a conversation between celestial beings. What is the relationship of the "time, times and half a time" (v. 7; cf. NIV text note and 7:25), the "1,290 days" and "1,365 days" (vv. 11–12), and the "2,300 evenings and mornings" (8:14)? Apparently the answer is that God alone knows. Twice Daniel was told, "Go your way" (vv. 9,13). God has determined an end, but Daniel wasn't supposed to figure it all out. As the angel told Daniel, our eternal rest and reward are coming, but for now we too are to "go [our] way." God gave Daniel (and desires to give all his followers) the confidence to persist in the light of continuing persecution and trouble.

Both Daniel and Revelation end by leaving God's people with a future, end-times hope. For us this hope isn't based on wishful thinking but on faith (see Heb. 11:1) in the realities of Jesus' death and resurrection (see 1 Cor. 15). Our faith in these past events gives us certain hope for the future, which fills us with confidence in a troubled present. Because we know something better is coming, we can enjoy today. God is in control!

INTRODUCTION TO

Hosea

AUTHOR

This book identifies its contents as "the word of the LORD that came to Hosea son of Beeri" (1:1). Hosea was a prophet to the northern kingdom of Israel between 753 and 715 B.C., the period during which the capital city of Samaria fell to the Assyrians (722 B.C.). Whether Hosea himself wrote this book or someone else recorded his words is uncertain.

DATE WRITTEN

Hosea was probably written about 715 B.C.

ORIGINAL READERS

Hosea initially delivered his message of doom orally to the northern kingdom of Israel. After the fall of Samaria, his words were transcribed to scrolls as a record of prophecy fulfilled and as a warning of judgment, a call to repentance, and a promise of restoration.

TIMELINE

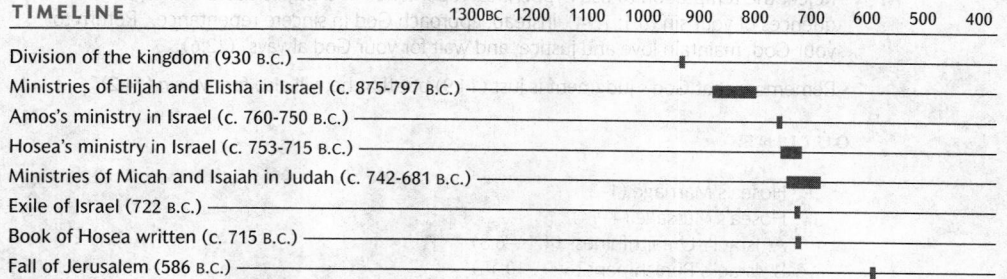

	1300BC	1200	1100	1000	900	800	700	600	500	400
Division of the kingdom (930 B.C.)										
Ministries of Elijah and Elisha in Israel (c. 875-797 B.C.)										
Amos's ministry in Israel (c. 760-750 B.C.)										
Hosea's ministry in Israel (c. 753-715 B.C.)										
Ministries of Micah and Isaiah in Judah (c. 742-681 B.C.)										
Exile of Israel (722 B.C.)										
Book of Hosea written (c. 715 B.C.)										
Fall of Jerusalem (586 B.C.)										

THEMES

Hosea describes the prophet Hosea's marriage, mandated by God, to an adulterous woman. His life portrayed God's love for his people in spite of their unfaithfulness to him. The book recounts the sin of the northern kingdom of Israel, Israel's defeat by Assyria as judgment for that sin, and God's future restoration of his people. Hosea includes the following themes:

1. *God's faithfulness, mercy, and unfailing love.* Hosea's love for his adulterous wife represents God's love for the Israelites (1:2). Their unfaithfulness, or spiritual adultery (4:13–14; 5:4; 9:1), is contrasted with God's love (2:19; 6:6; 10:12; 12:6) and faithfulness to his covenant (2:23; 14:1–9). God's covenantal relationship with his people is likened to the intimacy experienced in marriage (2:2–5; 3:3; 4:10–19; 5:3–7; 6:10; 8:9; 9:1), reinforcing the theme of God's passionate love for his people.

2. *Judgment for sin.* At the root of Israel's idolatry was her failure to acknowledge God (2:8,13,20; 4:1,6; 5:4; 6:3,6; 13:4). The people's unfaithfulness would result in the punishment of exile (7:16; 8:14; 9:3,6,17; 11:5).

3. *Repentance and restoration.* God wouldn't leave his people under judgment and in exile forever. He could heal Israel of the wounds caused by her disobedience and reestablish her people in the land (14:1–9). the book of Hosea demonstrates the recurring theme that repentance brings restoration (1:10–11; 2:14–23; 3:5; 11:10–11; 14:4–7).

FAITH IN ACTION

The pages of Hosea contain life lessons and role models of faith—people who challenge believers to put their faith in action.

Role Models

- HOSEA (3:1–2) obeyed God and bought back his adulterous wife as an example of God's love for his wayward people. In submission to God, the prophet endured a difficult, emotionally painful life. What is God asking you to do for him? Does the assignment seem beyond you? How can Hosea encourage you?

- THE WISE PERSON (14:1–9) accepts God's call to return to him and receive his forgiveness. Have you wandered from God? Return to him today, seek his forgiveness, and receive his love and blessing.

Challenges

- God sometimes calls us to do difficult things (1:2–3). Determine to obey him, even when you don't understand his purpose.

- Resolve not be unfaithful to God by going after other "lovers" (2:5), like secular, ungodly principles and philosophies (2:5–7). Guard especially against the lure of materialism (2:5).

- Acknowledge that God is the One who has given you your wealth and blessings (2:8).

- Guard against hypocrisy (4:14), aware that God sees everything.

- Reject the temptation to use hypocritical repentance as a way to avoid the negative consequences of your sin (6:1; 7:14). Instead, approach God in sincere repentance. "Return to your God; maintain love and justice, and wait for your God always" (12:6).

- Remember that God's judgment is just (14:9) but that he will also forgive sin (14:2).

OUTLINE

 I. Hosea's Marriage (1–3)
 II. Hosea's Message (4–14)
   A. Israel's Unfaithfulness (4:1—6:3)
   B. Israel's Punishment (6:4—10:15)
   C. God Is Faithful (11–14)

1:1
a Isa 1:1; Mic 1:1
b 2Ki 13:13
c Am 1:1

1 The word of the LORD that came to Hosea son of Beeri during the reigns of Uzziah, Jotham, Ahaz and Hezekiah, kings of Judah, *a* and during the reign of Jeroboam *b* son of Jehoash *a* king of Israel: *c*

a 1 Hebrew *Joash,* a variant of *Jehoash*

Hosea 1:1

Though the introduction to the book lists only one king from the northern kingdom of Israel (Jeroboam II, 793–753 B.C.), the list of kings from the southern kingdom of Judah demonstrates that Hosea preached during the reigns of several other northern kings, until just before Israel's exile to Assyria in 722 B.C. (2 Kings 17:1–6). Hosea's ministry in Israel came shortly after the preaching of Amos and partially overlapped with Micah's and Isaiah's ministries in Judah.

These were difficult times to be involved in prophetic ministry. The nation was falling apart before Hosea's eyes, and the ruling class lacked the caliber of leaders to provide a stable government. Most people who heard Hosea preach probably discounted his evaluation of the situation.

Hosea's Wife and Children

2When the LORD began to speak through Hosea, the LORD said to him, "Go, take to yourself an adulterous *d* wife and children of unfaithfulness, because the land is guilty of the vilest adultery *e* in departing from the LORD." 3So he married Gomer daughter of Diblaim, and she conceived and bore him a son.

4Then the LORD said to Hosea, "Call him Jezreel, *f* because I will soon punish the house of Jehu for the massacre at Jezreel, and I will put an end to the kingdom of Israel. 5In that day I will break Israel's bow in the Valley of Jezreel. *g*"

6Gomer *h* conceived again and gave birth to a daughter. Then the LORD said to Hosea, "Call her Lo-Ruhamah, *a* for I will no longer show love to the house of Israel, *i* that I should at all forgive them. 7Yet I will show love to the house of Judah; and I will save them—not by bow, *j* sword or battle, or by horses and horsemen, but by the LORD their God. *k*"

8After she had weaned Lo-Ruhamah, Gomer had another son. 9Then the LORD said, "Call him Lo-Ammi, *b* for you are not my people, and I am not your God.

10"Yet the Israelites will be like the sand on the seashore, which cannot be measured or counted. *l* In the place where it was said to them, 'You are not my people,' they will be called 'sons of the living God.' *m* 11The people of Judah and the people of Israel will be reunited, *n* and they will appoint one leader *o* and will come up out of the land, *p* for great will be the day of Jezreel.

2 "Say of your brothers, 'My people,' and of your sisters, 'My loved one.' *q*

Israel Punished and Restored

2 "Rebuke your mother, *r* rebuke her,
  for she is not my wife,
  and I am not her husband.
Let her remove the adulterous *s* look from her face
  and the unfaithfulness from between her breasts.
3Otherwise I will strip her naked

---

a 6 *Lo-Ruhamah* means *not loved.*   *b* 9 *Lo-Ammi* means *not my people.*

1:2 *d* Jer 3:1; Hos 2:2, 5; 3:1 *e* Dt 31:16; Jer 3:14; Eze 23:3-21; Hos 5:3
1:4 *f* 2Ki 10:1-14; Hos 2:22
1:5 *g* 2Ki 15:29
1:6 *h* ver 3 *i* Hos 2:4
1:7 *j* Ps 44:6 *k* Zec 4:6
1:10 *l* Ge 22:17; Jer 33:22 *m* ver 9; Ro 9:26*
1:11 *n* Isa 11:12,13 *o* Jer 23:5-8 *p* Eze 37:15-28
2:1 *q* ver 23
2:2 *r* ver 5; Isa 50:1; Hos 1:2 *s* Eze 23:45

📖 Little is known about this unique but interesting figure. Like many other minor Biblical characters, Hosea would, no doubt, have never anticipated that his name and prophecy would be known and studied thousands of years beyond his death. In much the same way God can and does use the service of Christians today. The outcome of some seemingly insignificant action on our part can make a difference in the course of later generations.

Hosea 1:2—2:1

In marrying an adulterous wife, Hosea submitted to God's will, setting himself up to experience a taste of God's pain and the depth of his love for undeserving people. Gomer symbolized the form of religion Israel's leaders promoted: worship of the Lord along with that of various idols.

The name "Jezreel" ("God scatters") emphasized the coming judgment on Israel's reigning dynasty as well as on the kingdom itself. "Lo-Ruhamah" ("not loved") revealed that God would end his tender feelings of deep affection that were foundational to his relationship with his people. And "Lo-Ammi" ("not my people") indicated that the covenant connection between God and Israel had been broken by their disobedience. The passage ends with a reversal of the meanings of these names. At one moment God rejected his people; in the next he accepted them back as covenant partners.

📖 God's mysterious plan for Hosea wasn't up for discussion or vote. The example of Hosea's obedience to the unusual circumstances God planned for him presents a challenge to all of us who desire to be faithful to the Lord's calling. By obediently following God's plan, Hosea came to understand and empathize in a much fuller way with God's deep hatred for sin and, at the same time, his unending love for those who deserve no compassion. To what degree do you share these attitudes?

That God commanded his prophet to love and marry a prostitute is shocking. How would a church respond today if its pastor or an elder were similarly called? What does this say about God's radical love for sin-stained people? Think about Jesus' ministry. How did he demonstrate care for society's outcasts? How can you follow in his steps?

Hosea 2:2–23

Two themes stand out in this passage. The shocking comparison of spiritual idolatry to sexual prostitution opens our eyes to how God views unfaithfulness. Sin is an outrage he can't overlook, a devastating betrayal of trust that goes to the heart of a relationship.

A second theme is the loving and just discipline of God, who openly confronts actions that threaten to undermine his covenant relationship with his people. But hope in God's eternal plans isn't destroyed by his people's

Compassion

1:2–3

Try to think of the most difficult situations in which to show compassion. Most likely your list will include cases where you have been personally wronged by someone who is now suffering as a result.

Among the many instances of Biblical compassion, both on the part of God and humans, one of the most astounding is Hosea's unwavering love for his unfaithful spouse, Gomer. The Bible uses the prophet's compassion as a parable of God's concern for an equally faithless nation, Israel. God's compassion was the fount from which Hosea's unlikely compassion flowed.

You may be tempted to think that the more garden variety of compassion for the world's faceless poor and needy is unremarkable. But consider:

- The world's suffering is so pervasive that we can't always handle the load. We suffer compassion fatigue and intentionally or unintentionally close ourselves off behind a thick wall of apathy.
- Another way to handle compassion overload is to think about compassion but avoid acting on the instinct. We acknowledge the needs but fail to follow through with actions appropriate to a Christian with God's heart for the world.

> **O**ur compassion capacity is greatly enhanced when we avoid being locked in by narrower thinking and feeling.

So how do we become compassionate Christians in thought *and* deed? Perhaps we can learn some lessons from Hosea's especially difficult case. The first thing to remember is that Hosea was a prophet— by definition willing to do whatever was required to carry God's message to his compatriots. We are not all prophets per se, but as Christians we all have a prophetic call, part of which involves a willingness to act on Christ's commands.

Second, we can learn from Hosea that there is always a bigger picture to consider. We rightly and naturally see life through our own eyes and feel it through our own senses. But Christians are to be willing to see and feel in relation to a wider, deeper perspective. Our compassion capacity is greatly enhanced when we avoid being locked in by narrower thinking and feeling. World Vision founder Bob Pierce put it this way: "Let my heart be broken by the things that break the heart of God."

Which leads to a third point—all the virtues of a world Christian are connected to and dependent on one another. Compassion is no exception. It's especially connected to two others:

- Humility. In order to feel deeply about the needs of others, we need to nudge aside our own needs a bit. This requires humility. When God instructed Hosea, "Go, take to yourself an adulterous wife" (Hos. 1:2), Hosea had to put aside much of his manly pride. He had to marry (and later reconcile with) someone whose behavior challenged his deeply ingrained senses of self-worth and community values. Gomer's actions made Hosea a community laughingstock. Compassion—act-compassion at least—often means that we act in ways that feel contrary to our own sense of legitimate pride.
- Generosity. Compassionate giving isn't an end in itself. It's intended to relieve others' suffering, not build up our own sense of well-being. The compassion of the world Christian is intended to glorify God.

and make her as bare as on the day she was born;[t]
I will make her like a desert,[u]
turn her into a parched land,
and slay her with thirst.
[4]I will not show my love to her children,[v]
because they are the children of adultery.
[5]Their mother has been unfaithful
and has conceived them in disgrace.
She said, 'I will go after my lovers,[w]
who give me my food and my water,
my wool and my linen, my oil and my drink.'[x]
[6]Therefore I will block her path with thornbushes;
I will wall her in so that she cannot find her way.[y]
[7]She will chase after her lovers but not catch them;
she will look for them but not find them.[z]
Then she will say,
'I will go back to my husband as at first,[a]
for then I was better off[b] than now.'
[8]She has not acknowledged[c] that I was the one
who gave her the grain, the new wine and oil,
who lavished on her the silver and gold—
which they used for Baal.[d]

[9]"Therefore I will take away my grain[e] when it ripens,
and my new wine[f] when it is ready.
I will take back my wool and my linen,
intended to cover her nakedness.
[10]So now I will expose her lewdness
before the eyes of her lovers;
no one will take her out of my hands.[g]
[11]I will stop[h] all her celebrations:
her yearly festivals, her New Moons,
her Sabbath days—all her appointed feasts.[i]
[12]I will ruin her vines[j] and her fig trees,
which she said were her pay from her lovers;
I will make them a thicket,[k]
and wild animals will devour them.[l]
[13]I will punish her for the days
she burned incense to the Baals;[m]
she decked herself with rings and jewelry,[n]
and went after her lovers,[o]
but me she forgot,[p]"

declares the LORD.

[14]"Therefore I am now going to allure her;
I will lead her into the desert
and speak tenderly to her.
[15]There I will give her back her vineyards,
and will make the Valley of Achor[a q] a door of hope.
There she will sing[b r] as in the days of her youth,[s]
as in the day she came up out of Egypt.[t]

[a] 15 *Achor* means *trouble*.   [b] 15 Or *respond*

2:3	[t] Eze 16:4,22 [u] Isa 32:13-14
2:4	[v] Eze 8:18
2:5	[w] Jer 3:6 [x] Jer 44:17-18
2:6	[y] Job 3:23; 19:8; La 3:9
2:7	[z] Hos 5:13 [a] Jer 2:2; 3:1 [b] Eze 16:8
2:8	[c] Isa 1:3 [d] Eze 16:15-19; Hos 8:4
2:9	[e] Hos 8:7 [f] Hos 9:2
2:10	[g] Eze 16:37
2:11	[h] Jer 7:34 [i] Isa 1:14; Jer 16:9; Hos 3:4; Am 8:10
2:12	[j] Isa 7:23; Jer 8:13 [k] Isa 5:6 [l] Hos 13:8
2:13	[m] Hos 11:2 [n] Eze 16:17 [o] Hos 4:13 [p] Hos 4:6; 8:14; 13:6
2:15	[q] Jos 7:24,26 [r] Ex 15:1-18 [s] Jer 2:2 [t] Hos 12:9

temporary failures. Hosea contrasted unfaithfulness and punishment with the allurement of a wonderful relationship with God, others, and all of creation (vv. 14–23).

Each of us is susceptible to self-deception, and we may not realize how deeply we have compromised our beliefs with the philosophies of our culture (see Jer. 17:9). It's important for us to immerse ourselves in God's Word so that our minds can be transformed by the Spirit's work (see Rom. 12:2). A belief system that accepts its culture's thinking and combines it with a few Bible verses looks and acts like an unholy prostitution of true faith.

2:17
u Ex 23:13; Ps 16:4
v Jos 23:7

2:18
w Job 5:22 *x* Isa 2:4
y Jer 23:6;
Eze 34:25

2:19
z Isa 62:4 *a* Isa 1:27

2:20
b Jer 31:34;
Hos 6:6; 13:4

2:21
c Isa 55:10;
Zec 8:12

2:22
d Jer 31:12;
Joel 2:19
2:23
e Jer 31:27
f Hos 1:6
g Hos 1:10
h Ro 9:25*;
1Pe 2:10

3:1
i Hos 1:2 / 2Sa 6:19

3:4
k Hos 13:11
l Da 11:31;
Hos 2:11
m Jdg 17:5-6;
Zec 10:2
3:5
n Eze 34:23-24
o Jer 50:4-5

16 "In that day," declares the LORD,
    "you will call me 'my husband';
    you will no longer call me 'my master.'*a*
17 I will remove the names of the Baals from her lips;*u*
    no longer will their names be invoked.*v*
18 In that day I will make a covenant for them
    with the beasts of the field and the birds of the air
    and the creatures that move along the ground.*w*
Bow and sword and battle
    I will abolish*x* from the land,
    so that all may lie down in safety.*y*
19 I will betroth*z* you to me forever;
    I will betroth you in*b* righteousness and justice,*a*
    in*c* love and compassion.
20 I will betroth you in faithfulness,
    and you will acknowledge*b* the LORD.

21 "In that day I will respond,"
    declares the LORD—
    "I will respond*c* to the skies,
    and they will respond to the earth;
22 and the earth will respond to the grain,
    the new wine and oil,*d*
    and they will respond to Jezreel.*d*
23 I will plant*e* her for myself in the land;
    I will show my love to the one I called 'Not my loved one.'*e**f*
I will say to those called 'Not my people,'*f* 'You are my people';*g*
    and they will say, 'You are my God.'*h* "

Hosea's Reconciliation With His Wife

3 The LORD said to me, "Go, show your love to your wife again, though she is loved by another and is an adulteress.*i* Love her as the LORD loves the Israelites, though they turn to other gods and love the sacred raisin cakes.*j*" 2 So I bought her for fifteen shekels*g* of silver and about a homer and a lethek*h* of barley. 3 Then I told her, "You are to live with*i* me many days; you must not be a prostitute or be intimate with any man, and I will live with*i* you." 4 For the Israelites will live many days without king or prince,*k* without sacrifice*l* or sacred stones, without ephod or idol.*m* 5 Afterward the Israelites will return and seek the LORD their God and David their king.*n* They will come trembling to the LORD and to his blessings in the last days.*o*

The Charge Against Israel

4 Hear the word of the LORD, you Israelites,
    because the LORD has a charge to bring

a 16 Hebrew *baal*   *b 19* Or *with*; also in verse 20   *c 19* Or *with*   *d 22* Jezreel means *God plants.*
f 23 Hebrew *Lo-Ruhamah*   *e 23* Hebrew *Lo-Ammi*   *g 2* That is, about 6 ounces (about 170 grams)
h 2 That is, probably about 10 bushels (about 330 liters)   *i 3* Or *wait for*

Hosea 3:1–5

The fact that Hosea "bought" Gomer means at the least that she had become indebted to someone, if not even that she had become a slave. The restoration of the relationship between Hosea and Gomer parallels that *between God and Israel.* No mention is made of punishment, only of Israel's living for "many days" without all those things that had led God's people away from himself. Just as Hosea cut Gomer off from those who had led her into adultery, so God would remove the factors that

had caused Israel to destroy her relationship with him.

In Hosea's payment to free Gomer from a debtor's bondage, we are reminded of Jesus' once-for-all payment of our eternal debt. No one has ever deserved God's love. His blessings may be interrupted by our unfaithfulness, but his love isn't thwarted by our rejection. God's love involves his commitment of faithfulness to his people. It's overpoweringly persuasive and nearly irresistible, able to soften and transform hearts—even hearts hardened by years of rejection.

against you who live in the land:
"There is no faithfulness, no love,
   no acknowledgment[p] of God in the land.
2 There is only cursing,[a] lying[q] and murder,[r]
   stealing[s] and adultery;
they break all bounds,
   and bloodshed follows bloodshed.
3 Because of this the land mourns,[b][t]
   and all who live in it waste away;[u]
the beasts of the field and the birds of the air
   and the fish of the sea are dying.[v]

4 "But let no man bring a charge,
   let no man accuse another,
for your people are like those
   who bring charges against a priest.[w]
5 You stumble[x] day and night,
   and the prophets stumble with you.
So I will destroy your mother[y]—
6   my people are destroyed from lack of knowledge.[z]

"Because you have rejected knowledge,
   I also reject you as my priests;
because you have ignored the law[a] of your God,
   I also will ignore your children.
7 The more the priests increased,
   the more they sinned against me;
they exchanged[c] their[d] Glory[b] for something disgraceful.[c]
8 They feed on the sins of my people
   and relish their wickedness.[d]
9 And it will be: Like people, like priests.[e]
   I will punish both of them for their ways
   and repay them for their deeds.[f]

10 "They will eat but not have enough;[g]
   they will engage in prostitution but not increase,
because they have deserted[h] the LORD
   to give themselves 11 to prostitution,[i]
to old wine and new,
   which take away the understanding[j] 12 of my people.
They consult a wooden idol[k]
   and are answered by a stick of wood.[l]
A spirit of prostitution leads them astray;[m]
   they are unfaithful to their God.
13 They sacrifice on the mountaintops

4:1
p Jer 7:28

4:2
q Hos 7:3; 10:4
r Hos 6:9 s Hos 7:1

4:3
t Jer 4:28 u Isa 33:9
v Jer 4:25; Zep 1:3

4:4
w Dt 17:12;
Eze 3:26
4:5
x Eze 14:7
y Hos 2:2
4:6
z Hos 2:13;
Mal 2:7-8
a Hos 8:1,12

4:7
b Hab 2:16
c Hos 10:1,6; 13:6

4:8
d Isa 56:11;
Mic 3:11
4:9
e Isa 24:2 f Jer 5:31;
Hos 8:13; 9:9,15

4:10
g Lev 26:26;
Mic 6:14
h Hos 7:14; 9:17

4:11
i Hos 5:4 j Pr 20:1

4:12
k Jer 2:27
l Hab 2:19
m Isa 44:20

---

a 2 That is, to pronounce a curse upon   b 3 Or *dries up*   c 7 Syriac and an ancient Hebrew scribal
tradition; Masoretic Text *I will exchange*   d 7 Masoretic Text; an ancient Hebrew scribal tradition *my*

Hosea 4:1–19

With chapter 4, the book of Hosea moves from a narration of Hosea's family life as a symbol of his message to God's legal "charge" or covenant lawsuit against his unfaithful people (cf. Mic. 6). A "spirit of prostitution" (v. 12; cf. 5:4) controlled the hearts of both priests and people, preventing them from acknowledging God as their Lord. The Israelites had given themselves over to common prostitution as well as to the sexual immorality that accompanied Baal worship (e.g., compare "harlots" and "shrine prostitutes" in v. 14).

What in our culture parallels Hosea's list of problems? He condemned anything that detracted from people's understanding of their relationship with God, anything or anyone other than God that people looked to for spiritual direction, anything that led to unfaithfulness to the Lord. This included doing the right thing in the wrong way or at the wrong place. Hosea also blasted sexually inappropriate behavior. If we have bought into the worldview of our secular culture, we—like the Israelites—need the stern warning Hosea proclaimed.

4:13
n Isa 1:29 o Jer 3:6;
Hos 11:2
p Jer 2:20; Am 7:17
q Hos 2:13

and burn offerings on the hills,
under oak,[n] poplar and terebinth,
where the shade is pleasant.[o]
Therefore your daughters turn to prostitution[p]
and your daughters-in-law to adultery.[q]

4:14
r ver 11

14 "I will not punish your daughters
when they turn to prostitution,
nor your daughters-in-law
when they commit adultery,
because the men themselves consort with harlots[r]
and sacrifice with shrine prostitutes—
a people without understanding will come to ruin!

15 "Though you commit adultery, O Israel,
let not Judah become guilty.

4:15
s Hos 9:15; 12:11;
Am 4:4

"Do not go to Gilgal;[s]
do not go up to Beth Aven.[a]
And do not swear, 'As surely as the LORD lives!'
16 The Israelites are stubborn,
like a stubborn heifer.
How then can the LORD pasture them

4:16
t Isa 5:17; 7:25

like lambs[t] in a meadow?
17 Ephraim is joined to idols;
leave him alone!
18 Even when their drinks are gone,
they continue their prostitution;
their rulers dearly love shameful ways.

4:19
u Hos 12:1; 13:15
v Isa 1:29

19 A whirlwind[u] will sweep them away,
and their sacrifices will bring them shame.[v]

Judgment Against Israel

5 "Hear this, you priests!
Pay attention, you Israelites!
Listen, O royal house!
This judgment is against you:

5:1
w Hos 6:9; 9:8

You have been a snare[w] at Mizpah,
a net spread out on Tabor.

5:2
x Hos 4:2
y Hos 9:15

2 The rebels are deep in slaughter.[x]
I will discipline all of them.[y]
3 I know all about Ephraim;
Israel is not hidden from me.

5:3
z Hos 6:10

Ephraim, you have now turned to prostitution;
Israel is corrupt.[z]

4 "Their deeds do not permit them
to return to their God.

---

a 15 *Beth Aven* means *house of wickedness* (a name for Bethel, which means *house of God*).

Hosea 5:1–15

Israel's sin had consequences. Hosea described how God as Judge would pronounce a "guilty" verdict on Israel, and particularly on her political and spiritual leaders. The Lord's ruling would include an announcement of war and a series of bold images of judgment on his people. God would destroy not just Israel but, eventually, Judah as well. Note that Hosea frequently used "Ephraim" as a synonym for Israel. The northern kingdom's largest tribe, Ephraim had come to be associated with the nation as a whole.

Sin causes conflicts and wars. If we avoid the "sin problem" and the "God solution," wars and interpersonal conflicts will fester. Hosea suggested that when God is excluded from the solution process, the problem may become aggravated. In fact, what people interpret as an earthly problem may be a divine fight—God versus out-of-control humans. The only resolution is to reject sin, seek God, and humbly plead for restoration.

A spirit of prostitution[a] is in their heart;
 they do not acknowledge[b] the LORD.
5 Israel's arrogance testifies[c] against them;
 the Israelites, even Ephraim, stumble in their sin;
Judah also stumbles with them.
6 When they go with their flocks and herds
 to seek the LORD,[d]
they will not find him;
 he has withdrawn[e] himself from them.
7 They are unfaithful[f] to the LORD;
 they give birth to illegitimate[g] children.
Now their New Moon festivals
 will devour[h] them and their fields.

8 "Sound the trumpet in Gibeah,[i]
 the horn in Ramah.[j]
Raise the battle cry in Beth Aven[a];[k]
 lead on, O Benjamin.
9 Ephraim will be laid waste
 on the day of reckoning.[l]
Among the tribes of Israel
 I proclaim what is certain.[m]
10 Judah's leaders are like those
 who move boundary stones.[n]
I will pour out my wrath[o] on them
 like a flood of water.
11 Ephraim is oppressed,
 trampled in judgment,
 intent on pursuing idols.[b][p]
12 I am like a moth[q] to Ephraim,
 like rot to the people of Judah.

13 "When Ephraim saw his sickness,
 and Judah his sores,
then Ephraim turned to Assyria,[r]
 and sent to the great king for help.[s]
But he is not able to cure[t] you,
 not able to heal your sores.[u]
14 For I will be like a lion[v] to Ephraim,
 like a great lion to Judah.
I will tear them to pieces and go away;
 I will carry them off, with no one to rescue them.[w]
15 Then I will go back to my place
 until they admit their guilt.
And they will seek my face;[x]
 in their misery[y] they will earnestly seek me.[z]"

Israel Unrepentant

6 "Come, let us return to the LORD.
 He has torn us to pieces[a]
  but he will heal us;
 he has injured us

---

[a] 8 *Beth Aven* means *house of wickedness* (a name for Bethel, which means *house of God*).
[b] 11 The meaning of the Hebrew for this word is uncertain.

Side references

5:4
[a] Hos 4:11
[b] Hos 4:6
5:5
[c] Hos 7:10
5:6
[d] Mic 6:6-7
[e] Pr 1:28; Isa 1:15; Eze 8:6
5:7
[f] Hos 6:7 [g] Hos 2:4
[h] Hos 2:11-12
5:8
[i] Hos 9:9; 10:9
[j] Isa 10:29
[k] Hos 4:15
5:9
[l] Isa 37:3; Hos 9:11-17
[m] Isa 46:10; Zec 1:6
5:10
[n] Dt 19:14
[o] Eze 7:8
5:11
[p] Hos 9:16; Mic 6:16
5:12
[q] Isa 51:8
5:13
[r] Hos 7:11; 8:9
[s] Hos 10:6
[t] Hos 14:3
[u] Jer 30:12
5:14
[v] Am 3:4 [w] Mic 5:8
5:15
[x] Hos 3:5 [y] Jer 2:27
[z] Isa 64:9
6:1
[a] Hos 5:14

Hosea 6:1—7:16

In 6:1–3 Hosea was quoting—or, more specifically, parodying—the Israelites' shallow and insincere "re-

pentance" (cf. 8:2). God's response began with a lament of disappointment (6:4–6). He loved Ephraim (Israel) and Judah dearly and didn't want to punish them, but he had

6:1
b Dt 32:39;
Jer 30:17; Hos 14:4
6:2
c Ps 30:5

but he will bind up our wounds. [b]

2 After two days he will revive us; [c]
  on the third day he will restore us,
  that we may live in his presence.

3 Let us acknowledge the LORD;
  let us press on to acknowledge him.
  As surely as the sun rises,
    he will appear;
  he will come to us like the winter rains, [d]
    like the spring rains that water the earth. [e]"

6:3
d Joel 2:23
e Ps 72:6
6:4
f Hos 11:8
g Hos 7:1; 13:3

4 "What can I do with you, Ephraim? [f]
  What can I do with you, Judah?
  Your love is like the morning mist,
    like the early dew that disappears. [g]

5 Therefore I cut you in pieces with my prophets,
  I killed you with the words of my mouth; [h]
  my judgments flashed like lightning upon you. [i]

6:5
h Jer 1:9-10; 23:29
i Heb 4:12
6:6
j Isa 1:11; Mt 9:13*;
12:7* k Hos 2:20

6 For I desire mercy, not sacrifice, [j]
  and acknowledgment [k] of God rather than burnt offerings.

7 Like Adam, [a] they have broken the covenant [l]—
  they were unfaithful [m] to me there.

6:7
l Hos 8:1 m Hos 5:7

8 Gilead is a city of wicked men,
  stained with footprints of blood.

9 As marauders lie in ambush for a man,
  so do bands of priests;
  they murder on the road to Shechem,
  committing shameful crimes. [n]

6:9
n Jer 7:9-10;
Eze 22:9; Hos 7:1
6:10
o Jer 5:30

10 I have seen a horrible [o] thing
  in the house of Israel.

---

a 7 Or As at Adam; or Like men

---

warned them, called them to wake up, and promised hope if they repented—all to no avail. When they failed to respond appropriately, what else could God do?

In the rest of this passage Hosea cited additional examples to prove that the Israelites had broken their covenant with God. Several sins stood out by repetition. God hates (1) deceit, plots, and lies; (2) violence and killing; and (3) failure to call on or turn to him. These failures prevent God from pouring out his blessings and eliminate the possibility of healing. Death, destruction, and ridicule are sin's only ultimate rewards.

📖 Just as in Hosea's time, convincing people today that they are sinners is the first step to getting right with God. In much of contemporary society, sin isn't defined by the moral absolutes revealed in the Bible. Without higher moral principles, almost nothing is seen as sin except a rejection of this permissive philosophy. The popular opinion is that the end justifies the means. Christian witness relies on the Holy Spirit's work in persuading people to turn away from such a worldview—not a wholesale rejection of culture, but of the godless beliefs and sinful behaviors it endorses (cf. John 16:7–11).

6:6

Seven Works of Mercy

The church has classically defined its social role around these seven

WORKS OF MERCY

1	2	3	4	5	6	7
Feed the hungry	Give drink to the thirsty	Take in the stranger	Clothe the naked	Tend the sick	Minister to prisoners	Bury the dead

Reflect for a few moments on Jesus' words in Matthew 25:31–46. When did you see your Lord hungry or thirsty or a stranger or needing clothes or sick or in prison? How do these activities demonstrate walking in humility with God?

There Ephraim is given to prostitution
and Israel is defiled. [p]

[11] "Also for you, Judah,
a harvest [q] is appointed.

7 [1] "Whenever I would restore the fortunes of my people,
whenever I would heal Israel,
the sins of Ephraim are exposed
and the crimes of Samaria revealed. [r]
They practice deceit, [s]
thieves break into houses, [t]
bandits rob in the streets;

[2] but they do not realize
that I remember [u] all their evil deeds.
Their sins engulf them; [v]
they are always before me.

[3] "They delight the king with their wickedness,
the princes with their lies. [w]

[4] They are all adulterers, [x]
burning like an oven
whose fire the baker need not stir
from the kneading of the dough till it rises.

[5] On the day of the festival of our king
the princes become inflamed with wine, [y]
and he joins hands with the mockers.

[6] Their hearts are like an oven; [z]
they approach him with intrigue.
Their passion smolders all night;
in the morning it blazes like a flaming fire.

[7] All of them are hot as an oven;
they devour their rulers.
All their kings fall,
and none of them calls [a] on me.

[8] "Ephraim mixes [b] with the nations;
Ephraim is a flat cake not turned over.

[9] Foreigners sap his strength, [c]
but he does not realize it.
His hair is sprinkled with gray,
but he does not notice.

[10] Israel's arrogance testifies against him, [d]
but despite all this
he does not return to the LORD his God
or search [e] for him.

[11] "Ephraim is like a dove, [f]
easily deceived and senseless—
now calling to Egypt,
now turning to Assyria. [g]

[12] When they go, I will throw my net [h] over them;
I will pull them down like birds of the air.
When I hear them flocking together,
I will catch them.

[13] Woe [i] to them,
because they have strayed [j] from me!
Destruction to them,
because they have rebelled against me!

6:10
[p] Hos 5:3

6:11
[q] Jer 51:33;
Joel 3:13

7:1
[r] Hos 6:4 [s] ver 13
[t] Hos 4:2

7:2
[u] Jer 14:10;
Hos 8:13 [v] Jer 2:19

7:3
[w] Hos 4:2; Mic 7:3
7:4
[x] Jer 9:2

7:5
[y] Isa 28:1,7

7:6
[z] Ps 21:9

7:7
[a] ver 16
7:8
[b] ver 11; Ps 106:35;
Hos 5:13

7:9
[c] Isa 1:7; Hos 8:7

7:10
[d] Hos 5:5 [e] Isa 9:13

7:11
[f] Hos 11:11
[g] Hos 5:13; 12:1

7:12
[h] Eze 12:13

7:13
[i] Hos 9:12
[j] Jer 14:10;
Eze 34:4-6;
Hos 9:17

I long to redeem them
    but they speak lies against me. [k]

14 They do not cry out to me from their hearts [l]
    but wail upon their beds.
They gather together [a] for grain and new wine [m]
    but turn away from me. [n]

15 I trained them and strengthened them,
    but they plot evil [o] against me.

16 They do not turn to the Most High;
    they are like a faulty bow. [p]
Their leaders will fall by the sword
    because of their insolent words.
For this they will be ridiculed [q]
    in the land of Egypt. [r]

Israel to Reap the Whirlwind

8 "Put the trumpet to your lips!
    An eagle [s] is over the house of the LORD
because the people have broken my covenant
    and rebelled against my law. [t]

2 Israel cries out to me,
    'O our God, we acknowledge you!'

3 But Israel has rejected what is good;
    an enemy will pursue him.

4 They set up kings without my consent;
    they choose princes without my approval. [u]
With their silver and gold
    they make idols [v] for themselves
    to their own destruction.

5 Throw out your calf-idol, O Samaria! [w]
    My anger burns against them.
How long will they be incapable of purity? [x]

6   They are from Israel!
This calf—a craftsman has made it;
    it is not God.
It will be broken in pieces,
    that calf of Samaria.

7 "They sow the wind
    and reap the whirlwind. [y]
The stalk has no head;
    it will produce no flour.

7:13
k ver 1; Mt 23:37
7:14
l Jer 3:10 m Am 2:8
n Hos 13:16

7:15
o Na 1:9,11

7:16
p Ps 78:9,57
q Eze 23:32
r Hos 9:3

8:1
s Dt 28:49; Jer 4:13
t Hos 4:6; 6:7

8:4
u Hos 13:10
v Hos 2:8

8:5
w Hos 10:5
x Jer 13:27

8:7
y Pr 22:8; Isa 66:15;
Hos 10:12-13;
Na 1:3

---

[a] 14 Most Hebrew manuscripts; some Hebrew manuscripts and Septuagint *They slash themselves*

Hosea 8:1–14

In chapter 8 Hosea pronounced judgment on Israel's [false] gods and government. In response to the impending attack from Assyria, the people briefly called out to God for help, claiming to know him (v. 2; cf. 6:1–3). But their pagan practices revealed their true allegiance. They had made idols of silver and gold, specifically the golden calves at Dan and Bethel (vv. 5–6; see 1 Kings 12:26–33). "Samaria" was the capital of the northern kingdom, *as well as another name for Israel.*

The agricultural proverb in verse 7 summarizes what every farmer knows: A harvest is directly related to that which was planted. Israel's sowing of friendly alliances with other nations would result in her reaping the whirl-wind of destruction.

The book of Hosea and other Scriptures tell us what displeases God—like inappropriate choices by politicians (see vv. 4,9,14). Some world leaders call on God to bless their countries, but government scandals around the world testify that he is often not nearly as important to them as the manipulation of facts to gain political advantage and reduce negative fallout.

Many passages in both Testaments clarify for us what *pleases* God (e.g., Deut. 6:5, Mic. 6:7–8; Heb. 11:6; 13:15–16). But Galatians 6:8 makes a key connection between appropriate motivation to make the right choice and the results of that choice: "The one who sows to please his sinful nature, from that nature will reap de-

Were it to yield grain,
    foreigners would swallow it up. *z*
[8] Israel is swallowed up; *a*
    now she is among the nations
    like a worthless *b* thing.
[9] For they have gone up to Assyria
    like a wild donkey wandering alone.
    Ephraim has sold herself to lovers.
[10] Although they have sold themselves among the nations,
    I will now gather them together. *c*
They will begin to waste away *d*
    under the oppression of the mighty king.

[11] "Though Ephraim built many altars for sin offerings,
    these have become altars for sinning. *e*
[12] I wrote for them the many things of my law,
    but they regarded them as something alien.
[13] They offer sacrifices given to me
    and they eat *f* the meat,
    but the LORD is not pleased with them.
Now he will remember *g* their wickedness
    and punish their sins: *h*
They will return to Egypt. *i*
[14] Israel has forgotten *j* his Maker
    and built palaces;
    Judah has fortified many towns.
But I will send fire upon their cities
    that will consume their fortresses." *k*

Punishment for Israel

9 Do not rejoice, O Israel;
    do not be jubilant *l* like the other nations.
For you have been unfaithful *m* to your God;
    you love the wages of a prostitute
    at every threshing floor.
[2] Threshing floors and winepresses will not feed the people;
    the new wine *n* will fail them.
[3] They will not remain *o* in the LORD's land;
    Ephraim will return to Egypt *p*
    and eat unclean *a* food in Assyria. *q*
[4] They will not pour out wine offerings to the LORD,
    nor will their sacrifices please *r* him.
Such sacrifices will be to them like the bread of mourners;
    all who eat them will be unclean. *s*

a 3 That is, ceremonially unclean

Cross references

8:7
z Hos 2:9
8:8
a Jer 51:34
b Jer 22:28

8:10
c Eze 16:37; 22:20
d Jer 42:2

8:11
e Hos 10:1; 12:11

8:13
f Jer 7:21 g Hos 7:2
h Hos 4:9
i Hos 9:3,6

8:14
j Dt 32:18;
Hos 2:13
k Jer 17:27

9:1
l Isa 22:12-13
m Hos 10:5

9:2
n Hos 2:9
9:3
o Lev 25:23
p Hos 8:13
q Eze 4:13;
Hos 7:11

9:4
r Jer 6:20; Hos 8:13
s Hag 2:13-14

---

struction; the one who sows to please the Spirit, from the Spirit will reap eternal life." As in Hosea 8:7, Paul presented the consequences of pleasing God as either a life-threatening or a life-giving decision.

Hosea 9:1—10:15

In the midst of a jubilant harvest festival, like the Feast of Tabernacles (cf. Lev. 23:40), Hosea admonished his listeners, shouting above the racket: "Stop the music! The party's over!" The people shouldn't have conducted their religious feasts like pagans; this too was an act of prostitution against God.

Israel's story started with positive images of God's joy at first entering into a covenant relationship with his people—an experience like stumbling upon sweet grapes in an arid desert or enjoying the first fruit from a fig tree (9:10a). But this joy abruptly turned to grief over the shameless idol worship into which they had fallen (9:10b; cf. 10:1).

Again (see previous "Here and Now"), the book of Hosea and other Scriptures reveal to us both what pleases *and* what displeases God. The Lord isn't pleased with attempts to worship without confession of sin (Isa. 59:1–2), nor is he fooled by self-righteous claims, flowery prayers, or hypocritical devotion (Amos 5:21–24; Zech. 7:1–12; Matt. 6:5–18).

This food will be for themselves;
it will not come into the temple of the LORD.

9:5
t Isa 10:3; Jer 5:31
u Hos 2:11

5 What will you do[t] on the day of your appointed feasts,[u]
on the festival days of the LORD?

6 Even if they escape from destruction,
Egypt will gather them,
and Memphis[v] will bury them.
Their treasures of silver will be taken over by briers,
and thorns[w] will overrun their tents.

9:6
v Isa 19:13
w Isa 5:6; Hos 10:8

7 The days of punishment[x] are coming,
the days of reckoning are at hand.
Let Israel know this.
Because your sins[y] are so many
and your hostility so great,
the prophet is considered a fool,[z]
the inspired man a maniac.

9:7
x Isa 34:8;
Jer 10:15; Mic 7:4
y Jer 16:18
z Isa 44:25; La 2:14;
Eze 14:9-10

8 The prophet, along with my God,
is the watchman over Ephraim,[a]
yet snares[a] await him on all his paths,
and hostility in the house of his God.

9:8
a Hos 5:1

9 They have sunk deep into corruption,
as in the days of Gibeah.[b]
God will remember[c] their wickedness
and punish them for their sins.

9:9
b Jdg 19:16-30;
Hos 5:8; 10:9
c Hos 8:13

10 "When I found Israel,
it was like finding grapes in the desert;
when I saw your fathers,
it was like seeing the early fruit on the fig tree.
But when they came to Baal Peor,[d]
they consecrated themselves to that shameful idol[e]
and became as vile as the thing they loved.

9:10
d Nu 25:1-5;
Ps 106:28-29
e Jer 11:13;
Hos 4:14
9:11
f Hos 4:7; 10:5
g ver 14

11 Ephraim's glory will fly away like a bird[f]—
no birth, no pregnancy, no conception.[g]

12 Even if they rear children,
I will bereave them of every one.
Woe[h] to them
when I turn away from them![i]

9:12
h Hos 7:13
i Dt 31:17

13 I have seen Ephraim, like Tyre,
planted in a pleasant place.[j]
But Ephraim will bring out
their children to the slayer."

9:13
j Eze 27:3

14 Give them, O LORD—
what will you give them?
Give them wombs that miscarry
and breasts that are dry.[k]

9:14
k ver 11; Lk 23:29

15 "Because of all their wickedness in Gilgal,[l]
I hated them there.
Because of their sinful deeds,[m]

9:15
l Hos 4:15
m Hos 7:2

---

a 8 Or The prophet is the watchman over Ephraim, / the people of my God

---

On the other hand, God *is* pleased when we "sow righteousness," which in turn allows him to bless us with his unfailing love (Hos. 10:12). He's also pleased when we seek him and trust in him rather than in our own abilities (Hos. 10:12–13). We can use these revelations as spiritual checkpoints: Has my behavior been just and righteous this week? Do I continually seek to know and have a deeper relationship with God? Do my daily actions demonstrate my trust in him?

I will drive them out of my house.
I will no longer love them;
    all their leaders are rebellious. [n]
16 Ephraim [o] is blighted,
    their root is withered,
    they yield no fruit. [p]
Even if they bear children,
    I will slay [q] their cherished offspring."

17 My God will reject them
    because they have not obeyed [r] him;
    they will be wanderers among the nations. [s]

10 Israel was a spreading vine; [t]
    he brought forth fruit for himself.
As his fruit increased,
    he built more altars; [u]
as his land prospered,
    he adorned his sacred stones. [v]
2 Their heart is deceitful, [w]
    and now they must bear their guilt. [x]
The LORD will demolish their altars [y]
    and destroy their sacred stones. [z]

3 Then they will say, "We have no king
    because we did not revere the LORD.
But even if we had a king,
    what could he do for us?"
4 They make many promises,
    take false oaths [a]
    and make agreements; [b]
therefore lawsuits spring up
    like poisonous weeds in a plowed field.
5 The people who live in Samaria fear
    for the calf-idol of Beth Aven. [a c]
Its people will mourn over it,
    and so will its idolatrous priests, [d]

[a] 5 *Beth Aven* means *house of wickedness* (a name for Bethel, which means *house of God*).

9:15 [n] Isa 1:23; Hos 4:9; 5:2
9:16 [o] Hos 5:11 [p] Hos 8:7 [q] ver 12
9:17 [r] Hos 4:10 [s] Dt 28:65; Hos 7:13
10:1 [t] Eze 15:2 [u] 1Ki 14:23 [v] Hos 8:11; 12:11
10:2 [w] 1Ki 18:21 [x] Hos 13:16 [y] ver 8 [z] Mic 5:13
10:4 [a] Hos 4:2 [b] Eze 17:19; Am 5:7
10:5 [c] Hos 5:8 [d] 2Ki 23:5

10:4

Chemicals by Health Effects

In the Bible poison was seen as coming mainly from weeds and plants. Modern technology has created a whole new class of toxins—some naturally refined, some artificially created, but all dealers of death if misused. Is our world a better place now than it was in Hosea's day? Perhaps "different" is a more apt description. Sin's manifestations change with time, but they are with us to stay until that glorious day when God ushers in the new heavens and the new earth (see Rev. 21:1).

Source: Worldwatch Institute, *State of the World 2002* (2002:87)

Health Effects	Main Chemicals
• Cancer	Arsenic, benzene chromium, vinyl chloride
• Cardiovascular diseases	Arsenic, cadmium, cobalt, lead
• Endocrine disruption	Aluminum, cadmium, DDT, lead, mercury, PCBs
• Nervous system/cognitive impairment	Aluminum, arsenic, lead, manganese, mercury
• Osteoporosis	Aluminum, cadmium, lead, selenium
• Reproductive effects	Arsenic, chlorine, chloroform, lead, mercury, nickel

those who had rejoiced over its splendor,
     because it is taken from them into exile. e
6 It will be carried to Assyria f
     as tribute for the great king. g
Ephraim will be disgraced; h
Israel will be ashamed of its wooden idols. a
7 Samaria and its king will float away i
     like a twig on the surface of the waters.
8 The high places of wickedness b j will be destroyed—
     it is the sin of Israel.
Thorns k and thistles will grow up
     and cover their altars. l
Then they will say to the mountains, "Cover us!"
     and to the hills, "Fall on us!" m

9 "Since the days of Gibeah, n you have sinned, O Israel,
     and there you have remained. c
Did not war overtake
     the evildoers in Gibeah?
10 When I please, I will punish o them;
     nations will be gathered against them
     to put them in bonds for their double sin.
11 Ephraim is a trained heifer
     that loves to thresh;
so I will put a yoke
     on her fair neck.
I will drive Ephraim,
     Judah must plow,
     and Jacob must break up the ground.
12 Sow for yourselves righteousness, p
     reap the fruit of unfailing love,
and break up your unplowed ground; q
     for it is time to seek r the LORD,
until he comes
     and showers righteousness s on you.
13 But you have planted wickedness,
     you have reaped evil, t
     you have eaten the fruit of deception.
Because you have depended on your own strength
     and on your many warriors, u
14 the roar of battle will rise against your people,
     so that all your fortresses will be devastated v—
as Shalman devastated Beth Arbel on the day of battle,
     when mothers were dashed to the ground with their children. w
15 Thus will it happen to you, O Bethel,
     because your wickedness is great.
When that day dawns,
     the king of Israel will be completely destroyed. x

God's Love for Israel

11 "When Israel was a child, I loved him,
     and out of Egypt I called my son. y
2 But the more I d called Israel,
     the further they went from me. e
They sacrificed to the Baals z

a 6 Or its counsel   b 8 Hebrew aven, a reference to Beth Aven (a derogatory name for Bethel)
c 9 Or there a stand was taken   d 2 Some Septuagint manuscripts; Hebrew they   e 2 Septuagint;
Hebrew them

and they burned incense to images. *a*
³ It was I who taught Ephraim to walk,
    taking them by the arms; *b*
but they did not realize
    it was I who healed *c* them.
⁴ I led them with cords of human kindness,
    with ties of love; *d*
I lifted the yoke *e* from their neck
    and bent down to feed *f* them.

⁵ "Will they not return to Egypt *g*
    and will not Assyria *h* rule over them
    because they refuse to repent?
⁶ Swords *i* will flash in their cities,
    will destroy the bars of their gates
    and put an end to their plans.
⁷ My people are determined to turn from me. *j*
    Even if they call to the Most High,
    he will by no means exalt them.

⁸ "How can I give you up, Ephraim? *k*
    How can I hand you over, Israel?
How can I treat you like Admah?
    How can I make you like Zeboiim? *l*
My heart is changed within me;
    all my compassion is aroused.
⁹ I will not carry out my fierce anger, *m*
    nor will I turn and devastate *n* Ephraim.
For I am God, and not man *o*—
    the Holy One among you.
I will not come in wrath. *a*
¹⁰ They will follow the LORD;
    he will roar like a lion.
When he roars,
    his children will come trembling from the west. *p*
¹¹ They will come trembling
    like birds from Egypt,
    like doves from Assyria. *q*
I will settle them in their homes," *r*
    declares the LORD.

Israel's Sin

¹² Ephraim has surrounded me with lies, *s*
    the house of Israel with deceit.
And Judah is unruly against God,
    even against the faithful Holy One.

---

a 9 Or *come against any city*

Cross-references

11:2 *a* 2Ki 17:15; Isa 65:7; Jer 18:15
11:3 *b* Dt 1:31; Hos 7:15 *c* Jer 30:17
11:4 *d* Jer 31:2-3 *e* Lev 26:13 *f* Ex 16:32; Ps 78:25
11:5 *g* Hos 7:16 *h* Hos 10:6
11:6 *i* Hos 13:16
11:7 *j* Jer 3:6-7; 8:5
11:8 *k* Hos 6:4 *l* Ge 14:8
11:9 *m* Dt 13:17; Jer 30:11 *n* Mal 3:6 *o* Nu 23:19
11:10 *p* Hos 6:1-3
11:11 *q* Isa 11:11 *r* Eze 28:26
11:12 *s* Hos 4:2

Hosea 11:1–11

Hosea portrayed two contrasting images: God the loving Father and Israel the stubborn, unrepentant son (rather than the unfaithful wife of chapters 1–3). But God couldn't bring himself to annihilate Israel as he had Admah and Zeboiim—obscure cities few remembered (see Deut. 29:23). Why not? His mind and heart were changed because his compassion was aroused. And he's holy, operating at a level above human action and existence. God had chosen to fulfill his sovereign plan, which was guided both by his love and his justice.

God's love is practically irresistible; it can soften and change the most rebellious people. He loves everyone in the world and doesn't want anyone to perish (John 3:16; 2 Peter 3:9). After a time of punishment, Israel would be restored (Hos. 11:10–11). God's love still brings about the transformation of people and the fulfillment of his promises. Nothing can frustrate God's plan to love people and enter into relationship with them.

12

12:1
t Eze 17:10
u 2Ki 17:4

12:2
v Mic 6:2 w Hos 4:9

12:3
x Ge 25:26
y Ge 32:24-29

12:4
z Ge 28:12-15;
35:15

12:5
a Ex 3:15

12:6
b Mic 6:8
c Hos 6:1-3; 10:12;
Mic 7:7

12:7
d Am 8:5

12:8
e Ps 62:10;
Rev 3:17

12:9
f Lev 23:43;
Hos 11:1 g Ne 8:17

12:10
h Eze 20:49
i 2Ki 17:13;
Jer 7:25
12:11
j Hos 6:8
k Hos 4:15
l Hos 8:11

12:12
m Ge 28:5
n Ge 29:18

12:13
o Ex 13:3;
Isa 63:11-14

1 Ephraim feeds on the wind;^{t}
  he pursues the east wind all day
  and multiplies lies and violence.
He makes a treaty with Assyria
  and sends olive oil to Egypt.^{u}
2 The LORD has a charge^v to bring against Judah;
  he will punish Jacob^a according to his ways
  and repay him according to his deeds.^{w}
3 In the womb he grasped his brother's heel;^{x}
  as a man he struggled^y with God.
4 He struggled with the angel and overcame him;
  he wept and begged for his favor.
He found him at Bethel^z
  and talked with him there—
5 the LORD God Almighty,
  the LORD is his name^a of renown!
6 But you must return to your God;
  maintain love and justice,^{b}
  and wait for your God always.^{c}

7 The merchant uses dishonest scales;^{d}
  he loves to defraud.
8 Ephraim boasts,
  "I am very rich; I have become wealthy.^{e}
With all my wealth they will not find in me
  any iniquity or sin."

9 "I am the LORD your God,
  ₗwho brought you₎ out of^b Egypt;^{f}
I will make you live in tents^g again,
  as in the days of your appointed feasts.
10 I spoke to the prophets,
  gave them many visions
  and told parables^h through them."^{i}

11 Is Gilead wicked?^{j}
  Its people are worthless!
Do they sacrifice bulls in Gilgal?^{k}
  Their altars will be like piles of stones
  on a plowed field.^{l}
12 Jacob fled to the country of Aram$^{c;m}$
  Israel served to get a wife,
  and to pay for her he tended sheep.^{n}
13 The LORD used a prophet to bring Israel up from Egypt,
  by a prophet he cared for him.^{o}

^{a} 2 Jacob means he grasps the heel (figuratively, he deceives). ^{b} 9 Or God / ever since you were in
^{c} 12 That is, Northwest Mesopotamia

Hosea 11:12—12:14

Using Jacob (Gen. 25–35) as an example, Hosea tried to persuade his audience to "return to [their] God" as Jacob had finally done, to exhibit steadfast love for the God who had made such great promises to (and through) Jacob, to follow the just practices of the law, and to wait for God in hard times (Hos. 12:6). They couldn't determine their own destiny through manipulation and dishonesty. They could only listen to God and learn from how he had dealt with Jacob.

To compensate for God's perceived weakness and their own inability to deal with reality, his people were lying, double-crossing, pretending, and twisting the truth to get what they wanted—in the process deceiving themselves into thinking they were without fault.

It's possible for us to think that we have a close relationship to God while we're cheating someone else. Even "good, religious" people sometimes practice deceit. But there is a direct relationship between our actions and our hearts. Those who consistently lie and cheat aren't demonstrating real love for God.

[14] But Ephraim has bitterly provoked him to anger;
 his Lord will leave upon him the guilt of his bloodshed[p]
 and will repay him for his contempt. [q]

The LORD's Anger Against Israel

13 When Ephraim spoke, men trembled;[r]
 he was exalted[s] in Israel.
 But he became guilty of Baal worship[t] and died.
[2] Now they sin more and more;
 they make idols for themselves from their silver,[u]
cleverly fashioned images,
 all of them the work of craftsmen.
It is said of these people,
 "They offer human sacrifice
 and kiss[a] the calf-idols. [v]"
[3] Therefore they will be like the morning mist,
 like the early dew that disappears,[w]
 like chaff[x] swirling from a threshing floor,[y]
 like smoke[z] escaping through a window.

[4] "But I am the LORD your God,
 ⌊who brought you⌋ out of[b] Egypt. [a]
You shall acknowledge no God but me,[b]
 no Savior[c] except me.
[5] I cared for you in the desert,
 in the land of burning heat.
[6] When I fed them, they were satisfied;
 when they were satisfied, they became proud;
 then they forgot me. [d]
[7] So I will come upon them like a lion,
 like a leopard I will lurk by the path.
[8] Like a bear robbed of her cubs, [e]
 I will attack them and rip them open.
Like a lion I will devour them;
 a wild animal will tear them apart. [f]

[9] "You are destroyed, O Israel,
 because you are against me,[g] against your helper. [h]
[10] Where is your king,[i] that he may save you?
 Where are your rulers in all your towns,
 of whom you said,
 'Give me a king and princes'?[j]
[11] So in my anger I gave you a king,
 and in my wrath I took him away. [k]
[12] The guilt of Ephraim is stored up,

---

[a] 2 Or "Men who sacrifice / kiss   [b] 4 Or God / ever since you were in

---

12:14
[p] Eze 18:13
[q] Da 11:18

13:1
[r] Jdg 12:1 [s] Jdg 8:1
[t] Hos 11:2

13:2
[u] Isa 46:6; Jer 10:4
[v] Isa 44:17-20

13:3
[w] Hos 6:4
[x] Isa 17:13
[y] Da 2:35 [z] Ps 68:2

13:4
[a] Hos 12:9
[b] Ex 20:3
[c] Isa 43:11;
45:21-22

13:6
[d] Dt 32:12-15;
Hos 2:13

13:8
[e] 2Sa 17:8
[f] Ps 50:22

13:9
[g] Jer 2:17-19
[h] Dt 33:29
13:10
[i] 2Ki 17:4 [j] 1Sa 8:6;
Hos 8:4

13:11
[k] 1Ki 14:10;
Hos 10:7

Hosea 13:1–16

This passage is about God's past grace to Israel and the death of Israel as a nation. God sees sin as rejection of and ingratitude for his gracious care in the past. Any feeling of human self-sufficiency that doesn't give the Lord credit for the marvelous things he has done is pride, which God hates. Israel would eventually be held accountable for her guilt (vv. 12,16). And no human rulers or leaders can protect people from the incredible power of God's wrath when the Judgment Day arrives (vv. 7–11). Yet death and destruction won't nullify God's plans. He has the final victory (v. 14).

The amazing declaration of God's power over death in verse 14 pictures one of his final acts of grace. Paul used this promise in 1 Corinthians 15:55 to remind followers of Christ that there is hope and life after death. Sin and death won't have the final victory over God's plan to redeem the world. In light of God's past, present, and future care for us, how should we live today? Can we simply forget what he has done and proudly act as though we can take care of things ourselves?

13:12
l Dt 32:34
13:13
m Isa 13:8;
Mic 4:9-10
n Isa 66:9

his sins are kept on record.*l*

13 Pains as of a woman in childbirth*m* come to him,
but he is a child without wisdom;
when the time arrives,
he does not come to the opening of the womb.*n*

13:14
o Ps 49:15;
Eze 37:12-13
p 1Co 15:55*

14 "I will ransom them from the power of the grave*a; o*
I will redeem them from death.
Where, O death, are your plagues?
Where, O grave,*a* is your destruction?*p*

"I will have no compassion,

13:15
q Hos 10:1
r Eze 19:12
s Jer 51:36
t Jer 20:5

15   even though he thrives*q* among his brothers.
An east wind*r* from the LORD will come,
blowing in from the desert;
his spring will fail
and his well dry up.*s*
His storehouse will be plundered*t*
of all its treasures.

13:16
u Hos 10:2
v Hos 7:14
w Hos 11:6
x 2Ki 8:12;
Hos 10:14
y 2Ki 15:16;
Isa 13:16

16 The people of Samaria must bear their guilt,*u*
because they have rebelled*v* against their God.
They will fall by the sword;*w*
their little ones will be dashed*x* to the ground,
their pregnant women*y* ripped open."

Repentance to Bring Blessing

14:1
z Hos 5:5

14 Return, O Israel, to the LORD your God.
Your sins have been your downfall!*z*
2 Take words with you
and return to the LORD.

a 14 Hebrew *Sheol*

Snapshots

13:14

Origen

Origen (c. 185–253?) was an early theologian, intellectual, and vigorous advocate of Christianity. Born in Alexandria of Christian parents who provided him a good education, he was thrust into active Christian service prior to the age of seventeen due to persecution and his father's martyrdom. By eighteen he was placed in charge of Christian education in a developing school. Origen, preferring the advanced classes, developed a comprehensive approach to knowledge, employing all the learned disciplines of his day. His skill appealed to the philosophical, many of whom converted to Christianity.

> Origen has been called the pioneer of mission studies.

Disagreement with his bishop prompted Origen to leave Alexandria for Caesarea in 231. While a presbyter there, he expanded his prolific literary output. He was imprisoned and tortured in 250 in a new wave of persecution, dying soon afterward at the age of seventy.

Origen has been called the pioneer of mission studies. His *De Principiis* ("on first principles") was the first theological treatise written from a reverent, intellectual perspective, and his commentaries brought the Bible into interaction with contemporary intellectual thought. Origen's approach to Christianity was inclusive; he embraced believers everywhere and traveled widely. Following his death, he was denounced as a heretic and never entered the calendar of saints.

Say to him:
"Forgive all our sins
and receive us graciously, *a*
that we may offer the fruit of our lips. *a b*
3 Assyria cannot save us;
we will not mount war-horses. *c*
We will never again say 'Our gods' *d*
to what our own hands have made,
for in you the fatherless *e* find compassion."

4 "I will heal *f* their waywardness
and love them freely, *g*
for my anger has turned away from them.
5 I will be like the dew to Israel;
he will blossom like a lily. *h*
Like a cedar of Lebanon *i*
he will send down his roots; *i*
6   his young shoots will grow.
His splendor will be like an olive tree, *k*
his fragrance like a cedar of Lebanon. *l*
7 Men will dwell again in his shade. *m*
He will flourish like the grain.
He will blossom like a vine,
and his fame will be like the wine *n* from Lebanon. *o*
8 O Ephraim, what more have I *b* to do with idols? *p*
I will answer him and care for him.
I am like a green pine tree;
your fruitfulness comes from me."

9 Who is wise? *q* He will realize these things.
Who is discerning? He will understand them. *r*
The ways of the LORD are right; *s*
the righteous walk *t* in them,
but the rebellious stumble in them.

a 2 Or *offer our lips as sacrifices of bulls*   *b 8* Or *What more has Ephraim*

14:2
a Mic 7:18-19
b Heb 13:15

14:3
c Ps 33:17; Isa 31:1
d Hos 8:6
e Ps 10:14; 68:5

14:4
f Hos 6:1
g Zep 3:17

14:5
h SS 2:1 *i* Isa 35:2
i Job 29:19

14:6
k Ps 52:8; Jer 11:16
l SS 4:11
14:7
m Ps 91:1-4
n Hos 2:22
o Eze 17:23

14:8
p ver 3

14:9
q Ps 107:43
r Pr 10:29; Isa 1:28
s Ps 111:7-8;
Zep 3:5; Ac 13:10
t Isa 26:7

Hosea 14:1–9

We don't know whether anyone actually prayed his model prayer of confession (vv. 2–3), but Hosea clearly revealed how God will respond when people turn to him: He will heal their waywardness, since they don't seem able on their own to resist the temptation to turn back the other way. People are inherently weak, unable to do what they should or even what they want to do (see Rom. 7). And sinning is more than a simple act of will. Past choices influence the pattern of later choices.

True repentance isn't bringing a gift to bribe or appease God, or a feeling of sorrow or shame about having gotten caught doing something wrong. It isn't about "turning over a new leaf" without a complete change of priorities and loyalties. It is about genuinely turning from a life of sin to serve God, and it's an essential part of God's plan to change this world and bring in his kingdom. Part of the reason we resist following God is that we think we can do a better job of directing our own lives. Hosea's final words urge us to make the best choice.

2:13 "RETURN TO THE LORD YOUR GOD, FOR HE IS GRACIOUS
AND COMPASSIONATE, SLOW TO ANGER AND ABOUNDING IN
LOVE."

INTRODUCTION TO
Joel

AUTHOR
The prophet Joel is identified as the book's author in 1:1.

DATE WRITTEN
The time of writing is unknown. Dates as early as 835 B.C. and as late as 400 B.C. have been suggested.

ORIGINAL READERS
Joel warned the people of Judah (the southern kingdom) of coming judgment and urged them to repent and turn to God.

TIMELINE

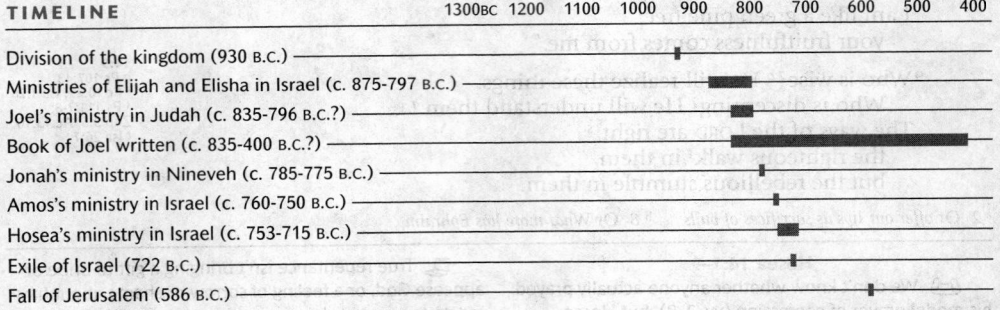

	1300BC	1200	1100	1000	900	800	700	600	500	400

Division of the kingdom (930 B.C.)
Ministries of Elijah and Elisha in Israel (c. 875-797 B.C.)
Joel's ministry in Judah (c. 835-796 B.C.?)
Book of Joel written (c. 835-400 B.C.?)
Jonah's ministry in Nineveh (c. 785-775 B.C.)
Amos's ministry in Israel (c. 760-750 B.C.)
Hosea's ministry in Israel (c. 753-715 B.C.)
Exile of Israel (722 B.C.)
Fall of Jerusalem (586 B.C.)

THEMES
Joel described the devastation caused by a locust plague and tied it to the coming day of judgment, referred to here and elsewhere in the prophetic books as the "day of the LORD." Joel revealed God's passionate concern for his people and his desire for intimacy with them. The book includes the following themes:

1. *Judgment.* Joel's description of the coming day of judgment on Israel foreshadowed a greater future judgment. The soon-coming judgment would be against God's own people, while the later, greater judgment would target their enemies. Joel described the judgment against Israel as the "great and dreadful day of the LORD" (2:31), "a day of darkness and gloom, a day of clouds and blackness" (2:2). The greater future judgment refers to a day when the nations will be held accountable for their treatment of God's people (3:2–16,19), who themselves will be protected and blessed (3:16–18,20–21).

2. *Repentance and salvation.* Joel called on everyone to repent: old and young (1:2–3; 2:16), drunkards (1:5), farmers (1:11), and priests (1:13; 2:17). Externals aren't enough (2:12); God requires sincere repentance (2:13). In response to heartfelt repentance and trust in his grace, love, and compassion (2:13), God forgives and restores (2:18–32). Most notable in this book is God's promise of the outpouring of the Holy Spirit on all people—young and old, men and women (2:28–29)—and the promise of salvation for "everyone who calls on the name of the LORD" (2:32).

FAITH IN ACTION
The pages of Joel contain life lessons and role models of faith—people who challenge believers to put their faith in action.

Role Models

- JOEL (2:12–14) warned God's people of coming judgment if they didn't repent and return to God. Do you know someone who needs a similar warning (or does it apply to you personally)? Will you allow God to use you to spread the message of his gracious gift of salvation through Jesus Christ?

- THOSE WHO CALL ON GOD (2:32) are saved and restored (3:17–21). Are you or is someone you know in need of deliverance? Turn to God today.

Challenges

- Fast for one day as a sign of penitence and humility (1:14; 2:15). Evaluate how the discipline of fasting helps you recognize your self-indulgent tendencies.

- Prepare yourself for Christ's return by keeping your heart humble (2:13). Humility is indeed a state of the heart, not an outward act that can be feigned.

- Now that the Holy Spirit has been given to the church (Acts 2:1–21), reflect on the ways the Spirit works in and through your life. Thank God for this precious privilege.

- Be energized to share the gospel with those around you, knowing that the day of judgment is near but that "everyone who calls on the name of the Lord will be saved" (2:32).

- Take comfort in knowing that, though Christ's return will bring judgment (3:1–16), it also will result in great blessing for God's people (3:17–21).

OUTLINE

I. The Locust Invasion and Call to Repentance (1:1—2:17)
   A. A Call to Mourning and Prayer (1:1–14)
   B. The Announcement of the Day of the Lord (1:15—2:11)
   C. A Call to Repentance and Prayer (2:12–17)
II. Salvation in the Day of the Lord (2:18—3:21)
   A. The Lord's Restoration of Judah (2:18–27)
   B. The Lord's Renewal of His People (2:28–32)
   C. The Coming of the Day of the Lord (3)

1

The word of the Lord that came[a] to Joel[b] son of Pethuel.

a Jer 1:2 *b* Ac 2:16

An Invasion of Locusts

2 Hear this,[c] you elders;
   listen, all who live in the land.[d]

1:2
c Hos 5:1 *d* Hos 4:1

Joel 1:1

Joel began his prophecy by simply identifying himself and his father/family. More importantly, he clearly declared the divine source of his message. The Old Testament prophets typically began their prophecies in much the same way. They were mouthpieces for God, not necessarily great intellectuals or skilled orators.

Not much is known about Joel's personal circumstances, except the little that can be gleaned from the book. The prophet Joel can't be identified with any of the 12 other figures in the Old Testament with the same name. Nor is he mentioned outside the books of Joel and Acts (Acts 2:16). Like the Lord's other prophets, he wasn't into self-promotion. How many of God's great servants came without pedigrees and ministered in relative obscurity? Can that be said of you as well?

Joel 1:2–12

Joel commanded the people—from the eldest downward—to give careful attention to his words. None could recall from previous experience such an intense

1435

Has anything like this ever happened in your days
  or in the days of your forefathers? [e]
[3] Tell it to your children, [f]
  and let your children tell it to their children,
  and their children to the next generation.
[4] What the locust swarm has left
  the great locusts have eaten;
what the great locusts have left
  the young locusts have eaten;
what the young locusts have left
  other locusts [a] have eaten. [g]

[5] Wake up, you drunkards, and weep!
  Wail, all you drinkers of wine; [h]
wail because of the new wine,
  for it has been snatched from your lips.
[6] A nation has invaded my land,
  powerful and without number; [i]
it has the teeth [j] of a lion,
  the fangs of a lioness.
[7] It has laid waste [k] my vines
  and ruined my fig trees. [l]
It has stripped off their bark
  and thrown it away,
  leaving their branches white.

1:2
e Joel 2:2
1:3
f Ex 10:2; Ps 78:4

1:4
g Dt 28:39; Na 3:15

1:5
h Joel 3:3

1:6
i Joel 2:2,11,25
j Rev 9:8

1:7
k Isa 5:6 l Am 4:9

---

[a] 4 The precise meaning of the four Hebrew words used here for locusts is uncertain.

---

and devastating calamity as the locust plague that had fallen on them. The prophet Amos mentioned the utter destruction left behind by a locust plague in the northern kingdom (Amos 4:9) but noted that there had been no resultant turning to God by the people. Joel recognized the seriousness of the situation: The locusts were in effect God's army in judgment on the southern kingdom (cf. 2:11,25).

Although Joel called for repentance, drunkenness (see v. 5) was the only specific sin mentioned in the book. It suggests a self-indulgent lifestyle (cf. Isa. 28:7–8; Amos 4:1) pursued by those who valued material things more than spiritual. The parallels with today's Western society are obvious and alarming. What evidences have you seen of disasters or economic slowdowns strengthening your church locally? The church nationally? Internationally? In what areas of the world today is the church seeing the healthiest levels of growth, both spiritually and numerically?

1:2–3

Biblical Attitudes Toward Children

The Bible makes clear that children are the future—of the world and of God's kingdom. Accordingly, they deserve to be treated with respect. Such respect involves:

Attention:
"When the chief priests and the teachers of the law . . . [heard] the children shouting in the temple area, 'Hosanna to the Son of David,' they were indignant. 'Do you hear what these children are saying?' they asked [Jesus]. 'Yes,' replied Jesus, 'have you never read, "From the lips of children and infants you have ordained praise"?' " (Matt. 21:15–16).

Caution:
"If anyone causes one of these little ones who believe in me to sin,

it would be better for him to have a large millstone hung around his neck and to be drowned in the depths of the sea" (Matt. 18:6).

Faithfulness:
"Children, obey your parents in the Lord . . . Fathers, do not exasperate your children" (Eph. 6:1).

Gratitude:
"Sons are a heritage from the LORD, children a reward from him . . . Blessed is the man whose quiver is full of them" Ps. 127:3,5).

Imitation:
"I tell you the truth, unless you change and become like little children, you will never enter the kingdom of heaven" (Matt. 18:23).

Training:
"Bring up [your children] in the training and instruction of the Lord" (Eph. 6:4).

Welcome:
"[Jesus said], 'Whoever welcomes a little child like this in my name welcomes me'" (Matt. 18:5).

8 Mourn like a virgin[a] in sackcloth[m]
grieving for the husband[b] of her youth.
9 Grain offerings and drink offerings[n]
are cut off from the house of the LORD.
The priests are in mourning,
those who minister before the LORD.
10 The fields are ruined,
the ground is dried up[c];[o]
the grain is destroyed,
the new wine[p] is dried up,
the oil fails.
11 Despair, you farmers,[q]
wail, you vine growers;
grieve for the wheat and the barley,
because the harvest of the field is destroyed.[r]
12 The vine is dried up
and the fig tree is withered;
the pomegranate, the palm and the apple tree—
all the trees of the field—are dried up.[s]
Surely the joy of mankind
is withered away.

A Call to Repentance

13 Put on sackcloth,[t] O priests, and mourn;
wail, you who minister[u] before the altar.

1:8 [m] ver 13; Isa 22:12; Am 8:10
1:9 [n] Hos 9:4; Joel 2:14,17
1:10 [o] Isa 24:4 [p] Hos 9:2
1:11 [q] Jer 14:3-4; Am 5:16 [r] Isa 17:11
1:12 [s] Hag 2:19
1:13 [t] Jer 4:8 [u] Joel 2:17

[a] 8 Or *young woman* [b] 8 Or *betrothed* [c] 10 Or *ground mourns*

Joel 1:13–20

Joel challenged Judah's spiritual leaders, the priests, to call for a "sacred assembly" (vv. 13–18) and then gave an example of a proper heart condition before God (vv. 19–20). The call for national prayer and fasting signaled an extraordinary event (cf. Neh. 9:1–3; Jer. 36:9).

Snapshots

1:11–12

Wang Chao and Lina

Scores of Chinese citizens emigrate to Canada annually seeking opportunity. But Wang Chao and his wife, Lina, returned to their native country to serve the poor. Chao entered the University of Montreal in 1990 to study urban planning and completed a Ph.D. five years later. Through the influence of a professor, he became a Christian. He married Lina, landed a job, and was eager to apply his skills. After years of hard work and frugality, life looked promising.

Then a Christian relief organization called. Was Chao interested in managing its first development project in southwest China? After months of discussion, reflection, and prayer, the couple decided to try it for six months.

In 1997, the Wangs arrived in Yunnan province. Living conditions were rudimentary. Chao and Lina, who had lived in major cities like Beijing, had never witnessed the struggles faced by farmers in Yunnan, many of whom owned only a pot and some firewood. Chao gradually won their confidence by listening to their concerns and ideas and working alongside them. "Every time I go into the community now, the people welcome me," says Chao.

> **Chao gradually won [the farmers'] confidence by listening to their concerns and ideas and working alongside them.**

After six months, the Wangs decided to stay on. When they do return to Canada, they will have the satisfaction of knowing they have helped thousands.

Come, spend the night in sackcloth,
    you who minister before my God;
for the grain offerings and drink offerings[v]
    are withheld from the house of your God.

14 Declare a holy fast;[w]
    call a sacred assembly.
Summon the elders
    and all who live in the land
to the house of the LORD your God,
    and cry out[x] to the LORD.

15 Alas for that[y] day!
    For the day of the LORD[z] is near;
    it will come like destruction from the Almighty.[a]

16 Has not the food been cut off[a]
    before our very eyes—
joy and gladness
    from the house of our God?[b]

17 The seeds are shriveled
    beneath the clods.[b][c]
The storehouses are in ruins,
    the granaries have been broken down,
    for the grain has dried up.
18 How the cattle moan!
    The herds mill about
because they have no pasture;
    even the flocks of sheep are suffering.

19 To you, O LORD, I call,[d]
    for fire[e] has devoured the open pastures[f]
    and flames have burned up all the trees of the field.

20 Even the wild animals pant for you;[g]
    the streams of water have dried up[h]
    and fire has devoured the open pastures.

An Army of Locusts

2 Blow the trumpet[j] in Zion;[i]
    sound the alarm on my holy hill.
Let all who live in the land tremble,
    for the day of the LORD[k] is coming.
It is close at hand[l]—

2 a day of darkness[m] and gloom,[n]
    a day of clouds and blackness.
Like dawn spreading across the mountains

---

a 15 Hebrew *Shaddai*   b 17 The meaning of the Hebrew for this word is uncertain.

But dreadful times called for decisive measures.

All the land had suffered an unprecedented locust invasion, apparently accompanied by a terrible drought. To Joel, God's message was plain: The barrenness of the land reflected the dryness and decay of the people's hearts. God had judged them. Even the animal world seemed to sense this (v. 20). How much more should the people! If their hearts were to remain unmoved and unrepentant, a worse judgment loomed ahead.

Many people refer indiscriminately to all natural disasters as "acts of God." Do you agree with this assessment? Clearly, not all catastrophes reflect God's disfavor.

Most of the time we are at a loss to account for the reasons behind earthquakes, hurricanes, droughts, and the like. But while they may not always be punishments, they almost always function as wakeup calls for those who are alert. What is your typical response when you hear of international or national crises?

Joel 2:1–11

Joel envisioned the invading locusts approaching "Zion" (Jerusalem, the capital of Judah). The "trumpet" was the shofar, made from a ram's horn and used here as a signal of imminent danger (cf. Jer. 4:5; 6:1; Ezek. 33:3). Its blast brought trembling fear to the people

a large and mighty army[o] comes,
    such as never was of old[p]
    nor ever will be in ages to come.

[3] Before them fire devours,
    behind them a flame blazes.
Before them the land is like the garden of Eden,[q]
    behind them, a desert waste[r]—
    nothing escapes them.
[4] They have the appearance of horses;[s]
    they gallop along like cavalry.
[5] With a noise like that of chariots[t]
    they leap over the mountaintops,
like a crackling fire[u] consuming stubble,
    like a mighty army drawn up for battle.

[6] At the sight of them, nations are in anguish;[v]
    every face turns pale.[w]
[7] They charge like warriors;
    they scale walls like soldiers.
They all march in line,
    not swerving[x] from their course.
[8] They do not jostle each other;
    each marches straight ahead.
They plunge through defenses
    without breaking ranks.
[9] They rush upon the city;
    they run along the wall.
They climb into the houses;
    like thieves they enter through the windows.[y]

[10] Before them the earth shakes,[z]
    the sky trembles,
the sun and moon are darkened,[a]
    and the stars no longer shine.[b]
[11] The LORD[c] thunders
    at the head of his army;
his forces are beyond number,
    and mighty are those who obey his command.
The day of the LORD is great;[d]
    it is dreadful.
    Who can endure it?[e]

Rend Your Heart

[12] "Even now," declares the LORD,
    "return[f] to me with all your heart,
    with fasting and weeping and mourning."

Cross references

2:2 o Joel 1:6 p Joel 1:2

2:3 q Ge 2:8 r Ps 105:34-35

2:4 s Rev 9:7

2:5 t Rev 9:9 u Isa 5:24; 30:30

2:6 v Isa 13:8 w Na 2:10

2:7 x Isa 5:27

2:9 y Jer 9:21
2:10 z Ps 18:7 a Mt 24:29 b Isa 13:10; Eze 32:8

2:11 c Joel 1:15 d Zep 1:14; Rev 18:8 e Eze 22:14

2:12 f Jer 4:1; Hos 12:6

(cf. Amos 3:6). Just as Isaiah had seen the Assyrians (Isa. 10:5–6; 13:4–5) and Jeremiah the Babylonians (Jer. 25:9; 43:10) as the Lord's weapons, so Joel saw the locusts as the Lord's army (v. 11; cf. Jos. 5:14; Ps. 68:17; Hab. 3:8–9)—the army with which he would come against his enemies in the day of the Lord (see Joel 3:9–11).

"The day of the LORD," a term found here in verses 1 and 11 and three other times in Joel (1:15; 2:31; 3:14), is a crucial concept in Scripture and the dominant theme of this book. The phrase often refers to God's critical intervention in history, such as through the invasion of locusts in Joel. It can also refer to Christ's return to con-

summate history (cf. Mal. 4:5; 1 Thess. 5:2; 2 Peter 3:10). At the end of this passage, Joel called the day of the Lord "dreadful" and asked, "Who can endure it?" Those of us who have responded to the gospel know that it truly is Good News: Trusting in Christ transforms that dreadful day for us into an event of deliverance and celebration.

Joel 2:12–17

Joel again summoned the people to repentance and prayer. In the last passage, he had given the command to "blow the trumpet in Zion" as an alarm (2:1); now he gave the same command, but as a call for a solemn assembly (v. 15; cf. 1:14). No one would be exempted from

2:13
g Ps 34:18;
Isa 57:15
h Job 1:20 / Ex 34:6
i Jer 18:8

13 Rend your heart [g]
  and not your garments. [h]
Return to the LORD your God,
  for he is gracious and compassionate,
slow to anger and abounding in love, [i]
  and he relents from sending calamity. [j]

2:14
k Jer 26:3
l Hag 2:19
m Joel 1:13

14 Who knows? He may turn [k] and have pity
  and leave behind a blessing [l]—
grain offerings and drink offerings [m]
  for the LORD your God.

2:15
n Nu 10:2
o Jer 36:9
p Joel 1:14

15 Blow the trumpet [n] in Zion,
  declare a holy fast, [o]
  call a sacred assembly. [p]

2:16
q Ex 19:10,22
r Ps 19:5

16 Gather the people,
  consecrate [q] the assembly;
bring together the elders,
  gather the children,
  those nursing at the breast.
Let the bridegroom [r] leave his room
  and the bride her chamber.

2:17
s Eze 8:16;
Mt 23:35
t Dt 9:26-29;
Ps 44:13
u Ps 42:3

17 Let the priests, who minister before the LORD,
  weep between the temple porch and the altar. [s]
Let them say, "Spare your people, O LORD.
  Do not make your inheritance an object of scorn, [t]
  a byword among the nations.
Why should they say among the peoples,
  'Where is their God?' [u] "

The LORD's Answer

2:18
v Zec 1:14

18 Then the LORD will be jealous [v] for his land
  and take pity on his people.

2:19
w Jer 31:12
x Eze 34:29

19 The LORD will reply [a] to them:

"I am sending you grain, new wine and oil, [w]
  enough to satisfy you fully;
never again will I make you
  an object of scorn [x] to the nations.

a 18,19 Or LORD was jealous . . . / and took pity . . . / 19The LORD replied

---

attending. The purpose was to implore God to spare his people—not just for their good but so that they, as God's "inheritance," might not be a disgrace before the world or his reputation be soiled by their evil deeds.

Verse 13 reminds us that God has compassion for all in need (cf. Jonah 4:2) and that he is a God of love who has revealed himself to people in redemptive grace (cf. Ex. 34:6–7). This is the *height* of his compassion. Its *length* is seen in his slowness to anger, its *breadth* in his righteous concern for humanity's spiritual welfare, and its *depth* in his willingness to reach down in forgiveness to humankind in its evil condition. Take a moment to reflect on this wonder. Then read Paul's stirring words in Romans 8:37–39.

Joel 2:18–27

Based on fulfillment of his instructions regarding repentance and worship in the previous passage, God promised to bless his people. The swarms of locusts were compared to a "northern army" (v. 20), since Is-

rael's most dreaded enemies (especially Assyria and Babylon) came from the north. God would restore what had been lost, so that neither land nor animals nor the people themselves need continue to live in fear. The people would experience such complete fullness that they would praise the Lord and experience the security he alone could give.

Does the word "jealous" sound like it could ever be a good thing? Joel said, in verse 18, that the Lord would be jealous for his land and people. Actually, *jealousy* is part of God's vocabulary of love. As part of the second commandment, God said, "You shall not bow down to [idols] or worship them; for I, the LORD your God, am a jealous God" (Ex. 20:5; cf. Joel 2:27). In Exodus 34:14 he even added that his "name is Jealous." How does it make you feel to know that God both blesses you and disciplines you because he's "jealous" for you? How does this concept expand your understanding of God?

20 "I will drive the northern army*y* far from you,
    pushing it into a parched and barren land,
with its front columns going into the eastern*z* sea*a*
    and those in the rear into the western sea.*b*
And its stench*a* will go up;
    its smell will rise."

Surely he has done great things.*c*
21   Be not afraid,*b* O land;
    be glad and rejoice.
Surely the LORD has done great things.*c*
22   Be not afraid, O wild animals,
    for the open pastures are becoming green.*d*
The trees are bearing their fruit;
    the fig tree and the vine yield their riches.*e*
23 Be glad, O people of Zion,
    rejoice*f* in the LORD your God,
for he has given you
    the autumn rains in righteousness.*d*
He sends you abundant showers,
    both autumn and spring rains,*g* as before.
24 The threshing floors will be filled with grain;
    the vats will overflow*h* with new wine*i* and oil.

25 "I will repay you for the years the locusts have eaten—
    the great locust and the young locust,
    the other locusts and the locust swarm*e*—
my great army that I sent among you.
26 You will have plenty to eat, until you are full,*j*
    and you will praise*k* the name of the LORD your God,
    who has worked wonders*l* for you;
never again will my people be shamed.
27 Then you will know that I am in Israel,
    that I am the LORD*m* your God,
    and that there is no other;
never again will my people be shamed.

The Day of the LORD

28 "And afterward,
    I will pour out my Spirit*n* on all people.
    Your sons and daughters will prophesy,

2:20
y Jer 1:14-15
z Zec 14:8
a Isa 34:3

2:21
b Isa 54:4;
Zep 3:16-17
c Ps 126:3

2:22
d Ps 65:12
e Joel 1:18-20

2:23
f Ps 149:2; Isa 12:6;
41:16; Hab 3:18;
Zec 10:7 *g* Lev 26:4

2:24
h Lev 26:10;
Mal 3:10 *i* Am 9:13

2:26
j Lev 26:5 *k* Isa 62:9
l Ps 126:3; Isa 25:1

2:27
m Joel 3:17

2:28
n Eze 39:29

a 20 That is, the Dead Sea   *b 20* That is, the Mediterranean   *c 20* Or *rise. / Surely it has done great things."*   *d 23* Or / *the teacher for righteousness:*   *e 25* The precise meaning of the four Hebrew words used here for locusts is uncertain.

Joel 2:28–32

If the previous section dealt with the near future, this one prophesied events further removed. In fact, the remainder of the book of Joel reveals God's ultimate intentions. Two primary thoughts are included: his promise of personal provision in the lives of his own (2:28–32) and the prediction of his final triumph on their behalf at the close of human history (ch. 3).

God intended to pour out his Holy Spirit, not just on selected individuals for particular tasks as he had done in the Old Testament, but on all believers. This would usher in a time of renewed spiritual activity (cf. Num. 11:24–29; 12:6). Along with the outpouring of the Spirit would come the outworking of salvation for those who

truly trusted God as their Redeemer (v. 32). Joel closed the chapter by balancing this with another truth. While salvation-deliverance will be the experience of those who truly "[call] on the name of the LORD," God himself will "call" or summon the remnant (those who have remained true to him).

At Pentecost (Acts 2:1–41) two streams of prophecy met and blended together. Christ's promise of the Spirit's coming was directly fulfilled (see Luke 24:49; John 14:16–18; 15:26; 16:7–15; Acts 1:4–5,8; 2:33), and Joel's prophecy became a partial reality. It awaits complete fulfillment in the miraculous signs heralding the Day of the Lord (Joel 2:30–31; Acts 2:19–20). Meanwhile, like an ever-rolling river, the central current of God's

your old men will dream dreams,
your young men will see visions.
29 Even on my servants,[o] both men and women,
    I will pour out my Spirit in those days.
30 I will show wonders in the heavens[p]
    and on the earth,[q]
    blood and fire and billows of smoke.
31 The sun will be turned to darkness[r]
    and the moon to blood
    before the coming of the great and dreadful day of the LORD.[s]
32 And everyone who calls
    on the name of the LORD will be saved;[t]
for on Mount Zion[u] and in Jerusalem
    there will be deliverance,[v]
    as the LORD has said,
among the survivors[w]
    whom the LORD calls.

The Nations Judged

3 "In those days and at that time,
    when I restore the fortunes[x] of Judah and Jerusalem,
2 I will gather all nations
    and bring them down to the Valley of Jehoshaphat.[a]
There I will enter into judgment[y] against them
    concerning my inheritance, my people Israel,

[a] 2 *Jehoshaphat* means *the LORD judges*; also in verse 12.

2:29
o 1Co 12:13;
Gal 3:28

2:30
p Lk 21:11
q Mk 13:24-25

2:31
r Mt 24:29
s Isa 13:9-10;
Mal 4:1,5

2:32
t Ac 2:17-21*;
Ro 10:13*
u Isa 46:13
v Ob 1:17
w Isa 11:11;
Mic 4:7; Ro 9:27

3:1
x Jer 16:15

3:2
y Eze 36:5

---

promise sweeps steadily onward toward that final shore. There the Great Controller of the flow of Earth's history will gather the various waves of prophecy to himself in total fulfillment.

Snapshots

2:28–29

Gregory the Illuminator

Gregory the Illuminator (c. 240–332) is known as the apostle to the Armenians. As a young man of aristocratic descent, he was forced to flee Persian-occupied Armenia. Exiled in Cappadocian Caesarea, he was converted to Christianity, returning home after the expulsion of the Persians to preach among the totally pagan population. King Trdat II arrested Gregory as an enemy of the gods, and he spent 15 agonizing years in a dungeon, during which time extensive and brutal persecution of Christians prevailed.

Then Trdat's sister saw Gregory in a dream. His face illuminated, he was calling for an end to the persecution. Gregory's prayers were instrumental in restoring Trdat's failing health and sanity—and prompting his conversion.

> More than a decade before Christianity gained tolerance in the Roman Empire, it became Armenia's state religion.

The converted king nominated Gregory as catholicus of the Armenian Church. With Trdat's encouragement and active participation, Christianity spread rapidly among the populace, with mass conversions, transformation of pagan temples into churches, and ordination of converted pagan priests. More than a decade before Christianity gained tolerance in the Roman Empire, it became Armenia's state religion. Legends of Gregory's feats—four million baptisms and four hundred Episcopal consecrations—are likely exaggerated, but his missionary zeal and success were indeed inspired.

for they scattered my people among the nations
    and divided up my land.
³They cast lots for my people
    and traded boys for prostitutes;
they sold girls for wine[z]
    that they might drink.

⁴"Now what have you against me, O Tyre and Sidon[a] and all you regions of Philistia? Are you repaying me for something I have done? If you are paying me back, I will swiftly and speedily return on your own heads what you have done.[b] ⁵For you took my silver and my gold and carried off my finest treasures to your temples.[c] ⁶You sold the people of Judah and Jerusalem to the Greeks, that you might send them far from their homeland.

⁷"See, I am going to rouse them out of the places to which you sold them,[d] and I will return on your own heads what you have done. ⁸I will sell your sons[e] and daughters to the people of Judah,[f] and they will sell them to the Sabeans, a nation far away." The LORD has spoken.

⁹Proclaim this among the nations:
    Prepare for war![g]
Rouse the warriors![h]
    Let all the fighting men draw near and attack.
¹⁰Beat your plowshares into swords
    and your pruning hooks[i] into spears.
Let the weakling[j] say,
    "I am strong!"
¹¹Come quickly, all you nations from every side,
    and assemble[k] there.

Bring down your warriors,[l] O LORD!

¹²"Let the nations be roused;
    let them advance into the Valley of Jehoshaphat,
for there I will sit
    to judge[m] all the nations on every side.
¹³Swing the sickle,
    for the harvest[n] is ripe.
Come, trample the grapes,
    for the winepress[o] is full
    and the vats overflow—
so great is their wickedness!"

¹⁴Multitudes, multitudes
    in the valley of decision!
For the day of the LORD[p] is near
    in the valley of decision.

3:3
z Am 2:6

3:4
a Mt 11:21
b Isa 34:8

3:5
c 2Ch 21:16-17

3:7
d Isa 43:5-6; Jer 23:8
3:8
e Isa 60:14
f Isa 14:2

3:9
g Isa 8:9 h Jer 46:4

3:10
i Isa 2:4; Mic 4:3
j Zec 12:8

3:11
k Eze 38:15-16; Zep 3:8 l Isa 13:3

3:12
m Isa 2:4
3:13
n Hos 6:11; Mt 13:39; Rev 14:15-19
o Rev 14:20

3:14
p Isa 34:2-8; Joel 1:15

Joel 3:1–16

Joel had a new and important announcement: In those future times (cf. 2:29) in which God will deal kindly with his covenant people (cf. Jer. 33:15–18), he will gather all nations together (cf. Zeph. 3:8) and judge them concerning their treatment of his own. The unchangeable God is still on the throne, directing all things to their appointed end (cf. Mic. 4:11–12).

The nations surrounding Judah are to gather for that final struggle that will close Earth's present history. In verse 13 God is pictured as sending his reapers into the harvest field (cf. Rev. 14:14–20) and to the winepress of judgment (Isa. 63:3). The nations are ripe for judgment. Their pitcher of wickedness is filled to overflowing.

In verses 14–16 the reader is transported to the scene of battle. The confused and clamoring throng of nations and the tumultuous uproar are vividly pictured (cf. Ezek. 38:21–23). The location, previously called "the Valley of Jehoshaphat" (vv. 2,12; cf. 2 Chron. 20:1–30), is now called "the valley of decision." In God's good grace you as a believer have likely made your decision long before this final day of reckoning. But the same can't necessarily be said of your brother-in-law, friend, neighbor, or coworker. Or of the millions, nearby and far away across the globe, who have never been told. Does this knowledge motivate your service in the kingdom of God?

15 The sun and moon will be darkened,
   and the stars no longer shine.
16 The LORD will roar from Zion
   and thunder from Jerusalem; *q*
   the earth and the sky will tremble. *r*
But the LORD will be a refuge for his people,
   a stronghold *s* for the people of Israel.

Blessings for God's People

17 "Then you will know that I, the LORD your God, *t*
   dwell in Zion, *u* my holy hill.
Jerusalem will be holy;
   never again will foreigners invade her.

18 "In that day the mountains will drip new wine,
   and the hills will flow with milk; *v*
all the ravines of Judah will run with water. *w*
A fountain will flow out of the LORD's house *x*
   and will water the valley of acacias. *a y*

19 But Egypt will be desolate,
   Edom a desert waste,
because of violence *z* done to the people of Judah,
   in whose land they shed innocent blood.
20 Judah will be inhabited forever *a*
   and Jerusalem through all generations.
21 Their bloodguilt, which I have not pardoned,
   I will pardon. *b*"

The LORD dwells in Zion!

---

a 18 Or Valley of Shittim

3:16
q Am 1:2
r Eze 38:19
s Jer 16:19

3:17
t Joel 2:27 *u* Isa 4:3

3:18
v Ex 3:8
w Isa 30:25; 35:6
x Rev 22:1-2
y Eze 47:1;
   Am 9:13

3:19
z Ob 1:10

3:20
a Am 9:15

3:21
b Eze 36:25

Joel 3:17–21

God promised to bless his people both negatively, by destroying their enemies, and positively, by giving them good things. Most importantly, in the Lord's end-times restoration of his people, he himself will "dwell" with them (vv. 17,21; cf. 2:27). Though a message of judgment, the book of Joel concluded with the blessings that will rest on the repentant, restored, and revitalized people of God.

The believer's destiny is to enjoy God's presence forever (Rev. 21:2–3). Already now we partake of that blessing in a limited measure through Christ's Spirit within us (John 16:7–14; 17:20–22; cf. Joel 2:28–29). Paul described the Holy Spirit as "a deposit guaranteeing our inheritance until the redemption of those who are God's possession" (Eph. 1:13–14; cf. 2 Cor. 1:22). May he be for us a conscious, ever-abiding presence that allows Christ's glory to shine through our lives!

INTRODUCTION TO
Amos

AUTHOR

Amos, a shepherd of Tekoa (a village about ten miles south of Jerusalem), wrote this book
(1:1). He was called by God to leave Judah and go to the northern kingdom of Israel (7:15) to
prophesy a message of judgment. He ministered in Israel from approximately 760 to 750 B.C.

DATE WRITTEN

The book of Amos was written between 760 and 750 B.C.

ORIGINAL READERS

Amos prophesied to the northern kingdom of Israel during a time of peace, success, and great
material prosperity.

TIMELINE

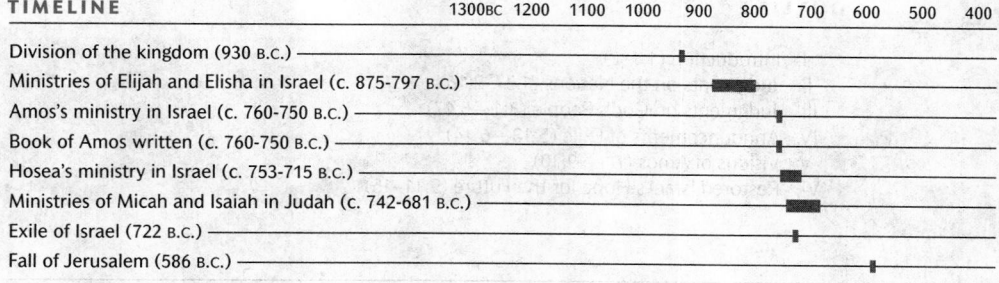

	1300BC	1200	1100	1000	900	800	700	600	500	400
Division of the kingdom (930 B.C.)										
Ministries of Elijah and Elisha in Israel (c. 875-797 B.C.)										
Amos's ministry in Israel (c. 760-750 B.C.)										
Book of Amos written (c. 760-750 B.C.)										
Hosea's ministry in Israel (c. 753-715 B.C.)										
Ministries of Micah and Isaiah in Judah (c. 742-681 B.C.)										
Exile of Israel (722 B.C.)										
Fall of Jerusalem (586 B.C.)										

THEMES

Amos describes the idolatry, self-indulgence, immorality, injustice, corruption, and oppression
of the poor in the northern kingdom of Israel. It includes the following themes:

1. *Social justice.* Amos demonstrated how periods of unusual prosperity can lead to spiritual
complacency and ethical laxity (6:1–6). Oppression of the poor (2:6–7a; 5:12; 8:4,6), injustice
in the courts (2:7a; 5:7,12; 6:12), sexual immorality (2:7b), religious abuses (2:8), violence
(3:10), idolatry (5:26), corrupt business practices (8:5)—all told the story: "The times [were]
evil" (5:13). Amos taught that true faith is expressed through actions, particularly those that
concern social justice.

2. *Judgment.* Injustice and exploitation of the poor will be punished (2:13–16; 6:8,14; 8:9—
9:10). Those who live opulently at the expense of others will lose everything they have
(3:15—4:3; 5:16–17; 6:4–7). God will expose the hypocrisy and false piety of his people (4:4–5;
5:21–23). But he calls them first to turn to him (5:4–6) and "live" (5:6). After judgment God
will restore his people (9:11–15).

FAITH IN ACTION

The pages of Amos contain life lessons and role models of faith—people who challenge believers to put their faith in action.

Role Models

• AMOS (7:10–17) was directed by the priest Amaziah to stop preaching, but he fearlessly continued to obey God, fulfilling his mission to bring God's message of judgment, hope, and restoration. Has someone tried to deter you from delivering God's message? How can Amos encourage you?

• THE RETURNING EXILES (9:14) would rebuild the ruins—ruins caused by judgment for their sin. What in your life has been broken because of sin and now needs rebuilding?

Challenges

• Expect God to use "ordinary" people in his service (1:1). He's just as likely to utilize a blue-collar worker as a pastor to relay his message.

• Evaluate your actions. Are you honest (5:12)? Do you seek justice for society's oppressed and vulnerable (2:6–7; 5:12)? Do you feign piety by using ill-gotten gain as an offering to God (2:8)? What do your actions reveal about your faith?

• Evaluate your lifestyle. Are you a "cow of Bashan" (4:1)—a wealthy, self-indulgent, spoiled, and/or demanding person who supports, allows, or overlooks oppression of others in order to protect your own lifestyle (5:11)? Are you complacently relying on materialism for your security (6:1–7)?

• Evaluate your "religion" (5:21–26). Does your faith express itself through deeds of justice and righteousness, or are you participating in special religious celebrations (5:21), the giving of monetary gifts (5:22), or superficial "acts of worship" (5:23) merely to appease your conscience?

OUTLINE

I. Introduction (1:1–2)
II. Judgments on the Nations (1:3—2:16)
III. Judgments on God's People (3:1—5:17)
IV. Announcements of Exile (5:18—6:14)
V. Visions of Amos (7:1—9:10)
VI. Restored Israel's Hope for the Future (9:11–15)

1:1
a 2Sa 14:2
b Zec 14:5
c 2Ch 26:23
d 2Ki 14:23
e Hos 1:1

1:2
f Isa 42:13
g Joel 3:16

1 The words of Amos, one of the shepherds of Tekoa *a*—what he saw concerning Israel two years before the earthquake, *b* when Uzziah *c* was king of Judah and Jeroboam *d* son of Jehoash *a* was king of Israel. *e*

²He said:

"The LORD roars *f* from Zion
and thunders from Jerusalem; *g*

a 1 Hebrew *Joash,* a variant of *Jehoash*

Amos 1:1–2

🔲 This introduction wasn't part of the message Amos spoke but likely was added to his sermons when they were put in written form. Unlike other prophets who made a living from their ministries, Amos was a shepherd and farmer (v. 1; 7:14–15). Though he was from the town of Tekoa, not far from Jerusalem, God sent him *from Judah to preach to the northern kingdom of Israel.* Based on the reference to Kings Uzziah and Jeroboam, we can surmise that Amos ministered around 750 B.C.

Verse 2 ominously announced the main theme of Amos's message. The earthquake mentioned in verse 1 was evidently seen as verification of the authority and truthfulness of this message.

📖 Three broad principles may be derived from this introduction: God (1) chooses regular people to communicate his words to others, (2) controls nature, and (3) reveals himself to humankind. The first principle doesn't suggest that God rejects people of status, power, and wealth but demonstrates that he is just as likely to use common, unpretentious people (cf. 1 Cor. 1:26–28). God

the pastures of the shepherds dry
    up, [a]
and the top of Carmel [h] withers." [i]

Judgment on Israel's Neighbors

[3]This is what the LORD says:

"For three sins of Damascus, [j]
    even for four, I will not turn back
    ⌞my wrath⌟. [k]
Because she threshed Gilead
    with sledges having iron teeth,
[4]I will send fire [l] upon the house of
    Hazael
    that will consume the fortresses [m]
    of Ben-Hadad. [n]
[5]I will break down the gate [o] of
    Damascus;
I will destroy the king who is in [b] the Valley of Aven [c]
and the one who holds the scepter in Beth Eden.
The people of Aram will go into exile to Kir, [p]"

                    says the LORD.

[6]This is what the LORD says:

"For three sins of Gaza, [q]
    even for four, I will not turn back ⌞my wrath⌟.
Because she took captive whole communities
    and sold them to Edom, [r]
[7]I will send fire upon the walls of Gaza
    that will consume her fortresses.
[8]I will destroy the king [d] of Ashdod [s]
    and the one who holds the scepter in Ashkelon.
I will turn my hand [t] against Ekron,
    till the last of the Philistines [u] is dead,"

                says the Sovereign LORD. [v]

[9]This is what the LORD says:

"For three sins of Tyre, [w]
    even for four, I will not turn back ⌞my wrath⌟.

---

a 2 Or *shepherds mourn*   b 5 Or *the inhabitants of*   c 5 *Aven* means *wickedness.*
d 8 Or *inhabitants*

Marginal references

1:2   h Am 9:3 i Jer 12:4
1:3   j Isa 8:4; 17:1-3   k Am 2:6
1:4   l Jer 49:27   m Jer 17:27   n 1Ki 20:1; 2Ki 6:24
1:5   o Jer 51:30   p 2Ki 16:9
1:6   q 1Sa 6:17; Zep 2:4   r Ob 1:11
1:8   s 2Ch 26:6   t Ps 81:14   u Eze 25:16   v Isa 14:28-32; Zep 2:4-7
1:9   w 1Ki 5:1; 9:11-14; Isa 23:1-18; Jer 25:22; Joel 3:4; Mt 11:21

Judgment on Israel's Neighbors (1:3)

Then: God judged Israel's neighbors—Assyria, Phoenicia, Aram, Ammon, Moab, Edom, and Egypt—for their specific sins.
Now: God judges all sinners the world over.

---

isn't as interested in our past successes or failures as in our present willingness to respond positively to his call.

Amos 1:3—2:5

Amos's message began with prophecies of judgment on eight nations (1:3—2:16), the last two being Judah and Israel. Each oracle began with "For three sins . . . even for four"—an expression meaning, "For their many sins, especially the one named."

Amos pronounced God's judgment on: (1) Aram (and its capital, Damascus), for war atrocities; (2) Philistia (and its major cities of Gaza, Ashdod, Ashkelon, and Ekron), for slave raids on defenseless villages; (3) Tyre, also for slave trafficking; (4) Edom (and its major cities, Teman and Bozrah)—Israel's "brother" through Esau (see Gen. 25:21–30; 27:38–40)—for years of hostility toward Israel; (5) Ammon (and its capital, Rabbah), for brutal genocide bred by territorial greed; (6) Moab, for

showing total disrespect for the dead; and (7) Judah (and its capital, Jerusalem), for rejecting God's law in general and worshiping false gods in particular.

These powerful messages of judgment provide insights concerning the principles guiding God's evaluation of governments and their policies. It's natural for tribes, nations, races, and other affiliate groups to act in their own political or economic interests and to favor their own members. But God judges people and nations who resort to torture, unreasonable seizure and imprisonment, slave trafficking, genocide, and murder. He hates these inhumane acts for their failure to treasure others as people created in his image and for their rejection of his plan for social relationships that promote peace and justice for all. They violate God's basic "Love your neighbor as yourself" law (cf. Luke 10:25–37), one of the guiding principles in the kingdom of God.

Because she sold whole communities of captives to Edom,
disregarding a treaty of brotherhood,

¹⁰ I will send fire upon the walls of Tyre
that will consume her fortresses. [x]"

1:10
x Zec 9:1-4

¹¹ This is what the LORD says:

"For three sins of Edom, [y]
even for four, I will not turn back ⌊my wrath⌋.
Because he pursued his brother with a sword,
stifling all compassion, [a]
because his anger raged continually
and his fury flamed unchecked, [z]
¹² I will send fire upon Teman [a]
that will consume the fortresses of Bozrah."

1:11
y Nu 20:14-21;
2Ch 28:17;
Jer 49:7-22
z Eze 25:12-14

1:12
a Ob 1:9-10

¹³ This is what the LORD says:

"For three sins of Ammon, [b]
even for four, I will not turn back ⌊my wrath⌋.
Because he ripped open the pregnant women [c] of Gilead
in order to extend his borders,
¹⁴ I will set fire to the walls of Rabbah [d]
that will consume her fortresses
amid war cries [e] on the day of battle,
amid violent winds on a stormy day.
¹⁵ Her king [b] will go into exile,
he and his officials together,"

1:13
b Jer 49:1-6;
Eze 21:28; 25:2-7
c Hos 13:16

1:14
d Dt 3:11 e Am 2:2

says the LORD.

2

This is what the LORD says:

"For three sins of Moab,
even for four, I will not turn back ⌊my wrath⌋.
Because he burned, as if to lime,
the bones of Edom's king,
² I will send fire upon Moab
that will consume the fortresses of Kerioth. [c]
Moab will go down in great tumult
amid war cries and the blast of the trumpet.
³ I will destroy her ruler [f]
and kill all her officials with him," [g]

2:3
f Ps 2:10 g Isa 40:23

says the LORD.

⁴ This is what the LORD says:

"For three sins of Judah, [h]
even for four, I will not turn back ⌊my wrath⌋.
Because they have rejected the law [i] of the LORD
and have not kept his decrees, [j]
because they have been led astray [k] by false gods, [d] [l]
the gods [e] their ancestors followed, [m]
⁵ I will send fire upon Judah
that will consume the fortresses of Jerusalem. [n]"

2:4
h 2Ki 17:19;
Hos 12:2 i Jer 6:19
j Eze 20:24
k Isa 9:16
l Isa 28:15
m 2Ki 22:13;
Jer 16:12

2:5
n Jer 17:27;
Hos 8:14

^a 11 Or *sword / and destroyed his allies*   ^b 15 Or */ Molech*; Hebrew *malcam*   ^c 2 Or *of her cities*
^d 4 Or *by lies*   ^e 4 Or *lies*

Amos 2:6–16

Amos had distinguished a fundamental difference between the type of sins the non-Israelite nations and Judah had committed (cf. 1:3—2:1 and 2:4): The other nations had violated basic laws of humanity, but Judah had broken its covenant with God. Now Amos turned to the northern kingdom of Israel, where he was ministering. While he would surely accuse Israel of sharing Judah's spiritual unfaithfulness, here he focused on Israel's social and moral sins.

Judgment on Israel

6 This is what the LORD says:

"For three sins of Israel,
even for four, I will not turn back ⌊my wrath⌋.
They sell the righteous for silver,
and the needy for a pair of sandals.[o]
7 They trample on the heads of the poor
as upon the dust of the ground
and deny justice to the oppressed.
Father and son use the same girl
and so profane my holy name.[p]
8 They lie down beside every altar
on garments taken in pledge.[q]
In the house of their god
they drink wine[r] taken as fines.

9 "I destroyed the Amorite[s] before them,
though he was tall as the cedars
and strong as the oaks.
I destroyed his fruit above
and his roots[t] below.

10 "I brought you up out of Egypt,[u]
and I led you forty years in the desert[v]
to give you the land of the Amorites.[w]
11 I also raised up prophets[x] from among your sons
and Nazirites[y] from among your young men.
Is this not true, people of Israel?"

declares the LORD.

12 "But you made the Nazirites drink wine
and commanded the prophets not to prophesy.[z]

13 "Now then, I will crush you
as a cart crushes when loaded with grain.
14 The swift will not escape,
the strong[a] will not muster their strength,
and the warrior will not save his life.[b]
15 The archer[c] will not stand his ground,
the fleet-footed soldier will not get away,
and the horseman will not save his life.
16 Even the bravest warriors[d]
will flee naked on that day,"

declares the LORD.

2:6 [o] Joel 3:3; Am 8:6
2:7 [p] Am 5:11-12; 8:4
2:8 [q] Ex 22:26 [r] Am 4:1; 6:6
2:9 [s] Nu 21:23-26; Jos 10:12 [t] Eze 17:9; Mal 4:1
2:10 [u] Ex 20:2; Am 3:1 [v] Dt 2:7 [w] Ex 3:8; Am 9:7
2:11 [x] Dt 18:18; Jer 7:25 [y] Nu 6:2-3; Jdg 13:5
2:12 [z] Isa 30:10; Jer 11:21; Am 7:12-13; Mic 2:6
2:14 [a] Jer 9:23 [b] Ps 33:16; Isa 30:16-17
2:15 [c] Eze 39:3
2:16 [d] Jer 48:41

Amos didn't mention just one sinful act, as in the earlier oracles against the foreign nations, but numerous ways in which the more powerful Israelites were oppressing the poor and sexually exploiting girls. Perhaps someone from the wealthy/ruling class would have been blind to the problems Amos identified. But the prophet's own humble background may have given him experience and insight into society's flaws, as well as a window into God's compassion for those who were suffering.

The oracles in chapters 1 and 2 highlight basic principles: (1) Every nation is accountable for its own rebellion against God. (2) An audience's common understanding of God and his ways can be used to evaluate the listeners' behavior. (3) Those who have received divine revelation will be evaluated according to what they know. (4) God holds people accountable if they exploit and oppress others. (5) Rebellion against God's design for healthy relationships erodes his reputation. (6) God fights on behalf of the oppressed.

Anyone tempted to take advantage of others, especially the poor and vulnerable, does well to remember that God hates every type of abuse or injustice and fights to deliver the innocent and powerless. The battle won't be won by the swift, brave, or mighty (Amos 2:14–16). It belongs to the Lord, and he stands opposed to those who oppress others (cf. Prov. 22:22–23). It's easier for us to insist that problems don't exist or are less serious when we ourselves are part of the problem. Listening carefully to people from other backgrounds can give us insight into our own behavior that we might not ordinarily recognize.

Serving the Poor

The prophet Isaiah boldly declared God's good news for the poor (Isa. 61:1–2), and Jesus himself took Isaiah's words as the text for his inaugural sermon at the outset of his earthly ministry (Luke 4:18–19) The range and volume of Old and New Testament materials that state God's concern for the poor and call God's people to action on their behalf suggest that the Biblical mandate to serve the poor is one of the major themes of Biblical faith.

An excellent resource for learning about conditions of the poor in the world today is the "PovertyNet" site of The World Bank Group (*www.worldbank.org/poverty/index.htm*). As that resource recognizes, poverty is more than a lack of economic resources. It's hunger, lack of shelter, being sick and unable to see a doctor, being unable to attend school and/or learn to read, not having a job, living each day in fear, or losing a child to illness brought about by unclean water.

> Perhaps we may simply resolve to find one tangible way in which we can make a difference by generously giving of ourselves.

The Old Testament books of the law (e.g., Lev. 19; 25) provided directions for the care of the poor. Certain regulations clearly intended to protect the poor, defined there not only as those without monetary resources, but also as widows, orphans, and aliens. Furthermore, the Old Testament prophets regularly took up the cause of the needy. These spokespersons for God admonished people in positions of power and security to attend to the welfare of the less fortunate among them. When the disadvantaged suffered oppression or neglect, the prophets denounced and condemned those responsible for that abuse. While Old Testament Wisdom Literature (especially Prov.) recognized that poverty may be the result of a person's own irresponsibility, there was also (as in Amos) a clear acknowledgment that the suffering of the poor may be caused by economic, political, and even religious exploitation.

In the New Testament, Jesus came ministering to the poor. He explicitly declared that he had come in the power of God's Spirit to preach Good News to them. He pronounced blessing on the needy, recognizing that their lack of worldly power could bring them into an intense spiritual relation to God because of their complete dependence on him (Luke 6:20–21). Jesus admonished his followers to care for the underprivileged—to give without thought of repayment and to attend to those suffering various sorts of oppression (Matt. 25:34–40). Jesus himself embodied God's compassion for the poor as he went about his earthly ministry. In the spirit of the Old Testament, the apostle James defined religion that is pure and undefiled in God's sight as benevolence toward orphans and widows (James 1:27). Then, in the spirit of Jesus, James declared that God chose the poor of the world to be rich in faith, heirs of God's kingdom (James 2:5).

God's desire for his people to care for the poor couldn't be clearer in Scripture. Nevertheless, many people with a genuine concern for faithful obedience to God's will still wonder what they are to do in light of the great problem poverty presents in the world today. One straightforward and effective course of action may be this: None of us is able to right every wrong or be involved with every good and godly cause. Perhaps we may simply resolve to find one tangible way in which we can make a difference by generously giving of ourselves—our time, talent, and resources—for the benefit of specific persons who suffer poverty in some identifiable way.

Marion L. Soards, professor of New Testament at Louisville Presbyterian Theological Seminary in Louisville, Kentucky

Witnesses Summoned Against Israel

3 Hear this word the LORD has spoken against you, O people of Israel—against the whole family I brought up out of Egypt:[e]

2 "You only have I chosen[f]
of all the families of the earth;
therefore I will punish you
for all your sins.[g]"

3 Do two walk together
unless they have agreed to do so?
4 Does a lion roar in the thicket
when he has no prey?[h]
Does he growl in his den
when he has caught nothing?
5 Does a bird fall into a trap on the ground
where no snare has been set?
Does a trap spring up from the earth
when there is nothing to catch?
6 When a trumpet sounds in a city,
do not the people tremble?
When disaster comes to a city,
has not the LORD caused it?[i]

7 Surely the Sovereign LORD does nothing
without revealing his plan[j]
to his servants the prophets.[k]

8 The lion has roared—
who will not fear?
The Sovereign LORD has spoken—
who can but prophesy?[l]

9 Proclaim to the fortresses of Ashdod
and to the fortresses of Egypt:
"Assemble yourselves on the mountains of Samaria;[m]
see the great unrest within her
and the oppression among her people."

10 "They do not know how to do right,[n]" declares the LORD,
"who hoard plunder[o] and loot in their fortresses."[p]

3:1 e Am 2:10
3:2 f Dt 7:6; Lk 12:47 g Jer 14:10
3:4 h Ps 104:21; Hos 5:14
3:6 i Isa 14:24-27; 45:7
3:7 j Ge 18:17; Da 9:22; Jn 15:15; Rev 10:7 k Jer 23:22
3:8 l Jer 20:9; Jnh 1:1-3; 3:1-3; Ac 4:20
3:9 m Am 4:1; 6:1
3:10 n Jer 4:22; Am 5:7; 6:12 o Hab 2:8 p Zep 1:9

Amos 3:1–15

Amos attempted to convince his audience to believe the disastrous news he had just announced in 2:6–16. God would indeed destroy Israel, his chosen people, because of their sinful rebellion. Amos asked a series of rhetorical questions in verses 3–6 to demonstrate that there is a cause behind every effect. There was a reason for God's plan to punish Israel; such things don't happen by chance.

In verse 9 Amos called for wealthy people in two foreign nations to serve as expert witnesses to the violence in Samaria (Israel). Amos indicted the Israelites "who hoard[ed] plunder and loot" through oppression (v. 10). Because of their sins, only a truncated remnant of Israel would survive (v. 12). The rich and powerful in Ashdod and Egypt were again summoned in verse 13 to testify against the rich and powerful in Israel. Further evidence of these Israelites' opulence was seen in their luxurious winter and summer houses (v. 12 indicates that some may even have maintained homes outside Israel, in Damascus).

God doesn't forbid us to gain riches or condemn people who are wealthy. In fact, he gives his people possessions and the ability to gain wealth (e.g., Deut. 8:6–18). Still, the Bible commands the wealthy not to put their trust in their riches and to use their resources to help the poor (1 Tim. 6:17–19).

God's opposition to inappropriate means of accumulating wealth through oppression of weaker people is a central emphasis in Amos's message—and a critical message for our day. Where do you see injustice today such as Amos described? What has God equipped you to do about it? At the very least, believers can pray, asking for God's light to break through such darkness. And your generosity to people in need can be one such light.

1451

11Therefore this is what the Sovereign Lord says:

> "An enemy will overrun the land;
>   he will pull down your strongholds
>   and plunder your fortresses. q"

12This is what the Lord says:

> "As a shepherd saves from the lion's r mouth
>   only two leg bones or a piece of an ear,
>   so will the Israelites be saved,
> those who sit in Samaria
>   on the edge of their beds
>   and in Damascus on their couches. a s"

13 "Hear this and testify t against the house of Jacob," declares the Lord, the Lord God Almighty.

14 "On the day I punish Israel for her sins,
>   I will destroy the altars of Bethel; u
> the horns of the altar will be cut off
>   and fall to the ground.
> 15 I will tear down the winter house v
>   along with the summer house; w
> the houses adorned with ivory x will be destroyed
>   and the mansions will be demolished,"

declares the Lord.

Israel Has Not Returned to God

4 Hear this word, you cows of Bashan y on Mount Samaria, z
>   you women who oppress the poor and crush the needy
>   and say to your husbands, "Bring us some drinks! a"
> 2The Sovereign Lord has sworn by his holiness:
>   "The time will surely come
> when you will be taken away b with hooks,

a 12 The meaning of the Hebrew for this line is uncertain.

4:1

The Faces of Malnutrition

The "cows of Bashan" sinned not only by denying food to the poor, but also by eating the excess themselves. One of the first decisions Daniel made as a captive in Babylon was to keep himself pure and healthy by refusing the rich fare he was offered (Dan. 1:8–16).

Malnutrition can take three forms:

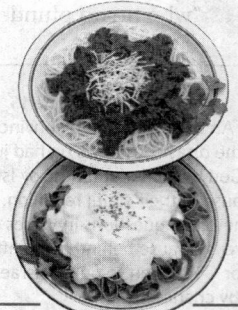

1. Eating too little food:
Insufficient food intake at its severest level ultimately results in starvation.

2. Eating poor food:
Eating the wrong foods or too much of only one food can lead to malnutrition, poor nutrition, and disease.

3. Eating too much food:
Overeating leads to obesity and related health concerns.

How sadly ironic that the scourge of malnutrition affects poor and rich alike—yet for vastly different reasons. What responsibility do you as a Christian have to help alleviate the problem caused by the first category? What about the second, in situations in which nutritious food is unavailable to people for economic reasons? What responsibility has God laid on you in terms of caring for and maintaining your own body—categories 2 and 3 (see 1 Cor. 6:19–20)?

the last of you with fishhooks.
³ You will each go straight out
    through breaks in the wall, ᶜ
    and you will be cast out toward Harmon, ᵃ"

                declares the LORD.

⁴ "Go to Bethel and sin;
    go to Gilgal ᵈ and sin yet more.
Bring your sacrifices every morning, ᵉ
    your tithes ᶠ every three years. ᵇᵍ
⁵ Burn leavened bread ʰ as a thank offering
    and brag about your freewill offerings ⁱ—
boast about them, you Israelites,
    for this is what you love to do,"

              declares the Sovereign LORD.

⁶ "I gave you empty stomachs ᶜ in every city
    and lack of bread in every town,
    yet you have not returned to me,"

              declares the LORD. ʲ

⁷ "I also withheld rain from you
    when the harvest was still three months away.
I sent rain on one town,
    but withheld it from another. ᵏ
One field had rain;
    another had none and dried up.
⁸ People staggered from town to town for water ˡ
    but did not get enough to drink,
    yet you have not returned ᵐ to me,"

              declares the LORD. ⁿ

⁹ "Many times I struck your gardens and vineyards,
    I struck them with blight and mildew. ᵒ
Locusts devoured your fig and olive trees, ᵖ
    yet you have not returned ᑫ to me,"

              declares the LORD.

¹⁰ "I sent plagues ʳ among you
    as I did to Egypt.

4:3
c Eze 12:5

4:4
d Hos 4:15
e Nu 28:3
f Dt 14:28
g Eze 20:39;
Am 5:21-22
4:5
h Lev 7:13
i Lev 22:18-21
4:6
j Isa 3:1; Jer 5:3;
Hag 2:17

4:7
k Ex 9:4,26;
Dt 11:17; 2Ch 7:13

4:8
l Eze 4:16-17
m Jer 3:7 n Jer 14:4

4:9
o Dt 28:22
p Joel 1:7
q Jer 3:10;
Hag 2:17

4:10
r Ex 9:3; Dt 28:27

ᵃ 3 Masoretic Text; with a different word division of the Hebrew (see Septuagint) *out, O mountain of oppression*   ᵇ 4 Or *tithes on the third day*   ᶜ 6 Hebrew *you cleanness of teeth*

Amos 4:1–13

The well-fed cattle raised in Bashan were considered the best breed in ancient Canaan. "Cows of Bashan," then, was a harsh but fitting symbol for Israel's wealthy, pampered, self-indulgent women, who maintained their lifestyles by exploiting the poor and speaking demandingly—even to their husbands.

Amos sarcastically called for *more* sinful worship at Israel's illegitimate worship shrines, an obvious putdown based on what was already happening (vv. 4–5). He next described how God had brought a series of covenant curses upon the people because they had never truly met him in their worship (vv. 6–11; see Lev. 26; Deut. 27–28). Five times the Lord repeated the refrain: "Yet you have not returned to me." Finally, the prophet thundered a warning: The people could no longer avoid God because he would soon come to meet *them*.

Self-focused people often lack the ability to "walk a mile in another's shoes" or to see life from another's perspective. What indulgent or self-focused practices is the Holy Spirit nudging you to set aside? Such sacrifices are not only pleasing to God, enhancing your relationship with him, but also nurture your compassion for people in need.

We don't offer burnt offerings or thank offerings in our churches today, but we do have a variety of symbolic worship traditions. Our prayers, songs, liturgies, and repeated acts can become just as dead as the meaningless sacrifices some offered in Israel. Genuine worship engages us in a relationship with God based on his self-revelation through Scripture and in good deeds that result from our encounter with him. The natural response of a believer to the glorious and fearful presence of a holy and all-powerful God is humble submission, reverence, service, and praise. This is part of what Amos had in mind when he talked about "returning to God."

I killed your young men with the sword,
    along with your captured horses.
I filled your nostrils with the stench of your camps,
    yet you have not returned to me,"

declares the LORD. ^s

4:10
s Isa 9:13

11 "I overthrew some of you
    as I ^a overthrew Sodom and Gomorrah. ^t
You were like a burning stick snatched from the fire,
    yet you have not returned to me,"

declares the LORD.

4:11
t Ge 19:24;
Jer 23:14

12 "Therefore this is what I will do to you, Israel,
    and because I will do this to you,
    prepare to meet your God, O Israel."

4:13
u Ps 65:6 v Da 2:28
w Mic 1:3
x Isa 47:4; Am 5:8,
27; 9:6

13 He who forms the mountains, ^u
    creates the wind,
    and reveals his thoughts ^v to man,
he who turns dawn to darkness,
    and treads the high places of the earth ^w—
    the LORD God Almighty is his name. ^x

A Lament and Call to Repentance

5:1
y Eze 19:1

5 Hear this word, O house of Israel, this lament ^y I take up concerning you:

5:2
z Jer 14:17
a Jer 50:32;
Am 8:14

2 "Fallen is Virgin ^z Israel,
    never to rise again,
deserted in her own land,
    with no one to lift her up. ^a"

3 This is what the Sovereign LORD says:

"The city that marches out a thousand strong for Israel
    will have only a hundred left;
the town that marches out a hundred strong
    will have only ten left. ^b"

5:3
b Isa 6:13; Am 6:9

4 This is what the LORD says to the house of Israel:

"Seek me and live; ^c

5:4
c Isa 55:3; Jer 29:13

5   do not seek Bethel,
do not go to Gilgal, ^d
    do not journey to Beersheba. ^e
For Gilgal will surely go into exile,
    and Bethel will be reduced to nothing. ^b ^f"

5:5
d 1Sa 11:14;
Am 4:4 e Am 8:14
f 1Sa 7:16

---

^a 11 Hebrew *God*   ^b 5 Or *grief;* or *wickedness;* Hebrew *aven,* a reference to Beth Aven (a derogatory name for Bethel)

Amos 5:1–17

Amos's wailing chant must have sent shivering shock waves through the nearly "dead" nation of Israel. He wanted to give the people a last-minute reality check, to convince them of their true status before God. Whether or not they knew it, they were enjoying their last few days of the good life. They were "fiddling" while their "Rome" was going up in smoke.

Since God is the sovereign power over nature and humanity, he establishes standards of justice for all people and administers judgment on those who practice injustice. Blessing, joy, security, and success aren't in-alienable rights but gifts of God's mercy. Our appreciation of life is heightened to the extent that we understand its preciousness—and precariousness.

Believers don't have to deny feelings of pain and loss; God has always been willing to listen to his people's cries. Amos, Job, and the psalmists, by voicing their grief, encourage us to face our deepest fears and distress. Underlying their sorrow was a faith that believed that God is trustworthy and understanding, that he can transform laments into assurance and praise. Attempts to stifle human complaints and expressions of grief to God make us view him as impotent to help and comfort us. They also discourage open and honest interaction between us and God.

6 Seek[g] the LORD and live,[h]
  or he will sweep through the house of Joseph like a fire;[i]
it will devour,
  and Bethel[j] will have no one to quench it.

7 You who turn justice into bitterness[k]
  and cast righteousness to the ground
8 (he who made the Pleiades and Orion,[l]
  who turns blackness into dawn[m]
  and darkens day into night,[n]
who calls for the waters of the sea
  and pours them out over the face of the land—
  the LORD is his name[o]—
9 he flashes destruction on the stronghold
  and brings the fortified city to ruin),[p]
10 you hate the one who reproves in court[q]
  and despise him who tells the truth.[r]

11 You trample on the poor[s]
  and force him to give you grain.
Therefore, though you have built stone mansions,[t]
  you will not live in them;
though you have planted lush vineyards,
  you will not drink their wine.[u]
12 For I know how many are your offenses
  and how great your sins.

You oppress the righteous and take bribes
  and you deprive the poor of justice in the courts.[v]
13 Therefore the prudent man keeps quiet in such times,
  for the times are evil.

14 Seek good, not evil,
  that you may live.
Then the LORD God Almighty will be with you,
  just as you say he is.
15 Hate evil,[w] love good;
  maintain justice in the courts.
Perhaps the LORD God Almighty will have mercy[x]
  on the remnant[y] of Joseph.

16 Therefore this is what the Lord, the LORD God Almighty, says:

"There will be wailing[z] in all the streets
  and cries of anguish in every public square.
The farmers[a] will be summoned to weep
  and the mourners to wail.
17 There will be wailing in all the vineyards,
  for I will pass through[b] your midst,"

says the LORD.[c]

The Day of the LORD

18 Woe to you who long
  for the day of the LORD![d]

Cross references

5:6
g Isa 55:6 h ver 14
i Dt 4:24 j Am 3:14

5:7
k Am 6:12

5:8
l Job 9:9
m Isa 42:16
n Ps 104:20;
Am 8:9
o Ps 104:6-9;
Am 4:13

5:9
p Mic 5:11
5:10
q Isa 29:21
r 1Ki 22:8

5:11
s Am 8:6 t Am 3:15
u Mic 6:15

5:12
v Isa 5:23; Am 2:6-7

5:15
w Ps 97:10; Ro 12:9
x Joel 2:14
y Mic 5:7,8

5:16
z Jer 9:17
a Joel 1:11

5:17
b Ex 12:12
c Isa 16:10;
Jer 48:33

5:18
d Joel 1:15

Amos 5:18–27

There was no sign of a positive response to Amos's lament in 5:1–17. Most people hadn't internalized his call to seek God. Some no doubt defended themselves, claiming that Amos was confused and be-lieving that the day of God's judgment would bring the destruction of their enemies, not of Israel. Amos attempted to destroy these false hopes of security and divine blessing. The expected great day would bring Israel only darkness and humiliation.

5:18
e Joel 2:2 f Isa 5:19,
30; Jer 30:7

5:19
g Job 20:24;
Isa 24:17-18;
Jer 15:2-3; 48:44
5:20
h Isa 13:10;
Zep 1:15
5:21
i Lev 26:31
j Isa 1:11-16

5:22
k Am 4:4; Mic 6:6-7
l Isa 66:3
5:23
m Am 6:5
5:24
n Jer 22:3 o Mic 6:8

5:25
p Isa 43:23
q Dt 32:17

5:27
r Am 4:13;
Ac 7:42-43*

6:1
s Lk 6:24 t Isa 32:9-
11

6:2
u Ge 10:10
v 2Ki 18:34
w 2Ch 26:6
x Na 3:8

Why do you long for the day of the Lord?
That day will be darkness, [e] not light. [f]

19 It will be as though a man fled from a lion
only to meet a bear,
as though he entered his house
and rested his hand on the wall
only to have a snake bite him. [g]

20 Will not the day of the Lord be darkness, not light—
pitch-dark, without a ray of brightness? [h]

21 "I hate, I despise your religious feasts; [i]
I cannot stand your assemblies. [j]

22 Even though you bring me burnt offerings and grain offerings,
I will not accept them.
Though you bring choice fellowship offerings, [a]
I will have no regard for them. [kl]

23 Away with the noise of your songs!
I will not listen to the music of your harps. [m]

24 But let justice [n] roll on like a river,
righteousness like a never-failing stream! [o]

25 "Did you bring me sacrifices [p] and offerings
forty years [q] in the desert, O house of Israel?

26 You have lifted up the shrine of your king,
the pedestal of your idols,
the star of your god [b]—
which you made for yourselves.

27 Therefore I will send you into exile beyond Damascus,"
says the Lord, whose name is God Almighty. [r]

Woe to the Complacent

6 Woe to you [s] who are complacent in Zion,
and to you who feel secure on Mount Samaria,
you notable men of the foremost nation,
to whom the people of Israel come! [t]

2 Go to Calneh [u] and look at it;
go from there to great Hamath, [v]
and then go down to Gath [w] in Philistia.
Are they better off than [x] your two kingdoms?
Is their land larger than yours?

3 You put off the evil day

---

a 22 Traditionally *peace offerings*   b 26 Or *lifted up Sakkuth your king / and Kaiwan your idols, / your star-gods*; Septuagint *lifted up the shrine of Molech / and the star of your god Rephan, / their idols*

Amos made no obvious connection between the Day of the Lord (vv. 18–20) and Israel's unacceptable worship (vv. 21–27), but their closeness in the text suggests a tie. If worship doesn't enhance spiritual character, it's only empty ritual and emotion. Justice among individuals should be a hallmark of God's people, a demonstration of their love for him and an expression of a profoundly loving, mutual relationship.

A complete Biblical view of God avoids the tendency to focus exclusively on any one of his characteristics to the exclusion or depreciation of the others. False or imbalanced ideas about God can turn worship into nothing more than playing church.

If the lives of believers don't overflow with justice and righteousness, God's kingdom isn't being pro-

claimed authentically. Justice and righteousness aren't optional traits we can choose to practice; they are key values that characterize the kingdom behavior of those of us who claim to love and follow God.

Amos 6:1–7

Both the people in Zion (Jerusalem), the capital of Judah, and those in Samaria, the capital of Israel, had deceived themselves with a false sense of security. Their leaders arrogantly viewed themselves as "notable men of the foremost nation" and took pride in the fact that others came to them for advice and help. But the Israelites were no better off than those in surrounding cities, who understood that they were vulnerable to attack and had to be prepared to defend themselves at all times.

Mother Teresa

Mother Teresa (1910–1997) served the poor in Calcutta, India. As a young girl she felt called to become a nun in India. But once there she received a "call within a call" to serve the utterly destitute. She received permission to start her own order of nuns, the Missionaries of Charity, whose sole purpose was to do "something beautiful for God" by offering free services to Calcutta's street people.

She summed up her work in the opening of the constitution of her order:

"Our *object* is to quench the thirst of Jesus Christ on the cross by dedicating ourselves freely to serve the poorest of the poor, according to the work and teaching of Our Lord, thus announcing the Kingdom in a special way;

"Our *special mission* is to work for the salvation and holiness of the poorest of the poor. As Jesus was sent by the Father, so he sends us, full of his spirit, to proclaim the gospel of his love and pity among the poorest of the poor throughout the world;

"Our *special task* will be to proclaim Jesus Christ to all peoples, above all to those who are in our care. We call ourselves Missionaries of Charity;

"God is Love. The missionary must be a missionary of love, must always be full of love in his soul, and must also spread it to the souls of others, whether Christian or not."

Mother Teresa reminds us of the prophet Amos. His clear call as God's representative: "Let justice roll on like a river, righteousness like a never-failing stream!" (5:24). She didn't just prophetically pronounce this need; she devoted her all to making her life and those of her coworkers model what it means to serve people with such a commitment to God's compassion.

> **M**other Teresa's model began with prayer—which led to faith, which led to love, which led to service.

Mother Teresa's call to service models how we are to hear and obey God's voice too. Her call went through four distinct steps: (1) She became intellectually interested in India's needs, reading all she could about what the church was already doing in that country and what more needed to be done. (2) She determined that one sign of a genuine call was being happy in the Lord just thinking about it. (3) She decided that she needed the support of a larger social group, the church. She found a group within the church, the Sisters of Loretto, who agreed to accept, train, and help her get to India, as well as to give her a community to live with once there. (4) She craved the support of a smaller social group—her family. Once they perceived her dedication, her family members agreed with her assessment of the situation. *Lesson: A call to serve and act on God's behalf needs to be fully explored.*

Mother Teresa often reflected that with Christ we can do anything—without him, nothing. Her life verse, prominently hung in the house where she and her coworkers lived, was "I thirst," one of Jesus' last words on the cross (John 19:28). She related it to the Lord's earlier words: "I was hungry and you gave me something to eat, I was thirsty and you gave me something to drink, I was a stranger and you invited me in" (Matt. 25:35).

Mother Teresa's model began with prayer—which led to faith, which led to love, which led to service. *Lesson: At the root of service to God is obedience motivated by compassion.* Mother Teresa loved and served the poor, because in that act she appropriately saw herself loving and serving Christ.

6:3
y Isa 56:12;
Am 9:10

6:4
z Eze 34:2-3;
Am 3:12

6:5
a Isa 5:12; Am 5:23
b 1Ch 15:16

6:6
c Am 2:8 d Eze 9:4

and bring near a reign of terror. [y]
⁴ You lie on beds inlaid with ivory
　 and lounge on your couches.
　 You dine on choice lambs
　 and fattened calves. [z]
⁵ You strum away on your harps [a] like David
　 and improvise on musical instruments. [b]
⁶ You drink wine [c] by the bowlful
　 and use the finest lotions,
　 but you do not grieve [d] over the ruin of Joseph.
⁷ Therefore you will be among the first to go into exile;
　 your feasting and lounging will end.

The LORD Abhors the Pride of Israel

6:8
e Ge 22:16;
Heb 6:13
f Lev 26:30
g Ps 47:4 h Am 4:2
i Dt 32:19

⁸ The Sovereign LORD has sworn by himself [e]—the LORD God Almighty declares:

"I abhor [f] the pride of Jacob [g]
　 and detest his fortresses;
I will deliver up [h] the city
　 and everything in it. [i]"

6:9
j Am 5:3
6:10
k 1Sa 31:12
l Am 8:3

⁹ If ten [j] men are left in one house, they too will die. ¹⁰ And if a relative who is to burn the bodies [k] comes to carry them out of the house and asks anyone still hiding there, "Is anyone with you?" and he says, "No," then he will say, "Hush! [l] We must not mention the name of the LORD."

6:11
m Am 3:15
n Isa 55:11

¹¹ For the LORD has given the command,
　 and he will smash the great house [m] into pieces
　 and the small house into bits. [n]

6:12
o Hos 10:4
p Am 5:7

¹² Do horses run on the rocky crags?
　 Does one plow there with oxen?
But you have turned justice into poison [o]
　 and the fruit of righteousness into bitterness [p]—

6:13
q Job 8:15;
Isa 28:14-15

¹³ you who rejoice in the conquest of Lo Debar [a]
　 and say, "Did we not take Karnaim [b] by our own strength? [q]"

6:14
r Jer 5:15

¹⁴ For the LORD God Almighty declares,
　 "I will stir up a nation [r] against you, O house of Israel,

---

[a] 13 *Lo Debar* means *nothing.*　　[b] 13 *Karnaim* means *horns; horn* here symbolizes strength.

The people of Israel imagined that they were "putting off" the day of judgment, but they were actually "bringing it near." Amos rebuked the upper class for its careless ease and security derived from wealth. The people's "feasting and lounging" would come to a sudden end as they would be "among the first to go into exile."

Security can lead to overconfidence, complacency, and carelessness—spiritually and physically. When situations change, people sometimes maintain their old attitudes of assurance and live with a false sense of reality. "Why do you feel so secure?" Amos asked. This is a question the church is called to address as well. What would your answer be—on both a personal and a corporate (church) level?

Some people can handle salary increases without becoming proud or dependent on money for their security. And some can live in beautiful homes and not derive their sense of importance from their possessions. We are wise to avoid judging others. Each of us is responsible to honestly analyze our own sources of pride and security.

Amos 6:8–14

To the sense of false security and pride arising from affluence (6:1–7), Amos added in this passage Israel's spirit of invincibility spawned by its "fortresses" (v. 8)—perhaps the palace-fortresses that were the status symbols of Israel's rich and famous—and past military victories (v. 13). But God would raise up a nation, which history would reveal to be Assyria, to oppress Israel from its northern to its southern tip (v. 14).

The frightening scene in verses 9–10, to be fulfilled when Israel would be invaded, may have been set in one of these palace-fortresses. The image is of a survivor cowering inside, his relative forbidding him to pray because God's wrath had fallen. The "great house" in verse 11 could have referred to the palace-fortresses, or the "great house" and "small house" may have pointed again to the summer and winter homes of the wealthy (see 3:13).

that will oppress you all the way
    from Lebo^a Hamath^s to the valley of the Arabah. ^t"

6:14
s 1Ki 8:65
t Am 3:11

Locusts, Fire and a Plumb Line

7 This is what the Sovereign LORD showed me: ^u He was preparing swarms of locusts ^v after the king's share had been harvested and just as the second crop was coming up. ²When they had stripped the land clean, ^w I cried out, "Sovereign LORD, forgive! How can Jacob survive? ^x He is so small! ^y"

7:1
u Am 8:1 v Joel 1:4

7:2
w Ex 10:15
x Isa 37:4
y Eze 11:13

³So the LORD relented. ^z

"This will not happen," the LORD said. ^a

7:3
z Dt 32:36;
Jer 26:19; Jnh 3:10
a Hos 11:8
7:4
b Isa 66:16
c Dt 32:22
7:5
d ver 1-2; Joel 2:17
7:6
e Jnh 3:10

⁴This is what the Sovereign LORD showed me: The Sovereign LORD was calling for judgment by fire; ^b it dried up the great deep and devoured ^c the land. ⁵Then I cried out, "Sovereign LORD, I beg you, stop! How can Jacob survive? He is so small! ^d"

⁶So the LORD relented. ^e

"This will not happen either," the Sovereign LORD said.

⁷This is what he showed me: The Lord was standing by a wall that had been built true to plumb, with a plumb line in his hand. ⁸And the LORD asked me, "What do you see, ^f Amos? ^g"

7:8
f Jer 1:11,13
g Isa 28:17; La 2:8;
Am 8:2 h 2Ki 21:13
i Jer 15:6; Eze 7:2-9

"A plumb line, ^h" I replied.

Then the Lord said, "Look, I am setting a plumb line among my people Israel; I will spare them no longer. ⁱ

    ⁹ "The high places of Isaac will be destroyed
        and the sanctuaries ^j of Israel will be ruined;
        with my sword I will rise against the house of Jeroboam. ^k"

7:9
j Lev 26:31
k 2Ki 15:9;
Isa 63:18; Hos 10:8

Amos and Amaziah

¹⁰Then Amaziah the priest of Bethel ^l sent a message to Jeroboam ^m king of Israel: "Amos is raising a conspiracy ⁿ against you in the very heart of Israel. The land cannot bear all his words. ^o ¹¹For this is what Amos is saying:

7:10
l 1Ki 12:32
m 2Ki 14:23
n Jer 38:4
o Jer 26:8-11

^a 14 Or *from the entrance to*

Modern Western materialism, like ancient Israelite acquisitiveness, tends to trust in tangible things more than in God. We can't, of course, totally remove ourselves from the physical aspects of living in the world. We can use material things in a good and controlled manner or overemphasize possessing things to gain fulfillment. Anyone with money and access to power is susceptible to the dangers of pride.

Amos pinpointed the danger of security based on military pride. It's natural for people living in countries with strong armies to feel a sense of patriotism when a battle is won. But the term "patriot" derives from expressions meaning "father" or "of one's father." Patriotism, even for Christians, can become a substitute for or dangerously co-mingled with belief in our Father God. And misplaced trust in anyone or anything but God alone is inconsistent with true Christian faith.

Amos 7:1–9

The divine message was now received through visions. God isn't a mindless, abstract principle or philosophy ruling by mechanical formulas; he's a personal, caring Ruler. In each of Amos's first two visions, the reversal of the intended plagues postponed God's wrath one more day. But the vision in verses 7–9 ended differently. Just as a builder tests the straightness of a wall with a plumb line, God exposed the true state of his people's moral character and covenant faithfulness by measuring them against his holy standards. They had run out of time; the Lord would "spare them no longer" (v. 8; cf. 8:2).

In the middle of this dynamic interaction, Amos interceded for those God planned to judge. God's people, both in the Bible and today, have repeatedly interceded for others and encouraged him to respond in grace and mercy rather than in wrath and judgment. Prayer to God is based on the reality that God wants a relationship with people, and our prayers are a continuing dialogue of relationship with him. God knows what will happen, but his gift of mercy still awaits our requests. When we intercede for others, we experience with them the agony of their situation, and compassion wells up within us. This can speak volumes to people who wonder whether anyone, and especially God, truly cares about their suffering.

Prayers of intercession aren't to be focused so much on those who want or "deserve" a better life as on those who deserve eternal damnation under God's wrath—on those without hope beyond prayers on their behalf. Maybe we can stay God's hand of judgment long enough to give them one more chance to respond to his grace. When did you last follow Scripture's example (cf. Num. 14:10–23; Luke 23:34; Rom. 9:1–5; 1 Tim. 2:1–4) by deeply interceding for an unsaved relative/friend, a family made vulnerable by poverty, or a troubled nation?

" 'Jeroboam will die by the sword,
    and Israel will surely go into exile,
        away from their native land.' "

¹²Then Amaziah said to Amos, "Get out, you seer! Go back to the land of Judah. Earn your bread there and do your prophesying there. *p* ¹³Don't prophesy anymore at Bethel, because this is the king's sanctuary and the temple of the kingdom. *q*"

¹⁴Amos answered Amaziah, "I was neither a prophet *r* nor a prophet's son, but I was a shepherd, and I also took care of sycamore-fig trees. ¹⁵But the LORD took me from tending the flock *s* and said to me, 'Go, prophesy to my people Israel.' *t* ¹⁶Now then, hear the word of the LORD. You say,

" 'Do not prophesy against *u* Israel,
    and stop preaching against the house of Isaac.'

¹⁷"Therefore this is what the LORD says:

" 'Your wife will become a prostitute *v* in the city,
    and your sons and daughters will fall by the sword.
Your land will be measured and divided up,
    and you yourself will die in a pagan *a* country.
And Israel will certainly go into exile,
    away from their native land.' *w* "

A Basket of Ripe Fruit

8 This is what the Sovereign LORD showed me: a basket of ripe fruit. ²"What do you see, *x* Amos? *y*" he asked.

"A basket of ripe fruit," I answered.

Then the LORD said to me, "The time is ripe for my people Israel; I will spare them no longer. *z*

³"In that day," declares the Sovereign LORD, "the songs in the temple will turn to wailing. *b a* Many, many bodies—flung everywhere! Silence! *b*"

⁴Hear this, you who trample the needy
    and do away with the poor *c* of the land, *d*

7:12
p Mt 8:34
7:13
q Am 2:12; Ac 4:18
7:14
r 2Ki 2:5; 4:38
7:15
s 2Sa 7:8
t Jer 7:1-2; Eze 2:3-4
7:16
u Eze 20:46; Mic 2:6

7:17
v Hos 4:13
w 2Ki 17:6; Eze 4:13; Hos 9:3

8:2
x Jer 24:3 *y* Am 7:8
z Eze 7:2-9

8:3
a Am 5:16
b Am 5:23; 6:10

8:4
c Pr 30:14
d Ps 14:4; Am 2:7

---

a 17 Hebrew *an unclean*   *b* 3 Or *"the temple singers will wail*

Amos 7:10–17

📖 Based on Amos's prophecy in 7:9, Amaziah, the priest of the sanctuary at Bethel, accused Amos of conspiracy. His quotation of Amos (v. 11) wasn't exact. He changed the prophet's warning against "the house of Jeroboam" into a direct threat on Jeroboam II himself. (Jeroboam died a natural death, but his family's dynasty ended when his son and successor Zechariah was assassinated; see 2 Kings 14:29; 15:10.)

Amaziah suggested a peaceable solution: Amos should back off and return to Judah before he caused any more problems. Amaziah's words implied that Amos was trying to get rich off the people of Israel with his wild prophecies. Amos responded by denying any connection with professional prophesying and affirming that he was a prophet only by divine calling. Then, along with repeating Israel's fate of exile, Amos condemned Amaziah personally. With the exile of the priest, the death of his children, and the loss of their property, his wife would be reduced to prostitution in order to survive.

💭 Amos's prophecies related to a specific people and historic situation, so we have to be careful about applying their judgments to specific situations today. Jesus himself didn't come to condemn people but to bring

them salvation (John 3:17), and our message is one of reconciliation with God (2 Cor. 5:20).

Christians in democratic societies today don't typically worry about life-threatening persecution. They face situations more like Amos's. Someone expresses an idea or belief, and someone else disagrees. Differences escalate, and one or the other chooses to attend a different church or find new friends (just as Amaziah encouraged Amos to go elsewhere). But Amos didn't take the path of least resistance in order to avoid conflict—and neither should we. From your reading of the New Testament, how was Paul's ministry similar to Amos's?

Amos 8:1–14

💭 The vision God gave Amos in verses 1–3 involved a play on words: Like ripe fruit, Israel was ready to be plucked in judgment. There would be no songs of thanksgiving during this gruesome "harvest" (cf. Lev. 23:39–40). This disaster would, in fact, lead to bitter mourning. The unimaginable transformation would drive the optimistic oppressors in Israel into deep depression—because God would cause it. And as his staggering judgment would result in the people's silence (v. 3), their search for comfort and direction would be answered by awful silence (vv. 11–12), since God had already spoken.

5saying,

> "When will the New Moon be over
>   that we may sell grain,
> and the Sabbath be ended
>   that we may market wheat?" —
> skimping the measure,
>   boosting the price
>   and cheating with dishonest scales, *e*
> 6buying the poor with silver
>   and the needy for a pair of sandals,
>   selling even the sweepings with the wheat. *f*

7The LORD has sworn by the Pride of Jacob: *g* "I will never forget *h* anything they have done.

> 8 "Will not the land tremble *i* for this,
>   and all who live in it mourn?
> The whole land will rise like the Nile;
>   it will be stirred up and then sink
>   like the river of Egypt. *j*

9"In that day," declares the Sovereign LORD,

> "I will make the sun go down at noon
>   and darken the earth in broad daylight. *k*
> 10I will turn your religious feasts into mourning
>   and all your singing into weeping.
> I will make all of you wear sackcloth *l*
>   and shave your heads.
> I will make that time like mourning for an only son *m*
>   and the end of it like a bitter day. *n*

11 "The days are coming," declares the Sovereign LORD,
>   "when I will send a famine through the land—
> not a famine of food or a thirst for water,
>   but a famine of hearing the words of the LORD. *o*
> 12Men will stagger from sea to sea
>   and wander from north to east,
> searching for the word of the LORD,
>   but they will not find it. *p*

13"In that day

> "the lovely young women and strong young men
>   will faint because of thirst. *q*
> 14They who swear by the shame *a* of Samaria,
>   or say, 'As surely as your god lives, O Dan,' *r*
>   or, 'As surely as the god *b* of Beersheba *s* lives'—
> they will fall,
>   never to rise again. *t*"

---

a 14 Or *by Ashima*; or *by the idol*   *b* 14 Or *power*

Cross references

8:5 *e* 2Ki 4:23; Ne 13:15-16; Hos 12:7; Mic 6:10-11
8:6 *f* Am 2:6
8:7 *g* Am 6:8; *h* Hos 8:13
8:8 *i* Hos 4:3 *j* Ps 18:7; Jer 46:8; Am 9:5
8:9 *k* Job 5:14; Isa 59:9-10; Jer 15:9; Am 5:8; Mic 3:6
8:10 *l* Jer 48:37 *m* Jer 6:26; Zec 12:10 *n* Eze 7:18
8:11 *o* 1Sa 3:1; 2Ch 15:3; Eze 7:26
8:12 *p* Eze 20:3,31
8:13 *q* Isa 41:17; Hos 2:3
8:14 *r* 1Ki 12:29 *s* Am 5:5 *t* Am 5:2

Amos's messages about God's justice interact head-on with real-life issues that permeate our lives—like making a living wage, feeding our families, and providing the basic necessities of life. God cares about motives, honesty, and fairness. Those who shortchange and overcharge may be clever—but they are his enemies (see vv. 4–7).

Though businesses need to make a profit, some meaningful questions might be: Are my career choices and business decisions based purely on a desire to make more money? How does my respect for God motivate my conduct in business settings? Does a servant attitude shape my interactions with customers? Clients? Colleagues? Direct reports? Employees? Do I demonstrate my love for Christ through generosity and selflessness?

Israel to Be Destroyed

9 I saw the Lord standing by the altar, and he said:

> "Strike the tops of the pillars
>   so that the thresholds shake.
> Bring them down on the heads [u] of all the people;
>   those who are left I will kill with the sword.
> Not one will get away,
>   none will escape.
> ² Though they dig down to the depths of the grave, [a] [v]
>   from there my hand will take them.
> Though they climb up to the heavens, [w]
>   from there I will bring them down. [x]
> ³ Though they hide themselves on the top of Carmel, [y]
>   there I will hunt them down and seize them. [z]
> Though they hide from me at the bottom of the sea,
>   there I will command the serpent to bite them. [a]
> ⁴ Though they are driven into exile by their enemies,
>   there I will command the sword [b] to slay them.
> I will fix my eyes upon them
>   for evil [c] and not for good. [d] [e]
>
> ⁵ The Lord, the LORD Almighty,
>   he who touches the earth and it melts, [f]
>   and all who live in it mourn—
> the whole land rises like the Nile,
>   then sinks like the river of Egypt [g]—
> ⁶ he who builds his lofty palace [b] in the heavens
>   and sets its foundation [c] on the earth,
> who calls for the waters of the sea
>   and pours them out over the face of the land—
>   the LORD is his name. [h]
>
> ⁷ "Are not you Israelites
>   the same to me as the Cushites [d] ?" [i]

declares the LORD.

> "Did I not bring Israel up from Egypt,
>   the Philistines from Caphtor [e] [j]
>   and the Arameans from Kir? [k]

9:1
u Ps 68:21

9:2
v Ps 139:8
w Jer 51:53
x Ob 1:4

9:3
y Am 1:2
z Ps 139:8-10
a Jer 16:16-17

9:4
b Lev 26:33;
Eze 5:12
c Jer 21:10
d Jer 39:16
e Jer 44:11

9:5
f Ps 46:2; Mic 1:4
g Am 8:8

9:6
h Ps 104:1-3,5-6,
13; Am 5:8

9:7
i Isa 20:4; 43:3
j Dt 2:23; Jer 47:4
k 2Ki 16:9; Isa 22:6;
Am 1:5; 2:10

ᵃ 2 Hebrew *to Sheol*   ᵇ 6 The meaning of the Hebrew for this phrase is uncertain.
ᶜ 6 The meaning of the Hebrew for this word is uncertain.   ᵈ 7 That is, people from the upper Nile region   ᵉ 7 That is, Crete

---

Amos 9:1–10

In this vision, Amos saw the Lord "standing by the altar." Normally we would assume that this referred to the temple in Jerusalem. But since Amos prophesied primarily against Israel, the sanctuary at Bethel may have been in view. Or perhaps the image wasn't of a literal temple. In that case it most likely represented the religion of the northern kingdom, which in the end would bring about the destruction of its adherents. At any rate, God was about to initiate judgment from the very place where the people expected to receive blessing.

Amos threw a theological grenade at his audience when he put the exodus of Israel—God's chosen people—on the same level as the movements of other nations (v. 7). The Israelites had been granted a covenant relationship with the Lord, but if they were unfaithful to that covenant their destruction was just as feasible as a pagan nation's. But this wasn't a blanket condemnation. God would judge each person individually, and not everyone would be killed. As a farmer uses a sieve at harvest, some of the grain—Israel's faithful remnant—would survive.

How easy is it for God's people to be self-deceived? We as church members can fall prey to thinking that we have a *right* to God's protection and blessing because of our past experiences with him. Peter reminded his readers that "it is time for judgment to begin with the family of God" (1 Peter 4:17). Amos's lesson is that behavior matters to God. Salvation is a gift of grace, but good works are to characterize our living in God's gracious kingdom (Eph. 2:8–10).

8 "Surely the eyes of the Sovereign LORD
   are on the sinful kingdom.
I will destroy it
   from the face of the earth—
yet I will not totally destroy
   the house of Jacob,"

9 "For I will give the command,
   and I will shake the house of Israel
   among all the nations
as grain^m is shaken in a sieve,ⁿ
   and not a pebble will reach the ground.
10 All the sinners among my people
   will die by the sword,
all those who say,
   'Disaster will not overtake or meet us.'^o

Israel's Restoration

11 "In that day I will restore
   David's fallen tent.
I will repair its broken places,
   restore its ruins,
   and build it as it used to be,^p
12 so that they may possess the remnant of Edom^q
   and all the nations that bear my name,^a^r"
      declares the LORD, who will do these things.^s

13 "The days are coming," declares the LORD,
   "when the reaper will be overtaken by the plowman^t
   and the planter by the one treading grapes.
New wine will drip from the mountains
   and flow from all the hills.^u
14 I will bring back my exiled^b people Israel;
   they will rebuild the ruined cities^v and live in them.
They will plant vineyards and drink their wine;
   they will make gardens and eat their fruit.^w
15 I will plant^x Israel in their own land,
   never again to be uprooted
   from the land I have given them,"

      says the LORD your God.^y

---

a 12 Hebrew; Septuagint *so that the remnant of men / and all the nations that bear my name may seek ˻the Lord˼*   b 14 Or *will restore the fortunes of my*

9:8
l Jer 44:27

9:9
m Lk 22:31
n Isa 30:28

9:10
o Am 6:3

9:11
p Ps 80:12
9:12
q Nu 24:18
r Isa 43:7
s Ac 15:16-17*

9:13
t Lev 26:5
u Joel 3:18

9:14
v Isa 61:4
w Jer 30:18; 31:28;
Eze 28:25-26

9:15
x Isa 60:21
y Jer 24:6;
Eze 34:25-28;
37:12,25

Amos 9:11–15

Amos's final words looked forward to Israel's restoration through the Messiah, in fulfillment of God's covenant with David (2 Sam. 7). This king would reign over a remnant of Israel's former enemies, of whom Edom is symbolic. Amos foresaw the conversion of Gentiles, an insight that helped the New Testament church decide to include Gentile converts into their fellowship (see Acts 15:13–18). In sharp contrast to Amos's earlier predictions, ruins, desolation, and breaches would be replaced by building, planting, and reaping in abundance. God would establish his eternal kingdom.

As at Pentecost, God will one day powerfully intervene and through his Spirit bring about the comple-

tion of his original plan for his world. He hasn't been confused in the intervening years, nor has he had to resort to a "Plan B." His original plan included curses and blessings (Gen. 12:3). The people of Amos's day felt the brunt of God's wrath. Those in the future would experience his gracious restoration.

Amos offered hope to the faithful who would suffer with the wicked when God destroyed Israel. His words also challenge unbelievers today with regard to their choices: Reject God and suffer the result, or turn to him and receive his offer of hope. Everyone needs hope in life—hope that isn't based on an "end-times" chart or eliminated by tough circumstances. God offers this hope to all who choose to believe in him.

INTRODUCTION TO
Obadiah

AUTHOR

The author of this book is Obadiah, an otherwise unknown prophet whose name means "the servant of the LORD."

DATE WRITTEN

The date of composition of this short book has long been debated. Some connect it with the invasion of Judah by the Philistines and Arabs (850–840 B.C.). Others relate the events to the fall of Jerusalem to the Babylonians (586 B.C.), which is more likely.

ORIGINAL READERS

Obadiah was written to condemn the Edomites for their treachery and violence toward the people of Judah and for their arrogance and indifference toward God.

TIMELINE

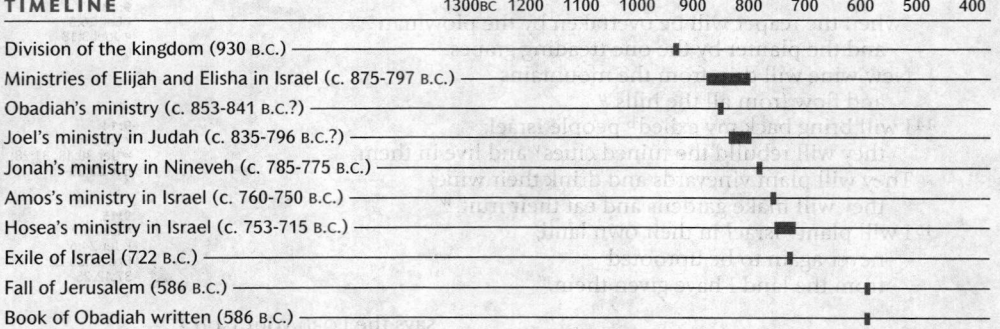

	1300BC	1200	1100	1000	900	800	700	600	500	400

Division of the kingdom (930 B.C.)

Ministries of Elijah and Elisha in Israel (c. 875-797 B.C.)

Obadiah's ministry (c. 853-841 B.C.?)

Joel's ministry in Judah (c. 835-796 B.C.?)

Jonah's ministry in Nineveh (c. 785-775 B.C.)

Amos's ministry in Israel (c. 760-750 B.C.)

Hosea's ministry in Israel (c. 753-715 B.C.)

Exile of Israel (722 B.C.)

Fall of Jerusalem (586 B.C.)

Book of Obadiah written (586 B.C.)

THEMES

Obadiah described the longstanding feud between God's people and the Edomites. The book predicted the destruction of Edom as God's vindication of his people. It includes the following themes:

1. *Judgment for Edom.* Edom was proud in her own security (v. 3) and gloated over Israel's defeat (v. 12; Ps. 137:7). Since the Edomites were related to the Israelites (v. 10), their violence against Israel and cruel indifference toward the people's suffering (vv. 10–11) were even more heinous. Conflict between Edom and Israel dated back to the patriarchal period, when their respective ancestors, the twin brothers Esau and Jacob, had been at odds. The fact that God had rejected Esau (Gen. 25:23; Mal. 1:2–3; Rom. 9:13) in no way excused Edom's disdain for Israel. The Old Testament contains other prophecies against Edom (Jer. 49:7–22; Lam. 4:21–22; Ezek. 25:12–14; 35:1–15), but Obadiah is the only book entirely dedicated to this purpose. The book of Obadiah assures God's people that God will punish those who abuse them.

2. *Deliverance and restoration for Israel.* Obadiah teaches that God is sovereign over all nations. Though the enemies of God's people may have momentary glimpses of glory, they will ultimately be defeated by God and their lands given to his people (vv. 19–21). Christians today are reminded of the book of Revelation, which informs believers that, while sometimes it appears that evil has the upper hand, Christ's return is certain and will result in the ultimate victory of righteousness.

FAITH IN ACTION
The pages of Obadiah contain life lessons and role models of faith—people who challenge believers to put their faith in action.

Role Models

• OBADIAH (v. 1) delivered a message of divine judgment against a proud, defiant, and treacherous people. Are you willing to be used by God for an unpleasant or unrewarding job?

• GOD'S PEOPLE (vv. 19–21) will be vindicated and rewarded by him. He will bless them and restore what's been stolen from them. Have you been wronged? Don't take matters into your own hands, but trust God to vindicate you.

Challenges

• Resolve to root out pride in your life; it's deceptive (v. 3) and will only bring you down (v. 4; Prov. 16:18). Those who seem invincible can't evade God's justice.

• Determine to confront injustice rather than stand by and allow it to happen (v. 11). Those who are indifferent to it are just as responsible as those actively engaged in it (v. 11).

• Do good to others, for "as you have done, it will be done to you" (v. 15).

• Don't gloat over someone else's suffering or take advantage of them in their unfortunate circumstances (11-14). Come to the aid of people affected by a disaster.

OUTLINE

I. Title and Introduction (1)
II. The Doom of Edom (2–14)
III. Edom in the Day of the Lord (15–21)

¹The vision of Obadiah.

This is what the Sovereign LORD says about Edom *a*—

We have heard a message from the LORD:
An envoy *b* was sent to the nations to say,
"Rise, and let us go against her for battle" *c*—

1:1
a Isa 63:1-6;
Jer 49:7-22;
Eze 25:12-14;
Am 1:11-12
b Isa 18:2
c Jer 6:4-5

Obadiah 1–21

Edom was another name for "Esau," Jacob's twin brother (Gen. 36:1,8,43; cf. Obad. 6,8–9,18–19,21). It also stood for Esau's descendants (Gen. 36:9,16–17, 31,43), whose blood relationship with Israel was mentioned repeatedly in the Old Testament (Num. 20:14; Deut. 23:7; Amos 1:11; Mal. 1:2; cf. Obad. 10,12). And it described the Edomites' land (Num. 20:23; 21:4; 34:3; cf. Obad. 18–21).

Edom's arrogance was grounded in its location "on the heights" (v. 3). Its natural defenses were imposing,

and it was defended by a series of fortresses. But its sense of security was deceptive. Though virtually impregnable to human forces, the country was utterly vulnerable before the wisdom and power of God.

The charge against Edom (v. 10) was "violence against your brother Jacob" (cf. Joel 3:19)—signifying both moral wrong and physical brutality, both of which had characterized the course of Edom's national relationship with Israel.

The first line of verse 15, referring to the all-important "day of the LORD," constitutes the core of Obadiah's

1:3
d Isa 16:6
e Isa 14:13-15;
Rev 18:7

2 "See, I will make you small among the nations;
  you will be utterly despised.
3 The pride *d* of your heart has deceived you,
  you who live in the clefts of the rocks *a*
  and make your home on the heights,
  you who say to yourself,
    'Who can bring me down to the ground?' *e*

1:4
f Hab 2:9
g Isa 14:13
h Job 20:6

4 Though you soar like the eagle
  and make your nest *f* among the stars,
  from there I will bring you down," *g*

declares the LORD. *h*

5 "If thieves came to you,
  if robbers in the night—
Oh, what a disaster awaits you—
  would they not steal only as much as they wanted?

1:5
i Dt 24:21

If grape pickers came to you,
  would they not leave a few grapes? *i*
6 But how Esau will be ransacked,
  his hidden treasures pillaged!

1:7
j Jer 30:14
k Ps 41:9

7 All your allies *j* will force you to the border;
  your friends will deceive and overpower you;
  those who eat your bread *k* will set a trap for you, *b*
  but you will not detect it.

1:8
l Job 5:12;
Isa 29:14
1:9
m Ge 36:11,34

8 "In that day," declares the LORD,
  "will I not destroy *l* the wise men of Edom,
  men of understanding in the mountains of Esau?
9 Your warriors, O Teman, *m* will be terrified,
  and everyone in Esau's mountains
  will be cut down in the slaughter.

1:10
n Joel 3:19
o Ps 137:7;
Am 1:11-12
p Eze 35:9

10 Because of the violence *n* against your brother Jacob, *o*
  you will be covered with shame;
  you will be destroyed forever. *p*
11 On the day you stood aloof
  while strangers carried off his wealth

1:11
q Na 3:10

  and foreigners entered his gates
  and cast lots *q* for Jerusalem,
  you were like one of them.
12 You should not look down on your brother
  in the day of his misfortune,

1:12
r Eze 35:15
s Pr 17:5 *t* Mic 4:11

  nor rejoice *r* over the people of Judah
  in the day of their destruction, *s*
  nor boast so much
  in the day of their trouble. *t*
13 You should not march through the gates of my people
  in the day of their disaster,

a 3 Or *of Sela*   *b 7* The meaning of the Hebrew for this clause is uncertain.

---

prophecy and provides its theological framework. The
localized disasters befalling Edom and Jerusalem
weren't isolated incidents. They marked the footsteps of
God himself, as he approached to set up for his people a
"kingdom that will never be destroyed" (Dan. 2:44). The
book's guiding principle was divine retribution: "As you
have done, it will be done to you."

Obadiah's vision ended with Judah restored to
its destined leadership of the nations and Mount Zion
exalted over the mountains of Esau. God is indeed Is-

rael's "king from of old" (Ps. 74:12). But the day is coming when his kingdom will be acknowledged universally,
when every knee shall bow (Phil. 2:10). Like Edom,
"every pretension that sets itself up against the knowledge of God" will be set aside (2 Cor. 10:15). "And the
kingdom will be the LORD's" (Obad. 21; cf. 1 Cor.
15:24–28; Rev. 11:15; 12:10; 22:1–5). What a day to anticipate! Are you doing all you can to invite and prepare
others to participate with you in this kingdom that has
no end?

nor look down on them in their calamity[u]
  in the day of their disaster,
nor seize their wealth
  in the day of their disaster.
14 You should not wait at the crossroads
  to cut down their fugitives,
nor hand over their survivors
  in the day of their trouble.

15 "The day of the LORD is near[v]
  for all nations.
As you have done, it will be done to you;
  your deeds[w] will return upon your own head.
16 Just as you drank on my holy hill,
  so all the nations will drink[x] continually;
they will drink and drink
  and be as if they had never been.
17 But on Mount Zion will be deliverance;[y]
  it will be holy,[z]
and the house of Jacob
  will possess its inheritance.
18 The house of Jacob will be a fire
  and the house of Joseph a flame;
the house of Esau will be stubble,
  and they will set it on fire and consume[a] it.
There will be no survivors
  from the house of Esau."

The LORD has spoken.

19 People from the Negev will occupy
  the mountains of Esau,
and people from the foothills will possess
  the land of the Philistines.[b]
They will occupy the fields of Ephraim and Samaria,[c]
  and Benjamin will possess Gilead.
20 This company of Israelite exiles who are in Canaan
  will possess ⌊the land⌋ as far as Zarephath;[d]
the exiles from Jerusalem who are in Sepharad
  will possess the towns of the Negev.[e]
21 Deliverers will go up on[a] Mount Zion
  to govern the mountains of Esau.
And the kingdom will be the LORD's.[f]

a 21 Or from

1:13
u Eze 35:5

1:15
v Eze 30:3
w Jer 50:29;
Hab 2:8

1:16
x Jer 25:15; 49:12

1:17
y Am 9:11-15
z Isa 4:3

1:18
a Zec 12:6

1:19
b Isa 11:14
c Jer 31:5

1:20
d 1Ki 17:9-10
e Jer 33:13

1:21
f Ps 22:28;
Zec 14:9,16;
Rev 11:15

4:10–11 "THE LORD SAID, '. . . NINEVEH HAS MORE THAN A HUNDRED AND TWENTY THOUSAND PEOPLE WHO CANNOT TELL THEIR RIGHT HAND FROM THEIR LEFT . . . SHOULD I NOT BE CONCERNED ABOUT THAT GREAT CITY?'"

INTRODUCTION TO
Jonah

AUTHOR
This book doesn't identify its author, but tradition has ascribed it to the prophet Jonah. It may be best understood as Jonah's autobiographical account of actual historical events.

DATE WRITTEN
The book was probably written between 785 and 750 B.C.

ORIGINAL READERS
Jonah was addressed to the northern kingdom (Israel) during the reign of Jeroboam II (793–753 B.C.), a time of great territorial and commercial expansion. Assyria, whose capital was Nineveh, was Israel's worst enemy at the time. The book of Jonah expresses God's concern for, and mercy toward, even the adversaries of his people.

TIMELINE

	1300BC	1200	1100	1000	900	800	700	600	500	400
Division of the kingdom (930 B.C.)										
Ministries of Elijah and Elisha in Israel (c. 875-797 B.C.)										
Jonah's ministry in Nineveh (c. 785-775 B.C.)										
Ministries of Amos and Hosea in Israel (c. 760-715 B.C.)										
Book of Jonah written (c. 785-750 B.C.)										
Micah's ministry in Judah (c. 742-687 B.C.)										
Isaiah's ministry in Judah (c. 740-681 B.C.)										
Exile of Israel (722 B.C.)										
Fall of Jerusalem (586 B.C.)										

THEMES
The book of Jonah describes the prophet Jonah's reluctant ministry to the people of Nineveh, Israel's hated enemy. It includes the following themes:

1. *God's sovereignty.* God is in control of life, nature, and circumstances (1:4,9,15,17; 2:10; 4:6–8). He's the God of *all* peoples, who is concerned about every nation and individual (4:11). He will bring his all-encompassing plan to completion.

2. *God's compassion and mercy.* God loves even the adversaries of his people and will show mercy when they repent (3:10; 4:2,11). He demands obedience (1:1–17) but is also the God of second chances.

3. *Mission.* We are called to proclaim God's message to the whole world (1:1–2; 3:1–2), even to those who oppose us (4:11; Matt. 5:44). As God's ambassadors (2 Cor. 5:20), we are to announce this call: "Be reconciled to God" (2 Cor. 5:20), for wickedness brings punishment (1:1–2; 3:4), but "salvation comes from the LORD" (2:10). Therefore, repent and seek God (3:5–9), a "compassionate God, slow to anger and abounding in love" (4:2).

FAITH IN ACTION

The pages of Jonah contain life lessons and role models of faith—people who challenge believers to put their faith in action.

Role Models

• JONAH (1:1–3; 3:1–3), despite his initial, drastic avoidance measures, eventually obeyed God and completed his mission. Is God asking you to do something distasteful? Be warned: It's better to obey God than to defy him.

• THE PEOPLE OF NINEVEH (3:5–9) responded with repentance and trusted God to be compassionate and merciful. Are you in need of God's mercy? Repent and trust in him. Pray for others, even those you consider to be enemies, to experience the great kindness of God. Look for ways to share the message of Christ with them.

Challenges

• Obey God—whether or not you want to (1:3). Don't run from his purpose for you.

• Don't exclude other people from participating in God's kingdom by judging whether or not they are "worthy" of salvation, for "salvation comes from the LORD" (2:9), who doesn't want "anyone to perish, but everyone to come to repentance" (2 Peter 3:9).

• Do more than confess your sin to God; give up your "evil ways" (3:8). Repentance calls for action (3:10).

• Resist and root out any prejudice or hatred in your life, for such attitudes are inconsistent with God's loving, compassionate nature (4:1–3,11) and will place a barrier in the way of your relationship both with him and with other people.

OUTLINE

I. Jonah Flees From God (1–2)
   A. Jonah's Commission and Flight (1:1–3)
   B. The Storm (1:4–6)
   C. Jonah's Disobedience Exposed (1:7–10)
   D. Jonah's Punishment and Deliverance (1:11—2:1; 2:10)
   E. Jonah's Prayer (2:2–9)
II. Jonah Reluctantly Fulfills His Mission (3–4)
   A. Jonah's Response (3:1–4)
   B. The Ninevites' Response (3:5–9)
   C. The Ninevites' Repentance (3:10—4:4)
   D. Jonah's Deliverance and Rebuke (4:5–11)

Jonah Flees From the LORD

1 The word of the LORD came to Jonah[a] son of Amittai:[b] 2 "Go to the great city of Nineveh[c] and preach against it, because its wickedness has come up before me."

3 But Jonah ran[d] away from the LORD and headed for Tarshish. He went down to

1:1
a Mt 12:39-41
b 2Ki 14:25
1:2
c Ge 10:11
1:3
d Ps 139:7

Jonah 1:1–17

Jonah's flight to Tarshish marked the beginning of a serious theological argument with God. The Lord commanded Jonah to preach against the wicked Ninevites, and Jonah suspected (as he would state in ch. 4) that God wanted to save Israel's archenemy and reconcile the Ninevites to himself. Jonah believed that God was serious, but he couldn't swallow this theology. God, in a counter-move, decided that Jonah would be swallowed by it!

God's difficult mercy found Jonah in the midst of a dramatic storm. It also found sailors, not looking for trouble, whose lives were imminently threatened. Hearing Jonah's witness and receiving the benefit of his self-sacrifice, they were delivered and turned to God in prayer, commitment (vows), and worship.

1:3
e Jos 19:46;
Ac 9:36,43

1:4
f Ps 107:23-26

1:5
g Ac 27:18-19

1:6
h Jnh 3:8
i Ps 107:28

1:7
j Jos 7:10-18;
1Sa 14:42

1:9
k Ac 17:24
l Ps 146:6

1:12
m 2Sa 24:17;
1Ch 21:17

1:13
n Pr 21:30

1:14
o Dt 21:8
p Ps 115:3

1:15
q Ps 107:29;
Lk 8:24

1:16
r Mk 4:41

1:17
s Mt 12:40; 16:4;
Lk 11:30

2:2
t Ps 18:6; 120:1

Joppa,[e] where he found a ship bound for that port. After paying the fare, he went aboard and sailed for Tarshish to flee from the LORD.

[4] Then the LORD sent a great wind on the sea, and such a violent storm arose that the ship threatened to break up.[f] [5] All the sailors were afraid and each cried out to his own god. And they threw the cargo into the sea to lighten the ship.[g]

But Jonah had gone below deck, where he lay down and fell into a deep sleep. [6] The captain went to him and said, "How can you sleep? Get up and call[h] on your god! Maybe he will take notice of us, and we will not perish."[i]

[7] Then the sailors said to each other, "Come, let us cast lots to find out who is responsible for this calamity."[j] They cast lots and the lot fell on Jonah.

[8] So they asked him, "Tell us, who is responsible for making all this trouble for us? What do you do? Where do you come from? What is your country? From what people are you?"

[9] He answered, "I am a Hebrew and I worship the LORD, the God of heaven,[k] who made the sea and the land.[l]"

[10] This terrified them and they asked, "What have you done?" (They knew he was running away from the LORD, because he had already told them so.)

[11] The sea was getting rougher and rougher. So they asked him, "What should we do to you to make the sea calm down for us?"

[12] "Pick me up and throw me into the sea," he replied, "and it will become calm. I know that it is my fault that this great storm has come upon you."[m]

[13] Instead, the men did their best to row back to land. But they could not, for the sea grew even wilder than before.[n] [14] Then they cried to the LORD, "O LORD, please do not let us die for taking this man's life. Do not hold us accountable for killing an innocent man,[o] for you, O LORD, have done as you pleased."[p] [15] Then they took Jonah and threw him overboard, and the raging sea grew calm.[q] [16] At this the men greatly feared[r] the LORD, and they offered a sacrifice to the LORD and made vows to him.

[17] But the LORD provided a great fish to swallow Jonah,[s] and Jonah was inside the fish three days and three nights.

Jonah's Prayer

2 From inside the fish Jonah prayed to the LORD his God. [2] He said:

"In my distress I called to the LORD,[t]
and he answered me.
From the depths of the grave[a] I called for help,

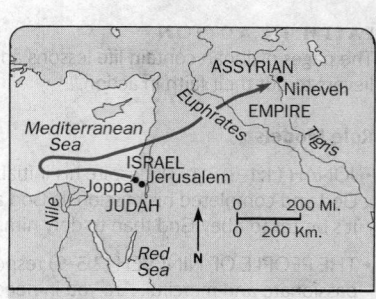

Jonah on the Run (1:3)

Then: Jonah fled to avoid doing what God wanted. He learned the hard way that it's impossible to run from God.

Now: Modern people don't think of running physically from God; instead we tend to avoid his call by blocking it from our minds.

---

a 2 Hebrew *Sheol*

Jonah began in protest by running away from God's call. His faith in God, though, is a real life example and source of hope for believers. Many who are called to difficult ministries or harsh environments struggle. Like Jonah, we might prefer to avoid certain people groups, nations, or types of ministry for something more comfortable or attractive. The world observes our struggle and may find itself attracted to a God so intimately involved in the affairs of his people. Who is watching you work through your relationship with God? Is it inviting them to faith?

Jonah 2:1–10

The amazing context of this poetic prayer is Jonah's gratitude while *inside* the fish. He had fully expected to die in the water. His thanksgiving from this unusual location was a proclamation of joy; God had delivered him in spite of his running. Though he wasn't yet on dry land, his faith had reached a new dimension of understanding.

Jesus used the "sign of Jonah" (Matt. 12:39–41) to refer to Jonah's (and his own) three days and three

and you listened to my cry.
³You hurled me into the deep,ᵘ
into the very heart of the seas,
and the currents swirled about me;
all your waves and breakers
swept over me.ᵛ
⁴I said, 'I have been banished
from your sight;ʷ
yet I will look again
toward your holy temple.'
⁵The engulfing waters threatened me,ᵃ
the deep surrounded me;
seaweed was wrapped around my head.ˣ
⁶To the roots of the mountains I sank down;
the earth beneath barred me in forever.
But you brought my life up from the pit,
O LORD my God.

⁷"When my life was ebbing away,
I rememberedʸ you, LORD,
and my prayerᶻ rose to you,
to your holy temple.ᵃ

⁸"Those who cling to worthless idolsᵇ
forfeit the grace that could be theirs.
⁹But I, with a song of thanksgiving,
will sacrificeᶜ to you.
What I have vowedᵈ I will make good.
Salvationᵉ comes from the LORD.'"

¹⁰And the LORD commanded the fish, and it vomited Jonah onto dry land.

Jonah Goes to Nineveh

3 Then the word of the LORD came to Jonahᶠ a second time: ²"Go to the great city of Nineveh and proclaim to it the message I give you."

³Jonah obeyed the word of the LORD and went to Nineveh. Now Nineveh was a very important city—a visit required three days. ⁴On the first day, Jonah started into the city. He proclaimed: "Forty more days and Nineveh will be overturned." ⁵The Ninevites believed God. They declared a fast, and all of them, from the greatest to the least, put on sackcloth.ᵍ

⁶When the news reached the king of Nineveh, he rose from his throne, took off

ᵃ 5 Or *waters were at my throat*

Side references:
2:3 ᵘ Ps 88:6 ᵛ Ps 42:7
2:4 ʷ Ps 31:22
2:5 ˣ Ps 69:1-2
2:7 ʸ Ps 77:11-12 ᶻ 2Ch 30:27 ᵃ Ps 11:4; 18:6
2:8 ᵇ 2Ki 17:15; Jer 10:8
2:9 ᶜ Ps 50:14,23; Hos 14:2 ᵈ Ecc 5:4-5 ᵉ Ps 3:8
3:1 ᶠ Jnh 1:1
3:5 ᵍ Da 9:3; Lk 11:32

nights in the belly of the fish/tomb. That a place of death would become a place of deliverance was in both cases completely unexpected. God is at work to save, even before those fleeing from him are aware of him. There is no place he isn't present. As Paul would declare so eloquently, nothing "will be able to separate us from the love of God that is in Christ Jesus our Lord" (Rom. 8:35–39).

Jonah had looked toward God (vv. 4,7), and this was enough for his deliverance. The Lord would deal later with his prophet's protest/running issues. God hears those who call to him in times of trouble. He accepted Jonah's thanks *and* his lack of repentance, because he accepted Jonah's protest as welcome dialogue. When have you struggled with God in prayer?

Jonah 3:1–10

Jonah's brusque message, "Forty more days and Nineveh will be overturned," could be taken two ways. The Hebrew word for "overturned" could mean (1) "turned over" or "overthrown"—that is, "destroyed"; or (2) "turned around"—meaning "brought to repentance." The conflict between the two is the primary subject of the book—and the essence of the argument between Jonah and God. God sent Jonah to Nineveh with a desire that the Ninevites would be overturned through their repentance. Jonah was willing to proclaim the double-edged message but hoped the result would be the Ninevites' annihilation.

That all of Nineveh was converted through Jonah's reluctant, half-hearted preaching seems less than credi-

3:6
h Job 2:8,13;
Eze 27:30-31
his royal robes, covered himself with sackcloth and sat down in the dust. *h* 7Then he issued a proclamation in Nineveh:

"By the decree of the king and his nobles:

3:7
i 2Ch 20:3
3:8
j Ps 130:1; Jnh 1:6
3:9
k 2Sa 12:22
l Joel 2:14
Do not let any man or beast, herd or flock, taste anything; do not let them eat or drink. *i* 8But let man and beast be covered with sackcloth. Let everyone call *j* urgently on God. Let them give up their evil ways and their violence. 9Who knows? *k* God may yet relent and with compassion turn *l* from his fierce anger so that we will not perish."

3:10
m Am 7:6
n Jer 18:8
o Ex 32:14
10When God saw what they did and how they turned from their evil ways, he had compassion *m* and did not bring upon them the destruction *n* he had threatened. *o*

Jonah's Anger at the LORD's Compassion

4:1
p ver 4; Lk 15:28
4 But Jonah was greatly displeased and became angry. *p* 2He prayed to the LORD, "O LORD, is this not what I said when I was still at home? That is why I was so quick to flee to Tarshish. I knew *q* that you are a gracious and compassionate God, slow to anger and abounding in love, *r* a God who relents from sending calamity. *s* 3Now, O LORD, take away my life, *t* for it is better for me to die *u* than to live."

4:2
q Jer 20:7-8
r Ex 34:6; Ps 86:5,
15 s Joel 2:13
4:3
t 1Ki 19:4
u Job 7:15
4:4
v Mt 20:11-15
4But the LORD replied, "Have you any right to be angry?" *v*

5Jonah went out and sat down at a place east of the city. There he made himself a shelter, sat in its shade and waited to see what would happen to the city. 6Then the LORD God provided a vine and made it grow up over Jonah to give shade for his head to ease his discomfort, and Jonah was very happy about the vine. 7But at dawn the next day God provided a worm, which chewed the vine so that it withered. *w* 8When the sun rose, God provided a scorching east wind, and the sun blazed on Jonah's head so that he grew faint. He wanted to die, and said, "It would be better for me to die than to live."

4:7
w Joel 1:12

9But God said to Jonah, "Do you have a right to be angry about the vine?"

---

ble. But the event was extraordinary, even supernatural. Similarly, Jesus' resurrection is deemed incredible by many today. The message of God's salvation and grace was, and is, considered foolishness.

When God calls us to a mission, the task and journey don't always make sense to us. Yet God is persistent. Why not take the time to reexamine the lives of Moses (Ex. 3:11—4:17), Elijah (1 Kings 19:1–18), and Jeremiah (Jer. 20:7–12)? We aren't told that Jonah was ever convinced by God's argument about the need to transform Nineveh.

The Ninevites' repentance was temporary. They reverted to their cruelty and pride and were overthrown (i.e., destroyed) in 612 B.C. The focus of the later book of Nahum would be prophecy of the Ninevites' destruction for their wickedness (cf. Nah. 3:2). A God interested in people who didn't sustain their repentance over time is an extravagant God who welcomes any who will turn to him. The book of Jonah isn't about the Ninevites' faith but about the reality that God cared enough to "turn around" their hearts. For the believing community, it stands as a reminder of the incredible love of the Creator for the creation and his radical willingness to seek out the most distant people and restore them to his grace.

Jonah 4:1–11

Jonah's confidence in *and* objection to God's mercy presents us with the complexity of faith in a God who can't be tamed, whose mercy and forgiveness can't

be controlled. Those who attempt to limit God's gracious actions share Jonah's protest: "Let me die now; your grace is too abundant. I want only the grace you offer to *me* and those I care about."

Jonah was happy about his first deliverance from the calamity of the sea (1:7; 2:9). He also was "very happy" about his deliverance from the discomfort of the sun (4:6). He wasn't at all pleased, though, about the Ninevites' deliverance from their destruction. The Lord used this contrast in his final—unanswered—question to his prophet.

While other prophets preached about a "faithful remnant" in Judah, Jonah reluctantly proclaimed a Creator whose concern for his remnant people didn't prevent his caring for other nations. The inclusion of this book in the Hebrew Bible was faithful to the broad vision given by God to Abraham in Genesis 12:3: "All peoples on earth will be blessed through you" (see also Isa. 42:6–7; 49:6). The book's viewpoint pushed the chosen people's range of vision wider at a time when the national consciousness threatened to narrow their view.

Each shelter (ship, fish, hut, vine, narrow worldview) failed Jonah, even when provided by God. We all seek security and salvation. Only when we fully rely on the God of Scripture and refuse to substitute temporary provisions for the true and lasting source of our security will we integrate the message of Jonah into our lives. Only then can we live securely between the false protection of "very happy" and "angry enough to die."

The Enduring Message of Jonah

 4:10–11

The story of Jonah is one the best known—and least understood—of Scripture. God called Jonah to travel to Nineveh to declare his merciful nature and to invite the people to turn from their self-destructive ways and find life. Jonah refused and ran away, but God arranged for a great fish to swallow him alive. Three days in solitary confinement gave Jonah time to rethink his response. The fish regurgitated Jonah onto a shoreline, God re-called, and Jonah complied. He traveled to Nineveh, preached to the people—who changed their lives—and became so angry about the outcome that he wanted to die.

The meaning of this remarkable story may be viewed from a few perspectives:

1. Some Israelites undoubtedly saw the Ninevites, despite their culture, knowledge, and power, as hopeless. These Jews believed that they were superior and that the Ninevite way of life was based entirely on lies and violence. They assumed that such an "evil society" couldn't possibly matter to Israel's God.

2. Jonah did *not* view the Ninevites as hopeless. He recognized that both the people *and their animals* mattered to God. But Jonah didn't like the Ninevites. He resisted his assignment because he knew, or suspected, that they would respond to God's invitation and that God would be gracious.

3. The Ninevites were important symbolically. Their name may serve today as a convenient shorthand term for all those who aren't like "good" church people, those with a shady past or shaky reputation. *That* includes just about all of us!

Some church leaders and members share a disposition to "write off" people who are different or threatening, consigning whole populations to the "hopeless" category. These believers can quickly list the "types" who would be impossible to redeem.

Others know that these people are redeemable but don't like it. They don't want "people like that in our church."

Yet Jesus prioritized outreach to lepers, paralytics, tax collectors, zealots, and other "hopeless" or "unclean" people. His apostles took the gospel to "barbarians" and even cannibals.

> **We don't have to like people to be used by God to reach them.**

In time, though, the church came to regard *rural* people as subhuman and unreachable—until St. Martin of Tours, in A.D. 371, demonstrated their reachability. The church also had come to regard "barbarians" as impossible to Christianize—until St. Patrick showed in A.D. 432 that even the Irish could be reached if approached appropriately. During the last 1,500 years, the same disease has mutated into many different forms.

Jonah's story and its message have much to teach us today:

1. Christians need to know that the Ninevites (and all peoples) matter to God.
2. The Good News of a compassionate God who can change people from within speaks to "closet Ninevites"—those of us who know, deep down, that our reputation is better than we deserve.
3. Not all people will respond to the gospel, but some will. We are called, to paraphrase Paul, to become all things to all people so that we might by all means save some (1 Cor. 9:22).
4. It's not always easy to reach and restore unbelieving populations. They often bring multiple problems to their new life of faith, and it takes time and effort to help them become whole. Paul's letters to the church in Corinth bear this out.
5. We don't have to like people to be used by God to reach them.
6. When "hopeless" people are reached and changed, the miracle catalyzes responsiveness in "regular" people, and a Christian movement ensues.

George G. Hunter III, professor of evangelism and church growth at Asbury Theological Seminary in Wilmore, Kentucky

"I do," he said. "I am angry enough to die."

4:11
x Jnh 1:2; 3:2
y Jnh 3:10

[10]But the LORD said, "You have been concerned about this vine, though you did not tend it or make it grow. It sprang up overnight and died overnight. [11]But Nineveh [x] has more than a hundred and twenty thousand people who cannot tell their right hand from their left, and many cattle as well. Should I not be concerned [y] about that great city?"

"Overturn" us, O God, this day. Turn us into new people with a heart for your peace. May we not hesitate to extend your offer of deliverance to our enemies. Turn us to repentance from our reliance on power and force (like the Ninevites). Speak to us as we sit on the hillside in safety (like Jonah), that we might learn from you for all our decisions. Overturn us for our sake, for the sake of your creation, and for the witness of your gospel in the world. Amen.

INTRODUCTION TO
Micah

AUTHOR
The prophet Micah wrote this book. He was a contemporary of Isaiah who ministered to the
people of Judah between 742 and 687 B.C.

DATE WRITTEN
The book of Micah was probably written between 740 and 710 B.C.

ORIGINAL READERS
Micah ministered primarily to the southern kingdom of Judah, but he also addressed the
northern kingdom of Israel, predicting the fall of Samaria (1:6) that would take place in 722
B.C. His message was aimed at greedy and oppressive landowners (2:1–5). They supported Israel's corrupt political and religious leaders, who had led the nation into moral decay.

TIMELINE

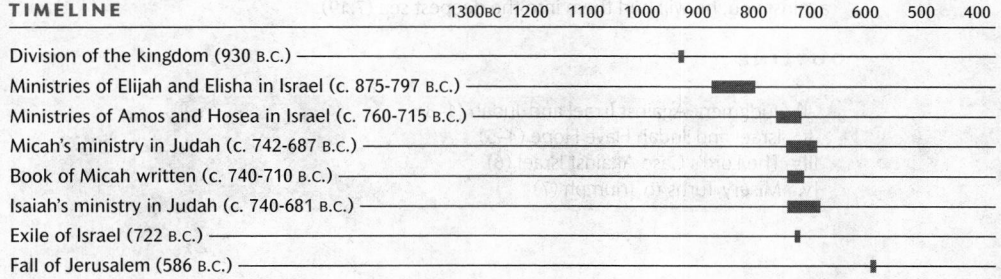

	1300BC	1200	1100	1000	900	800	700	600	500	400
Division of the kingdom (930 B.C.)										
Ministries of Elijah and Elisha in Israel (c. 875-797 B.C.)										
Ministries of Amos and Hosea in Israel (c. 760-715 B.C.)										
Micah's ministry in Judah (c. 742-687 B.C.)										
Book of Micah written (c. 740-710 B.C.)										
Isaiah's ministry in Judah (c. 740-681 B.C.)										
Exile of Israel (722 B.C.)										
Fall of Jerusalem (586 B.C.)										

THEMES
Micah demonstrates the balancing of God's justice and mercy. God punishes the wicked but
saves and restores those who repent. Micah includes the following themes:

1. *Judgment against oppressors.* Micah predicted that God would justly judge "the sins of the
house of Israel" (1:5). Both Israel's and Judah's landowners and religious and political leaders
had abused their power and conspired to do evil (2:1; 7:3), coveted and defrauded others of
their property (2:2; 6:10), stolen and plundered (2:8), hated good and loved evil (3:2), oppressed the poor (3:3), despised justice and distorted truth (3:9), accepted bribes (3:11; 7:3),
used their religious positions for profit (3:11), engaged in dishonest business practices (6:11),
acted with violence and deceit (6:12), and murdered their own people (7:2). God would bring
disaster upon Samaria (1:6–7), Jerusalem (1:12; 3:12; 4:10), the greedy landowners (2:3–5),
the corrupted leaders (3:4), and the false prophets (3:5–7).

2. *Restoration.* Micah declared that after judgment God would mercifully forgive and restore
his people (7:9). He would bring them back from exile in Babylon (4:10) and restore
Jerusalem's dominion (4:8,13). God is the same today. He pardons sin and forgives his people
(7:18). He has compassion on those who repent and will "tread our sins underfoot and hurl all
our iniquities into the depths of the sea" (7:19).

3. *Justice.* Micah asked a deceptively simple question: "What does the LORD require of you?" (6:8). The answer: "To act justly and to love mercy and to walk humbly with your God" (6:8). Israel had failed to live up to this divine expectation, and the nation would suffer the horrible consequences. God's requirements of social justice, mercy, and humble obedience still apply to us today, summed up by Jesus when he said, "Love the Lord your God . . . [and] love your neighbor as yourself" (Matt. 22:37–39).

FAITH IN ACTION

The pages of Micah contain life lessons and role models of faith—people who challenge believers to put their faith in action.

Role Models

- MICAH (3:1–4,11) denounced the leaders for their injustice and oppression of the people they were supposed to lead and care for. What are you doing to curtail injustice in your community?

- THE REMNANT (4:6; 7:18) would one day be healed and restored. Are you suffering? Are you burdened by your own sin? Accept and appropriate God's promises of forgiveness and restoration (7:18–19).

Challenges

- Don't lose sight of the vision of nations living together in mutual peace (4:2–3). Where possible, work for peace and reconciliation among people in conflict (Matt. 5:9).

- Evaluate yourself. Do you act justly, love mercy, and walk humbly with God (6:8)? If not, you are missing God's priorities.

- Receive God's compassion and forgiveness (7:18–19). He not only won't hold your sins against you; he will hurl them into the deepest sea (7:19).

OUTLINE

   I.   Judgment Against Israel and Judah (1–3)
   II. Israel and Judah Have Hope (4–5)
  III. The Lord's Case Against Israel (6)
  IV. Misery Turns to Triumph (7)

1:1
a Jer 26:18
b 1Ch 3:12
c 1Ch 3:13
d Hos 1:1 e Isa 1:1
1:2
f Ps 50:7 g Jer 6:19
h Ge 31:50;
Dt 4:26; Isa 1:2
i Ps 11:4

1 The word of the LORD that came to Micah of Moresheth [a] during the reigns of Jotham, [b] Ahaz [c] and Hezekiah, kings of Judah [d]—the vision [e] he saw concerning Samaria and Jerusalem.

² Hear, O peoples, all of you, [f]
   listen, O earth [g] and all who are in it,
that the Sovereign LORD may witness [h] against you,
   the Lord from his holy temple. [i]

Micah 1:1–2

The book of Micah opens with an announcement of its divine source, identification of the prophet, specification of the time period, and a notation of the subject of the prophecies. Micah was from Moresheth (*probably the "Moresheth Gath" of v. 14*), about 25 miles southwest of Jerusalem. His ministry likely extended from about 735 to 700 B.C., overlapping Isaiah's. Though Micah was from Judah, his prophetic revelations pertained to both the southern kingdom of Judah and the northern kingdom of Israel—represented, respectively, by their capitals of Jerusalem and Samaria.

The initial call to attention in verse 2 is surprisingly addressed to all the peoples of the earth. God, the universal King, comes from his "holy temple" in heaven (cf. v. 3) to administer justice in every nation.

Just as God witnessed the acts of people in Micah's lifetime, nothing escapes his notice today. The international chaos caused by ill-advised choices of

Judgment Against Samaria and Jerusalem

3 Look! The LORD is coming from his dwelling[j] place;
   he comes down and treads the high places of the earth.[k]
4 The mountains melt[l] beneath him
   and the valleys split apart,[m]
like wax before the fire,
   like water rushing down a slope.
5 All this is because of Jacob's transgression,
   because of the sins of the house of Israel.
What is Jacob's transgression?
   Is it not Samaria?[n]
What is Judah's high place?
   Is it not Jerusalem?

6 "Therefore I will make Samaria a heap of rubble,
   a place for planting vineyards.
I will pour her stones[o] into the valley
   and lay bare her foundations.[p]
7 All her idols[q] will be broken to pieces;
   all her temple gifts will be burned with fire;
   I will destroy all her images.[r]
Since she gathered her gifts from the wages of prostitutes,[s]
   as the wages of prostitutes they will again be used."

Weeping and Mourning

8 Because of this I will weep[t] and wail;
   I will go about barefoot and naked.
I will howl like a jackal
   and moan like an owl.
9 For her wound[u] is incurable;
   it has come to Judah.[v]
It[a] has reached the very gate[w] of my people,
   even to Jerusalem itself.
10 Tell it not in Gath[b];
   weep not at all.[c]
In Beth Ophrah[d]

1:3 j Isa 18:4 k Am 4:13
1:4 l Ps 46:2,6 m Nu 16:31; Na 1:5
1:5 n Am 8:14
1:6 o Am 5:11 p Eze 13:14
1:7 q Eze 6:6 r Dt 9:21 s Dt 23:17-18
1:8 t Isa 15:3
1:9 u Jer 46:11 v 2Ki 18:13 w Isa 3:26

---

a 9 Or He   b 10 Gath sounds like the Hebrew for tell.   c 10 Hebrew; Septuagint may suggest not in Acco. The Hebrew for in Acco sounds like the Hebrew for weep.   d 10 Beth Ophrah means house of dust.

---

leaders worldwide may bring harm or death to innocent people, but God isn't hoodwinked or unconcerned. He deals with individual and national sins in two ways: in surprising and undeserving grace and mercy—and in deserved justice.

Micah 1:3–7

Micah's initial judgment oracle culminated with a prediction of the northern kingdom's destruction (vv. 6–7), which was fulfilled during Micah's lifetime when Assyria conquered Israel in 722 B.C. He compared Israel's idolatry to prostitution, a common Old Testament metaphor. The wealth Israel had gained from her idolatry would be taken by the Assyrians to be used again in their own pagan worship.

Any thinking listener would have seen the unstated implications for Judah, since Judah's sins paralleled Israel's (v. 5). In fact, Micah sarcastically referred to Jerusalem as Judah's "high place"—a pagan shrine (cf. v. 3; see 2 Kings 16:1–4 regarding such idolatry at the time of Ahaz).

God witnessed sin among his chosen (and supposedly holy and separated; Ex. 19:3–6) people. He is equally displeased when he observes rebellion in his people today. The acts of bowing to our own ambitions, putting ourselves first, and loving our desires more than God's are veiled denials of his lordship and divinity. How do your acts and attitudes affirm God's kingship? Deny it? What concrete steps can you take to set things right?

Micah 1:8–16

In verse 8 Micah announced his determination to begin grieving over the fate of his people. The words of his funeral-like lament are found in verses 10–16. Israel's "incurable wound" of destruction at the hands of Assyria would spread like a cancer to the gate of Jerusalem. Micah chose several towns in or near Judah to include in his lament because puns (in Hebrew) could be made on their names (see NIV text notes). This was like saying: Watertown will be covered with water, and Washington will be washed away.

roll in the dust.

1:11
x Eze 23:29

11 Pass on in nakedness ˣ and shame,
    you who live in Shaphir. ᵃ
Those who live in Zaanan ᵇ
    will not come out.
Beth Ezel is in mourning;
    its protection is taken from you.

1:12
y Jer 14:19

12 Those who live in Maroth ᶜ writhe in pain,
    waiting for relief, ʸ
because disaster has come from the LORD,
    even to the gate of Jerusalem.

1:13
z Jos 10:3

13 You who live in Lachish, ᵈᶻ
    harness the team to the chariot.
You were the beginning of sin
    to the Daughter of Zion,
for the transgressions of Israel
    were found in you.

1:14
a 2Ki 16:8
b Jos 15:44
c Jer 15:18

14 Therefore you will give parting gifts ᵃ
    to Moresheth Gath.
The town of Aczib ᵉᵇ will prove deceptive ᶜ
    to the kings of Israel.

1:15
d Jos 15:44
e Jos 12:15

15 I will bring a conqueror against you
    who live in Mareshah. ᶠᵈ
He who is the glory of Israel
    will come to Adullam. ᵉ

1:16
f Job 1:20

16 Shave ᶠ your heads in mourning
    for the children in whom you delight;
make yourselves as bald as the vulture,
    for they will go from you into exile.

Man's Plans and God's

2:1
g Ps 36:4

2 Woe to those who plan iniquity,
    to those who plot evil on their beds! ᵍ
At morning's light they carry it out
    because it is in their power to do it.

2:2
h Isa 5:8

2 They covet fields ʰ and seize them,

ᵃ 11 *Shaphir* means *pleasant.*   ᵇ 11 *Zaanan* sounds like the Hebrew for *come out.*   ᶜ 12 *Maroth* sounds like the Hebrew for *bitter.*   ᵈ 13 *Lachish* sounds like the Hebrew for *team.*   ᵉ 14 *Aczib* means *deception.*   ᶠ 15 *Mareshah* sounds like the Hebrew for *conqueror.*

Prophetic laments voiced sorrow because the people hadn't responded to God's messengers. As a persuasive tool, the lament was a powerful alternative to accusations and condemnations. It conveyed identification and sympathy, not opposition and conflict. The speaker took the audience's side, expressing regret for what was about to happen.

📖 There is little talk in the church today about lamenting the world's hurting and lost. Moses, Amos, Micah, Jeremiah, Jesus, and Paul all found grief a fitting way to communicate their deep sorrow for those who would die outside of fellowship with God (cf. Num. 16:20–22; Jer. 8:18–22; Amos 5:1–27; Mic. 1:8–16; Matt. 23:37; Rom. 9:1–5). In the church, a lack of sorrow over those who resist or reject God's grace reveals our lack of compassion (2 Peter 3:9).

Micah 2:1–5
📖 This brief judgment woe follows the traditional

pattern (cf. Isa. 30:1–5; Amos 6:1–7): a cry of lament (v. 1a), a series of accusations (vv. 1b–2), and a statement of judgment (vv. 3–5). After the restoration of the nation, they would be excluded from participating in the redistribution of the land (v. 5). These rich land-grabbers would reap what they had sown.

📖 Covetousness gets to the root of sin because it exposes a person's deeply cherished inner desires and problems with self-control. Our rate of coveting can be measured by national consumer debt and consumer confidence numbers—skyrocketing figures in Western countries. But this plague isn't just economic; it has infiltrated our culture. Ads play upon people's lusts and desires. Coveting often underlies the plots of novels and movies and leads to crime and immorality in everyday life. Is there an antidote to this invasive force? How about generosity? The generous person is loosely attached to possessions and firmly connected to God and his kingdom.

and houses, and take them.
They defraud[i] a man of his home,
a fellowman of his inheritance.

2:2
i Jer 22:17

3Therefore, the LORD says:

"I am planning disaster[j] against this people,
from which you cannot save yourselves.
You will no longer walk proudly,[k]
for it will be a time of calamity.
4In that day men will ridicule you;
they will taunt you with this mournful song:
'We are utterly ruined;[l]
my people's possession is divided up.
He takes it from me!
He assigns our fields to traitors.' "

2:3
j Jer 18:11;
Am 3:1-2 k Isa 2:12

2:4
l Jer 4:13

5Therefore you will have no one in the assembly of the LORD
to divide the land[m] by lot.

2:5
m Jos 18:4

False Prophets

6"Do not prophesy," their prophets say.
"Do not prophesy about these things;
disgrace[n] will not overtake us.[o]"
7Should it be said, O house of Jacob:
"Is the Spirit of the LORD angry?
Does he do such things?"

2:6
n Mic 6:16
o Am 2:12

"Do not my words do good[p]
to him whose ways are upright?[q]
8Lately my people have risen up
like an enemy.
You strip off the rich robe
from those who pass by without a care,
like men returning from battle.
9You drive the women of my people
from their pleasant homes.[r]
You take away my blessing
from their children forever.
10Get up, go away!
For this is not your resting place,[s]
because it is defiled,[t]
it is ruined, beyond all remedy.
11If a liar and deceiver[u] comes and says,
'I will prophesy for you plenty of wine and beer,'
he would be just the prophet for this people![v]

2:7
p Ps 119:65
q Ps 15:2; 84:11

2:9
r Jer 10:20

2:10
s Dt 12:9
t Lev 18:25-29;
Ps 106:38-39

2:11
u Jer 5:31
v Isa 30:10

Micah 2:6–11

In this disputation exchange, the wealthy oppressors and their false prophets argued with Micah (and God) about his prophecy of 2:1–5 and his perception of the nature of God and of God's relationship to his covenant people. Micah's audience had misunderstood how God related to his people and had accepted pious phrases, half-truths, and unbalanced teachings that assured their own prosperity and security. Tragically, these deceptions caused them to fail to deal seriously with their responsibility to love and follow God completely and to treat their neighbors justly.

A sense of invulnerability can be a trap for religious people. The problem is aggravated by messages that concentrate exclusively on the Good News of God's love and forgiveness. It's right to emphasize God's compassion and patience and appropriate to tell a dying world about his love. But when believers ignore or deny a coming judgment (as Micah's listeners did), something is wrong. Respectful fear of God's righteous anger against sin is a healthy attitude for all people to share.

Deliverance Promised

2:12
w Mic 4:7; 5:7; 7:18

12 "I will surely gather all of you, O Jacob;
    I will surely bring together the remnant [w] of Israel.
I will bring them together like sheep in a pen,
    like a flock in its pasture;
    the place will throng with people.

2:13
x Isa 52:12

13 One who breaks open the way will go up before [x] them;
    they will break through the gate and go out.
Their king will pass through before them,
    the LORD at their head."

Leaders and Prophets Rebuked

3:1
y Jer 5:5

3 Then I said,

"Listen, you leaders [y] of Jacob,
    you rulers of the house of Israel.
Should you not know justice,
2   you who hate good and love evil;

3:2
z Ps 53:4; Eze 22:27
3:3
a Ps 14:4 b Zep 3:3
c Eze 11:7

who tear the skin from my people
    and the flesh from their bones; [z]
3 who eat my people's flesh, [a]
    strip off their skin
    and break their bones in pieces; [b]
who chop them up like meat for the pan,
    like flesh for the pot? [c]"

3:4
d Ps 18:41; Isa 1:15
e Dt 31:17

4 Then they will cry out to the LORD,
    but he will not answer them. [d]
At that time he will hide his face [e] from them
    because of the evil they have done.

5 This is what the LORD says:

3:5
f Isa 3:12; 9:16

"As for the prophets
    who lead my people astray, [f]

Micah 2:12–13

The first major section of Micah (1:1—2:13) ends with a salvation message offering hope for a remnant of survivors following God's judgment of exile. As Micah looked ahead, "Israel" in this case probably meant the whole nation, north and south. God promised that he wouldn't forget his people and that there would be a radical change in their situation in the future—when he (or possibly the Messiah) would go before them and become their King.

God has more than enough power to deliver and restore his people—though this passage, and others like it, doesn't promise that he will always deliver them from harm's way or always give them an obvious victory. Believers are called to stand fast in their faith, to wait for him to reveal the next step, and to rest in the assurance that he will do all he has promised. Does this kind of hope make sense? Yes, because God is in sovereign control of all that happens.

Micah 3:1–12

The references to Zion and Jerusalem (vv. 10,12) show that Micah had Judah in mind in this message to the leaders of "Israel" (vv. 1,9). The passage is comprised of

prophecies against (1) the civil leaders for relating to the people like cannibals (vv. 1–4); (2) the false prophets who denied God's coming judgment (vv. 5–7); and (3) the leaders, priests, and prophets for their corruption (vv. 8–12).

The oracles are unified by their condemnation of the leaders' unjust treatment of people and by a progression from God's silence when the leaders cried for his help (v. 4) to his silence when the false prophets looked for answers (vv. 6–7) to his refusal to intervene when Jerusalem and the temple were destroyed (v. 12).

Micah, filled with God's Spirit, spoke with conviction based on divine justice, whereas the false prophets based their words and actions on financial motives. Social and political power can pressure decision-makers to do what influential people want. The desire to be powerful and affluent can cause people in any age or culture to treat others unjustly in order to grasp the next higher level of status or authority. Micah's warnings set down key criteria for evaluating leadership in church, government, and civic organizations. But are the rest of us off the hook? How has the desire to advance affected your life in terms of your dealings with those around you—on lower, similar, and higher levels?

if one feeds them,
they proclaim 'peace';
if he does not,
they prepare to wage war against him.
6 Therefore night will come over you, without visions,
and darkness, without divination.[g]
The sun will set for the prophets,[h]
and the day will go dark for them.
7 The seers will be ashamed[i]
and the diviners disgraced.[j]
They will all cover their faces
because there is no answer from God."

8 But as for me, I am filled with power,
with the Spirit of the LORD,
and with justice and might,
to declare to Jacob his transgression,
to Israel his sin.[k]
9 Hear this, you leaders of the house of Jacob,
you rulers of the house of Israel,
who despise justice
and distort all that is right;[l]
10 who build[m] Zion with bloodshed,[n]
and Jerusalem with wickedness.[o]
11 Her leaders judge for a bribe,
her priests teach for a price,
and her prophets tell fortunes for money.[p]
Yet they lean upon the LORD and say,
"Is not the LORD among us?
No disaster will come upon us."[q]
12 Therefore because of you,
Zion will be plowed like a field,
Jerusalem will become a heap of rubble,[r]
the temple hill a mound overgrown with thickets.

The Mountain of the LORD

4 In the last days

the mountain[s] of the LORD's temple will be established
as chief among the mountains;
it will be raised above the hills,[t]
and peoples will stream to it.[u]

2 Many nations will come and say,

"Come, let us go up to the mountain of the LORD,[v]
to the house of the God of Jacob.[w]
He will teach us his ways,[x]
so that we may walk in his paths."
The law will go out from Zion,

3:6 [g] Isa 8:19-22 [h] Isa 29:10
3:7 [i] Mic 7:16 [j] Isa 44:25
3:8 [k] Isa 58:1
3:9 [l] Ps 58:1-2; Isa 1:23
3:10 [m] Jer 22:13 [n] Hab 2:12 [o] Eze 22:27
3:11 [p] Isa 1:23; Jer 6:13; Hos 4:8,18 [q] Jer 7:4
3:12 [r] Jer 26:18
4:1 [s] Zec 8:3 [t] Eze 17:22 [u] Ps 22:27; 86:9; Jer 3:17
4:2 [v] Jer 31:6 [w] Zec 2:11; 14:16 [x] Ps 25:8-9; Isa 54:13

Micah 4:1–5

These promises stand in sharp contrast to the judgments in chapter 3. This prophecy provided a vision of what God, through the Messiah (cf. Isa. 2:2–4) ultimately would do. It pointed forward to a time when people would experience God's presence in a completely new way. This era would inaugurate a new relationship between God and people, Israel and the nations, and humanity and nature. God's original purpose for humankind would be fulfilled as he brought his plan to completion.

God has a continuing plan to establish his kingdom. His vision includes, but extends far beyond, our personal salvation and the growth of our church. Our confident hope is that one day God will establish peace among nations and everyone will live without fear.

the word of the LORD from Jerusalem.

3 He will judge between many peoples
and will settle disputes for strong nations far and wide. y

They will beat their swords into plowshares
and their spears into pruning hooks. z

Nation will not take up sword against nation,
nor will they train for war anymore. a

4 Every man will sit under his own vine
and under his own fig tree, b

and no one will make them afraid, c
for the LORD Almighty has spoken. d

5 All the nations may walk
in the name of their gods; e

we will walk in the name of the LORD
our God for ever and ever. f

The LORD's Plan

6 "In that day," declares the LORD,

"I will gather the lame;
I will assemble the exiles g

and those I have brought to grief. h

7 I will make the lame a remnant, i
those driven away a strong nation.

The LORD will rule over them in Mount Zion
from that day and forever. j

8 As for you, O watchtower of the flock,
O stronghold a of the Daughter of Zion,

the former dominion will be restored k to you;
kingship will come to the Daughter of Jerusalem."

9 Why do you now cry aloud—
have you no king? l

Has your counselor perished,
that pain seizes you like that of a woman in labor? m

10 Writhe in agony, O Daughter of Zion,
like a woman in labor,

for now you must leave the city
to camp in the open field.

You will go to Babylon; n
there you will be rescued.

There the LORD will redeem o you
out of the hand of your enemies.

11 But now many nations

a 8 Or hill

Cross references (margin)

4:3
y Isa 11:4
z Joel 3:10 a Isa 2:4

4:4
b 1Ki 4:25
c Lev 26:6
d Isa 1:20; Zec 3:10

4:5
e 2Ki 17:29
f Jos 24:14-15;
Isa 26:8; Zec 10:12

4:6
g Ps 147:2
h Eze 34:13,16;
37:21; Zep 3:19

4:7
i Mic 2:12
j Da 7:14; Lk 1:33;
Rev 11:15

4:8
k Isa 1:26

4:9
l Jer 8:19
m Jer 30:6

4:10
n 2Ki 20:18;
Isa 43:14
o Isa 48:20

Micah 4:6-13

🔲 The image of God gathering his people as a shepherd might separate out his lame sheep represented a marvelous work of divine power and grace. The disabled individual in exile, who felt rejected and devalued, would be healed and join the precious remnant of God's surviving people. The weak exiles banished from their land would become a strong nation.

Verses 9–13 are a mixture of prophecies of judgment and salvation. To emphasize the foolishness of Judah's enemies, Micah contrasted their thoughts with God's. They thought they had a brilliant plan to gather at Jerusalem—but God would "gather" *them*. They wanted to destroy Judah's capital—but ultimately God would destroy *them*. They wanted to desecrate Zion and loot its temple—but Zion would end up "devoting" *their* wealth to God.

🔲 God doesn't abandon the weak and wounded, and neither should we. This attitude characterized Jesus, the "good shepherd" (John 10; cf. Mic. 5:4), who cared for society's sick and outcast. His strategy was to heal and lead them, to demonstrate that God's grace and love aren't based on human status or value systems. Does this kind of activity and attitude characterize the ministries you are involved in today?

are gathered against you.
They say, "Let her be defiled,
let our eyes gloat[p] over Zion!"
12 But they do not know
the thoughts of the LORD;
they do not understand his plan,[q]
he who gathers them like sheaves to the threshing floor.

13 "Rise and thresh, O Daughter of Zion,
for I will give you horns of iron;
I will give you hoofs of bronze
and you will break to pieces many nations."[r]

You will devote their ill-gotten gains to the LORD,
their wealth to the Lord of all the earth.

A Promised Ruler From Bethlehem

5 Marshal your troops, O city of troops,[a]
for a siege is laid against us.
They will strike Israel's ruler
on the cheek[s] with a rod.

2 "But you, Bethlehem[t] Ephrathah,[u]
though you are small among the clans[b] of Judah,
out of you will come for me
one who will be ruler over Israel,
whose origins[c] are from of old,[v]
from ancient times.[d][w]

3 Therefore Israel will be abandoned
until the time when she who is in labor gives birth
and the rest of his brothers return
to join the Israelites.

4 He will stand and shepherd his flock[x]
in the strength of the LORD,
in the majesty of the name of the LORD his God.
And they will live securely, for then his greatness[y]
will reach to the ends of the earth.

5 And he will be their peace.[z]

a 1 Or *Strengthen your walls, O walled city*   b 2 Or *rulers*   c 2 Hebrew *goings out*   d 2 Or *from days of eternity*

4:11 p La 2:16; Ob 1:12

4:12 q Isa 55:8; Ro 11:33-34

4:13 r Da 2:44

5:1 s La 3:30

5:2 t Jn 7:42 u Ge 48:7 v Ps 102:25 w Mt 2:6*

5:4 x Isa 40:11; 49:9; Eze 34:11-15,23; Mic 7:14 y Isa 52:13; Lk 1:32

5:5 z Isa 9:6; Lk 2:14; Col 1:19-20

Micah 5:1–5a

In verse 1 Micah apparently looked ahead to the Babylonians' siege of Jerusalem. In addition to destroying the city, the Babylonians would put out the eyes of Zedekiah, Judah's last king, and take him to Babylon (2 Kings 25:7). Micah's prophecy then took a 180-degree turn with a message of hope foreseeing the day when a strong ruler—whose "greatness will reach to the ends of the earth"—would arise from Bethlehem, the city of David (Ruth 4:11,17; 1 Sam. 16:1; 17:12). This reminded the people of the Messianic promise of the eternal reign of David's dynasty (2 Sam. 7:4–17; Ps. 2; 89:19–37; 132).

Verse 3 interrupted the flow of thought with the clarification that this ruler wouldn't come immediately; first there would be a period in which the nation would be abandoned to exile (cf. Mic. 4:10). Sometime after that a woman would give birth to this child who, like David his ancestor, would shepherd God's people by leading, protecting, and providing for their needs (cf. 2 Sam. 5:2; 7:7).

In a crisis, when people feel overwhelmed by circumstances beyond their control, it's easy to despair. Micah demonstrated that hope involves waiting, believing that a promise will come true, and retaining confidence in the One who made it.

For the person who has accepted Christ as Savior, Jesus' birth wonderfully confirms Micah's words (Matt. 2:6). This fulfillment provides assurance that other, as yet unfulfilled, aspects of this prophecy will also come true—that peace will prevail in our world. How can this confident expression alter how we live now?

Deliverance and Destruction

5:5
a Isa 8:7
b Isa 10:24-27

When the Assyrian invades*a* our land
　and marches through our fortresses,
we will raise against him seven shepherds,
　even eight leaders of men.*b*

5:6
c Ge 10:8
d Zep 2:13
e Na 2:11-13

⁶They will rule*a* the land of Assyria with the sword,
　the land of Nimrod*c* with drawn sword.*b d*
He will deliver us from the Assyrian
　when he invades our land
　and marches into our borders.*e*

5:7
f Mic 2:12
g Isa 44:4

⁷The remnant*f* of Jacob will be
　in the midst of many peoples
like dew from the LORD,
　like showers on the grass,*g*
which do not wait for man
　or linger for mankind.

a 6 Or *crush*　*b 6* Or *Nimrod in its gates*

Micah 5:5b–15

This passage is difficult to interpret. In verses 5b–6, Micah may have been quoting the people's boast that they, along with their allies (several "shepherds" or kings), would defeat the invading Assyrians (who would overrun Judah and threaten Jerusalem in 701 B.C.) and even go on the offensive and rule over all the territory of Assyria and Babylon ("the land of Nimrod"). Verses 7–8 corrected these brash statements. The dew analogy showed that Judah wasn't in control of her future, and

the lion symbol demonstrated that the nations weren't in charge of theirs. Following this interpretive approach to the passage, in verse 9 Micah spoke to God, by whose hand victory would come.

The prophecy in verses 10–15 again called for a purging of all false sources of trust and worship—of anything other than God himself. Walled cities, strong armies, and idols were of no value. God would destroy all these feeble human attempts to provide hope.

Snapshots

5:1–5a

Kalya = Peace

Joseph is the first-born son of his father's first wife. In Kenyan Pokot culture that means he shares with his father the responsibility of defending and feeding his family and its animals. No small task, since his father and his four wives have produced 24 children.

From the age of five, Joseph began developing a painful swelling in his left leg. His father took him to the mission clinic 40 kilometers away. But each time the walk itself cured the swelling. When Joseph was eight, his father decided that he was useless in terms of ability to herd livestock or defend against raids. He might as well attend the mission school. Joseph excelled. The swelling gradually disappeared, and his reluctant father allowed him to continue his education.

> "I have always wanted to go back and do my best for my people, because one day I might be asked, 'Why didn't you help?' "

After graduating from Daystar University in Nairobi, Joseph was hired as a peace monitor. He and his wife named their daughter Kalya: Pokot for "peace." "Everyone wondered about that name . . . People didn't see all the raiding and killing as a problem. It was just tradition.

"I have always wanted to go back and do my best for my people, because one day I might be asked, 'Why didn't you help?' I came back and am fulfilling my duty as the first-born, only not in the traditional way. . . . I am able to defend my family and my community through peace, not through war."

⁸The remnant of Jacob will be among the nations,
  in the midst of many peoples,
like a lion among the beasts of the forest, *ʰ*
  like a young lion among flocks of sheep,
which mauls and mangles *ⁱ* as it goes,
  and no one can rescue. *ʲ*
⁹Your hand will be lifted up *ᵏ* in triumph over your enemies,
  and all your foes will be destroyed.

¹⁰"In that day," declares the LORD,

"I will destroy your horses from among you
  and demolish your chariots. *ˡ*
¹¹I will destroy the cities *ᵐ* of your land
  and tear down all your strongholds. *ⁿ*
¹²I will destroy your witchcraft
  and you will no longer cast spells. *ᵒ*
¹³I will destroy your carved images
  and your sacred stones from among you;
you will no longer bow down
  to the work of your hands. *ᵖ*
¹⁴I will uproot from among you your Asherah poles *ᵃ �q*
  and demolish your cities.
¹⁵I will take vengeance *ʳ* in anger and wrath
  upon the nations that have not obeyed me."

The LORD's Case Against Israel

6 Listen to what the LORD says:

"Stand up, plead your case before the mountains; *ˢ*
  let the hills hear what you have to say.
²Hear, *ᵗ* O mountains, the LORD's accusation; *ᵘ*
  listen, you everlasting foundations of the earth.
For the LORD has a case against his people;
  he is lodging a charge *ᵛ* against Israel.

³"My people, what have I done to you?
  How have I burdened *ʷ* you? Answer me.

ᵃ 14 That is, symbols of the goddess Asherah

5:8
ʰ Ge 49:9
ⁱ Mic 4:13; Zec 10:5
ʲ Ps 50:22; Hos 5:14

5:9
ᵏ Ps 10:12

5:10
ˡ Hos 14:3; Zec 9:10
5:11
ᵐ Isa 6:11
ⁿ Hos 10:14; Am 5:9
5:12
ᵒ Dt 18:10-12; Isa 2:6; 8:19

5:13
ᵖ Eze 6:9; Zec 13:2
5:14
�q Ex 34:13

5:15
ʳ Isa 65:12

6:1
ˢ Ps 50:1; Eze 6:2

6:2
ᵗ Dt 32:1
ᵘ Hos 12:2
ᵛ Ps 50:7

6:3
ʷ Jer 2:5

📖 One factor that determines how people respond to a crisis is their belief about God's sovereignty in relation to "their" plans for the future. The tendency to depend on what "I/we" can do and the desire to control the future through "my/our" wisdom leaves no room for God to demonstrate his power, accomplish his plans, or demonstrate his glory.

People tend to develop their worldviews from their social relationships, but the church is responsible to give the world an accurate, Biblical picture of God. In our religiously diverse environment, we are to resist society's pressure to dilute or suppress our own beliefs. At the same time, belittling or demeaning others doesn't invite them into the kingdom. Our love for each other and compassion for all God's creation will point a watching world to the God who loved them so much that "he gave his one and only Son" (John 3:16).

Micah 6:1-8

📖 This chapter represents a courtroom scene in which God brought a covenant lawsuit against his people (cf. Deut. 32; Ps. 50; Jer. 2; Hos. 4). The mountains were called to be witnesses. In verses 6–7 the accused tried to defend themselves by explaining how faithful they had been to God. Their exaggerated rhetorical questions demanded a negative answer.

In responding to the people's questions, Micah stated that God had already communicated what he required. God's people are to act justly toward others in all their dealings, "love mercy" (remain loyal to God and the principles of covenantal life together with his community), and reject any presumptuous attitude of doing things their own way. Such a walk with God is humble in that it puts an individual's will in a secondary position and gives careful attention to doing God's will.

📖 These three broad requirements connect our day-to-day behavior to our religious faith. What we believe about God will shape our daily lives. What impact would it have on your life if this were to become your personal mission statement: "to act justly and to love mercy and to walk humbly with [my] God"?

Dorothy Day

Dorothy Day, founder of the Catholic Worker movement, demonstrated by her life and vision the power that results when passionate conviction unites with everyday actions.

Hers was a vision of distributive justice—a fair distribution of goods that counters individual greed and corporate power structures. She exhibited the contours of that vision by founding 33 hospitality houses. Here she welcomed the poor and could often be found peeling carrots or making beds rather than writing speeches or conversing with dignitaries.

Day's sense of justice developed during a difficult childhood, characterized by poverty and lack of familial affection. After her father refused her a place in the family home in New York City, she spent her young adult years wandering in search of a philosophy to support her idealism. Some would exclude her as a faith hero because of her radical politics and participation in the sexual revolution of the 1920s. But with the birth of her daughter in 1926, Day turned her back on communism and promiscuity, joining the Catholic Church of her childhood, to which she remained faithful until her death in 1980. Her passionate seeking had found a resting place in God.

Day spoke of her life as a long loneliness—reminiscent of the isolation experienced by the prophet Micah. Like Micah, she lived simply, speaking of justice to a rich and violent society. Like Micah she wandered mournful and barefoot through city streets, proclaiming a message no one wanted to hear.

> **Dorothy Day transformed practical acts of mercy into a movement.**

Day took up the cause of economic justice in the United States beginning in the 1920s, when prosperity seemed everlasting. But the Great Depression of the 1930s highlighted the need for distributive justice. Day, like Micah, criticized national leaders who supported injustice through violent means.

With Peter Maurin, Day established houses of hospitality where the poor could come and work, enjoy the fruits of their labor, and discuss the philosophical issues of the day. Following the Biblical injunction, she did more than preach against poverty; she fed and clothed the needy (James 1:22,27). Indeed, Dorothy Day transformed practical acts of mercy into a movement. The lessons she taught are those of the prophet Micah: to act justly, love mercy, and walk humbly with God (Mic. 6:8).

Day advocated justice. Even before her conversion experience in 1926, she worked as a journalist, becoming a regular correspondent for left-wing publications. She spoke her mind on current issues: women's suffrage, fair treatment of prisoners, and birth control. After her conversion, she gave up her common law husband, joined the church, and began searching for ways to articulate her new perspective. Collaborating with ex-peasant Frenchman Peter Maurin, she began publishing the *Catholic Worker* in 1933. The paper not only supported a neutral pacifism but advocated better conditions for the poor and spoke out for the rights of workers. *Lesson: Doing justice is the prerogative of people as well as nations.*

And Day loved mercy. Housing the homeless and feeding the hungry were for her a daily practice, not just a theory or theological principle. She advocated structural changes in government and labor organizations to help people provide for themselves. But she also organized and supported the hospitality houses that provided the model for soup kitchens throughout the United States. *Lesson: Acts of mercy go hand in hand with seeking justice.*

Finally, Day expressed humility in both her self-assessment and her actions. In her autobiography, *The Long Loneliness*, she credited others for her life's achievements. *Lesson: Humility characterizes the person who walks with God.*

⁴I brought you up out of Egypt
and redeemed you from the land of slavery.ˣ
I sent Mosesʸ to lead you,
also Aaronᶻ and Miriam.ᵃ
⁵My people, remember
what Balakᵇ king of Moab counseled
and what Balaam son of Beor answered.
Remember ⌊your journey⌋ from Shittimᶜ to Gilgal,ᵈ
that you may know the righteous actsᵉ of the LORD."

⁶With what shall I come before the LORD
and bow down before the exalted God?
Shall I come before him with burnt offerings,
with calves a year old?ᶠ
⁷Will the LORD be pleased with thousands of rams,ᵍ
with ten thousand rivers of oil?ʰ
Shall I offer my firstbornⁱ for my transgression,
the fruit of my body for the sin of my soul?ʲ
⁸He has showed you, O man, what is good.
And what does the LORD require of you?
To act justlyᵏ and to love mercy
and to walk humblyˡ with your God.ᵐ

Israel's Guilt and Punishment

⁹Listen! The LORD is calling to the city—
and to fear your name is wisdom—
"Heed the rod and the One who appointed it.ᵃ
¹⁰Am I still to forget, O wicked house,
your ill-gotten treasures
and the short ephah,ᵇ which is accursed?ⁿ
¹¹Shall I acquit a man with dishonest scales,ᵒ
with a bag of false weights?
¹²Her rich men are violent;ᵖ
her people are liarsᑫ

6:4
ˣ Dt 7:8 ʸ Ex 4:16
ᶻ Ps 77:20
ᵃ Ex 15:20
6:5
ᵇ Nu 22:5-6
ᶜ Nu 25:1
ᵈ Jos 5:9-10
ᵉ Jdg 5:11; 1Sa 12:7
6:6
ᶠ Ps 40:6-8; 51:16-17
6:7
ᵍ Isa 40:16
ʰ Ps 50:8-10
ⁱ Lev 18:21
ʲ 2Ki 16:3
6:8
ᵏ Isa 1:17; Jer 22:3
ˡ Isa 57:15
ᵐ Dt 10:12-13; 1Sa 15:22; Hos 6:6
6:10
ⁿ Eze 45:9-10; Am 3:10; 8:4-6
6:11
ᵒ Lev 19:36; Hos 12:7
6:12
ᵖ Isa 1:23 ᑫ Isa 3:8

ᵃ 9 The meaning of the Hebrew for this line is uncertain.   ᵇ 10 An ephah was a dry measure.

Micah 6:9–16

Having set the standards for proper covenant behavior in 6:8, God now raised specific examples, demonstrating that the people in Jerusalem had failed to live up to their covenant agreement. Because of Judah's infidelity, the present covenant relationship was unbearable to God. The only possible verdict for this lawsuit was "guilty as charged." To show the seriousness of the problem, Micah compared Judah to the northern kingdom under the reigns of Omri and Ahab, two wicked kings of Israel (see 1 Kings 16:25,30). The same tragedy

of ruin and exile that befell Israel would happen to Judah.

Are you ever tempted to separate your personal Christian life from the secular business of making a living? Christians sometimes become uncomfortable when the church starts talking about money. A discussion in our churches about business ethics might open the door to the less comfortable discussion about God's concern with all financial matters. God recognizes the connection between the "state of our soul" and our approach to money.

6:9

To Fear God's Name Is Wisdom

Fear is an attitude of anxiety or unrest. Some fears protect us from harm, but fear's only proper spiritual use, according to Scripture, is to open us up to a deepening faith in God. Reflect on this truth as you look up the following verses:

• Fear of natural phenomena	Ps. 91:5; Jonah 1:4–5
• Fear of unnatural phenomena, like thoughts, the unknown, or demons	Matt. 14:26–27
• Fear for ourselves: shame, persecution, or death	Ezra 4:4

Ironically, fear of God enables us to cope with these anxieties. Along with your love for God, do you maintain a healthy respect and awe of him?

6:12
r Jer 9:3
6:13
s Isa 1:7; 6:11
6:14
t Isa 9:20 u Isa 30:6

and their tongues speak deceitfully. *r*

13 Therefore, I have begun to destroy *s* you,
to ruin you because of your sins.
14 You will eat but not be satisfied; *t*
your stomach will still be empty. *a*
You will store up but save nothing, *u*
because what you save I will give to the sword.

6:15
v Dt 28:38;
Jer 12:13
w Am 5:11;
Zep 1:13
6:16
x 1Ki 16:25
y 1Ki 16:29-33
z Jer 7:24
a Jer 25:9
b Jer 51:51

15 You will plant but not harvest; *v*
you will press olives but not use the oil on yourselves,
you will crush grapes but not drink the wine. *w*
16 You have observed the statutes of Omri *x*
and all the practices of Ahab's *y* house,
and you have followed their traditions. *z*
Therefore I will give you over to ruin *a*
and your people to derision;
you will bear the scorn *b* of the nations. *b"*

Israel's Misery

7 What misery is mine!
I am like one who gathers summer fruit
at the gleaning of the vineyard;
there is no cluster of grapes to eat,
none of the early figs that I crave.

7:2
c Ps 12:1
d Mic 3:10
e Jer 5:26

2 The godly have been swept from the land; *c*
not one upright man remains.
All men lie in wait to shed blood; *d*
each hunts his brother with a net. *e*

7:3
f Pr 4:16

3 Both hands are skilled in doing evil; *f*
the ruler demands gifts,
the judge accepts bribes,
the powerful dictate what they desire—
they all conspire together.

7:4
g Eze 2:6
h Isa 22:5; Hos 9:7

4 The best of them is like a brier, *g*
the most upright worse than a thorn hedge.
The day of your watchmen has come,
the day God visits you.
Now is the time of their confusion. *h*

7:5
i Jer 9:4

5 Do not trust a neighbor;
put no confidence in a friend. *i*
Even with her who lies in your embrace

---

a 14 The meaning of the Hebrew for this word is uncertain.   *b 16* Septuagint; Hebrew *scorn due my people*

Micah 7:1–7

Micah began this final chapter with a lament over the sorrowful state of his society. Using the metaphor of a farmer going out to gather crops after the harvest was over, he expressed his disappointment with the absence of the righteous in the land. Deceit and manipulation in the highest levels of government were filtering down to poison the most basic bonds of trust. The institution of the family was even falling apart.

Verse 7 demonstrates an abrupt change of attitude and focus. Once the prophet moved his attention to God instead of the troubles all around him, a new sense of hope welled up inside him. The "watchman"/prophet (v. 4) would "watch" for the Lord his God, for there was no other possible source of life.

When Micah saw the powerful in his society exploiting the weak and realized that the glue of trust that had held the family together had disintegrated, he wept. How may we as the church and its individual members respond to this kind of social decay? Three applications come to mind: We can (1) reflect on whether God's love truly motivates us, (2) evaluate how we might positively impact our neighbors' lives, and (3) cry out to God for help.

Lamenting before God is different from complaining to other people. We can gain (or regain) hope by focusing not on the terrible plight of our world but on God, and especially on his ability as our "Savior" (v. 7) to deal with the insidious source of hopelessness—sin itself.

be careful of your words.
⁶ For a son dishonors his father,
    a daughter rises up against her mother, *j*
a daughter-in-law against her mother-in-law—
    a man's enemies are the members of his own household. *k*

⁷ But as for me, I watch in hope *l* for the LORD,
    I wait for God my Savior;
    my God will hear *m* me.

Israel Will Rise

⁸ Do not gloat over me, *n* my enemy!
    Though I have fallen, I will rise. *o*
Though I sit in darkness,
    the LORD will be my light. *p*
⁹ Because I have sinned against him,
    I will bear the LORD's wrath, *q*
until he pleads my case
    and establishes my right.
He will bring me out into the light;
    I will see his righteousness. *r*
¹⁰ Then my enemy will see it
    and will be covered with shame, *s*
she who said to me,
    "Where is the LORD your God?"
My eyes will see her downfall; *t*
    even now she will be trampled *u* underfoot
    like mire in the streets.

¹¹ The day for building your walls *v* will come,
    the day for extending your boundaries.
¹² In that day people will come to you
    from Assyria and the cities of Egypt,
even from Egypt to the Euphrates
    and from sea to sea
    and from mountain to mountain. *w*
¹³ The earth will become desolate because of its inhabitants,
    as the result of their deeds. *x*

Prayer and Praise

¹⁴ Shepherd *y* your people with your staff, *z*
    the flock of your inheritance,
which lives by itself in a forest,

Cross-references (margin)

7:6
j Eze 22:7
k Mt 10:35-36*

7:7
l Ps 130:5; Isa 25:9
m Ps 4:3

7:8
n Pr 24:17
o Ps 37:24;
Am 9:11 *p* Isa 9:2

7:9
q La 3:39-40
r Isa 46:13

7:10
s Ps 35:26
t Isa 51:23
u Zec 10:5

7:11
v Isa 54:11

7:12
w Isa 19:23-25

7:13
x Isa 3:10-11

7:14
y Mic 5:4 *z* Ps 23:4

Micah 7:8–13

In verses 8–10 Micah spoke as the representative voice of Judah. Though he was looking ahead to Jerusalem's destruction, which would occur in 586 B.C., Micah was actually expressing his trust in God's plan to forgive and restore his people. This was reinforced by his words of assurance addressed to the nation in verses 11–13. Micah accepted the inevitability of judgment but in faith believed that Israel would rise again—a transformation he didn't expect until after the people's hearts had been changed.

The hopelessness Micah expressed in the previous passage turned to hope because of his confidence that victory over sin was sure. Like the prophet, we too can remember that a relationship with God provides us with the certainty of a divine Advocate. Without this connection, there would be no hope of God's sovereign intervention into our circumstances. But with this relationship, we can be certain that the wait for salvation will end with rejoicing over the "enemy"—with light rather than darkness. God is pleading our cause, and he's motivated by the principles of righteousness and justice, not by the power or status of the one seeking help.

Micah 7:14–20

The yearning in Micah's prayer in verse 14 may have been the impetus for God's response in verse 15, recalling his deeds during the exodus from Egypt. The nations would be amazed and ashamed when they saw this demonstration of God's power (vv. 16–17).

This chapter that began in an atmosphere of gloom

7:14
a Jer 50:19

in fertile pasturelands. [a]
Let them feed in Bashan and Gilead [a]
as in days long ago.

7:15
b Ex 3:20; Ps 78:12

15 "As in the days when you came out of Egypt,
I will show them my wonders. [b]"

7:16
c Isa 26:11

16 Nations will see and be ashamed, [c]
deprived of all their power.
They will lay their hands on their mouths
and their ears will become deaf.

7:17
d Isa 25:3; 49:23;
59:19

17 They will lick dust like a snake,
like creatures that crawl on the ground.
They will come trembling out of their dens;
they will turn in fear [d] to the LORD our God
and will be afraid of you.

7:18
e Isa 43:25;
Jer 50:20
f Ps 103:8-13
g Mic 2:12
h Ex 34:9 i Ps 103:9
i Jer 32:41

18 Who is a God like you,
who pardons sin [e] and forgives [f] the transgression
of the remnant [g] of his inheritance? [h]
You do not stay angry [i] forever
but delight to show mercy. [i]

7:19
k Isa 43:25
l Jer 31:34

19 You will again have compassion on us;
you will tread our sins underfoot
and hurl all our iniquities [k] into the depths of the sea. [l]

7:20
m Dt 7:8; Lk 1:72

20 You will be true to Jacob,
and show mercy to Abraham,
as you pledged on oath to our fathers [m]
in days long ago.

[a] 14 Or in the middle of Carmel

---

ends in one of the most powerful statements of hope in the Old Testament. Micah's affirmation of faith in verses 18–20 serves as a moving conclusion to the book. Repentance makes it possible for the guilt of sin to be removed and for its power to be broken. God's steadfast covenant commitment, going back to Abraham (see Gen. 12:2–3; 22:17–18), would blossom again.

What we believe about God's character will shape how we live our lives. Micah recognized that God was a God of justice as well as of mercy. This passage dispels the common misunderstanding that the Old Testament portrays a God of wrath while the New presents one of love. We worship the God who calls us to live in a way that honors him—a God who delights in showing clemency.

INTRODUCTION TO
Nahum

AUTHOR
The prophet Nahum wrote this book (1:1).

DATE WRITTEN
The book of Nahum was written between 663 and 609 B.C.

ORIGINAL READERS
Nahum wrote to the people of Nineveh, the capital city of the ruthless Assyrians, and to the nation of Judah. His message of doom for Nineveh (approximately 100 years after the Ninevites' repentance under Jonah's ministry) was a comfort to the people of Judah, who had seen the northern kingdom of Israel defeated and carried into exile by the Assyrians and were themselves suffering under their vicious cruelty.

TIMELINE

	1300BC	1200	1100	1000	900	800	700	600	500	400
Ministries of Micah and Isaiah in Judah (c. 742-681 B.C.)							■			
Exile of Israel (722 B.C.)							▪			
Nahum's ministry (c. 663-612 B.C.)							■			
Zephaniah's ministry in Judah (c. 640-621 B.C.)							▪			
Book of Nahum written (c. 663-609 B.C.)							■			
Jeremiah's ministry in Judah (c. 626-585 B.C.)							■			
Habakkuk's ministry in Judah (c. 612-588 B.C.)							▪			
Fall of Jerusalem (586 B.C.)							▪			
Ministries of Haggai and Zechariah (c. 520-480 B.C.)									■	

THEMES
Nahum described the coming judgment on Nineveh. The book includes the following themes:

1. *Judgment.* According to the prophet, the instrument of Nineveh's destruction would be God himself (1:2–3,8,14–15). The Ninevites had failed to live in the light of their earlier repentance. Nahum made ample use of the divine warrior theme, the picture of God as a military figure who wages war against those who resist him. Nahum taught that God punishes violence (2:12; 3:1,4), idolatry (2:14), ruthless business practices (3:16), materialism (2:9; 3:4), and cruelty (3:19).

2. *Deliverance.* Nahum's prophecy of judgment was intended to bring hope to the people of Judah, who had suffered Assyrian abuse for many years. God cares for his people and will punish those who abuse them. He will protect them (1:7), free them from oppression (1:13,15), and restore them (2:2).

FAITH IN ACTION
The pages of Nahum contain life lessons and role models of faith—people who challenge believers to put their faith in action.

Role Models

- NAHUM (3:1–19) preached a message of doom against the representatives of the world power of his time, citing their violence and cruelty not only as crimes against humanity, but as sins against God himself. If called by God to do so, would you take the courageous step of confronting an authority who was abusing power?

- THOSE WHO TRUSTED IN GOD (1:7) found refuge in him; they were protected and avenged. Is God your refuge in times of trouble?

- THOSE WHO WAITED FOR THE LORD TO AVENGE THEM (1:15) heard the good news of peace proclaimed. Are you living under oppression or injustice? Trust God to bring you freedom (1:13) and peace (1:15).

Challenges

- Don't be lulled into focusing solely on God's loving side; he also is a God of vengeance (1:2): "The LORD is good, a refuge in times of trouble. He cares for those who trust in him, but with an overwhelming flood he will . . . pursue his foes into darkness" (1:7).

- Don't mistake God's patience for weakness; he *will* judge the wicked (1:3) and punish their "endless cruelty" (3:19).

- Don't be lured by the enticements of wealth and luxury (2:9; 3:4).

- Be courageous to do whatever God might ask of you.

OUTLINE

I. The Lord As Nineveh's Judge (1)
   A. God's Anger Against Nineveh (1:2–8)
   B. God's Judgment on Nineveh and Victory for Judah (1:9–15)
II. Nineveh's Fall (2)
   A. The Siege (2:1–10)
   B. The Desolation (2:11–13)
III. Woe to Nineveh (3)
   A. Nineveh's Sins (3:1–4)
   B. Nineveh's Coming Doom (3:5–19)

1:1
a Isa 13:1; 19:1;
Jer 23:33-34
b Jnh 1:2; Na 2:8;
Zep 2:13

1 An oracle*a* concerning Nineveh. *b* The book of the vision of Nahum the Elkoshite.

The LORD's Anger Against Nineveh

1:2
c Ex 20:5
d Dt 32:41; Ps 94:1

2 The LORD is a jealous*c* and avenging God;
   the LORD takes vengeance*d* and is filled with wrath.
The LORD takes vengeance on his foes
   and maintains his wrath against his enemies.

Nahum 1:1

The "oracle" ("burden" or "something lifted up") refers to Nahum's God-given message, "lifted" before the people. Oracles were often "against the nations" that threatened Judah (cf. Isa. 13:1; 15:1; 17:1; 19:1; 21:1; 23:1). The book communicates the oracle Nahum received in the form of a vision.

Nahum means "comfort" (the same Hebrew root appears in 3:10). This book may seem to be filled with doom and gloom, but God's justice on Assyria (represent-

ed by Nineveh, the capital of the Assyrian empire) was a message of comfort to Israel, who had suffered greatly at their hand. What do you know about the meaning of your name and how you received it? To what degree is this knowledge a source of motivation or comfort for you?

Nahum 1:2–15

Nahum's prophetic message began, in verses 2–6, with the revelation of God's power and divine nature in creation (cf. Rom. 1:18–20). This revelation was characterized preeminently by God's justice, expressed

3 The LORD is slow to anger[e] and great in power;
   the LORD will not leave the guilty unpunished.[f]
His way is in the whirlwind and the storm,
   and clouds[g] are the dust of his feet.
4 He rebukes the sea and dries it up;
   he makes all the rivers run dry.
Bashan and Carmel[h] wither
   and the blossoms of Lebanon fade.
5 The mountains quake[i] before him
   and the hills melt away.[j]
The earth trembles at his presence,
   the world and all who live in it.
6 Who can withstand his indignation?
   Who can endure[k] his fierce anger?
His wrath is poured out like fire;[l]
   the rocks are shattered[m] before him.

1:3
e Ne 9:17 f Ex 34:7
g Ps 104:3

1:4
h Isa 33:9

1:5
i Ex 19:18 j Mic 1:4

1:6
k Mal 3:2
l Jer 10:10
m 1Ki 19:11

in retribution and wrath that shook the entire creation. The mercy of God, for all its reality, was a counterpart to this awesome display of majesty.

Verse 7 proclaimed the Lord's fundamental goodness and care, while verses 8–9 declared the certainty of Nineveh's doom. Through the ministry of Jonah, Nineveh had formerly experienced the revelation and goodness of God. But she had later rejected it, the result being the darkness of judgment. Verse 11 is the most historically specific, referring to the king of Nineveh, who had plotted evil against God—which set the stage for the Lord's direct addresses to Nineveh and Judah in the rest of the chapter. This was the beginning of Judah's good news, of her *nahum* or "comfort."

Some Christians consider Nahum and other Old Testament texts presenting God as a warrior for justice (e.g., Ex. 15:1–21; Zech. 14:3–5) as being obsolete in light of the goodness of God revealed in Jesus. God *is* a God of love—whose fury is a direct response to evil actions that victimize the helpless. In Nahum's day, God exercised his vengeance to stop Nineveh's devastating cruelty, which no human power had been able to withstand.

Jesus' warfare, however, wasn't nationalistic but against human bondage to sin, death, and the evil one (Matt. 11:2–6; Mark 3:20–30; Luke 4:18–21). His crucifixion and resurrection gave new understanding to the ultimate love behind the warrior's use of force (Eph. 4:7–13; 6:10–20; Col. 2:8–15). Revelation 19:11–21 describes the

Snapshots

 1:7

William and Clementina (Rowe) Butler

William (1818–1899) and Clementina (1820–1913) Butler, founders of American Methodist missions in India and Mexico, were probably the best-known Methodist missionary couple of the late 19th century. William emigrated from Ireland to the United States in 1850. Already twice widowed, he wrote to a friend and supporter, Clementina Rowe of Ireland, who joined him in America. The two were married in 1854.

Two years later the couple sailed to India as missionaries. But the Sepoy Mutiny forced them to take refuge in the mountains, where they remained under siege for eight months. Afterward the couple opened orphanages for children left homeless by the rebellion.

The Butlers returned to the United States in 1865, where they enthusiastically promoted foreign missions. Clementina spurred Congregational and Methodist women to found societies to support single women missionaries.

In 1873 the couple again embarked on a foreign mission venture, this time to Mexico. As they had done in India, the Butlers established a printing press, schools, and a girls' orphanage and oversaw the construction of church buildings. Two children, John and Clementina, continued in their parents' footsteps.

> **T**he Butlers established a printing press, schools, and a girls' orphanage and oversaw the construction of church buildings.

1:7
n Jer 33:11 o Ps 1:6

7 The LORD is good, [n]
  a refuge in times of trouble.
He cares for [o] those who trust in him,
8   but with an overwhelming flood
he will make an end of ˻Nineveh˼;
  he will pursue his foes into darkness.

9 Whatever they plot against the LORD
he [a] will bring to an end;
  trouble will not come a second time.

1:10
p 2Sa 23:6
q Isa 5:24; Mal 4:1

10 They will be entangled among thorns [p]
  and drunk from their wine;
they will be consumed like dry stubble. [b] [q]
11 From you, ˻O Nineveh,˼ has one come forth
  who plots evil against the LORD
  and counsels wickedness.

12 This is what the LORD says:

1:12
r Isa 10:34
s Isa 54:6-8;
La 3:31-32

"Although they have allies and are numerous,
  they will be cut off [r] and pass away.
Although I have afflicted you, ˻O Judah,˼
  I will afflict you no more. [s]

1:13
t Isa 9:4

13 Now I will break their yoke [t] from your neck
  and tear your shackles away."

1:14
u Isa 14:22
v Mic 5:13
w Eze 32:22-23

14 The LORD has given a command concerning you, ˻Nineveh˼:
  "You will have no descendants to bear your name. [u]
I will destroy the carved images [v] and cast idols
  that are in the temple of your gods.
I will prepare your grave, [w]
  for you are vile."

1:15
x Isa 40:9; Ro 10:15
y Isa 52:7
z Lev 23:2-4
a Isa 52:1

15 Look, there on the mountains,
  the feet of one who brings good news, [x]
  who proclaims peace! [y]
Celebrate your festivals, [z] O Judah,
  and fulfill your vows.
No more will the wicked invade you; [a]
  they will be completely destroyed.

Nineveh to Fall

2:1
b Jer 51:20

2 An attacker [b] advances against you, ˻Nineveh˼.
  Guard the fortress,
  watch the road,
  brace yourselves,
  marshal all your strength!

---

[a] 9 Or *What do you foes plot against the LORD? / He*   [b] 10 The meaning of the Hebrew for this verse is uncertain.

---

final necessary battle, with the Lord triumphing over evil once and for all.

   When we read Nahum in this context, its military imagery becomes a pressing call to take refuge in Christ's cross. Living in the world of the Divine Warrior means a choice of suffering defeat alone and without a reference point or suffering death according to the model of Christ's dying warrior love. It means dying with him now, in defeat of our own rebellion—or without him later, in defeat of the same.

Nahum 2:1–13

   Nahum vividly described the destruction of the destroyers. He painted a word picture of the final battle to come between the Babylonians and Nineveh (Assyria) in 612 B.C. The prophet pictured in colorful detail Nineveh's battle preparations, followed by its unexpected fall. The chapter closes with a mock lament over the demise of the "lions' den" (Nineveh's walled city). The explanation? In God's words, "I am against you."
   Recalling how God delivers the oppressed is a long-

2 The LORD will restore^c the splendor^d of Jacob
    like the splendor of Israel,
though destroyers have laid them waste
    and have ruined their vines.

3 The shields of his soldiers are red;
    the warriors are clad in scarlet.^e
The metal on the chariots flashes
    on the day they are made ready;
    the spears of pine are brandished.^a
4 The chariots^f storm through the streets,
    rushing back and forth through the squares.
They look like flaming torches;
    they dart about like lightning.

5 He summons his picked troops,
    yet they stumble^g on their way.
They dash to the city wall;
    the protective shield is put in place.
6 The river gates^h are thrown open
    and the palace collapses.
7 It is decreed^b that the city
    be exiled and carried away.
Its slave girls moanⁱ like doves
    and beat upon their breasts.^j
8 Nineveh is like a pool,
    and its water is draining away.
"Stop! Stop!" they cry,
    but no one turns back.
9 Plunder the silver!
    Plunder the gold!
The supply is endless,
    the wealth from all its treasures!
10 She is pillaged, plundered, stripped!
    Hearts melt, knees give way,
    bodies tremble, every face grows pale.^k

11 Where now is the lions' den,^l
    the place where they fed their young,
where the lion and lioness went,
    and the cubs, with nothing to fear?
12 The lion killed^m enough for his cubs
    and strangled the prey for his mate,
filling his lairs with the kill
    and his dens with the prey.

13 "I am againstⁿ you,"
    declares the LORD Almighty.

2:2
^c Eze 37:23
^d Isa 60:15

2:3
^e Eze 23:14-15

2:4
^f Jer 4:13

2:5
^g Jer 46:12

2:6
^h Na 3:13

2:7
ⁱ Isa 59:11
^j Isa 32:12

2:10
^k Isa 29:22

2:11
^l Isa 5:29

2:12
^m Jer 51:34

2:13
ⁿ Jer 21:13; Na 3:5

---

^a 3 Hebrew; Septuagint and Syriac / *the horsemen rush to and fro*   ^b 7 The meaning of the Hebrew for this word is uncertain.

---

standing, valuable Biblical tradition for instilling hope in oppressed and abused peoples. The detailed description also waves a warning flag to the arrogant: God is against oppressors.

📖 Is God for or against us? The answer is both. God *is* against our willful rebellion. But his consistent attitude toward us is friendship, even while he stands opposed to our selfish, sinful nature.

Nineveh had failed to control its excessive wealth and power as it had its water supply through floodgates (used to regulate the flow from the city's impressive reservoir). Now God, through Babylon, had taken over control of the floodgates (v. 6). As a result, water and wealth were spilling out in unwanted ways; the city was drowning. This somber warning to those who use money without moderation is that God can and does make it drain away.

2:13
o Ps 46:9

"I will burn up your chariots in smoke,[o]
and the sword will devour your young lions.
I will leave you no prey on the earth.
The voices of your messengers
will no longer be heard."

Woe to Nineveh

3:1
p Eze 22:2;
Mic 3:10

3 Woe to the city of blood,[p]
full of lies,
full of plunder,
never without victims!
[2] The crack of whips,
the clatter of wheels,
galloping horses
and jolting chariots!
[3] Charging cavalry,
flashing swords
and glittering spears!
Many casualties,
piles of dead,

3:3
q 2Ki 19:35;
Isa 34:3

bodies without number,
people stumbling over the corpses[q]—
[4] all because of the wanton lust of a harlot,
alluring, the mistress of sorceries,[r]
who enslaved nations by her prostitution[s]
and peoples by her witchcraft.

3:4
r Isa 47:9
s Isa 23:17;
Eze 16:25-29

3:5
t Na 2:13
u Jer 13:22
v Isa 47:3

[5] "I am against[t] you," declares the LORD Almighty.
"I will lift your skirts[u] over your face.
I will show the nations your nakedness[v]
and the kingdoms your shame.

3:6
w Job 9:31
x 1Sa 2:30;
Jer 51:37
y Isa 14:16

[6] I will pelt you with filth,[w]
I will treat you with contempt[x]
and make you a spectacle.[y]
[7] All who see you will flee from you and say,
'Nineveh[z] is in ruins—who will mourn for her?'[a]
Where can I find anyone to comfort[b] you?"

3:7
z Na 1:1 a Jer 15:5
b Isa 51:19

3:8
c Am 6:2
d Jer 46:25
e Isa 19:6-9

[8] Are you better than[c] Thebes,[a d]
situated on the Nile,[e]
with water around her?
The river was her defense,
the waters her wall.

3:9
f 2Ch 12:3

[9] Cush[b f] and Egypt were her boundless strength;

a 8 Hebrew *No Amon*   b 9 That is, the upper Nile region

Nahum 3:1–19

The theme of chapter 3 is the end of Nineveh's "endless cruelty" (v. 19). Nahum described her coming woe in three parts: her cruelty and exposure (vv. 1–7), her defenselessness (vv. 8–13), and her corrupt infrastructure and the joy of the surrounding nations over her fall (vv. 14–19).

The horrifying killing of babies (v. 10) is hard for us to understand. Remember that the baby Jesus was the target of the same strategy as "dashing on the rocks" (Matt. 2:13–18). God's ownership of responsibility took on flesh. He became vulnerable to violence, going so far

as a torturous death as an abandoned criminal.

To dismiss the slaughter of innocents as the work of evil people doesn't put it out of mind. Nor does it settle the issue of innocent suffering today. Our limited perspective doesn't allow us a complete understanding of evil. When Job questioned God about his suffering, God finally answered by posing to him a series of questions (Job 38:1—41:34), to which Job acknowledged, "I spoke of things I did not understand" (42:2). Believers stand in faith that God's good kingdom will eventually come "on earth as it is in heaven" (Matt. 6:10). Until then we can with the Spirit's help "overcome evil with good" (Rom. 12:21).

Put[g] and Libya[h] were among her allies.
10 Yet she was taken captive[i]
    and went into exile.
Her infants were dashed[j] to pieces
    at the head of every street.
Lots were cast for her nobles,
    and all her great men were put in chains.
11 You too will become drunk;[k]
    you will go into hiding[l]
    and seek refuge from the enemy.

12 All your fortresses are like fig trees
    with their first ripe fruit;
when they are shaken,
    the figs[m] fall into the mouth of the eater.
13 Look at your troops—
    they are all women![n]
The gates[o] of your land
    are wide open to your enemies;
    fire has consumed their bars.[p]

14 Draw water for the siege,[q]
    strengthen your defenses![r]
Work the clay,
    tread the mortar,
    repair the brickwork!
15 There the fire will devour you;
    the sword will cut you down
    and, like grasshoppers, consume you.
Multiply like grasshoppers,
    multiply like locusts![s]
16 You have increased the number of your merchants
    till they are more than the stars of the sky,
but like locusts they strip the land
    and then fly away.
17 Your guards are like locusts,[t]
    your officials like swarms of locusts
    that settle in the walls on a cold day—
but when the sun appears they fly away,
    and no one knows where.

18 O king of Assyria, your shepherds[a] slumber;[u]
    your nobles lie down to rest.[v]
Your people are scattered[w] on the mountains
    with no one to gather them.
19 Nothing can heal your wound;[x]
    your injury is fatal.
Everyone who hears the news about you
    claps his hands[y] at your fall,
for who has not felt
    your endless cruelty?

a 18 Or rulers

3:9
g Eze 27:10
h Eze 30:5
3:10
i Isa 20:4
j Isa 13:16;
Hos 13:16
3:11
k Isa 49:26
l Isa 2:10

3:12
m Isa 28:4

3:13
n Isa 19:16;
Jer 50:37 o Na 2:6
p Isa 45:2

3:14
q 2Ch 32:4 r Na 2:1

3:15
s Joel 1:4

3:17
t Jer 51:27

3:18
u Ps 76:5-6
v Isa 56:10
w 1Ki 22:17

3:19
x Jer 30:13; Mic 1:9
y Job 27:23;
La 2:15; Zep 2:15

INTRODUCTION TO
Habakkuk

AUTHOR
The prophet Habakkuk, a contemporary of Jeremiah, wrote this book.

DATE WRITTEN
The book of Habakkuk was probably written between 610 and 605 B.C.

ORIGINAL READERS
The book of Habakkuk is a dialogue between God and Habakkuk that was composed for the people of Judah. Habakkuk was troubled by Judah's idolatry, indifference to God, and social injustice. He wondered how long God would ignore the wickedness of his people. God responded by revealing that his judgment would come through the Babylonians. This perplexed Habakkuk even more. How could a just God use the Babylonians, a people even more wicked than Judah, to punish his people?

TIMELINE

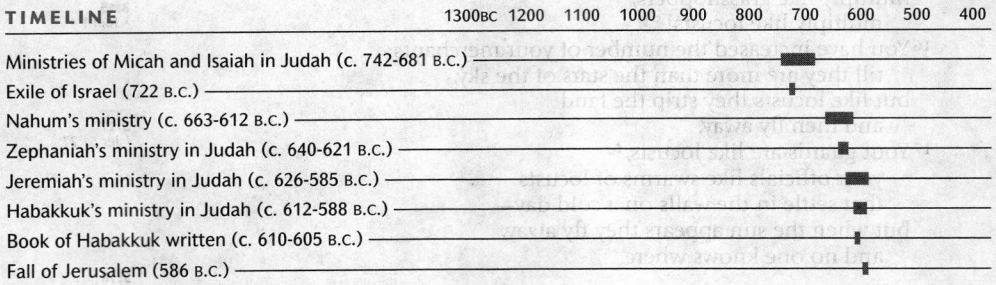

	1300BC	1200	1100	1000	900	800	700	600	500	400
Ministries of Micah and Isaiah in Judah (c. 742-681 B.C.)										
Exile of Israel (722 B.C.)										
Nahum's ministry (c. 663-612 B.C.)										
Zephaniah's ministry in Judah (c. 640-621 B.C.)										
Jeremiah's ministry in Judah (c. 626-585 B.C.)										
Habakkuk's ministry in Judah (c. 612-588 B.C.)										
Book of Habakkuk written (c. 610-605 B.C.)										
Fall of Jerusalem (586 B.C.)										

THEMES
The book of Habakkuk describes the prophet Habakkuk's struggle to understand God's justice in the face of wickedness, oppression, and injustice. It includes the following themes:

1. *Justice.* Habakkuk affirmed that God is holy and just (1:12–13; 3:3), never indifferent to sin and injustice. He will eventually punish the wicked (1:5–11; 2:2–20) and has in fact fixed an "appointed time" (2:3) in history for revealing his justice and judgment on evil. Like Habakkuk, God's faithful people today often wonder why the wicked seem to go unpunished. The book of Habakkuk apprises us that the current situation isn't the true and ultimate state of things. We may have to wait for vindication, but it certainly will come.

2. *Faith.* Faith is needed to endure injustice (2:4). Even when life seems confusing, we are to wait patiently for God's deliverance, trusting that he will eventually make all things right (2:3). "The righteous will live by his faith" (2:4), not by what is evident or appears to be true (1:4; see Heb. 11:1). As Abraham waited patiently for God to fulfill his promise (Heb. 6:13–15)— and as Habakkuk and the faithful remnant were to wait for him to respond in justice (2:3;

3:16)—so we are to wait in faith for God to carry out his purposes (Rom. 1:17; 5:1–2). Hebrews 11:13 and 39 remind us that those listed in this roster of faith died without having seen the promises of God fulfilled in their lifetimes.

FAITH IN ACTION
The pages of Habakkuk contain life lessons and role models of faith—people who challenge believers to put their faith in action.

Role Models

• HABAKKUK (1:2–4; 2:12—2:1) was honest with God about his doubts and questions. Are you being straightforward with God? He can handle your concerns and questions and wants authenticity from you, not pious clichés.

• HABAKKUK (3:2,17–19) came to a new level of reverence and awe of God. That revelation of God gave him faith to endure adversity with the certain hope of God's faithfulness and goodness. Is the current state of this world testing your faith in a just God? Resolve to know God better, so you can trust him increasingly to do what's right.

Challenges

• Pour out your heart (and your complaints) to God when you are frustrated with his seeming indifference to injustice and evil (1:2–4; 1:12—2:1). Don't be afraid to ask questions of God, recognizing that the problem isn't with God but with your limited understanding of him and his ways (Job 38:1–7; 40:8–14; Isa. 55:8–9).

• Determine to express your faith in, and praise to, God (3:1–19), trusting him to work things out in his time and in his way.

• Trust God to turn your doubt to faith. When God reveals himself to you (3:2–6), you will be able to praise him regardless of your situation (3:16–19).

OUTLINE

I. Habakkuk's First Question (1:1–4)
II. God's Answer (1:5–11)
III. Habakkuk's Second Question (1:12—2:1)
IV. God's Answer (2:2–20)
V. Habakkuk's Prayer (3)

1
The oracle*ᵃ* that Habakkuk the prophet received.

1:1
ᵃ Na 1:1

Habakkuk's Complaint

²How long, O LORD, must I call for help,
but you do not listen?*ᵇ*

1:2
ᵇ Ps 13:1-2; 22:1-2

Habakkuk 1:1

"The oracle that Habakkuk the prophet received" was given to him as a conversation with the Lord. The inspired oracle (message or "burden") included both sides of the conversation: Habakkuk's questions, God's responses, and Habakkuk's concluding prayer/song in chapter 3.

Habakkuk's hard-hitting, "in your face" questions and complaints were integral to the oracle the prophet received—implying that even his questioning was Spirit-inspired. Honest dialogue with God is neces-sary for a relationship with him. And the problems we face in living a life of faith in a secular society aren't easi-ly resolved. How many of us have "mastered" the art of petitioning God, of asking for what we think is reason-able or even expected? But how often do we ask him ag-onizing questions about complex issues—and then wait patiently for his response?

Habakkuk 1:2–4

Habakkuk's complaint began like a lament from the Psalms or the book of Job. Injustice was its theme. The likely historical context was the corruption of Judah's

1:2
c Jer 14:9

1:3
d ver 13 e Jer 20:8
f Ps 55:9

1:4
g Ps 119:126
h Job 19:7;
Isa 1:23; 5:20;
Eze 9:9

1:5
i Isa 29:9
j Ac 13:41*

1:6
k 2Ki 24:2
l Jer 13:20

1:7
m Isa 18:7;
Jer 39:5-9

Or cry out to you, "Violence!"
but you do not save?[c]
[3] Why do you make me look at injustice?
Why do you tolerate[d] wrong?
Destruction and violence[e] are before me;
there is strife,[f] and conflict abounds.
[4] Therefore the law[g] is paralyzed,
and justice never prevails.
The wicked hem in the righteous,
so that justice is perverted.[h]

The LORD's Answer

[5] "Look at the nations and watch—
and be utterly amazed.[i]
For I am going to do something in
your days
that you would not believe,
even if you were told.[j]
[6] I am raising up the Babylonians,[a][k]
that ruthless and impetuous
people,
who sweep across the whole earth
to seize dwelling places not their
own.[l]
[7] They are a feared and dreaded people;[m]

The Babylonian Empire (1:6)
Then: Babylonia has supported settled
life from as early as the sixth millennium B.C.
Now: The Iraqi culture remains vital and
powerful today.

a 6 Or *Chaldeans*

government under the cruel and oppressive King Jehoiakim (cf. 2 Kings 23:34–37; Jer. 22:13–19). Justice was
perverted because the rich controlled the courts
through bribery (cf. Mic. 3:11; 7:3). Habakkuk wanted
to know why his pleas to God for justice were falling on
deaf ears (cf. Gen. 18:20–21; Ex. 2:23–25; 22:22–24).

We frequently find ourselves complaining about
needs in our own lives, but how often do we lament injustices in the world that are falling on others? Direct dialogue with God is the believer's profound privilege. Reflect on your own prayer life. To what extent do you
plead with God on behalf of the children and women in

Snapshots

1:2–4

Albert John Mbumbi Luthuli

Albert Luthuli (1899–1967), a Zulu Christian leader, was born into a Christian family in
Groutville, South Africa, home of that country's mission station of the American Board of
Commissioners for Foreign Missions. In 1921 Luthuli became the first
African to become a teacher-training instructor in South Africa. In
1934 he was appointed a chief and returned to Groutville to aid his
people. He served as a deacon in the Groutville church, as well as
chairman of the Bantu Congregational Church.

**[Luthuli] was awarded the
Nobel Peace Prize for his
tireless efforts on behalf of
South Africa's native
population.**

Luthuli became involved in his country's political struggles and
was elected president of the African National Congress in 1952, at
which time he was banned by the new Afrikaner Nationalist regime.
He led the ANC Defiance Campaign in the late 50s. Arrested for treason in 1957, Luthuli was exonerated in 1961 but banished to
Groutville. In 1960 he was awarded the Nobel Peace Prize for his tireless efforts on behalf of
South Africa's native population.

they are a law to themselves
and promote their own honor.
⁸Their horses are swifterⁿ than leopards,
fiercer than wolves at dusk.
Their cavalry gallops headlong;
their horsemen come from afar.
They fly like a vulture swooping to devour;
⁹ they all come bent on violence.
Their hordes^a advance like a desert wind
and gather prisoners^o like sand.
¹⁰They deride kings
and scoff at rulers.^p
They laugh at all fortified cities;
they build earthen ramps and capture them.
¹¹Then they sweep past like the wind^q and go on—
guilty men, whose own strength is their god."^r

Habakkuk's Second Complaint

¹²O LORD, are you not from everlasting?
My God, my Holy One,^s we will not die.
O LORD, you have appointed^t them to execute judgment;
O Rock, you have ordained them to punish.
¹³Your eyes are too pure to look on evil;
you cannot tolerate wrong.^u
Why then do you tolerate the treacherous?
Why are you silent while the wicked
swallow up those more righteous than themselves?

^a 9 The meaning of the Hebrew for this word is uncertain.

1:8
n Jer 4:13

1:9
o Hab 2:5

1:10
p 2Ch 36:6

1:11
q Jer 4:11-12
r Da 4:30

1:12
s Isa 31:1 t Isa 10:6

1:13
u La 3:34-36

---

our world who are the victims of oppression and injustice? We have been invited to come "with confidence to the throne of grace" for the help we—and others—need with life's struggles (cf. Heb. 4:14–16).

Habakkuk 1:5–11

🔖 The Lord's initial words in verse 5 prepared Habakkuk for the message to come. God challenged the prophet to believe the unbelievable: The Lord was raising up the ruthless Babylonians to conquer Judah. Habakkuk had brought up a local problem (Judah's sinfulness), but God answered with an international scenario.

📖 God's first interest isn't our prosperity or political power. He would rather destroy what we hold dear (in hope of eventually accomplishing his greater purpose) than see us prosper in political security while

chasing our own whims. As the Lord of the nations God can use whomever he pleases to fulfill his purposes. Can you see ways today in which God might be using nations, even unbelieving ones, to chastise his people and call them to greater faithfulness?

Habakkuk 1:12—2:1

🔖 God's words sounded wrong to Habakkuk, so he quoted to God what he knew about God, "You are from everlasting," adding in the same breath, "We will not die." Since God is eternal, the prophet reasoned, his people must also endure. Immediately, though, he stated that he believed the Lord concerning the Babylonians. In this one verse Habakkuk moved from astonished denial to acceptance. Though Jerusalem would be captured and God's people exiled, they would survive as a people. "We will not die" became a cry of hope for the future.

1:5

Belief and Identity

Habakkuk was searching for the meaning of God's ways, and in the process the meaning of his own life. Such existential concerns have engaged and troubled human beings from earliest history. Which of the following statements do you find most satisfying? Which provides you comfort?

Descartes: "I think, therefore I am."

Tertullian: "I believe because it is absurd."

Anselm: "I believe in order that I may understand."

Tolstoy: "I believe."

Mbiti: "I am because we are."

William James: "I believe, therefore I am."

Paul: "I know whom I have believed" (2 Tim. 2:12).

¹⁴ You have made men like fish in the sea,
    like sea creatures that have no ruler.

1:15
v Isa 19:8
w Jer 16:16

¹⁵ The wicked foe pulls all of them up with hooks, ^v
    he catches them in his net, ^w
he gathers them up in his dragnet;
    and so he rejoices and is glad.

1:16
x Jer 44:8

¹⁶ Therefore he sacrifices to his net
    and burns incense ^x to his dragnet,
for by his net he lives in luxury
    and enjoys the choicest food.

1:17
y Isa 14:6; 19:8

¹⁷ Is he to keep on emptying his net,
    destroying nations without mercy? ^y

2:1
z Isa 21:8
a Ps 48:13
b Ps 85:8 c Ps 5:3

2

I will stand at my watch ^z
    and station myself on the ramparts; ^a
I will look to see what he will say ^b to me,
    and what answer I am to give to this complaint. ^{a c}

The LORD's Answer

² Then the LORD replied:

2:2
d Rev 1:19

"Write ^d down the revelation
    and make it plain on tablets
so that a herald ^b may run with it.

2:3
e Da 8:17; 10:14
f Ps 27:14
g Eze 12:25;
Heb 10:37-38

³ For the revelation awaits an appointed time;
    it speaks of the end ^e
    and will not prove false.
Though it linger, wait ^f for it;
    it ^c will certainly come and will not delay. ^g

2:4
h Ro 1:17*;
Gal 3:11*;
Heb 10:37-38*
2:5
i Pr 20:1 j Pr 27:20;
30:15-16

⁴ "See, he is puffed up;
    his desires are not upright—
    but the righteous will live by his faith ^{d h}—
    ⁵ indeed, wine ⁱ betrays him;
    he is arrogant and never at rest.
Because he is as greedy as the grave ^e
    and like death is never satisfied, ^j
he gathers to himself all the nations
    and takes captive all the peoples.

2:6
k Isa 14:4 / Am 2:8

⁶ "Will not all of them taunt ^k him with ridicule and scorn, saying,

" 'Woe to him who piles up stolen goods
    and makes himself wealthy by extortion! ^l
How long must this go on?'
    ⁷ Will not your debtors ^f suddenly arise?

---

^a 1 Or and what to answer when I am rebuked   ^b 2 Or so that whoever reads it   ^c 3 Or Though he
linger, wait for him; / he   ^d 4 Or faithfulness   ^e 5 Hebrew Sheol   ^f 7 Or creditors

---

Yet what Habakkuk knew about the Babylonians didn't fit with what he knew about God. Habakkuk felt that God hadn't answered his first question, "Why do you tolerate wrong?" (v. 3). So he rephrased it: "You cannot tolerate wrong. Why then do you tolerate the treacherous?" (v. 13). In the rest of the chapter, Habakkuk expanded the question with a fishing metaphor.

Usually we view judgment as something to be feared, but Habakkuk saw it as something for which to hope. He knew that God is a God of justice and that one day he will stop the treacherous and those who become rich at others' expense, "destroying nations without mercy" (v. 17). For whom in our world today is Habakkuk's view of God's judgment good news? For whom isn't it?

Habakkuk 2:2–20

Habakkuk 2 recounts the Lord's revelation of the fall of Babylon. The foolishness of puffed-up desire (v. 4) led to five "woes" from the mouths of Babylon's captives or threatened victims, particularly Judah. The woes condemned the Babylonians' (1) greed for con-

Will they not wake up and make you tremble?
Then you will become their victim. *m*

8 Because you have plundered many nations,
the peoples who are left will plunder you. *n*
For you have shed man's blood; *o*
you have destroyed lands and cities and everyone in them.

9 "Woe to him who builds *p* his realm by unjust gain
to set his nest on high,
to escape the clutches of ruin!
10 You have plotted the ruin *q* of many peoples,
shaming *r* your own house and forfeiting your life.
11 The stones *s* of the wall will cry out,
and the beams of the woodwork will echo it.

12 "Woe to him who builds a city with bloodshed *t*
and establishes a town by crime!
13 Has not the LORD Almighty determined
that the people's labor is only fuel for the fire, *u*
that the nations exhaust themselves for nothing? *v*
14 For the earth will be filled with the knowledge of the glory *w* of the LORD,
as the waters cover the sea. *x*

15 "Woe to him who gives drink to his neighbors,
pouring it from the wineskin till they are drunk,
so that he can gaze on their naked bodies.
16 You will be filled with shame *y* instead of glory.
Now it is your turn! Drink and be exposed *a*! *z*
The cup *a* from the LORD's right hand is coming around to you,
and disgrace will cover your glory.
17 The violence *b* you have done to Lebanon will overwhelm you,
and your destruction of animals will terrify you. *c*
For you have shed man's blood; *d*
you have destroyed lands and cities and everyone in them.

18 "Of what value is an idol, *e* since a man has carved it?
Or an image that teaches lies?
For he who makes it trusts in his own creation;
he makes idols that cannot speak. *f*
19 Woe to him who says to wood, 'Come to life!'
Or to lifeless stone, 'Wake up!' *g*
Can it give guidance?
It is covered with gold and silver; *h*
there is no breath in it.
20 But the LORD is in his holy temple; *i*
let all the earth be silent *j* before him. "

---

a 16 Masoretic Text; Dead Sea Scrolls, Aquila, Vulgate and Syriac (see also Septuagint) *and stagger*

Cross references (right margin):

2:7
m Pr 29:1

2:8
n Isa 33:1;
Zec 2:8-9
o ver 17

2:9
p Jer 22:13

2:10
q Jer 26:19 r ver 16

2:11
s Jos 24:27;
Lk 19:40

2:12
t Mic 3:10

2:13
u Isa 50:11
v Isa 47:13

2:14
w Nu 14:21
x Isa 11:9

2:16
y ver 10 z La 4:21
a Isa 51:22

2:17
b Jer 51:35
c Jer 50:15 d ver 8

2:18
e Jer 5:21
f Ps 115:4-5;
Jer 10:14

2:19
g 1Ki 18:27
h Jer 10:4

2:20
i Ps 11:4 j Isa 41:1

---

quest (vv. 6–8); (2) pride in their building projects accomplished at others' expense (vv. 9–11); (3) self-centered injustice (vv. 12–13); (4) violence in stripping others of their possessions and dignity (vv. 15–17); and (5) idol worship (vv. 18–19).

These woes stand in contrast to the righteous living by faith (v. 4). The insatiable pursuit of wealth, status, or consumerism is like being drunk with wine; its satisfaction is false and gives no rest (v. 5). Babylon didn't rest till it had taken all of the cultures of the ancient world captive and brought their treasures home

(cf. Ps. 137). Our world remains under the bondage of greed and death.

Can you imagine a world where the "knowledge of the glory of the Lord" will cover the earth "as waters cover the sea"? In this new world injustice, greed, extortion, and bloodshed won't be tolerated. This kingdom will have a high standard indeed: holiness (v. 20). Believers who have responded to this King's rule have already embarked on the journey to see this spiritual reality become physical. We live under our Lord's command: "Be holy, because I am holy" (cf. 1 Peter 1:15–16).

Habakkuk's Prayer

3 A prayer of Habakkuk the prophet. On *shigionoth*.[a]

3:2
k Ps 44:1
l Ps 119:120
m Ps 85:6 n Isa 54:8

2 Lord, I have heard[k] of your fame;
  I stand in awe[l] of your deeds, O Lord.
Renew[m] them in our day,
  in our time make them known;
  in wrath remember mercy.[n]

3 God came from Teman,
  the Holy One from Mount Paran. *Selah*[b]
His glory covered the heavens
  and his praise filled the earth.[o]

3:3
o Ps 48:10

4 His splendor was like the sunrise;
  rays flashed from his hand,
  where his power was hidden.
5 Plague went before him;
  pestilence followed his steps.
6 He stood, and shook the earth;
  he looked, and made the nations tremble.
The ancient mountains crumbled
  and the age-old hills collapsed.[p]
His ways are eternal.

3:6
p Ps 114:1-6

7 I saw the tents of Cushan in distress,
  the dwellings of Midian[q] in anguish.[r]

3:7
q Jdg 7:24-25
r Ex 15:14
3:8
s Ex 7:20 t Ps 68:17

8 Were you angry with the rivers,[s] O Lord?
  Was your wrath against the streams?
Did you rage against the sea
  when you rode with your horses
  and your victorious chariots?[t]
9 You uncovered your bow,
  you called for many arrows.[u] *Selah*
You split the earth with rivers;
10   the mountains saw you and writhed.

3:9
u Ps 7:12-13

Torrents of water swept by;
  the deep roared[v]
  and lifted its waves[w] on high.
11 Sun and moon stood still[x] in the heavens

3:10
v Ps 98:7 w Ps 93:3
3:11
x Jos 10:13

---

a 1 Probably a literary or musical term also in verses 9 and 13   b 3 A word of uncertain meaning; possibly a musical term;

Habakkuk 3:1–19

This prayer or song created and maintained hope in the face of a calamitous future and provided a lasting resource for survival following the devastation of an enemy attack. Habakkuk demonstrated the geography of hope in two ways: *looking back* by reciting the Lord's victories on Israel's behalf (cf. Deut. 26:11; Ps. 78; Acts 7) and *looking up* at creation's wonders as a sign of the Creator's presence and power (cf. Ps. 19:1–6; Rom. 1:18–20).

Concluding his hymn of past remembrance, Habakkuk was shaken as he accepted the mystery of God's way in the world (v. 16). He knew that Judah would be delivered, but only after great crises. Habakkuk's faith found renewed vigor. His concluding lines are likely the most loved in the entire book. They illustrate a person who

has begun to "live by faith" (2:4). Habakkuk called for four movements of the heart: accepting God's judgment (v. 16), accepting deprivation as a consequence of sin (v. 17), resolving to rejoice in the Lord in all circumstances (v. 18), and experiencing the gifts of confidence and hope from God (v. 18).

We can learn much from Habakkuk's extended dialogue with the Lord. With him we can ask difficult questions (1:2–4) and be persistent in questioning and seeking God (1:12—2:1). We can be historically grounded in God's mighty acts of deliverance (3:2–15). We are also invited to join Habakkuk in his profound faith (3:16–19). His humanity and joy are a model and a challenge. May we be witnesses, like Habakkuk, to God's purposes in a world dominated by corruption. May God's kingdom come also to us.

at the glint of your flying arrows, *y*
at the lightning of your flashing spear.
¹²In wrath you strode through the earth
and in anger you threshed *z* the nations.
¹³You came out to deliver *a* your people,
to save your anointed one.
You crushed *b* the leader of the land of wickedness,
you stripped him from head to foot.
¹⁴With his own spear you pierced his head
when his warriors stormed out to scatter us, *c*
gloating as though about to devour
the wretched *d* who were in hiding.
¹⁵You trampled the sea with your horses,
churning the great waters. *e*

¹⁶I heard and my heart pounded,
my lips quivered at the sound;
decay crept into my bones,
and my legs trembled.
Yet I will wait patiently for the day of calamity
to come on the nation invading us.
¹⁷Though the fig tree does not bud
and there are no grapes on the vines,
though the olive crop fails
and the fields produce no food, *f*
though there are no sheep in the pen
and no cattle in the stalls, *g*
¹⁸yet I will rejoice in the LORD, *h*
I will be joyful in God my Savior.

¹⁹The Sovereign LORD is my strength; *i*
he makes my feet like the feet of a deer,
he enables me to go on the heights. *j*

For the director of music. On my stringed instruments.

Selah

3:11
y Ps 18:14

3:12
z Isa 41:15
3:13
a Ps 20:6; 28:8
b Ps 68:21; 110:6

3:14
c Jdg 7:22
d Ps 64:2-5

3:15
e Ex 15:8; Ps 77:19

3:17
f Joel 1:10-12, 18
g Jer 5:17

3:18
h Isa 61:10; Php 4:4

3:19
i Dt 33:29;
Ps 46:1-5
j Dt 32:13;
2Sa 22:34; Ps 18:33

3:9 "THEN WILL I PURIFY THE LIPS OF THE PEOPLES, THAT ALL OF
THEM MAY CALL ON THE NAME OF THE LORD AND SERVE HIM
SHOULDER TO SHOULDER."

INTRODUCTION TO
Zephaniah

AUTHOR
The prophet Zephaniah, a contemporary of Nahum and Jeremiah, wrote this book.

DATE WRITTEN
This book was probably written between 635 and 630 B.C.

ORIGINAL READERS
Zephaniah wrote to the people of Judah to warn them of God's impending judgment, to urge them to repent, and to give them hope of restoration.

TIMELINE

	1300BC	1200	1100	1000	900	800	700	600	500	400
Ministries of Micah and Isaiah in Judah (c. 742-681 B.C.)										
Exile of Israel (722 B.C.)										
Nahum's ministry (c. 663-612 B.C.)										
Zephaniah's ministry in Judah (c. 640-621 B.C.)										
Book of Zephaniah written (c. 635-630 B.C.)										
Jeremiah's ministry in Judah (c. 626-585 B.C.)										
Habakkuk's ministry in Judah (c. 612-588 B.C.)										
Fall of Jerusalem (586 B.C.)										

THEMES
Zephaniah describes the prophet Zephaniah's ministry to the people of Judah. It warns of impending judgment and promises a future society of justice. It includes the following themes:

1. *Judgment.* Zephaniah's main theme was the imminent coming of the "day of the LORD" (1:7,14). That day would be one of universal judgment (1:2–3), as well as of specific judgment against Judah (1:4–6) and other nations (2:4-15). The book emphasizes that mixing worship of God with idolatry (1:4–6) brings destruction (1:9–13) but that seeking God in humility brings salvation (2:1–3).

2. *Restoration.* Zephaniah taught that judgment would be followed by restoration. God would purify his own (3:9), bring rejoicing to Jerusalem (3:14–17), and restore both his people and Jerusalem's glory (3:18–20).

FAITH IN ACTION
The pages of Zephaniah contain life lessons and role models of faith—people who challenge believers to put their faith in action.

Role Models

• THE MEEK AND THE HUMBLE (3:12) put their trust in God. Do these attributes define you? How would you rate your level of trust in God?

- THE PEOPLE COMPRISING THE REMNANT (3:13) were characterized as people who spoke no lies, were without deceit, and were unafraid. Had you been alive in Zephaniah's day, would you, based on this description, have been among their ranks?

Challenges

- Resolve not to be double-minded in your worship of God: Don't mix your allegiance to him with homage to other things, like power, prestige, money, or fame (1:4–5).

- Seek God and his direction (1:6). Ask him to be involved in your life and decisions.

- Look forward to the day when people from all nations will worship and serve God "shoulder to shoulder" (2:11; 3:9).

- Desire humility and righteousness (2:3), trusting God to save you (3:12,17).

- Meditate on what it means for God to delight in you, quiet you with his love, and rejoice over you with singing (3:17).

OUTLINE

   I.   Introduction: Announcement of Total Judgment (1:1–3)
   II. The Day of the Lord Coming on Judah and the Nations (1:4–18)
   III. God's Judgment on the Nations (2:1—3:8)
   IV. The Promise of Redemption (3:9–20)

1 The word of the LORD that came to Zephaniah son of Cushi, the son of Gedaliah, the son of Amariah, the son of Hezekiah, during the reign of Josiah*a* son of Amon king of Judah:

1:1
a 2Ki 22:1;
2Ch 34:1-35:25

Warning of Coming Destruction

2 "I will sweep away everything
    from the face of the earth,"*b*

                                                    declares the LORD.

1:2
b Ge 6:7

3 "I will sweep away both men and animals;

Zephaniah 1:1

📖 Zephaniah prophesied during the reign of King Josiah (640–609 B.C.)—probably relatively early during that period, before Josiah's spiritual reforms. Zephaniah belonged to a faithful and believing family, if the naming of the children is any indication. All the ancestors listed here except his father had names that included "the LORD" (Cushi means "my Ethiopian"; perhaps Zephaniah's grandmother was from ancient Ethiopia). Hezekiah means "the LORD is my strength," Amariah "the LORD speaks," Gedaliah "the LORD is great," and Zephaniah "the LORD hides" or "the LORD protects."

📖 Assuming that the Hezekiah mentioned here was King Hezekiah, Zephaniah was the great, great grandson of one of Judah's best kings. Zephaniah's name may indicate that his parents prayed for his protection at the time of his birth during the reign of the wicked Manasseh—who would have seen Zephaniah, a person of royal blood, as a threat to the throne. Naming a child in Old Testament times was serious business. A name's meaning, not its popularity or sound, was all-important. Some Christians today choose their children's names in this Biblical tradition. Who do you know whose name is special in this way?

Zephaniah 1:2–3

📖 Zephaniah foresaw a radical housecleaning ("sweeping away") of the whole world, but he would go on to describe what *wasn't* to be destroyed (2:6–7,9,11, 14; 3:12,20). What can we make of this? Would the earth be destroyed or not? Not in Zephaniah. A summary of his perspective is offered in 3:8–10. The consuming fire wouldn't bring annihilation but purification, the destruction of societal structures of corruption, rebellion, and false worship that hindered spiritual life.

📖 God sounded angry in Zephaniah 1. In fact, this chapter may be the most vivid description of his anger in the entire Bible. The intense language and detailed descriptions of Jerusalem's defeat demonstrate that God was more than angry. He was enraged—as angry as he could be. But can we see through the severity of his wrath to his long-term concern for us? The harshness of his anger is a measure of how deeply he cares about our well-being.

1:3
c Jer 4:25 d Hos 4:3

I will sweep away the birds of the air[c]
and the fish of the sea.
The wicked will have only heaps of rubble[a]
when I cut off man from the face of the earth,"[d]

declares the LORD.

Against Judah

1:4
e Jer 6:12
f Mic 5:13
g Hos 10:5

[4] "I will stretch out my hand[e] against Judah
and against all who live in Jerusalem.
I will cut off from this place every remnant of Baal,[f]
the names of the pagan and the idolatrous priests[g]—
[5] those who bow down on the roofs
to worship the starry host,
those who bow down and swear by the LORD
and who also swear by Molech,[b][h]

1:5
h Jer 5:7
1:6
i Isa 1:4; Jer 2:13
j Isa 9:13 k Hos 7:7
1:7
l Hab 2:20;
Zec 2:13 m ver 14;
Isa 13:6 n Isa 34:6;
Jer 46:10

[6] those who turn back from following[i] the LORD
and neither seek[j] the LORD nor inquire[k] of him.
[7] Be silent[l] before the Sovereign LORD,
for the day of the LORD[m] is near.
The LORD has prepared a sacrifice;[n]
he has consecrated those he has invited.

1:8
o Isa 24:21
p Jer 39:6

[8] On the day of the LORD's sacrifice
I will punish[o] the princes
and the king's sons[p]
and all those clad
in foreign clothes.
[9] On that day I will punish
all who avoid stepping on the threshold,[c]
who fill the temple of their gods
with violence and deceit.[q]

1:9
q Am 3:10

[10] "On that day," declares the LORD,
"a cry will go up from the Fish Gate,[r]
wailing from the New Quarter,
and a loud crash from the hills.

1:10
r 2Ch 33:14

[11] Wail,[s] you who live in the market district[d];
all your merchants will be wiped out,
all who trade with[e] silver will be ruined.[t]

1:11
s Jas 5:1 t Hos 9:6

[12] At that time I will search Jerusalem with lamps
and punish those who are complacent,[u]
who are like wine left on its dregs,[v]

1:12
u Am 6:1
v Jer 48:11

a 3 The meaning of the Hebrew for this line is uncertain.   b 5 Hebrew *Malcam*, that is, Milcom
c 9 See 1 Samuel 5:5.   d 11 Or *the Mortar*   e 11 Or *in*

Zephaniah 1:4–13

Zephaniah launched into a list of Judah's offenses, all involving misuse of worship and trust in wealth. Verses 7–9 begin with a call to worship the Lord, who had taken it upon himself to prepare the sacrifice and consecrate those he had invited. But it becomes clear that the leaders of Jerusalem were themselves consecrated as the sacrifice. God's willingness to sacrifice his beloved city shows that his kingdom wasn't political. It was a kingdom of love and faithfulness between himself and his people.

God's self-satisfied people preferred the stability and security of wealth to trust in him. They had stopped believing he would act at all. Their attention and confidence had turned toward their own accomplishments, to building houses and planting vineyards—the very activities God would cut off.

The nuclear fallout shelters of the sixties may seem silly in retrospect, but we still trust in all kinds of "shelters" of our own making: "securities," insurance policies, 401Ks, tax shelters, vaccinations, alarm systems, "fail-safe" investments, military preparedness. Believers through the ages have often lived lives of "practical atheism." "God won't do anything—good or bad" (see v. 12), they convince themselves, "so we had better act on our own behalf." The Day will expose the utter foolishness of crouching under such flimsy structures for shelter.

who think, 'The Lord will do nothing,[w]
  either good or bad.'
13 Their wealth will be plundered,[x]
  their houses demolished.
They will build houses
  but not live in them;
they will plant vineyards
  but not drink the wine.[y]

The Great Day of the Lord

14 "The great day of the Lord[z] is near[a]—
  near and coming quickly.
Listen! The cry on the day of the Lord will be bitter,
  the shouting of the warrior there.
15 That day will be a day of wrath,
  a day of distress and anguish,
a day of trouble and ruin,
  a day of darkness and gloom,
  a day of clouds and blackness,[b]
16 a day of trumpet and battle cry[c]
  against the fortified cities
  and against the corner towers.[d]
17 I will bring distress on the people
  and they will walk like blind[e] men,
  because they have sinned against the Lord.
Their blood will be poured out[f] like dust
  and their entrails like filth.[g]
18 Neither their silver nor their gold
  will be able to save them
  on the day of the Lord's wrath.[h]
In the fire of his jealousy
  the whole world will be consumed,[i]
for he will make a sudden end
  of all who live in the earth.[i]"

2 Gather together,[k] gather together,
  O shameful[l] nation,
2 before the appointed time arrives
  and that day sweeps on like chaff,[m]
before the fierce anger[n] of the Lord comes upon you,
  before the day of the Lord's wrath comes upon you.
3 Seek[o] the Lord, all you humble of the land,
  you who do what he commands.

1:12
w Eze 8:12
1:13
x Jer 15:13
y Dt 28:30,39;
Am 5:11; Mic 6:15

1:14
z ver 7; Joel 1:15
a Eze 7:7

1:15
b Isa 22:5; Joel 2:2
1:16
c Jer 4:19 d Isa 2:15

1:17
e Isa 59:10 f Ps 79:3
g Jer 9:22

1:18
h Eze 7:19 i ver 2-3;
Zep 3:8 j Ge 6:7

2:1
k 2Ch 20:4;
Joel 1:14 l Jer 3:3;
6:15
2:2
m Isa 17:13;
Hos 13:3 n La 4:11

2:3
o Am 5:6

Zephaniah 1:14—2:3

Zephaniah's description left no doubt about the horror to befall Jerusalem in the final Babylonian invasion of 587 B.C. Anyone who believed his warning would have been highly motivated to participate in King Josiah's reforms, wouldn't they? But self-sufficient, successful, accomplished people can be hard to move.

In 2:3 God called the humble and obedient of the land—and only them—to seek him. No promise of shelter was offered from "the day"—just a "perhaps." Even for them it was the eleventh hour for finding shelter. The "humble" weren't just people with a "good attitude." The word's most basic meaning is "poor," "weak," or "afflicted." Those who saw their need for God's shelter were the humble and wise ones.

God gives some of us more than we need so we can give to those with less. When we participate in this discipline, we share in his work. God must find it frustrating to deal with people who trust in him only until he blesses them with wealth or fame. His greatest successes can become his worst failures because of their material success! As Zephaniah shows, nothing grieves God more.

Almost everyone wants to be a "survivor." Christians want to be included in the humble, obedient "remnant" that will survive, even in the Day of the Lord. The test is in what we do with the words "perhaps you will be sheltered." Zephaniah asks us to trust that God's "perhaps" is more certain than any security this world has to offer.

2:3
p Ps 45:4;
Am 5:14-15
q Ps 57:1

Seek righteousness, seek humility;[p]
perhaps you will be sheltered[q]
on the day of the LORD's anger.

Against Philistia

2:4
r Am 1:6,7-8;
Zec 9:5-7

4 Gaza[r] will be abandoned
and Ashkelon left in ruins.
At midday Ashdod will be emptied
and Ekron uprooted.

2:5
s Eze 25:16
t Am 3:1
u Isa 14:30

5 Woe to you who live by the sea,
O Kerethite[s] people;
the word of the LORD is against you,[t]
O Canaan, land of the Philistines.

"I will destroy you,
and none will be left."[u]

2:6
v Isa 5:17

6 The land by the sea, where the Kerethites[a] dwell,
will be a place for shepherds and sheep pens.[v]
7 It will belong to the remnant of the house of Judah;
there they will find pasture.
In the evening they will lie down
in the houses of Ashkelon.

2:7
w Ps 126:4;
Jer 32:44

The LORD their God will care for them;
he will restore their fortunes.[b][w]

Against Moab and Ammon

2:8
x Jer 48:27
y Eze 25:3

8 "I have heard the insults[x] of Moab
and the taunts of the Ammonites,
who insulted[y] my people
and made threats against their land.
9 Therefore, as surely as I live,"
declares the LORD Almighty, the God of Israel,
"surely Moab[z] will become like Sodom,[a]
the Ammonites[b] like Gomorrah—
a place of weeds and salt pits,
a wasteland forever.
The remnant of my people will plunder[c] them;
the survivors of my nation will inherit their land. [d]"

2:9
z Isa 15:1-16:14;
Jer 48:1-47
a Dt 29:23
b Jer 49:1-6;
Eze 25:1-7
c Isa 11:14
d Am 2:1-3

a 6 The meaning of the Hebrew for this word is uncertain.   b 7 Or will bring back their captives

Zephaniah 2:4–7

Chapter 2 began with the possibility that a remnant that sought the Lord would survive (vv. 1–3) and now went on to announce that survivors would live again in the land (vv. 6–7,9). The clearing and cleansing of the earth is described in the rest of the chapter.

Zephaniah declared the cities and open spaces of the Philistines (also called Kerethites) forfeit. Then came the surprise: Shepherds and sheep would live there after the destruction. This was Zephaniah's first mention of Judah's remnant—and his first word of certain hope.

Not only would the remnant graze their flocks in former Philistine pastures, but these humble survivors would "find pasture" (v. 7) themselves as God's "sheep" (cf. Ps. 23; 100:3; John 10:11–16). The arrogant of Judah built houses but wouldn't live in them (Zeph. 1:13). Now the Lord would provide houses built by another arrogant people for the remnant to "lie down in" each evening (Zeph. 2:7). They would daily understand that their

homes were gifts from God and not the products of their own power. Do you view all that you have and are as God's provision—and totally depend upon him as your all-sufficient Shepherd?

Zephaniah 2:8–11

God had given Moab and Ammon, Israel's "cousins" through Abraham's nephew Lot (Gen. 19:30–38), territory east of the Jordan River. The hundreds of years of history between these nations and Israel were filled with hostility (Num. 22:1–6; Judg. 3:12–14; 11:12–33; Ezek. 25:2–7). After verse 10, the audience would have expected more prophetic doom. Instead, Zephaniah stated an amazing revelation: As part of his response to their pride, God would be "awesome" to the Moabites and Ammonites. And "the nations on every shore" would worship the Lord. God doesn't merely want to wipe out arrogance and self-sufficiency but to replace them with true worship in every land.

Service and Humility

2:2–3

More than any other single way the grace of humility is worked into our lives through the discipline of service. Humility, as we all know, is one of those virtues that is never gained by seeking it. The more we pursue it the more distant it becomes. To think we have it is sure evidence that we don't. Therefore most of us assume there is nothing we can do to gain this prized Christian virtue—and so we do nothing.

But there *is* something we can do. We do not need to go through life faintly hoping that some day humility may fall upon our heads. Of all the classical spiritual disciplines, service is the most conducive to the growth of humility. When we set out on a consciously chosen course of action that accents the good of others and is for the most part a hidden work, a deep change occurs in our spirit.

Nothing *disciplines* the inordinate desires of the flesh like service, and nothing *transforms* the desires of the flesh like serving in hiddenness. The flesh whines against service but screams against hidden service. It strains and pulls for honor and recognition. It will devise subtle, religiously acceptable means to call attention to the service rendered. If we stoutly refuse to give in to this lust of the flesh we crucify it. Every time we crucify the flesh we crucify our pride and arrogance.

> **Joyous hidden service to others is an acted prayer of thanksgiving.**

. . . The strictest daily discipline is necessary to hold [our] passions in check. The flesh must learn the painful lesson that it has no rights of its own. It is the work of hidden service that will accomplish this self-abasement.

. . . The result then of . . . daily discipline of the flesh will be the rise of the grace of humility. It will slip in on us unawares. Though we do not sense its presence, we are aware of a fresh zest and exhilaration with living. We wonder at the new sense of confidence that marks our activities. Although the demands of life are as great as ever, we live in a new sense of unhurried peace. People whom we once only envied we now view with compassion, for we see not only their position but their pain. People whom we would have passed over we now see and find to be delightful individuals. We feel a new spirit of identification with the outcasts, the "offscourings" of the earth (1 Cor. 4:13, RSV).

Even more than the transformation that is occurring within us we are aware of a deeper love and joy in God. Our days are punctuated with spontaneous breathings of praise and adoration. Joyous hidden service to others is an acted prayer of thanksgiving. We seem to be directed by a new Control Center—and so we are.

Richard J. Foster, writer on Christian spirituality
Source: Richard J. Foster, *Celebration of Discipline* (San Francisco: Harper & Row, 1978), 113–115

2:10
e Isa 16:6
f Jer 48:27
2:11
g Joel 2:11
h Zep 1:4 i Zep 3:9

10 This is what they will get in return for their pride, [e]
for insulting [f] and mocking the people of the LORD Almighty.
11 The LORD will be awesome [g] to them
when he destroys all the gods [h] of the land.
The nations on every shore will worship him, [i]
every one in its own land.

Against Cush

2:12
j Isa 18:1; 20:4
k Jer 46:10

12 "You too, O Cushites, [a][j]
will be slain by my sword. [k]"

Against Assyria

13 He will stretch out his hand against
the north
and destroy Assyria,

2:13
l Na 1:1 m Mic 5:6

leaving Nineveh [l] utterly desolate
and dry as the desert. [m]
14 Flocks and herds will lie down there,
creatures of every kind.

2:14
n Isa 14:23

The desert owl [n] and the screech owl
will roost on her columns.
Their calls will echo through the
windows,
rubble will be in the doorways,
the beams of cedar will be exposed.

2:15
o Isa 32:9 p Isa 47:8
q Eze 28:2
r Na 3:19

15 This is the carefree [o] city
that lived in safety. [p]
She said to herself,
"I am, and there is none besides me." [q]
What a ruin she has become,
a lair for wild beasts!
All who pass by her scoff [r]
and shake their fists.

The Assyrian Empire (2:13)
Then: In its heyday, from 911–609 B.C.,
Assyria represented the largest political configuration in the Middle East.
Now: The heartland of Assyria lay in what is now northern Iraq, in the upper regions surrounding the Tigris River.

a 12 That is, people from the upper Nile region

The Lord's opposition to the arrogant has the purpose of (eventually) bringing hope. The hope of salvation is to remove our self-reliance and pride and cause us to cast ourselves on the mercy of God. The meek will inherit the earth (v. 9; Matt. 5:5), and God's faithfulness to the humble assures their survival beyond the violence of the arrogant. Humility is an attribute of the Bible's greatest figures (Num. 12:3), and the healing of societies and communities through humbling ourselves before God (2 Chron. 7:14). Why not take a moment to affirm that posture in your heart right now?

Zephaniah 2:12

Cush, located south of Egypt, was also known as Ethiopia (not to be confused with modern Ethiopia, which is located farther to the southeast). In 715 B.C. a Cushite named Shabako gained control of Egypt. Since Egypt was ruled from that time until 663 B.C. by a Cushite dynasty, Zephaniah may have included both Cush and Egypt in this single-verse prophecy. "My sword" was probably a reference to Babylon.

Zephaniah's brief mention of the Cushites may have reflected his personal grief. His father, Cushi, was probably part Ethiopian (perhaps named so by an

Ethiopian mother). Sometimes sin's consequences (either natural consequences or direct intervention by God) affect us personally, through those we love. When this happens we can rely only on God's mercies and enduring love for all his creation, very much including people from every tribe and nation.

Zephaniah 2:13–15

Zephaniah predicted the destruction of Assyria and its capital, Nineveh. This proud city would become a home, not for the arrogant Ninevites, but for a humbler creation—the wild animals. Assyrian power and cruelty were legendary. No one could imagine their defeat soon to come in 612 B.C. at the hands of the Babylonians.

Zephaniah began his figurative description of the ruined city at the top with the columns, where the birds would roost. He moved down to the windows, where they would call, and to the doorways, where rubble would rest. Finally, plaster would fall from the cedar beams, leaving their created glory visible. Only what was of God would remain. This chapter's accounts of the clearing of the nations from the earth prepared it for a new beginning. The land, its animals, and a humble remnant would be renewed by God.

The Future of Jerusalem

3 Woe to the city of oppressors, [s]
   rebellious and defiled! [t]
² She obeys [u] no one,
   she accepts no correction. [v]
She does not trust in the LORD,
   she does not draw near [w] to her God.
³ Her officials are roaring lions,
   her rulers are evening wolves, [x]
   who leave nothing for the morning.
⁴ Her prophets are arrogant;
   they are treacherous [y] men.
Her priests profane the sanctuary
   and do violence to the law. [z]
⁵ The LORD within her is righteous;
   he does no wrong. [a]
Morning by morning he dispenses his justice,
   and every new day he does not fail,
   yet the unrighteous know no shame.

⁶ "I have cut off nations;
   their strongholds are demolished.
I have left their streets deserted,
   with no one passing through.
Their cities are destroyed; [b]
   no one will be left—no one at all.
⁷ I said to the city,
   'Surely you will fear me
   and accept correction!'
Then her dwelling would not be cut off,
   nor all my punishments come upon her.
But they were still eager
   to act corruptly [c] in all they did.
⁸ Therefore wait [d] for me," declares the LORD,
   "for the day I will stand up to testify. [a]
I have decided to assemble the nations, [e]
   to gather the kingdoms
and to pour out my wrath on them—
   all my fierce anger.
The whole world will be consumed [f]
   by the fire of my jealous anger.

⁹ "Then will I purify the lips of the peoples,

---

[a] 8 Septuagint and Syriac; Hebrew *will rise up to plunder*

3:1	[s] Jer 6:6
	[t] Eze 23:30
3:2	[u] Jer 22:21
	[v] Jer 7:28
	[w] Ps 73:28; Jer 5:3
3:3	[x] Eze 22:27
3:4	[y] Jer 9:4
	[z] Eze 22:26
3:5	[a] Dt 32:4
3:6	[b] Lev 26:31
3:7	[c] Hos 9:9
3:8	[d] Ps 27:14
	[e] Joel 3:2
	[f] Zep 1:18

Have you experienced God's peace in visiting reserves set aside for wild animals or perhaps in walking among the ruins of Rome, Greece, or other ancient lands? The land and all non-human life in it witness to the Creator by their purity. Without humanity the creation is pristine, a witness to God's glory (Ps. 19:1–6; cf. Job 38–41). Only the human creation rebels against God. There are always environmental consequences to sin (Gen. 3:17–19; Lev. 26:21–22). In Zephaniah they are dramatic (1:2–3).

Zephaniah 3:1–20

Chapter 3 began with two points regarding Jerusalem's judgment: (1) The city's sins of arrogance and corruption were described (vv. 1–5)—sins against both God and people. (2) The Lord described the futile warnings he had given (vv. 6–8), but Jerusalem wouldn't accept correction. Therefore, "the whole world [would] be consumed."

But the chapter ended, again in two parts, with Jerusalem's joy: (1) God promised that the nations would be purified, the scattered remnant restored, and Jerusalem purged (vv. 9–13). (2) Zephaniah envisioned Jerusalem's day of joy (vv. 14–20); the people would sing in security because the Lord would be near to them.

If Jerusalem today could be a city of peace between cultures and races, peace would be possible for

1513

3:9
g Zep 2:11
h Isa 19:18
3:10
i Ps 68:31 i Isa 60:7

3:11
k Joel 2:26-27

3:12
l Isa 14:32 m Na 1:7

3:13
n Isa 10:21; Mic 4:7
o Ps 119:3
p Rev 14:5
q Eze 34:15;
Zep 2:7
r Eze 34:25-28

3:14
s Zec 2:10
t Isa 12:6

that all of them may call[g] on the name of the LORD
    and serve[h] him shoulder to shoulder.
10 From beyond the rivers of Cush[a][i]
    my worshipers, my scattered people,
    will bring me offerings.[j]
11 On that day you will not be put to shame[k]
    for all the wrongs you have done to me,
because I will remove from this city
    those who rejoice in their pride.
Never again will you be haughty
    on my holy hill.
12 But I will leave within you
    the meek[l] and humble,
    who trust[m] in the name of the LORD.
13 The remnant[n] of Israel will do no wrong;[o]
    they will speak no lies,[p]
    nor will deceit be found in their mouths.
They will eat and lie down[q]
    and no one will make them afraid.[r]"

14 Sing, O Daughter of Zion;[s]
    shout aloud,[t] O Israel!
Be glad and rejoice with all your heart,
    O Daughter of Jerusalem!
15 The LORD has taken away your punishment,
    he has turned back your enemy.

a 10 That is, the upper Nile region

the whole world. People of many ethnic backgrounds have immigrated to Israel, and various cultures surround it. Nations throughout the world are affected by war and peace in the Middle East. The call to pray for Jerusalem's peace (Ps. 122:6) is relevant today as a cry for the reconciliation and unity of all cultures. Such peace would be a source of hope for unity everywhere.

In Jesus we have reason to sing Zephaniah's song of joy (3:14). We have the Lord in our midst (v. 17). Sorrows are removed (v. 18) through prayer. The oppressions of sin and death (v. 19) are relieved by the power of his forgiveness and resurrection from the dead. Do you feel a song stirring within?

3:20

Population

"All the peoples of the earth" was a more metaphorical phrase for Zephaniah than for the demographers of today. How current population growth is perceived depends on how you measure it. There are three principle ways:

Source: American Association for the Advancement of Science (2002:14–15)

Total numbers:
The raw number of people in the world: currently at 6.4 billion and climbing

Annual additions:
The number of people added each year. The birth rate peaked in about 1990 (at 86 million per year) and has steadily declined since (currently at about 75 million per year).

Growth rates:
The rate of growth reached its peak between 1965 and 1970 (at 2.1 percent per year) and has steeply declined to about 1.2 percent per year.

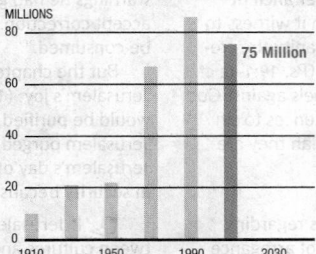

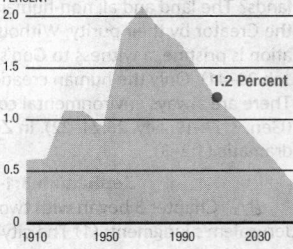

The Lord, the King of Israel, is with you;[u]
  never again will you fear[v] any harm.
16 On that day they will say to Jerusalem,
  "Do not fear, O Zion;
  do not let your hands hang limp.[w]
17 The Lord your God is with you,
  he is mighty to save.[x]
He will take great delight[y] in you,
  he will quiet you with his love,
  he will rejoice over you with singing."

18 "The sorrows for the appointed feasts
  I will remove from you;
  they are a burden and a reproach to you.[a]
19 At that time I will deal
  with all who oppressed you;
I will rescue the lame
  and gather those who have been scattered.[z]
I will give them praise[a] and honor
  in every land where they were put to shame.
20 At that time I will gather you;
  at that time I will bring[b] you home.
I will give you honor[c] and praise
  among all the peoples of the earth
when I restore your fortunes[b][d]
  before your very eyes,"

                            says the Lord.

3:15 u Eze 37:26-28 v Isa 54:14
3:16 w Job 4:3; Isa 35:3-4; Heb 12:12
3:17 x Isa 63:1 y Isa 62:4
3:19 z Eze 34:16; Mic 4:6 a Isa 60:18
3:20 b Jer 29:14; Eze 37:12 c Isa 56:5; 66:22 d Joel 3:1

a 18 Or "I will gather you who mourn for the appointed feasts; / your reproach is a burden to you
b 20 Or I bring back your captives

INTRODUCTION TO
Haggai

AUTHOR
This book was written by the prophet Haggai, who worked with Zechariah to encourage the returning exiles to complete the rebuilding of the temple in Jerusalem.

DATE WRITTEN
Haggai's messages were given during a four-month period in 520 B.C.

ORIGINAL READERS
Zerubbabel had returned to Jerusalem in 538 B.C. with about 50,000 Jews to rebuild the temple. Over the years they had become discouraged by opposition and had abandoned the project. Haggai's messages were given to encourage the Jews to complete the temple rebuilding project.

TIMELINE

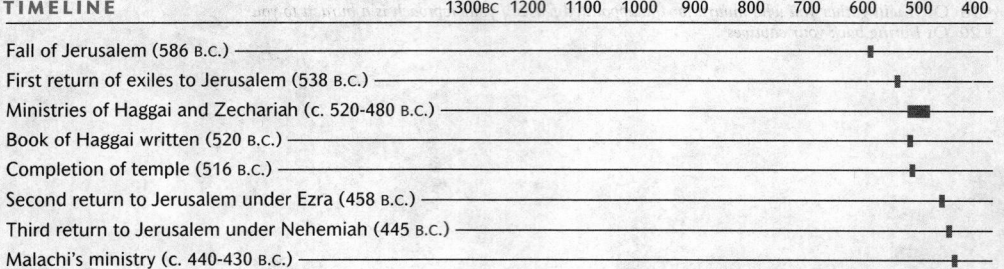

	1300BC	1200	1100	1000	900	800	700	600	500	400
Fall of Jerusalem (586 B.C.)										
First return of exiles to Jerusalem (538 B.C.)										
Ministries of Haggai and Zechariah (c. 520-480 B.C.)										
Book of Haggai written (520 B.C.)										
Completion of temple (516 B.C.)										
Second return to Jerusalem under Ezra (458 B.C.)										
Third return to Jerusalem under Nehemiah (445 B.C.)										
Malachi's ministry (c. 440-430 B.C.)										

THEMES
Haggai spoke to a discouraged people who had misplaced their priorities. He directed them to think about what they were doing (or, more appropriately, what they *weren't* doing), get their priorities straight, and work wholeheartedly for God. The book of Haggai contains the following themes:

1. *Priorities.* The people had neglected the rebuilding of God's temple while focusing on constructing beautiful homes for themselves (1:2–4,9). Haggai instructed them that God's temple and work should be their top priority. They were to "give careful thought" (1:5,7; 2:15,18) to their ways, for God's pleasure and honor were to be their overriding goals (1:8).

2. *Obedience.* When the people disobeyed God, there were consequences (1:6,11; 2:16–17). But when they followed him (1:12), he provided the enthusiasm (1:14), strength (2:4–5), and resources (2:8) to do his will. God promised that if they were obedient, he would bless them with his presence (2:9), peace (2:9), and prosperity (2:19).

FAITH IN ACTION
The pages of Haggai contain life lessons and role models of faith—people who challenge believers to put their faith in action.

Role Models

• HAGGAI (1:4–9) boldly rebuked the Jews for caring only for their own needs while ignoring the rebuilding of God's temple. Have you put your needs above God's mission? Or are your priorities aligned with his?

• ZERUBBABEL (THE GOVERNOR) AND JOSHUA (THE HIGH PRIEST) (1:12) responded in obedience to Haggai's message and began to work on the temple (1:14). When you are corrected, do you respond positively, or do you take a defensive stance?

Challenges

• Take a few moments to evaluate your life. Is it fulfilling, meaningful, rewarding? If not, perhaps you have misplaced your priorities (1:9–11). Determine to put God first in your life (Matt. 6:33). Commit to doing his work and fulfilling his purpose for you, believing that everything else will fall into place.

• As a steward of God's gifts (talents, time, treasure), use his resources wisely. Don't neglect the work God has called you to do by channeling his resources toward your own selfish ends (1:9; 2:15–19a).

• Believe that God has chosen you (2:23). Don't be afraid to cast your all into whatever task God has called you to do. He will encourage you along the way (2:4), help you complete the job (2:7–9), and bless you for your obedience and service (2:19b).

OUTLINE

I.   First Message: The Call to Rebuild the Temple (1:1–11)
II. The Response of Zerubbabel and the People (1:12–15)
III. Second Message: The Promised Glory (2:1–9)
IV. Third Message: A Defiled People Blessed (2:10–19)
V.   Fourth Message: The Promise to Zerubbabel (2:20–23)

A Call to Build the House of the LORD

1 In the second year of King Darius, *a* on the first day of the sixth month, the word of the LORD came through the prophet Haggai *b* to Zerubbabel *c* son of Shealtiel, governor *d* of Judah, and to Joshua *a e* son of Jehozadak, *f* the high priest:

2 This is what the LORD Almighty says: "These people say, 'The time has not yet come for the LORD's house to be built.' "

3 Then the word of the LORD came through the prophet Haggai: *g* 4 "Is it a time for

a 1 A variant of Jeshua; here and elsewhere in Haggai

1:1 *a* Ezr 4:24 *b* Ezr 5:1 *c* Mt 1:12-13 *d* Ezr 5:3 *e* Ezr 2:2 *f* 1Ch 6:15; Ezr 3:2

1:3 *g* Ezr 5:1

Haggai 1:1–15

Haggai received a series of prophetic messages during a four-month period in 520 B.C. The first one came on "the first day of the sixth month," on August 29. Haggai's call to rebuild the temple didn't represent the first initiative to restore this structure. According to Ezra 5:13–16, the project had begun immediately following the decree of Cyrus in 538 B.C. (cf. Ezra 1). Although the returned exiles had rebuilt the foundation shortly thereafter (Ezra 3:8–11), they had allowed opposition to prevent them from making further progress on the temple itself (Ezra 4:23–24).

The people were experiencing futility in all their labor (Hag. 1:6,9–11). Because of neglecting the Lord's temple, they were reaping the negative consequences of covenant unfaithfulness, as God had clearly warned them through Moses (Lev. 26:18–20; Deut. 28:15,38–40; cf. Mic. 6:13–15). God required the people to respond, but their action was linked to God's purposes. Ultimately they were to act, not to avoid another curse on their crops but for the pleasure and glory of God (Hag. 1:8).

You may not worry about a famine of food, but you might struggle with the lack of a job or a spiritual drought. Drought of any kind and especially spiritual dryness can become an opportunity to listen to God's challenges to your way of life. What are your top priorities? What are the most important issues in your fellowship of believers? Do your primary concerns enhance God's pleasure and give him glory? Does your life reflect a "kingdom" orientation (cf. Matt. 6:33)?

What Are Your Priorities?

When the Jews returned to Israel from Babylon in 538 B.C., they began immediately to rebuild God's temple (Ezra 3). But no sooner had the foundation been laid than Samaritan opposition suspended progress (Ezra 4:24)—for almost 20 years. By the time Haggai began preaching, indifference had set in. But the prophet's stinging rebuke, "Is it a time for you yourselves to be living in your paneled houses, while this house remains a ruin?" (Hag. 1:4), brought the issue into stark focus.

True, the Israelites were battling for survival. Politically they were weak, bullied by neighbors and subjugated under a foreign power. Drought, diseased crops, failing harvests, and, no doubt, taxation all added to their woes. The temptation was pressing to neglect their responsibility to God. But "paneled houses" didn't exactly connote destitution. Moreover, Haggai (1:5–11) reminded them that their problems were largely of their own making. By neglecting the temple, they had neglected to honor God, violating their covenant promises and bringing judgment upon themselves (cf. 1:10ff.; Deut. 28:14,37ff.).

> **T**he lives of those who think in terms of kingdom priorities will have genuine Christian impact.

Haggai's challenge is echoed throughout the Bible—most clearly articulated by Jesus' call to "seek first [God's] kingdom and his righteousness, and all these things will be given to you as well" (Matt. 6:33). Among other issues, putting God first means focusing on world evangelization and caring for the poor and oppressed. These priorities are to be integrated into our whole life but especially affect our finances and career choices.

Christians in a world of plenty easily forget that many live under crushing poverty, both materially and spiritually. Nearly four billion people worldwide live on less than $2 a day, and on the spiritual front, more than four billion don't know Jesus Christ as Lord and Savior. Can we as Christians truly honor God by giving priority to our homes, often palatial in comparison with those of the poor, while ignoring our responsibly to world missions and the suffering of others?

The question of priority relates also to our career choices. For many middle-class Christians, these decisions are governed by monetary rewards and social status. Yet the lives of those who think in terms of kingdom priorities will have genuine Christian impact.

The greatest evangelist of 20th-century China, John Sung, sailed through his university studies in America, earning a PhD in less than six years. But he knew God had called him to preach the gospel. Relinquishing the prospect of a brilliant academic career, he returned to China in 1927. During his 15-year ministry, tens of thousands came to Christ and hundreds of churches in Southeast Asia revived.

Similarly, a diminutive Albanian girl, Agnes Bojaxhiu, with none of the brilliance of John Sung, traveled as a nun and a teacher to India. After some years she went to live and work among the poorest of Calcutta's poor. Thus was born the inspiring ministry of Mother Teresa, through which thousands of broken lives were touched and transformed by Christ.

Living a life of ordered priorities is part and parcel of our Christian calling. Without it our lives become purposeless and we end up as self-indulgent "couch potatoes." How would we respond to Haggai's question (Hag. 1:4) today? Only by putting God first can our lives acquire a powerful, transforming relevance for the world and for his glory!

Hwa Yung, director of the Centre for the Study of Christianity in Asia at Trinity Theological College in Singapore

you yourselves to be living in your paneled houses,[h] while this house remains a ruin?'"

5Now this is what the LORD Almighty says: "Give careful thought[j] to your ways. 6You have planted much, but have harvested little.[k] You eat, but never have enough. You drink, but never have your fill. You put on clothes, but are not warm. You earn wages,[l] only to put them in a purse with holes in it."

7This is what the LORD Almighty says: "Give careful thought to your ways. 8Go up into the mountains and bring down timber and build the house, so that I may take pleasure[m] in it and be honored," says the LORD. 9"You expected much, but see, it turned out to be little. What you brought home, I blew away. Why?" declares the LORD Almighty. "Because of my house, which remains a ruin,[n] while each of you is busy with his own house. 10Therefore, because of you the heavens have withheld their dew and the earth its crops.[o] 11I called for a drought[p] on the fields and the mountains, on the grain, the new wine, the oil and whatever the ground produces, on men and cattle, and on the labor of your hands.[q]"

12Then Zerubbabel[r] son of Shealtiel, Joshua son of Jehozadak, the high priest, and the whole remnant[s] of the people obeyed[t] the voice of the LORD their God and the message of the prophet Haggai, because the LORD their God had sent him. And the people feared[u] the LORD.

13Then Haggai, the LORD's messenger, gave this message of the LORD to the people: "I am with[v] you," declares the LORD. 14So the LORD stirred up the spirit of Zerubbabel[w] son of Shealtiel, governor of Judah, and the spirit of Joshua son of Jehozadak, the high priest, and the spirit of the whole remnant[x] of the people. They came and began to work on the house of the LORD Almighty, their God, 15on the twenty-fourth day of the sixth month[y] in the second year of King Darius.

The Promised Glory of the New House

2 On the twenty-first day of the seventh month, the word of the LORD came through the prophet Haggai: 2"Speak to Zerubbabel son of Shealtiel, governor of Judah, to Joshua son of Jehozadak, the high priest, and to the remnant of the people. Ask them, 3'Who of you is left who saw this house[z] in its former glory? How does it look to you now? Does it not seem to you like nothing?[a] 4But now be strong, O Zerubbabel,' declares the LORD. 'Be strong,[b] O Joshua son of Jehozadak, the high priest. Be strong, all you people of the land,' declares the LORD, 'and work.

1:4
h 2Sa 7:2 i ver 9;
Jer 33:12
1:5
j La 3:40
1:6
k Dt 28:38
l Hag 2:16;
Zec 8:10

1:8
m Ps 132:13-14
1:9
n ver 4

1:10
o Lev 26:19;
Dt 28:23
1:11
p Dt 28:22;
1Ki 17:1 q Hag 2:17

1:12
r ver 1 s ver 14;
Isa 1:9; Hag 2:2
t Isa 50:10
u Dt 31:12

1:13
v Mt 28:20; Ro 8:31
1:14
w Ezr 5:2 x ver 12

1:15
y ver 1

2:3
z Ezr 3:12
a Zec 4:10

2:4
b 1Ch 28:20;
Zec 8:9; Eph 6:10

Haggai 2:1–9

 Now that the people and their leaders had responded to Haggai's first message (1:12–15), the prophet brought a very different one about a month after work had resumed on the temple. Instead of laying ultimatums on a disobedient people, he delivered encouragement to a discouraged but faithful people. Haggai relayed support from God in two forms: (1) The Lord encouraged the people's actions and attitude by telling them to be strong—"For I am with you" (v. 4; cf. 1:13). (2) God motivated the people by reminding them that, because his Spirit was among them, they needn't fear.

1:5–6

Who Are the Poor?

BASIC NECESSITIES	HOUSEHOLD AND INCOME THRESHOLD	LONGEVITY, KNOWLEDGE, STANDARD OF LIVING
1	2	3
People who lack adequate access to life's basic necessities: water, food, clothing, shelter.[1]	People falling below thresholds set according to the number of people living in a household and measured by the level of money income (before taxes), excluding capital gains and non-cash benefits (like public housing, Medicaid, and food stamps).[2]	The Human Poverty Index (HPI) measures deprivations in three dimensions of human life—longevity, knowledge, and a decent standard of living.[3]

Sources: [1] McGrath (1999:1668) [2] U.S. Census Bureau (2002:441–444) [3] United Nations Development Programme, *Human Development Report 2002* (2002:265)

2:4
c 2Sa 5:10; Ac 7:9
2:5
d Ex 29:46
e Ne 9:20; Isa 63:11
2:6
f Isa 10:25
g Heb 12:26*
2:7
h Isa 60:7
2:9
i Ps 85:9

For I am with[c] you,' declares the LORD Almighty. [5]'This is what I covenanted with you when you came out of Egypt.[d] And my Spirit[e] remains among you. Do not fear.'

[6] "This is what the LORD Almighty says: 'In a little while[f] I will once more shake the heavens and the earth,[g] the sea and the dry land. [7]I will shake all nations, and the desired of all nations will come, and I will fill this house[h] with glory,' says the LORD Almighty. [8]'The silver is mine and the gold is mine,' declares the LORD Almighty. [9]'The glory[i] of this present house will be greater than the glory of the former house,' says the LORD Almighty. 'And in this place I will grant peace,' declares the LORD Almighty."

Blessings for a Defiled People

2:10
j ver 1

[10]On the twenty-fourth day of the ninth month,[j] in the second year of Darius, the word of the LORD came to the prophet Haggai: [11] "This is what the LORD Almighty

2:11
k Lev 10:10-11;
Dt 17:8-11; Mal 2:7

says: 'Ask the priests[k] what the law says: [12]If a person carries consecrated meat in the fold of his garment, and that fold touches some bread or stew, some wine, oil

2:12
l Lev 6:27; Mt 23:19

or other food, does it become consecrated?' "

The priests answered, "No."

[13]Then Haggai said, "If a person defiled by contact with a dead body touches one of these things, does it become defiled?"

2:13
m Lev 22:4-6

"Yes," the priests replied, "it becomes defiled.[m]"

[14]Then Haggai said, " 'So it is with this people and this nation in my sight,' declares the LORD. 'Whatever they do and whatever they offer[n] there is defiled.

2:14
n Isa 1:13
2:15
o Hag 1:5
p Ezr 3:10
q Ezr 4:24

[15] " 'Now give careful thought[o] to this from this day on[a]—consider how things were before one stone was laid[p] on another in the LORD's temple.[q] [16]When anyone came to a heap of twenty measures, there were only ten. When anyone went to a wine vat to draw fifty measures, there were only twenty.[r] [17]I struck all the work of your hands[s] with blight,[t] mildew and hail, yet you did not turn to me,' declares the

2:16
r Hag 1:6
2:17
s Hag 1:11
t Dt 28:22;
1Ki 8:37; Am 4:9

a 15 Or to the days past

The Lord intensified his assurance of his presence with his people by promising to fill the rebuilt temple with his glory. In fact, the glory of Zerubbabel's temple would be greater than that of Solomon's, a reality fulfilled when Jesus the Messiah entered it (cf. Luke 2:25–38).

Not only does this passage focus on God's action on behalf of his people; it also emphasizes his presence among them. This shows us the supreme importance of nurturing the presence of God in our lives both individually and corporately—not only in the focused rhythms of individual and corporate spiritual disciplines, but also through a sustained consciousness of God's abiding presence with us throughout our days and weeks. It's tempting in the midst of trying circumstances to forego our accustomed spiritual rhythms, but these are the times we need them more than ever.

Haggai 2:10–19

God instructed Haggai to ask the priests questions about transmitting holiness and defilement. Ceremonial uncleanness was passed on much more easily than holiness. The Lord's point: Even though the people were back in the Holy Land, that holiness didn't make them pure. They needed to obey God, particularly with regard to rebuilding the temple.

1:6,10–11

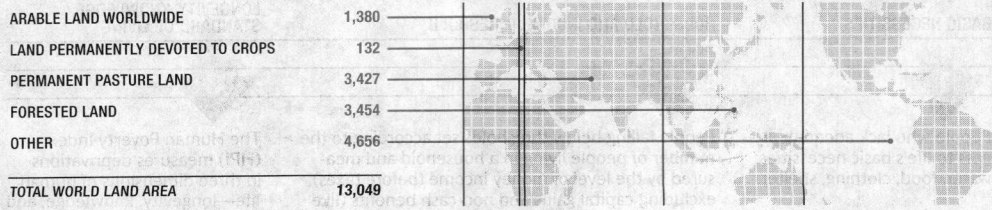

World Land Use

Good soil in which to plant crops is and has always been a blessing from God—a blessing that, for whatever reason, isn't being enjoyed in many parts of the world today.

MILLION HECTARES	(a hectare is an area of 10,000 square meters, equivalent to 2.47 acres.)
ARABLE LAND WORLDWIDE	1,380
LAND PERMANENTLY DEVOTED TO CROPS	132
PERMANENT PASTURE LAND	3,427
FORESTED LAND	3,454
OTHER	4,656
TOTAL WORLD LAND AREA	13,049

What challenges does this grim reality present for the caring Christian in a land of plenty?

Source: American Association for the Advancement of Science (2002:72)

LORD. [u] 18'From this day on, from this twenty-fourth day of the ninth month, give careful thought to the day when the foundation [v] of the LORD's temple was laid. Give careful thought: 19Is there yet any seed left in the barn? Until now, the vine and the fig tree, the pomegranate and the olive tree have not borne fruit.

" 'From this day on I will bless you.' "

Zerubbabel the LORD's Signet Ring

20The word of the LORD came to Haggai a second time on the twenty-fourth day of the month: 21"Tell Zerubbabel [w] governor of Judah that I will shake the heavens and the earth. 22I will overturn royal thrones and shatter the power of the foreign kingdoms. [x] I will overthrow chariots [y] and their drivers; horses and their riders will fall, each by the sword of his brother. [z]

23" 'On that day,' declares the LORD Almighty, 'I will take you, my servant [a] Zerubbabel son of Shealtiel,' declares the LORD, 'and I will make you like my signet ring, for I have chosen you,' declares the LORD Almighty."

2:17
u Am 4:6
2:18
v Zec 8:9

2:21
w Ezr 5:2

2:22
x Da 2:44
y Mic 5:10
z Jdg 7:22
2:23
a Isa 43:10

The Israelites' poor harvests were related to their sin (see "There and Then" for 1:1–15). In verse 18, the Lord stated that the same potential for blessing had existed at the time when the foundation of the temple was laid in 536 B.C. (Ezra 3:11). This was a warning not to fail again. God concluded by saying that, because of the people's response to Haggai's message, future abundance was assured (cf. Mal. 3:10).

It's easy within the church today to bring our sacrifices, whether our verbal worship, our material contributions, or our gifts and abilities, and yet be walking in disobedience—due either to a heart that is disengaged from God or a pattern of life contrary to his standards. God's blessing to us is received in and through Jesus Christ: the foundation of the church and the stronghold of an obedient people. Jesus affirmed this, saying, "If you love me, you will obey what I command" (John 14:15).

Haggai 2:20–23

Haggai's final message showed that God's promise of blessing in the immediate future (e.g., abundant crops) was but the firstfruits of a far greater blessing. In addition to being made governor of Judah by the reigning Persians, Zerubbabel was the rightful heir to the throne of David (1 Chron. 3:17–19; Matt. 1:13). God promised to shake the universe, overthrow human power, and appoint the Davidic line to its due place as ruler over the world.

The image of the signet ring reminds believers of all times that they have no power without the God who sends them forth in his name. Haggai 2 focuses on the perseverance of the Jerusalem community through the difficult and discouraging early days of rebuilding the temple. In our world of short attention spans and split-second communication, we have lost patience with "hanging in there." But God declares his blessing for those who do, revealing that such determination will ultimately bear fruit in the transformation of the cosmos. Do we as the church realize this? Have we grasped the truth that God's plan is to work through us as his people to bring about his rule and justice on Earth?

INTRODUCTION TO
Zechariah

AUTHOR

The book identifies its author as "Zechariah son of Berekiah, the son of Iddo" (1:1). Zechariah, a contemporary of Haggai, was a priest and prophet.

DATE WRITTEN

Zechariah was probably written in 520 B.C.

ORIGINAL READERS

Zechariah encouraged the Jews who had returned from exile in Babylon to complete the rebuilding of the temple. He also prophesied concerning Jerusalem's future place in God's kingdom.

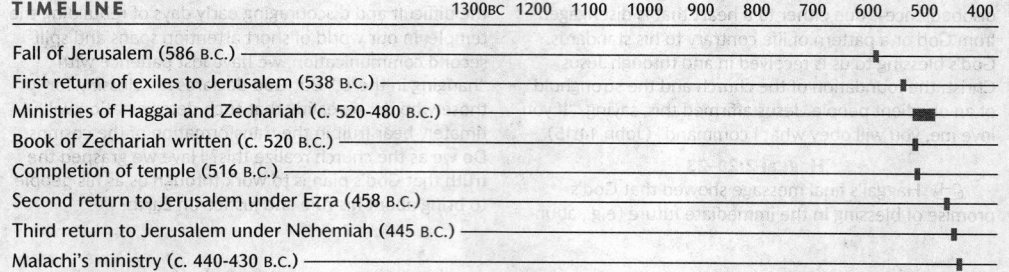

TIMELINE	1300BC	1200	1100	1000	900	800	700	600	500	400

Fall of Jerusalem (586 B.C.)
First return of exiles to Jerusalem (538 B.C.)
Ministries of Haggai and Zechariah (c. 520-480 B.C.)
Book of Zechariah written (c. 520 B.C.)
Completion of temple (516 B.C.)
Second return to Jerusalem under Ezra (458 B.C.)
Third return to Jerusalem under Nehemiah (445 B.C.)
Malachi's ministry (c. 440-430 B.C.)

THEMES

Zechariah was written as an encouraging message to a people who had lost their sense of identity and purpose in God's plan. It includes the following themes:

1. *Israel's near future.* The first eight chapters of Zechariah fit its historical setting and focus on the near future of the restored Jewish community. Zechariah encouraged the returnees as they struggled to rebuild the temple. He called them to repent of their sin (1:2–6) and exhorted them to exhibit compassion and mercy toward the vulnerable (7:4–14). Zechariah's night visions expressed God's continuing concern for the protection and restoration of his people (1:16–17,20; 2:11–12; 8:3–23) and the importance of Zerubbabel and Joshua in God's plan (3:1—14; 6:9–15).

2. *Israel's distant future.* The last six chapters of Zechariah focus on the distant future of the restored Jewish community. These prophecies reveal God's plan to bring blessings to Jerusalem: God would avenge his people by destroying their enemies (9:1–8); Israel's king would arrive in Jerusalem, ushering in a time of peace (9:9–17); and God would gather his scattered people (10:1—11:3). The final chapters culminate in a vision of God's ultimate victory over those who continued to resist his will (12:1–9) and his cleansing of the land and people (13:1–9). The Divine Warrior will return, and all humans will submit to his rule (14:1–21).

of a coming king and an ultimate, divine victory over evil points not only to Christ's earthly ministry, but also to his ultimate return as described in the book of Revelation.

FAITH IN ACTION

The pages of Zechariah contain life lessons and role models of faith—people who challenge believers to put their faith in action.

Role Models

- ZECHARIAH (1:1–6) used the past lessons of their forefathers to warn God's people to repent. Are you learning from your mistakes and those of your parents and grandparents?

- THE PEOPLE (1:6) repented, acknowledging their sin. Do you pray that those who are in rebellion against God will repent and turn to him?

- ZERUBBABEL (4:6–9) was strengthened by the Holy Spirit to accomplish the task of temple reconstruction. What special job has God entrusted to you? Are you trusting him to give you the strength to follow it through to completion?

- JOSHUA (3:1–10) represents both the Old Testament priesthood and the New Testament priesthood of believers, who depend on Christ's atoning blood for cleansing. Do you picture yourself spiritually dressed in "filthy clothes" or in "rich garments" (3:3)? Be aware that our reality doesn't always match our perceptions.

Challenges

- Briefly review your family history. What lessons can you learn from the sins of your ancestors (1:2–6)? Turn away from any ingrained sins in your family line and steer your family back to God and his ways (1:3–4).

- Remember to rely on the Spirit, not on your own strength or ability (4:6).

- Evaluate your religious life. Practice godly obedience, not empty religious rituals (7:4–6).

- Resolve to obey God's command to practice social justice: "Administer true justice; show mercy and compassion to one another. Do not oppress the widow or the fatherless, the alien or the poor. In your hearts do not think evil of each other" (7:9–10).

- Cultivate a vision for your city or neighborhood that includes the safety and well-being of children (8:5). Work locally and globally to make it a reality.

- When you experience days of discouragement, remember that you are like a jewel in God's crown (9:16). At times it may be difficult to see your place in his cosmic plan, but hold to the truth that God has a glorious purpose for your life, a purpose that will one day be fully revealed.

OUTLINE

I. A Call to Repentance (1:1–6)
II. Eight Night Visions and Prophecies (1:7—6:8)
III. The Crowning of Joshua the High Priest (6:9–15)
IV. Fasting and the Future (7–8)
V. The Advent and Rejection of Messiah (9–11)
VI. The Advent and Reception of Messiah (12–14)

A Call to Return to the LORD

1:1
a Ezr 4:24; 6:15
b Ezr 5:1
c Mt 23:35;
Lk 11:51 d ver 7;
Ne 12:4
1:2
e 2Ch 36:16
1:3
f Mal 3:7; Jas 4:8
1:4
g 2Ch 36:15
h Ps 106:6
i 2Ch 24:19;
Ps 78:8; Jer 6:17

1 In the eighth month of the second year of Darius,ᵃ the word of the LORD came to the prophet Zechariah ᵇ son of Berekiah, ᶜ the son of Iddo:ᵈ

² "The LORD was very angryᵉ with your forefathers. ³Therefore tell the people: This is what the LORD Almighty says: 'Return to me,' declares the LORD Almighty, 'and I will return to you,'ᶠ says the LORD Almighty. ⁴Do not be like your forefathers,ᵍ to whom the earlier prophets proclaimed: This is what the LORD Almighty says: 'Turn from your evil waysʰ and your evil practices.' But they would not listen or pay attention to me,ⁱ declares the LORD. ⁵Where are your forefathers now? And the prophets, do they live forever? ⁶But did not my words and my decrees, which I commanded my servants the prophets, overtake your forefathers?

1:6
j Jer 12:14-17;
La 2:17

"Then they repented and said, 'The LORD Almighty has done to us what our ways and practices deserve,ʲ just as he determined to do.' "

The Man Among the Myrtle Trees

⁷On the twenty-fourth day of the eleventh month, the month of Shebat, in the second year of Darius, the word of the LORD came to the prophet Zechariah son of Berekiah, the son of Iddo.

1:8
k Rev 6:4
l Zec 6:2-7

⁸During the night I had a vision—and there before me was a man riding a redᵏ horse! He was standing among the myrtle trees in a ravine. Behind him were red, brown and white horses.ˡ

1:9
m Zec 4:1,4-5

⁹I asked, "What are these, my lord?"

The angelᵐ who was talking with me answered, "I will show you what they are."

1:10
n Zec 6:5-8

¹⁰Then the man standing among the myrtle trees explained, "They are the ones the LORD has sent to go throughout the earth."ⁿ

1:11
o Isa 14:7

¹¹And they reported to the angel of the LORD, who was standing among the myrtle trees, "We have gone throughout the earth and found the whole world at rest and in peace."ᵒ

1:12
p Da 9:2
1:13
q Zec 4:1

¹²Then the angel of the LORD said, "LORD Almighty, how long will you withhold mercy from Jerusalem and from the towns of Judah, which you have been angry with these seventyᵖ years?" ¹³So the LORD spoke kind and comforting words to the angel who talked with me.ۥ

1:14
r Joel 2:18; Zec 8:2
1:15
s Jer 48:11
t Ps 123:3-4;
Am 1:11
1:16
u Zec 8:3
v Zec 2:1-2

¹⁴Then the angel who was speaking to me said, "Proclaim this word: This is what the LORD Almighty says: 'I am very jealousʳ for Jerusalem and Zion, ¹⁵but I am very angry with the nations that feel secure.ˢ I was only a little angry, but they added to the calamity.'ᵗ

¹⁶"Therefore, this is what the LORD says: 'I will returnᵘ to Jerusalem with mercy, and there my house will be rebuilt. And the measuring lineᵛ will be stretched out over Jerusalem,' declares the LORD Almighty.

1:17
w Isa 51:3
x Isa 14:1
y Zec 2:12

¹⁷"Proclaim further: This is what the LORD Almighty says: 'My towns will again overflow with prosperity, and the LORD will again comfortʷ Zion and chooseˣ Jerusalem.' "ʸ

Zechariah 1:1–6

📖 Zechariah's opening message, dated according to the reign of the Persian king Darius I, occurred in October-November 520 B.C. Zechariah, who came from a priestly family, was born in Babylonia but was part of the first group of exiles to return to Judah in about 538 B.C. He joined forces with and followed up the ministry of the prophet Haggai, who encouraged the returnees by revealing God's plan to establish his rule and identified the rebuilding of the temple as the initial phase of this plan (Hag. 2:1–9,20–23). Zechariah took restoration to another level by calling the people to covenant renewal alongside their rebuilding project—as evidenced in his charge here to "return" to the Lord.

🕮 Biblical repentance is a matter of turning to as well as turning from—an abandonment into the arms of a God passionate for relationship with us. Such repentance isn't just focused on behavioral patterns but on relational patterns: The issue is Someone to know, not just some way to act.

Zechariah 1:7–17

📖 Zechariah described his eight "night visions," which he received on February 15, 519 B.C., in chapters 1–6. The report of the reconnaissance mission in this first vision appeared to be positive, as the angelic envoys "found the whole world at rest and in peace." But this was hardly comforting to the angel of the Lord. While the Persian Empire as a whole was secure at this time,

1:17

Jesus taught us to pray "Give us this day our daily bread." But people want it via a job, not a handout. Productive economic activity can be a means to enhance and support Christian ministry. This phenomenon has seen successful implementation since the apostle Paul first discussed his own work habits in his letters to young churches. He made it clear that people are to work for their living (2 Thess. 3:10). But this isn't easy in a world where poverty and unemployment abound. Models are needed that combine business with a clear focus on a holistic Christian outreach.

Consider the following six models of economic ministry:

Business Incubators—the creation of new businesses for street teens, recovering addicts, and alcoholics. The Puerta de Esperanza program in Mexico teaches men to make wooden tortilla presses. A related youth center instructs homeless teenagers in making puppets and stuffed animals. As home businesses generate income, the equipment is paid for and funds are used for new enterprises.

Ministry Businesses—the development of self-sustaining service enterprises like Christian clinics, dental offices, schools, and bookstores, where the ministry charges a fee for services. Some of these projects, like the Clinica Biblica (hospital) in Costa Rica, have grown to handle multi-million dollar budgets. The Colegio Latinoamericano (elementary and high school) in Cartageña serves over 800 students.

Foreign Direct Investment—funds provided from overseas for investor-designed projects that bring special markets, technology, or other proprietary information to developing countries through integration with Christian missions. They provide employment for local church members and a context for mission activity for U.S. businesspeople.

Endowment Enterprises—for the support of Christian ministry in the field. The Granja Roblealto, a chicken and pig farm in Costa Rica created to support children's ministries, employs more the 90 people. In 1999 it channeled more than $200,000 to local Christian day care centers.

Tent Making Enterprises—to provide legal entry, financial support, and ministry opportunity for expatriates. For example, a Mexican family can minister in another country by setting up a retail store, which provides income and a context for ministry. This economic methodology is especially relevant to indigenous (local) missions movements. Sadly, the financial foundation based on donor support is often weak.

Micro Credit Programs—Latin American Mission has started revolving loan programs, like the OPDS program in Barranquilla, Colombia, a LAM affiliate ministry with assignment of one missionary family. Small loans averaging $350 allow impoverished people, many displaced by Colombia's civil war, to support their families by opening a business. The economic programs are integrated with church outreach and direct evangelistic ministry.

> There is currently a vital interest in the potential of micro credit and job creation programs with Christian missions.

The type of productive activity varies in these programs, but there are common economic training issues: how to identify the business idea, where to obtain funding, definition of ownership, management oversight, and marketing. New mission staff members are being recruited, promoting the creation of a new type of missionary-consultant able to provide business training. The organization of enterprise as a ministry is a serious matter requiring definition of technologies, prior determination of profit distribution, and connections with ministry or church institutions.

There is currently a vital interest in the potential of micro credit and job creation programs with Christian missions. Like health and education programs, these development tools have tremendous ministry outreach potential, ever more relevant in a world where poverty and unemployment are rampant.

David R. Befus, president of Latin America Mission in Miami, Florida

Four Horns and Four Craftsmen

18Then I looked up—and there before me were four horns! 19I asked the angel who was speaking to me, "What are these?"

He answered me, "These are the horns *z* that scattered Judah, Israel and Jerusalem."

20Then the LORD showed me four craftsmen. 21I asked, "What are these coming to do?"

He answered, "These are the horns that scattered Judah so that no one could raise his head, but the craftsmen have come to terrify them and throw down these horns of the nations who lifted up their horns *a* against the land of Judah to scatter its people." *b*

A Man With a Measuring Line

2 Then I looked up—and there before me was a man with a measuring line in his hand! 2I asked, "Where are you going?"

He answered me, "To measure Jerusalem, to find out how wide and how long it is." *c*

3Then the angel who was speaking to me left, and another angel came to meet him 4and said to him: "Run, tell that young man, 'Jerusalem will be a city without walls *d* because of the great number *e* of men and livestock in it. 5And I myself will be a wall *f* of fire around it,' declares the LORD, 'and I will be its glory *g* within.'

6"Come! Come! Flee from the land of the north," declares the LORD, "for I have scattered you to the four winds of heaven," *h* declares the LORD.

1:19
z Am 6:13

1:21
a Ps 75:4
b Ps 75:10

2:2
c Eze 40:3;
Rev 21:15

2:4
d Eze 38:11
e Isa 49:20;
Jer 30:19; 33:22
2:5
f Isa 26:1
g Rev 21:23
2:6
h Eze 17:21

---

the Israelites in Judah were oppressed and still under foreign domination.

The angel of the Lord cried out, "LORD Almighty, how long will you withhold mercy?" This kind of question was familiar to the Jews from its use in the laments of the Psalter (cf. Ps. 6:3; 74:10; 80:4; 90:13). God responded with "kind and comforting words"—referring to his jealous love for his people and to his anger against the nations he had used to punish them—but who had gone too far in doing so.

📖 Faith in God's sovereignty is essential for us as Christians as we await Christ's return. The words of the apostles in the book of Acts were a powerful expression of such faith. Fresh from persecution they "raised their voices together in prayer to God," beginning with the simple cry, "Sovereign Lord" (Acts 4:23–30). May this be our cry as his people!

Zechariah 1:18–21

📖 With the proclamation of the Lord still ringing in their ears—a proclamation that offered hope to Judah and warning to her enemies—Zechariah's audience now entered a second visionary scene. It continued God's response to the cry of the angel of the Lord ("How long?") in 1:12, promising that the nations that had mistreated his people would in turn be destroyed by other nations.

📖 The ultimate symbol for helplessness (the lifelong experience of many of the exiles) is Christ's incarnation. He came into the world in a defenseless state and conquered the forces of evil through the helplessness of the cross. This is the basis for our vulnerable life of faith, an example to us as we take up our own crosses and follow him. The weak things of the world conquer, not because they are weak, but because of the necessity of faith. Helplessness forces us to trust in

the only One who can rescue us.

Zechariah 2:1–13

📖 The Jews who had returned to the land were involved in restoring the temple (Ezra 3–6; Hag. 1–2) and rebuilding their homes (Hag. 1). The thought of reconstructing a protective wall around the city would have been natural (this would occur later under Nehemiah's leadership; Neh. 2–6). For two reasons, though, God saw the measuring of the city, the first step in building a wall, as opposed to his agenda: (1) He planned to fill Jerusalem with a multitude no wall could contain, and (2) he himself planned to shelter the city.

Verses 6–13 appear to have been a challenge given to those still in exile. This prophetic message called the people to respond to God's initial work and promise by returning to Jerusalem, where he pledged his presence. But Zechariah threw in a zinger: He expanded the scope of the community to include "many nations."

📖 It's critical that we learn to dream outside the boxes that limit our vision of the kingdom's potential. Sometimes these boxes are created by well-meaning people trying to protect God from losing face. They place artificial limitations on what God actually does today. But we as his people are called to bear witness to the miraculous God of Scripture. Other boxes are constructed by fearful people trying to preserve their community from change. The walls in this particular vision would have protected Jerusalem from foreign nations, at the same time limiting these nations from access to God.

From the outset of redemptive history, God has had a global vision (see Gen. 12:3). We as Christians are saved out of this world by God's grace into a relationship with him by his Spirit. But this same Spirit propels us back into the world as instruments of God's grace to bring the "nations" into covenant relationship with him.

7"Come, O Zion! Escape, you who live in the Daughter of Babylon!"[i] 8For this is what the LORD Almighty says: "After he has honored me and has sent me against the nations that have plundered you—for whoever touches you touches the apple of his eye— 9I will surely raise my hand against them so that their slaves will plunder them.[a][k] Then you will know that the LORD Almighty has sent me.[l]

10"Shout and be glad, O Daughter of Zion.[m] For I am coming,[n] and I will live among you,"[o] declares the LORD. 11"Many nations will be joined with the LORD in that day and will become my people. I will live among you and you will know that the LORD Almighty has sent me to you. 12The LORD will inherit[p] Judah as his portion in the holy land and will again choose[q] Jerusalem. 13Be still[r] before the LORD, all mankind, because he has roused himself from his holy dwelling."

Clean Garments for the High Priest

3 Then he showed me Joshua[b][s] the high priest standing before the angel of the LORD, and Satan[c][t] standing at his right side to accuse him. 2The LORD said to Satan, "The LORD rebuke you,[u] Satan! The LORD, who has chosen[v] Jerusalem, rebuke you! Is not this man a burning stick snatched from the fire?"[w]

3Now Joshua was dressed in filthy clothes as he stood before the angel. 4The angel said to those who were standing before him, "Take off his filthy clothes."

Then he said to Joshua, "See, I have taken away your sin,[x] and I will put rich garments[y] on you."

5Then I said, "Put a clean turban[z] on his head." So they put a clean turban on his head and clothed him, while the angel of the LORD stood by.

6The angel of the LORD gave this charge to Joshua: 7"This is what the LORD Almighty says: 'If you will walk in my ways and keep my requirements, then you will govern my house[a] and have charge of my courts, and I will give you a place among these standing here.

8" 'Listen, O high priest Joshua and your associates seated before you, who are men symbolic[b] of things to come: I am going to bring my servant, the Branch.[c] 9See, the stone I have set in front of Joshua! There are seven eyes[d] on that one stone,[d] and I will engrave an inscription on it,' says the LORD Almighty, 'and I will remove the sin[e] of this land in a single day.

10" 'In that day each of you will invite his neighbor to sit under his vine and fig tree,'[f] declares the LORD Almighty."

The Gold Lampstand and the Two Olive Trees

4 Then the angel who talked with me returned and wakened[g] me, as a man is wakened from his sleep.[h] 2He asked me, "What do you see?"[i]

I answered, "I see a solid gold lampstand[j] with a bowl at the top and seven

[a] 8,9 Or *says after . . . eye:* [9]"I . . . *plunder them.*"   [b] 1 A variant of *Jeshua*; here and elsewhere in Zechariah   [c] 1 *Satan* means *accuser.*   [d] 9 Or *facets*

Cross references

2:7
[i] Isa 48:20

2:8
[j] Dt 32:10

2:9
[k] Isa 14:2 [l] Zec 4:9

2:10
[m] Zep 3:14
[n] Zec 9:9
[o] Lev 26:12;
Zec 8:3

2:12
[p] Dt 32:9; Ps 33:12;
Jer 10:16
[q] Zec 1:17

2:13
[r] Hab 2:20

3:1
[s] Hag 1:1; Zec 6:11
[t] Ps 109:6

3:2
[u] Jude 1:9
[v] Isa 14:1
[w] Am 4:11;
Jude 1:23

3:4
[x] Eze 36:25;
Mic 7:18 [y] Isa 52:1;
Rev 19:8

3:5
[z] Ex 29:6

3:7
[a] Dt 17:8-11;
Eze 44:15-16

3:8
[b] Eze 12:11
[c] Isa 4:2

3:9
[d] Isa 28:16
[e] Jer 50:20

3:10
[f] 1Ki 4:25; Mic 4:4

4:1
[g] Da 8:18
[h] Jer 31:26

4:2
[i] Jer 1:13
[j] Ex 25:31; Rev 1:12

Zechariah 3:1–10

In this vision the high priest Joshua ("Jeshua" in Ezra and Nehemiah) represented the sinful nation of Israel (see vv. 8–9). The basis of Satan's accusation was Joshua's impurity, but his defender was none other than the Lord himself. Taking off his filthy clothes deprived Joshua of his priestly office but was also symbolic of the removal of sin. Putting a clean turban on his head reinstated him to his high-priestly function so that Israel once again had a divinely authorized priestly mediator.

God pointed to Joshua as the forerunner of "my servant, the Branch"—a combination of two well-known references to the Messiah (e.g., 6:12; Isa. 4:2; 11:1; 42:1; Jer. 23:5; 33:15). The "stone" was probably another Messianic metaphor (cf. Ps. 118:22; Isa. 8:14; 28:16; Dan. 2:35,45). Zechariah looked ahead to the day when the

Lord, through the Messiah, would graciously remove his people's sin.

Zechariah 3 witnesses to God's continuing pursuit of his people. Joshua was a sorry sight, unworthy to be within Israel's camp, let alone the divine council of heaven. But God declared a new start by his grace—the same grace by which we are called to faithfulness. God's provision of the prophetic word in Zechariah 3 parallels his provision to us of immediate access through Jesus Christ to the "throne of grace" (Heb. 4:16). The call to Joshua applies to each of us as members of God's community of priests within our world.

Zechariah 4:1–14

The two olive trees in this vision (vv. 3,12) represented Joshua the priest (see ch. 3) and Zerubbabel,

4:2
k Rev 4:5
4:3
l ver 11; Rev 11:4

4:5
m Zec 1:9
4:6
n Ezr 5:2
o Isa 11:2-4;
Hos 1:7

4:7
p Jer 51:25
q Ps 118:22

4:9
r Ezr 3:11 s Ezr 3:8;
6:15; Zec 6:12
t Zec 2:9
4:10
u Hag 2:3
v Zec 3:9; Rev 5:6

4:11
w ver 3; Rev 11:4

4:14
x Ex 29:7; 40:15;
Da 9:24-26;
Zec 3:1-7

5:1
y Eze 2:9; Rev 5:1

5:3
z Isa 24:6; 43:28;
Mal 3:9; 4:6
a Ex 20:15; Mal 3:8
b Isa 48:1

lights[k] on it, with seven channels to the lights. [3]Also there are two olive trees[l] by it, one on the right of the bowl and the other on its left."

[4]I asked the angel who talked with me, "What are these, my lord?"

[5]He answered, "Do you not know what these are?"

"No, my lord," I replied.[m]

[6]So he said to me, "This is the word of the LORD to Zerubbabel:[n] 'Not by might nor by power, but by my Spirit,'[o] says the LORD Almighty.

[7]"What[a] are you, O mighty mountain? Before Zerubbabel you will become level ground.[p] Then he will bring out the capstone[q] to shouts of 'God bless it! God bless it!' "

[8]Then the word of the LORD came to me: [9]"The hands of Zerubbabel have laid the foundation[r] of this temple; his hands will also complete it.[s] Then you will know that the LORD Almighty has sent me[t] to you.

[10]"Who despises the day of small things?[u] Men will rejoice when they see the plumb line in the hand of Zerubbabel.

"(These seven are the eyes[v] of the LORD, which range throughout the earth.)"

[11]Then I asked the angel, "What are these two olive trees[w] on the right and the left of the lampstand?"

[12]Again I asked him, "What are these two olive branches beside the two gold pipes that pour out golden oil?"

[13]He replied, "Do you not know what these are?"

"No, my lord," I said.

[14]So he said, "These are the two who are anointed[x] to[b] serve the Lord of all the earth."

The Flying Scroll

5 I looked again—and there before me was a flying scroll![y]

[2]He asked me, "What do you see?"

I answered, "I see a flying scroll, thirty feet long and fifteen feet wide.[c]"

[3]And he said to me, "This is the curse[z] that is going out over the whole land; for according to what it says on one side, every thief[a] will be banished, and according to what it says on the other, everyone who swears falsely[b] will be banished. [4]The LORD Almighty declares, 'I will send it out, and it will enter the house of the thief

---

[a] 7 Or *Who*   [b] 14 Or *two who bring oil and*   [c] 2 Hebrew *twenty cubits long and ten cubits wide* (about 9 meters long and 4.5 meters wide)

---

governor of Judah and rightful heir to the throne of David (1 Chron. 3:17–19; Hag. 1:1; 2:2; Matt. 1:13). The bowl providing fuel for the lampstand signified an abundant supply of oil, thus symbolizing the fullness of God's power through his Spirit (v. 2; cf. v. 6). This power would enable Zerubbabel in the rebuilding of the temple. The combination of the priestly and royal offices pointed ultimately to the Messianic King-Priest—Jesus—and his ministry (cf. 6:13; Ps. 110; Heb. 7).

This chapter calls the church of today back to the empowerment of God's Spirit for its life and mission. In contrast to the situation in Zechariah's time, the Spirit's activity has been greatly expanded to involve the church as a whole. We as the church's body and as individual members are called to do all we can, gifted by God's Spirit, to accomplish his mission in this world. This is a mission in which we can joyfully participate.

Zechariah 5:1–4

After a series of visions proclaiming hope, this one packed a warning. A large scroll was flying in the air,

unrolled like a banner for all to read. Like the two tablets of the law (Ex. 32:15), the scroll was inscribed on both sides (cf. Ezek. 2:9–10; Rev. 5:1)—one side bearing the eighth commandment regarding stealing and the other the third commandment regarding false witness. Though theft and perjury may have been the most common forms of lawbreaking at the time, they were probably intended as representative sins; the people of Judah had been guilty of breaking the whole law (cf. James 2:10). Those within the covenant community couldn't ignore or abuse God's law and expect to escape discipline.

We can filter this vision through the perspective of Christ's call to "love your neighbor as yourself." In what ways—outright, subtle, or through ignorance or indifference—might you have "stolen" from others or perverted justice? Most Christians don't actively exploit the economic system, but that doesn't let us off the hook. Ignoring poverty or minority injustice is just as serious in God's eyes as avoiding taxes or underpaying employees. What can you do today to better love one neighbor as you love yourself?

and the house of him who swears falsely by my name. It will remain in his house and destroy it, both its timbers and its stones. *c* "

The Woman in a Basket

5Then the angel who was speaking to me came forward and said to me, "Look up and see what this is that is appearing."

6I asked, "What is it?"

He replied, "It is a measuring basket. *a*" And he added, "This is the iniquity *b* of the people throughout the land."

7Then the cover of lead was raised, and there in the basket sat a woman! 8He said, "This is wickedness," and he pushed her back into the basket and pushed the lead cover down over its mouth. *d*

9Then I looked up—and there before me were two women, with the wind in their wings! They had wings like those of a stork, *e* and they lifted up the basket between heaven and earth.

10"Where are they taking the basket?" I asked the angel who was speaking to me.

11He replied, "To the country of Babylonia *c f* to build a house *g* for it. When it is ready, the basket will be set there in its place." *h*

Four Chariots

6 I looked up again—and there before me were four chariots *i* coming out from between two mountains—mountains of bronze! 2The first chariot had red horses, the second black, *j* 3the third white, *k* and the fourth dappled—all of them powerful. 4I asked the angel who was speaking to me, "What are these, my lord?"

5The angel answered me, "These are the four spirits *d l* of heaven, going out from standing in the presence of the Lord of the whole world. 6The one with the black horses is going toward the north country, the one with the white horses toward the west, *e* and the one with the dappled horses toward the south."

7When the powerful horses went out, they were straining to go throughout the earth. *m* And he said, "Go throughout the earth!" So they went throughout the earth.

8Then he called to me, "Look, those going toward the north country have given my Spirit *f* rest *n* in the land of the north."

A Crown for Joshua

9The word of the LORD came to me: 10"Take ˻silver and gold˼ from the exiles Heldai, Tobijah and Jedaiah, who have arrived from Babylon. *o* Go the same day to the

Cross references (margin):

5:4
c Lev 14:34-45; Hab 2:9-11; Mal 3:5

5:8
d Mic 6:11

5:9
e Lev 11:19

5:11
f Ge 10:10
g Jer 29:5,28
h Da 1:2

6:1
i ver 5

6:2
j Rev 6:5
6:3
k Rev 6:2
6:5
l Eze 37:9; Mt 24:31; Rev 7:1

6:7
m Zec 1:10

6:8
n Eze 5:13; 24:13

6:10
o Ezr 7:14-16; Jer 28:6

a 6 Hebrew *an ephah;* also in verses 7-11   *b* 6 Or *appearance*   *c* 11 Hebrew *Shinar*   *d* 5 Or *winds*
e 6 Or *horses after them*   *f* 8 Or *spirit*

Zechariah 5:5–11

Whereas the first vision in chapter 5 confronted covenant unfaithfulness in human relationships, the second dealt with covenant unfaithfulness in the people's relationship with God. The Lord is a jealous God who won't tolerate any rival. Babylonia (a land of idolatry), not Judah (where God desired to live with his people), was an appropriate place for wickedness (v. 10). Only after being purged of its evil would Judah truly be the "holy land" (2:12).

Purity of *affection* lies at the core of true worship. We don't need to abandon all our pursuits and retreat to a monastery to ensure that our hearts are focused on God alone. But we are called to initiate and maintain a life orientation with Christ as its center and goal. Paul expressed this well in Colossians 3:17: "Whatever you do, whether in word or deed, do it all in the name of the Lord Jesus, giving thanks to God the Father through him."

Zechariah 6:1–8

This revelation closed the string of night visions. It was clearly intended to remind the audience of the vision in 1:8–17, which featured various colored horses patrolling the earth. God again assured his people that he was in control of world events and would exact justice on the nations that oppressed Israel. For those still in exile it was an incentive to return to the promised land (cf. Zech. 2), signaling a new phase in redemptive history. For those who had returned it was a reminder of God's grace, especially important as they pursued the rebuilding of the temple in a volatile environment (cf. Ezra 2–6).

Application of this vision for Christians has past, present, and future implications. God has continued to rescue (redeem) his people. Jesus Christ represented both the exiled community, longing for release, and God waging war on their behalf. Christ suffered and died as the ultimate child of the exile under the Babylon of his day (Rome). But he rose in resurrection victory—the

6:11 [p] Ps 21:3 [q] Zec 3:1 [r] Ezr 3:2 **6:12** [s] Isa 4:2; Zec 3:8 [t] Ezr 3:8-10; Zec 4:6-9 **6:13** [u] Ps 110:4 **6:15** [v] Isa 60:10 [w] Zec 2:9-11 [x] Isa 58:12; Jer 7:23; Zec 3:7

house of Josiah son of Zephaniah. 11Take the silver and gold and make a crown,[p]
and set it on the head of the high priest, Joshua[q] son of Jehozadak.[r] 12Tell him this
is what the LORD Almighty says: 'Here is the man whose name is the Branch,[s] and
he will branch out from his place and build the temple of the LORD.[t] 13It is he who
will build the temple of the LORD, and he will be clothed with majesty and will sit
and rule on his throne. And he will be a priest[u] on his throne. And there will be harmony between the two.' 14The crown will be given to Heldai,[a] Tobijah, Jedaiah and
Hen[b] son of Zephaniah as a memorial in the temple of the LORD. 15Those who are
far away will come and help to build the temple of the LORD,[v] and you will know
that the LORD Almighty has sent me to you.[w] This will happen if you diligently
obey[x] the LORD your God."

Justice and Mercy, Not Fasting

7:1 [y] Ne 1:1 **7:2** [z] Jer 26:19; Zec 8:21 **7:3** [a] Zec 12:12-14 [b] Jer 52:12-14; Zec 8:19 **7:5** [c] Isa 58:5 **7:7** [d] Zec 1:4 [e] Jer 22:21 [f] Jer 17:26 **7:9** [g] Zec 8:16

7 In the fourth year of King Darius, the word of the LORD came to Zechariah on
the fourth day of the ninth month, the month of Kislev.[y] 2The people of Bethel had sent Sharezer and Regem-Melech, together with their men, to entreat[z] the
LORD 3by asking the priests of the house of the LORD Almighty and the prophets,
"Should I mourn[a] and fast in the fifth[b] month, as I have done for so many years?"
4Then the word of the LORD Almighty came to me: 5"Ask all the people of the land
and the priests, 'When you fasted[c] and mourned in the fifth and seventh months
for the past seventy years, was it really for me that you fasted? 6And when you were
eating and drinking, were you not just feasting for yourselves? 7Are these not the
words the LORD proclaimed through the earlier prophets[d] when Jerusalem and its
surrounding towns were at rest[e] and prosperous, and the Negev and the western
foothills[f] were settled?' "
8And the word of the LORD came again to Zechariah: 9"This is what the LORD Almighty says: 'Administer true justice;[g] show mercy and compassion to one anoth-

[a] 14 Syriac; Hebrew *Helem* [b] 14 Or *and the gracious one, the*

turning point of redemptive history and the foundation of our faith.

The New Testament encourages us to expect ultimate victory: Christ gathering his exiled people from the four winds (Mark 13:26–27). Our Divine Warrior will appear, bringing final justice to Earth (Rev. 19). For those of us living between the past "already" and the future "not yet," Zechariah 6:1–8 provides a comforting revelation of God's intentions. It prompts our praise, stimulates our hope, and calls us to entrust ourselves into the hands of our gracious, sovereign God.

Zechariah 6:9–15

The immediate situation of the unfinished temple rebuilding project appears to provide the context for this prophetic act. The visions of chapters 3 and 4 were concerned with the high priest and the civil governor in the Davidic line. Here Zechariah linked the message of those two visions to the Messianic King-Priest. Zerubbabel and Joshua represented two separate offices; but "the Branch"—the Messiah (see "There and Then" for ch. 3)—was to hold both offices (v. 13).

In 3:5, Joshua had received the high priest's turban. Now he was given an ornate crown (v. 11). The royal crowning of the high priest foreshadowed the culmination of Old Testament prophecy: the coronation of the Messianic King-Priest (cf. Heb. 7:1–3; Rev. 19:12).

Our main purpose as God's redeemed people is the restoration of his rule in this world. Christ's death and resurrection extended God's rule beyond the confines of temple and land. It is now expressed through a community of people—us—in whom he is present. This new way of extending his rule makes God's temple mobile and portable. We sometimes miss the greatest opportunities for extending God's reign in the world by limiting our vision to Christian "professionals." God has called *each* of us to bring his presence into the entire world through word and deed. What particular role are you playing?

Zechariah 7:1–14

The occasion of these prophetic messages, nearly two years after the eight night visions, was a question raised by a delegation from Bethel ("I," in v. 3, was used in a collective sense). They had observed days of fasting in commemoration of the destruction of Jerusalem. But now that the prophesied 70 years of exile (cf. Jer. 25:11–12) were almost over and the temple nearly rebuilt, did they still have to fast?

The Lord cast doubt on the people's sincerity: They had turned what should have been a time of prayer and genuine repentance into a time of self-pity. If their spiritual devotion had been sincere, it would have been expressed in kindness, mercy, and special regard for widows, orphans, strangers, and the poor.

In the wake of the exile there was doubtless a degree of sincere contrition in the observance of these fast days, but they had largely become a formality. The

er. [10]Do not oppress the widow or the fatherless, the alien[h] or the poor. In your hearts do not think evil of each other.'[i]

[11]"But they refused to pay attention; stubbornly they turned their backs and stopped up their ears.[j] [12]They made their hearts as hard as flint[k] and would not listen to the law or to the words that the LORD Almighty had sent by his Spirit through the earlier prophets.[l] So the LORD Almighty was very angry.[m]

[13]" 'When I called, they did not listen;[n] so when they called, I would not listen,'[o] says the LORD Almighty.[p] [14]'I scattered[q] them with a whirlwind[r] among all the nations, where they were strangers. The land was left so desolate behind them that no one could come or go. This is how they made the pleasant land desolate.'[s] "

The LORD Promises to Bless Jerusalem

8 Again the word of the LORD Almighty came to me. [2]This is what the LORD Almighty says: "I am very jealous for Zion; I am burning with jealousy for her."

[3]This is what the LORD says: "I will return[t] to Zion and dwell in Jerusalem.[u] Then Jerusalem will be called the City of Truth, and the mountain of the LORD Almighty will be called the Holy Mountain."

[4]This is what the LORD Almighty says: "Once again men and women of ripe old age will sit in the streets of Jerusalem,[v] each with cane in hand because of his age. [5]The city streets will be filled with boys and girls playing there.[w]"

[6]This is what the LORD Almighty says: "It may seem marvelous to the remnant of this people at that time,[x] but will it seem marvelous to me?[y]" declares the LORD Almighty.

[7]This is what the LORD Almighty says: "I will save my people from the countries of the east and the west.[z] [8]I will bring them back[a] to live in Jerusalem; they will be my people,[b] and I will be faithful and righteous to them as their God."

[9]This is what the LORD Almighty says: "You who now hear these words spoken by the prophets[c] who were there when the foundation was laid for the house of the LORD Almighty, let your hands be strong[d] so that the temple may be built. [10]Before that time there were no wages[e] for man or beast. No one could go about his business safely because of his enemy, for I had turned every man against his neighbor. [11]But now I will not deal with the remnant of this people as I did in the past,"[f] declares the LORD Almighty.

[12]"The seed will grow well, the vine will yield its fruit,[g] the ground will produce its crops,[h] and the heavens will drop their dew.[i] I will give all these things as an inheritance[j] to the remnant of this people. [13]As you have been an object of cursing[k] among the nations, O Judah and Israel, so will I save you, and you will be a blessing.[l] Do not be afraid, but let your hands be strong."

[14]This is what the LORD Almighty says: "Just as I had determined to bring disas-

Cross references

7:10
h Ex 22:21
i Ex 22:22; Isa 1:17

7:11
j Jer 8:5; 11:10; 17:23
7:12
k Jer 17:1; Eze 11:19 / Ne 9:29
m Da 9:12
7:13
n Pr 1:24 o Isa 1:15; Jer 11:11; 14:12; Mic 3:4 p Pr 1:28
7:14
q Dt 4:27; 28:64-67
r Jer 23:19
s Jer 44:6

8:3
t Zec 1:16
u Zec 2:10

8:4
v Isa 65:20
8:5
w Jer 30:20; 31:13

8:6
x Ps 118:23; 126:1-3
y Jer 32:17,27

8:7
z Ps 107:3; Isa 11:11; 43:5
8:8
a Zec 10:10
b Eze 11:19-20; 36:28; Zec 2:11
8:9
c Ezr 5:1 d Hag 2:4
8:10
e Hag 1:6

8:11
f Isa 12:1

8:12
g Joel 2:22
h Ps 67:6
i Ge 27:28
j Ob 1:17
8:13
k Jer 42:18
l Ge 12:2

---

people wanted God's blessing and assumed that prayer and fasting would move him in that direction. Our religious activities, too, can become extensions of our personal agendas—efforts to gain God's promises and rewards while ignoring his warnings and discipline. But God still demands repentance, even as he extends grace to us through Christ's death and resurrection.

Zechariah called his generation to practice social justice. God still calls us, as individuals and communities, to champion righteousness in society. This means taking seriously his call to become lawyers, social workers, psychologists, and teachers, in order to communicate and enact God's justice in our culture. It also means realigning our churches' priorities. Scripture's constant theme is that true devotion will be expressed in our care for those less fortunate than ourselves.

Zechariah 8:1–23

In contrast to the ending of chapter 7, this chapter is comprised of ten promises of blessing, each beginning with "This is what the LORD (Almighty) says." Contained in this positive vision of God's intentions for his people are specific calls to obedience in verses 9 and 16–17. In response to a repentant, obedient people pursuing justice, the Lord would bless Jerusalem and Judah, once again taking up residence in the city. Fasts would be replaced with feasts. God's people weren't to form a "holy huddle," cut off from the world and critical of outsiders. This blessed community was to be a community of blessing to surrounding peoples (v. 13), as God had long ago promised Abraham (Gen. 22:18).

What would it take for our city streets to be safe places for boys and girls to play (v. 5)? This is a fitting symbol of nearly everyone's longing and for the impact of God's coming kingdom. What might it mean for your church to help create a safe place in its neighborhood for children to play?

A Counterintuitive Calling

Being a prophet is counterintuitive. It means unquestioning obedience to God by saying unpopular things that typically lead to persecution from powerful people. Consider Haggai. On August 29, 520 B.C., God told him to confront his fellow Jews with their slackness in rebuilding the temple. He went to the prince, Zerubbabel, and the high priest, Joshua. His compatriot Zechariah, perhaps inspired by Haggai's courage, joined in the prophetic task two months later. Their message: "You seem to have the energy you need to build your own houses, but the Lord's house still lies in blackened ruins. Let's get busy."

Intriguingly, these confrontive messages didn't sow discord. They brought comfort. The overall response to the prophets' calls was also counterintuitive—action, reconnection with God, and relationship renewal. How and why could a message so tactless, so politically incorrect, so socially inappropriate produce such positive results?

If both prophetic identity and the results of prophetic work are counterintuitive, perhaps the problem is with our intuition. Maybe we are not reading the signs right. Maybe we are not speaking the Lord's words but spouting conventional wisdom. Maybe.

It's just possible, though, that prophetic work and the results of prophecy are *supposed* to be counterintuitive. After all, not everyone is called to be a prophet. If the sociology of the Old Testament is any indication, it appears that numerous prophets were odd ducks. We are all called to be apostles of the word, but how long has it been since you met someone who claimed a prophetic calling?

One way to clarify the uniqueness of the prophetic task is to look at the question in modern terms. Who are today's candidates for prophethood?

> There is more to being a prophet than doing what a group of people thinks is good.

How about corporate whistleblowers? They are people who not only discover illegal behavior on the part of the corporations they work for but decide to risk their careers by going public with their knowledge. Officially we endorse this behavior and try to protect such people through our laws. But do we really like what they do? We are sometimes more sympathetic with the fallen leaders ("There but for the grace of God go I!") than with the moralistic tattletales. A test: Name a recent whistleblower.

Are such informants prophets? It seems there is more to prophethood than the courage to act on moral indignation. Do we need to ask first whether their motivation was honest, a calling of God?

How about the leaders of regulating agencies and groups? When Ralph Nader fought for seat belt laws, he wasn't combating illegalities but human ignorance. People's refusal to do what was good for them—or their persistence in continuing harmful behavior—was the problem he addressed. Is it a prophetic function to save us from our own follies? Do we first need to ask about the relationship between those so-called follies and God's will?

And what about activists like those concerned with the degradation of our environment? These are people who choose to address patterns of long-term, failed policies. We are using up our natural resources at unacceptable rates. Yet because that rate of consumption is part of what makes our lives so materially comfortable, we are as a society reluctant to cut back. Activists call us to do just that.

Does this make them prophets?

There is more to being a prophet than doing what a group of people thinks is good. Prophets are to do what God thinks is good—and what God calls them to do. Prophets aren't just doers of the Word—they must first be hearers. Like Haggai and Zechariah.

ter[m] upon you and showed no pity when your fathers angered me," says the LORD Almighty, [15]"so now I have determined to do good[n] again to Jerusalem and Judah. Do not be afraid. [16]These are the things you are to do: Speak the truth[o] to each other, and render true and sound judgment in your courts;[p] [17]do not plot evil[q] against your neighbor, and do not love to swear falsely.[r] I hate all this," declares the LORD.

[18]Again the word of the LORD Almighty came to me. [19]This is what the LORD Almighty says: "The fasts of the fourth,[s] fifth,[t] seventh[u] and tenth[v] months will become joyful[w] and glad occasions and happy festivals for Judah. Therefore love truth[x] and peace."

[20]This is what the LORD Almighty says: "Many peoples and the inhabitants of many cities will yet come, [21]and the inhabitants of one city will go to another and say, 'Let us go at once to entreat[y] the LORD and seek the LORD Almighty. I myself am going.' [22]And many peoples and powerful nations will come to Jerusalem to seek the LORD Almighty and to entreat him."[z]

[23]This is what the LORD Almighty says: "In those days ten men from all languages and nations will take firm hold of one Jew by the hem of his robe and say, 'Let us go with you, because we have heard that God is with you.' "[a]

Judgment on Israel's Enemies

An Oracle

9 The word of the LORD is against the land of Hadrach
  and will rest upon Damascus[b]—
for the eyes of men and all the tribes of Israel
  are on the LORD—[a]
[2]and upon Hamath[c] too, which borders on it,

---

[a] 1 Or *Damascus. / For the eye of the LORD is on all mankind, / as well as on the tribes of Israel,*

8:14
m Jer 31:28;
Eze 24:14
8:15
n ver 13; Jer 29:11;
Mic 7:18-20
8:16
o Ps 15:2; Eph 4:25
p Zec 7:9
8:17
q Pr 3:29
r Pr 6:16-19
8:19
s Jer 39:2
t Jer 52:12
u 2Ki 25:25
v Jer 52:4
w Ps 30:11 x ver 16
8:21
y Zec 7:2
8:22
z Ps 117:1; Isa 60:3;
Zec 2:11
8:23
a Isa 45:14;
1Co 14:25

9:1
b Isa 17:1

9:2
c Jer 49:23

Zechariah 9:1–8

 The remainder of the book of Zechariah contains two undated oracles (chs. 9–11 and 12–14), though they probably came from Zechariah's old age (shortly after 480 B.C.). For the most part these prophecies appear to foretell the more distant future, particularly the arrival of the great Messianic era.

This opening scene described the Lord as Divine Warrior marching south to Jerusalem, defeating Israel's traditional enemies. As history shows, the agent of God's judgment was Alexander the Great. After defeating the Persians in 333 B.C., Alexander moved swiftly toward

---

Snapshots

8:23

Jesus Speaks My Language!

Campus Crusade's *Jesus Film* has been viewed by more than 4.9 billion people, translated into 766 languages, and shown in 236 countries. Complete with a specially created evangelistic close, the film has proved the ideal tool for missionary teams on every continent for presenting the message of Jesus Christ.

After viewing the picture, 52 people from the communities of Anyinofi, Seneso, and Aboabogya, Ghana, chose to give their lives to Jesus—who spoke in the film in the Twi and Konkomba local languages. Those who, due to shyness, opted not to come forward after the showing found their way into community churches the following Sunday, filling them to the brim.

"I didn't know Jesus speaks my language!" marveled Adjoa, a thirty-six year old mother of four from Seneso. "I would have become a Christian long ago."

> The *[Jesus Film]* has proved the ideal tool for missionary teams on every continent for presenting the message of Jesus Christ.

9:2
d Eze 28:1-19

9:3
e Job 27:16;
Eze 28:4

9:4
f Isa 23:1;
Eze 26:3-5; 28:18

9:8
g Isa 52:1; 54:14

9:9
h Isa 9:6-7; 43:3-11;
Jer 23:5-6;
Zep 3:14-15;
Zec 2:10
i Mt 21:5*;
Jn 12:15*

9:10
j Hos 1:7; 2:18;
Mic 4:3; 5:10;
Zec 10:4

and upon Tyre[d] and Sidon, though they are very skillful.
3 Tyre has built herself a stronghold;
　　she has heaped up silver like dust,
　　and gold like the dirt of the streets. [e]
4 But the Lord will take away her possessions
　　and destroy her power on the sea,
　　and she will be consumed by fire.[f]
5 Ashkelon will see it and fear;
　　Gaza will writhe in agony,
　　and Ekron too, for her hope will wither.
　Gaza will lose her king
　　and Ashkelon will be deserted.
6 Foreigners will occupy Ashdod,
　　and I will cut off the pride of the Philistines.
7 I will take the blood from their mouths,
　　the forbidden food from between their teeth.
　Those who are left will belong to our God
　　and become leaders in Judah,
　　and Ekron will be like the Jebusites.
8 But I will defend my house
　　against marauding forces.
　Never again will an oppressor overrun my people,
　　for now I am keeping watch. [g]

The Coming of Zion's King

9 Rejoice greatly, O Daughter of Zion!
　　Shout, Daughter of Jerusalem!
　See, your king[a] comes to you,
　　righteous and having salvation, [h]
　　gentle and riding on a donkey,
　　on a colt, the foal of a donkey. [i]
10 I will take away the chariots from Ephraim
　　and the war-horses from Jerusalem,
　　and the battle bow will be broken.[j]
　He will proclaim peace to the nations.

a 9 Or King

Egypt. Yet, on coming to Jerusalem, he refused to destroy it. Verse 8 attributes the city's protection to God's miraculous intervention. The words "Never again," especially in light of the Romans' future destruction of Jerusalem in A.D. 70, evidently anticipated either the second advent of the Messiah or the invulnerability of the church (cf. Matt. 16:18).

In verses 6–7 the Lord said that he would remove the pride and idolatry of the Philistines—enemies of Israel. Though most of them would be destroyed, a remnant would "belong to God and become leaders in Judah." God's including of Philistines among his people demonstrated his intention to bless all nations through Abraham. This wasn't an easy message for Jews who had suffered for generations at the hands of this ancient enemy. Nor is it easy for Christians today. In our pursuit of truth, justice, and redemption, we may be tempted to villainize enemies of the faith to the point of relishing their damnation. But our actions are to embody God's truth in indiscriminate acts of love. God wants to bless *all* people through us.

Today there are Palestinian believers (possible descendants of the ancient Philistines) who are our brothers and sisters in Christ. Though political realities might prevent their leadership right now, the possibility exists for the future fulfillment of Zechariah's vision.

Zechariah 9:9–13

The Gospels quote verse 9 in relationship to Jesus' Triumphal Entry into Jerusalem (Matt. 21:5; John 12:15). In contrast to Alexander's empire, which was founded on bloodshed, the Messianic King would establish a universal kingdom of peace (cf. Isa. 2:4; 9:5–7; Mic. 5:10–11). A donkey, a lowly animal of peace, was an appropriate choice (contrast the war-horse of v. 10).

Before this Davidic King could reign in peace, he first had to restore his people and conquer their enemies. The initial fulfillment of verse 13 was apparently to be found in the conflict in the 2nd century B.C. between the Maccabees ("Zion") and the Seleucids of Syria ("Greece" after the breakup of Alexander's empire). But the complete fulfillment looks beyond that: God's people *will* gain the victory over their enemies.

His rule will extend from sea to sea
  and from the River[a] to the ends of the earth.[b][k]
11 As for you, because of the blood of my covenant[l] with you,
  I will free your prisoners[m] from the waterless pit.
12 Return to your fortress,[n] O prisoners of hope;
  even now I announce that I will restore twice as much to you.
13 I will bend Judah as I bend my bow
  and fill it with Ephraim.[o]
  I will rouse your sons, O Zion,
  against your sons, O Greece,[p]
  and make you like a warrior's sword.[q]

The LORD Will Appear

14 Then the LORD will appear over them;[r]
  his arrow will flash like lightning.[s]
  The Sovereign LORD will sound the trumpet;
  he will march in the storms[t] of the south,
15   and the LORD Almighty will shield[u] them.
  They will destroy
  and overcome with slingstones.
  They will drink and roar as with wine;
  they will be full like a bowl
  used for sprinkling[c] the corners[v] of the altar.
16 The LORD their God will save them on that day
  as the flock of his people.
  They will sparkle in his land
  like jewels in a crown.[w]
17 How attractive and beautiful they will be!
  Grain will make the young men thrive,
  and new wine the young women.

The LORD Will Care for Judah

10 Ask the LORD for rain in the springtime;
  it is the LORD who makes the storm clouds.
  He gives showers of rain to men,
  and plants of the field to everyone.

[a] 10 That is, the Euphrates   [b] 10 Or *the end of the land*   [c] 15 Or *bowl, / like*

Right column refs:
9:10 k Ps 72:8
9:11 l Ex 24:8 m Isa 42:7
9:12 n Joel 3:16
9:13 o Isa 49:2 p Joel 3:6 q Jer 51:20
9:14 r Isa 31:5 s Ps 18:14; Hab 3:11 t Isa 21:1; 66:15
9:15 u Isa 37:35; Zec 12:8 v Ex 27:2
9:16 w Isa 62:3; Jer 31:11

God extends his mighty rule through the weakness of a humble King who died on a cross. As Christ's suffering brought about the world's redemption, so the application of that redemption in later generations comes through the suffering of the Christian community. On local, national, and international scenes, churches are to be known for their servanthood and humility. They are to assume the societal functions rejected by others and communicate Christ's values through their love expressed for people.

Zechariah 9:14–17

Though the Apocryphal book of 1 Maccabees likely records an initial fulfillment of verse 15, the phrase "on that day" (v. 16) gives the passage an eschatological, or end times, tone. The passage closes with images of vitality as the land brings forth plenty (grain, new wine) to sustain a new generation (young men and women). This promised blessing is fulfilled ultimately in the "great multitude" pictured in Revelation 7. Interestingly, the members of that throng hold palm branches in their hands,

reminiscent of Jesus' entry into Jerusalem as the fulfillment of Zechariah 9:9.

Protected by God, the people gained victory—not with the sophisticated weapons that had been removed from the kingdom (v. 10) but with the lowly sling, an allusion to David's triumph over Goliath (v. 15; cf. 1 Sam. 17:48–50). It isn't surprising that not only the Messianic King but also the people were linked to David in Zechariah 9, as the Lord limited their military action to slingstones. Like David of old, we are to rely on God alone for victory. As the church and as individual believers, we are called to approach life with the attitude that only God can grant us success in our endeavors. Is that your position?

Zechariah 10:1—11:3

The people, led astray like sheep without a shepherd, lacked spiritual leadership (cf. Mark 6:34). But God himself would shepherd his flock. Verse 4 is probably Messianic: The Messiah would come from Judah

10:2
x Eze 21:21
y Eze 34:5; Hos 3:4;
Mt 9:36

2 The idols [x] speak deceit,
　　diviners see visions that lie;
they tell dreams that are false,
　　they give comfort in vain.
Therefore the people wander like sheep
　　oppressed for lack of a shepherd. [y]

10:3
z Jer 25:34

3 "My anger burns against the shepherds,
　　and I will punish the leaders; [z]
for the LORD Almighty will care
　　for his flock, the house of Judah,
　　and make them like a proud horse in battle.

10:4
a Isa 22:23
b Zec 9:10

4 From Judah will come the cornerstone,
　　from him the tent peg, [a]
　　from him the battle bow, [b]
　　from him every ruler.

10:5
c 2Sa 22:43
d Am 2:15;
Hag 2:22

5 Together they [a] will be like mighty men
　　trampling the muddy streets in battle. [c]
Because the LORD is with them,
　　they will fight and overthrow the horsemen. [d]

6 "I will strengthen the house of Judah
　　and save the house of Joseph.

10:6
e Zec 8:7-8
f Zec 13:9

I will restore them
　　because I have compassion on them. [e]
They will be as though
　　I had not rejected them,
for I am the LORD their God
　　and I will answer [f] them.

10:7
g Zec 9:15

7 The Ephraimites will become like mighty men,
　　and their hearts will be glad as with wine. [g]
Their children will see it and be joyful;
　　their hearts will rejoice in the LORD.

10:8
h Isa 5:26
i Jer 33:22;
Eze 36:11

8 I will signal [h] for them
　　and gather them in.
Surely I will redeem them;
　　they will be as numerous [i] as before.

10:9
j Eze 6:9

9 Though I scatter them among the peoples,
　　yet in distant lands they will remember me. [j]
They and their children will survive,
　　and they will return.

10:10
k Isa 11:11
l Jer 50:19
m Isa 49:19

10 I will bring them back from Egypt
　　and gather them from Assyria. [k]
I will bring them to Gilead [l] and Lebanon,
　　and there will not be room [m] enough for them.
11 They will pass through the sea of trouble;

---

a 4,5 Or ruler, all of them together. / 5 They

(cf. Gen. 49:10; Jer. 30:21; Mic. 5:2). He is here called "the cornerstone" (cf. 3:9; Isa. 28:16; Eph. 2:20).

Zechariah foresaw a reunification of the southern kingdom (Judah) and northern (Joseph/Ephraim). The reason for their restoration would be God's tender compassion. Not only would Judah be like mighty men, but so also would Ephraim, resulting in great joy. Egypt and Assyria, two ancient oppressors of God's chosen people, were probably intended to represent all the regions to which the Israelites had been dispersed.

Only through the Messianic leadership of the Davidic Ruler, Jesus, could the unity Zechariah visualized become reality: Through his death and resurrection Jesus Christ rescued Jews and Gentiles alike from the kingdom of darkness and delivered them into his kingdom of light. In so doing he created a community of love and peace, united in allegiance to the Father, redemption through Jesus Christ, and empowerment by the Holy Spirit. Ephesians 4:1–6 describes in detail the unity believers are to experience in growing measure.

the surging sea will be subdued
and all the depths of the Nile will dry up. [n]
Assyria's pride [o] will be brought down
and Egypt's scepter [p] will pass away.
[12] I will strengthen them in the LORD
and in his name they will walk, [q]"

declares the LORD.

11

Open your doors, O Lebanon, [r]
so that fire may devour your cedars!
[2] Wail, O pine tree, for the cedar has fallen;
the stately trees are ruined!
Wail, oaks of Bashan;
the dense forest [s] has been cut down!
[3] Listen to the wail of the shepherds;
their rich pastures are destroyed!
Listen to the roar of the lions;
the lush thicket of the Jordan is ruined! [t]

Two Shepherds

[4] This is what the LORD my God says: "Pasture the flock marked for slaughter.
[5] Their buyers slaughter them and go unpunished. Those who sell them say, 'Praise
the LORD, I am rich!' Their own shepherds do not spare them. [u] [6] For I will no longer have pity on the people of the land," declares the LORD. "I will hand everyone
over to his neighbor [v] and his king. They will oppress the land, and I will not rescue them from their hands." [w]

[7] So I pastured the flock marked for slaughter, particularly the oppressed of the
flock. Then I took two staffs and called one Favor and the other Union, and I pastured the flock. [8] In one month I got rid of the three shepherds.

The flock detested me, and I grew weary of them [9] and said, "I will not be your
shepherd. Let the dying die, and the perishing perish. [x] Let those who are left eat one
another's flesh."

[10] Then I took my staff called Favor [y] and broke it, revoking [z] the covenant I had
made with all the nations. [11] It was revoked on that day, and so the afflicted of the
flock who were watching me knew it was the word of the LORD.

[12] I told them, "If you think it best, give me my pay; but if not, keep it." So they
paid me thirty pieces of silver. [a]

[13] And the LORD said to me, "Throw it to the potter"—the handsome price at
which they priced me! So I took the thirty pieces of silver and threw them into the
house of the LORD to the potter. [b]

Cross references

10:11 [n] Isa 19:5-7; 51:10 [o] Zep 2:13 [p] Eze 30:13

10:12 [q] Mic 4:5

11:1 [r] Eze 31:3

11:2 [s] Isa 32:19

11:3 [t] Jer 2:15; 50:44

11:5 [u] Jer 50:7; Eze 34:2-3

11:6 [v] Zec 14:13 [w] Isa 9:19-21; Jer 13:14; Mic 5:8; 7:2-6

11:9 [x] Jer 15:2; 43:11

11:10 [y] ver 7 [z] Ps 89:39; Jer 14:21

11:12 [a] Ex 21:32; Mt 26:15

11:13 [b] Mt 27:9-10*; Ac 1:18-19

Zechariah 11:4–17

We see in this passage a series of prophetic acts, dramatizing the rejection of the coming Messianic Shepherd-King and the resulting judgment of Israel. Zechariah was first instructed to act out the role of a good shepherd for the flock (i.e., Israel). He gave special attention to the "oppressed" (or "afflicted") of the flock. At least part of the fulfillment of the "slaughter" likely came in A.D. 70 with the Romans' destruction of Jerusalem.

With the Shepherd of the Lord's choice removed from the scene, a foolish and worthless shepherd would replace him. Zechariah acted out the role of such a bad shepherd, thus signifying that a selfish, corrupt, and greedy leader would arise and afflict the flock. While the arrival of this counterfeit shepherd may have found a

partial fulfillment in one or more historical leaders, it seems that the ultimate fulfillment of the prophecy awaits the rise of the final Antichrist (cf. Dan. 11:36–39; 2 Thess. 2:3–10; Rev. 13:1–8).

Zechariah 11 was key for the early church's understanding of Christ's ministry. Jesus was God's Shepherd who cared for the flock, protecting it from disinterested and abusive owners. For 30 pieces of silver Jesus was removed from leadership, rejected alike by flock (Jewish nation), shepherds (Jewish religious leaders), and owners (Romans). But Christ's death was followed by his resurrection and ascension, ushering in a new age for the remnant flock of Israel, the church. As Christians we return regularly to the salvation story, allowing it to inform and stimulate our faith, worship, and action.

14Then I broke my second staff called Union, breaking the brotherhood between Judah and Israel.

15Then the LORD said to me, "Take again the equipment of a foolish shepherd. 16For I am going to raise up a shepherd over the land who will not care for the lost, or seek the young, or heal the injured, or feed the healthy, but will eat the meat of the choice sheep, tearing off their hoofs.

11:17
c Jer 23:1
d Eze 30:21-22
e Jer 23:1

17 "Woe to the worthless shepherd,[c]
    who deserts the flock!
May the sword strike his arm[d] and his right eye!
    May his arm be completely withered,
    his right eye totally blinded!"[e]

Jerusalem's Enemies to Be Destroyed

An Oracle

12:1
f Isa 42:5; Jer 51:15
g Ps 102:25;
Heb 1:10
h Isa 57:16
12:2
i Ps 75:8 i Isa 51:23
k Zec 14:14
12:3
l Zec 14:2
m Da 2:34-35
n Mt 21:44

12:4
o Ps 76:6

12:6
p Isa 10:17-18;
Zec 11:1 q Ob 1:18

12:7
r Jer 30:18;
Am 9:11
12:8
s Joel 3:16;
Zec 9:15 t Ps 82:6
u Mic 7:8
12:9
v Zec 14:2-3

12 This is the word of the LORD concerning Israel. The LORD, who stretches out the heavens,[f] who lays the foundation of the earth,[g] and who forms the spirit of man[h] within him, declares: 2"I am going to make Jerusalem a cup[i] that sends all the surrounding peoples reeling.[j] Judah[k] will be besieged as well as Jerusalem. 3On that day, when all the nations[l] of the earth are gathered against her, I will make Jerusalem an immovable rock[m] for all the nations. All who try to move it will injure[n] themselves. 4On that day I will strike every horse with panic and its rider with madness," declares the LORD. "I will keep a watchful eye over the house of Judah, but I will blind all the horses of the nations.[o] 5Then the leaders of Judah will say in their hearts, 'The people of Jerusalem are strong, because the LORD Almighty is their God.'

6"On that day I will make the leaders of Judah like a firepot[p] in a woodpile, like a flaming torch among sheaves. They will consume[q] right and left all the surrounding peoples, but Jerusalem will remain intact in her place.

7"The LORD will save the dwellings of Judah first, so that the honor of the house of David and of Jerusalem's inhabitants may not be greater than that of Judah.[r] 8On that day the LORD will shield[s] those who live in Jerusalem, so that the feeblest among them will be like David, and the house of David will be like God,[t] like the Angel of the LORD going before[u] them. 9On that day I will set out to destroy all the nations that attack Jerusalem.[v]

Mourning for the One They Pierced

12:10
w Isa 44:3;
Eze 39:29;
Joel 2:28-29

10"And I will pour out on the house of David and the inhabitants of Jerusalem a spirit[a] of grace and supplication.[w] They will look on[b] me, the one they have

[a] 10 Or the Spirit   [b] 10 Or to

Zechariah 12:1–9

As a unit, Zechariah 12–14 presents God's plan to cleanse his people and defeat the nations in a future day. The prophecy began by describing a siege of Jerusalem and Judah by opposing forces—a conflict of global proportions. God would use Judah's leaders to bring the first phase of victory for Judah and Jerusalem. He would save the "dwellings" of Judah first, granting them the same honor as the royal house and city. In the second phase of victory, God would use Jerusalem and the house of David as a fighting force.

This passage affirms an ongoing role for covenant leadership, while urging the full participation of the entire community. The New Testament witnesses to the development of leadership within the church. But these leaders are to define themselves in terms of the larger community in whom God dwells and which he

uses to accomplish his purposes. This wider community of believers is in turn to view its leaders not simply as professional ministers but as equippers of a whole community of ministers.

Zechariah 12:10–14

Accompanying the deliverance from external forces, just described, would be internal renewal. The Lord promised to "pour out" upon the nation "a spirit of grace and supplication." In light of the second NIV text note on verse 10, the emphasis seems to be on looking "to" the Messiah in faith (cf. Num. 21:9; John 3:14–15). The apostle John saw the "piercing" of the Messiah to be at least partly fulfilled at the crucifixion (John 19:34,37; cf. Isa. 53:5).

The mourning included the house of David and his son Nathan (cf. 2 Sam. 5:14; Luke 3:31) and the house of Levi and his grandson Shimei (cf. Num. 3:17–18,21).

pierced,ˣ and they will mourn for him as one mourns for an only child, and grieve bitterly for him as one grieves for a firstborn son. ¹¹On that day the weeping in Jerusalem will be great, like the weeping of Hadad Rimmon in the plain of Megiddo.ʸ ¹²The land will mourn,ᶻ each clan by itself, with their wives by themselves: the clan of the house of David and their wives, the clan of the house of Nathan and their wives, ¹³the clan of the house of Levi and their wives, the clan of Shimei and their wives, ¹⁴and all the rest of the clans and their wives.

Cleansing From Sin

13 "On that day a fountainᵃ will be opened to the house of David and the inhabitants of Jerusalem, to cleanseᵇ them from sin and impurity.

²"On that day, I will banish the names of the idolsᶜ from the land, and they will be remembered no more," declares the Lᴏʀᴅ Almighty. "I will remove both the prophetsᵈ and the spirit of impurity from the land. ³And if anyone still prophesies, his father and mother, to whom he was born, will say to him, 'You must die, because you have told lies in the Lᴏʀᴅ's name.' When he prophesies, his own parents will stab him.ᵉ

⁴"On that day every prophet will be ashamedᶠ of his prophetic vision. He will not put on a prophet's garmentᵍ of hairʰ in order to deceive. ⁵He will say, 'I am not a prophet. I am a farmer; the land has been my livelihood since my youth.ᵃ ⁱ ⁶If someone asks him, 'What are these wounds on your body ᵇ?' he will answer, 'The wounds I was given at the house of my friends.'

The Shepherd Struck, the Sheep Scattered

⁷"Awake, O sword,ʲ against my shepherd,ᵏ
   against the man who is close to me!"
   declares the Lᴏʀᴅ Almighty.
"Strike the shepherd,
   and the sheep will be scattered,ˡ
   and I will turn my hand against the little ones.
⁸In the whole land," declares the Lᴏʀᴅ,
   "two-thirds will be struck down and perish;
   yet one-third will be left in it.ᵐ
⁹This third I will bring into the fire;ⁿ
   I will refine them like silverᵒ
   and test them like gold.
They will callᵖ on my name

ᵃ 5 Or *farmer; a man sold me in my youth*   ᵇ 6 Or *wounds between your hands*

12:10
ˣ Jn 19:34,37*; Rev 1:7
12:11
ʸ 2Ki 23:29
12:12
ᶻ Mt 24:30; Rev 1:7

13:1
ᵃ Jer 17:13
ᵇ Ps 51:2; Heb 9:14
13:2
ᶜ Ex 23:13; Eze 36:25; Hos 2:17
ᵈ 1Ki 22:22; Jer 23:14-15

13:3
ᵉ Dt 13:6-11; 18:20; Jer 23:34; Eze 14:9
13:4
ᶠ Jer 6:15; Mic 3:6-7 ᵍ Mt 3:4
ʰ 2Ki 1:8; Isa 20:2
13:5
ⁱ Am 7:14

13:7
ʲ Jer 47:6
ᵏ Isa 40:11; 53:4; Eze 37:24
ˡ Mt 26:31*; Mk 14:27*

13:8
ᵐ Eze 5:2-4,12
13:9
ⁿ Mal 3:2
ᵒ Isa 48:10; 1Pe 1:6-7
ᵖ Ps 50:15

While the repentance and mourning were led by the civil (royal) and religious leaders, they extended to "all the rest of the clans" in the nation.

The kind of repentance encouraged in these verses is rooted in covenant relationship. The focus isn't on turning from a list of inappropriate behaviors but on mourning over our mistreatment of God. This is primarily a relational issue arising from our unfaithfulness to him, a theme introduced at the beginning of Zechariah and captured in God's simple cry through his prophet: "Return to me . . . and I will return to you" (1:3).

Guilt is often used to motivate repentance. But Zechariah (using the translation in the first NIV text note on v. 10) informs us that "the Spirit of grace and supplication" stimulates our response. The incentive for penitence doesn't come from within ourselves. It's based on an operation of God within our hearts—in New Testament language, on the Holy Spirit at work within our lives.

Zechariah 13:1–6

Verse 1 emphasizes one of the provisions of the new covenant (Jer. 31:34; cf. Ezek. 36:25; Zech. 3:4–9). Not only would there be personal cleansing from sin, but the land would be purged of idols and false prophets—constant snares to Israel (10:2–3; Ezek. 13:1—14:11; cf. Matt. 24:4–5,23–24).

The Hebrew for "stab" (v. 3) is the same as the word for "pierced" in 12:10, possibly indicating that the motivations for piercing the Messiah would now be directed toward the false prophets. Because of these stern measures, a false prophet would be reluctant to identify himself as such. If a suspicious person noticed wounds on his body and inquired about them—apparently suspecting that they had been self-inflicted as part of idolatrous worship (cf. Lev. 19:28; Deut. 14:1; 1 Kings 18:28)—he would claim that he had received them in a scuffle with friends.

The promise of cleansing in Zechariah 13:1 reminds us of God's provision for forgiveness through

13:9
q Zec 10:6
r Jer 30:22
s Jer 29:12

14:1
t Isa 13:9; Mal 4:1

14:2
u Isa 13:6; Zec 13:8
14:3
v Zec 9:14-15
14:4
w Eze 11:23

14:5
x Am 1:1 y Isa 29:6;
66:15-16
z Mt 16:27; 25:31
14:6
a Isa 13:10;
Jer 4:23
14:7
b Jer 30:7
c Rev 21:23-25;
22:5 d Isa 30:26
14:8
e Eze 47:1-12;
Jn 7:38; Rev 22:1-2
f Joel 2:20

and I will answer ^{q} them;
I will say, 'They are my people,' ^{r}
and they will say, 'The LORD is our God.' ^{s} "

The LORD Comes and Reigns

14 A day of the LORD ^{t} is coming when your plunder will be divided among you.

^{2}I will gather all the nations to Jerusalem to fight against it; the city will be captured, the houses ransacked, and the women raped. Half of the city will go into exile, but the rest of the people will not be taken from the city. ^{u}

^{3}Then the LORD will go out and fight ^{v} against those nations, as he fights in the day of battle. ^{4}On that day his feet will stand on the Mount of Olives, ^{w} east of Jerusalem, and the Mount of Olives will be split in two from east to west, forming a great valley, with half of the mountain moving north and half moving south. ^{5}You will flee by my mountain valley, for it will extend to Azel. You will flee as you fled from the earthquake $^{a\,x}$ in the days of Uzziah king of Judah. Then the LORD my God will come, ^{y} and all the holy ones with him. ^{z}

^{6}On that day there will be no light, ^{a} no cold or frost. ^{7}It will be a unique ^{b} day, without daytime or nighttime ^{c}—a day known to the LORD. When evening comes, there will be light. ^{d}

^{8}On that day living water ^{e} will flow out from Jerusalem, half to the eastern ^{f} sea ^{b} and half to the western sea, ^{c} in summer and in winter.

---

^{a} 5 Or ^{5}My mountain valley will be blocked and will extend to Azel. It will be blocked as it was blocked because of the earthquake ^{b} 8 That is, the Dead Sea ^{c} 8 That is, the Mediterranean

---

Christ's death on the cross and of our need to embrace this provision through faith. But this can't be separated from the ongoing process of purification so essential to our life in the Spirit. We *are* cleansed, are *being* cleansed, and *will be* cleansed.

Zechariah 13:7–9

In 11:17 the worthless shepherd was to be struck. Now it's the good shepherd—the Messiah (cf. 12:10). When this shepherd is struck, the sheep (cf. 10:3) are scattered, in part as fulfillment of the curses for covenant disobedience (Deut. 28:64; 29:24–25). This part of 13:7 was quoted by Jesus not long before his arrest (Matt. 26:31; Mark 14:27) and applied to the scatter-

ing of the disciples (Matt. 26:56). At any rate, God would discipline his flock ("little ones") to purify them. The result of this refining process would be restoration of the covenant relationship between God and his people.

The Christian life is all about a relationship with God, a relationship with key characteristics: (1) It's intimate and personal. (2) It's exclusive, involving faithfulness to God's covenant demands. Israel's struggle was that it loved the privileges—but not the responsibilities—of this relationship. (3) It's communal—between "us and God," not simply "me and God." Does your Christian life reflect a healthy balance among these three principles?

14:8

Water

Water is "living" in the sense that it sustains life. It's vital to the earth's future that this essential resource be conserved. A seven-minute shower uses about 15 gallons of water (approximately 5,475 gallons/year if repeated on a daily basis). University of California agricultural specialists estimate that it takes 5,214 gallons of water to produce a pound of beef. By simply forgoing five quarter-pound hamburgers, you could save enough water for a year's worth of showers.

Water required to produce one pound of:	GALLONS	REPRESENTS 100 GALLONS OF WATER
BEEF	5,214	
PORK	1,630	
CHICKEN	815	
APPLES	49	
CARROTS	33	
WHEAT	25	
POTATOES	24	
TOMATOES	23	
LETTUCE	23	

Source: University of California Agriculture and Natural Resources (*www.ucanr.org/search*)

9 The LORD will be king over the whole earth.[g] On that day there will be one LORD,
and his name the only name.[h]
10 The whole land, from Geba[i] to Rimmon, south of Jerusalem, will become like
the Arabah. But Jerusalem will be raised up[j] and remain in its place,[k] from the Benjamin Gate to the site of the First Gate, to the Corner Gate, and from the Tower of
Hananel to the royal winepresses. 11 It will be inhabited; never again will it be destroyed. Jerusalem will be secure.[l]
12 This is the plague with which the LORD will strike all the nations that fought
against Jerusalem: Their flesh will rot while they are still standing on their feet, their
eyes will rot in their sockets, and their tongues will rot in their mouths.[m] 13 On that
day men will be stricken by the LORD with great panic. Each man will seize the hand
of another, and they will attack each other.[n] 14 Judah[o] too will fight at Jerusalem.
The wealth of all the surrounding nations will be collected[p]—great quantities of
gold and silver and clothing. 15 A similar plague[q] will strike the horses and mules,
the camels and donkeys, and all the animals in those camps.
16 Then the survivors from all the nations that have attacked Jerusalem will go up
year after year to worship the King, the LORD Almighty, and to celebrate the Feast
of Tabernacles.[r] 17 If any of the peoples of the earth do not go up to Jerusalem to
worship the King, the LORD Almighty, they will have no rain.[s] 18 If the Egyptian people do not go up and take part, they will have no rain. The LORD[a] will bring on them
the plague he inflicts on the nations that do not go up to celebrate the Feast of Tabernacles.[t] 19 This will be the punishment of Egypt and the punishment of all the nations that do not go up to celebrate the Feast of Tabernacles.
20 On that day HOLY TO THE LORD will be inscribed on the bells of the horses, and
the cooking pots[u] in the LORD's house will be like the sacred bowls[v] in front of the
altar. 21 Every pot in Jerusalem and Judah will be holy[w] to the LORD Almighty, and
all who come to sacrifice will take some of the pots and cook in them. And on that
day[x] there will no longer be a Canaanite[b][y] in the house of the LORD Almighty.[z]

14:9 [g] Dt 6:4; Isa 45:24; Rev 11:15 [h] Eph 4:5-6
14:10 [i] 1Ki 15:22 [j] Jer 30:18; Am 9:11 [k] Zec 12:6
14:11 [l] Eze 34:25-28
14:12 [m] Lev 26:16; Dt 28:22
14:13 [n] Zec 11:6
14:14 [o] Zec 12:2 [p] Isa 23:18
14:15 [q] ver 12
14:16 [r] Isa 60:6-9
14:17 [s] Jer 14:4; Am 4:7
14:18 [t] ver 12
14:20 [u] Eze 46:20 [v] Zec 9:15
14:21 [w] Ro 14:6-7; 1Co 10:31 [x] Ne 8:10 [y] Zec 9:8 [z] Eze 44:9

[a] *18* Or *part, then the LORD* [b] *21* Or *merchant*

Zechariah 14:1–21

The ultimate goal of all history is the Lord's personal appearance and reign (cf. vv. 4–5 with Matt. 25:31; Acts 1:11–12; 1 Thess. 3:13). But before the full manifestation of his kingdom, the Earth must experience the throes of birth pangs. This passage pictures God disciplining Jerusalem through the nations, after which he would turn around and fight against them. Their defeat would lead to their submission to this King, demonstrated by their yearly pilgrimage to Jerusalem for the Feast of Tabernacles. The festival speaks of the final, joyful regathering of Israel, as well as of the ingathering of the nations.

In verses 20–21 the nature of the Messianic kingdom is depicted: It would be characterized by complete holiness. "Canaanite" represents anyone who was spiritually or morally unclean—anyone not included among the chosen people of God (cf. Isa. 35:8; Ezek. 43:7; 44:9; Rev. 21:22–27; see also NIV text note for Zech. 14:21 and Matt. 21:12–13).

Christ calls us to balance two aspects of our faith: holiness and mission. Such balance is often attempted by focusing attention on each one in isolation from the other, but a healthier approach is to acknowledge the intimate connection between the two. In Zechariah 14 God purified his people, establishing them as a holy community through which the nations could enter into communion with himself. God brings the nations to their knees through his sovereign acts of power—then draws them into the life of his holy community to worship before his throne.

INTRODUCTION TO
Malachi

AUTHOR

The authorship of Malachi is debated. It's uncertain whether Malachi is the author's name or whether it was used as a title; prophets were called messengers of the Lord, and the term "Malachi" means "my message."

DATE WRITTEN

The book of Malachi was probably written about 430 B.C.

ORIGINAL READERS

Malachi was written to the Jews who had returned from Babylon. The temple in Jerusalem had by this time been rebuilt (516 B.C.), but the people had fallen into a state of spiritual apathy. They were disillusioned about their future and skeptical of God's promises.

TIMELINE

	1300BC	1200	1100	1000	900	800	700	600	500	400
Fall of Jerusalem (586 B.C.)								■		
First return of exiles to Jerusalem (538 B.C.)									■	
Ministries of Haggai and Zechariah (c. 520-480 B.C.)									■	
Completion of temple (516 B.C.)									■	
Second return to Jerusalem under Ezra (458 B.C.)									■	
Third return to Jerusalem under Nehemiah (445 B.C.)									■	
Malachi's ministry (c. 440-430 B.C.)									■	
Book of Malachi written (c. 430 B.C.)									■	

THEMES

Malachi describes the complacency, hypocrisy, disillusionment, and indifference of God's people after the temple in Jerusalem had been rebuilt. It includes the following themes:

1. *Israel's unfaithfulness.* Malachi rebuked the people of Israel for their lapse into unfaithfulness. The priests had shown contempt for God's name by offering diseased or imperfect animals (1:6–14) and by violating the covenant (2:1–9). The men of Israel had married idolatrous Gentile women and had broken the marriage covenants by divorcing their Israelite wives (2:10–16). The people weren't honoring God with the tithe (3:8–12). The book of Malachi demonstrates that God demands our best (1:7–8)—both in our service and in our lives. What we give and how we live reflect the degree of our love for and commitment to him.

2. *Judgment.* God will judge those who practice evil (2:17—3:5; 4:1) but save and reward those who honor him (3:16–18; 4:2–3). Our service to God is important and will be remembered and rewarded (3:13–18).

FAITH IN ACTION

The pages of Malachi contain life lessons that challenge believers to put their faith in action.

Role Models

- THOSE WHO FEAR THE LORD (3:16–17) are God's treasured possession. He will save them from judgment. Do you perceive yourself as God's "treasured possession"?

- THOSE WHO REVERE GOD'S NAME (4:2) will be saved and renewed. Do you respect God? If so, in what ways does your life reflect your attitude?

Challenges

- Determine to honor God by giving him only your best, not your castoffs (1:6–14). Put God, not things or other people, first in your life.

- Choose to honor your relational commitments, particularly those made within the covenant of marriage (2:15–16).

- Don't complain against God and question his fairness (2:17; 3:14). God won't forget your service but will eventually reward you (3:16–17; 4:2). One day all people will be justly judged (3:18).

- Honor God with your financial and material blessings (3:8–12). Don't give as an afterthought or out of a sense of obligation.

- Choose to be honest in your work and treat the helpless with kindness and justice (3:5).

OUTLINE

I. God's Covenant Love for Israel (1:1–5)
II. Israel's Unfaithfulness Rebuked (1:6—2:16)
   A. The Unfaithfulness of the Priests (1:6—2:9)
   B. The Unfaithfulness of the People (2:10–16)
III. The Lord's Coming (2:17—4:6)
   A. His Coming Will Bring Purification and Judgment (2:17—3:5)
   B. Repentance Is Appropriate Preparation for the Lord's Coming (3:6–18)
   C. The Day of the Lord Is Certain to Come (4)

1

An oracle:[a] The word[b] of the LORD to Israel through Malachi.[a]

1:1
a Na 1:1 b 1Pe 4:11

Jacob Loved, Esau Hated

2 "I have loved[c] you," says the LORD.
"But you ask, 'How have you loved us?'

1:2
c Dt 4:37

---

a 1 *Malachi* means *my messenger.*

Malachi 1:1

🕮 This verse is like the opening verses of other prophetic books or of chapters within such books (cf. Isa. 13; 15; 17; 19; 21; 22; 23; Nah. 1; Hab. 1; Zech. 9; 12). It tells the three barest minimum facts about the "oracle" or message: (1) It was from God, (2) for Israel, (3) with Malachi as its agent.

The similarity between the sins denounced in Nehemiah and those condemned in Malachi suggests that the two leaders were contemporaries. Malachi may have been written after the book of Nehemiah, named after the individual who was appointed governor of Judah by the king of Persia but who returned to Persia in 433 B.C.

📖 Have you ever thought about the tremendous responsibility involved in being required to convey a direct message from God? Malachi was the last in a long string of faithful Old Testament prophets, many of whom carried out their work in obscurity and in the face of opposition. But he was by no means God's last prophet. Each of us as a believer carries a prophetic role. How does Jesus' Great Commission (Matt. 28:16–20) speak to you in terms of your God-given responsibility in this area? Your message is from God, and you are his agent. Who is on the receiving end?

Malachi 1:2–5

🕮 Malachi's prophecy begins with the beautiful words "I have loved you"—the first of seven such dialogues between God and Israel in Malachi (cf. 1:6,7; 2:14,17; 3:7b–8,13b–14). We don't know for sure whether the people overtly expressed doubt about God's love for

1543

1:2
d Ro 9:13*
1:3
e Isa 34:10
f Eze 35:3-9
1:4
g Isa 9:10
h Eze 25:12-14

"Was not Esau Jacob's brother?" the LORD says. "Yet I have loved Jacob, *d* 3but Esau I have hated, and I have turned his mountains into a wasteland *e* and left his inheritance to the desert jackals. *f*"

4Edom may say, "Though we have been crushed, we will rebuild *g* the ruins."

But this is what the LORD Almighty says: "They may build, but I will demolish. They will be called the Wicked Land, a people always under the wrath of the LORD. *h*

1:5
i Ps 35:27; Mic 5:4
j Am 1:11-12

5You will see it with your own eyes and say, 'Great *i* is the LORD—even beyond the borders of Israel!' *j*

Blemished Sacrifices

1:6
k Isa 1:2 l Job 5:17

6"A son honors his father, and a servant his master. If I am a father, where is the honor due me? If I am a master, where is the respect *k* due me?" says the LORD Almighty. *l* "It is you, O priests, who show contempt for my name.

1:7
m ver 12; Lev 21:6

"But you ask, 'How have we shown contempt for your name?'

7"You place defiled food *m* on my altar.

"But you ask, 'How have we defiled you?'

1:8
n Lev 22:22;
Dt 15:21
o Isa 43:23

"By saying that the LORD's table is contemptible. 8When you bring blind animals for sacrifice, is that not wrong? When you sacrifice crippled or diseased animals, *n* is that not wrong? Try offering them to your governor! Would he be pleased with you? Would he accept you?" says the LORD Almighty. *o*

1:9
p Lev 23:33-44

9"Now implore God to be gracious to us. With such offerings *p* from your hands, will he accept you?"—says the LORD Almighty.

1:10
q Hos 5:6
r Isa 1:11-14;
Jer 14:12
1:11
s Isa 60:6-7; Rev 8:3

10"Oh, that one of you would shut the temple doors, so that you would not light useless fires on my altar! I am not pleased *q* with you," says the LORD Almighty, "and I will accept no offering *r* from your hands. 11My name will be great among the nations, from the rising to the setting of the sun. In every place incense *s* and pure offerings will be brought to my name, because my name will be great among the nations," says the LORD Almighty.

1:12
t ver 7
1:13
u Isa 43:22-24

12"But you profane it by saying of the Lord's table, 'It is defiled,' and of its food, *t* 'It is contemptible.' 13And you say, 'What a burden!' *u* and you sniff at it contemptuously," says the LORD Almighty.

"When you bring injured, crippled or diseased animals and offer them as sacrifices, should I accept them from your hands?" says the LORD. 14"Cursed is the cheat

---

them. But Malachi wrote a century after the exiles' return from Babylon, and God's people may have been experiencing despair born of unfulfilled hopes. The glorious future announced by the prophets, including the post-exilic prophets Haggai and Zechariah, hadn't been realized.

If the Israelites doubted God's love for them, they could have contrasted his relationship with them with that of their relatives the Edomites. While not stated explicitly in Genesis 25:23, in his sovereignty God had chosen Jacob over his older brother, Esau (also known as Edom)—a choice that in a sense amounted to "hating" Esau. In Romans 9:13 Paul quoted this verse in expressing the concept of divine election.

As human beings we are completely unable to comprehend how God could choose to favor one individual (like Jacob) and reject another (like Esau). The same question may occur to readers mulling over the sparse details in Genesis 4 about God's acceptance of Abel's gift but not Cain's. Our limited minds lack the capacity to understand God's ways, but we believe they are right and perfect. Someday the gray areas will pop into focus for us. Until then, we can take confidence in the simple truth that "God so loved the world that he gave his one and only Son, that whoever believes in him shall not perish but have eternal life" (John 3:16).

Malachi 1:6–14

The temple priests, who were closest to sacred things, had defaulted in the most central obligation of all—that of honoring God. And if the leadership failed, what could the people be expected to do? Spiritual leaders have often run the risk of treating sacred things as ordinary. Intimate familiarity with holy matters can too easily lead to treating them with indifference.

In verse 10 God expressed his wish that the temple would go out of business! As long as it wasn't serving as a meeting place for God and people, why should self-deceiving rituals continue to go on there? Not only were the sacrifices ineffective, but the priests and people had been lulled into thinking that their deeds were winning God's approval.

In verse 11 God told his faithless priests that others in different places and later times would bring acceptable offerings and give him the worship he demanded. Christians don't bring God incense and sacrificial animals. But Revelation 5:8 reminds us that incense corresponds to prayer, and Hebrews 13:15–16 states that "a sacrifice of praise" is "the fruit of lips that confess his name." So Christians are among those about whom Malachi spoke. Take a moment to read and rejoice with Peter's ringing affirmation in 1 Peter 2:9.

who has an acceptable male in his flock and vows to give it, but then sacrifices a blemished animal[v] to the Lord. For I am a great king,[w]" says the LORD Almighty, "and my name is to be feared among the nations.

Admonition for the Priests

2 "And now this admonition is for you, O priests.[x] [2]If you do not listen, and if you do not set your heart to honor my name," says the LORD Almighty, "I will send a curse[y] upon you, and I will curse your blessings. Yes, I have already cursed them, because you have not set your heart to honor me.

[3]"Because of you I will rebuke[a] your descendants[b]; I will spread on your faces the offal[z] from your festival sacrifices, and you will be carried off with it.[a] [4]And you will know that I have sent you this admonition so that my covenant with Levi[b] may continue," says the LORD Almighty. [5]"My covenant was with him, a covenant[c] of life and peace,[d] and I gave them to him; this called for reverence and he revered me and stood in awe of my name. [6]True instruction[e] was in his mouth and nothing false was found on his lips. He walked with me in peace and uprightness, and turned many from sin.[f]

[7]"For the lips of a priest[g] ought to preserve knowledge, and from his mouth men should seek instruction[h]—because he is the messenger[i] of the LORD Almighty. [8]But you have turned from the way and by your teaching have caused many to stumble;[j] you have violated the covenant with Levi," says the LORD Almighty. [9]"So I have caused you to be despised[k] and humiliated before all the people, because you have not followed my ways but have shown partiality in matters of the law."

Judah Unfaithful

[10]Have we not all one Father[c]?[l] Did not one God create us? Why do we profane the covenant[m] of our fathers by breaking faith with one another?

[11]Judah has broken faith. A detestable thing has been committed in Israel and in Jerusalem: Judah has desecrated the sanctuary the LORD loves, by marrying[n] the daughter of a foreign god.[o] [12]As for the man who does this, whoever he may be,

---

a 3 Or *cut off* (see Septuagint)   b 3 Or *will blight your grain*   c 10 Or *father*

Cross references

1:14
v Lev 22:18-21
w 1Ti 6:15

2:1
x ver 7

2:2
y Dt 28:20

2:3
z Ex 29:14
a 1Ki 14:10
2:4
b Nu 3:12
2:5
c Dt 33:9
d Nu 25:12
2:6
e Dt 33:10
f Jer 23:22;
Jas 5:19-20
2:7
g Jer 18:18
h Lev 10:11
i Nu 27:21
2:8
j Jer 18:15

2:9
k 1Sa 2:30

2:10
l 1Co 8:6 m Ex 19:5

2:11
n Ne 13:23
o Ezr 9:1; Jer 3:7-9

Malachi 2:1–9

In Malachi's day, instead of turning people *from* sin, the priests were, by word and deed, turning them *to* sin (v. 8). It seems inconceivable that those who should have stood for righteousness actually practiced and promoted sin. How the unbelieving world must have delighted to behold that spectacle! First Timothy 3:7 and James 3:1 both address this topic. James stated, "Not many of you should presume to be teachers, my brothers, because you know that we who teach will be judged more strictly."

Christians today still cringe when evangelists, pastors, and priests succumb to the temptation to fall into gross sins. A secular media delights in such "breaking" news, and religious detractors nod knowingly, their preconceptions about hypocrisy confirmed to their satisfaction and beyond. What safeguards has your pastor or congregation put in place to eliminate the opportunity for such tragedy? How often do we as Christians pray that the enemy's influence will be hindered in the lives of prominent and visible believers he so delights to attack?

Malachi 2:10–16

This passage begins and ends with references to "breaking faith." Two examples of such sins are addressed: intermarriage with other nations and divorce. Ezra and Nehemiah also dealt with this problem of intermarriage with nonbelievers (Ezra 9:1–2; Neh. 13:23–27). Hand in hand with this sin went an inevitable compromise of true religion. "The daughter of a foreign god" (v. 11) may mean that Israelite men had married foreigners or that they had adopted all or part of a pagan religion. Hosea had often mixed the ideas of idolatry and adultery, of physical and spiritual intermarriage.

" 'I hate divorce,' says the LORD God of Israel" (v. 16). Many today would accuse Malachi of having a rigid view of marriage and divorce. But the covenant made between a man and a woman in the presence of God is a solemn matter (cf. Matt. 19:6).

The mixture of the ideas of intermarriage and "desecrating the sanctuary" (v. 11) reminds us of Paul's string of strong rhetorical questions in 2 Corinthians 6:14–16: "Do not be yoked together with unbelievers. For what do righteousness and wickedness have in common? Or what fellowship can light have with darkness? What harmony is there between Christ and Belial? What does a believer have in common with an unbeliever? What agreement is there between the temple of God and idols?" Paul wasn't advocating isolation from the unbelieving world. But our truly intimate relationships are to be reserved for those who share our faith.

2:12
p Eze 24:21
q Mal 1:10

2:13
r Jer 14:12

2:14
s Pr 5:18

2:15
t Ge 2:24;
Mt 19:4-6
u 1Co 7:14

2:16
v Dt 24:1;
Mt 5:31-32; 19:4-9

2:17
w Isa 43:24

3:1
x Isa 40:3;
Mt 11:10*;
Mk 1:2*; Lk 7:27*

3:2
y Eze 22:14;
Rev 6:17
z Zec 13:9;
Mt 3:10-12
3:3
a Da 12:10
b Isa 1:25
3:4
c 2Ch 7:12;
Ps 51:19; Mal 1:11
d 2Ch 7:3
3:5
e Jer 7:9
f Lev 19:13; Jas 5:4
g Ex 22:22

3:6
h Nu 23:19;
Jas 1:17
3:7
i Jer 7:26; Ac 7:51
j Zec 1:3

may the LORD cut him off[p] from the tents of Jacob[a]—even though he brings offerings[q] to the LORD Almighty.

13Another thing you do: You flood the LORD's altar with tears. You weep and wail because he no longer pays attention[r] to your offerings or accepts them with pleasure from your hands. 14You ask, "Why?" It is because the LORD is acting as the witness between you and the wife of your youth,[s] because you have broken faith with her, though she is your partner, the wife of your marriage covenant.

15Has not ⌊the LORD⌋ made them one?[t] In flesh and spirit they are his. And why one? Because he was seeking godly offspring.[b][u] So guard yourself in your spirit, and do not break faith with the wife of your youth.

16"I hate divorce,[v]" says the LORD God of Israel, "and I hate a man's covering himself[c] with violence as well as with his garment," says the LORD Almighty.

So guard yourself in your spirit, and do not break faith.

The Day of Judgment

17You have wearied[w] the LORD with your words.

"How have we wearied him?" you ask.

By saying, "All who do evil are good in the eyes of the LORD, and he is pleased with them" or "Where is the God of justice?"

3 "See, I will send my messenger, who will prepare the way before me.[x] Then suddenly the Lord you are seeking will come to his temple; the messenger of the covenant, whom you desire, will come," says the LORD Almighty.

2But who can endure[y] the day of his coming? Who can stand when he appears? For he will be like a refiner's fire[z] or a launderer's soap. 3He will sit as a refiner and purifier of silver;[a] he will purify[b] the Levites and refine them like gold and silver. Then the LORD will have men who will bring offerings in righteousness, 4and the offerings[c] of Judah and Jerusalem will be acceptable to the LORD, as in days gone by, as in former years.[d]

5"So I will come near to you for judgment. I will be quick to testify against sorcerers, adulterers and perjurers,[e] against those who defraud laborers of their wages,[f] who oppress the widows[g] and the fatherless, and deprive aliens of justice, but do not fear me," says the LORD Almighty.

Robbing God

6"I the LORD do not change.[h] So you, O descendants of Jacob, are not destroyed. 7Ever since the time of your forefathers you have turned away[i] from my decrees and have not kept them. Return to me, and I will return to you,"[j] says the LORD Almighty.

a 12 Or 12May the LORD cut off from the tents of Jacob anyone who gives testimony in behalf of the man who does this   b 15 Or 15But the one ⌊who is our father⌋ did not do this, not as long as life remained in him. And what was he seeking? An offspring from God   c 16 Or his wife

---

Malachi 2:17—3:5

The people had given up on God and had grown spiritually cynical and morally corrupt. God's "messenger" (3:1) would be John the Baptist (see Matt. 11:10; Mark 1:2; Luke 1:76). The "Lord" and "messenger of the covenant" who would then follow was none other than Jesus Christ, the Son of God. He would come to purify (v. 3) and judge (v. 5).

Malachi's indictment against oppressors of widows, orphans, and aliens reflected his interest in social justice. Like all true ministers of God, Malachi couldn't separate responsibilities toward God from those toward the people of his creation. The number of laws in the Pentateuch (first five OT books) and elsewhere for the protection of widows, orphans, and foreigners/aliens suggests that it must have been common and/or easy to exploit such people.

How does your culture "deprive aliens of justice"? The criminal justice system in the United States guarantees them just treatment, but what of the private sector? Do you complain about jobs going to immigrants? About the helping hand of government assistance initially enjoyed by refugees? About the number of doctors, telemarketers, and retail associates with foreign-sounding names and accents? Our attitudes come through regardless of our words. Just as Moses and Joshua repeatedly reminded the Israelites, most U.S. citizens are descended from immigrant groups. What can you do to help those making every effort to adjust to our often bewildering culture?

Malachi 3:6—18

God was (and is) pledged to attend to those who earnestly seek him (cf. Jer. 29:13). His invitation in

"But you ask, 'How are we to return?'
8"Will a man rob God? Yet you rob me.
"But you ask, 'How do we rob you?'
"In tithes[k] and offerings. 9You are under a curse—the whole nation of you—because you are robbing me. 10Bring the whole tithe into the storehouse,[l] that there
may be food in my house. Test me in this," says the LORD Almighty, "and see if I will
not throw open the floodgates[m] of heaven and pour out so much blessing that you
will not have room enough for it. 11I will prevent pests from devouring your crops,
and the vines in your fields will not cast their fruit," says the LORD Almighty.
12"Then all the nations will call you blessed,[n] for yours will be a delightful land,"[o]
says the LORD Almighty.
13"You have said harsh things[p] against me," says the LORD.
"Yet you ask, 'What have we said against you?'
14"You have said, 'It is futile[q] to serve God. What did we gain by carrying out his
requirements and going about like mourners[r] before the LORD Almighty? 15But now
we call the arrogant blessed. Certainly the evildoers[s] prosper, and even those who
challenge God escape.' "
16Then those who feared the LORD talked with each other, and the LORD listened
and heard.[t] A scroll[u] of remembrance was written in his presence concerning those
who feared the LORD and honored his name.
17"They will be mine," says the LORD Almighty, "in the day when I make up my
treasured possession.[a][v] I will spare[w] them, just as in compassion a man spares his
son who serves him. 18And you will again see the distinction between the righteous[x] and the wicked, between those who serve God and those who do not.

The Day of the LORD

4 "Surely the day is coming;[y] it will burn like a furnace. All the arrogant and every evildoer will be stubble,[z] and that day that is coming will set them on fire,"
says the LORD Almighty. "Not a root or a branch will be left to them. 2But for you
who revere my name, the sun of righteousness[a] will rise with healing[b] in its wings.
And you will go out and leap[c] like calves released from the stall. 3Then you will
trample[d] down the wicked; they will be ashes[e] under the soles of your feet on the
day when I do these things," says the LORD Almighty.
4"Remember the law[f] of my servant Moses, the decrees and laws I gave him at Horeb for all Israel.

3:8 [k] Ne 13:10-12
3:10 [l] Ne 13:12 [m] 2Ki 7:2
3:12 [n] Isa 61:9 [o] Isa 62:4
3:13 [p] Mal 2:17
3:14 [q] Ps 73:13 [r] Isa 58:3
3:15 [s] Jer 7:10
3:16 [t] Ps 34:15 [u] Ps 56:8
3:17 [v] Dt 7:6 [w] Ps 103:13; Isa 26:20
3:18 [x] Ge 18:25
4:1 [y] Joel 2:31 [z] Isa 5:24; Ob 1:18
4:2 [a] Lk 1:78; Eph 5:14 [b] Isa 30:26 [c] Isa 35:6
4:3 [d] Job 40:12 [e] Eze 28:18
4:4 [f] Ps 147:19

[a] 17 Or *Almighty, "my treasured possession, in the day when I act*

verse 7 to return ("repent" or "convert") was met with a cynical question: *"How?"* Malachi didn't grace this question with an answer: His whole book and ministry were about telling people how to get right with God.

The remedy for Israel was to start doing what was right—to bring the whole tithe into the storehouse. The temple served as a warehouse for the produce Israel brought. The Levites distributed it for sacrificial purposes, for their own needs, and for emergencies.

In verse 16 Malachi portrayed God as listening to those who feared him. What they were saying we don't know, but we can assume that it was an expression of love and worship. Then comes the remarkable statement: "A scroll of remembrance was written in his presence concerning those who feared the LORD." This idea of God's keeping written records appears occasionally in the Old Testament. Perhaps its most beautiful expression is found in Isaiah 49:16: "See, I have engraved you on the palms of my hands."

"Storehouse tithing" (separate from personal charity or gifts to Christian friends or institutions) has a sound basis in verse 10. Paul would later instruct New Testament believers on the necessity of regularly and proportionately setting aside support for God's ongoing work (cf. 1 Cor. 16:1–2). The Old Testament tithe isn't an upper limit. We as Christians are urged to *"excel in the grace of giving"* (2 Cor. 8:7, emphasis added). After all, we owe everything to the One who for our sake "made himself nothing" (Phil. 2:7; cf. 2 Cor. 8:9).

Malachi 4:1–6

The end-times theme of the Day of the Lord looms large in the Old Testament prophets (cf. Isa. 13:6; Jer. 46:10; Joel 2:31; Zeph. 1:14—2:3) and also appears in the New Testament (cf. Matt. 24–25; Rom. 2:5; 2 Peter 3:10; Rev. 16:14). Verse 1 focuses on the fate of the wicked and verse 2 on the blessed future of the righteous, who, enlightened and healed, will "leap like calves" frisking about in their newfound freedom. An added reward is described in verse 3: The righteous will trample the wicked on the great judgment day (cf. Mic. 2:12–13).

The final three verses give us two somewhat unrelat-

4:5
g Mt 11:14; Lk 1:17
h Joel 2:31
4:6
i Lk 1:17 *i* Isa 11:4;
Rev 19:15 *k* Zec 5:3

⁵ "See, I will send you the prophet Elijah*g* before that great and dreadful day of the LORD comes. *h* ⁶ He will turn the hearts of the fathers to their children, *i* and the hearts of the children to their fathers; or else I will come and strike*j* the land with a curse." *k*

ed "appendixes" to the book. Verses 5–6, like 3:1, look ahead to John the Baptist preparing the way for the Messiah (Luke 1:17; cf. Matt. 11:13–14; 17:12–13; Mark 9:11–13).

📖 Chances are the picture of trampling the wicked doesn't appear on your radar screen as a pleasurable future prospect. But imagine for a moment, no matter what your physical limitations or natural emotional re-

straint, leaping like a calf released from the stall. What a beautiful picture of the unreserved freedom we as Christians will one day enjoy, though the spiritual reality is being released in us to a more limited degree now! Do you find it difficult to look forward to heaven? Does the picture the Bible presents seem too blurred? Perhaps the less we imagine now of the wonders to come, the more amazing the reality will be.

Snapshots

4:2

Susan

Susan, a Friend of Families from Ghana, is passionate about her work. Her role is to act as an intermediary between the families in a designated rural community and their U.S. sponsors. She accomplishes this expertly, sensitizing her clients about life issues and about the community development projects with which they are mutually involved.

Every day, Susan visits at least five families in the Anyinofi district. She enjoys sharing the gospel with them and assisting them in replying to their mail. She also discusses with family members such issues as health, education, agriculture, nutrition, sanitation, and microenterprise development (entrepreneurial business ventures). Susan recently took part in the distribution of worm expellers and other medicines during a maternal and health exercise with her district health management team. She also mobilizes the youth for HIV/AIDS education and cleanup campaigns to promote a healthy and environmentally conscious neighborhood.

"**M**y comfort is when I am able to interact with the children and share the gospel with them."

Like other native Ghanian workers, Susan says she is faced with challenges, one of which is the inaccessibility of the roads during the rainy season. Despite this, she reflects, "My comfort is when I am able to interact with the children and share the gospel with them."

From Malachi to Christ

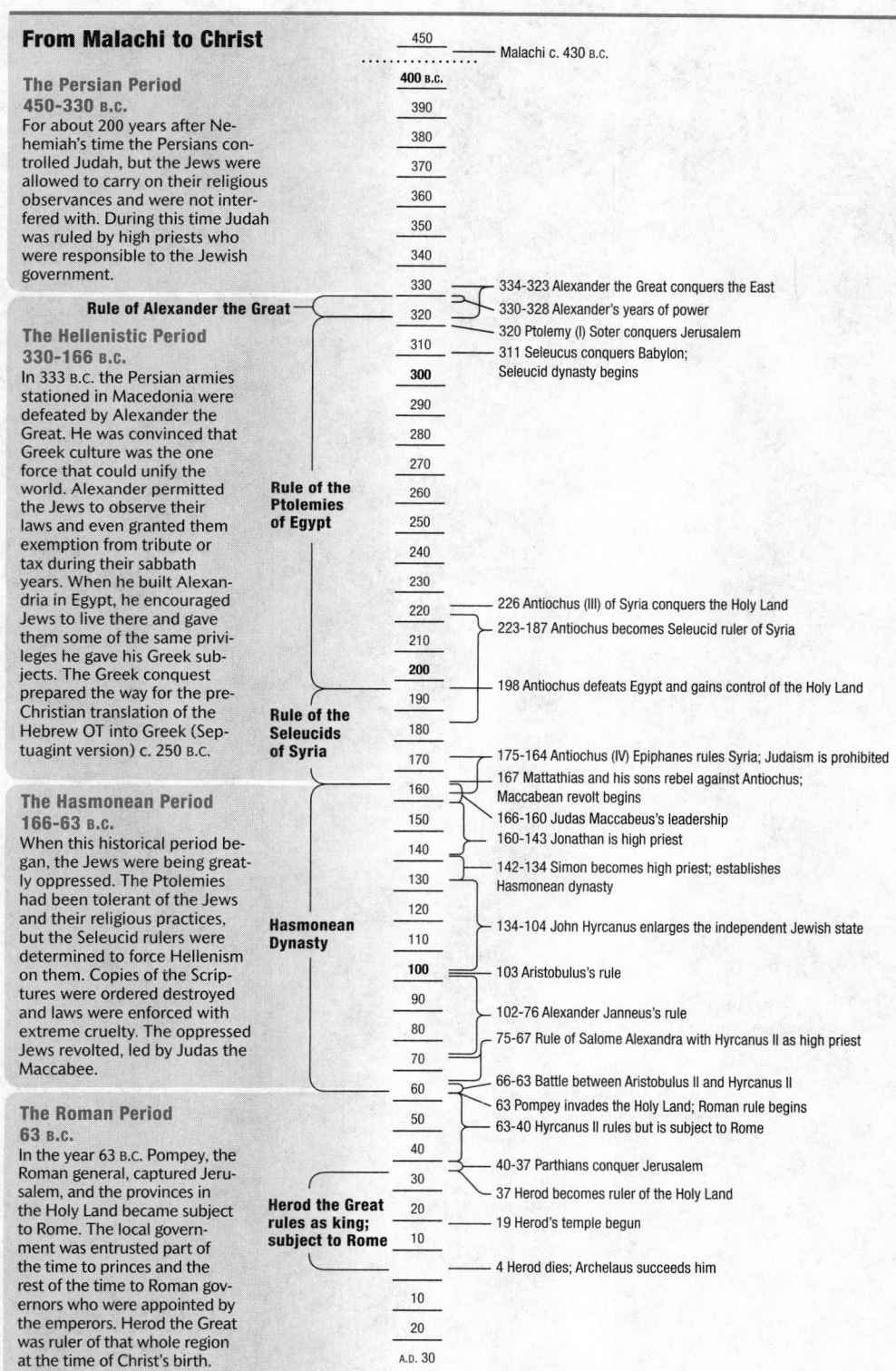

450
.... Malachi c. 430 B.C.

400 B.C.

390

380

370

360

350

340

330 —— 334-323 Alexander the Great conquers the East

320 —— 330-328 Alexander's years of power

—— 320 Ptolemy (I) Soter conquers Jerusalem

310 —— 311 Seleucus conquers Babylon;
Seleucid dynasty begins

300

290

280

270

260

250

240

230

220 —— 226 Antiochus (III) of Syria conquers the Holy Land

—— 223-187 Antiochus becomes Seleucid ruler of Syria

210

200

—— 198 Antiochus defeats Egypt and gains control of the Holy Land

190

180

170 —— 175-164 Antiochus (IV) Epiphanes rules Syria; Judaism is prohibited

167 Mattathias and his sons rebel against Antiochus;
160 Maccabean revolt begins

—— 166-160 Judas Maccabeus's leadership

150 —— 160-143 Jonathan is high priest

140

—— 142-134 Simon becomes high priest; establishes
130 Hasmonean dynasty

120

—— 134-104 John Hyrcanus enlarges the independent Jewish state
110

100 —— 103 Aristobulus's rule

90

—— 102-76 Alexander Janneus's rule
80
—— 75-67 Rule of Salome Alexandra with Hyrcanus II as high priest

70

—— 66-63 Battle between Aristobulus II and Hyrcanus II
60
—— 63 Pompey invades the Holy Land; Roman rule begins
50 —— 63-40 Hyrcanus II rules but is subject to Rome

40

—— 40-37 Parthians conquer Jerusalem
30
—— 37 Herod becomes ruler of the Holy Land

20

—— 19 Herod's temple begun
10

—— 4 Herod dies; Archelaus succeeds him

10

20

A.D. 30

The Persian Period
450-330 B.C.

For about 200 years after Nehemiah's time the Persians controlled Judah, but the Jews were allowed to carry on their religious observances and were not interfered with. During this time Judah was ruled by high priests who were responsible to the Jewish government.

Rule of Alexander the Great

The Hellenistic Period
330-166 B.C.

In 333 B.C. the Persian armies stationed in Macedonia were defeated by Alexander the Great. He was convinced that Greek culture was the one force that could unify the world. Alexander permitted the Jews to observe their laws and even granted them exemption from tribute or tax during their sabbath years. When he built Alexandria in Egypt, he encouraged Jews to live there and gave them some of the same privileges he gave his Greek subjects. The Greek conquest prepared the way for the pre-Christian translation of the Hebrew OT into Greek (Septuagint version) c. 250 B.C.

Rule of the Ptolemies of Egypt

Rule of the Seleucids of Syria

The Hasmonean Period
166-63 B.C.

When this historical period began, the Jews were being greatly oppressed. The Ptolemies had been tolerant of the Jews and their religious practices, but the Seleucid rulers were determined to force Hellenism on them. Copies of the Scriptures were ordered destroyed and laws were enforced with extreme cruelty. The oppressed Jews revolted, led by Judas the Maccabee.

Hasmonean Dynasty

The Roman Period
63 B.C.

In the year 63 B.C. Pompey, the Roman general, captured Jerusalem, and the provinces in the Holy Land became subject to Rome. The local government was entrusted part of the time to princes and the rest of the time to Roman governors who were appointed by the emperors. Herod the Great was ruler of that whole region at the time of Christ's birth.

Herod the Great rules as king; subject to Rome

1549

The New Testament

INTRODUCTION TO
Matthew

AUTHOR

The author of this Gospel was most probably Matthew (Levi), the man who left his tax office to follow Jesus (9:9; 10:3; cf. Mark 2:13–17).

DATE WRITTEN

Matthew was probably written between A.D. 70 and 80.

ORIGINAL READERS

Matthew's original readers were predominately Jews who already believed in Jesus and confessed him as the Son of God (14:33; 16:16; 27:54).

TIMELINE

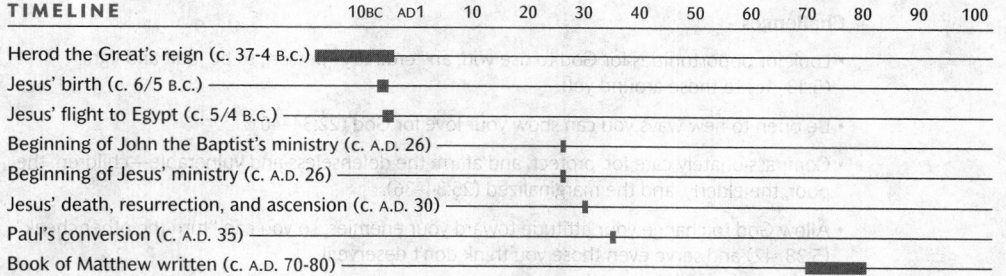

	10BC	AD1	10	20	30	40	50	60	70	80	90	100
Herod the Great's reign (c. 37-4 B.C.)												
Jesus' birth (c. 6/5 B.C.)												
Jesus' flight to Egypt (c. 5/4 B.C.)												
Beginning of John the Baptist's ministry (c. A.D. 26)												
Beginning of Jesus' ministry (c. A.D. 26)												
Jesus' death, resurrection, and ascension (c. A.D. 30)												
Paul's conversion (c. A.D. 35)												
Book of Matthew written (c. A.D. 70-80)												

THEMES

Matthew contains the following themes:

1. *Jesus is the Messiah.* Matthew clearly taught that Jesus was the fulfillment of Old Testament promises, especially that of the coming Messiah (King). Jesus was presented as king shortly after his birth (2:11–12) and was proven to be so in his resurrection (28:1–10). Matthew used the phrase "kingdom of heaven" 32 times, highlighting Jesus' kingly authority and power. But while many expected Jesus to be king of Israel, Matthew revealed him as King of heaven and Earth.

2. *Righteousness.* Citizens of the kingdom of heaven are called to be righteous, and ethical issues are a major focus in Matthew. Jesus' first recorded words in Matthew had to do with fulfilling righteousness (3:15). He demanded that his disciples invest their treasures in God's kingdom, not in earthly possessions. Love for others is also emphasized. The world's way of returning good for good or evil for evil isn't God's way; God returns *good* for evil. According to Matthew, mercy and forgiveness are to be paramount virtues in a Christian's life. Mercy dictates love for fellow human beings (5:7; 6:2–4,12,14–15) and directly affects a believer's relationship to God (9:9–13; 12:1–8; 23:23). The failure to exercise mercy results in final judgment (18:21–35).

3. *The believer's commission.* In its closing verses (28:16–20) Matthew reveals the plan for the expansion of the kingdom of heaven. Believers are to be "salt" and "light" (5:13–16), spreading the Good News of the kingdom to all the world.

FAITH IN ACTION

The pages of Matthew contain life lessons and role models of faith—people who challenge believers to put their faith in action.

Role Models

• JOSEPH (1:18–25; 2:13–15) displayed integrity, compassion, and mercy, obeying God despite the personal cost to himself. If God is calling you to a thankless or difficult task, how can Joseph inspire you to trust God's guidance?

• JOHN THE BAPTIST (3:1–12; 11:1–19) lived an unusual lifestyle that pointed people to Jesus. How can you live in a way that intentionally points others to Christ?

• THE ROMAN CENTURION'S (8:5–13) faith impressed Jesus, who used the comments of this representative of the foreign occupation as a teaching moment for the disciples. What models of faith or exemplary living outside the believing community or your social group have impressed you? What have they taught you?

• MATTHEW (9:9) followed Jesus immediately when he was called. What has been your response when you have sensed God calling or directing you?

• MARY OF BETHANY (26:6–13) revealed her deep love for Jesus in an extravagant act of worship. Have you been criticized for openly expressing your devotion to Jesus? What has his response been to your love?

Challenges

• Look for opportunities for God to use you, an "ordinary" person, to be "salt and light" (5:13–16) to those around you.

• Be open to new ways you can show your love for God (22:34–40).

• Compassionately care for, protect, and affirm the defenseless and vulnerable—children, the poor, the elderly, and the marginalized (25:34–36).

• Allow God to change your attitude toward your enemies, so you can "turn the other cheek" (5:38–42) and serve even those you think don't deserve it.

• Be alert to what you can learn about faith from people you might normally write off—those outside your ethnic group, social circle, or the fellowship of believers.

• Be open to the unique mission God has for you as Christ's disciple. Follow the Spirit's leading as you join others in advancing God's kingdom (4:18–20; 19:16–22).

OUTLINE

   I. Jesus' Childhood (1–2)
  II. The Beginnings of Jesus' Ministry (3:1—4:11)
      A. John the Baptist (3)
      B. The Temptation (4:1–11)
 III. Jesus' Ministry in Galilee (4:12—14:12)
      A. His Early Ministry (4:12–25)
      B. The Sermon on the Mount (5–7)
      C. Miracles (8–9)
      D. Ministry (10:1—14:12)
 IV. Ministry in Other Areas (14:13—17:21)
  V. Jesus Returns to Galilee (17:22—18:35)
 VI. Jesus' Ministry in Judea and Perea (19–20)

VII. Passion Week (21–27)
  A. The Triumphal Entry (21:1–11)
  B. The Cleansing of the Temple (21:12–17)
  C. Questions From the Jewish Leaders (21:18—23:39)
  D. The Olivet Discourse (24—25)
  E. The Anointing of Jesus' Feet (26:1–13)
  F. The Arrest, Trials, and Death of Jesus (26:14—27:66)
VIII. The Resurrection (28)

The Genealogy of Jesus

1 A record of the genealogy of Jesus Christ the son of David, [a] the son of Abraham: [b]

2 Abraham was the father of Isaac, [c]
  Isaac the father of Jacob, [d]
  Jacob the father of Judah and his brothers, [e]
3 Judah the father of Perez and Zerah, whose mother was Tamar, [f]
  Perez the father of Hezron,
  Hezron the father of Ram,
4 Ram the father of Amminadab,
  Amminadab the father of Nahshon,
  Nahshon the father of Salmon,
5 Salmon the father of Boaz, whose mother was Rahab,
  Boaz the father of Obed, whose mother was Ruth,
  Obed the father of Jesse,
6 and Jesse the father of King David. [g]

David was the father of Solomon, whose mother had been Uriah's wife, [h]
7 Solomon the father of Rehoboam,
  Rehoboam the father of Abijah,
  Abijah the father of Asa,
8 Asa the father of Jehoshaphat,
  Jehoshaphat the father of Jehoram,
  Jehoram the father of Uzziah,
9 Uzziah the father of Jotham,
  Jotham the father of Ahaz,
  Ahaz the father of Hezekiah,
10 Hezekiah the father of Manasseh, [i]
  Manasseh the father of Amon,
  Amon the father of Josiah,
11 and Josiah the father of Jeconiah [a] and his brothers at the time of the exile to Babylon. [j]

a 11 That is, Jehoiachin; also in verse 12

1:1
a 2Sa 7:12-16;
Isa 9:6,7; 11:1;
Jer 23:5,6; Mt 9:27;
Lk 1:32,69; Ro 1:3;
Rev 22:16
b Ge 22:18;
Gal 3:16
1:2
c Ge 21:3,12
d Ge 25:26
e Ge 29:35
1:3
f Ge 38:27-30
1:6
g 1Sa 16:1; 17:12
h 2Sa 12:24
1:10
i 2Ki 20:21
1:11
j 2Ki 24:14-16;
Jer 27:20; Da 1:1,2

Matthew 1:1–17

Like most people today, 1st-century Hebrews kept extensive records of a family's ancestry (cf. 1 Chron. 1–9). These were used for practical and legal purposes—to establish a person's heritage, inheritance, legitimacy, and rights. Luke followed the traditional approach of tracing lineage through males (Luke 3:23–38), but Matthew radically innovated. Throughout his Gospel he stressed the coming of God's kingdom to all nations. Here, in the geneaology, he scandalously included four women, three of whom were outsiders to Israel. The kingdom includes people of all nations, and Matthew recognized women as central in God's purposes.

Try asking people to trace back their lineage. Many will draw a blank after their grandparents. We tend to live as self-defined individuals, not as members of a community. For one thing, we find ourselves in a mobile world where many grow up far from extended family. God's kingdom establishes a new community into which all who follow Christ are adopted and which includes people from every nation. How does this genealogy help you understand your faith roots and the new "family" into which you have been incorporated?

1555

12 After the exile to Babylon:
    Jeconiah was the father of Shealtiel,[k]
    Shealtiel the father of Zerubbabel,[l]
13 Zerubbabel the father of Abiud,
    Abiud the father of Eliakim,
    Eliakim the father of Azor,
14 Azor the father of Zadok,
    Zadok the father of Akim,
    Akim the father of Eliud,
15 Eliud the father of Eleazar,
    Eleazar the father of Matthan,
    Matthan the father of Jacob,
16 and Jacob the father of Joseph, the husband of Mary,[m] of whom was born
    Jesus, who is called Christ.[n]

17 Thus there were fourteen generations in all from Abraham to David, fourteen
from David to the exile to Babylon, and fourteen from the exile to the Christ.[a]

[a] 17 Or *Messiah.* "The Christ" (Greek) and "the Messiah" (Hebrew) both mean "the Anointed One."

1:12
[k] 1Ch 3:17
[l] 1Ch 3:19; Ezr 3:2

1:16
[m] Lk 1:27
[n] Mt 27:17

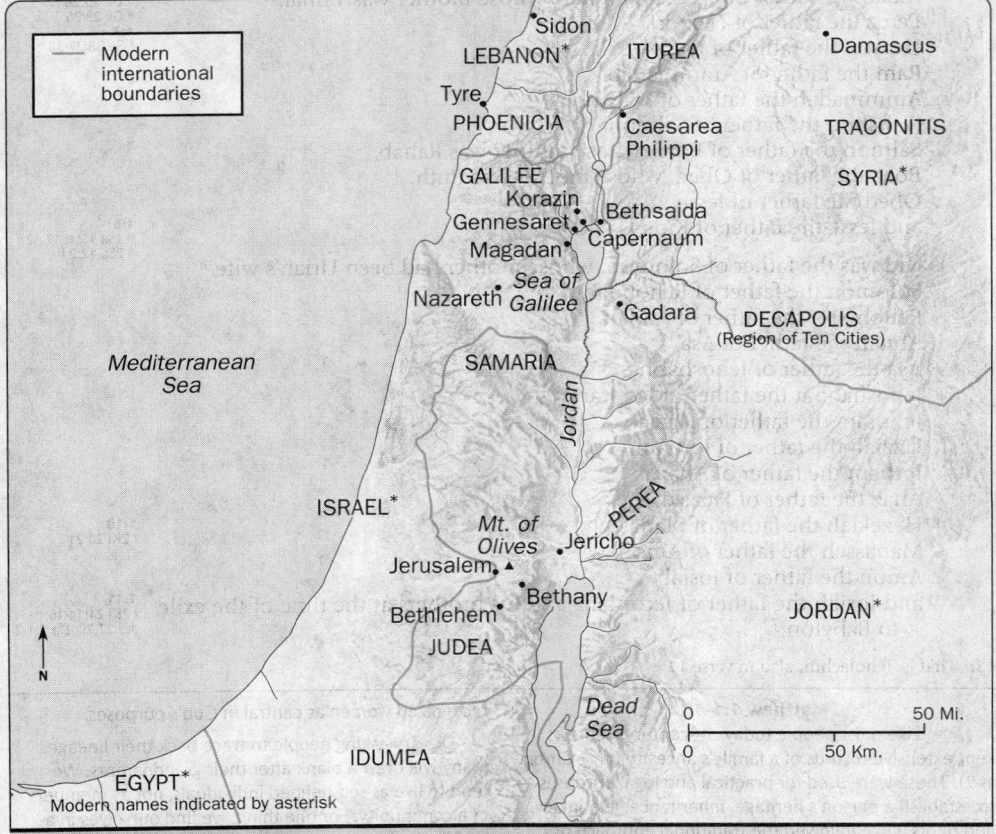

Setting of the Gospels (1:1)

Then: *Area divided by fluid tribal boundaries that grew larger and smaller as the fortunes of individual tribes waxed and waned. Geographical features important for boundaries.*

Now: *Area divided by political considerations. Straight boundary lines between countries created nations based on balance of power more than on geographical features. Egyptian, Israeli, Lebanese, Syrian, and Jordanian boundaries set primarily after World War I.*

The Birth of Jesus Christ

18This is how the birth of Jesus Christ came about: His mother Mary was pledged to be married to Joseph, but before they came together, she was found to be with child through the Holy Spirit.*o* 19Because Joseph her husband was a righteous man and did not want to expose her to public disgrace, he had in mind to divorce*p* her quietly.

20But after he had considered this, an angel of the Lord appeared to him in a dream and said, "Joseph son of David, do not be afraid to take Mary home as your wife, because what is conceived in her is from the Holy Spirit. 21She will give birth to a son, and you are to give him the name Jesus,*a q* because he will save his people from their sins."*r*

22All this took place to fulfill what the Lord had said through the prophet: 23"The virgin will be with child and will give birth to a son, and they will call him Immanuel"*b s*—which means, "God with us."

24When Joseph woke up, he did what the angel of the Lord had commanded him and took Mary home as his wife. 25But he had no union with her until she gave birth to a son. And he gave him the name Jesus.*t*

a 21 Jesus is the Greek form of *Joshua,* which means *the LORD saves.*   *b 23* Isaiah 7:14

1:18
o Lk 1:35
1:19
p Dt 24:1

1:21
q Lk 1:31 r Lk 2:11;
Ac 5:31; 13:23,28

1:23
s Isa 7:14; 8:8,10

1:25
t ver 21

Matthew 1:18–25

The terms "husband" and "wife" (1:19–20,24) were used during a second stage of a betrothal (engagement), involving official arrangements and a formal prenuptial agreement before witnesses. At this point, sexual unfaithfulness was considered adultery, the penalty for which was death by stoning (Lev. 20:10; Deut. 22:23–24). Joseph planned to opt for a private divorce—the only choice that would allow him to maintain his personal righteousness according to the Law of Moses and yet save Mary from public disgrace and possible death.

The angel dramatically announced to Joseph that the child's conception was from the Holy Spirit, not from Joseph (which he knew personally) or some other man (which he might have suspected). Old Testament writers repeatedly referred to the Spirit of God as the agent of God's power. Here, at the introduction to the story of Jesus, we are also introduced to the Spirit as a distinct person in the Trinity.

Joseph stood in the line of other figures whose pursuit of godliness meant risking misunderstanding and ridicule. Following God's will often means embracing people others reject, as Joseph embraced Mary. Obedience to God can be costly. We are all acquainted with

---

Snapshots

1:22

Emmanuel

Emmanuel means "God with us." And he often is with us, as Mother Teresa described it, "in a most distressing disguise."

Three-year-old Emmanuel lives near Monrovia, Liberia, a West African country that has endured 14 years of civil war. Emmanuel has spent most of his short life fleeing with his mother from one refugee camp to another. He has been malnourished for most of that time.

During the summer of 2003, as the war in his country was drawing to a close, Emmanuel was living in the hallway of a high school with his mother, his baby sister, and 14,000 others who had lost their homes. By then, Emmanuel was close to death. Fortunately, a Christian relief and development ministry built a feeding center for malnourished children at the high school—the only hope for Emmanuel's survival.

> Jesus tells us that when we serve the poor—and the children—we are serving him.

Jesus tells us that when we serve the poor—and the children—we are serving him. In a real sense, little Emmanuel is indeed "God with us." Who represents "the least of these" in your life? How can thinking of this person as Christ in a "distressing disguise" change your response to them?

The Visit of the Magi

2 After Jesus was born in Bethlehem in Judea,[u] during the time of King Herod,[v] Magi[a] from the east came to Jerusalem ²and asked, "Where is the one who has been born king of the Jews?[w] We saw his star[x] in the east[b] and have come to worship him."

³When King Herod heard this he was disturbed, and all Jerusalem with him. ⁴When he had called together all the people's chief priests and teachers of the law, he asked them where the Christ[c] was to be born. ⁵"In Bethlehem[y] in Judea," they replied, "for this is what the prophet has written:

⁶ " 'But you, Bethlehem, in the land of Judah,
  are by no means least among the rulers of Judah;
for out of you will come a ruler
  who will be the shepherd of my people Israel.'[d][z]

⁷Then Herod called the Magi secretly and found out from them the exact time the star had appeared. ⁸He sent them to Bethlehem and said, "Go and make a careful search for the child. As soon as you find him, report to me, so that I too may go and worship him."

⁹After they had heard the king, they went on their way, and the star they had seen in the east[e] went ahead of them until it stopped over the place where the child was. ¹⁰When they saw the star, they were overjoyed. ¹¹On coming to the house, they saw the child with his mother Mary, and they bowed down and worshiped him.[a] Then they opened their treasures and presented him with gifts[b] of gold and of incense and of myrrh. ¹²And having been warned[c] in a dream[d] not to go back to Herod, they returned to their country by another route.

The Escape to Egypt

¹³When they had gone, an angel[e] of the Lord appeared to Joseph in a dream.[f] "Get up," he said, "take the child and his mother

Cross references (margin)

2:1 u Lk 2:4-7 v Lk 1:5
2:2 w Jer 23:5; Mt 27:11; Mk 15:2; Jn 1:49; 18:33-37 x Nu 24:17
2:5 y Jn 7:42
2:6 z 2Sa 5:2; Mic 5:2
2:11 a Isa 60:3 b Ps 72:10
2:12 c Heb 11:7 d ver 13,19,22; Mt 27:19
2:13 e Ac 5:19 f ver 12,19,22

Escape to Egypt (2:13)

Then: Joseph, Mary, and Jesus had to flee to Egypt to avoid Jesus being killed by King Herod. They sought refuge in a safe "political" climate.

Now: In the modern world people move from one country to another for the same reasons: protection from hostile powers (refugees) and to seek better economic living conditions (migrants).

Map labels

Nazareth
Mediterranean Sea
Jerusalem
Gaza
Bethlehem
EGYPT
0   200 Mi.
0   200 Km.
N

---

a 1 Traditionally *Wise Men*   b 2 Or *star when it rose*   c 4 Or *Messiah*   d 6 Micah 5:2
e 9 Or *seen when it rose*

---

individuals whose hearts have become pure in the midst of controversies surrounding their everyday lives—from Christian leaders to homemakers, from business leaders to store greeters. Who stands out in your mind?

Matthew 2:1–12

Herod's rule was marked by splendid buildings on one hand and murderous, iron rule on the other. He was "disturbed" by the Magis' announcement because he knew he wasn't the rightful heir to Israel's throne, having usurped power by aligning himself with Rome. The Magis' visit likely made him fear that invading forces from the east might join others within Israel to replace him with a king from the true line of the anticipated Messiah. We might have expected the religious leaders to celebrate the birth of Israel's king. But they had aligned themselves politically with Herod. If his power base was threatened, so was theirs.

The Messiah's kingdom isn't just spiritual; it threatens all human powers. In the final analysis, there is room for only one King. Religious and political leaders often align themselves together in an effort to secure their position and power. As we take stock of our ambitions, we are wise to take a sober look at our response to Jesus. Are you ready to acknowledge his presence in *all* life's details, or do your personal desires and loyalties to your own nation sometimes get in the way?

Matthew 2:13–18

Like other tyrants throughout history, Herod was willing to do anything to maintain his power—even massacre children! The kingly gifts Mary and Joseph received from the Magi were no doubt soon put to good use. They were some of the most valuable, transportable, and marketable items of the day, perfect to sustain refugees in another country. By noting how this flight to

and escape to Egypt. Stay there until I tell you, for Herod is going to search for the child to kill him."

¹⁴So he got up, took the child and his mother during the night and left for Egypt, ¹⁵where he stayed until the death of Herod. And so was fulfilled what the Lord had said through the prophet: "Out of Egypt I called my son." ᵃ ᵍ

¹⁶When Herod realized that he had been outwitted by the Magi, he was furious, and he gave orders to kill all the boys in Bethlehem and its vicinity who were two years old and under, in accordance with the time he had learned from the Magi. ¹⁷Then what was said through the prophet Jeremiah was fulfilled:

> ¹⁸"A voice is heard in Ramah,
> weeping and great mourning,
> Rachel weeping for her children
> and refusing to be comforted,
> because they are no more." ᵇ ʰ

The Return to Nazareth

¹⁹After Herod died, an angel of the Lord appeared in a dream ⁱ to Joseph in Egypt ²⁰and said, "Get up, take the child and his mother and go to the land of Israel, for those who were trying to take the child's life are dead."

²¹So he got up, took the child and his mother and went to the land of Israel. ²²But when he heard that Archelaus was reigning in Judea in place of his father Herod, he was afraid to go there. Having been warned in a dream, ʲ he withdrew to the district of Galilee, ᵏ ²³and he went and lived in a town called Nazareth. ˡ So was fulfilled ᵐ what was said through the prophets: "He will be called a Nazarene." ⁿ

ᵃ 15 Hosea 11:1   ᵇ 18 Jer. 31:15

2:15
ᵍ Ex 4:22,23;
Hos 11:1

2:18
ʰ Jer 31:15

2:19
ⁱ ver 12,13,22

2:22
ʲ ver 12,13,19;
Mt 27:19 ᵏ Lk 2:39
2:23
ˡ Lk 1:26;
Jn 1:45,46
ᵐ Mt 1:22
ⁿ Mk 1:24

Egypt actually was fulfilling a prophecy, Matthew underscored God's power over all human powers.

🔲 When human power and politics collide with God's way, children often suffer most. Refugees around the world who are victims of political conflict take comfort that Jesus also was a refugee. Children who are victims of human ambition encounter a Messiah who identified fully with their suffering. The incarnate God was a refugee, driven into exile by politically-inspired violence against children.

Matthew 2:19–23

🔲 No Old Testament prophecy uses the exact words "He will be called a Nazarene." But several

prophecies relate to wordplays associated with the words "Nazareth" and "Nazarene." Perhaps Nazareth was originally settled by people from David's line, who gave the village a Messianic name—tied in meaning to the hope of the coming "Branch" of Isaiah 11:1. But Nazareth never rose from obscurity. By Jesus' day "Nazarene" had become a derogatory term for a person from any remote area (cf. John 1:45–46)—something like our "yokel."

🔲 "Nazarene" was for Jesus a title of honor. He was the long-awaited, redemptive, Messianic Branch. But it also was a label of scorn for Israel's despised, suffering servant (cf. Isa. 53:3). Similarly, "Christian" is for us a name of honor—but also of scorn and sometimes

2:16

The Slaughter of Innocents

As Matthew 2:16 tells us, Jesus was born into a land of dying children.

King Herod ordered the murder of thousands of children under the age of two (some estimate that as many as 30,000 boys died).

We still live in a world of dying children. Today, *every day of the year,* 30,000 children under the age of five die of preventable causes.

The greatest child killers:

HUNGER

20 million children

Hunger: 20 million children under the age of 15 die each year from hunger-related diseases.[1]

DISEASE

15 million children

Disease: 15 million children die each year from preventable diseases, most because of lack of immunizations.[2]

ABUSE

1 million children

Emotional and Physical Abuse: Over one million children are forcibly involved in sex trade each year.[3]

WAR

200,000 children

War: On average, over 200,000 children are currently fighting in one of the world's wars.[4]

Sources: [1] Smith (1999:18) [2] World Vision Australia (2003:23) [3] Bellamy (2001:44) [4] Smith (1999:56)

John the Baptist Prepares the Way

3:1
o Lk 1:13,57-66;
3:2-19
3:2
p Da 2:44; Mt 4:17;
6:10; Lk 11:20;
21:31; Jn 3:3,5;
Ac 1:3,6
3:3
q Isa 40:3; Mal 3:1;
Lk 1:76; Jn 1:23

3 In those days John the Baptist⁰ came, preaching in the Desert of Judea ²and saying, "Repent, for the kingdom of heavenᵖ is near." ³This is he who was spoken of through the prophet Isaiah:

"A voice of one calling in the desert,
'Prepare the way for the Lord,
    make straight paths for him.' "ᵃq

3:4
r 2Ki 1:8
s Lev 11:22

⁴John's clothes were made of camel's hair, and he had a leather belt around his waist.ʳ His food was locustsˢ and wild honey. ⁵People went out to him from Jerusalem and all Judea and the whole region of the Jordan. ⁶Confessing their sins, they were baptized by him in the Jordan River.

3:7
t Mt 12:34; 23:33
u Ro 1:18; 1Th 1:10
3:8
v Ac 26:20

⁷But when he saw many of the Pharisees and Sadducees coming to where he was baptizing, he said to them: "You brood of vipers!ᵗ Who warned you to flee from the coming wrath?ᵘ ⁸Produce fruit in keeping with repentance.ᵛ ⁹And do not think you can say to yourselves, 'We have Abraham as our father.' I tell you that out of these stones God can raise up children for Abraham. ¹⁰The ax is already at the root of the trees, and every tree that does not produce good fruit will be cut down and thrown into the fire.ʷ

3:10
w Mt 7:19;
Lk 13:6-9;
Jn 15:2,6

3:11
x Mk 1:8 y Isa 4:4;
Ac 2:3,4
3:12
z Mt 13:30

¹¹"I baptize you withᵇ water for repentance. But after me will come one who is more powerful than I, whose sandals I am not fit to carry. He will baptize you with the Holy Spiritˣ and with fire.ʸ ¹²His winnowing fork is in his hand, and he will clear his threshing floor, gathering his wheat into the barn and burning up the chaff with unquenchable fire."ᶻ

The Baptism of Jesus

3:13
a Mk 1:4

¹³Then Jesus came from Galilee to the Jordan to be baptized by John.ᵃ ¹⁴But John tried to deter him, saying, "I need to be baptized by you, and do you come to me?"

¹⁵Jesus replied, "Let it be so now; it is proper for us to do this to fulfill all righteousness." Then John consented.

ᵃ 3 Isaiah 40:3   ᵇ 11 Or in

---

maltreatment. Persecution worldwide is on the increase. Every society has people it regards with derision as lacking in sophistication or failing to fit in with expected norms. Here we see God himself identifying with those others ridiculed. Still today, he shares their humiliation—and uses it redemptively.

Matthew 3:1–12

📖 John the Baptist appears prominently in all four Gospels. The term "kingdom of heaven" shows up 33 times in Matthew and is interchangeable with the expression "kingdom of God" in the other Gospels. It describes the radical in-breaking of God's will and way into the world. John called people to repent and turn from everything contrary to the kingdom and to embrace God's reign over every aspect of life.

Like his Old Testament prophetic predecessors, John called the political and religious leaders of Israel to special accountability—to lead as examples to the flock of Israel. If faith in God is genuine, it will be seen in the fruit of changed lives.

📖 Religious pedigree doesn't guarantee participation in the kingdom of heaven. To be born into a Christian home today is a tremendous privilege that carries an equal responsibility. By opening our hearts to God and enabling us to live fully for and before him, the Spirit produces in and through us the fruit of the kind of life

John called for. What kind and quality of fruit are God and others discerning in your life today?

Matthew 3:13-17

📖 John had prepared his listeners for a powerful figure coming with the might of the Holy Spirit and the judgment of fire (vv. 11–12). But Matthew stated simply that "Jesus came from Galilee"—a solitary figure from an insignificant agricultural region. Jesus exercised his divine might and judgment in humility, taking that judgment upon himself. Through submitting to baptism, the sinless Savior identified with sinful people in their need for cleansing and salvation.

Jesus' baptism would "fulfill all righteousness." God's prophesied saving activity was being inaugurated in Jesus' ministry, which would culminate in his death on the cross.

📖 In our day humility isn't highly esteemed. We relate much better to rights. The picture John and Jesus give every age is the incongruity of their humility in relation to the significance of their roles. We don't like to give up our appearance of importance. But Jesus exercised his power through humility, bearing our sin without sinning himself, from baptism to crucifixion. If we are to walk in his way, our self-promotion and pride must be washed from us in the waters of baptism and the power of the cross.

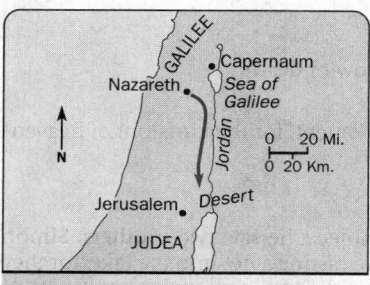

Temptation of Jesus (4:1)

Then: The Judean desert was a place for solitude and spiritual discipline. In Jesus' case this meant a literal wilderness where few living beings could survive for long.

Now: We still recognize the wilderness or desert as a place for spiritual growth. With the gradual disappearance of real wilderness areas, however, we often have to create artificial places of refuge for separation and solitude.

[16]As soon as Jesus was baptized, he went up out of the water. At that moment heaven was opened, and he saw the Spirit of God [b] descending like a dove and lighting on him. [17]And a voice from heaven [c] said, "This is my Son, [d] whom I love; with him I am well pleased." [e]

The Temptation of Jesus

4 Then Jesus was led by the Spirit into the desert to be tempted by the devil. [2]After fasting forty days and forty nights, [f] he was hungry. [3]The tempter [g] came to him and said, "If you are the Son of God, [h] tell these stones to become bread."

[4]Jesus answered, "It is written: 'Man does not live on bread alone, but on every word that comes from the mouth of God.'[a]" [i]

[5]Then the devil took him to the holy city [j] and had him stand on the highest point of the temple. [6]"If you are the Son of God," he said, "throw yourself down. For it is written:

" 'He will command his angels concerning you,
and they will lift you up in their hands,
so that you will not strike your foot against a stone.'[b]" [k]

[7]Jesus answered him, "It is also written: 'Do not put the Lord your God to the test.'[c]" [l]

[8]Again, the devil took him to a very high mountain and showed him all the kingdoms of the world and their splendor. [9]"All this I will give you," he said, "if you will bow down and worship me."

[10]Jesus said to him, "Away from me, Satan! [m] For it is written: 'Worship the Lord your God, and serve him only.'[d]" [n]

[11]Then the devil left him, and angels came and attended him. [o]

Jesus Begins to Preach

[12]When Jesus heard that John had been put in prison, [p] he returned to Galilee. [q] [13]Leaving Nazareth, he went and lived in Capernaum, [r] which was by the lake in the area of Zebulun and Naphtali— [14]to fulfill what was said through the prophet Isaiah:

[15] "Land of Zebulun and land of Naphtali,
the way to the sea, along the Jordan,
Galilee of the Gentiles—

3:16 b Isa 11:2; 42:1
3:17 c Mt 17:5; Jn 12:28 d Pe 2:7; 2Pe 1:17,18 e Isa 42:1; Mt 12:18; 17:5; Mk 1:11; 9:7; Lk 9:35
4:2 f Ex 34:28; 1Ki 19:8
4:3 g 1Th 3:5 h Mt 3:17; Jn 5:25; Ac 9:20
4:4 i Dt 8:3
4:5 j Ne 11:1; Da 9:24; Mt 27:53
4:6 k Ps 91:11,12
4:7 l Dt 6:16
4:10 m 1Ch 21:1 n Dt 6:13
4:11 o Mt 26:53; Lk 22:43; Heb 1:14
4:12 p Mt 14:3 q Mk 1:14
4:13 r Mk 1:21; Lk 4:23,31; Jn 2:12; 4:46,47

---

[a] 4 Deut. 8:3   [b] 6 Psalm 91:11,12   [c] 7 Deut. 6:16   [d] 10 Deut. 6:13

Matthew 4:1–11

The Spirit of God led Jesus into the desert to be tempted. Satan's temptations were used by God to help Jesus define what kind of Messiah he would be. How would he use his power? The devil tempted him to exercise it for material gain, religious control, and political domination. But Jesus' victorious encounter with the enemy confirmed that Christ was not only the Son of God but also the suffering Messiah, triumphing over evil through faith in God and through choosing the path of weakness.

We are often tempted to use our faith in God for material, religious, or political advantage. Reflect on your own prayer life. For what have you prayed recently? Are there ways you have sought to use God for your own gain? How do Jesus' three responses to the devil guide your own use of power and guidance from Scripture in response to your basic needs?

Matthew 4:12–17

"The way to the sea" was the trade route through the tribal territories of Zebulun (including Nazareth) and Naphtali (including Capernaum) to the Mediterranean. Ever since this region had been reduced to an Assyrian province in 732 B.C. (see 2 Kings 15:29), it had experienced turmoil and a strong Gentile influence.

4:16
s Isa 9:1,2; Lk 2:32

4:17
t Mt 3:2

4:18
u Mt 15:29;
Mk 7:31; Jn 6:1
v Mt 16:17,18
4:19
w Mk 10:21,28,52

4:21
x Mt 20:20
4:23
y Mk 1:39; Lk 4:15,
44 z Mt 9:35; 13:54;
Mk 1:21; Lk 4:15;
Jn 6:59 a Mk 1:14
b Mt 3:2; Ac 20:25
c Mt 8:16; 15:30;
Ac 10:38
4:24
d Lk 2:2
e Mt 8:16,28; 9:32;
15:22; Mk 1:32;
5:15,16,18
f Mt 17:15
g Mt 8:6; 9:2;
Mk 2:3
4:25
h Mk 3:7,8; Lk 6:17

16 the people living in darkness
   have seen a great light;
on those living in the land of the shadow of death
   a light has dawned." a s

17 From that time on Jesus began to preach, "Repent, for the kingdom of heaven t is near."

The Calling of the First Disciples

18 As Jesus was walking beside the Sea of Galilee, u he saw two brothers, Simon called Peter v and his brother Andrew. They were casting a net into the lake, for they were fishermen. 19 "Come, follow me," w Jesus said, "and I will make you fishers of men." 20 At once they left their nets and followed him.

21 Going on from there, he saw two other brothers, James son of Zebedee and his brother John. x They were in a boat with their father Zebedee, preparing their nets. Jesus called them, 22 and immediately they left the boat and their father and followed him.

Jesus Heals the Sick

23 Jesus went throughout Galilee, y teaching in their synagogues, z preaching the good news a of the kingdom, b and healing every disease and sickness among the people. c 24 News about him spread all over Syria, d and people brought to him all who were ill with various diseases, those suffering severe pain, the demon-possessed, e those having seizures, f and the paralyzed, g and he healed them. 25 Large crowds from Galilee, the Decapolis, b Jerusalem, Judea and the region across the Jordan followed him. h

a 16 Isaiah 9:1,2   b 25 That is, the Ten Cities

It was the land of outcasts, its inhabitants "the people living in darkness." Here, where the darkness was most dense, these Jews and Gentiles would be first to glimpse the great light of God's deliverance in Jesus. But Jesus' message was like John's: To enter the kingdom they first had to repent.

📖 The kingdom of God brings light to those who feel lost and life to those feeling shrouded by death. Many today perceive themselves as outcasts, sitting in darkness, surrounded by death. Can you identify some of them? What would it mean for the light and life of Christ to dawn in their lives through something *you* might do?

Matthew 4:18–22

Matthew seems to have assumed that these first disciples were already acquainted with Jesus. Still, their response was remarkable evidence of his powerful Messianic authority. Without army, sword, or the backing of the religious establishment, Jesus' authority as the kingdom inaugurator demanded unqualified obedience. He called, and these two sets of brothers immediately joined him as partners in his kingdom enterprise.

📖 Christ's followers throughout the centuries have struggled with the temptation to simply add faith in Jesus onto their agendas, rather than allowing their lives to be transformed. Jesus called simple fishermen to move their focus from fish to people. Everything changed in their lives! As Jesus' disciples, we have the privilege of carrying the gospel to those all around us who are attempting to navigate dark and dangerous waters.

Matthew 4:23–25

Matthew emphasized the impact of Jesus' comprehensive, healing ministry by stacking up a list of illnesses. The kingdom's arrival was confirmed by Jesus' power over all realms of human existence—spiritual, physical, emotional, social, and economic. Many of the individuals listed would have been social outcasts, living in economic destitution. To be healed of their illnesses meant restoration to society and livelihood. No wonder Jesus generated such a stir in Israel with his message of the kingdom's arrival. His ministry wasn't just in words, but in life and deeds—providing people with tangible signs of the kingdom.

📖 Jesus first conducted his public ministry in Galilee. Someone familiar with Israel's history might have expected the Messiah to focus on Jerusalem—the center of religious power, prestige, and prophetic hope. Galilee represented all the places not to visit in that society. But once again in Matthew we see God turning marginal places and people into the center of his kingdom. This kingdom pertains to every aspect of life, not just our souls! Today, Jesus is as fully at home in a tent city or shantytown as he is in a shopping mall, government office, or on Wall Street. What would it mean in each of these settings for the kingdom's healing power to transform lives?

The Beatitudes

5 Now when he saw the crowds, he went up on a mountainside and sat down. His disciples came to him, ²and he began to teach them, saying:

³ "Blessed are the poor in spirit,
    for theirs is the kingdom of heaven. *ⁱ*
⁴ Blessed are those who mourn,
    for they will be comforted. *ʲ*
⁵ Blessed are the meek,
    for they will inherit the earth. *ᵏ*
⁶ Blessed are those who hunger and thirst for righteousness,
    for they will be filled. *ˡ*
⁷ Blessed are the merciful,

5:3
ⁱ ver 10,19;
Mt 25:34
5:4
ʲ Isa 61:2,3;
Rev 7:17
5:5
ᵏ Ps 37:11; Ro 4:13
5:6
ˡ Isa 55:1,2

Matthew 5:1–12

In his introduction to the Sermon on the Mount, the Beatitudes, Jesus proclaimed the character of citizens in the kingdom of God. Kingdom life contradicts the values most people hold dear; God's blessing typically rests on unlikely people. The poor, hungry, mourning, and persecuted are the ones who will experience the kingdom in its fullness. These pithy statements define reality in such a way that our world's usual order of things is shown to be upside-down in God's eyes. Throughout his ministry Jesus stressed such reversals and ironies.

The characteristics of the Beatitudes aren't self-produced, nor can we simply learn or imitate them in an attempt to integrate them into our lives. They are by-products of a life energized by the Spirit. They are, like the listing Paul gave in Galatians 5:22–23, the fruit of the Spirit. How might you cooperate with the Spirit to see these marks of a disciple become more real in your life?

 5:1–12

The Beatitudes

Eight primary statements of blessing make up the Beatitudes. The ninth (5:11–12) is an extension of the eighth Beatitude, and it applies to Jesus' disciples who experience persecution. The chart below outlines the Beatitudes' messages.

Beatitude	Summary
1. "Blessed are the poor in spirit, for theirs is the kingdom of heaven."	The "poor" are those who have few resources from an economic standpoint but also those who are spiritually and emotionally in need of God's help. The kingdom belongs to those who recognize that they have no resources—material or otherwise—by which to better their position in God's eyes.
2. "Blessed are those who mourn, for they will be comforted."	The loss of anything a person counts valuable produces mourning. A disciple will mourn the things that break God's heart—sin, oppression, etc.
3. "Blessed are the meek, for they will inherit the earth."	The domineering, aggressive, harsh, and tyrannical can't experience a kingdom characterized by gentleness. Meek people who proclaim the Good News and announce the arrival of God's favor have already entered into their spiritual inheritance.
4. "Blessed are those who hunger and thirst for righteousness, for they will be filled."	People who are hungry and thirsty are in dire need; they will die if not helped. Such is the passion of a disciple. The ultimate source of righteousness is God himself. Those in relationship with him have their deepest desire for righteousness or justice satisfied.
5. "Blessed are the merciful, for they will be shown mercy."	Those who demonstrate forgiveness toward the guilty and kindness for the hurting and needy are merciful. Showing mercy is a heart attitude that opens a person to receive the offer of mercy Jesus proclaims in the gospel.
6. "Blessed are the pure in heart, for they will see God."	Purity describes a person who demonstrates single-minded loyalty to God in every area of life. Those who exemplify such undivided devotion to God will be rewarded with their greatest hope—gazing into his face.
7. "Blessed are the peacemakers, for they will be called sons of God."	Peacemakers bring the good news that "God reigns" and that he can mend every broken relationship people experience. God's children reflect his character as they carry Jesus' peacemaking mission to the world.
8. "Blessed are those who are persecuted because of righteousness, for theirs is the kingdom of heaven."	Jesus comforts those who suffer undeserved persecution because of a stand for righteousness. Such ill treatment can involve any measure designed to harm the one who is doing good. The reward here far outweighs the hazard. However, that reward is realized in heaven, not necessarily on Earth.

Source: NIV Application Commentary, Matthew (2004)

5:8
m Ps 24:3,4
n Heb 12:14;
Rev 22:4

for they will be shown mercy.
8 Blessed are the pure in heart, *m*
    for they will see God. *n*
9 Blessed are the peacemakers,
    for they will be called sons of God. *o*
10 Blessed are those who are persecuted because of righteousness, *p*
    for theirs is the kingdom of heaven.

5:9
o ver 44,45;
Ro 8:14
5:10
p 1Pe 3:14

11 "Blessed are you when people insult you, *q* persecute you and falsely say all kinds of evil against you because of me. 12 Rejoice and be glad, *r* because great is your reward in heaven, for in the same way they persecuted the prophets who were before you. *s*

5:11
q 1Pe 4:14
5:12
r Ac 5:41; 1Pe 4:13,
16 s Mt 23:31,37;
Ac 7:52; 1Th 2:15

Salt and Light

13 "You are the salt of the earth. But if the salt loses its saltiness, how can it be made salty again? It is no longer good for anything, except to be thrown out and trampled by men. *t*

14 "You are the light of the world. *u* A city on a hill cannot be hidden. 15 Neither do people light a lamp and put it under a bowl. Instead they put it on its stand, and it gives light to everyone in the house. *v* 16 In the same way, let your light shine before men, that they may see your good deeds and praise *w* your Father in heaven.

5:13
t Mk 9:50;
Lk 14:34,35
5:14
u Jn 8:12
5:15
v Mk 4:21; Lk 8:16
5:16
w Mt 9:8

The Fulfillment of the Law

17 "Do not think that I have come to abolish the Law or the Prophets; I have not come to abolish them but to fulfill them. *x* 18 I tell you the truth, until heaven and earth disappear, not the smallest letter, not the least stroke of a pen, will by any means disappear from the Law until everything is accomplished. *y* 19 Anyone who breaks one of the least of these commandments *z* and teaches others to do the same will be called least in the kingdom of heaven, but whoever practices and teaches these commands will be called great in the kingdom of heaven. 20 For I tell you that unless your righteousness surpasses that of the Pharisees and the teachers of the law, you will certainly not enter the kingdom of heaven.

5:17
x Ro 3:31

5:18
y Lk 16:17
5:19
z Jas 2:10

Murder

21 "You have heard that it was said to the people long ago, 'Do not murder, *a a* and anyone who murders will be subject to judgment.' 22 But I tell you that anyone who is angry with his brother *b* will be subject to judgment. *b* Again, anyone who says to

5:21
a Ex 20:13; Dt 5:17

5:22
b 1Jn 3:15

a 21 Exodus 20:13   b 22 Some manuscripts *brother without cause*

Matthew 5:13–16

Salt had a variety of natural qualities and everyday uses in the ancient world. The lamp used in a typical one-room home was small, giving off only modest light. For maximum benefit, it was placed on a stand. With these two metaphors, Jesus focused on his disciples. He revealed the nature of kingdom life in those who belong to him, the impact of that life on a watching world, and the responsibility of his followers to the world as they await the coming of God's kingdom in its fullness.

Much "salt" and "light" witness is accomplished in and through life's ordinariness. We might think in more dramatic terms—of activities like preaching or participating on a missions trip. But we, as Jesus' disciples, are to live our everyday lives so we can positively and *exclusively be identified as kingdom individuals*. The transformation of our daily activities will cause people to praise our Father in heaven. Ask God to help you be salt and light today. Then be on the alert for the opportunities he places in your path in answer to your prayer.

Matthew 5:17–20

Jesus made the religious establishment edgy and angry. At the center was their suspicion that he wasn't fully orthodox in his commitment to the Old Testament. Here he set the record straight. He didn't simply affirm one Jewish school of thought or offer another application of the ancient law to his own time and place. He gave the authoritative interpretation of the Old Testament's intended meaning. God's will for humanity found its realization in Jesus.

The issues surrounding the Christian's relationship to the Old Testament (law) are complex, but some principles are helpful. (1) The law reveals God's will for people. (2) It was given to point out our sinfulness and need for God and to lead us to Christ. (3) Jesus objected not to the law but to misinterpretations of it. (4) Jesus fulfilled the law and, as the perfect God-man, became the example for us to live rightly before God and one another. (5) Jesus interpreted the law, distinguishing between binding principles and temporary, symbolic rituals.

his brother, 'Raca,'[a] is answerable to the Sanhedrin.[c] But anyone who says, 'You fool!' will be in danger of the fire of hell.[d]

23 "Therefore, if you are offering your gift at the altar and there remember that your brother has something against you, 24 leave your gift there in front of the altar. First go and be reconciled to your brother; then come and offer your gift.

25 "Settle matters quickly with your adversary who is taking you to court. Do it while you are still with him on the way, or he may hand you over to the judge, and the judge may hand you over to the officer, and you may be thrown into prison. 26 I tell you the truth, you will not get out until you have paid the last penny.[b]

Adultery

27 "You have heard that it was said, 'Do not commit adultery.'[c][e] 28 But I tell you that anyone who looks at a woman lustfully has already committed adultery with her in his heart.[f] 29 If your right eye causes you to sin,[g] gouge it out and throw it away. It is better for you to lose one part of your body than for your whole body to be thrown into hell. 30 And if your right hand causes you to sin, cut it off and throw it away. It is better for you to lose one part of your body than for your whole body to go into hell.

Divorce

31 "It has been said, 'Anyone who divorces his wife must give her a certificate of divorce.'[d][h] 32 But I tell you that anyone who divorces his wife, except for marital unfaithfulness, causes her to become an adulteress, and anyone who marries the divorced woman commits adultery.[i]

5:22
c Mt 26:59 d Jas 3:6

5:27
e Ex 20:14; Dt 5:18

5:28
f Pr 6:25
5:29
g Mt 18:6,8,9;
Mk 9:42-47

5:31
h Dt 24:1-4

5:32
i Lk 16:18

a 22 An Aramaic term of contempt   b 26 Greek *kodrantes*   c 27 Exodus 20:14   d 31 Deut. 24:1

Matthew 5:21–26

Verses 21–48 are commonly called "the antitheses." Six times Jesus declared the opposite of popular viewpoints. In so doing he demonstrated how the Old Testament should be interpreted and applied and, thus, how the Law and the Prophets were to be fulfilled.

Jesus cited three ways people can "murder" someone else without committing homicide: (1) By expressing inappropriate anger that degrades a person's value. (2) By name-calling that insults an individual (*Raca* in Aramaic means "empty-headed"). (3) By name-calling that calls someone's character into question. The term "you fool" carried moral connotations (cf. Prov. 10:23). In this "antithesis" Jesus revealed the law's intent: to guide us in the attitudes and behaviors that nurture life-giving relationships.

A principle we teach our little ones early is that words can wound. The important feature of the first "antithesis" is its emphasis on the dignity of every human being created in God's image. Not only are we not to take the physical life of another, we are not to do anything that demeans his or her dignity. We can't truly worship with the knowledge that we have treated another wrongly.

Matthew 5:27–30

Adultery is serious, both because it fractures the union between a man and a woman, which reflects the image of God, and because it violates a covenant of faithfulness that reflects God's character. Jesus' reaffirmation of the Old Testament commitment to the unity of the marriage bond took it to its deepest intended meaning. Life in the kingdom of heaven produces disciples who live out human relations, including marriage, in the way God designed them.

It's one thing for a spouse never to have committed adultery, but quite another for him or her to have faithfully avoided violating the marriage by flirting, dabbling in pornography, or even looking at someone else with lustful appreciation. For marriage partners to give themselves solely to their mates is to treat them with the dignity they deserve as persons created in God's image. Jesus calls us to be severely honest with ourselves in this area, to commit ourselves to our husbands and wives with single-minded devotion.

Matthew 5:31–32

God sees marriage as permanent, but sometimes the union is violated so severely as to be irreversibly shattered. The Greek word translated here as "marital unfaithfulness" is less specific than adultery but means more than something frivolous. It includes any sinful activity that intentionally divides the relationship. Jesus affirmed the sacredness of marriage but allowed divorce to protect the non-offending partner and the marriage relationship from being reduced to a vulgar sham.

The point of the third "antithesis" (see "There and Then" for vv. 21–26) is for us to treat the marriage covenant so sacredly that it's never broken except when the most extreme conditions make it impossible to remain married. A man and woman entering marriage commit themselves to each other as one indivisible unit. To stay firmly committed—in actions, words, thoughts, emotions, and priorities—is to experience the fullness of relationship God designed for spouses.

Oaths

5:33
i Lev 19:12
k Nu 30:2;
Dt 23:21;
Mt 23:16-22
5:34
l Jas 5:12
m Isa 66:1;
Mt 23:22
5:35
n Ps 48:2
5:37
o Jas 5:12
p Mt 6:13; 13:19,
38; Jn 17:15;
2Th 3:3;
1Jn 2:13,14; 3:12;
5:18,19
5:38
q Ex 21:24;
Lev 24:20; Dt 19:21
5:39
r Lk 6:29; Ro 12:17,
19; 1Co 6:7;
1Pe 3:9
5:42
s Dt 15:8; Lk 6:30
5:43
t Lev 19:18
u Dt 23:6
5:44
v Lk 6:27,28; 23:34;
Ac 7:60; Ro 12:14;
1Co 4:12; 1Pe 2:23
5:45
w ver 9 x Job 25:3
5:46
y Lk 6:32
5:48
z Lev 19:2;
1Pe 1:16

33 "Again, you have heard that it was said to the people long ago, 'Do not break your oath,[i] but keep the oaths you have made to the Lord.'[k] 34 But I tell you, Do not swear at all:[l] either by heaven, for it is God's throne;[m] 35 or by the earth, for it is his footstool; or by Jerusalem, for it is the city of the Great King.[n] 36 And do not swear by your head, for you cannot make even one hair white or black. 37 Simply let your 'Yes' be 'Yes,' and your 'No,' 'No';[o] anything beyond this comes from the evil one.[p]

An Eye for an Eye

38 "You have heard that it was said, 'Eye for eye, and tooth for tooth.'[a][q] 39 But I tell you, Do not resist an evil person. If someone strikes you on the right cheek, turn to him the other also.[r] 40 And if someone wants to sue you and take your tunic, let him have your cloak as well. 41 If someone forces you to go one mile, go with him two miles. 42 Give to the one who asks you, and do not turn away from the one who wants to borrow from you.[s]

Love for Enemies

43 "You have heard that it was said, 'Love your neighbor[b][t] and hate your enemy.'[u] 44 But I tell you: Love your enemies[c] and pray for those who persecute you,[v] 45 that you may be sons[w] of your Father in heaven. He causes his sun to rise on the evil and the good, and sends rain on the righteous and the unrighteous.[x] 46 If you love those who love you, what reward will you get?[y] Are not even the tax collectors doing that? 47 And if you greet only your brothers, what are you doing more than others? Do not even pagans do that? 48 Be perfect, therefore, as your heavenly Father is perfect.[z]

---

[a] 38 Exodus 21:24; Lev. 24:20; Deut. 19:21   [b] 43 Lev. 19:18   [c] 44 Some late manuscripts enemies, bless those who curse you, do good to those who hate you

---

Matthew 5:33–37

Jesus went to the heart of the law's intent regarding oaths when he called on his disciples not to swear "at all." He was talking about using God's name, or substitutes for it, to guarantee the truth of a statement. His followers are to be people of such integrity of character and truthfulness of heart that whatever they say is absolutely believable and dependable—without the backing of an oath.

Jesus didn't say all oaths are wrong. He himself testified under oath at his trial (26:63–64). In court a person operates under the jurisdiction of governing authorities who are carrying out human law. This "antithesis" (see "There and Then" for vv. 21–26) is another test of the heart. A dependable heart speaks dependable words. And when we are being honest, we are liberated to trust each other.

Matthew 5:38–42

In the fifth "antithesis" (see "There and Then" for vv. 21–26), Jesus used four illustrations from his disciples' everyday lives to emphasize how they could serve even those who took advantage of them. The first scene was about insult—striking a cheek was more an insult than it was an act of violence. The second shifted to a legal setting—bringing a lawsuit. The third was a military scene—conscripting a civilian to serve the needs of a soldier. The last dealt with people who begged or freeloaded. Jesus widened the law's obligation (cf. Deut. 15:7–11) with powerful images of generosity.

Jesus lived what he proclaimed, becoming our supreme example (cf. 1 Peter 2:20–25). Our obligation as disciples isn't to retaliate for evil or to protect ourselves and our interests (cf. Rom. 12:17–21). Our role is to serve, both those we think deserve it and those we assume don't! This principle causes discomfort for those of us in cultures concerned with individual rights. We don't have to let people walk all over us (cf. Acts 22:22–29; 2 Thess. 3:10–12). But a disciple's ultimate goal is servanthood—thinking about others ahead of oneself.

Matthew 5:43–48

Jesus called his disciples to move beyond arbitrary boundary markers (family, friends, etc.) to love all persons, even adversaries and rivals. This is the character of God, and it would cause others to see in them God's "family resemblance." This sixth "antithesis" (see "There and Then" for vv. 21–26) took Jesus' disciples to the pinnacle of understanding God's purpose for their lives—to express the very character of God ("be perfect"). His followers would demonstrate, as kingdom subjects, lives of a totally different quality, characterized by a righteousness that would surpass that of their religious leaders (cf. v. 20).

As his disciples, we are empowered to love people as Jesus does—enough to reach out to them with his message of reconciliation. Love may be defined as an unconditional commitment to an imperfect person, in which we give ourselves to seek the best for the other and to bring the relationship to God's intended purpose.

Giving to the Needy

6 "Be careful not to do your 'acts of righteousness' before men, to be seen by them. [a] If you do, you will have no reward from your Father in heaven.

2 "So when you give to the needy, do not announce it with trumpets, as the hypocrites do in the synagogues and on the streets, to be honored by men. I tell you the truth, they have received their reward in full. 3 But when you give to the needy, do not let your left hand know what your right hand is doing, 4 so that your giving may be in secret. Then your Father, who sees what is done in secret, will reward you. [b]

Prayer

5 "And when you pray, do not be like the hypocrites, for they love to pray standing [c] in the synagogues and on the street corners to be seen by men. I tell you the truth, they have received their reward in full. 6 But when you pray, go into your room, close the door and pray to your Father, [d] who is unseen. Then your Father, who sees what is done in secret, will reward you. 7 And when you pray, do not keep on babbling [e] like pagans, for they think they will be heard because of their many words. [f] 8 Do not be like them, for your Father knows what you need [g] before you ask him.

9 "This, then, is how you should pray:

" 'Our Father in heaven,
hallowed be your name,
10 your kingdom [h] come,
your will be done [i]
on earth as it is in heaven.
11 Give us today our daily bread. [j]
12 Forgive us our debts,
as we also have forgiven our debtors. [k]
13 And lead us not into temptation, [l]
but deliver us from the evil one. [a'] [m]

14 For if you forgive men when they sin against you, your heavenly Father will also

a 13 Or *from evil*; some late manuscripts *one*, / *for yours is the kingdom and the power and the glory forever. Amen.*

Reference column

6:1
a Mt 23:5

6:4
b ver 6,18;
Col 3:23,24

6:5
c Mk 11:25;
Lk 18:10-14
6:6
d 2Ki 4:33

6:7
e Ecc 5:2
f 1Ki 18:26-29
6:8
g ver 32

6:10
h Mt 3:2 i Mt 26:39

6:11
j Pr 30:8

6:12
k Mt 18:21-35
6:13
l Jas 1:13
m Mt 5:37

Matthew 6:1–4

In 6:1—7:12 Jesus taught his disciples how kingdom righteousness works itself out in three primary areas of everyday life: *public* religious life (6:1–18), *personal*, interior life (6:19–34), and *interpersonal* relationships (7:1–12).

Poverty was widespread in ancient agricultural societies, as it is today, and the people of Israel took seriously the obligation to provide for the poor (cf. Deut. 15:11). Jesus seemed to assume his disciples would practice generosity. "To do mercy" had become an expression for caring for the poor by giving alms. But Jesus cautioned, "Do not announce it with trumpets" (in today's terms, "Don't toot your own horn"). Jesus may have been expressing concern about protecting both the dignity of the recipients of the help and the hearts of those who gave.

Jesus had urged his disciples to "let your light shine before men, that they may see your good deeds and praise your Father in heaven" (5:16). This may seem to contradict 6:1, but the crux of the issue was the disciples' motive for doing good in public. In the former case, Jesus knew they might be afraid of persecution (5:10), so he called them to think of God's glory as their motive. Here, he warned against religious vanity. Over a century ago

A.B. Bruce offered us a formula that still works: "Show when tempted to *hide*, hide when tempted to *show*."

Matthew 6:5–15

Pious Jews prayed publicly at set times—usually morning, afternoon, and evening (cf. Ps. 55:17; Dan. 6:10; Acts 3:1). Jesus focused on the intimacy of communion with God in a person's heart, which is central to all prayer. He didn't condemn public prayer and prayed in public himself (Matt. 14:19; 15:36). In fact, he instructed his disciples to address God as "*our* Father" (emphasis added), implying a community or family approach. But when praying publicly, as in giving alms (6:1–4), disciples were and are to guard their motivation.

Jesus' model prayer isn't a formula or rote words to be rattled off mindlessly. Yet its elements (vv. 9–13) encompass all primary aspects of prayer. A central reality is that in prayer we bring the depth of our needs to the depth of our trustworthy God. Jesus centered his prayer in his disciples' longing for God's kingdom to come fully on Earth. What would this mean for someone trapped in poverty, a child soldier, or an adolescent prostitute? Jesus developed this theme further in his so-called "high priestly prayer" (John 17), as did Paul in his prayers for the churches (e.g., Eph. 3:14–21).

6:14
n Mt 18:21-35;
Mk 11:25,26;
Eph 4:32; Col 3:13
6:15
o Mt 18:35
6:16
p Isa 58:5
6:18
q ver 4,6
6:19
r Pr 23:4; Heb 13:5
s Jas 5:2,3
6:20
t Mt 19:21;
Lk 12:33; 18:22;
1Ti 6:19 u Lk 12:33
6:21
v Lk 12:34
6:24
w Lk 16:13
6:25
x ver 27,28,31,34;
Lk 10:41; 12:11,22;
Php 4:6; 1Pe 5:7
6:26
y Job 38:41;
Ps 147:9
z Mt 10:29-31
6:27
a Ps 39:5

forgive you. n 15 But if you do not forgive men their sins, your Father will not forgive your sins. o

Fasting

16 "When you fast, do not look somber p as the hypocrites do, for they disfigure their faces to show men they are fasting. I tell you the truth, they have received their reward in full. 17 But when you fast, put oil on your head and wash your face, 18 so that it will not be obvious to men that you are fasting, but only to your Father, who is unseen; and your Father, who sees what is done in secret, will reward you. q

Treasures in Heaven

19 "Do not store up for yourselves treasures on earth, r where moth and rust destroy, s and where thieves break in and steal. 20 But store up for yourselves treasures in heaven, t where moth and rust do not destroy, and where thieves do not break in and steal. u 21 For where your treasure is, there your heart will be also. v

22 "The eye is the lamp of the body. If your eyes are good, your whole body will be full of light. 23 But if your eyes are bad, your whole body will be full of darkness. If then the light within you is darkness, how great is that darkness!

24 "No one can serve two masters. Either he will hate the one and love the other, or he will be devoted to the one and despise the other. You cannot serve both God and Money. w

Do Not Worry

25 "Therefore I tell you, do not worry x about your life, what you will eat or drink; or about your body, what you will wear. Is not life more important than food, and the body more important than clothes? 26 Look at the birds of the air; they do not sow or reap or store away in barns, and yet your heavenly Father feeds them. y Are you not much more valuable than they? z 27 Who of you by worrying can add a single hour to his life a? a

a 27 Or single cubit to his height

Matthew 6:16–18

As was the case with their giving to the poor, Jesus assumed his followers would fast. "Disfigure" here refers to disguising one's face to publicize physical hardships endured while fasting. During the fasting period religious individuals of Jesus' day might somehow have marked their faces, remained ungroomed, or sprinkled ashes on their heads and faces. This was a deceptive way of letting others see and appreciate their extensive efforts to increase their godliness.

When we fast in the right spirit, we allow God to disclose to us those habits and attitudes that hold us back, so that we might "run swiftly" and "adhere closely" to God's grace. The ideal goes beyond mere penance or self-punishment. Fasting provides us opportunity to focus on our deepest hungers—"blessed are those who hunger and thirst for righteousness" (5:6). Like giving to the needy and praying (vv. 1–15), fasting is a private matter between us and God. Jesus didn't prohibit corporate (group) fasting—a custom later mentioned in the book of Acts (13:1–3; 14:23). But even the fasts of a believing community are to be conducted in the privacy of the heart, with no church (or member) boasting about the practice.

Matthew 6:19–24

The "upside-down" character qualities of the "blessed" in God's kingdom have from Jesus' time resulted in upside-down approaches to material goods and

wealth. God created people for more than the acquisition and accumulation of things. The treasure of his kingdom is and has from the start been so great and so permanent that a life goal of pursuing lesser treasures is foolish and pointless.

In themselves, there is nothing wrong with the material blessings God provides. In fact, we have seen how Jesus encourages us to help others gain access to them. Wealth and possessions have at least three positive purposes in Scripture: They allow us (1) to provide for our families (1 Tim. 5:8); (2) to help those in need, especially other Christians (Gal. 6:9–10); and (3) to encourage and support God's work in spreading the gospel of the kingdom both at home and around the world (1 Cor. 9:7–14). If we put Jesus at the center of our lives, we can appropriately use all the blessings of life, while avoiding the modern idol of materialism.

Matthew 6:25–34

After hearing Jesus' words in the previous passage, listeners may have worried, *If I choose God as my Master and trust him as my source of security, who will take care of my earthly needs?* Jesus was talking to people consumed by life's daily struggles. Like many in our world today, much of their routine was spent trying to eke out a hand-to-mouth existence. But the kind of anxiety Jesus was referring to is based on a lack of trust in God and on misguided goals. Rich and poor alike are called to focus

28 "And why do you worry about clothes? See how the lilies of the field grow. They do not labor or spin. 29 Yet I tell you that not even Solomon in all his splendor *b* was dressed like one of these. 30 If that is how God clothes the grass of the field, which is here today and tomorrow is thrown into the fire, will he not much more clothe you, O you of little faith? *c* 31 So do not worry, saying, 'What shall we eat?' or 'What shall we drink?' or 'What shall we wear?' 32 For the pagans run after all these things, and your heavenly Father knows that you need them. *d* 33 But seek first his kingdom and his righteousness, and all these things will be given to you as well. *e* 34 Therefore do not worry about tomorrow, for tomorrow will worry about itself. Each day has enough trouble of its own.

Judging Others

7 "Do not judge, or you too will be judged. *f* 2 For in the same way you judge others, you will be judged, and with the measure you use, it will be measured to you. *g*

3 "Why do you look at the speck of sawdust in your brother's eye and pay no attention to the plank in your own eye? 4 How can you say to your brother, 'Let me take the speck out of your eye,' when all the time there is a plank in your own eye? 5 You hypocrite, first take the plank out of your own eye, and then you will see clearly to remove the speck from your brother's eye.

6 "Do not give dogs what is sacred; do not throw your pearls to pigs. If you do, they may trample them under their feet, and then turn and tear you to pieces.

Ask, Seek, Knock

7 "Ask and it will be given to you; *h* seek and you will find; knock and the door will be opened to you. 8 For everyone who asks receives; he who seeks finds; *i* and to him who knocks, the door will be opened.

9 "Which of you, if his son asks for bread, will give him a stone? 10 Or if he asks for a fish, will give him a snake? 11 If you, then, though you are evil, know how to give good gifts to your children, how much more will your Father in heaven give

6:29
b 1Ki 10:4-7

6:30
c Mt 8:26; 14:31; 16:8
6:32
d ver 8
6:33
e Mt 19:29; Mk 10:29-30

7:1
f Lk 6:37; Ro 14:4,10,13; 1Co 4:5; Jas 4:11,12
7:2
g Mk 4:24; Lk 6:38

7:7
h Mt 21:22; Mk 11:24; Jn 14:13,14; 15:7,16; 16:23,24; Jas 1:5-8; 4:2,3; 1Jn 3:22; 5:14,15
7:8
i Pr 8:17; Jer 29:12,13

---

on the most important issue of life—seeking God's kingdom, with its righteousness and justice.

📖 Have you ever thought of *worry* as an idol? It occurs when we take our eyes off Jesus—substituting fear for faith, pursuing the wrong goals, and depending on our own efforts to control our environment and circumstances. Jesus' examples from the natural world show that his disciples are to operate on unique values. When we pursue God's kingdom and righteousness in our daily priorities and activities, we will experience a new quality of freedom and discover that our most important needs are met by our faithful heavenly Father. How does seeking the righteousness and justice of God's coming kingdom as your life goal impact your attitudes and ambitions—whether you are rich or poor?

Matthew 7:1–6

📖 Jesus had spent considerable time indicting the religious leaders for their hypocrisy (6:1–18). Now he turned and confronted any tendency among his followers toward self-righteousness and a critical spirit. Disciples do have a responsibility to help each other remove the "specks" of sin from their lives (cf. 18:15–20), but note that Jesus focused on *response* to fellow disciples. To be effective, such "help" only helps if it comes from a humble and self-examined life that has already removed its personal "plank" of self-righteous judgment.

📖 Twice this passage requires us to balance seemingly opposite truths. We are not to judge, yet we are to be wisely discerning. Second, we are not to give the holy to "dogs," but we are to lovingly proclaim the gospel, even to our enemies (5:44–45). We are to be utterly realistic about others, recognizing their inadequacies but still reflecting on God's utter love for them. Jesus' followers, now as then, are to be known for their discerning love, not their self-righteous judgments.

Matthew 7:7–12

📖 Jesus' teaching on prayer and the so-called "Golden Rule" (v. 12) describes the two dimensions of discipleship—how we relate both to God and others. God can be trusted completely, and people are to be loved freely. This section of the Sermon on the Mount is for good reason one of the best known, for it summarizes the distinctive nature of Jesus' teaching.

📖 Total confidence in prayer and total commitment to care for others are unique and defining marks of Jesus' disciples. Many people believe they must manipulate and maneuver around God to get what they want. Jesus said simply to ask and trust. God will provide what we need because he's good. Many religions promote the inverse of the "Golden Rule"—don't do to others what you don't want them to do to you. Though this principle isn't bad in and of itself, Jesus went much further: We are to take the initiative in providing for others what we ourselves would like to have.

7:12
j Lk 6:31
k Ro 13:8-10;
Gal 5:14
good gifts to those who ask him! ¹²So in everything, do to others what you would have them do to you,*j* for this sums up the Law and the Prophets.*k*

The Narrow and Wide Gates

7:13
l Lk 13:24
¹³"Enter through the narrow gate.*l* For wide is the gate and broad is the road that leads to destruction, and many enter through it. ¹⁴But small is the gate and narrow the road that leads to life, and only a few find it.

A Tree and Its Fruit

7:15
m Jer 23:16;
Mt 24:24;
Mk 13:22; Lk 6:26;
2Pe 2:1; 1Jn 4:1;
Rev 16:13
n Ac 20:29
7:16
o Mt 12:33; Lk 6:44
p Jas 3:12
7:19
q Mt 3:10
7:21
r Hos 8:2; Mt 25:11
s Ro 2:13; Jas 1:22
¹⁵"Watch out for false prophets.*m* They come to you in sheep's clothing, but inwardly they are ferocious wolves.*n* ¹⁶By their fruit you will recognize them.*o* Do people pick grapes from thornbushes, or figs from thistles?*p* ¹⁷Likewise every good tree bears good fruit, but a bad tree bears bad fruit. ¹⁸A good tree cannot bear bad fruit, and a bad tree cannot bear good fruit. ¹⁹Every tree that does not bear good fruit is cut down and thrown into the fire.*q* ²⁰Thus, by their fruit you will recognize them.

²¹"Not everyone who says to me, 'Lord, Lord,'*r* will enter the kingdom of heaven, but only he who does the will of my Father who is in heaven.*s* ²²Many will say to

7:22
t Mt 10:15
u 1Co 13:1-3
7:23
v Ps 6:8;
Mt 25:12,41;
Lk 13:25-27
me on that day,*t* 'Lord, Lord, did we not prophesy in your name, and in your name drive out demons and perform many miracles?'*u* ²³Then I will tell them plainly, 'I never knew you. Away from me, you evildoers!'*v*

The Wise and Foolish Builders

7:24
w Jas 1:22-25
²⁴"Therefore everyone who hears these words of mine and puts them into practice*w* is like a wise man who built his house on the rock. ²⁵The rain came down, the streams rose, and the winds blew and beat against that house; yet it did not fall, because it had its foundation on the rock. ²⁶But everyone who hears these words of mine and does not put them into practice is like a foolish man who built his

Matthew 7:13–14

📖 The image of two paths was common in Judaism. Sometimes the analogy was of separate roads leading in opposite directions—to paradise or hell. At other times a narrow path of life's hardships was pictured as ultimately leading to a broad path of eternal blessing. In Jesus' use of this imagery the broad gate and road were inviting—offering excellent conditions for those following the cultural norms of the religious leaders. But the security and comfort of going with the flow was (and still is) deceiving, in this case ending in "destruction" (cf. 2 Peter 3:7; Rev. 17:8).

📖 Jesus' invitation isn't to the path of popularity. We can't discover God's will by appealing to the majority, because our ways aren't necessarily God's (cf. Isa. 55:8–9). "Everybody does it" is seldom a helpful guideline for the Christian. Jesus calls us to courageously commit to him as the entrance to the road of life in the kingdom of heaven. Should we choose to accept his invitation, we will meet there the community of disciples with whom we share a common appreciation for kingdom values and fellowship.

Matthew 7:15–23

📖 What a person says and does reveals who he or she is (James 3:9–12). A vine or tree will produce fruit consistent with its nature—good to good, bad to bad. *Jesus admonished his disciples to be "fruit inspectors"* of those passing themselves off as prophets.

Jesus never emphasized externals as signs of genuineness. He demanded inward allegiance to God's will, which produces the good fruit of a changed life. In accomplishing his goals, God may use a person who professes Jesus' name but whose stand isn't genuine. The ultimate revelation of the authenticity of a person's life and testimony will come at the time of judgment.

📖 As Jesus concludes his Sermon on the Mount, all humanity stands before him. He asks each person: "What will *you* do with me? Will you come to me and allow your inner attitudes and outer behavior to be absolutely transformed? Or will you continue trying to add faith in God onto your life and asking God to bless your own ambitions and pursuits?" Life in God's kingdom changes our priorities in work and play, relationships and commitments, stewardship and service. The consequence of rejecting kingdom citizenship is severe: rejection by Jesus on the last day.

Matthew 7:24–29

📖 The Sea of Galilee served as a natural setting for this closing parable. The sand ringing the lake was rock hard during the hot summer. But a wise builder would dig down, as far as ten feet below the surface sand to the bedrock, knowing this was the only way to erect a foundation able to withstand winter flooding. Jesus' audience would readily have understood the parable's surface meaning. But were they willing to reject the secure yet shallow, shifting sands of their religious leadership? Would they abandon their pursuit of temporarily comfortable circumstances, choosing instead Jesus' words and way as the underpinning of their lives?

house on sand. ²⁷The rain came down, the streams rose, and the winds blew and beat against that house, and it fell with a great crash."

²⁸When Jesus had finished saying these things, ˣ the crowds were amazed at his teaching, ʸ ²⁹because he taught as one who had authority, and not as their teachers of the law.

The Man With Leprosy

8 When he came down from the mountainside, large crowds followed him. ²A man with leprosy ᵃᶻ came and knelt before him ᵃ and said, "Lord, if you are willing, you can make me clean."

³Jesus reached out his hand and touched the man. "I am willing," he said. "Be clean!" Immediately he was cured ᵇ of his leprosy. ⁴Then Jesus said to him, "See that you don't tell anyone. ᵇ But go, show yourself to the priest and offer the gift Moses commanded, ᶜ as a testimony to them."

The Faith of the Centurion

⁵When Jesus had entered Capernaum, a centurion came to him, asking for help. ⁶"Lord," he said, "my servant lies at home paralyzed and in terrible suffering."

⁷Jesus said to him, "I will go and heal him."

⁸The centurion replied, "Lord, I do not deserve to have you come under my roof. But just say the word, and my servant will be healed. ᵈ ⁹For I myself am a man under authority, with soldiers under me. I tell this one, 'Go,' and he goes; and that one, 'Come,' and he comes. I say to my servant, 'Do this,' and he does it."

¹⁰When Jesus heard this, he was astonished and said to those following him, "I tell you the truth, I have not found anyone in Israel with such great faith. ᵉ ¹¹I say to you that many will come from the east and the west, ᶠ and will take their places at the feast with Abraham, Isaac and Jacob in the kingdom of heaven. ᵍ ¹²But the subjects of the kingdom ʰ will be thrown outside, into the darkness, where there will be weeping and gnashing of teeth." ⁱ

ᵃ 2 The Greek word was used for various diseases affecting the skin—not necessarily leprosy.
ᵇ 3 Greek made clean

Cross references

7:28
ˣ Mt 11:1; 13:53; 19:1; 26:1
ʸ Mt 13:54; Mk 1:22; 6:2; Lk 4:32; Jn 7:46

8:2
ᶻ Lk 5:12 ᵃ Mt 9:18; 15:25; 18:26; 20:20

8:4
ᵇ Mt 9:30; Mk 5:43; 7:36; 8:30
ᶜ Lev 14:2-32

8:8
ᵈ Ps 107:20

8:10
ᵉ Mt 15:28
8:11
ᶠ Ps 107:3; Isa 49:12; 59:19; Mal 1:11 ᵍ Lk 13:29
8:12
ʰ Mt 13:38
ⁱ Mt 13:42,50; 22:13; 24:51; 25:30; Lk 13:28

📖 James Montgomery Boice cited two mistakes people can make with respect to the choice Jesus presented in this parable. One is to claim they need no foundation. The other is to insist that any foundation will do. We see the former attitude in modern skepticism about absolute truth, and the second in the pursuit of the "easy way," "quick fixes," immediate pleasure. The solid rock that already has provided stability, security, and hope for two millennia is Jesus—and him alone. Building our lives on him is the only firm foundation.

Matthew 8:1–4

📖 Our picture of leprosy brings to mind the dreaded and debilitating Hansen's disease, but other skin conditions may have been regarded as leprosy. The Old Testament provided specific guidelines for the examination and treatment of skin diseases (see Lev. 13–14), which were in general considered highly contagious. In reaching out to touch the leper Jesus reversed Old Testament purity laws. Instead of becoming unclean himself, he cleansed the man with his healing hand and spiritual purity.

📖 Jesus has the authority to break down all social boundaries that create spiritual barriers, freeing society's "lepers" to approach him. His first action following his great sermon was to do the socially unimaginable—touch a leper. His simple but moving "I am willing" says it all regarding God's response to everyone who feels unclean and unacceptable.

Matthew 8:5–13

📖 Not only is this an astonishing account of Jesus healing a person from a distance, it's also a staggering reversal of ethnic and religious expectations. Already at this early stage of Jesus' ministry, not just any Gentile was healed, but the servant of one of the Jews' military oppressors! Furthermore, Jesus revealed the promise of Gentiles being included in the kingdom of heaven, and Jews were warned of exclusion from God's redemption program if they didn't repent. These factors must have shocked Jesus' audience, as well as starkly reminded Matthew's readers of the true nature of discipleship.

📖 Jesus has authority to break down ethnic barriers. So the centurion came, acknowledging "Lord, I am not worthy" but immediately moving to "Just say the word, and my servant will be healed." "Lord, I'm unworthy" is our lead-in statement as we approach Christ for salvation and deliverance. But from this humble stance we may confidently claim all God's promises, available to us through Christ's atoning death (Heb. 4:16). They are for people from every nation, even those others might regard as oppressors.

13Then Jesus said to the centurion, "Go! It will be done just as you believed it would."*j* And his servant was healed at that very hour.

8:13
j Mt 9:22

Jesus Heals Many

14When Jesus came into Peter's house, he saw Peter's mother-in-law lying in bed with a fever. 15He touched her hand and the fever left her, and she got up and began to wait on him.

16When evening came, many who were demon-possessed were brought to him, and he drove out the spirits with a word and healed all the sick.*k* 17This was to fulfill*l* what was spoken through the prophet Isaiah:

8:16
k Mt 4:23,24
8:17
l Mt 1:22 *m* Isa 53:4

> "He took up our infirmities
> and carried our diseases."*a m*

The Cost of Following Jesus

18When Jesus saw the crowd around him, he gave orders to cross to the other side of the lake.*n* 19Then a teacher of the law came to him and said, "Teacher, I will follow you wherever you go."

20Jesus replied, "Foxes have holes and birds of the air have nests, but the Son of Man*o* has no place to lay his head."

21Another disciple said to him, "Lord, first let me go and bury my father."
22But Jesus told him, "Follow me,*p* and let the dead bury their own dead."

8:18
n Mk 4:35

8:20
o Da 7:13;
Mt 12:8,32,40;
16:13,27,28; 17:9;
19:28; Mk 2:10;
8:31
8:22
p Mt 4:19

Jesus Calms the Storm

23Then he got into the boat and his disciples followed him. 24Without warning, a furious storm came up on the lake, so that the waves swept over the boat. But Jesus was sleeping. 25The disciples went and woke him, saying, "Lord, save us! We're going to drown!"

a 17 Isaiah 53:4

Matthew 8:14–17

Jesus had already crossed purity and ethnic boundaries (vv. 1–13). Now in the third healing miracle in this section he breached a gender boundary to heal another person marginalized in Jewish society—a woman, Peter's mother-in-law. Her response indicated instantaneous gratitude.

Matthew once again emphasized that Jesus' life and ministry are the fulfillment of the Old Testament, specifying that his healing ministry fulfilled a prophecy from one of Isaiah's servant songs (Isa. 53:5). All sickness and death are rooted in the entrance of sin into human existence. Now Jesus' inauguration of the kingdom of heaven began to reverse the cycle of suffering and death—beginning with society's marginalized and outcast.

In the Messiah's presence, social and ethnic barriers are breached and suffering and disease disappear. The kingdom of heaven doesn't just assure us of a new future; its coming renovates our lives in the present. Do we live with the realization that Jesus offers us and our societies spiritual, as well as social and physical, transformation? The unassuming but grateful response of Peter's mother-in-law was strikingly understated; yet the message is powerful.

Matthew 8:18–22

In these two accounts Jesus cautioned his hearers against making bold promises to follow him without fully meaning it. It was common in Jesus' day for a rabbi's disciples to live with and follow their teacher. Rather

than accepting vague assertions, Jesus described the unrestricted nature of "wherever." And instead of inviting people to follow him at some future time, Jesus graphically described the implications of "now."

In light of the extreme obligation of caring for the dead, Jesus' response to the second man would have been shocking. This prospective disciple may actually have wanted to postpone his commitment for the foreseeable future. Jesus was saying that the spiritually dead could bury the physically dead—while the spiritually alive served in God's kingdom.

Not all who encounter Jesus' authority respond with trust and allegiance to his person and mission. Some come with mixed motives and find discipleship a threat to their comfortable lifestyles. Others come with dual loyalties and find that commitment to Jesus threatens their social and cultural acceptability. Jesus deserves our awe and reverence, but he also demands that we follow him wherever and whenever he calls, regardless of the cost or of a possible threat to our reputation or to the status quo.

Matthew 8:23–27

Crossing the Sea of Galilee after dark was common for fishermen, who used trammel nets throughout the night. The lake's low-lying setting results in sudden, violent storms that produce waves seven feet or higher. This must have been a powerful storm for these seasoned boaters to be afraid. Their terrified reaction was in itself remarkable. But Jesus' calming of the raging

26He replied, "You of little faith,*q* why are you so afraid?" Then he got up and rebuked the winds and the waves, and it was completely calm.*r*

27The men were amazed and asked, "What kind of man is this? Even the winds and the waves obey him!"

The Healing of Two Demon-possessed Men

28When he arrived at the other side in the region of the Gadarenes,*a* two demon-possessed*s* men coming from the tombs met him. They were so violent that no one could pass that way. 29"What do you want with us,*t* Son of God?" they shouted. "Have you come here to torture us before the appointed time?"*u*

30Some distance from them a large herd of pigs was feeding. 31The demons begged Jesus, "If you drive us out, send us into the herd of pigs."

32He said to them, "Go!" So they came out and went into the pigs, and the whole herd rushed down the steep bank into the lake and died in the water. 33Those tending the pigs ran off, went into the town and reported all this, including what had happened to the demon-possessed men. 34Then the whole town went out to meet Jesus. And when they saw him, they pleaded with him to leave their region.*v*

Jesus Heals a Paralytic

9 Jesus stepped into a boat, crossed over and came to his own town.*w* 2Some men brought to him a paralytic,*x* lying on a mat. When Jesus saw their faith,*y* he said to the paralytic, "Take heart,*z* son; your sins are forgiven."*a*

3At this, some of the teachers of the law said to themselves, "This fellow is blaspheming!"*b*

4Knowing their thoughts,*c* Jesus said, "Why do you entertain evil thoughts in your hearts? 5Which is easier: to say, 'Your sins are forgiven,' or to say, 'Get up and walk'? 6But so that you may know that the Son of Man*d* has authority on earth to forgive sins . . . ." Then he said to the paralytic, "Get up, take your mat and go home." 7And the man got up and went home. 8When the crowd saw this, they were filled with awe; and they praised God,*e* who had given such authority to men.

---

a 28 Some manuscripts *Gergesenes*; others *Gerasenes*

8:26
q Mt 6:30 *r* Ps 65:7; 89:9; 107:29

8:28
s Mt 4:24

8:29
t Jdg 11:12; 2Sa 16:10; 1Ki 17:18; Mk 1:24; Lk 4:34; Jn 2:4 *u* 2Pe 2:4

8:34
v Lk 5:8; Ac 16:39

9:1
w Mt 4:13

9:2
x Mt 4:24 *y* ver 22 *z* Jn 16:33 *a* Lk 7:48

9:3
b Mt 26:65; Jn 10:33

9:4
c Ps 94:11; Mt 12:25; Lk 6:8; 9:47; 11:17

9:6
d Mt 8:20

9:8
e Mt 5:16; 15:31; Lk 7:16; 13:13; 17:15; 23:47; Jn 15:8; Ac 4:21; 11:18; 21:20

---

storm demonstrated to their astonishment that he had authority not just over diseases and social customs—but over nature itself.

📖 As a human being Jesus was likely tired after an exhausting day, but with divine power he quieted the storm by a mere word of command. Jesus challenges all of us to look clearly at him as the fully divine and fully human Messiah, to allow him to amaze us and move us to follow him as his true disciples. Like our predecessors in the boat, we do well, despite our assumed self-sufficiency, to trust him in every circumstance.

Matthew 8:28–34

🕮 Having demonstrated Jesus' authority over disease, ethnic barriers, gender and social customs, and nature itself, Matthew now disclosed Christ's power over evil and the demonic. The demons' plea to move into the swine would have been welcome to Jews, who considered "unclean" pigs on a par with demons. But this incident took place in Gentile territory; the pigs were most likely being raised commercially. The request of the townspeople for Jesus to leave was a sad commentary on their values. As one commentator stated, "All down the ages the world has been refusing Jesus because it prefers the pigs."

📖 Some people become so fixated on the consequences of Jesus' authoritative assault on the powers of

this world that they are threatened by the personal implications if they allow him to move into their lives. This issue becomes most urgent in remote areas of our world where people acknowledge the role of evil as a built-in feature of everyday life. How real is demonic evil to you? Might your cultural bias "move" it further away than it actually is?

Matthew 9:1–8

🕮 A further dimension of Jesus' authority was now disclosed—his right and ability to forgive sins! The teachers of the law rightly perceived in Jesus' statement to the paralyzed man an outright claim to divinity. The crowds still didn't get the message, though. They thought this authority had been given to "men" (v. 8), not exclusively to "the Son of Man" (v. 6). But Matthew's later readers recognized that in Jesus an entirely new era had dawned—the age of forgiveness of sins, the reason for which he had been born (1:21).

📖 Jesus' claims threaten the very core of many people's worldview. They flatly refuse to shift their thinking and belief structure to allow him the authoritative role in their lives he deserves and demands. Still today, when we are exposed to the reality of Jesus' identity and ability, our only appropriate response is unqualified trust in him regarding all aspects of life and allegiance to him above everything else. This passage says nothing about the faith of the paralyzed man—only of his friends. Still

The Calling of Matthew

9 As Jesus went on from there, he saw a man named Matthew sitting at the tax collector's booth. "Follow me," he told him, and Matthew got up and followed him.

10 While Jesus was having dinner at Matthew's house, many tax collectors and "sinners" came and ate with him and his disciples. **11** When the Pharisees saw this, they asked his disciples, "Why does your teacher eat with tax collectors and 'sinners'?"[f]

12 On hearing this, Jesus said, "It is not the healthy who need a doctor, but the sick. **13** But go and learn what this means: 'I desire mercy, not sacrifice.'[a][g] For I have not come to call the righteous, but sinners."[h]

Jesus Questioned About Fasting

14 Then John's disciples came and asked him, "How is it that we and the Pharisees fast,[i] but your disciples do not fast?"

15 Jesus answered, "How can the guests of the bridegroom mourn while he is with

9:11
f Mt 11:19; Lk 5:30; 15:2; Gal 2:15

9:13
g Hos 6:6; Mic 6:6-8; Mt 12:7
h 1Ti 1:15

9:14
i Lk 18:12

[a] 13 Hosea 6:6

---

today, we have the privilege of believing *on behalf of others* and of bringing them to Jesus.

Matthew 9:9–13

Matthew may have collected tolls from commercial traffic or taxes for the fish caught on the Sea of Galilee—a heavy toll to extract from struggling Galileans. The population probably considered him a traitor, selling out his own people to the Romans. But Jesus reached out to blatant sinners and social outcasts, even calling this one—who would eventually write this Gospel—to be an apostle (10:1–4; Acts 1:13). Those who were preoccupied with preserving their own righteousness were scandalized by Jesus' welcome of this traitorous sinner. The way of God is the way of mercy, not the sacrifice of ourselves or others in pursuit of a self-made righteousness.

The greatest miracle is often the one least noticed—that of forgiveness. When Jesus called Matthew, he made a momentous announcement about his kingdom mission—to bring healing to a sin-sickened world. His compassion continues to extend to despised and neglected individuals. Each of us has the incredible privilege of being instruments of his healing and compassion.

Matthew 9:14–17

The disciples of John the Baptist couldn't understand why Jesus' disciples didn't regularly fast as a sign of repentance or an indication of their spiritual discipline. Jesus' reply: The arrival of the kingdom had brought to fulfillment God's promises to Israel, making this a time of rejoicing. Fasting would be appropriate later on. Jesus hadn't come to shore up the traditional practices of the Jews but to offer an entirely new approach to God.

Spiritual growth doesn't come automatically from observing spiritual disciplines. In fact, they are worthless unless they express our humble desire to grow in the Father's likeness (5:48—6:18). Traditions are human designs intended to apply Biblical principles to everyday life—not commands from God. They become stifling if we allow them to become more important than Scripture itself.

9:9–13

Jesus and Food

Food is often mentioned in stories about Jesus' life. Sometimes Jesus offered food to those in need. At other times he used it as a metaphor in his teachings. Sometimes meals with Jesus became teaching times, and sometimes eating food with others served a ritual purpose. Some examples:

Fasted for forty days and nights: Food not the most important thing in life; need can be temporarily suspended in favor of spiritual pursuits.	Matt. 4:1
Multiplied food—feeding of five thousand: Meeting spiritual and physical needs together	Matt. 14:13–21
Ate with "sinners": Jesus demonstrated that relationships are more important than rituals.	Matt. 9:9–13
Served the Last Supper: Food can be used in a symbolic way, in this case to remind us of Jesus' sacrifice for us.	Luke 22:7–38
Called the bread of life: Only Jesus can satisfy our spiritual needs.	John 6:35
Offered the bread of life: We have a resource to offer the world, greater than any physical resources/needs.	John 6:51
Cooked fish for disciples on beach: Preparation of food for others an ideal opportunity to serve	John 21
Broke bread with disciples: When they ate together, their spiritual eyes were opened.	John 21:12–13

them?[j] The time will come when the bridegroom will be taken from them; then they will fast.[k]

9:15
j Jn 3:29
k Ac 13:2,3; 14:23

16 "No one sews a patch of unshrunk cloth on an old garment, for the patch will pull away from the garment, making the tear worse. 17 Neither do men pour new wine into old wineskins. If they do, the skins will burst, the wine will run out and the wineskins will be ruined. No, they pour new wine into new wineskins, and both are preserved."

A Dead Girl and a Sick Woman

18 While he was saying this, a ruler came and knelt before him[l] and said, "My daughter has just died. But come and put your hand on her,[m] and she will live." 19 Jesus got up and went with him, and so did his disciples.

9:18
l Mt 8:2 m Mk 5:23

20 Just then a woman who had been subject to bleeding for twelve years came up behind him and touched the edge of his cloak.[n] 21 She said to herself, "If I only touch his cloak, I will be healed."

9:20
n Mt 14:36;
Mk 3:10

22 Jesus turned and saw her. "Take heart, daughter," he said, "your faith has healed you."[o] And the woman was healed from that moment.[p]

23 When Jesus entered the ruler's house and saw the flute players and the noisy crowd,[q] 24 he said, "Go away. The girl is not dead[r] but asleep."[s] But they laughed at him. 25 After the crowd had been put outside, he went in and took the girl by the hand, and she got up. 26 News of this spread through all that region.[t]

9:22
o Mk 10:52;
Lk 7:50; 17:19;
18:42 p Mt 15:28
9:23
q 2Ch 35:25;
Jer 9:17,18
9:24
r Ac 20:10
s Jn 11:11-14
9:26
t Mt 4:24

Jesus Heals the Blind and Mute

27 As Jesus went on from there, two blind men followed him, calling out, "Have mercy on us, Son of David!"[u]

9:27
u Mt 15:22;
Mk 10:47;
Lk 18:38-39

28 When he had gone indoors, the blind men came to him, and he asked them, "Do you believe that I am able to do this?"

"Yes, Lord," they replied.

29 Then he touched their eyes and said, "According to your faith will it be done to you"; [v] 30 and their sight was restored. Jesus warned them sternly, "See that no one knows about this."[w] 31 But they went out and spread the news about him all over that region.[x]

9:29
v ver 22
9:30
w Mt 8:4

32 While they were going out, a man who was demon-possessed[y] and could not talk[z] was brought to Jesus. 33 And when the demon was driven out, the man who had been mute spoke. The crowd was amazed and said, "Nothing like this has ever been seen in Israel."[a]

9:31
x ver 26; Mk 7:36
9:32
y Mt 4:24
z Mt 12:22-24

34 But the Pharisees said, "It is by the prince of demons that he drives out demons."[b]

9:33
a Mk 2:12
9:34
b Mt 12:24;
Lk 11:15

Matthew 9:18–26

Both Mark and Luke identified this "ruler" as Jairus, a synagogue official. His faith was strong enough to believe Jesus could raise his daughter from the dead—which is precisely what the Healer did. Touching a corpse rendered a person "unclean," but Jesus restored the girl to life, transforming uncleanness to purity. The hemorrhaging woman, considered ritually unclean, was excluded from social and religious relations. Her faith had brought her to the place where God could heal her. By making her healing public with his announcement, Jesus removed the public stigma of her condition and smoothed the way for her reentry into social and religious life.

As we see the needs of people all around us, we can allow our hearts to feel deeply for and with them. But we can't stop there. To care we have to get close to them. If we do that, we will be forced to confront social stigmas. When has this happened to you? How did you deal with the situation?

Matthew 9:27–34

Blindness was one of the grimmest maladies in the ancient world—considered only a little less serious than death. These men understood Jesus' true identity and addressed him as "Son of David"—the first time he had been called by this title. They connected Jesus with the prophecies of the Messianic descendant of David, who would heal blindness (Isa. 29:18; 35:5; 42:7). And they asked specifically for that gift. Jesus' temporary demand for secrecy (v. 30) was a regular aspect of his ministry (see "There and Then" for 12:15–21).

The phenomenon of demon possession in some way prohibited the man from speaking (see also 12:22). The exorcism of the demon, along with the healing of the man's muteness, powerfully demonstrated that the kingdom of heaven had arrived.

"Columbine," "9/11," and "Washington-area snipers" have become shorthand reminders that evil is real. Our world lies in the grip of sin, and the evil one is

The Workers Are Few

9:35
c Mt 4:23
9:36
d Mt 14:14
e Nu 27:17;
Eze 34:5,6;
Zec 10:2; Mk 6:34
9:37
f Jn 4:35 g Lk 10:2

35 Jesus went through all the towns and villages, teaching in their synagogues, preaching the good news of the kingdom and healing every disease and sickness. c 36 When he saw the crowds, he had compassion on them, d because they were harassed and helpless, like sheep without a shepherd. e 37 Then he said to his disciples, "The harvest f is plentiful but the workers are few. g 38 Ask the Lord of the harvest, therefore, to send out workers into his harvest field."

Jesus Sends Out the Twelve

10:1
h Mk 3:13-15;
Lk 9:1

10 He called his twelve disciples to him and gave them authority to drive out evil a spirits h and to heal every disease and sickness.

a 1 Greek unclean

---

still at large. But into the scene Jesus comes to offer hope—for you and me and that insolent neighbor down the block. He doesn't come with more religious tradition or demand that we earn the right to his healing. He comes with mercy and grace to save us and others from our helpless state. How can we keep such stupendous news to ourselves?

Matthew 9:35–38

Jesus manifested the Good News of the kingdom by his words of proclamation, deeds of healing, and life of compassion. He grieved over the multitudes of people who felt helpless, harassed, and leaderless. Rather than being overwhelmed to the point of incapacitation or total discouragement by the extent of people's needs, Jesus recognized the great opportunity to bring hope. Instead of responding by himself, he called his people to join in this harvest.

We are not called to respond to the world's needs with resources limited to our own initiative and strength. Jesus calls us to pray, to ask for help from the God who commissioned us for our task. What difference does this make in both our motive and our capacity? Who are some of the people in our world today who feel helpless and harassed? What would it mean for them to encounter in word, deed, and life the fullness of God's kingdom?

Matthew 10:1–42

Jesus' mission was by now well established. He had announced his central message (4:17), assembled his circle of coworkers (4:18–22), articulated his standard of discipleship (chs. 5–7), and demonstrated his authoritative power (chs. 8–9). Now was the time to expand his influence by sending out his disciples with the same message and power. Jesus would send them first to Israel but also would prepare them for a worldwide

---

Snapshots

9:35–36

Giovanna

Parents in the highlands of Peru can't regularly take their children to the doctor. To get to the hospital, families have to travel between three and five hours. The transportation and hospital charges amount to approximately 30 soles (U.S. $8.50)—the same amount they could make selling two pounds of corn (enough to purchase ample food and household supplies). Even if they do see a doctor, they seldom have the funds necessary to obtain prescribed medications.

In response to the needs in this area, one Christian group provided donated medicine and medical supplies . . . to a local hospital and clinic.

Due to a congenital malformation, eleven-year-old Giovanna had suffered ear infections from age six on. When the situation became chronic, she needed costly antibiotics. But she was unable to complete the treatment plan because her parents couldn't afford to follow through. Her condition progressed to the point that she began losing her hearing and missing too much school.

In response to the needs in this area, one Christian group provided medicine and medical supplies such as gloves, alcohol, and gauze to a local hospital and clinic. Thanks to this generous gift, antibiotics like amoxicillin and ceforoxine were administered to patients like Giovanna. All told, some 160,000 people benefited from this generous gift.

Cry, the Beloved Continent: Don't Let AIDS Steal African Children's Future

9:35–36

Visiting a Christian care facility in Johannesburg for those with advanced AIDS, I saw children with matchstick arms and vacant eyes lying in beds awaiting their next seizure. New advances in treatment offer hope for some, but many die. One nearby community that used to average two funerals per week now has 75.

But who wants to hear about AIDS in Africa? Relief agencies face that question while trying to raise funds to fight this world health catastrophe. Americans, overwhelmed by the magnitude of Africa's problems, wonder if anything can help. Many can't help thinking, "They deserve it." After all, doesn't AIDS in Africa spread mainly through sexual promiscuity?

The visitor to Africa finds a different sexual landscape. In some countries, adolescent boys celebrate their rite of passage into adulthood with a public circumcision ceremony, afterward marking their adult status with sexual exploits. The continent has a long history of polygamy, and in places like South Africa the practice of separating male workers from their families has further broken down marital ties.

Nobody is exempt: In confidential surveys by World Vision, 72 percent of South African pastors admit to extramarital affairs, averaging three to four partners each. Yet finger-wagging doesn't help. One well-meaning American stirred up a hornets' nest lecturing to African church leaders about the sinful aspects of the epidemic. In Uganda, some churches won't marry a couple unless both test negative for the virus, thus driving young couples away from the church.

Nor does denial help. In South Africa, with the world's largest number of people living with HIV/AIDS, President Thabo Mbeki has questioned the link between AIDS and HIV. He declared that he personally knew of no one who had died of AIDS. That may be technically true (AIDS lowers the body's resistance to other diseases that kill), but his attitude has set back the work of health educators.

AIDS workers face a Herculean task. In parts of Africa, life expectancy has sunk from 65 to 37. In some countries half the population under 15 will die within ten years. Imagine a teacher looking at the fresh faces in her classroom, knowing that half will soon be in the grave.

Self-stigma, which keeps infected people from testing or treatment, is another obstacle. When Botswana (with a 38 percent HIV infection rate—the world's highest) offered free AIDS medication, only one percent of the population responded.

> This [crisis] is one of compassion, requiring not a change in laws and government, but of hearts.

An HIV-infected worker who contracted the virus through a blood transfusion told me, "To those who lack compassion for Africans because 'they deserve it,' I remind them that half the infections come about when a promiscuous partner infects someone 'innocent' and unsuspecting." HIV frequently is passed on to a newly conceived child, or a child becomes one of Africa's millions orphaned by AIDS.

South Africa is the country where you will most likely hear words of hope and transformation. Larger-than-life heroes like Desmond Tutu and Nelson Mandela inspire the nation with the power of grace and reconciliation. AIDS presents a wholly different crisis from the previously entrenched apartheid government. That was a crisis of theology and of justice. This is one of compassion, requiring not a change in laws and government, but of hearts.

We can look at the children with stolen dreams, at an entire continent whose future hangs in the balance, and question God. Or we can look at the same problems and realize this is God's question to us: Who cares about AIDS in Africa?

Philip Yancey, Christian author and editor-at-large for *Christianity Today* magazine in Carol Stream, Illinois
Source: Adapted from "Cry, the Beloved Continent: Don't Let AIDS Steal African Children's Future," *Christianity Today* 48, no. 3 (March 2004):112

10:4
i Mt 26:14-16, 25,
47; Jn 13:2, 26, 27
10:5
j 2Ki 17:24; Lk 9:52;
Jn 4:4-26, 39, 40;
Ac 8:5, 25
10:6
k Jer 50:6;
Mt 15:24
10:7
l Mt 3:2
10:9
m Lk 22:35
10:10
n 1Ti 5:18
10:12
o 1Sa 25:6

10:14
p Ne 5:13;
Lk 10:11; Ac 13:51
10:15
q 2Pe 2:6
r Mt 12:36; 2Pe 2:9;
1Jn 4:17
s Mt 11:22, 24
10:16
t Lk 10:3 *u* Ro 16:19
10:17
v Mt 5:22
w Mt 23:34;
Mk 13:9; Ac 5:40;
26:11
10:18
x Ac 25:24-26
10:19
y Ex 4:12
10:20
z Ac 4:8
10:21
a ver 35, 36;
Mic 7:6
10:22
b Mt 24:13;
Mk 13:13
10:24
c Lk 6:40; Jn 13:16;
15:20
10:25
d Mk 3:22

10:26
e Mk 4:22; Lk 8:17

10:28
f Isa 8:12, 13;
Heb 10:31
10:30
g 1Sa 14:45;
2Sa 14:11;
Lk 21:18; Ac 27:34
10:31
h Mt 12:12
10:32
i Ro 10:9
10:33
j Mk 8:38; 2Ti 2:12

2These are the names of the twelve apostles: first, Simon (who is called Peter) and his brother Andrew; James son of Zebedee, and his brother John; 3Philip and Bartholomew; Thomas and Matthew the tax collector; James son of Alphaeus, and Thaddaeus; 4Simon the Zealot and Judas Iscariot, who betrayed him. *i*

5These twelve Jesus sent out with the following instructions: "Do not go among the Gentiles or enter any town of the Samaritans. *j* 6Go rather to the lost sheep of Israel. *k* 7As you go, preach this message: 'The kingdom of heaven *l* is near.' 8Heal the sick, raise the dead, cleanse those who have leprosy, *a* drive out demons. Freely you have received, freely give. 9Do not take along any gold or silver or copper in your belts; *m* 10take no bag for the journey, or extra tunic, or sandals or a staff; for the worker is worth his keep. *n*

11 "Whatever town or village you enter, search for some worthy person there and stay at his house until you leave. 12As you enter the home, give it your greeting. *o* 13If the home is deserving, let your peace rest on it; if it is not, let your peace return to you. 14If anyone will not welcome you or listen to your words, shake the dust off your feet *p* when you leave that home or town. 15I tell you the truth, it will be more bearable for Sodom and Gomorrah *q* on the day of judgment *r* than for that town. *s* 16I am sending you out like sheep among wolves. *t* Therefore be as shrewd as snakes and as innocent as doves. *u*

17 "Be on your guard against men; they will hand you over to the local councils *v* and flog you in their synagogues. *w* 18On my account you will be brought before governors and kings *x* as witnesses to them and to the Gentiles. 19But when they arrest you, do not worry about what to say or how to say it. *y* At that time you will be given what to say, 20for it will not be you speaking, but the Spirit of your Father *z* speaking through you.

21 "Brother will betray brother to death, and a father his child; children will rebel against their parents *a* and have them put to death. 22All men will hate you because of me, but he who stands firm to the end will be saved. *b* 23When you are persecuted in one place, flee to another. I tell you the truth, you will not finish going through the cities of Israel before the Son of Man comes.

24 "A student is not above his teacher, nor a servant above his master. *c* 25It is enough for the student to be like his teacher, and the servant like his master. If the head of the house has been called Beelzebub, *b* *d* how much more the members of his household!

26 "So do not be afraid of them. There is nothing concealed that will not be disclosed, or hidden that will not be made known. *e* 27What I tell you in the dark, speak in the daylight; what is whispered in your ear, proclaim from the roofs. 28Do not be afraid of those who kill the body but cannot kill the soul. Rather, be afraid of the One *f* who can destroy both soul and body in hell. 29Are not two sparrows sold for a penny *c*? Yet not one of them will fall to the ground apart from the will of your Father. 30And even the very hairs of your head are all numbered. *g* 31So don't be afraid; you are worth more than many sparrows. *h*

32 "Whoever acknowledges me before men, *i* I will also acknowledge him before my Father in heaven. 33But whoever disowns me before men, I will disown him before my Father in heaven. *j*

34 "Do not suppose that I have come to bring peace to the earth. I did not come to bring peace, but a sword. 35For I have come to turn

---

a 8 The Greek word was used for various diseases affecting the skin—not necessarily leprosy.
b 25 Greek *Beezeboul* or *Beelzeboul*   *c* 29 Greek *an assarion*

---

mission. Here we see another staggering truth: The Lord of creation had (and still has) entrusted people to manifest in life, word, deed, and sign the coming of the kingdom of God. God could have chosen any number of various methods. He chose us.

📖 Christians today, like the Twelve, are everyday

people who have been asked to participate in the coming of the kingdom of God in an alien and hostile world. Together we are the church, the body of Jesus Christ. Whether we serve in public honor, in the humility of obscurity, or in the suffering of persecution, we, like the Twelve, have been handpicked by the Master for service.

" 'a man against his father,
    a daughter against her mother,
   a daughter-in-law against her mother-in-law[k]—
36   a man's enemies will be the members of his own household.'[a][l]

37"Anyone who loves his father or mother more than me is not worthy of me; anyone who loves his son or daughter more than me is not worthy of me;[m] 38 and anyone who does not take his cross and follow me is not worthy of me.[n] 39 Whoever finds his life will lose it, and whoever loses his life for my sake will find it.[o]

40"He who receives you receives me,[p] and he who receives me receives the one who sent me.[q] 41 Anyone who receives a prophet because he is a prophet will receive a prophet's reward, and anyone who receives a righteous man because he is a righteous man will receive a righteous man's reward. 42 And if anyone gives even a cup of cold water to one of these little ones because he is my disciple, I tell you the truth, he will certainly not lose his reward."[r]

Jesus and John the Baptist

11 After Jesus had finished instructing his twelve disciples,[s] he went on from there to teach and preach in the towns of Galilee.[b]

2 When John heard in prison[t] what Christ was doing, he sent his disciples 3 to ask him, "Are you the one who was to come,[u] or should we expect someone else?"

4 Jesus replied, "Go back and report to John what you hear and see: 5 The blind receive sight, the lame walk, those who have leprosy[c] are cured, the deaf hear, the dead are raised, and the good news is preached to the poor.[v] 6 Blessed is the man who does not fall away on account of me."[w]

7 As John's[x] disciples were leaving, Jesus began to speak to the crowd about John: "What did you go out into the desert to see? A reed swayed by the wind? 8 If not,

---

a 36 Micah 7:6   b 1 Greek *in their towns*   c 5 The Greek word was used for various diseases affecting the skin—not necessarily leprosy.

10:35
k ver 21
10:36
l Mic 7:6

10:37
m Lk 14:26
10:38
n Mt 16:24;
Lk 14:27
10:39
o Lk 17:33;
Jn 12:25
10:40
p Mt 18:5; Gal 4:14
q Lk 9:48; Jn 12:44;
13:20

10:42
r Mt 25:40;
Mk 9:41; Heb 6:10

11:1
s Mt 7:28

11:2
t Mt 14:3
11:3
u Ps 118:26;
Jn 11:27;
Heb 10:37

11:5
v Isa 35:4-6; 61:1;
Lk 4:18,19
11:6
w Mt 13:21
11:7
x Mt 3:1

Matthew 11:1–19

As God's prophet preparing the way for the Messiah, John the Baptist knew Jesus was the One. But languishing in prison awaiting execution didn't connect with his expectations of the judgment he thought the Messiah's arrival would bring. Jesus' reply forced John to take a hard look at the facts of Christ's ministry and to adjust his expectations to fit God's reality. Jesus was bringing the Messianic kingdom in a different way than John—and others—had expected. Rather than through the violent overthrow of evil, it was coming as person after person—blind, outcast, sick, and captive—experienced for themselves the life-transforming Good News.

Questions about God's ways are natural and normal. The fact is that those ways typically don't coincide with ours. We take our cues from Jesus as to how best to respond in the lives of the suffering: (1) Act with compassion, not condemnation; (2) refuse to allow a sufferer's vulnerable questions to cancel out in our minds their years of dedicated service; and (3) help them see the reality of God's Word, especially in Jesus' ministry (cf. Isa. 35:5–6; 61:1). When have you been on either end—giving or receiving—of such a relationship?

10:14–42

Persecution

Jesus didn't pretend Christian service would be pain-free. In Matthew 10 he warned his disciples that persecution will come but that he will supply the words and strength for those who are faithful. Millions of Christians throughout history have believed this promise and given their lives because of their faith. The largest documented groups of martyred Christians:

	MILLION(S)	
1921–1980 Soviet prison camps	20	✝✝✝✝✝✝✝✝✝✝✝✝✝✝✝✝✝✝✝✝
1214 Genghis Kahn (Central Asia)	4	✝✝✝✝
1358 Tamerlane (Southwest Asia)	4	✝✝✝✝
1929–1937 Stalin (Soviet Russia)	2.7	✝✝✝
1939 Hitler (Nazi Germany)	1	✝

✝ REPRESENTS 1 MILLION MARTYRED CHRISTIANS

Note: Other serious situations, in such places as Sudan, China, and North Korea, currently exist that may impact these figures.

Source: Barrett and Johnson (2001:399)

11:9
y Mt 21:26; Lk 1:76

what did you go out to see? A man dressed in fine clothes? No, those who wear fine clothes are in kings' palaces. 9Then what did you go out to see? A prophet?y Yes, I tell you, and more than a prophet. 10This is the one about whom it is written:

11:10
z Mal 3:1; Mk 1:2

" 'I will send my messenger ahead of you,
   who will prepare your way before you.' a z

11I tell you the truth: Among those born of women there has not risen anyone greater than John the Baptist; yet he who is least in the kingdom of heaven is greater than he. 12From the days of John the Baptist until now, the kingdom of heaven has been forcefully advancing, and forceful men lay hold of it. 13For all the Prophets and the Law prophesied until John. 14And if you are willing to accept it, he is the Elijah who was to come.a 15He who has ears, let him hear.b

11:14
a Mal 4:5;
Mt 17:10-13;
Mk 9:11-13;
Lk 1:17; Jn 1:21
11:15
b Mt 13:9,43;
Mk 4:23; Lk 14:35;
Rev 2:7

16"To what can I compare this generation? They are like children sitting in the marketplaces and calling out to others:

17 " 'We played the flute for you,
      and you did not dance;
   we sang a dirge,
      and you did not mourn.'

11:18
c Mt 3:4 d Lk 1:15
11:19
e Mt 9:11

18For John came neither eatingc nor drinking,d and they say, 'He has a demon.' 19The Son of Man came eating and drinking, and they say, 'Here is a glutton and a drunkard, a friend of tax collectors and "sinners." ' e But wisdom is proved right by her actions."

Woe on Unrepentant Cities

20Then Jesus began to denounce the cities in which most of his miracles had been performed, because they did not repent. 21"Woe to you, Korazin! Woe to you, Bethsaida! f If the miracles that were performed in you had been performed in Tyre and Sidon, g they would have repented long ago in sackcloth and ashes. h 22But I tell you, it will be more bearable for Tyre and Sidon on the day of judgment than for you.i 23And you, Capernaum,j will you be lifted up to the skies? No, you will go down to the depths.b k If the miracles that were performed in you had been performed in Sodom, it would have remained to this day. 24But I tell you that it will be more bearable for Sodom on the day of judgment than for you."l

11:21
f Mk 6:45; Lk 9:10;
Jn 12:21
g Mt 15:21;
Lk 6:17; Ac 12:20
h Jnh 3:5-9
11:22
i ver 24; Mt 10:15
11:23
j Mt 4:13
k Isa 14:13-15
11:24
l Mt 10:15

Rest for the Weary

25At that time Jesus said, "I praise you, Father,m Lord of heaven and earth, because you have hidden these things from the wise and learned, and revealed them to little children.n 26Yes, Father, for this was your good pleasure.
27"All things have been committed to meo by my Father.p No one knows the Son

11:25
m Lk 22:42;
Jn 11:41
n 1Co 1:26-29
11:27
o Mt 28:18
p Jn 3:35; 13:3;
17:2

a 10 Mal. 3:1   b 23 Greek Hades

Matthew 11:20–24

Jesus turned up the heat by denouncing by name the towns that had rejected his message. Korazin, Bethsaida, and Capernaum were the villages in which most of his miracles had been performed. They had experienced the greatest opportunity to hear the message and see it validated by miracles, but their privilege hadn't led to repentance. The judgment of these predominantly Jewish cities would be greater than that of the infamously sinful cities of the ancient world.

Do you think of discipleship to Jesus as a privilege? How about citizenship in the kingdom of heaven? It's easy for us to take for granted our relationship to Jesus, our peace with the Father, and the reality of the church's position as the body of Christ. We may even forget that it was out of God's voluntary love and sacrifice

that our current spiritual existence has been made possible—or that the life we enjoy is richer than that of any who lived before Jesus.

Matthew 11:25–30

The contrast in verses 25–26 was between those whose pride and self-sufficiency had caused them to reject Jesus' message and those whose humility and recognition of need had allowed them to be open. Jesus would use his teaching in parables as a way to test people's hearts.

The image of a yoke was commonly used in the Old Testament to describe Israel's subjection to foreign oppression (Lev. 26:13; Isa. 10:24–27). By Jesus' time, it also had become a metaphor in Judaism for the law. Jesus' invitation was a stark contrast to the military burden of foreign oppressors or the religious burden imposed by the Pharisees.

except the Father, and no one knows the Father except the Son and those to whom he the Son chooses to reveal him. *q*

28 "Come to me, *r* all you who are weary and burdened, and I will give you rest. 29 Take my yoke upon you and learn from me, *s* for I am gentle and humble in heart, and you will find rest for your souls. *t* 30 For my yoke is easy and my burden is light." *u*

Lord of the Sabbath

12 At that time Jesus went through the grainfields on the Sabbath. His disciples were hungry and began to pick some heads of grain *v* and eat them. 2 When the Pharisees saw this, they said to him, "Look! Your disciples are doing what is unlawful on the Sabbath." *w*

3 He answered, "Haven't you read what David did when he and his companions were hungry? *x* 4 He entered the house of God, and he and his companions ate the consecrated bread—which was not lawful for them to do, but only for the priests. *y* 5 Or haven't you read in the Law that on the Sabbath the priests in the temple desecrate the day *z* and yet are innocent? 6 I tell you that one*a* greater than the temple is here. *a* 7 If you had known what these words mean, 'I desire mercy, not sacrifice,'*b b* you would not have condemned the innocent. 8 For the Son of Man *c* is Lord of the Sabbath."

9 Going on from that place, he went into their synagogue, 10 and a man with a shriveled hand was there. Looking for a reason to accuse Jesus, they asked him, "Is it lawful to heal on the Sabbath?" *d*

11 He said to them, "If any of you has a sheep and it falls into a pit on the Sabbath, will you not take hold of it and lift it out? *e* 12 How much more valuable is a man than a sheep! *f* Therefore it is lawful to do good on the Sabbath."

13 Then he said to the man, "Stretch out your hand." So he stretched it out and it was completely restored, just as sound as the other. 14 But the Pharisees went out and plotted how they might kill Jesus. *g*

God's Chosen Servant

15 Aware of this, Jesus withdrew from that place. Many followed him, and he healed all their sick, *h* 16 warning them not to tell who he was. *i* 17 This was to fulfill what was spoken through the prophet Isaiah:

a 6 Or *something*; also in verses 41 and 42   b 7 Hosea 6:6

11:27
q Jn 10:15
11:28
r Jn 7:37
11:29
s Jn 13:15; Php 2:5; 1Pe 2:21; 1Jn 2:6
t Jer 6:16
11:30
u 1Jn 5:3

12:1
v Dt 23:25
12:2
w ver 10; Lk 13:14; 14:3; Jn 5:10; 7:23; 9:16
12:3
x 1Sa 21:6
12:4
y Lev 24:5,9
12:5
z Nu 28:9,10; Jn 7:22,23
12:6
a ver 41,42
12:7
b Hos 6:6; Mic 6:6-8; Mt 9:13
12:8
c Mt 8:20
12:10
d ver 2; Lk 13:14; 14:3; Jn 9:16
12:11
e Lk 14:5
12:12
f Mt 10:31
12:14
g Mt 26:4; 27:1; Mk 3:6; Lk 6:11; Jn 5:18; 11:53
12:15
h Mt 4:23
12:16
i Mt 8:4

📖 Discipleship relieves us from legalism, but it's not lawlessness. In fact, Jesus' interpretation of the law was even more demanding than that of the Pharisees! He calls us to fulfill the law from the obedience of our hearts, not simply by external activity (5:21–47)—and to be "perfect" (5:48). Yet Jesus' discipleship is an easy yoke because his teaching and the gift of the Spirit equip us to live out God's will in the way he designed us to live. His "burden" makes life's load manageable (cf. Gal. 6:5).

Matthew 12:1–14

🕮 To a Pharisee, "what is unlawful" could have referred either to a Scriptural command or to a rabbi's interpretation of that command. The disciples could have been cited for violating any of several rabbinic taboos. But the Mosaic Law made provision for hungry people to eat from a neighbor's field. Jesus' Old Testament examples made the Pharisees' accusation immaterial. He demonstrated that the higher principle wasn't abstaining from activity on the Sabbath but doing good.

📖 As Lord of the Sabbath, Jesus had the right to interpret its intent. He brings rest to God's people through the easy yoke and light burden of discipleship (11:28–30).

But that doesn't make the call to be disciples something easy or allow for an irresponsible failure to do good. Followers of Jesus don't simply abstain from doing evil; we actively seek to do good. Jesus illustrated in his actions what it means for God to desire mercy, not sacrifice.

Matthew 12:15–21

🕮 Jesus carefully avoided stirring up in the crowds a misunderstanding of his Messianic identity. The typical Israelite hoped for liberation from Rome and a Messiah who would restore the dignity of David's kingdom. Matthew showed that Jesus was indeed the Messiah—who would come *meekly* to bring justice to the nations. He pictured the Servant Messiah from Isaiah's prophecy (Isa. 42:1–4), the One who invites those most in need—the harassed, helpless, weary, and burdened—to receive healing, freedom, and hope as they enter his kingdom. Compare this list with those who initially followed David (1 Sam. 22:2).

📖 In the midst of mounting opposition, Matthew inserted a powerful vision of Jesus, the Servant, balancing strength with gentleness, conviction with compassion, commitment to do what is right with a refusal to beat others down. If our witness to them is to be com-

12:18
j Mt 3:17

18 "Here is my servant whom I have chosen,
    the one I love, in whom I delight;[j]
I will put my Spirit on him,
    and he will proclaim justice to the nations.
19 He will not quarrel or cry out;
    no one will hear his voice in the streets.
20 A bruised reed he will not break,
    and a smoldering wick he will not snuff out,
    till he leads justice to victory.

12:21
k Isa 42:1-4

21   In his name the nations will put their hope." [a][k]

Jesus and Beelzebub

12:22
l Mt 4:24; 9:32-33
12:23
m Mt 9:27
12:24
n Mk 3:22
o Mk 9:34
12:25
p Mt 9:4

22 Then they brought him a demon-possessed man who was blind and mute, and Jesus healed him, so that he could both talk and see.[l] 23 All the people were astonished and said, "Could this be the Son of David?"[m]

24 But when the Pharisees heard this, they said, "It is only by Beelzebub,[b][n] the prince of demons, that this fellow drives out demons."[o]

25 Jesus knew their thoughts[p] and said to them, "Every kingdom divided against itself will be ruined, and every city or household divided against itself will not stand. 26 If Satan[q] drives out Satan, he is divided against himself. How then can his kingdom stand? 27 And if I drive out demons by Beelzebub, by whom do your people[r] drive them out? So then, they will be your judges. 28 But if I drive out demons by the Spirit of God, then the kingdom of God has come upon you.

12:26
q Mt 4:10
12:27
r Ac 19:13

29 "Or again, how can anyone enter a strong man's house and carry off his possessions unless he first ties up the strong man? Then he can rob his house.

12:30
s Mk 9:40; Lk 11:23
12:31
t Mk 3:28,29;
Lk 12:10

30 "He who is not with me is against me, and he who does not gather with me scatters.[s] 31 And so I tell you, every sin and blasphemy will be forgiven men, but the blasphemy against the Spirit will not be forgiven.[t] 32 Anyone who speaks a word against the Son of Man will be forgiven, but anyone who speaks against the Holy Spirit will not be forgiven, either in this age[u] or in the age to come.[v]

12:32
u Tit 2:12
v Mk 10:30;
Lk 20:34,35;
Eph 1:21; Heb 6:5
12:33
w Mt 7:16,17;
Lk 6:43,44
12:34
x Mt 3:7; 23:33
y Mt 15:18; Lk 6:45

33 "Make a tree good and its fruit will be good, or make a tree bad and its fruit will be bad, for a tree is recognized by its fruit.[w] 34 You brood of vipers,[x] how can you who are evil say anything good? For out of the overflow of the heart the mouth speaks.[y] 35 The good man brings good things out of the good stored up in him, and the evil man brings evil things out of the evil stored up in him. 36 But I tell you that men will have to give account on the day of judgment for every careless word they have spoken. 37 For by your words you will be acquitted, and by your words you will be condemned."

The Sign of Jonah

12:38
z Mt 16:1;
Mk 8:11,12;
Lk 11:16; Jn 2:18;
6:30; 1Co 1:22

38 Then some of the Pharisees and teachers of the law said to him, "Teacher, we want to see a miraculous sign from you."[z]

---

a 21 Isaiah 42:1-4   b 24 Greek *Beezeboul* or *Beelzeboul*; also in verse 27

---

pelling, those who hurt us need to see this Jesus in us (cf. 2 Cor. 3:18). We are to act, think, speak, and bear the fruit of the Spirit (Gal. 5:22–23) as Jesus did in each encounter. What image of Jesus are you projecting to those who have hurt you? The Spirit is eager to empower us to represent him accurately.

Matthew 12:22–37

Ancient exorcists used a variety of incantations and spells; potions and herbs; and material articles, like rings, to try to manipulate the spirit world. Jesus commanded demons from his own authority—and they immediately submitted. The Pharisees attributed Jesus' power to Satan. This charge of practicing magic under the influence of Satan was punishable by stoning.

Jesus defended his ministry of exorcism with two short parables (vv. 25,29) and followed up with two scathing denunciations of the Pharisees (vv. 30–32,33–37). The logical conclusion was that if the man had been delivered and healed, the source of Jesus' power had to have been God in his battle against Satan's kingdom.

By attributing the work and power of the Spirit to Satan, these Pharisees dishonored God and rejected his offer of forgiveness. Apparently Jesus knew their hardened hearts had reached the point of no return. "Blasphemy against the Holy Spirit" can only be committed today by people who reject the Spirit's ministry of leading them to salvation. To speak against Jesus implies a lack of understanding of who he is. By yielding to the Spirit, a person can overcome this obstacle, repent, and find forgiveness.

39He answered, "A wicked and adulterous generation asks for a miraculous sign! But none will be given it except the sign of the prophet Jonah. *a* **40**For as Jonah was three days and three nights in the belly of a huge fish, *b* so the Son of Man *c* will be three days and three nights in the heart of the earth. *d* **41**The men of Nineveh *e* will stand up at the judgment with this generation and condemn it; for they repented at the preaching of Jonah, *f* and now one *a* greater than Jonah is here. **42**The Queen of the South will rise at the judgment with this generation and condemn it; for she came *g* from the ends of the earth to listen to Solomon's wisdom, and now one greater than Solomon is here.

43"When an evil *b* spirit comes out of a man, it goes through arid places seeking rest and does not find it. **44**Then it says, 'I will return to the house I left.' When it arrives, it finds the house unoccupied, swept clean and put in order. **45**Then it goes and takes with it seven other spirits more wicked than itself, and they go in and live there. And the final condition of that man is worse than the first. *h* That is how it will be with this wicked generation."

Jesus' Mother and Brothers

46While Jesus was still talking to the crowd, his mother *i* and brothers *j* stood outside, wanting to speak to him. **47**Someone told him, "Your mother and brothers are standing outside, wanting to speak to you." *c*

48He replied to him, "Who is my mother, and who are my brothers?" **49**Pointing to his disciples, he said, "Here are my mother and my brothers. **50**For whoever does the will of my Father in heaven *k* is my brother and sister and mother."

The Parable of the Sower

13 That same day Jesus went out of the house *l* and sat by the lake. **2**Such large crowds gathered around him that he got into a boat *m* and sat in it, while all

a 41 Or *something*; also in verse 42   *b* 43 Greek *unclean*   *c* 47 Some manuscripts do not have verse 47.

12:39
a Mt 16:4; Lk 11:29
12:40
b Jnh 1:17
c Mt 8:20
d Mt 16:21
12:41
e Jnh 1:2 *f* Jnh 3:5

12:42
g 1Ki 10:1; 2Ch 9:1

12:45
h 2Pe 2:20

12:46
i Mt 1:18;
2:11,13,14,20;
Lk 1:43; 2:33,34,48,
51; Jn 2:1,5; 19:25,
26 / Mt 13:55;
Jn 2:12; 7:3,5;
Ac 1:14; 1Co 9:5;
Gal 1:19
12:50
k Jn 15:14

13:1
l ver 36; Mt 9:28
13:2
m Lk 5:3

Matthew 12:38–45

The Pharisees wanted an on-demand, spectacular display to convince them that Jesus' power was from God. But they weren't asking in faith. If they had been open to God's message, they would already have accepted Jesus as Messiah. Instead, they used his earlier miracles as the basis for their charge that he was a satanic tool. The only other sign Jesus would give them pointed to God's coming judgment.

Jesus made a final point via a parable featuring a person who was exorcised but didn't come to Jesus and enter the kingdom. Without kingdom transformation, a "cleaned-up" person is vulnerable to renewed and persistent attack by the demon world. He or she can easily end up in worse shape than before. But if the person does receive Jesus, Satan will flee from God's presence in this disciple's life (cf. James 4:7; 1 Jn. 4:1–4).

Why did the Pharisees and teachers of the law challenge and oppose Jesus? Why couldn't they recognize the hand of God in his ministry? Unfortunately, there is something of the Pharisee in each of us. When we challenge, ignore, or dismiss Jesus' role in our own lives, we may, at least temporarily, be more like his detractors than we care to admit.

Matthew 12:46–50

We know from Mark's Gospel that Jesus' family had come from Nazareth because of reports of the commotion his ministry was causing. They wanted to take

control of Jesus and escort him home, thinking he was out of his mind (Mark 3:21). But Jesus wouldn't let family loyalty deter him from his Messianic ministry. He hadn't come to abolish the family (cf. Matt. 15:3–9), but he demonstrated the primacy of commitment to himself and the kingdom of heaven. This places believers in a new spiritual family—with membership based on doing the Father's will.

Jesus broadened his gender references to include women as his disciples. Within Judaism at that time, only men could become disciples of a rabbi and study the Torah. But with Jesus, any person who responded to the gospel and believed on him for eternal life was (and is) his disciple.

The importance of obeying the Father's will is central to this passage. Tom White, director of The Voice of the Martyrs, understands this necessity, which he saw exemplified in the suffering endured by Christians. He wrote, "I was in the central highlands in Vietnam when someone remarked about how the Christians suffer here. One Vietnamese Christian remarked, 'Suffering is not the worst thing that can happen to us. Disobedience to God is the worst thing.'" Are you able with conviction to echo this claim?

Matthew 13:1–23

The crowds were a mixed group. Some leaned toward discipleship, some toward opposition, and others rode the fence. But the parables forced a decision. God

1583

the people stood on the shore. 3 Then he told them many things in parables, saying: "A farmer went out to sow his seed. 4 As he was scattering the seed, some fell
along the path, and the birds came and ate it up. 5 Some fell on rocky places, where
it did not have much soil. It sprang up quickly, because the soil was shallow. 6 But
when the sun came up, the plants were scorched, and they withered because they
had no root. 7 Other seed fell among thorns, which grew up and choked the plants.
8 Still other seed fell on good soil, where it produced a crop—a hundred,[n] sixty or
thirty times what was sown. 9 He who has ears, let him hear."[o]

10 The disciples came to him and asked, "Why do you speak to the people in parables?"

11 He replied, "The knowledge of the secrets of the kingdom of heaven has been
given to you,[p] but not to them. 12 Whoever has will be given more, and he will have
an abundance. Whoever does not have, even what he has will be taken from him.[q]
13 This is why I speak to them in parables:

"Though seeing, they do not see;
  though hearing, they do not hear or understand.[r]

14 In them is fulfilled the prophecy of Isaiah:

" 'You will be ever hearing but never understanding;
  you will be ever seeing but never perceiving.
15 For this people's heart has become calloused;
  they hardly hear with their ears,
  and they have closed their eyes.
Otherwise they might see with their eyes,
  hear with their ears,
  understand with their hearts
and turn, and I would heal them.'[a][s]

16 But blessed are your eyes because they see, and your ears because they hear.[t] 17 For
I tell you the truth, many prophets and righteous men longed to see what you see[u]
but did not see it, and to hear what you hear but did not hear it.

18 "Listen then to what the parable of the sower means: 19 When anyone hears the
message about the kingdom[v] and does not understand it, the evil one[w] comes and
snatches away what was sown in his heart. This is the seed sown along the path.
20 The one who received the seed that fell on rocky places is the man who hears the
word and at once receives it with joy. 21 But since he has no root, he lasts only a short
time. When trouble or persecution comes because of the word, he quickly falls
away.[x] 22 The one who received the seed that fell among the thorns is the man who
hears the word, but the worries of this life and the deceitfulness of wealth[y] choke
it, making it unfruitful. 23 But the one who received the seed that fell on good soil
is the man who hears the word and understands it. He produces a crop, yielding a
hundred, sixty or thirty times what was sown."[z]

The Parable of the Weeds

24 Jesus told them another parable: "The kingdom of heaven is like[a] a man who
sowed good seed in his field. 25 But while everyone was sleeping, his enemy came

13:8 n Ge 26:12
13:9 o Mt 11:15
13:11 p Mt 11:25; 16:17; 19:11; Jn 6:65; 1Co 2:10,14; Col 1:27; 1Jn 2:20,27
13:12 q Mt 25:29; Lk 19:26
13:13 r Dt 29:4; Jer 5:21; Eze 12:2
13:15 s Isa 6:9,10; Jn 12:40; Ac 28:26,27; Ro 11:8
13:16 t Mt 16:17
13:17 u Jn 8:56; Heb 11:13; 1Pe 1:10-12
13:19 v Mt 4:23 w Mt 5:37
13:21 x Mt 11:6
13:22 y Mt 19:23; 1Ti 6:9,10,17
13:23 z ver 8
13:24 a ver 31,33,45,47; Mt 18:23; 20:1; 22:2; 25:1; Mk 4:26,30

a *15* Isaiah 6:9,10

knew those who would "steel" themselves against his truth—and also those who would respond favorably. We see here the clear interplay between God's sovereignty and people's responsibility to choose his ways.

Through his parables Jesus revealed to his disciples the secrets of the kingdom of God, making known that during this age (continuing through our day) that the kingdom exists in a hidden form. It's a covert, undercover operation (cf. vv. 31–33), not the overpowering political and militaristic display of God's rule many expected. The parables reveal what it means for us as Jesus' disciples to live as kingdom subjects in a world that isn't yet experiencing the fully consummated kingdom of God.

Matthew 13:24–30

Zizanion, a kind of weed referred to as "darnel" or "tares," has poisonous seeds but looks like wheat in its early stages of growth. Yet it's easily distinguishable at harvest. Jesus didn't fault the servants for failing to pre-

and sowed weeds among the wheat, and went away. 26When the wheat sprouted and formed heads, then the weeds also appeared.

27"The owner's servants came to him and said, 'Sir, didn't you sow good seed in your field? Where then did the weeds come from?'

28" 'An enemy did this,' he replied.

"The servants asked him, 'Do you want us to go and pull them up?'

29" 'No,' he answered, 'because while you are pulling the weeds, you may root up the wheat with them. 30Let both grow together until the harvest. At that time I will tell the harvesters: First collect the weeds and tie them in bundles to be burned; then gather the wheat and bring it into my barn.' "b

The Parables of the Mustard Seed and the Yeast

31He told them another parable: "The kingdom of heaven is likec a mustard seed,d which a man took and planted in his field. 32Though it is the smallest of all your seeds, yet when it grows, it is the largest of garden plants and becomes a tree, so that the birds of the air come and perch in its branches."e

33He told them still another parable: "The kingdom of heaven is likef yeast that a woman took and mixed into a large amounta of flourg until it worked all through the dough."h

34Jesus spoke all these things to the crowd in parables; he did not say anything to them without using a parable.i 35So was fulfilled what was spoken through the prophet:

> "I will open my mouth in parables,
> I will utter things hidden since the creation of the world."bj

The Parable of the Weeds Explained

36Then he left the crowd and went into the house. His disciples came to him and said, "Explain to us the parablek of the weeds in the field."

a 33 Greek *three satas* (probably about 1/2 bushel or 22 liters) b 35 Psalm 78:2

13:30
b Mt 3:12

13:31
c ver 24
d Mt 17:20; Lk 17:6

13:32
e Ps 104:12;
Eze 17:23; 31:6;
Da 4:12
13:33
f ver 24 g Ge 18:6
h Gal 5:9

13:34
i Mk 4:33; Jn 16:25

13:35
j Ps 78:2;
Ro 16:25,26;
1Co 2:7; Eph 3:9;
Col 1:26

13:36
k Mt 15:15

---

vent the crime or encourage them to worry about the presence of evil in their midst. He would later explain the meaning of the parable to his disciples at their request (see vv. 36–43).

📖 We won't see the uprooting or elimination of evil until the end of this age. Instead, there will be a mixed nature in the world. Evil derives from the evil one, and we are to expect spiritual warfare as we live in an environment contaminated by evil. But there looms on history's horizon both certain rescue for Jesus' disciples and certain judgment for those aligned with Satan. Jesus' disciples aren't called out of the world. We are promised his continual prayer for the Father's protecting hand upon us (cf. John 17:15–19).

Matthew 13:31–35

📖 The smallness of the mustard seed as a metaphor for the kingdom no doubt shocked Jesus' audience, who expected God's kingdom to be great and expansive. But Jesus emphasized that an inconspicuous beginning would grow into external greatness. Scripture almost always uses yeast as a negative image. But Jesus cited it to symbolize the positive, hidden permeation of the kingdom of heaven into an unsuspecting world.

📖 The kingdom of heaven enters our lives in small, unassuming ways. God isn't preoccupied with power and prestige. Though initially inconspicuous and hidden, the kingdom grows to transform everything, as yeast transforms dough. As kingdom citizens we are to be salt and light to the world (5:13–16). We seek to bring people into a loving community within the church. But our popularity, or lack of it, will never be the final gauge of the kingdom's real influence.

Matthew 13:36–43

📖 The explanation of the parable of the wheat and weeds is unique for the way in which Jesus identified the main elements of the story, leading to a conclusion about the end times. His clarification helps us interpret other parables. But several elements aren't defined here (e.g., the servants and their sleep in v. 25), and it isn't necessarily true that every detail in a parable has significant meaning. Do you think it's possible for us to read too much into a parable? A good guideline might be to exercise caution with respect to connections that go beyond the explanations Jesus offered.

📖 Jesus stated that "the field is the world," reminding us of the coexistence of believers and unbelievers on Earth. But there is a secondary application to the church. The parable of the wheat and weeds makes us aware of Satan's attempts to infiltrate the church. We are to be on guard and pray against those plans. Satan will operate in this world until the judgment. But we can reduce his influence by being confident in God's final judgment of evil and by allowing the Spirit to produce in us the fruit of righteousness, so that we can "shine like the sun."

1585

13:37
l Mt 8:20
13:38
m Jn 8:44,45;
1Jn 3:10
13:39
n Joel 3:13
o Mt 24:3; 28:20
p Rev 14:15
13:41
q Mt 8:20
r Mt 24:31
13:42
s ver 50; Mt 8:12
13:43
t Da 12:3
u Mt 11:15

37He answered, "The one who sowed the good seed is the Son of Man.[l] 38The field is the world, and the good seed stands for the sons of the kingdom. The weeds are the sons of the evil one,[m] 39and the enemy who sows them is the devil. The harvest[n] is the end of the age,[o] and the harvesters are angels.[p]

40"As the weeds are pulled up and burned in the fire, so it will be at the end of the age. 41The Son of Man[q] will send out his angels,[r] and they will weed out of his kingdom everything that causes sin and all who do evil. 42They will throw them into the fiery furnace, where there will be weeping and gnashing of teeth.[s] 43Then the righteous will shine like the sun[t] in the kingdom of their Father. He who has ears, let him hear.[u]

The Parables of the Hidden Treasure and the Pearl

13:44
v ver 24 w Isa 55:1;
Php 3:7,8

44"The kingdom of heaven is like[v] treasure hidden in a field. When a man found it, he hid it again, and then in his joy went and sold all he had and bought that field.[w]

13:45
x ver 24

45"Again, the kingdom of heaven is like[x] a merchant looking for fine pearls. 46When he found one of great value, he went away and sold everything he had and bought it.

The Parable of the Net

13:47
y ver 24 z Mt 22:10

47"Once again, the kingdom of heaven is like[y] a net that was let down into the lake and caught all kinds[z] of fish. 48When it was full, the fishermen pulled it up on the shore. Then they sat down and collected the good fish in baskets, but threw the bad away. 49This is how it will be at the end of the age. The angels will come and

13:49
a Mt 25:32
13:50
b Mt 8:12

separate the wicked from the righteous[a] 50and throw them into the fiery furnace, where there will be weeping and gnashing of teeth.[b]

51"Have you understood all these things?" Jesus asked.

"Yes," they replied.

52He said to them, "Therefore every teacher of the law who has been instructed about the kingdom of heaven is like the owner of a house who brings out of his storeroom new treasures as well as old."

A Prophet Without Honor

13:53
c Mt 7:28
13:54
d Mt 4:23

53When Jesus had finished these parables,[c] he moved on from there. 54Coming to his hometown, he began teaching the people in their synagogue,[d] and they

---

Matthew 13:44–46

People in ancient times commonly hid valuables in fields, for instance when a marauding army approached. If the homeowner didn't survive the invasion, the treasure might go unclaimed for generations. Jesus wasn't addressing the ethical issue of stealthily buying land known to contain treasure. His point was to reveal to his disciples that pursuing the kingdom was of higher value than anything else.

In the second story we find a merchant—apparently a wholesale pearl dealer on a business trip—deliberately searching for fine pearls. The issue wasn't about buying one's way into the kingdom but about recognizing its superlative value and the unreserved self-surrender needed to obtain it. The religious leaders of Jesus' day were the experts qualified to understand the kingdom's value. But they were sidelined by hypocrisy and a desire for a pious reputation and honor from people (6:2,5,16).

Has your wonder over life in God's kingdom become stale, slipping into a take-it-for-granted complacency? If a person has always known the Good News, he or she may not fully appreciate its value. Think about how you might make kingdom truths relevant for today.

Do you need a renewed infusion of Jesus in your own faith experience?

Matthew 13:47–52

Jesus used the metaphor of the net as another way to describe the end-of-the-age judgment in which the good will be separated from the bad (cf. vv. 40–43). When he asked his disciples (some of whom were fishermen by trade) whether they understood, he had in mind their comprehension of both explained and unexplained parables. They hadn't fully understood earlier (vv. 10,36), but now their "yes" was swift and confident. Again Jesus stressed that his disciples need not judge evil. That is God's work.

Which parable, if any, in this chapter has left you with more questions than answers? Some of us tend to "get it" right away, while others need another example or explanation. Jesus taught, prodded, explained, questioned, and told another story—all to help this group of learners understand. We, too, can read these stories and come away scratching our heads. Yet by his Holy Spirit he reveals the truths they contain. And he will continue to help us see new layers of meaning—reading after reading (cf. John 14:26).

were amazed.[e] "Where did this man get this wisdom and these miraculous powers?" they asked. 55"Isn't this the carpenter's son?[f] Isn't his mother's[g] name Mary, and aren't his brothers James, Joseph, Simon and Judas? 56Aren't all his sisters with us? Where then did this man get all these things?" 57And they took offense[h] at him.

But Jesus said to them, "Only in his hometown and in his own house is a prophet without honor."[i]

58And he did not do many miracles there because of their lack of faith.

John the Baptist Beheaded

14 At that time Herod[j] the tetrarch heard the reports about Jesus,[k] 2and he said to his attendants, "This is John the Baptist;[l] he has risen from the dead! That is why miraculous powers are at work in him."

3Now Herod had arrested John and bound him and put him in prison[m] because of Herodias, his brother Philip's wife,[n] 4for John had been saying to him: "It is not lawful for you to have her."[o] 5Herod wanted to kill John, but he was afraid of the people, because they considered him a prophet.[p]

6On Herod's birthday the daughter of Herodias danced for them and pleased Herod so much 7that he promised with an oath to give her whatever she asked. 8Prompted by her mother, she said, "Give me here on a platter the head of John the Baptist." 9The king was distressed, but because of his oaths and his dinner guests, he ordered that her request be granted 10and had John beheaded[q] in the prison. 11His head was brought in on a platter and given to the girl, who carried it to her mother. 12John's disciples came and took his body and buried it.[r] Then they went and told Jesus.

Jesus Feeds the Five Thousand

13When Jesus heard what had happened, he withdrew by boat privately to a solitary place. Hearing of this, the crowds followed him on foot from the towns. 14When Jesus landed and saw a large crowd, he had compassion on them[s] and healed their sick.[t]

13:54
e Mt 7:28
13:55
f Lk 3:23; Jn 6:42
g Mt 12:46
13:57
h Jn 6:61 i Lk 4:24;
Jn 4:44

14:1
j Mk 8:15;
Lk 3:1,19; 13:31;
23:7,8; Ac 4:27;
12:1 k Lk 9:7-9
14:2
l Mt 3:1
14:3
m Mt 4:12; 11:2
n Lk 3:19,20
14:4
o Lev 18:16; 20:21
14:5
p Mt 11:9

14:10
q Mt 17:12

14:12
r Ac 8:2

14:14
s Mt 9:36 t Mt 4:23

Matthew 13:53–58

At the beginning of Jesus' ministry, the townspeople in Nazareth had been outraged by his inclusion of Gentiles in God's salvation plan (Luke 4:16–30). Now they were amazed at his supposed wisdom and the reports of the miracles he had demonstrated throughout Galilee. Like the Pharisees in Capernaum (Matt. 12:24), they questioned the source of his power. Familiar with his human roots, they determined he couldn't be anyone special. The old expression was true in this instance—familiarity breeds contempt.

Do you give people a chance to prove themselves, or do you judge them based on past performance or others' perceptions? If a person hasn't been particularly striking or gifted at one point in life, then family, friends, and neighbors often won't let them (or don't want them to) grow into something more significant. How does application of the Golden Rule (7:12) relate to this situation?

Matthew 14:1–12

When Herod Antipas married Herodias, the popular John the Baptist publicly condemned him for marrying his half-brother's wife (who was also his half-niece). Such a marriage would have been considered an incestuous affront to God's law (Lev. 18:16; 20:21). John was a threat to Herod politically, so Herod had him arrested to counter his influence with the people.

The kingdom of God can be a threat to people in power. Desiring popularity over truth and power over righteousness, people may resort to force and violence against those who call their ways into question. Around the world followers of Christ are experiencing violence and persecution for living out the way of God. Do you know people who have suffered for doing what is right or have been a threat to those whose way of life was wrong?

Matthew 14:13–21

All four Gospels record this miracle, but only Matthew noted that the number 5,000 included only men. The total number of people may have stretched to 10,000 or more. The remote region offered no food for the people, but neither would such abundant staples likely have been on hand in the nearby villages. Jesus gave the problem back to the disciples by instructing them to provide the crowd with something to eat. In so doing, he demonstrated the importance of compassion, as well as pointing out God's reliance on us to fulfill his purposes.

Even Jesus needed time alone, but he didn't let his needs stifle his compassion. He responded to all needs of people, not just "spiritual ones," curing diseases and feeding their hungers. We learn in the feeding of the 5,000 that he's adequate to meet any need, no matter how "impossible" the circumstances. When we act in his service to respond to the needs of others, he will give us all the resources we require.

15As evening approached, the disciples came to him and said, "This is a remote place, and it's already getting late. Send the crowds away, so they can go to the villages and buy themselves some food."

16Jesus replied, "They do not need to go away. You give them something to eat."

17"We have here only five loaves*u* of bread and two fish," they answered.

18"Bring them here to me," he said. 19And he directed the people to sit down on the grass. Taking the five loaves and the two fish and looking up to heaven, he gave thanks and broke the loaves.*v* Then he gave them to the disciples, and the disciples gave them to the people. 20They all ate and were satisfied, and the disciples picked up twelve basketfuls of broken pieces that were left over. 21The number of those who ate was about five thousand men, besides women and children.

Jesus Walks on the Water

22Immediately Jesus made the disciples get into the boat and go on ahead of him to the other side, while he dismissed the crowd. 23After he had dismissed them, he went up on a mountainside by himself to pray.*w* When evening came, he was there alone, 24but the boat was already a considerable distance*a* from land, buffeted by the waves because the wind was against it.

25During the fourth watch of the night Jesus went out to them, walking on the lake. 26When the disciples saw him walking on the lake, they were terrified. "It's a ghost,"*x* they said, and cried out in fear.

27But Jesus immediately said to them: "Take courage!*y* It is I. Don't be afraid."*z*

28"Lord, if it's you," Peter replied, "tell me to come to you on the water."

29"Come," he said.

Then Peter got down out of the boat, walked on the water and came toward Jesus. 30But when he saw the wind, he was afraid and, beginning to sink, cried out, "Lord, save me!"

31Immediately Jesus reached out his hand and caught him. "You of little faith,"*a* he said, "why did you doubt?"

32And when they climbed into the boat, the wind died down. 33Then those who were in the boat worshiped him, saying, "Truly you are the Son of God."*b*

a 24 Greek many stadia

Side references

14:17
u Mt 16:9

14:19
v 1Sa 9:13;
Mt 26:26; Mk 8:6;
Lk 24:30; Ac 2:42;
27:35; 1Ti 4:4

14:23
w Lk 3:21

14:26
x Lk 24:37
14:27
y Mt 9:2; Ac 23:11
z Da 10:12;
Mt 17:7; 28:10;
Lk 1:13,30; 2:10;
Ac 18:9; 23:11;
Rev 1:17

14:31
a Mt 6:30

14:33
b Ps 2:7; Mt 4:3

Matthew 14:22–36

 The disciples assumed that what they saw walking on the water was sinister. Jewish superstition held that the appearance of a spirit at night spelled disaster. Jesus' words "It is I" (lit., "I am") alluded both to God's voice from the burning bush (Ex. 3:14) and to the voice of assurance to Israel of his identity and presence as Savior (Isa. 43:10–13). Jesus even has authority over creation, which he demonstrated by walking on a windswept lake that immediately became calm when he climbed into their boat. The story is capped off with the disciples worshiping him and proclaiming his identity: "Truly you are the Son of God."

Jesus calls us to come to him, regardless of how threatening or difficult our circumstances may seem. The key as we do so is to remember who he is and to keep our eyes fully on him. When we forget that, or shift our gaze, we may drown in our circumstances. What does this mean for you? Around the world many people feel as though they are drowning in difficulties. What one or two things, small as they may seem, can you do to help?

14:25–31

Jesus and WATER

Water was an important part of Jesus' life and teachings. Jesus frequently used water as a metaphor, and bodies of water (e.g., the Sea of Galilee and the Jordan River) were often backdrops for events in his life. Some examples:

1. Baptized in the Jordan	Matt. 3:13–17
2. Turned water into wine	John 2:3–11
3. Offered living water	John 4:10; Rev. 7:17
4. Knew where to fish	Luke 5:4
5. Calmed stormy water	Luke 8:24
6. Walked on water	Matt. 14:25–31
7. Thirsted for water on the cross	John 19:28

34When they had crossed over, they landed at Gennesaret. 35And when the men of that place recognized Jesus, they sent word to all the surrounding country. People brought all their sick to him 36and begged him to let the sick just touch the edge of his cloak, *c* and all who touched him were healed.

Clean and Unclean

15 Then some Pharisees and teachers of the law came to Jesus from Jerusalem and asked, 2"Why do your disciples break the tradition of the elders? They don't wash their hands before they eat!" *d*

3Jesus replied, "And why do you break the command of God for the sake of your tradition? 4For God said, 'Honor your father and mother' *a e* and 'Anyone who curses his father or mother must be put to death.' *b f* 5But you say that if a man says to his father or mother, 'Whatever help you might otherwise have received from me is a gift devoted to God,' 6he is not to 'honor his father*c*' with it. Thus you nullify the word of God for the sake of your tradition. 7You hypocrites! Isaiah was right when he prophesied about you:

8 " 'These people honor me with their lips,
    but their hearts are far from me.
9They worship me in vain;
    their teachings are but rules taught by men.' *g d h* "

10Jesus called the crowd to him and said, "Listen and understand. 11What goes into a man's mouth does not make him 'unclean,'*i* but what comes out of his mouth, that is what makes him 'unclean.' "*j*

12Then the disciples came to him and asked, "Do you know that the Pharisees were offended when they heard this?"

13He replied, "Every plant that my heavenly Father has not planted*k* will be pulled up by the roots. 14Leave them; they are blind guides.*e l* If a blind man leads a blind man, both will fall into a pit." *m*

15Peter said, "Explain the parable to us."*n*

16"Are you still so dull?"*o* Jesus asked them. 17"Don't you see that whatever enters the mouth goes into the stomach and then out of the body? 18But the things that come out of the mouth come from the heart,*p* and these make a man 'unclean.' 19For out of the heart come evil thoughts, murder, adultery, sexual immorality, theft, false testimony, slander. *q* 20These are what make a man 'unclean';*r* but eating with unwashed hands does not make him 'unclean.' "

The Faith of the Canaanite Woman

21Leaving that place, Jesus withdrew to the region of Tyre and Sidon. *s* 22A Canaanite woman from that vicinity came to him, crying out, "Lord, Son of David, *t* have mercy on me! My daughter is suffering terribly from demon-possession."*u*

14:36
c Mt 9:20

15:2
d Lk 11:38

15:4
e Ex 20:12; Dt 5:16; Eph 6:2 *f* Ex 21:17; Lev 20:9

15:9
g Col 2:20-22
h Isa 29:13; Mal 2:2

15:11
i Ac 10:14,15
j ver 18

15:13
k Isa 60:21; 61:3; Jn 15:2
15:14
l Mt 23:16,24; Ro 2:19 *m* Lk 6:39
15:15
n Mt 13:36
15:16
o Mt 16:9

15:18
p Mt 12:34; Lk 6:45; Jas 3:6
15:19
q Gal 5:19-21
15:20
r Ro 14:14

15:21
s Mt 11:21
15:22
t Mt 9:27 *u* Mt 4:24

a 4 Exodus 20:12; Deut. 5:16   *b* 4 Exodus 21:17; Lev. 20:9   *c* 6 Some manuscripts *father or his mother*   *d* 9 Isaiah 29:13   *e* 14 Some manuscripts *guides of the blind*

Matthew 15:1–20

The "tradition of the elders" was a reference to Old Testament interpretations made by earlier rabbis and passed on orally to later generations. By focusing on conformity to their traditions, the Pharisees were able to select the commands of Scripture they would obey, thus neglecting some of its clear directives. They lived with the appearance of purity, while their hearts and attitudes were foul. Jesus confronted them with the reality that outer purity is an expression of inner attitudes and desires.

Have you noticed how many times Jesus used examples of needy persons or of people's use of their resources/income/treasure to teach a lesson? The point of

Jesus' lesson here is that we are not to be selective about what portions of God's Word we choose to obey, while allowing our religious or human traditions to take precedence. Jesus repeatedly warned about the very religious often living with impure motives. Still today, this is often expressed in how such people use their resources and treat or regard people in need.

Matthew 15:21–28

"Lost sheep of Israel" (cf. 10:5–6) didn't indicate lost sheep *within* Israel, as though some were lost and others weren't, but the lost sheep *who were* the house of Israel. Jesus went first to Israel to fulfill the promises made to the nation (cf. Isa. 53:6–8). Only then could the Gentiles glorify God for his promises to his people (cf. Rom.

²³Jesus did not answer a word. So his disciples came to him and urged him, "Send her away, for she keeps crying out after us."

15:24
v Mt 10:6, 23;
Ro 15:8
15:25
w Mt 8:2

²⁴He answered, "I was sent only to the lost sheep of Israel." ^v

²⁵The woman came and knelt before him. ^w "Lord, help me!" she said.

²⁶He replied, "It is not right to take the children's bread and toss it to their dogs."

²⁷"Yes, Lord," she said, "but even the dogs eat the crumbs that fall from their masters' table."

15:28
x Mt 9:22

²⁸Then Jesus answered, "Woman, you have great faith! ^x Your request is granted." And her daughter was healed from that very hour.

Jesus Feeds the Four Thousand

²⁹Jesus left there and went along the Sea of Galilee. Then he went up on a mountainside and sat down. ³⁰Great crowds came to him, bringing the lame, the blind, the crippled, the mute and many others, and laid them at his feet; and he healed

15:30
y Mt 4:23

them. ^y ³¹The people were amazed when they saw the mute speaking, the crippled made well, the lame walking and the blind seeing. And they praised the God of Israel. ^z

15:31
z Mt 9:8
15:32
a Mt 9:36

³²Jesus called his disciples to him and said, "I have compassion for these people; ^a they have already been with me three days and have nothing to eat. I do not want to send them away hungry, or they may collapse on the way."

³³His disciples answered, "Where could we get enough bread in this remote place to feed such a crowd?"

³⁴"How many loaves do you have?" Jesus asked.

"Seven," they replied, "and a few small fish."

15:36
b Mt 14:19

³⁵He told the crowd to sit down on the ground. ³⁶Then he took the seven loaves and the fish, and when he had given thanks, he broke them ^b and gave them to the disciples, and they in turn to the people. ³⁷They all ate and were satisfied. Afterward

15:37
c Mt 16:10

the disciples picked up seven basketfuls of broken pieces that were left over. ^c ³⁸The number of those who ate was four thousand, besides women and children. ³⁹After Jesus had sent the crowd away, he got into the boat and went to the vicinity of Magadan.

The Demand for a Sign

16:1
d Ac 4:1 e Mt 12:38

16 The Pharisees and Sadducees ^d came to Jesus and tested him by asking him to show them a sign from heaven. ^e

---

15:8–12). Our Lord didn't demonstrate ethnic bigotry against Gentiles. But he acknowledged that God's promises would *first* be fulfilled among Abraham's descendants, through whom the whole world would eventually be blessed (Gen. 12:3; 17:3–8). Jesus held up as an example the great faith of a non-Jew, this time one of Israel's despised, historic enemies, a Canaanite woman (28:19).

📖 "Great faith" (v. 28) doesn't imply a large quantity of faith but an unshakable determination to trust God's Word and will against all odds and adverse circumstances. This woman's openness to Jesus' identity and mission allowed his healing ministry to operate in her situation. Her example offers hope to men and women of every generation. Jesus' compassionate care challenges our prejudices against and disregard for people we might otherwise be tempted to regard as unworthy.

Matthew 15:29–39

📖 Matthew reported Jesus' return to Galilee, and Mark specified that he went to the Decapolis (Mark 7:31)—a predominantly Gentile region marked by ten cities. Here he performed many miracles, authenticating his message that the kingdom of God had arrived. When

contrasted against the preceding story, the dropping of "crumbs" to the Gentile mother and daughter prepared for Jesus' turning to Gentiles with the bread and fish of the miraculous feeding of the 4,000. Gentiles were increasingly experiencing the same fullness of the kingdom as Jews: their lame walking, blind seeing, deaf hearing, and hungry being fed.

📖 The coming of God's kingdom breaks down all social barriers and transforms all aspects of life. Jesus' kingdom isn't just a spiritual reality. Our deepest needs and hungers are met and transformed. The blessing of God continually moves to those willing to admit their hunger and need and seek his righteousness.

Matthew 16:1–4

📖 Back in Jewish territory, Jesus and his disciples were confronted again by the Pharisees, this time joined by the Sadducees (see "There and Then" for 22:23–33). Usually bitter opponents, the two groups formed alliances when they perceived a threat to their leadership. Looking to trip Jesus up, they asked him for a sign—to use against him. Jesus called them to account for failing to recognize the signs of his identity and mission he had already dis-

2He replied,[a] "When evening comes, you say, 'It will be fair weather, for the sky is red,' 3and in the morning, 'Today it will be stormy, for the sky is red and overcast.' You know how to interpret the appearance of the sky, but you cannot interpret the signs of the times.[f] 4A wicked and adulterous generation looks for a miraculous sign, but none will be given it except the sign of Jonah."[g] Jesus then left them and went away.

The Yeast of the Pharisees and Sadducees

5When they went across the lake, the disciples forgot to take bread. 6"Be careful," Jesus said to them. "Be on your guard against the yeast of the Pharisees and Sadducees."[h]

7They discussed this among themselves and said, "It is because we didn't bring any bread."

8Aware of their discussion, Jesus asked, "You of little faith,[i] why are you talking among yourselves about having no bread? 9Do you still not understand? Don't you remember the five loaves for the five thousand, and how many basketfuls you gathered?[j] 10Or the seven loaves for the four thousand, and how many basketfuls you gathered?[k] 11How is it you don't understand that I was not talking to you about bread? But be on your guard against the yeast of the Pharisees and Sadducees." 12Then they understood that he was not telling them to guard against the yeast used in bread, but against the teaching of the Pharisees and Sadducees.[l]

Peter's Confession of Christ

13When Jesus came to the region of Caesarea Philippi, he asked his disciples, "Who do people say the Son of Man is?"

14They replied, "Some say John the Baptist;[m] others say Elijah; and still others, Jeremiah or one of the prophets."[n]

15"But what about you?" he asked. "Who do you say I am?"

16Simon Peter answered, "You are the Christ,[b] the Son of the living God."[o]

17Jesus replied, "Blessed are you, Simon son of Jonah, for this was not revealed to you by man,[p] but by my Father in heaven. 18And I tell you that you are Peter,[c][q] and on this rock I will build my church,[r] and the gates of Hades[d] will not overcome it.[e] 19I will give you the keys[s] of the kingdom of heaven; whatever you bind on earth will be[f] bound in heaven, and whatever you loose on earth will be[f] loosed in heaven."[t] 20Then he warned his disciples not to tell anyone[u] that he was the Christ.

16:3
f Lk 12:54-56
16:4
g Mt 12:39

16:6
h Lk 12:1

16:8
i Mt 6:30

16:9
j Mt 14:17-21
16:10
k Mt 15:34-38

16:12
l Ac 4:1

16:14
m Mt 3:1; 14:2
n Mk 6:15; Jn 1:21
16:16
o Mt 4:3; Ps 42:2; Jn 11:27; Ac 14:15; 2Co 6:16; 1Th 1:9; 1Ti 3:15; Heb 10:31; 12:22
16:17
p 1Co 15:50; Gal 1:16; Eph 6:12; Heb 2:14
16:18
q Jn 1:42
r Eph 2:20
16:19
s Isa 22:22; Rev 3:7
t Mt 18:18; Jn 20:23
16:20
u Mk 8:30

---

a 2 Some early manuscripts do not have the rest of verse 2 and all of verse 3.   b 16 Or Messiah; also in verse 20   c 18 Peter means rock.   d 18 Or hell   e 18 Or not prove stronger than it
f 19 Or have been

---

played (cf. 11:2–6). Because of their evil intention, the only other sign he would give them would be one of God's coming judgment: a comparison between Jonah's days in the whale and Jesus' burial and resurrection (cf. 12:40).

📖 Throughout chapter 16, Matthew would call his readers to view Jesus from God's perspective. The religious leaders wanted signs of Jesus' Messianic identity on their terms. Still today, some seek to test Jesus, or accept him only on their own terms before they will believe. Jesus is uncompromising. Those desiring to understand him can't appeal to any other authority or experience to test or prove his truthfulness.

Matthew 16:5–12

📖 The disciples had neglected to bring provisions for what now appeared to be an extended trip. Jesus used the occasion to instruct them about the Pharisees and Sadducees who had just tried to trap him. He had already used yeast as a positive metaphor to represent the permeating nature of the kingdom of heaven

(13:33). Here he used it negatively to indicate how the evil of corruption can penetrate that which is good (e.g., Ex. 12:8,15–20). The earlier parable of the mystery of the kingdom should have prepared the disciples to understand that he was again referring symbolically to yeast.

📖 The disciples had witnessed two miraculous feedings. They had heard the clause in Jesus' model prayer, "Give us today our daily bread" (6:11), as well as his admonition not to worry about food (6:25–34). They should have been ready to allow Jesus to provide their material needs. When have you found yourself so preoccupied by temporal concerns that you forgot about God's faithfulness? Each of us is called to live with a challenging balance: appropriate attention to daily responsibilities, but ultimate dependency on God's providential care.

Matthew 16:13–20

📖 Jesus' statement about "keys" had to do with entrance into the kingdom of heaven. God alone can grant forgiveness of sins and kingdom entry, but Peter

Jesus Predicts His Death

21 From that time on Jesus began to explain to his disciples that he must go to Jerusalem and suffer many things *v* at the hands of the elders, chief priests and teachers of the law, and that he must be killed and on the third day *w* be raised to life. *x*

22 Peter took him aside and began to rebuke him. "Never, Lord!" he said. "This shall never happen to you!"

23 Jesus turned and said to Peter, "Get behind me, Satan! *y* You are a stumbling block to me; you do not have in mind the things of God, but the things of men."

24 Then Jesus said to his disciples, "If anyone would come after me, he must deny himself and take up his cross and follow me. *z* 25 For whoever wants to save his life *a* will lose it, but whoever loses his life for me will find it. *a* 26 What good will it be for a man if he gains the whole world, yet forfeits his soul? Or what can a man give in exchange for his soul? 27 For the Son of Man *b* is going to come *c* in his Father's glory with his angels, and then he will reward each person according to what he has done. *d* 28 I tell you the truth, some who are standing here will not taste death before they see the Son of Man coming in his kingdom."

The Transfiguration

17 After six days Jesus took with him Peter, James and John the brother of James, and led them up a high mountain by themselves. 2 There he was transfigured before them. His face shone like the sun, and his clothes became as white as the light. 3 Just then there appeared before them Moses and Elijah, talking with Jesus.

4 Peter said to Jesus, "Lord, it is good for us to be here. If you wish, I will put up three shelters—one for you, one for Moses and one for Elijah."

5 While he was still speaking, a bright cloud enveloped them, and a voice from the cloud said, "This is my Son, whom I love; with him I am well pleased. *e* Listen to him!" *f*

---

a 25 The Greek word means either *life* or *soul*; also in verse 26.

Margin references

16:21
v Mk 10:34;
Lk 17:25 *w* Jn 2:19
x Mt 17:22,23;
27:63; Mk 9:31;
Lk 9:22; 18:31-33;
24:6,7
16:23
y Mt 4:10

16:24
z Mt 10:38;
Lk 14:27
16:25
a Jn 12:25
16:27
b Mt 8:20 *c* Ac 1:11
d Job 34:11;
Ps 62:12; Jer 17:10;
Ro 2:6; 2Co 5:10;
Rev 22:12

17:5
e Mt 3:17; 2Pe 1:17
f Ac 3:22,23

---

was given authority to declare the terms. This representative disciple who made the first personal confession of Jesus' identity (v. 16) would soon open that kingdom door by preaching the gospel—first to Jews at Pentecost (Acts 2), then to Gentiles (Acts 10). Peter stood in contrast to the Pharisees, who shut the door for people trying to enter (Matt. 23:13).

📖 The door to the kingdom Peter opened will remain open until Jesus returns (cf. Acts 1:11). Today we have the privilege of inviting people inside. This gives new meaning to the ministry of hospitality and the phrase in Psalm 84:10 about being a "doorkeeper" in the house of God. We obviously want to make the invitation attractive. But the call remains clear. We are to set our minds on the divine, not on human things. Faith in Jesus can't simply be inserted on top of our other commitments. Entrance into the kingdom means submitting everything to doing God's will.

Matthew 16:21–28

⚕ At the start of Jesus' ministry, Satan had tried to tempt him away from the Father's will (4:1–11). Now Satan used Peter—the same Peter who had just received an amazing revelation from God (16:17)—to try to hinder Jesus' mission. Peter had his own ideas about the Messiah's path, but he needed to know God's plans. There were, and are, only two choices: God's way or Satan's. God's ways are often quite different from human ways—and diametrically opposed to Satan's propositions.

📖 The cross was for Jesus, and remains for us who follow him, our primary symbol of doing the Father's will. It involves both the negative—"denying self" (our own will for our life)—and the positive—"taking up the cross" (accepting God's will) and "following Jesus" (putting it into practice).

It's easy for us to judge Peter. But if we are honest with ourselves, we will see our own tendencies to be swayed by our circumstances. We need to appreciate deeply the powerful, courageous stand and role Peter played in the outworking of salvation history. To do God's will, our only choice is to yield ourselves consistently to his leading in every area of life.

Matthew 17:1–13

⚕ Both Moses and Elijah had experienced mountaintop visions of God's glory (Ex. 24:15–18; 1 Kings 19:8–18). Elijah had been taken directly to heaven (2 Kings 2:11–12), and rabbinic tradition says the same of Moses (cf. Deut. 34:5–6). Malachi 4:4–6 mentions them together: The law came through Moses, and the prophet Elijah would precede the day of the Lord. Their appearance together on the mountain underscored the greatness of Jesus, who surpassed both the Law and the Prophets as the One declared to be God's Son (Matt. 17:5).

The disciples were so close to Jesus physically that they couldn't understand the immensity of his incarnation (his taking on our human nature). It took the transfiguration to shake them into seeing that what Peter had

6When the disciples heard this, they fell facedown to the ground, terrified. 7But Jesus came and touched them. "Get up," he said. "Don't be afraid."[g] 8When they looked up, they saw no one except Jesus.

9As they were coming down the mountain, Jesus instructed them, "Don't tell anyone[h] what you have seen, until the Son of Man[i] has been raised from the dead."[j]

10The disciples asked him, "Why then do the teachers of the law say that Elijah must come first?"

11Jesus replied, "To be sure, Elijah comes and will restore all things.[k] 12But I tell you, Elijah has already come,[l] and they did not recognize him, but have done to him everything they wished.[m] In the same way the Son of Man is going to suffer[n] at their hands." 13Then the disciples understood that he was talking to them about John the Baptist.

The Healing of a Boy With a Demon

14When they came to the crowd, a man approached Jesus and knelt before him. 15"Lord, have mercy on my son," he said. "He has seizures[o] and is suffering greatly. He often falls into the fire or into the water. 16I brought him to your disciples, but they could not heal him."

17"O unbelieving and perverse generation," Jesus replied, "how long shall I stay with you? How long shall I put up with you? Bring the boy here to me." 18Jesus rebuked the demon, and it came out of the boy, and he was healed from that moment.

19Then the disciples came to Jesus in private and asked, "Why couldn't we drive it out?"

20He replied, "Because you have so little faith. I tell you the truth, if you have faith[p] as small as a mustard seed,[q] you can say to this mountain, 'Move from here to there' and it will move.[r] Nothing will be impossible for you.[a]"

22When they came together in Galilee, he said to them, "The Son of Man[s] is going to be betrayed into the hands of men. 23They will kill him,[t] and on the third day[u] he will be raised to life."[v] And the disciples were filled with grief.

The Temple Tax

24After Jesus and his disciples arrived in Capernaum, the collectors of the two-drachma tax[w] came to Peter and asked, "Doesn't your teacher pay the temple tax[b]?"
25"Yes, he does," he replied.

---

[a] 20 Some manuscripts you. 21But this kind does not go out except by prayer and fasting. [b] 24 Greek the two drachmas

---

Cross references:
- 17:7 [g] Mt 14:27
- 17:9 [h] Mk 8:30 [i] Mt 8:20 [j] Mt 16:21
- 17:11 [k] Mal 4:6; Lk 1:16,17
- 17:12 [l] Mt 11:14 [m] Mt 14:3,10 [n] Mt 16:21
- 17:15 [o] Mt 4:24
- 17:20 [p] Mt 21:21 [q] Mt 13:31; Mk 11:23; Lk 17:6 [r] 1Co 13:2
- 17:22 [s] Mt 8:20
- 17:23 [t] Ac 2:23; 3:13 [u] Mt 16:21 [v] Mt 16:21
- 17:24 [w] Ex 30:13

---

said was true (16:16). Jesus wasn't just divinely endowed—he was divine.

🖳 Like the disciples, our worldview is radically transformed when we place Jesus at its center. Not only our thoughts, but also our daily priorities and activities, are then evaluated in light of Jesus' revelation. The Father instructed the disciples to "listen to him!" That means being attuned to his concrete, practical guidance for the way we live—how much television and what kinds of movies we watch, how we budget our income, the respect we show our family members, the kind of car we drive, our style of clothing, the words we speak. How is your lifestyle different because you are Jesus' disciple?

Matthew 17:14–23

🖳 Immediately following the extraordinary encounter with God in the transfiguration, Jesus' disciples were confronted with the demonic. This account reveals a holistic understanding of the interplay between spiritual and natural forces in this world. Not all illness or disease is the direct result of demonic activity, but the fallenness of this world does impact our entire being.

After the disciples heard Jesus condemn his generation for lack of faith, they questioned him in private about their own inability to heal the boy. Jesus reinforced the same theme: their "little faith."

🖳 Move a mountain? Faith is confidence that we can do whatever God calls us to do—even seemingly absurd things from the world's viewpoint. It's not the amount of our faith that works miracles. It's the focus of that faith on Jesus, who will work miracles through us according to his will. Jesus' point was that anyone with any amount of faith can do remarkable things—if that is what God has called them to do. In his strength we can accomplish anything he wills (cf. Phil. 4:13; 1 Jn. 5:14–15). What has God enabled you to do for him?

Matthew 17:24–27

🖳 Unlike Matthew, who had collected taxes for the occupying Roman forces (9:9), these tax collectors represented the Jewish religious establishment in Jerusalem overseeing the temple and its tax (cf. Ex. 30:13–14; Neh. 10:32–33). Since the temple was his Father's house, Jesus was exempt from paying the tax. By

17:25
x Mt 22:17-21;
Ro 13:7

When Peter came into the house, Jesus was the first to speak. "What do you think, Simon?" he asked. "From whom do the kings of the earth collect duty and taxes[x]—from their own sons or from others?"

26 "From others," Peter answered.

17:27
y Jn 6:61

"Then the sons are exempt," Jesus said to him. 27 "But so that we may not offend[y] them, go to the lake and throw out your line. Take the first fish you catch; open its mouth and you will find a four-drachma coin. Take it and give it to them for my tax and yours."

The Greatest in the Kingdom of Heaven

18 At that time the disciples came to Jesus and asked, "Who is the greatest in the kingdom of heaven?"

18:3
z Mt 19:14; 1Pe 2:2
a Mt 3:2
18:4
b Mk 9:35
18:5
c Mt 10:40
18:6
d Mt 5:29
e Mk 9:42; Lk 17:2

2 He called a little child and had him stand among them. 3 And he said: "I tell you the truth, unless you change and become like little children,[z] you will never enter the kingdom of heaven.[a] 4 Therefore, whoever humbles himself like this child is the greatest in the kingdom of heaven.[b]

5 "And whoever welcomes a little child like this in my name welcomes me.[c] 6 But if anyone causes one of these little ones who believe in me to sin,[d] it would be better for him to have a large millstone hung around his neck and to be drowned in the depths of the sea.[e]

18:7
f Lk 17:1
18:8
g Mt 5:29;
Mk 9:43,45
18:9
h Mt 5:29 i Mt 5:22

7 "Woe to the world because of the things that cause people to sin! Such things must come, but woe to the man through whom they come![f] 8 If your hand or your foot causes you to sin,[g] cut it off and throw it away. It is better for you to enter life maimed or crippled than to have two hands or two feet and be thrown into eternal fire. 9 And if your eye causes you to sin,[h] gouge it out and throw it away. It is better for you to enter life with one eye than to have two eyes and be thrown into the fire of hell.[i]

The Parable of the Lost Sheep

18:10
j Ge 48:16; Ps 34:7;
Ac 12:11,15;
Heb 1:14

10 "See that you do not look down on one of these little ones. For I tell you that their angels[j] in heaven always see the face of my Father in heaven.[a] 12 "What do you think? If a man owns a hundred sheep, and one of them wan-

a 10 Some manuscripts *heaven.* 11*The Son of Man came to save what was lost.*

---

extension, his disciples, now part of the Father's family (Matt. 12:48–50), were too. After Jesus' coming sacrifice there would be no need for the temple system. Jesus and the disciples paid the tax not from obligation but to avoid offending the conscience of those Jews who hadn't yet experienced liberation through him.

Have you ever set aside something you were rightfully entitled to in order to benefit someone else? True freedom is the ability to sacrifice ourselves for the good of others (cf. Rom. 14:13—15:4). The kingdom life that characterizes the church and us as disciples in this world isn't about asserting our rights. We have been set free *from* sin, *to* serve. As the reformer Martin Luther (1483–1546) stated, "A Christian . . . is the most free lord of all, and subject to none; a Christian . . . is the most dutiful servant of all, and subject to every one."

Matthew 18:1–9

Jesus celebrated the humility inherent in a child's defenselessness and vulnerability. He used this as a visual aid to contrast the world's greatness with the kingdom's (cf. 5:3–10). What's more, he stressed that our response to God will be measured in part by how we treat children. God's judgment on those who abuse the defenseless and vulnerable is so severe that people in all

eras are wise to resort even to extreme measures to avoid inflicting such harm.

We are wise not to jump too quickly from Jesus' statements about children to their broader applications. Jesus commented on the defenselessness of actual children. Take a few moments to think about how your society and others around the world treat the very young. If Jesus cautioned people against harming a disciple, how do you think he views those who abuse or take advantage of children? As his disciple, what could you do to make a difference for one or more of these vulnerable little ones?

Matthew 18:10–14

In the midst of the crowds, Jesus stressed God's tender regard for individuals, and especially for the vulnerable, lost, and neglected. As the Father pursues everyone, desiring none to be lost, so Jesus warned his followers to care for the defenseless. No mention is given in his parable as to whether the sheep was lost by its own fault—or even stupidity. No blame is suggested, no judgment cast. The Father has compassion on all—and he calls his followers to do the same.

Do we as Christians truly live up to our sad reputation of "shooting our own wounded"? It's sometimes

ders away, will he not leave the ninety-nine on the hills and go to look for the one that wandered off? 13And if he finds it, I tell you the truth, he is happier about that one sheep than about the ninety-nine that did not wander off. 14In the same way your Father in heaven is not willing that any of these little ones should be lost.

A Brother Who Sins Against You

15 "If your brother sins against you, *a* go and show him his fault, *k* just between the two of you. If he listens to you, you have won your brother over. 16But if he will not listen, take one or two others along, so that 'every matter may be established by the testimony of two or three witnesses.' *b l* 17If he refuses to listen to them, tell it to the church; *m* and if he refuses to listen even to the church, treat him as you would a pagan or a tax collector. *n*

18"I tell you the truth, whatever you bind on earth will be *c* bound in heaven, and whatever you loose on earth will be *c* loosed in heaven. *o*

19"Again, I tell you that if two of you on earth agree about anything you ask for, it will be done for you *p* by my Father in heaven. 20For where two or three come together in my name, there am I with them."

a 15 Some manuscripts do not have *against you.*   *b* 16 Deut. 19:15   *c* 18 Or *have been*

18:15
k Lev 19:17;
Lk 17:3; Gal 6:1;
Jas 5:19,20
18:16
l Nu 35:30; Dt 17:6;
19:15; Jn 8:17;
2Co 13:1; 1Ti 5:19;
Heb 10:28
18:17
m 1Co 6:1-6
n Ro 16:17;
2Th 3:6,14
18:18
o Mt 16:19;
Jn 20:23
18:19
p Mt 7:7

easiest to beat down a fallen brother or sister, punishing them for a lack of faithfulness or trying to get even with other believers for the hurts they have caused. But the church is accountable to the Shepherd for attempting to restore those who have gone astray. Jesus calls us to reach out to such people so they can return to fruitfulness in the Christian community. What experience do you have in dealing with a straying believer? What was the outcome?

Matthew 18:15–20
Jesus called his disciples (now the church) to be the center-point of reconciliation. Avoiding the extremes of either ignoring or escalating conflict, he outlined a careful process for healing hurts and mending torn lives.

This reconciliation has eternal consequences, binding evil and releasing healing justice and righteousness on Earth and in heaven.

Few ministries are more urgently needed in our broken societies, communities, and homes than the work of reconciliation. Identify some situations in your own experience that need to have evil and brokenness bound and the healing power of reconciliation released. Two guidelines are important: (1) The goal is restoration of relationship, and (2) the ultimate source of the discipline is God himself. Jesus calls us to gather together and pray in his name that the world might experience his reconciling life.

18:19–20

Jesus' Messages in Matthew's Gospel

Matthew had a special interest in Jesus' messages (sermons or discourses). Mark and Luke summarized several of them. John's Gospel records the extended Upper Room Discourse Jesus gave on the night before his crucifixion (John 13–17). But Matthew has preserved five major messages. When viewed together, they describe the kind of disciple who will develop when taught to obey the teaching of these messages.

Message	Passage	Focus	Teaching
1. Sermon on the Mount	Matt. 5–7	Kingdom life	Unpacks what it means for Jesus' disciples to live out radical kingdom values in their everyday world
2. Mission Mandate	Matt. 10	Missions	Specifies how Jesus' disciples are to go and live out the message of the gospel of the kingdom in a hostile world
3. Parable Discourse	Matt. 13	Unseen nature of God's kingdom	Reveals what it means for Jesus' disciples to live as kingdom subjects in a world where (1) God's power is known and available to believers, but (2) non-believers live in ignorance or denial of this hidden kingdom's existence
4. Community Prescription	Matt. 18	A kingdom built on community	Focuses on discipleship to Jesus expressed through a faith community that lives in humility, purity, accountability, forgiveness, and reconciliation
5. Future Forecast (Olivet Discourse)	Matt. 24–25	Waiting and preparation for kingdom to come	Describes how Jesus' disciples are to live each day as travelers in this world, preparing for his return in power

Source: NIV Application Commentary, Matthew (2004)

The Parable of the Unmerciful Servant

18:21
q Mt 6:14 *r* Lk 17:4
18:22
s Ge 4:24
18:23
t Mt 13:24
u Mt 25:19
18:25
v Lk 7:42
w Lev 25:39;
2Ki 4:1; Ne 5:5,8

18:26
x Mt 8:2

21Then Peter came to Jesus and asked, "Lord, how many times shall I forgive my brother when he sins against me?*q* Up to seven times?"*r*

22Jesus answered, "I tell you, not seven times, but seventy-seven times.*a s*

23"Therefore, the kingdom of heaven is like*t* a king who wanted to settle accounts*u* with his servants. **24**As he began the settlement, a man who owed him ten thousand talents*b* was brought to him. **25**Since he was not able to pay,*v* the master ordered that he and his wife and his children and all that he had be sold*w* to repay the debt.

26"The servant fell on his knees before him.*x* 'Be patient with me,' he begged, 'and I will pay back everything.' **27**The servant's master took pity on him, canceled the debt and let him go.

28"But when that servant went out, he found one of his fellow servants who owed him a hundred denarii.*c* He grabbed him and began to choke him. 'Pay back what you owe me!' he demanded.

29"His fellow servant fell to his knees and begged him, 'Be patient with me, and I will pay you back.'

30"But he refused. Instead, he went off and had the man thrown into prison until he could pay the debt. **31**When the other servants saw what had happened, they were greatly distressed and went and told their master everything that had happened.

32"Then the master called the servant in. 'You wicked servant,' he said, 'I canceled all that debt of yours because you begged me to. **33**Shouldn't you have had mercy on your fellow servant just as I had on you?' **34**In anger his master turned him over to the jailers to be tortured, until he should pay back all he owed.

18:35
y Mt 6:14; Jas 2:13

35"This is how my heavenly Father will treat each of you unless you forgive your brother from your heart."*y*

Divorce

19:1
z Mt 7:28
19:2
a Mt 4:23
19:3
b Mt 5:31

19 When Jesus had finished saying these things,*z* he left Galilee and went into the region of Judea to the other side of the Jordan. **2**Large crowds followed him, and he healed them*a* there.

3Some Pharisees came to him to test him. They asked, "Is it lawful for a man to divorce his wife*b* for any and every reason?"

---

a 22 Or *seventy times seven*   *b 24* That is, millions of dollars   *c 28* That is, a few dollars

---

Matthew 18:21–35

The standard teaching within Judaism (based on Job 33:29–30; Amos 1:3; 2:6) was that three instances of forgiveness reflected a forgiving spirit. Peter's offer to more than double that number was generous, probably reflecting his desire for the completeness the number seven usually represented. Jesus' response, in essence that Peter was to forgive countless times, was astonishing. Jesus offered the rationale for this unheard of concept in his parable: The reality of the forgiveness Peter himself had received would be demonstrated in the way he forgave others (cf. 6:14–15).

Jesus advocated the unqualified expulsion of all we hold against others. The world can't understand this value because hurt is real in offended relationships. We don't want to be used, to be vulnerable again. We *do* want to get even with our abusers. Many states in the U.S. have adopted a "three strikes and you are out" law. But God's unqualified forgiveness impacts all our relationships. Mercy experienced produces mercy demonstrated. How has this been true in your life? Can you personally attest to the freedom forgiveness offers, to the forgiver as well as to the forgiven?

Matthew 19:1–12

Divorce isn't a morally neutral option. It evidences hardness of heart. The Pharisees had focused on the wrong issue. They weren't looking at God's original intention (Gen. 2:24; Mal. 2:15–16) but at Moses' prescription for dealing with sin (Deut. 24:1–4). With the arrival of the gospel of the kingdom, the reversal of the fallen order had begun—implying the redemption of marriages as well. Hard hearts could be regenerated and the divorce certificate (except in the case of marital unfaithfulness) made obsolete.

Is there a relationship in your life that needs healing? Jesus doesn't condemn you. Chapters 18–20 reveal the antidote for hurting and hardened hearts—a combination of humility, purity, accountability, discipline, reconciliation, restoration, and forgiveness—whether the hard heart is within a marriage or a church. This spiritual medicine penetrates to our deepest needs and affects all our relationships. God's healing can draw back together estranged disciples of all backgrounds.

4 "Haven't you read," he replied, "that at the beginning the Creator 'made them male and female,'[a][c] 5 and said, 'For this reason a man will leave his father and mother and be united to his wife, and the two will become one flesh'[b]? [d] 6 So they are no longer two, but one. Therefore what God has joined together, let man not separate."

7 "Why then," they asked, "did Moses command that a man give his wife a certificate of divorce and send her away?"[e]

8 Jesus replied, "Moses permitted you to divorce your wives because your hearts were hard. But it was not this way from the beginning. 9 I tell you that anyone who divorces his wife, except for marital unfaithfulness, and marries another woman commits adultery."[f]

10 The disciples said to him, "If this is the situation between a husband and wife, it is better not to marry."

11 Jesus replied, "Not everyone can accept this word, but only those to whom it has been given.[g] 12 For some are eunuchs because they were born that way; others were made that way by men; and others have renounced marriage[c] because of the kingdom of heaven. The one who can accept this should accept it."

The Little Children and Jesus

13 Then little children were brought to Jesus for him to place his hands on them[h] and pray for them. But the disciples rebuked those who brought them.

14 Jesus said, "Let the little children come to me, and do not hinder them, for the kingdom of heaven belongs[i] to such as these."[j] 15 When he had placed his hands on them, he went on from there.

The Rich Young Man

16 Now a man came up to Jesus and asked, "Teacher, what good thing must I do to get eternal life[k]?"[l]

17 "Why do you ask me about what is good?" Jesus replied. "There is only One who is good. If you want to enter life, obey the commandments."[m]

18 "Which ones?" the man inquired.

Jesus replied, " 'Do not murder, do not commit adultery,[n] do not steal, do not give false testimony, 19 honor your father and mother,'[d][o] and 'love your neighbor as yourself.'[e]"[p]

20 "All these I have kept," the young man said. "What do I still lack?"

---

[a] 4 Gen. 1:27   [b] 5 Gen. 2:24   [c] 12 Or *have made themselves eunuchs*   [d] 19 Exodus 20:12-16;
Deut. 5:16-20   [e] 19 Lev. 19:18

Cross references

19:4
[c] Ge 1:27; 5:2
19:5
[d] Ge 2:24;
1Co 6:16; Eph 5:31

19:7
[e] Dt 24:1-4;
Mt 5:31

19:9
[f] Mt 5:32; Lk 16:18

19:11
[g] Mt 13:11;
1Co 7:7-9,17

19:13
[h] Mk 5:23

19:14
[i] Mt 25:34
[j] Mt 18:3; 1Pe 2:2

19:16
[k] Mt 25:46
[l] Lk 10:25

19:17
[m] Lev 18:5

19:18
[n] Jas 2:11
19:19
[o] Ex 20:12-16;
Dt 5:16-20
[p] Lev 19:18;
Mt 5:43

Matthew 19:13–15

The very weakness of children often makes them most receptive to Jesus' words. Before hardening of the heart sets in from experiencing life's hurts, vulnerable children have always been open to learning to trust the gospel's message of hope and salvation. Jesus' gentle kindness to them, his compassionate touch, and his protective and affirming words elevated them to being valuable people in the kingdom.

All humans are equally precious to Jesus, and this picture of his tender touch on the little children has become an emblem of missionary and humanitarian efforts for the church throughout history. The community of disciples sees in Jesus' actions a picture of how to devote itself to the spiritual and physical care not only of children, but of all those who are vulnerable, hurting, and on society's fringes.

Matthew 19:16–30

The young man had almost certainly given to the poor in the past. But when this act is done out of abundance, it can give the benefactor a heightened sense of power and personal pride. Jesus called him to address the central lack in his life. The man's wealth had become his means to identity, power, purpose, and meaning—in a real sense, his god. Jesus called him to exchange the god of wealth for following Jesus as the one true God. Peter got the point of Jesus' words—partly. His response showed that he, too, was motivated by less than pure "treasure in heaven" (v. 21).

What rules your life? Where do your thoughts typically turn in an idle moment? The gods of pleasure-seeking and materialism aren't new. Augustine, one of the giants of church history, struggled in this area. After coming to faith, he wrote: "The very toys of toys and vanities of vanities . . . still held me." After reading Paul's words in Romans 13:13–14, he was set free: "No further would I read; nor needed I: for instantly . . . by a light . . . serenity infused into my heart, all the darkness of doubt vanished away."

19:21
q Mt 5:48
r Lk 12:33; Ac 2:45;
4:34-35 s Mt 6:20

19:23
t Mt 13:22;
1Ti 6:9,10

19:26
u Ge 18:14;
Job 42:2; Jer 32:17;
Zec 8:6; Lk 1:37;
18:27; Ro 4:21
19:27
v Mt 4:19
19:28
w Mt 20:21; 25:31
x Lk 22:28-30;
Rev 3:21; 4:4; 20:4
19:29
y Mt 6:33; 25:46
19:30
z Mt 20:16;
Mk 10:31; Lk 13:30

21 Jesus answered, "If you want to be perfect, *q* go, sell your possessions and give to the poor, *r* and you will have treasure in heaven. *s* Then come, follow me."

22 When the young man heard this, he went away sad, because he had great wealth.

23 Then Jesus said to his disciples, "I tell you the truth, it is hard for a rich man *t* to enter the kingdom of heaven. 24 Again I tell you, it is easier for a camel to go through the eye of a needle than for a rich man to enter the kingdom of God."

25 When the disciples heard this, they were greatly astonished and asked, "Who then can be saved?"

26 Jesus looked at them and said, "With man this is impossible, but with God all things are possible." *u*

27 Peter answered him, "We have left everything to follow you! *v* What then will there be for us?"

28 Jesus said to them, "I tell you the truth, at the renewal of all things, when the Son of Man sits on his glorious throne, *w* you who have followed me will also sit on twelve thrones, judging the twelve tribes of Israel. *x* 29 And everyone who has left houses or brothers or sisters or father or mother*a* or children or fields for my sake will receive a hundred times as much and will inherit eternal life. *y* 30 But many who are first will be last, and many who are last will be first. *z*

The Parable of the Workers in the Vineyard

20:1
a Mt 13:24
b Mt 21:28,33

20 "For the kingdom of heaven is like*a* a landowner who went out early in the morning to hire men to work in his vineyard. *b* 2 He agreed to pay them a denarius for the day and sent them into his vineyard.

3 "About the third hour he went out and saw others standing in the marketplace doing nothing. 4 He told them, 'You also go and work in my vineyard, and I will pay you whatever is right.' 5 So they went.

"He went out again about the sixth hour and the ninth hour and did the same thing. 6 About the eleventh hour he went out and found still others standing around. He asked them, 'Why have you been standing here all day long doing nothing?'

7 " 'Because no one has hired us,' they answered.

"He said to them, 'You also go and work in my vineyard.'

20:8
c Lev 19:13;
Dt 24:15

8 "When evening came, *c* the owner of the vineyard said to his foreman, 'Call the workers and pay them their wages, beginning with the last ones hired and going on to the first.'

9 "The workers who were hired about the eleventh hour came and each received a denarius. 10 So when those came who were hired first, they expected to receive more. But each one of them also received a denarius. 11 When they received it, they began to grumble*d* against the landowner. 12 'These men who were hired last worked only one hour,' they said, 'and you have made them equal to us who have borne the burden of the work and the heat*e* of the day.'

20:11
d Jnh 4:1

20:12
e Jnh 4:8; Lk 12:55;
Jas 1:11
20:13
f Mt 22:12; 26:50

13 "But he answered one of them, 'Friend, *f* I am not being unfair to you. Didn't you agree to work for a denarius? 14 Take your pay and go. I want to give the man who was hired last the same as I gave you. 15 Don't I have the right to do what I want with my own money? Or are you envious because I am generous?' *g*

20:15
g Dt 15:9; Mk 7:22
20:16
h Mt 19:30

16 "So the last will be first, and the first will be last." *h*

---

a 29 Some manuscripts *mother or wife*

Matthew 20:1–16

The question the landowner asked in verse 15, "Are you envious?" literally means "Is your eye evil?" The "evil eye" in the ancient world coveted what belonged to another. The laborer couldn't be thankful because he was blinded by self-centered envy. If a disciple's eyes are fixed on earthly, material treasure as the basis for personal value, significance, and earthly security, his or her service will inevitably be compromised. Is your "eye evil"? Why not approach the Author of all good about your situation and attitude?

If you think you deserve recognition for your time, diligence, and service commitment, you have lost the value of what you have done. Jesus made it utterly clear in this parable that all of us are saved only by God's grace. All who respond to the grace of God in Jesus' kingdom invitation are equal as disciples. We are to be careful not to measure our worth by what we have done or sacrificed. Our calling is of grace, and a grateful heart will serve without thought of reward or comparison to others. As the landowner pointed out, an unthankful heart will question God's wisdom and fairness and become poisoned by envy.

Jesus Again Predicts His Death

[17] Now as Jesus was going up to Jerusalem, he took the twelve disciples aside and said to them, [18] "We are going up to Jerusalem,[i] and the Son of Man[j] will be betrayed to the chief priests and the teachers of the law.[k] They will condemn him to death [19] and will turn him over to the Gentiles to be mocked and flogged[l] and crucified.[m] On the third day[n] he will be raised to life!"[o]

A Mother's Request

[20] Then the mother of Zebedee's sons[p] came to Jesus with her sons and, kneeling down,[q] asked a favor of him.

[21] "What is it you want?" he asked.

She said, "Grant that one of these two sons of mine may sit at your right and the other at your left in your kingdom."[r]

[22] "You don't know what you are asking," Jesus said to them. "Can you drink the cup[s] I am going to drink?"

"We can," they answered.

[23] Jesus said to them, "You will indeed drink from my cup,[t] but to sit at my right or left is not for me to grant. These places belong to those for whom they have been prepared by my Father."

[24] When the ten heard about this, they were indignant[u] with the two brothers. [25] Jesus called them together and said, "You know that the rulers of the Gentiles lord it over them, and their high officials exercise authority over them. [26] Not so with you. Instead, whoever wants to become great among you must be your servant,[v] [27] and whoever wants to be first must be your slave— [28] just as the Son of Man[w] did not come to be served, but to serve,[x] and to give his life as a ransom[y] for many."

Two Blind Men Receive Sight

[29] As Jesus and his disciples were leaving Jericho, a large crowd followed him. [30] Two blind men were sitting by the roadside, and when they heard that Jesus was going by, they shouted, "Lord, Son of David,[z] have mercy on us!"

20:18
[i] Lk 9:51 / Mt 8:20
[k] Mt 16:21; 27:1,2
20:19
[l] Mt 16:21
[m] Ac 2:23
[n] Mt 16:21
[o] Mt 16:21

20:20
[p] Mt 4:21 [q] Mt 8:2

20:21
[r] Mt 19:28

20:22
[s] Isa 51:17,22;
Jer 49:12;
Mt 26:39,42;
Mk 14:36; Lk 22:42;
Jn 18:11
20:23
[t] Ac 12:2; Rev 1:9

20:24
[u] Lk 22:24,25

20:26
[v] Mt 23:11;
Mk 9:35
20:28
[w] Mt 8:20
[x] Lk 22:27;
Jn 13:13-16;
2Co 8:9; Php 2:7
[y] Isa 53:10;
Mt 26:28; 1Ti 2:6;
Tit 2:14; Heb 9:28;
1Pe 1:18,19

20:30
[z] Mt 9:27

Matthew 20:17–19

With the fateful events in Jerusalem only weeks away, Jesus took aside the Twelve to discuss his coming suffering. This was the third of four predictions Jesus made about his arrest and crucifixion (see 16:21; 17:22–23; 26:2). But the drama was heightened by his first direct references to the Jewish religious leaders condemning him to death and the Gentiles carrying out the execution.

How could the disciples have missed, or dismissed, so pointed a statement? God's way of saving through suffering, judging through being judged, exercising power through accepting weakness, is alien to our ways. Like the disciples, we too easily fail to recognize God's sovereignty expressed through weakness. The disciples' difficulty in understanding reminds us to guard against becoming so familiar with the way of the cross that we take it for granted.

Matthew 20:20–28

A "servant" (diakonos) worked for hire to maintain the master's home and property. A "slave" (doulos), on the other hand, was forced into service (although the NIV often translates doulos as "servant"). Paul used both titles to describe himself and others who gave their lives for the welfare of humanity and the church. John would later call himself a doulos of Jesus (Rev. 1:1), as would

Peter (2 Peter 1:1) and Jesus' own brothers (James 1:1; Jude 1).

How often aren't we preoccupied with our own position and status? This blinds us to what God is doing and saying in our midst. Convinced of the recognition we deserve, we become blinded to our own weakness and vulnerability. There never will be any higher position for us: We are all equal brothers and sisters under one Father and equal disciples following one Teacher and Master (23:8–12). Our position is established; we are called to turn the world's pattern of greatness upside down and find our value serving other's needs and living servant lives.

Matthew 20:29–34

Mark and Luke spoke of only one blind beggar (Mark 10:46; Luke 18:35), whom Mark identified as Bartimaeus—apparently the more prominent of the two. The blind men understood Jesus to be the "Son of David" and asked for Messianic mercy to heal them. Jesus was experiencing increasing rejection from his own people, but he continued to have compassion for those in need. Jesus likely asked "What do you want me to do for you?" in order to stimulate the blind men's faith. But the question also demonstrated his servant mindset (cf. Matt. 20:28).

It's sobering to ponder the wonder—and incongruity—of Jesus serving us. He deserved all the honor humanity could give him, but he thought first of human

31The crowd rebuked them and told them to be quiet, but they shouted all the louder, "Lord, Son of David, have mercy on us!"

32Jesus stopped and called them. "What do you want me to do for you?" he asked.

33"Lord," they answered, "we want our sight."

34Jesus had compassion on them and touched their eyes. Immediately they received their sight and followed him.

The Triumphal Entry

21 As they approached Jerusalem and came to Bethphage on the Mount of Olives, *a* Jesus sent two disciples, 2saying to them, "Go to the village ahead of you, and at once you will find a donkey tied there, with her colt by her. Untie them and bring them to me. 3If anyone says anything to you, tell him that the Lord needs them, and he will send them right away."

4This took place to fulfill what was spoken through the prophet:

5 "Say to the Daughter of Zion,
  'See, your king comes to you,
gentle and riding on a donkey,
  on a colt, the foal of a donkey.' " *a b*

6The disciples went and did as Jesus had instructed them. 7They brought the donkey and the colt, placed their cloaks on them, and Jesus sat on them. 8A very large crowd spread their cloaks *c* on the road, while others cut branches from the trees and spread them on the road. 9The crowds that went ahead of him and those that followed shouted,

"Hosanna *b* to the Son of David!" *d*

"Blessed is he who comes in the name of the Lord!" *c e*

"Hosanna *b* in the highest!" *f*

10When Jesus entered Jerusalem, the whole city was stirred and asked, "Who is this?"

11The crowds answered, "This is Jesus, the prophet *g* from Nazareth in Galilee."

Jesus at the Temple

12Jesus entered the temple area and drove out all who were buying *h* and selling there. He overturned the tables of the money changers *i* and the benches of those

a 5 Zech. 9:9   *b* 9 A Hebrew expression meaning "Save!" which became an exclamation of praise; also in verse 15   *c* 9 Psalm 118:26

Cross-references (margin):

21:1
a Mt 24:3; 26:30; Mk 14:26; Lk 19:37; 21:37; 22:39; Jn 8:1; Ac 1:12

21:5
b Isa 62:11; Zec 9:9

21:8
c 2Ki 9:13

21:9
d ver 15; Mt 9:27
e Ps 118:26;
Mt 23:39 *f* Lk 2:14

21:11
g Lk 7:16,39; 24:19;
Jn 1:21,25; 6:14;
7:40

21:12
h Dt 14:26
i Ex 30:13

---

needs, relinquishing all that was rightfully his to give himself in service to the world's hurting and blind. As we experience his ministry in our lives, our values are transformed so we can serve those around us. As you consider this challenge, try dropping to your knees—literally or in spirit. Strip away all that makes you "important," and consider yourself a servant—of Jesus and of others.

Matthew 21:1–11

Through what we call the "Triumphal Entry," Jesus intentionally declared his Messianic identity to Israel. His descent from the Mount of Olives into Jerusalem evoked images of Zechariah's prophecy of God fighting, with his feet on the Mount of Olives, on Israel's behalf (Zech. 14:3–21). Further excitement would be stirred by Jesus riding on a colt, fulfilling Zechariah's prophecy of the Messianic King coming to liberate his people (Zech. 9:9). There is no mistaking that Jesus proceeded into Jerusalem as the anticipated King, the Messianic Son of

David. But his entry was "triumphant" in a paradoxical sense: His victory would come by way of a cross.

Many in the crowd could only think of physical and military liberation. They cried "Hosanna" now, but they would soon see that Jesus wasn't bringing the kind of freedom they desired and quickly change their chant to "Crucify him!" (27:22). Why do you offer praise to Jesus? Do you love him simply and sincerely? Do you worship him for who he really is? Or do you actually care more about how he might help fulfill your own aspirations and dreams?

Matthew 21:12–17

Israel failed to understand the temple's significance. This failure wasn't just of conducting sacrifices in the wrong way, profiteering from the poor, or personal corruption among the priesthood. Jesus' critique was that ritual itself was obscuring authentic communion with God.

selling doves.[j] 13"It is written," he said to them, " 'My house will be called a house
of prayer,'[a][k] but you are making it a 'den of robbers.'[b]"[l]
14The blind and the lame came to him at the temple, and he healed them.[m] 15But
when the chief priests and the teachers of the law saw the wonderful things he did
and the children shouting in the temple area, "Hosanna to the Son of David,"[n] they
were indignant.[o]
16"Do you hear what these children are saying?" they asked him.
"Yes," replied Jesus, "have you never read,

> " 'From the lips of children and infants
> you have ordained praise'[c]?"[p]

17And he left them and went out of the city to Bethany,[q] where he spent the night.

The Fig Tree Withers

18Early in the morning, as he was on his way back to the city, he was hungry.
19Seeing a fig tree by the road, he went up to it but found nothing on it except
leaves. Then he said to it, "May you never bear fruit again!" Immediately the tree
withered.[r]
20When the disciples saw this, they were amazed. "How did the fig tree wither so
quickly?" they asked.
21Jesus replied, "I tell you the truth, if you have faith and do not doubt,[s] not only
can you do what was done to the fig tree, but also you can say to this mountain,
'Go, throw yourself into the sea,' and it will be done. 22If you believe, you will receive whatever you ask for[t] in prayer."

The Authority of Jesus Questioned

23Jesus entered the temple courts, and, while he was teaching, the chief priests
and the elders of the people came to him. "By what authority[u] are you doing these
things?" they asked. "And who gave you this authority?"

21:12 j Lev 1:14 **21:13** k Isa 56:7 l Jer 7:11 **21:14** m Mt 4:23 **21:15** n ver 9; Mt 9:27 o Lk 19:39 **21:16** p Ps 8:2 **21:17** q Mt 26:6; Mk 11:1; Lk 24:50; Jn 11:1,18; 12:1 **21:19** r Isa 34:4; Jer 8:13 **21:21** s Mt 17:20; Lk 17:6; 1Co 13:2; Jas 1:6 **21:22** t Mt 7:7 **21:23** u Ac 4:7; 7:27

a *13* Isaiah 56:7 b *13* Jer. 7:11 c *16* Psalm 8:2

Of the Gospel writers, Matthew alone mentioned Jesus' temple healings. The Jewish authorities typically restricted the lame, blind, deaf, or mute from full temple access to symbolize the purity expected in those approaching God. These healings demonstrated that, as the One greater than the temple (12:6), Jesus, the perfect high priest, welcomed those considered unclean and unworthy into God's presence, there to be made clean. Once again Jesus stressed the example of children in leading God's people in worship.

After reading this passage, we can't avoid the question: How much of our religious activity is purely self-serving ritual? Conversely, what percentage of our everyday routine is conducted in open consciousness of Jesus' presence, in communion with him? By focusing on the temple's real purpose, Jesus opened the door for healing. Are there people you regard as the "wrong kind," whose presence in your worship service would seem "unfitting" or uncomfortable? Might a certain amount of discomfort be exactly what the church needs to promote healthy self-reflection and awareness?

Matthew 21:18–22

Was Jesus temperamental? After reading Matthew 21:12–19, you might come to that conclusion. But Jesus' action in cursing the fig tree was symbolic, not reactive. Just as a fig tree's fruitfulness was a sign of health, so fruitfulness was a sign of Israel's covenant faithfulness. Judgment was at hand for Israel. The nation, especially represented by its religious leadership, had perverted temple practices and failed to repent at the arrival of the Messiah and the kingdom of heaven.

Human beings were created to carry out God's will—to enter into a discipleship relationship to him, to demonstrate fruit in a life of faith empowered by prayer and service. When we live in this manner, our lives become one continual act of worship. Our faith in Jesus impacts their every aspect, in the marketplace or in meditation, on the freeway or in a gym, walking the neighbor's dog or waking with our spouse at our side. In all things we are to live a worshipful life that gives adoration, praise, and glory to Jesus, bearing fruit for the kingdom.

Matthew 21:23–27

Most likely on Tuesday morning of Holy Week, Jesus returned to the temple. The religious leaders hadn't endorsed John the Baptist, who had condemned them for failing to repent (cf. 3:7–10). Besides, John had pointed to Jesus as the Messiah (cf. 3:11–17). Their admitting this truth would have validated Jesus' authority. But they were spiritually dishonest—hypocrites—for failing to acknowledge the truth they knew and for hardening their hearts against God's revelation.

The world hates a hypocrite. Each of us has a vital responsibility to represent our Savior and Lord accurately and consistently. If our testimony is flawed by

24 Jesus replied, "I will also ask you one question. If you answer me, I will tell you by what authority I am doing these things. 25 John's baptism—where did it come from? Was it from heaven, or from men?"

They discussed it among themselves and said, "If we say, 'From heaven,' he will ask, 'Then why didn't you believe him?' 26 But if we say, 'From men'—we are afraid of the people, for they all hold that John was a prophet." v

27 So they answered Jesus, "We don't know."

Then he said, "Neither will I tell you by what authority I am doing these things.

The Parable of the Two Sons

28 "What do you think? There was a man who had two sons. He went to the first and said, 'Son, go and work today in the vineyard.' w

29 " 'I will not,' he answered, but later he changed his mind and went.

30 "Then the father went to the other son and said the same thing. He answered, 'I will, sir,' but he did not go.

31 "Which of the two did what his father wanted?"

"The first," they answered.

Jesus said to them, "I tell you the truth, the tax collectors x and the prostitutes y are entering the kingdom of God ahead of you. 32 For John came to you to show you the way of righteousness, z and you did not believe him, but the tax collectors a and the prostitutes b did. And even after you saw this, you did not repent c and believe him.

The Parable of the Tenants

33 "Listen to another parable: There was a landowner who planted d a vineyard. He put a wall around it, dug a winepress in it and built a watchtower. e Then he rented the vineyard to some farmers and went away on a journey. f 34 When the harvest time approached, he sent his servants g to the tenants to collect his fruit.

35 "The tenants seized his servants; they beat one, killed another, and stoned a third. h 36 Then he sent other servants i to them, more than the first time, and the tenants treated them the same way. 37 Last of all, he sent his son to them. 'They will respect my son,' he said.

38 "But when the tenants saw the son, they said to each other, 'This is the heir. j Come, let's kill him k and take his inheritance.' l 39 So they took him and threw him out of the vineyard and killed him.

40 "Therefore, when the owner of the vineyard comes, what will he do to those tenants?"

Cross references (margin)

21:26
v Mt 11:9; Mk 6:20

21:28
w ver 33; Mt 20:1

21:31
x Lk 7:29 y Lk 7:50

21:32
z Mt 3:1-12
a Lk 3:12,13; 7:29
b Lk 7:36-50
c Lk 7:30

21:33
d Ps 80:8 e Isa 5:1-7
f Mt 25:14,15

21:34
g Mt 22:3

21:35
h 2Ch 24:21;
Mt 23:34,37;
Heb 11:36,37
21:36
i Mt 22:4
21:38
j Heb 1:2
k Mt 12:14 l Ps 2:8

---

word, silence, action, or inaction, an unforgiving world will call our bluff. God's reputation is at stake. Can those of us who follow Christ afford to discredit the gospel by our own hypocrisy?

Matthew 21:28–32

The son who initially refused to comply with the father's directive but then obeyed was like those in Israel who were disobedient to the law, like the tax collectors and prostitutes. When John the Baptist announced the arrival of the kingdom of God and its implications, they repented. By contrast, the religious leaders were like the son who verbally consented but did nothing. They were externally obedient to the law, but when God sent his messenger, John, they ignored his warnings.

We, too, must address Jesus' question, "Which of the two did what his father wanted?" Those who truly repent will obey God—and by their obedience show their repentance. In the final analysis, the fruit of our lives demonstrates whether or not we are submissive to God's message.

Matthew 21:33–46

The religious leaders had neither acknowledged Jesus publicly as God's Son nor publicly condemned him for fear of the crowds (cf. vv. 45–46). But Jesus foretold their line of attack. They would condemn him for being a Messianic pretender and would have him killed by the Gentiles, thinking that would enable them to retain their claim to religious authority. He had been telling his disciples of his death at the hands of the religious leaders (16:21; 17:23; 20:18–19). Now he told the leaders themselves in parable form.

The privileged role of the religious leaders in caring for God's "vineyard" was being taken away. Israel's special role in the establishment of God's kingdom also would be removed and given to all believers. The church, a nation of gathered people, includes both Jews and Gentiles. Its establishment hasn't abolished God's promises made to Israel (cf. Rom. 11:25–32). But it does point to the transition of leadership and prominence given to the church in the outworking of God's kingdom initiative today.

Walking With Jesus Through the Holy (Passion) Week

Modern Calendar Day	Event	Scripture
• Saturday	Arrival in Bethany	John 12:1
	Evening celebration—Mary anoints Jesus	John 12:2–8; cf. Matt. 26:6–13
• Sunday	Triumphal entry into Jerusalem	Matt. 21:1–11; Mark 11:1–10; Luke 19:28–44; John 12:12–18
	Jesus surveys temple area	Mark 11:11
	Return to Bethany	Matt. 21:17; Mark 11:11
• Monday	Cursing the fig tree	Matt. 21:18–22; cf. Mark 11:12–14
	Cleansing the temple	Matt. 21:12–13; Mark 11:15–17; Luke 19:45–48
	Miracles and challenges in the temple	Matt. 21:14–16; Mark 11:18
	Return to Bethany	Matt. 21:17; Mark 11:19
• Tuesday	Reaction to cursing the fig tree	Matt. 21:20–22; Mark 11:20–21
	Debates with religious leaders in Jerusalem and teaching in the temple	Matt. 21:23—23:39; Mark 11:27—12:44
	Teaching about end times on the Mount of Olives on return to Bethany	Matt. 24:1—25:46; Mark 13:1–37
• Wednesday	Jesus and disciples remain in Bethany for fellowship ("Silent Wednesday")	None
	Judas returns alone to Jerusalem to make preparations for betrayal	Matt. 26:14–16; Mark 14:10–11; Luke 22:1–6
• Thursday	Preparations for Passover	Matt. 26:17–19; Mark 14:12–16: Luke 22:7–13
	Passover meal and Last Supper (after sundown)	Matt. 26:20–35; Mark 12:17–25; Luke 22:14–38
	Upper Room Discourses	John 13–17
	Prayer in the Garden of Gethsemane	Matt. 26:36–46; Mark 14:32–42; Luke 22:39–46
• Friday	Betrayal and arrest (perhaps after midnight)	Matt. 26:47–56; Mark 14:43–52; Luke 22:47–53; John 18:1–11
	Jewish trial—Jesus appears before Annas, Caiaphas, and partial Sanhedrin, and (perhaps after sunrise) the fully assembled Sanhedrin	Matt. 26:57—27:2; Mark 14:53—15:1; Luke 22:54–65; John 18:12–27
	Roman trial—Jesus appears in three phases before Pilate, Herod Antipas, and back to Pilate	Matt. 27:2–26; Mark 15:2–15; Luke 22:66—23:25; John 18:28—19:16
	Crucifixion (approximately 9:00 A.M. to 3:00 P.M.)	Matt. 27:27–66; Mark 15:16–39; Luke 23:26–49; John 19:17–37
	Burial	Matt. 27:57–61; Mark 15:42–47; Luke 23:50–56; John 19:38–42
• Saturday	Guard placed at the tomb	Matt. 27:62–66
• Sunday	Resurrection	Matt. 28:1–8; Mark 16:1–8; Luke 24:1–12; John 20:1–18
	Resurrection appearances	Matt. 28:9–20; Luke 24:13–53; John 20:19—21:25

Source: NIV Application Commentary, Matthew (2004)

41 "He will bring those wretches to a wretched end,"*m* they replied, "and he will rent the vineyard to other tenants,*n* who will give him his share of the crop at harvest time."

42 Jesus said to them, "Have you never read in the Scriptures:

" 'The stone the builders rejected
has become the capstone*a*;
the Lord has done this,
and it is marvelous in our eyes'*b*?*o*

43 "Therefore I tell you that the kingdom of God will be taken away from you*p* and given to a people who will produce its fruit. 44 He who falls on this stone will be broken to pieces, but he on whom it falls will be crushed."*c q*

45 When the chief priests and the Pharisees heard Jesus' parables, they knew he was talking about them. 46 They looked for a way to arrest him, but they were afraid of the crowd because the people held that he was a prophet.*r*

The Parable of the Wedding Banquet

22 Jesus spoke to them again in parables, saying: 2 "The kingdom of heaven is like*s* a king who prepared a wedding banquet for his son. 3 He sent his servants*t* to those who had been invited to the banquet to tell them to come, but they refused to come.

4 "Then he sent some more servants*u* and said, 'Tell those who have been invited that I have prepared my dinner: My oxen and fattened cattle have been butchered, and everything is ready. Come to the wedding banquet.'

5 "But they paid no attention and went off—one to his field, another to his business. 6 The rest seized his servants, mistreated them and killed them. 7 The king was enraged. He sent his army and destroyed those murderers*v* and burned their city.

8 "Then he said to his servants, 'The wedding banquet is ready, but those I invited did not deserve to come. 9 Go to the street corners*w* and invite to the banquet anyone you find.' 10 So the servants went out into the streets and gathered all the people they could find, both good and bad,*x* and the wedding hall was filled with guests.

11 "But when the king came in to see the guests, he noticed a man there who was not wearing wedding clothes. 12 'Friend,'*y* he asked, 'how did you get in here without wedding clothes?' The man was speechless.

13 "Then the king told the attendants, 'Tie him hand and foot, and throw him outside, into the darkness, where there will be weeping and gnashing of teeth.'*z*

14 "For many are invited, but few are chosen."*a*

Paying Taxes to Caesar

15 Then the Pharisees went out and laid plans to trap him in his words. 16 They sent their disciples to him along with the Herodians.*b* "Teacher," they said, "we

a 42 Or *cornerstone*   *b 42* Psalm 118:22,23   *c 44* Some manuscripts do not have verse 44.

Matthew 22:1–14

This parable falls into three sections: God's judgment on those who rejected Jesus' invitation to repent and enter the kingdom, a description of those who would be invited to replace them, and the requirements for kingdom participation.

The striking, almost frightening, point of the parable (and the two previous ones) is that those most severely condemned were "insiders." The religious leaders received Jesus' kingdom invitation along with the rest of the people of Israel, but they were blinded from seeing the truth. The one who did respond but was condemned for not wearing the appropriate garment likely represented insiders like Judas Iscariot, who would betray Jesus from within his inner circle.

Unfortunately, many who identify themselves as "Christians" today don't live as true members of the kingdom. God's desire is for all people to enter into that kingdom. He will pursue "outsiders" to encourage them to come in. But some who assume special privilege may ultimately be shocked to find themselves outside.

Matthew 22:15–22

Jesus wasn't attempting to wiggle out of a sticky riddle by countering with one of his own. Behind his words were some profound implications. (1) He hadn't come as a military or political threat to the established rulers of this world. (2) Those who responded to his kingdom invitation would continue to have obligations to governing authorities. (3) God as Creator has

know you are a man of integrity and that you teach the way of God in accordance with the truth. You aren't swayed by men, because you pay no attention to who they are. [17]Tell us then, what is your opinion? Is it right to pay taxes[c] to Caesar or not?"

[18]But Jesus, knowing their evil intent, said, "You hypocrites, why are you trying to trap me? [19]Show me the coin used for paying the tax." They brought him a denarius, [20]and he asked them, "Whose portrait is this? And whose inscription?"

[21]"Caesar's," they replied.

Then he said to them, "Give to Caesar what is Caesar's,[d] and to God what is God's." [22]When they heard this, they were amazed. So they left him and went away.[e]

Marriage at the Resurrection

[23]That same day the Sadducees,[f] who say there is no resurrection,[g] came to him with a question. [24]"Teacher," they said, "Moses told us that if a man dies without having children, his brother must marry the widow and have children for him.[h] [25]Now there were seven brothers among us. The first one married and died, and since he had no children, he left his wife to his brother. [26]The same thing happened to the second and third brother, right on down to the seventh. [27]Finally, the woman died. [28]Now then, at the resurrection, whose wife will she be of the seven, since all of them were married to her?"

[29]Jesus replied, "You are in error because you do not know the Scriptures[i] or the power of God. [30]At the resurrection people will neither marry nor be given in marriage;[j] they will be like the angels in heaven. [31]But about the resurrection of the dead—have you not read what God said to you, [32]'I am the God of Abraham, the God of Isaac, and the God of Jacob'[a]?[k] He is not the God of the dead but of the living."

[33]When the crowds heard this, they were astonished at his teaching.[l]

The Greatest Commandment

[34]Hearing that Jesus had silenced the Sadducees,[m] the Pharisees got together. [35]One of them, an expert in the law,[n] tested him with this question: [36]"Teacher, which is the greatest commandment in the Law?"

[37]Jesus replied: "'Love the Lord your God with all your heart and with all your

[a] 32 Exodus 3:6

Cross references:
22:17 c Mt 17:25
22:21 d Ro 13:7
22:22 e Mk 12:12
22:23 f Ac 4:1 g Ac 23:8; 1Co 15:12
22:24 h Dt 25:5,6
22:29 i Jn 20:9
22:30 j Mt 24:38
22:32 k Ex 3:6; Ac 7:32
22:33 l Mt 7:28
22:34 m Ac 4:1
22:35 n Lk 7:30; 10:25; 11:45; 14:3

sovereign right over all creation and everything in it. What belongs to "Caesar" is Caesar's only secondarily.

Our allegiance to God isn't to make us reluctant as citizens to pay our dues to "Caesar." But neither should our allegiance to "Caesar" ever infringe on our loyalty to God. When the kingdoms of this world violate the demands of God's kingdom, the penetrating command of Peter and the other apostles comes into play: "We must obey God rather than men!" (Acts 5:29). Have you found yourself in a situation, or can you identify situations in our world today in which the two "ways" were or are clearly in conflict?

Matthew 22:23–33

Once the disciples of the Pharisees and the Herodians had taken their whack at Jesus, the Sadducees stepped up. They didn't believe in the resurrection because they accepted only the books of Moses (first five OT books). Jesus' reference to angels had a double edge, since the Sadducees also denied their existence (cf. Acts 23:8). The Sadducees, Jesus contended, should have recognized the rest of the Old Testament as Scripture. He cited a clinching argument from Exodus—a book that was part of their authoritative base. He also pointed out that God's power lies behind the resurrection.

How well do you "know the Scriptures [and] the power of God" (v. 29)? It's vital for us to grasp the whole teaching of Scripture, not just selections or books we find easy to understand, comforting, or compatible with our worldview. And we need to know the power of God which, in addition to resurrecting the dead, can make a difference in this world—changing lives, healing anguished souls, breaking the chains of addictions, enabling marriages to last and flourish. God's power is for every Christian, everywhere, every day, and every hour.

Matthew 22:34–40

Competition among the religious leaders to trounce Jesus in debate was heating up. Now the Pharisees tried to trip him up theologically, using a topic of regular debate among the rabbis—that of distinguishing between the weighty and light commandments. Jesus quoted from Deuteronomy 6:5 and Leviticus 19:18, both well-known and accepted principles. The entire Old Testament hinges on this Great Commandment: to love God and others with every aspect of our life.

The legal expert was looking for an all-encompassing formula for obeying God's will. If we truly love God with all our heart, soul, and mind, our entire person is focused on giving ourselves to him. More than anything else, we want intimacy with God and a heart of

soul and with all your mind.'ᵃ ᵒ ³⁸This is the first and greatest commandment. ³⁹And the second is like it: 'Love your neighbor as yourself.'ᵇ ᵖ ⁴⁰All the Law and the Prophets hang on these two commandments."ᵠ

Whose Son Is the Christ?

⁴¹While the Pharisees were gathered together, Jesus asked them, ⁴²"What do you think about the Christ ᶜ? Whose son is he?"

"The son of David,"ʳ they replied.

⁴³He said to them, "How is it then that David, speaking by the Spirit, calls him 'Lord'? For he says,

⁴⁴ " 'The Lord said to my Lord:
"Sit at my right hand
until I put your enemies
under your feet." 'ᵈ ˢ

⁴⁵If then David calls him 'Lord,' how can he be his son?" ⁴⁶No one could say a word in reply, and from that day on no one dared to ask him any more questions. ᵗ

Seven Woes

23 Then Jesus said to the crowds and to his disciples: ²"The teachers of the lawᵘ and the Pharisees sit in Moses' seat. ³So you must obey them and do everything they tell you. But do not do what they do, for they do not practice what they preach. ⁴They tie up heavy loads and put them on men's shoulders, but they themselves are not willing to lift a finger to move them. ᵛ

⁵"Everything they do is done for men to see: ʷ They make their phylacteriesᵉ ˣ wide and the tassels on their garmentsʸ long; ⁶they love the place of honor at banquets and the most important seats in the synagogues;ᶻ ⁷they love to be greeted in the marketplaces and to have men call them 'Rabbi.'ᵃ

⁸"But you are not to be called 'Rabbi,' for you have only one Master and you are all brothers. ⁹And do not call anyone on earth 'father,' for you have one Father, ᵇ and he is in heaven. ¹⁰Nor are you to be called 'teacher,' for you have one Teacher, the Christ. ᶜ ¹¹The greatest among you will be your servant. ᶜ ¹²For whoever exalts himself will be humbled, and whoever humbles himself will be exalted. ᵈ

ᵃ 37 Deut. 6:5   ᵇ 39 Lev. 19:18   ᶜ 42,10 Or *Messiah*   ᵈ 44 Psalm 110:1   ᵉ 5 That is, boxes containing Scripture verses, worn on forehead and arm

Cross references (left margin)

22:37
o Dt 6:5
22:39
p Lev 19:18;
Mt 5:43; 19:19;
Gal 5:14
22:40
q Mt 7:12

22:42
r Mt 9:27

22:44
s Ps 110:1; Ac 2:34,
35; 1Co 15:25;
Heb 1:13; 10:13
22:46
t Mk 12:34;
Lk 20:40

23:2
u Ezr 7:6,25;
Ne 8:4
23:4
v Lk 11:46;
Ac 15:10; Gal 6:13
23:5
w Mt 6:1,2,5,16
x Ex 13:9; Dt 6:8
y Nu 15:38;
Dt 22:12
23:6
z Lk 11:43; 14:7;
20:46
23:7
a ver 8; Mk 9:5;
10:51; Jn 1:38,49
23:9
b Mal 1:6; Mt 7:11
23:11
c Mt 20:26;
Mk 9:35
23:12
d Lk 14:11

---

obedience. We love our neighbors by giving ourselves to them, helping them to experience everything in life we desire for ourselves. Do you see these two commandments as a burden—or as a liberating orientation to the life Jesus intended (see "Here and Now" for 11:25–30)? How does this summary of life in the kingdom as absolute love for God and others impact your understanding of God's will for your life?

Matthew 22:41–46

📖 The Jews didn't generally believe the coming Messiah would be divine. And Jesus was far more than what the Pharisees had understood the "son of David" would be. He was more than a human descendant of David. Since the Pharisees didn't adequately understand the Old Testament prophecies regarding the Messiah, they couldn't possibly comprehend who Jesus was. Failing to grasp the depth of the identity of the Messiah, they completely missed Jesus' relationship to God.

💻 If Jesus is truly the One he declares himself to be—and we believe he is—we have a unique message for the world. He's unlike any other figure ever to walk the earth. He's not just a messenger or physical appearance of God. He's the fully divine, yet fully human Son of God. None of us can afford to ignore the implications of Jesus' identity for our personal lives. He demands nothing less than to be accepted, served, and worshiped as Lord (cf. Phil. 2:9–11).

Matthew 23:1–39

📖 The "heavy loads" (v. 4) referred to the oral tradition (see "There and Then" for 15:1–20), a distinctive feature of the Pharisees' brand of Judaism. It was intended to make the Old Testament relevant to life situations, but its massive obligations were far more burdensome than Scripture itself. Jesus rejected this emphasis on external conformity to relatively petty rules and this preoccupation with appearing pious before others. More important were inner desires and attitudes, with fulfilling the "weightier matters" of justice, mercy, and faith.

💻 The section of warnings (vv. 1–12) confronts temptations to which believers today can fall prey: demands for legalistic performance of Christian duty, pretentious displays of piety, and exploitation of titles and positions of honor.

The Role of the Law in Helping the Poor and Oppressed

22:37–40

In Matthew 22:37–40, when Christ was asked by a lawyer which commandment was most important, he replied: " 'Love the Lord your God with all your heart and with all your soul and with all your mind.' This is the first and greatest commandment. And the second is like it: 'Love your neighbor as yourself.' "

Christ emphasized dedicating our whole self to serving God by loving our fellow human beings and treating them with the same measure of concern and respect we want for ourselves. If we strive to accomplish this, we can be of great service to God.

Helping the less fortunate is a recurrent theme throughout both Testaments. Proverbs 31:8–9 instructs: "Speak up for those who cannot speak for themselves, for the rights of all who are destitute. Speak up and judge fairly; defend the rights of the poor and needy."

As Christ announced in the synagogue in Nazareth in Luke 4:18–19: " 'The Spirit of the Lord . . . has anointed me to preach good news to the poor. He has sent me to proclaim freedom for the prisoners . . . to proclaim the year of the Lord's favor.' "

God calls us to take up the cause of the despised and helpless in our chaotic world. But what does it mean to help such people? Certainly more than just prayer or lip service. In Luke 10, the Good Samaritan helped the injured man by bandaging his wounds and taking him to a place where he could recover. He even left money for extended care. He went far out of his way to help a fellow human being who had fallen on hard times. Christ's application is explicit: "Go and do likewise."

Being a Good Samaritan means showing love to everyone in need—including the oppressed. Our neighbors include people who are harassed, jailed, and tortured for their beliefs, as well as the economically disadvantaged. Being a Good Samaritan means giving to the poor and beyond until it hurts—in other words, giving *sacrificially*.

Christ's directives apply to every person. But some—like lawyers—possess special skills or influence that can be particularly effective in assisting the needy. Such individuals, especially those who are Christians, have a unique responsibility to act as Good Samaritans.

Legal systems in free countries can be effective tools for assisting the oppressed. If not for effective use of the courts, the African-American civil rights movement in the United States might have been stalled. There is nothing wrong with seeking legal recourse, with following Christ's example to "release the oppressed" (Luke 4:18).

Even the apostle Paul, well-versed in the law, used the legal system to vindicate his rights. A prisoner at the time, he was tried before Festus, the Roman procurator of Judea. Paul proclaimed in Acts 25:11: "If . . . I am guilty of doing anything deserving death, I do not refuse to die. But if the charges brought against me by these Jews are not true, no one has the right to hand me over to them. I appeal to Caesar!" Not finding anything in Paul worthy of death or imprisonment, Festus was inclined to release him. But due to Paul's appeal to Caesar, Festus was compelled instead to send the apostle to Rome, where Paul could continue to preach (Acts 25:12).

Each of us has the privilege and responsibility to rise above our own self-interest and work for the interests of others less fortunate than ourselves. As Albert Einstein once observed, "Only a life lived for others is worth living."

> **B**eing a Good Samaritan means giving to the poor and beyond until it hurts—in other words, giving *sacrificially*.

John W. Whitehead, president of the Rutherford Institute, based in Charlottesville, Virginia

23:13
e ver 15,23,25,27,
29 f Lk 11:52

23:15
g Ac 2:11; 6:5;
13:43 h Mt 5:22

23:16
i ver 24; Mt 15:14
j Mt 5:33-35

23:17
k Ex 30:29

23:19
l Ex 29:37

23:21
m 1Ki 8:13; Ps 26:8
23:22
n Ps 11:4; Mt 5:34

23:23
o Lev 27:30
p Mic 6:8; Lk 11:42

23:24
q ver 16

23:25
r Mk 7:4 s Lk 11:39

23:27
t Lk 11:44; Ac 23:3

23:29
u Lk 11:47,48

23:31
v Ac 7:51-52
23:32
w 1Th 2:16
23:33
x Mt 3:7; 12:34
y Mt 5:22
23:34
z 2Ch 36:15,16;
Lk 11:49 a Mt 10:17
b Mt 10:23
23:35
c Ge 4:8; Heb 11:4
d Zec 1:1
e 2Ch 24:21
23:36
f Mt 10:23; 24:34
23:37
g 2Ch 24:21;
Mt 5:12
23:38
h 1Ki 9:7,8;
Jer 22:5
23:39
i Ps 118:26; Mt 21:9

13 "Woe to you, teachers of the law and Pharisees, you hypocrites! e You shut the kingdom of heaven in men's faces. You yourselves do not enter, nor will you let those enter who are trying to. a f

15 "Woe to you, teachers of the law and Pharisees, you hypocrites! You travel over land and sea to win a single convert, g and when he becomes one, you make him twice as much a son of hell h as you are.

16 "Woe to you, blind guides! i You say, 'If anyone swears by the temple, it means nothing; but if anyone swears by the gold of the temple, he is bound by his oath.' j 17 You blind fools! Which is greater: the gold, or the temple that makes the gold sacred? k 18 You also say, 'If anyone swears by the altar, it means nothing; but if anyone swears by the gift on it, he is bound by his oath.' 19 You blind men! Which is greater: the gift, or the altar that makes the gift sacred? l 20 Therefore, he who swears by the altar swears by it and by everything on it. 21 And he who swears by the temple swears by it and by the one who dwells m in it. 22 And he who swears by heaven swears by God's throne and by the one who sits on it. n

23 "Woe to you, teachers of the law and Pharisees, you hypocrites! You give a tenth o of your spices—mint, dill and cummin. But you have neglected the more important matters of the law—justice, mercy and faithfulness. p You should have practiced the latter, without neglecting the former. 24 You blind guides! q You strain out a gnat but swallow a camel.

25 "Woe to you, teachers of the law and Pharisees, you hypocrites! You clean the outside of the cup and dish, r but inside they are full of greed and self-indulgence. s 26 Blind Pharisee! First clean the inside of the cup and dish, and then the outside also will be clean.

27 "Woe to you, teachers of the law and Pharisees, you hypocrites! You are like whitewashed tombs, t which look beautiful on the outside but on the inside are full of dead men's bones and everything unclean. 28 In the same way, on the outside you appear to people as righteous but on the inside you are full of hypocrisy and wickedness.

29 "Woe to you, teachers of the law and Pharisees, you hypocrites! You build tombs for the prophets u and decorate the graves of the righteous. 30 And you say, 'If we had lived in the days of our forefathers, we would not have taken part with them in shedding the blood of the prophets.' 31 So you testify against yourselves that you are the descendants of those who murdered the prophets. v 32 Fill up, then, the measure w of the sin of your forefathers!

33 "You snakes! You brood of vipers! x How will you escape being condemned to hell? y 34 Therefore I am sending you prophets and wise men and teachers. Some of them you will kill and crucify; z others you will flog in your synagogues a and pursue from town to town. b 35 And so upon you will come all the righteous blood that has been shed on earth, from the blood of righteous Abel c to the blood of Zechariah son of Berekiah, d whom you murdered between the temple and the altar. e 36 I tell you the truth, all this will come upon this generation. f

37 "O Jerusalem, Jerusalem, you who kill the prophets and stone those sent to you, g how often I have longed to gather your children together, as a hen gathers her chicks under her wings, but you were not willing. 38 Look, your house is left to you desolate. h 39 For I tell you, you will not see me again until you say, 'Blessed is he who comes in the name of the Lord.' b " i

a 13 Some manuscripts to. 14 Woe to you, teachers of the law and Pharisees, you hypocrites! You devour widows' houses and for a show make lengthy prayers. Therefore you will be punished more severely.
b 39 Psalm 118:26

Followers of Christ can learn some positive lessons from the "woes" (vv. 13–32): Be a doorway to the kingdom; make converts to Christ, not to our own regulations and traditions; maintain personal accountability; and be motivated in your service from the inside out.

God's will for people is clear, and he grieves when we walk in another direction. We live as kingdom citizens when we walk by faith in God, seek justice for the oppressed, and manifest mercy when we are wronged. Are there ways in which this clarifies God's call in your life?

Signs of the End of the Age

24 Jesus left the temple and was walking away when his disciples came up to him to call his attention to its buildings. [2] "Do you see all these things?" he asked. "I tell you the truth, not one stone here will be left on another;[j] every one will be thrown down."

[3] As Jesus was sitting on the Mount of Olives,[k] the disciples came to him privately. "Tell us," they said, "when will this happen, and what will be the sign of your coming and of the end of the age?"

[4] Jesus answered: "Watch out that no one deceives you. [5] For many will come in my name, claiming, 'I am the Christ,[a]' and will deceive many.[l] [6] You will hear of wars and rumors of wars, but see to it that you are not alarmed. Such things must happen, but the end is still to come. [7] Nation will rise against nation, and kingdom against kingdom.[m] There will be famines[n] and earthquakes in various places. [8] All these are the beginning of birth pains.

[9] "Then you will be handed over to be persecuted[o] and put to death,[p] and you will be hated by all nations because of me. [10] At that time many will turn away from the faith and will betray and hate each other, [11] and many false prophets[q] will appear and deceive many people. [12] Because of the increase of wickedness, the love of most will grow cold, [13] but he who stands firm to the end will be saved.[r] [14] And this gospel of the kingdom[s] will be preached in the whole world[t] as a testimony to all nations, and then the end will come.

[15] "So when you see standing in the holy place[u] 'the abomination that causes desolation,'[b][v] spoken of through the prophet Daniel—let the reader understand— [16] then let those who are in Judea flee to the mountains. [17] Let no one on the roof of his house[w] go down to take anything out of the house. [18] Let no one in the field go back to get his cloak. [19] How dreadful it will be in those days for pregnant women and nursing mothers![x] [20] Pray that your flight will not take place in winter or on the Sabbath. [21] For then there will be great distress, unequaled from the beginning of the world until now—and never to be equaled again.[y] [22] If those days had not been cut short, no one would survive, but for the sake of the elect[z] those days will be shortened. [23] At that time if anyone says to you, 'Look, here is the Christ!' or, 'There he is!' do not believe it.[a] [24] For false Christs and false prophets will appear and perform great signs and miracles[b] to deceive even the elect—if that were possible. [25] See, I have told you ahead of time.

[26] "So if anyone tells you, 'There he is, out in the desert,' do not go out; or, 'Here he is, in the inner rooms,' do not believe it. [27] For as lightning[c] that comes from the east is visible even in the west, so will be the coming of the Son of Man.[d] [28] Wherever there is a carcass, there the vultures will gather.[e]

[29] "Immediately after the distress of those days

"'the sun will be darkened,
    and the moon will not give its light;
the stars will fall from the sky,
    and the heavenly bodies will be shaken.'[c][f]

---

[a] 5 Or *Messiah*; also in verse 23   [b] 15 Daniel 9:27; 11:31; 12:11   [c] 29 Isaiah 13:10; 34:4

24:2
j Lk 19:44

24:3
k Mt 21:1

24:5
l ver 11,23,24;
1Jn 2:18

24:7
m Isa 19:2
n Ac 11:28

24:9
o Mt 10:17
p Jn 16:2
24:11
q Mt 7:15

24:13
r Mt 10:22
24:14
s Mt 4:23 t Lk 2:1;
4:5; Ac 11:28; 17:6;
Ro 10:18; Col 1:6,
23; Rev 3:10; 16:14
24:15
u Ac 6:13
v Da 9:27; 11:31;
12:11
24:17
w 1Sa 9:25;
Mt 10:27; Lk 12:3;
Ac 10:9
24:19
x Lk 23:29

24:21
y Da 12:1; Joel 2:2
24:22
z ver 24,31

24:23
a Lk 17:23; 21:8
24:24
b 2Th 2:9-11;
Rev 13:13

24:27
c Lk 17:24
d Mt 8:20

24:28
e Lk 17:37

24:29
f Isa 13:10; 34:4;
Eze 32:7;
Joel 2:10,31;
Zep 1:15;
Rev 6:12,13; 8:12

Matthew 24:1–35

This passage begins the Olivet Discourse (24:1—25:46), spoken by Jesus from the Mount of Olives in response to the disciples' questions in verse 3. The way they posed their questions seems to indicate their assumption that the temple's destruction and the end of the age were inseparable. Jesus did allude to the temple's destruction—which would occur some 40 years later in A.D. 70—but he also was symbolically forecasting end-time events. The near event, the destruction of Jerusalem by the Romans, served as a symbol for others more distant.

"The end" will come after the gospel has been preached to all nations (v. 14). This doesn't mean we are to preach the Good News to force Christ's return. But his second coming and the consummation of the kingdom are connected with this requirement. God's will is that all people encounter the kingdom through others. In fact, the end of this age won't come until that has occurred. Some Christians seem more preoccupied with reading the "signs of the times" than with doing all they can to expose those who haven't heard to the gospel message.

24:30
g Da 7:13; Rev 1:7
24:31
h Mt 13:41
i Isa 27:13;
Zec 9:14;
1Co 15:52;
1Th 4:16; Rev 8:2;
10:7; 11:15
24:33
j Jas 5:9
24:34
k Mt 16:28; 23:36
24:35
l Mt 5:18

30 "At that time the sign of the Son of Man will appear in the sky, and all the nations of the earth will mourn. They will see the Son of Man coming on the clouds of the sky, g with power and great glory. 31And he will send his angels h with a loud trumpet call, i and they will gather his elect from the four winds, from one end of the heavens to the other.

32 "Now learn this lesson from the fig tree: As soon as its twigs get tender and its leaves come out, you know that summer is near. 33Even so, when you see all these things, you know that it a is near, right at the door. j 34I tell you the truth, this generation b will certainly not pass away until all these things have happened. k 35Heaven and earth will pass away, but my words will never pass away. l

The Day and Hour Unknown

24:36
m Ac 1:7
24:37
n Ge 6:5; 7:6-23
24:38
o Mt 22:30

36 "No one knows about that day or hour, not even the angels in heaven, nor the Son, c but only the Father. m 37As it was in the days of Noah, n so it will be at the coming of the Son of Man. 38For in the days before the flood, people were eating and drinking, marrying and giving in marriage, o up to the day Noah entered the ark; 39and they knew nothing about what would happen until the flood came and took them all away. That is how it will be at the coming of the Son of Man. 40Two men will be in the field; one will be taken and the other left. p 41Two women will be grinding with a hand mill; one will be taken and the other left. q

24:40
p Lk 17:34
24:41
q Lk 17:35

42 "Therefore keep watch, because you do not know on what day your Lord will come. r 43But understand this: If the owner of the house had known at what time of night the thief was coming, s he would have kept watch and would not have let his house be broken into. 44So you also must be ready, t because the Son of Man will come at an hour when you do not expect him.

24:42
r Mt 25:13;
Lk 12:40
24:43
s Lk 12:39
24:44
t 1Th 5:6
24:45
u Mt 25:21,23

45 "Who then is the faithful and wise servant, u whom the master has put in charge of the servants in his household to give them their food at the proper time? 46It will be good for that servant whose master finds him doing so when he returns. v 47I tell you the truth, he will put him in charge of all his possessions. w 48But suppose that servant is wicked and says to himself, 'My master is staying away a long time,' 49and he then begins to beat his fellow servants and to eat and drink with drunkards. x 50The master of that servant will come on a day when he does not expect him and at an hour he is not aware of. 51He will cut him to pieces and assign him a place with the hypocrites, where there will be weeping and gnashing of teeth. y

24:46
v Rev 16:15
24:47
w Mt 25:21,23
24:49
x Lk 21:34
24:51
y Mt 8:12

The Parable of the Ten Virgins

25:1
z Mt 13:24
a Lk 12:35-38;
Ac 20:8; Rev 4:5
b Rev 19:7; 21:2
25:2
c Mt 24:45
25:5
d 1Th 5:6

25 "At that time the kingdom of heaven will be like z ten virgins who took their lamps a and went out to meet the bridegroom. b 2Five of them were foolish and five were wise. c 3The foolish ones took their lamps but did not take any oil with them. 4The wise, however, took oil in jars along with their lamps. 5The bridegroom was a long time in coming, and they all became drowsy and fell asleep. d

6 "At midnight the cry rang out: 'Here's the bridegroom! Come out to meet him!'

7 "Then all the virgins woke up and trimmed their lamps. 8The foolish ones said to the wise, 'Give us some of your oil; our lamps are going out.' e

25:8
e Lk 12:35

a 33 Or he   b 34 Or race   c 36 Some manuscripts do not have nor the Son.

Matthew 24:36–51

📖 Jesus didn't give up his deity when he took on human flesh, but he voluntarily limited the use of his divine attributes so he could experience human life in its entirety (cf. Phil. 2:6–7; Heb. 4:14–16). It wasn't the Father's will for Jesus to know the date of his return during his time on Earth.

In light of the unknown day or hour of his return, Jesus used a series of analogies and parables to warn his disciples to be prepared. He showed the contrast between true and false believers and addressed the consequences for those who choose not to follow him.

📖 Since Biblical prophecy is permeated with impending judgment (see, e.g., v. 51), our belief in Jesus' return ought to fuel a vigorous involvement in missions and evangelism. When we are gripped with the reality that the eternal destiny of individuals is at stake, we will move our study of prophecy beyond speculation, debate, or curiosity. Active participation in reaching out to a lost world enables people around the globe to be prepared to meet the Lord when he returns. Are you impelled by a sense of urgency to enable others to encounter the Good News of the kingdom through your life, deed, and word?

9 " 'No,' they replied, 'there may not be enough for both us and you. Instead, go to those who sell oil and buy some for yourselves.'

10 "But while they were on their way to buy the oil, the bridegroom arrived. The virgins who were ready went in with him to the wedding banquet. *f* And the door was shut.

11 "Later the others also came. 'Sir! Sir!' they said. 'Open the door for us!'

12 "But he replied, 'I tell you the truth, I don't know you.'

13 "Therefore keep watch, because you do not know the day or the hour. *g*

The Parable of the Talents

14 "Again, it will be like a man going on a journey, *h* who called his servants and entrusted his property to them. 15 To one he gave five talents *a* of money, to another two talents, and to another one talent, each according to his ability. *i* Then he went on his journey. 16 The man who had received the five talents went at once and put his money to work and gained five more. 17 So also, the one with the two talents gained two more. 18 But the man who had received the one talent went off, dug a hole in the ground and hid his master's money.

19 "After a long time the master of those servants returned and settled accounts with them. *j* 20 The man who had received the five talents brought the other five. 'Master,' he said, 'you entrusted me with five talents. See, I have gained five more.'

21 "His master replied, 'Well done, good and faithful servant! You have been faithful with a few things; I will put you in charge of many things. *k* Come and share your master's happiness!'

22 "The man with the two talents also came. 'Master,' he said, 'you entrusted me with two talents; see, I have gained two more.'

23 "His master replied, 'Well done, good and faithful servant! You have been faithful with a few things; I will put you in charge of many things. *l* Come and share your master's happiness!'

24 "Then the man who had received the one talent came. 'Master,' he said, 'I knew that you are a hard man, harvesting where you have not sown and gathering where you have not scattered seed. 25 So I was afraid and went out and hid your talent in the ground. See, here is what belongs to you.'

26 "His master replied, 'You wicked, lazy servant! So you knew that I harvest where I have not sown and gather where I have not scattered seed? 27 Well then, you

---

a *15* A talent was worth more than a thousand dollars.

25:10
f Rev 19:9

25:13
g Mt 24:42,44;
Mk 13:35; Lk 12:40

25:14
h Mt 21:33;
Lk 19:12
25:15
i Mt 18:24,25

25:19
j Mt 18:23

25:21
k ver 23;
Mt 24:45,47;
Lk 16:10

25:23
l ver 21

Matthew 25:1–13

Jesus' true disciples will be ready for his return. The destiny of those who aren't ready is outside the shut door. The previous and following parables both speak of hell as the destination for those who don't "watch" correctly—who aren't properly prepared with salvation so they can accompany Jesus, "the bridegroom," when he arrives.

Themes of suddenness and preparedness both punctuate the Olivet Discourse. Four parables each emphasize a different aspect of preparedness: responsibility (24:45–51), readiness (25:1–13), productivity (25:14–30), and accountability (25:31–46). History will come to a climactic end when Jesus returns, accompanied by a separation between believers and unbelievers. It will be an either/or proposition, with no middle ground. How are you incorporating the four aspects of accountability into your Christian experience?

Matthew 25:14–30

The critical issue wasn't the total amount each servant earned but their faithful responsibility to exercise accountable stewardship over what they had been given. The first two were true disciples. But the third had a distorted image of and a negative attitude toward his master—both of which he used as an excuse for personal irresponsibility. False perceptions of God result in rationalizations for failing to enter into a loving and obedient relationship with him.

The English term "talent" came directly from this parable. In today's usage "talents" often refer to a person's natural abilities. Closer to the intent of the parable, the talents here symbolize the giftedness bestowed by God on each person who has been graced with kingdom life (cf. 1 Cor. 12:7). What particular talents has God given you? Do you feel you are using them to full capacity?

All that we are—whether naturally endowed or Spirit-bestowed—is to be employed in the service of the kingdom. Not everyone is born with the same capacities or blessed with the same gifts of the Spirit, yet each of us can be productive in our own unique way. All kingdom service is valuable, just as each servant is precious to God. We are responsible to be continuously prepared for Christ's return, all the while planning for the long haul and using our giftedness to advance the kingdom.

1611

Housing

25:34–40

Almost immediately after his ascension, Christ's followers began wondering when he would return. Continuing preoccupation with the last days and the end of our world as we know it is amazing, considering how often Jesus warned his disciples not to engage in such speculation.

In fact, the only reality Jesus claimed *not to know* was the precise date of the last, or judgment day. He instructs us simply to be alert and ready for the day the Son of God will return in glory. And yet the guessing game goes on, pulling in every generation. Cults spring up like mushrooms around leaders who claim to have done the math, to have pinpointed the precise date of the end of days. With great personal loss and public embarrassment, thousands of earnest disciples have found themselves gazing upward in vain on the "appointed" day.

This is, of course, a symptom of our human nature: We want to outsmart the Creator of the universe. This tendency is an unholy perversion of the holy desire, planted in every human heart, to know God intimately and understand his plan. God wants us to prepare for our Savior's return, but preparation isn't a matter of standing still, looking skyward, ticking off days on the calendar. Instead, he wants us to turn our attention to those around us who need our love, compassion, attention, and assistance.

> **F**eed the hungry and thirsty. Clothe the ragged. Visit the sick and incarcerated. To the extent that we do these things for the broken, bereft men, women, and children in our world, we do them to, and for, Christ himself.

This is the point of Matthew 25:35–40: On the last day, Jesus will sit on his glorious throne, with all the nations gathered before him, and separate the righteous from the unrighteous. There will be great praise—and severe punishment. How will Jesus sift out the pretenders from the true believers? Could there possibly be a clearer set of criteria than he lays out in these verses? Feed the hungry and thirsty. Clothe the ragged. Visit the sick and incarcerated. To the extent that we do these things for the broken, bereft men, women, and children in our world, we do them to, and for, Christ himself.

For more than 25 years I have been gripped by these verses, to the extent that I have built my life on them. When my wife, Linda, and I joined Koinonia Farm, a small Christian community in America's deep South, we looked around and saw many "strangers" living in abhorrent conditions. The Holy Spirit set us to work building houses in partnership with people on the margins of society, the edges of hopelessness. Habitat for Humanity, a movement to eliminate the disgrace of substandard housing, was born from the sweat of our brows and the passion of our prayers.

Today, I travel the world on a surging wave of support that can only be God-inspired. I'm humbled by our phenomenal growth: as of the beginning of 2002, more than 120,000 houses, built in partnership with more than 600,000 people in 80 nations. And a new house is completed currently at the rate of one every 26 minutes!

From north to south, east to west, anywhere two or more people are listening, I quote Jesus' words: "I was a stranger, and you invited me in." In to a simple, functional, healthful house, the foundation for human development. I firmly believe that if we as Christians engage in this kind of work for any stranger, we do it for Jesus. And when he comes again in glory, we will hear his words, "Come, you who are blessed of my Father, inherit the kingdom prepared for you."

Millard Fuller, founder and president of Habitat for Humanity International in Americus, Georgia

should have put my money on deposit with the bankers, so that when I returned I would have received it back with interest. [28] " 'Take the talent from him and give it to the one who has the ten talents. [29] For everyone who has will be given more, and he will have an abundance. Whoever does not have, even what he has will be taken from him. *m* [30] And throw that worthless servant outside, into the darkness, where there will be weeping and gnashing of teeth.' *n*

The Sheep and the Goats

[31] "When the Son of Man comes *o* in his glory, and all the angels with him, he will sit on his throne *p* in heavenly glory. [32] All the nations will be gathered before him, and he will separate *q* the people one from another as a shepherd separates the sheep from the goats. *r* [33] He will put the sheep on his right and the goats on his left.

[34] "Then the King will say to those on his right, 'Come, you who are blessed by my Father; take your inheritance, the kingdom *s* prepared for you since the creation of the world. *t* [35] For I was hungry and you gave me something to eat, I was thirsty and you gave me something to drink, I was a stranger and you invited me in, *u* [36] I needed clothes and you clothed me, *v* I was sick and you looked after me, *w* I was in prison and you came to visit me.' *x*

[37] "Then the righteous will answer him, 'Lord, when did we see you hungry and feed you, or thirsty and give you something to drink? [38] When did we see you a stranger and invite you in, or needing clothes and clothe you? [39] When did we see you sick or in prison and go to visit you?'

[40] "The King will reply, 'I tell you the truth, whatever you did for one of the least of these brothers of mine, you did for me.' *y*

[41] "Then he will say to those on his left, 'Depart from me, *z* you who are cursed, into the eternal fire *a* prepared for the devil and his angels. *b* [42] For I was hungry and you gave me nothing to eat, I was thirsty and you gave me nothing to drink, [43] I was a stranger and you did not invite me in, I needed clothes and you did not clothe me, I was sick and in prison and you did not look after me.'

[44] "They also will answer, 'Lord, when did we see you hungry or thirsty or a stranger or needing clothes or sick or in prison, and did not help you?'

[45] "He will reply, 'I tell you the truth, whatever you did not do for one of the least of these, you did not do for me.' *c*

[46] "Then they will go away to eternal punishment, but the righteous to eternal life. *d* *e*

The Plot Against Jesus

26 When Jesus had finished saying all these things, *f* he said to his disciples, [2] "As you know, the Passover *g* is two days away—and the Son of Man will be handed over to be crucified."

25:29 *m* Mt 13:12; Mk 4:25; Lk 8:18; 19:26
25:30 *n* Mt 8:12
25:31 *o* Mt 16:27; Lk 17:30 *p* Mt 19:28
25:32 *q* Mal 3:18 *r* Eze 34:17,20
25:34 *s* Mt 3:2; 5:3,10,19; 19:14; Ac 20:32; 1Co 15:50; Gal 5:21; Jas 2:5 *t* Heb 4:3; 9:26; Rev 13:8; 17:8
25:35 *u* Job 31:32; Isa 58:7; Eze 18:7; Heb 13:2
25:36 *v* Isa 58:7; Eze 18:7; Jas 2:15,16 *w* Jas 1:27 *x* 2Ti 1:16
25:40 *y* Pr 19:17; Mt 10:40,42; Heb 6:10; 13:2
25:41 *z* Mt 7:23 *a* Isa 66:24; Mt 3:12; 5:22; Mk 9:43,48; Lk 3:17; Jude 7 *b* 2Pe 2:4
25:45 *c* Pr 14:31; 17:5
25:46 *d* Mt 19:29; Jn 3:15,16,36; 17:2,3; Ro 2:7; Gal 6:8; 5:11,13,20 *e* Da 12:2; Jn 5:29; Ac 24:15; Ro 2:7,8; Gal 6:8
26:1 *f* Mt 7:28
26:2 *g* Jn 11:55; 13:1

Matthew 25:31–46

Jesus delineated a staggering—if not incriminating—criterion for the final judgment: how his people care for the hungry, thirsty, strangers, naked, sick, and imprisoned. Matthew had repeatedly stressed that if we love God we will, as an inevitable byproduct, also love others. In fact, if we don't love others, our love for God is in question. Love isn't a vague sentiment but a concrete action. And love in action is to be expressed not only toward our friends and family, but to the marginalized, suffering, and oppressed. When we care for such individuals, we are actually caring for Jesus. He so totally carries their injustice and pain that in loving them, we love him.

The "least of these brothers of mine" (v. 40) would seem to refer to those in need. Paul stated, "As we have opportunity, let us do good to all people, espe-cially to those who belong to the family of believers" (Gal. 6:10). Caring for the suffering and outcast is the mark of following Christ. Deeds of compassion and mercy aren't the means by which we enter the kingdom but the confirmation of our citizenship.

Matthew 26:1–5

Matthew identified the high priest as Caiaphas, the son-in-law of the previous high priest, Annas (who still wielded much influence). Appointed high priest in A.D. 18 by the Roman prefect Valerius Gratus, Pontius Pilate's predecessor, Caiaphas knew well how to maneuver the political scene. The reputation of the office had been ruined, since the Roman governor appointed and deposed the office-holder. The Jewish Qumran community (which produced the Dead Sea Scrolls) was especially critical of this Roman puppet, whom they called the "Wicked Priest."

26:3
h Ps 2:2 ¹ ver 57;
Jn 11:47-53;
18:13,14,24,28
26:4
j Mt 12:14
26:5
k Mt 27:24

³Then the chief priests and the elders of the people assembled[h] in the palace of the high priest, whose name was Caiaphas,[i] ⁴and they plotted to arrest Jesus in some sly way and kill him.[j] ⁵"But not during the Feast," they said, "or there may be a riot[k] among the people."

Jesus Anointed at Bethany

26:6
l Mt 21:17

⁶While Jesus was in Bethany[l] in the home of a man known as Simon the Leper, ⁷a woman came to him with an alabaster jar of very expensive perfume, which she poured on his head as he was reclining at the table.

⁸When the disciples saw this, they were indignant. "Why this waste?" they asked. ⁹"This perfume could have been sold at a high price and the money given to the poor."

26:11
m Dt 15:11

26:12
n Jn 19:40

¹⁰Aware of this, Jesus said to them, "Why are you bothering this woman? She has done a beautiful thing to me. ¹¹The poor you will always have with you,[m] but you will not always have me. ¹²When she poured this perfume on my body, she did it to prepare me for burial.[n] ¹³I tell you the truth, wherever this gospel is preached throughout the world, what she has done will also be told, in memory of her."

Judas Agrees to Betray Jesus

26:14
o ver 25,47;
Mt 10:4
26:15
p Ex 21:32;
Zec 11:12

¹⁴Then one of the Twelve—the one called Judas Iscariot[o]—went to the chief priests ¹⁵and asked, "What are you willing to give me if I hand him over to you?" So they counted out for him thirty silver coins.[p] ¹⁶From then on Judas watched for an opportunity to hand him over.

The Lord's Supper

26:17
q Ex 12:18-20

¹⁷On the first day of the Feast of Unleavened Bread,[q] the disciples came to Jesus and asked, "Where do you want us to make preparations for you to eat the Passover?" ¹⁸He replied, "Go into the city to a certain man and tell him, 'The Teacher says:

📖 The final scenes leading up to Jesus' arrest and crucifixion remind us that God is in control. He can use both enemies who plot against us and friends who desert us. Despite the downward spiral of events and his disappointment in people around him, Jesus resolutely moved forward. He trusted the Father's will even when his situation looked bleakest. We too are to continue to follow our convictions about God's will even through dark times. Have you trudged through some black canyon? Does your hindsight give you a better and bigger picture of God's grace now that the ordeal is over?

Matthew 26:6–13

📖 We know from John 12:3 that this woman who anointed Jesus was Mary, the sister of Martha and Lazarus. Jesus' words didn't relieve the disciples of responsibility to care for the poor. The poor would always be among them, and giving to them would be a perpetual duty (cf. Deut. 15:11; Matt. 6:2–4; 25:34–40). But Jesus emphasized that Mary was performing an act of homage that could only be done at this time (cf. Jesus' similar comment about fasting in 9:15). Mary had placed her Lord above all other values.

📖 Mary's example sets a precedent for us. The value of her perfume represented her belief in Jesus as her Messiah, the One who had inaugurated the kingdom of God and raised her brother from the dead. She gave all she had to anoint Jesus. What a memorable role model for us today, especially in light of our more complete understanding of his identity and mission. All our acts of service are to be expressions of worship and adoration.

Matthew 26:14–16

📖 In addition to Satan's influence (Luke 22:3–4), many other reasons have been suggested for Judas's treacherous act: greed and love of money; jealousy of the other disciples; an attempt to force Jesus to declare himself as Messiah; a vengeful spirit that arose when his worldly hopes for a prominent place in the kingdom were crushed. At the very least, he was likely disappointed in the spiritual nature of Jesus' Messiahship and decided to recoup the financial losses he had suffered in three "wasted" (cf. Matt. 26:8) years of following Jesus.

📖 Many people see the Christian life as wasted. Much like Esau, who devalued his birthright (Gen. 25:27–34), Judas lost sight of the value of a relationship to the Messiah and couldn't understand the way of the kingdom—triumph through sacrifice, strength through service. God's ways often seem so weak and foolish, sometimes even to us. We want a conquering king who wipes out all enemies. It takes spiritual insight to appreciate Christ's significance and the call of those who follow him (cf. 1 Cor. 2:6–10; 2 Cor. 4:4).

Matthew 26:17–30

📖 The Passover was Israel's celebration of God covenanting with his people to save them from bondage. Because they marked their homes with the blood of a lamb, God "passed-over" them in his judgment of sin (Ex. 12). What a powerful moment for Jesus' inauguration of the New Covenant! Jesus reconstituted the feast, saying in effect, "My own blood is the blood of the lamb" and "my own body is the unleavened bread we eat

My appointed time[r] is near. I am going to celebrate the Passover with my disciples at your house.' " ¹⁹So the disciples did as Jesus had directed them and prepared the Passover.

²⁰When evening came, Jesus was reclining at the table with the Twelve. ²¹And while they were eating, he said, "I tell you the truth, one of you will betray me."[s]

²²They were very sad and began to say to him one after the other, "Surely not I, Lord?"

²³Jesus replied, "The one who has dipped his hand into the bowl with me will betray me.[t] ²⁴The Son of Man will go just as it is written about him.[u] But woe to that man who betrays the Son of Man! It would be better for him if he had not been born."

²⁵Then Judas, the one who would betray him, said, "Surely not I, Rabbi?"[v] Jesus answered, "Yes, it is you."[a]

²⁶While they were eating, Jesus took bread, gave thanks and broke it,[w] and gave it to his disciples, saying, "Take and eat; this is my body."

²⁷Then he took the cup, gave thanks and offered it to them, saying, "Drink from it, all of you. ²⁸This is my blood of the[b] covenant,[x] which is poured out for many for the forgiveness of sins.[y] ²⁹I tell you, I will not drink of this fruit of the vine from now on until that day when I drink it anew with you[z] in my Father's kingdom."

³⁰When they had sung a hymn, they went out to the Mount of Olives.[a]

Jesus Predicts Peter's Denial

³¹Then Jesus told them, "This very night you will all fall away on account of me,[b] for it is written:

" 'I will strike the shepherd,
    and the sheep of the flock will be scattered.'[cc]

³²But after I have risen, I will go ahead of you into Galilee."[d]

³³Peter replied, "Even if all fall away on account of you, I never will."

³⁴"I tell you the truth," Jesus answered, "this very night, before the rooster crows, you will disown me three times."[e]

³⁵But Peter declared, "Even if I have to die with you,[f] I will never disown you." And all the other disciples said the same.

Gethsemane

³⁶Then Jesus went with his disciples to a place called Gethsemane, and he said to them, "Sit here while I go over there and pray." ³⁷He took Peter and the two sons of Zebedee[g] along with him, and he began to be sorrowful and troubled. ³⁸Then

26:18
r Jn 7:6,8,30;
12:23; 13:1; 17:1

26:21
s Lk 22:21-23;
Jn 13:21

26:23
t Ps 41:9; Jn 13:18
26:24
u Isa 53; Da 9:26;
Mk 9:12;
Lk 24:25-27,46;
Ac 17:2,3; 26:22,23
26:25
v Mt 23:7
26:26
w Mt 14:19;
1Co 10:16

26:28
x Ex 24:6-8;
Heb 9:20
y Mt 20:28; Mk 1:4
26:29
z Ac 10:41
26:30
a Mt 21:1;
Mk 14:26

26:31
b Mt 11:6
c Zec 13:7;
Jn 16:32

26:32
d Mt 28:7,10,16

26:34
e ver 75; Jn 13:38
26:35
f Jn 13:37

26:37
g Mt 4:21

---

a 25 Or "You yourself have said it"   b 28 Some manuscripts the new   c 31 Zech. 13:7

---

tonight." As the Passover meal was a central feast for Jews in celebrating the first covenant, "the Lord's Supper" is the celebration of the New.

📖 The Lord's Supper has at least six dimensions. It causes us to look (1) *backward* (to the history of salvation that prompted the Passover meal and to Jesus' accomplishment of salvation as a finished act); (2) *forward* (to the time we will enjoy the consummation of the kingdom and the fellowship of drinking the cup with Jesus); (3) *inward* (in self-examination, as we face our own sin and captivity); (4) *upward* (remembering that the story ended with Jesus' resurrection and ascension, not his death and burial); (5) *around* (to appreciate our participation in the body of Christ); and (6) *outward* (to a world dying without the Good News). Our feast is incomplete until people from every tribe and tongue can join us.

Matthew 26:31–35
🔍 The expression "fall away on account of me" (cf.

11:6) indicates that this night would bring an extreme test of the disciples' loyalty to Jesus. They wouldn't cease being his disciples, but they would fail the test of courage to stand up for him. Later they would be strengthened to become the courageous foundation of the church—but that strengthening would come through failure and after having been filled with the Holy Spirit (Acts 2).

📖 How easy is it for you to come to God in repentance, especially after a major failure? The difference between Judas and Peter (and the rest of the disciples) was demonstrated by their behavior *after* their failures. Judas, seized with remorse (but not repentance), took his own life (see "There and Then" for 27:1–10). Peter and the others faltered, but their repentance brought them back to Jesus for restoration (see John 21 for Peter's story). Even betraying or denying Christ can be forgiven on the basis of genuine repentance (a change of heart followed by right action).

26:38
h Jn 12:27
i ver 40,41

26:39
j Mt 20:22 k ver 42;
Ps 40:6-8; Isa 50:5;
Jn 5:30; 6:38
26:40
l ver 38
26:41
m Mt 6:13

he said to them, "My soul is overwhelmed with sorrow[h] to the point of death. Stay here and keep watch with me."[i]

39 Going a little farther, he fell with his face to the ground and prayed, "My Father, if it is possible, may this cup[j] be taken from me. Yet not as I will, but as you will."[k]

40 Then he returned to his disciples and found them sleeping. "Could you men not keep watch with me[l] for one hour?" he asked Peter. 41 "Watch and pray so that you will not fall into temptation.[m] The spirit is willing, but the body is weak."

42 He went away a second time and prayed, "My Father, if it is not possible for this cup to be taken away unless I drink it, may your will be done."

43 When he came back, he again found them sleeping, because their eyes were heavy. 44 So he left them and went away once more and prayed the third time, saying the same thing.

26:45
n ver 18

45 Then he returned to the disciples and said to them, "Are you still sleeping and resting? Look, the hour[n] is near, and the Son of Man is betrayed into the hands of sinners. 46 Rise, let us go! Here comes my betrayer!"

Jesus Arrested

47 While he was still speaking, Judas, one of the Twelve, arrived. With him was a large crowd armed with swords and clubs, sent from the chief priests and the elders of the people. 48 Now the betrayer had arranged a signal with them: "The one I kiss

26:49
o ver 25

is the man; arrest him." 49 Going at once to Jesus, Judas said, "Greetings, Rabbi!"[o] and kissed him.

26:50
p Mt 20:13; 22:12

50 Jesus replied, "Friend,[p] do what you came for."[a]

Then the men stepped forward, seized Jesus and arrested him. 51 With that, one

26:51
q Lk 22:36,38
r Jn 18:10

of Jesus' companions reached for his sword,[q] drew it out and struck the servant of the high priest, cutting off his ear.[r]

26:52
s Ge 9:6; Rev 13:10
26:53
t 2Ki 6:17; Da 7:10;
Mt 4:11
26:54
u ver 24

52 "Put your sword back in its place," Jesus said to him, "for all who draw the sword will die by the sword.[s] 53 Do you think I cannot call on my Father, and he will at once put at my disposal more than twelve legions of angels?[t] 54 But how then would the Scriptures be fulfilled[u] that say it must happen in this way?"

26:55
v Mk 12:35;
Lk 21:37;
Jn 7:14,28; 18:20
26:56
w ver 24

55 At that time Jesus said to the crowd, "Am I leading a rebellion, that you have come out with swords and clubs to capture me? Every day I sat in the temple courts teaching,[v] and you did not arrest me. 56 But this has all taken place that the writings of the prophets might be fulfilled."[w] Then all the disciples deserted him and fled.

Before the Sanhedrin

26:57
x ver 3

57 Those who had arrested Jesus took him to Caiaphas,[x] the high priest, where the teachers of the law and the elders had assembled. 58 But Peter followed him at a dis-

---

a 50 Or "Friend, why have you come?"

Matthew 26:36–46

Once at Gethsemane, Jesus asked to be alone with the three disciples who had been especially close to him—Peter and the brothers James and John (cf. 17:1), referred to here as "the two sons of Zebedee." Jesus wanted them to share in his overwhelming sorrow as he faced the cross. It may be difficult for us to grasp that the Son of God relied even partially on human relationships to sustain him in his time of greatest need. But this realization deepens our understanding of what it meant for him to take on our human nature (cf. Phil. 2:5–8) and for us to share in the fellowship of his suffering.

You may have been laid off from work. Your child may have been diagnosed with autism. You may have sustained an injury that wiped out your life's dream. Any number of pitfalls can threaten our stability. We may ask for support from friends, family, and our faith community. But our real strength comes when, with the people who

support us, we draw before God in prayer. God doesn't ask us to bear our own, or others', suffering alone. We do this as a community, in collaboration with him.

Matthew 26:47–56

Even at this point of deepest crisis, the disciples didn't understand the way of the kingdom. When Jesus was under attack, their instinct was to use force to defend him (and themselves). "Turning the other cheek" seemed irrelevant at that moment. Yet God's way isn't that of force and violence. Violence begets more violence, Jesus said. Even the angelic armies were restrained by God's hand.

Judas betrayed Jesus with the kiss of friendship. It's easy for us to betray him too, refusing to accept his way as right. History is filled with illustrations of how "those who take up the sword perish by it." What does it mean in our present world of violence and terror to walk the way of Jesus' kingdom?

tance, right up to the courtyard of the high priest. [y] He entered and sat down with the guards[z] to see the outcome.

[59]The chief priests and the whole Sanhedrin[a] were looking for false evidence against Jesus so that they could put him to death. [60]But they did not find any, though many false witnesses[b] came forward.

Finally two[c] came forward [61]and declared, "This fellow said, 'I am able to destroy the temple of God and rebuild it in three days.'"[d]

[62]Then the high priest stood up and said to Jesus, "Are you not going to answer? What is this testimony that these men are bringing against you?" [63]But Jesus remained silent.[e]

The high priest said to him, "I charge you under oath[f] by the living God:[g] Tell us if you are the Christ,[a] the Son of God."

[64]"Yes, it is as you say," Jesus replied. "But I say to all of you: In the future you will see the Son of Man sitting at the right hand of the Mighty One[h] and coming on the clouds of heaven."[i]

[65]Then the high priest tore his clothes[j] and said, "He has spoken blasphemy! Why do we need any more witnesses? Look, now you have heard the blasphemy. [66]What do you think?"

"He is worthy of death,"[k] they answered.

[67]Then they spit in his face and struck him with their fists.[l] Others slapped him [68]and said, "Prophesy to us, Christ. Who hit you?"[m]

Peter Disowns Jesus

[69]Now Peter was sitting out in the courtyard, and a servant girl came to him. "You also were with Jesus of Galilee," she said.

[70]But he denied it before them all. "I don't know what you're talking about," he said.

[71]Then he went out to the gateway, where another girl saw him and said to the people there, "This fellow was with Jesus of Nazareth."

[72]He denied it again, with an oath: "I don't know the man!"

[73]After a little while, those standing there went up to Peter and said, "Surely you are one of them, for your accent gives you away."

[a] 63 Or Messiah; also in verse 68

26:58 [y] Jn 18:15 [z] Jn 7:32,45,46
26:59 [a] Mt 5:22
26:60 [b] Ps 27:12; 35:11; Ac 6:13 [c] Dt 19:15
26:61 [d] Jn 2:19
26:63 [e] Mt 27:12,14 [f] Lev 5:1 [g] Mt 16:16
26:64 [h] Ps 110:1 [i] Da 7:13; Rev 1:7
26:65 [j] Mk 14:63
26:66 [k] Lev 24:16; Jn 19:7
26:67 [l] Mt 16:21; 27:30
26:68 [m] Lk 22:63-65

Matthew 26:57–68

The focus had been on the "chief priests and elders of the people" (vv. 3,47), probably a select group of Caiaphas's allies. Now the "whole Sanhedrin" or ecclesiastical court—70 members plus the high priest—was gathered. When a capital case was considered, the sages required that 23 members be present for a quorum. Scholars have long noted the irregularities of the Jewish legal proceedings against Jesus, among them: (1) a trial held at night; (2) at the high priest's home; (3) on the eve of a festival day; (4) beginning with reasons for conviction instead of acquittal; (4) based on false and contradictory witnesses; and (5) the verdict rendered on the day of trial.

Caiaphas hadn't only lied and manipulated the truth to have Jesus executed; he had violated the Jewish procedures he ascribed to as high priest—making him a kind of "super" hypocrite. There was no help for him due to his hardness of heart, demonstrated in his refusal to repent. The downward spiral of those who violate their own principles is described in Romans 1:18–32 (esp. vv. 28–32). These are strong words, but full of truth for those with ears to hear.

Matthew 26:69–75

Peter's three denials were likely spread out over a period of hours, with the threat level intensifying each time: (1) He was personally challenged by a servant girl. (2) Another girl spoke against him to the bystanders. (3) The bystanders confronted him. The poignancy of Peter's self-revelation is stated starkly: "He went outside and wept bitterly." Peter's grief was a recognition of his emptiness; he had thrown away all that had given him a new identity as Jesus' disciple. But the weeping was also the first sign of his repentance. Have you ever wept over a disservice or failure to your Lord?

Why did Peter deny Jesus, whom he vowed to follow even to his own death (v. 35)? Think carefully about your answer. Periods of stress or transition can place even the strongest of us at an overwhelming disadvantage. Jesus had told Peter, "Satan has asked to sift you as wheat" (Luke 22:31). And the enemy's desire hasn't changed: the failure of every believer's faith. But we are assured that Jesus continuously intercedes for us (cf. Heb. 7:24–25). Even in our most vulnerable moments or seasons, we can be confident in his presence and faith in us.

74Then he began to call down curses on himself and he swore to them, "I don't know the man!"

Immediately a rooster crowed. 75Then Peter remembered the word Jesus had spoken: "Before the rooster crows, you will disown me three times."*n* And he went outside and wept bitterly.

26:75
n ver 34; Jn 13:38

Judas Hangs Himself

27 Early in the morning, all the chief priests and the elders of the people came to the decision to put Jesus to death.*o* 2They bound him, led him away and handed him over*p* to Pilate, the governor. *q*

3When Judas, who had betrayed him,*r* saw that Jesus was condemned, he was seized with remorse and returned the thirty silver coins*s* to the chief priests and the elders. 4"I have sinned," he said, "for I have betrayed innocent blood."

"What is that to us?" they replied. "That's your responsibility."*t*

5So Judas threw the money into the temple*u* and left. Then he went away and hanged himself.*v*

6The chief priests picked up the coins and said, "It is against the law to put this into the treasury, since it is blood money." 7So they decided to use the money to buy the potter's field as a burial place for foreigners. 8That is why it has been called the Field of Blood*w* to this day. 9Then what was spoken by Jeremiah the prophet was fulfilled:*x* "They took the thirty silver coins, the price set on him by the people of Israel, 10and they used them to buy the potter's field, as the Lord commanded me."*a y*

27:1
o Mt 12:14;
Mk 15:1; Lk 22:66
27:2
p Mt 20:19
q Mk 15:1; Lk 13:1;
Ac 3:13; 1Ti 6:13
27:3
r Mt 10:4
s Mt 26:14,15
27:4
t ver 24
27:5
u Lk 1:9,21
v Ac 1:18

27:8
w Ac 1:19
27:9
x Mt 1:22
27:10
y Zec 11:12,13;
Jer 32:6-9

Jesus Before Pilate

11Meanwhile Jesus stood before the governor, and the governor asked him, "Are you the king of the Jews?"*z*

"Yes, it is as you say," Jesus replied.

12When he was accused by the chief priests and the elders, he gave no answer.*a* 13Then Pilate asked him, "Don't you hear the testimony they are bringing against you?"*b* 14But Jesus made no reply,*c* not even to a single charge—to the great amazement of the governor.

15Now it was the governor's custom at the Feast to release a prisoner*d* chosen by the crowd. 16At that time they had a notorious prisoner, called Barabbas. 17So when the crowd had gathered, Pilate asked them, "Which one do you want me to release to you: Barabbas, or Jesus who is called Christ?"*e* 18For he knew it was out of envy that they had handed Jesus over to him.

27:11
z Mt 2:2

27:12
a Mt 26:63;
Mk 14:61; Jn 19:9
27:13
b Mt 26:62
27:14
c Mk 14:61
27:15
d Jn 18:39

27:17
e ver 22; Mt 1:16

a 10 See Zech. 11:12,13; Jer. 19:1-13; 32:6-9.

Matthew 27:1–10

Matthew showed the depth of Judas's remorse but stopped short of saying he repented. The word "remorse" (*metamelomai*) is different from the normal word for repentance (*metanoeo*). Repentance is a change of heart. Remorse, a weaker emotion, means feeling regret. Had Judas truly repented, he would have been impelled to seek forgiveness from God. Instead, he turned to the chief priests and elders.

Paul differentiated between repentance and mere remorse: "Godly sorrow brings repentance that leads to salvation and leaves no regret, but worldly sorrow brings death" (2 Cor. 7:10). Why would Paul say that remorse (worldly sorrow) is lethal? Because it's self-centered sorrow over sin's consequences—not God-centered sorrow over its evil. Take a moment to ask the Lord to keep your heart softened, God-centered, and quick to repent.

Matthew 27:11–26

Here we find three fascinating accounts recorded only in Matthew: Pilate's warning based on his wife's dream; his attempt to "wash his hands" of the guilt of Jesus' blood; and the crowd's response: "Let his blood be on us and on our children!" These people were so convinced that Jesus deserved death that they brashly claimed responsibility. Pilate tried halfheartedly and unsuccessfully to escape accountability. Soon afterward, Peter would make a sweeping indictment for Jesus' death: of his fellow Jews in general, their leaders in particular, and the Romans (Acts 2:23,36; 3:17).

The Jewish mob declared a truth incredibly beyond their understanding: They and their children would share in the responsibility for taking Jesus' life, but his "blood"—his sacrificial death—would be sufficient and available for their salvation and for that of all future generations. Their words provide no excuse for anti-Semitism. We all stand in need of redemption through faith in Christ's blood (Rom. 3:22–25; cf. Eph. 2:11–13). In the hauntingly poignant words of a hymn: "Twas I, Lord Jesus. I it was denied thee. I crucified thee!"

19 While Pilate was sitting on the judge's seat,[f] his wife sent him this message:
"Don't have anything to do with that innocent[g] man, for I have suffered a great deal
today in a dream[h] because of him."
20 But the chief priests and the elders persuaded the crowd to ask for Barabbas and
to have Jesus executed.[i]
21 "Which of the two do you want me to release to you?" asked the governor.
"Barabbas," they answered.
22 "What shall I do, then, with Jesus who is called Christ?"[j] Pilate asked.
They all answered, "Crucify him!"
23 "Why? What crime has he committed?" asked Pilate.
But they shouted all the louder, "Crucify him!"
24 When Pilate saw that he was getting nowhere, but that instead an uproar[k] was
starting, he took water and washed his hands[l] in front of the crowd. "I am innocent
of this man's blood,"[m] he said. "It is your responsibility!"[n]
25 All the people answered, "Let his blood be on us and on our children!"[o]
26 Then he released Barabbas to them. But he had Jesus flogged,[p] and handed him
over to be crucified.

The Soldiers Mock Jesus

27 Then the governor's soldiers took Jesus into the Praetorium[q] and gathered the
whole company of soldiers around him. 28 They stripped him and put a scarlet robe
on him,[r] 29 and then twisted together a crown of thorns and set it on his head. They
put a staff in his right hand and knelt in front of him and mocked him. "Hail, king
of the Jews!" they said.[s] 30 They spit on him, and took the staff and struck him on
the head again and again.[t] 31 After they had mocked him, they took off the robe and
put his own clothes on him. Then they led him away to crucify him.[u]

The Crucifixion

32 As they were going out,[v] they met a man from Cyrene,[w] named Simon, and
they forced him to carry the cross.[x] 33 They came to a place called Golgotha (which
means The Place of the Skull).[y] 34 There they offered Jesus wine to drink, mixed with
gall;[z] but after tasting it, he refused to drink it. 35 When they had crucified him, they
divided up his clothes by casting lots.[a][a] 36 And sitting down, they kept watch[b] over
him there. 37 Above his head they placed the written charge against him: THIS IS
JESUS, THE KING OF THE JEWS. 38 Two robbers were crucified with him,[c] one on his right
and one on his left. 39 Those who passed by hurled insults at him, shaking their

27:19 [f] Jn 19:13 [g] ver 24 [h] Ge 20:6; Nu 12:6; 1Ki 3:5; Job 33:14-16; Mt 1:20; 2:12,13, 19,22
27:20 [i] Ac 3:14
27:22 [j] Mt 1:16
27:24 [k] Mt 26:5 [l] Ps 26:6 [m] Dt 21:6-8 [n] ver 4
27:25 [o] Jos 2:19; Ac 5:28
27:26 [p] Isa 53:5; Jn 19:1
27:27 [q] Jn 18:28,33; 19:9
27:28 [r] Jn 19:2
27:29 [s] Isa 53:3; Jn 19:2,3
27:30 [t] Mt 16:21; 26:67
27:31 [u] Isa 53:7
27:32 [v] Heb 13:12 [w] Ac 2:10; 6:9; 11:20; 13:1 [x] Mk 15:21; Lk 23:26
27:33 [y] Jn 19:17
27:34 [z] ver 48; Ps 69:21
27:35 [a] Ps 22:18
27:36 [b] ver 54
27:38 [c] Isa 53:12

[a] *35* A few late manuscripts *lots that the word spoken by the prophet might be fulfilled: "They divided my garments among themselves and cast lots for my clothing"* (Psalm 22:18)

Matthew 27:27–31

Roman soldiers in Jerusalem at the time were known to play a cruel game with condemned prisoners, especially revolutionary brigands. The prisoner was dressed up like a burlesque king and used as a game pawn. With each roll of "dice" the prisoner "king" moved around a game board etched in the floor. For the entertainment of the troops, they hurled verbal and physical abuse at the mock king. The charges against Jesus (vv. 11,37) made him "fair" game for this torturous pastime.

Suffering is a reality each of us must master—or at least avoid being mastered by. But Jesus' suffering shows us a new dimension of our own. Jesus suffered for what *we* did, and that brings us humbly to consider our own pain. Does your every creak and strain cause you to focus on furthering your life's purpose in establishing the reality of the kingdom of God in the lives of others? Or does it cause you to complain about your misfortunes?

Matthew 27:32–44

If Jesus really was the Son of God, the religious leaders reasoned, God wouldn't allow him to die on a cross. A crucified Messiah was unthinkable. So for them a final proof of his identity would be God's rescue of his Son. But as Jesus had earlier declared, the definitive sign of who he was would be his resurrection—which would also be a sign of God's judgment on these religious leaders (12:39–41). To truly save humanity, Jesus had to pursue his life's mission to the very end.

What comes to mind when you hear the word *cross*? For some of us it may primarily indicate a piece of jewelry, for others the difficulties we have to bear. For still others it produces an emotional reaction as we think of Jesus hanging between two criminals. Matthew calls us to recognize that the cross represents Jesus' entire earthly ministry, allows us an intimate look into the Savior's heart for this world, and symbolizes God's work in our lives as well.

d Ps 22:7; 109:25;
La 2:15
27:40
e Mt 26:61; Jn 2:19
f ver 42 *g* Mt 4:3,6
27:42
h Jn 1:49; 12:13
i Jn 3:15
27:43
j Ps 22:8

heads *d* 40 and saying, "You who are going to destroy the temple and build it in three days, *e* save yourself! *f* Come down from the cross, if you are the Son of God!" *g*

41 In the same way the chief priests, the teachers of the law and the elders mocked him. 42 "He saved others," they said, "but he can't save himself! He's the King of Israel! *h* Let him come down now from the cross, and we will believe *i* in him. 43 He trusts in God. Let God rescue him *j* now if he wants him, for he said, 'I am the Son of God.' " 44 In the same way the robbers who were crucified with him also heaped insults on him.

The Death of Jesus

27:45
k Am 8:9
27:46
l Ps 22:1

45 From the sixth hour until the ninth hour darkness *k* came over all the land. 46 About the ninth hour Jesus cried out in a loud voice, "*Eloi, Eloi,* *a* *lama sabachthani?*"—which means, "My God, my God, why have you forsaken me?" *b l*

47 When some of those standing there heard this, they said, "He's calling Elijah."

27:48
m ver 34; Ps 69:21

48 Immediately one of them ran and got a sponge. He filled it with wine vinegar, *m* put it on a stick, and offered it to Jesus to drink. 49 The rest said, "Now leave him alone. Let's see if Elijah comes to save him."

27:50
n Jn 19:30
27:51
o Ex 26:31-33;
Heb 9:3,8 *p* ver 54

50 And when Jesus had cried out again in a loud voice, he gave up his spirit. *n*

51 At that moment the curtain of the temple *o* was torn in two from top to bottom. The earth shook and the rocks split. *p* 52 The tombs broke open and the bodies of many holy people who had died were raised to life. 53 They came out of the tombs, and after Jesus' resurrection they went into the holy city *q* and appeared to many people.

27:53
q Mt 4:5
27:54
r ver 36 *s* Mt 4:3;
17:5

54 When the centurion and those with him who were guarding *r* Jesus saw the earthquake and all that had happened, they were terrified, and exclaimed, "Surely he was the Son *c* of God!" *s*

27:55
t Lk 8:2,3
27:56
u Mk 15:47;
Lk 24:10; Jn 19:25

55 Many women were there, watching from a distance. They had followed Jesus from Galilee to care for his needs. *t* 56 Among them were Mary Magdalene, Mary the mother of James and Joses, and the mother of Zebedee's sons. *u*

The Burial of Jesus

27:60
v Mt 27:66; 28:2;
Mk 16:4

57 As evening approached, there came a rich man from Arimathea, named Joseph, who had himself become a disciple of Jesus. 58 Going to Pilate, he asked for Jesus' body, and Pilate ordered that it be given to him. 59 Joseph took the body, wrapped it in a clean linen cloth, 60 and placed it in his own new tomb *v* that he had cut out of the rock. He rolled a big stone in front of the entrance to the tomb and went away. 61 Mary Magdalene and the other Mary were sitting there opposite the tomb.

a 46 Some manuscripts *Eli, Eli*   *b 46* Psalm 22:1   *c 54* Or *a son*

Matthew 27:45–56

Of Jesus' seven cries from the cross, Matthew recorded only the one in verse 46—spoken originally in Aramaic and translated by Matthew into Greek. This wasn't the "It is finished" (John 19:30) cry of victory that ultimately came from Jesus' completion of his atoning sacrifice. Matthew focused on Jesus' feelings of abandonment on the cross. Bearing the full weight of human sin, he felt acutely and completely the separation our sin causes between us and God. The suffering of physical pain Jesus endured was only a small part of the agony of feeling cut off from the Father.

The enormity of Jesus' crucifixion tempts us to minimize its horror. But we may not underrate the outrageousness of the cross. It was there that the God-man *bore humanity's load of sin and experienced ultimate* separation from God, while retaining in his consciousness a painful intimacy with his Father. Is it hard for you to stir up the same emotion you felt when you first learned of Jesus' death for you?

Matthew 27:57–61

Joseph stands in sharp contrast to the 11 male disciples who had forsaken Jesus. Given his membership in the Sanhedrin (cf. Luke 23:50–51), it couldn't have been easy for him to follow Jesus. But when all the men had fled, God enabled Joseph and the two Marys to buck the religious establishment, provide leadership, and put their lives on the line. Joseph went so far as to relinquish his family tomb to the Master.

Some time earlier, another rich man had walked sadly away upon realization that Jesus must be his sole Master (19:16–22). It's harder, Jesus had noted to his disciples after the man's disheartened departure, for a rich man to be saved than for a camel to go through the eye of a needle. But, as Jesus declared in the same breath, all things are possible with God (19:23–26). The faithfulness of Mary Magdalene and the other Mary demonstrates that those society tends to disregard—like women and the marginalized—are welcome in God's eyes.

The Guard at the Tomb

62The next day, the one after Preparation Day, the chief priests and the Pharisees went to Pilate. 63"Sir," they said, "we remember that while he was still alive that deceiver said, 'After three days I will rise again.' w 64So give the order for the tomb to be made secure until the third day. Otherwise, his disciples may come and steal the body and tell the people that he has been raised from the dead. This last deception will be worse than the first."

65"Take a guard," x Pilate answered. "Go, make the tomb as secure as you know how." 66So they went and made the tomb secure by putting a seal y on the stone z and posting the guard. a

The Resurrection

28 After the Sabbath, at dawn on the first day of the week, Mary Magdalene and the other Mary b went to look at the tomb.

2There was a violent earthquake, c for an angel d of the Lord came down from heaven and, going to the tomb, rolled back the stone and sat on it. 3His appearance was like lightning, and his clothes were white as snow. e 4The guards were so afraid of him that they shook and became like dead men.

5The angel said to the women, "Do not be afraid, f for I know that you are looking for Jesus, who was crucified. 6He is not here; he has risen, just as he said. g Come and see the place where he lay. 7Then go quickly and tell his disciples: 'He has risen from the dead and is going ahead of you into Galilee. h There you will see him.' Now I have told you."

8So the women hurried away from the tomb, afraid yet filled with joy, and ran to tell his disciples. 9Suddenly Jesus met them. i "Greetings," he said. They came to him, clasped his feet and worshiped him. 10Then Jesus said to them, "Do not be afraid. Go and tell my brothers j to go to Galilee; there they will see me."

The Guards' Report

11While the women were on their way, some of the guards k went into the city and reported to the chief priests everything that had happened. 12When the chief priests had met with the elders and devised a plan, they gave the soldiers a large sum of money, 13telling them, "You are to say, 'His disciples came during the night and stole him away while we were asleep.' 14If this report gets to the governor, l we will satisfy him and keep you out of trouble." 15So the soldiers took the money and did

---

27:63
w Mt 16:21

27:65
x ver 66; Mt 28:11
27:66
y Da 6:17 z ver 60;
Mt 28:2 a Mt 28:11

28:1
b Mt 27:56
28:2
c Mt 27:51
d Jn 20:12
28:3
e Da 10:6; Mk 9:3;
Jn 20:12
28:5
f ver 10; Mt 14:27
28:6
g Mt 16:21

28:7
h ver 10,16;
Mt 26:32

28:9
i Jn 20:14-18

28:10
j Jn 20:17; Ro 8:29;
Heb 2:11-13,17

28:11
k Mt 27:65,66

28:14
l Mt 27:2

Matthew 27:62–66

🔑 The chief priests and Pharisees went to Pilate to make sure the dead man didn't arouse more support after his death. The disciples somehow failed to recall Jesus' prediction of rising again after three days, but the religious leaders apparently sensed that the excitement wasn't over.

The seal was a security device, likely a cord attached both to the stone (cf. v. 60) and to the tomb, with wax imprinted with the Roman seal anchoring both ends so that tampering could be detected (cf. Dan. 6:17). The soldiers standing guard added additional security. The religious leaders and Pilate went to great lengths to prevent a hoax about Jesus' resurrection. Instead they unintentionally provided another witness to its reality.

📖 Our emphasis today is typically on the empty tomb, not the cross—and rightly so. The unoccupied tomb is a permanent reminder that Jesus' work on the cross has effectively canceled the penalty for our sins. As Paul declared, "If Christ has not been raised, your faith is futile; you are still in your sins" (1 Cor. 15:17).

But in our rush to reach the tomb, we need to resist the temptation to hurtle headlong past the cross. We find in its shadows an example—not of mindless self-abasement but of the heart of Jesus. Some call it "cruciformity"—the experience of dying and rising with Christ. This experience embarks us on a lifelong journey of conformity to his image, a kingdom life expressed in faith, love, power, and hope (cf. 1 Cor. 2:2; Gal. 2:20; Phil. 3:10). Have you lingered for a while at the foot of the cross?

Matthew 28:1–10

🔑 Once again women were elevated by God to positions of leadership. God used women as witnesses, not just of Jesus' crucifixion but also of his resurrection. Several of them had observed Jesus' death and burial (vv. 55–56,61), and they were the first to see the empty tomb and meet the resurrected Christ. They were designated by both the angel and Jesus to carry their witness to the other disciples—the first to testify to the reality of the resurrection. These women had come to the tomb expecting to confirm the death of their hopes. They found instead life and hope beyond their wildest dreams.

Cross-cultural Mission

28:19–20

Harry Emerson Fosdick observed that nobody goes to church "to discover what happened to the Jebusites." While the Bible centers on one people—the Jews, and then upon the "New Israel," the church—the world at that time included Jebusites, Hittites, Ninevites, and scores of other peoples. Our world includes about 30,000 people groups.

Biblical writers often stress our mission to reach Earth's "peoples." God promised Abraham that his descendents would bless "all peoples on earth" (Gen. 12:1–3). Isaiah declared that Israel was raised up to bring "salvation to the ends of the earth" (Isa. 49:6). Jesus' Great Commission (Matt. 28: 19–20) to "go and make disciples of all nations" reinforces this sacred calling.

Christianity isn't the only religion inviting others into its ranks. Judaism welcomes "Gentile" converts, and Islam is proactively mission-minded. Christianity's approach, though, is different. Judaism expects Gentiles to become culturally kosher, and Islam shapes converts into an Arabic cultural mold. But, ideally, Christian mission adapts to the tongues and cultures of the people it seeks to reach. This became official policy early in the Christian movement, with the decisions of the Jerusalem Council reported in Acts 15. It's voiced in Paul's reflection in 1 Corinthians 9:22: "I have become all things to all men so that by all possible means I might save some."

> There may be nothing more meaningful for us as Christians than helping to plant or advance an indigenous church in another culture.

Most Christians realize that cross-cultural mission necessitates learning and using the host population's language. But a sensitive approach also requires Christ's ambassadors to understand and employ other features of their culture. A culture is like an iceberg: partly visible (behaviors) but substantially invisible (assumptions, values, beliefs). Edward T. Hall views culture as "the silent language." Meaning is communicated (or lost) in *every way* people express themselves. According to Geert Hofstede, intercultural communication requires adapting the forms by which we communicate our message to the host population's "software of the mind." Indigenous Christianity is the indispensable means by which we can extend the Good News of the incarnation to include them.

Many new missionaries seriously underestimate the importance of culture and the complexity of cross-cultural communication. Most who "wing it" fail. But those who take the time to learn to make sense of cultural differences typically succeed.

Even with preparation, cross-cultural living is at first demanding and exhausting. A person needs to navigate his or her daily life by a totally new cultural "map." Almost everything—from greeting people to mailing a letter to buying bread to getting the news—requires thought, decision, and effort. In time, though, one adjusts and becomes a bi-cultural servant of the people. Effective missionaries don't necessarily win many converts on their own; the converts themselves become bridges to their cultural peers.

There is no shortcut to understanding the people in an unfamiliar society. But when they begin to sense that we understand them, want to understand them, or even understand people *like* them, they may risk believing that our God understands *them*. At that point they become more open to his revelation.

There may be nothing more meaningful for us as Christians than helping to plant or advance an indigenous church in another culture. As the gospel's meaning is expressed in their language, music, art, architecture, and style, some of the people will discover faith, experience life change, and become agents of hope to their peers—and even to other peoples. And we gain a deeper understanding of the gospel's meaning through the experience of interpreting it *cross-culturally* than we ever could by staying home.

George G. Hunter III, professor of evangelism and church growth at Asbury Theological Seminary in Wilmore, Kentucky

as they were instructed. And this story has been widely circulated among the Jews to this very day.

The Great Commission

[16]Then the eleven disciples went to Galilee, to the mountain where Jesus had told them to go.[m] [17]When they saw him, they worshiped him; but some doubted. [18]Then Jesus came to them and said, "All authority in heaven and on earth has been given to me.[n] [19]Therefore go and make disciples of all nations,[o] baptizing them in[a] the name of the Father and of the Son and of the Holy Spirit,[p] [20]and teaching[q] them to obey everything I have commanded you. And surely I am with you[r] always, to the very end of the age."[s]

[a] 19 Or *into*; see Acts 8:16; 19:5; Rom. 6:3; 1 Cor. 1:13; 10:2 and Gal. 3:27.

28:16
m ver 7,10;
Mt 26:32
28:18
n Da 7:13,14;
Lk 10:22; Jn 3:35;
17:2; 1Co 15:27;
Eph 1:20-22;
Php 2:9,10
28:19
o Mk 16:15,16;
Lk 24:47; Ac 1:8;
14:21 *p* Ac 2:38;
8:16; Ro 6:3,4
28:20
q Ac 2:42
r Mt 18:20;
Ac 18:10
s Mt 13:39

📖 Throughout his ministry Jesus placed men and women in a position of equality, a status denied most women in 1st-century Israel. Since women were the first to bear witness to the resurrection, they were regarded as coworkers with men in the community of faith. There are divisions among Christians over the role of women in the church today. Such arguments aside, what does it mean to you that Jesus entrusted this valuable message first to women?

Matthew 28:11–15

📖 Why did the religious leaders continue to try to prevent verification of Jesus' Messianic identity? They believed Jesus' ministry was satanically empowered (12:22–24) and thought they were doing the right thing in keeping another event from deceiving the people. When their use of violence didn't work, they resorted to bribery. Yet the Good News, then and now, is that God can break through any hard heart, as demonstrated in the earliest days of the church when even priests became obedient disciples of Jesus (Acts 6:7).

📖 Sometimes "good news" sounds—and is—too good to be true. Doubt in Jesus' resurrection is a given in this world. But we who know the Good News owe it to those who don't to defend the reality of the resurrection. We do this best not through clever arguments, but by living with bold hope. Knowing that Jesus has risen, we can face all suffering, sin, and evil with courage and confidence. In Peter's words, "Always be prepared to give an answer to everyone who asks you to give the reason for the hope that you have" (1 Peter 3:15). Has someone asked you why you are so hopeful? How might you explain more effectively your reasons for eternal optimism?

Matthew 28:16–20

📖 In his "Great Commission" Jesus summed up his purpose on Earth. The placement of this summation at the end of his Gospel indicates Matthew's purpose in writing. The all-inclusive nature of Jesus' command is indicated by the repetition of the adjective *pas* ("all"): "all authority," "all nations," "all things" (NIV "everything"), "all the days" (NIV "always"). This commission is comprehensive—indicating Jesus' authority over all political and spiritual powers, the extent of his kingdom to all ethnic groups, and the expectation that his followers will obey all aspects of his teaching.

📖 Disciples of Christ live with bold confidence and humble conviction; he has authority over all things and nations, and we seek to obey him in everything we do. Jesus' final saying assures us that we can indeed faithfully live as kingdom citizens; he promises unconditionally to be with us. Jesus' arrival began the greatest revolution the world has ever known: the transformation of human hearts—and of every aspect of human society. It's our privilege to participate in the coming of his kingdom into every corner of the world.

INTRODUCTION TO
Mark

AUTHOR
The earliest testimony connects this Gospel to Mark, also known as John Mark. (John was his
Jewish name; Mark [Marcus] his Roman one.) John Mark wasn't one of the Twelve but was a
relative of Barnabas (Col. 4:10) and companion of Peter (Acts 12:12–13; 1 Peter 5:13).

DATE WRITTEN
Mark was probably written between A.D. 50 and 70.

ORIGINAL READERS
Mark addressed his Gospel to Gentile Christians facing increasingly trying conditions in Rome.

TIMELINE

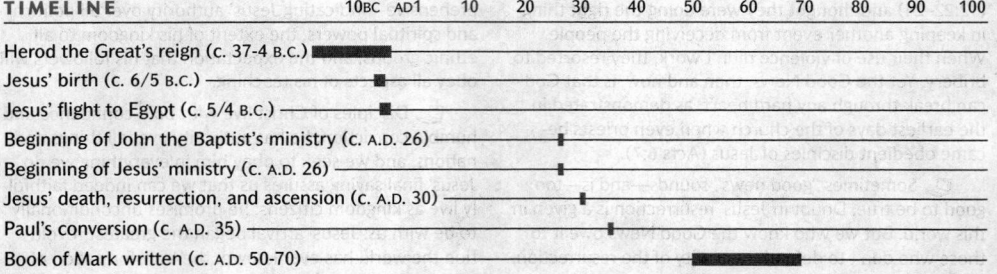

TIMELINE	10BC AD1	10	20	30	40	50	60	70	80	90	100
Herod the Great's reign (c. 37-4 B.C.)											
Jesus' birth (c. 6/5 B.C.)											
Jesus' flight to Egypt (c. 5/4 B.C.)											
Beginning of John the Baptist's ministry (c. A.D. 26)											
Beginning of Jesus' ministry (c. A.D. 26)											
Jesus' death, resurrection, and ascension (c. A.D. 30)											
Paul's conversion (c. A.D. 35)											
Book of Mark written (c. A.D. 50-70)											

THEMES
Mark wrote to tell others about Jesus. His themes include the following:

1. *Jesus, the Son of God.* Mark's account reveals Jesus' authority (a) as a teacher (1:21–22);
(b) to forgive sins (2:5–12); and (c) over the Sabbath (2:27–28), unclean spirits (3:20–27), nature (4:35–41; 6:45–52), the law (7:1–20), the temple (11:12–19,27–33; 12:1–12), and the mystery of the kingdom of God (4:10–11).

2. *Jesus, the Son of Man.* Jesus didn't shrink from ritual defilement, physical contamination, or
moral pollution. His loving touch displayed his compassion and accessibility, as well as God's
concern for our bodily health.

3. *Jesus, the Messiah.* Jesus' suffering, rejection, and death were central to God's way of salvation. Mark revealed the disciples' initial inability to recognize Jesus' Messianic identity and
role, as well as their later reluctance to accept that the Messiah had to suffer and die.

4. *Jesus, a model of suffering.* Jesus spoke openly of his suffering and death and warned his
disciples that they also would face tribulation. Mark clearly portrayed the rigors of discipleship—both then and now. Jesus expects his disciples to deny themselves, endure suffering,
and take up their own crosses (8:34–38), leaving everything behind to follow him (1:18;
10:17–22,28–31,49–50).

5. *Jesus, Savior of all who believe.* Jesus is the Savior of all who receive him by faith. Mark's Gospel focuses on Jesus' ministry in Gentile regions, explains Jewish terms and customs, records the confession of faith of a Gentile (15:39) and the sending of the first Gentile missionary (5:18–19), and calls the temple "a house of prayer for *all* nations" (11:17, emphasis added).

FAITH IN ACTION
The pages of Mark contain life lessons and role models of faith—people who challenge believers to put their faith in action.

Role Models

- JESUS (1:40–42; 5:24–34; 7:24–30; 8:1–8) displayed compassion and mercy to all, including the poor, the socially ostracized, and ordinary people in need. How is God calling you to respond as a servant to those around you?

- THE DEMON-POSSESSED MAN (5:1–20), after having been set free from the bondage of demonic control, went with joy to tell others what Jesus had done for him. From what has Jesus freed you? What has been your response?

- THE GREEK (SYROPHOENICIAN) WOMAN (7:24–30) wouldn't be deterred from seeking deliverance/healing for her daughter. How does her example encourage you?

- PETER (8:27–30) boldly expressed the truth that Jesus is the Christ. Who do *you* say Jesus is? Who have you told?

- BARTIMAEUS (10:46–52) threw aside his one possession, his cloak, to follow Jesus. What is Jesus calling you to leave behind—a possession, habit, person, attitude—as you follow him?

Challenges

- Be ready for God to move through you—ready with the message of salvation, regardless of the personal cost (8:34—9:1).

- Allow God to use you to show his love and compassion for others by bringing healing and wholeness to those around you (1:40–42).

- Be willing to confront the injustice of a domineering system that opts for violent "solutions" or "benign neglect" of society's most vulnerable (7:1–23; 10:13–16).

- Live your life from the perspective that greatness in God's kingdom is expressed by service and sacrifice (10:43–45).

OUTLINE

  I. The Beginnings of Jesus' Ministry (1:1–13)
  II. Jesus' Ministry in Galilee (1:14—6:29)
      A. His Early Ministry (1:14—3:12)
      B. His Later Ministry (3:13—6:29)
  III. Ministry in Other Areas (6:30—9:32)
  IV. Final Ministry in Galilee (9:33–50)
  V. Jesus' Ministry in Judea and Perea (10)
  VI. The Passion of Jesus (11:1—14:11)
      A. The Triumphal Entry (11:1–11)
      B. The Cleansing of the Temple (11:12–19)
      C. Last Questions From the Jewish Leaders (11:20—12:44)
      D. The Olivet Discourse (13)
      E. The Anointing of Jesus' Head (14:1–11)
  VII. The Arrest, Trial, and Death of Jesus (14:12—15:47)
  VIII. The Resurrection of Jesus (16)

John the Baptist Prepares the Way

1:1
a Mt 4:3

1

¹The beginning of the gospel about Jesus Christ, the Son of God. ª*a*

²It is written in Isaiah the prophet:

1:2
b Mal 3:1;
Mt 11:10; Lk 7:27

"I will send my messenger ahead of you,
     who will prepare your way"*b b*—
³ "a voice of one calling in the desert,
    'Prepare the way for the Lord,
        make straight paths for him.' "*c c*

1:3
c Isa 40:3; Jn 1:23
1:4
d Mt 3:1 *e* Ac 13:24
f Lk 1:77

⁴And so John *d* came, baptizing in the desert region and preaching a baptism of repentance*e* for the forgiveness of sins.*f* ⁵The whole Judean countryside and all the people of Jerusalem went out to him. Confessing their sins, they were baptized by him in the Jordan River. ⁶John wore clothing made of camel's hair, with a leather belt around his waist, and he ate locusts*g* and wild honey. ⁷And this was his message: "After me will come one more powerful than I, the thongs of whose sandals

1:6
g Lev 11:22

ª *1* Some manuscripts do not have *the Son of God.*   ᵇ *2* Mal. 3:1   ᶜ *3* Isaiah 40:3

Mark 1:1–8

Mark's presentation of the gospel is concise and energetic, opening with a quotation from Isaiah about the preparation for the Messiah (vv. 2–3). John the Baptist appears here out of nowhere, baptizing and preaching a message of repentance. But this Scripture quotation underscores that both John and Jesus were the fulfillment of God's plan.

Other than a brief quotation in Mark 6:18, verses 7–8 of this passage constitute John's only speaking part in this Gospel. Mark's interest in John's preaching centered around John's announcement that One more powerful than himself was coming, One who would baptize with the Spirit. In fact, John wound up an executed prisoner. Though Jesus ranked him with the mighty, John believed his limited power and prestige didn't even qualify him to function as Jesus' slave. What would it mean for you to approach Christ in the spirit of John the Baptist?

1:1–11

Great Encouragers in the Bible

John the Baptist wasn't the only person in the Bible who recognized one aspect of his role to be that of supporting someone else. Following are other outstanding examples. Notice that being an encourager doesn't necessarily mean a life of anonymity:

Jonathan: When his father Saul was pursuing David with murderous intent, Jonathan sought out his friend David in the wilderness to help him "find strength in God" (1 Sam. 23:16).	
Servant girl: She encouraged Naaman's wife to advise her husband to seek out Elisha for healing from leprosy (2 Kings 5:2–4).	
Hezekiah: This king encouraged the priests and Levites to follow closely the word of the Lord (2 Chron. 30:22).	
Elizabeth: Elizabeth blessed the newly pregnant Mary for believing God's word (Luke 1:39–45). This undoubtedly encouraged Mary, who would be exposed to the shame of having become pregnant while unwed (Matt. 1:19).	
John the Baptist: John recognized that though his own work was important, Jesus' would be more important (Matt. 3:11).	
Paul: Paul recognized that encouragement is reciprocal, that people encourage one another in turn (Rom. 1:11–12).	
Barnabas: Joseph of Cyprus became so well known for his encouragement of others that his friends nicknamed him Son of Encouragement (Barnabas) (Acts 4:36; 11:22–23).	
Timothy: Part of Timothy's ministry was to encourage "young" believers as they grew in the faith (1 Thess. 3:2; 2 Tim. 4:2).	
Jesus: "Peace I leave with you; my peace I give you. I do not give to you as the world gives. Do not let your hearts be troubled and do not be afraid" (John 14:27).	

I am not worthy to stoop down and untie.[h] 8I baptize you with[a] water, but he will baptize you with the Holy Spirit."[i]

The Baptism and Temptation of Jesus

9At that time Jesus came from Nazareth[j] in Galilee and was baptized by John in the Jordan. 10As Jesus was coming up out of the water, he saw heaven being torn open and the Spirit descending on him like a dove.[k] 11And a voice came from heaven: "You are my Son,[l] whom I love; with you I am well pleased."

12At once the Spirit sent him out into the desert, 13and he was in the desert forty days, being tempted by Satan.[m] He was with the wild animals, and angels attended him.

The Calling of the First Disciples

14After John was put in prison, Jesus went into Galilee,[n] proclaiming the good news of God.[o] 15"The time has come,"[p] he said. "The kingdom of God is near. Repent and believe the good news!"[q]

16As Jesus walked beside the Sea of Galilee, he saw Simon and his brother Andrew casting a net into the lake, for they were fishermen. 17"Come, follow me," Jesus said, "and I will make you fishers of men." 18At once they left their nets and followed him.

19When he had gone a little farther, he saw James son of Zebedee and his brother John in a boat, preparing their nets. 20Without delay he called them, and they left their father Zebedee in the boat with the hired men and followed him.

Jesus Drives Out an Evil Spirit

21They went to Capernaum, and when the Sabbath came, Jesus went into the synagogue and began to teach.[r] 22The people were amazed at his teaching, because he taught them as one who had authority, not as the teachers of the law.[s] 23Just then a man in their synagogue who was possessed by an evil[b] spirit cried out, 24"What do you want with us,[t] Jesus of Nazareth?[u] Have you come to destroy us? I know who you are—the Holy One of God!"[v]

---

[a] 8 Or in   [b] 23 Greek unclean; also in verses 26 and 27

1:7
[h] Ac 13:25
1:8
[i] Isa 44:3; Joel 2:28; Ac 1:5; 2:4; 11:16; 19:4-6
1:9
[j] Mt 2:23
1:10
[k] Jn 1:32
1:11
[l] Mt 3:17
1:13
[m] Mt 4:10
1:14
[n] Mt 4:12 [o] Mt 4:23
1:15
[p] Gal 4:4; Eph 1:10 [q] Ac 20:21
1:21
[r] Mt 4:23; Mk 10:1
1:22
[s] Mt 7:28,29
1:24
[t] Mt 8:29 [u] Mt 2:23; Lk 24:19; Ac 24:5 [v] Lk 1:35; Jn 6:69; Ac 3:14

Mark 1:9–13

From the throng that tramped out to John from Judea and Jerusalem (v. 5), the focus shifts to One who hailed from Nazareth in Galilee. As with John, Mark told us nothing about Jesus' pedigree or birth—nothing about heavenly signs, strange callers bringing gifts, or childhood incidents that clue us in to his less- (or more-) than-ordinary childhood. Unlike the urban sophisticates from Jerusalem, Jesus emerged from a dot on the map. This son of man from Nowhere—the Messiah from Eternity—arrived on the scene without fanfare.

When you read the Gospels, do you tend to focus more on Jesus' human or divine nature? We glimpse here the mysterious balance between the two: humble submission to John's baptism contrasted with thundering affirmation from heaven; forty days of raw temptation culminating in the ministry of angels. In both scenarios Jesus identified with sinners, just as he would later die for us. We can take comfort when we pass through our own desert experiences: Jesus has been there and knows the way. All we have to do is follow.

Mark 1:14–20

Mark doesn't tell us why Jesus singled out four fishermen to be his disciples or why they responded so readily. The more "fleshed out" accounts in Luke and John (Luke 5:1–11; John 1:35–37) make more sense to modern readers. We want some rational explanation for these men's behavior—something like the fishing industry having dried up or their having been itching for the Messiah to oust the Roman oppressors. But by not preparing us to expect these fishermen to follow, Mark may deliberately have underscored the force of Jesus' call.

Preaching comes to crowds, but the call to follow comes to individuals. We can easily be tempted to avoid full commitment as disciples by the illusion that our real needs are physical—resulting in an excessive concern for material security. But Jesus can deliver us from bondage to material concerns (like the desire to preserve our standard of living). He gives us a vision that there is more to life than a net bulging with wriggling fish or a comfortable income. Does your life revolve around following Jesus and serving others for his sake?

Mark 1:21–28

Mark emphasized the power—not the content—of Jesus' teaching. His first readers knew Jesus' authority derived from God's Spirit. At this point, though, only demons and angels (cf. v. 13) fathomed the mysteries of the unseen world. They knew Jesus wasn't just another exorcist, but the One God had sent to break Satan's rule. Yet the dumbfounded witnesses to this demon's expulsion remained in the dark about the source of Jesus' power and mission.

Mark, like other New Testament writers, took demons for granted. Many of us today are uncomfort-

1:25
w ver 34
1:26
x Mk 9:20
1:27
y Mk 10:24,32
1:28
z Mt 9:26

25 "Be quiet!" said Jesus sternly. "Come out of him!" [w] 26 The evil spirit shook the man violently and came out of him with a shriek. [x]

27 The people were all so amazed [y] that they asked each other, "What is this? A new teaching—and with authority! He even gives orders to evil spirits and they obey him." 28 News about him spread quickly over the whole region [z] of Galilee.

1:29
a ver 21,23

Jesus Heals Many

1:31
b Lk 7:14

29 As soon as they left the synagogue, [a] they went with James and John to the home of Simon and Andrew. 30 Simon's mother-in-law was in bed with a fever, and they told Jesus about her. 31 So he went to her, took her hand and helped her up. [b] The fever left her and she began to wait on them.

1:32
c Mt 4:24
1:34
d Mt 4:23
e Mk 3:12;
Ac 16:17,18

32 That evening after sunset the people brought to Jesus all the sick and demon-possessed. [c] 33 The whole town gathered at the door, 34 and Jesus healed many who had various diseases. [d] He also drove out many demons, but he would not let the demons speak because they knew who he was. [e]

---

able with this subject, though we ask questions like "What's gotten into him?" or "What's come over you?" Since demons avoid detection on scientific radar screens, we easily dismiss incidents like this as primitive misdiagnoses. At the opposite extreme are those who brand much they fail to understand as demonic in origin. Both views risk trivializing a potent evil that wages war with God and infects everything in this fallen world.

Mark 1:29–34

Mark introduced the second sign pointing to the identity of the God/man: acts of physical healing. He differentiated between Jesus' power to heal and to liberate the demon-possessed (see v. 34). Those afflicted with demons weren't "healed"; instead, the demons

went out of them. The presence of an evil spirit indicated that a spiritual force had taken internal control, to twist and maim a human life and alienate the person from God and others.

Peter's mother-in-law was the first in Mark's account to receive physical healing. Her immediate ability and desire to "wait on them" signified not only her physical wholeness but also her spiritual responsiveness to Jesus. Such an act of love is significant: The angels had offered Jesus the same kind of assistance in the desert (v. 13). Serving is characteristic of discipleship—and the natural response of a grateful person. How are you living out your thanks for Christ's blessings?

Snapshots

1:18

The Cambridge Seven

Montagu Beauchamp, William W. Cassels, Dixon E. Hoste, Arthur Polhill-Turner, Cecil Polhill-Turner, Stanley P. Smith, and Charles T. Studd gave up everything to join Hudson Taylor and the China Inland Mission (CIM) in 1885.

Smith, a key member of the Cambridge rowing team, had participated in street evangelism and in D.L. Moody's 1884 London campaign. In China he often worked with the national Christian leader Hsi Shengmo, engaging in ministry to opium addicts as well as in rural evangelism and leadership training.

Studd was considered an outstanding cricket player. His decision to give up a substantial inheritance, as well as his sport, created a sensation in the press. He embraced CIM's radical model of incarnational ministry, which impacted later efforts in India and what is now the Democratic Republic of the Congo. He eventually founded Heart of Africa Mission, today called World Evangelization for Christ.

> [Studd's] decision to give up a substantial inheritance, as well as his sport, created a sensation in the press.

Another cricketeer, Cecil Polhill-Turner, returned from China in 1900 in ill health and inherited an estate in 1903. He used his resources to fund Pentecostal outreach at home and abroad.

Hoste evangelized in rural Shansi villages, eventually becoming CIM's general director. He was imprisoned by the Japanese (1941–45) and died shortly thereafter in London.

Jesus Prays in a Solitary Place

[35] Very early in the morning, while it was still dark, Jesus got up, left the house and went off to a solitary place, where he prayed.[f] [36] Simon and his companions went to look for him, [37] and when they found him, they exclaimed: "Everyone is looking for you!"

[38] Jesus replied, "Let us go somewhere else—to the nearby villages—so I can preach there also. That is why I have come."[g] [39] So he traveled throughout Galilee, preaching in their synagogues[h] and driving out demons.[i]

A Man With Leprosy

[40] A man with leprosy[a] came to him and begged him on his knees,[j] "If you are willing, you can make me clean."

[41] Filled with compassion, Jesus reached out his hand and touched the man. "I am willing," he said. "Be clean!" [42] Immediately the leprosy left him and he was cured.

[43] Jesus sent him away at once with a strong warning: [44] "See that you don't tell this to anyone.[k] But go, show yourself to the priest[l] and offer the sacrifices that Moses commanded for your cleansing,[m] as a testimony to them." [45] Instead he went out and began to talk freely, spreading the news. As a result, Jesus could no longer enter a town openly but stayed outside in lonely places.[n] Yet the people still came to him from everywhere.[o]

Jesus Heals a Paralytic

2 A few days later, when Jesus again entered Capernaum, the people heard that he had come home. [2] So many[p] gathered that there was no room left, not even outside the door, and he preached the word to them. [3] Some men came, bringing to him a paralytic,[q] carried by four of them. [4] Since they could not get him to Jesus

---

1:35
f Lk 3:21

1:38
g Isa 61:1
1:39
h Mt 4:23 i Mt 4:24

1:40
j Mk 10:17

1:44
k Mt 8:4 l Lev 13:49
m Lev 14:1-32

1:45
n Lk 5:15,16
o Mk 2:13; Lk 5:17;
Jn 6:2

2:2
p ver 13; Mk 1:45

2:3
q Mt 4:24

---

[a] 40 The Greek word was used for various diseases affecting the skin—not necessarily leprosy.

Mark 1:35–39

Once again, this time subtly, Jesus met temptation in a solitary place. Peter and his companions interrupted his prayer time to urge him to return to what they saw as his scene of personal triumph. The people of Capernaum were looking for him because of the miracles—not because of his words—and the disciples were anxious to accommodate this popularity surge. But Jesus didn't intend a repeat engagement; he instead sought seclusion to prepare himself through prayer to move forward in his mission to preach the kingdom.

Unlike Jesus, who prayed *before* moving into action, the disciples were more interested in action than prayer. Can you identify with this tension? Do the demands and opportunities of "life" and Christian service tempt you to spring into action before preparing your heart and mind before God? If this has been the way you function, you may experience temporary "success" in ministry efforts, but it won't be sustainable. Why not? Because you have deluded yourself into thinking prayer and preparation are optional.

Mark 1:40–45

If a priest declared a person leprous, the sufferer was excluded from the community by divine decree (Lev. 13:45–46). Leprosy was considered a primary source of spiritual uncleanness. Like a corpse, a leper could transfer ritual impurity to people through touch. The leper in this story broke through the religious barrier. He risked believing Jesus had both the power and desire to heal him. Jesus' compassion came through in his touch—probably the first this social outcast had experienced in a long time. By calling him to present himself to the priest, Jesus not only healed his disease but restored him to the religious and social community.

Jesus' willingness to reach out and touch the untouchable squelched any doubt about his eagerness or ability to heal, or about the scope of his compassion. Leprosy wasn't just a physical disease—these people were social rejects, the wrong kind of people for the "godly" to be around. The Messiah was for all people, even outsiders. Our culture has taboos about touch that leave many people in desperate isolation. But we who bear Christ's name are called to break out of our cocoons; to minister in that name to the untouchables in our disease-ridden, sin-sick world; and as God restores their bodies, to help restore their damaged relationships.

Mark 2:1–12

Jesus recognized the determined faith that led the paralytic's friends to go to so much trouble. Mark didn't record the reaction of the sick man or his friends to the unexpected words "Your sins are forgiven." But he did call attention to the scornful silence of the teachers of the law. Proof that Jesus spoke for God came in his response to their unexpressed criticism. He skirted the blasphemy issue with a question of his own, in effect, "Which is easier—to make a theological statement about the forgiveness of sins or to provide solid proof this man's sins have been forgiven?"

Imagine yourself as one or another of the characters in this story. What would it take to motivate you

Compassion

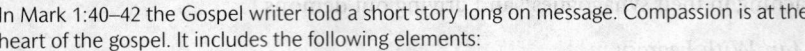

In Mark 1:40–42 the Gospel writer told a short story long on message. Compassion is at the heart of the gospel. It includes the following elements:

Hearing and Seeing

Compassion begins with hearing and seeing. The man approached Jesus, who heard his cry and looked at him. We need to look around us into the eyes of those who are in pain, forgotten, sidelined.

Not everyone engages in this kind of hearing and seeing. Some stay safely away from the places where the poor subsist. They turn off or tune out the news of shanty towns and refugee camps. It's not so much that they don't care as that they want to avoid distress.

Jesus went where the poor, sick, and demon-possessed lived. Compassion begins with going where the pain is and listening for its call.

Feeling

If we are willing to see and hear, we also must be willing to feel. The Greek word for compassion comes from a word associated with the spleen or intestine. Leprosy's marring impact on a human life wrenched Jesus' gut in a visceral way.

To be compassionate we must be truly human, deeply moved by pity.

> The Biblical Christian needs to *do* compassion in a way that demonstrates how the gospel addresses human suffering.

Acting

Hearing, seeing, and feeling are the launching pads for compassion—not compassion itself. Jesus *acted*. In the familiar parable of the good Samaritan (Luke 10:30–37), the Samaritan crossed the road, setting aside his timetable, ignoring his ethnicity, and risking his security. Pity becomes compassion only when we act on it.

The action Jesus took wasn't simply soothing. He didn't just relieve the leper's pain, bind his wounds, and move on. He healed him and instructed him to go to the temple for ritual cleansing, for restoration to his rightful place in his community.

The Message

Jesus didn't have to touch the leper to heal him. Words alone would have been enough—*if healing had been enough*. But in the leper, Jesus saw more than just a man whose body was marred by disease. He saw a human being who had been rejected by the community and cast out. The religious and social establishment believed this exclusion to be both right and *required by God*.

Healing wasn't enough. The deeper social issue had to be addressed as well. Jesus' decision to touch a "defiled" man added a message to his act of compassion.

Radical Critique

The Biblical Christian needs to *do* compassion in a way that demonstrates how the gospel addresses human suffering. For example, we are to show compassion to refugees, yet do so in a way that unmasks the human greed or hunger for power that created the conflict from which they fled.

Again, compassion without gospel comment concerning the causes of human suffering isn't Biblical compassion. The gospel calls us through word and action to beckon a fallen world toward the kingdom and its values.

Bryant L. Myers, vice president of World Vision International in Monrovia, California

because of the crowd, they made an opening in the roof above Jesus and, after digging through it, lowered the mat the paralyzed man was lying on. [5]When Jesus saw their faith, he said to the paralytic, "Son, your sins are forgiven." [r]

2:5
r Lk 7:48

[6]Now some teachers of the law were sitting there, thinking to themselves, [7] "Why does this fellow talk like that? He's blaspheming! Who can forgive sins but God alone?" [s]

2:7
s Isa 43:25

[8]Immediately Jesus knew in his spirit that this was what they were thinking in their hearts, and he said to them, "Why are you thinking these things? [9]Which is easier: to say to the paralytic, 'Your sins are forgiven,' or to say, 'Get up, take your mat and walk'? [10]But that you may know that the Son of Man [t] has authority on earth to forgive sins . . ." He said to the paralytic, [11] "I tell you, get up, take your mat and go home." [12]He got up, took his mat and walked out in full view of them all. This amazed everyone and they praised God, [u] saying, "We have never seen anything like this!" [v]

2:10
t Mt 8:20

2:12
u Mt 9:8 v Mt 9:33

The Calling of Levi

[13]Once again Jesus went out beside the lake. A large crowd came to him, [w] and he began to teach them. [14]As he walked along, he saw Levi son of Alphaeus sitting at the tax collector's booth. "Follow me," [x] Jesus told him, and Levi got up and followed him.

2:13
w Mk 1:45; Lk 5:15;
Jn 6:2

2:14
x Mt 4:19

[15]While Jesus was having dinner at Levi's house, many tax collectors and "sinners" were eating with him and his disciples, for there were many who followed him. [16]When the teachers of the law who were Pharisees [y] saw him eating with the "sinners" and tax collectors, they asked his disciples: "Why does he eat with tax collectors and 'sinners'?" [z]

2:16
y Ac 23:9 z Mt 9:11

[17]On hearing this, Jesus said to them, "It is not the healthy who need a doctor, but the sick. I have not come to call the righteous, but sinners." [a]

2:17
a Lk 19:10; 1Ti 1:15

Jesus Questioned About Fasting

[18]Now John's disciples and the Pharisees were fasting. [b] Some people came and asked Jesus, "How is it that John's disciples and the disciples of the Pharisees are fasting, but yours are not?"

2:18
b Mt 6:16-18;
Ac 13:2

[19]Jesus answered, "How can the guests of the bridegroom fast while he is with

---

to struggle up a roof, hefting a dead weight, and then dig your way through it to bring another to the source of healing? How hard would it be for you to recruit three partners? What is there about a crowd that squelches such motivation? What in you is like a teacher of the law—a skeptical observer who doesn't expect God to work "outside the box"? To what degree are you like the paralytic, craving healing and a word of forgiveness?

Mark 2:13–17

Levi, a.k.a. Matthew, was stationed at an intersection of trade routes to collect tolls and customs for Rome. In addition to being labeled traitors, tax collectors were notorious for their dishonesty. Levi responded to Jesus' call as promptly as the fishermen had (1:16–20), but his obedience marked an even more radical break with his past. Next we find Jesus eating at Levi's home, along with other tax collectors and "sinners." Jesus identified with and reached out to society's misfits and pariahs.

This episode reveals at least four significant truths: (1) Sinners don't need to *do* anything to be worthy of God's love. (2) Jesus doesn't excuse, but wants to change, sinful lifestyles. (3) Jesus makes no value distinctions between persons. (4) Jesus doesn't fear contamination by sinners. Instead, he "contaminates" them with God's love, grace, and power. Has it occurred to you that you are responsible to bring Jesus to people, not just to bring people to Jesus? How does this model change your outlook?

Mark 2:18–22

The question about fasting prompted two answers. (1) The kingdom of God, Jesus pointed out, is like a wedding party, not a funeral wake. It's inappropriate to fast in the presence of such joy. (2) The "new" Jesus brought was incompatible with the old. The old—represented by the condemnation and exclusion of sinners in the previous controversy (vv. 15–17) and the practice of fasting in this debate—couldn't contain the new. Both would be ruined if they were forcibly combined.

This discussion regarding fasting moves us to question the purposes of our religious traditions. The following motivations are to be rejected (see Col. 2:16–23): (1) any sacrifice of life's earthly pleasures as an attempt to gain favor with God or achieve eternal life; (2) any observance done simply to conform to external rules; (3) any spiritual exercise that aims to set us apart from and above others. Do you practice spiritual disciplines, like fasting, from sincere inner conviction? What purpose(s) do such disciplines serve in your life?

2:20
c Lk 17:22

them? They cannot, so long as they have him with them. 20But the time will come when the bridegroom will be taken from them, c and on that day they will fast.

21"No one sews a patch of unshrunk cloth on an old garment. If he does, the new piece will pull away from the old, making the tear worse. 22And no one pours new wine into old wineskins. If he does, the wine will burst the skins, and both the wine and the wineskins will be ruined. No, he pours new wine into new wineskins."

Lord of the Sabbath

2:23
d Dt 23:25
2:24
e Mt 12:2

23One Sabbath Jesus was going through the grainfields, and as his disciples walked along, they began to pick some heads of grain. d 24The Pharisees said to him, "Look, why are they doing what is unlawful on the Sabbath?" e

---

Mark 2:23—3:6

📖 This passage recounts two Sabbath controversies. The Pharisees, acting as self-proclaimed religion police, spotted the disciples plucking grain as they strolled through a field. The law allowed anyone (particularly the needy) to pluck grain without a sickle in a neighbor's field (Deut. 23:25). But the Pharisees arbitrarily classified this as harvesting—a Sabbath violation. The second

2:16

Jewish Sects

Pharisees	Their roots can be traced to Hasidim of the the second century B.C.
	1. Along with the Torah, they accepted as equally inspired and authoritative all material contained within the oral tradition.
	2. On free will and determination, they held to a mediating view that made it impossible for either free will or the sovereignty of God to cancel out the other.
	3. They accepted a rather highly developed hierarchy of angels and demons.
	4. They believed in the resurrection of the dead.
	5. They believed in the immortality of the soul and in reward and retribution after death.
	6. They were champions of human equality.
	7. The emphasis of their teaching was ethical rather than theological.
Sadducees	They probably had their beginning during the Hasmonean period (166-63 B.C.). Their demise occurred c. A.D. 70 with the fall of Jerusalem and the destruction of the temple.
	1. They denied that the oral law was authoritative and binding.
	2. They interpreted the Mosaic Law more literally than did the Pharisees.
	3. They were very exacting in Levitical purity.
	4. They attributed everything to free will.
	5. They argued that there is neither resurrection of the dead nor a future life.
	6. They rejected belief in angels and demons.
	7. They rejected the idea of a spiritual world.
	8. They considered only the five books of Moses (Gen.–Deut.) to be canonical Scripture.
Essenes	They probably originated among the Hasidim, along with the Pharisees, from whom they later separated (I Macc. 2:42; 7:13. Maccabees is an Apocryphal book that isn't a part of the traditional Protestant canon). They were a group of very strict and zealous Jews who took part with the Maccabeans in a revolt against the Syrians, c. 165-155 B.C.
	1. They strictly observed the purity laws of the Torah.
	2. They practiced communal ownership of property.
	3. They had a strong sense of mutual responsibility.
	4. Daily worship was important, along with daily study of their sacred scriptures.
	5. Solemn oaths of piety and obedience had to be taken.
	6. Sacrifices were offered on holy days and during sacred seasons.
	7. Marriage wasn't condemned in principle but was avoided.
	8. They attributed everything that happened to fate.
Zealots	They originated during the reign of Herod the Great c. 6 B.C. and were exterminated at Masada in A.D. 73.
	1. They opposed payment of tribute for taxes to a pagan emperor because they believed that allegiance was due to God alone.
	2. They were fiercely loyal to Jewish tradition.
	3. They believed in violence as long as it accomplished a good end.
	4. They were opposed to use of the Greek language in the Holy Land.

25 He answered, "Have you never read what David did when he and his companions were hungry and in need? 26 In the days of Abiathar the high priest, *f* he entered the house of God and ate the consecrated bread, which is lawful only for priests to eat. *g* And he also gave some to his companions." *h*

27 Then he said to them, "The Sabbath was made for man, *i* not man for the Sabbath. *j* 28 So the Son of Man *k* is Lord even of the Sabbath."

3 Another time he went into the synagogue, *l* and a man with a shriveled hand was there. 2 Some of them were looking for a reason to accuse Jesus, so they watched him closely *m* to see if he would heal him on the Sabbath. *n* 3 Jesus said to the man with the shriveled hand, "Stand up in front of everyone."

4 Then Jesus asked them, "Which is lawful on the Sabbath: to do good or to do evil, to save life or to kill?" But they remained silent.

5 He looked around at them in anger and, deeply distressed at their stubborn hearts, said to the man, "Stretch out your hand." He stretched it out, and his hand was completely restored. 6 Then the Pharisees went out and began to plot with the Herodians *o* how they might kill Jesus. *p*

Crowds Follow Jesus

7 Jesus withdrew with his disciples to the lake, and a large crowd from Galilee followed. *q* 8 When they heard all he was doing, many people came to him from Judea, Jerusalem, Idumea, and the regions across the Jordan and around Tyre and Sidon. *r* 9 Because of the crowd he told his disciples to have a small boat ready for him, to keep the people from crowding him. 10 For he had healed many, *s* so that those with diseases were pushing forward to touch him. *t* 11 Whenever the evil *a* spirits saw him, they fell down before him and cried out, "You are the Son of God." *u* 12 But he gave them strict orders not to tell who he was. *v*

The Appointing of the Twelve Apostles

13 Jesus went up on a mountainside and called to him those he wanted, and they came to him. *w* 14 He appointed twelve—designating them apostles *b x*—that they

---

a 11 Greek *unclean*; also in verse 30   *b* 14 Some manuscripts do not have *designating them apostles*.

Cross references (right margin):
- 2:26 *f* 1Ch 24:6; 2Sa 8:17 *g* Lev 24:5-9 *h* 1Sa 21:1-6
- 2:27 *i* Ex 23:12; Dt 5:14 *j* Col 2:16
- 2:28 *k* Mt 8:20
- 3:1 *l* Mt 4:23; Mk 1:21
- 3:2 *m* Mt 12:10 *n* Lk 14:1
- 3:6 *o* Mt 22:16; Mk 12:13 *p* Mt 12:14
- 3:7 *q* Mt 4:25
- 3:8 *r* Mt 11:21
- 3:10 *s* Mt 4:23 *t* Mt 9:20
- 3:11 *u* Mt 4:3; Mk 1:23,24
- 3:12 *v* Mt 8:4; Mk 1:24,25,34; Ac 16:17,18
- 3:13 *w* Mt 5:1
- 3:14 *x* Mk 6:30

---

instance of "Sabbath violation" revealed how easily well-intentioned rules can get in the way of helping people! This incident revealed more about Jesus' opponents than about the Sabbath.

The church and culture of our day have reacted against the strict religiosity that marked the observance of the Lord's Day in earlier generations. But Jesus never criticized treating the Sabbath as holy. He simply affirmed this set-apart day as an occasion to do good, not just a time to relax or avoid doing wrong. The question isn't whether or not something is allowed; it's whether an activity helps others. Doing good is always expected of Christians, regardless of the day of the week or hour of the day.

Mark 3:7–12

Jesus couldn't dodge his own popularity. The sick no longer waited for his touch but threw themselves on him. The crowds, Mark stated, "[fell] upon him" while the evil spirits "[fell] before him." Try to imagine the pandemonium! The demons continued to blurt out Jesus' identity, and Jesus continued to order them to be quiet. Why? The time hadn't come for the clear revelation of who he was. Plus, raving demons can never be agents of revelation. Jesus' silencing of evil spirits demonstrated his power over them.

Played out here are two inadequate responses to Jesus and his identity. (1) The crowd swarmed him not because of what he said but what he did. No doubt you are grateful for God's physical and material blessings, but do you ever catch yourself following him for the benefit package he offers? (2) The demons correctly recognized Jesus as the Son of God, but didn't turn from sin to him. To what degree does your head knowledge about Jesus and his ways outpace the loyalty of your heart or the integrity of your actions?

Mark 3:13–19

The mission of the Twelve was twofold. (1) They were delegated to "be with him"—to witness Jesus' ministry, learn from him, and pass on and authenticate the truth about his life (see Luke 1:2). (2) They were to extend Jesus' work by proclaiming good news, including the driving out of the forces of evil. But these tasks weren't limited to the Twelve (see 5:18–20; 9:38–40). Their *unique* function and privilege was being with Jesus.

What about you? What natural outcomes might you expect from quality time simply spent in Christ's company? Being with Jesus is harder than we might think. Hanging around (or *onto*) him isn't the same as being *with* him. The latter means we follow where he leads and share with him the toil, harassment, and bitterness of suffering. As bearers of the Good News, we are "bad news" for the forces of evil. Therefore, we are to expect opposition, temptation, and obstacles.

3:15
y Mt 10:1
3:16
z Jn 1:42

might be with him and that he might send them out to preach 15and to have authority to drive out demons.y 16These are the twelve he appointed: Simon (to whom he gave the name Peter);z 17James son of Zebedee and his brother John (to them he gave the name Boanerges, which means Sons of Thunder); 18Andrew, Philip, Bartholomew, Matthew, Thomas, James son of Alphaeus, Thaddaeus, Simon the Zealot 19and Judas Iscariot, who betrayed him.

Jesus and Beelzebub

3:20
a ver 7 b Mk 6:31

20Then Jesus entered a house, and again a crowd gathered,a so that he and his disciples were not even able to eat.b 21When his family heard about this, they went to take charge of him, for they said, "He is out of his mind."c

3:21
c Jn 10:20;
Ac 26:24
3:22
d Mt 15:1
e Mt 10:25; 11:18;
12:24; Jn 7:20;
8:48,52; 10:20
f Mk 9:34

22And the teachers of the law who came down from Jerusalemd said, "He is possessed by Beelzebuba!e By the prince of demons he is driving out demons."f

3:23
g Mk 4:2 h Mt 4:10

23So Jesus called them and spoke to them in parables:g "How can Satanh drive out Satan? 24If a kingdom is divided against itself, that kingdom cannot stand. 25If a house is divided against itself, that house cannot stand. 26And if Satan opposes himself and is divided, he cannot stand; his end has come. 27In fact, no one can enter a strong man's house and carry off his possessions unless he first ties up the strong man. Then he can rob his house.i 28I tell you the truth, all the sins and blasphemies of men will be forgiven them. 29But whoever blasphemes against the Holy Spirit will never be forgiven; he is guilty of an eternal sin."j

3:27
i Isa 49:24,25

3:29
j Mt 12:31,32;
Lk 12:10

30He said this because they were saying, "He has an evil spirit."

Jesus' Mother and Brothers

3:31
k ver 21

31Then Jesus' mother and brothers arrived.k Standing outside, they sent someone in to call him. 32A crowd was sitting around him, and they told him, "Your mother and brothers are outside looking for you."

33"Who are my mother and my brothers?" he asked.

34Then he looked at those seated in a circle around him and said, "Here are my mother and my brothers! 35Whoever does God's will is my brother and sister and mother."

a 22 Greek Beezeboul or Beelzeboul

Mark 3:20–30

Jesus' behavior was generating such controversy that even his family tried to get him to calm down and not be so extreme. Jerusalem's power brokers thought the disturbing rumors about this popular teacher and healer warranted sending deputies to investigate and discredit his ministry. The teachers of the law conceded that Jesus could cast out demons but insisted that his success came from a relationship to Satan. For such indictments Jesus no longer responded to his opponents with direct statements (cf. 2:10,28). Instead, he spoke in parables (3:23)—drawing out the absurdity of their accusations and opening the way to truth.

Mark continually bombards us with the question of the hour: "Who is Jesus?" In this section, Jesus is either the Son of God who liberates the possessed, or he is possessed—an agent of Satan. What does it take to convince skeptics in our culture that Jesus is God's Son? When we encounter someone hardened to the gospel, it's usually best to follow Jesus' example of sharing thought-provoking ideas—ideas that tease the mind into discovering truth for itself. We will never "defeat" cynics

in debate. But God may use us in influencing them to seriously consider Christ's claims.

Mark 3:31–35

Jesus' response to his family's visit ran counter to the accepted wisdom of the time. In the 1st-century world, family was the basis of a person's social and economic life, the source of his or her identity. But life under God isn't defined by position within a biological family, which in Jesus' day had everything to do with preservation of the family line, wealth, and honor. We owe ultimate devotion to God—the head of a new, spiritual family of faith. Membership in this radically new family, as we see here, had (and has) its costs.

In our society, where many feel isolated, it's important to stress the positive aspects of this passage. Who are your "brothers and sisters"? Some of us may be forced to disengage from family relationships that would strangle our commitment to God, but every Christian needs a "family" of special people "related" to each other through mutual devotion. As the church, we have an added responsibility to seek out the lonely —not only to help them heal but to create new family relationships within the dynamic faith community.

The Parable of the Sower

4 Again Jesus began to teach by the lake.[l] The crowd that gathered around him was so large that he got into a boat and sat in it out on the lake, while all the people were along the shore at the water's edge. [2]He taught them many things by parables,[m] and in his teaching said: [3]"Listen! A farmer went out to sow his seed.[n] [4]As he was scattering the seed, some fell along the path, and the birds came and ate it up. [5]Some fell on rocky places, where it did not have much soil. It sprang up quickly, because the soil was shallow. [6]But when the sun came up, the plants were scorched, and they withered because they had no root. [7]Other seed fell among thorns, which grew up and choked the plants, so that they did not bear grain. [8]Still other seed fell on good soil. It came up, grew and produced a crop, multiplying thirty, sixty, or even a hundred times."[o]

[9]Then Jesus said, "He who has ears to hear, let him hear."[p]

[10]When he was alone, the Twelve and the others around him asked him about the parables. [11]He told them, "The secret of the kingdom of God[q] has been given to you. But to those on the outside[r] everything is said in parables [12]so that,

"'they may be ever seeing but never perceiving,
and ever hearing but never understanding;
otherwise they might turn and be forgiven!'[a][s]

[13]Then said to them, "Don't you understand this parable? How then will you understand any parable? [14]The farmer sows the word.[t] [15]Some people are like seed along the path, where the word is sown. As soon as they hear it, Satan[u] comes

[a] 12 Isaiah 6:9,10

Cross references

4:1 / Mk 2:13; 3:7
4:2 m ver 11; Mk 3:23
4:3 n ver 26
4:8 o Jn 15:5; Col 1:6
4:9 p ver 23; Mt 11:15
4:11 q Mt 3:2 r 1Co 5:12,13; Col 4:5; 1Th 4:12; 1Ti 3:7
4:12 s Isa 6:9,10; Mt 13:13-15
4:14 t Mk 16:20; Lk 1:2; Ac 4:31; 8:4; 16:6; 17:11; Php 1:14
4:15 u Mt 4:10

Mark 4:1–20

This parable foretold a continuing misunderstanding about Jesus' words and deeds, as well as the "harvest" that would occur among those who did understand and respond. When the Twelve and the others around Jesus asked about his parables, his reply set them apart from outsiders: To them had been given the mystery of the kingdom! Those entrusted with this secret would eventually see the kingdom's steady advance—not just through miracles, but in suffering and persecution.

Soil can't change its character, but we can. This parable challenges us to a "soil" test. (1) Sometimes we are like the hard ground on the path. Nothing soaks in. (2) Sometimes we are like soil that nourishes only a shallow root system. Any hint of trouble or mistreatment shrivels our faith. (3) Sometimes the weeds of materialism threaten to choke out our struggling sprouts of commitment. The same seed falls on all soil. If the gospel is to bear fruit in our lives, we are to be ready for change. What fertilizer can you add to the soil of your heart in order to be more receptive to kingdom ways?

 4:1–9

Good Land

In the parable of the sower (Mark 4:1–9), Jesus used agriculture to make a spiritual point: To grow spiritually we need nurturing "soil." Paul used a similar idea in Ephesians 3:17, insisting that Christians should be "rooted and grounded in love" (KJV).

These references also remind us today that we are running out of good soil in which to grow crops.

In Jesus' time over 90 percent of people were engaged in agriculture.

In 1960, 60 percent of the world's people were engaged in agriculture.

By 2000, only 40 percent of people worldwide were engaged in agriculture.

Source: American Association for the Advancement of Science (2002:73)

In Jesus' time there was an unlimited supply of arable soil in which to grow crops—the only limitations were access and politics. Today, farmers are still limited by access and politics but have the added woe that half the world's once arable land has become unfit for farming through pollution, growing urbanization, dried up water sources, unjust land policies, and other causes. Although increased agricultural productivity of arable acres allows us to produce adequate food sources, the diminishing of arable land will have devastating long-term effects.

and takes away the word that was sown in them. 16Others, like seed sown on rocky places, hear the word and at once receive it with joy. 17But since they have no root, they last only a short time. When trouble or persecution comes because of the word, they quickly fall away. 18Still others, like seed sown among thorns, hear the word; 19but the worries of this life, the deceitfulness of wealth *v* and the desires for other things come in and choke the word, making it unfruitful. 20Others, like seed sown on good soil, hear the word, accept it, and produce a crop—thirty, sixty or even a hundred times what was sown."

4:19
v Mt 19:23; 1Ti 6:9, 10, 17; 1Jn 2:15-17

A Lamp on a Stand

21He said to them, "Do you bring in a lamp to put it under a bowl or a bed? Instead, don't you put it on its stand? *w* 22For whatever is hidden is meant to be disclosed, and whatever is concealed is meant to be brought out into the open. *x* 23If anyone has ears to hear, let him hear." *y*

24"Consider carefully what you hear," he continued. "With the measure you use, it will be measured to you—and even more. *z* 25Whoever has will be given more; whoever does not have, even what he has will be taken from him." *a*

4:21
w Mt 5:15
4:22
x Jer 16:17; Mt 10:26; Lk 8:17; 12:2
4:23
y ver 9; Mt 11:15
4:24
z Mt 7:2; Lk 6:38
4:25
a Mt 13:12; 25:29

The Parable of the Growing Seed

26He also said, "This is what the kingdom of God is like. *b* A man scatters seed on the ground. 27Night and day, whether he sleeps or gets up, the seed sprouts and grows, though he does not know how. 28All by itself the soil produces grain—first the stalk, then the head, then the full kernel in the head. 29As soon as the grain is ripe, he puts the sickle to it, because the harvest has come." *c*

4:26
b Mt 13:24

4:29
c Rev 14:15

The Parable of the Mustard Seed

30Again he said, "What shall we say the kingdom of God is like, *d* or what parable shall we use to describe it? 31It is like a mustard seed, which is the smallest seed

4:30
d Mt 13:24

Mark 4:21–25

The purpose of a lamp—or parable—is to shed light. But for the time being secrecy was the order of the "night." Not because anything was wrong with the lamp, but because God wanted it that way. Sometimes, the act of hiding something makes it plain. God's glory was revealed indirectly through parables, weakness, suffering, and death. The mystery of Jesus' identity would become clear after his death and resurrection. But even then many would be clueless, their eyes blinded by the world's razzle-dazzle, their ears deafened by its incessant racket (2 Cor. 4:4).

The related parable of the measure is short, but long enough to include a warning and a promise. Are you careful how you listen—and respond—to Jesus' words? If you snub the truth by blocking it out, or if you hear without listening, you have everything to lose. But if you listen with your heart, risking faith in what still lies partially hidden, you have everything to gain. What steps can you take to make sure you are attentive and eager to follow through when God's Word is being preached?

Mark 4:26–29

Ever wonder what it takes for seeds to produce a crop? The growth process is a mystery. In the same way, the hidden kingdom of God will one day spring forth, ripe and mature. The kingdom is already here; this "harvest" likely represents the final judgment (cf. Joel 3:13). This imagery for God's reign is deceptively ordi-

nary. That is why so many overlook it, underestimate it, and shrug off its claim on their lives.

Do you ever doubt God's control? Parables like this give us confidence: Even though the kingdom lies hidden, it's working "underground" to produce the harvest God intends. We do well to remember this when we feel the Spirit has gone on vacation. God's kingdom works powerfully, independent of our skill or strength. And it often works invisibly, like a seed sprouting below ground level. Try for a moment to picture our world as Jesus sees it, with seeds sown everywhere in preparation for the harvest.

Mark 4:30–34

Jesus didn't compare the kingdom of God to a miniscule mustard seed but to *what happens to* that seed. It holds within itself the power to transform itself dramatically into something we can't ignore—an impressive plant (Matthew and Luke say a "tree"). God's way of working in the world may appear small and insignificant. But his kingdom will one day transform all of life and provide a home for multitudes beyond our ability to count. Many observers in his day would never have guessed that Jesus' inconspicuous presence displayed God's awesome power and dominion. By the time of the kingdom's final stage, it will be too late for those who couldn't, or wouldn't, see what God was doing all along.

The parables in verses 21–34 can fill us with confidence about the condition of God's kingdom, assure us that its success won't depend solely on our efforts, and

you plant in the ground. [32]Yet when planted, it grows and becomes the largest of all garden plants, with such big branches that the birds of the air can perch in its shade."

[33]With many similar parables Jesus spoke the word to them, as much as they could understand. [e] [34]He did not say anything to them without using a parable. [f] But when he was alone with his own disciples, he explained everything.

Jesus Calms the Storm

[35]That day when evening came, he said to his disciples, "Let us go over to the other side." [36]Leaving the crowd behind, they took him along, just as he was, in the boat. [g] There were also other boats with him. [37]A furious squall came up, and the waves broke over the boat, so that it was nearly swamped. [38]Jesus was in the stern, sleeping on a cushion. The disciples woke him and said to him, "Teacher, don't you care if we drown?"

[39]He got up, rebuked the wind and said to the waves, "Quiet! Be still!" Then the wind died down and it was completely calm.

[40]He said to his disciples, "Why are you so afraid? Do you still have no faith?" [h]

[41]They were terrified and asked each other, "Who is this? Even the wind and the waves obey him!"

The Healing of a Demon-possessed Man

5 They went across the lake to the region of the Gerasenes. [a] [2]When Jesus got out of the boat, [i] a man with an evil [b] spirit [j] came from the tombs to meet him. [3]This man lived in the tombs, and no one could bind him any more, not even with a chain. [4]For he had often been chained hand and foot, but he tore the chains apart and broke the irons on his feet. No one was strong enough to subdue him. [5]Night and day among the tombs and in the hills he would cry out and cut himself with stones.

[6]When he saw Jesus from a distance, he ran and fell on his knees in front of him. [7]He shouted at the top of his voice, "What do you want with me, [k] Jesus, Son of the

Side notes:
4:33 e Jn 16:12
4:34 f Jn 16:25
4:36 g ver 1; Mk 3:9; 5:2,21; 6:32,45
4:40 h Mt 14:31; Mk 16:14
5:2 i Mk 4:1 j Mk 1:23
5:7 k Mt 8:29

---

[a] 1 Some manuscripts *Gadarenes*; other manuscripts *Gergesenes*   [b] 2 Greek *unclean*; also in verses 8 and 13

---

encourage us to exercise patient faith. Does your eagerness for kingdom fulfillment make you want to hurry? Would you like to plow the field, plant the seed, reap the harvest, thresh the grain, and bake the cake in a single worship service? If so, now might be a good time to rethink your focus: Might your well-intentioned activity to some degree be a smoke screen hiding a lack of trust in *God's ability* to get the job done?

Mark 4:35–41

Jesus was understandably exhausted after a demanding day of ministry. Still, his ability to sleep in the midst of a raging storm was a sign of trust in God (cf. Ps. 3:5; 4:8). The disciples, though, interpreted it as indifference to their safety. That Jesus was able to muzzle the storm with a word revealed his power to do what only the Creator could do. Still, their fear intensified—shifting from the storm to this mysterious person with God-like control of the sea. Would their terror turn to absolute trust in this Deliverer? At this point, Mark leaves us hanging.

When hurricanes howl through our lives and world—when we lose jobs, health, or loved ones; when famines strike, wars rage, and the innocent suffer—we may accuse Jesus of being asleep at the helm. Fear leads us to suspect God really doesn't care. The emphasis in this scene is on who Jesus is, not on how he rescued his phobic disciples from danger. Storms are an unavoidable

part of life. This story helps us learn to trust in a Savior who doesn't always deliver us *from* storms—but always leads us *through* them.

Mark 5:1–20

Mark puts us on the edge of our seats with this confrontation between Jesus and the evil spirits controlling this ravaged man. They called on the name of God to keep the Son of God off their backs. But "unclean" spirits and animals were both wiped out in one fell swoop—leaving one cleansed, and grateful, human being. Sadly, the townspeople begged Jesus to leave; they were more comfortable with the evil forces and an unclean herd that secured their standard of living than with the One who could drive them out. The liberated man, though, became a passionate evangelist.

We typically label broken, "demonized" persons as dangerous. We deny any responsibility for their condition, shifting the blame for their problems onto them, their dysfunctional backgrounds, and/or their incurable mental instability. The solution goes beyond preaching to them or providing more government programs, better housing, or prison reform. The transformed life found in God's kingdom includes effective evangelism and changing the contexts and systems that hold people in bondage. Sometimes these changes threaten our own way of life.

5:7
l Mt 4:3; Lk 1:32;
6:35; Ac 16:17;
Heb 7:1
5:9
m ver 15

Most High God?[l] Swear to God that you won't torture me!" [8]For Jesus had said to him, "Come out of this man, you evil spirit!"

[9]Then Jesus asked him, "What is your name?"

"My name is Legion,"[m] he replied, "for we are many." [10]And he begged Jesus again and again not to send them out of the area.

[11]A large herd of pigs was feeding on the nearby hillside. [12]The demons begged Jesus, "Send us among the pigs; allow us to go into them." [13]He gave them permission, and the evil spirits came out and went into the pigs. The herd, about two thousand in number, rushed down the steep bank into the lake and were drowned.

5:15
n ver 9 o ver 16,18;
Mt 4:24

[14]Those tending the pigs ran off and reported this in the town and countryside, and the people went out to see what had happened. [15]When they came to Jesus, they saw the man who had been possessed by the legion[n] of demons,[o] sitting there, dressed and in his right mind; and they were afraid. [16]Those who had seen it told the people what had happened to the demon-possessed man—and told about the pigs as well. [17]Then the people began to plead with Jesus to leave their region.

5:19
p Mt 8:4
5:20
q Mt 4:25; Mk 7:31

[18]As Jesus was getting into the boat, the man who had been demon-possessed begged to go with him. [19]Jesus did not let him, but said, "Go home to your family and tell them[p] how much the Lord has done for you, and how he has had mercy on you." [20]So the man went away and began to tell in the Decapolis[a][q] how much Jesus had done for him. And all the people were amazed.

A Dead Girl and a Sick Woman

5:21
r Mt 9:1 s Mk 4:1
5:22
t ver 35,36,38;
Lk 13:14; Ac 13:15;
18:8,17
5:23
u Mt 19:13; Mk 6:5;
7:32; 8:23; 16:18;
Lk 4:40; 13:13;
Ac 6:6
5:25
v Lev 15:25-30
5:28
w Mt 9:20
5:29
x ver 34
5:30
y Lk 5:17; 6:19

[21]When Jesus had again crossed over by boat to the other side of the lake,[r] a large crowd gathered around him while he was by the lake.[s] [22]Then one of the synagogue rulers,[t] named Jairus, came there. Seeing Jesus, he fell at his feet [23]and pleaded earnestly with him, "My little daughter is dying. Please come and put your hands on[u] her so that she will be healed and live." [24]So Jesus went with him.

A large crowd followed and pressed around him. [25]And a woman was there who had been subject to bleeding[v] for twelve years. [26]She had suffered a great deal under the care of many doctors and had spent all she had, yet instead of getting better she grew worse. [27]When she heard about Jesus, she came up behind him in the crowd and touched his cloak, [28]because she thought, "If I just touch his clothes,[w] I will be healed." [29]Immediately her bleeding stopped and she felt in her body that she was freed from her suffering.[x]

[30]At once Jesus realized that power[y] had gone out from him. He turned around in the crowd and asked, "Who touched my clothes?"

[31]"You see the people crowding against you," his disciples answered, "and yet you can ask, 'Who touched me?' "

[32]But Jesus kept looking around to see who had done it. [33]Then the woman, knowing what had happened to her, came and fell at his feet and, trembling with fear, told him the whole truth. [34]He said to her, "Daughter, your faith has healed you.[z] Go in peace[a] and be freed from your suffering."

5:34
z Mt 9:22
a Ac 15:33
5:35
b ver 22

[35]While Jesus was still speaking, some men came from the house of Jairus, the synagogue ruler.[b] "Your daughter is dead," they said. "Why bother the teacher any more?"

---

[a] 20 That is, the Ten Cities

Mark 5:21–43

The story of the raising of Jairus's 12-year-old daughter wraps around that of the healing of the woman suffering from a hemorrhage for 12 years. The main characters occupied opposite ends of the social, economic, and religious spectrum. Jairus was a man of means and influence, a male synagogue leader with a large household. By contrast, the nameless woman's condition had left her ritually unclean, socially ostracized, and financially depleted. The one common denominator: Both had heard about Jesus and desperately needed his healing touch.

Sometimes our attention is so focused on "important" or powerful people that we block the way for "little people" to make their way to Jesus. The woman had to press her way through the crowds. What does it mean for us to clear the way for people to touch Jesus? When have you been desperate for that touch? Have you felt confident to ask him, or do you feel inadequate and undeserving (common "side effects" of a troubled situation)? God doesn't require "perfect" faith. Faith can be bold—or laced with fear. What counts for it to be effective is that it be directed exclusively toward Jesus and God.

³⁶Ignoring what they said, Jesus told the synagogue ruler, "Don't be afraid; just believe."

³⁷He did not let anyone follow him except Peter, James and John the brother of James. *c* ³⁸When they came to the home of the synagogue ruler, *d* Jesus saw a commotion, with people crying and wailing loudly. ³⁹He went in and said to them, "Why all this commotion and wailing? The child is not dead but asleep." *e* ⁴⁰But they laughed at him.

After he put them all out, he took the child's father and mother and the disciples who were with him, and went in where the child was. ⁴¹He took her by the hand *f* and said to her, *"Talitha koum!"* (which means, "Little girl, I say to you, get up!"). *g* ⁴²Immediately the girl stood up and walked around (she was twelve years old). At this they were completely astonished. ⁴³He gave strict orders not to let anyone know about this, *h* and told them to give her something to eat.

A Prophet Without Honor

6 Jesus left there and went to his hometown, *i* accompanied by his disciples. ²When the Sabbath came, *j* he began to teach in the synagogue, *k* and many who heard him were amazed. *l*

"Where did this man get these things?" they asked. "What's this wisdom that has been given him, that he even does miracles! ³Isn't this the carpenter? Isn't this Mary's son and the brother of James, Joseph, *a* Judas and Simon? *m* Aren't his sisters here with us?" And they took offense at him. *n*

⁴Jesus said to them, "Only in his hometown, among his relatives and in his own house is a prophet without honor." *o* ⁵He could not do any miracles there, except lay his hands on *p* a few sick people and heal them. ⁶And he was amazed at their lack of faith.

Jesus Sends Out the Twelve

Then Jesus went around teaching from village to village. *q* ⁷Calling the Twelve to him, *r* he sent them out two by two *s* and gave them authority over evil *b* spirits. *t*

⁸These were his instructions: "Take nothing for the journey except a staff—no bread, no bag, no money in your belts. ⁹Wear sandals but not an extra tunic. ¹⁰Whenever you enter a house, stay there until you leave that town. ¹¹And if any

---

a 3 Greek *Joses,* a variant of *Joseph*   *b 7* Greek *unclean*

Mark 6:1–6a

Jesus returned to his hometown, only to find that his early acquaintances "knew" all there was to know about him—and more! The scandal of the gospel showed itself again: "How does this nobody dare rise above his roots? How can an unknown have the audacity to perform miracles and spout 'wisdom'? How can somebody so *local* be God's anointed?" Jesus' rejection here pointed ahead to his rude dismissal by the people he had come to save—a denial that would culminate on a cross in Jerusalem.

When have you felt rejected, out-of-place, or even hated because of your faith? Rejection and disappointment are common experiences of people sowing gospel seeds (cf. 4:14–19). Jesus was perplexed but not paralyzed. He cut his losses (no doubt mourned them, too!) and forged ahead to other villages and towns. We too can "move on" when our efforts to serve others and share Christ are snubbed. If you are intrigued, read ahead to Jesus' instructions to the Twelve in the next passage (v. 11).

Mark 6:6b–13

Like adding spokes to a wheel, Jesus expanded his mission by sending out the Twelve in various directions. They didn't travel first class. To embark on a mission dependent on the generosity of others for food and lodging is an expression of ultimate dependence on God for support. Jesus' disciples went out *as* the poor *to* the poor and hungry. Their mission also communicated dramatically the need for Israel to repent *now*. If the people were to reject the message, they would deprive themselves of the opportunity for healing and deliverance.

Often today we engage in mission work as the rich going to the poor. Our reliance on God can easily become veiled beneath our affluence. Jesus' instructions to the disciples are strong words for us: (1) As participants in Christ's work in the world, we go out as his voice and hands. The focus isn't to be on us, but on him. (2) We are to be so dedicated that personal comforts become inconsequential. No one will take us seriously if we claim to bring a life-or-death message while taking it easy. (3) Our mission isn't just a matter of broadcasting information but of bringing to effect all that is necessary to transform lives.

6:11
u Mt 10:14

6:12
v Lk 9:6
6:13
w Jas 5:14

place will not welcome you or listen to you, shake the dust off your feet[u] when you leave, as a testimony against them."

¹²They went out and preached that people should repent.[v] ¹³They drove out many demons and anointed many sick people with oil[w] and healed them.

John the Baptist Beheaded

6:14
x Mt 3:1

¹⁴King Herod heard about this, for Jesus' name had become well known. Some were saying,[a] "John the Baptist[x] has been raised from the dead, and that is why miraculous powers are at work in him."

6:15
y Mal 4:5
z Mt 21:11
a Mt 16:14;
Mk 8:28

¹⁵Others said, "He is Elijah."[y]

And still others claimed, "He is a prophet,[z] like one of the prophets of long ago."[a]

¹⁶But when Herod heard this, he said, "John, the man I beheaded, has been raised from the dead!"

6:17
b Mt 4:12; 11:2;
Lk 3:19,20

6:18
c Lev 18:16; 20:21

6:20
d Mt 11:9; 21:26

¹⁷For Herod himself had given orders to have John arrested, and he had him bound and put in prison.[b] He did this because of Herodias, his brother Philip's wife, whom he had married. ¹⁸For John had been saying to Herod, "It is not lawful for you to have your brother's wife."[c] ¹⁹So Herodias nursed a grudge against John and wanted to kill him. But she was not able to, ²⁰because Herod feared John and protected him, knowing him to be a righteous and holy man.[d] When Herod heard John, he was greatly puzzled[b]; yet he liked to listen to him.

6:21
e Est 1:3; 2:18
f Lk 3:1

²¹Finally the opportune time came. On his birthday Herod gave a banquet[e] for his high officials and military commanders and the leading men of Galilee.[f] ²²When the daughter of Herodias came in and danced, she pleased Herod and his dinner guests.

The king said to the girl, "Ask me for anything you want, and I'll give it to you."

6:23
g Est 5:3,6; 7:2

²³And he promised her with an oath, "Whatever you ask I will give you, up to half my kingdom."[g]

²⁴She went out and said to her mother, "What shall I ask for?"

"The head of John the Baptist," she answered.

²⁵At once the girl hurried in to the king with the request: "I want you to give me right now the head of John the Baptist on a platter."

²⁶The king was greatly distressed, but because of his oaths and his dinner guests, he did not want to refuse her. ²⁷So he immediately sent an executioner with orders to bring John's head. The man went, beheaded John in the prison, ²⁸and brought back his head on a platter. He presented it to the girl, and she gave it to her mother. ²⁹On hearing of this, John's disciples came and took his body and laid it in a tomb.

Jesus Feeds the Five Thousand

6:30
h Mt 10:2; Lk 9:10;
17:5; 22:14; 24:10;
Ac 1:2,26 i Lk 9:10

³⁰The apostles[h] gathered around Jesus and reported to him all they had done and taught.[i] ³¹Then, because so many people were coming and going that they did not

---

[a] 14 Some early manuscripts *He was saying*   [b] 20 Some early manuscripts *he did many things*

Mark 6:14–29

🔲 Mark interrupted his report on the disciples' mission with a flashback, recalling the execution of John the Baptist. John died as a consequence of his public criticism of Herod's unlawful marriage to his brother's wife (vv. 17–19). The sending out of the Twelve (vv. 7–13) and their return (v. 30) sandwich the account of John's death. This bracketing suggests that what happened to John also would happen to others who preached the message of repentance in a hostile world. Those in power would often feel threatened by the kingdom's approach.

📖 The sobering story of John's death throws cold water on the rush of excitement from the disciples' fruitful mission (vv. 12–13). Jesus still sends us into a dangerous world, much of which remains under the domination

of evil powers. Many believers today still face persecution—even martyrdom—for taking a stand against sin and injustice. Are you willing to take that stand, publicly, with or without the possibility of consequences much more serious than indifference?

Mark 6:30–44

🔲 The feeding of the 5,000 in this "remote place" suggests several Biblical themes. (1) It recalls the Israelites' exodus and feeding in the desert. (2) It echoes miracles of Elijah (1 Kings 17:7–15) and Elisha (2 Kings 4:42–44). (3) Jesus had brought the disciples across the sea for some much needed R & R; God's provision of rest in the desert recurs in Scripture. (4) Psalm 23 ties in with the story: Jesus had compassion on the people because they were like sheep without a shepherd. (5) It foreshadows Jesus' actions at the Last Supper (see 14:22).

even have a chance to eat,[j] he said to them, "Come with me by yourselves to a quiet place and get some rest."

[32]So they went away by themselves in a boat[k] to a solitary place. [33]But many who saw them leaving recognized them and ran on foot from all the towns and got there ahead of them. [34]When Jesus landed and saw a large crowd, he had compassion on them, because they were like sheep without a shepherd.[l] So he began teaching them many things.

[35]By this time it was late in the day, so his disciples came to him. "This is a remote place," they said, "and it's already very late. [36]Send the people away so they can go to the surrounding countryside and villages and buy themselves something to eat."

[37]But he answered, "You give them something to eat."[m]

They said to him, "That would take eight months of a man's wages[a]! Are we to go and spend that much on bread and give it to them to eat?"

[38]"How many loaves do you have?" he asked. "Go and see."

When they found out, they said, "Five—and two fish."[n]

[39]Then Jesus directed them to have all the people sit down in groups on the green grass. [40]So they sat down in groups of hundreds and fifties. [41]Taking the five loaves and the two fish and looking up to heaven, he gave thanks and broke the loaves.[o] Then he gave them to his disciples to set before the people. He also divided the two fish among them all. [42]They all ate and were satisfied, [43]and the disciples picked up twelve basketfuls of broken pieces of bread and fish. [44]The number of the men who had eaten was five thousand.

Jesus Walks on the Water

[45]Immediately Jesus made his disciples get into the boat[p] and go on ahead of him to Bethsaida,[q] while he dismissed the crowd. [46]After leaving them, he went up on a mountainside to pray.[r]

[47]When evening came, the boat was in the middle of the lake, and he was alone on land. [48]He saw the disciples straining at the oars, because the wind was against them. About the fourth watch of the night he went out to them, walking on the lake. He was about to pass by them, [49]but when they saw him walking on the lake, they thought he was a ghost.[s] They cried out, [50]because they all saw him and were terrified.

Immediately he spoke to them and said, "Take courage! It is I. Don't be afraid."[t] [51]Then he climbed into the boat[u] with them, and the wind died down.[v] They were completely amazed, [52]for they had not understood about the loaves; their hearts were hardened.[w]

[53]When they had crossed over, they landed at Gennesaret and anchored there.[x] [54]As soon as they got out of the boat, people recognized Jesus. [55]They ran throughout that whole region and carried the sick on mats to wherever they heard he was. [56]And wherever he went—into villages, towns or countryside—they placed the sick in the marketplaces. They begged him to let them touch even the edge of his cloak,[y] and all who touched him were healed.

[a] 37 Greek take two hundred denarii

Cross references (margin):

6:31 j Mk 3:20
6:32 k ver 45; Mk 4:36
6:34 l Mt 9:36
6:37 m 2Ki 4:42-44
6:38 n Mt 15:34; Mk 8:5
6:41 o Mt 14:19
6:45 p ver 32 q Mt 11:21
6:46 r Lk 3:21
6:49 s Lk 24:37
6:50 t Mt 14:27
6:51 u ver 32 v Mk 4:39
6:52 w Mk 8:17-21
6:53 x Jn 6:24,25
6:56 y Mt 9:20

📖 Jesus' invitation, "Come with me by yourselves to a quiet place and get some rest," is vital for weary Christians. We can't serve others 24/7. But this story also demonstrates that when we do try to get away we often encounter more "hungry" people. The fact is that, even when we are drained physically and financially, we still have resources to help others. The next time you feel like asking God to "send the people away," first "go and see" how many loaves you still have and count on God's ability to multiply them.

Mark 6:45–56

Separated from their Master, the disciples were in a struggle—it was them against the waves. The storm hadn't thrown these seasoned sailors into a panic—but the sight of Jesus did. When Jesus came walking across the water, he shared in the unlimited power of the Creator. This event was an *epiphany*, a surprise self-disclosure of Jesus' deity to his bewildered disciples. They didn't follow a mere prophet, but the very Son of God. This miracle made it plain: God himself has visited us in the flesh.

📖 Do you ever find yourself in such a whirlwind of activity that you feel like the disciples—rowing furiously against the wind but getting nowhere ("spinning your wheels," we might call it)? We can become so involved in the task at hand that we fail to see the revelation of Christ's power or the care he's giving us.

Clean and Unclean

7 The Pharisees and some of the teachers of the law who had come from Jerusalem gathered around Jesus and 2saw some of his disciples eating food with hands that were "unclean,"z that is, unwashed. 3(The Pharisees and all the Jews do not eat unless they give their hands a ceremonial washing, holding to the tradition of the elders.a 4When they come from the marketplace they do not eat unless they wash. And they observe many other traditions, such as the washing of cups, pitchers and kettles.a)b

5So the Pharisees and teachers of the law asked Jesus, "Why don't your disciples live according to the tradition of the eldersc instead of eating their food with 'unclean' hands?"

6He replied, "Isaiah was right when he prophesied about you hypocrites; as it is written:

> " 'These people honor me with their lips,
> but their hearts are far from me.
> 7They worship me in vain;
> their teachings are but rules taught by men.'b d

8You have let go of the commands of God and are holding on to the traditions of men."e

9And he said to them: "You have a fine way of setting aside the commands of God in order to observec your own traditions!f 10For Moses said, 'Honor your father and your mother,'d g and, 'Anyone who curses his father or mother must be put to death.'e h 11But you sayi that if a man says to his father or mother: 'Whatever help you might otherwise have received from me is Corban' (that is, a gift devoted to God), 12then you no longer let him do anything for his father or mother. 13Thus you nullify the word of Godj by your traditionk that you have handed down. And you do many things like that."

14Again Jesus called the crowd to him and said, "Listen to me, everyone, and understand this. 15Nothing outside a man can make him 'unclean' by going into him. Rather, it is what comes out of a man that makes him 'unclean.'f"

17After he had left the crowd and entered the house, his disciples asked himl about this parable. 18"Are you so dull?" he asked. "Don't you see that nothing that enters a man from the outside can make him 'unclean'? 19For it doesn't go into his heart but into his stomach, and then out of his body." (In saying this, Jesus declared all foodsm "clean.")n

20He went on: "What comes out of a man is what makes him 'unclean.' 21For from within, out of men's hearts, come evil thoughts, sexual immorality, theft, murder, adultery, 22greed,o malice, deceit, lewdness, envy, slander, arrogance and folly. 23All these evils come from inside and make a man 'unclean.' "

Cross references (side margin)

7:2 z Ac 10:14,28; 11:8; Ro 14:14
7:3 a ver 5,8,9,13; Lk 11:38
7:4 b Mt 23:25; Lk 11:39
7:5 c ver 3; Gal 1:14; Col 2:8
7:7 d Isa 29:13
7:8 e ver 3
7:9 f ver 3
7:10 g Ex 20:12; Dt 5:16 h Ex 21:17; Lev 20:9
7:11 i Mt 23:16,18
7:13 j Heb 4:12 k ver 3
7:17 l Mk 9:28
7:19 m Ro 14:1-12; Col 2:16; 1Ti 4:3-5 n Ac 10:15
7:22 o Mt 20:15

---

a 4 Some early manuscripts *pitchers, kettles and dining couches*   b 6,7 Isaiah 29:13   c 9 Some manuscripts *set up*   d 10 Exodus 20:12; Deut. 5:16   e 10 Exodus 21:17; Lev. 20:9   f 15 Some early manuscripts *'unclean.'* 16*If anyone has ears to hear, let him hear.*

Mark 7:1–23

The Pharisees struggled to impose on the people their vision of morality and obedience to the law. The disagreement about hand washing wasn't about hygiene but about purity—an issue high on their agenda. They must have been galled that a popular, prophetic figure like Jesus was acting in a "religiously incorrect" manner. His seemingly cavalier attitude threatened their vision of a smooth running, holy community. "The tradition of the elders" was unscriptural law. The Pharisees may have been particularly defensive about washing hands since the rule had no Biblical basis.

Every community has to apply Scripture to life, and traditions inevitably develop as a result. We need to be careful not to belittle 1st-century Judaism, when our own brand of Christianity also can be "dead" and legalistic. We can mechanically obey regulations and believe doctrines. But we wind up with a religion that affects our hands but never touches our hearts. How can you ensure that what you do is solidly based on loving and believing?

Chap. 7

Purity is a condition of beauty. Something pure exists in its essential nature: undefiled, un-blemished, uncontaminated. An entire department of the U.S. government, the Food and Drug Administration, exists as a purity watchdog. Its guidelines spell out how much impurity manufacturers can get away with—and it's a little alarming. Coffee beans, for instance, won't be withdrawn from the market unless an average of ten percent or more are insect-infested. Generally, if something's good we want it to exist in its pure state: oxygen without fumes, snow without slush.

This is supremely true for people. Old Testament purity codes were some of the most fiercely observed commands of Scripture by those who took righteousness seriously. Wise spiritual minds have always understood that God desires a pure heart, an unblemished con-science.

But what is purity? Many debates between Jesus and religious leaders (like this one in Mark 7) centered around this question. Jesus insisted on a definition that focused on the heart and will—a person's interior—as opposed to external or ritual purity.

This has an extra-ordinary impact on how we deal with people. Some of the greatest crimes against humanity are defended by the language of purity. Genocide, for example, is identified as "ethnic cleansing." Many religious leaders of Jesus' day believed that a con-cern for purity meant they had to exclude and avoid people they con-sidered impure. But Jesus rightly saw himself as called to include and embrace just such people. The Pharisees believed the world's impuri-ty might infect them. Jesus knew the purity within himself could "in-fect" the world.

> For a human being to be pure, the *inside* of the tree—its sap, the unceasing, largely automatic flow of thoughts and feelings—must be changed.

What did Paul mean when he said that "to the pure, all things are pure" (Titus 1:15)? Jesus used a simple picture (check out his anal-ogy to trees in Luke 6:43–45). A constant flow of thoughts and feelings goes on inside each of us. These inner workings take on patterns, tendencies that determine our fruit—the things we say and do on the outside. For a human being to be pure, the *inside* of the tree—its sap, the unceasing, largely automatic flow of thoughts and feelings—must be changed.

There is a world of difference between authentic purity and behavior modification. A fundamental mistake people make in spiritual life is aiming at behavioral change. They don't know how to take concrete, practical steps to allow God to change the stream of their thoughts and emotions.

The goal isn't learning to squelch "negative" human emotions. It's uncorrupted minds and consciences. The desert fathers called impure thoughts *logismoi*: false beliefs and mis-guided desires that shape the people Paul described to Titus: "They claim to know God, but by their actions they deny him" (Titus 1:16).

A pure mind relentlessly brings your situation into God's presence. When challenged, you remember he's your partner. When confused, you instinctively call out for guidance. When rejected, you immediately recall his love, so you don't have to appease or hurt some-one else back.

This kind of purity can't be soiled—not because it's naïve or ignorant, but because it's stronger and more robust than corruption and rot. Though none of us will reach it perfectly in this life, it's the hope of the world. It's not acquired by avoiding the world, but it *enables* us to engage it. It can embrace every human being—and bring redemption.

Blessed are the pure in heart, for they shall see God.

John Ortberg, teaching pastor at Menlo Park Presbyterian Church in Menlo Park, California

The Faith of a Syrophoenician Woman

7:24
p Mt 11:21

24 Jesus left that place and went to the vicinity of Tyre. [a][p] He entered a house and did not want anyone to know it; yet he could not keep his presence secret. 25 In fact, as soon as she heard about him, a woman whose little daughter was possessed by an evil[b] spirit[q] came and fell at his feet. 26 The woman was a Greek, born in Syrian Phoenicia. She begged Jesus to drive the demon out of her daughter.

7:25
q Mt 4:24

27 "First let the children eat all they want," he told her, "for it is not right to take the children's bread and toss it to their dogs."

28 "Yes, Lord," she replied, "but even the dogs under the table eat the children's crumbs."

29 Then he told her, "For such a reply, you may go; the demon has left your daughter."

30 She went home and found her child lying on the bed, and the demon gone.

The Healing of a Deaf and Mute Man

7:31
r ver 24; Mt 11:21
s Mt 4:18 t Mt 4:25;
Mk 5:20
7:32
u Mt 9:32; Lk 11:14
v Mk 5:23

31 Then Jesus left the vicinity of Tyre[r] and went through Sidon, down to the Sea of Galilee[s] and into the region of the Decapolis.[c][t] 32 There some people brought to him a man who was deaf and could hardly talk,[u] and they begged him to place his hand on[v] the man.

7:33
w Mk 8:23
7:34
x Mk 6:41; Jn 11:41
y Mk 8:12

33 After he took him aside, away from the crowd, Jesus put his fingers into the man's ears. Then he spit[w] and touched the man's tongue. 34 He looked up to heaven[x] and with a deep sigh[y] said to him, *"Ephphatha!"* (which means, "Be opened!"). 35 At this, the man's ears were opened, his tongue was loosened and he began to speak plainly.[z]

7:35
z Isa 35:5,6
7:36
a Mt 8:4

36 Jesus commanded them not to tell anyone.[a] But the more he did so, the more they kept talking about it. 37 People were overwhelmed with amazement. "He has done everything well," they said. "He even makes the deaf hear and the mute speak."

Jesus Feeds the Four Thousand

8 During those days another large crowd gathered. Since they had nothing to eat, Jesus called his disciples to him and said, 2 "I have compassion for these peo-

[a] 24 Many early manuscripts *Tyre and Sidon*   [b] 25 Greek *unclean*   [c] 31 That is, the Ten Cities

Mark 7:24–30

Jesus' conversation with this Gentile woman took some unexpected turns: (1) He wasn't the accommodating gentleman we would have expected. He dismissed her appeal with what sounds to modern ears like a sharp insult. (2) She understood, though, his use of the word "first": Gentiles had to wait their turn. But because she believed her turn *would* come, she refused to take no for an answer. (3) The disciples had trouble receiving the kingdom as "little children" (10:13–15), but this woman was ready to receive it in any way it might arrive. Thus, what at first appeared to be a racist slur actually demonstrated Jesus' commitment that all people, regardless of race or gender, might experience the fullness of the kingdom.

God didn't send Jesus to reward the deserving but to serve the needy—those of us who admit we are entitled to nothing, yet trust God's mercy for everything. This woman humbly begged for crumbs from the Jews' bread. She didn't resent their share of God's blessing, didn't display the "you-owe-me" attitude prevalent today. On the other hand, she assertively sought needed help for her daughter. How do you find the balance between humbly requesting and selfishly claiming God's best for your life? Are there people you treat as though they are unworthy of your attention—or even of God's compassion?

Mark 7:31–37

Jesus continued to minister in Gentile territory. Just as the Jewish crowds in Galilee brought him their sick, so a Gentile crowd led a deaf-mute to him. Jesus often healed people with a simple word. But he couldn't speak to someone who couldn't hear. Instead he acted out what he intended to do for the man. Then Jesus looked up to heaven, the source of his power, and sighed deeply, a gesture of prayer. At last Jesus did speak: "Be opened!" The man could immediately both hear and speak.

We can easily be deafened to God's voice by the earsplitting competition in our culture—noise pollution is all around us, from the blaring vibrations of music to the scream of sirens to the endless hum of human chatter. Are your ears open and attentive so you can hear the word of God clearly enough to repeat it to others? And since you are surrounded by a spiritually deaf world, are you *acting out* the Good News in a "sign language" universally understood—through deeds of kindness?

ple;[b] they have already been with me three days and have nothing to eat. [3]If I send them home hungry, they will collapse on the way, because some of them have come a long distance."

[4]His disciples answered, "But where in this remote place can anyone get enough bread to feed them?"

[5]"How many loaves do you have?" Jesus asked.

"Seven," they replied.

[6]He told the crowd to sit down on the ground. When he had taken the seven loaves and given thanks, he broke them and gave them to his disciples to set before the people, and they did so. [7]They had a few small fish as well; he gave thanks for them also and told the disciples to distribute them.[c] [8]The people ate and were satisfied. Afterward the disciples picked up seven basketfuls of broken pieces that were left over.[d] [9]About four thousand men were present. And having sent them away, [10]he got into the boat with his disciples and went to the region of Dalmanutha.

[11]The Pharisees came and began to question Jesus. To test him, they asked him for a sign from heaven.[e] [12]He sighed deeply[f] and said, "Why does this generation ask for a miraculous sign? I tell you the truth, no sign will be given to it." [13]Then he left them, got back into the boat and crossed to the other side.

The Yeast of the Pharisees and Herod

[14]The disciples had forgotten to bring bread, except for one loaf they had with them in the boat. [15]"Be careful," Jesus warned them. "Watch out for the yeast[g] of the Pharisees[h] and that of Herod."[i] [16]They discussed this with one another and said, "It is because we have no bread."

[17]Aware of their discussion, Jesus asked them: "Why are you talking about having no bread? Do you still not see or understand? Are your hearts hardened?[j] [18]Do you have eyes but fail to see, and ears but fail to hear? And don't you remember? [19]When I broke the five loaves for the five thousand, how many basketfuls of pieces did you pick up?"

"Twelve,"[k] they replied.

[20]"And when I broke the seven loaves for the four thousand, how many basketfuls of pieces did you pick up?"

They answered, "Seven."[l]

[21]He said to them, "Do you still not understand?"[m]

8:2
[b] Mt 9:36
8:7
[c] Mt 14:19
8:8
[d] ver 20
8:11
[e] Mt 12:38
8:12
[f] Mk 7:34
8:15
[g] 1Co 5:6-8
[h] Lk 12:1 [i] Mt 14:1; Mk 12:13
8:17
[j] Isa 6:9,10; Mk 6:52
8:19
[k] Mt 14:20; Mk 6:41-44; Lk 9:17; Jn 6:13
8:20
[l] ver 6-9; Mt 15:37
8:21
[m] Mk 6:52

Mark 8:1–13

In 7:24–30, the healing of the woman's daughter introduced the novel idea that Gentiles might be fed spiritually without stealing bread from the Jews. This second account in Mark's Gospel of a miraculous feeding was set in Gentile country. The miracle signified that Jesus isn't simply *a* messiah—he's *the* Messiah, extending his kingdom offer beyond Israel. The disciples, demonstrating a deplorable lack of short-term memory, failed to recognize that they had enough in Jesus to feed the entire world.

Like the feeding of the 5,000 (6:35–44), this incident emphasized a dynamic combination of spiritual teaching and social concern. Jesus offered the bread of life to feed the soul *and* physical bread to fill the stomach. Presenting Bible lessons to famished crowds and sending them away hungry does too little. But satiating their appetites without feeding their souls also misses the mark. Ministry that *works* meets both spiritual and physical needs. Jesus didn't demonstrate that one is more important than the other. Both are integral to the kingdom.

Mark 8:14–21

In the Old Testament, yeast or leaven symbolized corruption and the infectious power of evil. Jesus was using couched language to warn his disciples not to fall victim to the unbelief of the Pharisees and Herod. Unfortunately, anxiety about their next meal rendered them clueless to his meaning. Jesus expressed concern about their squabbling over loaves and then quickly recapped recent events. They could do the math, since they had helped distribute the food and gather up the leftovers. Yet they had become fixated on the means to fix lunch for 13.

Several dangers arise when we become, like the disciples, focused on concerns about our material well-being: (1) We may doubt Jesus' power to provide enough and be tempted to look to alternative sources ("yeasts"). (2) We might vent anxiety by quarreling with others, undermining community. (3) The never-ending pursuit of "daily bread" can distract us from obeying God's will. If we lift our eyes above our earthbound quest for life's "stuff," we will see that God provides all we need in Jesus.

The Healing of a Blind Man at Bethsaida

8:22
n Mt 11:21
o Mk 10:46; Jn 9:1

22They came to Bethsaida,[n] and some people brought a blind man[o] and begged Jesus to touch him. 23He took the blind man by the hand and led him outside the

8:23
p Mk 7:33
q Mk 5:23

village. When he had spit[p] on the man's eyes and put his hands on[q] him, Jesus asked, "Do you see anything?"

24He looked up and said, "I see people; they look like trees walking around."

25Once more Jesus put his hands on the man's eyes. Then his eyes were opened, his sight was restored, and he saw everything clearly. 26Jesus sent him home, saying, "Don't go into the village.[a]"

Peter's Confession of Christ

8:28
r Mt 3:1 s Mal 4:5

27Jesus and his disciples went on to the villages around Caesarea Philippi. On the way he asked them, "Who do people say I am?"

28They replied, "Some say John the Baptist;[r] others say Elijah;[s] and still others, one of the prophets."

8:29
t Jn 6:69; 11:27
8:30
u Mt 8:4; 16:20;
17:9; Mk 9:9;
Lk 9:21

29"But what about you?" he asked. "Who do you say I am?"
Peter answered, "You are the Christ.[b]"[t]

30Jesus warned them not to tell anyone about him.[u]

Jesus Predicts His Death

8:31
v Mt 8:20
w Mt 16:21
x Mt 27:1,2
y Ac 2:23; 3:13
z Mt 16:21
a Mt 16:21
8:32
b Jn 18:20
8:33
c Mt 4:10

31He then began to teach them that the Son of Man[v] must suffer many things[w] and be rejected by the elders, chief priests and teachers of the law,[x] and that he must be killed[y] and after three days[z] rise again.[a] 32He spoke plainly[b] about this, and Peter took him aside and began to rebuke him.

33But when Jesus turned and looked at his disciples, he rebuked Peter. "Get behind me, Satan!"[c] he said. "You do not have in mind the things of God, but the things of men."

8:34
d Mt 10:38;
Lk 14:27

34Then he called the crowd to him along with his disciples and said: "If anyone would come after me, he must deny himself and take up his cross and follow me.[d]

a 26 Some manuscripts *Don't go and tell anyone in the village*   b 29 Or *Messiah.* "The Christ" (Greek) and "the Messiah" (Hebrew) both mean "the Anointed One."

Mark 8:22–26

Since the blind man didn't recover his sight immediately, we get the impression his blindness was stubborn and hard to cure. But Mark's context, which portrays Jesus' struggle to get his disciples to see *anything*, gives this unusual, two-stage healing added significance. The blind man's healing occurred between two examples of the disciples' blindness (8:14–21 and 8:31–33). This physical healing of blindness prepares us for the spiritual healing of the disciples' sight, which would also come gradually and with difficulty.

Mark's Gospel does its work when we identify with the disciples' blindness. They saw dimly, through a glass coated with the dust of traditional ways and views and warped by the curvature of their own dreams and ambitions. We are no less in need of healing before we can see what God is doing—and the cure may not "take" on the first try. What "dust" or "warping" has affected your spiritual lenses?

Mark 8:27–30

This pivotal passage falls at the very center of Mark's Gospel—between the first half, where Jesus' power was prominent, and the second, where his weakness was evident. Peter's response to Jesus' critical question represented a significant leap of faith, especially in light of the Jewish expectations of the Christ, or Messi-

ah. In the 1st century most Jews believed he would be a royal figure God would empower to physically deliver Israel from its oppressors, in this case the power of Rome.

Many people "respectfully" slide Jesus into categories that allow them to evade God's claim on their lives. They admire him for his politically correct sayings and agree with turning the other cheek, declining to cast the first stone, and loving their neighbor. But the Jesus Mark presented and the church confesses wasn't just a Galilean holy man, a kind teacher, a passionate prophet, a peasant leader. Nor was he a wandering philosopher calling people to live according to common sense and natural law. *He's the Son of God.* What is *your* answer to his question: "But what about you? Who do you say I am?"

Mark 8:31—9:1

Peter had begun to understand that Jesus must be the Messiah, but he didn't have a clue how his Lord's suffering tied into Jesus' identity. Jesus proceeded to lay out the expectations of discipleship. The vivid imagery of danger and sacrifice must have sounded strange before his death and resurrection. But Jesus didn't want a convoy of followers who marveled at his deeds but failed to follow his example. Ironically, the only way to experience the fullness of life is to die to all claims to our life. In the procession Jesus envisioned, disciples would follow after their Master—each in turn carrying a cross.

35For whoever wants to save his life[a] will lose it, but whoever loses his life for me and for the gospel will save it. [e] 36What good is it for a man to gain the whole world, yet forfeit his soul? 37Or what can a man give in exchange for his soul? 38If anyone is ashamed of me and my words in this adulterous and sinful generation, the Son of Man[f] will be ashamed of him[g] when he comes[h] in his Father's glory with the holy angels."

9 And he said to them, "I tell you the truth, some who are standing here will not taste death before they see the kingdom of God come[i] with power."[j]

The Transfiguration

2After six days Jesus took Peter, James and John[k] with him and led them up a high mountain, where they were all alone. There he was transfigured before them. 3His clothes became dazzling white,[l] whiter than anyone in the world could bleach them. 4And there appeared before them Elijah and Moses, who were talking with Jesus.

5Peter said to Jesus, "Rabbi,[m] it is good for us to be here. Let us put up three shelters—one for you, one for Moses and one for Elijah." 6(He did not know what to say, they were so frightened.)

7Then a cloud appeared and enveloped them, and a voice came from the cloud:[n] "This is my Son, whom I love. Listen to him!"[o]

8Suddenly, when they looked around, they no longer saw anyone with them except Jesus.

9As they were coming down the mountain, Jesus gave them orders not to tell anyone[p] what they had seen until the Son of Man[q] had risen from the dead. 10They kept the matter to themselves, discussing what "rising from the dead" meant.

11And they asked him, "Why do the teachers of the law say that Elijah must come first?"

12Jesus replied, "To be sure, Elijah does come first, and restores all things. Why then is it written that the Son of Man[r] must suffer much[s] and be rejected?[t] 13But I tell you, Elijah has come,[u] and they have done to him everything they wished, just as it is written about him."

The Healing of a Boy With an Evil Spirit

14When they came to the other disciples, they saw a large crowd around them and

a 35 The Greek word means either *life* or *soul*; also in verse 36.

Cross references

8:35
e Jn 12:25

8:38
f Mt 8:20
g Mt 10:33; Lk 12:9
h 1Th 2:19

9:1
i Mk 13:30;
Lk 22:18 j Mt 24:30;
25:31

9:2
k Mt 4:21

9:3
l Mt 28:3

9:5
m Mt 23:7

9:7
n Ex 24:16
o Mt 3:17

9:9
p Mk 8:30
q Mt 8:20

9:12
r Mt 8:20
s Mt 16:21
t Lk 23:11
9:13
u Mt 11:14

You may be tempted to flee from Jesus' strong words: (1) to retreat from the embarrassment of standing up for your faith; (2) to be free to seek worldly security rather than sacrificing your life for Christ and others; or (3) to avoid Jesus' requirements by substituting a more user-friendly brand of discipleship. You may want personal choices, not eternal imperatives. Are you at times tempted to approach the Christian life in a consumer mode, asking "What am *I* going to get from this?" What would it take for you to fully embrace Jesus' hard demands of discipleship?

Mark 9:2–13

"After six days" connects the transfiguration to the previous event—where Peter confessed Jesus to be the Christ and Jesus revealed his future suffering and the requirement that his disciples follow his example. The account ends with Jesus again speaking of his suffering (v. 12). The transfiguration confirmed that the suffering Jesus would endure wasn't incompatible with his glory. For a brief moment, the disciples glimpsed the truth; divine glory penetrated the dark cloud of their confusion.

Who wouldn't have preferred to be with Peter, James, and John—basking in mountaintop glory—rather than plodding along with the other disciples below? After having failed to help a boy plagued with demonic seizures, they found themselves surrounded by argumentative opponents and an edgy crowd (vv. 14–18). We spend much of our lives in the valley of anxiety, failure, and frustration. But recalling an experience where the truth blazed before us can carry us through the dark times when faith is challenged from inside and out. What memory of an encounter with God has kept you going?

Mark 9:14–32

Jesus had given his disciples authority over evil spirits (6:7,13), yet they couldn't drive out the demon that possessed this boy. Later, they reviewed their failure privately with Jesus (v. 28). His response, "This kind can come out only by prayer," implies that they had failed because they hadn't prayed sufficiently—if at all. (Maybe they had argued instead!) The prayer Jesus had in mind wasn't some magical invocation but a natural dialogue, based on a close and enduring relationship with God and expressing trust and confidence in him.

the teachers of the law arguing with them. ¹⁵As soon as all the people saw Jesus, they were overwhelmed with wonder and ran to greet him.

¹⁶"What are you arguing with them about?" he asked.

¹⁷A man in the crowd answered, "Teacher, I brought you my son, who is possessed by a spirit that has robbed him of speech. ¹⁸Whenever it seizes him, it throws him to the ground. He foams at the mouth, gnashes his teeth and becomes rigid. I asked your disciples to drive out the spirit, but they could not."

¹⁹"O unbelieving generation," Jesus replied, "how long shall I stay with you? How long shall I put up with you? Bring the boy to me."

²⁰So they brought him. When the spirit saw Jesus, it immediately threw the boy into a convulsion. He fell to the ground and rolled around, foaming at the mouth. ᵛ

²¹Jesus asked the boy's father, "How long has he been like this?"

"From childhood," he answered. ²²"It has often thrown him into fire or water to kill him. But if you can do anything, take pity on us and help us."

²³"'If you can'?" said Jesus. "Everything is possible for him who believes." ʷ

²⁴Immediately the boy's father exclaimed, "I do believe; help me overcome my unbelief!"

²⁵When Jesus saw that a crowd was running to the scene,ˣ he rebuked the evilᵃ spirit. "You deaf and mute spirit," he said, "I command you, come out of him and never enter him again."

²⁶The spirit shrieked, convulsed him violently and came out. The boy looked so much like a corpse that many said, "He's dead." ²⁷But Jesus took him by the hand and lifted him to his feet, and he stood up.

²⁸After Jesus had gone indoors, his disciples asked him privately,ʸ "Why couldn't we drive it out?"

²⁹He replied, "This kind can come out only by prayer.ᵇ"

³⁰They left that place and passed through Galilee. Jesus did not want anyone to know where they were, ³¹because he was teaching his disciples. He said to them, "The Son of Manᶻ is going to be betrayed into the hands of men. They will kill him,ᵃ and after three daysᵇ he will rise."ᶜ ³²But they did not understand what he meantᵈ and were afraid to ask him about it.

Who Is the Greatest?

³³They came to Capernaum.ᵉ When he was in the house,ᶠ he asked them, "What were you arguing about on the road?" ³⁴But they kept quiet because on the way they had argued about who was the greatest.ᵍ

³⁵Sitting down, Jesus called the Twelve and said, "If anyone wants to be first, he must be the very last, and the servant of all."ʰ

³⁶He took a little child and had him stand among them. Taking him in his arms,ⁱ he said to them, ³⁷"Whoever welcomes one of these little children in my name wel-

Cross references (margin)

9:20 ᵛ Mk 1:26
9:23 ʷ Mt 21:21; Mk 11:23; Jn 11:40
9:25 ˣ ver 15
9:28 ʸ Mk 7:17
9:31 ᶻ Mt 8:20 ᵃ ver 12; Ac 2:23; 3:13 ᵇ Mt 16:21 ᶜ Mt 16:21
9:32 ᵈ Lk 2:50; 9:45; 18:34; Jn 12:16
9:33 ᵉ Mt 4:13 ᶠ Mk 1:29
9:34 ᵍ Lk 22:24
9:35 ʰ Mt 18:4; 20:26; Mk 10:43; Lk 22:26
9:36 ⁱ Mk 10:16

ᵃ 25 Greek *unclean*   ᵇ 29 Some manuscripts *prayer and fasting*

How do you react to failure? As we attempt to use our lives and gifts to serve others, we generally see failure as a bad thing—to be avoided at all costs. But failure can be a positive, learning opportunity. It can lead to a teachable moment, heightening our awareness of our need for total dependence on God and for taking the time to pray. "I do believe; help me overcome my unbelief" is as necessary a plea for us as helpers as it is for those we seek to help.

Mark 9:33–37

Jesus had just informed the Twelve that he was "going to be betrayed into the hands of men" (v. 31). Instead of worrying about who might betray him, they sparred with each other about their ratings with him. Their bickering opened the door for Jesus' teaching on selfless service. He presented them with two paradoxes:

(1) The one who wants to be first must become last and the servant of all. (2) When we serve those without status, we welcome Jesus and the One who sent him. Mark pictured a community with no kingpins and no nobodies (see 1 Cor. 12:12–26).

Jesus used a child to represent the disrespected, discarded, and ignored—the people on the fringes, the unsophisticated, the ones nobody misses when they are absent. But these "little ones" aren't irrelevant to our Lord. God works through them, and Jesus ministered to them and calls us to do the same. In fact, how we respond to those who seem insignificant indicates how we will respond to Jesus. Identify one or two "little" people in your circle of acquaintance. What might Christ want you to do to serve and welcome them?

comes me; and whoever welcomes me does not welcome me but the one who sent me." [j]

9:37
j Mt 10:40

Whoever Is Not Against Us Is for Us

38 "Teacher," said John, "we saw a man driving out demons in your name and we told him to stop, because he was not one of us." [k]

9:38
k Nu 11:27-29

39 "Do not stop him," Jesus said. "No one who does a miracle in my name can in the next moment say anything bad about me, 40for whoever is not against us is for us. [l] 41 I tell you the truth, anyone who gives you a cup of water in my name because you belong to Christ will certainly not lose his reward. [m]

9:40
l Mt 12:30;
Lk 11:23
9:41
m Mt 10:42

Causing to Sin

42 "And if anyone causes one of these little ones who believe in me to sin, [n] it would be better for him to be thrown into the sea with a large millstone tied around his neck. [o] 43 If your hand causes you to sin, [p] cut it off. It is better for you to enter life maimed than with two hands to go into hell, [q] where the fire never goes out. [a] [r] 45 And if your foot causes you to sin, [s] cut it off. It is better for you to enter life crippled than to have two feet and be thrown into hell. [b] [t] 47 And if your eye causes you to sin, [u] pluck it out. It is better for you to enter the kingdom of God with one eye than to have two eyes and be thrown into hell, [v] 48where

9:42
n Mt 5:29
o Mt 18:6; Lk 17:2
9:43
p Mt 5:29
q Mt 5:30; 18:8
r Mt 25:41
9:45
s Mt 5:29 t Mt 18:8

9:47
u Mt 5:29
v Mt 5:29; 18:9

> " 'their worm does not die,
> and the fire is not quenched.' [c] [w]

9:48
w Isa 66:24;
Mt 25:41
9:49
x Lev 2:13
9:50
y Mt 5:13;
Lk 14:34,35
z Col 4:6
a Ro 12:18;
2Co 13:11;
1Th 5:13

49 Everyone will be salted [x] with fire.

50 "Salt is good, but if it loses its saltiness, how can you make it salty again? [y] Have salt in yourselves, [z] and be at peace with each other." [a]

Divorce

10 Jesus then left that place and went into the region of Judea and across the Jordan. [b] Again crowds of people came to him, and as was his custom, he taught them. [c]

10:1
b Mk 1:5; Jn 10:40;
11:7 c Mt 4:23;
Mk 2:13; 4:2;
6:6,34
10:2
d Mk 2:16

2 Some Pharisees [d] came and tested him by asking, "Is it lawful for a man to divorce his wife?"

3 "What did Moses command you?" he replied.

---

a 43 Some manuscripts out, 44where / " 'their worm does not die, / and the fire is not quenched.'
b 45 Some manuscripts hell, 46where / " 'their worm does not die, / and the fire is not quenched.'
c 48 Isaiah 66:24

Mark 9:38–41

📖 The disciples had recently bungled an exorcism (vv. 14–18), yet they didn't hesitate to obstruct someone who was successful but not a member of their "official" team. Jesus threw open the door to include on his side all who weren't against him. But his statement "whoever is not against us is for us" must be understood in its context. Neutrality is impossible—a reality intensified when believers face hostility.

📖 The disciples wanted exclusive rights to Jesus' name, as if they owned the copyright. This same attitude crops up today when we regard our own church as the true one, seeking to confine God's work to our personal endeavors. If we can't do it, we don't want anyone else to, either. Genuine humility understands that God can use anyone and applauds others who are successful for him. How do you, and others in your congregation, view the other churches in your community? Do you pray—sincerely and wholeheartedly—for their success?

Mark 9:42–50

📖 Jesus had just promised a reward to outsiders willing to show others a bare minimum of goodwill (v. 41). We can conclude from his exaggerated statement in verse 42 that God makes people's active care for the little ones now a criterion for his judgment of them in the future. Jesus continued to use exaggeration in a string of proverbs to follow, warning the disciples that they needed to be more worried about the evil in themselves than they were about outsiders.

📖 Jesus didn't literally intend for us to mutilate our bodies, but we are left to determine what he does require. If not hand, foot, and eye, what are we to "cut off" to keep from harming others or ourselves? For some of us, getting rid of our television(s) or cell phone would seem almost as painful as plucking out an eye. Jesus often chose harsh metaphors to alert potential disciples of real danger to their spiritual lives. Let's be careful not to mute the imagery and muffle the alarm.

10:4
e Dt 24:1-4;
Mt 5:31
10:5
f Ps 95:8; Heb 3:15
10:6
g Ge 1:27; 5:2
10:8
h Ge 2:24;
1Co 6:16

4They said, "Moses permitted a man to write a certificate of divorce and send her away." e

5"It was because your hearts were hard f that Moses wrote you this law," Jesus replied. 6"But at the beginning of creation God 'made them male and female.' a g 7'For this reason a man will leave his father and mother and be united to his wife, b 8and the two will become one flesh.' c h So they are no longer two, but one. 9Therefore what God has joined together, let man not separate."

10When they were in the house again, the disciples asked Jesus about this. 11He answered, "Anyone who divorces his wife and marries another woman commits adultery against her. i 12And if she divorces her husband and marries another man, she commits adultery." j

10:11
i Mt 5:32; Lk 16:18
10:12
j Ro 7:3;
1Co 7:10,11

The Little Children and Jesus

13People were bringing little children to Jesus to have him touch them, but the disciples rebuked them. 14When Jesus saw this, he was indignant. He said to them, "Let the little children come to me, and do not hinder them, for the kingdom of God belongs to such as these. k 15I tell you the truth, anyone who will not receive the kingdom of God like a little child will never enter it." l 16And he took the children in his arms, m put his hands on them and blessed them.

10:14
k Mt 25:34
10:15
l Mt 18:3
10:16
m Mk 9:36

The Rich Young Man

10:17
n Mk 1:40
o Lk 10:25;
Ac 20:32

17As Jesus started on his way, a man ran up to him and fell on his knees n before him. "Good teacher," he asked, "what must I do to inherit eternal life?" o

18"Why do you call me good?" Jesus answered. "No one is good—except God alone. 19You know the commandments: 'Do not murder, do not commit adultery,

---

a 6 Gen. 1:27   b 7 Some early manuscripts do not have *and be united to his wife.*   c 8 Gen. 2:24

Mark 10:1–12

Through their testing on the subject of divorce, the Pharisees probably wanted to expose Jesus as a misguided teacher who ignored Scripture and common sense. They responded to his counter question by citing Deuteronomy 24:1–4. Jesus argued that Moses' command was an accommodation designed to reduce the fallout from divorce. If this law had its roots in people's hardness of heart, Jesus reasoned, it couldn't reflect God's perfect will. Jesus viewed marriage as an unbreakable, "one-flesh" union (cf. Gen. 2:21–24; Eph. 5:28–31).

How have you personally been impacted by divorce? Can we hold up a high standard of the sanctity of marriage—at the same time recognizing that a broken marriage is no different from any other sin, except that it's public and has many unwanted and unseen effects? Can we affirm Jesus' strong words here—at the same time exercising the principle of redemption that governed his ministry to broken and repentant people?

Mark 10:13–16

In the ancient world, children had little status. Considered property, they were easily pushed aside. In fact, an unwanted child could literally be thrown away. But God works most powerfully in weakness. Those who are "like a little child" or "poor in spirit" (Matt. 5:3) are most open to accepting God's reign. While some may consider children liabilities, Jesus stated that he reveals *himself through the little ones in our midst.* Children are to be at the center of his people's care and concern.

Children worldwide continue to be abused, discarded, and discounted. They have less international pro-

tection than an endangered species! As Christians, we are called to do everything we can to combat child labor, child pornography, harmful advertising aimed at the very young, and the abuse of children at all societal levels. The treatment of children is the primary barometer humanitarian organizations often use to evaluate the relative health of a region. This passage indicates that the quality of our care for children is also God's barometer.

Mark 10:17–31

This man saw himself as already good and acceptable to God, but he was concerned about any fine print he might have overlooked. We learn that he was rich only from Mark's report of the man's disappointment at Jesus' response. Jesus further astounded the disciples by observing that the rich have a hard time entering the kingdom. Salvation comes from a divine, not a human, source. But since the man asked for something *he* could do, Jesus obliged. To enter the kingdom we are to submit to God's rule in every aspect of life.

There are twin pitfalls to avoid in applying this passage: (1) the desire to whittle away Jesus' radical demand about possessions to make it more "reasonable" (acceptable) and (2) the inclination to make it apply to somebody else. Jesus didn't categorically reject being wealthy or this affluent individual himself. The central issue is our ultimate loyalty. The burning question is whether material possessions own our heart's allegiance and encumber our lives. Are there ways in which your dependency on possessions and pursuit of wealth are keeping you from trusting God fully and actively pursuing his will?

do not steal, do not give false testimony, do not defraud, honor your father and
mother.'[a]"[p]
20"Teacher," he declared, "all these I have kept since I was a boy."
21Jesus looked at him and loved him. "One thing you lack," he said. "Go, sell everything you have and give to the poor,[q] and you will have treasure in heaven.[r] Then
come, follow me."[s]
22At this the man's face fell. He went away sad, because he had great wealth.
23Jesus looked around and said to his disciples, "How hard it is for the rich[t] to
enter the kingdom of God!"
24The disciples were amazed at his words. But Jesus said again, "Children, how
hard it is[b] to enter the kingdom of God![u] 25It is easier for a camel to go through
the eye of a needle than for a rich man to enter the kingdom of God."[v]
26The disciples were even more amazed, and said to each other, "Who then can
be saved?"
27Jesus looked at them and said, "With man this is impossible, but not with God;
all things are possible with God."[w]
28Peter said to him, "We have left everything to follow you!"[x]
29"I tell you the truth," Jesus replied, "no one who has left home or brothers or
sisters or mother or father or children or fields for me and the gospel 30will fail to
receive a hundred times as much[y] in this present age (homes, brothers, sisters,
mothers, children and fields—and with them, persecutions) and in the age to
come,[z] eternal life.[a] 31But many who are first will be last, and the last first."[b]

Jesus Again Predicts His Death

32They were on their way up to Jerusalem, with Jesus leading the way, and the disciples were astonished, while those who followed were afraid. Again he took the
Twelve[c] aside and told them what was going to happen to him. 33"We are going up
to Jerusalem,"[d] he said, "and the Son of Man[e] will be betrayed to the chief priests
and teachers of the law.[f] They will condemn him to death and will hand him over
to the Gentiles, 34who will mock him and spit on him, flog him[g] and kill him.[h]
Three days later[i] he will rise."[j]

The Request of James and John

35Then James and John, the sons of Zebedee, came to him. "Teacher," they said,
"we want you to do for us whatever we ask."

10:19 [p] Ex 20:12-16; Dt 5:16-20
10:21 [q] Ac 2:45 [r] Mt 6:20; Lk 12:33 [s] Mt 4:19
10:23 [t] Ps 52:7; 62:10; 1Ti 6:9,10,17
10:24 [u] Mt 7:13,14
10:25 [v] Lk 12:16-20
10:27 [w] Mt 19:26
10:28 [x] Mt 4:19
10:30 [y] Mt 6:33 [z] Mt 12:32 [a] Mt 25:46
10:31 [b] Mt 19:30
10:32 [c] Mk 3:16-19
10:33 [d] Lk 9:51 [e] Mt 8:20 [f] Mt 27:1,2
10:34 [g] Mt 16:21 [h] Ac 2:23; 3:13 [i] Mt 16:21 [j] Mt 16:21

[a] *19* Exodus 20:12-16; Deut. 5:16-20 [b] *24* Some manuscripts *is for those who trust in riches*

Mark 10:32–34

Jesus had been leading his disciples on the road, and he now identified their destination as Jerusalem. He went there as the Messiah—not in triumph, but to die. The disciples, bewildered and still worried about the order of their procession (see 9:33–34; 10:37,41), trailed behind. Jesus predicted for the third time his coming death and resurrection, this time providing more specific details. As he drew nearer the site of his ordeal, the disciples drew no closer to understanding his mission.

Mark here depicted the disciples as preoccupied with power, achievement, and personal ambition. They wanted a Messiah who would move beyond suffering and death to fulfill their expectations and guarantee their success. But Jesus can never be understood apart from the necessity of his pain. To know and understand him requires us to accept his destiny as a Messiah who suffered (and died) for others—and then to embrace the same destiny for ourselves. What does it mean for you to share in Jesus' sufferings so you may also share in his glory (see Rom. 8:17; Phil. 3:10–11)?

Mark 10:35–45

Jesus had been talking about all he was about to give (vv. 32–34). But the Zebedee brothers came with a shopping list of all they wanted to *get*. Jesus responded with grace to their brazen request. James and John would share his fate of suffering (see Acts 12:2), but the Father hadn't put Jesus in charge of seating arrangements in the kingdom. This scene, tragic-comical as it is to us, prompted Jesus to give instructions on the nature of discipleship. He still invites his followers to be great—great servants to each other!

Jesus' life and teaching turns the worldly understanding of greatness on its head. Self-giving service is the only greatness God recognizes. We can conduct our own attitude check by examining how we respond when asked to perform a task we might see as beneath our dignity. This story also compels us to evaluate our requests to God. Would we look like the disciples in this passage if some of our prayer requests were to be made public?

10:37
k Mt 19:28
10:38
l Job 38:2
m Mt 20:22
n Lk 12:50

³⁶"What do you want me to do for you?" he asked.

³⁷They replied, "Let one of us sit at your right and the other at your left in your glory." *k*

³⁸"You don't know what you are asking," *l* Jesus said. "Can you drink the cup *m* I drink or be baptized with the baptism I am baptized with?" *n*

³⁹"We can," they answered.

Jesus said to them, "You will drink the cup I drink and be baptized with the baptism I am baptized with, *o* ⁴⁰but to sit at my right or left is not for me to grant. These places belong to those for whom they have been prepared."

10:39
o Ac 12:2; Rev 1:9

⁴¹When the ten heard about this, they became indignant with James and John. ⁴²Jesus called them together and said, "You know that those who are regarded as rulers of the Gentiles lord it over them, and their high officials exercise authority over them. ⁴³Not so with you. Instead, whoever wants to become great among you must be your servant, *p* ⁴⁴and whoever wants to be first must be slave of all. ⁴⁵For even the Son of Man did not come to be served, but to serve, *q* and to give his life as a ransom for many." *r*

10:43
p Mk 9:35
10:45
q Mt 20:28
r Mt 20:28

Blind Bartimaeus Receives His Sight

⁴⁶Then they came to Jericho. As Jesus and his disciples, together with a large crowd, were leaving the city, a blind man, Bartimaeus (that is, the Son of Timaeus), was sitting by the roadside begging. ⁴⁷When he heard that it was Jesus of Nazareth, *s* he began to shout, "Jesus, Son of David, *t* have mercy on me!"

10:47
s Mk 1:24 t Mt 9:27

⁴⁸Many rebuked him and told him to be quiet, but he shouted all the more, "Son of David, have mercy on me!"

⁴⁹Jesus stopped and said, "Call him."

So they called to the blind man, "Cheer up! On your feet! He's calling you." ⁵⁰Throwing his cloak aside, he jumped to his feet and came to Jesus.

⁵¹"What do you want me to do for you?" Jesus asked him.

The blind man said, "Rabbi, *u* I want to see."

⁵²"Go," said Jesus, "your faith has healed you." *v* Immediately he received his sight and followed *w* Jesus along the road.

10:51
u Mt 23:7
10:52
v Mt 9:22
w Mt 4:19

The Triumphal Entry

11:1
x Mt 21:17
y Mt 21:1

11 As they approached Jerusalem and came to Bethphage and Bethany *x* at the Mount of Olives, *y* Jesus sent two of his disciples, ²saying to them, "Go to the village ahead of you, and just as you enter it, you will find a colt tied there, which

---

Mark 10:46–52

Blind Bartimaeus somehow knew the man passing by was more than a popular prophet and miracle worker. He cried out to him as the "Son of David," a title that affirmed Jesus' Messianic mission. As Jesus moved closer to Jerusalem and his shameful death, his identity as the Messiah needed to be sounded loud and clear. Bartimaeus's cry prepared for Jesus' dramatic entry into Jerusalem (11:1–11). And his faith transformed him into a person who saw—and followed—Jesus. God used this "nobody" to announce his Son's approach.

Jesus asked the sons of Zebedee and Bartimaeus the identical question, "What do you want me to do for you?" (vv. 36,51). This is still the most important question God asks us—and the one to which we are most prone to give the wrong answer. James and John wanted to sit on thrones and reign with Jesus in triumph. Bartimaeus wanted only to see. Jesus can heal physical blindness, but more than that he wants to heal spiritual blindness. What do you want Jesus to do for you?

Mark 11:1–11

Jesus had consistently avoided calling attention to himself, yet now he arranged an entrance into Jerusalem that encouraged public scrutiny. But the crowd's infectious enthusiasm only temporarily shut out the looming catastrophe Mark prepared us to expect. The crowd, led by Jesus' followers, shouted nationalistic slogans about the restoration of the power and glory of the Davidic kingdom. But Jesus' entrance pointed to a different kind of triumph—more powerful than any kingly monarchy and farther-reaching than the narrow borders of Israel or even the Roman Empire.

As churchgoers, we still memorialize Jesus' grand entrance into Jerusalem, typically on Palm Sunday. A week later, we return on Easter to celebrate his glorious resurrection. But how many of us take part in the special services in between, those commemorating the significant events of Passion Week? To hail Jesus properly means to acknowledge him as the One who came to die for us. The crowd, thinking Jesus would save

no one has ever ridden. *z* Untie it and bring it here. ³If anyone asks you, 'Why are you doing this?' tell him, 'The Lord needs it and will send it back here shortly.' "

⁴They went and found a colt outside in the street, tied at a doorway. *a* As they untied it, ⁵some people standing there asked, "What are you doing, untying that colt?" ⁶They answered as Jesus had told them to, and the people let them go. ⁷When they brought the colt to Jesus and threw their cloaks over it, he sat on it. ⁸Many people spread their cloaks on the road, while others spread branches they had cut in the fields. ⁹Those who went ahead and those who followed shouted,

"Hosanna! *a* "

"Blessed is he who comes in the name of the Lord!" *b b*

¹⁰"Blessed is the coming kingdom of our father David!"

"Hosanna in the highest!" *c*

¹¹Jesus entered Jerusalem and went to the temple. He looked around at everything, but since it was already late, he went out to Bethany with the Twelve. *d*

Jesus Clears the Temple

¹²The next day as they were leaving Bethany, Jesus was hungry. ¹³Seeing in the distance a fig tree in leaf, he went to find out if it had any fruit. When he reached it, he found nothing but leaves, because it was not the season for figs. *e* ¹⁴Then he said to the tree, "May no one ever eat fruit from you again." And his disciples heard him say it.

¹⁵On reaching Jerusalem, Jesus entered the temple area and began driving out those who were buying and selling there. He overturned the tables of the money changers and the benches of those selling doves, ¹⁶and would not allow anyone to carry merchandise through the temple courts. ¹⁷And as he taught them, he said, "Is it not written:

" 'My house will be called
    a house of prayer for all nations' *c*? *f*

But you have made it 'a den of robbers.' *d" g*

¹⁸The chief priests and the teachers of the law heard this and began looking for a way to kill him, for they feared him, *h* because the whole crowd was amazed at his teaching. *i*

¹⁹When evening came, they *e* went out of the city. *j*

The Withered Fig Tree

²⁰In the morning, as they went along, they saw the fig tree withered from the roots. ²¹Peter remembered and said to Jesus, "Rabbi, *k* look! The fig tree you cursed has withered!"

a 9 A Hebrew expression meaning "Save!" which became an exclamation of praise; also in verse 10   *b 9* Psalm 118:25,26   *c 17* Isaiah 56:7   *d 17* Jer. 7:11   *e 19* Some early manuscripts *he*

Cross references (margin)

11:2 *z* Nu 19:2; Dt 21:3; 1Sa 6:7
11:4 *a* Mk 14:16
11:9 *b* Ps 118:25,26; Mt 23:39
11:10 *c* Lk 2:14
11:11 *d* Mt 21:12,17
11:13 *e* Lk 13:6-9
11:17 *f* Isa 56:7 *g* Jer 7:11
11:18 *h* Mt 21:46; Mk 12:12; Lk 20:19 *i* Mt 7:28
11:19 *j* Lk 21:37
11:21 *k* Mt 23:7

---

them from their political enemies, shouted "Hosanna—save us!" But what we really need is for him to save us from *ourselves*.

Mark 11:12–19

Many motives have been suggested for Jesus' actions in the temple courtyard (vv. 15–17). Whatever they were, this scene clearly portrayed his anger against those who exploit others, especially in the name of religion. He couldn't stand to watch simple but sincere people cheated for religious profit. He condemned corruption that mistreated even the most holy things. The temple was the central institution of Israel's religious, political, and economic life. To attack something so important, so holy, so entrenched, took enormous courage—and it sealed Jesus' fate (cf. v. 18).

Many around the world today live under unjust political, religious, and/or economic situations and are unable to protect themselves. What can you do? If your answer is "I'm not sure" or "probably nothing," talk to your pastor or surf the net. Opportunities for Christian service and advocacy abound. Does fear of being labeled a religious "fanatic" or "kook" hold you back? Before you answer, consider Proverbs 29:7 and Jesus' example in this passage.

11:23
l Mt 21:21

11:24
m Mt 7:7
11:25
n Mt 6:14

22"Have[a] faith in God," Jesus answered. 23"I tell you the truth, if anyone says to this mountain, 'Go, throw yourself into the sea,' and does not doubt in his heart but believes that what he says will happen, it will be done for him.[l] 24Therefore I tell you, whatever you ask for in prayer, believe that you have received it, and it will be yours.[m] 25And when you stand praying, if you hold anything against anyone, forgive him, so that your Father in heaven may forgive you your sins.[b][n]

The Authority of Jesus Questioned

27They arrived again in Jerusalem, and while Jesus was walking in the temple courts, the chief priests, the teachers of the law and the elders came to him. 28"By what authority are you doing these things?" they asked. "And who gave you authority to do this?"

29Jesus replied, "I will ask you one question. Answer me, and I will tell you by what authority I am doing these things. 30John's baptism—was it from heaven, or from men? Tell me!"

31They discussed it among themselves and said, "If we say, 'From heaven,' he will ask, 'Then why didn't you believe him?' 32But if we say, 'From men' . . ." (They

11:32
o Mt 11:9

feared the people, for everyone held that John really was a prophet.)[o]

33So they answered Jesus, "We don't know."

Jesus said, "Neither will I tell you by what authority I am doing these things."

The Parable of the Tenants

12:1
p Isa 5:1-7

12 He then began to speak to them in parables: "A man planted a vineyard.[p] He put a wall around it, dug a pit for the winepress and built a watchtower. Then he rented the vineyard to some farmers and went away on a journey. 2At harvest time he sent a servant to the tenants to collect from them some of the fruit of the vineyard. 3But they seized him, beat him and sent him away empty-handed. 4Then he sent another servant to them; they struck this man on the head and treat-

---

a 22 Some early manuscripts *If you have*   *b 25* Some manuscripts *sins.* 26*But if you do not forgive, neither will your Father who is in heaven forgive your sins.*

Mark 11:20–26

The fig tree incident (vv. 12–14 and 20–25) surrounds and interprets Jesus' bold action in the temple (vv. 15–19). A fig tree full of leaves would normally also have figs, but this one didn't. Surprisingly, Jesus didn't rehabilitate the tree. He cursed it. The unfruitful fig tree represented the barrenness of temple-centered Judaism, which was unprepared to accept Jesus' Messianic reign. Time was coming to an end for fruitless trees and faithless temples.

Some Bible scholars assume the fig tree incident was included by Mark as a prop to hold up the traditional sayings about prayer and forgiveness. Others view the scene as integrated, seeing that the sayings reveal the essence of the new order that replaced the old. This new order, of which we are a part, is based on faith in God that overcomes insurmountable odds (vv. 22–23), is sustained by grace (v. 24), and is characterized by forgiveness (v. 25). But even without a temple, this new community will pray. How do you participate in the prayers of God's people?

Mark 11:27–33

As was his custom, Jesus fended off his adversaries with a counter question. They asked by what authority he could assail the temple system (vv. 15–17); he asked about John the Baptist's authority. Jesus aligned

himself with John, who had come preaching a baptism of repentance that bypassed temple ritual (see 1:4–5). By suspending judgment, these religious leaders managed to save face before the people, but at the same time they demonstrated their rejection of both John and Jesus as God's messengers.

Do you resent someone else's authority or popularity? Are some of your actions driven by fear of people rather than of God? Are you more interested in your status or position than in welcoming the changes God wants for your life? These are hard-hitting questions, but Jesus plays hardball with us—for *our* sakes! He wants nothing more than our honest assessment, followed up with appropriate action.

Mark 12:1–12

Jesus continued to respond to the Jewish leaders' challenge of his authority (11:27–33), bringing matters to a head. He had told his disciples the chief priests and teachers of the law would kill him (10:33). Now he informed the rulers themselves—in allegory form. They didn't need coaching to see that they were the target of his parable. Their understanding of its implications only heightened the enormity of their guilt. There is no question they moved ahead with their plot with premeditated malice.

ed him shamefully. [5] He sent still another, and that one they killed. He sent many others; some of them they beat, others they killed.

[6] "He had one left to send, a son, whom he loved. He sent him last of all, [q] saying, 'They will respect my son.'

[7] "But the tenants said to one another, 'This is the heir. Come, let's kill him, and the inheritance will be ours.' [8] So they took him and killed him, and threw him out of the vineyard.

[9] "What then will the owner of the vineyard do? He will come and kill those tenants and give the vineyard to others. [10] Haven't you read this scripture:

> " 'The stone the builders rejected
>   has become the capstone[a]; [r]
> [11] the Lord has done this,
>   and it is marvelous in our eyes'[b]?" [s]

[12] Then they looked for a way to arrest him because they knew he had spoken the parable against them. But they were afraid of the crowd; [t] so they left him and went away. [u]

Paying Taxes to Caesar

[13] Later they sent some of the Pharisees and Herodians [v] to Jesus to catch him [w] in his words. [14] They came to him and said, "Teacher, we know you are a man of integrity. You aren't swayed by men, because you pay no attention to who they are; but you teach the way of God in accordance with the truth. Is it right to pay taxes to Caesar or not? [15] Should we pay or shouldn't we?"

But Jesus knew their hypocrisy. "Why are you trying to trap me?" he asked. "Bring me a denarius and let me look at it." [16] They brought the coin, and he asked them, "Whose portrait is this? And whose inscription?"

"Caesar's," they replied.

[17] Then Jesus said to them, "Give to Caesar what is Caesar's and to God what is God's." [x]

And they were amazed at him.

Marriage at the Resurrection

[18] Then the Sadducees, [y] who say there is no resurrection, [z] came to him with a question. [19] "Teacher," they said, "Moses wrote for us that if a man's brother dies and leaves a wife but no children, the man must marry the widow and have children for his brother. [a] [20] Now there were seven brothers. The first one married and

---

[a] 10 Or cornerstone   [b] 11 Psalm 118:22,23

Side references:

12:6
[q] Heb 1:1-3

12:10
[r] Ac 4:11

12:11
[s] Ps 118:22,23

12:12
[t] Mk 11:18
[u] Mt 22:22

12:13
[v] Mt 22:16; Mk 3:6
[w] Mt 12:10

12:17
[x] Ro 13:7

12:18
[y] Ac 4:1 [z] Ac 23:8;
1Co 15:12

12:19
[a] Dt 25:5

The world of the wicked tenants was a lot like ours—riddled with meaningless violence, rife with broken contracts, acknowledging no sense of right or wrong. God may at times seem like an absentee landlord—a foolish one at that. People "get away with" injustice, oppression, and murder, and God's messengers continue to be persecuted. All is not as it seems, though. God is gracious, but his patience won't last forever. We can move ahead in our Christian service with confidence, certain he will win even when it seems he's already lost.

Mark 12:13–17

Jesus' interrogators baited their trap by asking a yes or no question about an explosive issue—paying taxes to the occupying Romans. Since his critics produced the coin, Jesus exposed that they had no qualms about bringing an image of Caesar (and his pretension to deity) into God's temple. "Give to Caesar what is Caesar's and to God what is God's" didn't mean Caesar had control of the political sphere and God of the religious. The

coin was Caesar's idol—and he could have it back!

How do you fulfill your responsibility to God *and* government? Taxes are a trivial matter compared to our debt to God. As Jesus would point out in the next passage, we owe God the love of our heart, soul, mind, and strength, as well as a genuine, loving concern for our fellow human beings (vv. 29–31). We may owe Caesar a percentage of our money, but we who bear God's image owe God everything we have and all we are.

Mark 12:18-27

The Sadducees considered only the Pentateuch (first five books of the Bible) to be Scripture and didn't believe in resurrection since the Pentateuch doesn't mention it. They tried to lure Jesus with a teasing challenge based on a technicality: the law of levirate (priestly) marriage. Jesus told them what *not* to expect in heaven, offering no frame of reference for what life after death *will* be like. He corrected them on two counts—their view of the resurrection and their Biblical ignorance.

died without leaving any children. 21The second one married the widow, but he also died, leaving no child. It was the same with the third. 22In fact, none of the seven left any children. Last of all, the woman died too. 23At the resurrection a whose wife will she be, since the seven were married to her?"

24Jesus replied, "Are you not in error because you do not know the Scriptures b or the power of God? 25When the dead rise, they will neither marry nor be given in marriage; they will be like the angels in heaven. c 26Now about the dead rising—have you not read in the book of Moses, in the account of the bush, how God said to him, 'I am the God of Abraham, the God of Isaac, and the God of Jacob'b? d 27He is not the God of the dead, but of the living. You are badly mistaken!"

The Greatest Commandment

28One of the teachers of the law e came and heard them debating. Noticing that Jesus had given them a good answer, he asked him, "Of all the commandments, which is the most important?"

29"The most important one," answered Jesus, "is this: 'Hear, O Israel, the Lord our God, the Lord is one. c 30Love the Lord your God with all your heart and with all your soul and with all your mind and with all your strength.' d f 31The second is this: 'Love your neighbor as yourself.' e g There is no commandment greater than these."

32"Well said, teacher," the man replied. "You are right in saying that God is one and there is no other but him. h 33To love him with all your heart, with all your understanding and with all your strength, and to love your neighbor as yourself is more important than all burnt offerings and sacrifices." i

34When Jesus saw that he had answered wisely, he said to him, "You are not far from the kingdom of God." j And from then on no one dared ask him any more questions. k

Whose Son Is the Christ?

35While Jesus was teaching in the temple courts, l he asked, "How is it that the teachers of the law say that the Christ f is the son of David? m 36David himself, speaking by the Holy Spirit, n declared:

" 'The Lord said to my Lord:
"Sit at my right hand

a 23 Some manuscripts resurrection, when men rise from the dead,   b 26 Exodus 3:6   c 29 Or the Lord our God is one Lord   d 30 Deut. 6:4,5   e 31 Lev. 19:18   f 35 Or Messiah

Cross-references: 12:24 b 2Ti 3:15-17; 12:25 c 1Co 15:42,49,52; 12:26 d Ex 3:6; 12:28 e Lk 10:25-28; 20:39; 12:30 f Dt 6:4,5; 12:31 g Lev 19:18; Mt 5:43; 12:32 h Dt 4:35,39; Isa 45:6,14; 46:9; 12:33 i 1Sa 15:22; Hos 6:6; Mic 6:6-8; Heb 10:8; 12:34 j Mt 3:2 k Mt 22:46; Lk 20:40; 12:35 l Mt 26:55 m Mt 9:27; 12:36 n 2Sa 23:2

How do you envision heaven? One danger in trying to picture resurrection life is that our image often matches our wishes for an earthly paradise—with human beings at the center. Rather than expending effort trying to imagine heavenly life, why not commit yourself to a close tie now to your heavenly Father, who keeps his promises? When the resurrection comes, you will see and glorify the God who gave you life—and who at that moment will show you its unimaginable finale: fullness of life in him.

Mark 12:28–34

Jesus' statement that no other command is greater than these two could mean the others simply spell out different ways to apply these overarching principles. Or the implication may be more radical: These are the only two commands that really matter. Paul reflected this same radical understanding in Romans 13:8: "He who loves his fellowman [other people] has fulfilled the law."

Our love for God and neighbor is the only fitting response to God's love for us. He doesn't love only certain parts of us, so we are to love him with our whole selves. But if we don't show love to others, we can hardly claim to love God (see 1 Jn. 4:19–21). This is one of those challenges from Jesus that is both simple and comprehensive. With God, it's all or nothing. Do you find yourself in "full compliance"—or trying to straddle the fence? How do you demonstrate your love to God and to people?

Mark 12:35–40

Jesus pointed out the faulty understanding of the teachers of the law regarding the Messiah. Then he denounced them as a group: (1) They wore special clothing to set themselves apart from others and boost their authority. (2) They basked in the esteem of those of lesser status. (3) They used their position to prey on the weak and vulnerable ("Devouring widows' houses" probably refers to mismanagement of their estates). (4) Instead of being humbly directed to God, their prayers were spoken to impress those listening.

until I put your enemies
   under your feet.' ' ^a ^o

12:36
o Ps 110:1;
Mt 22:44

³⁷David himself calls him 'Lord.' How then can he be his son?"
The large crowd^p listened to him with delight.

12:37
p Jn 12:9

³⁸As he taught, Jesus said, "Watch out for the teachers of the law. They like to walk around in flowing robes and be greeted in the marketplaces, ³⁹and have the most important seats in the synagogues and the places of honor at banquets. ^q ⁴⁰They devour widows' houses and for a show make lengthy prayers. Such men will be punished most severely."

12:39
q Lk 11:43

The Widow's Offering

⁴¹Jesus sat down opposite the place where the offerings were put^r and watched the crowd putting their money into the temple treasury. Many rich people threw in large amounts. ⁴²But a poor widow came and put in two very small copper coins,^b worth only a fraction of a penny.^c

12:41
r 2Ki 12:9; Jn 8:20

⁴³Calling his disciples to him, Jesus said, "I tell you the truth, this poor widow has put more into the treasury than all the others. ⁴⁴They all gave out of their wealth; but she, out of her poverty, put in everything—all she had to live on." ^s

12:44
s 2Co 8:12

^a 36 Psalm 110:1   ^b 42 Greek *two lepta*   ^c 42 Greek *kodrantes*

Loving others (v. 31) doesn't mean never confronting them with their errors. After all, Jesus didn't shy away from opposing the powerful religious establishment, zeroing in on their dress-for-success mentality, pompous religiosity, and callous disregard for the poor. How comfortable are you at rebuking another believer (Luke 17:3)? Would Jesus identify similar flaws in your life (Matt. 7:1–5)? How do you weave Paul's direction in 1 Timothy 5:1 and Titus 2:15 into the mix?

Mark 12:41–44

Jesus situated himself opposite the temple treasury, where there were 13 trumpet-shaped offering boxes. He disregarded the wealthy donors who threw in large sums, accompanied by loud clangs. Instead, he singled out a poor widow whose offering made only a tiny clink. While the religious leaders may have preferred the big gifts, in the divine currency exchange these can swiftly deflate to nothing. The rich gave from their abundance, but they didn't sacrifice their abundance. The woman, by contrast, gave God her entire heart, soul, and substance.

We can draw at least three principles from the widow's example: (1) Jesus praises those who give because they seek *God*—not benefits from God. (2) So-called little gifts may outshine those of substantially greater monetary value. (3) Assuming the rich were offering God their tithes, this incident revealed a continuing problem with an attitude about tithing. Does your focus tend to be on how much you give, or on how much you keep—and how you spend it?

12:38–42

The Dangers of Professional Religious Service

In this passage Jesus summed up the dangers that lurk for professional and "career" Christians—for those who formally spend their lives serving in the church or in a ministry. At its best, this calling is one of the most satisfying and fulfilling ways to serve God. In the worst case scenario, though, such leaders may give in to the pitfalls of:

Pride: walking "around in flowing robes" (v. 38)	Respect or recognition: being "greeted in the marketplaces" (v. 38)	Power: having "the most important seats in the synagogues and the places of honor at banquets" (v. 39)	Greed: "Devour(ing) widows' houses" (v. 40)	Phoniness: "for a show mak[ing] lengthy prayers" (v. 40)

Religious leaders risk an extra measure of punishment (v. 40) if they succumb to these enticements. As with all temptations, though, God offers us the grace to resist.

Signs of the End of the Age

13 As he was leaving the temple, one of his disciples said to him, "Look, Teacher! What massive stones! What magnificent buildings!"

2 "Do you see all these great buildings?" replied Jesus. "Not one stone here will be left on another; every one will be thrown down." [t]

3 As Jesus was sitting on the Mount of Olives [u] opposite the temple, Peter, James, John [v] and Andrew asked him privately, 4 "Tell us, when will these things happen? And what will be the sign that they are all about to be fulfilled?"

5 Jesus said to them: "Watch out that no one deceives you. [w] 6 Many will come in my name, claiming, 'I am he,' and will deceive many. 7 When you hear of wars and rumors of wars, do not be alarmed. Such things must happen, but the end is still to come. 8 Nation will rise against nation, and kingdom against kingdom. There will be earthquakes in various places, and famines. These are the beginning of birth pains.

9 "You must be on your guard. You will be handed over to the local councils and flogged in the synagogues. [x] On account of me you will stand before governors and kings as witnesses to them. 10 And the gospel must first be preached to all nations. 11 Whenever you are arrested and brought to trial, do not worry beforehand about what to say. Just say whatever is given you at the time, for it is not you speaking, but the Holy Spirit. [y]

12 "Brother will betray brother to death, and a father his child. Children will rebel against their parents and have them put to death. [z] 13 All men will hate you because of me, [a] but he who stands firm to the end will be saved. [b] 14 "When you see 'the abomination that causes desolation' [a c] standing where it [b] does not belong—let the reader understand—then let those who are in Judea flee to the mountains. 15 Let no one on the roof of his house go down or enter the house to take anything out. 16 Let no one in the field go back to get his cloak. 17 How dreadful it will be in those days for pregnant women and nursing mothers! [d] 18 Pray that this will not take place in winter, 19 because those will be days of distress unequaled from the beginning, when God created the world, [e] until now—and never to be equaled again. [f] 20 If the Lord had not cut short those days, no one would survive. But for the sake of the elect, whom he has chosen, he has shortened them. 21 At that time if anyone says to you, 'Look, here is the Christ [c]!' or, 'Look, there he is!' do not believe it. [g] 22 For false Christs and false prophets [h] will appear and perform signs and miracles [i] to deceive the elect—if that were possible. 23 So be on your guard; [j] I have told you everything ahead of time.

24 "But in those days, following that distress,

" 'the sun will be darkened,
    and the moon will not give its light;
25 the stars will fall from the sky,
    and the heavenly bodies will be shaken.' [d k]

26 "At that time men will see the Son of Man coming in clouds [l] with great pow-

Cross references (margin)

13:2 t Lk 19:44
13:3 u Mt 21:1 v Mt 4:21
13:5 w ver 22; Jer 29:8; Eph 5:6; 2Th 2:3, 10-12; 1Ti 4:1; 2Ti 3:13; 1Jn 4:6
13:9 x Mt 10:17
13:11 y Mt 10:19,20; Lk 12:11,12
13:12 z Mic 7:6; Mt 10:21; Lk 12:51-53
13:13 a Jn 15:21 b Mt 10:22
13:14 c Da 9:27; 11:31; 12:11
13:17 d Lk 23:29
13:19 e Mk 10:6 f Da 9:26; 12:1; Joel 2:2
13:21 g Lk 17:23; 21:8
13:22 h Mt 7:15 i Jn 4:48; 2Th 2:9,10
13:23 j 2Pe 3:17
13:25 k Isa 13:10; 34:4; Mt 24:29
13:26 l Da 7:13; Mt 16:27; Rev 1:7

---

a 14 Daniel 9:27; 11:31; 12:11   b 14 Or he; also in verse 29   c 21 Or Messiah
d 25 Isaiah 13:10; 34:4

Mark 13:1–31

Tension had been building from Jesus' confrontations with his opponents in the temple. Now the hostile examiners retreated into the background, and Jesus left the temple, never to return. As he departed, he predicted its destruction. Then, just prior to his own suffering, he forecast that of his disciples—linking the two. *But Jesus confidently assured them that ultimate victory would fall hard on the heels of great tragedy and a full measure of suffering. Even though torn apart by tribulation, the saints will one day be re-gathered by God.*

Jesus' words help us understand what it means to be a persecuted Christian. In each generation, there will be Christians who undergo severe trials. Jesus declared that the advancement of God's kingdom and the suffering of his people are mysteriously bound together. Those of us who want to be heirs to God's glory, gathered with all believers, have to be ready to embrace the affliction that comes first. Are you prepared? Are you already experiencing hardship related to your commitment to Christ?

er and glory. 27And he will send his angels and gather his elect from the four winds, from the ends of the earth to the ends of the heavens. *m*

28"Now learn this lesson from the fig tree: As soon as its twigs get tender and its leaves come out, you know that summer is near. 29Even so, when you see these things happening, you know that it is near, right at the door. 30I tell you the truth, this generation *a n* will certainly not pass away until all these things have happened. *o* 31Heaven and earth will pass away, but my words will never pass away. *p*

The Day and Hour Unknown

32"No one knows about that day or hour, not even the angels in heaven, nor the Son, but only the Father. *q* 33Be on guard! Be alert *b*! *r* You do not know when that time will come. 34It's like a man going away: He leaves his house and puts his servants *s* in charge, each with his assigned task, and tells the one at the door to keep watch.

35"Therefore keep watch because you do not know when the owner of the house will come back—whether in the evening, or at midnight, or when the rooster crows, or at dawn. 36If he comes suddenly, do not let him find you sleeping. 37What I say to you, I say to everyone: 'Watch!' " *t*

Jesus Anointed at Bethany

14 Now the Passover *u* and the Feast of Unleavened Bread were only two days away, and the chief priests and the teachers of the law were looking for some sly way to arrest Jesus and kill him. *v* 2"But not during the Feast," they said, "or the people may riot."

3While he was in Bethany, *w* reclining at the table in the home of a man known as Simon the Leper, a woman came with an alabaster jar of very expensive perfume, made of pure nard. She broke the jar and poured the perfume on his head. *x*

4Some of those present were saying indignantly to one another, "Why this waste of perfume? 5It could have been sold for more than a year's wages *c* and the money given to the poor." And they rebuked her harshly.

6"Leave her alone," said Jesus. "Why are you bothering her? She has done a beautiful thing to me. 7The poor you will always have with you, and you can help them any time you want. *y* But you will not always have me. 8She did what she could. She poured perfume on my body beforehand to prepare for my burial. *z* 9I tell you the truth, wherever the gospel is preached throughout the world, *a* what she has done will also be told, in memory of her."

13:27
m Zec 2:6

13:30
n Lk 17:25 *o* Mk 9:1
13:31
p Mt 5:18

13:32
q Ac 1:7; 1Th 5:1,2
13:33
r 1Th 5:6
13:34
s Mt 25:14

13:37
t Lk 12:35-40

14:1
u Jn 11:55; 13:1
v Mt 12:14

14:3
w Mt 21:17
x Lk 7:37-39

14:7
y Dt 15:11
14:8
z Jn 19:40
14:9
a Mt 24:14;
Mk 16:15

---

a 30 Or *race*   *b* 33 Some manuscripts *alert and pray*   *c* 5 Greek *than three hundred denarii*

Mark 13:32–37

Jesus stated that the time of the end is hidden. That information is so classified that only God the Father is privy to it (see Acts 1:7). Key to the parable of the doorkeeper is that the servants had no advance knowledge of when the master would return. Servants must endure the tests of absence and uncertainty. What kind of servant requires a master to look constantly over his shoulder to make sure the job is done faithfully and properly?

The end will come suddenly, both for believers and unbelievers. God has given us plenty of instruction on how to live as disciples in this world but doesn't deem it vital for us to know exactly what will happen before the end comes. As disciples, our primary task is to share the Good News of the kingdom by loving God with our whole lives and others as ourselves. When Christ returns, he won't quiz us to see whose date predictions were closest. He will want to know what we have done to manifest God's love for people and to live the life of discipleship.

Mark 14:1–11

This woman's act of extraordinary adoration at the house of Simon the leper stands in sharp contrast to the hatred of the chief priests and teachers of the law and to Judas's treachery. A similar anointing scene is found in Luke 7:36–40 at the house of Simon the Pharisee. Ancient custom suggests that Jesus should have been anointed more than once as a guest. The woman lovingly sacrificed her precious gift, equaling a year's wages. She held back nothing in pouring out her life in love for Jesus.

This story calls us to reflect on the proper focus of our generosity. All our giving is to be an expression of love for Jesus. How do we most effectively show this love? This woman's action was good, said Jesus, because she was anointing him for his burial. Now, since he's died and risen, it may be more fitting for us to direct some of our gifts to mission service and to the poor. As we offer to them, we give to our Savior (see Matt. 25:40).

14:10
b Mk 3:16-19
c Mt 10:4

10Then Judas Iscariot, one of the Twelve, *b* went to the chief priests to betray Jesus to them. *c* 11They were delighted to hear this and promised to give him money. So he watched for an opportunity to hand him over.

The Lord's Supper

14:12
d Ex 12:1-11;
Dt 16:1-4; 1Co 5:7

12On the first day of the Feast of Unleavened Bread, when it was customary to sacrifice the Passover lamb, *d* Jesus' disciples asked him, "Where do you want us to go and make preparations for you to eat the Passover?"

13So he sent two of his disciples, telling them, "Go into the city, and a man carrying a jar of water will meet you. Follow him. 14Say to the owner of the house he enters, 'The Teacher asks: Where is my guest room, where I may eat the Passover with my disciples?' 15He will show you a large upper room, *e* furnished and ready.

14:15
e Ac 1:13

Make preparations for us there."

16The disciples left, went into the city and found things just as Jesus had told them. So they prepared the Passover.

17When evening came, Jesus arrived with the Twelve. 18While they were reclining at the table eating, he said, "I tell you the truth, one of you will betray me—one who is eating with me."

19They were saddened, and one by one they said to him, "Surely not I?"

14:20
f Jn 13:18-27
14:21
g Mt 8:20
14:22
h Mt 14:19

20"It is one of the Twelve," he replied, "one who dips bread into the bowl with me. *f* 21The Son of Man *g* will go just as it is written about him. But woe to that man who betrays the Son of Man! It would be better for him if he had not been born."

22While they were eating, Jesus took bread, gave thanks and broke it, *h* and gave it to his disciples, saying, "Take it; this is my body."

14:23
i 1Co 10:16
14:24
j Mt 26:28
14:25
k Mt 3:2
14:26
l Mt 21:1

23Then he took the cup, gave thanks and offered it to them, and they all drank from it. *i*

24"This is my blood of the *a* covenant, *j* which is poured out for many," he said to them. 25"I tell you the truth, I will not drink again of the fruit of the vine until that day when I drink it anew in the kingdom of God." *k*

26When they had sung a hymn, they went out to the Mount of Olives. *l*

Jesus Predicts Peter's Denial

27"You will all fall away," Jesus told them, "for it is written:

14:27
m Zec 13:7

" 'I will strike the shepherd,
and the sheep will be scattered.' *b m*

a 24 Some manuscripts *the new*   *b* 27 Zech. 13:7

Mark 14:12–26

At Jewish meals, the head of the family would take bread to be eaten, lift it up, and praise God for his provision. After an Amen response, the bread would be broken, mediating the blessing to everyone who would partake. The same was true of the wine. By stating "This is my body," Jesus said in effect, "This is myself." To the people around the table, a person's body represented or encompassed the whole person. Mark was clear that all drank from one cup. Drinking the cup of someone meant entering into a communion relationship with that person, to the point of sharing his or her destiny, for good or ill.

The Lord's Supper works for good, but it's no magic ritual. It reminds us of who we are, what our story and values are, and who claims us as his own. It confronts our five physical senses: We see, hear, taste, smell, and touch what it meant for Christ to die for us. It also binds together the past, present, and future. We experience Jesus' death for us and the power of our sins being forgiven in the present. We also look forward to the future celebration in God's kingdom, when all will acknowledge Jesus as Lord. Next time you partake of the communion supper, reflect on these truths.

Mark 14:27–31

Jesus taught and lived with more authority than anyone else in history, but soon his small band of devotees would be thrown into confusion and flee in all directions. Just as Jesus was about to fully identify himself with us in our sin, his disciples were about to fully desert him. Peter disputed Jesus' words in a spirit of rivalry, insisting he would prove himself more trustworthy than the others.

Peter's problem was twofold: He was overly confident in his own commitment and excessively reliant on his own power. The other disciples were all too eager to follow his lead: They too would always be true to Jesus! How about you? Are you tempted to favorably compare your own spiritual faithfulness to someone else's commitment? Do you rely on your own strength to remain loyal to Jesus? Or are you prepared for a cross?

28But after I have risen, I will go ahead of you into Galilee."[n]
29Peter declared, "Even if all fall away, I will not."
30"I tell you the truth," Jesus answered, "today—yes, tonight—before the rooster crows twice[a] you yourself will disown me three times."[o]
31But Peter insisted emphatically, "Even if I have to die with you,[p] I will never disown you." And all the others said the same.

Gethsemane

32They went to a place called Gethsemane, and Jesus said to his disciples, "Sit here
while I pray." 33He took Peter, James and John[q] along with him, and he began to
be deeply distressed and troubled. 34"My soul is overwhelmed with sorrow to the
point of death,"[r] he said to them. "Stay here and keep watch."
35Going a little farther, he fell to the ground and prayed that if possible the
hour[s] might pass from him. 36"*Abba*,[b] Father,"[t] he said, "everything is possible for
you. Take this cup[u] from me. Yet not what I will, but what you will."[v]
37Then he returned to his disciples and found them sleeping. "Simon," he said
to Peter, "are you asleep? Could you not keep watch for one hour? 38Watch and pray
so that you will not fall into temptation.[w] The spirit is willing, but the body is
weak."[x]
39Once more he went away and prayed the same thing. 40When he came back,
he again found them sleeping, because their eyes were heavy. They did not know
what to say to him.
41Returning the third time, he said to them, "Are you still sleeping and resting?
Enough! The hour[y] has come. Look, the Son of Man is betrayed into the hands of
sinners. 42Rise! Let us go! Here comes my betrayer!"

Jesus Arrested

43Just as he was speaking, Judas,[z] one of the Twelve, appeared. With him was a

14:28 [n] Mk 16:7
14:30 [o] ver 66-72; Lk 22:34; Jn 13:38
14:31 [p] Lk 22:33; Jn 13:37
14:33 [q] Mt 4:21
14:34 [r] Jn 12:27
14:35 [s] ver 41; Mt 26:18
14:36 [t] Ro 8:15; Gal 4:6 [u] Mt 20:22 [v] Mt 26:39
14:38 [w] Mt 6:13 [x] Ro 7:22,23
14:41 [y] ver 35; Mt 26:18
14:43 [z] Mt 10:4

[a] *30* Some early manuscripts do not have *twice*. [b] *36* Aramaic for *Father*

Mark 14:32–42

As Jesus faced the dreadful prospect before him, he acknowledged his overpowering distress through prayer. In Gethsemane, though, Jesus encountered heaven's dreadful silence. There was no reassuring voice proclaiming, "You are my Son, whom I love" (1:11; 9:7). God had already spoken. Jesus overcame the silence, fought off the human temptation to do as *he* willed, and acquiesced to the Father's will. He wouldn't evade God's plan either by slipping away into the darkness or resorting to violence. He would accept "this cup"—nails driven through his flesh into a cross.

Can you imagine yourself agreeing willingly to be a sacrificial lamb? How would you approach the situation? Jesus had already handed himself over to death by his words and actions in the temple (Mark 11–12). This Scriptural glimpse shows us the transition between Jesus as "actor" to one waiting to be acted upon. Passivity following a life of involvement and the prospect of being at the mercy of others are hard things for many to accept. Jesus demonstrated that crying out to God to be spared these crosses is normal. For believers, prayer may be the *one* activity that best prepares us to face life's darkest moments.

14:32–42

Prayer in the Garden

Jesus' prayer for deliverance from crucifixion is one of many Scriptural examples of prayer. Some others:

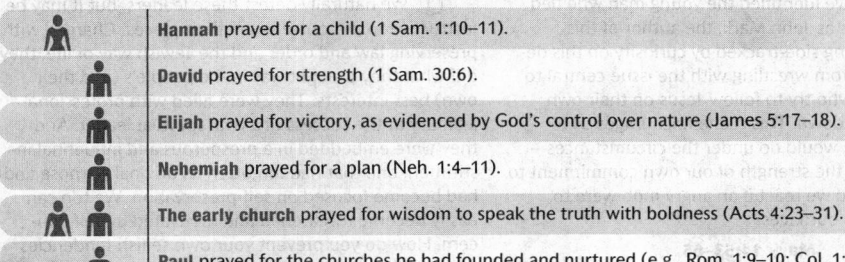

- **Hannah** prayed for a child (1 Sam. 1:10–11).
- **David** prayed for strength (1 Sam. 30:6).
- **Elijah** prayed for victory, as evidenced by God's control over nature (James 5:17–18).
- **Nehemiah** prayed for a plan (Neh. 1:4–11).
- **The early church** prayed for wisdom to speak the truth with boldness (Acts 4:23–31).
- **Paul** prayed for the churches he had founded and nurtured (e.g., Rom. 1:9–10; Col. 1:9).

crowd armed with swords and clubs, sent from the chief priests, the teachers of the law, and the elders.

⁴⁴Now the betrayer had arranged a signal with them: "The one I kiss is the man; arrest him and lead him away under guard." ⁴⁵Going at once to Jesus, Judas said, "Rabbi!" ^a and kissed him. ⁴⁶The men seized Jesus and arrested him. ⁴⁷Then one of those standing near drew his sword and struck the servant of the high priest, cutting off his ear.

⁴⁸"Am I leading a rebellion," said Jesus, "that you have come out with swords and clubs to capture me? ⁴⁹Every day I was with you, teaching in the temple courts, ^b and you did not arrest me. But the Scriptures must be fulfilled." ^c ⁵⁰Then everyone deserted him and fled. ^d

⁵¹A young man, wearing nothing but a linen garment, was following Jesus. When they seized him, ⁵²he fled naked, leaving his garment behind.

Before the Sanhedrin

⁵³They took Jesus to the high priest, and all the chief priests, elders and teachers of the law came together. ⁵⁴Peter followed him at a distance, right into the courtyard of the high priest. ^e There he sat with the guards and warmed himself at the fire. ^f

⁵⁵The chief priests and the whole Sanhedrin ^g were looking for evidence against Jesus so that they could put him to death, but they did not find any. ⁵⁶Many testified falsely against him, but their statements did not agree.

⁵⁷Then some stood up and gave this false testimony against him: ⁵⁸"We heard him say, 'I will destroy this man-made temple and in three days will build another, ^h not made by man.' " ⁵⁹Yet even then their testimony did not agree.

⁶⁰Then the high priest stood up before them and asked Jesus, "Are you not going to answer? What is this testimony that these men are bringing against you?" ⁶¹But Jesus remained silent and gave no answer. ⁱ

Again the high priest asked him, "Are you the Christ, ^a the Son of the Blessed One?" ^j

⁶²"I am," said Jesus. "And you will see the Son of Man sitting at the right hand of the Mighty One and coming on the clouds of heaven." ^k

⁶³The high priest tore his clothes. ^l "Why do we need any more witnesses?" he asked. ⁶⁴"You have heard the blasphemy. What do you think?"

^a 61 Or Messiah

Mark 14:43–52

The sorry performance of Jesus' disciples—particularly Judas—in this crucial moment dominates the scene of his arrest. A kiss reflecting mutual trust and affection is still common in the Near East, corresponding to the handshake of the Western world (see Luke 7:45). Rabbis were customarily greeted by their disciples with a kiss. Judas gave Jesus no sign that their fellowship had been broken. He turned him over to certain execution with a warm gesture of love, turning a sign of intimacy and goodwill into one of betrayal and death.

Many have identified the young man who fled into the darkness as John Mark, the author of this Gospel. But getting side-tracked by curiosity on this detail prevents us from wrestling with the issue central to Mark: Disciples who try to follow Jesus on their own steam will break down. This scene encourages us to imagine what we would do under the circumstances—and to reflect on the strength of our own commitment to Jesus. How would we react if an angry mob were to wave weapons in our faces?

Mark 14:53–65

The two charges that emerged from this hearing had to do with the temple and the Messiah. They would resurface as taunts at the cross: (1) "So! You who are going to destroy the temple and build it in three days, come down from the cross and save yourself!" (15:29–30) and (2) "Let this Christ, this King of Israel, come down now from the cross, that we may see and believe" (15:32). Two events occurred at Jesus' death that paralleled these taunts: (1) The temple veil was torn from top to bottom (15:38), and (2) a Roman centurion confessed, "Surely this man was the Son of God!" (15:39).

We naturally detest these leaders, but it may be instructive to put ourselves in their places. Charged with preserving law and order and the Jewish way of life, they did what they thought was in the people's (and their own) best interests. They were filled with professional jealousy at the success of a rival spiritual leader. And they were embedded in a prosperous and influential institution, one that had forgotten its original purpose and had become focused on self-preservation. We too can easily become threatened and motivated by self-concern. How do you prevent your own selfish tendencies from leading you down a path to spiritual disaster?

They all condemned him as worthy of death. [m] [65] Then some began to spit at him; they blindfolded him, struck him with their fists, and said, "Prophesy!" And the guards took him and beat him. [n]

Peter Disowns Jesus

[66] While Peter was below in the courtyard, [o] one of the servant girls of the high priest came by. [67] When she saw Peter warming himself, [p] she looked closely at him.

"You also were with that Nazarene, Jesus," [q] she said.

[68] But he denied it. "I don't know or understand what you're talking about," [r] he said, and went out into the entryway. [a]

[69] When the servant girl saw him there, she said again to those standing around, "This fellow is one of them." [70] Again he denied it. [s]

After a little while, those standing near said to Peter, "Surely you are one of them, for you are a Galilean." [t]

[71] He began to call down curses on himself, and he swore to them, "I don't know this man you're talking about." [u]

[72] Immediately the rooster crowed the second time. [b] Then Peter remembered the word Jesus had spoken to him: "Before the rooster crows twice [c] you will disown me three times." [v] And he broke down and wept.

Jesus Before Pilate

15 Very early in the morning, the chief priests, with the elders, the teachers of the law [w] and the whole Sanhedrin, [x] reached a decision. They bound Jesus, led him away and handed him over to Pilate. [y]

[2] "Are you the king of the Jews?" [z] asked Pilate.

"Yes, it is as you say," Jesus replied.

[3] The chief priests accused him of many things. [4] So again Pilate asked him, "Aren't you going to answer? See how many things they are accusing you of."

[5] But Jesus still made no reply, [a] and Pilate was amazed.

[6] Now it was the custom at the Feast to release a prisoner whom the people requested. [7] A man called Barabbas was in prison with the insurrectionists who had

---

14:64 [m] Lev 24:16
14:65 [n] Mt 16:21

14:66 [o] ver 54
14:67 [p] ver 54 [q] Mk 1:24

14:68 [r] ver 30,72

14:70 [s] ver 30,68,72 [t] Ac 2:7

14:71 [u] ver 30,72

14:72 [v] ver 30,68

15:1 [w] Mt 27:1; Lk 22:66 [x] Mt 5:22 [y] Mt 27:2

15:2 [z] ver 9,12,18,26; Mt 2:2

15:5 [a] Mk 14:61

---

[a] 68 Some early manuscripts *entryway and the rooster crowed*   [b] 72 Some early manuscripts do not have *the second time.*   [c] 72 Some early manuscripts do not have *twice.*

Mark 14:66–72

Peter's courtyard trial took place just as his Lord's was happening inside. While Jesus was under fire within, Peter warmed himself by the fire outside (vv. 54,67). Jesus, under immense pressure and hostility that would seal his fate (vv. 61–62), readily confessed to his identity as the Messiah. Peter caved in under mild pressure and lied to save himself. The rooster was the perfect image of Peter's cocky boastfulness in verse 29. Yet its crowing snapped Peter into awareness of what he had just done.

We never know when our faith or allegiance might be tested. It's conceivable, though improbable, that we too might get burned by a fiery ordeal as we warm ourselves by an inviting fire. Few of us today are forced to choose between Christ and imprisonment or execution. Our denials of Christ take more subtle forms—like timid silence. Maybe we don't speak up when others sarcastically dismiss the Christian faith. Or we try to blend into the crowd of our Master's enemies, not wanting to be singled out as different or rock any boats. But this scene challenges us to stand out from others—by standing up for our Lord. The men in this situation all deserted Jesus. Only the women who followed

him accompanied him to the cross (see 15:40).

Mark 15:1–15

A Roman governor wouldn't have put a Jew on trial for his life simply on a charge of religious blasphemy (see 14:61–64). Thus, the chief priests presented the accusations against Jesus in a way Pilate would have to take seriously. If Jesus claimed to be a king, he would be guilty of a crime against Rome. Jesus' silence amazed Pilate, but he couldn't release someone who refused to deny such a serious allegation. Jesus fittingly left it to God to provide the answers, both to the charges and to the evil amassed against him.

Many people today are like Pilate. They prefer Jesus to the envious, malicious chief priests and the violent Barabbas. But that is as far as it goes. They see no harm in Jesus, but they see nothing else either—including a reason to risk anything for him. Two crucial things we can do on their behalf are: (1) to seek to demonstrate by our words and actions the impact Christ has had on our lives and (2) to pray for a breakthrough in their understanding—to help them realize that Jesus isn't simply "the king of the Jews" (v. 9) but the "King of kings" (Rev. 17:14; 19:16) and Lord of all!

committed murder in the uprising. [8]The crowd came up and asked Pilate to do for them what he usually did.

15:9
b ver 2

[9]"Do you want me to release to you the king of the Jews?"[b] asked Pilate, [10]knowing it was out of envy that the chief priests had handed Jesus over to him. [11]But the chief priests stirred up the crowd to have Pilate release Barabbas[c] instead.

15:11
c Ac 3:14

[12]"What shall I do, then, with the one you call the king of the Jews?" Pilate asked them.

[13]"Crucify him!" they shouted.

[14]"Why? What crime has he committed?" asked Pilate.

But they shouted all the louder, "Crucify him!"

[15]Wanting to satisfy the crowd, Pilate released Barabbas to them. He had Jesus flogged,[d] and handed him over to be crucified.

15:15
d Isa 53:6

The Soldiers Mock Jesus

15:16
e Jn 18:28,33; 19:9

[16]The soldiers led Jesus away into the palace[e] (that is, the Praetorium) and called together the whole company of soldiers. [17]They put a purple robe on him, then twisted together a crown of thorns and set it on him. [18]And they began to call out to him, "Hail, king of the Jews!"[f] [19]Again and again they struck him on the head with a staff and spit on him. Falling on their knees, they paid homage to him. [20]And when they had mocked him, they took off the purple robe and put his own clothes on him. Then they led him out[g] to crucify him.

15:18
f ver 2

15:20
g Heb 13:12

The Crucifixion

15:21
h Mt 27:32
i Ro 16:13
j Mt 27:32; Lk 23:26

[21]A certain man from Cyrene,[h] Simon, the father of Alexander and Rufus,[i] was passing by on his way in from the country, and they forced him to carry the cross.[j] [22]They brought Jesus to the place called Golgotha (which means The Place of the Skull). [23]Then they offered him wine mixed with myrrh,[k] but he did not take it. [24]And they crucified him. Dividing up his clothes, they cast lots[l] to see what each would get.

15:23
k ver 36; Ps 69:21;
Pr 31:6
15:24
l Ps 22:18

[25]It was the third hour when they crucified him. [26]The written notice of the charge against him read: THE KING OF THE JEWS.[m] [27]They crucified two robbers with him, one on his right and one on his left.[a] [29]Those who passed by hurled insults

15:26
m ver 2

a 27 Some manuscripts left, [28]and the scripture was fulfilled which says, "He was counted with the lawless ones" (Isaiah 53:12)

Mark 15:16–20

Jesus' Jewish captors despised him as a false messiah, and now a whole company of Roman soldiers mocked him as a false king. Their ridicule probably expressed as much contempt for the Jews, who had no official king, as for Jesus. Their mockery implied that this pitiful, weak figure was exactly the king the Jews deserved. These soldiers unknowingly, though, stumbled onto the truth. Here indeed was the King before whom every knee will bow, the One every tongue will one day confess (Phil. 2:10–11).

Mark's Passion account (summary of Jesus' final week) represents a dramatic turnabout from Jesus' earlier ministry style—a new passivity. Jesus no longer initiated the action but had become the object of others' actions (the subject of only 9 verbs but the object of 56). He was stolidly silent, answering nothing, taking nothing—except the lashes to his back, the blows to his head, and the spit on his face. We can learn from Jesus how to endure insult and suffering with grace, trusting in God to eventually vindicate us. When has your silence or inactivity been an effective form of witness?

Mark 15:21–32

The account of Jesus' crucifixion is filled with irony. (1) Jesus, who had resisted all political overtones during his ministry, was executed as a political messiah—"The king of the Jews." (2) Jesus had spent his life in the company of sinners; now he died flanked by two of them. (3) Scoffers spouted their scorn, inadvertently proclaiming the truth: His death did destroy the temple made with hands but built a new one without hands, and he saved others by refusing to save himself. (4) Traditional symbols had been reversed: Weakness signified power, and death had become the means of life.

The cross was the point at which the blind rage of hell and humanity against God was unleashed with a horrible intensity, with both the religious and irreligious inflicting their wounds on the heart of God. The question of the old spiritual, "Were you there when they crucified my Lord?" can only be answered "Yes." The gospel story identifies the sins of Jesus' accusers that put him on this cross: pride, envy, jealousy, betrayal, cruelty, greed, indifference, cowardice, and murder. Ours, too, are added to that infamous list (see John 1:29).

at him, shaking their heads[n] and saying, "So! You who are going to destroy the temple and build it in three days, [o] 30come down from the cross and save yourself!"

31In the same way the chief priests and the teachers of the law mocked him[p] among themselves. "He saved others," they said, "but he can't save himself! 32Let this Christ,[a][q] this King of Israel,[r] come down now from the cross, that we may see and believe." Those crucified with him also heaped insults on him.

The Death of Jesus

33At the sixth hour darkness came over the whole land until the ninth hour.[s] 34And at the ninth hour Jesus cried out in a loud voice, *"Eloi, Eloi, lama sabachthani?"*—which means, "My God, my God, why have you forsaken me?"[b][t]

35When some of those standing near heard this, they said, "Listen, he's calling Elijah."

36One man ran, filled a sponge with wine vinegar,[u] put it on a stick, and offered it to Jesus to drink. "Now leave him alone. Let's see if Elijah comes to take him down," he said.

37With a loud cry, Jesus breathed his last.[v]

38The curtain of the temple was torn in two from top to bottom.[w] 39And when the centurion,[x] who stood there in front of Jesus, heard his cry and[c] saw how he died, he said, "Surely this man was the Son[d] of God!"[y]

40Some women were watching from a distance.[z] Among them were Mary Magdalene, Mary the mother of James the younger and of Joses, and Salome.[a] 41In Galilee these women had followed him and cared for his needs. Many other women who had come up with him to Jerusalem were also there.[b]

The Burial of Jesus

42It was Preparation Day (that is, the day before the Sabbath).[c] So as evening approached, 43Joseph of Arimathea, a prominent member of the Council,[d] who was himself waiting for the kingdom of God,[e] went boldly to Pilate and asked for Jesus' body. 44Pilate was surprised to hear that he was already dead. Summoning the centurion, he asked him if Jesus had already died. 45When he learned from the

---

a 32 Or *Messiah*   b 34 Psalm 22:1   c 39 Some manuscripts do not have *heard his cry and*
d 39 Or *a son*

Side references:

15:29
n Ps 22:7; 109:25
o Mk 14:58; Jn 2:19
15:31
p Ps 22:7

15:32
q Mk 14:61 r ver 2

15:33
s Am 8:9

15:34
t Ps 22:1

15:36
u ver 23; Ps 69:21

15:37
v Jn 19:30
15:38
w Heb 10:19,20
15:39
x ver 45
y Mk 1:1,11; 9:7;
Mt 4:3
15:40
z Ps 38:11
a Mk 16:1;
Lk 24:10; Jn 19:25
15:41
b Mt 27:55,56;
Lk 8:2,3

15:42
c Mt 27:62;
Jn 19:31
15:43
d Mt 5:22 e Mt 3:2;
Lk 2:25,38

Mark 15:33–41

When Jesus died so ignominiously, the religious leaders no doubt felt confirmed in their prejudice that God hadn't sent him. Surely God would never have allowed the Messiah, David's ultimate successor and Israel's hope, to die this way. The confession from the leader of the Roman soldiers, therefore, came as a shock. This Gentile officer's awed statement meant that Jesus' full identity was inseparably linked to his death. It marked the beginning of the fulfillment of Psalm 22:27: "All the families of the nations will bow down before him."

Jesus' forsaken cry from the cross, a quotation from Psalm 22:1, recalled an Old Testament "lament." Such prayers called out to God in distress and presented a frank complaint against him. Yet they concluded with thanksgiving and confidence that God had heard. No one can go through life and not feel isolated at times from God and others. But we may feel free at any time to express our true emotions to him, particularly our frustration and anger. Jesus' cry on the cross revealed a faith that wouldn't let go of God, even when deluged by the greatest suffering.

Mark 15:42–47

Joseph of Arimathea was a member of the Sanhedrin, which condemned Jesus to death. Now he surprisingly took the initiative in securing Jesus' body for burial. The fact that he was the third exceptional character to emerge from the enemy camp reminds us to guard against pigeonholing people based on their past allegiances. First came the teacher of the law Jesus commended as not being far from the kingdom of God (12:28–34). Then the centurion who confessed Jesus as the Son of God (15:39). And now Joseph, who courageously asked for Jesus' body and buried it at his own expense.

A faithful group of women stood with Jesus at the end (v. 40). And now at least two of them witnessed his burial. Mark commended their past service (v. 41). In fact, the only ones Mark cited as caring for Jesus' needs during his lifetime were angels (1:13), Peter's mother-in-law (1:31), and these women—who would, in the next passage, also attempt to serve him in death. Though the church has at times denied women positions of leadership, the Gospels remind us that they are often among the most faithful followers of Christ. The question gnawing at our hearts is how we would have responded, given the same opportunity. Are you ministering *to Jesus now* by serving "the least of these" (Matt. 25:40)?

15:45
f ver 39
15:46
g Mk 16:3
15:47
h ver 40

centurion *f* that it was so, he gave the body to Joseph. ⁴⁶So Joseph bought some linen cloth, took down the body, wrapped it in the linen, and placed it in a tomb cut out of rock. Then he rolled a stone against the entrance of the tomb. *g* ⁴⁷Mary Magdalene and Mary the mother of Joses *h* saw where he was laid.

The Resurrection

16:1
i Lk 23:56;
Jn 19:39,40
16:3
j Mk 15:46

16 When the Sabbath was over, Mary Magdalene, Mary the mother of James, and Salome bought spices *i* so that they might go to anoint Jesus' body. ²Very early on the first day of the week, just after sunrise, they were on their way to the tomb ³and they asked each other, "Who will roll the stone away from the entrance of the tomb?" *j*

16:5
k Jn 20:12
16:6
l Mk 1:24

⁴But when they looked up, they saw that the stone, which was very large, had been rolled away. ⁵As they entered the tomb, they saw a young man dressed in a white robe *k* sitting on the right side, and they were alarmed.

⁶"Don't be alarmed," he said. "You are looking for Jesus the Nazarene, *l* who was crucified. He has risen! He is not here. See the place where they laid him. ⁷But go, tell his disciples and Peter, 'He is going ahead of you into Galilee. There you will see him, *m* just as he told you.' " *n*

16:7
m Jn 21:1-23
n Mk 14:28

⁸Trembling and bewildered, the women went out and fled from the tomb. They said nothing to anyone, because they were afraid.

[The earliest manuscripts and some other ancient witnesses do not have Mark 16:9-20.]

16:9
o Jn 20:11-18

⁹When Jesus rose early on the first day of the week, he appeared first to Mary Magdalene, *o* out of whom he had driven seven demons. ¹⁰She went and told those who had been with him and who were mourning and weeping. ¹¹When they heard that Jesus was alive and that she had seen him, they did not believe it. *p*

16:11
p ver 13,14;
Lk 24:11
16:12
q Lk 24:13-32

¹²Afterward Jesus appeared in a different form to two of them while they were walking in the country. *q* ¹³These returned and reported it to the rest; but they did not believe them either.

16:14
r Lk 24:36-43
16:15
s Mt 28:18-20;
Lk 24:47,48
16:16
t Jn 3:16,18,36;
Ac 16:31

¹⁴Later Jesus appeared to the Eleven as they were eating; he rebuked them for their lack of faith and their stubborn refusal to believe those who had seen him after he had risen. *r*

¹⁵He said to them, "Go into all the world and preach the good news to all creation. *s* ¹⁶Whoever believes and is baptized will be saved, but whoever does not believe will be condemned. *t* ¹⁷And these signs will accompany those who believe:

Mark 16:1–8

Mark's Gospel begins with God's messenger announcing what God was about to do (1:2–8) and closes with God's messenger announcing what he had already done. Luke described the clothing of both messengers. The camel hair outfit of John the prophet contrasts with the white robe of the angel. The "way" is important in both settings. In the opening scene, the way was to be prepared. In the final, it had been prepared, and the disciples were to follow where Jesus had gone before them.

The resurrection wasn't the end of the story, but its beginning.

None of the four Gospels describes the resurrection. It was prophesied in advance, symbolized by the transfiguration, and announced after the fact. Mark didn't answer the prying questions both skeptics and seekers might raise today: When did Jesus arise? How? In what form? Where's the evidence? Faith rests on the proclamation of the resurrection and leads to the really important questions: Where is he now—and how can I find him?

16:15–16

Witnessing Through the Years

As Mark 16:15–16 tells us, Jesus calls Christians to witness to their faith.

Millions have obeyed his call, from the year 33 A.D. through the early years of 2000 A.D.:

2,041,757,000 lay missionaries

257,393,000 professional Christian workers (pastoral workers, home and foreign missionaries)

Presently serving around the world:

642,297,000 lay missionaries

5,500,000 professional Christian workers (pastoral workers, home and foreign missionaries)

Source: Barrett and Johnson (2001:31)

In my name they will drive out demons;ᵘ they will speak in new tongues;ᵛ ¹⁸they will pick up snakesʷ with their hands; and when they drink deadly poison, it will not hurt them at all; they will place their hands onˣ sick people, and they will get well."

¹⁹After the Lord Jesus had spoken to them, he was taken up into heavenʸ and he sat at the right hand of God.ᶻ ²⁰Then the disciples went out and preached everywhere, and the Lord worked with them and confirmed his word by the signs that accompanied it.

16:17
ᵘ Mk 9:38; Lk 10:17;
Ac 5:16; 8:7; 16:18;
19:13-16 ᵛ Ac 2:4;
10:46; 19:6;
1Co 12:10,28,30
16:18
ʷ Lk 10:19;
Ac 28:3-5 ˣ Ac 6:6
16:19
ʸ Lk 24:50,51;
Jn 6:62; Ac 1:9-11;
1Ti 3:16 ᶻ Ps 110:1;
Ro 8:34; Col 3:1;
Heb 1:3; 12:2

Mark 16:9–20

According to Bible scholars, Mark's Gospel ended at verse 8 (since the two oldest manuscripts end here), or possibly his original ending was lost. Still, verses 9–20 serve as a valuable testimony to the vitality of the early church. As the disciples "went out and preached," Jesus "worked with them" (v. 20). How could Jesus do this *after* he had ascended? The key is in three little words in verse 17: "in my name." As the disciples shared their lives and experiences, they used Jesus' name—in effect calling on the power behind that name. In consequence, miraculous "signs" occurred, Jesus' words were confirmed, and lives were changed.

Much of the speculation regarding verses 9–20 concerns the possibility that the early church may have been uncomfortable with Mark's abrupt ending to the Gospel. After extensive study of all manuscripts, many scholars believe that one or more scribes took a hand at "writing a more appropriate ending," using the information from Matthew, Luke, and John's Gospels to avoid their own discomfort and to "fill in the blanks" for future generations. Still, the book through verse 20 is included in the New Testament canon—the authorized Scripture of the church. How does this information affect your reading of Mark and all Scripture? Does this small controversy discourage you or press you to delve deeper into the mystery of faith?

INTRODUCTION TO
Luke

AUTHOR

The third Gospel doesn't identify its author, but tradition has identified him as Luke, the beloved physician (Col. 4:14; cf. 2 Tim. 4:11; Philem. 24). The opening lines of the book (1:1–4) reveal that Luke wrote as a historian, not as a firsthand observer of the events he recorded.

DATE WRITTEN

Luke was probably written between A.D. 59 and 63.

ORIGINAL READERS

Luke directly addressed someone named Theophilus (1:3). But his Gospel, the most comprehensive of the four, was written to strengthen the faith of all believers. Some think Theophilus (God-lover) may represent a group of people.

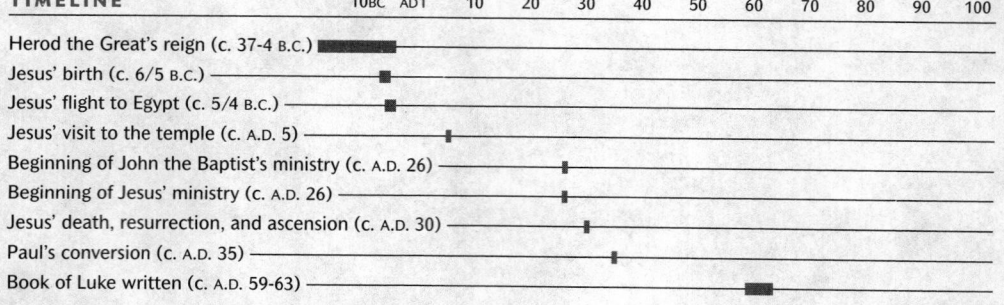

TIMELINE	10BC AD1	10	20	30	40	50	60	70	80	90	100
Herod the Great's reign (c. 37-4 B.C.)											
Jesus' birth (c. 6/5 B.C.)											
Jesus' flight to Egypt (c. 5/4 B.C.)											
Jesus' visit to the temple (c. A.D. 5)											
Beginning of John the Baptist's ministry (c. A.D. 26)											
Beginning of Jesus' ministry (c. A.D. 26)											
Jesus' death, resurrection, and ascension (c. A.D. 30)											
Paul's conversion (c. A.D. 35)											
Book of Luke written (c. A.D. 59-63)											

THEMES

Luke's primary purpose was to record an accurate, comprehensive account of Jesus' life, but other concerns also are evident in his narrative. Luke's themes include:

1. *The universality of the gospel.* Luke's account of Jesus' birth, ministry, death, and resurrection emphasizes that the gospel is intended for all peoples, including Gentiles (2:14,32).

2. *Concern for social outcasts.* Luke's Gospel underscores Jesus' particular concern for social outcasts, women, and the poor. Jesus' first public sermon recorded in Luke (4:16–21) cited Isaiah 61:1–2 in proclaiming good news to the poor, freedom for the prisoners, healing for the blind, and release for the oppressed (4:18–19).

3. *Repentance.* The vocabulary of repentance is prominent in Luke, as manifested in the parable of the lost son (15:11–32), the parable of the tax collector and the Pharisee (18:9–14), and the story of Zacchaeus (19:1–10). Repentance requires a fundamental reorientation toward God, which then leads to reconciliation of human relationships.

4. *Wealth.* Luke stressed the ethical aspects of the Christian life, making it clear that repentance involves a change in attitude that reveals itself in how a person handles money (3:10–14).

FAITH IN ACTION

The pages of Luke are filled with life lessons and role models of faith—people who challenge believers to put faith in action.

Role Models

• MARY (1:26–38), Jesus' mother, obeyed God's calling despite innuendo, scandal, public censure, and ridicule. Is God calling you to take on a servant role? Is sacrifice involved? Can you with Mary affirm unreservedly, "I am the Lord's servant" (1:38)?

• MEN WHO CARRIED A PARALYZED MAN TO JESUS (5:17–26) let him down into a crowded area through the roof so he could be healed. They demonstrated compassion and care for one who wouldn't otherwise have been able to obtain access to Jesus because of his disability. How do you care for the disabled around you? How can you make their way easier?

• THE GOOD SAMARITAN (10:30–37) defied an ancient tradition of prejudicial hatred and acted as a loving instrument of reconciliation when he helped a man in distress. Are there "undesirable" people in your community you had just as soon avoid? How can you instead reach out to them?

• MARY (10:38–42), the sister of Lazarus, yearned to be close to Jesus despite the social taboos of the day. Is Jesus calling you to set aside preconceived notions, customs, or traditions to make him your priority?

• ZACCHAEUS (19:1–10) was a truly repentant sinner who took reconciliation seriously. Is there someone in your life with whom you need to make restitution or amends?

• A WIDOW (21:1-4) gave "all she had to live on," while others donated from their abundance. Is there sacrifice involved in what you offer the Lord?

Challenges

• Cultivate new relationships that allow you to be a "giver," not a "taker" (10:25–37; 12:13–21).

• Look for opportunities to share your wealth (money, time, talents, abilities) with others (19:11–27; 21:1–4).

• Step out of your comfort zone by seeking ways to facilitate reconciliation between races, genders, and social classes (7:36–50).

• Perform simple acts of kindness (5:18–19).

OUTLINE

   I. The Births of John and Jesus (1–2)
  II. The Beginnings of Jesus' Ministry (3:1—4:13)
     A. John the Baptist (3:1–20)
     B. Jesus Is Baptized (3:21–22)
     C. Jesus' Genealogy (3:23–38)
     D. Jesus Is Tempted (4:1–13)
  III. Jesus' Ministry in Galilee (4:14—9:9)
     A. His Early Ministry in Galilee (4:14—5:39)
     B. His Later Ministry (6:1—9:9)
  IV. Ministry in Other Areas (9:10—13:21)
   V. Jesus' Ministry in and Around Perea (13:22—19:27)
  VI. The Passion of Jesus (19:28—24:53)
     A. His Triumphal Entry (19:28–44)
     B. The Cleansing of the Temple (19:45–48)
     C. Last Questions From the Jewish Leaders (20)

D. The Olivet Discourse (21)

E. The Last Supper (22:1–38)

F. The Prayer in Gethsemane (22:39–46)

G. Jesus' Arrest, Trial, and Crucifixion (22:47—23:56)

H. Jesus' Resurrection (24:1–49)

I. The Ascension (24:50–53)

Introduction

1 Many have undertaken to draw up an account of the things that have been fulfilled[a] among us, 2just as they were handed down to us by those who from the first[a] were eyewitnesses[b] and servants of the word.[c] 3Therefore, since I myself have carefully investigated everything from the beginning, it seemed good also to me to write an orderly account[d] for you, most excellent[e] Theophilus,[f] 4so that you may know the certainty of the things you have been taught.[g]

The Birth of John the Baptist Foretold

5In the time of Herod king of Judea[h] there was a priest named Zechariah, who belonged to the priestly division of Abijah;[i] his wife Elizabeth was also a descendant of Aaron. 6Both of them were upright in the sight of God, observing all the Lord's commandments and regulations blamelessly.[j] 7But they had no children, because Elizabeth was barren; and they were both well along in years.

8Once when Zechariah's division was on duty and he was serving as priest before God,[k] 9he was chosen by lot, according to the custom of the priesthood, to go into the temple of the Lord and burn incense.[l] 10And when the time for the burning of incense came, all the assembled worshipers were praying outside.[m]

11Then an angel[n] of the Lord appeared to him, standing at the right side of the altar of incense.[o] 12When Zechariah saw him, he was startled and was gripped with fear.[p] 13But the angel said to him: "Do not be afraid,[q] Zechariah; your prayer has been heard. Your wife Elizabeth will bear you a son, and you are to give him the name John.[r] 14He will be a joy and delight to you, and many will rejoice because of his birth,[s] 15for he will be great in the sight of the Lord. He is never to take wine or other fermented drink,[t] and he will be filled with the Holy Spirit even from birth.[b][u] 16Many of the people of Israel will he bring back to the Lord their God.

a 1 Or been surely believed   b 15 Or from his mother's womb

1:2
a Mk 1:1; Jn 15:27; Ac 1:21,22
b Heb 2:3; 1Pe 5:1; 2Pe 1:16; 1Jn 1:1
c Mk 4:14
1:3
d Ac 11:4
e Ac 24:3; 26:25
f Ac 1:1
1:4
g Jn 20:31
1:5
h Mt 2:1
i 1Ch 24:10
1:6
j Ge 7:1; 1Ki 9:4
1:8
k 1Ch 24:19; 2Ch 8:14
1:9
l Ex 30:7,8; 1Ch 23:13; 2Ch 29:11
1:10
m Lev 16:17
1:11
n Ac 5:19
o Ex 30:1-10
1:12
p Jdg 6:22,23; 13:22
1:13
q ver 30; Mt 14:27
r ver 60,63
1:14
s ver 58
1:15
t Nu 6:3; Jdg 13:4; Lk 7:33 *u* Jer 1:5; Gal 1:15

Luke 1:1–4

Luke told us four things about his work: (1) He had "investigated" the story. (2) He had gone back to "the beginning," starting with John the Baptist. (3) He had been thorough, having studied "everything" (much material in Luke's account isn't found in the other three). (4) He had worked "carefully" to tell the story clearly. In calling his account "orderly," Luke meant that he had tried to relate the story logically. This includes some arrangement of his material by topics or themes (events aren't necessarily in chronological order).

Luke stressed that God acted *in history through Jesus*. God also wants us to see that the Jesus story isn't just about him, but about us. Luke reassured us that we belong in relationship with God in his new community—the church. Third, we can trust his Gospel. Luke worked under the Spirit's inspiration, carefully passing on this account from those who had seen the events firsthand. We can have confidence in the message and in the certain basis of our faith.

Luke 1:5–25

Luke's announcement of John's birth: (1) was similar to previous announcements of the births of special children (Gen. 17:15–17; 25:21–23; Judg. 13:2–21); (2) shows that John had a special place in God's plan; and (3) contains an underlying thread of drama. We enter vicariously into the disappointment in the lives of these "blameless" servants of God who had lived so many years with the "disgrace" of childlessness.

Elizabeth teaches us to take our grief over disappointments to God—and our rejoicing over resolutions to him as well. Zechariah demonstrated how God leads and instructs his own in difficult times. Underestimating God can be as dangerous for us as open rebellion. Our sin may not be a matter of *doing* wrong but of *being* hesitant to trust fully. When have you been "deprived" of one thing because God had something better for you around the corner?

17And he will go on before the Lord, v in the spirit and power of Elijah, w to turn the hearts of the fathers to their children x and the disobedient to the wisdom of the righteous—to make ready a people prepared for the Lord."

18Zechariah asked the angel, "How can I be sure of this? I am an old man and my wife is well along in years." y

19The angel answered, "I am Gabriel. z I stand in the presence of God, and I have been sent to speak to you and to tell you this good news. 20And now you will be silent and not able to speak a until the day this happens, because you did not believe my words, which will come true at their proper time."

21Meanwhile, the people were waiting for Zechariah and wondering why he stayed so long in the temple. 22When he came out, he could not speak to them. They realized he had seen a vision in the temple, for he kept making signs b to them but remained unable to speak.

23When his time of service was completed, he returned home. 24After this his wife Elizabeth became pregnant and for five months remained in seclusion. 25"The Lord has done this for me," she said. "In these days he has shown his favor and taken away my disgrace c among the people."

The Birth of Jesus Foretold

26In the sixth month, God sent the angel Gabriel d to Nazareth, e a town in Galilee, 27to a virgin pledged to be married to a man named Joseph, f a descendant of David. The virgin's name was Mary. 28The angel went to her and said, "Greetings, you who are highly favored! The Lord is with you."

29Mary was greatly troubled at his words and wondered what kind of greeting this might be. 30But the angel said to her, "Do not be afraid, g Mary, you have found favor with God. 31You will be with child and give birth to a son, and you are to give him the name Jesus. h 32He will be great and will be called the Son of the Most High. i The Lord God will give him the throne of his father David, 33and he will reign over the house of Jacob forever; his kingdom j will never end." k

34"How will this be," Mary asked the angel, "since I am a virgin?"

35The angel answered, "The Holy Spirit will come upon you, l and the power of the Most High m will overshadow you. So the holy one n to be born will be called a the Son of God. o 36Even Elizabeth your relative is going to have a child in her old age, and she who was said to be barren is in her sixth month. 37For nothing is impossible with God." p

38"I am the Lord's servant," Mary answered. "May it be to me as you have said." Then the angel left her.

Mary Visits Elizabeth

39At that time Mary got ready and hurried to a town in the hill country of Judea, q 40where she entered Zechariah's home and greeted Elizabeth. 41When Elizabeth heard Mary's greeting, the baby leaped in her womb, and Elizabeth was filled with the Holy Spirit. 42In a loud voice she exclaimed: "Blessed are you among women, r

a 35 Or So the child to be born will be called holy,

1:17 v ver 76 w Mt 11:14 x Mal 4:5,6
1:18 y ver 34; Ge 17:17
1:19 z ver 26; Da 8:16; 9:21; Mt 18:10
1:20 a Eze 3:26
1:22 b ver 62
1:25 c Ge 30:23; Isa 4:1
1:26 d ver 19 e Mt 2:23
1:27 f Mt 1:16,18,20; Lk 2:4
1:30 g ver 13; Mt 14:27
1:31 h Isa 7:14; Mt 1:21,25; Lk 2:21
1:32 i ver 35,76; Mk 5:7
1:33 j Mt 28:18 k Da 2:44; 7:14,27; Mic 4:7; Heb 1:8
1:35 l Mt 1:18 m ver 32,76 n Mk 1:24 o Mt 4:3
1:37 p Mt 19:26
1:39 q ver 65
1:42 r Jdg 5:24

Luke 1:26–38

Luke demonstrated that God's plan advances in stages—in this case through the birth announcements of John and Jesus. He also revealed the character of those surrounding these miracle births. All the figures involved are positive examples of spirituality as they responded to what God was doing through and among them. Mary was the person God unexpectedly chose to mother his Son incarnate. A humble teenager, she was a model of availability and willingness to serve. Aren't those the most basic characteristics any of us can offer God?

This passage comments on five themes: (1) the character of God's heart—he loves the humble in spirit;

(2) the certainty that he will fulfill his promises—nothing is impossible for him; (3) the importance of our willingness to serve God—with a trust that takes us beyond our human limitations; (4) the significance of the Virgin Birth in confirming Jesus' divinity; and (5) the importance of sexual faithfulness throughout our lives. How significant is each theme in the "scheme" of your life?

Luke 1:39–45

Two major characters "met" symbolically through their mothers. John the Baptist began "pointing to" Jesus even from the womb, just as verses 15–17 had predicted. Three points were central in Elizabeth's testimony: (1) Joy and blessing came her way because she

and blessed is the child you will bear! 43But why am I so favored, that the mother of my Lord should come to me? 44As soon as the sound of your greeting reached my ears, the baby in my womb leaped for joy. 45Blessed is she who has believed that what the Lord has said to her will be accomplished!"

Mary's Song

46And Mary said:

> "My soul glorifies the Lord *s*
> 47   and my spirit rejoices in God my Savior, *t*
> 48for he has been mindful
>   of the humble state of his servant. *u*
>   From now on all generations will call me blessed, *v*
> 49   for the Mighty One has done great things *w* for me—
>   holy is his name. *x*
> 50His mercy extends to those who fear him,
>   from generation to generation. *y*
> 51He has performed mighty deeds with his arm; *z*
>   he has scattered those who are proud in their inmost thoughts.
> 52He has brought down rulers from their thrones
>   but has lifted up the humble.
> 53He has filled the hungry with good things *a*
>   but has sent the rich away empty.
> 54He has helped his servant Israel,
>   remembering to be merciful *b*
> 55to Abraham and his descendants *c* forever,
>   even as he said to our fathers."

56Mary stayed with Elizabeth for about three months and then returned home.

The Birth of John the Baptist

57When it was time for Elizabeth to have her baby, she gave birth to a son. 58Her neighbors and relatives heard that the Lord had shown her great mercy, and they shared her joy.

1:46
s Ps 34:2,3
1:47
t 1Ti 1:1; 2:3
1:48
u Ps 138:6
v Lk 11:27
1:49
w Ps 71:19
x Ps 111:9
1:50
y Ex 20:6;
Ps 103:17
1:51
z Ps 98:1; Isa 40:10
1:53
a Ps 107:9
1:54
b Ps 98:3
1:55
c Ge 17:19;
Ps 132:11; Gal 3:16

---

believed God does what he says. (2) Mary's child was especially blessed—at the very center of God's fresh, exhilarating activity. (3) She was amazed at being part of these astounding events.

📖 Luke aimed directly at our hearts in these stories. As believers, we too have the opportunity to be "blessed" by believing what God has said will come to pass. In fact, beyond opportunity, we have an *obligation* to take the Lord at his word, to recognize his involvement in our lives. As the child leaped in Elizabeth's womb, so our hearts will leap when we are attuned to God's blessings. What good gifts come immediately to your mind?

Luke 1:46–56

📖 That Mary's hymn was a praise psalm is indicated by verses 46b–47 (notice Hannah's similar focus in 1 Sam. 2:1; cf. Ps. 35:9). In verses 46–49 Mary offered personal praise for her specific situation. The rest of the hymn extolled God's activity in broad terms. A shift of tenses from present (v. 46b–47) to past (v. 48a) to future (v. 48b) shows the broadening sweep of her basis for praise. Mary would be honored "from now on" by "all generations" as a model recipient of God's grace and mercy (vv. 49–50).

📖 We may tend to view the rich and famous as divinely favored. Yet the text makes clear that God honors the poor and humble, really seeing those we easily overlook. Mary's hymn heralded the focus of the Messiah's ministry—on lifting up the lowly, honoring the humble, and feeding the hungry. Many ministries committed to reaching those disregarded by society lack the glamour of celebrity status—but they please God. How could you become involved in such a blessed endeavor?

Luke 1:57–66

📖 The events surrounding John's birth and naming point to his unusual nature. The open-ended question "What then is this child going to be?" prompted Luke's early readers to reflect on this special infant. We have largely lost the sense of drama and irony today, perhaps due to our familiarity with the story or our distance from this ancient culture. But the sequence, with its surprising twists, would have piqued the interest of Luke's first readers. The story, though, is just getting interesting. Stay tuned, Luke implied: There is more to come about this special child—and the One to follow!

📖 Zechariah, a man of lifelong faith, still had much to learn about trusting God. God revealed to him

⁵⁹On the eighth day they came to circumcise^d the child, and they were going to name him after his father Zechariah, ⁶⁰but his mother spoke up and said, "No! He is to be called John."^{e}

⁶¹They said to her, "There is no one among your relatives who has that name."

⁶²Then they made signs^f to his father, to find out what he would like to name the child. ⁶³He asked for a writing tablet, and to everyone's astonishment he wrote, "His name is John."^{g} ⁶⁴Immediately his mouth was opened and his tongue was loosed, and he began to speak,^{h} praising God. ⁶⁵The neighbors were all filled with awe, and throughout the hill country of Judea^i people were talking about all these things. ⁶⁶Everyone who heard this wondered about it, asking, "What then is this child going to be?" For the Lord's hand was with him.^{j}

Zechariah's Song

⁶⁷His father Zechariah was filled with the Holy Spirit and prophesied:^{k}

⁶⁸ "Praise be to the Lord, the God of Israel,^{l}
   because he has come and has redeemed his people.^{m}
⁶⁹ He has raised up a horn$^{a\,n}$ of salvation for us
   in the house of his servant David^o
⁷⁰ (as he said through his holy prophets of long ago),^{p}
⁷¹ salvation from our enemies
   and from the hand of all who hate us—
⁷² to show mercy to our fathers^q
   and to remember his holy covenant,^{r}
⁷³   the oath he swore to our father Abraham:^{s}
⁷⁴ to rescue us from the hand of our enemies,
   and to enable us to serve him^t without fear
⁷⁵   in holiness and righteousness^u before him all our days.

⁷⁶ And you, my child, will be called a prophet^v of the Most High;^{w}
   for you will go on before the Lord to prepare the way for him,^{x}
⁷⁷ to give his people the knowledge of salvation
   through the forgiveness of their sins,^{y}
⁷⁸ because of the tender mercy of our God,
   by which the rising sun^z will come to us from heaven
⁷⁹ to shine on those living in darkness
   and in the shadow of death,^{a}
   to guide our feet into the path of peace."

⁸⁰And the child grew and became strong in spirit;^{b} and he lived in the desert until he appeared publicly to Israel.

^{a} 69 *Horn* here symbolizes strength.

1:59
d Ge 17:12; Lev 12:3; Lk 2:21; Php 3:5
1:60
e ver 13,63
1:62
f ver 22
1:63
g ver 13,60
1:64
h ver 20
1:65
i ver 39
1:66
j Ge 39:2; Ac 11:21

1:67
k Joel 2:28
1:68
l Ps 72:18
m Ps 111:9; Lk 7:16
1:69
n 1Sa 2:1,10; Ps 18:2; 89:17; 132:17; Eze 29:21
o Mt 1:1
1:70
p Jer 23:5
1:72
q Mic 7:20
r Ps 105:8,9; 106:45; Eze 16:60
1:73
s Ge 22:16-18
1:74
t Heb 9:14
1:75
u Eph 4:24
1:76
v Mt 11:9
w ver 32,35
x ver 17; Mal 3:1
1:77
y Jer 31:34; Mk 1:4
1:78
z Mal 4:2
1:79
a Isa 9:2; 59:9; Mt 4:16; Ac 26:18
1:80
b Lk 2:40,52

---

through the sign of silence that the time to speak had passed. The same lesson applies to each of us today. There is a time to be silent before God and a time to speak, both to and for him. He wants us to journey through both seasons in faithful obedience. When has God broken through your silence to speak to you in some meaningful way?

Luke 1:67–80

Just as Mary's song (vv. 46–55) is known as the *Magnificat*, this second hymn in Luke is identified as the *Benedictus* (each represents the opening word of its Latin translation). Whereas Mary's hymn spoke in personal and general terms, Zechariah's anticipated and previewed the careers of the two children divine destiny was bringing together. Zechariah's hymn focused on the person to whom John would point—the One promised long ago to rescue and bless any who would turn to him.

Zechariah's hymn is a grand overview of God's fulfillment of his promised salvation and deliverance. The Messiah guides those who follow him onto the path of peace (v. 79). Entry onto this path takes only a moment, but salvation isn't a momentary proposition. It's a lifelong journey, involving every aspect of our lives, an excursion guided by our allegiance to Christ, the source of true light. Our Messiah still goes before us, guiding us in the way of God.

2:1
c Mt 22:17; Lk 3:1
d Mt 24:14

2:2
e Mt 4:24

2:4
f Jn 7:42

2:9
g Lk 1:11; Ac 5:19

2:10
h Mt 14:27
2:11
i Mt 1:21; Jn 4:42;
Ac 5:31 j Mt 1:16;
16:16,20; Jn 11:27;
Ac 2:36
2:12
k 1Sa 2:34;
2Ki 19:29; Isa 7:14

2:14
l Lk 1:79; Ro 5:1;
Eph 2:14,17

The Birth of Jesus

2 In those days Caesar Augustus[c] issued a decree that a census should be taken of the entire Roman world.[d] 2(This was the first census that took place while Quirinius was governor of Syria.)[e] 3And everyone went to his own town to register.

4So Joseph also went up from the town of Nazareth in Galilee to Judea, to Bethlehem[f] the town of David, because he belonged to the house and line of David. 5He went there to register with Mary, who was pledged to be married to him and was expecting a child. 6While they were there, the time came for the baby to be born, 7and she gave birth to her firstborn, a son. She wrapped him in cloths and placed him in a manger, because there was no room for them in the inn.

The Shepherds and the Angels

8And there were shepherds living out in the fields nearby, keeping watch over their flocks at night. 9An angel[g] of the Lord appeared to them, and the glory of the Lord shone around them, and they were terrified. 10But the angel said to them, "Do not be afraid.[h] I bring you good news of great joy that will be for all the people. 11Today in the town of David a Savior[i] has been born to you; he is Christ[a][j] the Lord. 12This will be a sign[k] to you: You will find a baby wrapped in cloths and lying in a manger."

13Suddenly a great company of the heavenly host appeared with the angel, praising God and saying,

14 "Glory to God in the highest,
 and on earth peace[l] to men on whom his favor rests."

15When the angels had left them and gone into heaven, the shepherds said to one another, "Let's go to Bethlehem and see this thing that has happened, which the Lord has told us about."

Jesus Is Born (2:4)

Then: Bethlehem was a village of fewer than 1,000 people, located six miles south of Jerusalem.

Now: It's a bustling, historically significant town of 22,000.

---

a 11 Or *Messiah.* "The Christ" (Greek) and "the Messiah" (Hebrew) both mean "the Anointed One"; also in verse 26.

Luke 2:1–7

📖 The circumstances of Jesus' birth were so humble that it's hard at first to appreciate the implications of this inconspicuous labor and delivery. When his parents wrapped Jesus in cloths and laid him in a prickly feeding trough, Christ's humble "emptying" had already begun (Phil. 2:5–8). The God/man lived without pretense, totally devoid of the trappings of wealth and societal power. From the moment he was born, Jesus began to pay the price for our redemption, carrying our sorrow and humiliation. The dignity of this event came exclusively from the identity of the person lying in the manger.

📖 What criteria do you use to measure the worth of a person—any person? This most modest of births for the most exalted figure ever born demonstrates that life's true value is found in life itself, not in the trimmings or trappings that come with it. The utter humility surrounding Jesus' birth sends a major challenge to our cultures, which often fail to perceive the sanctity of life or the tracings of God's fingers in "lowborn" or obscure people.

Luke 2:8–20

📖 Through the appearance and announcement of the angels heaven met and greeted the average person, represented by these unassuming shepherds. The poor and marginalized were elevated by the coming of the Messiah. The proclamation of "good news of great joy that will be for all the people" indicated that all humanity would be impacted by Jesus' coming. The notes of praise that have dominated the opening scenes fittingly continue in this section.

📖 In a real sense, Jesus' story is our story—told *to* us and *for* us, just as if we had been among the shepherds that night near Bethlehem. Their journey to see "this thing" needs to be every person's quest to see what God is up to in Jesus. Does your sense of wonder begin to match theirs? The best way you can show the extent of your amazement is with a response of faithful living, including ample contributions of grateful praise and willing service.

Jesus they hurried off and found Mary and Joseph, and the baby, who was lying in the manger. When they had seen him, they spread the word concerning what and all who heard it were amazed at what them in their hearts the Shepherds returned glorifying and praising God for all the things they had heard and seen, which were just as they had been told

Is There Room in Your Inn?

 2:7

A powerful image pervades my thinking during Advent. Indeed I hope it hovers over me for the rest of my life. "There was no room for them in the inn," Luke tells us (2:7). So the Creator of the universe was born in a stable.

All this is familiar, so familiar we hardly stop to think much about it—however astonishingly true it is. Our children perform simple skits about the cattle making room for Jesus, but the meaning fails to penetrate deeply into our souls.

Something more happens for me in Advent—thanks to a powerful sermon my pastor, Leonard Dow, preached several years ago. He connected this passage with the story of Jesus' visit to Mary and Martha. (That may be a common connection in the history of preaching, but I don't remember hearing it made before.) While Mary sat listening at Jesus' feet, Martha rushed madly around the house frantically doing all kinds of good things so the food and lodging would be just right. Finally, her growing frustration that Mary was doing nothing to help erupted in an angry demand that Jesus order Mary to get working.

> **The inn of our lives is too full for Jesus to find room. Our frantic busyness pushes him away.**

Jesus' answer speaks clearly to busy, type-A Christian activists rushing around so furiously to promote justice and peace that they have little time left for quiet meditation and contemplative prayer: " 'Martha, Martha,' the Lord answered, 'you are worried and upset about many things, but only one thing is needed. Mary has chosen what is better, and it will not be taken away from her' " (Luke 10:41–42).

That sermon hit hard just where I needed it. Sure, I wrote immediately after the original Chicago Declaration on Evangelical Social Concern (1973) that prayer was perhaps the one thing most needed by evangelical social activists. But to this day, I still struggle to find the time. We try to build a 24/7 relationship with Christ with a miserly investment of one and a quarter hours of sitting at his feet on a Sunday morning. The inn of our lives is too full for Jesus to find room. Our frantic busyness pushes him away.

This Advent, I have resolved to hold before me the image of sitting quietly at the feet of my Lord, just listening, learning, and waiting for directions. Theoretically, as much as I know my heart, I want to do only what Christ wants me to do. I don't want to attend one more meeting, give one more speech, organize one more urgent campaign, or write one more book unless my Lord wants me to. But if that is truly the case, why is it so much easier for me to rush into another activity and pack the day with important calls than to take real time just to sit at his feet listening for direction?

My desire is to change. I hope I learn to pray as much as Christ wants me to pray. I'm determined to discover how to make prayer and dependence on the Spirit more central to my life and the work of Evangelicals for Social Action.

I don't pretend I can easily switch from imitating Martha to following Mary. But I ask the Lord to change me.

May it be true this Advent—and for the rest of my life—that there is less and less frenzied worry about making good things happen, and more and more sitting prayerfully, listening at Jesus' feet. Lord, my longing is to have room in my heart for you.

Ronald J. Sider, professor of theology, holistic ministry, and public policy at Eastern Seminary in Philadelphia and president of Evangelicals for Social Action in Wynnewood, Pennsylvania

16So they hurried off and found Mary and Joseph, and the baby, who was lying in the manger. 17When they had seen him, they spread the word concerning what had been told them about this child, 18and all who heard it were amazed at what the shepherds said to them. 19But Mary treasured up all these things and pondered them in her heart. *m* 20The shepherds returned, glorifying and praising God *n* for all the things they had heard and seen, which were just as they had been told.

2:19
m ver 51
2:20
n Mt 9:8

Jesus Presented in the Temple

2:21
o Lk 1:59 *p* Lk 1:31

21On the eighth day, when it was time to circumcise him, *o* he was named Jesus, the name the angel had given him before he had been conceived. *p*

2:22
q Lev 12:2-8

22When the time of their purification according to the Law of Moses *q* had been completed, Joseph and Mary took him to Jerusalem to present him to the Lord 23(as it is written in the Law of the Lord, "Every firstborn male is to be consecrated to the Lord" a), *r* 24and to offer a sacrifice in keeping with what is said in the Law of the Lord: "a pair of doves or two young pigeons." b s

2:23
r Ex 13:2,12,15;
Nu 3:13
2:24
s Lev 12:8
2:25
t Lk 1:6 *u* ver 38;
Isa 52:9; Lk 23:51

25Now there was a man in Jerusalem called Simeon, who was righteous and devout. *t* He was waiting for the consolation of Israel, *u* and the Holy Spirit was upon him. 26It had been revealed to him by the Holy Spirit that he would not die before he had seen the Lord's Christ. 27Moved by the Spirit, he went into the temple courts. When the parents brought in the child Jesus to do for him what the custom of the Law required, *v* 28Simeon took him in his arms and praised God, saying:

2:27
v ver 22

2:29
w ver 26 *x* Ac 2:24

29 "Sovereign Lord, as you have promised, *w*
   you now dismiss c your servant in peace. *x*
30 For my eyes have seen your salvation, *y*
31   which you have prepared in the sight of all people,
32 a light for revelation to the Gentiles
   and for glory to your people Israel." *z*

2:30
y Isa 52:10; Lk 3:6

2:32
z Isa 42:6; 49:6;
Ac 13:47; 26:23

2:34
a Mt 12:46
b Isa 8:14;
Mt 21:44; 1Co 1:23;
2Co 2:16; 1Pe 2:7,8

33The child's father and mother marveled at what was said about him. 34Then Simeon blessed them and said to Mary, his mother: *a* "This child is destined to cause the falling *b* and rising of many in Israel, and to be a sign that will be spoken against, 35so that the thoughts of many hearts will be revealed. And a sword will pierce your own soul too."

2:36
c Ac 21:9

36There was also a prophetess, *c* Anna, the daughter of Phanuel, of the tribe of Asher. She was very old; she had lived with her husband seven years after her marriage, 37and then was a widow until she was eighty-four. d d She never left the temple but worshiped night and day, fasting and praying. *e* 38Coming up to them at that very moment, she gave thanks to God and spoke about the child to all who were looking forward to the redemption of Jerusalem. *f*

2:37
d 1Ti 5:9 *e* Ac 13:3;
14:23; 1Ti 5:5

2:38
f ver 25; Isa 40:2;
Lk 1:68; 24:21

39When Joseph and Mary had done everything required by the Law of the Lord, they returned to Galilee to their own town of Nazareth. *g* 40And the child grew and became strong; he was filled with wisdom, and the grace of God was upon him. *h*

2:39
g ver 51; Mt 2:23
2:40
h ver 52; Lk 1:80

The Boy Jesus at the Temple

2:41
i Ex 23:15;
Dt 16:1-8

41Every year his parents went to Jerusalem for the Feast of the Passover. *i* 42When

---

a 23 Exodus 13:2,12   b 24 Lev. 12:8   c 29 Or *promised, / now dismiss*   d 37 Or *widow for eighty-four years*

Luke 2:21–40

Mary and Joseph engaged in the prescribed Jewish rites of purification after Jesus' birth and traveled to Jerusalem to present the baby to God. Whereas the shepherds had symbolized the average person on the street, Simeon, the first prophetic witness, was a wise elder who had walked throughout his long life with God. Anna too had given herself full-time to a ministry of intercession for many years. What an honor for these patient, older believers to be singled out in this way!

Once again God spoke through people proclaiming the unexpected focus of the Messiah's ministry. These two wise elders proclaimed that the Messiah was for the Gentiles as well as for Israel, that his ministry would be opposed rather than eagerly welcomed, and that even his mother would suffer. We prefer to have our leaders speak words that affirm us and make us feel comfortable. How can we prepare ourselves to hear messages that surprise and challenge us?

he was twelve years old, they went up to the Feast, according to the custom. [43]After the Feast was over, while his parents were returning home, the boy Jesus stayed behind in Jerusalem, but they were unaware of it. [44]Thinking he was in their company, they traveled on for a day. Then they began looking for him among their relatives and friends. [45]When they did not find him, they went back to Jerusalem to look for him. [46]After three days they found him in the temple courts, sitting among the teachers, listening to them and asking them questions. [47]Everyone who heard him was amazed[j] at his understanding and his answers. [48]When his parents saw him, they were astonished. His mother[k] said to him, "Son, why have you treated us like this? Your father[l] and I have been anxiously searching for you."

[49]"Why were you searching for me?" he asked. "Didn't you know I had to be in my Father's house?"[m] [50]But they did not understand what he was saying to them. [n]

[51]Then he went down to Nazareth with them[o] and was obedient to them. But his mother treasured all these things in her heart.[p] [52]And Jesus grew in wisdom and stature, and in favor with God and men.[q]

John the Baptist Prepares the Way

3 In the fifteenth year of the reign of Tiberius Caesar—when Pontius Pilate[r] was governor of Judea, Herod[s] tetrarch of Galilee, his brother Philip tetrarch of Iturea and Traconitis, and Lysanias tetrarch of Abilene— [2]during the high priesthood of Annas and Caiaphas,[t] the word of God came to John[u] son of Zechariah[v] in the desert. [3]He went into all the country around the Jordan, preaching a baptism of repentance for the forgiveness of sins.[w] [4]As is written in the book of the words of Isaiah the prophet:

"A voice of one calling in the desert,
'Prepare the way for the Lord,
    make straight paths for him.
[5]Every valley shall be filled in,
    every mountain and hill made low.
The crooked roads shall become straight,
    the rough ways smooth.
[6]And all mankind will see God's salvation.' "[a][x]

[7]John said to the crowds coming out to be baptized by him, "You brood of vi-

[a] 6 Isaiah 40:3-5

2:47
j Mt 7:28
2:48
k Mt 12:46
l Lk 3:23; 4:22
2:49
m Jn 2:16
2:50
n Mk 9:32
2:51
o ver 39; Mt 2:23
p ver 19
2:52
q ver 40; 1Sa 2:26; Lk 1:80
3:1
r Mt 27:2 s Mt 14:1
3:2
t Mt 26:3; Jn 18:13; Ac 4:6 u Mt 3:1
v Lk 1:13
3:3
w ver 16; Mk 1:4
3:6
x Ps 98:2; Isa 40:3-5; 42:16; 52:10; Lk 2:30

Luke 2:41–52

In Jesus' day it wasn't unusual for students to gather at the feet of their rabbis to discuss theology, often in a question-and-answer, discussion format. Even at this tender age Jesus showed amazing knowledge of the things of God. In fact, the onlookers were astonished at his understanding—the same reaction that would come later in response to his miraculous work (8:56). Early in life the developing Jesus already knew that his relationship with the Father was unique.

Jesus understood the priority of being in "his Father's house." Our time spent before him "in the temple," at his feet in the Word, or using our hands for him in ministry may baffle people who have different priorities. Yet having a hunger to grow and understand more about the ways of God is one of the greatest gifts we can have. What has nourished your desire to grow in your relationship with God? Have your choices caused others to engage you in conversations that have allowed you to point them to Jesus?

Luke 3:1–20

Ministering in the desert in fulfillment of Isaiah's prophecy, John preached "a baptism of repentance for the forgiveness of sins." His ministry at and in the Jordan River prepared people for God's salvation by opening their hearts to respond to the coming Messiah (1:15–17,76–77). That is why, in citing Isaiah 40:3–5, Luke mentioned leveling the obstacles in the way of God's arrival. If the creation bowed to God's coming, can't people of all ages trust him to work in human hearts to do the same?

Recognizing our accountability to God can be either suffocating or liberating. The realization smothers us when we insist on continuing to sin. But it frees us when we turn to God for forgiveness and experience the blessings of obedience. John's message still applies. God isn't only concerned with our "spiritual" lives. Walking his way impacts every daily aspect of our life. The fruits worthy of repentance include: (1) sharing what we have with the needy, (2) feeding the hungry, (3) refusing to cheat in our business dealings, and (4) making sure we never use our power to oppress the vulnerable. How are you doing in each of these basic areas?

3:7
y Mt 12:34; 23:33
z Ro 1:18
3:8
a Isa 51:2; Lk 19:9;
Jn 8:33,39;
Ac 13:26; Ro 4:1,
11,12,16,17;
Gal 3:7
3:9
b Mt 3:10
3:10
c ver 12,14;
Ac 2:37; 16:30
3:11
d Isa 58:7
3:12
e Lk 7:29
3:13
f Lk 19:8
3:14
g Ex 23:1;
Lev 19:11

3:15
h Mt 3:1
i Jn 1:19,20;
Ac 13:25
3:16
j ver 3; Mk 1:4
k Jn 1:26,33;
Ac 1:5; 11:16; 19:4
3:17
l Isa 30:24
m Mt 13:30; 25:41

3:19
n ver 1

3:20
o Mt 14:3,4;
Mk 6:17-18

3:21
p Mt 14:23;
Mk 1:35; 6:46;
Lk 5:16; 6:12; 9:18,
28; 11:1
3:22
q Isa 42:1;
Jn 1:32,33;
Ac 10:38 r Mt 3:17
s Mt 3:17
3:23
t Mt 4:17; Ac 1:1
u Lk 1:27

pers![y] Who warned you to flee from the coming wrath?[z] **8**Produce fruit in keeping with repentance. And do not begin to say to yourselves, 'We have Abraham as our father.'[a] For I tell you that out of these stones God can raise up children for Abraham. **9**The ax is already at the root of the trees, and every tree that does not produce good fruit will be cut down and thrown into the fire."[b]

10"What should we do then?"[c] the crowd asked.

11John answered, "The man with two tunics should share with him who has none, and the one who has food should do the same."[d]

12Tax collectors also came to be baptized.[e] "Teacher," they asked, "what should we do?"

13"Don't collect any more than you are required to,"[f] he told them.

14Then some soldiers asked him, "And what should we do?"

He replied, "Don't extort money and don't accuse people falsely[g]—be content with your pay."

15The people were waiting expectantly and were all wondering in their hearts if John[h] might possibly be the Christ.[a][i] **16**John answered them all, "I baptize you with[b] water.[j] But one more powerful than I will come, the thongs of whose sandals I am not worthy to untie. He will baptize you with the Holy Spirit and with fire.[k] **17**His winnowing fork[l] is in his hand to clear his threshing floor and to gather the wheat into his barn, but he will burn up the chaff with unquenchable fire."[m] **18**And with many other words John exhorted the people and preached the good news to them.

19But when John rebuked Herod[n] the tetrarch because of Herodias, his brother's wife, and all the other evil things he had done, **20**Herod added this to them all: He locked John up in prison.[o]

The Baptism and Genealogy of Jesus

21When all the people were being baptized, Jesus was baptized too. And as he was praying,[p] heaven was opened **22**and the Holy Spirit descended on him[q] in bodily form like a dove. And a voice came from heaven: "You are my Son,[r] whom I love; with you I am well pleased."[s]

23Now Jesus himself was about thirty years old when he began his ministry.[t] He was the son, so it was thought, of Joseph,[u]

the son of Heli, **24**the son of Matthat,
the son of Levi, the son of Melki,
the son of Jannai, the son of Joseph,
25the son of Mattathias, the son of Amos,
the son of Nahum, the son of Esli,
the son of Naggai, **26**the son of Maath,
the son of Mattathias, the son of Semein,
the son of Josech, the son of Joda,

a 15 Or *Messiah*   b 16 Or *in*

Luke 3:21–38

🕊 As he anointed him for ministry, God identified Jesus as his Son. This event confirmed or authorized Jesus' ministry—not by *making* him something he wasn't before, but by *recognizing* that the Son would now actively exercise the authority he had possessed from the beginning. Matthew opened his book with Jesus' genealogy, but Luke sandwiched it between Jesus' baptism as Son and the devil's testing. Why? To answer the burning question: Is Jesus qualified to be God's promised Son—the Messiah?

📖 You are unaccustomed to hearing God speak in an audible voice. But he still talks to you. The Spirit resident in your heart directs you—especially as you seek God's guidance in prayer and consultation with Scripture. When we are new creatures in Christ, the Spirit echoes the words the Father spoke to the Son: "Behold my beloved child, in whom I'm pleased." The Good News we receive and proclaim to all people, especially to those who feel unworthy and outcast, is that because of Jesus Christ, God is pleased with us. He may communicate with you through the words of other people, often caring believers. That is why Christian community, where the fellowship of the Spirit takes place, is so important. How strategically are you positioned to "hear" God speak? Are the two of you close enough that you immediately recognize his voice (cf. John 10:5)?

27 the son of Joanan, the son of Rhesa,
   the son of Zerubbabel, ᵛ the son of Shealtiel,
   the son of Neri, 28 the son of Melki,
   the son of Addi, the son of Cosam,
   the son of Elmadam, the son of Er,
29 the son of Joshua, the son of Eliezer,
   the son of Jorim, the son of Matthat,
   the son of Levi, 30 the son of Simeon,
   the son of Judah, the son of Joseph,
   the son of Jonam, the son of Eliakim,
31 the son of Melea, the son of Menna,
   the son of Mattatha, the son of Nathan, ʷ
   the son of David, 32 the son of Jesse,
   the son of Obed, the son of Boaz,
   the son of Salmon, ᵃ the son of Nahshon,
33 the son of Amminadab, the son of Ram, ᵇ
   the son of Hezron, the son of Perez, ˣ
   the son of Judah, 34 the son of Jacob,
   the son of Isaac, the son of Abraham,
   the son of Terah, the son of Nahor, ʸ
35 the son of Serug, the son of Reu,
   the son of Peleg, the son of Eber,
   the son of Shelah, 36 the son of Cainan,
   the son of Arphaxad, ᶻ the son of Shem,
   the son of Noah, the son of Lamech, ᵃ
37 the son of Methuselah, the son of Enoch,
   the son of Jared, the son of Mahalalel,
   the son of Kenan, 38 the son of Enosh,
   the son of Seth, the son of Adam,
   the son of God. ᵇ

The Temptation of Jesus

4 Jesus, full of the Holy Spirit, ᶜ returned from the Jordan ᵈ and was led by the Spirit ᵉ in the desert, 2 where for forty days ᶠ he was tempted by the devil. He ate nothing during those days, and at the end of them he was hungry.

3 The devil said to him, "If you are the Son of God, tell this stone to become bread."

4 Jesus answered, "It is written: 'Man does not live on bread alone.' ᶜ ᵍ

5 The devil led him up to a high place and showed him in an instant all the kingdoms of the world. ʰ 6 And he said to him, "I will give you all their authority and splendor, for it has been given to me, ⁱ and I can give it to anyone I want to. 7 So if you worship me, it will all be yours."

8 Jesus answered, "It is written: 'Worship the Lord your God and serve him only.' ᵈ ʲ

9 The devil led him to Jerusalem and had him stand on the highest point of the temple. "If you are the Son of God," he said, "throw yourself down from here. 10 For it is written:

ᵃ 32 Some early manuscripts *Sala*   ᵇ 33 Some manuscripts *Amminadab, the son of Admin, the son of Arni*; other manuscripts vary widely.   ᶜ 4 Deut. 8:3   ᵈ 8 Deut. 6:13

Sidebar references:

3:27 ᵛ Mt 1:12

3:31 ʷ 2Sa 5:14; 1Ch 3:5

3:33 ˣ Ru 4:18-22; 1Ch 2:10-12

3:34 ʸ Ge 11:24,26

3:36 ᶻ Ge 11:12 ᵃ Ge 5:28-32

3:38 ᵇ Ge 5:1,2,6-9

4:1 ᶜ ver 14,18 ᵈ Lk 3:3,21 ᵉ Lk 2:27
4:2 ᶠ Ex 34:28; 1Ki 19:8

4:4 ᵍ Dt 8:3

4:5 ʰ Mt 24:14
4:6 ⁱ Jn 12:31; 14:30; 1Jn 5:19

4:8 ʲ Dt 6:13

Luke 4:1–13

Jesus, "full of the Holy Spirit," was "led by the Spirit in the desert" (v. 1). His successful encounter there with the devil reveals his thorough dedication to God's itinerary and travel guide. Jesus would take only the road God asked him to follow—no shortcuts, detours, or back doors. He knew that a successful walk *with* God depends on allowing him to act as guide and escort.

Jesus' temptations were unique, yet Satan and his forces use the same basic strategies with us. He tries to offer "shortcuts" in which we use God to gain material, social, and even spiritual power. When have you experienced run-ins with the enemy? Did you identify his role in the situation at the time? Were they frontal assaults, or did he take a more subtle approach? Were you, like Jesus, able to resist and move ahead down the road that leads to life?

" 'He will command his angels concerning you
to guard you carefully;
11 they will lift you up in their hands,
so that you will not strike your foot against a stone.' a" k

12 Jesus answered, "It says: 'Do not put the Lord your God to the test.' b" l
13 When the devil had finished all this tempting, m he left him n until an opportune time.

4:11
k Ps 91:11,12
4:12
l Dt 6:16
4:13
m Heb 4:15
n Jn 14:30

Jesus Rejected at Nazareth

4:14
o Mt 4:12 p Mt 9:26
4:15
q Mt 4:23

14 Jesus returned to Galilee o in the power of the Spirit, and news about him spread through the whole countryside. p 15 He taught in their synagogues, q and everyone praised him.

4:16
r Mt 2:23
s Mt 13:54

16 He went to Nazareth, r where he had been brought up, and on the Sabbath day he went into the synagogue, s as was his custom. And he stood up to read. 17 The scroll of the prophet Isaiah was handed to him. Unrolling it, he found the place where it is written:

4:18
t Jn 3:34

18 "The Spirit of the Lord is on me, t
because he has anointed me
to preach good news to the poor.
He has sent me to proclaim freedom for the prisoners
and recovery of sight for the blind,
to release the oppressed,

4:19
u Lev 25:10;
Isa 61:1,2
4:20
v ver 17; Mt 26:55

19 to proclaim the year of the Lord's favor." c u

20 Then he rolled up the scroll, gave it back to the attendant and sat down. v The eyes of everyone in the synagogue were fastened on him, 21 and he began by saying to them, "Today this scripture is fulfilled in your hearing."

a 11 Psalm 91:11,12   b 12 Deut. 6:16   c 19 Isaiah 61:1,2

Luke 4:14–30

Luke placed Jesus' sermon in his hometown of Nazareth as the inaugural message for his ministry. Jesus' choice of Isaiah as his subject caused a stir. All Israel believed this passage not only to be the text that would announce the Messiah's coming, but also the one that instituted the Year of the Jubilee ("the year of the Lord's favor"). When the Messiah came, everyone was to get a new beginning—the poor, the oppressed, the blind, and the indebted. When Jesus cited outsiders as recipients of God's blessing, he provoked rage. His ministry began with people trying to kill him!

The gospel message is ideally suited to poor people and those who know their need. The self-sufficient, well-to-do often live with a false sense of security and control. The Messiah makes all things new, and his reign pertains to every aspect of our lives—physical, social, spiritual, financial. This Good News, as the angel announced at Jesus' birth, is "for all the people" (2:10), especially those who feel like outsiders to God's blessing. How might people in your fellowship respond if Jesus were to preach this message from your pulpit?

4:18–19

Jesus' Ministry

Jesus quoted some verses from the book of Isaiah to outline the focus of his ministry. Each point can be understood both spiritually and physically:

✓ Task	Spiritual	Physical
1. Preach the gospel to the poor.	Tell the story of Jesus.	Live out the story by helping the needy.
2. Proclaim release to the captives.	Teach that sin's bondage is over.	Fight for freedom for all.
3. Recovery of sight to the blind	Help remove ignorance of God.	Provide medical help for the sick.
4. Set free those who are oppressed.	Release people from sin's grasp.	Help remove injustice from the world.
5. Proclaim the year of the Lord.	Instill hope in the spiritually dead.	Work so humans everywhere may thrive.

22All spoke well of him and were amazed at the gracious words that came from his lips. "Isn't this Joseph's son?" they asked. *w*

23Jesus said to them, "Surely you will quote this proverb to me: 'Physician, heal yourself! Do here in your hometown *x* what we have heard that you did in Capernaum.' " *y*

24"I tell you the truth," he continued, "no prophet is accepted in his hometown. *z* 25I assure you that there were many widows in Israel in Elijah's time, when the sky was shut for three and a half years and there was a severe famine throughout the land. *a* 26Yet Elijah was not sent to any of them, but to a widow in Zarephath in the region of Sidon. *b* 27And there were many in Israel with leprosy *a* in the time of Elisha the prophet, yet not one of them was cleansed—only Naaman the Syrian." *c*

28All the people in the synagogue were furious when they heard this. 29They got up, drove him out of the town, *d* and took him to the brow of the hill on which the town was built, in order to throw him down the cliff. 30But he walked right through the crowd and went on his way. *e*

Jesus Drives Out an Evil Spirit

31Then he went down to Capernaum, *f* a town in Galilee, and on the Sabbath began to teach the people. 32They were amazed at his teaching, *g* because his message had authority. *h*

33In the synagogue there was a man possessed by a demon, an evil *b* spirit. He cried out at the top of his voice, 34"Ha! What do you want with us, *i* Jesus of Nazareth? *j* Have you come to destroy us? I know who you are *k*—the Holy One of God!" *l*

35"Be quiet!" Jesus said sternly. *m* "Come out of him!" Then the demon threw the man down before them all and came out without injuring him.

36All the people were amazed *n* and said to each other, "What is this teaching? With authority *o* and power he gives orders to evil spirits and they come out!" 37And the news about him spread throughout the surrounding area. *p*

Jesus Heals Many

38Jesus left the synagogue and went to the home of Simon. Now Simon's mother-in-law was suffering from a high fever, and they asked Jesus to help her. 39So he bent over her and rebuked *q* the fever, and it left her. She got up at once and began to wait on them.

40When the sun was setting, the people brought to Jesus all who had various kinds of sickness, and laying his hands on each one, *r* he healed them. *s* 41Moreover, demons

a 27 The Greek word was used for various diseases affecting the skin—not necessarily leprosy.
b 33 Greek *unclean*; also in verse 36

4:22
w Mt 13:54,55; Jn 6:42; 7:15
4:23
x ver 16
y Mk 1:21-28; 2:1-12
4:24
z Mt 13:57; Jn 4:44
4:25
a 1Ki 17:1; 18:1; Jas 5:17,18
4:26
b 1Ki 17:8-16; Mt 11:21
4:27
c 2Ki 5:1-14
4:29
d Nu 15:35; Ac 7:58; Heb 13:12
4:30
e Jn 8:59; 10:39
4:31
f ver 23; Mt 4:13
4:32
g Mt 7:28 *h* ver 36; Mt 7:29
4:34
i Mt 8:29 *j* Mk 1:24
k Jas 2:19 *l* ver 41; Mk 1:24
4:35
m ver 39,41; Mt 8:26; Lk 8:24
4:36
n Mt 7:28 *o* ver 32; Mt 7:29; Mt 10:1
4:37
p ver 14; Mt 9:26
4:39
q ver 35,41
4:40
r Mk 5:23 *s* Mt 4:23

Luke 4:31–37

The first of Jesus' miracles Luke recorded was an exorcism. This makes sense, since Jesus' primary opponents were the spiritual forces of evil: Demons get 23 dishonorable mentions in this Gospel. Jews had long believed their Messiah would crush demonic power, and Jesus had already sparred with Satan in the desert. Now he faced off against the devil's cohorts. Jesus' work, including casting out of demons, authenticated him as the unique, set-apart One from God (cf. Acts 10:38).

As we participate in the coming of Christ's kingdom, we too engage in spiritual battle. Jesus' authority is complete—authoritative teaching, but also power over evil, illness, injustice, and death. Our proclamation of the gospel isn't simply done with words. We do it as the Spirit manifests the power of Christ in our lives and deeds. Have you considered how you and your church family might demonstrate Jesus' compassion to those suffering

from demonic oppression or mental illness? What would such a ministry look like in your community?

Luke 4:38–44

Jesus' sermon in Capernaum was similar to the one he had preached at Nazareth (vv. 16–21)—a word of release and fulfillment. Luke didn't define the kingdom of God here, but the message of release in Luke 4 suggests that it's a "place" of deliverance, where the forces of evil can be overcome. Stay tuned, Luke seemed to be saying, quoting Jesus in verse 43. This cryptic kingdom reference piques our interest, and we won't be disappointed. "This is why I was sent," Jesus stated simply.

Jesus came to proclaim and inaugurate his kingdom. Not a place with geographic boundaries, it's present wherever God's grace and power breaks the control of Satan, evil, sin, suffering, and injustice. We have the privilege of participating in God's continuing activity of overwhelming Satan's "kingdom" and infusing it with good.

came out of many people, shouting, "You are the Son of God!" [t] But he rebuked [u] them and would not allow them to speak, [v] because they knew he was the Christ. [a]

42 At daybreak Jesus went out to a solitary place. The people were looking for him and when they came to where he was, they tried to keep him from leaving them. 43 But he said, "I must preach the good news of the kingdom of God [w] to the other towns also, because that is why I was sent." 44 And he kept on preaching in the synagogues of Judea. [b][x]

The Calling of the First Disciples

5 One day as Jesus was standing by the Lake of Gennesaret, [c] with the people crowding around him and listening to the word of God, [y] 2 he saw at the water's edge two boats, left there by the fishermen, who were washing their nets. 3 He got into one of the boats, the one belonging to Simon, and asked him to put out a little from shore. Then he sat down and taught the people from the boat. [z]

4 When he had finished speaking, he said to Simon, "Put out into deep water, and let down [d] the nets for a catch." [a]

5 Simon answered, "Master, [b] we've worked hard all night and haven't caught anything. [c] But because you say so, I will let down the nets."

6 When they had done so, they caught such a large number of fish that their nets began to break. [d] 7 So they signaled their partners in the other boat to come and help them, and they came and filled both boats so full that they began to sink.

8 When Simon Peter saw this, he fell at Jesus' knees and said, "Go away from me, Lord; I am a sinful man!" [e] 9 For he and all his companions were astonished at the catch of fish they had taken, 10 and so were James and John, the sons of Zebedee, Simon's partners.

Then Jesus said to Simon, "Don't be afraid; [f] from now on you will catch men." 11 So they pulled their boats up on shore, left everything and followed him. [g]

The Man With Leprosy

12 While Jesus was in one of the towns, a man came along who was covered with leprosy. [e][h] When he saw Jesus, he fell with his face to the ground and begged him, "Lord, if you are willing, you can make me clean."

13 Jesus reached out his hand and touched the man. "I am willing," he said. "Be clean!" And immediately the leprosy left him.

[a] 41 Or Messiah   [b] 44 Or the land of the Jews; some manuscripts Galilee   [c] 1 That is, Sea of Galilee   [d] 4 The Greek verb is plural.   [e] 12 The Greek word was used for various diseases affecting the skin—not necessarily leprosy.

Cross-reference column
4:41 [t] Mt 4:3 [u] ver 35 [v] Mt 8:4

4:43 [w] Mt 3:2

4:44 [x] Mt 4:23

5:1 [y] Mk 4:14; Heb 4:12

5:3 [z] Mt 13:2

5:4 [a] Jn 21:6
5:5 [b] Lk 8:24,45; 9:33,49; 17:13 [c] Jn 21:3

5:6 [d] Jn 21:11

5:8 [e] Ge 18:27; Job 42:6; Isa 6:5

5:10 [f] Mt 14:27
5:11 [g] ver 28; Mt 4:19

5:12 [h] Mt 8:2

Luke 5:1–11

A carpenter/itinerant preacher informed a fisherman that it was time to fish—and he complied. Conditions weren't favorable, but the effort was successful—so successful that the "system" was ill-equipped to handle the intake. Peter failed at first to realize that admitting his limitation was the one prerequisite needed for service; only then could he truly depend on God. But his subsequent confession of sin became his résumé for service. Jesus' call to ministry marked a radical career change for him and his companions.

Peter's professional training and instincts told him there was little chance of a successful catch. But he staked his obedience on Jesus' reputation. Such willingness to follow where Jesus leads may go against the grain of culture, custom, common sense, or accepted "wisdom." But sometimes God stretches us, exercising the muscles of our faith by taking us to surprising places in surprising ways. How willing are you to go wherever and do whatever Jesus asks?

Luke 5:12–16

The leper's request raised the question of Jesus' willingness—not ability—to heal. Lepers were regarded as social and religious outcasts beyond the reach of God's mercy. The very fact that this man approached and addressed Jesus at all took grit. Before declaring his willingness and announcing the man cleansed, Jesus touched him—a stroke of compassion and acceptance that must have sent a thrill coursing through the veins of a contaminated, shunned sufferer (cf. Lev. 13:46; Num. 19:22).

In Jesus' day leprosy, or any contagious skin disease, was viewed as a reflection of sin. So to watching eyes, the Lord reached out and touched a sinner, not just a leper. Similarly, the argument today that AIDS victims have often been engaged in serious sin isn't a rationale for a cold shoulder or lack of response from Christians. Jesus came to save people from sin, of which the very presence of sickness on Earth is a natural consequence. How willing are you to follow in his footsteps, to touch society's untouchables?

14Then Jesus ordered him, "Don't tell anyone,*i* but go, show yourself to the priest and offer the sacrifices that Moses commanded*j* for your cleansing, as a testimony to them."

5:14
i Mt 8:4
j Lev 14:2-32

15Yet the news about him spread all the more,*k* so that crowds of people came to hear him and to be healed of their sicknesses. 16But Jesus often withdrew to lonely places and prayed.*l*

5:15
k Mt 9:26

5:16
l Mt 14:23; Lk 3:21

Jesus Heals a Paralytic

17One day as he was teaching, Pharisees and teachers of the law,*m* who had come from every village of Galilee and from Judea and Jerusalem, were sitting there. And the power of the Lord was present for him to heal the sick.*n* 18Some men came carrying a paralytic on a mat and tried to take him into the house to lay him before Jesus. 19When they could not find a way to do this because of the crowd, they went up on the roof and lowered him on his mat through the tiles into the middle of the crowd, right in front of Jesus. 20When Jesus saw their faith, he said, "Friend, your sins are forgiven."*o*

5:17
m Mt 15:1; Lk 2:46
n Mk 5:30; Lk 6:19

5:20
o Lk 7:48,49

21The Pharisees and the teachers of the law began thinking to themselves, "Who is this fellow who speaks blasphemy? Who can forgive sins but God alone?"*p* 22Jesus knew what they were thinking and asked, "Why are you thinking these things in your hearts? 23Which is easier: to say, 'Your sins are forgiven,' or to say, 'Get up and walk'? 24But that you may know that the Son of Man*q* has authority on earth to forgive sins . . ." He said to the paralyzed man, "I tell you, get up, take your mat and go home." 25Immediately he stood up in front of them, took what he had been lying on and went home praising God. 26Everyone was amazed and gave praise to God.*r* They were filled with awe and said, "We have seen remarkable things today."

5:21
p Isa 43:25

5:24
q Mt 8:20

5:26
r Mt 9:8

The Calling of Levi

27After this, Jesus went out and saw a tax collector by the name of Levi sitting at his tax booth. "Follow me,"*s* Jesus said to him, 28and Levi got up, left everything and followed him.*t*

5:27
s Mt 4:19
5:28
t ver 11; Mt 4:19

29Then Levi held a great banquet for Jesus at his house, and a large crowd of tax collectors*u* and others were eating with them. 30But the Pharisees and the teachers of the law who belonged to their sect*v* complained to his disciples, "Why do you eat and drink with tax collectors and 'sinners'?"*w* 31Jesus answered them, "It is not the healthy who need a doctor, but the sick. 32I have not come to call the righteous, but sinners to repentance."*x*

5:29
u Lk 15:1
5:30
v Ac 23:9 *w* Mt 9:11

5:32
x Jn 3:17

Jesus Questioned About Fasting

33They said to him, "John's disciples*y* often fast and pray, and so do the disciples of the Pharisees, but yours go on eating and drinking."

5:33
y Lk 7:18; Jn 1:35; 3:25,26

Luke 5:17–26

Jesus asked the Pharisees to ponder a question: Is it easier to declare sins forgiven or to tell a paraplegic to get up and walk? Neither is easy, but the Pharisees knew that only God can forgive sins. With his authority over sin and suffering, Jesus scandalized and amazed them all.

If Jesus were to give you a complete physical, how would you be likely to fare? Today we tend to leave sin out of the health equation, zeroing in on chemicals, physiology, and biology. Jesus' later words about a man born blind (John 9:1–3) warn against *always* making a sin-health connection. But the fact is that we are *whole* persons—sometimes unwell because we are unwise. Whatever the relationship, God is committed to healing our souls and our bodies.

Luke 5:27–32

Jesus called Levi to "follow" him, to become his disciple. Our Lord was demonstrating that tax collectors (regarded as corrupt conspirators with the occupying Roman government), like fishermen (vv. 8–11), can enter into an intimate relationship with God and leadership in the kingdom. Pharisees, on the other hand, sought to preserve their righteousness by avoiding "sinners." Jesus was clear that God draws close to those who know their need.

Levi's life took a 180-degree turn because of Jesus; he couldn't wait to introduce him to his friends. Jesus extended himself toward others beyond the "clique" of his disciples. Have you been willing to do the same? It's easy for us as Christians to limit our social circle to fellow church members or to those we think are acceptable and "good." Is God calling you to invite into your home and life those beyond your normal Christian circle?

5:34
z Jn 3:29

5:35
a Lk 9:22; 17:22;
Jn 16:5-7

34 Jesus answered, "Can you make the guests of the bridegroom^z fast while he is with them? 35 But the time will come when the bridegroom will be taken from them;^{a} in those days they will fast."

36 He told them this parable: "No one tears a patch from a new garment and sews it on an old one. If he does, he will have torn the new garment, and the patch from the new will not match the old. 37 And no one pours new wine into old wineskins. If he does, the new wine will burst the skins, the wine will run out and the wineskins will be ruined. 38 No, new wine must be poured into new wineskins. 39 And no one after drinking old wine wants the new, for he says, 'The old is better.' "

Lord of the Sabbath

6:1
b Dt 23:25

6:2
c Mt 12:2

6:3
d 1Sa 21:6
6:4
e Lev 24:5,9
6:5
f Mt 8:20
6:6
g ver 1

6:7
h Mt 12:10
i Mt 12:2
6:8
j Mt 9:4

6 One Sabbath Jesus was going through the grainfields, and his disciples began to pick some heads of grain, rub them in their hands and eat the kernels.^{b} 2 Some of the Pharisees asked, "Why are you doing what is unlawful on the Sabbath?"^{c}

3 Jesus answered them, "Have you never read what David did when he and his companions were hungry?^{d} 4 He entered the house of God, and taking the consecrated bread, he ate what is lawful only for priests to eat.^{e} And he also gave some to his companions." 5 Then Jesus said to them, "The Son of Man^f is Lord of the Sabbath."

6 On another Sabbath^g he went into the synagogue and was teaching, and a man was there whose right hand was shriveled. 7 The Pharisees and the teachers of the law were looking for a reason to accuse Jesus, so they watched him closely^h to see if he would heal on the Sabbath.^{i} 8 But Jesus knew what they were thinking^j and said to the man with the shriveled hand, "Get up and stand in front of everyone." So he got up and stood there.

9 Then Jesus said to them, "I ask you, which is lawful on the Sabbath: to do good or to do evil, to save life or to destroy it?"

6:11
k Jn 5:18

10 He looked around at them all, and then said to the man, "Stretch out your hand." He did so, and his hand was completely restored. 11 But they were furious^k and began to discuss with one another what they might do to Jesus.

The Twelve Apostles

6:12
l Lk 3:21
6:13
m Mk 6:30
6:15
n Mt 9:9

12 One of those days Jesus went out to a mountainside to pray, and spent the night praying to God.^{l} 13 When morning came, he called his disciples to him and chose twelve of them, whom he also designated apostles:^{m} 14 Simon (whom he named Peter), his brother Andrew, James, John, Philip, Bartholomew, 15 Matthew,^{n} Thomas, James son of Alphaeus, Simon who was called the Zealot, 16 Judas son of James, and Judas Iscariot, who became a traitor.

Luke 5:33–39

After answering the Pharisees' question about fasting, Jesus backed up his reply with three illustrations: (1) The image of the new and old garment shows that blending what Jesus brings with the old ways creates a destructive mix. (2) The picture of new and old wineskins reveals that Jesus was more than a reformer of Judaism; he had come to refashion it into something fresh. (3) Jesus' final analogy used a common proverb to indicate his expectation that many would continue to resist change at all cost.

Jesus ushered in a new era, one in which we still share. The new way focuses on changed character expressed in changed conduct—not just on the externals of relating to God—and on more serious concerns about the condition of the heart and just treatment of others, both within and outside the community. How do you assess your spiritual life? What qualities describe your relationships with God and other people?

Luke 6:1–11

Luke's placement of this incident (after the passage about Jesus' new way) was no accident. This event showed a radically new approach to Sabbath issues—new wine going into new wineskins. Implied in the scribes' and Pharisees' attitudes toward the man with the shriveled hand was the assumption that he could live with his chronic condition until after the Sabbath. Jesus approached the Sabbath from a relational angle. The ironic edge to his question in verse 9 insinuated that *failure to act* would have constituted evil.

Jesus implied that Sabbath observance is futile without a servant attitude. His healing act demonstrated the priority God places on showing mercy—as soon as opportunity arises. The Jewish leaders, preoccupied by a Sabbath "violation," ignored the restoration. Our natural reaction is to judge these hardhearted men. But more to the point, how quick are we to show mercy—on Sunday or any other day God has made?

Blessings and Woes

[17] He went down with them and stood on a level place. A large crowd of his disciples was there and a great number of people from all over Judea, from Jerusalem, and from the coast of Tyre and Sidon, [o] [18] who had come to hear him and to be healed of their diseases. Those troubled by evil[a] spirits were cured, [19] and the people all tried to touch him, [p] because power was coming from him and healing them all. [q]

[20] Looking at his disciples, he said:

> "Blessed are you who are poor,
>   for yours is the kingdom of God. [r]
> [21] Blessed are you who hunger now,
>   for you will be satisfied. [s]
> Blessed are you who weep now,
>   for you will laugh. [t]
> [22] Blessed are you when men hate you,
>   when they exclude you[u] and insult you[v]
>   and reject your name as evil,
>   because of the Son of Man. [w]

[23] "Rejoice in that day and leap for joy, [x] because great is your reward in heaven. For that is how their fathers treated the prophets. [y]

> [24] "But woe to you who are rich, [z]
>   for you have already received your comfort. [a]
> [25] Woe to you who are well fed now,
>   for you will go hungry. [b]
> Woe to you who laugh now,
>   for you will mourn and weep. [c]
> [26] Woe to you when all men speak well of you,
>   for that is how their fathers treated the false prophets. [d]

Love for Enemies

[27] "But I tell you who hear me: Love your enemies, do good to those who hate you, [e] [28] bless those who curse you, pray for those who mistreat you. [f] [29] If someone strikes you on one cheek, turn to him the other also. If someone takes your cloak, do not stop him from taking your tunic. [30] Give to everyone who asks you, and if

---

[a] 18 Greek *unclean*

6:17 o Mt 4:25; 11:21; Mk 3:7,8

6:19 p Mt 9:20 q Mt 14:36; Mk 5:30; Lk 5:17

6:20 r Mt 25:34

6:21 s Isa 55:1,2; Mt 5:6 t Isa 61:2,3; Mt 5:4; Rev 7:17

6:22 u Jn 9:22; 16:2 v Isa 51:7 w Jn 15:21

6:23 x Mt 5:12 y Mt 5:12

6:24 z Jas 5:1 a Lk 16:25

6:25 b Isa 65:13 c Pr 14:13

6:26 d Mt 7:15

6:27 e ver 35; Mt 5:44; Ro 12:20 6:28 f Mt 5:44

Luke 6:12–16

Rising opposition signaled the need for Jesus to organize his followers. He selected the Twelve in preparation for missions to come (see 9:1–6), as well as in anticipation of his future departure through death, resurrection, and ascension. He intended to build the disciples' character to the point where they could lead the church he would leave behind. The setting of Jesus' selection was no accident. He had spent the entire previous night in prayer, so his selection was set in a context of communion with God.

"The Twelve" included fishermen and a tax collector. Jesus no doubt consciously selected a diverse—and balanced—group, whose central bond was himself. The new community he builds today is as varied as his embrace is wide, and we can rejoice in that diversity. Jesus doesn't want or expect us all to be the same. Is prayer a unifying factor in your congregation? Is your commonality based on your sameness or on your mutual commitment to Christ? Are you personally willing to embrace diversity?

Luke 6:17–26

The Sermon on the Plain (vv. 20–49) is Luke's equivalent to Matthew's Sermon on the Mount. Jesus reversed the common understanding of who would be blessed. The poor, hungry, weeping, and despised—not the rich, satisfied, laughing, and applauded—would receive God's blessing. In fact, he uttered a "woe" of warning to the rest.

Why would God single out the poor and issue stark warnings to the rich? For one thing, Jesus was affirming the dignity of people the world treats as worthless. If God honors and cares for the poor, hungry, sorrowful, and rejected, shouldn't we do the same? God is committed to social as well as spiritual transformation. He seeks to redeem the whole person, to create a compassionate community concerned with all dimensions of life.

6:30
g Dt 15:7,8,10;
Pr 21:26
6:31
h Mt 7:12
6:32
i Mt 5:46

6:34
j Mt 5:42
6:35
k ver 27 l Ro 8:14
m Mk 5:7

6:36
n Jas 2:13
o Mt 5:48; 6:1;
Lk 11:2; 12:32;
Ro 8:15; Eph 4:6;
1Pe 1:17; 1Jn 1:3;
3:1
6:37
p Mt 7:1 q Mt 6:14

6:38
r Ps 79:12;
Isa 65:6,7
s Mt 7:2; Mk 4:24
6:39
t Mt 15:14
6:40
u Mt 10:24;
Jn 13:16

6:44
v Mt 12:33

6:45
w Pr 4:23;
Mt 12:34,35;
Mk 7:20

anyone takes what belongs to you, do not demand it back. g 31 Do to others as you would have them do to you. h

32 "If you love those who love you, what credit is that to you? i Even 'sinners' love those who love them. 33 And if you do good to those who are good to you, what credit is that to you? Even 'sinners' do that. 34 And if you lend to those from whom you expect repayment, what credit is that to you? j Even 'sinners' lend to 'sinners,' expecting to be repaid in full. 35 But love your enemies, do good to them, k and lend to them without expecting to get anything back. Then your reward will be great, and you will be sons l of the Most High, m because he is kind to the ungrateful and wicked. 36 Be merciful, n just as your Father o is merciful.

Judging Others

37 "Do not judge, and you will not be judged. p Do not condemn, and you will not be condemned. Forgive, and you will be forgiven. q 38 Give, and it will be given to you. A good measure, pressed down, shaken together and running over, will be poured into your lap. r For with the measure you use, it will be measured to you." s

39 He also told them this parable: "Can a blind man lead a blind man? Will they not both fall into a pit? t 40 A student is not above his teacher, but everyone who is fully trained will be like his teacher. u

41 "Why do you look at the speck of sawdust in your brother's eye and pay no attention to the plank in your own eye? 42 How can you say to your brother, 'Brother, let me take the speck out of your eye,' when you yourself fail to see the plank in your own eye? You hypocrite, first take the plank out of your eye, and then you will see clearly to remove the speck from your brother's eye.

A Tree and Its Fruit

43 "No good tree bears bad fruit, nor does a bad tree bear good fruit. 44 Each tree is recognized by its own fruit. v People do not pick figs from thornbushes, or grapes from briers. 45 The good man brings good things out of the good stored up in his heart, and the evil man brings evil things out of the evil stored up in his heart. For out of the overflow of his heart his mouth speaks. w

---

Luke 6:27–36

Following words of invitation and warning, Jesus addressed the disciples' ethical character. Fundamental to ethics is love—not like the world's, but a unique love that endures. The love Jesus commands isn't abstract but demonstrates itself, even to enemies, in concrete action. Judgment is always to be left in God's hands. The greatest possible resolution of conflict is for us to help transform an enemy into a friend of God through our positive acts of love.

To do what Jesus asks requires relational contact with the outside world. To be struck on the cheek implies being within striking distance. To give to beggars (or the destitute) means knowing where to find them. To love in a way that doesn't maneuver for a payback is to offer the world a radically new concept of attitude and behavior. How wide is your circle? God calls us to take the initiative and "do to others as we would have them do to us." This requires broadening our circle for Jesus' sake.

Luke 6:37–42

Just before this, Jesus had called his followers to be like God (v. 36) in terms of their willingness to offer mercy—a tall order! One concrete thing they weren't to do in imitation of God was judge others. God generously honors compassion. And Jesus denounced a critical spir-

it by pointing out our tendency to be hypocritically aware of a minor flaw in someone else while ignoring our own glaring deficiency.

A hypercritical spirit isn't any more open to love than a hypocritical one; it constantly evaluates everyone around it. Judgment is God's territory, but that doesn't mean we are exempt from all accountability. Jesus calls us to self-accountability. Are you able to receive rebuke and honestly approach the Lord for removal of your "beam"? The homes, communities, and nations of our world are fractured by remembered hurts and the inability to forgive. Christ's followers are to be marked by our forgiving, non-judgmental spirit. This will empower us to be agents of God's reconciling love.

Luke 6:43–45

How can we know another person's character? Jesus says to check out the fruit. His agricultural illustrations, drawn from everyday life in his day, depict two basic types of people—good (fruitful) and bad (unfruitful). Pointing out that Christians aren't perfect, just forgiven, only expresses part of the Good News. God wants to change us and produce through us the fruit that characterizes his life. The world needs people who know God and live out their faith in such a way that others can't miss the compelling evidence.

The Wise and Foolish Builders

46 "Why do you call me, 'Lord, Lord,'[x] and do not do what I say?[y] 47 I will show you what he is like who comes to me and hears my words and puts them into practice.[z] 48 He is like a man building a house, who dug down deep and laid the foundation on rock. When a flood came, the torrent struck that house but could not shake it, because it was well built. 49 But the one who hears my words and does not put them into practice is like a man who built a house on the ground without a foundation. The moment the torrent struck that house, it collapsed and its destruction was complete."

The Faith of the Centurion

7 When Jesus had finished saying all this[a] in the hearing of the people, he entered Capernaum. 2 There a centurion's servant, whom his master valued highly, was sick and about to die. 3 The centurion heard of Jesus and sent some elders of the Jews to him, asking him to come and heal his servant. 4 When they came to Jesus, they pleaded earnestly with him, "This man deserves to have you do this, 5 because he loves our nation and has built our synagogue." 6 So Jesus went with them.

He was not far from the house when the centurion sent friends to say to him: "Lord, don't trouble yourself, for I do not deserve to have you come under my roof. 7 That is why I did not even consider myself worthy to come to you. But say the word, and my servant will be healed.[b] 8 For I myself am a man under authority, with soldiers under me. I tell this one, 'Go,' and he goes; and that one, 'Come,' and he comes. I say to my servant, 'Do this,' and he does it."

9 When Jesus heard this, he was amazed at him, and turning to the crowd following him, he said, "I tell you, I have not found such great faith even in Israel." 10 Then the men who had been sent returned to the house and found the servant well.

Jesus Raises a Widow's Son

11 Soon afterward, Jesus went to a town called Nain, and his disciples and a large crowd went along with him. 12 As he approached the town gate, a dead person was being carried out—the only son of his mother, and she was a widow. And a large

---

6:46
x Jn 13:13
y Mal 1:6; Mt 7:21

6:47
z Lk 8:21; 11:28; Jas 1:22-25

7:1
a Mt 7:28

7:7
b Ps 107:20

📖 Jesus declared that we are what we produce, especially when it comes to our words. Stated simply, we are what we say. Our mouth is a litmus test of who we are spiritually. If you were to evaluate the character and tone of your daily speech, would it register like acid on litmus paper? Or would it indicate the sweet presence of a person secure in God's care? As James testified, we need to learn how to control our tongues (James 3:1–12). Where does your speech fall on the acidic-sweet continuum?

Luke 6:46–49

🔗 Jesus closed his sermon by turning to the issue of his authority. Any disciple who respects Jesus is obligated to do what he says. How could his followers otherwise call him "Lord"? To drive home his point, Jesus used a parable, drawing on imagery from Ezekiel 13:10–16. Nobody would dispute the foolishness of building a house without a foundation. What about a life?

📖 Our loyalty as disciples comes down to responding to Jesus in terms of what we *do*. Simply calling Jesus "Lord" holds little weight unless we live in obedience to him as Lord. If we obey him, we will be able to stand up to the harsh realities of life in a fallen world. By contrast, to ignore his teaching is to set ourselves up for tragic loss. As sad as it would be to lose our homes in a flood, it would be infinitely sadder for our lives to be swept away because we have failed to live God's way.

Luke 7: 1–10

🔗 The scenario here is interesting and possibly unusual. This Roman centurion sent a delegation of *Jewish* elders to ask Jesus to heal his dying slave. These messengers not only brought the man's request but lobbied on his behalf: The centurion loved Israel and had contributed to building the local synagogue. The question raised was significant on two levels: Would Jesus minister to someone from outside Israel, and would he help a wealthy individual? Jesus not only did both, he went on to hold up this non-Jewish outsider as the greatest example of faith he had seen.

📖 This Gentile soldier and the Jewish emissaries together served as an example of mutual respect overcoming cultural and ethnic barriers and religious prejudices. As our communities become more diverse, we need to appreciate other cultures. Our warmth and openness can build new bridges for the gospel where we might before have been isolated from each other through fear or ignorance. How can you employ whatever degree of power and wealth you possess to serve—not use—other people?

7:13
c ver 19; Lk 10:1;
13:15; 17:5; 22:61;
24:34; Jn 11:2

7:14
d Mt 9:25; Mk 1:31;
Lk 8:54; Jn 11:43;
Ac 9:40

7:16
e Lk 1:65 f Mt 9:8
g ver 39; Mt 21:11
h Lk 1:68

7:17
i Mt 9:26

7:18
j Mt 3:1 k Lk 5:33

7:21
l Mt 4:23

7:22
m Isa 29:18,19;
35:5,6; 61:1,2;
Lk 4:18

7:26
n Mt 11:9

7:27
o Mal 3:1;
Mt 11:10; Mk 1:2

7:28
p Mt 3:2

7:29
q Mt 21:32; Mk 1:5;
Lk 3:12

crowd from the town was with her. 13When the Lord c saw her, his heart went out to her and he said, "Don't cry."

14Then he went up and touched the coffin, and those carrying it stood still. He said, "Young man, I say to you, get up!" d 15The dead man sat up and began to talk, and Jesus gave him back to his mother.

16They were all filled with awe e and praised God. f "A great prophet g has appeared among us," they said. "God has come to help his people." h 17This news about Jesus spread throughout Judea a and the surrounding country. i

Jesus and John the Baptist

18John's j disciples k told him about all these things. Calling two of them, 19he sent them to the Lord to ask, "Are you the one who was to come, or should we expect someone else?"

20When the men came to Jesus, they said, "John the Baptist sent us to you to ask, 'Are you the one who was to come, or should we expect someone else?' "

21At that very time Jesus cured many who had diseases, sicknesses l and evil spirits, and gave sight to many who were blind. 22So he replied to the messengers, "Go back and report to John what you have seen and heard: The blind receive sight, the lame walk, those who have leprosy b are cured, the deaf hear, the dead are raised, and the good news is preached to the poor. m 23Blessed is the man who does not fall away on account of me."

24After John's messengers left, Jesus began to speak to the crowd about John: "What did you go out into the desert to see? A reed swayed by the wind? 25If not, what did you go out to see? A man dressed in fine clothes? No, those who wear expensive clothes and indulge in luxury are in palaces. 26But what did you go out to see? A prophet? n Yes, I tell you, and more than a prophet. 27This is the one about whom it is written:

" 'I will send my messenger ahead of you,
who will prepare your way before you.' c o

28I tell you, among those born of women there is no one greater than John; yet the one who is least in the kingdom of God p is greater than he."

29(All the people, even the tax collectors, when they heard Jesus' words, acknowledged that God's way was right, because they had been baptized by John. q 30But the

---

a 17 Or *the land of the Jews*   b 22 The Greek word was used for various diseases affecting the skin—not necessarily leprosy.   c 27 Mal. 3:1

Luke 7:11–17

The Old Testament prophets Elijah and Elisha had also miraculously raised the sons of bereaved mothers (1 Kings 17:17–24; 2 Kings 4:8–37). Jesus stopped this funeral procession and touched the burial plank—a gesture leaving him ritually unclean (Num. 19:11,16). But by doing so, he expressed his compassionate concern. In contrast to Elijah and Elisha, who stretched themselves out on the bodies, Jesus had only to utter a word. The crowd fittingly—but shortsightedly—concluded that he too was "a great prophet."

Jesus demonstrated another dimension of his authority—over death! His compassion extends to grieving widows. Sometimes our most effective response to another's pain is a simple act of kindness, not a solution or remedy. Simply touching the coffin showed Jesus' willingness to identify with—not back away from—the situation. Africa today is filled with grieving widows and children, their lives thrust into misery and poverty through AIDS. The church has the privilege of reaching out and touching them with Jesus' compassion, gentleness, and power.

Luke 7:18–35

John's question in verse 19 may surprise you. Jesus wasn't the type of Messiah he had expected. Nor had he likely envisioned pacing in a prison cell, adrenalin still pumping to get on with the program. So he sent a contingent to Jesus just to make sure he was in fact the Christ. But Jesus' failure to fulfill the politically-charged expectations for the coming Messiah didn't mean his ministry lacked authority. The marks of his Messianic kingdom were all-encompassing—transforming the lives of people spiritually, physically, and socially. Yet Jesus knew some would be offended by these changes among society's poor and outcast.

When John confronted him point blank about his identity, Jesus simply pointed to his actions. Unlike mere words, the undeniable results of in-depth ministry speak volumes. Jesus confirmed John's Messianic hopes, allowing John to deduce who he was based on the lives he had impacted. What criteria do you use to evaluate a ministry? How about your own?

Pharisees and experts in the law^r rejected God's purpose for themselves, because they had not been baptized by John.)

^{31}"To what, then, can I compare the people of this generation? What are they like? ^{32}They are like children sitting in the marketplace and calling out to each other:

" 'We played the flute for you,
    and you did not dance;
we sang a dirge,
    and you did not cry.'

^{33}For John the Baptist came neither eating bread nor drinking wine,^{s} and you say, 'He has a demon.' ^{34}The Son of Man came eating and drinking, and you say, 'Here is a glutton and a drunkard, a friend of tax collectors and "sinners." '^{t} ^{35}But wisdom is proved right by all her children."

7:30
^{r} Mt 22:35

7:33
^{s} Lk 1:15

7:34
^{t} Lk 5:29,30; 15:1,2

Jesus Anointed by a Sinful Woman

^{36}Now one of the Pharisees invited Jesus to have dinner with him, so he went to the Pharisee's house and reclined at the table. ^{37}When a woman who had lived a sinful life in that town learned that Jesus was eating at the Pharisee's house, she brought an alabaster jar of perfume, ^{38}and as she stood behind him at his feet weeping, she began to wet his feet with her tears. Then she wiped them with her hair, kissed them and poured perfume on them.

Luke 7:36–50

Lest we think Jesus was always at odds with the Pharisees, Luke noted that he went home to dinner with them. Hospitality was a sign of friendship and the home a haven. Into this home of a pious, ritually pure Pharisee burst a woman, most likely a prostitute—an "unclean" sinner—who responded in faith and represented the hope that the most disreputable of sinners can find God. Simon the Pharisee revealed how *not* to approach the issue of flagrant sin and its practitioners. And Jesus supplied the commentary, relationally and theologically, to what had taken place.

The woman expressed herself not in a loud voice but by silent action. Based on your experience, what approximate mix of testimony and service do you see as optimal for piquing the interest of nonbelievers in the Good News? Regarding the Pharisees' response, do you ever catch yourself subtly walling people off from God—assuming they are beyond his reach, or at least spiritually and socially unacceptable in your home and life? Or do you do all you can, relying on the unlimited power of the Holy Spirit, to lead them into the sphere of God's forgiveness?

7:36–50

Extravagant Devotion

The Bible is filled with examples of people (like this woman in Luke 7) who committed (or were asked to commit) extravagant acts for God. Some of the more memorable:

	Noah undertook a monstrous building project (Gen. 6).
	Abraham was willing to offer Isaac as a sacrifice (Gen. 22:1–19).
	Moses challenged the mighty pharaoh of Egypt (Ex. 4:18—12:31).
	Rahab harbored the Israelite spies (Josh. 2; 6:22–25).
	David fought Goliath (1 Sam. 17).
	Jonah preached to the Ninevites—finally (Jonah 3).
	Esther, at the risk of her life, interceded for her people (Est. 4–5; 7–8).
	Shadrach, Meshach, and Abednego defied the king's command to worship an image (Dan. 3).
	Jesus told a rich young man to sell all he had for the poor (Luke 18:18–30).
	Stephen boldly preached the gospel and was martyred by religious authorities (Acts 6:8—8:1).

³⁹When the Pharisee who had invited him saw this, he said to himself, "If this man were a prophet, ^u he would know who is touching him and what kind of woman she is—that she is a sinner."

⁴⁰Jesus answered him, "Simon, I have something to tell you."

"Tell me, teacher," he said.

⁴¹"Two men owed money to a certain moneylender. One owed him five hundred denarii, ^a and the other fifty. ⁴²Neither of them had the money to pay him back, so he canceled the debts of both. Now which of them will love him more?"

⁴³Simon replied, "I suppose the one who had the bigger debt canceled."

"You have judged correctly," Jesus said.

⁴⁴Then he turned toward the woman and said to Simon, "Do you see this woman? I came into your house. You did not give me any water for my feet, ^v but she wet my feet with her tears and wiped them with her hair. ⁴⁵You did not give me a kiss, ^w but this woman, from the time I entered, has not stopped kissing my feet. ⁴⁶You did not put oil on my head, ^x but she has poured perfume on my feet. ⁴⁷Therefore, I tell you, her many sins have been forgiven—for she loved much. But he who has been forgiven little loves little."

⁴⁸Then Jesus said to her, "Your sins are forgiven." ^y

⁴⁹The other guests began to say among themselves, "Who is this who even forgives sins?"

⁵⁰Jesus said to the woman, "Your faith has saved you; ^z go in peace." ^a

The Parable of the Sower

8 After this, Jesus traveled about from one town and village to another, proclaiming the good news of the kingdom of God. ^b The Twelve were with him, ²and also some women who had been cured of evil spirits and diseases: Mary (called Magdalene) ^c from whom seven demons had come out; ³Joanna the wife of Cuza, the manager of Herod's ^d household; Susanna; and many others. These women were helping to support them out of their own means.

⁴While a large crowd was gathering and people were coming to Jesus from town after town, he told this parable: ⁵"A farmer went out to sow his seed. As he was scattering the seed, some fell along the path; it was trampled on, and the birds of the air ate it up. ⁶Some fell on rock, and when it came up, the plants withered because they had no moisture. ⁷Other seed fell among thorns, which grew up with it and choked the plants. ⁸Still other seed fell on good soil. It came up and yielded a crop, a hundred times more than was sown."

When he said this, he called out, "He who has ears to hear, let him hear." ^e

⁹His disciples asked him what this parable meant. ¹⁰He said, "The knowledge of the secrets of the kingdom of God has been given to you, ^f but to others I speak in parables, so that,

" 'though seeing, they may not see;
though hearing, they may not understand.' ^{b g}

¹¹"This is the meaning of the parable: The seed is the word of God. ^h ¹²Those along the path are the ones who hear, and then the devil comes and takes away the

Margin references

7:39
u ver 16; Mt 21:11

7:44
v Ge 18:4; 19:2;
43:24; Jdg 19:21;
Jn 13:4-14; 1Ti 5:10
7:45
w Lk 22:47,48;
Ro 16:16
7:46
x Ps 23:5; Ecc 9:8

7:48
y Mt 9:2

7:50
z Mt 9:22; Mk 5:34;
Lk 8:48 a Ac 15:33

8:1
b Mt 4:23

8:2
c Mt 27:55,56
8:3
d Mt 14:1

8:8
e Mt 11:15

8:10
f Mt 13:11 g Isa 6:9;
Mt 13:13,14

8:11
h Heb 4:12

---

^a 41 A denarius was a coin worth about a day's wages.   ^b 10 Isaiah 6:9

Luke 8:1–15

Contributors to Jesus' ministry spanned gender and social scales. A pattern (grace received, ministry given) emerges in the exemplary responses of these women. Luke underscored that these faithful female disciples provided financially for Jesus and the others. Regarding the parable of the soils, we are wise to remember that fruit doesn't sprout overnight. Jesus' teaching doesn't look at a person's reaction to God and his Word in a single moment, but over a period of time. Response is the product of a process—a lifelong journey.

These women stand out in history as positive examples of women in leadership who served the Master with whatever resources they had. No matter who or what we are, each of us has more to give than we realize. A careful assessment of our unique, individual gifts will allow us all to engage in creative, satisfying, seed-sowing ministry. What a privilege, responsibility—and wonder—that Jesus works through *us*.

word from their hearts, so that they may not believe and be saved. [13]Those on the
rock are the ones who receive the word with joy when they hear it, but they have
no root. They believe for a while, but in the time of testing they fall away.[i] [14]The
seed that fell among thorns stands for those who hear, but as they go on their way
they are choked by life's worries, riches[j] and pleasures, and they do not mature.
[15]But the seed on good soil stands for those with a noble and good heart, who hear
the word, retain it, and by persevering produce a crop.

A Lamp on a Stand

[16]"No one lights a lamp and hides it in a jar or puts it under a bed. Instead, he
puts it on a stand, so that those who come in can see the light.[k] [17]For there is nothing hidden that will not be disclosed, and nothing concealed that will not be
known or brought out into the open.[l] [18]Therefore consider carefully how you listen. Whoever has will be given more; whoever does not have, even what he thinks
he has will be taken from him."[m]

Jesus' Mother and Brothers

[19]Now Jesus' mother and brothers came to see him, but they were not able to get
near him because of the crowd. [20]Someone told him, "Your mother and brothers[n]
are standing outside, wanting to see you."

[21]He replied, "My mother and brothers are those who hear God's word and put
it into practice."[o]

Jesus Calms the Storm

[22]One day Jesus said to his disciples, "Let's go over to the other side of the lake."
So they got into a boat and set out. [23]As they sailed, he fell asleep. A squall came down
on the lake, so that the boat was being swamped, and they were in great danger.
[24]The disciples went and woke him, saying, "Master, Master,[p] we're going to
drown!"

He got up and rebuked[q] the wind and the raging waters; the storm subsided, and
all was calm.[r] [25]"Where is your faith?" he asked his disciples.

8:13 [i] Mt 11:6
8:14 [j] Mt 19:23; 1Ti 6:9,10,17
8:16 [k] Mt 5:15; Mk 4:21; Lk 11:33
8:17 [l] Mt 10:26; Mk 4:22; Lk 12:2
8:18 [m] Mt 13:12; 25:29; Lk 19:26
8:20 [n] Jn 7:5
8:21 [o] Lk 6:47; 11:28; Jn 14:21
8:24 [p] Lk 5:5 [q] Lk 4:35,39,41 [r] Ps 107:29; Jnh 1:15

Luke 8:16–18

Jesus called people to respond to the light—in light of the dire consequences of not doing so. The function of light, and Jesus' message, is to make the hidden visible. He switched metaphors from sight to hearing, cautioning his audience to listen with care; they were accountable for what they did with what they heard. Whoever "has"—in terms of receiving and responding to revelation—will receive more revelation (and responsibility). But those who refuse to respond will lose what they thought they had.

God still holds us accountable for what we do with his Word. Hearing (or reading) it well is crucial. He's put his revelation on a lampstand. The secrets of our hearts and the hidden aspects of our lives will one day be disclosed. If we have heard and internalized the truth, we will live in its light.

Luke 8:19–21

Jesus' family consists of those who *hear* and *do* God's Word—a common Scriptural pairing (6:46–49; James 1:22–25). His remark recapped his messages about listening and responding in the preceding parables.

The application is straightforward: Don't just listen to or study God's Word—apply it. *Do* it. The life of faith involves more than intellectual and theological understanding (getting it). God's will for us is that we be so responsive to him that we reflect his character. This is what it means to be conformed to the image of Christ (cf. Rom. 12:1–2). In following Christ we enter a new "family"—those who bear the family resemblance marked by the life of Christ.

Luke 8:22–25

The disciples needed to understand that their Teacher's authority extended to all of creation. They did the right thing in turning to Jesus for help, but their cry that they were about to die revealed a deplorable weakness of faith. Had they understood God's care and the implication of Jesus' remark that they *were going to the other side of the lake*, they would have realized that divine providence never takes a break.

Our point of connection may be with the disciples' feelings of helplessness about where Jesus had led them. Ravaging events in our lives may leave us feeling vulnerable, even to the point of doubting God's goodness. God has never promised us uninterrupted sunshine, placid waters, or clear sailing. But he does promise the resources to navigate white water. Jesus has authority over anything and everything we might experience. Imagine people whose lives feel besieged by storms of illness, political chaos, and war. What would it mean for Jesus to calm their storm?

In fear and amazement they asked one another, "Who is this? He commands even the winds and the water, and they obey him."

The Healing of a Demon-possessed Man

26They sailed to the region of the Gerasenes, a which is across the lake from Galilee. 27When Jesus stepped ashore, he was met by a demon-possessed man from the town. For a long time this man had not worn clothes or lived in a house, but had lived in the tombs. 28When he saw Jesus, he cried out and fell at his feet, shouting at the top of his voice, "What do you want with me, s Jesus, Son of the Most High God? t I beg you, don't torture me!" 29For Jesus had commanded the evil b spirit to come out of the man. Many times it had seized him, and though he was chained hand and foot and kept under guard, he had broken his chains and had been driven by the demon into solitary places.

30Jesus asked him, "What is your name?"

"Legion," he replied, because many demons had gone into him. 31And they begged him repeatedly not to order them to go into the Abyss. u

32A large herd of pigs was feeding there on the hillside. The demons begged Jesus to let them go into them, and he gave them permission. 33When the demons came out of the man, they went into the pigs, and the herd rushed down the steep bank into the lake v and was drowned.

34When those tending the pigs saw what had happened, they ran off and reported this in the town and countryside, 35and the people went out to see what had happened. When they came to Jesus, they found the man from whom the demons had gone out, sitting at Jesus' feet, w dressed and in his right mind; and they were afraid. 36Those who had seen it told the people how the demon-possessed x man had been cured. 37Then all the people of the region of the Gerasenes asked Jesus to leave them, y because they were overcome with fear. So he got into the boat and left.

38The man from whom the demons had gone out begged to go with him, but Jesus sent him away, saying, 39"Return home and tell how much God has done for you." So the man went away and told all over town how much Jesus had done for him.

A Dead Girl and a Sick Woman

40Now when Jesus returned, a crowd welcomed him, for they were all expecting him. 41Then a man named Jairus, a ruler of the synagogue, z came and fell at Jesus' feet, pleading with him to come to his house 42because his only daughter, a girl of about twelve, was dying.

As Jesus was on his way, the crowds almost crushed him. 43And a woman was

---

Margin references:

8:28
s Mt 8:29 t Mk 5:7

8:31
u Rev 9:1,2,11; 11:7; 17:8; 20:1,3

8:33
v ver 22,23

8:35
w Lk 10:39
8:36
x Mt 4:24

8:37
y Ac 16:39

8:41
z ver 49; Mk 5:22

---

a 26 Some manuscripts *Gadarenes;* other manuscripts *Gergesenes;* also in verse 37   b 29 Greek *unclean*

Luke 8:26–39

📖 The detailed description of the demon-possessed man demonstrates the destructive power of these evil spirits. He had totally withdrawn from society, existing naked among the tombs. Inhuman strength prevented him from being restrained. The incident involving the pigs also indicates the impact of demonic influence—in this case, the destruction of life. Though the demons themselves remained invisible, the effect of their presence in the pigs illustrates how dangerous they can be.

💻 Our world toys with spiritual forces. The lure of the demonic has taken on a popular air. Much of our music and many of our movies are laden with innuendo—and false and unscriptural information—about the spirit world. As Christians, we recognize the reality of the demonic but trust that Jesus has authority over all the supernatural powers that oppose God and destroy, deface, defeat, and deform life.

Luke 8:40–56

📖 Jesus' power over the twin enemies of disease and death showcased his sovereignty over life itself. These related stories, one enfolded within the other, together make a strong statement. As with the other miracles recorded in Luke's Gospel, the emphasis was on Jesus' authority. But the combination also raises another theme—faith. Take a moment to compare and contrast the faith of these two dissimilar pleaders. The woman and Jairus reflected different aspects of growing in faith and understanding.

💻 Faith rightly seizes the initiative to claim God's promises, but it must sometimes be patient. In one sense faith forges full speed ahead; in another it forces us to curb our natural impulsiveness. How would you evaluate your effectiveness in this balancing act—exercising a vibrant faith that impacts the affairs of your life, while at the same time waiting on the Lord's timing?

LUKE 9:4

there who had been subject to bleeding[a] for twelve years,[a] but no one could heal her. [44]She came up behind him and touched the edge of his cloak,[b] and immediately her bleeding stopped.

[45]"Who touched me?" Jesus asked.

When they all denied it, Peter said, "Master,[c] the people are crowding and pressing against you."

[46]But Jesus said, "Someone touched me;[d] I know that power has gone out from me."[e]

[47]Then the woman, seeing that she could not go unnoticed, came trembling and fell at his feet. In the presence of all the people, she told why she had touched him and how she had been instantly healed. [48]Then he said to her, "Daughter, your faith has healed you.[f] Go in peace."[g]

[49]While Jesus was still speaking, someone came from the house of Jairus, the synagogue ruler.[h] "Your daughter is dead," he said. "Don't bother the teacher any more."

[50]Hearing this, Jesus said to Jairus, "Don't be afraid; just believe, and she will be healed."

[51]When he arrived at the house of Jairus, he did not let anyone go in with him except Peter, John and James,[i] and the child's father and mother. [52]Meanwhile, all the people were wailing and mourning[j] for her. "Stop wailing," Jesus said. "She is not dead but asleep."[k]

[53]They laughed at him, knowing that she was dead. [54]But he took her by the hand and said, "My child, get up!"[l] [55]Her spirit returned, and at once she stood up. Then Jesus told them to give her something to eat. [56]Her parents were astonished, but he ordered them not to tell anyone what had happened.[m]

Jesus Sends Out the Twelve

9 When Jesus had called the Twelve together, he gave them power and authority to drive out all demons[n] and to cure diseases,[o] [2]and he sent them out to preach the kingdom of God[p] and to heal the sick. [3]He told them: "Take nothing for the journey—no staff, no bag, no bread, no money, no extra tunic.[q] [4]Whatever

[a] 43 Many manuscripts *years, and she had spent all she had on doctors*

8:43
[a] Lev 15:25-30
8:44
[b] Mt 9:20

8:45
[c] Lk 5:5

8:46
[d] Mt 14:36; Mk 3:10 [e] Lk 5:17; 6:19

8:48
[f] Mt 9:22
[g] Ac 15:33

8:49
[h] ver 41

8:51
[i] Mt 4:21
8:52
[j] Lk 23:27
[k] Lk 9:24; Jn 11:11,13

8:54
[l] Lk 7:14

8:56
[m] Mt 8:4

9:1
[n] Mt 10:1
[o] Mt 4:23; Lk 5:17
9:2
[p] Mt 3:2
9:3
[q] Lk 10:4; 22:35

Luke 9:1–9

Jesus intended to permeate the nation of Israel with the message of kingdom hope. He commissioned the Twelve to minister on his behalf in the towns and villages. He sent them out with the same authority he exercised, enabling them to preach the kingdom, drive out demons, and heal the sick. Jesus' ministry was, and is, one of word and deed. And he still empowers his followers to serve in both these critical areas.

9:1–9

Spiritual Trips

Jesus sent out the 12 disciples to preach the kingdom of God and heal the sick. Most of our trips are either for business or pleasure. Sometimes we are called to take what might be called spiritual trips. Planning and executing such a trip calls for a unique approach:

	Business Trip	**Pleasure Trip**	**Spiritual Trip**
1. Motivation:	Boss's request or business need	Pleasure seeking	God's call
2. Planning:	Assistant sets itinerary.	Guidebook choices	Faith in the unknown
3. Authority:	Company	Personal	Holy Spirit
4. Agenda:	Company business	Enjoyment	Serve/build/heal/pray/provide relief
5. Resources:	Host business	Tourist office	Local church or mission organization
6. Luggage:	Carry-on bags	Checked luggage	As little as possible physically/ much spiritually/relief supplies

1693

house you enter, stay there until you leave that town. [5]If people do not welcome you, shake the dust off your feet when you leave their town, as a testimony against them." [r] [6]So they set out and went from village to village, preaching the gospel and healing people everywhere.

[7]Now Herod[s] the tetrarch heard about all that was going on. And he was perplexed, because some were saying that John[t] had been raised from the dead,[u] [8]others that Elijah had appeared,[v] and still others that one of the prophets of long ago had come back to life.[w] [9]But Herod said, "I beheaded John. Who, then, is this I hear such things about?" And he tried to see him.[x]

Jesus Feeds the Five Thousand

[10]When the apostles[y] returned, they reported to Jesus what they had done. Then he took them with him and they withdrew by themselves to a town called Bethsaida,[z] [11]but the crowds learned about it and followed him. He welcomed them and spoke to them about the kingdom of God,[a] and healed those who needed healing.

[12]Late in the afternoon the Twelve came to him and said, "Send the crowd away so they can go to the surrounding villages and countryside and find food and lodging, because we are in a remote place here."

[13]He replied, "You give them something to eat."

They answered, "We have only five loaves of bread and two fish—unless we go and buy food for all this crowd." [14](About five thousand men were there.)

But he said to his disciples, "Have them sit down in groups of about fifty each." [15]The disciples did so, and everybody sat down. [16]Taking the five loaves and the two fish and looking up to heaven, he gave thanks and broke them.[b] Then he gave them to the disciples to set before the people. [17]They all ate and were satisfied, and the disciples picked up twelve basketfuls of broken pieces that were left over.

Peter's Confession of Christ

[18]Once when Jesus was praying[c] in private and his disciples were with him, he asked them, "Who do the crowds say I am?"

[19]They replied, "Some say John the Baptist;[d] others say Elijah; and still others, that one of the prophets of long ago has come back to life."[e]

[20]"But what about you?" he asked. "Who do you say I am?"

9:5
r Mt 10:14

9:7
s Mt 14:1 t Mt 3:1
u ver 19

9:8
v Mt 11:14
w ver 19; Jn 1:21

9:9
x Lk 23:8

9:10
y Mk 6:30
z Mt 11:21

9:11
a ver 2; Mt 3:2

9:16
b Mt 14:19

9:18
c Lk 3:21

9:19
d Mt 3:1 e ver 7,8

These two fundamental prongs of ministry span the time between Jesus' day and ours. Ministering to people's immediate, obvious needs while announcing the Good News remains as effective a combination now as then. To teach that God loves sinners means little unless we demonstrate that compassion through meeting human needs. How are you involved—through your own efforts, your local church, and/or organizations you support—in Christ's ongoing ministry of word and deed?

Luke 9:10–17
The feeding of the five thousand is the only miracle recorded in all four Gospels (cf. Matt. 14:13–21; Mark 6:32–44; John 6:5–13). This event intertwines a rich tapestry of themes that weave throughout Jesus' ministry, including compassion for all human needs—physical and spiritual, control over creation, the ability to sustain life, and the involvement of others in responding to people's needs. In a sense, this incident provides a cameo portrait of God's grace and provision. This provision was channeled through the disciples, whom Jesus had just *commissioned to share the kingdom message* (vv. 1–6).

In what ways have you reached out to people? The possibilities are endless, but one dynamic is constant: An effective effort finds its source in Jesus.

Whether you minister through a hospital visit, cooking a meal for a family in need, or making yourself available just to listen—when you seek to provide in Jesus' name what *he* offers, you bring an indelible picture of God's compassion to those you serve.

Luke 9:18–27
Peter needed further instruction, but his confession (why was it so amazing?) was a crucial turning point. It set the stage for Jesus to prepare his followers for his suffering to come. This concept of enduring affliction was foreign to the traditional Jewish concept of the Messiah. The Jews looked for a deliverer, not a suffering servant—though Isaiah's prophecies should have prepared them (cf. Isa. 52:13—53:12).

Jesus walked a path his disciples are still called to follow. In cultures enjoying religious tolerance, suffering today is more subtle. Discipleship in our experience no longer extracts the cost it carried in Jesus' day, or still carries in many parts of our world. In fact, it's possible to operate in such a closed Christian circle that we completely avoid meaningful interaction with and rejection by the world. But isolated discipleship isn't what Jesus has in mind for us. Pray today for Christians in another nation who are being persecuted for their faith.

Peter answered, "The Christ ^a of God." ^f

²¹Jesus strictly warned them not to tell this to anyone. ^g ²²And he said, "The Son of Man^h must suffer many thingsⁱ and be rejected by the elders, chief priests and teachers of the law,^j and he must be killed^k and on the third day^l be raised to life." ^m

²³Then he said to them all: "If anyone would come after me, he must deny himself and take up his cross daily and follow me. ⁿ ²⁴For whoever wants to save his life will lose it, but whoever loses his life for me will save it. ^o ²⁵What good is it for a man to gain the whole world, and yet lose or forfeit his very self? ²⁶If anyone is ashamed of me and my words, the Son of Man will be ashamed of him^p when he comes in his glory and in the glory of the Father and of the holy angels. ^q ²⁷I tell you the truth, some who are standing here will not taste death before they see the kingdom of God."

The Transfiguration

²⁸About eight days after Jesus said this, he took Peter, John and James^r with him and went up onto a mountain to pray. ^s ²⁹As he was praying, the appearance of his face changed, and his clothes became as bright as a flash of lightning. ³⁰Two men, Moses and Elijah, ³¹appeared in glorious splendor, talking with Jesus. They spoke about his departure,^t which he was about to bring to fulfillment at Jerusalem. ³²Peter and his companions were very sleepy, ^u but when they became fully awake, they saw his glory and the two men standing with him. ³³As the men were leaving Jesus, Peter said to him, "Master, ^v it is good for us to be here. Let us put up three shelters—one for you, one for Moses and one for Elijah." (He did not know what he was saying.)

³⁴While he was speaking, a cloud appeared and enveloped them, and they were afraid as they entered the cloud. ³⁵A voice came from the cloud, saying, "This is my Son, whom I have chosen;^w listen to him." ^x ³⁶When the voice had spoken, they found that Jesus was alone. The disciples kept this to themselves, and told no one at that time what they had seen. ^y

The Healing of a Boy With an Evil Spirit

³⁷The next day, when they came down from the mountain, a large crowd met him. ³⁸A man in the crowd called out, "Teacher, I beg you to look at my son, for he is my only child. ³⁹A spirit seizes him and he suddenly screams; it throws him into convulsions so that he foams at the mouth. It scarcely ever leaves him and is destroying him. ⁴⁰I begged your disciples to drive it out, but they could not."

^a 20 Or Messiah

9:20
f Jn 1:49; 6:66-69; 11:27
9:21
g Mt 16:20; Mk 8:30
9:22
h Mt 8:20
i Mt 16:21
j Mt 27:1,2
k Ac 2:23; 3:13
l Mt 16:21
m Mt 16:21
9:23
n Mt 10:38; Lk 14:27
9:24
o Jn 12:25
9:26
p Mt 10:33; Lk 12:9; 2Ti 2:12
q Mt 16:27

9:28
r Mt 4:21 s Lk 3:21

9:31
t 2Pe 1:15
9:32
u Mt 26:43

9:33
v Lk 5:5

9:35
w Isa 42:1
x Mt 3:17
9:36
y Mt 17:9

Luke 9:28–36

Jesus' transfiguration was significant in at least two ways: (1) It emphasized who and what he was. Jesus the Messiah functioned like Moses and Elijah, two of the greatest Old Testament prophets. Yet in his presence the two were mere witnesses. The voice of God himself proclaimed Jesus' identity: his own and only Son, the chosen One. (2) God's command to listen to his Son summed up the disciples' responsibility. There was no need for three memorial booths—only a call to listen to one voice.

Worship is at the heart of our life in Christ. There are times in worship when we are faced with the sheer wonder and awe of who God is, and our best response is silence. The disciples kept silent about what they had seen. When in worship have you been struck silent in awe? What is needed in our corporate worship to create a context where people can encounter God in all his holiness?

Luke 9:37–45

Meanwhile, back on the flatlands, the nine remaining disciples struggled with a failed exorcism. They still had a stiff learning curve. Their impotence, based on their attempt to work on their own steam, surfaced vividly here. This was the first in a series of incidents, extending to verse 56, in which the disciples needed correction. The voice in the cloud (v. 35) had been a timely reminder: Jesus' disciples were (and are) to listen to him.

Our need to trust God's ability to overcome evil is as great now as ever. Faith stands up to the spiritual opposition Christians will inevitably face. With all the spiritual resources available to us in Christ, there is no reason for sin to prevail in our lives or for demonic forces to gain a foothold. Why not take a moment to list these resources (see Eph. 1:18–23; 6:10–18)? Pretty impressive, aren't they? Let's be honest: Failure to draw on them is spiritual neglect.

9:41
z Dt 32:5

41"O unbelieving and perverse generation,"z Jesus replied, "how long shall I stay with you and put up with you? Bring your son here."

42Even while the boy was coming, the demon threw him to the ground in a convulsion. But Jesus rebuked the evila spirit, healed the boy and gave him back to his father. 43And they were all amazed at the greatness of God.

9:44
a ver 22
9:45
b Mk 9:32

While everyone was marveling at all that Jesus did, he said to his disciples, 44"Listen carefully to what I am about to tell you: The Son of Man is going to be betrayed into the hands of men."g 45But they did not understand what this meant. It was hidden from them, so that they did not grasp it,b and they were afraid to ask him about it.

Who Will Be the Greatest?

9:46
c Lk 22:24
9:47
d Mt 9:4
9:48
e Mt 10:40
f Mk 9:35
9:49
g Lk 5:5

46An argument started among the disciples as to which of them would be the greatest.c 47Jesus, knowing their thoughts,d took a little child and had him stand beside him. 48Then he said to them, "Whoever welcomes this little child in my name welcomes me; and whoever welcomes me welcomes the one who sent me.e For he who is least among you all—he is the greatest."f

49"Master," g said John, "we saw a man driving out demons in your name and we tried to stop him, because he is not one of us."

9:50
h Mt 12:30;
Lk 11:23

50"Do not stop him," Jesus said, "for whoever is not against you is for you."h

Samaritan Opposition

9:51
i Mk 16:19
j Lk 13:22; 17:11;
18:31; 19:28
9:52
k Mt 10:5
9:54
l Mt 4:21
m 2Ki 1:10,12

51As the time approached for him to be taken up to heaven,i Jesus resolutely set out for Jerusalem.j 52And he sent messengers on ahead, who went into a Samaritank village to get things ready for him; 53but the people there did not welcome him, because he was heading for Jerusalem. 54When the disciples James and Johnl saw this, they asked, "Lord, do you want us to call fire down from heaven to destroy themb?"m 55But Jesus turned and rebuked them, 56andc they went to another village.

The Cost of Following Jesus

9:57
n ver 51

57As they were walking along the road,n a man said to him, "I will follow you wherever you go."

a 42 Greek unclean   b 54 Some manuscripts them, even as Elijah did   c 55,56 Some manuscripts them. And he said, "You do not know what kind of spirit you are of, for the Son of Man did not come to destroy men's lives, but to save them." 56And

---

Luke 9:46–50

📖 Two brief incidents close Luke's report on the Galilean phase of Jesus' ministry. In the first, Jesus responded to the disciples' haggling for position. He made clear that stature in his eyes is the reverse of normal human measures of power. The least are greatest. Ultimately, how we treat children will be the measure of how much we welcome Jesus into our lives and society.

📖 We may think ancient people were somehow different from ourselves, but a look at the disciples' tendency to compete in trying to build an elite ministry makes them look pretty familiar. Our own culture is highly competitive, but Jesus' words and attitudes confront head on our inclination toward assertive pride. When the least is the greatest, the quest for greatness is reversed. What would an outsider understand about your picture of greatness by examining the ways you, and your society, treat children?

Luke 9:51–56

📖 Jews typically despised Samaritans and avoided their territory, but Jesus intended to minister to them on

his way to Jerusalem. The Samaritans for their part had a practice of refusing to provide overnight shelter to Jewish pilgrims heading for Jerusalem. These townspeople rejected Jesus and his messengers, and the brothers James and John reacted with fiery anger. Luke didn't record Jesus' words of rebuke to his disciples; the company simply moved on. Now wasn't the time for judgment, but a time to offer grace and warn about accountability.

📖 Rejection is hard to take, but Jesus' perspective here is an effective model for the church, as well as for us as individual disciples. Elsewhere Jesus spoke of judgment, but it would occur in a future era—when he returns to show his authority (v. 26; 17:26–37). Vindication isn't appropriate now. Some Christians express deep anger at an unfeeling world. But to be a servant of the gospel isn't to highlight judgment or long for its execution. It's to seek to save lives as long as God allows.

Luke 9:57–62

📖 Discipleship isn't a casual affair to Jesus, as this series of three encounters shows. It requires focused, sacrificial commitment. The central action verb in this

58 Jesus replied, "Foxes have holes and birds of the air have nests, but the Son of Man o has no place to lay his head."

59 He said to another man, "Follow me." p

But the man replied, "Lord, first let me go and bury my father."

60 Jesus said to him, "Let the dead bury their own dead, but you go and proclaim the kingdom of God." q

61 Still another said, "I will follow you, Lord; but first let me go back and say good-by to my family." r

62 Jesus replied, "No one who puts his hand to the plow and looks back is fit for service in the kingdom of God."

Jesus Sends Out the Seventy-two

10 After this the Lord s appointed seventy-two a others t and sent them two by two u ahead of him to every town and place where he was about to go. v 2 He told them, "The harvest is plentiful, but the workers are few. Ask the Lord of the harvest, therefore, to send out workers into his harvest field. w 3 Go! I am sending you out like lambs among wolves. x 4 Do not take a purse or bag or sandals; and do not greet anyone on the road.

5 "When you enter a house, first say, 'Peace to this house.' 6 If a man of peace is

a 1 Some manuscripts seventy; also in verse 17

9:58
o Mt 8:20
9:59
p Mt 4:19

9:60
q Mt 3:2

9:61
r 1Ki 19:20

10:1
s Lk 7:13
t Lk 9:1,2,51,52
u Mk 6:7
v Mt 10:1

10:2
w Mt 9:37,38;
Jn 4:35
10:3
x Mt 10:16

---

passage is *follow* (vv. 57,59,61). Potential disciples initiated the encounter in two of these scenarios, while Jesus made the first move in the third. But the point in each case was the same: If Jesus' followers opt for discipleship, everything else is secondary. Nothing is to stand in the way of following Jesus.

Is your spiritual pager on—all the time? The implications of discipleship haven't changed: Following Jesus isn't a leisure time pursuit or a part-time, side job. It's a permanent commitment, placing us on call for God and other people, 24/7. Those who want to pursue spirituality as a hobby, or simply keep faith in Jesus alongside all their other commitments, won't discover its blessing.

Luke 10:1–24

Jesus entrusted to his followers the privilege not only of proclaiming the Good News but of manifesting signs of the kingdom. The fact that such workers emerged as a result of intercession (v. 2) implies that God is Lord of the harvest. Now as then, he leads the mission and sends out workers into the field.

Snapshots

 9:58

Aung Lin

When Aung Lin followed some other children into a Christian drop-in center for street children in the city of Mandalay in Myanmar, he didn't just find a place to stay—he found a home.

Early in life, Aung Lin had lost four siblings to illness, his father to crime, and his mother to malaria. During this turbulent period, he could fall back on a few literacy courses but no formal schooling. When his father was finally released from prison, his new wife mistreated Aung Lin, forcing him into child labor. To escape the abuse, he fled to the streets, where he filled his days by scavenging for plastic bottles or cardboard he could sell for money. Each day, he accumulated just enough to buy some food.

At the center, life was different. Aung Lin was given a warm bed, the chance to learn, and needed medical attention. No longer shouldering the relentless burden of anxiety over hunger, he spends his days playing football, doing homework, and helping with household chores.

"I wear clean clothes, sleep in a safe place, and am receiving food and a good education," says Aung Lin, now fifteen. "I am in good hands."

> "**I wear clean clothes, sleep in a safe place, and am receiving food and a good education . . . I am in good hands.**"

10:7
y Mt 10:10;
1Co 9:14; 1Ti 5:18

10:8
z 1Co 10:27
10:9
a Mt 3:2; 10:7

10:11
b Mt 10:14;
Mk 6:11 *c* ver 9
10:12
d Mt 10:15
e Mt 11:24
10:13
f Lk 6:24-26
g Rev 11:3

10:15
h Mt 4:13

10:16
i Mt 10:40; Jn 13:20
10:17
j ver 1 *k* Mk 16:17

10:18
l Mt 4:10
m Isa 14:12;
Rev 9:1; 12:8,9
10:19
n Mk 16:18;
Ac 28:3-5
10:20
o Ex 32:32;
Ps 69:28; Da 12:1;
Php 4:3;
Heb 12:23;
Rev 13:8; 20:12;
21:27
10:21
p 1Co 1:26-29
10:22
q Mt 28:18
r Jn 1:18

10:24
s 1Pe 1:10-12

10:25
t Mt 19:16;
Lk 18:18

10:27
u Dt 6:5
v Lev 19:18;
Mt 5:43

there, your peace will rest on him; if not, it will return to you. [7]Stay in that house, eating and drinking whatever they give you, for the worker deserves his wages. [y] Do not move around from house to house.

[8]"When you enter a town and are welcomed, eat what is set before you. [z] [9]Heal the sick who are there and tell them, 'The kingdom of God [a] is near you.' [10]But when you enter a town and are not welcomed, go into its streets and say, [11]'Even the dust of your town that sticks to our feet we wipe off against you. [b] Yet be sure of this: The kingdom of God is near.' [c] [12]I tell you, it will be more bearable on that day for Sodom [d] than for that town. [e]

[13]"Woe to you, [f] Korazin! Woe to you, Bethsaida! For if the miracles that were performed in you had been performed in Tyre and Sidon, they would have repented long ago, sitting in sackcloth [g] and ashes. [14]But it will be more bearable for Tyre and Sidon at the judgment than for you. [15]And you, Capernaum, [h] will you be lifted up to the skies? No, you will go down to the depths. [a]

[16]"He who listens to you listens to me; he who rejects you rejects me; but he who rejects me rejects him who sent me." [i]

[17]The seventy-two [j] returned with joy and said, "Lord, even the demons submit to us in your name." [k]

[18]He replied, "I saw Satan [l] fall like lightning from heaven. [m] [19]I have given you authority to trample on snakes [n] and scorpions and to overcome all the power of the enemy; nothing will harm you. [20]However, do not rejoice that the spirits submit to you, but rejoice that your names are written in heaven." [o]

[21]At that time Jesus, full of joy through the Holy Spirit, said, "I praise you, Father, Lord of heaven and earth, because you have hidden these things from the wise and learned, and revealed them to little children. [p] Yes, Father, for this was your good pleasure.

[22]"All things have been committed to me by my Father. [q] No one knows who the Son is except the Father, and no one knows who the Father is except the Son and those to whom the Son chooses to reveal him." [r]

[23]Then he turned to his disciples and said privately, "Blessed are the eyes that see what you see. [24]For I tell you that many prophets and kings wanted to see what you see but did not see it, and to hear what you hear but did not hear it." [s]

The Parable of the Good Samaritan

[25]On one occasion an expert in the law stood up to test Jesus. "Teacher," he asked, "what must I do to inherit eternal life?" [t]

[26]"What is written in the Law?" he replied. "How do you read it?"

[27]He answered: " 'Love the Lord your God with all your heart and with all your soul and with all your strength and with all your mind' [b]; [u] and, 'Love your neighbor as yourself.' [c]" [v]

---

[a] 15 Greek *Hades*   [b] 27 Deut. 6:5   [c] 27 Lev. 19:18

📖 Jesus said little about method and avoided a canned message. The disciples were to attend to needs—to reveal God's power and share where it came from. Many of us are intimidated about sharing the Good News because we are afraid we won't know what to say. We are hesitant to respond to others' needs out of fear we will be overwhelmed and our response will be inadequate. But Jesus instructed the 72 simply to give of themselves and point to God.

Luke 10:25–37

📖 The expert on Jewish law wanted to shrink from (and shirk) his responsibility by identifying a select, elite few as his neighbors. Jesus instructed him through the Samaritan's example, "Let the neighbor be *you*." Rather than worrying about categorizing those around them, Jesus' followers are called to be neighborly to anyone in need. By reversing the perspective, Jesus changed both the question and the answer: Who is Jesus' disciple in relation to all others? A neighbor to anyone in need.

📖 It's easy to conclude that the task of dealing with the world's pain is so vast we can't even make a dent. But such thinking can become an excuse for indifference and inaction. Being neighborly doesn't mean we have to meet every need we see, but we can pitch in wherever and whenever we reasonably can. If the church can become the nucleus for "neighborhood watches" and "neighborhood associations," we will be amazed at the amount of spiritual good we "neighbors" can accomplish together.

What Jesus asked of the young man in this story was radical. Jews of that day wouldn't even speak to Samaritans. This group was despised as a heathen minority. They had been deposited in the area by the Assyrians for the expressed purpose of serving as a living buffer between the Assyrians and the Israelites in the 7th century B.C. A modern equivalent might be a Washington D.C. attorney inviting an undocumented immigrant out to lunch.

How can we hope to go and do likewise? First, start slow. We need an ongoing program of small commitments that will prepare us for the big opportunities to come. For example, begin by committing yourself to meeting someone new each week. Look around you at all the people who seek and need recognition. Make it a specific agenda item in your appointment book.

Second, read about models of faith who have lived their lives by being neighborly to the unwanted. Here are three examples:

Richard Valdemar remembers a high school friend who vowed he would return and build a better neighborhood in the barrios of Los Angeles. "He went off to Yale and got a law degree and became a big success, but he didn't live up to that promise." Richard had made that same vow himself—but he did come back. He's now a member of an elite county sheriff unit that helps violent street gangs avoid trouble. Though he earns less than he could have made in private industry, Valdemar's only regret is that so many who leave the poor, Hispanic neighborhoods have no feeling for those who remain.

Life at the girls' school in India was fulfilling enough until Agnes Bojaxhiu received "the message" in 1946. "Quit the cloistered existence and plunge into Calcutta's slums," she was instructed. Thus began a crusade that earned a Nobel Peace Prize in 1979 for Mother Teresa. From collecting abandoned babies out of the garbage to building leprosariums, the Missionaries of Charity are committed to serving others "as themselves." The order functions worldwide with 1,800 nuns, 250 brothers, and thousands of workers serving in 30 countries.

> We need an ongoing program of small commitments that will prepare us for the big opportunities to come.

Hazel Hudson saw and filled a need. In 1972, parents in a Black neighborhood in Chicago were concerned about the growing number of youth gangs. So a local church opened a private school for youngsters. But they needed a principal. Though Hazel had served only as a community representative for the Chicago Public Schools, she was picked for that job. Hazel returned to college and then poured herself into the task for 12 to 14 hours a day. "This is my life—working with people and caring about them and watching people grow."

Go and do likewise.

Ted Engstrom, former president of World Vision U.S. in Federal Way, Washington

Love Your Neighbor

The legal expert had come to Jesus to inquire about the afterlife. He may have been trying to embarrass the young rabbi, but Jesus went along with his game, asking him how he read the Mosaic Law. Jesus acknowledged his correct answer, commenting that if he did this he would indeed live. But the expert pushed his advantage too far when he asked Jesus to identify his neighbor. Jesus' answer has come to be known as the parable of the good Samaritan (Luke 10:25–37).

The world is haunted by the poignant question uttered by an African American after having been beaten by police officers in Los Angeles: "Can't we just all get along?" This is the issue among child victims of rape in Africa and thousands of displaced children from East Timor; among children whose limbs have been blown off by land mines in Bosnia and Afghanistan and thousands of AIDS victims in Africa. It remains the unanswered question among the victims of mindless or state-sponsored "terrorism" around the globe. One writer has observed that "the world is coming reluctantly together and falling precipitously apart at the very same time."

> Jesus' parable contains the essence of the Christian response to "neighborliness" and holds a key to the most radical motivation for action on behalf of the victims of oppression and discrimination: *love*.

It's been advocated that the most dangerous four-letter word in America is *hate*. That message is based upon recurring outbreaks of murder and mayhem aimed at persons whose color and/or lifestyles are deemed unacceptable by the perpetrators of such crimes. Racism often is the prevailing attitude in such cases. Or the motivation may be related to class distinctions and the struggle for power in the arenas of business and housing. In this light, perhaps a more dangerous four-letter word is *them*. Dr. W.E.B. Dubois, one of America's foremost scholars and for many years the leading intellectual among African American academics, is best known for his prophesy that the dividing line in human relations at the end of this past century would be color.

Racism has become an ideology. Westerners like to argue that it's a global reality. But what is being defined as racism among non-Western peoples may more accurately be labeled tribalism. This isn't to deny the volatility of such tribalism. Violence and genocide are all too familiar realities at the beginning of a new century.

The world is in the grip of violence spurred on by racist and tribal ideologies. When it's convenient for nations to intimidate their neighbors for the vested interests of wealth and power, racism becomes a part of nationalism, usually profiting those whose wealth is at stake. When re-enforced by institutionalized power, it becomes terrorism, which denies people the rights to belong and to have.

At the core of all these cultures—Western and non-Western alike—is religion: those various fundamentalisms both holding people together and driving them apart. Jesus' parable contains the essence of the Christian response to "neighborliness" and holds a key to the most radical motivation for action on behalf of the victims of oppression and discrimination: *love*.

Most of Earth's people would probably agree that we all should just get along. So why don't we? Because neighborliness isn't just a rational matter. Becoming a merciful neighbor as Jesus commanded requires a conversion, a transformation so radical it leaves old habits and ideologies behind. Old tribal allegiances would have to be severely readjusted. Political alliances would need revitalization, as Jesus became Lord and Savior. It's critical in the midst of our fallen humanity that the church continue to affirm its call to radical discipleship and passionate, loving evangelism.

Bill Pannell, professor of urban studies at Fuller Theological Seminary in Pasadena, California

28 "You have answered correctly," Jesus replied. "Do this and you will live." *w*

29 But he wanted to justify himself, *x* so he asked Jesus, "And who is my neighbor?"

30 In reply Jesus said: "A man was going down from Jerusalem to Jericho, when he fell into the hands of robbers. They stripped him of his clothes, beat him and went away, leaving him half dead. 31 A priest happened to be going down the same road, and when he saw the man, he passed by on the other side. *y* 32 So too, a Levite, when he came to the place and saw him, passed by on the other side. 33 But a Samaritan, *z* as he traveled, came where the man was; and when he saw him, he took pity on him. 34 He went to him and bandaged his wounds, pouring on oil and wine. Then he put the man on his own donkey, took him to an inn and took care of him. 35 The next day he took out two silver coins *a* and gave them to the innkeeper. 'Look after him,' he said, 'and when I return, I will reimburse you for any extra expense you may have.'

36 "Which of these three do you think was a neighbor to the man who fell into the hands of robbers?"

37 The expert in the law replied, "The one who had mercy on him."

Jesus told him, "Go and do likewise."

At the Home of Martha and Mary

38 As Jesus and his disciples were on their way, he came to a village where a woman named Martha *a* opened her home to him. 39 She had a sister called Mary, *b* who sat at the Lord's feet *c* listening to what he said. 40 But Martha was distracted by all the preparations that had to be made. She came to him and asked, "Lord, don't you care *d* that my sister has left me to do the work by myself? Tell her to help me!"

41 "Martha, Martha," the Lord answered, "you are worried *e* and upset about many things, 42 but only one thing is needed. *b f* Mary has chosen what is better, and it will not be taken away from her."

Jesus' Teaching on Prayer

11 One day Jesus was praying *g* in a certain place. When he finished, one of his disciples said to him, "Lord, *h* teach us to pray, just as John taught his disciples."

2 He said to them, "When you pray, say:

---

a 35 Greek *two denarii*   *b 42* Some manuscripts *but few things are needed—or only one*

10:28
w Lev 18:5; Ro 7:10
10:29
x Lk 16:15

10:31
y Lev 21:1-3
10:33
z Mt 10:5

10:38
a Jn 11:1; 12:2
10:39
b Jn 11:1; 12:3
c Lk 8:35
10:40
d Mk 4:38
10:41
e Mt 6:25-34; Lk 12:11,22
10:42
f Ps 27:4

11:1
g Lk 3:21
h Jn 13:13

Luke 10:38–42

Martha was performing a worthy task, but she was consumed with what her sister was doing. Jesus didn't criticize her work ethic but her critical attitude. His emotion-filled reply to Martha's challenge, in which he spoke her name twice, showed love and concern for both sisters. Jesus indicated, though, how appropriate it was for Mary to sit before him. She had chosen a needful thing—under the circumstances, a better thing—and she would be rewarded for time well spent with her Lord.

This incident illustrates a crucial principle for disciples of any era: Effective discipleship involves a balance between serving (physical) and being served (spiritual). Mary demonstrated the importance of reflecting on what Jesus teaches. Today that translates into time spent in the Word and the church's instruction. It also involves moments of awed silence before God. Are you sometimes tempted to continue feeding others at the expense of taking in your necessary ration of soul food? Or do you only sit in church, ready to be filled and fed but failing to contribute through your service to the body of Christ?

Luke 11:1–13

Jesus began this teaching on prayer by telling his followers what to pray. It's critical to recognize that God is both very present and totally involved when his children pray. Next, Jesus instructed them how to approach prayer: with a spirit of dependence and humility, looking for God's gracious provision. Jesus then presented a parable, emphasizing that God is approachable, generous, and ready to hear requests.

If a human being responds generously to the earthly requests of her neighbor, surely a gracious God will respond to our petitions about our spiritual needs. God wants bold—even "shameless"—prayer. Not in the sense of coming to him in a greedy spirit with our every whim or wish, but in making use of the access he gives us to call on him for spiritual development. The answer, of course, is up to God and may not appear in packaging we will immediately recognize.

11:2
i Mt 3:2

" 'Father,[a]
hallowed be your name,
    your kingdom[i] come.[b]
³Give us each day our daily bread.
⁴Forgive us our sins,
    for we also forgive everyone who sins against us.[c][j]
And lead us not into temptation.'[d] "[k]

11:4
j Mt 18:35;
Mk 11:25
k Mt 26:41;
Jas 1:13

⁵Then he said to them, "Suppose one of you has a friend, and he goes to him at midnight and says, 'Friend, lend me three loaves of bread, ⁶because a friend of mine on a journey has come to me, and I have nothing to set before him.'

⁷"Then the one inside answers, 'Don't bother me. The door is already locked, and my children are with me in bed. I can't get up and give you anything.' ⁸I tell you, though he will not get up and give him the bread because he is his friend, yet because of the man's boldness[e] he will get up and give him as much as he needs.[l]

11:8
l Lk 18:1-6
11:9
m Mt 7:7

⁹"So I say to you: Ask and it will be given to you;[m] seek and you will find; knock and the door will be opened to you. ¹⁰For everyone who asks receives; he who seeks finds; and to him who knocks, the door will be opened.

¹¹"Which of you fathers, if your son asks for[f] a fish, will give him a snake instead? ¹²Or if he asks for an egg, will give him a scorpion? ¹³If you then, though you are evil, know how to give good gifts to your children, how much more will your Father in heaven give the Holy Spirit to those who ask him!"

Jesus and Beelzebub

11:14
n Mt 9:32,33
11:15
o Mk 3:22
p Mt 9:34
11:16
q Mt 12:38
11:17
r Mt 9:4
11:18
s Mt 4:10

¹⁴Jesus was driving out a demon that was mute. When the demon left, the man who had been mute spoke, and the crowd was amazed.[n] ¹⁵But some of them said, "By Beelzebub,[g][o] the prince of demons, he is driving out demons."[p] ¹⁶Others tested him by asking for a sign from heaven.[q]

¹⁷Jesus knew their thoughts[r] and said to them: "Any kingdom divided against itself will be ruined, and a house divided against itself will fall. ¹⁸If Satan[s] is divided against himself, how can his kingdom stand? I say this because you claim that I drive out demons by Beelzebub. ¹⁹Now if I drive out demons by Beelzebub, by whom do your followers drive them out? So then, they will be your judges. ²⁰But if I drive out demons by the finger of God,[t] then the kingdom of God[u] has come to you.

11:20
t Ex 8:19 u Mt 3:2

²¹"When a strong man, fully armed, guards his own house, his possessions are safe. ²²But when someone stronger attacks and overpowers him, he takes away the armor in which the man trusted and divides up the spoils.

11:23
v Mt 12:30;
Mk 9:40; Lk 9:50

²³"He who is not with me is against me, and he who does not gather with me, scatters.[v]

²⁴"When an evil[h] spirit comes out of a man, it goes through arid places seeking rest and does not find it. Then it says, 'I will return to the house I left.' ²⁵When it arrives, it finds the house swept clean and put in order. ²⁶Then it goes and takes seven other

a 2 Some manuscripts *Our Father in heaven*   b 2 Some manuscripts *come. May your will be done on earth as it is in heaven.*   c 4 Greek *everyone who is indebted to us*   d 4 Some manuscripts *temptation but deliver us from the evil one*   e 8 Or *persistence*   f 11 Some manuscripts *for bread, will give him a stone; or if he asks for*   g 15 Greek *Beezeboul* or *Beelzeboul*; also in verses 18 and 19   h 24 Greek *unclean*

Luke 11:14–28
Jesus claimed that his miracles in general, and his exorcisms in particular, revealed God's victorious rule. Our Lord established his position as the stronger man who overcomes the power of the evil one. Though skirmishes with Satan are still being fought, the ultimate victory described here is part of a fundamental perspective Jesus wanted his disciples and opponents to appreciate. Neutrality is impossible; revelation missed brings a person one step closer to falling into destructive hands.

The theme of Jesus' victory speaks to every time period about his unparalleled authority. All that remains is for people to choose for (or against) him. Fence-sitting is a default position; to be undecided is to have already made a decision. But to decide that Jesus has been sent from God is to decide that "in him is life" (cf. John 1:4; 14:6). As an old church school song puts it: "One door and only one, and yet its sides are two. Inside and outside, on which side are you?"

spirits more wicked than itself, and they go in and live there. And the final condition of that man is worse than the first." [w]

27 As Jesus was saying these things, a woman in the crowd called out, "Blessed is the mother who gave you birth and nursed you." [x]

28 He replied, "Blessed rather are those who hear the word of God [y] and obey it." [z]

The Sign of Jonah

29 As the crowds increased, Jesus said, "This is a wicked generation. It asks for a miraculous sign, [a] but none will be given it except the sign of Jonah. [b] 30 For as Jonah was a sign to the Ninevites, so also will the Son of Man be to this generation. 31 The Queen of the South will rise at the judgment with the men of this generation and condemn them; for she came from the ends of the earth to listen to Solomon's wisdom, [c] and now one [a] greater than Solomon is here. 32 The men of Nineveh will stand up at the judgment with this generation and condemn it; for they repented at the preaching of Jonah, [d] and now one greater than Jonah is here.

The Lamp of the Body

33 "No one lights a lamp and puts it in a place where it will be hidden, or under a bowl. Instead he puts it on its stand, so that those who come in may see the light. [e] 34 Your eye is the lamp of your body. When your eyes are good, your whole body also is full of light. But when they are bad, your body also is full of darkness. 35 See to it, then, that the light within you is not darkness. 36 Therefore, if your whole body

---

[a] 31 Or *something*; also in verse 32

Cross references:
- 11:26 [w] 2Pe 2:20
- 11:27 [x] Lk 23:29
- 11:28 [y] Heb 4:12 [z] Pr 8:32; Lk 6:47; 8:21; Jn 14:21
- 11:29 [a] ver 16; Mt 12:38 [b] Jnh 1:17; Mt 16:4
- 11:31 [c] 1Ki 10:1; 2Ch 9:1
- 11:32 [d] Jnh 3:5
- 11:33 [e] Mt 5:15; Mk 4:21; Lk 8:16

Luke 11:29–32

On several occasions Jews asked for miraculous signs, but Jesus rejected their requests because of their flawed motives (cf. v. 16). In the Old Testament, both the Ninevites and the Queen of Sheba had believed the truth of God without physical evidence. The generation of Jews listening to Jesus' words lacked the faith of some Gentiles of previous eras. Someone infinitely greater than either Jonah (Ninevites) or Solomon (Queen of Sheba) had entered the scene, but they failed to heed his words.

Still today, to refuse Jesus is to face rejection in the final judgment—and the condemnation of previous generations who understood the unique opportunity Jesus' teaching provides. Jesus' words and the Spirit's witness of their truth in our hearts should be more than enough to convince us. We of all people are "without excuse" (Rom. 1:18–20) if we fail to allow the truth of God's Word to permeate our beings and motivate our service. To whose words do you give weight? A professor's? A relative's? A friend's? Those of Jesus? The truth shows itself in your actions.

Luke 11:33–36

Luke's Gospel continued to emphasize his disciples' obligation to respond faithfully to the revelation Jesus brought. Here Jesus compared his teaching to a lamp—in the ancient world a candle or some type of oil lamp. A person wouldn't go to the effort of lighting a lamp just to cover it up. Likewise, Jesus' teaching is light made available for all to see. But light has to be received by the eye—and what the eye lets into the mind defines the person. To take in light is to glow from the inside out.

11:33–36

Light to the World

As Christians we have light to offer a dark world. We don't hide our light under a basket but place it on a stand for all the world to see. Sometimes this means cooperating with secular organizations for divine purposes. Such cooperation is possible when certain conditions are present:

1. Clearly identified need
2. Biblically acceptable goal
3. Partners with a basic respect for Jesus
4. Available resources: people to participate, money/goods to contribute
5. Clear, simple agenda

Examples of possible cooperative actions:

Organization	Field of Cooperative Action
Parent-teacher associations	Educational values
D.A.R.E.	Fighting illegal drug use
Neighborhood watch	Crime prevention
Food pantries	Food for the hungry
Crisis pregnancy counseling centers	Teenage/unwanted pregnancy
Coffeehouses, drop-in centers	Preventing at-risk behavior in teens
MADD	Prevention of drunk driving

is full of light, and no part of it dark, it will be completely lighted, as when the light of a lamp shines on you."

Six Woes

37When Jesus had finished speaking, a Pharisee invited him to eat with him; so he went in and reclined at the table. *f* **38**But the Pharisee, noticing that Jesus did not first wash before the meal, *g* was surprised.

39Then the Lord *h* said to him, "Now then, you Pharisees clean the outside of the cup and dish, but inside you are full of greed and wickedness. *i* **40**You foolish people! *j* Did not the one who made the outside make the inside also? **41**But give what is inside ｟the dish｠ᵃ to the poor, *k* and everything will be clean for you. *l*

42"Woe to you Pharisees, because you give God a tenth *m* of your mint, rue and all other kinds of garden herbs, but you neglect justice and the love of God. *n* You should have practiced the latter without leaving the former undone. *o*

43"Woe to you Pharisees, because you love the most important seats in the synagogues and greetings in the marketplaces. *p*

44"Woe to you, because you are like unmarked graves, *q* which men walk over without knowing it."

45One of the experts in the law *r* answered him, "Teacher, when you say these things, you insult us also."

46Jesus replied, "And you experts in the law, woe to you, because you load people down with burdens they can hardly carry, and you yourselves will not lift one finger to help them. *s*

47"Woe to you, because you build tombs for the prophets, and it was your forefathers who killed them. **48**So you testify that you approve of what your forefathers did; they killed the prophets, and you build their tombs. *t* **49**Because of this, God in his wisdom *u* said, 'I will send them prophets and apostles, some of whom they will kill and others they will persecute.' *v* **50**Therefore this generation will be held responsible for the blood of all the prophets that has been shed since the beginning of the world, **51**from the blood of Abel *w* to the blood of Zechariah, *x* who was killed between the altar and the sanctuary. Yes, I tell you, this generation will be held responsible for it all. *y*

52"Woe to you experts in the law, because you have taken away the key to knowledge. You yourselves have not entered, and you have hindered those who were entering." *z*

53When Jesus left there, the Pharisees and the teachers of the law began to oppose him fiercely and to besiege him with questions, **54**waiting to catch him in something he might say. *a*

Warnings and Encouragements

12 Meanwhile, when a crowd of many thousands had gathered, so that they were trampling on one another, Jesus began to speak first to his disciples,

ᵃ 41 Or *what you have*

11:37
f Lk 7:36; 14:1
11:38
g Mk 7:3,4
11:39
h Lk 7:13
i Mt 23:25,26; Mk 7:20-23
11:40
j Lk 12:20; 1Co 15:36
11:41
k Lk 12:33
l Ac 10:15
11:42
m Lk 18:12
n Dt 6:5; Mic 6:8
o Mt 23:23
11:43
p Mt 23:6,7; Mk 12:38-39; Lk 14:7; 20:46
11:44
q Mt 23:27
11:45
r Mt 22:35
11:46
s Mt 23:4
11:48
t Mt 23:29-32; Ac 7:51-53
11:49
u 1Co 1:24,30; Col 2:3 *v* Mt 23:34
11:51
w Ge 4:8
x 2Ch 24:20,21
y Mt 23:35,36
11:52
z Mt 23:13
11:54
a Mt 12:10; Mk 12:13

📖 In our society, responsibility for truth has been abandoned to the black hole of shifting public opinion. Objective truth is anything but a given. In fact, it's considered politically incorrect to claim such truth exists. The church is called to present God's message in the public square and to make clear what's at stake. Public opinion notwithstanding, we do well to challenge unbelievers— and remind ourselves—that we live in a universe where, like it or not, we are responsible for our choices.

Luke 11:37–54

📖 Jesus' indictment of the Pharisees included two specific "sins of commission" (doing) in verse 39 and two specific "sins of omission" (failure to do) in verse 42: (1) They were full of greed in their use and view of re-

sources, and of wickedness in their violation of moral integrity. (2) They paid strict attention to external religious rites but neglected justice and the love of God. Jesus gave the Pharisees one specific challenge: Loosen the grip of greed and wickedness on your hearts by giving to the poor (v. 41).

📖 Some well-meaning but rule-driven Christians make sure every "i" is dotted and every "t" crossed. They also watch others with a hawk's eye to make sure they are acting properly. Is this the best use of our spiritual heritage? We are not to condone sin, yet we are to minister the message of reconciliation (cf. 2 Cor. 5:18–20). According to Jesus (v. 41), balance can be achieved in serving the poor. How balanced are you?

saying: "Be on your guard against the yeast of the Pharisees, which is hypocrisy. [b] [2]There is nothing concealed that will not be disclosed, or hidden that will not be made known. [c] [3]What you have said in the dark will be heard in the daylight, and what you have whispered in the ear in the inner rooms will be proclaimed from the roofs.

[4]"I tell you, my friends, [d] do not be afraid of those who kill the body and after that can do no more. [5]But I will show you whom you should fear: Fear him who, after the killing of the body, has power to throw you into hell. Yes, I tell you, fear him. [e] [6]Are not five sparrows sold for two pennies[a]? Yet not one of them is forgotten by God. [7]Indeed, the very hairs of your head are all numbered. [f] Don't be afraid; you are worth more than many sparrows. [g]

[8]"I tell you, whoever acknowledges me before men, the Son of Man will also acknowledge him before the angels of God. [h] [9]But he who disowns me before men will be disowned [i] before the angels of God. [10]And everyone who speaks a word against the Son of Man [j] will be forgiven, but anyone who blasphemes against the Holy Spirit will not be forgiven. [k]

[11]"When you are brought before synagogues, rulers and authorities, do not worry about how you will defend yourselves or what you will say, [l] [12]for the Holy Spirit will teach you at that time what you should say." [m]

The Parable of the Rich Fool

[13]Someone in the crowd said to him, "Teacher, tell my brother to divide the inheritance with me."

[14]Jesus replied, "Man, who appointed me a judge or an arbiter between you?" [15]Then he said to them, "Watch out! Be on your guard against all kinds of greed; a man's life does not consist in the abundance of his possessions." [n]

[16]And he told them this parable: "The ground of a certain rich man produced a good crop. [17]He thought to himself, 'What shall I do? I have no place to store my crops.'

[18]"Then he said, 'This is what I'll do. I will tear down my barns and build bigger ones, and there I will store all my grain and my goods. [19]And I'll say to myself, "You have plenty of good things laid up for many years. Take life easy; eat, drink and be merry."'

[20]"But God said to him, 'You fool! [o] This very night your life will be demanded from you. [p] Then who will get what you have prepared for yourself?' [q]

[21]"This is how it will be with anyone who stores up things for himself but is not rich toward God." [r]

[a] 6 Greek *two assaria*

12:1
b Mt 16:6,11,12; Mk 8:15
12:2
c Mk 4:22; Lk 8:17

12:4
d Jn 15:14,15
12:5
e Heb 10:31
12:7
f Mt 10:30
g Mt 12:12

12:8
h Lk 15:10
12:9
i Mk 8:38; 2Ti 2:12
12:10
j Mt 8:20
k Mt 12:31,32; Mk 3:28-29; 1Jn 5:16
12:11
l Mt 10:17,19; Mk 13:11; Lk 21:12,14
12:12
m Ex 4:12; Mt 10:20; Mk 13:11; Lk 21:15

12:15
n Job 20:20; 31:24; Ps 62:10

12:20
o Jer 17:11; Lk 11:40 p Job 27:8 q Ps 39:6; 49:10

12:21
r ver 33

Luke 12:1–12

A being who knows all a person's secrets is to be feared. Therefore, Jesus declared, his listeners should be afraid of the One with the power to consign them to hell—not of someone who could merely kill their body. Jesus brought up this issue because of the very real prospect of his disciples having to face the world's rejection for identifying with him. On the other hand, the "fear" (reverent awe) of God, as well as his presence, bring incredible comfort.

In a sense, Jesus called here for attitude—not action. He asks us to trust that he cares for us and will supply his Spirit's strength when we need it. To fear God means to respect his authority, trust in his care, and resist worrying about how others may react to us. Our Lord is aware not just of our secrets but of every minute detail of our lives. Can we doubt that someone who knows us so well will care for us?

Luke 12:13–21

Even legitimate sources of income can become opportunities for greed. This parable demonstrates how subtly greed can take over in a disciple's heart, multiplying itself just as surely as the acquisition of wealth only increases the desire for more. Richness toward God, on the other hand, means responding to life and blessing in a way that honors him—through compassionate service (Eph. 4:28; 1 Tim. 6:17–19).

Jesus didn't condemn wealth as such—only its misuse. But the implications of this text extend beyond what we do with what we have. Even in the Old Testament the grain the harvesters missed was left for those in need (Deut. 24:19–22)—a principle the rich fool ignored in storing up goods for his own use. Is it right for us to consume vast amounts of the world's resources while others have little or no access to such blessings? What actions can you take—large or small—to help restore balance?

Do Not Worry

22Then Jesus said to his disciples: "Therefore I tell you, do not worry about your life, what you will eat; or about your body, what you will wear. **23**Life is more than food, and the body more than clothes. **24**Consider the ravens: They do not sow or reap, they have no storeroom or barn; yet God feeds them. *s* And how much more valuable you are than birds! **25**Who of you by worrying can add a single hour to his life*a*? **26**Since you cannot do this very little thing, why do you worry about the rest?

27"Consider how the lilies grow. They do not labor or spin. Yet I tell you, not even Solomon in all his splendor *t* was dressed like one of these. **28**If that is how God clothes the grass of the field, which is here today, and tomorrow is thrown into the fire, how much more will he clothe you, O you of little faith! *u* **29**And do not set your heart on what you will eat or drink; do not worry about it. **30**For the pagan world runs after all such things, and your Father *v* knows that you need them. *w* **31**But seek his kingdom, *x* and these things will be given to you as well. *y*

32"Do not be afraid, *z* little flock, for your Father has been pleased to give you the kingdom. *a* **33**Sell your possessions and give to the poor. *b* Provide purses for yourselves that will not wear out, a treasure in heaven *c* that will not be exhausted, where no thief comes near and no moth destroys. *d* **34**For where your treasure is, there your heart will be also. *e*

Watchfulness

35"Be dressed ready for service and keep your lamps burning, **36**like men waiting for their master to return from a wedding banquet, so that when he comes and knocks they can immediately open the door for him. **37**It will be good for those servants whose master finds them watching when he comes. *f* I tell you the truth, he will dress himself to serve, will have them recline at the table and will come and wait on them. *g* **38**It will be good for those servants whose master finds them ready, even if he comes in the second or third watch of the night. **39**But understand this: If the owner of the house had known at what hour the thief *h* was coming, he would not have let his house be broken into. **40**You also must be ready, *i* because the Son of Man will come at an hour when you do not expect him."

41Peter asked, "Lord, are you telling this parable to us, or to everyone?"

42The Lord *j* answered, "Who then is the faithful and wise manager, whom the master puts in charge of his servants to give them their food allowance at the proper time? **43**It will be good for that servant whom the master finds doing so when he returns. **44**I tell you the truth, he will put him in charge of all his possessions. **45**But suppose the servant says to himself, 'My master is taking a long time in com-

a 25 Or single cubit to his height

Luke 12:22–34

Jesus *commanded* his followers to be constantly free of anxiety. If they didn't worry about life's provisions, they would have the energy and motivation to be generous with what God had given them. Accordingly, Jesus called for selling possessions and giving the proceeds to the poor—freeing up his followers from being controlled by their possessions and by worry over them. Such generosity God honors with indestructible "treasure in heaven"—his commendation and reward for service that pleases him.

The pursuit of materialistic goals and heaping up treasures on Earth *empties* our lives of God's most precious gifts: absolute trust in God and the honor of *serving those around us. The conflict between Jesus' call and that of our culture may explain why we tend to respond positively to his remarks about worry—all the while resisting what he says about the use of our re-

sources. Has this been the case for you?

Luke 12:35–48

Part of the treasure believers store up in heaven (v. 33) comes through faithful service. As they serve, they are aware that they will be accountable to the Lord when he returns. The Bible's teaching about the future exists not so much to inform Christians of the details as to prepare them to serve God daily. Grace doesn't eliminate accountability. He cares what his children do with his gifts, and at Jesus' return he will honor those who have been faithful.

Not everything in this passage warns of judgment. Is there a more amazing promise in Scripture than that the Master, upon finding the house well cared for, will turn around and *serve the servants* (v. 37)? Jesus' willingness to "dress himself to serve" (see John 13:3–5) will culminate in his glorious return. Christ wants us to become servants, like he is.

Side references:
12:24 *s* Job 38:41; Ps 147:9
12:27 *t* 1Ki 10:4-7
12:28 *u* Mt 6:30
12:30 *v* Lk 6:36 *w* Mt 6:8
12:31 *x* Mt 3:2 *y* Mt 19:29
12:32 *z* Mt 14:27 *a* Mt 25:34
12:33 *b* Mt 19:21; Ac 2:45 *c* Mt 6:20 *d* Jas 5:2
12:34 *e* Mt 6:21
12:37 *f* Mt 24:42,46; 25:13 *g* Mt 20:28
12:39 *h* Mt 6:19; 1Th 5:2; 2Pe 3:10; Rev 3:3; 16:15
12:40 *i* Mk 13:33; Lk 21:36
12:42 *j* Lk 7:13

ing,[j] and he then begins to beat the menservants and maidservants and to eat and drink and get drunk. [46]The master of that servant will come on a day when he does not expect him and at an hour he is not aware of.[k] He will cut him to pieces and assign him a place with the unbelievers.

[47]"That servant who knows his master's will and does not get ready or does not do what his master wants will be beaten with many blows.[l] [48]But the one who does not know and does things deserving punishment will be beaten with few blows.[m] From everyone who has been given much, much will be demanded; and from the one who has been entrusted with much, much more will be asked.

Not Peace but Division

[49]"I have come to bring fire on the earth, and how I wish it were already kindled! [50]But I have a baptism[n] to undergo, and how distressed I am until it is completed![o] [51]Do you think I came to bring peace on earth? No, I tell you, but division. [52]From now on there will be five in one family divided against each other, three against two and two against three. [53]They will be divided, father against son and son against father, mother against daughter and daughter against mother, mother-in-law against daughter-in-law and daughter-in-law against mother-in-law."[p]

Interpreting the Times

[54]He said to the crowd: "When you see a cloud rising in the west, immediately you say, 'It's going to rain,' and it does.[q] [55]And when the south wind blows, you say, 'It's going to be hot,' and it is. [56]Hypocrites! You know how to interpret the appearance of the earth and the sky. How is it that you don't know how to interpret this present time?[r]

[57]"Why don't you judge for yourselves what is right? [58]As you are going with your adversary to the magistrate, try hard to be reconciled to him on the way, or he may drag you off to the judge, and the judge turn you over to the officer, and the officer throw you into prison.[s] [59]I tell you, you will not get out until you have paid the last penny.[a][t]

Repent or Perish

13 Now there were some present at that time who told Jesus about the Galileans whose blood Pilate[u] had mixed with their sacrifices. [2]Jesus answered, "Do you think that these Galileans were worse sinners than all the other Galileans because they suffered this way?[v] [3]I tell you, no! But unless you repent, you too will

[a] 59 Greek *lepton*

12:46
[k] ver 40

12:47
[l] Dt 25:2
12:48
[m] Lev 5:17; Nu 15:27-30

12:50
[n] Mk 10:38
[o] Jn 19:30

12:53
[p] Mic 7:6; Mt 10:21

12:54
[q] Mt 16:2

12:56
[r] Mt 16:3

12:58
[s] Mt 5:25
12:59
[t] Mt 5:26; Mk 12:42

13:1
[u] Mt 27:2

13:2
[v] Jn 9:2,3

Luke 12:49–53

The fire image symbolizes judgment and purification (cf. 3:9,16). Jesus' message provided the way for people to make decisions about where they stood and gave them the opportunity to receive forgiveness (5:31–32). But before he could exercise such judgment and authority, he had to undergo his own "baptism"—in this case, a reference to his approaching death. The rejection he would suffer was only a portion of the tension introduced by his presence: Families would continue to be divided, as some opted for and others against him.

When you picture Jesus, do you think in terms of peace or conflict? Jesus brought and continues to bring peace, but a picture of him as the great peacemaker, *who sought peace at any cost*, is skewed. Jesus portrayed himself here as a figure who brings division and forces choices. His ministry confronts people, not harshly but directly, by calling them to account before God. Some are drawn to him; others turn away. He was and is the Great Divider, as well as the Prince of Peace.

Luke 12:54–59

Jesus called on those present to reflect on their perceptual skills. They could read "signs" to anticipate the weather. Yet they failed to discern the nature of events surrounding Jesus or to rightly assess his miracles and message. The illustration Jesus used came from everyday life—from a legal dispute over indebtedness. Jesus minced no words in urging his listeners to settle their accounts with God to avoid the grim prospect of judgment.

Some Christians try to package Jesus for our culture, as though sin were a minor topic on his agenda. As a result of trying to market Christ, the church softens its message on this point. In doing so, it distorts the gospel and fails to preach the Jesus who offers new life. To remove accountability to God for sin is to remove the power of grace. How do you handle the topic of sin when speaking to others about the new life Jesus offers?

13:4
w Jn 9:7,11

13:5
x Mt 3:2; Ac 2:38

13:6
y Isa 5:2; Jer 8:13;
Mt 21:19

13:7
z Mt 3:10

13:10
a Mt 4:23
13:11
b ver 16

13:13
c Mk 5:23
13:14
d Mt 12:2; Lk 14:3
e Mk 5:22 f Ex 20:9

13:15
g Lk 14:5
13:16
h Lk 3:8; 19:9
i Mt 4:10
13:17
j Isa 66:5

13:18
k Mt 3:2 l Mt 13:24

13:19
m Lk 17:6
n Mt 13:32

13:21
o 1Co 5:6

all perish. [4]Or those eighteen who died when the tower in Siloam[w] fell on them—do you think they were more guilty than all the others living in Jerusalem? [5]I tell you, no! But unless you repent,[x] you too will all perish."

[6]Then he told this parable: "A man had a fig tree, planted in his vineyard, and he went to look for fruit on it, but did not find any.[y] [7]So he said to the man who took care of the vineyard, 'For three years now I've been coming to look for fruit on this fig tree and haven't found any. Cut it down![z] Why should it use up the soil?'

[8]" 'Sir,' the man replied, 'leave it alone for one more year, and I'll dig around it and fertilize it. [9]If it bears fruit next year, fine! If not, then cut it down.' "

A Crippled Woman Healed on the Sabbath

[10]On a Sabbath Jesus was teaching in one of the synagogues,[a] [11]and a woman was there who had been crippled by a spirit for eighteen years.[b] She was bent over and could not straighten up at all. [12]When Jesus saw her, he called her forward and said to her, "Woman, you are set free from your infirmity." [13]Then he put his hands on her,[c] and immediately she straightened up and praised God.

[14]Indignant because Jesus had healed on the Sabbath,[d] the synagogue ruler[e] said to the people, "There are six days for work.[f] So come and be healed on those days, not on the Sabbath."

[15]The Lord answered him, "You hypocrites! Doesn't each of you on the Sabbath untie his ox or donkey from the stall and lead it out to give it water?[g] [16]Then should not this woman, a daughter of Abraham,[h] whom Satan[i] has kept bound for eighteen long years, be set free on the Sabbath day from what bound her?"

[17]When he said this, all his opponents were humiliated,[j] but the people were delighted with all the wonderful things he was doing.

The Parables of the Mustard Seed and the Yeast

[18]Then Jesus asked, "What is the kingdom of God[k] like?[l] What shall I compare it to? [19]It is like a mustard seed, which a man took and planted in his garden. It grew and became a tree,[m] and the birds of the air perched in its branches."[n]

[20]Again he asked, "What shall I compare the kingdom of God to? [21]It is like yeast that a woman took and mixed into a large amount[a] of flour until it worked all through the dough."[o]

a 21 Greek three satas (probably about 1/2 bushel or 22 liters)

Luke 13:1–9

The death that kills permanently isn't physical death but the "second death" sin produces (cf. Rev. 20:6; 21:8). Jesus' parable likely referred specifically to Israel as the fig tree. The issues of coming judgment and the short time to decide related to Israel's national status. Jesus' call to repent, though, is timeless—whether it's issued to the covenant nation of Israel or to individuals who need to enter into a relationship of grace and forgiveness with God.

Repentance is more than recognizing our error, regretting things we have done, or even apologizing. It's agreeing that a change of direction is required—and following through. Those who anticipate and rely on a deathbed repentance so they can "enjoy" life until the end usually don't care to repent—or lack the opportunity—when the end comes. Jesus calls us to respond today, before it's too late or we become too comfortable with sinful ways. What does true "enjoyment" of life mean to you?

Luke 13:10–17

Two major themes are addressed in this passage: (1) A watershed issue—the debate about Jesus' authority. If Jesus had the authority to heal, and God endorsed that

authority by giving him the power to heal on the Sabbath, the healing must have been of divine origin. (2) The battle with Satan, the source of the woman's bondage. Just as 10:18 and 11:14–23 tie Jesus' work to this cosmic conflict, so this text reflects Satan's diminishing authority.

The image of salvation as release from Satan's clutches is a positive picture in this text. Satan can damage us both physically and emotionally, causing us to depend on compulsive or destructive substances or behaviors. Whether the challenge is being "bent over" and "brought low" by alcohol, drugs, sex, or some other debilitating situation, Jesus' deliverance sets us free from the limitations with which Satan has chained us.

Luke 13:18–21

These two parables make the same point: The kingdom of God starts out small but will eventually cover the whole earth. Both the steady growth of the tree and the permeation of the loaf of bread from a pinch of yeast are inevitable. God's authority among his own extends itself as his Spirit moves to draw more people under the umbrella of his saving care. The crucial point about growth is a declaration about the protective presence of a caring God.

The Narrow Door

22Then Jesus went through the towns and villages, teaching as he made his way to Jerusalem. *p* 23Someone asked him, "Lord, are only a few people going to be saved?"

He said to them, 24"Make every effort to enter through the narrow door, *q* because many, I tell you, will try to enter and will not be able to. 25Once the owner of the house gets up and closes the door, you will stand outside knocking and pleading, 'Sir, open the door for us.'

"But he will answer, 'I don't know you or where you come from.' *r*

26"Then you will say, 'We ate and drank with you, and you taught in our streets.'

27"But he will reply, 'I don't know you or where you come from. Away from me, all you evildoers!' *s*

28"There will be weeping there, and gnashing of teeth, *t* when you see Abraham, Isaac and Jacob and all the prophets in the kingdom of God, but you yourselves thrown out. 29People will come from east and west *u* and north and south, and will take their places at the feast in the kingdom of God. 30Indeed there are those who are last who will be first, and first who will be last." *v*

Jesus' Sorrow for Jerusalem

31At that time some Pharisees came to Jesus and said to him, "Leave this place and go somewhere else. Herod *w* wants to kill you."

32He replied, "Go tell that fox, 'I will drive out demons and heal people today and tomorrow, and on the third day I will reach my goal.' *x* 33In any case, I must keep going today and tomorrow and the next day—for surely no prophet *y* can die outside Jerusalem!

34"O Jerusalem, Jerusalem, you who kill the prophets and stone those sent to you, how often I have longed to gather your children together, as a hen gathers her chicks under her wings, *z* but you were not willing! 35Look, your house is left to you desolate. *a* I tell you, you will not see me again until you say, 'Blessed is he who comes in the name of the Lord.' *a" b*

a 35 Psalm 118:26

13:22
p Lk 9:51

13:24
q Mt 7:13

13:25
r Mt 7:23; 25:10-12

13:27
s Mt 7:23; 25:41
13:28
t Mt 8:12

13:29
u Mt 8:11

13:30
v Mt 19:30

13:31
w Mt 14:1

13:32
x Heb 2:10
13:33
y Mt 21:11

13:34
z Mt 23:37
13:35
a Jer 12:17; 22:5
b Ps 118:26;
Mt 21:9; Lk 19:38

📖 The kingdom is found today wherever God's people are present. Its power is revealed in the transformation of lives that serve as a testimony to the living God (cf. Rom. 14:17–18). Manifesting the kingdom's presence isn't about constructing buildings or passing laws, but about honoring God with a quality of life directed powerfully by the work of his Spirit. The overriding priority of God's people is their commitment to live, to relate, and to serve in God-honoring ways. How is God's kingdom demonstrated in your life?

Luke 13:22–30

📖 Jesus' metaphorical answer to the question posed in this passage served as a warning to Israel. The kingdom was coming and people needed to respond immediately—before the door of opportunity slammed shut. Many of those originally invited, descendants of the ones to whom the original promise had come, would otherwise miss the blessing. What could be more tragic than closing yourself off to God's blessing and missing out—of being near, and yet so far away?

📖 Our culture views the road to heaven as a complex interstate highway system, offering dozens of routes and interchanges. Jesus used a more focused image: the narrow and soon-to-be-shut door. In Jesus' day, and ours, the door remains open to everyone. It's an equal-opportunity route marked out by God, not us. He wants us to

consciously enter into relationship with him—aware of our sins, our need for him, and the salvation Jesus has achieved for us. How does the world's any-road-will-do philosophy impact the sharing of the gospel?

Luke 13:31–35

📖 The Pharisees' statement appeared to be one of concern. The nuisance of Jesus' ministry would be eliminated if he were to turn tail and run. Jesus responded that *nothing* would stop him from completing his mission. Then he both lamented and warned Israel by referring to the city that represented her, Jerusalem. In a style suggestive of the prophets, he argued that judgment was inevitable. One of the tragedies of rejecting God's will is that people who do so get precisely what they ask for.

📖 Herod thought he could remove God's agent, and the Jewish leaders assumed they could make him go away. Similar efforts at intimidation occur today, ranging from cries that Christianity is outdated to attempts across the globe to threaten believers. God's ways, though, won't be thwarted. For the Christian, there is often victory in seeming defeat. Some of the strongest testimonies of God's faithfulness come from those who have over the centuries stood faithful in the midst of persecution. What account of a Christian martyr or missionary has moved you to a stronger stand for your faith?

14:1
c Lk 7:36; 11:37
d Mt 12:10
14:3
e Mt 22:35
f Mt 12:2
14:5
g Lk 13:15
14:7
h Lk 11:43
14:11
i Mt 23:12;
Lk 18:14
14:13
j ver 21
14:14
k Ac 24:15
14:15
l Isa 25:6; Mt 26:29;
Lk 13:29; Rev 19:9
m Mt 3:2

Jesus at a Pharisee's House

14 One Sabbath, when Jesus went to eat in the house of a prominent Pharisee, *c* he was being carefully watched. *d* 2There in front of him was a man suffering from dropsy. 3Jesus asked the Pharisees and experts in the law, *e* "Is it lawful to heal on the Sabbath or not?" *f* 4But they remained silent. So taking hold of the man, he healed him and sent him away.

5Then he asked them, "If one of you has a son*a* or an ox that falls into a well on the Sabbath day, will you not immediately pull him out?" *g* 6And they had nothing to say.

7When he noticed how the guests picked the places of honor at the table, *h* he told them this parable: 8"When someone invites you to a wedding feast, do not take the place of honor, for a person more distinguished than you may have been invited. 9If so, the host who invited both of you will come and say to you, 'Give this man your seat.' Then, humiliated, you will have to take the least important place. 10But when you are invited, take the lowest place, so that when your host comes, he will say to you, 'Friend, move up to a better place.' Then you will be honored in the presence of all your fellow guests. 11For everyone who exalts himself will be humbled, and he who humbles himself will be exalted." *i*

12Then Jesus said to his host, "When you give a luncheon or dinner, do not invite your friends, your brothers or relatives, or your rich neighbors; if you do, they may invite you back and so you will be repaid. 13But when you give a banquet, invite the poor, the crippled, the lame, the blind,*j* 14and you will be blessed. Although they cannot repay you, you will be repaid at the resurrection of the righteous." *k*

The Parable of the Great Banquet

15When one of those at the table with him heard this, he said to Jesus, "Blessed is the man who will eat at the feast*l* in the kingdom of God." *m*

16Jesus replied: "A certain man was preparing a great banquet and invited many guests. 17At the time of the banquet he sent his servant to tell those who had been invited, 'Come, for everything is now ready.'

18"But they all alike began to make excuses. The first said, 'I have just bought a field, and I must go and see it. Please excuse me.'

19"Another said, 'I have just bought five yoke of oxen, and I'm on my way to try them out. Please excuse me.'

a 5 Some manuscripts *donkey*

Luke 14:1–14

The imagery in verses 7–11 recalls Proverbs 25:6–7, which states that it's better for the host to invite you to a better seat than to assert yourself by trying to get his attention. Humility means resisting the urge toward social snobbery. Jesus expanded the call in verses 12–14 as he introduced another topic. He called his followers to serve those—the poor and needy—who couldn't repay their kindness. The best hospitality is *given*, not exchanged. Though the invited can't repay, divine commendation will come (cf. 1 Cor. 4:5).

Luke 14:7–14 treats two attitudes, humility and generosity, vital to Christian character. Many people assume that certain conditions in someone's life inevitably stem from that person's deficiencies. Ever hear this one: "People are poor because they are lazy"? This attitude doesn't encourage compassion toward those who, for instance, may have grown up without support or training. Genuine humility and generosity guard against a personally destructive and blinding perspective that ignores the needs and circumstances of "unimportant" people. What generalizations about a person or group of people have tripped you up?

Luke 14:15–24

This scene summarized all that Jesus had warned the Jews about in the last few chapters. Israel as a nation represented the initial banquet invitees, but her people were failing to RSVP. The time had come for the kingdom's arrival, and the celebration of its blessings would proceed as planned. The people who did come represented the spread of God's blessing beyond Israel's boundaries. God's people had missed their initial chance to sit at the table. The first had indeed become last (13:30).

How foolish to presume God will eventually bless us, either because he's not judging us right now or because we can always repent at the ninth hour (see also "Here and Now" for 13:1–9). The longer we refuse his offer, the more likely it won't interest us later on. This kind of self-sufficient pride explains why God's choosing of and sensitivity to the poor, lame, and blind were so important to Luke (4:18–19; 7:22–23). Those who know their need and position before God are the ones he will bring to himself (18:9–14; cf. 1 Cor. 1:26–31).

Hospitality

 14:12–14

Jesus' invitation to live in a radically new way extends to such ordinary activities as sharing meals. Though we are usually happy to include people we like and who are like us, in Luke 14:12–14 Jesus challenges our hospitality, pressing us to reach out to those on the fringes of community life.

Among the millions of hungry and destitute people in our world, some are additionally vulnerable. Whether through illness, personal misfortune, war, or natural disaster, they have lost the relationships that usually provide safety and security. They lack family connections and community to uphold or sustain them. Refugees, orphans, widows, homeless people, and those hidden away in institutions need more than food and shelter. They need relationships, friendships, and communities that will allow them to contribute and belong.

In this passage Jesus greatly expanded predictable, narrow definitions of hospitality. Typical hosts invite family, friends, and socially acceptable neighbors to their tables. In doing so, they solidify relationships, reinforce social boundaries, and anticipate return invitations. In contrast, hosts who look forward to the hospitality of God's kingdom welcome "the least," those ordinarily overlooked and excluded, unlikely ever to reciprocate.

Table fellowship followed a strict protocol in Jesus' day. Concerns about status and ritual cleanliness limited hospitality to the "right" kinds of people. Jesus' consistent, gracious invitations to outcasts and "sinners," his welcoming embrace of the least and the lost, was evident in his unqualified willingness to be both host and guest at their tables. His behavior rankled and threatened the secure in his society. Yet it powerfully proclaimed and embodied the hospitality of God's kingdom.

Luke 14:12–14 defines the difference between conventional and Christian hospitality. Welcoming needy strangers distinguished the early church from its surrounding environment, becoming a gospel hallmark. Based on Jesus' teaching and example, early Christian leaders criticized those who offered hospitality to get something in return, describing their motivation as "ambitious," a bid for personal advantage.

In many Biblical stories, God's blessing and presence are connected with hospitality to strangers. Abraham and Sarah welcomed three strangers who turned out to be angels (Gen. 18:1–15). The widow of Zarephath was rescued from famine when she shared her meager rations with Elijah (1 Kings 17:8–16). Jesus said that in the act of welcoming a stranger the Son of man himself is welcomed (Matt. 25:31–46). While the Bible and Christian tradition warn us against offering hospitality with the expectation of a return engagement, these stories also show us that generous hosts often do experience blessing and the mystery of God's presence (Heb. 13:2).

> **A**s we welcome others to our tables and into our lives, we remember, represent, and anticipate God's hospitality.

Sharing a meal is an expression of respect and equality. But our typical responses to hungry or needy people often allow us to maintain social distance and reinforce positions of inequality. We serve meals *to*, but don't sit down and eat *with*, homeless people; we stock food pantries and clothing closets but rarely share a coffee break or worship with the recipients of those services.

Some kinds of hunger can only be met through hospitality and personal welcome. Jesus expects us to share our resources but also asks us to share *ourselves*. Where and with whom we invest our time, as well as the people we welcome into our homes and churches, say a great deal about our values and commitments.

We all depend on God's grace and provision; we are all guests of a gracious and generous host. As we welcome others to our tables and into our lives, we remember, represent, and anticipate God's hospitality.

Christine D. Pohl, professor of social ethics at Asbury Theological Seminary in Wilmore, Kentucky

20 "Still another said, 'I just got married, so I can't come.'

21 "The servant came back and reported this to his master. Then the owner of the house became angry and ordered his servant, 'Go out quickly into the streets and alleys of the town and bring in the poor, the crippled, the blind and the lame.' [n]

22 " 'Sir,' the servant said, 'what you ordered has been done, but there is still room.'

23 "Then the master told his servant, 'Go out to the roads and country lanes and make them come in, so that my house will be full. 24 I tell you, not one of those men who were invited will get a taste of my banquet.' " [o]

The Cost of Being a Disciple

25 Large crowds were traveling with Jesus, and turning to them he said: 26 "If anyone comes to me and does not hate his father and mother, his wife and children, his brothers and sisters—yes, even his own life—he cannot be my disciple. [p] 27 And anyone who does not carry his cross and follow me cannot be my disciple. [q]

28 "Suppose one of you wants to build a tower. Will he not first sit down and estimate the cost to see if he has enough money to complete it? 29 For if he lays the foundation and is not able to finish it, everyone who sees it will ridicule him, 30 saying, 'This fellow began to build and was not able to finish.'

31 "Or suppose a king is about to go to war against another king. Will he not first sit down and consider whether he is able with ten thousand men to oppose the one coming against him with twenty thousand? 32 If he is not able, he will send a delegation while the other is still a long way off and will ask for terms of peace. 33 In the same way, any of you who does not give up everything he has cannot be my disciple. [r]

34 "Salt is good, but if it loses its saltiness, how can it be made salty again? [s] 35 It is fit neither for the soil nor for the manure pile; it is thrown out. [t]

"He who has ears to hear, let him hear." [u]

The Parable of the Lost Sheep

15 Now the tax collectors [v] and "sinners" were all gathering around to hear him. 2 But the Pharisees and the teachers of the law muttered, "This man welcomes sinners and eats with them." [w]

3 Then Jesus told them this parable: [x] 4 "Suppose one of you has a hundred sheep and loses one of them. Does he not leave the ninety-nine in the open country and go after the lost sheep until he finds it? [y] 5 And when he finds it, he joyfully puts it on his shoulders 6 and goes home. Then he calls his friends and neighbors together and says, 'Rejoice with me; I have found my lost sheep.' [z] 7 I tell you that in the

---

Marginal references:

14:21
n ver 13

14:24
o Mt 21:43;
Ac 13:46

14:26
p Mt 10:37;
Jn 12:25
14:27
q Mt 10:38; Lk 9:23

14:33
r Php 3:7,8
14:34
s Mk 9:50
14:35
t Mt 5:13
u Mt 11:15

15:1
v Lk 5:29

15:2
w Mt 9:11
15:3
x Mt 13:3
15:4
y Ps 23; 119:176;
Jer 31:10;
Eze 34:11-16;
Lk 5:32; 19:10
15:6
z ver 9

Luke 14:25–35

Discipleship requires that Jesus be the believer's highest priority in life. His will and the direction he leads were and are to be the forces that determine their life's direction. Jesus wants his disciples to bring to the journey an understanding of what following him requires and a resolve not to detour from the straight and narrow. If we are going to finish well, we will have to count the cost.

This text calls for serious self-reflection. Do I yield to the Lord in every area of my life—my possessions, my family—my very existence? Our lives as followers of Christ break down when we have allowed him to "convert" our souls, but not our finances, relationships, ambitions, or politics. Do I trust him to care for me? The wise builder submits to God's will in every aspect of life.

Luke 15:1–7

God is committed to finding the lost. Jesus addressed the contrast between this divine attitude and the temptation among some highly religious individuals to ignore such people. The Pharisees and teachers of the law couldn't believe he was spending so much time associating with "sinners." Such table fellowship represented, in their minds, a pollution of righteousness. But God's call *demands* that his people spend time seeking out the lost, lonely, hidden, and hiding.

It's easy to dismiss the people our culture has cast aside in contempt. AIDS sufferers, street people, and welfare recipients may be modern equivalents to the tax collectors and sinners of Jesus' world. But what about those who are just a little too backward, have too many personal problems, or lack social graces? Love compelled our Lord to reach out. Is there any reason our attitude toward such "lost sheep" should be any different?

same way there will be more rejoicing in heaven over one sinner who repents than over ninety-nine righteous persons who do not need to repent. [a]

The Parable of the Lost Coin

8 "Or suppose a woman has ten silver coins [a] and loses one. Does she not light a lamp, sweep the house and search carefully until she finds it? 9 And when she finds it, she calls her friends and neighbors together and says, 'Rejoice with me; I have found my lost coin.' [b] 10 In the same way, I tell you, there is rejoicing in the presence of the angels of God over one sinner who repents.'" [c]

The Parable of the Lost Son

11 Jesus continued: "There was a man who had two sons. [d] 12 The younger one said to his father, 'Father, give me my share of the estate.' [e] So he divided his property [f] between them.

13 "Not long after that, the younger son got together all he had, set off for a distant country and there squandered his wealth [g] in wild living. 14 After he had spent everything, there was a severe famine in that whole country, and he began to be in need. 15 So he went and hired himself out to a citizen of that country, who sent him to his fields to feed pigs. [h] 16 He longed to fill his stomach with the pods that the pigs were eating, but no one gave him anything.

17 "When he came to his senses, he said, 'How many of my father's hired men have food to spare, and here I am starving to death! 18 I will set out and go back to my father and say to him: Father, I have sinned [i] against heaven and against you. 19 I am no longer worthy to be called your son; make me like one of your hired men.' 20 So he got up and went to his father.

"But while he was still a long way off, his father saw him and was filled with compassion for him; he ran to his son, threw his arms around him and kissed him. [j]

21 "The son said to him, 'Father, I have sinned against heaven and against you. [k] I am no longer worthy to be called your son.' [b']

22 "But the father said to his servants, 'Quick! Bring the best robe [l] and put it on him. Put a ring on his finger [m] and sandals on his feet. 23 Bring the fattened calf and kill it. Let's have a feast and celebrate. 24 For this son of mine was dead and is alive again; [n] he was lost and is found.' So they began to celebrate. [o]

25 "Meanwhile, the older son was in the field. When he came near the house, he heard music and dancing. 26 So he called one of the servants and asked him what

---

15:7
[a] ver 10

15:9
[b] ver 6
15:10
[c] ver 7

15:11
[d] Mt 21:28
15:12
[e] Dt 21:17 [f] ver 30

15:13
[g] ver 30; Lk 16:1

15:15
[h] Lev 11:7

15:18
[i] Lev 26:40; Mt 3:2

15:20
[j] Ge 45:14,15;
46:29; Ac 20:37
15:21
[k] Ps 51:4

15:22
[l] Zec 3:4; Rev 6:11
[m] Ge 41:42

15:24
[n] Eph 2:1,5; 5:14;
1Ti 5:6 [o] ver 32

---

[a] 8 Greek *ten drachmas*, each worth about a day's wages   [b] 21 Some early manuscripts *son. Make me like one of your hired men.*

Luke 15:8–10

The second illustration in this chapter is similar. A woman systematically hunts for a lost coin—a denarius, a day's wage for the average worker. Her careful search consumes her until she finds the coin. Eureka! She's as exhilarated as the shepherd was, so much so that she calls her neighbors for an impromptu celebration. The point would have been clear to Jesus' listeners: The sinners with whom he was associating (vv. 1–2) were priceless to God.

Believers are called to engage the lost as valuable treasures. In our fast-moving culture, developing such relationships can be costly. Caring for people requires time and energy, like the shepherd's and the woman's searches. We may at times forget the treasure in others, but all of heaven breaks out in song when a lost child enters the kingdom.

Luke 15:11–32

This parable is often called "The Prodigal Son," but it's really about different reactions to the reckless spendthrift. The father depicts God. The lost son represents the sinner who repents. And the older son illustrates the attitude of the Pharisees who didn't want sinners to turn to God. What would you do, is Jesus' implied question, if you were in the older son's sandals? Would you be too preoccupied seething about the injustice to share in the joy of your brother's return?

God's attitude, not just the older brother's, is central to the parable, resulting in two important applications: (1) God eagerly pursues us and rejoices when we come home. Those of us with sensitive consciences need not doubt God's gracious desire to welcome us. (2) Jesus wants us to respond as the father called the older son to do—by pursuing sinners and welcoming them with joy upon their return. Do we believe God embraces those who turn to him—or are we afraid to press the issue? This text asks us to see that he does—and to rest in the encouragement such love and grace offers us.

was going on. 27 'Your brother has come,' he replied, 'and your father has killed the fattened calf because he has him back safe and sound.'

15:28
p Jnh 4:1

28 "The older brother became angry[p] and refused to go in. So his father went out and pleaded with him. 29 But he answered his father, 'Look! All these years I've been slaving for you and never disobeyed your orders. Yet you never gave me even a young goat so I could celebrate with my friends. 30 But when this son of yours who has squandered your property[q] with prostitutes[r] comes home, you kill the fattened calf for him!'

15:30
q ver 12,13
r Pr 29:3

31 " 'My son,' the father said, 'you are always with me, and everything I have is yours. 32 But we had to celebrate and be glad, because this brother of yours was dead and is alive again; he was lost and is found.' "[s]

15:32
s ver 24; Mal 3:17

The Parable of the Shrewd Manager

16 Jesus told his disciples: "There was a rich man whose manager was accused of wasting his possessions.[t] 2 So he called him in and asked him, 'What is this I hear about you? Give an account of your management, because you cannot be manager any longer.'

16:1
t Lk 15:13,30

3 "The manager said to himself, 'What shall I do now? My master is taking away my job. I'm not strong enough to dig, and I'm ashamed to beg— 4 I know what I'll do so that, when I lose my job here, people will welcome me into their houses.'

5 "So he called in each one of his master's debtors. He asked the first, 'How much do you owe my master?'

6 " 'Eight hundred gallons[a] of olive oil,' he replied.

"The manager told him, 'Take your bill, sit down quickly, and make it four hundred.'

7 "Then he asked the second, 'And how much do you owe?'

" 'A thousand bushels[b] of wheat,' he replied.

"He told him, 'Take your bill and make it eight hundred.'

8 "The master commended the dishonest manager because he had acted shrewdly. For the people of this world[u] are more shrewd[v] in dealing with their own kind than are the people of the light.[w] 9 I tell you, use worldly wealth[x] to gain friends for yourselves, so that when it is gone, you will be welcomed into eternal dwellings.[y]

16:8
u Ps 17:14
v Ps 18:26
w Jn 12:36;
Eph 5:8; 1Th 5:5
16:9
x ver 11,13
y Mt 19:21;
Lk 12:33

10 "Whoever can be trusted with very little can also be trusted with much,[z] and whoever is dishonest with very little will also be dishonest with much. 11 So if you have not been trustworthy in handling worldly wealth,[a] who will trust you with true riches? 12 And if you have not been trustworthy with someone else's property, who will give you property of your own?

16:10
z Mt 25:21,23;
Lk 19:17
16:11
a ver 9,13

13 "No servant can serve two masters. Either he will hate the one and love the other, or he will be devoted to the one and despise the other. You cannot serve both God and Money."[b]

16:13
b ver 9,11; Mt 6:24
16:14
c 1Ti 3:3 d Lk 23:35
16:15
e Lk 10:29
f 1Sa 16:7; Rev 2:23

14 The Pharisees, who loved money,[c] heard all this and were sneering at Jesus.[d] 15 He said to them, "You are the ones who justify yourselves[e] in the eyes of men, but God knows your hearts.[f] What is highly valued among men is detestable in God's sight.

a 6 Greek *one hundred batous* (probably about 3 kiloliters)   b 7 Greek *one hundred korous* (probably about 35 kiloliters)

Luke 16:1–15

Jesus used a negative example to make a positive point, making this parable more than usually difficult to interpret. Was he pointing out that the manager acted with foresight by reducing his debt, in hope of goodwill later? One way or another, the parable illustrates that believers are to use the resources God has put at their disposal wisely and generously. Money management for the Christian isn't an end but a means. It allows others to witness *acts* of caring from those who have told them God cares.

God's call to be generous means we are to be on the watch for valid ministries and legitimate needs. In addition to giving to local churches and ministries, we do well to look for broader opportunities—whether that entails involvement with feeding the hungry, enabling justice to come into the lives of victims of oppression, planting churches in non-Christian cultures, promoting education where family support for learning is minimal, or dealing with the needs of single mothers or of the elderly.

Additional Teachings

16 "The Law and the Prophets were proclaimed until John. *g* Since that time, the good news of the kingdom of God is being preached, *h* and everyone is forcing his way into it. 17 It is easier for heaven and earth to disappear than for the least stroke of a pen to drop out of the Law. *i*

18 "Anyone who divorces his wife and marries another woman commits adultery, and the man who marries a divorced woman commits adultery. *j*

The Rich Man and Lazarus

19 "There was a rich man who was dressed in purple and fine linen and lived in luxury every day. *k* 20 At his gate was laid a beggar *l* named Lazarus, covered with sores 21 and longing to eat what fell from the rich man's table. *m* Even the dogs came and licked his sores.

22 "The time came when the beggar died and the angels carried him to Abraham's side. The rich man also died and was buried. 23 In hell, *a* where he was in torment, he looked up and saw Abraham far away, with Lazarus by his side. 24 So he called to him, 'Father Abraham, *n* have pity on me and send Lazarus to dip the tip of his finger in water and cool my tongue, because I am in agony in this fire.' *o*

a 23 Greek *Hades*

16:16
g Mt 11:12,13
h Mt 4:23

16:17
i Mt 5:18

16:18
j Mt 5:31,32; 19:9;
Mk 10:11; Ro 7:2,3;
1Co 7:10,11

16:19
k Eze 16:49
16:20
l Ac 3:2
16:21
m Mt 15:27

16:24
n ver 30; Lk 3:8
o Mt 5:22

Luke 16:16–18

Our knowledge of God-endorsed values comes from both Testaments. Jesus recapped the ethical standards God desires. But those standards don't replace the values reflected by the Law and the Prophets. Instead, Jesus brings the *fulfillment* of the prophetic promises and the *hope* of the Law—to bring righteousness to God's people.

Jesus closed with a note about divorce to illustrate that the ethical call of the kingdom is rooted in an integrity that matches that of the Law and the Prophets. The point of this passage isn't to discuss possible grounds for divorce, as Matthew 5:31–32 and 1 Corinthians 7:12–16 do, but to illustrate the importance of personal commitments made in the new era. The commitment to marry is a promise to stay married. Just as God is faithful to his covenant with us, we are to be trustworthy in our promises to others.

Luke 16:19–31

This parable is unique to Luke and is also the only one to name any of its characters. It's interesting that the poor man was identified by name, while his wealthy counterpart remained anonymous. In this way Jesus personalized his level of concern for the poor man, while making clear that the rich man was a representative figure. God cares for each individual poor person and is fully aware of the plight, not just of "the needy" as a group, but of each disadvantaged individual.

Helping those in need doesn't have to be limited to donating money, though such funds can do much good. There are numerous organizations committed to aiding and educating the poor or giving children a chance to rise above debilitating backgrounds. Such organizations also seek donations of time and talent, because the people they touch need a stable environment with strong *personal* emotional support. How much of yourself—time, talent, or treasure—are you willing to give?

16:19–31

Moses and the Prophets

By telling the story of the rich man and the beggar, Jesus made clear the importance of witnessing to all who are alive. Everyone needs a chance to hear "Moses and the Prophets" (v. 29). Jesus left instructions for his disciples to tell the world the Good News (Luke 24:44–47; Acts 1:8). Thousands of Christian mission agencies exist to do exactly this. Five of the largest, with the number of missionaries they supported in 2000, are:

(Mission Agencies, Over $100 Million Annually / # of missionaries)   REPRESENTS 1,000 MISSIONARIES

Agency	#	
SOCIETY OF JESUS, OR JESUITS	24,421	
CAMPUS CRUSADE FOR CHRIST	6,698	
YOUTH WITH A MISSION	6,037	
SOCIETY OF THE DIVINE WORD	5,648	
SOUTHERN BAPTIST CONVENTION INTERNATIONAL MISSION BOARD	3,715	

Scale: 0 — 5,000 — 10,000 — 15,000 — 20,000

Source: Barrett and Johnson (2001:57)

Great Sins of Omission

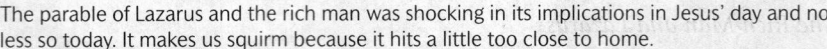

The parable of Lazarus and the rich man was shocking in its implications in Jesus' day and no less so today. It makes us squirm because it hits a little too close to home.

This rich man did nothing overtly to harm Lazarus—didn't beat, persecute, or evict him. Yet he failed to do anything to help Lazarus in his poverty.

A tendency of Christians today is to focus on *not* committing blatant sins—sins of commission. But how often do we reflect about our sins of omission (good things God calls us to do that we simply *omit* following through on)? This story makes us uncomfortable, challenging us with questions: What does God expect of his followers in relation to those around us? What should we do with the resources he's given us? What are the implications of wealth in a world with so much poverty and suffering?

God has high expectations for us as his followers. We are to be compassionate, concerned about "the least" in our world. We are stewards, not owners, of whatever resources God has entrusted to us, and it's our responsibility to invest them in ways that please God and are consistent with Biblical teaching.

> Lazarus's story is especially relevant today, as the chasm between rich and poor grows wider every year. Hasn't God also laid "beggars" at our gates?

God expects our actions to align with our faith professions. We are to "walk the walk," not just "talk the talk." James says that "faith by itself, if it is not accompanied by action, is dead" (James 2:17) and that "anyone, then, who knows the good he ought to do and doesn't do it, sins" (James 4:17). John repeats this theme in highly practical language: "If anyone has material possessions and sees his brother in need but has no pity on him, how can the love of God be in him?" (1 Jn. 3:17).

This principle is at the heart of the parable of the good Samaritan (Luke 10:25–37), perhaps one of the most profound moral teachings found in literature. Jesus told this story in answer to the question "Who is my neighbor?" posed by a legal expert.

In this parable a priest and Levite both see a man beaten and lying by the side of the road. But they turn away—sins of omission. A despised Samaritan does stop, binds up the man's wounds, and takes him to an inn to recover. This is loving one's neighbor—faith shown in tangible action, motivated by compassion. "Show me your faith without deeds, and I will show you my faith by what I do" (James 2:18).

Is this an argument for salvation by works and not by faith? No, but we can't avoid the reality that true faith is always evidenced by the fruit of the Spirit. Jesus underscored this: "By their fruit you will recognize them. Not everyone who says to me, 'Lord, Lord,' will enter the kingdom of heaven, but only he who does the will of my Father who is in heaven" (Matt. 7:20–21).

Lazarus's story is especially relevant today, as the chasm between rich and poor grows wider every year. Hasn't God also laid "beggars" at our gates?

> The bread which you keep belongs to the hungry; the coat which you preserve in your wardrobe, to the naked; those shoes which are rotting in your possession, to the shoeless; that gold which you have hidden in the ground, to the needy. Wherefore, as often as you are able to help others, and refuse, so often did you do them wrong.
>
> Augustine (A.D. 354–430), Bishop of Hippo (present-day Algeria)

Richard Stearns, president of World Vision U.S. in Federal Way, Washington

25 "But Abraham replied, 'Son, remember that in your lifetime you received your good things, while Lazarus received bad things, *p* but now he is comforted here and you are in agony. *q* 26And besides all this, between us and you a great chasm has been fixed, so that those who want to go from here to you cannot, nor can anyone cross over from there to us.'

27 "He answered, 'Then I beg you, father, send Lazarus to my father's house, 28for I have five brothers. Let him warn them, *r* so that they will not also come to this place of torment.'

29 "Abraham replied, 'They have Moses *s* and the Prophets; *t* let them listen to them.'

30 " 'No, father Abraham,' *u* he said, 'but if someone from the dead goes to them, they will repent.'

31 "He said to him, 'If they do not listen to Moses and the Prophets, they will not be convinced even if someone rises from the dead.' "

Sin, Faith, Duty

17 Jesus said to his disciples: "Things that cause people to sin *v* are bound to come, but woe to that person through whom they come. *w* 2It would be better for him to be thrown into the sea with a millstone tied around his neck than for him to cause one of these little ones *x* to sin. *y* 3So watch yourselves.

"If your brother sins, rebuke him, *z* and if he repents, forgive him. *a* 4If he sins against you seven times in a day, and seven times comes back to you and says, 'I repent,' forgive him." *b*

5The apostles *c* said to the Lord, *d* "Increase our faith!"

6He replied, "If you have faith as small as a mustard seed, *e* you can say to this mulberry tree, 'Be uprooted and planted in the sea,' and it will obey you. *f*

7 "Suppose one of you had a servant plowing or looking after the sheep. Would he say to the servant when he comes in from the field, 'Come along now and sit down to eat'? 8Would he not rather say, 'Prepare my supper, get yourself ready and wait on me *g* while I eat and drink; after that you may eat and drink'? 9Would he thank the servant because he did what he was told to do? 10So you also, when you have done everything you were told to do, should say, 'We are unworthy servants; we have only done our duty.' " *h*

Ten Healed of Leprosy

11 Now on his way to Jerusalem, *i* Jesus traveled along the border between Samaria and Galilee. *j* 12As he was going into a village, ten men who had leprosy *a* *k* met him. They stood at a distance *l* 13and called out in a loud voice, "Jesus, Master, *m* have pity on us!"

14When he saw them, he said, "Go, show yourselves to the priests." *n* And as they went, they were cleansed.

a 12 The Greek word was used for various diseases affecting the skin—not necessarily leprosy.

16:25
p Ps 17:14
q Lk 6:21,24,25

16:28
r Ac 2:40; 20:23;
1Th 4:6
16:29
s Lk 24:27,44;
Jn 5:45-47;
Ac 15:21 *t* Lk 4:17;
Jn 1:45
16:30
u ver 24; Lk 3:8

17:1
v Mt 5:29
w Mt 18:7

17:2
x Mk 10:24;
Lk 10:21 *y* Mt 5:29
17:3
z Mt 18:15
a Eph 4:32;
Col 3:13
17:4
b Mt 18:21,22
17:5
c Mk 6:30 *d* Lk 7:13
17:6
e Mt 13:31; 17:20;
Lk 13:19
f Mt 21:21; Mk 9:23

17:8
g Lk 12:37

17:10
h 1Co 9:16

17:11
i Lk 9:51
j Lk 9:51,52;
Jn 4:3,4
17:12
k Mt 8:2
l Lev 13:45,46
17:13
m Lk 5:5
17:14
n Lev 14:2; Mt 8:4

Luke 17:1–10

📖 This passage makes four points: (1) A warning (vv. 1–3a) treats the topic of causing someone else to sin. (2) This warning is serious, but it's equally important to forgive someone who has sinned against us (vv. 3b–4). (3) Another key discipleship characteristic is faith (vv. 5–6). (4) The final image is a short parable about serving (vv. 7–10). God honors our service (see 12:37), but obedience through serving isn't about merit badges but about faithfulness.

📖 It's vital that we avoid getting into a bargaining position with God. In fact, we are not to have a reward mentality at all. We serve God because of who he is and because he's worth serving. Service, obedience, and duty are natural outgrowths of a relationship with God and appreciation of his act of grace in saving us. Why do you practice Christian virtues?

Luke 17:11–19

📖 Only one of ten former lepers broke from the group and returned to Jesus. Overcome with gratitude, he fell at his healer's feet. Luke notes that the man was a Samaritan, one whose racial roots represented for the Jews insensitivity to God. Jesus simultaneously acclaimed this example of gratitude and pointed out that positive response to himself was possible from outside the nation of Israel. Do you struggle against preconceived notions of who God is likely to bless through your service?

17:15
o Mt 9:8
17:16
p Mt 10:5

17:19
q Mt 9:22

15 One of them, when he saw he was healed, came back, praising God o in a loud voice. 16 He threw himself at Jesus' feet and thanked him—and he was a Samaritan. p

17 Jesus asked, "Were not all ten cleansed? Where are the other nine? 18 Was no one found to return and give praise to God except this foreigner?" 19 Then he said to him, "Rise and go; your faith has made you well." q

The Coming of the Kingdom of God

17:20
r Mt 3:2
17:21
s ver 23

20 Once, having been asked by the Pharisees when the kingdom of God would come, r Jesus replied, "The kingdom of God does not come with your careful observation, 21 nor will people say, 'Here it is,' or 'There it is,' s because the kingdom of God is within a you."

17:22
t Mt 8:20
u Mt 9:15; Lk 5:35
17:23
v Mt 24:23;
Mk 13:21; Lk 21:8
17:24
w Mt 24:27
17:25
x Mt 16:21
y Lk 9:22; 18:32
z Mk 13:30;
Lk 21:32
17:26
a Ge 7:6-24
17:28
b Ge 19:1-28

22 Then he said to his disciples, "The time is coming when you will long to see one of the days of the Son of Man, t but you will not see it. u 23 Men will tell you, 'There he is!' or 'Here he is!' Do not go running off after them. v 24 For the Son of Man in his day b will be like the lightning, w which flashes and lights up the sky from one end to the other. 25 But first he must suffer many things x and be rejected y by this generation. z

26 "Just as it was in the days of Noah, a so also will it be in the days of the Son of Man. 27 People were eating, drinking, marrying and being given in marriage up to the day Noah entered the ark. Then the flood came and destroyed them all.

28 "It was the same in the days of Lot. b People were eating and drinking, buying and selling, planting and building. 29 But the day Lot left Sodom, fire and sulfur rained down from heaven and destroyed them all.

17:30
c Mt 10:23; 16:27;
24:3,27,37,39;
25:31; 1Co 1:7;
1Th 2:19; 2Th 1:7;
2:8; 2Pe 3:4;
Rev 1:7
17:31
d Mt 24:17,18;
Mk 13:15-16
17:32
e Ge 19:26
17:33
f Jn 12:25
17:35
g Mt 24:41
17:37
h Mt 24:28

30 "It will be just like this on the day the Son of Man is revealed. c 31 On that day no one who is on the roof of his house, with his goods inside, should go down to get them. Likewise, no one in the field should go back for anything. d 32 Remember Lot's wife! e 33 Whoever tries to keep his life will lose it, and whoever loses his life will preserve it. f 34 I tell you, on that night two people will be in one bed; one will be taken and the other left. 35 Two women will be grinding grain together; one will be taken and the other left. c g

37 "Where, Lord?" they asked.

He replied, "Where there is a dead body, there the vultures will gather." h

The Parable of the Persistent Widow

18:1
i Isa 40:31;
Lk 11:5-8; Ac 1:14;
Ro 12:12; Eph 6:18;
Col 4:2; 1Th 5:17

18 Then Jesus told his disciples a parable to show them that they should always pray and not give up. i 2 He said: "In a certain town there was a judge who

---

a 21 Or among   b 24 Some manuscripts do not have in his day.   c 35 Some manuscripts left.
36 Two men will be in the field; one will be taken and the other left.

📖 Expressing appreciation to God is an attitude and activity that has grown in the church in recent times, and that is good. Praise is important because it reestablishes our relationship with God on proper terms. But the thoughtless lack of response on the part of the nine reminds us how easy it is to take grace for granted. Why not take the time to deliberately reflect on what God has done for you—and to remember to thank him. You will become much more aware of his care as you purposely attune yourself to it.

📖 Attitudes in the church toward end-times theology span the spectrum. Some people devote their lives to trying to solve the "puzzle" of the "signs of the times"—and just how close we are to the end. On the other end are those who view such speculation as a waste of time and energy. Both are overreactions. The Bible devotes a good deal of space to the end times. Scripture provides a general outline about the future—but God's desire and design are for us to prepare our hearts, not our charts.

Luke 17:20–37

📖 The disciples of Jesus' day wouldn't personally see his return in power. The ultimate, authoritative manifestation of the Messiah was, and is, still coming. When the Son does arrive, the scene will be visible and obvious—like lightning flashing across the sky. But one crucial event needed to occur first: the Son of Man had to suffer. Suffering and rejection had to precede glory for Jesus.

Luke 18:1–8

📖 If God's saints minister in a world that refuses to accept them, how should they handle the injustice of that rejection? The answer comes in a call to pray persistently, without losing heart. If a judge who cares only for his own peace of mind hears and reacts to the wail of the nagging widow, how much more will a compassionate God listen and respond to the cries of his people!

neither feared God nor cared about men. ³And there was a widow in that town who kept coming to him with the plea, 'Grant me justice[j] against my adversary.'

⁴"For some time he refused. But finally he said to himself, 'Even though I don't fear God or care about men, ⁵yet because this widow keeps bothering me, I will see that she gets justice, so that she won't eventually wear me out with her coming!' "[k]

⁶And the Lord[l] said, "Listen to what the unjust judge says. ⁷And will not God bring about justice for his chosen ones, who cry out[m] to him day and night? Will he keep putting them off? ⁸I tell you, he will see that they get justice, and quickly. However, when the Son of Man[n] comes,[o] will he find faith on the earth?"

The Parable of the Pharisee and the Tax Collector

⁹To some who were confident of their own righteousness[p] and looked down on everybody else,[q] Jesus told this parable: ¹⁰"Two men went up to the temple to pray,[r] one a Pharisee and the other a tax collector. ¹¹The Pharisee stood up[s] and prayed about[a] himself: 'God, I thank you that I am not like other men—robbers, evildoers, adulterers—or even like this tax collector. ¹²I fast[t] twice a week and give a tenth[u] of all I get.'

¹³"But the tax collector stood at a distance. He would not even look up to heaven, but beat his breast[v] and said, 'God, have mercy on me, a sinner.'[w]

¹⁴"I tell you that this man, rather than the other, went home justified before God. For everyone who exalts himself will be humbled, and he who humbles himself will be exalted."[x]

The Little Children and Jesus

¹⁵People were also bringing babies to Jesus to have him touch them. When the disciples saw this, they rebuked them. ¹⁶But Jesus called the children to him and said, "Let the little children come to me, and do not hinder them, for the kingdom of God belongs to such as these. ¹⁷I tell you the truth, anyone who will not receive the kingdom of God like a little child[y] will never enter it."

The Rich Ruler

¹⁸A certain ruler asked him, "Good teacher, what must I do to inherit eternal life?"[z]

---

[a] 11 Or to

18:3 j Isa 1:17
18:5 k Lk 11:8
18:6 l Lk 7:13
18:7 m Ex 22:23; Ps 88:1; Rev 6:10
18:8 n Mt 8:20 o Mt 16:27
18:9 p Lk 16:15 q Isa 65:5
18:10 r Ac 3:1
18:11 s Mt 6:5; Mk 11:25
18:12 t Isa 58:3; Mt 9:14 u Mal 3:8; Lk 11:42
18:13 v Isa 66:2; Jer 31:19; Lk 23:48 w Lk 5:32; 1Ti 1:15
18:14 x Mt 23:12; Lk 14:11
18:17 y Mt 11:25; 18:3
18:18 z Lk 10:25

📖 This parable calls for unrelenting prayer. We are to pray earnestly for God's justice and the world's full redemption by his hand. Do we as a church community "wear God out" with such requests? The prayer in Scripture most like the one called for here appears in Acts 4:23–31. The church there asked for enablement to perform what God had called it to do, even in the face of fierce persecution.

Luke 18:9–14

📖 These two very different prayers represent two kinds of hearts. The marked contrast is seen both in the verbal and the body language of the two pray-ers. The real danger of pride is that it blinds people to their true standing before God. The prayer God hears is the call for mercy. Jesus explained why, stating one of the wonderful, topsy-turvy principles that characterize the Christian value system: Those who exalt themselves will be humbled, but the humble will be lifted up.

📖 Would you characterize yourself as humble? Humility is hard to discuss, because by its very nature it doesn't talk about itself. It simply gets out there and serves, often sacrificially and anonymously. It doesn't claim rights but tries to do what's right. It doesn't brag about integrity but demonstrates honesty. Sometimes Christians confuse humility with self-deprecation—an apologetic, timid approach to life. On the contrary, the truly humble Christian exudes a God-given joy and confidence that are attractive and inviting.

Luke 18:15–17

📖 In this short passage Jesus showed just how subtle humility is, while exhorting his disciples about the nature of true faith. He invited children to come to him because they were and are important people, people who represent by their open, trusting natures what the kingdom is all about. This is the opposite of how those in Jesus' day, and ours, tended to value others. Why do you suppose people are so often drawn to the powerful (cf. James 2:1–9)?

📖 When life slows down long enough for you to look around, are you ever moved by the sight of a child walking beside a parent? Whether or not you realize it, in that scene is a picture of a child of God with her Father. We are to place our hands in his and walk with him at our side, allowing him to direct our steps and keep us from falling. The kindness we show children is a measure of our childlikeness before God. Is your response to children like that of Jesus or more like that of the disciples'?

18:20
a Ex 20:12-16;
Dt 5:16-20; Ro 13:9

18:22
b Ac 2:45 c Mt 6:20

18:24
d Pr 11:28

18:27
e Mt 19:26
18:28
f Mt 4:19

18:30
g Mt 12:32
h Mt 25:46

18:31
i Lk 9:51 j Ps 22;
Isa 53 k Mt 8:20
18:32
l Lk 23:1
m Mt 16:21
n Ac 2:23
18:33
o Mt 16:21
p Mt 16:21
18:34
q Mk 9:32; Lk 9:45

18:35
r Lk 19:1

19"Why do you call me good?" Jesus answered. "No one is good—except God alone. 20You know the commandments: 'Do not commit adultery, do not murder, do not steal, do not give false testimony, honor your father and mother.' a" a

21"All these I have kept since I was a boy," he said.

22When Jesus heard this, he said to him, "You still lack one thing. Sell everything you have and give to the poor, b and you will have treasure in heaven. c Then come, follow me."

23When he heard this, he became very sad, because he was a man of great wealth. 24Jesus looked at him and said, "How hard it is for the rich to enter the kingdom of God! d 25Indeed, it is easier for a camel to go through the eye of a needle than for a rich man to enter the kingdom of God."

26Those who heard this asked, "Who then can be saved?"

27Jesus replied, "What is impossible with men is possible with God." e

28Peter said to him, "We have left all we had to follow you!" f

29"I tell you the truth," Jesus said to them, "no one who has left home or wife or brothers or parents or children for the sake of the kingdom of God 30will fail to receive many times as much in this age and, in the age to come, g eternal life." h

Jesus Again Predicts His Death

31Jesus took the Twelve aside and told them, "We are going up to Jerusalem, i and everything that is written by the prophets j about the Son of Man k will be fulfilled. 32He will be handed over to the Gentiles. l They will mock him, insult him, spit on him, flog him m and kill him. n 33On the third day o he will rise again." p

34The disciples did not understand any of this. Its meaning was hidden from them, and they did not know what he was talking about. q

A Blind Beggar Receives His Sight

35As Jesus approached Jericho, r a blind man was sitting by the roadside begging.

a 20 Exodus 20:12-16; Deut. 5:16-20

Luke 18:18–30

Jesus called on the man to sell everything he had and give to the poor. Then he challenged him to join with him in walking with God. This combination is crucial to understanding the nature of Jesus' reply. Would this man have preferred what Earth could afford or what God's kingdom had to offer? This wasn't a test of his works but a probing of his heart—an examination of his fundamental allegiance.

What was Jesus' view of wealth? This passage and the later example of Zacchaeus (19:1–10) show that the central issue isn't selling everything in order to know God. The critical question is Where does your trust reside? Are you secure in your stock portfolio—or in your God? Do you recognize that everything you have is his, that you are acting as his trustee? Are you a trustworthy personal representative of Earth's Creator and Owner?

Luke 18:31–34

These events were an integral part of God's master design, not a secondary or backup plan. As early as Isaiah 52:13—53:12, God had stated that his Servant would be rejected by his own people and put to death. It's often difficult to appreciate how shocking Jesus' road was for his group of friends. Their expectations for how the Messiah was "supposed" to triumph made it difficult for them to grasp Jesus' way of the suffering servant.

Part of the disciples' problem was their expectation of seeing something instant and awesome in terms of Jesus' kingdom inauguration. We sometimes handle God's promises similarly, clinging tenaciously to the "good parts" while shying away from the more demanding aspects. We prefer the victory to the agony, the crown to the nails and hammer. Yet God often molds and shapes victory through the heat and hammer of the forging process we dread (cf. James 1:2–3).

Luke 18:35–43

The exchange between Jesus and the blind man symbolizes much more than restoration of the physical ability to see. The man trusted that by asking the Son of David, the Messiah, to provide what God's power alone could deliver, his sight would be restored. Jesus not only opened his eyes but enabled him to follow Jesus down the road with his spiritual eyes fixed on God.

This social outcast, confronted with the "impossible" possibility of a close encounter with Jesus, risked stepping forward in the midst of public rebuke to engage him. He provides for us a model of trusting in Jesus, praising God after having received his grace, and following the Master. How willing would you have been to disregard public censure for the opportunity to receive the only gift that mattered? If you could have asked the now-sighted man what that gift was, what do you think he would have answered?

36When he heard the crowd going by, he asked what was happening. 37They told him, "Jesus of Nazareth is passing by."[s]

38He called out, "Jesus, Son of David,[t] have mercy[u] on me!"

39Those who led the way rebuked him and told him to be quiet, but he shouted all the more, "Son of David, have mercy on me!"[v]

40Jesus stopped and ordered the man to be brought to him. When he came near, Jesus asked him, 41"What do you want me to do for you?"

"Lord, I want to see," he replied.

42Jesus said to him, "Receive your sight; your faith has healed you."[w] 43Immediately he received his sight and followed Jesus, praising God. When all the people saw it, they also praised God.[x]

Zacchaeus the Tax Collector

19 Jesus entered Jericho[y] and was passing through. 2A man was there by the name of Zacchaeus; he was a chief tax collector and was wealthy. 3He wanted to see who Jesus was, but being a short man he could not, because of the crowd. 4So he ran ahead and climbed a sycamore-fig[z] tree to see him, since Jesus was coming that way.[a]

5When Jesus reached the spot, he looked up and said to him, "Zacchaeus, come down immediately. I must stay at your house today." 6So he came down at once and welcomed him gladly.

7All the people saw this and began to mutter, "He has gone to be the guest of a 'sinner.'"[b]

8But Zacchaeus stood up and said to the Lord,[c] "Look, Lord! Here and now I give half of my possessions to the poor, and if I have cheated anybody out of anything,[d] I will pay back four times the amount."[e]

9Jesus said to him, "Today salvation has come to this house, because this man, too, is a son of Abraham.[f] 10For the Son of Man came to seek and to save what was lost."[g]

The Parable of the Ten Minas

11While they were listening to this, he went on to tell them a parable, because he was near Jerusalem and the people thought that the kingdom of God[h] was going to appear at once.[i] 12He said: "A man of noble birth went to a distant country to have himself appointed king and then to return. 13So he called ten of his servants[j] and gave them ten minas.[a] 'Put this money to work,' he said, 'until I come back.'

a 13 A mina was about three months' wages.

Luke 19:1–10

Jesus gladly endorsed Zacchaeus's response of gratitude. God had reclaimed a lost child. Zacchaeus was now truly a son of Abraham—an image in which Paul delighted (cf. Rom. 4:16; Gal. 3:7). Even more exciting is the explanation in verse 10 of what Zacchaeus's change represented. The Son of Man had come to seek and save the lost. He had taken the initiative to single out Zacchaeus as a man who could experience God's acceptance, and Zacchaeus had embraced the opportunity. Can you picture heaven celebrating his restoration (cf. 15:10)?

The Christian faith is the ultimate "recovery" movement. What's recovered is the fundamental relationship with God that allows restoration in other areas to take place. After recognizing his failures, Zacchaeus not only confessed them publicly but went on to make restitution for his wrongs. The change in his heart expressed itself in a new openness toward needy people.

Such faith isn't an intellectual exercise; it's a worldview transformation.

Luke 19:11–27

This parable has a historical background. Both Herod in 40 B.C. and Archelaus in 4 B.C. went to Rome to receive ruling authority from the emperor. There was a public outcry against Archelaus, who was unpopular and received a less comprehensive ruling mandate.

In this "official" picture of Israel's rejection of Jesus, the third servant takes center stage. Here we see a hybrid, someone with a marginal association to the Messiah, whom he had never trusted as the One God had sent. The master's response to others shows him to be anything but "hard." The wicked servant has no clue to his master's true character, and his words reveal his ignorance. This one who has no trust in God's goodness, even though he or she has a connection to God, has no relationship with him and ends up with nothing.

18:37
s Lk 19:4
18:38
t ver 39; Mt 9:27
u Mt 17:15;
Lk 18:13
18:39
v ver 38

18:42
w Mt 9:22

18:43
x Mt 9:8; Lk 13:17

19:1
y Lk 18:35

19:4
z 1Ki 10:27;
1Ch 27:28; Isa 9:10
a Lk 18:37

19:7
b Mt 9:11
19:8
c Lk 7:13
d Lk 3:12,13
e Ex 22:1; Lev 6:4,5;
Nu 5:7; 2Sa 12:6

19:9
f Lk 3:8; 13:16;
Ro 4:16; Gal 3:7
19:10
g Eze 34:12,16;
Jn 3:17

19:11
h Mt 3:2 i Lk 17:20;
Ac 1:6

19:13
j Mk 13:34

14 "But his subjects hated him and sent a delegation after him to say, 'We don't want this man to be our king.'

15 "He was made king, however, and returned home. Then he sent for the servants to whom he had given the money, in order to find out what they had gained with it.

16 "The first one came and said, 'Sir, your mina has earned ten more.'

19:17
k Pr 27:18
l Lk 16:10

17 " 'Well done, my good servant!' *k* his master replied. 'Because you have been trustworthy in a very small matter, take charge of ten cities.' *l*

18 "The second came and said, 'Sir, your mina has earned five more.'

19 "His master answered, 'You take charge of five cities.'

19:21
m Mt 25:24
19:22
n 2Sa 1:16;
Job 15:6
o Mt 25:26

20 "Then another servant came and said, 'Sir, here is your mina; I have kept it laid away in a piece of cloth. 21 I was afraid of you, because you are a hard man. You take out what you did not put in and reap what you did not sow.' *m*

22 "His master replied, 'I will judge you by your own words, *n* you wicked servant! You knew, did you, that I am a hard man, taking out what I did not put in, and reaping what I did not sow? *o* 23 Why then didn't you put my money on deposit, so that when I came back, I could have collected it with interest?'

24 "Then he said to those standing by, 'Take his mina away from him and give it to the one who has ten minas.'

25 " 'Sir,' they said, 'he already has ten!'

19:26
p Mt 13:12; 25:29;
Lk 8:18

26 "He replied, 'I tell you that to everyone who has, more will be given, but as for the one who has nothing, even what he has will be taken away. *p* 27 But those enemies of mine who did not want me to be king over them—bring them here and kill them in front of me.' "

How well do you *know* the Master? Connection to the Christian community isn't what makes us a Christian. This parable illustrates that a Christian is someone who has a relationship of trust with Jesus. Is your relationship purely formal, or is it real?

Snapshots

19:11–27

Fanny Jackson Coppin

Educator and missionary Fanny Marion (Jackson) Coppin (1837–1913) was born into slavery, but an aunt paid for her emancipation. After completing a teaching course while working as a maid, she enrolled in Oberlin College.

As a student Fanny opened an evening literacy class for freed slaves. After graduating in 1865, she joined the faculty at the Quaker's Institute for Colored Youth in Philadelphia, teaching Latin, Greek, and mathematics. In five short years she became principal, leading programs specializing in training African-American teachers and business workers. Her innovations included a practice-teaching system and an industrial-training department.

Oppressed farm workers were paid in part with wine. Realizing its damaging impact on poor families, Fanny began speaking about temperance among black and "colored" women.

In 1881 Fanny married Levi Coppin, an African Methodist Episcopal minister in the U.S. who was later elected bishop of South Africa. There she often accompanied her husband to rural villages when he spoke. Oppressed farm workers were paid in part with wine. Realizing its damaging impact on poor families, Fanny began speaking about temperance among black and "colored" women. An educator at heart, she founded the Bethel Institute in Cape Town. The High and Training School of Baltimore was renamed the Fanny Jackson Coppin Normal School (now Coppin State College) in her memory.

The Triumphal Entry

28 After Jesus had said this, he went on ahead, going up to Jerusalem.[q] 29 As he approached Bethphage and Bethany[r] at the hill called the Mount of Olives,[s] he sent two
of his disciples, saying to them, 30 "Go to the village ahead of you, and as you enter
it, you will find a colt tied there, which no one has ever ridden. Untie it and bring it
here. 31 If anyone asks you, 'Why are you untying it?' tell him, 'The Lord needs it.' "
32 Those who were sent ahead went and found it just as he had told them.[t] 33 As
they were untying the colt, its owners asked them, "Why are you untying the colt?"
34 They replied, "The Lord needs it."
35 They brought it to Jesus, threw their cloaks on the colt and put Jesus on it. 36 As
he went along, people spread their cloaks[u] on the road.
37 When he came near the place where the road goes down the Mount of Olives,[v]
the whole crowd of disciples began joyfully to praise God in loud voices for all the
miracles they had seen:

38 "Blessed is the king who comes in the name of the Lord!"[a][w]

"Peace in heaven and glory in the highest!"[x]

39 Some of the Pharisees in the crowd said to Jesus, "Teacher, rebuke your disciples!"[y]
40 "I tell you," he replied, "if they keep quiet, the stones will cry out."[z]
41 As he approached Jerusalem and saw the city, he wept over it[a] 42 and said, "If
you, even you, had only known on this day what would bring you peace—but now
it is hidden from your eyes. 43 The days will come upon you when your enemies will
build an embankment against you and encircle you and hem you in on every
side.[b] 44 They will dash you to the ground, you and the children within your walls.[c]
They will not leave one stone on another,[d] because you did not recognize the time
of God's coming[e] to you."

Jesus at the Temple

45 Then he entered the temple area and began driving out those who were selling.
46 "It is written," he said to them, " 'My house will be a house of prayer'[b];[f] but you
have made it 'a den of robbers.'[c]"[g]
47 Every day he was teaching at the temple.[h] But the chief priests, the teachers of

19:28 [q] Mk 10:32; Lk 9:51
19:29 [r] Mt 21:17 [s] Mt 21:1
19:32 [t] Lk 22:13
19:36 [u] 2Ki 9:13
19:37 [v] Mt 21:1
19:38 [w] Ps 118:26; Lk 13:35 [x] Lk 2:14
19:39 [y] Mt 21:15,16
19:40 [z] Hab 2:11
19:41 [a] Isa 22:4; Lk 13:34,35
19:43 [b] Isa 29:3; Jer 6:6; Eze 4:2; 26:8; Lk 21:20
19:44 [c] Ps 137:9 [d] Mt 24:2; Mk 13:2; Lk 21:6 [e] 1Pe 2:12
19:46 [f] Isa 56:7 [g] Jer 7:11
19:47 [h] Mt 26:55

[a] *38* Psalm 118:26 [b] *46* Isaiah 56:7 [c] *46* Jer. 7:11

Luke 19:28–44

Luke's description of the Triumphal Entry quotes several Old Testament passages. The image of Jesus on the colt, for instance, recalls Zechariah 9:9. And circumstances were in some ways similar to the coronations of Kings Solomon (1 Kings 1:38–40) and Jehu (2 Kings 9:13). But Jesus didn't come in a Roman chariot with prancing steeds, the luxury limousine of his day. While the backdrop was regal, the ride on a humble animal denoted not a Messiah of raw power, but one of humility and service.

This portrait of the Messiah and how he went about making his claims says a lot about how we, as his church, portray him. Jesus embodied his evangelism with a humility of service that was represented even in the way he entered Jerusalem. He came in humility, allowing others to proclaim who he was. He preferred to let his actions reveal his identity. How can we truly be a community not just of testimony and words—but of presence and service among those we seek to reach?

Luke 19:45–48

The background to this event is crucial to understanding what took place. On the temple grounds, items necessary for sacrifices were sold: animals, wine, oil, salt, and doves. In addition, money was changed from Roman currency to the required Hebrew shekels in accordance with the law (Ex. 30:11–14). This exchange had a built-in surcharge, some of which probably went to the high priest's family. In Jesus' view, the temple had become an excessively commercial enterprise, not a place of worship and prayer.

Our culture may be correct when it accuses us of being too commercial about certain expressions of our Christian faith. Worship is a sacred trust, where commerce and hypocrisy have no place. Perhaps with the best of intentions, to reach more people for Christ, we have picked up on too many of our culture's advertising and marketing gimmicks and know-how. Think about the inconsistency between slick commercialism on the one hand and the Good News we share, along with the One we represent, on the other. What are some signs that an individual Christian or ministry may have crossed the line between relating to culture and "selling" the gospel?

19:47
i Mt 12:14;
Mk 11:18
the law and the leaders among the people were trying to kill him. [i] 48 Yet they could not find any way to do it, because all the people hung on his words.

The Authority of Jesus Questioned

20:1
j Mt 26:55 k Lk 8:1
20 One day as he was teaching the people in the temple courts[j] and preaching the gospel, [k] the chief priests and the teachers of the law, together with the elders, came up to him. 2 "Tell us by what authority you are doing these things," they said. "Who gave you this authority?" [l]

20:2
l Jn 2:18; Ac 4:7;
7:27

20:4
m Mk 1:4
3 He replied, "I will also ask you a question. Tell me, 4 John's baptism[m]—was it from heaven, or from men?"

20:6
n Lk 7:29 o Mt 11:9
5 They discussed it among themselves and said, "If we say, 'From heaven,' he will ask, 'Why didn't you believe him?' 6 But if we say, 'From men,' all the people[n] will stone us, because they are persuaded that John was a prophet." [o]

7 So they answered, "We don't know where it was from."

8 Jesus said, "Neither will I tell you by what authority I am doing these things."

The Parable of the Tenants

20:9
p Isa 5:1-7
q Mt 25:14
9 He went on to tell the people this parable: "A man planted a vineyard,[p] rented it to some farmers and went away for a long time. [q] 10 At harvest time he sent a servant to the tenants so they would give him some of the fruit of the vineyard. But the tenants beat him and sent him away empty-handed. 11 He sent another servant, but that one also they beat and treated shamefully and sent away empty-handed. 12 He sent still a third, and they wounded him and threw him out.

20:13
r Mt 3:17
13 "Then the owner of the vineyard said, 'What shall I do? I will send my son, whom I love;[r] perhaps they will respect him.'

14 "But when the tenants saw him, they talked the matter over. 'This is the heir,' they said. 'Let's kill him, and the inheritance will be ours.' 15 So they threw him out of the vineyard and killed him.

20:16
s Lk 19:27
"What then will the owner of the vineyard do to them? 16 He will come and kill those tenants[s] and give the vineyard to others."

When the people heard this, they said, "May this never be!"

17 Jesus looked directly at them and asked, "Then what is the meaning of that which is written:

20:17
t Ps 118:22;
Ac 4:11
" 'The stone the builders rejected
    has become the capstone[a][b]?[t]

---

a 17 Or cornerstone   b 17 Psalm 118:22

Luke 20:1–8

In response to Jesus' question, the Jewish leaders decided to play it safe. Their refusal to take a position left the door open for Jesus to refuse to commit himself—because the answer to their question about the source of his authority was obvious and inarguable. The time for debate was past. The leadership had made its decision, and those responsible needed to own up to it. Their inaction on this point was an indictment of their own evil actions.

What do you do when someone keeps asking the same question about the gospel but may have already decided to reject it? Jesus had responded numerous times in word and action to the question the Jewish leadership raised. The same is true for us. When we *have repeatedly and patiently shared the gospel over a long period*, there may come a time when words are no longer appropriate. Our role at that point is to urge the person to reflect on what's already been said.

Luke 20:9–19

This parable summarized the history of God's activity with Israel. Its placement here provides the answer to the questions in verses 1–8 about the origin of Jesus' authority. The image of the vineyard echoed Isaiah 5:1–7, where Israel was that vineyard. In Jesus' parable the tenants represented the Jews in general, but especially their leaders. The vineyard was soon to be placed in the care of "others" (v. 16)—that is, the Gentiles. This text seems harsh in portraying God's judgment of Israel, but note how patient and longsuffering God had been. Far from being a rash action, his punishment was the culmination of a long, even tedious process. God had sent numerous prophets to his people. Finally he had sent his Son.

Jesus wept as he entered Jerusalem; judgment isn't what God wants for humanity (19:41–44; 2 Peter 3:9). It comes only when we (the human race) fail to respond to God's compassion. Jesus asked his audience how the owner would respond to the killing of his son. The answer is something every person does well to consider carefully.

18Everyone who falls on that stone will be broken to pieces, but he on whom it falls will be crushed." *u*

19The teachers of the law and the chief priests looked for a way to arrest him *v* immediately, because they knew he had spoken this parable against them. But they were afraid of the people. *w*

Paying Taxes to Caesar

20Keeping a close watch on him, they sent spies, who pretended to be honest. They hoped to catch Jesus in something he said *x* so that they might hand him over to the power and authority of the governor. *y* 21So the spies questioned him: "Teacher, we know that you speak and teach what is right, and that you do not show partiality but teach the way of God in accordance with the truth. *z* 22Is it right for us to pay taxes to Caesar or not?"

23He saw through their duplicity and said to them, 24"Show me a denarius. Whose portrait and inscription are on it?"

25"Caesar's," they replied.

He said to them, "Then give to Caesar what is Caesar's, *a* and to God what is God's." 26They were unable to trap him in what he had said there in public. And astonished by his answer, they became silent.

The Resurrection and Marriage

27Some of the Sadducees, *b* who say there is no resurrection, *c* came to Jesus with a question. 28"Teacher," they said, "Moses wrote for us that if a man's brother dies and leaves a wife but no children, the man must marry the widow and have children for his brother. *d* 29Now there were seven brothers. The first one married a woman and died childless. 30The second 31and then the third married her, and in the same way the seven died, leaving no children. 32Finally, the woman died too. 33Now then, at the resurrection whose wife will she be, since the seven were married to her?"

34Jesus replied, "The people of this age marry and are given in marriage. 35But those who are considered worthy of taking part in that age *e* and in the resurrection from the dead will neither marry nor be given in marriage, 36and they can no longer die; for they are like the angels. They are God's children, *f* since they are children of the resurrection. 37But in the account of the bush, even Moses showed that the dead rise, for he calls the Lord 'the God of Abraham, and the God of Isaac, and the God of Jacob.' *a g* 38He is not the God of the dead, but of the living, for to him all are alive."

a 37 Exodus 3:6

20:18
u Isa 8:14,15
20:19
v Lk 19:47
w Mk 11:18

20:20
x Mt 12:10
y Mt 27:2

20:21
z Jn 3:2

20:25
a Lk 23:2; Ro 13:7

20:27
b Ac 4:1 c Ac 23:8;
1Co 15:12

20:28
d Dt 25:5

20:35
e Mt 12:32

20:36
f Jn 1:12; 1Jn 3:1-2

20:37
g Ex 3:6

Luke 20:20–26

👣 The question posed to Jesus was an either/or, but he responded with a both/and. Government has the right to exist and function, but its presence doesn't replace our allegiance to God (Rom. 13:1–7; 1 Peter 2:13–17). Jesus wasn't a political revolutionary who challenged Rome, nor was he an ardent nationalist. No one could have charged him with political subversion. He didn't step into the trap set for him, and the Jewish leadership recognized that its effort had failed. His enemies could only be silent in the face of Jesus' reply.

🔍 How is the church to view government? Does God look for or expect a "Christian nation"? If we mean that God wants the structures of society to relate to people in a way that honors God and humanity, the answer is definitely yes. But if we mean that God has a special contract of blessing with any given nation, the answer is no. The church—the place where God is especially at work today—transcends national boundaries (Phil. 3:3,20–21).

Luke 20:27–40

👣 The Sadducees accepted only the first five books of the Old Testament and didn't believe in bodily resurrection. Jesus' reply to their question was twofold. The hypothetical marriage dilemma was based on a misunderstanding of the afterlife, since marriage doesn't occur there. And Genesis *does* teach resurrection in the reference to the patriarchs Jesus cited. If God made promises related to the afterlife to these ancient forebears, the resurrection must be real. It's a fundamental doctrine of Christian hope.

🔍 We tend to think of ancient people as unsophisticated, gullible, and unscientific. But the Sadducees were "modern" people in an ancient time, questioning the existence both of the resurrection and of angels. They were committed materialists, dedicated to pursuing life on this earth. To the extent that you and I, or our children, are tempted by or subtly infected with that worldview, Paul comments: "If only for this life we have hope in Christ, we are to be pitied more than all men" (1 Cor. 15:19). On what does your hope rest?

20:40
h Mt 22:46;
Mk 12:34

39Some of the teachers of the law responded, "Well said, teacher!" 40And no one dared to ask him any more questions. h

Whose Son Is the Christ?

20:41
i Mt 1:1

41Then Jesus said to them, "How is it that they say the Christa is the Son of David? i 42David himself declares in the Book of Psalms:

" 'The Lord said to my Lord:
"Sit at my right hand

20:43
j Ps 110:1;
Mt 22:44

43until I make your enemies
a footstool for your feet." 'b j

44David calls him 'Lord.' How then can he be his son?"

45While all the people were listening, Jesus said to his disciples, 46"Beware of the teachers of the law. They like to walk around in flowing robes and love to be greeted in the marketplaces and have the most important seats in the synagogues and

20:46
k Lk 11:43

the places of honor at banquets. k 47They devour widows' houses and for a show make lengthy prayers. Such men will be punished most severely."

The Widow's Offering

21:1
l Mt 27:6; Jn 8:20

21 As he looked up, Jesus saw the rich putting their gifts into the temple treasury. l 2He also saw a poor widow put in two very small copper coins. c 3"I tell you the truth," he said, "this poor widow has put in more than all the others. 4All these people gave their gifts out of their wealth; but she out of her poverty put in all she had to live on." m

21:4
m 2Co 8:12

Signs of the End of the Age

5Some of his disciples were remarking about how the temple was adorned with beautiful stones and with gifts dedicated to God. But Jesus said, 6"As for what you

21:6
n Lk 19:44

see here, the time will come when not one stone will be left on another; n every one of them will be thrown down."

7"Teacher," they asked, "when will these things happen? And what will be the sign that they are about to take place?"

8He replied: "Watch out that you are not deceived. For many will come in my

21:8
o Lk 17:23

name, claiming, 'I am he,' and, 'The time is near.' Do not follow them. o 9When you hear of wars and revolutions, do not be frightened. These things must happen first, but the end will not come right away."

10Then he said to them: "Nation will rise against nation, and kingdom against

---

a 41 Or Messiah   b 43 Psalm 110:1   c 2 Greek two lepta

Luke 20:41–47

The before-and-after texts, as well as the parallel accounts in Matthew and Mark, show that "they" in verse 41 refers to the teachers of the law. Jesus pointed out that their understanding of the Messiah, "the Son of David," was incomplete. He then issued a final, public warning about the pride of these teachers. Such arrogance leads to an elevation of self that ends up seeing others (in this case widows) as inferior—available for use as pawns.

Jesus calls us to a mind-set that disregards titles. The more special we make ourselves, the less special God becomes in our eyes. As One who was both David's son and his Lord, Jesus deserved to be honored with an allegiance worthy of a king. Yet just before accepting the worst seat in the house (death on an accursed cross), our Lord declared that the service he expects of us is to be "not for profit." And exemptions don't exist.

Luke 21:1–4

God doesn't see things as humans do. People tend to appreciate the amount of a gift, not necessarily the sacrifice that went into the giving. As in other of Luke's texts, the example here came from a person on the fringe of society—a woman so humble as to be a cultural non-person. What others gave came from their excess. They wouldn't miss whatever they tossed into the collection. But this woman sacrificed what little she had, her last resource to live on. Jesus called that real giving.

How often do we miss seeing examples today of people in the most reduced circumstances having a better handle on generosity than those mired in materialism? Giving is the antidote to greed, a sure way to protect our hearts against selfishness. The humble poor have much to teach those of us with an abundance of resources but a calculating spirit. Our situations vary. What would sacrificial giving mean for you? Have you ever given past your last available resources? How has God seen you through?

kingdom.ᵖ ¹¹There will be great earthquakes, famines and pestilences in various places, and fearful events and great signs from heaven.ᵠ

¹²"But before all this, they will lay hands on you and persecute you. They will deliver you to synagogues and prisons, and you will be brought before kings and governors, and all on account of my name. ¹³This will result in your being witnesses to them.ʳ ¹⁴But make up your mind not to worry beforehand how you will defend yourselves.ˢ ¹⁵For I will give youᵗ words and wisdom that none of your adversaries will be able to resist or contradict. ¹⁶You will be betrayed even by parents, brothers, relatives and friends,ᵘ and they will put some of you to death. ¹⁷All men will hate you because of me.ᵛ ¹⁸But not a hair of your head will perish.ʷ ¹⁹By standing firm you will gain life.ˣ

²⁰"When you see Jerusalem being surrounded by armies,ʸ you will know that its desolation is near. ²¹Then let those who are in Judea flee to the mountains, let those in the city get out, and let those in the country not enter the city.ᶻ ²²For this is the time of punishmentᵃ in fulfillmentᵇ of all that has been written. ²³How dreadful it will be in those days for pregnant women and nursing mothers! There will be great distress in the land and wrath against this people. ²⁴They will fall by the sword and will be taken as prisoners to all the nations. Jerusalem will be trampledᶜ on by the Gentiles until the times of the Gentiles are fulfilled.

²⁵"There will be signs in the sun, moon and stars. On the earth, nations will be in anguish and perplexity at the roaring and tossing of the sea.ᵈ ²⁶Men will faint from terror, apprehensive of what is coming on the world, for the heavenly bodies will be shaken.ᵉ ²⁷At that time they will see the Son of Manᶠ coming in a cloudᵍ with power and great glory. ²⁸When these things begin to take place, stand up and lift up your heads, because your redemption is drawing near."ʰ

²⁹He told them this parable: "Look at the fig tree and all the trees. ³⁰When they sprout leaves, you can see for yourselves and know that summer is near. ³¹Even so, when you see these things happening, you know that the kingdom of Godⁱ is near.

³²"I tell you the truth, this generationᵃʲ will certainly not pass away until all these things have happened. ³³Heaven and earth will pass away, but my words will never pass away.ᵏ

³⁴"Be careful, or your hearts will be weighed down with dissipation, drunkenness and the anxieties of life,ˡ and that day will close on you unexpectedlyᵐ like a trap. ³⁵For it will come upon all those who live on the face of the whole earth. ³⁶Be always on the watch, and prayⁿ that you may be able to escape all that is about to happen, and that you may be able to stand before the Son of Man."

³⁷Each day Jesus was teaching at the temple,ᵒ and each evening he went outᵖ to spend the night on the hill called the Mount of Olives,ᵠ ³⁸and all the people came early in the morning to hear him at the temple.ʳ

Judas Agrees to Betray Jesus

22 Now the Feast of Unleavened Bread, called the Passover, was approaching,ˢ ²and the chief priests and the teachers of the law were looking for some way to get rid of Jesus,ᵗ for they were afraid of the people. ³Then Satanᵘ entered Judas,

ᵃ 32 Or *race*

Cross references (right margin):

21:10 ᵖ 2Ch 15:6; Isa 19:2
21:11 ᵠ Isa 29:6; Joel 2:30
21:13 ʳ Php 1:12
21:14 ˢ Lk 12:11
21:15 ᵗ Lk 12:12
21:16 ᵘ Lk 12:52,53
21:17 ᵛ Jn 15:21
21:18 ʷ Mt 10:30
21:19 ˣ Mt 10:22
21:20 ʸ Lk 19:43
21:21 ᶻ Lk 17:31
21:22 ᵃ Isa 63:4; Da 9:24-27; Hos 9:7 ᵇ Mt 1:22
21:24 ᶜ Isa 5:5; 63:18; Da 8:13; Rev 11:2
21:25 ᵈ 2Pe 3:10,12
21:26 ᵉ Mt 24:29
21:27 ᶠ Mt 8:20 ᵍ Rev 1:7
21:28 ʰ Lk 18:7
21:31 ⁱ Mt 3:2
21:32 ʲ Lk 11:50; 17:25
21:33 ᵏ Mt 5:18
21:34 ˡ Mk 4:19 ᵐ Lk 12:40,46; 1Th 5:2-7
21:36 ⁿ Mt 26:41
21:37 ᵒ Mt 26:55 ᵖ Mk 11:19 ᵠ Mt 21:1
21:38 ʳ Jn 8:2
22:1 ˢ Jn 11:55
22:2 ᵗ Mt 12:14
22:3 ᵘ Mt 4:10; Jn 13:2

Luke 21:5–38

📖 In Jesus' prophetic words about Jerusalem's coming destruction (A.D. 70 in the short term), we note similarities to Christ's expected return at the end of time. Old Testament prophets often mixed words related to short- and long-term fulfillment. This makes interpretation challenging, but the nearby and faraway events often mirror one another. As painful as the fall of Jerusalem would be, it wouldn't compare to the judgment to come. Yet Jesus' discourse still reassures believers that God is advancing his plan.

💻 We are to keep watch, stand fast, and trust God's timing, reassured that one day our deliverance will come. Events may be painful. Even our families may oppose us, and martyrdom may be real. We need the resolve to endure, a resolve supported by our assurance that God will make all things right for his children. We can't see our vindication, but we can "see" Jesus—the author and defender of our faith (Heb. 11:1; 12:1–2). He promises to return for us one day in power and glory. Are you looking, waiting, and serving in eager expectation?

Luke 22:1–6

📖 For the first time since 4:1–13, Satan is identified as an active player in the drama of Luke's Gospel.

22:3
v Mt 10:4
22:4
w ver 52; Ac 4:1;
5:24
22:5
x Zec 11:12
called Iscariot, v one of the Twelve. 4And Judas went to the chief priests and the officers of the temple guard w and discussed with them how he might betray Jesus. 5They were delighted and agreed to give him money. x 6He consented, and watched for an opportunity to hand Jesus over to them when no crowd was present.

The Last Supper

22:7
y Ex 12:18-20;
Dt 16:5-8;
Mk 14:12
22:8
z Ac 3:1,11;
4:13,19; 8:14
7Then came the day of Unleavened Bread on which the Passover lamb had to be sacrificed. y 8Jesus sent Peter and John, z saying, "Go and make preparations for us to eat the Passover."

9"Where do you want us to prepare for it?" they asked.

10He replied, "As you enter the city, a man carrying a jar of water will meet you. Follow him to the house that he enters, 11and say to the owner of the house, 'The Teacher asks: Where is the guest room, where I may eat the Passover with my disciples?' 12He will show you a large upper room, all furnished. Make preparations there."

22:13
a Lk 19:32
13They left and found things just as Jesus had told them. a So they prepared the Passover.

22:14
b Mk 6:30
c Mt 26:20;
Mk 14:17,18
22:15
d Mt 16:21
22:16
e Lk 14:15;
Rev 19:9
14When the hour came, Jesus and his apostles b reclined at the table. c 15And he said to them, "I have eagerly desired to eat this Passover with you before I suffer. d 16For I tell you, I will not eat it again until it finds fulfillment in the kingdom of God." e

17After taking the cup, he gave thanks and said, "Take this and divide it among you. 18For I tell you I will not drink again of the fruit of the vine until the kingdom of God comes."

22:19
f Mt 14:19
19And he took bread, gave thanks and broke it, f and gave it to them, saying, "This is my body given for you; do this in remembrance of me."

22:20
g Ex 24:8; Isa 42:6;
Jer 31:31-34;
Zec 9:11; 2Co 3:6;
Heb 8:6; 9:15
22:21
h Ps 41:9
22:22
i Mt 8:20 i Ac 2:23;
4:28
22:24
k Mk 9:34; Lk 9:46
22:26
l 1Pe 5:5
m Mk 9:35; Lk 9:48
20In the same way, after the supper he took the cup, saying, "This cup is the new covenant g in my blood, which is poured out for you. 21But the hand of him who is going to betray me is with mine on the table. h 22The Son of Man i will go as it has been decreed, i but woe to that man who betrays him." 23They began to question among themselves which of them it might be who would do this.

24Also a dispute arose among them as to which of them was considered to be greatest. k 25Jesus said to them, "The kings of the Gentiles lord it over them; and those who exercise authority over them call themselves Benefactors. 26But you are not to be like that. Instead, the greatest among you should be like the youngest, l and the one who rules like the one who serves. m 27For who is greater, the one who is at the table or the one who serves? Is it not the one who is at the table? But I am

---

He entered Judas. What this means isn't entirely clear. Was this a case of demon (in this case devil) possession? Did Judas invite the devil's presence in his life? At minimum it suggests satanic direction and influence. The remark showcases the cosmic dimensions of Jesus' mission: Even (and especially) the forces of evil had an opinion about him and desired nothing more than his removal from the scene.

No matter how Satan entrapped Judas, sin was the result. Sin is fundamentally a betrayal—not just of God, but of others injured by it. It even betrays the sinner as its destruction does its work. This passage isn't a history lesson. It's a study of human nature at its worst, revealing the form sin takes as it completes itself in action. Sin doesn't usually limit itself to a small sphere; it *has a ripple effect that impacts the lives of many others.*

Luke 22:7–38
The dialogue following the meal covered five areas: a prediction of betrayal, a discussion of greatness,

a mention of authority over Israel, a prediction of Peter's denials, and a discussion of preparations. Jesus was following typical form for a farewell meal in which a leader indicated the key principles he wished to see in the community he was leaving. How the disciples would handle power, authority, and rejection would mark them as a special kind of people, though they would be slow to get the message.

Jesus had much to say about humility and service. Verses 29–30 show that his disciples were indeed given authority—in their era and the one to come. But verses 24–27 contrast Jesus' thinking with the world's. Here, leaders get perks and receive service. They wield power and authority, at times assuming their might gives them the right to coerce others into action. Jesus' approach was directly opposite: Leadership isn't about wielding or flaunting self-interested authority. It's a responsibility and trust to exercise our skills and energies to serve those we lead. Who, and how, do you lead? Who, and how, do you serve?

among you as one who serves. [n] 28You are those who have stood by me in my trials. 29And I confer on you a kingdom, [o] just as my Father conferred one on me, 30so that you may eat and drink at my table in my kingdom [p] and sit on thrones, judging the twelve tribes of Israel. [q]

31"Simon, Simon, Satan has asked [r] to sift you [a] as wheat. [s] 32But I have prayed for you, [t] Simon, that your faith may not fail. And when you have turned back, strengthen your brothers." [u]

33But he replied, "Lord, I am ready to go with you to prison and to death." [v]

34Jesus answered, "I tell you, Peter, before the rooster crows today, you will deny three times that you know me."

35Then Jesus asked them, "When I sent you without purse, bag or sandals, [w] did you lack anything?"

"Nothing," they answered.

36He said to them, "But now if you have a purse, take it, and also a bag; and if you don't have a sword, sell your cloak and buy one. 37It is written: 'And he was numbered with the transgressors' [b]; [x] and I tell you that this must be fulfilled in me. Yes, what is written about me is reaching its fulfillment."

38The disciples said, "See, Lord, here are two swords."

"That is enough," he replied.

Jesus Prays on the Mount of Olives

39Jesus went out as usual [y] to the Mount of Olives, [z] and his disciples followed him. 40On reaching the place, he said to them, "Pray that you will not fall into temptation." [a] 41He withdrew about a stone's throw beyond them, knelt down [b] and prayed, 42"Father, if you are willing, take this cup [c] from me; yet not my will, but yours be done." [d] 43An angel from heaven appeared to him and strengthened him. [e] 44And being in anguish, he prayed more earnestly, and his sweat was like drops of blood falling to the ground. [c]

45When he rose from prayer and went back to the disciples, he found them asleep, exhausted from sorrow. 46"Why are you sleeping?" he asked them. "Get up and pray so that you will not fall into temptation." [f]

Jesus Arrested

47While he was still speaking a crowd came up, and the man who was called Judas, one of the Twelve, was leading them. He approached Jesus to kiss him, 48but Jesus asked him, "Judas, are you betraying the Son of Man with a kiss?"

49When Jesus' followers saw what was going to happen, they said, "Lord, should

---

22:27
[n] Mt 20:28;
Lk 12:37
22:29
[o] Mt 25:34;
2Ti 2:12
22:30
[p] Lk 14:15
[q] Mt 19:28
22:31
[r] Job 1:6-12
[s] Am 9:9
22:32
[t] Jn 17:9,15;
Ro 8:34
[u] Jn 21:15-17
22:33
[v] Jn 11:16
22:35
[w] Mt 10:9,10;
Lk 9:3; 10:4

22:37
[x] Isa 53:12

22:39
[y] Lk 21:37
[z] Mt 21:1
22:40
[a] Mt 6:13
22:41
[b] Lk 18:11
22:42
[c] Mt 20:22
[d] Mt 26:39
22:43
[e] Mt 4:11; Mk 1:13

22:46
[f] ver 40

---

[a] 31 The Greek is plural.   [b] 37 Isaiah 53:12   [c] 44 Some early manuscripts do not have verses 43 and 44.

Luke 22:39–46

Jesus turned from addressing his disciples to praying to his Father. The sincerity of his prayer reveals the depth and quality of his relationship with God. In the prayer we see both Jesus' agony and his desire to follow God's will, even at the cost of his life. The disciples, tragically underestimating the significance of this moment, fell asleep. What they really needed wasn't just physical rest but a renewed allegiance to God, who alone could prevent them from plunging into failure.

This text provides an example of how believers in every age can face life's inevitable trials. Trouble may force us to our knees, but too frequently life's hectic pace keeps us on the run and inhibits us from praying. This wasn't the case for Jesus. Prayer is vital, even—perhaps especially—in the most frantic of times. And Jesus wasn't just checking in with the Father. His words reflected integrity, pathos, and pain. Real prayer isn't a leisure time (or a bedtime) ritual. It's a participative, vital activity.

Luke 22:47–53

Jesus submitted to God's will (see v. 42) and refused any attempt to fight his way out of the situation. The healing of the servant's ear is the last miracle of Jesus' ministry Luke recorded. Ironically but movingly, Jesus healed to the very end. Even his enemies were beneficiaries.

There is something in Jesus' response and in the absence of violence that communicates a sense of confidence in God's sovereignty. A day is coming when Jesus will do battle (see Rev. 19:11–21), but we don't need to take up the sword for him now. Our call is to share the Word, love our neighbor, and work for the unity of believers. There is a subtle strength in facing persecution as Jesus did—resting in the active defense of our God.

22:49
g ver 38
we strike with our swords?"^{g} ^{50}And one of them struck the servant of the high priest, cutting off his right ear.

^{51}But Jesus answered, "No more of this!" And he touched the man's ear and healed him.

22:52
h ver 4

22:53
i Mt 26:55
j Jn 12:27
k Mt 8:12; Jn 1:5;
3:20
^{52}Then Jesus said to the chief priests, the officers of the temple guard,^{h} and the elders, who had come for him, "Am I leading a rebellion, that you have come with swords and clubs? ^{53}Every day I was with you in the temple courts,^{i} and you did not lay a hand on me. But this is your hour^j—when darkness reigns."^{k}

Peter Disowns Jesus

22:54
l Mt 26:57;
Mk 14:53
m Mt 26:58:
Mk 14:54; Jn 18:15
^{54}Then seizing him, they led him away and took him into the house of the high priest.^{l} Peter followed at a distance.^{m} ^{55}But when they had kindled a fire in the middle of the courtyard and had sat down together, Peter sat down with them. ^{56}A servant girl saw him seated there in the firelight. She looked closely at him and said, "This man was with him."

^{57}But he denied it. "Woman, I don't know him," he said.

^{58}A little later someone else saw him and said, "You also are one of them."

"Man, I am not!" Peter replied.

22:59
n Lk 23:6
^{59}About an hour later another asserted, "Certainly this fellow was with him, for he is a Galilean."^{n}

22:61
o Lk 7:13 p ver 34
^{60}Peter replied, "Man, I don't know what you're talking about!" Just as he was speaking, the rooster crowed. ^{61}The Lord^o turned and looked straight at Peter. Then Peter remembered the word the Lord had spoken to him: "Before the rooster crows today, you will disown me three times."^{p} ^{62}And he went outside and wept bitterly.

The Guards Mock Jesus

^{63}The men who were guarding Jesus began mocking and beating him. ^{64}They blindfolded him and demanded, "Prophesy! Who hit you?" ^{65}And they said many
22:65
q Mt 16:21
other insulting things to him.^{q}

Jesus Before Pilate and Herod

^{66}At daybreak the council^r of the elders of the people, both the chief priests and
22:66
r Mt 5:22 s Mt 27:1;
Mk 15:1
teachers of the law, met together,^{s} and Jesus was led before them. ^{67}"If you are the Christ,^{a}" they said, "tell us."

Jesus answered, "If I tell you, you will not believe me, ^{68}and if I asked you, you

^{a} 67 Or Messiah

Luke 22:54–62

Just as the rooster crowed, Jesus looked at Peter—a look indicating that he knew what Peter had just done. We can imagine the tender, tragic pathos in that penetrating gaze. Peter stumbled away, blinded by tears. The pain of his response expressed his real allegiance, a heart loyalty his fear-paralyzed brain hadn't allowed him to voice. Peter had experienced a major failure of nerve—a failure that would ultimately teach him to know himself as Jesus knew him, and to turn his life around for his Lord.

The church's goal is to restore its wounded. We could argue that Peter's denials should have disqualified him from any future leadership position. But Jesus had already set the stage for Peter's recovery, declaring that after Peter turned back, he was to strengthen his fellow believers (v. 32). Peter's failure was great. But his victory came through his restoration, made possible because Jesus forgives. How do you respond to believers who have failed?

Luke 22:63–65

Jesus' guards—probably the temple police who had arrested him—were having a heyday mocking this unusual and vulnerable prisoner. The game appears to have been an early version of blindman's buff. They blindfolded him and taunted him to "prophesy." One interpretation of Isaiah 11:2–4 was that the Messiah could judge by smell, without the need for sight. Luke told the story through pain-glazed eyes, using the Greek word for "insulting" from which we get our word *blasphemy*.

The guards were flip in their approach to Jesus. What experience have you had with people who have no time for religion and get a perverse "kick" out of mocking its "foolishness," "irrelevance," and "illegitimacy"? Tragically, what they treat as frivolous is life-and-death serious. Sin itself blinds people from properly perceiving its significance, and a vicious cycle is set in motion. Yet those who mock the faith, pretending to be above it, reveal their need for it.

would not answer.[t] [69] But from now on, the Son of Man will be seated at the right hand of the mighty God."[u]

[70] They all asked, "Are you then the Son of God?"[v]

He replied, "You are right in saying I am."[w]

[71] Then they said, "Why do we need any more testimony? We have heard it from his own lips."

23

Then the whole assembly rose and led him off to Pilate.[x] [2] And they began to accuse him, saying, "We have found this man subverting our nation.[y] He opposes payment of taxes to Caesar[z] and claims to be Christ,[a] a king."[a]

[3] So Pilate asked Jesus, "Are you the king of the Jews?"

"Yes, it is as you say," Jesus replied.

[4] Then Pilate announced to the chief priests and the crowd, "I find no basis for a charge against this man."[b]

[5] But they insisted, "He stirs up the people all over Judea[b] by his teaching. He started in Galilee[c] and has come all the way here."

[6] On hearing this, Pilate asked if the man was a Galilean.[d] [7] When he learned that Jesus was under Herod's jurisdiction, he sent him to Herod,[e] who was also in Jerusalem at that time.

[8] When Herod saw Jesus, he was greatly pleased, because for a long time he had been wanting to see him.[f] From what he had heard about him, he hoped to see him perform some miracle. [9] He plied him with many questions, but Jesus gave him no answer.[g] [10] The chief priests and the teachers of the law were standing there, vehemently accusing him. [11] Then Herod and his soldiers ridiculed and mocked him. Dressing him in an elegant robe,[h] they sent him back to Pilate. [12] That day Herod and Pilate became friends[i]—before this they had been enemies.

[13] Pilate called together the chief priests, the rulers and the people, [14] and said to them, "You brought me this man as one who was inciting the people to rebellion. I have examined him in your presence and have found no basis for your charges against him.[j] [15] Neither has Herod, for he sent him back to us; as you can see, he has done nothing to deserve death. [16] Therefore, I will punish him[k] and then release him.[c]"

[18] With one voice they cried out, "Away with this man! Release Barabbas to us!"[l] [19] (Barabbas had been thrown into prison for an insurrection in the city, and for murder.)

[20] Wanting to release Jesus, Pilate appealed to them again. [21] But they kept shouting, "Crucify him! Crucify him!"

[22] For the third time he spoke to them: "Why? What crime has this man committed? I have found in him no grounds for the death penalty. Therefore I will have him punished and then release him."[m]

[23] But with loud shouts they insistently demanded that he be crucified, and their shouts prevailed. [24] So Pilate decided to grant their demand. [25] He released the man who had been thrown into prison for insurrection and murder, the one they asked for, and surrendered Jesus to their will.

[a] 2 Or *Messiah*; also in verses 35 and 39   [b] 5 Or *over the land of the Jews*   [c] 16 Some manuscripts *him." [17] Now he was obliged to release one man to them at the Feast.*

22:68
[t] Lk 20:3-8
22:69
[u] Mk 16:19
22:70
[v] Mt 4:3
[w] Mt 27:11; Lk 23:3

23:1
[x] Mt 27:2; Mk 15:1; Jn 18:28
23:2
[y] ver 14 z Lk 20:22
[a] Jn 19:12

23:4
[b] ver 14,22,41; Mt 27:23; Jn 18:38; 1Ti 6:13; 2Co 5:21
23:5
[c] Mk 1:14
23:6
[d] Lk 22:59
23:7
[e] Mt 14:1; Lk 3:1

23:8
[f] Lk 9:9

23:9
[g] Mk 14:61

23:11
[h] Mk 15:17-19; Jn 19:2,3
23:12
[i] Ac 4:27

23:14
[j] ver 4
23:16
[k] ver 22; Mt 27:26; Jn 19:1; Ac 16:37; 2Co 11:23,24
23:18
[l] Ac 3:13,14

23:22
[m] ver 16

Luke 22:66—23:25

Luke recounted four trials preceding Jesus' crucifixion. The first was before the Sanhedrin, composed of leading Jews. Jesus then appeared—twice—before Pilate and once before a curious Herod. His first meeting with Pilate represented the Jewish attempt to solicit Roman help, since Roman authority was required to enact a death penalty. After their private meeting, Pilate, personally convinced of Jesus' innocence, allowed an agitated and vocal crowd to make his decision for him in the public trial that followed. Not justice, but the threat of an uprising, sent Jesus to the cross.

We hear nothing further of Barabbas, but in a real sense his story—which is also ours—explains Jesus. Jesus freed us by his death, just as Barabbas was freed in Jesus' stead. The Christian life is a statement of gratitude to the One who has taken our place.

The Crucifixion

23:26
n Mt 27:32
o Mk 15:21;
Jn 19:17

26As they led him away, they seized Simon from Cyrene, n who was on his way in from the country, and put the cross on him and made him carry it behind Jesus. o

23:27
p Lk 8:52
23:28
q Lk 19:41-44;
21:23,24
23:29
r Mt 24:19

27A large number of people followed him, including women who mourned and wailed p for him. 28Jesus turned and said to them, "Daughters of Jerusalem, do not weep for me; weep for yourselves and for your children. q 29For the time will come when you will say, 'Blessed are the barren women, the wombs that never bore and the breasts that never nursed!' r 30Then

23:30
s Isa 2:19;
Hos 10:8; Rev 6:16

" 'they will say to the mountains, "Fall on us!"
and to the hills, "Cover us!" ' a s

23:31
t Eze 20:47
23:32
u Isa 53:12;
Mt 27:38;
Mk 15:27; Jn 19:18
23:34
v Mt 11:25
w Mt 5:44
x Ps 22:18

31For if men do these things when the tree is green, what will happen when it is dry?" t 32Two other men, both criminals, were also led out with him to be executed. u 33When they came to the place called the Skull, there they crucified him, along with the criminals—one on his right, the other on his left. 34Jesus said, "Father, v forgive them, for they do not know what they are doing." b w And they divided up his clothes by casting lots. x

23:35
y Ps 22:17
z Isa 42:1
23:36
a Ps 22:7
b Ps 69:21;
Mt 27:48
23:37
c Lk 4:3,9
23:38
d Mt 2:2
23:39
e ver 35,37

35The people stood watching, and the rulers even sneered at him. y They said, "He saved others; let him save himself if he is the Christ of God, the Chosen One." z 36The soldiers also came up and mocked him. a They offered him wine vinegar b 37and said, "If you are the king of the Jews, c save yourself." 38There was a written notice above him, which read: THIS IS THE KING OF THE JEWS. d 39One of the criminals who hung there hurled insults at him: "Aren't you the Christ? Save yourself and us!" e

23:41
f ver 4
23:42
g Mt 16:27

40But the other criminal rebuked him. "Don't you fear God," he said, "since you are under the same sentence? 41We are punished justly, for we are getting what our deeds deserve. But this man has done nothing wrong." f 42Then he said, "Jesus, remember me when you come into your kingdom. c" g

23:43
h 2Co 12:3,4;
Rev 2:7

43Jesus answered him, "I tell you the truth, today you will be with me in paradise." h

Jesus' Death

23:44
i Am 8:9
23:45
j Ex 26:31-33;
Heb 9:3,8
k Heb 10:19,20
23:46
l Mt 27:50
m Ps 31:5; 1Pe 2:23
n Jn 19:30

44It was now about the sixth hour, and darkness came over the whole land until the ninth hour, i 45for the sun stopped shining. And the curtain of the temple j was torn in two. k 46Jesus called out with a loud voice, l "Father, into your hands I commit my spirit." m When he had said this, he breathed his last. n

a 30 Hosea 10:8   b 34 Some early manuscripts do not have this sentence.   c 42 Some manuscripts *come with your kingly power*

Luke 23:26–43

One dying criminal joined in taunting Jesus; the other made a serious request. He accepted Jesus' kingship, wanted to share in his kingdom, and wanted to be among the righteous in the judgment. Jesus' reply indicated that the criminal's request would be answered sooner than he might have dared hope. Jesus saved this individual even as the Savior hung helpless, brutally suspended from a cross.

The cross is at the heart of God's gracious offer of forgiveness to those who embrace it—to all who are willing to turn from the selfishness of sin. Reconciliation with God not only transforms our relationship with him but also alters the way we relate to others. Do you rest solidly and securely in the hands of a merciful heavenly Father? And are you quick to love and pray for those who mistreat you?

Luke 23:44–49

Jesus' final words—"Father, into your hands I commit my spirit"—came from verse 5 of Psalm 31, a psalm describing a righteous sufferer. Jesus' cry reflected his trust in the Father. What happened from this point on was up to God. The Roman centurion's declaration served as Luke's final commentary on the whole event—a clear vindication of Jesus from a most unlikely source.

Jesus' death was the darkest moment in human history. But immediately following the darkness the long-shut door of access to God flew open—permanently. The ripping of the temple curtain, which had guarded admittance to God, graphically demonstrated that no barrier continues to exist between us and the Father, so long as we approach him through Jesus. The heavens normally give a silent witness to God (Ps. 19:1–6). But when heaven spoke here, its "voice" was unforgettable. What does unlimited access to God mean for you?

47The centurion, seeing what had happened, praised God o and said, "Surely this was a righteous man." 48When all the people who had gathered to witness this sight saw what took place, they beat their breasts p and went away. 49But all those who knew him, including the women who had followed him from Galilee, q stood at a distance, r watching these things.

Jesus' Burial

50Now there was a man named Joseph, a member of the Council, a good and upright man, 51who had not consented to their decision and action. He came from the Judean town of Arimathea and he was waiting for the kingdom of God. s 52Going to Pilate, he asked for Jesus' body. 53Then he took it down, wrapped it in linen cloth and placed it in a tomb cut in the rock, one in which no one had yet been laid. 54It was Preparation Day, t and the Sabbath was about to begin.

55The women who had come with Jesus from Galilee u followed Joseph and saw the tomb and how his body was laid in it. 56Then they went home and prepared spices and perfumes. v But they rested on the Sabbath in obedience to the commandment. w

The Resurrection

24 On the first day of the week, very early in the morning, the women took the spices they had prepared x and went to the tomb. 2They found the stone rolled away from the tomb, 3but when they entered, they did not find the body of the Lord Jesus. y 4While they were wondering about this, suddenly two men in clothes that gleamed like lightning z stood beside them. 5In their fright the women bowed down with their faces to the ground, but the men said to them, "Why do you look for the living among the dead? 6He is not here; he has risen! Remember how he told you, while he was still with you in Galilee: a 7'The Son of Man b must be delivered into the hands of sinful men, be crucified and on the third day be raised again.' " c 8Then they remembered his words. d

9When they came back from the tomb, they told all these things to the Eleven and to all the others. 10It was Mary Magdalene, Joanna, Mary the mother of James, and the others with them e who told this to the apostles. f 11But they did not believe g the women, because their words seemed to them like nonsense. 12Peter, however, got up and ran to the tomb. Bending over, he saw the strips of linen lying by themselves, h and he went away, i wondering to himself what had happened.

23:47
o Mt 9:8

23:48
p Lk 18:13
23:49
q Lk 8:2 r Ps 38:11

23:51
s Lk 2:25,38

23:54
t Mt 27:62
23:55
u ver 49

23:56
v Mk 16:1; Lk 24:1
w Ex 12:16; 20:10

24:1
x Lk 23:56

24:3
y ver 23,24
24:4
z Jn 20:12

24:6
a Mt 17:22,23;
Mk 9:30-31;
Lk 9:22; 24:44
24:7
b Mt 8:20
c Mt 16:21
24:8
d Jn 2:22
24:10
e Lk 8:1-3 f Mk 6:30
24:11
g Mk 16:11
24:12
h Jn 20:3-7
i Jn 20:10

Luke 23:50–56

While many in Israel "fell" before Jesus, some also "rose" (2:34). Joseph and these women belonged to this second group. Joseph, a member of the Sanhedrin (Jewish council), may have been absent when this group had met earlier (22:66), or he was part of the minority in the vote at the mock trial. Scripture notes that he disagreed with the verdict. The women observed Joseph as he laid Jesus' body in the tomb, fully intending to return after the Sabbath to honor the Lord's body with spices and perfumes.

The resurrection should have been—but wasn't—anticipated. Jesus' body had been laid to rest, and the women expected it to remain there. It's not unusual for God to be active in our midst and even to tell us about what he's doing or going to do, only for us to miss the point. We get so locked into how things normally flow that we risk missing out when God is doing something beyond the ordinary. We are wise to be familiar with his promises. Otherwise, their fulfillment just might take us by surprise.

Luke 24:1–12

The empty tomb and Jesus' resurrection fulfilled some of the promises Jesus had made in Galilee, but that realization shocked the disciples. In fact, their early moments of discovery revealed their need to overcome a strong sense of doubt about the events. What emerged from the surprise, though, was the additional discovery that God's plan hadn't been derailed. The resurrection wasn't created by the church. Rather, the church was created by the resurrection.

The women were more responsive to what God had done, but the reaction of the Eleven makes them look as skeptical and "sophisticated" as any person today. They were usually characterized as open to miracles, but on this occasion they had to be persuaded. Their initial "show me" attitude fits well with the modern spirit. This reality calls for patience as we share the hope of the resurrection with others. Resurrection is a hard doctrine for many to believe. For that reason the Spirit needs to work in hearts as the gospel is shared.

On the Road to Emmaus

24:13
j Mk 16:12

13 Now that same day two of them were going to a village called Emmaus, about seven miles[a] from Jerusalem.[j] 14 They were talking with each other about everything that had happened. 15 As they talked and discussed these things with each other, Jesus himself came up and walked along with them;[k] 16 but they were kept from recognizing him.[l]

24:15
k ver 36
24:16
l Jn 20:14; 21:4

17 He asked them, "What are you discussing together as you walk along?"

24:18
m Jn 19:25

They stood still, their faces downcast. 18 One of them, named Cleopas,[m] asked him, "Are you only a visitor to Jerusalem and do not know the things that have happened there in these days?"

19 "What things?" he asked.

24:19
n Mk 1:24
o Mt 21:11

"About Jesus of Nazareth,"[n] they replied. "He was a prophet,[o] powerful in word and deed before God and all the people. 20 The chief priests and our rulers[p] handed him over

24:20
p Lk 23:13

24:21
q Lk 1:68; 2:38;
21:28 r Mt 16:21
24:22
s ver 1-10

to be sentenced to death, and they crucified him; 21 but we had hoped that he was the one who was going to redeem Israel.[q] And what is more, it is the third day[r] since all this took place. 22 In addition, some of our women amazed us.[s] They went to the tomb early this morning 23 but didn't find his body. They came and told us that they had seen a vision of angels, who said he was alive. 24 Then some of our companions went to the tomb and found it just as the women had said, but him they did not see."[t]

24:24
t ver 12

25 He said to them, "How foolish you are, and how slow of heart to believe all that the prophets have spoken! 26 Did not the Christ[b] have to suffer these things and then enter his glory?"[u] 27 And beginning with Moses[v] and all the Prophets,[w] he explained to them what was said in all the Scriptures concerning himself.[x]

24:26
u Heb 2:10;
1Pe 1:11
24:27
v Ge 3:15; Nu 21:9;
Dt 18:15 w Isa 7:14;
9:6; 40:10, 11; 53;
Eze 34:23; Da 9:24;
Mic 7:20; Mal 3:1
x Jn 1:45

28 As they approached the village to which they were going, Jesus acted as if he were going farther. 29 But they urged him strongly, "Stay with us, for it is nearly evening; the day is almost over." So he went in to stay with them.

24:30
y Mt 14:19
24:31
z ver 16
24:32
a Ps 39:3
b ver 27, 45

30 When he was at the table with them, he took bread, gave thanks, broke it[y] and began to give it to them. 31 Then their eyes were opened and they recognized him,[z] and he disappeared from their sight. 32 They asked each other, "Were not our hearts burning within us[a] while he talked with us on the road and opened the Scriptures[b] to us?"

33 They got up and returned at once to Jerusalem. There they found the Eleven and those with them, assembled together 34 and saying, "It is true! The Lord has risen and has appeared to Simon."[c] 35 Then the two told what had happened on the way, and how Jesus was recognized by them when he broke the bread.[d]

24:34
c 1Co 15:5
24:35
d ver 30, 31

---

[a] 13 Greek *sixty stadia* (about 11 kilometers)   [b] 26 Or *Messiah*; also in verse 46

On the Road to Emmaus (24:13)

Then: Like Bethlehem, the village of Emmaus was a six-mile walk from Jerusalem. Whereas Bethlehem lay south, Emmaus was west of the capital.

Now: The exact site is unknown, living on only in memory in the annual Walk to Emmaus devotional weekend (see chart on next page for detail).

Luke 24:13–35

The encounter between Jesus and the two disciples on the road to Emmaus is one of the most vivid accounts of a resurrection appearance. The story is unique to Luke and contains key themes of his Gospel: the importance of the promise of the Word, the status of Jesus as Prophet, and his Messianic role. The passage closes with another picture of table fellowship—a scenario Luke apparently enjoyed and appreciated. Jesus' revelations frequently came in this kind of intimate context.

It's no accident that Jesus was revealed as he sat enjoying table fellowship with these disciples. The table was the place for camaraderie in the ancient world. Still today, Jesus often reveals himself in life's basic, even mundane moments. He's at home in our homes, or elsewhere in the midst of our everyday activity. This image is replayed in the church through the Lord's Supper, which affirms Jesus' presence. As you partake of your next Communion meal, why not make a point of looking forward to the final banquet table and the full celebration of his salvation?

Jesus Appears to the Disciples

36While they were still talking about this, Jesus himself stood among them and said to them, "Peace be with you." *e*

37They were startled and frightened, thinking they saw a ghost. *f* **38**He said to them, "Why are you troubled, and why do doubts rise in your minds? **39**Look at my hands and my feet. It is I myself! Touch me and see; *g* a ghost does not have flesh and bones, as you see I have."

40When he had said this, he showed them his hands and feet. **41**And while they still did not believe it because of joy and amazement, he asked them, "Do you have anything here to eat?" **42**They gave him a piece of broiled fish, **43**and he took it and ate it in their presence. *h*

44He said to them, "This is what I told you while I was still with you: *i* Everything must be fulfilled *j* that is written about me in the Law of Moses, *k* the Prophets and the Psalms." *l*

45Then he opened their minds so they could understand the Scriptures. **46**He told them, "This is what is written: The Christ will suffer and rise from the dead on the third day, **47**and repentance and forgiveness of sins will be preached in his name *m* to all nations, *n* beginning at Jerusalem. **48**You are witnesses *o* of these things. **49**I am going to send you what my Father has promised; *p* but stay in the city until you have been clothed with power from on high."

24:36
e Jn 20:19,21,26; 14:27
24:37
f Mk 6:49
24:39
g Jn 20:27; 1Jn 1:1

24:43
h Ac 10:41
24:44
i Lk 9:45; 18:34
j Mt 16:21; Lk 9:22,44;
k ver 27 / Ps 2; 16; 22; 69; 72; 110; 118
24:47
m Ac 5:31; 10:43; 13:38 *n* Mt 28:19
24:48
o Ac 1:8; 2:32; 5:32; 13:31; 1Pe 5:1
24:49
p Jn 14:16; Ac 1:4

Luke 24:36–49

The momentum of Jesus' postresurrection appearances was building up, as one meeting followed another in rapid succession. As the disciples were sharing reports, Jesus himself suddenly and unaccountably stood among them. He gave further evidence, through partaking of a meal and inviting the disciples to touch him, that he was no mere apparition. Jesus then commissioned his followers to take the gospel to the world. But this wasn't something they could do in their own strength. They first had to receive power through the Spirit.

 This commission still applies to us as Jesus' faith community. The disciples testified to what they saw, and we bear witness both to their testimony and to our own experience of the resurrected Christ. But we need more than our own resources to share Jesus effectively. He's provided his Spirit for this express purpose. In fact, the disciples *waited* for Spirit empowerment before proceeding. For a convincing picture of the Spirit's effectiveness, contrast the Peter of the three denials with the Peter of the powerful sermons in Acts 2:14–41; 3:12–26; 4:8–14, etc.

24:13–35

Walk to Emmaus

The disciples' walk to the town of Emmaus has become a symbol for the process of discovering who Jesus is and what he means in our lives. Several denominations have organized programs that aid individual believers in discovering or rediscovering Jesus in their lives. Some examples and brief descriptions of their programs:

Walk to Emmaus (Methodist): The Walk to Emmaus is a spiritual renewal program intended to strengthen the local church through the development of Christian disciples and leaders. The Walk to Emmaus experience begins with a 72-hour short course in Christianity, comprised of 15 talks by lay speakers and clergy on the themes of God's grace, disciplines of Christian discipleship, and what it means to be the church. www.upperroom.org/emmaus/

Cursillo (Roman Catholic): The Cursillo Movement makes it possible for people to live out, together, the fundamentals of Christianity. It helps people discover and fulfill their personal vocations and promotes the creation of core groups of Christians who leaven (add spiritual "yeast" to) their environments with the gospel. Involvement in Cursillo (meaning "short course") often begins with a three-day weekend retreat. www.natl-cursillo.org

Stephen Ministries (Presbyterian): The mission of Stephen Ministries is to help congregations equip God's people for spiritual growth and Christ-centered, practical ministry in today's world. Participants take a training course called the Stephen's Series and engage in 50 hours of course work and continuing education. After this training they are commissioned as Stephen Ministers. www.stephenministries.org

Alpha Course (Episcopal): The Alpha Course is a 15-session program that runs over 10 weeks to provide a practical introduction to the Christian faith. It offers the opportunity to explore the meaning of life through a series of small-group discussions addressing issues related to the Christian faith. Each small group enjoys a simple meal together and participates in a short teaching and discussion. www.alpha-course.org

24:50
q Mt 21:17

The Ascension

50When he had led them out to the vicinity of Bethany, *q* he lifted up his hands and blessed them. 51While he was blessing them, he left them and was taken up into heaven. *r* 52Then they worshiped him and returned to Jerusalem with great joy. 53And they stayed continually at the temple, *s* praising God.

24:51
r 2Ki 2:11
24:53
s Ac 2:46

Luke 24:50–53

Luke closed his Gospel with a portrait of Jesus taking the disciples out to Bethany, lifting up his hands, blessing them, and departing upward into heaven. The ascension is summarized here and detailed in Acts 1:9–11, linking together Luke's two books. Jesus blessed the disciples as he left to continue his work—this time from God's right hand. They returned joyfully to the temple, the same place Luke's story had begun with the Zechariah account, to praise God for all that had taken place.

Luke's conclusion is open-ended. The disciples returned to Jerusalem to await the empowerment God would give so they could share Jesus with a needy world. Luke followed up with a sequel, an account of the church's early history as the disciples fulfilled the commission Jesus had given them. Yet even at the end of Acts, this commission remained only partially fulfilled. Around the world followers of Christ continue to live as witnesses to the kingdom with their words, deeds, character, and sacrifice.

INTRODUCTION TO
John

AUTHOR
Scholars, and early church tradition, have long held that this Gospel was written by the apostle John, Jesus' disciple, a firsthand witness to the events recorded.

DATE WRITTEN
John was probably written between A.D. 89 and 95.

ORIGINAL READERS
John was written to non-Jewish believers and questioning unbelievers struggling with popular
Greek philosophies that taught that Jesus was divine but not truly human.

TIMELINE

	10BC AD1	10	20	30	40	50	60	70	80	90	100
Herod the Great's reign (c. 37-4 B.C.)											
Jesus' birth (c. 6/5 B.C.)											
Jesus' flight to Egypt (c. 5/4 B.C.)											
Beginning of John the Baptist's ministry (c. A.D. 26)											
Beginning of Jesus' ministry (c. A.D. 26)											
Jesus' death, resurrection, and ascension (c. A.D. 30)											
Paul's conversion (c. A.D. 35)											
Book of John written (c. A.D. 89-95)											
John's exile on Patmos (c. A.D. 89-95)											

THEMES
The purpose of John is clearly stated in 20:31: "These are written that you may believe that
Jesus is the Christ, the Son of God, and that by believing you may have life in his name." The
following themes are highlighted in this book:

1. *Jesus is God.* John's Gospel identifies Jesus as the Word who was with God in the beginning
(1:1–2), the One who "came from the Father" (1:14) to make him known (1:18). It shows that
Jesus is "equal with God" (5:18) and records conversations in which he identified himself as
God (8:58; 9:35–37; 10:36; 14:9).

2. *Jesus is the Messiah.* The miracles recorded in John function primarily as "signs" pointing to
Jesus' Messianic identity. They had material results, but their spiritual significance was John's
primary focus. The miracles were signs of God's presence in Jesus' works and words. Each sign
called (and still calls) for a commitment: Who is this Jesus?

3. *Choose belief or unbelief.* Jesus' miracles fostered belief in some (2:11; 9:1–39; 11:1–44) but
only hardened the opposition of others (11:46–57). We say "Seeing is believing," but in John
believing is seeing.

FAITH IN ACTION

The pages of John are filled with life lessons and role models of faith—people who challenge believers to put faith in action.

Role Models

• NICODEMUS (3:1–21) set aside his preconceived ideas and beliefs to embrace faith in Jesus. He later was criticized for defending Jesus against the majority in the Sanhedrin (7:50–52). After Jesus' death, he publicly took his Lord's body and prepared it for burial (19:38–40). As your faith has grown, have you gained boldness in publicly proclaiming your faith in Jesus?

• THE SAMARITAN WOMAN (4:4–26,39–42) believed Jesus, altered her lifestyle, and shared the Good News with those around her, bringing many to faith in Christ. How has God changed your life? Have you enthusiastically shared your testimony with anyone recently?

• A BOY (6:1–15) donated his lunch, which Jesus used to feed a multitude. What small thing can you give or do for the Lord's use?

• MARTHA (11:17–27) believed Jesus despite her despair at her brother's death. Have you clung to your faith in the face of intense sorrow? Did it buoy you up in hope?

• THOMAS (20:24–28) displayed honesty, not unbelief, in his questioning of Jesus' resurrection. When Jesus answered his questions, Thomas responded with faith. Have you ever brought your doubts to Jesus? Were they put to rest by his loving response?

Challenges

• Look for "signs" around you that God is at work, and then find ways to display your faith in those situations.

• Give something small, but don't be surprised when the Lord uses it in a big way.

• Be on the lookout this week for opportunities to share your faith with others.

• If you are overwhelmed with sorrow, open your heart to God's healing and comfort.

• Bring your doubts to God and allow his Spirit to reassure your heart. Choose belief.

OUTLINE

   I. Prologue (1:1–18)
  II. Beginnings of Jesus' Ministry (1:19–51)
 III. Jesus' Ministry (2–11)
 IV. The Passion Week (12–19)
      A. The Anointing of Jesus' Feet by Mary (12:1–11)
      B. The Triumphal Entry (12:12–19)
      C. The Greeks Seek Jesus (12:20–36)
      D. Rejection by the Jews (12:37–50)
      E. Farewell Discourses (13–17)
      F. Jesus' Betrayal, Arrest, and Trial (18:1—19:15)
      G. The Crucifixion and Burial (19:16–42)
  V. The Resurrection (20:1–29)
 VI. Statement of Purpose (20:30–31)
VII. Epilogue (21)

The Word Became Flesh

1 In the beginning was the Word,[a] and the Word was with God,[b] and the Word was God.[c] 2He was with God in the beginning.[d]

3Through him all things were made; without him nothing was made that has been made.[e] 4In him was life,[f] and that life was the light[g] of men. 5The light shines in the darkness, but the darkness has not understood[a] it.[h]

6There came a man who was sent from God; his name was John.[i] 7He came as a witness to testify[j] concerning that light, so that through him all men might believe.[k] 8He himself was not the light; he came only as a witness to the light. 9The true light[l] that gives light to every man[m] was coming into the world.[b]

10He was in the world, and though the world was made through him,[n] the world did not recognize him. 11He came to that which was his own, but his own did not receive him. 12Yet to all who received him, to those who believed[o] in his name,[p] he gave the right to become children of God[q]— 13children born not of natural descent,[c] nor of human decision or a husband's will, but born of God.[r]

14The Word became flesh[s] and made his dwelling among us. We have seen his glory, the glory of the One and Only,[d] who came from the Father, full of grace and truth.[t]

15John testifies[u] concerning him. He cries out, saying, "This was he of whom I said, 'He who comes after me has surpassed me because he was before me.'"[v] 16From the fullness[w] of his grace we have all received one blessing after another. 17For the law was given through Moses;[x] grace and truth came through Jesus Christ.[y] 18No one has ever seen God,[z] but God the One and Only,[d,e,a] who is at the Father's side, has made him known.

[a] 5 Or darkness, and the darkness has not overcome   [b] 9 Or This was the true light that gives light to every man who comes into the world   [c] 13 Greek of bloods   [d] 14,18 Or the Only Begotten   [e] 18 Some manuscripts but the only (or only begotten) Son

1:1
[a] Rev 19:13
[b] Jn 17:5; 1Jn 1:2
[c] Php 2:6
1:2
[d] Ge 1:1
1:3
[e] 1Co 8:6; Col 1:16; Heb 1:2
1:4
[f] Jn 5:26; 11:25; 14:6 [g] Jn 8:12
1:5
[h] Jn 3:19
1:6
[i] Mt 3:1
1:7
[j] ver 15,19,32
[k] ver 12
1:9
[l] 1Jn 2:8 [m] Isa 49:6
1:10
[n] Heb 1:2
1:12
[o] ver 7 [p] 1Jn 3:23
[q] Gal 3:26
1:13
[r] Jn 3:6; Jas 1:18; 1Pe 1:23; 1Jn 3:9
1:14
[s] Gal 4:4; Php 2:7, 8; 1Ti 3:16; Heb 2:14 [t] Jn 14:6
1:15
[u] ver 7 [v] ver 30; Mt 3:11
1:16
[w] Eph 1:23; Col 1:19
1:17
[x] Jn 7:19 [y] ver 14
1:18
[z] Ex 33:20; Jn 6:46; Col 1:15; 1Ti 6:16
[a] Jn 3:16,18; 1Jn 4:9

John 1:1–18

The early church used the symbol of an eagle for the Gospel of John. Why? For one thing, its prologue (these inspiring opening verses) are high, soaring prose. With skill and delicacy, under the inspiration of the Holy Spirit, John handled profound issues in unforgettable, yet understandable language. This passage has been a foundation for the classic Christian explanation of Christ. Here divinity and humanity, revelation and sacrifice are each discussed by John with rich simplicity. The most extraordinary event of all time has occurred in Jesus. God's grace and truth are fully disclosed and explained to us in the life of this one divine man.

"The Word became flesh" discloses how God wants to communicate with us. The Message is accessible as a person—One who lived in the world and was touched and heard by many. This man Jesus is God himself! He became a human fully and eternally, delivering the reality of God to the world through his flesh and blood. A marker was placed in human history, and all humanity is now called to track time and progress by this post. Is Jesus the center of your life and history?

1:1–3

Twin Truths

Some Biblical truths are so vast and incomprehensible they require two tiers of human ideas (or the juxtaposition of contrasting ideas) to begin to express them. In John 1 we have one of these pairs: the Logos (God, the Word, the epitome of wisdom) and the logos (the Greek philosophical idea of human wisdom). In this instance, the author began with an assumption of the commonplace (logos) and then transformed the idea to talk about the highest and all-encompassing truth—God (Logos). Some additional examples:

Judgment	Mercy
God stands for justice and righteousness, yet his mercy is without limits (Ps. 85:10; "love" in NIV and "mercy" in KJV; Mic. 6:8).	

Wisdom	Foolishness
Both wisdom and foolishness (2 Cor. 12:11) can aid spiritual growth, yet both can also inhibit it (Prov. 8–10).	

Power	Presence
God is wholly "other" and above us. Yet he's at the same time with us and in us (Ps. 139; John 14:17).	

Strength	Weakness
God makes us strong through our weaknesses (2 Cor. 12:10).	

Faith	Works
We are saved by grace through faith but live our lives doing what God requires (Eph. 2:8–10; James 1–2).	

1:19
b Jn 2:18; 5:10, 16;
6:41, 52
1:20
c Jn 3:28;
Lk 3:15, 16
1:21
d Mt 11:14
e Dt 18:15

1:23
f Mt 3:1 g Isa 40:3

1:27
h ver 15, 30
1:28
i Jn 3:26; 10:40

1:29
j ver 36; Isa 53:7;
1Pe 1:19; Rev 5:6
1:30
k ver 15, 27

1:32
l Mt 3:16; Mk 1:10

1:33
m Mk 1:4
n Mt 3:11; Mk 1:8
1:34
o ver 49; Mt 4:3

1:35
p Mt 3:1
1:36
q ver 29

John the Baptist Denies Being the Christ

19 Now this was John's testimony when the Jews[b] of Jerusalem sent priests and Levites to ask him who he was. 20 He did not fail to confess, but confessed freely, "I am not the Christ." [a][c]

21 They asked him, "Then who are you? Are you Elijah?" [d]

He said, "I am not."

"Are you the Prophet?" [e]

He answered, "No."

22 Finally they said, "Who are you? Give us an answer to take back to those who sent us. What do you say about yourself?"

23 John replied in the words of Isaiah the prophet, "I am the voice of one calling in the desert,[f] 'Make straight the way for the Lord.'" [b][g]

24 Now some Pharisees who had been sent 25 questioned him, "Why then do you baptize if you are not the Christ, nor Elijah, nor the Prophet?"

26 "I baptize with[c] water," John replied, "but among you stands one you do not know. 27 He is the one who comes after me,[h] the thongs of whose sandals I am not worthy to untie."

28 This all happened at Bethany on the other side of the Jordan,[i] where John was baptizing.

Jesus the Lamb of God

29 The next day John saw Jesus coming toward him and said, "Look, the Lamb of God,[j] who takes away the sin of the world! 30 This is the one I meant when I said, 'A man who comes after me has surpassed me because he was before me.'[k] 31 I myself did not know him, but the reason I came baptizing with water was that he might be revealed to Israel."

32 Then John gave this testimony: "I saw the Spirit come down from heaven as a dove and remain on him.[l] 33 I would not have known him, except that the one who sent me to baptize with water[m] told me, 'The man on whom you see the Spirit come down and remain is he who will baptize with the Holy Spirit.'[n] 34 I have seen and I testify that this is the Son of God." [o]

Jesus' First Disciples

35 The next day John[p] was there again with two of his disciples. 36 When he saw Jesus passing by, he said, "Look, the Lamb of God!" [q]

a 20 Or *Messiah*. "The Christ" (Greek) and "the Messiah" (Hebrew) both mean "the Anointed One"; also in verse 25.   b 23 Isaiah 40:3   c 26 Or *in*; also in verses 31 and 33

John 1:19–28

John wasn't primarily concerned about the events surrounding the ministry of John the Baptist. He was beginning to tell someone else's story—that of Jesus Christ—by recalling insights from John the Baptist. This entire account is the "testimony" of Jesus' forerunner. It's as though we are in a courtroom setting, and the evidence for and against Jesus is being laid out before us.

Christians are sometimes tempted to promote themselves. As human beings, we want to be patted on the back for the great job we are doing to further Christ's kingdom cause. We do well at such times to notice John's reluctance to tout his own credentials. Three times he answered questions with simple negatives, limiting himself to words that pointed away from himself and toward the coming One. "He must become greater; I must become less" (John 3:30) goes against our human grain. How do you deal with this inner conflict?

John 1:29–34

This episode continues John the Baptist's testimony about Jesus. While previously he could only hint at Christ's coming, now he identified Jesus plainly. People today might assume that Jesus was called the Lamb of God because he was "nice" and gentle. But the title refers to his identity as the ultimate sacrifice to be offered to the Father for the sins of the world. John's understanding came through the Spirit's revelation—just as ours does. True knowledge of God is always beyond natural human reach: It's a gift of divine disclosure.

John 1 is a theological model for what it means to follow Christ. It urges *loving* God, but not at the expense of *knowing* him. John the Baptist not only experienced a burning desire to downplay himself and glorify Jesus—he also could give a correct explanation of who Jesus is. How does your Christian faith measure up in the critical areas of commitment and content? How effective can your witness be if one or the other component is weak or missing?

37When the two disciples heard him say this, they followed Jesus. 38Turning around, Jesus saw them following and asked, "What do you want?"

They said, "Rabbi"[r] (which means Teacher), "where are you staying?"

39"Come," he replied, "and you will see."

So they went and saw where he was staying, and spent that day with him. It was about the tenth hour.

40Andrew, Simon Peter's brother, was one of the two who heard what John had said and who had followed Jesus. 41The first thing Andrew did was to find his brother Simon and tell him, "We have found the Messiah" (that is, the Christ).[s] 42And he brought him to Jesus.

Jesus looked at him and said, "You are Simon son of John. You will be called[t] Cephas" (which, when translated, is Peter[a]).[u]

Jesus Calls Philip and Nathanael

43The next day Jesus decided to leave for Galilee. Finding Philip,[v] he said to him, "Follow me."[w]

44Philip, like Andrew and Peter, was from the town of Bethsaida.[x] 45Philip found Nathanael[y] and told him, "We have found the one Moses wrote about in the Law,[z] and about whom the prophets also wrote[a]—Jesus of Nazareth,[b] the son of Joseph."[c]

46"Nazareth! Can anything good come from there?"[d] Nathanael asked.

"Come and see," said Philip.

47When Jesus saw Nathanael approaching, he said of him, "Here is a true Israelite,[e] in whom there is nothing false."[f]

48"How do you know me?" Nathanael asked.

Jesus answered, "I saw you while you were still under the fig tree before Philip called you."

49Then Nathanael declared, "Rabbi,[g] you are the Son of God;[h] you are the King of Israel."[i]

50Jesus said, "You believe[b] because I told you I saw you under the fig tree. You shall see greater things than that." 51He then added, "I tell you[c] the truth, you[c] shall see heaven open,[j] and the angels of God ascending and descending[k] on the Son of Man."[l]

a 42 Both *Cephas* (Aramaic) and *Peter* (Greek) mean *rock.*   b 50 Or *Do you believe . . . ?*
c 51 The Greek is plural.

1:38 r ver 49; Mt 23:7
1:41 s Jn 4:25
1:42 t Ge 17:5,15 u Mt 16:18
1:43 v Mt 10:3; Jn 6:5-7; 12:21,22; 14:8,9 w Mt 4:19
1:44 x Mt 11:21; Jn 12:21
1:45 y Jn 21:2 z Lk 24:27 a Lk 24:27 b Mt 2:23; Mk 1:24 c Lk 3:23
1:46 d Jn 7:41,42,52
1:47 e Ro 9:4,6 f Ps 32:2
1:49 g ver 38; Mt 23:7 h ver 34; Mt 4:3 i Mt 2:2; 27:42; Jn 12:13
1:51 j Mt 3:16 k Ge 28:12 l Mt 8:20

John 1:35–42

John the Baptist encouraged two of his own disciples to follow Jesus. One was Andrew; the other isn't named. In Matthew, Mark, and Luke, the earliest converts to Jesus are identified as Andrew, Peter, James, and John (see Mark 1:16–20). The unnamed disciple in verse 37 may be a concealed reference to the apostle John, the author of this Gospel and likely the mystery person behind the title "the disciple whom Jesus loved" (13:23; 19:26; 20:2; 21:7,20). Had this John learned from John the Baptist the importance of deflecting attention from himself to Jesus?

People come to Jesus in different ways. Throughout this Gospel they'll be challenged to "come and see" (vv. 39,46). Conversion isn't just about knowing; it's about coming and entering into a personal relationship with Jesus.

John 1:43–51

John the Baptist, Andrew, and Philip intentionally brought others to Jesus. They spoke what they knew about him and encouraged others to share their experience. Philip invited Nathanael to "Come and see"—but Jesus had "seen" him already. This points to Jesus' supernatural knowledge, but also to God's sovereign awareness of his people. God has them in his sights long before they see or seek him. We don't "convert" people to faith. That is God's work.

Many people today can relate to the skeptic Nathanael. His snide remark in verse 46 expressed the cynicism of a man who hadn't yet met the compelling evidence that would win over his life. Evidence becomes convincing only when we encounter and engage it personally. We too have something convincing to show the world. Have you invited your friends, family members, coworkers, neighbors, or acquaintances to "come and see"? Does your lifestyle raise the question in people's minds to which Jesus is the answer?

Jesus Changes Water to Wine

2:1
m Jn 4:46; 21:2
n Mt 12:46

2 On the third day a wedding took place at Cana in Galilee. *m* Jesus' mother *n* was there, 2 and Jesus and his disciples had also been invited to the wedding. 3 When the wine was gone, Jesus' mother said to him, "They have no more wine."

2:4
o Jn 19:26
p Mt 8:29
q Mt 26:18; Jn 7:6

4 "Dear woman, *o* why do you involve me?" *p* Jesus replied. "My time *q* has not yet come."

John 2:1–11

John consistently referred to Jesus' mighty works as "signs." A miracle underscores power, but a sign reveals something significant beyond the "wow" factor of the spectacular. The signs in John's Gospel unveiled that God was at work in Jesus—and indeed present in him. John remarked that through this particular sign Jesus revealed his "glory." This essential affirmation moves straight to the center of what John asserted about Jesus. Radiating God's presence, Jesus reflected his glory (1:14).

In this his first sign, Jesus solved a straightforward problem, the kind of potential glitch that causes every prospective bride and groom to flinch. It's easy for

2:12–24

Justice

From the story of Jesus clearing the temple of financial swindlers and exploiters, it's clear he was a strong proponent of monetary justice (cf. Deut. 19:35; Prov. 20:23). But the Bible sets a standard for justice that goes far beyond issues of money. It paints a picture of what a just world should look like. Modern ministries often attempt to address the same issues through steps aimed at eliminating inequitable practices and unfair advantages.

WHAT BIBLICAL JUSTICE IS Eight Biblical Goals of Justice	WHAT MODERN JUSTICE MIGHT LOOK LIKE Eight Goals Set by International Consensus
1. Caring for the Poor: "[God] has lifted up the humble. He has filled the hungry with good things" (Luke 1:52–53; cf. 4:18–19).The righteous care about justice for the poor (Prov. 29:7; cf. 31:8–9).	1. Eradicate extreme poverty and hunger. Reduce by half the proportion of the 1.2 billion people living on less than $1/day by encouraging micro-loans for cottage-business owners and by helping people everywhere access jobs that pay a living wage. Reduce the number of people suffering from hunger by teaching/promoting sound agricultural methods in rural communities.
2. Education of Young in Ways of Righteousness: "Train a child in the way he should go" (Prov. 22:6; cf. Deut. 6:4–7).	2. Achieve the availability of primary education for every boy and girl by building schools, supplying school fees and supplies to the underprivileged, and encouraging governments to support education initiatives through their budgets.
3. Gender Equity: "Male and female he created them" (Gen. 1:27; cf. Gal. 3:28).	3. Promote gender equity and empower women to achieve their full potential, especially through literacy, small business training, and community organizing efforts.
4. Care for the Unborn and Very Young: "The midwives . . . feared God and . . . let the [baby] boys live" (Ex. 1:17; cf. Ps. 139:13–16). "Let the little children come to me" (Matt. 19:14).	4. Reduce child mortality. Reduce worldwide infant and under-five mortality rates through immunizations and good nutrition.
5. Just and Honorable Treatment of Your Parents and Older Persons: "Honor your father and your mother, so that you may live long in the land the LORD your God is giving you" (Ex. 20:12; cf. Deut. 28:50; Prov. 20:20).	5. Improve maternal health. Reduce maternal mortality ratios by three-quarters through basic health care for mothers.
6. Equal Opportunity for an Abundant Life: "I will heal my people and will let them enjoy abundant peace and security" (Jer. 33:6; cf. John 10:10).	6. Combat preventable diseases by providing basic health care, education, clean water, and sanitation to children and families.
7. Care for the Environment: "Be fruitful and increase in number; fill the earth and subdue it" (Gen. 1:28; cf. Ps. 8:6–8).	7. Ensure environmental sustainability through good farming techniques and other Earth-friendly measures.
8. Legal and Social Justice for All: "Administer true justice; show mercy and compassion to one another. Do not oppress the widow or the fatherless, the alien or the poor" (Zech. 7:9–10 cf. Ps. 82:2–4; Prov. 18:5).	8. Ensure governments' stability through legal measures that support people's basic rights and freedoms.

5His mother said to the servants, "Do whatever he tells you."[r]

6Nearby stood six stone water jars, the kind used by the Jews for ceremonial washing,[s] each holding from twenty to thirty gallons.[a]

7Jesus said to the servants, "Fill the jars with water"; so they filled them to the brim.

8Then he told them, "Now draw some out and take it to the master of the banquet."

They did so, 9and the master of the banquet tasted the water that had been turned into wine.[t] He did not realize where it had come from, though the servants who had drawn the water knew. Then he called the bridegroom aside 10and said, "Everyone brings out the choice wine first and then the cheaper wine after the guests have had too much to drink; but you have saved the best till now."

11This, the first of his miraculous signs,[u] Jesus performed at Cana in Galilee. He thus revealed his glory,[v] and his disciples put their faith in him.[w]

Jesus Clears the Temple

12After this he went down to Capernaum[x] with his mother and brothers[y] and his disciples. There they stayed for a few days.

13When it was almost time for the Jewish Passover,[z] Jesus went up to Jerusalem.[a] 14In the temple courts he found men selling cattle, sheep and doves, and others sitting at tables exchanging money. 15So he made a whip out of cords, and drove all from the temple area, both sheep and cattle; he scattered the coins of the money changers and overturned their tables. 16To those who sold doves he said, "Get these out of here! How dare you turn my Father's house[b] into a market!"

17His disciples remembered that it is written: "Zeal for your house will consume me."[b][c]

18Then the Jews demanded of him, "What miraculous sign can you show us to prove your authority to do all this?"[d]

19Jesus answered them, "Destroy this temple, and I will raise it again in three days."[e]

20The Jews replied, "It has taken forty-six years to build this temple, and you are going to raise it in three days?" 21But the temple he had spoken of was his body.[f] 22After he was raised from the dead, his disciples recalled what he had said.[g] Then they believed the Scripture and the words that Jesus had spoken.

23Now while he was in Jerusalem at the Passover Feast,[h] many people saw the miraculous signs he was doing and believed in his name.[c] 24But Jesus would not entrust himself to them, for he knew all men. 25He did not need man's testimony about man, for he knew what was in a man.[i]

---

[a] 6 Greek *two to three metretes* (probably about 75 to 115 liters) [b] 17 Psalm 69:9 [c] 23 Or *and believed in him*

2:5 r Ge 41:55
2:6 s Mk 7:3,4; Jn 3:25
2:9 t Jn 4:46
2:11 u ver 23; Jn 3:2; 4:48; 6:2,14,26,30; 12:37; 20:30; v Jn 1:14; w Ex 14:31
2:12 x Mt 4:13; y Mt 12:46
2:13 z Jn 11:55; a Dt 16:1-6; Lk 2:41
2:16 b Lk 2:49
2:17 c Ps 69:9
2:18 d Mt 12:38
2:19 e Mt 26:61; 27:40; Mk 14:58; 15:29
2:21 f 1Co 6:19
2:22 g Lk 24:5-8; Jn 12:16; 14:26
2:23 h ver 13
2:25 i Mt 9:4; Jn 6:61, 64; 13:11

---

us to spiritualize Christ's work, to conclude that he's solely in the business of saving souls and renewing lives. Do you really believe he's interested in the commonplace events, disappointments, hassles, slights, and hurts that characterize the hours of your day? The Cana story says yes. What a comfort and privilege that we can invite Christ into our practical dilemmas that seem embarrassingly inconsequential—and legitimately ask him to help.

John 2:12–25

In John's record, the first act of Jesus' life had been celebrative. But the second was confrontational and upsetting. Furniture was smashed; animals went running; coins flew from their scales. Yes, Jesus made a disturbance, but he was acting out the core of his prophetic message. The place of worship and prayer had been turned into a religious marketplace—an attempt at selling and buying God's favor. The sanctity of God's house had been compromised. At the very beginning of Jesus' ministry, John highlighted Jesus' proclamation that his own body is the temple at which his people encounter God and his favor.

Verses 23–25 assure us that Jesus knows entirely what's going on inside us and our churches. This story beckons us to inspect our own religious house—to imagine what would happen if Jesus were to visit. Would he be outraged by conflicts between choirs and contemporary worship teams? With struggles over whether or not to build? Over the color of the new carpeting? Even more, have we turned our religious activities into a business, seeking to earn or buy God's favor? What housekeeping is needed in the Spirit's closer residence—your heart?

Jesus Teaches Nicodemus

3:1
j Jn 7:50; 19:39
k Lk 23:13

3 Now there was a man of the Pharisees named Nicodemus,[j] a member of the Jewish ruling council.[k] [2]He came to Jesus at night and said, "Rabbi, we know you are a teacher who has come from God. For no one could perform the miraculous signs[l] you are doing if God were not with him."[m]

3:2
l Jn 9:16,33
m Ac 2:22; 10:38

[3]In reply Jesus declared, "I tell you the truth, no one can see the kingdom of God unless he is born again.[a][n]

3:3
n Jn 1:13; 1Pe 1:23

[4]"How can a man be born when he is old?" Nicodemus asked. "Surely he cannot enter a second time into his mother's womb to be born!"

[5]Jesus answered, "I tell you the truth, no one can enter the kingdom of God unless he is born of water and the Spirit.[o] [6]Flesh gives birth to flesh, but the Spirit[b] gives birth to spirit.[p] [7]You should not be surprised at my saying, 'You[c] must be born again.' [8]The wind blows wherever it pleases. You hear its sound, but you cannot tell where it comes from or where it is going. So it is with everyone born of the Spirit."

3:5
o Tit 3:5
3:6
p Jn 1:13;
1Co 15:50

[9]"How can this be?"[q] Nicodemus asked.

3:9
q Jn 6:52,60
3:10
r Lk 2:46
3:11
s Jn 1:18; 7:16,17
t ver 32

[10]"You are Israel's teacher,"[r] said Jesus, "and do you not understand these things? [11]I tell you the truth, we speak of what we know,[s] and we testify to what we have seen, but still you people do not accept our testimony.[t] [12]I have spoken to you of earthly things and you do not believe; how then will you believe if I speak of heavenly things? [13]No one has ever gone into heaven[u] except the one who came from heaven[v]—the Son of Man.[d] [14]Just as Moses lifted up the snake in the desert,[w] so the Son of Man must be lifted up,[x] [15]that everyone who believes[y] in him may have eternal life.[e]

3:13
u Pr 30:4; Ac 2:34;
Eph 4:8-10
v Jn 6:38,42
3:14
w Nu 21:8,9
x Jn 8:28; 12:32
3:15
y ver 16,36

[16]"For God so loved[z] the world that he gave his one and only Son,[f] that whoever believes in him shall not perish but have eternal life.[a] [17]For God did not send his Son into the world[b] to condemn the world, but to save the world through him.[c] [18]Whoever believes in him is not condemned,[d] but whoever does not believe stands condemned already because he has not believed in the name of God's one and only Son.[g][e] [19]This is the verdict: Light[f] has come into the world, but men loved darkness instead of light because their deeds were evil. [20]Everyone who does evil hates the light, and will not come into the light for fear that his deeds will be exposed.[g] [21]But whoever lives by the truth comes into the light, so that it may be seen plainly that what he has done has been done through God."[h]

3:16
z Ro 5:8; Eph 2:4;
1Jn 4:9,10 a ver 36;
Jn 6:29,40;
11:25,26
3:17
b Jn 6:29,57; 10:36;
11:42; 17:8,21;
20:21 c Jn 12:47;
1Jn 4:14
3:18
d Jn 5:24 e 1Jn 4:9
3:19
f Jn 1:4; 8:12
3:20
g Eph 5:11,13

John the Baptist's Testimony About Jesus

3:22
h Jn 4:2

[22]After this, Jesus and his disciples went out into the Judean countryside, where he spent some time with them, and baptized.[h] [23]Now John also was baptizing at

---

[a] 3 Or *born from above*; also in verse 7   [b] 6 Or *but spirit*   [c] 7 The Greek is plural.   [d] 13 Some manuscripts *Man, who is in heaven*   [e] 15 Or *believes may have eternal life in him*   [f] 16 Or *his only begotten Son*   [g] 18 Or *God's only begotten Son*   [h] 21 Some interpreters end the quotation after verse 15.

John 3:1–21

When Jesus challenged Nicodemus that he must be "born again" (or "born from above"), he was making a fundamental statement about human nature: Humanity is broken. God's work in the world isn't a question of fixing a part but of recreating the whole. Jesus described the needed process as nothing short of a new birth. True religion—and true spirituality—unite humanity with God's powerful Spirit, who overwhelms, transforms, and converts his people.

The longer we are in the church, the more we need stories of transformation. The gospel isn't just about forgiveness for a bad life but about the gift of new life. God not only accepts us in Christ. He changes us. Fresh accounts of such radical life changes remind us of the nature of the world (from which we are increasingly

isolated) and the power of God (about which we can become increasingly blasé). Churches benefit greatly from hearing people tell their own stories regularly. When did you last hear—or tell—an account of transformation in Christ?

John 3:22–36

Jesus and his followers moved into the countryside outside Jerusalem, where he conducted a ministry much like that of John the Baptist. This is the only record that Jesus had a baptizing ministry, though John 4:2 makes clear that Jesus' disciples, not Jesus himself, baptized people. The remark of John the Baptist's disciples in verse 26 reveals their envy of Jesus' growing popularity (cf. 4:1). The Baptist's response corrected the rivalry. Despite the loyalty and affections of his followers, John knew he must always play a secondary role.

Aenon near Salim, because there was plenty of water, and people were constantly coming to be baptized. 24(This was before John was put in prison.) *i* 25An argument developed between some of John's disciples and a certain Jew *a* over the matter of ceremonial washing. *j* 26They came to John and said to him, "Rabbi, *k* that man who was with you on the other side of the Jordan—the one you testified *l* about—well, he is baptizing, and everyone is going to him."

27To this John replied, "A man can receive only what is given him from heaven. 28You yourselves can testify that I said, 'I am not the Christ *b* but am sent ahead of him.' *m* 29The bride belongs to the bridegroom. *n* The friend who attends the bridegroom waits and listens for him, and is full of joy when he hears the bridegroom's voice. That joy is mine, and it is now complete. *o* 30He must become greater; I must become less.

31"The one who comes from above *p* is above all; the one who is from the earth belongs to the earth, and speaks as one from the earth. *q* The one who comes from heaven is above all. 32He testifies to what he has seen and heard, *r* but no one accepts his testimony. *s* 33The man who has accepted it has certified that God is truthful. 34For the one whom God has sent *t* speaks the words of God, for God *c* gives the Spirit *u* without limit. 35The Father loves the Son and has placed everything in his hands. *v* 36Whoever believes in the Son has eternal life, *w* but whoever rejects the Son will not see life, for God's wrath remains on him." *d*

Jesus Talks With a Samaritan Woman

4 The Pharisees heard that Jesus was gaining and baptizing more disciples than John, *x* 2although in fact it was not Jesus who baptized, but his disciples. 3When the Lord learned of this, he left Judea *y* and went back once more to Galilee.

4Now he had to go through Samaria. 5So he came to a town in Samaria called Sychar, near the plot of ground Jacob had given to his son Joseph. *z* 6Jacob's well was

a 25 Some manuscripts *and certain Jews* *b* 28 Or *Messiah* *c* 34 Greek *he* *d* 36 Some interpreters end the quotation after verse 30.

3:24
i Mt 4:12; 14:3
3:25
j Jn 2:6
3:26
k Mt 23:7 *l* Jn 1:7

3:28
m Jn 1:20,23
3:29
n Mt 9:15
o Jn 16:24; 17:13; Php 2:2; 1Jn 1:4; 2Jn 12
3:31
p ver 13 *q* Jn 8:23; 1Jn 4:5

3:32
r Jn 8:26; 15:15
s ver 11
3:34
t ver 17 *u* Mt 12:18; Lk 4:18; Ac 10:38

3:35
v Mt 28:18; Jn 5:20, 22; 17:2
3:36
w ver 15; Jn 5:24; 6:47

4:1
x Jn 3:22,26
4:3
y Jn 3:22

4:5
z Ge 33:19; 48:22; Jos 24:32

📖 John's followers had to expand their horizons, to transfer their allegiance to Jesus. The impulse to follow a charismatic religious leader and speaker is always with us. The problem sometimes rests with such individuals, and sometimes with the expectations of their followers, who may have a personal interest in elevating their leaders. If we are to submit to Jesus' authority and influence (the goal of all true Christian teachers and leaders), his spokespersons must always take a subordinate role. If God has given you a position of leadership, how easy has it been for you to live out this truth?

John 4:1–26

📖 In Jesus' day, a long-term tension smoldered between Judea and Samaria. Partly based on ethnicity and religion (the Samaritans were a mixed race who practiced an irregular form of Judaism), the conflict echoed centuries of political and ethnic clashes. Jews often avoided Samaria by crossing the Jordan and traveling on the east side. When John wrote that Jesus "had to go through Samaria," he was inferring that the necessity lay in Jesus' mission, not in geography.

📖 Samaria today may be viewed as a metaphor for the political and cultural boundaries that too often stand between us in the church and the needy people outside its doors. Jesus crossed such boundaries, and John 4 challenges us to take the same risk. Before stepping across our self-imposed borders, we need to identify them. For some of us this may mean moving to the inner

4:1–26

small
MEASURES

In the story of the Samaritan woman, Jesus challenged unjust social barriers by ignoring protocol and making an all-important contact—through a simple request for a drink of water. What are some small lead-ins or "minor" things you could do to begin to address seemingly insurmountable problems in the world today? Some examples from Jesus' life may give you some ideas:

• Jesus touching the leper during the healing act	Matt. 8:3
• Jesus picking grain on the Sabbath	Matt. 12:1–14
• Jesus' simple stories. Various parables in the Gospels	
• Jesus' lack of condemnation for the woman caught in adultery	John 8:3–11
• Jesus' washing of the disciples' feet	John 13:1–17
• Jesus' recognition of the widow's generosity	Mark 12:41–44

there, and Jesus, tired as he was from the journey, sat down by the well. It was about the sixth hour.

7When a Samaritan woman came to draw water, Jesus said to her, "Will you give me a drink?" 8(His disciples had gone into the town[a] to buy food.)

9The Samaritan woman said to him, "You are a Jew and I am a Samaritan[b] woman. How can you ask me for a drink?" (For Jews do not associate with Samaritans.[a])

10Jesus answered her, "If you knew the gift of God and who it is that asks you for a drink, you would have asked him and he would have given you living water."[c]

11"Sir," the woman said, "you have nothing to draw with and the well is deep. Where can you get this living water? 12Are you greater than our father Jacob, who gave us the well[d] and drank from it himself, as did also his sons and his flocks and herds?"

13Jesus answered, "Everyone who drinks this water will be thirsty again, 14but whoever drinks the water I give him will never thirst.[e] Indeed, the water I give him will become in him a spring of water[f] welling up to eternal life."[g]

15The woman said to him, "Sir, give me this water so that I won't get thirsty[h] and have to keep coming here to draw water."

16He told her, "Go, call your husband and come back."

17"I have no husband," she replied.

Jesus said to her, "You are right when you say you have no husband. 18The fact is, you have had five husbands, and the man you now have is not your husband. What you have just said is quite true."

19"Sir," the woman said, "I can see that you are a prophet.[i] 20Our fathers worshiped on this mountain,[j] but you Jews claim that the place where we must worship is in Jerusalem."[k]

21Jesus declared, "Believe me, woman, a time is coming[l] when you will worship the Father neither on this mountain nor in Jerusalem.[m] 22You Samaritans worship what you do not know;[n] we worship what we do know, for salvation is from the Jews.[o] 23Yet a time is coming and has now come[p] when the true worshipers will worship the Father in spirit[q] and truth, for they are the kind of worshipers the Father seeks. 24God is spirit,[r] and his worshipers must worship in spirit and in truth."

25The woman said, "I know that Messiah" (called Christ)[s] "is coming. When he comes, he will explain everything to us."

26Then Jesus declared, "I who speak to you am he."[t]

The Disciples Rejoin Jesus

27Just then his disciples returned[u] and were surprised to find him talking with a woman. But no one asked, "What do you want?" or "Why are you talking with her?"

28Then, leaving her water jar, the woman went back to the town and said to the people, 29"Come, see a man who told me everything I ever did.[v] Could this be the Christ[b]?"[w] 30They came out of the town and made their way toward him.

31Meanwhile his disciples urged him, "Rabbi,[x] eat something."

---

[a] 9 Or *do not use dishes Samaritans have used* [b] 29 Or *Messiah*

Cross references (margin):

4:8 a ver 5,39
4:9 b Mt 10:5; Lk 9:52,53
4:10 c Isa 44:3; Jer 2:13; Zec 14:8; Jn 7:37, 38; Rev 21:6; 22:1,17
4:12 d ver 6
4:14 e Jn 6:35 f Jn 7:38 g Mt 25:46
4:15 h Jn 6:34
4:19 i Mt 21:11
4:20 j Dt 11:29; Jos 8:33 k Lk 9:53
4:21 l Jn 5:28; 16:2 m Mal 1:11; 1Ti 2:8
4:22 n 2Ki 17:28-41 o Isa 2:3; Ro 3:1,2; 9:4,5
4:23 p Jn 5:25; 16:32 q Php 3:3
4:24 r Php 3:3
4:25 s Mt 1:16
4:26 t Jn 8:24; 9:35-37
4:27 u ver 8
4:29 v ver 17,18 w Mt 12:23; Jn 7:26,31
4:31 x Mt 23:7

---

city or to another country. For others it may involve making an effort to connect with that neighbor or coworker whose background is quite different from ours. Where is your "Samaria"?

John 4:27–38

This woman was part of a society where life was lived in public, and she was existing on the margins of her community—labeled by all as a sinner (see v. 18). Nevertheless, she took a tremendous risk. She returned to her town and started talking about Jesus, even though she had flaunted her unconcern about accepted morality for years. Strikingly, the townsfolk listened and responded. When people who have struggled with

morality meet God, their words may have an impact surpassing those of the devout or outwardly pious.

Once again John repeated his "come and see" theme. This time the invitation was to see the person who "knows everything I have done"—and still loves me! If Jesus' disciples would look around, they would see all about them people languishing from spiritual hunger and thirst. Surely the risk for us to invite others to "come and see" is no greater than for this woman, who shared her witness of Christ without concern about the reaction she would receive. When you witness to others, are you more concerned about their perception of you or about God's perception of and care for them?

The Samaritan Woman

 Chap. 4

The Gospels are clear that dividing people according to behavior, background, or other personal traits was never Jesus' way. John's fourth chapter describes a significant encounter between Jesus and a Samaritan woman.

She was known as promiscuous, having lived with five "husbands" in succession, and was condemned by her own people. She never went to the well during the cooler hours of the day with the other women but at noon, by herself. We can imagine the other women walking together, exchanging village gossip, and talking about their children or grandchildren while she watched from her window until they returned.

Furthermore, this woman was a Samaritan, a Jew whose ancestors were Abraham, Isaac, and Jacob and who worshiped the same God as all other Jews. But Samaritans were convinced that only five books (Gen. through Deut.) belonged in the Bible, and they recognized Moses as God's only prophet. They considered Mt. Gerizim, not the temple in Jerusalem, their holy place. When the Israelites returned from exile, they found that some of those who had stayed in Samaria had intermarried with Gentiles. These people were excluded from rebuilding Jerusalem.

The Samaritans were despised outcasts considered to have betrayed God. During Jesus' day, an Israelite on whom a Samaritan's shadow fell required ceremonial cleansing before entering the temple to worship!

One day while his disciples were away buying food, Jesus approached the Samaritan woman and asked, "Will you give me a drink?" Although its significance may not be obvious at first, this simple act was a startling demonstration against racial, gender, and religious prejudice.

All Southerners who lived during the time of racial segregation can recognize its bold nature. As a child, when my parents were away on a trip, I lived, ate, and slept with our African-American neighbors. My black boyhood friends and I played and fished together, plowed side by side with mules, and played on the same baseball team. But when I carried water to a group of people working in the field, it would have been inconceivable for black and white workers to drink from the same dipper. For Jesus to drink from the Samaritan woman's cup was a powerfully symbolic act of acceptance and friendship.

> **Jesus used just one cup of water to demonstrate the overcoming of prejudice. We have many opportunities to do the same.**

Amazed by Jesus' openness, the woman engaged him in conversation, and, after a few minutes of simple talk, became convinced Jesus was the Messiah.

During her brief encounter with Jesus, a miracle occurred—not a physical but a spiritual one. Because Jesus broke down all racial, social, and religious barriers between them, this woman became a messenger around whom the villagers gathered to hear the Good News about a man they would soon know as "the Savior of the world" (4:42). The encounter between Christ and the Samaritan woman is one of the most gratifying examples of salvation in the Bible. This woman was given what she needed most: acceptance, forgiveness, and a new life.

Unfortunately, we are usually quite comfortable with our prejudices. In my book *Turning Point,* I described the racial discrimination that existed over 30 years ago in the Deep South. At that time segregation was legally enforced. But although the laws have changed, our society now is almost as segregated as it was then.

Christians and believers of every faith have a responsibility to help break down barriers based on race, gender, religion, and other differences. Jesus used just one cup of water to demonstrate the overcoming of prejudice. We have many opportunities to do the same.

Jimmy Carter, former president of the United States
Source: Jimmy Carter, Living Faith (New York: Random House, 1996), 187–190

4:32
y Job 23:12; Mt 4:4;
Jn 6:27

4:34
z Mt 26:39; Jn 6:38;
17:4; 19:30
a Jn 19:30
4:35
b Mt 9:37; Lk 10:2
4:36
c Ro 1:13
d Mt 25:46

4:37
e Job 31:8;
Mic 6:15

4:39
f ver 5 g ver 29

4:42
h Lk 2:11; 1Jn 4:14

4:43
i ver 40
4:44
j Mt 13:57; Lk 4:24
4:45
k Jn 2:23

4:46
l Jn 2:1-11
4:47
m ver 3,54

4:48
n Da 4:2,3; Jn 2:11;
Ac 2:43; 14:3;
Ro 15:19;
2Co 12:12; Heb 2:4

32 But he said to them, "I have food to eat [y] that you know nothing about."

33 Then his disciples said to each other, "Could someone have brought him food?"

34 "My food," said Jesus, "is to do the will [z] of him who sent me and to finish his work. [a] 35 Do you not say, 'Four months more and then the harvest'? I tell you, open your eyes and look at the fields! They are ripe for harvest. [b] 36 Even now the reaper draws his wages, even now he harvests [c] the crop for eternal life, [d] so that the sower and the reaper may be glad together. 37 Thus the saying 'One sows and another reaps' [e] is true. 38 I sent you to reap what you have not worked for. Others have done the hard work, and you have reaped the benefits of their labor."

Many Samaritans Believe

39 Many of the Samaritans from that town [f] believed in him because of the woman's testimony, "He told me everything I ever did." [g] 40 So when the Samaritans came to him, they urged him to stay with them, and he stayed two days. 41 And because of his words many more became believers.

42 They said to the woman, "We no longer believe just because of what you said; now we have heard for ourselves, and we know that this man really is the Savior of the world." [h]

Jesus Heals the Official's Son

43 After the two days [i] he left for Galilee. 44 (Now Jesus himself had pointed out that a prophet has no honor in his own country.) [j] 45 When he arrived in Galilee, the Galileans welcomed him. They had seen all that he had done in Jerusalem at the Passover Feast, [k] for they also had been there.

46 Once more he visited Cana in Galilee, where he had turned the water into wine. [l] And there was a certain royal official whose son lay sick at Capernaum. 47 When this man heard that Jesus had arrived in Galilee from Judea, [m] he went to him and begged him to come and heal his son, who was close to death.

48 "Unless you people see miraculous signs and wonders," [n] Jesus told him, "you will never believe."

49 The royal official said, "Sir, come down before my child dies."

50 Jesus replied, "You may go. Your son will live."

The man took Jesus at his word and departed. 51 While he was still on the way, his servants met him with the news that his boy was living. 52 When he inquired as to

---

John 4:39–42

The Samaritans reentered the scene. Their faith was based initially on the woman's words, which underscored the value of human testimony to the work of God (17:20). Christian witness is a cooperative effort, in which the preparatory work of God joins with the believers' witness to what he has done and is doing in the world. Jesus and his followers agreed to remain there two days. Hearing Jesus for themselves, many Samaritans became convinced that he was indeed the long-awaited Messiah (v. 25), "the Savior of the world."

Jesus is indeed the Savior of *all* the world—in that his light shines for all (1:9). It's for "every nation, tribe, people, and language" (Rev. 7:9). Still, much of our world remains shrouded in ignorance, poverty, instability, and intolerance. Do you consider yourself lacking in *giftedness, time, or resources—unable to make a difference?* If so, you might do well to remind yourself of this unlikely candidate God chose as his witness—the "notorious" woman of Samaria.

John 4:43–54

Jesus returned to Cana, where he had previously turned water into wine at a wedding—the first of his "miraculous signs" (2:11). Now he healed an official's son. The official and his family believed, but Jesus critically addressed the Galileans in general: "Unless you people see miraculous signs and wonders, you will never believe." They had overlooked the sign Jesus had already given at the wedding. His point was sharp: They wanted miracles but didn't want to see what God was really doing among them (cf. 6:26).

God's desire to disclose himself in the natural world results in "signs." But merely hearing a witness or experiencing a miracle isn't enough. We may seek guidance from God, or for God to do a miracle that will benefit us, without seeking God or submitting to him. But God's revelation and signs unveil who *we* are, as well as who God is, in order to draw us into a relationship with him. Divine signs, like light, can be painful since they disclose what may be conveniently hidden in the darkness (3:19). But all this is for our healing and new birth.

the time when his son got better, they said to him, "The fever left him yesterday at the seventh hour."

⁵³Then the father realized that this was the exact time at which Jesus had said to him, "Your son will live." So he and all his household° believed.

⁵⁴This was the second miraculous signᵖ that Jesus performed, having come from Judea to Galilee.

The Healing at the Pool

5 Some time later, Jesus went up to Jerusalem for a feast of the Jews. ²Now there is in Jerusalem near the Sheep Gate�q a pool, which in Aramaicʳ is called Bethesdaᵃ and which is surrounded by five covered colonnades. ³Here a great number of disabled people used to lie—the blind, the lame, the paralyzed.ᵇ ⁵One who was there had been an invalid for thirty-eight years. ⁶When Jesus saw him lying there and learned that he had been in this condition for a long time, he asked him, "Do you want to get well?"

⁷"Sir," the invalid replied, "I have no one to help me into the pool when the water is stirred. While I am trying to get in, someone else goes down ahead of me."

⁸Then Jesus said to him, "Get up! Pick up your mat and walk."ˢ ⁹At once the man was cured; he picked up his mat and walked.

The day on which this took place was a Sabbath,ᵗ ¹⁰and so the Jewsᵘ said to the man who had been healed, "It is the Sabbath; the law forbids you to carry your mat."ᵛ

¹¹But he replied, "The man who made me well said to me, 'Pick up your mat and walk.'"

¹²So they asked him, "Who is this fellow who told you to pick it up and walk?"

¹³The man who was healed had no idea who it was, for Jesus had slipped away into the crowd that was there.

¹⁴Later Jesus found him at the temple and said to him, "See, you are well again. Stop sinningʷ or something worse may happen to you." ¹⁵The man went away and told the Jewsˣ that it was Jesus who had made him well.

Life Through the Son

¹⁶So, because Jesus was doing these things on the Sabbath, the Jews persecuted him. ¹⁷Jesus said to them, "My Father is always at his workʸ to this very day, and I, too, am working." ¹⁸For this reason the Jews tried all the harder to kill him;ᶻ not

---

ᵃ 2 Some manuscripts *Bethzatha*; other manuscripts *Bethsaida*   ᵇ 3 Some less important manuscripts *paralyzed—and they waited for the moving of the waters.* ⁴*From time to time an angel of the Lord would come down and stir up the waters. The first one into the pool after each such disturbance would be cured of whatever disease he had.*

4:53
° Ac 11:14
4:54
ᵖ ver 48; Jn 2:11

5:2
q Ne 3:1; 12:39
ʳ Jn 19:13,17,20;
20:16; Ac 21:40;
22:2; 26:14

5:8
ˢ Mt 9:5,6;
Mk 2:11; Lk 5:24

5:9
ᵗ Jn 9:14
5:10
ᵘ ver 16
ᵛ Ne 13:15-22;
Jer 17:21; Mt 12:2

5:14
ʷ Mk 2:5; Jn 8:11
5:15
ˣ Jn 1:19

5:17
ʸ Jn 9:4; 14:10
5:18
ᶻ Jn 7:1

John 5:1–15

Among the many at the pool of Bethesda awaiting healing that day, Jesus selected a particularly difficult case. Life for a paraplegic or quadriplegic is never easy, but imagine the obstacles in the 1st century. Problems of mobility, livelihood, personal hygiene, and social isolation began the list. People moved this man—who had been paralyzed for 38 years—from place to place. His meager income came from begging or from the charity of his friends and family.

Jesus' question "Do you wish to get well?" at first seems strange. *Of course*, we think. Yet sometimes people allow their identity to form around their problems. Removal of the difficulty necessitates re-forming their sense of who they are. Has this ever happened to you? Trying to help such people puts us at risk of getting sucked into their troubles.

As she embraced and loved the poorest of the poor

in Calcutta's streets, Mother Teresa encouraged her sisters to "let the poor eat you up." Needs like these look so overwhelming, but this is exactly the kind of place to which Jesus liked to go. What's the limit of your comfort zone in dealing personally with those with severe problems?

John 5:16–30

In verse 17 Jesus claimed remarkable authority, inferring that he, like his Father, couldn't and shouldn't refrain from deeds of compassion on the Sabbath. Key to the verses that follow is the understanding that Jesus was proclaiming his divine identity. He's the Son of God, the Father, the long-awaited "son of man" who brings in the Messianic judgment and kingdom (cf. Dan. 7:13). He does only the Father's will, and the Father has entrusted to him the judgment of the world. Whoever rejects the Son rejects the Father.

5:18
a Jn 10:30,33; 19:7
5:19
b ver 30; Jn 8:28
5:20
c Jn 3:35 *d* Jn 14:12
5:21
e Ro 4:17; 8:11
f Jn 11:25
5:22
g ver 27; Jn 9:39;
Ac 10:42; 17:31
5:23
h Lk 10:16;
1Jn 2:23
5:24
i Jn 3:18 *j* 1Jn 3:14
5:25
k Jn 4:23
l Jn 8:43,47
5:27
m ver 22; Ac 10:42;
17:31
5:28
n Jn 4:21
5:29
o Da 12:2; Mt 25:46
5:30
p ver 19 *q* Jn 8:16
r Mt 26:39; Jn 4:34;
6:38

only was he breaking the Sabbath, but he was even calling God his own Father, making himself equal with God. *a*

19 Jesus gave them this answer: "I tell you the truth, the Son can do nothing by himself; *b* he can do only what he sees his Father doing, because whatever the Father does the Son also does. 20 For the Father loves the Son *c* and shows him all he does. Yes, to your amazement he will show him even greater things than these. *d* 21 For just as the Father raises the dead and gives them life, *e* even so the Son gives life *f* to whom he is pleased to give it. 22 Moreover, the Father judges no one, but has entrusted all judgment to the Son, *g* 23 that all may honor the Son just as they honor the Father. He who does not honor the Son does not honor the Father, who sent him. *h*

24 "I tell you the truth, whoever hears my word and believes him who sent me has eternal life and will not be condemned; *i* he has crossed over from death to life. *j* 25 I tell you the truth, a time is coming and has now come *k* when the dead will hear *l* the voice of the Son of God and those who hear will live. 26 For as the Father has life in himself, so he has granted the Son to have life in himself. 27 And he has given him authority to judge *m* because he is the Son of Man.

28 "Do not be amazed at this, for a time is coming *n* when all who are in their graves will hear his voice 29 and come out—those who have done good will rise to live, and those who have done evil will rise to be condemned. *o* 30 By myself I can do nothing; *p* I judge only as I hear, and my judgment is just, *q* for I seek not to please myself but him who sent me. *r*

Testimonies About Jesus

5:31
s Jn 8:14
5:32
t ver 37; Jn 8:18
5:33
u Jn 1:7
5:34
v 1Jn 5:9
5:35
w 2Pe 1:19
5:36
x 1Jn 5:9
y Jn 14:11; 15:24
z Jn 3:17; 10:25
5:37
a Jn 8:18 *b* Dt 4:12;
1Ti 1:17; Jn 1:18
5:38
c 1Jn 2:14 *d* Jn 3:17
5:39
e Ro 2:17,18
f Lk 24:27,44;
Ac 13:27
5:41
g ver 44
5:44
h Ro 2:29
5:45
i Jn 9:28 *j* Ro 2:17

31 "If I testify about myself, my testimony is not valid. *s* 32 There is another who testifies in my favor, *t* and I know that his testimony about me is valid.

33 "You have sent to John and he has testified *u* to the truth. 34 Not that I accept human testimony; *v* but I mention it that you may be saved. 35 John was a lamp that burned and gave light, *w* and you chose for a time to enjoy his light.

36 "I have testimony weightier than that of John. *x* For the very work that the Father has given me to finish, and which I am doing, *y* testifies that the Father has sent me. *z* 37 And the Father who sent me has himself testified concerning me. *a* You have never heard his voice nor seen his form, *b* 38 nor does his word dwell in you, *c* for you do not believe the one he sent. *d* 39 You diligently study *a* the Scriptures *e* because you think that by them you possess eternal life. These are the Scriptures that testify about me, *f* 40 yet you refuse to come to me to have life.

41 "I do not accept praise from men, *g* 42 but I know you. I know that you do not have the love of God in your hearts. 43 I have come in my Father's name, and you do not accept me; but if someone else comes in his own name, you will accept him. 44 How can you believe if you accept praise from one another, yet make no effort to obtain the praise that comes from the only God *b*? *h*

45 "But do not think I will accuse you before the Father. Your accuser is Moses, *i* on whom your hopes are set. *j* 46 If you believed Moses, you would believe me, for

---

a 39 Or *Study diligently* (the imperative)   *b* 44 Some early manuscripts *the Only One*

📖 Jesus made an absolute claim. We live in a world of tolerance—where such "dogmatism" is rejected as divisive or arrogant. We hear, "It's fine to present Jesus as one way to God, but don't call him The Way." Maybe life isn't so different now than in Jesus' day, when people desired to kill him for his claims (v. 18). When and where have you encountered a hostile reaction to a claim of absolute truth? Have you allowed it to curb your enthusiasm for sharing the Good News?

John 5:31–47

📖 People of all times have tended to turn to religious traditions, prophetic leaders, and holy writings for guidance in life—but not necessarily to God himself. Jesus rebuked his listeners for looking for life in all the wrong places. His words were validated by his deeds and signs—all confirming him as the Son of God sent by the Father. Yet still many people wouldn't believe.

📖 Being "religious" isn't the point. Jesus calls us to "come" to him. We naturally apply passages like this one to Judaism and/or the unbelieving world. But aren't there times in our own lives when we fail to evidence love for God but still remain consistently and vigorously religious?

he wrote about me. [k] [47] But since you do not believe what he wrote, how are you going to believe what I say?" [l]

Jesus Feeds the Five Thousand

6 Some time after this, Jesus crossed to the far shore of the Sea of Galilee (that is, the Sea of Tiberias), [2] and a great crowd of people followed him because they saw the miraculous signs [m] he had performed on the sick. [3] Then Jesus went up on a mountainside [n] and sat down with his disciples. [4] The Jewish Passover Feast [o] was near.

[5] When Jesus looked up and saw a great crowd coming toward him, he said to Philip, [p] "Where shall we buy bread for these people to eat?" [6] He asked this only to test him, for he already had in mind what he was going to do.

[7] Philip answered him, "Eight months' wages [a] would not buy enough bread for each one to have a bite!"

[8] Another of his disciples, Andrew, Simon Peter's brother, [q] spoke up, [9] "Here is a boy with five small barley loaves and two small fish, but how far will they go among so many?" [r]

[10] Jesus said, "Have the people sit down." There was plenty of grass in that place, and the men sat down, about five thousand of them. [11] Jesus then took the loaves, gave thanks, [s] and distributed to those who were seated as much as they wanted. He did the same with the fish.

[12] When they had all had enough to eat, he said to his disciples, "Gather the pieces that are left over. Let nothing be wasted." [13] So they gathered them and filled twelve baskets with the pieces of the five barley loaves left over by those who had eaten.

[14] After the people saw the miraculous sign [t] that Jesus did, they began to say, "Surely this is the Prophet who is to come into the world." [u] [15] Jesus, knowing that they intended to come and make him king [v] by force, withdrew again to a mountain by himself. [w]

Jesus Walks on the Water

[16] When evening came, his disciples went down to the lake, [17] where they got into a boat and set off across the lake for Capernaum. By now it was dark, and Jesus had not yet joined them. [18] A strong wind was blowing and the waters grew rough. [19] When they had rowed three or three and a half miles, [b] they saw Jesus approaching the boat, walking on the water; [x] and they were terrified. [20] But he said to them,

[a] 7 Greek *two hundred denarii*   [b] 19 Greek *rowed twenty-five or thirty stadia* (about 5 or 6 kilometers)

Cross references

5:46 [k] Ge 3:15; Lk 24:27, 44; Ac 26:22
5:47 [l] Lk 16:29,31
6:2 [m] Jn 2:11
6:3 [n] ver 15
6:4 [o] Jn 2:13; 11:55
6:5 [p] Jn 1:43
6:8 [q] Jn 1:40
6:9 [r] 2Ki 4:43
6:11 [s] ver 23; Mt 14:19
6:14 [t] Jn 2:11
[u] Dt 18:15,18; Mt 11:3; 21:11
6:15 [v] Jn 18:36
[w] Mt 14:23; Mk 6:46
6:19 [x] Job 9:8

John 6:1–15

Throughout this chapter John dealt with the theme of sustenance, both material and spiritual. The crowd correctly interpreted the miracle of feeding the multitude as Messianic (v. 14). But verse 15 reflects a crass misunderstanding by the same audience: The people wanted to force Jesus to define his mission and work politically—to become a king who would rival the Herodians or the Romans. Jesus wanted no part of such a kingship.

The crowds' physical needs were obvious. Relief and social workers, as well as experienced missionaries and evangelists, know it all too well: If people's basic survival needs go unmet, the pursuit of any other ideal (religious or otherwise) collapses. Jesus recognized the interdependency of physical, social, and spiritual (as well as, in this passage, political) needs. In what ways is your church—and you personally—involved in caring for people as whole persons?

John 6:16–24

As in many Gospel stories, we see here an Old Testament motif: in this case a water miracle reminding us of Moses leading Israel through the sea (Ex. 13–15). When Jesus arrived at the boat, he identified himself with a term sure to evoke for his disciples further images of the Exodus story: "It is I." This phrase reflected God's covenant name—"I AM"—given to Moses at the burning bush (Ex. 3:14).

In combination with his previous miracle of multiplying the loaves and fish, Jesus was acting as God—feeding, protecting, rescuing, and guiding his followers by asserting his authority over the natural calamities surrounding them. Jesus calmed their fear simply by speaking to them. It was only after they recognized his voice that they were willing to take him into the boat. Take a moment to listen for Jesus' voice right now . . . and be ready to recognize and welcome him the next time a storm blows your way.

Sharing Lunch

He was just a kid hanging around the Master. He wasn't even counted in the 5,000.

"The crowd's hungry. Where shall we buy them food?" the Master asked as a test.

"Feeding this many people would cost eight month's wages," replied one disciple, who was good at math.

"I can share my lunch," said the kid who couldn't do the math. "I've got five barley loaves and two fish."

The Master smiled. "That is plenty, son. Thanks."

Then the Master gave thanks to God. And 5,000 men plus uncounted women and children ate their fill. Twelve baskets of leftovers, one for each disciple, reinforced the lesson.

Good things happen when you share your lunch.

The Brazilian pastor sat in the sun in his garden. It was a rare quiet moment. He was reading his Bible and praying. A tapping at the door broke his reverie.

He sat silently, hoping the person would tire and go away. The gentle tapping resumed. Grumpily he walked to the door, opening it with a scowl behind his face. It was a grimy kid with hard eyes. A street kid.

> **Good things happen when you share your lunch.**

"Sir, may I please have a little bread?" The pastor almost said no. And "Go away!" But he couldn't, so he said curtly, "Stay here!"

He went to his kitchen and wrapped a small piece of bread, returned, and handed it to the kid. "Here. Now don't bother me again."

Walking back toward his garden and his Bible, the pastor passed the window and glanced out. There was the boy, carefully dividing the bread into even smaller pieces, sharing them with three younger street kids.

Tears flowing, the pastor invited the children in. Begging for forgiveness, he shared bread, milk, and cheese. He asked their names and listened to their stories. Today in that Brazilian city every street kid knows there's a church and a pastor who will never turn them away.

Good things happen when you share your lunch.

Reviewing a recent bank statement, I noted a declining balance. I directed an angry rant toward my family. "Why can't we get control of our finances? Doesn't anyone realize we aren't made of money?"

The next day we sat at morning devotions. Midway through a short reading, a question and challenge broke through to me: "What did Jesus tell us to pray for when he taught his disciples to pray?"

"Give us this day our daily bread," the text replied. "Did you have breakfast today?" it went on. Yes, of course.

"Did you thank God for answering your prayer?" Oops.

The tirade of the evening before and the convicting questions came together in a rush. No, I hadn't thanked God for our daily bread. Or for a bank balance to worry about. Or a family to talk to.

I had focused on what was absent, not on what was present. I had lost the kingdom perspective. Had Jesus asked me how to feed the crowd, I would have answered just like Philip. Had I been that pastor, I would have wondered what my family would eat if I gave away our bread.

Three immediate applications come to mind: (1) We are called to be aware of what we have and to thank God. (2) In the kingdom good things happen when you share your lunch. (3) We are wise to listen to children (and the nameless and homeless). The Bible says they have important things to say.

Bryant L. Myers, vice president of World Vision International in Monrovia, California

"It is I; don't be afraid."[y] 21Then they were willing to take him into the boat, and
immediately the boat reached the shore where they were heading.
22The next day the crowd that had stayed on the opposite shore of the lake[z] realized that only one boat had been there, and that Jesus had not entered it with his
disciples, but that they had gone away alone.[a] 23Then some boats from Tiberias[b]
landed near the place where the people had eaten the bread after the Lord had giv-
en thanks.[c] 24Once the crowd realized that neither Jesus nor his disciples were there,
they got into the boats and went to Capernaum in search of Jesus.

Jesus the Bread of Life

25When they found him on the other side of the lake, they asked him, "Rabbi,[d]
when did you get here?"
26Jesus answered, "I tell you the truth, you are looking for me,[e] not because you
saw miraculous signs[f] but because you ate the loaves and had your fill. 27Do not
work for food that spoils, but for food that endures[g] to eternal life,[h] which the Son
of Man[i] will give you. On him God the Father has placed his seal[j] of approval."
28Then they asked him, "What must we do to do the works God requires?"
29Jesus answered, "The work of God is this: to believe[k] in the one he has sent."[l]
30So they asked him, "What miraculous sign[m] then will you give that we may see
it and believe you?[n] What will you do? 31Our forefathers ate the manna[o] in the desert; as it is written: 'He gave them bread from heaven to eat.'[a]"[p]
32Jesus said to them, "I tell you the truth, it is not Moses who has given you the
bread from heaven, but it is my Father who gives you the true bread from heaven.
33For the bread of God is he who comes down from heaven[q] and gives life to the
world."
34"Sir," they said, "from now on give us this bread."[r]
35Then Jesus declared, "I am the bread of life.[s] He who comes to me will never go
hungry, and he who believes in me will never be thirsty.[t] 36But as I told you, you have
seen me and still you do not believe. 37All that the Father gives me[u] will come to me,
and whoever comes to me I will never drive away. 38For I have come down from
heaven not to do my will but to do the will of him who sent me.[v] 39And this is the
will of him who sent me, that I shall lose none of all that he has given me,[w] but raise
them up at the last day.[x] 40For my Father's will is that everyone who looks to the Son
and believes in him shall have eternal life,[y] and I will raise him up at the last day."
41At this the Jews began to grumble about him because he said, "I am the bread that
came down from heaven." 42They said, "Is this not Jesus, the son of Joseph,[z] whose
father and mother we know?[a] How can he now say, 'I came down from heaven'?"[b]
43"Stop grumbling among yourselves," Jesus answered. 44"No one can come to
me unless the Father who sent me draws him,[c] and I will raise him up at the last
day. 45It is written in the Prophets: 'They will all be taught by God.'[b][d] Everyone who
listens to the Father and learns from him comes to me. 46No one has seen the Father except the one who is from God;[e] only he has seen the Father. 47I tell you the
truth, he who believes has everlasting life. 48I am the bread of life.[f] 49Your forefathers ate the manna in the desert, yet they died.[g] 50But here is the bread that comes

[a] *31* Exodus 16:4; Neh. 9:15; Psalm 78:24,25 [b] *45* Isaiah 54:13

6:20 [y] Mt 14:27
6:22 [z] ver 2 [a] ver 15-21
6:23 [b] ver 1 [c] ver 11
6:25 [d] Mt 23:7
6:26 [e] ver 24 [f] ver 30; Jn 2:11
6:27 [g] Isa 55:2 [h] ver 54; Mt 25:46; Jn 4:14 [i] Mt 8:20 [j] Ro 4:11; 1Co 9:2; 2Co 1:22; Eph 1:13; 4:30; 2Ti 2:19; Rev 7:3
6:29 [k] 1Jn 3:23 [l] Jn 3:17
6:30 [m] Jn 2:11 [n] Mt 12:38
6:31 [o] Nu 11:7-9 [p] Ex 16:4,15; Ne 9:15; Ps 78:24; 105:40
6:33 [q] ver 50
6:34 [r] Jn 4:15
6:35 [s] ver 48,51 [t] Jn 4:14
6:37 [u] ver 39; Jn 17:2,6,9,24
6:38 [v] Jn 4:34; 5:30
6:39 [w] Jn 10:28; 17:12; 18:9 [x] ver 40,44,54
6:40 [y] Jn 3:15,16
6:42 [z] Lk 4:22 [a] Jn 7:27,28 [b] ver 38,62
6:44 [c] ver 65; Jer 31:3; Jn 12:32
6:45 [d] Isa 54:13; Jer 31:33,34; Heb 8:10,11; 10:16
6:46 [e] Jn 1:18; 5:37; 7:29
6:48 [f] ver 35,51
6:49 [g] ver 31,58

John 6:25–59

The progression of John 6 moves from the physical (bread on a hillside) to the symbolic ("I am the bread of life") to the spiritual ("You must eat my flesh and drink my blood"). In his claim to be "the bread of life," Jesus identified himself with the Passover bread (v. 4), the heavenly manna. Jesus is the "living bread," just as before he had offered "living water" (4:10). In chapter 4 Jesus banished thirst; now he conquered hunger. "I am the bread of life" heads the list of seven "I am" sayings in John. Each of them reveals Jesus' divine identity in a unique way.

We are utterly dependent on food for survival. Uneaten food provides no nourishment. Similarly, Jesus proclaimed that our survival depends totally on him; we are to "eat him" if we are to have life. Our dependency on the life of Jesus inside us is more total than our reliance on food. Living in a consumer society fueled by sophisticated advertising and relative affluence, we have been given the means and motivation to pursue countless forms of "bread" that in the end can never satisfy. What does it mean for you to "eat" Jesus and live because of him?

6:50
h ver 33
6:51
i Heb 10:10
6:52
j Jn 7:43; 9:16;
10:19

6:53
k Mt 8:20
6:54
l ver 39

6:56
m Jn 15:4-7;
1Jn 3:24; 4:15
6:57
n Jn 3:17
6:58
o ver 49-51; Jn 3:36

6:60
p ver 66

6:61
q Mt 11:6
6:62
r Mk 16:19;
Jn 3:13; 17:5
6:63
s 2Co 3:6
6:64
t Jn 2:25
6:65
u ver 37,44
6:66
v ver 60
6:67
w Mt 10:2
6:68
x Mt 16:16
6:69
y Mk 8:29; Lk 9:20
6:70
z Jn 15:16,19
a Jn 13:27

7:1
b Jn 1:19 c Jn 5:18
7:2
d Lev 23:34;
Dt 16:16
7:3
e Mt 12:46

7:5
f Mk 3:21

down from heaven, [h] which a man may eat and not die. [51] I am the living bread that came down from heaven. If anyone eats of this bread, he will live forever. This bread is my flesh, which I will give for the life of the world." [i]

[52] Then the Jews began to argue sharply among themselves, [j] "How can this man give us his flesh to eat?"

[53] Jesus said to them, "I tell you the truth, unless you eat the flesh of the Son of Man [k] and drink his blood, you have no life in you. [54] Whoever eats my flesh and drinks my blood has eternal life, and I will raise him up at the last day. [l] [55] For my flesh is real food and my blood is real drink. [56] Whoever eats my flesh and drinks my blood remains in me, and I in him. [m] [57] Just as the living Father sent me [n] and I live because of the Father, so the one who feeds on me will live because of me. [58] This is the bread that came down from heaven. Your forefathers ate manna and died, but he who feeds on this bread will live forever." [o] [59] He said this while teaching in the synagogue in Capernaum.

Many Disciples Desert Jesus

[60] On hearing it, many of his disciples [p] said, "This is a hard teaching. Who can accept it?"

[61] Aware that his disciples were grumbling about this, Jesus said to them, "Does this offend you? [q] [62] What if you see the Son of Man ascend to where he was before! [r] [63] The Spirit gives life; [s] the flesh counts for nothing. The words I have spoken to you are spirit [a] and they are life. [64] Yet there are some of you who do not believe." For Jesus had known [t] from the beginning which of them did not believe and who would betray him. [65] He went on to say, "This is why I told you that no one can come to me unless the Father has enabled him." [u]

[66] From this time many of his disciples [v] turned back and no longer followed him.

[67] "You do not want to leave too, do you?" Jesus asked the Twelve. [w]

[68] Simon Peter answered him, [x] "Lord, to whom shall we go? You have the words of eternal life. [69] We believe and know that you are the Holy One of God." [y]

[70] Then Jesus replied, "Have I not chosen you, [z] the Twelve? Yet one of you is a devil!" [a] [71] (He meant Judas, the son of Simon Iscariot, who, though one of the Twelve, was later to betray him.)

Jesus Goes to the Feast of Tabernacles

7 After this, Jesus went around in Galilee, purposely staying away from Judea because the Jews [b] there were waiting to take his life. [c] [2] But when the Jewish Feast of Tabernacles [d] was near, [3] Jesus' brothers [e] said to him, "You ought to leave here and go to Judea, so that your disciples may see the miracles you do. [4] No one who wants to become a public figure acts in secret. Since you are doing these things, show yourself to the world." [5] For even his own brothers did not believe in him. [f]

a 63 Or *Spirit*

John 6:60–71

Jesus had just stunned his audience with words about eating his flesh and drinking his blood. His revelation that he himself was the bread from heaven had made the crowds grumble (v. 41), but this new emphasis offended even his own disciples. This difficult teaching sifted the wider group of Jesus' followers. Some fell away and refused to follow him any longer. It's even possible that Judas found this claim part of the driving force behind his own rebellion and betrayal.

Jesus used the most graphic image possible to emphasize that we can't live apart from him. We don't just believe in a savior who remains "outside" of us. Instead, his very life is to be within us. Yet our desire for independence and a merit derived from our own accomplishments is so great that we hold Jesus at a distance.

We believe in him for forgiveness of our failures but don't depend on him for every aspect of our life. Thus for us too, it's easy to find this teaching "difficult." Have you found yourself able to ask, with Peter: "Lord, to whom shall we go? You have the words of eternal life"?

John 7:1–13

About six months had passed between the Passover Feast (6:4) and the Feast of Tabernacles (7:2). Jesus had evidently been avoiding Judea due to the depth of hostility awaiting him there. We hear cynicism in the encouragement of Jesus' brothers for him to attend the autumn festival. They pushed him to assert his Messianic identity in full public view by performing miracles in Jerusalem. Jesus did attend the feast, making his entrance as quiet as possible. Later, at another Passover Feast, he would make a dramatic entry into Jerusalem.

⁶Therefore Jesus told them, "The right time^g for me has not yet come; for you any time is right. ⁷The world cannot hate you, but it hates me^h because I testify that what it does is evil.ⁱ ⁸You go to the Feast. I am not yet^a going up to this Feast, because for me the right time^j has not yet come." ⁹Having said this, he stayed in Galilee.

¹⁰However, after his brothers had left for the Feast, he went also, not publicly, but in secret. ¹¹Now at the Feast the Jews were watching for him^k and asking, "Where is that man?"

¹²Among the crowds there was widespread whispering about him. Some said, "He is a good man."

Others replied, "No, he deceives the people."^l ¹³But no one would say anything publicly about him for fear of the Jews.^m

Jesus Teaches at the Feast

¹⁴Not until halfway through the Feast did Jesus go up to the temple courts and begin to teach.ⁿ ¹⁵The Jews^o were amazed and asked, "How did this man get such learning^p without having studied?"^q

¹⁶Jesus answered, "My teaching is not my own. It comes from him who sent me.^r ¹⁷If anyone chooses to do God's will, he will find out^s whether my teaching comes from God or whether I speak on my own. ¹⁸He who speaks on his own does so to gain honor for himself,^t but he who works for the honor of the one who sent him is a man of truth; there is nothing false about him. ¹⁹Has not Moses given you the law? Yet not one of you keeps the law. Why are you trying to kill me?"^v

²⁰"You are demon-possessed,"^w the crowd answered. "Who is trying to kill you?"

²¹Jesus said to them, "I did one miracle, and you are all astonished. ²²Yet, because Moses gave you circumcision^x (though actually it did not come from Moses, but from the patriarchs),^y you circumcise a child on the Sabbath. ²³Now if a child can be circumcised on the Sabbath so that the law of Moses may not be broken, why are you angry with me for healing the whole man on the Sabbath? ²⁴Stop judging by mere appearances, and make a right judgment."^z

Is Jesus the Christ?

²⁵At that point some of the people of Jerusalem began to ask, "Isn't this the man they are trying to kill? ²⁶Here he is, speaking publicly, and they are not saying a

---

^a 8 Some early manuscripts do not have *yet*.

Cross references

7:6 — g Mt 26:18
7:7 — h Jn 15:18,19; i Jn 3:19,20
7:8 — j ver 6
7:11 — k Jn 11:56
7:12 — l ver 40,43
7:13 — m Jn 9:22; 12:42; 19:38
7:14 — n ver 28; Mt 26:55
7:15 — o Jn 1:19; p Ac 26:24; q Mt 13:54
7:16 — r Jn 3:11; 14:24
7:17 — s Ps 25:14; Jn 8:43
7:18 — t Jn 5:41; 8:50,54
7:19 — u Jn 1:17 v ver 1; Mt 12:14
7:20 — w Jn 8:48; 10:20
7:22 — x Lev 12:3; y Ge 17:10-14
7:24 — z Isa 11:3,4; Jn 8:15

📖 Even people who love us sometimes don't believe in us or in God's call on our lives. Have you experienced this? Opposing such a lack of trust takes enormous courage on our part, especially if, like Moses, we lack confidence in our ability to do the job (Ex. 3:11–14). Here Jesus knew he had to listen to the voice of his heavenly Father, not his earthly brothers. Do you get distracted from the course by others' influence (cf. Rom. 12:2)? How easy is it for you to resist even family pressure to follow what your heart tells you is God's intention for you?

John 7:14–24

📖 The debate of John 5 still dominated Jesus' interaction with these authorities. In this scene, they wanted to know where he had gone to school. Educational standards for rabbis were well established by Jesus' day. Advanced study under a rabbinic scholar was common (cf. Paul with Gamaliel in Acts 22:3). Jesus possessed no such credentials. Moreover, his authority stemmed directly from God. He was authorized to speak as he did because he bore the words of God, not religious tradition.

Jesus stressed the interdependence of obeying and knowing (v. 17): We know the truth by doing the truth.

📖 There was consistency between Jesus' words and his deeds, and so it must be for us. Our faith in Jesus will be expressed in obedience to his Word. Teaching and preaching do more than give us true ideas. The gospel isn't just "good views" but Good News. By the Spirit God emboldens us to live new lives. When we do, and we live differently from the prevailing norm, we shouldn't be surprised by opposition. Even the Son of God was accused of being demonic!

John 7:25–44

📖 The celebration of the Feast of Tabernacles included a daily procession from the temple to the Pool of Siloam. There a priest drew water that was then returned and poured out as an offering at the altar, accompanied by a recitation of Isaiah 12:3. On the final day of celebration, Jesus stepped into public view and made a startling pronouncement: "If anyone is thirsty, let him come to me and drink." Jesus fueled his antagonists' anger by offering himself as the source of "living water." Rather than promoting a religious experience with God that highlighted obedience to law, he offered the gift of intimacy with God that would lead to new life.

7:26
a ver 48
7:27
b Mt 13:55; Lk 4:22
7:28
c ver 14 *d* Jn 8:14
e Jn 8:26,42
7:29
f Mt 11:27
7:30
g ver 32,44;
Jn 10:39
7:31
h Jn 8:30 *i* Jn 2:11
7:33
j Jn 13:33; 16:16
k Jn 16:5,10,17,28
7:34
l Jn 8:21; 13:33
7:35
m Jas 1:1
n Jn 12:20; 1Pe 1:1
7:37
o Lev 23:36
p Isa 55:1;
Rev 22:17
7:38
q Isa 58:11
r Jn 4:10 *s* Jn 4:14
7:39
t Joel 2:28;
Ac 2:17,33
u Jn 20:22
v Jn 12:23;
13:31,32
7:40
w Mt 21:11; Jn 1:21
7:41
x ver 52; Jn 1:46
7:42
y Mt 1:1 *z* Mic 5:2;
Mt 2:5,6; Lk 2:4
7:43
a Jn 9:16; 10:19
7:44
b ver 30
7:46
c Mt 7:28
7:47
d ver 12
7:48
e Jn 12:42
7:50
f Jn 3:1; 19:39

word to him. Have the authorities *a* really concluded that he is the Christ *a*? 27But we know where this man is from; *b* when the Christ comes, no one will know where he is from."

28Then Jesus, still teaching in the temple courts, *c* cried out, "Yes, you know me, and you know where I am from. *d* I am not here on my own, but he who sent me is true. *e* You do not know him, 29but I know him *f* because I am from him and he sent me."

30At this they tried to seize him, but no one laid a hand on him, *g* because his time had not yet come. 31Still, many in the crowd put their faith in him. *h* They said, "When the Christ comes, will he do more miraculous signs *i* than this man?"

32The Pharisees heard the crowd whispering such things about him. Then the chief priests and the Pharisees sent temple guards to arrest him.

33Jesus said, "I am with you for only a short time, *j* and then I go to the one who sent me. *k* 34You will look for me, but you will not find me; and where I am, you cannot come." *l*

35The Jews said to one another, "Where does this man intend to go that we cannot find him? Will he go where our people live scattered *m* among the Greeks, *n* and teach the Greeks? 36What did he mean when he said, 'You will look for me, but you will not find me,' and 'Where I am, you cannot come'?"

37On the last and greatest day of the Feast, *o* Jesus stood and said in a loud voice, "If anyone is thirsty, let him come to me and drink. *p* 38Whoever believes in me, as *b* the Scripture has said, *q* streams of living water *r* will flow from within him." *s* 39By this he meant the Spirit, *t* whom those who believed in him were later to receive. *u* Up to that time the Spirit had not been given, since Jesus had not yet been glorified. *v*

40On hearing his words, some of the people said, "Surely this man is the Prophet." *w*

41Others said, "He is the Christ."

Still others asked, "How can the Christ come from Galilee? *x* 42Does not the Scripture say that the Christ will come from David's family *c y* and from Bethlehem, *z* the town where David lived?" 43Thus the people were divided *a* because of Jesus. 44Some wanted to seize him, but no one laid a hand on him. *b*

Unbelief of the Jewish Leaders

45Finally the temple guards went back to the chief priests and Pharisees, who asked them, "Why didn't you bring him in?"

46"No one ever spoke the way this man does," *c* the guards declared.

47"You mean he has deceived you also?" *d* the Pharisees retorted. 48"Has any of the rulers or of the Pharisees believed in him? *e* 49No! But this mob that knows nothing of the law—there is a curse on them."

50Nicodemus, *f* who had gone to Jesus earlier and who was one of their own num-

---

a 26 Or *Messiah*; also in verses 27, 31, 41 and 42   *b* 37,38 Or / *If anyone is thirsty, let him come to me.
/ And let him drink,* 38*who believes in me. / As*   *c* 42 Greek *seed*

📖 Isaiah portrayed the promise of the Spirit as water poured out on dry ground (Isa. 44:3; 55:1; 58:11). In a desert environment, water is as precious as life. We too need this precious commodity every day. What does it mean for you to drink from Jesus on a daily basis? How have you experienced the Spirit nourishing and refreshing you?

John 7:45—7:52

🔗 The temple police were impressed with Jesus to such a degree that they failed in their assignment to arrest him. But Jesus' opponents were adamant. Their contempt for the masses was well established. They refused to consider the common people truly pious. After all, such ignorant individuals couldn't possibly keep the law. The irony was that these were the very people who seemed to understand Jesus' true identity. Nicodemus, a Pharisee (cf. John 3:1–21), did speak up in Jesus' defense, urging caution.

📖 Throughout history people have sought to acclaim Jesus as a "good moral teacher" but have disregarded his claim to be the Son of God. John didn't leave us with that option. Jesus was indeed the best teacher ever. But his teaching was rejected as offensive—not simply affirmed as "good." In our desire to be accepted by others, and to have the Good News appear as attractive to them as possible, we may be tempted to "water down" the gospel. How would you summarize what the Pharisees found to be so offensive in Jesus' life and teaching at this point?

ber, asked, 51 "Does our law condemn anyone without first hearing him to find out what he is doing?"

52They replied, "Are you from Galilee, too? Look into it, and you will find that a prophet*a* does not come out of Galilee." *g*

7:52
g ver 41

[The earliest manuscripts and many other ancient witnesses do not have John 7:53—8:11.]

53Then each went to his own home.

8 But Jesus went to the Mount of Olives. *h* 2At dawn he appeared again in the temple courts, where all the people gathered around him, and he sat down to teach them. *i* 3The teachers of the law and the Pharisees brought in a woman caught in adultery. They made her stand before the group 4and said to Jesus, "Teacher, this woman was caught in the act of adultery. 5In the Law Moses commanded us to stone such women. *j* Now what do you say?" 6They were using this question as a trap, *k* in order to have a basis for accusing him. *l*

But Jesus bent down and started to write on the ground with his finger. 7When they kept on questioning him, he straightened up and said to them, "If any one of

8:1
h Mt 21:1
8:2
i ver 20; Mt 26:55

8:5
j Lev 20:10;
Dt 22:22
8:6
k Mt 22:15,18
l Mt 12:10

a 52 Two early manuscripts *the Prophet*

John 7:53—8:11

Evidence seems to indicate that this story was an independent account that circulated freely for some time and was only later placed here in John's Gospel. One way or another, this woman's portrait is powerful. Having been caught in the act of adultery, she was completely vulnerable—encircled by hostile men willing to stone her through their unyielding commitment to the law. The hypocrisy of the times was expressed in their violent condemnation of the woman, with no mention of the man involved. Certainly, she must have thought, this rabbi named Jesus would know and uphold the law. Instead, his mercy set her free in a manner she could never have expected.

Are you troubled that the Pharisees opted not to drag a woman *and a man* before Jesus? Sexual sins still today evoke a strong religious reaction, and this story probes our reflexes toward people who don't fit our religious expectations. Jesus wasn't committed simply to the requirements of the law, but to the care and transformation of the woman—and to every person who brings a debt of sin before him. As we encounter his amazing love and mercy through this story, he confronts any tendency in us toward self-righteous judgment of others. What does it mean for us not to throw stones but to encourage one another "to sin no more"?

8:1–11

Forgiveness

Jesus forgave the adulterous woman. And he told us to forgive repeatedly, "seventy-seven times" for the same offense if necessary (Matt. 18:22)—an answer in the spirit of "to infinity." What isn't/is Biblical forgiveness?

Forgiving *isn't*:

Pardoning:	Condoning:	Excusing:	Forgetting:	Denying:
This is a legal concept. Few of us have this power anyway.	Means justifying the offense. Wrong is wrong, even if the motive seems justifiable or some good comes of it.	Implies that the offender was helpless to do otherwise ("The Devil made me do it" mentality).	Usually impossible anyway.	A weak-minded, unhealthy reaction.

Forgiving *is*:

A change of attitude toward the offending person from negative to positive (Matt. 7:1–5).	A disposition that makes this kind of attitude change typical of our behavior, not unusual (Mark 12:30).	A characteristic of the church. Christ's united body should be a merciful social unit, where no one condemns (John 8:10–12). After all, each of us is a forgiven sinner.	An acknowledgement of all God has done for us (Matt. 6:12,14–15; 18:21–35).

8:7
m Dt 17:7
n Ro 2:1,22

you is without sin, let him be the first to throw a stone[m] at her."[n] 8Again he stooped down and wrote on the ground.

9At this, those who heard began to go away one at a time, the older ones first, until only Jesus was left, with the woman still standing there. 10Jesus straightened up and asked her, "Woman, where are they? Has no one condemned you?"

11"No one, sir," she said.

8:11
o Jn 3:17 p Jn 5:14

"Then neither do I condemn you,"[o] Jesus declared. "Go now and leave your life of sin."[p]

The Validity of Jesus' Testimony

8:12
q Jn 6:35 r Jn 1:4;
12:35 s Pr 4:18;
Mt 5:14

12When Jesus spoke again to the people, he said, "I am[q] the light of the world.[r] Whoever follows me will never walk in darkness, but will have the light of life."[s]

8:13
t Jn 5:31

13The Pharisees challenged him, "Here you are, appearing as your own witness; your testimony is not valid."[t]

8:14
u Jn 13:3; 16:28
v Jn 7:28; 9:29
8:15
w Jn 7:24 x Jn 3:17

14Jesus answered, "Even if I testify on my own behalf, my testimony is valid, for I know where I came from and where I am going.[u] But you have no idea where I come from[v] or where I am going. 15You judge by human standards;[w] I pass judgment on no one.[x] 16But if I do judge, my decisions are right, because I am not alone.

8:16
y Jn 5:30
8:17
z Dt 17:6; Mt 18:16
8:18
a Jn 5:37
8:19
b Jn 16:3 c Jn 14:7;
1Jn 2:23
8:20
d Mt 26:55
e Mk 12:41
f Mt 26:18; Jn 7:30

I stand with the Father, who sent me.[y] 17In your own Law it is written that the testimony of two men is valid.[z] 18I am one who testifies for myself; my other witness is the Father, who sent me."[a]

19Then they asked him, "Where is your father?"

"You do not know me or my Father,"[b] Jesus replied. "If you knew me, you would know my Father also."[c] 20He spoke these words while teaching[d] in the temple area near the place where the offerings were put.[e] Yet no one seized him, because his time had not yet come.[f]

8:21
g Eze 3:18
h Jn 7:34; 13:33

21Once more Jesus said to them, "I am going away, and you will look for me, and you will die[g] in your sin. Where I go, you cannot come."[h]

22This made the Jews ask, "Will he kill himself? Is that why he says, 'Where I go, you cannot come'?"

8:23
i Jn 3:31; 17:14
8:24
j Jn 4:26; 13:19

23But he continued, "You are from below; I am from above. You are of this world; I am not of this world.[i] 24I told you that you would die in your sins; if you do not believe that I am ⌊the one I claim to be⌋,[a][j] you will indeed die in your sins."

25"Who are you?" they asked.

8:26
k Jn 7:28 l Jn 3:32;
15:15

"Just what I have been claiming all along," Jesus replied. 26"I have much to say in judgment of you. But he who sent me is reliable,[k] and what I have heard from him I tell the world."[l]

8:28
m Jn 3:14; 5:19;
12:32

27They did not understand that he was telling them about his Father. 28So Jesus said, "When you have lifted up the Son of Man,[m] then you will know that I am ⌊the one I claim to be⌋ and that I do nothing on my own but speak just what the Father

8:29
n ver 16; Jn 16:32
o Jn 4:34; 5:30;
6:38
8:30
p Jn 7:31

has taught me. 29The one who sent me is with me; he has not left me alone,[n] for I always do what pleases him."[o] 30Even as he spoke, many put their faith in him.[p]

a 24 Or I am he; also in verse 28

John 8:12–30

Jesus was still at the Feast of Tabernacles, which was characterized by multiple themes. Harvest, drought, the coming winter darkness, and the desert wandering after the exodus all merged in spectacular ceremonies. Four stands, each holding four golden bowls, were placed in the heavily used court of women. These large bowls were filled with oil and lit during the feast. On this final day of Tabernacles, Jesus was teaching in the treasury located within the court of women. Imagine the scene as he stood beneath 16 lit bowls of oil, identifying himself as the true light not just of

Jerusalem, but of the whole world!

Since in John's Gospel Jesus is portrayed as the embodiment of God's presence in the world, it's not surprising that "light" is used 16 times to describe his work. John's letters continue this theme. Walking "in the light" is a description of discipleship (1 Jn. 1:7). Throughout Scripture, light is an image of illumination—of spiritual awareness and understanding. But most importantly, light characterizes Jesus. *He* is the light of the world. Are you drawn not only to the knowledge and direction Jesus provides, but to Christ himself as the source of that light?

The Children of Abraham

31To the Jews who had believed him, Jesus said, "If you hold to my teaching,[q] you are really my disciples. **32**Then you will know the truth, and the truth will set you free."[r]

33They answered him, "We are Abraham's descendants[a][s] and have never been slaves of anyone. How can you say that we shall be set free?"

34Jesus replied, "I tell you the truth, everyone who sins is a slave to sin.[t] **35**Now a slave has no permanent place in the family, but a son belongs to it forever.[u] **36**So if the Son sets you free, you will be free indeed. **37**I know you are Abraham's descendants. Yet you are ready to kill me,[v] because you have no room for my word. **38**I am telling you what I have seen in the Father's presence,[w] and you do what you have heard from your father.[b]"

39"Abraham is our father," they answered.

"If you were Abraham's children,"[x] said Jesus, "then you would[c] do the things Abraham did. **40**As it is, you are determined to kill me, a man who has told you the truth that I heard from God.[y] Abraham did not do such things. **41**You are doing the things your own father does."[z]

"We are not illegitimate children," they protested. "The only Father we have is God himself."[a]

The Children of the Devil

42Jesus said to them, "If God were your Father, you would love me,[b] for I came from God[c] and now am here. I have not come on my own;[d] but he sent me.[e] **43**Why is my language not clear to you? Because you are unable to hear what I say. **44**You belong to your father, the devil,[f] and you want to carry out your father's desire.[g] He was a murderer from the beginning, not holding to the truth, for there is no truth in him. When he lies, he speaks his native language, for he is a liar and the father of lies.[h] **45**Yet because I tell the truth,[i] you do not believe me! **46**Can any of you prove me guilty of sin? If I am telling the truth, why don't you believe me? **47**He who belongs to God hears what God says.[j] The reason you do not hear is that you do not belong to God."

The Claims of Jesus About Himself

48The Jews answered him, "Aren't we right in saying that you are a Samaritan[k] and demon-possessed?"[l]

49"I am not possessed by a demon," said Jesus, "but I honor my Father and you

---

8:31	q Jn 15:7; 2Jn 9
8:32	r Ro 8:2; Jas 2:12
8:33	s ver 37,39; Mt 3:9
8:34	t Ro 6:16; 2Pe 2:19
8:35	u Gal 4:30
8:37	v ver 39,40
8:38	w Jn 5:19,30; 14:10,24
8:39	x ver 37; Ro 9:7; Gal 3:7
8:40	y ver 26
8:41	z ver 38,44; a Isa 63:16; 64:8
8:42	b 1Jn 5:1; c Jn 16:27; 17:8 d Jn 7:28 e Jn 3:17
8:44	f 1Jn 3:8 g ver 38, 41 h Ge 3:4
8:45	i Jn 18:37
8:47	j Jn 18:37; 1Jn 4:6
8:48	k Mt 10:5 l ver 52; Jn 7:20

---

[a] 33 Greek *seed*; also in verse 37   [b] 38 Or *presence. Therefore do what you have heard from the Father.*
[c] 39 Some early manuscripts *"If you are Abraham's children," said Jesus, "then*

John 8:31–41

Jesus acknowledged that his listeners bore the bloodline of Abraham, but their attitude betrayed that their lives weren't guided by the Father. Blood ancestry doesn't guarantee spiritual lineage. Paul later made the same point (Gal. 4:21–31). True "Jewishness" was an inner reality (Rom. 2:28–29). The unrighteousness of the Jewish religious leaders placed in question their claim to possess any link to Abraham. Jesus implied that their activity pointed to another spiritual father!

Jesus' opponents claimed that their ancestry (historical and spiritual) had a direct bearing on their standing before God. After all, they possessed the traditions, heritage, temple, Scripture, and institutions. This temptation is timeless, affecting us as well. To what extent can our traditions become impediments to our hearing God's voice? To what degree do you rely on your religious heritage? Have you ever used it to insulate yourself from a prophetic word from God or from his work in the world today?

John 8:42–47

Jesus clearly described his own identity—as One sent by his Father. He contrasted this with the devil, whose power is manifested through deception and lies. What finally divided Jesus from the religious leaders was his ultimate claim about himself—this seemingly outrageous and unacceptable claim to unity with the Father.

It's a troubling question, but one to face squarely. If Jesus himself were to step into our century, stride into your church, pick up a religious symbol (as he did at the Feast of Tabernacles), and challenge its original meaning, would you bristle? Are there religious practices over which we fight and disagree in and between our churches? The devil works to keep us divided over Jesus and fighting over religious practice.

dishonor me. 50 I am not seeking glory for myself;[m] but there is one who seeks it,
and he is the judge. 51 I tell you the truth, if anyone keeps my word, he will never
see death."[n]
52 At this the Jews exclaimed, "Now we know that you are demon-possessed!
Abraham died and so did the prophets, yet you say that if anyone keeps your word,
he will never taste death. 53 Are you greater than our father Abraham?[o] He died, and
so did the prophets. Who do you think you are?"
54 Jesus replied, "If I glorify myself,[p] my glory means nothing. My Father, whom
you claim as your God, is the one who glorifies me.[q] 55 Though you do not know
him,[r] I know him.[s] If I said I did not, I would be a liar like you, but I do know him
and keep his word.[t] 56 Your father Abraham[u] rejoiced at the thought of seeing my
day; he saw it[v] and was glad."
57 "You are not yet fifty years old," the Jews said to him, "and you have seen Abraham!"
58 "I tell you the truth," Jesus answered, "before Abraham was born,[w] I am!"[x] 59 At
this, they picked up stones to stone him,[y] but Jesus hid himself,[z] slipping away
from the temple grounds.

Jesus Heals a Man Born Blind

9 As he went along, he saw a man blind from birth. 2 His disciples asked him,
"Rabbi,[a] who sinned,[b] this man[c] or his parents,[d] that he was born blind?"
3 "Neither this man nor his parents sinned," said Jesus, "but this happened so that
the work of God might be displayed in his life.[e] 4 As long as it is day,[f] we must do
the work of him who sent me. Night is coming, when no one can work. 5 While I
am in the world, I am the light of the world."[g]
6 Having said this, he spit[h] on the ground, made some mud with the saliva, and
put it on the man's eyes. 7 "Go," he told him, "wash in the Pool of Siloam"[i] (this
word means Sent). So the man went and washed, and came home seeing.[j]
8 His neighbors and those who had formerly seen him begging asked, "Isn't this
the same man who used to sit and beg?"[k] 9 Some claimed that he was.
Others said, "No, he only looks like him."
But he himself insisted, "I am the man."
10 "How then were your eyes opened?" they demanded.

8:50 [m] ver 54; Jn 5:41
8:51 [n] Jn 11:26
8:53 [o] Jn 4:12
8:54 [p] ver 50 [q] Jn 16:14; 17:1,5
8:55 [r] ver 19 [s] Jn 7:28, 29 [t] Jn 15:10
8:56 [u] ver 37,39 [v] Mt 13:17; Heb 11:13
8:58 [w] Jn 1:2; 17:5,24 [x] Ex 3:14
8:59 [y] Lev 24:16; Jn 10:31; 11:8 [z] Jn 12:36
9:2 [a] Mt 23:7 [b] ver 34; Lk 13:2; Ac 28:4 [c] Eze 18:20 [d] Ex 20:5; Job 21:19
9:3 [e] Jn 11:4
9:4 [f] Jn 11:9; 12:35
9:5 [g] Jn 1:4; 8:12; 12:46
9:6 [h] Mk 7:33; 8:23
9:7 [i] ver 11; 2Ki 5:10; Lk 13:4 [j] Isa 35:5; Jn 11:37
9:8 [k] Ac 3:2,10

John 8:48–59

The chapter climaxes at verse 58. Jesus made an absolute claim to preexistence, anchored in the "I am" language that characterizes John's Gospel. In this context "I am" has no object (as in "I am the light of the world"; 8:12). The two little words stand alone, clearly echoing the revelation of God's divine name in Exodus 3:14. To exist before Abraham's birth—and yet to stand there now before them—was Jesus' boldest claim to date. It recalled John's affirmation in 1:1–2 that the Word existed before the beginning of time.

There is something ultimate and final about Jesus' claims in this chapter: "I am the light of the world." "If the Son sets you free, you will be free indeed." "If anyone keeps my word, he will never see death." "Before Abraham was born, I am!" "Jesus" can't be an optional experience, an add-on to a religious system. He's the light, life, and the freedom everyone seeks. He's not just the bearer of these things—he *is* them. To embrace him, believe in him, and follow him mean that we acquire these qualities ourselves by being "in him." What do this light, life, and freedom mean to you, not just in theory, but in your day-to-day living?

John 9:1–12

Products of their time, Jesus' disciples assumed a cause-and-effect connection between sin and suffering (v. 34). So they probed the matter of who was responsible for this man having been born blind. The rabbis taught, based on Exodus 34:7, that if a person suffered from a physical ailment it must have been (1) because the individual's parents or grandparents had committed some sin or (2) because the sick person had sinned before birth. Jesus rejected this line of reasoning. He viewed this man's plight as an opportunity to do God's work.

When adversity strikes, we often try to attribute blame—someone's sin? God's will? Jesus circumvented the "why" question, in effect stating simply, "God wants to redeem the suffering and cause good to come out of it." Rather than being a barrier between us, one another, and God, suffering can become a bridge. Instead of casting us into darkness, it can draw us and other hurting people to the Light of the world. How have you seen God redeem suffering, turning darkness into light and bringing goodness out of evil? How does this impact your attitude toward suffering itself?

[11]He replied, "The man they call Jesus made some mud and put it on my eyes. He told me to go to Siloam and wash. So I went and washed, and then I could see."[l]

[12]"Where is this man?" they asked him.

"I don't know," he said.

The Pharisees Investigate the Healing

[13]They brought to the Pharisees the man who had been blind. [14]Now the day on which Jesus had made the mud and opened the man's eyes was a Sabbath.[m] [15]Therefore the Pharisees also asked him how he had received his sight.[n] "He put mud on my eyes," the man replied, "and I washed, and now I see."

[16]Some of the Pharisees said, "This man is not from God, for he does not keep the Sabbath."[o]

But others asked, "How can a sinner do such miraculous signs?" So they were divided.[p]

[17]Finally they turned again to the blind man, "What have you to say about him? It was your eyes he opened."

The man replied, "He is a prophet."[q]

[18]The Jews[r] still did not believe that he had been blind and had received his sight until they sent for the man's parents. [19]"Is this your son?" they asked. "Is this the one you say was born blind? How is it that now he can see?"

[20]"We know he is our son," the parents answered, "and we know he was born blind. [21]But how he can see now, or who opened his eyes, we don't know. Ask him. He is of age; he will speak for himself." [22]His parents said this because they were afraid of the Jews,[s] for already the Jews had decided that anyone who acknowledged that Jesus was the Christ[a] would be put out[t] of the synagogue.[u] [23]That was why his parents said, "He is of age; ask him."[v]

[24]A second time they summoned the man who had been blind. "Give glory to God,[b][w] they said. "We know this man is a sinner."[x]

[25]He replied, "Whether he is a sinner or not, I don't know. One thing I do know. I was blind but now I see!"

[26]Then they asked him, "What did he do to you? How did he open your eyes?"

[27]He answered, "I have told you already[y] and you did not listen. Why do you want to hear it again? Do you want to become his disciples, too?"

[28]Then they hurled insults at him and said, "You are this fellow's disciple! We are disciples of Moses![z] [29]We know that God spoke to Moses, but as for this fellow, we don't even know where he comes from."[a]

[30]The man answered, "Now that is remarkable! You don't know where he comes from, yet he opened my eyes. [31]We know that God does not listen to sinners. He listens to the godly man who does his will.[b] [32]Nobody has ever heard of opening the eyes of a man born blind. [33]If this man were not from God,[c] he could do nothing."

[34]To this they replied, "You were steeped in sin at birth;[d] how dare you lecture us!" And they threw him out.[e]

---

[a] 22 Or *Messiah*   [b] 24 A solemn charge to tell the truth (see Joshua 7:19)

Cross references (right margin):

9:11
[l] ver 7

9:14
[m] Jn 5:9
9:15
[n] ver 10

9:16
[o] Mt 12:2 [p] Jn 6:52; 7:43; 10:19

9:17
[q] Mt 21:11
9:18
[r] Jn 1:19

9:22
[s] Jn 7:13 [t] ver 34; Lk 6:22 [u] Jn 12:42; 16:2
9:23
[v] ver 21

9:24
[w] Jos 7:19 [x] ver 16

9:27
[y] ver 15

9:28
[z] Jn 5:45
9:29
[a] Jn 8:14

9:31
[b] Ge 18:23-32; Ps 34:15,16; 66:18; 145:19,20; Pr 15:29; Isa 1:15; 59:1,2; Jn 15:7; Jas 5:16-18; 1Jn 5:14,15
9:33
[c] ver 16; Jn 3:2
9:34
[d] ver.2 [e] ver 22,35; Isa 66:5

John 9:13–34

John presented four scenes in which questions were launched about the man and his healing. (1) First the neighbors investigated the event. They didn't reject the miracle but looked to the Pharisees, the established theological leaders, for answers. (2) The Pharisees questioned the man about the healing, but their chief concern was about a Sabbath violation. (3) The Pharisees turned to the man's parents to confirm that a miracle had indeed occurred. (4) The leaders questioned the man a second time. Sparks flew between the previously blind man (who supported Jesus) and the leaders (who didn't).

The cycle of interrogation ended with the formerly blind man experiencing the very thing his parents had feared: expulsion from the synagogue. John's Gospel leaves no doubt: Embracing Christ in faith has consequences: in some cases social isolation, punishment, even martyrdom. How might you have reacted if you had been this man or someone in his family? Would you have responded as he did—courageously holding to what you couldn't deny and suffering persecution as a result? Or would you have reacted like his parents—refusing to risk rejection, choosing not to "get involved"?

Spiritual Blindness

35 Jesus heard that they had thrown him out, and when he found him, he said, "Do you believe in the Son of Man?"

36 "Who is he, sir?" the man asked. "Tell me so that I may believe in him." *f*

37 Jesus said, "You have now seen him; in fact, he is the one speaking with you." *g*

38 Then the man said, "Lord, I believe," and he worshiped him. *h*

39 Jesus said, "For judgment *i* I have come into this world, *j* so that the blind will see *k* and those who see will become blind." *l*

40 Some Pharisees who were with him heard him say this and asked, "What? Are we blind too?" *m*

41 Jesus said, "If you were blind, you would not be guilty of sin; but now that you claim you can see, your guilt remains. *n*

The Shepherd and His Flock

10 "I tell you the truth, the man who does not enter the sheep pen by the gate, but climbs in by some other way, is a thief and a robber. 2 The man who enters by the gate is the shepherd of his sheep. *o* 3 The watchman opens the gate for him, and the sheep listen to his voice. *p* He calls his own sheep by name and leads them out. 4 When he has brought out all his own, he goes on ahead of them, and his sheep follow him because they know his voice. 5 But they will never follow a stranger; in fact, they will run away from him because they do not recognize a stranger's voice." 6 Jesus used this figure of speech, *q* but they did not understand what he was telling them.

7 Therefore Jesus said again, "I tell you the truth, I am the gate for the sheep. 8 All who ever came before me *r* were thieves and robbers, but the sheep did not listen to them. 9 I am the gate; whoever enters through me will be saved. *a* He will come in and go out, and find pasture. 10 The thief comes only to steal and kill and destroy; I have come that they may have life, and have it to the full.

11 "I am the good shepherd. *s* The good shepherd lays down his life for the sheep. *t* 12 The hired hand is not the shepherd who owns the sheep. So when he sees the wolf coming, he abandons the sheep and runs away. *u* Then the wolf attacks the flock and scatters it. 13 The man runs away because he is a hired hand and cares nothing for the sheep.

14 "I am the good shepherd; *v* I know my sheep *w* and my sheep know me— 15 just

Cross references

9:36
f Ro 10:14
9:37
g Jn 4:26
9:38
h Mt 28:9
9:39
i Jn 5:22 *j* Jn 3:19
k Lk 4:18 *l* Mt 13:13
9:40
m Ro 2:19
9:41
n Jn 15:22,24

10:2
o ver 11,14
10:3
p ver 4,5,14,16,27

10:6
q Jn 16:25

10:8
r Jer 23:1,2

10:11
s ver 14; Isa 40:11;
Eze 34:11-16,23;
Heb 13:20; 1Pe 5:4;
Rev 7:17 *t* Jn 15:13;
1Jn 3:16
10:12
u Zec 11:16,17
10:14
v ver 11 *w* ver 27

a 9 Or kept safe

John 9:35–41

📖 John 9 is a case study and magnificent summary of Jesus' message, beginning with his declaration in 8:12: "I am the light of the world. Whoever follows me will never walk in darkness, but will have the light of life." A man who had lived in darkness was miraculously given light. Physical healing had become a symbol for spiritual healing. But Jesus' opponents were immobilized by spiritual blindness. A striking reversal had occurred: The previously blind man had light and sight, while those arrayed against him groped in spiritual darkness.

📖 John 9 gives us all we need to properly identify Jesus. As the story progresses, the formerly blind man's understanding of Jesus moved forward as well. He went from describing his healer as the man Jesus (v. 11), to a prophet (v. 17), to one to be followed (v. 27), to one "from God" (v. 33), to the Lord who is worthy of worship (v. 38). How has your increasing knowledge of Jesus transformed your worship of him?

John 10:1–21

📖 People in Jesus' day were familiar with shepherds, both literally and as a metaphor for caretakers of God's people. It's important not to sentimentalize the image of the "good shepherd." This isn't just a portrait of a kindly man holding cuddly lambs. The shepherd's job was exhausting and hazardous. The most important feature of Jesus' role as shepherd is his willingness to die for his sheep, a repeated point in this passage.

📖 Jesus continued his confrontation with the religious leaders by contrasting them (and their desire to rob life from people) with himself, the shepherd who dies that the flock might have abundant life. He portrayed an intimate relationship between sheep and their shepherd: They recognize his voice and come running when he calls. The model for this closeness is the reciprocal love shared between the Son and the Father. Jesus' profound relationship with God models the intimacy he seeks with us, his followers (cf. 17:21). Take a moment to thank Jesus, the Good Shepherd, for laying down his life for you that you might experience life in all its fullness. Then listen for his voice. Do you unquestioningly follow him anywhere he leads?

as the Father knows me and I know the Father[x]—and I lay down my life for the sheep. [16]I have other sheep[y] that are not of this sheep pen. I must bring them also. They too will listen to my voice, and there shall be one flock[z] and one shepherd.[a] [17]The reason my Father loves me is that I lay down my life[b]—only to take it up again. [18]No one takes it from me, but I lay it down of my own accord.[c] I have authority to lay it down and authority to take it up again. This command I received from my Father."[d]

[19]At these words the Jews were again divided.[e] [20]Many of them said, "He is demon-possessed[f] and raving mad.[g] Why listen to him?"

[21]But others said, "These are not the sayings of a man possessed by a demon.[h] Can a demon open the eyes of the blind?"[i]

The Unbelief of the Jews

[22]Then came the Feast of Dedication[a] at Jerusalem. It was winter, [23]and Jesus was in the temple area walking in Solomon's Colonnade.[j] [24]The Jews[k] gathered around him, saying, "How long will you keep us in suspense? If you are the Christ,[b] tell us plainly."[l]

[25]Jesus answered, "I did tell you,[m] but you do not believe. The miracles I do in my Father's name speak for me,[n] [26]but you do not believe because you are not my sheep.[o] [27]My sheep listen to my voice; I know them,[p] and they follow me.[q] [28]I give them eternal life, and they shall never perish; no one can snatch them out of my hand.[r] [29]My Father, who has given them to me,[s] is greater than all[c];[t] no one can snatch them out of my Father's hand. [30]I and the Father are one."[u]

[31]Again the Jews picked up stones to stone him,[v] [32]but Jesus said to them, "I have shown you many great miracles from the Father. For which of these do you stone me?"

[33]"We are not stoning you for any of these," replied the Jews, "but for blasphemy, because you, a mere man, claim to be God."[w]

[34]Jesus answered them, "Is it not written in your Law,[x] 'I have said you are gods'[d]?[y] [35]If he called them 'gods,' to whom the word of God came—and the Scripture cannot be broken— [36]what about the one whom the Father set apart[z] as his very own[a] and sent into the world?[b] Why then do you accuse me of blasphemy because I said, 'I am God's Son'?[c] [37]Do not believe me unless I do what my Father does.[d] [38]But if I do it, even though you do not believe me, believe the miracles, that you may know and understand that the Father is in me, and I in the Father."[e] [39]Again they tried to seize him,[f] but he escaped their grasp.[g]

[40]Then Jesus went back across the Jordan[h] to the place where John had been baptizing in the early days. Here he stayed [41]and many people came to him. They said, "Though John never performed a miraculous sign,[i] all that John said about this man was true."[j] [42]And in that place many believed in Jesus.[k]

The Death of Lazarus

11 Now a man named Lazarus was sick. He was from Bethany,[l] the village of Mary and her sister Martha.[m] [2]This Mary, whose brother Lazarus now lay

10:15
x Mt 11:27
10:16
y Isa 56:8
z Jn 11:52;
Eph 2:11-19
a Eze 37:24;
1Pe 2:25
10:17
b ver 11,15,18
10:18
c Mt 26:53
d Jn 15:10;
Php 2:8; Heb 5:8
10:19
e Jn 7:43; 9:16
10:20
f Jn 7:20 g Mk 3:21
10:21
h Mt 4:24 i Ex 4:11;
Jn 9:32,33
10:23
j Ac 3:11; 5:12
10:24
k Jn 1:19
l Jn 16:25,29
10:25
m Jn 8:58 n Jn 5:36
10:26
o Jn 8:47
10:27
p ver 14 q ver 4
10:28
r Jn 6:39
10:29
s Jn 17:2,6,24
t Jn 14:28
10:30
u Jn 17:21-23
10:31
v Jn 8:59
10:33
w Lev 24:16;
Jn 5:18
10:34
x Jn 8:17; Ro 3:19
y Ps 82:6
10:36
z Jer 1:5 a Jn 6:69
b Jn 3:17
c Jn 5:17,18
10:37
d ver 25; Jn 15:24
10:38
e Jn 14:10,11,20;
17:21
10:39
f Jn 7:30 g Lk 4:30;
Jn 8:59
10:40
h Jn 1:28
10:41
i Jn 2:11; 3:30
j Jn 1:26,27,30,34
10:42
k Jn 7:31
11:1
l Mt 21:17
m Lk 10:38

---

a 22 That is, Hanukkah   b 24 Or Messiah   c 29 Many early manuscripts What my Father has given me is greater than all   d 34 Psalm 82:6

John 10:22–42

📖 This final section of chapter 10 is a critical revelation—Jesus' ultimate, public disclosure of his identity. Thus far Jesus hadn't made an explicit, public claim to be the Christ, though he had done this privately to the Samaritan woman (4:25–26) and the blind man (9:35–37). Given the explosive, highly politicized views of the Messiah, it isn't surprising that Jesus had used restraint so far. But his audience wanted a straight answer (v. 24), and, in claiming to be "one" with the Father, he couldn't have been more clear. This "blasphemy" demanded either stoning or submission.

💬 The root problem here was unbelief. These skeptics weren't Jesus' "sheep." Humans, of course, have the capacity to disbelieve, even when presented with the gospel truth. We are capable of resisting God's efforts on our behalf. As the late British writer C.S. Lewis once observed, there are only two sorts of people in the world: those who say to God "Thy will be done" and those to whom God says "Thy will be done." Jesus stressed that his works validated his words. What does it mean for you to have your witness about Christ confirmed by the quality of your life and deeds?

11:2
n Mk 14:3; Lk 7:38;
Jn 12:3
11:3
o ver 5,36

sick, was the same one who poured perfume on the Lord and wiped his feet with her hair. *n* ³So the sisters sent word to Jesus, "Lord, the one you love*o* is sick."

11:4
p ver 40; Jn 9:3

⁴When he heard this, Jesus said, "This sickness will not end in death. No, it is for God's glory*p* so that God's Son may be glorified through it." ⁵Jesus loved Martha and her sister and Lazarus. ⁶Yet when he heard that Lazarus was sick, he stayed where he was two more days.

11:7
q Jn 10:40
11:8
r Mt 23:7 *s* Jn 8:59;
10:31

⁷Then he said to his disciples, "Let us go back to Judea."*q*

⁸"But Rabbi,"*r* they said, "a short while ago the Jews tried to stone you,*s* and yet you are going back there?"

11:9
t Jn 9:4; 12:35

⁹Jesus answered, "Are there not twelve hours of daylight? A man who walks by day will not stumble, for he sees by this world's light.*t* ¹⁰It is when he walks by night that he stumbles, for he has no light."

11:11
u ver 3 *v* Ac 7:60

¹¹After he had said this, he went on to tell them, "Our friend*u* Lazarus has fallen asleep;*v* but I am going there to wake him up."

11:13
w Mt 9:24

¹²His disciples replied, "Lord, if he sleeps, he will get better." ¹³Jesus had been speaking of his death, but his disciples thought he meant natural sleep.*w*

¹⁴So then he told them plainly, "Lazarus is dead, ¹⁵and for your sake I am glad I was not there, so that you may believe. But let us go to him."

11:16
x Mt 10:3; Jn 14:5;
20:24-28; 21:2;
Ac 1:13

¹⁶Then Thomas*x* (called Didymus) said to the rest of the disciples, "Let us also go, that we may die with him."

Jesus Comforts the Sisters

11:17
y ver 6,39
11:18
z ver 1
11:19
a ver 31; Job 2:11
11:20
b Lk 10:38-42

¹⁷On his arrival, Jesus found that Lazarus had already been in the tomb for four days.*y* ¹⁸Bethany*z* was less than two miles*a* from Jerusalem, ¹⁹and many Jews had come to Martha and Mary to comfort them in the loss of their brother.*a* ²⁰When Martha heard that Jesus was coming, she went out to meet him, but Mary stayed at home.*b*

a 18 Greek *fifteen stadia* (about 3 kilometers)

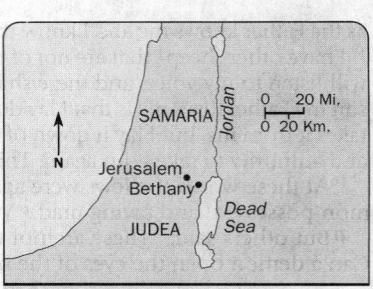

Jesus Raises Lazarus (11:1)
Then: The hamlet of Bethany was a two-mile walk from Jerusalem.
Now: Mention of Bethany still calls up associations with Lazarus, a symbol of God's love and of second chances.

John 11:1–16

When Jesus heard the report about Lazarus's illness, his response paralleled his comments about the man born blind (9:1–5). The final result of this seeming tragedy was that God would be glorified, not that death would gain the victory. Jesus wasn't denying Lazarus's death but demonstrating that death wouldn't gain the final word in this man's life. Lazarus's death wasn't by God's design, but God would use it for an opportunity to glorify his Son.

We live in an age that does its best to deny death. The process has been sanitized and taken over by professionals. This approach masks a profound anxiety even the prettiest funeral service can't disguise. In the life of the church, funeral services become potent opportunities for ministry. Here the raw vulnerability of our lives stands naked. We are confronted by a personal fate *we would rather not look at directly. Jesus* was about to graphically portray how the gospel transforms people's entire attitudes toward death.

John 11:17–37

Jesus gently corrected Martha so she would see that her hope was anchored not just to the far distant resurrection but to a present relationship with him. On the other hand, he didn't challenge her, "If you believe in the resurrection, why are you wasting your time and tears?" Nor did he say to Mary, "If you have victorious faith, you should stand clear-eyed and confident because I'm here." Jesus didn't try to short-circuit the sisters' grieving. Instead, he joined with them. As the Lord of life, he wept over death.

In some Christian circles Jesus' power over the grave is embraced with such conviction that those left behind feel they lack permission to mourn death's tragedy. To grieve, they are told, is to show a lack of faith; funerals are celebrations of eternal life and victory. While celebrating Christ's triumph over death, we can still mourn the loss of companionship with the person who has died. We can describe death as terrible without compromising the quality of our faith. Jesus himself wept at the pain death brought to one family. Death is a foe that in Christ is being defeated.

21"Lord," Martha said to Jesus, "if you had been here, my brother would not have died. *c* 22But I know that even now God will give you whatever you ask." *d*

23Jesus said to her, "Your brother will rise again."

24Martha answered, "I know he will rise again in the resurrection *e* at the last day."

25Jesus said to her, "I am the resurrection and the life. *f* He who believes in me will live, even though he dies; 26and whoever lives and believes in me will never die. Do you believe this?"

27"Yes, Lord," she told him, "I believe that you are the Christ, *a g* the Son of God, *h* who was to come into the world." *i*

28And after she had said this, she went back and called her sister Mary aside. "The Teacher *j* is here," she said, "and is asking for you." 29When Mary heard this, she got up quickly and went to him. 30Now Jesus had not yet entered the village, but was still at the place where Martha had met him. *k* 31When the Jews who had been with Mary in the house, comforting her, *l* noticed how quickly she got up and went out, they followed her, supposing she was going to the tomb to mourn there.

32When Mary reached the place where Jesus was and saw him, she fell at his feet and said, "Lord, if you had been here, my brother would not have died." *m*

33When Jesus saw her weeping, and the Jews who had come along with her also weeping, he was deeply moved *n* in spirit and troubled. *o* 34"Where have you laid him?" he asked.

"Come and see, Lord," they replied.

35Jesus wept. *p*

36Then the Jews said, "See how he loved him!" *q*

37But some of them said, "Could not he who opened the eyes of the blind man *r* have kept this man from dying?" *s*

Jesus Raises Lazarus From the Dead

38Jesus, once more deeply moved, *t* came to the tomb. It was a cave with a stone laid across the entrance. *u* 39"Take away the stone," he said.

"But, Lord," said Martha, the sister of the dead man, "by this time there is a bad odor, for he has been there four days." *v*

40Then Jesus said, "Did I not tell you that if you believed, *w* you would see the glory of God?" *x*

41So they took away the stone. Then Jesus looked up *y* and said, "Father, *z* I thank you that you have heard me. 42I knew that you always hear me, but I said this for the benefit of the people standing here, *a* that they may believe that you sent me." *b*

43When he had said this, Jesus called in a loud voice, "Lazarus, come out!" *c* 44The dead man came out, his hands and feet wrapped with strips of linen, *d* and a cloth around his face. *e*

Jesus said to them, "Take off the grave clothes and let him go."

The Plot to Kill Jesus

45Therefore many of the Jews who had come to visit Mary, *f* and had seen what Jesus did, *g* put their faith in him. *h* 46But some of them went to the Pharisees and

a 27 Or *Messiah*

11:21 *c* ver 32,37
11:22 *d* ver 41,42; Jn 9:31
11:24 *e* Da 12:2; Jn 5:28, 29; Ac 24:15
11:25 *f* Jn 1:4
11:27 *g* Lk 2:11 *h* Mt 16:16 *i* Jn 6:14
11:28 *j* Mt 26:18; Jn 13:13
11:30 *k* ver 20
11:31 *l* ver 19
11:32 *m* ver 21
11:33 *n* ver 38 *o* Jn 12:27
11:35 *p* Lk 19:41
11:36 *q* ver 3
11:37 *r* Jn 9:6,7 *s* ver 21,32
11:38 *t* ver 33 *u* Mt 27:60; Lk 24:2; Jn 20:1
11:39 *v* ver 17
11:40 *w* ver 23-25 *x* ver 4
11:41 *y* Jn 17:1 *z* Mt 11:25
11:42 *a* Jn 12:30 *b* Jn 3:17
11:43 *c* Lk 7:14
11:44 *d* Jn 19:40 *e* Jn 20:7
11:45 *f* ver 19 *g* Jn 2:23 *h* Ex 14:31; Jn 7:31

John 11:38–44

Jesus didn't ask God to raise Lazarus. He thanked him for having *already* answered his prayer. Jesus' faith in the Father was so great that he assumed the miracle was as good as done. The dramatic high point of the story was Jesus' call "in a loud voice" for Lazarus to come out. This wasn't a whisper or even a firm request. It was a shout of raw authority. We see here an important characteristic of Jesus' work: It's concrete. He's not just "the resurrection and the life" in an abstract sense. He brought life to a corpse that had been in a tomb for four days!

Jesus overrode the grim scene at Lazarus's grave with his own power. And he faced the specter of his own death with the confidence that the same power of God would rescue him from the grave. John 11 encourages us with strength from Christ to face our own mortality (or the death of someone near to us). Resurrection isn't a new principle now applied to human life; the Lord *who is resurrection* offers life where there was only the prospect of death. If you have been a believer for a long time, can you even imagine facing life without the assurance of an afterlife? If you are a newer Christian, what does this reality mean to you?

11:47
i ver 57 *j* Mt 26:3
k Mt 5:22 *l* Jn 2:11

told them what Jesus had done. [47]Then the chief priests and the Pharisees[i] called a meeting[j] of the Sanhedrin. [k]

"What are we accomplishing?" they asked. "Here is this man performing many miraculous signs. [l] [48]If we let him go on like this, everyone will believe in him, and then the Romans will come and take away both our place[a] and our nation."

11:49
m Mt 26:3 *n* ver 51;
Jn 18:13,14
11:50
o Jn 18:14

[49]Then one of them, named Caiaphas, [m] who was high priest that year, [n] spoke up, "You know nothing at all! [50]You do not realize that it is better for you that one man die for the people than that the whole nation perish." [o]

11:52
p Isa 49:6; Jn 10:16
11:53
q Mt 12:14
11:54
r Jn 7:1

[51]He did not say this on his own, but as high priest that year he prophesied that Jesus would die for the Jewish nation, [52]and not only for that nation but also for the scattered children of God, to bring them together and make them one. [p] [53]So from that day on they plotted to take his life. [q]

[54]Therefore Jesus no longer moved about publicly among the Jews. [r] Instead he withdrew to a region near the desert, to a village called Ephraim, where he stayed with his disciples.

11:55
s Ex 12:13,23,27;
Mt 26:1,2; Mk 14:1;
Jn 13:1
t 2Ch 30:17,18
11:56
u Jn 7:11

[55]When it was almost time for the Jewish Passover, [s] many went up from the country to Jerusalem for their ceremonial cleansing[t] before the Passover. [56]They kept looking for Jesus, [u] and as they stood in the temple area they asked one another, "What do you think? Isn't he coming to the Feast at all?" [57]But the chief priests and Pharisees had given orders that if anyone found out where Jesus was, he should report it so that they might arrest him.

Jesus Anointed at Bethany

12:1
v Jn 11:55
w Mt 21:17
12:2
x Lk 10:38-42
12:3
y Mk 14:3 *z* Jn 11:2

12 Six days before the Passover, [v] Jesus arrived at Bethany, [w] where Lazarus lived, whom Jesus had raised from the dead. [2]Here a dinner was given in Jesus' honor. Martha served, [x] while Lazarus was among those reclining at the table with him. [3]Then Mary took about a pint[b] of pure nard, an expensive perfume;[y] she poured it on Jesus' feet and wiped his feet with her hair. [z] And the house was filled with the fragrance of the perfume.

12:4
a Mt 10:4

[4]But one of his disciples, Judas Iscariot, who was later to betray him, [a] objected, [5]"Why wasn't this perfume sold and the money given to the poor? It was worth a year's wages. [c]" [6]He did not say this because he cared about the poor but because

---

[a] 48 Or *temple*   [b] 3 Greek *a litra* (probably about 0.5 liter)   [c] 5 Greek *three hundred denarii*

John 11:45–57

In his role as high priest, Caiaphas pointed to the last sacrificial Lamb in a prophecy he wasn't even aware he was making. John 11 is a profoundly ironic chapter. It climaxes in Jesus' gift of life to his dead friend Lazarus—and concludes with Jesus' enemies plotting his death (and soon Lazarus's as well; see 12:9–11). The Lord of life showed himself to be the victor over death, only to face death himself. He dispensed life while his enemies schemed to withdraw it.

This passage reminds us of a parable involving another "Lazarus." That passage ends with the words, "They will not be convinced even if someone rises from the dead" (Luke 16:31). Signs alone can't produce faith or transform lives. The experience of God's power isn't enough to persuade the human heart. (The event itself, not the One who worked it, can too easily become the object of faith.) While Christ has power over disease and death, this cautions us not to seek signs and wonders strictly for their own sake.

John 12:1–11

After Lazarus's raising, Jesus withdrew to Ephraim (11:54), probably a small town about 12 miles north of Jerusalem. But as the Passover approached, he returned to Bethany near Jerusalem and stayed with his friends Lazarus, Martha, and Mary. This family no doubt dreaded the looming tragedy of Jesus' arrest. Jesus had just raised Lazarus, and already people were trying to put both of them back into the grave. Feeling the weight of these momentous days, Mary anointed Jesus with a costly ointment. Such a gift (worth a year's wage for a day-laborer) was amazing.

The extravagance of Mary's action remains as problematic for us as it was for Judas and the other disciples (cf. Matt. 26:8–9). A year's income! Judas's complaint would no doubt have been echoed by many church members today. We can't physically duplicate Mary's gift, and she may not have known the eternal and worldwide significance of her action. (For that matter, neither did anyone else present, except Jesus.) But it's a mistake for us to think our sacrificial devotion is wasteful or insignificant. Jesus' difficult words in verse 8 make sense in the light of his death and resurrection. Our first calling is to give our life and all our resources to God. When we offer our very selves to Jesus, we'll also give them to the poor, among whom he is specially present. Our gifts to the needy are in reality offerings to him (cf. Matt. 25:31–46).

he was a thief; as keeper of the money bag,[b] he used to help himself to what was put into it.

[7]"Leave her alone," Jesus replied. "It was intended that she should save this perfume for the day of my burial.[c] [8]You will always have the poor among you,[d] but you will not always have me."

[9]Meanwhile a large crowd of Jews found out that Jesus was there and came, not only because of him but also to see Lazarus, whom he had raised from the dead.[e] [10]So the chief priests made plans to kill Lazarus as well, [11]for on account of him[f] many of the Jews were going over to Jesus and putting their faith in him.[g]

The Triumphal Entry

[12]The next day the great crowd that had come for the Feast heard that Jesus was on his way to Jerusalem. [13]They took palm branches and went out to meet him, shouting,

"Hosanna![a]"

"Blessed is he who comes in the name of the Lord!"[b][h]

"Blessed is the King of Israel!"[i]

[14]Jesus found a young donkey and sat upon it, as it is written,

[15] "Do not be afraid, O Daughter of Zion;
    see, your king is coming,
    seated on a donkey's colt."[c][j]

[16]At first his disciples did not understand all this.[k] Only after Jesus was glorified[l] did they realize that these things had been written about him and that they had done these things to him.

[17]Now the crowd that was with him[m] when he called Lazarus from the tomb and raised him from the dead continued to spread the word. [18]Many people, because they had heard that he had given this miraculous sign,[n] went out to meet him. [19]So the Pharisees said to one another, "See, this is getting us nowhere. Look how the whole world has gone after him!"[o]

Jesus Predicts His Death

[20]Now there were some Greeks[p] among those who went up to worship at the Feast. [21]They came to Philip, who was from Bethsaida[q] in Galilee, with a request. "Sir," they said, "we would like to see Jesus." [22]Philip went to tell Andrew; Andrew and Philip in turn told Jesus.

[23]Jesus replied, "The hour has come for the Son of Man to be glorified.[r] [24]I tell you the truth, unless a kernel of wheat falls to the ground and dies,[s] it remains only

a 13 A Hebrew expression meaning "Save!" which became an exclamation of praise
b 13 Psalm 118:25,26   c 15 Zech. 9:9

John 12:12–19

This scene is awash in political fervor. The palms, entry, and cries all remind us of John 6:14–15. After Jesus had fed the 5,000, the crowd had hailed him as "the Prophet" and intended to "make him king by force." But the crowd was cheering an imaginary Messianic hero who was a triumphant victor, not a humble servant. The people didn't realize the significance of their actions, but Jerusalem *was* celebrating the arrival of its King, despite the misguided motivations of the Jewish nationalists.

In some fashion the celebrants assumed Jesus and his movement would serve their cause. His failure to satisfy those visions (religious, political, and social) would lead to a cry for crucifixion one week later. How

often do we seek to use God to satisfy our own agendas—and find ourselves disappointed when he "fails" us?

John 12:20–36

Here "Greeks" who would become followers of Judaism wanted to "see Jesus." His meeting with them no doubt jeopardized his already strained status with his Jerusalem opponents. This event signaled the beginning of a "time" John had anticipated throughout his Gospel (2:4; 7:30; 8:20). The arrival of the Greeks on the scene marked the closing of a chapter for Jesus. He now belonged to the world beyond Judaism—to all people (v. 32). Jesus announced his great call to follow him and find life by losing it. Once again, the voice of the Father thundered forth from heaven.

12:6
b Jn 13:29

12:7
c Jn 19:40
12:8
d Dt 15:11

12:9
e Jn 11:43,44
12:11
f ver 17,18;
Jn 11:45 g Jn 7:31

12:13
h Ps 118:25,26
i Jn 1:49

12:15
j Zec 9:9

12:16
k Mk 9:32 l Jn 2:22;
7:39; 14:26

12:17
m Jn 11:42

12:18
n ver 11

12:19
o Jn 11:47,48

12:20
p Jn 7:35; Ac 11:20
12:21
q Mt 11:21; Jn 1:44

12:23
r Jn 13:32; 17:1
12:24
s 1Co 15:36

a single seed. But if it dies, it produces many seeds. 25The man who loves his life will lose it, while the man who hates his life in this world will keep it[t] for eternal life. 26Whoever serves me must follow me; and where I am, my servant also will be.[u] My Father will honor the one who serves me.

27"Now my heart is troubled,[v] and what shall I say? 'Father,[w] save me from this hour'?[x] No, it was for this very reason I came to this hour. 28Father, glorify your name!"

Then a voice came from heaven,[y] "I have glorified it, and will glorify it again." 29The crowd that was there and heard it said it had thundered; others said an angel had spoken to him.

30Jesus said, "This voice was for your benefit,[z] not mine. 31Now is the time for judgment on this world;[a] now the prince of this world[b] will be driven out. 32But I, when I am lifted up from the earth,[c] will draw all men to myself."[d] 33He said this to show the kind of death he was going to die.[e]

34The crowd spoke up, "We have heard from the Law that the Christ[a] will remain forever,[f] so how can you say, 'The Son of Man[g] must be lifted up'?[h] Who is this 'Son of Man'?"

35Then Jesus told them, "You are going to have the light[i] just a little while longer. Walk while you have the light,[j] before darkness overtakes you.[k] The man who walks in the dark does not know where he is going. 36Put your trust in the light while you have it, so that you may become sons of light."[l] When he had finished speaking, Jesus left and hid himself from them.[m]

The Jews Continue in Their Unbelief

37Even after Jesus had done all these miraculous signs[n] in their presence, they still would not believe in him. 38This was to fulfill the word of Isaiah the prophet:

"Lord, who has believed our message
    and to whom has the arm of the Lord been revealed?"[b][o]

39For this reason they could not believe, because, as Isaiah says elsewhere:

40"He has blinded their eyes
    and deadened their hearts,
so they can neither see with their eyes,
    nor understand with their hearts,
    nor turn—and I would heal them."[c][p]

41Isaiah said this because he saw Jesus' glory[q] and spoke about him.[r]

42Yet at the same time many even among the leaders believed in him.[s] But because of the Pharisees[t] they would not confess their faith for fear they would be put

a 34 Or *Messiah*   b 38 Isaiah 53:1   c 40 Isaiah 6:10

It's been noted that in America 11:00 A.M. on Sunday is the most segregated hour of the week. If we don't understand Jesus' radical mission and willingness to risk being seen with Gentiles in the Jewish temple, we can't comprehend his extreme love for the world. Are we who embrace Jesus' vision willing to take a risk parallel to his association with Greeks? How comfortable are you in reaching out to those who are unfamiliar and different? What might you have to "lose" by serving Jesus in this way? At the same time, how would you be "lifting Jesus up" before the eyes of the world?

John 12:37–50

John offered here a theological explanation for the unbelief of Judaism (vv. 37–43), followed by Jesus' final call for faith (vv. 44–50). Jesus' public work was com-

pleted. His signs had been displayed, his messages delivered. Yet for the most part his own people had failed to believe the Messenger sent by God. Some Jewish leaders did believe in Jesus (vv. 42–43). Yet they refused to make their faith public; many of their colleagues had no idea of their private stand (cf. 7:48–49).

John delivered a stinging rebuke to these "fearful believers": "They loved praise from men more than praise from God." To follow Jesus is to go and tell others and to obey his teaching—regardless of the social consequences. What does this say to men and women today who have privatized their faith, who are unwilling to "go public" among those with prestige and power? What role does reputation play in your willingness to obey Jesus and share the News?

out of the synagogue;[u] 43for they loved praise from men more than praise from God.[v]

44Then Jesus cried out, "When a man believes in me, he does not believe in me only, but in the one who sent me.[w] 45When he looks at me, he sees the one who sent me.[x] 46I have come into the world as a light,[y] so that no one who believes in me should stay in darkness.

47"As for the person who hears my words but does not keep them, I do not judge him. For I did not come to judge the world, but to save it.[z] 48There is a judge for the one who rejects me and does not accept my words; that very word which I spoke will condemn him[a] at the last day. 49For I did not speak of my own accord, but the Father who sent me commanded me[b] what to say and how to say it. 50I know that his command leads to eternal life. So whatever I say is just what the Father has told me to say."

Jesus Washes His Disciples' Feet

13 It was just before the Passover Feast.[c] Jesus knew that the time had come[d] for him to leave this world and go to the Father.[e] Having loved his own who were in the world, he now showed them the full extent of his love.[a]

2The evening meal was being served, and the devil had already prompted Judas Iscariot, son of Simon, to betray Jesus. 3Jesus knew that the Father had put all things under his power,[f] and that he had come from God[g] and was returning to God; 4so he got up from the meal, took off his outer clothing, and wrapped a towel around his waist. 5After that, he poured water into a basin and began to wash his disciples' feet,[h] drying them with the towel that was wrapped around him.

6He came to Simon Peter, who said to him, "Lord, are you going to wash my feet?"

7Jesus replied, "You do not realize now what I am doing, but later you will understand."[i]

8"No," said Peter, "you shall never wash my feet."

Jesus answered, "Unless I wash you, you have no part with me."

9"Then, Lord," Simon Peter replied, "not just my feet but my hands and my head as well!"

10Jesus answered, "A person who has had a bath needs only to wash his feet; his whole body is clean. And you are clean,[j] though not every one of you." 11For he knew who was going to betray him, and that was why he said not every one was clean.

12When he had finished washing their feet, he put on his clothes and returned

---

[a] 1 Or he loved them to the last

Cross references

12:42 u Jn 9:22
12:43 v Jn 5:44
12:44 w Mt 10:40; Jn 5:24
12:45 x Jn 14:9
12:46 y Jn 1:4; 3:19; 8:12; 9:5
12:47 z Jn 3:17
12:48 a Jn 5:45
12:49 b Jn 14:31
13:1 c Jn 11:55 d Jn 12:23 e Jn 16:28
13:3 f Mt 28:18 g Jn 8:42; 16:27,28, 30
13:5 h Lk 7:44
13:7 i ver 12
13:10 j Jn 15:3

John 13:1–17

As people of Jesus' time walked the dusty roads, shod only in sandals, their feet became dirt-encrusted. Etiquette demanded that, when a traveler entered a home as a guest, the host provide for the washing of his or her feet. This distasteful chore was generally delegated to the lowliest servant in the household. Jesus' startling act of kneeling with a towel to perform this menial task made a powerful visual statement of a servant atti-tude. As Jesus expressed it, if he had washed his disciples' feet, they ought to do the same for one another.

Few of our churches practice the tradition of foot washing. But Jesus provided in it a profound symbol of his call to servanthood. To follow Jesus is to seek the least desired or respected forms of service, not the positions of power and prestige. When have you experienced the blessing that comes from servant living (v. 17)?

13:1–17

Biblical humility

By washing his disciples' feet, Jesus modeled Biblical humility in at least three ways:

1. Respect:
Like Moses (cf. Num. 12:1–3), he showed the disciples the way a believ-er loves and respects others, no matter what their social, personal, or spiritual position.

2. Self-initiation:
Jesus acknowledged that though spiritual growth can't be forced, there is something we can do to initiate God's work in us (cf. Ps. 25:9; 1 Peter 5:5–6).

3. Community:
Jesus demonstrated that God's kingdom is made up of many persons in re-lationship, not of isolated, unrelated individuals (Phil. 2:1–3).

13:13
k Jn 11:28 r Lk 6:46;
1Co 12:3; Php 2:11
13:14
m 1Pe 5:5
13:15
n Mt 11:29
13:16
o Mt 10:24;
Lk 6:40; Jn 15:20
13:17
p Mt 7:24,25;
Lk 11:28; Jas 1:25
13:18
q ver 10 r Jn 15:16,
19 s Mt 26:23
t Jn 6:70 u Ps 41:9
13:19
v Jn 14:29; 16:4
w Jn 8:24
13:20
x Mt 10:40;
Lk 10:16
13:21
y Jn 12:27
z Mt 26:21
13:23
a Jn 19:26; 20:2;
21:7,20
13:25
b Jn 21:20

13:27
c Lk 22:3

13:29
d Jn 12:6

13:30
e Lk 22:53

13:31
f Jn 7:39
g Jn 14:13; 17:4;
1Pe 4:11
13:32
h Jn 17:1

13:33
i Jn 7:33,34
13:34
j 1Jn 2:7-11; 3:11
k Lev 19:18;
1Th 4:9; 1Pe 1:22
l Jn 15:12; Eph 5:2;
1Jn 4:10,11
13:35
m 1Jn 3:14; 4:20

to his place. "Do you understand what I have done for you?" he asked them. 13 "You call me 'Teacher'[k] and 'Lord,'[l] and rightly so, for that is what I am. 14 Now that I, your Lord and Teacher, have washed your feet, you also should wash one another's feet.[m] 15 I have set you an example that you should do as I have done for you.[n] 16 I tell you the truth, no servant is greater than his master,[o] nor is a messenger greater than the one who sent him. 17 Now that you know these things, you will be blessed if you do them.[p]

Jesus Predicts His Betrayal

18 "I am not referring to all of you;[q] I know those I have chosen.[r] But this is to fulfill the scripture: 'He who shares my bread[s] has lifted up his heel[t] against me.'[a][u]

19 "I am telling you now before it happens, so that when it does happen you will believe[v] that I am He.[w] 20 I tell you the truth, whoever accepts anyone I send accepts me; and whoever accepts me accepts the one who sent me."[x]

21 After he had said this, Jesus was troubled in spirit[y] and testified, "I tell you the truth, one of you is going to betray me."[z]

22 His disciples stared at one another, at a loss to know which of them he meant. 23 One of them, the disciple whom Jesus loved,[a] was reclining next to him. 24 Simon Peter motioned to this disciple and said, "Ask him which one he means."

25 Leaning back against Jesus, he asked him, "Lord, who is it?"[b]

26 Jesus answered, "It is the one to whom I will give this piece of bread when I have dipped it in the dish." Then, dipping the piece of bread, he gave it to Judas Iscariot, son of Simon. 27 As soon as Judas took the bread, Satan entered into him.[c]

"What you are about to do, do quickly," Jesus told him, 28 but no one at the meal understood why Jesus said this to him. 29 Since Judas had charge of the money,[d] some thought Jesus was telling him to buy what was needed for the Feast, or to give something to the poor. 30 As soon as Judas had taken the bread, he went out. And it was night.[e]

Jesus Predicts Peter's Denial

31 When he was gone, Jesus said, "Now is the Son of Man glorified[f] and God is glorified in him.[g] 32 If God is glorified in him,[b] God will glorify the Son in himself,[h] and will glorify him at once.

33 "My children, I will be with you only a little longer. You will look for me, and just as I told the Jews, so I tell you now: Where I am going, you cannot come.[i]

34 "A new command[j] I give you: Love one another.[k] As I have loved you, so you must love one another.[l] 35 By this all men will know that you are my disciples, if you love one another."[m]

36 Simon Peter asked him, "Lord, where are you going?"

a 18 Psalm 41:9   b 32 Many early manuscripts do not have *If God is glorified in him.*

John 13:18–30

John frequently mentioned Judas's betrayal (6:70–71; 12:4; 13:2,11,18,21,26–30). Jesus had chosen this man as one of his disciples. They had spent at least three years working together. The fact that Judas was the group's treasurer suggests that he held a place of trust and respect. Judas's departure at night was symbolic. Night represents the direct opposite of Jesus, the Light. Judas represented the temptation for all of us to try to get God to conform to our sense of what's best—and to hide our sins in the darkness. Jesus described this in 3:19: "Light has come into the world, but men loved darkness instead of light because their deeds were evil."

Throughout John's Gospel we are warned about the struggle between light and darkness. We have heard repeatedly about those who had chosen the darkness despite exposure to the light. Audiences had divided following Jesus' revelation of himself as the Light of the world. In Judas we see the danger of misunderstanding Jesus, of being seduced by our own dreams and visions. John invites us to reflect on the horror of Judas's choice.

John 13:31–38

After Judas's departure, Jesus spoke directly of his glorification—his impending death, resurrection, and ascension. Peter claimed eagerness to go with Jesus, even at the cost of his life. But Jesus prophesied that Peter's good intentions wouldn't hold when confronted with genuine danger. That the disciples were to love one another wasn't a "new commandment" (cf. Lev. 19:18). But that they were to love each other with the sort of love modeled by Jesus was dramatic. "As I have loved you" pointed back to Jesus' servant act of washing the disciples' feet.

Jesus replied, "Where I am going, you cannot follow now, [n] but you will follow later." [o]

[37] Peter asked, "Lord, why can't I follow you now? I will lay down my life for you."

[38] Then Jesus answered, "Will you really lay down your life for me? I tell you the truth, before the rooster crows, you will disown me three times! [p]

Jesus Comforts His Disciples

14 "Do not let your hearts be troubled. [q] Trust in God[a]; trust also in me. [2] In my Father's house are many rooms; if it were not so, I would have told you. I am going there [r] to prepare a place for you. [3] And if I go and prepare a place for you, I will come back and take you to be with me that you also may be where I am. [s] [4] You know the way to the place where I am going."

Jesus the Way to the Father

[5] Thomas [t] said to him, "Lord, we don't know where you are going, so how can we know the way?"

a 1 Or *You trust in God*

13:36
n ver 33; Jn 14:2
o Jn 21:18,19; 2Pe 1:14

13:38
p Jn 18:27

14:1
q ver 27

14:2
r Jn 13:33,36
14:3
s Jn 12:26

14:5
t Jn 11:16

📖 Nothing so astonishes our fractured world as a community in which radical, faithful, genuine love is shared among members. In the world's eyes, this is the authenticating mark of the truthfulness of the gospel. The church is a community of *love*, a circle of Christ-followers who invest in one another because Christ invested in us. Our love isn't based on the mutual attractiveness of church members, but on the model of Jesus, who washed the feet of everyone—including Judas.

John 14:1–4

👣 Our lives now and eternally are utterly encircled by God's faithfulness. In the midst of foretelling the disciples' betrayal of him, Jesus announced that none-theless he would come and lead them "home." Jesus is going to prepare a place (a "room") for his followers, and he'll take us there to be with him.

📖 Where do you call home? An anticipation of heaven builds in us an eternal vantage point. We live in a world that continually offers us temporary, time-bound securities and comforts, that keeps our eyes on the near horizon and denies the limitations of our mortality. Jesus was clear that earthly security is unreliable (Matt. 6:19–20). Our true home has already been built for us in heaven. Once we embrace the significance of this truth, our confidence to face this world's challenges, including death itself, is deepened.

Snapshots

  14:2–3

A Special Baptism

Seda, a grandmother in Armenia, voiced, "If children have the love and fear of God, they'll grow up honest and truthful . . . Justice and truth will always accompany them."

Her wish and that of many in the community was to have the children baptized. So a Christian aid group worked with the Armenian Apostolic Church to provide a baptismal service for 281 children in the area. Each received a package of presents and a handcrafted silver cross they wore with pride and excitement.

Eight-year-old Yervand expressed his thoughts, "I was really happy." Then he recited the Lord's Prayer, pronouncing each word with dancing eyes and a clear voice. Araksya, a mother of three, enthused, "I felt so wonderful that I can't explain it. Baptizing strengthens one's faith, and I'm so thankful that it was made possible for my daughters."

Most families in this impoverished area are without fathers at home; they have gone elsewhere to look for work. Yet the people have spiritual treasure to share. Seda reflected, "I would love for my children and everybody in the world to find themselves a place in God's home, to have love for God . . . and to find the right path in life."

> "I would love for my children and everybody in the world to find themselves a place in God's home, to have love for God . . . and to find the right path in life."

14:6
u Jn 10:9 v Jn 11:25

14:7
w Jn 8:19

14:9
x Jn 12:45;
Col 1:15; Heb 1:3

14:10
y Jn 10:38 z Jn 5:19

14:11
a Jn 5:36; 10:38
14:12
b Mt 21:21
c Lk 10:17
14:13
d Mt 7:7

14:15
e ver 21,23;
Jn 15:10; 1Jn 5:3
14:16
f Jn 15:26; 16:7
14:17
g Jn 15:26; 16:13;
1Jn 4:6 h 1Co 2:14
14:18
i ver 3,28
14:19
j Jn 7:33,34; 16:16
k Jn 6:57
14:20
l Jn 10:38
14:21
m 1Jn 5:3 n 1Jn 2:5
14:22
o Lk 6:16; Ac 1:13
p Ac 10:41
14:23
q ver 15 r 1Jn 2:24;
Rev 3:20

14:24
s Jn 7:16
14:26
t Jn 15:26; 16:7
u Ac 2:33
v Jn 16:13;
1Jn 2:20,27
w Jn 2:22

6 Jesus answered, "I am the way[u] and the truth and the life.[v] No one comes to the Father except through me. 7 If you really knew me, you would know[a] my Father as well.[w] From now on, you do know him and have seen him."

8 Philip said, "Lord, show us the Father and that will be enough for us."

9 Jesus answered: "Don't you know me, Philip, even after I have been among you such a long time? Anyone who has seen me has seen the Father.[x] How can you say, 'Show us the Father'? 10 Don't you believe that I am in the Father, and that the Father is in me?[y] The words I say to you are not just my own.[z] Rather, it is the Father, living in me, who is doing his work. 11 Believe me when I say that I am in the Father and the Father is in me; or at least believe on the evidence of the miracles themselves.[a] 12 I tell you the truth, anyone who has faith[b] in me will do what I have been doing.[c] He will do even greater things than these, because I am going to the Father. 13 And I will do whatever you ask[d] in my name, so that the Son may bring glory to the Father. 14 You may ask me for anything in my name, and I will do it.

Jesus Promises the Holy Spirit

15 "If you love me, you will obey what I command.[e] 16 And I will ask the Father, and he will give you another Counselor[f] to be with you forever— 17 the Spirit of truth.[g] The world cannot accept him,[h] because it neither sees him nor knows him. But you know him, for he lives with you and will be[b] in you. 18 I will not leave you as orphans; I will come to you.[i] 19 Before long, the world will not see me anymore, but you will see me.[j] Because I live, you also will live.[k] 20 On that day you will realize that I am in my Father,[l] and you are in me, and I am in you. 21 Whoever has my commands and obeys them, he is the one who loves me.[m] He who loves me will be loved by my Father,[n] and I too will love him and show myself to him."

22 Then Judas[o] (not Judas Iscariot) said, "But, Lord, why do you intend to show yourself to us and not to the world?"[p]

23 Jesus replied, "If anyone loves me, he will obey my teaching.[q] My Father will love him, and we will come to him and make our home with him.[r] 24 He who does not love me will not obey my teaching. These words you hear are not my own; they belong to the Father who sent me.[s]

25 "All this I have spoken while still with you. 26 But the Counselor,[t] the Holy Spirit, whom the Father will send in my name,[u] will teach you all things[v] and will remind you of everything I have said to you.[w] 27 Peace I leave with you; my peace I

---

a 7 Some early manuscripts *If you really have known me, you will know*   b 17 Some early manuscripts *and is*

John 14:5–14

📖 Jesus' answer to Thomas in verse 6 is the premier expression of the theology of John's Gospel: "I am the way and the truth and the life. No one comes to the Father except through me." Access to the Father's presence in heaven will be through Jesus alone. He's the only *Way*, the only One who can lead his followers to the places he's preparing (v. 3). This is true because he's the *Truth*, the authoritative representative and revealer of God. And those who follow Jesus will gain through him eternal *life* (cf. 11:25).

📖 Many today view all religions as offering variations on the same theme. People making exclusive claims to truth often find opponents who object not so much to the religious system advocated but to the "intolerant," "narrow-minded" nature of the claim. But Jesus doesn't just point the way—he *is* that Way. He doesn't just teach us truth—he *is* the Truth. Jesus doesn't represent one avenue to life—he *is* the Life. This is a restrictive claim that can't be compromised. In a

word, the human quest for God ends in the discovery of Jesus Christ.

John 14:15–31

📖 Jesus' teaching about our relationship with God reached its high point in these verses. The oneness he enjoyed with the Father would be paralleled by the unity the disciples would enjoy with him. The "counselor" was the promised Holy Spirit, who would guide and lead Christ's followers through the Son into intimacy with the Father. Here Jesus expanded on the meaning of the "home" he's preparing for us (v. 3). Not only will we be at home with God, but by the Spirit the Father and Son will be "at home" in us (v. 23). As the dwelling places of God, our love for and obedience to God are interwoven.

📖 The organizing theme of John 14 appears in verse 18: "I will not leave you as orphans; I will come to you." Throughout the chapter Jesus had assured his followers that, whatever might happen in the world, they would never be on their own. By the gift of the Spirit he would continue to shepherd and protect them. Orphans? Not us!

give you. *x* I do not give to you as the world gives. Do not let your hearts be troubled and do not be afraid.

28 "You heard me say, 'I am going away and I am coming back to you.' *y* If you loved me, you would be glad that I am going to the Father, *z* for the Father is greater than I. *a* 29 I have told you now before it happens, so that when it does happen you will believe. *b* 30 I will not speak with you much longer, for the prince of this world *c* is coming. He has no hold on me, 31 but the world must learn that I love the Father and that I do exactly what my Father has commanded me. *d*

"Come now; let us leave.

The Vine and the Branches

15 "I am the true vine, *e* and my Father is the gardener. 2 He cuts off every branch in me that bears no fruit, while every branch that does bear fruit he prunes *a* so that it will be even more fruitful. 3 You are already clean because of the word I have spoken to you. *f* 4 Remain in me, and I will remain in you. *g* No branch can bear fruit by itself; it must remain in the vine. Neither can you bear fruit unless you remain in me.

5 "I am the vine; you are the branches. If a man remains in me and I in him, he will bear much fruit; *h* apart from me you can do nothing. 6 If anyone does not remain in me, he is like a branch that is thrown away and withers; such branches are picked up, thrown into the fire and burned. *i* 7 If you remain in me and my words remain in you, ask whatever you wish, and it will be given you. *j* 8 This is to my Father's glory, *k* that you bear much fruit, showing yourselves to be my disciples. *l*

9 "As the Father has loved me, *m* so have I loved you. Now remain in my love. 10 If you obey my commands, *n* you will remain in my love, just as I have obeyed my Father's commands and remain in his love. 11 I have told you this so that my joy may be in you and that your joy may be complete. *o* 12 My command is this: Love each other as I have loved you. *p* 13 Greater love has no one than this, that he lay down his life for his friends. *q* 14 You are my friends *r* if you do what I command. *s* 15 I no longer call you servants, because a servant does not know his master's business. Instead, I have called you friends, for everything that I learned from my Father I have made known to you. *t* 16 You did not choose me, but I chose you and appointed you *u* to go and bear fruit—fruit that will last. Then the Father will give you whatever you ask in my name. 17 This is my command: Love each other. *v*

The World Hates the Disciples

18 "If the world hates you, *w* keep in mind that it hated me first. 19 If you belonged to the world, it would love you as its own. As it is, you do not belong to the world, but I have chosen you *x* out of the world. That is why the world hates you. *y*

a 2 The Greek for *prunes* also means *cleans*.

14:27
x Jn 16:33; Php 4:7; Col 3:15
14:28
y ver 2-4,18
z Jn 5:18
a Jn 10:29; Php 2:6
14:29
b Jn 13:19; 16:4
14:30
c Jn 12:31
14:31
d Jn 10:18; 12:49

15:1
e Isa 5:1-7

15:3
f Jn 13:10; 17:17; Eph 5:26
15:4
g Jn 6:56; 1Jn 2:6

15:5
h ver 16

15:6
i ver 2
15:7
j Mt 7:7
15:8
k Mt 5:16 *l* Jn 8:31
15:9
m Jn 17:23,24,26
15:10
n Jn 14:15
15:11
o Jn 17:13
15:12
p Jn 13:34
15:13
q Jn 10:11; Ro 5:7,8
15:14
r Lk 12:4 *s* Mt 12:50
15:15
t Jn 8:26
15:16
u Jn 6:70; 13:18
15:17
v ver 12

15:18
w 1Jn 3:13

15:19
x ver 16 *y* Jn 17:14

John 15:1–17

The picture of remaining (abiding) in Jesus in the same way a branch is attached to a vine aptly describes the life Jesus had been describing. The developing disciple, in whom the Father and the Son live through the Spirit, depends completely on Christ. A genuine spiritual encounter leads to a life that has Jesus' life running through its veins. Fruit becomes a sign of spiritual life and vitality. The fruit Jesus expected then—and still expects—from the branches is first and foremost love expressed in obedience.

Is discipleship a commitment to doctrinal beliefs about God and Jesus? Is it a way of life—or of *love*—that sets disciples apart from the world? Or is it an experience, a mystical, spiritual encounter that transforms? All three are true. Discipleship is a way of thinking (doc-trine) and living (ethics), as well as a supernatural experience (relationship). Neither doctrine nor ethics can alone define Christian discipleship. "Remaining in the vine"—experiencing Christ—is a nonnegotiable feature of following Jesus.

John 15:18—16:4

The disciples would be personally connected to God in the Spirit. But Jesus warned them about the conflicts they would encounter. His overriding theme is captured in John 15:20: "No servant is greater than his master." If Jesus experienced hostility, the same would be true of them. But Jesus would give them the "Counselor" or "Advocate." This is a judicial title for someone aiding in a legal argument. The Holy Spirit would strengthen the believers' witness, giving them the wisdom to live appropriately in the midst of life's trials.

15:20
z Jn 13:16
a 2Ti 3:12
15:21
b Mt 10:22
c Jn 16:3
15:22
d Jn 9:41; Ro 1:20

15:24
e Jn 5:36
15:25
f Ps 35:19; 69:4
15:26
g Jn 14:16
h Jn 14:26
i Jn 14:17 j 1Jn 5:7
15:27
k Lk 24:48; 1Jn 1:2;
4:14 l Lk 1:2
16:1
m Jn 15:18-27
n Mt 11:6
16:2
o Jn 9:22 p Isa 66:5;
Ac 26:9,10; Rev 6:9
16:3
q Jn 15:21; 17:25;
1Jn 3:1
16:4
r Jn 13:19

16:5
s Jn 7:33 t Jn 13:36;
14:5

16:7
u Jn 14:16,26;
15:26 v Jn 7:39
16:9
w Jn 15:22
16:10
x Ac 3:14; 7:52;
1Pe 3:18
16:11
y Jn 12:31
16:12
z Mk 4:33
16:13
a Jn 14:17
b Jn 14:26
16:15
c Jn 17:10

16:16
d Jn 7:33
e Jn 14:18-24

16:17
f ver 16 g ver 5

20 Remember the words I spoke to you: 'No servant is greater than his master.' [a][z] If they persecuted me, they will persecute you also. [a] If they obeyed my teaching, they will obey yours also. 21 They will treat you this way because of my name, [b] for they do not know the One who sent me. [c] 22 If I had not come and spoken to them, they would not be guilty of sin. Now, however, they have no excuse for their sin. [d] 23 He who hates me hates my Father as well. 24 If I had not done among them what no one else did, [e] they would not be guilty of sin. But now they have seen these miracles, and yet they have hated both me and my Father. 25 But this is to fulfill what is written in their Law: 'They hated me without reason.' [b][f]

26 "When the Counselor [g] comes, whom I will send to you from the Father, [h] the Spirit of truth [i] who goes out from the Father, he will testify about me. [j] 27 And you also must testify, [k] for you have been with me from the beginning. [l]

16 "All this [m] I have told you so that you will not go astray. [n] 2 They will put you out of the synagogue; [o] in fact, a time is coming when anyone who kills you will think he is offering a service to God. [p] 3 They will do such things because they have not known the Father or me. [q] 4 I have told you this, so that when the time comes you will remember [r] that I warned you. I did not tell you this at first because I was with you.

The Work of the Holy Spirit

5 "Now I am going to him who sent me, [s] yet none of you asks me, 'Where are you going?' [t] 6 Because I have said these things, you are filled with grief. 7 But I tell you the truth: It is for your good that I am going away. Unless I go away, the Counselor [u] will not come to you; but if I go, I will send him to you. [v] 8 When he comes, he will convict the world of guilt [c] in regard to sin and righteousness and judgment: 9 in regard to sin, [w] because men do not believe in me; 10 in regard to righteousness, [x] because I am going to the Father, where you can see me no longer; 11 and in regard to judgment, because the prince of this world [y] now stands condemned.

12 "I have much more to say to you, more than you can now bear. [z] 13 But when he, the Spirit of truth, [a] comes, he will guide you into all truth. [b] He will not speak on his own; he will speak only what he hears, and he will tell you what is yet to come. 14 He will bring glory to me by taking from what is mine and making it known to you. 15 All that belongs to the Father is mine. [c] That is why I said the Spirit will take from what is mine and make it known to you.

16 "In a little while [d] you will see me no more, and then after a little while you will see me." [e]

The Disciples' Grief Will Turn to Joy

17 Some of his disciples said to one another, "What does he mean by saying, 'In a little while you will see me no more, and then after a little while you will see me,' [f] and 'Because I am going to the Father'?" [g] 18 They kept asking, "What does he mean by 'a little while'? We don't understand what he is saying."

---

a 20 John 13:16   b 25 Psalms 35:19; 69:4   c 8 Or *will expose the guilt of the world*

Christians don't belong to the world and are wise not to expect its affection. On the contrary, persecution is a true sign of faithfulness to Christ. Jesus doesn't encourage us to *seek* persecution (it's not a merit badge proving we have been on the "front lines"), but he clearly warns us it will come. This is a far cry, though, from the motivation that drives most of us. To what extent is your goal often acceptance and affirmation? Does this at times lead you to keep your faith to yourself and conform to the world around you?

John 16:5–16

Jesus was putting the world on notice: Its guilt would be exposed. The Spirit would bring to light the true meaning of sin, righteousness, and judgment and would expose the world's fatal errors. Jesus' followers aren't given the function of judging the world. That is the role of the Holy Spirit.

Unfortunately, the church has often acted as the world's judge. Whenever it has, the world has quickly pointed out the church's own hypocrisy and failure to live differently from the world it criticizes. The work of the Spirit is to guide Jesus' followers into the truth so that our lives reflect his and to help the world see the error of its ways. How do you see the interrelationship of these two works of the Spirit in your own life?

19 Jesus saw that they wanted to ask him about this, so he said to them, "Are you asking one another what I meant when I said, 'In a little while you will see me no more, and then after a little while you will see me'? 20 I tell you the truth, you will weep and mourn *h* while the world rejoices. You will grieve, but your grief will turn to joy. *i* 21 A woman giving birth to a child has pain *j* because her time has come; but when her baby is born she forgets the anguish because of her joy that a child is born into the world. 22 So with you: Now is your time of grief, *k* but I will see you again *l* and you will rejoice, and no one will take away your joy. 23 In that day you will no longer ask me anything. I tell you the truth, my Father will give you whatever you ask in my name. *m* 24 Until now you have not asked for anything in my name. Ask and you will receive, and your joy will be complete. *n*

25 "Though I have been speaking figuratively, *o* a time is coming *p* when I will no longer use this kind of language but will tell you plainly about my Father. 26 In that day you will ask in my name. *q* I am not saying that I will ask the Father on your behalf. 27 No, the Father himself loves you because you have loved me *r* and have believed that I came from God. 28 I came from the Father and entered the world; now I am leaving the world and going back to the Father." *s*

29 Then Jesus' disciples said, "Now you are speaking clearly and without figures of speech. *t* 30 Now we can see that you know all things and that you do not even need to have anyone ask you questions. This makes us believe that you came from God."

31 "You believe at last!" *a* Jesus answered. 32 "But a time is coming, *u* and has come, when you will be scattered, *v* each to his own home. You will leave me all alone. Yet I am not alone, for my Father is with me. *w*

33 "I have told you these things, so that in me you may have peace. *x* In this world you will have trouble. *y* But take heart! I have overcome *z* the world."

Jesus Prays for Himself

17 After Jesus said this, he looked toward heaven *a* and prayed:

"Father, the time has come. Glorify your Son, that your Son may glorify you. *b* 2 For you granted him authority over all people that he might give eternal life to all those you have given him. *c* 3 Now this is eternal life: that they may know you, the only true God, and Jesus Christ, whom you have sent. *d* 4 I have brought you glory *e* on earth by completing the work you gave me to do. *f*

a 31 Or *"Do you now believe?"*

16:20
h Lk 23:27
i Jn 20:20
16:21
j Isa 26:17; 1Th 5:3
16:22
k ver 6 *l* ver 16

16:23
m Mt 7:7; Jn 15:16
16:24
n Jn 3:29; 15:11
16:25
o Mt 13:34; Jn 10:6
p ver 2
16:26
q ver 23,24
16:27
r Jn 14:21,23

16:28
s Jn 13:3

16:29
t ver 25

16:32
u ver 2,25
v Mt 26:31
w Jn 8:16,29

16:33
x Jn 14:27
y Jn 15:18-21
z Ro 8:37; 1Jn 4:4

17:1
a Jn 11:41
b Jn 12:23; 13:31,32

17:2
c ver 6,9,24; Da 7:14; Jn 6:37,39
17:3
d ver 8,18,21,23, 25; Jn 3:17
17:4
e Jn 13:31 *f* Jn 4:34

John 16:17–33

Jesus had represented the Father in the world (vv. 27–28; cf. 14:9). In him his disciples can draw close to the Father, asking freely for all they need. Verse 33 records Jesus' final words of comfort and reassurance to his disciples before his arrest. He had already referred to peace (14:27) and joy (vv. 20–22) as two gifts belonging to his followers. But they were to view these gifts together with the "trouble" they would have in the world. Still, no matter what the circumstances, Jesus' victory outweighs the jeopardy of the crisis.

We are interim citizens, living in the kingdom inaugurated by Christ yet yearning for its fulfillment. In this in-between citizenship we need to understand fully the nature of our lives. It's curious that Jesus spoke of peace, joy, and trouble in the same breath. The kind of peace he had in mind was peace *within* a storm. The peace of Jesus takes the struggles of the world seriously but keeps them in perspective. Jesus has conquered the world!

John 17:1–5

What did Jesus mean when he asked to be "glorified"? The Greek word *doxazo* has two sets of meanings: One is our common understanding—to praise, honor, or magnify. The other is to be solid, substantial, or strong. For Jesus the cross wasn't a place of shame but of honor. His oneness with God the Father meant that as he was glorified, so would be his Father. Also, through the brokenness of the cross, Jesus' followers would enter into the solidity of eternal life. Eternal life isn't just a place, but a relationship. To be in relationship with the Father and Son by the Spirit is to participate in the strength and the splendor of God!

Jesus' prayer covers all of John 17. In it John invites us to listen in on a divine conversation of the highest order. Jesus spoke of the completion of his tasks on Earth and prayed earnestly for his followers, both present and future. This prayer offers us a glimpse of who he truly is in relation to the Father. And it gives us a portrait of the things that were close to his heart in the last hours of his earthly life. If you knew you were fast approaching death, what issues do you suspect would occupy your heart and mind?

17:5
g Php 2:6 *h* Jn 1:2

17:6
i ver 26 *j* ver 2;
Jn 6:37,39

17:8
k ver 14,26
l Jn 16:27 *m* ver 3,
18,21,23,25;
Jn 3:17
17:9
n Lk 22:32
17:10
o Jn 16:15
17:11
p Jn 13:1 *q* Jn 7:33
r ver 21-23
s Jn 10:30

17:12
t Jn 6:39 *u* Jn 6:70

17:13
v Jn 3:29
17:14
w Jn 15:19
x Jn 8:23
17:15
y Mt 5:37

⁵And now, Father, glorify me in your presence with the glory I had with you *g* before the world began. *h*

Jesus Prays for His Disciples

⁶"I have revealed you ᵃ *i* to those whom you gave me *j* out of the world. They were yours; you gave them to me and they have obeyed your word. ⁷Now they know that everything you have given me comes from you. ⁸For I gave them the words you gave me *k* and they accepted them. They knew with certainty that I came from you, *l* and they believed that you sent me. *m* ⁹I pray for them. *n* I am not praying for the world, but for those you have given me, for they are yours. ¹⁰All I have is yours, and all you have is mine. *o* And glory has come to me through them. ¹¹I will remain in the world no longer, but they are still in the world, *p* and I am coming to you. *q* Holy Father, protect them by the power of your name—the name you gave me—so that they may be one *r* as we are one. *s* ¹²While I was with them, I protected them and kept them safe by that name you gave me. None has been lost *t* except the one doomed to destruction *u* so that Scripture would be fulfilled.

¹³"I am coming to you now, but I say these things while I am still in the world, so that they may have the full measure of my joy *v* within them. ¹⁴I have given them your word and the world has hated them, *w* for they are not of the world any more than I am of the world. *x* ¹⁵My prayer is not that you take them out of the world but that you protect them from the evil one. *y* ¹⁶They are not

---

ᵃ 6 Greek *your name*; also in verse 26

John 17:6–19

Now that Jesus' work was nearing completion, he prayed specifically for his immediate followers who would be left behind after he departed. His concerns: (1) He wanted them to remain united, to enjoy an intimacy and oneness like that he shared with the Father. (2) Their assignment of being sent into the world was dangerous, so Jesus prayed for their protection—particularly from Satan. (3) He also interceded for their sanctification or growth in holiness.

Jesus' disciples are "in the world but not of the world" (see v. 14) The issue isn't geographic but spiritual. All too often people who have called themselves "Christians" have been of the world but not really in it! Jesus prayed that his disciples might be sanctified by the truth. To be holy means to live a life so transformed by God that it expresses God's passions completely.

17:1–26

Jesus' PR🙏YERS

Jesus prayed often, upon many different occasions, for many different people, in many different ways. A few examples:

1. At his baptism (Luke 3:21–22).
We don't know the content of this prayer, but it was immediately followed by the Holy Spirit descending upon him in the form of a dove.

2. Before his temptation and public ministry launch (Luke 4:1–13).
The Bible doesn't explicitly state that Jesus prayed during his fast in the desert, but the two are often connected in Scripture (Neh. 1:4; Dan. 9:3; Luke 2:37; 5:33). We may conclude that he both fasted and prayed during this critical 40-day period.

3. Before choosing the disciples (Luke 6:12–13).
Jesus prayed all night before making crucial decisions about his key workers.

4. To teach others (Matt. 6:9–13).
Jesus presented the familiar Lord's Prayer as a model of how to pray when asked by his disciples for teaching on the subject.

5. Throughout his ministry (Luke 9:29).
Our Lord was a habitual pray-er.

6. Before his transfiguration (Luke 9:28–29).
Jesus took Peter, James, and John with him atop a mountain. While at prayer he was transfigured (his radiant appearance reflected the splendor of his divine majesty).

7. To bless children (Matt. 19:13–15).
People brought their children to Jesus for him to bless.

8. Before the raising of Lazarus (John 11:41–42).
In front of the open tomb, Jesus thanked God for hearing him. In the prayer he explicitly stated that he was praying for the hearers' benefit; he already knew Lazarus would emerge from the grave alive.

9. In the Garden of Gethsemane (Matt. 26:36).
Jesus first asked for God to spare him from crucifixion, then resigned himself to the Father's will.

10. For his disciples (John 17:1–26).
In his longest recorded prayer, Jesus asked God to glorify him in his final days and to bless his followers.

11. On the cross (Matt. 27:46).
In this poignant cry, Jesus asked the Father why he had forsaken him on the cross.

of the world, even as I am not of it.*z* *17*Sanctify*a* them by the truth; your word is truth.*a* *18*As you sent me into the world,*b* I have sent them into the world.*c* *19*For them I sanctify myself, that they too may be truly sanctified.

Jesus Prays for All Believers

20"My prayer is not for them alone. I pray also for those who will believe in me through their message, *21*that all of them may be one, Father, just as you are in me and I am in you.*d* May they also be in us so that the world may believe that you have sent me.*e* *22*I have given them the glory that you gave me, that they may be one as we are one:*f* *23*I in them and you in me. May they be brought to complete unity to let the world know that you sent me*g* and have loved them*h* even as you have loved me.

24"Father, I want those you have given me to be with me where I am,*i* and to see my glory,*j* the glory you have given me because you loved me before the creation of the world.*k*

25"Righteous Father, though the world does not know you,*l* I know you, and they know that you have sent me.*m* *26*I have made you known to them,*n* and will continue to make you known in order that the love you have for me may be in them*o* and that I myself may be in them."

Jesus Arrested

18 When he had finished praying, Jesus left with his disciples and crossed the Kidron Valley.*p* On the other side there was an olive grove,*q* and he and his disciples went into it.*r*

*2*Now Judas, who betrayed him, knew the place, because Jesus had often met there with his disciples.*s* *3*So Judas came to the grove, guiding*t* a detachment of soldiers and some officials from the chief priests and Pharisees.*u* They were carrying torches, lanterns and weapons.

*4*Jesus, knowing all that was going to happen to him,*v* went out and asked them, "Who is it you want?"*w*

5"Jesus of Nazareth," they replied.

"I am he," Jesus said. (And Judas the traitor was standing there with them.) *6*When Jesus said, "I am he," they drew back and fell to the ground.

*7*Again he asked them, "Who is it you want?"*x*

And they said, "Jesus of Nazareth."

8"I told you that I am he," Jesus answered. "If you are looking for me, then let

---

a 17 Greek *hagiazo (set apart for sacred use* or *make holy)*; also in verse 19

Cross references

17:16
z ver 14
17:17
a Jn 15:3
17:18
b ver 3,8,21,23,25
c Jn 20:21

17:21
d Jn 10:38 *e* ver 3, 8,18,23,25; Jn 3:17
17:22
f Jn 14:20
17:23
g Jn 3:17
h Jn 16:27

17:24
i Jn 12:26 / Jn 1:14
k ver 5; Mt 25:34

17:25
l Jn 15:21; 16:3
m ver 3,8,18,21,23; Jn 3:17; 7:29; 16:27
17:26
n ver 6 *o* Jn 15:9

18:1
p 2Sa 15:23
q ver 26 *r* Mt 26:36

18:2
s Lk 21:37; 22:39
18:3
t Ac 1:16 *u* ver 12

18:4
v Jn 6:64; 13:1,11
w ver 7

18:7
x ver 4

John 17:20–26

Jesus now prayed for his future followers—people he hadn't yet met, men and women across the ages. He prayed for their unity—not based simply on common beliefs or behaviors, but rather a unity found by participating in the very life of God. Because Jesus would be in them through the Spirit, they would become participants in the oneness of the Father, Son, and Spirit. That radically different kind of unity would cause the world to believe.

Jesus' prayer gives us insight into the nature of the relationship within God's *self*—within the "godhead." Incredibly, the prayer invites us into that circle of intimacy: "May they also be in us" (v. 21). How does this understanding of unity impact your view of your relationship with God and your approach to fellow believers?

John 18:1–11

Jesus' arrest didn't take him by surprise (v. 4). In fact, he stepped forward and initiated the interaction. Jesus identified himself using the "I am" formula seen

elsewhere in John's Gospel (e.g., 8:12,58)—which no doubt recalled God's divine name (see "There and Then" for 6:16–24). Upon hearing it, the soldiers and officials "drew back and fell to the ground." Jesus' words provoked a reaction his hearers themselves probably failed to understand—a Biblical response of holy fear before the Lord (Ezek. 1:28; Acts 26:14–15; Rev. 1:17). God had been revealed before mortals. The only possible response was to fall prostrate.

Jesus took charge of his own arrest. Twice he made the arresting party state that he was the one they wanted, thus protecting his followers from capture. Jesus functions as the good shepherd for us as well—not only laying down his life for us, his sheep, but also protecting us from wolves (10:11–12). Even in the darkest hour, Jesus is in control. And in the end, even his enemies will bow down and acknowledge him as Lord (Phil. 2:9–11). What difference does it make for you that Jesus is your Shepherd? Your Lord?

these men go." 9This happened so that the words he had spoken would be fulfilled: "I have not lost one of those you gave me."a y

10Then Simon Peter, who had a sword, drew it and struck the high priest's servant, cutting off his right ear. (The servant's name was Malchus.)

11Jesus commanded Peter, "Put your sword away! Shall I not drink the cupz the Father has given me?"

Jesus Taken to Annas

12Then the detachment of soldiers with its commander and the Jewish officialsa arrested Jesus. They bound him 13and brought him first to Annas, who was the father-in-law of Caiaphas,b the high priest that year. 14Caiaphas was the one who had advised the Jews that it would be good if one man died for the people.c

Peter's First Denial

15Simon Peter and another disciple were following Jesus. Because this disciple was known to the high priest,d he went with Jesus into the high priest's courtyard,e 16but Peter had to wait outside at the door. The other disciple, who was known to the high priest, came back, spoke to the girl on duty there and brought Peter in.

17"You are not one of his disciples, are you?" the girl at the door asked Peter. He replied, "I am not."f

18It was cold, and the servants and officials stood around a fireg they had made to keep warm. Peter also was standing with them, warming himself.h

The High Priest Questions Jesus

19Meanwhile, the high priest questioned Jesus about his disciples and his teaching.

20"I have spoken openly to the world," Jesus replied. "I always taught in synagoguesi or at the temple,j where all the Jews come together. I said nothing in secret.k 21Why question me? Ask those who heard me. Surely they know what I said."

a 9 John 6:39

John 18:12–14

Annas had been the high priest before being deposed by the Romans. His son-in-law Caiaphas held the office officially, though Annas retained a popular following. That John referred in the verses following this passage to Annas as high priest shouldn't confuse us. He clearly understood Caiaphas to be the ruling high priest. John reminded his readers of Caiaphas's unconscious prophecy in 11:50. The supreme irony of this statement can be appreciated in retrospect. It clearly reflects God's hand in the unfolding events leading to the crucifixion.

The image of an armed detachment of soldiers escorting one bound prisoner is ludicrous—what we would call "overkill." This picture underscores for us, though, the power of Satan and his evil cohorts in the world. Or, more to the point, their pitiful lack of power in the face of Jesus, our willing sacrificial Lamb. The truth is that no amount of force could have stopped God's perfect plan from moving forward (cf. 1 Cor. 2:8). What a powerful reminder that the One in us is infinitely greater than the one in the world (1 John 4:4)!

John 18:15–18

When Peter entered the courtyard, the young woman guarding the gate immediately inquired whether he was one of Jesus' disciples. Each of the Gospels notes that a young girl asked the question, and its form in the Greek implies a negative answer. She was cautious but curious, suggesting that she knew there were many who followed Jesus. Although Peter understandably felt vulnerable in the small courtyard swelling with people, it seems ironic that he lost his nerve when questioned by a servant girl.

Despite Peter's prominence and his role as custodian of the faith and leader among the disciples, he could still deny that faith. This is a warning. Actions of denial and faithlessness are always within reach of even the strongest disciple. Paul's words of caution in 1 Corinthians 10:12 come to mind: "If you think you are standing firm, be careful that you don't fall!" This incident doesn't address directly the larger issue of our eternal security in Christ (Peter was later restored into fellowship with Jesus in 21:1–19). When have you acted faithlessly, even if you didn't lose your faith?

John 18:19–24

In a formal Jewish trial, the judge didn't ask direct questions of the accused. Instead, he called witnesses whose words determined the outcome. If two or more agreed on the charge, the verdict was sealed. But this scene was more like a police interrogation than a trial. Jesus' sharp answer to the priest's direct question—pointing out that Annas should be talking to witnesses—unmasked Annas's attempt to make Jesus incriminate himself. In essence, Jesus was demanding a trial.

²²When Jesus said this, one of the officials *l* nearby struck him in the face. *m* "Is this the way you answer the high priest?" he demanded.

²³"If I said something wrong," Jesus replied, "testify as to what is wrong. But if I spoke the truth, why did you strike me?" *n* ²⁴Then Annas sent him, still bound, to Caiaphas *o* the high priest. *a*

Peter's Second and Third Denials

²⁵As Simon Peter stood warming himself, *p* he was asked, "You are not one of his disciples, are you?"

He denied it, saying, "I am not." *q*

²⁶One of the high priest's servants, a relative of the man whose ear Peter had cut off, *r* challenged him, "Didn't I see you with him in the olive grove?" *s* ²⁷Again Peter denied it, and at that moment a rooster began to crow. *t*

Jesus Before Pilate

²⁸Then the Jews led Jesus from Caiaphas to the palace of the Roman governor. *u* By now it was early morning, and to avoid ceremonial uncleanness the Jews did not enter the palace; *v* they wanted to be able to eat the Passover. *w* ²⁹So Pilate came out to them and asked, "What charges are you bringing against this man?"

³⁰"If he were not a criminal," they replied, "we would not have handed him over to you."

³¹Pilate said, "Take him yourselves and judge him by your own law."

"But we have no right to execute anyone," the Jews objected. ³²This happened so that the words Jesus had spoken indicating the kind of death he was going to die *x* would be fulfilled.

³³Pilate then went back inside the palace, *y* summoned Jesus and asked him, "Are you the king of the Jews?" *z*

³⁴"Is that your own idea," Jesus asked, "or did others talk to you about me?"

³⁵"Am I a Jew?" Pilate replied. "It was your people and your chief priests who handed you over to me. What is it you have done?"

a 24 Or (Now Annas had sent him, still bound, to Caiaphas the high priest.)

18:22
l ver 3 *m* Mt 16:21; Jn 19:3

18:23
n Mt 5:39; Ac 23:2-5

18:24
o ver 13; Mt 26:3

18:25
p ver 18 *q* ver 17

18:26
r ver 10 *s* ver 1

18:27
t Jn 13:38

18:28
u Mt 27:2; Mk 15:1; Lk 23:1 *v* ver 33; Jn 19:9 *w* Jn 11:55

18:32
x Mt 20:19; 26:2; Jn 3:14; 8:28; 12:32,33

18:33
y ver 28,29; Jn 19:9 *z* Lk 23:3; Mt 2:2

📖 There comes a point in our own dealings with hardened people at which further attempts at persuasion are pointless. God's truth stands on its own merit, and very few unsympathetic individuals are convicted of sin and drawn to the Savior on the basis of intellectual discussion or argument. At this point it's probably best for us to back off and allow our lives to tell the story of Jesus and his love, all the while relying on the Holy Spirit's convicting work (cf. 16:7–9). If you have tried unsuccessfully through your words to draw someone like this to the Lord, what tactic did you revert to? Have you seen results?

John 18:25–27

🔄 John returned to Peter's ongoing failings as a witness in the courtyard. His warming himself by the fire connected this scene with his first denial. Now the drama tightened. Around the fire stood "officials" (probably temple guards) and servants (v. 18). When they questioned Peter, he uttered a second denial. Then Peter's worries were confirmed: A relative of Malchus, the man Peter had attacked at Jesus' arrest (v. 10), spoke up. When Peter denied Jesus a third time, a rooster crowed, recalling Jesus' awful prediction of Peter's failure (13:38).

🔄 Perhaps what stands out most sharply in Peter's story is its aftermath: Jesus' continued interest in his fallen disciple. John reported later that the risen Jesus renewed his relationship with Peter (21:1–19). This com-plex, impulsive, and likable individual was a man still deeply loved—a man with work to do for his Master. Ours is a guilt-ridden age, with people's lives frequently broken by a sense of profound shame. If one medicine is needed in the lives of countless individuals, many of them Christians, it's the balm of forgiveness for their deepest shame.

John 18:28–40

🔄 Jesus' revelation that he was testifying to the truth served as an invitation for Pilate to believe in him. But Pilate's condemnation of Jesus was a condemnation of the Truth. Jesus had reversed positions with Pilate. Now Pilate had been challenged and carried the burden of response. His cynical question, "What is truth?" revealed his true position: Pilate couldn't recognize the things of God and would avoid the light (3:19–21). He didn't wait for an answer—because he didn't believe there was any.

🔄 While Annas and Caiaphas represent the betrayal of religious leadership, Pilate represents the betrayal of secular leadership that surrounds us today at every turn. How often do the Pilates of our world pursue a course of expediency, protecting their self-interest, using the "right" words, feigning an interest in truth? Yet when pressed to make a decision with moral consequences, they crumble. "What is truth?" is the question people ask when truth is the last thing they want to hear.

18:36
a Mt 3:2 b Mt 26:53
c Lk 17:21; Jn 6:15

18:37
d Jn 3:32 e Jn 8:47;
1Jn 4:6

18:38
f Lk 23:4; Jn 19:4,6

18:40
g Ac 3:14

19:1
h Dt 25:3; Isa 50:6;
53:5; Mt 27:26

19:3
i Mt 27:29
j Jn 18:22
19:4
k Jn 18:38 / ver 6;
Lk 23:4

19:5
m ver 2

19:6
n Ac 3:13 o ver 4;
Lk 23:4
19:7
p Lev 24:16
q Mt 26:63-66;
Jn 5:18; 10:33

19:9
r Jn 18:33
s Mk 14:61

19:11
t Ro 13:1
u Jn 18:28-30;
Ac 3:13

19:12
v Lk 23:2

19:13
w Mt 27:19 x Jn 5:2
19:14
y Mt 27:62
z Mk 15:25
a ver 19,21

19:16
b Mt 27:26;
Mk 15:15; Lk 23:25

36 Jesus said, "My kingdom *a* is not of this world. If it were, my servants would fight to prevent my arrest by the Jews. *b* But now my kingdom is from another place." *c*

37 "You are a king, then!" said Pilate.

Jesus answered, "You are right in saying I am a king. In fact, for this reason I was born, and for this I came into the world, to testify to the truth. *d* Everyone on the side of truth listens to me." *e*

38 "What is truth?" Pilate asked. With this he went out again to the Jews and said, "I find no basis for a charge against him. *f* 39 But it is your custom for me to release to you one prisoner at the time of the Passover. Do you want me to release 'the king of the Jews'?"

40 They shouted back, "No, not him! Give us Barabbas!" Now Barabbas had taken part in a rebellion. *g*

Jesus Sentenced to Be Crucified

19 Then Pilate took Jesus and had him flogged. *h* 2 The soldiers twisted together a crown of thorns and put it on his head. They clothed him in a purple robe 3 and went up to him again and again, saying, "Hail, king of the Jews!" *i* And they struck him in the face. *j*

4 Once more Pilate came out and said to the Jews, "Look, I am bringing him out *k* to you to let you know that I find no basis for a charge against him." *l* 5 When Jesus came out wearing the crown of thorns and the purple robe, *m* Pilate said to them, "Here is the man!"

6 As soon as the chief priests and their officials saw him, they shouted, "Crucify! Crucify!"

But Pilate answered, "You take him and crucify him. *n* As for me, I find no basis for a charge against him." *o*

7 The Jews insisted, "We have a law, and according to that law he must die, *p* because he claimed to be the Son of God." *q*

8 When Pilate heard this, he was even more afraid, 9 and he went back inside the palace. *r* "Where do you come from?" he asked Jesus, but Jesus gave him no answer. *s* 10 "Do you refuse to speak to me?" Pilate said. "Don't you realize I have power either to free you or to crucify you?"

11 Jesus answered, "You would have no power over me if it were not given to you from above. *t* Therefore the one who handed me over to you *u* is guilty of a greater sin."

12 From then on, Pilate tried to set Jesus free, but the Jews kept shouting, "If you let this man go, you are no friend of Caesar. Anyone who claims to be a king *v* opposes Caesar."

13 When Pilate heard this, he brought Jesus out and sat down on the judge's seat *w* at a place known as the Stone Pavement (which in Aramaic *x* is Gabbatha). 14 It was the day of Preparation *y* of Passover Week, about the sixth hour. *z*

"Here is your king," *a* Pilate said to the Jews.

15 But they shouted, "Take him away! Take him away! Crucify him!"

"Shall I crucify your king?" Pilate asked.

"We have no king but Caesar," the chief priests answered.

16 Finally Pilate handed him over to them to be crucified. *b*

John 19:1–16a

This passage bristles with irony. The soldiers mocked and abused the "king of the Jews." Pilate sarcastically stated, "Here is your king" (v. 14; cf. v. 5) and in the end agreed to crucify Jesus. The chief priests laid the groundwork for their own blasphemy. "We have no king but Caesar" was a direct contradiction of the Old Testament declaration that *God* alone was Israel's king (1 Sam. 8:7; 10:19)—and that the kings who did reign did so by divine appointment. By rejecting Jesus they rejected God himself. This was just as Jesus had predicted: "He who does not honor the Son does not hon-

or the Father, who sent him" (5:23).

This is indeed a story of tragedy. But it wasn't Jesus' tragedy. Our hearts are broken as we witness the futile efforts of people blinded by darkness, unable to recognize the true King in their midst. God is in control of history—even this hostile, darkened chapter of history that seemingly offered no hope. If God could demonstrate glory and accomplish his purposes here, when to the observer everything seemed like defeat and disaster, our history can be no different. What hour in your life has he transformed from calamity to glory (cf. 12:23)?

The Crucifixion

So the soldiers took charge of Jesus. [17]Carrying his own cross,[c] he went out to the place of the Skull[d] (which in Aramaic[e] is called Golgotha). [18]Here they crucified him, and with him two others[f]—one on each side and Jesus in the middle.

[19]Pilate had a notice prepared and fastened to the cross. It read: JESUS OF NAZARETH,[g] THE KING OF THE JEWS.[h] [20]Many of the Jews read this sign, for the place where Jesus was crucified was near the city,[i] and the sign was written in Aramaic, Latin and Greek. [21]The chief priests of the Jews protested to Pilate, "Do not write 'The King of the Jews,' but that this man claimed to be king of the Jews."[j]

[22]Pilate answered, "What I have written, I have written."

[23]When the soldiers crucified Jesus, they took his clothes, dividing them into four shares, one for each of them, with the undergarment remaining. This garment was seamless, woven in one piece from top to bottom.

[24]"Let's not tear it," they said to one another. "Let's decide by lot who will get it." This happened that the scripture might be fulfilled[k] which said,

> "They divided my garments among them
> and cast lots for my clothing."[a][l]

So this is what the soldiers did.

[25]Near the cross[m] of Jesus stood his mother,[n] his mother's sister, Mary the wife of Clopas, and Mary Magdalene.[o] [26]When Jesus saw his mother[p] there, and the disciple whom he loved[q] standing nearby, he said to his mother, "Dear woman, here is your son," [27]and to the disciple, "Here is your mother." From that time on, this disciple took her into his home.

The Death of Jesus

[28]Later, knowing that all was now completed,[r] and so that the Scripture would be fulfilled,[s] Jesus said, "I am thirsty." [29]A jar of wine vinegar[t] was there, so they soaked a sponge in it, put the sponge on a stalk of the hyssop plant, and lifted it to Jesus' lips. [30]When he had received the drink, Jesus said, "It is finished."[u] With that, he bowed his head and gave up his spirit.

[31]Now it was the day of Preparation,[v] and the next day was to be a special Sabbath. Because the Jews did not want the bodies left on the crosses[w] during the Sab-

[a] 24 Psalm 22:18

19:17
[c] Ge 22:6; Lk 14:27; 23:26 [d] Lk 23:33 [e] Jn 5:2
19:18
[f] Lk 23:32

19:19
[g] Mk 1:24 [h] ver 14,21
19:20
[i] Heb 13:12

19:21
[j] ver 14

19:24
[k] ver 28,36,37; Mt 1:22 [l] Ps 22:18

19:25
[m] Mt 27:55,56; Mk 15:40,41; Lk 23:49 [n] Mt 12:46 [o] Lk 24:18
19:26
[p] Mt 12:46 [q] Jn 13:23

19:28
[r] ver 30; Jn 13:1 [s] ver 24,36,37
19:29
[t] Ps 69:21
19:30
[u] Lk 12:50; Jn 17:4

19:31
[v] ver 14,42 [w] Dt 21:23; Jos 8:29; 10:26,27

John 19:16b–27

It was customary for the Romans to provide a public, written notice of a criminal's name and activity. In this case, it was written in (1) Aramaic, which the Jews would understand; (2) Latin, the language of the Romans; and (3) Greek, the universal language of the Mediterranean world. It comes as no surprise that the chief priests were furious and insulted, realizing that the sign implied a sarcastic endorsement by Rome of Jesus' royal (indeed, divine) identity. But for the first time in the story, Pilate stood up to them. He refused to publish a lie, even though he lacked the courage to act on the truth. Thus Jesus' kingship was revealed.

John made Jesus' regal glory central to his account. The title over the cross—JESUS OF NAZARETH, THE KING OF THE JEWS—made the imagery obvious. It's not that Jesus was *merely* king over Israel. He was and is a *global, international* King. In God's eyes the notice included countless other languages: Russian, Swahili, Swedish, Arabic, Spanish, Japanese, Hindi . . . Pilate's notice rightly suggested that there was no limit. Is Jesus' kingship all-important in your life? Without any limits?

John 19:28–37

Throughout the trial sequence John had portrayed Jesus as the victorious King, the One who knew more than his captors and controlled the events. The same scenario appears in the story of the cross. What Jesus knew about the finality of his work (v. 28) he now uttered aloud: "It is finished" (v. 30). This confirmed the sense throughout the story that Jesus was accomplishing what he intended. He wasn't a victim but a servant doing God's bidding. This wasn't a cry of desolation or resignation ("At last it's over!") but an announcement of triumph ("It's accomplished!").

"It is finished" is our signal that God has succeeded in accomplishing everything he designed to do in the life of his Son. In Jesus Christ, God himself was at work demonstrating his love for us, revealing his will for our lives, and bringing about a reconciliation that needs no supplement. Jesus' victory is the basis of our security. Our confidence in God and the assurance of our salvation can't be anchored in our religious performance. "It is finished." What was needed to satisfy God ought to satisfy us as well. This is the Good News of the gospel.

bath, they asked Pilate to have the legs broken and the bodies taken down. 32The soldiers therefore came and broke the legs of the first man who had been crucified with Jesus, and then those of the other. x 33But when they came to Jesus and found that he was already dead, they did not break his legs. 34Instead, one of the soldiers pierced y Jesus' side with a spear, bringing a sudden flow of blood and water. z 35The man who saw it a has given testimony, and his testimony is true. b He knows that he tells the truth, and he testifies so that you also may believe. 36These things happened so that the scripture would be fulfilled: c "Not one of his bones will be broken," a d 37and, as another scripture says, "They will look on the one they have pierced." b e

The Burial of Jesus

38Later, Joseph of Arimathea asked Pilate for the body of Jesus. Now Joseph was a disciple of Jesus, but secretly because he feared the Jews. With Pilate's permission, he came and took the body away. 39He was accompanied by Nicodemus, f the man who earlier had visited Jesus at night. Nicodemus brought a mixture of myrrh and aloes, about seventy-five pounds. c 40Taking Jesus' body, the two of them wrapped it, with the spices, in strips of linen. g This was in accordance with Jewish burial customs. h 41At the place where Jesus was crucified, there was a garden, and in the garden a new tomb, in which no one had ever been laid. 42Because it was the Jewish day of Preparation i and since the tomb was nearby, j they laid Jesus there.

The Empty Tomb

20 Early on the first day of the week, while it was still dark, Mary Magdalene k went to the tomb and saw that the stone had been removed from the entrance. l 2So she came running to Simon Peter and the other disciple, the one Jesus loved, m and said, "They have taken the Lord out of the tomb, and we don't know where they have put him!" n

3So Peter and the other disciple started for the tomb. o 4Both were running, but the other disciple outran Peter and reached the tomb first. 5He bent over and looked in p at the strips of linen q lying there but did not go in. 6Then Simon Peter, who was behind him, arrived and went into the tomb. He saw the strips of linen lying there, 7as well as the burial cloth that had been around Jesus' head. r The cloth was folded up by itself, separate from the linen. 8Finally the other disciple, who had

19:32
x ver 18

19:34
y Zec 12:10
z 1Jn 5:6,8

19:35
a Lk 24:48
b Jn 15:27; 21:24

19:36
c ver 24,28,37;
Mt 1:22 d Ex 12:46;
Nu 9:12; Ps 34:20

19:37
e Zec 12:10;
Rev 1:7

19:39
f Jn 3:1; 7:50

19:40
g Lk 24:12;
Jn 11:44; 20:5,7
h Mt 26:12

19:42
i ver 14,31
j ver 20,41

20:1
k ver 18; Jn 19:25
l Mt 27:60,66

20:2
m Jn 13:23 n ver 13

20:3
o Lk 24:12

20:5
p ver 11 q Jn 19:40

20:7
r Jn 11:44

---

a 36 Exodus 12:46; Num. 9:12; Psalm 34:20   b 37 Zech. 12:10   c 39 Greek *a hundred litrai* (about 34 kilograms)

John 19:38–42

Joseph was a wealthy (Matt. 27:57) member of the Sanhedrin, or supreme Jewish council (Mark 15:43). But he disagreed with Jesus' prosecution (Luke 23:50–51). Nicodemus also was a member of the Sanhedrin (3:1; 7:50–51). John's earlier description of these men sounded critical (cf. 12:42–43), but they redeemed their images here by honoring Jesus generously, publicly, and at great personal risk. Each could have been excommunicated from the synagogue and ousted from the Sanhedrin. Their definitive actions affected every aspect of their personal and professional lives.

As professionals with considerable social prestige and high visibility, Joseph and Nicodemus were deliberately stepping into the circle of true discipleship, joining the community of the faithful. The cross became for them, as for us, life's turning point. In Jesus' words, "I, when I am lifted up from the earth, will draw all [people] to myself" (John 12:32). Are you letting the world know your stand for the cross?

John 20:1–9

When Mary Magdalene discovered the empty tomb, she ran to tell Peter and "the other disciple"—John, the author of this Gospel. John's description of the grave clothes includes some unexpected details. If someone had simply stolen Jesus' body, the clothes would most likely have been missing, or at least strewn about the floor. But here was a baffling scenario in which the body was missing but the clothes appeared neatly folded. Seeing this, John "believed" Jesus had risen from the dead—though he wouldn't until later actually see Christ's resurrected body.

John provided the best evidence he could muster to persuade us that belief is both a reasonable choice and a necessary decision if we are to follow Jesus. The resurrection was the capstone event in Jesus' life. In fact, without this critical occurrence, the infrastructure of the Christian faith falls apart. See 1 Corinthians 15:12–20 for Paul's grim assessment of this unthinkable possibility. What priority does Christ's resurrection have in your life? Is it the pivotal reality around which everything else falls into place?

reached the tomb first,[s] also went inside. He saw and believed. [9](They still did not understand from Scripture[t] that Jesus had to rise from the dead.)[u]

Jesus Appears to Mary Magdalene

[10]Then the disciples went back to their homes, [11]but Mary stood outside the tomb crying. As she wept, she bent over to look into the tomb[v] [12]and saw two angels in white,[w] seated where Jesus' body had been, one at the head and the other at the foot.

[13]They asked her, "Woman, why are you crying?"[x]

"They have taken my Lord away," she said, "and I don't know where they have put him."[y] [14]At this, she turned around and saw Jesus standing there,[z] but she did not realize that it was Jesus.[a]

[15]"Woman," he said, "why are you crying?[b] Who is it you are looking for?"

Thinking he was the gardener, she said, "Sir, if you have carried him away, tell me where you have put him, and I will get him."

[16]Jesus said to her, "Mary."

She turned toward him and cried out in Aramaic,[c] "Rabboni!"[d] (which means Teacher).

[17]Jesus said, "Do not hold on to me, for I have not yet returned to the Father. Go instead to my brothers[e] and tell them, 'I am returning to my Father[f] and your Father, to my God and your God.'"

[18]Mary Magdalene[g] went to the disciples[h] with the news: "I have seen the Lord!" And she told them that he had said these things to her.

Jesus Appears to His Disciples

[19]On the evening of that first day of the week, when the disciples were together, with the doors locked for fear of the Jews,[i] Jesus came and stood among them and said, "Peace[j] be with you!"[k] [20]After he said this, he showed them his hands and side.[l] The disciples were overjoyed[m] when they saw the Lord.

[21]Again Jesus said, "Peace be with you![n] As the Father has sent me,[o] I am sending you."[p] [22]And with that he breathed on them and said, "Receive the Holy Spir-

20:8
s ver 4
20:9
t Mt 22:29; Jn 2:22
u Lk 24:26,46

20:11
v ver 5
20:12
w Mt 28:2,3;
Mk 16:5; Lk 24:4;
Ac 5:19
20:13
x ver 15 y ver 2
20:14
z Mt 28:9; Mk 16:9
a Lk 24:16; Jn 21:4
20:15
b ver 13

20:16
c Jn 5:2 d Mt 23:7

20:17
e Mt 28:10 f Jn 7:33

20:18
g ver 1
h Lk 24:10,22,23

20:19
i Jn 7:13
20:19
j Jn 14:27 k ver 21,
26; Lk 24:36-39
20:20
l Lk 24:39,40;
Jn 19:34
m Jn 16:20,22
20:21
n ver 19 o Jn 3:17
p Mt 28:19;
Jn 17:18

John 20:10–18

This section centers on Jesus' correction of Mary after she had apparently embraced him (cf. Matt. 28:9). This is typically interpreted as a statement about his transformed relationship with her. Mary thought Jesus' resurrection meant the resumption of normal relationships with his followers. In telling her not to hold on to him, Jesus was saying that his permanent "return" and presence were to come later, in another form. He was directing her away from his physical presence in preparation for the Spirit that would soon be given.

Jesus was being glorified, and his relationship with his followers had to change. Mary couldn't "hold on" to the way he had lived and worked with them but

---

20:21

The New Testament is clear that we are to witness to our faith. Witnessing, though, takes many forms—preaching, teaching, healing, helping the poor, friendship, lifestyle, and more. Because of the wide, 24/7 scope of action, it's important that we understand the four roots of witnessing so we can best determine how witnessing integrates into our individual and corporate community life:

Four Roots of
BIBLICAL WITNESS

A c t i o n ❶

The Great Commission (Matt. 28:19–20) tells us what to do: "Go and make disciples of all nations."

A t t i t u d e ❷

The Great Commandment (Mark 12:30–31) tells us the disposition we are to have: "Love the Lord your God with all your heart and with all your soul and with all your mind and with all your strength . . . Love your neighbor as yourself."

M o d e l ❸

Jesus is the great model (John 20:21) of what our task should be:"As the Father has sent me, I am sending you."

M e t h o d ❹

The great method (1 Peter 3:15) tells us how we are to go about our task: "Always be prepared to give an answer to everyone who asks you to give the reason for the hope that you have."

20:22
q Jn 7:39; Ac 2:38;
8:15-17; 19:2;
Gal 3:2
20:23
r Mt 16:19; 18:18
20:24
s Jn 11:16

it. *q* 23 If you forgive anyone his sins, they are forgiven; if you do not forgive them, they are not forgiven." *r*

Jesus Appears to Thomas

24 Now Thomas *s* (called Didymus), one of the Twelve, was not with the disciples when Jesus came. 25 So the other disciples told him, "We have seen the Lord!"

20:25
t ver 20 *u* Mk 16:11
20:26
v Jn 14:27 *w* ver 21

But he said to them, "Unless I see the nail marks in his hands and put my finger where the nails were, and put my hand into his side, *t* I will not believe." *u*

26 A week later his disciples were in the house again, and Thomas was with them. Though the doors were locked, Jesus came and stood among them and said, "Peace *v* be with you!" *w* 27 Then he said to Thomas, "Put your finger here; see my hands. Reach out your hand and put it into my side. Stop doubting and believe." *x*

20:27
x ver 25; Lk 24:40

28 Thomas said to him, "My Lord and my God!"

20:29
y Jn 3:15 *z* 1Pe 1:8
20:30
a Jn 2:11 *b* Jn 21:25
20:31
c Jn 3:15; 19:35
d Mt 4:3 *e* Mt 25:46

29 Then Jesus told him, "Because you have seen me, you have believed; *y* blessed are those who have not seen and yet have believed." *z*

30 Jesus did many other miraculous signs *a* in the presence of his disciples, which are not recorded in this book. *b* 31 But these are written that you may *a* believe *c* that Jesus is the Christ, the Son of God, *d* and that by believing you may have life in his name. *e*

Jesus and the Miraculous Catch of Fish

21:1
f Jn 20:19,26
g Jn 6:1
21:2
h Jn 11:16 *i* Jn 1:45
j Jn 2:1 *k* Mt 4:21

21 Afterward Jesus appeared again to his disciples, *f* by the Sea of Tiberias. *b g* It happened this way: 2 Simon Peter, Thomas *h* (called Didymus), Nathanael *i* from Cana in Galilee, *j* the sons of Zebedee, *k* and two other disciples were together. 3 "I'm going out to fish," Simon Peter told them, and they said, "We'll go with you." So they went out and got into the boat, but that night they caught nothing. *l*

21:3
l Lk 5:5

a 31 Some manuscripts *may continue to*   *b 1* That is, Sea of Galilee

needed a new perspective on the nature of intimacy with him. From now on it would be a spiritual closeness—realized in the coming of the Holy Spirit (vv. 21–23; cf. Acts 2:1–4). Our own coming to Christ also means discarding outmoded models about relating to God. As the "author and perfecter of our faith" (Heb. 12:2), Jesus defines the relationship. How readily do you adapt to changes initiated by God in your relationship with him?

John 20:19–23

This climactic passage begins with Jesus suddenly appearing to his frightened disciples. In 14:27 and 16:33 he had promised them the gift of peace. Now he delivered! Fast on the heels of their joy, Jesus charged them with a commission. As Jesus was God's special representative in the world, his disciples would become Jesus' agents. In verse 22 he voiced an astounding truth: Being commissioned to participate in God's work in the world means being empowered as Jesus was empowered—by receiving the Spirit.

Jesus framed his gift of the Spirit to his followers with two messages, both outlining aspects of the church's work in the world. We enter the world as bearers of peace and power. We are commissioned to participate in Jesus' mission, bearing the news of God's forgiveness of sins. The church doesn't have its own "mission." Rather, we as its members are sent by Jesus. This shapes our sense of confidence, authority, and purposefulness as we engage with the world.

John 20:24–31

Thomas, the skeptic, refused to believe until he had confirmed the reality for himself. Thomas's faith was

anchored in sight. This didn't necessarily mean it was blemished or weak. But he was privileged. Few would ever have the opportunity these disciples experienced. John's inclusion of this very human episode in his Gospel might be seen as a dramatic gift for cynics or pragmatists of all times.

Have you ever longed for proof of the resurrection, either for your own benefit or for help in convincing a skeptic? Thomas becomes a model for us, who read the story of Jesus from a distance and are challenged, sight unseen, to believe. This fortunate disciple got what he wanted and so believed. But he missed the blessing Jesus pronounces on those who believe even though they can't see or touch. This is precisely our position as we live out our lives and faith in today's world.

John 21:1–14

Unlike the rest of John's Gospel, the fishing miracle *wasn't* a compelling sign pointing unbelievers toward belief in the resurrected Christ. Chapter 21 is an epilogue addressed to the church, focusing on its relationship with the risen Christ and its ministry work in the world. Interestingly, Jesus had performed the same miracle once before at the same lake (see Luke 5:1–11). Early in his ministry he had gotten the disciples' attention with a dramatic catch of fish—an event that launched their joint ministry in Galilee. Now Jesus reclaimed their attention by evoking an old memory.

This miracle was no doubt a symbol as well as a surprise. Jesus was still the disciples' champion, providing for them in their daily struggles. But more, he wanted to direct their work. And with his help they would haul in

4Early in the morning, Jesus stood on the shore, but the disciples did not realize that it was Jesus. *m*

5He called out to them, "Friends, haven't you any fish?"

"No," they answered.

6He said, "Throw your net on the right side of the boat and you will find some." When they did, they were unable to haul the net in because of the large number of fish. *n*

7Then the disciple whom Jesus loved *o* said to Peter, "It is the Lord!" As soon as Simon Peter heard him say, "It is the Lord," he wrapped his outer garment around him (for he had taken it off) and jumped into the water. 8The other disciples followed in the boat, towing the net full of fish, for they were not far from shore, about a hundred yards. *a* 9When they landed, they saw a fire *p* of burning coals there with fish on it, *q* and some bread.

10Jesus said to them, "Bring some of the fish you have just caught."

11Simon Peter climbed aboard and dragged the net ashore. It was full of large fish, 153, but even with so many the net was not torn. 12Jesus said to them, "Come and have breakfast." None of the disciples dared ask him, "Who are you?" They knew it was the Lord. 13Jesus came, took the bread and gave it to them, and did the same with the fish. *r* 14This was now the third time Jesus appeared to his disciples *s* after he was raised from the dead.

Jesus Reinstates Peter

15When they had finished eating, Jesus said to Simon Peter, "Simon son of John, do you truly love me more than these?"

"Yes, Lord," he said, "you know that I love you." *t*

Jesus said, "Feed my lambs." *u*

16Again Jesus said, "Simon son of John, do you truly love me?"

He answered, "Yes, Lord, you know that I love you."

Jesus said, "Take care of my sheep." *v*

17The third time he said to him, "Simon son of John, do you love me?"

Peter was hurt because Jesus asked him the third time, "Do you love me?" *w* He said, "Lord, you know all things; *x* you know that I love you."

Jesus said, "Feed my sheep. *y* 18I tell you the truth, when you were younger you dressed yourself and went where you wanted; but when you are old you will stretch out your hands, and someone else will dress you and lead you where you do not want to go." 19Jesus said this to indicate the kind of death *z* by which Peter would glorify God. *a* Then he said to him, "Follow me!"

20Peter turned and saw that the disciple whom Jesus loved *b* was following them. (This was the one who had leaned back against Jesus at the supper and had said, "Lord, who is going to betray you?") *c* 21When Peter saw him, he asked, "Lord, what about him?"

22Jesus answered, "If I want him to remain alive until I return, *d* what is that to

21:4 *m* Lk 24:16; Jn 20:14
21:6 *n* Lk 5:4-7
21:7 *o* Jn 13:23
21:9 *p* Jn 18:18 *q* ver 10,13
21:13 *r* ver 9 21:14 *s* Jn 20:19,26
21:15 *t* Mt 26:33,35; Jn 13:37 *u* Lk 12:32
21:16 *v* Mt 2:6; Ac 20:28; 1Pe 5:2,3 21:17 *w* Jn 13:38 *x* Jn 16:30 *y* ver 16
21:19 *z* Jn 12:33; 18:32 *a* 2Pe 1:14 21:20 *b* ver 7; Jn 13:23 *c* Jn 13:25
21:22 *d* Mt 16:27; 1Co 4:5; Rev 2:25

a 8 Greek *about two hundred cubits* (about 90 meters)

"catches" beyond their wildest imaginings (cf. Acts 2:41). As Jesus worked under the Father's direction, we work at Jesus' direction. He'll do far more through us than anything we could ever have imagined (cf. Eph. 3:20).

John 21:15–25

Peter's restoration, begun with the miraculous catch of fish, was completed with this conversation. Possibly the last time Peter had stood over a charcoal fire had been the occasion of his denial of Jesus (18:18). Now Jesus bid him stand over another (21:9)—in the process reviewing old memories and removing their sting. The threefold invitation to affirm his love drowned out the echoes of Peter's triple betrayal. Jesus saw in

this fallen disciple genuine potential for good. He conveyed his forgiveness, renewed Peter's call to ministry, and predicted that Peter would follow him even to a martyr's death that would "glorify God."

We walk in faith as healed men and women who (1) understand well our personal histories (and handicaps), (2) have made our brokenness transparent before God, and (3) have been forgiven and transformed by the Spirit. We love others because we're loved by God. Like Jesus, we serve as good shepherds—loving and serving—even though this will lead us to places we never imagined going!

21:22
e ver 19
21:23
f Ac 1:16
21:24
g Jn 15:27
h Jn 19:35
21:25
i Jn 20:30

you? You must follow me." e 23 Because of this, the rumor spread among the brothers f that this disciple would not die. But Jesus did not say that he would not die; he only said, "If I want him to remain alive until I return, what is that to you?"

24 This is the disciple who testifies to these things g and who wrote them down. We know that his testimony is true. h

25 Jesus did many other things as well. i If every one of them were written down, I suppose that even the whole world would not have room for the books that would be written.

21:15–23

Feed My Sheep

Jesus minced no words: The sign that people truly love him is their willingness to help others. "Tend my sheep," he instructed simply, when the restored Peter affirmed three times his undying love. It was as though Jesus were saying, "Don't just tell me you love me; do something about it."

That "something" was helping others. All sheep need tending. But the flocks most in need today include:

Those without food:

Each night 800 million people around the globe, most of them women and children, go to bed hungry.

Those without economic security:

1.2 billion people worldwide live on less than $1 per day. The world's richest 1 percent together generate as much income as its poorest 57 percent.

37 MIL

18.5 MIL

The young:
70 percent of the world's births are into non-Christian homes.

70%

Exploited/abused children:

Half of the 37 million people displaced by conflict and persecution are children. More than 250 million children are working instead of attending school. More than 1 million children (most of them girls) will be forced to join the sex trade.

Source: Myers (2003:32,37,66–69,71)

Those without homes:

32 million people are either refugees or internally displaced within their own countries.

The oppressed:
2.2 billion people survive under a yoke of oppression.

Those with HIV/AIDS:

Over 42 million people, the vast majority in Africa, live under a death threat from this dreaded disease. On this tragically hard-hit continent the most prevalent victims are women and young girls.

Those who haven't heard the Good News:

As of the beginning of the 21st century, 1.6 billion people had never heard the gospel message. Only 0.03 percent of the global income of all Christians is spent on mission efforts aimed at such people.

THAT IS 3 PENNIES FOR EVERY $100.00.

INTRODUCTION TO

Acts

AUTHOR

Acts nowhere identifies its author, but tradition from as early as the second century has held that the book was written by Luke as a sequel to his Gospel.

DATE WRITTEN

Acts was probably written between A.D. 63 and 70.

ORIGINAL READERS

Like the Gospel of Luke, the book of Acts was originally addressed to an individual named Theophilus. But it was clearly intended for all believers.

TIMELINE

	10BC	AD1	10	20	30	40	50	60	70	80	90	100
Jesus' life (c. 6/5 B.C.–A.D. 30)												
Paul's conversion (c. A.D. 35)												
Paul's first missionary journey (c. A.D. 46-48)												
Council at Jerusalem (c. A.D. 50-51)												
Paul's second missionary journey (c. A.D. 50-52)												
Paul's third missionary journey (c. A.D. 53-57)												
Paul's fourth missionary journey (c. A.D. 62-67)												
Paul's imprisonment and death in Rome (c. A.D. 67-68)												
Book of Acts written (c. A.D. 63–70)												

THEMES

The Gospel of Luke records what Jesus *began* to do and teach. Acts describes what he *continued* to do and teach through the Holy Spirit. Luke's primary purpose in writing Acts was to record a true historical account of the expansion of the early church. The Holy Spirit's role was central to that mission. Acts includes the following themes:

1. *The Holy Spirit's empowerment for witness.* The central theme in Acts is the Spirit's power and witness. Peter and John asserted, "We cannot help speaking about what we have seen and heard" (4:20). Believers today aren't eyewitnesses to Christ in the flesh, but we are empowered by the Spirit to *experience* Christ in our hearts. This propels us to share him with others.

2. *Community.* Acts reveals a united, caring community of believers who enjoyed not only a common belief and worship, but also a common experience as they shared their possessions and themselves with one another (2:42–47; 4:32–37). Spirituality is inseparable from social responsibility, and we are to use God's gifts to meet others' needs (see 1 Tim. 6:17–18).

3. *Reconciliation.* Despite the oneness of the faith community, conflicts did arise. Rather than split into two groups, the Christians achieved unity by implementing a program of caring for their needy. The church is to be inclusive: Jews and Gentiles (10:23–48)—even Samaritans (8:4–24)—were members of Christ's body. Christ's Spirit brings harmony and reconciliation.

4. *Persecution.* The Holy Spirit not only empowers believers to withstand opposition and suffering (6:10) but also enables the spread of the gospel, despite persecution (8:1–4; 11:19–21). Mistreatment for the sake of the faith actually spreads the gospel and builds up the faith of those who suffer, validating them as Christ's disciples (John 15:18—16:4).

FAITH IN ACTION

The pages of Acts are filled with life lessons and role models of faith—people who challenge believers to put their faith in action.

Role Models

• PETER AND JOHN (3:1–10) treated the needy man with respect and dignity. They offered more than money, spreading the gift of healing given them by the Spirit. What non-monetary gift are you able and prepared to offer someone in need?

• BARNABAS (4:36–37; 9:27) displayed a spirit of generosity and encouragement. What spirit characterizes your actions? Who can you encourage this week?

• DEACONS (6:1–6) distributed resources, so church unity wouldn't be disrupted by inequality between "haves" and "have-nots." Does your church maintain a fund for helping the needy? Have you contributed recently, either in general or for a specific cause?

• STEPHEN (7:54–60) forgave his persecutors as he gave his life for the gospel. Is there someone you need to forgive?

• BELIEVERS (11:19–21) continued to spread the gospel despite persecution. When you face opposition, what is your typical response? How are you encouraged by the believers in Acts?

• PAUL was willing to serve the church sacrificially and suffer for the gospel (20:19; 2 Cor. 4:8–12; 11:16—12:10). To what is Christ calling you as you fulfill your commission to be his witness to the world?

Challenges

• All Christians are called to be Christ's witnesses. Look for opportunities to share your unique testimony with someone this week. Depend on the Spirit to give you the words to effectively share what Christ has done for you.

• Observe the needs of those in your local church. Determine how you can share your gifts (money, time, talents, attention) with others.

• Seek ways to be a peacemaker in your church, your community, and the world.

• Ask God daily for a fresh filling of his Spirit to strengthen your faith and give you courage to withstand life's pressures and trials, enabling you to be a faithful witness to those around you.

OUTLINE

I. The Beginnings of the Church (1–12)
  A. The Church in Jerusalem (1–7)
  B. The Church Is Scattered (8:1—9:31)
  C. The Church Spreads to the Gentiles (9:32—12:25)
II. Paul's Missionary Journeys (13:1—21:16)
  A. Paul's First Missionary Journey (13–14)
  B. The Jerusalem Conference (15:1–35)
  C. Paul's Second Missionary Journey (15:36—18:22)
  D. Paul's Third Missionary Journey (18:23—21:16)
III. Paul's Arrest and Imprisonment (21:17—28:31)

Jesus Taken Up Into Heaven

1 In my former book,[a] Theophilus, I wrote about all that Jesus began to do and to teach[b] [2]until the day he was taken up to heaven,[c] after giving instructions[d] through the Holy Spirit to the apostles[e] he had chosen.[f] [3]After his suffering, he showed himself to these men and gave many convincing proofs that he was alive. He appeared to them[g] over a period of forty days and spoke about the kingdom of God. [4]On one occasion, while he was eating with them, he gave them this command: "Do not leave Jerusalem, but wait for the gift my Father promised, which you have heard me speak about.[h] [5]For John baptized with[a] water, but in a few days you will be baptized with the Holy Spirit."

[6]So when they met together, they asked him, "Lord, are you at this time going to restore[i] the kingdom to Israel?"

[7]He said to them: "It is not for you to know the times or dates the Father has set

[a] 5 Or in

1:1
a Lk 1:1-4 b Lk 3:23
1:2
c ver 9,11;
Mk 16:19
d Mt 28:19,20
e Mk 6:30
f Jn 13:18
1:3
g Mt 28:17;
Lk 24:34,36;
Jn 20:19,26; 21:1,
14; 1Co 15:5-7
1:4
h Lk 24:49;
Jn 14:16; Ac 2:33
1:6
i Mt 17:11

Acts 1:1–11

Though this book is often called "the Acts of the Apostles," Luke introduced in the first verses its real heart—the acts of the Holy Spirit through the apostles. Jesus' instructions to his apostles focused on the kingdom of God and were given "through the Holy Spirit" (v. 2). Luke's central themes were the Spirit's power and witness manifesting God's kingdom among Jesus' disciples. Though the apostles' initial concern was the restoration of Israel's kingdom, they came to discover that the kingdom of God is for all people, everywhere. Verse 8 outlines and summarizes Acts. And it serves, with its geographic references, as a "table of contents" for the rest of the book.

We can't witness to Christ in our own power and according to our own plans. Rather, we too must "wait" for the Spirit to come with his *dunamos* (dynamite or power). Too often the church has taken a sequential view of witnessing: First we take care of our own town and country, then go to the ends of the world. In so doing, we easily avoid the "Samaritans"—people of an ethnic or cultural background different from our own—right in our midst. As we participate in God's mission, the Spirit propels us across all barriers, as witnesses to everyone of God's coming kingdom.

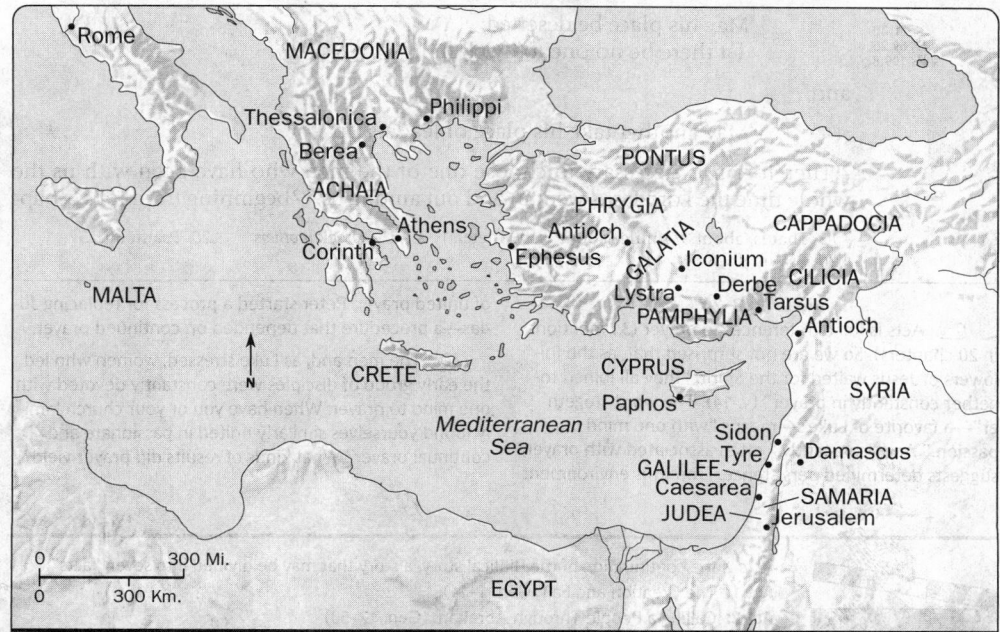

Setting of Acts (1:2)
Then: The Roman provinces of the time were Italy, Illyricum, Moesia, Macedonia, Thrace, Achaia, Bithynia, Pontus, Galatia, Asia, Lycia, Pamphylia, Cilicia, Cappadocia, Syria, and the Kingdom of Herod (not all included on this map).
Now: Modern nations located on these sites are Israel, Lebanon, Syria, Turkey, Greece, Macedonia, and Italy.

1:7
j Mt 24:36
1:8
k Ac 2:1-4
l Lk 24:48 *m* Ac 8:1-25 *n* Mt 28:19
1:9
o ver 2

by his own authority.*j* 8But you will receive power when the Holy Spirit comes on you;*k* and you will be my witnesses*l* in Jerusalem, and in all Judea and Samaria,*m* and to the ends of the earth."*n*

9After he said this, he was taken up*o* before their very eyes, and a cloud hid him from their sight.

1:10
p Lk 24:4; Jn 20:12
1:11
q Ac 2:7 *r* Mt 16:27

10They were looking intently up into the sky as he was going, when suddenly two men dressed in white*p* stood beside them. 11"Men of Galilee,"*q* they said, "why do you stand here looking into the sky? This same Jesus, who has been taken from you into heaven, will come back*r* in the same way you have seen him go into heaven."

Matthias Chosen to Replace Judas

1:12
s Lk 24:52 *t* Mt 21:1

12Then they returned to Jerusalem*s* from the hill called the Mount of Olives,*t* a Sabbath day's walk*a* from the city. 13When they arrived, they went upstairs to the

1:13
u Ac 9:37; 20:8
v Mt 10:2-4; Mk 3:16-19; Lk 6:14-16
1:14
w Ac 2:42; 6:4
x Lk 23:49,55
y Mt 12:46
1:16
z ver 20 *a* Jn 13:18

room*u* where they were staying. Those present were Peter, John, James and Andrew; Philip and Thomas, Bartholomew and Matthew; James son of Alphaeus and Simon the Zealot, and Judas son of James.*v* 14They all joined together constantly in prayer,*w* along with the women*x* and Mary the mother of Jesus, and with his brothers.*y*

15In those days Peter stood up among the believers*b* (a group numbering about a hundred and twenty) 16and said, "Brothers, the Scripture had to be fulfilled*z* which the Holy Spirit spoke long ago through the mouth of David concerning Judas,*a* who served as guide for those who arrested Jesus— 17he was one of our

1:17
b Jn 6:70,71
c ver 25

number*b* and shared in this ministry."*c*

1:18
d Mt 26:14,15
e Mt 27:3-10

18(With the reward*d* he got for his wickedness, Judas bought a field;*e* there he fell headlong, his body burst open and all his intestines spilled out. 19Everyone in Jerusalem heard about this, so they called that field in their language Akeldama, that is, Field of Blood.)

20"For," said Peter, "it is written in the book of Psalms,

1:20
f Ps 69:25
g Ps 109:8

> " 'May his place be deserted;
>   let there be no one to dwell in it,'*cf*

and,

> " 'May another take his place of leadership.'*dg*

21Therefore it is necessary to choose one of the men who have been with us the whole time the Lord Jesus went in and out among us, 22beginning from John's bap-

---

a 12 That is, about 3/4 mile (about 1,100 meters)   *b 15* Greek *brothers*   *c 20* Psalm 69:25
d 20 Psalm 109:8

Acts 1:12–26

Acts is full of references to prayer (31 mentions in 20 chapters). So we are not surprised that, as the followers of Jesus waited for the Spirit, "they all joined together constantly in prayer" (v. 14). The word "together"—a favorite of Luke's—means "with one mind or passion." And "constantly," often associated with prayer, suggests determined persistence. From this environment

of united prayer, Peter started a process for replacing Judas—a procedure that depended on continued prayer.

The men and, as Luke stressed, women who led the early group of disciples were constantly devoted with one mind to prayer. When have you or your church family found yourselves similarly united in passionate and continual prayer? What kinds of results did prayer yield?

1:1–11

The Divine Drama

Acts is the continuation of the Biblical story, a story that may be divided into seven "acts":

Act 1: The Creation and Fall (Gen. 1–11)
Act 2: Calling a People Through Abraham (Gen. 12–50)
Act 3: Rescuing and Separating a People (the Exodus to the Exile)
Act 4: Maintaining God's Holiness (the Exile)
Act 5: Saving All People (Jesus in the Gospels)
Act 6: Gathering the Church (Acts and the New Testament Letters)
Act 7: Renewing All Creation (Revelation)

Source: Moreau (2004:29)

tism ^{h} to the time when Jesus was taken up from us. For one of these must become a witness ^{i} with us of his resurrection."

^{23}So they proposed two men: Joseph called Barsabbas (also known as Justus) and Matthias. ^{24}Then they prayed, ^{j} "Lord, you know everyone's heart. ^{k} Show us which of these two you have chosen ^{25}to take over this apostolic ministry, which Judas left to go where he belongs." ^{26}Then they cast lots, and the lot fell to Matthias; so he was added to the eleven apostles. ^{l}

The Holy Spirit Comes at Pentecost

2 When the day of Pentecost ^{m} came, they were all together ^{n} in one place. ^{2}Suddenly a sound like the blowing of a violent wind came from heaven and filled the whole house where they were sitting. ^{o} ^{3}They saw what seemed to be tongues of fire that separated and came to rest on each of them. ^{4}All of them were filled with the Holy Spirit and began to speak in other tongues $^{a\,p}$ as the Spirit enabled them.

^{5}Now there were staying in Jerusalem God-fearing ^{q} Jews from every nation un-

^{a} 4 Or *languages*; also in verse 11

1:22
^{h} Mk 1:4 ^{i} ver 8

1:24
^{j} Ac 6:6; 14:23
^{k} 1Sa 16:7;
Jer 17:10; Ac 15:8;
Rev 2:23
1:26
^{l} Ac 2:14

2:1
^{m} Lev 23:15,16;
Ac 20:16 ^{n} Ac 1:14

2:2
^{o} Ac 4:31

2:4
^{p} Mk 16:17;
1Co 12:10
2:5
^{q} Ac 8:2

Acts 2:1–13

The "tongues" were the spiritual gift of communication; all present could understand what was being said in their mother tongue. The proclamation of the kingdom began with "the ends of the earth." The nations, divided over language after the Tower of Babel (see Gen. 11), were now united, despite their diverse languages, by the Holy Spirit. God knows that the language of birth is the language of a person's heart. And he's seen to it that the gospel is translatable so that hearts can be

changed. The result? About three thousand people were "added to their number that day" (v. 41).

The gospel honors our ethnic and cultural diversity, while surmounting our divisions over differences. Rather than making everyone worship and talk alike, the Spirit meets and unites us in our rich variety. How has your church dealt with ethnic and cultural diversity? How have you witnessed the Spirit giving the gift of communication to proclaim God's deeds of power to people from a different background than your own?

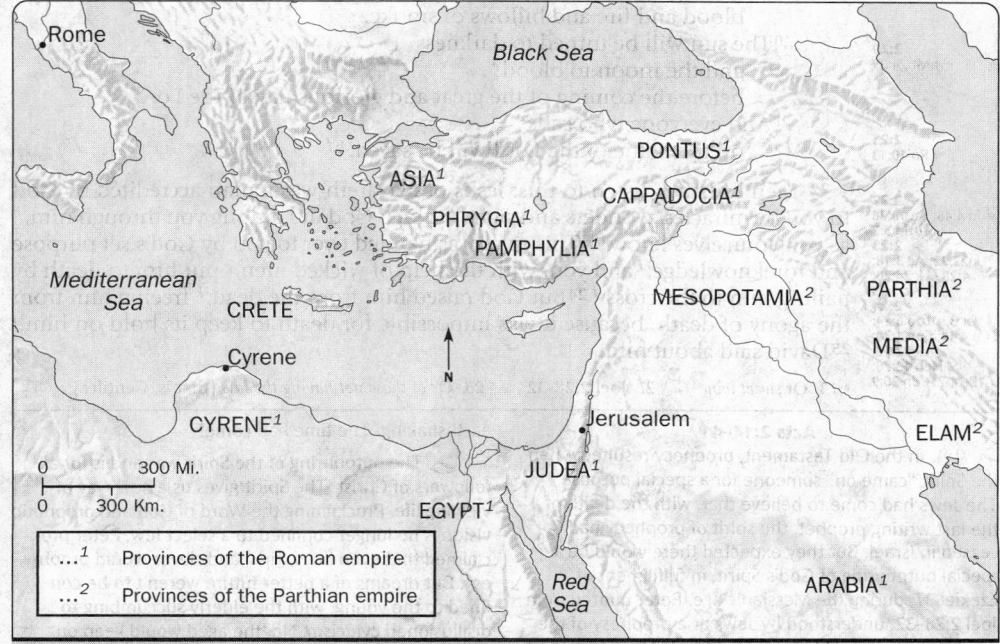

Jews From Every Nation (2:5)

Then: This area covered the region only much later referred to as Palestine, as well as Asia Minor, Macedonia, Greece, and Italy.

Now: Israel, Lebanon, Syria, Turkey, Greece, and Italy share this land mass.

2:7
r ver 12 s Ac 1:11

2:9
t 1Pe 1:1 u Ac 18:2
v Ac 16:6; Ro 16:5;
1Co 16:19; 2Co 1:8
2:10
w Ac 16:6; 18:23
x Ac 13:13; 15:38
y Mt 27:32

2:13
z 1Co 14:23

der heaven. ⁶When they heard this sound, a crowd came together in bewilderment, because each one heard them speaking in his own language. ⁷Utterly amazed,ʳ they asked: "Are not all these men who are speaking Galileans?ˢ ⁸Then how is it that each of us hears them in his own native language? ⁹Parthians, Medes and Elamites; residents of Mesopotamia, Judea and Cappadocia,ᵗ Pontusᵘ and Asia,ᵛ ¹⁰Phrygiaʷ and Pamphylia,ˣ Egypt and the parts of Libya near Cyrene;ʸ visitors from Rome ¹¹(both Jews and converts to Judaism); Cretans and Arabs—we hear them declaring the wonders of God in our own tongues!" ¹²Amazed and perplexed, they asked one another, "What does this mean?"

¹³Some, however, made fun of them and said, "They have had too much wine.ᵃ"ᶻ

Peter Addresses the Crowd

¹⁴Then Peter stood up with the Eleven, raised his voice and addressed the crowd: "Fellow Jews and all of you who live in Jerusalem, let me explain this to you; listen carefully to what I say. ¹⁵These men are not drunk, as you suppose. It's only nine in the morning!ᵃ ¹⁶No, this is what was spoken by the prophet Joel:

2:15
a 1Th 5:7

2:17
b Isa 44:3; Jn 7:37-
39; Ac 10:45
c Ac 21:9

¹⁷ " 'In the last days, God says,
   I will pour out my Spirit on all people.ᵇ
Your sons and daughters will prophesy,ᶜ
   your young men will see visions,
   your old men will dream dreams.
¹⁸Even on my servants, both men and women,
   I will pour out my Spirit in those days,
   and they will prophesy.ᵈ

2:18
d Ac 21:9-12

¹⁹I will show wonders in the heaven above
   and signs on the earth below,
   blood and fire and billows of smoke.
²⁰The sun will be turned to darkness
   and the moon to bloodᵉ
before the coming of the great and glorious day of the Lord.
²¹And everyone who calls
   on the name of the Lord will be saved.'ᵇ ᶠ

2:20
e Mt 24:29

2:21
f Ro 10:13

²²"Men of Israel, listen to this: Jesus of Nazareth was a man accredited by God to you by miracles, wonders and signs,ᵍ which God did among you through him,ʰ as you yourselves know. ²³This man was handed over to you by God's set purpose and foreknowledge;ⁱ and you, with the help of wicked men,ᶜ put him to death by nailing him to the cross.ʲ ²⁴But God raised him from the dead,ᵏ freeing him from the agony of death, because it was impossible for death to keep its hold on him.ˡ ²⁵David said about him:

2:22
g Jn 4:48; Ac 10:38
h Jn 3:2
2:23
i Lk 22:22; Ac 3:18;
4:28 j Lk 24:20;
Ac 3:13
2:24
k ver 32; 1Co 6:14;
2Co 4:14; Eph 1:20;
Col 2:12;
Heb 13:20;
1Pe 1:21 l Jn 20:9

ᵃ 13 Or *sweet wine*   ᵇ 21 Joel 2:28-32   ᶜ 23 Or *of those not having the law* (that is, Gentiles)

Acts 2:14–41

In the Old Testament, prophecy resulted when the Spirit "came on" someone for a special purpose. The Jews had come to believe that, with the death of the last writing prophet, the spirit of prophecy had ceased in Israel. But they expected there would be a special outpouring of God's Spirit, in fulfillment of Ezekiel 37, during the Messianic age. Peter quoted from Joel 2:28–32, understood by Jews as a prophesy of the inauguration of the Messianic age. The gift of the Spirit was no longer confined to priests and prophets. Now young and old, men and women, slaves and free were being given the capacity to live life according to a different vision. Peter's message to a patient people was earthshaking: The time had come!

The outpouring of the Spirit was and is for all followers of Christ. The Spirit gives us a new way of viewing life. Proclaiming the Word of God and prophetic vision is no longer confined to a select few. Peter proclaimed that even boys, girls, and slaves would prophesy. But dreams of a better future weren't to be confined to the young, with the elderly succumbing to disillusioned cynicism. No, the aged would keep on dreaming. Even fearful fishermen could be transformed into courageous leaders. Intimidated no more (cf. Luke 22:54–62), Peter boldly witnessed to Christ and the kingdom. Are you, with the Spirit's support, following his example?

" 'I saw the Lord always before me.
     Because he is at my right hand,
          I will not be shaken.
26 Therefore my heart is glad and my tongue rejoices;
     my body also will live in hope,
27 because you will not abandon me to the grave,
     nor will you let your Holy One see decay. *m*
28 You have made known to me the paths of life;
     you will fill me with joy in your presence.' *a*

29 "Brothers, I can tell you confidently that the patriarch *n* David died and was buried, *o* and his tomb is here *p* to this day. 30 But he was a prophet and knew that God had promised him on oath that he would place one of his descendants on his throne. *q* 31 Seeing what was ahead, he spoke of the resurrection of the Christ, *b* that he was not abandoned to the grave, nor did his body see decay. *r* 32 God has raised this Jesus to life, *s* and we are all witnesses *t* of the fact. 33 Exalted *u* to the right hand of God, *v* he has received from the Father *w* the promised Holy Spirit *x* and has poured out *y* what you now see and hear. 34 For David did not ascend to heaven, and yet he said,

" 'The Lord said to my Lord:
     "Sit at my right hand
35 until I make your enemies
     a footstool for your feet." ' *c z*

36 "Therefore let all Israel be assured of this: God has made this Jesus, whom you crucified, both Lord and Christ." *a*

37 When the people heard this, they were cut to the heart and said to Peter and the other apostles, "Brothers, what shall we do?" *b*

38 Peter replied, "Repent and be baptized, *c* every one of you, in the name of Jesus Christ for the forgiveness of your sins. *d* And you will receive the gift of the Holy Spirit. 39 The promise is for you and your children *e* and for all who are far off *f*—for all whom the Lord our God will call."

40 With many other words he warned them; and he pleaded with them, "Save yourselves from this corrupt generation." *g* 41 Those who accepted his message were baptized, and about three thousand were added to their number that day.

The Fellowship of the Believers

42 They devoted themselves to the apostles' teaching and to the fellowship, to the

---

2:27
m ver 31; Ac 13:35

2:29
n Ac 7:8,9
o 1Ki 2:10;
Ac 13:36 *p* Ne 3:16

2:30
q 2Sa 7:12;
Ps 132:11
2:31
r Ps 16:10
2:32
s ver 24 *t* Ac 1:8
2:33
u Php 2:9
v Mk 16:19
w Ac 1:4 *x* Jn 7:39;
14:26 *y* Ac 10:45

2:35
z Ps 110:1;
Mt 22:44

2:36
a Lk 2:11

2:37
b Lk 3:10,12,14
2:38
c Ac 8:12,16,36,38;
22:16 *d* Lk 24:47;
Ac 3:19
2:39
e Isa 44:3
f Ac 10:45;
Eph 2:13

2:40
g Dt 32:5

---

a 28 Psalm 16:8-11   *b 31* Or *Messiah.* "The Christ" (Greek) and "the Messiah" (Hebrew) both mean "the Anointed One"; also in verse 36.   *c 35* Psalm 110:1

Acts 2:42–47
 These verses provide a snapshot of early Christian community life. These same activities are often cited in the New Testament letters as essential aspects of Christian living. We are struck by the completeness of the community. It included caring for new believers; various elements of worship; miraculous wonders by the Spirit through the disciples; evangelistic outreach; concern for each other's material needs so that all were provided for; oneness in spirit; gatherings in the temple; and joyful, informal fellowship in homes.

2:41

Growth of the

The Christian church began after Jesus' death with 12 men huddled in an upstairs room in Jerusalem (A.D. 33). By 2000 Christianity had grown to become the largest religion in the world, with 2 billion members. Three thousand were added on the day of the first Pentecost in A.D. 33. In the decade from 1990 to 2000, an average of 65,000 people were added to the Christian church every day, either by birth or conversion.

Source: Barrett and Johnson (2001:31)

1793

2:42
h Ac 1:14
2:43
i Ac 5:12
2:44
j Ac 4:32
2:45
k Mt 19:21
2:46
l Lk 24:53; Ac 5:21,
42 m Ac 20:7
2:47
n Ro 14:18
o ver 41; Ac 5:14

3:1
p Lk 22:8 q Ac 2:46
r Ps 55:17
3:2
s Ac 14:8 t Lk 16:20
u Jn 9:8

3:6
v ver 16; Ac 4:10

3:8
w Ac 14:10
3:9
x Ac 4:16,21
3:10
y ver 2

3:11
z Lk 22:8
a Jn 10:23; Ac 5:12

3:13
b Ac 5:30

breaking of bread and to prayer. [h] 43Everyone was filled with awe, and many wonders and miraculous signs were done by the apostles. [i] 44All the believers were together and had everything in common. [j] 45Selling their possessions and goods, they gave to anyone as he had need. [k] 46Every day they continued to meet together in the temple courts. [l] They broke bread [m] in their homes and ate together with glad and sincere hearts, 47praising God and enjoying the favor of all the people. [n] And the Lord added to their number [o] daily those who were being saved.

Peter Heals the Crippled Beggar

3 One day Peter and John [p] were going up to the temple [q] at the time of prayer— at three in the afternoon. [r] 2Now a man crippled from birth [s] was being carried to the temple gate [t] called Beautiful, where he was put every day to beg [u] from those going into the temple courts. 3When he saw Peter and John about to enter, he asked them for money. 4Peter looked straight at him, as did John. Then Peter said, "Look at us!" 5So the man gave them his attention, expecting to get something from them.

6Then Peter said, "Silver or gold I do not have, but what I have I give you. In the name of Jesus Christ of Nazareth, [v] walk." 7Taking him by the right hand, he helped him up, and instantly the man's feet and ankles became strong. 8He jumped to his feet and began to walk. Then he went with them into the temple courts, walking and jumping, [w] and praising God. 9When all the people [x] saw him walking and praising God, 10they recognized him as the same man who used to sit begging at the temple gate called Beautiful, [y] and they were filled with wonder and amazement at what had happened to him.

Peter Speaks to the Onlookers

11While the beggar held on to Peter and John, [z] all the people were astonished and came running to them in the place called Solomon's Colonnade. [a] 12When Peter saw this, he said to them: "Men of Israel, why does this surprise you? Why do you stare at us as if by our own power or godliness we had made this man walk? 13The God of Abraham, Isaac and Jacob, the God of our fathers, [b] has glorified his servant

Our culture is so individualistic that this Biblical example of community may seem strange—even suspect—to us. It's been said that it's easier to *give* than to *share*. Once you give something away, your attachment to it ends. But sharing requires much more of your self—a long and steady commitment. What would it mean for your church community to "have everything in common" as the early church did?

Acts 3:1–10
Peter and John offered a timeless example of ministry meeting need: By engaging the crippled man through direct eye contact and treating him with respect and dignity, they acknowledged his worth. What they gave was of incomparably greater value than a few dollars in a cup. They offered him a reason to lift his head, the ability to stretch his legs—and jump, a permanent solution to begging, and an opportunity for a relationship with Christ.

Dignity and respect can't be bought. Donating money to solve a problem, while *good* in itself, may not always, in and of itself, be the *complete* solution. The poor and suffering need the dignity that comes from being treated as people—not just as objects of need. Engaging directly with those who suffer might be uncomfortable at first, but it's the only way to restore wholeness. Through it both givers and receivers discover their real value to God.

2:42–47

Nine Characteristics of a Healthy Church

In one short paragraph, Luke listed nine indicators of a healthy church. A healthy church:

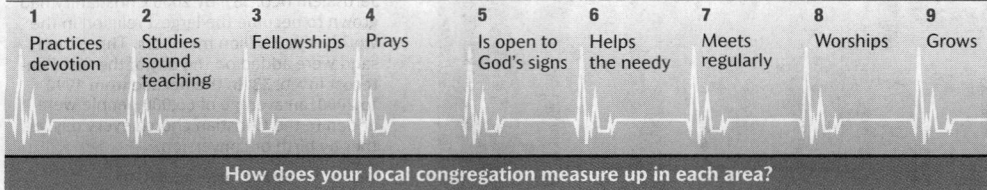

1	2	3	4	5	6	7	8	9
Practices devotion	Studies sound teaching	Fellowships	Prays	Is open to God's signs	Helps the needy	Meets regularly	Worships	Grows

How does your local congregation measure up in each area?

Jesus. You handed him over to be killed, and you disowned him before Pilate, [c] though he had decided to let him go. [d] 14You disowned the Holy[e] and Righteous One[f] and asked that a murderer be released to you. [g] 15You killed the author of life, but God raised him from the dead. [h] We are witnesses of this. 16By faith in the name of Jesus, this man whom you see and know was made strong. It is Jesus' name and the faith that comes through him that has given this complete healing to him, as you can all see.

17"Now, brothers, I know that you acted in ignorance, [i] as did your leaders. [j] 18But this is how God fulfilled what he had foretold[k] through all the prophets, [l] saying that his Christ[a] would suffer. [m] 19Repent, then, and turn to God, so that your sins may be wiped out, [n] that times of refreshing may come from the Lord, 20and that he may send the Christ, who has been appointed for you—even Jesus. 21He must remain in heaven[o] until the time comes for God to restore everything, [p] as he promised long ago through his holy prophets. [q] 22For Moses said, 'The Lord your God will raise up for you a prophet like me from among your own people; you must listen to everything he tells you.' [r] 23Anyone who does not listen to him will be completely cut off from among his people.' [b][s]

24"Indeed, all the prophets[t] from Samuel on, as many as have spoken, have foretold these days. 25And you are heirs[u] of the prophets and of the covenant[v] God made with your fathers. He said to Abraham, 'Through your offspring all peoples on earth will be blessed.' [c][w] 26When God raised up[x] his servant, he sent him first[y] to you to bless you by turning each of you from your wicked ways."

Peter and John Before the Sanhedrin

4 The priests and the captain of the temple guard[z] and the Sadducees[a] came up to Peter and John while they were speaking to the people. 2They were greatly disturbed because the apostles were teaching the people and proclaiming in Jesus the resurrection of the dead. [b] 3They seized Peter and John, and because it was evening, they put them in jail[c] until the next day. 4But many who heard the message believed, and the number of men grew[d] to about five thousand.

5The next day the rulers, [e] elders and teachers of the law met in Jerusalem. 6Annas the high priest was there, and so were Caiaphas, [f] John, Alexander and the other men of the high priest's family. 7They had Peter and John brought before them and began to question them: "By what power or what name did you do this?"

8Then Peter, filled with the Holy Spirit, said to them: "Rulers and elders of the

---

a 18 Or Messiah; also in verse 20   b 23 Deut. 18:15,18,19   c 25 Gen. 22:18; 26:4

Cross references (right margin):

3:13 c Mt 27:2 d Lk 23:4
3:14 e Mk 1:24; Ac 4:27 f Ac 7:52 g Mk 15:11; Lk 23:18-25
3:15 h Ac 2:24
3:17 i Lk 23:34 j Ac 13:27
3:18 k Ac 2:23 l Lk 24:27 m Ac 17:2,3; 26:22,23
3:19 n Ac 2:38
3:21 o Ac 1:11 p Mt 17:11 q Lk 1:70
3:22 r Dt 18:15,18; Ac 7:37
3:23 s Dt 18:19
3:24 t Lk 24:27
3:25 u Ac 2:39 v Ro 9:4, 5 w Ge 12:3; 22:18; 26:4; 28:14
3:26 x ver 22; Ac 2:24 y Ac 13:46; Ro 1:16
4:1 z Lk 22:4 a Mt 3:7
4:2 b Ac 17:18
4:3 c Ac 5:18
4:4 d Ac 2:41
4:5 e Lk 23:13
4:6 f Mt 26:3; Lk 3:2

Acts 3:11–26

The crowd's astonishment provided a launching pad for Peter's speech. He began by deflecting the glory away from himself and John. People often associate miracles with personal power, or at least claim that God uses individuals because they are holy or great. Peter vigorously refuted this idea: This healing had been accomplished "by faith in the name of Jesus"—a faith that in the first place "comes through him" (v. 16). As in his Pentecost sermon (2:14–40), Peter emphasized the name of "Jesus" (repeated eight times in Acts 3–4).

None of us deserves the ministry we have been given (2 Cor. 4:1). Yet God has invited and gifted us to participate in his own work. Peter repeated God's promise to Abraham. Now, through those who believe in Jesus as adopted descendants of Abraham, "all the peoples on earth will be blessed." How do you personally take the attention off your own "power or godliness" and place it back on Jesus?

Acts 4:1–22

Peter and John weren't professionally qualified, yet they boldly and eloquently conducted their own defense before this legal assembly. The Sanhedrin already knew these men had been with Jesus. But their performance reminded these Jewish leaders how the two had been influenced by Christ, who also had "taught . . . as one who had authority" (Mark 1:22). Luke described effective ministry in the New Testament era: speaking from the fullness of the Spirit and a thorough knowledge of Scripture.

Salvation coming only through Jesus grates against the inclusive, tolerant mood in our society. It's sheer arrogance, many people think, to hold this position. But there is room neither for arrogance nor for lack of confidence among those who follow Christ. To accept the Good News is to humbly admit that Christ alone can help us. We can boldly say that Jesus is the only way—because he said so (cf. John 14:6). How do you infuse a humble attitude into your sharing of the message about salvation through Jesus alone?

4:8
g ver 5; Lk 23:13
4:9
h Ac 3:6
4:10
i Ac 2:24

4:11
j Ps 118:22;
Isa 28:16; Mt 21:42

4:12
k Mt 1:21;
Ac 10:43; 1Ti 2:5
4:13
l Lk 22:8
m Mt 11:25

4:15
n Mt 5:22
4:16
o Jn 11:47
p Ac 3:6-10

4:18
q Ac 5:40
4:19
r Ac 5:29

4:21
s Ac 5:26 *t* Mt 9:8

4:25
u Ac 1:16

4:26
v Ps 2:1,2; Da 9:25;
Lk 4:18; Ac 10:38;
Heb 1:9
4:27
w Mt 14:1
x Mt 27:2; Lk 23:12
y ver 30
4:28
z Ac 2:23
4:29
a ver 13,31;
Ac 9:27; 14:3;
Php 1:14
4:30
b Jn 4:48 *c* ver 27

people![g] [9]If we are being called to account today for an act of kindness shown to a cripple[h] and are asked how he was healed, [10]then know this, you and all the people of Israel: It is by the name of Jesus Christ of Nazareth, whom you crucified but whom God raised from the dead,[i] that this man stands before you healed. [11]He is

" 'the stone you builders rejected,
which has become the capstone.[a][b][j]

[12]Salvation is found in no one else, for there is no other name under heaven given to men by which we must be saved."[k]

[13]When they saw the courage of Peter and John[l] and realized that they were unschooled, ordinary men,[m] they were astonished and they took note that these men had been with Jesus. [14]But since they could see the man who had been healed standing there with them, there was nothing they could say. [15]So they ordered them to withdraw from the Sanhedrin[n] and then conferred together. [16]"What are we going to do with these men?"[o] they asked. "Everybody living in Jerusalem knows they have done an outstanding miracle,[p] and we cannot deny it. [17]But to stop this thing from spreading any further among the people, we must warn these men to speak no longer to anyone in this name."

[18]Then they called them in again and commanded them not to speak or teach at all in the name of Jesus.[q] [19]But Peter and John replied, "Judge for yourselves whether it is right in God's sight to obey you rather than God.[r] [20]For we cannot help speaking about what we have seen and heard."

[21]After further threats they let them go. They could not decide how to punish them, because all the people[s] were praising God[t] for what had happened. [22]For the man who was miraculously healed was over forty years old.

The Believers' Prayer

[23]On their release, Peter and John went back to their own people and reported all that the chief priests and elders had said to them. [24]When they heard this, they raised their voices together in prayer to God. "Sovereign Lord," they said, "you made the heaven and the earth and the sea, and everything in them. [25]You spoke by the Holy Spirit through the mouth of your servant, our father David:[u]

" 'Why do the nations rage
and the peoples plot in vain?
[26]The kings of the earth take their stand
and the rulers gather together
against the Lord
and against his Anointed One.[c][d][v]

[27]Indeed Herod[w] and Pontius Pilate[x] met together with the Gentiles and the people[e] of Israel in this city to conspire against your holy servant Jesus,[y] whom you anointed. [28]They did what your power and will had decided beforehand should happen.[z] [29]Now, Lord, consider their threats and enable your servants to speak your word with great boldness.[a] [30]Stretch out your hand to heal and perform miraculous signs and wonders[b] through the name of your holy servant Jesus."[c]

[a] 11 Or *cornerstone*   [b] 11 Psalm 118:22   [c] 26 That is, Christ or Messiah   [d] 26 Psalm 2:1,2
[e] 27 The Greek is plural.

Acts 4:23–31

We receive from the book of Acts rich guidance about prayer in difficult times: (1) Unity of believers is a key theme in Acts. Not surprisingly, it's noted especially in times of crisis. (2) It's to be focused on God's sovereignty and saturated in Scripture. (3) The early Christians' request had to do with obedience—that they might continue to witness with courage. (4) They also asked God to perform miracles by which people's hearts might be opened to the gospel.

How often do you pray for protection from opposition and suffering? The early church asked instead for boldness to proclaim the gospel and power to perform miracles. As you petition God for your own needs, those of hurting people, and those of the worldwide church as it faces fierce opposition, include a request for God to pour out his boldness and power.

31After they prayed, the place where they were meeting was shaken.*d* And they were all filled with the Holy Spirit and spoke the word of God boldly.*e*

The Believers Share Their Possessions

32All the believers were one in heart and mind. No one claimed that any of his possessions was his own, but they shared everything they had.*f* 33With great power the apostles continued to testify*g* to the resurrection*h* of the Lord Jesus, and much grace was upon them all. 34There were no needy persons among them. For from time to time those who owned lands or houses sold them,*i* brought the money from the sales 35and put it at the apostles' feet,*j* and it was distributed to anyone as he had need.*k*

36Joseph, a Levite from Cyprus, whom the apostles called Barnabas*l* (which means Son of Encouragement), 37sold a field he owned and brought the money and put it at the apostles' feet.*m*

Ananias and Sapphira

5 Now a man named Ananias, together with his wife Sapphira, also sold a piece of property. 2With his wife's full knowledge he kept back part of the money for himself, but brought the rest and put it at the apostles' feet.*n*

3Then Peter said, "Ananias, how is it that Satan*o* has so filled your heart*p* that you have lied to the Holy Spirit*q* and have kept for yourself some of the money you received for the land? 4Didn't it belong to you before it was sold? And after it was sold, wasn't the money at your disposal? What made you think of doing such a thing? You have not lied to men but to God."

5When Ananias heard this, he fell down and died.*r* And great fear*s* seized all who

Margin references
4:31 *d* Ac 2:2 *e* ver 29
4:32 *f* Ac 2:44
4:33 *g* Lk 24:48 *h* Ac 1:22
4:34 *i* Mt 19:21; Ac 2:45
4:35 *j* ver 37; Ac 5:2 *k* Ac 2:45; 6:1
4:36 *l* Ac 9:27; 1Co 9:6
4:37 *m* ver 35; Ac 5:2
5:2 *n* Ac 4:35,37
5:3 *o* Mt 4:10 *p* Jn 13:2, 27 *q* ver 9
5:5 *r* ver 10 *s* ver 11

Acts 4:32–37

Again Luke described the radical sharing this first Christian community practiced (see 2:44–45). "One in heart and mind" describes their unity. In fact, their sharing was so complete there were "no needy persons among them." But for this to happen, costly sacrifices had to be made. Private ownership continued in the church (cf. 5:4; 12:12). But when there was a need, those who could do so sold property and donated the proceeds to meet it.

Everything we have belongs first to God (cf. Ps. 24:1). The bottom line is that we are responsible to make sure no one in the body of Christ is in need (cf. 1 Tim. 6:17–19). A surprising reality is that Jesus had more to say about money than he did about heaven and hell. Christians have often thought that if they gave God a "tithe," whatever was left would be theirs to spend as they wished. The early church followed a different practice. How does its perspective challenge you?

Acts 5:1–11

This sobering story shows us how seriously God takes sin—in this case, the sin of lying. Ananias and Sapphira gave the appearance of being more generous than they really were; they "kept back" for themselves some of the money from a property sale. The two technically held on to their own money. But the Greek translation of the Old Testament uses this same word about Achan, who on the sly kept some of the booty from the spoils of war—plunder that had been devoted to God (Josh. 7:1). In Achan's case, as here, the sin was severely punished.

A distorted view of possessions and community is serious in God's sight, especially when it leads to deception. But we don't often, if at all, see God's judgment fall on us like this. Perhaps this example stands as his warning for all time. But we still place a high premium on appearances, and spiritual pride and lack of financial integrity remain problems. If we are honest, don't we tend to come down harder as a Christian community on sexual sins than on financial ones? In what ways does this forceful passage speak to you?

4:32–35

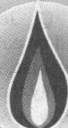

Six Ways of Witnessing

Chapters 2–4 teach us that there are many ways to witness to God's goodness and grace. Empowered by the Holy Spirit (2:1–14), we witness by:

1. Connecting our story to God's story (2:14–41).
2. Inviting others to join our fellowship (2:42–47).
3. Caring and interceding for the sick (3:1–10; 5:12–16).
4. Giving personal testimony (3:11–13).
5. Resisting unjust social systems (4:1–21; 5:17–42).
6. Sharing with the needy (4:32–37).

5:6
t Jn 19:40

5:8
u ver 2
5:9
v ver 3

5:10
w ver 5

5:11
x ver 5; Ac 19:17

5:12
y Ac 2:43 / Ac 4:32
a Ac 3:11
5:13
b Ac 2:47; 4:21

5:15
c Ac 19:12
5:16
d Mk 16:17

5:17
e Ac 15:5 / Ac 4:1

5:18
g Ac 4:3
5:19
h Mt 1:20; Lk 1:11;
Ac 8:26; 27:23
i Ac 16:26
5:20
j Jn 6:63,68
5:21
k Ac 4:5,6 / ver 27,
34,41; Mt 5:22

5:24
m Ac 4:1

heard what had happened. 6Then the young men came forward, wrapped up his body, t and carried him out and buried him.

7About three hours later his wife came in, not knowing what had happened. 8Peter asked her, "Tell me, is this the price you and Ananias got for the land?"

"Yes," she said, "that is the price." u

9Peter said to her, "How could you agree to test the Spirit of the Lord? v Look! The feet of the men who buried your husband are at the door, and they will carry you out also."

10At that moment she fell down at his feet and died. w Then the young men came in and, finding her dead, carried her out and buried her beside her husband. 11Great fear x seized the whole church and all who heard about these events.

The Apostles Heal Many

12The apostles performed many miraculous signs and wonders y among the people. And all the believers used to meet together z in Solomon's Colonnade. a 13No one else dared join them, even though they were highly regarded by the people. b 14Nevertheless, more and more men and women believed in the Lord and were added to their number. 15As a result, people brought the sick into the streets and laid them on beds and mats so that at least Peter's shadow might fall on some of them as he passed by. c 16Crowds gathered also from the towns around Jerusalem, bringing their sick and those tormented by evil a spirits, and all of them were healed. d

The Apostles Persecuted

17Then the high priest and all his associates, who were members of the party e of the Sadducees, f were filled with jealousy. 18They arrested the apostles and put them in the public jail. g 19But during the night an angel h of the Lord opened the doors of the jail i and brought them out. 20"Go, stand in the temple courts," he said, "and tell the people the full message of this new life." i

21At daybreak they entered the temple courts, as they had been told, and began to teach the people.

When the high priest and his associates k arrived, they called together the Sanhedrin l—the full assembly of the elders of Israel—and sent to the jail for the apostles. 22But on arriving at the jail, the officers did not find them there. So they went back and reported, 23"We found the jail securely locked, with the guards standing at the doors; but when we opened them, we found no one inside." 24On hearing this report, the captain of the temple guard and the chief priests m were puzzled, wondering what would come of this.

a 16 Greek unclean

Acts 5:12–16

The fear factor resulting from these deaths (vv. 5,10) didn't reduce the apostles' evangelistic effectiveness. Their miraculous ministry intensified, and they continued to gain new converts. Nor do we see here a cheapening of the gospel, with large numbers joining the church simply because of miracles. People realized that God's Spirit, while demonstrating awesome power, at the same time demanded responsibility and commitment—but still they came. The church didn't have to lower its standards to win the lost.

The early church showcased God's awesome holiness—provoking fear among outsiders—but also his power—making the Good News attractive. Preaching the gospel without stressing God's holiness has tragic consequences. We see people who claim to follow Christ happily continuing in the sins of their past lives. This projects to the world a faulty understanding of rebirth. What can individual Christians do to help restore balance?

Acts 5:17–42

This passage pulsates with the authority of the gospel. The apostles were arrested for witnessing, but after their miraculous release the angel sent them straight back to the temple to proclaim "the full message" (v. 20). They weren't to give in to the temptation to compromise. When asked to explain their actions, they used the opportunity to proclaim Christ. The authority of political and religious rulers is always subordinate to that of Christ. He is to be obeyed when human authorities demand something contrary to his will.

Jesus proclaimed that "all authority in heaven and on earth" had been given to him (Matt. 28:18). No demonic, political, or religious leader could claim authority that overruled God! Can you cite some situations today in which human authorities are ordering Christ's followers to remain silent and not proclaim the gospel? What price are his people paying when they obey God instead?

25Then someone came and said, "Look! The men you put in jail are standing in the temple courts teaching the people." 26At that, the captain went with his officers and brought the apostles. They did not use force, because they feared that the people*n* would stone them.

27Having brought the apostles, they made them appear before the Sanhedrin*o* to be questioned by the high priest. 28"We gave you strict orders not to teach in this name,"*p* he said. "Yet you have filled Jerusalem with your teaching and are determined to make us guilty of this man's blood."*q*

29Peter and the other apostles replied: "We must obey God rather than men!*r* 30The God of our fathers*s* raised Jesus from the dead*t*—whom you had killed by hanging him on a tree.*u* 31God exalted him to his own right hand*v* as Prince and Savior*w* that he might give repentance and forgiveness of sins to Israel.*x* 32We are witnesses of these things,*y* and so is the Holy Spirit,*z* whom God has given to those who obey him."

33When they heard this, they were furious*a* and wanted to put them to death. 34But a Pharisee named Gamaliel,*b* a teacher of the law,*c* who was honored by all the people, stood up in the Sanhedrin and ordered that the men be put outside for a little while. 35Then he addressed them: "Men of Israel, consider carefully what you intend to do to these men. 36Some time ago Theudas appeared, claiming to be somebody, and about four hundred men rallied to him. He was killed, all his followers were dispersed, and it all came to nothing. 37After him, Judas the Galilean appeared in the days of the census*d* and led a band of people in revolt. He too was killed, and all his followers were scattered. 38Therefore, in the present case I advise you: Leave these men alone! Let them go! For if their purpose or activity is of human origin, it will fail.*e* 39But if it is from God, you will not be able to stop these men; you will only find yourselves fighting against God."*f*

40His speech persuaded them. They called the apostles in and had them flogged.*g* Then they ordered them not to speak in the name of Jesus, and let them go.

41The apostles left the Sanhedrin, rejoicing*h* because they had been counted worthy of suffering disgrace for the Name.*i* 42Day after day, in the temple courts*j* and from house to house, they never stopped teaching and proclaiming the good news that Jesus is the Christ.*a*

The Choosing of the Seven

6 In those days when the number of disciples was increasing,*k* the Grecian Jews*l* among them complained against the Hebraic Jews because their widows*m* were being overlooked in the daily distribution of food.*n* 2So the Twelve gathered all the disciples together and said, "It would not be right for us to neglect the ministry of the word of God in order to wait on tables. 3Brothers,*o* choose seven men from among you who are known to be full of the Spirit and wisdom. We will turn this responsibility over to them 4and will give our attention to prayer*p* and the ministry of the word."

5This proposal pleased the whole group. They chose Stephen,*q* a man full of faith and of the Holy Spirit;*r* also Philip,*s* Procorus, Nicanor, Timon, Parmenas, and Nic-

a 42 Or *Messiah*

Side references:

5:26 *n* Ac 4:21
5:27 *o* Mt 5:22
5:28 *p* Ac 4:18
q Mt 23:35; 27:25; Ac 2:23,36; 3:14, 15; 7:52
5:29 *r* Ac 4:19
5:30 *s* Ac 3:13 *t* Ac 2:24 *u* Ac 10:39; 13:29; Gal 3:13; 1Pe 2:24
5:31 *v* Ac 2:33 *w* Lk 2:11 *x* Mt 1:21; Lk 24:47; Ac 2:38
5:32 *y* Lk 24:48 *z* Jn 15:26
5:33 *a* Ac 2:37; 7:54
5:34 *b* Ac 22:3 *c* Lk 2:46
5:37 *d* Lk 2:1,2
5:38 *e* Mt 15:13
5:39 *f* Pr 21:30; Ac 7:51; 11:17
5:40 *g* Mt 10:17
5:41 *h* Mt 5:12 *i* Jn 15:21
5:42 *j* Ac 2:46

6:1 *k* Ac 2:41 *l* Ac 9:29 *m* Ac 9:39,41 *n* Ac 4:35
6:3 *o* Ac 1:16
6:4 *p* Ac 1:14
6:5 *q* ver 8; Ac 11:19 *r* Ac 11:24 *s* Ac 8:5-40; 21:8

Acts 6:1–7

One of the strategies of our adversary is to divide believers. The Jerusalem community faced a serious unity problem. Jewish Christians from a Greek background believed that the widows of those with Hebrew roots were receiving preferential treatment. But their solution wasn't to split and worship separately. What they did do was so basic it might surprise us: They made sure the Grecians were well cared for. Note the qualities required in these first "deacons." It's striking that the early church had a daily program to make sure widows were provided with food.

Culturally diverse churches today risk misunderstandings and insensitivity. Yet overcoming these tensions demonstrates to a strife-torn world that Christ makes people one. Meeting the needs of those who can't provide for themselves demonstrates Christ's compassion. How does your church express multi-cultural and multi-generational unity and practical care for people's daily needs?

6:6
t Ac 1:24; 8:17;
13:3; 2Ti 1:6
u Nu 8:10; Ac 9:17;
1Ti 4:14
6:7
v Ac 12:24; 19:20

olas from Antioch, a convert to Judaism. ⁶They presented these men to the apostles, who prayed *t* and laid their hands on them. *u*

⁷So the word of God spread. *v* The number of disciples in Jerusalem increased rapidly, and a large number of priests became obedient to the faith.

Stephen Seized

6:8
w Jn 4:48
6:9
x Mt 27:32
y Ac 15:23,41;
22:3; 23:34 *z* Ac 2:9

⁸Now Stephen, a man full of God's grace and power, did great wonders and miraculous signs *w* among the people. ⁹Opposition arose, however, from members of the Synagogue of the Freedmen (as it was called)—Jews of Cyrene *x* and Alexandria as well as the provinces of Cilicia *y* and Asia. *z* These men began to argue with Stephen, ¹⁰but they could not stand up against his wisdom or the Spirit by whom he spoke. *a*

6:10
a Lk 21:15
6:11
b 1Ki 21:10
c Mt 26:59-61

¹¹Then they secretly *b* persuaded some men to say, "We have heard Stephen speak words of blasphemy against Moses and against God." *c*

6:12
d Mt 5:22
6:13
e Ac 21:28

¹²So they stirred up the people and the elders and the teachers of the law. They seized Stephen and brought him before the Sanhedrin. *d* ¹³They produced false witnesses, who testified, "This fellow never stops speaking against this holy place *e* and against the law. ¹⁴For we have heard him say that this Jesus of Nazareth will destroy this place and change the customs Moses handed down to us." *f*

6:14
f Ac 15:1; 21:21;
26:3; 28:17
6:15
g Mt 5:22

¹⁵All who were sitting in the Sanhedrin *g* looked intently at Stephen, and they saw that his face was like the face of an angel.

Stephen's Speech to the Sanhedrin

7:2
h Ac 22:1 *i* Ps 29:3
j Ge 11:31; 15:7

7 Then the high priest asked him, "Are these charges true?"

²To this he replied: "Brothers and fathers, *h* listen to me! The God of glory *i* appeared to our father Abraham while he was still in Mesopotamia, before he lived in Haran. *j* ³'Leave your country and your people,' God said, 'and go to the land I will show you.' ª*k*

7:3
k Ge 12:1

7:4
l Ge 12:5

⁴"So he left the land of the Chaldeans and settled in Haran. After the death of his father, God sent him to this land where you are now living. *l* ⁵He gave him no inheritance here, not even a foot of ground. But God promised him that he and his descendants after him would possess the land, *m* even though at that time Abraham had no child. ⁶God spoke to him in this way: 'Your descendants will be strangers in a country not their own, and they will be enslaved and mistreated four hundred years. *n* ⁷But I will punish the nation they serve as slaves,' God said, 'and afterward

7:5
m Ge 12:7; 17:8;
26:3

7:6
n Ex 12:40

ª 3 Gen. 12:1

Acts 6:8–15

Luke used interesting descriptors for Stephen, all involving fullness, completeness, a quality of bursting: "full of faith" (v. 5); "full of the Holy Spirit" (v. 5; 7:55); "full of God's grace and power" (v. 8). The Greek word for "grace" expresses being drawn into intimate relationship. Being filled with God's grace made Stephen a gracious person who cared for others. His opponents couldn't help but notice: "His face was like the face of an angel" (v. 15).

Stephen was selected to be one of the deacons, a table waiter serving the elderly. He became the church's first martyr, in part because he was a radical, fearlessly challenging the religious and political power brokers of his day. Yet when we get to know him, we see *balance, not recklessness*. What picture comes to mind when you think of a balanced Christian life? A bland existence—or a revolutionary life of following a revolutionary Lord? Moderation isn't negative, but balance in the Christian life is all about uncompromising obedience. In

what ways are you a radical follower of Christ?

Acts 7:1–53

Stephen's speech was a "defense"—not of himself but of the gospel. In the longest speech by someone other than Jesus recorded in the New Testament, Stephen recounted a history of Israel's response to the prophets. He made three key points: (1) God's activity wasn't limited to geographical Israel. (2) Worship acceptable to God wasn't confined to the Jerusalem temple. (3) The Jews had consistently rejected God's representatives. Stephen summed up this history as an indication of Jewish opposition to the Holy Spirit.

Stephen used the Jewish Scriptures as his source and authority, putting him in sync with his audience. His words may have been revolutionary, but they weren't new. Stephen didn't manufacture truth; he summarized nuggets of truth that were already accepted. His summary of Israel's response (vs. 51–53) was staggering. What can we learn from it about making sure we remain responsive to God's Word?

they will come out of that country and worship me in this place.'[a][o] 8Then he gave Abraham the covenant of circumcision.[p] And Abraham became the father of Isaac and circumcised him eight days after his birth.[q] Later Isaac became the father of Jacob,[r] and Jacob became the father of the twelve patriarchs.[s]

9 "Because the patriarchs were jealous of Joseph,[t] they sold him as a slave into Egypt.[u] But God was with him[v] 10and rescued him from all his troubles. He gave Joseph wisdom and enabled him to gain the goodwill of Pharaoh king of Egypt; so he made him ruler over Egypt and all his palace.[w]

11 "Then a famine struck all Egypt and Canaan, bringing great suffering, and our fathers could not find food.[x] 12When Jacob heard that there was grain in Egypt, he sent our fathers on their first visit.[y] 13On their second visit, Joseph told his brothers who he was,[z] and Pharaoh learned about Joseph's family. 14After this, Joseph sent for his father Jacob and his whole family,[a] seventy-five in all.[b] 15Then Jacob went down to Egypt, where he and our fathers died.[c] 16Their bodies were brought back to Shechem and placed in the tomb that Abraham had bought from the sons of Hamor at Shechem for a certain sum of money.[d]

17 "As the time drew near for God to fulfill his promise to Abraham, the number of our people in Egypt greatly increased.[e] 18Then another king, who knew nothing about Joseph, became ruler of Egypt.[f] 19He dealt treacherously with our people and oppressed our forefathers by forcing them to throw out their newborn babies so that they would die.[g]

20 "At that time Moses was born, and he was no ordinary child.[b] For three months he was cared for in his father's house.[h] 21When he was placed outside, Pharaoh's daughter took him and brought him up as her own son.[i] 22Moses was educated in all the wisdom of the Egyptians[j] and was powerful in speech and action.

23 "When Moses was forty years old, he decided to visit his fellow Israelites. 24He saw one of them being mistreated by an Egyptian, so he went to his defense and avenged him by killing the Egyptian. 25Moses thought that his own people would realize that God was using him to rescue them, but they did not. 26The next day Moses came upon two Israelites who were fighting. He tried to reconcile them by saying, 'Men, you are brothers; why do you want to hurt each other?'

27 "But the man who was mistreating the other pushed Moses aside and said, 'Who made you ruler and judge over us? 28Do you want to kill me as you killed the Egyptian yesterday?'[c] 29When Moses heard this, he fled to Midian, where he settled as a foreigner and had two sons.[k]

30 "After forty years had passed, an angel appeared to Moses in the flames of a burning bush in the desert near Mount Sinai. 31When he saw this, he was amazed at the sight. As he went over to look more closely, he heard the Lord's voice:[l] 32'I am the God of your fathers, the God of Abraham, Isaac and Jacob.'[d] Moses trembled with fear and did not dare to look.[m]

33 "Then the Lord said to him, 'Take off your sandals; the place where you are standing is holy ground.[n] 34I have indeed seen the oppression of my people in Egypt. I have heard their groaning and have come down to set them free. Now come, I will send you back to Egypt.'[e][o]

35 "This is the same Moses whom they had rejected with the words, 'Who made you ruler and judge?'[p] He was sent to be their ruler and deliverer by God himself, through the angel who appeared to him in the bush. 36He led them out of Egypt[q] and did wonders and miraculous signs in Egypt, at the Red Sea[f][r] and for forty years in the desert.

37 "This is that Moses who told the Israelites, 'God will send you a prophet like me from your own people.'[g][s] 38He was in the assembly in the desert, with the angel[t] who spoke to him on Mount Sinai, and with our fathers;[u] and he received living words[v] to pass on to us.[w]

39 "But our fathers refused to obey him. Instead, they rejected him and in their hearts turned back to Egypt.[x] 40They told Aaron, 'Make us gods who will go before

7:7
o Ex 3:12
7:8
p Ge 17:9-14
q Ge 21:2-4
r Ge 25:26
s Ge 29:31-35;
30:5-13, 17-24;
35:16-18, 22-26
7:9
t Ge 37:4, 11
u Ge 37:28;
Ps 105:17
v Ge 39:2, 21, 23
7:10
w Ge 41:37-43
7:11
x Ge 41:54
7:12
y Ge 42:1, 2
7:13
z Ge 45:1-4
7:14
a Ge 45:9, 10
b Ge 46:26, 27;
Ex 1:5; Dt 10:22
7:15
c Ge 46:5-7; 49:33;
Ex 1:6
7:16
d Ge 23:16-20;
33:18, 19; 50:13;
Jos 24:32
7:17
e Ex 1:7; Ps 105:24
7:18
f Ex 1:8
7:19
g Ex 1:10-22
7:20
h Ex 2:2; Heb 11:23
7:21
i Ex 2:3-10
7:22
j 1Ki 4:30; Isa 19:11
7:29
k Ex 2:11-15
7:31
l Ex 3:1-4
7:32
m Ex 3:6
7:33
n Ex 3:5; Jos 5:15
7:34
o Ex 3:7-10
7:35
p ver 27
7:36
q Ex 12:41; 33:1
r Ex 14:21
7:37
s Dt 18:15, 18;
Ac 3:22
7:38
t ver 53 u Ex 19:17
v Dt 32:45-47;
Heb 4:12 w Ro 3:2
7:39
x Nu 14:3, 4

a 7 Gen. 15:13,14   b 20 Or was fair in the sight of God   c 28 Exodus 2:14   d 32 Exodus 3:6
e 34 Exodus 3:5,7,8,10   f 36 That is, Sea of Reeds   g 37 Deut. 18:15

7:40
y Ex 32:1,23
7:41
z Ex 32:4-6;
Ps 106:19,20;
Rev 9:20
7:42
a Jos 24:20;
Isa 63:10
b Jer 19:13

us. As for this fellow Moses who led us out of Egypt—we don't know what has happened to him!' a y 41That was the time they made an idol in the form of a calf. They brought sacrifices to it and held a celebration in honor of what their hands had made. z 42But God turned away a and gave them over to the worship of the heavenly bodies. b This agrees with what is written in the book of the prophets:

" 'Did you bring me sacrifices and offerings
    forty years in the desert, O house of Israel?
43You have lifted up the shrine of Molech
    and the star of your god Rephan,
    the idols you made to worship.
Therefore I will send you into exile' b c beyond Babylon.

7:43
c Am 5:25-27
7:44
d Ex 38:21
e Ex 25:8,9,40

44"Our forefathers had the tabernacle of the Testimony d with them in the desert. It had been made as God directed Moses, according to the pattern he had seen. e

7:45
f Jos 3:14-17; 18:1;
23:9; 24:18; Ps 44:2
7:46
g 2Sa 7:8-16;
Ps 132:1-5

45Having received the tabernacle, our fathers under Joshua brought it with them when they took the land from the nations God drove out before them. f It remained in the land until the time of David, 46who enjoyed God's favor and asked that he might provide a dwelling place for the God of Jacob. c g 47But it was Solomon who built the house for him.

7:48
h 1Ki 8:27; 2Ch 2:6

48"However, the Most High does not live in houses made by men. h As the prophet says:

7:49
i Mt 5:34,35

49" 'Heaven is my throne,
    and the earth is my footstool. i
What kind of house will you build for me?
               says the Lord.
Or where will my resting place be?

7:50
j Isa 66:1,2

50Has not my hand made all these things?' d j

7:51
k Ex 32:9; 33:3,5
l Lev 26:41;
Dt 10:16; Jer 4:4;
9:26
7:52
m 2Ch 36:16;
Mt 5:12 n Ac 3:14;
1Th 2:15
7:53
o ver 38; Gal 3:19;
Heb 2:2
7:54
p Ac 5:33

51"You stiff-necked people, k with uncircumcised hearts l and ears! You are just like your fathers: You always resist the Holy Spirit! 52Was there ever a prophet your fathers did not persecute? m They even killed those who predicted the coming of the Righteous One. And now you have betrayed and murdered him n— 53you who have received the law that was put into effect through angels o but have not obeyed it."

The Stoning of Stephen

54When they heard this, they were furious p and gnashed their teeth at him. 55But Stephen, full of the Holy Spirit, looked up to heaven and saw the glory of God, and Jesus standing at the right hand of God. q 56"Look," he said, "I see heaven open r and the Son of Man s standing at the right hand of God."

7:55
q Mk 16:19
7:56
r Mt 3:16 s Mt 8:20

57At this they covered their ears and, yelling at the top of their voices, they all rushed at him, 58dragged him out of the city t and began to stone him. u Meanwhile, the witnesses laid their clothes v at the feet of a young man named Saul. w

7:58
t Lk 4:29
u Lev 24:14,16;
Dt 13:9 v Ac 22:20
w Ac 8:1
7:59
x Ps 31:5; Lk 23:46
7:60
y Ac 9:40 z Mt 5:44

59While they were stoning him, Stephen prayed, "Lord Jesus, receive my spirit." x 60Then he fell on his knees y and cried out, "Lord, do not hold this sin against them." z When he had said this, he fell asleep.

a 40 Exodus 32:1   b 43 Amos 5:25-27   c 46 Some early manuscripts *the house of Jacob*
d 50 Isaiah 66:1,2

Acts 7:54—8:1a

Luke recorded remarkable similarities between the deaths of Jesus and Stephen. Both were taken out of the city to be executed. Stephen's last words remind us of two of Jesus' statements from the cross: Stephen asked God to receive his spirit (cf. Luke 23:46) and not to "hold this sin against" his killers (cf. Luke 23:34). Stephen entered "the fellowship of sharing in [Jesus'] sufferings, becoming like him in his death" (Phil. 3:10).

Luke described the suffering Stephen as "full of the Holy Spirit" (5:55; see "There and Then" for 6:8–15). The Spirit also fills us, not only for ministry but also for suffering. Under what painful circumstances have you experienced him giving you a capacity and strength beyond what you thought possible? In Paul's unforgettable words, "*I* labor, struggling with all *his* energy, which so powerfully works *in me*" (Col. 1:29, emphasis added).

8

And Saul[a] was there, giving approval to his death.

The Church Persecuted and Scattered

On that day a great persecution broke out against the church at Jerusalem, and all except the apostles were scattered[b] throughout Judea and Samaria.[c] 2Godly men buried Stephen and mourned deeply for him. 3But Saul[d] began to destroy the church.[e] Going from house to house, he dragged off men and women and put them in prison.

Philip in Samaria

4Those who had been scattered[f] preached the word wherever they went.[g] 5Philip[h] went down to a city in Samaria and proclaimed the Christ[a] there. 6When the crowds heard Philip and saw the miraculous signs he did, they all paid close attention to what he said. 7With shrieks, evil[b] spirits came out of many,[i] and many paralytics and cripples were healed.[j] 8So there was great joy in that city.

---

a 5 Or Messiah   b 7 Greek unclean

8:1
a Ac 7:58
b Ac 11:19
c Ac 9:31

8:3
d Ac 7:58
e Ac 22:4,19; 26:10,11; 1Co 15:9; Gal 1:13,23; Php 3:6; 1Ti 1:13

8:4
f ver 1 g Ac 15:35
8:5
h Ac 6:5

8:7
i Mk 16:17
j Mt 4:24

Acts 8:1b–3

 As a result of the persecution that began with Stephen, the scattered believers "preached the word wherever they went" (v. 4). When Luke later described the early proclamation of the gospel to Gentiles outside Israel, he identified the missionaries as "those who had been scattered by the persecution in connection with Stephen" (11:19–21). Persecution became the catalyst for the next step in fulfilling Christ's commission to take the gospel to Jerusalem, Judea, Samaria, and the ends of the earth (cf. 1:8; "There and Then" for 1:1–11).

The apostle Paul would later call Christians to maintain joy in the midst of pain or persecution, trusting the One working behind the scenes for our good (cf. Rom. 8:28). If you are struggling now, how about trying this perspective on for size? Concerning his imprisonment, Paul told the Philippians, "I want you to know . . . that what has happened to me has really served to advance the gospel" (Phil. 1:12–13; cf. Col. 1:24). God can use our suffering to propel his kingdom forward. In fact, persecution is an *expected* cost of discipleship (cf. John 15:18—16:4).

Snapshots

7:59—8:1

Auca Five

Friends Jim Elliot and Peter Fleming had long discussed finding a way to reach an elusive South American tribe, the Auca—a Quicha word for "wild men"—now known by their tribal name, Waorani. The two sailed for Ecuador in 1952 to fulfill their dream and were later joined by Elliot's Wheaton college buddy Ed McCully. Waiting for an opportunity to make contact with the tribe, the group ministered among the Quicha tribe.

Nate Saint, a Missionary Aviation Fellowship pilot, made many flights over the jungle, serving as a supply link to missionaries in remote locales. On one of these flights in 1955, he located a Waorani village. For 12 weeks he, Elliott, and McCully made weekly flights over the village, dropping gifts according to a system he had devised (one of many techniques Saint developed that have become standards in missions aviation work).

> Eventually about half of the tribe received Christ, including the five killers, three of whom became pastors and evangelists.

Finally Elliot, Fleming, McCully, and Saint, along with Roger Youderian, made contact with three Waoranis along the Curaray River. In January, 1956, they expected another friendly meeting but were killed by tribesmen with spears. Eventually about half of the tribe received Christ, including the five killers, three of whom became pastors and evangelists.

Witness

Acts is a book about witness. Chapter 8 describes early believers fleeing their homes because of a wave of persecution (v. 1). Far from being intimidated, "those who had been scattered preached the word wherever they went" (v. 4). These refugees and internally displaced persons for Christ had become witnesses, a scenario repeated countless times in history. Situations people consider bleak, hopeless, and less than ideal for evangelism still are often transformed by Christians into fertile opportunities for Christlike service. I have seen this happen many times in Sri Lanka, which has been engulfed in a bloody civil war for over 20 years.

In Acts, some of the scattered converts went to Samaria, a region typically avoided by Jews because of their own ethnic prejudice. Philip had a fruitful ministry there (vv. 5–8). His work helped remove the barriers of bigotry that divided people—a prominent New Testament theme. After stating that Christ had died for all, Paul said, "From now on we regard no one from a worldly point of view" (2 Cor. 5:14–16). Social criteria such as race, caste, class, and wealth don't matter any more.

> **E**ffective evangelism requires us to get close to non-Christians, observing and learning their doubts and aspirations.

Perhaps the "great joy in that [Samaritan] city" (v. 8) was due in part to Christian love breaking down intolerance and animosity among the various peoples of that region. I have experienced such joy when traveling during wartime for ministry in areas where the Sri Lankan people view those of my race as enemies. We participate together in the exhilarating unity in Christ that goes deeper than the wounds of war.

Sadly, some committed to Christ have over the years neglected to stress this barrier-breaking feature of the gospel. They have birthed new generations of Christians who continue to be biased despite testifying to new life in Christ. Paul addressed discrimination in Athens when he challenged the Greek belief in ethnic superiority by proclaiming that all humans come from the same stock (17:26).

In an unexpected angel encounter, Philip was commanded to leave his effective field of ministry in Samaria to embark on a 50-mile trek to Gaza. On the way he met an Ethiopian eunuch (8:26–38). Philip encountered this foreigner reading a prophecy about Jesus which, he confessed, he couldn't understand. Philip's attempt to answer the Ethiopian's question gave him an opportunity to present the gospel.

Still today, an effective way to initiate witness for Christ is to address the questions people are asking and show how Christ answers them. But because the thought patterns of non-Christians are often so different from ours, we may find it hard to identify and relate to their questions and qualms—concluding that they have none. But they do, and we need to get familiar before we can recognize them. Effective evangelism requires us to get close to non-Christians, observing and learning their doubts and aspirations. Because Jesus is the Creator's solution to the problems of the human race, the deepest desires of all people can be fully satisfied only in Christ.

Ajith Fernando, national director of Youth for Christ in Sri Lanka

Simon the Sorcerer

[9]Now for some time a man named Simon had practiced sorcery[k] in the city and amazed all the people of Samaria. He boasted that he was someone great,[l] [10]and all the people, both high and low, gave him their attention and exclaimed, "This man is the divine power known as the Great Power."[m] [11]They followed him because he had amazed them for a long time with his magic. [12]But when they believed Philip as he preached the good news of the kingdom of God[n] and the name of Jesus Christ, they were baptized,[o] both men and women. [13]Simon himself believed and was baptized. And he followed Philip everywhere, astonished by the great signs and miracles[p] he saw.

[14]When the apostles in Jerusalem heard that Samaria[q] had accepted the word of God, they sent Peter and John[r] to them. [15]When they arrived, they prayed for them that they might receive the Holy Spirit,[s] [16]because the Holy Spirit had not yet come upon any of them;[t] they had simply been baptized into[a] the name of the Lord Jesus.[u] [17]Then Peter and John placed their hands on them,[v] and they received the Holy Spirit.

[18]When Simon saw that the Spirit was given at the laying on of the apostles' hands, he offered them money [19]and said, "Give me also this ability so that everyone on whom I lay my hands may receive the Holy Spirit."

[20]Peter answered: "May your money perish with you, because you thought you could buy the gift of God with money![w] [21]You have no part or share in this ministry, because your heart is not right[x] before God. [22]Repent of this wickedness and pray to the Lord. Perhaps he will forgive you for having such a thought in your heart. [23]For I see that you are full of bitterness and captive to sin."

[24]Then Simon answered, "Pray to the Lord for me[y] so that nothing you have said may happen to me."

[25]When they had testified and proclaimed the word of the Lord, Peter and John returned to Jerusalem, preaching the gospel in many Samaritan villages.[z]

Philip and the Ethiopian

[26]Now an angel[a] of the Lord said to Philip, "Go south to the road—the desert road—that goes down from Jerusalem to Gaza." [27]So he started out, and on his way he met an Ethiopian[b][b] eunuch,[c] an important official in charge of all the treasury

---

8:9
k Ac 13:6 l Ac 5:36

8:10
m Ac 14:11; 28:6

8:12
n Ac 1:3 o Ac 2:38

8:13
p ver 6; Ac 19:11
8:14
q ver 1 r Lk 22:8

8:15
s Ac 2:38
8:16
t Ac 19:2
u Mt 28:19; Ac 2:38
8:17
v Ac 6:6

8:20
w 2Ki 5:16; Da 5:17; Mt 10:8; Ac 2:38
8:21
x Ps 78:37

8:24
y Ex 8:8; Nu 21:7; 1Ki 13:6

8:25
z ver 40

8:26
a Ac 5:19

8:27
b Ps 68:31; 87:4; Zep 3:10
c Isa 56:3-5

---

a 16 Or in   b 27 That is, from the upper Nile region

Acts 8:4–8

The Samaritans were a mixed race—a blend of Jews left behind after Israel's exile and Gentiles forcibly settled in the region by Assyria (2 Kings 17:24). Their religion was based on the Pentateuch (first five OT books), but "pure" Jews still viewed them with contempt (cf. John 4:4–9). Philip, a Grecian Jew, brought the Good News to the Samaritans. In preaching Jesus as the Christ (v. 5), he tapped into their expectation of a coming Messiah (John 4:25–26). The Samaritans joyfully responded.

Jerusalem Jews tended to distrust Grecian Christians like Stephen and Philip, so Philip could relate to the "second class" Samaritans. Still today, outcast people respond better to the Good News when they can identify with its bearer. God can use our vulnerability and human struggles to touch and move the hearts of seekers. The Spirit gave Philip a three-fold ministry: to proclaim Christ, perform miracles, and produce joy!

Acts 8:9–25

Even people who don't follow Christ can at times perform signs and wonders that amaze people. Pharaoh's magicians could replicate many of the wonders God did through Moses (Ex. 7:11). So spiritual power alone isn't a sign of God's blessing. Sadly, those drawn to power may seek to use even God's power to expand their own influence.

Simon's attempt to buy power with money catches our attention. In our world, money's the currency that counts—but God wants our submissive hearts. In what ways have you been tempted to seek spiritual power for your personal gain?

Acts 8:26–40

Philip's encounter with the Ethiopian offers us an effective evangelistic model. Philip: twice obeyed God's promptings; discovered that the Ethiopian had been prepared by God even before he spoke to him; began his witness with a question and then encouraged the Ethiopian to ask questions; based his witness on Scripture; made Jesus the focal point of his message; overcame cultural and ethnic differences; and invited a response. Once again Luke recorded the witness to the gospel *beginning at the ends* of the earth. The church in Ethiopia, and thus in Africa, dates from the 1st century A.D.

8:27
d 1Ki 8:41-43;
Jn 12:20
8:29
e Ac 10:19; 11:12;
13:2; 20:23; 21:11

of Candace, queen of the Ethiopians. This man had gone to Jerusalem to worship,[d] 28and on his way home was sitting in his chariot reading the book of Isaiah the prophet. 29The Spirit told[e] Philip, "Go to that chariot and stay near it."

30Then Philip ran up to the chariot and heard the man reading Isaiah the prophet. "Do you understand what you are reading?" Philip asked.

31"How can I," he said, "unless someone explains it to me?" So he invited Philip to come up and sit with him.

32The eunuch was reading this passage of Scripture:

> "He was led like a sheep to the slaughter,
> and as a lamb before the shearer is silent,
> so he did not open his mouth.
> 33 In his humiliation he was deprived of justice.
> Who can speak of his descendants?
> For his life was taken from the earth." [a][f]

8:33
f Isa 53:7,8

8:35
g Mt 5:2
h Lk 24:27; Ac 17:2;
18:28; 28:23

34The eunuch asked Philip, "Tell me, please, who is the prophet talking about, himself or someone else?" 35Then Philip began[g] with that very passage of Scripture[h] and told him the good news about Jesus.

8:36
i Ac 10:47

36As they traveled along the road, they came to some water and the eunuch said, "Look, here is water. Why shouldn't I be baptized?"[b][i] 38And he gave orders to stop the chariot. Then both Philip and the eunuch went down into the water and Philip baptized him. 39When they came up out of

8:39
j 1Ki 18:12;
2Ki 2:16; Eze 3:12,
14; 8:3; 11:1,24;
43:5; 2Co 12:2

the water, the Spirit of the Lord suddenly took Philip away,[j] and the eunuch did not see him again, but went on his way rejoicing. 40Philip, however, appeared at Azotus and traveled about, preaching the gospel in all the towns[k] until he reached Caesarea.[l]

8:40
k ver 25 / Ac 10:1,
24; 12:19; 21:8,16;
23:23,33;
25:1,4,6,13

Saul's Conversion

9:1
m Ac 8:3

9 Meanwhile, Saul was still breathing out murderous threats against the Lord's disciples.[m] He went to the high priest 2and asked him for letters to the synagogues in Damascus, so that if he found any there who belonged to the Way,[n] whether men or women, he might take them as prisoners to Jerusalem. 3As he neared Damascus on his journey, suddenly a light from heaven flashed

9:2
n Ac 19:9,23; 22:4;
24:14,22

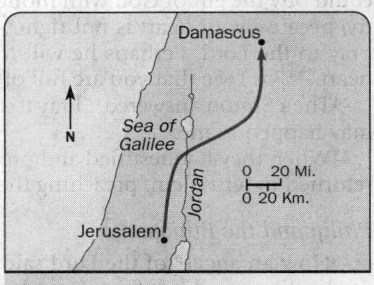

Saul in Damascus (9:3)

Then: Damascus was one of oldest continuously occupied towns in the world.

Now: This still-thriving city, the capital of Syria, is home to 1.7 million people.

---

a 33 Isaiah 53:7,8   b 36 Some late manuscripts *baptized?"* 37Philip said, "If you believe with all your heart, you may." The eunuch answered, "I believe that Jesus Christ is the Son of God."

📖 Boldness begins with a decision to *obey* the call to witness. Philip took a risk in approaching this stranger, but he was obeying an inner voice. The more we learn to rely on the Spirit's prompting, the more we will come to recognize and trust it. Discerning how God is at work in people's lives and learning to ask the right questions are as important as the words we speak and the answers we give. Our witness is only as effective as people's openness. Therefore listening and discerning are foundational. Then, when God prompts us to speak up, he gives us the courage—and the words—we need.

Acts 9:1–19a

📖 His spectacular confrontation with Jesus radically altered Saul's life. He received both a conversion and a commission—a change and a charge. Through Ananias, the Lord told Saul that he would take the Good

News to Gentiles, kings, and the people of Israel—and that he would suffer greatly for Jesus. But he couldn't, and wouldn't, do so without first receiving Christ's power. Once again Luke underscored the Spirit's work in preparing someone for service. Our life as witnesses is simply our participation in that work. Ananias came so that Saul might "see again and be filled with the Holy Spirit" (v. 17).

📖 It's possible for us to stress the blessings of our conversion (change) so much that we forget all about our commission (charge). *All* Christians are called to be Christ's witnesses—a task that involves risk and suffering. Suffering for Christ is basic to faith (cf. 2 Tim. 3:12; 1 Pet. 4:12–16). How and when have you experienced hardship, inconvenience, sacrifice, or ridicule for the Name? How has this strengthened you for your faith journey?

around him.[o] [4]He fell to the ground and heard a voice say to him, "Saul, Saul, why do you persecute me?"

[5]"Who are you, Lord?" Saul asked.

"I am Jesus, whom you are persecuting," he replied. [6]"Now get up and go into the city, and you will be told what you must do."[p]

[7]The men traveling with Saul stood there speechless; they heard the sound[q] but did not see anyone.[r] [8]Saul got up from the ground, but when he opened his eyes he could see nothing. So they led him by the hand into Damascus. [9]For three days he was blind, and did not eat or drink anything.

[10]In Damascus there was a disciple named Ananias. The Lord called to him in a vision,[s] "Ananias!"

"Yes, Lord," he answered.

[11]The Lord told him, "Go to the house of Judas on Straight Street and ask for a man from Tarsus[t] named Saul, for he is praying. [12]In a vision he has seen a man named Ananias come and place his hands on[u] him to restore his sight."

[13]"Lord," Ananias answered, "I have heard many reports about this man and all the harm he has done to your saints[v] in Jerusalem.[w] [14]And he has come here with authority from the chief priests[x] to arrest all who call on your name."

[15]But the Lord said to Ananias, "Go! This man is my chosen instrument[y] to carry my name before the Gentiles[z] and their kings[a] and before the people of Israel. [16]I will show him how much he must suffer for my name."[b]

[17]Then Ananias went to the house and entered it. Placing his hands on[c] Saul, he said, "Brother Saul, the Lord—Jesus, who appeared to you on the road as you were coming here—has sent me so that you may see again and be filled with the Holy Spirit." [18]Immediately, something like scales fell from Saul's eyes, and he could see again. He got up and was baptized, [19]and after taking some food, he regained his strength.

Saul in Damascus and Jerusalem

Saul spent several days with the disciples[d] in Damascus.[e] [20]At once he began to preach in the synagogues[f] that Jesus is the Son of God.[g] [21]All those who heard him were astonished and asked, "Isn't he the man who raised havoc in Jerusalem among those who call on this name?[h] And hasn't he come here to take them as prisoners to the chief priests?"[i] [22]Yet Saul grew more and more powerful and baffled the Jews living in Damascus by proving that Jesus is the Christ.[a][j]

[23]After many days had gone by, the Jews conspired to kill him, [24]but Saul learned of their plan.[k] Day and night they kept close watch on the city gates in order to kill him. [25]But his followers took him by night and lowered him in a basket through an opening in the wall.[l]

[26]When he came to Jerusalem,[m] he tried to join the disciples, but they were all afraid of him, not believing that he really was a disciple. [27]But Barnabas[n] took him and brought him to the apostles. He told them how Saul on his journey had seen the Lord and that the Lord had spoken to him,[o] and how in Damascus he had preached fearlessly in the name of Jesus.[p] [28]So Saul stayed with them and moved about freely in Jerusalem, speaking boldly in the name of the Lord. [29]He talked and

[a] 22 Or *Messiah*

Acts 9:19b–31

Saul didn't venture back to Jerusalem until three years after his conversion (see Gal. 1:17–18). What mixed feelings he must have had in returning to the city he loved. He knew that his former associates would shun him and that his fellow disciples would be afraid of him. One of the pivotal "buts" of Acts introduces God's solution (v. 27): Barnabas advocated for Saul, taking him not just to the larger group of disciples but accompanying him into the inner circle of the apostles.

The risk Barnabas took was immense. But he represented the gospel of Christ—and a faith based on love. Risking belief in others, possibly at the expense of our own reputations, is one expression of love. Just as the Spirit is our counselor and supporter, so we are empowered by him to advocate for others. We all need people who believe in us. The gospel isn't just for the popular and the praised but for the feared and despised as well. The church is a community that welcomes outcasts. But for this to happen, we need supporters who will come alongside and draw people in.

9:29
q Ac 6:1
r 2Co 11:26
9:30
s Ac 1:16 t Ac 8:40
u ver 11
9:31
v Ac 8:1

debated with the Grecian Jews,^q but they tried to kill him.^r ³⁰When the brothers^s learned of this, they took him down to Caesarea^t and sent him off to Tarsus.^u

³¹Then the church throughout Judea, Galilee and Samaria^v enjoyed a time of peace. It was strengthened; and encouraged by the Holy Spirit, it grew in numbers, living in the fear of the Lord.

Aeneas and Dorcas

9:32
w ver 13

³²As Peter traveled about the country, he went to visit the saints^w in Lydda.

9:34
x Ac 3:6,16; 4:10

³³There he found a man named Aeneas, a paralytic who had been bedridden for eight years. ³⁴"Aeneas," Peter said to him, "Jesus Christ heals you.^x Get up and take care of your mat." Immediately Aeneas got up. ³⁵All those who lived in Lydda and

9:35
y 1Ch 5:16; 27:29; Isa 33:9; 35:2; 65:10 z Ac 11:21
9:36
a Jos 19:46; 2Ch 2:16; Ezr 3:7; Jnh 1:3; Ac 10:5
b 1Ti 2:10; Tit 3:8
9:37
c Ac 1:13
9:38
d Ac 11:26
9:39
e Ac 6:1

Sharon^y saw him and turned to the Lord.^z

³⁶In Joppa^a there was a disciple named Tabitha (which, when translated, is Dorcas^a), who was always doing good^b and helping the poor. ³⁷About that time she became sick and died, and her body was washed and placed in an upstairs room.^c ³⁸Lydda was near Joppa; so when the disciples^d heard that Peter was in Lydda, they sent two men to him and urged him, "Please come at once!"

³⁹Peter went with them, and when he arrived he was taken upstairs to the room. All the widows^e stood around him, crying and showing him the robes and other clothing that Dorcas had made while she was still with them.

9:40
f Mt 9:25
g Lk 22:41; Ac 7:60

⁴⁰Peter sent them all out of the room;^f then he got down on his knees^g and prayed. Turning toward the dead woman, he said, "Tabitha, get up." She opened her eyes, and seeing Peter she sat up. ⁴¹He took her by the hand and helped her to her feet. Then he called the believers and the widows and presented her to them alive. ⁴²This became known all over Joppa, and many people believed in the Lord. ⁴³Pe-

9:43
h Ac 10:6

ter stayed in Joppa for some time with a tanner named Simon.^h

Cornelius Calls for Peter

10:1
i Ac 8:40

10 At Caesareaⁱ there was a man named Cornelius, a centurion in what was known as the Italian Regiment. ²He and all his family were devout and God-

10:2
j ver 22,35; Ac 13:16,26
10:3
k Ac 3:1 l Ac 9:10
m Ac 5:19

fearing;^j he gave generously to those in need and prayed to God regularly. ³One day at about three in the afternoon^k he had a vision.^l He distinctly saw an angel^m of God, who came to him and said, "Cornelius!"

⁴Cornelius stared at him in fear. "What is it, Lord?" he asked.

The angel answered, "Your prayers and gifts to the poor have come up as a me-

10:4
n Mt 26:13
o Rev 8:4
10:5
p Ac 9:36
10:6
q Ac 9:43

morial offeringⁿ before God.^o ⁵Now send men to Joppa^p to bring back a man named Simon who is called Peter. ⁶He is staying with Simon the tanner,^q whose house is by the sea."

---

^a 36 Both *Tabitha* (Aramaic) and *Dorcas* (Greek) mean *gazelle.*

Acts 9:32–43

📖 *Hagios* (lit., "holy person," but often translated "believer" or "saint") appears three times in chapter 9 (vv. 13,32,41). The New Testament uses the word not for a class of people but for believers who belong fully to God. In a sense, all God's people are saints, expected to follow the way of the kingdom. Saintly character, holiness, and obedience are assumed in the "job" description.

📖 What a wonderful summary of a person's life: She "was always doing good and helping the poor" (v. 36)! The distinguishing mark of the church is our care for the needy. A good test of Christian character is how we treat society's "unimportant"—especially when no one else is looking. We all attend funerals and memorial services. But wouldn't it be a rich gift to have the poor and widows bring along to our service the "robes . . . and clothing" we had made for them (v. 39), commemorating how God had expressed Christ's compassion through us?

Acts 10:1–8

📖 Cornelius experienced his vision "at about three in the afternoon"—a traditional Jewish time of prayer. He and his family were "devout and God-fearing." "God-fearers" were probably non-Jews who attended the synagogue and honored Jewish laws and customs but who hadn't (in the case of men) been incorporated into the Jewish community through the rite of circumcision.

📖 The angelic messenger cited Cornelius's lively prayer life and generosity to the poor as "offerings" God had noticed. Churches today rightly emphasize worship, prayer, and studying the Word as foundational elements of the Christian life. But how well do you—and your church—balance these critical emphases with an equal focus on our role as God's agents to generously assist those in need?

Tabitha

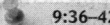 9:36–42

Tabitha "was always doing good and helping the poor" (Acts 9:36). We know little else about her, except that she was "a disciple," a member of the Christian community in Joppa, the ancient town on the Mediterranean coast, 35 miles west of Jerusalem, where hundreds of years earlier Jonah had embarked when running away from God.

Jesus reminded his disciples, "The poor you will always have with you" (Matt. 26:11, recalling Deut. 15:11). History has proved this true. Every society has its poor. Their relative numbers grow through famines, natural disasters, war, oppression, and injustice. Yet it's people like Tabitha, acting alone or through organized responses, who minister God's love to the poor, showing his special concern for all who suffer.

A widow or otherwise single woman, Tabitha was a disciple who put her faith into practice. Here as elsewhere in the New Testament we see that ministry wasn't restricted to apostles or officially appointed leaders.

What do we learn from Tabitha and her ministry—as well as her death and miraculous raising? This brief example teaches us key lessons:

Tabitha loved poor people. She wanted to help those in need, especially poor widows. *At its best, the church has consistently demonstrated this kind of God-inspired love and care.*

> **Though ministry to the poor can be controversial and spark opposition, love overflows to those who care for others.**

Tabitha was creative. A seamstress, she knew how to make clothing, and she used her creative gifts to help the poor. Her gifts became a channel of God's love to others. *God's Spirit can help the church be creative and effective in its ministry to the poor.*

Tabitha was vulnerable. We don't know what she died from, but it sounds as though her death was rather sudden. She was exposed to sickness and death as she served the poor. *Ministry to the poor may be risky and endanger our health.*

Tabitha was loved! A spirit of love breathes through this whole passage. The Christians in Joppa were shocked and saddened when Tabitha died. We sense the urgency in their message to Peter, "Please come at once!" One of the most moving passages in all the Bible is verse 39: "All the widows stood around . . . crying and showing Peter the robes and other clothing that Tabitha had made while she was still with them." *Though ministry to the poor can be controversial and spark opposition, love overflows to those who care for others.*

Interestingly, we know very little about the Joppa church and nothing of its leaders. Acts gives the names of only two disciples there: Tabitha, who ministered to the poor, and Simon the Tanner, who hosted Peter (Acts 9:43).

Tabitha's compassionate ministry reminds us of other Biblical examples. The wise woman described in Proverbs 31 "open[ed] her arms to the poor and extend[ed] her hands to the needy" (Prov. 31:20). Cornelius was commended for his "gifts to the poor" (Acts 10:4, 31), and Job also was known for his care for the disadvantaged (Job 29:12; 30:25). Proverbs 19:17 says that the person "who is kind to the poor lends to the LORD, and he will reward him for what he has done." Perhaps it was in fulfillment of this promise that God brought Tabitha back to life to continue her ministry.

God calls all his disciples—the whole church—to ministry, to show his love to the poor. Some are like Peter and Paul. But most are like Tabitha and Simon the Tanner—ordinary folks God uses to touch people in need.

Howard Snyder, professor of the history and theology of mission at Asbury Theological Seminary in Wilmore, Kentucky

10:8
r Ac 9:36

7When the angel who spoke to him had gone, Cornelius called two of his servants and a devout soldier who was one of his attendants. 8He told them everything that had happened and sent them to Joppa.r

Peter's Vision

10:9
s Mt 24:17
10:10
t Ac 22:17

9About noon the following day as they were on their journey and approaching the city, Peter went up on the roofs to pray. 10He became hungry and wanted something to eat, and while the meal was being prepared, he fell into a trance.t 11He saw heaven opened and something like a large sheet being let down to earth by its four corners. 12It contained all kinds of four-footed animals, as well as reptiles of the earth and birds of the air. 13Then a voice told him, "Get up, Peter. Kill and eat."

10:14
u Ac 9:5 v Lev 11:4-
8, 13-20; 20:25;
Dt 14:3-20;
Eze 4:14

14"Surely not, Lord!"u Peter replied. "I have never eaten anything impure or unclean."v

10:15
w Mt 15:11;
Ro 14:14,17,20;
1Co 10:25; 1Ti 4:3,
4; Tit 1:15

15The voice spoke to him a second time, "Do not call anything impure that God has made clean."w

16This happened three times, and immediately the sheet was taken back to heaven.

10:17
x ver 7,8

17While Peter was wondering about the meaning of the vision, the men sent by Corneliusx found out where Simon's house was and stopped at the gate. 18They called out, asking if Simon who was known as Peter was staying there.

10:19
y Ac 8:29

19While Peter was still thinking about the vision, the Spirit saidy to him, "Simon, threea men are looking for you. 20So get up and go downstairs. Do not hesitate to go with them, for I have sent them."z

10:20
z Ac 15:7-9

21Peter went down and said to the men, "I'm the one you're looking for. Why have you come?"

10:22
a ver 2 b Ac 11:14

22The men replied, "We have come from Cornelius the centurion. He is a righteous and God-fearing man,a who is respected by all the Jewish people. A holy angel told him to have you come to his house so that he could hear what you have to say."b 23Then Peter invited the men into the house to be his guests.

Peter at Cornelius's House

10:23
c Ac 1:16 d ver 45;
Ac 11:12
10:24
e Ac 8:40

The next day Peter started out with them, and some of the brothersc from Joppa went along.d 24The following day he arrived in Caesarea.e Cornelius was expecting them and had called together his relatives and close friends. 25As Peter entered the house, Cornelius met him and fell at his feet in reverence. 26But Peter made him get up. "Stand up," he said, "I am only a man myself."f

10:26
f Ac 14:15;
Rev 19:10

27Talking with him, Peter went inside and found a large gathering of people. 28He said to them: "You are well aware that it is against our law for a Jew to associate with a Gentile or visit him.g But God has shown me that I should not call any man impure or unclean.h 29So when I was sent for, I came without raising any objection. May I ask why you sent for me?"

10:28
g Jn 4:9; 18:28;
Ac 11:3 h Ac 15:8,9

30Cornelius answered: "Four days ago I was in my house praying at this hour, at three in the afternoon. Suddenly a man in shining clothes stood before me 31and

---

a 19 One early manuscript two; other manuscripts do not have the number.

Acts 10:9–23a

📖 At first Peter was revolted by God's command to eat "unclean" animals. For the Jews, dietary laws (see Lev. 20:24–26) were more than a matter of etiquette—they stood for survival and identity. But Peter's re-education was just beginning. This story is as much an account of Peter's conversion to the accessibility of the gospel for Gentiles as of Cornelius's conversion to Christ. Peter would soon realize that he wasn't to consider any people "unclean" (v. 28). After Jesus' discussion of clean and unclean objects in Mark 7:5–23, Mark noted, "In saying this, Jesus declared all foods 'clean.'" Peter finally

"got" Jesus' words—an understanding he probably later communicated to his young friend Mark, the Gospel writer.

🔖 Even mature Christians may need to realign themselves to keep up with God's unfolding plan and be liberated from prejudices and preconceptions that limit their understanding. It's easy for us to become so entrenched in tradition that we miss a point of obedience. In response to our well-intended resistance to untried ways comes a message from the living Christ: "Do not call anything impure that God has made clean."

said, 'Cornelius, God has heard your prayer and remembered your gifts to the poor. 32Send to Joppa for Simon who is called Peter. He is a guest in the home of Simon the tanner, who lives by the sea.' 33So I sent for you immediately, and it was good of you to come. Now we are all here in the presence of God to listen to everything the Lord has commanded you to tell us."

34Then Peter began to speak: "I now realize how true it is that God does not show favoritism [i] 35but accepts men from every nation who fear him and do what is right. [j] 36You know the message God sent to the people of Israel, telling the good news [k] of peace [l] through Jesus Christ, who is Lord of all. [m] 37You know what has happened throughout Judea, beginning in Galilee after the baptism that John preached— 38how God anointed [n] Jesus of Nazareth with the Holy Spirit and power, and how he went around doing good and healing [o] all who were under the power of the devil, because God was with him. [p]

39"We are witnesses [q] of everything he did in the country of the Jews and in Jerusalem. They killed him by hanging him on a tree, [r] 40but God raised him from the dead [s] on the third day and caused him to be seen. 41He was not seen by all the people, [t] but by witnesses whom God had already chosen—by us who ate [u] and drank with him after he rose from the dead. 42He commanded us to preach to the people [v] and to testify that he is the one whom God appointed as judge of the living and the dead. [w] 43All the prophets testify about him [x] that everyone [y] who believes in him receives forgiveness of sins through his name."

44While Peter was still speaking these words, the Holy Spirit came on [z] all who heard the message. 45The circumcised believers who had come with Peter [a] were astonished that the gift of the Holy Spirit had been poured out [b] even on the Gentiles. [c] 46For they heard them speaking in tongues [a][d] and praising God.

Then Peter said, 47"Can anyone keep these people from being baptized with water? [e] They have received the Holy Spirit just as we have." [f] 48So he ordered that they be baptized in the name of Jesus Christ. [g] Then they asked Peter to stay with them for a few days.

Peter Explains His Actions

11 The apostles and the brothers [h] throughout Judea heard that the Gentiles also had received the word of God. 2So when Peter went up to Jerusalem, the circumcised believers [i] criticized him 3and said, "You went into the house of uncircumcised men and ate with them." [j]

---

a 46 Or *other languages*

Cross references

10:34
i Dt 10:17;
2Ch 19:7;
Job 34:19; Ro 2:11;
Gal 2:6; Eph 6:9;
Col 3:25; 1Pe 1:17
10:35
j Ac 15:9
10:36
k Ac 13:32 / Lk 2:14
m Mt 28:18;
Ro 10:12
10:38
n Ac 4:26 o Mt 4:23
p Jn 3:2
10:39
q Ac 24:48
r Ac 5:30
10:40
s Ac 2:24
10:41
t Jn 14:17,22
u Lk 24:43;
Jn 21:13
10:42
v Mt 28:19,20
w Jn 5:22;
Ac 17:31; Ro 14:9;
2Co 5:10; 2Ti 4:1;
1Pe 4:5
10:43
x Isa 53:11
y Ac 15:9
10:44
z Ac 8:15,16;
11:15; 15:8
10:45
a ver 23 b Ac 2:33,
38 c Ac 11:18
10:46
d Mk 16:17
10:47
e Ac 8:36
f Ac 11:17
10:48
g Ac 2:38; 8:16
11:1
h Ac 1:16
11:2
i Ac 10:45
11:3
j Ac 10:25,28;
Gal 2:12

Acts 10:23b–48

Peter readily admitted that he had been wrong about his prejudices. When he preached to the crowd, he publicly confessed his life-changing discovery: God shows no favoritism. The willingness to acknowledge and repent of past biases has always gone a long way in healing relationships ruptured by this sin. Public confession by Christian leaders builds bridges rather than discrediting authority. It opens an ideal ministry opportunity for the repentant Christian with those he or she once viewed in a misguided way.

Peter's openness to change depended on his willingness to step outside his cultural and religious comfort zone. There is a lot of talk today about being on the cutting edge. But cutting-edge ministry relies on cutting-edge identification. Many kingdom advances are made in the difficult and uncomfortable situations into which our love for people pulls—or pushes—us, situations compelling us to be with people we may previously have considered "unclean" or unacceptable.

Acts 11:1–18

There was unmistakable evidence these Gentiles had been converted. Peter didn't hesitate to baptize them immediately (10:47–48), reasoning, *I acted in obedience to God's call to me. Now they are having an experience just like we had, which we know was from God.* Nonetheless, his obedience got Peter into trouble. His friends and fellow believers criticized him for welcoming outsiders into the church.

Do you sometimes get frustrated with people who don't take to new ministry ideas or opportunities as readily as you do? Criticism from cautious or skeptical Christians often accompanies creative ministry. We are wise (and Biblical) to take seriously the whole community—especially our well-meaning critics—working to get the majority on board for innovative ministry approaches, no matter how inefficient this approach may seem. Rather than being defensive and impatient, we do well to follow Peter's example—to explain "everything to them precisely as it . . . had happened" (v. 4) and to confess, "Who [am] I to think that I could oppose God?" (v. 17).

11:5
k Ac 9:10; 10:9-32

4Peter began and explained everything to them precisely as it had happened: 5"I was in the city of Joppa praying, and in a trance I saw a vision.*k* I saw something like a large sheet being let down from heaven by its four corners, and it came down to where I was. 6I looked into it and saw four-footed animals of the earth, wild beasts, reptiles, and birds of the air. 7Then I heard a voice telling me, 'Get up, Peter. Kill and eat.'

8"I replied, 'Surely not, Lord! Nothing impure or unclean has ever entered my mouth.'

11:9
l Ac 10:15

9"The voice spoke from heaven a second time, 'Do not call anything impure that God has made clean.'*l* 10This happened three times, and then it was all pulled up to heaven again.

11:12
m Ac 8:29
n Ac 15:9; Ro 3:22

11"Right then three men who had been sent to me from Caesarea stopped at the house where I was staying. 12The Spirit told*m* me to have no hesitation about going with them.*n* These six brothers also went with me, and we entered the man's house. 13He told us how he had seen an angel appear in his house and say, 'Send to Joppa for Simon who is called Peter. 14He will bring you a message through which you and all your household*o* will be saved.'

11:14
o Jn 4:53; Ac 16:15, 31-34; 1Co 1:11,16
11:15
p Ac 10:44 *q* Ac 2:4
11:16
r Mk 1:8; Ac 1:5
11:17
s Ac 10:45,47

15"As I began to speak, the Holy Spirit came on*p* them as he had come on us at the beginning.*q* 16Then I remembered what the Lord had said: 'John baptized with*a* water, but you will be baptized with the Holy Spirit.'*r* 17So if God gave them the same gift as he gave us,*s* who believed in the Lord Jesus Christ, who was I to think that I could oppose God?"

11:18
t Ro 10:12,13; 2Co 7:10

18When they heard this, they had no further objections and praised God, saying, "So then, God has granted even the Gentiles repentance unto life."*t*

The Church in Antioch

11:19
u Ac 8:1,4 *v* ver 26, 27; Ac 13:1; 18:22; Gal 2:11
11:20
w Ac 4:36
x Mt 27:32
11:21
y Lk 1:66 *z* Ac 2:47
11:22
a Ac 4:36
11:23
b Ac 13:43; 14:26; 20:24

19Now those who had been scattered by the persecution in connection with Stephen*u* traveled as far as Phoenicia, Cyprus and Antioch,*v* telling the message only to Jews. 20Some of them, however, men from Cyprus*w* and Cyrene,*x* went to Antioch and began to speak to Greeks also, telling the good news about the Lord Jesus. 21The Lord's hand was with them,*y* and a great number of people believed and turned to the Lord.*z*

22News of this reached the ears of the church at Jerusalem, and they sent Barnabas*a* to Antioch. 23When he arrived and saw the evidence of the grace of God,*b* he

a 16 Or *in*

Acts 11:19–30

In Antioch "the disciples were called Christians first" (v. 26). This term was probably applied to them by the city's non-Christian population, possibly as a derogatory label meaning "little messiahs." Christ is the Greek word for Messiah—a redeemer the Jews thought they still awaited. According to the historian Josephus, a severe famine occurred in Judah (affecting Jerusalem) in A.D. 46. This young fellowship's financial gift to the "mother" church in Jerusalem demonstrated the

---

 11:19–21

A Model for Urban Ministry

In chapters 11 and 13 Luke noted eight characteristics of successful urban ministry, using the church in Antioch as the model. Since today 65 percent of all Christians live in cities, and by the year 2015 five cities will have populations of 20 million or more (Tokyo, Bombay [Mumbai], Lagos, Dhaka, and Sao Paulo), Christians face an increasingly urgent need to learn what makes urban ministry work.

65% of all CHRISTIANS live in cities

Source: Gallagher (2004:144–156)

1. **Lay Leadership:** Leadership represents people in the church (11:20).

2. **Every Member Ministries:** A church isn't just about good leadership, but about all members doing their part (11:23).

3. **Care for New Believers:** A church and its leaders need to invest enough time to teach people (11:25).

4. **Witness to Oneness in Christ:** The believers in Antioch were noticed and called Christians; people pay attention to what's happening (11:26).

5. **Compassion for the Poor:** People in need are fed as part of the church's ministry (11:28).

6. **Balanced Leadership:** Leaders exercise a variety of gifts (13:1).

7. **Overcoming Racial and Ethnic Barriers:** The people mentioned in the Antiochene story heralded from many cultures, yet worked together efficiently (11:9).

8. **Mission for Others:** This church sent Barnabas and Paul on a missionary venture to South Asia (13:2)—a model for churches in all settings.

Barnabas

Barnabas, the Son of Encouragement (Acts 4:36), was sent by the church in Jerusalem to establish a relationship with the converts in Antioch. In so doing he demonstrated two of the characteristics of God that are revealed by the work of the church: encouragement and outreach.

The church is intended to reflect God's love as revealed in Jesus Christ and to extend the gospel throughout the world. Without God's love, there is no message, only prideful meddling. And without the vision for outreach there is no motive, only selfish narrowness.

Barnabas was sent. He didn't decide on his own to undertake this task. He moved across cultural lines, likely dealing with a language barrier in order to partner with the new Christians in Antioch.

As soon as Barnabas began participating in this church, he realized that the good reports heard in Jerusalem were true. Thus encouraged, Barnabas proceeded to Tarsus to invite Saul—later called Paul the apostle—to join in the new work (11:22–26).

> **G**odly encouragement isn't motivated by fear or a preference for the safe and easy way out.

The encourager rarely works alone. Invitations are extended and resources and assignments shared. Then the encourager and his or her companions partner with those to whom they have been sent. This pattern is still important today for those who carry out assistance and development work.

What can we learn from Barnabas? We can imagine his disappointment when the skittish Jerusalem church was unwilling to take a chance on Saul after his conversion on the Damascus road. Saul of Tarsus had been a vicious enemy of the Christians and was still mistrusted because of the danger he had once represented. But encouragers don't give up. Just as soon as he saw the importance of the work in Antioch, Barnabas brought Saul into the action, launching Paul as this fledgling apostle began his pioneering career as the greatest ever personal example of Christian outreach and vision (9:26–31; 13:1–52).

What can we learn about other encouragers? Throughout the Bible encouragement is a character trait of believers. God encourages us both individually and as members of his body. And he encourages his people to encourage others. Can you cite one or two stories in the Bible that come out differently because an encourager intervened at just the right time? Godly encouragement isn't motivated by fear or a preference for the safe and easy way out. It's an outcome of generous good-will for others, as Jesus taught.

Reading the Bible provides encouragement. As we ask God to reveal himself, thereby shoring us up through our study, a focus on the encouragement that uplifts and inspires godly risk-taking becomes our source of spiritual strength. Consider the way God's voice influenced Abraham, Joseph, Moses, Joshua, Naomi, Jonathan, Daniel, Elizabeth, Jesus, Peter, John, and Paul.

Following is a short list of texts to encourage would-be encouragers. Studying the circumstances of each of these passages can provide valuable insight on this vital topic: Numbers 6:22–27, 1 Samuel 19:1–7, 1 Kings 8:54–61, 1 Chronicles 16:1–36, Psalm 23:1–6, 14:22, 20:1–2, 28:15, Romans 12:8, Ephesians 3:14–21, Colossians 4:7–8, 1 Thessalonians 2:10–12, and Hebrews 13:20–21.

Ted Ward, professor emeritus of Trinity Evangelical Divinity School in Deerfield, Illinois, and Michigan State University in East Lansing, Michigan

11:23
c Ac 14:22
11:24
d ver 21; Ac 5:14
11:25
e Ac 9:11
11:26
f Ac 6:1,2; 13:52
g Ac 26:28;
1Pe 4:16
11:27
h Ac 13:1; 15:32;
1Co 12:28,29;
Eph 4:11
11:28
i Ac 21:10
j Mt 24:14
k Ac 18:2
11:29
l ver 26
m Ro 15:26;
2Co 9:2 n Ac 1:16
11:30
o Ac 14:23
p Ac 12:25
12:2
q Mt 4:21
12:3
r Ac 24:27
s Ex 12:15; 23:15

12:5
t Eph 6:18

12:6
u Ac 21:33
12:7
v Ac 5:19
w Ac 16:26

12:9
x Ac 9:10

12:10
y Ac 5:19; 16:26

12:11
z Lk 15:17
a Ps 34:7; Da 3:28;
6:22; 2Co 1:10;
2Pe 2:9

was glad and encouraged them all to remain true to the Lord with all their hearts. [c] [24]He was a good man, full of the Holy Spirit and faith, and a great number of people were brought to the Lord. [d]

[25]Then Barnabas went to Tarsus [e] to look for Saul, [26]and when he found him, he brought him to Antioch. So for a whole year Barnabas and Saul met with the church and taught great numbers of people. The disciples [f] were called Christians first [g] at Antioch.

[27]During this time some prophets [h] came down from Jerusalem to Antioch. [28]One of them, named Agabus, [i] stood up and through the Spirit predicted that a severe famine would spread over the entire Roman world. [j] (This happened during the reign of Claudius.) [k] [29]The disciples, [l] each according to his ability, decided to provide help [m] for the brothers [n] living in Judea. [30]This they did, sending their gift to the elders [o] by Barnabas and Saul. [p]

Peter's Miraculous Escape From Prison

12 It was about this time that King Herod arrested some who belonged to the church, intending to persecute them. [2]He had James, the brother of John, [q] put to death with the sword. [3]When he saw that this pleased the Jews, [r] he proceeded to seize Peter also. This happened during the Feast of Unleavened Bread. [s] [4]After arresting him, he put him in prison, handing him over to be guarded by four squads of four soldiers each. Herod intended to bring him out for public trial after the Passover.

[5]So Peter was kept in prison, but the church was earnestly praying to God for him. [t]

[6]The night before Herod was to bring him to trial, Peter was sleeping between two soldiers, bound with two chains, [u] and sentries stood guard at the entrance. [7]Suddenly an angel [v] of the Lord appeared and a light shone in the cell. He struck Peter on the side and woke him up. "Quick, get up!" he said, and the chains fell off Peter's wrists. [w]

[8]Then the angel said to him, "Put on your clothes and sandals." And Peter did so. "Wrap your cloak around you and follow me," the angel told him. [9]Peter followed him out of the prison, but he had no idea that what the angel was doing was really happening; he thought he was seeing a vision. [x] [10]They passed the first and second guards and came to the iron gate leading to the city. It opened for them by itself, [y] and they went through it. When they had walked the length of one street, suddenly the angel left him.

[11]Then Peter came to himself [z] and said, "Now I know without a doubt that the Lord sent his angel and rescued me [a] from Herod's clutches and from everything the Jewish people were anticipating."

[12]When this had dawned on him, he went to the house of Mary the mother of

compassionate spirit catching on rapidly in a congregation that would itself soon become "mother" to a Gentile missions effort involving many congregations (13:1–3).

In a partnership approach to missions, two churches contribute to each other from their economic, cultural, intellectual, and spiritual riches (cf. Rom. 1:11–12). Such partnerships challenge our donor-recipient mentality—a pattern that defines two roles: giver and taker. Rather than being composed of one-way relationships between rich/poor, helper/helpee, First World/Third World, the Christian community is a global family of brothers and sisters who, at least ideally, bring to each other whatever is needed.

Acts 12:1–19a

This chapter is rich in irony. During the Passover, while the Jews celebrated their rescue from captivity through God's intervention (see Ex. 12:31–42), a herald of God's ultimate act of deliverance was taken into captivity—to please the Jews. Both Peter and the praying church initially failed to believe their prayers had been answered. And Herod responded with extreme measures to Peter's "escape," which deflated his ego.

Luke's side-by-side placement of James's death and Peter's deliverance highlights contrasting ways God may express his sovereignty in times of trouble. Just as the disciples earnestly prayed for Peter's release, we too can ask God for physical deliverance. Like James and Peter, we are to remain faithful and expectantly obedient—regardless of the immediate or long-term outcome. Though the church was "earnestly praying to God" for Peter, its members were surprised that God answered. We too can become so discouraged by difficulties that we lose our expectation that God will act.

John, also called Mark,[b] where many people had gathered and were praying.[c] 13Peter knocked at the outer entrance, and a servant girl named Rhoda came to answer the door.[d] 14When she recognized Peter's voice, she was so overjoyed[e] she ran back without opening it and exclaimed, "Peter is at the door!"

15"You're out of your mind," they told her. When she kept insisting that it was so, they said, "It must be his angel."[f]

16But Peter kept on knocking, and when they opened the door and saw him, they were astonished. 17Peter motioned with his hand[g] for them to be quiet and described how the Lord had brought him out of prison. "Tell James[h] and the brothers[i] about this," he said, and then he left for another place.

18In the morning, there was no small commotion among the soldiers as to what had become of Peter. 19After Herod had a thorough search made for him and did not find him, he cross-examined the guards and ordered that they be executed.[j]

Herod's Death

Then Herod went from Judea to Caesarea[k] and stayed there a while. 20He had been quarreling with the people of Tyre and Sidon;[l] they now joined together and sought an audience with him. Having secured the support of Blastus, a trusted personal servant of the king, they asked for peace, because they depended on the king's country for their food supply.[m]

21On the appointed day Herod, wearing his royal robes, sat on his throne and delivered a public address to the people. 22They shouted, "This is the voice of a god, not of a man." 23Immediately, because Herod did not give praise to God, an angel of the Lord struck him down,[n] and he was eaten by worms and died.

24But the word of God continued to increase and spread.[o]

25When Barnabas[p] and Saul had finished their mission,[q] they returned from[a] Jerusalem, taking with them John, also called Mark.[r]

Barnabas and Saul Sent Off

13 In the church at Antioch[s] there were prophets[t] and teachers: Barnabas,[u] Simeon called Niger, Lucius of Cyrene, Manaen (who had been brought up

[a] 25 Some manuscripts to

Acts 12:19b–25

We don't know the exact cause of Herod's repulsive death. It underscored God's judgment on any leader who allows others to regard him or her as the "voice of . . . [God], not of . . . man" (v. 22). Immediately after recording Herod's death, Luke reported on church growth. He used this customary summary to mark the end of one sphere of the church's engagement in God's mission. Acts 6:7 marks the transition from Jerusalem to Judea and Samaria. Verse 24 in turn marks the shift to Asia, and 19:20 to Rome.

The church continued to thrive after the death of this tyrant. Verse 24 stops short of establishing a cause-and-effect relationship, but growth in the "body" can occur after removal of restrictions. Still, the church often finds strength and solidarity during repression and persecution. For a modern example, you might want to study church growth in China or India over the last 60 years. Considering the circumstances in varying locations around the globe, what is God doing today to cause the church to flourish? Some suggest a law of "spiritual" thermodynamics—the greater the heat the greater the expansion!

Acts 13:1–3

Luke highlighted the ethnic and cultural diversity in Antioch, where the disciples of Christ were first called Christians (11:26). Barnabas, a Jerusalem Jew, originally hailed from Cyprus (4:36). Simeon is a Jewish name, but he was called Niger, meaning "black." Lucius was from Cyrene in North Africa. The note regarding Manaen (another Jewish name) suggests that he was a foster brother or close childhood friend of Herod the tetrarch—who beheaded John the Baptist. Saul, an educated Jew and former Pharisee originally from Tarsus, receives last mention. The world's attention was drawn to this little community of disciples because theirs was the only place in Roman society where Jews, Greeks, Gentiles, slaves, men, and women could gather together as equals.

Racial, ethnic, caste, and economic divisions create enormous tensions and conflicts in societies around the world. Whether its members are educated or illiterate, from one or another ethnic background, rich or poor, the church worldwide can exhibit a unity amid diversity that is attractive and effective in witnessing to the gospel's power to make us one. Are our mono-ethnic, mono-cultural churches robbing the world of the chance to witness one of the most compelling proofs of the truthfulness of the gospel?

13:1
v Mt 14:1
13:2
w Ac 8:29
x Ac 14:26
y Ac 22:21
13:3
z Ac 6:6 a Ac 14:26

with Herod[v] the tetrarch) and Saul. [2]While they were worshiping the Lord and fasting, the Holy Spirit said,[w] "Set apart for me Barnabas and Saul for the work[x] to which I have called them."[y] [3]So after they had fasted and prayed, they placed their hands on them[z] and sent them off.[a]

On Cyprus

13:4
b ver 2,3 c Ac 4:36
13:5
d Ac 9:20
e Ac 12:12
13:6
f Ac 8:9 g Mt 7:15
13:7
h ver 8,12;
Ac 19:38

[4]The two of them, sent on their way by the Holy Spirit,[b] went down to Seleucia and sailed from there to Cyprus. [c] [5]When they arrived at Salamis, they proclaimed the word of God in the Jewish synagogues. [d] John[e] was with them as their helper.
[6]They traveled through the whole island until they came to Paphos. There they met a Jewish sorcerer[f] and false prophet[g] named Bar-Jesus, [7]who was an attendant of the proconsul,[h] Sergius Paulus. The proconsul, an intelligent man, sent for Barnabas and Saul because he wanted to hear the word of God. [8]But Elymas the sorcerer[i] (for that is what his name means) opposed them and tried to turn the proconsul[j] from the faith. [k] [9]Then Saul, who was also called Paul, filled with the Holy Spirit, [l] looked straight at Elymas and said, [10]"You are a child of the devil[m] and an enemy of everything that is right! You are full of all kinds of deceit and trickery. Will you never stop perverting the right ways of the Lord?[n] [11]Now the hand of the Lord is against you.[o] You are going to be blind, and for a time you will be unable to see the light of the sun."

13:8
i Ac 8:9 / ver 7
k Ac 6:7
13:9
l Ac 4:8
13:10
m Mt 13:38; Jn 8:44
n Hos 14:9
13:11
o Ex 9:3; 1Sa 5:6,7;
Ps 32:4

Immediately mist and darkness came over him, and he groped about, seeking someone to lead him by the hand. [12]When the proconsul[p] saw what had happened, he believed, for he was amazed at the teaching about the Lord.

13:12
p ver 7

In Pisidian Antioch

13:13
q ver 6 r Ac 12:12
13:14
s Ac 14:19,21
t Ac 16:13
u Ac 9:20
13:15
v Ac 15:21

[13]From Paphos,[q] Paul and his companions sailed to Perga in Pamphylia, where John[r] left them to return to Jerusalem. [14]From Perga they went on to Pisidian Antioch. [s] On the Sabbath[t] they entered the synagogue[u] and sat down. [15]After the reading from the Law[v] and the Prophets, the synagogue rulers sent word to them, saying, "Brothers, if you have a message of encouragement for the people, please speak."

13:16
w Ac 12:17
13:17
x Ex 6:6,7; Dt 7:6-8
13:18
y Dt 1:31 z Ac 7:36
13:19
a Dt 7:1
b Jos 19:51

[16]Standing up, Paul motioned with his hand[w] and said: "Men of Israel and you Gentiles who worship God, listen to me! [17]The God of the people of Israel chose our fathers; he made the people prosper during their stay in Egypt, with mighty power he led them out of that country, [x] [18]he endured their conduct[a][y] for about forty years in the desert, [z] [19]he overthrew seven nations in Canaan[a] and gave their land to his people[b] as their inheritance. [20]All this took about 450 years.

13:20
c Jdg 2:16
d 1Sa 3:19,20

"After this, God gave them judges[c] until the time of Samuel the prophet. [d] [21]Then

---

[a] 18 Some manuscripts *and cared for them*

Acts 13:4–12

📖 Paul was "filled with the Holy Spirit" when he rebuked Elymas. This was no error on his part, but an example of effective use of his spiritual gifts, through which he communicated a direct and specific word of judgment from God. Verse 12 credits the faith of Sergius Paulus to his observation of the consequences of Elymas's opposition and to his amazement at the apostles' teaching.

💻 We live in an age of tolerance—of everything, that is, but absolute truth! Yet we do well to remember the church's commitment "to contend for the faith that was once for all entrusted to the saints" (Jude 3). This task remains urgent in light of Christ's call to "snatch others from the fire and save them" (Jude 23). The gospel is still the *only* way to salvation, and our task is pressing. However, when we speak, it must be in response to the Spirit's prompting, moving beyond our own opinions and prejudices.

Acts 13:13–52

📖 The Gentile converts in Antioch recognized the gospel message as God's truth and rejoiced even after the ministry team had been forced to leave. When people come to Christ, their first motivation may be to meet a need. But they stay on because they recognize they have embraced the truth. When we realize truth is at the heart of the Good News, we have a security and joy that can weather life's storms.

💻 The God of the universe is acting according to a gradually unfolding plan. No matter how baffled and frustrated we may feel, we can rest securely, knowing there is meaning to life's puzzle! Tracing God's hand in the history of the human race is a powerful encouragement. God is the Lord of all nations, and the church exists for the salvation of all people. If you were to track God's involvement in your life, how would you describe the hills, valleys, and turning points? Is the big picture beginning to make more sense?

the people asked for a king, *e* and he gave them Saul *f* son of Kish, of the tribe of Benjamin, *g* who ruled forty years. 22After removing Saul, *h* he made David their king. *i* He testified concerning him: 'I have found David son of Jesse a man after my own heart; *j* he will do everything I want him to do.'

23 "From this man's descendants *k* God has brought to Israel the Savior *l* Jesus, *m* as he promised. *n* 24Before the coming of Jesus, John preached repentance and baptism to all the people of Israel. *o* 25As John was completing his work, *p* he said: 'Who do you think I am? I am not that one. *q* No, but he is coming after me, whose sandals I am not worthy to untie.' *r*

26 "Brothers, children of Abraham, and you God-fearing Gentiles, it is to us that this message of salvation *s* has been sent. 27The people of Jerusalem and their rulers did not recognize Jesus, *t* yet in condemning him they fulfilled the words of the prophets *u* that are read every Sabbath. 28Though they found no proper ground for a death sentence, they asked Pilate to have him executed. *v* 29When they had carried out all that was written about him, *w* they took him down from the tree *x* and laid him in a tomb. *y* 30But God raised him from the dead, *z* 31and for many days he was seen by those who had traveled with him from Galilee to Jerusalem. *a* They are now his witnesses *b* to our people.

32 "We tell you the good news: *c* What God promised our fathers *d* 33he has fulfilled for us, their children, by raising up Jesus. As it is written in the second Psalm:

" 'You are my Son;
today I have become your Father.' *a'* *b* *e*

34The fact that God raised him from the dead, never to decay, is stated in these words:

" 'I will give you the holy and sure blessings promised to David.' *c* *f*

35So it is stated elsewhere:

" 'You will not let your Holy One see decay.' *d* *g*

36 "For when David had served God's purpose in his own generation, he fell asleep; he was buried with his fathers *h* and his body decayed. 37But the one whom God raised from the dead did not see decay.

38 "Therefore, my brothers, I want you to know that through Jesus the forgiveness of sins is proclaimed to you. *i* 39Through him everyone who believes is justified from everything you could not be justified from by the law of Moses. *j* 40Take care that what the prophets have said does not happen to you:

41 " 'Look, you scoffers,
wonder and perish,
for I am going to do something in your days
that you would never believe,
even if someone told you.' *e"* *k*

42As Paul and Barnabas were leaving the synagogue, *l* the people invited them to speak further about these things on the next Sabbath. 43When the congregation was dismissed, many of the Jews and devout converts to Judaism followed Paul and Barnabas, who talked with them and urged them to continue in the grace of God. *m*

44On the next Sabbath almost the whole city gathered to hear the word of the Lord. 45When the Jews saw the crowds, they were filled with jealousy and talked abusively *n* against what Paul was saying. *o*

46Then Paul and Barnabas answered them boldly: "We had to speak the word of God to you first. *p* Since you reject it and do not consider yourselves worthy of eternal life, we now turn to the Gentiles. *q* 47For this is what the Lord has commanded us:

a 33 Or *have begotten you*   *b* 33 Psalm 2:7   *c* 34 Isaiah 55:3   *d* 35 Psalm 16:10
e 41 Hab. 1:5

13:21
e 1Sa 8:5, 19
f 1Sa 10:1
g 1Sa 9:1,2
13:22
h 1Sa 15:23,26
i 1Sa 16:13;
Ps 89:20
j 1Sa 13:14
13:23
k Mt 1:1 *l* Lk 2:11
m Mt 1:21 *n* ver 32
13:24
o Mk 1:4
13:25
p Ac 20:24
q Jn 1:20 *r* Mt 3:11;
Jn 1:27
13:26
s Ac 4:12
13:27
t Ac 3:17
u Lk 24:27
13:28
v Mt 27:20-25;
Ac 3:14
13:29
w Lk 18:31
x Ac 5:30
y Lk 23:53
13:30
z Mt 28:6; Ac 2:24
13:31
a Mt 28:16
b Lk 24:48
13:32
c Ac 5:42
d Ac 26:6; Ro 4:13
13:33
e Ps 2:7

13:34
f Isa 55:3

13:35
g Ps 16:10; Ac 2:27

13:36
h 1Ki 2:10; Ac 2:29

13:38
i Lk 24:47; Ac 2:38
13:39
j Ro 3:28

13:41
k Hab 1:5
13:42
l ver 14

13:43
m Ac 11:23; 14:22

13:45
n Ac 18:6; 1Pe 4:4;
Jude 10 *o* 1Th 2:16
13:46
p ver 26; Ac 3:26
q Ac 18:6; 22:21;
28:28

13:47
r Lk 2:32 s Isa 49:6

" 'I have made you[a] a light for the Gentiles,[r]
that you[a] may bring salvation to the ends of the earth.'[b]"[s]

48When the Gentiles heard this, they were glad and honored the word of the Lord; and all who were appointed for eternal life believed.

49The word of the Lord spread through the whole region. 50But the Jews incited the God-fearing women of high standing and the leading men of the city. They stirred up persecution against Paul and Barnabas, and expelled them from their re-

13:50
t 1Th 2:16
13:51
u Mt 10:14; Ac 18:6
v Ac 14:1,19,21;
2Ti 3:11

gion.[t] 51So they shook the dust from their feet[u] in protest against them and went to Iconium.[v] 52And the disciples were filled with joy and with the Holy Spirit.

14:1
w Ac 13:51

In Iconium

14 At Iconium[w] Paul and Barnabas went as usual into the Jewish synagogue. There they spoke so effectively that a great number of Jews and Gentiles believed. 2But the Jews who refused to believe stirred up the Gentiles and poisoned their minds against the brothers. 3So Paul and Barnabas spent considerable time there, speaking boldly[x] for the Lord, who confirmed the message of his grace by enabling them to do miraculous signs and wonders.[y] 4The people of the city were divided; some sided with the Jews, others with the apostles.[z] 5There was a plot afoot among the Gentiles and Jews, together with their leaders, to mistreat them and stone them.[a] 6But they found out about it and fled[b] to the Lycaonian cities of Lystra and Derbe and to the surrounding country, 7where they continued to preach[c] the good news.[d]

14:3
x Ac 4:29 y Jn 4:48;
Heb 2:4
14:4
z Ac 17:4,5
14:5
a ver 19
14:6
b Mt 10:23
14:7
c Ac 16:10
d ver 15,21

In Lystra and Derbe

14:8
e Ac 3:2

8In Lystra there sat a man crippled in his feet, who was lame from birth[e] and had never walked. 9He listened to Paul as he was speaking. Paul looked directly at him, saw that he had faith to be healed[f] 10and called out, "Stand up on your feet!" At that, the man jumped up and began to walk.[g]

14:9
f Mt 9:28,29
14:10
g Ac 3:8

11When the crowd saw what Paul had done, they shouted in the Lycaonian language, "The gods have come down to us in human form!"[h] 12Barnabas they called Zeus, and Paul they called Hermes because he was the chief speaker. 13The priest of Zeus, whose temple was just outside the city, brought bulls and wreaths to the city gates because he and the crowd wanted to offer sacrifices to them.

14:11
h Ac 8:10; 28:6

14:14
i Mk 14:63

14But when the apostles Barnabas and Paul heard of this, they tore their clothes[i] and rushed out into the crowd, shouting: 15"Men, why are you doing this? We too are only men,[j] human like you. We are bringing you good news,[k] telling you to turn

14:15
j Ac 10:26; Jas 5:17
k ver 7,21;
Ac 13:32

---

a 47 The Greek is singular.   b 47 Isaiah 49:6

Acts 14:1–7

Luke continually emphasized that the gospel isn't just powerful words. The Spirit also produces signs and wonders. Physical and social healing were and still are integral to spiritual proclamation. When the reign of God enters a community, spiritual as well as social and physical transformation occurs. Deeds of love and power "confirm[ed] the message" (v. 3).

Christians today are divided over whether verbal witness or social concern should be the church's main priority. As the primary agent in mission, the Spirit of God enables both simultaneously. Words and work, proclamation and deeds of power, lives of boldness and hope are all characteristic marks of effective witness.

Acts 14:8–20

Zeus, the most popular god in Galatia, was regularly linked with Hermes. The response of the Lystrans may be traced to a legend: Zeus and Hermes once visited the Phrygian hill country, disguised as ordinary men.

They were turned away from a thousand homes but finally welcomed into the humble abode of an elderly couple. The gods turned that house into a temple and destroyed the houses of all who had rejected them.

This was the first time the gospel was offered to people not previously influenced by the Jewish faith. Luke suggested a key to ministering to such a group: Begin at the beginning, explaining who God is. Other suggestions appear in his report on Paul's later ministry in Athens (17:16–34).

In our celebrity-oriented society, the church can easily fall into the temptation to elevate our leaders into a special status of godliness and power. Barnabas and Paul's humble rebuke is well-placed on the lips of all Christian leaders: "Why are you doing this? We too are only men, human like you." (v. 15). Jesus admonished his followers that the first shall be last, and the greatest the least. Our appropriate focus isn't on ourselves as the witnesses, but on the Good News we have the privilege of bringing.

from these worthless things *l* to the living God, *m* who made heaven and earth *n* and sea and everything in them. *o* ¹⁶In the past, he let *p* all nations go their own way. *q* ¹⁷Yet he has not left himself without testimony: *r* He has shown kindness by giving you rain from heaven and crops in their seasons; *s* he provides you with plenty of food and fills your hearts with joy." ¹⁸Even with these words, they had difficulty keeping the crowd from sacrificing to them.

¹⁹Then some Jews *t* came from Antioch and Iconium *u* and won the crowd over. They stoned Paul *v* and dragged him outside the city, thinking he was dead. ²⁰But after the disciples *w* had gathered around him, he got up and went back into the city. The next day he and Barnabas left for Derbe.

The Return to Antioch in Syria

²¹They preached the good news in that city and won a large number of disciples. Then they returned to Lystra, Iconium *x* and Antioch, ²²strengthening the disciples and encouraging them to remain true to the faith. *y* "We must go through many hardships *z* to enter the kingdom of God," they said. ²³Paul and Barnabas appointed elders *a a* for them in each church and, with prayer and fasting, *b* committed them to the Lord, *c* in whom they had put their trust. ²⁴After going through Pisid-

a 23 Or *Barnabas ordained elders;* or *Barnabas had elders elected*

14:15 *l* 1Sa 12:21; 1Co 8:4; 1Th 1:9 *m* Mt 16:16 *n* Ge 1:1; Jer 14:22 *o* Ps 146:6; Rev 14:7
14:16 *p* Ac 17:30 *q* Ps 81:12; Mic 4:5
14:17 *r* Ac 17:27; Ro 1:20 *s* Dt 11:14; Job 5:10; Ps 65:10
14:19 *t* Ac 13:45 *u* Ac 13:51 *v* 2Co 11:25; 2Ti 3:11
14:20 *w* ver 22,28; Ac 11:26
14:21 *x* Ac 13:51
14:22 *y* Ac 11:23; 13:43 *z* Jn 16:33; 1Th 3:3; 2Ti 3:12
14:23 *a* Ac 11:30; Tit 1:5 *b* Ac 13:3 *c* Ac 20:32

Acts 14:21–28

 Their return trip took Paul and Barnabas back through the three towns they had just visited: Lystra, Iconium, and Pisidian Antioch. They had been forced out of one of them (13:50) and had fled the other two (14:6,20). But this time they had a new program: follow-up care of the converts. Their agenda involved strengthening the disciples, encouraging them to remain true to the faith, warning them about approaching hardship, and setting up leadership teams.

Paul and Barnabas weren't short-term missionaries who failed to develop long-term relationships. They continued to care for the people they met on their journeys. Part of that care involved encouraging their leaders, people who could shepherd the flock through suffering: "We must go through many hardships to enter the kingdom of God" (v. 22). That wouldn't make an appealing ad campaign for a "seeker sensitive" approach, but suffering is integral to our growth in godliness. That is why the commissioning of leaders occurred through prayer and fasting (cf. Acts 1:24–25; 6:5–6; 13:1–3; 14:23).

Snapshots

14:19–20

Ki-Poong

Pioneer Presbyterian missionary Samuel A. Moffett (1864–1939) might not have selected Ki-Poong Yi (1865–1942) as a candidate for missionary/martyr on their first meeting. At the time, Ki-Poong was stoning him! But the Lord had other plans. Ki-Poong eventually responded to the gospel preached by a Korean evangelist and was baptized by missionary W.L. Swallen.

In 1907 Ki-Poong was one of the first seven graduates of Presbyterian Theological Seminary, a school established by Moffett, who stressed intensive Bible study and evangelism for all believers. These seven were ordained at the founding meeting of the first presbytery of the Presbyterian Church of Korea that same year. Ki-Poong immediately volunteered as a missionary and was sent to one of the Korean islands where people had resisted the gospel. He was stoned there for his witness but, like Paul in Acts 14, didn't die.

> [Ki-Poong] was stoned there for his witness but, like Paul in Acts 14, didn't die.

In 1921 Ki-Poong was elected moderator of the general assembly of the Korean Presbyterian Church. In the 1930s tensions arose between the Japanese governor and church leaders in Pyongyang over whether Christian students should be required to participate in non-Christian religious ceremonies. Ki-Poong was arrested for his stand against the Japanese government, imprisoned, and tortured. He died from the injuries he sustained.

ia, they came into Pamphylia, [25]and when they had preached the word in Perga, they went down to Attalia.

14:26
d Ac 11:19
e Ac 15:40
f Ac 13:1,3
14:27
g Ac 15:4,12; 21:19
h 1Co 16:9;
2Co 2:12; Col 4:3;
Rev 3:8

[26]From Attalia they sailed back to Antioch,[d] where they had been committed to the grace of God[e] for the work they had now completed.[f] [27]On arriving there, they gathered the church together and reported all that God had done through them[g] and how he had opened the door[h] of faith to the Gentiles. [28]And they stayed there a long time with the disciples.

The Council at Jerusalem

15:1
i ver 24; Gal 2:12
j ver 5; Gal 5:2,3
k Ac 6:14

15 Some men[i] came down from Judea to Antioch and were teaching the brothers: "Unless you are circumcised,[j] according to the custom taught by Moses,[k] you cannot be saved." [2]This brought Paul and Barnabas into sharp dispute and debate with them. So Paul and Barnabas were appointed, along with some other believers, to go up to Jerusalem[l] to see the apostles and elders[m] about this question. [3]The church sent them on their way, and as they traveled through Phoenicia and Samaria, they told how the Gentiles had been converted.[n] This news made all the brothers very glad. [4]When they came to Jerusalem, they were welcomed by the church and the apostles and elders, to whom they reported everything God had done through them.[o]

[5]Then some of the believers who belonged to the party of the Pharisees stood

15:2
l Gal 2:2
m Ac 11:30
15:3
n Ac 14:27
15:4
o ver 12; Ac 14:27

Acts 15:1–21

If this council met after the confrontation when Peter was rebuked by Paul (Gal. 2:11–21), it was to Peter's credit that he took Paul and Barnabas's side. No doubt passions ran high, but the generous Christian character of the leaders shone through. In arguing for the full inclusion of Gentiles into the church, both Peter's and Paul's reasoning and experiences were shown to be in harmony with Scripture (vv. 14–18).

The debate at the council focused on whether Gentiles needed to become Jews before they could follow Christ. The decision was an adamant no! There isn't a cultural pattern to which all Christians must conform. Today, rather than being perceived as a "Jewish" religion, Christianity is often viewed as "Western." What are some "Western" cultural forms that overlay people's understanding of the gospel? What are some "non-negotiable" essentials all people who follow Christ are to share in common?

15:1–2

God's Call to Missions

There are several different levels at which God calls his people to missions—and at least one approach (the first, below) well-meaning Christians from the days of Acts on have adopted in an apparent misunderstanding of the Spirit's intent:

	Change Agent	Cultural Change Desired	Personal Change Desired	Method(s) Used	Attitude Toward Others
1. Proselytism	Missionaries	Adopt missionary's culture	Change beliefs	Proclamation	Triumphal, aggressive, patronizing
(Most missionaries today avoid this approach, which is widely viewed to be ineffective and misguided.)					
2. Mission	Missionaries and all Christians	Modify indigenous culture	Reorient life to gospel values	Tell gospel story, plant churches, meet social needs, meet physical needs	Loving, personal, restrained, sensitive
3. Evangelism	Church	Expose to gospel	Consider gospel's claims	Institutional programs	Managerial
4. Witness	Individuals	Exchange cultural gifts	Mutually enlarged worldview	Lifestyle, interpersonal dialogue	Accepting, appreciative

Proselytism: Attempts to make others "like me" religiously, culturally, intellectually, and/or personally
Mission: Participation in God's purpose to establish his kingdom on Earth
Evangelism: The church's organized activity of spreading the gospel in circumstances it can control
Witness: Living our life so that gospel values are evident to all we meet

up and said, "The Gentiles must be circumcised and required to obey the law of
Moses."
6 The apostles and elders met to consider this question. 7 After much discussion,
Peter got up and addressed them: "Brothers, you know that some time ago God
made a choice among you that the Gentiles might hear from my lips the message
of the gospel and believe. 8 God, who knows the heart,[p] showed that he accepted
them by giving the Holy Spirit to them,[q] just as he did to us. 9 He made no distinction between us and them,[r] for he purified their hearts by faith.[s] 10 Now then, why
do you try to test God by putting on the necks of the disciples a yoke[t] that neither
we nor our fathers have been able to bear? 11 No! We believe it is through the
grace[u] of our Lord Jesus that we are saved, just as they are."
12 The whole assembly became silent as they listened to Barnabas and Paul telling about the miraculous signs and wonders[v] God had done among the Gentiles
through them.[w] 13 When they finished, James[x] spoke up: "Brothers, listen to me.
14 Simon[a] has described to us how God at first showed his concern by taking from
the Gentiles a people for himself. 15 The words of the prophets are in agreement
with this, as it is written:

16 " 'After this I will return
and rebuild David's fallen tent.
Its ruins I will rebuild,
and I will restore it,
17 that the remnant of men may seek the Lord,
and all the Gentiles who bear my name,
says the Lord, who does these things'[b][y]
18 that have been known for ages.[c]

19 "It is my judgment, therefore, that we should not make it difficult for the Gentiles who are turning to God. 20 Instead we should write to them, telling them to abstain from food polluted by idols,[z] from sexual immorality,[a] from the meat of
strangled animals and from blood.[b] 21 For Moses has been preached in every city
from the earliest times and is read in the synagogues on every Sabbath."[c]

The Council's Letter to Gentile Believers

22 Then the apostles and elders, with the whole church, decided to choose some
of their own men and send them to Antioch with Paul and Barnabas. They chose
Judas (called Barsabbas) and Silas,[d] two men who were leaders among the brothers. 23 With them they sent the following letter:

The apostles and elders, your brothers,

To the Gentile believers in Antioch,[e] Syria and Cilicia:[f]

Greetings.[g]

15:8 [p] Ac 1:24 [q] Ac 10:44,47
15:9 [r] Ac 10:28,34; 11:12 [s] Ac 10:43
15:10 [t] Mt 23:4; Gal 5:1
15:11 [u] Ro 3:24; Eph 2:5-8
15:12 [v] Jn 4:48 [w] Ac 14:27
15:13 [x] Ac 12:17
15:17 [y] Am 9:11,12
15:20 [z] 1Co 8:7-13; 10:14-28; Rev 2:14, 20 [a] 1Co 10:7,8 [b] ver 29; Ge 9:4; Lev 3:17; Dt 12:16,23
15:21 [c] Ac 13:15; 2Co 3:14,15
15:22 [d] ver 27,32,40
15:23 [e] ver 1 [f] ver 41 [g] Ac 23:25,26; Jas 1:1

[a] *14* Greek *Simeon,* a variant of *Simon;* that is, Peter [b] *17* Amos 9:11,12 [c] *17,18* Some manuscripts *things'— / 18known to the Lord for ages is his work*

Acts 15:22–35

Maintaining ritual purity was important to many New Testament Jews. So the issue of table fellowship with Gentiles, especially when non-kosher food was offered, was a serious concern. Believers interested in maintaining openhearted fellowship didn't have to eat the same foods, but it was critical that they respect each others' scruples. Paul's warning against sexual immorality also was necessary because some areas, like Antioch, were notorious for promiscuity.

In Romans 14 and 1 Corinthians 8, Paul recommended sensitivity to the possibility of putting a stumbling block in someone else's way. Living out our convictions may involve tempering our actions with love—doing things differently from our inclinations. We are wise to be generous in our dealings with others, accommodating those with sensitive consciences, even when we view an issue as non-essential. What practice(s) in your life might upset an onlooking seeker or fellow believer? What adjustment might you make for someone who objected to those activities? Have you had occasion to act on this principle?

15:24
h ver 1; Gal 1:7;
5:10
15:26
i Ac 9:23-25; 14:19

15:28
j Ac 5:32

15:29
k ver 20; Ac 21:25

15:33
l Mk 5:34;
Ac 16:36;
1Co 16:11
15:35
m Ac 8:4

15:36
n Ac 13:4,13,14,51;
14:1,6,24,25
15:37
o Ac 12:12
15:38
p Ac 13:13

15:40
q ver 22 r Ac 11:23
15:41
s ver 23 t Ac 6:9
u Ac 16:5

16:1
v Ac 14:6
w Ac 17:14; 18:5;
19:22; Ro 16:21;
1Co 4:17; 2Co 1:1,
19; 1Th 3:2,6;
1Ti 1:2,18;
2Ti 1:2,5,6
16:2
x ver 40 y Ac 13:51
16:3
z Gal 2:3
16:4
a Ac 11:30

24We have heard that some went out from us without our authorization and disturbed you, troubling your minds by what they said. h 25So we all agreed to choose some men and send them to you with our dear friends Barnabas and Paul— 26men who have risked their lives i for the name of our Lord Jesus Christ. 27Therefore we are sending Judas and Silas to confirm by word of mouth what we are writing. 28It seemed good to the Holy Spirit j and to us not to burden you with anything beyond the following requirements: 29You are to abstain from food sacrificed to idols, from blood, from the meat of strangled animals and from sexual immorality. k You will do well to avoid these things.

Farewell.

30The men were sent off and went down to Antioch, where they gathered the church together and delivered the letter. 31The people read it and were glad for its encouraging message. 32Judas and Silas, who themselves were prophets, said much to encourage and strengthen the brothers. 33After spending some time there, they were sent off by the brothers with the blessing of peace l to return to those who had sent them. a 35But Paul and Barnabas remained in Antioch, where they and many others taught and preached m the word of the Lord.

Disagreement Between Paul and Barnabas

36Some time later Paul said to Barnabas, "Let us go back and visit the brothers in all the towns n where we preached the word of the Lord and see how they are doing." 37Barnabas wanted to take John, also called Mark, o with them, 38but Paul did not think it wise to take him, because he had deserted them p in Pamphylia and had not continued with them in the work. 39They had such a sharp disagreement that they parted company. Barnabas took Mark and sailed for Cyprus, 40but Paul chose Silas q and left, commended by the brothers to the grace of the Lord. r 41He went through Syria s and Cilicia, t strengthening the churches. u

Timothy Joins Paul and Silas

16 He came to Derbe and then to Lystra, v where a disciple named Timothy w lived, whose mother was a Jewess and a believer, but whose father was a Greek. 2The brothers x at Lystra and Iconium y spoke well of him. 3Paul wanted to take him along on the journey, so he circumcised him because of the Jews who lived in that area, for they all knew that his father was a Greek. z 4As they traveled from town to town, they delivered the decisions reached by the apostles and elders a in

a 33 Some manuscripts them, 34but Silas decided to remain there

Acts 15:36–41

One mark of the Bible's authenticity is its inclusion of accounts of leaders' weaknesses and failures. God's Word isn't an "authorized biography" that only portrays people's virtues. In the midst of the call to unity and love, Paul and Barnabas had such a sharp disagreement that they parted ways. Later on the two became colleagues again (1 Cor. 9:6; Col. 4:10), and Paul came to appreciate John Mark so much that he asked specifically for him toward the end of his life (2 Tim. 4:11; cf. Col. 4:10; Philem. 24). The sovereignty of God, who works out his purposes in spite of and even through human weakness, was revealed as two teams set out—with four people carrying the message.

This passage doesn't give us an excuse to quarrel, but it does provide comfort when we have disagreements that don't immediately end in friendly resolutions. It also instills hope. God enabled Paul and Barnabas to reunite, and he can do the same in our divisions and dis-

agreements. We are wise to avoid doing or saying hurtful things during an argument—especially making public statements that might create permanent ill will or show a lack of respect for our Christian family members.

Acts 16:1–5

Timothy needed to win the respect of Jewish Christians, and circumcision would open doors for him to evangelize Jews. If Timothy hadn't been half Jewish, Paul wouldn't have insisted on this ritual (see Gal. 2:3). Paul's battle was against the insistence that circumcision be a condition for full inclusion of Gentiles among the people of God.

Timothy sacrificed his rights to build a bridge to others, even though this caused him pain and humiliation. What would you be willing to do, give, or give up to identify with a person or group for whom you felt called to care? Sometimes we need to let go of our symbols of identity and worth in order to enter into others' lives.

Jerusalem[b] for the people to obey.[c] [5]So the churches were strengthened[d] in the faith and grew daily in numbers.

Paul's Vision of the Man of Macedonia

[6]Paul and his companions traveled throughout the region of Phrygia[e] and Galatia,[f] having been kept by the Holy Spirit from preaching the word in the province of Asia.[g] [7]When they came to the border of Mysia, they tried to enter Bithynia, but the Spirit of Jesus[h] would not allow them to. [8]So they passed by Mysia and went down to Troas.[i] [9]During the night Paul had a vision[j] of a man of Macedonia[k] standing and begging him, "Come over to Macedonia and help us." [10]After Paul had seen the vision, we[l] got ready at once to leave for Macedonia, concluding that God had called us to preach the gospel[m] to them.

Lydia's Conversion in Philippi

[11]From Troas[n] we put out to sea and sailed straight for Samothrace, and the next day on to Neapolis. [12]From there we traveled to Philippi,[o] a Roman colony and the leading city of that district of Macedonia.[p] And we stayed there several days. [13]On the Sabbath[q] we went outside the city gate to the river, where we expected to find a place of prayer. We sat down and began to speak to the women who had gathered there. [14]One of those listening was a woman named Lydia, a dealer in purple cloth from the city of Thyatira,[r] who was a worshiper of God. The Lord opened her heart[s] to respond to Paul's message. [15]When she and the members of her household[t] were baptized, she invited us to her home. "If you consider me a believer in the Lord," she said, "come and stay at my house." And she persuaded us.

Paul and Silas in Prison

[16]Once when we were going to the place of prayer,[u] we were met by a slave girl who had a spirit[v] by which she predicted the future. She earned a great deal of money for her owners by fortune-telling. [17]This girl followed Paul and the rest of us, shouting, "These men are servants of the Most High God,[w] who are telling you the way to be saved." [18]She kept this up for many days. Finally Paul became so troubled that he turned around and said to the spirit, "In the name of Jesus Christ I command you to come out of her!" At that moment the spirit left her.[x]

16:4
b Ac 15:2
c Ac 15:28,29
16:5
d Ac 9:31; 15:41

16:6
e Ac 18:23
f Ac 18:23; Gal 1:2; 3:1 g Ac 2:9

16:7
h Ro 8:9; Gal 4:6
16:8
i ver 11; 2Co 2:12; 2Ti 4:13
16:9
j Ac 9:10
k Ac 20:1,3
16:10
l ver 10-17
m Ac 14:7

16:11
n ver 8
16:12
o Ac 20:6; Php 1:1; 1Th 2:2 p ver 9
16:13
q Ac 13:14

16:14
r Rev 1:11
s Lk 24:45
16:15
t Ac 11:14

16:16
u ver 13 v Dt 18:11; 1Sa 28:3,7

16:17
w Mk 5:7

16:18
x Mk 16:17

Acts 16:6–10

📖 Not only did God lead Paul, but he also blocked his way. Twice he disrupted Paul's planned itinerary—to lead him to the place God wanted him to go.

Verse 10 introduces the pronoun "we," suggesting that Paul and Luke may have met or joined forces at Troas. Some scholars believe Luke joined the team as a doctor due to Paul's health concerns (cf. Gal. 4:13).

📖 How do you respond when your plans fall through and God seems to close a door? With discouragement or enthusiasm? Have you ever paid attention to a dream, believing that through it God might be speaking to you? For whatever reason, our proposals might not suit his big-picture plan. If the Spirit's cues move us in a different—even opposite—direction from what we had in mind, we are wise to eagerly set out on the new course before us.

Acts 16:11–15

📖 God is the ultimate evangelist: "The Lord [opened Lydia's] heart to respond to Paul's message" (v. 14). Lydia was obviously a person of stature and credibility; her faith led to the baptism of her whole household. Her leadership gifts were evident as she invited Paul and company to stay at her home. This apparently

took some persuading, possibly because Paul's vision had been of a *man* asking for help. Also, as a Jew he may have been hesitant to stay in the home of a woman.

📖 We often approach the Christian faith individually and institutionally. We think in terms of "going to church," not of "being the church." Homes were central to the life of the early church. Beyond being centers for hospitality, they were places for teaching, worship, fellowship, and witness. Life was lived in community, so that when Lydia believed, her whole household did as well. What's the role of community in your life, and how can your home be used as a place of ministry?

Acts 16:16–40

📖 The treatment the team received after the deliverance of the slave girl was impermissible for Roman citizens. After having been stripped, flogged, and sentenced without a trial, these men were sent to a maximum security area ("inner cell"). Prisoners in stocks had to sleep sitting or lying on the floor. Changing positions was nearly impossible. Rather than simply thinking of himself, Paul wanted to encourage a "civil society" ruled by law. Thus he remained in jail and demanded that society be properly governed.

16:19
y ver 16; Ac 19:25,
26 z Ac 15:22
a Ac 8:3; 17:6;
21:30; Jas 2:6
16:20
b Ac 17:6
16:21
c ver 12 d Est 3:8

16:22
e 2Co 11:25;
1Th 2:2
16:23
f ver 27,36
16:24
g Job 13:27; 33:11;
Jer 20:2,3; 29:26
16:25
h Eph 5:19
16:26
i Ac 4:31 j Ac 12:10
k Ac 12:7

16:27
l Ac 12:19

16:30
m Ac 2:37

16:31
n Ac 11:14
16:33
o ver 25

16:34
p Ac 11:14

16:36
q ver 23,27
r Ac 15:33

16:37
s Ac 22:25-29

16:38
t Ac 22:29
16:39
u Mt 8:34
16:40
v ver 14 w ver 2;
Ac 1:16

17:1
x ver 11,13;
Php 4:16; 1Th 1:1;
2Th 1:1; 2Ti 4:10
17:2
y Ac 9:20
z Ac 13:14
a Ac 8:35
17:3
b Lk 24:26; Ac 3:18

[19]When the owners of the slave girl realized that their hope of making money[y] was gone, they seized Paul and Silas[z] and dragged[a] them into the marketplace to face the authorities. [20]They brought them before the magistrates and said, "These men are Jews, and are throwing our city into an uproar[b] [21]by advocating customs unlawful for us Romans[c] to accept or practice."[d]

[22]The crowd joined in the attack against Paul and Silas, and the magistrates ordered them to be stripped and beaten.[e] [23]After they had been severely flogged, they were thrown into prison, and the jailer[f] was commanded to guard them carefully. [24]Upon receiving such orders, he put them in the inner cell and fastened their feet in the stocks.[g]

[25]About midnight Paul and Silas were praying and singing hymns[h] to God, and the other prisoners were listening to them. [26]Suddenly there was such a violent earthquake that the foundations of the prison were shaken.[i] At once all the prison doors flew open,[j] and everybody's chains came loose.[k] [27]The jailer woke up, and when he saw the prison doors open, he drew his sword and was about to kill himself because he thought the prisoners had escaped.[l] [28]But Paul shouted, "Don't harm yourself! We are all here!"

[29]The jailer called for lights, rushed in and fell trembling before Paul and Silas. [30]He then brought them out and asked, "Sirs, what must I do to be saved?"[m]

[31]They replied, "Believe in the Lord Jesus, and you will be saved—you and your household."[n] [32]Then they spoke the word of the Lord to him and to all the others in his house. [33]At that hour of the night[o] the jailer took them and washed their wounds; then immediately he and all his family were baptized. [34]The jailer brought them into his house and set a meal before them; he[p] was filled with joy because he had come to believe in God—he and his whole family.

[35]When it was daylight, the magistrates sent their officers to the jailer with the order: "Release those men." [36]The jailer[q] told Paul, "The magistrates have ordered that you and Silas be released. Now you can leave. Go in peace."[r]

[37]But Paul said to the officers: "They beat us publicly without a trial, even though we are Roman citizens,[s] and threw us into prison. And now do they want to get rid of us quietly? No! Let them come themselves and escort us out."

[38]The officers reported this to the magistrates, and when they heard that Paul and Silas were Roman citizens, they were alarmed.[t] [39]They came to appease them and escorted them from the prison, requesting them to leave the city.[u] [40]After Paul and Silas came out of the prison, they went to Lydia's house,[v] where they met with the brothers[w] and encouraged them. Then they left.

In Thessalonica

17 When they had passed through Amphipolis and Apollonia, they came to Thessalonica,[x] where there was a Jewish synagogue. [2]As his custom was, Paul went into the synagogue,[y] and on three Sabbath[z] days he reasoned with them from the Scriptures,[a] [3]explaining and proving that the Christ[a] had to suffer[b] and

a 3 Or Messiah

📖 Christ breaks down barriers that separate humans and creates a new community, his body. Possibly by way of demonstration, Luke showcased three diverse converts from Philippi: a (single?) businesswoman, a slave girl in bondage to an evil spirit, and a Roman jailer. God was establishing through the early church a new kind of society, where divisions over race, class, and gender didn't exist. How would your own fellowship compare to this new kind of society founded in Philippi?

Acts 17:1–9

🔷 Dubbing Paul and Silas "men who have caused trouble all over the world" was severe. But turmoil does often result when the gospel challenges people to change their lives. The agitation usually originates with those who feel threatened. The events here may have occurred in the spring of A.D. 50, shortly after Claudius expelled Jews from Rome (in 49) following riots associated with Jews and Christians. The authorities would have wanted to avoid such problems, and the Jewish opponents would have exploited those fears.

📖 Tragically, Christians are often viewed as being no different from anyone else—except that they think they are forgiven. In many places in the world conformity, not criticism, characterizes the church's role in society. But the gospel message is so radical that many will

rise from the dead. *c* "This Jesus I am proclaiming to you is the Christ, *a" d* he said. 4Some of the Jews were persuaded and joined Paul and Silas, *e* as did a large number of God-fearing Greeks and not a few prominent women.

5But the Jews were jealous; so they rounded up some bad characters from the marketplace, formed a mob and started a riot in the city. *f* They rushed to Jason's *g* house in search of Paul and Silas in order to bring them out to the crowd. *b* 6But when they did not find them, they dragged *h* Jason and some other brothers before the city officials, shouting: "These men who have caused trouble all over the world *i* have now come here, *j* 7and Jason has welcomed them into his house. They are all defying Caesar's decrees, saying that there is another king, one called Jesus." *k* 8When they heard this, the crowd and the city officials were thrown into turmoil. 9Then they made Jason *l* and the others post bond and let them go.

In Berea

10As soon as it was night, the brothers sent Paul and Silas away to Berea. *m* On arriving there, they went to the Jewish synagogue. 11Now the Bereans were of more noble character than the Thessalonians, *n* for they received the message with great eagerness and examined the Scriptures *o* every day to see if what Paul said was true. 12Many of the Jews believed, as did also a number of prominent Greek women and many Greek men.

13When the Jews in Thessalonica learned that Paul was preaching the word of God at Berea, they went there too, agitating the crowds and stirring them up. 14The brothers immediately sent Paul to the coast, but Silas *p* and Timothy *q* stayed at Berea. 15The men who escorted Paul brought him to Athens *r* and then left with instructions for Silas and Timothy to join him as soon as possible. *s*

In Athens

16While Paul was waiting for them in Athens, he was greatly distressed to see that the city was full of idols. 17So he reasoned in the synagogue *t* with the Jews and the God-fearing Greeks, as well as in the marketplace day by day with those who happened to be there. 18A group of Epicurean and Stoic philosophers began to dispute with him. Some of them asked, "What is this babbler trying to say?" Others remarked, "He seems to be advocating foreign gods." They said this because Paul was

a 3 Or *Messiah*   *b* 5 Or *the assembly of the people*

17:3
c Lk 24:46
d Ac 9:22; 18:28
17:4
e Ac 15:22

17:5
f ver 13; 1Th 2:16
g Ro 16:21

17:6
h Ac 16:19
i Mt 24:14
j Ac 16:20

17:7
k Lk 23:2; Jn 19:12

17:9
l ver 5

17:10
m ver 13; Ac 20:4

17:11
n ver 1 *o* Lk 16:29;
Jn 5:39

17:14
p Ac 15:22
q Ac 16:1
17:15
r ver 16,21,22;
Ac 18:1; 1Th 3:1
s Ac 18:5

17:17
t Ac 9:20

---

continue to see it as a cause that has "turned the world upside down" (v. 6, KJV).

Acts 17:10–15

Did Luke's praise of the Bereans mean that they deserved salvation more than others? *No one deserves to be saved,* you may rightly object—*We have all sinned* (cf. Rom. 3:22–23). The Bereans were praised because they willingly admitted their need with an eagerness to hear from God and to receive and believe what they heard. Jesus in his ministry had looked for that same hunger for God (cf. Matt. 5:5; 18:3–4).

What motivates you to study the Bible? At the heart of a living faith is a burning desire to pore over Scripture to learn more and more. Salvation comes through faith—and so, in turn, does Christian growth. Bible study that pleases God stems from an attitude that acknowledges, "I'm hungry, and you alone can satisfy me. I will approach your Book with the urgency of a famished baby frantically groping for its mother's milk" (cf. 1 Peter 2:2).

Acts 17:16–34

In Athens Paul ministered in three diverse arenas: in the synagogue to Jews, in the marketplace ("street evangelism"), and in an academy—to the leaders of an intellectual city. The Areopagus was the main administrative body and chief court in Athens, representing that society's intellectual elite. Many view Paul's message as a model of cross-cultural communication. Paul sensitively used his hearers' beliefs and even quoted from their own religious writings to build a bridge, while at the same time presenting the gospel as the fulfillment of their longings. He discerned how God was at work in their lives to prepare them for the gospel.

Effective communication requires knowing what others are thinking, as well as what God is doing in their lives. Because God is at work among all people, it's appropriate to build off their existing beliefs and longings, rather than assuming they know nothing of value. This requires us to become knowledgeable about the viewpoints and practices of other people. We don't "bring" the presence of God into people's lives when we share Christ. Nonetheless, the gospel challenges people to change, and we needn't be surprised when they reject us and our message.

17:18
u ver 31,32; Ac 4:2
17:19
v ver 22 w Mk 1:27

17:23
x Jn 4:22

17:24
y Isa 42:5; Ac 14:15
z Dt 10:14;
Mt 11:25 a Ac 7:48

17:25
b Ps 50:10-12;
Isa 42:5

17:26
c Dt 32:8;
Job 12:23
17:27
d Dt 4:7; Jer 23:23,
24; Ac 14:17
17:28
e Job 12:10;
Da 5:23
17:29
f Isa 40:18-20;
Ro 1:23
17:30
g Ac 14:16; Ro 3:25
h ver 23; 1Pe 1:14
i Lk 24:47;
Tit 2:11,12
17:31
j Mt 10:15 k Ps 9:8;
96:13; 98:9
l Ac 10:42
m Ac 2:24
17:32
n ver 18,31
17:34
o ver 19,22
18:1
p Ac 17:15
q Ac 19:1; 1Co 1:2;
2Co 1:1,23;
2Ti 4:20
18:2
r Ro 16:3;
1Co 16:19; 2Ti 4:19
s Ac 11:28
18:3
t Ac 20:34;
1Co 4:12; 1Th 2:9;
2Th 3:8
18:4
u Ac 13:14
18:5
v Ac 15:22
w Ac 16:1
x Ac 16:9; 17:14,15
y ver 28; Ac 17:3
18:6
z Ac 13:45
a 2Sa 1:16;
Eze 18:13; 33:4
b Ac 20:26
c Ac 13:46

preaching the good news about Jesus and the resurrection. [u] 19Then they took him and brought him to a meeting of the Areopagus, [v] where they said to him, "May we know what this new teaching[w] is that you are presenting? 20You are bringing some strange ideas to our ears, and we want to know what they mean." 21(All the Athenians and the foreigners who lived there spent their time doing nothing but talking about and listening to the latest ideas.)

22Paul then stood up in the meeting of the Areopagus and said: "Men of Athens! I see that in every way you are very religious. 23For as I walked around and looked carefully at your objects of worship, I even found an altar with this inscription: TO AN UNKNOWN GOD. Now what you worship as something unknown[x] I am going to proclaim to you.

24"The God who made the world and everything in it[y] is the Lord of heaven and earth[z] and does not live in temples built by hands. [a] 25And he is not served by human hands, as if he needed anything, because he himself gives all men life and breath and everything else. [b] 26From one man he made every nation of men, that they should inhabit the whole earth; and he determined the times set for them and the exact places where they should live. [c] 27God did this so that men would seek him and perhaps reach out for him and find him, though he is not far from each one of us. [d] 28'For in him we live and move and have our being.'[e] As some of your own poets have said, 'We are his offspring.'

29"Therefore since we are God's offspring, we should not think that the divine being is like gold or silver or stone—an image made by man's design and skill. [f] 30In the past God overlooked[g] such ignorance,[h] but now he commands all people everywhere to repent. [i] 31For he has set a day when he will judge[j] the world with justice[k] by the man he has appointed. [l] He has given proof of this to all men by raising him from the dead." [m]

32When they heard about the resurrection of the dead, [n] some of them sneered, but others said, "We want to hear you again on this subject." 33At that, Paul left the Council. 34A few men became followers of Paul and believed. Among them was Dionysius, a member of the Areopagus, [o] also a woman named Damaris, and a number of others.

In Corinth

18 After this, Paul left Athens[p] and went to Corinth. [q] 2There he met a Jew named Aquila, a native of Pontus, who had recently come from Italy with his wife Priscilla, [r] because Claudius[s] had ordered all the Jews to leave Rome. Paul went to see them, 3and because he was a tentmaker as they were, he stayed and worked with them. [t] 4Every Sabbath[u] he reasoned in the synagogue, trying to persuade Jews and Greeks.

5When Silas[v] and Timothy[w] came from Macedonia, [x] Paul devoted himself exclusively to preaching, testifying to the Jews that Jesus was the Christ. [a][y] 6But when the Jews opposed Paul and became abusive, [z] he shook out his clothes in protest and said to them, "Your blood be on your own heads! [a] I am clear of my responsibility. [b] From now on I will go to the Gentiles." [c]

7Then Paul left the synagogue and went next door to the house of Titius Justus,

a 5 Or Messiah; also in verse 28

Acts 18:1–17

God reassured Paul through a vision, promising to protect him and encouraging him that God had "many people [laos] in the city." Laos was the usual term for Israelites as the people of God. What a confirmation for Paul that God's "people" now included all believers!

Luke introduced the proconsul Gallio, a well-known Roman figure, whose position in Achaia was cited in an inscription in Delphi, dated around A.D. 52, and in the writings of his famous brother, the philosopher Seneca.

Gallio's positive response to Paul was a key building block in the church's case for a strong legal standing in the empire.

God often uses good friends and manual work to encourage us. Paul settled down in Corinth for a year and a half with his good friends Aquila, Priscilla, Silas, and Timothy, making tents and teaching the gospel. We are not just "spiritual beings"; friendship and fruitful work are integral to our wholeness. How has God used these gifts to bring encouragement in your life?

a worshiper of God. *d* 8 Crispus, *e* the synagogue ruler, *f* and his entire household *g* believed in the Lord; and many of the Corinthians who heard him believed and were baptized.

9 One night the Lord spoke to Paul in a vision: "Do not be afraid; keep on speaking, do not be silent. 10 For I am with you, *h* and no one is going to attack and harm you, because I have many people in this city." 11 So Paul stayed for a year and a half, teaching them the word of God.

12 While Gallio was proconsul of Achaia, *i* the Jews made a united attack on Paul and brought him into court. 13 "This man," they charged, "is persuading the people to worship God in ways contrary to the law."

14 Just as Paul was about to speak, Gallio said to the Jews, "If you Jews were making a complaint about some misdemeanor or serious crime, it would be reasonable for me to listen to you. 15 But since it involves questions about words and names and your own law *j*—settle the matter yourselves. I will not be a judge of such things." 16 So he had them ejected from the court. 17 Then they all turned on Sosthenes *k* the synagogue ruler and beat him in front of the court. But Gallio showed no concern whatever.

Priscilla, Aquila and Apollos

18 Paul stayed on in Corinth for some time. Then he left the brothers *l* and sailed for Syria, accompanied by Priscilla and Aquila. Before he sailed, he had his hair cut off at Cenchrea *m* because of a vow he had taken. *n* 19 They arrived at Ephesus, *o* where Paul left Priscilla and Aquila. He himself went into the synagogue and reasoned with the Jews. 20 When they asked him to spend more time with them, he declined. 21 But as he left, he promised, "I will come back if it is God's will." *p* Then he set sail from Ephesus. 22 When he landed at Caesarea, *q* he went up and greeted the church and then went down to Antioch. *r*

23 After spending some time in Antioch, Paul set out from there and traveled from place to place throughout the region of Galatia *s* and Phrygia, strengthening all the disciples. *t*

24 Meanwhile a Jew named Apollos, *u* a native of Alexandria, came to Ephesus. He was a learned man, with a thorough knowledge of the Scriptures. 25 He had been instructed in the way of the Lord, and he spoke with great fervor *a v* and taught about Jesus accurately, though he knew only the baptism of John. *w* 26 He began to speak boldly in the synagogue. When Priscilla and Aquila heard him, they invited him to their home and explained to him the way of God more adequately.

27 When Apollos wanted to go to Achaia, *x* the brothers *y* encouraged him and wrote to the disciples there to welcome him. On arriving, he was a great help to those who by grace had believed. 28 For he vigorously refuted the Jews in public debate, proving from the Scriptures *z* that Jesus was the Christ. *a*

Paul in Ephesus

19 While Apollos was at Corinth, *b* Paul took the road through the interior and arrived at Ephesus. *c* There he found some disciples 2 and asked them, "Did you receive the Holy Spirit when *b* you believed?"

---

a 25 Or *with fervor in the Spirit*   *b* 2 Or *after*

Column notes (right margin)

18:7
d Ac 16:14
18:8
e 1Co 1:14
f Mk 5:22
g Ac 11:14
18:10
h Mt 28:20

18:12
i ver 27

18:15
j Ac 23:29;
25:11,19
18:17
k 1Co 1:1

18:18
l Ac 1:16 *m* Ro 16:1
n Nu 6:2,5,18;
Ac 21:24
18:19
o ver 21,24;
1Co 15:32

18:21
p Ro 1:10;
1Co 4:19; Jas 4:15
18:22
q Ac 8:40
r Ac 11:19

18:23
s Ac 16:6
t Ac 14:22;
15:32,41
18:24
u Ac 19:1;
1Co 1:12; 3:5,6,22;
4:6; 16:12; Tit 3:13
18:25
v Ro 12:11
w Ac 19:3

18:27
x ver 12 *y* ver 18

18:28
z Ac 17:2 *a* ver 5;
Ac 9:22

19:1
b Ac 18:1
c Ac 18:19

Acts 18:18–28

Paul's third missionary journey began from Antioch with return visits to Galatia and Phrygia. Galatia had been evangelized during Paul's first journey. Phrygia is mentioned two other times in Acts (2:10; 16:6). Paul's purpose for these return engagements? "Strengthening all the disciples."

People in Paul's day typically cut or shaved their hair after following through on a vow. Paul may have taken this vow in connection with the vision he had received (18:9–10). If so, cutting his hair was an act of thanksgiving for his protection and for the positive response of the Corinthians to the gospel.

Vows, like magical charms, can be misused: *If I do this, God will be obligated to do something for me.* But a vow can positively symbolize our commitment to God and his work in us. If Paul's focus was thanksgiving, his vow touched on an important area we may be prone to neglect. A spiritual vow can be a visual symbol—a bookmark—reminding us to put first things first.

They answered, "No, we have not even heard that there is a Holy Spirit."

3So Paul asked, "Then what baptism did you receive?"

"John's baptism," they replied.

4Paul said, "John's baptism was a baptism of repentance. He told the people to believe in the one coming after him, that is, in Jesus."[d] 5On hearing this, they were baptized into[a] the name of the Lord Jesus. 6When Paul placed his hands on them,[e] the Holy Spirit came on them,[f] and they spoke in tongues[b][g] and prophesied. 7There were about twelve men in all.

8Paul entered the synagogue[h] and spoke boldly there for three months, arguing persuasively about the kingdom of God.[i] 9But some of them[j] became obstinate; they refused to believe and publicly maligned the Way.[k] So Paul left them. He took the disciples[l] with him and had discussions daily in the lecture hall of Tyrannus. 10This went on for two years,[m] so that all the Jews and Greeks who lived in the province of Asia[n] heard the word of the Lord.

11God did extraordinary miracles[o] through Paul, 12so that even handkerchiefs and aprons that had touched him were taken to the sick, and their illnesses were cured[p] and the evil spirits left them.

13Some Jews who went around driving out evil spirits[q] tried to invoke the name of the Lord Jesus over those who were demon-possessed. They would say, "In the name of Jesus,[r] whom Paul preaches, I command you to come out." 14Seven sons of Sceva, a Jewish chief priest, were doing this. 15⌞One day⌟ the evil spirit answered them, "Jesus I know, and I know about Paul, but who are you?" 16Then the man who had the evil spirit jumped on them and overpowered them all. He gave them such a beating that they ran out of the house naked and bleeding.

17When this became known to the Jews and Greeks living in Ephesus,[s] they were all seized with fear,[t] and the name of the Lord Jesus was held in high honor. 18Many of those who believed now came and openly confessed their evil deeds. 19A number who had practiced sorcery brought their scrolls together and burned them publicly. When they calculated the value of the scrolls, the total came to fifty thousand drachmas.[c] 20In this way the word of the Lord spread widely and grew in power.[u]

21After all this had happened, Paul decided to go to Jerusalem,[v] passing through Macedonia[w] and Achaia.[x] "After I have been there," he said, "I must visit Rome also."[y] 22He sent two of his helpers,[z] Timothy[a] and Erastus,[b] to Macedonia, while he stayed in the province of Asia[c] a little longer.

The Riot in Ephesus

23About that time there arose a great disturbance about the Way.[d] 24A silversmith named Demetrius, who made silver shrines of Artemis, brought in no little business

---

Cross references (margin)

19:4 d Jn 1:7; Ac 13:24,25
19:6 e Ac 6:6; 8:17 f Ac 2:4 g Mk 16:17; Ac 10:46
19:8 h Ac 9:20 i Ac 1:3; 28:23
19:9 j Ac 14:4 k ver 23; Ac 9:2 l ver 30; Ac 11:26
19:10 m Ac 20:31 n ver 22,26,27
19:11 o Ac 8:13
19:12 p Ac 5:15
19:13 q Mt 12:27 r Mk 9:38
19:17 s Ac 18:19 t Ac 5:5,11
19:20 u Ac 6:7; 12:24
19:21 v Ac 20:16,22; Ro 15:25 w Ac 16:9 x Ac 18:12 y Ro 15:24,28
19:22 z Ac 13:5 a Ac 16:1 b Ro 16:23; 2Ti 4:20 c ver 10,26,27
19:23 d Ac 9:2

---

[a] 5 Or in   [b] 6 Or other languages   [c] 19 A drachma was a silver coin worth about a day's wages.

Acts 19:1–22

Ephesus was different from other cities Paul had visited: A few believers and "semi-believers" were already there. But Paul wasn't content with a smattering of Christians. He wanted everyone to hear the Good News. His success rate? During his 27-plus-months' stay, he succeeded in exposing the entire population of the province of Asia to the message of Christ.

Every culture has unique aspects that hold people back from God, bind them to some form of evil or false belief—or make them open to the gospel. It's helpful to view the incidents in Ephesus as examples of power encounters with demonic forces. A *power encounter* is a situation in which God decisively manifests his authority over all other forces.

Throughout the world the truth of the gospel is being confirmed through miraculous power encounters. Bold confrontations with evil, illness, and even death are occurring, demonstrating Christ's authority over all other powers. In Ephesus, the gospel of the kingdom was known as "the Way" (v. 9). Following Christ isn't adhering to a set of beliefs but walking in a way that overrules all lesser authorities and powers that are contrary to God's way.

Acts 19:23–41

Luke described one more episode from Paul's lengthy ministry in Ephesus. This riot—and its conclusion in the Christians' acquittal—reinforced Luke's recurrent theme of opposition to the gospel (here called "great disturbance about the Way").

Though the legal system wasn't influenced by the early church, several times it protected Christians from unfair treatment. Shortly after this incident Paul wrote to the Christians in Rome about the state's positive contribution (see Rom. 13:3–5). In Ephesus his friendly relationship with the officials may have helped him obtain a fair trial.

for the craftsmen. 25He called them together, along with the workmen in related trades, and said: "Men, you know we receive a good income from this business. *e* 26And you see and hear how this fellow Paul has convinced and led astray large numbers of people here in Ephesus*f* and in practically the whole province of Asia. He says that man-made gods are no gods at all. *g* 27There is danger not only that our trade will lose its good name, but also that the temple of the great goddess Artemis will be discredited, and the goddess herself, who is worshiped throughout the province of Asia and the world, will be robbed of her divine majesty."

28When they heard this, they were furious and began shouting: "Great is Artemis of the Ephesians!" *h* 29Soon the whole city was in an uproar. The people seized Gaius*i* and Aristarchus, *j* Paul's traveling companions from Macedonia, *k* and rushed as one man into the theater. 30Paul wanted to appear before the crowd, but the disciples would not let him. 31Even some of the officials of the province, friends of Paul, sent him a message begging him not to venture into the theater.

32The assembly was in confusion: Some were shouting one thing, some another. *l* Most of the people did not even know why they were there. 33The Jews pushed Alexander to the front, and some of the crowd shouted instructions to him. He motioned*m* for silence in order to make a defense before the people. 34But when they realized he was a Jew, they all shouted in unison for about two hours: "Great is Artemis of the Ephesians!"

35The city clerk quieted the crowd and said: "Men of Ephesus, *n* doesn't all the world know that the city of Ephesus is the guardian of the temple of the great Artemis and of her image, which fell from heaven? 36Therefore, since these facts are undeniable, you ought to be quiet and not do anything rash. 37You have brought these men here, though they have neither robbed temples*o* nor blasphemed our goddess. 38If, then, Demetrius and his fellow craftsmen have a grievance against anybody, the courts are open and there are proconsuls. *p* They can press charges. 39If there is anything further you want to bring up, it must be settled in a legal assembly. 40As it is, we are in danger of being charged with rioting because of today's events. In that case we would not be able to account for this commotion, since there is no reason for it." 41After he had said this, he dismissed the assembly.

Through Macedonia and Greece

20 When the uproar had ended, Paul sent for the disciples*q* and, after encouraging them, said good-by and set out for Macedonia. *r* 2He traveled through that area, speaking many words of encouragement to the people, and finally arrived in Greece, 3where he stayed three months. Because the Jews made a plot against him*s* just as he was about to sail for Syria, he decided to go back through Macedonia. *t* 4He was accompanied by Sopater son of Pyrrhus from Berea, Aristarchus*u* and Secundus from Thessalonica, *v* Gaius*w* from Derbe, Timothy*x* also, and Tychicus*y* and Trophimus*z* from the province of Asia. 5These men went on ahead and wait-

Cross references

19:25
e Ac 16:16,19,20

19:26
f Ac 18:19
g Dt 4:28; Ps 115:4; Isa 44:10-20; Jer 10:3-5; Ac 17:29; 1Co 8:4; Rev 9:20

19:28
h Ac 18:19
19:29
i Ac 20:4; Ro 16:23; 1Co 1:14 *j* Ac 20:4; 27:2; Col 4:10; Phm 24 *k* Ac 16:9

19:32
l Ac 21:34

19:33
m Ac 12:17

19:35
n Ac 18:19

19:37
o Ro 2:22

19:38
p Ac 13:7,8,12

20:1
q Ac 11:26
r Ac 16:9
20:3
s ver 19; Ac 9:23, 24; 23:12,15,30; 25:3; 2Co 11:26
t Ac 16:9
20:4
u Ac 19:29
v Ac 17:1
w Ac 19:29
x Ac 16:1
y Eph 6:21; Col 4:7; 2Ti 4:12; Tit 3:12
z Ac 21:29; 2Ti 4:20

Government intervention may be necessary for Christian activity to go on. God's people have used this option effectively throughout history (consider Joseph, Daniel, Esther, and Nehemiah). We may legitimately capitalize upon the esteem Christians have won with government officials, courts, etc., to represent Christ's cause and highlight the need for justice at home or abroad. As Christians work to establish civil societies governed fairly by the rule of law, they are providing the world with one more sign of God's kingdom.

Acts 20:1–6

Encouragement is key to this chapter. The Greek verb "to encourage" appears in verses 1, 2, and 12, and verses 18–35 sample the content of Paul's encouragement. The wording in verse 2 suggests that he

spent considerable time in Macedonia, during which he wrote 2 Corinthians. By now Paul had established churches in a good portion of the Greek world. His plan from that point was to reach the Latin world, possibly using Rome as his base of operations.

The shift in verse 5 from a third to first person viewpoint may be confusing. Luke resumed another "we" section (see "There and Then" for 16:11–15). He had been left at Philippi in chapter 16 and had apparently remained there. Now he rejoined the party to accompany Paul to Jerusalem.

Christian witness is always personal, and personal encouragement is at the heart of effective ministry. Individual encouragement can multiply the resolve of a discouraged or weary person (cf. Gal. 6:9). Who could use a heartening call from you today?

20:5
a Ac 16:10
b Ac 16:8
20:6
c Ac 16:12
d Ac 16:8
20:7
e 1Co 16:2;
Rev 1:10

20:8
f Ac 1:13

20:10
g 1Ki 17:21;
2Ki 4:34
h Mt 9:23,24
20:11
i ver 7

ed for us *a* at Troas. *b* 6But we sailed from Philippi *c* after the Feast of Unleavened Bread, and five days later joined the others at Troas, *d* where we stayed seven days.

Eutychus Raised From the Dead at Troas

7On the first day of the week *e* we came together to break bread. Paul spoke to the people and, because he intended to leave the next day, kept on talking until midnight. 8There were many lamps in the upstairs room *f* where we were meeting. 9Seated in a window was a young man named Eutychus, who was sinking into a deep sleep as Paul talked on and on. When he was sound asleep, he fell to the ground from the third story and was picked up dead. 10Paul went down, threw himself on the young man *g* and put his arms around him. "Don't be alarmed," he said. "He's alive!" *h* 11Then he went upstairs again and broke bread *i* and ate. After talking until daylight, he left. 12The people took the young man home alive and were greatly comforted.

Paul's Farewell to the Ephesian Elders

13We went on ahead to the ship and sailed for Assos, where we were going to take Paul aboard. He had made this arrangement because he was going there on foot. 14When he met us at Assos, we took him aboard and went on to Mitylene. 15The next day we set sail from there and arrived off Kios. The day after that we crossed over to Samos, and on the following day arrived at Miletus. *j* 16Paul had decided to sail past Ephesus *k* to avoid spending time in the province of Asia, for he was in a hurry to reach Jerusalem, *l* if possible, by the day of Pentecost. *m*

20:15
j ver 17; 2Ti 4:20
20:16
k Ac 18:19
l Ac 19:21
m Ac 2:1; 1Co 16:8
20:17
n Ac 11:30
20:18
o Ac 18:19-21;
19:1-41
20:19
p ver 3
20:20
q ver 27
20:21
r Ac 18:5 *s* Ac 2:38
t Ac 24:24; 26:18;
Eph 1:15; Col 2:5;
Phm 5
20:22
u ver 16
20:23
v Ac 21:4
w Ac 9:16

17From Miletus, Paul sent to Ephesus for the elders *n* of the church. 18When they arrived, he said to them: "You know how I lived the whole time I was with you, *o* from the first day I came into the province of Asia. 19I served the Lord with great humility and with tears, although I was severely tested by the plots of the Jews. *p* 20You know that I have not hesitated to preach anything *q* that would be helpful to you but have taught you publicly and from house to house. 21I have declared to both Jews *r* and Greeks that they must turn to God in repentance *s* and have faith in our Lord Jesus. *t*

22"And now, compelled by the Spirit, I am going to Jerusalem, *u* not knowing what will happen to me there. 23I only know that in every city the Holy Spirit warns me *v* that prison and hardships are facing me. *w* 24However, I consider my life worth noth-

---

Acts 20:7–12

The raising of Eutychus reminds us of two resurrections performed, respectively, through Elijah and Elisha in the Old Testament (1 Kings 17:17–24; 2 Kings 4:32–37). Paul's embrace of the young man may have been an extension of the common practice of laying hands on a person during the act of healing. This is the last of eight Biblical accounts of the dead being raised.

We find here the first clear reference to believers meeting for worship on the first day of the week, but we are not sure whether Sunday worship had already become a regular practice. Luke's method of counting days wasn't Jewish, which measured from sundown to sundown, but Roman, which counted from midnight to midnight.

Some view the death of Eutychus as an illustration that there is no such thing as a good, long sermon! Others see in the story people's passion to receive good teaching, hunger for fellowship, and recognition of the gospel's radical power. These particular believers met together for almost 24 hours for fellowship and teaching! In many places in the world today believers walk for hours and gather for long periods to be nourished by fellowship and the Word.

Acts 20:13–38

Paul's address to the Ephesian elders is our only record of a speech he gave to believers. Its content is similar to his letters (also to believers). Paul defended his behavior, presenting it as an example to the elders; gave a charge, along with a warning; and committed his hearers to God.

Paul cited his willingness to suffer for the gospel in an attempt to encourage the elders to be faithful to their task. This was a common theme with Paul (cf. 2 Cor. 4:8–12; Gal. 6:17; Eph. 4:1). Similar encouragement comes from Hebrews: "Consider [Jesus] who endured such opposition from sinful men, *so that you will not grow weary and lose heart*" (Heb. 12:3, emphasis added).

We often find it difficult to motivate one another to serve others, let alone suffer, for Christ. Three insights from this passage can help: (1) Recognizing the greatness of Christ's cause can fire us, as a natural response, with a willingness to take on suffering. (2) Leaders can motivate others by their example of sacrificial service, by not working for personal gain or security. (3) And we can continually commit one another to God's grace, reminding each other of his faithfulness.

ing to me,^x if only I may finish the race and complete the task^y the Lord Jesus has given me^z—the task of testifying to the gospel of God's grace.

²⁵"Now I know that none of you among whom I have gone about preaching the kingdom will ever see me again.^a ²⁶Therefore, I declare to you today that I am innocent of the blood of all men.^b ²⁷For I have not hesitated to proclaim to you the whole will of God.^c ²⁸Keep watch over yourselves and all the flock of which the Holy Spirit has made you overseers.^{a d} Be shepherds of the church of God,^b which he bought with his own blood. ²⁹I know that after I leave, savage wolves^e will come in among you and will not spare the flock.^f ³⁰Even from your own number men will arise and distort the truth in order to draw away disciples^g after them. ³¹So be on your guard! Remember that for three years^h I never stopped warning each of you night and day with tears.ⁱ

³²"Now I commit you to God^j and to the word of his grace, which can build you up and give you an inheritance^k among all those who are sanctified.^l ³³I have not coveted anyone's silver or gold or clothing.^m ³⁴You yourselves know that these hands of mine have supplied my own needs and the needs of my companions.ⁿ ³⁵In everything I did, I showed you that by this kind of hard work we must help the weak, remembering the words the Lord Jesus himself said: 'It is more blessed to give than to receive.'"

³⁶When he had said this, he knelt down with all of them and prayed.^o ³⁷They all wept as they embraced him and kissed him.^p ³⁸What grieved them most was his statement that they would never see his face again.^q Then they accompanied him to the ship.

On to Jerusalem

21 After we^r had torn ourselves away from them, we put out to sea and sailed straight to Cos. The next day we went to Rhodes and from there to Patara. ²We found a ship crossing over to Phoenicia,^s went on board and set sail. ³After sighting Cyprus and passing to the south of it, we sailed on to Syria. We landed at Tyre, where our ship was to unload its cargo. ⁴Finding the disciples^t there, we stayed with them seven days. Through the Spirit^u they urged Paul not to go on to Jerusalem. ⁵But when our time was up, we left and continued on our way. All the disciples and their wives and children accompanied us out of the city, and there on the beach we knelt to pray.^v ⁶After saying good-by to each other, we went aboard the ship, and they returned home.

⁷We continued our voyage from Tyre^w and landed at Ptolemais, where we greeted the brothers^x and stayed with them for a day. ⁸Leaving the next day, we reached Caesarea^y and stayed at the house of Philip^z the evangelist,^a one of the Seven. ⁹He had four unmarried daughters who prophesied.^b

¹⁰After we had been there a number of days, a prophet named Agabus^c came down from Judea. ¹¹Coming over to us, he took Paul's belt, tied his own hands and

---

20:24
x Ac 21:13
y 2Co 4:1 z Gal 1:1;
Tit 1:3
20:25
a ver 38
20:26
b Ac 18:6
20:27
c ver 20
20:28
d 1Pe 5:2
20:29
e Mt 7:15 f ver 28
20:30
g Ac 11:26
20:31
h Ac 19:10 / ver 19
20:32
j Ac 14:23
k Eph 1:14;
Col 1:12; 3:24;
Heb 9:15; 1Pe 1:4
l Ac 26:18
20:33
m 1Sa 12:3;
1Co 9:12; 2Co 7:2;
11:9; 12:14-17
20:34
n Ac 18:3

20:36
o Lk 22:41; Ac 21:5
20:37
p Lk 15:20
20:38
q ver 25

21:1
r Ac 16:10

21:2
s Ac 11:19

21:4
t Ac 11:26 u ver 11;
Ac 20:23

21:5
v Ac 20:36

21:7
w Ac 12:20
x Ac 1:16
21:8
y Ac 8:40 z Ac 6:5;
8:5-40 a Eph 4:11;
2Ti 4:5
21:9
b Lk 2:36; Ac 2:17
21:10
c Ac 11:28

---

^a 28 Traditionally bishops   ^b 28 Many manuscripts of the Lord

---

Acts 21:1–16

"Through the Spirit" the Christians in Tyre urged Paul not to go on to Jerusalem. How do we reconcile this with Paul's statement that his trip there was "compelled by the Spirit" (20:22)? The Christians in Tyre received a prophecy that Paul would have trouble in Jerusalem. From that they may have inferred that the Spirit was prompting him not to go there. But Paul placed the Spirit's prediction about coming persecution alongside his urging that he proceed to Jerusalem.

Luke provided an unadorned glimpse of the early Christian community at work, seen especially in his repetition of the believers' response to Paul. He recorded warm affection with weeping, embracing, and kissing

(20:37), making it hard for Paul to leave. Even Paul's newfound friends in Tyre expressed loving attachment as they came with their families to send off him and his team and to pray kneeling on the beach.

Each of us, if we are obedient to Christ, will face "death" of some sort; the cross is a nonnegotiable requirement of discipleship (cf. Matt. 16:24). Even our Christian loved ones may fail to understand or appreciate the path we are taking. If they oppose us, it's most likely not because they reject God's ways. They may in misplaced love want to help us avoid pain. We owe it to them to explain what lies behind our decisions and help them understand and accept our choices. In what areas of life have you experienced this?

21:11
d ver 33 e 1Ki 22:11

21:13
f Ac 20:24
g Ac 9:16

21:16
h Ac 8:40 i ver 3,4

21:17
j Ac 15:4
21:18
k Ac 15:13
l Ac 11:30
21:19
m Ac 14:27
n Ac 1:17

21:20
o Ac 22:3; Ro 10:2;
Gal 1:14
p Ac 15:1,5
21:21
q ver 28 r Ac 15:19-
21; 1Co 7:18,19
s Ac 6:14

21:23
t Ac 18:18
21:24
u ver 26; Ac 24:18
v Ac 18:18

21:25
w Ac 15:20,29

21:26
x Nu 6:13-20;
Ac 24:18

21:27
y Ac 24:18; 26:21

feet with it and said, "The Holy Spirit says, 'In this way the Jews of Jerusalem will bind ^{d} the owner of this belt and will hand him over to the Gentiles.' " ^{e}

^{12}When we heard this, we and the people there pleaded with Paul not to go up to Jerusalem. ^{13}Then Paul answered, "Why are you weeping and breaking my heart? I am ready not only to be bound, but also to die ^{f} in Jerusalem for the name of the Lord Jesus." ^{g} ^{14}When he would not be dissuaded, we gave up and said, "The Lord's will be done."

^{15}After this, we got ready and went up to Jerusalem. ^{16}Some of the disciples from Caesarea ^{h} accompanied us and brought us to the home of Mnason, where we were to stay. He was a man from Cyprus ^{i} and one of the early disciples.

Paul's Arrival at Jerusalem

^{17}When we arrived at Jerusalem, the brothers received us warmly. ^{j} ^{18}The next day Paul and the rest of us went to see James, ^{k} and all the elders ^{l} were present. ^{19}Paul greeted them and reported in detail what God had done among the Gentiles ^{m} through his ministry. ^{n}

^{20}When they heard this, they praised God. Then they said to Paul: "You see, brother, how many thousands of Jews have believed, and all of them are zealous ^{o} for the law. ^{p} ^{21}They have been informed that you teach all the Jews who live among the Gentiles to turn away from Moses, ^{q} telling them not to circumcise their children ^{r} or live according to our customs. ^{s} ^{22}What shall we do? They will certainly hear that you have come, ^{23}so do what we tell you. There are four men with us who have made a vow. ^{t} ^{24}Take these men, join in their purification rites ^{u} and pay their expenses, so that they can have their heads shaved. ^{v} Then everybody will know there is no truth in these reports about you, but that you yourself are living in obedience to the law. ^{25}As for the Gentile believers, we have written to them our decision that they should abstain from food sacrificed to idols, from blood, from the meat of strangled animals and from sexual immorality." ^{w}

^{26}The next day Paul took the men and purified himself along with them. Then he went to the temple to give notice of the date when the days of purification would end and the offering would be made for each of them. ^{x}

Paul Arrested

^{27}When the seven days were nearly over, some Jews from the province of Asia saw Paul at the temple. They stirred up the whole crowd and seized him, ^{y} ^{28}shouting, "Men of Israel, help us! This is the man who teaches all men everywhere against our

---

Acts 21:17–26

🔍 Was Paul being inconsistent or hypocritical in purifying himself with Jewish Christians who were fulfilling a vow? The opposition in his letters to works of the law was all about the belief that they were a requirement for salvation. Paul certainly wasn't opposed to God's law itself (cf. Rom. 3:31). His words in 1 Corinthians 9:20 state his position well: "I became like one under the law . . . . so as to win those under the law." Paul's actions in this passage were in line with that approach.

📖 God doesn't call us to cling to our privileges, preferences, or priorities. Paul consented in practice for himself and his companions to undergo a purification ritual that he didn't believe was necessary because he valued community over some of his personal convictions. When we are secure in God's grace, we can participate in religious ceremonies others think are essential, even if we don't. How might this impact your response to divisions and differences within your church, and in the larger body of Christ?

Acts 21:27–36

🔍 Notices in Greek and Latin were attached to the barrier between the inner and outer temple courts, warning Gentiles of the death penalty for going any further. The Roman authorities were so anxious to appease the Jews in this regard that they authorized execution even if the offender was a Roman citizen. Verse 36 sounds hauntingly familiar to us. Luke must have shivered at the recollection that some 27 years earlier another crowd had shouted "Away with this man!" at a spot nearby (see Luke 23:18).

📖 The temple complex included a "court of the Gentiles" where all people could come and worship. It was this area that Jesus had cleansed from its use as a religious marketplace that kept Gentiles from drawing near in worship. Though Paul was falsely accused of bringing Trophimus with him into the temple, his entire ministry was spent clearing the way for all people to draw near to the living Temple, Jesus. Are there barriers of prejudice or custom in your fellowship that make it harder for "outsiders" to find access to God?

people and our law and this place. And besides, he has brought Greeks into the temple area and defiled this holy place." [z] 29(They had previously seen Trophimus [a] the Ephesian [b] in the city with Paul and assumed that Paul had brought him into the temple area.)

30The whole city was aroused, and the people came running from all directions. Seizing Paul, [c] they dragged him [d] from the temple, and immediately the gates were shut. 31While they were trying to kill him, news reached the commander of the Roman troops that the whole city of Jerusalem was in an uproar. 32He at once took some officers and soldiers and ran down to the crowd. When the rioters saw the commander and his soldiers, they stopped beating Paul. [e]

33The commander came up and arrested him and ordered him to be bound [f] with two [g] chains. [h] Then he asked who he was and what he had done. 34Some in the crowd shouted one thing and some another, [i] and since the commander could not get at the truth because of the uproar, he ordered that Paul be taken into the barracks. [j] 35When Paul reached the steps, [k] the violence of the mob was so great he had to be carried by the soldiers. 36The crowd that followed kept shouting, "Away with him!" [l]

Paul Speaks to the Crowd

37As the soldiers were about to take Paul into the barracks, [m] he asked the commander, "May I say something to you?"

"Do you speak Greek?" he replied. 38"Aren't you the Egyptian who started a revolt and led four thousand terrorists out into the desert [n] some time ago?" [o]

39Paul answered, "I am a Jew, from Tarsus [p] in Cilicia, [q] a citizen of no ordinary city. Please let me speak to the people."

40Having received the commander's permission, Paul stood on the steps and motioned [r] to the crowd. When they were all silent, he said to them in Aramaic [a]: [s]

22 1"Brothers and fathers, [t] listen now to my defense."

2When they heard him speak to them in Aramaic, [u] they became very quiet.

Then Paul said: 3"I am a Jew, [v] born in Tarsus [w] of Cilicia, but brought up in this city. Under [x] Gamaliel [y] I was thoroughly trained in the law of our fathers [z] and was just as zealous [a] for God as any of you are today. 4I persecuted [b] the followers of this Way to their death, arresting both men and women and throwing them into prison, [c] 5as also the high priest and all the Council [d] can testify. I even obtained letters from them to their brothers [e] in Damascus, [f] and went there to bring these people as prisoners to Jerusalem to be punished.

6"About noon as I came near Damascus, suddenly a bright light from heaven flashed around me. [g] 7I fell to the ground and heard a voice say to me, 'Saul! Saul! Why do you persecute me?'

8" 'Who are you, Lord?' I asked.

" 'I am Jesus of Nazareth, whom you are persecuting,' he replied. 9My companions saw the light, [h] but they did not understand the voice [i] of him who was speaking to me.

10" 'What shall I do, Lord?' I asked.

" 'Get up,' the Lord said, 'and go into Damascus. There you will be told all that

[a] 40 Or possibly Hebrew; also in 22:2

Cross references (right column)

21:28
z Mt 24:15;
Ac 24:5,6
21:29
a Ac 20:4
b Ac 18:19

21:30
c Ac 26:21
d Ac 16:19

21:32
e Ac 23:27
21:33
f ver 11 g Ac 12:6
h Ac 20:23;
Eph 6:20; 2Ti 2:9
21:34
i Ac 19:32 j ver 37;
Ac 23:10,16,32
21:35
k ver 40

21:36
l Lk 23:18;
Jn 19:15; Ac 22:22

21:37
m ver 34

21:38
n Mt 24:26
o Ac 5:36
21:39
p Ac 9:11 q Ac 22:3

21:40
r Ac 12:17 s Jn 5:2
22:1
t Ac 7:2
22:2
u Ac 21:40
22:3
v Ac 21:39
w Ac 9:11
x Lk 10:39
y Ac 5:34 z Ac 26:5
a Ac 21:20
22:4
b Ac 8:3
c ver 19,20
22:5
d Lk 22:66
e Ac 13:26 f Ac 9:2

22:6
g Ac 9:3

22:9
h Ac 26:13 i Ac 9:7

Acts 21:37—22:21

📖 A new detail in Paul's repeated accounts of his calling and conversion was this description of his vision in the Jerusalem temple. Paul had expressed to God his desire to stay in Jerusalem and witness to the Jews, but this wasn't to be. Luke's earlier description of the circumstances surrounding Paul's departure from Jerusalem had been from a different perspective (9:29–30). This isn't the only example in Acts of divine direction and human initiative working together (cf. 16:11–15).

📖 Ironically, the Jews' traditionalism made them reject the truth about the Messiah that flowed naturally from that tradition. Throughout church history, traditionalists have at times mistreated those who have launched out into new directions, even if these approaches were permitted and even suggested by their traditions. What role has tradition played in the life of your congregation? Your family? When have you been called to change a tradition in response to God's call?

22:10
j Ac 16:30
22:11
k Ac 9:8
22:12
l Ac 9:17
m Ac 10:22
22:14
n Ac 3:13
o 1Co 9:1; 15:8
p Ac 7:52
22:15
q Ac 23:11; 26:16
22:16
r Ac 2:38
s Heb 10:22
t Ro 10:13
22:17
u Ac 9:26
v Ac 10:10
22:19
w ver 4; Ac 8:3
x Mt 10:17
22:20
y Ac 7:57-60; 8:1
22:21
z Ac 9:15; 13:46
22:22
a Ac 21:36
b Ac 25:24
22:23
c Ac 7:58
d 2Sa 16:13
22:24
e Ac 21:34 f ver 29
22:25
g Ac 16:37
22:29
h ver 24,25;
Ac 16:38

you have been assigned to do.'[j] ¹¹My companions led me by the hand into Damascus, because the brilliance of the light had blinded me.[k]

¹²"A man named Ananias came to see me.[l] He was a devout observer of the law and highly respected by all the Jews living there.[m] ¹³He stood beside me and said, 'Brother Saul, receive your sight!' And at that very moment I was able to see him.

¹⁴"Then he said: 'The God of our fathers[n] has chosen you to know his will and to see[o] the Righteous One[p] and to hear words from his mouth. ¹⁵You will be his witness[q] to all men of what you have seen and heard. ¹⁶And now what are you waiting for? Get up, be baptized[r] and wash your sins away,[s] calling on his name.'[t]

¹⁷"When I returned to Jerusalem[u] and was praying at the temple, I fell into a trance[v] ¹⁸and saw the Lord speaking. 'Quick!' he said to me. 'Leave Jerusalem immediately, because they will not accept your testimony about me.'

¹⁹" 'Lord,' I replied, 'these men know that I went from one synagogue to another to imprison[w] and beat[x] those who believe in you. ²⁰And when the blood of your martyr[a] Stephen was shed, I stood there giving my approval and guarding the clothes of those who were killing him.'[y]

²¹"Then the Lord said to me, 'Go; I will send you far away to the Gentiles.' "[z]

Paul the Roman Citizen

²²The crowd listened to Paul until he said this. Then they raised their voices and shouted, "Rid the earth of him![a] He's not fit to live!"[b]

²³As they were shouting and throwing off their cloaks[c] and flinging dust into the air,[d] ²⁴the commander ordered Paul to be taken into the barracks.[e] He directed[f] that he be flogged and questioned in order to find out why the people were shouting at him like this. ²⁵As they stretched him out to flog him, Paul said to the centurion standing there, "Is it legal for you to flog a Roman citizen who hasn't even been found guilty?"[g]

²⁶When the centurion heard this, he went to the commander and reported it. "What are you going to do?" he asked. "This man is a Roman citizen."

²⁷The commander went to Paul and asked, "Tell me, are you a Roman citizen?"
"Yes, I am," he answered.

²⁸Then the commander said, "I had to pay a big price for my citizenship."
"But I was born a citizen," Paul replied.

²⁹Those who were about to question him withdrew immediately. The commander himself was alarmed when he realized that he had put Paul, a Roman citizen,[h] in chains.

a 20 Or witness

Acts 22:22-29

Before Paul arrived in Jerusalem, he had been given ample warning from God that he would be persecuted, and he came prepared to suffer (20:23–24; 21:4,10–13). But he wasn't a masochist who took on suffering unnecessarily. He indicated his willingness to die in Jerusalem (21:13), but when the Romans tried to scourge him to get him to talk, he rightly appealed to his citizenship to halt the process.

As representatives of a just God, we as believers are committed to combating injustice—even if it's against us. Paul stated elsewhere that it's better to be wronged or cheated than to appeal to secular courts against *other believers* (1 Cor. 6:6–7). But we can appeal to the law for protection if we are attacked in a way that clearly violates the law of the land. Most countries have laws against prisoner abuse or the mistreatment of women and children in forced prostitution or labor. A

powerful ministry of the church is to encourage the just and fair rule of law.

Acts 22:30—23:11

Paul's outburst was triggered by the high priest's illegal command that those standing near Paul strike him on the mouth. Striking someone prior to a conviction was unjust. In this case, Paul hadn't even been properly charged. His comment about Ananias proved to be prophetic; within ten years the high priest was forced to flee to Herod's palace and was killed.

Paul's first line of defense before the Sanhedrin having failed, he adopted a new tack. At stake was the resurrection of the dead, a doctrine accepted by the Pharisees but not the Sadducees (see "There and Then" for Matt. 22:23–32). Paul wasn't just using his skills to divide the group but was pointing to the heart of the gospel. Jesus' resurrection fulfilled the Pharisees' belief. Every Pharisee should logically have become a Christian!

Before the Sanhedrin

30The next day, since the commander wanted to find out exactly why Paul was being accused by the Jews, [i] he released him[j] and ordered the chief priests and all the Sanhedrin[k] to assemble. Then he brought Paul and had him stand before them.

23 Paul looked straight at the Sanhedrin[l] and said, "My brothers,[m] I have fulfilled my duty to God in all good conscience[n] to this day." **2**At this the high priest Ananias[o] ordered those standing near Paul to strike him on the mouth.[p] **3**Then Paul said to him, "God will strike you, you whitewashed wall![q] You sit there to judge me according to the law, yet you yourself violate the law by commanding that I be struck!"[r]

4Those who were standing near Paul said, "You dare to insult God's high priest?"

5Paul replied, "Brothers, I did not realize that he was the high priest; for it is written: 'Do not speak evil about the ruler of your people.'[a]"[s]

6Then Paul, knowing that some of them were Sadducees and the others Pharisees, called out in the Sanhedrin, "My brothers,[t] I am a Pharisee,[u] the son of a Pharisee. I stand on trial because of my hope in the resurrection of the dead."[v] **7**When he said this, a dispute broke out between the Pharisees and the Sadducees, and the assembly was divided. **8**(The Sadducees say that there is no resurrection,[w] and that there are neither angels nor spirits, but the Pharisees acknowledge them all.)

9There was a great uproar, and some of the teachers of the law who were Pharisees[x] stood up and argued vigorously. "We find nothing wrong with this man,"[y] they said. "What if a spirit or an angel has spoken to him?"[z] **10**The dispute became so violent that the commander was afraid Paul would be torn to pieces by them. He ordered the troops to go down and take him away from them by force and bring him into the barracks.[a]

11The following night the Lord stood near Paul and said, "Take courage![b] As you have testified about me in Jerusalem, so you must also testify in Rome."[c]

The Plot to Kill Paul

12The next morning the Jews formed a conspiracy and bound themselves with an oath not to eat or drink until they had killed Paul.[d] **13**More than forty men were involved in this plot. **14**They went to the chief priests and elders and said, "We have taken a solemn oath not to eat anything until we have killed Paul.[e] **15**Now then, you and the Sanhedrin[f] petition the commander to bring him before you on the pretext of wanting more accurate information about his case. We are ready to kill him before he gets here."

16But when the son of Paul's sister heard of this plot, he went into the barracks[g] and told Paul.

---

[a] 5 Exodus 22:28

22:30 [i] Ac 23:28; [j] Ac 21:33; [k] Mt 5:22
23:1 [l] Ac 22:30; [m] Ac 22:5; [n] Ac 24:16; 1Co 4:4; 2Co 1:12; 2Ti 1:3; Heb 13:18
23:2 [o] Ac 24:1; [p] Jn 18:22
23:3 [q] Mt 23:27; [r] Lev 19:15; Dt 25:1,2; Jn 7:51
23:5 [s] Ex 22:28
23:6 [t] Ac 22:5 [u] Ac 26:5; Php 3:5 [v] Ac 24:15, 21; 26:8
23:8 [w] Mt 22:23
23:9 [x] Mk 2:16 [y] ver 29; Ac 25:25; 26:31 [z] Ac 22:7,17,18
23:10 [a] Ac 21:34
23:11 [b] Ac 18:9 [c] Ac 19:21; 28:23
23:12 [d] ver 14,21,30; Ac 25:3
23:14 [e] ver 12
23:15 [f] ver 1; Ac 22:30
23:16 [g] ver 10; Ac 21:34

More than once God had to curb Paul's personal ambitions (see 16:6–10; 22:17–21). But Paul had a burning desire to go to Rome (Rom. 1:10–15; 15:22–32)—an ambition God confirmed in a vision. It's good to dream big dreams—as long as we are willing to place them on God's altar and bow to his sovereignty. But earthly desires can cloud godly ambitions. It may be difficult for us to distinguish between the two, so God may send obstacles to alert us to danger. We can even ask for such confirmation if we are unsure!

Acts 23:12–22

When Paul said he had lost "all things" (from a human standpoint) because of the gospel (Phil. 3:4–8), this must have included his family. His father, probably a wealthy person, had likely disowned him. But something of family affection must have remained for his sister's

son to take the risk of uncovering the plot of this murderous group.

Standing up for the right against the established authorities in Paul's day (as in ours) often involved the willingness to take risks. The fanatics who took a vow to kill Paul were matched by his nephew's commitment to save him.

Paul was prepared to die, but it's not an act of faithlessness or cowardice to appeal through legitimate means to escape the consequences of persecution. When we encourage those in power to do what's right we help strengthen society's moral fabric. Our world is filled with fanatics willing to kill in the name of their religious beliefs. Paul's nephew illustrates the gospel's call to be willing to risk our lives to save those of others.

23:18
h Eph 3:1

17Then Paul called one of the centurions and said, "Take this young man to the commander; he has something to tell him." 18So he took him to the commander. The centurion said, "Paul, the prisoner,h sent for me and asked me to bring this young man to you because he has something to tell you."

19The commander took the young man by the hand, drew him aside and asked, "What is it you want to tell me?"

23:20
i ver 1 j ver 14,15
23:21
k ver 13 l ver 12,14

20He said: "The Jews have agreed to ask you to bring Paul before the Sanhedrini tomorrow on the pretext of wanting more accurate information about him.j 21Don't give in to them, because more than fortyk of them are waiting in ambush for him. They have taken an oath not to eat or drink until they have killed him.l They are ready now, waiting for your consent to their request."

22The commander dismissed the young man and cautioned him, "Don't tell anyone that you have reported this to me."

Paul Transferred to Caesarea

23:23
m Ac 8:40 n ver 33
23:24
o ver 26,33;
Ac 24:1-3,10; 25:14

23Then he called two of his centurions and ordered them, "Get ready a detachment of two hundred soldiers, seventy horsemen and two hundred spearmena to go to Caesaream at nine tonight.n 24Provide mounts for Paul so that he may be taken safely to Governor Felix."o

25He wrote a letter as follows:

23:26
p Lk 1:3; Ac 24:3;
26:25 q Ac 15:23

26Claudius Lysias,

To His Excellency,p Governor Felix:

Greetings.q

23:27
r Ac 21:32
s Ac 21:33
t Ac 22:25-29

27This man was seized by the Jews and they were about to kill him,r but I came with my troops and rescued him,s for I had learned that he is a Roman citizen.t 28I wanted to know why they were accusing him, so I brought him to

23:28
u Ac 22:30
23:29
v Ac 18:15; 25:19
w ver 9; Ac 26:31
23:30
x ver 20,21
y Ac 20:3 z ver 35;
Ac 24:19; 25:16

their Sanhedrin.u 29I found that the accusation had to do with questions about their law,v but there was no charge against himw that deserved death or imprisonment. 30When I was informedx of a ploty to be carried out against the man, I sent him to you at once. I also ordered his accusersz to present to you their case against him.

23:32
a ver 23 b Ac 21:34
23:33
c ver 23,24
d Ac 8:40 e ver 26

31So the soldiers, carrying out their orders, took Paul with them during the night and brought him as far as Antipatris. 32The next day they let the cavalrya go on with him, while they returned to the barracks.b 33When the cavalryc arrived in Caesarea,d they delivered the letter to the governore and handed Paul over to him. 34The governor read the letter and asked what province he was from. Learning that he was

23:34
f Ac 6:9; 21:39
23:35
g ver 30; Ac 24:19;
25:16 h Ac 24:27

from Cilicia,f 35he said, "I will hear your case when your accusersg get here." Then he ordered that Paul be kept under guardh in Herod's palace.

a 23 The meaning of the Greek for this word is uncertain.

Acts 23:23–35

The commander embellished his story about having rescued Paul after discovering his Roman citizenship, specifically mentioning that there was no charge against Paul deserving of death or imprisonment. Luke's emphasis on Paul's blamelessness before the Roman law is a major theme in this part of Acts.

Moving a prisoner for his or her own safety or to avoid possible violence or the threat of a riot is a tactic still used today. The commander made every possible provision for Paul's security, sending him off in the company of 470 armed soldiers under cover of darkness. For

the third time Paul left a city secretly, at night (cf. Damascus, 9:25; Thessalonica, 17:10).

The importance of the letter lay in the commander's declaration of Paul's innocence. Compare similar comments by Gallio (18:14–15), the city executive of Ephesus (19:40), Pharisees (23:9), Festus (25:25), and Herod Agrippa II (26:31–32). Considering the moral crisis we face today, it's critical that the church and individual Christians be blameless before the world. Our reputations are reflections on Christ, and Jesus' harshest criticism fell on the Pharisees, who preached one thing and practiced another (cf. Matt. 23).

The Trial Before Felix

24 Five days later the high priest Ananias[i] went down to Caesarea with some of the elders and a lawyer named Tertullus, and they brought their charges[j] against Paul before the governor.[k] 2When Paul was called in, Tertullus presented his case before Felix: "We have enjoyed a long period of peace under you, and your foresight has brought about reforms in this nation. 3Everywhere and in every way, most excellent[l] Felix, we acknowledge this with profound gratitude. 4But in order not to weary you further, I would request that you be kind enough to hear us briefly.

5"We have found this man to be a troublemaker, stirring up riots[m] among the Jews[n] all over the world. He is a ringleader of the Nazarene[o] sect[p] 6and even tried to desecrate the temple;[q] so we seized him. 8By[a] examining him yourself you will be able to learn the truth about all these charges we are bringing against him."

9The Jews joined in the accusation,[r] asserting that these things were true.

10When the governor[s] motioned for him to speak, Paul replied: "I know that for a number of years you have been a judge over this nation; so I gladly make my defense. 11You can easily verify that no more than twelve days[t] ago I went up to Jerusalem to worship. 12My accusers did not find me arguing with anyone at the temple,[u] or stirring up a crowd[v] in the synagogues or anywhere else in the city. 13And they cannot prove to you the charges they are now making against me.[w] 14However, I admit that I worship the God of our fathers[x] as a follower of the Way,[y] which they call a sect.[z] I believe everything that agrees with the Law and that is written in the Prophets,[a] 15and I have the same hope in God as these men, that there will be a resurrection[b] of both the righteous and the wicked.[c] 16So I strive always to keep my conscience clear[d] before God and man.

17"After an absence of several years, I came to Jerusalem to bring my people gifts for the poor[e] and to present offerings. 18I was ceremonially clean[f] when they found me in the temple courts doing this. There was no crowd with me, nor was I involved in any disturbance.[g] 19But there are some Jews from the province of Asia, who ought to be here before you and bring charges if they have anything against me.[h] 20Or these who are here should state what crime they found in me when I stood before the Sanhedrin— 21unless it was this one thing I shouted as I stood in their presence: 'It is concerning the resurrection of the dead that I am on trial before you today.' "[i]

22Then Felix, who was well acquainted with the Way, adjourned the proceedings. "When Lysias the commander comes," he said, "I will decide your case." 23He ordered the centurion to keep Paul under guard[j] but to give him some freedom[k] and permit his friends to take care of his needs.[l]

24Several days later Felix came with his wife Drusilla, who was a Jewess. He sent for Paul and listened to him as he spoke about faith in Christ Jesus.[m] 25As Paul discoursed on righteousness, self-control[n] and the judgment[o] to come, Felix was

---

[a] 6-8 Some manuscripts *him and wanted to judge him according to our law.* 7But the commander, Lysias, came and with the use of much force snatched him from our hands 8and ordered his accusers to come before you. By

---

24:1
[i] Ac 23:2
[j] Ac 23:30,35
[k] Ac 23:24
24:3
[l] Lk 1:3; Ac 23:26; 26:25
24:5
[m] Ac 16:20; 17:6
[n] Ac 21:28
[o] Mk 1:24 [p] ver 14; Ac 26:5; 28:22
24:6
[q] Ac 21:28
24:9
[r] 1Th 2:16
24:10
[s] Ac 23:24
24:11
[t] Ac 21:27; ver 1
24:12
[u] Ac 25:8; 28:17 [v] ver 18
24:13
[w] Ac 25:7
24:14
[x] Ac 3:13 [y] Ac 9:2 [z] ver 5 [a] Ac 26:6, 22; 28:23
24:15
[b] Ac 23:6; 28:20 [c] Da 12:2; Jn 5:28, 29
24:16
[d] Ac 23:1
24:17
[e] Ac 11:29,30; Ro 15:25-28,31; 1Co 16:1-4,15; 2Co 8:1-4; Gal 2:10
24:18
[f] Ac 21:26 [g] ver 12
24:19
[h] Ac 23:30
24:21
[i] Ac 23:6
24:23
[j] Ac 23:35 [k] Ac 28:16 [l] Ac 23:16; 27:3
24:24
[m] Ac 20:21
24:25
[n] Gal 5:23; 2Pe 1:6 [o] Ac 10:42

Acts 24:1–27

Felix should have released Paul but was reluctant to stir up the Jews and hoped to secure a bribe from him. Beyond that, the governor enjoyed talking with his prisoner. Still, their discussions scared him—which he covered up with a "couldn't care less" front. Felix's delaying tactics dragged on for two years, at which time he was removed from office. Luke left no doubt that Felix thought Paul innocent of crimes against the state.

Luke provided details of Felix's response, not just to Paul's legal case but also to his message. Once again Paul had the opportunity to preach the truth of the gospel to political rulers (cf. Luke's account of Paul's conversation with Agrippa in 26:25–29). The Bible is concerned with the conversion of all people, including the rich and powerful.

In some parts of the world Christians willingly return to prison because there they have the opportunity freely and boldly to proclaim Christ. Having already relinquished everything, they have nothing more to lose. We are called to always be ready to account for the hope that is in us. If you were arrested for the crime of following Christ, would there be sufficient evidence to convict you?

afraid and said, "That's enough for now! You may leave. When I find it convenient, I will send for you." [26]At the same time he was hoping that Paul would offer him a bribe, so he sent for him frequently and talked with him.

[27]When two years had passed, Felix was succeeded by Porcius Festus,[p] but because Felix wanted to grant a favor to the Jews,[q] he left Paul in prison.[r]

The Trial Before Festus

25 Three days after arriving in the province, Festus went up from Caesarea[s] to Jerusalem, [2]where the chief priests and Jewish leaders appeared before him and presented the charges against Paul.[t] [3]They urgently requested Festus, as a favor to them, to have Paul transferred to Jerusalem, for they were preparing an ambush to kill him along the way. [4]Festus answered, "Paul is being held[u] at Caesarea, and I myself am going there soon. [5]Let some of your leaders come with me and press charges against the man there, if he has done anything wrong."

[6]After spending eight or ten days with them, he went down to Caesarea, and the next day he convened the court[v] and ordered that Paul be brought before him. [7]When Paul appeared, the Jews who had come down from Jerusalem stood around him, bringing many serious charges against him,[w] which they could not prove.[x]

[8]Then Paul made his defense: "I have done nothing wrong against the law of the Jews or against the temple[y] or against Caesar."

[9]Festus, wishing to do the Jews a favor,[z] said to Paul, "Are you willing to go up to Jerusalem and stand trial before me there on these charges?"[a]

[10]Paul answered: "I am now standing before Caesar's court, where I ought to be tried. I have not done any wrong to the Jews, as you yourself know very well. [11]If, however, I am guilty of doing anything deserving death, I do not refuse to die. But if the charges brought against me by these Jews are not true, no one has the right to hand me over to them. I appeal to Caesar!"[b]

[12]After Festus had conferred with his council, he declared: "You have appealed to Caesar. To Caesar you will go!"

Festus Consults King Agrippa

[13]A few days later King Agrippa and Bernice arrived at Caesarea[c] to pay their respects to Festus. [14]Since they were spending many days there, Festus discussed Paul's case with the king. He said: "There is a man here whom Felix left as a prisoner.[d] [15]When I went to Jerusalem, the chief priests and elders of the Jews brought charges against him[e] and asked that he be condemned.

[16]"I told them that it is not the Roman custom to hand over any man before he has faced his accusers and has had an opportunity to defend himself against their

---

Cross references (margin):

24:27
p Ac 25:1,4,9,14
q Ac 12:3; 25:9
r Ac 23:35; 25:14

25:1
s Ac 8:40

25:2
t ver 15; Ac 24:1

25:4
u Ac 24:23

25:6
v ver 17

25:7
w Mk 15:3; Lk 23:2, 10; Ac 24:5,6
x Ac 24:13

25:8
y Ac 6:13; 24:12; 28:17

25:9
z Ac 24:27 a ver 20

25:11
b ver 21,25; Ac 26:32; 28:19

25:13
c Ac 8:40

25:14
d Ac 24:27

25:15
e ver 2; Ac 24:1

Acts 25:1–12

The Roman justice system had served Paul well under Gallio (18:14–16) but couldn't operate for his good in Caesarea because of the influence of powerful locals. Paul must have felt this problem wouldn't be as serious in Rome. Besides, the Lord had told him he would testify there (23:11).

Roman law was a good system Christians used for protection, yet officials were reluctant to antagonize their constituency. Luke used the word *favor* three times (24:27; 25:3,9): Once the Jewish leaders asked for a favor; twice the Roman officials granted them one. Paul was forced to look for a more promising climate for a fair trial. Felix must have been relieved by Paul's appeal to Caesar; he could wash his hands of an awkward case.

In what ways have you as a Christian been involved with the legal system? Regardless of your role or position, do you feel justice was served? Even the best legal system is administered by fallible—and fallen—individuals. Leadership in such a system is an important Christian calling, and those who have responded deserve the support and encouragement of the Christian community. With the emergence of numerous new nations in the past decades, many Christians have been involved in writing constitutions and formulating laws.

Acts 25:13–22

The "king Agrippa" here was Herod Agrippa II, son of Herod Agrippa I (see Acts 12). Paul acknowledged that Agrippa was "well acquainted with all the Jewish customs and controversies" (26:3). Romans would naturally have consulted him on religious matters.

Festus was at a loss to interpret the accusations against Paul, stemming, as they did, from Paul's claim that, in Festus's words, "a dead man named Jesus" was in fact alive. Both Agrippa and Festus were curious about the case, possibly lured by its entertainment value. Jesus' crucifixion and resurrection were in Paul's day "foolishness to [many] Gentiles."

charges.[f] 17When they came here with me, I did not delay the case, but convened the court the next day and ordered the man to be brought in.[g] 18When his accusers got up to speak, they did not charge him with any of the crimes I had expected. 19Instead, they had some points of dispute[h] with him about their own religion[i] and about a dead man named Jesus who Paul claimed was alive. 20I was at a loss how to investigate such matters; so I asked if he would be willing to go to Jerusalem and stand trial there on these charges.[j] 21When Paul made his appeal to be held over for the Emperor's decision, I ordered him held until I could send him to Caesar."[k]

22Then Agrippa said to Festus, "I would like to hear this man myself."

He replied, "Tomorrow you will hear him."[l]

Paul Before Agrippa

23The next day Agrippa and Bernice[m] came with great pomp and entered the audience room with the high ranking officers and the leading men of the city. At the command of Festus, Paul was brought in. 24Festus said: "King Agrippa, and all who are present with us, you see this man! The whole Jewish community[n] has petitioned me about him in Jerusalem and here in Caesarea, shouting that he ought not to live any longer.[o] 25I found he had done nothing deserving of death,[p] but because he made his appeal to the Emperor[q] I decided to send him to Rome. 26But I have nothing definite to write to His Majesty about him. Therefore I have brought him before all of you, and especially before you, King Agrippa, so that as a result of this investigation I may have something to write. 27For I think it is unreasonable to send on a prisoner without specifying the charges against him."

26 Then Agrippa said to Paul, "You have permission to speak for yourself."[r] So Paul motioned with his hand and began his defense: 2"King Agrippa, I consider myself fortunate to stand before you today as I make my defense against all the accusations of the Jews, 3and especially so because you are well acquainted with all the Jewish customs[s] and controversies.[t] Therefore, I beg you to listen to me patiently.

4"The Jews all know the way I have lived ever since I was a child,[u] from the beginning of my life in my own country, and also in Jerusalem. 5They have known me for a long time[v] and can testify, if they are willing, that according to the strictest sect of our religion, I lived as a Pharisee.[w] 6And now it is because of my hope[x] in what God has promised our fathers[y] that I am on trial today. 7This is the promise our twelve tribes[z] are hoping to see fulfilled as they earnestly serve God day and night.[a] O king, it is because of this hope that the Jews are accusing me.[b] 8Why should any of you consider it incredible that God raises the dead?[c]

9"I too was convinced[d] that I ought to do all that was possible to oppose[e] the name of Jesus of Nazareth.[f] 10And that is just what I did in Jerusalem. On the authority of the chief priests I put many of the saints[g] in prison,[h] and when they were

25:16 [f] ver 4,5; Ac 23:30
25:17 [g] ver 6,10
25:19 [h] Ac 18:15; 23:29 [i] Ac 17:22
25:20 [j] ver 9
25:21 [k] ver 11,12
25:22 [l] Ac 9:15
25:23 [m] ver 13; Ac 26:30
25:24 [n] ver 2,3,7 [o] Ac 22:22
25:25 [p] Ac 23:9 [q] ver 11
26:1 [r] Ac 9:15; 25:22
26:3 [s] ver 7; Ac 6:14 [t] Ac 25:19
26:4 [u] Gal 1:13,14; Php 3:5
26:5 [v] Ac 22:3 [w] Ac 23:6; Php 3:5
26:6 [x] Ac 23:6; 24:15; 28:20 [y] Ac 13:32; Ro 15:8
26:7 [z] Jas 1:1 [a] 1Th 3:10; 1Ti 5:5 [b] ver 2
26:8 [c] Ac 23:6
26:9 [d] 1Ti 1:13 [e] Jn 16:2 [f] Jn 15:21
26:10 [g] Ac 9:13 [h] Ac 8:3; 9:2,14,21

Jesus' resurrection victory is pivotal to the Christian faith, yet in our practical world people find it hard to visualize how such an event (even if they acknowledge it did occur) could affect their lives. The answer to today's moral and ethical poverty isn't more instruction on how to live. Rather, we need the power of Christ's new creation pouring through our lives and transforming our character, values, and behavior. The gospel isn't just words and ideas, but the power of grace expressed in love. Only this will authenticate the miracle of the resurrection before a skeptical world.

Acts 25:23—26:32

Paul zeroed in on Agrippa with a direct challenge: "Do you believe the prophets?" (26:27). As an expert on Jewish Scripture, this king knew what Paul was talking about. But he couldn't afford to make connections between what he knew and what Paul was saying

because then he would be forced to make a decision about the gospel. His choice? To brush off the challenge with a cagey comeback.

God's work in the world includes both divine and human activity. He's engaged in the entire process, calling, commissioning, equipping, and protecting his ambassadors. We have the privilege of obediently participating in his work.

Some Christians, appealing to God's wisdom being higher than ours (Isa. 55:8–9), feel we should avoid using reason in approaching people for Christ. Yet we are called to love God with our minds, as well as with our hearts and strength. Thus we may legitimately appeal to logic as we discuss spiritual matters: "Come now, let us reason together" invited Isaiah (Isa. 1:18). Has the use of reason been effective in your life of faith and your communication of the gospel to others?

26:10
i Ac 22:20
26:11
j Mt 10:17

put to death, I cast my vote against them. *i* **11**Many a time I went from one synagogue to another to have them punished, *j* and I tried to force them to blaspheme. In my obsession against them, I even went to foreign cities to persecute them.

12"On one of these journeys I was going to Damascus with the authority and commission of the chief priests. **13**About noon, O king, as I was on the road, I saw a light from heaven, brighter than the sun, blazing around me and my companions.

26:14
k Ac 9:7

14We all fell to the ground, and I heard a voice *k* saying to me in Aramaic, *a* 'Saul, Saul, why do you persecute me? It is hard for you to kick against the goads.'

15"Then I asked, 'Who are you, Lord?'

" 'I am Jesus, whom you are persecuting,' the Lord replied. **16**'Now get up and

26:16
l Eze 2:1; Da 10:11
m Ac 22:14,15
26:17
n Jer 1:8,19
o Ac 9:15
26:18
p Isa 35:5
q Isa 42:7,16;
Eph 5:8; Col 1:13;
1Pe 2:9 *r* Lk 24:47;
Ac 2:38
s Ac 20:21,32
26:20
t Ac 9:19-25
u Ac 9:26-29;
22:17-20 *v* Ac 9:15;
13:46 *w* Ac 3:19
x Mt 3:8; Lk 3:8
26:21
y Ac 21:27,30
z Ac 21:31
26:22
a Lk 24:27,44;
Ac 10:43; 24:14
26:23
b 1Co 15:20,23;
Col 1:18; Rev 1:5
c Lk 2:32
26:24
d Jn 10:20;
1Co 4:10 *e* Jn 7:15
26:25
f Ac 23:26
26:26
g ver 3

stand on your feet. *l* I have appeared to you to appoint you as a servant and as a witness of what you have seen of me and what I will show you. *m* **17**I will rescue you *n* from your own people and from the Gentiles. *o* I am sending you to them **18**to open their eyes *p* and turn them from darkness to light, *q* and from the power of Satan to God, so that they may receive forgiveness of sins *r* and a place among those who are sanctified by faith in me.' *s*

19"So then, King Agrippa, I was not disobedient to the vision from heaven. **20**First to those in Damascus, *t* then to those in Jerusalem *u* and in all Judea, and to the Gentiles *v* also, I preached that they should repent *w* and turn to God and prove their repentance by their deeds. *x* **21**That is why the Jews seized me *y* in the temple courts and tried to kill me. *z* **22**But I have had God's help to this very day, and so I stand here and testify to small and great alike. I am saying nothing beyond what the prophets and Moses said would happen *a*— **23**that the Christ *b* would suffer and, as the first to rise from the dead, *b* would proclaim light to his own people and to the Gentiles." *c*

24At this point Festus interrupted Paul's defense. "You are out of your mind, *d* Paul!" he shouted. "Your great learning *e* is driving you insane."

25"I am not insane, most excellent *f* Festus," Paul replied. "What I am saying is true and reasonable. **26**The king is familiar with these things, *g* and I can speak freely to him. I am convinced that none of this has escaped his notice, because it was not done in a corner. **27**King Agrippa, do you believe the prophets? I know you do."

26:28
h Ac 11:26

28Then Agrippa said to Paul, "Do you think that in such a short time you can persuade me to be a Christian?" *h*

26:29
i Ac 21:33
26:30
j Ac 25:23

29Paul replied, "Short time or long—I pray God that not only you but all who are listening to me today may become what I am, except for these chains." *i*

30The king rose, and with him the governor and Bernice *j* and those sitting with them. **31**They left the room, and while talking with one another, they said, "This man is not doing anything that deserves death or imprisonment." *k*

26:31
k Ac 23:9
26:32
l Ac 28:18
m Ac 25:11

32Agrippa said to Festus, "This man could have been set free *l* if he had not appealed to Caesar." *m*

Paul Sails for Rome

27:1
n Ac 16:10
o Ac 18:2; 25:12,25
p Ac 10:1

27 When it was decided that we *n* would sail for Italy, *o* Paul and some other prisoners were handed over to a centurion named Julius, who belonged to the Imperial Regiment. *p* **2**We boarded a ship from Adramyttium about to sail for ports along the coast of the province of Asia, *q* and we put out to sea. Aristarchus, *r* a Macedonian *s* from Thessalonica, *t* was with us.

27:2
q Ac 2:9 *r* Ac 19:29
s Ac 16:9 *t* Ac 17:1

27:3
u Mt 11:21 *v* ver 43
w Ac 24:23; 28:16

3The next day we landed at Sidon; *u* and Julius, in kindness to Paul, *v* allowed him to go to his friends so they might provide for his needs. *w* **4**From there we put out

---

a 14 Or *Hebrew*   *b* 23 Or *Messiah*

Acts 27:1–12

📖 A helpful resource for studying this passage is a book written more than a century ago by James Smith, *The Voyage and Shipwreck of St. Paul.* An experienced yachtsman and classical scholar, Smith verified the accuracy of Luke's account of the voyage, commenting that "no sailor would have written in a style so little like that

of a sailor; no man not a sailor could have written a narrative of a sea voyage so consistent in all its parts, unless from actual observation."

It's surprising to find 60 verses (27:1—28:16) devoted to a journey in a historical/theological book. The writing is so intense we almost feel we are there. This gripping account demonstrates Acts' historical reliability.

to sea again and passed to the lee of Cyprus because the winds were against us.[x] [5]When we had sailed across the open sea off the coast of Cilicia[y] and Pamphylia, we landed at Myra in Lycia. [6]There the centurion found an Alexandrian ship[z] sailing for Italy[a] and put us on board. [7]We made slow headway for many days and had difficulty arriving off Cnidus. When the wind did not allow us to hold our course,[b] we sailed to the lee of Crete,[c] opposite Salmone. [8]We moved along the coast with difficulty and came to a place called Fair Havens, near the town of Lasea.

[9]Much time had been lost, and sailing had already become dangerous because by now it was after the Fast.[a][d] So Paul warned them, [10]"Men, I can see that our voyage is going to be disastrous and bring great loss to ship and cargo, and to our own lives also."[e] [11]But the centurion, instead of listening to what Paul said, followed the advice of the pilot and of the owner of the ship. [12]Since the harbor was unsuitable to winter in, the majority decided that we should sail on, hoping to reach Phoenix and winter there. This was a harbor in Crete, facing both southwest and northwest.

The Storm

[13]When a gentle south wind began to blow, they thought they had obtained what they wanted; so they weighed anchor and sailed along the shore of Crete. [14]Before very long, a wind of hurricane force,[f] called the "northeaster," swept down from the island. [15]The ship was caught by the storm and could not head into the wind; so we gave way to it and were driven along. [16]As we passed to the lee of a small island called Cauda, we were hardly able to make the lifeboat secure. [17]When the men had hoisted it aboard, they passed ropes under the ship itself to hold it together. Fearing that they would run aground[g] on the sandbars of Syrtis, they lowered the sea anchor and let the ship be driven along. [18]We took such a violent battering from the storm that the next day they began to throw the cargo overboard.[h] [19]On the third day, they threw the ship's tackle overboard with their own hands. [20]When neither sun nor stars appeared for many days and the storm continued raging, we finally gave up all hope of being saved.

[21]After the men had gone a long time without food, Paul stood up before them and said: "Men, you should have taken my advice[i] not to sail from Crete;[j] then you would have spared yourselves this damage and loss. [22]But now I urge you to keep up your courage,[k] because not one of you will be lost; only the ship will be destroyed. [23]Last night an angel[l] of the God whose I am and whom I serve[m] stood beside me[n] [24]and said, 'Do not be afraid, Paul. You must stand trial before Caesar;[o] and God has graciously given you the lives of all who sail with you.'[p] [25]So keep up your courage,[q] men, for I have faith in God that it will happen just as he told me.[r] [26]Nevertheless, we must run aground[s] on some island."[t]

The Shipwreck

[27]On the fourteenth night we were still being driven across the Adriatic[b] Sea, when about midnight the sailors sensed they were approaching land. [28]They took

---

[a] 9 That is, the Day of Atonement (Yom Kippur)   [b] 27 In ancient times the name referred to an area extending well south of Italy.

Cross references

27:4
[x] ver 7
27:5
[y] Ac 6:9
27:6
[z] Ac 28:11 [a] ver 1
27:7
[b] ver 4
[c] ver 12,13,21

27:9
[d] Lev 16:29-31; 23:27-29; Nu 29:7

27:10
[e] ver 21

27:14
[f] Mk 4:37

27:17
[g] ver 26,39

27:18
[h] ver 19,38; Jnh 1:5

27:21
[i] ver 10 [j] ver 7

27:22
[k] ver 25,36
27:23
[l] Ac 5:19 [m] Ro 1:9 [n] Ac 18:9; 23:11; 2Ti 4:17
27:24
[o] Ac 23:11 [p] ver 44
27:25
[q] ver 22,36
[r] Ro 4:20,21
27:26
[s] ver 17,39
[t] Ac 28:1

📖 Paul and his team would have avoided the storm had the ship's officers heeded his words of wisdom. Christ doesn't immunize Christians from problems others in the world also face. Sometimes he miraculously delivers us; sometimes he gives us courage to endure disaster. Have you thanked him for performing miracles in your life, and for his grace that provided endurance when a miracle wasn't his choice (2 Cor. 12:7–10)?

Acts 27:13–26

🔄 We have witnessed again and again in Acts God working out his purposes in the face of human sinfulness. Here he worked despite nature's unpredictability and hu-

man errors in judgment (vv. 12,14). God spoke to Paul at a crucial time so he could maintain his courage and trust in God's sovereignty when others were panicking.

📖 What does a positive outlook in hard times have to do with courage? What role does your faith play? The verb here translated "to keep up [one's] courage" appears only three times in the New Testament—twice here and again in James 5:13 (there meaning "to be happy"). The word carries the idea of being in good spirits. Even as a prisoner Paul didn't hesitate to make known his faith in God or to demonstrate by word and action its influence on his perspective.

soundings and found that the water was a hundred and twenty feet[a] deep. A short time later they took soundings again and found it was ninety feet[b] deep. 29Fearing that we would be dashed against the rocks, they dropped four anchors from the stern and prayed for daylight. 30In an attempt to escape from the ship, the sailors let the lifeboat[u] down into the sea, pretending they were going to lower some anchors from the bow. 31Then Paul said to the centurion and the soldiers, "Unless these men stay with the ship, you cannot be saved."[v] 32So the soldiers cut the ropes that held the lifeboat and let it fall away.

33Just before dawn Paul urged them all to eat. "For the last fourteen days," he said, "you have been in constant suspense and have gone without food—you haven't eaten anything. 34Now I urge you to take some food. You need it to survive. Not one of you will lose a single hair from his head."[w] 35After he said this, he took some bread and gave thanks to God in front of them all. Then he broke it[x] and began to eat. 36They were all encouraged[y] and ate some food themselves. 37Altogether there were 276 of us on board. 38When they had eaten as much as they wanted, they lightened the ship by throwing the grain into the sea.[z]

39When daylight came, they did not recognize the land, but they saw a bay with a sandy beach,[a] where they decided to run the ship aground if they could. 40Cutting loose the anchors,[b] they left them in the sea and at the same time untied the ropes that held the rudders. Then they hoisted the foresail to the wind and made for the beach. 41But the ship struck a sandbar and ran aground. The bow stuck fast and would not move, and the stern was broken to pieces by the pounding of the surf.[c]

42The soldiers planned to kill the prisoners to prevent any of them from swimming away and escaping. 43But the centurion wanted to spare Paul's life[d] and kept them from carrying out their plan. He ordered those who could swim to jump overboard first and get to land. 44The rest were to get there on planks or on pieces of the ship. In this way everyone reached land in safety.[e]

Ashore on Malta

28 Once safely on shore, we[f] found out that the island[g] was called Malta. 2The islanders showed us unusual kindness. They built a fire and welcomed us all because it was raining and cold. 3Paul gathered a pile of brushwood and, as he put it on the fire, a viper, driven out by the heat, fastened itself on his hand. 4When the islanders saw the snake hanging from his hand,[h] they said to each other, "This man must be a murderer; for though he escaped from the sea, Justice has not allowed him to live."[i] 5But Paul shook the snake off into the fire and suffered no ill effects.[j] 6The people expected him to swell up or suddenly fall dead, but after waiting a long time and seeing nothing unusual happen to him, they changed their minds and said he was a god.[k]

7There was an estate nearby that belonged to Publius, the chief official of the is-

[a] 28 Greek twenty orguias (about 37 meters)   [b] 28 Greek fifteen orguias (about 27 meters)

Acts 27:27–44
Luke presented Paul as an example of leadership in tough circumstances. Though a prisoner, Paul rose to the occasion and gradually became more and more influential as a leader. Paul was an agent of hope, a prisoner who could have taken advantage of a confusing situation but chose instead to be a servant.

When have your actions, with or without words, raised someone else's spirits in a bleak situation? Paul invited people to picnic in the midst of the storm. One of the most powerful messages we can give the world is that because God is sovereign, a gloom-and-doom mentality is neither necessary nor appropriate. Through constructive and meaningful actions, Christians can influence society by inspiring hope in others.

Acts 28:1–10
The assumption that Paul was a murderer was typical of people who see all misfortune as punishment. When nothing happened to him following the snake bite, the same superstition led them to change their verdict: Far from being considered a criminal, Paul was proclaimed a god!

A servant lifestyle characterized Paul's ministry—whether he was working for his own food so as not to be a burden on others (see 20:17-35) or, as now, by gathering firewood. Our deeds don't have to be unusual or outstanding. Our willingness to serve in little things opens doors in ways we might never dream.

land. He welcomed us to his home and for three days entertained us hospitably. [8]His father was sick in bed, suffering from fever and dysentery. Paul went in to see him and, after prayer,[l] placed his hands on him and healed him.[m] [9]When this had happened, the rest of the sick on the island came and were cured. [10]They honored us in many ways and when we were ready to sail, they furnished us with the supplies we needed.

Arrival at Rome

[11]After three months we put out to sea in a ship that had wintered in the island. It was an Alexandrian ship[n] with the figurehead of the twin gods Castor and Pollux. [12]We put in at Syracuse and stayed there three days. [13]From there we set sail and arrived at Rhegium. The next day the south wind came up, and on the following day we reached Puteoli. [14]There we found some brothers[o] who invited us to spend a week with them. And so we came to Rome. [15]The brothers[p] there had heard that we were coming, and they traveled as far as the Forum of Appius and the Three Taverns to meet us. At the sight of these men Paul thanked God and was encouraged. [16]When we got to Rome, Paul was allowed to live by himself, with a soldier to guard him.[q]

Paul Preaches at Rome Under Guard

[17]Three days later he called together the leaders of the Jews.[r] When they had assembled, Paul said to them: "My brothers,[s] although I have done nothing against our people[t] or against the customs of our ancestors,[u] I was arrested in Jerusalem and handed over to the Romans. [18]They examined me[v] and wanted to release me,[w] because I was not guilty of any crime deserving death.[x] [19]But when the Jews objected, I was compelled to appeal to Caesar[y]—not that I had any charge to bring against my own people. [20]For this reason I have asked to see you and talk with you. It is because of the hope of Israel[z] that I am bound with this chain."[a]

[21]They replied, "We have not received any letters from Judea concerning you, and none of the brothers[b] who have come from there has reported or said anything bad about you. [22]But we want to hear what your views are, for we know that people everywhere are talking against this sect."[c]

[23]They arranged to meet Paul on a certain day, and came in even larger numbers to the place where he was staying. From morning till evening he explained and declared to them the kingdom of God[d] and tried to convince them about Jesus[e] from the Law of Moses and from the Prophets.[f] [24]Some were convinced by what he said, but others would not believe.[g] [25]They disagreed among themselves and began to leave after Paul had made this final statement: "The Holy Spirit spoke the truth to your forefathers when he said through Isaiah the prophet:

28:8 l Jas 5:14,15 m Ac 9:40

28:11 n Ac 27:6

28:14 o Ac 1:16
28:15 p Ac 1:16

28:16 q Ac 24:23; 27:3

28:17 r Ac 25:2 s Ac 22:5 t Ac 25:8 u Ac 6:14

28:18 v Ac 22:24 w Ac 26:31,32 x Ac 23:9
28:19 y Ac 25:11
28:20 z Ac 26:6,7 a Ac 21:33

28:21 b Ac 22:5

28:22 c Ac 24:5,14

28:23 d Ac 19:8 e Ac 17:3 f Ac 8:35
28:24 g Ac 14:4

Acts 28:11–16

Paul must have felt drained as he approached the end of his trip on foot. When he saw the Roman Christians who had trekked out to meet him, he thanked God and was encouraged. Their own long walk from Rome was a sacrificial expression of kindness and good will. Similarly, when we "go out of our way" to welcome, affirm, or assist fellow believers, our actions cheer them.

Christians who have boldly and publicly stood for Christ testify how support from fellow Christians has encouraged them. A note or card of appreciation, a dinner invitation, an offer of assistance, or a simple pat on the back may be just what a person involved in a lonely battle for God needs to overcome discouragement. Each of us can be Christ's hands and feet to fellow believers. Who might need you? What could you do? Where might some small act of love be appreciated?

Acts 28:17–31

Luke ended Acts abruptly, summarizing what had happened throughout this second and final section of the book, focusing on the impact of the gospel on Gentiles (11:19—28:31). As we turn the last page, we're left with an unforgettable glimpse of Paul chained to a soldier, busily "unchaining" the gospel as he shared it with the many who came to him.

Does the Spirit want to communicate to us through Luke's conclusion something about what we're to do with the gospel? Former U.S. Senate Chaplain Lloyd Ogilvie thought so: "The abrupt ending leaves us with the challenge and opportunity to allow the Spirit to write the next chapter in the Book of Acts today in and through us!" An appropriate prayer at this moment might be, "What can I do for you, Lord?" What are the next sections of "the Acts of the Holy Spirit through the followers of Christ" that God wants to write based on your life?

26 " 'Go to this people and say,
   "You will be ever hearing but never understanding;
      you will be ever seeing but never perceiving."
   27 For this people's heart has become calloused;[h]
      they hardly hear with their ears,
      and they have closed their eyes.
   Otherwise they might see with their eyes,
      hear with their ears,
      understand with their hearts
   and turn, and I would heal them.'[a][i]

28:27
[h] Ps 119:70
[i] Isa 6:9,10

28:28
[j] Lk 2:30 [k] Ac 13:46

28 "Therefore I want you to know that God's salvation[j] has been sent to the Gentiles,[k] and they will listen!"[b]

30 For two whole years Paul stayed there in his own rented house and welcomed all who came to see him. 31 Boldly and without hindrance he preached the kingdom of God[l] and taught about the Lord Jesus Christ.

28:31
[l] ver 23; Mt 4:23

[a] 27 Isaiah 6:9,10   [b] 28 Some manuscripts *listen!" 29After he said this, the Jews left, arguing vigorously among themselves.*

28:30

The Ends of the Earth

The curtain closes on Acts with Paul preaching "without hindrance" in the powerful city of Rome. In a sense, the end of Acts was the prelude to the history of the Christian movement to the rest of the world. That world was complex in Paul's day. Today it's more so, with many different layers of cultures, nations, ethnic groups, and religions. A Biblical division of today's complexity might look like this:

Countries/Nations (*laos*)	Over 300
Cultures (*ethnos*)	Over 30 thousand
Languages (*glossa*)	Over 12 thousand
Individuals (*anthropos*)	Over 6 billion

INTRODUCTION TO
Romans

AUTHOR

That the apostle Paul is the author of this letter is unquestioned. The book's opening verse identifies him as such (1:1), and its closing chapter states that the letter was dictated by Paul to a secretary named Tertius (16:22).

DATE WRITTEN

Romans was probably written in A.D. 57.

ORIGINAL READERS

Paul's original readers were the believers—both Jews and Gentiles, but predominately Gentiles (1:13)—in Rome. Paul introduced himself to the Roman church—a church he hadn't personally founded—and explained why he intended to visit.

TIMELINE

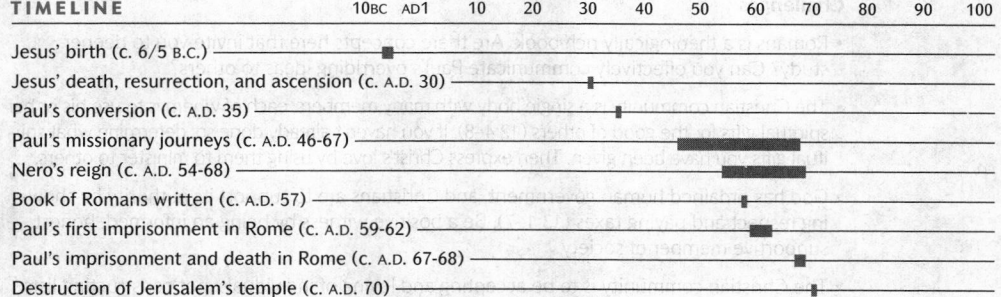

	10BC AD1	10	20	30	40	50	60	70	80	90	100
Jesus' birth (c. 6/5 B.C.)											
Jesus' death, resurrection, and ascension (c. A.D. 30)											
Paul's conversion (c. A.D. 35)											
Paul's missionary journeys (c. A.D. 46-67)											
Nero's reign (c. A.D. 54-68)											
Book of Romans written (c. A.D. 57)											
Paul's first imprisonment in Rome (c. A.D. 59-62)											
Paul's imprisonment and death in Rome (c. A.D. 67-68)											
Destruction of Jerusalem's temple (c. A.D. 70)											

THEMES

In order to gain credibility with and assistance from the church in Rome, it was essential that Paul provide its members with his credentials and a summary of his teachings. His focus centered on the following:

1. *God's faithfulness.* A central theme of Romans is God's covenant faithfulness. His fidelity to his promise to Abraham is revealed in salvation on the basis of faith. Both Jews and Gentiles find righteousness before God through faith in Jesus (3:21–26).

2. *Righteousness.* Neither Jew nor Gentile is righteous before God; each, apart from Christ, is under his wrath (2:1—3:20). But there is Good News available to everyone: Through Jesus' death, God credits *his own* righteousness to all who believe and rely on his promise of salvation in Jesus Christ (3:21—5:21). This righteousness is a gift—not earned by human effort or through obedience to Old Testament law. Through their union with Jesus, the power of the Holy Spirit still enables Christians to live righteous lives here and now (6:1—8:39).

3. *Reconciliation.* Romans is marked by Paul's concern for racial reconciliation and cross-cultural sensitivity. His advice on resolving internal conflicts in the church (14:1—15:6) lifted up Christ's attitude as the example for our own (15:1–6). Paul reiterated Jesus' teaching that love of neighbor fulfills the law's intent (13:8–10). His exhortation on treatment of enemies (12:17–21) was intended to turn hostility into friendship, in the hope that loving responses would burn away hatred.

FAITH IN ACTION

The pages of Romans contain life lessons and role models of faith—people who challenge believers to put faith in action.

Role Models

• PAUL spent much of his life working for racial reconciliation. How can you be used by God to work toward this goal in your community?

• PHOEBE (16:1–2) worked tirelessly as a "servant of the church." To what ministry is God calling you in your local church?

• SAINTS OF MACEDONIA AND ACHAIA (15:25–27) contributed to the needs of impoverished believers in Jerusalem. Do you give to help the poor?

• PRISCILLA AND AQUILA (16:3–4) risked their lives for the gospel. Is God directing you to engage in a ministry that might jeopardize your very life? How can you be encouraged by the example of this godly couple?

• TERTIUS (16:22) wrote out Paul's letter to the Romans. Is there someone you can help?

• GAIUS (16:23) provided hospitality to Tertius and others in the church. When was the last time you offered hospitality to assist fellow church members?

Challenges

• Romans is a theologically rich book. Are there concepts here that invite you to deeper study? Can you effectively communicate Paul's overriding ideas to others?

• The Christian community is a single body with many members, each of whom is to use his or her spiritual gifts for the good of others (12:4–8). If you haven't already done so, determine what spiritual gifts you have been given. Then express Christ's love by using them to minister to others.

• God has ordained human government, and Christians are to support its authority by showing respect and paying taxes (13:1–7). Be a positive witness by being an informed, honest, supportive member of society.

• The Christian community is to be accepting and loving of individuals, not constructing lists of "dos and don'ts" by which to judge one another (14:1–23). Examine your attitudes toward fellow believers, and determine to express love, not judgment.

• Paul devoted a whole section of this letter to talking about people (ch. 16). How important are the people in your life—your friends, family, fellowship body? How about sending "thank you" notes to those people who have in some special way helped or influenced your Christian journey?

OUTLINE

   I. Introduction (1:1–15)
  II. Theme: Righteousness From God (1:16–17)
 III. The Unrighteousness of All Humankind (1:18—3:20)
 IV. Justification (3:21—5:21)
     A. Righteousness Comes Only Through Christ (3:21–26)
     B. Righteousness Is Received by Faith (3:27—4:25)
     C. Peace and Joy Are Fruits of Righteousness (5:1–11)
     D. Death Through Adam, Life Through Christ (5:12–21)

V. Sanctification (6–8)
   A. Slaves to Sin or Slaves to Righteousness (6)
   B. The Struggle With Sin (7)
   C. The Spirit-Empowered Life (8)
VI. God's Righteousness Vindicated: The Problem of Israel's Rejection (9–11)
   A. God's Sovereign Choice (9:1–29)
   B. Israel's Unbelief (9:30—10:21)
   C. The Remnant and the Ingrafted Branches (11)
VII. Righteousness Practiced (12:1—15:13)
VIII. Conclusion (15:14—16:27)

1 Paul, a servant of Christ Jesus, called to be an apostle[a] and set apart[b] for the gospel of God[c]— [2]the gospel he promised beforehand through his prophets in the Holy Scriptures[d] [3]regarding his Son, who as to his human nature[e] was a descendant of David, [4]and who through the Spirit[a] of holiness was declared with power to be the Son of God[b] by his resurrection from the dead: Jesus Christ our Lord. [5]Through him and for his name's sake, we received grace and apostleship to call people from among all the Gentiles[f] to the obedience that comes from faith. [g] [6]And you also are among those who are called to belong to Jesus Christ. [h]

1:1 *a* 1Co 1:1 *b* Ac 9:15 *c* 2Co 11:7
1:2 *d* Gal 3:8
1:3 *e* Jn 1:14
1:5 *f* Ac 9:15 *g* Ac 6:7
1:6 *h* Rev 17:14
1:7 *i* Ro 8:39 *j* 1Co 1:3

[7]To all in Rome who are loved by God[i] and called to be saints:

Grace and peace to you from God our Father and from the Lord Jesus Christ.[j]

Paul's Longing to Visit Rome

[8]First, I thank my God through Jesus Christ for all of you, [k] because your faith is being reported all over the world.[l] [9]God, whom I serve[m] with my whole heart in preaching the gospel of his Son, is my witness[n] how constantly I remember you [10]in my prayers at all times; and I pray that now at last by God's will the way may be opened for me to come to you. [o]

1:8 *k* 1Co 1:4 *l* Ro 16:19
1:9 *m* 2Ti 1:3 *n* Php 1:8
1:10 *o* Ro 15:32
1:11 *p* Ro 15:23

[11]I long to see you[p] so that I may impart to you some spiritual gift to make you strong— [12]that is, that you and I may be mutually encouraged by each other's faith. [13]I do not

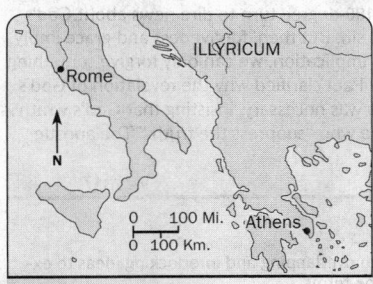

The Church in Rome (1:7)

Then: Rome, the center of the Roman Empire, had a population of 650,000.

Now: The capital of Italy, Rome is home to three million people. The Vatican, the papal headquarters of the Roman Catholic Church, is located there.

---

a 4 Or *who as to his spirit*   *b* 4 Or *was appointed to be the Son of God with power*

Romans 1:1–7

Ancient letters typically began with a simple identification of the sender, the recipients, and a greeting. New Testament letters follow this pattern, often adding distinctly Christian touches. But in no other New Testament letter does the author elaborate as much as Paul did in Romans. Maybe because he was writing to a church he had never visited, Paul spent six verses identifying himself before mentioning his audience and extending them a greeting.

In verse 5 Paul connected God's saving grace and his own apostolic calling. Our ability to serve God and his people in specific ways is a product of his unmerited favor toward us. Grace is God loving us so much in

Jesus Christ that he has accepted us as we are. But it's also God loving us too much to leave us that way. Thus, Paul also connected grace with obedience. He himself was called to bring about the obedience that comes from faith.

Romans 1:8–17

As Paul reflected on the ministry he hoped to have in Rome, he naturally turned his attention to his plans for such a visit. He wanted the Romans to understand that his failure to visit them previously had been due to lack of opportunity. Paul's desire to preach in Rome was motivated not by a desire to expand his personal "territory" but by his deep sense of obligation that all people encounter the gospel.

1:13
q Ro 15:22,23
1:14
r 1Co 9:16
1:15
s Ro 15:20
1:16
t 2Ti 1:8 *u* 1Co 1:18
v Ac 3:26 *w* Ro 2:9,
10
1:17
x Ro 3:21
y Hab 2:4;
Gal 3:11;
Heb 10:38

want you to be unaware, brothers, that I planned many times to come to you (but have been prevented from doing so until now) *q* in order that I might have a harvest among you, just as I have had among the other Gentiles.

¹⁴I am obligated *r* both to Greeks and non-Greeks, both to the wise and the foolish. ¹⁵That is why I am so eager to preach the gospel also to you who are at Rome. *s*

¹⁶I am not ashamed of the gospel, *t* because it is the power of God *u* for the salvation of everyone who believes: first for the Jew, *v* then for the Gentile. *w* ¹⁷For in the gospel a righteousness from God is revealed, *x* a righteousness that is by faith from first to last, *a* just as it is written: "The righteous will live by faith." *b y*

God's Wrath Against Mankind

1:18
z Eph 5:6; Col 3:6

¹⁸The wrath of God *z* is being revealed from heaven against all the godlessness and wickedness of men who suppress the truth by their wickedness, ¹⁹since what may

---

a 17 Or *is from faith to faith*   *b 17* Hab. 2:4

Paul's summary of the gospel in verses 16–17 is one of the most concise and profound in Scripture. These verses transformed the life of the reformer Martin Luther (1483–1546). Our righteousness is a gift from God in Jesus Christ through faith, not something we can create or establish through our own merit.

The gospel isn't just true ideas, but life-transforming power. That transformation is rooted in the truth that our lives are made acceptable to God because of Jesus Christ, not because of our own performance or accomplishments. In our performance-evaluating society this is staggering news. We may be able to accept that we are saved by grace through faith. But we tend to live by a

non-Biblical formula: saved by grace, justified by works. When the truth that we are justified by *grace through faith* sinks into our hearts, we can't help but feel the same joyous obligation to tell all people the Good News.

Romans 1:18–32

Verse 18 comes as a surprise. Paul had just announced his theme: the gospel of God's saving grace. He now made a 180-degree turn to dire news about God's wrath against sin. But then, forgiveness and grace imply judgment. By implication, we can only forgive something that is wrong. Paul clarified why the revelation of God's righteousness was necessary, insisting that God's wrath falls on people who "suppress the truth." The apostle

1:17

Theological Terms in Romans

Romans is Paul's most theologically rich letter. Paul taught the following seven overlapping and interlocking ideas to explain human relationships with God. Paul often used a contrast to illustrate the terms.

Term	Meaning	Text	Contrast
1. Justification	The declaration of being right with, or righteous before, God	"The result of one act of righteousness was justification that brings life for all men" (Rom. 5:12–21).	Adam/Jesus
2. Faith	A constant outlook of trust toward God	"The righteous will live by faith" (Rom. 1:16–17).	Unbelief/Faith
3. Sin	A wrong relationship with God; a lack of faith in God; a violation of God's law	"All have sinned and fall short of the glory of God" (Rom. 3:23).	Flesh/Spirit
4. Grace	God's undeserved favor toward sinful humans	"Through [Christ] we have gained access by faith into this grace in which we now stand" (Rom 5:2–8).	Law/Grace
5. Salvation	Transformation of an individual's sinful nature; deliverance from the power and effects of sin; an eternal relationship with God	"It is with your heart that you believe and are justified, and it is with your mouth that you confess and are saved" (Rom. 10:10).	Sin/Salvation
6. Election	God's choice to bring individuals to salvation through faith in Jesus Christ	"I will have mercy on whom I have mercy" (Rom. 9:14–24).	Death/Life
7. Righteousness	Being in a right relationship with God	"This righteousness from God comes through faith in Jesus Christ to all who believe" (Rom. 3:22; cf. 9:26).	Disobedience/Obedience

be known about God is plain to them, because God has made it plain to them. [a]
20For since the creation of the world God's invisible qualities—his eternal power and divine nature—have been clearly seen, being understood from what has been made, [b] so that men are without excuse.

21For although they knew God, they neither glorified him as God nor gave thanks to him, but their thinking became futile and their foolish hearts were darkened. [c] 22Although they claimed to be wise, they became fools [d] 23and exchanged the glory of the immortal God for images [e] made to look like mortal man and birds and animals and reptiles.

24Therefore God gave them over [f] in the sinful desires of their hearts to sexual impurity for the degrading of their bodies with one another. [g] 25They exchanged the truth of God for a lie, [h] and worshiped and served created things [i] rather than the Creator—who is forever praised. [j] Amen.

26Because of this, God gave them over [k] to shameful lusts. [l] Even their women exchanged natural relations for unnatural ones. [m] 27In the same way the men also abandoned natural relations with women and were inflamed with lust for one another. Men committed indecent acts with other men, and received in themselves the due penalty for their perversion. [n]

28Furthermore, since they did not think it worthwhile to retain the knowledge of God, he gave them over [o] to a depraved mind, to do what ought not to be done. 29They have become filled with every kind of wickedness, evil, greed and depravity. They are full of envy, murder, strife, deceit and malice. They are gossips, [p] 30slanderers, God-haters, insolent, arrogant and boastful; they invent ways of doing evil; they disobey their parents; [q] 31they are senseless, faithless, heartless, [r] ruthless. 32Although they know God's righteous decree that those who do such things deserve death, [s] they not only continue to do these very things but also approve [t] of those who practice them.

God's Righteous Judgment

2 You, therefore, have no excuse, [u] you who pass judgment on someone else, for at whatever point you judge the other, you are condemning yourself, because you who pass judgment do the same things. [v] 2Now we know that God's judgment against those who do such things is based on truth. 3So when you, a mere man, pass judgment on them and yet do the same things, do you think you will escape God's judgment? 4Or do you show contempt for the riches [w] of his kindness, [x] tolerance [y] and patience, [z] not realizing that God's kindness leads you toward repentance? [a]

5But because of your stubbornness and your unrepentant heart, you are storing up wrath against yourself for the day of God's wrath, when his righteous judgment [b] will be revealed. 6God "will give to each person according to what he has done." [a][c]

[a] 6 Psalm 62:12; Prov. 24:12

1:19
a Ac 14:17

1:20
b Ps 19:1-6

1:21
c Jer 2:5;
Eph 4:17,18
1:22
d 1Co 1:20,27
1:23
e Ps 106:20;
Jer 2:11; Ac 17:29
1:24
f Eph 4:19
g 1Pe 4:3
1:25
h Isa 44:20
i Jer 10:14 / Ro 9:5
1:26
k ver 24,28
l 1Th 4:5
m Lev 18:22,23

1:27
n Lev 18:22; 20:13

1:28
o ver 24,26

1:29
p 2Co 12:20

1:30
q 2Ti 3:2
1:31
r 2Ti 3:3
1:32
s Ro 6:23
t Ps 50:18;
Lk 11:48; Ac 8:1;
22:20

2:1
u Ro 1:20
v 2Sa 12:5-7;
Mt 7:1,2

2:4
w Ro 9:23; Eph 1:7,
18; 2:7 x Ro 11:22
y Ro 3:25 z Ex 34:6
a 2Pe 3:9
2:5
b Jude 6
2:6
c Ps 62:12;
Mt 16:27

---

was talking about a deliberate act. People can't suppress or hold back what they don't know, but they can and often do deny what's evident around them.

📖 God's anger isn't like the egoistic and unpredictable anger attributed to the mythic gods with whom Paul's Roman audience was familiar. Wrath is God's response to the corruption and distortion of his good creation because of sin. Two extremes are at work in the world today. Some view God as distant, remote, and unapproachable. Others, in an era of awakened "spirituality," see him as a kindly, even "harmless" being, who passively accepts all people regardless of their beliefs and behavior.

Romans 2:1–16
📖 Paul was all-inclusive in his proclamation of human guilt. No one escapes—neither Gentiles who never

knew God's law nor Jews who presumed to hold a place of religious superiority as God's "chosen" people. The Jews' possession of the law gave them no advantage. It's doing, not having, the law that counts. And when judged in terms of living according to God's law, everyone is guilty. No one except Jesus has ever lived the way God created people to live.

📖 Paul's warning about presuming on God's grace is just as relevant for us as Christians as it was for the Jews of his time. Paul leveled the playing field: All will be judged impartially by God.

Paul's idea of natural law (vv. 12–16) helps us establish a foundation for universal moral norms and positive law—law that won't be undermined by society's whims or the majority's convenience. Regardless of social conventions, everyone knows deep inside what's right. God's law is "written on their hearts" (v. 15).

2:7
d ver 10
e 1Co 15:53,54
2:8
f 2Th 2:12
2:9
g 1Pe 4:17

2:10
h ver 9
2:11
i Ac 10:34
2:12
j Ro 3:19;
1Co 9:20,21
2:13
k Jas 1:22,23,25
2:14
l Ac 10:35

2:16
m Ecc 12:14
n Ac 10:42
o Ro 16:25

2:17
p ver 23; Mic 3:11;
Ro 9:4

2:21
q Mt 23:3,4
2:22
r Ac 19:37
2:23
s ver 17
2:24
t Isa 52:5;
Eze 36:22
2:25
u Gal 5:3 v Jer 4:4
2:26
w Ro 8:4
x 1Co 7:19
2:27
y Mt 12:41,42

2:28
z Mt 3:9; Jn 8:39;
Ro 9:6,7 a Gal 6:15

2:29
b Php 3:3; Col 2:11
c Ro 7:6 d Jn 5:44;
1Co 4:5; 2Co 10:18;
1Th 2:4; 1Pe 3:4

3:2
e Dt 4:8; Ps 147:19

[7]To those who by persistence in doing good seek glory, honor [d] and immortality, [e] he will give eternal life. [8]But for those who are self-seeking and who reject the truth and follow evil, [f] there will be wrath and anger. [9]There will be trouble and distress for every human being who does evil: first for the Jew, then for the Gentile; [g] [10]but glory, honor and peace for everyone who does good: first for the Jew, then for the Gentile. [h] [11]For God does not show favoritism. [i]

[12]All who sin apart from the law will also perish apart from the law, and all who sin under the law [j] will be judged by the law. [13]For it is not those who hear the law who are righteous in God's sight, but it is those who obey [k] the law who will be declared righteous. [14](Indeed, when Gentiles, who do not have the law, do by nature things required by the law, [l] they are a law for themselves, even though they do not have the law, [15]since they show that the requirements of the law are written on their hearts, their consciences also bearing witness, and their thoughts now accusing, now even defending them.) [16]This will take place on the day when God will judge men's secrets [m] through Jesus Christ, [n] as my gospel [o] declares.

The Jews and the Law

[17]Now you, if you call yourself a Jew; if you rely on the law and brag about your relationship to God; [p] [18]if you know his will and approve of what is superior because you are instructed by the law; [19]if you are convinced that you are a guide for the blind, a light for those who are in the dark, [20]an instructor of the foolish, a teacher of infants, because you have in the law the embodiment of knowledge and truth— [21]you, then, who teach others, do you not teach yourself? You who preach against stealing, do you steal? [q] [22]You who say that people should not commit adultery, do you commit adultery? You who abhor idols, do you rob temples? [r] [23]You who brag about the law, [s] do you dishonor God by breaking the law? [24]As it is written: "God's name is blasphemed among the Gentiles because of you." [a] [t]

[25]Circumcision has value if you observe the law, [u] but if you break the law, you have become as though you had not been circumcised. [v] [26]If those who are not circumcised keep the law's requirements, [w] will they not be regarded as though they were circumcised? [x] [27]The one who is not circumcised physically and yet obeys the law will condemn you [y] who, even though you have the [b] written code and circumcision, are a lawbreaker.

[28]A man is not a Jew if he is only one outwardly, [z] nor is circumcision merely outward and physical. [a] [29]No, a man is a Jew if he is one inwardly; and circumcision is circumcision of the heart, by the Spirit, [b] not by the written code. [c] Such a man's praise is not from men, but from God. [d]

God's Faithfulness

3 What advantage, then, is there in being a Jew, or what value is there in circumcision? [2]Much in every way! First of all, they have been entrusted with the very words of God. [e]

[a] 24 Isaiah 52:5; Ezek. 36:22   [b] 27 Or who, by means of a

---

Romans 2:17–29

In criticizing his fellow Jews, Paul leveled an attack on all "nominal" faith. People who call themselves believers but don't live according to faith "[dishonor] God" and cause unbelievers to "blaspheme" his name (vv. 23–24). A true believer is determined not by birthright but by inner commitment to God and outer conformity to his will. It's easy in religious contexts to seek the praise of other members of the faith community. But all that really counts is praise from God (v. 29).

History is littered with the debris of Jewish-Christian debates and arguments. We can only share the conclusion of this former Jewish Pharisee, Paul: Jewish

people need to hear and respond to the gospel just as much as anyone else. Similarly, there may be many people who call themselves "Christians" because of culture and birth who are only so outwardly. Can you think of situations where God's name is "blasphemed" because people who call themselves Christians aren't living like it? Mahatma Gandhi was once asked what it would take for India to become Christian. His response was compelling: "All it would take is for Christians to be Christian."

Romans 3:1–8

Paul knew his argument in chapter 2 might suggest that the Jews' privileges had been revoked—and his knowledge of human nature told him that some Gentile

[3]What if some did not have faith?[f] Will their lack of faith nullify God's faithfulness?[g] [4]Not at all! Let God be true,[h] and every man a liar.[i] As it is written:

"So that you may be proved right when you speak
  and prevail when you judge."[a][j]

[5]But if our unrighteousness brings out God's righteousness more clearly, what shall we say? That God is unjust in bringing his wrath on us? (I am using a human argument.)[k] [6]Certainly not! If that were so, how could God judge the world?[l] [7]Someone might argue, "If my falsehood enhances God's truthfulness and so increases his glory,[m] why am I still condemned as a sinner?" [8]Why not say—as we are being slanderously reported as saying and as some claim that we say—"Let us do evil that good may result"?[n] Their condemnation is deserved.

No One Is Righteous

[9]What shall we conclude then? Are we any better[b]? Not at all! We have already made the charge that Jews and Gentiles alike are all under sin.[o] [10]As it is written:

"There is no one righteous, not even one;
11   there is no one who understands,
       no one who seeks God.
12 All have turned away,
       they have together become worthless;
   there is no one who does good,
       not even one."[c][p]
13 "Their throats are open graves;
       their tongues practice deceit."[d][q]
   "The poison of vipers is on their lips."[e][r]
14   "Their mouths are full of cursing and bitterness."[f][s]
15 "Their feet are swift to shed blood;
16   ruin and misery mark their ways,
17 and the way of peace they do not know."[g]
18   "There is no fear of God before their eyes."[h][t]

[19]Now we know that whatever the law says,[u] it says to those who are under the law,[v] so that every mouth may be silenced and the whole world held accountable

a [4] Psalm 51:4   b [9] Or *worse*   c [12] Psalms 14:1-3; 53:1-3; Eccles. 7:20   d [13] Psalm 5:9
e [13] Psalm 140:3   f [14] Psalm 10:7   g [17] Isaiah 59:7,8   h [18] Psalm 36:1

3:3
f Heb 4:2 g 2Ti 2:13
3:4
h Jn 3:33
i Ps 116:11
j Ps 51:4
3:5
k Ro 6:19; Gal 3:15
3:6
l Ge 18:25
3:7
m ver 4
3:8
n Ro 6:1
3:9
o ver 19,23;
Gal 3:22
3:12
p Ps 14:1-3
3:13
q Ps 5:9 r Ps 140:3
3:14
s Ps 10:7
3:18
t Ps 36:1
3:19
u Jn 10:34
v Ro 2:12

Christians would be eager to support this conclusion. So he quickly countered that line of thought. The Jews' special rights gave them no advantage over Gentiles in the judgment, but that didn't mean they had no privileges. They had no immunity from judgment. But the blessing of knowing God's Word is a double-edged sword: God promises blessing for obedience—and judgment on disobedience.

📖 The tendency of Jews in Paul's day to assume that the covenant insured them against judgment has parallels in the church. Christians do indeed have security: If we truly have faith in Christ and live as his disciples, we can be confident of appearing before him in glory. But the Word also makes clear that our eternal glory rests on a life of obedience (cf. 8:12–13). Paul warns us as believers not to so presume on the grace we have received that we fail to make every effort to live in loving obedience to Christ. What does this kind of obedience look like for you?

Romans 3:9–20
🔑 Having specified what the law *can't* do—bring

people into relationship with God—Paul went on to reveal what it *does* accomplish: Through it "we become conscious of sin." By setting before people a detailed record of God's will, the law makes them vividly aware of their failure to live as God intends.

Paul asserted that all people are "under sin," in the sense of being "under" domination or slavery. The choice isn't between freedom apart from Christ and submission to Christ. We are all slaves—either of sin or of righteousness. The human plight isn't that people commit sins or even that they are in the habit of doing so. It's that they are prisoners to sin.

📖 Many thinkers throughout history have believed that humanity's basic problem is ignorance. The solution? Knowledge. Western culture is steeped in humanism, the belief that people can improve their lot as new generations learn more. But Scripture's analysis is radically different: People, by nature (i.e., without God), are sinners—addicted to sin, imprisoned under it, unable to free themselves by anything they can do.

to God. 20Therefore no one will be declared righteous in his sight by observing the law; *w* rather, through the law we become conscious of sin. *x*

3:20
w Ac 13:39;
Gal 2:16 *x* Ro 7:7

Righteousness Through Faith

21But now a righteousness from God, *y* apart from law, has been made known, to which the Law and the Prophets testify. *z* 22This righteousness from God comes through faith *a* in Jesus Christ to all who believe. There is no difference, *b* 23for all have sinned and fall short of the glory of God, 24and are justified freely by his grace *c* through the redemption *d* that came by Christ Jesus. 25God presented him as a sacrifice of atonement, *a e* through faith in his blood. *f* He did this to demonstrate his justice, because in his forbearance he had left the sins committed beforehand unpunished *g*— 26he did it to demonstrate his justice at the present time, so as to be just and the one who justifies those who have faith in Jesus.

3:21
y Ro 1:17; 9:30
z Ac 10:43
3:22
a Ro 9:30
b Ro 10:12;
Gal 3:28; Col 3:11
3:24
c Ro 4:16; Eph 2:8
d Eph 1:7,14;
Col 1:14; Heb 9:12
3:25
e 1Jn 4:10
f Heb 9:12,14
g Ac 17:30
3:27
h Ro 2:17,23; 4:2;
1Co 1:29-31;
Eph 2:9
3:28
i ver 20,21;
Ac 13:39; Eph 2:9
3:29
j Ro 9:24
3:30
k Gal 3:8

27Where, then, is boasting? *h* It is excluded. On what principle? On that of observing the law? No, but on that of faith. 28For we maintain that a man is justified by faith apart from observing the law. *i* 29Is God the God of Jews only? Is he not the God of Gentiles too? Yes, of Gentiles too, *j* 30since there is only one God, who will justify the circumcised by faith and the uncircumcised through that same faith. *k* 31Do we, then, nullify the law by this faith? Not at all! Rather, we uphold the law.

Abraham Justified by Faith

4 What then shall we say that Abraham, our forefather, discovered in this matter? 2If, in fact, Abraham was justified by works, he had something to boast about—but not before God. *l* 3What does the Scripture say? "Abraham believed God, and it was credited to him as righteousness." *b m*

4Now when a man works, his wages are not credited to him as a gift, *n* but as an obligation. 5However, to the man who does not work but trusts God who justifies

4:2
l 1Co 1:31
4:3
m ver 5,9,22;
Ge 15:6; Gal 3:6;
Jas 2:23
4:4
n Ro 11:6

a 25 Or *as the one who would turn aside his wrath, taking away sin*   *b 3* Gen. 15:6; also in verse 22

Romans 3:21–31

📖 The Protestant reformer Martin Luther (1483–1546) identified verses 21–26 as "the chief point, and the very central place of the Epistle, and of the whole Bible." Paul brought together in a few verses many important theological ideas: God's righteousness, justification, the shift in salvation history, faith, sin, redemption, grace, atonement, forgiveness, and God's justice. Here he explained why Christ's coming means Good News for everyone: We are all needy, sinful people.

Paul drew on several dimensions of human experience. "Justification" is the language of the courtroom: what a judge does when he declares a defendant not guilty. "Redemption" comes from the world of commerce and slavery: One could redeem slaves by purchasing their freedom. "Sacrifice for atonement" obviously is the language of religion: the giving of an offering to take the place of the guilty.

📖 These verses don't focus on a change in the way we may *feel* but on the difference in who we *are* in God's sight—a basic theme of Romans. Paul would say more on this subject in chapters 5–8. But he laid the foundation here by reminding us of the great turning point in history: the revelation of God's righteousness in Christ. *This pivotal event inaugurated a new age in which a restored relationship with God—and through Christ with one another—is available to all.*

Romans 4:1–25

📖 The story of God's promise to Abraham, first is-

sued when God called him to leave his home but renewed and elaborated on several occasions, was familiar to Roman Jews and Christians. But Paul's word choice is interesting: God promised that Abraham would be the "heir of the world" (v. 13). Even before Abraham and Sarah had children, God had spoken of the "many nations" that would come from this couple as though they already existed.

Paul argued that *Abraham's faith* in response to God's promise (Gen. 17:5) was the basis for his righteousness. Law had nothing to do with his stature or God's promise to him. In Jewish thought, a distinction remained between Abraham's descendants—covenant participants—and the nations, who also received benefits through Abraham in some unspecified way. Paul broke down that distinction: Gentiles along with Jews are Abraham's "offspring," equal recipients with Jews of God's covenant blessings.

📖 As Paul explained the gospel in Romans, *faith* is the heart of the matter. The apostle said three things about faith in verses 13–22, which together go a long way toward filling out its meaning: Faith (1) is distinct from the law (an openness to *receive*, not a mandate to *do*); (2) has power because of the One in whom we place our trust; and (3) is based on God's Word, not on the evidence of our senses. But don't let #1 trip you up. Faith isn't simply a noun, *belief*, but a verb, *to live in trusting obedience*. Compare this with James's comments on this two-pronged issue in James 1:22–25.

the wicked, his faith is credited as righteousness. [6]David says the same thing when he speaks of the blessedness of the man to whom God credits righteousness apart from works:

[7]"Blessed are they
  whose transgressions are forgiven,
  whose sins are covered.
[8]Blessed is the man
  whose sin the Lord will never count against him."[a][o]

[9]Is this blessedness only for the circumcised, or also for the uncircumcised?[p] We have been saying that Abraham's faith was credited to him as righteousness.[q] [10]Under what circumstances was it credited? Was it after he was circumcised, or before? It was not after, but before! [11]And he received the sign of circumcision, a seal of the righteousness that he had by faith while he was still uncircumcised.[r] So then, he is the father[s] of all who believe[t] but have not been circumcised, in order that righteousness might be credited to them. [12]And he is also the father of the circumcised who not only are circumcised but who also walk in the footsteps of the faith that our father Abraham had before he was circumcised.

[13]It was not through law that Abraham and his offspring received the promise[u] that he would be heir of the world,[v] but through the righteousness that comes by faith. [14]For if those who live by law are heirs, faith has no value and the promise is worthless,[w] [15]because law brings wrath.[x] And where there is no law there is no transgression.[y]

[16]Therefore, the promise comes by faith, so that it may be by grace[z] and may be guaranteed[a] to all Abraham's offspring—not only to those who are of the law but also to those who are of the faith of Abraham. He is the father of us all. [17]As it is written: "I have made you a father of many nations."[b][b] He is our father in the sight of God, in whom he believed—the God who gives life[c] to the dead and calls[d] things that are not[e] as though they were.

[18]Against all hope, Abraham in hope believed and so became the father of many nations,[f] just as it had been said to him, "So shall your offspring be."[c][g] [19]Without weakening in his faith, he faced the fact that his body was as good as dead[h]—since he was about a hundred years old[i]—and that Sarah's womb was also dead.[j] [20]Yet he did not waver through unbelief regarding the promise of God, but was strengthened in his faith and gave glory to God,[k] [21]being fully persuaded that God had power to do what he had promised.[l] [22]This is why "it was credited to him as righteousness."[m] [23]The words "it was credited to him" were written not for him alone, [24]but also for us,[n] to whom God will credit righteousness—for us who believe in him[o] who raised Jesus our Lord from the dead.[p] [25]He was delivered over to death for our sins[q] and was raised to life for our justification.

Peace and Joy

5 Therefore, since we have been justified through faith,[r] we[d] have peace with God through our Lord Jesus Christ, [2]through whom we have gained access[s] by faith into this grace in which we now stand.[t] And we[d] rejoice in the hope[u] of the glory of God. [3]Not only so, but we[d] also rejoice in our sufferings,[v] because we know that suffering produces perseverance;[w] [4]perseverance, character; and character, hope.

[a]8 Psalm 32:1,2   [b]17 Gen. 17:5   [c]18 Gen. 15:5   [d]1,2,3 Or let us

4:8
[o] Ps 32:1,2;
2Co 5:19
4:9
[p] Ro 3:30 [q] ver 3

4:11
[r] Ge 17:10,11
[s] ver 16,17; Lk 19:9
[t] Ro 3:22

4:13
[u] Gal 3:16,29
[v] Ge 17:4-6

4:14
[w] Gal 3:18
4:15
[x] Ro 7:7-25;
1Co 15:56; 2Co 3:7;
Gal 3:10; Ro 7:12
[y] Ro 3:20; 7:7
4:16
[z] Ro 3:24 [a] Ro 15:8
4:17
[b] Ge 17:5 [c] Jn 5:21
[d] Isa 48:13
[e] 1Co 1:28

4:18
[f] ver 17 [g] Ge 15:5
4:19
[h] Heb 11:11,12
[i] Ge 17:17
[j] Ge 18:11

4:20
[k] Mt 9:8
4:21
[l] Ge 18:14;
Heb 11:19
4:22
[m] ver 3
4:24
[n] Ro 15:4;
1Co 9:10; 10:11
[o] Ro 10:9 [p] Ac 2:24
4:25
[q] Isa 53:5,6;
Ro 5:6,8
5:1
[r] Ro 3:28
5:2
[s] Eph 2:18
[t] 1Co 15:1
[u] Heb 3:6
5:3
[v] Mt 5:12
[w] Jas 1:2,3

Romans 5:1–11

Paul mentioned many topics in these verses, but one surfaces as his unifying focal point: hope for final salvation. Suffering, far from being a threat to hope, can spur it. Hope is certain not just because it's based on God's work but because it's rooted in his love.

The peace in Christ God gives believers, then and now, has many aspects. First is the "peace of God," an inner sense of security and serenity that wells up in their hearts when they appreciate the blessings they enjoy in Christ (see, e.g., Phil. 4:7). Second is "peace with God," the position Christians enjoy because God has reconciled them to himself (see esp. Eph. 2:14,15,17; cf. Rom. 2:10; 8:6; 14:17). Paul undoubtedly had in mind the Hebrew word shalom, which communicates multi-dimensional harmony: with God, within ourselves, with others, and even with the natural creation. Such peace is total well-being.

5:5
x Php 1:20
y Ac 2:33
5:6
z Gal 4:4 *a* Ro 4:25

5:8
b Jn 15:13;
1Pe 3:18
5:9
c Ro 3:25 *d* Ro 1:18
5:10
e Ro 11:28;
Col 1:21 *f* 2Co 5:18,
19; Col 1:20,22
g Ro 8:34

⁵And hope^x does not disappoint us, because God has poured out his love into our hearts by the Holy Spirit, ^y whom he has given us.

⁶You see, at just the right time, ^z when we were still powerless, Christ died for the ungodly. ^a ⁷Very rarely will anyone die for a righteous man, though for a good man someone might possibly dare to die. ⁸But God demonstrates his own love for us in this: While we were still sinners, Christ died for us. ^b

⁹Since we have now been justified by his blood, ^c how much more shall we be saved from God's wrath ^d through him! ¹⁰For if, when we were God's enemies, ^e we were reconciled ^f to him through the death of his Son, how much more, having been reconciled, shall we be saved through his life! ^g ¹¹Not only is this so, but we also rejoice in God through our Lord Jesus Christ, through whom we have now received reconciliation.

People won't find peace until they find peace with God. Lack of such peace is the basic human predicament. Sinful humanity is in a state of dis-ease, hostility with God and ourselves. People attribute many different meanings to the word *peace*, but almost everyone wants it. They want to be "at peace" with themselves and hope one day to "rest in peace." Thus Paul began most of his letters by greeting people with God's grace and peace. Many church traditions "pass the peace" during worship. What does it mean for us to be bearers of peace to others?

5:10–11

A Recipe for Reconciliation

Ingredients:

Christ's reconciling role
Believers are one in Christ, reconciled to God (restored to friendship, harmony, and peace) through Jesus (Eph. 2:11–22).

Christ has made possible peace between God and humans and has begun the restoration of harmony in the physical world—a process to be completed when he returns (Col. 1:19–22).

Through Christ our sinful nature's hostility against God has been ended (Rom. 5:10–11).

The believer's role
Christ has made us his ambassadors, making his appeal for humanity's reconciliation to God through us (2 Cor. 5:11–21).

Restoration of harmony starts with those closest to us (Matt. 5:21–24).

God expects us to love him and others—two overarching commandments (Mark 12:28–34).

We can't love God if we hate other people (1 Jn. 2:9–11; 3:11–24; 4:7–11).

Jesus prayed that believers might be brought to complete unity—a process of which we are a part (John 17:20–23).

Love for God and others is a continuing "debt" we spend our whole lives paying off (Rom. 13:8).

Models to follow
The good Samaritan—unconditional love *from* the despised underdog (Luke 10:25–37)

Peter and Cornelius—mutual openness to previous "enemies" and to radical change (Acts 10:9–35)

Jesus—deliberate "blindness" to human distinctions and prejudice (Gal. 3:26–29)

Putting it all together:

Step 1: Forgive
- Love your enemies and pray for those who persecute you (Matt. 5:43–48).
- Forgive continuously and relentlessly, just as you have been forgiven (Matt. 6:9–15; 18:21–35).

Step 2: Restore
- A slave (and new Christian) voluntarily returning to his master; Paul offering to make restitution (make good, repay, or restore) and calling for unity (the book of Philem.)
- Zacchaeus paying back those he had cheated far beyond their expectations (Luke 19:1–10)
- Righting our wrongs against others (Ex. 21:12–36)

Step 3: Live a godly life
- God's power is freely available in all its fullness to us who believe (Eph. 1:18–21).
- Christ's power gives us everything we need for living godly lives (2 Peter 1:3).

Step 4: Be humble, accepting, and embracing
- We are to imitate Christ's humility, demonstrated in his taking on our human nature (Phil. 2:1–11).
- We are to follow his example in accepting others as he accepted us. Christ shared in our humanity, enabling our union with him in a spiritual family (Heb. 2:9–18).
- We are to embrace all kinds of people. Christ created one new and united humanity, having broken down barriers of hostility and prejudice (Eph. 2:14–16).

Racial Reconciliation

 5:10

Reconciliation is costly. It cost Jesus his life to mend our relationship to God (Rom. 5:10; Col. 1:19–22). Now Christ calls us to a similar ministry (2 Cor. 5:19). True restoration with another will cost us our hoarded craving for vengeance. Said Pope Paul VI: "A love of reconciliation is not weakness or cowardice. It demands courage, nobility, generosity, sometimes heroism, an overcoming of oneself rather than of one's adversary."

Christ brings us to a screeching halt outside the church door with his devastating question: "Does your brother or sister have anything against you?" If the answer is yes, he spins us around and sends us back. "First go and be reconciled to your brother; then come and offer your gift" (Matt. 5:24).

The Rwandan conflict of 1994 between Hutus and Tutsis added its cruel chapter to our racially divided age. A country with a convoluted history of racial tensions, Rwanda erupted into violence overnight. One hundred days later up to one million people had been hacked, shot, clubbed, raped, or burned to death. Still today the country is reeling. Is reconciliation possible there? Jesus insists that it is—especially for believers.

Most of us find it easier to believe we can be restored through Christ to a relationship with God than that we can be reconciled through Christ to other people. The righting of long-standing racial wrongs may sound in particular like an impossible request. Yet Christ calls us his ambassadors of reconciliation (2 Cor. 5:20) and has a personal message for each of us: Christ died not only to reconcile me, a sinner, to a holy God, but to reconcile me to any estranged brother or sister.

One Rwandan story proves it's possible. Years after the genocide, Deborah still felt the sting of her son's death. Daily she asked God to help her to move on. One morning, answering a knock, she faced a young Hutu man. "I killed your son," he said simply. "Take me to the authorities and let them deal with me. I haven't slept since the night I shot him. Every time I lie down I see you praying, and I know it's for me."

Deborah stared at her son's murderer—clearly a hurting young man who had been used as a pawn by Hutu extremists. With the power of him "who has made the two one and has destroyed the barrier, the dividing wall of hostility" (Eph. 2:14), she opened her arms, offering him not only forgiveness but an invitation to join her family. Surely Rwanda, as Deborah's story spreads, is one step closer to national healing.

Cross-racial understanding begins by letting Christ search our hearts and reveal to us anyone, of whatever ethnic or racial background, from whom we are alienated. Repentance, forgiveness, and reparation are possible through the power of him who died to destroy all walls of hostility (Eph. 2:16, 2 Peter 1:3).

True resolution comes about when godly relationships are formed (Eph. 2:15). Croatian theologian Miroslav Volf rightly notes that reconciliation succeeds only when we receive another in a way that expands our own identity, as Deborah and the young man did when they assumed new mother/son roles. Jesus reconciled us to the Father by taking on our humanity. Now he has committed the ministry of reconciliation to *us* (2 Cor. 5:18)—the church, his people. May we be unflinchingly obedient to that call and willing to pay whatever price may be exacted of us.

> Cross-racial understanding begins by letting Christ search our hearts and reveal to us anyone, of whatever ethnic or racial background, from whom we are alienated.

Michael Cassidy, founder and international team leader of African Enterprise in Monrovia, California

Source: World Vision Australia, *Rwanda's Gift to the World*, VHS, Stormfront Video, 2001

5:12
h ver 15,16,17;
1Co 15:21,22
i Ge 2:17; 3:19;
Ro 6:23

5:13
j Ro 4:15

5:14
k 1Co 15:22,45

5:15
l ver 12,18,19
m Ac 15:11

5:17
n ver 12

5:18
o ver 12 p Ro 4:25

5:19
q ver 12 r Php 2:8

5:20
s Ro 7:7,8; Gal 3:19
t 1Ti 1:13,14
5:21
u ver 12,14

6:1
v ver 15; Ro 3:5,8
6:2
w Col 3:3,5;
1Pe 2:24
6:3
x Mt 28:19

6:4
y Col 2:12 z Ro 7:6;
Gal 6:15; Eph 4:22-
24; Col 3:10
6:5
a 2Co 4:10;
Php 3:10,11
6:6
b Eph 4:22; Col 3:9
c Gal 2:20;
Col 2:12,20
d Ro 7:24

Death Through Adam, Life Through Christ

12Therefore, just as sin entered the world through one man,[h] and death through sin,[i] and in this way death came to all men, because all sinned— 13for before the law was given, sin was in the world. But sin is not taken into account when there is no law.[j] 14Nevertheless, death reigned from the time of Adam to the time of Moses, even over those who did not sin by breaking a command, as did Adam, who was a pattern of the one to come.[k]

15But the gift is not like the trespass. For if the many died by the trespass of the one man,[l] how much more did God's grace and the gift that came by the grace of the one man, Jesus Christ,[m] overflow to the many! 16Again, the gift of God is not like the result of the one man's sin: The judgment followed one sin and brought condemnation, but the gift followed many trespasses and brought justification. 17For if, by the trespass of the one man, death[n] reigned through that one man, how much more will those who receive God's abundant provision of grace and of the gift of righteousness reign in life through the one man, Jesus Christ.

18Consequently, just as the result of one trespass was condemnation for all men,[o] so also the result of one act of righteousness was justification[p] that brings life for all men. 19For just as through the disobedience of the one man[q] the many were made sinners, so also through the obedience[r] of the one man the many will be made righteous.

20The law was added so that the trespass might increase.[s] But where sin increased, grace increased all the more,[t] 21so that, just as sin reigned in death,[u] so also grace might reign through righteousness to bring eternal life through Jesus Christ our Lord.

Dead to Sin, Alive in Christ

6 What shall we say, then? Shall we go on sinning so that grace may increase?[v] 2By no means! We died to sin;[w] how can we live in it any longer? 3Or don't you know that all of us who were baptized[x] into Christ Jesus were baptized into his death? 4We were therefore buried with him through baptism into death in order that, just as Christ was raised from the dead[y] through the glory of the Father, we too may live a new life.[z]

5If we have been united with him like this in his death, we will certainly also be united with him in his resurrection.[a] 6For we know that our old self[b] was crucified with him[c] so that the body of sin[d] might be done away with,[a] that we should no longer be slaves to sin— 7because anyone who has died has been freed from sin.

a 6 Or be rendered powerless

Romans 5:12–21

Paul sketched the world's spiritual history in the broadest of strokes: Adam in his sin had sealed the fate of all people. Now Christ, the "second Adam," enables people to escape that fate and draw near to God. But, Jews of Paul's day might have objected, what about all God had done for Israel? Paul argued that the law brought no relief from the curse of sin and death. In fact, the loss of ignorance only made people more responsible. Sin had "increased," but God's grace had more than compensated.

The doctrine of "original sin" (the Bible's teaching about the relationship between Adam's first sin and the sin and death of all people) seems to some today to be irrational or unjust. But what better explanation for the extent and persistence of "crimes against humanity"? When will we realize that serial murders or genocide aren't exceptional? They manifest the hatred and enmity that have characterized human beings since Adam's fall.

Romans 6:1–14

In chapter 5, Paul had assured believers that their new relationship with God would result in salvation from God's wrath in the judgment. Because they were in Christ, they (and we today) could be confident of the eternal life he had secured for them. But what did this new relationship mean for their lives in the present? Since they were saved by grace through faith, did it matter what they did? Absolutely! It's helpful to remember that Christ has set believers free both from the penalty and the power of sin.

Paul used the image of baptism to describe the change God's grace makes in us. The "old self" is crucified and buried with Christ, so that we might be united and raised with him to new life (cf. 2 Cor. 5:17; Eph. 4:22–24; Col. 3:9–11) Verses 12–14 suggest that since sin no longer controls our lives, we are free to obey God rather than our natural impulses. Does freedom to obey sound like a contradiction? Remember, Paul said we were either slaves to obey sin or free to obey God.

8Now if we died with Christ, we believe that we will also live with him. 9For we know that since Christ was raised from the dead, *e* he cannot die again; death no longer has mastery over him. *f* 10The death he died, he died to sin *g* once for all; but the life he lives, he lives to God.

11In the same way, count yourselves dead to sin *h* but alive to God in Christ Jesus. 12Therefore do not let sin reign in your mortal body so that you obey its evil desires. 13Do not offer the parts of your body to sin, as instruments of wickedness, *i* but rather offer yourselves to God, as those who have been brought from death to life; and offer the parts of your body to him as instruments of righteousness. *j* 14For sin shall not be your master, because you are not under law, *k* but under grace. *l*

Slaves to Righteousness

15What then? Shall we sin because we are not under law but under grace? By no means! 16Don't you know that when you offer yourselves to someone to obey him as slaves, you are slaves to the one whom you obey—whether you are slaves to sin, *m* which leads to death, *n* or to obedience, which leads to righteousness? 17But thanks be to God *o* that, though you used to be slaves to sin, you wholeheartedly obeyed the form of teaching *p* to which you were entrusted. 18You have been set free from sin *q* and have become slaves to righteousness.

19I put this in human terms *r* because you are weak in your natural selves. Just as you used to offer the parts of your body in slavery to impurity and to ever-increasing wickedness, so now offer them in slavery to righteousness *s* leading to holiness. 20When you were slaves to sin, *t* you were free from the control of righteousness. 21What benefit did you reap at that time from the things you are now ashamed of? Those things result in death! *u* 22But now that you have been set free from sin *v* and have become slaves to God, *w* the benefit you reap leads to holiness, and the result is eternal life. 23For the wages of sin is death, *x* but the gift of God is eternal life *y* in *a* Christ Jesus our Lord.

An Illustration From Marriage

7 Do you not know, brothers *z*—for I am speaking to men who know the law— that the law has authority over a man only as long as he lives? 2For example, by law a married woman is bound to her husband as long as he is alive, but if her husband dies, she is released from the law of marriage. *a* 3So then, if she marries another man while her husband is still alive, she is called an adulteress. But if her hus-

a *23 Or through*

Cross references

6:9 *e* Ac 2:24 *f* Rev 1:18
6:10 *g* ver 2
6:11 *h* ver 2
6:13 *i* ver 16,19; Ro 7:5 *j* Ro 12:1; 1Pe 2:24
6:14 *k* Gal 5:18 *l* Ro 3:24
6:16 *m* Jn 8:34; 2Pe 2:19 *n* ver 23
6:17 *o* Ro 1:8; 2Co 2:14 *p* 2Ti 1:13
6:18 *q* ver 7,22; Ro 8:2
6:19 *r* Ro 3:5 *s* ver 13
6:20 *t* ver 16
6:21 *u* ver 23
6:22 *v* ver 18 *w* 1Co 7:22; 1Pe 2:16
6:23 *x* Ge 2:17; Ro 5:12; Gal 6:7,8; Jas 1:15 *y* Mt 25:46
7:1 *z* Ro 1:13
7:2 *a* 1Co 7:39

Romans 6:15–23

Paul continued to proclaim that believers are set free from sin, but he shifted his emphasis slightly. Freedom was his dominant theme in verses 1–14, but slavery now took center stage. In using this imagery, Paul both reminded his readers of their former state and encouraged them to recognize what they had become in Christ. His focus was on the transfer from one state of "slavery" (negative) to another (positive). The slavery image had its limitations, but Paul's point still comes through clearly. See "There and Then" notes in Philemon for a discussion of slavery in the Roman Empire.

Notice in this chapter the interplay between what God does and what he calls us to do. One thing is clear in Romans: What we are called to do grows out of what God has done for us. We are not asked to wage a war against sin with the hope that God will take our side. God takes the initiative, acting in grace to help his people and then asking us to respond in obedience. To use a common phrase, Christians are called to "become

what they are." In what ways are you in a process of *becoming*? What progress in your faith have you seen over time?

Romans 7:1–6

Much in this passage parallels chapter 6: As believers "die to sin" (6:2) and are set free from it (6:6), so they die to the law (7:4) and are set free from it (v. 6). As freedom from sin leads to serving God and producing fruit pleasing to him (6:18–22), so freedom from the law leads to serving "in the new way of the Spirit" (7:6) and producing "fruit to God" (v. 4). Paul addressed the Christian's relationship to two of the key powers of the old regime: sin and the Mosaic Law.

Some scholars insist that verses 2–3 prove that remarriage on any basis other than the death of a spouse is adulterous. But others don't believe these verses may be applied this way. Both Roman and Jewish law allowed for remarriage after a legitimate divorce. Paul wasn't teaching about marriage or divorce but was illustrating the point that believers have "died" to the law.

7:4
b Ro 8:2; Gal 2:19
c Col 1:22

7:5
d Ro 7:7-11
e Ro 6:13

7:6
f Ro 2:29; 2Co 3:6

7:7
g Ro 3:20; 4:15
h Ex 20:17; Dt 5:21
7:8
i ver 11 / Ro 4:15;
1Co 15:56

7:10
k Lev 18:5;
Lk 10:26-28;
Ro 10:5; Gal 3:12
7:11
l Ge 3:13
7:12
m 1Ti 1:8

7:14
n 1Co 3:1
o 1Ki 21:20,25;
2Ki 17:17
7:15
p ver 19; Gal 5:17
7:16
q ver 12
7:17
r ver 20
7:18
s ver 25
7:19
t ver 15
7:20
u ver 17
7:21
v ver 23,25
7:22
w Eph 3:16 x Ps 1:2
7:23
y Gal 5:17; Jas 4:1;
1Pe 2:11
7:24
z Ro 6:6; 8:2

band dies, she is released from that law and is not an adulteress, even though she marries another man. ⁴So, my brothers, you also died to the law ᵇ through the body of Christ, ᶜ that you might belong to another, to him who was raised from the dead, in order that we might bear fruit to God. ⁵For when we were controlled by the sinful nature, ᵃ the sinful passions aroused by the law ᵈ were at work in our bodies, ᵉ so that we bore fruit for death. ⁶But now, by dying to what once bound us, we have been released from the law so that we serve in the new way of the Spirit, and not in the old way of the written code. ᶠ

Struggling With Sin

⁷What shall we say, then? Is the law sin? Certainly not! Indeed I would not have known what sin was except through the law. ᵍ For I would not have known what coveting really was if the law had not said, "Do not covet." ᵇ ʰ ⁸But sin, seizing the opportunity afforded by the commandment, ⁱ produced in me every kind of covetous desire. For apart from law, sin is dead. ʲ ⁹Once I was alive apart from law; but when the commandment came, sin sprang to life and I died. ¹⁰I found that the very commandment that was intended to bring life ᵏ actually brought death. ¹¹For sin, seizing the opportunity afforded by the commandment, deceived me, ˡ and through the commandment put me to death. ¹²So then, the law is holy, and the commandment is holy, righteous and good. ᵐ

¹³Did that which is good, then, become death to me? By no means! But in order that sin might be recognized as sin, it produced death in me through what was good, so that through the commandment sin might become utterly sinful.

¹⁴We know that the law is spiritual; but I am unspiritual, ⁿ sold ᵒ as a slave to sin. ¹⁵I do not understand what I do. For what I want to do I do not do, but what I hate I do. ᵖ ¹⁶And if I do what I do not want to do, I agree that the law is good. ᑫ ¹⁷As it is, it is no longer I myself who do it, but it is sin living in me. ʳ ¹⁸I know that nothing good lives in me, that is, in my sinful nature. ᶜˢ For I have the desire to do what is good, but I cannot carry it out. ¹⁹For what I do is not the good I want to do; no, the evil I do not want to do—this I keep on doing. ᵗ ²⁰Now if I do what I do not want to do, it is no longer I who do it, but it is sin living in me that does it. ᵘ

²¹So I find this law at work: ᵛ When I want to do good, evil is right there with me. ²²For in my inner being ʷ I delight in God's law; ˣ ²³but I see another law at work in the members of my body, waging war ʸ against the law of my mind and making me a prisoner of the law of sin at work within my members. ²⁴What a wretched man I am! Who will rescue me from this body of death? ᶻ ²⁵Thanks be to God— through Jesus Christ our Lord!

---

a 5 Or *the flesh*; also in verse 25   b 7 Exodus 20:17; Deut. 5:21   c 18 Or *my flesh*

We as Christians, saved from sin by Christ's sacrifice, are no longer under Old Testament law. But that law still serves an important function for us. One reason we continue to read the Old Testament law is to guide us in our interpretation of the New Testament. Many specific laws that fit the context of ancient Israel seem irrelevant in our culture, but God's *moral* will for people as spelled out in the Ten Commandments can never change.

Romans 7:7–25

Paul anticipated the direction his readers might take. He headed them off from drawing what might seem the logical conclusion of his argument in verses 1–6. "The law," he affirmed, "is holy, and the commandment is holy, righteous and good" (v. 12). The law may have had a disastrous effect, but the fault wasn't with the law. The culprit was sin, which used God's good law to bring death.

This passage is one of the most controversial in Romans. Since early in church history, Christians have debated two questions: (1) Was Paul truly writing about himself or using "I" language to represent a group of people? (2) Whose experience was he describing? Three basic answers have been proposed: (a) a non-Christian's (in this context, a Jew under the law), (b) a mature believer's, or (c) an immature Christian's.

Whatever our view of the controversial issues of Romans 7, it's critical that we avoid misusing the text to justify sin or stagnation in the Christian life—the attitude that says, "I'm really struggling with a sin, and it keeps getting the best of me. But that is alright; Paul had the same problem." Paul may indeed have had that problem, but that doesn't make a complacent attitude appropriate—for Paul or for us. What sin trips you up on a consistent basis? How have you dealt with it? Passively? With self-condemnation? With denial? Or with warfare prayer?

So then, I myself in my mind am a slave to God's law, but in the sinful nature a slave to the law of sin.

Life Through the Spirit

8 Therefore, there is now no condemnation[a] for those who are in Christ Jesus,[ab] [2]because through Christ Jesus the law of the Spirit of life[c] set me free[d] from the law of sin[e] and death. [3]For what the law was powerless[f] to do in that it was weakened by the sinful nature,[b] God did by sending his own Son in the likeness of sinful man[g] to be a sin offering.[ch] And so he condemned sin in sinful man,[d] [4]in order that the righteous requirements of the law might be fully met in us, who do not live according to the sinful nature but according to the Spirit.[i]

[5]Those who live according to the sinful nature have their minds set on what that nature desires;[j] but those who live in accordance with the Spirit have their minds set on what the Spirit desires.[k] [6]The mind of sinful man[e] is death, but the mind controlled by the Spirit is life[l] and peace; [7]the sinful mind[f] is hostile to God.[m] It does not submit to God's law, nor can it do so. [8]Those controlled by the sinful nature cannot please God.

[9]You, however, are controlled not by the sinful nature but by the Spirit, if the Spirit of God lives in you.[n] And if anyone does not have the Spirit of Christ,[o] he does not belong to Christ. [10]But if Christ is in you,[p] your body is dead because of sin, yet your spirit is alive because of righteousness. [11]And if the Spirit of him who raised Jesus from the dead[q] is living in you, he who raised Christ from the dead will also give life to your mortal bodies[r] through his Spirit, who lives in you.

[12]Therefore, brothers, we have an obligation—but it is not to the sinful nature, to live according to it. [13]For if you live according to the sinful nature, you will die; but if by the Spirit you put to death the misdeeds of the body, you will live,[s] [14]because those who are led by the Spirit of God[t] are sons of God.[u] [15]For you did not receive a spirit that makes you a slave again to fear,[v] but you received the Spirit of sonship.[g] And by him we cry, "Abba,[h] Father."[w] [16]The Spirit himself testifies with our spirit[x] that we are God's children. [17]Now if we are children, then we are heirs[y]—heirs of God and co-heirs with Christ, if indeed we share in his sufferings in order that we may also share in his glory.[z]

Future Glory

[18]I consider that our present sufferings are not worth comparing with the glory that will be revealed in us.[a] [19]The creation waits in eager expectation for the sons of God to be revealed. [20]For the creation was subjected to frustration, not by its own choice, but by the will of the one who subjected it,[b] in hope [21]that[i] the creation it-

8:1
a ver 34 b ver 39;
Ro 16:3
8:2
c 1Co 15:45
d Ro 6:18 e Ro 7:4
8:3
f Ac 13:39;
Heb 7:18 g Php 2:7
h Heb 2:14,17
8:4
i Gal 5:16
8:5
j Gal 5:19-21
k Gal 5:22-25
8:6
l Gal 6:8
8:7
m Jas 4:4
8:9
n 1Co 6:19; Gal 4:6
o Jn 14:17;
1Jn 4:13
8:10
p Gal 2:20;
Eph 3:17; Col 1:27
8:11
q Ac 2:24 r Jn 5:21
8:13
s Gal 6:8
8:14
t Gal 5:18
u Jn 1:12; Rev 21:7
8:15
v 2Ti 1:7; Heb 2:15
w Mk 14:36;
Gal 4:5,6
8:16
x Eph 1:13
8:17
y Ac 20:32; Gal 4:7
z 1Pe 4:13
8:18
a 2Co 4:17;
1Pe 4:13
8:20
b Ge 3:17-19

---

a 1 Some later manuscripts Jesus, who do not live according to the sinful nature but according to the Spirit,
b 3 Or the flesh; also in verses 4, 5, 8, 9, 12 and 13   c 3 Or man, for sin   d 3 Or in the flesh
e 6 Or mind set on the flesh   f 7 Or the mind set on the flesh   g 15 Or adoption   h 15 Aramaic for
Father   i 20,21 Or subjected it in hope. 21For

Romans 8:1–17

Romans 8 has been called the "inner sanctuary within the cathedral of Christian faith." It sets before Christians in all ages some of the most wonderful blessings they enjoy as believers: being freed from God's condemnation; filled with his own Spirit; liberated from sin's power; adopted into his family; destined for resurrection and glory; and full of hope because of his love and promise to bring good in every circumstance of life.

Having the Holy Spirit's "mind-set" is the crucial step between living around the Spirit and living according to the Spirit. Cultivating a Spirit-led, Spirit-filled disposition of heart and mind is necessary if we are to live in a God-pleasing manner. How are you forming your mind? What are you putting in it? If you are serious about pro-

gressing in the Christian life, it's critical to nourish your mind each day with wholesome spiritual food.

Romans 8:18–27

The theme of this passage is the future glory of believers and all of creation. At the end of verse 17 Paul reminded his readers that they needed to share in Christ's sufferings if they expected to share in his glory. The sin of Adam and Eve impacted all of creation, and it won't be free until people are redeemed. Paul made two basic points about this glory: (1) It's the climax in God's plan both for his people and for his creation generally. (2) God himself provides what believers need in order to wait eagerly and patiently. The Spirit helps them pray, and God has promised them a glory that already exists in heaven—for which they are to simply wait in hope.

8:21
c Ac 3:21; 2Pe 3:13;
Rev 21:1
8:22
d Jer 12:4

8:23
e 2Co 5:5
f 2Co 5:2,4
g Gal 5:5
8:24
h 1Th 5:8

self will be liberated from its bondage to decay[c] and brought into the glorious freedom of the children of God.

22We know that the whole creation has been groaning[d] as in the pains of childbirth right up to the present time. 23Not only so, but we ourselves, who have the firstfruits of the Spirit,[e] groan[f] inwardly as we wait eagerly[g] for our adoption as sons, the redemption of our bodies. 24For in this hope we were saved.[h] But hope that is seen is no hope at all. Who hopes for what he already has? 25But if we hope for what we do not yet have, we wait for it patiently.

God intends to liberate, or redeem, the created world, along with his own children. This points Christians in the direction of care for creation. Properly understood, concern for the environment is a natural, God-given mandate for the Christian. God created the world, pronounced it good, and entrusted its care to human beings. What are you doing or can you do to make the physical world a more beautiful or healthier place?

8:18–27

The Creation Groans

An audit of our world's environment reveals that the Biblical "groaning of creation" continues, despite steps taken to address the most serious problems. And yet God remains the sovereign Creator/Provider, and some positive trends emerge.

Water
- At current consumption rates it is possible that up to 3 billion people could be short of drinkable water by 2032.
- Although more people have safe drinking water today than ten years ago, many do not have enough (up to 40 percent) for comfortable living conditions.

And yet: People enjoying improved quality water increased from 4.1 billion to 4.9 billion in the last ten years.

Soil
- At least 15 percent of the earth's surface has already been damaged by human activities.
- Ten percent of once tillable soil has been lost to overgrazing, deforestation, and development.

And yet: 10 percent of Earth's land is in protected areas, five times as much as 30 years ago.

Disease
- There are 4 billion cases of preventable diarrhea each year, causing 2.2 million deaths per year.
- Two billion people are at risk from malaria, with 2 million dying annually from this disease.

And yet: From 1970–2000 the under-age-five global mortality rate fell from 96 to 56 per 1000 births.

Pollution
- Experts estimate that concentrations of carbon dioxide in the air will double by 2050.
- Half the world's rivers are seriously depleted and polluted.

And yet: The hole in the ozone layer is being repaired because of an 85 percent reduction in 114 countries in the use of harmful chemicals.

Resource Management
- One third of the world's fish stocks are depleted or over-harvested.
- One fifth of the world's population consumes 90 percent of its resources.

And yet: In some countries the abandonment of farmlands has allowed forests to recover.

Population
- Worldwide, 1 billion urban dwellers live in slums; another 1 billion will be living in cities by 2010.
- Somewhat less than one half of the earth's population (approximately 2.5–3 billion people) lives on less than $2 per day.

And yet: While Earth's population continues to increase in terms of total numbers of people, growth rates in most parts of the world have declined since the 1980s.

Extinction of Animals
- 1,183 species of birds (12 percent of the world's total) are threatened with extinction.
- 1,130 species of mammals (25 percent of the world's total) are threatened with extinction.

And yet: A moratorium on commercial whaling since 1986 is allowing that species to recover.

Now take a moment to read Psalm 145, especially verse 17, to understand God's heart for the world.

Source: Global Environment Outlook 3 (2002)

26In the same way, the Spirit helps us in our weakness. We do not know what we ought to pray for, but the Spirit himself intercedes for us[i] with groans that words cannot express. 27And he who searches our hearts[j] knows the mind of the Spirit, because the Spirit intercedes for the saints in accordance with God's will.

More Than Conquerors

28And we know that in all things God works for the good of those who love him,[a] who[b] have been called[k] according to his purpose. 29For those God foreknew[l] he also predestined[m] to be conformed to the likeness of his Son,[n] that he might be the firstborn among many brothers. 30And those he predestined,[o] he also called; those he called, he also justified;[p] those he justified, he also glorified.[q]

31What, then, shall we say in response to this?[r] If God is for us, who can be against us?[s] 32He who did not spare his own Son,[t] but gave him up for us all—how will he not also, along with him, graciously give us all things? 33Who will bring any charge[u] against those whom God has chosen? It is God who justifies. 34Who is he that condemns? Christ Jesus, who died[v]—more than that, who was raised to life— is at the right hand of God[w] and is also interceding for us.[x] 35Who shall separate us from the love of Christ? Shall trouble or hardship or persecution or famine or nakedness or danger or sword?[y] 36As it is written:

"For your sake we face death all day long;
    we are considered as sheep to be slaughtered."[c][z]

37No, in all these things we are more than conquerors[a] through him who loved us.[b] 38For I am convinced that neither death nor life, neither angels nor demons,[d] neither the present nor the future, nor any powers,[c] 39neither height nor depth, nor anything else in all creation, will be able to separate us from the love of God[d] that is in Christ Jesus our Lord.

God's Sovereign Choice

9 I speak the truth in Christ—I am not lying,[e] my conscience confirms[f] it in the Holy Spirit— 2I have great sorrow and unceasing anguish in my heart. 3For I could wish that I myself[g] were cursed[h] and cut off from Christ for the sake of my

---

[a] 28 Some manuscripts And we know that all things work together for good to those who love God
[b] 28 Or works together with those who love him to bring about what is good—with those who
[c] 36 Psalm 44:22   [d] 38 Or nor heavenly rulers

Cross references

8:26
[i] Eph 6:18
8:27
[j] Rev 2:23

8:28
[k] 1Co 1:9; 2Ti 1:9
8:29
[l] Ro 11:2
[m] Eph 1:5,11
[n] 1Co 15:49; 2Co 3:18; Php 3:21; 1Jn 3:2
8:30
[o] Eph 1:5,11
[p] 1Co 6:11
[q] Ro 9:23
8:31
[r] Ro 4:1 [s] Ps 118:6
8:32
[t] Jn 3:16; Ro 4:25; 5:8
8:33
[u] Isa 50:8,9
8:34
[v] Ro 5:6-8
[w] Mk 16:19
[x] Heb 7:25; 9:24; 1Jn 2:1
8:35
[y] 1Co 4:11
8:36
[z] Ps 44:22; 2Co 4:11
8:37
[a] 1Co 15:57
[b] Gal 2:20; Rev 1:5; 3:9
8:38
[c] Eph 1:21; 1Pe 3:22
8:39
[d] Ro 5:8
9:1
[e] 2Co 11:10; Gal 1:20; 1Ti 2:7
[f] Ro 1:9
9:3
[g] Ex 32:32
[h] 1Co 12:3; 16:22

Romans 8:28–39

Rhetoric (the art of speaking, and particularly the science of persuasion) was important in the ancient Greco-Roman world. Paul's language in verses 31–39 was *rhetorical*—chosen to move or convince the reader. In asking repeated rhetorical questions, Paul was trying to draw his audience into the discussion. Questions and answers follow without pause, giving the paragraph a flavor of solemn proclamation. With regard to the lists in verses 35 and 38–39, Paul made his point effectively by going into specifics about what was included in *nothing!*—the implied answer to his questions.

Christians find immeasurable comfort in the promise of Romans 8:28, but it's important to clear away some common misconceptions. The promise isn't that God causes all things, or that all things work together for good (a familiar translation) but that God works for our good in all things. Not every difficult experience will lead to something good in a material or circumstantial sense. The ultimate spiritual good is God's glory, and he is glorified when his children live as Jesus did and attain the glory he has destined for them. God doesn't allow any suffering to be wasted. Because he has authority over all things, he redeems evil and tragedy, causing it to bear positive fruit in our lives.

Paul's unqualified assertion that *nothing*—including any spiritual being—can separate us from Christ can't be overemphasized by and to Christians today.

Romans 9:1–29

For Paul, there could be no Good News in Christ unless what God had done in the Son had become part of the one master plan the Old Testament reveals. Paul wanted his readers to understand that God's work in the gospel perfectly fulfilled the Old Testament promises. The Jews needed this message, but Gentile Christians also needed to see that their faith had roots sunk deeply into Old Testament soil.

The many direct references and allusions to Moses throughout chapters 9–11 suggest that Paul saw Moses as a model for his own position as mediator between God and Israel. But in verse 3 Paul went further: He offered to suffer God's curse on Israel's behalf. Moses' story had a happy ending for God's people, and Paul may have foreseen a long-term positive end to his own struggle for the salvation of the Jewish people.

9:3
i Ro 11:14
9:4
j Ex 4:22 *k* Ge 17:2;
Ac 3:25; Eph 2:12
l Ps 147:19
m Heb 9:1
n Ac 13:32
9:5
o Mt 1:1-16 *p* Jn 1:1
q Ro 1:25
9:6
r Ro 2:28,29;
Gal 6:16
9:7
s Ge 21:12;
Heb 11:18
9:8
t Ro 8:14
9:9
u Ge 18:10,14
9:10
v Ge 25:21
9:11
w Ro 8:28
9:12
x Ge 25:23
9:13
y Mal 1:2,3
9:14
z 2Ch 19:7

9:15
a Ex 33:19
9:16
b Eph 2:8

9:17
c Ex 9:16
9:18
d Ex 4:21
9:19
e Ro 11:19
f 2Ch 20:6; Da 4:35
9:20
g Isa 64:8
h Isa 29:16
9:21
i 2Ti 2:20
9:22
j Ro 2:4
9:23
k Ro 2:4 *l* Ro 8:30
9:24
m Ro 8:28
n Ro 3:29
9:25
o Hos 2:23;
1Pe 2:10

9:26
p Hos 1:10

9:27
q Ge 22:17;
Hos 1:10

brothers, those of my own race,[i] [4]the people of Israel. Theirs is the adoption as sons;[j] theirs the divine glory, the covenants,[k] the receiving of the law,[l] the temple worship[m] and the promises.[n] [5]Theirs are the patriarchs, and from them is traced the human ancestry of Christ,[o] who is God over all,[p] forever praised![a][q] Amen.

[6]It is not as though God's word had failed. For not all who are descended from Israel are Israel.[r] [7]Nor because they are his descendants are they all Abraham's children. On the contrary, "It is through Isaac that your offspring will be reckoned."[b][s] [8]In other words, it is not the natural children who are God's children,[t] but it is the children of the promise who are regarded as Abraham's offspring. [9]For this was how the promise was stated: "At the appointed time I will return, and Sarah will have a son."[c][u]

[10]Not only that, but Rebekah's children had one and the same father, our father Isaac.[v] [11]Yet, before the twins were born or had done anything good or bad—in order that God's purpose[w] in election might stand: [12]not by works but by him who calls—she was told, "The older will serve the younger."[d][x] [13]Just as it is written: "Jacob I loved, but Esau I hated."[e][y]

[14]What then shall we say? Is God unjust? Not at all![z] [15]For he says to Moses,

"I will have mercy on whom I have mercy,
and I will have compassion on whom I have compassion."[f][a]

[16]It does not, therefore, depend on man's desire or effort, but on God's mercy.[b] [17]For the Scripture says to Pharaoh: "I raised you up for this very purpose, that I might display my power in you and that my name might be proclaimed in all the earth."[g][c] [18]Therefore God has mercy on whom he wants to have mercy, and he hardens whom he wants to harden.[d]

[19]One of you will say to me:[e] "Then why does God still blame us? For who resists his will?"[f] [20]But who are you, O man, to talk back to God? "Shall what is formed say to him who formed it,[g] 'Why did you make me like this?' "[h][h] [21]Does not the potter have the right to make out of the same lump of clay some pottery for noble purposes and some for common use?[i]

[22]What if God, choosing to show his wrath and make his power known, bore with great patience[j] the objects of his wrath—prepared for destruction? [23]What if he did this to make the riches of his glory[k] known to the objects of his mercy, whom he prepared in advance for glory[l]— [24]even us, whom he also called,[m] not only from the Jews but also from the Gentiles?[n] [25]As he says in Hosea:

"I will call them 'my people' who are not my people;
and I will call her 'my loved one' who is not my loved one,"[i][o]

[26]and,

"It will happen that in the very place where it was said to them,
'You are not my people,'
they will be called 'sons of the living God.' "[j][p]

[27]Isaiah cries out concerning Israel:

"Though the number of the Israelites be like the sand by the sea,[q]

[a] 5 Or *Christ, who is over all. God be forever praised!* Or *Christ. God who is over all be forever praised!*
[b] 7 Gen. 21:12   [c] 9 Gen. 18:10,14   [d] 12 Gen. 25:23   [e] 13 Mal. 1:2,3   [f] 15 Exodus 33:19
[g] 17 Exodus 9:16   [h] 20 Isaiah 29:16; 45:9   [i] 25 Hosea 2:23   [j] 26 Hosea 1:10

Interpreters have traditionally assumed that Israel's plight (vv. 1–5) was her failure to accept salvation in Jesus. But some theologians point out that Paul didn't suggest that the Jewish people were no longer the people of God. Rather, they say, by attempting to keep their special relationship with God to themselves, Jews refused to acknowledge that God would offer salvation to Gentiles. Paul was implicitly warning Christians of all times who are uninterested in reaching others with God's Good News or ministering Christ's love to a hurting world. His passion to see his fellow Jews come to Christ was compelling—if it would have helped, he would have gone to hell for them!

Can God be trusted? This was Paul's ultimate question in chapters 9–11. Verse 6 states his conclusion: God is utterly trustworthy and all-powerful. Nothing can keep him from doing what he has promised to do.

only the remnant will be saved.ʳ
²⁸For the Lord will carry out
  his sentence on earth with speed and finality."ᵃˢ

²⁹It is just as Isaiah said previously:

"Unless the Lord Almightyᵗ
  had left us descendants,
we would have become like Sodom,
  we would have been like Gomorrah."ᵇᵘ

Israel's Unbelief

³⁰What then shall we say? That the Gentiles, who did not pursue righteousness, have obtained it, a righteousness that is by faith;ᵛ ³¹but Israel, who pursued a law of righteousness,ʷ has not attained it.ˣ ³²Why not? Because they pursued it not by faith but as if it were by works. They stumbled over the "stumbling stone."ʸ ³³As it is written:

"See, I lay in Zion a stone that causes men to stumble
  and a rock that makes them fall,
and the one who trusts in him will never be put to shame."ᶜᶻ

10 Brothers, my heart's desire and prayer to God for the Israelites is that they may be saved. ²For I can testify about them that they are zealousᵃ for God, but their zeal is not based on knowledge. ³Since they did not know the righteousness that comes from God and sought to establish their own, they did not submit to God's righteousness.ᵇ ⁴Christ is the end of the lawᶜ so that there may be righteousness for everyone who believes.ᵈ

⁵Moses describes in this way the righteousness that is by the law: "The man who does these things will live by them."ᵈᵉ ⁶But the righteousness that is by faithᶠ says: "Do not say in your heart, 'Who will ascend into heaven?'ᵉᵍ (that is, to bring Christ down) ⁷"or 'Who will descend into the deep?'ᶠ" (that is, to bring Christ up from the dead). ⁸But what does it say? "The word is near you; it is in your mouth and in your

---

ᵃ 28 Isaiah 10:22,23   ᵇ 29 Isaiah 1:9   ᶜ 33 Isaiah 8:14; 28:16   ᵈ 5 Lev. 18:5
ᵉ 6 Deut. 30:12   ᶠ 7 Deut. 30:13

Cross References

9:27 ʳ Ro 11:5
9:28 ˢ Isa 10:22,23
9:29 ᵗ Jas 5:4 ᵘ Isa 1:9; Dt 29:23; Isa 13:19; Jer 50:40
9:30 ᵛ Ro 1:17; 10:6; Gal 2:16; Php 3:9; Heb 11:7
9:31 ʷ Isa 51:1; Ro 10:2, 3 ˣ Gal 5:4
9:32 ʸ 1Pe 2:8
9:33 ᶻ Isa 28:16; Ro 10:11
10:2 ᵃ Ac 21:20
10:3 ᵇ Ro 1:17
10:4 ᶜ Gal 3:24; Ro 7:1-4 ᵈ Ro 3:22
10:5 ᵉ Lev 18:5; Ne 9:29; Eze 20:11, 13,21; Ro 7:10
10:6 ᶠ Ro 9:30 ᵍ Dt 30:12

Romans 9:30–33

Ignorant of God's promises and excluded from the covenant, Gentiles had previously failed to pursue a right relationship with God. But when God reached out to them in grace, they responded in faith. The people of Israel, on the other hand, tended to focus narrowly on the works of the law and missed the larger demand to submit to God in faith. Paul pictured a walker so intent on pursuing a goal that she stumbled over a rock. Israel, nearsightedly concentrating on the law, had missed Christ, the "stone" God had placed in her path to get her to look up, see the big picture, and get back on track.

The logical conclusion from these verses is that Christians are to offer the gospel to all people, everywhere. Some groups propose sending missionaries only where there is some indication people might respond. Decisions about where to allocate resources are never easy, but we simply can't predict where God's Spirit will find a warm reception. Have you heard about missionaries who toiled a lifetime for a handful of converts—followed by an explosion of conversions in the following generation(s)? How about those who went in with low expectations and saw an immediate, unprecedented response? For what country or within what group of people are you consistently praying to see God move?

Romans 10:1–21

Paul faulted the Jews on two counts: for failing (1) to see that God was doing something new with the Gentiles and (2) to seek a relationship with him in the right way. Verse 3 refers to both problems. In failing to submit to God's righteousness, the Jews were guilty of missing the decisive turn in salvation history that had come with Christ. But in seeking to establish their own righteousness, they also were guilty of relying on their own works.

Romans 10:14–21 teaches that response to God's Word is the only way to salvation and that sending out people to proclaim that Word is God's chosen way of bringing it "to the ends of the world." Because salvation is relational—being drawn together by the Spirit through faith in the Son into the communion of the Father—its only effective method of communication is relational. Yet like Paul's Jewish audience, we too easily turn inward, neglecting the millions around us and around the world who have never heard the News. What an awesome privilege we have to participate in God's glory by showing people the way into the kingdom!

heart,"[a][h] that is, the word of faith we are proclaiming: [9]That if you confess[i] with your mouth, "Jesus is Lord," and believe in your heart that God raised him from the dead,[j] you will be saved. [10]For it is with your heart that you believe and are justified, and it is with your mouth that you confess and are saved. [11]As the Scripture says, "Anyone who trusts in him will never be put to shame."[b][k] [12]For there is no difference between Jew and Gentile[l]—the same Lord is Lord of all[m] and richly blesses all who call on him, [13]for, "Everyone who calls on the name of the Lord[n] will be saved."[c][o]

[14]How, then, can they call on the one they have not believed in? And how can they believe in the one of whom they have not heard? And how can they hear without someone preaching to them? [15]And how can they preach unless they are sent? As it is written, "How beautiful are the feet of those who bring good news!"[d][p]

[16]But not all the Israelites accepted the good news. For Isaiah says, "Lord, who has believed our message?"[e][q] [17]Consequently, faith comes from hearing the message,[r] and the message is heard through the word of Christ.[s] [18]But I ask: Did they not hear? Of course they did:

> "Their voice has gone out into all the earth,
>   their words to the ends of the world."[f][t]

[19]Again I ask: Did Israel not understand? First, Moses says,

> "I will make you envious[u] by those who are not a nation;
>   I will make you angry by a nation that has no understanding."[g][v]

[20]And Isaiah boldly says,

> "I was found by those who did not seek me;
>   I revealed myself to those who did not ask for me."[h][w]

[21]But concerning Israel he says,

> "All day long I have held out my hands
>   to a disobedient and obstinate people."[i][x]

The Remnant of Israel

11 I ask then: Did God reject his people? By no means![y] I am an Israelite myself, a descendant of Abraham,[z] from the tribe of Benjamin.[a] [2]God did not reject his people, whom he foreknew.[b] Don't you know what the Scripture says in the passage about Elijah—how he appealed to God against Israel: [3]"Lord, they have killed your prophets and torn down your altars; I am the only one left, and they are trying to kill me"[j][c] [4]And what was God's answer to him? "I have reserved for myself seven thousand who have not bowed the knee to Baal."[k][d] [5]So too, at the present time there is a remnant[e] chosen by grace. [6]And if by grace, then it is no longer by works;[f] if it were, grace would no longer be grace.[l]

Cross references (margin)

10:8
[h] Dt 30:14
10:9
[i] Mt 10:32; Lk 12:8
[j] Ac 2:24
10:11
[k] Isa 28:16; Ro 9:33
10:12
[l] Ro 3:22,29
[m] Ac 10:36
10:13
[n] Ac 2:21
[o] Joel 2:32
10:15
[p] Isa 52:7; Na 1:15
10:16
[q] Isa 53:1; Jn 12:38
10:17
[r] Gal 3:2,5
[s] Col 3:16
10:18
[t] Ps 19:4; Mt 24:14; Col 1:6,23; 1Th 1:8
10:19
[u] Ro 11:11,14
[v] Dt 32:21
10:20
[w] Isa 65:1; Ro 9:30
10:21
[x] Isa 65:2
11:1
[y] 1Sa 12:22; Jer 31:37
[z] 2Co 11:22
[a] Php 3:5
11:2
[b] Ro 8:29
11:3
[c] 1Ki 19:10,14
11:4
[d] 1Ki 19:18
11:5
[e] Ro 9:27
11:6
[f] Ro 4:4

Footnotes

[a] 8 Deut. 30:14   [b] 11 Isaiah 28:16   [c] 13 Joel 2:32   [d] 15 Isaiah 52:7   [e] 16 Isaiah 53:1
[f] 18 Psalm 19:4   [g] 19 Deut. 32:21   [h] 20 Isaiah 65:1   [i] 21 Isaiah 65:2   [j] 3 1 Kings 19:10,14
[k] 4 1 Kings 19:18   [l] 6 Some manuscripts *be grace. But if by works, then it is no longer grace; if it were, work would no longer be work.*

Romans 11:1–10

Central to Jewish tradition was a distinction between corporate (group) and individual election. Deuteronomy 7:6 represented the first—the binding, covenant agreement between God and Israel (group). As Israel's history progressed, though, Jews continued to rebel against God. From this came the concept of the "remnant": those individual Israelites who remained committed to God. Paul intertwined these strands: Only those Jews God had chosen by grace were truly his people—the "Israel [individuals] within Israel [group]" (see 9:6) God had created.

Some Jews in Paul's day made the mistake of assuming that God's election of Israel guaranteed spiritual benefits to every individual member of the nation regardless of their faith and obedience. Some in the church today have a similar attitude. Such people assume salvation as long as they can claim external credits like baptism, confirmation, church attendance, participation in worship services, and acts of service. Such activities may be expected of Christians as acts of gratitude and expressions of love for God. But they aren't a ticket to heaven.

7What then? What Israel sought so earnestly it did not obtain, g but the elect did. The others were hardened, h 8as it is written:

"God gave them a spirit of stupor,
    eyes so that they could not see
    and ears so that they could not hear, i
to this very day." a j

9And David says:

"May their table become a snare and a trap,
    a stumbling block and a retribution for them.
10 May their eyes be darkened so they cannot see,
    and their backs be bent forever." b k

Ingrafted Branches

11Again I ask: Did they stumble so as to fall beyond recovery? Not at all! l Rather, because of their transgression, salvation has come to the Gentiles m to make Israel envious. n 12But if their transgression means riches for the world, and their loss means riches for the Gentiles, o how much greater riches will their fullness bring!

13I am talking to you Gentiles. Inasmuch as I am the apostle to the Gentiles, p I make much of my ministry 14in the hope that I may somehow arouse my own people to envy q and save r some of them. 15For if their rejection is the reconciliation s of the world, what will their acceptance be but life from the dead? t 16If the part of the dough offered as firstfruits u is holy, then the whole batch is holy; if the root is holy, so are the branches.

17If some of the branches have been broken off, v and you, though a wild olive shoot, have been grafted in among the others w and now share in the nourishing sap from the olive root, 18do not boast over those branches. If you do, consider this: You do not support the root, but the root supports you. x 19You will say then, "Branches were broken off so that I could be grafted in." 20Granted. But they were broken off because of unbelief, and you stand by faith. y Do not be arrogant, z but be afraid. a 21For if God did not spare the natural branches, he will not spare you either.

22Consider therefore the kindness b and sternness of God: sternness to those who fell, but kindness to you, provided that you continue c in his kindness. Otherwise, you also will be cut off. d 23And if they do not persist in unbelief, they will be grafted in, for God is able to graft them in again. e 24After all, if you were cut out of an olive tree that is wild by nature, and contrary to nature were grafted into a cultivated olive tree, how much more readily will these, the natural branches, be grafted into their own olive tree!

All Israel Will Be Saved

25I do not want you to be ignorant f of this mystery, g brothers, so that you may

a 8 Deut. 29:4; Isaiah 29:10   b 10 Psalm 69:22,23

Romans 11:11–24

Paul asked rhetorically whether the situation with regard to Israel was permanent. His answer was a resounding no. God had brought about Israel's rejection to further his plan for salvation history. This plan brought salvation to the Gentiles but would ultimately benefit Israel as well. Paul went through the cycle of Jewish rejection to Gentile blessing back again to Jewish blessing three times—and twice again in verses 25–32. See "Here and Now" to follow.

The intermediate phase of this cycle—Gentile blessing—has lasted for almost two thousand years. But the amount of time between events isn't Scripture's concern. With the first coming of Christ and the outpouring

of the Spirit accomplished, now is the time for the church to participate in the coming of the kingdom to all nations. The next event of the timetable will be Christ's glorious return. We, like Paul, still await that day when Israel's unbelief and rejection will be replaced by faith and acceptance.

Paul's language suggests that the "olive tree" represents not national Israel but the "true Israel," the "Israel within Israel" described in 9:6. Ultimately, there is only one people of God—and the church hasn't "replaced" Israel. In fact, as the New Testament community of faith, the church is "Israel"—an Israel including individual Gentiles and Jews. The church is a spiritual entity, made up of people from every nation, including Israel.

11:7 g Ro 9:31 h ver 25; Ro 9:18
11:8 i Mt 13:13-15 j Dt 29:4; Isa 29:10
11:10 k Ps 69:22,23
11:11 l ver 1 m Ac 13:46 n Ro 10:19
11:12 o ver 25
11:13 p Ac 9:15
11:14 q ver 11; Ro 10:19 r 1Co 1:21; 1Ti 2:4; Tit 3:5
11:15 s Ro 5:10 t Lk 15:24,32
11:16 u Lev 23:10,17; Nu 15:18-21
11:17 v Jer 11:16; Jn 15:2 w Ac 2:39; Eph 2:11-13
11:18 x Jn 4:22
11:20 y 1Co 10:12; 2Co 1:24 z Ro 12:16; 1Ti 6:17 a 1Pe 1:17
11:22 b Ro 2:4 c 1Co 15:2; Heb 3:6 d Jn 15:2
11:23 e 2Co 3:16
11:25 f Ro 1:13 g Ro 16:25

11:25
h Ro 12:16 i ver 7;
Ro 9:18 j Lk 21:24

not be conceited:[h] Israel has experienced a hardening[i] in part until the full number of the Gentiles has come in.[j] 26And so all Israel will be saved, as it is written:

> "The deliverer will come from Zion;
> he will turn godlessness away from Jacob.
> 27 And this is[a] my covenant with them
> when I take away their sins."[b][k]

11:27
k Isa 27:9;
Heb 8:10,12
11:28
l Ro 5:10 m Dt 7:8;
10:15; Ro 9:5
11:29
n Ro 8:28
o Heb 7:21
11:30
p Eph 2:2
11:32
q Ro 3:9

28As far as the gospel is concerned, they are enemies[l] on your account; but as far as election is concerned, they are loved on account of the patriarchs,[m] 29for God's gifts and his call[n] are irrevocable.[o] 30Just as you who were at one time disobedient[p] to God have now received mercy as a result of their disobedience, 31so they too have now become disobedient in order that they too may now[c] receive mercy as a result of God's mercy to you. 32For God has bound all men over to disobedience[q] so that he may have mercy on them all.

Doxology

11:33
r Ro 2:4 s Ps 92:5
t Job 11:7

> 33Oh, the depth of the riches[r] of the wisdom and[d] knowledge of God![s]
> How unsearchable his judgments,
> and his paths beyond tracing out![t]

11:34
u Isa 40:13,14;
Job 15:8; 36:22;
1Co 2:16
11:35
v Job 35:7
11:36
w 1Co 8:6;
Col 1:16; Heb 2:10
x Ro 16:27

> 34"Who has known the mind of the Lord?
> Or who has been his counselor?"[e][u]
> 35"Who has ever given to God,
> that God should repay him?"[f][v]
> 36For from him and through him and to him are all things.[w]
> To him be the glory forever! Amen.[x]

Living Sacrifices

12:1
y Eph 4:1 z Ro 6:13,
16,19; 1Pe 2:5
12:2
a 1Pe 1:14
b 1Jn 2:15

12 Therefore, I urge you,[y] brothers, in view of God's mercy, to offer your bodies as living sacrifices,[z] holy and pleasing to God—this is your spiritual[g] act of worship. 2Do not conform[a] any longer to the pattern of this world,[b] but be trans-

a 27 Or will be   b 27 Isaiah 59:20,21; 27:9; Jer. 31:33,34   c 31 Some manuscripts do not have now.   d 33 Or riches and the wisdom and the   e 34 Isaiah 40:13   f 35 Job 41:11   g 1 Or reasonable

Romans 11:25–32

In these verses Paul brought the argument of chapters 9–11 to its climax. He let his readers in on a "mystery," the heart of which is found in 11:26. But Paul wasn't really saying anything new. The salvation of all Israel was simply one of the stages in the sequence he had already outlined: Jewish rejection, followed by Gentile inclusion, followed once again by Jewish inclusion.

Some interpreters believe that, through the revelation of a mystery, Paul had come to understand that Israel would be saved in a special way, apart from Christ, based on God's unbreakable covenant with his people. It's impossible to support this view from the text. Paul had spent most of Romans describing the gospel, through which salvation is offered to Jews and Gentiles. But the heart of that gospel is Christ (1:3–4) and his atoning sacrifice for all people (3:21–26). No one can be saved apart from faith in Jesus.

Romans 11:33–36

The doxology that ends this section of Romans was the natural outpouring of Paul's praise to God, whose wisdom and knowledge far surpasses our understanding. All things were created by, through, and for God. This concept of God as source, sustainer, and goal

of all things may reflect Greek Stoic philosophy. But whatever its origins, it expresses well what the Bible teaches about God's greatness and the totality of our dependence on him.

God's thoughts and plans are far more intricate and marvelous than we could ever begin to imagine! This reality calls on us to exercise humility in seeking to understand God and his Word. On this side of glory, all our knowledge is uncertain and tentative. Humility, willingness to listen, respect for others, and praise and wonder are appropriate attitudes as we seek to grasp the depths of God's character and truth. Do these attitudes accurately describe your approach to the incredible treasure you have in his Word?

Romans 12:1–8

Paul now turned his full attention to the gospel's ethical implications. The "therefore" in verse 1 gathered up all his teaching in the book so far and confronted his readers with the all-important question: "So what?" Paul answered in 12:1—15:13 by touching on several key areas where Christians need to display in their actions the reality of God's salvation through Christ.

Scholars claim that in the ancient world religion was sacrifice. The popularity of sacrifice in ancient religion,

formed by the renewing of your mind.*c* Then you will be able to test and approve what God's will is*d*—his good, pleasing and perfect will.

3For by the grace given me*e* I say to every one of you: Do not think of yourself more highly than you ought, but rather think of yourself with sober judgment, in accordance with the measure of faith God has given you. 4Just as each of us has one body with many members, and these members do not all have the same function,*f* 5so in Christ we who are many form one body,*g* and each member belongs to all the others. 6We have different gifts,*h* according to the grace given us. If a man's gift is prophesying, let him use it in proportion to his*a* faith.*i* 7If it is serving, let him serve; if it is teaching, let him teach;*j* 8if it is encouraging, let him encourage;*k* if it is contributing to the needs of others, let him give generously;*l* if it is leadership, let him govern diligently; if it is showing mercy, let him do it cheerfully.

a 6 Or *in agreement with the*

12:2
c Eph 4:23
d Eph 5:17
12:3
e Ro 15:15; Gal 2:9; Eph 4:7

12:4
f 1Co 12:12-14; Eph 4:16
12:5
g 1Co 10:17
12:6
h 1Co 7:7; 12:4,8-10 *i* 1Pe 4:10,11
12:7
j Eph 4:11
12:8
k Ac 15:32
l 2Co 9:5-13

---

though, often led to abuses. People thought all they had to do to please their god was to offer a sacrifice, regardless of their sincerity. Both Jewish and pagan authors in Paul's day warned about this attitude. Paul made a similar point in verses 1–2: Worship that pleases God is "informed"—offered by Christians who understand who God is, what he has given believers in the gospel, and what he demands in return.

In 12:3—15:13, Paul unpacked some specific components of God's will. First, we live out our transformed existence in community. Central to our community life is a fair and sober estimate of ourselves in line with the Christian faith and the gifts God has given us

and those around us. What benefits does worshiping alongside other believers offer—to God and to yourself? How important are fellow Christians to you socially? Do you feel you have achieved a healthy balance in this regard?

Romans 12:1–2 is one of the Bible's best-known passages—and deservedly so. We find here an excellent description of the essence of the believer's response to God's grace. Our obedience is the product of God's work in our lives, not something we manufacture on our own. It contrasts a "living sacrifice" as our spiritual act of worship against the Old Testament's physical, dead-animal sacrifices.

 12:1–2

Service

Romans 12–14 tells us how we are to live out our faith each day. Paul cited five areas of life that can be channeled to God's service:

1. Selflessness (12:1–8)
* Worship God: This helps us avoid worshiping ourselves or other idols!
* Be transformed: Don't conform to worldly practices and standards but open yourself up for God to change you in ways that will honor him.
* Act responsibly: Measure your service on the basis of *your* gifts, not someone else's.

5. Care for the Weak (ch. 14)
* Follow Christ's example: He came to us in our weakness to bring us salvation.
* Leave judgments about the "why" of their circumstances to God: It's not our place to judge.
* Don't offend weaker people by doing anything that might cause them to question the Christian faith.
* Do everything you can to build people up—not tear them down.

2. Sincere Love for Christ's Body (12:9–21)
* Honor others above yourself: Be humble, not conceited.
* Serve the Lord with joy: Keep your priorities on track by making this a focus.
* Be openhanded: Share what you have with believers in need.
* Be hospitable: Widen your circle by associating with people who have disabilities or are from different social or ethnic groups.
* Live in peace with people: Don't take revenge when you have been wronged.

GOD'S service

4. Love of Neighbor (13:8–14)
* Avoid sinning against others: Steer clear of adultery, murder, theft, coveting, drunkenness, conflict, and jealousy.
* Your good actions will witness to the love of Christ. This may result in your neighbor's salvation!

3. Good Citizenship (13:1–7)
* Unless their actions are contrary to God's rules for living, obey governmental authorities.
* Have goodness as your goal. Work to create and maintain fear-free communities.
* Pay your taxes.

Love

9 Love must be sincere.[m] Hate what is evil; cling to what is good. 10 Be devoted to
one another in brotherly love.[n] Honor one another above yourselves.[o] 11 Never be
lacking in zeal, but keep your spiritual fervor,[p] serving the Lord. 12 Be joyful in
hope,[q] patient in affliction,[r] faithful in prayer. 13 Share with God's people who are
in need. Practice hospitality.[s]

14 Bless those who persecute you;[t] bless and do not curse. 15 Rejoice with those
who rejoice; mourn with those who mourn.[u] 16 Live in harmony with one another.[v] Do not be proud, but be willing to associate with people of low position.[a] Do
not be conceited.[w]

17 Do not repay anyone evil for evil.[x] Be careful to do what is right in the eyes of
everybody.[y] 18 If it is possible, as far as it depends on you, live at peace with everyone.[z] 19 Do not take revenge,[a] my friends, but leave room for God's wrath, for it is
written: "It is mine to avenge; I will repay,"[b][b] says the Lord. 20 On the contrary:

> "If your enemy is hungry, feed him;
> if he is thirsty, give him something to drink.
> In doing this, you will heap burning coals on his head."[c][c]

21 Do not be overcome by evil, but overcome evil with good.

Submission to the Authorities

13 Everyone must submit himself to the governing authorities,[d] for there is no
authority except that which God has established.[e] The authorities that exist have been established by God. 2 Consequently, he who rebels against the authority is rebelling against what God has instituted, and those who do so will bring
judgment on themselves. 3 For rulers hold no terror for those who do right, but for
those who do wrong. Do you want to be free from fear of the one in authority? Then

12:9 [m] 1Ti 1:5
12:10 [n] Heb 13:1 [o] Php 2:3
12:11 [p] Ac 18:25
12:12 [q] Ro 5:2 [r] Heb 10:32,36
12:13 [s] 1Ti 3:2
12:14 [t] Mt 5:44
12:15 [u] Job 30:25
12:16 [v] Ro 15:5 [w] Jer 45:5; Ro 11:25
12:17 [x] Pr 20:22 [y] 2Co 8:21
12:18 [z] Mk 9:50; Ro 14:19
12:19 [a] Lev 19:18; Pr 20:22; 24:29 [b] Dt 32:35
12:20 [c] Pr 25:21,22; Mt 5:44; Lk 6:27
13:1 [d] Tit 3:1; 1Pe 2:13,14 [e] Da 2:21; Jn 19:11

[a] 16 Or *willing to do menial work* [b] 19 Deut. 32:35 [c] 20 Prov. 25:21,22

Romans 12:9–21

Verse 9 begins a noticeable change in style (short sentences, a seemingly random series of commands, and little structure). Paul moved rapidly and with little clear continuity of subject matter through a list of basic Christian rules of moral conduct. Even if these verses can't be unified around one topic, they share a focus: the call for a humble and peaceable attitude, both toward Christians (vv. 10,13,16) and non-Christians (vv. 14,17–21).

Compare this passage with Matthew 5:44 and Luke 6:27–28. The way Paul wove references from Jesus' teachings into his own exhortations is typical of how early Christians absorbed Jesus' words into their own ethical tradition. Like Jesus, Paul called on Christians to turn the other cheek and display concern for others—far beyond the expected boundaries of human love.

Love is the most important way of expressing the nature of the Christian life. The New Testament puts it at the heart of what it means to live as a Christian in relationship to other people. The problem with love, though, is that it can be a vague term. Biblical love is a choice, an act of the will, not an emotion. It's easy to like certain people without loving them. But how well do *you love those you find it impossible to like?*

Of the various manifestations of love Paul touched on here, none receives more attention than the absence of retaliation. The desire for revenge is deeply rooted in our sinful nature. It's celebrated in books and movies and displayed daily in aggressive highway driving. But we as Christians are called to go beyond refraining from doing evil to those who harm us. We are to do them good. Seeking peace—to the extent of our ability to control a situation—is a primary value in God's kingdom.

Romans 13:1–7

While this section may seem at first glance to be out-of-place, it does contribute to Paul's description of the transformed living expected of believers in the new era of redemption. From the church's early beginnings, the gospel's radical demands to avoid conformity to this world were taken too far by some overly enthusiastic believers, who scorned such institutions as marriage and the government. The apostles fought this extremism, pointing out that earthly authorities and institutions were appointed by God for the good of people.

Scripture seems in some cases to present *disobedience* to secular rulers as a virtue. Classic instances include Peter and John (see Acts 4:19–20; cf. Acts 5:29) and the three Hebrews facing Nebuchadnezzar (Dan. 3). Paul provided three marks of rulers, all established by God. Rulers who are to be obeyed reward good behavior (v. 3), punish evil actions (v. 4), and live as God's servants (v. 6). Such leaders recognize that they too are subject and accountable to a higher authority. Paul's heritage supplied him with a robust belief that God appoints secular rulers for his purposes, as well as a proud heritage of resistance to evil rulers.

do what is right and he will commend you.[f] 4For he is God's servant to do you good. But if you do wrong, be afraid, for he does not bear the sword for nothing. He is God's servant, an agent of wrath to bring punishment on the wrongdoer.[g] 5Therefore, it is necessary to submit to the authorities, not only because of possible punishment but also because of conscience.

6This is also why you pay taxes, for the authorities are God's servants, who give their full time to governing. 7Give everyone what you owe him: If you owe taxes, pay taxes;[h] if revenue, then revenue; if respect, then respect; if honor, then honor.

Love, for the Day Is Near

8Let no debt remain outstanding, except the continuing debt to love one another, for he who loves his fellowman has fulfilled the law.[i] 9The commandments, "Do not commit adultery," "Do not murder," "Do not steal," "Do not covet,"[a][j] and whatever other commandment there may be, are summed up in this one rule: "Love your neighbor as yourself."[b][k] 10Love does no harm to its neighbor. Therefore love is the fulfillment of the law.[l]

11And do this, understanding the present time. The hour has come[m] for you to wake up from your slumber,[n] because our salvation is nearer now than when we first believed. 12The night is nearly over; the day is almost here.[o] So let us put aside the deeds of darkness[p] and put on the armor[q] of light. 13Let us behave decently, as in the daytime, not in orgies and drunkenness, not in sexual immorality and debauchery, not in dissension and jealousy.[r] 14Rather, clothe yourselves with the Lord Jesus Christ,[s] and do not think about how to gratify the desires of the sinful nature.[c]

The Weak and the Strong

14 Accept him whose faith is weak,[t] without passing judgment on disputable matters. 2One man's faith allows him to eat everything, but another man, whose faith is weak, eats only vegetables. 3The man who eats everything must not look down on[u] him who does not, and the man who does not eat everything must not condemn[v] the man who does, for God has accepted him. 4Who are you to judge someone else's servant?[w] To his own master he stands or falls. And he will stand, for the Lord is able to make him stand.

a 9 Exodus 20:13-15,17; Deut. 5:17-19,21   b 9 Lev. 19:18   c 14 Or the flesh

13:3
f 1Pe 2:14
13:4
g 1Th 4:6

13:7
h Mt 17:25; 22:17, 21; Lk 23:2

13:8
i ver 10; Jn 13:34; Gal 5:14; Col 3:14
13:9
j Ex 20:13-15,17; Dt 5:17-19,21
k Lev 19:18; Mt 19:19
13:10
l ver 8; Mt 22:39,40
13:11
m 1Co 7:29-31; 10:11 n Eph 5:14; 1Th 5:5,6
13:12
o 1Jn 2:8
p Eph 5:11
q Eph 6:11,13
13:13
r Gal 5:20,21
13:14
s Gal 3:27; 5:16; Eph 4:24

14:1
t Ro 15:1; 1Co 8:9-12

14:3
u Lk 18:9 v Col 2:16

14:4
w Jas 4:12

The key question people ask of this passage is "Where's the exception?" It may help to recognize that *submission* is a broader term than *obedience*: To submit is to accept our subordinate place in a hierarchy established by God. Paul assumed that our ultimate submission would be to God. No human being can ever stand as the final authority for a believer. Have you ever felt it necessary to engage in some form of civil disobedience, resistance, or protest on the basis of your Christian beliefs?

Romans 13:8–14

Jesus summarized the law, built on the twin foundations of love for God and for neighbor. He charged his followers to teach all that *he* had taught them (Matt. 28:18–20). Paul seems to have been referring extensively to Jesus' teaching throughout this part of Romans. Specifically here, he built on Jesus' summary of the Mosaic Law to love God and neighbor.

A recurring theme among Christians is the relationship between love and law. Am I to decide what to do in a given situation by looking for a commandment to guide me, or should I do what seems to be the loving choice? God wants sincere love: an honest, consistent concern for other people that spills over into loving actions. When we live and love rightly, we can't help but obey whatever commandments he has given us. God doesn't speak with two voices. What he requires of us is what his Spirit inspires in us.

A great gap can exist between who we *are* as believers and how we *live*. Many in the church need a "wake-up call" about their participation in activities the Bible forbids: immoral sexual practices, excessive drinking, jealousy and prolonged conflict with others, etc. Holiness is both a gift and a choice. God gives it, but we decide whether to live holy lives and allow God to transform our affections, intentions, and actions.

Romans 14:1—15:13

In this lengthy passage, Paul rebuked Roman Christians for judging one another, particularly with regard to "neutral" or nonessential matters—life's gray areas. The community was divided into two groups, the "weak" and the "strong" in faith (cf. 15:1). The weak were those (mainly Jewish) Christians who couldn't bring themselves to abandon the requirements of the law they had observed all their lives. They weren't necessarily lesser Christians. But Paul insisted that the judgmental attitudes on both sides give way to tolerance and mutual respect.

14:5
x Gal 4:10

14:6
y Mt 14:19;
1Co 10:30,31;
1Ti 4:3,4
14:7
z 2Co 5:15;
Gal 2:20
14:8
a Php 1:20
14:9
b Rev 1:18
c 2Co 5:15

14:10
d 2Co 5:10

14:11
e Isa 45:23;
Php 2:10,11
14:12
f Mt 12:36; 1Pe 4:5
14:13
g Mt 7:1

14:14
h Ac 10:15
i 1Co 8:7

14:15
j Eph 5:2
k 1Co 8:11
14:16
l 1Co 10:30
14:17
m 1Co 8:8
n Ro 15:13
14:18
o 2Co 8:21
14:19
p Ps 34:14;
Ro 12:18;
Heb 12:14
q Ro 15:2;
2Co 12:19
14:20
r ver 15
s 1Co 8:9-12
14:21
t 1Co 8:13
14:22
u 1Jn 3:21
14:23
v ver 5

⁵One man considers one day more sacred than another;ˣ another man considers every day alike. Each one should be fully convinced in his own mind. ⁶He who regards one day as special, does so to the Lord. He who eats meat, eats to the Lord, for he gives thanks to God;ʸ and he who abstains, does so to the Lord and gives thanks to God. ⁷For none of us lives to himself aloneᶻ and none of us dies to himself alone. ⁸If we live, we live to the Lord; and if we die, we die to the Lord. So, whether we live or die, we belong to the Lord. ᵃ

⁹For this very reason, Christ died and returned to lifeᵇ so that he might be the Lord of both the dead and the living. ᶜ ¹⁰You, then, why do you judge your brother? Or why do you look down on your brother? For we will all stand before God's judgment seat. ᵈ ¹¹It is written:

" 'As surely as I live,' says the Lord,
'every knee will bow before me;
every tongue will confess to God.' "ᵃᵉ

¹²So then, each of us will give an account of himself to God.ᶠ

¹³Therefore let us stop passing judgmentᵍ on one another. Instead, make up your mind not to put any stumbling block or obstacle in your brother's way. ¹⁴As one who is in the Lord Jesus, I am fully convinced that no foodᵇ is unclean in itself.ʰ But if anyone regards something as unclean, then for him it is unclean. ⁱ ¹⁵If your brother is distressed because of what you eat, you are no longer acting in love.ʲ Do not by your eating destroy your brother for whom Christ died. ᵏ ¹⁶Do not allow what you consider good to be spoken of as evil. ˡ ¹⁷For the kingdom of God is not a matter of eating and drinking, ᵐ but of righteousness, peace and joy in the Holy Spirit, ⁿ ¹⁸because anyone who serves Christ in this way is pleasing to God and approved by men. ᵒ

¹⁹Let us therefore make every effort to do what leads to peaceᵖ and to mutual edification. �q ²⁰Do not destroy the work of God for the sake of food. ʳ All food is clean, but it is wrong for a man to eat anything that causes someone else to stumble. ˢ ²¹It is better not to eat meat or drink wine or to do anything else that will cause your brother to fall. ᵗ

²²So whatever you believe about these things keep between yourself and God. Blessed is the man who does not condemnᵘ himself by what he approves. ²³But the man who has doubtsᵛ is condemned if he eats, because his eating is not from faith; and everything that does not come from faith is sin.

ᵃ 11 Isaiah 45:23   ᵇ 14 Or that nothing

📖 Paul taught several principles that still apply: (1) We are to try to understand and respect where other people are coming from. (2) Christians who aren't convinced a practice is right for them shouldn't do it. (3) We are to avoid causing anyone to stumble. When we are confronted with believers who have such scruples, we need to modify our expression of freedom because of love. Liberty is wonderful, but love is greater.

Paul called on Christians everywhere to turn away from any traditions contrary to God's revealed will. But he encouraged us to take a slow and loving approach with regard to those that aren't clearly sinful.

Key to interpreting Romans is understanding its personal and community emphases. Paul clearly stressed the personal, concentrating on justification by faith, sanctification, and the duties of the individual believer. Yet he also described our life as a community and the need for reconciliation. Through the Good News of Jesus, God is both *transforming* individuals and *forming* a community.

Romans 15:14–22

🔗 Paul pictured himself as a priest, using the gospel as the means by which he offered his Gentile converts as an offering acceptable to God. He didn't claim a monopoly on the priesthood or deny that other Christians also might be priests. Paul's priesthood, like ours, is a participation in Christ's. Through signs, wonders, and the Spirit's power, Christ prepared this offering (vv. 18–19). The result wasn't simply the faith of the Gentiles, but their obedience in word and deed (v. 18).

📖 Paul gave all the credit for his ministry to the Lord. Christ worked through him by the power of the Spirit. When God enables us to do something good, it's fine to "boast" about it—as long as the focus isn't on us. Instead, it's to be on God at work in and through us. We did indeed struggle and work, using our creativity, commitment, and obedience in word and deed. But we rightly view ourselves as participants in God's work. When have you found yourself boasting about what God had accomplished in and through you? How did you manage to maintain a humble, grateful perspective?

15 We who are strong ought to bear with the failings of the weak[w] and not to please ourselves. ²Each of us should please his neighbor for his good,[x] to build him up.[y] ³For even Christ did not please himself[z] but, as it is written: "The insults of those who insult you have fallen on me."[a][a] ⁴For everything that was written in the past was written to teach us,[b] so that through endurance and the encouragement of the Scriptures we might have hope.

⁵May the God who gives endurance and encouragement give you a spirit of unity[c] among yourselves as you follow Christ Jesus, ⁶so that with one heart and mouth you may glorify the God and Father[d] of our Lord Jesus Christ.

⁷Accept one another,[e] then, just as Christ accepted you, in order to bring praise to God. ⁸For I tell you that Christ has become a servant of the Jews[b][f] on behalf of God's truth, to confirm the promises[g] made to the patriarchs ⁹so that the Gentiles[h] may glorify God[i] for his mercy, as it is written:

"Therefore I will praise you among the Gentiles;
    I will sing hymns to your name."[c][j]

¹⁰Again, it says,

"Rejoice, O Gentiles, with his people."[d][k]

¹¹And again,

"Praise the Lord, all you Gentiles,
    and sing praises to him, all you peoples."[e][l]

¹²And again, Isaiah says,

"The Root of Jesse[m] will spring up,
    one who will arise to rule over the nations;
    the Gentiles will hope in him."[f][n]

¹³May the God of hope fill you with all joy and peace[o] as you trust in him, so that you may overflow with hope by the power of the Holy Spirit.[p]

Paul the Minister to the Gentiles

¹⁴I myself am convinced, my brothers, that you yourselves are full of goodness,[q] complete in knowledge[r] and competent to instruct one another. ¹⁵I have written you quite boldly on some points, as if to remind you of them again, because of the grace God gave me[s] ¹⁶to be a minister of Christ Jesus to the Gentiles[t] with the priestly duty of proclaiming the gospel of God,[u] so that the Gentiles might become an offering[v] acceptable to God, sanctified by the Holy Spirit.

¹⁷Therefore I glory in Christ Jesus[w] in my service to God.[x] ¹⁸I will not venture to speak of anything except what Christ has accomplished through me in leading the Gentiles[y] to obey God[z] by what I have said and done— ¹⁹by the power of signs and miracles,[a] through the power of the Spirit.[b] So from Jerusalem[c] all the way around

---

[a] 3 Psalm 69:9   [b] 8 Greek *circumcision*   [c] 9 2 Samuel 22:50; Psalm 18:49   [d] 10 Deut. 32:43
[e] 11 Psalm 117:1   [f] 12 Isaiah 11:10

15:1
w Ro 14:1; Gal 6:1,2; 1Th 5:14
15:2
x 1Co 10:33
y Ro 14:19
15:3
z 2Co 8:9 a Ps 69:9
15:4
b Ro 4:23,24
15:5
c Ro 12:16; 1Co 1:10
15:6
d Rev 1:6
15:7
e Ro 14:1
15:8
f Mt 15:24; Ac 3:25, 26 g 2Co 1:20
15:9
h Ro 3:29 i Mt 9:8 j 2Sa 22:50; Ps 18:49
15:10
k Dt 32:43
15:11
l Ps 117:1
15:12
m Rev 5:5
n Isa 11:10; Mt 12:21
15:13
o Ro 14:17
p ver 19; 1Co 2:4; 1Th 1:5
15:14
q Eph 5:9
r 2Pe 1:12
15:15
s Ro 12:3
15:16
t Ac 9:15; Ro 11:13
u Ro 1:1 v Isa 66:20
15:17
w Php 3:3
x Heb 2:17
15:18
y Ac 15:12; 21:19; Ro 1:5 z Ro 16:26
15:19
a Jn 4:48; Ac 19:11
b ver 13
c Ac 22:17-21

Romans 15:23–33

Paul's concern in 15:22–29 was to explain why it was taking him so long to get to Rome and why, when he did arrive, he didn't intend to stay long. He had to fulfill his commission to bring the gospel where the name of Christ hadn't yet been heard, and Spain was a fertile field. But a stop in Rome would be necessary for him to secure logistical support for this new outreach. Paul first needed to visit Jerusalem, though, to bring the money he had collected from Gentile churches for the impoverished saints there. He asked the Romans to join him in praying for the success of this venture.

In this case, spiritual learning had passed from the poorer to the richer group. Throughout church history, this has frequently been the case. The gospel has moved surprisingly often from the margins, from the poor and outsiders, to the centers of power and wealth. We as Western Christians don't necessarily owe our spiritual existence to those in poverty around the world, but we can learn much from our brothers and sisters in Christ who have fewer material resources than we do. And Paul made clear in 12:13 the obligation of rich believers to help their poorer counterparts. What can you personally do for or in conjunction with less affluent Christians, at home or abroad? What might you expect to learn from them?

to Illyricum, I have fully proclaimed the gospel of Christ. ²⁰It has always been my ambition to preach the gospel where Christ was not known, so that I would not be building on someone else's foundation. *d* ²¹Rather, as it is written:

> "Those who were not told about him will see,
> and those who have not heard will understand." *a e*

²²This is why I have often been hindered from coming to you. *f*

Paul's Plan to Visit Rome

²³But now that there is no more place for me to work in these regions, and since I have been longing for many years to see you, *g* ²⁴I plan to do so when I go to Spain. *h* I hope to visit you while passing through and to have you assist me on my journey there, after I have enjoyed your company for a while. ²⁵Now, however, I am on my way to Jerusalem *i* in the service *j* of the saints there. ²⁶For Macedonia *k* and Achaia *l* were pleased to make a contribution for the poor among the saints in Jerusalem. ²⁷They were pleased to do it, and indeed they owe it to them. For if the Gentiles have shared in the Jews' spiritual blessings, they owe it to the Jews to share with them their material blessings. *m* ²⁸So after I have completed this task and have made sure that they have received this fruit, I will go to Spain and visit you on the way. ²⁹I know that when I come to you, *n* I will come in the full measure of the blessing of Christ.

³⁰I urge you, brothers, by our Lord Jesus Christ and by the love of the Spirit, *o* to join me in my struggle by praying to God for me. *p* ³¹Pray that I may be rescued *q* from the unbelievers in Judea and that my service in Jerusalem may be acceptable to the saints there, ³²so that by God's will *r* I may come to you *s* with joy and together with you be refreshed. *t* ³³The God of peace *u* be with you all. Amen.

Personal Greetings

16 I commend *v* to you our sister Phoebe, a servant *b* of the church in Cenchrea. *w* ²I ask you to receive her in the Lord *x* in a way worthy of the saints and to give her any help she may need from you, for she has been a great help to many people, including me.

³Greet Priscilla *c* and Aquila, *y* my fellow workers in Christ Jesus. *z* ⁴They risked their lives for me. Not only I but all the churches of the Gentiles are grateful to them. ⁵Greet also the church that meets at their house. *a*
Greet my dear friend Epenetus, who was the first convert *b* to Christ in the province of Asia.
⁶Greet Mary, who worked very hard for you.
⁷Greet Andronicus and Junias, my relatives *c* who have been in prison with me. They are outstanding among the apostles, and they were in Christ before I was.
⁸Greet Ampliatus, whom I love in the Lord.
⁹Greet Urbanus, our fellow worker in Christ, *d* and my dear friend Stachys.

---

a 21 Isaiah 52:15   *b* 1 Or *deaconess*   *c* 3 Greek *Prisca*, a variant of *Priscilla*

15:20
d 2Co 10:15,16

15:21
e Isa 52:15

15:22
f Ro 1:13

15:23
g Ac 19:21;
Ro 1:10,11
15:24
h ver 28
15:25
i Ac 19:21
j Ac 24:17
15:26
k Ac 16:9; 2Co 8:1
l Ac 18:12

15:27
m 1Co 9:11

15:29
n Ro 1:10,11

15:30
o Gal 5:22
p 2Co 1:11;
Col 4:12
15:31
q 2Th 3:2
15:32
r Ac 18:21
s Ro 1:10,13
t 1Co 16:18
15:33
u Ro 16:20;
2Co 13:11; Php 4:9;
1Th 5:23;
Heb 13:20
16:1
v 2Co 3:1
w Ac 18:18
16:2
x Php 2:29
16:3
y Ac 18:2
z ver 7,9,10

16:5
a 1Co 16:19;
Col 4:15; Phm 2
b 1Co 16:15

16:7
c ver 11,21

16:9
d ver 3

Romans 16:1–27

Historian Peter Lampe has studied the names in Romans 16 and concluded that most were Gentiles, freed slaves, or descendants of freed slaves. Paul specifically mentioned at least two groups of slaves: the household servants of Aristobulus and those of Narcissus. What little evidence we have suggests that a large percentage of early Christians came from the "lower" classes.

Of the twenty-seven Christians Paul greeted, ten were women. Women (1) made up a significant part of the early Christian church; (2) have the same access to God as men (e.g., Gal. 3:28; 1 Peter 3:7); and (3) engaged in significant ministry. Paul commended six of them—Phoebe, Priscilla, Junias, Tryphena, Tryphosa, and Persis—for their labor in the Lord.

God has a special concern for the poor, downtrodden, and helpless. This point emerges many times in Luke's Gospel and is reaffirmed in the New Testament letters (see esp. James 2:5–6; 5:1–11). The church is called to offer help to those in our world who most need it.

The ministry of women in the contemporary church has become a "hot" topic. Whatever view we hold, it's helpful to remember that, as Paul observed in this passage, every believer has essential contributions to make to the life of the body and to God's work in the world.

¹⁰Greet Apelles, tested and approved in Christ.
Greet those who belong to the household of Aristobulus.
¹¹Greet Herodion, my relative. ^e
Greet those in the household of Narcissus who are in the Lord.
¹²Greet Tryphena and Tryphosa, those women who work hard in the Lord.
Greet my dear friend Persis, another woman who has worked very hard in the Lord.
¹³Greet Rufus, chosen in the Lord, and his mother, who has been a mother to me, too.
¹⁴Greet Asyncritus, Phlegon, Hermes, Patrobas, Hermas and the brothers with them.
¹⁵Greet Philologus, Julia, Nereus and his sister, and Olympas and all the saints ^f with them. ^g
¹⁶Greet one another with a holy kiss. ^h
All the churches of Christ send greetings.

¹⁷I urge you, brothers, to watch out for those who cause divisions and put obstacles in your way that are contrary to the teaching you have learned. ⁱ Keep away from them. ^j ¹⁸For such people are not serving our Lord Christ, but their own appetites. ^k By smooth talk and flattery they deceive ^l the minds of naive people. ¹⁹Everyone has heard ^m about your obedience, so I am full of joy over you; but I want you to be wise about what is good, and innocent about what is evil. ⁿ

²⁰The God of peace ^o will soon crush ^p Satan under your feet.
The grace of our Lord Jesus be with you. ^q

²¹Timothy, ^r my fellow worker, sends his greetings to you, as do Lucius, ^s Jason ^t and Sosipater, my relatives. ^u

²²I, Tertius, who wrote down this letter, greet you in the Lord.

²³Gaius, whose hospitality I and the whole church here enjoy, sends you his greetings.
Erastus, ^v who is the city's director of public works, and our brother Quartus send you their greetings. ^a

²⁵Now to him who is able ^w to establish you by my gospel ^x and the proclamation of Jesus Christ, according to the revelation of the mystery ^y hidden for long ages past, ²⁶but now revealed and made known through the prophetic writings by the command of the eternal God, so that all nations might believe and obey him— ²⁷to the only wise God be glory forever through Jesus Christ! Amen. ^z

^a 23 Some manuscripts *their greetings.* ²⁴*May the grace of our Lord Jesus Christ be with all of you. Amen.*

16:11
^e ver 7,21

16:15
^f ver 2 ^g ver 14

16:16
^h 1Co 16:20;
2Co 13:12;
1Th 5:26

16:17
ⁱ Gal 1:8,9; 1Ti 1:3;
6:3 / 2Th 3:6,14;
2Jn 10
16:18
^k Php 3:19 ^l Col 2:4
16:19
^m Ro 1:8
ⁿ Mt 10:16;
1Co 14:20
16:20
^o Ro 15:33
^p Ge 3:15
^q 1Th 5:28
16:21
^r Ac 16:1 ^s Ac 13:1
^t Ac 17:5 ^u ver 7,11

16:23
^v Ac 19:22

16:25
^w Eph 3:20
^x Ro 2:16 ^y Eph 1:9;
Col 1:26,27

16:27
^z Ro 11:36

INTRODUCTION TO

1 Corinthians

AUTHOR

Early church fathers, as well as the letter itself (1:1), acknowledge Paul as the author of
1 Corinthians.

DATE WRITTEN

First Corinthians was probably written in A.D. 54 or 55.

ORIGINAL READERS

Paul wrote this letter to the believers in Corinth.

TIMELINE

	10BC	AD1	10	20	30	40	50	60	70	80	90	100
Jesus' life (c. 6/5 B.C.–A.D. 30)												
Paul's conversion (c. A.D. 35)												
Paul's missionary journeys (c. A.D. 46-67)												
Paul's stay in Corinth (c. A.D. 50-52)												
Nero's reign (c. A.D. 54-68)												
Book of 1 Corinthians written (c. A.D. 54-55)												
Paul's first imprisonment in Rome (c. A.D. 59-62)												
Paul's imprisonment and death in Rome (c. A.D. 67-68)												

THEMES

This letter was prompted by oral reports from Chloe's household about infighting in the church
(1:11). The Corinthians also had sent Paul a letter (7:1), probably carried by Stephanas
(16:15–18), that presented various questions and introduced certain concerns. Paul's themes include:

1. *Divisions.* Corinthian society was riddled with competitive individualism, an attitude that
spilled over into relationships within the church. Feuding groups developed around rival leading figures who may have been the hosts of different house churches. Paul admonished those
who fancied themselves "spiritual" (3:1), "mature" (2:6), and "wise" (3:18; 4:10). He reminded
them that God uses the weak, low, and despised in the world, and the things that "are not," to
bring about change in the wise, the strong, and the things that "are" (1:18–31).

2. *Christian conduct.* Correct living is rooted in correct thinking. Paul addressed the problem
of sexual immorality and the dangers and advantages of sexual asceticism (5:1–13; 6:12—
7:40). He also pointed out the detrimental effects of Christians suing one another in pagan
(secular) courts (6:1–11) and the evils of association with blatant idolatry (8:1—11:1).

3. *Worship.* Paul addressed practices in worship (11:2–16; 14:26–40), the character of the
Lord's Supper (11:17–34), and the nature and use of spiritual gifts (12:1—14:40). He viewed
the church as one large, extended family in which all members share their resources with one

another. Worship is to be orderly and offered in a manner that honors God. To be useful, it must be uplifting and unifying.

4. *Resurrection.* In denying the resurrection, the Corinthians almost certainly weren't denying life after death; this was a belief held by virtually everyone in the ancient world. They were disputing the Jewish and Christian doctrine of *bodily* resurrection in favor of a Greek form of belief that limited the afterlife to disembodied immortality of the soul. The reality of the bodily resurrection gives hope and confidence to every believer. We live today knowing that we will spend eternity with Christ.

FAITH IN ACTION

The pages of 1 Corinthians contain life lessons and role models of faith—people who challenge believers to put faith in action.

Role Models

- PAUL demonstrated fearlessness in tackling the big issues of the day. Are there concerns in your local church that need to be addressed? How can you follow Paul's example in working for unity?

- APOLLOS (3:5–9), Paul's fellow worker in the gospel, helped nurture the Corinthian church. Do you appreciate those in other fellowships or denominations of the body of Christ who contribute to your Christian journey and help spread the gospel in your community?

- STEPHANAS (16:15–17) devoted himself and his household to the service of the church. He went where he was needed, supplied what was lacking, and refreshed the spirits of those to whom he ministered. How can you be of service to your church and its leaders?

Challenges

- Do all you can to bring peace and unity to your local church.

- Demonstrate an attitude of acceptance and love to the "have-nots" in your church and community.

- Measure your spirituality by the love you express to others.

- Evaluate your lifestyle, turning from behaviors or attitudes that aren't Christlike, so that your life can be a witness to the world of Christ's love.

- Minister through words and actions to the pastor(s) of your local church.

OUTLINE

   I. Introduction: Greeting and Thanksgiving (1:1–9)
  II. Divisions in the Church (1:10—4:21)
 III. Moral Problems in the Church (5–6)
     A. Need for Church Discipline (5)
     B. Lawsuits Among Believers (6:1–11)
     C. Sexual Immorality (6:12–20)
 IV. Questions About Marriage (7)
  V. Questions About Christian Freedom (8:1—11:1)
 VI. Questions About Worship (11:2—14:40)
VII. Questions About the Resurrection (15)
VIII. Questions About Collections for the Church (16:1–9)
 IX. Conclusion (16:10–24)

1:1
a Ro 1:1; Eph 1:1
b 2Co 1:1
c Ac 18:17

1:2
d Ac 18:1 *e* Ro 1:7

1:3
f Ro 1:7

1:4
g Ro 1:8

1:5
h 2Co 9:11
i 2Co 8:7
1:6
j Rev 1:2

1:7
k Php 3:20;
Tit 2:13; 2Pe 3:12
1:8
l 1Th 3:13
1:9
m 1Jn 1:3
n Isa 49:7; 1Th 5:24

1 Paul, called to be an apostle[a] of Christ Jesus by the will of God,[b] and our brother Sosthenes,[c]

[2] To the church of God in Corinth,[d] to those sanctified in Christ Jesus and called[e] to be holy, together with all those everywhere who call on the name of our Lord Jesus Christ—their Lord and ours:

[3] Grace and peace to you from God our Father and the Lord Jesus Christ.[f]

Thanksgiving

[4] I always thank God for you[g] because of his grace given you in Christ Jesus. [5] For in him you have been enriched[h] in every way—in all your speaking and in all your knowledge[i]— [6] because our testimony[j] about Christ was confirmed in you. [7] Therefore you do not lack any spiritual gift as you eagerly wait for our Lord Jesus Christ to be revealed.[k] [8] He will keep you strong to the end, so that you will be blameless[l] on the day of our Lord Jesus Christ. [9] God, who has called you into fellowship with his Son Jesus Christ our Lord,[m] is faithful.[n]

Divisions in the Church

[10] I appeal to you, brothers, in the name of our Lord Jesus Christ, that all of you agree with one another so that there may be no divisions among you and that you may be perfectly united in mind and thought. [11] My brothers, some from Chloe's household have informed me that there are quarrels among you. [12] What I mean is

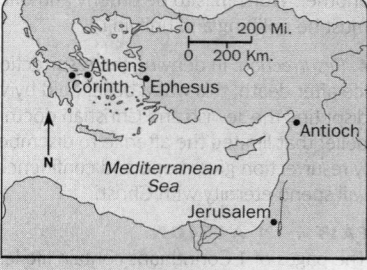

The Church in Corinth (1:2)
Then: Corinth was a bustling trading port of 100,000.
Now: It still exists as a small village in Greece.

1 Corinthians 1:1–3

The concerns Paul would address in this letter are introduced in his greeting through the ways in which he partially broke with the normal conventions for 1st-century letters. Two themes are highlighted: (1) His concern about asserting his authority (which had been rejected by some in Corinth [v. 12]) is evidenced by his unusual amount of elaboration ("called," "apostle," and "the will of God"). (2) He included declarations about the Corinthians' spiritual state and God's purposes for them.

Paul addressed the Corinthian Christians as a group—"the church" or assembly of those God had saved. "Sanctified" has to do with being separated or set apart for God—"called to be holy." Paul was reminding the Corinthians of their identity and calling. He then stressed their interconnection with believers everywhere.

A major theme of Paul's letter was that the manner in which the Corinthians lived impacted Christians everywhere. He went on to generalize to include all Christians. When you think of unity in Christ, does the picture in your mind's eye include a historical dimension? You are closely connected with your "peers" in Christ—but also part of a continuous string of believers since this first generation of Christianity.

1 Corinthians 1:4–9

Paul's statement of thanksgiving focused on what God had done in the Corinthians' lives, not on what they were doing. How could he be so positive about a church full of divisions and abuses even of these gifts? Because God had given the Corinthian believers grace, enriched them in every way, gifted them, strengthened them, and promised they would be blameless. And he would remain faithful to his promises to perfect his people, however immature they might seem to be.

Paul focused on God's faithfulness, not on people's fickleness. His combination of authority and tact set a model for Christian leaders of every age. He managed to avoid heavy-handed authoritarianism on the one hand and detachment on the other.

Viewing people from the perspective of who God is making them into in Christ transforms our entire attitude. And focusing on our interdependence as the body of Christ transforms our commitment. Scripture doesn't envision Christians apart from a local church, nor the local body apart from the entire church.

1 Corinthians 1:10–17

Paul went on to address four problems plaguing the Corinthian church—factions (1:10—4:21), incest (5:1–13), lawsuits (6:1–11), and sexual immorality in general (6:12–20). His initial reply to reports of factions consisted of three rhetorical questions: (1) Since Christ isn't divided, how could his people be? (2) Since no mere human (Jesus was both human and divine) was crucified for the world's sins, how could Christians exalt mortal authorities? (3) Since baptism is in Jesus' name, how could believers lift up anyone else?

this: One of you says, "I follow Paul";[o] another, "I follow Apollos";[p] another, "I follow Cephas[a]";[q] still another, "I follow Christ."

[13]Is Christ divided? Was Paul crucified for you? Were you baptized into[b] the name of Paul?[r] [14]I am thankful that I did not baptize any of you except Crispus[s] and Gaius,[t] [15]so no one can say that you were baptized into my name. [16](Yes, I also baptized the household of Stephanas;[u] beyond that, I don't remember if I baptized anyone else.) [17]For Christ did not send me to baptize,[v] but to preach the gospel—not with words of human wisdom,[w] lest the cross of Christ be emptied of its power.

Christ the Wisdom and Power of God

[18]For the message of the cross is foolishness to those who are perishing,[x] but to us who are being saved it is the power of God.[y] [19]For it is written:

"I will destroy the wisdom of the wise;
    the intelligence of the intelligent I will frustrate."[c z]

[20]Where is the wise man?[a] Where is the scholar? Where is the philosopher of this age? Has not God made foolish[b] the wisdom of the world? [21]For since in the wisdom of God the world through its wisdom did not know him, God was pleased through the foolishness of what was preached to save those who believe. [22]Jews demand miraculous signs[c] and Greeks look for wisdom, [23]but we preach Christ crucified: a stumbling block[d] to Jews and foolishness[e] to Gentiles, [24]but to those whom God has called,[f] both Jews and Greeks, Christ the power of God and the wisdom of God.[g] [25]For the foolishness[h] of God is wiser than man's wisdom, and the weakness[i] of God is stronger than man's strength.

[26]Brothers, think of what you were when you were called. Not many of you were wise by human standards; not many were influential; not many were of noble birth. [27]But God chose[j] the foolish[k] things of the world to shame the wise; God chose the weak things of the world to shame the strong. [28]He chose the lowly things of this world and the despised things—and the things that are not[l]—to nullify the things that are, [29]so that no one may boast before him.[m] [30]It is because of him that you are in Christ Jesus, who has become for us wisdom from God—that is, our righteousness,[n] holiness and redemption.[o] [31]Therefore, as it is written: "Let him who boasts boast in the Lord."[d p]

[a] 12 That is, Peter   [b] 13 Or in; also in verse 15   [c] 19 Isaiah 29:14   [d] 31 Jer. 9:24

Cross references

1:12
o 1Co 3:4,22
p Ac 18:24
q Jn 1:42
1:13
r Mt 28:19
1:14
s Ac 18:8; Ro 16:23
t Ac 19:29
1:16
u 1Co 16:15
1:17
v Jn 4:2
w 1Co 2:1,4,13

1:18
x 2Co 2:15
y Ro 1:16

1:19
z Isa 29:14

1:20
a Isa 19:11,12
b Job 12:17;
Ro 1:22

1:22
c Mt 12:38
1:23
d Lk 2:34; Gal 5:11
e 1Co 2:14
1:24
f Ro 8:28 g ver 30;
Col 2:3
1:25
h ver 18 i 2Co 13:4

1:27
j Jas 2:5 k ver 20

1:28
l Ro 4:17
1:29
m Eph 2:9
1:30
n Jer 23:5,6;
2Co 5:21 o Ro 3:24;
Eph 1:7,14
1:31
p Jer 9:23,24;
2Co 10:17

Paul avoided taking sides. His goal was harmony. He couldn't request a unanimous perspective or require consistent practice on every issue. This was especially true in light of his emphasis on the diversity of spiritual gifts in chapters 12–14. Paul rejected any demand for Christian "clones." But cooperation, mutual concern, peaceful coexistence, edification in love—all these are positive antidotes to division.

The church's disunity remains one of the biggest scandals compromising Christian witness today. In John 17 Jesus prayed that his disciples might be united, and in Galatians 3:28 and Ephesians 3:6 Paul called for unity despite the greatest sociological divisions of the ancient Middle East—Jew versus Gentile, slave versus free, men versus women. The witness of a united church extends to the most powerful anti-Christian forces of the universe (Eph. 3:9–10). The only way this unity can impact a non-Christian world is for it to be visible. Why do you think unity is such a powerful witness to the work of Jesus Christ? How can you, within your sphere of influence, make sure this witness isn't compromised?

1 Corinthians 1:18—2:5

Paul argued that God's ways are radically different from people's. Human wisdom and power shun God's ways as foolish and pathetic. Indeed, God's power is different, exercised through what appears to be weakness—the cross. Those his Spirit touches and converts, from whatever ethnic background, find in the cross both godly wisdom and power to transform their lives. The fact that the gospel seems foolish by human standards doesn't discount it. The ways of an all-knowing and all-powerful God are far above human ways (Isa. 55:8–9).

Paul identified the type of people God calls—the powerless and weak—as majority members of the church. Whatever gifts and strengths we have that count in God's eyes aren't of our own creation. No one can legitimately boast in them. Yet no one is powerless or worthless, either. Christ is our wisdom, our righteousness, our holiness, and our redemption. As a result, we needn't worry about our own weakness and inadequacy. As we focus on Christ and especially on Christ bearing our sin on the cross, we can live with confidence and boldness.

2:1
q 1Co 1:17
2:2
r Gal 6:14;
1Co 1:23
2:3
s Ac 18:1-18
2:4
t Ro 15:19
2:5
u 2Co 4:7; 6:7

2:6
v Eph 4:13;
Php 3:15; Heb 5:14
w 1Co 1:20

2:8
x Ac 7:2; Jas 2:1

2:9
y Isa 64:4; 65:17
2:10
z Mt 13:11;
Eph 3:3,5
a Jn 14:26
2:11
b Jer 17:9
c Pr 20:27

2:12
d Ro 8:15
e 1Co 1:20,27
2:13
f 1Co 1:17

2 When I came to you, brothers, I did not come with eloquence or superior wisdom*q* as I proclaimed to you the testimony about God.*a* 2For I resolved to know nothing while I was with you except Jesus Christ and him crucified.*r* 3I came to you*s* in weakness and fear, and with much trembling. 4My message and my preaching were not with wise and persuasive words, but with a demonstration of the Spirit's power,*t* 5so that your faith might not rest on men's wisdom, but on God's power.*u*

Wisdom From the Spirit

6We do, however, speak a message of wisdom among the mature,*v* but not the wisdom of this age*w* or of the rulers of this age, who are coming to nothing. 7No, we speak of God's secret wisdom, a wisdom that has been hidden and that God destined for our glory before time began. 8None of the rulers of this age understood it, for if they had, they would not have crucified the Lord of glory.*x* 9However, as it is written:

> "No eye has seen,
>   no ear has heard,
>   no mind has conceived
>   what God has prepared for those who love him"*b**y*—

10but God has revealed*z* it to us by his Spirit.*a*

The Spirit searches all things, even the deep things of God. 11For who among men knows the thoughts of a man*b* except the man's spirit*c* within him? In the same way no one knows the thoughts of God except the Spirit of God. 12We have not received the spirit*d* of the world*e* but the Spirit who is from God, that we may understand what God has freely given us. 13This is what we speak, not in words taught us by human wisdom*f* but in words taught by the Spirit, expressing spiritual truths in spiritual words.*c* 14The man without the Spirit does not accept the things that come

---

a 1 Some manuscripts *as I proclaimed to you God's mystery*   *b* 9 Isaiah 64:4   *c* 13 Or *Spirit, interpreting spiritual truths to spiritual men*

---

1 Corinthians 2:6–16

Greek society was preoccupied with wisdom, looking to philosophers and rulers as the fount of insight. Paul radically challenged this. Because God's wisdom is different from the world's, people are wise only by the gift of God's Spirit. True wisdom isn't confined to those society regards as powerful and influential. The humble believer who relies utterly on God's Spirit is the source of the deepest wisdom.

In this passage the wise person is identified as the one who lives focused on the crucified Christ as Savior. Through the Spirit we actually share in the "mind of God" and teach the truths of God. What does it mean for you to rely utterly on the Spirit to discern God's truth and mind? How can Scripture guide you to make sure the Spirit is leading you into the truth?

1:30

Wisdom

In chapter one Paul put the wisdom of "wise men" in perspective. God, he said, makes the wisdom of humans appear foolish. In 1:30 Paul acknowledged Jesus as the model of a wise man. Compare Jesus' actions with what one study referred to as the four dimensions of wise people:

1. Knowledge of the human condition— *of our fallen nature and need to learn from our mistakes.*	**2. Skill in using knowledge—** *sense of when to give/withhold advice.*	**3. Knowledge about the importance of life's contexts—** *the understanding that priorities change and conflicts among priorities are common.*	**4. Empathy—** *the ability to feel with, not simply sorry for, another.*
Jesus understood Nicodemus and his situation perfectly (John 3).	Because of his uncanny ability in this area, Jesus was constantly being sought out by others for aid (Mark 10:17–31).	Jesus' actions illustrated his shifting priorities as God's mission developed over time (Luke 3:41–52; 4:1–13; 9:37–45; 18:31–34; 22:39–46).	Known for his compassion, Jesus still managed to avoid syrupy, sentimental sympathy. He was able to put himself in another's sandals, to pinpoint and meet his/her need. He understood precisely what the woman at the well needed (John 4).

Source: Snyder (2002:327–347)

from the Spirit of God, for they are foolishness[g] to him, and he cannot understand them, because they are spiritually discerned. [15]The spiritual man makes judgments about all things, but he himself is not subject to any man's judgment:

[16] "For who has known the mind of the Lord
    that he may instruct him?"[a][h]

But we have the mind of Christ.[i]

On Divisions in the Church

3 Brothers, I could not address you as spiritual[j] but as worldly[k]—mere infants[l] in Christ. [2]I gave you milk, not solid food,[m] for you were not yet ready for it.[n] Indeed, you are still not ready. [3]You are still worldly. For since there is jealousy and quarreling[o] among you, are you not worldly? Are you not acting like mere men? [4]For when one says, "I follow Paul," and another, "I follow Apollos,"[p] are you not mere men?

[5]What, after all, is Apollos? And what is Paul? Only servants, through whom you came to believe—as the Lord has assigned to each his task. [6]I planted the seed,[q] Apollos watered it, but God made it grow. [7]So neither he who plants nor he who waters is anything, but only God, who makes things grow. [8]The man who plants and the man who waters have one purpose, and each will be rewarded according to his own labor.[r] [9]For we are God's fellow workers;[s] you are God's field,[t] God's building.[u]

[10]By the grace God has given me,[v] I laid a foundation[w] as an expert builder, and someone else is building on it. But each one should be careful how he builds. [11]For no one can lay any foundation other than the one already laid, which is Jesus Christ.[x] [12]If any man builds on this foundation using gold, silver, costly stones, wood, hay or straw, [13]his work will be shown for what it is,[y] because the Day[z] will bring it to light. It will be revealed with fire, and the fire will test the quality of each man's work. [14]If what he has built survives, he will receive his reward. [15]If it is burned up, he will suffer loss; he himself will be saved, but only as one escaping through the flames.[a]

[16]Don't you know that you yourselves are God's temple[b] and that God's Spirit lives in you? [17]If anyone destroys God's temple, God will destroy him; for God's temple is sacred, and you are that temple.

[18]Do not deceive yourselves. If any one of you thinks he is wise[c] by the standards of this age, he should become a "fool" so that he may become wise. [19]For the wisdom of this world is foolishness[d] in God's sight. As it is written: "He catches the wise in their craftiness"[b][e] [20]and again, "The Lord knows that the thoughts of the wise are futile."[c][f] [21]So then, no more boasting about men! [g] All things are yours,[h] [22]whether Paul or Apollos or Cephas[d][i] or the world or life or death or the present or the future[j]—all are yours, [23]and you are of Christ,[k] and Christ is of God.

Apostles of Christ

4 So then, men ought to regard us as servants of Christ and as those entrusted[l] with the secret things[m] of God. [2]Now it is required that those who have been given a trust must prove faithful. [3]I care very little if I am judged by you or by any

---

[a] 16 Isaiah 40:13   [b] 19 Job 5:13   [c] 20 Psalm 94:11   [d] 22 That is, Peter

---

2:14
[g] 1Co 1:18

2:16
[h] Isa 40:13
[i] Jn 15:15

3:1
[j] 1Co 2:15
[k] Ro 7:14; 1Co 2:14
[l] Heb 5:13
3:2
[m] Heb 5:12-14; 1Pe 2:2 [n] Jn 16:12
3:3
[o] 1Co 1:11; Gal 5:20
3:4
[p] 1Co 1:12

3:6
[q] Ac 18:4-11

3:8
[r] Ps 62:12
3:9
[s] 2Co 6:1 [t] Isa 61:3
[u] Eph 2:20-22; 1Pe 2:5
3:10
[v] Ro 12:3
[w] Ro 15:20
3:11
[x] Isa 28:16; Eph 2:20
3:13
[y] 1Co 4:5
[z] 2Th 1:7-10

3:15
[a] Jude 23
3:16
[b] 1Co 6:19; 2Co 6:16

3:18
[c] Isa 5:21; 1Co 8:2

3:19
[d] 1Co 1:20,27
[e] Job 5:13
3:20
[f] Ps 94:11
3:21
[g] 1Co 4:6 [h] Ro 8:32
3:22
[i] 1Co 1:12 [j] Ro 8:38
3:23
[k] 1Co 15:23; 2Co 10:7; Gal 3:29
4:1
[l] 1Co 9:17; Tit 1:7
[m] Ro 16:25

---

1 Corinthians 3:1–23

Chapter 3 addresses a key to overcoming divisions in the church: recognizing the equal, humble, and yet exalted position of all Christians in Christ. By the Spirit in Christ God is making us into holy temples, his own dwelling places. Therefore, we are to be careful how we live and treat one another. Paul didn't assume that every church member was a true disciple of Jesus and warned about following human leaders rather than Christ.

All believers are being knit together into a sacred temple, God's dwelling place. This truth enables rejected, marginalized, and suffering disciples, who today form a majority of Christians worldwide, to live with dignity and hope in the midst of pain. It also confronts ambitious, ego-driven people with a warning: Watch out; you are building your life on a weak foundation. How does regarding yourself as God's temple impact your attitude toward yourself, your church community, and suffering Christians everywhere?

4:4
n Ro 2:13
4:5
o Mt 7:1,2; Ro 2:1
p Ro 2:29

human court; indeed, I do not even judge myself. [4]My conscience is clear, but that does not make me innocent. [n] It is the Lord who judges me. [5]Therefore judge nothing[o] before the appointed time; wait till the Lord comes. He will bring to light what is hidden in darkness and will expose the motives of men's hearts. At that time each will receive his praise from God. [p]

4:6
q 1Co 1:19,31;
3:19,20 r 1Co 1:12
4:7
s Jn 3:27; Ro 12:3,6
4:8
t Rev 3:17,18

[6]Now, brothers, I have applied these things to myself and Apollos for your benefit, so that you may learn from us the meaning of the saying, "Do not go beyond what is written." [q] Then you will not take pride in one man over against another. [r] [7]For who makes you different from anyone else? What do you have that you did not receive? [s] And if you did receive it, why do you boast as though you did not?

[8]Already you have all you want! Already you have become rich! [t] You have become kings—and that without us! How I wish that you really had become kings so that we might be kings with you! [9]For it seems to me that God has put us apostles

4:9
u Ro 8:36
v Heb 10:33
4:10
w 1Co 1:18;
Ac 17:18
x 1Co 3:18
y 1Co 2:3
4:11
z Ro 8:35;
2Co 11:23-27
4:12
a Ac 18:3 b 1Pe 3:9
4:13
c La 3:45
4:14
d 1Th 2:11

on display at the end of the procession, like men condemned to die[u] in the arena. We have been made a spectacle[v] to the whole universe, to angels as well as to men. [10]We are fools for Christ, [w] but you are so wise in Christ! [x] We are weak, but you are strong! [y] You are honored, we are dishonored! [11]To this very hour we go hungry and thirsty, we are in rags, we are brutally treated, we are homeless. [z] [12]We work hard with our own hands. [a] When we are cursed, we bless;[b] when we are persecuted, we endure it; [13]when we are slandered, we answer kindly. Up to this moment we have become the scum of the earth, the refuse[c] of the world.

[14]I am not writing this to shame you, but to warn you, as my dear children. [d] [15]Even though you have ten thousand guardians in Christ, you do not have many

4:15
e 1Co 9:12,14,18,
23
4:16
f 1Co 11:1;
Php 3:17; 1Th 1:6;
2Th 3:7,9
4:17
g 1Ti 1:2
h 1Co 7:17
4:19
i 2Co 1:15,16
j Ac 18:21

fathers, for in Christ Jesus I became your father through the gospel. [e] [16]Therefore I urge you to imitate me. [f] [17]For this reason I am sending to you Timothy, my son[g] whom I love, who is faithful in the Lord. He will remind you of my way of life in Christ Jesus, which agrees with what I teach everywhere in every church. [h]

[18]Some of you have become arrogant, as if I were not coming to you. [19]But I will come to you very soon, [i] if the Lord is willing,[j] and then I will find out not only how these arrogant people are talking, but what power they have. [20]For the kingdom of God is not a matter of talk but of power. [21]What do you prefer? Shall I come to you

4:21
k 2Co 1:23; 13:2,10

with a whip, [k] or in love and with a gentle spirit?

Expel the Immoral Brother!

5:1
l Lev 18:8; Dt 22:30
5:2
m 2Co 7:7-11

5 It is actually reported that there is sexual immorality among you, and of a kind that does not occur even among pagans: A man has his father's wife. [l] [2]And you are proud! Shouldn't you rather have been filled with grief[m] and have put out of

---

1 Corinthians 4:1–21

📖 Paul was correcting an imbalance in the Corinthians' approach to leaders. The gospel's continual theme is that church leaders are servants and fellow sufferers, who lead by example and exercise authority as tender guardians. Paul contrasted his own suffering and mistreatment with the pride, exercise of power, and idolization often associated with leaders.

🔎 Paul didn't provide an attractive picture of leaders (v. 13). His emphasis on God's power being exercised through apparent weakness and suffering, as demonstrated on the cross, transformed his entire attitude toward pride, position, power, and suffering. Sadly, we who experience the most widespread material comfort of any culture in history often have a poor understanding of the positive value of affliction.

Much of Paul's suffering was due to the dangers of itinerant ministry in the ancient world. Today these conditions prevail in many places, where ministers can expect to be bi-vocational; poorly paid; and required to

travel long distances to small, scattered outposts of believers. What can you (as a congregation and an individual or family) do to directly aid an overseas church leader? How does Paul's portrayal of leadership impact your own approach?

1 Corinthians 5:1–13

📖 Appealing to the Jews' practice of purifying their homes from all leavened bread prior to the Passover feast, Paul stressed that serious sin can infect a whole congregation. Passover reminded him of Christ as the believer's perfect sacrifice. Jesus' atonement frees every Christian—not *to* sin but *from* sin. Paul called his audience to "become what they were"—to act according to the way God had already *chosen to consider* them in Christ. This meant putting away all forms of evil and behaving in ways that conformed to God's true standards.

Fellow church members, Paul urged, were to continue to reach out to and urge repentance from a person engaged in serious sin. But church relationships can't continue unchanged so long as the individual refuses to

your fellowship the man who did this? [3]Even though I am not physically present, I am with you in spirit. [n] And I have already passed judgment on the one who did this, just as if I were present. [4]When you are assembled in the name of our Lord Jesus[o] and I am with you in spirit, and the power of our Lord Jesus is present, [5]hand this man over[p] to Satan, so that the sinful nature[a] may be destroyed and his spirit saved on the day of the Lord.

[6]Your boasting is not good. [q] Don't you know that a little yeast[r] works through the whole batch of dough?[s] [7]Get rid of the old yeast that you may be a new batch without yeast—as you really are. For Christ, our Passover lamb, has been sacrificed. [t] [8]Therefore let us keep the Festival, not with the old yeast, the yeast of malice and wickedness, but with bread without yeast, [u] the bread of sincerity and truth.

[9]I have written you in my letter not to associate[v] with sexually immoral people— [10]not at all meaning the people of this world[w] who are immoral, or the greedy and swindlers, or idolaters. In that case you would have to leave this world. [11]But now I am writing you that you must not associate with anyone who calls himself a brother but is sexually immoral or greedy, an idolater[x] or a slanderer, a drunkard or a swindler. With such a man do not even eat.

[12]What business is it of mine to judge those outside[y] the church? Are you not to judge those inside?[z] [13]God will judge those outside. "Expel the wicked man from among you."[b][a]

Lawsuits Among Believers

6 If any of you has a dispute with another, dare he take it before the ungodly for judgment instead of before the saints?[b] [2]Do you not know that the saints will judge the world?[c] And if you are to judge the world, are you not competent to judge trivial cases? [3]Do you not know that we will judge angels? How much more the things of this life! [4]Therefore, if you have disputes about such matters, appoint as judges even men of little account in the church![c] [5]I say this to shame you. [d] Is it possible that there is nobody among you wise enough to judge a dispute between believers?[e] [6]But instead, one brother goes to law against another—and this in front of unbelievers![f]

[7]The very fact that you have lawsuits among you means you have been completely defeated already. Why not rather be wronged? Why not rather be cheated?[g] [8]Instead, you yourselves cheat and do wrong, and you do this to your brothers. [h]

[a] 5 Or *that his body; or that the flesh*   [b] 13 Deut. 17:7; 19:19; 21:21; 22:21,24; 24:7
[c] 4 Or *matters, do you appoint as judges men of little account in the church?*

Cross references
5:3 [n] Col 2:5
5:4 [o] 2Th 3:6
5:5 [p] 1Ti 1:20
5:6 [q] Jas 4:16 [r] Mt 16:6,12 [s] Gal 5:9
5:7 [t] Mk 14:12; 1Pe 1:19
5:8 [u] Ex 12:14,15; Dt 16:3
5:9 [v] Eph 5:11; 2Th 3:6,14
5:10 [w] 1Co 10:27
5:11 [x] 1Co 10:7,14
5:12 [y] Mk 4:11 [z] ver 3-5; 1Co 6:1-4
5:13 [a] Dt 13:5
6:1 [b] Mt 18:17
6:2 [c] Mt 19:28; Lk 22:30
6:5 [d] 1Co 4:14 [e] Ac 1:15
6:6 [f] 2Co 6:14,15
6:7 [g] Mt 5:39,40
6:8 [h] 1Th 4:6

---

acknowledge wrongdoing. The point of barring such persons from fellowship is twofold: to shock them by the severity of the church's disapproval and to stimulate them to change their behavior. Such "dis-fellowshipping" is a last resort.

Even our secular world finds incest offensive. The unacceptability of its occurrence in Christian circles is apparent, and the need when it does come to light for loving but firm discipline remains great.

The Biblical definition of *immorality* covers the full range of humanity's sinful behavior, and Paul stressed that disciplinary action is necessary in situations involving fraud, greed, idolatry, cheating, and abusive and addictive behaviors. The church is a holy temple, the Spirit's dwelling place. A holy congregation, one that cleans its own house to preserve its purity but doesn't expect the same standards of obedience from the unsaved, can profoundly impact an unholy world.

1 Corinthians 6:1–11

Paul turned to a discussion of how the judicial process was to work within the church. The sin of the group he was addressing involved the practice of suing fellow Christians in secular courts. Paul made two main points: (1) If disputes require intervention, it should occur within the Christian community, and (2) it's better to accept being wronged than to demand compensation in *either* a secular or a Christian context.

Our society rivals ancient Corinth in its passion for suing people. Paul didn't address whether or not Christians may sue non-Christians or secular institutions like corporations or the government. His focus was first on prohibiting Christians from suing other believers in secular courts and second on questioning the legitimacy of any lawsuit between believers. There is also is a key difference between seeking justice for others who have been wronged (cf. Isa. 10:1–2) and trying to avenge injustices against ourselves.

The concept of giving up our rights goes against our cultural grain. Yet from the Sermon on the Mount on this is a fundamental calling of the gospel. God doesn't give us what we actually deserve. We are wise to proceed with caution in demanding from others what we think we deserve.

9 Do you not know that the wicked will not inherit the kingdom of God?[i] Do not be deceived:[j] Neither the sexually immoral nor idolaters nor adulterers nor male prostitutes nor homosexual offenders 10 nor thieves nor the greedy nor drunkards nor slanderers nor swindlers will inherit the kingdom of God. 11 And that is what some of you were.[k] But you were washed,[l] you were sanctified,[m] you were justified in the name of the Lord Jesus Christ and by the Spirit of our God.

Sexual Immorality

12 "Everything is permissible for me"—but not everything is beneficial.[n] "Everything is permissible for me"—but I will not be mastered by anything. 13 "Food for the stomach and the stomach for food"—but God will destroy them both.[o] The body is not meant for sexual immorality, but for the Lord, and the Lord for the body. 14 By his power God raised the Lord from the dead, and he will raise us also.[p] 15 Do you not know that your bodies are members of Christ himself?[q] Shall I then take the members of Christ and unite them with a prostitute? Never! 16 Do you not know that he who unites himself with a prostitute is one with her in body? For it is said, "The two will become one flesh."[a][r] 17 But he who unites himself with the Lord is one with him in spirit.[s]

18 Flee from sexual immorality.[t] All other sins a man commits are outside his body, but he who sins sexually sins against his own body.[u] 19 Do you not know that your body is a temple[v] of the Holy Spirit, who is in you, whom you have received from God? You are not your own;[w] 20 you were bought at a price.[x] Therefore honor God with your body.

Marriage

7 Now for the matters you wrote about: It is good for a man not to marry.[b][y] 2 But since there is so much immorality, each man should have his own wife, and each woman her own husband. 3 The husband should fulfill his marital duty to his wife,[z] and likewise the wife to her husband. 4 The wife's body does not belong to her alone but also to her husband. In the same way, the husband's body does not belong to him alone but also to his wife. 5 Do not deprive each other except by mutual consent and for a time,[a] so that you may devote yourselves to prayer. Then come together again so that Satan[b] will not tempt you[c] because of your lack of self-con-

6:9 [i] Gal 5:21 [j] 1Co 15:33; Jas 1:16
6:11 [k] Eph 2:2 [l] Ac 22:16 [m] 1Co 1:2
6:12 [n] 1Co 10:23
6:13 [o] Col 2:22
6:14 [p] Ro 6:5; Eph 1:19,20
6:15 [q] Ro 12:5
6:16 [r] Ge 2:24; Mt 19:5; Eph 5:31
6:17 [s] Jn 17:21-23; Gal 2:20
6:18 [t] 2Co 12:21; 1Th 4:3,4; Heb 13:4 [u] Ro 6:12
6:19 [v] Jn 2:21 [w] Ro 14:7,8
6:20 [x] Ac 20:28; 1Co 7:23; 1Pe 1:18, 19; Rev 5:9
7:1 [y] ver 8,26
7:3 [z] Ex 21: 10; 1Pe 3:7
7:5 [a] Ex 19:15; 1Sa 21:4,5 [b] Mt 4:10 [c] 1Th 3:5

[a] *16* Gen. 2:24 [b] *1* Or *"It is good for a man not to have sexual relations with a woman."*

---

1 Corinthians 6:12–20

Paul began this passage by quoting two Corinthian slogans. He gave them limited endorsement but then substantially qualified them. The apostle went on to discuss sexual immorality in general, but particularly as manifested in prostitution, for which Corinth was infamous. Sex for hire has all too frequently epitomized the abuse of human beings by those with no commitment to their greater good. Paul's approach to our bodies, and thus to sexuality, was rooted in his conviction that underlies the entire letter: They are temples of the Holy Spirit (v. 19).

Because sex reflects the most intimate of interpersonal relations among humans, it's to be reserved for marriage—the most permanent of interpersonal commitments.

Many cultures of our world, and especially those in the West, are preoccupied with sex. Sex trafficking—the selling of children and women into forced prostitution—is a horrific crime destroying the lives of millions of women and children every year. Paul's perspective impacts this totally. Our bodies aren't our own, to do with as our desires and pleasures dictate. They belong to Christ and have been made sacred, holy dwelling places of God's Spirit. Beyond sexuality, what implications does this perspective have in terms of how you care for your body?

1 Corinthians 7:1–40

Here Paul addressed a list of questions pertaining to "the household code." In light of believers' bodies being temples of God, how were they to order their intimate relationships—marriage, singleness, divorce, slavery? Paul emphasized three implications: Christians are to (1) fulfill the responsibilities of their present situation (vv. 5,17,20,26,40); (2) live in all situations as Christ's slaves (v. 22); and (3) live in the knowledge that the time is short, impelling them to use the things of the world without becoming engrossed in them (v. 31).

Sexual asceticism remains in Roman Catholic circles, which require celibacy for priests and various religious orders. Protestants at times have gone to the opposite extreme, inappropriately disapproving of or being suspicious of the single life. Some churches decline to hire unmarried pastors, and many single adults testify to being treated as second-class citizens within their congregations. A balanced approach is important if we are to respect God's unique calling and purpose for each life.

trol. ⁶I say this as a concession, not as a command. *d* ⁷I wish that all men were as I am. *e* But each man has his own gift from God; one has this gift, another has that. *f*

⁸Now to the unmarried and the widows I say: It is good for them to stay unmarried, as I am. *g* ⁹But if they cannot control themselves, they should marry, *h* for it is better to marry than to burn with passion.

¹⁰To the married I give this command (not I, but the Lord): A wife must not separate from her husband. *i* ¹¹But if she does, she must remain unmarried or else be reconciled to her husband. And a husband must not divorce his wife.

¹²To the rest I say this (I, not the Lord):*j* If any brother has a wife who is not a believer and she is willing to live with him, he must not divorce her. ¹³And if a woman has a husband who is not a believer and he is willing to live with her, she must not divorce him. ¹⁴For the unbelieving husband has been sanctified through his wife, and the unbelieving wife has been sanctified through her believing husband. Otherwise your children would be unclean, but as it is, they are holy. *k*

¹⁵But if the unbeliever leaves, let him do so. A believing man or woman is not bound in such circumstances; God has called us to live in peace. *l* ¹⁶How do you know, wife, whether you will save *m* your husband? *n* Or, how do you know, husband, whether you will save your wife?

¹⁷Nevertheless, each one should retain the place in life that the Lord assigned to him and to which God has called him. *o* This is the rule I lay down in all the churches. *p* ¹⁸Was a man already circumcised when he was called? He should not become uncircumcised. Was a man uncircumcised when he was called? He should not be circumcised. *q* ¹⁹Circumcision is nothing and uncircumcision is nothing. *r* Keeping God's commands is what counts. ²⁰Each one should remain in the situation which he was in when God called him. *s* ²¹Were you a slave when you were called? Don't let it trouble you—although if you can gain your freedom, do so. ²²For he who was a slave when he was called by the Lord is the Lord's freedman; *t* similarly, he who was a free man when he was called is Christ's slave. *u* ²³You were bought at a price; *v* do not become slaves of men. ²⁴Brothers, each man, as responsible to God, should remain in the situation God called him to. *w*

²⁵Now about virgins: I have no command from the Lord, *x* but I give a judgment as one who by the Lord's mercy *y* is trustworthy. ²⁶Because of the present crisis, I think that it is good for you to remain as you are. *z* ²⁷Are you married? Do not seek a divorce. Are you unmarried? Do not look for a wife. ²⁸But if you do marry, you have not sinned; and if a virgin marries, she has not sinned. But those who marry will face many troubles in this life, and I want to spare you this.

²⁹What I mean, brothers, is that the time is short. *a* From now on those who have wives should live as if they had none; ³⁰those who mourn, as if they did not; those who are happy, as if they were not; those who buy something, as if it were not theirs to keep; ³¹those who use the things of the world, as if not engrossed in them. For this world in its present form is passing away. *b*

³²I would like you to be free from concern. An unmarried man is concerned about the Lord's affairs *c*—how he can please the Lord. ³³But a married man is concerned about the affairs of this world—how he can please his wife— ³⁴and his interests are divided. An unmarried woman or virgin is concerned about the Lord's affairs: Her aim is to be devoted to the Lord in both body and spirit. *d* But a married woman is concerned about the affairs of this world—how she can please her husband. ³⁵I am saying this for your own good, not to restrict you, but that you may live in a right way in undivided *e* devotion to the Lord.

³⁶If anyone thinks he is acting improperly toward the virgin he is engaged to, and if she is getting along in years and he feels he ought to marry, he should do as he

7:6
d 2Co 8:8
7:7
e ver 8; 1Co 9:5
f Mt 19:11,12;
Ro 12:6;
1Co 12:4,11
7:8
g ver 1,26
7:9
h 1Ti 5:14
7:10
i Mal 2:14-16;
Mt 5:32; 19:3-9;
Mk 10:11; Lk 16:18
7:12
j ver 6,10;
2Co 11:17
7:14
k Mal 2:15
7:15
l Ro 14:19;
1Co 14:33
7:16
m Ro 11:14
n 1Pe 3:1
7:17
o Ro 12:3
p 1Co 4:17; 14:33;
2Co 8:18; 11:28
7:18
q Ac 15:1,2
7:19
r Ro 2:25-27;
Gal 5:6; 6:15;
Col 3:11
7:20
s ver 24
7:22
t Jn 8:32,36;
Phm 16 *u* Eph 6:6
7:23
v 1Co 6:20
7:24
w ver 20
7:25
x ver 6; 2Co 8:8
y 2Co 4:1;
1Ti 1:13,16
7:26
z ver 1,8
7:29
a ver 31;
Ro 13:11,12
7:31
b 1Jn 2:17
7:32
c 1Ti 5:5
7:34
d Lk 2:37
7:35
e Ps 86:11

Both outright and subtle forms of slavery still exist in parts of the developing world, particularly as children are sold into prostitution or as child laborers. Addictions and "isms" enslave others, predominantly in wealthier nations. Against all of these we as Christ's followers can be a voice for freedom. People suffering under oppressive governments and impoverished by unjust economic policies also need to hear from us that the gospel holds out hope for their physical and spiritual circumstances.

7:36
f ver 28

7:38
g Heb 13:4

7:39
h Ro 7:2,3
i 2Co 6:14

7:40
j ver 25

wants. He is not sinning. *f* They should get married. [37] But the man who has settled the matter in his own mind, who is under no compulsion but has control over his own will, and who has made up his mind not to marry the virgin—this man also does the right thing. [38] So then, he who marries the virgin does right, *g* but he who does not marry her does even better. *a*

[39] A woman is bound to her husband as long as he lives. *h* But if her husband dies, she is free to marry anyone she wishes, but he must belong to the Lord. *i* [40] In my judgment, *j* she is happier if she stays as she is—and I think that I too have the Spirit of God.

Food Sacrificed to Idols

8:1
k Ac 15:20
l Ro 15:14

8:2
m 1Co 3:18
n 1Co 13:8,9,12;
1Ti 6:4

8:3
o Ro 8:29; Gal 4:9

8:4
p ver 1,7,10
q 1Co 10:19
r Dt 6:4; Eph 4:6

8:5
s 2Th 2:4

8:6
t Mal 2:10
u Ro 11:36
v Eph 4:5 *w* Jn 1:3

8 Now about food sacrificed to idols: *k* We know that we all possess knowledge. *b l* Knowledge puffs up, but love builds up. [2] The man who thinks he knows something *m* does not yet know as he ought to know. *n* [3] But the man who loves God is known by God. *o*

[4] So then, about eating food sacrificed to idols: *p* We know that an idol is nothing at all in the world *q* and that there is no God but one. *r* [5] For even if there are so-called gods, *s* whether in heaven or on earth (as indeed there are many "gods" and many "lords"), [6] yet for us there is but one God, the Father, *t* from whom all things came *u* and for whom we live; and there is but one Lord, *v* Jesus Christ, through whom all things came *w* and through whom we live.

8:7
x Ro 14:14;
1Co 10:28

8:8
y Ro 14:17

8:9
z Gal 5:13
a Ro 14:1

8:11
b Ro 14:15,20

8:12
c Mt 18:6

[7] But not everyone knows this. Some people are still so accustomed to idols that when they eat such food they think of it as having been sacrificed to an idol, and since their conscience is weak, *x* it is defiled. [8] But food does not bring us near to God; *y* we are no worse if we do not eat, and no better if we do.

[9] Be careful, however, that the exercise of your freedom does not become a stumbling block *z* to the weak. *a* [10] For if anyone with a weak conscience sees you who have this knowledge eating in an idol's temple, won't he be emboldened to eat what has been sacrificed to idols? [11] So this weak brother, for whom Christ died, is destroyed *b* by your knowledge. [12] When you sin against your brothers *c* in this way and wound their weak conscience, you sin against Christ. [13] Therefore, if what I eat causes my brother to fall into sin, I will never eat meat again, so that I will not cause him to fall. *d*

8:13
d Ro 14:21

a 36-38 Or [36] *If anyone thinks he is not treating his daughter properly, and if she is getting along in years, and he feels she ought to marry, he should do as he wants. He is not sinning. He should let her get married.* [37] *But the man who has settled the matter in his own mind, who is under no compulsion but has control over his own will, and who has made up his mind to keep the virgin unmarried—this man also does the right thing.* [38] *So then, he who gives his virgin in marriage does right, but he who does not give her in marriage does even better.*   *b* 1 Or *"We all possess knowledge," as you say*

---

1 Corinthians 8:1–13

Most meat sold in the Corinthian marketplace came from sacrificial animals that had been slaughtered at pagan temple ceremonies. Did these rituals somehow automatically taint the food? Could Christians buy it? Could they eat it if it was offered to them at friends' homes? What about social events—weddings, business lunches? The issue clearly wasn't as simple as it might have seemed at first glance.

Common contemporary issues we can compare to "eating meat sacrificed to idols" have to do with involvement in activities that may or may not be offensive to others or lead them astray. These may include drinking alcohol, wearing certain styles of clothing, choosing various forms of entertainment, smoking, buying lottery tickets, and participating in other forms of gambling. Paul made it clear that Christians are to

behave in ways most likely to lead to others' salvation (see esp. 9:19–23). Three timeless principles dominate this discussion: (1) What's safe for one Christian may not be for another; (2) true discernment requires love *and* knowledge; and (3) believers have no right to demand freedoms that might hurt or offend those around them.

1 Corinthians 9:1–27

Some Corinthians doubted Paul's authority because he didn't accept payment for his services (cf. 2 Cor. 11:7), unlike itinerant Greco-Roman philosophers and religious teachers who supported themselves by various means. Powerful patrons in the church would have preferred that Paul accept their money rather than relying on tent-making—with the implied understanding that he would in turn give them respect and political/social support or clout.

The Rights of an Apostle

9 Am I not free? Am I not an apostle?[e] Have I not seen Jesus our Lord?[f] Are you not the result of my work in the Lord?[g] **2**Even though I may not be an apostle to others, surely I am to you! For you are the seal[h] of my apostleship in the Lord.

3This is my defense to those who sit in judgment on me. **4**Don't we have the right to food and drink?[i] **5**Don't we have the right to take a believing wife[j] along with us, as do the other apostles and the Lord's brothers[k] and Cephas[a]? **6**Or is it only I and Barnabas[l] who must work for a living?

7Who serves as a soldier at his own expense? Who plants a vineyard[m] and does not eat of its grapes? Who tends a flock and does not drink of the milk? **8**Do I say this merely from a human point of view? Doesn't the Law say the same thing? **9**For it is written in the Law of Moses: "Do not muzzle an ox while it is treading out the grain."[b][n] Is it about oxen that God is concerned?[o] **10**Surely he says this for us, doesn't he? Yes, this was written for us,[p] because when the plowman plows and the thresher threshes, they ought to do so in the hope of sharing in the harvest.[q] **11**If we have sown spiritual seed among you, is it too much if we reap a material harvest from you?[r] **12**If others have this right of support from you, shouldn't we have it all the more?

But we did not use this right.[s] On the contrary, we put up with anything rather than hinder[t] the gospel of Christ. **13**Don't you know that those who work in the temple get their food from the temple, and those who serve at the altar share in what is offered on the altar?[u] **14**In the same way, the Lord has commanded that those who preach the gospel should receive their living from the gospel.[v]

15But I have not used any of these rights.[w] And I am not writing this in the hope that you will do such things for me. I would rather die than have anyone deprive me of this boast.[x] **16**Yet when I preach the gospel, I cannot boast, for I am compelled to preach.[y] Woe to me if I do not preach the gospel! **17**If I preach voluntarily, I have a reward;[z] if not voluntarily, I am simply discharging the trust committed to me.[a] **18**What then is my reward? Just this: that in preaching the gospel I may offer it free of charge,[b] and so not make use of my rights in preaching it.

19Though I am free[c] and belong to no man, I make myself a slave to everyone,[d] to win as many as possible.[e] **20**To the Jews I became like a Jew, to win the Jews.[f] To those under the law I became like one under the law (though I myself am not under the law), so as to win those under the law. **21**To those not having the law I became like one not having the law[g] (though I am not free from God's law but am under Christ's law), so as to win those not having the law. **22**To the weak I became weak, to win the weak. I have become all things to all men[h] so that by all possible means I might save some.[i] **23**I do all this for the sake of the gospel, that I may share in its blessings.

24Do you not know that in a race all the runners run, but only one gets the prize? Run[j] in such a way as to get the prize. **25**Everyone who competes in the games goes into strict training. They do it to get a crown that will not last; but we do it to get a crown that will last forever.[k] **26**Therefore I do not run like a man running aimlessly; I do not fight like a man beating the air. **27**No, I beat my body[l] and make it my slave so that after I have preached to others, I myself will not be disqualified for the prize.

---

a 5 That is, Peter   b 9 Deut. 25:4

9:1
e 2Co 12:12
f 1Co 15:8
g 1Co 3:6; 4:15
9:2
h 2Co 3:2,3

9:4
i 1Th 2:6
9:5
j 1Co 7:7,8
k Mt 12:46
9:6
l Ac 4:36
9:7
m Dt 20:6; Pr 27:18

9:9
n Dt 25:4; 1Ti 5:18
o Dt 22:1-4
9:10
p Ro 4:23,24
q 2Ti 2:6

9:11
r Ro 15:27

9:12
s Ac 18:3
t 2Co 11:7-12

9:13
u Lev 6:16,26;
Dt 18:1
9:14
v Mt 10:10;
1Ti 5:18
9:15
w Ac 18:3
x 2Co 11:9,10
9:16
y Ro 1:14; Ac 9:15
9:17
z 1Co 3:8,14
a Gal 2:7; Col 1:25
9:18
b 2Co 11:7; 12:13
9:19
c ver 1 d Gal 5:13
e Mt 18:15; 1Pe 3:1
9:20
f Ac 16:3; 21:20-26;
Ro 11:14

9:21
g Ro 2:12,14

9:22
h 1Co 10:33
i Ro 11:14

9:24
j Gal 2:2; 2Ti 4:7;
Heb 12:1
9:25
k Jas 1:12; Rev 2:10
9:27
l Ro 8:13

In life's morally gray areas, Paul bent over backward to be sensitive to the non-Christian values of society so as not to hinder people from accepting the gospel. He changed the *forms* of his message in relevant ways, while preserving the integrity of its *content*.

In this passage Paul outlined one of his passionate priorities, as well as his decisions about the complex ethical issues the early church faced—like slavery, divorce, and the role of women in leadership. "Though I am free . . . I make myself a slave to everyone to win as many as possible" (v. 19). "I have become all things to all people so that by all possible means I might save some" (v. 22). Paul's priority was on causing minimum offense among non-believers so that God could bring them to faith and the new life found in Christ. How might this guide the church today in its approach to ethical issues in society?

Billy Graham

Evangelist William Franklin "Billy" Graham (1918–) has preached the gospel message to more people than anyone else in history. His evangelistic crusades have spanned the globe.

Although conservative in theology, he has long advocated the necessity for Christians to fully engage the world, not only with the gospel message of conversion but also with social service. As Richard Pierard reported in an article in *Modern American Protestantism and Its World*, Graham once asserted, "The fruit of rebirth is neighbor love, expressed in social service," adding that "social service without conversion is absurd." Graham further pointed out that "a great section of the church" feels these should go hand-in-hand, going on to state, "I am one of them."

Graham over the course of his fifty-plus years of ministry has consistently been ranked by Americans in the top five of "most admired" men. Clearly Americans, Christian and otherwise, view him as a trailblazer. Why? And what can we learn from his example?

> The fruit of rebirth is neighbor love, expressed in social service.

Billy Graham's goal has always been to preach the gospel to as many people as possible. Whatever he has done may be analyzed only after it's been filtered through that goal. In this sense he is a prime modern manifestation of the apostle Paul's comment, "Though I am free and belong to no man, I make myself a slave to everyone to win as many as possible."

This Pauline stance on the part of Graham explains what some have called his commitment to "local ecumenism." Graham has insisted throughout his ministry that his crusades are to be supported by a diverse coalition of local churches. Increasingly, this has included Roman Catholics. More than any other evangelical, Graham also has reached out to the world's Jewish communities. In 1966 he spoke of Jesus Christ before the General Assembly of the National Council of Churches at its annual meeting in Miami Beach, Florida. Lesson: *We are to be focused on preaching Christian faith, not strictly Roman Catholic or Protestant or Evangelical or Orthodox faith.*

At the meeting in Miami Beach, Graham affirmed the need for two kinds of conversion: one from the world to Christ, the second expressed as an overt display of the fruits of being a Spirit-filled Christian. For Graham this has meant shifting his focus from an intensely introverted United States base to a concern for the whole world. This is both a geographical and a spiritual widening. And these two have led to a methodological flexibility that has grown as the years have marched on. Lesson: *The gospel changes people's relations, both to Christ and to the world.*

A hero of the faith is to be flexible—a risk-taker, not only in the face of the world's problems but also in response to his or her own Christian community. As the years have progressed, Billy Graham has changed his mind about numerous issues, most notably the politics of the former Soviet-bloc and nuclear armament. As world conditions changed, Graham traveled to the former Soviet Union to preach, even though this decision cost him some support from certain sectors of his constituency. And he became an outspoken critic of the nuclear arms race, foreseeing the dangers of the world's headlong rush to mass destruction. Lesson: *A trailblazer is willing to take risks.*

Warnings From Israel's History

10 For I do not want you to be ignorant of the fact, brothers, that our forefathers were all under the cloud[m] and that they all passed through the sea.[n] 2They were all baptized into Moses in the cloud and in the sea. 3They all ate the same spiritual food 4and drank the same spiritual drink; for they drank from the spiritual rock[o] that accompanied them, and that rock was Christ. 5Nevertheless, God was not pleased with most of them; their bodies were scattered over the desert.[p]

6Now these things occurred as examples[a] to keep us from setting our hearts on evil things as they did. 7Do not be idolaters,[q] as some of them were; as it is written: "The people sat down to eat and drink and got up to indulge in pagan revelry."[b][r] 8We should not commit sexual immorality, as some of them did—and in one day twenty-three thousand of them died.[s] 9We should not test the Lord, as some of them did—and were killed by snakes.[t] 10And do not grumble, as some of them did[u]—and were killed[v] by the destroying angel.[w]

11These things happened to them as examples and were written down as warnings for us, on whom the fulfillment of the ages has come.[x] 12So, if you think you are standing firm,[y] be careful that you don't fall! 13No temptation has seized you except what is common to man. And God is faithful;[z] he will not let you be tempted beyond what you can bear.[a] But when you are tempted, he will also provide a way out so that you can stand up under it.

Idol Feasts and the Lord's Supper

14Therefore, my dear friends, flee from idolatry. 15I speak to sensible people; judge for yourselves what I say. 16Is not the cup of thanksgiving for which we give thanks a participation in the blood of Christ? And is not the bread that we break a participation in the body of Christ?[b] 17Because there is one loaf, we, who are many, are one body,[c] for we all partake of the one loaf.

18Consider the people of Israel: Do not those who eat the sacrifices[d] participate in the altar? 19Do I mean then that a sacrifice offered to an idol is anything, or that an idol is anything?[e] 20No, but the sacrifices of pagans are offered to demons,[f] not to God, and I do not want you to be participants with demons. 21You cannot drink the cup of the Lord and the cup of demons too; you cannot have a part in both the Lord's table and the table of demons.[g] 22Are we trying to arouse the Lord's jealousy?[h] Are we stronger than he?[i]

The Believer's Freedom

23"Everything is permissible"—but not everything is beneficial.[j] "Everything is

---

a 6 Or *types*; also in verse 11   b 7 Exodus 32:6

10:1
m Ex 13:21
n Ex 14:22,29

10:4
o Ex 17:6;
Nu 20:11; Ps 78:15
10:5
p Nu 14:29;
Heb 3:17
10:7
q ver 14
r Ex 32:4,6,19

10:8
s Nu 25:1-9
10:9
t Nu 21:5,6
10:10
u Nu 16:41
v Nu 16:49
w Ex 12:23
10:11
x Ro 13:11
10:12
y Ro 11:20
10:13
z 1Co 1:9 a 2Pe 2:9

10:16
b Mt 26:26-28
10:17
c Ro 12:5;
1Co 12:27
10:18
d Lev 7:6,14,15
10:19
e 1Co 8:4
10:20
f Dt 32:17;
Ps 106:37; Rev 9:20

10:21
g 2Co 6:15,16
10:22
h Dt 32:16,21
i Ecc 6:10; Isa 45:9

10:23
j 1Co 6:12

---

1 Corinthians 10:1–13

Paul illustrated the danger of failing to exercise strict self-control in the Christian life (see 9:24–27). He used numerous examples of spiritual blessings received and sins committed by the Israelites during their wilderness wanderings to warn the Corinthians against succumbing to the temptations of idolatry, sexual immorality, and testing God.

When faced with temptation, we are not to wallow in self-pity, assuming that no one understands our dilemma. Paul encouraged us with three truths: (1) Others have experienced the same temptations before us, (2) God is faithful, and (3) he won't let us be tempted beyond what we can withstand but will provide a way out if we are willing to choose it. God provides us the ability to be victorious over whatever tempts us—a way *through*—not necessarily a removal *of*, the temptation.

1 Corinthians 10:14–22

These verses return to the topic with which chapter 8 began—eating idol meat—contrasting this practice with eating the body and blood of Christ in communion. Paul made one absolute prohibition: Eating idol meat in the context of explicitly pagan worship services was always wrong. The common loaf of communion, on the other hand, demonstrated to the Corinthians their unity in Christ, which also separated them from false religion.

Morally neutral activities can lead to immorality. And what tempts one individual may not even remotely interest another. Recognizing that we have been made one, as the body of Christ, can keep us as believers from personally falling into either sin or legalism, as well as from leading others astray.

k ver 33; Ro 15:1,2;
1Co 13:5;
Php 2:4,21
10:25
l Ac 10:15; 1Co 8:7
10:26
m Ps 24:1
10:27
n Lk 10:7
10:28
o 1Co 8:7,10-12
10:29
p Ro 14:16;
1Co 9:1,19
10:30
q Ro 14:6
10:31
r Col 3:17; 1Pe 4:11
10:32
s Ac 24:16
t Ac 20:28
10:33
u Ro 15:2; 1Co 9:22
v Ro 11:14
11:1
w 1Co 4:16

11:2
x ver 17,22
y 1Co 4:17
z 1Co 15:2,3;
2Th 2:15
11:3
a Eph 1:22
b Ge 3:16; Eph 5:23
c 1Co 3:23

11:5
d Ac 21:9
e Dt 21:12

11:7
f Ge 1:26; Jas 3:9
11:8
g Ge 2:21-23;
1Ti 2:13

permissible"—but not everything is constructive. 24Nobody should seek his own good, but the good of others. k

25Eat anything sold in the meat market without raising questions of conscience, l 26for, "The earth is the Lord's, and everything in it." am

27If some unbeliever invites you to a meal and you want to go, eat whatever is put before youn without raising questions of conscience. 28But if anyone says to you, "This has been offered in sacrifice," then do not eat it, both for the sake of the man who told you and for conscience' sakebo— 29the other man's conscience, I mean, not yours. For why should my freedomp be judged by another's conscience? 30If I take part in the meal with thankfulness, why am I denounced because of something I thank God for?q

31So whether you eat or drink or whatever you do, do it all for the glory of God. r 32Do not cause anyone to stumble, s whether Jews, Greeks or the church of Godt— 33even as I try to please everybody in every way. u For I am not seeking my own good but the good of many, so that they may be saved. v 1Follow my example, w as I follow the example of Christ.

11

Propriety in Worship

2I praise youx for remembering me in everythingy and for holding to the teachings, c just as I passed them on to you. z

3Now I want you to realize that the head of every man is Christ, a and the head of the woman is man, b and the head of Christ is God. c 4Every man who prays or prophesies with his head covered dishonors his head. 5And every woman who prays or prophesiesd with her head uncovered dishonors her head—it is just as though her head were shaved. e 6If a woman does not cover her head, she should have her hair cut off; and if it is a disgrace for a woman to have her hair cut or shaved off, she should cover her head. 7A man ought not to cover his head, d since he is the image f and glory of God; but the woman is the glory of man. 8For man did not come from woman, but woman from man; g 9neither was man created for woman, but

a 26 Psalm 24:1   b 28 Some manuscripts conscience' sake, for "the earth is the Lord's and everything in it"   c 2 Or traditions   d 4-7 Or 4Every man who prays or prophesies with long hair dishonors his head. 5And every woman who prays or prophesies with no covering of hair on her head dishonors her head—she is just like one of the "shorn women." 6If a woman has no covering, let her be for now with short hair, but since it is a disgrace for a woman to have her hair shorn or shaved, she should grow it again. 7A man ought not to have long hair

1 Corinthians 10:23—11:1

This passage restates one last time the twin principles of freedom and restraint, now in the context of seeking both the good of others and God's glory. Paul's underlying motive, already expressed in 9:19–23, was the salvation of as many as possible. He included this discussion of his own actions and motives so that the Corinthians might imitate him carefully, to the extent that he modeled Christlike behavior.

If someone were to be offended no matter what Paul did, he would rather that person be a fellow Christian, already secure in the Savior's love, than an unbeliever who might turn away from Christ as a result. This was consistent with the lifestyle of Jesus, who mingled with "tax-collectors and sinners," angering the religious establishment (cf. Mark 2:16–17).

Christian models and mentors are desperately needed today. How would someone live if he or she were to imitate you? Who is watching you? What are some ways you could make yourself available to a young person, coworker, family member, or neighbor who could follow your Christian example?

1 Corinthians 11:2–16

Based on their newfound freedom in Christ, women in the Corinthian church were praying and prophesying. Christian tradition from Pentecost on had approved of such practice (Acts 2:17–18), and it readily fit Paul's emphasis on freedom. But these women, as they spoke in worship, were apparently flaunting social convention by sending ambiguous signals about their sexuality or religious commitment through inappropriate hairstyles or lack of headdress. Paul encouraged them to exercise restraint. Knowledge is to be tempered with love.

Most interpreters agree on a timeless principle from this controversial passage: Christians aren't to blur all distinctions between the sexes, either in terms of appearance or bearing. Most also agree that there is nothing inherently moral or immoral about head coverings or hairstyles. A caution: We are wise to be sensitive to the social messages associated with particular fashions. Husbands and wives are to carefully guard against sending signals that suggest that they are either unmarried or disloyal to their spouses.

woman for man.[h] 10For this reason, and because of the angels, the woman ought to have a sign of authority on her head.

11In the Lord, however, woman is not independent of man, nor is man independent of woman. 12For as woman came from man, so also man is born of woman. But everything comes from God.[i] 13Judge for yourselves: Is it proper for a woman to pray to God with her head uncovered? 14Does not the very nature of things teach you that if a man has long hair, it is a disgrace to him, 15but that if a woman has long hair, it is her glory? For long hair is given to her as a covering. 16If anyone wants to be contentious about this, we have no other practice—nor do the churches of God.[j]

The Lord's Supper

17In the following directives I have no praise for you,[k] for your meetings do more harm than good. 18In the first place, I hear that when you come together as a church, there are divisions[l] among you, and to some extent I believe it. 19No doubt there have to be differences among you to show which of you have God's approval.[m] 20When you come together, it is not the Lord's Supper you eat, 21for as you eat, each of you goes ahead without waiting for anybody else.[n] One remains hungry, another gets drunk. 22Don't you have homes to eat and drink in? Or do you despise the church of God[o] and humiliate those who have nothing?[p] What shall I say to you? Shall I praise you[q] for this? Certainly not!

23For I received from the Lord[r] what I also passed on to you:[s] The Lord Jesus, on the night he was betrayed, took bread, 24and when he had given thanks, he broke it and said, "This is my body, which is for you; do this in remembrance of me." 25In the same way, after supper he took the cup, saying, "This cup is the new covenant[t] in my blood;[u] do this, whenever you drink it, in remembrance of me." 26For whenever you eat this bread and drink this cup, you proclaim the Lord's death until he comes.

27Therefore, whoever eats the bread or drinks the cup of the Lord in an unworthy manner will be guilty of sinning against the body and blood of the Lord.[v] 28A man ought to examine himself[w] before he eats of the bread and drinks of the cup. 29For anyone who eats and drinks without recognizing the body of the Lord eats and drinks judgment on himself. 30That is why many among you are weak and sick, and a number of you have fallen asleep. 31But if we judged ourselves, we would not come under judgment.[x] 32When we are judged by the Lord, we are being disciplined[y] so that we will not be condemned with the world.

33So then, my brothers, when you come together to eat, wait for each other. 34If anyone is hungry,[z] he should eat at home,[a] so that when you meet together it may not result in judgment.

And when I come[b] I will give further directions.

Spiritual Gifts

12 Now about spiritual gifts,[c] brothers, I do not want you to be ignorant. 2You know that when you were pagans,[d] somehow or other you were influenced

11:9 h Ge 2:18
11:12 i Ro 11:36
11:16 j 1Co 7:17
11:17 k ver 2,22
11:18 l 1Co 1:10-12; 3:3
11:19 m 1Jn 2:19
11:21 n 2Pe 2:13; Jude 12
11:22 o 1Co 10:32 p Jas 2:6 q ver 2,17
11:23 r Gal 1:12 s 1Co 15:3
11:25 t Lk 22:20 u 1Co 10:16
11:27 v Heb 10:29
11:28 w 2Co 13:5
11:31 x Ps 32:5; 1Jn 1:9
11:32 y Ps 94:12; Heb 12:7-10; Rev 3:19
11:34 z ver 21 a ver 22 b 1Co 4:19
12:1 c Ro 1:11; 1Co 14:1,37
12:2 d Eph 2:11,12; 1Pe 4:3

1 Corinthians 11:17–34

Instead of sharing in a common communion meal, some in the church gorged themselves and got drunk at the expense of those who came later or had less. Jude 12 addresses a similar problem, using the early Christian term "love feasts" for these meals, which ended with celebration of the Lord's Supper. Paul didn't object to the wealthy enjoying ampler or more delicate fare in the privacy of their homes. But in this church setting their perceived gluttony at the expense of the "have-nots" was inappropriate and unkind.

Preparation for and partaking of Communion are to be accompanied by self-examination. Christians are called to consider sinful behaviors they might be exhibiting, their attitudes toward the needy, and any rifts in

their relationships. Jesus' words regarding a somewhat comparable situation are relevant here: "If you are offering your gift at the altar and there remember that your brother has something against you, leave your gift there in front of the altar. First go and be reconciled to your brother; then come and offer your gift" (Matt. 5:23–24).

Many churches appropriately include an offering for the needy as part of their Communion celebration. Since we are one body in Christ, the needs of one part of that body impact the whole. Messages that accompany the celebration of the Lord's Supper appropriately emphasize the plight of poor Christians around the world and the need to be generous in aiding the marginalized, both at home and abroad.

12:2
e Ps 115:5;
Jer 10:5; Hab 2:18,
19; 1Th 1:9
12:3
f Ro 9:3 g Jn 13:13
h 1Jn 4:2,3
12:4
i Ro 12:4-8;
Eph 4:11; Heb 2:4
12:6
j Eph 4:6
12:7
k Eph 4:12
12:8
l 1Co 2:6 m 2Co 8:7
12:9
n Mt 17:19,20;
2Co 4:13
o ver 28,30
12:10
p Gal 3:5 q 1Jn 4:1
r Mk 16:17
12:11
s ver 4

and led astray to mute idols. e 3Therefore I tell you that no one who is speaking by the Spirit of God says, "Jesus be cursed," f and no one can say, "Jesus is Lord," g except by the Holy Spirit. h

4There are different kinds of gifts, but the same Spirit. i 5There are different kinds of service, but the same Lord. 6There are different kinds of working, but the same God j works all of them in all men.

7Now to each one the manifestation of the Spirit is given for the common good. k 8To one there is given through the Spirit the message of wisdom, l to another the message of knowledge m by means of the same Spirit, 9to another faith n by the same Spirit, to another gifts of healing o by that one Spirit, 10to another miraculous powers, p to another prophecy, to another distinguishing between spirits, q to another speaking in different kinds of tongues, a r and to still another the interpretation of tongues. a 11All these are the work of one and the same Spirit, s and he gives them to each one, just as he determines.

One Body, Many Parts

12:12
t Ro 12:5 u ver 27
12:13
v Eph 2:18
w Gal 3:28;
Col 3:11
x Jn 7:37-39

12The body is a unit, though it is made up of many parts; and though all its parts are many, they form one body. t So it is with Christ. u 13For we were all baptized by b one Spirit v into one body—whether Jews or Greeks, slave or free w—and we were all given the one Spirit to drink. x

14Now the body is not made up of one part but of many. 15If the foot should say, "Because I am not a hand, I do not belong to the body," it would not for that reason cease to be part of the body. 16And if the ear should say, "Because I am not an eye, I do not belong to the body," it would not for that reason cease to be part of the body. 17If the whole body were an eye, where would the sense of hearing be? If the whole body were an ear, where would the sense of smell be? 18But in fact God has arranged y the parts in the body, every one of them, just as he wanted them to

12:18
y ver 28

a 10 Or *languages*; also in verse 28   b 13 Or *with*; or in

---

1 Corinthians 12:1–11

Corinthian worship services tended to be chaotic. The church's freethinking wing apparently equated spirituality with the exercise of the more spectacular spiritual gifts. Spiritual gifts, said Paul, are (1) bestowed freely by the Spirit's grace, (2) intended to be used in a Christ-like attitude of servanthood, and (3) result from God's powerful working in a person's life. Because the Holy Spirit determines who gets which gifts, they are not to be used to mark out anyone for special status within the church.

Paul's discussion of spiritual gifts is timely for our day. The squabbling among Corinthian believers and contemporary debates over the charismatic movement sound familiar. On the positive side, there are promising signs that churches are focusing on spiritual gifts, as well as recovering the Biblical model of "every-member" ministry. How would you assess your own spiritual gifts? Are you putting them to good use?

Once an individual is reasonably aware of how he or she has been gifted, that person needs an outlet for service. This fact has staggering implications for the way churches, both in Paul's day and ours, may best be organized. Leaders can encourage members to exercise their gifts and help each person to find ways of using them, both within the local body of believers and in the larger contexts of community and societal ministry.

1 Corinthians 12:12–31a

Paul developed an extended metaphor of the church as Christ's body. We see a pattern as he followed up an initial statement of the metaphor (v. 12) by moving from the theme of unity (v. 13) to that of diversity (v. 14). Then he turned it around, discussing, and then describing in more detail first diversity (vv. 15–20) and then unity (vv. 21–26). There were two reasons for his advocating diversity within unity: (1) The believers in Corinth, and elsewhere in the ancient world, came from diverse ethnic and socioeconomic backgrounds. (2) They would all "get it": After all, diversity within unity is exactly how a human body works.

Paul's model seriously challenges those paradigms of church growth that stress grouping common backgrounds and interests—keeping people with others who are "like" them. Perhaps at certain foundational levels, outreach and fellowship occur best among those most like ourselves. But the most dynamic evangelistic power of the gospel comes when the world is forced to sit up and take notice that people are loving each other in ways it can't explain.

Church is to be a place where people gather and get along for more than just human reasons. As diverse people who have been baptized by one Spirit into one body, the church surmounts the walls of division and discrimination society has erected between people. What are you, and/or your church, doing to express your oneness in the midst of the ethnic and social diversity that characterize Christ's body?

Passionate Service

12:4–7

An important element in determining where and how to serve God is your passion. James Dobson, Luis Palau, John Perkins, and R.C. Sproul are all respected Christian leaders. Each has a ministry with national or international impact. Yet each is directed to a different audience. Why? Because each has a different passion.

James Dobson, founder of Focus on the Family ministries and radio program, is passionate about family. If you get him talking about the family, you had better have time to listen. There is nothing he would rather discuss than the family's condition, needs, value, and future. He applies all his gifts to building it up.

Luis Palau, international evangelist, has a passion for the lost. What turns his crank are stadiums full of people who need the Lord. He goes from crusade to crusade, country to country, reaching the lost: "Give me the gospel and some good music, and we will do damage in enemy territory."

John Perkins, founder of Voice of Calvary Ministries, is passionate about minorities and the inner-city needy. He devotes his gifts to setting up programs to help them find dignity and self-esteem through meaningful employment opportunities.

R.C. Sproul, respected theologian and author, passionately studies and teaches the deepest truths of the Christian faith. He likes to get small groups of seminarians together to discuss the existence of God. After that, he moves on to the heavy stuff! More than once, while listening to R.C., I have felt like the train left me standing at the station. But that is his passion.

These are multi-gifted men who could serve in many other ways. Why don't they? Because their specific passions call them to specific ministries, and they love what they do. If they tried to swap ministries, they couldn't do it authentically—not because they lack the gifts, but because they lack the passions.

Do you know your passion? If not, ask yourself these questions:

What local, global, political, social, or church issues stir you emotionally?

What group of people do you feel most attracted to?

What area of need is of ultimate importance to you?

If you knew you couldn't fail, what would you do with your life?

What area of your church's ministry would you most like to influence?

Answering these questions may help you detect a passion for unwed mothers, the poor, unbelievers, youth, discipleship, the sick, or business executives. You may notice that this passion is related to your heritage or past experiences.

Once you determine your passion, think of ways to use your gifts to promote it. If it's for middle schoolers and your gift is helping, offer your services to your church's youth director—to set up equipment, chauffeur students, or do mailings.

If your passion is for young moms and your gift is teaching, start a Bible study for them. If your gift is helping, volunteer to watch their children during the study. If your gift is mercy, prepare meals for them when they are sick.

There are endless different ways to serve. In Paul's words, "There are different kinds of gifts, but the same Spirit. There are different kinds of service, but the same Lord" (1 Cor. 12:4–5).

> **O**nce you determine your passion, think of ways to use your gifts to promote it.

Bill Hybels, pastor of Willow Creek Community Church in Barrington, Illinois
Source: Bill Hybels, *Honest to God?* (Grand Rapids, Mich.: Zondervan, 1990), 112–113

12:18
z ver 11
12:20
a ver 12,14

be. [z] 19If they were all one part, where would the body be? 20As it is, there are many parts, but one body. [a]

21The eye cannot say to the hand, "I don't need you!" And the head cannot say to the feet, "I don't need you!" 22On the contrary, those parts of the body that seem to be weaker are indispensable, 23and the parts that we think are less honorable we treat with special honor. And the parts that are unpresentable are treated with special modesty, 24while our presentable parts need no special treatment. But God has combined the members of the body and has given greater honor to the parts that lacked it, 25so that there should be no division in the body, but that its parts should have equal concern for each other. 26If one part suffers, every part suffers with it; if one part is honored, every part rejoices with it.

12:27
b Eph 1:23; 4:12;
Col 1:18,24
c Ro 12:5
12:28
d 1Co 10:32
e Eph 4:11 f ver 9
g Ro 12:6-8
h ver 10
12:30
i ver 10
12:31
j 1Co 14:1,39

27Now you are the body of Christ, [b] and each one of you is a part of it. [c] 28And in the church [d] God has appointed first of all apostles, [e] second prophets, third teachers, then workers of miracles, also those having gifts of healing, [f] those able to help others, those with gifts of administration, [g] and those speaking in different kinds of tongues. [h] 29Are all apostles? Are all prophets? Are all teachers? Do all work miracles? 30Do all have gifts of healing? Do all speak in tongues[a]? [i] Do all interpret? 31But eagerly desire[b] [j] the greater gifts.

Love

13:1
k ver 8

And now I will show you the most excellent way.

13:2
l 1Co 14:2
m 1Co 12:9
n Mt 17:20; 21:21
13:3
o Mt 6:2 p Da 3:28

13 If I speak in the tongues[c] [k] of men and of angels, but have not love, I am only a resounding gong or a clanging cymbal. 2If I have the gift of prophecy and can fathom all mysteries [l] and all knowledge, and if I have a faith [m] that can move mountains, [n] but have not love, I am nothing. 3If I give all I possess to the poor[o] and surrender my body to the flames,[d] [p] but have not love, I gain nothing.

13:4
q 1Th 5:14
13:5
r 1Co 10:24
13:6
s 2Th 2:12 t 2Jn 4;
3Jn 3,4
13:8
u ver 2 v ver 1

4Love is patient, [q] love is kind. It does not envy, it does not boast, it is not proud. 5It is not rude, it is not self-seeking, [r] it is not easily angered, it keeps no record of wrongs. 6Love does not delight in evil [s] but rejoices with the truth. [t] 7It always protects, always trusts, always hopes, always perseveres.

13:9
w ver 12; 1Co 8:2
13:10
x Php 3:12

8Love never fails. But where there are prophecies, [u] they will cease; where there are tongues, [v] they will be stilled; where there is knowledge, it will pass away. 9For we know in part [w] and we prophesy in part, 10but when perfection comes, [x] the imperfect disappears. 11When I was a child, I talked like a child, I thought like a child, I reasoned like a child. When I became a man, I put childish ways behind me. 12Now we see but a poor reflection as in a mirror; then we shall see face to face. [y] Now I know in part; then I shall know fully, even as I am fully known. [z]

13:12
y Ge 32:30;
2Co 5:7; 1Jn 3:2
z 1Co 8:3
13:13
a Gal 5:5,6
b 1Co 16:14

13And now these three remain: faith, hope and love. [a] But the greatest of these is love. [b]

---

[a] 30 Or other languages   [b] 31 Or But you are eagerly desiring   [c] 1 Or languages   [d] 3 Some early manuscripts body that I may boast

---

1 Corinthians 12:31b—13:13

📖 Love is more important than any of the spiritual gifts. Without it they are not just watered down but *worthless*. Chapter 13:4–7 describes love's nature, in language designed to point out how poorly the Corinthians were measuring up. Verses 8–13 highlight the temporary nature of the gifts, contrasted with love's permanence. The entire passage is poetic in nature, with an elaborate structure of symmetry and parallelism comparable to that found in the Psalms.

Paul didn't classify love itself as a spiritual gift. It's the fundamental Christian virtue—Number One on the list of the "fruit" of the Spirit (Gal. 5:22)—that must be present with all the gifts if they are to be used in ways that please God and have eternal value. Whatever inspi-

ration it may have as a self-contained hymn to love, Paul wanted chapter 13 to help solve a specific problem: the destructive way the Corinthians were using their spiritual gifts.

📖 The need for genuine, Christ-like love remains as great today as ever. Yet one of our most difficult problems is defining love. Popular culture uses the word to mean just about everything *except* what the Bible means by it. Even Christians are easily misled into thinking of love as primarily a feeling, something unintentional you fall into and out of. Scripture defines love as, first of all, an *action*, an unconditional commitment, a sacrifice of self-interest, an unbreakable promise. Paul described 16 separate love actions in this passage. In which of these would you particularly like the Spirit to help you grow?

Gifts of Prophecy and Tongues

14 Follow the way of love[c] and eagerly desire[d] spiritual gifts,[e] especially the gift of prophecy. [2]For anyone who speaks in a tongue[a][f] does not speak to men but to God. Indeed, no one understands him; he utters mysteries[g] with his spirit.[b] [3]But everyone who prophesies speaks to men for their strengthening,[h] encouragement and comfort. [4]He who speaks in a tongue[i] edifies himself, but he who prophesies[j] edifies the church. [5]I would like every one of you to speak in tongues,[c] but I would rather have you prophesy.[k] He who prophesies is greater than one who speaks in tongues,[c] unless he interprets, so that the church may be edified.

[6]Now, brothers, if I come to you and speak in tongues, what good will I be to you, unless I bring you some revelation[l] or knowledge or prophecy or word of instruction?[m] [7]Even in the case of lifeless things that make sounds, such as the flute or harp, how will anyone know what tune is being played unless there is a distinction in the notes? [8]Again, if the trumpet does not sound a clear call, who will get ready for battle?[n] [9]So it is with you. Unless you speak intelligible words with your tongue, how will anyone know what you are saying? You will just be speaking into the air. [10]Undoubtedly there are all sorts of languages in the world, yet none of them is without meaning. [11]If then I do not grasp the meaning of what someone is saying, I am a foreigner to the speaker, and he is a foreigner to me. [12]So it is with you. Since you are eager to have spiritual gifts, try to excel in gifts that build up the church.

[13]For this reason anyone who speaks in a tongue should pray that he may interpret what he says. [14]For if I pray in a tongue, my spirit prays, but my mind is unfruitful. [15]So what shall I do? I will pray with my spirit, but I will also pray with my

[a] 2 Or *another language*; also in verses 4, 13, 14, 19, 26 and 27   [b] 2 Or *by the Spirit*   [c] 5 Or *other languages*; also in verses 6, 18, 22, 23 and 39

14:1
[c] 1Co 16:14
[d] ver 39; 1Co 12:31
[e] 1Co 12:1
14:2
[f] Mk 16:17
[g] 1Co 13:2
14:3
[h] ver 4,5,12,17,26; Ro 14:19
14:4
[i] Mk 16:17
[j] 1Co 13:2
14:5
[k] Nu 11:29
14:6
[l] ver 26; Eph 1:17
[m] Ro 6:17
14:8
[n] Nu 10:9; Jer 4:19

---

1 Corinthians 14:1–25

 In chapter 14 Paul climaxed his discussion of spiritual gifts by encouraging the Corinthians to prefer prophecy to tongues. But he acknowledged a place for both, as well as for the other gifts, if they are made understandable (vv. 1–25) and exercised in an orderly fashion (vv. 26–40). Paul gave a higher priority to prophecy because (1) it involves other people, as well as addressing God, and (2) it edifies and improves the whole assembly, not just the individual speaker.

Prophecy is the proclamation of a message from God. The church is called to consider thoughtfully what God wants to say to a particular congregation at a particular time, yet be sensitive enough to the Spirit to say what seems most appropriate for that audience. It's essential for us to make sure our messages "strengthen, encourage and comfort" (v. 3).

Around the world the Spirit is intervening to liberate particular individuals from a fruitless devotional time, lifeless worship, or inconsistent relationship with the Lord. The gospel isn't just an idea or set of beliefs; it's transforming power through the Spirit for new life in Christ.

13:13

L♥VE 1 Corinthians 13 is widely considered the greatest love passage in the Bible. It identifies various and diverse qualities of this complex attitude, emotion, and Christian virtue:

Patient: Love is the basic component of friendship and mutual tolerance, the superglue that alone holds people, society, Christians, and a diverse world together. Given the sinful nature of people, maintaining an attitude of love requires the staying power of persistent patience (v. 4).

Painful: Love is self-sacrificing (v. 3).

Pliant: Love is kind, easily moved to compassion and concern (v. 4).

Promotional: Love identifies the other party's need above one's own (v. 4). Jealousy and prideful, self-serving attitudes can't coexist with its truly "other-centered" mentality (v. 5).

Peace loving: Love forgives and "forgets," refusing to nurse grudges and keeping short accounts (v. 5).

Passionate: Love presupposes deep attraction and warm affection, whether to a spouse, an intimate friend, or brothers and sisters in the Lord and humanity in general (vv. 6–7).

Powerful: Love trusts implicitly, protects, and never fails (vv. 7–8).

Paramount: Because our God is defined as "love" itself (1 John 4:8), this quality stands alone as the greatest, the overriding Christian virtue (v. 13).

14:15
o Eph 5:19;
Col 3:16
14:16
p Dt 27:15-26;
1Ch 16:36; Ne 8:6;
Ps 106:48;
Rev 5:14; 7:12
q 1Co 11:24

14:20
r Eph 4:14;
Heb 5:12,13;
1Pe 2:2 *s* Ro 16:19
14:21
t Jn 10:34
u Isa 28:11,12

14:22
v ver 1

14:23
w Ac 2:13

14:25
x Isa 45:14;
Zec 8:23

14:26
y 1Co 12:7-10
z Eph 5:19 *a* ver 6
b Ro 14:19

14:29
c 1Co 12:10

14:32
d 1Jn 4:1
14:33
e ver 40 *f* Ac 9:13
14:34
g 1Ti 2:11,12
h Ge 3:16

mind; I will sing[o] with my spirit, but I will also sing with my mind. [16]If you are praising God with your spirit, how can one who finds himself among those who do not understand[a] say "Amen"[p] to your thanksgiving,[q] since he does not know what you are saying? [17]You may be giving thanks well enough, but the other man is not edified.

[18]I thank God that I speak in tongues more than all of you. [19]But in the church I would rather speak five intelligible words to instruct others than ten thousand words in a tongue.

[20]Brothers, stop thinking like children.[r] In regard to evil be infants,[s] but in your thinking be adults. [21]In the Law[t] it is written:

"Through men of strange tongues
   and through the lips of foreigners
I will speak to this people,
   but even then they will not listen to me,"[b][u]

                              says the Lord.

[22]Tongues, then, are a sign, not for believers but for unbelievers; prophecy,[v] however, is for believers, not for unbelievers. [23]So if the whole church comes together and everyone speaks in tongues, and some who do not understand[c] or some unbelievers come in, will they not say that you are out of your mind?[w] [24]But if an unbeliever or someone who does not understand[d] comes in while everybody is prophesying, he will be convinced by all that he is a sinner and will be judged by all, [25]and the secrets of his heart will be laid bare. So he will fall down and worship God, exclaiming, "God is really among you!"[x]

Orderly Worship

[26]What then shall we say, brothers? When you come together, everyone[y] has a hymn,[z] or a word of instruction,[a] a revelation, a tongue or an interpretation. All of these must be done for the strengthening[b] of the church. [27]If anyone speaks in a tongue, two—or at the most three—should speak, one at a time, and someone must interpret. [28]If there is no interpreter, the speaker should keep quiet in the church and speak to himself and God.

[29]Two or three prophets should speak, and the others should weigh carefully what is said.[c] [30]And if a revelation comes to someone who is sitting down, the first speaker should stop. [31]For you can all prophesy in turn so that everyone may be instructed and encouraged. [32]The spirits of prophets are subject to the control of prophets.[d] [33]For God is not a God of disorder[e] but of peace.

As in all the congregations of the saints,[f] [34]women should remain silent in the churches. They are not allowed to speak, but must be in submission,[g] as the Law[h] says. [35]If they want to inquire about something, they should ask their own husbands at home; for it is disgraceful for a woman to speak in the church.

---

[a] 16 Or *among the inquirers*   [b] 21 Isaiah 28:11,12   [c] 23 Or *some inquirers*   [d] 24 Or *or some inquirer*

---

1 Corinthians 14:26–40

👥 If understandability is a priority for the gathered community, how should worship proceed? Verse 26 endorsed the Corinthians' preference for worshiping in a highly participatory and spontaneous fashion, with opportunity provided for anyone led by the Spirit to contribute. This didn't mean every person present exercised all the gifts, or even that all exercised at least one in every service. But opportunity was made available for all *whom the Spirit led on any given occasion to contribute.*

Many believers point out cultural and situational factors underlying Paul's commands in verses 34–35 regarding women. He had already noted that God had gifted women with the capacity to prophesy and pray

in public (11:5). So rather than intending to silence women totally in the church, Paul may have been referring to interfering chatter or to the promotion of false teaching.

📖 This chapter ends with plain words—that are nevertheless ignored by large sections of the contemporary church. Many noncharismatics flatly denounce tongues, while many charismatics seldom worship in an orderly manner. If Christians were to obey Paul's commands, most of the divisiveness over this issue could be prevented. And Paul's dominant concern for the mutual strengthening of believers would be enhanced. How open are you to variations in worship styles among God's diverse people?

36Did the word of God originate with you? Or are you the only people it has reached? 37If anybody thinks he is a prophet[i] or spiritually gifted, let him acknowledge that what I am writing to you is the Lord's command.[j] 38If he ignores this, he himself will be ignored.[a]

39Therefore, my brothers, be eager[k] to prophesy, and do not forbid speaking in tongues. 40But everything should be done in a fitting and orderly[l] way.

The Resurrection of Christ

15 Now, brothers, I want to remind you of the gospel[m] I preached to you, which you received and on which you have taken your stand. 2By this gospel you are saved,[n] if you hold firmly[o] to the word I preached to you. Otherwise, you have believed in vain.

3For what I received[p] I passed on to you[q] as of first importance[b]: that Christ died for our sins[r] according to the Scriptures,[s] 4that he was buried, that he was raised[t] on the third day[u] according to the Scriptures,[v] 5and that he appeared to Peter,[c][w] and then to the Twelve.[x] 6After that, he appeared to more than five hundred of the brothers at the same time, most of whom are still living, though some have fallen asleep. 7Then he appeared to James, then to all the apostles,[y] 8and last of all he appeared to me also,[z] as to one abnormally born.

9For I am the least of the apostles[a] and do not even deserve to be called an apostle, because I persecuted[b] the church of God. 10But by the grace of God I am what I am, and his grace to me[c] was not without effect. No, I worked harder than all of them[d]—yet not I, but the grace of God that was with me.[e] 11Whether, then, it was I or they, this is what we preach, and this is what you believed.

The Resurrection of the Dead

12But if it is preached that Christ has been raised from the dead, how can some of you say that there is no resurrection of the dead?[f] 13If there is no resurrection of the dead, then not even Christ has been raised. 14And if Christ has not been raised,[g] our preaching is useless and so is your faith. 15More than that, we are then found to be false witnesses about God, for we have testified about God that he raised Christ from the dead.[h] But he did not raise him if in fact the dead are not raised. 16For if the dead are not raised, then Christ has not been raised either. 17And if

---

[a] 38 Some manuscripts *If he is ignorant of this, let him be ignorant*   [b] 3 Or *you at the first*
[c] 5 Greek *Cephas*

14:37 [i] 2Co 10:7 [j] 1Jn 4:6
14:39 [k] 1Co 12:31
14:40 [l] ver 33
15:1 [m] Ro 2:16
15:2 [n] Ro 1:16 [o] Ro 11:22
15:3 [p] Gal 1:12 [q] 1Co 11:23 [r] Isa 53:5; 1Pe 2:24 [s] Lk 24:27; Ac 26:22,23
15:4 [t] Ac 2:24 [u] Mt 16:21 [v] Ac 2:25,30,31
15:5 [w] Lk 24:34 [x] Mk 16:14
15:7 [y] Lk 24:33,36,37; Ac 1:3,4
15:8 [z] Ac 9:3-6,17; 1Co 9:1
15:9 [a] Eph 3:8; 1Ti 1:15 [b] Ac 8:3
15:10 [c] Ro 12:3 [d] 2Co 11:23 [e] Php 2:13
15:12 [f] Ac 17:32; 23:8; 2Ti 2:18
15:14 [g] 1Th 4:14
15:15 [h] Ac 2:24

---

1 Corinthians 15:1–11

This first part of chapter 15 restates the reality of Christ's bodily resurrection. Paul began by reminding the Corinthians of what they should have remembered. He rehearsed the foundational Christian creed or confession he had first taught them. And verses 9–11 highlight Paul's own unique role as an after-the-fact witness to the risen and ascended Lord (see Acts 9:1–19).

The resurrection is central to the Christian faith. Paul's emphasis on it here doesn't contradict 2:2; Jesus' death and resurrection are inseparable. To counteract those who played down Jesus' weakness and servanthood, Paul stressed the crucifixion. But to refute those who denied a future material hope for believers and for the cosmos, he emphasized Jesus' resurrection.

The reality of Jesus' death and resurrection in space and time, as bona fide historical events, sets the gospel apart from other religions. The Christian faith lives or dies on the truth of Christ's resurrection.

1 Corinthians 15:12–34

The position of some in the Corinthian church is specified in verse 12, and it was to this challenge that Paul responded. By denying the resurrection, these Corinthians almost certainly weren't denying life after death—virtually everyone in the ancient world believed in that. They were disputing the Jewish and Christian doctrine of *bodily* resurrection, in favor of one of the Greek forms of belief that limited the afterlife to disembodied immortality of the soul (cf. 2 Tim. 2:17–18).

Have you ever thought of heaven as an ethereal kind of existence to which you don't really look forward? We as Christians believe in the resurrection of the *body*. We won't understand either life here on Earth, or that to come in heaven, if we don't grasp the implications of this truth.

Previous generations have often lampooned some Christians for being so heavenly minded that they were no earthly good. But ours is a generation in which many Christians are so earthly minded that they seem to be little or no heavenly good. Our society—Christians often as much as anyone else—has become preoccupied with physical health, dieting, recreation, and fitness, all at the expense of anything close to a comparable concern for spiritual health and salvation.

Christ has not been raised, your faith is futile; you are still in your sins.[i] 18Then those also who have fallen asleep in Christ are lost. 19If only for this life we have hope in Christ, we are to be pitied more than all men.[j]

20But Christ has indeed been raised from the dead,[k] the firstfruits[l] of those who have fallen asleep.[m] 21For since death came through a man,[n] the resurrection of the dead comes also through a man. 22For as in Adam all die, so in Christ all will be made alive.[o] 23But each in his own turn: Christ, the firstfruits;[p] then, when he comes,[q] those who belong to him. 24Then the end will come, when he hands over the kingdom[r] to God the Father after he has destroyed all dominion, authority and power.[s] 25For he must reign until he has put all his enemies under his feet.[t] 26The last enemy to be destroyed is death.[u] 27For he "has put everything under his feet."[a][v] Now when it says that "everything" has been put under him, it is clear that this does not include God himself, who put everything under Christ.[w] 28When he has done this, then the Son himself will be made subject to him who put everything under him,[x] so that God may be all in all.[y]

29Now if there is no resurrection, what will those do who are baptized for the dead? If the dead are not raised at all, why are people baptized for them? 30And as for us, why do we endanger ourselves every hour?[z] 31I die every day[a]—I mean that, brothers—just as surely as I glory over you in Christ Jesus our Lord. 32If I fought wild beasts[b] in Ephesus[c] for merely human reasons, what have I gained? If the dead are not raised,

> "Let us eat and drink,
> for tomorrow we die."[b][d]

33Do not be misled: "Bad company corrupts good character." 34Come back to your senses as you ought, and stop sinning; for there are some who are ignorant of God—I say this to your shame.

The Resurrection Body

35But someone may ask,[e] "How are the dead raised? With what kind of body will they come?"[f] 36How foolish![g] What you sow does not come to life unless it dies.[h] 37When you sow, you do not plant the body that will be, but just a seed, perhaps of wheat or of something else. 38But God gives it a body as he has determined, and to each kind of seed he gives its own body.[i] 39All flesh is not the same: Men have one kind of flesh, animals have another, birds another and fish another. 40There are also heavenly bodies and there are earthly bodies; but the splendor of the heavenly bodies is one kind, and the splendor of the earthly bodies is another. 41The sun has one kind of splendor, the moon another and the stars another; and star differs from star in splendor.

42So will it be[j] with the resurrection of the dead. The body that is sown is perishable, it is raised imperishable; 43it is sown in dishonor, it is raised in glory;[k] it is

a 27 Psalm 8:6   b 32 Isaiah 22:13

---

1 Corinthians 15:35–58

Paul described the implications of the bodily resurrection in three ways. Verses 36 through the beginning of 44 use analogies from the created world to describe the resurrection body. The end of verse 44 through verse 49 argue for the need of a heavenly body from the existence of an earthly body. Verses 50–57 describe why such transformation is necessary. Paul closed with commands to stand firm in true belief and action.

The biological continuity between seed and plant would remain hidden were it not for the recurring cause-and-effect relationship between planting a seed and seeing new life sprout in that very place. So we may expect some kind of ongoing personal identity between natural

and spiritual bodies but still look forward to substantial physical change in our resurrection body. Paul reminded his readers that the resurrection hope keeps believers in every place and time from despair and helps them stay faithful in Christian service.

The ultimate defeat of death can speak volumes to those who continue to live in fear of it today. Christians have nothing to dread. They may grieve the loss of loved ones and experience anxiety about the unknown factors surrounding their own deaths. But neither reaction ought to be like those "who have no hope" (1 Thess. 4:13). This hope of the resurrection arms us with a confidence that allows us to stand firm and unshakeable, whatever our circumstances.

sown in weakness, it is raised in power; 44it is sown a natural body, it is raised a spiritual body.*l*

If there is a natural body, there is also a spiritual body. 45So it is written: "The first man Adam became a living being"*a;m* the last Adam,*n* a life-giving spirit.*o* 46The spiritual did not come first, but the natural, and after that the spiritual. 47The first man was of the dust of the earth,*p* the second man from heaven.*q* 48As was the earthly man, so are those who are of the earth; and as is the man from heaven, so also are those who are of heaven.*r* 49And just as we have borne the likeness of the earthly man,*s* so shall we*b* bear the likeness of the man from heaven.*t*

50I declare to you, brothers, that flesh and blood*u* cannot inherit the kingdom of God, nor does the perishable inherit the imperishable. 51Listen, I tell you a mystery:*v* We will not all sleep, but we will all be changed*w*— 52in a flash, in the twinkling of an eye, at the last trumpet. For the trumpet will sound,*x* the dead*y* will be raised imperishable, and we will be changed. 53For the perishable must clothe itself with the imperishable,*z* and the mortal with immortality. 54When the perishable has been clothed with the imperishable, and the mortal with immortality, then the saying that is written will come true: "Death has been swallowed up in victory."*c a*

55 "Where, O death, is your victory?
    Where, O death, is your sting?"*d b*

56The sting of death is sin,*c* and the power of sin is the law.*d* 57But thanks be to God!*e* He gives us the victory through our Lord Jesus Christ.*f*

58Therefore, my dear brothers, stand firm. Let nothing move you. Always give yourselves fully to the work of the Lord,*g* because you know that your labor in the Lord is not in vain.

a 45 Gen. 2:7   *b 49* Some early manuscripts *so let us*   *c 54* Isaiah 25:8   *d 55* Hosea 13:14

15:44
l ver 50

15:45
m Ge 2:7 *n* Ro 5:14
o Jn 5:21; Ro 8:2
15:47
p Ge 2:7; 3:19
q Jn 3:13,31

15:48
r Php 3:20,21
15:49
s Ge 5:3 *t* Ro 8:29
15:50
u Jn 3:3,5

15:51
v 1Co 13:2
w Php 3:21
15:52
x Mt 24:31
y Jn 5:25
15:53
z 2Co 5:2,4

15:54
a Isa 25:8;
Rev 20:14

15:55
b Hos 13:14

15:56
c Ro 5:12 *d* Ro 4:15
15:57
e 2Co 2:14
f Ro 8:37

15:58
g 1Co 16:10

Snapshots

  15:58

Apostle of the Indies

Bartolomé de Las Casas (1484–1566) is known as the Apostle of the Indies. Raised in Seville, Spain, he went to the Americas in 1502 as an *encomendero*, an official licensed to take tribute from New World tribes. After experiencing a deep conversion and being influenced by the Dominicans (who denounced the Spaniards for abusing native tribes), he entered the priesthood, dedicating his life to serving Native Americans.

The pen was a mighty weapon in Las Casas' cause. His tract "The Only Method of Attracting All Peoples to the True Faith" (1537) stressed the importance of peace in evangelizing native tribal peoples. His major works, *Historia de las Indias* and *Apologética Historia*, were published posthumously.

Later in life Las Casas saw some fruit from his labor. Pope Paul III declared in his bull *Sublimis Deus* (1537) that New World "Indians" were rational beings with the same rights as European Christians. And in 1542 the Spanish Crown limited the powers of encomenderos.

Some scholars think Las Casas inflated numbers and exaggerated abuses, rendering his historical works inaccurate. Whether or not this is true, it's indisputable that he helped European powers reverse policies that oppressed "Indians" and broadened the world's understanding of human rights.

> [Las Casas] helped European powers reverse policies that oppressed "Indians" and broadened the world's understanding of human rights.

The Collection for God's People

16 Now about the collection[h] for God's people:[i] Do what I told the Galatian[j] churches to do. 2On the first day of every week,[k] each one of you should set aside a sum of money in keeping with his income, saving it up, so that when I come no collections will have to be made.[l] 3Then, when I arrive, I will give letters of introduction to the men you approve[m] and send them with your gift to Jerusalem. 4If it seems advisable for me to go also, they will accompany me.

Personal Requests

5After I go through Macedonia, I will come to you[n]—for I will be going through Macedonia.[o] 6Perhaps I will stay with you awhile, or even spend the winter, so that you can help me on my journey,[p] wherever I go. 7I do not want to see you now and make only a passing visit; I hope to spend some time with you, if the Lord permits.[q] 8But I will stay on at Ephesus[r] until Pentecost,[s] 9because a great door for effective work has opened to me,[t] and there are many who oppose me.

10If Timothy[u] comes, see to it that he has nothing to fear while he is with you, for he is carrying on the work of the Lord,[v] just as I am. 11No one, then, should refuse to accept him.[w] Send him on his way in peace[x] so that he may return to me. I am expecting him along with the brothers.

12Now about our brother Apollos:[y] I strongly urged him to go to you with the brothers. He was quite unwilling to go now, but he will go when he has the opportunity.

13Be on your guard; stand firm[z] in the faith; be men of courage; be strong.[a] 14Do everything in love.[b]

15You know that the household of Stephanas[c] were the first converts[d] in Achaia,[e] and they have devoted themselves to the service of the saints. I urge you, brothers, 16to submit[f] to such as these and to everyone who joins in the work, and labors at it. 17I was glad when Stephanas, Fortunatus and Achaicus arrived, because

16:1
h Ac 24:17
i Ac 9:13 / Ac 16:6
16:2
k Ac 20:7
l 2Co 9:4,5
16:3
m 2Co 8:18,19
16:5
n 1Co 4:19
o Ac 19:21
16:6
p Ro 15:24
16:7
q Ac 18:21
16:8
r Ac 18:19 s Ac 2:1
16:9
t Ac 14:27
16:10
u Ac 16:1
v 1Co 15:58
16:11
w 1Ti 4:12
x Ac 15:33
16:12
y Ac 18:24;
1Co 1:12
16:13
z Gal 5:1; Php 1:27;
1Th 3:8; 2Th 2:15
a Eph 6:10
16:14
b 1Co 14:1
16:15
c 1Co 1:16
d Ro 16:5
e Ac 18:12
16:16
f Heb 13:17

---

1 Corinthians 16:1–4

Many Jewish Christians in Jerusalem were impoverished (cf. Rom. 15:26), and Paul spent considerable energy on his third missionary journey raising funds on their behalf from various Gentile churches in Europe and the Roman province of Asia. But in addition to alleviating physical suffering, Paul undoubtedly saw the collection as an opportunity to promote unity and to pay a spiritual debt the Gentile congregations owed their "mother church" in Jerusalem (Rom. 15:27). He also hoped to demonstrate the genuineness of Gentile Christianity to skeptical Jewish Christians (cf. Acts 24:17).

Paul's two primary rationales for this collection provide the major foci of Christian giving in every age—supporting fellow believers and helping to meet the physical and spiritual needs of the world's dispossessed. Paul's phrase "in keeping with his income" reminds us of the New Testament emphasis on a weekly, "equal" sacrifice. Each is to give in proportion to his or her income.

The amount of money required annually to relieve the worst suffering in the two-thirds of the world that is desperately poor is far exceeded by the billions of dollars Americans spend each year on cosmetics, sports, and entertainment. A better understanding and more consistent application of the Biblical call to stewardship and the principles of faith-based financial management are acutely needed in today's Western church. Governments aren't in a position to present the type of complete antidote to spiritual and physical ills churches and Christians can. The body of Christ has been entrusted by God with all that is necessary to alleviate the most severe forms of human suffering, as well as to witness to the gospel among every community on Earth.

1 Corinthians 16:5–18

Paul's desire to spend a full winter in Corinth may have been realized, even if it was delayed by a year. His motivation was at least twofold: (1) He wanted a significant period of time with the Corinthians in hopes of improving the situation in the church, and (2) he hoped to avoid having to travel in treacherous weather during that season of the year in which the high seas were generally impassable and travel overland was arduous.

Paul's desires reflect his concern to spend "quantity" (as well as "quality") time with his spiritual children. As he consistently did in his ministry, he wanted to revisit this church he had founded for follow-up ministry and discipleship. Paul was never content to evangelize, make converts, and move on—even when it meant risking his life to return to cities in which he had previously ministered.

No packaged discipleship program can substitute for quality time spent with other Christians. This is all the more true in our fast-paced, fractured urban society. In verses 13–14 Paul concisely summarized the qualities of a mature disciple. He also affirmed people who "refreshed" his and others' spirits (v. 18). What does it mean for us to bring refreshment to others?

they have supplied what was lacking from you. *g* 18For they refreshed *h* my spirit and yours also. Such men deserve recognition. *i*

Final Greetings

19The churches in the province of Asia send you greetings. Aquila and Priscilla *a j* greet you warmly in the Lord, and so does the church that meets at their house. *k*
20All the brothers here send you greetings. Greet one another with a holy kiss. *l*
21I, Paul, write this greeting in my own hand. *m*
22If anyone does not love the Lord *n*—a curse *o* be on him. Come, O Lord *b*! *p*
23The grace of the Lord Jesus be with you. *q*
24My love to all of you in Christ Jesus. Amen. *c*

a 19 Greek *Prisca*, a variant of *Priscilla*   *b 22* In Aramaic the expression *Come, O Lord* is *Marana tha.*
c 24 Some manuscripts do not have *Amen.*

16:17
g 2Co 11:9;
Php 2:30
16:18
h Phm 7 *i* Php 2:29

16:19
j Ac 18:2 *k* Ro 16:5

16:20
l Ro 16:16
16:21
m Gal 6:11;
Col 4:18
16:22
n Eph 6:24 *o* Ro 9:3
p Rev 22:20
16:23
q Ro 16:20

---

1 Corinthians 16:19–24

Verses 19–20 conveyed greetings to the Corinthian church from four groups of believers: (1) the various churches in the province of Asia (present-day western Turkey); (2) Paul's good friends Aquila and Priscilla; (3) the specific house church that met in their home; and (4) Paul's other immediate companions in ministry.

After verse 20, Paul stopped dictating his letter to his *amanuensis* (secretary). As was his custom, he picked up pen and papyrus himself to write the closing words in his own hand (cf. Gal. 6:11; Col. 4:18; 2 Thess. 3:17; other ancient letter writers did the same). Despite the strong language of verse 22, Paul closed on a note of love and encouragement profoundly needed in fractured Corinth. He had been stern with these believers, but he ended his letter with an assurance of his love. "Faithful are the wounds of a friend" (Prov. 27:6).

Fittingly, Paul concluded with one final reminder of the crucial importance of "grace" and "love" to the Christian life. We continue to need—and crave—both. If our generation has sometimes removed God from the concept of love, it has at least correctly captured the centrality of love for human existence. Only one truly life- and world-changing love exists, and it's found in Jesus Christ.

INTRODUCTION TO
2 Corinthians

AUTHOR
Because of this letter's internal evidence (1:1; 10:1), writing style, and autobiographical information, Paul's authorship has been undisputed.

DATE WRITTEN
Second Corinthians was probably written in A.D. 55.

ORIGINAL READERS
Paul wrote this letter to the believers in Corinth.

TIMELINE

	10BC	AD1	10	20	30	40	50	60	70	80	90	100
Jesus' life (c. 6/5 B.C.–A.D. 30)												
Paul's conversion (c. A.D. 35)												
Paul's missionary journeys (c. A.D. 46-67)												
Council at Jerusalem (c. A.D. 50-51)												
Nero's reign (c. A.D. 54-68)												
Book of 2 Corinthians written (c. A.D. 55)												
Paul's first imprisonment in Rome (c. A.D. 59-62)												
Paul's imprisonment and death in Rome (c. A.D. 67-68)												

THEMES
This letter, like 1 Corinthians, was written to deal with problems and dissension in the church in Corinth. Paul's themes include the following:

1. *Ministry of Reconciliation.* Paul's love for the Corinthians was evidenced by his joy at their repentance and renewed commitment to him (7:9), his pride in them (1:14; 7:4), and his hope for their future (1:7). Paul's desire and goal was reconciliation—between himself and the Corinthians; among the Corinthian church members; and, most importantly, between God and human beings. Paul explained that this "ministry of reconciliation" (5:18) is also the ministry of every believer. Believers, as "Christ's ambassadors" (5:20), are to implore sinners to be reconciled to God through Jesus Christ.

2. *Generosity in giving.* Paul encouraged the Corinthians to renew their commitment to the collection for the believers in Jerusalem (8:1—9:15). The Jerusalem project offered the Corinthians a chance to participate in something greater than themselves. Paul taught that charity is an act of obedience, results in eternal reward, and brings glory to God. Those who give solely in the hope of attaining greater material prosperity will harvest only spiritual poverty. God often rewards generosity with material abundance to make it possible for people to be even more generous.

3. *Defense of Paul's apostleship.* Some in the Corinthian church had become alienated from Paul by the presence and influence of boastful rivals. Paul defended his apostleship and made a fervent appeal for them to renew their commitment to him. The breach between Paul and some Corinthians wasn't simply over theological issues but had its roots in Corinthian cultural values that clashed with Christian values. Christians, then and now, live under the sign of the cross, which revolutionizes worldly values and ambitions. Paul called believers back to the reality of Christ crucified, a message that reveals God's power in humility.

FAITH IN ACTION

The pages of 2 Corinthians contain life lessons and role models of faith—people who challenge believers to put faith in action.

Role Models

- PAUL (12:7–10) delighted in his weaknesses, knowing that they revealed God's glory, power, and grace.

- THE CORINTHIANS (7:4–13) repented when confronted and brought joy and encouragement to Paul.

- MACEDONIAN BELIEVERS (8:1–5) gave generously to the Jerusalem Fund out of their "extreme poverty."

- TITUS (8:6,16–19,23) was the enthusiastic co-administrator of the Jerusalem Fund, accepting the responsibility in response to the churches' request.

Challenges

- Seek opportunities to bring reconciliation to those in your church, your community, and the world.

- As an ambassador for Christ (5:20), use every opportunity to point others to him.

- Look for ways to become a generous giver to those in need, remembering that your reward will be eternal.

- Try to view your weaknesses in a new light—as a means for God to show his grace, power, and glory in and through you.

- If you are given or accept a financial responsibility, see to it that you follow through with integrity (8:20–21).

OUTLINE

I. Introduction: Greeting and Thanksgiving (1:1–11)
II. Paul's Explanation of His Conduct and Apostolic Ministry (1:12—7:16)
   A. Paul's Integrity (1:12—2:4)
   B. The Need for Forgiveness (2:5–11)
   C. Ministers of the New Covenant (2:12–17)
   D. Ministers Made Competent by the Spirit (3:1–11)
   E. Transformed Into His Likeness (3:12—4:6)
   F. Treasure in Jars of Clay (4:7–16a)
   G. The Prospects of Our Heavenly Dwelling (4:16b—5:10)
   H. The Ministry of Reconciliation (5:11—6:10)
   I. Paul's Appeal to the Corinthians (6:11—7:4)
   J. Titus's Good Report (7:5–16)
III. The Collection for the Christians at Jerusalem (8–9)
IV. Paul's Vindication of His Apostolic Authority (10–13)
   A. Defense of His Ministry (10)
   B. Paul Compared to False Apostles (11–12)
   C. Final Warnings (13:1–10)
V. Conclusion (13:11–14)

1:1
a 1Co 1:1; Eph 1:1;
Col 1:1; 2Ti 1:1
b 1Co 10:32
c Ac 18:12
1:2
d Ro 1:7

1:3
e Eph 1:3; 1Pe 1:3
1:4
f 2Co 7:6,7,13

1:5
g 2Co 4:10;
Col 1:24
1:6
h 2Co 4:15
1:7
i Ro 8:17

1:8
j 1Co 15:32

1:9
k Jer 17:5,7
1:10
l Ro 15:31
1:11
m Ro 15:30;
Php 1:19
n 2Co 4:15

1:12
o Ac 23:1
p 2Co 2:17
q 1Co 2:1,4,13

1:14
r 1Co 1:8

1 Paul, an apostle of Christ Jesus by the will of God, *a* and Timothy our brother,

To the church of God *b* in Corinth, together with all the saints throughout Achaia: *c*

2 Grace and peace to you from God our Father and the Lord Jesus Christ. *d*

The God of All Comfort

3 Praise be to the God and Father of our Lord Jesus Christ, *e* the Father of compassion and the God of all comfort, 4 who comforts us *f* in all our troubles, so that we can comfort those in any trouble with the comfort we ourselves have received from God. 5 For just as the sufferings of Christ flow over into our lives, *g* so also through Christ our comfort overflows. 6 If we are distressed, it is for your comfort and salvation; *h* if we are comforted, it is for your comfort, which produces in you patient endurance of the same sufferings we suffer. 7 And our hope for you is firm, because we know that just as you share in our sufferings, *i* so also you share in our comfort.

8 We do not want you to be uninformed, brothers, about the hardships we suffered *j* in the province of Asia. We were under great pressure, far beyond our ability to endure, so that we despaired even of life. 9 Indeed, in our hearts we felt the sentence of death. But this happened that we might not rely on ourselves but on God, *k* who raises the dead. 10 He has delivered us from such a deadly peril, *l* and he will deliver us. On him we have set our hope that he will continue to deliver us, 11 as you help us by your prayers. *m* Then many will give thanks *n* on our *a* behalf for the gracious favor granted us in answer to the prayers of many.

Paul's Change of Plans

12 Now this is our boast: Our conscience *o* testifies that we have conducted ourselves in the world, and especially in our relations with you, in the holiness and sincerity *p* that are from God. We have done so not according to worldly wisdom *q* but according to God's grace. 13 For we do not write you anything you cannot read or understand. And I hope that, 14 as you have understood us in part, you will come to understand fully that you can boast of us just as we will boast of you in the day of the Lord Jesus. *r*

a 11 Many manuscripts *your*

2 Corinthians 1:1–2

There were two kinds of apostles in the early church: (1) the original "twelve apostles," (called "disciples" in the Gospels) sent out by Jesus during his ministry and later confirmed by the resurrected Christ, and (2) those "apostles" sent out by churches. Such missionaries derived their authority from the other apostles and the sending churches. Paul was unique in that he stood in, or between, these classes (see Acts 13:1–3). But this combination caused him problems. Those rejecting his apostleship denied his calling by the resurrected Christ and discredited his authority.

Some people today see Paul's claim to speak for Christ according to God's will as arrogant or self-promoting. It's critical to remember that Paul wrote with the authority of God himself. As an apostle he represented not his own will, but the will of God and the character of Christ. This issue is of life-or-death importance: To reject Paul's credibility is to reject the very One who authorized his mission and calling.

2 Corinthians 1:3–11

Paul's prayer of praise in verses 3–7 is a carefully crafted expression of his main points. It provides a key to his theme, perspective, and purpose in this letter. His desire was to defend his apostolic ministry in the face of those who called his legitimacy into question, primarily because of his apparent weakness and suffering. Paul talked about comfort more than any other New Testament author. Why? Because he also talked more about and experienced more suffering. Comfort for Paul wasn't the absence of pain, but the presence of God, who strengthens his children in and through suffering.

The comfort/suffering equation is a kind of "spiritual math." The measure of God's comfort matched the measure of Paul's suffering, with the result that others were comforted to that same degree (Paul's suffering + God's comfort = comfort for others). Hope for the future creates comfort in the present. It wasn't *in spite of*, but *in* and *through* Paul's suffering that his legitimacy as an apostle was established.

The capacity of believers to live with trust (v. 9), integrity (1:12—2:4), and mercy (2:5–11) *in the midst of* adversity manifests the coming of the kingdom of God and the reality of Jesus' death and resurrection. The life and teaching of a pastor, reproduced in the faith of people in the midst of their own sufferings, is one way God grows his church. Has an instance in your own life shown this to be true?

15Because I was confident of this, I planned to visit you[s] first so that you might benefit twice.[t] 16I planned to visit you on my way[u] to Macedonia and to come back to you from Macedonia, and then to have you send me on my way to Judea. 17When I planned this, did I do it lightly? Or do I make my plans in a worldly manner[v] so that in the same breath I say, "Yes, yes" and "No, no"?

18But as surely as God is faithful,[w] our message to you is not "Yes" and "No." 19For the Son of God, Jesus Christ, who was preached among you by me and Silas[a] and Timothy, was not "Yes" and "No," but in him it has always[x] been "Yes." 20For no matter how many promises[y] God has made, they are "Yes" in Christ. And so through him the "Amen"[z] is spoken by us to the glory of God. 21Now it is God who makes both us and you stand firm in Christ. He anointed[a] us, 22set his seal of ownership on us, and put his Spirit in our hearts as a deposit, guaranteeing what is to come.[b]

23I call God as my witness[c] that it was in order to spare you[d] that I did not return to Corinth. 24Not that we lord it over[e] your faith, but we work with you for

2 your joy, because it is by faith you stand firm.[f] 1So I made up my mind that I would not make another painful visit to you.[g] 2For if I grieve you,[h] who is left to make me glad but you whom I have grieved? 3I wrote as I did[i] so that when I came I should not be distressed[j] by those who ought to make me rejoice. I had confidence[k] in all of you, that you would all share my joy. 4For I wrote you[l] out of great distress and anguish of heart and with many tears, not to grieve you but to let you know the depth of my love for you.

Forgiveness for the Sinner

5If anyone has caused grief,[m] he has not so much grieved me as he has grieved all of you, to some extent—not to put it too severely. 6The punishment[n] inflicted on him by the majority is sufficient for him. 7Now instead, you ought to forgive and comfort him,[o] so that he will not be overwhelmed by excessive sorrow. 8I urge you, therefore, to reaffirm your love for him. 9The reason I wrote you was to see if you would stand the test and be obedient in everything.[p] 10If you forgive anyone, I also forgive him. And what I have forgiven—if there was anything to forgive—I have forgiven in the sight of Christ for your sake, 11in order that Satan[q] might not outwit us. For we are not unaware of his schemes.[r]

Ministers of the New Covenant

12Now when I went to Troas[s] to preach the gospel of Christ[t] and found that the

[a] 19 Greek *Silvanus*, a variant of *Silas*

Cross references

1:15
s 1Co 4:19
t Ro 1:11,13; 15:29
1:16
u 1Co 16:5-7
1:17
v 2Co 10:2,3
1:18
w 1Co 1:9
1:19
x Heb 13:8
1:20
y Ro 15:8
z 1Co 14:16
1:21
a 1Jn 2:20,27
1:22
b 2Co 5:5
1:23
c Ro 1:9; Gal 1:20
d 1Co 4:21;
2Co 2:1,3; 13:2,10
1:24
e 1Pe 5:3
f Ro 11:20;
1Co 15:1
2:1
g 2Co 1:23
2:2
h 2Co 7:8
2:3
i 2Co 7:8,12
j 2Co 12:21
k 8:22;
Gal 5:10
2:4
l 2Co 7:8,12
2:5
m 1Co 5:1,2
2:6
n 1Co 5:4,5
2:7
o Gal 6:1; Eph 4:32
2:9
p 2Co 10:6
2:11
q Mt 4:10
r Lk 22:31; 2Co 4:4;
1Pe 5:8,9
2:12
s Ac 16:8 t Ro 1:1

---

2 Corinthians 1:12—2:4

In response to the Corinthians' doubts about Paul's reliability, he proclaimed the source of his commitment and confidence. All God's promises are fulfilled in Christ, and the Spirit is God's guarantee in believers' lives that one day they will see them fully completed.

Galileo's discovery that the earth revolves around the sun caused a revolution in people's thinking. Similarly, we need to understand the Bible in a new way: It's not fundamentally about us, but about God. When we are confronted about major life decisions, the question isn't "What do I need and how can I ask God to help me?" but "What are God's promises and how does he want to work through me and this situation to bring them to life?" God is faithful, and Christ is his great "yes" to us! Therefore, it's imperative that our focus be fully on him.

2 Corinthians 2:5–11

Paul addressed here a church discipline issue. He didn't mention specifics, but the offense must have involved some sort of slander against himself and his apostolic relationship with the Corinthians. Most of them had initially sided with the slanderer. But later, after the majority had repented (2:4; 7:8–13), they grieved with Paul because of the offender's influence over them. And they punished him, most likely by excluding him from their fellowship. Paul was now adamant that the community forgive, comfort, and reaffirm its love for that individual. Failure to forgive opens a door for Satan.

Paul followed five guiding principles that apply directly in such situations today: (1) Christ's body is interconnected (this grief, punishment, and forgiveness weren't private matters). (2) There will be judgment and punishment, forgiveness and reconciliation within that body. (3) The exercise of faith includes the courage to punish and the willingness to forgive. (4) Christ's lordship leads to forgiving others for their sakes, not seeking vengeance for our own pain. (5) A lack of forgiveness allows Satan an inroad to carry out his schemes among God's people.

2:12
u Ac 14:27
2:13
v 2Co 7:5
w 2Co 7:6,13;
12:18
2:14
x Ro 6:17 y Eph 5:2;
Php 4:18

2:15
z 1Co 1:18
2:16
a Lk 2:34
b 2Co 3:5,6
2:17
c 2Co 4:2 d 1Co 5:8
e 2Co 1:12
3:1
f 2Co 5:12; 12:11
g Ac 18:27
3:2
h 1Co 9:2

3:3
i Ex 24:12 j Pr 3:3;
Jer 31:33;
Eze 11:19
3:4
k Eph 3:12
3:5
l 1Co 15:10
3:6
m Lk 22:20
n Jn 6:63

3:7
o Ex 34:29-35
3:9
p ver 7 q Ro 1:17;
3:21,22

3:12
r Eph 6:19
3:13
s ver 7; Ex 34:33

Lord had opened a door[u] for me, 13I still had no peace of mind,[v] because I did not find my brother Titus[w] there. So I said good-by to them and went on to Macedonia.

14But thanks be to God,[x] who always leads us in triumphal procession in Christ and through us spreads everywhere the fragrance[y] of the knowledge of him. 15For we are to God the aroma of Christ among those who are being saved and those who are perishing.[z] 16To the one we are the smell of death;[a] to the other, the fragrance of life. And who is equal to such a task?[b] 17Unlike so many, we do not peddle the word of God for profit.[c] On the contrary, in Christ we speak before God with sincerity,[d] like men sent from God.[e]

3 Are we beginning to commend ourselves[f] again? Or do we need, like some people, letters of recommendation[g] to you or from you? 2You yourselves are our letter, written on our hearts, known and read by everybody.[h] 3You show that you are a letter from Christ, the result of our ministry, written not with ink but with the Spirit of the living God, not on tablets of stone[i] but on tablets of human hearts.[j]

4Such confidence[k] as this is ours through Christ before God. 5Not that we are competent in ourselves to claim anything for ourselves, but our competence comes from God.[l] 6He has made us competent as ministers of a new covenant[m]—not of the letter but of the Spirit; for the letter kills, but the Spirit gives life.[n]

The Glory of the New Covenant

7Now if the ministry that brought death, which was engraved in letters on stone, came with glory, so that the Israelites could not look steadily at the face of Moses because of its glory,[o] fading though it was, 8will not the ministry of the Spirit be even more glorious? 9If the ministry that condemns men[p] is glorious, how much more glorious is the ministry that brings righteousness![q] 10For what was glorious has no glory now in comparison with the surpassing glory. 11And if what was fading away came with glory, how much greater is the glory of that which lasts!

12Therefore, since we have such a hope, we are very bold.[r] 13We are not like Moses, who would put a veil over his face[s] to keep the Israelites from gazing at it while

---

2 Corinthians 2:12—3:6

Paul's concern over Titus, who was bringing news about how the Corinthians had responded to Paul's "tearful" letter (cf. 2:4), illustrates the suffering he bore as an apostle. Just as his concern for Titus and the Corinthians had originally led him to Troas, so now his anxiety for them propelled him on to Macedonia (cf. 7:5–7).

But Paul returned to his theme: Hardship or opposition pales in comparison to our confidence in Christ. To illustrate this he used images drawn from the military and the marketplace. In all things God always leads his own in triumph in Christ. When a victorious Roman army returned home, the captives marched in parade with the conquerors. The flowers along the route smelled life-giving for the victors but represented the aroma of defeat for the vanquished. Switching to the marketplace, Paul rebuked those accusing him of peddling God's word for profit.

Paul's convictions about his own ministry can prompt soul-searching in Christians today. Ask yourself: Do I show a growing trust in God's sovereignty over the circumstances of my life? Do I increasingly reflect the peace and praise that come from understanding the role of suffering in my circumstances? Do I demonstrate loving actions that flow from a willingness to give up my rights for the sake of others? Do I evidence the Spirit's transforming work by my eagerness to stand for the

truth? Does my life model for others what it means to imitate Christ?

We can't manufacture the transformation Paul describes. It's the result of a miraculous invasion of our lives by the power and presence of God himself. Our confidence in our ability to live boldly for Christ doesn't reside in our own power but in the power of the Spirit in us.

2 Corinthians 3:7–18

The *similarity* between the calls of Moses and Paul contrasts with the *differences* between their ministries. Moses needed a veil to cover his face, first to protect others from seeing God's glory on it, then to hide the fact that the glory was disappearing. But Paul was free to preach the gospel, knowing that the present revelation of God's glory—the message of Christ—didn't have to be veiled. We can live with bold hope because the Spirit is transforming us more and more into Christ's image.

As followers of Christ, we don't have to put on a "spiritual show," hiding our sin and trying to look more pious and godly than we are. Nor are we to live with resignation, passively accepting our sinful desires and actions as if there was nothing we could do about them. Rather, we live with bold hope because God is in the process of transforming us. We long to grow and are eager to change. Instead of bondage to a set of behavioral codes, we live in the life-giving freedom of the Spirit, hungry to be changed ever more fully into Christ's image.

the radiance was fading away. 14But their minds were made dull,[t] for to this day the
same veil remains when the old covenant[u] is read.[v] It has not been removed, because only in Christ is it taken away. 15Even to this day when Moses is read, a veil
covers their hearts. 16But whenever anyone turns to the Lord,[w] the veil is taken
away.[x] 17Now the Lord is the Spirit,[y] and where the Spirit of the Lord is, there is freedom.[z] 18And we, who with unveiled faces all reflect[a][a] the Lord's glory,[b] are being
transformed into his likeness[c] with ever-increasing glory, which comes from the
Lord, who is the Spirit.

Treasures in Jars of Clay

4 Therefore, since through God's mercy[d] we have this ministry, we do not lose
heart. 2Rather, we have renounced secret and shameful ways;[e] we do not use
deception, nor do we distort the word of God.[f] On the contrary, by setting forth the
truth plainly we commend ourselves to every man's conscience[g] in the sight of God.
3And even if our gospel[h] is veiled,[i] it is veiled to those who are perishing.[j] 4The
god[k] of this age has blinded[l] the minds of unbelievers, so that they cannot see the
light of the gospel of the glory of Christ, who is the image of God. 5For we do not
preach ourselves,[m] but Jesus Christ as Lord, and ourselves as your servants[n] for
Jesus' sake. 6For God, who said, "Let light shine out of darkness,"[b][o] made his light
shine in our hearts[p] to give us the light of the knowledge of the glory of God in the
face of Christ.

7But we have this treasure in jars of clay[q] to show that this all-surpassing power
is from God[r] and not from us. 8We are hard pressed on every side,[s] but not crushed;
perplexed, but not in despair; 9persecuted,[t] but not abandoned;[u] struck down, but
not destroyed.[v] 10We always carry around in our body the death of Jesus, so that the
life of Jesus may also be revealed in our body.[w] 11For we who are alive are always
being given over to death for Jesus' sake,[x] so that his life may be revealed in our
mortal body. 12So then, death is at work in us, but life is at work in you.[y]

13It is written: "I believed; therefore I have spoken."[c][z] With that same spirit of
faith we also believe and therefore speak, 14because we know that the one who
raised the Lord Jesus from the dead will also raise us with Jesus[a] and present us with
you in his presence.[b] 15All this is for your benefit, so that the grace that is reaching
more and more people may cause thanksgiving[c] to overflow to the glory of God.

16Therefore we do not lose heart. Though outwardly we are wasting away, yet inwardly[d] we are being renewed[e] day by day. 17For our light and momentary troubles
are achieving for us an eternal glory that far outweighs them all.[f] 18So we fix our
eyes not on what is seen, but on what is unseen.[g] For what is seen is temporary, but
what is unseen is eternal.

Our Heavenly Dwelling

5 Now we know that if the earthly[h] tent[i] we live in is destroyed, we have a building from God, an eternal house in heaven, not built by human hands. 2Mean-
while we groan,[j] longing to be clothed with our heavenly dwelling,[k] 3because

3:14 [t] Ro 11:7,8 [u] Ac 13:15 [v] ver 6
3:16 [w] Ro 11:23 [x] Ex 34:34
3:17 [y] Isa 61:1,2 [z] Jn 8:32
3:18 [a] 1Co 13:12 [b] 2Co 4:4,6 [c] Ro 8:29
4:1 [d] 1Co 7:25
4:2 [e] 1Co 4:5 [f] 2Co 2:17 [g] 2Co 5:11
4:3 [h] 2Co 2:12 [i] 2Co 3:14 [j] 1Co 1:18
4:4 [k] Jn 12:31 [l] 2Co 3:14
4:5 [m] 1Co 1:13 [n] 1Co 9:19
4:6 [o] Ge 1:3 [p] 2Pe 1:19
4:7 [q] Job 4:19; 2Co 5:1 [r] 1Co 2:5
4:8 [s] 2Co 7:5
4:9 [t] Jn 15:20 [u] Heb 13:5 [v] Ps 37:24
4:10 [w] Ro 6:5
4:11 [x] Ro 8:36
4:12 [y] 2Co 13:9
4:13 [z] Ps 116:10
4:14 [a] 1Th 4:14 [b] Eph 5:27
4:15 [c] 2Co 1:11
4:16 [d] Ro 7:22 [e] Col 3:10
4:17 [f] Ro 8:18; 1Pe 1:6,7
4:18 [g] Ro 8:24; Heb 11:1
5:1 [h] 1Co 15:47 [i] 2Pe 1:13,14
5:2 [j] ver 4; Ro 8:23 [k] 1Co 15:53,54

[a] *18* Or *contemplate* [b] *6* Gen. 1:3 [c] *13* Psalm 116:10

2 Corinthians 4:1–18

Just as Paul wasn't daunted by suffering because he served the God of all comfort, so he wasn't thwarted by his own weakness. His focus wasn't on himself or his circumstances but on Jesus Christ and his own role as Christ's servant. Regardless of any suffering or weakness Paul experienced, he was but a clay jar through whom God would display his all-surpassing power.

"Glory" is a great word that conveys not just the ideas of splendor and praise, but also substance and solidity. To be glorious is to be pure, solid, complete, and luminous. It's to be refined into "pure gold." The weight of our problems is nothing compared to that of the glory that lies before us.

Being Christian implies for us a different way of thinking and living. A true comparison between the suffering now and the glory to be revealed leads to the conclusion that no one can out-serve or out-give God. Whatever we give up in the present (our time, resources, preferred lifestyles—even our lives) pales in comparison to what God will grant us. This eternal perspective makes all the difference as we interact in love with a desperately needy world.

when we are clothed, we will not be found naked. [4]For while we are in this tent, we groan and are burdened, because we do not wish to be unclothed but to be clothed with our heavenly dwelling,[l] so that what is mortal may be swallowed up by life. [5]Now it is God who has made us for this very purpose and has given us the Spirit as a deposit, guaranteeing what is to come.[m]

[6]Therefore we are always confident and know that as long as we are at home in the body we are away from the Lord. [7]We live by faith, not by sight.[n] [8]We are confident, I say, and would prefer to be away from the body and at home with the Lord.[o] [9]So we make it our goal to please him,[p] whether we are at home in the body or away from it. [10]For we must all appear before the judgment seat of Christ, that each one may receive what is due him[q] for the things done while in the body, whether good or bad.

The Ministry of Reconciliation

[11]Since, then, we know what it is to fear the Lord,[r] we try to persuade men. What we are is plain to God, and I hope it is also plain to your conscience.[s] [12]We are not trying to commend ourselves to you again,[t] but are giving you an opportunity to take pride in us,[u] so that you can answer those who take pride in what is seen rath-

5:4
l 1Co 15:53,54

5:5
m Ro 8:23;
2Co 1:22

5:7
n 1Co 13:12

5:8
o Php 1:23
5:9
p Ro 14:18
5:10
q Mt 16:27;
Ro 14:10; Eph 6:8

5:11
r Heb 10:31;
Jude 23 s 2Co 4:2

5:12
t 2Co 3:1
u 2Co 1:14

---

2 Corinthians 5:1–10

Paul compared a Christian's body to a frail tent, compared to the solid home that awaits us (see John 14:2). Certainly believers of all times have struggled in these tents. But rather than death being the ultimate threat to life, our lives now will one day "be swallowed up by life" (v. 4). In light of the infinitely more solid and glorious life to come after death, Paul had only one goal: to please God.

Death is the foe of human existence. Humanity's greatest deception is and has always been the thought that this life is all there is, that there is no eternity, let alone a judgment at its gateway. The life-changing impact of *knowing* there is a future reality and a judgment to come in the presence of Christ remains as radical in

the 21st century as it was in the first. This knowledge fuels a life lived not for the present, but for the Lord. What practical differences has this knowledge made in your life?

2 Corinthians 5:11—6:2

Some scholars believe Paul's use of the word "reconciliation" came from the ancient secular world, where it was a diplomatic term referring to the harmony established between enemies by peace treaties. As "Christ's ambassador," Paul was sent to announce that God had established a "peace treaty" with his enemies.

But God's way of establishing peace is far more radical than human treaties. The treaty he offered wasn't through a negotiated agreement or even an amnesty. Rather, Christ bore all the judgment and enmity on be-

---

4:16–18

Witness

Chapters three and four comprise one of Paul's most eloquent descriptions of the mission of the Christian church. It applied to the church in Corinth, and it applies to the church today. The contemporary church, though, does its work for the Master on a much larger stage. **Within the next 24 hours** worldwide:

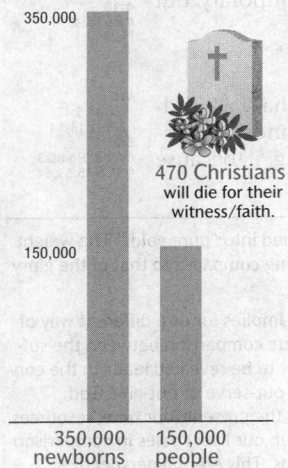

470 Christians will die for their witness/faith.

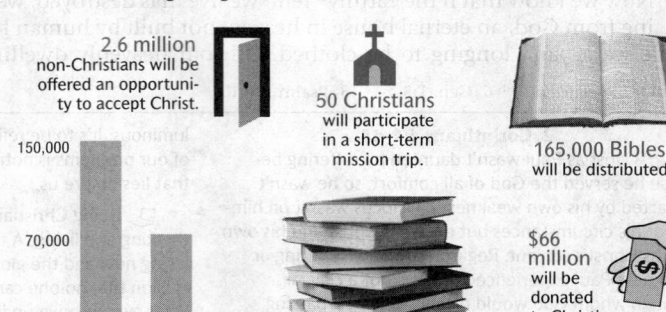

2.6 million non-Christians will be offered an opportunity to accept Christ.

50 Christians will participate in a short-term mission trip.

165,000 Bibles will be distributed.

$66 million will be donated to Christian causes.

350,000 newborns will first see the light of day.	150,000 people will breathe their last breath.	150,000 people will choose a non-Christian religion.
		70,000 people will be converted to Christianity.

7 new books or articles on evangelization will be published.

⌐Source: Barrett and Johnson (2001:8)

er than in what is in the heart. 13 If we are out of our mind,[v] it is for the sake of God;
if we are in our right mind, it is for you. 14 For Christ's love compels us, because we
are convinced that one died for all, and therefore all died.[w] 15 And he died for all,
that those who live should no longer live for themselves[x] but for him who died for
them and was raised again.
16 So from now on we regard no one from a worldly[y] point of view. Though we
once regarded Christ in this way, we do so no longer. 17 Therefore, if anyone is in
Christ, he is a new creation;[z] the old has gone, the new has come![a] 18 All this is from
God, who reconciled us to himself through Christ[b] and gave us the ministry of reconciliation: 19 that God was reconciling the world to himself in Christ, not counting men's sins against them.[c] And he has committed to us the message of reconciliation. 20 We are therefore Christ's ambassadors,[d] as though God were making his
appeal through us. We implore you on Christ's behalf: Be reconciled to God. 21 God
made him who had no sin[e] to be sin[a] for us, so that in him we might become the
righteousness of God.[f]

6 As God's fellow workers[g] we urge you not to receive God's grace in vain. 2 For
he says,

> "In the time of my favor I heard you,
> and in the day of salvation I helped you."[b][h]

I tell you, now is the time of God's favor, now is the day of salvation.

Paul's Hardships

3 We put no stumbling block in anyone's path,[i] so that our ministry will not be
discredited. 4 Rather, as servants of God we commend ourselves in every way: in
great endurance; in troubles, hardships and distresses; 5 in beatings, imprisonments[j] and riots; in hard work, sleepless nights and hunger;[k] 6 in purity, understanding, patience and kindness; in the Holy Spirit[l] and in sincere love; 7 in truthful
speech[m] and in the power of God; with weapons of righteousness[n] in the right hand
and in the left; 8 through glory and dishonor,[o] bad report and good report; genuine, yet regarded as impostors;[p] 9 known, yet regarded as unknown; dying,[q] and yet
we live on;[r] beaten, and yet not killed; 10 sorrowful, yet always rejoicing;[s] poor, yet
making many rich;[t] having nothing, and yet possessing everything.[u]
11 We have spoken freely to you, Corinthians, and opened wide our hearts to you.[v]
12 We are not withholding our affection from you, but you are withholding yours
from us. 13 As a fair exchange—I speak as to my children[w]—open wide your hearts
also.

5:13 [v] 2Co 11:1,16,17
5:14 [w] Gal 2:20
5:15 [x] Ro 14:7-9
5:16 [y] 2Co 11:18
5:17 [z] Gal 6:15 [a] Isa 65:17; Rev 21:4,5
5:18 [b] Ro 5:10; Col 1:20
5:19 [c] Ro 4:8
5:20 [d] 2Co 6:1; Eph 6:20
5:21 [e] Heb 4:15; 1Pe 2:22,24; 1Jn 3:5 [f] Ro 1:17
6:1 [g] 1Co 3:9; 2Co 5:20
6:2 [h] Isa 49:8
6:3 [i] Ro 14:13,20; 1Co 9:12; 10:32
6:5 [j] 2Co 11:23-25 [k] 1Co 4:11
6:6 [l] 1Th 1:5
6:7 [m] 2Co 4:2 [n] 2Co 10:4; Eph 6:10-18
6:8 [o] 1Co 4:10 [p] Mt 27:63
6:9 [q] Ro 8:36 [r] 2Co 1:8-10; 4:10,11
6:10 [s] 2Co 7:4 [t] 2Co 8:9 [u] Ro 8:32; 1Co 3:21
6:11 [v] 2Co 7:3
6:13 [w] 1Co 4:14

[a] 21 Or *be a sin offering* [b] 2 Isaiah 49:8

half of everyone else. The conflict is over! Now, for the Christian to enter into the peace of that reconciliation, there is only one thing necessary: to die to ourselves and be reborn as new creatures in Christ!

In transferring Paul's gospel to our day, we do well to emphasize the powerful, life-changing nature of Jesus' death. To be reconciled to God in Christ is an act of sovereign restoration and creative power as magnificent and miraculous as the creation (cf. 4:4–6 with 5:17). The gospel is God's action in Christ to make us right with God—not simply by accepting us but by transforming us. At certain times in history political leaders have negotiated a cease fire, but the soldiers, who hadn't yet received this news at the front, went on fighting. Our privilege as ambassadors for Christ is to race to the front and tell everyone of the reconciliation available in him for the asking.

2 Corinthians 6:3–13

Paul used a father image to describe his relationship to the Corinthians. His heart for them seems to have been bursting with a father's love and even jealously. Paul provided one of the most complete summaries in any of his letters of the qualities that characterized his life. All he asked of these believers in return was their love.

The contemporary significance of Paul's defense was threefold. (1) Each of us is called to live for others as we participate in the life of Christ (5:15). (2) This means we will be willing to suffer for others (cf. 4:1–18). The suffering of the righteous is distinguished by the transforming and sustaining power of God's presence in their lives. People God calls to suffer for others aren't called to masochism but to mission. (3) A genuine love looks forward to a genuine response. Paul's confidence in the truth led him to expect that those who knew God would open their hearts to Paul as well.

Reconciliation

This may be the Bible's most succinct passage on reconciliation. It's presented in two parts: (1) becoming a new creation in and through Christ, who satisfied God's need for holiness through his blood-covering of our sins; and (2) receiving the charge to continue this ministry, to be agents of restoration in the world. Neither God's grace nor human responsibility has ever been elevated higher!

Reconciliation requires costly grace and incomprehensible love. Some years ago, during Easter week, I sat in a slum kitchen in Danang, Vietnam, listening to a fifteen-year-old boy sing love songs about his native land. He was flanked by adoring parents, applauding his every move. He needed all the support he could get; he was totally blind and severely mentally impaired.

Over the course of an evening, the story emerged. During the last desperate days of the Vietnam War, the boy's mother had a brief affair, leaving her pregnant. By the time the baby was born, her guilt was such that she attempted—with near success—to kill him.

Her husband followed to where she was attempting to bury the baby alive. Frantically, he uncovered the child. He took the injured baby home, gave him his name, forgave his wife, and kept the family intact. Over the years, a gift emerged in the young child. He could sing! In the midst of Passion Week, far from home, we were treated to this gift.

> **We pursue reconciliation through Christ's massive prompt of grace.**

Echoes of another event, 2000 years earlier, were unmistakable. Difficult days had produced a horrific sin. Guilt demanded the sacrifice of the innocent. But the grave couldn't hold the body. The Father rescued the Son, forgave sinners, established a new identity—a new creation—and looked on proudly as the love song was sung. An Easter song! The song of reconciliation.

In a world of shattered hopes, false promises, war, poverty, and disease, the God-man's modeling of divine reconciliation has never been needed more. We are profoundly grateful for what he demonstrated at Calvary. In this ultimate exercise of unmerited favor, there were two specific acts of grace. Christ forgave those responsible. The victim initiated reconciliation before the perpetrator had even thought of repentance. And God turned his back on his Son— so he would never again have to turn away from another child! Such grace is costly, such love incomprehensible. There is nothing easy about the ministry of reconciliation.

But Calvary wasn't the first intimation of a reconciled relationship. Hints emerge as early as the first chapters of Genesis. "The earth was formless and empty" (Gen. 1:2), but God penetrated the darkness and created a perfect universe. Adam and Eve opted for the forbidden fruit, but God covered their newly discovered nakedness with animal skins—the first sacrifice. Cain killed Abel but was given a divine mark of protection to ease his life as a fugitive. A common language was lost at Babel, and the ensuing multiple tribes became nations, out of which God called one to be his witness to a fallen world.

The baton has been passed. We have been entrusted with the ministry of reconciliation. What an awesome responsibility! This is more than a process, more than a program. We grab the baton out of obedience. We pursue reconciliation through Christ's massive prompt of grace. It's this spirituality that incarnates our commitment to the One who made the supreme commitment to us. This witness continues to bring hope to a broken world.

Robert Seiple, former U.S. Ambassador of Religious Freedom, former president of World Vision U.S., and founder and chairman of the board of the Institute for Global Engagement in St. David's, Pennsylvania

Do Not Be Yoked With Unbelievers

¹⁴Do not be yoked together^x with unbelievers. For what do righteousness and wickedness have in common? Or what fellowship can light have with darkness?^y ¹⁵What harmony is there between Christ and Belial^a? What does a believer^z have in common with an unbeliever? ¹⁶What agreement is there between the temple of God and idols? For we are the temple^a of the living God. As God has said: "I will live with them and walk among them, and I will be their God, and they will be my people."^b ^b

¹⁷"Therefore come out from them^c
and be separate,

says the Lord.

Touch no unclean thing,
and I will receive you."^{c d}
¹⁸"I will be a Father to you,
and you will be my sons and daughters,^e

says the Lord Almighty."^d

7 Since we have these promises,^f dear friends, let us purify ourselves from everything that contaminates body and spirit, perfecting holiness out of reverence for God.

Paul's Joy

²Make room for us in your hearts.^g We have wronged no one, we have corrupted no one, we have exploited no one. ³I do not say this to condemn you; I have said before that you have such a place in our hearts^h that we would live or die with you. ⁴I have great confidence in you; I take great pride in you. I am greatly encouraged; in all our troubles my joy knows no bounds.ⁱ

⁵For when we came into Macedonia,^j this body of ours had no rest, but we were harassed at every turn^k—conflicts on the outside, fears within.^l ⁶But God, who comforts the downcast,^m comforted us by the coming of Titus,ⁿ ⁷and not only by his coming but also by the comfort you had given him. He told us about your longing

6:14
x 1Co 5:9,10
y Eph 5:7,11;
1Jn 1:6
6:15
z Ac 5:14
6:16
a 1Co 3:16
b Lev 26:12;
Jer 32:38;
Eze 37:27
6:17
c Rev 18:4
d Isa 52:11
6:18
e Isa 43:6
7:1
f 2Co 6:17,18
7:2
g 2Co 6:12,13
7:3
h 2Co 6:11,12
7:4
i 2Co 6:10
7:5
j 2Co 2:13
k 2Co 4:8
l Dt 32:25
7:6
m 2Co 1:3,4
n ver 13; 2Co 2:13

---

^a 15 Greek *Beliar*, a variant of *Belial*   ^b 16 Lev. 26:12; Jer. 32:38; Ezek. 37:27   ^c 17 Isaiah 52:11; Ezek. 20:34,41   ^d 18 2 Samuel 7:14; 7:8

---

2 Corinthians 6:14—7:1

📖 Paul called on his readers in 6:14,17 and 7:1 to flee anything that might keep them from being "reconciled to God" (5:20). Positively, this meant having an open heart toward Paul (6:13; cf. 7:2–4). Negatively, it meant separating from those who rejected him and the gospel and closing their ears to those preaching a "different gospel" (cf. 11:4). Nothing less than the true message of the new covenant, the genuine presence of the Spirit, and the identity of God's people was at stake.

Paul pleaded with the Corinthians not to be "yoked together" with unbelievers. He was referring to any kind of association that might significantly form an individual's identity. Determining whether someone is "yoked together" with another is a judgment call. The answer depends on the degree, significance, purpose, and level of self-identification involved in one person's relationship with another.

📖 Our desire to live holy lives isn't to get God to love us. Rather, God loves us so much he has made us his own sons and daughters in Christ. As members of his family we want our lives to bring honor to our Father. This is God's great promise to us fulfilled in Christ. In

response, we are eager to rid our lives of anything that might contaminate them.

2 Corinthians 7:2–16

📖 In light of the still-raging controversy, Paul had been addressing the Corinthian church as a whole, focusing on the defense of his life and teaching. But most of its members had already repented in response to his previous letter (cf. 2:3–4; 7:8–13). In 7:2–9:15, the apostle addressed this majority, focusing on their responsibilities as Christians. He was no longer speaking as the guardian defending his faith. He was the pastor admonishing his flock.

📖 Confronting sin and calling God's people to repentance are vital tasks for Christians, and especially their leaders. Yet in many places this kind of activity has become uncomfortable and uncommon. Paul made it clear that having the courage to take such a stand is an essential expression of Christian love and leadership. But he expressed this in the context of his constant affirmation of the Corinthians—taking great pride and having great confidence in them (v. 4). He wasn't their critic but their loving undershepherd!

for me, your deep sorrow, your ardent concern for me, so that my joy was greater than ever.

8 Even if I caused you sorrow by my letter, *o* I do not regret it. Though I did regret it—I see that my letter hurt you, but only for a little while— 9 yet now I am happy, not because you were made sorry, but because your sorrow led you to repentance. For you became sorrowful as God intended and so were not harmed in any way by us. 10 Godly sorrow brings repentance that leads to salvation *p* and leaves no regret, but worldly sorrow brings death. 11 See what this godly sorrow has produced in you: what earnestness, what eagerness to clear yourselves, what indignation, what alarm, what longing, what concern, *q* what readiness to see justice done. At every point you have proved yourselves to be innocent in this matter. 12 So even though I wrote to you, *r* it was not on account of the one who did the wrong *s* or of the injured party, but rather that before God you could see for yourselves how devoted to us you are. 13 By all this we are encouraged.

In addition to our own encouragement, we were especially delighted to see how happy Titus *t* was, because his spirit has been refreshed by all of you. 14 I had boasted to him about you, *u* and you have not embarrassed me. But just as everything we said to you was true, so our boasting about you to Titus *v* has proved to be true as well. 15 And his affection for you is all the greater when he remembers that you were all obedient, *w* receiving him with fear and trembling. *x* 16 I am glad I can have complete confidence in you. *y*

Generosity Encouraged

8 And now, brothers, we want you to know about the grace that God has given the Macedonian *z* churches. 2 Out of the most severe trial, their overflowing joy and their extreme poverty welled up in rich generosity. 3 For I testify that they gave as much as they were able, *a* and even beyond their ability. Entirely on their own, 4 they urgently pleaded with us for the privilege of sharing in this service *b* to the saints. *c* 5 And they did not do as we expected, but they gave themselves first to the Lord and then to us in keeping with God's will. 6 So we urged *d* Titus, *e* since he had earlier made a beginning, to bring also to completion *f* this act of grace on your part. 7 But just as you excel in everything *g*—in faith, in speech, in knowledge, *h* in complete earnestness and in your love for us *a*—see that you also excel in this grace of giving.

8 I am not commanding you, *i* but I want to test the sincerity of your love by comparing it with the earnestness of others. 9 For you know the grace of our Lord Jesus Christ, *j* that though he was rich, yet for your sakes he became poor, *k* so that you through his poverty might become rich.

10 And here is my advice *l* about what is best for you in this matter: Last year you were the first not only to give but also to have the desire to do so. *m* 11 Now finish the work, so that your eager willingness *n* to do it may be matched by your comple-

---

a 7 Some manuscripts *in our love for you*

---

2 Corinthians 8:1–15

The generosity Paul encouraged in chapters 8 and 9 wasn't to be an "add-on" or extra credit for those who were serious about their faith. Instead, the Corinthians' generosity in giving to the collection for needy Christians in Jerusalem was to be a visible expression of the gospel's impact on their lives.

Paul emphasized that the attitude in giving is more important than the amount. He stressed that the Macedonians' generosity resulted from their joy. The progression in verse 2 is from grace to joy to giving, not the other way around. Yet Paul noted that these Christians gave from their poverty, not their abundance, offering more than they could afford to give.

The ideal of resource equity is as difficult for us as it was for the Corinthians. But that shouldn't keep us from adjusting our behavior to reflect the truth of Scripture. Wealthier Christians have a God-given mandate to help support their poorer counterparts around the world. A scaled-back lifestyle and regular giving to those in need will help those of us who have "gathered much" not to have too much—and those who have "gathered little" to have enough to survive.

Paul's advice to the Corinthian believers—and ultimately to us—boils down to this: Give (1) your entire lives to the Lord; (2) your resources as an act of joyous privilege, not burdensome duty; and (3) more than you can afford to give—not just the surplus skimmed from the top.

tion of it, according to your means. ¹²For if the willingness is there, the gift is acceptable according to what one has, *o* not according to what he does not have.

¹³Our desire is not that others might be relieved while you are hard pressed, but that there might be equality. ¹⁴At the present time your plenty will supply what they need, *p* so that in turn their plenty will supply what you need. Then there will be equality, ¹⁵as it is written: "He who gathered much did not have too much, and he who gathered little did not have too little." *a q*

Titus Sent to Corinth

¹⁶I thank God, *r* who put into the heart *s* of Titus *t* the same concern I have for you. ¹⁷For Titus not only welcomed our appeal, but he is coming to you with much enthusiasm and on his own initiative. *u* ¹⁸And we are sending along with him the brother *v* who is praised by all the churches *w* for his service to the gospel. *x* ¹⁹What is more, he was chosen by the churches to accompany us *y* as we carry the offering, which we administer in order to honor the Lord himself and to show our eagerness to help. *z* ²⁰We want to avoid any criticism of the way we administer this liberal gift. ²¹For we are taking pains to do what is right, not only in the eyes of the Lord but also in the eyes of men. *a*

²²In addition, we are sending with them our brother who has often proved to us in many ways that he is zealous, and now even more so because of his great confidence in you. ²³As for Titus, he is my partner *b* and fellow worker *c* among you; as for our brothers, *d* they are representatives of the churches and an honor to Christ. ²⁴Therefore show these men the proof of your love and the reason for our pride in you, *e* so that the churches can see it.

9 There is no need *f* for me to write to you about this service to the saints. *g* ²For I know your eagerness to help, and I have been boasting *h* about it to the Macedonians, telling them that since last year *i* you in Achaia *j* were ready to give; and your enthusiasm has stirred most of them to action. ³But I am sending the brothers in order that our boasting about you in this matter should not prove hollow, but that you may be ready, as I said you would be. *k* ⁴For if any Macedonians *l* come with me and find you unprepared, we—not to say anything about you—would be ashamed of having been so confident. ⁵So I thought it necessary to urge the brothers to visit you in advance and finish the arrangements for the generous gift you had promised. Then it will be ready as a generous gift, *m* not as one grudgingly given. *n*

Sowing Generously

⁶Remember this: Whoever sows sparingly will also reap sparingly, and whoever sows generously will also reap generously. *o* ⁷Each man should give what he has de-

---

a 15 Exodus 16:18

Cross references

8:12 *o* Mk 12:43,44; Lk 21:3
8:14 *p* 2Co 9:12
8:15 *q* Ex 16:18
8:16 *r* 2Co 2:14 *s* Rev 17:17 *t* 2Co 2:13
8:17 *u* ver 6
8:18 *v* 2Co 12:18 *w* 1Co 7:17 *x* 2Co 2:12
8:19 *y* 1Co 16:3,4 *z* ver 11,12
8:21 *a* Ro 12:17; 14:18
8:23 *b* Phm 17 *c* Php 2:25 *d* ver 18,22
8:24 *e* 2Co 7:4,14; 9:2
9:1 *f* 1Th 4:9 *g* 2Co 8:4
9:2 *h* 2Co 7:4,14 *i* 2Co 8:10 *j* Ac 18:12
9:3 *k* 1Co 16:2
9:4 *l* Ro 15:26
9:5 *m* Php 4:17 *n* 2Co 12:17,18
9:6 *o* Pr 11:24,25; 22:9; Gal 6:7,9

---

2 Corinthians 8:16—9:5

The importance of the monetary collection within Paul's argument in 2 Corinthians can't be overestimated. The practical point of this book is expressed in chapters 8–9. Those Corinthians who hadn't accepted the grace of God in vain (6:1–2), as evidenced by their repentance (7:9–11), were to prepare for Paul's third visit by purifying the church (6:14—7:1) and completing the collection (8:1—9:15).

We follow Paul's lead by focusing on God's grace as the basis for our giving. But we are to resist the temptation to turn the necessity of giving into a voluntary opportunity to "do something great for God." Giving to others is never about contributing back to God for what he has done for us. We are to give as much as we can to meet as many needs as we can in order to glorify God as much as we can. Is your primary aim in giving to advance God's glory within his world?

2 Corinthians 9:6–15

The basis of Paul's appeal for money was the history of redemption. His call to the Corinthians to give was driven by his conviction that under the new covenant God was revealing himself in and through the lives of his people. One expression of Christians' joy in God's grace that brings him great glory is their giving freely and generously to others. The Corinthians' participation in giving to those in need wasn't "for the church." It was evidence that they *were* the church.

The fact that we give freely to those in need doesn't mean our giving is optional. Giving to others is a demonstration of the righteousness of God in our lives, apart from which there could be no salvation (vv. 9–11). Grace-driven generosity is a thermometer of our spiritual health. Asking how much we should give for the poor reveals that we haven't yet gained a Biblical perspective on the subject.

9:7
p Ex 25:2; 2Co 8:12
q Dt 15:10
r Ro 12:8
9:8
s Eph 3:20
t Php 4:19

9:9
u Ps 112:9
9:10
v Isa 55:10
w Hos 10:12

9:11
x 1Co 1:5
y 2Co 1:11
9:12
z 2Co 8:14
a 2Co 1:11

9:13
b 2Co 8:4 *c* Mt 9:8
d 2Co 2:12

9:15
e 2Co 2:14
f Ro 5:15,16

10:1
g Mt 11:29
h Gal 5:2

10:2
i 1Co 4:21;
2Co 13:2,10

cided in his heart to give,*p* not reluctantly or under compulsion,*q* for God loves a cheerful giver.*r* 8And God is able*s* to make all grace abound to you, so that in all things at all times, having all that you need,*t* you will abound in every good work. 9As it is written:

> "He has scattered abroad his gifts to the poor;
>   his righteousness endures forever." *a u*

10Now he who supplies seed to the sower and bread for food*v* will also supply and increase your store of seed and will enlarge the harvest of your righteousness. *w* 11You will be made rich*x* in every way so that you can be generous on every occasion, and through us your generosity will result in thanksgiving to God.*y*

12This service that you perform is not only supplying the needs*z* of God's people but is also overflowing in many expressions of thanks to God.*a* 13Because of the service*b* by which you have proved yourselves, men will praise God*c* for the obedience that accompanies your confession of the gospel of Christ,*d* and for your generosity in sharing with them and with everyone else. 14And in their prayers for you their hearts will go out to you, because of the surpassing grace God has given you. 15Thanks be to God*e* for his indescribable gift!*f*

Paul's Defense of His Ministry

10 By the meekness and gentleness*g* of Christ, I appeal to you—I, Paul,*h* who am "timid" when face to face with you, but "bold" when away! 2I beg you that when I come I may not have to be as bold*i* as I expect to be toward some peo-

a 9 Psalm 112:9

---

2 Corinthians 10:1–18

📖 Paul employed a touch of irony by linking the "meekness and gentleness" of Christ with "boldness," "war," "weapons," "power," and "strongholds." Paul's purpose was to destroy the defenses that had been erected by those who preached a "different gospel" alto-

---

Snapshots

9:2

Joining Forces

Despite winter's chill, the color orange blossomed in mid-February all over a Christian university campus. It wasn't spring's early arrival but hundreds of Seattle Pacific University students donning orange t-shirts to take a stand on an epidemic killing millions around the world: AIDS. When SPU students heard the alarming global statistics about AIDS—millions orphaned and life expectancy in many countries plummeting—they decided to raise the alarm. Joining forces, more than 200 students hosted a week of fairs, concerts, workshops, and volunteer opportunities to call their classmates to action.

> **The event was replicated at Christian colleges across the United States—all because two college students were obedient to God's call to care for those in need.**

Two SPU students, convinced that peers could make a difference for many young people sick and orphaned by AIDS, initiated the event that attracted more than 500 students. Participants learned, brainstormed, volunteered, and planned for future activities. "The most rewarding aspect was speaking to students whose hearts were changed and challenged by these events," co-organizer Lisa stated. *"So many students left with a greater understanding and a desire to take action."*

The excitement didn't end on SPU's campus. The event was replicated at Christian colleges across the United States—all because two college students were obedient to God's call to care for those in need.

ple who think that we live by the standards of this world. ³For though we live in the world, we do not wage war as the world does. ⁴The weapons we fight with[j] are not the weapons of the world. On the contrary, they have divine power[k] to demolish strongholds.[l] ⁵We demolish arguments and every pretension that sets itself up against the knowledge of God,[m] and we take captive every thought to make it obedient[n] to Christ. ⁶And we will be ready to punish every act of disobedience, once your obedience is complete.[o]

⁷You are looking only on the surface of things.[a][p] If anyone is confident that he belongs to Christ,[q] he should consider again that we belong to Christ just as much as he.[r] ⁸For even if I boast somewhat freely about the authority the Lord gave us for building you up rather than pulling you down,[s] I will not be ashamed of it. ⁹I do not want to seem to be trying to frighten you with my letters. ¹⁰For some say, "His letters are weighty and forceful, but in person he is unimpressive[t] and his speaking amounts to nothing."[u] ¹¹Such people should realize that what we are in our letters when we are absent, we will be in our actions when we are present.

¹²We do not dare to classify or compare ourselves with some who commend themselves.[v] When they measure themselves by themselves and compare themselves with themselves, they are not wise. ¹³We, however, will not boast beyond proper limits, but will confine our boasting to the field God has assigned to us,[w] a field that reaches even to you. ¹⁴We are not going too far in our boasting, as would be the case if we had not come to you, for we did get as far as you[x] with the gospel of Christ.[y] ¹⁵Neither do we go beyond our limits by boasting of work done by others.[b][z] Our hope is that, as your faith continues to grow,[a] our area of activity among you will greatly expand, ¹⁶so that we can preach the gospel in the regions beyond

---

a 7 Or *Look at the obvious facts*   b 13-15 Or *¹³We, however, will not boast about things that cannot be measured, but we will boast according to the standard of measurement that the God of measure has assigned us—a measurement that relates even to you. ¹⁴ . . . ¹⁵Neither do we boast about things that cannot be measured in regard to the work done by others.*

10:4
j 2Co 6:7 k 1Co 2:5
l Jer 1:10;
2Co 13:10

10:5
m Isa 2:11,12;
1Co 1:19
n 2Co 9:13
10:6
o 2Co 2:9; 7:15
10:7
p Jn 7:24
q 1Co 1:12; 3:23;
14:37 r 2Co 11:23
10:8
s 2Co 13:10

10:10
t 1Co 2:3; Gal 4:13,
14 u 1Co 1:17

10:12
v 2Co 3:1

10:13
w ver 15,16

10:14
x 1Co 3:6
y 2Co 2:12
10:15
z Ro 15:20
a 2Th 1:3

---

gether. What made these teachers so dangerous was that their charisma and flair for presentation tended to make their false "gospel" attractive.

Instead of acting with immediate anger when offended, as the world would have done, Paul used weapons that had "divine power" for bringing about genuine repentance and endurance in faith. Just as Christ's meekness isn't to be misinterpreted to mean that he ignored or was overcome by sin and evil, so Paul's restraint isn't to be seen as cowardice. He was living the way of God's powerful victory through humble, obedient service.

"We don't wage war as the world does" (v. 3). Self-promotion and self-defense aren't kingdom ways. Rather, we know that every life and thought will, in Christ's powerful tenderness, be taken captive to make it obedient to Christ (v. 5). With this strong confidence we are neither boastful nor passive but persistently and gently bold.

9:12

Generosity

Paul reminds us in 2 Corinthians 9:12 that we give because God models generosity ("He has given freely to the poor"; Ps. 112:9). This model was fleshed out in Jesus, who, "though he was rich, yet for your sakes he became poor, so that you through his poverty might become rich" (8:9). Paul offers several guidelines in chapters 8 and 9 for our Christian giving:

Give freely: "Then it will be . . . a generous gift, not . . . one grudgingly given" (9:5).

Give voluntarily: "Entirely on their own, they urgently pleaded with us for the privilege of sharing" (8:3).

Give sacrificially: "Their overflowing joy and their extreme poverty welled up in rich generosity" (8:2).

Give with a big heart and open hands: "Whoever sows generously will also reap generously" (9:6).

Give faithfully: "Each [one] should give what he has decided in his heart to give" (9:7).

Give gladly: "God loves a cheerful giver" (9:7).

Give without thinking about your own needs: "God is able to make all grace abound to you" (9:8).

Give as part of your spiritual commitment: "Just as you excel in everything—in faith, in speech, in knowledge . . . see that you also excel in this grace of giving" (8:7).

Give expecting great returns on your gift: "You will be made rich in every way so that you can be generous on every occasion" (9:11).

Give understanding that God will multiply your gift: "He . . . will enlarge the harvest of your righteousness" (9:10).

you.[b] For we do not want to boast about work already done in another man's territory. [17]But, "Let him who boasts boast in the Lord."[a c] [18]For it is not the one who commends himself[d] who is approved, but the one whom the Lord commends.[e]

Paul and the False Apostles

11 I hope you will put up with[f] a little of my foolishness;[g] but you are already doing that. [2]I am jealous for you with a godly jealousy. I promised you to one husband,[h] to Christ, so that I might present you[i] as a pure virgin to him. [3]But I am afraid that just as Eve was deceived by the serpent's cunning,[j] your minds may somehow be led astray from your sincere and pure devotion to Christ. [4]For if someone comes to you and preaches a Jesus other than the Jesus we preached,[k] or if you receive a different spirit[l] from the one you received, or a different gospel[m] from the one you accepted, you put up with it easily enough. [5]But I do not think I am in the least inferior to those "super-apostles."[n] [6]I may not be a trained speaker,[o] but I do have knowledge.[p] We have made this perfectly clear to you in every way.

[7]Was it a sin[q] for me to lower myself in order to elevate you by preaching the gospel of God to you free of charge?[r] [8]I robbed other churches by receiving support from them[s] so as to serve you. [9]And when I was with you and needed something, I was not a burden to anyone, for the brothers who came from Macedonia supplied what I needed. I have kept myself from being a burden to you[t] in any way, and will continue to do so. [10]As surely as the truth of Christ is in me,[u] nobody in the regions of Achaia[v] will stop this boasting[w] of mine. [11]Why? Because I do not love you? God knows I do![x] [12]And I will keep on doing what I am doing in order to cut the ground from under those who want an opportunity to be considered equal with us in the things they boast about.

[13]For such men are false apostles,[y] deceitful[z] workmen, masquerading as apostles of Christ.[a] [14]And no wonder, for Satan himself masquerades as an angel of light. [15]It is not surprising, then, if his servants masquerade as servants of righteousness. Their end will be what their actions deserve.[b]

Paul Boasts About His Sufferings

[16]I repeat: Let no one take me for a fool.[c] But if you do, then receive me just as you would a fool, so that I may do a little boasting. [17]In this self-confident boasting I am not talking as the Lord would,[d] but as a fool. [18]Since many are boasting in the way the world does, I too will boast.[e] [19]You gladly put up with fools since you are so wise![f] [20]In fact, you even put up with anyone who enslaves you[g] or ex-

a 17 Jer. 9:24

---

2 Corinthians 11:1–15

📖 Paul intentionally remained an "amateur" when it came to public speaking. Why? Because he viewed his calling to be proclamation, not persuasion or manipulation. He did whatever it took not to be confused with entertainers/public speakers, who were the crowns of a liberal education in the ancient world—the movie stars of their day.

Paul's practice of self-support went beyond duty for the sake of the gospel. What his opponents considered a "sin" was the very thing for which Paul expected to be commended by God. The Macedonians' gifts to the apostle and his own self-support made it possible for Paul not to "burden" the Corinthians. His "robbing" other churches for the sake of his ministry in Corinth was an expression of Christ-like love, both on Paul's part and on the part of those who had given.

📖 Imagine the reaction in your church if congregations in a poor, developing country were to pay part of your pastor's salary and he were to work at another full-

time or part-time job, refusing to accept contributions for support from your church. What would this say about the giving churches? How would your congregation receive your pastor's ministry? How might this affect your personal spending and giving habits? Far fetched? Probably. But speculation on this scenario might be eye-opening.

2 Corinthians 11:16–33

📖 It had become necessary for Paul to boast like his opponents, but it made him extremely uncomfortable. Since the rebellious Corinthians so easily put up with false apostles, who were truly fools, he argued that they should bear with him while he played the fool as well. Paul considered all boasting foolish. He had grown up steeped in Jewish wisdom tradition (cf. Prov. 1:7; 18:2), familiar with the picture of the classic "fool" who refuses to acknowledge or praise God. On the other hand, he hated the false boasting of the arrogant, consistently condemned by Old Testament prophets as an affront to God's glory.

ploits you or takes advantage of you or pushes himself forward or slaps you in the face. 21To my shame I admit that we were too weak[h] for that!

What anyone else dares to boast about—I am speaking as a fool—I also dare to boast about.[i] 22Are they Hebrews? So am I.[j] Are they Israelites? So am I.[k] Are they Abraham's descendants? So am I. 23Are they servants of Christ? (I am out of my mind to talk like this.) I am more. I have worked much harder,[l] been in prison more frequently,[m] been flogged more severely, and been exposed to death again and again. 24Five times I received from the Jews the forty lashes[n] minus one. 25Three times I was beaten with rods,[o] once I was stoned,[p] three times I was shipwrecked, I spent a night and a day in the open sea, 26I have been constantly on the move. I have been in danger from rivers, in danger from bandits, in danger from my own countrymen,[q] in danger from Gentiles; in danger in the city,[r] in danger in the country, in danger at sea; and in danger from false brothers.[s] 27I have labored and toiled and have often gone without sleep; I have known hunger and thirst and have often gone without food;[t] I have been cold and naked. 28Besides everything else, I face daily the pressure of my concern for all the churches. 29Who is weak, and I do not feel weak? Who is led into sin, and I do not inwardly burn?

30If I must boast, I will boast of the things that show my weakness.[u] 31The God and Father of the Lord Jesus, who is to be praised forever,[v] knows that I am not lying. 32In Damascus the governor under King Aretas had the city of the Damascenes guarded in order to arrest me.[w] 33But I was lowered in a basket from a window in the wall and slipped through his hands.[x]

Paul's Vision and His Thorn

12 I must go on boasting.[y] Although there is nothing to be gained, I will go on to visions and revelations[z] from the Lord. 2I know a man in Christ who fourteen years ago was caught up[a] to the third heaven.[b] Whether it was in the body or out of the body I do not know—God knows.[c] 3And I know that this man— whether in the body or apart from the body I do not know, but God knows— 4was caught up to paradise.[d] He heard inexpressible things, things that man is not permitted to tell. 5I will boast about a man like that, but I will not boast about myself, except about my weaknesses. 6Even if I should choose to boast, I would not be a fool,[e] because I would be speaking the truth. But I refrain, so no one will think more of me than is warranted by what I do or say.

7To keep me from becoming conceited because of these surpassingly great revelations, there was given me a thorn in my flesh,[f] a messenger of Satan, to torment me. 8Three times I pleaded with the Lord to take it away from me.[g] 9But he said to me, "My grace is sufficient for you, for my power[h] is made perfect in weakness." Therefore I will boast all the more gladly about my weaknesses, so that Christ's power may rest on me. 10That is why, for Christ's sake, I delight in weaknesses, in insults, in hardships,[i] in persecutions,[j] in difficulties. For when I am weak, then I am strong.[k]

11:21
h 2Co 10:1,10
i Php 3:4
11:22
j Php 3:5 k Ro 9:4
11:23
l 1Co 15:10
m Ac 16:23;
2Co 6:4,5
11:24
n Dt 25:3
11:25
o Ac 16:22
p Ac 14:19
11:26
q Ac 9:23; 14:5
r Ac 21:31 s Gal 2:4
11:27
t 1Co 4:11,12;
2Co 6:5
11:30
u 1Co 2:3
11:31
v Ro 9:5
11:32
w Ac 9:24
11:33
x Ac 9:25
12:1
y 2Co 11:16,30
z ver 7
12:2
a Ac 8:39
b Eph 4:10
c 2Co 11:11
12:4
d Lk 23:43; Rev 2:7
12:6
e 2Co 11:16
12:7
f Nu 33:55
12:8
g Mt 26:39,44
12:9
h Php 4:13
12:10
i 2Co 6:4 / Ro 5:3;
2Th 1:4 k 2Co 13:4

Paul's boasting, in his weakness wasn't just a satire of his opponents but a positive expression of his own calling. Regardless of cultural pressures to do otherwise, we also are free to boast only in what God has done in and through us. We are to give him credit for all we are and do, since everything is a gift from him. Are you sometimes tempted to take credit for what God has done?

2 Corinthians 12:1–10

Flaunting his visions would have led Paul to cut out the heart of the gospel by exalting himself at its expense. Have you ever noticed that Paul referred to his "surpassingly great" visions and revelations but then only shared one of them? He knew that even such experiences can't compare to a genuine boast in the Lord (cf. 2 Cor. 10:17–18).

Paul's boasting in his weakness challenges our (1) tendency to elevate and mimic Christian celebrities based on their "spiritual experiences" and "power"; (2) preoccupation with self; and (3) very definition of spirituality. In view of Jesus' suffering and death, our own greatest experiences of Christ's grace and power often come through times of weakness. When has this been true for you? What have you learned during such periods about God's ability and willingness to meet your needs and those of others?

12:11
l 2Co 11:1
m 2Co 11:5
n 1Co 15:9,10

12:12
o Jn 4:48
12:13
p 1Co 9:12,18
q 2Co 11:7
12:14
r 2Co 13:1
s 1Co 4:14,15
t Pr 19:14

12:15
u Php 2:17; 1Th 2:8
12:16
v 2Co 11:9

12:18
w 2Co 8:6,16
x 2Co 8:18

12:19
y Ro 9:1 *z* 2Co 10:8
12:20
a 2Co 2:1-4
b 1Co 4:21
c 1Co 1:11; 3:3
d Gal 5:20
e Ro 1:29
f 1Co 14:33
12:21
g 2Co 2:1,4
h 2Co 13:2

13:1
i 2Co 12:14
j Dt 19:15;
Mt 18:16
13:2
k 2Co 1:23
l 2Co 12:21
13:3
m Mt 10:20;
1Co 5:4
13:4
n Php 2:7,8;
1Pe 3:18 *o* Ro 1:4;
6:4 *p* ver 9
13:5
q 1Co 11:28
r Jn 6:6

Paul's Concern for the Corinthians

11 I have made a fool of myself,[l] but you drove me to it. I ought to have been commended by you, for I am not in the least inferior to the "super-apostles,"[m] even though I am nothing.[n] **12** The things that mark an apostle—signs, wonders and miracles[o]—were done among you with great perseverance. **13** How were you inferior to the other churches, except that I was never a burden to you?[p] Forgive me this wrong![q]

14 Now I am ready to visit you for the third time,[r] and I will not be a burden to you, because what I want is not your possessions but you. After all, children should not have to save up for their parents,[s] but parents for their children.[t] **15** So I will very gladly spend for you everything I have and expend myself as well.[u] If I love you more, will you love me less? **16** Be that as it may, I have not been a burden to you.[v] Yet, crafty fellow that I am, I caught you by trickery! **17** Did I exploit you through any of the men I sent you? **18** I urged[w] Titus to go to you and I sent our brother[x] with him. Titus did not exploit you, did he? Did we not act in the same spirit and follow the same course?

19 Have you been thinking all along that we have been defending ourselves to you? We have been speaking in the sight of God[y] as those in Christ; and everything we do, dear friends, is for your strengthening.[z] **20** For I am afraid that when I come[a] I may not find you as I want you to be, and you may not find me as you want me to be.[b] I fear that there may be quarreling,[c] jealousy, outbursts of anger, factions,[d] slander, gossip,[e] arrogance and disorder.[f] **21** I am afraid that when I come again my God will humble me before you, and I will be grieved[g] over many who have sinned earlier[h] and have not repented of the impurity, sexual sin and debauchery in which they have indulged.

Final Warnings

13 This will be my third visit to you.[i] "Every matter must be established by the testimony of two or three witnesses."[a][j] **2** I already gave you a warning when I was with you the second time. I now repeat it while absent: On my return I will not spare[k] those who sinned earlier[l] or any of the others, **3** since you are demanding proof that Christ is speaking through me.[m] He is not weak in dealing with you, but is powerful among you. **4** For to be sure, he was crucified in weakness,[n] yet he lives by God's power.[o] Likewise, we are weak[p] in him, yet by God's power we will live with him to serve you.

5 Examine yourselves[q] to see whether you are in the faith; test yourselves.[r] Do you

a 1 Deut. 19:15

---

2 Corinthians 12:11–21

In 12:14, Paul announced his upcoming third visit to Corinth (cf. 1:15—2:1; 9:3–5). His readiness to return reflected the changed situation in this church. Now that the majority had repented in response to his "tearful letter" (2:4,9; 7:4–16), the apostle would return to strengthen the faithful (6:14—7:2), complete the collection as evidence of their repentance (chs. 8–9), and sift out those still in rebellion (cf. 10:1–6; 13:1–4). This was Paul's last attempt to keep the rebellious minority from God's coming judgment.

Christian growth is a lifelong process, not an overnight transformation. When it comes to completing the work God has begun in our lives, we can't put him on our timetable. Often our slow rate of change is part of our school of faith, teaching us to depend totally on the only One who can help us. If 2 Corinthians reveals anything about Paul, it's his long-suffering patience with God's people. How willing are you to "suffer" along with someone else's stumbling progress? Might this give you added confidence in God's patience when you fumble or fall?

2 Corinthians 13:1–10

A growing transformation into God's image marks the lives of those on whom God has "set his seal of ownership" by pouring out his Spirit in their hearts (1:22). The way God's people work out their trust in his provision in Christ in their daily lives is by obeying his commands. To "accept Christ" is to obey God's call to be like him. The effect flows naturally from the cause.

Sometimes our response to the sting of conscience is to "try harder." But Paul did something we might easily pass over in the process of making a concerted effort on our own: He *prayed*. Obedience to God's commands flows from and is made possible by his gracious presence in our lives—a presence we can invite daily through prayer. How regularly does prayer come to your mind as a first—or even last—resort?

not realize that Christ Jesus is in you[s]—unless, of course, you fail the test? 6 And I
trust that you will discover that we have not failed the test. 7 Now we pray to God
that you will not do anything wrong. Not that people will see that we have stood
the test but that you will do what is right even though we may seem to have failed.
8 For we cannot do anything against the truth, but only for the truth. 9 We are glad
whenever we are weak but you are strong; and our prayer is for your perfection.[t]
10 This is why I write these things when I am absent, that when I come I may not
have to be harsh in my use of authority—the authority the Lord gave me for building you up, not for tearing you down.[u]

Final Greetings

11 Finally, brothers,[v] good-by. Aim for perfection, listen to my appeal, be of one
mind, live in peace.[w] And the God of love and peace[x] will be with you.
12 Greet one another with a holy kiss.[y] 13 All the saints send their greetings.[z]
14 May the grace of the Lord Jesus Christ,[a] and the love of God,[b] and the fellowship of the Holy Spirit[c] be with you all.

13:5 [s] Ro 8:10
13:9 [t] ver 11
13:10 [u] 2Co 10:8
13:11 [v] 1Th 4:1; 2Th 3:1 [w] Mk 9:50 [x] Ro 15:33; Eph 6:23
13:12 [y] Ro 16:16
13:13 [z] Php 4:22
13:14 [a] Ro 16:20; 2Co 8:9 [b] Ro 5:5; Jude 21 [c] Php 2:1

2 Corinthians 13:11–14

In his conclusion Paul spelled out four commands: aim for perfection, listen to his appeal, be of one mind, and live in peace. Keeping them doesn't make a person a Christian. But being a Christian means pursuing these qualities. Paul's closing admonitions, greetings, and benedictions reflect the reconciliation for which he longed (5:20—6:2; 10:1–2), prayed (13:7), and labored as a minister of the new covenant (2:17; 6:3–10)—and toward which he had written this letter (13:10).

God's act of grace in the mercy of the cross—by which he grants us his presence in Christ through the Spirit—is the all-sufficient ground of our life with God. And God's presence with his people here and now brings with it the promise to sustain us through this life and bring us into his presence in the age to come. As God's sons and daughters in Christ, we trust him with our lives. Faith doesn't get any stronger than this. Do you also trust God with the little details of your life? He is interested in their every aspect.

13:5

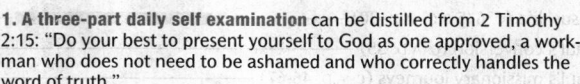

Self Examination

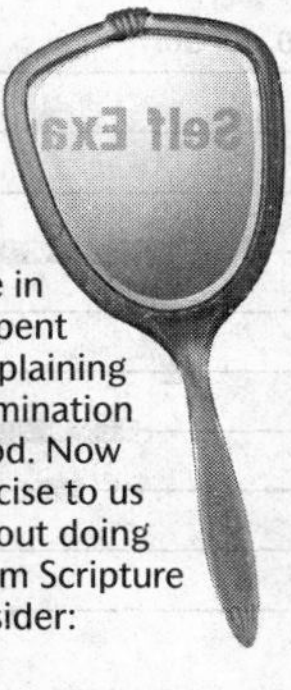

Paul urged people to examine themselves to see whether they were in the faith (13:5). He had spent much of 2 Corinthians explaining the results of his self-examination as an apostle called of God. Now he recommends the exercise to us all. How might you go about doing this? Several methods from Scripture suggest themselves. Consider:

1. **A three-part daily self examination** can be distilled from 2 Timothy 2:15: "Do your best to present yourself to God as one approved, a workman who does not need to be ashamed and who correctly handles the word of truth."

2. **At the end of every day** ask yourself three questions: Is God honored by what I did today? Am I satisfied with my work? Have I studied the Bible today?

3. **Use the Ten Commandments** in Exodus 20 as an outline for a self-examination at the end of the day.

4. **Different parts of the Sermon on the Mount** in Matthew 5 lend themselves as criteria for living a holy life. Consider especially the Beatitudes.

5. **The fruits of the spirit** in Galatians 5:22–23 should be evident in a faithful Christian's life. Ask yourself what evidences you see in your own life.

INTRODUCTION TO
Galatians

AUTHOR

The apostle Paul wrote Galatians (1:1). His authorship has never been seriously questioned.

DATE WRITTEN

Galatians was probably written between A.D. 48 and 53.

ORIGINAL READERS

We are uncertain of the original recipients of this letter. Some scholars hold that the churches addressed in this letter were those founded by Paul and Barnabas (Acts 14:1–23) in southern Galatia (Iconium, Lystra, and Derbe). Others believe that the addressees were believers in northern Galatia in the region of Ancyra. These churches would have been founded by Paul during a journey that may be alluded to in Acts (see Acts 16:6; 18:23).

TIMELINE

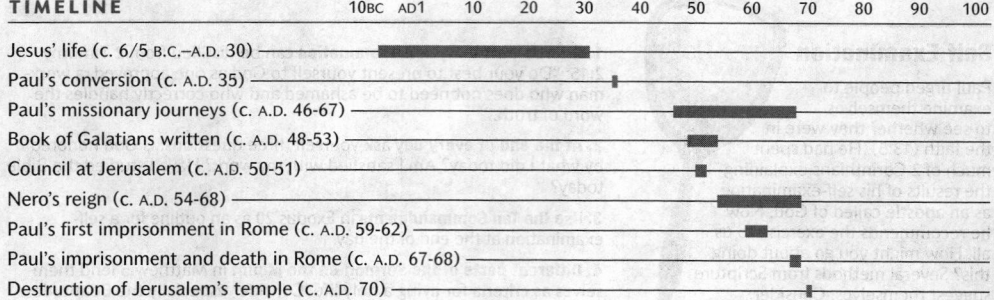

	10BC AD1	10	20	30	40	50	60	70	80	90	100
Jesus' life (c. 6/5 B.C.–A.D. 30)											
Paul's conversion (c. A.D. 35)											
Paul's missionary journeys (c. A.D. 46-67)											
Book of Galatians written (c. A.D. 48-53)											
Council at Jerusalem (c. A.D. 50-51)											
Nero's reign (c. A.D. 54-68)											
Paul's first imprisonment in Rome (c. A.D. 59-62)											
Paul's imprisonment and death in Rome (c. A.D. 67-68)											
Destruction of Jerusalem's temple (c. A.D. 70)											

THEMES

Troublemakers, traditionally identified as Judaizers (Jewish legalists), claimed that Gentiles not only had to believe in Christ for salvation, but also had to live under the Jewish law and practice circumcision. Paul's letter includes the following themes:

1. *Paul's apostleship.* Paul vigorously defended his apostolic calling (1:1,15; 2:1–10) and his gospel (1:11–12). He wasn't trying to protect his wounded reputation as an apostle, but was defending the truth of the gospel as it had been revealed to him by Christ. He had been set apart by God to "preach [Christ] among the Gentiles" (1:16).

2. *Salvation by faith alone.* Paul had been given a particular message: Gentiles are saved on the basis of faith alone (3:8–9), not by keeping the law (5:1–6). The promise to Abraham was fulfilled in Christ, and Gentiles become Abraham's seed and heirs of the promise through their faith in Christ (3:26–29). Paul's definition of the truth of the gospel affirms God's universal grace for all people: In Christ there is "neither Jew nor Greek, slave nor free, male nor female, for . . . all [are] one in Christ Jesus" (3:28). Justification by faith, a doctrine central to this letter, creates harmonious community. We are all joined to Christ as equals.

3. *Legalism versus freedom.* Believers don't need to be under the law to lead ethical lives (5:1—6:16). The Spirit, whom they receive when they believe (3:1–3), empowers them to live the way God wants (5:16–17,22–25). The law can't produce the fruit of the Spirit (5:22–23) or restrain people from sinning. It identifies sin and pronounces God's judgment (3:19–24). Through the law people see their need for forgiveness, which is found only in Christ. Christ died to set people free from the law and the power of sin (3:13–14). It's through the believer's union with Christ that he or she is truly set free. This liberation isn't freedom to sin, but freedom to "serve one another in love" (5:13).

4. *A Spirit-empowered life.* This theme is stressed throughout Paul's letters, but with particular force in Galatians. Believers aren't to rely on their own power to live the Christian life. It's "foolish" (3:3) to think this might even be possible. The Spirit-led Christian doesn't live for self (5:16) but allows the fruit of the Spirit—love, joy, peace, patience, kindness, goodness, faithfulness, gentleness, and self-control—to shine through his or her everyday activities (5:22–23).

FAITH IN ACTION

The pages of Galatians contain life lessons and role models of faith—people who challenge believers to put faith in action.

Role Models

- ABRAHAM (3:6) "believed God, and it was credited to him as righteousness." Have you trusted in Christ alone for forgiveness?

- PAUL (2:11–21) confronted Peter, an important church leader, for a particular incidence of hypocrisy and gospel compromise. Is there someone in your church who has gotten "off track" in their lifestyle or beliefs? How can this situation be addressed Biblically and sensitively?

- JAMES, PETER, AND JOHN (2:9) offered the "right hand of fellowship" to Paul when they recognized that he had been called to his ministry. How are you supporting others in their ministries?

Challenges

- Salvation comes by faith alone, not by works. Christ alone can offer forgiveness and a restored relationship with God. If this is already a reality for you, how have you shared the Good News recently?

- Doing good deeds and following a list of "dos and don'ts" won't earn God's favor. If you have believed this deception, repent and turn to God in faith. Stay close to Jesus and depend on the Holy Spirit's guidance in order to remain free.

- Living in freedom means living a righteous life by the power of the Spirit. Evaluate your lifestyle. How do your "works" give evidence of your faith? Are you living a life of service?

- There is equality in Christ. Evaluate your prejudices toward others. How can you change your negative attitudes, accept others, and be more inclusive?

- Find ways to celebrate your faith and freedom in Christ by loving others. "The only thing that counts is faith expressing itself through love" (5:6).

- Conduct a "fruit inspection" of your life. How are you measuring up to the qualities listed in 5:22–23? Are you sufficiently nurtured in the Word, in worship, and in the fellowship of the saints to produce a good crop? Are you allowing the Spirit to exhibit these qualities through you?

OUTLINE

  I. Introduction: Greeting and Denunciation (1:1–9)
  II. Paul Defends His Authority (1:10—2:21)
  III. Paul Defends the Doctrine of Liberty and Faith (3–4)
  IV. Paul Defends the Gospel of Freedom (5:1—6:10)
      A. The Principle of Freedom in Christ (5:1–12)
      B. Live by the Spirit, Not by the Flesh (5:13–26)
      C. Bearing Each Other's Burdens (6:1–10)
  V. Conclusion (6:11–18)

1:1
a Ac 9:15 b Ac 2:24

1:2
c Php 4:21
d Ac 16:6; 1Co 16:1

1:3
e Ro 1:7
1:4
f Mt 20:28; Ro 4:25;
Gal 2:20 g Php 4:20

1:5
h Ro 11:36

1:6
i Gal 5:8 j 2Co 11:4

1:7
k Ac 15:24;
Gal 5:10
1:8
l 2Co 11:4 m Ro 9:3

1:9
n Ro 16:17

1:10
o Ro 2:29; 1Th 2:4

1:11
p 1Co 15:1
1:12
q ver 1 r ver 16

1:13
s Ac 26:4,5 t Ac 8:3

1 Paul, an apostle—sent not from men nor by man, but by Jesus Christ[a] and God the Father, who raised him from the dead[b]— ²and all the brothers with me,[c]

To the churches in Galatia:[d]

³Grace and peace to you from God our Father and the Lord Jesus Christ,[e] ⁴who gave himself for our sins[f] to rescue us from the present evil age, according to the will of our God and Father,[g] ⁵to whom be glory for ever and ever. Amen.[h]

The Church in Galatia (1:2)
Then: Galatia was a Roman province.
Now: It designates an area in central Turkey.

No Other Gospel

⁶I am astonished that you are so quickly deserting the one who called[i] you by the grace of Christ and are turning to a different gospel[j]— ⁷which is really no gospel at all. Evidently some people are throwing you into confusion[k] and are trying to pervert the gospel of Christ. ⁸But even if we or an angel from heaven should preach a gospel other than the one we preached to you,[l] let him be eternally condemned![m] ⁹As we have already said, so now I say again: If anybody is preaching to you a gospel other than what you accepted,[n] let him be eternally condemned!

¹⁰Am I now trying to win the approval of men, or of God? Or am I trying to please men?[o] If I were still trying to please men, I would not be a servant of Christ.

Paul Called by God

¹¹I want you to know, brothers,[p] that the gospel I preached is not something that man made up. ¹²I did not receive it from any man,[q] nor was I taught it; rather, I received it by revelation[r] from Jesus Christ.

¹³For you have heard of my previous way of life in Judaism,[s] how intensely I persecuted the church of God and tried to destroy it.[t] ¹⁴I was advancing in Judaism beyond many Jews of my own age and was extremely zealous for the traditions of my

---

Galatians 1:1–5

📖 Paul's introduction to Galatians has two parts: salutation (vv. 1–5) and occasion for writing (vv. 6–9). The salutation includes Paul's authority, the group to whom his letter is addressed, those who were with Paul, and his greeting of grace and peace. Paul expanded the greeting by directing the Galatians' focus on who God is and what he's done. We worship the God who gives grace and peace, who gave himself to rescue us from sin and evil.

📖 The Christian life is first and foremost about God—not us. Paul stressed the abundance of what God has done on our behalf in Christ—drawn us into relationship with himself, knit our lives back into harmony, and delivered us from domination by the evil around us. We are not alone or trapped. God hasn't merely given the orders and then sat back waiting for our obedience. Rather, he takes the initiative to draw us into the fullness of life and freedom of intimate relationship for which he created us.

Galatians 1:6–10

📖 The Galatians had taken it upon themselves to switch positions on a crucial subject: the means of acceptance with God and Christ's role in that acceptance.

They were arguing that God's grace and Christ's finished work weren't enough. They wanted to revert to living in B.C. days on an A.D. calendar. But supplementing the gospel of Christ with the old Mosaic Law didn't make their position stronger or better. The result was a perversion of the truth and a compromised message.

📖 The basic human religious impulse is to seek to make our lives acceptable by what we do. Somehow it's so hard for us to believe that our salvation is complete in Christ. Surely, it must somehow depend on us! Thus, like the Galatians, we are tragically tempted to turn to an "un-gospel." Why do you think it's so hard for us to accept the fullness of God's gift of grace and peace? What has helped you to live more fully in that freedom?

Galatians 1:11–24

📖 Jerusalem played just as crucial a role in first-century Christianity as it did for ancient Judaism. The apostles were based there much of the time, and in that city resided much of the authority and knowledge needed for the development of Christian thinking. The Judaizers in Paul's day—those he argued against in this letter—insisted that Christian converts also needed to convert to Judaism. They may have claimed that this was being taught by the elders in Jerusalem.

fathers.[u] [15]But when God, who set me apart from birth[a][v] and called me[w] by his grace, was pleased [16]to reveal his Son in me so that I might preach him among the Gentiles,[x] I did not consult any man,[y] [17]nor did I go up to Jerusalem to see those who were apostles before I was, but I went immediately into Arabia and later returned to Damascus.

[18]Then after three years,[z] I went up to Jerusalem[a] to get acquainted with Peter[b] and stayed with him fifteen days. [19]I saw none of the other apostles—only James,[b] the Lord's brother. [20]I assure you before God that what I am writing you is no lie.[c] [21]Later I went to Syria and Cilicia.[d] [22]I was personally unknown to the churches of Judea[e] that are in Christ. [23]They only heard the report: "The man who formerly persecuted us is now preaching the faith[f] he once tried to destroy." [24]And they praised God[g] because of me.

Paul Accepted by the Apostles

2 Fourteen years later I went up again to Jerusalem,[h] this time with Barnabas. I took Titus along also. [2]I went in response to a revelation and set before them the gospel that I preach among the Gentiles.[i] But I did this privately to those who seemed to be leaders, for fear that I was running or had run my race[j] in vain. [3]Yet not even Titus,[k] who was with me, was compelled to be circumcised, even though he was a Greek.[l] [4]⌊This matter arose⌋ because some false brothers[m] had infiltrated our ranks to spy on[n] the freedom[o] we have in Christ Jesus and to make us slaves. [5]We did not give in to them for a moment, so that the truth of the gospel[p] might remain with you.

[6]As for those who seemed to be important[q]—whatever they were makes no difference to me; God does not judge by external appearance[r]—those men added nothing to my message. [7]On the contrary, they saw that I had been entrusted with the task[s] of preaching the gospel to the Gentiles,[c][t] just as Peter[u] had been to the Jews.[d] [8]For God, who was at work in the ministry of Peter as an apostle[v] to the Jews, was also at work in my ministry as an apostle to the Gentiles. [9]James, Peter[e][w] and John, those reputed to be pillars,[x] gave me and Barnabas[y] the right hand of fellowship when they recognized the grace given to me.[z] They agreed that we should go to the Gentiles, and they to the Jews. [10]All they asked was that we should continue to remember the poor,[a] the very thing I was eager to do.

Paul Opposes Peter

[11]When Peter[b] came to Antioch,[c] I opposed him to his face, because he was clearly in the wrong. [12]Before certain men came from James, he used to eat with the

---

[a] 15 Or *from my mother's womb*   [b] 18 Greek *Cephas*   [c] 7 Greek *uncircumcised*   [d] 7 Greek
circumcised; also in verses 8 and 9   [e] 9 Greek *Cephas*; also in verses 11 and 14

1:14
[u] Mt 15:2
1:15
[v] Isa 49:1,5; Jer 1:5
[w] Ac 9:15
1:16
[x] Gal 2:9
[y] Mt 16:17
1:18
[z] Ac 9:22,23
[a] Ac 9:26,27
1:19
[b] Mt 13:55
1:20
[c] Ro 9:1
1:21
[d] Ac 6:9
1:22
[e] 1Th 2:14
1:23
[f] Ac 6:7
1:24
[g] Mt 9:8
2:1
[h] Ac 15:2

2:2
[i] Ac 15:4,12
[j] 1Co 9:24;
Php 2:16
2:3
[k] 2Co 2:13
[l] Ac 16:3; 1Co 9:21
2:4
[m] 2Co 11:26
[n] Jude 4 [o] Ac 15:1;
Gal 5:1,13
2:5
[p] ver 14
2:6
[q] Gal 6:3 [r] Ac 10:34

2:7
[s] 1Th 2:4; 1Ti 1:11
[t] Ac 9:15
[u] ver 9,11,14
2:8
[v] Ac 1:25
2:9
[w] ver 7,11,14
[x] 1Ti 3:15 [y] Ac 4:36
[z] Ro 12:3
2:10
[a] Ac 24:17

2:11
[b] ver 7,9,14
[c] Ac 11:19

📖 Periodic attitude checks are in order for all of us who want to serve in Christ's name. Is it possible we are giving the impression that, to be Christians, others must look just like us? The truth of Paul's teaching is binding on all Christians. (1) The gospel of Christ can't be restricted to one nation or cultural group. (2) If others disapprove of us when we know God approves, we are to close our eyes to their disapproval. (3) We are to regularly examine our expressions of the gospel and our lifestyle. Are yours and those of your church consistent with Scripture?

Galatians 2:1–10

📖 Paul's gospel was a direct revelation from Christ, independent of the Jerusalem apostles. This section concerns (1) Paul's presentation of his message, (2) the opposition to that message, and (3) the unity expressed by the Jerusalem pillars and Paul over that message. The parties had reached a consensus: Paul was called to preach to the Gentiles and Peter to the Jews.

"What" they preached was the same; the difference regarded "to whom."

📖 Many in the church expect all Christians to be alike—from the clothes they wear to the Bible translations they carry, from the schools they attend to the stores they patronize, from the political views they embrace to the kinds of cars they buy. But fundamental to Christian unity is the recognition of different callings and movements within the church of Christ. The one nonnegotiable to characterize all followers of Christ must be care for the poor (v. 10). What a striking distinctive! When people outside the church look at us, is this what they notice? How well is your church living out this remarkable characteristic of believers?

Galatians 2:11–21

📖 Peter, who had been willing to shed the laws of Judaism (food and table restrictions) in Antioch, in order

2:12
d Ac 11:3 e Ac 11:2

Gentiles.^d But when they arrived, he began to draw back and separate himself from the Gentiles because he was afraid of those who belonged to the circumcision group.^e 13The other Jews joined him in his hypocrisy, so that by their hypocrisy even Barnabas^f was led astray.

2:13
f ver 1; Ac 4:36

2:14
g ver 5 h ver 7,9,11
i Ac 10:28

14When I saw that they were not acting in line with the truth of the gospel,^g I said to Peter^h in front of them all, "You are a Jew, yet you live like a Gentile and not like a Jew.ⁱ How is it, then, that you force Gentiles to follow Jewish customs?"

2:15
j Php 3:4,5
k 1Sa 15:18

2:16
l Ac 13:39; Ro 9:30

15 "We who are Jews by birth^j and not 'Gentile sinners'^k 16know that a man is not justified by observing the law, but by faith in Jesus Christ.^l So we, too, have put our faith in Christ Jesus that we may be justified by faith in Christ and not by observing the law, because by observing the law no one will be justified.

2:17
m ver 15 n Gal 3:21

2:19
o Ro 7:4 p Ro 6:10,
11, 14; 2Co 5:15

2:20
q Ro 6:6 r 1Pe 4:2
s Mt 4:3 t Ro 8:37
u Gal 1:4

2:21
v Gal 3:21

17 "If, while we seek to be justified in Christ, it becomes evident that we ourselves are sinners,^m does that mean that Christ promotes sin? Absolutely not!ⁿ 18If I rebuild what I destroyed, I prove that I am a lawbreaker. 19For through the law I died to the law^o so that I might live for God.^p 20I have been crucified with Christ^q and I no longer live, but Christ lives in me.^r The life I live in the body, I live by faith in the Son of God,^s who loved me^t and gave himself for me.^u 21I do not set aside the grace of God, for if righteousness could be gained through the law,^v Christ died for nothing!"^a

Faith or Observance of the Law

3:1
w Gal 5:7
x 1Co 1:23

3 You foolish Galatians! Who has bewitched you?^w Before your very eyes Jesus Christ was clearly portrayed as crucified.^x 2I would like to learn just one thing from you: Did you receive the Spirit by observing the law, or by believing what you heard?^y 3Are you so foolish? After beginning with the Spirit, are you now trying to attain your goal by human effort? 4Have you suffered so much for nothing—if it really was for nothing? 5Does God give you his Spirit and work miracles^z among you because you observe the law, or because you believe what you heard?

3:2
y Ro 10:17

3:5
z 1Co 12:10

a 21 Some interpreters end the quotation after verse 14.

---

to enjoy a new-found fellowship with Gentile Christians, later abandoned this stance when Jewish believers from Jerusalem showed up. The sharing of a common meal was a visible and powerful symbol of what Paul was teaching young churches: "You are all one in Christ Jesus" (3:28). But this symbol was publicly damaged by Peter's return to an insistence that Gentile Christians had to live like Jews.

At stake here was the gospel's very essence. Are Christians saved by grace through faith—yet justified by their works, or are all aspects of salvation and justification complete in Christ? Lest Paul be accused by the Judaizers of advocating "cheap grace," he concluded by summarizing how believers enter into the freedom of God's grace—by being crucified with Christ!

There is a certain safety and respectability in being regulated by law. When a questionable practice arises, we can consult the rule book for the answer. But life in the Spirit isn't so predictable.

We need to let the gospel of God's grace have its full implications in our lives. Are we (even subtly or unintentionally) preventing other racial groups from enjoying God's grace? Discriminating against other cultures or social groups? Building (or failing to knock down) walls between the sexes? Preventing the younger—or older—generation from feeling important and needed in our congregation? As we die to our self-justified lives and allow the life of Christ to be lived out in us, we encounter the rich freedom and open fellowship with others to

which we are called. Without this, "Christ died for nothing!" (v. 21).

Galatians 3:1–14

Paul's argument in verses 1–5 proceeded from experience. In essence he asked, "Did your conversion and Christian living come through your association with the Law of Moses? Or did they occur through faith in Christ?"

Paul contended that justification (becoming right with God) comes by faith, through the Spirit in Christ, not by law-abiding behavior or good works. This principle isn't new: Acceptance by God solely on the basis of faith, and Gentiles being accepted on the same basis as Jews—both are realities as old as Abraham. Besides, rather than producing justification, the law produces a curse. Why? Because no one under it has ever kept it perfectly (except for Christ, who was both fully God and fully human).

Before Paul, conversion to Judaism meant that people had to become naturalized Jews. But Paul saw in the gospel that anyone, through Jesus Christ by faith, can become part of the "people of God" without leaving his or her own culture and conforming to a Jewish way of life. A common instinct is to insist that others become like us if we are to accept their experience of God as true. Unfortunately, "Western" civilization has at times been equated with "Christian" civilization. Are there expressions of this assumption in your "world" that are in need of changing?

6Consider Abraham: "He believed God, and it was credited to him as righteousness."[a][a] 7Understand, then, that those who believe[b] are children of Abraham. 8The Scripture foresaw that God would justify the Gentiles by faith, and announced the gospel in advance to Abraham: "All nations will be blessed through you."[b][c] 9So those who have faith[d] are blessed along with Abraham, the man of faith.

10All who rely on observing the law are under a curse, for it is written: "Cursed is everyone who does not continue to do everything written in the Book of the Law."[c][e] 11Clearly no one is justified before God by the law, because, "The righteous will live by faith."[d][f] 12The law is not based on faith; on the contrary, "The man who does these things will live by them."[e][g] 13Christ redeemed us from the curse of the law[h] by becoming a curse for us, for it is written: "Cursed is everyone who is hung on a tree."[f][i] 14He redeemed us in order that the blessing given to Abraham might come to the Gentiles through Christ Jesus,[j] so that by faith we might receive the promise of the Spirit.[k]

The Law and the Promise

15Brothers, let me take an example from everyday life. Just as no one can set aside or add to a human covenant that has been duly established, so it is in this case. 16The promises were spoken to Abraham and to his seed.[l] The Scripture does not say "and to seeds," meaning many people, but "and to your seed,"[g] meaning one person, who is Christ. 17What I mean is this: The law, introduced 430 years[m] later, does not set aside the covenant previously established by God and thus do away with the promise. 18For if the inheritance depends on the law, then it no longer depends on a promise;[n] but God in his grace gave it to Abraham through a promise.

19What, then, was the purpose of the law? It was added because of transgressions[o] until the Seed[p] to whom the promise referred had come. The law was put into effect through angels[q] by a mediator.[r] 20A mediator,[s] however, does not represent just one party; but God is one.

21Is the law, therefore, opposed to the promises of God? Absolutely not![t] For if a law had been given that could impart life, then righteousness would certainly have come by the law.[u] 22But the Scripture declares that the whole world is a prisoner of sin,[v] so that what was promised, being given through faith in Jesus Christ, might be given to those who believe.

23Before this faith came, we were held prisoners[w] by the law, locked up until faith should be revealed. 24So the law was put in charge to lead us to Christ[h][x] that we might be justified by faith.[y] 25Now that faith has come, we are no longer under the supervision of the law.

3:6
[a] Ge 15:6; Ro 4:3
3:7
[b] ver 9
3:8
[c] Ge 12:3; Ac 3:25
3:9
[d] ver 7; Ro 4:16
3:10
[e] Dt 27:26; Jer 11:3
3:11
[f] Hab 2:4; Gal 2:16; Heb 10:38
3:12
[g] Lev 18:5; Ro 10:5
3:13
[h] Gal 4:5
[i] Dt 21:23; Ac 5:30
3:14
[j] Ro 4:9,16 [k] ver 2; Joel 2:28; Ac 2:33

3:16
[l] Lk 1:55; Ro 4:13,16
3:17
[m] Ge 15:13,14; Ex 12:40

3:18
[n] Ro 4:14
3:19
[o] Ro 5:20 [p] ver 16
[q] Ac 7:53
[r] Ex 20:19
3:20
[s] Heb 8:6; 9:15; 12:24
3:21
[t] Gal 2:17
[u] Gal 2:21

3:22
[v] Ro 3:9-19; 11:32

3:23
[w] Ro 11:32
3:24
[x] Ro 10:4
[y] Gal 2:16

[a] 6 Gen. 15:6   [b] 8 Gen. 12:3; 18:18; 22:18   [c] 10 Deut. 27:26   [d] 11 Hab. 2:4   [e] 12 Lev. 18:5
[f] 13 Deut. 21:23   [g] 16 Gen. 12:7; 13:15; 24:7   [h] 24 Or *charge until Christ came*

Galatians 3:15–25

God hadn't given the law to Moses until 430 years *after* his original covenant with Abraham. So the Abrahamic covenant had been established solely by faith. The covenant relationship God had with the Galatians through Christ was based squarely on those ancient promises to Abraham. Like that long-ago, unalterable covenant, it too was based on faith, not works.

Paul argued that the Judaizers—those who wanted Gentile believers to become Jews and practice the Jewish laws of Moses—were wrong. They failed to understand *why* God had given the law in the first place. So they didn't realize that imposing it on believers after Christ had come was a major step backward.

God's way has always been salvation through faith. But faith is expressed in obedience to God. The Ju-

daizers had tragically reversed the order, making salvation possible through obedience. As a result the law in their minds had been distorted into a means of salvation, not an expression of what it means to live a saved life. "Now that faith [through Christ] has come, we are no longer under the supervision of the law" (v. 25), because it's fulfilled in Christ and the Spirit. The law still (1) gives us a summary of God's moral will for us and (2) convicts people of sin. But life in the Spirit is our primary mode of operation as we seek to live obediently before God.

In his emphasis that justification (being made right with God) is by faith (Gal. 3:6–9), Paul had no disagreement with James, who asserted that justification comes about by works in conjunction with faith (James 2:14–26). Justification is by faith—but saving faith is a faith that *works!*

Sons of God

3:26
z Ro 8:14
3:27
a Mt 28:19; Ro 6:3
b Ro 13:14
3:28
c Col 3:11
d Jn 10:16; 17:11;
Eph 2:14,15
3:29
e 1Co 3:23 f ver 16

26You are all sons of God z through faith in Christ Jesus, 27for all of you who were baptized into Christ a have clothed yourselves with Christ. b 28There is neither Jew nor Greek, slave nor free, c male nor female, for you are all one in Christ Jesus. d 29If you belong to Christ, e then you are Abraham's seed, and heirs according to the promise. f

4:3
g Gal 2:4
h Col 2:8,20
4:4
i Mk 1:15; Eph 1:10
j Jn 1:14 k Lk 2:27
4:5
l Jn 1:12
4:6
m Ro 5:5
n Ro 8:15,16
4:7
o Ro 8:17

4 What I am saying is that as long as the heir is a child, he is no different from a slave, although he owns the whole estate. 2He is subject to guardians and trustees until the time set by his father. 3So also, when we were children, we were in slavery g under the basic principles of the world. h 4But when the time had fully come, i God sent his Son, born of a woman, j born under law, k 5to redeem those under law, that we might receive the full rights l of sons. 6Because you are sons, God sent the Spirit of his Son into our hearts, m the Spirit who calls out, "Abba, a Father." n 7So you are no longer a slave, but a son; and since you are a son, God has made you also an heir. o

Paul's Concern for the Galatians

4:8
p 1Co 1:21;
Eph 2:12; 1Th 4:5
q 2Ch 13:9;
Isa 37:19
4:9
r 1Co 8:3 s ver 3
t Col 2:20
4:10
u Ro 14:5
4:11
v 1Th 3:5
4:12
w Gal 6:18
4:13
x 1Co 2:3

8Formerly, when you did not know God, p you were slaves to those who by nature are not gods. q 9But now that you know God—or rather are known by God r— how is it that you are turning back to those weak and miserable principles? Do you wish to be enslaved s by them all over again? t 10You are observing special days and months and seasons and years! u 11I fear for you, that somehow I have wasted my efforts on you. v

12I plead with you, brothers, w become like me, for I became like you. You have done me no wrong. 13As you know, it was because of an illness x that I first preached the gospel to you. 14Even though my illness was a trial to you, you did not treat me with contempt or scorn. Instead, you welcomed me as if I were an angel of God, as

a 6 Aramaic for *Father*

Galatians 3:26—4:7

This passage was Paul's third argument supporting his claim, based on Christ's revelation: Acceptance by and a relationship with God, for all people, are based on faith. This time Paul used the analogy of "sonship": (1) Faith in Christ makes a person a "son of God" (3:28). This gives people, regardless of race, class, or gender, a new identity—that of Jesus Christ, with whom they share "sonship." (2) Such a person through association with Christ also is a spiritual descendant of Abraham and, through adoption, (3) an "[heir] according to the promise" (v. 29).

Being a "son" of God for Paul wasn't a status reserved for males. The term meant being intimate with God. According to Paul, a "son of God" learns to call God "Daddy" (*Abba*; see 4:6) because God has given his Spirit to his "sons." Jewish children used this term to show both intimacy and respect.

3:23–25

Christian Human Rights

Paul wrote about Christians' freedom from the law under which they had lived for so long. Today we enjoy that same spiritual freedom in Christ. But if Paul were writing in the 21st century, we can assume he would also champion the right of Christians everywhere to express their faith in the public sphere. That freedom might be cast in the form of Christian human rights.

As CHRISTIANS,
we proclaim that everyone on Earth has the right to:

I. *Hear and understand the gospel of Jesus Christ (Matt. 28:19).*

II. *Have a Bible available in their own language (2 Tim. 3:16–17).*

III. *Have access to a Christian fellowship that can meet freely (Acts 2:42–47; Heb. 10:25).*

IV. *Enjoy the basic necessities of life: food, clean water, clothing, shelter, health care, an elementary education, and a livable income (Phil. 4:19).*

V. *Lead a productive life of fulfillment—spiritually, mentally, socially, emotionally, and physically (Ps. 138:8; John 10:10).*

if I were Christ Jesus himself.[y] 15What has happened to all your joy? I can testify that, if you could have done so, you would have torn out your eyes and given them to me. 16Have I now become your enemy by telling you the truth?[z]

17Those people are zealous to win you over, but for no good. What they want is to alienate you ⌐from us⌐, so that you may be zealous for them. 18It is fine to be zealous, provided the purpose is good, and to be so always and not just when I am with you.[a] 19My dear children,[b] for whom I am again in the pains of childbirth until Christ is formed in you,[c] 20how I wish I could be with you now and change my tone, because I am perplexed about you!

Hagar and Sarah

21Tell me, you who want to be under the law, are you not aware of what the law says? 22For it is written that Abraham had two sons, one by the slave woman[d] and the other by the free woman.[e] 23His son by the slave woman was born in the ordinary way;[f] but his son by the free woman was born as the result of a promise.[g]

24These things may be taken figuratively, for the women represent two covenants. One covenant is from Mount Sinai and bears children who are to be slaves: This is Hagar. 25Now Hagar stands for Mount Sinai in Arabia and corresponds to the present city of Jerusalem, because she is in slavery with her children. 26But the Jerusalem that is above[h] is free, and she is our mother. 27For it is written:

"Be glad, O barren woman,
    who bears no children;
break forth and cry aloud,
    you who have no labor pains;
because more are the children of the desolate woman
    than of her who has a husband."[a][i]

28Now you, brothers, like Isaac, are children of promise. 29At that time the son born in the ordinary way[j] persecuted the son born by the power of the Spirit.[k] It is the same now. 30But what does the Scripture say? "Get rid of the slave woman and her son, for the slave woman's son will never share in the inheritance with the free woman's son."[b][l] 31Therefore, brothers, we are not children of the slave woman, but of the free woman.

a 27 Isaiah 54:1   b 30 Gen. 21:10

4:14
y Mt 10:40

4:16
z Am 5:10

4:18
a ver 13, 14
4:19
b 1Co 4:15
c Eph 4:13

4:22
d Ge 16:15
e Ge 21:2
4:23
f Ro 9:7,8
g Ge 18:10-14;
Heb 11:11

4:26
h Heb 12:22;
Rev 3:12

4:27
i Isa 54:1

4:29
j ver 23 k Ge 21:9

4:30
l Ge 21:10

📖 Paul provided the theological foundation for overcoming any view of women as inferior, or any prejudice based on people's ethnic background or social class. The church is a radically new kind of society because all members, equally, are "clothed" with Jesus Christ and experience the same freedoms and responsibilities as "sons" of God.

Galatians 4:8–20

📖 Paul considered the final step of the Galatians' zigzag move from idolatry to Christianity and back to Judaism as no different from a venture back into idolatry and slavery.

Verses 12–20 present an emotional appeal. But Paul also could, when necessary, be reasoned and complex in his argumentation, as well as deeply personal. Paul's love for the Galatians was so deep that he compared himself to a mother in childbirth—in labor to see Christ formed in them (v. 19).

📖 Paul's plea for the Galatians to become like him was a common theme in his letters. (See 1 Cor. 4:8–21; 10:23—11:1; Gal. 4:12, Phil. 3: 7—4:1; 4:9, 1 Thess. 1:4–10, and 2 Thess. 3:6–15.) He was willing to let his life be scrutinized, for his words were only as valid as his character and deeds. Paul could exhort and rebuke—from his tender love. What do you think of the apostle's pleas? Do they seem arrogant, or do you see him as making a legitimate request from a humble spirit?

Galatians 4:21–31

📖 Paul continued his theme of women in labor by playing the game of ancestry with the Judaizers. They claimed that a true child of God had to be a descendant of Sarah—and that the line of the Gentiles went back to Hagar. But Paul showed that Hagar's son was the "son of slavery." Consequently, those who adhered to the slavery of the law were following Ishmael's tradition. True children of God, those who aren't tied to the rigid strictures of law, are in the line of Sarah and Isaac—and of freedom in Christ.

📖 Many hesitate about giving their lives in full obedience to Christ, fearing they will lose their freedom. Many Christians seem to live in bondage to a set of burdens and duties. In essence, Paul proclaimed to both, "We are no longer slaves but children who have freely received the promised inheritance."

5:1
m Jn 8:32
n 1Co 16:13
o Ac 15:10; Gal 2:4
5:2
p Ac 15:1
5:3
q Gal 3:10

5:4
r Heb 12:15;
2Pe 3:17
5:5
s Ro 8:23,24
5:6
t 1Co 7:19
u 1Th 1:3
5:7
v 1Co 9:24
w Gal 3:1
5:8
x Ro 8:28; Gal 1:6
5:9
y 1Co 5:6
5:10
z 2Co 2:3
a Php 3:15
b Gal 1:7
5:11
c Gal 4:29; 6:12
d 1Co 1:23
5:12
e ver 10
5:13
f 1Co 8:9; 1Pe 2:16
g 1Co 9:19;
Eph 5:21
5:14
h Lev 19:18;
Mt 22:39
5:16
i Ro 8:2,4-6,9,14
j ver 24
5:17
k Ro 8:5-8
l Ro 7:15-23
5:18
m Ro 6:14; 1Ti 1:9
5:19
n 1Co 6:18
5:21
o Ro 13:13

Freedom in Christ

5 It is for freedom that Christ has set us free.*m* Stand firm,*n* then, and do not let yourselves be burdened again by a yoke of slavery.*o*

²Mark my words! I, Paul, tell you that if you let yourselves be circumcised,*p* Christ will be of no value to you at all. ³Again I declare to every man who lets himself be circumcised that he is obligated to obey the whole law.*q* ⁴You who are trying to be justified by law have been alienated from Christ; you have fallen away from grace.*r* ⁵But by faith we eagerly await through the Spirit the righteousness for which we hope.*s* ⁶For in Christ Jesus neither circumcision nor uncircumcision has any value.*t* The only thing that counts is faith expressing itself through love.*u*

⁷You were running a good race.*v* Who cut in on you*w* and kept you from obeying the truth? ⁸That kind of persuasion does not come from the one who calls you.*x* ⁹"A little yeast works through the whole batch of dough."*y* ¹⁰I am confident*z* in the Lord that you will take no other view.*a* The one who is throwing you into confusion*b* will pay the penalty, whoever he may be. ¹¹Brothers, if I am still preaching circumcision, why am I still being persecuted?*c* In that case the offense*d* of the cross has been abolished. ¹²As for those agitators,*e* I wish they would go the whole way and emasculate themselves!

¹³You, my brothers, were called to be free. But do not use your freedom to indulge the sinful nature*a;f* rather, serve one another*g* in love. ¹⁴The entire law is summed up in a single command: "Love your neighbor as yourself."*b h* ¹⁵If you keep on biting and devouring each other, watch out or you will be destroyed by each other.

Life by the Spirit

¹⁶So I say, live by the Spirit,*i* and you will not gratify the desires of the sinful nature.*j* ¹⁷For the sinful nature desires what is contrary to the Spirit, and the Spirit what is contrary to the sinful nature.*k* They are in conflict with each other, so that you do not do what you want.*l* ¹⁸But if you are led by the Spirit, you are not under law.*m*

¹⁹The acts of the sinful nature are obvious: sexual immorality,*n* impurity and debauchery; ²⁰idolatry and witchcraft; hatred, discord, jealousy, fits of rage, selfish ambition, dissensions, factions ²¹and envy; drunkenness, orgies, and the like.*o* I warn

---

a 13 Or *the flesh*; also in verses 16, 17, 19 and 24   *b 14* Lev. 19:18

Galatians 5:1–15

Paul's call for freedom was the essence of his message to the Galatians. Christ's work freed Jews from the law's curse and allowed Gentiles to enjoy the same liberation by breaking their chains to disobedience and sin. It's impossible to overstate the centrality of freedom in this letter. Paul applied his thesis to circumcision, the most blatant issue facing Gentile Christians of his time. Submitting to circumcision, he argued, meant abandoning Jesus and God's grace. Living in freedom, on the other hand, meant refusing to indulge the sinful nature but living in love.

Freedom, today, is used as a synonym for independence, autonomy, and personal sovereignty. Or it implies the breaking down of social structures seen as oppressive or obstacles to equality and justice. Still another definition is highly individualistic: the freedom of self-actualization, sometimes referred to as psychological freedom.

Paul's *emphases* were on freedom *from* the law's curse and freedom for all to be part of God's family (3:28). Ironically, for him freedom involved "slavery to God and his will"—*not* doing whatever he wanted. Such freedom begins in a relationship with God through

Christ and in the Spirit—*not* in a lack of accountability for our lives. It's *inter*dependence—not *in*dependence. In Christ we are freed *from* sin *for* obedience, from self-indulgence for serving one another in love. What does a Biblical view of freedom in Christ mean for you?

Galatians 5:16–26

For Paul, a life of freedom equated to a life lived in the Spirit. Those who have surrendered to Christ have crucified their sinful nature and have no business being involved in its works. People who have been given life by the Spirit will bear in their lives the fruit of the Spirit, not the fruit of sin.

Paul knew that a Spirit-controlled person will live a holy life. Lest we foolishly turn back on ourselves, strenuously trying to appear holy and be obedient, Paul reminded us of the way to freedom and new life: "Those who belong to Christ have crucified the sin nature with its passions and desires" (v. 24).

Life in the Spirit of Christ isn't marked just by the sinful things we don't do (see the list of the acts of our sinful nature in vv. 19–21) but by the fruit we bear. This fruit isn't produced by us but by the Spirit of Christ in us. To bear Christ's fruit we need Christ's life, and this comes only by being crucified with him.

you, as I did before, that those who live like this will not inherit the kingdom of God.

22But the fruit[p] of the Spirit is love,[q] joy, peace, patience, kindness, goodness, faithfulness, 23gentleness and self-control.[r] Against such things there is no law. 24Those who belong to Christ Jesus have crucified the sinful nature[s] with its passions and desires.[t] 25Since we live by the Spirit, let us keep in step with the Spirit. 26Let us not become conceited,[u] provoking and envying each other.

Doing Good to All

6 Brothers, if someone is caught in a sin, you who are spiritual[v] should restore him gently. But watch yourself, or you also may be tempted. 2Carry each other's burdens, and in this way you will fulfill the law of Christ.[w] 3If anyone thinks he is something[x] when he is nothing, he deceives himself. 4Each one should test his own actions. Then he can take pride in himself, without comparing himself to somebody else, 5for each one should carry his own load.

6Anyone who receives instruction in the word must share all good things with his instructor.[y]

7Do not be deceived:[z] God cannot be mocked. A man reaps what he sows.[a] 8The one who sows to please his sinful nature, from that nature[a] will reap destruction;[b] the one who sows to please the Spirit, from the Spirit will reap eternal life.[c] 9Let us not become weary in doing good,[d] for at the proper time we will reap a harvest if we do not give up.[e] 10Therefore, as we have opportunity, let us do good[f] to all people, especially to those who belong to the family[g] of believers.

Not Circumcision but a New Creation

11See what large letters I use as I write to you with my own hand![h]

12Those who want to make a good impression outwardly are trying to compel you to be circumcised.[i] The only reason they do this is to avoid being persecuted[j] for the cross of Christ. 13Not even those who are circumcised obey the law,[k] yet they want you to be circumcised that they may boast about your flesh.[l] 14May I never boast except in the cross of our Lord Jesus Christ, through which[b] the world has

---

a 8 Or *his flesh, from the flesh*   b 14 Or *whom*

5:22
p Mt 7:16-20;
Eph 5:9
q Col 3:12-15
5:23
r Ac 24:25
5:24
s Ro 6:6 t ver 16,17
5:26
u Php 2:3

6:1
v 1Co 2:15

6:2
w Ro 15:1; Jas 2:8
6:3
x Ro 12:3; 1Co 8:2

6:6
y 1Co 9:11,14
6:7
z 1Co 6:9 a 2Co 9:6
6:8
b Job 4:8; Hos 8:7
c Jas 3:18
6:9
d 1Co 15:58
e Rev 2:10
6:10
f Pr 3:27 g Eph 2:19

6:11
h 1Co 16:21

6:12
i Ac 15:1 j Gal 5:11

6:13
k Ro 2:25 l Php 3:3

Galatians 6:1–10

Paul illustrated Christian living within a community guided by freedom in the Spirit. Spiritual people are to bear each other's burdens (moral problems and sins) in humility, financially support their teachers, and recognize that God will hold them accountable for how they have treated others. This passage touches again on helping those in need (cf. 2:10). The practice of assisting the poor was so ingrained in the early Christian church that it often required only the briefest of reminders in the epistles.

Two themes from this passage, mutual accountability and personal responsibility, militate against Western individualism. These values force us to reach out to others. They call us to abandon the impulse of letting others do their own thing and push us to become involved in their lives. They also force the neighbor to be approachable: To be a neighbor means to be both neighborly and open to neighborliness. Which of these two qualities have you, as a neighbor, been more likely to emphasize? Does the call to openness catch you off guard?

Paul says God will judge us on the basis of our lives. To be sure, our acceptance with God is based on Jesus' work on our behalf. But for God to assess whether we are attached to Christ, he will scan the evidence of our lives. Don't underestimate God's demand on your life by

minimizing the judgment. Behind it stands a holy and loving God who will always act in accordance with his love and holiness. What practical evidence points to your faith in Christ?

Galatians 6:11–18

Paul ended his letter with a signature, concluding summary, and benediction. His conclusion doesn't contain the greetings, request for prayer, or doxology sections typical of his other letters, and in no other Pauline letter do we find such an emphasis on a summary. Two points may be considered: (1) If Galatians was Paul's first letter (as some believe), no pattern had yet been established; and (2) the conclusions to Paul's letters don't follow patterns in the sense of set habits.

Who in our world are the primary targets of Paul's arguments in Galatians? The answer isn't a specific group, whether defined religiously, racially, sexually, or culturally. It does no good to point fingers at others; the problem is far more subtle than that. The target for the message of Galatians today is anyone who undervalues Jesus Christ as the all-sufficient Savior and/or minimizes the power of the Holy Spirit as the all-sufficient Guide. These are serious matters, worthy of serious reflection on the part of every Christian.

6:14
m Ro 6:2,6
6:15
n 1Co 7:19
o 2Co 5:17
6:17
p Isa 44:5; 2Co 1:5
6:18
q Ro 16:20
r 2Ti 4:22

been crucified to me, and I to the world. *m* ¹⁵Neither circumcision nor uncircumcision means anything; *n* what counts is a new creation. *o* ¹⁶Peace and mercy to all who follow this rule, even to the Israel of God.

¹⁷Finally, let no one cause me trouble, for I bear on my body the marks*p* of Jesus.

¹⁸The grace of our Lord Jesus Christ*q* be with your spirit, *r* brothers. Amen.

6:10

Do Good to All People

Many Christians take very seriously Paul's admonition in 6:10 to do good to all people. They support associations, sometimes called nongovernmental organizations (NGOs), whose charter it is to help poor people with relief and developmental aid. But Old Testament concepts of what constituted "doing good" were already in the portfolio of the Galatian readers of Paul's letter, so he didn't need to spell them out. Proverbs 3:27 generally instructed, "Do not withhold good from those who deserve it, when it is in your power to act." Jesus' great parable about the sheep and goats in Matthew 25:31-46 listed some of the good deeds for which kingdom believers would be rewarded. Here's a list of the kinds of help many organizations provide:

Provision	Principle	Scripture
• Food	Let the poor glean.	Lev. 19:9-10; Prov. 6:31; 22:9
• Hospitality	Take care of strangers.	Gen. 18:1-8; Lev. 19:10; Heb. 13:2
• Clean water	Well water is precious.	Gen. 21:22-31; Prov. 25:21,26
• Shelter	Live in tents/houses.	Prov. 3:33; Isa. 4:6; 25:4
• Education	Seek wisdom/understanding.	Prov. 4:5-7; 7:10-11; 22:6; 23:12
• Health care	Don't lead blind astray.	Lev. 19:14; Deut. 27:18; Ps. 103:3
• Emergency relief	Help during a disaster.	Prov. 17:5,17; Luke 10:33-35
• Justice	Don't use dishonest scales.	Deut. 26:13-16; Prov. 17:15
• Property rights	Don't move ancient boundaries.	Deut. 27:17; Prov. 23:10-11
• Livable wages	Workers deserve their wages.	Deut. 24:6,14-15; Luke 10:7
• Fair economic policies	Don't charge exorbitant interest.	Deut. 23:19-20; Prov. 28:8
• Improved farming practices	Rest agricultural land.	Lev. 25:1-7; Prov. 27:18,23
• Sanitation	Bury waste outside the camp.	Deut. 23:12-14

INTRODUCTION TO
Ephesians

AUTHOR
Ephesians was written by the apostle Paul (1:1; 3:1).

DATE WRITTEN
This letter was probably written between A.D. 60 and 62, during Paul's imprisonment in Rome (Acts 28).

ORIGINAL READERS
It was addressed to believers in Ephesus, the capital of the province of Asia.

TIMELINE

	10BC AD1	10	20	30	40	50	60	70	80	90	100
Jesus' life (c. 6/5 B.C.–A.D. 30)											
Paul's conversion (c. A.D. 35)											
Paul's missionary journeys (c. A.D. 46-67)											
Council at Jerusalem (c. A.D. 50-51)											
Nero's reign (c. A.D. 54-68)											
Paul's first imprisonment in Rome (c. A.D. 59-62)											
Book of Ephesians written (c. A.D. 60-62)											
Paul's imprisonment and death in Rome (c. A.D. 67-68)											
Destruction of Jerusalem's temple (c. A.D. 70)											

THEMES
Paul sought to explain that the church, as the people of God, is both the goal and the instrument of achieving God's purpose of bringing "all things in heaven and on earth together under one head, even Christ" (1:10). Paul's letter focuses on two aspects of unity:

1. *The basis for unity.* God's eternal purpose, stated in 1:10, above, is evidenced in, and accomplished through, the church. Christians are chosen to be "holy and blameless" before God (1:4), were created in Christ Jesus "to do good works" (2:10), and have been called to be members of a united "household" (2:19). By his death Christ destroyed every "barrier" and "dividing wall" (2:14) that separated human beings, so believers can have true unity as members of "one body" (3:6). Through the church the "mystery" (1:9; 3:3–6) that all believers share a common identity as the one family of God is revealed and fulfilled (3:9–10).

2. *Maintaining unity.* Church unity isn't just an ideal; it's a reality to be experienced. Paul gave practical instructions for realizing and maintaining this unity. Old patterns of thinking and behavior, which were characterized by futility, darkness, and sensuality (4:17–19), had to be "put off" (4:25). Instead, believers were to live in a manner consistent with their salvation in Christ (4:1). Then, as now, Christians were to be humble, gentle, and patient (4:2), submitting to one another out of reverence for Christ (5:21). These behavioral changes are possible as they imi-

tate Christ's self-sacrificing love and service (5:1–2) and access God's power, which enables them to resist and defeat their spiritual enemies (6:10–18).

FAITH IN ACTION

The pages of Ephesians contain life lessons and role models of faith—people who challenge believers to put faith in action.

Role Models

• THE EPHESIANS (1:15) were known for their faith and "love for all the saints." What sets apart your local church? What would you like its mark to be?

• PAUL (1:16–23; 3:14–19) gave thanks for the church and prayed for its members' spiritual enrichment, understanding, and unity. Do you pray for your congregation and each individual's spiritual growth and understanding? Do you intercede for unity in your local church? How are you promoting peace in your church and community?

• APOSTLES, PROPHETS, EVANGELISTS, AND PASTOR-TEACHERS (4:11) are gifts given by Christ to lead and develop believers for effective ministry in the church. How can you demonstrate your support of and appreciation for these gifts placed by Christ in your local fellowship? How are they important to your Christian life?

• JESUS (5:2) modeled love and self-sacrifice. Are these characteristics apparent in your life and church community?

Challenges

• Develop programs in your church that express love—first to other believers and then to those in the broader community—so that your church will be known for its love.

• Pray for spiritual understanding and unity in your local church and among Christian churches around the world.

• The "church" is more than a building, and it includes more than your particular congregation or denomination. Pray for an understanding of the implications of church unity and the means by which it can be accomplished.

• Reach out to other Christian churches to promote unity through the "bond of peace" (4:3).

OUTLINE

I. Greeting (1:1–2)
II. The Divine Purpose (1:3—3:21)
   A. Made Alive in Christ by Grace (1:3—2:10)
   B. Jew and Gentile Made One in Christ (2:11–18)
   C. Jew and Gentile United in One Household in Christ (2:19–22)
   D. Paul as a Minister to the Gentiles (3:1–13)
   E. Paul's Prayer for the Ephesians (3:14–21)
III. Practical Instruction (4:1—6:20)
IV. Conclusion (6:21–24)

1 Paul, an apostle^a of Christ Jesus by the will of God,^b

To the saints in Ephesus,^a the faithful^{b c} in Christ Jesus:

²Grace and peace to you from God our Father and the Lord Jesus Christ.^d

Spiritual Blessings in Christ

³Praise be to the God and Father of our Lord Jesus Christ,^e who has blessed us in the heavenly realms^f with every spiritual blessing in Christ. ⁴For he chose us in him before the creation of the world to be holy and blameless^g in his sight. In love^h ⁵he^c predestinedⁱ us to be adopted as his sons through Jesus Christ, in accordance with his pleasure^j and will— ⁶to the praise of his glorious grace, which he has freely given us in the One

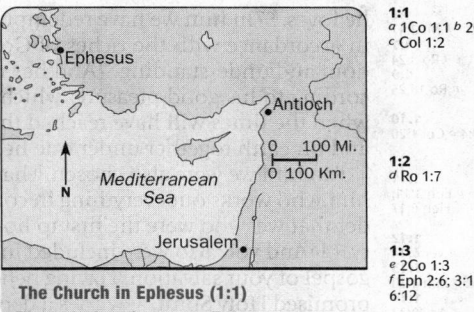

1:1
^a 1Co 1:1 ^b 2Co 1:1
^c Col 1:2

1:2
^d Ro 1:7

1:3
^e 2Co 1:3
^f Eph 2:6; 3:10;
6:12

1:4
^g Eph 5:27;
Col 1:22
^h Eph 4:2,15,16
1:5
ⁱ Ro 8:29,30
^j 1Co 1:21

The Church in Ephesus (1:1)
Then: A city of 200,000, Ephesus was renowned for its traders and silver-smiths.
Now: The Turkish city of Selcuk occupies the site.

---

^a *1 Some early manuscripts do not have* in Ephesus. ^b *1 Or* believers who are ^c *4,5 Or* sight in love. *5*He

---

Ephesians 1:1–2

Letters in the ancient world followed a set form: identification of the writer and addressees, greeting, prayer or wish for health, body, and closing. Christian writers "Christianized" the form by changing or expanding the traditional elements. The author and recipients are described by their relationship to Christ. And instead of the standard greeting (*chairein*), through a play on words Paul here changed his greeting to read "grace [*charis*] and peace to you from God our Father and the Lord Jesus Christ."

Paul's adaptation of his culture's letter form for specifically Christian letters raises a crucial question: How do culture and gospel relate? The gospel defines life for Christians, but our life is lived out in a culture that also seeks to define us. It's important that we understand the culture we live in and decide which aspects to adapt and enjoy—and which to reject. Our expression of the gospel in our culture must be a natural outflow of the depth of our relationship with Christ, not just a borrowing of "religious" words. How "at home" are you as a Christian in your culture and society?

Snapshots

 1:4–5

Sebastian

Married for ten years, Lucia and Petru's greatest sorrow was that they couldn't have children. But this couple's prayers were answered when a Christian ministry operating in their native country of Romania initiated a foster care program in which they enrolled.

About the time they finished their training, Sebastian was born to a teenage mom. Sebi, as they call him, was placed as a foster child with Lucia and Petru. "When we first saw the little one, we . . . knew that he was our son," confessed Lucia. But the road to adoption was bumpy. Eventually, though, the adoption was finalized.

Petru was initially leery of emotional involvement, fearing things might not work out. But his resistance soon melted. Now he proudly enthuses, "I took him out . . . to the city. Everyone was looking and smiling at Sebi. A few stopped and congratulated me for having such a wonderful son."

> **S**ebi's parents are overwhelmed with love.

The ministry's staff keeps tabs on the family, answering their questions and helping them adapt to their new situation. Visitors to their home can't help but notice two things: This has become a family—happy, warm, and united. And Sebi's parents are overwhelmed with love.

1:6
k Mt 3:17
1:7
l Ro 3:24
1:9
m Ro 16:25
1:10
n Gal 4:4 o Col 1:20
1:11
p Eph 3:11; Heb 6:17
1:12
q ver 6,14
1:13
r Col 1:5 s Eph 4:30
1:14
t Ac 20:32

he loves.[k] [7]In him we have redemption[l] through his blood, the forgiveness of sins, in accordance with the riches of God's grace [8]that he lavished on us with all wisdom and understanding. [9]And he[a] made known to us the mystery[m] of his will according to his good pleasure, which he purposed in Christ, [10]to be put into effect when the times will have reached their fulfillment[n]—to bring all things in heaven and on earth together under one head, even Christ.[o]

[11]In him we were also chosen,[b] having been predestined according to the plan of him who works out everything in conformity with the purpose[p] of his will, [12]in order that we, who were the first to hope in Christ, might be for the praise of his glory.[q] [13]And you also were included in Christ when you heard the word of truth,[r] the gospel of your salvation. Having believed, you were marked in him with a seal,[s] the promised Holy Spirit, [14]who is a deposit guaranteeing our inheritance[t] until the redemption of those who are God's possession—to the praise of his glory.

Thanksgiving and Prayer

1:15
u Col 1:4
1:16
v Ro 1:8
1:17
w Jn 20:17
x Col 1:9
1:18
y Ac 26:18; 2Co 4:6

[15]For this reason, ever since I heard about your faith in the Lord Jesus and your love for all the saints,[u] [16]I have not stopped giving thanks for you,[v] remembering you in my prayers. [17]I keep asking that the God of our Lord Jesus Christ, the glorious Father,[w] may give you the Spirit[c] of wisdom[x] and revelation, so that you may know him better. [18]I pray also that the eyes of your heart may be enlightened[y] in order that you may know the hope to which he has called you, the riches of his glo-

---

[a] 8,9 Or *us. With all wisdom and understanding,* [9]*he*   [b] 11 Or *were made heirs*   [c] 17 Or *a spirit*

Ephesians 1:3–14

📖 Paul's opening prayer contains an extended doxology or blessing (vv. 3–14), a thanksgiving (vv. 15–16), and an intercessory prayer (vv. 17–23). The first three chapters of Ephesians are filled with worship—virtually doctrine set to music. "Heavenly realms" (v. 3) doesn't refer to a physical location but to a spiritual reality—God's world, in which believers share and which evil forces seek to attack.

📖 Christians live in two realities at the same time: our physical world and the "heavenly realms" in Christ. How difficult it must have been for these early Christians to think of themselves as "in" a person who had been alive with them only a few years earlier and whose earthly brothers they knew. Similarly, how difficult is it for us to think of ourselves as "in Christ," when we often explain salvation as having invited Christ into our hearts, to live *in us*?

Ephesians 1:15–23

📖 This is Paul's only letter to combine a doxology with a prayer of thanks and intercession for others. Paul's petition for the continuing work of God in his readers grew out of his thanks for what God had already accomplished in them. Since the themes of prayer for others in these verses also are present in 3:14–21, it's worthwhile to compare the two passages. Another valuable study is to examine the extensive parallels between this passage and Colossians 1:3–12, 15–20.

The emotional tone of verses 15–16 reflects Paul's encouragement over the news he had received about his readers' faith and love, as well as the depth of relationship he felt with many people he had likely never met. (Paul was either writing a circular letter to churches in addition to the one at Ephesus, or the church at Ephesus had grown extensively since his prolonged stay there.) Paul's example encouraged his readers to pray continually for all God's people.

1:3–14

The Image of God

In chapters one and two, Paul taught us that because we are in Christ we have a new identity (Eph. 1:3–14). Having been created in the image or likeness of God, we now recapture our true nature. Because we are new in Christ, that image comes alive again. *Created. Fallen. Redeemed.* That is our story: God's Good News on the most personal—and global—levels (Eph. 4:22–24).

See also "*Imago Dei*" on page 4, Genesis 1:26.

Created
- We were created in the image of God (Gen. 1:26–27).

Fallen
- The image of God as displayed in human beings was disfigured through the fall (Rom. 3:23).
- The fall resulted in strife and contention between humanity and creation (Gen. 3:17–19).
- As a result, people exploited others in God's creation—and creation itself (Deut. 22:6–7).

Redeemed
- Jesus Christ is God, and he is the image of God—we see God through him (Phil. 2:6; Col. 1:15).

- He is also the perfect human being (John 1:4; Heb. 1:3).
- God's image is renewed in those who are united with Jesus (Rom. 8:29).
- Complete restoration is coming in the future (1 Cor. 15:49).
- The Christian life is a process of transformation (2 Cor. 3:18).

Consequences
- Christians respect all human life (Gen. 9:6; James 3:9).
- Christians exercise proper care of creation (Gen. 1:26; Ps. 8:3–8).
- Christians imitate God's love and justice (Deut. 10:17–19; Matt. 5:48).

rious inheritance in the saints, [19]and his incomparably great power for us who believe. That power[z] is like the working of his mighty strength,[a] [20]which he exerted in Christ when he raised him from the dead[b] and seated him at his right hand in the heavenly realms, [21]far above all rule and authority, power and dominion, and every title[c] that can be given, not only in the present age but also in the one to come. [22]And God placed all things under his feet[d] and appointed him to be head[e] over everything for the church, [23]which is his body, the fullness of him who fills everything in every way.

Made Alive in Christ

2 As for you, you were dead in your transgressions and sins,[f] [2]in which you used to live[g] when you followed the ways of this world and of the ruler of the kingdom of the air,[h] the spirit who is now at work in those who are disobedient.[i] [3]All of us also lived among them at one time, gratifying the cravings of our sinful nature[aj] and following its desires and thoughts. Like the rest, we were by nature objects of wrath. [4]But because of his great love for us, God, who is rich in mercy, [5]made us alive with Christ even when we were dead in transgressions[k]—it is by grace you have been saved.[l] [6]And God raised us up with Christ and seated us with him[m] in the heavenly realms[n] in Christ Jesus, [7]in order that in the coming ages he might show the incomparable riches of his grace, expressed in his kindness[o] to us in Christ Jesus. [8]For it is by grace you have been saved,[p] through faith—and this not from yourselves, it is the gift of God— [9]not by works,[q] so that no one can boast.[r] [10]For we are God's workmanship, created[s] in Christ Jesus to do good works,[t] which God prepared in advance for us to do.

One in Christ

[11]Therefore, remember that formerly you who are Gentiles by birth and called "uncircumcised" by those who call themselves "the circumcision" (that done in the body by the hands of men)[u]— [12]remember that at that time you were separate from Christ, excluded from citizenship in Israel and foreigners to the covenants of the promise,[v] without hope[w] and without God in the world. [13]But now in Christ Jesus you who once were far away have been brought near[x] through the blood of Christ.[y]

---

[a] 3 Or our flesh

1:19
z Col 1:29
a Eph 6:10
1:20
b Ac 2:24
1:21
c Php 2:9,10
1:22
d Mt 28:18
e Eph 4:15; 5:23

2:1
f ver 5; Col 2:13
2:2
g Col 3:7
h Jn 12:31;
Eph 6:12 / Eph 5:6
2:3
i Gal 5:16

2:5
k ver 1 / ver 8;
Ac 15:11
2:6
m Eph 1:20
n Eph 1:3
2:7
o Tit 3:4
2:8
p ver 5
2:9
q 2Ti 1:9 r 1Co 1:29
2:10
s Eph 4:24
t Tit 2:14

2:11
u Col 2:11

2:12
v Gal 3:17
w 1Th 4:13
2:13
x ver 17; Ac 2:39
y Col 1:20

📖 This text implies the kind of community the church should be: (1) a worldwide, caring community—we are unified with all other believers; (2) a praying community—we acknowledge who "owns the house"; (3) a thinking community—our wisdom is practical knowledge for right living; (4) a community that understands—what Christ has done affects our present and future; (5) a confident community—we live in Christ's victory over sin; and (6) a community of power—we live and minister in the powerful authority Christ gave his disciples.

Ephesians 2:1–10

📖 This passage is one of the clearest, most expressive, and best loved descriptions of salvation in the New Testament. It contains the first of several "formerly-now" contrasts, which distinguish between a life of sin and alienation before Christ and a life of faith in him. Paul acknowledged that God's work in the Ephesian believers prepared them to do the good works he anticipated they would engage in. The connection between *being* and *doing* is a strong emphasis in this book.

📖 In your heart of hearts, do you believe yourself to be as bad as the picture Paul paints? Is the life you so carefully groom really meaningless without God? Or, on the other hand, do you find it hard to believe the facts are as good as Paul says? Can God really love you so deeply, and are you really exalted with Christ in the heavenly realms? The message here is about value and hope. Without God people have little of either. We are so highly valued by God that not only has he made and redeemed us, but he has created us to bear fruit through good works in Christ.

Ephesians 2:11–22

📖 This passage is one of only a few in Paul's letters to discuss the doctrine of *reconciliation*, the restoration of broken relationships. Romans 5:10–11 focuses on reconciliation between God and sinners, who in their unredeemed state are his "enemies." In 2 Corinthians 5:18–21 we learn that God reconciles us/the world to himself and gives us a ministry of reconciliation. In Colossians 1:19–20 we receive the news that God reconciles to himself all things on Earth and in heaven. Here in Ephesians 2:16 we read about a *double reconciliation*—between God and humanity and with regard to all that divides us as people—expressed through the wall separating Jews and Gentiles.

2:14
z 1Co 12:13
2:15
a Col 1:21,22
b Col 2:14
c Gal 3:28
2:16
d Col 1:20,22

2:17
e Ps 148:14;
Isa 57:19
2:18
f Eph 3:12
g Col 1:12
h 1Co 12:13
2:19
i ver 12 / Php 3:20
k Gal 6:10
2:20
l Mt 16:18;
Rev 21:14
m 1Pe 2:4-8
2:21
n 1Co 3:16,17
3:1
o Ac 23:18; Eph 4:1

3:2
p Col 1:25
3:3
q Ro 16:25
r 1Co 2:10
3:4
s 2Co 11:6
3:5
t Ro 16:26
3:6
u Gal 3:29
v Eph 2:15,16
3:7
w 1Co 3:5
x Eph 1:19
3:8
y 1Co 15:9

3:9
z Ro 16:25

3:10
a 1Co 2:7
b 1Pe 1:12
c Eph 1:21

3:12
d Eph 2:18
e Heb 4:16

3:14
f Php 2:10

3:16
g Col 1:11
h Ro 7:22

14For he himself is our peace, who has made the two one[z] and has destroyed the barrier, the dividing wall of hostility, 15by abolishing in his flesh[a] the law with its commandments and regulations.[b] His purpose was to create in himself one[c] new man out of the two, thus making peace, 16and in this one body to reconcile both of them to God through the cross,[d] by which he put to death their hostility. 17He came and preached peace to you who were far away and peace to those who were near.[e] 18For through him we both have access[f] to the Father[g] by one Spirit.[h]

19Consequently, you are no longer foreigners and aliens,[i] but fellow citizens[j] with God's people and members of God's household,[k] 20built on the foundation[l] of the apostles and prophets, with Christ Jesus himself as the chief cornerstone.[m] 21In him the whole building is joined together and rises to become a holy temple[n] in the Lord. 22And in him you too are being built together to become a dwelling in which God lives by his Spirit.

Paul the Preacher to the Gentiles

3 For this reason I, Paul, the prisoner[o] of Christ Jesus for the sake of you Gentiles—

2Surely you have heard about the administration of God's grace that was given to me[p] for you, 3that is, the mystery[q] made known to me by revelation,[r] as I have already written briefly. 4In reading this, then, you will be able to understand my insight[s] into the mystery of Christ, 5which was not made known to men in other generations as it has now been revealed by the Spirit to God's holy apostles and prophets.[t] 6This mystery is that through the gospel the Gentiles are heirs[u] together with Israel, members together of one body,[v] and sharers together in the promise in Christ Jesus.

7I became a servant of this gospel[w] by the gift of God's grace given me through the working of his power.[x] 8Although I am less than the least of all God's people,[y] this grace was given me: to preach to the Gentiles the unsearchable riches of Christ, 9and to make plain to everyone the administration of this mystery,[z] which for ages past was kept hidden in God, who created all things. 10His intent was that now, through the church, the manifold wisdom of God[a] should be made known[b] to the rulers and authorities[c] in the heavenly realms, 11according to his eternal purpose which he accomplished in Christ Jesus our Lord. 12In him and through faith in him we may approach God[d] with freedom and confidence.[e] 13I ask you, therefore, not to be discouraged because of my sufferings for you, which are your glory.

A Prayer for the Ephesians

14For this reason I kneel[f] before the Father, 15from whom his whole family[a] in heaven and on earth derives its name. 16I pray that out of his glorious riches he may strengthen you with power[g] through his Spirit in your inner being,[h] 17so that

---

a 15 Or whom all fatherhood

We as Christians can too easily forget that our vertical relationship with God is bound to be expressed in horizontal relationships with other people. We *create* barriers among races, nations, religions, genders, social and economic classes, denominations, communities, and families. Differentiation is necessary for identity, but the human tendency to erect walls is a distortion and a sin. Diversity and uniqueness don't have to lead to division. Peace is unexpectedly both *destructive* and *constructive*. Division and hostility have to be destroyed for unity and peace to be established. The foundation *has already been laid in Christ*, in whom all people are united.

Ephesians 3:1–13

Paul's view of his sufferings as his readers' "glory" may seem strange. But he saw his imprisonment as part of his service for Christ, a service that put the Gentiles' spiritual needs ahead of his own comfort and safety. If Paul was in prison for preaching to them, that meant someone was fighting on their side. His confinement shouldn't have discouraged them. What if no one had been willing to risk imprisonment for ministry to the Gentiles?

Your hardship probably won't be like Paul's, but your identification with the cross isn't optional and will be costly. Chances are you are willing to expend enormous energy and resources to care for a highly valued person or prized possession. Do you value the gospel enough to endure hardship for it? Are you willing to suffer belittlement, financial sacrifice, or personal risk? Can you see yourself, like Paul, dying to yourself and rising with Christ in service to others?

Christ may dwell in your hearts[i] through faith. And I pray that you, being rooted[j] and established in love, [18]may have power, together with all the saints, to grasp how wide and long and high and deep[k] is the love of Christ, [19]and to know this love that surpasses knowledge—that you may be filled[l] to the measure of all the fullness of God.[m]

[20]Now to him who is able[n] to do immeasurably more than all we ask or imagine, according to his power that is at work within us, [21]to him be glory in the church and in Christ Jesus throughout all generations, for ever and ever! Amen.[o]

Unity in the Body of Christ

4 As a prisoner[p] for the Lord, then, I urge you to live a life worthy[q] of the calling you have received. [2]Be completely humble and gentle; be patient, bearing with one another[r] in love.[s] [3]Make every effort to keep the unity[t] of the Spirit through the bond of peace. [4]There is one body and one Spirit[u]—just as you were called to one hope when you were called— [5]one Lord, one faith, one baptism; [6]one God and Father of all, who is over all and through all and in all.[v]

[7]But to each one of us[w] grace has been given[x] as Christ apportioned it. [8]This is why it[a] says:

> "When he ascended on high,
> he led captives[y] in his train
> and gave gifts to men."[b][z]

[9](What does "he ascended" mean except that he also descended to the lower, earthly regions[c]? [10]He who descended is the very one who ascended higher than all the heavens, in order to fill the whole universe.) [11]It was he who gave some to be apostles,[a] some to be prophets, some to be evangelists,[b] and some to be pastors and teachers, [12]to prepare God's people for works of service, so that the body of Christ[c] may be built up [13]until we all reach unity[d] in the faith and in the knowledge of the Son of God and become mature,[e] attaining to the whole measure of the fullness of Christ.

[14]Then we will no longer be infants,[f] tossed back and forth by the waves,[g] and blown here and there by every wind of teaching and by the cunning and craftiness of men in their deceitful scheming.[h] [15]Instead, speaking the truth in love, we will in all things grow up into him who is the Head,[i] that is, Christ. [16]From him the

[a] 8 Or *God*   [b] 8 Psalm 68:18   [c] 9 Or *the depths of the earth*

3:17 [i] Jn 14:23 [j] Col 1:23
3:18 [k] Job 11:8,9
3:19 [l] Col 2:10 [m] Eph 1:23
3:20 [n] Ro 16:25
3:21 [o] Ro 11:36

4:1 [p] Eph 3:1 [q] Php 1:27; Col 1:10
4:2 [r] Col 3:12,13 [s] Eph 1:4
4:3 [t] Col 3:14
4:4 [u] 1Co 12:13
4:6 [v] Ro 11:36
4:7 [w] 1Co 12:7,11 [x] Ro 12:3
4:8 [y] Col 2:15 [z] Ps 68:18

4:11 [a] 1Co 12:28 [b] Ac 21:8
4:12 [c] 1Co 12:27
4:13 [d] ver 3,5 [e] Col 1:28

4:14 [f] 1Co 14:20 [g] Jas 1:6 [h] Eph 6:11

4:15 [i] Eph 1:22

Ephesians 3:14–21

Paul returned to prayer to explain his desire for his readers. He wanted them to be strengthened by God's Spirit so they might intimately know Christ's presence and love. If this happened all else would fall into place. Love brings movement and causes things to happen. The ethic of chapters 4–6 has its foundation in this prayer.

That love is central to the prayer is no accident. Now we see how the hostility mentioned in 2:14–16 was erad-

---

4:3–6

Unity in the Body of Christ

Paul was focusing on unity within the local body of Christ. The fledgling church hadn't yet spread far. But it's never been more important than today for the worldwide body of believers (approximately one third of Earth's population!) to move toward this goal. Though diverse in many ways—culture, worship practices, church organizations—all Christians confess Jesus as both Lord and the only Way of salvation.

Source: Barrett and Johnson (2001:15)

NON-CHRISTIANS: 4 BILLION

World Population: 6 Billion

ALL CHRISTIANS: SLIGHTLY MORE THAN 2 BILLION	
ROMAN CATHOLICS	1 BILLION
PROTESTANTS	350 MILLION
INDEPENDENTS	350 MILLION
ORTHODOX	225 MILLION
ANGLICANS	80 MILLION

4:16
j Col 2:19

whole body, joined and held together by every supporting ligament, grows[j] and builds itself up in love, as each part does its work.

Living as Children of Light

4:17
k Ro 1:21
4:18
l Ro 1:21
m Eph 2:12
n 2Co 3:14
4:19
o 1Ti 4:2 *p* Ro 1:24
q Col 3:5

[17] So I tell you this, and insist on it in the Lord, that you must no longer live as the Gentiles do, in the futility of their thinking.[k] [18] They are darkened in their understanding[l] and separated from the life of God[m] because of the ignorance that is in them due to the hardening of their hearts.[n] [19] Having lost all sensitivity,[o] they have given themselves over[p] to sensuality[q] so as to indulge in every kind of impurity, with a continual lust for more.

[20] You, however, did not come to know Christ that way. [21] Surely you heard of him and were taught in him in accordance with the truth that is in Jesus. [22] You were

4:22
r 1Pe 2:1 *s* Ro 6:6

4:23
t Col 3:10
4:24
u Ro 6:4 *v* Eph 2:10
4:25
w Zec 8:16
x Ro 12:5

taught, with regard to your former way of life, to put off[r] your old self,[s] which is being corrupted by its deceitful desires; [23] to be made new in the attitude of your minds;[t] [24] and to put on the new self,[u] created to be like God in true righteousness and holiness.[v]

[25] Therefore each of you must put off falsehood and speak truthfully[w] to his neighbor, for we are all members of one body.[x] [26] "In your anger do not sin"[a]: Do not let the sun go down while you are still angry, [27] and do not give the devil a foot-

4:28
y Ac 20:35
z 1Th 4:11
a Lk 3:11

hold. [28] He who has been stealing must steal no longer, but must work,[y] doing something useful with his own hands,[z] that he may have something to share with those in need.[a]

4:29
b Col 3:8

[29] Do not let any unwholesome talk come out of your mouths,[b] but only what is helpful for building others up according to their needs, that it may benefit those

4:30
c 1Th 5:19
d Ro 8:23

who listen. [30] And do not grieve the Holy Spirit of God,[c] with whom you were sealed for the day of redemption.[d] [31] Get rid of all bitterness, rage and anger, brawl-

4:31
e Col 3:8
4:32
f Mt 6:14, 15

ing and slander, along with every form of malice.[e] [32] Be kind and compassionate to one another, forgiving each other, just as in Christ God forgave you.[f]

---

[a] 26 Psalm 4:4

---

icated. The love of Christ destroyed the antagonism both between humanity and God and between various groups of people. Love is no mere feeling—it's the power of God that surpasses our puny understanding to fill us with God's very fullness. No wonder Paul closed by breaking into a great doxology of praise (vv. 20–21)!

📖 To know Christ is to know his love. The experience of God's love and the wonder and worship that result from it provide the nurture and stability that create confidence and trust. Christians today need time for reflecting, for remembering, for pondering matters too deep for our limited knowledge. Some activities of our busy lives may need to be laid aside, but the contemplative part of faith isn't one of them. How regularly do you spend quality time engaged in worship, praise, and appreciation of God?

Ephesians 4:1–16

📖 No other New Testament passage describes the church in action quite like this one. Christianity is a God-directed, Christ-defined, others-oriented faith. Ancient Greek culture (like our society) often viewed humility, meekness, gentleness, and self-sacrifice in negative terms, as weaknesses. But Paul taught that the love experienced in Christ is to be extended to others. Christians, as *part of each other*, are to receive, think about, serve, love, build up, submit to, and encourage one another.

📖 Have you tried functioning as a go-it-alone Christian? If so, did you sense a disconnect between your faith and your lifestyle? Christianity is relational. Our faith offers a strong basis for positive interactions with other human beings, simply because we share the distinction of being persons created in God's image. But relations among Christians have a broader foundation. We share an identity in Christ, the experience of Christ, the values determined by Christ. Most of the vices listed in the New Testament's ethical instructions are sins that disrupt community. Most of the virtues promote unity.

Ephesians 4:17—5:21

📖 Some ancient Greeks believed that desires corrupted and destroyed life and therefore sought to be free of desire. In fact, they viewed passions as diseases of the mind. Living free of desire was considered the mark of wisdom and maturity. But no one can achieve this status. The solution isn't the rejection of desires but their subjection to God.

📖 While much of the world lacks basic necessities of life, many in the West want what they don't need, gauging success by accumulation of money and possessions—positive and useful in themselves, but heavy baggage and terrible masters. The more we allow our desires to control us the more corrupting they become. This passage ignites a bomb under our self-centered thinking.

5 Be imitators of God, [g] therefore, as dearly loved children [2]and live a life of love, just as Christ loved us and gave himself up for us [h] as a fragrant offering and sacrifice to God. [i]

[3]But among you there must not be even a hint of sexual immorality, or of any kind of impurity, or of greed, [j] because these are improper for God's holy people. [4]Nor should there be obscenity, foolish talk or coarse joking, which are out of place, but rather thanksgiving. [k] [5]For of this you can be sure: No immoral, impure or greedy person—such a man is an idolater [l]—has any inheritance in the kingdom of Christ and of God. [a][m] [6]Let no one deceive you with empty words, for because of such things God's wrath [n] comes on those who are disobedient. [7]Therefore do not be partners with them.

[8]For you were once [o] darkness, but now you are light in the Lord. Live as children of light [p] [9](for the fruit [q] of the light consists in all goodness, righteousness and truth) [10]and find out what pleases the Lord. [11]Have nothing to do with the fruitless deeds of darkness, but rather expose them. [12]For it is shameful even to mention what the disobedient do in secret. [13]But everything exposed by the light [r] becomes visible, [14]for it is light that makes everything visible. This is why it is said:

> "Wake up, O sleeper, [s]
>   rise from the dead, [t]
> and Christ will shine on you." [u]

[15]Be very careful, then, how you live—not as unwise but as wise, [16]making the most of every opportunity, [v] because the days are evil. [w] [17]Therefore do not be foolish, but understand what the Lord's will is. [x] [18]Do not get drunk on wine, [y] which leads to debauchery. Instead, be filled with the Spirit. [z] [19]Speak to one another with psalms, hymns and spiritual songs. [a] Sing and make music in your heart to the Lord, [20]always giving thanks [b] to God the Father for everything, in the name of our Lord Jesus Christ.

[21]Submit to one another [c] out of reverence for Christ.

Wives and Husbands

[22]Wives, submit to your husbands [d] as to the Lord. [e] [23]For the husband is the head of the wife as Christ is the head of the church, [f] his body, of which he is the Savior. [24]Now as the church submits to Christ, so also wives should submit to their husbands in everything.

[25]Husbands, love your wives, [g] just as Christ loved the church and gave himself up for her [h] [26]to make her holy, cleansing [b] her by the washing [i] with water through the word, [27]and to present her to himself as a radiant church, without stain or wrinkle or any other blemish, but holy and blameless. [j] [28]In this same way, husbands ought to love their wives [k] as their own bodies. He who loves his wife loves himself. [29]After all, no one ever hated his own body, but he feeds and cares for it, just as

---

[a] 5 Or kingdom of the Christ and God   [b] 26 Or having cleansed

---

Cross references (margin):

5:1 [g] Lk 6:36
5:2 [h] Gal 1:4 [i] 2Co 2:15; Heb 7:27
5:3 [j] Col 3:5
5:4 [k] ver 20
5:5 [l] Col 3:5 [m] 1Co 6:9
5:6 [n] Ro 1:18
5:8 [o] Eph 2:2 [p] Lk 16:8
5:9 [q] Gal 5:22
5:13 [r] Jn 3:20,21
5:14 [s] Ro 13:11 [s] Jn 5:25 [u] Isa 60:1
5:16 [v] Col 4:5 [w] Eph 6:13
5:17 [x] Ro 12:2; 1Th 4:3
5:18 [y] Pr 20:1 [z] Lk 1:15
5:19 [a] Ac 16:25; Col 3:16
5:20 [b] Ps 34:1
5:21 [c] Gal 5:13
5:22 [d] Ge 3:16; 1Pe 3:1,5,6 [e] Eph 6:5
5:23 [f] 1Co 11:3; Eph 1:22
5:25 [g] Col 3:19 [h] ver 2
5:26 [i] Ac 22:16
5:27 [j] Eph 1:4; Col 1:22
5:28 [k] ver 25

Ephesians 5:22–33

"House codes" is the label assigned to those sections of Ephesians, Colossians, and 1 Peter that give instructions to wives and husbands, children and parents, and slaves and masters. Unlike secular "house codes" of the day, those in the New Testament focused on the responsibilities of the more powerful persons in society (husbands, parents, and masters) toward the dependent and vulnerable.

Paul didn't directly attack slavery or society's views on women and children. He focused on the gospel, in which "there is neither . . . slave nor free, male nor female" (Gal. 3:28). Differences still existed, but they had no value: All are one in Christ and share the task of living lives motivated by Christ.

Ask yourself how the world has changed for wives, children, and the downtrodden. How does it need to change further, both close to home and abroad? What implications of the gospel still need the most work? What role can you play?

Paul expected Christians to submit to each other. He had in mind rejecting self-centeredness and working for the good of others. Our society emphasizes independence, looking out for number one. To a lesser (and conflicting?) degree, it touts the value of equality. In what ways is mutual submission a stronger ideal? How does it work out in practice, not just between spouses but in other relationships as well? Does this attitude and behavior characterize believers you know? Does it describe your approach to other people?

Christ does the church— [30]for we are members of his body.[l] [31]"For this reason a man will leave his father and mother and be united to his wife, and the two will become one flesh."[a][m] [32]This is a profound mystery—but I am talking about Christ and the church. [33]However, each one of you also must love his wife[n] as he loves himself, and the wife must respect her husband.

Children and Parents

6 Children, obey your parents in the Lord, for this is right.[o] [2]"Honor your father and mother"—which is the first commandment with a promise— [3]"that it may go well with you and that you may enjoy long life on the earth."[b][p]

[4]Fathers, do not exasperate your children;[q] instead, bring them up in the training and instruction of the Lord.[r]

[a] 31 Gen. 2:24   [b] 3 Deut. 5:16

Side references:
5:30 / 1Co 12:27
5:31 m Ge 2:24; Mt 19:5; 1Co 6:16
5:33 n ver 25
6:1 o Col 3:20
6:3 p Ex 20:12
6:4 q Col 3:21
r Ge 18:19; Dt 6:7

Ephesians 6:1–4

Parental anger was (and is) out, and nurturing was in. Concern over the anger of children is emphasized because of the destruction smoldering resentment can cause in the family and society. Can you think of some Biblical examples of disastrous results of unresolved anger in children? What about Absalom (2 Samuel 13–18)? Too often children of every era have been targets for parental hostility or neglect. Parents wield power, simply on the basis of their superior strength and intellect. Will it be used negatively to destroy or positively to enhance?

Too many people, including Christians, have a public and a private persona. They may appear in public as warm, congenial, godly people—but be tyrants at home. How often aren't you at your worst with the people closest to you? We owe it to those we love to live out the humility, tolerant love, and mutual submission of the gospel, especially in the comfortable confines of our homes, behind conveniently closed doors. The most important witness we have is at stake—our witness within our families.

5:15–17

Be Very Careful How You Live

Paul instructed us as children of light to produce the fruit of light—fruit that reflects goodness, righteousness, and truth. He also warned Christians of all ages not to have anything to do with the fruitless deeds of darkness. Instead we are called to expose those deeds to the light. Whenever and wherever we encounter evil in this world, we are not to be shy about exposing it. Our world is full of two kinds of fruit. We can do much to promote that which, having passed God's rigorous inspection, is stamped with his "Sonkist" seal of approval:

Fruit of Light

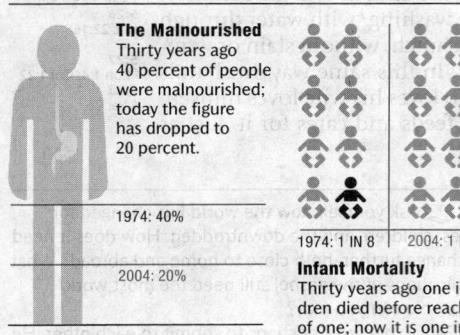

The Malnourished
Thirty years ago 40 percent of people were malnourished; today the figure has dropped to 20 percent.

1974: 40%
2004: 20%

1974: 1 IN 8   2004: 1 IN 16

Infant Mortality
Thirty years ago one in eight children died before reaching the age of one; now it is one in sixteen.

Unclean Water
Thirty years ago 75 percent of people had little access to clean water; today the problem affects only *slightly more than* 25 percent.

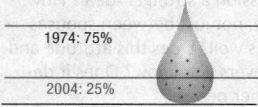

1974: 75%
2004: 25%

Illiteracy
Thirty years ago global illiteracy was at 53 percent; today it's 20 percent.

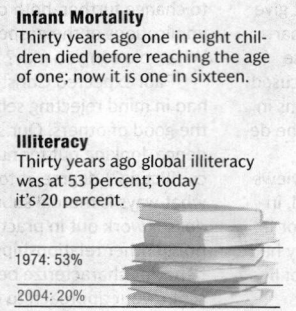

1974: 53%
2004: 20%

Fruit of Darkness

Poverty
Somewhat less than 50 percent of the world's population lives on less than $2 per day.

HIV / AIDS
Over 42 million people are living under the death threat of HIV/AIDS.

Rich and Poor
The disparity between rich and poor is alarming: 60 percent of the world's income is generated by North America, Germany, and Japan.

WORLD'S INCOME

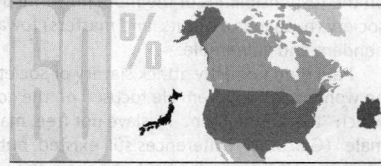

Source: Yancey, *Christianity Today* (May 2004:88)

Slaves and Masters

[5]Slaves, obey your earthly masters with respect[s] and fear, and with sincerity of heart,[t] just as you would obey Christ.[u] [6]Obey them not only to win their favor when their eye is on you, but like slaves of Christ, doing the will of God from your heart. [7]Serve wholeheartedly, as if you were serving the Lord, not men,[v] [8]because you know that the Lord will reward everyone for whatever good he does,[w] whether he is slave or free.

[9]And masters, treat your slaves in the same way. Do not threaten them, since you know that he who is both their Master and yours[x] is in heaven, and there is no favoritism with him.

The Armor of God

[10]Finally, be strong in the Lord[y] and in his mighty power.[z] [11]Put on the full armor of God[a] so that you can take your stand against the devil's schemes. [12]For our struggle is not against flesh and blood, but against the rulers, against the authorities,[b] against the powers[c] of this dark world and against the spiritual forces of evil in the heavenly realms.[d] [13]Therefore put on the full armor of God, so that when the day of evil comes, you may be able to stand your ground, and after you have done everything, to stand. [14]Stand firm then, with the belt of truth buckled around your waist,[e] with the breastplate of righteousness in place,[f] [15]and with your feet fitted with the readiness that comes from the gospel of peace.[g] [16]In addition to all this, take up the shield of faith,[h] with which you can extinguish all the flaming arrows of the evil one. [17]Take the helmet of salvation[i] and the sword of the Spirit, which is the word of God.[j] [18]And pray in the Spirit on all occasions[k] with all kinds of prayers and requests.[l] With this in mind, be alert and always keep on praying for all the saints.

[19]Pray also for me,[m] that whenever I open my mouth, words may be given me so that I will fearlessly[n] make known the mystery of the gospel, [20]for which I am an ambassador[o] in chains.[p] Pray that I may declare it fearlessly, as I should.

Final Greetings

[21]Tychicus,[q] the dear brother and faithful servant in the Lord, will tell you every-

6:5
s 1Ti 6:1 t Col 3:22
u Eph 5:22
6:7
v Col 3:23
6:8
w Col 3:24
6:9
x Job 31:13,14
6:10
y 1Co 16:13
z Eph 1:19
6:11
a Ro 13:12
6:12
b Eph 1:21
c Ro 8:38 d Eph 1:3
6:14
e Isa 11:5
f Isa 59:17
6:15
g Isa 52:7
6:16
h 1Jn 5:4
6:17
i Isa 59:17
j Heb 4:12
6:18
k Lk 18:1
l Mt 26:41; Php 1:4
6:19
m 1Th 5:25
n Ac 4:29; 2Co 3:12
6:20
o 2Co 5:20
p Ac 21:33
6:21
q Ac 20:4

Ephesians 6:5–9

In the Greek and Roman world slavery was considered an economic and practical necessity, an assumed part of life. It's possible that up to one-third of the people living in Greece and Rome were slaves in Paul's day. People became slaves through birth, parental selling or abandonment, captivity in war, inability to pay debts, and voluntary attempts to better their conditions. Race wasn't a factor.

The directions Paul gave to slaves didn't upset the cultural order but were still extremely radical. Slave owners were losing control; Christian slaves had a higher allegiance than to their owners. They had become slaves of Christ, serving him and doing God's will. What's more, Christian owners were to treat them the same way the slaves were to treat their masters. In dealing with other people they, like us, were really dealing with Christ (cf. Matt. 25:40).

The message of this text naturally moves from ancient slavery to modern employer-employee relations, but it pushes us far beyond that. Its theology concerns who we really are, what motivates us, who we seek to please, and how we use power. Everything we do involves a direct encounter with Jesus Christ. For us as Christians, no act is mundane, no person unimportant.

All of us stand on equal footing with the same Lord—who cares deeply how we treat each other and will hold us accountable. Think about the variety of relationships in your life. How important to you are ranks, titles, and roles? Do you treat people differently based on such considerations?

Ephesians 6:10–20

In this final section of the body of his letter, Paul effectively summarized and challenged his readers. They needed to be prepared, as if for battle. Why? Because right living doesn't just happen, and opposition is certain. Paul acknowledged evil as an active force and sought to motivate his readers to make real—even in the midst of demonic powers—all that his letter had been saying about their identity in Christ.

Does it surprise you to hear that Christians aren't called to tranquility but to war? We are called to peace, yes—but peace in the midst of struggle. This peace doesn't render us inactive but makes us ready to do God's will. We need most of all a sense of urgency, an awareness of the conflict, a sense of our own danger. If driving defensively is necessary in our cars, staying alert and avoiding error are compulsory in life. Are you paying careful attention as you negotiate potential pitfalls?

6:22
r Col 4:7-9

6:23
s Gal 6:16; 1Pe 5:14

thing, so that you also may know how I am and what I am doing. 22I am sending him to you for this very purpose, that you may know how we are, *r* and that he may encourage you.

23Peace *s* to the brothers, and love with faith from God the Father and the Lord Jesus Christ. 24Grace to all who love our Lord Jesus Christ with an undying love.

Ephesians 6:21–24

This final section had two purposes: to affirm Tychicus and the additional message he would deliver, and to close the letter formally with a benediction/ blessing extending peace and grace to the readers. The instructions concerning Tychicus are repeated almost verbatim in Colossians 4:7–8. In all likelihood Colossians, Ephesians, and Philemon were written at about the same time and carried by Tychicus to their destinations.

Paul's benediction focused on God and Christ as the joint sources of peace, love, faithfulness, and grace. God provides everything we as Christians need through Christ—bringing us full circle back to the beginning of the letter (see 1:3). God expects a loving response from us—living worthy of the gift! What does this overriding attitude and behavior look like to you?

INTRODUCTION TO
Philippians

AUTHOR
Paul identified himself as the author of this letter (1:1), and the early church unanimously attributed it to him.

DATE WRITTEN
The letter to the Philippians was probably written between A.D. 60 and 62, during Paul's imprisonment in Rome (Acts 28).

ORIGINAL READERS
Paul wrote this letter to the believers in Philippi. The city was located at the gateway between
Europe and Asia and was like a miniature Rome with a large number of Roman citizens.

TIMELINE

	10BC AD1	10	20	30	40	50	60	70	80	90	100
Jesus' life (c. 6/5 B.C.–A.D. 30)											
Paul's conversion (c. A.D. 35)											
Paul's missionary journeys (c. A.D. 46-67)											
Council at Jerusalem (c. A.D. 50-51)											
Nero's reign (c. A.D. 54-68)											
Paul's first imprisonment in Rome (c. A.D. 59-62)											
Book of Philippians written (c. A.D. 60-62)											
Paul's imprisonment and death in Rome (c. A.D. 67-68)											
Destruction of Jerusalem's temple (c. A.D. 70)											

THEMES
Paul wrote this letter to explain his imprisonment and to thank and encourage the Philippians. He included the following themes:

1. *Joy.* Paul modeled joy in the midst of suffering and guided the Philippians in their situation
of persecution (1:27–30; 2:14–16). He expressed joy in their "partnership in the gospel"
(1:4–5), unity (2:2), preaching of the gospel (1:18), faith (1:25), relationship to Christ (1:26; see
3:1; 4:4,10), and suffering and service (2:17). His joy derived from his union with Christ (3:8;
4:12–13), his communion with other Christians (1:4–5), and the promise of the resurrection
(3:10–11,20–21).

2. *Humility.* Believers are to imitate Christ, who modeled humility (2:3–4) by emptying himself
in order to obey God and serve others, even to the point of death on the cross (2:8). Both
Timothy and Epaphroditus exemplified the selfless attitude Paul wanted the community to
emulate (2:19–30). In contrast, Euodia and Syntyche were at odds with one another (4:2–3).

3. *Thanksgiving.* Paul commended Epaphroditus for his life-endangering service to him. He also acknowledged and thanked the Philippians for their missionary partnership and gift to him. Paul had served them sacrificially (2:17), and they had responded in kind. He commended them for their Christian maturity, affirmed that they had received spiritual benefits from giving, and assured them of God's reward. Paul did more than express gratitude; he showed what such sharing means in the life of the Christian community.

FAITH IN ACTION

The pages of Philippians contain life lessons and role models of faith—people who challenge believers to put faith in action.

Role Models

- PAUL (1:12–14) courageously and fearlessly endured suffering in order to advance the gospel. He had learned the secret of living life in plenty or in want—through Christ's strength (4:12–13). How strong is your faith? Do you suspect it could withstand the test of persecution? Are you content no matter what your material circumstances?

- TIMOTHY (2:19–23) took a "genuine interest" (2:20) in the Philippians and served Paul selflessly. Is there someone or some group you are being called to serve? Are you motivated by a "genuine interest" or by "selfish ambition"?

- EPAPHRODITUS (2:25–30) risked his life for the "work of Christ" (2:30). Is God calling you to an area of ministry that might involve personal danger? How can you be encouraged by the example of this godly servant?

- THE PHILIPPIANS (4:10–18) generously shared in Paul's "troubles" (4:14) by supporting him financially, emotionally, and spiritually. Do you regularly share in the ministries of others by generously offering such support?

Challenges

- Find opportunities to share in the ministries of others.

- Examine your "contentment quotient." Are you satisfied with what you have?

- Look for ways to be of service to a pastor or missionary involved in full-time ministry.

- Pray for an attitude of humility and self-sacrifice, one that looks first to the interests of others.

- Ask God to strengthen your faith so you will be able to courageously and fearlessly endure suffering for the sake of the gospel.

OUTLINE

   I. Greeting, Thanksgiving, and Prayer (1:1–11)
  II. Paul's Circumstances (1:12–26)
 III. Exhortations (1:27—2:18)
     A. Live a Life Worthy of the Gospel (1:27–30)
     B. Be Imitators of Christ in Attitude and Action (2:1–18)
 IV. Messengers of the Gospel (2:19–30)
     A. Timothy (2:19–24)
     B. Epaphroditus (2:25–30)
  V. Warnings Against Legalists and Libertines (3:1—4:1)
     A. Paul's Testimony Against Legalists (3:1–16)
     B. Paul's Testimony Against Libertines (3:17—4:1)
 VI. Final Exhortations, Thanks, and Conclusion (4:2–23)

1 Paul and Timothy,[a] servants of Christ Jesus,

To all the saints[b] in Christ Jesus at Philippi,[c] together with the overseers[a][d] and deacons:[e]

2 Grace and peace to you from God our Father and the Lord Jesus Christ.[f]

Thanksgiving and Prayer

3 I thank my God every time I remember you.[g] 4 In all my prayers for all of you, I always pray[h] with joy 5 because of your partnership[i] in the gospel from the first day[j] until now, 6 being confident of this, that he who began a good work in you will carry it on to completion until the day of Christ Jesus.[k]

7 It is right[l] for me to feel this way about all of you, since I have you in my heart;[m] for whether I am in chains[n] or defending[o] and confirming the gospel, all of you share in God's grace with me. 8 God can testify[p] how I long for all of you with the affection of Christ Jesus.

9 And this is my prayer: that your love[q] may abound more and more in knowledge and depth of insight, 10 so that you may be able to discern what is best and may be pure and blameless until the day of Christ,[r] 11 filled with the fruit of righteousness[s] that comes through Jesus Christ—to the glory and praise of God.

Paul's Chains Advance the Gospel

12 Now I want you to know, brothers, that what has happened to me has really served to advance the gospel. 13 As a result, it has become clear throughout the whole palace guard[b] and to everyone else that I am in chains[t] for Christ. 14 Because of my chains,[u] most of the brothers in the Lord have been encouraged to speak the word of God more courageously and fearlessly.

15 It is true that some preach Christ out of envy and rivalry, but others out of goodwill. 16 The latter do so in love, knowing that I am put here for the defense of the gospel.[v] 17 The former preach Christ out of selfish ambition,[w] not sincerely, supposing that they can stir up trouble for me while I am in chains.[c] 18 But what does it

The Church in Philippi (1:1)
Then: Gold and silver mines nearby made Philippi a wealthy town.
Now: The Greek city of Kavalla is located nine miles from the ruins of Philippi.

1:1
a Ac 16:1; 2Co 1:1
b Ac 9:13
c Ac 16:12 d 1Ti 3:1
e 1Ti 3:8
1:2
f Ro 1:7
1:3
g Ro 1:8
1:4
h Ro 1:10
1:5
i Ac 2:42; Php 4:15
j Ac 16:12-40
1:6
k ver 10; 1Co 1:8
1:7
l 2Pe 1:13
m 2Co 7:3 n ver 13, 14,17; Ac 21:33
o ver 16
1:8
p Ro 1:9
1:9
q 1Th 3:12
1:10
r ver 6; 1Co 1:8
1:11
s Jas 3:18
1:13
t ver 7,14,17
1:14
u ver 7,13,17
1:16
v ver 7,12
1:17
w Php 2:3
x ver 7,13,14

---

a 1 Traditionally *bishops*   b 13 Or *whole palace*   c 16,17 Some late manuscripts have verses 16 and 17 in reverse order.

Philippians 1:1–2

Paul's letters follow the expected format and outline of the day, but he modified the customs, allowing him to apply the grand themes of his theology to the concrete situations of individual churches. So skillful was Paul at such adaptation that the reader can often discover his primary concerns by examining his opening paragraphs. Philippians 1:1–11 is a great example of this principle in operation.

The term "saints" in Paul's letters refers to the status of all believers as the people God has called out from among others and set apart for a special purpose. Paul described the two dimensions of believers' identities: saints and servants. We are people of special worth and calling, as expressed by our living as servants of Christ—giving up all rights and privileges created through positions of power and influence.

Philippians 1:3–11

In the first part of this section (vv. 3–8), Paul reported to the Philippians his continual gratitude to God for them, along with reasons for his thankfulness. In the second part (vv. 9–11) he informed this church that he pleaded the cause of its members before God. Paul described the content of his prayers on their behalf—that they might grow spiritually in every way: in knowledge, discernment, purity, and righteousness. Every aspect of believers' lives—mind, attitudes, and behavior—are to be transformed by God's love in Christ. The result: God receives glory and praise.

Even though he was writing from prison, Paul lived with utter confidence. As in Paul's case, God will complete the good work he has begun in us. Though he was confined by chains, nothing could restrain Paul's trust and prayer. How do the topics of your prayer life compare to Paul's? Fill in the names of some people about whom you are concerned. Then pray on their behalf Paul's prayer in verses 9–11.

matter? The important thing is that in every way, whether from false motives or true, Christ is preached. And because of this I rejoice.

Yes, and I will continue to rejoice, [19]for I know that through your prayers[y] and the help given by the Spirit of Jesus Christ,[z] what has happened to me will turn out for my deliverance.[a] [20]I eagerly expect[a] and hope that I will in no way be ashamed, but will have sufficient courage[b] so that now as always Christ will be exalted in my body,[c] whether by life or by death.[d] [21]For to me, to live is Christ[e] and to die is gain. [22]If I am to go on living in the body, this will mean fruitful labor for me. Yet what shall I choose? I do not know! [23]I am torn between the two: I desire to depart[f] and be with Christ,[g] which is better by far; [24]but it is more necessary for you that I remain in the body. [25]Convinced of this, I know that I will remain, and I will continue with all of you for your progress and joy in the faith, [26]so that through my being with you again your joy in Christ Jesus will overflow on account of me.

[27]Whatever happens, conduct yourselves in a manner worthy[h] of the gospel of Christ. Then, whether I come and see you or only hear about you in my absence, I will know that you stand firm[i] in one spirit, contending[j] as one man for the faith of the gospel [28]without being frightened in any way by those who oppose you. This is a sign to them that they will be destroyed, but that you will be saved—and that by God. [29]For it has been granted to you[k] on behalf of Christ not only to believe on him, but also to suffer[l] for him, [30]since you are going through the same struggle[m] you saw[n] I had, and now hear[o] that I still have.

Imitating Christ's Humility

2 If you have any encouragement from being united with Christ, if any comfort from his love, if any fellowship with the Spirit,[p] if any tenderness and compassion,[q] [2]then make my joy complete[r] by being like-minded,[s] having the same love, being one[t] in spirit and purpose. [3]Do nothing out of selfish ambition or vain con-

---

[a] 19 Or *salvation*

Philippians 1:12–30

📖 Paul's comments on suffering in verses 27–30 are difficult to transfer from his world to ours, for at least two reasons: (1) Believers in modern Western democracies know little or nothing of the kind of suffering Paul described—though we can support our brothers and

2:3

Models of Biblical Humility

🧍	**Jacob** admitted his unworthiness to receive God's blessings (Gen. 32:10).
🧍	**Joseph** acknowledged God as the source of his strength (Gen. 41:15–16).
🧍	**Moses** was known as the most humble man on Earth (Num. 12:3).
🧍	**Saul** recognized his unworthiness for leadership (1 Sam. 9:21).
🧍	**David** felt unworthy to marry the king's daughter (1 Sam. 18:18; 2 Sam. 7:18).
🧍	**Solomon** knew he couldn't measure up to his father's greatness (1 Kings 3:7).
🧍	**Mary** didn't feel worthy to be the mother of Jesus—but accepted the role (Luke 1:48).
🧍	**Elizabeth** felt incompetent to counsel Mary—but did it anyway (Luke 1:43).
🧍	**John the Baptist** recognized his limited role as the preparer of the way (Matt. 3:13–15; John 3:30).
🧍	**A sinful woman** gave Jesus the respect he was due (Luke 7:37–38).
🧍	**Paul** acknowledged himself to be the worst of all sinners, yet forgiven by God (1 Tim. 1:15).

Cross-reference margin notes

1:19
y 2Co 1:11
z Ac 16:7
1:20
a Ro 8:19 b ver 14
c 1Co 6:20
d Ro 14:8
1:21
e Gal 2:20

1:23
f 2Ti 4:6 g Jn 12:26;
2Co 5:8

1:27
h Eph 4:1
i 1Co 16:13
j Jude 3

1:29
k Mt 5:11,12
l Ac 14:22
1:30
m Col 2:1; 1Th 2:2
n Ac 16:19-40
o ver 13

2:1
p 2Co 13:14
q Col 3:12
2:2
r Jn 3:29 s Php 4:2
t Ro 12:16

ceit, *u* but in humility consider others better than yourselves. *v* 4Each of you should look not only to your own interests, but also to the interests of others.

5Your attitude should be the same as that of Christ Jesus: *w*

6Who, being in very nature*a* God, *x*
did not consider equality with God*y* something to be grasped,
7but made himself nothing,
taking the very nature*b* of a servant, *z*
being made in human likeness. *a*
8And being found in appearance as a man,
he humbled himself

a 6 Or in the form of *b 7 Or the form*

2:3
u Gal 5:26
v Ro 12:10; 1Pe 5:5
2:5
w Mt 11:29
2:6
x Jn 1:1 *y* Jn 5:18
2:7
z Mt 20:28
a Jn 1:14; Heb 2:17

---

sisters across the globe who endure similar circumstances. (2) Paul's claim that suffering is a gift can easily be misunderstood to mean that it's inherently good. Paul didn't mean that God is the author of suffering. But God in his sovereignty uses it to serve his own good purposes.

Verses 27–30 provide perspective for persecuted believers everywhere. Theologian Karl Barth commented on this passage: "Christians do not strive 'against' anybody (nor *for* anybody either!), but *for the faith*." The Christian way is to refuse retaliation and to live such exemplary lives that our persecutors not only become ashamed of their conduct but want to become believers themselves. Have you been involved in situations with this kind of result?

Philippians 2:1–11

Paul turned in verses 1–4 from the problem of withstanding persecution from the outside to healing the strife within the Philippian church. If the Philippians were to participate successfully with him in the struggle to advance the gospel, they had to be unified in mind, love, and spirit and humbly place the interests of fellow believers above their own.

Verses 6–11 are among the most informative statements in the Bible on the nature of Christ's incarnation (entry into the world in human form). The passage speaks of Christ's preexistence, his equality with God, and the costly nature of his identification with humanity. It also provides insight into Christ's status after his incarnation and the future submission of all created beings to his authority.

Christ's willingness to come to Earth in human form represents the opposite of the human drive to dominate, and Paul called the church to follow that example. This is difficult in our culture. Have you at times found yourself tempted to attach great—even ultimate—value to wealth, glamour, power, or prestige? Have you wanted to achieve such an end so badly that you were willing to belittle or trample on someone else? Appealing to the Holy Spirit for the power to overcome is our best recourse in such situations.

 2:4

How to Develop Humility

The Bible tells us how to be humble (James 4:10). How can you cultivate humility?

1 By forgiving (Col. 3:12-13)
Ask yourself: How good am I at forgiving? Since there is an experiential link between humility and forgiveness, you can indirectly measure your "humility quotient" by your speed and ability to forgive others for their wrongdoings to yourself and others. Do you keep short accounts or hold long-standing resentments?

2 By asking *What is my place in the world?* (Phil. 2:3)
Write out an honest assessment. Include the contributions you make, the factors that limit you from changing things by yourself, and a list of the people you need in your life. Don't forget to include those people who rub you the wrong way or whose disabilities or illnesses test your patience or inspire your life.

3 By wondering *Are people threatened by me?* (Luke 18:9-14)
Others feel less threatened by humble people; boastful, arrogant behavior often results in social disapproval.

4 By remembering my mistakes (2 Chron. 7:14; Ps. 51)
Experts tell us that people are remarkably successful at remembering their own successes, while tending to blame their failures on others. Humble people acknowledge their faults. Check out King David's prayer in 2 Samuel 7:18–29.

5 By being willing to let God be God (Ps. 25:9; Mic. 6:8)
Acknowledge God's supremacy in all things.

Source: Snyder (2002:446–458)

Incarnational Identification

In this passage from Philippians we are given a picture of the incarnation—God becoming a human being. We see that it's more than a theological doctrine. It's a model for cross-cultural ministry.

Paul, writing from his prison cell in Rome, instructed the church at Philippi to have the same attitude as Christ. His words are poignant advice for us as well. In cross-cultural ministry many factors increase success (like knowledge, training, and experience), but no credential is more important than having the attitude of Jesus when we approach others.

Humility is the single most important ingredient for cross-cultural witnesses in community development. Paul pointed out that Jesus has God's nature—but he didn't try to become or remain equal with his heavenly Father. This is the mystery of the incarnation (God taking on human flesh). How could Jesus be 100% human and at the same time 100% divine?

Jesus freely, without hesitation, gave up all he had to become a servant, appearing as a human being among us. He didn't come as a generic human being but appeared as a Jew, shaped and molded by 1st-century, Roman-occupied Jewish culture. This meant that Jesus spoke Aramaic with the low-prestige accent common to Galilee. He avoided eating pork and other foods prohibited by the Torah. The God of the universe was manifested through Jesus, who was embedded in this particular culture.

The incarnation tells us that God isn't afraid of using culture to communicate with us. S.D. Gordon once observed, "Jesus is God spelled out in language human beings can understand." As the incarnation tells us something about God's nature, it also becomes a model for ministry in our own time. In the same way that God entered Jewish culture in the person of Jesus, we must be willing to enter the culture of the people among whom we serve, to speak their language, adjust our lifestyle to theirs, understand their worldview and religious values, and laugh and weep with them. Community development occurs best when it's done "incarnationally."

> When we take the incarnation seriously, it frequently means downward mobility.

The same process of incarnation, of God taking on humanity, occurs every time the gospel crosses a new cultural, linguistic, or religious frontier. If God's mission was achieved by Jesus' incarnation, and Jesus in turn said to his disciples and to us, "As the Father has sent me, I am sending you" (John 20:21), what does this mean for a model of mission, of cross-cultural, community development work? We start with where people are, because this is where God started with us in order to transform us into what he wanted us to become. When we take the incarnation seriously, it frequently means downward mobility. For Jesus it led to crucifixion, and we too will have to die to many things in our life—among them our prejudices, lifestyle, and agenda of what we want to do for God. Maybe even our physical life. When we take the incarnation seriously in ministry, we bow at the cross in humility before we wave the flag of patriotism. The incarnation as a mission model means we are to give up our cultural preferences and not seek to impose them on another culture.

If we follow this lesson from Philippians, we will model Jesus in our ministry. Jesus always met people where they lived, accepted them as he found them, and never left them the same. This is our challenge in identifying with the people we serve and among whom we live.

Darrell Whiteman, dean of the E. Stanley Jones School of World Mission and Evangelism at Asbury Theological Seminary in Wilmore, Kentucky

and became obedient to death [b]—
   even death on a cross!
[9] Therefore God exalted him [c] to the highest place
   and gave him the name that is above every name, [d]
[10] that at the name of Jesus every knee should bow, [e]
   in heaven and on earth and under the earth, [f]
[11] and every tongue confess that Jesus Christ is Lord, [g]
   to the glory of God the Father.

Shining as Stars

[12] Therefore, my dear friends, as you have always obeyed—not only in my presence, but now much more in my absence—continue to work out your salvation with fear and trembling, [h] [13] for it is God who works in you [i] to will and to act according to his good purpose.

[14] Do everything without complaining [j] or arguing, [15] so that you may become blameless and pure, children of God [k] without fault in a crooked and depraved generation, [l] in which you shine like stars in the universe [16] as you hold out [a] the word of life—in order that I may boast on the day of Christ that I did not run or labor for nothing. [m] [17] But even if I am being poured out like a drink offering [n] on the sacrifice [o] and service coming from your faith, I am glad and rejoice with all of you. [18] So you too should be glad and rejoice with me.

Timothy and Epaphroditus

[19] I hope in the Lord Jesus to send Timothy to you soon, [p] that I also may be

---

[a] 16 Or *hold on to*

Cross references (right margin):
2:8
[b] Mt 26:39;
Jn 10:18; Heb 5:8
2:9
[c] Ac 2:33; Heb 2:9
[d] Eph 1:20,21
2:10
[e] Ro 14:11
[f] Mt 28:18
2:11
[g] Jn 13:13
2:12
[h] 2Co 7:15
2:13
[i] Ezr 1:5
2:14
[j] 1Co 10:10;
1Pe 4:9
2:15
[k] Mt 5:45,48;
Eph 5:1
2:15
[l] Ac 2:40
2:16
[m] 1Th 2:19
2:17
[n] 2Ti 4:6
[o] Ro 15:16
2:19
[p] ver 23

Philippians 2:12–18

After this great hymn of praise ascending to heaven, Paul dove back down to Earth with very practical implications for the Philippians: (1) He encouraged them, in light of Christ's triumph and example, to continue their obedience, knowing that God would enable them. (2) He urged them to avoid "complaining" and "arguing." (3) Their witness in the world depended on this; only if they were "blameless" and "pure" could they demonstrate Christ's life to the world.

Jesus, in one of his last recorded prayers, asked God to protect the unity of his disciples and went on to cover those who would believe through their witness (John 17:1–26). Like Paul, Jesus spoke of the unity of believers in the same breath as the effectiveness of the church's testimony (John 17:23). This unity isn't abstract—like a friendly feeling or recognition of common beliefs—but visible. Sadly, the church too often fails to show the world concrete expressions of its oneness, whether the problem manifests itself in the form of church splits or believers' complaints and gossip.

Philippians 2:19–30

Israel served as a negative example of how complaining and arguing can tarnish a witness

---

2:14–16

The Roads to Contentment

In Hebrews 4 the author reminds us to make sure we rest as God did on the seventh day of creation. Sabbath observance leads to contentment—the Sabbath road to contentment. Other Biblical roads to contentment:

The Road to Israel:
Ruth, by leaving her people to settle in a foreign land, teaches us that we can become content by accepting God-ordained changes in our lives (Ruth 1).

The Road to Shiloh:
Hannah, who kept her promise to dedicate her child to God's service, teaches us that faithfulness leads to contentment (1 Sam. 1–2).

The Road to Jerusalem:
David, in accepting God's punishment for his flagrant sins, learned that contentment comes through obedience (2 Sam. 12).

The Road to Wisdom:
In Proverbs 1–3, Solomon urged his readers to embrace wisdom as the way to peace and contentment in life.

The Road to Bethlehem:
Mary found contentment by embracing her role as the mother of Jesus (Luke 1). What is God's road for you?

The Road to Rome:
Paul, on his way to an uncertain future in Rome, teaches us that we can be content even when we don't know our fate (1 Cor. 15:55).

The Road to Ministry:
Timothy learned that holy living—godliness—leads not necessarily to financial gain but invariably to contentment (1 Tim. 6:6).

2:20
q 1Co 16:10
2:21
r 1Co 10:24; 13:5

2:22
s 1Co 4:17; 1Ti 1:2
2:23
t ver 19
2:24
u Php 1:25

2:25
v Php 4:3 w Phm 2
x Php 4:18
2:26
y Php 1:8

2:29
z 1Co 16:18;
1Ti 5:17
2:30
a 1Co 16:17

cheered when I receive news about you. 20I have no one else like him, q who takes a genuine interest in your welfare. 21For everyone looks out for his own interests, r not those of Jesus Christ. 22But you know that Timothy has proved himself, because as a son with his father s he has served with me in the work of the gospel. 23I hope, therefore, to send him as soon as I see how things go with me. t 24And I am confident u in the Lord that I myself will come soon.

25But I think it is necessary to send back to you Epaphroditus, my brother, fellow worker v and fellow soldier, w who is also your messenger, whom you sent to take care of my needs. x 26For he longs for all of you y and is distressed because you heard he was ill. 27Indeed he was ill, and almost died. But God had mercy on him, and not on him only but also on me, to spare me sorrow upon sorrow. 28Therefore I am all the more eager to send him, so that when you see him again you may be glad and I may have less anxiety. 29Welcome him in the Lord with great joy, and honor men like him, z 30because he almost died for the work of Christ, risking his life to make up for the help you could not give me. a

No Confidence in the Flesh

3:2
b Ps 22:16,20
3:3
c Ro 2:28,29;
Gal 6:15; Col 2:11

3 Finally, my brothers, rejoice in the Lord! It is no trouble for me to write the same things to you again, and it is a safeguard for you. 2Watch out for those dogs, b those men who do evil, those mutilators of the flesh. 3For it is we who are the circumcision, c we who worship by the Spirit of God,

---

(cf. vv. 14–15 with Ex. 16:6–8 and Deut. 32:5). Paul's discussion of Timothy and Epaphroditus was more than a travelogue. It was an illustration of how two fellow believers were putting into practice the way of life Paul wanted the Philippians to follow. The gospel's ethical principles ask no more than God gives the power to obey.

The church throughout history has been plagued by those who fail to allow the gospel to move from their heads and hearts to their hands and feet. Against this unhealthy separation of faith and action, the apostle held out the examples of Timothy, Epaphroditus, and Paul himself. All three understood that Christian commitment means letting go of protecting our own interests and instead seeking the best for others. A divided commitment to the gospel, as Jesus never tired of stressing, is no commitment at all. Without being harder on yourself than your Lord would be, how would you assess your belief/behavior ratio?

Philippians 3:1–11

Paul expressed concern that "Judaizing" missionaries would come to Philippi. Their "gospel" mixed the notion of faith in Christ for salvation with the idea that all who wanted to belong to God's people had to accept the yoke of the Jewish law. (Paul's strongest words against this group are found in Galatians.) Paul's desire to warn his brothers and sisters of this danger accounts for the change in tone at verse 2—a change that, though surprising in a letter as cheerful as Philippians, is consistent with the straightforward language of 1:17 and 2:21.

The primary point of the passage is clear: Righ-

2:17–18

How Giving Helps the Giver

Increases our joy	**Increases our understanding**	**Enhances our work**	**Increases our contentment**	**Increases our opportunity for blessing**
Helping others can be an intensely gratifying experience (cf. 1 Chron. 29:17–18; Ps. 27:6b; Prov. 21:15; Acts 20:35; 2 Cor. 8:2).	Giving makes us more appreciative of the needy and diverse. Those appointed as deacons to help with the distribution of food to Greek and Hebraic Jewish widows learned much from their service (Acts 6:1-7).	Giving leads to the development of work values that shape and define our careers. Before his encounter with Jesus, Zacchaeus didn't give, but took. As a result, he despaired of his lifestyle. Jesus recommended he change his ways (Luke 19:5).	Giving reduces stress, feelings of alienation, and guilt. Because of a lifetime of service, Paul was able to say in Philippians 4:12 that he had "learned the secret of being content."	The Philippian and Corinthian churches were promised blessing as a result of their giving (2 Cor. 9:10; Phil. 4:19; cf. Prov. 19:17; Matt. 25:34–36).

1 Joy   2 Understanding   3 Work   4 Contentment   5 Blessing

Source: Stukas (1999:1–19)

who glory in Christ Jesus, and who put no confidence in the flesh— 4though I myself have reasons for such confidence.

If anyone else thinks he has reasons to put confidence in the flesh, I have more: 5circumcised *d* on the eighth day, of the people of Israel, *e* of the tribe of Benjamin, *f* a Hebrew of Hebrews; in regard to the law, a Pharisee; *g* 6as for zeal, persecuting the church; *h* as for legalistic righteousness, *i* faultless.

7But whatever was to my profit I now consider loss *j* for the sake of Christ. 8What is more, I consider everything a loss compared to the surpassing greatness of knowing *k* Christ Jesus my Lord, for whose sake I have lost all things. I consider them rubbish, that I may gain Christ 9and be found in him, not having a righteousness of my own that comes from the law, *l* but that which is through faith in Christ—the righteousness that comes from God and is by faith. *m* 10I want to know Christ and the power of his resurrection and the fellowship of sharing in his sufferings, *n* becoming like him in his death, *o* 11and so, somehow, to attain to the resurrection *p* from the dead.

Pressing on Toward the Goal

12Not that I have already obtained all this, or have already been made perfect, *q* but I press on to take hold *r* of that for which Christ Jesus took hold of me. *s* 13Brothers, I do not consider myself yet to have taken hold of it. But one thing I do: Forgetting what is behind *t* and straining toward what is ahead, 14I press on *u* toward the goal to win the prize for which God has called *v* me heavenward in Christ Jesus.

15All of us who are mature *w* should take such a view of things. *x* And if on some point you think differently, that too God will make clear to you. 16Only let us live up to what we have already attained.

17Join with others in following my example, *y* brothers, and take note of those who live according to the pattern we gave you. 18For, as I have often told you before and now say again even with tears, *z* many live as enemies of the cross of Christ. *a* 19Their destiny is destruction, their god is their stomach, *b* and their glory is in their shame. *c* Their mind is on earthly things. *d* 20But our citizenship *e* is in heaven. *f* And we eagerly await a Savior from there, the Lord Jesus Christ, *g* 21who, by the power *h* that enables him to bring everything under his control, will transform our lowly bodies *i* so that they will be like his glorious body. *j*

4 Therefore, my brothers, you whom I love and long for, *k* my joy and crown, that is how you should stand firm *l* in the Lord, dear friends!

Exhortations

2I plead with Euodia and I plead with Syntyche to agree with each other *m* in the Lord. 3Yes, and I ask you, loyal yokefellow, *a* help these women who have contend-

a 3 Or *loyal Syzygus*

Cross references

3:5
d Lk 1:59
e 2Co 11:22
f Ro 11:1 *g* Ac 23:6
3:6
h Ac 8:3 *i* Ro 10:5
3:7
j Mt 13:44; Lk 14:33
3:8
k Eph 4:13; 2Pe 1:2
3:9
l Ro 10:5 *m* Ro 9:30
3:10
n Ro 8:17
o Ro 6:3-5
3:11
p Rev 20:5,6

3:12
q 1Co 13:10
r 1Ti 6:12
s Ac 9:5,6
3:13
t Lk 9:62
3:14
u Heb 6:1 *v* Ro 8:28

3:15
w 1Co 2:6
x Gal 5:10
3:17
y 1Co 4:16; 1Pe 5:3
3:18
z Ac 20:31
a Gal 6:12
3:19
b Ro 16:18
c Ro 6:21
d Ro 8:5,6
3:20
e Eph 2:19 *f* Col 3:1
g 1Co 1:7
3:21
h Eph 1:19
i 1Co 15:43-53
j Col 3:4
4:1
k Php 1:8
l 1Co 16:13;
Php 1:27

4:2
m Php 2:2

---

teousness before God comes solely from God. Any attempt to base our lives on human requirements, or to measure our worth by our accomplishments and performance, amounts to a rejection of the whole gospel. Such a message, Paul says elsewhere, is "a different gospel—which is really no gospel at all" (Gal. 1:6–7; cf. 2 Cor. 11:4).

If we seek everything, we end up with nothing. If we seek the one "thing," Jesus Christ, we gain all. Apart from Christ everything else is rubbish—the term Paul used is literally "manure." Paul's focus was singular, and nothing would get in his way. He wanted to know Christ and express in his life the quality of righteousness found only through faith in him. Rather than devoting himself to security and comfort, Paul refused to view suffering as an obstacle to his goal. How does this relate to the way you live today?

Philippians 3:12—4:1

Paul argued that there are only two kinds of citizens: those bound to Earth who are controlled by their own appetites, and those of heaven who seek Christ's transformation of their desires and behavior. One lifestyle ends in destruction, the other in glory. Paul urged the Philippians to imitate him and others who followed his pattern of behavior. Was it brash for him to urge the Philippians to try to be like himself? Not when we recognize that he and others were worthy of copying only insofar as *they* followed Christ's example (1 Cor. 11:1; 1 Thess. 1:6).

This passage challenges us to reflect on our own citizenship. Are we trying to have it both ways—calling Christ our Savior for heaven but letting our own appetites and desires on Earth function as our "lord"? Setting our mind on heavenly things doesn't mean we are

ed at my side in the cause of the gospel, along with Clement and the rest of my fellow workers, whose names are in the book of life.

4:4
n Ro 12:12; Php 3:1
4:5
o Heb 10:37;
Jas 5:8,9
4:6
p Mt 6:25-34
q Eph 6:18
4:7
r Isa 26:3; Jn 14:27;
Col 3:15

[n] 4Rejoice in the Lord always. I will say it again: Rejoice![n] 5Let your gentleness be evident to all. The Lord is near.[o] 6Do not be anxious about anything,[p] but in everything, by prayer and petition, with thanksgiving, present your requests to God.[q] 7And the peace of God,[r] which transcends all understanding, will guard your hearts and your minds in Christ Jesus.

8Finally, brothers, whatever is true, whatever is noble, whatever is right, whatever is pure, whatever is lovely, whatever is admirable—if anything is excellent or praiseworthy—think about such things. 9Whatever you have learned or received or heard from me, or seen in me—put it into practice.[s] And the God of peace[t] will be with you.

4:9
s Php 3:17
t Ro 15:33

Thanks for Their Gifts

4:10
u 2Co 11:9

10I rejoice greatly in the Lord that at last you have renewed your concern for me.[u] Indeed, you have been concerned, but you had no opportunity to show it. 11I am not saying this because I am in need, for I have learned to be content[v] whatever the

4:11
v 1Ti 6:6,8

no earthly good. Rather, our Savior brings everything in our lives and world under his control, transforming us into his likeness.

Philippians 4:2–9

The disagreement between the two women Paul singled out by name in verse 2 may have been at the bottom of the disunity that had concerned him throughout the letter. The clause translated "agree with each other" is nearly identical in the Greek to his call in 2:2 to be "like-minded." Euodia and Syntyche needed to put each other's interests first and, "in the Lord," to drop their quarrel. When have you let go of a dispute "in the Lord"? Did God help the two of you to establish/reestablish a healthy relationship?

Christian unity is to be worked out, one quarrel at a time. No discrepancy is to exist between what we believe and what we practice. If we confess, according to the Apostles' Creed, belief in the "communion of saints," we obligate ourselves to work for reconciliation whenever relationships within the church are broken. Once again Paul demonstrated the centrality of prayer to this work of reconciliation and transformation. Substitute the names of people you know who are in conflict or discouraged. Then pray for them.

4:8

Television Time

True, noble, right, pure, lovely, admirable, excellent, praiseworthy. What an inspiring—and intimidating—list of adjectives for parents to consider in terms of their children's exposure to this world. Overall, how does TV fare in terms of meeting Paul's (and God's) tough standards? If you are a parent, what steps are you taking to ensure that your kids' television viewing is as positive and nurturing an experience as possible?

The average youth living in the U.S. watches television **25 HOURS** a week and plays computer games an additional **7 HOURS.**

Kids spend more time watching television than at any other activity except sleep.

44 percent of kids say they watch something different when they are alone than with their parents (25 percent choose MTV).

55 percent of children have a television in their bedroom.

62 percent of children (ages 6 to 10) think sex on television influences kids to have sex when they are young.

66 percent of children (ages 6 to 10) say their peers are influenced by television shows.

Television reaches children at a **younger age and for more time** than any other socializing institution except the family.

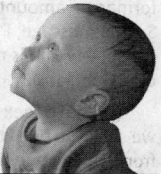

60% 62%

Teenagers are almost as likely to get **sex information** (about sex choices) from television (60 percent) as from a health care provider (62 percent).

Source: American Academy of Pediatrics (June 1995:6)

circumstances. ¹²I know what it is to be in need, and I know what it is to have plenty. I have learned the secret of being content in any and every situation, whether well fed or hungry, ʷ whether living in plenty or in want. ˣ ¹³I can do everything through him who gives me strength. ʸ

¹⁴Yet it was good of you to share ᶻ in my troubles. ¹⁵Moreover, as you Philippians know, in the early days ᵃ of your acquaintance with the gospel, when I set out from Macedonia, not one church shared with me in the matter of giving and receiving, except you only; ᵇ ¹⁶for even when I was in Thessalonica, ᶜ you sent me aid again and again when I was in need. ᵈ ¹⁷Not that I am looking for a gift, but I am looking for what may be credited to your account. ᵉ ¹⁸I have received full payment and even more; I am amply supplied, now that I have received from Epaphroditus ᶠ the gifts you sent. They are a fragrant ᵍ offering, an acceptable sacrifice, pleasing to God. ¹⁹And my God will meet all your needs ʰ according to his glorious riches ⁱ in Christ Jesus.

²⁰To our God and Father ʲ be glory for ever and ever. Amen. ᵏ

Final Greetings

²¹Greet all the saints in Christ Jesus. The brothers who are with me ˡ send greetings. ²²All the saints ᵐ send you greetings, especially those who belong to Caesar's household.

²³The grace of the Lord Jesus Christ ⁿ be with your spirit. Amen. ᵃ

ᵃ 23 Some manuscripts do not have *Amen.*

4:12 w 1Co 4:11 x 2Co 11:9
4:13 y 2Co 12:9
4:14 z Php 1:7
4:15 a Php 1:5 b 2Co 11:8,9
4:16 c Ac 17:1 d 1Th 2:9
4:17 e 1Co 9:11,12
4:18 f Php 2:25 g 2Co 2:14
4:19 h Ps 23:1; 2Co 9:8 i Ro 2:4
4:20 j Gal 1:4 k Ro 11:36
4:21 l Gal 1:2
4:22 m Ac 9:13
4:23 n Ro 16:20

Philippians 4:10–20

Paul proclaimed the secret to contentment, at the same time affirming the Philippians' provision for his needs. Their aid to him demonstrated their partnership with him in the work of the gospel and their progress in Christ-likeness.

How many truly contented people do you know? What would it mean for you to understand and live the key to contentment Paul described in verses 11–13? Wealthy believers are wise to beware of money's ability to gain the upper hand. Wealth can deceive us into dishonest dealings with others and, more subtly, into thinking we are well off because we are good. Yet neither the presence nor absence of resources will make us truly content. The most powerful antidote to these deceptions is giving generously to those in need. Where do you stand on the serving God/serving money continuum?

Philippians 4:21–23

Paul's final greetings encouraged the church's unity one last time. The phrasing of his personal greetings was unique in its stress on each member of the congregation without distinction. The NIV doesn't capture this nuance, but the words *all* and *saints* are singular in Greek. Translated more literally, the sentence says "Greet every saint in Christ Jesus." Just as Paul had stressed unity, here he emphasized the equal worth before God of every believer.

Paul's stress on individual believers is highly relevant in anonymous, urban cultures. Too many Christians feel invisible and peripheral, resulting in spiritual apathy and lack of fruit. We do well to seek fellowship with, and encourage participation from, "wallflower" Christians. Christ's body is the one arena of life in an already alienated world in which isolation is surmounted. God's gracious dealings with us are to be evident by our vital relationships with others in his body. What can you do to gently lead a lonely individual or family into the welcoming circle of God's family?

INTRODUCTION TO
Colossians

AUTHOR
The letter identifies its author as the apostle Paul (1:1; 4:18).

DATE WRITTEN:
Colossians was probably written between A.D. 60 and 62.

ORIGINAL READERS
This letter was written to the believers in Colosse. The church there had been planted by
Paul's coworker Epaphras (1:7; 4:12), who joined Paul while he was under house arrest in
Rome (4:12; Philem. 23; see Acts 28:16–31). This letter was written by Paul during that impris-
onment.

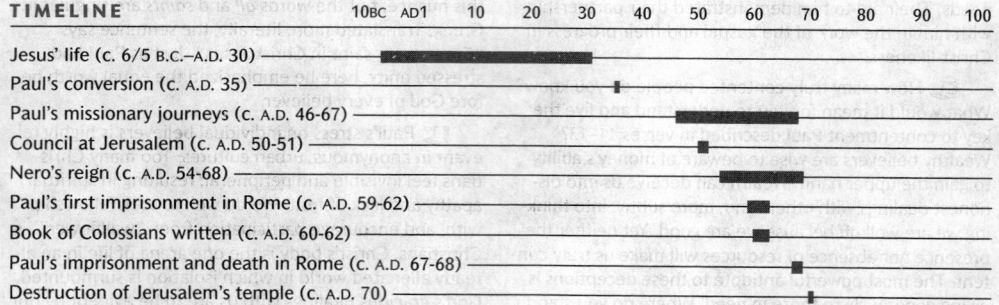

TIMELINE	10BC AD1	10	20	30	40	50	60	70	80	90	100
Jesus' life (c. 6/5 B.C.–A.D. 30)											
Paul's conversion (c. A.D. 35)											
Paul's missionary journeys (c. A.D. 46-67)											
Council at Jerusalem (c. A.D. 50-51)											
Nero's reign (c. A.D. 54-68)											
Paul's first imprisonment in Rome (c. A.D. 59-62)											
Book of Colossians written (c. A.D. 60-62)											
Paul's imprisonment and death in Rome (c. A.D. 67-68)											
Destruction of Jerusalem's temple (c. A.D. 70)											

THEMES
A religious ideology that mixed Greek philosophy with Judaism threatened the Colossian
church. Paul's letter, an argument against that heresy, includes the following themes:

1. *A warning against heresy.* The Colossian heresy stressed the importance of (a) circumcision
(2:11); (b) dietary regulations (2:16); (c) ritual observances like festivals, Sabbaths, and New
Moons (2:16); (d) asceticism (2:21,23); (e) the worship of angels (2:18); and (f) secret knowledge through mystical experiences (2:18). Paul labeled this heresy a vain deceit based on human tradition (2:8) and the "basic principles of this world" (2:8,20). It denied Christ's sufficien-
cy and belittled the Christians' hope in his finished work on the cross.

2. *The supremacy of Christ.* In refuting the Colossian heresy, Paul affirmed that (a) Christ is God
(1:15; 2:9); (b) Christ is the Creator of *all* things (1:16); (c) all the fullness of God dwells in
Christ (1:19; 2:9); (d) Christ is superior to the angels (2:10,15); (e) Christ is the head of the
church (1:18), through whom believers have "fullness" (2:10); (f) in Christ all the requirements
of the Mosaic Law—including circumcision, dietary regulations, and ceremonial observances—
have been met (2:11,16–17); (g) asceticism leads to pride and has no value (2:23), but a life
"hidden with Christ" (3:3) brings glory (3:4); and (h) Christ is the "mystery of God" (2:2; see
1:25–27; 4:3); no other secret knowledge is necessary.

3. *Christian living.* Paul insisted that the believer's union with Christ (3:1–4) results in holy living. He outlined clear standards (3:5–17) that prescribe attitudes—submission, love, service, obedience, conscientious work, and fairness—that were to govern relationships within family and church. His instructions reveal a special concern for weaker or powerless members—wives, children, slaves—and recognize the importance of giving back. Leadership is to be exercised, but domination is unacceptable.

FAITH IN ACTION
The pages of Colossians are filled with life lessons and role models of faith—people who challenge believers to put faith in action.

Role Models

• PAUL (1:28–29) took his role of warning and teaching seriously. His goal was the spiritual growth of others. Do you sometimes hesitate to warn others about wrong thinking? Why are warnings so critical to the church? What are your goals when warning others?

• TYCHICUS (4:7) is pictured as "a dear brother, a faithful minister and fellow servant in the Lord." How do you want to be portrayed by others?

• ONESIMUS (4:9) is described as "faithful." How can you display this quality in your family, church, and community? How do your actions reflect your character?

• EPAPHRAS (4:12–13) was "always wrestling in prayer" for the Colossian believers. How regularly do you pray? When was the last time you "wrestled" in prayer, interceding with God for a fellow Christian?

Challenges

• Evaluate your beliefs about Christ and his supremacy. Seriously study the book of Colossians to nail down the truths of Christ and his finished work on your behalf.

• Paul worked with *Christ's* energy to reach his ministry goal of bringing others to spiritual maturity (1:28–29). Analyze your ministry commitments, measuring the level of energy *you* expend. Choose to let *Christ's* energy fuel your ministry to others.

• Christian households are to function according to the basic guidelines of love, submission, service, and obedience. Meet with your family this week and determine how you can make these characteristics a central focus of your relationships.

• Prayer is crucial for developing spiritual maturity. How devoted are you to this vital discipline? Commit to making it a daily priority.

OUTLINE

I. Greeting, Thanksgiving, and Prayer (1:1–14)
II. Christ Is Supreme (1:15–23)
III. Paul's Ministry (1:24—2:7)
IV. Freedom From Human Regulations Through Life in Christ (2:8–23)
  A. Warning Concerning False Teaching (2:8–15)
  B. Ritual and Asceticism Not Standards of Maturity (2:16–19)
  C. The False Practice of Asceticism (2:20–23)
V. Rules for Holy Living (3:1—4:6)
  A. Put to Death the Old Self and Put On the New Self (3:1–17)
  B. Rules for Christian Households (3:18—4:1)
  C. Further Instructions (4:2–6)
VI. Final Greetings and Conclusion (4:7–18)

1:1
a 1Co 1:1 *b* 2Co 1:1

1 Paul, an apostle[a] of Christ Jesus by the will of God,[b] and Timothy our brother,

²To the holy and faithful[a] brothers in Christ at Colosse:

1:2
c Col 4:18 *d* Ro 1:7

Grace[c] and peace to you from God our Father.[b][d]

Thanksgiving and Prayer

1:3
e Ro 1:8

³We always thank God,[e] the Father of our Lord Jesus Christ, when we pray for you, ⁴because we have heard of your faith in Christ

1:4
f Gal 5:6 *g* Eph 1:15
1:5
h 1Th 5:8; Tit 1:2
i 1Pe 1:4

Jesus and of the love[f] you have for all the saints[g]— ⁵the faith and love that spring from the hope[h] that is stored up for you in heaven[i] and that you have already heard about in the

1:6
j Ro 10:18
k Jn 15:16

word of truth, the gospel ⁶that has come to you. All over the world[j] this gospel is bearing fruit[k] and growing, just as it has been doing among you since the day you heard it and understood God's grace in all its

1:7
l Phm 23 *m* Col 4:7
1:8
n Ro 15:30

truth. ⁷You learned it from Epaphras,[l] our dear fellow servant, who is a faithful minister[m] of Christ on our[c] behalf, ⁸and who also told us of your love in the Spirit.[n]

1:9
o Eph 1:15
p Eph 5:17
q Eph 1:17

⁹For this reason, since the day we heard about you,[o] we have not stopped praying for you and asking God to fill you with the knowledge of his will[p] through all spiritual wisdom and understanding.[q] ¹⁰And we pray this in order

1:10
r Eph 4:1

that you may live a life worthy[r] of the Lord and may please him in every way: bearing fruit in every good work, growing in the knowledge of God, ¹¹being

1:11
s Eph 3:16
t Eph 4:2
1:12
u Eph 5:20
v Ac 20:32

strengthened with all power[s] according to his glorious might so that you may have great endurance and patience,[t] and joyfully ¹²giving thanks to the Father,[u] who has qualified you[d] to share in the inheritance[v] of the saints in the kingdom

1:13
w Ac 26:18
x Eph 6:12;
2Pe 1:11 *y* Mt 3:17
1:14
z Ro 3:24 *a* Eph 1:7

of light. ¹³For he has rescued us from the dominion of darkness[w] and brought us into the kingdom[x] of the Son he loves,[y] ¹⁴in whom we have redemption,[e][z] the forgiveness of sins.[a]

---

a 2 Or *believing*   *b 2* Some manuscripts *Father and the Lord Jesus Christ*   *c 7* Some manuscripts *your*   *d 12* Some manuscripts *us*   *e 14* A few late manuscripts *redemption through his blood*

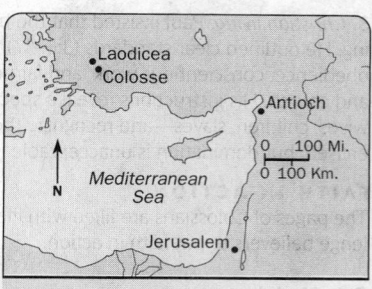

The Church in Colosse (1:2)
Then: Colosse was known for its soft wool and dyed cloth.
Now: The site housing the city's ruins is located near the Turkish village of Honaz.

Colossians 1:1–2

📖 Paul introduced this letter by focusing on the foundations: who he was—an apostle by the will of God; who the Colossians were—holy and faithful in Christ; and who God is—the One who gives us grace and peace.

📖 Paul's assertion that his apostolic calling came "by the will of God" reflected his conviction that Christ had called and empowered him for a special purpose. But Paul didn't see himself as set apart for a high office from which he could issue divine directives (see 1 Cor. 4:9). God had assigned him a task, not a status. Believers today, no matter what our vocation or station in life, are still called by God. In that calling we are to be holy—marked and set apart by the Spirit of God, and faithful—utterly obedient and persistent.

Colossians 1:3–14

📖 The thanksgiving theme is important to this letter, appearing in 1:3, 12, 2:7, 3:15–17, and 4:2. In verses 3–8 Paul gave thanks for three developments: (1) the Colossians' faithful acceptance of the gospel, expressed in their love for others; (2) the universal impact of the gospel as it influenced the whole world; and (3) the solid

foundation Epaphras had laid for them in the true gospel.

In verses 9–14 Paul prayed that God would fill the Colossians with the knowledge of his will through spiritual wisdom and discernment, and with the strength to obey that will—bearing fruit in good works, enduring with patient joy, and bringing pleasure to God. For Paul, understanding God's will involved recognizing how (1) Christ is the fulfillment of God's redemptive purposes (1:27; 2:2), (2) God's salvation is available to all people, and (3) God intends for Christians to live and serve in whatever situation they find themselves.

📖 Verses 10–12 list four behaviors pleasing to God: (1) "Bearing fruit in every good work"—good works reveal our spiritual health; (2) "growing in the knowledge of God"—knowing him leads us deeper into fulfilling his purposes; (3) "being strengthened with all power according to his glorious might"—resurrection power enables our obedience; and (4) "joyfully giving thanks"—gratitude for what God has done to shape our lives. Why not take an objective inventory of your own Christian life in these four critical areas. Are you faring better in some than in others?

The Supremacy of Christ

15 He is the image [b] of the invisible God, [c] the firstborn over all creation. 16 For by him all things were created: [d] things in heaven and on earth, visible and invisible, whether thrones or powers or rulers or authorities; [e] all things were created by him and for him. [f] 17 He is before all things, [g] and in him all things hold together. 18 And he is the head [h] of the body, the church; he is the beginning and the firstborn from among the dead, [i] so that in everything he might have the supremacy. 19 For God was pleased [j] to have all his fullness [k] dwell in him, 20 and through him to reconcile [l] to himself all things, whether things on earth or things in heaven, [m] by making peace through his blood, [n] shed on the cross.

21 Once you were alienated from God and were enemies [o] in your minds [p] because of [a] your evil behavior. 22 But now he has reconciled you by Christ's physical body [q] through death to present you holy in his sight, without blemish and free from ac-

[1:15]
[b] 2Co 4:4 [c] Jn 1:18
[1:16]
[d] Jn 1:3 [e] Eph 1:20, 21 [f] Ro 11:36
[1:17]
[g] Jn 1:2
[1:18]
[h] Eph 1:22
[i] Ac 26:23; Rev 1:5
[1:19]
[j] Eph 1:5 [k] Jn 1:16
[1:20]
[l] 2Co 5:18
[m] Eph 1:10
[n] Eph 2:13
[1:21]
[o] Ro 5:10 [p] Eph 2:3
[1:22]
[q] Ro 7:4

---

[a] 21 Or minds, as shown by

Colossians 1:15–23

 Many ancients felt forsaken by God. Their local gods seemed totally impotent before the might of Rome and lost in its vast and growing empire. How could such people stem the tide of chaos they believed was threatening to engulf their world?

Paul called Christ "the image of the invisible God." In Greek philosophy, an image wasn't distinct from the object it represented. As God's representation and representative, Christ clarified people's notions of God (1 Tim. 1:17; 6:16). In Christ believers see (1) who God is—Creator and Redeemer; (2) what he's like—a God of mercy and love; and (3) what he's done—sent his Son to rescue people from darkness and bring about the recon-

ciliation of all creation. Notice that God's character is completely consistent with his actions.

The mood of many people today parallels the despair in Paul's time. The anxiety of the ancients over their world's chaos is similar to our fears. God's gracious purposes for this world are being worked out. A merciful, loving God, not chance, determines our destiny.

We can witness to our world with its technological wizardry and terrors, with its great economic prosperity and despair, that our universe isn't godless. Jesus Christ has authority over all powers—political, spiritual, and natural. God has reconciled all things in heaven and on Earth through the cross.

Snapshots

1:19–20

Reconciliation

World War II brought Phil, an American soldier, to Iwo Jima to face the enemy. But when he saw Japanese prisoners behind barbed wire, Phil befriended them. After a massive landmine nearly killed him, Phil believed God had a special work for him to do—return to Japan—this time to share the peace of Christ.

Around the same time, a Japanese soldier named Ogata lay deeply depressed from losing his sight. When another Japanese man challenged him to follow Christ, Ogata despaired, "Why would God want me when I can't see?" When Ogata learned that this man also was blind, he trusted that God had plans for his life.

Ogata became a pastor and eventually met Phil. They served the Lord side-by-side for 30 years—quietly demonstrating the peace of Christ.

One summer, God used the two to tangibly demonstrate his reconciling power. As Ogata shared his wartime experiences, Phil stood by his side. "This man here was my mortal enemy. But God made him my brother in Christ, closer than my own family." Ogata threw his arm around Phil's shoulder—affection unthinkable in Japanese culture. The entire audience spontaneously stood up and cheered, affirming the truth so dramatically revealed.

> [The two men] served the Lord side-by-side for 30 years—quietly demonstrating the peace of Christ.

1:22
r Eph 5:27
1:23
s Eph 3:17 t ver 5
u Ro 10:18 v ver 25;
1Co 3:5

1:24
w 2Co 1:5
1:25
x ver 23 y Eph 3:2
1:26
z Ro 16:25

1:27
a Mt 13:11

1:28
b Col 3:16
c 1Co 2:6,7
d Eph 5:27
1:29
e 1Co 15:10
f Col 2:1 g Eph 1:19
2:1
h Col 1:29; 4:12
i Rev 1:11
2:2
j Col 4:8

2:3
k Ro 11:33;
1Co 1:24,30
2:4
l Ro 16:18
2:5
m 1Th 2:17
n 1Co 14:40
o 1Pe 5:9

2:6
p Col 1:10
2:7
q Eph 3:17

cusation[r]— 23if you continue in your faith, established[s] and firm, not moved from the hope[t] held out in the gospel. This is the gospel that you heard and that has been proclaimed to every creature under heaven,[u] and of which I, Paul, have become a servant.[v]

Paul's Labor for the Church

24Now I rejoice in what was suffered for you, and I fill up in my flesh what is still lacking in regard to Christ's afflictions,[w] for the sake of his body, which is the church. 25I have become its servant[x] by the commission God gave me[y] to present to you the word of God in its fullness— 26the mystery[z] that has been kept hidden for ages and generations, but is now disclosed to the saints. 27To them God has chosen to make known[a] among the Gentiles the glorious riches of this mystery, which is Christ in you, the hope of glory.

28We proclaim him, admonishing[b] and teaching everyone with all wisdom,[c] so that we may present everyone perfect[d] in Christ. 29To this end I labor,[e] struggling[f] with all his energy, which so powerfully works in me.[g]

2 I want you to know how much I am struggling[h] for you and for those at Laodicea,[i] and for all who have not met me personally. 2My purpose is that they may be encouraged in heart[j] and united in love, so that they may have the full riches of complete understanding, in order that they may know the mystery of God, namely, Christ, 3in whom are hidden all the treasures of wisdom and knowledge.[k] 4I tell you this so that no one may deceive you by fine-sounding arguments.[l] 5For though I am absent from you in body, I am present with you in spirit[m] and delight to see how orderly[n] you are and how firm[o] your faith in Christ is.

Freedom From Human Regulations Through Life With Christ

6So then, just as you received Christ Jesus as Lord,[p] continue to live in him, 7rooted[q] and built up in him, strengthened in the faith as you were taught, and overflowing with thankfulness.

Colossians 1:24—2:5

In the Colossians' pagan religious environment, the word *mystery* referred to rites and symbols hidden from the uninitiated. Paul used the word in a more Jewish sense (see "Here and Now," below). The mystery he referred to related to God's purposes, which can only be imparted by divine revelation. Humans, no matter how clever, can't know or discover such mystery on their own. In just seven words Paul summed up the secret of the cosmos, which all philosophers, sages, wise men, and religious seekers have pursued since the beginning—"Christ in you, the hope of glory."

Paul's use of "mystery" may confuse modern readers, who think in terms of a puzzle. His usage differed in three ways: (1) In the Old Testament, the "mystery" was kept hidden, but it has now been disclosed to the "saints" (likely all believers; cf. Eph. 3:3–9). (2) The word *mystery* in Jewish tradition meant God's secret plans for the last days. The "mystery" has to do with the assurance of being welcomed by God and enabled to experience life in all its fullness. (3) This mystery isn't found in complex philosophical truths, but in a Person. And this person isn't lost in history but is present among—and even in—us: Jesus Christ. Our goal is to see everyone made complete and whole in Christ.

Colossians 2:6–23

Since Christ is the fullness of God, argued Paul, and all believers are in him, they have all the fullness humans can possess. Boastful Corinthians faced the danger of thinking they had already arrived in Christ (1 Cor. 4:8). The opposite was true of the Colossians. Their opponents had tried to persuade them that the fullness they yearned for was unattainable. Paul countered that they already possessed in Christ all the completeness they could ever need.

A certain contingent in the Colossian church was promoting a philosophy of asceticism (strict self-denial as a form of spiritual discipline). Asceticism, countered Paul, is a futile attempt to defeat the flesh—and no match for the cross. Christianity is rooted in history, and the Colossians had "received" all the facts about salvation. Now they needed to allow these realities to permeate their souls and burst forth in thanksgiving to God. By doing so, they would become less vulnerable to the "put downs" and "come ons" of competing beliefs.

We can't be sure which "philosophy" Paul was attacking, but the text provides clues about its nature. We are wise to be wary of anything that: (1) judges and disqualifies others according to human measures; (2) substitutes sham battles for the real struggle with sin Jesus has already won for us; (3) makes subjective feelings or mysticism more important than Jesus' crucifixion and resurrection; (4) places more importance on divine intermediaries, like angels, than on Christ; or (5) cuts people off from Christ or his people.

[8]See to it that no one takes you captive through hollow and deceptive philosophy,[r] which depends on human tradition and the basic principles of this world[s] rather than on Christ.

[9]For in Christ all the fullness of the Deity lives in bodily form, [10]and you have been given fullness in Christ, who is the head[t] over every power and authority. [11]In him you were also circumcised,[u] in the putting off of the sinful nature,[a][v] not with a circumcision done by the hands of men but with the circumcision done by Christ, [12]having been buried with him in baptism and raised with him[w] through your faith in the power of God, who raised him from the dead.[x]

[13]When you were dead in your sins[y] and in the uncircumcision of your sinful nature,[b] God made you[c] alive with Christ. He forgave us all our sins, [14]having canceled the written code, with its regulations,[z] that was against us and that stood opposed to us; he took it away, nailing it to the cross.[a] [15]And having disarmed the powers and authorities,[b] he made a public spectacle of them, triumphing over them[c] by the cross.[d]

[16]Therefore do not let anyone judge you[d] by what you eat or drink,[e] or with regard to a religious festival,[f] a New Moon celebration[g] or a Sabbath day.[h] [17]These are a shadow of the things that were to come;[i] the reality, however, is found in Christ. [18]Do not let anyone who delights in false humility[j] and the worship of angels disqualify you for the prize.[k] Such a person goes into great detail about what he has seen, and his unspiritual mind puffs him up with idle notions. [19]He has lost connection with the Head,[l] from whom the whole body, supported and held together by its ligaments and sinews, grows as God causes it to grow.[m]

[20]Since you died with Christ to the basic principles of this world,[n] why, as though you still belonged to it, do you submit to its rules:[o] [21]"Do not handle! Do not taste! Do not touch!"? [22]These are all destined to perish[p] with use, because they are based on human commands and teachings.[q] [23]Such regulations indeed have an appearance of wisdom, with their self-imposed worship, their false humility and their harsh treatment of the body, but they lack any value in restraining sensual indulgence.

Rules for Holy Living

3 Since, then, you have been raised with Christ, set your hearts on things above, where Christ is seated at the right hand of God. [2]Set your minds on things above, not on earthly things.[r] [3]For you died,[s] and your life is now hidden with Christ in God. [4]When Christ, who is your[e] life, appears,[t] then you also will appear with him in glory.[u]

[5]Put to death, therefore, whatever belongs to your earthly nature: sexual immorality, impurity, lust, evil desires and greed,[v] which is idolatry.[w] [6]Because of these, the wrath of God[x] is coming.[f] [7]You used to walk in these ways, in the life you once lived.[y] [8]But now you must rid yourselves[z] of all such things as these: anger, rage, malice, slander,[a] and filthy language from your lips.[b] [9]Do not lie to each other,[c] since you have taken off your old self with its practices [10]and have put on the new self, which is being renewed[d] in knowledge in the image of its Creator.[e] [11]Here there

---

[a] 11 Or *the flesh*   [b] 13 Or *your flesh*   [c] 13 Some manuscripts *us*   [d] 15 Or *them in him*
[e] 4 Some manuscripts *our*   [f] 6 Some early manuscripts *coming on those who are disobedient*

2:8
r 1Ti 6:20 s Gal 4:3
2:10
t Eph 1:22
2:11
u Ro 2:29; Php 3:3
v Gal 5:24
2:12
w Ro 6:5 x Ac 2:24
2:13
y Eph 2:1,5
2:14
z Eph 2:15
a 1Pe 2:24
2:15
b Eph 6:12
c Lk 10:18
2:16
d Ro 14:3,4
e Ro 14:17
f Ro 14:5
g 1Ch 23:31
h Gal 4:10
2:17
i Heb 8:5
2:18
j ver 23 k Php 3:14
2:19
l Eph 1:22
m Eph 4:16
2:20
n Gal 4:3,9
o ver 14,16
2:22
p 1Co 6:13
q Isa 29:13;
Mt 15:9; Tit 1:14

3:2
r Php 3:19,20
3:3
s Ro 6:2; 2Co 5:14
3:4
t 1Co 1:7
u 1Pe 1:13; 1Jn 3:2
3:5
v Eph 5:3 w Eph 5:5
3:6
x Ro 1:18
3:7
y Eph 2:2
3:8
z Eph 4:22
a Eph 4:31
b Eph 4:29
3:9
c Eph 4:22,25
3:10
d Ro 12:2; Eph 4:23
e Eph 2:10

Colossians 3:1–17

Dying was for Paul the doorway to fullness of life. Christ doesn't just save our life; he *is* our life. To find that life we must allow his Spirit to put to death all that is contrary to Christ. There is no alternative. Being raised with Christ, both then and now, leads to new life for believers—a life that embraces people regardless of class or culture.

Being moral isn't identical to being Christian. Yet we can't claim to be Christian if we ignore morality. Our behavior as Christians becomes an advertisement of what being in Christ does in a person's life. Unbelievers should see a clear distinction in the way believers handle sexuality and anger, treat others from diverse backgrounds, and practice forgiveness and generosity. Once again Paul stressed the central truth that in Christ all the ethnic and social walls that divide people are broken down. Our community-creating love for people is one of the most persuasive proofs of the gospel to the world. Have you had the experience of encountering someone only briefly and "knowing" that person was a Christian? What clued you in?

3:11
f Ro 10:12
g 1Co 7:19
h Gal 3:28
i Eph 1:23
3:12
j Php 2:3 *k* 2Co 6:6;
Gal 5:22,23
3:13
l Eph 4:2
m Eph 4:32
3:14
n 1Co 13:1-13
o Eph 4:3
3:15
p Jn 14:27
3:16
q Ro 10:17
r Col 1:28
s Eph 5:19
3:17
t 1Co 10:31
u Eph 5:20

3:18
v Eph 5:22

is no Greek or Jew,*f* circumcised or uncircumcised,*g* barbarian, Scythian, slave or free,*h* but Christ is all,*i* and is in all.

12Therefore, as God's chosen people, holy and dearly loved, clothe yourselves with compassion, kindness, humility,*j* gentleness and patience.*k* 13Bear with each other*l* and forgive whatever grievances you may have against one another. Forgive as the Lord forgave you.*m* 14And over all these virtues put on love,*n* which binds them all together in perfect unity.*o*

15Let the peace of Christ*p* rule in your hearts, since as members of one body you were called to peace. And be thankful. 16Let the word of Christ*q* dwell in you richly as you teach and admonish one another with all wisdom,*r* and as you sing psalms, hymns and spiritual songs with gratitude in your hearts to God.*s* 17And whatever you do,*t* whether in word or deed, do it all in the name of the Lord Jesus, giving thanks*u* to God the Father through him.

Rules for Christian Households

18Wives, submit to your husbands,*v* as is fitting in the Lord. 19Husbands, love your wives and do not be harsh with them. 20Children, obey your parents in everything, for this pleases the Lord. 21Fathers, do not embitter your children, or they will become discouraged. 22Slaves, obey your earthly masters in everything; and do it, not only when their

---

Colossians 3:18—4:1

Paul's inclusion of instructions on home life served a theological function. The presence of these household rules drew attention to two truths: (1) Christ's lordship finds expression in the routine experiences of life, and (2) the call to the Colossians to set their minds on things above didn't allow them to brush aside family and social obligations.

The family is the place where, under Christ's

lordship, we learn to control our anger, rage, abusive language, and lying so that peace might reign (cf. 3:8–9,15). It's the first place where we learn to practice the virtues listed in 3:12–14. Do you also find it to be the most difficult place? If so, why? The new life enables submissiveness that puts others first, love that refuses to grow bitter or harsh, obedience, supportive and encouraging parenting, devotion to doing work well, and fairness and justice in dealing with others.

3:10

Our Story From Colossians 3

God designed humans to:

Obey him. "Put to death . . . whatever belongs to your earthly nature" (3:5).

Enjoy fellowship with him. "Your life is now hidden with Christ in God" (v. 3).

Represent him. "Whatever you do, whether in word or deed, do it all in the name of the Lord Jesus" (v. 17).

Imitate him. "Put on the new self, which is being renewed in knowledge in the image of its Creator" (v. 10).

Glorify him. "Sing psalms, hymns and spiritual songs with gratitude in your hearts to God" (v. 16).

We carry out these functions within our different spheres of influence:

Individuals	Couples	Families	Workplace ("slaves" and "masters")	Churches
"As God's chosen people, holy and dearly loved, clothe yourselves with compassion, kindness, humility, gentleness and patience" (v. 12).	"Wives, submit to your husbands, as is fitting in the Lord. Husbands, love your wives and do not be harsh with them" (vv. 18–19).	"Children, obey your parents in everything, for this pleases the Lord. Fathers, do not embitter your children, or they will become discouraged" (vv. 20–21).	"Whatever you do, work at it with all your heart, as working for the Lord, not for men . . . It is the Lord Christ you are serving . . . Masters, provide your slaves with what is right and fair, because you know that you also have a Master in heaven" (vv. 23,24; 4:1).	"Here there is no Greek or Jew . . . slave or free, but Christ is all, and is in all" (v. 11).

Source (for Five Spheres): Vardell (1998:470)

eye is on you and to win their favor, but with sincerity of heart and reverence for the Lord. [23] Whatever you do, work at it with all your heart, as working for the Lord, not for men, [24] since you know that you will receive an inheritance[w] from the Lord as a reward. It is the Lord Christ you are serving. [25] Anyone who does wrong will be repaid for his wrong, and there is no favoritism.[x]

4 Masters, provide your slaves with what is right and fair, because you know that you also have a Master in heaven.

Further Instructions

[2] Devote yourselves to prayer,[y] being watchful and thankful. [3] And pray for us, too, that God may open a door[z] for our message, so that we may proclaim the mystery of Christ, for which I am in chains.[a] [4] Pray that I may proclaim it clearly, as I should. [5] Be wise[b] in the way you act toward outsiders;[c] make the most of every opportunity.[d] [6] Let your conversation be always full of grace,[e] seasoned with salt,[f] so that you may know how to answer everyone.[g]

3:24
w Ac 20:32
3:25
x Ac 10:34

4:2
y Lk 18:1
4:3
z Ac 14:27
a Eph 6:19,20
4:5
b Eph 5:15
c Mk 4:11
d Eph 5:16
4:6
e Eph 4:29
f Mk 9:50
g 1Pe 3:15

Colossians 4:2–6

Paul's concluding words reveal his driving concern for the advancement of the gospel throughout the world. He asked the Colossian believers to pray not for his deliverance but that his work might be even more effective. We don't know how his prayers were answered, but we are aware that his imprisonment forced him to write letters that have blessed far more lives than he could ever have reached had he been free to speak in person.

Paul's admonitions apply directly to us. *Devoting ourselves to prayer* is a far cry from repeating in rote fashion a formula prayer or rattling off a shopping list of desires, dreams, or thoughtless requests. We too need to be attuned for God's responses, remembering to thank him specifically for his blessings. And we do well to be alert to the content and tone of even our casual conversations, "making the most of every opportunity" to help others encounter Christ.

 3:16

Bible Study

Paul advocated paying diligent attention to God's Word. For his original audience that meant the Old Testament and recollections, passed on orally, of Jesus' life and teachings. For us it means the whole Bible—both Old and New Testaments.

In 3:16, Paul seems to have suggested that some of this study be done in group settings, by "teach[ing] and admonish[ing] one another." Preparation for and leading a group Bible study might include these steps:

 **Preparation**

 Leading the Group

1. Ask for the Spirit's guidance in understanding the passage and preparing for fruitful discussion (John 16:13).

2. Read the passage.

3. Reread it, several times if necessary, focusing each time on a different aspect.

4. Read the passage in several different translations if possible. Make comparative notes you feel might enhance understanding.

5. List questions that occur to you or that might emerge from a reading of the passage.

6. Be prepared as much as possible with answers, using other texts, if necessary, for clarification of the issue(s). Bible dictionaries, commentaries, study guides, atlases, and so on can provide you with valuable information.

1. Begin on time.

2. Open with prayer. Ask for praise reports before prayer. This encourages an attitude of thanksgiving as you approach your time in the Word.

3. Ask for a volunteer to read the passage (1 Tim. 4:13). You may want to read and discuss it in sections.

4. Invite questions, reflections, and observations.

5. When questions arise, wait for answers from within the group. Resist the temptation to answer them yourself.

6. When discussion lags, introduce the questions that occurred to you in your preparation.

7. Encourage everyone to participate.

8. Receive all answers encouragingly. Expand on them or ask related, leading questions as appropriate.

9. If discussion goes off on a tangent, record the issue on a "parking lot" list and deal with it later.

10. As necessary, tactfully discourage talkative members from dominating. Calling on quieter individuals in a non-threatening way may resolve the problem. Setting a time limit for responses also can curb overly lengthy contributions.

11. Close with prayer. If participants share prayer requests, encourage them to write them down between meetings.

Final Greetings

4:7
h Ac 20:4
i Eph 6:21,22

4:8
j Eph 6:21,22
4:9
k Phm 10
4:10
l Ac 19:29
m Ac 4:36

4:12
n Col 1:7; Phm 23
o Ro 15:30
p 1Co 2:6

4:13
q Col 2:1
4:14
r 2Ti 4:11; Phm 24
s 2Ti 4:10
4:15
t Ro 16:5
4:16
u 2Th 3:14
4:17
v Phm 2 *w* 2Ti 4:5

4:18
x 1Co 16:21
y Heb 13:3
z 1Ti 6:21; 2Ti 4:22;
Tit 3:15; Heb 13:25

⁷Tychicus *h* will tell you all the news about me. He is a dear brother, a faithful minister and fellow servant *i* in the Lord. ⁸I am sending him to you for the express purpose that you may know about our *a* circumstances and that he may encourage your hearts. *j* ⁹He is coming with Onesimus, *k* our faithful and dear brother, who is one of you. They will tell you everything that is happening here.

¹⁰My fellow prisoner Aristarchus *l* sends you his greetings, as does Mark, the cousin of Barnabas. *m* (You have received instructions about him; if he comes to you, welcome him.) ¹¹Jesus, who is called Justus, also sends greetings. These are the only Jews among my fellow workers for the kingdom of God, and they have proved a comfort to me. ¹²Epaphras, *n* who is one of you and a servant of Christ Jesus, sends greetings. He is always wrestling in prayer for you, *o* that you may stand firm in all the will of God, mature *p* and fully assured. ¹³I vouch for him that he is working hard for you and for those at Laodicea *q* and Hierapolis. ¹⁴Our dear friend Luke, *r* the doctor, and Demas *s* send greetings. ¹⁵Give my greetings to the brothers at Laodicea, and to Nympha and the church in her house. *t*

¹⁶After this letter has been read to you, see that it is also read *u* in the church of the Laodiceans and that you in turn read the letter from Laodicea.

¹⁷Tell Archippus: *v* "See to it that you complete the work you have received in the Lord." *w*

¹⁸I, Paul, write this greeting in my own hand. *x* Remember *y* my chains. Grace be with you. *z*

ᵃ 8 Some manuscripts *that he may know about your*

Colossians 4:7–18

📖 Paul's list of coworkers reveals specifics about his ministry: (1) It was a team effort. (2) Paul inspired love and loyalty; any picture of him as an embattled and embittered loner is mistaken. (3) Early Christians relied on a network of friends.

📖 No one lives out the Christian life in a vacuum. No matter how high our profile, there are those tireless coworkers and assistants who come behind us. No matter how lowly our status, we may approach our calling with confidence, knowing we are indispensable links in God's chain of mercy. And underlying the entire process is the wonder of our absolute equality. Onesimus, the runaway slave, and Luke, the dear doctor, shared equal honor in Paul's affections and in God's sight.

INTRODUCTION TO
1 Thessalonians

AUTHOR
The apostle Paul wrote this letter.

DATE WRITTEN
Paul probably wrote this letter between A.D. 50 and 51.

ORIGINAL READERS
Paul wrote to the new believers in Thessalonica, a major military and commercial port located along the Egnatian Way (an important Roman road connecting Asia Minor with the Adriatic Sea). Thessalonica had a population of about 200,000, making it the largest city in Macedonia.

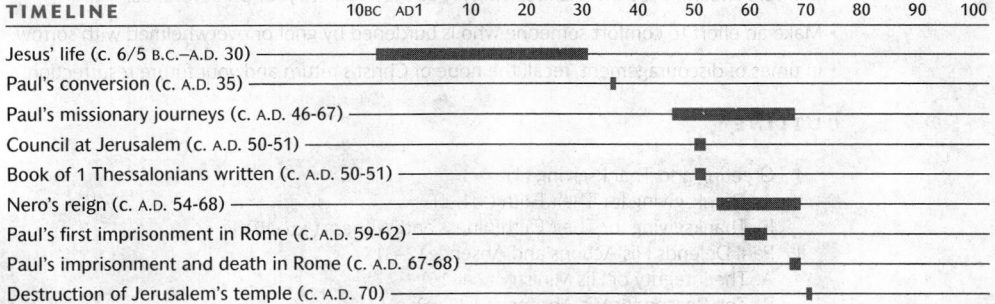

TIMELINE	10BC AD1	10	20	30	40	50	60	70	80	90	100
Jesus' life (c. 6/5 B.C.–A.D. 30)											
Paul's conversion (c. A.D. 35)											
Paul's missionary journeys (c. A.D. 46-67)											
Council at Jerusalem (c. A.D. 50-51)											
Book of 1 Thessalonians written (c. A.D. 50-51)											
Nero's reign (c. A.D. 54-68)											
Paul's first imprisonment in Rome (c. A.D. 59-62)											
Paul's imprisonment and death in Rome (c. A.D. 67-68)											
Destruction of Jerusalem's temple (c. A.D. 70)											

THEMES
Paul wrote this letter to express his joy in the Thessalonians' faith and to encourage them in the midst of persecution. His themes include:

1. *Persecution.* Paul applauded the Thessalonians for their progress in the faith and urged them to stay the course (4:1,10; 5:11). He also asserted that the trials believers endure because of their faith aren't just the chance happenings that occasionally arise. In a world hostile to the Christian message, suffering for the faith is to be expected: "You know quite well that we were destined for them" (3:3).

2. *Christ's return.* Paul assured the Thessalonians that believers who have died will be raised first at Christ's return. Regarding the time and date of this event, Paul likened it to the unexpected arrival of a thief in the night (5:2) and the certain, but often sudden, arrival of a baby (5:3). Believers are to be "alert and self-controlled" (5:6), not caught off guard when the Lord returns or entangled by worldly affairs in the interim.

3. *Christian living.* While believers await the Lord's coming, they are to live holy lives (4:1–12). They are not to engage in sexual immorality (4:3) but are to love each other, live quiet lives, respect the rights of others, and work to support themselves (4:9–12). They are to encourage

and help each other and be patient and kind to everyone (5:14). While a moral life isn't a pre-condition for acceptance by God, an immoral lifestyle is irreconcilable with being a Christian.

FAITH IN ACTION

The pages of 1 Thessalonians contain life lessons and role models of faith—people who challenge believers to put faith in action.

Role Models

- PAUL (2:1–2) shared the gospel with the Thessalonians "in spite of strong opposition." Have you ever sensed opposition to the gospel message from your family, friends, or community? What is your best course of action when faced with insults and ridicule?

- TIMOTHY (3:2) was sent to the Thessalonians to strengthen and encourage them. Who can you strengthen and encourage this week?

- THE THESSALONIANS (1:6; 3:9) welcomed the message of the gospel despite "severe suffering" and brought great joy to Paul because of their strong faith in the face of persecution. Have you considered how your faith can be a blessing to someone else who needs encouragement?

Challenges

- Suffering is a normal part of the Christian life (3:3). Evaluate your expectations of life. Are they realistic? Are you surprised when life becomes difficult? Work to realign your thinking so it conforms to this Biblical view of the Christian life.

- If you are going through a time of suffering, mentally picture your loved ones and spiritual mentors cheering you on and receiving joy as they witness your perseverance.

- Make an effort to comfort someone who is burdened by grief or overwhelmed with sorrow.

- In times of discouragement, recall the hope of Christ's return and your future resurrection.

OUTLINE

I. Greeting and Thanksgiving (1)
   A. Thanksgiving for Their Faith (1:1–4)
   B. Thanksgiving for Their Faithfulness and Witness (1:5–10)
II. Paul Defends His Actions and Absence (2–3)
   A. The Integrity of His Ministry (2:1–16)
   B. The Reason for His Absence (2:17—3:10)
   C. Prayer (3:11–13)
III. Exhortations (4:1—5:22)
   A. Live to Please God (4:1–12)
   B. Take Hope in the Promise of Christ's Coming (4:13—5:11)
   C. Final Instructions (5:12–22)
IV. Concluding Prayer, Greeting, and Benediction (5:23–28)

1:1
a Ac 16:1; 2Th 1:1
b Ac 17:1 *c* Ro 1:7

1 Paul, Silas*a* and Timothy,*a*

To the church of the Thessalonians*b* in God the Father and the Lord Jesus Christ: Grace and peace to you.*b c*

a 1 Greek *Silvanus,* a variant of *Silas*   *b 1* Some early manuscripts *you from God our Father and the Lord Jesus Christ*

---

1 Thessalonians 1:1
📖 This verse forms a complete unit, the "prescript" or introduction. It identifies the senders and re-cipients and conveys Paul's expression of goodwill. This is the simplest and most culturally typical opening of all Paul's letters.

Thanksgiving for the Thessalonians' Faith

2We always thank God for all of you,[d] mentioning you in our prayers. 3We continually remember before our God and Father your work produced by faith,[e] your labor prompted by love, and your endurance inspired by hope in our Lord Jesus Christ.

4For we know, brothers loved by God, that he has chosen you, 5because our gospel[f] came to you not simply with words, but also with power, with the Holy Spirit and with deep conviction. You know how we lived among you for your sake. 6You became imitators of us[g] and of the Lord; in spite of severe suffering,[h] you welcomed the message with the joy given by the Holy Spirit.[i] 7And so you became a model to all the believers in Macedonia and Achaia. 8The Lord's message rang out from you not only in Macedonia and Achaia—your faith in God has become known everywhere.[j] Therefore we do not need to say anything about it, 9for they themselves report what kind of reception you gave us. They tell how you turned to God from idols[k] to serve the living and true God, 10and to wait for his Son from heaven, whom he raised from the dead[l]—Jesus, who rescues us from the coming wrath.[m]

Paul's Ministry in Thessalonica

2 You know, brothers, that our visit to you[n] was not a failure. 2We had previously suffered[o] and been insulted in Philippi, as you know, but with the help of

The Church in Thessalonica (1:1)

Then: Thessalonica was a thriving metropolis of 200,000.
Now: The city still exists as the Macedonian city of Thessalonika, population 750,000.

1:2 [d] Ro 1:8
1:3 [e] 2Th 1:11
1:5 [f] 2Th 2:14
1:6 [g] 1Co 4:16 [h] Ac 17:5-10 [i] Ac 13:52
1:8 [j] Ro 1:8; 10:18
1:9 [k] 1Co 12:2; Gal 4:8
1:10 [l] Ac 2:24 [m] Ro 5:9
2:1 [n] 1Th 1:5,9
2:2 [o] Ac 16:22; Php 1:30

Paul's primary emphasis in his prescript seems to have been the centrality and importance of God for the life of the church. The phrases and words he linked together remind us that the church has no life apart from God's saving work in Christ. This work is rooted in God's grace and results in "peace" (a restored relationship) with God. The gift of the Spirit evidences this.

Over against the self-centeredness of our culture stands Paul's opening verse, with its emphasis on God and Jesus. The church wouldn't even exist apart from God's saving work in Christ. It's not just another organization designed to meet our needs. It's nothing less than the people of God. As such, we are called together by him for his worship and glory, commissioned to spread his Good News and infiltrate the world in his name as channels of his mercy and goodness. Is this a good description of your local congregation/fellowship?

1 Thessalonians 1:2–10

In his opening thanksgiving, Paul alluded to several themes that would arise later in the letter: love for fellow believers (4:9–10), hope for the future (4:13—5:11), advice about the Holy Spirit and prophecy (5:19–22), holiness (4:3–8), and watchfulness (5:1–11).

The familiar trio of faith, love, and hope (cf. 1 Cor. 13:13) functioned for Paul as a shorthand summary of the essentials of Christianity. *Faith* is the assurance that God has acted in Christ to save his people. *Love* is the present expression and experience of the restored relationship between God and his people. And *hope* is the

confidence that "he who began a good work in you will carry it on to completion" (Phil. 1:6).

Paul's descriptions of this congregation touch on several important points. This was a community (1) rooted in God's grace, love, and election (see chart at Romans 1:17 for theological definitions); (2) committed to Jesus Christ; (3) empowered by the Holy Spirit; (4) bearing witness to the gospel; (5) characterized by faith, love, and hope; and (6) clearly different from that of other religions. What is your definition of a Christian "community"? How is it similar to or different from the one Paul described?

1 Thessalonians 2:1–16

In verses 1–12 Paul mentioned four of his own attitudes and behaviors he wanted the Thessalonians (and all Christians) to imitate. Paul had modeled a clear sense of (1) correct priorities, (2) concern for the integrity of the gospel, (3) love and commitment for those to whom he had ministered, and (4) the goal toward which he was working.

Some readers have concluded from verses 13–16 that Paul was anti-Semitic. But his comments expressed a theological disagreement with some Jews about the identity of the Messiah, not an attack on an entire category of people (to which he belonged). His words also must be taken together with other passages (e.g., Rom. 9–11) for a fuller understanding of his viewpoint. Finally, this passage was a *description* of certain opponents at a given point in time, not a *prescription* for the attitudes of other Christians in other times and circumstances.

2:3
p 2Co 2:17
2:4
q Gal 2:7 *r* Gal 1:10
2:5
s Ac 20:33 *t* Ro 1:9

2:6
u 1Co 9:1,2
2:7
v ver 11

2:8
w 2Co 12:15;
1Jn 3:16
2:9
x Ac 18:3 *y* 2Th 3:8
2:10
z 1Th 1:5
a 2Co 1:12
2:11
b ver 7; 1Co 4:14
2:12
c Eph 4:1
2:13
d 1Th 1:2
e Heb 4:12

2:14
f Gal 1:22
g Ac 17:5; 2Th 1:4
2:15
h Ac 2:23 *i* Mt 5:12

2:16
j Ac 13:45,50
k Mt 23:32

2:17
l 1Co 5:3; Col 2:5
m 1Th 3:10
2:18
n Mt 4:10
o Ro 1:13; 15:22
2:19
p Php 4:1
q 2Co 1:14
r Mt 16:27;
1Th 3:13
2:20
s 2Co 1:14

our God we dared to tell you his gospel in spite of strong opposition. [3]For the appeal we make does not spring from error or impure motives,[p] nor are we trying to trick you. [4]On the contrary, we speak as men approved by God to be entrusted with the gospel.[q] We are not trying to please men[r] but God, who tests our hearts. [5]You know we never used flattery, nor did we put on a mask to cover up greed[s]—God is our witness.[t] [6]We were not looking for praise from men, not from you or anyone else.

As apostles[u] of Christ we could have been a burden to you, [7]but we were gentle among you, like a mother caring for her little children.[v] [8]We loved you so much that we were delighted to share with you not only the gospel of God but our lives as well,[w] because you had become so dear to us. [9]Surely you remember, brothers, our toil and hardship; we worked[x] night and day in order not to be a burden to anyone[y] while we preached the gospel of God to you.

[10]You are witnesses,[z] and so is God, of how holy,[a] righteous and blameless we were among you who believed. [11]For you know that we dealt with each of you as a father deals with his own children,[b] [12]encouraging, comforting and urging you to live lives worthy[c] of God, who calls you into his kingdom and glory.

[13]And we also thank God continually[d] because, when you received the word of God,[e] which you heard from us, you accepted it not as the word of men, but as it actually is, the word of God, which is at work in you who believe. [14]For you, brothers, became imitators of God's churches in Judea,[f] which are in Christ Jesus: You suffered from your own countrymen[g] the same things those churches suffered from the Jews, [15]who killed the Lord Jesus[h] and the prophets[i] and also drove us out. They displease God and are hostile to all men [16]in their effort to keep us from speaking to the Gentiles[j] so that they may be saved. In this way they always heap up their sins to the limit.[k] The wrath of God has come upon them at last.[a]

Paul's Longing to See the Thessalonians

[17]But, brothers, when we were torn away from you for a short time (in person, not in thought),[l] out of our intense longing we made every effort to see you.[m] [18]For we wanted to come to you—certainly I, Paul, did, again and again—but Satan[n] stopped us.[o] [19]For what is our hope, our joy, or the crown[p] in which we will glory[q] in the presence of our Lord Jesus when he comes?[r] Is it not you? [20]Indeed, you are our glory[s] and joy.

a 16 Or them fully

It's a healthful exercise for church members and those involved in humanitarian efforts to step back periodically and ask: Why are we offering this program, or why are we involved in this activity? Too often programs that once started with a clear goal continue on because of habit, or just because "that's the way we've always done things." Well-defined goals can help us assess and perhaps redirect our efforts.

Christians should continue to insist that discrimination is wrong. Prejudice against, hostility toward, or attacks on any group simply because they share a common set of racial, ethnic, social, cultural, religious, or genetic characteristics is blatant sin.

1 Thessalonians 2:17—3:5

A theme throughout this letter, but especially in 2:17—3:13, is that of friendship. Here we see a reflection of Paul's deep concern for the Thessalonians, setting the stage for the advice and appeals to follow in chapters 4–5. In Paul's day, a "superior" could write a letter of friendship to an "inferior" as a basis for making a request. Thus Paul's words not only expressed to the Thessalonians his feelings for them but also prepared the way for the rest of his letter.

Christians living as a minority in a culture whose controlling values are opposed to the gospel can expect persecution. The situation in the West is complex. While a majority of the population claims to be Christian, some of society's most dominant and deeply held values clearly aren't. Moreover, in certain broadly influential subcultures, like the academic community, the news and entertainment industry, and the arts, Christians are clearly outnumbered, and their voices are too often squelched and snubbed.

An honest employee is fired for blowing the whistle on corruption. A law enforcement officer is ostracized because he refuses to cover up the misconduct of another officer. A young Christian is excluded from family activities because she's embarrassed family members by working in the inner city rather than taking a "good job." Teenagers lose social status for taking a stand against alcohol, drugs, or sexual promiscuity. Families who resist a consumer mentality are rejected by neighbors and friends. What forms has persecution taken for you?

3 So when we could stand it no longer,[t] we thought it best to be left by ourselves in Athens.[u] 2We sent Timothy, who is our brother and God's fellow worker[a] in spreading the gospel of Christ, to strengthen and encourage you in your faith, 3so that no one would be unsettled by these trials. You know quite well that we were destined for them.[v] 4In fact, when we were with you, we kept telling you that we would be persecuted. And it turned out that way, as you well know.[w] 5For this reason, when I could stand it no longer,[x] I sent to find out about your faith. I was afraid that in some way the tempter[y] might have tempted you and our efforts might have been useless.[z]

Timothy's Encouraging Report

6But Timothy has just now come to us from you[a] and has brought good news about your faith and love.[b] He has told us that you always have pleasant memories of us and that you long to see us, just as we also long to see you. 7Therefore, brothers, in all our distress and persecution we were encouraged about you because of your faith. 8For now we really live, since you are standing firm[c] in the Lord. 9How can we thank God enough for you[d] in return for all the joy we have in the presence of our God because of you? 10Night and day we pray[e] most earnestly that we may see you again[f] and supply what is lacking in your faith.

11Now may our God and Father himself and our Lord Jesus clear the way for us to come to you. 12May the Lord make your love increase and overflow for each other[g] and for everyone else, just as ours does for you. 13May he strengthen your hearts so that you will be blameless[h] and holy in the presence of our God and Father when our Lord Jesus comes[i] with all his holy ones.

Living to Please God

4 Finally, brothers,[j] we instructed you how to live in order to please God,[k] as in fact you are living. Now we ask you and urge you in the Lord Jesus to do this more and more. 2For you know what instructions we gave you by the authority of the Lord Jesus.

3It is God's will that you should be sanctified: that you should avoid sexual immorality;[l] 4that each of you should learn to control his own body[b][m] in a way that

---

[a] 2 Some manuscripts *brother and fellow worker;* other manuscripts *brother and God's servant*
[b] 4 Or *learn to live with his own wife;* or *learn to acquire a wife*

3:1
[t] ver 5 [u] Ac 17:15
3:3
[v] Ac 9:16; 14:22
3:4
[w] 1Th 2:14
3:5
[x] ver 1 [y] Mt 4:3
[z] Gal 2:2; Php 2:16
3:6
[a] Ac 18:5 [b] 1Th 1:3
3:8
[c] 1Co 16:13
3:9
[d] 1Th 1:2
3:10
[e] 2Ti 1:3 [f] 1Th 2:17
3:12
[g] 1Th 4:9,10
3:13
[h] 1Co 1:8
[i] 1Th 2:19
4:1
[j] 2Co 13:11
[k] 2Co 5:9
4:3
[l] 1Co 6:18
4:4
[m] 1Co 7:2,9

---

1 Thessalonians 3:6–13

Paul had sent Timothy to inquire about the Thessalonians' "faith" (v. 5) but had received a bonus in Timothy's report: a commendation of both their "faith and love" (v. 6). "What is lacking" in their faith was most likely Paul's reference to instruction they still needed, perhaps on specific points of doctrine and conduct—not to some kind of spiritual or ethical defect.

The God-centered emphasis of Paul's prayer calls attention to the tension that runs throughout the letter between divine activity and human responsibility (cf. v. 12 with 4:10). Paul emphasized God's grace and initiative but never ceased to instruct his audience (see 5:12–22, with its 17 commands). For Paul, the emphasis lay with God's prior action, followed by their response as an outworking or expression of their faith.

Paul's prayer in verses 9–13 offers us a model, suggesting at least four ways we can go about interceding for other Christians: (1) with thanksgiving, (2) that they might be strengthened through their loving service, (3) from an eternal perspective, and (4) out of our deep and sincere love for them. Why not take a moment to pray for someone who is on your heart today, making sure to incorporate these steps?

1 Thessalonians 4:1–12

A wide range of sexual values and practices existed in Paul's day in Greek and Roman society. For Paul, sexual activity wasn't just an insignificant, private function involving consenting adults. It impacted a person's relationship both with God (cf. 1 Cor. 6:12–20) and with other people (1 Thess. 4:6). Sexual behavior as God intended it was and is a matter of giving to, not taking from. Paul offered people from diverse backgrounds a sexual standard based on what they shared—a relationship with God.

Paul sought to establish clear standards of community conduct (holiness and honor) and to promote a community attitude among believers. He consistently used insider/outsider language: e.g., "brothers" (a term for men and women within the Christian community) versus those "who do not know God." In this way he encouraged a sense of congregational identity and established a clear boundary between the church and the larger culture.

Paul believed that genuine love and concern for others influence—even determine—individual decisions. His words challenge us to reconsider what it means to love our neighbor in light of two closely related choices:

4:5
n Ro 1:26
o Eph 4:17
4:6
p 1Co 6:8
q Heb 13:4
4:7
r Lev 11:44;
1Pe 1:15
4:8
s Ro 5:5; Gal 4:6
4:9
t Ro 12:10
u 1Th 5:1
v Jn 13:34
4:10
w 1Th 1:7
x 1Th 3:12
4:11
y Eph 4:28;
2Th 3:10-12
4:12
z Mk 4:11
4:13
a Eph 2:12
4:14
b 1Co 15:18
4:15
c 1Co 15:52
4:16
d Mt 24:31
e 1Co 15:23;
2Th 2:1
4:17
f 1Co 15:52
g Ac 1:9; Rev 11:12
h Jn 12:26
5:1
i Ac 1:7 / 1Th 4:9
5:2
k 1Co 1:8
l 2Pe 3:10
5:4
m Ac 26:18; 1Jn 2:8
5:6
n Ro 13:11

is holy and honorable, [5] not in passionate lust[n] like the heathen, [o] who do not know God; [6] and that in this matter no one should wrong his brother or take advantage of him. [p] The Lord will punish men for all such sins, [q] as we have already told you and warned you. [7] For God did not call us to be impure, but to live a holy life. [r] [8] Therefore, he who rejects this instruction does not reject man but God, who gives you his Holy Spirit. [s]

[9] Now about brotherly love[t] we do not need to write to you, [u] for you yourselves have been taught by God to love each other. [v] [10] And in fact, you do love all the brothers throughout Macedonia. [w] Yet we urge you, brothers, to do so more and more. [x]

[11] Make it your ambition to lead a quiet life, to mind your own business and to work with your hands, [y] just as we told you, [12] so that your daily life may win the respect of outsiders[z] and so that you will not be dependent on anybody.

The Coming of the Lord

[13] Brothers, we do not want you to be ignorant about those who fall asleep, or to grieve like the rest of men, who have no hope. [a] [14] We believe that Jesus died and rose again and so we believe that God will bring with Jesus those who have fallen asleep in him. [b] [15] According to the Lord's own word, we tell you that we who are still alive, who are left till the coming of the Lord, will certainly not precede those who have fallen asleep. [c] [16] For the Lord himself will come down from heaven, with a loud command, with the voice of the archangel and with the trumpet call of God, [d] and the dead in Christ will rise first. [e] [17] After that, we who are still alive and are left[f] will be caught up together with them in the clouds[g] to meet the Lord in the air. And so we will be with the Lord[h] forever. [18] Therefore encourage each other with these words.

5 Now, brothers, about times and dates[i] we do not need to write to you, [j] [2] for you know very well that the day of the Lord[k] will come like a thief in the night. [l] [3] While people are saying, "Peace and safety," destruction will come on them suddenly, as labor pains on a pregnant woman, and they will not escape.

[4] But you, brothers, are not in darkness[m] so that this day should surprise you like a thief. [5] You are all sons of the light and sons of the day. We do not belong to the night or to the darkness. [6] So then, let us not be like others, who are asleep, [n] but let us be alert and self-controlled. [7] For those who sleep, sleep at night, and those

---

our occupation and our spending habits. His words invite hard questions: Is accumulating wealth more important to me than working to serve others? What would it mean for me to make spending decisions based on "brotherly love"? Take a moment to review Jesus' words in Luke 12:48 about people to whom much has been given.

1 Thessalonians 4:13—5:11

In considering Paul's words in 4:13–18, it's helpful to remember that: (1) he was dealing with a fairly narrow question—the fate of believers who died before Christ's return. (2) His expectations of what God and Jesus would do in the future were grounded in what they had done in the past. (3) He wrote for the sake of the living, to show that what Christians believe ought to shape how they live, even in the face of death. (4) His purpose wasn't to answer all questions but to equip the Thessalonians to encourage one another.

In 5:1–11 Paul also made several points: (1) No one knows when the "day of the Lord" will come. (2) To unbelievers, Christ's return will be absolutely unexpected. (3) Believers have security of salvation based on the death (and, by implication, resurrection) of Jesus. (4) For them, Christ's second coming will mean life together

with him. (5) Christians are to stay alert and disciplined, encouraging and building each other up in faith, hope, and love.

People are naturally curious about the future. Add God to the mix, and it's easy to understand why conjecture about Jesus' return is so attractive. There are, though, negative aspects associated with this fascination. Speculation (1) about when Jesus will return is largely a waste of time (Matt. 24:36,42); (2) about dates can lead to behavior that brings ridicule to the gospel; (3) feeds the development of a crisis mentality with regard to Jesus' return; and (4) keeps some Christians from fully engaging in the present.

Behind the intense interest in our day in death and its aftermath lies a personal concern: What will happen to *me* when I die? The Thessalonian Christians' version of that question was: What will happen to me if I die before Jesus comes back? There are at least two aspects of Paul's answer that need emphasis today: The future of believers (being "with the Lord forever") isn't about a place but a relationship, and death for us isn't an end but a transition to eternity with the Lord.

Holiness and the Poor

 4:9–12

On December 17, 2001, the Fifth Avenue Presbyterian Church went to federal court to stop the police from enforcing a new policy of ejecting homeless people from its property. That church is located amid some of the most exclusive stores and hotels in New York City. It asked for an emergency order to protect the 20 to 30 people sleeping nightly on its steps. It operates a homeless shelter, but its license limits occupancy to 10. Since many other homeless people began sleeping on the premises, the congregation decided to make them welcome. They couldn't house them within the church, but they provided them with space, bathrooms, and a place to warm up in the morning. But in the middle of the night on December 4, police arrived and gave these hapless people the choice of leaving, going to a city shelter, or being arrested.

Peter described the church as God's "chosen people, a royal priesthood, a holy nation" (1 Peter 2:9). And Paul assumed its members understood the need to care for others: "About brotherly love we do not need to write to you, for you yourselves have been taught by God to love each other" (1 Thess. 4:9). If there is no obvious difference between Christians and non-Christians, something's seriously wrong. One way Scripture describes the difference is holiness. Peter made the case dramatically: "Just as he who called you is holy, so be holy in all you do" (1 Peter 1:15).

There are no exceptions to the call. Every Christian from every nation is called to be holy. Scripture's witness is that salvation in Christ isn't limited to forgiveness of sins. It also has the power to break sin's control in our lives and conform us into the likeness of Christ. Jesus wants disciples, not admirers (see Rom. 8:29).

Holiness isn't optional for Christians. There should be about us something distinctive in the way we work, rear our children, relate to our parents, witness and share the gospel, spend our money, care for the poor and oppressed. There should be something distinctive in our personal morality and ethical commitments.

According to recent United Nations studies, on an average day 34,000 children under five die of hunger or preventable diseases related to malnutrition. Eight hundred million people around the globe are undernourished, among them 160 million children five years old or younger.

Seventy percent of the world's poor are women. Since they are the primary caregivers of children in most of the world, their children also are poor and hungry. We haven't solved the problem of undernourished children, even in a developed country like the United States, where 31 million are "food-insecure," according to the United Nations, and 10 million chronically hungry. In 1998, 13.8 million families with children in the United States received food stamps.

> In our passion to scrub ourselves clean, we often narrow the scope of Christian concern.

John Wesley stated, "The gospel of Christ knows no religion but social, no holiness but social." Holiness demands that we pay attention to the poor and oppressed. Unfortunately, we too easily restrict our understanding of the call to holiness to personal morality. In our passion to scrub ourselves clean, we often narrow the scope of Christian concern. We know from the Old Testament prophets that God enacted fearsome judgment on a people who would "sell the poor for a pair of shoes" (Amos 2:6). We also know from Jesus himself that our judgment will be based on our response to "the least of these" (Matt. 25:40).

Maxie Dunnam, chancellor of Asbury Theological Seminary in Wilmore, Kentucky

5:7
o Ac 2:15; 2Pe 2:13
5:8
p Eph 6:14
q Ro 8:24
r Eph 6:17
5:9
s 2Th 2:13,14
5:10
t 2Co 5:15

5:12
u 1Ti 5:17;
Heb 13:17
5:13
v Mk 9:50
5:14
w 2Th 3:6,7,11
x Ro 14:1
5:15
y 1Pe 3:9
z Gal 6:10;
Eph 4:32
5:16
a Php 4:4
5:19
b Eph 4:30
5:20
c 1Co 14:1-40
5:21
d 1Co 14:29;
1Jn 4:1
5:23
e Ro 15:33
5:24
f 1Co 1:9
5:25
g Eph 6:19
5:26
h Ro 16:16
5:27
i Col 4:16
5:28
j Ro 16:20

who get drunk, get drunk at night. *o* 8But since we belong to the day, let us be self-controlled, putting on faith and love as a breastplate, *p* and the hope of salvation *q* as a helmet. *r* 9For God did not appoint us to suffer wrath but to receive salvation through our Lord Jesus Christ. *s* 10He died for us so that, whether we are awake or asleep, we may live together with him. *t* 11Therefore encourage one another and build each other up, just as in fact you are doing.

Final Instructions

12Now we ask you, brothers, to respect those who work hard among you, who are over you in the Lord *u* and who admonish you. 13Hold them in the highest regard in love because of their work. Live in peace with each other. *v* 14And we urge you, brothers, warn those who are idle, *w* encourage the timid, help the weak, *x* be patient with everyone. 15Make sure that nobody pays back wrong for wrong, *y* but always try to be kind to each other *z* and to everyone else.

16Be joyful always; *a* 17pray continually; 18give thanks in all circumstances, for this is God's will for you in Christ Jesus.

19Do not put out the Spirit's fire; *b* 20do not treat prophecies *c* with contempt. 21Test everything. *d* Hold on to the good. 22Avoid every kind of evil.

23May God himself, the God of peace, *e* sanctify you through and through. May your whole spirit, soul and body be kept blameless at the coming of our Lord Jesus Christ. 24The one who calls you is faithful *f* and he will do it.

25Brothers, pray for us. *g* 26Greet all the brothers with a holy kiss. *h* 27I charge you before the Lord to have this letter read to all the brothers. *i*

28The grace of our Lord Jesus Christ be with you. *j*

---

1 Thessalonians 5:12–28

Verses 12–22 were first directed to the community. This isn't to suggest they had nothing to say to individuals—just that this application was indirect. Paul was trying to develop in the entire congregation a sense of responsibility toward leaders (vv. 12–13), individuals (vv. 14–15), God (vv. 16–18), and the Spirit (vv. 19–22).

Paul reminded his audience in verse 23 that sanctification (the process of growing in holiness) is both a gift and a goal. It's a gift of grace: At conversion believers have already passed from death to life and are new creations in Christ (2 Cor. 5:17), in whom they stand before God blamelessly. Yet it's also a goal (cf. 3:13) they are called to live out in their daily lives.

Most of the time we are "nice" to one another and coexist without open strife. But do you at times catch yourself placing a higher value on superficial harmony than on genuine peace? Do you try so hard not to upset or disturb someone else that you avoid the hard work it takes to maintain a relationship? Paul's command to live in peace with one another refers not just to the absence of conflict but to the presence of positive, healthy relationships.

Paul's closing verses invite us to reflect on a theme that has been running beneath the surface throughout his letter. And he restated another theme that has been clear since his opening verse. The first is the importance of remembering what God has done, the second the centrality of God for the life of the church.

5:18

An Attitude of GRATITUDE

Is the Biblical injunction to be thankful *in* (not necessarily *for*) all circumstances (5:18) realistic? Modern studies seem to point in that direction. Studies of people who score high on measures of gratitude show that they are able to distill lessons even from bad experiences for which they are appreciative:

Opportunities: An attitude of gratitude helps people see beyond tragedies to opportunities.

Skills: Difficult circumstances force people to develop life skills, for which gratitude is appropriate.

Blessing: The ability to perceive and identify blessings is a wonderful strength only humans can possess.

Contrast Effects: A harsh winter makes an individual more grateful for a mild spring.

Ways of Coping: Gratitude is an effective way of dealing with stressful life situations.

"Redemption Sequences": Gratitude can make the telling of life stories move naturally from trying times to triumphant times.

Mental Flexibility: Grateful people are less defensive and more open to life.

Source: Snyder (2002:467)

INTRODUCTION TO

2 Thessalonians

AUTHOR
The apostle Paul is the letter's stated author (1:1; 3:17).

DATE WRITTEN
Second Thessalonians was probably written in A.D. 51 or 52, shortly after 1 Thessalonians
(see 2:15).

ORIGINAL READERS
Paul wrote this letter to the new believers in Thessalonica, a major military and commercial
port located along the Egnatian Way (an important Roman road connecting Asia Minor with
the Adriatic Sea). Thessalonica had a population of about 200,000, making it the largest city in
Macedonia.

TIMELINE

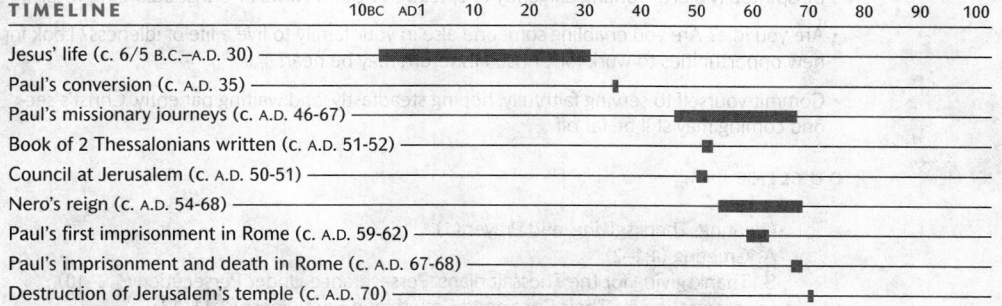

	10BC AD1	10	20	30	40	50	60	70	80	90	100
Jesus' life (c. 6/5 B.C.–A.D. 30)											
Paul's conversion (c. A.D. 35)											
Paul's missionary journeys (c. A.D. 46-67)											
Book of 2 Thessalonians written (c. A.D. 51-52)											
Council at Jerusalem (c. A.D. 50-51)											
Nero's reign (c. A.D. 54-68)											
Paul's first imprisonment in Rome (c. A.D. 59-62)											
Paul's imprisonment and death in Rome (c. A.D. 67-68)											
Destruction of Jerusalem's temple (c. A.D. 70)											

THEMES
Second Thessalonians includes the following themes:

1. *Christ's return.* Some of the Thessalonians had developed an unhealthy anxiety about
Christ's return and had been duped by those who claimed it had already occurred (2:2). Paul
stated that Christ's coming will be preceded by the arrival of an antichrist figure, who will unleash a season of unprecedented hostility to God, incite widespread rebellion, and delude
many through satanic signs and wonders. He will be a self-deifying figure who will exalt himself over other deities, seek to destroy Christ's work, and beguile those who are perishing
(2:4–12).

2. *Vigilance until Christ's return.* Paul reminded the church that it had been chosen for salvation through sanctification by God and must stand firm to the end (2:13–17). Since God will
inflict vengeance on those who afflict the faithful, Christians are to wait patiently and faithfully
for Christ's return. The end could come at any time, and Paul called his audience (and us) to
be spiritually vigilant. Watchfulness has nothing to do with calculating the precise moment of

Christ's coming. It's expressed by diligent work for Christ. Attentive Christians will persevere by faith, love, and hope. Paul admonished idlers (3:11) who were making a nuisance of themselves to other Christians and tainting the church's reputation in the community. Christians aren't to be idle while they await the Lord's return.

FAITH IN ACTION

The pages of 2 Thessalonians are filled with life lessons and role models of faith—people who challenge believers to put faith in action.

Role Models

• SILAS (1:1), mentioned here (and in 1 Thess. 1:1), was on the ministry team with Paul and Timothy. Do you partner with others in ministry? How are teams useful in spreading the gospel today? In what ways are you a team player?

• THE THESSALONIANS (1:3–4) were praised by Paul for their growing faith, increasing love, and perseverance in the face of persecution. How can they be an example to you?

• PAUL (3:1–5) continued to spread the gospel despite opposition (3:1–5). Does opposition or ridicule tempt you to keep the Good News to yourself? How can your endurance be a testimony to others?

Challenges

• If you are not part of a ministry team, join one. If you haven't been active in your team lately, determine to reengage and be a contributing member. Teams are most effective when all members pull their weight.

• Evaluate your attitudes about the nearness of Christ's return. Determine to have a balanced view of that great, anticipated event.

• Be spiritually alert, working diligently to spread the Good News of Christ before his return.

• Are you idle? Are you enabling someone else in your family to live a life of idleness? Look for new opportunities to work for Christ. His return may be near!

• Commit yourself to serving faithfully, hoping steadfastly, and waiting patiently. Christ's second coming may still be far off.

OUTLINE

I. Greeting, Thanksgiving, and Prayer (1)
  A. Greeting (1:1–2)
  B. Thanksgiving for the Thessalonians' Perseverance Under Persecution (1:3–10)
  C. Intercession for Their Continued Growth and Fruitfulness (1:11–12)
II. Instruction Regarding Jesus' Coming and Christian Conduct (2)
  A. The Role of the Man of Lawlessness (2:1–12)
  B. Admonition to Stand Firm (2:13–15)
  C. Prayer for God's Enabling in Life and Ministry (2:16–17)
III. Request for Prayer and Warning Against Idleness (3:1–15)
  A. Paul's Request for Himself (3:1–3)
  B. Warning Concerning Laziness and Idleness (3:4–15)
IV. Final Greetings and Benediction (3:16–18)

1

Paul, Silas[a] and Timothy,[a]

To the church of the Thessalonians in God our Father and the Lord Jesus Christ:

[2]Grace and peace to you from God the Father and the Lord Jesus Christ.[b]

Thanksgiving and Prayer

[3]We ought always to thank God for you, brothers, and rightly so, because your faith is growing more and more, and the love every one of you has for each other is increasing.[c] [4]Therefore, among God's churches we boast[d] about your perseverance and faith[e] in all the persecutions and trials you are enduring.[f]

[5]All this is evidence[g] that God's judgment is right, and as a result you will be counted worthy of the kingdom of God, for which you are suffering. [6]God is just: He will pay back trouble to those who trouble you[h] [7]and give relief to you who are troubled, and to us as well. This will happen when the Lord Jesus is revealed from heaven in blazing fire with his powerful angels.[i] [8]He will punish those who do not know God[j] and do not obey the gospel of our Lord Jesus.[k] [9]They will be punished with everlasting destruction[l] and shut out from the presence of the Lord and from the majesty of his power[m] [10]on the day[n] he comes to be glorified[o] in his holy people and to be marveled at among all those who have believed. This includes you, because you believed our testimony to you.[p]

[11]With this in mind, we constantly pray for you, that our God may count you worthy[q] of his calling, and that by his power he may fulfill every good purpose of yours and every act prompted by your faith.[r] [12]We pray this so that the name of our Lord Jesus may be glorified in you,[s] and you in him, according to the grace of our God and the Lord Jesus Christ.[b]

The Man of Lawlessness

2

Concerning the coming of our Lord Jesus Christ and our being gathered to him,[t] we ask you, brothers, [2]not to become easily unsettled or alarmed by some

---

[a] 1 Greek *Silvanus*, a variant of *Silas*   [b] 12 Or *God and Lord, Jesus Christ*

1:1
[a] Ac 16:1; 1Th 1:1
1:2
[b] Ro 1:7
1:3
[c] 1Th 3:12
1:4
[d] 2Co 7:14
[e] 1Th 1:3
[f] 1Th 2:14
1:5
[g] Php 1:28
1:6
[h] Col 3:25; Rev 6:10
1:7
[i] 1Th 4:16; Jude 14
1:8
[j] Gal 4:8 [k] Ro 2:8
1:9
[l] Php 3:19; 2Pe 3:7
[m] 2Th 2:8
1:10
[n] 1Co 3:13
[o] Jn 17:10
[p] 1Co 1:6
1:11
[q] ver 5 [r] 1Th 1:3
1:12
[s] Php 2:9-11
2:1
[t] Mk 13:27; 1Th 4:15-17

---

2 Thessalonians 1:1–2

Paul's introduction is nearly identical to that found in 1 Thessalonians 1:1. The exceptions are the addition of "our" to "Father" (typical of the rest of his letters) and the explicit identification of the source of the "grace and peace" as "God the Father and the Lord Jesus Christ." Paul consistently took the team approach, represented here by his mention of the work of Silas and Timothy in helping to establish the Thessalonian congregation.

Team leadership isn't appropriate for every congregation. But where it's feasible, it offers important advantages: (1) Accountability to other members reduces the chance of a leader falling into sin. (2) Even in cases of significant moral failure in a leader, the presence of a team reduces the odds that the failure will devastate the congregation. (3) In the New Testament the critical issue isn't office or formal structure but giftedness (of all members). In this respect team leadership models the New Testament ideal of what the church is.

2 Thessalonians 1:3–12

The growth, dedication, and faith demonstrated by the Thessalonians together evidenced that they were indeed a part of God's people. Paul interpreted the fact that they were not only persevering and trusting, but also growing and increasing in spite of persecution, as a

sign of God's blessing.

Some members of this congregation had become convinced that the "day of the Lord" had already arrived (2:2)—and had in light of this misconception begun to question God's justice. Paul responded by insisting that God is just and that the rightness of his judgment will become evident to all "when the Lord Jesus is revealed from heaven."

The range of choices in our culture has multiplied to the point that the difference between similar options often seems—or is—superficial. This makes it hard for many people to understand how one decision can have eternal consequences. But when the time of judgment comes, those and only those who have believed and placed their trust in Christ will be with him forever. How can you convey the urgency of a decision for Christ to those around you who may consider one option as good as another?

What can those of us who aren't experiencing persecution do for the sake of the gospel? Some suggestions: Pray for and encourage persecuted Christians. Question organizations that provide aid to oppressive governments, encouraging them to review each country's human rights conditions as an eligibility requirement. Lobby your own government officials to express concern for the plight of persecuted believers worldwide.

2:2
u 2Th 3:17
v 1Co 1:8
2:3
w Eph 5:6-8
x Da 7:25; 8:25;
11:36; Rev 13:5,6
2:4
y 1Co 8:5
z Isa 14:13,14;
Eze 28:2

prophecy, report or letter[u] supposed to have come from us, saying that the day of the Lord[v] has already come. 3Don't let anyone deceive you[w] in any way, for that day will not come, until the rebellion occurs and the man of lawlessness[a] is revealed,[x] the man doomed to destruction. 4He will oppose and will exalt himself over everything that is called God[y] or is worshiped, so that he sets himself up in God's temple, proclaiming himself to be God.[z]

5Don't you remember that when I was with you I used to tell you these things? 6And now you know what is holding him back, so that he may be revealed at the proper time. 7For the secret power of lawlessness is already at work; but the one who now holds it back will continue to do so till he is taken out of the way. 8And then

2:8
a Isa 11:4;
Rev 19:15

the lawless one will be revealed, whom the Lord Jesus will overthrow with the breath of his mouth[a] and destroy by the splendor of his coming. 9The coming of

2:9
b Mt 24:24; Jn 4:48
2:10
c 1Co 1:18
2:11
d Ro 1:28

the lawless one will be in accordance with the work of Satan displayed in all kinds of counterfeit miracles, signs and wonders,[b] 10and in every sort of evil that deceives those who are perishing.[c] They perish because they refused to love the truth and so be saved. 11For this reason God sends them[d] a powerful delusion so that they will

2:12
e Ro 1:32

believe the lie 12and so that all will be condemned who have not believed the truth but have delighted in wickedness.[e]

Stand Firm

2:13
f Eph 1:4 g 1Th 5:9
h 1Pe 1:2

13But we ought always to thank God for you, brothers loved by the Lord, because from the beginning God chose you[b][f] to be saved[g] through the sanctifying work of the Spirit[h] and through belief in the truth. 14He called you to this through our gos-

2:15
i 1Co 16:13
j 1Co 11:2

pel, that you might share in the glory of our Lord Jesus Christ. 15So then, brothers, stand firm[i] and hold to the teachings[c] we passed on to you,[j] whether by word of mouth or by letter.

2:16
k Jn 3:16
2:17
l 1Th 3:2 m 2Th 3:3

16May our Lord Jesus Christ himself and God our Father, who loved us[k] and by his grace gave us eternal encouragement and good hope, 17encourage[l] your hearts and strengthen[m] you in every good deed and word.

a 3 Some manuscripts *sin*   b 13 Some manuscripts *because God chose you as his firstfruits*
c 15 Or *traditions*

2 Thessalonians 2:1–12

Belief on the part of some members of the congregation that the "day of the Lord" had already arrived had generated anxiety (see "There and Then" for 1:3–12). It also may have spurred questions about the significance of their afflictions and about God's justice. Paul informed the Thessalonians that this day couldn't yet have arrived because certain events and developments had to occur first. He urged them to stand firm and hold fast to his earlier teachings.

The "rebellion" and the appearance of "the man of lawlessness" ("antichrist" in 1 Jn. 2:18 or "beast" in Rev. 13) would precede Christ's return and his gathering up of believers to be with him. In laying out a sequence of events, was Paul contradicting his earlier statement in 1 Thessalonians 5:2 that "the day of the Lord will come like a thief in the night"? Paul had been referring there only to unbelievers. Believers, he wrote, "are not in darkness so that this day should surprise [them]" (1 Thess. 5:4).

Christians need to be ready to experience persecution and distress for the gospel. Paul emphasized that we ought to be prepared for such experiences even before the appearance of the antichrist (an event subject to much speculation): "The secret power of lawlessness is

already at work" (v. 7). We can find encouragement even in the midst of turmoil. Why? Because in the end, Jesus will win and vindicate those who are his. Try for a moment to imagine life without the knowledge of Christ's ultimate victory. Does this increase your sense of urgency to witness to those who don't cling to this hope?

2 Thessalonians 2:13–17

The important little word "but" that opens this passage contrasts the fate of those "who are perishing" (v. 10) with that of the Thessalonian believers, who were "loved by the Lord" and chosen by God for salvation. Paul's goal was to reassure them regarding their destiny (salvation), in contrast to that of their oppressors. Regardless of the efforts of the coming "lawless one" to deceive them, their salvation was secure in God's hand.

Paul urged his readers to hold tightly to the teachings they had received from the apostles. Contemporary society is awash in false and deceptive "information." No idea, it seems, is too outrageous to find an outlet. Sadly, many professing Christians read and accept Scripture selectively. They twist, ignore, supplement, or replace it, finding sophisticated ways to reject it while appearing to follow it. Are you clinging tightly to *all* the Bible's inspired words?

Request for Prayer

3 Finally, brothers, *n* pray for us *o* that the message of the Lord *p* may spread rapidly and be honored, just as it was with you. ²And pray that we may be delivered from wicked and evil men, *q* for not everyone has faith. ³But the Lord is faithful, *r* and he will strengthen and protect you from the evil one. *s* ⁴We have confidence *t* in the Lord that you are doing and will continue to do the things we command. ⁵May the Lord direct your hearts *u* into God's love and Christ's perseverance.

Warning Against Idleness

⁶In the name of the Lord Jesus Christ, *v* we command you, brothers, to keep away from *w* every brother who is idle *x* and does not live according to the teaching *a* you received from us. *y* ⁷For you yourselves know how you ought to follow our example. *z* We were not idle when we were with you, ⁸nor did we eat anyone's food without paying for it. On the contrary, we worked *a* night and day, laboring and toil-

a 6 Or *tradition*

3:1
n 1Th 4:1
o 1Th 5:25
p 1Th 1:8
3:2
q Ro 15:31
3:3
r 1Co 1:9 *s* Mt 5:37
3:4
t 2Co 2:3
3:5
u 1Ch 29:18

3:6
v 1Co 5:4
w Ro 16:17
x ver 7,11
y 1Co 11:2
3:7
z 1Co 4:16
3:8
a Ac 18:3; Eph 4:28

---

2 Thessalonians 3:1–5

Paul's first request in verses 1–2 was on behalf of the gospel. The second was for the gospel messengers: that Paul and his companions might "be delivered from wicked and evil men." Paul was referring to people who maliciously obstructed the gospel, like those in Thessalonica who had instigated a riot to hinder Paul from preaching the gospel when he had first visited the city (see Acts 17:5).

At first glance, there may seem to be tension in Paul's epistles to the Thessalonians between divine activity and human responsibility (2:13,15; 3:3–4; cf. 1:11; see also 1 Thess. 3:12; 4:10). The order in which Paul presented these realities was always divine action (grace) followed by human response (faith). For Paul, these crucial concepts weren't competing but complementary.

Christianity, for Paul and for us, isn't a quick-fix treatment or short-term solution for human ills. It's been described instead as "a long walk in the same direction." The writer of Hebrews expressed this idea when he encouraged his readers to "run with perseverance the race marked out for us" (Heb. 12:1), for "we have come to share in Christ if we hold firmly until the end the confidence we had at first" (Heb. 3:14). Has the outworking of your Christian faith looked more like a series of sprints or a marathon?

2 Thessalonians 3:6–15

Work is fundamental to life because it provides the means for sustaining it. Congregations have an obligation to care for their members in need, and individuals who *can* work are obligated to do so to avoid becoming a burden on others. This second point was for Paul no minor matter: Refusal to work was a breach of conduct serious enough to call for discipline.

Snapshots

 2:16–17

Mary Jane

The youngest of seven children, Mary Jane grew up amidst poverty and hardship in her native Philippines. When she was twelve, her father died of a heart attack. Her mother deserted the family a few years later for another man. But as a child who had been sponsored through a Christian organization, Mary Jane never lost hope.

Earlier, when Mary Jane's sponsor sent her a gift of $250 (U.S.), the timing couldn't have been better. Her father was in the hospital, suffering from kidney disease. The gift paid his hospital bill.

"I thank my sponsor for his generosity and support. He is an inspiration to me," Mary Jane enthuses. She credits her sponsor for encouraging her and for opening her eyes to the blessings around her.

Now in her second year of college, Mary Jane is working toward her Bachelor of Arts degree in education. She wants to encourage others the way she was encouraged. "I want to focus on helping children and finding ways to improve life for them."

> [Mary Jane] credits her sponsor for encouraging her and for opening her eyes to the blessings around her.

3:9
b 1Co 9:4-14
c ver 7
3:10
d 1Th 3:4
e 1Th 4:11
3:11
f ver 6,7; 1Ti 5:13
3:12
g 1Th 4:1
h 1Th 4:11;
Eph 4:28
3:13
i Gal 6:9

3:14
j ver 6
3:15
k Gal 6:1; 1Th 5:14

3:16
l Ro 15:33 m Ru 2:4

3:17
n 1Co 16:21

3:18
o Ro 16:20

ing so that we would not be a burden to any of you. 9We did this, not because we do not have the right to such help, b but in order to make ourselves a model for you to follow. c 10For even when we were with you, d we gave you this rule: "If a man will not work, e he shall not eat."

11We hear that some among you are idle. They are not busy; they are busybodies. f 12Such people we command and urge in the Lord Jesus Christ g to settle down and earn the bread they eat. h 13And as for you, brothers, never tire of doing what is right. i

14If anyone does not obey our instruction in this letter, take special note of him. Do not associate with him, j in order that he may feel ashamed. 15Yet do not regard him as an enemy, but warn him as a brother. k

Final Greetings

16Now may the Lord of peace l himself give you peace at all times and in every way. The Lord be with all of you. m

17I, Paul, write this greeting in my own hand, n which is the distinguishing mark in all my letters. This is how I write.

18The grace of our Lord Jesus Christ be with you all. o

📖 The connection between work and sustenance is under attack in Western cultures. Policies designed to provide a "safety net" for those in need have frequently done so in a way that has discouraged people receiving assistance from working. Can you think of ways a government might reduce the detrimental effects of such well-intentioned programs? The "entertainment" culture, professional sports, new forms of financial speculation, and gambling also have weakened the bond between "working" and "eating."

Donor fatigue. Volunteer burnout. These terms are unfortunately familiar to organizations that help those in need. This text doesn't specify *how* to ensure that we "never tire of doing what is right" (v. 13). But we understand from Paul's remark in Galatians 6:9–10 that believers are to consistently demonstrate a spirit of generosity and care for the needy.

2 Thessalonians 3:16–18

Paul ended his letter as he had begun—with the spotlight squarely on Jesus Christ. The future of all Christians rests entirely on the power and faithfulness of God as revealed through Jesus. Christians of every era are to persevere in faith (1:4) and await with eternal encouragement and good hope (2:16) the revelation from heaven of the Lord Jesus himself (1:7).

📖 In his benediction in verse 16 Paul prayed that the Lord Jesus might grant the Thessalonians "peace at all times and in every way." Peace, for Paul, encompassed a state of well-being and wholeness characterized by reconciled relationships with God, others in the congregation, and those outside the faith community. Are you experiencing this peace? What about your church? Your city or community? The larger society in which you live? How can you promote peace at these various levels?

INTRODUCTION TO
1 Timothy

AUTHOR
This letter identifies its author as the apostle Paul (1:1).

DATE WRITTEN
Paul probably wrote this letter between A.D. 63 and 65.

ORIGINAL READER
Paul wrote to Timothy, whom he had sent to the church in Ephesus to combat the false teaching that had arisen there. Timothy occupied a special place in Paul's heart as his coworker, emissary, traveling companion, and "true son in the faith" (1:2).

TIMELINE

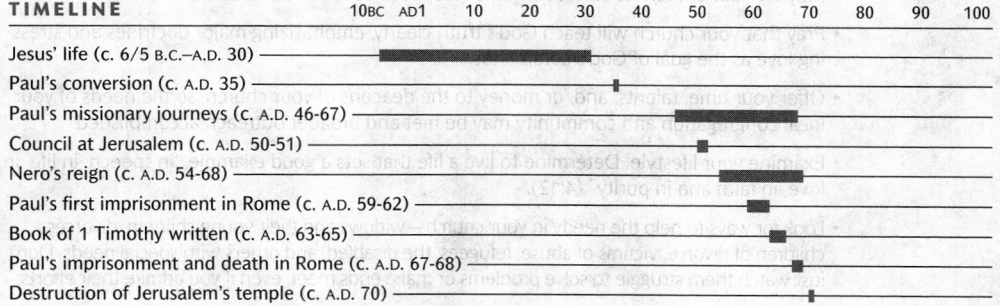

TIMELINE	10BC	AD1	10	20	30	40	50	60	70	80	90	100

Jesus' life (c. 6/5 B.C.–A.D. 30)
Paul's conversion (c. A.D. 35)
Paul's missionary journeys (c. A.D. 46-67)
Council at Jerusalem (c. A.D. 50-51)
Nero's reign (c. A.D. 54-68)
Paul's first imprisonment in Rome (c. A.D. 59-62)
Book of 1 Timothy written (c. A.D. 63-65)
Paul's imprisonment and death in Rome (c. A.D. 67-68)
Destruction of Jerusalem's temple (c. A.D. 70)

THEMES
Paul's first letter to Timothy includes the following themes:

1. *Sound doctrine.* False teachers who showed an unhealthy fascination with myths and genealogies (1:4; 4:7) and a preoccupation with the law (1:7) had infiltrated the church in Ephesus. They prohibited marriage and the eating of certain foods (4:3) and taught that the final resurrection had already taken place (1:20; see 2 Tim. 2:18). To combat these false teachings, Timothy was to teach only what is trustworthy, sound, and good (1:9–11; 3:9; 4:6; 6:3–4).

2. *Right living.* The false teachers were intent on stirring up controversy and prone to speculation (1:4,6; 6:4,20), deception (4:1–2), and greed (6:5). Though unqualified, they promoted themselves as authorities (1:7). They weren't governed by the principle of love but devoted themselves to self-aggrandizement. To combat this, Paul instructed Timothy to "set an example for the believers in speech, in life, in love, in faith and in purity" (4:12).

3. *Evangelism.* Paul's concern for the church's successful evangelism lies at the heart of his commands. He showed a particular sensitivity to Christian misbehavior producing a negative reaction from society (5:14; 6:1; cf. 5:8). The conduct of Christians must be above reproach because it has a direct effect on the success of their evangelism. Christians aren't called to es-

cape the world but to be obedient to God within it. Paul emphasized fulfilling family roles, marrying, having children, caring well for the family, managing households, and providing for widows and relatives.

4. *Church leaders.* Church leaders need to reach for even higher standards than what is expected of persons holding similarly important positions in contemporary society. The church is to be directed by leaders who are morally above reproach and who administer their own households well (3:1–13). Warnings against immoral practices and materialism apply to all members (6:7–10,17–19).

FAITH IN ACTION

The pages of 1 Timothy contain life lessons and role models of faith—people who challenge believers to put faith in action.

Role Models

• PAUL (1:2) was Timothy's spiritual mentor, providing him with seasoned counsel and guidance. To whom can you go for spiritual advice? To whom can you be a spiritual mentor?

• ELDERS AND DEACONS (3:1–13) are to lead congregations by their example. If you are a leader, how is your life measuring up to the qualifications listed here? If you are not, are you ready to step up to a leadership position?

• TIMOTHY (6:11) was called a "man of God." Do you aspire to be known as a man or woman of God? How can Timothy be an example to you?

Challenges

• Pray for your church leaders, asking that they receive spiritual wisdom and discernment.

• Pray that your church will teach God's truth clearly, emphasizing major doctrines and stressing love as the goal of God's commands.

• Offer your time, talents, and/or money to the deacons of your church, so the needs of your local congregation and community may be met and broader outreach accomplished.

• Examine your lifestyle. Determine to live a life that sets a good example "in speech, in life, in love, in faith and in purity" (4:12).

• Look for ways to help the needy in your church—widows and their young children, divorcés, children of divorce, victims of abuse, refugees, the disabled, and others with special needs. Don't just watch them struggle to solve problems or make ends meet, even if you admire their efforts.

OUTLINE

    I.   Greeting (1:1–2)

   II. Warning Against False Teachers (1:3–11)

  III. The Lord's Grace to Paul (1:12–17)

  IV. The Purpose of Paul's Instructions to Timothy (1:18–20)

   V. Instructions Concerning the Church (2:1—4:5)

      A. Guidelines for Public Worship (2:1–15)

      B. Qualifications for Overseers and Deacons (3:1–13)

      C. The Purpose of the Letter (3:14–16)

      D. Dealing With False Teaching (4:1–5)

  VI. Timothy's Responsibilities (4:6—6:19)

      A. Personal Life (4:6–16)

      B. Relationships With Others (5:1—6:2)

      C. More on False Teachers (6:3–5)

      D. The Love of Money (6:6–10)

      E. Paul's Charge to Timothy (6:11–16)

      F. Command to the Rich (6:17–19)

 VII. Conclusion (6:20–21)

1 Paul, an apostle of Christ Jesus by the command of God[a] our Savior and of Christ Jesus our hope,[b]

[2]To Timothy[c] my true son[d] in the faith:

Grace, mercy and peace from God the Father and Christ Jesus our Lord.

Warning Against False Teachers of the Law

[3]As I urged you when I went into Macedonia, stay there in Ephesus[e] so that you may command certain men not to teach false doctrines[f] any longer [4]nor to devote themselves to myths[g] and endless genealogies. These promote controversies[h] rather than God's work—which is by faith. [5]The goal of this command is love, which comes from a pure heart[i] and a good conscience and a sincere faith.[j] [6]Some have wandered away from these and turned to meaningless talk. [7]They want to be teachers of the law, but they do not know what they are talking about or what they so confidently affirm.

[8]We know that the law is good[k] if one uses it properly. [9]We also know that law[a] is made not for the righteous but for lawbreakers and rebels,[l] the ungodly and sinful, the unholy and irreligious; for those who kill their fathers or mothers, for murderers, [10]for adulterers and perverts, for slave traders and liars and perjurers—and for whatever else is contrary to the sound doctrine[m] [11]that conforms to the glorious gospel of the blessed God, which he entrusted to me.[n]

The Lord's Grace to Paul

[12]I thank Christ Jesus our Lord, who has given me strength,[o] that he considered me faithful, appointing me to his service. [13]Even though I was once a blasphemer and a persecutor[p] and a violent man, I was shown mercy because I acted in igno-

---

[a] 9 Or *that the law*

1:1
a Tit 1:3 *b* Col 1:27
1:2
c Ac 16:1 *d* 2Ti 1:2;
Tit 1:4
1:3
e Ac 18:19
f Gal 1:6,7
1:4
g 1Ti 4:7; Tit 1:14
h 1Ti 6:4
1:5
i 2Ti 2:22 *j* 1Ti 1:5
1:8
k Ro 7:12
1:9
l Gal 3:19
1:10
m 2Ti 4:3; Tit 1:9
1:11
n Gal 2:7
1:12
o Php 4:13
1:13
p Ac 8:3

---

1 Timothy 1:1–2

We are so used to thinking of Jesus as our Savior that the term applied to *God* in verse 1 catches our attention. The phrase "God our Savior" occurs only five times in the Old Testament and six in the New. In Titus 1:3 the phrase also appears in the salutation, linked with the word "command." Such words give Paul's openings a weight of authority and majesty. The God who had repeatedly brought about the salvation of Israel had the authority to command Paul regarding the preservation of the faith.

In verse 1 the command comes from God *and* Christ Jesus. The Biblical view is that there is only one God, existing in three persons. Christ is God in his *nature* and the Son in his *person*.

The word *grace* is important in the Christian vocabulary. But it often fails to communicate to the Biblically uninitiated (saying "grace be with you" to someone unfamiliar with Scripture would be as meaningless as announcing "the Force be with you" to someone who had never seen *Star Wars*). On the other hand, the word has become so familiar through such hymns as "Amazing Grace" that it's lost much of its meaning. The ancient Greek usage of the word implied a "superior" welcoming and accepting a "subordinate" into intimate relationship and favor.

1 Timothy 1:3–11

Timothy was at Ephesus when it became clear to Paul that conditions there were critically unhealthy because of false teaching by immoral persons. Paul

urged Timothy to stay on there and command those false teachers to discontinue their activities.

Verses 8–11 indirectly address the function of Old Testament law for New Testament believers. Christians are no longer "under" the law. But they are bound by gratitude to the law of love (a summary statement of the spirit of the law) Jesus spelled out in Matthew 22:37–39. See also Jesus' expansion of the love principle to the rich young man (Matt. 19:16–20). Verses 9–10 are surprising. Paul in Romans 1:19 referred in a similar context to "men who suppress the truth by their wickedness." God's good law is explicit—a clear indictment against those who deliberately flaunt its spirit.

We need to include enough Biblical instruction in our preaching and worship to provide a foundation on which seekers and new believers can ground their faith. The church bears responsibility to see to it that new Christians are given the background they lack as quickly as possible, to equip them to identify and resist deviation from Scriptural truth. The church, while growing rapidly in many places in the world, too often lacks trained leadership. The faith of believers in such settings is frequently passionate—they are willing to die for Christ—but their grasp of the gospel and its implications for all aspects of life is limited.

1 Timothy 1:12–20

God had shown mercy to Paul for his early, anti-Christian activity because Paul had acted "in ignorance and unbelief." That doesn't mean that God excuses anyone who acts without knowledge before coming to faith.

1:13
q Ac 26:9
1:14
r Ro 5:20 s 2Ti 1:13
1:15
t 1Ti 3:1; 2Ti 2:11;
Tit 3:8
1:16
u ver 13
1:17
v Rev 15:3
w Col 1:15
x Ro 11:36
1:18
y 1Ti 4:14 z 2Ti 2:3
1:19
a 1Ti 6:21
1:20
b 2Ti 2:17
c 2Ti 4:14
d 1Co 5:5
2:2
e Ezr 6:10; Ro 13:1
2:4
f Eze 18:23,32
g Tit 2:11
h 2Ti 2:25
2:5
i Ro 3:29,30
j Gal 3:20
2:6
k 1Co 1:6 l 1Ti 6:15
2:7
m 2Ti 1:11
n Ac 9:15;
Eph 3:7,8
2:8
o Ps 134:2;
Lk 24:50
2:9
p 1Pe 3:3
2:11
q 1Co 14:34

rance and unbelief.[q] [14]The grace of our Lord was poured out on me abundantly,[r] along with the faith and love that are in Christ Jesus.[s]

[15]Here is a trustworthy saying[t] that deserves full acceptance: Christ Jesus came into the world to save sinners—of whom I am the worst. [16]But for that very reason I was shown mercy[u] so that in me, the worst of sinners, Christ Jesus might display his unlimited patience as an example for those who would believe on him and receive eternal life. [17]Now to the King[v] eternal, immortal, invisible,[w] the only God, be honor and glory for ever and ever. Amen.[x]

[18]Timothy, my son, I give you this instruction in keeping with the prophecies once made about you,[y] so that by following them you may fight the good fight,[z] [19]holding on to faith and a good conscience. Some have rejected these and so have shipwrecked their faith.[a] [20]Among them are Hymenaeus[b] and Alexander,[c] whom I have handed over to Satan[d] to be taught not to blaspheme.

Instructions on Worship

2 I urge, then, first of all, that requests, prayers, intercession and thanksgiving be made for everyone— [2]for kings and all those in authority,[e] that we may live peaceful and quiet lives in all godliness and holiness. [3]This is good, and pleases God our Savior, [4]who wants[f] all men[g] to be saved and to come to a knowledge of the truth.[h] [5]For there is one God[i] and one mediator[j] between God and men, the man Christ Jesus, [6]who gave himself as a ransom for all men—the testimony[k] given in its proper time.[l] [7]And for this purpose I was appointed a herald and an apostle—I am telling the truth, I am not lying—and a teacher[m] of the true faith to the Gentiles.[n]

[8]I want men everywhere to lift up holy hands[o] in prayer, without anger or disputing.

[9]I also want women to dress modestly, with decency and propriety, not with braided hair or gold or pearls or expensive clothes,[p] [10]but with good deeds, appropriate for women who profess to worship God.

[11]A woman should learn in quietness and full submission.[q] [12]I do not permit a

---

But it does showcase his sovereign mercy and power in reaching out to one such person, Saul of Tarsus (Paul). This passionate apostle-to-be had sought to honor God by trying to wipe out the Christians when he thought *they* were blaspheming (see Acts 7:60—8:3).

People like Hymenaeus and Alexander have managed to infiltrate Christian groups throughout the ages. The expressions "shipwrecked" and "handed over to Satan" hammer home the seriousness of heresy. The repetition of phrases combining sound doctrine with integrity of character isn't just a major distinctive of Paul's Pastoral Letters (1 and 2 Tim. and Titus). It's his legacy to all who serve the Lord.

Truth is worth celebrating; we will always number ourselves among those sinners for whom Christ came! Therefore, as we confront errors in others' beliefs and practices, we are wise to do so with confidence in God's "unlimited patience." The church needs to practice a delicate balancing act of patient, confident, non-condescending, gentle wooing of those whose understanding of the gospel is inadequate.

1 Timothy 2:1–15

Verses 1–7 show that God takes no pleasure in people dying without salvation, but the passage doesn't teach that he will save people regardless of their stance toward Christ. The way of salvation is singular—there is only one Mediator—Jesus Christ. As for anyone who

hasn't learned enough about the Good News to make a meaningful decision, believers can only fall back on Abraham's rhetorical question, "Will not the Judge of all the earth do right?" (Gen. 18:25).

Verses 12–15 have received much attention in recent years. Some believe that Paul restricted women in all circumstances and cultures from teaching or exercising authority over men. Others hold that Paul's prohibitions are not normative at all times and in all places.

Paul's restriction on women teaching certainly made sense in a world that refused to give women teachers a hearing and where most women weren't educated. The New Testament hadn't yet been completed, so people were dependent on the authoritative, spoken word. Today when someone teaches from Scripture, he or she may be challenged or corrected by anyone with an open Bible. The teachers or leaders have no authority in themselves; the authority is in the Word they declare and under which they stand.

Don't allow the debate over the issue of women in church leadership roles to obscure for you the broad teachings in this passage: God's will is that everyone be saved through the one Mediator, Jesus Christ. We enter into a religiously plural world with humble confidence. We don't possess the truth—the Truth, Jesus Christ, possesses us! We don't want anything in our behavior to discredit the gospel.

woman to teach or to have authority over a man; she must be silent. [13]For Adam was formed first, then Eve.[r] [14]And Adam was not the one deceived; it was the woman who was deceived and became a sinner.[s] [15]But women[a] will be saved[b] through childbearing—if they continue in faith, love[t] and holiness with propriety.

Overseers and Deacons

3 Here is a trustworthy saying:[u] If anyone sets his heart on being an overseer,[c][v] he desires a noble task. [2]Now the overseer must be above reproach,[w] the husband of but one wife, temperate, self-controlled, respectable, hospitable,[x] able to teach,[y] [3]not given to drunkenness, not violent but gentle, not quarrelsome,[z] not a lover of money.[a] [4]He must manage his own family well and see that his children obey him with proper respect.[b] [5](If anyone does not know how to manage his own family, how can he take care of God's church?)[c] [6]He must not be a recent convert, or he may become conceited[d] and fall under the same judgment as the devil. [7]He must also have a good reputation with outsiders, so that he will not fall into disgrace and into the devil's trap.[e]

[8]Deacons,[f] likewise, are to be men worthy of respect, sincere, not indulging in much wine,[g] and not pursuing dishonest gain. [9]They must keep hold of the deep truths of the faith with a clear conscience.[h] [10]They must first be tested; and then if there is nothing against them, let them serve as deacons.

2:13	r Ge 2:7,22; 1Co 11:8
2:14	s Ge 3:1-6,13; 2Co 11:3
2:15	t 1Ti 1:14
3:1	u 1Ti 1:15 v Ac 20:28
3:2	w Tit 1:6-8 x Ro 12:13 y 2Ti 2:24
3:3	z 2Ti 2:24 a Heb 13:5; 1Pe 5:2
3:4	b Tit 1:6
3:5	c 1Co 10:32
3:6	d 1Ti 6:4
3:7	e 2Ti 2:26
3:8	f Php 1:1 g Tit 2:3
3:9	h 1Ti 1:19

a 15 Greek *she*   b 15 Or *restored*   c 1 Traditionally *bishop*; also in verse 2

---

1 Timothy 3:1–16

Elders and overseers didn't represent distinct categories in the early church, but it was important for Christians to grasp the need for recognized, authoritative church leaders. Paul and Barnabas appointed elders with amazing rapidity on the return trip of their first missionary journey (Acts 14:23), even though this meant assigning people young in the faith. Some provision had to be made to continue the appointment process outside Paul's personal presence.

The hymn in verse 16 no doubt reminded the Ephesian believers about the indestructible foundation of the church. The doctrine of Christ (Christology) is the unchanging center of Christian theology.

Many Christians today think of church leadership in administrative terms. Elders' meetings are times for decision-making, resulting in a perception that pastoral care is outside their area of responsibility. But Paul instructed the Ephesian elders in Acts 20:28 to "be shepherds," and the pastoral ministry of elders is vital in today's church. Deacons are to care for people in practical and spiritual ways and handle financial affairs without greed or deceit. Jesus' teaching about letting our lights shine (Matt. 5:16) is for all Christians, but deacons play a special role in fulfilling this ideal on behalf of a congregation.

2:5–6

Six Questions of Bible Study

A Biblical passage may be studied in various ways. Each passage has the potential to ask and answer different questions, often making it more meaningful with every reading. Following are six basic types of approaches/questions to ask of the passage:

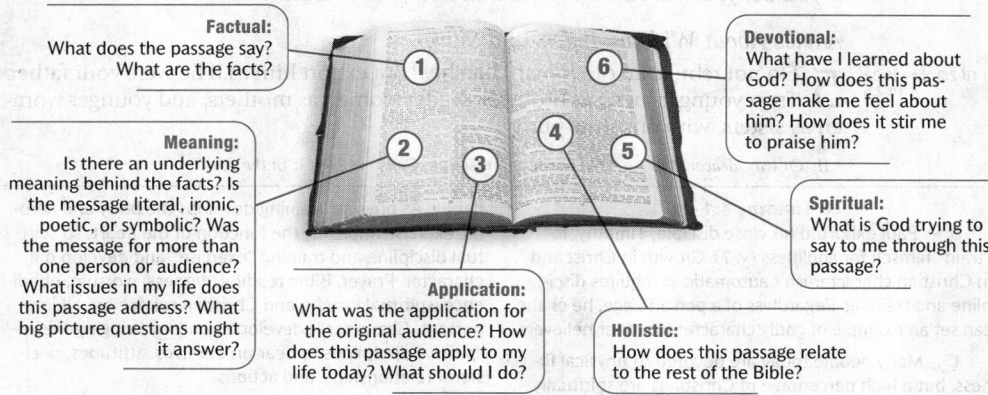

Factual: What does the passage say? What are the facts?

Devotional: What have I learned about God? How does this passage make me feel about him? How does it stir me to praise him?

Meaning: Is there an underlying meaning behind the facts? Is the message literal, ironic, poetic, or symbolic? Was the message for more than one person or audience? What issues in my life does this passage address? What big picture questions might it answer?

Spiritual: What is God trying to say to me through this passage?

Application: What was the application for the original audience? How does this passage apply to my life today? What should I do?

Holistic: How does this passage relate to the rest of the Bible?

3:11
i 2Ti 3:3; Tit 2:3
3:12
j ver 4

3:15
k ver 5; Eph 2:21
3:16
l Ro 16:25
m Jn 1:14
n Col 1:23
o Mk 16:19

4:1
p Jn 16:13 *q* 2Ti 3:1
r 2Th 2:3
4:2
s Eph 4:19
4:3
t Heb 13:4
u Col 2:16
v Ge 1:29
w Ro 14:6
4:4
x Ro 14:14-18

4:6
y 1Ti 1:10
4:7
z 2Ti 2:16

4:8
a 1Ti 6:6 *b* Ps 37:9,
11; Mk 10:29,30
4:9
c 1Ti 1:15

4:11
d 1Ti 5:7; 6:2
4:12
e Tit 2:7; 1Pe 5:3
f 1Ti 1:14

4:14
g 1Ti 1:18 *h* Ac 6:6;
2Ti 1:6

5:1
i Tit 2:2 *j* Lev 19:32
k Tit 2:6

[11] In the same way, their wives[a] are to be women worthy of respect, not malicious talkers[i] but temperate and trustworthy in everything.

[12] A deacon must be the husband of but one wife and must manage his children and his household well.[j] [13] Those who have served well gain an excellent standing and great assurance in their faith in Christ Jesus.

[14] Although I hope to come to you soon, I am writing you these instructions so that, [15] if I am delayed, you will know how people ought to conduct themselves in God's household, which is the church[k] of the living God, the pillar and foundation of the truth. [16] Beyond all question, the mystery[l] of godliness is great:

> He[b] appeared in a body,[c][m]
> was vindicated by the Spirit,
> was seen by angels,
> was preached among the nations,[n]
> was believed on in the world,
> was taken up in glory.[o]

Instructions to Timothy

4 The Spirit[p] clearly says that in later times[q] some will abandon the faith and follow deceiving spirits[r] and things taught by demons. [2] Such teachings come through hypocritical liars, whose consciences have been seared as with a hot iron.[s] [3] They forbid people to marry[t] and order them to abstain from certain foods,[u] which God created[v] to be received with thanksgiving[w] by those who believe and who know the truth. [4] For everything God created is good,[x] and nothing is to be rejected if it is received with thanksgiving, [5] because it is consecrated by the word of God and prayer.

[6] If you point these things out to the brothers, you will be a good minister of Christ Jesus, brought up in the truths of the faith[y] and of the good teaching that you have followed. [7] Have nothing to do with godless myths and old wives' tales;[z] rather, train yourself to be godly. [8] For physical training is of some value, but godliness has value for all things,[a] holding promise for both the present life[b] and the life to come. [9] This is a trustworthy saying[c] that deserves full acceptance [10] (and for this we labor and strive), that we have put our hope in the living God, who is the Savior of all men, and especially of those who believe.

[11] Command and teach these things.[d] [12] Don't let anyone look down on you because you are young, but set an example[e] for the believers in speech, in life, in love, in faith[f] and in purity. [13] Until I come, devote yourself to the public reading of Scripture, to preaching and to teaching. [14] Do not neglect your gift, which was given you through a prophetic message[g] when the body of elders laid their hands on you.[h]

[15] Be diligent in these matters; give yourself wholly to them, so that everyone may see your progress. [16] Watch your life and doctrine closely. Persevere in them, because if you do, you will save both yourself and your hearers.

Advice About Widows, Elders and Slaves

5 Do not rebuke an older man[i] harshly,[j] but exhort him as if he were your father. Treat younger men[k] as brothers, [2] older women as mothers, and younger women as sisters, with absolute purity.

---

[a] 11 Or *way, deaconesses*   [b] 16 Some manuscripts *God*   [c] 16 Or *in the flesh*

---

1 Timothy 4:1–16

Paul exhorted his close disciple, Timothy, to "train" himself for godliness (v. 7). Growth in Christ and in Christian character isn't automatic. It requires discipline and training. Regardless of a person's age, he or she can set an example of godly character for other believers.

Many people today are devoted to physical fitness, but a high percentage of Christians are spiritually flabby. As physical training develops the body and aerobic exercise improves the function of the heart, so spiritual discipline and training "exercise" and develop our character. Prayer, Bible reading, witness, worship, obedience, spiritual insight, and Christian service are all important. Character is developed only by bringing these spiritual disciplines to bear on our lives, attitudes, decisions, relationships, and actions.

3 Give proper recognition to those widows who are really in need.[l] 4 But if a widow has children or grandchildren, these should learn first of all to put their religion
into practice by caring for their own family and so repaying their parents and
grandparents,[m] for this is pleasing to God.[n] 5 The widow who is really in need[o] and
left all alone puts her hope in God[p] and continues night and day to pray[q] and to
ask God for help. 6 But the widow who lives for pleasure is dead even while she
lives.[r] 7 Give the people these instructions,[s] too, so that no one may be open to
blame. 8 If anyone does not provide for his relatives, and especially for his immediate family, he has denied[t] the faith and is worse than an unbeliever.
9 No widow may be put on the list of widows unless she is over sixty, has been
faithful to her husband,[a] 10 and is well known for her good deeds,[u] such as bringing up children, showing hospitality, washing the feet[v] of the saints, helping those
in trouble[w] and devoting herself to all kinds of good deeds.
11 As for younger widows, do not put them on such a list. For when their sensual

5:3
[l] ver 5,16
5:4
[m] Eph 6:1,2
[n] 1Ti 2:3
5:5
[o] ver 3,16
[p] 1Co 7:34; 1Pe 3:5
[q] Lk 2:37
5:6
[r] Lk 15:24
5:7
[s] 1Ti 4:11
5:8
[t] 2Pe 2:1; Jude 4; Tit 1:16
5:10
[u] Ac 9:36; 1Ti 6:18; 1Pe 2:12 [v] Lk 7:44
[w] ver 16

[a] 9 Or *has had but one husband*

1 Timothy 5:1—6:2

In ancient Rome life expectancy was much less than it is today. We may assume that there were more unmarried women than available men in the Ephesian congregation and that some of these women had become financially destitute. Paul's discussion of the care of widows is complex. His general concern was how the church should address their needs—social, personal, and religious. Paul defined widows who were "really in need" as those who had no family members to care for them, who trusted God, and who didn't live for worldly pleasure.

Paul stressed to Timothy that the church should accept responsibility for widows. By extension, this includes in our situation divorcées, children of divorce, victims of abuse, refugees, the disabled, and others with special needs. There are resources available today that weren't even conceived of in Paul's time. But governments aren't able to, and shouldn't, do it all. The church is still a "household," the family of God. What is your particular branch of the family doing for its less self-sufficient members?

With regard to moral failure among church leaders, several observations are relevant: (1) Circumstances are often complicated by the existence of heavy ministry demands and increasing family tensions. (2) When a pastor has lacked stable, loving support and moral encouragement in early life or is tired, busy with evening meetings, or occupied in counseling people with sexual problems, temptations can be strong. (3) The pastor is a likely target for the enemy of our souls (see James 1:13–15). (4) Understanding and counseling can't replace definitive action on the part of the church.

Snapshots

4:12

Loving Kakolo

Can teens living in the United States make a difference around the world? Absolutely! When a group of high school students from Chicago set their minds and hearts on showing Jesus' love to Zambian children orphaned by AIDS, who could have imagined their efforts would make a tangible difference!

They sacrificed new prom dresses and flowers, gave up Christmas presents, sponsored a basketball tournament, and more—all with the selfless spirit of donating the money saved or earned to these vulnerable children across the ocean. The result? About $80,000 (U.S.) to literally transform the community of Kakolo, Zambia—in the form of a new school building, a well to provide clean water for the village, improved health care, agricultural training, blankets, and more!

Making use of their love for those with fewer resources, faith that God would help them accomplish their goal, and purity of heart, God was able to do more than they had ever hoped or dreamed. What an unforgettable testimony to the way he can and does use his willing people of any age when they seek to do his work!

Making use of their love . . . faith . . . and purity of heart, God was able to do more than they had ever hoped or dreamed.

Widows and Service

5:3–16

As in Bible times, the poorest of the poor in the world today are widows and their children. The greater degree of poverty for women compared to men occurs for many reasons, among them the fact that women take primary responsibility for child care. Most refugees are female. Women are more likely than men to flee from abusive relationships. Even though women, statistically, do most of the world's work, they control far less of its resources. On a global level, women typically work longer hours than men, with much of their labor unpaid. The patriarchal nature of many societies means females are less valued than males. They receive less nutritious food, education, and medical care and are more frequently victims of abortion and infanticide.

Among poor women, widows are often the most vulnerable. Not only do they lack male bread-winners or protectors, but in traditional African and southern Asian societies they may be blamed for their husbands' deaths. In this situation they become outcasts, subject to long-term punishment or community abuse. Yet women tend to live longer than men.

Remember the story of Tabitha in Acts 9:36–42? She's the only New Testament woman for whom the feminine form of the Greek word for "disciple" was used. She was valued by Joppa's believers for her service to the poor. Her work among needy widows illustrates the nature and importance of servanthood within grassroots, subsistence-level communities.

> In many parts of the world the church is the community of the faithful poor, most of whom are women.

The early church attracted widows because it empowered them by helping them sustain themselves. Through his parables, Jesus honored widows as models of faithfulness (Mark 12:41-44; Luke 18:1-8). Because the Good News didn't link spiritual worth to gender, marital, or social status (1 Cor. 7:25–28; Gal. 2:6; 3:28), widows were treated with dignity in the church (1 Cor. 7:39–40). Disputes over their care led to the appointment of deacons (Acts 6:1–6). Wealthy women became facilitators and sponsors for poor widows, as well as official patrons of the apostles (e.g. Acts 16:14–15).

The widows who grieved over Tabitha showed Peter the clothing she had made them. Tabitha had herself been a widow involved in charitable service to her less fortunate peers; she had probably led the community of widows in income-generating clothing production. Christian widows who declined to remarry often devoted their time and wealth to the church. As widows helped each other and the other needy people in their communities, organized groups of celibate women became vitally important to the early church's well-being. In Christian tradition Peter, who raised Tabitha from the dead, became the patron saint of widows. But by healing Tabitha, Peter didn't create a climate of dependency. Instead, as an outside resource person, he intervened at the request of the local community.

Throughout the third world, groups of women are the backbone of the church's faithful service to the poor. Mothers' Unions in African churches provide economic and social support for poor women in their congregations. Deaconesses in the Philippines visit the sick and disadvantaged. Chinese women lead house churches, and mothers in Latin American churches organize demonstrations for clean water and basic family services.

Serving the poor means nurturing their capabilities, empowering them on their own terms. Christ's followers are to respect and care for widows and others the larger society tends to neglect and abuse. Just as Peter discovered in Joppa, in many parts of the world the church is the community of the faithful poor, most of whom are women.

Dana L. Robert, Truman Collins Professor of World Mission at Boston University School of Theology in Boston, Massachusetts
Sources: *The World's Women, 1995: Trends and Statistics* (New York: United Nations, 1995); Linda Schmittroth, ed. *Statistical Record of Women Worldwide* (New York: Gale Research, 1995)

desires overcome their dedication to Christ, they want to marry. [12]Thus they bring judgment on themselves, because they have broken their first pledge. [13]Besides, they get into the habit of being idle and going about from house to house. And not only do they become idlers, but also gossips and busybodies, [x] saying things they ought not to. [14]So I counsel younger widows to marry, [y] to have children, to manage their homes and to give the enemy no opportunity for slander. [z] [15]Some have in fact already turned away to follow Satan. [a]

[16]If any woman who is a believer has widows in her family, she should help them and not let the church be burdened with them, so that the church can help those widows who are really in need. [b]

[17]The elders [c] who direct the affairs of the church well are worthy of double honor, [d] especially those whose work is preaching and teaching. [18]For the Scripture says, "Do not muzzle the ox while it is treading out the grain," [a] [e] and "The worker deserves his wages." [b] [f] [19]Do not entertain an accusation against an elder [g] unless it is brought by two or three witnesses. [h] [20]Those who sin are to be rebuked [i] publicly, so that the others may take warning. [j]

[21]I charge you, in the sight of God and Christ Jesus [k] and the elect angels, to keep these instructions without partiality, and to do nothing out of favoritism.

[22]Do not be hasty in the laying on of hands, [l] and do not share in the sins of others. [m] Keep yourself pure.

[23]Stop drinking only water, and use a little wine [n] because of your stomach and your frequent illnesses.

[24]The sins of some men are obvious, reaching the place of judgment ahead of them; the sins of others trail behind them. [25]In the same way, good deeds are obvious, and even those that are not cannot be hidden.

6

All who are under the yoke of slavery should consider their masters worthy of full respect, [o] so that God's name and our teaching may not be slandered. [p] [2]Those who have believing masters are not to show less respect for them because they are brothers. [q] Instead, they are to serve them even better, because those who benefit from their service are believers, and dear to them. These are the things you are to teach and urge on them. [r]

Love of Money

[3]If anyone teaches false doctrines [s] and does not agree to the sound instruction [t] of our Lord Jesus Christ and to godly teaching, [4]he is conceited and understands nothing. He has an unhealthy interest in controversies and quarrels about words [u] that result in envy, strife, malicious talk, evil suspicions [5]and constant friction between men of corrupt mind, who have been robbed of the truth [v] and who think that godliness is a means to financial gain.

[6]But godliness with contentment [w] is great gain. [x] [7]For we brought nothing into the world, and we can take nothing out of it. [y] [8]But if we have food and clothing, we will be content with that. [z] [9]People who want to get rich [a] fall into temptation and a trap [b] and into many foolish and harmful desires that plunge men into ruin and destruction. [10]For the love of money [c] is a root of all kinds of evil. Some peo-

---

[a] 18 Deut. 25:4   [b] 18 Luke 10:7

5:13
[x] 2Th 3:11
5:14
[y] 1Co 7:9 [z] 1Ti 6:1
5:15
[a] Mt 4:10

5:16
[b] ver 3-5
5:17
[c] Ac 11:30
[d] Php 2:29;
1Th 5:12
5:18
[e] Dt 25:4;
[f] Lev 19:13;
Dt 24:14, 15;
Mt 10:10; Lk 10:7;
1Co 9:14
5:19
[g] Ac 11:30
[h] Mt 18:16
5:20
[i] 2Ti 4:2; Tit 1:13
[j] Dt 13:11
5:21
[k] 1Ti 6:13; 2Ti 4:1
5:22
[l] Ac 6:6 [m] Eph 5:11
5:23
[n] 1Ti 3:8

6:1
[o] Eph 6:5; Tit 2:9;
1Pe 2:18 [p] Tit 2:5,8
6:2
[q] Phm 16 [r] 1Ti 4:11

6:3
[s] 1Ti 1:3 [t] 1Ti 1:10
6:4
[u] 2Ti 2:14

6:5
[v] Tit 1:15

6:6
[w] Php 4:11;
Heb 13:5 [x] 1Ti 4:8
6:7
[y] Job 1:21; Ecc 5:15
6:8
[z] Heb 13:5
6:9
[a] Pr 15:27 [b] 1Ti 3:7
6:10
[c] 1Ti 3:3

---

1 Timothy 6:3–10

Pursuing ministry as a means toward financial gain pollutes the gospel message. Paul's point in verses 9–10 is that the *desire* for wealth is wrong. Three phrases make this clear (emphases added): (1) "people who *want* to get rich," (2) "the *love* of money is a root of all kinds of evil," and (3) "some people, *eager* for money." The love of money is one of many roots of evil. To clarify a common misperception, though, Paul was saying that it's a root of *all kinds* of evil, not of *all evil*.

How many Christians today are truly content with "food and clothing"? A good exercise to keep your spiritual checkbook "in balance" might be to draw a chart with two columns, one labeled "need" and the other "want." You could then list in the appropriate columns your home with its market value, your car(s), an inventory of your clothes and shoes, etc. You might decide to present your list before God in prayer, determined to take appropriate action as a result of your evaluation. Many of us could downsize significantly and still live more than comfortably, with more to give to those in need.

6:10
d Jas 5:19

ple, eager for money, have wandered from the faith[d] and pierced themselves with many griefs.

Paul's Charge to Timothy

6:11
e 2Ti 3:17 *f* 2Ti 2:22
6:12
g 1Co 9:25,26;
1Ti 1:18 *h* Php 3:12

6:13
i Jn 18:33-37
j 1Ti 5:21

6:15
k 1Ti 1:11 *l* 1Ti 1:17
m Rev 17:14; 19:16
6:16
n 1Ti 1:17 *o* Jn 1:18

[11] But you, man of God,[e] flee from all this, and pursue righteousness, godliness, faith, love,[f] endurance and gentleness. [12] Fight the good fight[g] of the faith. Take hold of[h] the eternal life to which you were called when you made your good confession in the presence of many witnesses. [13] In the sight of God, who gives life to everything, and of Christ Jesus, who while testifying before Pontius Pilate[i] made the good confession, I charge you[j] [14] to keep this command without spot or blame until the appearing of our Lord Jesus Christ, [15] which God will bring about in his own time—God, the blessed[k] and only Ruler,[l] the King of kings and Lord of lords,[m] [16] who alone is immortal[n] and who lives in unapproachable light, whom no one has seen or can see.[o] To him be honor and might forever. Amen.

6:17
p Lk 12:20,21
q 1Ti 4:10
r Ac 14:17
6:18
s 1Ti 5:10
t Ro 12:8,13
6:19
u Mt 6:20
6:20
v 2Ti 1:12,14
w 2Ti 2:16

6:21
x 2Ti 2:18
y Col 4:18

[17] Command those who are rich in this present world not to be arrogant nor to put their hope in wealth,[p] which is so uncertain, but to put their hope in God,[q] who richly provides us with everything for our enjoyment.[r] [18] Command them to do good, to be rich in good deeds,[s] and to be generous and willing to share.[t] [19] In this way they will lay up treasure for themselves[u] as a firm foundation for the coming age, so that they may take hold of the life that is truly life.

[20] Timothy, guard what has been entrusted[v] to your care. Turn away from godless chatter[w] and the opposing ideas of what is falsely called knowledge, [21] which some have professed and in so doing have wandered from the faith.[x]

Grace be with you.[y]

---

1 Timothy 6:11–21

In verses 17–19 Paul returned to the subject of wealth. Just as he had instructed Timothy to take hold of eternal life (v. 12), so he commanded the affluent to "take hold of the life that is truly life" (v. 19). Early Christian churches didn't lack members of the upper, wealthier class. Regardless of how they had gained their wealth, they needed instructions on how to use it in a Christian manner: (1) Such people were to recognize that wealth is temporary. (2) Rather than being arrogant they were to "do good" and "be generous and willing to share." (3) And they weren't to "put their hope in wealth" because it's "so uncertain."

Christians hold varying views on what constitutes spirituality and how it's attained. Some are activists, engaging in spiritual exercises or programs. Oth-

ers more passively emphasize abiding in Christ. For Paul, spirituality involved *doing*: "Flee," "pursue," "take hold," and "fight" are all active verbs. The development of our Christian character involves both wise decisions and swift obedience on our part. Pause a moment to reflect on taking hold of the life that is truly life. What do these words mean for you?

All we are and have is God's. Those with money have a special opportunity to put their hope in God, who "richly provides us with everything for our enjoyment." All of us have the freedom to share our wealth. Added to this privilege is the opportunity of "taking hold of eternal life" by using the material blessings of our earthly life to do good. What forms has doing good taken for you? To what new "good" might God be calling you?

INTRODUCTION TO

2 Timothy

AUTHOR
The apostle Paul is the letter's stated author (1:1).

DATE WRITTEN
Second Timothy was probably written in A.D. 66 or 67.

ORIGINAL READER
Paul wrote this letter to Timothy (1:2) from prison (1:16; 2:9). Timothy was still in Ephesus
(see 4:19), where Paul had previously left him (1 Tim. 1:3). Timothy occupied a special place
in Paul's heart as his coworker, emissary, traveling companion, and "true son in the faith"
(1 Tim. 1:2).

TIMELINE

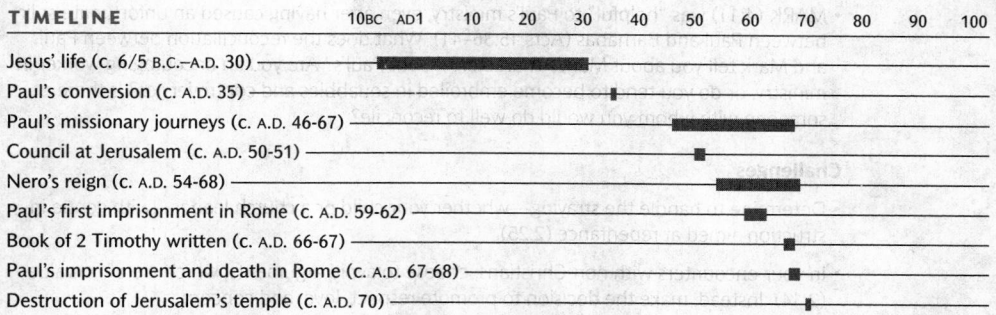

TIMELINE	10BC AD1	10	20	30	40	50	60	70	80	90	100
Jesus' life (c. 6/5 B.C.–A.D. 30)											
Paul's conversion (c. A.D. 35)											
Paul's missionary journeys (c. A.D. 46-67)											
Council at Jerusalem (c. A.D. 50-51)											
Nero's reign (c. A.D. 54-68)											
Paul's first imprisonment in Rome (c. A.D. 59-62)											
Book of 2 Timothy written (c. A.D. 66-67)											
Paul's imprisonment and death in Rome (c. A.D. 67-68)											
Destruction of Jerusalem's temple (c. A.D. 70)											

THEMES
Paul knew that his life was coming to an end (4:6) and that this would most likely be his last
letter. He used the opportunity to give Timothy some final advice and warnings. His themes
include:

1. *Encouragement to persevere.* Paul encouraged Timothy to continue the mission of evangelism (4:2). He directed his young protégé to hold fast to the traditions he had received
(1:3–14; 2:1–9; 3:14–15) and set himself up as a model for Timothy to emulate (1:8,13; 2:3;
3:10–11; 4:6–8). This letter teaches that the truth isn't just something to believe but a path to
follow (cf. 2:18). Faithfully living the Christian life and proclaiming the gospel isn't an easy
road, for it involves persecution (3:12). But God's faithfulness (2:11; 4:17–18) and the promise
of a righteous reward (4:8) enable believers to endure mistreatment.

2. *Rely on the authority of Scripture.* Timothy had been trained from early childhood in the
Scriptures (3:14), which helped him respond to the truth of Jesus Christ. Paul emphasized the
importance of handling the Scriptures correctly (2:15), their authority (3:16), and their importance in developing disciples capable of serving others (3:16–17).

3. *Warning against false teachers.* Paul warned Timothy about false teachers who stir up quarrels over senseless controversies (2:23) and seek to deceive (3:6). They indulge in "godless chatter" (2:16) and propagate muddy theology, like the belief that the final resurrection was already past (2:17–18). By contrast, the Lord's servants are to hold to sound doctrine and not engage in pointless quarrels. They are to be kind to everyone, teach sound doctrine, and gently and patiently instruct opponents in the truth rather than seeking to crush them (2:24–26).

FAITH IN ACTION

The pages of 2 Timothy are filled with life lessons and role models of faith—people who challenge believers to put faith in action.

Role Models

- TIMOTHY (1:5) had a "sincere faith," grounded in sound teaching (3:10–11,14–15). How can you mature spiritually into a person of "sincere faith"?

- LOIS AND EUNICE (1:5) nurtured Timothy in the faith during his infancy and youth. How can you do the same for your children or those of others?

- ONESIPHORUS (1:16–18; 4:19) took great pains to find Paul in Rome, ministering to and standing by him in the later days of his incarceration (4:10,16). Earlier he had also been of help to Paul and Timothy in Ephesus, Onesiphorus's hometown. How can you help minister to those who are imprisoned for the faith today? If effort is required, will you persevere?

- PAUL (4:7–8), despite suffering and persecution, had "fought the good fight" and "finished the race." How does his example encourage you?

- LUKE (4:11) was the only one who remained at Paul's side. How does loyal friendship display a person's faith and character?

- MARK (4:11) was "helpful" to Paul's ministry, even after having caused an unfortunate split between Paul and Barnabas (Acts 15:36–41). What does the reconciliation between Paul and Mark tell you about Mark's character? About Paul's? Are you an encouraging worker in ministry, or do you tend to become embroiled in squabbles and controversies? Is there someone with whom you would do well to reconcile?

Challenges

- Determine to handle the straying—whether your child or a church leader—with gentle instruction aimed at repentance (2:25).

- In your encounters with non-Christians, choose to avoid arguments, which are of no value (2:14). Instead, make the decision to promote respect, love, and concern.

- Evaluate your progress in the Christian life. If you can't say "I have fought the good fight" (4:7), resolve to make the necessary changes to get back into the fray.

- Remember Christians worldwide who are imprisoned for their faith. Find ways to help them, even though it may require considerable effort on your part (1:16–18).

- Look for opportunities to prove your loyalty to friends in need. Let no friend of yours ever have to complain, "No one came to my support, but everyone deserted me" (4:16).

- If you face loneliness or lack of support, take courage from the truth that the Lord will always stand at your side and give you strength (4:17).

OUTLINE

I. Introduction (1:1–4)
II. Paul's Concern for Timothy (1:5–14)
III. Paul's Situation (1:15–18)
IV. Special Instructions to Timothy (2)
   A. Charge to Be Strong (2:1–13)
   B. Charge to Be a Workman Approved by God (2:14–26)

V. Warning About the Last Days (3)
   A. Evil Times of the Last Days (3:1–9)
   B. Holding to the Truth in Evil Times (3:10–17)
VI. Paul's Departing Remarks (4:1–8)
   A. Final Charge to Timothy (4:1–5)
   B. The Waiting Crown of Righteousness (4:6–8)
VII. Final Requests, Greetings, and Benediction (4:9–22)

1 Paul, an apostle of Christ Jesus by the will of God, [a] according to the promise of life that is in Christ Jesus, [b]

2 To Timothy, [c] my dear son: [d]

Grace, mercy and peace from God the Father and Christ Jesus our Lord.

Encouragement to Be Faithful

3 I thank God, [e] whom I serve, as my forefathers did, with a clear conscience, as night and day I constantly remember you in my prayers. [f] 4 Recalling your tears, [g] I long to see you, [h] so that I may be filled with joy. 5 I have been reminded of your sin-

1:1
a 2Co 1:1
b Eph 3:6; 1Ti 6:19
1:2
c Ac 16:1 d 1Ti 1:2

1:3
e Ro 1:8 f Ro 1:10
1:4
g Ac 20:37
h 2Ti 4:9

---

2 Timothy 1:1–2

In 2 Timothy Paul connected his apostleship with the "will of God, according to the promise of life that is in Christ Jesus." As in Titus, the salutation includes the idea of life. And, like Paul's other Pastoral Letters (1 Tim. and Titus), the salutation and the verses that follow provide a realistic picture of the author and the recipient.

In verse 2 Paul identified Timothy as his "dear son." We as Christians are related to each other as

brothers and sisters in Christ and, as such, share one another's joys and sufferings and overlook distinctions that might otherwise divide us. Paul's expression here reminds us of another vital relationship believers can share: that of father (grandfather)/son, or mother (grandmother)/daughter. In our complex and confusing age, the mentor/disciple relationship between seasoned and less mature Christians is critical. Can you identify one particular person as your close relative in Christ? How has that relationship enriched your faith?

Snapshots

1:5

Transforming an Artless World

No stranger to travel, Suzanne has employed her art background to lead tours throughout the world. When presented with the opportunity to take a very different trip to Kenya, Suzanne jumped at the chance. Soon she realized that no gallery or museum had touched her as much as the artless world of Nairobi's slums. There, God presented her with a gift that changed Suzanne's life. Through relationships with women who struggle to raise families in dire poverty, this woman of wealth and intellect gleaned lessons of eternal value: joy, gratitude, and—most of all—faith.

A few years later, Suzanne returned to Kenya with her grown daughter, Kristen. Soon Kristen's own seismic life-shift began to shake her priorities. A successful consultant, Kristen returned home to exchange the boardroom for the classroom, where she could weave threads about caring for people in need into her lessons.

Suzanne and Kristen continue to visit Kenya regularly and provide monthly financial support for six Kenyan children. They also help organize fund-raising events to help the poor around the world. "How did my life change?" Kristen asks. "My mother took me to Africa to break my heart. She succeeded, and I can't thank her enough."

> "**My** mother took me to Africa to break my heart. She succeeded, and I can't thank her enough."

1:5
i 1Ti 1:5 *j* Ac 16:1

1:6
k 1Ti 4:14
1:7
l Ro 8:15

1:8
m Mk 8:38; Ro 1:16
n Eph 3:1
o 2Ti 2:3,9; 4:5
1:9
p Ro 8:28

1:10
q Eph 1:9
r 1Co 15:26,54

1:11
s 1Ti 2:7

1:12
t 1Ti 6:20 *u* ver 18

1:13
v Tit 1:9 *w* 1Ti 1:14

1:14
x Ro 8:9

1:15
y 2Ti 4:10,11,16

1:16
z 2Ti 4:19

1:18
a Heb 6:10
2:1
b Eph 6:10
2:2
c 2Ti 1:13
d 1Ti 6:12
2:3
e 1Ti 1:18

2:5
f 1Co 9:25

2:8
g Ac 2:24 *h* Mt 1:1
i Ro 2:16
2:9
j Ac 9:16
2:10
k Col 1:24
l 2Co 4:17

2:11
m Ro 6:2-11

2:12
n Ro 8:17; 1Pe 4:13

cere faith, *i* which first lived in your grandmother Lois and in your mother Eunice *j* and, I am persuaded, now lives in you also. 6For this reason I remind you to fan into flame the gift of God, which is in you through the laying on of my hands. *k* 7For God did not give us a spirit of timidity, *l* but a spirit of power, of love and of self-discipline.

8So do not be ashamed *m* to testify about our Lord, or ashamed of me his prisoner. *n* But join with me in suffering for the gospel, *o* by the power of God, 9who has saved us and called *p* us to a holy life—not because of anything we have done but because of his own purpose and grace. This grace was given us in Christ Jesus before the beginning of time, 10but it has now been revealed *q* through the appearing of our Savior, Christ Jesus, who has destroyed death *r* and has brought life and immortality to light through the gospel. 11And of this gospel I was appointed a herald and an apostle and a teacher. *s* 12That is why I am suffering as I am. Yet I am not ashamed, because I know whom I have believed, and am convinced that he is able to guard *t* what I have entrusted to him for that day. *u*

13What you heard from me, keep *v* as the pattern of sound teaching, with faith and love in Christ Jesus. *w* 14Guard the good deposit that was entrusted to you—guard it with the help of the Holy Spirit who lives in us. *x*

15You know that everyone in the province of Asia has deserted me, *y* including Phygelus and Hermogenes.

16May the Lord show mercy to the household of Onesiphorus, *z* because he often refreshed me and was not ashamed of my chains. 17On the contrary, when he was in Rome, he searched hard for me until he found me. 18May the Lord grant that he will find mercy from the Lord on that day! You know very well in how many ways he helped me *a* in Ephesus.

2 You then, my son, be strong *b* in the grace that is in Christ Jesus. 2And the things you have heard me say *c* in the presence of many witnesses *d* entrust to reliable men who will also be qualified to teach others. 3Endure hardship with us like a good soldier *e* of Christ Jesus. 4No one serving as a soldier gets involved in civilian affairs—he wants to please his commanding officer. 5Similarly, if anyone competes as an athlete, he does not receive the victor's crown *f* unless he competes according to the rules. 6The hardworking farmer should be the first to receive a share of the crops. 7Reflect on what I am saying, for the Lord will give you insight into all this.

8Remember Jesus Christ, raised from the dead, *g* descended from David. *h* This is my gospel, *i* 9for which I am suffering *j* even to the point of being chained like a criminal. But God's word is not chained. 10Therefore I endure everything *k* for the sake of the elect, that they too may obtain the salvation that is in Christ Jesus, with eternal glory. *l*

11Here is a trustworthy saying:

If we died with him,
 we will also live with him; *m*
12if we endure,
 we will also reign with him. *n*

---

2 Timothy 1:3—2:13

There is a touching quality here that is absent from 1 Timothy and Titus, the other Pastoral Letters. Paul's two letters to Timothy appear together in the New Testament, but the tone of 2 Timothy leads many to place it chronologically after Titus as Paul's final written words. The sense of urgency in 1 Timothy against the forces of evil is past. That doesn't mean all opposition was gone: Already in 1:15 Paul reflected on his unhappy circumstances and feelings of abandonment. And the presence of evil and heresy at Ephesus comes through clearly in the rest of the letter.

Churches and Christian institutions today are

meeting a new kind of volunteer: more and more people who grew up in non-Christian families. It's never too late, of course, to foster the development of character and wisdom in God's servants. But we don't want to forfeit opportunities for early nurturing, like that Timothy received from his godly mother and grandmother. If you were raised in a Christian home, what memories do you savor of parents or grandparents passing the faith along? If your upbringing was in a non-Christian environment, what good qualities were instilled? Where might you need help in godly living or character development? Have you identified a Christian mentor or joined an accountability group to help you?

> If we disown him,
>> he will also disown us;[o]
> 13 if we are faithless,
>> he will remain faithful,[p]
>> for he cannot disown himself.

A Workman Approved by God

14 Keep reminding them of these things. Warn them before God against quarreling about words;[q] it is of no value, and only ruins those who listen. 15 Do your best to present yourself to God as one approved, a workman who does not need to be ashamed and who correctly handles the word of truth.[r] 16 Avoid godless chatter,[s] because those who indulge in it will become more and more ungodly. 17 Their teaching will spread like gangrene. Among them are Hymenaeus[t] and Philetus, 18 who have wandered away from the truth. They say that the resurrection has already taken place, and they destroy the faith of some.[u] 19 Nevertheless, God's solid foundation stands firm,[v] sealed with this inscription: "The Lord knows those who are his,"[a][w] and, "Everyone who confesses the name of the Lord[x] must turn away from wickedness."

20 In a large house there are articles not only of gold and silver, but also of wood and clay; some are for noble purposes and some for ignoble.[y] 21 If a man cleanses himself from the latter, he will be an instrument for noble purposes, made holy, useful to the Master and prepared to do any good work.[z]

22 Flee the evil desires of youth, and pursue righteousness, faith, love[a] and peace, along with those who call on the Lord out of a pure heart.[b] 23 Don't have anything to do with foolish and stupid arguments, because you know they produce quarrels. 24 And the Lord's servant must not quarrel; instead, he must be kind to everyone, able to teach, not resentful.[c] 25 Those who oppose him he must gently instruct, in the hope that God will grant them repentance leading them to a knowledge of the truth,[d] 26 and that they will come to their senses and escape from the trap of the devil,[e] who has taken them captive to do his will.

Godlessness in the Last Days

3 But mark this: There will be terrible times in the last days.[f] 2 People will be lovers of themselves, lovers of money,[g] boastful, proud,[h] abusive, disobedient to their parents,[i] ungrateful, unholy, 3 without love, unforgiving, slanderous, without

a 19 Num. 16:5 (see Septuagint)

Cross references:
2:12 o Mt 10:33
2:13 p Nu 23:19; Ro 3:3
2:14 q 1Ti 6:4
2:15 r Eph 1:13; Jas 1:18
2:16 s Tit 3:9
2:17 t 1Ti 1:20
2:18 u 1Ti 1:19
2:19 v Isa 28:16 w Jn 10:14 x 1Co 1:2
2:20 y Ro 9:21
2:21 z 2Ti 3:17
2:22 a 1Ti 1:14; 6:11 b 1Ti 1:5
2:24 c 1Ti 3:2,3
2:25 d 1Ti 2:4
2:26 e 1Ti 3:7
3:1 f 1Ti 4:1
3:2 g 1Ti 3:3 h Ro 1:30 i Ro 1:30

---

2 Timothy 2:14–26

After the encouragement in verses 1–10 and the lofty saying of verses 11–13, we find ourselves plunged back into the world of the Ephesian church with its heretical teachers. Yet there is no disconnect here. Verse 14 looks back: "Keep reminding them of these things." Timothy's reminding had to be accompanied by warning. Verse 25 describes the goal: gentle instruction aimed at repentance.

Paul was more concerned with handling doctrinal controversy in general than with discussing particular departures from truth. Timothy, as a shepherd concerned with protecting the flock from wolves, needed tactics for dealing with—not annihilating—the opposition. If he had allowed himself to be drawn into heated debates, he would have been distracted from his primary focus, at risk of taking the low road of human quarreling and vulnerable to loss of respect. Squabbling isn't productive; it "only ruins those who listen" (v. 14).

Ask a person on the street what Christians stand for, and you may get an answer like "anti-this,

anti-that." Paul and Timothy were of course anti-heresy and anti-godlessness. But Timothy wasn't to be argumentative like the false teachers. He was to avoid quarreling that might have put him at risk of developing a sub-Christian reputation. In your encounters with nonbelievers, do you emphasize the positives—the pros, blessings, and privileges of your faith—while making certain not to compromise on necessary standards? Do you avoid arguing and promote instead respect, love, and compassion?

2 Timothy 3:1–9

The people Paul described as consumed by their own vices had "a form of godliness." This doesn't necessarily mean they were in the church, but Paul's counsel to Timothy to "have nothing to do with them" suggests that they may have been. Paul stressed in 1 Corinthians 5:9–11 that believers are to distance themselves from immoral people in the *church*, not the world.

"Lovers of themselves" walk through countless cultures and levels of society. "Bad as I wanna be" and

3:4
i 1Ti 3:6

self-control, brutal, not lovers of the good, ⁴treacherous, rash, conceited,ⁱ lovers of pleasure rather than lovers of God— ⁵having a form of godliness but denying its power. Have nothing to do with them.

3:6
k Jude 4

⁶They are the kind who worm their wayᵏ into homes and gain control over weak-willed women, who are loaded down with sins and are swayed by all kinds of evil desires, ⁷always learning but never able to acknowledge the truth. ⁸Just as Jannes and

---

"Having my way" are now acceptable public declarations—but they are not new. Even though we may evaluate self-esteem as a valid and healthy Christian attitude, the terminology has been abused by some. How do you avoid the fine line between a healthy self-image and unbiblical pride (cf. Prov. 16:18-19; 1 Peter 5:5)?

It's possible for us as Christians to become so preoccupied with evils outside the church that we miss shady "operators" within. Those of us who home school, send our children to Christian schools/colleges, and encourage our young people to attend church activities may develop a false sense of security. What safeguards can a church put in place to avoid tragedies involving sexual offenders, financial predators, or other dangerous insiders? Can we effectively teach our church family trust and caution at the same time?

2:15

Bible Study Programs

There are many structured programs that can help you study the Bible, either in a group setting or on your own. A few of the better known programs:

Back to the Bible www.backtothebible.org	Started as a radio ministry in 1939, this program may now be accessed through television, online, or even on a handheld computer. All programs are designed for personal study. The ministry offers a "Bible Read Me Plan" providing a schedule for reading through the Bible in one year. Several approaches are available: historical sequence, read-through-the-Bible approach, combining Old Testament and New Testament readings, and a blended approach.
Bethel Series www.bethelseries.org	This forty-year-old program was designed to help congregations engage in organized, sustained Bible study. Trained teachers from within the congregation facilitate six different seven-week Bible study segments.
Neighborhood Bible Study www.neighborhoodbiblestudy.org	A leader in small group Bible study programs, this one is designed especially for neighborhood groups. In its 40 years of ministry, NBS has developed 35 different Bible study guides that can be tailored by topic, book of the Bible, and makeup of group.
Disciple www.umph.org/disciple	This is a high-commitment Bible study program for congregational use. Participants are asked to read the Bible and related questions for at least one hour per day. Each week's reading is then processed in 90–120 minute classes, each of which begins with a 10–15 minute video discussing the themes of the readings.
Kerygma www.kerygma.com	This program, begun in 1977, emphasizes studying the Bible as a unified whole. Each reading is related to the Bible's overarching story and is integrated into the larger context of overall Biblical teaching. There are two main programs, each taking place in a group setting at church. One involves weekly two-hour sessions for two semesters (34 weeks) and the other 30 weekly one-hour sessions.
Walk Thru the Bible www.walkthruthebible.org	Begun in 1976 by Bruce Wilkinson, Walk Thru the Bible offers seminars, literature, videos, and broadcasts to enable people to read through the Bible individually. The program emphasizes the big picture of the Bible, giving users a sense of the whole Biblical story and message.
Bible Study Fellowship www.bsfinternational.org	Begun in 1958 by A. Wetherall Johnson, Bible Study Fellowship features a seven-year study schedule covering Genesis; Romans; Matthew; the lives of Moses, John, Israel, and the Minor Prophets; and Acts. The study program uses a fourfold approach: (1) daily study questions for personal Bible study; (2) discussion groups; (3) lectures on application for daily living; and (4) notes on Biblical texts for further information. The organization offers a variety of classes, both for daytime and evening, for women, men, young adults, and children.

Jambres opposed Moses,[l] so also these men oppose[m] the truth—men of depraved minds,[n] who, as far as the faith is concerned, are rejected. [9]But they will not get very far because, as in the case of those men,[o] their folly will be clear to everyone.

Paul's Charge to Timothy

[10]You, however, know all about my teaching,[p] my way of life, my purpose, faith, patience, love, endurance, [11]persecutions, sufferings—what kinds of things happened to me in Antioch,[q] Iconium and Lystra, the persecutions I endured.[r] Yet the Lord rescued me from all of them.[s] [12]In fact, everyone who wants to live a godly life in Christ Jesus will be persecuted,[t] [13]while evil men and impostors will go from bad to worse,[u] deceiving and being deceived. [14]But as for you, continue in what you have learned and have become convinced of, because you know those from whom you learned it,[v] [15]and how from infancy[w] you have known the holy Scriptures,[x] which are able to make you wise[y] for salvation through faith in Christ Jesus. [16]All Scripture is God-breathed[z] and is useful for teaching,[a] rebuking, correcting and training in righteousness, [17]so that the man of God[b] may be thoroughly equipped for every good work.[c]

4 In the presence of God and of Christ Jesus, who will judge the living and the dead,[d] and in view of his appearing and his kingdom, I give you this charge:[e] [2]Preach[f] the Word;[g] be prepared in season and out of season; correct, rebuke[h] and encourage—with great patience and careful instruction. [3]For the time will come when men will not put up with sound doctrine.[i] Instead, to suit their own desires, they will gather around them a great number of teachers to say what their itching ears want to hear. [4]They will turn their ears away from the truth and turn aside to myths.[j] [5]But you, keep your head in all situations, endure hardship,[k] do the work of an evangelist,[l] discharge all the duties of your ministry.

[6]For I am already being poured out like a drink offering,[m] and the time has come for my departure.[n] [7]I have fought the good fight,[o] I have finished the race,[p] I have kept the faith. [8]Now there is in store for me[q] the crown of righteousness, which the Lord, the righteous Judge, will award to me on that day[r]—and not only to me, but also to all who have longed for his appearing.

Personal Remarks

[9]Do your best to come to me quickly, [10]for Demas,[s] because he loved this world,[t] has deserted me and has gone to Thessalonica. Crescens has gone to Galatia,[u] and

3:8
l Ex 7:11 m Ac 13:8
n 1Ti 6:5
3:9
o Ex 7:12

3:10
p 1Ti 4:6
3:11
q Ac 13:14,50
r 2Co 11:23-27
s Ps 34:19
3:12
t Ac 14:22
3:13
u 2Ti 2:16
3:14
v 2Ti 1:13
3:15
w 2Ti 1:5 x Jn 5:39
y Ps 119:98,99
3:16
z 2Pe 1:20,21
a Ro 4:23,24
3:17
b 1Ti 6:11
c 2Ti 2:21
4:1
d Ac 10:42
e 1Ti 5:21
4:2
f 1Ti 4:13 g Gal 6:6
h 1Ti 5:20; Tit 1:13; 2:15
4:3
i 1Ti 1:10
4:4
j 1Ti 1:4
4:5
k 2Ti 1:8 l Ac 21:8
4:6
m Php 2:17
n Php 1:23
4:7
o 1Ti 1:18
p 1Co 9:24
4:8
q Col 1:5 r 2Ti 1:12

4:10
s Col 4:14
t 1Jn 2:15 u Ac 16:6

---

2 Timothy 3:10—4:8

Second Timothy 3:14–17 is one of the Bible's strongest statements about itself. The "holy Scriptures" Timothy studied in his Jewish upbringing were what we know as the Old Testament. But Peter's mention of Paul's writings among the "Scriptures" (2 Peter 3:16) shows that the early church already viewed such apostolic letters to be as authoritative as the Old Testament.

Paul's autobiographical notes in 1 and 2 Timothy and Titus served multiple purposes. They demonstrated the sovereign grace of God in his life, acknowledged that faithful service brings suffering, and provided a model for his young protégés. Paul was now ready to close his second letter to Timothy. Second Timothy 4:1–8 includes a charge to Timothy and a further reflection on Paul's life of service. In verses 6–8 it becomes painfully clear that the apostle expected imminent execution for his faith.

In 4:3 Paul predicted that the time when people preferred heresy *would* come. And in verse 6 he declared that the time for his own departure *had already* come. Apparently Paul had no doubt that his personal fate had been sealed, and this offered him opportunity

for a self-portrait. He was a servant of God who, though he had only done his duty (Luke 17:10), expected to hear his Master's "well done" (Luke 19:17). His words "I have fought the good fight, I have finished the race, I have kept the faith" have spurred generations of God's servants to do the same. Are you comfortable proclaiming the triumphant words of this faithful servant? If not, there is still time to get into the race, doing what God has called you to accomplish.

2 Timothy 4:9–18

To what extent may we draw principles from Paul's comments on the various people he mentioned in this passage? We know Paul wrote under the Spirit's inspiration. Since this isn't true for us, his public citing of faults doesn't necessarily give us free rein to comment negatively on other people, particularly in a non-private setting. Yet there is benefit in recognizing that certain universal characteristics and behavioral patterns reappear in the global church in spite of cultural differences.

Paul wrote in the shadow of death row. The faces behind these names were no doubt vivid to him. The same may be true today of those whose successes

v Col 4:14
w 2Ti 1:15
x Ac 12:12
y Ac 20:4
z Ac 19:33
a Ro 12:19

b Ac 7:60
c Ac 23:11
d Ac 9:15
e Ps 121:7
f Ro 11:36

g Ac 18:2
h Ac 19:22
i Ac 20:4
j ver 9
k Gal 6:18; Phm 25
l Col 4:18

4:11
4:12
4:14
4:16
4:17
4:18
4:19
4:20
4:21
4:22

Titus to Dalmatia. [11]Only Luke[v] is with me.[w] Get Mark[x] and bring him with you, because he is helpful to me in my ministry. [12]I sent Tychicus[y] to Ephesus. [13]When you come, bring the cloak that I left with Carpus at Troas, and my scrolls, especially the parchments.

[14]Alexander[z] the metalworker did me a great deal of harm. The Lord will repay him for what he has done.[a] [15]You too should be on your guard against him, because he strongly opposed our message.

[16]At my first defense, no one came to my support, but everyone deserted me. May it not be held against them.[b] [17]But the Lord stood at my side[c] and gave me strength, so that through me the message might be fully proclaimed and all the Gentiles might hear it.[d] And I was delivered from the lion's mouth. [18]The Lord will rescue me from every evil attack[e] and will bring me safely to his heavenly kingdom. To him be glory for ever and ever. Amen.[f]

Final Greetings

[19]Greet Priscilla[a] and Aquila[g] and the household of Onesiphorus. [20]Erastus[h] stayed in Corinth, and I left Trophimus[i] sick in Miletus. [21]Do your best to get here before winter.[j] Eubulus greets you, and so do Pudens, Linus, Claudia and all the brothers.

[22]The Lord be with your spirit.[k] Grace be with you.[l]

---

[a] 19 Greek *Prisca*, a variant of *Priscilla*

---

and failures, faithfulness or defection encourage or plague you to the end of your days. We serve the Lord today in the environment of persons whose comings and goings permanently affect our life and ministry. We, like Paul, do well to learn how to acknowledge our peers and team members as we seek to minister for our Lord. Who would you mention specifically if you were to find yourself in a similar situation? How have these individuals affected you, and why have they made such an impression?

2 Timothy 4:19–22

Only God knows the number of people who have read the names of Demas, Crescens, Titus, Luke, Mark, Tychicus, Alexander, Priscilla, Aquila, Onesiphorus, Erastus, Trophimus, Eubulus, Pudens, Linus, and Claudia and have seen in them the faces of those who have affected their own lives for good or ill. The pathetic words "no one came to my support, but everyone

deserted me" (v. 16) have no doubt been true over the ages of many forgotten saints. But so has the ringing affirmation "but the Lord stood at my side and gave me strength" (v. 17).

Saying farewell is a good and thoughtful act on the part of a person facing death. Paul was giving Timothy closure on their relationship. He wasn't courting death but was *ready* to die. That readiness speaks volumes to us as we confront our own mortality.

Many people resist dealing with advancing age and death. Sadly, they lose the opportunity to offer or receive last words of support or forgiveness. It's a blessed person who has the love of a warm household like that of Onesiphorus (cf. 1:16), a dear friend like Trophimus, or a sweet longing to see someone "before winter." Our personal winters may arrive at any stage of life, but it's always appropriate to seek the presence of friends and offer them our blessing.

3:8 "I WANT YOU TO STRESS THESE THINGS, SO THAT THOSE
WHO HAVE TRUSTED IN GOD MAY BE CAREFUL TO DEVOTE
THEMSELVES TO DOING WHAT IS GOOD."

INTRODUCTION TO
Titus

AUTHOR
The apostle Paul is the letter's stated author (1:1).

DATE WRITTEN
This letter was probably written between A.D. 63 and 65.

ORIGINAL READER
This letter was written to Titus (1:4), a Gentile Christian (see Gal. 2:1–3) who had probably been converted through Paul's ministry. Titus had traveled with Paul and become his trusted associate. Paul and Titus had visited Crete, an island in the Mediterranean Sea. When Paul departed, he left Titus behind to continue the ministry, organize the churches, and appoint elders (1:5).

TIMELINE

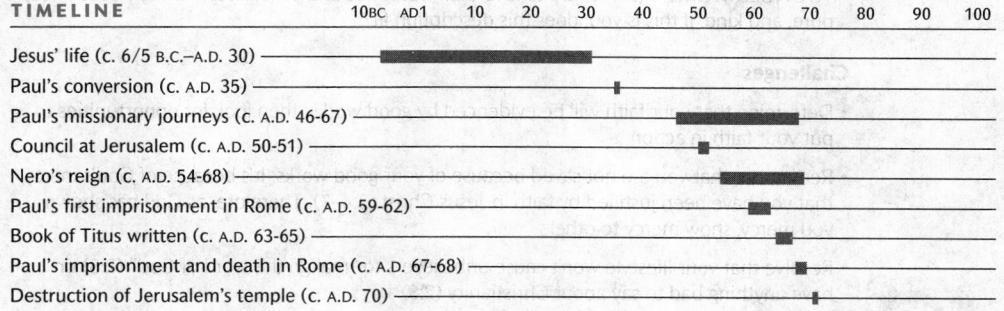

TIMELINE	10BC	AD1	10	20	30	40	50	60	70	80	90	100
Jesus' life (c. 6/5 B.C.–A.D. 30)												
Paul's conversion (c. A.D. 35)												
Paul's missionary journeys (c. A.D. 46-67)												
Council at Jerusalem (c. A.D. 50-51)												
Nero's reign (c. A.D. 54-68)												
Paul's first imprisonment in Rome (c. A.D. 59-62)												
Book of Titus written (c. A.D. 63-65)												
Paul's imprisonment and death in Rome (c. A.D. 67-68)												
Destruction of Jerusalem's temple (c. A.D. 70)												

THEMES
Titus contains the following themes:

1. *Church leaders.* Cretan culture was known for its moral decadence (1:12), and Paul instruct-ed Titus that leaders in the church must be above reproach as examples to others of the Christian life. When Christians are guilty of immoral behavior, they discredit the truth of the gospel they proclaim. The criteria for leaders require that they combine sound doctrine and a firm grasp of the Word with exemplary lives. Paul warned Titus not to appoint leaders who were arrogant, hot tempered, or greedy. Leaders are to be "self-controlled, upright, holy and disciplined" (1:8).

2. *Self-control and integrity make the gospel attractive.* Paul also instructed Titus on how to di-rect various other groups besides the leaders—older men (2:2); older women, who also taught younger women (2:3–5); younger men (2:6)—all were to exhibit self-control. Slaves (2:9–10), like today's employees, were to be respectful and honest. Paul insisted that Chris-tians are "to slander no one, to be peaceable and considerate, and to show true humility to-ward all men" (3:2). No person of any race, gender, or station in life is excluded. Christians are to be truthful, gentle, temperate, and devoted to good works (2:7,14; 3:1,8). The gospel has a

civilizing effect on all aspects of a Christian's life (2:11–14), including relationships within the home (2:4–5).

3. *False teachers.* Titus also had to contend with false teachers, about whom Paul spoke harshly (1:10–16). Those who caused dissension and started quarrels about interpretations were to be rebuked and silenced (1:11,13). Paul clearly valued unity within the community and condemned anyone who threatened it.

FAITH IN ACTION
The pages of Titus contain life lessons and role models of faith—people who challenge believers to put faith in action.

Role Models

- PAUL (1:5) was a spiritual mentor to Titus. He spent time and energy training Titus, delegated ministry responsibilities to him, and supported him with advice and encouragement. Are you in a position to be a spiritual mentor to someone in your church community?

- TITUS (1:5) was a trusted, responsible young leader (2:6–8). Can you be depended upon when placed in a position of leadership?

- OLDER MEN (2:2) are to be worthy of respect, self-controlled, and sound in faith. If you fall into this category, how well does this description fit you?

- YOUNGER MEN (2:6–8) are to be self-controlled. If you are a young man, does this adjective describe you?

- OLDER WOMEN (2:3–5) are to be reverent, kind, self-controlled, and teach what is good. If you are a woman in the second half of your life, is this a fitting portrayal of you?

- YOUNGER WOMEN (2:4–5) are to love their husbands and children and be self-controlled, pure, and kind. If this is you, does this description fit?

Challenges

- Determine that your faith will be evidenced by good works; then look for opportunities to put your faith in action.

- Remember that you are not saved because of your good works. It's because of God's mercy that you have been justified by faith in Jesus Christ (3:4–7). Therefore, as God has shown you mercy, show mercy to others.

- Resolve that your lifestyle won't cause unbelievers to "malign the word of God" (2:5) or have anything bad to say about Christianity (2:8).

- Be a witness in your community by being a good citizen in society, supporting and obeying government officials, and working honestly.

- Value unity in your church community by being a peacemaker and by warning those who are divisive.

- As a believer, see to it that you are self-controlled and honest. Others will notice!

OUTLINE

I. Greeting (1:1–4)
II. Concerning Elders (1:5–9)
    A. Where to Appoint Elders (1:5)
    B. Qualifications of Elders (1:6–9)
III. Concerning False Teachers (1:10–16)
IV. Concerning Various Groups in the Congregation (2)
    A. Teaching for Different Groups (2:1–10)
    B. Grace as the Foundation for Christian Living (2:11–14)
    C. Charge to Titus (2:15)

V. Concerning Believers in General (3:1–8)
  A. Believers as Citizens (3:1–2)
  B. Doing What Is Good (3:3–8)
VI. Concerning Response to Spiritual Error (3:9–11)
VII. Conclusion (3:12–15)

1 Paul, a servant of God [a] and an apostle of Jesus Christ for the faith of God's elect and the knowledge of the truth [b] that leads to godliness— [2] a faith and knowledge resting on the hope of eternal life, [c] which God, who does not lie, promised before the beginning of time, [d] [3] and at his appointed season [e] he brought his word to light [f] through the preaching entrusted to me [g] by the command of God our Savior, [h]

[4] To Titus, [i] my true son in our common faith:

Grace and peace from God the Father and Christ Jesus our Savior.

Titus's Task on Crete

[5] The reason I left you in Crete [j] was that you might straighten out what was left unfinished and appoint [a] elders [k] in every town, as I directed you. [6] An elder must be blameless, [l] the husband of but one wife, a man whose children believe and are not open to the charge of being wild and disobedient. [7] Since an overseer [b][m] is entrusted with God's work, [n] he must be blameless—not overbearing, not quick-tempered, not given to drunkenness, not violent, not pursuing dishonest gain. [o] [8] Rather he must be hospitable, [p] one who loves what is good, [q] who is self-controlled, upright, holy and disciplined. [9] He must hold firmly [r] to the trustworthy message as it has been taught, so that he can encourage others by sound doctrine [s] and refute those who oppose it.

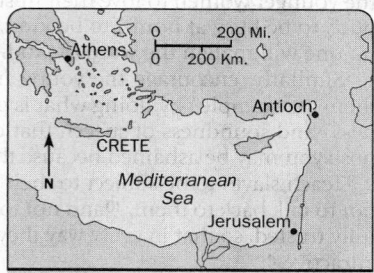

Titus's Task on Crete (1:5)
Then: Crete was a Roman province of mostly farmers and fruit growers.
Now: The Greek island of Crete is home to 600,000 people.

[a] 5 Or *ordain* [b] 7 Traditionally *bishop*

1:1
[a] Ro 1:1 [b] 1Ti 2:4
1:2
[c] 2Ti 1:1 [d] 2Ti 1:9
1:3
[e] 1Ti 2:6 [f] 2Ti 1:10
[g] 1Ti 1:11 [h] Lk 1:47
1:4
[i] 2Co 2:13
1:5
[j] Ac 27:7
[k] Ac 11:30
1:6
[l] 1Ti 3:2
1:7
[m] 1Ti 3:1 [n] 1Co 4:1
[o] 1Ti 3:3,8
1:8
[p] 1Ti 3:2 [q] 2Ti 3:3
1:9
[r] 1Ti 1:19 [s] 1Ti 1:10

Titus 1:1–4

📖 Paul's letter to Titus was likely written soon after 1 Timothy and well before 2 Timothy (Paul's other two Pastoral Letters). As with Timothy in Ephesus, Paul had left Titus on the island of Crete to organize the church there and deal with a crisis situation of false teachers who had infiltrated its ranks. The false teachings at both Ephesus and Crete could only be corrected by a clear presentation of the truth. The same emphasis that characterizes 1 Timothy—the blending of sound doctrine with godly living—is important in Titus and expressed already in verse 1.

📖 This letter, like those to Timothy, insists that the Christian gospel be backed up by right living—by lives characterized by "godliness." This was important in Crete, and it's equally imperative today, whether in the United States, Sierra Leone, or Iraq, whether at a football game, in a boardroom, or at a mission compound.

Christianity is tied to the ongoing revelation and historical activity of God among his special people.

Jesus didn't come in a vacuum. The eternal life proclaimed in the gospel was "promised before the beginning of time" and brought to light in that gospel. The history of Israel and the Messianic prophecies provide a solid foundation for the gospel and play an important role in Christian witness. What priority does your church place on Old Testament readings and teachings? Are you familiar and comfortable with these books?

Titus 1:5–16

📖 Paul had visited Crete briefly en route to Rome as a prisoner (Acts 27:7–15), and the existence of a Christian community there probably drew him back after his release. The group of believers was apparently not well organized, and Paul left Titus to remedy the situation, in part by appointing responsible leadership.

Verses 10–16 introduce the false teachers who had to be opposed by doctrinally informed elders. The presence of Jews throughout the ancient world, many of

1:10
t 1Ti 1:6 u Ac 11:2

1:11
v 2Ti 3:6
1:12
w Ac 17:28
x Ac 2:11
1:13
y 2Co 13:10
z Tit 2:2
1:14
a 1Ti 1:4 b Col 2:22
1:15
c Ro 14:14,23

1:16
d 1Jn 2:4

¹⁰For there are many rebellious people, mere talkers*t* and deceivers, especially those of the circumcision group. *u* ¹¹They must be silenced, because they are ruining whole households*v* by teaching things they ought not to teach—and that for the sake of dishonest gain. ¹²Even one of their own prophets*w* has said, "Cretans*x* are always liars, evil brutes, lazy gluttons." ¹³This testimony is true. Therefore, rebuke*y* them sharply, so that they will be sound in the faith*z* ¹⁴and will pay no attention to Jewish myths*a* or to the commands*b* of those who reject the truth. ¹⁵To the pure, all things are pure, but to those who are corrupted and do not believe, nothing is pure. *c* In fact, both their minds and consciences are corrupted. ¹⁶They claim to know God, but by their actions they deny him. *d* They are detestable, disobedient and unfit for doing anything good.

What Must Be Taught to Various Groups

2:1
e 1Ti 1:10
2:2
f Tit 1:13

2 You must teach what is in accord with sound doctrine. *e* ²Teach the older men to be temperate, worthy of respect, self-controlled, and sound in faith,*f* in love and in endurance.

2:3
g 1Ti 3:8

³Likewise, teach the older women to be reverent in the way they live, not to be slanderers or addicted to much wine,*g* but to teach what is good. ⁴Then they can train the younger women to love their husbands and children, ⁵to be self-controlled and pure, to be busy at home, to be kind, and to be subject to their husbands,*h* so that no one will malign the word of God. *i*

2:5
h Eph 5:22 i 1Ti 6:1
2:6
j 1Ti 5:1
2:7
k 1Ti 4:12

⁶Similarly, encourage the young men*j* to be self-controlled. ⁷In everything set them an example*k* by doing what is good. In your teaching show integrity, seriousness ⁸and soundness of speech that cannot be condemned, so that those who oppose you may be ashamed because they have nothing bad to say about us. *l*

2:8
l 1Pe 2:12
2:9
m Eph 6:5
2:10
n Mt 5:16

⁹Teach slaves to be subject to their masters in everything, *m* to try to please them, not to talk back to them, ¹⁰and not to steal from them, but to show that they can be fully trusted, so that in every way they will make the teaching about God our Savior attractive. *n*

2:11
o 1Ti 2:4
2:12
p Tit 3:3 q 2Ti 3:12
2:13
r 2Pe 1:1

¹¹For the grace of God that brings salvation has appeared to all men. *o* ¹²It teaches us to say "No" to ungodliness and worldly passions,*p* and to live self-controlled, upright and godly lives*q* in this present age, ¹³while we wait for the blessed hope—the glorious appearing of our great God and Savior, Jesus Christ, *r* ¹⁴who gave him-

---

whom bought into "Jewish myths," provided a network through which those who taught nonbiblical stories and other deviant teachings could circulate their errors. The substitution of human commands for those of God was apparently even more pervasive than the following of myths and genealogies (cf. 3:9; 1 Tim. 1:4). Basic to both is the rejection of truth.

📖 People everywhere share some common hopes and fears. Yet particular belief systems, values, and popular philosophies generate differing worldviews. Paul used individualized approaches as he attempted to reach Jews, barbarians, Gentiles, the wise, slaves, and Cretans. Christians in all times and places have been entrusted with a gospel that must be meaningfully explained and applied if it's to communicate. This principle goes beyond the context of foreign missions. How have you tailored your presentation of God's truth to reach different audiences and subcultures? Have you found it difficult for people to separate folk wisdom or cultural practice from true faith and sound doctrine?

Titus 2:1–15

📖 Verses 2–10 reinforce Paul's command in verse 1: A Christian's moral character is to be consistent with

sound doctrine. God is glorified not only through praise and worship but also in the loving deeds of those who profess faith in Christ. While Paul had repeatedly stressed the importance of moral character and good works to Timothy, Titus, and the church leaders, this quality of behavior was and is expected of every believer. Good works can never save people. But they, along with their professions of faith in Christ, are irrefutable evidence of salvation.

📖 Christians are to work hard to live so as not to cause unbelievers to "malign the word of God," have anything "bad to say about us," or find Christianity unattractive. Do these criteria describe your lifestyle?

The wide availability of the Christian gospel in many cultures today is an amazing reality. True, many of Earth's inhabitants still haven't heard the name of Christ. But the grace of God has "appeared" to an immense number of people worldwide, with unexpected responsiveness even among many who have traditionally been opposed and hostile. In spite of flaws and misunderstandings in our presentations, God's grace has powerfully brought the saving word of the gospel to millions. Why not pray for a group of people today who have had little or no access to the Good News?

self for us to redeem us from all wickedness and to purify for himself a people that are his very own,[s] eager to do what is good.[t]

15These, then, are the things you should teach. Encourage and rebuke with all authority. Do not let anyone despise you.

Doing What Is Good

3 Remind the people to be subject to rulers and authorities,[u] to be obedient, to be ready to do whatever is good,[v] 2to slander no one,[w] to be peaceable and considerate, and to show true humility toward all men.

3At one time we too were foolish, disobedient, deceived and enslaved by all kinds of passions and pleasures. We lived in malice and envy, being hated and hating one another. 4But when the kindness[x] and love of God our Savior appeared,[y] 5he saved us, not because of righteous things we had done,[z] but because of his mercy. He saved us through the washing of rebirth and renewal[a] by the Holy Spirit, 6whom he poured out on us[b] generously through Jesus Christ our Savior, 7so that, having been justified by his grace,[c] we might become heirs[d] having the hope[e] of eternal life.[f] 8This is a trustworthy saying.[g] And I want you to stress these things, so that those who have trusted in God may be careful to devote themselves to doing what is good.[h] These things are excellent and profitable for everyone.

9But avoid foolish controversies and genealogies and arguments and quarrels[i] about the law, because these are unprofitable and useless. 10Warn a divisive person once, and then warn him a second time. After that, have nothing to do with him.[j] 11You may be sure that such a man is warped and sinful; he is self-condemned.

Final Remarks

12As soon as I send Artemas or Tychicus[k] to you, do your best to come to me at Nicopolis, because I have decided to winter there.[l] 13Do everything you can to help Zenas the lawyer and Apollos[m] on their way and see that they have everything they need. 14Our people must learn to devote themselves to doing what is

2:14
s Ex 19:5 t Eph 2:10

3:1
u Ro 13:1 v 2Ti 2:21
3:2
w Eph 4:31;
2Ti 2:24

3:4
x Eph 2:7 y Tit 2:11
3:5
z Eph 2:9 a Ro 12:2

3:6
b Ro 5:5
3:7
c Ro 3:24 d Ro 8:17
e Ro 8:24 f Tit 1:2
3:8
g 1Ti 1:15
h Tit 2:14

3:9
i 1Ti 1:4; 2Ti 2:14

3:10
j Ro 16:17

3:12
k Ac 20:4
l 2Ti 4:9,21
3:13
m Ac 18:24

Titus 3:1–11

Verse 4 provides the same kind of gracious interruption Paul used in Ephesians 2:4: "Because of his great love for us, God, who is rich in mercy . . ." Paul finished his sentiment in verses 5–10. In both instances, the operative words are *mercy*, *love*, *grace*, and *kindness* (see Eph. 2:7). And each time we read that God "saved" us (Christians of all ages). In Ephesians we learn that he raised us up and seated us with Christ in the heavenly realms. Here he washes, renews, justifies, and gives us "the hope of eternal life." Both passages conclude with Paul's call to good works (see Eph. 2:10).

Verses 1 and 8 both speak of doing good. Church members can make immense strides in their community witness if they discuss together the spiritual climate in their neighborhoods and strategize how they may better implement the gospel of Christ in their own lives. Has it occurred to you that there are not only distinctive ways to *witness* in different communities, but distinctive ways to *be a witness?* The story of a changed life or an act of kindness can have immense power to turn people to Christ.

Titus 3:12–15

Paul's final remarks include personal requests,

greetings, and a benediction. His every instruction about doctrine, every warning about heresy, and every encouragement to holiness and good works is effective only as it's realized in the lives of people. One of the joys of heaven will be to meet 1st-century slaves and their masters, medieval peasants and their lords, business people from India, teachers from the Czech Republic, and computer scientists from Asia—all testifying to the grace of God in their lives. The Christian's joy in any age is the opportunity to bring the love of Christ to people.

Behind every statistic is a person. The personal nature of Paul's letter reminds us of his tender care for people. Christian agencies that are engaged in church planting or in relief and community development may use statistics to generate interest, but their ultimate focus is on individual people. As we partner with these organizations, together we can "devote ourselves to doing what is good." No one wants "to live an unproductive life." One of the greatest gifts we can give other people is the spiritual, educational, and economic resources they need on a daily basis, thereby enabling them, in turn, to devote themselves to doing good to others.

3:14
n ver 8

good, *n* in order that they may provide for daily necessities and not live unproductive lives.

3:15
o 1Ti 1:2 *p* Col 4:18

15 Everyone with me sends you greetings. Greet those who love us in the faith. *o*
Grace be with you all. *p*

Snapshots

3:14

Mirriam

Mirriam, a remarkable Zambian woman, is turning a small chicken farm into hope for the future and a means of helping her extended family and others.

> Caring for her own family
> has motivated Mirriam to
> help others in her position.

With an investment of 80 chicks from a Christian group, Mirriam
will turn a small profit from breeding and selling the poultry at market,
about U.S. $62 in the first round. The continued earnings will help
support and pay school fees for Mirriam's daughter and the three orphaned nieces and nephew living with her.

Caring for her own family has motivated Mirriam to help others
in her position. She notes, "AIDS has brought so many problems to
our community . . . We need to work together to fight this." So she also volunteers (with the
same group that invested in her business) as an in-home caregiver, looking in on 18 families
with children made vulnerable by HIV/AIDS, to see that their needs are met.

While she's out helping others, her fifteen-year-old nephew, Reuben, tends their growing
poultry farm. Mirriam sees this as an added blessing: He's learning a skill.

"Now I want to expand this business . . . that is the future for us," she asserts.

Verse 6 "BE ACTIVE IN SHARING YOUR FAITH, SO THAT YOU
WILL HAVE A FULL UNDERSTANDING OF EVERY GOOD THING
WE HAVE IN CHRIST."

INTRODUCTION TO
Philemon

AUTHOR
The letter identifies its author as the apostle Paul (v. 1), and this has never been seriously
questioned.

DATE WRITTEN
This letter was probably written between A.D. 60 and 62, during Paul's imprisonment in Rome,
at about the same time Ephesians and Colossians were written.

ORIGINAL READERS
Paul wrote this letter primarily to Philemon, but it's also addressed to Apphia (possibly Philemon's wife), Archippus (see Col. 4:17), and the members of the church in Colosse. Philemon
was a slave owner whose slave Onesimus had run away (vv. 11,15,18)—a crime punishable
under Roman law by death. Onesimus had met Paul in Rome and become a believer through
Paul's ministry. Paul entreated Philemon to forgive Onesimus and receive him back as a Christian brother.

TIMELINE

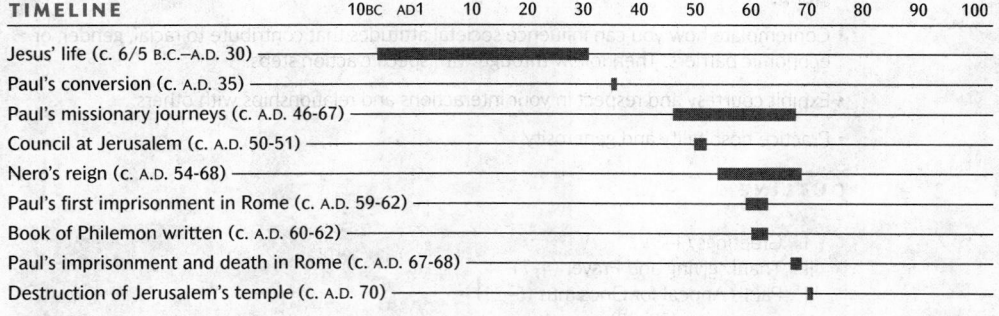

	10BC AD1	10	20	30	40	50	60	70	80	90	100
Jesus' life (c. 6/5 B.C.–A.D. 30)											
Paul's conversion (c. A.D. 35)											
Paul's missionary journeys (c. A.D. 46-67)											
Council at Jerusalem (c. A.D. 50-51)											
Nero's reign (c. A.D. 54-68)											
Paul's first imprisonment in Rome (c. A.D. 59-62)											
Book of Philemon written (c. A.D. 60-62)											
Paul's imprisonment and death in Rome (c. A.D. 67-68)											
Destruction of Jerusalem's temple (c. A.D. 70)											

THEMES
Philemon includes the following themes:

1. *Forgiveness.* Paul asked Philemon to accept his formerly troublesome slave as he would accept Paul himself, extending the same forgiving love to Onesimus that he himself had received from God (see Col. 3:13). Their reconciliation was so important that it took precedence
over Paul's wish to have Onesimus remain with himself (v. 13). This letter parallels Jesus' parable of the lost son (Luke 15:11–32). It speaks of failure, intercession, repentance, forgiveness,
and restoration. Regardless of how they might have been wronged, genuine disciples are to
relate to fellow believers with grace, forgiveness, and encouragement.

2. *Equality in Christ.* Being joined in Christ redefines all human relationships. In Christ there is no
distinction between slave and free. All are brothers and sisters in the Lord. Rather than exerting
his authority to bend Philemon's will to his own (v. 8), Paul made an appeal based on Philemon's
new relationship with Onesimus as "a brother in the Lord" (v. 16). Philemon was free to do what-

ever his conscience dictated, but his decision was to be informed by the gospel and his relationship to Paul, who had led him to Christ (v. 19). Paul didn't overtly challenge the slavery system, but neither did he sanctify it as part of God's design. Instead, he focused on how conversion fundamentally transforms personal relationships with others and with God. He laid down universal principles that, when taken seriously, ultimately topple the foundations of injustice in any form.

FAITH IN ACTION
The letter to Philemon contains life lessons and role models of faith—people who challenge believers to put faith in action.

Role Models

- PAUL (v. 10) called Onesimus his "son." When Onesimus came to Paul, Paul didn't see him as a criminal or slave, but as a soul in need of the Savior. How do you view people on society's margins?

- PHILEMON (v. 5) was known for his faith and love. What qualities do others associate with you?

- ONESIMUS (v. 11) served Paul during Paul's imprisonment and became very useful to him. He didn't allow his past to become an excuse to remain useless. How can God use you, regardless or even in spite of your past?

- ARCHIPPUS (v. 2) served the fellowship in Colosse by holding church meetings in his home. Do you practice hospitality and generosity with the material things God has entrusted to your care?

Challenges

- Examine your relationships. Is there someone you need to forgive? Choose to do so rather than to punish.

- Allow Christ to work through you to bring reconciliation between individuals and people groups.

- Contemplate how you can influence societal attitudes that contribute to racial, gender, or economic barriers. Then follow through with specific action steps.

- Exhibit courtesy and respect in your interactions and relationships with others.

- Practice hospitality and generosity.

OUTLINE

I. Greetings (1–3)
II. Thanksgiving and Prayer (4–7)
III. Paul's Appeal for Onesimus (8–21)
IV. Conclusion (22–25)

---

a ver 9,23; Eph 3:1
b 2Co 1:1
c Php 2:25
2
d Col 4:17
e Php 2:25
f Ro 16:5

¹Paul, a prisoner*ᵃ* of Christ Jesus, and Timothy our brother,*ᵇ*

To Philemon our dear friend and fellow worker,*ᶜ* ²to Apphia our sister, to Archippus*ᵈ* our fellow soldier*ᵉ* and to the church that meets in your home:*ᶠ*

³Grace to you and peace from God our Father and the Lord Jesus Christ.

Philemon 1–3

Many have wondered why this short letter is included in the Bible. It teaches no profound doctrinal truth. In fact, in sending Onesimus back to his owner, Paul appeared at first glance to be endorsing the practice of slavery. Alarmingly, Philemon was free to punish the runaway Onesimus, now Paul's brother in Christ, with death. With possibly one-third of the Roman population enslaved, Paul had to be tactful in how he approached this subject.

Thanksgiving and Prayer

[4]I always thank my God[g] as I remember you in my prayers, [5]because I hear about your faith in the Lord Jesus and your love for all the saints.[h] [6]I pray that you may be active in sharing your faith, so that you will have a full understanding of every good thing we have in Christ. [7]Your love has given me great joy and encouragement,[i] because you, brother, have refreshed[j] the hearts of the saints.

Paul's Plea for Onesimus

[8]Therefore, although in Christ I could be bold and order you to do what you ought to do, [9]yet I appeal to you on the basis of love. I then, as Paul—an old man and now also a prisoner[k] of Christ Jesus— [10]I appeal to you for my son[l] Onesimus,[a][m] who became my son while I was in chains. [11]Formerly he was useless to you, but now he has become useful both to you and to me.

[12]I am sending him—who is my very heart—back to you. [13]I would have liked to keep him with me so that he could take your place in helping me while I am in chains for the gospel. [14]But I did not want to do anything without your consent, so that any favor you do will be spontaneous and not forced.[n] [15]Perhaps the reason he was separated from you for a little while was that you might have him back for good— [16]no longer as a slave, but better than a slave, as a dear brother.[o] He is very dear to me but even dearer to you, both as a man and as a brother in the Lord.

[17]So if you consider me a partner,[p] welcome him as you would welcome me. [18]If he has done you any wrong or owes you anything, charge it to me. [19]I, Paul, am writing this with my own hand. I will pay it back—not to mention that you owe me your very self. [20]I do wish, brother, that I may have some benefit from you in the

4
g Ro 1:8
5
h Eph 1:15; Col 1:4

7
i 2Co 7:4,13
j ver 20

9
k ver 1,23
10
l 1Co 4:15
m Col 4:9

14
n 2Co 9:7; 1Pe 5:2

16
o Mt 23:8; 1Ti 6:2

17
p 2Co 8:23

a 10 *Onesimus* means *useful.*

Tactful he was. In a few brief words, Paul effectively undermined the entire system of slavery, stressing that he too was a prisoner in chains, accused of violating the laws and subject to the authority of Rome.

📖 Most of us wouldn't appreciate our congregation overhearing our personal correspondence suggesting how we could dispose of our property or reconcile with another member. Our culture encourages us to regard religion as a private matter, but Paul thought otherwise. The apostle viewed Christians as living and acting out of a communal context, in which trust and respect are paramount virtues (see Acts 2:42–47).

Individual Christians don't exist in a vacuum. When we're joined to Christ, we're at the same time joined to other believers. The reconciliation of a disloyal slave with his master as brothers in Christ—the theme of Philemon—recasts all relationships and reflects Christ's reconciliation of all things (Col. 1:20). We're not to view others in terms of their social class or the wrong they may have done to us. With which fellow church member have you experienced differences? Has the issue been fully resolved? Where in the world does this reconciling, relationship-transforming power of the gospel most need to be manifested?

Philemon 4–7

📖 Paul told Philemon, a member of the Colossian church, that he prayed for him regularly—and he told him why. The "your" in verse 5 is singular; Paul was directing his remarks to Philemon, who alone had the power to grant his request. Paul wasn't trying to soften up Philemon. He regularly offered congratulatory thanksgivings in his letters, and his tribute to Philemon

for his faith and love was identical to his praise of all the Colossians (Col. 1:4).

📖 Would you agree with a definition of the church as a gathering of people who share common religious views? Paul saw church membership as something far more. In this letter he showed how two households, the natural and the spiritual, intersect. He understood that what Philemon decided to do with his unfaithful slave would have consequences for his whole house church. Things haven't changed in this regard: A leader's responses to the demands of love in everyday decisions directly affect the spiritual health of the whole congregation.

Philemon 8–25

📖 The Roman imperial economy depended on slaves for labor. Slaves had no legal status, and a runaway could be severely whipped, branded on the face, chained, forced to wear an iron neck collar, or restrained by having his or her legs broken. Slaves also could be sold to the mines or sentenced to death. Any concern for a slave's welfare was usually practical, motivated by the owner's self-interest.

Paul delicately referred to Onesimus as a new convert. He underscored this slave's value to himself by musing that he would like to keep Onesimus with him. He formally asked Philemon to receive Onesimus back as a brother. Knowing Philemon's affection for Paul, Paul simply instructed him to receive Onesimus as though he were receiving Paul himself. Any debt Onesimus owed, Philemon was encouraged to charge to Paul. Knowing that Philemon wouldn't dream of executing Paul, Paul was confident of his compliance.

Reconciliation Among Christians

Paul faced a tough problem when he sat down to write Philemon: how to convince him to accept Onesimus back, not as a runaway slave but as a Christian brother. Philemon had much to forgive. But Onesimus also must have struggled with the idea of reconciling with the man who had the right to punish or kill him.

The Christian community faces a similar dilemma. How can people with much to forgive learn to think of each other as members of the same family? Growing up in Mississippi in the 1950s and 60s, I learned that Christians in the white community had a hard time loving Christians in the black community. Many churches that supported and sent missionaries to Africa wouldn't allow me, a black man, to sit in their pews. My dream of attending a Christian liberal arts college in 1965 was thwarted: Most weren't open to black students. Two years later I was finally accepted at a college in Southern California. When I left Mississippi, I vowed never to return.

But God brought me back in 1971. For a number of years I have been working with an organization called Mission Mississippi. Our mission is to take Paul's message to Philemon to the whole church in Mississippi.

> **H**ow can people with much to forgive learn to think of each other as members of the same family?

We say we love all the saints, but we have often predetermined who they are. Our mental picture of the Christian family is easily restricted to people who look and talk like us and live in the same neighborhood. But God also has called us to love very different saints. He wants us to live together in love, not in some abstract way but in a visible, outward manifestation of his love for the church (John 17:23).

Being Christian means undergoing a continuous, radical transformation. In 2 Corinthians 5:17, Paul taught that as Christians we have become "a new creation." He saw us clothed in Jesus' righteousness and, because of Christ's finished work on the cross and resurrection, equal in righteousness and honor.

The New Testament church struggled continually with this newfound unity and equality. Jews resented Greeks for gaining God's favor without first having followed the law. Greeks disliked Jews for their superior attitude. Paul and the other apostles were constantly arbitrating disputes, reminding this new family that all who had been baptized into Christ had *clothed* themselves with him. Neither gender nor occupation nor financial status nor cultural difference nor the color of one's skin was to be a barrier to Christian unity (see Gal. 3:27–28).

Lack of such unity is a worldwide problem. In Ireland, Catholics and Protestants are in tension. In Central America, class divisions rock the church. In Africa, tribal divisions make Christian oneness seem like a distant dream. The wounds are deep, the need for reconciliation profound. Unless the Christian community works intentionally to build bridges around the fact that there is *one* Savior, Spirit, and destination, the chasms will grow deeper and wider. How can this be done?

1. Pray for people racially and culturally different from yourself, asking God to open your heart to appreciate his image in all people.

2. Read books by authors, especially Christians, from a different ethnic or racial background.

3. Develop a one-on-one relationship with a Christian from another race, culture, or denomination.

4. Seek opportunities to sit under the leadership of someone you don't know.

5. Pray that God will lead you to others who desire Christian unity. Then begin a Bible study.

6. Stay at the table long enough to get to know those who are racially and culturally diverse, no matter how different your opinions may be.

Dolphus Weary, executive director of Mission Mississippi, a faith-based program in Jackson, Mississippi, that cultivates racial tolerance by facilitating church-to-church dialogue

Lord; refresh *q* my heart in Christ. ²¹Confident *r* of your obedience, I write to you, knowing that you will do even more than I ask.

²²And one thing more: Prepare a guest room for me, because I hope to be *s* restored to you in answer to your prayers. *t*

²³Epaphras, *u* my fellow prisoner in Christ Jesus, sends you greetings. ²⁴And so do Mark, *v* Aristarchus, *w* Demas *x* and Luke, my fellow workers.
²⁵The grace of the Lord Jesus Christ be with your spirit. *y*

20
q ver 7
21
r 2Co 2:3
22
s Php 1:25; 2:24
t 2Co 1:11
23
u Col 1:7
24
v Ac 12:12
w Ac 19:29
x Col 4:14
25
y 2Ti 4:22

Some Christians today see Paul's silence on the inequities of slavery as a deplorable blind spot. But his attitude may have been based on a recognition that the system wouldn't be changed unless the attitudes on which it was based were transformed. Paul knew the existing social order was deeply flawed (see Rom. 1:18–32) but expected the present scheme of things to pass away (1 Cor. 7:29–31). What glaring inequities characterize your own or other societies around the world? How can you work *within the system* to prepare for change?

Do you sometimes feel overwhelmed, even immobilized, by social evils? How, you ask, can one individual possibly do anything to alleviate so much suffering? Paul here helped *one* slave and contributed to the church's understanding of the importance of the equality of believers in Christ. You too can ask God to lead you to that one oppressed person who needs your friendship and loving hand. God's Spirit will transform the world as, one believer at a time, we open ourselves up to be agents of his justice.

INTRODUCTION TO
Hebrews

AUTHOR

The author of Hebrews is unknown. Paul, Luke, Clement of Rome, Barnabas, Apollos, Epaphras, Silas, Philip, Priscilla, and others have been suggested. The author was well schooled in the Old Testament, acquainted with his audience, capable of writing excellent Greek, and a friend of Timothy (13:23).

DATE WRITTEN

Hebrews was probably written between A.D. 60 and 70.

ORIGINAL READERS

Hebrews was written to Jewish believers who spoke Greek and probably used the Septuagint (the Greek translation of the OT). They had heard the testimony of eyewitnesses to Christ (2:3) and were undergoing persecution (10:32–34; 13:3).

TIMELINE

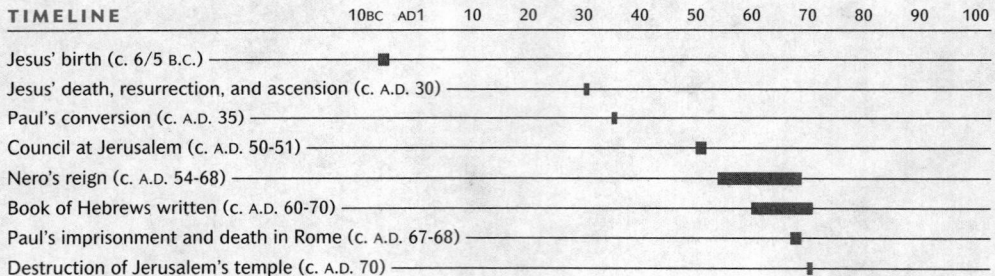

	10BC AD1	10	20	30	40	50	60	70	80	90	100
Jesus' birth (c. 6/5 B.C.)											
Jesus' death, resurrection, and ascension (c. A.D. 30)											
Paul's conversion (c. A.D. 35)											
Council at Jerusalem (c. A.D. 50-51)											
Nero's reign (c. A.D. 54-68)											
Book of Hebrews written (c. A.D. 60-70)											
Paul's imprisonment and death in Rome (c. A.D. 67-68)											
Destruction of Jerusalem's temple (c. A.D. 70)											

THEMES

Hebrews contains the following themes:

1. *The superiority of Christ.* Hebrews presents Christ as superior to the prophets (1:1–2), angels (1:4–6), Moses (3:3), Joshua (4:8), the Old Testament priesthood and the high priest (4:14—5:10; 7:1–28), the old covenant, the sacrificial system, and the sanctuary where God was approached (8:1—10:18). Christ is the agent of creation (1:2), "the radiance of God's glory and the exact representation of his being" (1:3), honored above angels (1:4–14), sinless (4:15; 7:26–28), and eternal (7:3,24). Yet he also shares our humanity (2:14–18) and is a sympathetic high priest (4:15; 5:7–10) and the sacrifice for our sins (7:27; 9:12,26,28; 10:10).

2. *Perseverance.* Believers are called to a heavenward journey (3:1) and a heavenly country (11:16), the new Jerusalem (12:22). But the journey will be dangerous. Christians must undergo testing, just as the wilderness generation did. "Today" is the time of decision, because God's call always requires a response and carries a time limit. If we are to enter the rest prepared for us (4:11), we are to obey (4:7), hold fast to our confession in Jesus (4:14), approach the throne of grace with boldness (4:16; 10:22), run the race (12:1), fix our eyes on Jesus (12:2), and venture "outside the camp" (13:13)—beyond religious traditions.

3. *Faith pleases God.* Chapter 11 emphasizes a faith that is exercised in numerous large and small ways. We are to follow the Old Testament examples of people whose lives demonstrated a living, active faith.

4. *Discipline comes to God's children.* Hardship is the means God uses to discipline his children. Difficulties can take many forms, but the believer is to endure them all. As our heavenly Father, God disciplines us for our good in order to produce "a harvest of righteousness and peace" (12:1–13).

5. *Christian living.* Christians are to show hospitality to strangers and remember those in prison (13:1–3). They are to refrain from sexual immorality (13:4), guard against the love of money (13:5), do good and share with others (13:16), obey their leaders and submit to their authority (13:17), and pray (13:18–19).

FAITH IN ACTION

The pages of Hebrews contain life lessons and role models of faith—people who challenge believers to put faith in action.

Role Models

- JESUS (1:1–4) is the best example of godly living, superior in every way. Do you model yourself after him?

- ENOCH (11:5) pleased God by faith. Is the Lord pleased with the outworkings of your faith?

- NOAH (11:7) built an ark on faith. Have you been called to an act of obedience that seems illogical or unreasonable? How can Noah's example encourage you?

- ABRAHAM (11:8–12) ventured from his homeland by faith, not knowing where he was going. Is God asking you to trust him as he leads you into a new, uncertain endeavor?

- MOSES (11:24–28) refused the privileged life of a prince, choosing instead to be mistreated, because he was "looking ahead to his [faith] reward" (11:26). Is God calling you to give up a life of privilege to serve him?

- RAHAB (11:31) welcomed the Israelite spies by faith and was spared when Jericho fell. Is God asking you to take the risk of helping a stranger?

Challenges

- Christ is superior to everyone and everything else. Pray for spiritual discernment, that you may see the deceptions of the world.

- Be sensitive to non-Christians who feel that Christianity invalidates their beliefs by proclaiming Jesus as the only way to God. Respect them and their traditions, but be ready to humbly articulate the truth of the gospel.

- Welcome hardships that come your way. God uses them to train his children.

- Be open to the unconventional ways God may want to use you to display your faith.

- Live an ethical, moral life that is a visible proclamation of your faith to the world.

- In this fast-paced society, find your "rest" (peace) in your relationship with Jesus, allowing him to lead you into God's very presence.

OUTLINE

I.   The Superiority of God's New Revelation (1:1–4)
II. Christ Is Superior to the Angels (1:5—2:18)
     A. Biblical Evidence of Christ's Superiority (1:5–14)
     B. The Danger of Neglecting the Truth About Christ (2:1–4)
     C. Further Biblical Evidence of Christ's Superiority (2:5–18)
III. Christ Is Superior to Moses (3:1—4:13)
     A. Christ the Son; Moses the Servant (3:1–6)
     B. Warning Against Unbelief (3:7—4:13)

IV. Christ Is Superior to the Aaronic Priests (4:14—7:28)
   A. Access to the Throne of Grace Through Our High Priest (4:14–16)
   B. Jesus' Qualifications as a Priest (5:1–10)
   C. Exhortation to Become Spiritually Mature (5:11—6:12)
   D. Confident Hope as an Anchor for the Soul (6:13–20)
   E. Christ and Melchizedek (7)
V. The Superior Sacrificial Work of Our High Priest (8–10)
   A. A Better Covenant (8)
   B. A Better Sanctuary (9:1–12)
   C. A Better Sacrifice (9:13—10:18)
   D. Exhortations (10:19–39)
VI. Application: Stand Fast (11–12)
   A. Examples From the Past (11)
   B. Discipline's Role in Developing Faith (12:1–11)
   C. Warning Concerning Consequences of Sin (12:12–17)
   D. Danger of Refusing This Message (12:18–29)
VII. Conclusion (13)

The Son Superior to Angels

1:1
a Jn 9:29; Heb 2:2,
3 *b* Ac 2:30
c Nu 12:6,8
1:2
d Ps 2:8 *e* Jn 1:3
1:3
f Jn 1:14 *g* Col 1:17
h Heb 7:27
i Mk 16:19

1 In the past God spoke[a] to our forefathers through the prophets[b] at many times and in various ways,[c] 2but in these last days he has spoken to us by his Son, whom he appointed heir[d] of all things, and through whom[e] he made the universe. 3The Son is the radiance of God's glory[f] and the exact representation of his being, sustaining all things[g] by his powerful word. After he had provided purification for sins,[h] he sat down at the right hand of the Majesty in heaven.[i] 4So he became as much superior to the angels as the name he has inherited is superior to theirs.[j]

1:4
j Eph 1:21;
Php 2:9,10

5For to which of the angels did God ever say,

1:5
k Ps 2:7 *l* 2Sa 7:14

"You are my Son;
   today I have become your Father[a]"[b]?[k]

Or again,

"I will be his Father,
   and he will be my Son"[c]?[l]

1:6
m Heb 10:5
n Dt 32:43 (LXX
and DSS); Ps 97:7

6And again, when God brings his firstborn into the world,[m] he says,

"Let all God's angels worship him."[d][n]

7In speaking of the angels he says,

a 5 Or *have begotten you*   b 5 Psalm 2:7   c 5 2 Samuel 7:14; 1 Chron. 17:13   d 6 Deut. 32:43
(see Dead Sea Scrolls and Septuagint)

Hebrews 1:1–14

🔲🔲 The unidentified author of Hebrews opened with a majestic overture, eloquent and theologically packed. This opening statement (vv. 1–4 form a single Greek sentence) contrasts the revelation in the Old Testament with that in the New, focusing on and climaxing in the person of God's Son—Heir, Agent of creation, Sustainer of the universe, Savior, and Sovereign—who now sits at God's right hand.

Hebrews was likely an early Christian sermon, crafted by someone accustomed to worshiping in a Greek-speaking synagogue and educated in the Greek and Roman institutions of the day. Both the Greek and Roman traditions emphasized an appropriate beginning, in which the speaker was to present the main topic(s) of his speech or sermon and seek to rivet the audience's attention.

🔲 Warm-hearted, practical Christianity is to be encouraged. Yet theology and practice are both vital to Christians. Can you explain why you believe as you do by using Scripture, as well as by describing your salvation experience?

Often we view the world as "out of control" or, at least, as dominated by evil. In verses 5–14 the author used a chain of Old Testament quotations, focusing on Jesus' superior position in order to draw the audience to Christ's unsurpassed authority.

"He makes his angels winds,
 his servants flames of fire." [a][o]

8But about the Son he says,

"Your throne, O God, will last for ever and ever,
 and righteousness will be the scepter of your kingdom.
9You have loved righteousness and hated wickedness;
 therefore God, your God, has set you above your companions[p]
 by anointing you with the oil[q] of joy." [b]

10He also says,

"In the beginning, O Lord, you laid the foundations of the earth,
 and the heavens are the work of your hands.
11They will perish, but you remain;
 they will all wear out like a garment.[r]
12You will roll them up like a robe;
 like a garment they will be changed.
But you remain the same,[s]
 and your years will never end." [c][t]

13To which of the angels did God ever say,

"Sit at my right hand
until I make your enemies
a footstool[u] for your feet" [d]?[v]

14Are not all angels ministering spirits[w] sent to serve those who will inherit salvation?[x]

Warning to Pay Attention

2 We must pay more careful attention, therefore, to what we have heard, so that we do not drift away. 2For if the message spoken[y] by angels[z] was binding, and every violation and disobedience received its just punishment,[a] 3how shall we escape if we ignore such a great salvation?[b] This salvation, which was first announced by the Lord,[c] was confirmed to us by those who heard him.[d] 4God also testified to it by signs, wonders and various miracles,[e] and gifts of the Holy Spirit[f] distributed according to his will.[g]

Jesus Made Like His Brothers

5It is not to angels that he has subjected the world to come, about which we are speaking. 6But there is a place where someone has testified:

1:7
[o] Ps 104:4

1:9
[p] Php 2:9
[q] Isa 61:1,3

1:11
[r] Isa 34:4

1:12
[s] Heb 13:8
[t] Ps 102:25-27

1:13
[u] Jos 10:24; Heb 10:13
[v] Ps 110:1

1:14
[w] Ps 103:20
[x] Heb 5:9

2:2
[y] Heb 1:1
[z] Dt 33:2; Ac 7:53
[a] Heb 10:28

2:3
[b] Heb 10:29
[c] Heb 1:2 [d] Lk 1:2

2:4
[e] Jn 4:48 [f] 1Co 12:4
[g] Eph 1:5

---

[a] 7 Psalm 104:4 [b] 9 Psalm 45:6,7 [c] 12 Psalm 102:25-27 [d] 13 Psalm 110:1

Hebrews 2:1–4

Having established Christ's supreme authority, the preacher confronted listeners with their responsibility not to drift away, while stressing the solidity of such a "great salvation." A frequent theme of this book is the total reliability of hope in Christ—and the need to hold fast to it. The author counseled caution: If those who were disobedient to the older revelation—the Law of Moses given through angels (Acts 7:38,53; Gal. 3:19)—were punished, those who turned away from salvation offered in Christ surely wouldn't escape.

Do you think the idea of God punishing people for sin is overly harsh or outdated? Some do. Yet the reality of just punishment for disobedience is woven throughout the Old Testament (Ps. 62:12; Prov. 24:12; Ezek. 7:3, 27; cf. Jer. 11:11) and was emphasized by

Jesus (Matt. 5:22; 16:27; 23:14; 25:41–46). In fact, the foundation for God's just punishment is his holy character and divine love. The Scriptures show sin as a force that moves people away from holiness and God's presence. If God is light, love, and life, then apart from him lie only darkness and death.

Hebrews 2:5–18

In verses 5–9 the preacher quoted Psalm 8. In addition to its references to the Son's supremacy, this passage discusses his coming to Earth and taking on a "status" lower than that of the angels. Jesus walked the earth as a human before being exalted back to heaven. In verses 10–18 the author explained that the incarnation (Jesus' coming to Earth as a human) was necessary for his identification with our suffering.

2:6
h Job 7:17

"What is man that you are mindful of him,
    the son of man that you care for him?[h]
7 You made him a little[a] lower than the angels;
    you crowned him with glory and honor
8   and put everything under his feet."[b][i]

2:8
i Ps 8:4-6;
1Co 15:25

In putting everything under him, God left nothing that is not subject to him. Yet at present we do not see everything subject to him. 9 But we see Jesus, who was made a little lower than the angels, now crowned with glory and honor[j] because he suffered death,[k] so that by the grace of God he might taste death for everyone.[l]

2:9
j Ac 2:33; 3:13;
Php 2:9 k Php 2:7-9
l Jn 3:16; 2Co 5:15

10 In bringing many sons to glory, it was fitting that God, for whom and through whom everything exists,[m] should make the author of their salvation perfect through suffering.[n] 11 Both the one who makes men holy and those who are made holy[o] are of the same family. So Jesus is not ashamed to call them brothers.[p] 12 He says,

2:10
m Ro 11:36
n Lk 24:26;
Heb 7:28
2:11
o Heb 10:10
p Mt 28:10;
Jn 20:17

"I will declare your name to my brothers;
    in the presence of the congregation I will sing your praises."[c][q]

2:12
q Ps 22:22

13 And again,

"I will put my trust in him."[d][r]

2:13
r Isa 8:17 s Isa 8:18;
Jn 10:29

And again he says,

"Here am I, and the children God has given me."[e][s]

14 Since the children have flesh and blood, he too shared in their humanity[t] so that by his death he might destroy[u] him who holds the power of death—that is, the devil[v]—15 and free those who all their lives were held in slavery by their fear[w] of death. 16 For surely it is not angels he helps, but Abraham's descendants. 17 For this reason he had to be made like his brothers[x] in every way, in order that he might become a merciful[y] and faithful high priest[z] in service to God,[a] and that he might

2:14
t Jn 1:14
u 1Co 15:54-57;
2Ti 1:10 v 1Jn 3:8

2:15
w 2Ti 1:7

2:17
x Php 2:7 y Heb 5:2
z Heb 4:14,15;
7:26,28 a Heb 5:1

---

a 7 Or *him for a little while*; also in verse 9   b 8 Psalm 8:4-6   c 12 Psalm 22:22
d 13 Isaiah 8:17   e 13 Isaiah 8:18

Does the problem of pain ever lead you to question God? Is there an ongoing or intermittent struggle between your faith and your feelings? Christian writer Larry Crabb noted, "We have become committed to relieving the pain behind our problems rather than . . . to wrestle more passionately with the character and purposes of God. *Feeling better has become more important than finding God.* And worse, we assume that people who find God always feel better." The difficulty lies in our living between Christ's exaltation and his second coming, when we "do not [yet] see everything subject to him." Straining to "see Jesus," our eternal reference point, will keep our perspective on course.

2:15

FROM FEAR TO COURAGE

Studies have shown that we are more afraid of something new, manufactured, forced, sudden, or unfamiliar than we are of older, natural things, even when statistically speaking the older things have the potential to cause more damage:

	More fear (Less danger)	Less fear (More danger)
New rather than something that has been around	SARS, West Nile Virus	Flu, HIV/AIDS
Manufactured rather than natural	Nuclear waste radiation	Sun radiation
Imposed (forced on us) rather than chosen	Air pollution	Smoking
Sudden danger rather than slow, insidious danger	Shark attack	Heart disease
Controlled by someone else	Riding in an airplane	Driving a car

The writer of Hebrews tells us not that "the only thing to fear is fear itself" (Franklin Delano Roosevelt) but that the only One to "fear" (in the sense of awe and reverence) is God. God has rendered powerless all fears, even the greatest of human fears, the fear of death (2:15). "The fear of the LORD is the beginning of knowledge" (Prov. 1:7).

make atonement for[a] the sins of the people. [18]Because he himself suffered when he was tempted, he is able to help those who are being tempted.[b]

Jesus Greater Than Moses

3 Therefore, holy brothers,[c] who share in the heavenly calling, fix your thoughts on Jesus, the apostle and high priest[d] whom we confess.[e] [2]He was faithful to the one who appointed him, just as Moses was faithful in all God's house.[f] [3]Jesus has been found worthy of greater honor than Moses, just as the builder of a house has greater honor than the house itself. [4]For every house is built by someone, but God is the builder of everything. [5]Moses was faithful as a servant[g] in all God's house,[h] testifying to what would be said in the future. [6]But Christ is faithful as a son[i] over God's house. And we are his house,[j] if we hold on[k] to our courage and the hope[l] of which we boast.

Warning Against Unbelief

[7]So, as the Holy Spirit says:[m]

> "Today, if you hear his voice,
> [8]   do not harden your hearts
>   as you did in the rebellion,
>   during the time of testing in the desert,
> [9]where your fathers tested and tried me
>   and for forty years saw what I did.[n]
> [10]That is why I was angry with that generation,
>   and I said, 'Their hearts are always going astray,
>   and they have not known my ways.'
> [11]So I declared on oath in my anger,
>   'They shall never enter my rest.'"[o][b][p]

[12]See to it, brothers, that none of you has a sinful, unbelieving heart that turns away from the living God. [13]But encourage one another daily,[q] as long as it is called Today, so that none of you may be hardened by sin's deceitfulness.[r] [14]We have come to share in Christ if we hold firmly[s] till the end the confidence we had at first. [15]As has just been said:

> "Today, if you hear his voice,
>   do not harden your hearts
>   as you did in the rebellion."[c][t]

---

[a] 17 Or *and that he might turn aside God's wrath, taking away*
[b] 11 Psalm 95:7-11
[c] 15 Psalm 95:7,8

Cross-references column:

2:18
b Heb 4:15

3:1
c Heb 2:11
d Heb 2:17
e Heb 4:14
3:2
f Nu 12:7

3:5
g Ex 14:31 *h* ver 2; Nu 12:7
3:6
i Heb 1:2
j 1Co 3:16
k Ro 11:22 / Ro 5:2
3:7
m Heb 9:8

3:9
n Ac 7:36

3:11
o Heb 4:3,5
p Ps 95:7-11

3:13
q Heb 10:24,25
r Eph 4:22
3:14
s ver 6

3:15
t ver 7,8; Ps 95:7,8

Hebrews 3:1–6

Since believers are "children" (2:13), they need a model of someone who has lived out the faithfulness of a son. Jesus, God's Son, provides an example superior to that of the greatest Old Testament figures. As Creator, Jesus has greater authority than Moses. The author built on Moses' greatness but asserted that Jesus must be the object of the Christian's ultimate focus.

People tend to exalt superstars, not true heroes. Today our cultural heroes are often people who can dribble, sprint, sing, dance, or act. This kind of fuzzy thinking by Christians can lead us to follow the wrong sort of example. The author here pointed to Moses. Who are your heroes of the faith, both past and contemporary? How have they inspired your faith? Courage? Holiness? Persistence?

Hebrews 3:7–19

Verses 7–19 consist of a quotation from and commentary on Psalm 95:7–11. The hearers weren't to follow the example of those who had fallen in the desert but were to hold firmly to their Christian confidence, keeping their hearts impressionable, yielded, and vigilant against sin. They were to encourage one another "today," while they had opportunity to respond obediently to God's voice.

This chapter promotes five principles of faithfulness: (1) A healthy focus on Christ encourages faithfulness. (2) Faithfulness is volitional (a choice), as well as emotional and intellectual. (3) Sinfulness and unbelief can hinder faithfulness. (4) The faithful persevere in commitment until the end. (5) Faithfulness is a community affair, with each believer depending on the others for encouragement.

To some, Hebrews' emphasis on a well-paced faith may seem out of step with our instant-oriented society. Yet obedience to God is to be lived out in the daily, sometime mundane experiences of life over time, often without immediate reward or acknowledgement for our efforts. Hebrews 3 challenges us as believers to take seriously our commitment to Christ and to remain faithful to him as a life pattern.

¹⁶Who were they who heard and rebelled? Were they not all those Moses led out of Egypt?^u ¹⁷And with whom was he angry for forty years? Was it not with those who sinned, whose bodies fell in the desert?^v ¹⁸And to whom did God swear that they would never enter his rest^w if not to those who disobeyed^a?^x ¹⁹So we see that they were not able to enter, because of their unbelief.^y

A Sabbath-Rest for the People of God

4 Therefore, since the promise of entering his rest still stands, let us be careful that none of you be found to have fallen short of it.^z ²For we also have had the gospel preached to us, just as they did; but the message they heard was of no value to them, because those who heard did not combine it with faith.^b^a ³Now we who have believed enter that rest, just as God has said,

"So I declared on oath in my anger,
'They shall never enter my rest.' "^c^b

And yet his work has been finished since the creation of the world. ⁴For somewhere he has spoken about the seventh day in these words: "And on the seventh day God rested from all his work."^d^c ⁵And again in the passage above he says, "They shall never enter my rest."^d

⁶It still remains that some will enter that rest, and those who formerly had the gospel preached to them did not go in, because of their disobedience.^e ⁷Therefore God again set a certain day, calling it Today, when a long time later he spoke through David, as was said before:

"Today, if you hear his voice,
do not harden your hearts."^e^f

⁸For if Joshua had given them rest,^g God would not have spoken^h later about another day. ⁹There remains, then, a Sabbath-rest for the people of God; ¹⁰for anyone who enters God's rest also rests from his own work, just as God did from his.ⁱ ¹¹Let us, therefore, make every effort to enter that rest, so that no one will fall by following their example of disobedience.^j

¹²For the word of God^k is living and active.^l Sharper than any double-edged sword,^m it penetrates even to dividing soul and spirit, joints and marrow; it judges the thoughts and attitudes of the heart.ⁿ ¹³Nothing in all creation is hidden from God's sight.^o Everything is uncovered and laid bare before the eyes of him to whom we must give account.

Jesus the Great High Priest

¹⁴Therefore, since we have a great high priest who has gone through the heavens,^f^p Jesus the Son of God, let us hold firmly to the faith we profess.^q ¹⁵For we do not have a high priest who is unable to sympathize with our weaknesses, but we have one who has been tempted in every way, just as we are^r—yet was without sin.^s

---

^a 18 Or *disbelieved*   ^b 2 Many manuscripts *because they did not share in the faith of those who obeyed*   ^c 3 Psalm 95:11; also in verse 5   ^d 4 Gen. 2:2   ^e 7 Psalm 95:7,8   ^f 14 Or *gone into heaven*

Marginal references:

3:16
u Nu 14:2
3:17
v Nu 14:29;
Ps 106:26
3:18
w Nu 14:20-23
x Heb 4:6
3:19
y Jn 3:36

4:1
z Heb 12:15
4:2
a 1Th 2:13

4:3
b Ps 95:11;
Heb 3:11

4:4
c Ge 2:2,3;
Ex 20:11
4:5
d Ps 95:11

4:6
e Heb 3:18

4:7
f Ps 95:7,8;
Heb 3:7,8,15
4:8
g Jos 22:4
h Heb 1:1

4:10
i ver 4

4:11
j Heb 3:18
4:12
k 1Pe 1:23
l Jer 23:29
m Eph 6:17;
Rev 1:16
n 1Co 14:24,25
4:13
o Ps 33:13-15

4:14
p Heb 6:20
q Heb 3:1

4:15
r Heb 2:18
s 2Co 5:21

Hebrews 4:1–13

The author saw some of the original audience as poised between entering God's rest and turning back to a spiritual desert. Some hearers were casual in their evaluation of salvation and the consequences of rejecting it (cf. 2:1–3). The author wanted to impress on them the real opportunity that lay before those who were willing to take God at his word and move forward in obedience to lay hold of his promise of rest.

Fast-paced living conceals God's invitation to rest. At the same time true rest can't be found simply in ceasing from labor. Spiritual wandering and restlessness aren't new problems. Jesus observed a wearied humanity and invited, "Come to me . . . and I will give you rest" (Matt. 11:28). Still today he offers the ultimate source for rest to everyone—a right relationship with God. Ask yourself: Do I project to those watching a sense of hurry, frustration, and hassle? Or do I convey the confidence of someone who has found rest in God?

Hebrews 4:14—5:10

After the powerful description of Jesus as a compassionate high priest, the author invited the readers to "approach the throne of grace." Christians are to draw near to God with unabashed openness, since he alone is their true source of mercy and grace, the One who will "help us in our time of need."

Using the Bible in Life

 4:12

The author of Hebrews describes the Bible as "living and active . . . sharper than any double-edged sword." We are called to move beyond reading it or even meditating upon it; we are to take the next step, employing its wisdom to critique life and determine courses of action. The question is how.

Subtle differences in the ways people appeal to and use the Bible in ethical reflection seem endless. But the great variety of uses—ranging from irresponsible to responsible—people make of Scripture in deliberations about morality fall into four basic categories: *proof-texts, parallels, principles,* and *paradigms.*

Proof-texts. People may point to a "proving" text in the Bible in an effort to establish or validate an argument, idea, or action—even though the Biblical material referred to at times may have at best a questionable relevance to the matter at hand.

Parallels. Biblical material is used this way when people refer to a passage, usually a sentence or story, they see as in some way analogous to a context other than that of the original Biblical text.

Principles. A Biblical text is used to establish a principle when someone derives from it a directive or standard they can then cite to make an ethical decision, either in relation to a particular situation or to general practice. More than proof-texts and parallels, principles formed and articulated from Scriptural perspectives can provide insight and guidance for serious ethical reflection.

> **At various times and in various places the Bible speaks *directly, indirectly,* or *not at all* about matters of ethical significance.**

Paradigms. Biblical texts yielding examples or patterns that may offer ethical guidance for life situations are usually identified as paradigms. Paradigmatic passages typically present pictures, most often in the form of stories, that can serve as examples, models, or precedents for thinking about ethical issues.

Because the models communicated through paradigms are often complex, this kind of text may have a unique capacity to inspire, inform, and guide our decision-making efforts. As is always the case with Biblical materials, the best use of Scripture in reflection on matters of morality comes when we pay attention to two areas: (1) the plain sense of the texts (what do they say, period, in and of themselves, in isolation from the material before and after?) and (2) their place in their original Biblical contexts (what do they say in the framework of the time, place, and unique situation in which they were written?).

At various times and in various places the Bible speaks *directly, indirectly,* or *not at all* about matters of ethical significance. Scripturally based reflections about right and wrong engage Biblical statements that seem pertinent to the issues by using a range of approaches. Because there are diverse ways of reading and responding to the Bible, people attempting to make moral decisions on a Biblical basis are wise to (1) summarize their understanding of the Scriptural statement, (2) recognize that—and how—others might interpret the material differently, and (3) be able to articulate how and why they feel this particular passage impacts their process of ethical reflection.

Marion L. Soards, professor of New Testament at Louisville Presbyterian Theological Seminary in Louisville, Kentucky

16Let us then approach the throne of grace with confidence, so that we may receive mercy and find grace to help us in our time of need.

5 Every high priest is selected from among men and is appointed to represent them in matters related to God, to offer gifts and sacrifices[t] for sins.[u] 2He is able to deal gently with those who are ignorant and are going astray,[v] since he himself is subject to weakness.[w] 3This is why he has to offer sacrifices for his own sins, as well as for the sins of the people.[x]

4No one takes this honor upon himself; he must be called by God, just as Aaron was.[y] 5So Christ also did not take upon himself the glory[z] of becoming a high priest. But God said[a] to him,

"You are my Son;
today I have become your Father.[a]"[b]

6And he says in another place,

"You are a priest forever,
in the order of Melchizedek."[cc]

7During the days of Jesus' life on earth, he offered up prayers and petitions with loud cries and tears[d] to the one who could save him from death, and he was heard because of his reverent submission.[e] 8Although he was a son, he learned obedience from what he suffered[f] 9and, once made perfect,[g] he became the source of eternal salvation for all who obey him 10and was designated by God to be high priest[h] in the order of Melchizedek.[i]

Warning Against Falling Away

11We have much to say about this, but it is hard to explain because you are slow to learn. 12In fact, though by this time you ought to be teachers, you need someone to teach you the elementary truths[j] of God's word all over again. You need milk, not solid food![k] 13Anyone who lives on milk, being still an infant,[l] is not acquainted with the teaching about righteousness. 14But solid food is for the mature,[m] who by constant use have trained themselves to distinguish good from evil.[n]

6 Therefore let us leave[o] the elementary teachings[p] about Christ and go on to maturity, not laying again the foundation of repentance from acts that lead to death,[dq] and of faith in God, 2instruction about baptisms,[r] the laying on of hands,[s]

5:1 [t] Heb 8:3 [u] Heb 7:27
5:2 [v] Heb 2:18 [w] Heb 7:28
5:3 [x] Heb 7:27; 9:7
5:4 [y] Ex 28:1
5:5 [z] Jn 8:54 [a] Heb 1:1 [b] Ps 2:7
5:6 [c] Ps 110:4; Heb 7:17,21
5:7 [d] Mt 27:46,50 [e] Mk 14:36
5:8 [f] Php 2:8
5:9 [g] Heb 2:10
5:10 [h] ver 5 [i] ver 6
5:12 [j] Heb 6:1 [k] 1Co 3:2; 1Pe 2:2
5:13 [l] 1Co 14:20
5:14 [m] 1Co 2:6 [n] Isa 7:15
6:1 [o] Php 3:12-14 [p] Heb 5:12 [q] Heb 9:14
6:2 [r] Jn 3:25 [s] Ac 6:6

---

[a] 5 Or *have begotten you*   [b] 5 Psalm 2:7   [c] 6 Psalm 110:4   [d] 1 Or *from useless rituals*

The claims that Christ "learned obedience" and was "made perfect" don't suggest that he had been disobedient and flawed before (cf. 4:15). Jesus walked obediently all the way to the end of the path to which the Father had called him. The author's point was this: If suffering bore fruit in the life of the great high priest, then his followers weren't to fear or flee it.

📖 If you have found your grip on faith slipping, have you examined your view of Jesus? Do you have a clear picture of him and his high priestly role on your behalf? Our sympathetic high priest experienced the temptation to bolt and run. He's joined us in our humanness and now invites us to join him at the throne of grace.

Jesus' high priesthood represents open access to God. Rather than a heavenly bouncer who stands between God and humanity, Jesus as our go-between escorts us to God, ripping away the obstacles that had prevented our free access to his presence. Are you taking him up on his invitation of admission to God's throne?

Hebrews 5:11—6:12

📖 The preacher in 5:11—6:3 called upon the hearers to grapple with their spiritual immaturity. Growth doesn't occur automatically, and believers are called to move beyond the basics and train themselves to discern between good and evil. Spiritual growth is a universal aspect of the Christian experience. And a believer's development includes a process of moving toward maturity, grounded in the faithful teaching of God's Word.

Hebrews 6:4–12 is one of the most disputed passages in the New Testament. In the Jewish literature of the day, repentance was God's gift, and the author viewed the person and work of Jesus as the specific embodiment of that repentance. It's "impossible" then for someone who has fallen away to repent: There is nowhere else to go after having rejected Christ.

📖 Faith in Christ isn't an insurance policy on heaven. It's a living relationship with Christ as we draw near through him to the throne of grace. How often have you thought of the Christian life as something for which you "trained" in righteousness? Where are you in your spiritual diet—still on baby food or eating solids?

the resurrection of the dead,[t] and eternal judgment. [3]And God permitting,[u] we will do so.

[4]It is impossible for those who have once been enlightened,[v] who have tasted the heavenly gift,[w] who have shared in the Holy Spirit,[x] [5]who have tasted the goodness of the word of God and the powers of the coming age, [6]if they fall away, to be brought back to repentance,[y] because[a] to their loss they are crucifying the Son of God all over again and subjecting him to public disgrace.

[7]Land that drinks in the rain often falling on it and that produces a crop useful to those for whom it is farmed receives the blessing of God. [8]But land that produces thorns and thistles is worthless and is in danger of being cursed.[z] In the end it will be burned.

[9]Even though we speak like this, dear friends,[a] we are confident of better things in your case—things that accompany salvation. [10]God is not unjust; he will not forget your work and the love you have shown him as you have helped his people and continue to help them.[b] [11]We want each of you to show this same diligence to the very end, in order to make your hope[c] sure. [12]We do not want you to become lazy, but to imitate[d] those who through faith and patience[e] inherit what has been promised.[f]

The Certainty of God's Promise

[13]When God made his promise to Abraham, since there was no one greater for him to swear by, he swore by himself,[g] [14]saying, "I will surely bless you and give you many descendants."[b][h] [15]And so after waiting patiently, Abraham received what was promised.[i]

---

[a] 6 Or *repentance while*   [b] 14 Gen. 22:17

6:2
[t] Ac 17:18,32
6:3
[u] Ac 18:21
6:4
[v] Heb 10:32
[w] Eph 2:8 [x] Gal 3:2
6:6
[y] 2Pe 2:21;
1Jn 5:16
6:8
[z] Ge 3:17,18;
Isa 5:6
6:9
[a] 1Co 10:14
6:10
[b] Mt 10:40,42;
25:40; 1Th 1:3
6:11
[c] Heb 3:6
6:12
[d] Heb 13:7
[e] 2Th 1:4; Jas 1:3;
Rev 13:10
[f] Heb 10:36
6:13
[g] Ge 22:16; Lk 1:73
6:14
[h] Ge 22:17
6:15
[i] Ge 21:5

Hebrews 6:13–20

The "inner sanctuary behind the curtain" refers to the Most Holy Place, the place of God's presence. Under the old covenant only the high priest could go behind the curtain in the tabernacle (later temple) separating the outer part of the Holy Place from the inner—and then only once a year on the Day of Atonement. This barrier was torn away in the new covenant. The salvation of believers' souls rests firmly in the eternal, high-priestly work of Christ, by which he has entered into God's presence on our behalf and made a way for us to follow.

Snapshots

 6:10

Dorcas

In a rural community in Ghana, Dorcas can't walk down the road without being stopped by someone with a question.

"Do you have any school uniforms? My child's is torn and I need a replacement."

"Have you been traveling? I haven't seen you in a couple of days."

For Dorcas, questions come with the territory. In college, she studied sociology, psychology, and community development. Now, as a community worker tending to the needs of 185 families, she's endeared herself to more than 700 people. They care passionately for this woman who has devoted herself to serving them in the name of Christ.

Each morning Dorcas visits at least ten families to assess their needs and offer encouragement. In the afternoon she does paperwork and in the evening attends a community meeting or church service.

Dorcas is hopeful about her clients' futures. "They are making steady progress," she asserts. Instrumental in helping this community claw its way out of poverty, Dorcas says simply that helping others has been a blessing: "It gives me joy to know that people's lives are being transformed through my little efforts."

> "It gives me joy to know that people's lives are being transformed through my little efforts."

6:16
j Ex 22:11
6:17
k Ps 110:4
l Heb 11:9
6:18
m Nu 23:19; Tit 1:2
n Heb 3:6

6:19
o Lev 16:2;
Heb 9:2,3,7
6:20
p Heb 4:14
q Heb 2:17
r Heb 5:6

7:1
s Mk 5:7
t Ge 14:18-20

7:3
u ver 6 *v* Mt 4:3
7:4
w Ac 2:29
x Ge 14:20

7:5
y Nu 18:21,26
7:6
z Ge 14:19,20
a Ro 4:13

7:8
b Heb 5:6; 6:20

7:11
c ver 18,19;
Heb 8:7 *d* Heb 10:1
e ver 17
7:13
f ver 11 *g* ver 14
7:14
h Isa 11:1; Mt 1:3;
Lk 3:33

¹⁶Men swear by someone greater than themselves, and the oath confirms what is said and puts an end to all argument.ʲ ¹⁷Because God wanted to make the unchangingᵏ nature of his purpose very clear to the heirs of what was promised,ˡ he confirmed it with an oath. ¹⁸God did this so that, by two unchangeable things in which it is impossible for God to lie,ᵐ we who have fled to take hold of the hopeⁿ offered to us may be greatly encouraged. ¹⁹We have this hope as an anchor for the soul, firm and secure. It enters the inner sanctuary behind the curtain,ᵒ ²⁰where Jesus, who went before us, has entered on our behalf.ᵖ He has become a high priest�q forever, in the order of Melchizedek.ʳ

Melchizedek the Priest

7 This Melchizedek was king of Salem and priest of God Most High.ˢ He met Abraham returning from the defeat of the kings and blessed him,ᵗ ²and Abraham gave him a tenth of everything. First, his name means "king of righteousness"; then also, "king of Salem" means "king of peace." ³Without father or mother, without genealogy,ᵘ without beginning of days or end of life, like the Son of Godᵛ he remains a priest forever.

⁴Just think how great he was: Even the patriarchʷ Abraham gave him a tenth of the plunder!ˣ ⁵Now the law requires the descendants of Levi who become priests to collect a tenth from the peopleʸ—that is, their brothers—even though their brothers are descended from Abraham. ⁶This man, however, did not trace his descent from Levi, yet he collected a tenth from Abraham and blessedᶻ him who had the promises.ᵃ ⁷And without doubt the lesser person is blessed by the greater. ⁸In the one case, the tenth is collected by men who die; but in the other case, by him who is declared to be living.ᵇ ⁹One might even say that Levi, who collects the tenth, paid the tenth through Abraham, ¹⁰because when Melchizedek met Abraham, Levi was still in the body of his ancestor.

Jesus Like Melchizedek

¹¹If perfection could have been attained through the Levitical priesthood (for on the basis of it the law was given to the people),ᶜ why was there still need for another priest to comeᵈ—one in the order of Melchizedek,ᵉ not in the order of Aaron? ¹²For when there is a change of the priesthood, there must also be a change of the law. ¹³He of whom these things are said belonged to a different tribe,ᶠ and no one from that tribe has ever served at the altar.ᵍ ¹⁴For it is clear that our Lord descended from Judah,ʰ and in regard to that tribe Moses said nothing about priests. ¹⁵And

---

📖 Hebrews brings a fresh perspective to our age of hopelessness. Life is more than what we see on the surface. Our hope isn't in our circumstances but in Jesus Christ, who in fact *is* that hope. His "oaths" help us see beyond our limitations to his limitless power and provisions. Our age asks, "Is there more?" The Christian conviction rings out: "Yes, and our hope is utterly reliable."

Hebrews 7:1–10

📖 For the first Christians, what we call the Old Testament comprised the sum total of God's Word. Preaching among these Christians was based on the new covenant teachings about and from Christ, anchored in those Old Testament Scriptures. Here the writer to the Hebrews briefly explained Genesis 14:17–20, demonstrating connections between Melchizedek and Jesus. Also highlighted are key points suggested by Psalm 110:4 (quoted directly in vv. 17,21) that strengthen the association between the two figures.

The priest Melchizedek foreshadowed the heavenly high priest, Jesus Christ. Melchizedek was "like the Son of God" in that he "remains a priest forever." This was in contrast to the Levitical priesthood, which clearly had a beginning and an end.

📖 We readily refer to Jesus as our Savior, Lord, and even friend—but how often do you picture him as the "king of righteousness" and "king of peace?" In our broken, warring world, Jesus is indeed the King of justice and peace. Spend some time praying for the reign of King Jesus to penetrate the troubled places of our world.

Hebrews 7:11–28

📖 In Jesus' appointment as high priest, believers (then and now) have a new and superior model for approaching God. The author wanted the hearers to understand what this cataclysmic change meant for their relationship with God through Christ, for worship, and for endurance in Christian obedience. Jesus' authority doesn't stem from his ancestry or from his good deeds. Rather, he's the eternal mediator between God and people because of his "indestructible life." Whereas the dead offerings of human priests were temporary, needing regular repetition, Jesus' offering of himself was perfect and permanent.

what we have said is even more clear if another priest like Melchizedek appears, [16]one who has become a priest not on the basis of a regulation as to his ancestry but on the basis of the power of an indestructible life. [17]For it is declared:

> "You are a priest forever,
>   in the order of Melchizedek." [a][i]

[18]The former regulation is set aside because it was weak and useless[j] [19](for the law made nothing perfect),[k] and a better hope is introduced, by which we draw near to God.[l]

[20]And it was not without an oath! Others became priests without any oath, [21]but he became a priest with an oath when God said to him:

> "The Lord has sworn
>   and will not change his mind:[m]
> 'You are a priest forever.' "[b][n]

[22]Because of this oath, Jesus has become the guarantee of a better covenant.[o]

[23]Now there have been many of those priests, since death prevented them from continuing in office; [24]but because Jesus lives forever, he has a permanent priesthood.[p] [25]Therefore he is able to save completely[c] those who come to God[q] through him, because he always lives to intercede for them.[r]

[26]Such a high priest meets our need—one who is holy, blameless, pure, set apart from sinners,[s] exalted above the heavens.[t] [27]Unlike the other high priests, he does not need to offer sacrifices[u] day after day, first for his own sins,[v] and then for the sins of the people. He sacrificed for their sins once for all[w] when he offered himself.[x] [28]For the law appoints as high priests men who are weak;[y] but the oath, which came after the law, appointed the Son,[z] who has been made perfect[a] forever.

The High Priest of a New Covenant

8 The point of what we are saying is this: We do have such a high priest,[b] who sat down at the right hand of the throne of the Majesty in heaven, [2]and who serves in the sanctuary, the true tabernacle[c] set up by the Lord, not by man.

[3]Every high priest is appointed to offer both gifts and sacrifices,[d] and so it was necessary for this one also to have something to offer.[e] [4]If he were on earth, he would not be a priest, for there are already men who offer the gifts prescribed by the law.[f] [5]They serve at a sanctuary that is a copy[g] and shadow[h] of what is in heaven. This is why Moses was warned[i] when he was about to build the tabernacle: "See

---

[a] 17 Psalm 110:4   [b] 21 Psalm 110:4   [c] 25 Or forever

7:17
[i] Ps 110:4; ver 21; Heb 5:6
7:18
[j] Ro 8:3
7:19
[k] Ac 13:39; Ro 3:20; Heb 9:9
[l] Heb 4:16

7:21
[m] 1Sa 15:29
[n] Ps 110:4

7:22
[o] Heb 8:6

7:24
[p] ver 28
7:25
[q] ver 19 [r] Ro 8:34

7:26
[s] 2Co 5:21
[t] Heb 4:14
7:27
[u] Heb 5:1
[v] Heb 5:3
[w] Heb 9:12,26,28
[x] Eph 5:2; Heb 9:14,28
7:28
[y] Heb 5:2
[z] Heb 1:2
[a] Heb 2:10
8:1
[b] Heb 2:17
8:2
[c] Heb 9:11,24
8:3
[d] Heb 5:1
[e] Heb 9:14
8:4
[f] Heb 5:1
8:5
[g] Heb 9:23
[h] Col 2:17; Heb 10:1
[i] Heb 11:7; 12:25

📖 It's no exaggeration to characterize the Bible as an interconnected network of texts about relationships. In it we find love and hate, joy and grief, hope and despair. And behind all the individual lives stands the Priest, the Life, the Story, the Lover, the One who from before time has envisioned, cultivated, and nurtured a meaningful relationship with each of us. How has your network of relationships been affected by your relationship with Christ? Have you gained new ones? Lost others? Have your attitudes and actions influenced anyone to faith in Christ?

Hebrews 8:1–13

🔖 In verses 1–5 the writer continued to contrast the Levitical priests and the exalted Son, now examining the locales of their ministries—the earthly and heavenly realms. The system of the Old Testament priests was earthly and law-bound. And their tabernacle was only a copy or shadow of the true place of worship in heaven. The author quoted Jeremiah 31:31–34, pointing out that the new covenant "is founded on better promises" (v. 6).

The second covenant replaces the first.

The original hearers of Hebrews probably were drawn to Judaism's advantages. The author addressed them concerning the much greater value of the new covenant in Christ. We miss the intended impact of Hebrews 8 if we fail to understand the value of Old Testament Judaism.

📖 Using Hebrews 8, we can explain to those outside the faith that God offers everyone a meaningful covenant with himself. For his part, he agrees to be our God, to allow us to know him, to transform our hearts and minds, and to forgive and "forget" our sin. This is the gospel in a nutshell.

How can we relate to people who feel that our faith, by definition, sets theirs aside? Consider these suggestions: (1) Respect other people and their religious traditions, avoiding a superior attitude. (2) Be ready to articulate what you believe, and then proclaim the gospel boldly. (3) Maintain an uncompromising commitment to act ethically and morally as an example of godly living.

8:5
j Ex 25:40
8:6
k Lk 22:20
l Heb 7:22

to it that you make everything according to the pattern shown you on the mountain." *a j* 6But the ministry Jesus has received is as superior to theirs as the covenant *k* of which he is mediator *l* is superior to the old one, and it is founded on better promises.

8:7
m Heb 7:11,18

7For if there had been nothing wrong with that first covenant, no place would have been sought for another. *m* 8But God found fault with the people and said *b*:

8:8
n Jer 31:31

"The time is coming, declares the Lord,
    when I will make a new covenant *n*
with the house of Israel
    and with the house of Judah.

8:9
o Ex 19:5,6

9It will not be like the covenant
    I made with their forefathers *o*
when I took them by the hand
    to lead them out of Egypt,
because they did not remain faithful to my covenant,
    and I turned away from them,
                                        declares the Lord.

10This is the covenant I will make with the house of Israel
    after that time, declares the Lord.

8:10
p 2Co 3:3;
Heb 10:16
q Zec 8:8

I will put my laws in their minds
    and write them on their hearts. *p*
I will be their God,
    and they will be my people. *q*

8:11
r Isa 54:13; Jn 6:45

11No longer will a man teach his neighbor,
    or a man his brother, saying, 'Know the Lord,'
because they will all know me, *r*
    from the least of them to the greatest.

8:12
s Heb 10:17
t Ro 11:27
8:13
u 2Co 5:17

12For I will forgive their wickedness
    and will remember their sins no more. *s" c t*

13By calling this covenant "new," he has made the first one obsolete; *u* and what is obsolete and aging will soon disappear.

Worship in the Earthly Tabernacle

9:1
v Ex 25:8
9:2
w Ex 25:8,9
x Ex 25:31-39
y Ex 25:23-29
z Lev 24:5-8
9:3
a Ex 26:31-33
9:4
b Ex 30:1-5
c Ex 25:10-22
d Ex 16:32,33
e Nu 17:10
9:5
f Ex 25:17-19

9 Now the first covenant had regulations for worship and also an earthly sanctuary. *v* 2A tabernacle *w* was set up. In its first room were the lampstand, *x* the table *y* and the consecrated bread; *z* this was called the Holy Place. 3Behind the second curtain was a room called the Most Holy Place, *a* 4which had the golden altar of incense *b* and the gold-covered ark of the covenant. *c* This ark contained the gold jar of manna, *d* Aaron's staff that had budded, *e* and the stone tablets of the covenant. 5Above the ark were the cherubim of the Glory, *f* overshadowing the atonement cover. *d* But we cannot discuss these things in detail now.

a 5 Exodus 25:40   *b 8* Some manuscripts may be translated *fault and said to the people.*
c 12 Jer. 31:31-34   *d 5* Traditionally *the mercy seat*

Hebrews 9:1–10

The basic problem with the old covenant was the sacrificial system's inability to resolve personal guilt. The outer room of the tabernacle illustrates the limitation of that covenant. The general populace couldn't draw near to God because provision hadn't yet been made for their consciences to be cleansed. Ultimately the conscience, not physical space, prevents intimacy with God.

We see in this text three truths about God's nature and activity: (1) He wants people to approach him. (2) His holiness makes him particular about how people approach him. (3) The details of worship surrounding the priestly ministry of the tabernacle contrasted God's holiness with people's sinfulness.

Are you comfortable admitting that your sin separates you from God? Or does the idea offend your pride? A look at Jesus shows us that holiness means wholeness. It involves separation from sin and submission to the Father's will. God can bring fullness to our lives only when sin's humanity-sapping power has been broken. In the true and ultimate Holy Place we will find in God the living Presence, true wholeness, true beauty and rightness, and true humanity for which we long all our lives.

6When everything had been arranged like this, the priests entered regularly[g] into the outer room to carry on their ministry. 7But only the high priest entered[h] the inner room, and that only once a year,[i] and never without blood, which he offered for himself[j] and for the sins the people had committed in ignorance. 8The Holy Spirit was showing[k] by this that the way[l] into the Most Holy Place had not yet been disclosed as long as the first tabernacle was still standing. 9This is an illustration for the present time, indicating that the gifts and sacrifices being offered[m] were not able to clear the conscience of the worshiper. 10They are only a matter of food[n] and drink[o] and various ceremonial washings—external regulations[p] applying until the time of the new order.

The Blood of Christ

11When Christ came as high priest[q] of the good things that are already here,[a r] he went through the greater and more perfect tabernacle[s] that is not man-made, that is to say, not a part of this creation. 12He did not enter by means of the blood of goats and calves;[t] but he entered the Most Holy Place[u] once for all[v] by his own blood, having obtained eternal redemption. 13The blood of goats and bulls and the ashes of a heifer[w] sprinkled on those who are ceremonially unclean sanctify them so that they are outwardly clean. 14How much more, then, will the blood of Christ, who through the eternal Spirit[x] offered himself unblemished to God, cleanse our consciences[y] from acts that lead to death,[b z] so that we may serve the living God!

15For this reason Christ is the mediator[a] of a new covenant, that those who are called may receive the promised eternal inheritance—now that he has died as a ransom to set them free from the sins committed under the first covenant.[b]

16In the case of a will,[c] it is necessary to prove the death of the one who made it, 17because a will is in force only when somebody has died; it never takes effect while the one who made it is living. 18This is why even the first covenant was not put into effect without blood.[c] 19When Moses had proclaimed every commandment of the law to all the people, he took the blood of calves, together with water, scarlet wool and branches of hyssop, and sprinkled the scroll and all the people.[d] 20He said, "This is the blood of the covenant, which God has commanded you to keep."[d e] 21In the same way, he sprinkled with the blood both the tabernacle and everything used in its ceremonies. 22In fact, the law requires that nearly everything be cleansed with blood,[f] and without the shedding of blood there is no forgiveness.[g]

23It was necessary, then, for the copies[h] of the heavenly things to be purified with these sacrifices, but the heavenly things themselves with better sacrifices than these. 24For Christ did not enter a man-made sanctuary that was only a copy of the true one;[i] he entered heaven itself, now to appear for us in God's presence. 25Nor did he enter heaven to offer himself again and again, the way the high priest enters the Most Holy Place[j] every year with blood that is not his own.[k] 26Then Christ would have had to suffer many times since the creation of the world.[l] But now he has appeared once for all[m] at the end of the ages to do away with sin by the sacrifice of himself. 27Just as man is destined to die once,[n] and after that to face judgment,[o]

9:6
g Nu 28:3
9:7
h Lev 16:11-19
i Lev 16:34
j Heb 5:2,3
9:8
k Heb 3:7 l Jn 14:6;
Heb 10:19,20

9:9
m Heb 5:1
9:10
n Lev 11:2-23
o Col 2:16
p Heb 7:16

9:11
q Heb 2:17
r Heb 10:1
s Heb 8:2

9:12
t Heb 10:4 u ver 24
v Heb 7:27

9:13
w Nu 19:9,17,18

9:14
x 1Pe 3:18
y Tit 2:14;
Heb 10:2,22
z Heb 6:1
9:15
a 1Ti 2:5
b Heb 7:22

9:18
c Ex 24:6-8

9:19
d Ex 24:6-8
9:20
e Ex 24:8; Mt 26:28

9:22
f Lev 8:15
g Lev 17:11
9:23
h Heb 8:5

9:24
i Heb 8:2

9:25
j Heb 10:19
k ver 7,8
9:26
l Heb 4:3
m Heb 7:27
9:27
n Ge 3:19
o 2Co 5:10

a 11 Some early manuscripts *are to come*   b 14 Or *from useless rituals*   c 16 Same Greek word as *covenant*; also in verse 17   d 20 Exodus 24:8

Hebrews 9:11–28

The writer demonstrated three ways in which Christ's covenant offering is superior to Old Testament animal sacrifices: (1) The blood of the offering (vv. 13–22) was Jesus' own; (2) the place was in heaven (vv. 23–24), not an earthly tabernacle; and (3) the offering was eternal (vv. 25–28). This passage also refers to three "appearances" of Christ: (1) his past coming when he obtained our redemption (v. 11), (2) his present availability in God's presence on our behalf (v. 24), and (3) his future appearance to bring final salvation to all who await his coming (v. 28).

Some people today pick and choose ideas to incorporate into their individual moral systems. But contrary to popular opinion, God doesn't grade on a curve or judge us in comparison to others. Our good deeds can never outweigh our bad, and we can't please him just by avoiding "serious" sins. Today's Christians have the privilege of allowing the cross and the redemption it bears to transform their lives. Jesus willingly paid the penalty for everybody's sins. Such love astounds those who hear of it, especially when it's manifest through the lives of people who have been changed by it.

9:28
p Tit 2:13
q 1Pe 2:24
r 1Co 1:7

[28] so Christ was sacrificed once to take away the sins of many people; and he will appear a second time, *p* not to bear sin, *q* but to bring salvation to those who are waiting for him. *r*

Christ's Sacrifice Once for All

10:1
s Heb 8:5
t Heb 9:11
u Heb 9:23
v Heb 7:19

10 The law is only a shadow *s* of the good things *t* that are coming—not the realities themselves. *u* For this reason it can never, by the same sacrifices repeated endlessly year after year, make perfect *v* those who draw near to worship. [2] If it could, would they not have stopped being offered? For the worshipers would have been cleansed once for all, and would no longer have felt guilty for their sins. [3] But those sacrifices are an annual reminder of sins, *w* [4] because it is impossible for the blood of bulls and goats *x* to take away sins.

10:3
w Heb 9:7
10:4
x Heb 9:12,13
10:5
y Heb 1:6
z 1Pe 2:24

[5] Therefore, when Christ came into the world, *y* he said:

> "Sacrifice and offering you did not desire,
>   but a body you prepared for me; *z*
> [6] with burnt offerings and sin offerings
>   you were not pleased.

10:7
a Jer 36:2
b Ps 40:6-8

> [7] Then I said, 'Here I am—it is written about me in the scroll *a*—
>   I have come to do your will, O God.'" *a b*

10:8
c ver 5,6; Mk 12:33
10:9
d ver 7
10:10
e Jn 17:19
f Heb 2:14;
1Pe 2:24
g Heb 7:27
10:11
h Heb 5:1 / ver 1,4

[8] First he said, "Sacrifices and offerings, burnt offerings and sin offerings you did not desire, nor were you pleased with them" *c* (although the law required them to be made). [9] Then he said, "Here I am, I have come to do your will." *d* He sets aside the first to establish the second. [10] And by that will, we have been made holy *e* through the sacrifice of the body *f* of Jesus Christ once for all. *g*

[11] Day after day every priest stands and performs his religious duties; again and again he offers the same sacrifices, *h* which can never take away sins. *i* [12] But when this priest had offered for all time one sacrifice for sins, he sat down at the right hand of God. [13] Since that time he waits for his enemies to be made his footstool, *j* [14] because by one sacrifice he has made perfect *k* forever those who are being made holy.

10:13
i Heb 1:13
10:14
k ver 1

10:15
l Heb 3:7

[15] The Holy Spirit also testifies *l* to us about this. First he says:

> [16] "This is the covenant I will make with them
>   after that time, says the Lord.
>   I will put my laws in their hearts,
>   and I will write them on their minds." *b m*

10:16
m Jer 31:33;
Heb 8:10

[17] Then he adds:

> "Their sins and lawless acts
>   I will remember no more." *c n*

10:17
n Heb 8:12

[18] And where these have been forgiven, there is no longer any sacrifice for sin.

a 7 Psalm 40:6-8 (see Septuagint)   *b 16* Jer. 31:33   *c 17* Jer. 31:34

Hebrews 10:1–18

The author began with a problem: the limited ability of the law and its required sacrifices to deal with sin. The answer came in the person of Jesus Christ. As foretold in the quote from Psalm 40:6–8, Jesus' sacrifice of his own body was God's way of making his people holy. Our high priest's act of sitting down at God's right hand indicates the finality of that sacrifice. By it Jesus made all believers for all time perfect and holy in God's sight.

Most religions require some form of sacrificial "doing" to win divine favor. But at the heart of the Chris-

tian faith stands the truth that God has done something for us, through the sacrifice of his Son, that we could never have done for ourselves. He's taken away our sins, forgiven us completely, and now relates to us intimately and eternally. As covenant people, we are pronounced "not guilty" before God and drawn into a life-changing relationship with him. God is holy love, and as we abide in Christ by the Spirit we share in Christ's holiness. Former priests could only act from the outside of people's lives. But Christ, our high priest, puts God's laws on our hearts (v. 16).

A Call to Persevere

19 Therefore, brothers, since we have confidence to enter the Most Holy Place[o] by the blood of Jesus, 20 by a new and living way[p] opened for us through the curtain,[q] that is, his body, 21 and since we have a great priest[r] over the house of God, 22 let us draw near to God[s] with a sincere heart in full assurance of faith, having our hearts sprinkled to cleanse us from a guilty conscience[t] and having our bodies washed with pure water. 23 Let us hold unswervingly to the hope[u] we profess, for he who promised is faithful.[v] 24 And let us consider how we may spur one another on toward love and good deeds. 25 Let us not give up meeting together,[w] as some are in the habit of doing, but let us encourage one another[x]—and all the more as you see the Day approaching.

26 If we deliberately keep on sinning[y] after we have received the knowledge of the truth, no sacrifice for sins is left, 27 but only a fearful expectation of judgment and of raging fire[z] that will consume the enemies of God. 28 Anyone who rejected the law of Moses died without mercy on the testimony of two or three witnesses.[a] 29 How much more severely do you think a man deserves to be punished who has trampled the Son of God under foot,[b] who has treated as an unholy thing the blood of the covenant[c] that sanctified him, and who has insulted the Spirit[d] of grace?[e] 30 For we know him who said, "It is mine to avenge; I will repay,"[a][f] and again, "The Lord will judge his people."[b][g] 31 It is a dreadful thing to fall into the hands of the living God.[h]

32 Remember those earlier days after you had received the light,[i] when you stood your ground in a great contest in the face of suffering.[j] 33 Sometimes you were publicly exposed to insult and persecution;[k] at other times you stood side by side with those who were so treated.[l] 34 You sympathized with those in prison[m] and joyfully accepted the confiscation of your property, because you knew that you yourselves had better and lasting possessions.[n]

35 So do not throw away your confidence; it will be richly rewarded. 36 You need to persevere[o] so that when you have done the will of God, you will receive what he has promised. 37 For in just a very little while,

> "He who is coming[p] will come and will not delay.[q]
38   But my righteous one[c] will live by faith.[r]
>   And if he shrinks back,
>   I will not be pleased with him."[d]

39 But we are not of those who shrink back and are destroyed, but of those who believe and are saved.

By Faith

11 Now faith is being sure of what we hope for and certain of what we do not see.[s] 2 This is what the ancients were commended for.[t]

---

a 30 Deut. 32:35   b 30 Deut. 32:36; Psalm 135:14   c 38 One early manuscript *But the righteous*
d 38 Hab. 2:3,4

Cross references

10:19 o Eph 2:18; Heb 9:8,12,25
10:20 p Heb 9:8; q Heb 9:3
10:21 r Heb 2:17
10:22 s Heb 7:19; t Eze 36:25; Heb 9:14
10:23 u Heb 3:6; v 1Co 1:9
10:25 w Ac 2:42; x Heb 3:13
10:26 y Nu 15:30; 2Pe 2:20
10:27 z Isa 26:11; 2Th 1:7; Heb 9:27
10:28 a Dt 17:6,7; Heb 2:2
10:29 b Heb 6:6; c Mt 26:28; d Eph 4:30; Heb 6:4 e Heb 2:3
10:30 f Dt 32:35; Ro 12:19; g Dt 32:36
10:31 h Mt 16:16
10:32 i Heb 6:4; j Php 1:29,30
10:33 k 1Co 4:9; l Php 4:14; 1Th 2:14
10:34 m Heb 13:3; n Heb 11:16
10:36 o Lk 21:19; Heb 12:1
10:37 p Mt 11:3; q Rev 22:20
10:38 r Ro 1:17; Gal 3:11
11:1 s Ro 8:24; 2Co 4:18
11:2 t ver 4,39

Hebrews 10:19–39

This entire letter rotates around the "therefore" that begins this section. In light of the confidence with which Christians in all ages can approach God, knowing of his deep, forgiving love for us in Christ, we eagerly draw near. What's more, this relationship isn't just an individual matter. We are to encourage one another in love—expressed in kind deeds. Our works don't earn our forgiveness or God's love. But because of the empowering love we have received from God through Christ we are free to express our love in our actions.

How lenient or easy-going is God? One of English writer C.S. Lewis's favorite comments about Aslan, the Christ figure in his Chronicles of Narnia, is "He is not a tame lion." The great foolishness of an individual walking away from Christ's offer lies in this: There is no other means for dealing with sin and drawing near to God. Thus, we call one another to persevere with courage, to be nourished by love, and to draw near with hope.

Hebrews 11:1–40

Hebrews 11, often referred to as the great "Hall of Faith," has become through the centuries one of the church's best-loved portions of Scripture. Poetic in its cadence, panoramic in its historical sweep, and relevant in its challenge, this chapter calls believers of every generation to faithful endurance by use of testimonies from the

3 By faith we understand that the universe was formed at God's command, u so that what is seen was not made out of what was visible.

4 By faith Abel offered God a better sacrifice than Cain did. By faith he was commended as a righteous man, when God spoke well of his offerings. v And by faith he still speaks, even though he is dead. w

5 By faith Enoch was taken from this life, so that he did not experience death; he could not be found, because God had taken him away. x For before he was taken, he was commended as one who pleased God. 6 And without faith it is impossible to please God, because anyone who comes to him y must believe that he exists and that he rewards those who earnestly seek him.

7 By faith Noah, when warned about things not yet seen, in holy fear built an ark z to save his family. a By his faith he condemned the world and became heir of the righteousness that comes by faith.

8 By faith Abraham, when called to go to a place he would later receive as his inheritance, b obeyed and went, c even though he did not know where he was going. 9 By faith he made his home in the promised land d like a stranger in a foreign country; he lived in tents, e as did Isaac and Jacob, who were heirs with him of the same promise. f 10 For he was looking forward to the city g with foundations, h whose architect and builder is God.

11 By faith Abraham, even though he was past age—and Sarah herself was barren i—was enabled to become a father j because he a considered him faithful who had made the promise. 12 And so from this one man, and he as good as dead, k came descendants as numerous as the stars in the sky and as countless as the sand on the seashore. l

13 All these people were still living by faith when they died. They did not receive the things promised; m they only saw them and welcomed them from a distance. n And they admitted that they were aliens and strangers on earth. o 14 People who say such things show that they are looking for a country of their own. 15 If they had been thinking of the country they had left, they would have had opportunity to return. p 16 Instead, they were longing for a better country—a heavenly one. q Therefore God is not ashamed r to be called their God, s for he has prepared a city t for them.

17 By faith Abraham, when God tested him, offered Isaac as a sacrifice. u He who had received the promises was about to sacrifice his one and only son, 18 even though God had said to him, "It is through Isaac that your offspring b will be reckoned." c v 19 Abraham reasoned that God could raise the dead, w and figuratively speaking, he did receive Isaac back from death.

20 By faith Isaac blessed Jacob and Esau in regard to their future. x

21 By faith Jacob, when he was dying, blessed each of Joseph's sons, y and worshiped as he leaned on the top of his staff.

22 By faith Joseph, when his end was near, spoke about the exodus of the Israelites from Egypt and gave instructions about his bones. z

23 By faith Moses' parents hid him for three months after he was born, a because they saw he was no ordinary child, and they were not afraid of the king's edict. b

24 By faith Moses, when he had grown up, refused to be known as the son of Pharaoh's daughter. c 25 He chose to be mistreated d along with the people of God rath-

---

a 11 Or By faith even Sarah, who was past age, was enabled to bear children because she   b 18 Greek seed
c 18 Gen. 21:12

---

lives of ancient saints. The author challenged the audience to live lives of faith, according to the pattern of the great heroes of faith.

Faith as "defined" by Hebrews 11 has several essential elements. It: (1) involves confident action; (2) is action taken in response to the unseen God and his promises; (3) involves God's working extraordinary miracles in the lives of ordinary people; (4) works in a variety of situations; (5) may have a variety of outcomes; and (6) is always rewarded by God.

📖 This passage is undeniably beautiful, but it challenges many of our assumptions. If God is just (fair), why were some delivered because of faithful actions while others experienced torture or horrible deaths? Why did some prosper materially and others experience severe hardship and poverty? To what extent have you connected faithfulness with security and comfort? How does the perspective on the rewards of faith portrayed in this passage challenge you? Who are some heroes of faith you know personally, today?

Demonstrations of Devotion

 11:6

All you have to do is reach out and touch Jesus, "because power [is] coming from him and healing them all" (Luke 6:19). But for some reason we don't even try.

Does this sound right to you? You have nothing to give God but problems. All you have to offer him is your hurt. You want to accept his gift of grace, but you feel unworthy of his sacrifice.

Maybe that has kept you from coming to God. Oh, you have taken a step or two in his direction. But then you saw the other people who follow him. They seemed so clean, so neat, so trim and fit in their faith. So you hesitated.

If that description fits, read the story of the nameless woman in Mark 5. She, considered unclean by her culture, demonstrated her devotion to Jesus by touching the hem of the Savior's garment. And that slight gesture moved Jesus to heal her. She was a shame-struck, penniless outcast who clung to her hunch that he could and her hope that he would.

Isn't that what faith is all about? A conviction that he can and that he will. Sounds similar to the definition of faith given by the Bible: "Without faith no one can please God. Anyone who comes to God must believe that he is real and that he rewards those who truly want to find him" (Heb. 11:6).

Not too complicated, is it? Faith is the belief that God is real and that God is good. Faith isn't a mystical experience or a midnight vision or a voice in the forest . . . It's a choice to believe that the One who made it all hasn't left it all and that he still sends light into shadows and responds to gestures of faith.

Faith is not the belief that God will do what you want. Faith is the belief that God will do what is right. God is always near and always available. Just waiting for your touch. So let him know. Demonstrate your devotion:

Write a letter.
Ask forgiveness.
Confess.
Be baptized.
Feed a hungry person.
Pray.
Teach.
Go.

Do something that reveals your faith. For faith with no effort is no faith at all. God will respond. He has never rejected a genuine gesture of faith. Never.

God honors radical, risk-taking faith. When arks are built, lives are saved. When soldiers march, Jerichos tumble. When staffs are raised, seas still open. When a lunch is shared, thousands are fed. And when a garment is touched—whether by the hand of an anemic woman in Galilee or by the prayers of a beggar in Bangladesh—Jesus stops. So make your choice, announce your faith to God, and demonstrate your devotion.

> **F**aith is not the belief that God will do what you want. Faith is the belief that God will do what is right.

Max Lucado, pulpit minister of Oak Hills Church of Christ in San Antonio, Texas, and author of over 30 books
Source: Max Lucado, *The Gift for All People: Thoughts on God's Great Grace* (Sisters, Ore.: Multnomah, 1999), 121–123

11:26
e Heb 13:13
f Heb 10:35
11:27
g Ex 12:50,51

11:28
h Ex 12:21-23

11:29
i Ex 14:21-31

11:30
j Jos 6:12-20

11:31
k Jos 2:1,9-14;
6:22-25; Jas 2:25
11:32
l Jdg 4-5
m 1Sa 16:1,13
n 1Sa 1:20
11:33
o 2Sa 7:11; 8:1-3
p Da 6:22
11:34
q 2Ki 20:7
r Jdg 15:8
11:35
s 1Ki 17:22,23
11:36
t Jer 20:2
u Ge 39:20
11:37
v 2Ch 24:21
w 1Ki 19:10
x 2Ki 1:8
11:38
y 1Ki 18:4
11:39
z ver 2,4 *a* ver 13

er than to enjoy the pleasures of sin for a short time. 26He regarded disgrace*e* for the sake of Christ as of greater value than the treasures of Egypt, because he was looking ahead to his reward.*f* 27By faith he left Egypt,*g* not fearing the king's anger; he persevered because he saw him who is invisible. 28By faith he kept the Passover and the sprinkling of blood, so that the destroyer of the firstborn would not touch the firstborn of Israel.*h*

29By faith the people passed through the Red Sea*a* as on dry land; but when the Egyptians tried to do so, they were drowned.*i*

30By faith the walls of Jericho fell, after the people had marched around them for seven days.*j*

31By faith the prostitute Rahab, because she welcomed the spies, was not killed with those who were disobedient.*b k*

32And what more shall I say? I do not have time to tell about Gideon, Barak,*l* Samson, Jephthah, David,*m* Samuel*n* and the prophets, 33who through faith conquered kingdoms,*o* administered justice, and gained what was promised; who shut the mouths of lions,*p* 34quenched the fury of the flames, and escaped the edge of the sword; whose weakness was turned to strength;*q* and who became powerful in battle and routed foreign armies.*r* 35Women received back their dead, raised to life again.*s* Others were tortured and refused to be released, so that they might gain a better resurrection. 36Some faced jeers and flogging,*t* while still others were chained and put in prison.*u* 37They were stoned*c;v* they were sawed in two; they were put to death by the sword.*w* They went about in sheepskins and goatskins,*x* destitute, persecuted and mistreated— 38the world was not worthy of them. They wandered in deserts and mountains, and in caves*y* and holes in the ground.

39These were all commended*z* for their faith, yet none of them received what had been promised.*a* 40God had planned something better for us so that only together with us would they be made perfect.

God Disciplines His Sons

12 Therefore, since we are surrounded by such a great cloud of witnesses, let us throw off everything that hinders and the sin that so easily entangles, and let us run*b* with perseverance*c* the race marked out for us. 2Let us fix our eyes on Jesus, the author and perfecter of our faith, who for the joy set before him endured the cross,*d* scorning its shame,*e* and sat down at the right hand of the throne of God. 3Consider him who endured such opposition from sinful men, so that you will not grow weary*f* and lose heart.

4In your struggle against sin, you have not yet resisted to the point of shedding your blood.*g* 5And you have forgotten that word of encouragement that addresses you as sons:

"My son, do not make light of the Lord's discipline,
    and do not lose heart when he rebukes you,
6because the Lord disciplines those he loves,*h*
    and he punishes everyone he accepts as a son."*d i*

12:1
b 1Co 9:24
c Heb 10:36

12:2
d Php 2:8,9
e Heb 13:13
12:3
f Gal 6:9

12:4
g Heb 10:32-34

12:6
h Ps 94:12;
Rev 3:19
i Pr 3:11,12

a 29 That is, Sea of Reeds   *b* 31 Or *unbelieving*   *c* 37 Some early manuscripts *stoned; they were put to the test;*   *d* 6 Prov. 3:11,12

Hebrews 12:1–13

The author encouraged the readers to persevere through difficult experiences by using two illustrations—a long-distance race and parental discipline. The race is pictured as challenging and God's discipline as unpleasant. Christ-following is costly (cf. Luke 14:28). But the believers' focus isn't on hardship but on Jesus, the One who began—and will complete—their faith. He guarantees they will cross the finish line! Thus the believer embraces the need for endurance and wise choices with the perspective that outward challenges are lovingly used by the Father for his or her good.

Do you sometimes turn a deaf ear to God's "pain language" or strain to hear his message through your difficulties? Our pain can deafen us to God's background music that calls us to sing joyfully of what he can do *in* and *through* us, even while others seek to do harm *to* us (cf. Acts 16:16–34). Have you asked him to discipline your ears to hear and to help you receive what he wants to teach you through your hurtful experiences?

Faith Is Demonstrated by Activity

In Hebrews 11, Old Testament individuals and groups are cited as examples of faith, based on their actions.

	Individual/Group	Faith-inspired activity
	Abel	Offered a better sacrifice than Cain.
	Enoch	Lived in a manner that pleased God.
	Noah	In holy fear, built an ark to save his family.
	Abraham	Obeyed God's summons, though he didn't know the destination. Made his home in the promised land. Was willing to offer Isaac as a sacrifice. Reasoned that God could raise Isaac from the dead.
	Abraham, Sarah	Became parents well past their child-bearing years.
	Abraham, Isaac, Jacob	Lived in tents.
	All listed above	Lived by faith until they died. Welcomed God's promises from a distance. Admitted that they were aliens and strangers on Earth.
	Isaac	Blessed Jacob and Esau in regard to the future.
	Jacob	Blessed each of Joseph's sons.
	Joseph	Spoke of the exodus to come and gave instructions about his bones.
	Moses' parents	Hid Moses after he was born. Saw that their son was a child of promise.
	Moses	Refused to be known as the son of Pharoah's daughter. Chose to be mistreated with God's people rather than to enjoy the pleasures of sin. Regarded disgrace for God's sake as of greater value than the treasures of Egypt. Left Egypt, not fearing Pharoah's anger. Saw him who is invisible. Kept the Passover.
	The people of Israel	Passed through the Red Sea. Marched around the walls of Jericho and saw them fall.
	Rahab	Welcomed the Israelite spies.
	Gideon, Barak, Samson, Jepthah, David, Samuel, and the prophets	Conquered kingdoms. Administered justice. Gained what was promised. Shut the mouths of lions. Quenched the fury of flames. Escaped the edge of the sword. Became powerful in battle and routed foreign armies.
	Women	Received back their dead.
	Others	Refused release from torture. Faced jeers and flogging. Submitted to imprisonment. Allowed themselves to be stoned, sawed in two, and put to death by the sword. Accepted destitution, persecution, and mistreatment. Accepted delayed gratification of God's great promise (Christ).
	You	What faith-inspired activities in your life could be added to the chart?

12:7
j Dt 8:5
12:8
k 1Pe 5:9
12:9
l Nu 16:22
m Isa 38:16
12:10
n 2Pe 1:4
12:11
o Isa 32:17;
Jas 3:17,18
12:12
p Isa 35:3
12:13
q Pr 4:26 *r* Gal 6:1

[7] Endure hardship as discipline; God is treating you as sons.[j] For what son is not disciplined by his father? [8] If you are not disciplined (and everyone undergoes discipline),[k] then you are illegitimate children and not true sons. [9] Moreover, we have all had human fathers who disciplined us and we respected them for it. How much more should we submit to the Father of our spirits[l] and live![m] [10] Our fathers disciplined us for a little while as they thought best; but God disciplines us for our good, that we may share in his holiness.[n] [11] No discipline seems pleasant at the time, but painful. Later on, however, it produces a harvest of righteousness and peace[o] for those who have been trained by it.

[12] Therefore, strengthen your feeble arms and weak knees.[p] [13] "Make level paths for your feet,"[a][q] so that the lame may not be disabled, but rather healed.[r]

Warning Against Refusing God

12:14
s Ro 14:19
t Ro 6:22 *u* Mt 5:8
12:15
v Gal 5:4; Heb 3:12
12:16
w Ge 25:29-34
12:17
x Ge 27:30-40

[14] Make every effort to live in peace with all men[s] and to be holy;[t] without holiness no one will see the Lord.[u] [15] See to it that no one misses the grace of God[v] and that no bitter root grows up to cause trouble and defile many. [16] See that no one is sexually immoral, or is godless like Esau, who for a single meal sold his inheritance rights as the oldest son.[w] [17] Afterward, as you know, when he wanted to inherit this blessing, he was rejected. He could bring about no change of mind, though he sought the blessing with tears.[x]

12:18
y Ex 19:12-22;
Dt 4:11
12:19
z Ex 20:18
a Ex 20:19; Dt 5:5,
25
12:20
b Ex 19:12,13
12:22
c Gal 4:26
d Heb 11:10
12:23
e Lk 10:20 *f* Ps 94:2
g Php 3:12

[18] You have not come to a mountain that can be touched and that is burning with fire; to darkness, gloom and storm;[y] [19] to a trumpet blast[z] or to such a voice speaking words that those who heard it begged that no further word be spoken to them,[a] [20] because they could not bear what was commanded: "If even an animal touches the mountain, it must be stoned."[b][b] [21] The sight was so terrifying that Moses said, "I am trembling with fear."[c]

[22] But you have come to Mount Zion, to the heavenly Jerusalem,[c] the city[d] of the living God. You have come to thousands upon thousands of angels in joyful assembly, [23] to the church of the firstborn, whose names are written in heaven.[e] You have come to God, the judge of all men,[f] to the spirits of righteous men made perfect,[g]

12:24
h Ge 4:10;
Heb 11:4

[24] to Jesus the mediator of a new covenant, and to the sprinkled blood that speaks a better word than the blood of Abel.[h]

12:25
i Heb 8:5; 11:7
j Heb 2:2,3
12:26
k Ex 19:18
l Hag 2:6
12:27
m 1Co 7:31;
2Pe 3:10
12:28
n Da 2:44

[25] See to it that you do not refuse him who speaks. If they did not escape when they refused him who warned[i] them on earth, how much less will we, if we turn away from him who warns us from heaven?[j] [26] At that time his voice shook the earth,[k] but now he has promised, "Once more I will shake not only the earth but also the heavens."[d][l] [27] The words "once more" indicate the removing of what can be shaken[m]—that is, created things—so that what cannot be shaken may remain.

[28] Therefore, since we are receiving a kingdom that cannot be shaken,[n] let us be

---

[a] 13 Prov. 4:26   [b] 20 Exodus 19:12,13   [c] 21 Deut. 9:19   [d] 26 Haggai 2:6

Hebrews 12:14–29

Verses 14–17 hint at a critical problem among the addressees: disunity. The dissension seems to have stemmed from friction caused by those who had abandoned Christian commitment. Having missed out on God's grace, they had brought bitterness into the church. By abandoning the hope of God's inheritance, these bitter persons were following the example of Esau, who afterward, "when he wanted to inherit this blessing . . . was rejected."

Two mountains highlight the stark contrasts between the old and the new covenants. The new covenant believers addressed in Hebrews "[had] not come" to the old covenant mountain, Sinai, but to the new mountain, Zion. They were citizens of the heavenly Jerusalem, in fellowship with thousands of celebrating angels, members of the church on Earth, and believers who had already died. Most important, they had come to Jesus, whose blood had cleansed them.

The analogies of the foreboding Mount Sinai and the festive Mount Zion couldn't be more up-to-date. Each represents a way of viewing our relationship with God. The author wasn't interested in physical movement and literal mountains but with where the listeners were in relation to God.

The "call to come" has always been central to the church's message. But it's important for us to think about which mountain we are calling people to. Sometimes we boom and flash with the darkness of Sinai more than we sing and gather people to the light of Zion. Are we calling people to a set of rules or to grace? Are we summoning them to drudgery or to joy? Are we heralding a religion or a relationship with the living God?

thankful, and so worship God acceptably with reverence and awe, [o] 29for our "God is a consuming fire." [a][p]

Concluding Exhortations

13 Keep on loving each other as brothers. [q] 2Do not forget to entertain strangers, [r] for by so doing some people have entertained angels without knowing it. [s] 3Remember those in prison [t] as if you were their fellow prisoners, and those who are mistreated as if you yourselves were suffering.

4Marriage should be honored by all, and the marriage bed kept pure, for God will judge the adulterer and all the sexually immoral. [u] 5Keep your lives free from the love of money and be content with what you have, [v] because God has said,

> "Never will I leave you;
> never will I forsake you." [b][w]

6So we say with confidence,

> "The Lord is my helper; I will not be afraid.
> What can man do to me?" [c]

7Remember your leaders, [x] who spoke the word of God to you. Consider the outcome of their way of life and imitate [y] their faith. 8Jesus Christ is the same yesterday and today and forever. [z]

9Do not be carried away by all kinds of strange teachings. [a] It is good for our hearts to be strengthened [b] by grace, not by ceremonial foods, [c] which are of no value to those who eat them. 10We have an altar from which those who minister at the tabernacle have no right to eat. [d]

11The high priest carries the blood of animals into the Most Holy Place as a sin offering, but the bodies are burned outside the camp. [e] 12And so Jesus also suffered outside the city gate [f] to make the people holy through his own blood. 13Let us, then, go to him outside the camp, bearing the disgrace he bore. [g] 14For here we do not have an enduring city, but we are looking for the city that is to come. [h]

15Through Jesus, therefore, let us continually offer to God a sacrifice [i] of praise—the fruit of lips [j] that confess his name. 16And do not forget to do good and to share with others, [k] for with such sacrifices [l] God is pleased.

17Obey your leaders and submit to their authority. They keep watch over you [m] as men who must give an account. Obey them so that their work will be a joy, not a burden, for that would be of no advantage to you.

18Pray for us. [n] We are sure that we have a clear conscience [o] and desire to live honorably in every way. 19I particularly urge you to pray so that I may be restored to you soon. [p]

20May the God of peace, [q] who through the blood of the eternal covenant [r] brought back from the dead [s] our Lord Jesus, that great Shepherd of the sheep, [t] 21equip you with everything good for doing his will, and may he work in us [u] what

---

[a] 29 Deut. 4:24   [b] 5 Deut. 31:6   [c] 6 Psalm 118:6,7

12:28
o Heb 13:15
12:29
p Dt 4:24

13:1
q Ro 12:10;
1Pe 1:22
13:2
r Mt 25:35
s Ge 18:1-33
13:3
t Mt 25:36;
Col 4:18
13:4
u 1Co 6:9
13:5
v Php 4:11
w Dt 31:6,8; Jos 1:5

13:7
x ver 17,24
y Heb 6:12
13:8
z Heb 1:12
13:9
a Eph 4:14
b Col 2:7 c Col 2:16
13:10
d 1Co 9:13; 10:18

13:11
e Ex 29:14;
Lev 16:27
13:12
f Jn 19:17
13:13
g Heb 11:26
13:14
h Php 3:20;
Heb 12:22
13:15
i 1Pe 2:5 j Hos 14:2
13:16
k Ro 12:13
l Php 4:18
13:17
m Isa 62:6;
Ac 20:28
13:18
n 1Th 5:25
o Ac 23:1
13:19
p Phm 22
13:20
q Ro 15:33
r Isa 55:3;
Eze 37:26; Zec 9:11
s Ac 2:24 t Jn 10:11
13:21
u Php 2:13

Hebrews 13:1–25

The author concluded with a series of practical guidelines on how his hearers might serve God and live out a persevering faith. The first five (vv. 1–6) provided general instructions, while the remaining seven (vv. 7–19) revolved around the community's relationship with its leaders, ending with the author's personal appeal for prayer. The benediction (vv. 20–21) was probably the ending of the original sermon. The closing (vv. 22–25) may have been an addendum added when the author sent the manuscript by courier.

C.S. Lewis once remarked, "He who has God and everything has no more than he who has God alone." The truth of this statement and freedom from the love of money can escape rich and poor alike. The poor struggle against the grasping demands of daily existence. The rich experience the drowning out of God's promises by their super supply of material things. Both positions can lead people to reject God.

The life of the Spirit and the life of the street are to be integrated in the Christian experience. Through devoted living the gospel's truth is proclaimed in a thousand varied voices. God finds pleasure and builds his kingdom through ethical practices in financial management, healthy marital relationships, the nurture of children, integrity in the workplace, care for the burdened or oppressed, and sharing with others. What are you doing to put a smile on God's face?

13:21
v 1Jn 3:22
w Ro 11:36

is pleasing to him, [v] through Jesus Christ, to whom be glory for ever and ever. Amen. [w]

13:22
x 1Pe 5:12
13:23
y Ac 16:1
13:24
z ver 7,17
a Ac 18:2

22Brothers, I urge you to bear with my word of exhortation, for I have written you only a short letter. [x]

23I want you to know that our brother Timothy [y] has been released. If he arrives soon, I will come with him to see you.

24Greet all your leaders [z] and all God's people. Those from Italy [a] send you their greetings.

13:25
b Col 4:18

25Grace be with you all. [b]

13:20–21

Biblical Prayers of Blessing

Prayer	Reference
1. "The LORD bless you and keep you; the LORD make his face shine upon you and be gracious to you; the LORD turn his face toward you and give you peace."	Num. 6:24–26
2. "May the LORD our God be with us as he was with our fathers; may he never leave us nor forsake us. May he turn our hearts to him, to walk in all his ways and to keep the commands . . . he gave our fathers."	1 Kings 8:57–58
3. "Restore us, O God; make your face shine upon us, that we may be saved."	Ps. 80:3
4. "Grace and peace to you from God our Father and from the Lord Jesus Christ."	Rom. 1:7
5. "May the grace of the Lord Jesus Christ, and the love of God, and the fellowship of the Holy Spirit be with you all."	2 Cor. 13:14
6. "May the God of peace, who through the blood of the eternal covenant brought back from the dead our Lord Jesus, that great Shepherd of the sheep, equip you with everything good for doing his will, and may he work in us what is pleasing to him, through Jesus Christ, to whom be glory for ever and ever. Amen."	Heb. 13:20–21
7. "To him who is able to keep you from falling and to present you before his glorious presence without fault and with great joy—to the only God our Savior be glory, majesty, power and authority, through Jesus Christ our Lord, before all ages, now and forevermore! Amen."	Jude 24–25

INTRODUCTION TO
James

AUTHOR
James, the half-brother of Jesus, is the author of this epistle (1:1). He was a leader of the Jerusalem church (Gal. 1:19) and presided over the council of Jerusalem (see Acts 15:1–29). James didn't at first believe in Jesus (see John 7:5) but was later converted, perhaps when Jesus appeared to him after the resurrection (1 Cor. 15:7).

DATE WRITTEN
James was probably written between A.D. 40 and 50.

ORIGINAL READERS
James wrote to the "twelve tribes scattered among the nations" (1:1), a phrase that may refer to Jewish Christians who were scattered throughout the Roman world because of persecution (see Acts 8:1).

TIMELINE

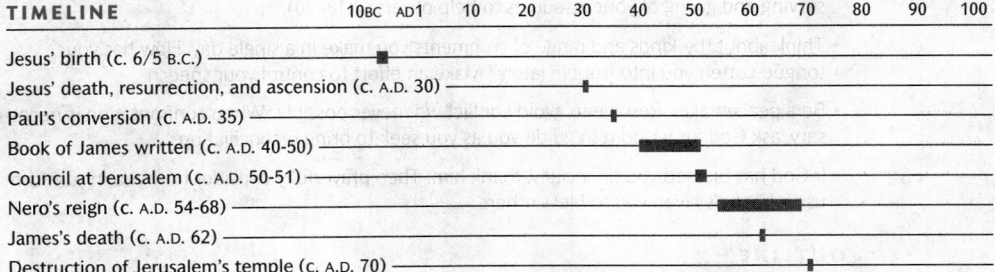

	10BC	AD1	10	20	30	40	50	60	70	80	90	100
Jesus' birth (c. 6/5 B.C.)												
Jesus' death, resurrection, and ascension (c. A.D. 30)												
Paul's conversion (c. A.D. 35)												
Book of James written (c. A.D. 40-50)												
Council at Jerusalem (c. A.D. 50-51)												
Nero's reign (c. A.D. 54-68)												
James's death (c. A.D. 62)												
Destruction of Jerusalem's temple (c. A.D. 70)												

THEMES
The book of James contains the following themes:

1. *Genuine faith.* James's statement that "a person is justified by what he does and not by faith alone" isn't a contradiction of Paul's teaching that salvation is based solely on faith (see Gal. 3:6–14). James is contrasting two kinds of faith: a genuine faith marked by sincere trust in Christ and a religious "faith" characterized simply by intellectual agreement. A "faith" that knows for certain that God exists but fails to trust him isn't faith at all, and it can't save. Genuine, saving faith will transform lives and be demonstrated through good deeds.

2. *Good deeds.* "Deeds" in James is another term for "fruit" or acts of Christian love. Jesus taught that genuine faith will produce "good fruit" (Matt. 7:17) and warned that many who call him "Lord" won't enter heaven (Matt. 7:21–23). Genuine faith doesn't show partiality to the rich while exploiting the poor (2:1–6). It doesn't mouth pious, empty sentiments of good-will to the poor. Genuine faith offers aid to the needy (2:14–16) and manifests itself in compassion for orphans and widows in distress (1:27).

3. *Genuine wisdom.* James contrasted two kinds of wisdom. False wisdom produces envy and selfish ambition (3:14). Genuine wisdom results in humility, deeds of mercy, and right conduct (3:13). Wisdom helps Christians control their speech (3:1–12) and promotes peace, consideration, submission, mercy, good deeds, impartiality, and sincerity (3:17).

FAITH IN ACTION

The pages of James contain life lessons and role models of faith—people who challenge believers to put faith in action.

Role Models

- ABRAHAM (2:21–24) demonstrated his faith by his actions. Test yours to see if it's genuine. In what concrete ways are you acting on it?

- RAHAB (2:25) displayed faith in God when, despite her fear, she hid the spies. Are you facing a situation requiring extraordinary courage? How can Rahab be an encouragement for you?

- PEACEMAKERS (3:18) "raise a harvest of righteousness." How can you fill this role with respect to those around you?

- ELIJAH (5:17) prayed earnestly, and as a consequence it didn't rain for three-and-a-half years. Is God prompting you to pray for something "impossible"? What can you learn from Elijah?

Challenges

- Examine your local church's attitudes toward the poor and those from diverse backgrounds. Determine to warmly welcome people from all backgrounds and walks of life into your church community.

- Look for concrete ways to share God's concern for "orphans and widows" (1:27)—those people on the social and economic fringes who are at risk of harm.

- Rather than debate the faith-versus-works issue, find ways to demonstrate your faith by serving and giving of your resources to help others (2:18–20).

- Think about the kinds and range of comments you make in a single day. How has your tongue gotten you into trouble lately? Make an effort to control your speech.

- Be a peacemaker. Resolve to avoid conflict whenever possible. When confrontation is necessary, ask God for wisdom to guide you as you seek to bring reconciliation.

- If God has blessed you financially, thank him. Then prayerfully consider how you in turn can use what he's given you to bless others.

OUTLINE

   I. Greeting (1:1)
  II. Trials and Temptations (1:2–18)
      A. Facing Trials and Temptations (1:2–12)
      B. God as the Giver of Good Gifts, Not as Tempter (1:13–18)
 III. Listening and Doing (1:19–27)
  IV. Favoritism Forbidden (2:1–13)
   V. Faith and Deeds (2:14–26)
  VI. Taming the Tongue (3:1–12)
 VII. Two Kinds of Wisdom (3:13–18)
VIII. Warning Against Worldliness (4:1—5:6)
      A. Selfishness (4:1–3)
      B. Friendship With the World (4:4)
      C. Pride (4:5–10)
      D. Slander (4:11–12)
      E. Boasting (4:13–17)
      F. Selfishness (5:1–6)
  IX. Miscellaneous Exhortations (5:7–20)

1 James,[a] a servant of God[b] and of the Lord Jesus Christ,

To the twelve tribes[c] scattered[d] among the nations:

Greetings.

Trials and Temptations

[2]Consider it pure joy, my brothers, whenever you face trials of many kinds,[e] [3]because you know that the testing of your faith develops perseverance. [4]Perseverance must finish its work so that you may be mature and complete, not lacking anything. [5]If any of you lacks wisdom, he should ask God,[f] who gives generously to all without finding fault, and it will be given to him.[g] [6]But when he asks, he must believe and not doubt,[h] because he who doubts is like a wave of the sea, blown and tossed by the wind. [7]That man should not think he will receive anything from the Lord; [8]he is a double-minded man,[i] unstable in all he does.

[9]The brother in humble circumstances ought to take pride in his high position. [10]But the one who is rich should take pride in his low position, because he will pass away like a wild flower.[j] [11]For the sun rises with scorching heat and withers[k] the plant; its blossom falls and its beauty is destroyed.[l] In the same way, the rich man will fade away even while he goes about his business.

[12]Blessed is the man who perseveres under trial, because when he has stood the test, he will receive the crown of life[m] that God has promised to those who love him.[n]

[13]When tempted, no one should say, "God is tempting me." For God cannot be tempted by evil, nor does he tempt anyone; [14]but each one is tempted when, by his own evil desire, he is dragged away and enticed. [15]Then, after desire has conceived, it gives birth to sin;[o] and sin, when it is full-grown, gives birth to death.[p]

[16]Don't be deceived,[q] my dear brothers.[r] [17]Every good and perfect gift is from above,[s] coming down from the Father of the heavenly lights, who does not change[t] like shifting shadows. [18]He chose to give us birth[u] through the word of truth, that we might be a kind of firstfruits[v] of all he created.

Listening and Doing

[19]My dear brothers, take note of this: Everyone should be quick to listen, slow to speak[w] and slow to become angry, [20]for man's anger does not bring about the righteous life that God desires. [21]Therefore, get rid of[x] all moral filth and the evil that is so prevalent and humbly accept the word planted in you,[y] which can save you.

1:1
a Ac 15:13 b Tit 1:1
c Ac 26:7
d Dt 32:26; Jn 7:35;
1Pe 1:1
1:2
e Mt 5:12; 1Pe 1:6
1:5
f 1Ki 3:9,10;
Pr 2:3-6 g Mt 7:7
1:6
h Mk 11:24
1:8
i Jas 4:8
1:10
j 1Co 7:31;
1Pe 1:24
1:11
k Ps 102:4,11
l Isa 40:6-8
1:12
m 1Co 9:25
n Jas 2:5
1:15
o Job 15:35;
Ps 7:14 p Ro 6:23
1:16
q 1Co 6:9 r ver 19
1:17
s Jn 3:27
t Nu 23:19; Mal 3:6
1:18
u Jn 1:13
v Eph 1:12;
Rev 14:4
1:19
w Pr 10:19
1:21
x Eph 4:22
y Eph 1:13

James 1:1

📖 James knew he had been given authority by the church to write this forceful letter. In his day and age—when a majority of the Roman-conquered world lived in slavery or poverty—most people saw authority as oppressive. But James turned the common understanding of authority on its head. Authority properly exercised is *service*—to God and others.

📖 Servant leadership means resolving to accomplish God's will, with compassion, in the best interests of others. Who is under your authority? What practical differences would it make if you were to consciously pair your authority with servanthood, like James and Jesus did? "Whoever wants to be great among you must be your servant," Jesus declared. "For even the Son of Man did not come to be served, but to serve" (Mark 10:43,45). When have you experienced the joy of giving away a piece of your life for someone else?

James 1:2–18

📖 James no doubt drew on Jesus' teachings, including the Sermon on the Mount. For instance, verse 12 reads like the Beatitudes (Matt. 5:3–12). James made three points in this passage: (1) Prayer and God's wisdom are necessary to negotiate successfully life's minefield of trials and the questions they raise in Christians' minds (vv. 2–8). (2) Poverty and wealth affect a believer's spiritual life in surprising ways (vv. 9–11). (3) God, the author of every good gift, isn't to blame when Christians fail to stand firm in times of trial (vv. 12–18).

📖 How recently have you asked the big questions: Why is my life so hard? Why did God let this happen to me? What difference does my faith make? James didn't give easy answers, but he made some observations: God is a generous giver, even to the undeserving, and what he's really looking for is character development. James had thought-provoking words for poor (v. 9; cf. 2:5) and rich (vv. 10–11) alike. What does it mean for you personally that Christ rules such an "upside-down" kingdom? What lasting values are high on your priority list?

22Do not merely listen to the word, and so deceive yourselves. Do what it says. 23Anyone who listens to the word but does not do what it says is like a man who looks at his face in a mirror 24and, after looking at himself, goes away and immediately forgets what he looks like. 25But the man who looks intently into the perfect law that gives freedom,*z* and continues to do this, not forgetting what he has heard, but doing it—he will be blessed in what he does.*a*

26If anyone considers himself religious and yet does not keep a tight rein on his tongue,*b* he deceives himself and his religion is worthless. 27Religion that God our Father accepts as pure and faultless is this: to look after*c* orphans and widows*d* in their distress and to keep oneself from being polluted by the world.*e*

Favoritism Forbidden

2 My brothers, as believers in our glorious*f* Lord Jesus Christ, don't show favoritism.*g* 2Suppose a man comes into your meeting wearing a gold ring and fine clothes, and a poor man in shabby clothes also comes in. 3If you show special attention to the man wearing fine clothes and say, "Here's a good seat for you," but say to the poor man, "You stand there" or "Sit on the floor by my feet," 4have you not discriminated among yourselves and become judges*h* with evil thoughts?

5Listen, my dear brothers:*i* Has not God chosen those who are poor in the eyes of the world*j* to be rich in faith*k* and to inherit the kingdom he promised those who love him?*l* 6But you have insulted the poor.*m* Is it not the rich who are exploiting you? Are they not the ones who are dragging you into court?*n* 7Are they not the ones who are slandering the noble name of him to whom you belong?

8If you really keep the royal law found in Scripture, "Love your neighbor as yourself,"*a**o* you are doing right. 9But if you show favoritism,*p* you sin and are convicted by the law as lawbreakers.*q* 10For whoever keeps the whole law and yet stumbles at just one point is guilty of breaking all of it.*r* 11For he who said, "Do not commit

a 8 Lev. 19:18

Marginal references

1:25
z Jas 2:12
a Jn 13:17

1:26
b Ps 34:13;
1Pe 3:10

1:27
c Mt 25:36
d Isa 1:17,23
e Ro 12:2

2:1
f 1Co 2:8
g Lev 19:15

2:4
h Jn 7:24

2:5
i Jas 1:16,19
j 1Co 1:26-28
k Lk 12:21
l Jas 1:12

2:6
m 1Co 11:22
n Ac 8:3

2:8
o Lev 19:18

2:9
p ver 1 q Dt 1:17

2:10
r Mt 5:19; Gal 3:10

James 1:19–27

James called for an active faith, and God's gift of salvation irresistibly prods believers of all eras toward good behavior. When they are humbly open to his Word, they let it shape their characters until the natural result is good works. James specifically pointed out a believer's responsibility to share God's concern for "orphans and widows"—for people on the social, economic, and legal fringes who are at risk of exploitation (cf. Deut. 10:18–19).

James closed this passage with three action items. These points, which continue to be tough challenges today, involve: (1) controlling our speech, (2) looking after society's voiceless and vulnerable, and (3) avoiding the spiritual pollution of our fallen world. Take a moment to hold up your behavior in these areas to the mirror of God's Word. Are you ready to face the challenges waiting for you when you walk away?

James 2:1–13

The early church could have given the wealthy a chance to demonstrate their superiority. But for James, favoring the rich and belittling the poor were obvious examples of failure to "keep . . . from being polluted by the world" (1:27). These attitudes are incompatible with the gospel.

How do matters like education, profession, clothing, and social polish affect how you and others in your church view people? James warned us about the subtle power such outward symbols can have over the Christian community. Does your church warmly welcome people from all backgrounds and walks of life? Can you think of suggestions for how your congregation (and you yourself) could do better? When you or other people from your church engage personally with those who are poor—either at home or abroad—how can you make sure their dignity is honored?

1:22–25

Theories of How to Apply the Bible to Everyday Life

The Two Step:
First attempt to understand the text in its context, then apply it to your life (premise for the "There and Then" and "Here and Now" notes system in this Bible).

The One Step:
If you really understand the text, you already know how to apply it.

The Glide Step:
Understanding and application are distinct, but neither is prior to the other. Instead, they inform each other.

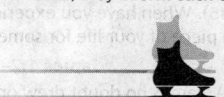

adultery,"ᵃˢ also said, "Do not murder."ᵇᵗ If you do not commit adultery but do commit murder, you have become a lawbreaker.

¹²Speak and act as those who are going to be judged by the law that gives freedom,ᵘ ¹³because judgment without mercy will be shown to anyone who has not been merciful.ᵛ Mercy triumphs over judgment!

Faith and Deeds

¹⁴What good is it, my brothers, if a man claims to have faith but has no deeds?ʷ Can such faith save him? ¹⁵Suppose a brother or sister is without clothes and daily food.ˣ ¹⁶If one of you says to him, "Go, I wish you well; keep warm and well fed," but does nothing about his physical needs, what good is it?ʸ ¹⁷In the same way, faith by itself, if it is not accompanied by action, is dead.

¹⁸But someone will say, "You have faith; I have deeds."

Show me your faith without deeds,ᶻ and I will show you my faith by what I do.ᵃ ¹⁹You believe that there is one God.ᵇ Good! Even the demons believe thatᶜ—and shudder.

ᵃ 11 Exodus 20:14; Deut. 5:18   ᵇ 11 Exodus 20:13; Deut. 5:17

2:11
ˢ Ex 20:14; Dt 5:18
ᵗ Ex 20:13; Dt 5:17

2:12
ᵘ Jas 1:25
2:13
ᵛ Mt 5:7; 18:32-35

2:14
ʷ Mt 7:26; Jas 1:22-25

2:15
ˣ Mt 25:35,36
2:16
ʸ 1Jn 3:17,18

2:18
ᶻ Ro 3:28 ᵃ Jas 3:13
2:19
ᵇ Dt 6:4 ᶜ Mt 8:29; Lk 4:34

James 2:14–26

James made a statement that sounds audacious: "Faith" not backed by concrete action doesn't lead to salvation! James and Paul didn't disagree on this subject, as many have thought. (For Paul's view see Eph. 2:8–10.) But James argued that true faith *always* and *inevitably* shows itself in good deeds. After claiming that faith and deeds go together, Jesus had earlier voiced a similar sobering warning: Many who call him "Lord" won't enter heaven (Matt. 7:15–23).

James presented a clear illustration to make his point. "Suppose a brother or sister is without clothes and daily food." It doesn't take much to see that "Go, I wish you well; keep warm and well fed" alone won't meet the need. Thanks to modern media, we are constantly exposed to "brothers and sisters" worldwide in destitute circumstances. We may tend to feel overwhelmed, vaguely guilty—and above all, helpless. But guilt that doesn't lead to changed behavior doesn't help, and we may not be as helpless as we think. What *one* thing can you do to couple your faith with action in this area? Could it be that God has entrusted Christ's followers with all that is needed to eliminate severe poverty in the world?

Snapshots

1:27

A Love Affair for Jesus

In the early 1990s members of Christ Presbyterian Church of Minneapolis visited Rakai, Uganda. Riveted by the impact of AIDS and the needs of orphaned children, the congregation asked what it could do to bring transformation to this impoverished, isolated community. Soon a love affair began to grow between the church and the people of Rakai. More than a dozen years later, this faithful congregation is still supporting Rakai by praying and providing support for its orphans. The relationships continue to grow as church representatives visit Rakai annually.

The success of this venture may be directly attributed to the work of the Holy Spirit, as well as to a heart within the congregation to seek out what God would have them do in the world. Because of this growing, successful, and sustainable relationship, this church has gone on to support other mission efforts, both domestically and abroad. One of the pastors stated that his church "now recognizes that it can have an impact that ripples beyond its immediate congregation. It's the miracle of God's children being empowered to carry out the ministry of Jesus."

> [This] church "now recognizes that it can have an impact that ripples beyond its immediate congregation. It's the miracle of God's children being empowered to carry out the ministry of Jesus."

2:20
d ver 17,26

2:21
e Ge 22:9,12

2:22
f Heb 11:17
g 1Th 1:3

2:23
h Ge 15:6; Ro 4:3
i 2Ch 20:7; Isa 41:8

2:25
j Heb 11:31

2:26
k ver 17,20

3:2
l 1Ki 8:46; Jas 2:10
m 1Pe 3:10
n Mt 12:37
o Jas 1:26

3:3
p Ps 32:9

3:5
q Ps 12:3,4

3:6
r Pr 26:27
s Mt 15:11,18,19

3:8
t Ps 140:3; Ro 3:13

3:9
u Ge 1:26,27;
1Co 11:7

20 You foolish man, do you want evidence that faith without deeds is useless a? d 21 Was not our ancestor Abraham considered righteous for what he did when he offered his son Isaac on the altar? e 22 You see that his faith and his actions were working together, f and his faith was made complete by what he did. g 23 And the scripture was fulfilled that says, "Abraham believed God, and it was credited to him as righteousness," b h and he was called God's friend. i 24 You see that a person is justified by what he does and not by faith alone.

25 In the same way, was not even Rahab the prostitute considered righteous for what she did when she gave lodging to the spies and sent them off in a different direction? j 26 As the body without the spirit is dead, so faith without deeds is dead. k

Taming the Tongue

3 Not many of you should presume to be teachers, my brothers, because you know that we who teach will be judged more strictly. 2 We all stumble l in many ways. If anyone is never at fault in what he says, m he is a perfect man, n able to keep his whole body in check. o

3 When we put bits into the mouths of horses to make them obey us, we can turn the whole animal. p 4 Or take ships as an example. Although they are so large and are driven by strong winds, they are steered by a very small rudder wherever the pilot wants to go. 5 Likewise the tongue is a small part of the body, but it makes great boasts. q Consider what a great forest is set on fire by a small spark. 6 The tongue also is a fire, r a world of evil among the parts of the body. It corrupts the whole person, s sets the whole course of his life on fire, and is itself set on fire by hell.

7 All kinds of animals, birds, reptiles and creatures of the sea are being tamed and have been tamed by man, 8 but no man can tame the tongue. It is a restless evil, full of deadly poison. t

9 With the tongue we praise our Lord and Father, and with it we curse men, who have been made in God's likeness. u 10 Out of the same mouth come praise and curs-

a 20 Some early manuscripts *dead*   b 23 Gen. 15:6

James 3:1–12

🔖 James returned to the subject of proper speech (cf. 1:19–21,26). Verbal attacks, like favoritism (cf. 2:1–13), are lethal to a faith community. He made three points: (1) Small items—the tongue in this case—can and often do control a larger whole. (2) The source of evil is hell, Satan's stronghold. (3) When the Christian's tongue is influenced by hell's forces, the result is severe "double-mindedness"—a situation in which the same tongue praises God but curses people he's made in his likeness.

📖 Think about the range of comments you make in a single day. What words have you been proud of in the last few days? How has your tongue gotten you into trouble lately? We all struggle to keep our tongues in check. For instance, we may speak and sing words of praise to God during a worship service—and then make barbed comments about a fellow worshiper or leader during dinner afterward. Out of the same mouth (see vv. 9–10)! In James's words: "This should not be."

2:14–17

Faith and Good Works

Faith is the foundation. Works are the houses (Matt. 7:26).

GOOD WORKS	Are part of God's nature (Jer. 32:36–40).	Are unnatural to sinful people (Rom. 3:9–18).	Are expected by God of his people (Gal. 6:9–10).	Please God (Heb. 13:16).	Will be rewarded (John 5:28–29).	Are evidences of God's grace (2 Cor. 9:8).

F A I T H

Is confidence in and commitment to Jesus Christ (John 14:1).	Is acting on God's promises (Heb. 11:1–40).	Is demonstrated in good deeds (James 2:14–26).	Is the basis for salvation (Eph. 2:8–9).	Marks powerful ministries (Acts 11:24).	Is a gift from God (John 6:63–65; Rom. 12:3).	Is strengthened through testing (Rom. 4:1–21).

ing. My brothers, this should not be. [11]Can both fresh water and salt[a] water flow from the same spring? [12]My brothers, can a fig tree bear olives, or a grapevine bear figs?[v] Neither can a salt spring produce fresh water.

Two Kinds of Wisdom

[13]Who is wise and understanding among you? Let him show it[w] by his good life, by deeds done in the humility that comes from wisdom. [14]But if you harbor bitter envy and selfish ambition[x] in your hearts, do not boast about it or deny the truth.[y] [15]Such "wisdom" does not come down from heaven[z] but is earthly, unspiritual, of the devil.[a] [16]For where you have envy and selfish ambition, there you find disorder and every evil practice.

[17]But the wisdom that comes from heaven[b] is first of all pure; then peace-loving, considerate, submissive, full of mercy[c] and good fruit, impartial and sincere.[d] [18]Peacemakers who sow in peace raise a harvest of righteousness.[e]

Submit Yourselves to God

4 What causes fights and quarrels[f] among you? Don't they come from your desires that battle[g] within you? [2]You want something but don't get it. You kill and covet, but you cannot have what you want. You quarrel and fight. You do not have,

[a] 11 Greek bitter (see also verse 14)

3:12
v Mt 7:16

3:13
w Jas 2:18

3:14
x ver 16 y Jas 5:19
3:15
z Jas 1:17 a 1Ti 4:1

3:17
b 1Co 2:6 c Lk 6:36
d Ro 12:9

3:18
e Pr 11:18;
Isa 32:17

4:1
f Tit 3:9 g Ro 7:23

James 3:13–18

James contrasted two opposite "wisdoms." False wisdom produces envy and selfish ambition. True wisdom results in humility and deeds of mercy. When James encouraged his readers to "sow in peace," he was referring to an Old Testament notion—*shalom*, a state of wholeness, health, completion. As a common greeting or blessing it expressed a wish for prosperity, physical health, salvation, and harmonious relationships. Justice, righteousness, and peace are central to God's character. They are to characterize the Christian community as well.

Are you energized by heated debate, or do you avoid conflict and controversy? The second approach may seem to lead to peace, but the byproducts of "peace at any price" often include superficial relationships, insincerity, and pervasive "niceness" (an appearance of peace). Absence of conflict is only the bottom layer of peace. Peace that leads to righteousness isn't afraid of exerting "tough love" (cf. Eph. 4:15). It refuses to let go of justice or compromise God's wisdom. What can you do to promote real peace within your sphere of influence?

James 4:1–12

The church James addressed was threatened by earthly passions, like ambition, envy, pride, and jealousy. Because these attitudes and behaviors are self-interested, they lead believers away from their true goal. James's readers needed to repent and choose a relationship with God over "friendship with the world." To "come near to God" and to "wash [our] hands" remind us of Israel's priests cleansing themselves before entering God's presence (cf. Ex. 30:17–21).

2:20–24

The Relationship Between Faith and Action

Faith alone.
At certain times in church history, when spiritual living has been judged to be too much a matter of right action, or spiritual benefits have been offered for contributions to the church, faith alone has been emphasized. This was one of the main issues of the Protestant Reformation. See Romans 5:1.

Action alone.
At other times, a reluctance to act on the basis of faith has led to charges of withdrawal from the world. This has made faithful living seem unrelated to the needs of the world and has led to renewed emphasis on the need for fruits of the Spirit. The book of James was written to counter this trend.

Faith is the root; action is the fruit.
Genuine faith should motivate us to do things consistent with the nature of that faith. Jesus cursed the fig tree because what it was "doing" (failing to produce figs) was inconsistent with its nature. As faithful disciples of Jesus Christ, we should do the things reflected in the Biblical fruits of the Spirit as listed in Galatians 5:22. See also Ephesians 2:8–10.

Action develops compassion.
The American psychologist William James taught that actions produce feelings. If you want to love the unlovely, he said, do loving things for them—even when you don't feel like it. The feelings will come. The Bible tells us to love our enemies (Matt. 5:44–48). Sometimes we must act in the confidence that the love will come later (1 Cor. 13:1–13).

Both faith and action are part of a disciple's life in Jesus Christ.

4:3
h Ps 18:41
i 1Jn 3:22; 5:14
4:4
j Jas 1:27
k 1Jn 2:15
l Jn 15:19

because you do not ask God. ³When you ask, you do not receive, [h] because you ask with wrong motives, [i] that you may spend what you get on your pleasures.

⁴You adulterous people, don't you know that friendship with the world [j] is hatred toward God? [k] Anyone who chooses to be a friend of the world becomes an enemy of God. [l] ⁵Or do you think Scripture says without reason that the spirit he caused to live in us envies intensely? [a] ⁶But he gives us more grace. That is why Scripture says:

4:6
m Ps 138:6;
Pr 3:34; Mt 23:12
4:7
n Eph 4:27;
1Pe 5:6-9
4:8
o 2Ch 15:2
p Isa 1:16 q Jas 1:8
4:9
r Lk 6:25
4:11
s 1Pe 2:1 t Mt 7:1
u Jas 1:22

> "God opposes the proud
>   but gives grace to the humble." [b] [m]

⁷Submit yourselves, then, to God. Resist the devil, [n] and he will flee from you. ⁸Come near to God and he will come near to you. [o] Wash your hands, [p] you sinners, and purify your hearts, you double-minded. [q] ⁹Grieve, mourn and wail. Change your laughter to mourning and your joy to gloom. [r] ¹⁰Humble yourselves before the Lord, and he will lift you up.

¹¹Brothers, do not slander one another. [s] Anyone who speaks against his brother or judges him [t] speaks against the law and judges it. When you judge the law, you are not keeping it, [u] but sitting in judgment on it. ¹²There is only one Lawgiver and

4:12
v Mt 10:28
w Ro 14:4

Judge, the one who is able to save and destroy. [v] But you—who are you to judge your neighbor? [w]

Boasting About Tomorrow

4:13
x Pr 27:1

¹³Now listen, you who say, "Today or tomorrow we will go to this or that city, spend a year there, carry on business and make money." [x] ¹⁴Why, you do not even know what will happen tomorrow. What is your life? You are a mist that appears

4:14
y Job 7:7; Ps 102:3
4:15
z Ac 18:21
4:16
a 1Co 5:6
4:17
b Lk 12:47; Jn 9:41

for a little while and then vanishes. [y] ¹⁵Instead, you ought to say, "If it is the Lord's will, [z] we will live and do this or that." ¹⁶As it is, you boast and brag. All such boasting is evil. [a] ¹⁷Anyone, then, who knows the good he ought to do and doesn't do it, sins. [b]

Warning to Rich Oppressors

5:1
c Lk 6:24
5:2
d Job 13:28;
Mt 6:19,20
5:3
e ver 7,8

5 Now listen, you rich people, [c] weep and wail because of the misery that is coming upon you. ²Your wealth has rotted, and moths have eaten your clothes. [d] ³Your gold and silver are corroded. Their corrosion will testify against you and eat your flesh like fire. You have hoarded wealth in the last days. [e] ⁴Look! The wages you failed to pay

---

a 5 Or that God jealously longs for the spirit that he made to live in us; or that the Spirit he caused to live in us longs jealously   b 6 Prov. 3:34

📖 In this letter appealing to action and service, James also emphasized the anchor of our faith—intimacy with God. How well do you know God? Do you see yourself in relationship to him as an acquaintance, business associate, lobbyist, petitioner, servant, debtor—son or daughter? Coming near to God is more than resolving to improve our spiritual lives. It's entering his presence, living there, being comfortable, being at home. What difference does this make in your life of Christian service?

📖 What's your bedrock of security? Are your behavior, mind, and heart in alignment on this issue, or do you find yourself vacillating—in James's terms, being "double-minded" (cf. 1:8; 4:8)? Like a mist, prosperity, job security, health, family, and countless other false foundations can disappear even as we grasp them. What concrete steps can you take to ensure you are holding on—single-mindedly and single-heartedly—to a permanent hope founded on your life in Christ?

James 4:13–17

🔄 James addressed some traveling merchants within the church. He wasn't arguing against making money but against a smug, self-assured attitude, revealing a mind-set in which making money outstripped devotion to God in importance. Underlying this was another sin: Many hadn't caught a vision of the poor in the church as sisters and brothers. They had ignored and sidestepped them, showing favoritism to the well-heeled. There was no observable difference in their lives for having come to know Jesus.

James 5:1–6

🔄 James shifted his attention from the merchant to the landowning class. In the ancient world, rural land holdings and their produce were the source of real wealth. A prosperous landowner in James's culture was, by definition, an exploiter of the poor. In characteristic fashion James threw out a controversial observation: A life of self-absorbed, irresponsible luxury is nothing short of murder! The rich, he charged, had seen the poverty around them but had failed to take action.

Sharing God's Compassion

 5:1–6

These verses are just a sampling of the hundreds in the Bible about God's concern for the poor and oppressed. If we want to share God's compassion, we must understand four Biblical truths about the needy.

1. The Sovereign of history works to lift up the disadvantaged. Consider the exodus. Again and again God intervened because he hated Israel's oppression (Ex. 3:7–8; 6:5–7). Annually at the harvest festival his people repeated this confession: "The Egyptians mistreated us . . . Then we cried out to the LORD, the God of our fathers, and the LORD heard our voice and saw our misery, toil and oppression. So the LORD brought us out of Egypt" (Deut. 26:6–8).

2. Sometimes God tears down rich and powerful people: "The Lord . . . has filled the hungry with good things but has sent the rich away empty" (Luke 1:46,53). And "listen, you rich people, weep and wail because of the misery that is coming upon you" (James 5:1).

God has created a gorgeous world and has placed humans here to revel in its splendor and produce an abundance of good things. He has no prejudice against rich or poor (Deut. 10:17–18). But when the wealthy oppress or neglect the needy, God is furious.

What if we work hard and create wealth in just ways? God is pleased—as long as we remember to share. When we hoard our blessings, he treats us the same way he does those who exploit the have-nots. God judges societies by their treatment of people at the bottom of the socio-economic ladder.

3. God identifies with the poor so strongly that caring for them is tantamount to helping him. "Whoever is kind to the poor lends to the LORD" (Prov. 19:17a). But anyone "who oppresses the poor shows contempt for their Maker" (Prov. 14:31). Jesus' parable of the sheep and goats is the ultimate commentary on these proverbs: "Whatever you did for one of the least of these brothers of mine, you did for me" (Matt. 25:40).

4. God's faithful people share his concern for the underprivileged. God commanded the Israelites not to treat widows, orphans, and foreigners the way the Egyptians had treated them but to love them instead (Ex. 22:21–24; Deut. 15:13–15).

> God judges societies by their treatment of people at the bottom of the socio-economic ladder.

But the Bible goes one shocking step further. If we don't imitate God's concern for the poor, we are not really his people. When Israel failed to correct repression and defend widows, Isaiah equated the nation with Gomorrah's pagan population (Isa. 1:10–17). Jesus was harsher still. To those who don't feed the hungry and clothe the naked, he will utter a terrible judgment: "Depart from me, you who are cursed, into the eternal fire prepared for the devil and his angels" (Matt. 25:41).

Imagine the stunning impact if even a quarter of today's Christians would begin to care about justice as the Bible says we should. Skeptics would reconsider Christianity. Revival would break out. Untold numbers would come to Christ. Church planting would accelerate. Global tensions would decrease. Our Creator and Redeemer would rejoice.

God doesn't love the poor more than the rich. But he longs for wholeness, goodness, and joy for every person. Poverty crushes the bodies, minds, and spirits of billions of people the Creator loves as his image-bearing children. That is why God longs for us to share his compassion for the less fortunate.

Ronald J. Sider, professor of theology, holistic ministry, and public policy at Eastern Seminary in Philadelphia and president of Evangelicals for Social Action in Wynnewood, Pennsylvania
Source: Part of this article is adapted (with permission) from Chapter 9 of Ronald Sider's *Living Like Jesus: Eleven Essentials for Growing a Genuine Faith* (Grand Rapids, Mich.: Baker, 1999).

5:4
f Lev 19:13
g Dt 24:15
h Ro 9:29
5:5
i Am 6:1 j Jer 12:3;
25:34
5:6
k Heb 10:38

the workmen[f] who mowed your fields are crying out against you. The cries[g] of the harvesters have reached the ears of the Lord Almighty.[h] 5You have lived on earth in luxury and self-indulgence. You have fattened yourselves[i] in the day of slaughter.[a][j] 6You have condemned and murdered innocent men,[k] who were not opposing you.

Patience in Suffering

5:7
l Dt 11:14; Jer 5:24
5:8
m Ro 13:11;
1Pe 4:7
5:9
n Jas 4:11
o 1Co 4:5; 1Pe 4:5
p Mt 24:33
5:10
q Mt 5:12
5:11
r Mt 5:10
s Job 1:21,22; 2:10
t Job 42:10,12-17
u Nu 14:18
5:12
v Mt 5:34-37

7Be patient, then, brothers, until the Lord's coming. See how the farmer waits for the land to yield its valuable crop and how patient he is for the autumn and spring rains.[l] 8You too, be patient and stand firm, because the Lord's coming is near.[m] 9Don't grumble against each other, brothers,[n] or you will be judged. The Judge[o] is standing at the door![p]

10Brothers, as an example of patience in the face of suffering, take the prophets[q] who spoke in the name of the Lord. 11As you know, we consider blessed[r] those who have persevered. You have heard of Job's perseverance[s] and have seen what the Lord finally brought about.[t] The Lord is full of compassion and mercy.[u]

12Above all, my brothers, do not swear—not by heaven or by earth or by anything else. Let your "Yes" be yes, and your "No," no, or you will be condemned.[v]

The Prayer of Faith

5:13
w Ps 50:15
x Col 3:16
5:14
y Mk 6:13
5:16
z Mt 3:6 a 1Pe 2:24
b Jn 9:31
5:17
c Ac 14:15
d 1Ki 17:1; Lk 4:25
5:18
e 1Ki 18:41-45
5:19
f Jas 3:14
g Mt 18:15
5:20
h Ro 11:14
i 1Pe 4:8

13Is any one of you in trouble? He should pray.[w] Is anyone happy? Let him sing songs of praise.[x] 14Is any one of you sick? He should call the elders of the church to pray over him and anoint him with oil[y] in the name of the Lord. 15And the prayer offered in faith will make the sick person well; the Lord will raise him up. If he has sinned, he will be forgiven. 16Therefore confess your sins[z] to each other and pray for each other so that you may be healed.[a] The prayer of a righteous man is powerful and effective.[b]

17Elijah was a man just like us.[c] He prayed earnestly that it would not rain, and it did not rain on the land for three and a half years.[d] 18Again he prayed, and the heavens gave rain, and the earth produced its crops.[e]

19My brothers, if one of you should wander from the truth[f] and someone should bring him back,[g] 20remember this: Whoever turns a sinner from the error of his way will save[h] him from death and cover over a multitude of sins.[i]

a 5 Or yourselves as in a day of feasting

How is appreciation for money different from love of money? Is the difference a matter of degree, or does it affect your outlook, value system, and behavior? God doesn't despise the rich. But he cares deeply and personally how we handle our wealth. In Matthew 25:31–46 Jesus said that he considered our reaction to the hungry, thirsty, poor, sick, and imprisoned to be our response to *him*. If God has blessed you financially, thank him. Then consider prayerfully how you can bless others with the means he's put at your disposal.

James 5:7–12

James focused in the previous passage on the victims of oppression, leading to two points: (1) Patience allows believers to grow through difficult times. (2) Christians aren't to judge others, even if these people are the source of their hardship. James urged his audience to remember God's generosity and live in humility and compassion—as Jesus did. But, he wasn't afraid to remind them, God also is Judge. This was less a threat than the warning of a dear friend. Christ's return will have two-pronged consequences: judgment and reward.

Who has taken advantage of you? Are you withholding forgiveness? If you have forgiven, what difference has this made in your relationship with God? With this person, if you are still in contact? With yourself? The wealthy exploiters James referred to hadn't even asked for forgiveness. Yet James directed the poor to let it go. In refusing to forgive we sink to the level of those who have wronged us (cf. Matt. 6:14–15; 7:1–2). But by patient endurance we progress toward spiritual maturity.

James 5:13–20

Here surfaces James's passion for true spiritual community. He encouraged his readers to confess their sins to each other and pray for one another. This is important for at least two reasons: (1) In order to combat the forces of arrogance and conflict in the church, James urged public openness and vulnerability. Confession of wrongs committed against sisters and brothers is a sure path to interpersonal healing. (2) Moses, Daniel, Nehemiah, and, of course, Jesus, identified themselves with the people's sins.

How would you feel about sharing your sins and failings with another believer? How comfortable would you be listening to another Christian's confession and praying for him or her? Have you recently been involved in either exchange? Through James, God calls us to push through our hesitancy and willingly shoulder a responsibility that may not feel like it's technically ours. In this way we become the community of the faithful.

INTRODUCTION TO

1 Peter

AUTHOR
The author of this epistle identified himself as "Peter, an apostle of Jesus Christ" (1:1).

DATE WRITTEN
This letter was probably written in Rome between A.D. 60 and 64, at a time when persecution
was imminent or intensifying.

ORIGINAL READERS
This letter was written as a circular epistle to churches located in "Pontus, Galatia, Cappadocia, Asia and Bithynia" (1:1), regions in modern Turkey. Believers in those areas were suffering
persecution for their faith (1:6; 4:12–19; 5:9–10).

TIMELINE

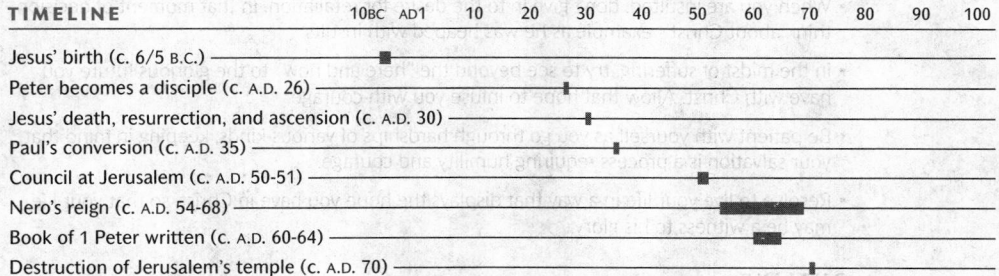

	10BC AD1	10	20	30	40	50	60	70	80	90	100
Jesus' birth (c. 6/5 B.C.)											
Peter becomes a disciple (c. A.D. 26)											
Jesus' death, resurrection, and ascension (c. A.D. 30)											
Paul's conversion (c. A.D. 35)											
Council at Jerusalem (c. A.D. 50-51)											
Nero's reign (c. A.D. 54-68)											
Book of 1 Peter written (c. A.D. 60-64)											
Destruction of Jerusalem's temple (c. A.D. 70)											

THEMES
First Peter contains the following themes:

1. *The believer's new identity.* Peter's goal was to encourage believers suffering persecution.
He did this by reminding them of the Christian hope and of their new identity in Christ. Because of God's great mercy (1:3), believers have been given new life (1:3), a "living hope" (1:3;
see 1:13,21; 3:15), and an eternal inheritance (1:4). They are now "the people of God" (2:10).
Because of the glorious future reserved for them (1:13), they are to rejoice (1:6,8; 4:13) and be
encouraged in the midst of suffering.

2. *Suffering for doing good.* Though believers may experience "all kinds of trials" (1:6) and
face slander (2:12), the "ignorant talk of foolish men" (2:15), malicious verbal attacks (3:16),
abuse (4:4), and insults (4:14), they are to stand firm in the faith (5:9). After they have suffered
a "little while" (5:10), God will "restore [them] and make [them] strong, firm and steadfast"
(5:10). Suffering acts as a purifying fire to prove the genuineness of faith (1:7). It also gives
Christians an opportunity to bear witness to their hope (3:15). When they suffer unjustly,
they are to follow Christ's example (2:21). They are never to retaliate (2:23; 3:9) but are to
persist in doing what's right (2:15,20; 3:6,17), living with joy (1:6,8; 4:13,16) and hope
(1:3,13,21; 3:15).

3. *Christian living.* Christians are to live lives befitting their conversion. Peter pictured salvation as a process (1:9; 2:2) into which believers grow from their daily faithfulness under pressure. They are to strive toward personal holiness (1:13–21) out of reverent fear of God (1:17–21) and to display their faith by loving others (1:22). Their salvation is to affect their social relationships (2:11—3:7) with believers as well as nonbelievers (1:22—3:12; 5:1–9).

FAITH IN ACTION

The pages of 1 Peter are filled with life lessons and role models of faith—people who challenge believers to put faith in action.

Role Models

- SARAH (3:6) did what was right and didn't give in to fear. Are you tempted to cave in because of your current situation? How can Sarah inspire you to trust God?

- PETER (5:12) wrote to encourage suffering believers and testify to the great mercy and grace of God. Whom have you encouraged lately?

- SILAS (5:12) was called a "faithful brother" by Peter. Are you a loyal friend? How can your faithfulness both encourage your Christian friends and witness to your non-Christian friends?

- MARK (5:13) was called "my son" by Peter, implying that Peter had led Mark to Christ. How many spiritual "sons" and "daughters" do you have?

Challenges

- Make a list that describes your new identity in Christ. Meditate on it when you become discouraged.

- When you are insulted, don't give in to the desire for retaliation. In that moment of decision, think about Christ's example as he was heaped with insults.

- In the midst of suffering, try to see beyond the "here and now" to the glorious future you have with Christ. Allow that hope to infuse you with courage.

- Be patient with yourself as you go through hardships of various kinds, keeping in mind that your salvation is a process requiring humility and courage.

- Resolve to live your life in a way that displays the hope you have in Christ, so that your life may be a witness to his glory.

OUTLINE

   I. Greeting (1:1–12)
  II. Exhortations to Holy Living (1:13—5:11)
     A. Self-Control and Holiness (1:13—2:3)
     B. The Conduct of the People of God (2:4–12)
     C. Submission to Authority (2:13—3:7)
     D. Suffering for Doing Good (3:8–17)
     E. Armed With the Attitude of Christ (3:18—4:6)
     F. Conduct in View of the End of All Things (4:7–11)
     G. Suffering for Being a Christian (4:12–19)
     H. Exhortations to Elders (5:1–4)
     I. Exhortations to Young Men (5:5–11)
  III. The Purpose of the Letter (5:12)
  IV. Closing Greeting (5:13–14)

1 Peter, an apostle of Jesus Christ, [a]

To God's elect, [b] strangers in the world, scattered throughout Pontus, Galatia, Cappadocia, Asia and Bithynia, [c] 2who have been chosen according to the foreknowledge [d] of God the Father, through the sanctifying work of the Spirit, [e] for obedience to Jesus Christ and sprinkling by his blood: [f]

Grace and peace be yours in abundance.

Praise to God for a Living Hope

3Praise be to the God and Father of our Lord Jesus Christ! [g] In his great mercy [h] he has given us new birth into a living hope through the resurrection of Jesus Christ from the dead, [i] 4and into an inheritance that can never perish, spoil or fade—kept in heaven for you, [j] 5who through faith are shielded by God's power [k] until the coming of the salvation that is ready to be revealed in the last time. 6In this you greatly rejoice, [l] though now for a little while [m] you may have had to suffer grief in all kinds of trials. [n] 7These have come so that your faith—of greater worth than gold, which perishes even though refined by fire [o]—may be proved genuine [p] and may result in praise, glory and honor when Jesus Christ is revealed. [q] 8Though you have not seen him, you love him; and even though you do not see him now, you believe in him [r] and are filled with an inexpressible and glorious joy, 9for you are receiving the goal of your faith, the salvation of your souls. [s]

10Concerning this salvation, the prophets, who spoke [t] of the grace that was to come to you, searched intently and with the greatest care, [u] 11trying to find out the time and circumstances to which the Spirit of Christ [v] in them was pointing when he predicted the sufferings of Christ and the glories that would follow. 12It was revealed to them that they were not serving themselves but you, when they spoke of the things that have now been told you by those who have preached the gospel to you [w] by the Holy Spirit sent from heaven. Even angels long to look into these things.

1:1
a 2Pe 1:1
b Mt 24:22
c Ac 16:7

1:2
d Ro 8:29
e 2Th 2:13
f Heb 10:22; 12:24

1:3
g 2Co 1:3; Eph 1:3
h Tit 3:5; Jas 1:18
i 1Co 15:20

1:4
j Col 1:5
1:5
k Jn 10:28
1:6
l Ro 5:2 m 1Pe 5:10
n Jas 1:2
1:7
o Job 23:10;
Ps 66:10; Pr 17:3
p Jas 1:3 q Ro 2:7

1:8
r Jn 20:29

1:9
s Ro 6:22
1:10
t Mt 26:24
u Mt 13:17
1:11
v 2Pe 1:21

1:12
w ver 25

---

1 Peter 1:1–2

Peter's salutation here is one of the richest opening greetings of any New Testament letter. It contains both a penetrating description of the readers and a theological explanation of how they had become Christians. Its themes are central to the letter itself: the status of God's people and the salvation God provides for them.

The term "strangers" in this context refers to people in lowly conditions, who reside in an area without the legal protection and rights provided to citizens or who stay in one place for only a brief time. The Christians of Asia Minor were considered strangers either because (1) they were from already-marginalized social castes or (2) by becoming Christians they were joining a disenfranchised group.

This greeting gives us Peter's general perspective on and for Christians who find themselves excluded and oppressed socially: Their primary group is God's family, not their society. Their basic means of coping with stress and persecution is to see themselves as God's people being prepared for his final kingdom (cf. 1:3–12). Persecution for you may have taken a more subtle form (see "Here and Now" to follow), if you are even aware of it. In what ways is God preparing you for ultimate kingdom citizenship?

1 Peter 1:3–12

These ten verses form one massive run-on sentence in the Greek. But Peter was both elegantly and profoundly expressive of the grandeur of his subject: salvation. The passage is a eulogy to the Father that overflows into a fuller eulogy touching on (1) the joyful realization of salvation and the anticipation of its complete fulfillment, (2) how that expectation could sustain suffering Christians, and (3) how privileged they could feel about being able to enjoy that salvation after many millennia of waiting.

In your opinion, might the apparent lack of suffering in the West today relate to a lack of nerve on the part of the church to challenge our contemporary world with the message of the cross? Do we live according to the teachings of Jesus with uncompromising rigor? While the Bible never stipulates that every Christian in every age will suffer, Paul did say that "everyone who wants to live a godly life in Christ Jesus will be persecuted" (2 Tim. 3:12). This is a general principle rooted in the nature of a fallen world.

The message of the need for salvation may not be popular, but our world both needs and deserves to hear it clearly. God has brought his Son into the world so that all might have opportunity to know the liberating truth and find meaning in life. Are you sharing the Good News willingly and gladly?

Be Holy

13Therefore, prepare your minds for action; be self-controlled; set your hope fully on the grace to be given you when Jesus Christ is revealed. 14As obedient children, do not conform[x] to the evil desires you had when you lived in ignorance.[y] 15But just as he who called you is holy, so be holy in all you do;[z] 16for it is written: "Be holy, because I am holy."[a][a]

17Since you call on a Father who judges each man's work impartially,[b] live your lives as strangers here in reverent fear.[c] 18For you know that it was not with perishable things such as silver or gold that you were redeemed[d] from the empty way of life handed down to you from your forefathers, 19but with the precious blood of Christ, a lamb[e] without blemish or defect.[f] 20He was chosen before the creation of the world,[g] but was revealed in these last times[h] for your sake. 21Through him you believe in God,[i] who raised him from the dead and glorified him, and so your faith and hope are in God.

22Now that you have purified[j] yourselves by obeying the truth so that you have sincere love for your brothers, love one another deeply,[k] from the heart.[b] 23For you have been born again,[l] not of perishable seed, but of imperishable, through the living and enduring word of God.[m] 24For,

> "All men are like grass,
>> and all their glory is like the flowers of the field;
> the grass withers and the flowers fall,
> 25   but the word of the Lord stands forever."[c][n]

And this is the word that was preached to you.

2 Therefore, rid yourselves[o] of all malice and all deceit, hypocrisy, envy, and slander[p] of every kind. 2Like newborn babies, crave pure spiritual milk,[q] so that by it you may grow up[r] in your salvation, 3now that you have tasted that the Lord is good.[s]

The Living Stone and a Chosen People

4As you come to him, the living Stone[t]—rejected by men but chosen by God and precious to him—5you also, like living stones, are being built[u] into a spiritual house[v] to be a holy priesthood,[w] offering spiritual sacrifices acceptable to God through Jesus Christ.[x] 6For in Scripture it says:

> "See, I lay a stone in Zion,
>> a chosen and precious cornerstone,[y]

1:14
x Ro 12:2
y Eph 4:18
1:15
z 2Co 7:1; 1Th 4:7
1:16
a Lev 11:44,45
1:17
b Ac 10:34
c Heb 12:28
1:18
d Mt 20:28; 1Co 6:20
1:19
e Jn 1:29 f Ex 12:5
1:20
g Eph 1:4
h Heb 9:26
1:21
i Ro 4:24
1:22
j Jas 4:8 k Jn 13:34; Heb 13:1
1:23
l Jn 1:13
m Heb 4:12
1:25
n Isa 40:6-8
2:1
o Eph 4:22
p Jas 4:11
2:2
q 1Co 3:2
r Eph 4:15,16
2:3
s Heb 6:5
2:4
t ver 7
2:5
u 1Co 3:9
v 1Ti 3:15
w Isa 61:6
x Php 4:18; Heb 13:15
2:6
y Eph 2:20

a 16 Lev. 11:44,45; 19:2   b 22 Some early manuscripts from a pure heart   c 25 Isaiah 40:6-8

---

1 Peter 1:13—2:3

📖 Ethical living in a Christian context begins with a belief in the fallen nature of humans, not in their inherent goodness. Peter reminded his readers that they had been saved from slavery to their former, empty religious traditions (1:18), given a new life and a living hope (1:3–5), and purified (1:22). People are in need of repair, restoration, and reformation—all fully provided in the salvation Christ offers.

📖 Ethical behavior must either originate within ourselves (through reason, intuition, or conscience) or from the outside (through revelation, an established code of ethics, or law). The proper motive for moral living comes from God's work of grace. A life pleasing to God finds its blueprint in the Bible's pages. How tragic when "good" and "moral" people lack the one relationship that alone will make them acceptable to God!

1 Peter 2:4–12

📖 The spiritual connection of Peter's readers to the living Stone was the foundation of the spiritual house they were forming. His words here about Jesus Christ were fundamental to his understanding not only of Jesus, but also of the Christian life. Jesus was rejected by human beings but chosen by God, just as Peter's readers, who were being rejected by their society, were now part of God's family.

📖 Peter's message in verses 11–12: Live holy lives in the midst of secular chaos, and let God take care of the results. Peter was calling the churches in Asia Minor to a lifestyle radically different from that of their surrounding culture. This was part of their strategy for pleasing God and coping with their environment. This call to holiness is no different today. The contemporary church is more under the influence of our modern culture than many of us realize. Aside from your commute to church, what visibly distinguishes you from your unbelieving neighbors?

and the one who trusts in him
will never be put to shame." [a][z]

7 Now to you who believe, this stone is precious. But to those who do not believe, [a]

"The stone the builders rejected
has become the capstone, [b]" [c][b]

8 and,

"A stone that causes men to stumble
and a rock that makes them fall." [d][c]

They stumble because they disobey the message—which is also what they were destined for. [d]

9 But you are a chosen people, [e] a royal priesthood, a holy nation, [f] a people belonging to God, that you may declare the praises of him who called you out of darkness into his wonderful light. [g] 10 Once you were not a people, but now you are the people of God; [h] once you had not received mercy, but now you have received mercy.

11 Dear friends, I urge you, as aliens and strangers in the world, to abstain from sinful desires, [i] which war against your soul. [j] 12 Live such good lives among the pagans that, though they accuse you of doing wrong, they may see your good deeds [k] and glorify God [l] on the day he visits us.

Submission to Rulers and Masters

13 Submit yourselves for the Lord's sake to every authority [m] instituted among men: whether to the king, as the supreme authority, 14 or to governors, who are sent by him to punish those who do wrong [n] and to commend those who do right. [o] 15 For it is God's will [p] that by doing good you should silence the ignorant talk of foolish men. [q] 16 Live as free men, [r] but do not use your freedom as a cover-up for evil; live as servants of God. [s] 17 Show proper respect to everyone: Love the brotherhood of believers, [t] fear God, honor the king. [u]

18 Slaves, submit yourselves to your masters with all respect, [v] not only to those who are good and considerate, [w] but also to those who are harsh. 19 For it is commendable if a man bears up under the pain of unjust suffering because he is conscious of God. [x] 20 But how is it to your credit if you receive a beating for doing wrong and endure it? But if you suffer for doing good and you endure it, this is commendable before God. [y] 21 To this [z] you were called, because Christ suffered for you, leaving you an example, [a] that you should follow in his steps.

22 "He committed no sin,
and no deceit was found in his mouth." [e][b]

23 When they hurled their insults at him, he did not retaliate; when he suffered, he made no threats. [c] Instead, he entrusted himself [d] to him who judges justly. 24 He himself bore our sins [e] in his body on the tree, so that we might die to sins [f] and live for righteousness; by his wounds you have been healed. [g] 25 For you were like sheep going astray, [h] but now you have returned to the Shepherd [i] and Overseer of your souls.

[a] 6 Isaiah 28:16   [b] 7 Or *cornerstone*   [c] 7 Psalm 118:22   [d] 8 Isaiah 8:14   [e] 22 Isaiah 53:9

2:6
z Isa 28:16
2:7
a 2Co 2:16
b Ps 118:22

2:8
c Isa 8:14; 1Co 1:23
d Ro 9:22

2:9
e Dt 10:15
f Isa 62:12
g Ac 26:18

2:10
h Hos 1:9,10

2:11
i Gal 5:16 j Jas 4:1
2:12
k Php 2:15;
1Pe 3:16 l Mt 5:16;
9:8

2:13
m Ro 13:1
2:14
n Ro 13:4 o Ro 13:3
2:15
p 1Pe 3:17 q ver 12
2:16
r Jn 8:32 s Ro 6:22

2:17
t Ro 12:10
u Ro 13:7
2:18
v Eph 6:5
w Jas 3:17

2:19
x 1Pe 3:14,17

2:20
y 1Pe 3:17
2:21
z Ac 14:22
a Mt 16:24

2:22
b Isa 53:9

2:23
c Isa 53:7
d Lk 23:46
2:24
e Heb 9:28 f Ro 6:2
g Isa 53:5;
Heb 12:13; Jas 5:16
2:25
h Isa 53:6 i Jn 10:11

---

1 Peter 2:13–25

The meaning of "submit" in the Greek is "to order oneself under, or according to, a given relationship" or "to live according to the governmental order." Clearly here the notion of submitting to the government is secondary to that of obeying God (1:2,14,22) and doing his will (v. 15). In spite of their freedom in Christ, though, Christians are to live according to governmental order.

Preacher Jonathan Edwards (1703–1758) sug-

gested a strategy for Christians in public life. His points: Christians (1) have a responsibility beyond the church walls; (2) can join with nonbelievers to work toward common moral goals; (3) are to support their governments but be ready to criticize if the occasion demands; (4) do well to remember that politics are relatively unimportant in the long run; (5) are wise to beware of national pride; and (6) are called to care for the poor. Ask yourself: What reputation have Christians gained in the marketplace or political arena today? Is it God-honoring?

Civility

The Bible recognizes that courtesy doesn't come easily, but its writers do insist we work at it. Hebrews 12:14 is a case in point. We are to "make every effort to live in peace with all men." Indeed, the writer adds, to do so is to cultivate the holiness that will make our lives pleasing to God. Peter urged a similar pattern: "Show proper respect to everyone" (1 Peter 2:17) and be sure that, when you are expressing your deepest convictions to others, you do so "with gentleness and respect" (3:15).

"Civility" (courtesy or respect) comes from *civitas*, meaning "city." When ancient philosophers first started to discuss civility, they thought about the kinds of things that happen in a city, where people regularly encounter others different from themselves. The "public square" is where we bump into strangers, people with whom we have no "natural" ties of kinship or friendship. But we are still to treat them with respect and kindness.

> **The hardest part of cultivating kindness is consistently reminding ourselves that at the heart of the Christian message is the insistence that we are all sinners.**

Cultivating civility continues to be an urgent matter. We are probably more aware of human diversity now than the ancients were. *In*civility (discourtesy or rudeness) is a major problem. This is obvious from some of the world's highly publicized conflicts: Jew versus Arab in the Middle East, Protestant versus Catholic in Northern Ireland, ethnic strife, tribal warfare, confrontations between persons who advocate different lifestyles, "culture wars." But incivility also is present in our daily routines: "road rage," arguments over parking spaces, teasing and bullying on school playgrounds.

This kind of teaching appears in the Old Testament, where the Israelites were regularly instructed to act with kindness and mercy toward people with whom they had little in common. Old Testament writers insisted that God cared about "strangers" or "sojourners"—resident aliens or people just passing through. Leviticus 19 was emphatic. God's people were to attend to the needs of strangers, loving them as they loved their own kind. The Israelites weren't to forget that they had been strangers in Egypt—and that God had heard their cries for help in the midst of their suffering.

Theologian Martin Marty expressed the problem in an interesting light. Many people who are civil, he observed, don't have very strong convictions—and many with strong convictions aren't very civil. The world needs people with *convicted civility*. All will benefit when Christians in particular are deliberate and intentional in their courtesy, when they respect all those with whom they rub shoulders, regardless of belief and lifestyle differences.

Being civil doesn't mean compromising what we believe. In fact, the hardest part of cultivating kindness is consistently reminding ourselves that at the heart of the Christian message is the insistence that we are all sinners, all alike regularly tempted to arrogance and self-centeredness. Psalm 139 contains an important lesson about civility. The Psalmist got quite passionate about his realization that many people live lives displeasing to God. "Do I not hate those who hate you, O LORD," he asked emphatically, "and abhor those who rise up against you?" (v. 21). But when he realized the need to look at his own life, he changed his tone: "Search me, O God, and know my heart . . . See if there is any offensive way in me" (vv. 23–24). If we would all make this plea on a regular basis, how much easier we would find it to respond obediently to God's call to civility.

Richard Mouw, president of Fuller Theological Seminary in Pasadena, California

Wives and Husbands

3 Wives, in the same way be submissive[j] to your husbands[k] so that, if any of them do not believe the word, they may be won over[l] without words by the behavior of their wives, 2when they see the purity and reverence of your lives. 3Your beauty should not come from outward adornment, such as braided hair and the wearing of gold jewelry and fine clothes.[m] 4Instead, it should be that of your inner self,[n] the unfading beauty of a gentle and quiet spirit, which is of great worth in God's sight. 5For this is the way the holy women of the past who put their hope in God[o] used to make themselves beautiful. They were submissive to their own husbands, 6like Sarah, who obeyed Abraham and called him her master.[p] You are her daughters if you do what is right and do not give way to fear.

7Husbands,[q] in the same way be considerate as you live with your wives, and treat them with respect as the weaker partner and as heirs with you of the gracious gift of life, so that nothing will hinder your prayers.

Suffering for Doing Good

8Finally, all of you, live in harmony with one another; be sympathetic, love as brothers,[r] be compassionate and humble.[s] 9Do not repay evil with evil[t] or insult with insult,[u] but with blessing, because to this[v] you were called so that you may inherit a blessing.[w] 10For,

"Whoever would love life
    and see good days
must keep his tongue from evil
    and his lips from deceitful speech.
11He must turn from evil and do good;
    he must seek peace and pursue it.
12For the eyes of the Lord are on the righteous
    and his ears are attentive to their prayer,
but the face of the Lord is against those who do evil."[a][x]

13Who is going to harm you if you are eager to do good?[y] 14But even if you should suffer for what is right, you are blessed.[z] "Do not fear what they fear[b]; do not be frightened."[c][a] 15But in your hearts set apart Christ as Lord. Always be prepared to give an answer[b] to everyone who asks you to give the reason for the hope that you

---

[a] 12 Psalm 34:12-16   [b] 14 Or *not fear their threats*   [c] 14 Isaiah 8:12

Cross references

3:1 [j] 1Pe 2:18 [k] Eph 5:22 [l] 1Co 7:16; 9:19

3:3 [m] Isa 3:18-23; 1Ti 2:9
3:4 [n] Ro 7:22
3:5 [o] 1Ti 5:5
3:6 [p] Ge 18:12

3:7 [q] Eph 5:25-33

3:8 [r] Ro 12:10 [s] 1Pe 5:5
3:9 [t] Ro 12:17 [u] 1Pe 2:23 [v] 1Pe 2:21 [w] Heb 6:14

3:12 [x] Ps 34:12-16

3:13 [y] Pr 16:7
3:14 [z] 1Pe 2:19,20; 4:15,16 [a] Isa 8:12,13
3:15 [b] Col 4:6

---

1 Peter 3:1–7

Peter no doubt encountered and associated with a large number of women whose husbands weren't yet Christians. His call to "be submissive" was followed by the reason: to win their spouses to faith on the basis of their behavior. Culture in Asia Minor permitted many freedoms to women, including some kinds of religious freedom. But when a woman struck out on her own and joined a religion different from her husband's, that could be seen as an act of insubordination.

The reality is that men have dominated church history, and much of world culture remains patriarchal/hierarchical. For this reason and others, many have seen in this passage a call for suppression of women by men. To maintain a credible witness, Christians are to live under the social order. But, in part due to the gospel's impact, many cultural norms around the world have changed. Peter's comment that husbands' spiritual lives might be hindered if they treat their wives poorly offers a chilling corrective to any notion that Scripture encourages male dominance. Viewed in this light, the instruc-

tion to wives and husbands is similar—treat your spouses in such a way that both they and you can grow in Christ.

1 Peter 3:8–22

This final section of Peter's "household codes" (guidelines for social groups) expressed his concern for everyone in the churches and exhorted Christians on their overall behavior. Peter outlined the ethical principles required of believers in a world that opposed their lifestyle and their very existence. Psalm 34, which he quoted, is particularly suitable for a situation of harassment and persecution.

The local church is intended to be the model in its community of what it means to live harmoniously, lovingly, righteously, and peacefully. All people have a need for community, driven by their divinely implanted yearning for love. The church of Jesus Christ is to be precisely that: the living incarnation of the love of Christ expressed to one another and to the world. Is your church a welcoming presence? Does it attempt to function as an integral part of its neighborhood?

3:16
c Heb 13:18
d 1Pe 2:12,15
3:17
e 1Pe 2:15
f 1Pe 2:20
3:18
g 1Pe 2:21
h Col 1:22; 1Pe 4:1
i 1Pe 4:6
3:19
j 1Pe 4:6
3:20
k Ge 6:3,5,13,14
l Heb 11:7
3:21
m Tit 3:5 n 1Pe 1:3

3:22
o Mk 16:19
p Ro 8:38

have. But do this with gentleness and respect, ¹⁶keeping a clear conscience,ᶜ so that those who speak maliciously against your good behavior in Christ may be ashamed of their slander.ᵈ ¹⁷It is better, if it is God's will,ᵉ to suffer for doing goodᶠ than for doing evil. ¹⁸For Christ died for sinsᵍ once for all, the righteous for the unrighteous, to bring you to God. He was put to death in the bodyʰ but made alive by the Spirit,ⁱ ¹⁹through whomᵃ also he went and preached to the spirits in prisonʲ ²⁰who disobeyed long ago when God waited patiently in the days of Noah while the ark was being built.ᵏ In it only a few people, eight in all, were savedˡ through water, ²¹and this water symbolizes baptism that now saves youᵐ also—not the removal of dirt from the body but the pledgeᵇ of a good conscience toward God. It saves you by the resurrection of Jesus Christ,ⁿ ²²who has gone into heaven and is at God's right handᵒ—with angels, authorities and powers in submission to him.ᵖ

Living for God

4:2
q Ro 6:2

4 Therefore, since Christ suffered in his body, arm yourselves also with the same attitude, because he who has suffered in his body is done with sin. ²As a result, he does not live the rest of his earthly life for evil human desires,�q but rather for the

---

ᵃ 18,19 Or *alive in the spirit,* ¹⁹*through which*   ᵇ 21 Or *response*

---

1 Peter 4:1–11

🔖 In verses 1–6 Peter focused on the effects of suffering on the Christian life. After calling his audience to be like Christ, the apostle gave a reason for suffering like Christ: "because he who has suffered in his body is done with sin." As Christians in any age know only too well, we won't stop sinning during this earthly life (1 Jn. 1:8). But neither are we ruled or mastered by our old sin natures (Rom. 6:2,11,14). The most likely interpretation of Peter's difficult expression is that Christians get their priorities in order and grow spiritually by undergoing persecution.

📖 As Christians we look forward to the Day: (1) when Christ will be praised by all; (2) when God will be acknowledged by all to be God; (3) when the lion will lie down with the lamb; (4) when swords will be re-forged into instruments of peace; and (5) when peoples of all nations, tribes, and languages will be eternally united, putting millennia of hostilities and prejudices permanently aside. But this will happen only as a result of God's grace and intervention in history. However hard we may work for justice and peace, only God can bring the desired changes. And so we continue to work and pray: "May your kingdom come."

3:21

Symbolic Actions

Baptism in 1 Peter 3:21 is seen as a symbol of salvation in Jesus Christ. This is perhaps the most prominent of a number of symbolic actions taken for different spiritual meanings in the Bible. A more inclusive listing:

Symbol	Spiritual Meaning	Scripture
• Tearing garments	a symbol of anger or sorrow	Gen. 37:29,34; Matt. 26:65
• Sprinkling blood	a sign of covenant	Deut. 24:6; Heb. 9:20–21
• Sprinkling dust on the head	a symbol of grief	Josh. 7:6; Job 2:12
• Anointing	a symbol of empowerment by God's Spirit	1 Sam. 16:3; Isa. 61:1; Luke 4:18
• Washing hands	a symbol of innocence or purification	Ps. 24:4; Matt. 27:24; James 4:8
• Lifting of hands	a symbol of prayer	Ps. 63:4; Lam. 3:41; 1 Tim. 2:8
• Sitting in sackcloth	a symbol of repentance	Ps. 69:11; Isa. 22:12; Jonah 3:5–6
• Spitting	a symbol of contempt	Isa. 50:6; Matt. 26:67
• Shaking off dust	a symbol of protest or rejection	Matt. 10:14; Acts 13:51
• The Lord's Supper	a symbol of union with Christ	Matt. 26:26–29; 1 Cor. 11:23–26
• Baptism	a symbol of salvation in Jesus Christ	Acts 22:16; Rom. 6:3–4; 1 Peter 3:21
• Covering the head	a symbol of submission	1 Cor. 11:3–10

will of God. [3]For you have spent enough time in the past[r] doing what pagans choose to do—living in debauchery, lust, drunkenness, orgies, carousing and detestable idolatry. [4]They think it strange that you do not plunge with them into the same flood of dissipation, and they heap abuse on you.[s] [5]But they will have to give account to him who is ready to judge the living and the dead.[t] [6]For this is the reason the gospel was preached even to those who are now dead,[u] so that they might be judged according to men in regard to the body, but live according to God in regard to the spirit.

[7]The end of all things is near.[v] Therefore be clear minded and self-controlled so that you can pray. [8]Above all, love each other deeply,[w] because love covers over a multitude of sins.[x] [9]Offer hospitality to one another without grumbling.[y] [10]Each one should use whatever gift he has received to serve others,[z] faithfully[a] administering God's grace in its various forms. [11]If anyone speaks, he should do it as one speaking the very words of God. If anyone serves, he should do it with the strength God provides,[b] so that in all things God may be praised[c] through Jesus Christ. To him be the glory and the power for ever and ever. Amen.

Suffering for Being a Christian

[12]Dear friends, do not be surprised at the painful trial you are suffering,[d] as though something strange were happening to you. [13]But rejoice that you participate in the sufferings of Christ, so that you may be overjoyed when his glory is revealed.[e] [14]If you are insulted because of the name of Christ, you are blessed,[f] for the Spirit of glory and of God rests on you. [15]If you suffer, it should not be as a murderer or thief or any other kind of criminal, or even as a meddler. [16]However, if you suffer as a Christian, do not be ashamed, but praise God that you bear that name.[g] [17]For it is time for judgment to begin with the family of God;[h] and if it begins with us, what will the outcome be for those who do not obey the gospel of God?[i] [18]And,

> "If it is hard for the righteous to be saved,
> what will become of the ungodly and the sinner?"[a][j]

[19]So then, those who suffer according to God's will should commit themselves to their faithful Creator and continue to do good.

To Elders and Young Men

5 To the elders among you, I appeal as a fellow elder,[k] a witness[l] of Christ's sufferings and one who also will share in the glory to be revealed: [m] [2]Be shepherds of God's flock[n] that is under your care, serving as overseers—not because you must, but because you are willing, as God wants you to be; not greedy for money,[o] but

[a] 18 Prov. 11:31

4:3 r Eph 2:2
4:4 s 1Pe 3:16
4:5 t Ac 10:42; 2Ti 4:1
4:6 u 1Pe 3:19
4:7 v Ro 13:11
4:8 w 1Pe 1:22
x Pr 10:12
4:9 y Php 2:14
4:10 z Ro 12:6,7
a 1Co 4:2
4:11 b Eph 6:10
c 1Co 10:31
4:12 d 1Pe 1:6,7
4:13 e Ro 8:17
4:14 f Mt 5:11
4:16 g Ac 5:41
4:17 h Jer 25:29
i 2Th 1:8
4:18 j Pr 11:31; Lk 23:31
5:1 k Ac 11:30
l Lk 24:48
m 1Pe 1:5,7; Rev 1:9
5:2 n Jn 21:16 o 1Ti 3:3

---

1 Peter 4:12–19

Paul taught that his own sufferings completed those of Jesus (Col. 1:24). And Peter saw the sufferings of ordinary believers as a special bond with their Lord. But this attitude is only a preparation: Injustice and difficulty can be turned into celebration when Christians understand that Jesus endured the same. But even that celebration is nothing compared with the abundant joy they will experience when Christ's glory is revealed to vindicate God's people and usher them into his pure joy, peace, and love (cf. Rom. 8:18–21).

We owe respect to our brothers and sisters throughout the world and church history who have truly suffered in the name of Jesus. What examples are on your mind and heart? Still, this text speaks to our situation when we lose status because of our allegiance to Christ. Whenever our Christian commitment leads to shame or loss of social standing and influence, we are to endure with joy. When has this happened to you? How did you react or respond? Was joy in any way a component? If not, how could it have been?

1 Peter 5:1–11

Satan's assaults may be understood here as his attempts to get Christians to crumble in the face of persecution. His other devices include (1) tempting us to sin (Gen. 3:1–6); (2) accusing us and making us doubt our standing before God (Job 1:6–12; Rev. 12:10); (3) opposing God's will (Matt. 13:19); (4) confusing our minds (2 Cor. 4:4); (5) inciting people to acts of magic and idolatry (Acts 8:9–11; 19:19; 1 Cor. 10:14–21); (6) dominating people to the point of demon possession (Mark 5:1–20); and (7) infiltrating political and social institutions so they become tools of oppression (Dan. 10; John 8:44).

5:3
p Eze 34:4
q Php 3:17
5:4
r 1Co 9:25
5:5
s Eph 5:21
t Pr 3:34; Jas 4:6

eager to serve; ³not lording it over*ᵖ* those entrusted to you, but being examples*q* to the flock. ⁴And when the Chief Shepherd appears, you will receive the crown of glory*r* that will never fade away.

⁵Young men, in the same way be submissive*ˢ* to those who are older. All of you, clothe yourselves with humility toward one another, because,

> "God opposes the proud
>   but gives grace to the humble." *ᵃ ᵗ*

5:6
u Jas 4:10
5:7
v Ps 37:5; Mt 6:25
w Heb 13:5
5:8
x Job 1:7
5:9
y Jas 4:7 *z* Col 2:5
a Ac 14:22
5:10
b 2Co 4:17
c 2Th 2:17
5:11
d Ro 11:36

⁶Humble yourselves, therefore, under God's mighty hand, that he may lift you up in due time.*ᵘ* ⁷Cast all your anxiety on him*ᵛ* because he cares for you.*ʷ*

⁸Be self-controlled and alert. Your enemy the devil prowls around*ˣ* like a roaring lion looking for someone to devour. ⁹Resist him,*ʸ* standing firm in the faith,*ᶻ* because you know that your brothers throughout the world are undergoing the same kind of sufferings.*ᵃ*

¹⁰And the God of all grace, who called you to his eternal glory*ᵇ* in Christ, after you have suffered a little while, will himself restore you and make you strong,*ᶜ* firm and steadfast. ¹¹To him be the power for ever and ever. Amen.*ᵈ*

Final Greetings

5:12
e 2Co 1:19

¹²With the help of Silas,*ᵇ ᵉ* whom I regard as a faithful brother, I have written to

---

ᵃ 5 Prov. 3:34   *ᵇ 12* Greek *Silvanus*, a variant of *Silas*

Peter's alternative to domineering leadership was an exemplary lifestyle. When a Christian leader can stand up in all humility and ask others to follow as he or she follows Christ (cf. 1 Cor. 11:1), that leader is doing exactly what God has asked. What Christian leaders do you know who are worthy of being followed?

God is stronger than Satan. He can reclaim any who have been demonized (Matt. 8:32; 17:18) and permit his people to escape the devil's lures (Luke 4:1–13; 1 Cor.

10:13; Eph. 6:10–18). The everyday trust we exercise protects us from Satan's assaults against God and his people. The temptation to deny association with Jesus can be overcome when we remember that God is Judge, that others have endured the same kind of suffering, and that someday God will bring about total justice.

1 Peter 5:12–14

Our letters begin with greetings. Peter's ended that way: "She who is in Babylon, chosen together with

5:8–9

The Three Worlds

Peter made it clear that Christians are to live godly lives. There are plenty of challenges facing us as we look at the world before us—challenges that demand thoughtful prioritization and implementation. What conclusions do you draw from the statistics below? What changes might you suggest?

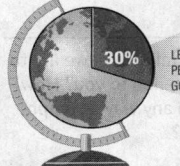

30% — LESS THAN 50% OF THESE PEOPLE HAVE HEARD THE GOSPEL

40% — MORE THAN 50% OF THESE PEOPLE HAVE HEARD THE GOSPEL

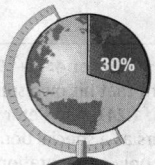

30%

The Un-evangelized World
1. Definition: Comprises 30% of the global population. Less than 50% of these people have heard the gospel.
2. 38 countries. The percentage of Christians in their populations is very low.
3. Represents 1.6 billion un-evangelized people.
4. Controls 12% of global income.
5. 10,200 foreign missionaries have been sent from these countries.

The Evangelized, Non-Christian World
1. Definition: Comprises 40% of the global population. More than 50% of these people have heard the gospel.
2. 59 countries. Less than 60% of the population is Christian.
3. Represents 2.4 billion evangelized non-Christians.
4. Controls 35% of global income.
5. 103,100 foreign missionaries have been sent from these countries.

The Christian World
1. Definition: Comprises 30% of the global population (2 billion people).
2. 141 countries. More than 60% of the population professes to be Christian.
3. Controls 53% of global income.
4. 99.9% of Christians' income is spent on themselves; .09% on the evangelized, non-Christian world; .01% on the un-evangelized world.
5. 306,200 foreign missionaries have been sent from these countries.

Source: Barrett and Johnson (2001:52)

you briefly,[f] encouraging you and testifying that this is the true grace of God. Stand fast in it.

13 She who is in Babylon, chosen together with you, sends you her greetings, and so does my son Mark.[g] 14 Greet one another with a kiss of love.[h]

Peace[i] to all of you who are in Christ.

5:12
f Heb 13:22
5:13
g Ac 12:12
5:14
h Ro 16:16
i Eph 6:23

---

you, sends you her greetings, and so does my son Mark." Because Old Testament Babylon was a notorious place of sin, that city's name had become shorthand for any place known for its wickedness. Peter also may have used it here to describe any place where Christians had been deported from their homeland of Judea. In either case, the description fit Rome, and early Christian tradition confirms that Peter wrote from there.

As we come to the end of a marvelous letter, we are confronted with the call to responsible living in our world. No matter how many adjustments we have to make as we read Peter's letter, we are anchored by the common salvation that transforms our behavior, challenged to obey and live with integrity within our society and culture, and expected to live as members of the family of God.

3:9 "THE LORD IS NOT SLOW IN KEEPING HIS PROMISE . . . . HE IS
PATIENT WITH YOU, NOT WANTING ANYONE TO PERISH, BUT
EVERYONE TO COME TO REPENTANCE."

INTRODUCTION TO
2 Peter

AUTHOR
The author identified himself as the apostle Peter (1:1).

DATE WRITTEN
This epistle was probably written between A.D. 64 and 68, near the end of Peter's life (1:13–15).

ORIGINAL READERS
This letter was addressed to Christians to warn them against false teaching (2:1). If 3:1 is a reference to 1 Peter, then Christians in Asia Minor were the recipients of both epistles (see the introduction to 1 Peter). If 3:1 doesn't refer to 1 Peter, then the identity of this epistle's addressees is uncertain.

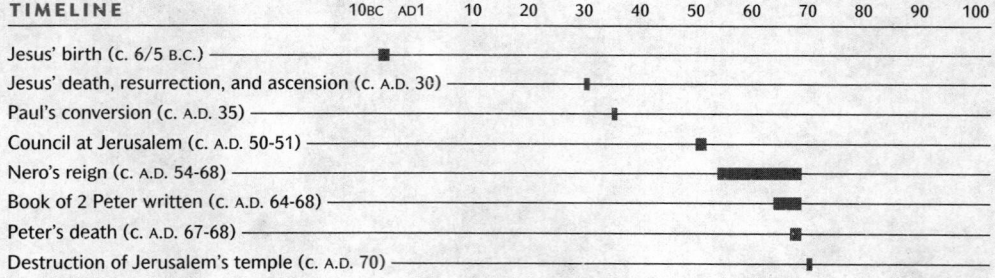

TIMELINE

	10BC	AD1	10	20	30	40	50	60	70	80	90	100

Jesus' birth (c. 6/5 B.C.)

Jesus' death, resurrection, and ascension (c. A.D. 30)

Paul's conversion (c. A.D. 35)

Council at Jerusalem (c. A.D. 50-51)

Nero's reign (c. A.D. 54-68)

Book of 2 Peter written (c. A.D. 64-68)

Peter's death (c. A.D. 67-68)

Destruction of Jerusalem's temple (c. A.D. 70)

THEMES
Second Peter contains the following themes:

1. *Spiritual Growth.* As Peter faced the end of his life (1:13–15), he predicted impending calamities and expressed concern that his readers might remain faithful and keep growing in discipleship. Peter began by focusing on believers' blessings in Christ (1:3–4), which are sufficient for "everything" (1:3) they need for life and godliness. Because of these blessings, believers are to work toward spiritual maturity, adding to their faith godly character in "increasing measure" (1:8). Godly character includes goodness, knowledge, self-control, perseverance, godliness, kindness, and love (1:5–6).

2. *False teaching.* Peter sounded the alarm about false teachers, who posed a major threat to the faithfulness of believers. These particular false teachers were greedy exploiters who relied on cleverly invented stories and slyly introduced destructive heresies (2:1–3). Peter declared that their condemnation and destruction were certain (2:3–10). Until Christ's return, there will continue to be "lawless men" (3:17) who despise authority, are brazen and arrogant (2:10), *and spew slanderous blasphemy* (2:11). These "ignorant and unstable people distort [the truth of Scripture] to their own destruction" (3:16). Believers are to guard against such teachings, remember the truth (1:3–15), and rely on the testimony and teachings of the apostles, as well as the prophecies of Scripture (1:16–21).

3. *The certainty of Christ's return.* Peter warned against scoffers who abandon the hope of Christ's coming in judgment (3:3–4). They mistakenly assume that since nothing has changed since the creation of the world, the day of the Lord has simply been a delusion. But just as God brought judgment on the world through the flood, so his judgment will come on the present heavens and earth (3:4–7). The delay of divine judgment is a revelation of God's patience; he's allowing time for repentance (3:9). Since the return of the Lord Jesus is certain, believers are to prepare themselves through faithful, ethical living (3:11–16).

FAITH IN ACTION

The pages of 2 Peter contain life lessons and role models of faith—people who challenge believers to put faith in action.

Role Models

- PETER (1:13–15), knowing his death was near, was energized to clarify the truths of the gospel to those he loved. Is declaring the gospel truth a priority in your life?

- BIBLICAL WRITERS (1:19–21) laid aside their own agendas and allowed the Holy Spirit to speak his message through them. When someone asks for your advice, do you simply give your opinion or allow the Holy Spirit to guide your conversation? Can you easily lay aside your personal agenda and allow God's Spirit to lead you?

- PAUL (3:15) was given wisdom by God to declare the truths of Scripture. In light of the fact that you have been given "everything" you need for life and godliness (1:3), do you believe God has given you wisdom to declare the truths of the gospel?

Challenges

- Evaluate your Christian character. Make every effort to grow spiritually in ever-increasing measure.

- Determine to resist the temptation to abandon the truth of the gospel for new and seductive teachings that suit society's preferences.

- Resolve to stand for the truth when others attempt to shed features of the Christian faith they consider to be outmoded or embarrassing—particularly those commands related to sexual ethics.

- Practice laying aside your own ideas, thoughts, and plans, while allowing the Holy Spirit to lead you in a new direction or speak his mind through you.

- Examine your belief in Christ's return. Has his delay led you to develop a sense of apathy regarding your Christian life?

OUTLINE

I. Introduction (1:1–2)
II. Knowing God (1:3–21)
   A. Know Your Calling (1:3–11)
   B. Know the Scriptures (1:12–21)
III. Warning Against False Teachers (2)
   A. Their Coming Predicted (2:1–3a)
   B. God Will Judge Them (2:3b–9)
   C. Some Characteristics (2:10–22)
IV. The Fact of Christ's Return (3:1–16)
   A. Peter's Purpose in Writing Restated (3:1–2)
   B. The Coming of Scoffers (3:3–7)
   C. The Certainty of Christ's Return (3:8–10)
   D. Exhortations Based on the Fact of Christ's Return (3:11–16)
V. Concluding Remarks (3:17–18)

1:1
a Ro 1:1 b 1Pe 1:1
c Ro 3:21-26
d Tit 2:13

1 Simon Peter, a servant[a] and apostle of Jesus Christ,[b]

To those who through the righteousness[c] of our God and Savior Jesus Christ[d] have received a faith as precious as ours:

1:2
e Php 3:8

[2]Grace and peace be yours in abundance through the knowledge of God and of Jesus our Lord.[e]

Making One's Calling and Election Sure

1:3
f 1Pe 1:5
g 1Th 2:12
1:4
h 2Co 7:1
i Eph 4:24;
Heb 12:10; 1Jn 3:2
j 2Pe 2:18-20

[3]His divine power[f] has given us everything we need for life and godliness through our knowledge of him who called us[g] by his own glory and goodness. [4]Through these he has given us his very great and precious promises,[h] so that through them you may participate in the divine nature[i] and escape the corruption in the world caused by evil desires.[j]

1:5
k Col 2:3
1:6
l Ac 24:25 m ver 3
1:7
n 1Th 3:12
1:8
o Jn 15:2; Tit 3:14
1:9
p 1Jn 2:11
q Eph 5:26

[5]For this very reason, make every effort to add to your faith goodness; and to goodness, knowledge;[k] [6]and to knowledge, self-control;[l] and to self-control, perseverance; and to perseverance, godliness;[m] [7]and to godliness, brotherly kindness; and to brotherly kindness, love.[n] [8]For if you possess these qualities in increasing measure, they will keep you from being ineffective and unproductive[o] in your knowledge of our Lord Jesus Christ. [9]But if anyone does not have them, he is nearsighted and blind,[p] and has forgotten that he has been cleansed from his past sins.[q]

1:10
r 2Pe 3:17

[10]Therefore, my brothers, be all the more eager to make your calling and election sure. For if you do these things, you will never fall,[r] [11]and you will receive a rich welcome into the eternal kingdom of our Lord and Savior Jesus Christ.

1:12
s Php 3:1; 1Jn 2:21

Prophecy of Scripture

[12]So I will always remind you of these things,[s] even though you know them and are firmly established in the truth you now have. [13]I think it is right to refresh your memory as long as I live in the tent of this body,[t] [14]because I know that I will soon

1:13
t 2Co 5:1,4

---

2 Peter 1:1–2

When God chose to communicate the gospel message to the world, he chose human beings as his instruments. Had God sent his Son into *our* world, those entrusted with the Good News might have communicated it through radio announcements, TV "infomercials," and a "Good News Home Page" on the Internet. In the 1st-century context, gospel ambassadors used synagogue sermons, marketplace discussion groups, and letters.

"Growing in knowledge" is key to this letter. Biblical *knowing* is highly personal. Old Testament writers used the term to describe intimate relations between two people. The New Testament makes similar use of the word, as when Paul asserted that "Jesus knew no sin" (2 Cor. 5:21). Peter said that his readers would only enjoy "grace and peace in abundance" as they grew in their relationship to God and Jesus. How well do you really know God? Are you growing in knowledge, or have you reached a plateau?

2 Peter 1:3–11

In verses 3–4, Peter laid the groundwork for the main point in his mini-sermon by reminding his readers that God has provided Christians with the power to live godly lives. In verses 5–9 he stated his key point: Christians *need* to live godly lives. And, just in case his audience missed the connection, he spelled it out: It's "for this very reason"—that is, God's provision of all we need—that we are to seek spiritual maturity.

New Testament authors adapted literary forms from their culture as they communicated the Good News. One of these, the *sorites*, linked together virtues or vices in a series (see, e.g., Rom. 5:3–4). The ancient writer didn't necessarily list the vices or virtues in a particular order. All the virtues in verses 5–7 are important, and Christians were and are to exhibit each of them "in increasing measure."

"Participating in the divine nature" is a precious privilege. Through our union with Christ and the indwelling presence of the Holy Spirit, we share in God's holy nature. It's precisely "for that reason" that we are called to *progress* in holiness and godliness. We need to understand both the divine and human sides of this sanctifying (growing) process. Jesus took upon himself our human nature so that by the Spirit in him we might participate in his divine nature! God by the Spirit makes us holy, and we, by our choices, participate in becoming holy. Is your participation observable?

2 Peter 1:12–21

Peter knew how prone believers can be to lose the fine edge of their zeal for godliness. He promised to encourage these Christians "as long as [he lived] in the tent of [his] body." Many scholars classify 2 Peter as a "testament"—a book, or part of a book, in which a person makes a final speech from his or her deathbed. Peter announced that he was near death, addressed an audience that was close to him, asked his hearers to remember his teaching and example, predicted the future, and made moral appeals.

put it aside, [u] as our Lord Jesus Christ has made clear to me. [v] 15And I will make every effort to see that after my departure [w] you will always be able to remember these things.

16We did not follow cleverly invented stories when we told you about the power and coming of our Lord Jesus Christ, but we were eyewitnesses of his majesty. [x] 17For he received honor and glory from God the Father when the voice came to him from the Majestic Glory, saying, "This is my Son, whom I love; with him I am well pleased." [a][y] 18We ourselves heard this voice that came from heaven when we were with him on the sacred mountain. [z]

19And we have the word of the prophets made more certain, and you will do well to pay attention to it, as to a light [a] shining in a dark place, until the day dawns and the morning star [b] rises in your hearts. 20Above all, you must understand that no prophecy of Scripture came about by the prophet's own interpretation. 21For prophecy never had its origin in the will of man, but men spoke from God [c] as they were carried along by the Holy Spirit. [d]

False Teachers and Their Destruction

2 But there were also false prophets [e] among the people, just as there will be false teachers among you. [f] They will secretly introduce destructive heresies, even denying the sovereign Lord [g] who bought them [h]—bringing swift destruction on themselves. 2Many will follow their shameful ways and will bring the way of truth into disrepute. 3In their greed these teachers will exploit you [i] with stories they have made up. Their condemnation has long been hanging over them, and their destruction has not been sleeping.

a 17 Matt. 17:5; Mark 9:7; Luke 9:35

1:14
u 2Ti 4:6
v Jn 21:18,19
1:15
w Lk 9:31

1:16
x Mt 17:1-8

1:17
y Mt 3:17
1:18
z Mt 17:6

1:19
a Ps 119:105
b Rev 22:16

1:21
c 2Ti 3:16
d 2Sa 23:2; Ac 1:16;
1Pe 1:11

2:1
e Dt 13:1-3 f 1Ti 4:1
g Jude 4
h 1Co 6:20

2:3
i 2Co 2:17; 1Th 2:5

In verses 16–21 Peter turned to the issue he felt his readers most needed to remember: Christ's return in glory and judgment at the end of history. Peter could have been referring to Christ's first "coming": his incarnation and powerful, redeeming ministry. But the word "coming" is used throughout the New Testament as shorthand for Christ's return—so much so that the Greek word, *parousia* ("coming"), has become part of our theological vocabulary.

As Jesus recognized, the Holy Spirit reminds us of the truths of the gospel (John 14:26). But God's Word is the source of that reminder. Peter was indirectly suggesting that the repetition of gospel truth, in word and in acted "memorials" like the Lord's Supper, is necessary for a vital Christian experience. What significance does the celebration of communion have in your Christian life?

A persistent concern for Christians has been how to explain the truth of the gospel and convince people to respond appropriately. Some scholars focus on evidence. Others argue that no amount of confirmation will convince someone whose mind has been blinded by Satan. Evidence without the work of the Spirit, sought through prayer and the Word, is useless. But a refusal to appeal to fact flies in the face of the historical nature of revelation and the witness of early Christians.

2 Peter 2:1–22

The New Testament predicted a short time of particular distress immediately preceding Christ's return (see 2 Thess. 2:3–11). But New Testament writers more typically portrayed the entire period from Jesus' ascension to his second coming as a time of tribulation. The apostles and early Christians were convinced that they were already living in "the last days" (see Acts 2:16–21). So it was natural for Peter to apply Jesus' predictions from Matthew 24 to the false teachers disturbing the security of the church in his day.

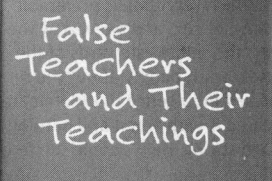

False Teachers and Their Teachings

What are some Biblical examples of false teachings?
1. Teaching that we don't have to follow God's commandments (Matt. 5:19)
2. Teaching that denies the Lordship of Jesus Christ (2 Peter 2:1)
3. Teaching that the day of the Lord has already come and gone (1 Thess. 2:1)
4. Teaching that allows acts of immorality (Rev. 2:14)

Where do false teachings come from?
1. Evil spirits (1 Jn. 4:1–2)
2. False teachers (2 Peter 2:1–3)
How do we recognize false teaching?
1. By its content (1 Jn. 4:2–3)
2. By the teacher's lifestyle (Matt. 7:15–20)
3. By the effects of the teaching (1 Tim. 6:3–5)

What question can we ask to unmask false teachers?
1. Do you believe Jesus Christ has come in the flesh from God and that he's Lord (1 Cor. 12:31; 1 Jn. 4:2)?

2:4
i Jude 6; Rev 20:1,2
2:5
k 2Pe 3:6
l Heb 11:7;
1Pe 3:20
2:6
m Ge 19:24,25
n Nu 26:10; Jude 7
2:7
o Ge 19:16
p 2Pe 3:17
2:9
q 1Co 10:13
2:10
r 2Pe 3:3 s Jude 8
2:11
t Jude 9
2:12
u Jude 10
2:13
v Ro 13:13
w 1Co 11:20,21;
Jude 12
2:14
x ver 18 y ver 3
z Eph 2:3
2:15
a Nu 22:4-20;
Jude 11
2:16
b Nu 22:21-30
2:17
c Jude 12
d Jude 13
2:18
e Jude 16
2:19
f Jn 8:34; Ro 6:16
2:20
g 2Pe 1:2
h Mt 12:45
2:21
i Heb 6:4-6
2:22
j Pr 26:11
3:1
k 2Pe 1:13

[4]For if God did not spare angels when they sinned, but sent them to hell,[a] putting them into gloomy dungeons[b] to be held for judgment;[i] [5]if he did not spare the ancient world[k] when he brought the flood on its ungodly people, but protected Noah, a preacher of righteousness, and seven others;[l] [6]if he condemned the cities of Sodom and Gomorrah by burning them to ashes,[m] and made them an example[n] of what is going to happen to the ungodly; [7]and if he rescued Lot,[o] a righteous man, who was distressed by the filthy lives of lawless men[p] [8](for that righteous man, living among them day after day, was tormented in his righteous soul by the lawless deeds he saw and heard)— [9]if this is so, then the Lord knows how to rescue godly men from trials[q] and to hold the unrighteous for the day of judgment, while continuing their punishment.[c] [10]This is especially true of those who follow the corrupt desire[r] of the sinful nature[d] and despise authority.

Bold and arrogant, these men are not afraid to slander celestial beings;[s] [11]yet even angels, although they are stronger and more powerful, do not bring slanderous accusations against such beings in the presence of the Lord.[t] [12]But these men blaspheme in matters they do not understand. They are like brute beasts, creatures of instinct, born only to be caught and destroyed, and like beasts they too will perish.[u]

[13]They will be paid back with harm for the harm they have done. Their idea of pleasure is to carouse in broad daylight.[v] They are blots and blemishes, reveling in their pleasures while they feast with you.[e][w] [14]With eyes full of adultery, they never stop sinning; they seduce[x] the unstable; they are experts in greed[y]—an accursed brood![z] [15]They have left the straight way and wandered off to follow the way of Balaam[a] son of Beor, who loved the wages of wickedness. [16]But he was rebuked for his wrongdoing by a donkey—a beast without speech—who spoke with a man's voice and restrained the prophet's madness.[b]

[17]These men are springs without water[c] and mists driven by a storm. Blackest darkness is reserved for them.[d] [18]For they mouth empty, boastful words[e] and, by appealing to the lustful desires of sinful human nature, they entice people who are just escaping from those who live in error. [19]They promise them freedom, while they themselves are slaves of depravity—for a man is a slave to whatever has mastered him.[f] [20]If they have escaped the corruption of the world by knowing[g] our Lord and Savior Jesus Christ and are again entangled in it and overcome, they are worse off at the end than they were at the beginning.[h] [21]It would have been better for them not to have known the way of righteousness, than to have known it and then to turn their backs on the sacred command that was passed on to them.[i] [22]Of them the proverbs are true: "A dog returns to its vomit,"[f][j] and, "A sow that is washed goes back to her wallowing in the mud."

The Day of the Lord

3 Dear friends, this is now my second letter to you. I have written both of them as reminders[k] to stimulate you to wholesome thinking. [2]I want you to recall

---

[a] 4 Greek *Tartarus*   [b] 4 Some manuscripts *into chains of darkness*   [c] 9 Or *unrighteous for punishment until the day of judgment*   [d] 10 Or *the flesh*   [e] 13 Some manuscripts *in their love feasts*   [f] 22 Prov. 26:11

We live in a time when nearly everything is tolerated—except intolerance. In such a climate of opinion, Christians often find it uncomfortable and difficult to take a stand for absolute truth. If we follow the trend of defending our faith on a practical basis—something like "Going to church has helped my family"—we become less concerned about truth. This opens the door for false teachers to enter our ranks and prey upon those who don't know much about what they believe and why. If you were asked point blank to explain and defend your stand on these critical issues, do you know in advance what you would say?

Scripture is clear that every person is subject to someone or something. Which servitude is preferable? Attracted by power, money, or sex, and swayed by media images, many answer: the self. As stewards of the gospel, we can aggressively warn people about the terrible consequences of the self-indulgence that dominates our culture. Peter compared it with vomit and bathing in mud. Such images, though strong, help people see free expression for just what it is.

2 Peter 3:1–18
Having reminded his readers of the requirements of Christ and the apostles, Peter went on in verses

the words spoken in the past by the holy prophets and the command given by our Lord and Savior through your apostles.

³First of all, you must understand that in the last days^l scoffers will come, scoffing and following their own evil desires.^m ⁴They will say, "Where is this 'coming' he promised?^n Ever since our fathers died, everything goes on as it has since the beginning of creation."^o ⁵But they deliberately forget that long ago by God's word^p the heavens existed and the earth was formed out of water and by water.^q ⁶By these waters also the world of that time was deluged and destroyed.^r ⁷By the same word the present heavens and earth are reserved for fire,^s being kept for the day of judgment and destruction of ungodly men.

⁸But do not forget this one thing, dear friends: With the Lord a day is like a thousand years, and a thousand years are like a day.^t ⁹The Lord is not slow in keeping his promise,^u as some understand slowness. He is patient^v with you, not wanting anyone to perish, but everyone to come to repentance.^w

¹⁰But the day of the Lord will come like a thief.^x The heavens will disappear with a roar; the elements will be destroyed by fire, and the earth and everything in it will be laid bare.^a ^y

¹¹Since everything will be destroyed in this way, what kind of people ought you to be? You ought to live holy and godly lives ¹²as you look forward^z to the day of God and speed its coming.^b ^a That day will bring about the destruction of the heavens by fire, and the elements will melt in the heat.^b ¹³But in keeping with his promise we are looking forward to a new heaven and a new earth,^c the home of righteousness.

¹⁴So then, dear friends, since you are looking forward to this, make every effort to be found spotless, blameless^d and at peace with him. ¹⁵Bear in mind that our Lord's patience^e means salvation,^f just as our dear brother Paul also wrote you with the wisdom that God gave him.^g ¹⁶He writes the same way in all his letters, speaking in them of these matters. His letters contain some things that are hard to understand, which ignorant and unstable^h people distort, as they do the other Scriptures,^i to their own destruction.

¹⁷Therefore, dear friends, since you already know this, be on your guard^j so that you may not be carried away by the error^k of lawless men and fall from your secure position.^l ¹⁸But grow in the grace and knowledge of our Lord and Savior Jesus Christ.^m To him be glory both now and forever! Amen.

---

^a 10 Some manuscripts *be burned up*   ^b 12 Or *as you wait eagerly for the day of God to come*

3:3
l 1Ti 4:1
m 2Pe 2:10; Jude 18
3:4
n Isa 5:19; Eze 12:22; Mt 24:48 *o* Mk 10:6
3:5
p Ge 1:6,9; Heb 11:3 *q* Ps 24:2
3:6
r Ge 7:21,22
3:7
s ver 10,12; 2Th 1:7
3:8
t Ps 90:4
3:9
u Hab 2:3; *v* Ro 2:4
w 1Ti 2:4
3:10
x Lk 12:39; 1Th 5:2
y Mt 24:35; Rev 21:1

3:12
z 1Co 1:7 *a* Ps 50:3
b ver 10

3:13
c Isa 65:17; 66:22; Rev 21:1

3:14
d 1Th 3:13
3:15
e Ro 2:4 *f* ver 9
g Eph 3:3

3:16
h 2Pe 2:14 *i* ver 2

3:17
i 1Co 10:12
k 2Pe 2:18 *l* Rev 2:5

3:18
m 2Pe 1:11

3–4 to suggest why such a reminder was so urgently needed: The false teachers were mocking the idea of Christ's return in glory. Here Peter brought together two of the most important issues in his letter: their skepticism about Christ's return (cf. 1:16–21) and their rejection of holy living (ch. 2). Chapter 3:18 is key. In it Peter summarized his root concern and desire: that his readers, resisting heresy, continue to grow spiritually, becoming more and more like Christ.

Peter predicted the destruction of the universe and the coming of a "new heaven and a new earth." But it's difficult to tell whether we are to expect replacement or transformation of the existing world. Jesus spoke of the renewal of all things (Matt. 19:28), Peter seems to have suggested this in Acts 3:21, and Paul talked about creation being liberated from bondage to decay (Rom. 8:21). But in Revelation 21 John apparently referred to replacement (v. 1) and renewal (v. 5) in the same passage.

Peter accused false teachers of promoting the belief that "everything goes on as it has since the beginning." This attitude is similar to the theory of evolution. Its destructive assumption, that history operates through blind chance, dismisses the intervention of a personal God. Christians can unconsciously pick up this view, accepting an image of a closed universe that leaves little or no room for God to act and to reveal himself.

As we look back at verses 3–13, we as Christians do well to (1) remember the "bottom-line" purpose of end-times theology—to make us better Christians here and now; and (2) understand the nature of the relationship between teaching about the world to come and living and serving in the present. Our end-times beliefs inevitably affect our ethics. Can you think of concrete ways in which this is true for you?

INTRODUCTION TO
1 John

AUTHOR

The author of this epistle didn't identify himself, but evidence indicates he was almost certainly the apostle John.

DATE WRITTEN

This epistle was probably written between A.D. 85 and 95.

ORIGINAL READERS

The precise identity of the Christians to whom John wrote is unknown.

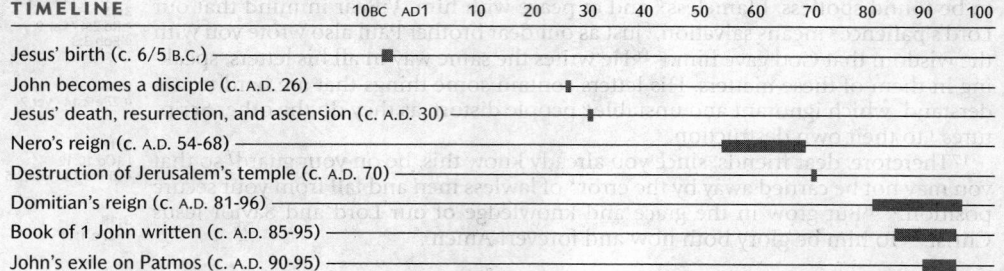

TIMELINE		10BC	AD1	10	20	30	40	50	60	70	80	90	100
Jesus' birth (c. 6/5 B.C.)													
John becomes a disciple (c. A.D. 26)													
Jesus' death, resurrection, and ascension (c. A.D. 30)													
Nero's reign (c. A.D. 54-68)													
Destruction of Jerusalem's temple (c. A.D. 70)													
Domitian's reign (c. A.D. 81-96)													
Book of 1 John written (c. A.D. 85-95)													
John's exile on Patmos (c. A.D. 90-95)													

THEMES

First John contains the following themes:

1. *The incarnation.* John wrote this epistle to warn Christians of false teachers, or "antichrists" (2:18), from within the church who denied that Jesus had come in the flesh (2:22; 4:2–3). John insisted that the Christ isn't some supernatural apparition disguised as a human; he's a historical person, Jesus of Nazareth. Christians can determine whether a teacher is a false prophet by testing the "spirits" (4:1): "Every spirit that acknowledges that Jesus Christ has come in the flesh is from God" (4:2). John stated that those who are from God also acknowledge that Jesus is the Son of God (4:15). The test of Biblical Christianity is belief in the full humanity and full divinity of Jesus Christ.

2. *Love.* The key command of this beautiful little book is the call to love (3:11,23; 4:11,21). John's definition of love? "God is love" (4:8,16), and God showed his great love for us by sending "his one and only Son into the world that we might live through him" (4:9), receive forgiveness (4:10), and be called his children (3:1). Christians are to follow Christ's example by loving one another (3:10–11) and caring for those in need (3:17), even to the point of laying down their lives for one another (3:16). Since "love comes from God" (4:7), genuine love can only be expressed as God lives in us (4:12) and we in him (4:16). "In this way, love is made complete among us so that we will have confidence on the day of judgment, because in this world we are like him" (4:17). The command: "Whoever loves God must also love his brother [or sister]" (4:21).

3. *Christian certainties.* John stated that Christians can be certain of the following: (1) Jesus is the Son of God (5:5); (2) they have eternal life through him (5:11); (3) God hears and answers their prayers (5:14); (4) they are no longer in bondage to sin but are kept safe by God from the evil one (5:18); (5) they are children of God (5:19); (6) they can know God through his Son Jesus Christ (5:20); and (7) Jesus is "the true God" (5:20).

FAITH IN ACTION

The pages of 1 John contain life lessons and role models of faith—people who challenge believers to put faith in action.

Role Models

- THE "DEAR CHILDREN" (2:12) were forgiven through Jesus Christ and know the Father. Have you taken to heart the implications of your forgiveness if you belong to Christ?

- THE "FATHERS" (2:13–14) had a more intimate knowledge of God. Do you know him up close and personal through his Son Jesus Christ?

- THE "YOUNG MEN" (2:13–14) were strong, and the Word of God lived in them so that they could overcome the evil one. What victory have you experienced in terms of overcoming the world through your faith in Jesus Christ (see 5:4–5)?

- GOD is love (4:7–21). He freely lavished his love on us (3:1) by sending "his one and only Son" to die for our sins. How is God's love your example? As 3:17 asks: "If anyone has material possessions and sees his brother in need but has no pity on him, how can the love of God be in him?"

Challenges

- Learn to articulate your belief in the full humanity and full divinity of Christ. Perhaps this will require some extra study on your part.

- In a time of praise, thank God for his great love for you. Divide a page into two columns. In one column, list the many blessings you have because of his love. In the other, list concrete activities that demonstrate that you live in God's love (4:18).

- Using 1 John 5, make a list of the certainties you have as a Christian. Focus on them when you are tempted, discouraged, or in need of assurance.

- Love is action, not just words. Determine to demonstrate your love for others this week by practicing loving acts of kindness.

OUTLINE

I. The Reality of the Incarnation (1:1–4)
II. Fellowship With the Father and the Son (1:5—2:28)
   A. Walking in the Light as the Basis of Fellowship (1:5—2:11)
   B. A Digression (2:12–14)
   C. Love of the World as a Hindrance to Fellowship (2:15–17)
   D. Denial of Christ as a Hindrance to Fellowship (2:18–28)
III. Children of God (2:29—4:6)
   A. What a Child of God Looks Like (2:29—3:24)
   B. What a Child of God Knows (4:1–6)
IV. God Is Love (4:7—5:12)
V. Great Christian Certainties (5:13–21)

1:1
a Jn 1:2 *b* Jn 1:14;
2Pe 1:16 *c* Jn 20:27

1:2
d Jn 1:1-4; 1Ti 3:16

1:3
e 1Co 1:9
1:4
f 1Jn 2:1 *g* Jn 3:29

1:5
h 1Jn 3:11

1:6
i 2Co 6:14
j Jn 3:19-21

1:7
k Heb 9:14; Rev 1:5

The Word of Life

1 That which was from the beginning, *a* which we have heard, which we have seen with our eyes, *b* which we have looked at and our hands have touched *c*—this we proclaim concerning the Word of life. 2The life appeared; *d* we have seen it and testify to it, and we proclaim to you the eternal life, which was with the Father and has appeared to us. 3We proclaim to you what we have seen and heard, so that you also may have fellowship with us. And our fellowship is with the Father and with his Son, Jesus Christ. *e* 4We write this *f* to make our *a* joy complete. *g*

Walking in the Light

5This is the message we have heard *h* from him and declare to you: God is light; in him there is no darkness at all. 6If we claim to have fellowship with him yet walk in the darkness, *i* we lie and do not live by the truth. *j* 7But if we walk in the light, as he is in the light, we have fellowship with one another, and the blood of Jesus, his Son, purifies us from all *b* sin. *k*

a 4 Some manuscripts *your*   *b* 7 Or *every*

1 John 1:1–4

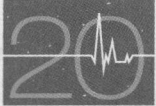 A careful reader of John will note echoes of the prologue to his Gospel in the opening of this letter. In both introductions, the *logos* or Word of God is central, and yet the two are complementary, not parallel. In John's Gospel we learn about the history and work of the Word (Jesus Christ) in creation, his incarnation (coming to Earth in human flesh), his rejection, and the eternal life he offered. Now John took up two themes: the reality of Christ's incarnation and its importance for salvation.

The purpose of John's letter was fellowship. A right understanding of Jesus informs Christians how to live and function with one another. Knowing the historical Jesus and continuing to bear witness to him is to be at the center of believers' lives together. Jesus Christ as God-in-the-flesh can't be marginalized.

John didn't see Jesus' ascension as the end of Christ's earthly presence. The Holy Spirit given to his followers was indeed *the* Spirit of Christ (3:24; 4:13). The Spirit makes Christ's life present within us. If Jesus is only a doctrine, our witness will be hollow. But if he's a person with whom we are in relationship through the Holy Spirit, our testimony will be potent.

Christian fellowship is triangular: Through the Spirit my life is in fellowship with Christ, your life is in fellowship with Christ, and my life is in fellowship with you. The union we enjoy with Christ becomes the adhesive that binds the church together. This is the nature of a genuinely Christ-centered fellowship.

1 John 1:5—2:14

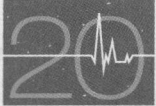 The "If we claim" statements in 1:6, 8, and 10 and the corresponding "But if" contrasts in verses 7, 9, and 2:1 are variations on the same theme. If God is removed from the world and unaffected by earthly concerns, then behavior outside the spiritual context is unimportant. Not so, countered John. A good God expects good people; a God of light expects lives permeated by that light.

1:6–10

Questions

The book of 1 John notes 20 vital signs to help you take your spiritual pulse. Answer the following questions as honestly as you can, realizing that you haven't yet reached a state of perfection:

1. Do you walk in God's light (1 Jn. 1:6)?

2. Do you enjoy fellowship with God's family (1:7)?

3. Can you identify your own sinfulness (1:8,10)?

4. Do you live in obedience to God's Word (2:3,5)?

5. Are you endeavoring to break the world's hold on you (2:15)?

6. Do you do things that are right in God's eyes (2:29)?

7. Do you eagerly await the Lord's return (3:2)?

8. Do you desire to live a life of purity (3:3)?

9. Have you noticed in yourself a growing dissatisfaction with sinful behavior (3:6–10; 5:18)?

10. Do you have a genuine love for other believers (3:14; 4:7)?

11. Do you demonstrate your love in word and deed (3:18–19)?

12. Is your conscience guilt-free (3:21–22)?

13. Is the presence of the Holy Spirit evident in your life (3:24; 4:13)?

14. Can you distinguish truth from error (4:6)?

15. Do you confess that Jesus is God the Son (4:15)?

16. Do you believe that Jesus is the Christ (2:22–23; 5:1)?

17. Do you exhibit "overcoming faith" (5:4–5)?

18. Do you believe the promise of God (5:9–10,12)?

19. Do you trust God's word (5:13)?

20. Have you received understanding from the Son of God (5:20)?

Source: Kroll (1999)

[8]If we claim to be without sin,[l] we deceive ourselves and the truth is not in us.[m] [9]If we confess our sins, he is faithful and just and will forgive us our sins[n] and purify us from all unrighteousness. [10]If we claim we have not sinned, we make him out to be a liar[o] and his word has no place in our lives.[p]

2 My dear children,[q] I write this to you so that you will not sin. But if anybody does sin, we have one who speaks to the Father in our defense[r]—Jesus Christ, the Righteous One. [2]He is the atoning sacrifice for our sins,[s] and not only for ours but also for[a] the sins of the whole world.

[3]We know that we have come to know him if we obey his commands.[t] [4]The man who says, "I know him," but does not do what he commands is a liar, and the truth is not in him.[u] [5]But if anyone obeys his word,[v] God's love[b] is truly made complete in him.[w] This is how we know we are in him: [6]Whoever claims to live in him must walk as Jesus did.[x]

[7]Dear friends, I am not writing you a new command but an old one, which you have had since the beginning.[y] This old command is the message you have heard. [8]Yet I am writing you a new command;[z] its truth is seen in him and you, because the darkness is passing[a] and the true light[b] is already shining.[c]

[9]Anyone who claims to be in the light but hates his brother is still in the darkness. [10]Whoever loves his brother lives in the light,[d] and there is nothing in him[c] to make him stumble. [11]But whoever hates his brother is in the darkness and walks around in the darkness; he does not know where he is going, because the darkness has blinded him.[e]

[12]I write to you, dear children,
because your sins have been forgiven on account of his name.
[13]I write to you, fathers,
because you have known him who is from the beginning.
I write to you, young men,
because you have overcome the evil one.[f]
I write to you, dear children,
because you have known the Father.
[14]I write to you, fathers,
because you have known him who is from the beginning.
I write to you, young men,
because you are strong,[g]
and the word of God lives in you,[h]
and you have overcome the evil one.[i]

[a] 2 Or He is the one who turns aside God's wrath, taking away our sins, and not only ours but also
[b] 5 Or word, love for God [c] 10 Or it

1:8 l Pr 20:9; Jas 3:2 m 1Jn 2:4
1:9 n Ps 32:5; 51:2
1:10 o 1Jn 5:10 p 1Jn 2:14
2:1 q ver 12,13,28 r Ro 8:34; Heb 7:25
2:2 s Ro 3:25
2:3 t Jn 14:15
2:4 u 1Jn 1:6,8
2:5 v Jn 14:21,23 w 1Jn 4:12
2:6 x Mt 11:29; 1Pe 2:21
2:7 y 1Jn 3:11,23; 2Jn 5,6
2:8 z Jn 13:34 a Ro 13:12 b Jn 1:9 c Eph 5:8; 1Th 5:5
2:10 d 1Jn 3:14
2:11 e Jn 12:35
2:13 f ver 14
2:14 g Eph 6:10 h Jn 5:38; 1Jn 1:10 i ver 13

God is eager to forgive, but what puts his generosity within reach? Jesus "speaks to the Father in our defense" (2:1). The basis of his case comes from his sacrifice on the cross, by which our sins were covered and God's righteous anger appeased. Jesus supplied what was needed for our pardon. His righteousness made his sacrifice powerful enough to benefit the whole world (cf. Heb. 7:26–28).

Are you convinced that fallenness is characteristic of the human experience? Or do you see sin as the result of poor choices, inferior education, or deprived childhoods? Or is it both? John understood that we are captive to sin. Just beneath our veneer of respectability is a crippling disease. Our impulse is to repair brokenness, rebuild esteem, and affirm grace. But John's impetus was to remind people to be humble. He focus on the necessity for forgiveness. We sometimes focus only on its results—healing and grace.

Often religious life, whether in the form of Eastern or New Age mysticism or even in some expressions of the Christian faith, disconnects religion from day-to-day life. This attitude invites a religious schizophrenia—the idea that people have two, essentially disconnected, lives—spiritual and physical. But viewing Jesus as working on our behalf today gives a new dimension to our spirituality—and a new impetus for us to confess and reject such disastrous thinking.

1 John 2:15–17
If we misunderstand what John meant by "world," we will miss his point. "World" to him wasn't the world of people—for "God so loved" that world (John 3:16). Nor was it the created world—for God made it and pronounced it "good" (Gen. 1:31). Rather, John's "world" was that of sin—characterized by crav-

Do Not Love the World

2:15
j Ro 12:2 *k* Jas 4:4

15Do not love the world or anything in the world.*j* If anyone loves the world, the love of the Father is not in him.*k* 16For everything in the world—the cravings of sinful man,*l* the lust of his eyes*m* and the boasting of what he has and does—comes not from the Father but from the world. 17The world and its desires pass away,*n* but the man who does the will of God lives forever.

2:16
l Ro 13:14
m Pr 27:20
2:17
n 1Co 7:31

Warning Against Antichrists

2:18
o ver 22; 1Jn 4:3;
2Jn 7 *p* 1Jn 4:1
2:19
q Ac 20:30
r 1Co 11:19

18Dear children, this is the last hour; and as you have heard that the antichrist is coming,*o* even now many antichrists have come.*p* This is how we know it is the last hour. 19They went out from us,*q* but they did not really belong to us. For if they had belonged to us, they would have remained with us; but their going showed that none of them belonged to us.*r*

2:20
s 2Co 1:21
t Mk 1:24
u Jn 14:26
2:21
v 2Pe 1:12; Jude 5

20But you have an anointing*s* from the Holy One,*t* and all of you know the truth.*a u* 21I do not write to you because you do not know the truth, but because you do know it*v* and because no lie comes from the truth. 22Who is the liar? It is the man who denies that Jesus is the Christ. Such a man is the antichrist—he denies the Father and the Son.*w* 23No one who denies the Son has the Father; whoever acknowledges the Son has the Father also.*x*

2:22
w 2Jn 7
2:23
x Jn 8:19; 1Jn 4:15

2:24
y Jn 14:23

24See that what you have heard from the beginning remains in you. If it does, you also will remain in the Son and in the Father.*y* 25And this is what he promised us—even eternal life.

2:26
z 2Jn 7
2:27
a ver 20

26I am writing these things to you about those who are trying to lead you astray.*z* 27As for you, the anointing*a* you received from him remains in you, and you do not need anyone to teach you. But as his anointing teaches you about all things and as that anointing is real, not counterfeit—just as it has taught you, remain in him.

Children of God

2:28
b ver 1 *c* 1Jn 3:2
d 1Jn 4:17
e 1Th 2:19
2:29
f 1Jn 3:7

28And now, dear children,*b* continue in him, so that when he appears*c* we may be confident*d* and unashamed before him at his coming.*e*

29If you know that he is righteous,*f* you know that everyone who does what is right has been born of him.

3:1
g Jn 3:16 *h* Jn 1:12

3 How great is the love*g* the Father has lavished on us, that we should be called children of God!*h* And that is what we are! The reason the world does not know

---

a 20 Some manuscripts *and you know all things*

---

ings, lust, and boasting. All of this is contrary to how God made the physical world—or us. If we love God we won't love that kind of world.

📖 Only by aligning with Christ and doing the will of God can we be freed from the allure of the world that is contrary to the love of God.

The enticements of wealth and power have unfortunately invaded the church. When secular, worldly power forms the basis for Christian leadership, ungodly values make the church vulnerable. Christians can avoid trouble by discerning corrupting influences, erecting boundaries against false values, and voicing potent, compelling claims for the truth. Have you set definite boundaries between the world's systems and practices and your Christian faith and values?

1 John 2:18–27

📖 Suddenly John turned up the heat, warning against "antichrists," "the last hour," and those leading people astray. He explicitly described those in this church who had brought these divisions—former disciples who had left the fold and yet continued to wreak havoc. John

had already revealed the false teachers' threats along moral or ethical lines. Now he addressed doctrinal error.

📖 What do we do when schism (rift or division) holds us in its grip? John's response is crucial. Focus on Christ. It's in him that we are united, and by recognizing Jesus as our Savior, the Messiah, we are drawn by the Spirit into relationship with the Father and Son and through God with one another. John referred frequently to an "anointing"—the presence of the Spirit knitting our lives to Christ. He warned that anyone who denies Jesus as the Christ isn't from God.

1 John 2:28—3:10

📖📖 "Rebirth" (2:29) inspired John to reflect on the splendor of God's love for sinners. The Greek term translated "How great" implies a love so unearthly that Christians barely expect its result: "We are called children of God" (cf. Matt. 5:9). Our rebirth is into Christ, and the mark of this will be doing what's right. This is an act of legitimization, like a father who by naming his children makes a permanent claim to identity and relationship with them.

2:15

The need for a vital evangelicalism is proportionate to the world in need. The days are as hectic as Nero's Rome, and they demand attention as immediate as Luke's Macedonia.

The divine order involves a supernatural principle, a creative force that enters society from outside its natural sources of uplift, and regenerates humanity. In that divine reversal of the self-defeating sinfulness of man is the only real answer to our problems—of whatever political, economic, or sociological nature. Is there political unrest? Seek first not a Republican [or Democrat] or a labor victory, but the kingdom of God and his righteousness. Then there will be added—not necessarily a Republican [or Democrat] or labor victory, but—political rest.

Is there economic unrest? Seek first not increased wages coupled with shorter hours but divine righteousness; this latter norm will involve fairness for both labor and management. But there will be added not only the solutions of the problems of the economic man, but also those of the spiritual man.

There is no satisfying rest for modern civilization if it is found in a context of spiritual unrest. This is but another way of declaring that the gospel of redemption is the most pertinent message for our modern weariness.

But that does not mean that we cannot cooperate in securing relatively higher goods, when this is the loftiest commitment we can evoke from humanity, providing we do so with appropriate warning of the inadequacy and instability of such solutions. The supernatural, regenerative grace of God, offered to the regenerate, does not prevent his natural grace to all people, regenerate and unregenerate alike.

Because he brings rivers of living water to the redeemed, he does not on that account withhold the rain from the unjust and the just alike. The realm of special grace does not preclude that of common grace. Just so, without minimizing the redemptive message, the church ministers by its message to those who stop short of commitment, as well as to regenerate believers.

The implication of this for evangelicalism seems clear. The battle against evil in all its forms must be pressed unsparingly; we must pursue the enemy in politics, in economics, in science, in ethics—everywhere, in every field, we must pursue relentlessly. But when we have singled out the enemy—when we have disentangled him from those whose company he has kept and whom he has misled—we must meet the foe head-on, girded in the gospel armor.

Others may resist him with inadequate weapons; they do not understand aright the nature of the foe, nor the requirements for victory. We join with them in battle, seeking all the while more clearly to defeat the enemy, and more precisely to state the redemptive formula.

> The battle against evil in all its forms must be pressed unsparingly; we must pursue the enemy in politics, in economics, in science, in ethics—everywhere, in every field.

Carl F.H. Henry, founding editor of *Christianity Today* magazine and former lecturer at-large for World Vision U.S. in Federal Way, Washington
Source: Adapted from Carl F.H. Henry's *The Uneasy Conscience of Modern Fundamentalism* (1947), 85–86

3:1
i Jn 16:3

3:2
j Ro 8:29; 2Pe 1:4
k 2Co 3:18

3:3
l 2Co 7:1; 2Pe 3:13, 14

3:4
m 1Jn 5:17

3:5
n 2Co 5:21

3:6
o ver 9 *p* 3Jn 11
q 1Jn 2:4

3:7
r 1Jn 2:1 *s* 1Jn 2:26
t 1Jn 2:29

3:8
u Jn 8:44

3:9
v Jn 1:13
w 1Jn 5:18
x 1Pe 1:23

3:10
y 1Jn 4:8

3:11
z 1Jn 1:5
a Jn 13:34,35;
2Jn 5

3:12
b Ge 4:8

3:13
c Jn 15:18,19;
17:14

3:14
d Jn 5:24 *e* 1Jn 2:9

3:15
f Mt 5:21,22;
Jn 8:44
g Gal 5:20,21

3:16
h Jn 15:13

3:17
i Dt 15:7,8
j 1Jn 4:20

3:18
k 1Jn 2:1
l Eze 33:31; Ro 12:9

3:21
m 1Jn 5:14

3:22
n Mt 7:7 *o* Jn 8:29

3:23
p Jn 6:29
q Jn 13:34

us is that it did not know him.[i] 2Dear friends, now we are children of God, and what we will be has not yet been made known. But we know that when he appears,[a] we shall be like him,[j] for we shall see him as he is.[k] 3Everyone who has this hope in him purifies himself,[l] just as he is pure.

4Everyone who sins breaks the law; in fact, sin is lawlessness.[m] 5But you know that he appeared so that he might take away our sins. And in him is no sin.[n] 6No one who lives in him keeps on sinning.[o] No one who continues to sin has either seen him[p] or known him.[q]

7Dear children,[r] do not let anyone lead you astray.[s] He who does what is right is righteous, just as he is righteous.[t] 8He who does what is sinful is of the devil,[u] because the devil has been sinning from the beginning. The reason the Son of God appeared was to destroy the devil's work. 9No one who is born of God[v] will continue to sin,[w] because God's seed[x] remains in him; he cannot go on sinning, because he has been born of God. 10This is how we know who the children of God are and who the children of the devil are: Anyone who does not do what is right is not a child of God; nor is anyone who does not love[y] his brother.

Love One Another

11This is the message you heard[z] from the beginning: We should love one another.[a] 12Do not be like Cain, who belonged to the evil one and murdered his brother.[b] And why did he murder him? Because his own actions were evil and his brother's were righteous. 13Do not be surprised, my brothers, if the world hates you.[c] 14We know that we have passed from death to life,[d] because we love our brothers. Anyone who does not love remains in death.[e] 15Anyone who hates his brother is a murderer,[f] and you know that no murderer has eternal life in him.[g]

16This is how we know what love is: Jesus Christ laid down his life for us. And we ought to lay down our lives for our brothers.[h] 17If anyone has material possessions and sees his brother in need but has no pity on him,[i] how can the love of God be in him?[j] 18Dear children,[k] let us not love with words or tongue but with actions and in truth.[l] 19This then is how we know that we belong to the truth, and how we set our hearts at rest in his presence 20whenever our hearts condemn us. For God is greater than our hearts, and he knows everything.

21Dear friends, if our hearts do not condemn us, we have confidence before God[m] 22and receive from him anything we ask,[n] because we obey his commands and do what pleases him.[o] 23And this is his command: to believe[p] in the name of his Son, Jesus Christ, and to love one another as he commanded us.[q] 24Those who

---

[a] 2 Or *when it is made known*

John's bold statements in 3:6–9 have led to debates about God's expectations for "perfection"—and to personal struggles for many Christians. The NIV's translation of the Greek terms related to "sin" is helpful. The use of the present tense suggests continuous, repeated activity. John wasn't saying that Christians don't sin. But ongoing, habitual sin can find no place in a genuine believer's life. What destructive habits have you, with the Spirit's help, been able to put behind you? If you are still struggling, don't give up. Claim the promise of forgiveness in 1:9 and read Romans 7:7–25 to understand that all Christians struggle against their sin nature.

1 John 3:11–24

Those who exhibit love for Christ's family demonstrate that they are already enjoying the promised eternal life. Such love is a tangible sign of Christ's saving work in progress. "Love" that fails to take the form of action on others' behalf is nothing more than religious talk. No doubt the ongoing church conflict fueled John's concern. Religious weapons were being used with devastating consequences, and he was eager for his community to exhibit *visible* signs of love—love demonstrated in acts of kindness.

Our assurance of faith is anchored in God alone, never in our own ability to generate feelings of confidence. Because of the wonder of God's overwhelming love, we are propelled to love others. Because love isn't a mere feeling, but concrete action, we love in deed. Our capacity to love others confirms for us that we have "passed from death to life."

One measure of love within the church is the degree to which people blessed with resources distribute that wealth within the community and beyond. A church isn't a loving community if the rich are simply *friendly* to the poor. Imagine all churches being places where Christ's love is sewn generously—not just metaphorically, but also financially! Imagine if churches in the West were propelled by the love of God to demonstrate that love tangibly, to brothers and sisters who are struggling around the world in life-destroying poverty!

obey his commands live in him,ʳ and he in them. And this is how we know that he lives in us: We know it by the Spirit he gave us.ˢ

3:24
ʳ 1Jn 2:6 ˢ 1Jn 4:13

Test the Spirits

4 Dear friends, do not believe every spirit, but test the spirits to see whether they are from God, because many false prophets have gone out into the world.ᵗ ²This is how you can recognize the Spirit of God: Every spirit that acknowledges that Jesus Christ has come in the fleshᵘ is from God,ᵛ ³but every spirit that does not acknowledge Jesus is not from God. This is the spirit of the antichrist,ʷ which you have heard is coming and even now is already in the world.

4:1
ᵗ 2Pe 2:1; 1Jn 2:18

4:2
ᵘ Jn 1:14; 1Jn 2:23
ᵛ 1Co 12:3
4:3
ʷ 1Jn 2:22; 2Jn 7

⁴You, dear children, are from God and have overcome them, because the one who is in youˣ is greater than the one who is in the world.ʸ ⁵They are from the worldᶻ and therefore speak from the viewpoint of the world, and the world listens to them. ⁶We are from God, and whoever knows God listens to us; but whoever is not from God does not listen to us.ᵃ This is how we recognize the Spiritᵃ of truthᵇ and the spirit of falsehood.

4:4
ˣ Ro 8:31
ʸ Jn 12:31
4:5
ᶻ Jn 15:19
4:6
ᵃ Jn 8:47 ᵇ Jn 14:17

ᵃ 6 Or spirit

---

1 John 4:1–6

 Christians are to judge whether a particular teaching fits what they know to be true about Jesus. If Christ isn't central, suspicion is in order. Lest believers become overcome by fear about the evil one, John reminded them that God has overcome the world and is greater than any evil in it.

Many Christians are eager to tell how they feel about an issue but can't necessarily give a Biblically reasoned argument on the topic. How well does your church equip its members to "test the spirits" of the day? John's call is to build mature believers who can use their theological understanding to spot intruders bent on causing confusion and chaos in the church.

How do we cultivate a discerning spirit without being judgmental? The answer may be found in the delicate balance of this letter. The first half speaks of light (1:1—3:10) and the second of love (3:11—5:12). We are to first come into the light—understand and appreciate the full meaning of Christ's person and work on Earth. Then that Light can inform our actions, so that we will lovingly and humbly serve our community of faith while contending for the truth. Our struggle, after all, isn't against people but against evil spiritual forces (cf. Eph. 6:12).

Snapshots

3:18

María

Striding along the narrow, meandering streets in Lota, Chile, María passes through the city of her birth, which she has never considered leaving. Largely due to the circumstances of her own background, she's deeply committed to her work in a Christian community development project.

At age nine María sold bread door to door and sometimes worked as a *chinchorrera*, gathering coal from the beaches to sell. When she was thirteen, though, she stopped working at her father's insistence to focus on her education. As the result of hard work and family sacrifices, she eventually finished college with a degree in social work.

After college María began working in the project as an assistant. Today she leads a project team that strives for better living conditions and educational opportunities for Lota's children and families.

The team has faced difficulties, including danger on the streets, yet María is convinced they have made life better for people. The team remains committed to its goals: "We need resources . . . Perhaps we are asking a lot, but we have a lot to offer too. We . . . are willing to offer all our time and work to make it possible that Lota moves forward," she asserted with passion.

> "We . . . are willing to offer all our time and work to make it possible that Lota moves forward."

God's Love and Ours

7 Dear friends, let us love one another,[c] for love comes from God. Everyone who loves has been born of God and knows God.[d] **8** Whoever does not love does not know God, because God is love.[e] **9** This is how God showed his love among us: He sent his one and only Son[a] into the world that we might live through him.[f] **10** This is love: not that we loved God, but that he loved us[g] and sent his Son as an atoning sacrifice for[b] our sins.[h] **11** Dear friends, since God so loved us,[i] we also ought to love one another. **12** No one has ever seen God;[j] but if we love one another, God lives in us and his love is made complete in us.[k]

13 We know that we live in him and he in us, because he has given us of his Spirit.[l] **14** And we have seen and testify[m] that the Father has sent his Son to be the Savior of the world.[n] **15** If anyone acknowledges that Jesus is the Son of God,[o] God lives in him and he in God. **16** And so we know and rely on the love God has for us.

God is love.[p] Whoever lives in love lives in God, and God in him.[q] **17** In this way, love is made complete[r] among us so that we will have confidence on the day of judgment, because in this world we are like him. **18** There is no fear in love. But perfect love drives out fear,[s] because fear has to do with punishment. The one who fears is not made perfect in love.

19 We love because he first loved us.[t] **20** If anyone says, "I love God," yet hates his brother,[u] he is a liar.[v] For anyone who does not love his brother, whom he has seen,[w] cannot love God, whom he has not seen.[x] **21** And he has given us this command: Whoever loves God must also love his brother.[y]

Faith in the Son of God

5 Everyone who believes that Jesus is the Christ[z] is born of God,[a] and everyone who loves the father loves his child as well.[b] **2** This is how we know that we love the children of God: by loving God and carrying out his commands.[c] **3** This is love for God: to obey his commands. And his commands are not burdensome,[d] **4** for everyone born of God overcomes[e] the world. This is the victory that has overcome the world, even our faith. **5** Who is it that overcomes the world? Only he who believes that Jesus is the Son of God.

6 This is the one who came by water and blood[f]—Jesus Christ. He did not come

---

[a] 9 Or *his only begotten Son*   [b] 10 Or *as the one who would turn aside his wrath, taking away*

Cross references (left margin):

4:7
c 1Jn 3:11 d 1Jn 2:4
4:8
e ver 7, 16
4:9
f Jn 3:16, 17;
1Jn 5:11
4:10
g Ro 5:8, 10
h 1Jn 2:2
4:11
i Jn 3:16
4:12
j Jn 1:18; 1Ti 6:16
k 1Jn 2:5
4:13
l 1Jn 3:24
4:14
m Jn 15:27
n Jn 3:17
4:15
o Ro 10:9
4:16
p ver 8 q 1Jn 3:24
4:17
r 1Jn 2:5
4:18
s Ro 8:15
4:19
t ver 10
4:20
u 1Jn 2:9 v 1Jn 2:4
w 1Jn 3:17 x ver 12
4:21
y Mt 5:43

5:1
z 1Jn 2:22
a Jn 1:13; 1Jn 2:23
b Jn 8:42
5:2
c Jn 14:15; 2Jn 6
5:3
d Mt 11:30
5:4
e Jn 16:33

5:6
f Jn 19:34

---

1 John 4:7–21

Spiritual rebirth and divine knowledge (see 3:9) were no doubt among the claims promoted by those who had left the church and continued to cause division. Through a simple test of spiritual maturity, John defeated in one stroke his opponents' spiritual claims. The test? Love one another. This is the mark, John stressed, of authentic discipleship. Through love we confirm that God "lives in us" and that his love is completed in our lives.

God's generous affection and love, demonstrated in Christ, compel us on the basis of gratitude to obey. The presence of Christ in us by the Holy Spirit empowers this obedience. Genuine love can't be exhibited in any community unless it reflects God's love, unless it's rooted in an experience of being loved. When John said "God is love" (vv. 8,16), he was stating more than that God is loving or even that he loves us. All God's activity is loving—because love is the essence of who he is.

1 John 5:1–12

Verse 6 is one of the most perplexing verses in John's letters. The majority of interpreters see water and blood as summing up the totality of Jesus' humanity and ministry on Earth. His baptism (water) and crucifixion (blood) frame his ministry. John's opponents may have taught that the heavenly Christ descended on the man Jesus at baptism but departed before he was crucified. Hence, John explained, Jesus came, not only by baptismal water but also through the blood of the cross.

In verses 7–8 John added the Spirit to "the water and the blood," affirming the three as sharing one view. The background here may have been Jewish law, where at least two witnesses were required in order to confirm some testimony (Deut. 19:15; John 8:17–18). Jesus' trial illustrated this well. The Sanhedrin's witnesses couldn't agree (Mark 14:56–59). But John pointed to three witnesses—all in accord!

We as Christians can't stress too highly that the mystery of God's work on our behalf is anchored in the cross. Jesus isn't just one example of God's revealed wisdom—not *a* wisdom that can stand alongside other religious systems. Christ is *the* wisdom of God (1 Cor. 1:24), and this wisdom was manifested in his sacrificial death. The victory of the Christian life is about power—transformation through rebirth—that defeats the impulses that once controlled us. Has your insistence that Christ is *the only* way to God offended anyone to whom you have witnessed? Why do you think the cross is such a stumbling block for some people?

by water only, but by water and blood. And it is the Spirit who testifies, because the Spirit is the truth. [g] [7]For there are three[h] that testify: [8]the[a] Spirit, the water and the blood; and the three are in agreement. [9]We accept man's testimony, [i] but God's testimony is greater because it is the testimony of God,[j] which he has given about his Son. [10]Anyone who believes in the Son of God has this testimony in his heart. [k] Anyone who does not believe God has made him out to be a liar, [l] because he has not believed the testimony God has given about his Son. [11]And this is the testimony: God has given us eternal life, and this life is in his Son. [m] [12]He who has the Son has life; he who does not have the Son of God does not have life. [n]

Concluding Remarks

[13]I write these things to you who believe in the name of the Son of God[o] so that you may know that you have eternal life. [p] [14]This is the confidence[q] we have in approaching God: that if we ask anything according to his will, he hears us.[r] [15]And if we know that he hears us—whatever we ask—we know[s] that we have what we asked of him.

[16]If anyone sees his brother commit a sin that does not lead to death, he should pray and God will give him life. [t] I refer to those whose sin does not lead to death. There is a sin that leads to death. [u] I am not saying that he should pray about that. [v] [17]All wrongdoing is sin, [w] and there is sin that does not lead to death. [x]

[18]We know that anyone born of God does not continue to sin; the one who was born of God keeps him safe, and the evil one cannot harm him. [y] [19]We know that we are children of God, [z] and that the whole world is under the control of the evil one. [a] [20]We know also that the Son of God has come and has given us understanding, [b] so that we may know him who is true. [c] And we are in him who is true—even in his Son Jesus Christ. He is the true God and eternal life. [d]

[21]Dear children, keep yourselves from idols. [e]

[a] 7,8 Late manuscripts of the Vulgate *testify in heaven: the Father, the Word and the Holy Spirit, and these three are one.* [8]*And there are three that testify on earth: the* (not found in any Greek manuscript before the fourteenth century)

5:6
g Jn 14:17
5:7
h Mt 18:16
5:9
i Jn 5:34
j Mt 3:16,17; Jn 8:17,18
5:10
k Ro 8:16; Gal 4:6
l Jn 3:33
5:11
m Jn 1:4; 1Jn 2:25
5:12
n Jn 3:15,16,36
5:13
o 1Jn 3:23
p Jn 20:31; 1Jn 1:1,2
5:14
q 1Jn 3:21 r Mt 7:7
5:15
s ver 18,19,20
5:16
t Jas 5:15
u Heb 6:4-6; 10:26
v Jer 7:16
5:17
w 1Jn 3:4 x 1Jn 2:1
5:18
y Jn 14:30
5:19
z 1Jn 4:6 a Gal 1:4
5:20
b Lk 24:45 c Jn 17:3
d ver 11
5:21
e 1Co 10:14; 1Th 1:9

---

1 John 5:13–21

True Christians, who have been "born of God" and are protected from the evil one, don't engage in the kind of sustained, willful denial of God and Jesus that leads to death (cf. v. 16). John's encouraging words about prayer, eternal life, and Christ's nurturing protection climaxed his pastoral effort. He wanted his readers to be confident—not victimized—Christians. John not only affirmed his care for his followers but added that they needed to watch out for one another. Through their joint efforts John envisioned a self-sustaining, mutually encouraging community.

How do you balance the practical realities of prayer (e.g., that you don't always receive the answer you want) with Scripture's unequivocal promises (cf. Mark 11:21–24; John 14:13–14,16; 15:7,16; 16:23–24)? These promises aren't formulas to bring about our wishes, but they are not wishful thinking either. John had in mind a union between us and the Holy Spirit, a blending so intimate that it ultimately expresses itself in one voice. When he said we are to pray "in Jesus' name," he understood that we have become one with Jesus, that our will has been transformed to his. With God stepping so deeply inside our lives, and we into his, we have complete confidence that our prayers will be answered.

INTRODUCTION TO
2 John

AUTHOR

The author of this epistle, who referred to himself only as "the elder" (v. 1), has traditionally
been identified as the apostle John.

DATE WRITTEN

This letter was probably written between A.D. 85 and 95.

ORIGINAL READERS

It was addressed to "the chosen lady" (v. 1), also called "dear lady" (v. 5). This address may be
a reference to a Christian woman and her family or to an individual, female leader of a house
church (see Col. 4:15). Some have suggested that since she's unnamed, this is a metaphorical
reference to a sister church in a nearby town. In this case, the "children of your chosen sister"
(v. 13) would refer to the members of another local church.

TIMELINE

	10BC	AD1	10	20	30	40	50	60	70	80	90	100
Jesus' birth (c. 6/5 B.C.)	■											
John becomes a disciple (c. A.D. 26)					■							
Jesus' death, resurrection, and ascension (c. A.D. 30)					■							
Nero's reign (c. A.D. 54-68)								▬▬				
Destruction of Jerusalem's temple (c. A.D. 70)									■			
Domitian's reign (c. A.D. 81-96)										▬▬▬		
Book of 2 John written (c. A.D. 85-95)											▬▬	
John's exile on Patmos (c. A.D. 90-95)											▬	

THEMES

Second John contains the following themes:

1. *Warning against false teaching.* This epistle was written to warn against the same false
teaching John opposed in his first letter (see the introduction to 1 John). These false teachers
appear to have been traveling preachers who denied that Jesus had come in the flesh (v. 7).
John warned the recipients of his letter not to receive these troublemakers (v. 10), because offering them hospitality would have meant aiding them in their "wicked work" (v. 11).

2. *Truth.* Truth is an important theme in the writings of John—mentioned 52 times in his
Gospel and 22 times in his three short epistles. John stated the following regarding truth: (1)
Jesus is full of truth (John 1:14); (2) truth comes from Jesus (John 1:17); (3) truth sets us free
(John 8:34); (4) Jesus "came into the world to testify to the truth" (John 18:37); (5) we are to
live by the truth (1 Jn. 1:6); (6) truth can be known (2 Jn. 1); (7) the truth of Christ is in us
(v. 2); and (8) if a person doesn't live the truth, the truth doesn't live in that person (vv. 1–2).

3. *Love.* Like 1 John, this letter emphasizes the command to love one another. This is the command John's audience had heard from the beginning, and it's the test of a true believer. John's command to love doesn't contradict his directive to refuse hospitality to false teachers. Issues of truth are too important to compromise.

FAITH IN ACTION
Second John contains life lessons and role models of faith—people who challenge believers to put faith in action.

Role Models

• JOHN (v. 1) loved "the chosen lady and her children . . . in the truth." Do you express love to your fellow Christians and take joy in their spiritual growth?

• THE "CHOSEN LADY" lived in the truth (v. 1) and led her children to also walk in it (v. 4). If you are a parent, church school teacher, pastor, or other leader, are you leading those entrusted to your care in the way of truth? Is this a priority for you?

• THE "CHILDREN" (v. 4) OF THE "CHOSEN LADY" (v. 1) were walking in the truth. Are your family members—both biological and spiritual—doing the same?

Challenges

• Know the Bible, the "word of truth" (2 Tim. 2:15), so you will be able to identify teachings that *aren't* truth.

• Resolve never to compromise the truths of the Bible or misuse the Bible for your own purposes.

• Determine to live the truth and love others.

OUTLINE

    I. Greeting (1–3)
   II. Commendation (4)
  III. Counsel and Warning (5–11)
   IV. Conclusion (12–13)

---

[1]The elder,[a]

To the chosen[b] lady and her children, whom I love in the truth—and not I only, but also all who know the truth[c]— [2]because of the truth,[d] which lives in us[e] and will be with us forever:

[3]Grace, mercy and peace from God the Father and from Jesus Christ,[f] the Father's Son, will be with us in truth and love.

[4]It has given me great joy to find some of your children walking in the truth,[g] just

1
a 3Jn 1 b Ro 16:13
c Jn 8:32

2
d 2Pe 1:12
e 1Jn 1:8

3
f Ro 1:7

4
g 3Jn 3,4

---

2 John 1–13

Second John was a message "from the front lines," like a scrap of war correspondence discovered long after the battle has passed. The tension implied in 1 John takes on a desperate tone in this letter. John wrote with two purposes: to encourage and support his followers' commitment to the truth and to warn them about the need to protect themselves from their opponents. A personal letter, 2 John follows conventional 1st-century form. This is different from 1 John, which isn't a letter as much as a public theological statement.

The recipients of John's letter were under heavy attack. In some cases, the threats were subtle. But in others, agents from Satan were making inroads into the church to win an audience and a following. John used strong language—"deceivers," "antichrist," "do not . . . welcome him"—because the church's very existence was at stake. An error in interpreting this letter today is to adopt John's stern warnings while neglecting their original context.

as the Father commanded us. [5]And now, dear lady, I am not writing you a new command but one we have had from the beginning.[h] I ask that we love one another. [6]And this is love:[i] that we walk in obedience to his commands. As you have heard from the beginning, his command is that you walk in love.

[7]Many deceivers, who do not acknowledge Jesus Christ[j] as coming in the flesh, have gone out into the world.[k] Any such person is the deceiver and the antichrist.[l] [8]Watch out that you do not lose what you have worked for, but that you may be rewarded fully.[m] [9]Anyone who runs ahead and does not continue in the teaching of Christ does not have God; whoever continues in the teaching has both the Father and the Son.[n] [10]If anyone comes to you and does not bring this teaching, do not take him into your house or welcome him.[o] [11]Anyone who welcomes him shares[p] in his wicked work.

[12]I have much to write to you, but I do not want to use paper and ink. Instead, I hope to visit you and talk with you face to face,[q] so that our joy may be complete.

[13]The children of your chosen[r] sister send their greetings.

Marginal references:

5
[h] 1Jn 2:7; 3:11
6
[i] 1Jn 2:5
7
[j] 1Jn 2:22; 4:2,3
[k] 1Jn 4:1 [l] 1Jn 2:18
8
[m] 1Co 3:8
9
[n] 1Jn 2:23
10
[o] Ro 16:17
11
[p] 1Ti 5:22
12
[q] 3Jn 13,14
13
[r] ver 1

Verse 5 "DEAR FRIEND, YOU ARE FAITHFUL IN WHAT YOU ARE
DOING FOR THE BROTHERS, EVEN THOUGH THEY ARE
STRANGERS TO YOU."

INTRODUCTION TO

3 John

AUTHOR

The author of this epistle, who referred to himself only as "the elder" (v. 1), has traditionally
been identified as the apostle John.

DATE WRITTEN

This letter was probably written between A.D. 85 and 95.

ORIGINAL READER

John wrote this letter to his friend Gaius. Gaius was a common Roman name, and it isn't
known whether the Gaius addressed here is to be identified with any other New Testament
person bearing that name (see Acts 19:29; 20:4; Rom. 16:23; 1 Cor. 1:14).

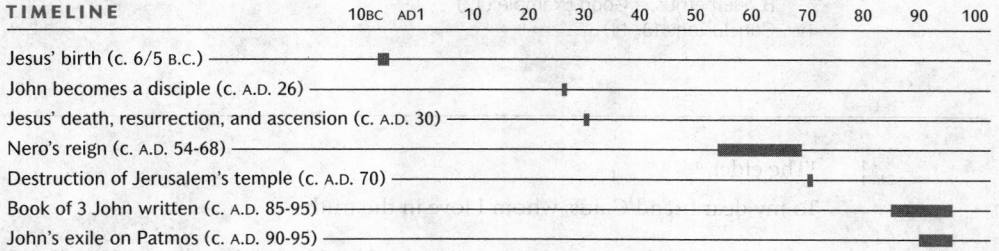

TIMELINE	10BC	AD1	10	20	30	40	50	60	70	80	90	100
Jesus' birth (c. 6/5 B.C.)												
John becomes a disciple (c. A.D. 26)												
Jesus' death, resurrection, and ascension (c. A.D. 30)												
Nero's reign (c. A.D. 54-68)												
Destruction of Jerusalem's temple (c. A.D. 70)												
Book of 3 John written (c. A.D. 85-95)												
John's exile on Patmos (c. A.D. 90-95)												

THEMES

Third John contains the following themes:

1. *Hospitality.* John praised Gaius for his hospitality and condemned Diotrephes for refusing to
show hospitality to "the brothers." Diotrephes' behavior may have been at least partly what
John had in mind when he referred in 1 John 3:15–17 to hating fellow Christians. Itinerant
Christian preachers were dependent upon the hospitality of Christians among whom they ministered. Believers offered Christian missionaries lodging, received their teaching, and helped
them with provisions for the next stage of their travels. This hospitality built up networks between the scattered churches and fostered a sense of solidarity. The local churches saw themselves as belonging to the one church united around the foundational truth of the gospel.

2. *Truth.* Demetrius, who is otherwise unknown, was probably the bearer of this letter. He was
to be received because he manifested the truth (v. 12). We can assume that he passed the
ethical tests of faith outlined in 1 John. For further information on John's theme of truth, see
the themes listed in the introduction to 2 John.

FAITH IN ACTION

Third John contains life lessons and role models of faith—people who challenge believers to
put faith in action.

Role Models

- JOHN (v. 3) received joy from hearing of Gaius's good deeds. Are you happy when others do good deeds, are thought well of, and are growing in their faith? Or do you gossip maliciously and prevent others from doing good, as Diotrephes did (vv. 9–10)?

- GAIUS (vv. 3,6) was commended by John for his faithfulness to the truth, his love, and his help to "the brothers." What are you known for?

- DEMETRIUS (v. 12) was well spoken of because of his commitment to truth. Are you someone with a reputation for speaking, teaching, and living truth?

Challenges

- Look for opportunities to open your home to traveling Christian workers in need of temporary housing.

- Find ways to support the pastor(s) of your local church.

- Examine your attitudes toward other Christians who are hospitable. Encourage them and thank them for their sacrifices.

- If you are a leader in your local church, determine to use your authority for good, not evil.

OUTLINE

   I. Greeting (1–2)
  II. Commendation of Gaius (3–8)
 III. Exhortation to Gaius (9–12)
     A. Diotrephes: a Bad Example (9–11)
     B. Demetrius: a Good Example (12)
 IV. Conclusion (13–14)

---

1 The elder,[a]

a 2Jn 1

To my dear friend Gaius, whom I love in the truth.

2 Dear friend, I pray that you may enjoy good health and that all may go well with you, even as your soul is getting along well. **3** It gave me great joy to have some brothers[b] come and tell about your faithfulness to the truth and how you continue to walk in the truth.[c] **4** I have no greater joy than to hear that my children[d] are walking in the truth.

b ver 5,10 *c* 2Jn 4
d 1Co 4:15; 1Jn 2:1

5 Dear friend, you are faithful in what you are doing for the brothers, even though they are strangers to you.[e] **6** They have told the church about your love. You will do well to send them on their way in a manner worthy of God. **7** It was for the sake of the Name[f] that they went out, receiving no help from the pagans.[g] **8** We ought therefore to show hospitality to such men so that we may work together for the truth.

e Ro 12:13; Heb 13:2
f Jn 15:21 *g* Ac 20:33,35

9 I wrote to the church, but Diotrephes, who loves to be first, will have nothing to do with us. **10** So if I come,[h] I will call attention to what he is doing, gossiping

h 2Jn 12

---

3 John 1–14

🕮 Third John was a brief note dashed off to one heroic Christian. Gaius was standing firm while his community was struggling under the pressure of a single antagonist, Diotrephes, a powerful church leader who had gained control and rejected John's authority. The Christian community under John's influence was evidently made up of scattered congregations who had brought in some converts who had no knowledge of apostolic tradition. When a source of authority—like the apostolic elder, John—stepped forward, some resisted submitting. Third John raises some interesting issues about conflict resolution and pastoral leadership.

maliciously about us. Not satisfied with that, he refuses to welcome the brothers. [i]
He also stops those who want to do so and puts them out of the church. [j]

[11] Dear friend, do not imitate what is evil but what is good. [k] Anyone who does
what is good is from God. [l] Anyone who does what is evil has not seen God. [m] [12] Demetrius is well spoken of by everyone [n]—and even by the truth itself. We also speak
well of him, and you know that our testimony is true. [o]

[13] I have much to write you, but I do not want to do so with pen and ink. [14] I hope
to see you soon, and we will talk face to face. [p]

Peace to you. The friends here send their greetings. Greet the friends there by
name. [q]

10
[i] ver 5 [j] Jn 9:22,34

11
[k] Ps 37:27
[l] 1Jn 2:29
[m] 1Jn 3:6,9,10

12
[n] 1Ti 3:7 [o] Jn 21:24

14
[p] 2Jn 12 [q] Jn 10:3

John used three strategies pastors today can follow in conflict situations: (1) Don't retreat, but remain in contact with the group. (2) Find an ally (like Gaius) who can give objective, wise counsel. (3) Personally confront your opponent. The failure of pastors (or church members) to stand for truth and to act in sincere, courageous love compromises a congregation's health.

The situation reflected in 3 John raises numerous questions. How should the church plan for confrontations? What processes are to be in place to ensure that all concerns are heard fairly and objectively? Will the pastor experience a solo, head-on confrontation? Should today's church take severe measures against people like Diotrephes, as implied in verses 10–11? Are we in theory ready and in practice able to do so?

INTRODUCTION TO
Jude

AUTHOR

The writer identified himself as "Jude . . . a brother of James" (1:1). Though there are several persons in the New Testament with the name James, it's likely that this James was the half-brother of Jesus, who became a follower of Christ after the resurrection (1 Cor. 15:7) and emerged as a church leader (cf. Acts 12:17; 15:13–21; Gal. 2:9; see also Introduction to James). James and Jude (Greek, "Judas") are listed as Jesus' brothers in Matthew 13:55.

DATE WRITTEN

If 2 Peter makes use of Jude, which is a commonly accepted view, then this epistle was probably written around A.D. 65 or earlier.

ORIGINAL READERS

The original recipients of this letter are unknown. The epistle of Jude may have been a circular letter to a number of churches.

THEMES

Jude contains the following themes:

1. *Warning against false teachers.* Jude's primary focus was the ethical dangers posed by false teachers who denied Christ's lordship by using Christian freedom and God's grace as a "license for immorality" (v. 4). These false teachers were "grumblers and faultfinders" (v. 16), scoffers who followed their own ungodly desires and natural instincts (vv. 18–19). They had also used the sacred fellowship meal to indulge their own cravings (v. 12).

2. *Christian behavior.* Jude's letter emphasizes the lordship of Christ (vv. 4,9,14–15,25). Submitting to Christ's lordship demands moral behavior. Christian freedom isn't a hall pass to do whatever we wish. Behavior will bring either judgment or reward. Christians are to trust their safekeeping to Christ (vv. 1,24) and keep themselves in God's love (v. 21). The letter concludes with admonitions that show how Christians can resist the lures of false teachers and rescue their victims (vv. 20–23). They are to build themselves up in the foundational teachings of the faith, pray, remain faithful to God, and be merciful to others.

FAITH IN ACTION

Jude contains life lessons and role models of faith—people who challenge believers to put faith in action.

Role Models

• JUDE (v. 3) encouraged Christians to "contend for the faith" by adhering to the message taught by the apostles and living a life faithful to that message. Do you encourage other Christians to hold to the teachings of Scripture and live lives worthy of the gospel?

- THE ARCHANGEL MICHAEL (v. 9), a powerful angel of God, didn't use his own authority but appealed to God's lordship when he confronted the devil. Do you at times misuse your position in an attempt to usurp God's authority, or do you readily and consistently acknowledge God's authority over situations and people?

Challenges

- Study the Bible so you can defend the truth of the gospel when confronted with false teachings.
- Evaluate your attitude regarding Christian freedom to determine whether your behavior is in line with Christ's lordship.
- Gently counsel those who have sincere questions about faith (v. 22).
- Directly confront those who've believed error so they may instead learn the truth (v. 23).
- Exercise concerned care and caution with those who've fallen into unbelief and sin. Be wary of being influenced by them (v. 23).
- Use verses 24–25 as a model to write your own statement of praise to God.

OUTLINE

    I. Introduction (1–2)
    II. Occasion for the Letter (3–4)
    III. Warning Against False Teachers (5–16)
    IV. Exhortation to Believers (17–23)
    V. Concluding Doxology (24–25)

¹Jude, *a* a servant of Jesus Christ and a brother of James,

To those who have been called, *b* who are loved by God the Father and kept by *a* Jesus Christ: *c*

²Mercy, peace and love be yours in abundance. *d*

The Sin and Doom of Godless Men

³Dear friends, although I was very eager to write to you about the salvation we share, *e* I felt I had to write and urge you to contend *f* for the faith that was once for

1
a Mt 13:55; Ac 1:13
b Ro 1:6,7
c Jn 17:12

2
d 2Pe 1:2

3
e Tit 1:4 *f* 1Ti 6:12

a 1 Or for; or in

Jude 1–2

There are six different Judes in the New Testament, but the author of this letter was almost certainly Jesus' brother (see Mark 6:3). Like Jesus' other brothers, Jude didn't follow him during his earthly ministry but now identified himself as a "servant of Jesus Christ." When Jude put "Jesus Christ" in place of "the Lord" or "God," he communicated something of immense importance—that Jesus had a relationship to him like that of God to Moses and David. This is even more impressive when we remember that Jude grew up in the same household as Jesus. Surely an event as spectacular as the resurrection had been necessary to lead Jude to view his own brother as equal to God.

Texts in which Jesus is called "God" (like John 1:1; 20:28; Rom. 9:5, Titus 2:13, and 2 Peter 1:1) are important. More significantly, early Christians came to act toward and speak to Jesus as God. They worshiped him (Heb. 1:6), applied Old Testament verses about God to him (Rom. 10:13), and prayed to him (Acts 7:59).

Particularly striking is Jude's description of his readers as "kept by Jesus Christ." This is precisely what Jesus had prayed for: "Holy Father, protect [keep] them by the power of your name—the name you gave me—so that they may be one as we are one" (John 17:11b). We naturally pay attention to God's grace in conversion and joyfully anticipate its renewed manifestation in Christ's return. But do you at times lose sight of God's grace of preservation in the face of depression, temptation, or crisis?

Jude 3–16

Imagine Jude preparing to write joyfully about salvation when he learned about a serious threat to his

4
g Gal 2:4 *h* Tit 1:16;
2Pe 2:1

5
i Nu 14:29;
Ps 106:26

6
j 2Pe 2:4,9
7
k Dt 29:23 *l* 2Pe 2:6

8
m 2Pe 2:10
9
n Da 10:13,21
o Zec 3:2

10
p 2Pe 2:12
11
q Ge 4:3-8;
1Jn 3:12 *r* 2Pe 2:15
s Nu 16:1-3,31-35
12
t 2Pe 2:13;
1Co 11:20-22
u Pr 25:14;
2Pe 2:17 *v* Eph 4:14
w Mt 15:13
13
x Isa 57:20
y Php 3:19
z 2Pe 2:17
14
a Ge 5:18,21-24
b Dt 33:2; Da 7:10
15
c 2Pe 2:6-9
d 1Ti 1:9
16
e 2Pe 2:18

17
f 2Pe 3:2
18
g 1Ti 4:1 *h* 2Pe 2:1

19
i 1Co 2:14,15

all entrusted to the saints. ⁴For certain men whose condemnation was written about ᵃ long ago have secretly slipped in among you. ᵍ They are godless men, who change the grace of our God into a license for immorality and deny Jesus Christ our only Sovereign and Lord. ʰ

⁵Though you already know all this, I want to remind you that the Lord ᵇ delivered his people out of Egypt, but later destroyed those who did not believe. ⁱ ⁶And the angels who did not keep their positions of authority but abandoned their own home—these he has kept in darkness, bound with everlasting chains for judgment on the great Day. ʲ ⁷In a similar way, Sodom and Gomorrah and the surrounding towns ᵏ gave themselves up to sexual immorality and perversion. They serve as an example of those who suffer the punishment of eternal fire. ˡ

⁸In the very same way, these dreamers pollute their own bodies, reject authority and slander celestial beings. ᵐ ⁹But even the archangel Michael, ⁿ when he was disputing with the devil about the body of Moses, did not dare to bring a slanderous accusation against him, but said, "The Lord rebuke you!" ᵒ ¹⁰Yet these men speak abusively against whatever they do not understand; and what things they do understand by instinct, like unreasoning animals—these are the very things that destroy them. ᵖ

¹¹Woe to them! They have taken the way of Cain; �q they have rushed for profit into Balaam's error; ʳ they have been destroyed in Korah's rebellion. ˢ

¹²These men are blemishes at your love feasts, ᵗ eating with you without the slightest qualm—shepherds who feed only themselves. They are clouds without rain, ᵘ blown along by the wind; ᵛ autumn trees, without fruit and uprooted ʷ—twice dead. ¹³They are wild waves of the sea, ˣ foaming up their shame; ʸ wandering stars, for whom blackest darkness has been reserved forever. ᶻ

¹⁴Enoch, ᵃ the seventh from Adam, prophesied about these men: "See, the Lord is coming with thousands upon thousands of his holy ones ᵇ ¹⁵to judge ᶜ everyone, and to convict all the ungodly of all the ungodly acts they have done in the ungodly way, and of all the harsh words ungodly sinners have spoken against him." ᵈ ¹⁶These men are grumblers and faultfinders; they follow their own evil desires; they boast ᵉ about themselves and flatter others for their own advantage.

A Call to Persevere

¹⁷But, dear friends, remember what the apostles of our Lord Jesus Christ foretold. ᶠ ¹⁸They said to you, "In the last times ᵍ there will be scoffers who will follow their own ungodly desires." ʰ ¹⁹These are the men who divide you, who follow mere natural instincts and do not have the Spirit. ⁱ

ᵃ 4 Or *men who were marked out for condemnation*   ᵇ 5 Some early manuscripts *Jesus*

---

readers' faith—false teachers. Jude implied that these teachers claimed to be Christian but noted that they somehow abused the grace of God in Christ. Accusations about their immoral lifestyle lay at the heart of his critique. His chosen term, "godless," has become a keynote of his epistle. Yet Jude's purpose was positive: to encourage true believers to display godliness.

Jude's second example of judgment (v. 6) leaves us wondering. A popular tradition about angels who sinned was associated with the reference in Genesis 6:1–4 to "sons of God" who came down to Earth and cohabitated with "daughters of men." Jewish interpreters had built an extensive story, identifying the "sons of God" as angels and attributing much (or even all) evil in our world to their influence. These stories were elaborated in 1 Enoch, a book not included in the Protestant canon, written between the time of the Old and New Testaments. Since Jude quoted from this book in verses 14–15, verse 6 can be interpreted in light of this passage.

Jude's dependence on Jewish sources apart from the Old Testament has been a cause of controversy. In addition to quoting 1 Enoch in verses 14–15, in verse 9 Jude cited a story from another book (The Assumption of Moses or The Testament of Moses) never accepted as canonical by any religious group. Jude may have viewed the story as legend and used it as illustration.

As believers, we look forward eagerly to Christ's coming. But Jude reminded us that Christ will come to judge. There's a note of urgency in this letter, an urgency that propels us into mission. The gospel is Good News, and we are entrusted with letting all people hear and see the transforming impact of life in Christ.

Jude 17–23
Jude urged faithful believers to reach out to three different groups. They were to (1) "be merciful to those in doubt" (v. 22); (2) reach out to those who had gone further down the road led by the false teachers;

20But you, dear friends, build yourselves up*j* in your most holy faith and pray in the Holy Spirit.*k* 21Keep yourselves in God's love as you wait*l* for the mercy of our Lord Jesus Christ to bring you to eternal life.

22Be merciful to those who doubt; 23snatch others from the fire and save them;*m* to others show mercy, mixed with fear—hating even the clothing stained by corrupted flesh.*n*

Doxology

24To him who is able*o* to keep you from falling and to present you before his glorious presence*p* without fault*q* and with great joy— 25to the only God*r* our Savior be glory, majesty, power and authority, through Jesus Christ our Lord, before all ages, now and forevermore!*s* Amen.*t*

20
j Col 2:7 *k* Eph 6:18
21
l Tit 2:13; 2Pe 3:12
23
m Am 4:11;
Zec 3:2-5 *n* Rev 3:4

24
o Ro 16:25
p 2Co 4:14
q Col 1:22
25
r Jn 5:44; 1Ti 1:17
s Heb 13:8
t Ro 11:36

---

and (3) show mercy to (likely by praying for) the false teachers themselves, as well as for church members who had been swayed by them. But believers were at the same time to "fear" the subtle influence of the false teachers, being cautious yet loving in their contacts.

📖 Some Christians view this accusatory letter as being overly negative. But Jude was writing not to the false teachers themselves but to faithful Christians needing reassurance and instruction while facing godlessness in the church. Jude instructed them to (1) remember that the apostles had predicted false teaching; (2) devote themselves to their own spiritual growth; and (3) reach out to those affected by false teaching—all important considerations for Christians today.

Why, you may ask, do I need to "keep myself in God's love" (v. 21) if I'm already being "kept by Jesus Christ" (v. 1)? Jude reflects the balance between God's sovereignty and human responsibility. God in his grace exerts his power and influence to "keep" us in his love. But the world bombards us with trials and temptations, and our sinful nature wants to drag us back to the old

way of life. God provides all we need to resist these forces, but we are responsible to take advantage of the spiritual resources he puts at our disposal.

Jude 24–25

📖 Jude's doxology is frequently used by pastors as a blessing. Why? Because it's one of the longest and most beautiful in the New Testament. Jude expanded the usual "form." Some of his additions may have been picked up from traditional wording, but others relate back to themes from his letter. Absent are the typical greetings and prayer requests that close other New Testament letters. This omission gives this brief book the flavor of a sermon.

📖 Reciting the glowing affirmation of the doxology creates in our minds a fresh picture of the all-consuming power and wonder of God. By meditating on these words, we are drawn to worship our awesome God. In the midst of struggles and conflicts—both in the world and in the church—God is able to keep us from falling. This assuring hope propels us into the world with the Good News.

INTRODUCTION TO
Revelation

AUTHOR

The author identified himself as John (1:1,4,9; 22:8), and authorship of Revelation has been attributed to the apostle John from as early as the 2nd century. He's believed to have been exiled to Patmos (an island not far from Ephesus that was used as a Roman penal settlement) on the basis of his testimony about Jesus (1:9).

DATE WRITTEN

Revelation was probably written between A.D. 90 and 96.

ORIGINAL READERS

Revelation is addressed to seven churches in Asia Minor (modern Turkey)—Ephesus, Smyrna, Pergamum, Thyatira, Sardis, Philadelphia, and Laodicea. Roman persecution of Christians (1:9; 2:10,13; 3:10) was widespread at the time, and false teachings were prominent in the churches.

TIMELINE

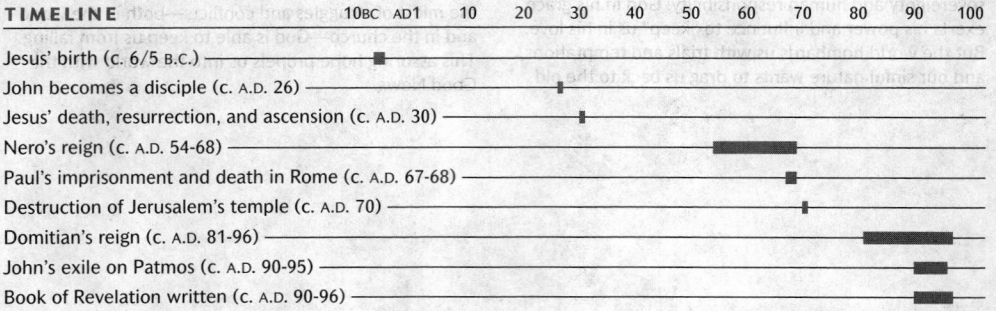

	10BC AD1	10	20	30	40	50	60	70	80	90	100
Jesus' birth (c. 6/5 B.C.)											
John becomes a disciple (c. A.D. 26)											
Jesus' death, resurrection, and ascension (c. A.D. 30)											
Nero's reign (c. A.D. 54-68)											
Paul's imprisonment and death in Rome (c. A.D. 67-68)											
Destruction of Jerusalem's temple (c. A.D. 70)											
Domitian's reign (c. A.D. 81-96)											
John's exile on Patmos (c. A.D. 90-95)											
Book of Revelation written (c. A.D. 90-96)											

THEMES

The book of Revelation is apocalyptic ("unveiled," "disclosed," or "revealed") literature. It's a book of prophecy (1:3; 22:7,10,18–19) that begins in the form of a circular letter to seven churches and moves to a report of prophetic visions intermixed with narrative and instruction. Revelation's primary themes include:

1. *God is in control.* God is in heaven, and while all isn't yet right with the world, it soon will be. God has long ago determined the world's destiny. John's visions penetrate the barrier that separates the heavenly realm from the earthly world and reveal the heavenly reality that will triumph over earthly illusion. Your knowledge of the Old Testament is helpful for understanding Revelation's symbolism. Events in the Old Testament are seen as reflecting recurring patterns in history. As God has resolved past conflicts, so he will bring present animosities to resolution.

2. *Jesus will return.* The final deliverance will occur at Christ's return. It will be preceded by a period of unprecedented distress symbolized by images of childbirth; military conflict; and supernatural, cosmic catastrophes. The new age won't come as the result of human activity, nor will it evolve from this present age. It will result from God's direct intervention. Revelation warns its readers to evaluate the present in light of the future age, in which evil will be judged and destroyed and the righteous rewarded. Humans must decide now whose side they will choose—that of God, who will triumph in the end, or of Satan and the world's champions, who may prevail momentarily but are destined for eternal destruction. John's purpose wasn't just to reveal events to come but to encourage believers to remain faithful under extreme pressure.

3. *Salvation is for all who will receive it.* Salvation is not exclusive to any people group or nation. All are invited. People from every "nation, tribe, people and language" stand before the Lamb and proclaim his praise (7:9–10). Tragically, some from every nation will choose not to follow him, aligning themselves instead with Satan's servant, the beast (13:1–8).

FAITH IN ACTION
The pages of Revelation contain life lessons and role models of faith—people who challenge believers to put faith in action.

Role Models

- JOHN (1:9) suffered persecution and exile for his faith. Are you willing to testify to your faith even if it means severe consequences?

- MICHAEL (12:7–9) and his angels fought and prevailed against Satan and his angels. Are you aware of and actively engaged in the spiritual battle being waged for the souls of people around you?

- CHRISTIANS IN EPHESUS (2:2–3) worked hard, persevered, refused to tolerate wicked teachers who taught false doctrine, and endured hardships—all without growing weary. Is this a fitting description of you and your local church?

- CHRISTIANS IN PERGAMUM (2:13) refused to renounce their faith in the face of persecution but remained true to Christ. What can you learn from their example?

- CHRISTIANS IN THYATIRA (2:19) put their love and faith into action through deeds and acts of service. What have you done lately to demonstrate your faith and love?

- CHRISTIANS IN PHILADELPHIA (2:8), despite their "little strength," kept Christ's word and refused to deny his name. How can their endurance, in spite of their limited strength (2:8), encourage you when you face trials?

- THE SAINTS (12:11), despite great opposition and even the threat of death (17:6), overcome "by the blood of the Lamb and by the word of their testimony." Is your commitment to Christ strong enough to face this ultimate challenge?

Challenges

- Paul had once commended the Ephesians for their faith and love for God and others (Eph. 1:15), but they had forsaken that love (2:4). Evaluate your journey of faith. Determine to love both Christ and others with the same intensity you had at first.

- Depend on God's power and faithfulness as you seek to obey Christ's command to "be faithful, even to the point of death" (2:10). Pray for Christians around the world who face death for their faith.

- When you are tempted to compromise your faith, when you think you have no strength left to endure, just "hold on to what you have" (2:25).

- Resolve that you won't be like the church members in Sardis who had a reputation for being alive but were really dead (3:1). Examine your Christian faith and life for hypocrisy. "Wake up! Strengthen what remains and is about to die" (3:2).

OUTLINE

   I.   Introduction (1:1–8)
  II.   Jesus and the Seven Churches (1:9—3:22)
 III. The Throne, the Scroll, and the Lamb (4–5)
 IV. The Seven Seals (6:1—8:1)
  V.   The Seven Trumpets (8:2—11:19)
 VI. The Conflict With Satan (12–14)
VII. The Seven Bowls (15–16)
VIII. The Fall of Babylon (17:1—19:5)
 IX. The Wedding of the Lamb (19:6–10)
  X.   The Rider (19:11–21)
 XI. The Thousand Years (20:1–6)
XII. Satan's Doom (20:7–10)
XIII. Great White Throne Judgment (20:11–15)
XIV. New Heaven, New Earth, New Jerusalem (21:1—22:5)
 XV. Conclusion (22:6–21)

Prologue

1:1
a Rev 22:16

1 The revelation of Jesus Christ, which God gave him to show his servants what must soon take place. He made it known by sending his angel *a* to his servant John,

1:2
b 1Co 1:6;
Rev 12:17

²who testifies to everything he saw—that is, the word of God and the testimony of Jesus Christ. *b* ³Blessed is the one who reads the words of this prophecy, and blessed

1:3
c Lk 11:28

are those who hear it and take to heart what is written in it, *c* because the time is near.

Greetings and Doxology

⁴John,

To the seven churches in the province of Asia:

1:4
d Rev 3:1; 4:5

1:5
e Rev 3:14
f Col 1:18
g Rev 17:14

Grace and peace to you from him who is, and who was, and who is to come, and from the seven spirits *a d* before his throne, ⁵and from Jesus Christ, who is the faithful witness, *e* the firstborn from the dead, *f* and the ruler of the kings of the earth. *g*

a 4 Or the sevenfold Spirit

Revelation 1:1–3

📖 Though an apostle, John identified himself not in terms of his authority over the churches but as a servant of God, a title often applied to Old Testament prophets (cf. Jer. 29:19). This title could reflect honor as well as submission: Servants of powerful masters like Caesar often enjoyed more prestige than aristocrats. John didn't attribute the revelation to any special merit of his own but testified "to everything he saw"—"the word of God and the testimony of Jesus Christ," the central figure in Revelation.

💻 Does launching into a study of Revelation intimidate you? Readers of Revelation over the centuries have found it helpful to identify either with John as the messenger or with the people to whom Jesus was sending his message. Those using either method receive the *mention of John as verification of the book's authority* and an invitation to pay careful attention to its content. John's openness to the Spirit, humility as God's servant, and obedience in speaking a less-than-popular message provide a model for believers of every era.

Revelation 1:4–8

📖 The leading council of Asiarchs (cf. Acts 19:31, "officials of the province") met each year in a revolving succession of seven strategic Asian cities. These were the same cities to which John wrote, with the exception that he replaced Cyzicus, far to the north, with the more central Thyatira. Ephesus, the first city John mentioned (1:11; 2:1), was the most important, but also the first to which a messenger from Patmos, 40 to 50 miles away in the Aegean Sea, would have come.

💻 That John's book was first sent to the most strategic cities of Asia Minor, with the assumption that its message would spread from there, invites us to think strategically about our plans to spread God's message within our communities and throughout the world. Ask yourself: Why does Islam now predominate in a region where Christianity took firm hold and once flourished? Some scholars believe the church destroyed itself with doctrinal infighting and ethnic divisions. What does this say to you about engaging strategically and being truly "Christian" where you live?

To him who loves us and has freed us from our sins by his blood, [6]and has made us to be a kingdom and priests[h] to serve his God and Father—to him be glory and power for ever and ever! Amen.[i]

> [7]Look, he is coming with the clouds,[j]
>   and every eye will see him,
>   even those who pierced him;
> and all the peoples of the earth
>   will mourn[k] because of him.
>   So shall it be! Amen.

[8]"I am the Alpha and the Omega,"[l] says the Lord God, "who is, and who was, and who is to come, the Almighty."[m]

One Like a Son of Man

[9]I, John, your brother and companion in the suffering[n] and kingdom and patient endurance[o] that are ours in Jesus, was on the island of Patmos because of the word of God and the testimony of Jesus. [10]On the Lord's Day I was in the Spirit,[p] and I heard behind me a loud voice like a trumpet,[q] [11]which said: "Write on a scroll what you see and send it to the seven churches:[r] to Ephesus, Smyrna, Pergamum, Thyatira, Sardis,[s] Philadelphia and Laodicea."

[12]I turned around to see the voice that was speaking to me. And when I turned I saw seven golden lampstands,[t] [13]and among the lampstands was someone "like a son of man,"[a][u] dressed in a robe reaching down to his feet and with a golden sash around his chest.[v] [14]His head and hair were white like wool, as white as snow, and his eyes were like blazing fire.[w] [15]His feet were like bronze glowing in a furnace,[x] and his voice was like the sound of rushing waters.[y] [16]In his right hand he held seven stars,[z] and out of his mouth came a sharp double-edged sword.[a] His face was like the sun shining in all its brilliance.

[17]When I saw him, I fell at his feet[b] as though dead. Then he placed his right hand on me and said: "Do not be afraid. I am the First and the Last.[c] [18]I am the Living One; I was dead,[d] and behold I am alive for ever and ever! And I hold the keys of death and Hades.[f]

[19]"Write, therefore, what you have seen, what is now and what will take place later. [20]The mystery of the seven stars that you saw in my right hand and of the seven

---

[a] 13 Daniel 7:13

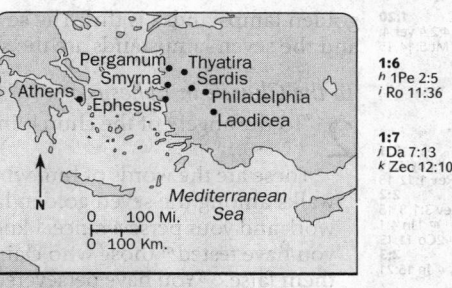

The Seven Churches (1:4)

Then: The seven churches specifically addressed by the risen Christ through John were located in Ephesus, Smyrna, Pergamum, Thyatira, Sardis, Philadelphia, and Laodicea.

Now: See "Here and Now" note for Revelation 1:9–20.

1:6
h 1Pe 2:5
i Ro 11:36

1:7
j Da 7:13
k Zec 12:10

1:8
l Rev 21:6
m Rev 4:8

1:9
n Php 4:14
o 2Ti 2:12

1:10
p Rev 4:2 q Rev 4:1

1:11
r ver 4,20 s Rev 3:1

1:12
t Ex 25:31-40; Zec 4:2

1:13
u Eze 1:26; Da 7:13; 10:16
v Da 10:5; Rev 15:6

1:14
w Da 7:9; 10:6; Rev 19:12

1:15
x Da 10:6
y Eze 43:2; Rev 14:2

1:16
z Rev 2:1; 3:1
a Isa 49:2; Heb 4:12; Rev 2:12,16

1:17
b Eze 1:28; Da 8:17,18
c Isa 41:4; 44:6; 48:12; Rev 22:13

1:18
d Ro 6:9 e Rev 4:9, 10 f Rev 20:1

Revelation 1:9–20

Jesus made his appearance among the lampstands, which represented seven specific churches. Throughout the ancient Mediterranean world, a seven-branched lampstand, or menorah, stood as a recognizable symbol of Israel and Judaism. The fact that each local congregation was symbolized by a lampstand likely suggested to John the larger church, the full people of God.

In ancient palaces, the one holding the keys was an important official—the only person controlling access into the king's presence. "Death and Hades" together represent death's power; as Jesus had told Peter (cf. Matt. 16:18). Because of his victory on the cross, Jesus holds these powerful keys.

Writer William Ramsey noted that the two cities in Revelation currently uninhabited were locations of the two churches Jesus most severely rebuked (Sardis and Laodicea). The two that held out longest before the Turkish conquest were the only two Christ unreservedly praised (Smyrna and Philadelphia). And Ephesus was literally moved to another site, just as Jesus through John had threatened this church with removal from its spiritual place (v. 5). Parallels between the cities' geo-political situations and the spiritual conditions of their churches may be coincidental, but they illustrate a principle: The church represents its culture.

How do you envision Jesus? Some people have tried to use this passage to identify Jesus' physical or ethnic features. But its point was to declare his power—not describe his complexion. He's the reigning Lord of the universe, the One with power over life and death. That awesome power is available to strengthen, correct, and encourage us as we participate in his mission, spreading the gospel of God's redeeming love for humanity.

1:20
g Zec 4:2 h ver 4,
11 i Mt 5:14,15

golden lampstands*g* is this: The seven stars are the angels*a* of the seven churches,*h* and the seven lampstands are the seven churches.*i*

To the Church in Ephesus

2 "To the angel*b* of the church in Ephesus write:

2:1
i Rev 1:16
k Rev 1:12,13
2:2
l Rev 3:1,8,15
m 1Jn 4:1
n 2Co 11:13
2:3
o Jn 15:21

These are the words of him who holds the seven stars in his right hand*j* and walks among the seven golden lampstands:*k* 2I know your deeds,*l* your hard work and your perseverance. I know that you cannot tolerate wicked men, that you have tested*m* those who claim to be apostles but are not, and have found them false.*n* 3You have persevered and have endured hardships for my name,*o* and have not grown weary.

2:4
p Mt 24:12
2:5
q ver 16,22
r Rev 1:20

4Yet I hold this against you: You have forsaken your first love.*p* 5Remember the height from which you have fallen! Repent*q* and do the things you did at first. If you do not repent, I will come to you and remove your lampstand*r* from its place. 6But you have this in your favor: You hate the practices of the

2:6
s ver 15
2:7
t Mt 11:15; Rev 3:6,
13,22 u Ge 2:9;
Rev 22:2,14,19
v Lk 23:43

Nicolaitans,*s* which I also hate.

7He who has an ear, let him hear*t* what the Spirit says to the churches. To him who overcomes, I will give the right to eat from the tree of life,*u* which is in the paradise*v* of God.

To the Church in Smyrna

2:8
w Rev 1:11
x Rev 1:17
y Rev 1:18

8"To the angel of the church in Smyrna*w* write:

These are the words of him who is the First and the Last,*x* who died and came to life again.*y* 9I know your afflictions and your poverty—yet you are

2:9
z Jas 2:5 a Rev 3:9
b Mt 4:10
2:10
c Rev 3:10

rich!*z* I know the slander of those who say they are Jews and are not,*a* but are a synagogue of Satan.*b* 10Do not be afraid of what you are about to suffer. I tell you, the devil will put some of you in prison to test you,*c* and you will suffer

a 20 Or *messengers*   b 1 Or *messenger*; also in verses 8, 12 and 18

Revelation 2:1–7

The fatal flaw in the Ephesians' behavior was their lack of love. Some interpreters have understood "forsaken your first love" to refer to a diminished love for God. But more commentators today understand the phrase as referring to the church members' love for one another (cf. John 13:34–35; Eph. 1:15; Col 1:4; 2 Thess. 1:3). Who the Nicolaitans were and what they taught have been lost in history.

Love is to be the hallmark of the community of believers. This church rightly "hated the sin" but apparently neglected to "love the sinner." Have you caught yourself avoiding those either in or outside the faith whose lifestyles or worship traditions differ from yours? Even

when dealing with clear cases of believers who err, the Bible calls us to offer correction with love and grace (2 Tim. 2:24–26). What do you hear the Spirit saying to you?

Revelation 2:8–11

The earliest Christians were Jews, and their Gentile converts viewed themselves as belonging to the truest form of Judaism. These Christians believed that obedience to Jesus was as necessary as obedience to Moses' law had been in the past. They regarded Jews who rejected Jesus as apostate from the true faith of Israel.

In Smyrna "overcoming" meant withstanding persecution. Jewish teaching already identified martyrdom with overcoming, but Revelation underlined the image of the triumphant Lion as a slain Lamb (5:5–6,9,12).

2:1—3:22

Understanding the Letters to the Churches

Each of the letters in chapters 2–3 is a prophetic word from Jesus through the Spirit, who was inspiring John. "These are the words" (2:1) is literally "Thus says," a standard Biblical prophetic messenger form (e.g.,

Acts 21:11; also used *hundreds of times by the OT prophets*). Each letter follows a similar pattern, balancing praise and reproof:

- "To the angel of the church in [a given city], write:"

- "Jesus [depicted in glory, often in terms from 1:13–18] says:"

- "I know . . ." (in most instances some form of praise)

- "But I have this against you . . ." (offers some reproof, where applicable)

- "The one who has ears must pay attention to what the Spirit says"

- An end-times promise

Source: NIV Application Commentary, Revelation (2000)

To the Church That Endures Persecution

2:8–10

To the angel of the church of the despised, incarcerated, separated, raped, and martyred; the persecuted church. These are the words of him who knows your patient endurance, understands your distress, and like you has been faithful to the shedding of his own precious blood.

You say you are isolated, cut off, that no one acknowledges your state. I see the terrors you face: the raids of your house churches in Laos, Indonesia, and China; the assault and murder of your leadership in Iran, India, and Chechnya; the indiscriminate bombing and enslavement that ravage your villages in Sudan.

I register every tear cried, record each longing conceived, hear each desperate plea confessed. I identify intimately with your plight. I haven't forgotten you. Nor have many others who, although unfamiliar with the gravity of your suffering, draw hope and strength from your noble sacrifices for me. I have revealed your plight to your brothers and sisters in Christ and have called thousands of churches to pray for you and to serve you.

You say you are afraid. Recognize what you have that can't be taken away. I have given you new life, an irrepressible joy, and an ever-present Spirit. Your transforming faith in me can't be crushed but instead shines like a lighthouse, drawing those who sincerely search for the Way, the Truth, and the Life.

You say you are losing hope. Know that these afflictions aren't the final word, that I'm sovereign and just. In time, I will repay. Although these tribulations threaten to overwhelm you, I have prepared an eternal place of peace for you, a permanent sanctuary of refreshment and true freedom that begins the moment you recognize me as Lord and serve me as King. I am with you always.

Beware of those who come from outside your fellowship, who masquerade as teachers of the church but elevate personal comfort over godly obedience. Many travel from long distances and present themselves as spiritual masters of the faith, proclaiming that temporal health and security are your due. Don't listen to them. Theirs is a false teaching, only shackling you to the unrequited masters of greed and disquiet. In the midst of your suffering, I will prove to be your only true peace and anchor.

Beware of those who are among you, immature in their belief, who mix notions contrary to my word with selected elements of saving truth. Like weeds among healthy grain, their subtle heresies pollute your fellowship, leading many to believe there are means other than a relationship with me to ensure eternity. Strive to know my Word and remain rooted in my loving commands.

I delight in your resourcefulness with little, your dignity in suffering, your joyful endurance in the midst of adversity. These things give witness to a power above all earthly kingdoms, a source of strength stronger than the might of any human power.

Remain faithful, and I will raise you up in victory. Patiently endure, for I won't tarry long.

> I delight in your resourcefulness with little, your dignity in suffering, your joyful endurance in the midst of adversity.

Steve Haas, vice president of World Vision U.S. in Federal Way, Washington

2:10
d Da 1:12,14
e ver 13

persecution for ten days. *d* Be faithful, *e* even to the point of death, and I will give you the crown of life.

2:11
f Rev 20:6,14; 21:8

11 He who has an ear, let him hear what the Spirit says to the churches. He who overcomes will not be hurt at all by the second death. *f*

To the Church in Pergamum

2:12
g Rev 1:11
h Rev 1:16

12 "To the angel of the church in Pergamum *g* write:

These are the words of him who has the sharp, double-edged sword. *h* 13 I know where you live—where Satan has his throne. Yet you remain true to my name. You did not renounce your faith in me, *i* even in the days of Antipas, my faithful witness, who was put to death in your city—where Satan lives. *j*

2:13
i Rev 14:12 *j* ver 9, 24

2:14
k ver 20 *l* 2Pe 2:15
m 1Co 6:13

14 Nevertheless, I have a few things against you: *k* You have people there who hold to the teaching of Balaam, *l* who taught Balak to entice the Israelites to sin by eating food sacrificed to idols and by committing sexual immorality. *m*

2:15
n ver 6

15 Likewise you also have those who hold to the teaching of the Nicolaitans. *n*

2:16
o 2Th 2:8; Rev 1:16

16 Repent therefore! Otherwise, I will soon come to you and will fight against them with the sword of my mouth. *o*

2:17
p Jn 6:49,50
q Isa 62:2
r Rev 19:12

17 He who has an ear, let him hear what the Spirit says to the churches. To him who overcomes, I will give some of the hidden manna. *p* I will also give him a white stone with a new name *q* written on it, known only to him who receives it. *r*

To the Church in Thyatira

2:18
s Rev 1:11
t Rev 1:14,15

18 "To the angel of the church in Thyatira *s* write:

These are the words of the Son of God, whose eyes are like blazing fire and whose feet are like burnished bronze. *t* 19 I know your deeds, *u* your love and faith, your service and perseverance, and that you are now doing more than you did at first.

2:19
u ver 2

2:20
v 1Ki 16:31; 21:25; 2Ki 9:7

20 Nevertheless, I have this against you: You tolerate that woman Jezebel, *v* who calls herself a prophetess. By her teaching she misleads my servants into sexual immorality and the eating of food sacrificed to idols. 21 I have given her time *w* to repent of her immorality, but she is unwilling. *x* 22 So I will cast her

2:21
w Ro 2:4 *x* Rev 9:20

📖 Suffering reminds us of what really matters, forces us to depend radically on God, and purifies our obedience to his will. We are called to be "overcomers." Rather than living as victims of our circumstances, making excuses for our limitations, we bear the life of the One who is the First and the Last, who died and came to life again. Whether or not we have material riches, we are rich. Around the world there are followers of Christ living in poverty and oppression—but bold and rich in their courageous faith. How might the Spirit be calling you to step out as an "overcomer"?

Revelation 2:12–17

📖 The church in Pergamum faced external and internal opposition. Any of several pagan connections may apply to "Satan's throne." But the greatest threat to this church was Pergamum's identity as Asia's official center of emperor worship. For Christians there, "overcoming" meant continuing steadfast in the face of opposition. It especially involved standing against compromise with the world and doing their best to purge such teachings and practices from their ranks.

📖 Many Christians in the rest of the world mourn how quickly the West has shifted from being a source of blessing to becoming a self-centered "mission field," ex-

porting ungodly values through its entertainment media. When we as Christians adopt the world's values instead of valuing the kingdom, we forfeit our role as Christ's witnesses. If we support what the world promotes and live as it does, to what can we invite unbelievers in conversion?

Revelation 2:18–29

📖 Thyatira was known for its merchants, crafts, and trade guilds (cf. Acts 16:14). Shopkeepers or craftsmen risked loss of income by refusing to join guilds, whose meetings included common meals dedicated to patron deities. Aspects of emperor worship also affected nearly every guild. This situation likely contributed to "Jezebel's" appeal. This false prophetess, claiming to offer "deep secrets," deceived and misled God's people, advocating participation in local civic and commercial life despite the inevitable compromise with paganism.

📖 The Bible doesn't demand conformity on every point. No matter how strongly individual believers feel about styles of dress, end-times teachings, women in ministry, spiritual gifts, and the like, we are to recognize that those with different views can still be committed Christians. We appropriately draw a line in the sand, though, on issues that involve spiritual life and death, like participation in idolatry or sexual immorality.

on a bed of suffering, and I will make those who commit adultery^y with her suffer intensely, unless they repent of her ways. ²³I will strike her children dead. Then all the churches will know that I am he who searches hearts and minds,^z and I will repay each of you according to your deeds. ²⁴Now I say to the rest of you in Thyatira, to you who do not hold to her teaching and have not learned Satan's so-called deep secrets (I will not impose any other burden on you):^a ²⁵Only hold on to what you have^b until I come.

²⁶To him who overcomes and does my will to the end, I will give authority over the nations^c—

²⁷'He will rule them with an iron scepter;^d
he will dash them to pieces like pottery'^{a e}—

just as I have received authority from my Father. ²⁸I will also give him the morning star.^f ²⁹He who has an ear, let him hear^g what the Spirit says to the churches.

To the Church in Sardis

3 "To the angel^b of the church in Sardis write:

These are the words of him who holds the seven spirits^{c h} of God and the seven stars.ⁱ I know your deeds;^j you have a reputation of being alive, but you are dead.^k ²Wake up! Strengthen what remains and is about to die, for I have not found your deeds complete in the sight of my God. ³Remember, therefore, what you have received and heard; obey it, and repent.^l But if you do not wake up, I will come like a thief,^m and you will not know at what time I will come to you.

⁴Yet you have a few people in Sardis who have not soiled their clothes.ⁿ They will walk with me, dressed in white,^o for they are worthy. ⁵He who overcomes will, like them, be dressed in white. I will never blot out his name from the book of life,^p but will acknowledge his name before my Father^q and his angels. ⁶He who has an ear, let him hear^r what the Spirit says to the churches.

To the Church in Philadelphia

⁷"To the angel of the church in Philadelphia^s write:

These are the words of him who is holy and true,^t who holds the key of David.^u What he opens no one can shut, and what he shuts no one can open. ⁸I know your deeds. See, I have placed before you an open door^v that no one can shut. I know that you have little strength, yet you have kept my word and have not denied my name.^w ⁹I will make those who are of the synagogue of Satan,^x

---

2:22
y Rev 17:2; 18:9
2:23
z 1Sa 16:7;
Jer 11:20; Ac 1:24;
Ro 8:27

2:24
a Ac 15:28
2:25
b Rev 3:11
2:26
c Ps 2:8; Rev 3:21
2:27
d Rev 12:5
e Isa 30:14;
Jer 19:11

2:28
f Rev 22:16
2:29
g ver 7

3:1
h Rev 1:4 i Rev 1:16
j Rev 2:2 k 1Ti 5:6

3:3
l Rev 2:5
m 2Pe 3:10

3:4
n Jude 23
o Rev 4:4; 6:11;
7:9,13,14

3:5
p Rev 20:12
q Mt 10:32
3:6
r Rev 2:7

3:7
s Rev 1:11
t 1Jn 5:20
u Isa 22:22;
Mt 16:19

3:8
v Ac 14:27
w Rev 2:13

3:9
x Rev 2:9

---

^a 27 Psalm 2:9   ^b 1 Or *messenger*; also in verses 7 and 14   ^c 1 Or *the sevenfold Spirit*

Revelation 3:1–6

Sardis was full of sophisticated paganism. The lack of mention of persecution probably reflects the secure position of its Jewish community. Jesus' followers evidently coexisted peacefully with the synagogue community and city establishment. Unaccustomed to opposition, they had grown comfortable in their relationship with the world. Their spiritual state (deadness) kept them from realizing that Jesus' resurrection power was available to them.

Satan didn't have to pressure the Sardian Christians with persecution or temptation. They probably thought of themselves as spiritually vital, but their church was already dead. Jesus' wake-up call applies to everyone; all must be ready for Christ's return and judgment. But the warning is most relevant to sleeping churches—those guided more by their culture than by Jesus' voice or any sense of future reckoning with him. It's important not to downplay the text's blunt warning. Our faith in the Bible as God's Word requires us to revise our thinking to fit the text, not the reverse.

Revelation 3:7–13

The Philadelphian believers were like the Jewish Christians for whom John wrote his Gospel. Many had likely been expelled from their synagogues, similar to the formerly blind man of John 9:34. But Jesus had defended that man as one of his sheep, noting that he himself had the right to determine who belonged to his people (John 10:1–15). Despite Jesus' praise for the Philadelphian Christians' perseverance to this point, "it isn't over until it's over." They had to continue holding fast to what they had.

3:9
y Isa 49:23
z Isa 43:4
3:10
a 2Pe 2:9
b Rev 2:10
c Rev 6:10; 17:8
3:11
d Rev 2:25
e Rev 2:10
3:12
f Gal 2:9
g Rev 14:1; 22:4
h Rev 21:2, 10

who claim to be Jews though they are not, but are liars—I will make them come and fall down at your feet[y] and acknowledge that I have loved you.[z] [10]Since you have kept my command to endure patiently, I will also keep you[a] from the hour of trial that is going to come upon the whole world to test[b] those who live on the earth.[c]

[11]I am coming soon. Hold on to what you have,[d] so that no one will take your crown.[e] [12]Him who overcomes I will make a pillar[f] in the temple of my God. Never again will he leave it. I will write on him the name of my God[g] and the name of the city of my God, the new Jerusalem,[h] which is coming down out of heaven from my God; and I will also write on him my new name. [13]He who has an ear, let him hear what the Spirit says to the churches.

To the Church in Laodicea

[14]"To the angel of the church in Laodicea write:

3:14
i Col 1:16, 18
3:15
j Ro 12:11

3:17
k Hos 12:8; 1Co 4:8

3:18
l Rev 16:15

3:19
m Pr 3:12;
Heb 12:5, 6
n Rev 2:5
3:20
o Mt 24:33
p Lk 12:36
q Jn 14:23
3:21
r Mt 19:28
s Rev 5:5
3:22
t Rev 2:7

These are the words of the Amen, the faithful and true witness, the ruler of God's creation.[i] [15]I know your deeds, that you are neither cold nor hot.[j] I wish you were either one or the other! [16]So, because you are lukewarm—neither hot nor cold—I am about to spit you out of my mouth. [17]You say, 'I am rich; I have acquired wealth and do not need a thing.'[k] But you do not realize that you are wretched, pitiful, poor, blind and naked. [18]I counsel you to buy from me gold refined in the fire, so you can become rich; and white clothes to wear, so you can cover your shameful nakedness;[l] and salve to put on your eyes, so you can see.

[19]Those whom I love I rebuke and discipline.[m] So be earnest, and repent.[n] [20]Here I am! I stand at the door[o] and knock. If anyone hears my voice and opens the door,[p] I will come in[q] and eat with him, and he with me.

[21]To him who overcomes, I will give the right to sit with me on my throne,[r] just as I overcame[s] and sat down with my Father on his throne. [22]He who has an ear, let him hear[t] what the Spirit says to the churches."

The Throne in Heaven

4:1
u Rev 1:10

4 After this I looked, and there before me was a door standing open in heaven. And the voice I had first heard speaking to me like a trumpet[u] said, "Come up

---

📖 That these Christians had little social power (v. 8) counted in their favor before God. Power is easily abused, but weakness leads to dependence upon God's power (cf. 2 Cor. 12:9). One insight from Christians in poor countries draws on the Biblical emphasis of God's special concern for the broken. He promises to live with and embrace the hurting and humble, but he's far from the proud and self-sufficient (Ps. 51:17; Isa. 57:15; 66:2; James 4:6). God judges each of us not on the power we start out with, but on what we do with that which he's given us. On whose power do you depend?

Revelation 3:14–22

📖 The Christians in Laodicea probably shared their neighbors' pride over the city's self-sufficiency. But they presumably also shared a distaste for its water supply. Lacking access to cold water from the mountains or hot water from the nearby springs in Hierapolis, Laodicea had to pipe in lukewarm water. Jesus told this self-satisfied church, "I want water that will refresh me, but you remind me of the water you complain about. You make me want to spit you out."

Jesus didn't reject these believers. He wanted to have dinner with them—an image associated with intimacy in the ancient world. Inviting Jesus in for a meal during his ministry years would have been a gesture of hospitality not uncommon even from an acquaintance. Can a Christian who calls Jesus "Lord" do any less?

📖 Jesus' personalized invitation reveals how easily Christians can shut him out of their lives by their own self-sufficiency. The sad truth is that, as our brothers and sisters in Christ suffer and die for their faith in many lands, we in the West share only a small percentage of our resources with them. Our material wealth can prove a source of spiritual poverty, blinding us to the needs of others and pressuring us to conform to the society around us. We who live in abundance can use what remains of this season of plenty not to increase our luxury but to serve God's purposes among the nations. What part can you play in such a radical turnaround?

Revelation 4:1–11

📖 Jewish tradition suggested that God created the world for the sake of humanity or for Israel, but Christians see his ultimate purpose in Christ's saving work. The emperor Domitian expected worship as "lord and god." But the heavenly choirs of angels and the redeemed people hail the true "Lord and God"—the One who created and rules over his universe.

here,^{v} and I will show you what must take place after this."^{w} ^{2}At once I was in the Spirit,^{x} and there before me was a throne in heaven^y with someone sitting on it. ^{3}And the one who sat there had the appearance of jasper and carnelian. A rainbow,^{z} resembling an emerald, encircled the throne. ^{4}Surrounding the throne were twenty-four other thrones, and seated on them were twenty-four elders.^{a} They were dressed in white^b and had crowns of gold on their heads. ^{5}From the throne came flashes of lightning, rumblings and peals of thunder.^{c} Before the throne, seven lamps^d were blazing. These are the seven spirits^{a}^{e} of God. ^{6}Also before the throne there was what looked like a sea of glass,^{f} clear as crystal.

In the center, around the throne, were four living creatures,^{g} and they were covered with eyes, in front and in back. ^{7}The first living creature was like a lion, the second was like an ox, the third had a face like a man, the fourth was like a flying eagle.^{h} ^{8}Each of the four living creatures had six wings^i and was covered with eyes all around, even under his wings. Day and night they never stop saying:

> "Holy, holy, holy
> is the Lord God Almighty,^{j}
> who was, and is, and is to come."^{k}

^{9}Whenever the living creatures give glory, honor and thanks to him who sits on the throne^l and who lives for ever and ever, ^{10}the twenty-four elders^m fall down before him^n who sits on the throne,^{o} and worship him who lives for ever and ever. They lay their crowns before the throne and say:

> ^{11} "You are worthy, our Lord and God,
> to receive glory and honor and power,^{p}
> for you created all things,
> and by your will they were created
> and have their being."^{q}

The Scroll and the Lamb

5 Then I saw in the right hand of him who sat on the throne^r a scroll with writing on both sides^s and sealed^t with seven seals. ^{2}And I saw a mighty angel proclaiming in a loud voice, "Who is worthy to break the seals and open the scroll?" ^{3}But no one in heaven or on earth or under the earth could open the scroll or even look inside it. ^{4}I wept and wept because no one was found who was worthy to open

---

^{a} 5 Or *the sevenfold Spirit*

Cross references

4:1
^{v} Rev 11:12
^{w} Rev 1:19
4:2
^{x} Rev 1:10 ^{y} Isa 6:1;
Eze 1:26-28; Da 7:9
4:3
^{z} Eze 1:28
4:4
^{a} Rev 11:16
^{b} Rev 3:4,5
4:5
^{c} Rev 8:5; 16:18
^{d} Zec 4:2 ^{e} Rev 1:4
4:6
^{f} Rev 15:2 ^{g} Eze 1:5

4:7
^{h} Eze 1:10; 10:14
4:8
^{i} Isa 6:2 ^{j} Isa 6:3;
Rev 1:8 ^{k} Rev 1:4

4:9
^{l} Ps 47:8

4:10
^{m} ver 4
^{n} Rev 5:8,14
^{o} ver 2

4:11
^{p} Rev 5:12
^{q} Rev 10:6

5:1
^{r} ver 7,13
^{s} Eze 2:9,10
^{t} Isa 29:11; Da 12:4

📖 Many Western Christians think of Christianity as the heritage of the Western world, despite its continuing decline here. Sadly, many in Africa (where Christianity is growing fastest) and elsewhere still believe the lie that it's a Western religion. Meanwhile, in its Middle Eastern birthplace our faith struggles to regain a foothold. The apostle needed to remind his audience that the church wasn't for Israel alone. And we do well to remember that no culture or region has a permanent claim on the gospel.

Revelation 5:1–14

📖 Most ancient people wrote on one side of a scroll, using the back only if they ran out of space. Clearly this book has much to say. Legal documents were usually closed by listing witnesses and were sealed shut with wax over the threads that tied the scroll shut. The witnesses would press their seals into this wax. Seals reserved the contents for the rightful recipient(s)—as authenticated and attested by the witnesses.

Horns appeared on Passover lambs, but John's symbolism went further. In prophetic literature they some-

times represented power (Dan. 7:7–24). Here, though, the power wasn't human, but that of the seven spirits of God (Rev. 5:6). This brings to mind an ancient prophecy that the Jewish king would prevail not by human strength but by the power of the Spirit (Zech. 3:9; 4:6,10).

📖 John wept at the prospect of the world without a heavenly advocate. We already know Jesus as our champion. But Revelation unfolds its message not in theological language but in graphic images that confront us with the familiar gospel message in a new way. Do you see the church at large, with God's help, finding creative, fresh ways to communicate his message to new generations? What about your own congregation?

Jesus was filled with the Spirit for his earthly ministry (Matt. 3:16), and he foretold that the same would happen to his disciples (Acts 1:8). Does it surprise you that his activity in heaven also is Spirit empowered? What needs to change for you to depend more on the Holy Spirit and less on yourself?

5:5
u Ge 49:9
v Isa 11:1,10;
Ro 15:12;
Rev 22:16
5:6
w Jn 1:29
x Zec 4:10

the scroll or look inside. 5Then one of the elders said to me, "Do not weep! See, the Lion[u] of the tribe of Judah, the Root of David,[v] has triumphed. He is able to open the scroll and its seven seals."

6Then I saw a Lamb,[w] looking as if it had been slain, standing in the center of the throne, encircled by the four living creatures and the elders. He had seven horns and seven eyes,[x] which are the seven spirits[a] of God sent out into all the earth. 7He came

5:7
y ver 1

and took the scroll from the right hand of him who sat on the throne.[y] 8And when he had taken it, the four living creatures and the twenty-four elders fell down be-

5:8
z Rev 14:2
a Ps 141:2
5:9
b Ps 40:3
c Rev 4:11
d Heb 9:12
e 1Co 6:20

fore the Lamb. Each one had a harp[z] and they were holding golden bowls full of incense, which are the prayers[a] of the saints. 9And they sang a new song:[b]

"You are worthy[c] to take the scroll
and to open its seals,
because you were slain,
and with your blood[d] you purchased[e] men for God
from every tribe and language and people and nation.

5:10
f 1Pe 2:5

10You have made them to be a kingdom and priests[f] to serve our God,
and they will reign on the earth."

5:11
g Da 7:10;
Heb 12:22

11Then I looked and heard the voice of many angels, numbering thousands upon thousands, and ten thousand times ten thousand.[g] They encircled the throne and the living creatures and the elders. 12In a loud voice they sang:

5:12
h Rev 4:11
5:13
i ver 3; Php 2:10
j Rev 6:16
k 1Ch 29:11

"Worthy is the Lamb, who was slain,
to receive power and wealth and wisdom and strength
and honor and glory and praise!"[h]

13Then I heard every creature in heaven and on earth and under the earth[i] and on the sea, and all that is in them, singing:

"To him who sits on the throne and to the Lamb[j]
be praise and honor and glory and power,
for ever and ever!"[k]

5:14
l Rev 4:9
m Rev 4:10; 19:4

14The four living creatures said, "Amen,"[l] and the elders fell down and worshiped.[m]

The Seals

6:1
n Rev 5:6 o Rev 5:1
p Rev 4:6,7
q Rev 14:2; 19:6
6:2
r Zec 6:3;
Rev 19:11
s Zec 6:11;
Rev 14:14 t Ps 45:4
6:3
u Rev 4:7
6:4
v Zec 6:2

6 I watched as the Lamb[n] opened the first of the seven seals.[o] Then I heard one of the four living creatures[p] say in a voice like thunder,[q] "Come!" 2I looked, and there before me was a white horse![r] Its rider held a bow, and he was given a crown,[s] and he rode out as a conqueror bent on conquest.[t]

3When the Lamb opened the second seal, I heard the second living creature[u] say, "Come!" 4Then another horse came out, a fiery red one.[v] Its rider was given pow-

a 6 Or the sevenfold Spirit

Revelation 6:1–17

The opening of the first four seals presents the notorious four horsemen of the Apocalypse as fierce images of terrifying judgment. The judgments threatened by the horsemen are those Jesus said would characterize the present age (Mark 13:7–8).

The fifth seal presents the martyrs who have suffered at the hands of a hostile world, crying out for vindication. And the sixth portrays the fate of the world at the hands of God, whose agents it has martyred. Together these testimonies provide encouragement to believers to stand as witnesses regardless of any opposition they may face.

Skeptics of Christianity have asked whether Christians can work to prevent and/or combat the effects

of plagues and famines when they believe these hardships to be judgments sent by God. But John the Baptist, John the apostle, and James, all prophets of judgment, defined true repentance before God by our commitment to care for others' needs (Luke 3:11; 1 Jn. 3:17-18; James 2:14–17, respectively). How would Jesus, who focused on the lost and the outcasts of his day and who fed the hungry crowds, evaluate our priorities?

In many countries, such as China, Indonesia, Sudan, India, Iran, and Pakistan, the credibility of the gospel is being enhanced by the quality of the life of Christ's followers—and by their willingness to die for their faith. What does this reality stir in your heart? How will it affect your Christian witness?

er to take peace from the earth [w] and to make men slay each other. To him was given a large sword.

[5]When the Lamb opened the third seal, I heard the third living creature [x] say, "Come!" I looked, and there before me was a black horse! [y] Its rider was holding a pair of scales in his hand. [6]Then I heard what sounded like a voice among the four living creatures, [z] saying, "A quart [a] of wheat for a day's wages, [b] and three quarts of barley for a day's wages, [b] and do not damage [a] the oil and the wine!"

[7]When the Lamb opened the fourth seal, I heard the voice of the fourth living creature [b] say, "Come!" [8]I looked, and there before me was a pale horse! [c] Its rider was named Death, and Hades [d] was following close behind him. They were given power over a fourth of the earth to kill by sword, famine and plague, and by the wild beasts of the earth. [e]

[9]When he opened the fifth seal, I saw under the altar [f] the souls of those who had been slain [g] because of the word of God and the testimony they had maintained. [10]They called out in a loud voice, "How long, [h] Sovereign Lord, holy and true, [i] until you judge the inhabitants of the earth and avenge our blood?" [j] [11]Then each of them was given a white robe, [k] and they were told to wait a little longer, until the number of their fellow servants and brothers who were to be killed as they had been was completed. [l]

[12]I watched as he opened the sixth seal. There was a great earthquake. [m] The sun turned black [n] like sackcloth made of goat hair, the whole moon turned blood red, [13]and the stars in the sky fell to earth, [o] as late figs drop from a fig tree [p] when shaken by a strong wind. [14]The sky receded like a scroll, rolling up, and every mountain and island was removed from its place. [q]

[15]Then the kings of the earth, the princes, the generals, the rich, the mighty, and every slave and every free man hid in caves and among the rocks of the mountains. [r] [16]They called to the mountains and the rocks, "Fall on us [s] and hide us from the face of him who sits on the throne and from the wrath of the Lamb! [17]For the great day [t] of their wrath has come, and who can stand?" [u]

[a] 6 Greek *a choinix* (probably about a liter) [b] 6 Greek *a denarius*

6:4 [w] Mt 10:34
6:5 [x] Rev 4:7 [y] Zec 6:2
6:6 [z] Rev 4:6,7 [a] Rev 9:4
6:7 [b] Rev 4:7
6:8 [c] Zec 6:3 [d] Hos 13:14 [e] Jer 15:2,3; Eze 5:12,17
6:9 [f] Rev 14:18; 16:7 [g] Rev 20:4
6:10 [h] Zec 1:12 [i] Rev 3:7 [j] Rev 19:2
6:11 [k] Rev 3:4 [l] Heb 11:40
6:12 [m] Rev 16:18 [n] Mt 24:29
6:13 [o] Mt 24:29; Rev 8:10; 9:1 [p] Isa 34:4
6:14 [q] Jer 4:24; Rev 16:20
6:15 [r] Isa 2:10,19,21
6:16 [s] Hos 10:8; Lk 23:30
6:17 [t] Zep 1:14,15; Rev 16:14 [u] Ps 76:7

6:1–8

Judgment and the Four Horsemen

The judgments threatened by the four horsemen were judgments Jesus had said would characterize the present (church) age (Mark 13:7–8). The list of four plagues resembles some from the Old Testament (Deut. 32:24; 2 Chron. 20:9; Jer. 15:2; Ezek. 5:17; 14:21). But this passage most directly recalls Zechariah 1:8–11, where many riders on horses of different colors represented the Lord's patrol, reporting back to him about quiet on the earth. Later, in Zechariah 6:1–8, God sent out four chariots, each drawn by horses of different colors, as his patrol—more impressive than the Persian patrols from which the image may have derived.

Horse	Rider	Purpose	Implications today
White	Has bow and arrow; given a crown	Conquest	Wins people's hearts
Red	Has power to destroy peace; given a large sword	Make people kill each other	Wars, conflicts
Black	Pair of scales	Economic instability	Increased disparity between rich (luxuries like oil and wine) and poor (who lack resources to buy food)
Pale	Named Death, with Hades following close behind	Both have power over ¼ of Earth	Kills by sword (violence) and famine, plagues, and wild beasts (epidemics)

Source: NIV Application Commentary, Revelation (2000)

144,000 Sealed

7:1
v Da 7:2

7 After this I saw four angels standing at the four corners of the earth, holding back the four winds[v] of the earth to prevent any wind from blowing on the land or on the sea or on any tree. ²Then I saw another angel coming up from the east, having the seal of the living God. He called out in a loud voice to the four angels who had been given power to harm the land and the sea: ³"Do not harm[w] the land or the sea or the trees until we put a seal on the foreheads[x] of the servants of our God." ⁴Then I heard the number[y] of those who were sealed: 144,000[z] from all the tribes of Israel.

7:3
w Rev 6:6
x Eze 9:4; Rev 22:4

7:4
y Rev 9:16
z Rev 14:1,3

⁵From the tribe of Judah 12,000 were sealed,
from the tribe of Reuben 12,000,
from the tribe of Gad 12,000,
⁶from the tribe of Asher 12,000,
from the tribe of Naphtali 12,000,
from the tribe of Manasseh 12,000,
⁷from the tribe of Simeon 12,000,
from the tribe of Levi 12,000,
from the tribe of Issachar 12,000,
⁸from the tribe of Zebulun 12,000,
from the tribe of Joseph 12,000,
from the tribe of Benjamin 12,000.

The Great Multitude in White Robes

7:9
a Rev 5:9 b ver 15

⁹After this I looked and there before me was a great multitude that no one could count, from every nation, tribe, people and language,[a] standing before the throne[b] and in front of the Lamb. They were wearing white robes and were holding palm branches in their hands. ¹⁰And they cried out in a loud voice:

7:10
c Ps 3:8; Rev 12:10;
19:1

"Salvation belongs to our God,[c]
who sits on the throne,
and to the Lamb."

7:11
d Rev 4:4 e Rev 4:6
f Rev 4:10

¹¹All the angels were standing around the throne and around the elders[d] and the four living creatures.[e] They fell down on their faces[f] before the throne and worshiped God, ¹²saying:

Revelation 7:1–8

Chapter 7 provides an intermission between the sixth and seventh seals and builds suspense. The identity of the 144,000 is open to question. The text suggests a census, typically used in the Old Testament to assess military preparedness (Num. 1; 26; 1 Chron. 27). This vision may represent an end-time army, prepared for spiritual battle—possibly the same army that returns with Jesus in 19:14, clothed with the righteous acts of the saints. Other factors in Revelation suggest that John may have been adapting the pattern of a Jewish end-time remnant to represent all believers in Jesus—Jews and Gentiles alike.

Three principles come to light when we read this passage in its context. (1) God views believers as his army, yet we triumph through sharing the Lamb's suffering (Rom. 8:17; 2 Tim. 2:11–13). (2) We have nothing to fear. God, who is sovereign over creation, can protect us from trouble. (3) God views us—Gentile and Jewish believers alike—as his people. In sealing us, he proudly marks us as his own. Have you ever envisioned yourself visibly marked, sealed, or branded as belonging to Jesus?

Revelation 7:9–17

If the first vision of the 144,000 (vv. 1–8) portrays symbolically God's end-time spiritual army, then this second is a more literal interpretation of the first. All of us as God's people are his soldiers. We vanquish our foes not by killing them but by praising God in their midst and by suffering persecution and even martyrdom at their hands. In this, we are like our Lord. That the multitude is countless probably echoes the promise to the patriarchs. But here, in contrast to the first vision, the promised multitude is gathered from all nations.

This picture of the 144,000 as God's martyr army challenges us. He's called us to take the news of our King outside the church walls—to strike offensively, even as we stand defensively. Few of us think of martyrdom as a privilege. Yet if we must die, wouldn't we want our deaths to bring God as much glory as possible? John's vision, taken seriously, may invite inner conflict for those of us too comfortable with the world. Have you given serious thought to what you would do if faced with martyrdom for your faith? The classic *Fox's Book of Martyrs* provides inspiring reading about those who have walked this path before us.

"Amen!
Praise and glory
and wisdom and thanks and honor
and power and strength
be to our God for ever and ever.
Amen!" [g]

[13] Then one of the elders asked me, "These in white robes—who are they, and where did they come from?"

[14] I answered, "Sir, you know."

And he said, "These are they who have come out of the great tribulation; they have washed their robes [h] and made them white in the blood of the Lamb. [i] [15] Therefore,

"they are before the throne of God [j]
    and serve him [k] day and night in his temple; [l]
and he who sits on the throne will spread his tent over them. [m]
[16] Never again will they hunger;
    never again will they thirst.
The sun will not beat upon them,
    nor any scorching heat. [n]
[17] For the Lamb at the center of the throne will be their shepherd; [o]
he will lead them to springs of living water.
And God will wipe away every tear from their eyes." [p]

The Seventh Seal and the Golden Censer

8 When he opened the seventh seal, [q] there was silence in heaven for about half an hour.

[2] And I saw the seven angels [r] who stand before God, and to them were given seven trumpets.

[3] Another angel, [s] who had a golden censer, came and stood at the altar. He was given much incense to offer, with the prayers of all the saints, [t] on the golden altar [u] before the throne. [4] The smoke of the incense, together with the prayers of the saints, went up before God [v] from the angel's hand. [5] Then the angel took the censer, filled it with fire from the altar, [w] and hurled it on the earth; and there came peals of thunder, [x] rumblings, flashes of lightning and an earthquake. [y]

The Trumpets

[6] Then the seven angels who had the seven trumpets [z] prepared to sound them. [7] The first angel sounded his trumpet, and there came hail and fire [a] mixed with

Cross references (right margin)

7:12
g Rev 5:12-14

7:14
h Rev 22:14
i Heb 9:14; 1Jn 1:7

7:15
j ver 9 k Rev 22:3
l Rev 11:19
m Isa 4:5,6;
Rev 21:3

7:16
n Isa 49:10

7:17
o Ps 23:1; Jn 10:11
p Isa 25:8; Rev 21:4

8:1
q Rev 6:1

8:2
r ver 6-13;
Rev 9:1,13; 11:15

8:3
s Rev 7:2 t Rev 5:8
u Ex 30:1-6;
Heb 9:4; Rev 9:13

8:4
v Ps 141:2

8:5
w Lev 16:12,13
x Rev 4:5
y Rev 6:12

8:6
z ver 2
8:7
a Eze 38:22

Revelation 8:1–5

The "silence in heaven" provides a dramatic interlude between the judgments of the seals and the trumpets. As fresh prayers for vindication are added to other prayers, judgment is set in motion. The sufferings and prayers of God's people invite his intervention, even if his timing doesn't always coincide with ours (Ex. 2:23–25; Luke 18:7). What takes place in heaven clearly affects what happens on Earth (and vice versa). We can't always see the results, but countless judgments come in direct response to human prayers.

Other texts refer to the world's silence before God at the Day of Judgment (Zeph. 1:7; Zech. 2:13; cf. Rev. 18:22–23). That its clamor will one day be hushed offers Christians encouragement. The arrogance of politics, academia, the media, and other elite groups who ridicule or ignore God will fall silent. The text also has a word for those who blame God for the world's injustices,

while trivializing sin.

That judgment comes in response to prayer renews our motivation to pray. For suffering people, the prospect of judgment on a repressive world brings hope. God is, among other attributes, a God of justice and wrath. And he gives us the moral clarity to take sides when clear examples of oppression are taking place. What motivates you to pray?

Revelation 8:6—9:21

The trumpet judgments resemble the plagues in Exodus (see Ex. 9:23–24; 7:20–21; 10:22; 10:13–14, in that order). By referring to them indirectly and to God's protection of his ancient people (Rev. 9:4), John reminded us that God's work in history offers future assurance. If God judged the oppressors of our spiritual ancestors, he will overturn the powers that seek to crush his people in every age.

The monstrosities from the Abyss may represent

8:7
b ver 7-12;
Rev 9:15,18; 12:4
c Rev 9:4
8:8
d Jer 51:25 *e* ver 7
f Rev 16:3
8:9
g ver 7
8:10
h Isa 14:12;
Rev 6:13; 9:1
i Rev 14:7; 16:4
8:11
j ver 7 *k* Jer 9:15;
23:15
8:12
l ver 7
m Ex 10:21-23;
Rev 6:12,13
8:13
n Rev 14:6; 19:17
o Rev 9:12; 11:14

9:1
p Rev 8:10
q ver 2,11; Lk 8:31
9:2
r Ge 19:28;
Ex 19:18
s Joel 2:2,10
9:3
t Ex 10:12-15
u ver 5,10
9:4
v Rev 6:6 *w* Rev 8:7
x Rev 7:2,3
9:5
y ver 10 *z* ver 3

9:6
a Job 3:21; Jer 8:3;
Rev 6:16
9:7
b Joel 2:4 *c* Da 7:8

9:8
d Joel 1:6

9:9
e Joel 2:5
9:10
f ver 3,5,19
9:11
g ver 1,2

9:12
h Rev 8:13

9:13
i Ex 30:1-3 / Rev 8:3
9:14
k Rev 16:12

9:15
l ver 18

9:16
m Rev 5:11; 7:4

blood, and it was hurled down upon the earth. A third *b* of the earth was burned up, a third of the trees were burned up, and all the green grass was burned up. *c*

⁸The second angel sounded his trumpet, and something like a huge mountain, *d* all ablaze, was thrown into the sea. A third *e* of the sea turned into blood, *f* ⁹a third *g* of the living creatures in the sea died, and a third of the ships were destroyed.

¹⁰The third angel sounded his trumpet, and a great star, blazing like a torch, fell from the sky *h* on a third of the rivers and on the springs of water *i* — ¹¹the name of the star is Wormwood. *a* A third *j* of the waters turned bitter, and many people died from the waters that had become bitter. *k*

¹²The fourth angel sounded his trumpet, and a third of the sun was struck, a third of the moon, and a third of the stars, so that a third *l* of them turned dark. *m* A third of the day was without light, and also a third of the night.

¹³As I watched, I heard an eagle that was flying in midair *n* call out in a loud voice: "Woe! Woe! Woe *o* to the inhabitants of the earth, because of the trumpet blasts about to be sounded by the other three angels!"

9 The fifth angel sounded his trumpet, and I saw a star that had fallen from the sky to the earth. *p* The star was given the key to the shaft of the Abyss. *q* ²When he opened the Abyss, smoke rose from it like the smoke from a gigantic furnace. *r* The sun and sky were darkened *s* by the smoke from the Abyss. ³And out of the smoke locusts *t* came down upon the earth and were given power like that of scorpions *u* of the earth. ⁴They were told not to harm *v* the grass of the earth or any plant or tree, *w* but only those people who did not have the seal of God on their foreheads. *x* ⁵They were not given power to kill them, but only to torture them for five months. *y* And the agony they suffered was like that of the sting of a scorpion *z* when it strikes a man. ⁶During those days men will seek death, but will not find it; they will long to die, but death will elude them. *a*

⁷The locusts looked like horses prepared for battle. *b* On their heads they wore something like crowns of gold, and their faces resembled human faces. *c* ⁸Their hair was like women's hair, and their teeth were like lions' teeth. *d* ⁹They had breastplates like breastplates of iron, and the sound of their wings was like the thundering of many horses and chariots rushing into battle. *e* ¹⁰They had tails and stings like scorpions, and in their tails they had power to torment people for five months. *f* ¹¹They had as king over them the angel of the Abyss, *g* whose name in Hebrew is Abaddon, and in Greek, Apollyon. *b*

¹²The first woe is past; two other woes are yet to come. *h*

¹³The sixth angel sounded his trumpet, and I heard a voice coming from the horns *c i* of the golden altar that is before God. *j* ¹⁴It said to the sixth angel who had the trumpet, "Release the four angels who are bound at the great river Euphrates." *k* ¹⁵And the four angels who had been kept ready for this very hour and day and month and year were released to kill a third of mankind. *l* ¹⁶The number of the mounted troops was two hundred million. I heard their number. *m*

---

a 11 That is, Bitterness   *b 11 Abaddon* and *Apollyon* mean *Destroyer.*   *c 13* That is, projections

---

either a human army or a host of evil forces unleashed to wreak havoc. That God limits their destructiveness, both in force (9:6) and duration (9:10), suggests his mercy and underlines his sovereignty. But God also intensifies the victims' pain by preventing their death, so we can't read this limitation as a decrease in the judgment's severity.

The killing of one-third of the world's population is catastrophic. But it's less severe than the massacres reflected in many other apocalyptic traditions. Often in Revelation God inflicts judgments on a minority (one-third or a tenth), hoping others will repent. The death of one-third of the world's population is definitely judgment, but it also reflects mercy on the two-thirds who are spared.

📖 Today we might terrify some people by talking about a pervasively destructive computer virus. To the

atmospheric calamity of hail we can add floods, blizzards, ice storms, earthquakes, fires, hurricanes, tornadoes, mudslides, smog, acid rain, and global warming. Water pollution and a shrinking supply of drinking water are serious problems in some areas. We are unaccustomed to thinking of environmental judgments of God. But has it occurred to you that some of them may be?

The Bible is useful for teaching (2 Tim. 3:16), but specific passages are helpful for particular circumstances. Passages like this shake us from our complacency. They provide a reality check, destroying our fantasy that life will always continue as it is. And they summon us to recognize and work to alleviate the terrible suffering in the world around us.

[17]The horses and riders I saw in my vision looked like this: Their breastplates were fiery red, dark blue, and yellow as sulfur. The heads of the horses resembled the heads of lions, and out of their mouths[n] came fire, smoke and sulfur.[o] [18]A third of mankind was killed[p] by the three plagues of fire, smoke and sulfur[q] that came out of their mouths. [19]The power of the horses was in their mouths and in their tails; for their tails were like snakes, having heads with which they inflict injury.

[20]The rest of mankind that were not killed by these plagues still did not repent of the work of their hands;[r] they did not stop worshiping demons,[s] and idols of gold, silver, bronze, stone and wood—idols that cannot see or hear or walk.[t] [21]Nor did they repent[u] of their murders, their magic arts,[v] their sexual immorality[w] or their thefts.

The Angel and the Little Scroll

10 Then I saw another mighty angel[x] coming down from heaven. He was robed in a cloud, with a rainbow above his head; his face was like the sun,[y] and his legs were like fiery pillars.[z] [2]He was holding a little scroll, which lay open in his hand. He planted his right foot on the sea and his left foot on the land, [3]and he gave a loud shout like the roar of a lion. When he shouted, the voices of the seven thunders[a] spoke. [4]And when the seven thunders spoke, I was about to write; but I heard a voice from heaven say, "Seal up what the seven thunders have said and do not write it down."[b]

[5]Then the angel I had seen standing on the sea and on the land raised his right hand to heaven.[c] [6]And he swore by him who lives for ever and ever, who created the heavens and all that is in them, the earth and all that is in it, and the sea and all that is in it,[d] and said, "There will be no more delay![e] [7]But in the days when the seventh angel is about to sound his trumpet, the mystery[f] of God will be accomplished, just as he announced to his servants the prophets."

[8]Then the voice that I had heard from heaven[g] spoke to me once more: "Go, take the scroll that lies open in the hand of the angel who is standing on the sea and on the land."

[9]So I went to the angel and asked him to give me the little scroll. He said to me, "Take it and eat it. It will turn your stomach sour, but in your mouth it will be as sweet as honey."[h] [10]I took the little scroll from the angel's hand and ate it. It tasted as sweet as honey in my mouth, but when I had eaten it, my stomach turned sour. [11]Then I was told, "You must prophesy[i] again about many peoples, nations, languages and kings."

The Two Witnesses

11 I was given a reed like a measuring rod[j] and was told, "Go and measure the temple of God and the altar, and count the worshipers there. [2]But exclude the outer court;[k] do not measure it, because it has been given to the Gentiles.[l] They will trample on the holy city[m] for 42 months.[n] [3]And I will give power to my two

Cross-references

9:17
[n] Rev 11:5 [o] ver 18

9:18
[p] ver 15 [q] ver 17

9:20
[r] Dt 31:29 [s] 1Co 10:20 [t] Ps 115:4-7; 135:15-17; Da 5:23
9:21
[u] Rev 2:21 [v] Rev 18:23 [w] Rev 17:2,5

10:1
[x] Rev 5:2 [y] Mt 17:2; Rev 1:16 [z] Rev 1:15

10:3
[a] Rev 4:5

10:4
[b] Da 8:26; 12:4,9; Rev 22:10
10:5
[c] Da 12:7

10:6
[d] Rev 4:11; 14:7 [e] Rev 16:17
10:7
[f] Ro 16:25
10:8
[g] ver 4

10:9
[h] Jer 15:16; Eze 2:8–3:3
10:11
[i] Eze 37:4,9

11:1
[j] Eze 40:3; Rev 21:15
11:2
[k] Eze 40:17,20 [l] Lk 21:24 [m] Rev 21:2 [n] Da 7:25; Rev 13:5

Revelation 10:1–11

It's possible that the "little scroll" is the book whose seals were broken in 6:1—8:1. Eating the scroll suggests internalizing its contents, enabling the eater to prophesy (see Ezek. 3:1). The fact that it turned bitter in John's stomach probably points to its sad content (cf. Ezek. 2:10). In contrast to Ezekiel, who was to deliver a message only to Israel, John and the two witnesses (Rev. 11:3,9) would prophesy to many.

This passage connects to us at several points: (1) The awesomeness of the obedient angel implies that God rules all supernatural forces. (2) The thunders reveal that some matters aren't yet ours to know. (3) The promise of "no more delay" reminds us that waiting won't last forever. (4) We are to follow John's example, obeying even when the message we are called to proclaim is bitter or makes no sense to us. (5) The message of Revelation concerns "many peoples"; no one is exempt from its warnings.

Revelation 11:1–14

Scholars debate the identity and time period of the two witnesses. The figures from the past to which they allude are easier to determine: The olive trees and lampstands recall the godly leaders Joshua and Zerubbabel (Zech. 4). Calling down fire and bringing about a drought hearkens back to Elijah. And turning water into blood and sending other plagues points to Moses. The two witnesses most likely represent the prophetic witness of the church as a whole.

witnesses,[o] and they will prophesy for 1,260 days, clothed in sackcloth."[p] 4These
are the two olive trees[q] and the two lampstands that stand before the Lord of the
earth.[r] 5If anyone tries to harm them, fire comes from their mouths and devours
their enemies.[s] This is how anyone who wants to harm them must die.[t] 6These men
have power to shut up the sky so that it will not rain during the time they are prophesying; and they have power to turn the waters into blood[u] and to strike the earth
with every kind of plague as often as they want.

7Now when they have finished their testimony, the beast[v] that comes up from the
Abyss will attack them,[w] and overpower and kill them. 8Their bodies will lie in the
street of the great city, which is figuratively called Sodom[x] and Egypt, where also
their Lord was crucified.[y] 9For three and a half days men from every people, tribe,
language and nation will gaze on their bodies and refuse them burial.[z] 10The inhabitants of the earth[a] will gloat over them and will celebrate by sending each other
gifts,[b] because these two prophets had tormented those who live on the earth.
11But after the three and a half days a breath of life from God entered them,[c] and
they stood on their feet, and terror struck those who saw them. 12Then they heard
a loud voice from heaven saying to them, "Come up here."[d] And they went up to
heaven in a cloud,[e] while their enemies looked on.

13At that very hour there was a severe earthquake[f] and a tenth of the city collapsed. Seven thousand people were killed in the earthquake, and the survivors were
terrified and gave glory[g] to the God of heaven.[h]

14The second woe has passed; the third woe is coming soon.[i]

11:3 [o] Rev 1:5 [p] Ge 37:34
11:4 [q] Ps 52:8; Jer 11:16; Zec 4:3, 11 [r] Zec 4:14
11:5 [s] 2Ki 1:10; Jer 5:14 [t] Nu 16:29,35
11:6 [u] Ex 7:17,19
11:7 [v] Rev 13:1-4 [w] Da 7:21
11:8 [x] Isa 1:9 [y] Heb 13:12
11:9 [z] Ps 79:2,3
11:10 [a] Rev 3:10 [b] Est 9:19,22
11:11 [c] Eze 37:5,9,10,14
11:12 [d] Rev 4:1 [e] 2Ki 2:11; Ac 1:9
11:13 [f] Rev 6:12 [g] Rev 14:7 [h] Rev 16:11
11:14 [i] Rev 8:13

The two witnesses provide a model for us, just as do other men and women of God (cf. 1 Cor. 10:11; 11:1). God's servants who proclaim his Word can't always expect deliverance (cf. Heb. 11:39). We are to be Spirit-empowered witnesses to the world, ready to pay any cost and utterly dependent on God's power to accomplish his purposes. In the end God vindicates his servants in the sight of those who have ridiculed them (vv. 11–13). This is a frequent Biblical pattern (Ps. 23:5).

Some of those who scorn our message now may repent later. God's judgments get people's attention, but there is no guarantee they will soften their hearts and respond. The appropriate time for repentance is always "now" (cf. 2 Cor. 6:2). Have you been able to effectively communicate this urgency in your personal witness?

11:18

Signs of Discontent

We live in a world filled with discontentment. Some of the signs:

Family Discord
In 1998, 2,256,000 American couples were married and 1,135,000 couples divorced.[2]

2,256,000
COUPLES
MARRIED
1,135,000
COUPLES
DIVORCED

Crime

24.2 million people in the United States were the victims of crime in 2001.[1]

Addictions
In 2001, the rate of illicit drug use in the United States was 8.7 percent for all males over 12 years of age and 5.5 percent for all females over 12 years of age.[3]

2001 Rate of illicit drug use
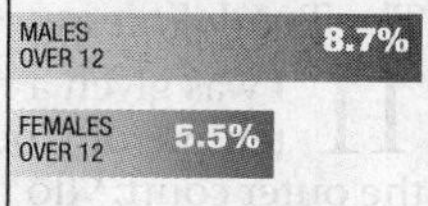
MALES
OVER 12
8.7%
FEMALES
OVER 12
5.5%

Suicide
Over **29,000** Americans committed suicide in 2000.[4]

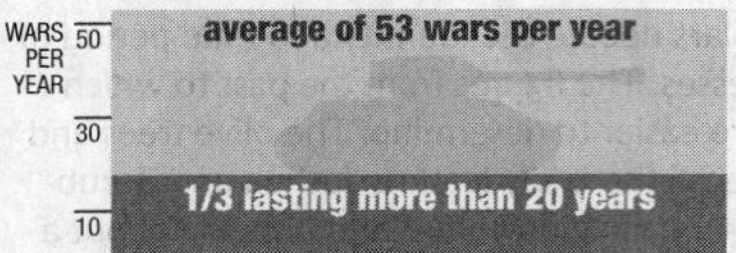
WARS
PER
YEAR
50
30
10
average of 53 wars per year
1/3 lasting more than 20 years
1990
1995
2000

Wars
From 1990 to 2000 an average of 53 wars were fought each year. One-third of those wars have lasted more than 20 years.[5]

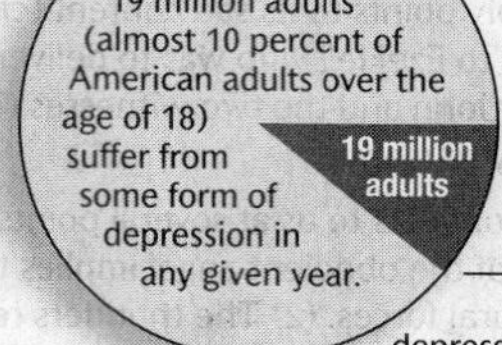
19 million
adults
Depression
19 million adults (almost 10 percent of American adults over the age of 18) suffer from some form of depression in any given year.

1 in 6 suffers serious depression at some point in life.[6]

Sources: [1] U.S. Census Bureau (2002:189) [2] U.S. Census Bureau (2000:59) [3] Wurman (2000:150) [4] Wurman (2000:75) [5] World Almanac (2003:94) [6] Smith (1999:58)

The Seventh Trumpet

15The seventh angel sounded his trumpet,*j* and there were loud voices*k* in heaven, which said:

"The kingdom of the world has become the kingdom of our Lord and
of his Christ,*l*
and he will reign for ever and ever."*m*

16And the twenty-four elders,*n* who were seated on their thrones before God, fell on their faces and worshiped God, 17saying:

"We give thanks to you, Lord God Almighty,*o*
the One who is and who was,
because you have taken your great power
and have begun to reign.*p*
18The nations were angry;*q*
and your wrath has come.
The time has come for judging the dead,
and for rewarding your servants the prophets*r*
and your saints and those who reverence your name,
both small and great*s*—
and for destroying those who destroy the earth."

19Then God's temple*t* in heaven was opened, and within his temple was seen the ark of his covenant. And there came flashes of lightning, rumblings, peals of thunder, an earthquake and a great hailstorm.*u*

The Woman and the Dragon

12 A great and wondrous sign appeared in heaven: a woman clothed with the sun, with the moon under her feet and a crown of twelve stars on her head. 2She was pregnant and cried out in pain*v* as she was about to give birth. 3Then another sign appeared in heaven: an enormous red dragon with seven heads and ten

11:15
j Rev 10:7
k Rev 16:17; 19:1
l Rev 12:10
m Da 2:44; 7:14,27

11:16
n Rev 4:4

11:17
o Rev 1:8
p Rev 19:6

11:18
q Ps 2:1 *r* Rev 10:7
s Rev 19:5

11:19
t Rev 15:5,8
u Rev 16:21

12:2
v Gal 4:19

Revelation 11:15–19

The seventh trumpet fits the occasion: Trumpets were blown when a new king ascended his throne. Scripture promised that the Messiah would "reign for ever" (v. 15; cf. Isa. 9:7), Daniel emphasized the final triumph of God's kingdom over world empires (Dan. 2:44), and Jews stressed that God and his people would reign in the world to come. The kingdom "of our Lord and of his Christ" recalls Psalm 2:2, where the nations who challenge the Lord and his Anointed One will ultimately be crushed.

The earth is the Lord's (Ps. 24:1; Rev. 11:15), and those who destroy it challenge his rule. Environmental ruin harms not only the rest of creation but also people, starting with the poor. Those who corrupt or abuse God's creation in any age attract judgment.

Those who face grief or hardship in the world can find comfort in these verses. This world belongs to God, and he will right all wrongs on the Day of Judgment, shattering all opposition. This passage also invites worship as we contemplate God's coming rule. And it reminds us that God will reward (or punish; 6:15–17) both small and great.

Many environmentalists focus on the problem of global warming, but far more immediate threats include unsafe drinking water and the improper dumping of waste. How we treat other people's property reflects our

level of respect for them. What does your treatment of and concern for his creation (human and otherwise) say about your estimation of God?

Revelation 12:1—13:1a

For John the woman probably represented Israel or its faithful remnant, since the prophets often pictured righteous Israel as the mother of the restored future remnant (Isa. 54:1; 66:7–10; Mic. 4:9–10; 5:3)—an image they mixed with that of Israel as a bride (Isa. 62:5). In Jewish tradition Zion or Jerusalem often appeared as a mother. In one passage, God promised the suffering, pregnant Israel that she would truly bear new life in the time of the resurrection, the day of God's wrath in which he would slay the serpent (Isa. 26:17—27:1).

Michael was Israel's guardian and defender (Dan. 10:13,21), despite certain limitations to his power (Dan. 12:1; Jude 9). Here, though, Michael and his forces, representing the heavenly victory won by Christ on Earth, cast down Satan's forces. Satan's being hurled to Earth ended his position of privilege in God's court. His loss of "place" (12:8) contrasts with the "place" of refuge (12:5, 14) God provides his own persecuted people.

Our battle is spiritual, God is sovereign, and the devil's time is limited. The fact that Revelation recycles the ancient serpent of Genesis (v. 9; Gen. 3:1–15) for its day underlines the continuity of the enemy throughout history.

horns [w] and seven crowns [x] on his heads. [4] His tail swept a third [y] of the stars out of the sky and flung them to the earth. [z] The dragon stood in front of the woman who was about to give birth, so that he might devour her child [a] the moment it was born. [5] She gave birth to a son, a male child, who will rule all the nations with an iron scepter. [b] And her child was snatched up to God and to his throne. [6] The woman fled into the desert to a place prepared for her by God, where she might be taken care of for 1,260 days. [c]

[7] And there was war in heaven. Michael and his angels fought against the dragon, [d] and the dragon and his angels fought back. [8] But he was not strong enough, and they lost their place in heaven. [9] The great dragon was hurled down—that ancient serpent [e] called the devil, [f] or Satan, who leads the whole world astray. [g] He was hurled to the earth, [h] and his angels with him.

[10] Then I heard a loud voice in heaven [i] say:

"Now have come the salvation and the power and the kingdom of our
    God,
  and the authority of his Christ.
For the accuser of our brothers, [j]
  who accuses them before our God day and night,
  has been hurled down.
[11] They overcame him
  by the blood of the Lamb [k]
  and by the word of their testimony; [l]
they did not love their lives so much
  as to shrink from death. [m]
[12] Therefore rejoice, you heavens [n]
  and you who dwell in them!
But woe [o] to the earth and the sea, [p]
  because the devil has gone down to you!
He is filled with fury,
  because he knows that his time is short."

[13] When the dragon [q] saw that he had been hurled to the earth, he pursued the woman who had given birth to the male child. [r] [14] The woman was given the two wings of a great eagle, [s] so that she might fly to the place prepared for her in the desert, where she would be taken care of for a time, times and half a time, [t] out of the serpent's reach. [15] Then from his mouth the serpent spewed water like a river, to overtake the woman and sweep her away with the torrent. [16] But the earth helped the woman by opening its mouth and swallowing the river that the dragon had spewed out of his mouth. [17] Then the dragon was enraged at the woman and went off to make war [u] against the rest of her offspring [v]—those who obey God's commandments [w] and hold to the testimony of Jesus. [x] [1] And the dragon [a] stood on the shore of the sea.

13

The Beast out of the Sea

And I saw a beast coming out of the sea. [y] He had ten horns and seven heads, [z] with ten crowns on his horns, and on each head a blasphemous name. [a] [2] The beast I saw resembled a leopard, [b] but had feet like those of a bear [c] and a mouth like that

---

a [1] Some late manuscripts And I

We are unequipped for life in the real world if we are blind to spiritual battle. But we are disabled for life if we are preoccupied with it. This passage affirms that the enemy is defeated. He knows his time is short. There are three keys in verse 11 to the accuser being overcome: God's people (1) claimed the blood of the Lamb; (2) proclaimed the Word; and (3) weren't afraid of dying. How does this relate to your encounter with the adversary?

Revelation 13:1b–10

Many believed at the time of John's revelation that the cruel emperor Nero would come back as the final antichrist. But John spoke of an oppressor after the current one (17:8). The issue is more the pattern than the person—the "secret power of lawlessness" rather than a "man of lawlessness" (2 Thess. 2:3,7). The behavior of evil rulers throughout history fits this sad pattern.

12:3 w Da 7:7,20; Rev 13:1; x Rev 19:12
12:4 y Rev 8:7 z Da 8:10 a Mt 2:16
12:5 b Ps 2:9; Rev 2:27
12:6 c Rev 11:2
12:7 d ver 3
12:9 e Ge 3:1-7 f Mt 25:41 g Rev 20:3,8,10 h Lk 10:18; Jn 12:31
12:10 i Rev 11:15 j Job 1:9-11; Zec 3:1
12:11 k Rev 7:14 l Rev 6:9 m Lk 14:26
12:12 n Ps 96:11; Isa 49:13; Rev 18:20 o Rev 8:13 p Rev 10:6
12:13 q ver 3 r ver 5
12:14 s Ex 19:4 t Da 7:25
12:17 u Rev 11:7 v Ge 3:15 w Rev 14:12 x Rev 1:2
13:1 y Da 7:1-6; Rev 15:2 z Rev 12:3 a Da 11:36; Rev 17:3
13:2 b Da 7:6 c Da 7:5

Spiritual Warfare

Revelation 12:7–9 portrays spiritual warfare in the heavens corresponding to Christ's triumph on the earth (12:5,10). Clearly this indicates that our battle is spiritual (cf. Eph. 1:21; 6:1–17), a reality recognized early in Scripture. The following describes some of the Bible's major spiritual battles. The list isn't exhaustive.

Battlefield/ Text	Type of Encounter	Stakes	People's Use or Disuse of Spiritual Resources/Gifts	Supernatural Intervention	Outcome
Garden of Eden (Gen. 3:1–24)	Temptation; direct confrontation with Satan	Humanity's innocence or sinful nature	Lack of obedience to God's command; lack of faith in God's word	God speaking to Adam (2:15–17); cherubim guarding Eden and protecting access to the tree of life	Satan won this victory. As a result, humanity was infected with a sinful nature.
Jericho (Josh. 5:13—6:27)	Taking a city	Israel's confidence in taking the promised land	Obedience to God's explicit directions for taking the city; faith	Captain of the Lord's host appearing to Joshua; God speaking to Joshua	The walls of Jericho fell, and the Israelites took the city.
Valley near the hill of Moreh (Judg. 7:1–25)	Battle against enemy forces	Israel's freedom from Midianite oppression	Obedience to God's directions; overhearing enemy's dream and its interpretation; faith	God speaking to Gideon; God giving dream to enemy and causing enemy's confusion	Israel routed the fleeing army.
Valley of Elah (1 Sam. 17:1–58)	Battle against enemy forces	Establishment of David as God's anointed and defeat of the Philistines	Fear on part of Israel's army; David's faith and willingness to fight in God's name	God helping David kill Goliath	Israel's army defeated the Philistines.
Mount Carmel (1 Kings 18:16–46)	Confrontation with false prophets	God's reputation over that of false gods; Israelite worship	Elijah's challenge to false prophets in God's name; faith; prayer; prophecy. Elijah's killing of false prophets	God answering Elijah's prayer and consuming the sacrifice, including the altar, in a spectacular display of power; God energizing Elijah with power to outrun Ahab's chariot	The people acknowledged the Lord.
Unknown (2 Kings 6:8–17)	Enemy attempt to kill God's prophet	Elisha's life; God's prophetic voice in Israel	Faith; prayer to open servant's eyes and to strike the enemy blind, as well as to give back their sight	God giving Elisha prophetic knowledge of the enemy king's war plans; God opening the eyes of Elisha's servant; Elisha's servant seeing chariots of fire protecting them; God answering Elisha's prayers	Elisha led his blinded enemies to Samaria. The enemy army was fed, not destroyed. The enemy king stopped raiding Israel.
Plain of Dura, province of Babylon (Dan. 3:1–30)	King demanding Israelite worship of false God	Worship of God versus an idol; testimony about God to King Nebuchadnezzar	Defied king by obeying commandment not to worship other gods; faith	God keeping three Hebrews from harm in the fiery furnace; Christ's pre-incarnate appearance	The three Hebrews were cast into the fire. The king acknowledged God's greatness.
Desert (Matt. 4:1–11; Mark 1:12–13; Luke 4:1–13)	Temptation; direct confrontation with Satan	Jesus' mission on Earth	Filled with the Holy Spirit; fasting; reliance on and obedience to the Word of God	Angelic appearance	Jesus resisted Satan's three temptations.
Garden of Gethsemene; the cross; the resurrection (Matt. 26:36—28:15; Mark 14:32—16:13; Luke 22:39—24:35; John 18:1—19:23; cf. 1 Cor. 2:7–8; Col. 1:15–22; 2:13–15)	Inner conflict to submit to God's will; direct confrontation with Satan and his forces	Jesus' submission to the Father's will; the plan of salvation for all humanity	Obedience to God's will; filled with the Holy Spirit; prayer; faith; healing (of Malchus); prophecy (thief on the cross); endurance of intense physical, mental, and spiritual suffering	Angelic appearance	Jesus submitted to his arrest and was crucified. God raised him from the dead. The plan of salvation was accomplished in every detail.

Source: NIV Application Commentary, Revelation (2000)

The Image of God in Human Beings

Theologians and preachers agree that the "image of God" (Gen. 1:26) is potentially the most fundamental notion Christianity and Judaism have to offer the world. But it's imperative that we first examine the Biblical texts to understand just what's meant by "image of God."

Humans, male and female, stand tall as the climax of creation because they alone have a nature that includes the "image of God." Scholars have debated the distinction between being made *in* God's image and being *the actual* image of God, and we should probably listen to them. But important as that distinction might be, the fact that humans are made in God's image is a *constitutional*, not just a developmental, difference.

Second, this image of God is evidently passed from human to human through natural reproduction, as we infer from Genesis 5:3, where Seth bears the image of his father, Adam. We should observe here that the fall (Gen. 3), regardless of what it did to humans or how it impacted the image of God, didn't erase that image in humans. After all, it was after the fall that Seth acquired the image of God from his father, Adam.

> The "measure of humans" isn't an abstract definition or set of commandments: It's the very person, practice, and life of Jesus Christ.

Third, the image of God implies fundamental respect for all other human beings. This is an uncontestable inference from Genesis 9:6, where murder is prohibited because humans are God's image-bearers—while the killing of animals isn't. Murder is an action by humans against God, not just against other humans.

Fourth, in the New Testament "image of God" takes on the goal of spiritual development for Christians. The apostle Paul developed this notion. He placed the concept of "image of God" smack-dab in the middle of his understanding that the death and resurrection of Jesus Christ set off a restoration work, a new creation, and the beginning of the return to Eden, to Paradise (Rom. 8:19–21; 1 Cor 15:24–28).

Fifth, the highpoint of Christian perceptions of the image of God is that Jesus Christ is God's perfect image, as the second Adam. The "measure of humans" isn't an abstract definition or set of commandments: It's the very person, practice, and life of Jesus Christ (1 Cor. 15:45–49). In him we see not someone made *in* God's image, but the actual image of God himself (Col. 1:15). George Carey called Jesus the "Paradigm Man," leaving the wonderfully tantalizing suggestion that Adam and Eve, and all humans, are to be understood in light of Christ—not the other way around. Christology (the study of Christ) underlies anthropology (the study of people).

Finally, in the Revelation John described the final work of Satan as an attempt to make an "image" of the beast. *We are led to think of this as a copy of God's perfect image in his Son, Jesus Christ.*

In short, we can say that the image of God is the special nature of human beings. Why? Because they are formed in accordance with God's nature, a nature that finds its most perfect expression in Jesus Christ. This leads to the ultimate glorification of Christians. But, tragically, it also finds its most hideous expression in Satan's cheap copy, the beast (antichrist).

Scot McKnight, Karl A. Olsson Professor of Religious Studies at North Park University in Chicago, Illinois

of a lion.[d] The dragon gave the beast his power and his throne and great authority.[e] 3 One of the heads of the beast seemed to have had a fatal wound, but the fatal wound had been healed.[f] The whole world was astonished[g] and followed the beast. 4 Men worshiped the dragon because he had given authority to the beast, and they also worshiped the beast and asked, "Who is like[h] the beast? Who can make war against him?"

5 The beast was given a mouth to utter proud words and blasphemies[i] and to exercise his authority for forty-two months.[j] 6 He opened his mouth to blaspheme God, and to slander his name and his dwelling place and those who live in heaven.[k] 7 He was given power to make war[l] against the saints and to conquer them. And he was given authority over every tribe, people, language and nation.[m] 8 All inhabitants of the earth[n] will worship the beast—all whose names have not been written in the book of life[o] belonging to the Lamb that was slain from the creation of the world.[a][p]

9 He who has an ear, let him hear.[q]

10 If anyone is to go into captivity,
    into captivity he will go.
If anyone is to be killed[b] with the sword,
    with the sword he will be killed.[r]

This calls for patient endurance and faithfulness[s] on the part of the saints.[t]

The Beast out of the Earth

11 Then I saw another beast, coming out of the earth. He had two horns like a lamb, but he spoke like a dragon. 12 He exercised all the authority[u] of the first beast on his behalf,[v] and made the earth and its inhabitants worship the first beast,[w] whose fatal wound had been healed.[x] 13 And he performed great and miraculous signs,[y] even causing fire to come down from heaven[z] to earth in full view of men. 14 Because of the signs[a] he was given power to do on behalf of the first beast, he deceived[b] the inhabitants of the earth. He ordered them to set up an image in honor of the beast who was wounded by the sword and yet lived. 15 He was given power to give breath to the image of the first beast, so that it could speak and cause all who refused to worship the image to be killed.[c] 16 He also forced everyone, small and great,[d] rich and poor, free and slave, to receive a mark on his right hand or on his

---

[a] 8 Or written from the creation of the world in the book of life belonging to the Lamb that was slain
[b] 10 Some manuscripts anyone kills

13:2 [d] Da 7:4 [e] Rev 16:10
13:3 [f] ver 12, 14 [g] Rev 17:8
13:4 [h] Ex 15:11
13:5 [i] Da 7:8,11,20,25; 11:36; 2Th 2:4 [j] Rev 11:2
13:6 [k] Rev 12:12
13:7 [l] Da 7:21; Rev 11:7 [m] Rev 5:9
13:8 [n] Rev 3:10 [o] Rev 3:5; 20:12 [p] Mt 25:34
13:9 [q] Rev 2:7
13:10 [r] Jer 15:2; 43:11 [s] Heb 6:12 [t] Rev 14:12
13:12 [u] ver 4 [v] ver 14 [w] Rev 14:9,11 [x] ver 3
13:13 [y] Mt 24:24 [z] 1Ki 18:38; Rev 20:9
13:14 [a] 2Th 2:9,10 [b] Rev 12:9
13:15 [c] Da 3:3-6
13:16 [d] Rev 19:5

This passage testifies to the awfulness to which humans can descend in following the devil's ways (Eph. 2:1–3). The world's Neros, Hitlers, Idi Amins, and Saddam Husseins; the trafficking in human flesh; the genocides that happen with horrifying frequency—all testify to the reality of demonic power amplifying human sin and crushing moral restraint. How do you respond when you hear of an evil outbreak in some part of the world? Prayer may seem like a weak or insignificant response, yet Revelation stresses the impact of the saints' prayers (5:8). And God uses our weakness to display his strength (cf. 2 Cor. 12:9–10). What other responses might be appropriate for you?

Revelation 13:11–18

Amid much speculation about the identity of the second beast, two points are clear: (1) The second character is dedicated to promoting worship of the first; (2) Although deceitful, this second beast has a religious quality; elsewhere in Revelation he's referred to as "the false prophet" (16:13; 19:20; 20:10). Most interpreters see a connection between the second beast and the emperor worship of John's day.

Some scholars think the significance of the number associated with the beast was apparent to the first audience. The fact that verse 18 invites the hearer to interpret the riddle implies that the answer was available to believers in the seven churches.

Even in Christian circles we confront the temptation to compromise our values. Job security often carries more weight in our thinking than justice. Every time we purchase something we don't need just because our neighbors have it, we have "bought into" the world's system. If status and materialism so entice us, how will we stand against persecution?

Satan and his followers like to imitate God. This means that those who don't embrace the complete message of the cross and its suffering are susceptible to being taken in by a counterfeit. What counterfeit schemes have you seen crop up recently? What makes them effective in deceiving people?

13:16
e Rev 14:9
13:17
f Rev 14:9
g Rev 14:11; 15:2
13:18
h Rev 17:9
i Rev 15:2; 21:17

forehead,[e] [17]so that no one could buy or sell unless he had the mark,[f] which is the name of the beast or the number of his name. [g]

[18]This calls for wisdom. [h] If anyone has insight, let him calculate the number of the beast, for it is man's number.[i] His number is 666.

The Lamb and the 144,000

14:1
j Rev 5:6 k Ps 2:6
l Rev 7:4
m Rev 3:12

14 Then I looked, and there before me was the Lamb,[j] standing on Mount Zion,[k] and with him 144,000[l] who had his name and his Father's name[m] written on their foreheads. [2]And I heard a sound from heaven like the roar of rushing waters[n] and like a loud peal of thunder. The sound I heard was like that of harpists playing their harps. [o] [3]And they sang a new song[p] before the throne and before the four living creatures and the elders. No one could learn the song except the 144,000[q] who had been redeemed from the earth. [4]These are those who did not defile themselves with women, for they kept themselves pure.[r] They follow the Lamb wherever he goes. They were purchased from among men[s] and offered as firstfruits[t] to God and the Lamb. [5]No lie was found in their mouths;[u] they are blameless.[v]

14:2
n Rev 1:15
o Rev 5:8
14:3
p Rev 5:9 q ver 1
14:4
r 2Co 11:2; Rev 3:4
s Rev 5:9 t Jas 1:18
14:5
u Ps 32:2; Zep 3:13
v Eph 5:27

The Three Angels

14:6
w Rev 8:13
x Rev 3:10
y Rev 13:7
14:7
z Rev 15:4
a Rev 11:13
b Rev 8:10

[6]Then I saw another angel flying in midair, [w] and he had the eternal gospel to proclaim to those who live on the earth[x]—to every nation, tribe, language and people.[y] [7]He said in a loud voice, "Fear God[z] and give him glory,[a] because the hour of his judgment has come. Worship him who made the heavens, the earth, the sea and the springs of water."[b]

14:8
c Isa 21:9; Jer 51:8
d Rev 17:2,4;
18:3,9

[8]A second angel followed and said, "Fallen! Fallen is Babylon the Great,[c] which made all the nations drink the maddening wine of her adulteries."[d]

14:9
e Rev 13:14
14:10
f Isa 51:17;
Jer 25:15
g Rev 18:6

[9]A third angel followed them and said in a loud voice: "If anyone worships the beast and his image[e] and receives his mark on the forehead or on the hand, [10]he, too, will drink of the wine of God's fury,[f] which has been poured full strength into the cup of his wrath. [g] He will be tormented with burning sulfur in the presence of the holy angels and of the Lamb. [11]And the smoke of their torment rises for ever and ever. [h] There is no rest day or night for those who worship the beast and his image, or for anyone who receives the mark of his name." [12]This calls for patient endur-

14:11
h Isa 34:10;
Rev 19:3

Revelation 14:1–5

Why are the 144,000 celibate? As a portrait of God's army ready for holy war, they resemble Israel's troops who kept themselves from women prior to battle (cf. Deut. 23:10; 1 Sam. 21:5; 2 Sam. 11:11). Revelation also portrays unrepentant humanity as a prostitute (Rev. 17:1–5) and those faithful to Christ as a pure spouse (19:7; 21:2,9). These 144,000 have refused to commit immorality with Babylon.

The spirit of the Roman Empire (Babylon) is alive today, claiming tolerance of many gods but suppressing dissent from those who preach the truth of the one God and his Son, Jesus Christ. The message of purity makes a strong point: Christians are to remain faithful to Christ if they wish to be prepared for and engage in the Lamb's holy war. Unlike the world (13:7), believers can't indulge in divided interests. No lie was found on the lips of the Lamb's army. Its members were blameless. How do you stay disentangled from the world's system *when it so easily claims others' allegiance?*

Revelation 14:6–13

The term "gospel" may not simply refer to the "Good News" of Jesus. In the prophetic tradition, "good

news" included announcements of judgment on the enemies of God's people (Nah. 1:15). The Greek word translated "maddening" here and in 18:3 can mean passion, but normally in Revelation it refers to anger (cf. 12:12; 15:1,7: 16:1). God's wine can be seen as righteous anger (judgment) against the "adulteries" Babylon has brought on the nations. Ancients typically diluted every part of wine with two parts water, except to get drunk. But God administers this wine of his anger at "full strength."

Does God hate sinners? No. He loves them so much he sent his Son to die for them (John 3:16). Is God angry at what sin has done to his creation? Yes. The image of God's cup of wrath is frightening, and John didn't water it down. This message is comforting to persecuted Christians, reminding them that God will judge their oppressors. But Revelation was written not just to persecuted churches but also to those in relative security and prosperity. Do we downplay the reality of God's judgment and anger over sin? Think about how you can communicate this message, at the same time affirming God's great love for people. Do you think it's possible for you to effectively do both?

ance on the part of the saints[i] who obey God's commandments and remain faithful to Jesus.

13Then I heard a voice from heaven say, "Write: Blessed are the dead who die in the Lord[j] from now on."

"Yes," says the Spirit, "they will rest from their labor, for their deeds will follow them."

The Harvest of the Earth

14I looked, and there before me was a white cloud, and seated on the cloud was one "like a son of man"[a][k] with a crown[l] of gold on his head and a sharp sickle in his hand. 15Then another angel came out of the temple and called in a loud voice to him who was sitting on the cloud, "Take your sickle[m] and reap, because the time to reap has come, for the harvest[n] of the earth is ripe." 16So he who was seated on the cloud swung his sickle over the earth, and the earth was harvested.

17Another angel came out of the temple in heaven, and he too had a sharp sickle. 18Still another angel, who had charge of the fire, came from the altar and called in a loud voice to him who had the sharp sickle, "Take your sharp sickle and gather the clusters of grapes from the earth's vine, because its grapes are ripe." 19The angel swung his sickle on the earth, gathered its grapes and threw them into the great winepress of God's wrath.[o] 20They were trampled in the winepress[p] outside the city,[q] and blood flowed out of the press, rising as high as the horses' bridles for a distance of 1,600 stadia.[b]

Seven Angels With Seven Plagues

15 I saw in heaven another great and marvelous sign:[r] seven angels[s] with the seven last plagues[t]—last, because with them God's wrath is completed. 2And I saw what looked like a sea of glass[u] mixed with fire and, standing beside the sea, those who had been victorious over the beast and his image[v] and over the number of his name. They held harps given them by God 3and sang the song of Moses[w] the servant of God and the song of the Lamb:

> "Great and marvelous are your deeds,[x]
>   Lord God Almighty.
> Just and true are your ways,[y]
>   King of the ages.

a 14 Daniel 7:13   b 20 That is, about 180 miles (about 300 kilometers)

Side references

14:12 i Rev 13:10
14:13 j 1Co 15:18; 1Th 4:16
14:14 k Da 7:13; Rev 1:13 l Rev 6:2
14:15 m Joel 3:13 n Jer 51:33
14:19 o Rev 19:15
14:20 p Isa 63:3 q Heb 13:12; Rev 11:8
15:1 r Rev 12:1,3 s Rev 16:1 t Lev 26:21
15:2 u Rev 4:6 v Rev 13:14
15:3 w Ex 15:1; Dt 32:4 x Ps 111:2 y Ps 145:17

Revelation 14:14–20

This passage develops an image from Joel's prophecy (Joel 3:13) about final judgment on the nations. Some commentators suggest that only the second image applies strictly to judgment and that the grain harvest includes the evangelism and gathering of God's people (see Mark 4:20,29). Either way, the meaning of the second vision is plain. The wicked are gathered grapes crushed into wine in God's winepress. They must drink the wine of his wrath—ultimately their own blood (v. 20; cf. 14:10; 16:6).

Do you avoid trying to "scare" people into the kingdom? In a culture in revolt against authority and skeptical of threats, emphasizing God's love and grace may indeed be effective. But John (and other NT writers) had no scruples about presenting spiritual realities. Effective ad campaigns against drug abuse, drunk driving, and smoking often emphasize horrific results of these behaviors. Considering the eternal consequences at stake, there remain occasions when a no-holds-barred approach is appropriate (see Acts 24:25).

Revelation 15:1–8

Early Christian literature is unanimous that there is no conversion apart from faith in Christ, and Revelation portrays the destruction of the nations. So it's likely that their turning in verse 4 refers to the repentant among them. Some take this as the majority who weren't killed, hence predicting the conversion of much of the world (cf. 11:13, if it refers to the world rather than to Jewish people). But as the beast has a kingdom from all peoples (13:7–8), so does Christ. A remnant from all nations will worship him.

This text provides a graphic model of spiritual warfare. Ironically, we overcome by being physically defeated and by enduring the world's torment. As theologian George E. Ladd notes, "The Beast had conquered them in martyrdom but in that same martyrdom *they had conquered the Beast*, for he had been utterly unable to make them deny Christ. This is their victory: loyalty to Christ in tribulation." Has your loyalty to Christ's cause stood up to Satan's attempts to manipulate you?

15:4
z Jer 10:7
a Isa 66:23

4 Who will not fear you, O Lord, [z]
    and bring glory to your name?
For you alone are holy.
All nations will come
    and worship before you, [a]
for your righteous acts have been revealed."

15:5
b Rev 11:19
c Nu 1:50
15:6
d Rev 14:15 e ver 1
f Rev 1:13
15:7
g Rev 4:6

15:8
h Isa 6:4 i Ex 40:34,
35; 1Ki 8:10,11;
2Ch 5:13,14

5 After this I looked and in heaven the temple, [b] that is, the tabernacle of the Testimony, [c] was opened. 6 Out of the temple [d] came the seven angels with the seven plagues. [e] They were dressed in clean, shining linen and wore golden sashes around their chests. [f] 7 Then one of the four living creatures [g] gave to the seven angels seven golden bowls filled with the wrath of God, who lives for ever and ever. 8 And the temple was filled with smoke [h] from the glory of God and from his power, and no one could enter the temple [i] until the seven plagues of the seven angels were completed.

The Seven Bowls of God's Wrath

16:1
j Rev 15:1

16:2
k Rev 8:7
l Ex 9:9-11
m Rev 13:15-17

16 Then I heard a loud voice from the temple saying to the seven angels, [j] "Go, pour out the seven bowls of God's wrath on the earth." 2 The first angel went and poured out his bowl on the land, [k] and ugly and painful sores [l] broke out on the people who had the mark of the beast and worshiped his image. [m]

16:3
n Ex 7:17-21;
Rev 8:8,9
16:4
o Rev 8:10
p Ex 7:17-21
16:5
q Rev 15:3
r Rev 1:4 s Rev 15:4

3 The second angel poured out his bowl on the sea, and it turned into blood like that of a dead man, and every living thing in the sea died. [n]

4 The third angel poured out his bowl on the rivers and springs of water, [o] and they became blood. [p] 5 Then I heard the angel in charge of the waters say:

"You are just in these judgments, [q]
    you who are and who were, [r] the Holy One, [s]
    because you have so judged;

16:6
t Isa 49:26;
Rev 17:6
16:7
u Rev 6:9
v Rev 15:3; 19:2

6 for they have shed the blood of your saints and prophets,
    and you have given them blood to drink [t] as they deserve."

7 And I heard the altar [u] respond:

"Yes, Lord God Almighty,
    true and just are your judgments." [v]

16:8
w Rev 8:12
x Rev 14:18
16:9
y ver 11,21
z Rev 2:21
a Rev 11:13
16:10
b Rev 13:2
c Rev 9:2
16:11
d ver 9,21

8 The fourth angel [w] poured out his bowl on the sun, and the sun was given power to scorch people with fire. [x] 9 They were seared by the intense heat and they cursed the name of God, [y] who had control over these plagues, but they refused to repent [z] and glorify him. [a]

10 The fifth angel poured out his bowl on the throne of the beast, [b] and his kingdom was plunged into darkness. [c] Men gnawed their tongues in agony 11 and cursed [d]

Revelation 16:1–21

Most of the bowls, like the trumpets, recall the plagues in Exodus 7:14—12:30. As God protected his people during the plagues, he will shield them from his judgments (7:1–8; 12:6,16). He sends judgments not only to vindicate his oppressed people, but also to catch the world's attention and offer the opportunity for repentance.

The devil and his agents seemingly gather the nations together to battle against God. But they are really being gathered for God's great day—that of their own destruction (cf. 19:15–18; 20:8–9). The gathering of the wicked for destruction is a common end-time image (Joel 3:9–16; Mic. 4:11–13; Zeph. 3:8; Zech. 12:3; 14:2–3).

Many people dislike talking about divine judgment. But to depict God as kind but never firm diminishes the nature of his love and denies his limitless power and lordship over a world of suffering. A god who never judges what's wrong isn't really a god of love.

Throughout history political leaders have portrayed their enemies as evil. This has encouraged prejudice and permitted violence against them. After all, the argument goes, they are not really people—they are evil tyrants, animals, haters of life. As those entrusted with the gospel, we are to be careful not to promote retaliation, prejudice, or hatred of any people (leaders included) for whom Christ died. What attitudes and actions are appropriate for a Christian faced with the evils of terrorism, violence, or oppressive governments and political groups?

the God of heaven[e] because of their pains and their sores,[f] but they refused to repent of what they had done.[g]

[12]The sixth angel poured out his bowl on the great river Euphrates,[h] and its water was dried up to prepare the way for the kings from the East.[i] [13]Then I saw three evil[a] spirits that looked like frogs; they came out of the mouth of the dragon,[j] out of the mouth of the beast[k] and out of the mouth of the false prophet.[l] [14]They are spirits of demons[m] performing miraculous signs, and they go out to the kings of the whole world, to gather them for the battle[n] on the great day of God Almighty.

[15]"Behold, I come like a thief! Blessed is he who stays awake[o] and keeps his clothes with him, so that he may not go naked and be shamefully exposed."

[16]Then they gathered the kings together to the place that in Hebrew[p] is called Armageddon.[q]

[17]The seventh angel poured out his bowl into the air,[r] and out of the temple[s] came a loud voice[t] from the throne, saying, "It is done!"[u] [18]Then there came flashes of lightning, rumblings, peals of thunder[v] and a severe earthquake.[w] No earthquake like it has ever occurred since man has been on earth,[x] so tremendous was the quake. [19]The great city[y] split into three parts, and the cities of the nations collapsed. God remembered[z] Babylon the Great[a] and gave her the cup filled with the wine of the fury of his wrath.[b] [20]Every island fled away and the mountains could not be found.[c] [21]From the sky huge hailstones[d] of about a hundred pounds each fell upon men. And they cursed God on account of the plague of hail,[e] because the plague was so terrible.

The Woman on the Beast

17 One of the seven angels[f] who had the seven bowls[g] came and said to me, "Come, I will show you the punishment[h] of the great prostitute,[i] who sits on many waters.[j] [2]With her the kings of the earth committed adultery and the inhabitants of the earth were intoxicated with the wine of her adulteries."[k]

[3]Then the angel carried me away in the Spirit into a desert.[l] There I saw a woman sitting on a scarlet beast that was covered with blasphemous names[m] and had seven heads and ten horns.[n] [4]The woman was dressed in purple and scarlet, and was glittering with gold, precious stones and pearls.[o] She held a golden cup[p] in her hand, filled with abominable things and the filth of her adulteries. [5]This title was written on her forehead:

MYSTERY

BABYLON THE GREAT[q]

THE MOTHER OF PROSTITUTES

AND OF THE ABOMINATIONS OF THE EARTH.

[6]I saw that the woman was drunk with the blood of the saints,[r] the blood of those who bore testimony to Jesus.

When I saw her, I was greatly astonished. [7]Then the angel said to me: "Why are you astonished? I will explain to you the mystery[s] of the woman and of the beast she rides, which has the seven heads and ten horns.[t] [8]The beast, which you saw,

---

[a] 13 Greek *unclean*

Cross references

16:11
[e] Rev 11:13 [f] ver 2
[g] Rev 2:21
16:12
[h] Rev 9:14
[i] Isa 41:2
16:13
[j] Rev 12:3
[k] Rev 13:1
[l] Rev 19:20
16:14
[m] 1Ti 4:1
[n] Rev 17:14
16:15
[o] Lk 12:37
16:16
[p] Rev 9:11
[q] 2Ki 23:29,30
16:17
[r] Eph 2:2
[s] Rev 14:15
[t] Rev 11:15
[u] Rev 21:6
16:18
[v] Rev 4:5
[w] Rev 6:12
[x] Da 12:1
16:19
[y] Rev 17:18
[z] Rev 18:5
[a] Rev 14:8
[b] Rev 14:10
16:20
[c] Rev 6:14
16:21
[d] Rev 11:19
[e] Ex 9:23-25

17:1
[f] Rev 15:1
[g] Rev 21:9
[h] Rev 16:19
[i] Rev 19:2
[j] Jer 51:13
17:2
[k] Rev 14:8; 18:3
17:3
[l] Rev 12:6,14
[m] Rev 13:1
[n] Rev 12:3
17:4
[o] Rev 18:16
[p] Jer 51:7; Rev 18:6

17:5
[q] Rev 14:8

17:6
[r] Rev 18:24

17:7
[s] ver 5 [t] ver 3

Revelation 17:1–18

Coins and other artwork depicted many an ancient city as a wealthy goddess enthroned beside a river. Literal Babylon lived by "many waters" (Jer. 51:13), as did most other ancient cities, including Rome. The "waters" may symbolize international power.

In more ways than one, Babylon was "dressed to kill." Her purple and scarlet clothing indicated wealth. The gold, precious stones, and pearls further contributed to her splendor. John saw a high-class prostitute who had intoxicated the nations with her hard-to-resist

immorality (v. 2) but was herself drunk with the blood of the saints (v. 6).

Is there really "honor among thieves"? That the ten kings turn on the prostitute shows something about the world's loyalties. God often allows the wicked to destroy themselves (cf. Judg. 7:22; 2 Chron. 20:23). Such a falling out, a dividing of Satan against Satan, is inevitable before the end. From the short vantage point of our lives, justice may seem delayed. But from the long perspective of eternity, the power of oppressors will be brought to an end. Which perspective is easier for you to adopt?

17:8
u Rev 13:10
v Rev 3:10
w Rev 13:8
x Rev 13:3

17:9
y Rev 13:18

17:11
z ver 8

17:12
a Rev 12:3
b Rev 18:10,17,19

17:13
c ver 17
17:14
d Rev 16:14
e 1Ti 6:15;
Rev 19:16
f Mt 22:14

17:15
g Isa 8:7 h Rev 13:7

17:16
i Rev 18:17,19
j Eze 16:37,39
k Rev 19:18
l Rev 18:8
17:17
m Rev 10:7
17:18
n Rev 16:19

18:1
o Rev 17:1
p Rev 10:1
q Eze 43:2

18:2
r Rev 14:8
s Isa 13:21,22;
Jer 50:39

18:3
t Rev 14:8
u Rev 17:2
v Eze 27:9-25
w ver 7,9

once was, now is not, and will come up out of the Abyss and go to his destruction. [u] The inhabitants of the earth [v] whose names have not been written in the book of life [w] from the creation of the world will be astonished [x] when they see the beast, because he once was, now is not, and yet will come.

9 "This calls for a mind with wisdom. [y] The seven heads are seven hills on which the woman sits. 10 They are also seven kings. Five have fallen, one is, the other has not yet come; but when he does come, he must remain for a little while. 11 The beast who once was, and now is not, [z] is an eighth king. He belongs to the seven and is going to his destruction.

12 "The ten horns [a] you saw are ten kings who have not yet received a kingdom, but who for one hour [b] will receive authority as kings along with the beast. 13 They have one purpose and will give their power and authority to the beast. [c] 14 They will make war [d] against the Lamb, but the Lamb will overcome them because he is Lord of lords and King of kings [e]—and with him will be his called, chosen [f] and faithful followers."

15 Then the angel said to me, "The waters [g] you saw, where the prostitute sits, are peoples, multitudes, nations and languages. [h] 16 The beast and the ten horns you saw will hate the prostitute. They will bring her to ruin [i] and leave her naked; [j] they will eat her flesh [k] and burn her with fire. [l] 17 For God has put it into their hearts to accomplish his purpose by agreeing to give the beast their power to rule, until God's words are fulfilled. [m] 18 The woman you saw is the great city [n] that rules over the kings of the earth."

The Fall of Babylon

18 After this I saw another angel [o] coming down from heaven. [p] He had great authority, and the earth was illuminated by his splendor. [q] 2 With a mighty voice he shouted:

> "Fallen! Fallen is Babylon the Great! [r]
> She has become a home for demons
> and a haunt for every evil [a] spirit,
> a haunt for every unclean and detestable bird. [s]
> 3 For all the nations have drunk
> the maddening wine of her adulteries. [t]
> The kings of the earth committed adultery with her, [u]
> and the merchants of the earth grew rich [v] from her excessive
> luxuries." [w]

4 Then I heard another voice from heaven say:

a 2 Greek *unclean*

Revelation 18:1–24

The exiled Jewish Christian prophet had the audacity to write a funeral dirge over the mightiest empire in the world. He might as well have issued a press release. This thinly veiled attack on Rome could have brought the early church unwanted scrutiny and more persecution. It may not seem so reckless from our armchairs or pews. But John's act must have appeared to his contemporary believers as courageous and full of faith—or as an invitation to mass martyrdom!

Rome's mercantile empire made it rich. Most of its people, though poor themselves, were seduced by its greatness. The problem may not have been its wealth per se but unequal opportunity. The luxury items (vv. 12–13) represent status symbols or a squandering of resources at the expense of others' essential needs. This passage also addresses the arrogance of considering one's country indestructible (v. 8).

How do you react when Christian leaders take a bold, public stand against sin and injustice in your culture? Are you vaguely embarrassed or even angered? Do you dislike mopping up afterward and facing uncomfortable questions from friends, family, and coworkers? Hebrews 11:24–26 cites the example of Moses, who gave up his culture's approval to be identified with God's people. How do John's and Moses' examples encourage you?

Christians today have the opportunity to address many of the injustices enumerated in this chapter, including economic exploitation. Instead of blaming the poor for their impoverishment or a government for its bad choices, we can remember God's mercy and invest our resources, participating in the coming of God's kingdom by serving people's spiritual and physical needs.

> "Come out of her, my people,[x]
> > so that you will not share in her sins,
> > so that you will not receive any of her plagues;

[5] for her sins are piled up to heaven,[y]
> and God has remembered[z] her crimes.

[6] Give back to her as she has given;
> pay her back[a] double for what she has done.
> Mix her a double portion from her own cup.[b]

[7] Give her as much torture and grief
> as the glory and luxury she gave herself.[c]
> In her heart she boasts,
> > 'I sit as queen; I am not a widow,
> > and I will never mourn.'[d]

[8] Therefore in one day[e] her plagues will overtake her:
> death, mourning and famine.
> She will be consumed by fire,[f]
> for mighty is the Lord God who judges her.

[9] "When the kings of the earth who committed adultery with her[g] and shared her luxury see the smoke of her burning,[h] they will weep and mourn over her.[i] [10]Terrified at her torment, they will stand far off[j] and cry:

> " 'Woe! Woe, O great city,[k]
> > O Babylon, city of power!
> In one hour[l] your doom has come!'

[11] "The merchants[m] of the earth will weep and mourn over her because no one buys their cargoes any more[n]— [12]cargoes of gold, silver, precious stones and pearls; fine linen, purple, silk and scarlet cloth; every sort of citron wood, and articles of every kind made of ivory, costly wood, bronze, iron and marble;[o] [13]cargoes of cinnamon and spice, of incense, myrrh and frankincense, of wine and olive oil, of fine flour and wheat; cattle and sheep; horses and carriages; and bodies and souls of men.[p]

[14] "They will say, 'The fruit you longed for is gone from you. All your riches and splendor have vanished, never to be recovered.' [15]The merchants who sold these things and gained their wealth from her[q] will stand far off, terrified at her torment. They will weep and mourn[r] [16]and cry out:

> " 'Woe! Woe, O great city,
> > dressed in fine linen, purple and scarlet,
> > and glittering with gold, precious stones and pearls!'[s]

[17] In one hour[t] such great wealth has been brought to ruin!'[u]

"Every sea captain, and all who travel by ship, the sailors, and all who earn their living from the sea,[v] will stand far off. [18]When they see the smoke of her burning, they will exclaim, 'Was there ever a city like this great city?'[w] [19]They will throw dust on their heads,[x] and with weeping and mourning cry out:

> " 'Woe! Woe, O great city,
> > where all who had ships on the sea
> > became rich through her wealth!
> In one hour she has been brought to ruin!'[y]

[20] Rejoice over her, O heaven![z]
> Rejoice, saints and apostles and prophets!
> God has judged her for the way she treated you.' "[a]

[21] Then a mighty angel[b] picked up a boulder the size of a large millstone and threw it into the sea,[c] and said:

> "With such violence
> > the great city of Babylon will be thrown down,
> > never to be found again.

18:4
x Isa 48:20;
Jer 50:8; 2Co 6:17

18:5
y Jer 51:9
z Rev 16:19

18:6
a Ps 137:8;
Jer 50:15,29
b Rev 14:10; 16:19

18:7
c Eze 28:2-8
d Isa 47:7,8;
Zep 2:15

18:8
e ver 10; Isa 47:9;
Jer 50:31,32
f Rev 17:16

18:9
g Rev 17:2,4
h ver 18; Rev 19:3
i Eze 26:17,18
18:10
j ver 15,17
k ver 16,19
l Rev 17:12

18:11
m Eze 27:27 n ver 3

18:12
o Rev 17:4

18:13
p Eze 27:13;
1Ti 1:10

18:15
q ver 3 r Eze 27:31

18:16
s Rev 17:4
18:17
t ver 10
u Rev 17:16
v Eze 27:28-30

18:18
w Eze 27:32;
Rev 13:4
18:19
x Jos 7:6; Eze 27:30
y Rev 17:16

18:20
z Jer 51:48;
Rev 12:12
a Rev 19:2

18:21
b Rev 5:2
c Jer 51:63

18:22
d Isa 24:8;
Eze 26:13
e Jer 25:10

22 The music of harpists and musicians, flute players and trumpeters,
  will never be heard in you again. *d*
No workman of any trade
  will ever be found in you again.
The sound of a millstone
  will never be heard in you again. *e*

23 The light of a lamp
  will never shine in you again.
The voice of bridegroom and bride
  will never be heard in you again. *f*
Your merchants were the world's great men. *g*
  By your magic spell *h* all the nations were led astray.

18:23
f Jer 7:34; 16:9;
25:10 g Isa 23:8
h Na 3:4

18:24
i Rev 16:6; 17:6
j Jer 51:49

24 In her was found the blood of prophets and of the saints, *i*
  and of all who have been killed on the earth." *j*

Hallelujah!

19

19:1
k Rev 11:15
l Rev 7:10
m Rev 4:11

After this I heard what sounded like the roar of a great multitude *k* in heaven shouting:

"Hallelujah!
Salvation *l* and glory and power *m* belong to our God,
2   for true and just are his judgments.
He has condemned the great prostitute
  who corrupted the earth by her adulteries.
He has avenged on her the blood of his servants." *n*

19:2
n Dt 32:43;
Rev 6:10

3 And again they shouted:

19:3
o Isa 34:10;
Rev 14:11
19:4
p Rev 4:4 q Rev 4:6
r Rev 5:14

"Hallelujah!
The smoke from her goes up for ever and ever." *o*

4 The twenty-four elders *p* and the four living creatures *q* fell down *r* and worshiped God, who was seated on the throne. And they cried:

"Amen, Hallelujah!"

5 Then a voice came from the throne, saying:

19:5
s Ps 134:1
t Rev 11:18; 20:12

"Praise our God,
  all you his servants, *s*
you who fear him,
  both small and great!" *t*

19:6
u Rev 11:15

6 Then I heard what sounded like a great multitude, *u* like the roar of rushing waters and like loud peals of thunder, shouting:

"Hallelujah!
  For our Lord God Almighty reigns.
7 Let us rejoice and be glad
  and give him glory!
For the wedding of the Lamb *v* has come,

19:7
v Mt 22:2; 25:10;
Eph 5:32

Revelation 19:1–10

The angel disallows John's worship and declares that he, too, is simply acting as God's messenger. Many of John's Jewish contemporaries believed that the Spirit of prophecy had been suppressed but would return during the Messianic age. The activity of the Spirit in testifying about Jesus throughout the book of Revelation attested to his identity as the true Lord and Israel's Messiah.

Have you ever thought of yourself as a prophet?

Verse 10 reminds us that the Spirit empowers us all to speak about Jesus Christ; thus all believers are potential prophets. Some Christians rank the anointing of others based on their demonstration of particular spiritual gifts, but Christ gave all of us his Spirit to testify about him (Acts 1:8). We are all called to speak God's truth to human power—in bold humility and courageous gentleness. Every Christian who witnesses about Jesus experiences this empowerment (cf. 1 Cor. 12:3). Take a moment to reflect on the implications of this privilege.

and his bride[w] has made herself ready.
 8 Fine linen, bright and clean,
 was given her to wear."
(Fine linen stands for the righteous acts[x] of the saints.)

9 Then the angel said to me,[y] "Write:[z] 'Blessed are those who are invited to the wedding supper of the Lamb!' "[a] And he added, "These are the true words of God."[b]

10 At this I fell at his feet to worship him.[c] But he said to me, "Do not do it! I am a fellow servant with you and with your brothers who hold to the testimony of Jesus. Worship God![d] For the testimony of Jesus[e] is the spirit of prophecy."

The Rider on the White Horse

11 I saw heaven standing open and there before me was a white horse, whose rider[f] is called Faithful and True.[g] With justice he judges and makes war.[h] 12 His eyes are like blazing fire,[i] and on his head are many crowns.[j] He has a name written on him that no one knows but he himself.[k] 13 He is dressed in a robe dipped in blood,[l] and his name is the Word of God.[m] 14 The armies of heaven were following him, riding on white horses and dressed in fine linen,[n] white and clean. 15 Out of his mouth comes a sharp sword[o] with which to strike down[p] the nations. "He will rule them with an iron scepter."[a][q] He treads the winepress[r] of the fury of the wrath of God Almighty. 16 On his robe and on his thigh he has this name written:[s]

KING OF KINGS AND LORD OF LORDS.[t]

17 And I saw an angel standing in the sun, who cried in a loud voice to all the birds[u] flying in midair,[v] "Come,[w] gather together for the great supper of God, 18 so that you may eat the flesh of kings, generals, and mighty men, of horses and their riders, and the flesh of all people,[x] free and slave, small and great."

19 Then I saw the beast and the kings of the earth[y] and their armies gathered together to make war against the rider on the horse and his army. 20 But the beast was captured, and with him the false prophet[z] who had performed the miraculous signs on his behalf.[a] With these signs he had deluded those who had received the mark of the beast and worshiped his image. The two of them were thrown alive into the fiery lake[b] of burning sulfur.[c] 21 The rest of them were killed with the sword[d] that came out of the mouth of the rider on the horse,[e] and all the birds[f] gorged themselves on their flesh.

The Thousand Years

20 And I saw an angel coming down out of heaven,[g] having the key[h] to the Abyss and holding in his hand a great chain. 2 He seized the dragon, that ancient serpent, who is the devil, or Satan,[i] and bound him for a thousand years.[j] 3 He threw him into the Abyss, and locked and sealed[k] it over him, to keep him from de-

a 15 Psalm 2:9

Notes (side column)

19:7 w Rev 21:2,9
19:8 x Rev 15:4
19:9 y ver 10 z Rev 1:19 a Lk 14:15 b Rev 21:5; 22:6
19:10 c Rev 22:8 d Ac 10:25,26; Rev 22:9 e Rev 12:17
19:11 f Rev 6:2 g Rev 3:14 h Isa 11:4
19:12 i Rev 1:14 / Rev 6:2 k Rev 2:17
19:13 l Isa 63:2,3 m Jn 1:1
19:14 n ver 8
19:15 o Rev 1:16 p Isa 11:4; 2Th 2:8 q Ps 2:9; Rev 2:27 r Rev 14:20
19:16 s ver 12 t Rev 17:14
19:17 u ver 21 v Rev 8:13 w Eze 39:17
19:18 x Eze 39:18-20
19:19 y Rev 16:14,16
19:20 z Rev 16:13 a Rev 13:12 b Da 7:11; Rev 20:10,14,15; 21:8 c Rev 14:10
19:21 d ver 15 e ver 11,19 f ver 17
20:1 g Rev 10:1 h Rev 1:18
20:2 i Rev 12:9 j 2Pe 2:4
20:3 k Da 6:17

Revelation 19:11–21

If God's angel messenger in verse 10 was the wrong one to worship, verses 11–16 abruptly and immediately reveal the proper object of worship. Heaven opens and Jesus appears. Here, at his second coming, Christ "judges and makes war"—a final response to the worshipers of the beast who have asked, "Who is like the beast? Who can make war against him?" (13:4). All along God has allowed the beast and his followers to wage war against God's people on Earth (11:7; 12:17; 13:7). Now the time has come for these evil forces to make war on the Lamb himself—and be destroyed (vv. 19–21; cf. 17:14).

Images like those in this chapter and others in the Bible have unfortunately prompted some Christians to acts

of violence. They have paid too little attention to Jesus' teachings on non-retaliation and loving God and neighbors. But like Peter who drew his sword in the garden (Matt. 26:50–53; John 18:10–11), they didn't understand the believer's real struggle. We wage a spiritual battle against spiritual forces (cf. Eph. 6:12). We are to practice justice and mercy (Matt. 23:23) and pray for Christ's kingdom to come in its fullness on Earth (Matt. 6:10).

Revelation 20:1–6

Interpreters of this chapter are divided among three schools of thought. Premillennialists believe that Jesus will return to establish a thousand-year kingdom on Earth. Amillennialists believe the thousand-year kingdom symbolizes the present (church) age. And postmil-

20:3
l Rev 12:9

ceiving the nations *l* anymore until the thousand years were ended. After that, he must be set free for a short time.

20:4
m Da 7:9 *n* Rev 6:9
o Rev 13:12
p Rev 13:16

4I saw thrones *m* on which were seated those who had been given authority to judge. And I saw the souls of those who had been beheaded *n* because of their testimony for Jesus and because of the word of God. They had not worshiped the beast *o* or his image and had not received his mark on their foreheads or their hands. *p* They came to life and reigned with Christ a thousand years. 5(The rest of the dead did not come to life until the thousand years were ended.) This is the first resurrection. *q* 6Blessed *r* and holy are those who have part in the first resurrection. The second death *s* has no power over them, but they will be priests *t* of God and of Christ and will reign with him *u* for a thousand years.

20:5
q Lk 14:14;
Php 3:11
20:6
r Rev 14:13
s Rev 2:11 *t* Rev 1:6
u ver 4

Satan's Doom

20:7
v ver 2
20:8
w ver 3,10
x Eze 38:2; 39:1
y Rev 16:14
z Heb 11:12
20:9
a Eze 38:9,16
b Eze 38:22; 39:6
20:10
c Rev 19:20
d Rev 14:10,11

7When the thousand years are over, *v* Satan will be released from his prison 8and will go out to deceive the nations *w* in the four corners of the earth—Gog and Magog *x*—to gather them for battle. *y* In number they are like the sand on the seashore. *z* 9They marched across the breadth of the earth and surrounded *a* the camp of God's people, the city he loves. But fire came down from heaven *b* and devoured them. 10And the devil, who deceived them, *c* was thrown into the lake of burning sulfur, where the beast and the false prophet had been thrown. They will be tormented day and night for ever and ever. *d*

The Dead Are Judged

20:11
e Rev 4:2

11Then I saw a great white throne *e* and him who was seated on it. Earth and sky fled from his presence, and there was no place for them. 12And I saw the dead, great and small, standing before the throne, and books were opened. *f* Another book was opened, which is the book of life. *g* The dead were judged according to what they had done *h* as recorded in the books. 13The sea gave up the dead that were in it, and death and Hades *i* gave up the dead *j* that were in them, and each person was judged according to what he had done. 14Then death *k* and Hades were thrown into the lake of fire. The lake of fire is the second death. 15If anyone's name was not found written in the book of life, *l* he was thrown into the lake of fire.

20:12
f Da 7:10 *g* Rev 3:5
h Jer 17:10;
Mt 16:27; Rev 2:23
20:13
i Rev 6:8 *j* Isa 26:19
20:14
k 1Co 15:26
20:15
l ver 12

---

lennialists believe that Christians will help establish the thousand-year kingdom on Earth prior to Jesus' return.

📖 Interpretive distinctions about the millennium don't affect the most important issues in Revelation. Whether in a temporary, intermediate kingdom or in the new heaven and the new earth, we will be with Christ, and Christ's reign will be fully established on Earth. Jesus will raise those who have endured hardship for him, and they will reign with him (cf. 2 Tim. 2:11–12).

We face the same difficulty as ancient readers of Old Testament prophetic books: Descriptions of Jesus' first coming were blended with those of his (still) future kingdom, causing them to misunderstand his mission and teaching (cf. Acts 1:6–7). Rather than warring among ourselves over the chronology of the end-times, our calling is to live together in resolute hope and to manifest, in the midst of the present age, signs of that coming kingdom.

Revelation 20:7–10

🕮 Some scholars have suggested that Satan's release represents his own "second coming," mocking Jesus' future return to Earth. If so, in God's providence it becomes merely the stage for his final destruction. John's image of Gog and Magog comes from Ezekiel 38 and 39. Revelation draws on the warning in Ezekiel 39:6

that God will hurl fire on Magog, and especially on the threat of 38:22 that he will cast hailstones and burning sulfur on Gog's army. God will defend his people and be glorified through this army's final destruction.

📖 Do you ever feel discouraged or overwhelmed in the heat of spiritual battle? God's defense of a city that embodies the heritage of his people points to his love and faithfulness toward us. Though we may be outnumbered, God's purposes will ultimately triumph. Even when the battle against evil seems futile, we know that victory belongs to the Lord—and that it's assured.

Revelation 20:11–15

🕮 The scene of a battle judgment gives way to the final judgment before God's throne. That there is "no place" for earth or sky reveals the drama of God's appearance as Judge and paves the way for the new heaven and earth (21:1). No one can see God in his glory and live (Ex. 33:20). But in the new creation, his servants will see his face (Rev. 22:4–5).

📖 Skeptics have charged Christians with living for a "pie in the sky" hope while neglecting pressing issues in the present. But Biblical hope summons us to holy lives (Titus 2:12–13; 1 Peter 1:13–16; 1 Jn. 3:3). The heavenly books in this passage remind us that our deeds in this life matter in eternity.

The New Jerusalem

21 Then I saw a new heaven and a new earth, [m] for the first heaven and the first earth had passed away, and there was no longer any sea. [2]I saw the Holy City, the new Jerusalem, coming down out of heaven from God, [n] prepared as a bride beautifully dressed for her husband. [3]And I heard a loud voice from the throne saying, "Now the dwelling of God is with men, and he will live with them. They will be his people, and God himself will be with them and be their God. [o] [4]He will wipe every tear from their eyes. [p] There will be no more death [q] or mourning or crying or pain, [r] for the old order of things has passed away."

[5]He who was seated on the throne [s] said, "I am making everything new!" Then he said, "Write this down, for these words are trustworthy and true." [t]

[6]He said to me: "It is done. [u] I am the Alpha and the Omega, [v] the Beginning and the End. To him who is thirsty I will give to drink without cost from the spring of the water of life. [w] [7]He who overcomes will inherit all this, and I will be his God and he will be my son. [8]But the cowardly, the unbelieving, the vile, the murderers, the sexually immoral, those who practice magic arts, the idolaters and all liars [x]—their place will be in the fiery lake of burning sulfur. This is the second death." [y]

[9]One of the seven angels who had the seven bowls full of the seven last plagues [z] came and said to me, "Come, I will show you the bride, [a] the wife of the Lamb." [10]And he carried me away [b] in the Spirit [c] to a mountain great and high, and showed me the Holy City, Jerusalem, coming down out of heaven from God. [11]It shone with the glory of God, [d] and its brilliance was like that of a very precious jewel, like a jas-

21:1
m Isa 65:17;
2Pe 3:13
21:2
n Heb 11:10; 12:22;
Rev 3:12
21:3
o 2Co 6:16
21:4
p Rev 7:17
q 1Co 15:26;
Rev 20:14
r Isa 35:10; 65:19
21:5
s Rev 4:9; 20:11
t Rev 19:9
21:6
u Rev 16:17
v Rev 1:8; 22:13
w Jn 4:10
21:8
x 1Co 6:9
y Rev 2:11
21:9
z Rev 15:1,6,7
a Rev 19:7
21:10
b Rev 17:3
c Rev 1:10
21:11
d Rev 15:8; 22:5

Revelation 21:1–27

The cubic shape of the new Jerusalem (v. 16) brings to mind the Most Holy Place (1 Kings 6:19–20). The entire city will be the place where believers will experience God's presence in its full intensity. The church is already a temple (Eph. 2:19–22), but our future experience will be like its holiest part, inviting continual worship and enjoyment of God's presence.

The city of gold may reflect Eden (cf. Gen. 2:11–12), but more likely it represents the commonness of what is now regarded as wealth, a stark contrast with the gold decorations of "wealthy" Rome, or "Babylon" (Rev. 17:4; 18:12,16). The description of the gold as being like glass matches no refining process known to humankind, reflecting instead God's incomparable glory.

John used the image of the new Jerusalem as Christ's bride to convey a message of God's intimacy with and love for his people. Our hope is founded in the conviction that one day all sorrows will cease and all injustices will end. God will wipe away all tears. There will be no more mourning, crying, or death. God will dwell among us and make all things new. In the same intimacy as Adam and Eve walked with God in the first garden, all of God's redeemed will walk with him in the new City.

Jesus said, "Where your treasure is, there your heart will be also" (Matt. 6:21). With this treasure before us, we are freed from clinging to or devoting our lives to second-rate treasures. The Spirit wants to manifest through us signs of what that glorious new city will be like. As we wipe away tears and ease others' pain, we show people God's redeeming love.

21:1–4

The Messianic Banquet   This feast is a symbol of the blessings God is going to give us in the age to come. Sometimes it's pictured as a marriage feast between Jesus (the groom) and the church as both bride and guests.

The Promise:
"The LORD Almighty will prepare a feast of rich food for all peoples, a banquet of aged wine—the best of meats and the finest of wines" (Isa. 25:6).

The Meaning:

Spiritual blessing: "Blessed is the man who will eat at the feast in the kingdom of God" (Luke 14:15).

Spiritual satisfaction: "My soul will be satisfied as with the richest of foods" (Ps. 63:5).

Fellowship with God: "Here I am! I stand at the door and knock. If anyone hears my voice and opens the door, I will come in and eat with him, and he with me" (Rev. 3:20).

Celebrating God's goodness: "Celebrate the Feast to the LORD your God at the place the LORD will choose" (Deut. 16:15).

The Invitation: "Come, I will show you the bride, the wife of the Lamb" (Rev. 21:9).

21:11
e Rev 4:6

21:12
f Eze 48:30-34

21:15
g Rev 11:1

21:18
h ver 11 i ver 21
21:19
j Isa 54:11,12

21:20
k Rev 4:3

21:21
l ver 18
21:22
m Jn 4:21,23
n Rev 1:8 o Rev 5:6
21:23
p Isa 24:23;
60:19,20;
Rev 22:5

per, clear as crystal. e 12It had a great, high wall with twelve gates, and with twelve angels at the gates. On the gates were written the names of the twelve tribes of Israel. f 13There were three gates on the east, three on the north, three on the south and three on the west. 14The wall of the city had twelve foundations, and on them were the names of the twelve apostles of the Lamb.

15The angel who talked with me had a measuring rod g of gold to measure the city, its gates and its walls. 16The city was laid out like a square, as long as it was wide. He measured the city with the rod and found it to be 12,000 stadia a in length, and as wide and high as it is long. 17He measured its wall and it was 144 cubits b thick, c by man's measurement, which the angel was using. 18The wall was made of jasper, h and the city of pure gold, as pure as glass. i 19The foundations of the city walls were decorated with every kind of precious stone. j The first foundation was jasper, the second sapphire, the third chalcedony, the fourth emerald, 20the fifth sardonyx, the sixth carnelian, k the seventh chrysolite, the eighth beryl, the ninth topaz, the tenth chrysoprase, the eleventh jacinth, and the twelfth amethyst. d 21The twelve gates were twelve pearls, each gate made of a single pearl. The great street of the city was of pure gold, like transparent glass. l

22I did not see a temple m in the city, because the Lord God Almighty n and the Lamb o are its temple. 23The city does not need the sun or the moon to shine on it, for the glory of God gives it light, p and the Lamb is its lamp. 24The nations will walk

a 16 That is, about 1,400 miles (about 2,200 kilometers)   b 17 That is, about 200 feet (about 65 meters)   c 17 Or high   d 20 The precise identification of some of these precious stones is uncertain.

Snapshots

21:4

My Dear Teacher

Javsaa was a favorite teacher at a Christian center for street children in Mongolia. It was a shock to all when she suddenly became ill and within a few weeks died of Hepatitis B. Seventeen-year-old Naranbatt, a former runaway and pickpocket, summed up her students' feelings in a sensitive poem, an excerpt of which is shared here:

> Your honor and the work you did is lifted high to the sky.

My Dear Teacher
by Naranbatt

You'll never see the sunrise again or feel the wind blow.
Dear teacher, you left everything because your unexpected time
   had come.
You'll never feel the moisture of a single drop of rain again or see
   the mist
Which falls on the high mountain.

Dear teacher, even your rebukes were like a lesson to me.
Your personality was very tender. Even your soul is in my mind.
Your teaching gave me realization of my potential.

I will keep you in my heart forever and your lessons in my mind.
With my mind I want to recall you from the heavens.

Dear teacher, you left sorrow and unexpected suffering for us.
Your honor and the work you did is lifted high to the sky.

by its light, and the kings of the earth will bring their splendor into it. [q] [25]On no day will its gates ever be shut, [r] for there will be no night there. [s] [26]The glory and honor of the nations will be brought into it. [27]Nothing impure will ever enter it, nor will anyone who does what is shameful or deceitful, [t] but only those whose names are written in the Lamb's book of life.

The River of Life

22 Then the angel showed me the river of the water of life, as clear as crystal, [u] flowing [v] from the throne of God and of the Lamb [2]down the middle of the great street of the city. On each side of the river stood the tree of life, [w] bearing twelve crops of fruit, yielding its fruit every month. And the leaves of the tree are for the healing of the nations. [x] [3]No longer will there be any curse. [y] The throne of God and of the Lamb will be in the city, and his servants will serve him. [z] [4]They will see his face, [a] and his name will be on their foreheads. [b] [5]There will be no more night. [c] They will not need the light of a lamp or the light of the sun, for the Lord God will give them light. [d] And they will reign for ever and ever. [e]

[6]The angel said to me, [f] "These words are trustworthy and true. [g] The Lord, the God of the spirits of the prophets, [h] sent his angel [i] to show his servants the things that must soon take place."

21:24
q Isa 60:3,5
21:25
r Isa 60:11
s Zec 14:7; Rev 22:5
21:27
t Isa 52:1; Joel 3:17; Rev 22:14,15

22:1
u Rev 4:6
v Eze 47:1; Zec 14:8
22:2
w Rev 2:7
x Eze 47:12
22:3
y Zec 14:11
z Rev 7:15
22:4
a Mt 5:8 b Rev 14:1
22:5
c Rev 21:25
d Rev 21:23
e Da 7:27; Rev 20:4
22:6
f Rev 1:1
g Rev 19:9; 21:5
h Heb 12:9 i ver 16

Revelation 22:1–6

That the tree is "for the healing of the nations" reminds us that representatives of all peoples will follow the Lamb in this age and constitute the nations in their ideal character in the world to come, bringing gifts from all cultures to worship Jesus (21:24). The single tree and street may point to the fact that God has provided only one source of life and one "way" into the new Jerusalem.

The tree for healing suggests that we, as God's people, will depend on Christ for all eternity. The picture is an invitation: Let anyone who wills come and taste God's paradise. Anyone choosing to miss out on this promise does so at great personal loss (22:14–15).

21:8

Vice List

The list of those excluded from the new Jerusalem (21:8) appears in related forms in 21:27 and 22:15. Vice lists were a common literary form in ancient texts, but Revelation tailors this list to specific issues confronting John's audience.

Vice	Definition
1. Cowards	People who fear persecution (2:10) more than they revere God (11:18; 14:7; 15:4; 19:5)
2. Unbelievers	People who prove faithless, unwilling to maintain their faith in the midst of testing (2:13,19; 13:10; 14:12)
3. Vile persons	The word *vile* describes something abominable or disgusting to God; people who engage in two sins: sexual immorality (Lev. 18:22–29; Deut. 22:5; 23:18; 24:4; 1 Kings 14:24; Jer. 13:27; Mal. 2:11) and, more frequently, idolatry (over 40 times in the OT); or those who compromise(d) with the cult of the emperor or other forms of paganism and worldliness
4. Murderers	Broad, but includes those who kill God's saints (2:13, 6:11; 13:10,15). Also may include those who betray fellow saints (2:9; 3:9), refuse to love enough to refrain from betraying others (cf. 1 Jn. 3:14–16), or refuse to meet a fellow believer's needs (1 Jn. 3:17)
5. Sexually immoral	In Revelation points to spiritual immorality (2:14,20; 17:1–2,5,15–16; 18:3,9; 19:2) but also to physical immorality associated with paganism. In either case, unfaithfulness in sharp contrast to the purity of the bride, the holy city, and the city's inhabitants (14:4; 19:7–8; 21:2)
6. Practitioners of magic arts	Those under the world's seductive signs (13:13–14) and perhaps even its seductive power (18:23), or those who use any deceptive tools of demons (9:20–21; Gal. 5:20)
7. Idolaters	Those who had succumbed to the demands of the imperial cult or worshiped the idols of the world system (2:14,20; cf. 1 Jn. 5:2–10); those who worshiped the image of the beast (13:15)
8. Liars	Not only false prophets (2:2; cf. 1 Jn. 2:22) like Balaam and Jezebel (2:14,20), but also those who falsely claim to follow the truth (3:9; cf. 1 Jn. 2:4; 4:20), in contrast to the saints (14:5)

Source: *NIV Application Commentary, Revelation* (2000)

22:7
j Rev 3:11 k Rev 1:3

22:8
l Rev 1:1
m Rev 19:10

22:9
n ver 10,18,19
o Rev 19:10

22:10
p Da 8:26; Rev 10:4
q Rev 1:3

22:11
r Eze 3:27;
Da 12:10

22:12
s ver 7,20
t Isa 40:10

22:13
u Rev 1:8
v Rev 1:17
w Rev 21:6

22:14
x Rev 2:7
y Rev 21:12
z Rev 21:27

22:15
a 1Co 6:9,10;
Gal 5:19-21;
Col 3:5,6 b Php 3:2

22:16
c Rev 1:1 d Rev 1:4
e Rev 5:5
f 2Pe 1:19;
Rev 2:28

22:17
g Rev 2:7

22:18
h Dt 4:2; Pr 30:6
i Rev 15:6-16:21

22:19
j Dt 4:2

22:20
k Rev 1:2
l 1Co 16:22

22:21
m Ro 16:20

Jesus Is Coming

7 "Behold, I am coming soon! [j] Blessed [k] is he who keeps the words of the prophecy in this book."

8 I, John, am the one who heard and saw these things. [l] And when I had heard and seen them, I fell down to worship at the feet [m] of the angel who had been showing them to me. 9 But he said to me, "Do not do it! I am a fellow servant with you and with your brothers the prophets and of all who keep the words of this book. [n] Worship God!" [o]

10 Then he told me, "Do not seal up [p] the words of the prophecy of this book, because the time is near. [q] 11 Let him who does wrong continue to do wrong; let him who is vile continue to be vile; let him who does right continue to do right; and let him who is holy continue to be holy." [r]

12 "Behold, I am coming soon! [s] My reward is with me, [t] and I will give to everyone according to what he has done. 13 I am the Alpha and the Omega, [u] the First and the Last, [v] the Beginning and the End. [w]

14 "Blessed are those who wash their robes, that they may have the right to the tree of life [x] and may go through the gates [y] into the city. [z] 15 Outside [a] are the dogs, [b] those who practice magic arts, the sexually immoral, the murderers, the idolaters and everyone who loves and practices falsehood.

16 "I, Jesus, [c] have sent my angel to give you [a] this testimony for the churches. [d] I am the Root [e] and the Offspring of David, and the bright Morning Star." [f]

17 The Spirit [g] and the bride say, "Come!" And let him who hears say, "Come!" Whoever is thirsty, let him come; and whoever wishes, let him take the free gift of the water of life.

18 I warn everyone who hears the words of the prophecy of this book: If anyone adds anything to them, [h] God will add to him the plagues described in this book. [i] 19 And if anyone takes words away [j] from this book of prophecy, God will take away from him his share in the tree of life and in the holy city, which are described in this book.

20 He who testifies to these things [k] says, "Yes, I am coming soon." Amen. Come, Lord Jesus. [l]

21 The grace of the Lord Jesus be with God's people. [m] Amen.

a 16 The Greek is plural.

Revelation 22:7–21

This passage offers final testimonies from God, the Lamb, the Spirit, the bride, and the prophets who speak to the bride for the Spirit, supporting the message of God's revelation to John. John also mentioned his own name for the first time since chapter 1, and for the same reason: to provide eyewitness testimony, much as he did in his Gospel (John 19:35; 21:24). Those who heed this true prophecy will be rewarded; Jesus is "coming soon" to compensate each according to his or her deeds.

Revelation closes with a prayer: "Come, Lord Jesus." Roughly the same plea in Aramaic, *Marana tha* ("Come, O Lord"), appears in 1 Corinthians 16:22. This suggests that these words reflect the longing of even the earliest churches.

If celebrity endorsements can prompt people to buy certain products, how much more do the testimonies in this passage influence you to consider the message of Revelation? This book is often left unopened by Christians due to confusion over its symbolic content. But the promised blessing for its reading (1:3), as well as the endorsements in this passage, provide strong reasons for all Christians to reconsider any hesitancy.

This passage repeatedly emphasizes that Jesus is "coming soon." We are called to be ready for Christ's coming, watching and eagerly anticipating that day. If the thought of his return generates anxiety, it's because we have become too attached to this world and its values. Do you find yourself longing to see your Lord, in all his glory, face-to-face? "Marana tha." Come quickly, O Lord!

Study Helps

Table of Weights and Measures, 2111

Reading Tracks, 2112

Study Guides, 2120

Subject Index, 2132

Index to Charts, 2141

Index to Articles, 2144

Index to Snapshots, 2146

Bibliography, 2148

Concordance, 2150

Colophon, 2316

Study Helps

Table of Weights and Measures, 2111

Reading Tables, 2112

Study Guides, 2120

Subject Index, 2132

Index to Charts, 2141

Index to Articles, 2144

Index to Snapshots, 2146

Bibliography, 2148

Concordance, 2150

Colophon, 2356

Table of Weights and Measures

	BIBLICAL UNIT	APPROXIMATE AMERICAN EQUIVALENT	APPROXIMATE METRIC EQUIVALENT
WEIGHTS	talent (60 minas)	75 pounds	34 kilograms
	mina (50 shekels)	$1^1/_4$ pounds	0.6 kilogram
	shekel (2 bekas)	$^2/_5$ ounce	11.5 grams
	pim ($^2/_3$ shekel)	$^1/_3$ ounce	7.6 grams
	beka (10 gerahs)	$^1/_5$ ounce	5.5 grams
	gerah	$^1/_{50}$ ounce	0.6 gram
LENGTH	cubit	18 inches	0.5 meter
	span	9 inches	23 centimeters
	handbreadth	3 inches	8 centimeters
CAPACITY			
Dry Measure	cor [homer] (10 ephahs)	6 bushels	220 liters
	lethek (5 ephahs)	3 bushels	110 liters
	ephah (10 omers)	$^3/_5$ bushel	22 liters
	seah ($^1/_3$ ephah)	7 quarts	7.3 liters
	omer ($^1/_{10}$ ephah)	2 quarts	2 liters
	cab ($^1/_{18}$ ephah)	1 quart	1 liter
Liquid Measure	bath (1 ephah)	6 gallons	22 liters
	hin ($^1/_6$ bath)	4 quarts	4 liters
	log ($^1/_{72}$ bath)	$^1/_3$ quart	0.3 liter

The figures of the table are calculated on the basis of a shekel equaling 11.5 grams, a cubit equaling 18 inches and an ephah equaling 22 liters. The quart referred to is either a dry quart (slightly larger than a liter) or a liquid quart (slightly smaller than a liter), whichever is applicable. The ton referred to in the footnotes is the American ton of 2,000 pounds.

This table is based upon the best available information, but it is not intended to be mathematically precise; like the measurement equivalents in the footnotes, it merely gives approximate amounts and distances. Weights and measures differed somewhat at various times and places in the ancient world. There is uncertainty particularly about the ephah and the bath; further discoveries may shed more light on these units of capacity.

Reading Tracks

Living the Christian Life

The Christian life begins with God's Holy Spirit. It doesn't begin with things we do—human faith, human wisdom, human deeds—but with God reaching out to us.

The Christian life continues, though, with us. We respond to God's Holy Spirit by shaping our hearts to God's desires, building our minds to think his thoughts, and acting in ways that will build his kingdom.

HEART SHAPING

We respond to God's Holy Spirit with faith, hope, and love—faith that is both humble and wise, hope that creates courage and leads to encouragement, and love that is shown in compassion and generosity. Thus we build hearts shaped by Christian virtue.

MIND BUILDING

Our experience, of course, demands reflection. What can our feelings toward God mean? Theological deliberation, the process of formulating and organizing our knowledge about God, comes in the "middle of the day" of the Christian life. It's neither the morning star nor the setting sun, neither the first word nor the last. Theology's greatest virtues are to connect and unify. Without theology, untended emotions are in danger of devouring the very life they create. Without theology, good deeds can choke with self-righteousness. Without a theory or system or formulation of what we believe, without a series of checks and balances, we'd never act, but only react.

ACTION PRODUCING

But act we do. And act we must. Our actions make all of us heroes of the faith. Only actions—Corrie ten Boom-like actions, Lincolnesque actions, actions of the Billy Graham sort—set us apart from the world. When we act in Christ's name on behalf of the "least" of his children, we truly live the Christian life.

At this point, statistics and balance sheets and strategic planning become sanctified in the Christian life. The reason is this: Not just any act will do. Christians act to meet great needs. What the world needs and what the Christian life provides aren't insignificant actions but world-shaping, life-changing deeds that make the world a better place in which to live.

THE BIBLE

The Bible is our teacher. In order to grow in the Christian life, we need a map to show us the way. We read the Bible to understand God. In the Bible we find descriptions of our faith, hope, and love. Reading the Bible helps us define the purposes for which God has created us.

What follows are reading tracks that will lead you through the stages of the Christian life. They begin with God and end with us acting on God's behalf in the world.

The sections of the reading track can be used in several ways:

- Read the passages through from beginning to end—from heart shaping to mind building to action producing.
- Pick one of the three sections for an in-depth, focused study.
- Use the material selectively for your personal devotions.
- Use the material in your small group for discussion starters.

If you'd like to study how each of these Biblical themes applies to everyday life in the 21st century, choose a topic that particularly interests you and find the corresponding study guide on pages 2120–2131.

HEART SHAPING

Humility (an attitude of reverence for, dependence on, and obedience to God)

Reasons for humility
For renewal (Lev. 26:41–42; Ps. 44:25–26)
For reward (2 Sam. 7:8; Prov. 18:12; Luke 1:52; James 4:10)
In recognition of our status (Prov. 3:34–35; Rom. 12:3)
Because God commands it (Mic. 6:8; 1 Peter 5:5–6)
As a reflection of Christ (Phil. 2:1–11)

Some Biblical examples of humility
Jacob (Gen. 32:10)
Joseph (Gen. 41:15–16)
Moses (Num. 12:3)
David (1 Sam. 18:18; 2 Sam. 7:18)
Solomon (1 Kings 3:7)
Daniel (Dan. 2:30)
John the Baptist (Matt. 3:13–14)
Elizabeth (Luke 1:43)
Mary (Luke 1:48)
Sinful woman (Luke 7:37–38)
Women at the tomb (Luke 23:55–56)
Martha and Mary (John 12:2–3)
Paul (1 Tim. 1:15)

Wisdom (the quality of knowledge, discernment, and understanding that is characteristic of God himself)

Definition of wisdom
To fear God (Job 28:28)
To have knowledge of God (Prov. 30:3)
To know God personally (Eph. 1:17)

Components of wisdom
Discernment (Gen. 41:39; Ps. 107:43; Hos. 14:9)
Skills and abilities (Ex. 28:3; 36:1)
Political astuteness (Est. 1:13; Prov. 21:22)
Integrity in daily living (Prov. 14:8; Eccl. 12:11; James 3:17)
Supernatural knowledge (Dan. 5:12)

Sources of wisdom
God (Gen. 41:16; Job 12:13; Prov. 3:19–20; 8:12,22–23; Eph. 1:17; James 3:17)
God's Word (Ps. 19:7; 119:5–6; Prov. 1:1–6)
Parents (Prov. 1:8; 3:11–12; 6:20–22)
Sound teaching (Prov. 9:9)
The human spirit (Rom. 8:16)
Prayer (James 1:5)
Accepting/rejecting wisdom (Prov. 1:20–25; 8:10–12; 10:8; 1 Thess. 4:7–8)

Results of rejecting wisdom
Abusive behavior (Prov. 3:29–30)
Rebellion (Prov. 5:12–14)
Laziness (Prov. 6:9–11)
Deceit (Prov. 6:12–15; Dan. 2:8–9)
Adultery (Prov. 6:32)
Ruin and death (Prov. 7:24–27; 8:36; 9:17–18)
Pride and self-deception (Isa. 47:10)
Error (1 Cor. 1:21)
Foolishness (1 Cor. 3:19–20)
Dissension (1 Tim. 6:3–5)
Envy and selfishness (James 3:14–16)

Characteristics of godly wisdom
Accepts instruction (Prov. 1:5; 9:9; 13:10; 15:31)
Instructs others (Prov. 4:1–2; Eccl. 12:9; Eph. 6:4; 1 Tim. 1:18)
Gives security and protection (Prov. 4:6; Eccl. 8:5)
Brings prosperity (Prov. 8:18; Jer. 10:21)
Results in justice (Prov. 8:20)
Leads to life (Prov. 15:24; Dan. 12:3)

Rewards of seeking wisdom
Discretion (Prov. 1:4; 5:1–2)
Knowledge (Prov. 1:23)
Knowledge of God (Prov. 2:1–6)
Protection (Prov. 2:13–16)
Health (Prov. 3:7–8; 4:22; 9:11)
Peace (Prov. 3:17)
Blessing (Prov. 3:18; 8:18)
Life (Prov. 3:21–22; 4:4)
Honor (Prov. 4:7–9)
Joy (Prov. 29:3)

Biblical examples of wise people
Joseph (Gen. 41:39–40; Acts 7:10)
Joshua (Deut. 34:9)
David (2 Sam. 14:20)
Solomon (1 Kings 3:28)
Daniel (Dan. 2:19–23)
Paul (2 Peter 3:15)

Courage (the ability to act bravely under difficult conditions)

Reasons to desire courage
Necessity for leaders (Deut. 1:21; 31:7)
Commanded by God (Josh. 1:6–9; Matt. 14:25–27)
Demonstrates God's calling (1 Sam. 17:32; Acts 4:13)

Occasions that require Christian courage
Praying (Gen. 18:27–28; Rom. 8:15; Heb. 4:14–16)
Seeking God's blessing (Gen. 32:24–26; Luke 8:43–47)
Confronting sin (2 Sam. 12:7–13; Mark 6:18; Gal. 2:11)
Accomplishing God's calling (1 Chron. 22:11–13; Acts 20:22–24; Phil. 1:20; Heb. 11:8)
Facing personal pressure (Ps. 46:1–3; Matt. 14:27; Acts 13:44–46; 1 Cor. 16:13)
Witnessing (Matt. 10:19–26; Acts 4:18–20; 2 Tim. 4:17)

Encouragement (giving someone else the confidence and courage to live out their faith)

Essentials of Christian encouragement
Must be received in the spirit it is given (Gen. 37:34–35)
Includes exhortation or warning (2 Chron. 32:6–8; Luke 3:18; Eph. 4:1; Col. 1:28; 1 Thess. 2:11–12)
Commanded (Isa. 35:3–4; Mark 6:50; Heb. 12:12)

Sources of encouragement
Prayer (Ps. 10:17; Rom. 15:30)
God's Word (Ps. 119:105; John 14:26; Rom. 15:4)
God's promises (Isa. 44:21–22; John 17:26)
God's grace (John 1:16; Rom. 11:22)
God's Spirit (Acts 4:29–31)
Other believers (2 Cor. 7:4,12–13; Eph. 6:22; Phil. 1:14; 1 Thess. 3:6–7)

Biblical examples of people who were encouragers
Jonathan (1 Sam. 23:16)
King Hezekiah (2 Chron. 30:22)
Jesus (John 14:27)
Barnabas (Acts 4:36; 11:22–23)
Paul (Rom. 1:11–12)
Paul's friends (1 Cor. 16:17–18; Col. 1:4–8)
Timothy (1 Thess. 3:2; 1 Tim. 5:1)

Prayers for encouragement
Romans 15:5–6
Colossians 1:9–12
2 Thessalonians 2:16–17

Compassion (care and concern usually displayed by acts of kindness to those in distress)

Characteristics of Christian compassion
Limited (Ex. 34:6–7; Matt. 12:46–49; Rom. 9:14–16)

God-inspired (Ps. 146:6–9; Jer. 42:12; Dan. 1:9; John 14:12; Rom. 9:15; 2 Cor. 1:3)
Requires action (Isa. 58:6–7; John 13:12–17; James 2:15–16; 1 Peter 3:8–9)
Vital requirement of Christian character (Eph. 4:32; Col. 3:12)

Objects of Christian compassion
The bereaved (Gen. 37:35; Ruth 2:11; Job 29:13; Luke 7:11–15; John 11:19; Rom. 12:15)
The oppressed (Ex. 22:27; Job 29:15–17; Ps. 82:3–4; Luke 4:18)
The lonely (Ruth 4:13–15; 1 Sam. 2:18–21; Eccl. 4:10–11; Luke 7:11–15; 2 Cor. 7:6)
Children (1 Kings 3:26; Isa. 66:13; Mark 10:14–16; 1 Tim. 5:10)
Prisoners (2 Chron. 28:15; Ps. 79:11; Matt. 25:36; Luke 4:18; Acts 16:33–34; Heb. 13:3)
The sick (Job 2:11–13; Ps. 35:13–14; Matt. 14:14; Mark 1:41; Acts 5:15–16; James 5:15)
The poor (Job 29:12; Ps. 82:3; Zech. 7:9–10; Luke 4:18)
Widows and orphans (Job 29:12–13; Ps. 68:5; Zech. 7:9–10; John 14:18; Acts 9:36–39; 1 Tim. 5:3; James 1:27)
The needy (Job 29:16; Ps. 82:4; Prov. 14:21; Matt. 15:32; 1 Jn. 3:17)
The harassed and helpless (Ezek. 34:15–16; Matt. 9:36; John 21:16)
Sinners (Luke 6:37; 15:2; John 8:10–11; Rom. 8:33–34; 2 Cor. 2:7–8; Gal. 6:1; James 5:16)

Generosity (the free and liberal bestowal on others of wealth, possessions, or food)
God as primary model of generosity
God's gifts (Gen. 17:5–8; Ps. 84:11; John 16:23; 1 Cor. 12:4–5; 2 Cor. 9:8–11)
Creation (Ps. 65:9–13; 89:8–11)
Provision (Ps. 78:12–16; Acts 14:17)
Salvation (Ps. 85:1–3,8–9; Isa. 44:24–28; Eph. 1:7)
Wisdom (Prov. 1:20–23; Eph. 1:8; James 1:5)
Comfort (Isa. 40:1; 2 Cor. 1:5)
Jesus (Matt. 10:7–8; John 17:26)
Sanctification (2 Peter 1:2–3)
Human demonstrations of generosity
Giving in worship (Ex. 34:22; Matt. 26:6–7; Rom. 12:1)
Giving gifts (1 Kings 10:13; Prov. 18:16; Luke 21:1–4; 1 Cor. 16:17)
Acts of mercy (Prov. 11:16; Luke 10:33–35; 15:21–24)
Giving in general (Prov. 19:17; Matthew 7:11; Acts 4:32–37; 1 Tim. 6:18)
Giving to the church (1 Cor. 16:1–2; 2 Cor. 9:12–13; Phil. 4:16)
Rewards for generosity (Prov. 18:16; Mal. 3:10; Acts 9:36–42; 2 Cor. 9:6; Phil. 4:18–19)

MIND BUILDING

Imago Dei (humanity created in the image, or likeness, of God)
Biblical statement of this reality (Gen. 1:26–27)
Implications
Stewardship of all creation (Gen. 1:26; Ps. 8:3–8)
Respect for all human life (Gen. 9:6; James 3:9)
Imitation of God's love and justice (Deut. 10:17–19; Matt. 5:48)
Imago Dei *disfigured*
Resulting in contention with creation (Gen. 3:17–19; Rom. 8:20–21)

Resulting in exploitation of nature (Deut. 22:6–7)
As a result of the fall (Rom. 3:23)
Imago Dei *restored*
Imago Dei restored in union with Jesus (Rom. 8:29)
Complete restoration of *imago dei* in the future (1 Cor. 15:49)
Christian life as a process of transformation (2 Cor. 3:18)
Jesus Christ as the image of God (Phil. 2:6; Col. 1:15; Heb. 1:3)
Jesus Christ as the perfect human being (Heb. 4:15)

Fallen World (the departure by creation, including human beings, from the standards set by God)
Essentials of the fall
Defined as the first sin by Adam and Eve (Gen. 3:1–7)
Caused by disobedience (Gen. 2:16–17; 3:6; Hos. 6:7)
Resulted from the temptation and deception of Satan (Gen. 3:1–4,13; 2 Cor. 11:3)
Results of the fall
Impaired relationship with God (Gen. 3:22–23)
Broken relationships with humans (Gen. 4:1–8; Rom. 1:18–32)
Damaged relationship with creation (Gen. 3:17–19; Rom. 8:19–21)
Death (Rom. 5:12)
Inclination toward sin, despite ability to choose between right and wrong (James 1:13–15; 1 Jn. 2:15–17)

Reconciliation (the restoration of fellowship between God and humanity and creation)
The process of reconciliation
God initiates it (Rom. 5:6–8; 8:3; 2 Cor. 5:18–19)
Jesus is the means (Rom. 5:15–19; 2 Cor. 5:14–15; Eph. 2:14–18; Heb. 9:28)
Humans must respond (Rom. 8:12–17; 2 Cor. 5:19–21; 7:10–11; Eph. 5:1)
Results of reconciliation
Peace with God (Acts 10:36,43; Rom. 5:1; Phil. 4:7; 1 Thess. 5:23–24)
Access to God (Rom. 5:2; Eph. 3:6; Heb. 4:16; 10:19–22)
Joy in partnership with God (Rom. 5:2; Phil. 1:3–6; 1 Thess. 3:7–9)
Adoption as God's child (Rom. 8:15–16; Gal. 4:4–7; Heb. 2:10–12; 1 Jn. 3:1)
Peace within creation (Col. 1:20)
Hope (Heb. 6:18–20; 1 Jn. 3:2–3)

Love of Neighbor (Scripture's instruction to love one another)
Reasons for loving our neighbor
Commanded by God (Lev. 19:18; Gal. 5:14; 1 Jn. 3:23)
Models God's love (Hos. 2:21–23; John 13:34; 1 Jn. 4:7–12)
Fulfills the law (Rom. 13:10; Gal. 5:14)
Maintains fellowship (Phil. 4:10–14; 1 Thess. 3:6; Heb. 10:25; 1 Peter 4:8)
Promotes service (Phil. 4:17; 1 Thess. 2:8–9; Heb. 6:10–11)
Helps us know God (1 Jn. 1:2–8; 2:2–11)
Ways to express love for our neighbor
Care for the sick (Matt. 10:1; 25:36)
Meet material needs (Matt. 25:37–40; Rom. 12:13)
Practice hospitality (Luke 14:12–14)
Obey God (Luke 18:22; 1 Jn. 2:3–6)
Be sincere (Rom. 12:9–10)

Biblical examples of those who showed love for others
Abraham for Lot (Gen. 14:14–16)
Abraham for Sodom (Gen. 18:20–33)
Moses for the Israelites (Ex. 32:31–32)
Jonathan for David (1 Sam. 18:3)
Esther for the Jews (Est. 4:6–16)
An unknown woman for Jesus (Luke 7:36–50)
The Good Samaritan for a stranger (Luke 10:29–37)
Paul for the churches (2 Cor. 1:3–6; 12:15;
Gal. 4:19; Phil. 1:3,7)

Spiritual Formation (the process of believers growing in their faith)

Essential nature of spiritual formation
God desires and expects spiritual growth
(Matt. 5:48, Rom. 8:29–30)
We must make the effort (Rom. 8:12–14;
Phil. 2:12; 2 Peter 1:5–9)
God supplies the resources (Rom. 8:26–27;
Phil. 2:13; 2 Peter 1:3)
The goal is to become like Christ (Rom. 8:29;
Eph. 4:13–15)

Evidences of spiritual growth
Understanding (Ps. 119:27; 1 Cor. 2:2; Col. 3:2–10)
Love (Luke 6:27–35; Rom. 12:9–10; Col. 3:14;
1 Thess. 3:12)
Mercy (Luke 6:36)
Forgiveness (Luke 6:37; Eph. 4:32; Col. 3:13)
Grace (Luke 6:37–38; Rom. 14:13; 2 Cor. 1:12;
2 Peter 3:18)
Fruitfulness (Luke 6:43–45; John 15:16;
Gal. 5:22–23; Col. 3:12)
Faith (Rom. 14:1–3; Eph. 6:16; 2 Thess. 1:3)
Holiness (2 Cor. 7:1; Eph. 4:24; 5:25–27)
Contentment (Phil. 4:11–12; 1 Tim. 6:6)

Tools for spiritual growth
Scripture (Josh. 1:8; Eph. 6:17; 2 Tim. 3:16–17)
Meditation (Ps. 119:27; Phil. 4:8; Heb. 3:1)
Prayer (Matt. 6:13; Rom. 12:12; Eph. 3:14–17; 6:18;
Phil. 4:6)
The Holy Spirit (Rom. 8:26–27; 1 Cor. 2:4–5,10;
Eph. 3:16–18)
Relationships with believers (1 Cor. 12:4–6,12;
2 Cor. 1:6–7)

Stewardship (the careful use, control, and management of the possessions entrusted to us)

Possessions of which we're stewards
Creation (Gen. 1:28; 2:15; 1 Cor. 6:20)
Material possessions (Deut. 8:17–18;
Matt. 25:14–30; Luke 16:10–13)
Time (Ps. 90:12; Matt. 24:45–51)
The gospel (Luke 24:45–47; John 6:68–69;
1 Cor. 4:1–2)
Spiritual gifts (1 Cor. 12:7–11; 14:1; 1 Peter 4:10–11)

Actions that reveal our stewardship
Expressing care and concern (Gen. 2:15;
Matt. 25:40; Heb. 10:34; James 2:15–17)
Giving ourselves to God (Est. 4:15–16; 2 Cor. 12:14)
Giving to the needy (Prov. 14:21,31; Matt. 19:21;
Luke 19:8; Acts 4:32–35; 6:1–3; 2 Cor. 8:1–5;
Eph. 4:28; 1 Jn. 3:17)
Working diligently (Dan. 6:1–3; 1 Thess. 4:11–12;
5:12–13)

Service (the ministry all creatures owe their Creator and humanity)

Reasons to serve
Out of obedience to God (Deut. 10:12; 11:13;
Rom. 1:25; 1 Tim. 6:17–18; Heb. 13:16;
1 Peter 4:10)

To aid human development, order, and peace
(Deut. 11:13–15)
As a sign of our love for God and neighbor
(Josh. 22:4–5; Gal. 5:13–14)
To build God's kingdom (Josh. 24:13–14;
Rom. 12:5–7; 1 Peter 4:11)
Because God is worthy of our service and praise
(Ps. 148:7–12; Rev. 5:10)
It is the purpose of our freedom (Rom. 7:6;
1 Cor. 7:22–23; Gal. 5:13; Heb. 9:14)
In view of God's promised rewards (Gal. 6:8–10;
Eph. 6:7–8; Heb. 10:33–35)

Correct attitude of those who serve
Kindness (Gal. 4:14; Eph. 4:32)
Gentleness (Gal. 6:1; Eph. 4:2; 1 Thess. 2:7)
Humility (Eph. 4:2; Col. 3:17; 1 Peter 5:5–6)
Patience (Col. 3:13; 1 Thess. 5:14)

Ways to serve
Supply material needs (Deut. 8:17–18; Acts 6:2–3;
1 Tim. 5:8)
Worship God (Ps. 150; Heb. 13:15; Rev. 5:12–14)
Provide pastoral leadership (Acts 20:28;
1 Tim. 3:1; 1 Peter 5:2–3)
Share burdens (Acts 20:35; Gal. 6:2)
Practice hospitality (Rom. 12:13; Phil. 2:29;
1 Peter 4:9)
Pray (Col. 1:9–12; 1 Tim. 2;1,8; James 5:16;
1 Peter 4:7)
Teach and admonish (Col. 3:16; 1 Tim. 4:6,13;
5:17)
Encourage (1 Thess. 5:11; Heb. 10:24)

Biblical examples of service
Abigail (1 Sam. 40–41)
Elijah (1 Kings 18:15)
Elisha (2 Kings 3:14; 5:16)
Old Testament priests (2 Chron. 13:10)
Jesus (Matt. 20:28)
Sinful woman (Luke 7:37–38)
Women at the tomb (Luke 23:55–56)
Martha and Mary (John 12:2–3)
Paul (Rom. 1:9; 2 Cor. 11:8; Col. 1:23)

ACTION PRODUCING

Children (gifts from God to be loved, cared for, and trained)

Needs of children
Education (Ex. 10:2; 12:26–27; 13:14–15;
Prov. 1:8–9; Joel 1:1–3; Eph. 6:4)
Provision and protection (1 Sam. 2:19; Matt. 2:13;
7:9–11)
Role models (1 Sam. 3:1; 1 King 9:4; 2 Chron. 17:3;
Ps. 128:1–4; 2 Tim. 1:5; 3:14–15)
Discipline (Prov. 13:24; Heb. 12:7–11)
Love, affection, and nurturing (Matt. 19:13–15;
Mark 10:16; Luke 18:15; Titus 2:4)

Correct attitudes to have regarding children
Be grateful for them (Ps. 113:9; 127:3)
Imitate them (Matt. 11:25; Luke 18:17)
Welcome them (Matt. 18:5; 19:13–15)
Protect them (Matt. 18:6)
Cherish them (Luke 2:19,51)
Be patient with them (Eph. 6:4)

Notable children of the Bible
Joseph (Gen. 37:3)
Moses (Ex. 2:7–8)
Samson (Judg. 13:2–25)
Samuel (1 Sam. 1)
David (1 Sam. 16:11–13)
Son of the widow of Zarephath (1 Kings 17:7–23)

Son of the Shunammite woman (2 Kings 4:8–37)
The slave girl of Naaman's wife (2 Kings 5:2–6)
Demon-possessed boy (Mark 9:17–27)
John the Baptist (Luke 1:13–17,57–66,80)
Jesus (Luke 2:34–52)
Jairus's daughter (Luke 8:49–56)
Timothy (2 Tim. 1:5; 3:14–15)

Disease (an illness or other condition that prevents people achieving their full potential)

Causes of disease
Sin (Gen. 3:16–17; James 5:15)
Judgment (Deut. 28:20–21; Ps. 107:17; 1 Cor. 11:29–30)
Accident (2 Kings 4:39–40)
Testing (Job 2:4–6)
Aging (2 Cor. 4:16)

Appropriate responses to various diseases (our own and others')
Isolation if contagious (Lev. 13:9)
Submission to God (Job 13:15; 2 Cor. 12:8–10)
Compassion and care (Matt. 25:36; Luke 10:30–37)
Prayer (James 5:14–15)

Sources of healing
God (Ex. 15:26; Isa. 30:26; Jer. 33:6)
Priests (Lev. 14:1–31; Matt. 8:4)
Prophets (1 Kings 17:17–24; 2 Kings 5:10,14)
Medicine/remedies (Ezek. 30:21; 1 Tim. 5:23)
Jesus Christ (Matt. 8:2–3; Mark 1:32–34; Luke 4:40; 8:26–36)
Apostles (Matt. 10:1; Luke 9:6; Acts 5:12–16)
Doctors (Luke 4:23)
The Holy Spirit (Luke 5:17)
Followers of Jesus (Luke 10:8–9)
The church (1 Cor. 12:8–9,28)

Examples of diseases mentioned in the Bible
Leprosy (Num. 12:10; Luke 17:11–19)
Tumors (Deut. 28:27; 1 Sam. 5:6)
Insanity (Deut. 28:28; 1 Sam. 21:13; Dan. 4:33–34)
Boils/sores (Deut. 28:35; Job 2:7; Luke 16:20)
Depression (1 Kings 19:4; Ps. 42:5–11; Prov. 13:12; 2 Cor. 1:8–9)
Fever (Job 30:30; Luke 4:38; Acts 28:8)
Paralysis (Matt. 4:24; 8:6; 9:2)
Demon possession (Matt. 4:24; 8:28; 9:32–33)
Seizures (Matt. 4:24; 17:15; Mark 9:17–18)
General disease (Matt. 8:17)
Hemorrhaging (Matt. 9:20)
Blindness (Matt. 9:27; John 9:1)
Dysentery (Acts 28:8)

Education (the imparting of spiritual, intellectual, moral, and social instruction)

Components of godly education
Fear of the Lord (Ps. 111:10; Heb. 2:1–4)
Knowledge (Prov. 9:9; 24:4–5)
Discipline (Prov. 10:17; 12:1; 15:32; Heb. 12:11)
Faith (John 14:10–12; Heb. 11:3)
Truth (2 Cor. 10:5; Col. 2:2–4; 1 Tim. 6:20–21)

Places where godly education occurs
Home (Deut. 6:4–9)
Worship (Deut. 31:9–13; Josh. 8:34–35; Acts 5:42; 1 Cor. 11:23–26; 14:26–33)
The church (1 Cor. 14:19,23–25)

Sources of godly education
Priests (1 Sam. 1:24–28; Mal. 2:7)
Prophets (2 Chron. 26:5; Heb. 1:1)
God (Ps. 25:12; Prov. 2:6–9; Heb. 8:10–11)
Parents (Prov. 1:8; Eph. 6:4; 2 Tim. 3:14–15)
Jesus (John 14:24; Heb. 1:1–3)

The Holy Spirit (John 14:26; 1 Cor. 12:1–3; 2 Tim. 1:13–14)
Apostles (Acts 5:42; Eph. 6:19)
Conscience (Rom. 2:14–15; 1 Cor. 11:27–33)
Lay teachers (1 Cor. 14:3–5; 2 Tim. 2:2)
Scripture (2 Tim. 3:16–17)
Elders (Titus 1:6–9; 2:1–15)

Products of godly education
Discernment (Prov. 9:6; 10:13; Hos. 14:9)
Joy in practical living (Prov. 10:1,9)
Hope (Prov. 24:14)
Right relationship with God (Prov. 30:7–9)
Political astuteness (Eccl. 9:14–18)

Hunger (a state of emptiness reflecting a lack of physical or spiritual food)

Causes of hunger
Punishment for sin (Gen. 3:17–19; Lev. 26:23–26)
Famine (Gen. 41:56; Ps. 63:1; Amos 8:11–12)
Fasting (Ps. 109:24; Matt. 4:2)

Effects of hunger
Moral degradation (Lev. 26:27–29; Deut. 28:53; Isa. 9:20; Jer. 19:9)
Physical deterioration (Job 30:3)
Obsession with food (Isa. 29:8; Rom. 14:20–21)

God's provision for the hungry
Natural (Gen. 8:22; Zech. 8:12)
Miraculous (Ex. 16:12–15; Matt. 14:15–21; 15:32–38; John 21:1–11)
Spiritual (Matt. 5:6; John 6:35; Rom. 14:17)

Injustice (the unfair or ill treatment of others)

Sources of injustice
Rulers (Ps. 58: 1–2; Isa. 1:23; Jer. 22:13–17; Mic. 3:1–3,9–11; Hab. 2:9)
Social structures (Eccl. 5:8; Isa. 3:14–15; Mic. 1:5)
Sin (Amos 5:12; Matt. 15:19–20; Eph. 4:17–19; 5:11–12)
Religious leaders (Matt. 23:1–4; 26:3–5; Luke 11:46; Acts 4:1–3; 23:1–3)
Satan (John 8:44; 13:26–27; 1 Jn. 3:10)
Principalities and powers (Eph. 6:12)

Environments in which injustice occurs
Courts of law (Ex. 23:2–3; Prov. 24:23–24; Amos 2:7; 5:10,12; Hab. 1:3–4)
Government (Ps. 82:1–4; Isa. 10:1–2; Ezek. 34:1–4)
Business (Prov. 28:8; Hos. 12:7; Amos 2:6; 8:5–6; Hab. 2:9; James 5:1–6)
Community (Isa. 59:14–15; Amos 2:7; Jonah 3:8)
Family life (Amos 2:7; 4:1; Mark 7:9–13)

Some Biblical examples of injustice
Slavery (Gen. 37:26–28; Ex. 1:11–14)
False accusations (Gen. 39:6–20)
Oppression of the helpless (Ex. 1:11; Ezek. 22:29; Amos 4:1; 5:11–12)
Perjury (Ex. 23:1)
Slander (Ps. 31:13; Jer. 6:28; Ezek. 36:3; 1 Peter 2:1)
Violence (Ps. 58:2; Isa. 59:3–7; Jer. 6:7; Ezek. 8:17; 18:10–13; 45:9; Joel 3:19; Obad. 10; Hab. 1:3,9; Acts 21:35)
Usury (Prov. 28:8)
Dishonesty (Isa. 59:4,14–15; Mic. 2:2; Eph. 4:25)
Rebellion against God (Isa. 59:12–13)

God's attitude toward injustice (which we should imitate)
God's people are to hate injustice (Ex. 22:1–9; Prov. 22:22; Mark 12:31)
God helps victims of injustice (Deut. 1:30–31; Ps. 12:5; Mic. 2:1–3)

God hates injustice (Prov. 6:16–19; Amos 2:6–7;
5:21–24)
God will restore justice (Isa. 1:26–27; 32:16; 33:5;
Mic. 5:1–5a)
God hates human complacency toward injustice
(Amos 6:1–6; Obad. 10–15)
God will punish those who are unjust
(Amos 8:7–14; Obad. 10–15; Mic. 2:3–4;
Nah. 1:2–6; Hab. 2:6–8)

Mission (actions that bear witness to the Good News
of what God has done for his people)

God's vehicles of mission
Old Testament Israel (Gen. 18:18)
Jesus Christ (Isa. 42:6; 49:6; Matt. 8:11; Luke 2:32;
John 10:16; Acts 26:23)
The church (Matt. 28:18–20; Luke 9:1;
John 20:21–22; Acts 13:47)
The Holy Spirit (John 14:26; 16:13; Acts 13:2)

Tasks of mission
Making disciples (Matt. 28:19–20; Acts 2:41–42)
Healing (Luke 9:2)
Proclaiming the gospel (Acts 20:24)
Bringing honor to God (Eph. 3:10–11)

Audiences of mission
Jews (Matt. 10:5–6; Acts 11:19)
Everyone (Matt. 24:14; 28:19; Luke 24:47)
Samaritans (Acts 8:4–8)
Gentiles (Acts 9:15; 13:46–47; Rom. 11:13;
15:15–16)

Those called to mission
Those sent to other people groups
(2 Kings 17:27–28; Amos 7:15; Jonah 1:1–2;
Acts 11:19–20)
All God's people (Ps. 96:2–3; Mark 16:15)

Receiving the call to mission
Given by God (Isa. 6:8–9; Jer. 1:4–10;
Acts 8:26–35; 22:21)
Compelled by the message of the Bible
(Acts 4:18–20; 1 Cor. 9:16; 2 Cor. 5:14)
Through circumstances in our lives (Acts 8:4;
18:1–2)
Confirmed by the church (Acts 13:2–3; Gal. 2:7–9)

Peace (the state of harmony available to believers through
a right relationship with God)

Those with whom we should have peace
God (Job 22:21; Isa. 26:3; 27:5; Rom. 5:1;
Col. 1:19–20)
Self (Ps. 4:8; Prov. 14:30)
Others (Matt. 5:9,24; Mark 9:50; Rom. 12:18;
14:19; 1 Cor. 7:15)
Creation (1 Tim. 4:4)

Some reasons for lack of peace
Suffering (Job 3:24–26; 2 Cor. 1:8)
Fear of death (Ps. 55:4–5; Isa. 57:2)
Oppression (Ps. 56:2–3)
Unfulfilled longing (Prov. 13:12)
Envy (Prov. 14:30)
Strife (Prov. 17:1)
Disobedience (Isa. 48:18)
Wickedness (Isa. 48:22; 57:20–21; 59:2,8;
Rom. 3:17)
Denial of truth (Jer. 6:14; Ezek. 13:10)
Burdens of life (Matt. 11:28–29)

How peace is acquired
Through obedience to God's Word (Lev. 26:3–6;
Ps. 119:165)
As a blessing from God (Ps. 29:11; 85:8; Isa. 66:12;
2 Cor. 1:3–4)

Through human pursuit and effort (Ps. 34:14;
Rom. 14:19; 2 Tim. 2:22; 1 Peter 3:11;
2 Peter 3:14)
Through wisdom (Prov. 3:17)
As a result of faithful living (Prov. 16:7; Isa. 57:2)
Through discipline (Prov. 29:17; Heb. 12:11)
Through trust in God (Isa. 26:3)
Through Jesus Christ (Isa. 53:5; John 14:27;
Rom. 5:1; Eph. 2:14; Col. 1:20)
Through God's healing (Isa. 57:18–19; 60:17–19;
Jer. 33:6; Luke 8:43–48)
Through the Holy Spirit (Rom. 14:17; Gal. 5:22)

Benefits of peace
Safety (Ps. 4:8; Prov. 1:33; Jer. 33:6; Ezek. 34:25)
Harmonious living (Ps. 133:1; Rom. 12:17–19)
God's presence (Isa. 41:10; Matt. 28:20; Gal. 4:6)
Hope (Rom. 5:1–2; 15:13)

Pollution (environmental corruption caused by the failure
of human beings to exercise the responsibility God delegated to them for the well-being of the earth)

*Responsibility for creation delegated by God
to human beings*
God's ownership of creation (Ex. 19:5–6;
Ps. 24:1–2; 50:9–12; Isa. 44:24)
Its care delegated to humankind (Gen. 1:26–28;
Ps. 8:6; 115:16; Heb. 2:6–8)
God's caring supervision (Ps. 65:9–13; 104:10–14;
Luke 12:24–28)
Creation's praise of God (Ps. 19:1; 89:5; 96:1;
148:3; Isa. 44:23; 55:12)

Caring for creation
Responsibility toward animals (Ex. 23:4–5,12;
Prov. 12:10; James 3:7)
Responsibility for natural resources (Lev. 25:1–7;
Deut. 20:19)
Repairing environmental damage (Ex. 23:10–11;
Lev. 25:1–7; Neh. 10:31)

Restoration of creation
(Acts 3:21; Rom. 8:19–21; 2 Peter 3:13;
Rev. 21:1–4; 22:1)

Population (human beings, the pinnacle of God's creation,
charged to be fruitful and multiply as well as manage
and care for the rest of creation)

Why God created human beings
As the apex, or high point, of creation
(Gen. 1:26–27; 5:1–2)
To care for creation (Gen. 1:26–28; 2:15;
Heb. 2:5–8)
To be fruitful and multiply (Gen. 1:28)
To commune with God (Gen. 3:8–9; Ex. 33:11;
Deut. 5:4; John 14:1–3; Rev. 21:3)
To give praise and glory to God (Ps. 145:10–12;
Eph. 1:12; Rev. 19:5)
To bring delight to God (Ps. 149:4)
To reign with God forever (Rev. 20:4; 22:5)

God's value of the human race
(Gen. 1:31; Ps. 8:3–6; John 3:16–17; Eph. 2:4–7)

Lessons related to childbirth
Parenthood is a blessing (Gen. 1:28; 4:1;
Ps. 127:3–5)
God controls the events of childbirth
(Gen. 17:16–19; Ps. 139:13,16; Isa. 49:5)
Fertility as a sign of God's blessing (Ex. 23:25–26;
Isa. 48:18–19)
Children are a gift of God (1 Sam. 2:20–21;
Ps. 127:3; Prov. 17:6)
Childbirth as a symbol of self-giving love
(Isa. 49:15; Gal. 4:19)

Poverty (lack of the basic necessities of life, such as water, food, clothing, shelter)

Some prominent groups of poor people in the Bible
Slaves (Ex. 23:12; Lev. 25:39)
Orphans (Deut. 10:18; 14:28–29)
Aliens (Deut. 24:17–21)
Widows (1 Kings 17:10–12; Jer. 18:21; Mark 12:41–44; Luke 7:11–15; 1 Tim. 5:3,9–10,16)
The oppressed (Ps. 9:9; 146:7; Prov. 15:15; Eccl. 4:1; Isa. 1:17; 58:10)
The spiritually poor (Ps. 34:6; Matt. 9:12–13; Luke 6:20–21)

Causes of poverty
Sin (Gen. 3:17–19)
Famine (Gen. 45:11; Acts 7:11)
God's judgment (Deut. 28:48)
Oppression (Judg. 6:5–6; Job 20:19; Isa. 1:7; James 5:1–6)
Misfortune (Job 1:13–21)
Idleness (Prov. 6:9–11; 20:13; 24:30–34; 2 Thess. 3:6–12)
Lack of discipline (Prov. 13:18; 21:5,20)
Loose living (Prov. 21:17; 23:21; Luke 15:13–14)
Debt (Prov. 22:7; Matt. 18:23–25)
Neglect of God's work (Hag. 1:9–11)

Effects of poverty
Crime (Prov. 6:30; 30:8–9)
Ruin (Prov. 10:15; 23:21; 24:33–34)
Shame (Prov. 14:20; Luke 16:3)
Misery (Prov. 31:7)

Proper attitudes to have toward the poor
Justice (Ex. 23:6; 2 Sam. 12:1–6; Prov. 22:22–23)
Bestowal of special rights (Lev. 19:9–10; 25:5–6)
Generosity (Deut. 15:7–8; Prov. 22:9; Matt. 6:1–4)
Compassion (Matt. 15:32; 18:26–27)
Care (Luke 3:11; 19:8; Eph. 4:28; 1 Tim. 5:3)

Persons/things that can help the poor
Relatives (Gen. 45:9–11; Lev. 25:25; 1 Tim. 5:16)
The rich (Deut. 15:7–8; Luke 14:13–14; 18:22; Eph. 4:28; 1 Tim. 6:18)
God (Ps. 35:10; Prov. 22:22–23; Matt. 6:28–30; Luke 18:7–8)
Jesus Christ (Isa. 61:1; Luke 4:18; 22:27)
The church (Gal. 2:10; James 2:1–9)
Work (Eph. 4:28; 2 Thess. 3:10; Titus 3:14)

Religion (a set of beliefs, a form of worship, ritual, prayer, and a code of moral behavior)

Different aspects of religion
Belief (Gen. 15:6; Heb. 11:6)
Worship (Gen. 24:26–27; Isa. 44:15; Acts 17:22–23)
Ritual (Ex. 23:14; Lev. 23:41; 1 Kings 12:32; Mark 7:3–4; Gal. 1:14)
Prayer (Isa. 44:17; Luke 2:37)
Code of behavior (Neh. 9:13–14; Mark 10:17–20)

How to identify a false religious practice
Worship of demons (Deut. 32:17)
Worship of humans or man-made things (Jer. 2:11; Acts 14:8–15; 17:29; Rom. 1:22,25)
Worship of secular authorities (Rev. 13:4)
Immoral practices encouraged/expected (1 Kings 14:23–24; Hos. 4:13–14)
Human sacrifices offered (2 Kings 17:17; Ps. 106:37–38)
Practices don't provide help in time of need (1 Sam. 12:21; Isa. 37:12; Jer. 14:22)
Practices based on human traditions, myths, or philosophies (Col. 2:8,20–23)

Signs of good religious practice
Purity/holiness (James 1:27; 1 Peter 1:15)
High moral standards (Dan. 6:4; 1 Cor. 5:11; 7:19; Phil. 1:27; 1 Peter 2:12)
Good works (Eph. 2:10; 1 Tim. 5:4; James 2:14–17; 3:13; 1 Peter 2:12)

Water (that colorless, odorless liquid essential for the sustenance of life)

Uses of water in the Bible
For washing (Gen. 18:4; Lev. 8:6; Matt. 27:24)
To sustain life (Gen. 21:8–21; 1 Kings 17:1–11; Mark 9:41)
As a sign from God (Gen. 24:34–50; 1 Sam. 12:16–18; 2 Kings 3:4–20)
For cooking (Ex. 12:9)
To irrigate crops (Lev. 26:4; James 5:17–18)
For drinking (2 Sam. 23:15–16; John 4:4–7)
In baptism (John 1:31)

Sources of water
Rivers (Gen. 2:10–14; Ex. 4:9; Rev. 8:10–11)
Floods (Gen. 7:17–24; Job 20:28; 22:16)
Wells (Gen. 26:19–22; Ex. 2:15–17; Isa. 37:25)
Springs (Ex. 15:27; Deut. 8:7; Josh. 15:19; 2 Chron. 32:3; James 3:11–12)
Rain (Lev. 26:4; Judg. 5:4; Ps. 68:7–10)
Cisterns (2 Chron. 26:10; Jer. 2:13; 14:3)

Things water symbolizes in the Bible
Judgment (Gen. 6:17; 7:7; Ex. 14:26–30; Jer. 47:2; 1 Peter 3:20–21)
Blessing (Deut. 8:7; Isa. 35:6–7; 43:19–20; Jer. 2:13; Zech. 14:8)
Affliction (2 Sam. 22:17; Ps. 68:1–4; Isa. 30:20; 43:2)
Salvation (Isa. 12:3; 49:10; 55:1; John 4:10; 1 Peter 3:20–21)
The Holy Spirit (Isa. 44:3; John 7:38–39)
Cleansing from sin (Ezek. 36:25; Eph. 5:26; Heb. 10:22)
Eternal life (John 4:10–14; Rev. 21:6; 22:1,17)
Baptism (Rom. 6:4; 1 Peter 3:20–21)

BUILDING TOOLS

Bible Study (an essential means by which believers are nurtured in faith and led to spiritual maturity)

The basic principles of Bible study
Scripture is sufficient for life (Deut. 4:1–2; Prov. 30:5–6)
Scripture is explained in order to be clearly understood (Neh. 8:8; Ps. 119:130; Luke 24:27)
Scripture is upheld as leading to maturity in faith (2 Tim. 3:16)

Reasons to study Scripture
To increase reverence for God (Deut. 17:18–19)
To learn about God's works (Ps. 111:2)
To foster hope (Ps. 119:81; Rom. 15:4; Col. 1:5)
To gain wisdom (Ps. 119:98–99,104; Prov. 2:1–5; 2 Tim. 3:15)
To learn about human activity, achievement, and wisdom (Eccl. 1:13–14; 1 Cor. 10:11)
To understand the salvation message (Acts 8:32–35; 17:2–3; 28:23)
To determine truth (Acts 17:11; 2 Tim. 2:15)

Ways to promote understanding of the Bible
Public reading (Ex. 24:7; Deut. 31:11–13; Neh. 8:1–8; 1 Tim. 4:13)
Thoughtful meditation (Josh. 1:8; Ps. 1:2; 119:15,48,97,148)
Private study (Acts 17:11; 2 Tim. 2:15)

Prayer (fellowship with God expressed in adoration, thanksgiving, confession, and intercession)

Some Biblical examples of those who interceded (prayed) for others
Moses prayed for the Israelites (Deut. 9:18–19)
Samuel prayed for Israel (1 Sam. 7:5–9)
Job prayed for his friends (Job 42:8–9)
Jesus urged prayer for enemies (Matt. 5:44)
Paul encouraged prayer for one another (Eph. 6:18)
Paul advocated prayer for rulers (1 Tim. 2:1–2)

Some Biblical examples of prayers that changed things
Hannah's prayer for a child (1 Sam. 1:10–20)
David's prayer for an end to a plague on Israel (2 Sam. 24:25)
Elijah's prayer for victory (1 Kings 17:1; James 5:17–18)
Nehemiah's prayer for a plan (Neh. 1:1–4)
Jesus' prayer for people to believe in him (John 11:41–42)
Believers' prayer for evangelistic boldness (Acts 4:23–31)
Paul's prayers for the churches (Rom. 1:9–10; Col. 1:9)

How to pray
Simply (Matt. 6:7–8)
Without pretentious display (Matt. 6:5–6)
Any time/all the time (Dan. 6:10; Mark 1:35; Luke 6:12; Eph. 6:18)
Anywhere/everywhere (John 4:21–24)
Accompanied, at times, by fasting (2 Sam. 12:15–16; Neh. 1:4; Dan. 9:3; Acts 13:2–3)

Postures used in prayer
Arms outstretched (Ex. 9:29; 2 Chron. 6:12–13; Ezra 9:5)
Sitting (2 Sam. 7:18)
Standing (1 Kings 8:22; Luke 18:11,13)
Kneeling (1 Kings 8:54; Ezra 9:5; Ps. 95:6; Luke 22:41; Acts 20:36; 21:5)
Prostrate (2 Chron. 20:18)
Hands raised (Lam. 3:41; 1 Tim. 2:8)

Relationships (an innate human need to enjoy fellowship with God and other people)

Those with whom humans are to be in relationship
One another (Gen. 2:18; 2 Cor. 13:11; 1 Jn. 1:7)
God (Ex. 29:45; 33:11; John 14:23; 2 Cor. 6:16; 1 Jn. 1:3; Rev. 21:3)

Characteristics of Christian fellowship
Unity in worship (Ps. 55:13–14; Eph. 5:19; Col. 3:16)
Common blessings (Ps. 106:4–5)
Agreement in prayer (Matt. 18:19–20)
Common purpose/mission (John 17:21–23; 1 Cor. 12:21–26; Phil. 2:1–2)
Sense of community (Acts 1:14; 2:1,42,44–47)
Mutual encouragement (Rom. 1:12; 15:1–2; Gal. 6:2; 1 Thess. 5:11; Heb. 10:24–25)
Common inheritance (Rom. 8:17; Col. 1:12)
Acceptance (Rom. 15:7)
Harmony (1 Cor. 1:10; 1 Peter 3:8)
Interdependence (1 Cor. 12:21–26)

Witness (the task of declaring what has happened)
What?
Sharing the gospel (Luke 24:46–48)
Who?
All God's people (1 Peter 2:9; 3:15)
Where?
At home, as individuals, in groups (Mark 5:18–19; John 1:40–41; Acts 17:17)
When?
All the time (Rom. 10:9–10; 1 Peter 3:15)
How?
By personal testimony (John 4:28–29; Acts 22:3–8)
By explaining the Scriptures (Acts 8:30–35)
By using prophetic gifts (1 Cor. 14:24–25)
By answering questions (1 Peter 3:15)
Through holy living (Matt. 5:16)
Through acts of devotion (Matt. 26:6–7)
Through writing (John 20:31)
With what attitude?
Love (Mark 10:21)
Respect (Acts 26:1–3; 1 Peter 3:15)
Urgency (2 Cor. 5:20)
Confidence (Eph. 6:19–20)

Study Guides

The following Study Guides may be used in church school classes and small group discussions, as well as in personal Bible study. They are short and suggestive, intended to be shaped by teachers, Bible study leaders, and seekers for their own purposes. A brief Bible study session, for example, may not include enough time to use all the resources included in the guide. Don't hesitate to pick and choose what will best serve your personal or group study needs.

The guides follow the same overall outline of the Reading Tracks and may be used in conjunction with them. You might also want to consider using the subject index and concordance to follow as resources to flesh out areas of the guides.

HEART SHAPING

Study Guide on Humility

Our Western culture puts a lot of emphasis on self-esteem, self-gratification, self-promotion, self-fulfillment, and (who could forget?) self-help. It's about self, self, and more self. Children and teenagers are often said to think the world revolves around them, but adults aren't much different. Unlike a generation ago, when the word *conceited* would have come to mind, people today who think highly of themselves are often highly thought of.

The Bible counsels us to see things from a different perspective.

- Read Philippians 2:3 and review the chart "Models of Biblical Humility" at Philippians 2:3, page 1944.

Since the Bible values humility, how can we develop this trait?

- Review the chart "How to Develop Humility" at Philippians 2:4, page 1945.

HEART-SHAPING QUESTIONS:
Do you consider yourself a humble person? Is humility a character trait you value? Read through the section on humility in the Reading Tracks (p. 2113) and list some reasons for you to seek to develop this quality. Pray a prayer of humility, such as the one found in Psalm 123:1–3.

MIND-BUILDING BLOCKS:
What is the Biblically correct view of who you are in Christ? Read Romans 12:3 with 1 Corinthians 6:9–11 and 1 John 3:1–3. Review the chart "Biblical Humility" at John 13:1–17, page 1769, to see how Jesus demonstrated humility.

ACTION-PRODUCING EXERCISES:
Summarize the article "Service and Humility" at Zephaniah 2:2–3, page 1511. How can serving others help you to develop humility? How can you become involved in service in your community? Read the article "Incarnational Identification" at Philippians 2:5–8, page 1946. Why is humility important in witnessing?

REMEMBER:
"Humility and the fear of the LORD bring wealth and honor and life" (Prov. 22:4).

Study Guide on Wisdom

Everyone wants to be considered wise, but not many people actually are. Wisdom seems to be a rare and elusive quality these days. In order to be wise, do you have to start by being smart? Old? Experienced with suffering? What exactly are the criteria? *Wisdom* seems pretty hard to define—and acquiring it seems even harder.

The Bible talks a lot about wisdom.

- Read Job 28:28, Proverbs 30:3, and Ephesians 1:17 to discover the Bible's definition of wisdom. Then review the chart "The Wise Man According to Proverbs: An Outline" at Proverbs 1:1–7, page 977, and summarize the various aspects of wisdom.

HEART-SHAPING QUESTIONS:
In which areas of life do you display wisdom? In which areas are you lacking in this trait? Read the article "Wisdom" at 1 Kings 3:16–28, page 495. What warnings can you take from Solomon's life?

MIND-BUILDING BLOCKS:
Read the article "Wisdom" at Proverbs 1:1–7, page 978. Why is wisdom so difficult to acquire? Read through the section on wisdom in the Reading Tracks (p. 2113). What are some sources of wisdom?

ACTION-PRODUCING EXERCISES:
Review the chart "Discerning God's Will" at Ruth 1:22, page 392. How can you exercise godly wisdom in your daily life? Review the chart "Wisdom" at 1 Corinthians 1:30, page 1878, to learn how Jesus demonstrated wisdom in his life.

REMEMBER:
"If any of you lacks wisdom, he should ask God, who gives generously to all without finding fault, and it will be given to him" (James 1:5).

Study Guide on Courage

We all live with fear, and some people have this emotion as their constant companion. Do you fear for your life, safety, health, children, spouse, and/or future success? Or perhaps you're afraid of something as "silly" as the dark. We'd all like to beat our fears, but we often give up even

trying to conquer them. Why? Is courage a genetic trait that you either have or don't have? Can you develop it?

The Bible has a lot to say about courage.

- Read Joshua 1:6–9. Then review the chart "Act With Courage" at 2 Chronicles 19:11, page 663, to understand what courage is. Surprisingly, courage isn't synonymous with fearlessness.

HEART-SHAPING QUESTIONS:
Fear is something all people face. Of what are you afraid? Review the charts "To Fear God's Name Is Wisdom" at Micah 6:9, page 1487, and "From Fear to Courage" at Hebrews 2:15, page 2008. What surprising facts did you learn about fear?

MIND-BUILDING BLOCKS:
Do you question your ability to act with courage? Read the article "Courage" at Joshua 1:6–7, page 318, to learn some reassuring things about the subject. Then reflect on the Snapshot "Do No Fear: Johanna Veenstra" at Psalm 44:22, page 860. How does her example encourage you to act with courage?

ACTION-PRODUCING EXERCISES:
You face situations daily that require courage. Review the chart "Be Strong and Courageous" at Joshua 1:6–11, page 317, and make a list of some everyday situations that require this character quality. Then read through the section on courage in the Reading Tracks (p. 2113) to supplement your list.

REMEMBER:
"When I am afraid, I will trust in [God]" (Ps. 56:3).

Study Guide on Encouragement

Life is hard. That's a fact. We all have times when we need encouragement, when we crave for someone to come alongside us with a comforting or uplifting word. But sometimes it's difficult to know how to be an encourager. What if we express it wrong? What if we make things worse?

The Bible commands us to encourage one another, and it gives us many wonderful examples of encouragers.

- Read 2 Timothy 4:2 and review the chart "Great Encouragers in the Bible" at Mark 1:1–11, page 1626. Being a good encourager is more than being a cheerleader. It's acting as an extension of God's love, a love that dispenses encouragement or comfort in conjunction with wisdom.

HEART-SHAPING QUESTIONS:
Do you feel ill-equipped to take on the role of an encourager? No matter what our situation, we can encourage someone else. As Christians, we have many useful resources at our disposable to help us in this endeavor. Read through the section on encouragement in the Reading Tracks (p. 2113). What are some sources of encouragement?

MIND-BUILDING BLOCKS:
Read the article "Barnabas" at Acts 11:22, page 1813. What can you learn from Barnabas about being an encourager? How can the Bible encourage you to do better in this vital area?

ACTION-PRODUCING EXERCISES:
Review the chart "Encourage Others in the Lord's Service" at 2 Chronicles 35:2, page 686, to discover some ways you can lift up the people around you. Remem-

ber, encouragement comes in many forms. To whom can you be a blessing today?

REMEMBER:
"May our Lord Jesus Christ himself and God our Father, who loved us and by his grace gave us eternal encouragement and good hope, encourage your hearts and strengthen you in every good deed and word" (2 Thess. 2:16–17).

Study Guide on Compassion

Turn on the television or open the newspaper, and you'll be glaringly reminded of the desperate needs of people everywhere. So why do so many people, including Christians, live as though compassion is optional?

The Bible goes to elaborate lengths to display the compassion of God, and it's blatantly clear that Christians are to follow his example.

- Read Exodus 34:6 and Psalm 103:8 to learn more about God's compassion. Then read Zechariah 7:9 and Ephesians 4:32 to learn about your responsibility to be compassionate.

HEART-SHAPING QUESTIONS:
Do you consider yourself a compassionate person? More telling, would others describe you that way? Review the chart "Why Should We Be Compassionate?" at Isaiah 58:6–10, page 1177. Then read the article "Sharing God's Compassion" at James 5:2–6, page 2035. Do these articles depict compassion as a merely optional trait for a believer?

MIND-BUILDING BLOCKS:
Do you *see* the needs of people around you? Sometimes with our hectic schedules we're tempted to put on our blinders just to make it through. Read through the section on compassion in the Reading Tracks (pp. 2113–2114) and review the chart "People in Need of Christian Care and Protection" at Leviticus 19:1, page 179. Then read the article "Compassion" at Mark 1:40–42, page 1630. What are the differences between pity and compassion and between feelings and actions?

ACTION-PRODUCING EXERCISES:
How can you step out of your "comfort zone" to minister compassionately to others? Read the articles "Compassion" at Hosea 1:2–3, page 1416; "Mother Teresa" at Amos 5:24, page 1457; and "Tabitha" at Acts 9:36–42, page 1809. Then reflect on the Snapshot "Bob Pierce" at Isaiah 61:1–3, page 1183. How do these examples inspire you to a life devoted to compassionately meeting the needs of others?

REMEMBER:
"Finally, *all of you*, live in harmony with one another; be sympathetic, love as brothers, be compassionate and humble" (1 Peter 3:8, emphasis added).

Study Guide on Generosity

We all know the joy of giving a gift that is truly appreciated. We also know that the price of the gift is often inconsequential to the receiver. After all, as the saying goes, "It's the thought that counts." So why do we cling to the misconception that only people with wealth can afford to be generous?

The Bible points out that a "generous" gift has nothing to do with its price.

• Read Mark 12:41–44 and 2 Corinthians 8:12.

HEART-SHAPING QUESTIONS:

Giving is both a requirement and a blessing. How can both be true? Review the charts "Gifts to God" at Exodus 35:5, page 139, and "Biblical Attitudes Toward the Poor" at Proverbs 22:22–23, page 1015. Why should you give? Then review the chart "How Giving Helps the Giver" at Philippians 2:17–18, page 1948. What are some rewards of giving?

MIND-BUILDING BLOCKS:

Trying to meet the needs of people around you can be overwhelming. Read the article "Serving the Poor" at Amos 2:6–7, page 1450. How can you make a difference to some of the many needy people in our world? Review the chart "Generosity" at 2 Corinthians 9:12, page 1913. What are some Scriptural guidelines for giving?

ACTION-PRODUCING EXERCISES:

Read through the section on generosity in the Reading Tracks (p. 2114) and review the chart "Do Good to All People" at Galatians 6:10, page 1928. How can you give generously in a way that is unique to you?

Read the Snapshot "Loving Kakolo" at 1 Timothy 4:12, page 1981, to see how a group of Chicago teenagers found their giving "niche." Then read "Mary Jane" at 2 Thessalonians 2:16–17, page 1973, to see how a receiver of someone's generosity was immeasurably blessed.

REMEMBER:

"Each man should give what he has decided in his heart to give, not reluctantly or under compulsion, for God loves a cheerful giver" (2 Cor. 9:7).

MIND BUILDING

Study Guide on *Imago Dei*

Christianity teaches us not only that God created every human being in the world but that he created each of them in his own image. In a world where it's common to denigrate other human beings—to call them aliens, enemies, pagans, and worse—this teaching has far-reaching implications. Whenever we meet another human being we're to remember that this person has, like ourselves, been made by our God in his own image.

The Bible tells us that the *imago Dei* (image of God) makes human beings unique, different in a very basic way from both animals and angels:

Read "The Image of God in Human Beings" article at Revelation 13:13–15, page 2094. Then read through the passages in the Reading Track on page 2114 that summarizes the Bible's teaching on the subject.

Because the Bible teaches that we're all made in God's image, we have a different view of both ourselves and others, especially marginalized peoples.

• See the "New Identities" article at Ezekiel 37:11–14, page 1368, and the "Belief and Identity" chart at Habakkuk 1:5, page 1501.

HEART-SHAPING QUESTIONS:

Read "The Antidote for Meaningless" article at Psalm 8:3–9, page 817, and then express in your own words how the way you feel about yourself as God's "image carrier" affects the way you view other people.

MIND-BUILDING BLOCKS:

Both the *"Imago Dei"* chart at Genesis 1:26, page 4, and "The Image of God" chart at Ephesians 1:3–14, page 1932, outline what the Bible teaches about the image of God, suggesting questions the teaching raises. Formulate your own list of questions that this reality raises in your mind.

ACTION-PRODUCING EXERCISES:

The story of Mirza at 2 Samuel 9:1–13, page 459, reminds us that God loves all people equally. Are there people in your life who would benefit from realizing they are carriers of God's image? How might you go about convincing them?

Hamedi, whose story is told at Jeremiah 22:2–3, page 1238, is a Palestinian living in Israel. How might the *imago Dei* change the way Palestinians and Israelis view one another?

REMEMBER:

"God created man in his own image, in the image of God he created him; male and female he created them" (Gen. 1:27).

Study Guide on Fallen World

Briefly peruse the morning newspaper and jot down some of the bad things that happened yesterday. This list will illustrate what the Bible means when it says we live in a fallen world.

The Bible tells us that God made the world good—in fact, very good. Traces of that goodness can still be found in all of creation. But facets of that creation at times seem to be overwhelmed by evil:

• The Reading Track on page 2114 summarizes the Biblical teaching on our fallen world.

The article "Fine Hammered Steel of Woe" at Ecclesiastes 12:13–14, page 1052, points out how difficult it can be to identify good and evil in this world when the two conflicting forces are so mixed up in all we do and in all the people we meet. Much of the Christian life is spent learning discernment—the ability to tell the difference between good and evil.

HEART-SHAPING QUESTIONS:

How do you distinguish between the good and the bad things that happen to you? Does knowing that your friends are created in God's image and yet fallen make you judgmental about them? Or sympathetic? From a Biblical perspective, what view do you see as appropriate?

MIND-BUILDING BLOCKS:

Review the following charts: "Natural Disasters" at Genesis 6:7, page 12; "Tower of Babel" at Genesis 11:8–9, page 20; "Vision" at Numbers 13:17–20, page 219; "Blessings and Curses" at Deuteronomy 30:19–20, page 305; "Signs of Discontent" at Revelation 11:18, page 2090; and "Vice List" at Revelation 21:8, page 2107. Some of the world's evils illustrated in these charts are easy to see. Which might not be so readily visible? Do you think we as Christians have the ability to eliminate some of these "structures of sin"?

ACTION-PRODUCING EXERCISES:

In "Do Not Love the World" at 1 John 2, page 2059, the author cautions us against deliberately associating with evil. If human beings, even at their best, are confusing mixtures of good and evil, what precautions should we take in relating to them?

What lessons can we learn from reading the story of Aleksandr Men at 2 Chronicles 34:3, page 684?

REMEMBER:
"Every good and perfect gift is from above" (James 1:17).

Study Guide on Reconciliation

Television, newspapers, and magazines remind us daily of violence in our world. Wars, rumors of wars, crimes, workplace conflicts, even family tensions—everywhere we turn we see the need for reconciliation.

The Bible tells us that reconciliation is needed.

- Read 2 Corinthians 5:18–19, as well as the "Reconciliation" article at 2 Corinthians 5:17–20, page 1908.

The Bible tells us that reconciliation is possible. If we look beyond the media-reported violence, we do find stories of this kind of reconciliation in our world.
At Colossians 1:19–20, read the story of two men who served the Lord side by side for 30 years—all the while quietly demonstrating the peace of Christ.

HEART-SHAPING QUESTIONS:
What feelings do you experience when you've been wronged? How do you move beyond those emotions to a willingness to forgive? See Matthew 18:21ff.

MIND-BUILDING BLOCKS:
Do you understand how reconciliation works? Read through the section on reconciliation in the Reading Tracks (p. 2114), and then summarize the Biblical approach to conflict resolution.

ACTION-PRODUCING EXERCISES:
Near Romans 4 you will find a "Recipe for Reconciliation." Summarize in your own words what steps you must take to bring about reconciliation. How can the essay "Racial Reconciliation" at Romans 5:10, page 1855, serve as a model for reconciliation in your own life? What can you do today to bring about reconciliation in some corner of your world?

REMEMBER:
"All this is from God, who reconciled us to himself through Christ and gave us the ministry of reconciliation" (2 Cor. 5:18).

Study Guide on Love of Neighbor

The Bible is full of references to loving our *neighbors*. But in Leviticus 17 we're also told to offer hospitality to *strangers*. And by the time we get to the gospel of Matthew, we're instructed to extend our love as far as our *enemies* (Matt. 5:44). Soon afterward Jesus was telling people that all God's requirements in this regard are summed up in one phrase: "Love your neighbor *as [you love] yourself*" (Rom. 13:9, emphasis added).

The Christian life is all about loving other people. Simple enough. Now on to the hard part. How do we accomplish this? Especially when our fallen natures seem to tug us in the opposite direction.

- Read through the passages for the Reading Track on pages 2114–2115. Because the Bible places so much emphasis on love of neighbor, our first priority is to come to grips with this as the fundamental building block of living the Christian life.

It won't do just to talk about or even understand it. We're to *do* it.

HEART-SHAPING QUESTIONS:
What is your favorite Biblical story on this subject? Many think immediately of the parable of the good Samaritan. If that was your response, do you have a second favorite? Why does this account appeal to you?

MIND-BUILDING BLOCKS:
Has 1 Corinthians 13 influenced the way you treat other people? Or does this passage seem to apply almost exclusively to wedding services and burgeoning romantic relationships? Check out the "Love" chart at 1 Corinthians 13:13, page 1893, for some applications.

ACTION-PRODUCING EXERCISES:
Who are you called to love today? Read the "Love Your Neighbor" article at Luke 10:25–37, page 1700. Love can take many forms. Read "Elijah and the Widow at Zarephath" at 1 Kings 17:7–15, page 524. What is unusual about the love expressed in this story? Can you think of some other atypical features of true, Biblical love?
Do the "Grace" Snapshot at Deuteronomy 4:9, page 267, and the "Paulina" Snapshot at Jeremiah 30:17, page 1252, give you any ideas for action? What are they?

REMEMBER:
"Love is patient, love is kind. It does not envy, it does not boast, it is not proud. It is not rude, it is not self-seeking, it is not easily angered, it keeps no record of wrongs" (1 Cor. 13:4–5).

Study Guide on Spiritual Formation

We're saved by God's grace. And we live by that grace. These gifts of grace are comforting and freeing, but we can't escape that part of the Christian life that seems like good, old-fashioned, hard work. That's what spiritual formation sometimes seems like. God has buried the pearl of great price somewhere in a field and told us which field it's in, but we still have to go digging to find it.

The Bible tells us that spiritual formation is important, that when we're growing in Christian living we see increases in our lives of faith, love, understanding, contentment, and forgiveness.
In order to more fully understand what the Bible says about this process, read through the Reading Track on spiritual formation on page 2115.

Because the Bible clues us in that this is important, we need to spend significant time in thinking about and acting upon the Biblical principles of spiritual formation.

- See the "Spiritual Formation" chart at 1 Samuel 3:19–20, page 405.

HEART-SHAPING QUESTIONS:
When asked about spiritual formation in their lives, people seem to vacillate between two poles: great excitement over the challenge of living godly lives—or overwhelming guilt over feeling unable to do enough. Which pole are you closer to today? Do you need your heart broken anew (see "Transforming an Artless World" at 2 Tim. 1:5, p. 1987), or do you need to be inspired (see "The Girl Preacher" at Ezra 8:2–3, p. 705)?

MIND-BUILDING BLOCKS:
Attempting to live holy lives can rivet our focus on trying to keep laws. See "Outdated Laws?" at Leviticus 13:47–59, page 170. How have you involved your church community in your process of spiritual formation? Also, look at the "Stress" chart at 2 Samuel 23:3–4, page 481. What are some "spiritual stressors" for you?

ACTION-PRODUCING EXERCISES:
Assess where you are spiritually. Use one of the exercises suggested in the "Self Examination" chart at 2 Corinthians 13:5, page 1917. Or consider the "20 Questions" at 1 John 1:6–10, page 2056. Then figure out where you want to go. Stories of what others have done can be inspiring. What Biblical characters have particularly captivated you? What qualities in their lives would you like to emulate?

Finally, figure out what you'll do to get there. Read the article titled "Service and Humility" at Zephaniah 2:2–3, page 1511. Consider even the smallest of actions, recognizing that these can ultimately be some of the most earth-shattering (see the "Symbolic Actions" chart at 1 Peter 3:21, p. 2044). The spiritual practices we choose are important, but the attitude with which we undertake them is key. See the "Faith and Good Works" chart at James 2:14–17, page 2032.

REMEMBER:
"We have an obligation—but it is not to the sinful nature" (Rom. 8:12).

Study Guide on Stewardship

For many Christians *stewardship* can be a turn-off word. You may associate it with regular church fund-raising campaigns. Unfortunately, an official definition doesn't help much with this perception: "the careful use, control, and management of the possessions entrusted to one." But properly understood, stewardship is central to the Christian life.

The Bible reminds us that we're trustees of much more than money. We're also caretakers of the creation, representatives of the gospel, and stewards of non-monetary, material possessions. Further, we're entrusted with the proper use of whatever unique gifts and abilities—and of the time—God has given to each of us.

• Read through the Reading Track on page 2115 to learn the Bible's take on each of these responsibilities.

God's Word goes on to tell us what to do with those things of which we're trustees. We're to care for them, share them, give them away, and work to accumulate (in the best sense) and improve them.

• Read the "Stewardship" article at 1 Chronicles 29:10–20, page 637.

HEART-SHAPING QUESTIONS:
We're stewards of our relationships with others, as well as of the world. After reading "Our Story From Colossians 3" at Colossians 3:10, page 1958, ask yourself the question: Am I being a good steward of my relationships? Read the story of Valentin at Proverbs 27:26–27, page 1024. In this short *Snapshot*, tabulate the ways in which Valentin was shown to be a good steward of what God had entrusted to him.

MIND-BUILDING BLOCKS:
Read John Calvin's summary of the "Right Use of God's Gifts" at Ecclesiastes 5:18–19, page 1043. Then check out the chart on "Bad Counting, Good Counting" at 2 Samuel 24:10, page 485. Think of a particularly good gift God has given to you. Are you being a faithful steward of it? How might you do better?

ACTION-PRODUCING EXERCISES:
Read the "Biblical Instruction to the Rich" chart at Psalm 49:1–2, page 865. Use it as a checklist for measuring your approaches to stewardship. List three ways in which you're being a good steward—and three areas where improvement might be called for.

In the Bible's economy, small isn't necessarily inferior to large. After looking at the "Small Measures" chart at John 4:1–26, page 1747, identify some small measures you might take to become a better steward.

The chart titled "Do Good to All People" at Galatians 6:10, page 1928, reminds us that stewardship isn't negative (like burying our talents in the sand for safekeeping) but a positive principle of making good use of what God has given us.

REMEMBER:
"All this abundance . . . comes from [God's] hand, and all of it belongs to [him]" (1 Chron. 29:16).

Study Guide on Service

Christianity isn't just a right way of thinking but an all-encompassing way of life. Christian teachings aren't real in our lives until we act on the basis of what we learn from them. Christianity is faith in action.

The Bible tells us that all human beings owe their Creator a ministry of service—first to God and then to humanity and the rest of creation. That service can take many forms:

• Read the "World Renewal" article at Isaiah 65:17–25, page 1191, for one illustration of service to God and humanity. Then examine the "Service" chart at Romans 12:1–2, page 1867, for a list of five specific areas of life that can be used to serve God.

As Christians, we're to leave no stone unturned in finding ways to help our neighbors, especially the poor, disadvantaged, sick, and mistreated.

• Read through the Reading Track on page 2115 for a list of Biblical principles on and examples of serving others.

The Bible is filled with examples of profuse, beyond-the-call-of-duty service.

• See the "Extravagant Devotion" chart at Luke 7:36–50, page 1689, as well as the "Demonstrations of Devotion" chart at Hebrews 11:6, page 2021.

HEART-SHAPING QUESTIONS:
Service to others is based on service to God. When we get our hearts right toward God, out attitudes toward others fall into line. Read Genet's story at Exodus 15:2, page 107; she states that "there is nothing on this earth that satisfies me more than singing and praising my Lord."

Charles Mully (see "A Stolen Car and a Changed Life" Snapshot at Job 24:1–11, p. 784) prayed to God for two years before starting a children's ministry. When you want to do good for others, do you begin with some moments of praise to God? What are some different ways you might go about doing this?

Be aware that potential pitfalls may lurk behind our desires to serve others, particularly if we're doing so in an "official" ("full-time Christian service") capacity. See chart titled "the Dangers of Professional Religious Service" at Mark 12:38–42, page 1657.

MIND-BUILDING BLOCKS:
Effective service requires: (1) obedience (see chart at Deut. 4:1–2, p. 266); (2) a sense of God's direction (see "Discerning God's Will" chart at Ruth 1:22, p. 392); (3) judgment as to what particular aspect of service will complement what others around us are already doing (see "Seven Works of Mercy" chart at Hos. 6:6, p. 1422, for categories of service); and (4) perseverance (see "William Wilberforce" article at Gen. 6:8–9, p. 13).

ACTION-PRODUCING EXERCISES:
Acts of service aren't just performed alone but also in community. Is your community (e.g., your church) committed to service? See the chart at Nehemiah 9:26–31, "Signs of a Stagnant Congregation," page 727, to help you discern the state of your community in this regard.

Use the chart "Obey God and Serve Him" at Job 36:11, page 798, to answer the questions What kinds of things am I doing to serve God? and What (or what else) could I be doing?

REMEMBER:
"Do not merely listen to the word, and so deceive yourselves. Do what it says" (James 1:22).

ACTION PRODUCING

Study Guide on Children

"As the children go, so goes a society." If such is the measure we use for the health of a society, we have many sick social orders in our world today. Considered on a global level, with different risk factors taken into account depending upon location and culture, the pat statement that our children are dying isn't too far from the truth. As "The Slaughter of Innocents" chart at Matthew 2:16, page 1559, poignantly shows, the most innocent among us are often the most abused.

The Bible, as well as concerned adults in our own society, stresses that children need attention, authenticity, training, consistent discipline, and welcome. Jesus made a point of welcoming children, and he voiced particularly sharp warnings against neglecting these little ones.

- Read the "Look With Compassion on Children" chart at Isaiah 13:18, page 1098, and the "Biblical Attitudes Toward Children" chart at Joel 1:2–3, page 1436. How are the children in your community doing when measured against these Biblical benchmarks? Then read the "Blessing the Children" article at Psalm 144:12, page 966.

Because the Bible says we're to care for children, we're obligated to act.

- Not all of us can do as much as Amy Carmichael did for the orphans of India (see article at Ex. 22:22–23, p. 118), but each of us can do something. The stories of Geoffrey (Gen. 50:18–21, p. 81) and Angela Miyanda (Job 29:12–13, p. 789) remind us of the plight of street children all over the world. What can each of us, no matter where we find ourselves, do to help?

HEART-SHAPING QUESTIONS:
Read about the Bamboo Shoots Street Children's Center in Phnom Penh, Cambodia (2 Sam. 7:10, p. 456). Then scan the statistics about United States children at risk in the chart at Job 1:5, page 754. The reality is that children all over the world need our help. How can we decide when and where and how to go about alleviating their pain? How can we have our hearts broken by the things that break God's heart? (See story of Bob Pierce at Isa. 61:1–3, p. 1183.)

MIND-BUILDING BLOCKS:
Read through the Reading Track on pages 2115–2116 and summarize in your own words what the Bible has to say about children. Then compare your findings with statistics on what is happening to children today (see charts on child labor at 1 Sam. 2:18, p. 402, and sobering statistics at Prov. 8:32, p. 990). Why is there such a disparity between what the Bible recommends and what is actually happening?

ACTION-PRODUCING EXERCISES:
The Bible offers numerous examples of exceptional children who were used in big ways by God (see "Gifted Children of the Bible" chart at Prov. 17:6, p. 1005). How can these models inspire us to treat children better?

How can we help provide proper nutrition for the world's children? See the sobering "Child Starvation" chart at Lamentations 2:19, page 1302, for a list of factors aiding good nutrition.

Is television viewing good or bad for children? See charts near 2 Kings 2 ("Child Violence," p. 541) and Philippians 4 ("Television Time," p. 1950).

REMEMBER:
"Jesus said: 'Let the little children come to me'" (Matt. 19:14).

Study Guide on Disease

Jesus conducted an ongoing healing ministry, and so should we. Our Lord was concerned with both spiritual and physical healing, and we should be, too. This has never been more urgent than today, as a scourge of unparalleled proportions sweeps the earth: HIV/AIDS (see "Cry, the Beloved Continent" article at Matt. 9:35–36, p. 1577, as well as the "HIV/AIDS" chart at 2 Chron. 26:21, p. 673). What is the church's responsibility in the face of this and other deadly diseases?

The Bible says that our responsibility is to facilitate healing. "The sick" are mentioned often in the Bible, and its passages don't compartmentalize physical versus spiritual disease the way we moderns do.

- Read through the Reading Track on disease on page 2116.

Because the Bible says we're to facilitate healing, we should begin by acknowledging the ongoing presence and potency of disease in the world today.

- See "The Plagues" chart at Exodus 7:1–5, page 94, for reference to the pestilences that struck Egypt as signposts pointing to the "plagues" we experience today. What are the lessons, both positive and negative, to be learned from this comparison?

HEART-SHAPING QUESTIONS:
Disease strikes indiscriminately, affecting society's "high" and "low" alike. Read the story of Agness at

Psalm 23:4–6, page 834. What emotions does this Snapshot stir up in you? What about the feelings you have as you read the inspiring story about Kakolo, a village in Zambia (1 Tim. 4:12, p. 1981)? What might account for your markedly different responses?

MIND-BUILDING BLOCKS:
How does the form God's healing takes today differ from some of the forms it took in the Bible? See "The Bronze Snake" chart at Numbers 21:4–9, page 231. The changes in form are well-illustrated by the dramatic differences between the way the 1st-century mindset viewed blood and the way we see it today. What are some continuities between the two views? (See also the "Shed Blood" chart at Deut. 12:23, p. 279.)

Using malaria (see chart at Isa. 7:18, p. 1085) as an illustration, at what point in the disease/healing process can we as Christians make the most effective contributions to the health of victims or potential victims?

ACTION-PRODUCING EXERCISES:
Jesus healed others (e.g., Matt. 8:2–3). What do his actions mean for us? Our Lord also commissioned his associates to heal (Matt. 10:1). What can we learn from these early healers? Finally, we're called to be healers today (1 Cor. 12:8–9). What can you do to live up to this calling?

REMEMBER:
"[Jesus] took up our infirmities and carried our diseases" (Matt. 8:17).

Study Guide on Education

Education provides the key to reversing many of the world's woes. Too many young people, however, don't have access to a good education. Christians have traditionally placed a high priority on learning. Jesus modeled this for us with his performance as a young boy in the temple, the educational institution of his day (Luke 2:41–52).

The Bible says that a good education provides us with numerous benefits, primary among them the wisdom to know and obey God.

* Read through the Reading Track on page 2116 to gain a renewed sense of the important role instruction plays in living the Christian life.

Because the Bible teaches that education is important, Christians are to do whatever is required to instruct their children (and continue their own ongoing learning process). One of the primary building blocks of education is literacy, the ability to read and write.

* Read "Literacy: An Open Door" at Daniel 1:3–4 and 17 on page 1390.

HEART-SHAPING QUESTIONS:
Read the moving poem "My Dear Teacher" at Revelation 21:4, page 2106. What do such poignant sentiments toward a beloved teacher tell us about the importance of education? What feelings does this tribute stir in you? What, if anything, will it inspire you to do?

MIND-BUILDING BLOCKS:
The importance of on-the-job training is underscored by the information in the "Learner Retention" chart at Proverbs 31:1–9, page 1029. Learners typically retain only 10 percent of what they *hear* but 90 percent of

what they *do*. The lessons of faith are learned more from our putting them into action than from our passive listening. Further, many of the measures of the quality of life have an educational component (see "Quality of Life" chart at Isa. 11:1–11, p. 1094).

For us as Christians, one of the primary values of education is the opportunity to learn to identify false teachers and teachings (see "False Teachers and Their Teachings" chart at 2 Peter 2:1–3, p. 2051).

ACTION-PRODUCING EXERCISES:
"Educational Opportunity," the chart at 1 Samuel 2:26, page 403, lists some of the challenges in providing education for all by identifying statistical shortcomings. Draft a list of possible "solutions" to these challenges, and suggest ways each individual Christian can contribute to solving the problems.

Education takes place on many levels and in many settings. After reading the "Groups" chart at Proverbs 22:17, page 1014, make a list of memorable educational moments in your life, indicating the groups and settings in which they occurred.

REMEMBER:
"Wise men store up knowledge" (Prov. 10:14).

Study Guide on Hunger

One of the early Bible stories we learn—and one we almost inevitably remember—is that of God providing manna from heaven when the Israelites were in danger of starving to death in the wilderness (Ex. 16). There is no more powerful image of God taking care of his children than the picture of him being, and providing, "the bread of life" (see "Jesus and Food," Matt. 9:9–13, p. 1574). It would seem, then, that there could be no more powerful witness to God's providential care than for us as Christians to help feed hungry people.

The Bible states what at first glance may seem obvious: People don't live on bread [or food] alone. But helping the hungry attain food still is given high priority in scores of Scripture passages.

* Read through the Reading Track on hunger on page 2116. Also see "Hunger in the Bible" at Exodus 16:2–3, page 109.

The Bible calls on us to help *all* people find food—"If your enemy is hungry, feed him" (Rom. 12:20). The statistics found in the "Hunger" chart at Ruth 2:8, page 393, indicate that we won't have any trouble finding hungry people. The fact is that they're everywhere, in every land and society.

* Read the "Hospitality" article at Luke 14:12–14, page 1711.

HEART-SHAPING QUESTIONS:
Read Doxer's story at Judges 5:24–25, page 363. Does it make you feel hopeful? Why or why not? Either way, there are some positive signs on the hunger-satisfaction front. See the chart at Isaiah 58:6–7, "Easing the Hunger Equation," page 1176. What overriding problems remain unsolved?

MIND-BUILDING BLOCKS:
Malnutrition is not just about too little food. Not surprisingly for most of us, steeped as we are in media coverage about the rampant nutritional deficiencies in our fast-food culture, it can take different forms. Read the chart at Amos 4:1, page 1452, for a summary.

ACTION-PRODUCING EXERCISES:

There are many ways to reduce or alleviate hunger. Some of them involve providing actual, material food, while others entail offering educational opportunities and an overall healthy environment in which people can live. See the "Malnutrition" chart at Ruth 3:17–18, page 395.

In addition, *hunger* can refer to many other needs besides the gnawing of an empty stomach (see second paragraph in this section, on previous page, as well as the "Feed My Sheep" chart at John 21:15–23, p. 1786).

Read the "Kingdom Business" article at Zechariah 1:17, page 1525, and summarize how it's the business of the kingdom to reduce hunger.

REMEMBER:

"Feed my sheep" (John 21:17).

Study Guide on Injustice

Injustice refers to the unnecessary and deliberate mistreatment of others. In a fallen world, injustice can take many forms. It also has many roots, ranging from satanic influence to unjust political structures to individual sins.

The Bible is clear that God won't stand for injustice. This stance isn't just a decision God has made; it's an integral part of his very nature. God is, by definition, just.

- Read through the Reading Track on injustice on pages 2116–2117. Then read the "God's Rescue Plan" article at Psalm 10:17–18, page 820.

Because the Bible makes it clear that God desires and stands for justice, it goes without saying that we as his representatives are to want and work toward the same goal.

- Read the stories of Josefa Andrianaivoravelona at Psalm 17:7–9, page 825; Armida at Psalm 138:6–7, page 960; and Judy at Isaiah 13:14, page 1097. What justice issues do these stories raise? List five principles of justice gleaned from these Snapshots.

HEART-SHAPING QUESTIONS:

The American civil rights movement was led by Dr. Martin Luther King. Jr., who based his appeals for justice for African Americans in part on Old Testament prophetic literature. See the article on this 20th-century faith hero at Exodus 4:10–11, page 89. Also read the story of Moses leading the Israelites out of Egypt, beginning at Exodus 12:31. List situations in the world today that require the kinds of prophetic leadership Dr. King and Moses displayed.

MIND-BUILDING BLOCKS:

Many social concerns today, as in every era, call for the administration of justice. See the chart titled "Major Social Concerns in the Covenant" at Deuteronomy 26:16–19, page 298. Some of the more pressing include situations regarding:

Refugees: See chart at Exodus 13:18, page 105.

Persecution: See chart at Matthew 10:14–42, page 1579.

Bad government: See charts at Exodus 21:1, page 116, and Judges 21:25, page 388.

Warfare: See chart at Isaiah 1:16–17, page 1073.

Human rights: See chart at Galatians 3:23–25, page 1924.

ACTION-PRODUCING EXERCISES:

The first step in addressing an unjust situation is to formulate a clear picture of the problem and a vision for its solution. The second step, though, is equally as important: the willingness and courage to act based on the vision. The two steps are often artificially separated. See "Vision" chart at Numbers 13:17–20, page 219.

Read the various quality of life measures listed in the chart at Isaiah 11:1–11, page 1094. What role does justice play in these measures?

Biblical justice isn't synonymous with political and humanitarian justice, but there are strong similarities between them, with Biblical justice often providing the rational for political justice. Read the "Justice" chart at John 2:12–24, page 1742. In what ways can Christians impact these two lists of justice principles?

REMEMBER:

"What does the LORD require of you? To act justly and to love mercy and to walk humbly with your God" (Mic. 6:8).

Study Guide on Mission

Although God has used and continues to use many vehicles of mission—for instance Israel, Jesus Christ, the Holy Spirit, and the church—the most important point to make about mission is that God's *nature* entails it. God created, redeems, and sustains all missional activities. He is continuously at work in the world he created. Human mission is all about trying to discern how God is working at any particular time and in any given place and then jumping on board.

The Bible tells us that the tasks of getting on board with God's mission are many, including healing, making disciples, telling the gospel story, and fighting for justice. Each is not only worthy but necessary.

- Read through the Reading Track on mission on page 2117.

Even though the Bible specifies multiple goals of mission, the temptation is to emphasize one to the exclusion of the rest. We typically tend to prioritize the area our particular sector of the church endorses—or one that we're particularly good at or comfortable with.

- Read "Cross-cultural Mission" at Matthew 28:19–20, page 1622, and "Incarnational Identification" at Philippians 2:5–8, page 1946. How would you summarize each of these authors' views of mission?

The temptation exists to employ improper methods in mission-oriented activities.

- See "God's Call to Missions" chart at Acts 15:1–2, page 1820.

HEART-SHAPING QUESTIONS:

Read the essay about Catherine Booth at Judges 7:7–8, page 366. How would you describe her vision of mission? How do you feel about her efforts? Now review the stories of Salih Abdul Masih at Exodus 18:20, page 113, and of Origen at Hosea 13:14, page 1432. Did these stories teach you anything new about God's perspective on missions?

MIND-BUILDING BLOCKS:

As "The Poor and the Lost" chart at Ezekiel 18:12–13, page 1334, shows, a large percentage of the poor are also in need of the gospel story. What implications

does this have for the church's overall missions task and strategy? The history of missions has ranged from the Old Testament prophets and their unique task (see "Isaiah, Which Will It Be?" article at Isa. 1:17, p. 1074) to the millions of cross cultural mission workers throughout the history of the church (see "Witnessing Through the Years" chart at Mark 16:15–16, p. 1666) to today's configuration (see "Moses and the Prophets" chart at Luke 16:19–31, p. 1715). What brand of mission workers do we most need in the 21st century?

ACTION-PRODUCING EXERCISES:
The "Light to the World" chart at Luke 11:33–36, page 1703, lists come possible cooperative mission activities Christians might undertake. Add three more possibilities to this list.

Review "The Three Worlds" chart at 1 Peter 5:8–9, page 2046, noting the paradigm that divides the world into three spheres: the Christian world; the evangelized, non-Christian world; and the unevangelized world. To which sector is God calling you?

REMEMBER:
"Always be prepared to give an answer to everyone who asks you to give the reason for the hope that you have. But do this with gentleness and respect" (1 Peter 3:15).

Study Guide on Peace

"Peace, peace . . . when there is no peace." Jeremiah's lament (8:11) describes perfectly the less than perfect political situation in today's world. Never before in the history of humankind have more people been committed to peace. Yet wars and conflicts persist and proliferate (see "Number of Wars in the World by Year" chart at Jer. 8:11, p. 1214). As nuclear weapons fall into the hands of terrorists and rogue states, can Christians in good conscience support war—when the total annihilation of God's creation may be at stake?

The Bible says that peace is preferable to war—and that it's one of the goals of the kingdom of God. Because of this, Christians are to be committed to peace and work for it tirelessly at national, local, and interpersonal levels.

- Read through the Reading Track on page 2117 to see what the Bible says about peace. Then read the article about Corrie ten Boom at 2 Kings 11:1–4, page 558. The actions of this courageous woman on behalf of persecuted Europeans during World War II have inspired Christians ever since.

HEART-SHAPING QUESTIONS:
Read "Another Dangerous Day" at Lamentations 3:31–36, page 1305, as well as the Snapshot at Micah 5:1–5a, page 1484. What did these individuals do to help bring about Biblical peace? What ideas do these stories trigger in your mind about how each of us, in our own limited contexts, can contribute to peace?

MIND-BUILDING BLOCKS:
War has been a feature of human existence almost continuously since humans began to exist, but its overall cost in terms of resources and human lives is increasing along with the increasing effectiveness of weapons. See "Wars" chart at Joshua 9:1–2, page 328. Also, war has become more encompassing in more than just nuclear terms. Increasingly, women and children are being drawn into the conflict. See "Women in the Military" chart at Judges 4:4–5, page 360.

ACTION-PRODUCING EXERCISES:
Does the solution lie with the nations of the world? What insight does the "Nations" chart at Deuteronomy 16:18–20, page 284, shed on this issue?

Peace also is desperately needed at the micro level, between and among individuals. Review the chart "Ineffective Ways of Dealing With Conflict" at 1 Kings 20:1–12, page 529. What might be some more effective approaches for reducing interpersonal conflict and creating interpersonal peace?

Review "The Nobel Peace Prize" chart at Isaiah 32:17–18, page 1127. Why do you suspect that more religious people in general and Christians in particular haven't won the Nobel Peace Prize?

REMEMBER:
"Since we have been justified through faith, we have peace with God through our Lord Jesus Christ" (Rom. 5:1).

Study Guide on Pollution

God delegated to human beings the responsibility for the well-being of the earth. But people have only been partially successful at this task. Currently, humanity is challenged with several growing crises, most of which can be categorized as pollution problems: air unfit to breathe; water too dirty to drink; land too poisoned to grow crops; an atmosphere too thin to protect from harmful rays; and garbage, garbage everywhere—with no place to put it all.

"Fill the earth and subdue it," the Bible instructs in Genesis 1. But Scripture doesn't tell us to *overfill* the earth, nor does it say to "subdue" it to death!

- Read through the Reading Track on pollution on page 2117. Then read the "Be Fruitful and Multiply" article at Genesis 1:28, page 6. What do you think God intended by his mandate for people to subdue the earth?

HEART-SHAPING QUESTIONS:
One way to begin to appreciate the need for action is to rekindle our awe of God's creation. Review the chart "Fearfully and Wonderfully Made" at Psalm 139:13–14, page 961. What does the incredible diversity of God's creation mean for us who are charged with caring for it?

MIND-BUILDING BLOCKS:
Our lack of care can be traced to more than just overuse. It's also due to our unwise use of polluting agents. Review the chart "Chemicals by Health Effects" at Hosea 10:4, page 1427. What is our responsibility as Christians in the face of such misuse and danger? To what extent are we responsible for others' actions—or lack of positive or preventative action? What can be done?

Consider the information in the chart on "World Land Use" at Haggai 1:6 and 10–11, page 1520, as well as on "Good Land" at Mark 4:1–9, page 1635. What challenges do the realities of shrinking arable land and a decreasing number of farmers present to the caring Christian?

ACTION-PRODUCING EXERCISES:
The chart "The Creation Groans" at Romans 8:18–27, page 1860, outlines the good and the bad aspects of our ecosystem's current status. Consider in turn each of the eight areas of challenge and suggest ways we as Christians might act to help to address the situations.

REMEMBER:
"He who was seated on the throne said, 'I am making everything new!'" (Rev. 21:5).

Study Guide on Population

Human beings are the pinnacle of God's creation, charged both to be fruitful and multiply *and* to manage and care for the rest of creation. Sadly, human history reflects that we've done better overall at multiplying than at care taking. And at a certain point multiplying begins to be counter-productive to caring for the creation. We do well to clarify what the Bible says about population growth.

God's Word is clear that children are a blessing (Ps. 127:3–5) and a gift from God (1 Sam. 2:20–21).

• Read through the Reading Track on population on page 2117.

But providing any child with a quality upbringing inevitably necessitates caring for a world whose resources are stretched to the limit by the number of people it is called to sustain.

• Read "Be Fruitful and Increase" at Genesis 1:28, page 6.

HEART-SHAPING QUESTIONS:
Read about what two motivated college students did in the face of the needs of HIV/AIDS stricken people across the globe (at 2 Cor. 9:2, p. 1912). Ironically, population growth can also be accompanied by rapid population decline, as is the case with Africa's devastating AIDS crisis. What does "growth" mean in this particular Snapshot?

MIND-BUILDING BLOCKS:
There are many ways to count the people in our world. The simplest is to tabulate the raw number, currently about six billion. We can also count by annual growth rates. See "Population" chart at Zephaniah 3:20, page 1514. But there are other ways of counting:
By number of people in need: See chart at Leviticus 19:1, page 179.
By income: See chart at Numbers 4:1–3, page 202.
By characteristics of Christians: See chart at Psalm 18:29, page 827.
By church growth: See chart at Acts 2:41, page 1793.
By countries, cultures, and languages: See chart at Acts 28:30, page 1844.
By religious affiliation: See chart at Ephesians 4:3–6, page 1935.

ACTION-PRODUCING EXERCISES:
Different segments of the population have different needs when it comes to ministry. The chart at Acts 11:19–21, page 1812, for example, details some of the specific needs of an urban population. What type of ministry are you involved in? What are the unique characteristics and needs of the people you work with?

REMEMBER:
"Be fruitful and increase in number; fill the earth and subdue it" (Gen. 1:28).

Study Guide on Poverty

Poverty is especially prevalent today among women and the elderly. The story of Grandma Varsenik (at Isa. 1:17, p. 1075) is a parable of what happens to so many in our world.

Read through the Reading Track on poverty on page 2118. The Bible spells out that we are to treat the poor by:
Paying attention to them and their needs (Deut. 15:7–8)
Caring for them (Luke 3:11)
Showing them compassion (Prov. 22:22–23)
Exercising humble generosity (Matt. 6:2)
Administering justice to them (Ex. 23:6–7)
Granting them special rights, where it's appropriate (Lev. 19:9–10)

• Read the "World Renewal" article at Isaiah 65:17–25, page 1191. What do you think of the author's breakdown of 13 shackles that keep poor people poor?

HEART-SHAPING QUESTIONS:
How did the story of Grandma Varsenik (first paragraph, above) make you feel? Sorry or ready to do something to relieve the suffering so many similar grandmas face?
Read the article by Mother Teresa at Isaiah 55:1–3, page 1171. What do you think about her statement that today's biggest disease is poverty?

MIND-BUILDING BLOCKS:
There is no strict or across-the-board standard of poverty. The situation varies from place to place. See Haggai 1 for several different ways of defining poverty. The "Uneven Distribution of Wealth in the United States" chart at Jeremiah 22:1–5, page 1237, highlights the extent of this problem in the United States, a country with one of the highest average incomes in the world.

ACTION-PRODUCING EXERCISES:
Read "Serving the Poor" at Amos 2:6–7, page 1450. The author points out that God's desire for his people to care for the poor couldn't possibly be made clearer in Scripture. What do you think of his prescription that each of us needs to find a tangible way to help the poor? What is your way?
What do you see as the implications of the fact that the poorest people of the world are also the least evangelized—and vice versa? (See chart at Ezek. 18:12–13, p. 1334.)

REMEMBER:
"The man with two tunics should share with him who has none" (Luke 3:11).

Study Guide on Water

Water is colorless, odorless, and largely tasteless. In short, it's a pretty unremarkable substance—at first glance. But this understated, unspectacular liquid is essential to life. Without water we die—it's as simple as that. No wonder the Bible has so much to say about water, both literally and figuratively.

The Bible tells us that water sustains life (Mark 9:41) and that it's a sign from God that represents blessing (Gen. 24:34–50).

• Read the Reading Track on page 2118 that summarizes the Bible's teaching on water.

But the Bible also uses water as a symbol of some of the most important elements of the Christian life: salvation (Isa. 12:3) and life itself (Jer. 17:13), to mention only two. Because the Bible has so much to say about this life-giving liquid, we recognize that water is important in Christian living both as a symbol of the extraordinary power of

Christianity and as a way of showing love and concern for the millions of people in this world who have little access to clean water—equating to a perilous connection to life itself.

HEART-SHAPING QUESTIONS:
Read "Water for Joateca" at Genesis 26:19–22, page 43. Can you imagine having to go to such lengths just to get water? Read the story of Yetisha ("Water for Ethiopia") at Numbers 19:7–8, page 229. How can public policy either hinder or enhance the availability of clean water? Finally, read the story of Mwajuma ("A Life Source") at Joshua 15:16–19, page 339. Did you ever realize that locating and lugging water could be practically a full-time job?

MIND-BUILDING BLOCKS:
Notice the many times Jesus spoke about water (see "Jesus and Water" chart at Matt. 14:25–31, p. 1588). From our Lord's references to water as both an idea and a material necessity, we see a picture of the perfect balance between the spiritual and the material in the Christian life.

ACTION-PRODUCING EXERCISES:
Read the chart "Costs of Clean Water" at Nehemiah 9:15, page 726. What can we as Christians do to help avert crises related to lack of access to clean, safe drinking water?

We hear and read much about the importance of conserving clean water. Too often, though, we're unaware of the hidden uses of water that make it such a precious commodity. Read the "Water" chart at Zechariah 14:8 for one such insight.

REMEMBER:
"For the LORD your God is bringing you into a good land—a land with streams and pools of water" (Deut. 8:7).

BUILDING TOOLS

Study Guide on Bible Study

As Christians, we know we're supposed to study the Bible. But we're often intimidated by the idea of reading God's Word, interpreting it, and applying it to contemporary issues—and doing those things in a group setting can be even more threatening. How can you get the most out of your Bible reading? What types of Bible study groups are available to you? In what setting might you feel most comfortable?

The Bible tells us that we're to study Scripture and clearly understand its teachings.

- Read 1 Samuel 3:21 to determine the primary reason for doing so. Check out 2 Timothy 3:16 and read through the section on Bible study in the Reading Tracks (p. 2118) to discover other benefits of spending time in the Word.

HEART-SHAPING QUESTIONS:
Do you use the Bible as your primary source of guidance? Does reading Scripture have a place of priority in your daily schedule? Read the articles "Can We Learn Lessons From Esther?" at Esther 4:12–14 (p. 743) and "Using the Bible in Life" at Hebrews 4:12 (p. 2011) to discover how to read the Bible for daily guidance. Review the chart "Theories of How to Apply the Bible to Everyday Life" at James 1:22–25, page 2030. Why would it be advantageous to use different theo-

ries of application depending upon the type of passage being studied?

MIND-BUILDING BLOCKS:
Review the charts "Four Questions to Ask of a Biblical Text" at Nehemiah 8:1–3 (p. 724) and "Six Questions of Bible Study" at 1 Timothy 2:5–6 (p. 1979) to learn about different ways to approach a Bible text.

ACTION-PRODUCING EXERCISES:
Investigate possible Bible study groups you might wish to join. Review the chart "Bible Study Programs" at 2 Timothy 2:15, page 1990, to discover different programs that may be available to you. To learn how to enhance a group's effectiveness and/or to efficiently lead a Bible study, review the charts "Groups" at Proverbs 22:17, page 1014, and "Bible Study" at Colossians 3:16, page 1959.

REMEMBER:
"Do not merely listen to [or read] the word, and so deceive yourselves. Do what it says" (James 1:22).

Study Guide on Prayer

We say that prayer is powerful, but, down deep, do we really believe it? Do we pray—both in frequency and fervency—as though our prayers will truly make a difference? How did prayer become so disconnected from our daily lives? More importantly, how can we make this privilege and discipline a daily priority?

The Bible offers many precious promises regarding prayer.

- For a few of them, read John 14:13–14, 1 John 3:21–22, and 1 John 5:14–15.

Read through the section on prayer in the Reading Tracks (p. 2119) for some Biblical examples of prayers that have changed situations and lives.

HEART-SHAPING QUESTIONS:
Did you know that you can pray in any situation and express any emotion—even anger or resentment at God? Review the chart "Types of Prayer" at 1 Kings 8:22–53, page 504. What does it teach you about when you can/should pray? Review the charts "Times of Prayer" at 2 Kings 23:30, page 580, and "Regular Prayer" at Daniel 6:10–11, page 1400, to learn about scheduling times of prayer throughout your day.

MIND-BUILDING BLOCKS:
Study some Biblical examples of prayer by reviewing the charts "Prayer in the Garden" at Mark 14:32–42 (p. 1661), "Jesus' Prayers" at John 17:1–26 (p. 1776), and "Biblical Prayers of Blessing" at Hebrews 13:20–21 (p. 2026). How do these examples inspire you to make prayer a regular part of your day?

ACTION-PRODUCING EXERCISES:
Set aside specific times each day for prayer, and become more aware of opportunities throughout the day to "shoot off" prayers to God in the midst of your regular activities. Read the articles "Abraham Lincoln" at 2 Samuel 24:1–4 (p. 484), "Forgiving—and Forgiven" at Psalm 19:12–14 (p. 830), and "The Mission of Prayer" at Psalm 149:4–5 (p. 972) to learn how other people have integrated prayer into their daily schedules.

REMEMBER:
"Pray continually" (1 Thess. 5:17).

Study Guide on Relationships

Conflict is rampant, and it's everywhere—between countries, tribes, political parties, families, and even churches. Sadly, many of our individual relationships are fraught with conflict. How can we live at peace with one another? How can we find reconciliation and healing?

While the Bible is filled with accounts of family conflicts and relational tragedies, its primary themes are love, reconciliation, and unity.

- Read Matthew 22:37–39, Colossians 3:13, and Hebrews 12:14. Then read through the section on relationships in the Reading Tracks (p. 2119).

HEART-SHAPING QUESTIONS:

With whom are you currently "in relationship"? Review the chart "Relationships" at 2 Samuel 12:11–12 and 14 (p. 462) to recognize the surprising scope of your relationships. What is your current method of dealing with disagreements or disputes? Review the chart "Ineffective Ways of Dealing With Conflict" at 1 Kings 20:1–12, page 529, to consider some possibly more effective approaches and strategies.

MIND-BUILDING BLOCKS:

Several attitudes are essential for building and maintaining healthy relationships with other people. Read about some of them in the articles and charts listed below:

Compassion	"Shared Suffering" at Job 7:25–30, page 762
Respect	"The Antidote for Meaninglessness" at Psalm 8:3–9, page 817
Humility	"Civility" at 1 Peter 2:17; 3:15, page 2042

ACTION-PRODUCING EXERCISES:

Think about someone whose relational qualities you admire. How does that person treat those around him or her? Review the chart "The Wise Man According to Proverbs: An Outline" at Proverbs 1:1–7, page 977, to learn the key elements for developing successful relationships. Review the chart "A Recipe for Reconciliation" at Romans 5:10–11, page 1854. Identify a personal relationship that needs reconciliation, and ask God to help you change your attitudes and behaviors so you can positively influence the situation.

REMEMBER:

"If it is possible, as far as it depends on you, live at peace with everyone" (Rom. 12:18).

Study Guide on Witness

Witnessing is a scary word to many people. It just isn't their "thing," and they would rather be involved in other aspects of ministry. Is witnessing really that important—or effective? What forms can it take? Can God really use *you*?

Witnessing was a major focus of the New Testament church—and still needs to be in the church today.

- Read Matthew 28:18–20, Jesus' last directive to his followers.

HEART-SHAPING QUESTIONS:

Does *every* Christian have to be involved in witnessing? Is the need really that great? Review the charts "The Poor and the Lost" at Ezekiel 18:12–13 (p. 1334), "The Ends of the Earth" at Acts 28:30 (p. 1844), "Witness" at 2 Corinthians 4:16–18 (p. 1906), and "The Three Worlds" at 1 Peter 5:8–9 (p. 2046). Are you needed in God's witnessing program?

MIND-BUILDING BLOCKS:

Review the charts "Four Roots of Biblical Witness" at John 20:21 (p. 1783), "Six Ways of Witnessing" at Acts 4:32–35 (p. 1797), and "God's Call to Mission" at Acts 15:1–2 (p. 1820). Then read through the section on witnessing in the Reading Tracks (p. 2119) to learn about some other ways you can witness. Remember that a proper attitude is necessary when witnessing. Read the "Henry Martyn" Snapshot at Genesis 18:18 (p. 30) and the articles "The Enduring Message of Jonah" at Jonah 4:10–11 (p. 1473), "Cross-cultural Mission" at Matthew 28:19–20 (p. 1622), "Witness" at Acts 8:1 (p. 1804), and "Incarnational Identification" at Philippians 2:5–8 (p. 1946) to discover the importance of respect, obedience, acceptance, and humility in witnessing.

ACTION-PRODUCING EXERCISES:

Seek God's "calling" for your life. Read the Snapshots "Grace" at Deuteronomy 4:9 (p. 267), "Joining in God's Program" at Isaiah 43:18–19 (p. 1148), and "Joining Forces" at 2 Corinthians 9:2 (p. 1912) to see how others have discovered their "calling." Take a risk. Be obedient. Look for an adventure.

REMEMBER:

"I pray that you may be active in sharing your faith, so that you will have a full understanding of every good thing we have in Christ" (Philem. 6).

Subject Index

The Subject Index to follow is intended to help focus your study of particular topics addressed in the book introductions, articles, charts, "Snapshots" (stories and sketches), and maps in this Bible.

Accepting Others

"Henry Martyn," p. 30 (Gen. 18:18); "Love Your Neighbor" (chart), p. 176 (Lev. 17:8,10,13,15); Introduction to Joshua, p. 315; Introduction to Ruth, p. 390; Introduction to Romans, p. 1845; "Reconciliation Among Christians," p. 2002 (Philem. 16)

AIDS

"The Plagues" (chart), p. 94 (Ex. 7:1–5); "HIV/AIDS" (chart), p. 673 (2 Chron. 26:21); "A Place for Children," p. 789 (Job 29:12–13); "A Positive Outlook," p. 834 (Ps. 23:4–6); "Cry, the Beloved Continent: Don't Let AIDS Steal African Children's Future," p. 1577 (Matt. 9:35–36); "Feed My Sheep" (chart), p. 1786 (John 21:15–23); "Joining Forces," p. 1912 (2 Cor. 9:2); "Loving Kakolo," p. 1981 (1 Tim. 4:12); "Mirriam," p. 1998 (Titus 3:14); "A Love Affair for Jesus," p. 2031 (James 1:27)

Anger, God's

"God's Anger" (chart), p. 372 (Judg. 9:56–57)

Atonement

Introduction to Leviticus, p. 151; Introduction to Zechariah, p. 1522

Attributes of God

Introduction to Psalms, p. 808; Introduction to Lamentations, p. 1295

Bible/Bible Study

"Gideons Bibles" (chart), p. 364 (Judg. 6:14); "Four Questions to Ask of a Biblical Text" (chart), p. 724 (Neh. 8:1–3); "Can We Learn Lessons From Esther?" p. 743 (Est. 4:12–14); "Transfer of Use," p. 906 (Ps. 86:5–6); "Groups" (chart), p. 1014 (Prov. 22:17); "Six Biblical Sources for Application" (chart), p. 1059 (Song 2:3–13); "English Bible Major Translation Timeline" (chart), p. 1139 (Isa. 40:8); "Visions of Truth," p. 1313 (Ezek. 1:1); "Bible Study" (chart), p. 1959 (Col. 3:16); "Six Questions of Bible Study" (chart), p. 1979 (1 Tim. 2:5–6); "Bible Study Programs" (chart), p. 1990 (2 Tim. 2:15); "Using the Bible in Life," p. 2011 (Heb. 4:12); "Theories of How to Apply the Bible to Everyday Life" (chart), p. 2030 (James 1:22–25)

Blessings

Introduction to 2 Kings, p. 537; Introduction to 1 Chronicles, p. 585; Introduction to 2 Chronicles, p. 639; Introduction to Joel, p. 1434

Introduction to Zechariah, p. 1522; "The Beatitudes" (chart), p. 1563 (Matt. 5:1–12); "Biblical Prayers of Blessing" (chart), p. 2026 (Heb. 13:20–21)

Blood

"Shed Blood" (chart), p. 279 (Deut. 12:23)

Busyness

"Is There Room in Your Inn?" p. 1675 (Luke 2:7)

Change

Introduction to 2 Kings, p. 537; "Ki-Poong," p. 1819 (Acts 14:19–20)

Children

"Be Fruitful and Increase," p. 6 (Gen. 1:28); "Geoffrey," p. 81 (Gen. 50:18–21); "Amy Carmichael," p. 118 (Ex. 22:22–23); "Grace," p. 267 (Deut. 4:9); "Lee," p. 295 (Deut. 24:17); "Vali," p. 397 (Ruth 4:14–16); "Child Labor" (chart), p. 402 (1 Sam. 2:18); "Bamboo Shoots Street Children's Center," p. 456 (2 Sam. 7:10); "Mirza," p. 459 (2 Sam. 9:1–13); "Television Violence" (chart), p. 541 (2 Kings 2:23); "The Girl Preacher," p. 705 (Ezra 8:2–3); "Friend of Family," p. 714 (Neh. 2:10); "United States Children at Risk" (chart), p. 754 (Job 1:5); "A Stolen Car and a Changed Life," p. 784 (Job 24:1–11); "A Place for Children," p. 789 (Job 29:12–13); "Jacquiline," p. 883 (Ps. 68:5–6a); "Blessing the Children," p. 966 (Ps. 144:12); "Sobering Stats on Children" (chart), p. 990 (Prov. 8:32); "Isaac," p. 992 (Prov. 10:1); "Gifted Children of the Bible" (chart), p. 1005 (Prov. 17:6); "Learner Retention" (chart), p. 1029 (Prov. 31:1–9); "Reflections of a Sponsored Child," p. 1040 (Eccl. 4:10–12); "Look With Compassion on Children" (chart), p. 1098 (Isa. 13:18); "Hamedi," p. 1238 (Jer. 22:2–3); "Child Starvation" (chart), p. 1302 (Lam. 2:19); "Biblical Attitudes Toward Children" (chart), p. 1436 (Joel 1:2–3); "Susan," p. 2548 (Mal. 4:2); "Emmanuel," p. 1557 (Matt. 1:22); "The Slaughter of Innocents" (chart), p. 1559 (Matt. 2:16); "Giovanna," p. 1576 (Matt. 9:35–36); "Aung Lin," p. 1697 (Luke 9:58); "A Special Baptism," p. 1771 (John 14:2–3); "Feed My Sheep" (chart), p. 1786 (John 21:15–23); "Sebastian," p. 1931 (Eph. 1:4–5); "Television Time" (chart), p. 1950 (Phil. 4:8); "Mary Jane," p. 1973 (2 Thess. 2:16–17)

Choices

Introduction to Deuteronomy, p. 258; "Discerning God's Will" (chart), p. 392 (Ruth 1:22); "Abraham Lincoln," p. 484 (2 Sam. 24:1–4); "Can We Learn Lessons From Esther?" p. 743 (Est. 4:12–14); "Joining in God's Program," p. 1148 (Isa. 43:18–19); Introduction to John, p. 1737

Christ's Return

"World Renewal," p. 1191 (Isa. 65:17–25); Introduction to 1 Thessalonians, p. 1961; Introduction to 2 Thessalonians, p. 1969; Introduction to 2 Peter, p. 2048; Introduction to Revelation, p. 2074

Christmas

"Is There Room in Your Inn?" p. 1675 (Luke 2:7)

Church Growth

"Bad Counting, Good Counting" (chart), p. 485 (2 Sam. 24:10); "Building Churches," p. 699 (Ezra 4:4–5); "Signs of a Stagnant Congregation" (chart), p. 727 (Neh. 9:26–31); "Profile of World Christianity" (chart), p. 827

(Ps. 18:29); "Growth of the Church" (chart), p. 1793 (Acts 2:41); "Nine Characteristics of a Healthy Church" (chart), p. 1794 (Acts 2:42–47); "A Model for Urban Ministry" (chart), p. 1812 (Acts 11:19–21); "The Ends of the Earth" (chart), p. 1844 (Acts 28:30)

Community
"Outdated Laws?" p. 170 (Lev. 13:47–59); "Relationships" (chart), p. 462 (2 Sam. 12:11–12,14); "Ineffective Ways of Dealing With Conflict" (chart), p. 529 (1 Kings 20:1–12); "The Wise Man According to Proverbs: An Outline" (chart), p. 977 (Prov. 1:1–7); "Groups" (chart), p. 1014 (Prov. 22:17); Introduction to Acts, p. 1787; Introduction to Romans, p. 1845; Introduction to Ephesians, p. 1929

Compassion, God's
Introduction to 2 Kings, p. 537; Introduction to Lamentations, p. 1295; "Compassion," p. 1416 (Hos. 1:2–3); Introduction to Jonah, p. 1468; "The Enduring Message of Jonah," p. 1473 (Jonah 4:10–11); "Sharing God's Compassion," p. 2035 (James 5:2–6)

Compassion, Human
"People in Need of Christian Care and Protection" (chart), p. 179 (Lev. 19:1); Introduction to 2 Samuel, p. 444; Introduction to 2 Kings, p. 537; Introduction to Job, p. 751; Introduction to Psalms, p. 808; "Biblical Attitudes Toward the Poor" (chart), p. 1015 (Prov. 22:22–23); "Look With Compassion on Children" (chart), p. 1098 (Isa. 13:18); "Why Should We Be Compassionate?" (chart), p. 1177 (Isa. 58:6–10); "Bob Pierce," p. 1183 (Isa. 61:1–3); "Compassion," p. 1416 (Hos. 1:2–3); "Mother Teresa," p. 1457 (Amos 5:24); "Compassion," p. 1630 (Mark 1:40–42); "Tabitha," p. 1809 (Acts 9:36–42); "Sharing God's Compassion," p. 2035 (James 5:2–6)

Complaining
Introduction to Numbers, p. 195; Introduction to Malachi, p. 1542

Compromise
Introduction to Judges, p. 353; Introduction to 2 Kings, p. 537; Introduction to Ezra, p. 691; Introduction to Esther, p. 736; Introduction to Ezekiel, p. 1310; Introduction to Daniel, p. 1387; Introduction to 2 Peter, p. 2048; Introduction to 2 John, p. 2064; Introduction to Revelation, p. 2074

Confession
Introduction to 2 Samuel, p. 444; Introduction to 1 Chronicles, p. 585; Introduction to 2 Chronicles, p. 639; Introduction to Psalms, p. 808; Introduction to Jonah, p. 1468

Confronting Others
"Be Strong and Courageous" (chart), p. 317 (Josh. 1:6–11); Introduction to 2 Samuel, p. 444; "Ineffective Ways of Dealing With Conflict" (chart), p. 529 (1 Kings 20:1–12); Introduction to Job, p. 751; "A Counterintuitive Calling," p. 1532 (Zech. 8:9–11); Introduction to 1 Corinthians, p. 1874; Introduction to Galatians, p. 1918; Introduction to Colossians, p. 1952; Introduction to 2 Timothy, p. 1985; Introduction to James, p. 2027; Introduction to Jude, p. 2070

Contentment
Introduction to Numbers, p. 195; "Obey God and Serve Him" (chart), p. 798 (Job 36:11); Introduction to Ecclesiastes, p. 1032; Introduction to Song of Songs, p. 1054; "The Roads to Contentment" (chart), p. 1947 (Phil. 2:14–16); "Signs of Discontent" (chart), p. 2090 (Rev. 11:18)

Cooperation
"Groups" (chart), p. 1014 (Prov. 22:17); "Light to the World" (chart), p. 1703 (Luke 11:33–36)

Courage
Introduction to Exodus, p. 82; Introduction to Joshua, p. 315; "Courage," p. 318 (Josh. 1:6–7); "Be Strong and Courageous" (chart), p. 317 (Josh. 1:6–11); "Act With Courage" (chart), p. 663 (2 Chron. 19:11); Introduction to Esther, p. 736; Introduction to Job, p. 751; "Do Not Fear: Johanna Veenstra," p. 860 (Ps. 44:22); Introduction to John, p. 1737; "From Fear to Courage" (chart), p. 2008 (Heb. 2:15)

Covenant(s)
Introduction to Exodus, p. 82; Introduction to Deuteronomy, p. 258; "Major Social Concerns in the Covenant" (chart), p. 298 (Deut. 26:16–19); Introduction to 2 Samuel, p. 444; Introduction to 1 Kings, p. 487; Introduction to 1 Chronicles, p. 585; Introduction to 2 Chronicles, p. 639

Creation
Introduction to Genesis, p. 1; "Days of Creation" (chart), p. 7 (Gen. 2:1–2); "Fearfully and Wonderfully Made" (chart), p. 961 (Ps. 139:13–14); "The Creation Groans" (chart), p. 1860 (Rom. 8:18–27)

Cultural Diversity
"Henry Martyn," p. 30 (Gen. 18:18); "Love Your Neighbor" (chart), p. 176 (Lev. 17:8,10,13,15); "Cross-cultural Mission," p. 1622 (Matt. 28:19–20); "Billy Graham," p. 1886 (1 Cor. 9:19–23); "Apostle of the Indies," p. 1897 (1 Cor. 15:58); "Incarnational Identification," p. 1946 (Phil. 2:5–8); "Reconciliation Among Christians," p. 2002 (Philem. 16)

Death
"Natural Disasters" (chart), p. 12 (Gen. 6:7); "The Top 24 Causes of Christian Deaths" (chart), p. 314 (Deut. 34:5); Introduction to 2 Kings, p. 537; Introduction to 2 Chronicles, p. 639; Introduction to Nehemiah, p. 711; Introduction to Ecclesiastes, p. 1032; "The Slaughter of Innocents" (chart), p. 1559 (Matt. 2:16); Introduction to John, p. 1737; Introduction to 2 Peter, p. 2048; "My Dear Teacher," p. 2106 (Rev. 21:4)

Deliverance
Introduction to Exodus, p. 82; "Deliverance From Bondage," p. 87 (Ex. 3:7–10); "Frederick Douglass," p. 734 (Neh. 13:14); Introduction to Esther, p. 736; Introduction to Obadiah, p. 1464; Introduction to Nahum, p. 1491

Devotion to God, wholehearted
"William Wilberforce," p. 13 (Gen. 6:8–9); Introduction to 2 Kings, p. 537; Introduction to 1 Chronicles, p. 585; Introduction to 2 Chronicles, p. 639; "Righteous Kings," p. 1197 (Jer. 1:1–3); Introduction to Daniel, p. 1387; "Extravagant Devotion" (chart), p. 1689 (Luke 7:36–50)

Discipleship
"Spiritual Formation" (chart), p. 405 (1 Sam. 3:19–20); "Jesus' Messages in Matthew's Gospel" (chart), p. 1595 (Matt. 18:19–20); Introduction to Mark, p. 1624; "Walk to Emmaus" (chart), p. 1735 (Luke 24:13–35); "Self Examination" (chart), p. 1917 (2 Cor. 13:5); "20 Questions" (chart), p. 2056 (1 Jn. 1:6–10)

Disease
"The Bronze Snake" (chart), p. 231 (Num. 21:4–9); "Malaria" (chart), p. 1085 (Isa. 7:18); "Paulina," p. 1252 (Jer. 30:17); "New Identities," p. 1368 (Ezek. 37:11–14); "Chemicals by Health Effects" (chart), p. 1427 (Hos. 10:4)

Education

"New Beginnings in Francisco de Opalaca," p. 191 (Lev. 26:3–6); "Grace," p. 267 (Deut. 4:9); "Educational Opportunity" (chart), p. 403 (1 Sam. 2:26); "Friend of Family," p. 714 (Neh. 2:10); "Temka School," p. 841 (Ps. 30:4–7); "Betsey Stockton," p. 987 (Prov. 6:23); "A Struggle and a Dream," p. 1024 (Prov. 27:26–27); "Learner Retention" (chart), p. 1029 (Prov. 31:1–9); "K'ang Ch'eng, Gertrude Howe, and Shih Mei-yü," p. 1031 (Prov. 31:29–30); "Education" (chart), p. 1093 (Isa. 11:1–3); "Martha," p. 1363 (Ezek. 34:26–27); "Literacy: An Open Door," p. 1390 (Dan. 1:3–4,17); "Kalya = Peace," p. 1484 (Mic. 5:1–5a)

Emotions

"Godly Emotions?" (chart), p. 757 (Job 3:1–16)

Encouragement

"Encourage Others in the Lord's Service" (chart), p. 686 (2 Chron. 35:2); "Groups" (chart), p. 1014 (Prov. 22:17); "Great Encouragers in the Bible" (chart), p. 1626 (Mark 1:1–11); Introduction to Acts, p. 1787; "Barnabas," p. 1813 (Acts 11:22); Introduction to 1 Thessalonians, p. 1961; Introduction to 2 Timothy, p. 1985

Environmental Responsibility

Introduction to Genesis, p. 1; "Be Fruitful and Increase," p. 6 (Gen. 1:28); "Water for Joateca," p. 43 (Gen. 26:19–22); "A Life Source," p. 339 (Josh. 15:16–19); "Costs of Clean Water" (chart), p. 726 (Neh. 9:15); "Chemicals by Health Effects" (chart), p. 1427 (Hos. 10:4); "World Land Use" (chart), p. 1520 (Hag. 1:6,10–11); "Water" (chart), p. 1540 (Zech. 14:8); "The Creation Groans" (chart), p. 1860 (Rom. 8:18–27)

Equality

"Henry Martyn," p. 30 (Gen. 18:18); Introduction to Exodus, p. 82; "Rev. Martin Luther King, Jr." p. 89 (Ex. 4:10–11); "Love Your Neighbor" (chart), p. 176 (Lev. 17:8,10,13,15); Introduction to Joshua, p. 315; "A Life Source," p. 339 (Josh. 15:16–19); "Catherine Booth," p. 366 (Judg. 7:7–8); "Mirza," p. 459 (2 Sam. 9:1–13); "Frederick Douglass," p. 734 (Neh. 13:14); "Hamedi," p. 1238 (Jer. 22:2–3); Introduction to Mark, p. 1624; Introduction to Acts, p. 1787; Introduction to Galatians, p. 1918; Introduction to Ephesians, p. 1929; Introduction to Titus, p. 1993; Introduction to Philemon, p. 1999

Ethics

"Outdated Laws?" p. 170 (Lev. 13:47–59); "Abraham Lincoln," p. 484 (2 Sam. 24:1–4); "Can We Learn Lessons From Esther?" p. 743 (Est. 4:12–14); "Wisdom," p. 978 (Prov. 1:1–7); Introduction to Matthew, p. 1553; "The Beatitudes" (chart), p. 1563 (Matt. 5:1–12); "Using the Bible in Life," p. 2011 (Heb. 4:12)

Evangelism

"Henry Martyn," p. 30 (Gen. 18:18); "Salih Abdul Masih," p. 113 (Ex. 18:20); "Grace," p. 267 (Deut. 4:9); "Be Strong and Courageous" (chart), p. 318 (Josh. 1:6–11); "Catherine Booth," p. 366 (Judg. 7:7–8); "Aleksandr Men," p. 684 (2 Chron. 34:3); "The Girl Preacher," p. 705 (Ezra 8:2–3); "Reflections of a Sponsored Child," p. 1040 (Eccl. 4:10–12); Introduction to Ezekiel, p. 1310; "The Poor and the Lost," p. 1334 (Ezek. 18:12–13); "New Identities," p. 1368 (Ezek. 37:11–14); Introduction to Joel, p. 1434; Introduction to Jonah, p. 1468; "The Enduring Message of Jonah," p. 1473 (Jonah 4:10–11); "William and Clementina (Rowe) Butler," p. 1493 (Nah. 1:7); "Jesus Speaks My Language!" p. 1533 (Zech. 8:23); Introduction to Matthew, p. 1553; "Witnessing Through the Years" (chart), p. 1666 (Mark 16:15–14); "Moses and the Prophets" (chart), p. 1715 (Luke 16:19–31); Introduction to John, p. 1737; "Four Roots of Biblical Witness" (chart), p. 1783 (John 20:21); Introduction to Acts, p. 1787; "Six Ways of Witnessing" (chart), p. 1797 (Acts 4:32–35); "Auca Five," p. 1803 (Acts 7:59—8:1); "Witness," p. 1804 (Acts 8:1); "A Model for Urban Ministry" (chart), p. 1812 (Acts 11:19–21); "God's Call to Mission" (chart), p. 1820 (Acts 15:1–2); "The Ends of the Earth" (chart), p. 1844 (Acts 28:30); "Billy Graham," p. 1886 (1 Cor. 9:19–23); "Apostle of the Indies," p. 1897 (1 Cor. 15:58); Introduction to 2 Corinthians, p. 1900; "Witness" (chart), p. 1906 (2 Cor. 4:16–18); "Incarnational Identification," p. 1946 (Phil. 2:5–8); Introduction to 1 Thessalonians, p. 1961; Introduction to 2 Thessalonians, p. 1969; Introduction to 1 Timothy, p. 1975; "The Three Worlds" (chart), p. 2046 (1 Peter 5:8–9); Introduction to 2 Peter, p. 2048

Faith

"Be Strong and Courageous" (chart), p. 318 (Josh. 1:6–11); Introduction to Ruth, p. 390; Introduction to 2 Kings, p. 537; Introduction to 2 Chronicles, p. 639; Introduction to Ezra, p. 691; Introduction to Ezekiel, p. 1310; Introduction to Daniel, p. 1387; Introduction to Habakkuk, p. 1498; "Belief and Identity" (chart), p. 1501 (Hab. 1:5); Introduction to Luke, p. 1668; Introduction to John, p. 1737; Introduction to Galatians, p. 1918; Introduction to Hebrews, p. 2004; "Demonstrations of Devotion," p. 2021 (Heb. 11:6); "Faith Is Demonstrated by Activity" (chart), p. 2023 (Heb. 11:32–34); Introduction to James, p. 2027; "Faith and Good Works" (chart), p. 2032 (James 2:14–17); "The Relationship Between Faith and Action" (chart), p. 2033 (James 2:20–24)

Faith Into Action

"Corrie ten Boom," p. 558 (2 Kings 11:1–4); Introduction to Nehemiah, p. 711; "The Eternal Now and the Temporal Now," p. 844 (Ps. 31:14–16); Introduction to Proverbs, p. 974; "Isaiah, Which Will It Be?" p. 1074 (Isa. 1:17); Introduction to Jeremiah, p. 1194; "Frances Elizabeth Caroline Willard," p. 1198 (Jer. 1:10); Introduction to Amos, p. 1445; "Mother Teresa," p. 1457 (Amos 5:24); "Dorothy Day," p. 1486 (Mic. 6:8); "The Beatitudes" (chart), p. 1563 (Matt. 5:1–12); "Jesus' Ministry" (chart), p. 1680 (Luke 4:18–19); "Feed My Sheep" (chart), p. 1786 (John 21:15–23); "Service" (chart), p. 1867 (Rom. 12:1–2); Introduction to Galatians, p. 1918; "Be Very Careful How You Live" (chart), p. 1938 (Eph. 5:15–17); "Holiness and the Poor," p. 1967 (1 Thess. 4:9–12); Introduction to Titus, p. 1993; "Demonstrations of Devotion," p. 2021 (Heb. 11:6); "Faith Is Demonstrated by Activity" (chart), p. 2023 (Heb. 11:32–34); Introduction to James, p. 2027; "Faith and Good Works" (chart), p. 2032 (James 2:14–17); "The Relationship Between Faith and Action" (chart), p. 2033 (James 2:20–24)

Faithfulness, God's

Introduction to Numbers, p. 195; Introduction to Joshua, p. 315; Introduction to Judges, p. 353; Introduction to Hosea, p. 1413; Introduction to Romans, p. 1845

Faithfulness, Human

Introduction to Ruth, p. 390; Introduction to 1 Kings, p. 487; Introduction to Jeremiah, p. 1194; Introduction to Colossians, p. 1952

False Teachers

"Apostasy" (chart), p. 370 (Judg. 8:33–35); Introduction to 2 Timothy, p. 1985; Introduction to Titus, p. 1993; Introduction to 2 Peter, p. 2048; "False Teachers and Their Teachings" (chart), p. 2051 (2 Peter 2:1–3); Introduction to 2 John, p. 2064; Introduction to Jude, p. 2070;

"To the Church That Endures Persecution," p. 2079 (Rev. 2:8–10)

Family Conflict
Introduction to Genesis, p. 1; "Relationships" (chart), p. 462 (2 Sam. 12:11–12,14)

Farming
"Joseph Sold Into Egypt" (map), p. 61 (Gen. 37:28); "New Beginnings in Francisco de Opalaca," p. 191 (Lev. 26:3–6); "Friend of Family," p. 714 (Neh. 2:10); "A Struggle and a Dream," p. 1024 (Prov. 27:26–27); "World Land Use" (chart), p. 1520 (Hag. 1:6,10–11); "Good Land" (chart), p. 1635 (Mark 4:1–9)

Fasting
Introduction to Joel, p. 1434; "Jesus and Food" (chart), p. 1574 (Matt. 9:9–13)

Fear
Introduction to 2 Chronicles, p. 639; "Act With Courage" (chart), p.663 (2 Chron. 19:11); "Do Not Fear: Johanna Veenstra," p. 860 (Ps. 44:22); Introduction to Isaiah, p. 1070; "To Fear God's Name Is Wisdom" (chart), p. 1475 (Mic. 6:9); Introduction to John, p. 1737; "From Fear to Courage" (chart), p. 2008 (Heb. 2:15); Introduction to 1 Peter, p. 2037

Feasts
"Ancient Israelite and Contemporary Christian Feasts" (chart), p. 185 (Lev. 23:1)

Forgiveness
Introduction to 2 Samuel, p. 444; Introduction to 1 Chronicles, p. 585; Introduction to 2 Chronicles, p. 639; "Forgiving—and Forgiven," p. 830 (Ps. 19:12–14); Introduction to Hosea, p. 1413; Introduction to Micah, p. 1475; "Forgiveness" (chart), p. 1757 (John 8:1–11); Introduction to Acts, p. 1787; "Racial Reconciliation," p. 1855 (Rom. 5:10); "A Recipe for Reconciliation" (chart), p. 1854 (Rom. 5:10–11); "Reconciliation," p. 1908 (2 Cor. 5:17–20); "Reconciliation," p. 1955 (Col. 1:19–20); Introduction to Philemon, p. 1999; "Reconciliation Among Christians," p. 2002 (Philem. 16); Introduction to 1 John, p. 2054

Freedom
"Rev. Martin Luther King, Jr." p. 89 (Ex. 4:10–11); "Freedom" (chart), p. 388 (Judg. 21:25); "Frederick Douglass," p. 734 (Neh. 13:14); "The 13 Shackles," p. 1182 (Isa. 61:1–3a); "Christian Human Rights" (chart), p. 1924 (Gal. 3:23–25)

Friendship
Introduction to 1 Samuel, p. 398; "Relationships" (chart), p. 462 (2 Sam. 12:11–12,14); "Ineffective Ways of Dealing With Conflict" (chart), p. 529 (1 Kings 20:1–12); Introduction to 2 Timothy, p. 1985; Introduction to 1 Peter, p. 2037

Giving
"Gifts to God" (chart), p. 139 (Ex. 35:5); Introduction to Numbers, p. 195; Introduction to Ezra, p. 691; Introduction to Proverbs, p. 974; "Biblical Attitudes Toward the Poor" (chart), p. 1015 (Prov. 22:22–23); "Compassion," p. 1416 (Hos. 1:2–3); "Serving the Poor," p. 1450 (Amos 2:6–7); Introduction to 2 Corinthians, p. 1900; "Generosity" (chart), p. 1913 (2 Cor. 9:12); Introduction to Philippians, p. 1941; "How Giving Helps the Giver" (chart), p. 1948 (Phil. 2:17–18); "Mary Jane," p. 1973 (2 Thess. 2:16–17); "Loving Kakolo," p. 1981 (1 Tim. 4:12)

Goodness, God's
Introduction to Job, p. 751; "Transfer of Use," p. 906 (Ps. 86:5–6)

Government
"Layers of Legislation" (chart), p. 116 (Ex. 2:1); "Nations" (chart), p. 284 (Deut. 16:18–20); "Freedom" (chart), p. 388 (Judg. 21:25)

Grace, God's
Introduction to Judges, p. 353; "Reconciliation," p. 1908 (2 Cor. 5:17–20)

Guidance
Introduction to Numbers, p. 195; Introduction to Joshua, p. 315; "Discerning God's Will" (chart), p. 392 (Ruth 1:22); Introduction to 1 Chronicles, p. 585; "Can We Learn Lessons From Esther?" p. 743 (Est. 4:12–14); "Joining in God's Program," p. 1148 (Isa. 43:18–19); Introduction to Zephaniah, p. 1506; Introduction to Matthew, p. 1553; Introduction to 1 Timothy, p. 1975

Healing
Introduction to 2 Kings, p. 537; "New Identities," p. 1368 (Ezek. 37:11–14)

Heaven
"Three Heavens" (chart), p. 505 (1 Kings 8:27)

Helping Others
"Love Your Neighbor" (chart), p. 176 (Lev. 17:8,10,13,15); "People in Need of Christian Care and Protection" (chart), p. 179 (Lev. 19:1); "As Poor as the Poor," p. 1171 (Isa. 55:1–3); "New Identities," p. 1368 (Ezek. 37:11–14); "The Role of the Law in Helping the Poor and Oppressed," p. 1607 (Matt. 22:37); "The Cambridge Seven," p. 1628 (Mark 1:18); "Who Is Our Neighbor?" p. 1699 (Luke 10:25–37); "Great Sins of Omission," p. 1716 (Luke 16:19–31); "Fanny Jackson Coppin," p. 1722 (Luke 19:11–27); "Sharing Lunch," p. 1752 (John 6:1–14); "Feed My Sheep" (chart), p. 1786 (John 21:15–23); "Do Good to All People" (chart), p. 1928 (Gal. 6:10); "Mirriam," p. 1998 (Titus 3:14); "Dorcas," p. 2013 (Heb. 6:10)

Holiness, God's
Introduction to 1 Samuel, p. 398

Holiness/Righteousness, Human
Introduction to Leviticus, p. 151; Introduction to Matthew, p. 1553; "Purity," p. 1643 (Mark 7); Introduction to Romans, p. 2074; Introduction to Colossians, p. 1952; "Holiness and the Poor," p. 1967 (1 Thess. 4:9–12)

Honesty
Introduction to Psalms, p. 808; Introduction to Jeremiah, p. 1194; Introduction to Habakkuk, p. 1498; Introduction to John, p. 1737

Hope
Introduction to Numbers, p. 195; "Elijah and the Widow at Zarephath," p. 524 (1 Kings 17:7–15); Introduction to Lamentations, p. 1295; Introduction to Ezekiel, p. 1310; Introduction to Nahum, p. 1491; Introduction to Habakkuk, p. 1498; Introduction to Zechariah, p. 1522; Introduction to 1 Peter, p. 2037

Hospitality
"Hospitality," p. 1711 (Luke 14:12–14); Introduction to Hebrews, p. 2004; Introduction to 3 John, p. 2067

Human Rights
"Major Social Concerns in the Covenant" (chart), p. 298 (Deut. 26:16–19); "Christian Human Rights" (chart), p. 1924 (Gal. 3:23–25)

Humility
"Wisdom," p. 495 (1 Kings 3:16–28); Introduction to 2 Kings, p. 537; Introduction to Nehemiah, p. 711; "Compassion," p. 1416 (Hos. 1:2–3); Introduction to

Joel, p. 1434; "Dorothy Day," p. 1475 (Mic. 6:8); Introduction to Zephaniah, p. 1506; "Service and Humility," p. 1511 (Zeph. 2:2–3); "Biblical Humility" (chart), p. 1769 (John 13:1–17); Introduction to Philippians, p. 1941; "Models of Biblical Humility" (chart), p. 1944 (Phil. 2:3); "How to Develop Humility" (chart), p. 1945 (Phil. 2:4); "Incarnational Identification," p. 1946 (Phil. 2:5–8)

Hunger
"Hunger in the Bible" (chart), p. 109 (Ex. 16:2–3); Milk Money," p. 363 (Judg. 5:24–25); "Hunger" (chart), p. 393 (Ruth 2:8); "Malnutrition" (chart), p. 395 (Ruth 3:17–18); "Sobering Stats on Children" (chart), p. 990 (Prov. 8:32); "Joining in God's Program," p. 1148 (Isa. 43:18–19); "As Poor as the Poor," p. 1171 (Isa. 55:1–3); "Easing the Hunger Equation" (chart), p. 1176 (Isa. 58:6–7); "Child Starvation" (chart), p. 1302 (Lam. 2:19); "Martha," p. 1363 (Ezek. 34:26–27); "The Faces of Malnutrition" (chart), p. 1452 (Amos 4:1); "Feed My Sheep" (chart), p. 1786 (John 21:15–23)

Hypocrisy
Introduction to Judges, p. 353; Introduction to Isaiah, p. 1070; Introduction to Hosea, p. 1413; Introduction to Amos, p. 1445; "The Dangers of Professional Religious Service" (chart), p. 1657 (Mark 12:38–42); Introduction to Revelation, p. 2074

Idolatry
"Apostasy" (chart), p. 370 (Judg. 8:33–35); Introduction to 2 Kings, p. 537; Introduction to Isaiah, p. 1070; Introduction to Ezekiel, p. 1310; Introduction to Hosea, p. 1413

Image of God
Introduction to Genesis, p. 1; *Imago Dei* (chart), p. 4 (Gen. 1:26); "Relationships" (chart), p. 462 (2 Sam. 12:11–12,14); "The Antidote for Meaninglessness," p. 817 (Ps. 8:3–9); "The Image of God" (chart), p. 1932 (Eph. 1:3–14); "The Image of God in Human Beings," p. 2094 (Rev. 13:13–15)

Injustice
Introduction to 2 Chronicles, p. 639; Introduction to Nehemiah, p. 711; "Frederick Douglass," p. 734 (Neh. 13:14); "God's Rescue Plan," p. 820 (Ps. 10:17–18); Introduction to Ecclesiastes, p. 1032; Introduction to Isaiah, p. 1070; "The 13 Shackles," p. 1182 (Isa. 61:1–3a); Introduction to Jeremiah, p. 1194; Introduction to Amos, p. 1445; Introduction to Obadiah, p. 1464; Introduction to Micah, p. 1475; Introduction to Habakkuk, p. 1498; Introduction to Mark, p. 1624

Integrity
Introduction to 2 Samuel, p. 444; "Abraham Lincoln," p. 484 (2 Sam. 24:1–4); Introduction to Proverbs, p. 974; Introduction to Daniel, p. 1387

Joy
"Service and Humility," p. 1511 (Zeph. 2:2–3); Introduction to Philippians, p. 1941

Judging Others
Introduction to Genesis, p. 1; "Judgment," p. 746 (Est. 7:3–4); Introduction to Job, p. 751; Introduction to Jonah, p. 1468; Introduction to Romans, p. 1845

Judgment
Introduction to 2 Samuel, p. 444; Introduction to 2 Kings, p. 537; Introduction to 2 Chronicles, p. 639; Introduction to Isaiah, p. 1070; Introduction to Jeremiah, p. 1194; Introduction to Lamentations, p. 1295; Introduction to Ezekiel, p. 1310; "Daniel in Babylon" (map), p. 1387 (Dan. 1:6); Introduction to Hosea, p.

1413; Introduction to Joel, p. 1434; Introduction to Amos, p. 1445; "Judgment on Israel's Neighbors" (map), p. 1447 (Amos 1:3); Introduction to Obadiah, p. 1464; Introduction to Micah, p. 1475; Introduction to Nahum, p. 1491; Introduction to Zephaniah, p. 1506; Introduction to Malachi, p. 1542; "Twin Truths" (chart), p. 1739 (John 1:1–3); "Judgment and the Four Horsemen" (chart), p. 2085 (Rev. 6:1–8); "Vice List" (chart), p. 2107 (Rev. 21:8)

Justice, God's
Introduction to Exodus, p. 82; Introduction to Numbers, p. 195; Introduction to Job, p. 751; Introduction to Ecclesiastes, p. 1032; Introduction to Hosea, p. 1413; Introduction to Habakkuk, p. 1498

Justice, Human
"Frederick Douglass," p. 734 (Neh. 13:14); "Biblical Attitudes Toward the Poor" (chart), p. 1015 (Prov. 22:22–23); "Isaiah, Which Will It Be?" p. 1074 (Isa. 1:17); "Mother Teresa," p. 1457 (Amos 5:24); "Dorothy Day," p. 1486 (Mic. 6:8); "The Role of the Law in Helping the Poor and Oppressed," p. 1607 (Matt. 22:37); "Justice" (chart), p. 1742 (John 2:12–24)

Kindness
Introduction to Ruth, p. 390; Introduction to 2 Samuel, p. 444; Introduction to Proverbs, p. 974; Introduction to Malachi, p. 1542; Introduction to Luke, p. 1668; "Civility," p. 2042 (1 Peter 2:17; 3:15)

Law, God's
"Outdated Laws?" p. 170 (Lev. 13:47–59); "Eight Terms for God's Law in Psalm 119" (chart), p. 941 (Ps. 119:1–8)

Laws
"Layers of Legislation" (chart), p. 116 (Ex. 21:1); "Outdated Laws?" p. 170 (Lev. 13:47–59); "Major Social Concerns in the Covenant" (chart), p. 298 (Deut. 26:16–19)

Leadership
Introduction to Numbers, p. 195; "Vision" (chart), p. 219 (Num. 13:17–20); Introduction to Judges, p. 353; Introduction to 1 Samuel, p. 398; Introduction to 2 Samuel, p. 444; "Abraham Lincoln," p. 484 (2 Sam. 24:1–4); Introduction to 1 Kings, p. 487; Introduction to 2 Chronicles, p. 639; "Building Churches," p. 699 (Ezra 4:4–5); "Righteous Kings," p. 1197 (Jer. 1:1–3); "The Dangers of Professional Religious Service" (chart), p. 1657 (Mark 12:38–42); Introduction to 1 Timothy, p. 1975; Introduction to Titus, p. 1993

Legalism
Introduction to Galatians, p. 1918; Introduction to Colossians, p. 1952; Introduction to 1 Timothy, p. 1975

Love, God's
Introduction to Deuteronomy, p. 258; Introduction to Job, p. 751; Introduction to Psalms, p. 808; "Visions of Truth," p. 1310 (Ezek. 1:1); Introduction to Hosea, p. 1413; Introduction to 1 John, p. 2054

Love, Human
Introduction to Song of Songs, p. 1054; "Billy Graham," p. 1886 (1 Cor. 9:19–23); "Love" (chart), p. 1893 (1 Cor. 13:13); Introduction to Ephesians, p. 1929; Introduction to 1 John, p. 2054; Introduction to 2 John, p. 2064

Loyalty, Human
Introduction to Ruth, p. 390; Introduction to 1 Samuel, p. 398; Introduction to 2 Samuel, p. 444; Introduction to 1 Kings, p. 487; Introduction to 1 Chronicles, p. 585; Introduction to Proverbs, p. 974; Introduction to 2 Timothy, p. 1985; Introduction to 1 Peter, p. 2037

Marriage

Introduction to Song of Songs, p. 1054; Introduction to Malachi, p. 1542

Mercy, God's

Introduction to Numbers, p. 195; Introduction to Hosea, p. 1413; Introduction to Jonah, p. 1468; "Twin Truths" (chart), p. 1739 (John 1:1–3)

Mercy, Human

Introduction to Exodus, p. 82; Introduction to Deuteronomy, p. 258; "Seven Works of Mercy" (chart), p. 1413 (Hos. 6:6); "Dorothy Day," p. 1486 (Mic. 6:8); "The Beatitudes" (chart), p. 1563 (Matt. 5:1–12); Introduction to Jude, p. 2070

Messiah

Introduction to Matthew, p. 1553; Introduction to Mark, p. 1624; Introduction to John, p. 1737

Miracles

Introduction to 1 Kings, p. 487; Introduction to 2 Kings, p. 538

Mission

"William Wilberforce," p. 13 (Gen. 6:8–9); "Henry Martyn," p. 30 (Gen. 18:18); "Rev. Martin Luther King, Jr." p. 89 (Ex. 4:10–11); "Amy Carmichael," p. 118 (Ex. 22:22–23); "Catherine Booth," p. 366 (Judg. 7:7–8); Introduction to 1 Chronicles, p. 585; "The Mission of Prayer," p. 972 (Ps. 149:4–5); Introduction to Isaiah, p. 1070; "Joining in God's Program," p. 1148 (Isa. 43:18–19); "Frances Elizabeth Caroline Willard," p. 1198 (Jer. 1:10); Introduction to Ezekiel, p. 1310; Introduction to Jonah, p. 1468; Introduction to Matthew, p. 1553; "Cross-cultural Mission," p. 1622 (Matt. 28:19–20); "Witnessing Through the Years" (chart), p. 1666 (Mark 16:15–14); "Jesus' Ministry" (chart), p. 1680 (Luke 4:18–19); "Spiritual Trips" (chart), p. 1693 (Luke 9:1–9); "Moses and the Prophets" (chart), p. 1715 (Luke 16:19–31); "Four Roots of Biblical Witness" (chart), p. 1783 (John 20:21); "Auca Five," p. 1803 (Acts 7:59—8:1); "A Model for Urban Ministry" (chart), p. 1812 (Acts 11:19–21); "God's Call to Mission" (chart), p. 1820 (Acts 15:1–2); "The Ends of the Earth" (chart), p. 1844 (Acts 28:30); "Witness" (chart), p. 1906 (2 Cor. 4:16–18); "Joining Forces," p. 1912 (2 Cor. 9:2); "Incarnational Identification," p. 1946 (Phil. 2:5–8); "Reconciliation," p. 1955 (Col. 1:19–20); "Transforming an Artless World," p. 1987 (2 Tim. 1:5)

Moses

Introduction to Exodus, p. 82

Obedience

"William Wilberforce," p. 13 (Gen. 6:8–9); Introduction to Exodus, p. 82; Introduction to Deuteronomy, p. 258; "Obedience" (chart), p. 266 (Deut. 4:1–2); "Be Strong and Courageous" (chart), p. 317 (Josh. 1:6–11); Introduction to 1 Samuel, p. 398; Introduction to 2 Kings, p. 537; Introduction to 2 Chronicles, p. 639; "Act With Courage" (chart), p. 663 (2 Chron. 19:11); Introduction to Esther, p. 736; "Obey God and Serve Him" (chart), p. 798 (Job 36:11); Introduction to Jeremiah, p. 1194; Introduction to Hosea, p. 1413; Introduction to Jonah, p. 1468; "Jonah on the Run" (map), p. 1470 (Jonah 1:3); Introduction to Haggai, p. 1516; "A Counterintuitive Calling," p. 1532 (Zech. 8:9–11); Introduction to Matthew, p. 1553; "Extravagant Devotion" (chart), p. 1689 (Luke 7:36–50)

Offerings, Old Testament

"Offerings" (chart), p. 153 (Lev. 1:1–2)

Parenting

Introduction to 1 Samuel, p. 398; "Learner Retention" (chart), p. 1029 (Prov. 31:1–9); "Visions of Truth," p. 1313 (Ezek. 1:1); Introduction to 2 Timothy, p. 1985

Passion Week

"Walking With Jesus Through the Holy (Passion) Week" (chart), p. 1603 (Matt. 21–28)

Patience, God's

Introduction to Nahum, p. 1491

Peace/Peacemakers

Introduction to 1 Samuel, p. 398; Introduction to Isaiah, p. 1070; "The Nobel Peace Prize" (chart), p. 1127 (Isa. 32:17–18); "Kalya = Peace," p. 1484 (Mic. 5:1–5a); "Albert John Mbumbi Luthuli," p. 1500 (Hab. 1:2–4); "The Beatitudes" (chart), p. 1563 (Matt. 5:1–12); Introduction to Acts, p. 1787; Introduction to James, p. 2027

Persecution/Opposition

Introduction to Deuteronomy, p. 258; "Building Churches," p. 699 (Ezra 4:4–5); Introduction to Nehemiah, p. 711; "Josefa Andrianaivoravelona," p. 825 (Ps. 17:7–9); "Origen," p. 1432 (Hos. 13:14); "Gregory the Illuminator," p. 1442 (Joel 2:28–29); Introduction to Amos, p. 1445; "The Beatitudes" (chart), p. 1563 (Matt. 5:1–12); "Persecution" (chart), p. 1579 (Matt. 10:14–42); Introduction to Acts, p. 1787; "Ki-Poong," p. 1819 (Acts 14:19–20); Introduction to Philippians, p. 1941; Introduction to 1 Thessalonians, p. 1961; Introduction to 2 Thessalonians, p. 1969; Introduction to 2 Timothy, p. 1985; "To the Church That Endures Persecution," p. 2079 (Rev. 2:8–10)

Perseverance

Introduction to 2 Timothy, p. 1985; Introduction to Hebrews, p. 2004; Introduction to Revelation, p. 2074; "To the Church That Endures Persecution," p. 2079 (Rev. 2:8–10)

Perspective

"Understanding Genesis" (chart), p. 65 (Gen. 40:20–22); "Vision" (chart), p. 219 (Num. 13:17–20); Introduction to Judges, p. 353; Introduction to 2 Kings, p. 537; Introduction to 1 Chronicles, p. 585; Introduction to Job, p. 751; "Do Not Fear: Johanna Veenstra," p. 860 (Ps. 44:22); "Right Use of God's Gifts," p. 1043 (Eccl. 5:18–19); "Fine Hammered Steel of Woe," p. 1052 (Eccl. 12:13–14); Introduction to Daniel, p. 1387; "Compassion," p. 1413 (Hos. 1:2–3); Introduction to Jonah, p. 1468; Introduction to Mark, p. 1624

Poor, Helping the

Introduction to Genesis, p. 1; "Deliverance From Bondage," p. 87 (Ex. 3:7–10); "Amy Carmichael," p. 118 (Ex. 22:22–23); "People in Need of Christian Care and Protection" (chart), p. 179 (Lev. 19:1); "New Beginnings in Francisco de Opalaca," p. 191 (Lev. 26:3–6); "Water for Ethiopia," p. 229 (Num. 19:7–8); Introduction to Deuteronomy, p. 258; "Lee," p. 295 (Deut. 24:17); "Catherine Booth," p. 366 (Judg. 7:7–8); Introduction to Ruth, p. 390; "Elijah and the Widow at Zarephath," p. 524 (1 Kings 17:7–15); Introduction to Job, p. 751; "A Stolen Car and a Changed Life," p. 784 (Job 24:1–11); Introduction to Psalms, p. 808; "Biblical Attitudes Toward the Poor" (chart), p. 1015 (Prov. 22:22–23); "Reflections of a Sponsored Child," p. 1040 (Eccl. 4:10–12); "Isaiah, Which Will It Be?" p. 1074 (Isa. 1:17); "As Poor as the Poor," p. 1171 (Isa. 55:1–3); "The 13 Shackles," p. 1182 (Isa. 61:1–3a); "Seven Works of Mercy" (chart), p. 1422 (Hos. 6:6); "Wang Chao and Lina," p. 1437 (Joel 1:11–12); "Serving the Poor," p. 1450 (Amos 2:6–7); "Dorothy Day," p. 1486 (Mic. 6:8); "Who

Are the Poor?" (chart), p. 1519 (Hag. 1:5–6); Introduction to Zechariah, p. 1522; "Kingdom Business," p. 1525 (Zech. 1:17); "Susan," p. 1548 (Mal. 4:2); Introduction to Matthew, p. 1553; "Emmanuel," p. 1557 (Matt. 1:22); "Jesus and Food" (chart), p. 1574 (Matt. 9:9–13); "Giovanna," p. 1576 (Matt. 9:35–36); "Housing," p. 1612 (Matt. 25:34–40); Introduction to Mark, p. 1624; Introduction to Luke, p. 1668; "Aung Lin," p. 1697 (Luke 9:58); "Sharing Lunch," p. 1752 (John 6:1–14); "Feed My Sheep" (chart), p. 1786 (John 21:15–23); "Tabitha," p. 1809 (Acts 9:36–42); "Holiness and the Poor," p. 1967 (1 Thess. 4:9–12); Introduction to 1 Timothy, p. 1975; "Loving Kakolo," p. 1981 (1 Tim. 4:12); "Widows and Service," p. 1982 (1 Tim. 5:3–16); "Transforming an Artless World," p. 1987 (2 Tim. 1:5); "Dorcas," p. 2013 (Heb. 6:10); Introduction to James, p. 2027; "Sharing God's Compassion," p. 2035 (James 5:2–6)

Potential for Service
"Rev. Martin Luther King, Jr." p. 89 (Ex. 4:10–11); Introduction to Judges, p. 353; "Catherine Booth," p. 366 (Judg. 7:7–8); "Corrie ten Boom," p. 558 (2 Kings 11:1–4); Introduction to Jeremiah, p. 1194; Introduction to Amos, p. 1445

Power, God's
Introduction to 1 Samuel, p. 398; "Transfer of Use," p. 906 (Ps. 86:5–6); "God Is in Control," p. 1411 (Dan. 12:9–10)

Power, Human
Introduction to 1 Chronicles, p. 585; "The Dangers of Professional Religious Service" (chart), p. 1657 (Mark 12:38–42)

Prayer
Introduction to Deuteronomy, p. 258; "Be Strong and Courageous" (chart), p. 317 (Josh. 1:6–11); "Catherine Booth," p. 366 (Judg. 7:7–8); Introduction to 1 Samuel, p. 398; "Abraham Lincoln," p. 484 (2 Sam. 24:1–4); "Types of Prayer" (chart), p. 504 (1 Kings 8:22–53); "Times of Prayer" (chart), p. 580 (1 Chron. 23:30); Introduction to 2 Chronicles, p. 639; Introduction to Ezra, p. 691; Introduction to Nehemiah, p. 711; Introduction to Psalms, p. 808; "Forgiving—and Forgiven," p. 830 (Ps. 19:12–14); "Transfer of Use," p. 906 (Ps. 86:5–6); "The Mission of Prayer," p. 972 (Ps. 149:4–5); Introduction to Daniel, p. 1387; "Regular Prayer," p. 1400 (Dan. 6:10–11); "Mother Teresa," p. 1457 (Amos 5:24); "Prayer in the Garden" (chart), p. 1661 (Mark 14:32–42); "Jesus' Prayers" (chart), p. 1776 (John 17:1–26); Introduction to Ephesians, p. 1929; Introduction to Colossians, p. 1952; Introduction to 1 Timothy, p. 1975; "Biblical Prayers of Blessing" (chart), p. 2026 (Heb. 13:20–21); Introduction to James, p. 2027; Introduction to Revelation, p. 2074

Pride
"Tower of Babel" (chart), p. 20 (Gen. 11:8–9); "Wisdom," p. 495 (1 Kings 3:16–28); Introduction to 2 Kings, p. 537; Introduction to 2 Chronicles, p. 639; Introduction to Daniel, p. 1387; Introduction to Obadiah, p. 1464; "The Dangers of Professional Religious Service" (chart), p. 1657 (Mark 12:38–42)

Priorities
Introduction to Numbers, p. 195; Introduction to Haggai, p. 1516; "What Are Your Priorities?" p. 1518 (Hag. 1:4); Introduction to Malachi, p. 1542

Prophets
Introduction to 2 Kings, p. 537; Introduction to 2 Chronicles, p. 639; "The Relevance of Old Testament Prophets" (chart), p. 1054 (before Isaiah introduction); "A Counterintuitive Calling," p. 1522 (Zech. 8:9–11)

Providence
Introduction to 1 Kings, p. 487; Introduction to 2 Chronicles, p. 639; Introduction to Esther, p. 736; Introduction to Job, p. 751; "God Is in Control," p. 1387 (Dan. 12:9–10)

Purpose
"Rev. Martin Luther King, Jr." p. 89 (Ex. 4:10–11); Introduction to 2 Kings, p. 537; Introduction to Esther, p. 736; "The Antidote for Meaninglessness," p. 817 (Ps. 8:3–9); Introduction to Isaiah, p. 1070; Introduction to Ezekiel, p. 1310; Introduction to Jonah, p. 1468; Introduction to Zechariah, p. 1522; Introduction to Matthew, p. 1553; Introduction to 2 Corinthians, p. 1900

Quality of Life
"Quality of Life" (chart), p. 1094 (Isa. 11:1–11)

Racism/Prejudice
"Henry Martyn," p. 30 (Gen. 18:18); "Rev. Martin Luther King, Jr." p. 89 (Ex. 4:10–11); Introduction to Numbers, p. 195; Introduction to Ruth, p. 390; "Frederick Douglass," p. 734 (Neh. 13:14); Introduction to Esther, p. 736; Introduction to Luke, p. 1668; "Love Your Neighbor," p. 1700 (Luke 10:25–37); "The Samaritan Woman," p. 1745 (John 4); Introduction to Romans, p. 1845; "Racial Reconciliation," p. 1855 (Rom. 5:10); Introduction to Titus, p. 1993

Reconciliation
"Rev. Martin Luther King, Jr." p. 89 (Ex. 4:10–11); "Ineffective Ways of Dealing With Conflict" (chart), p. 529 (1 Kings 20:1–12); Introduction to Acts, p. 1787; Introduction to Romans, p. 1845; "Racial Reconciliation," p. 1855 (Rom. 5:10); "A Recipe for Reconciliation" (chart), p. 1854 (Rom. 5:10–11); Introduction to 2 Corinthians, p. 1874; "Reconciliation," p. 1908 (2 Cor. 5:17–20); "Reconciliation," p. 1955 (Col. 1:19–20); "Reconciliation Among Christians," p. 2002 (Philem. 16)

Redemption
Introduction to Genesis, p. 1; "Shed Blood" (chart), p. 279 (Deut. 12:23); Introduction to Ruth, p. 390; "Daniel in Babylon" (map), p. 1387 (Dan. 1:6)

Regret
Introduction to Deuteronomy, p. 258

Relationship With God
Introduction to Exodus, p. 82; "Spiritual Formation" (chart), p. 405 (1 Sam. 3:19–20); Introduction to 1 Kings, p. 487; Introduction to 2 Kings, p. 537; Introduction to Psalms, p. 808; "Transfer of Use," p. 906 (Ps. 86:5–6); Introduction to Ecclesiastes, p. 1032; Introduction to Zephaniah, p. 1506

Repentance
Introduction to 2 Samuel, p. 444; Introduction to 1 Chronicles, p. 585; Introduction to 2 Chronicles, p. 639; Introduction to Jeremiah, p. 1194; Introduction to Lamentations, p. 1295; Introduction to Hosea, p. 1413; Introduction to Joel, p. 1434; Introduction to Jonah, p. 1468; Introduction to Luke, p. 1668

Respect
"Henry Martyn," p. 30 (Gen. 18:18); Introduction to Numbers, p. 195; Introduction to 1 Samuel, p. 398; "Mirza," p. 459 (2 Sam. 9:1–13); "Elijah and the Widow at Zarephath," p. 524 (1 Kings 17:7–15); "Shared Suffering," p. 762 (Job 7:25–30); "The Antidote for Meaninglessness," p. 817 (Ps. 8:3–9); "Biblical Humility" (chart), p. 1769 (John 13:1–17); Introduction to Acts, p. 1787; Introduction to Philemon, p. 1999; Introduction to Hebrews, p. 2004; "Civility," p. 2042 (1 Peter 2:17; 3:15)

Responsibility, Individual

"Be Fruitful and Increase," p. 6 (Gen. 1:28); Introduction to 1 Samuel, p. 398; "Judgment," p. 746 (Est. 7:3–4); Introduction to Ezekiel, p. 1310

Restoration

Introduction to Ezra, p. 691; Introduction to Nehemiah, p. 711; "World Renewal," p. 1191 (Isa. 65:17–25); Introduction to Jeremiah, p. 1194; Introduction to Ezekiel, p. 1310; "New Identities," p. 1368 (Ezek. 37:11–14); Introduction to Hosea, p. 1413; Introduction to Joel, p. 1434; Introduction to Obadiah, p. 1464 Introduction to Micah, p. 1475; Introduction to Zephaniah, p. 1506; "A Recipe for Reconciliation" (chart), p. 1854 (Rom. 5:10–11)

Resurrection

Introduction to 1 Corinthians, p. 1874

Revenge

Introduction to Genesis, p. 1; Introduction to 1 Samuel, p. 398; Introduction to Proverbs, p. 974; Introduction to Obadiah, p. 1464; Introduction to Matthew, p. 1553; Introduction to 1 Peter, p. 2037

Reverence for God

Introduction to Ecclesiastes, p. 1032; "To Fear God's Name Is Wisdom" (chart), p. 1475 (Mic. 6:9); Introduction to Habakkuk, p. 1498; Introduction to Malachi, p. 1542

Role Model

Introduction to 2 Chronicles, p. 639; "Who Is Our Neighbor?" p. 1699 (Luke 10:25–37); Introduction to 1 Timothy, p. 1975; Introduction to 2 Timothy, p. 1085; Introduction to Titus, p. 1993

Salvation

"New Identities," p. 1368 (Ezek. 37:11–14); Introduction to Mark, p. 1624; Introduction to Luke, p. 1668; Introduction to Galatians, p. 1918

Satan

Introduction to Job, p. 751

Self-denial/Self-sacrifice

Introduction to Leviticus, p. 151; Introduction to Esther, p. 736; "Do Not Fear: Johanna Veenstra," p. 860 (Ps. 44:22); "Paulina," p. 1252 (Jer. 30:17); Introduction to Joel, p. 1434; "Wang Chao and Lina," p. 1437 (Joel 1:11–12); "The Cambridge Seven," p. 1628 (Mark 1:18); "Maria," p. 2061 (1 Jn. 3:18)

Service

Introduction to Genesis, p. 1; "Amy Carmichael," p. 118 (Ex. 22:22–23); Introduction to Numbers, p. 195; "Water for Ethiopia," p. 229 (Num. 19:7–8); "Catherine Booth," p. 366 (Judg. 7:7–8); Introduction to 1 Samuel, p. 398; "Perine," p. 535 (1 Kings 22:17); Introduction to 2 Kings, p. 537; "Corrie ten Boom," p. 558 (2 Kings 11:1–4); Introduction to 2 Chronicles, p. 639; Introduction to Ezra, p. 691; Introduction to Nehemiah, p. 711; Introduction to Esther, p. 736; "Obey God and Serve Him" (chart), p. 798 (Job 36:11); "Of Works Done in Charity," p. 997 (Prov. 11:24–25); "Anna," p. 1013 (Prov. 22:6); Introduction to Isaiah, p. 1070; "Tension in Macedonia," p. 1097 (Isa. 13:14); "Salomey," p. 1166 (Isa. 52:7); "World Renewal," p. 1191 (Isa. 65:17–25); Introduction to Jeremiah, p. 1194; "Paulina," p. 1252 (Jer. 30:17); Introduction to Daniel, p. 1387; Introduction to Hosea, p. 1413; Introduction to Amos, p. 1445; "Serving the Poor," p. 1450 (Amos 2:6–7); "Mother Teresa," p. 1457 (Amos 5:24); Introduction to Jonah, p. 1468; Introduction to Micah, p. 1475; "Service and Humility," p. 1511 (Zeph. 2:2–3); Introduction to Haggai, p. 1516; Introduction to Zechariah, p. 1522; Introduction to Malachi, p.

1542; "Emmanuel," p. 1557 (Matt. 1:22); Introduction to Mark, p. 1624; "The Cambridge Seven," p. 1628 (Mark 1:18); "The Dangers of Professional Religious Service" (chart), p. 1657 (Mark 12:38–42); Introduction to Luke, p. 1668; "Small Measures" (chart), p. 1747 (John 4:1–26); Introduction to Acts, p. 1878; Introduction to Romans, p. 1845; "Service" (chart), p. 1867 (Rom. 12:1–2); Introduction to 1 Corinthians, p. 1874; "Billy Graham," p. 1886 (1 Cor. 9:19–23); "Passionate Service," p. 1891 (1 Cor. 12:4–7); Introduction to Ephesians, p. 1929; Introduction to Philippians, p. 1941; Introduction to 1 Timothy, p. 1975; "Widows and Service," p. 1982 (1 Tim. 5:3–16); "Dorcas," p. 2013 (Heb. 6:10); "A Love Affair for Jesus," p. 2031 (James 1:27); "Maria," p. 2061 (1 Jn. 3:18); "My Dear Teacher," p. 2106 (Rev. 21:4)

Sin

Introduction to Genesis, p. 1; "Nazirite Vow" (chart), p. 207 (Num. 6:1–8); "Blessings and Curses" (chart), p. 305 (Deut. 30:19–20); Introduction to 2 Samuel, p. 444; Introduction to 1 Chronicles, p. 585; Introduction to Ezekiel, p. 1310; Introduction to Zechariah, p. 1522; "Great Sins of Omission," p. 1716 (Luke 16:19–31); "Vice List" (chart), p. 2107 (Rev. 21:8)

Sovereignty, God's

Introduction to Ezra, p. 691; Introduction to Esther, p. 736; Introduction to Job, p. 751; Introduction to Isaiah, p. 1070; Introduction to Ezekiel, p. 1310; Introduction to Daniel, p. 1387; "God Is in Control," p. 1411 (Dan. 12:9–10); Introduction to Jonah, p. 1468; Introduction to Revelation, p. 2074

Spiritual Growth

"Spiritual Formation" (chart), p. 405 (1 Sam. 3:19–20); "Groups" (chart), p. 1014 (Prov. 22:17); "Self Examination" (chart), p. 1917 (2 Cor. 13:5); "20 Questions" (chart), p. 2056 (1 Jn. 1:6–10)

Spiritual Warfare

Introduction to Joshua, p. 315; "Be Strong and Courageous" (chart), p. 317 (Josh. 1:6–11); Introduction to Job, p. 751; "Do Not Love the World," p. 2059 (1 Jn. 2:15); "Spiritual Warfare" (chart), p. 2093 (Rev. 12:7–9)

Stewardship

Introduction to Genesis, p. 1; "Stewardship," p. 637 (1 Chron. 29:10–20); "Right Use of God's Gifts," p. 1043 (Eccl. 5:18–19); "Kingdom Business," p. 1525 (Zech. 1:17); "The Creation Groans" (chart), p. 1860 (Rom. 8:18–27)

Stress

"Stress" (chart), p. 481 (2 Sam. 23:3–4)

Suffering

"Be Strong and Courageous" (chart), p. 317 (Josh. 1:6–11); Introduction to Job, p. 751; "Shared Suffering," p. 762 (Job 7:25–30); "God's Rescue Plan," p. 820 (Ps. 10:17–18); Introduction to Isaiah, p. 1070; Introduction to Mark, p. 1624; Introduction to 1 Thessalonians, p. 1961; Introduction to 1 Peter, p. 2037

Supremacy of Christ

Introduction to Colossians, p. 1952; Introduction to Hebrews, p. 2004

Symbolism

"Symbols of Christianity" (chart), p. 16 (Gen. 9:13–16); "Symbols and Ceremonies," p. 140 (Ex. 35:1); "Symbolic Actions" (chart), p. 2044 (1 Peter 3:21); "The Messianic Banquet" (chart), p. 2105 (Rev. 21:1–4)

Tabernacle/Temple

Introduction to Exodus, p. 82; Introduction to 1 Chronicles, p. 585

Thankfulness

"Showing Gratitude" (chart), p. 371 (Judg. 8:35); "Varsenik," p. 1075 (Isa. 1:17); "Martha," p. 1363 (Ezek. 34:26–27); Introduction to Philippians, p. 1941; "An Attitude of Gratitude" (chart), p. 1968 (1 Thess. 5:18)

Trust

Introduction to Numbers, p. 195; Introduction to Judges, p. 353; Introduction to Ruth, p. 390; Introduction to 2 Chronicles, p. 639; Introduction to Isaiah, p. 1070; Introduction to Nahum, p. 1491; Introduction to Habakkuk, p. 1498

Truth

"Catherine Booth," p. 366 (Judg. 7:7–8); "Modern Attempts to Prove God's Existence" (chart), p. 759 (Job 5:8); "Modern Arguments Against God's Existence" (chart), p. 781 (Job 22:12–14); "Visions of Truth," p. 1313 (Ezek. 1:1); "Twin Truths" (chart), p. 1739 (John 1:1–3); Introduction to 2 John, p. 2064; Introduction to 3 John, p. 2067; Introduction to Jude, p. 2070

Unity

"Relationships" (chart), p. 462 (2 Sam. 12:11–12,14); Introduction to 1 Corinthians, p. 1874; Introduction to Ephesians, p. 1929; "Unity in the Body of Christ" (chart), p. 1935 (Eph. 4:3–6); Introduction to Titus, p. 1993; "Reconciliation Among Christians," p. 2002 (Philem. 16)

Using Your Gifts

Introduction to Exodus, p. 82; Introduction to Judges, p. 353; "Obey God and Serve Him" (chart), p. 798 (Job 36:11); "Right Use of God's Gifts," p. 1043 (Eccl. 5:18–19); Introduction to Jeremiah, p. 1194; Introduction to Daniel, p. 1387; Introduction to Haggai, p. 1516; Introduction to Matthew, p. 1553; Introduction to Acts, p. 1787; Introduction to Romans, p. 1845; "Passionate Service," p. 1891 (1 Cor. 12:4–7); Introduction to 1 Timothy, p. 1975

Vows

"Nazirite Vow" (chart), p. 207 (Num. 6:1–8)

War

"Wars" (chart), p. 328 (Josh. 9:1–2); "The Geneva Conventions" (chart), p. 1073 (Isa. 1:16–17); "Tension in Macedonia," p. 1097 (Isa. 13:14); "Number of Wars in the World by Year" (chart), p. 1214 (Jer. 8:11); "Hamedi," p. 1238 (Jer. 22:2–3); "Another Dangerous Day," p. 1305 (Lam. 3:31–36); "Emmanuel," p. 1557 (Matt. 1:22)

Warrior, God as

Introduction to Joshua, p. 315; Introduction to Nahum, p. 1491; Introduction to Zechariah, p. 1522

Water

"Abram's Journeys" (map), p. 22 (Gen. 12:4); "Great Rivers of the Bible" (chart), p. 26 (Gen. 15:18); "Water for Joateca," p. 43 (Gen. 26:19–22); "Joseph Sold Into Egypt" (map), p. 61 (Gen. 37:28); "Water for Ethiopia," p. 229 (Num. 19:7–8); "A Life Source," p. 339 (Josh. 15:16–19); "Costs of Clean Water" (chart), p. 726 (Neh. 9:15); "Water" (chart), p. 1540 (Zech. 14:8); "Jesus and Water" (chart), p. 1588 (Matt. 14:25–31)

Wealth

"Census Time" (chart), p. 202 (Num. 4:1–3); "Blessings and Curses" (chart), p. 305 (Deut. 30:19–20); "Stewardship," p. 637 (1 Chron. 29:10–20); Introduction to Proverbs, p. 974; "Uneven Distribution of Wealth in the United States" (chart), p. 1237 (Jer. 22:1–5); Introduction to Hosea, p. 1413; Introduction to Amos, p. 1445; Introduction to Luke, p. 1668

Wisdom/Discernment

"Discerning God's Will" (chart), p. 392 (Ruth 1:22); "Abraham Lincoln," p. 484 (2 Sam. 24:1–4); Introduction to 1 Kings, p. 487; "Wisdom," p. 495 (1 Kings 3:16–28); Introduction to 2 Chronicles, p. 639; Introduction to Ezra, p. 691; Introduction to Proverbs, p. 974; "The Wise Man According to Proverbs: An Outline" (chart), p. 977 (Prov. 1:1–7); "Wisdom," p. 978 (Prov. 1:1–7); Introduction to Ecclesiastes, p. 1032; "Famous Theological Wisdom Bytes" (chart), p. 1045 (Eccl. 7:24); "Intelligence" (chart), p. 1048 (Eccl. 9:11); "To Fear God's Name Is Wisdom" (chart), p. 1487 (Mic. 6:9); "Twin Truths" (chart), p. 1739 (John 1:1–3); "Wisdom" (chart), p. 1878 (1 Cor. 1:30); Introduction to James, p. 2027; Introduction to 2 Peter, p. 2048

Women

"Amy Carmichael," p. 118 (Ex. 22:22–23); "Women in the Military" (chart), p. 360 (Judg. 4:4–5); "Catherine Booth," p. 366 (Judg. 7:7–8); "Corrie ten Boom," p. 558 (2 Kings 11:1–4); "Do Not Fear: Johanna Veenstra," p. 860 (Ps. 44:22); "K'ang Ch'eng, Gertrude Howe, and Shih Mei-yü," p. 1031 (Prov. 31:29–30); "Varsenik," p. 1075 (Isa. 1:17); "Salomey," p. 1166 (Isa. 52:7); "Frances Elizabeth Caroline Willard," p. 1198 (Jer. 1:10); "Mother Teresa," p. 1457 (Amos 5:24); "Dorothy Day," p. 1486 (Mic. 6:8); "Widows and Service," p. 1982 (1 Tim. 5:3–16)

Words

"The Wise Man According to Proverbs: An Outline" (chart), p. 977 (Prov. 1:1–7)

Worship

"Genet," p. 107 (Ex. 15:2); Introduction to Leviticus, p. 151; "Outdated Laws?" p. 170 (Lev. 13:47–59); Introduction to 2 Samuel, p. 444; Introduction to 1 Kings, p. 487; Introduction to 1 Chronicles, p. 585; Introduction to 2 Chronicles, p. 639; Introduction to Nehemiah, p. 711; "Transfer of Use," p. 906 (Ps. 86:5–6); "Isaiah, Which Will It Be?" p. 1074 (Isa. 1:17); Introduction to Zephaniah, p. 1506; Introduction to Matthew, p. 1553; Introduction to 1 Corinthians, p. 1874

Index to Charts

Genesis 1:26 *Imago Dei* 4

Genesis 2:1–2 **Days of Creation** 7

Genesis 6:7 **Natural Disasters** 12

Genesis 9:13–16 **Symbols of Christianity** 16

Genesis 11:8–9 **Tower of Babel** 20

Genesis 15:18 **Great Rivers of the Bible** 26

Genesis 17:7 **Chronology of Bible Events** 28

Genesis 40:20–22 **Understanding Genesis** 65

Exodus 7:1–5 **The Plagues** 94

Exodus 13:18 **Refugees Then and Now** 105

Exodus 16:2–3 **Hunger in the Bible** 109

Exodus 21:1 **Layers of Legislation** 116

Exodus 35:5 **Gifts to God** 139

Leviticus 1:1–2 **Offerings** 153

Leviticus 16:8,10,13,15 **Love Your Neighbor** 176

Leviticus 19:1 **People in Need of Christian Care and Protection** 179

Leviticus 23:1 **Ancient Israelite and Contemporary Christian Feasts** 185

Numbers 4:1–3 **Census Time** 202

Numbers 6:1–8 **Nazirite Vow** 207

Numbers 13:17–20 **Vision** 219

Numbers 21:4–9 **The Bronze Snake** 231

Deuteronomy 4:1–2 **Obedience** 266

Deuteronomy 12:23 **Shed Blood** 279

Deuteronomy 16:18–20 **Nations** 284

Deuteronomy 26:16–19 **Major Social Concerns in the Covenant** 298

Deuteronomy 30:19–20 **Blessings and Curses** 305

Deuteronomy 34:5 **The Top 24 Causes of Christian Deaths** 314

Joshua 1:6–11 **Be Strong and Courageous** 317

Joshua 9:1–2 **Wars** 328

Judges 4:4–5 **Women in the Military** 360

Judges 6:14 **Gideons Bibles** 364

Judges 8:33–35 **Apostasy** 370

Judges 8:35 **Showing Gratitude** 371

Judges 9:56–57 **God's Anger** 372

Judges 21:25 **Freedom** 388

Ruth 1:22 **Discerning God's Will** 392

Ruth 2:8 **Hunger** 393

Ruth 3:17–18 **Malnutrition** 395

1 Samuel 2:18 **Child Labor** 402

1 Samuel 2:26 **Educational Opportunity** 403

1 Samuel 3:19–20 **Spiritual Formation** 405

1 Samuel 10:25 **Six Firsts of the Jewish People** 413

2 Samuel 12:11–12,14 **Relationships** 462

2 Samuel 23:3–4 **Stress** 481

2 Samuel 24:10 **Bad Counting, Good Counting** 485

1 Kings 8:22–53 **Types of Prayer** 504

1 Kings 8:27 **Three Heavens** 505

1 Kings 15:20 **Chronology of Foreign Kings** 519

1 Kings 20:1–12 **Ineffective Ways of Dealing With Conflict** 529

2 Kings 2:23 **Television Violence** 541

2 Kings 23:30 **Times of Prayer** 580

2 Chronicles 19:11 **Act With Courage** 663

2 Chronicles 26:21 **HIV/AIDS** 673

2 Chronicles 35:2 **Encourage Others in the Lord's Service** 686

Nehemiah 8:1–3 **Four Questions to Ask of a Biblical Text** 724

Nehemiah 9:15 **Costs of Clean Water** 726

Nehemiah 9:26–31 **Signs of a Stagnant Congregation** 727

Job 1:5 **United States Children at Risk** 754

Job 3:1–16 **Godly Emotions?** 757

Job 5:8 **Modern Attempts to Prove God's Existence** 759

Job 22:12–14 **Modern Arguments Against God's Existence** 781

Job 36:11 **Obey God and Serve Him** 789

Psalm 18:29 **Profile of World Christianity** 827

Psalm 49:1–2 **Biblical Instruction to the Rich** 865

Psalm 119:1–8 **Eight Terms for God's Law in Psalm 119** 941

Psalm 139:13–14 **Fearfully and Wonderfully Made** 961

Proverbs 1:1–7 **The Wise Man According to Proverbs: An Outline** 977

Proverbs 8:32 **Sobering Stats on Children** 990

Proverbs 17:6 **Gifted Children of the Bible** 1005

Proverbs 22:17 **Groups** 1014

Proverbs 22:22–23 **Biblical Attitudes Toward the Poor** 1015

Proverbs 31:1–9 **Learner Retention** 1029

Ecclesiastes 3:11 **Beauty** 1038

Ecclesiastes 7:24 **Famous Theological Wisdom Bytes** 1045

Ecclesiastes 9:11 **Intelligence** 1048

Song of Songs 2:3–13 **Six Biblical Sources for Application** 1059

Before Isaiah Introduction **The Relevance of Old Testament Prophets** 1069

Isaiah 1:16–17 **The Geneva Conventions** 1073

Isaiah 7:18 **Malaria** 1085

Isaiah 11:1–3 **Education** 1093

Isaiah 11:1–11 **Quality of Life** 1094

Isaiah 13:18 *Look With Compassion on Children* 1098

Isaiah 32:17–18 **The Nobel Peace Prize** 1127

Isaiah 40:8 **English Bible Major Translation Timeline** 1139

Isaiah 58:6–7 **Easing the Hunger Equation** 1176

Isaiah 58:6–10 **Why Should We Be Compassionate?** 1177

Jeremiah 8:11 **Number of Wars in the World by Year** 1214

Jeremiah 22:1–5 **Uneven Distribution of Wealth in the United States** 1237

Lamentations 2:19 **Child Starvation** 1302

Ezekiel 1:1 **Dates in Ezekiel** 1312

Ezekiel 18:12–13 **The Poor and the Lost** 1334

Daniel 6:10–11 **Regular Prayer** 1400

Hosea 6:6 **Seven Works of Mercy** 1422

Hosea 10:4 **Chemicals by Health Effects** 1427

Joel 1:2–3 **Biblical Attitudes Toward Children** 1436

Amos 4:1 **The Faces of Malnutrition** 1452

Micah 6:9 **To Fear God's Name Is Wisdom** 1487

Habakkuk 1:5 **Belief and Identity** 1501

Zephaniah 3:20 **Population** 1514

Haggai 1:5–6 **Who Are the Poor?** 1519

Haggai 1:6,10–11 **World Land Use** 1520

Zechariah 14:8 **Water** 1540

Between Testaments **From Malachi to Christ** 1549

Matthew 2:16 **The Slaughter of Innocents** 1559

Matthew 5:1–12 **The Beatitudes** 1563

Matthew 9:9–13 **Jesus and Food** 1574

Matthew 10:14–42 **Persecution** 1579

Matthew 14:25–31 **Jesus and Water** 1588

Matthew 18:19–20 **Jesus' Messages in Matthew's Gospel** 1595

Matthew 21–28 **Walking With Jesus Through the Holy (Passion) Week** 1603

Mark 1:1–11 **Great Encouragers in the Bible** 1626

Mark 2:16 **Jewish Sects** 1632

Mark 4:1–9 **Good Land** 1635

Mark 12:38–42 **The Dangers of Professional Religious Service** 1657

Mark 14:32–42   **Prayer in the Garden**   1661

Mark 16:15–16   **Witnessing Through the Years**   1666

Luke 4:18–19   **Jesus' Ministry**   1680

Luke 7:36–50   **Extravagant Devotion**   1689

Luke 9:1–9   **Spiritual Trips**   1693

Luke 11:33–36   **Light to the World**   1703

Luke 16:19–31   **Moses and the Prophets**   1715

Luke 24:13–35   **Walk to Emmaus**   1735

John 1:1–3   **Twin Truths**   1739

John 2:12–24   **Justice**   1742

John 4:1–26   **Small Measures**   1745

John 8:1–11   **Forgiveness**   1757

John 13:1–17   **Biblical Humility**   1769

John 17:1–26   **Jesus' Prayers**   1776

John 20:21   **Four Roots of Biblical Witness**   1783

John 21:15–23   **Feed My Sheep**   1786

Acts 1:1–11   **The Divine Drama**   1790

Acts 2:41   **Growth of the Church**   1793

Acts 2:42–47   **Nine Characteristics of a Healthy Church**   1794

Acts 4:32–35   **Six Ways of Witnessing**   1797

Acts 11:19–21   **A Model of Urban Ministry**   1812

Acts 15:1–2   **God's Call to Missions**   1820

Acts 28:30   **The Ends of the Earth**   1844

Romans 1:17   **Theological Terms in Romans**   1848

Romans 5:10–11   **A Recipe for Reconciliation**   1854

Romans 8:18–27   **The Creation Groans**   1860

Romans 12:1–2   **Service**   1867

1 Corinthians 1:30   **Wisdom**   1878

1 Corinthians 13:13   **Love**   1893

2 Corinthians 4:16–18   **Witness**   1906

2 Corinthians 9:12   **Generosity**   1913

2 Corinthians 13:5   **Self Examination**   1917

Galatians 3:23–25   **Christian Human Rights**   1924

Galatians 6:10   **Do Good to All People**   1928

Ephesians 1:3–14   **The Image of God**   1932

Ephesians 4:3–6   **Unity in the Body of Christ**   1935

Ephesians 5:15–17   **Be Very Careful How You Live**   1938

Philippians 2:3   **Models of Biblical Humility**   1944

Philippians 2:4   **How to Develop Humility**   1945

Philippians 2:14–16   **The Roads to Contentment**   1947

Philippians 2:17–18   **How Giving Helps the Giver**   1948

Philippians 4:8   **Television Time**   1950

Colossians 3:10   **Our Story From Colossians 3**   1958

Colossians 3:16   **Bible Study**   1959

1 Thessalonians 5:18   **An Attitude of Gratitude**   1968

1 Timothy 2:5–6   **Six Questions of Bible Study**   1979

2 Timothy 2:15   **Bible Study Programs**   1990

Hebrews 2:15   **From Fear to Courage**   2008

Hebrews 11:32–34   **Faith Is Demonstrated by Activity**   2023

Hebrews 13:20–21   **Biblical Prayers of Blessing**   2026

James 1:22–25   **Theories of How to Apply the Bible to Everyday Life**   2030

James 2:14–17   **Faith and Good Works**   2032

James 2:20–24   **The Relationship Between Faith and Action**   2033

1 Peter 3:21   **Symbolic Actions**   2044

1 Peter 5:8–9   **The Three Worlds**   2046

2 Peter 2:1–3   **False Teachers and Their Teachings**   2051

1 John 1:6–10   **20 Questions**   2056

Revelation 2:1—3:22   **Understanding the Letters to the Churches**   2078

Revelation 6:1–8   **Judgment and the Four Horsemen**   2085

Revelation 11:18   **Signs of Discontent**   2090

Revelation 12:7–9   **Spiritual Warfare**   2093

Revelation 21:1–4   **The Messianic Banquet**   2105

Revelation 21:8   **Vice List**   2107

Index to Articles

Genesis 1:28   **Be Fruitful and Increase**   6

Genesis 6:8–9   **William Wilberforce**   13

Exodus 3:7–10   **Deliverance From Bondage**   87

Exodus 4:10–11   **Rev. Martin Luther King, Jr.**   89

Exodus 22:22–23   **Amy Carmichael**   118

Exodus 35:1   **Symbols and Ceremonies**   140

Leviticus 13:47–59   **Outdated Laws?**   170

Joshua 1:6–7   **Courage**   318

Judges 7:7–8   **Catherine Booth**   366

2 Samuel 24:1–4   **Abraham Lincoln**   484

1 Kings 3:16–28   **Wisdom**   495

1 Kings 17:7–15   **Elijah and the Widow at Zarephath**   524

2 Kings 11:1–4   **Corrie ten Boom**   558

1 Chronicles 29:10–20   **Stewardship**   637

Ezra 4:4–5   **Building Churches**   699

Nehemiah 13:14   **Frederick Douglass**   734

Esther 4:12–14   **Can We Learn Lessons From Esther?**   743

Esther 7:3–4   **Judgment**   746

Job 7:25–30   **Shared Suffering**   762

Psalm 8:3–9   **The Antidote for Meaninglessness**   817

Psalm 10:17–18   **God's Rescue Plan**   820

Psalm 19:12–14   **Forgiving—and Forgiven**   830

Psalm 31:14–16   **The Eternal Now and the Temporal Now**   844

Psalm 86:5–6   **Transfer of Use**   906

Psalm 144:12   **Blessing the Children**   966

Psalm 149:4–5   **The Mission of Prayer**   972

Proverbs 1:1–7   **Wisdom**   978

Proverbs 11:24–25   **Of Works Done in Charity**   997

Ecclesiastes 5:18–19   **Right Use of God's Gifts**   1043

Ecclesiastes 12:13–14   **Fine Hammered Steel of Woe**   1052

Isaiah 1:17   **Isaiah, Which Will It Be?**   1074

Isaiah 55:1–3   **As Poor as the Poor**   1171

Isaiah 61:1–3a   **The 13 Shackles**   1182

Isaiah 65:17–25   **World Renewal**   1191

Jeremiah 1:1–3   **Righteous Kings**   1197

Jeremiah 1:10   **Frances Elizabeth Caroline Willard**   1198

Ezekiel 1:1   **Visions of Truth**   1313

Ezekiel 37:11–14   **New Identities**   1368

Daniel 1:3–4,17   **Literacy: An Open Door**   1390

Daniel 12:9–10   **God Is in Control**   1411

Hosea 1:2–3   **Compassion**   1416

Amos 2:6–7   **Serving the Poor**   1450

Amos 5:24   **Mother Teresa**   1457

Jonah 4:10–11   **The Enduring Message of Jonah**   1473

Micah 6:8   **Dorothy Day**   1486

Zephaniah 2:2–3   **Service and Humility**   1511

Haggai 1:4   **What Are Your Priorities?**   1518

Zechariah 1:17   **Kingdom Business**   1525

Zechariah 8:9–11   **A Counterintuitive Calling**   1532

Matthew 9:35–36   **Cry, the Beloved Continent: Don't Let AIDS Steal African Children's Future**   1577

Matthew 22:37   **The Role of the Law in Helping the Poor and Oppressed**   1607

Matthew 25:34–40   **Housing**   1612

Matthew 28:19–20   **Cross-cultural Mission**   1622

Mark 1:40–42   **Compassion**   1630

Mark 7   **Purity**   1643

Luke 2:7 **Is There Room in Your Inn?** 1675

Luke 10:25–37 **Who Is Our Neighbor?** 1699

Luke 10:25–37 **Love Your Neighbor** 1700

Luke 14:12–14 **Hospitality** 1711

Luke 16:19–31 **Great Sins of Omission** 1716

John 4 **The Samaritan Woman** 1747

John 6:1–14 **Sharing Lunch** 1752

Acts 8:1 **Witness** 1804

Acts 9:36–42 **Tabitha** 1809

Acts 11:22 **Barnabas** 1813

Romans 5:10 **Racial Reconciliation** 1855

1 Corinthians 9:19–23 **Billy Graham** 1886

1 Corinthians 12:4–7 **Passionate Service** 1891

2 Corinthians 5:17–20 **Reconciliation** 1908

Philippians 2:5–8 **Incarnational Identification** 1946

1 Thessalonians 4:9–12 **Holiness and the Poor** 1967

1 Timothy 5:3–16 **Widows and Service** 1982

Philemon 16 **Reconciliation Among Christians** 2002

Hebrews 4:12 **Using the Bible in Life** 2011

Hebrews 11:6 **Demonstrations of Devotion** 2021

James 5:2–6 **Sharing God's Compassion** 2035

1 Peter 2:17; 3:15 **Civility** 2042

1 John 2:15 **Do Not Love the World** 2059

Revelation 2:8–10 **To the Church That Endures Persecution** 2079

Revelation 13:13–15 **The Image of God in Human Beings** 2094

Index to Snapshots

Genesis 18:18 **Henry Martyn** 30

Genesis 26:19–22 **Water for Joateca** 43

Genesis 50:18–21 **Geoffrey** 81

Exodus 15:2 **Genet** 107

Exodus 18:20 **Salih Abdul Masih** 113

Leviticus 26:3–6 **New Beginnings in Francisco de Opalaca** 191

Numbers 19:7–8 **Water for Ethiopia** 229

Deuteronomy 4:9 **Grace** 267

Deuteronomy 24:17 **Lee** 295

Joshua 15:16–19 **A Life Source** 339

Judges 5:24–25 **Milk Money** 363

Ruth 4:14–16 **Vali** 397

2 Samuel 7:10 **Bamboo Shoots Street Children's Center** 456

2 Samuel 9:1–13 **Mirza** 459

1 Kings 22:17 **Perine** 535

2 Chronicles 34:3 **Aleksandr Men** 684

Ezra 8:2–3 **The Girl Preacher** 705

Nehemiah 2:10 **Friend of Family** 714

Job 24:1–11 **A Stolen Car and a Changed Life** 784

Job 29:12–13 **A Place for Children** 789

Psalm 17:7–9 **Josefa Andrianaivoravelona** 825

Psalm 23:4–6 **Agness: A Positive Outlook** 834

Psalm 30:4–7 **Temka School** 841

Psalm 44:22 **Do Not Fear: Johanna Veenstra** 860

Psalm 68:5–6a **Jacquiline** 883

Psalm 138:6–7 **A Long Trek to Nowhere?** 960

Proverbs 6:23 **Betsey Stockton** 987

Proverbs 10:1 **Isaac** 992

Proverbs 22:6 **Anna** 1013

Proverbs 27:26–27 **A Struggle and a Dream** 1024

Proverbs 31:29–30 **K'ang Ch'eng, Gertrude Howe, and Shih Mei-yü** 1031

Ecclesiastes 4:10–12 **Reflections of a Sponsored Child** 1040

Ecclesiastes 11:1–6 **Unexpected Disaster** 1050

Isaiah 1:17 **Varsenik** 1075

Isaiah 13:14 **Tension in Macedonia** 1097

Isaiah 43:18–19 **Joining in God's Program** 1148

Isaiah 52:7 **Salomey** 1166

Isaiah 61:1–3 **Bob Pierce** 1183

Jeremiah 22:2–3 **Hamedi** 1238

Jeremiah 30:17 **Paulina** 1252

Lamentations 3:31–36 **Another Dangerous Day** 1305

Ezekiel 34:26–27 **Martha** 1363

Ezekiel 36:23 **David Z. T. Yui** 1366

Hosea 13:14 **Origen** 1432

Joel 1:11–12 **Wang Chao and Lina** 1437

Joel 2:28–29 **Gregory the Illuminator** 1442

Micah 5:1–5a **Kalya = Peace** 1484

Nahum 1:7 **William and Clementina (Rowe) Butler** 1493

Habakkuk 1:2–4 **Albert John Mbumbi Luthuli** 1500

Zechariah 8:23 **Jesus Speaks My Language!** 1533

Malachi 4:2 **Susan** 1548

Matthew 1:22 **Emmanuel** 1557

Matthew 9:35–36 **Giovanna** 1576

Mark 1:18 **The Cambridge Seven** 1628

Luke 9:58 **Aung Lin** 1697

Luke 19:11–27 **Fanny Jackson Coppin** 1722

John 14:2–3 **A Special Baptism** 1771

Acts 7:59—8:1 **Auca Five** 1803

Acts 14:19–20 **Ki-Poong** 1819

1 Corinthians 15:58 **Apostle of the Indies** 1897

2 Corinthians 9:2 **Joining Forces** 1912

Ephesians 1:4–5 **Sebastian** 1931

Colossians 1:19–20 **Reconciliation** 1955

2 Thessalonians 2:16–17 **Mary Jane** 1973

1 Timothy 4:12 **Loving Kakolo** 1981

2 Timothy 1:5 **Transforming an Artless World** 1987

Titus 3:14 **Mirriam** 1998

Hebrews 6:10 **Dorcas** 2013

James 1:27 **A Love Affair for Jesus** 2031

1 John 3:18 **María** 2061

Revelation 21:4 **My Dear Teacher** 2106

Bibliography

Achtemeier, Paul J. *Harper's Bible Dictionary.* San Francisco: Harper & Row, 1985.

American Academy of Pediatrics. *AAP Policy Statement* (June 1995): 6.

American Association for the Advancement of Science. *AAAS Atlas of Population and Environment.* Berkley, Calif.: Univ. of California Press, 2002.

American Institute of Stress. *www.stress.org/job.* Accessed September 5, 2004.

Anderson, Gerald H., ed. *Biographical Dictionary of Christian Missions.* New York: Simon & Schuster Macmillan, 1998.

Banks, Robert. *Paul's Idea of Community: The Early House Churches in Their Cultural Setting.* Peabody, Mass.: Hendrickson, 1994.

Barash, David P. *Introduction to Peace Studies.* Belmont, Calif.: Wadsworth, 1991.

Barrett, David B., and Todd M. Johnson. *World Christian Trends AD 30–AD 2200: Interpreting the Annual Christian Megacensus.* Pasadena Calif.: William Carey Library, 2001.

Barrett, David B., George T. Kurian, and Todd M. Johnson. *World Christian Encyclopedia: A Comparative Survey of Churches and Religions in the Modern World,* 2nd ed. 2 vols. New York: Oxford, 2001.

Bellamy, Carol. *State of the World's Children 2001.* New York: UNICEF, 2001.

Brown, Lester R. *State of the World: A Worldwatch Institute Report on Progress Toward a Sustainable Society.* New York: W. W. Norton, 1994.

Calvin, John. *Golden Booklet of the True Christian Life.* Translated by Henry J. Van Andel. Grand Rapids, Mich.: Baker, 1952.

Carter, Jimmy. *Living Faith.* New York: Random House, 1996, 187–190.

Cozens, M. L. *A Handbook of Heresies.* New York: Sheed & Ward, 1959.

Doriani, Daniel M. *Putting the Truth to Work: The Theory and Practice of Biblical Application.* Phillipsburg, N.J.: P & R, 2001.

Eerdmans' Concise Bible Encyclopedia. Edited by Pat Alexander. Grand Rapids, Mich.: Eerdmans, 1980.

Eerdmans' Concise Bible Handbook. Edited by David Alexander and Pat Alexander. Grand Rapids, Mich.: Eerdmans, 1973.

Expositor's Bible Commentary, Psalms. Edited by Frank E. Gaebelein. Grand Rapids, Mich.: Zondervan, 1990.

Fendel, Lon. *William Wilberforce: Abolitionist, Politician, Writer.* Uhrichsville, Ohio: Barbour, 2002.

Food and Agriculture Organization of the United Nations. *www.fao.org.* Accessed September 5, 2004.

Foster, Richard J. *Celebration of Discipline.* San Francisco: Harper & Row, 1978.

Gabel, Medard, and Henry Bruner. *Global Inc.: An Atlas of the Multinational Corporation.* New York: New Press, 2002.

Galindo, Israel. *A Christian Educator's Book of Lists.* Macon, Georgia: Smyth & Helways, 2002.

Gallagher, Robert L., and Paul Hertig, eds. *Mission in Acts: Ancient Narratives in Contemporary Context.* Maryknoll, N.Y.: Orbis, 2004.

Gardner, Howard. *Frames of Mind: The Theory of Multiple Intelligences.* New York: Basic Books, 1985.

Gideons International. "About Us." *The Gideons International. www.gideons.org.*

Gleick, Peter H. *The World's Water 2002–2003: The Biennial Report on Freshwater Resources.* Washington D.C.: Island Press, 2002.

Global Environment Outlook 3. See United Nations Environment Programme.

Graham, Billy. *A Biblical Standard for Evangelists.* Minneapolis, Minn.: World Wide, 1984.

Henry, Carl F. H. *The Uneasy Conscience of Modern Fundamentalism.* Grand Rapids, Mich.: Eerdmans, 1947, 85–86.

Hosier, Helen K. *William and Catherine Booth: Founders of the Salvation Army.* Uhrichsville, Ohio: Barbour, 1982.

Hybels, Bill. *Honest to God?* Grand Rapids, Mich.: Zondervan, 1990, 112–113.

Izard, Carroll. *The Psychology of Emotions.* New York: Plenum, 1991.

Jenkins, Simon. *Bible Mapbook.* Belleville, Mich.: Lion, 1986.

Johnson, Paul. *A History of the Jews.* New York: Harper & Row, 1987.

Kelly, Thomas R. *A Testament of Devotion.* New York: Harper & Row, 1941.

Kroll, Woodrow. *7 Secrets to Spiritual Success.* Sisters, Ore.: Multnomah, 2000.

"The Longest Journey," *The Economist* (November 2, 2002): 4.

Lewis, C. S. *Letters to Malcolm: Chiefly on Prayer.* New York: Harcourt, Brace & World, 1963.

Lucado, Max. *The Gift for All People: Thoughts on God's Great Grace.* Sisters, Ore.: Multnomah, 1999, 121–123.

McGrath, Alister, ed. *NIV Thematic Reference Bible.* Grand Rapids, Mich.: Zondervan, 1999.

McWhirter, Norris, and Ross McWhirter. *1976 Guiness Book of World Records.* New York: Bantam, 1976.

Meeks, Wayne. *The First Urban Christians: The Social World of the Apostle Paul.* New Haven, Conn.: Yale Univ. Press, 1983.

Moreau, A. Scott, ed. *Evangelical Dictionary of World Missions.* Grand Rapids, Mich.: Baker, 2000.

Moreau, A. Scott, Gary R. Corwin, and Gary B. McGee. *Introducing World Missions: A Biblical, Historical, and Practical Survey.* Grand Rapids, Mich.: Baker, 2004.

Mulholland, Ken. *World Missions Today: What You Should Know About Global Ministries.* Wheaton, Ill.: Evangelical Training Association, 2000.

Myers, Bryant. *The New Context of World Mission.* Monrovia, Calif.: MARC, 1996.

———. *Exploring World Mission: Context and Challenges.* Monrovia, Calif.: World Vision International, 2003.

National Institute on Media and the Family. "Facts." *National Institute on Media and the Family. www.mediafamily.org/facts.* Accessed September 5, 2004.

"Natural Disasters: Earth, Wind and Water," *The Economist* (February 7, 2004): 28.

NIV Application Commentary. Edited by Terry C. Muck, 43 volumes (Genesis–Revelation). Grand Rapids, Mich.: Zondervan, 1990–2004.

Phillips, Rachael. *Frederick Douglass: Abolitionist and Reformer.* Uhrichsville, Ohio: Barbour, 2000.

Potter, Charles F. *Is That in the Bible?* Greenwich, Conn.: Fawcett, 1933.

"Primary School Attendance," *The Economist* (December 14, 2002): 98.

Schmittroth, Linda, ed. *Statistical Record of Women Worldwide.* New York: Gale Research, 1995.

"Sickness or Symptom? Child Labour Is Reviled—There Is Much Debate As To How It Can Be Reduced," *The Economist* (February 7, 2004): 69.

Sider, Ronald J. *Just Generosity: A New Vision for Overcoming Poverty in America.* Grand Rapids, Mich.: Baker, 1999.

———. Chapter 9 in *Living Like Jesus: Eleven Essentials for Growing a Genuine Faith.* Grand Rapids, Mich.: Baker, 1999.

Smith, Dan. *The State of the World Atlas.* 6th ed. New York: Penguin, 1999.

Snyder, C. R., and Shane J. Lopez, eds. *Handbook of Positive Psychology.* New York: Oxford, 2002.

Stott, John. *Why I Am a Christian.* Downers Grove, Ill.: InterVarsity, 2003, 106–107.

Stukas, A. A., E. G. Clary, and M. Snyder. "Service Learning: Who Benefits and Why?" *Social Policy Report* (1999): 1–19.

Teresa, Mother. *My Life for the Poor.* Ballantine, 1985, 53–55,57.

Thomas à Kempis. *The Imitation of Christ.* New York: Doubleday, 1989, 48–49.

United Nations Development Programme. *Human Development Report 2000: Human Rights and Human Development.* New York: Oxford, 2000.

———. *Human Development Report 2002: Deepening Democracy in a Fragmented World.* New York: Oxford, 2002.

———. *World Resources 2000–2001: People and Ecosystems—the Fraying Way of Life.* Edited by C. Rosen. San Diego: Elsevier Health Science, 2000.

United Nations Environment Programme. *Global Environment Outlook 3.* London, UK: Earthscan and UNEP, 2002.

University of California Agriculture and Natural Resources. *www.ucanr.org.*

U.S. Census Bureau. *Statistical Abstract of the United States 2002: The National Data Book.* Austin: Hoover Business, 2002.

U.S. Committee for Refugees. Refugee Report of December 31, 2002. *www.refugees.org.*

Vardell, M. "Curing Night Blindness," *Missiology* (1998): 470.

Wellman, Sam. *Amy Carmichael: A Life Abandoned to God.* Uhrichsville, Ohio: Barbour, 1998.

———. *Billy Graham: The Great Evangelist.* Uhrichsville, Ohio: Barbour, 1996.

———. *Mother Teresa: Missionary of Charity.* Uhrichsville, Ohio: Barbour, 1997.

———. *Corrie ten Boom: Heroine of Haarlem.* Uhrichsville, Ohio: Barbour, 1995.

Woolever, Cynthia, and Deborah Bruce. *A Field Guide to U.S. Congregations: Who's Going Where and Why.* Louisville: Westminster, 2002.

World Almanac and Book of Facts 2003, The. Edited by William McGeveran. New York: World Almanac, 2003.

World Bank. *World Bank Atlas 2000: From the World Development Indicators.* Washington D.C.: World Bank, 2001.

———. *World Bank Atlas 2002: From the World Development Indicators.* Washington D.C.: World Bank, 2002.

———. *World Development Indicators 2002.* Washington, D.C.: World Bank, 2002.

———. *World Development Report 2003: Sustainable Development in a Dynamic World: Transforming Institutions, Growth, and Quality of Life.* Washington D.C.: World Bank, 2003.

World Health Organization. *The World Health Report 2002: Reducing Risks, Promoting Healthy Life.* Geneva: WHO, 2002.

The World's Women, 1995: Trends and Statistics. New York: United Nations, 1995.

World Vision Australia. *Report: Children at Risk: Practical Approaches to Addressing Child Protection Issues in Cambodia, Indonesia, the Philippines, Sri Lanka, and Vietnam.* Melbourne, Australia: World Vision Australia, 2003.

———. *Rwanda's Gift to the World* (VHS), Stormfront Video, 2001.

Worldwatch Institute. *State of the World 2002.* New York: W. W. Norton, 2002.

———. *Vital Signs 2002: The Trends That Are Shaping Our Future.* New York: W. W. Norton, 2002.

Wright, John W., ed. *The New York Times Almanac 2003.* New York: Penguin, 2003.

Wurman, Richard Saul. *Understanding.* Newport, Rhode Island: TED Conferences, 2000.

Yancey, Philip. "Cry, the Beloved Continent: Don't Let AIDS Steal African Children's Future," *Christianity Today.* 48, no. 3 (March 2004): 112.

Yaukey, David, and Douglas L. Anderton. *Demography: The Study of Human Population.* Prospect Heights, Ill.: Waveland, 2001.

Concordance

This NIV Concordance is a condensation of *The NIV Complete Concordance*, taking over 35,000 references from the latter's 250,000. These 35,000 references have been selected as the most helpful for the average Bible student or layperson.

When determining whether or not to include a verse reference, we gave careful consideration to the passage in which the verse is located. We also encourage you to always consider the larger context of the passage, giving special attention to the flow of the thought from beginning to end. Whenever you look up a verse, your goal should be to discover the intended meaning of the verse in context. Do not use this concordance, or any concordance, merely as a *verse-finder*; it should also be used as a *passage-finder*. The contexts surrounding each entry are longer than those usually found in concordances; but even so, the context excerpts are too brief for study purposes. They serve only to help you locate familiar verses.

In some cases the usual short contextual phrases are ineffective in helping you locate a passage. This is especially true in studying key events in a Bible character's life. Therefore, we have incorporated 260 "block entries" in which we use descriptive phrases that mark the breadth of a passage containing episodes of that person's life. The descriptive phrases replace the brief context surrounding each occurrence of the name.

Often more than one Bible character has the same name. For example, there are more than thirty Zechariahs in the Bible. In these cases we have given the name a block entry, assigning each person a number (1), (2), etc., and have included a descriptive phrase to distinguish each. Insignificant names are not included.

In this concordance there are 1,239 key word entries that have an exhaustive list of every appearance of that word. When this occurs, the word or block entry is marked with an asterisk (*).

Two entries are marked with a dagger (†) and two with a double-dagger (‡). LORD† and LORD'S† list occurrences of the title "Lord," spelled "Lord" and "lord," "Lord's" and "lord's" in the NIV. LORD‡ and LORD'S‡ list occurrences of the proper name of God, *Yahweh*, spelled "LORD" and "LORD's" in the NIV. See the Preface to the New International Version on page xvi.

This mini-concordance includes some words not found in *The NIV Complete Concordance*. These words include: boy, boy's, boys, daughter, daughters, girl, man, man's, men, men's, people, peoples, woman, and women.

Since this concordance can only serve one translation—the New International Version—it is difficult for readers familiar with the Authorized Version to make the transition from its older, more archaic language to that of the NIV. We have tried, therefore, to make this transition a bit easier by including some forty-four prominent Authorized Version words and linking them to NIV words that have taken their place. We wish to thank Dr. Daniel E. Sauerwein of Multnomah Bible College for supplying the data for these additional words.

We pray that this concordance will be used by NIV readers to introduce them to the full scope of God's truth in every book of the Bible.

John R. Kohlenberger III
Edward W. Goodrick

AARON
Genealogy of (Ex 6:16–20; Jos 21:4, 10; 1Ch 6:3–15).
Priesthood of (Ex 28:1; Nu 17; Heb 5:1–4; 7), garments (Ex 28; 39), consecration (Ex 29), ordination (Lev 8).
Spokesman for Moses (Ex 4:14–16, 27–31; 7:1–2). Supported Moses' hands in battle (Ex 17:8–13). Built golden calf (Ex 32; Dt 9:20). Talked against Moses (Nu 12). Priesthood opposed (Nu 16); staff budded (Nu 17). Forbidden to enter land (Nu 20:1–12). Death (Nu 20:22–29; 33:38–39).

ABADDON*
Rev   9:11   whose name in Hebrew is *A*,

ABANDON (ABANDONED)
Dt   4:31   he will not *a* or destroy you
1Ki   6:13   and will not *a* my people Israel."
Ne   9:19   compassion you did not *a* them
      9:31   an end to them or *a* them,
Ps   16:10   you will not *a* me to the grave,
Ac   2:27   you will not *a* me to the grave,
1Ti   4: 1   in later times some will *a* the faith

ABANDONED (ABANDON)
Ge   24:27   who has not *a* his kindness
2Co   4: 9   persecuted, but not *a*; struck down,

ABBA*
Mk   14:36   "*A*, Father," he said, "everything is
Ro   8:15   And by him we cry, "*A*, Father."
Gal   4: 6   the Spirit who calls out, "*A*, Father

ABEDNEGO
Deported to Babylon with Daniel (Da 1:1–6). Name changed from Azariah (Da 1:7). Refused defilement by food (Da 1:8–20). Refused idol worship (Da 3:1–12); saved from furnace (Da 3:13–30).

ABEL
Second son of Adam (Ge 4:2). Offered proper sacrifice (Ge 4:4; Heb 11:4). Murdered by Cain (Ge 4:8; Mt 23:35; Lk 11:51; 1Jn 3:12).

ABHOR
Lev 26:30   of your idols, and I will *a* you.
Dt   7:26   Utterly *a* and detest it,
Ps   26: 5   I *a* the assembly of evildoers
    119:163   I hate and *a* falsehood
    139:21   and *a* those who rise up against you
Am   6: 8   "I *a* the pride of Jacob
Ro   2:22   You who *a* idols, do you rob

ABHORS (ABHOR)
Pr   11: 1   The LORD *a* dishonest scales,

ABIATHAR
High priest in days of Saul and David (1Sa 22; 2Sa 15; 1Ki 1–2; Mk 2:26). Escaped Saul's slaughter of priests (1Sa 22:18–23). Supported David in Absalom's revolt (2Sa 15:24–29). Supported Adonijah (1Ki 1:7–42); deposed by Solomon (1Ki 2:22–35; cf. 1Sa 2:31–35).

ABIGAIL
1. Sister of David (1Ch 2:16–17).
2. Wife of Nabal (1Sa 25:30); pled for his life with David (1Sa 25:14–35). Became David's wife after Nabal's death (1Sa 25:36–42); bore him Kileab (2Sa 3:3) also known as Daniel (1Ch 3:1).

ABIHU
Son of Aaron (Ex 6:23; 24:1, 9); killed for offering unauthorized fire (Lev 10; Nu 3:2–4; 1Ch 24:1–2).

ABIJAH
1. Second son of Samuel (1Ch 6:28); a corrupt judge (1Sa 8:1–5).
2. An Aaronic priest (1Ch 24:10; Lk 1:5).
3. Son of Jeroboam I of Israel; died as prophesied by Ahijah (1Ki 14:1–18).
4. Son of Rehoboam; king of Judah who fought Jeroboam I attempting to reunite the kingdom (1Ki 14:31–15:8; 2Ch 12:16–14:1; Mt 1:7).

ABILITY (ABLE)
Ex   35:34   tribe of Dan, the *a* to teach others.
Dt   8:18   for it is he who gives you the *a*
Ezr   2:69   According to their *a* they gave

Mt   25:15   one talent, each according to his *a*.
Ac   11:29   disciples, each according to his *a*,
2Co   1: 8   far beyond our *a* to endure,
      8: 3   were able, and even beyond their *a*.

ABIMELECH
1. King of Gerar who took Abraham's wife Sarah, believing her to be his sister (Ge 20). Later made a covenant with Abraham (Ge 21:22–33).
2. King of Gerar who took Isaac's wife Rebekah, believing her to be his sister (Ge 26:1–11). Later made a covenant with Isaac (Ge 26:12–31).
3. Son of Gideon (Jdg 8:31). Attempted to make himself king (Jdg 9).

ABISHAG*
Shunammite virgin; attendant of David in his old age (1Ki 1:1–15; 2:17–22).

ABISHAI
Son of Zeruiah, David's sister (1Sa 26:6; 1Ch 2:16). One of David's chief warriors (1Ch 11:15–21): against Edom (1Ch 18:12–13), Ammon (2Sa 10), Absalom (2Sa 18), Sheba (2Sa 20). Wanted to kill Saul (1Sa 26), killed Abner (2Sa 2:18–27; 3:22–39), wanted to kill Shimei (2Sa 16:5–13; 19:16–23).

ABLE (ABILITY ENABLE ENABLED ENABLES ENABLING)
Nu   14:16   'The LORD was not *a*
1Ch 29:14   that we should be *a* to give
2Ch   2: 6   who is *a* to build a temple for him,
Eze   7:19   and gold will not be *a* to save them
Da   3:17   the God we serve is *a* to save us
      4:37   walk in pride he is *a* to humble.
Mt   9:28   "Do you believe that I am *a*
Lk   13:24   will try to enter and will not be *a* to
     14:30   to build and was not *a* to finish.'
     21:15   none of your adversaries will be *a*
     21:36   and that you may be *a* to stand
Ac   5:39   you will not be *a* to stop these men;
Ro   8:39   will be *a* to separate us
     14: 4   for the Lord is *a* to make him stand
     16:25   to him who is *a* to establish you
2Co   9: 8   God is *a* to make all grace abound
Eph   3:20   him who is *a* to do immeasurably
      6:13   you may be *a* to stand your ground,
1Ti   3: 2   respectable, hospitable, *a* to teach,
2Ti   1:12   and am convinced that he is *a*
      2:24   kind to everyone, *a* to teach,
      3:15   which are *a* to make you wise
Heb   2:18   he is *a* to help those who are being
      7:25   he is *a* to save completely
Jas   3: 2   *a* to keep his whole body in check.
Jude :24   To him who is *a* to keep you
Rev   5: 5   He is *a* to open the scroll

ABNER
Cousin of Saul and commander of his army (1Sa 14:50; 17:55–57; 26). Made Ish-Bosheth king after Saul (2Sa 2:8–10), but later defected to David (2Sa 3:6–21). Killed Asahel (2Sa 2:18–32), for which he was killed by Joab and Abishai (2Sa 3:22–39).

ABOLISH (ABOLISHED ABOLISHING)
Hos   2:18   I will *a* from the land,
Mt   5:17   that I have come to *a* the Law

ABOLISHED (ABOLISH)
Gal   5:11   the offense of the cross has been *a*.

ABOLISHING* (ABOLISH)
Eph   2:15   by *a* in his flesh the law

ABOMINATION*
Da   11:31   set up the *a* that causes desolation.
     12:11   *a* that causes desolation is set up,
Mt   24:15   the holy place 'the *a* that causes
Mk   13:14   you see 'the *a* that causes

ABOUND (ABOUNDING)
2Co   9: 8   able to make all grace *a* to you,
      9: 8   you will *a* in every good work.
Php   1: 9   that your love may *a* more

ABOUNDING (ABOUND)
Ex   34: 6   slow to anger, *a* in love
Nu   14:18   *a* in love and forgiving sin
Ne   9:17   slow to anger and *a* in love.
Ps   86: 5   *a* in love to all who call to you.
     86:15   slow to anger, *a* in love,
    103: 8   slow to anger, *a* in love.
Joel 2:13   slow to anger and *a* in love,
Jnh   4: 2   slow to anger and *a* in love,

ABRAHAM
Abram, son of Terah (Ge 11:26–27), husband of Sarah (Ge 11:29).
Covenant relation with the LORD (Ge 12:1–3; 13:14–17; 15; 17; 22:15–18; Ex 2:24; Ne 9:8; Ps 105; Mic 7:20; Lk 1:68–75; Ro 4:9; Heb 6:13–15).
Called from Ur, via Haran, to Canaan (Ge 12:1; Ac 7:2–4; Heb 11:8–10). Moved to Egypt, nearly lost Sarah to Pharoah (Ge 12:10–20). Divided the land with Lot; settled in Hebron (Ge 13). Saved Lot from four kings (Ge 14:1–16); blessed by Melchizedek (Ge 14:17–20; Heb 7:1–20). Declared righteous by faith (Ge 15:6; Ro 4:3; Gal 3:6–9). Fathered Ishmael by Hagar (Ge 16).
Name changed from Abram (Ge 17:5; Ne 9:7). Circumcised (Ge 17; Ro 4:9–12). Entertained three visitors (Ge 18); promised a son by Sarah (Ge 18:9–15; 17:16). Questioned destruction of Sodom and Gomorrah (Ge 18:16–33). Moved to Gerar; nearly lost Sarah to Abimelech (Ge 20). Fathered Isaac by Sarah (Ge 21:1–7; Ac 7:8; Heb 11:11–12); sent away Hagar and Ishmael (Ge 21:8–21; Gal 4:22–30). Covenant with Abimelech (Ge 21:22–32). Tested by offering Isaac (Ge 22; Heb 11:17–19; Jas 2:21–24). Sarah died; bought field of Ephron for burial (Ge 23). Secured wife for Isaac (Ge 24). Fathered children by Keturah (Ge 25:1–6; 1Ch 1:32–33). Death (Ge 25:7–11).
Called servant of God (Ge 26:24), friend of God (2Ch 20:7; Isa 41:8; Jas 2:23), prophet (Ge 20:7), father of Israel (Ex 3:15; Isa 51:2; Mt 3:9; Jn 8:39–58).

ABSALOM
Son of David by Maacah (2Sa 3:3; 1Ch 3:2). Killed Amnon for rape of his sister Tamar; banished by David (2Sa 13). Returned to Jerusalem; received by David (2Sa 14). Rebelled against David; siezed kingdom (2Sa 15–17). Killed (2Sa 18).

ABSENT
Col   2: 5   though I am *a* from you in body,

ABSOLUTE*
1Ti   5: 2   women as sisters, with *a* purity.

ABSTAIN (ABSTAINS)
Ex   19:15   *A* from sexual relations."
Nu   6: 3   he must *a* from wine and other
Ac   15:20   them to *a* from food polluted
1Pe   2:11   to *a* from sinful desires,

ABSTAINS* (ABSTAIN)
Ro   14: 6   thanks to God; and he who *a*,

ABUNDANCE (ABUNDANT)
Ge   41:29   Seven years of great *a* are coming
Job 36:31   and provides food in *a*.
Ps   66:12   but you brought us to a place of *a*.
Ecc   5:12   but the *a* of a rich man
Isa 66:11   and delight in her overflowing *a*."
Jer   2:22   and use an *a* of soap,
Mt   13:12   given more, and he will have an *a*.
     25:29   given more, and he will have an *a*.
Lk   12:15   consist in the *a* of his possessions."
1Pe   1: 2   Grace and peace be yours in *a*.
2Pe   1: 2   yours in *a* through the knowledge
Jude : 2   peace and love be yours in *a*.

ABUNDANT (ABUNDANCE)
Dt   28:11   will grant you *a* prosperity—
     32: like a rain on tender plants.
Job 36:28   and *a* showers fall on mankind.
Ps   68: 9   You gave *a* showers, O God;
     78:15   gave them water as *a* as the seas;
    132:15   I will bless her with *a* provisions;
    145: 7   will celebrate your *a* goodness
Pr   12:11   works his land will have *a* food,

Pr　28:19　works his land will have *a* food,
Jer　33: 9　and will tremble at the *a* prosperity
Ro　 5:17　who receive God's *a* provision

ABUSIVE
2Ti　 3: 2　*a*, disobedient to their parents,

ABYSS*
Lk　 8:31　not to order them to go into the A.
Rev　 9: 1　the key to the shaft of the A.
　　　 9: 2　When he opened the A, smoke rose
　　　 9: 2　darkened by the smoke from the A.
　　　 9:11　king over them the angel of the A,
　　　11: 7　up from the A will attack them,
　　　17: 8　and will come up out of the A
　　　20: 1　having the key to the A
　　　20: 3　He threw him into the A,

ACCEPT (ACCEPTABLE ACCEPTANCE ACCEPTED ACCEPTS)
Ex　23: 8　"Do not *a* a bribe,
Dt　16:19　Do not *a* a bribe, for a bribe blinds
Job　42: 8　and I will *a* his prayer and not deal
Pr　10: 8　The wise in heart *a* commands,
　　19:20　Listen to advice and *a* instruction,
Ro　15: 7　*A* one another, then, just
Jas　 1:21　humbly *a* the word planted in you,

ACCEPTABLE (ACCEPT)
Pr　21: 3　is more *a* to the LORD

ACCEPTANCE* (ACCEPT)
Ro　11:15　what will their *a* be but life
1Ti　 1:15　saying that deserves full *a*:
　　　 4: 9　saying that deserves full *a*

ACCEPTED (ACCEPT)
Ge　 4: 7　will you not be *a*? But if you do not
Job　42: 9　and the LORD *a* Job's prayer.
Lk　 4:24　"no prophet is *a* in his hometown.
Gal　 1: 9　you a gospel other than what you *a*,

ACCEPTS (ACCEPT)
Ps　 6: 9　the LORD *a* my prayer.
Jn　13:20　whoever *a* anyone I send *a* me;
　　13:20　whoever *a* me *a* the one who sent

ACCESS
Ro　 5: 2　through whom we have gained *a*
Eph　 2:18　For through him we both have *a*

ACCOMPANIED (ACCOMPANY)
1Co　10: 4　from the spiritual rock that *a* them,
Jas　 2:17　if it is not *a* by action, is dead.

ACCOMPANIES (ACCOMPANY)
2Co　 9:13　obedience that *a* your confession

ACCOMPANY (ACCOMPANIED ACCOMPANIES)
Dt　28: 2　*a* you if you obey the LORD your
Mk　16:17　these signs will *a* those who believe
Heb　 6: 9　your case—things that *a* salvation.

ACCOMPLISH
Ecc　 2: 2　And what does pleasure *a*?"
Isa　44:28　and will *a* all that I please;
　　55:11　but will *a* what I desire

ACCORD
Nu　24:13　not do anything of my own *a*,
Jn　10:18　but I lay it down of my own *a*.
　　12:49　For I did not speak of my own *a*,

ACCOUNT (ACCOUNTABLE)
Ge　 2: 4　This is the *a* of the heavens
　　　 5: 1　This is the written *a* of Adam's line
　　　 6: 9　This is the *a* of Noah.
　　10: 1　This is the *a* of Shem, Ham
　　11:10　This is the *a* of Shem.
　　11:27　This is the *a* of Terah.
　　25:12　This is the *a* of Abraham's son
　　25:19　This is the *a* of Abraham's son
　　36: 1　This is the *a* of Esau (that is, Edom
　　36: 9　This is the *a* of Esau the father
　　37: 2　This is the *a* of Jacob.
Mt　12:36　to give *a* on the day of judgment
Lk　16: 2　Give an *a* of your management,
Ro　14:12　each of us will give an *a* of himself

Heb　 4:13　of him to whom we must give *a*.

ACCOUNTABLE* (ACCOUNT)
Eze　 3:18　and I will hold you *a* for his blood.
　　　 3:20　and I will hold you *a* for his blood.
　　33: 6　but I will hold the watchman *a*
　　33: 8　and I will hold you *a* for his blood.
　　34:10　and will hold them *a* for my flock.
Da　 6: 2　The satraps were made *a* to them
Jnh　 1:14　Do not hold us *a* for killing
Ro　 3:19　and the whole world held *a* to God.

ACCURATE
Dt　25:15　You must have *a* and honest
Pr　11: 1　but *a* weights are his delight.

ACCURSED (CURSE)
2Pe　 2:14　experts in greed—an *a* brood!

ACCUSATION (ACCUSE)
1Ti　 5:19　Do not entertain an *a*

ACCUSATIONS (ACCUSE)
2Pe　 2:11　do not bring slanderous *a*

ACCUSE (ACCUSATION ACCUSATIONS ACCUSER ACCUSES ACCUSING)
Pr　 3:30　Do not *a* a man for no reason—
Lk　 3:14　and don't *a* people falsely—

ACCUSER (ACCUSE)
Jn　 5:45　Your *a* is Moses, on whom your
Rev　12:10　For the *a* of our brothers,

ACCUSES (ACCUSE)
Job　40: 2　Let him who *a* God answer him!"
Rev　12:10　who *a* them before our God day

ACCUSING (ACCUSE)
Ro　 2:15　and their thoughts now *a*,

ACHAN*
　Sin at Jericho caused defeat at Ai; stoned (Jos 7; 22:20; 1Ch 2:7).

ACHE*
Pr　14:13　Even in laughter the heart may *a*,

ACHIEVE
Isa　55:11　*a* the purpose for which I sent it.

ACHISH
　King of Gath before whom David feigned insanity (1Sa 21:10–15). Later "ally" of David (2Sa 27–29).

ACKNOWLEDGE (ACKNOWLEDGED ACKNOWLEDGES)
Pr　 3: 6　in all your ways *a* him,
Jer　 3:13　Only *a* your guilt—
Hos　 6: 3　let us press on to *a*
Mt　10:32　*a* him before my Father in heaven.
Lk　12: 8　*a* him before the angels of God.
1Jn　 4: 3　spirit that does not *a* Jesus is not

ACKNOWLEDGED (ACKNOWLEDGE)
Lk　 7:29　*a* that God's way was right,

ACKNOWLEDGES* (ACKNOWLEDGE)
Ps　91:14　for he *a* my name.
Mt　10:32　"Whoever *a* me before men,
Lk　12: 8　whoever *a* me before men,
1Jn　 2:23　whoever *a* the Son has the Father
　　　 4: 2　Every spirit that *a* that Jesus Christ
　　　 4:15　If anyone *a* that Jesus is the Son

ACQUIRES (ACQUIRING)
Pr　18:15　of the discerning *a* knowledge;

ACQUIRING* (ACQUIRES)
Pr　 1: 3　for *a* a disciplined and prudent life,

ACQUIT (ACQUITTING)
Ex　23: 7　to death, for I will not *a* the guilty.

ACQUITTING* (ACQUIT)
Dt　25: 1　*a* the innocent and condemning
Pr　17:15　*A* the guilty and condemning

ACT (ACTION ACTIONS ACTIVE ACTIVITY ACTS)
Ps　119:126　It is time for you to *a*, O LORD;

ACTION (ACT)
2Co　 9: 2　has stirred most of them to *a*.
Jas　 2:17　if it is not accompanied by *a*,
1Pe　 1:13　minds for *a*; be self-controlled;

ACTIONS (ACT)
Mt　11:19　wisdom is proved right by her *a*."
Gal　 6: 4　Each one should test his own *a*.
Tit　 1:16　but by their *a* they deny him.

ACTIVE* (ACT)
Phm　 : 6　I pray that you may be *a*

Heb　 4:12　For the word of God is living and *a*

ACTIVITY (ACT)
Ecc　 3: 1　a season for every *a* under heaven:
　　　 3:17　for there will be a time for every *a*,

ACTS (ACT)
1Ch　16: 9　tell of all his wonderful *a*.
Ps　71:16　proclaim your mighty *a*,
　　71:24　tell of your righteous *a*
　　105: 2　tell of all his wonderful *a*.
　　106: 2　Who can proclaim the mighty *a*
　　145: 4　they will tell of your mighty *a*.
　　145:12　all men may know of your mighty *a*
　　150: 2　Praise him for his *a* of power;
Isa　64: 6　all our righteous *a* are like filthy
Mt　 6: 1　not to do your '*a* of righteousness'

ADAM
　1. First man (Ge 1:26–2:25; Ro 5:14; 1Ti 2:13). Sin of (Ge 3; Hos 6:7; Ro 5:12–21). Children of (Ge 4:1–5:5). Death of (Ge 5:5; Ro 5:12–21; 1Co 15:22).
　2. City (Jos 3:16).

ADD (ADDED)
Dt　 4: 2　Do not *a* to what I command you
　　12:32　do not *a* to it or take away from it.
Pr　 1: 5　let the wise listen and *a*
　　　 9: 9　he will *a* to his learning.
　　30: 6　Do not *a* to his words,
Mt　 6:27　by worrying can *a* a single hour
Lk　12:25　by worrying can *a* a single hour
Rev　22:18　God will *a* to him the plagues

ADDED (ADD)
Ecc　 3:14　nothing can be *a* to it and nothing
Ac　 2:47　Lord *a* to their number daily those
Ro　 5:20　The law was *a* so that the trespass
Gal　 3:19　It was *a* because of transgressions

ADDICTED*
Tit　 2: 3　to be slanderers or *a* to much wine,

ADMINISTRATION*
1Co　12:28　with gifts of *a*, and those speaking
Eph　 3: 2　Surely you have heard about the *a*
　　　 3: 9　to everyone the *a* of this mystery,

ADMIRABLE*
Php　 4: 8　whatever is lovely, whatever is *a*—

ADMIT
Hos　 5:15　until they *a* their guilt.

ADMONISH* (ADMONISHING)
Col　 3:16　and *a* one another with all wisdom,
1Th　 5:12　you in the Lord and who *a* you.

ADMONISHING* (ADMONISH)
Col　 1:28　*a* and teaching everyone

ADONIJAH
　1. Son of David by Haggith (2Sa 3:4; 1Ch 3:2). Attempted to be king after David; killed by Solomon's order (1Ki 1–2).
　2. Levite; teacher of the Law (2Ch 17:8).

ADOPTED (ADOPTION)
Eph　 1: 5　In love he predestined us to be *a*

ADOPTION* (ADOPTED)
Ro　 8:23　as we wait eagerly for our *a* as sons,
　　　 9: 4　Theirs is the *a* as sons; theirs

ADORE*
SS　 1: 4　How right they are to *a* you!

ADORNMENT* (ADORNS)
1Pe　 3: 3　should not come from outward *a*,

ADORNS* (ADORNMENT)
Ps　93: 5　holiness *a* your house
Isa　61:10　as a bride *a* herself with her jewels.
　　61:10　bridegroom *a* his head like a priest,

ADULTERER (ADULTERY)
Lev　20:10　both the *a* and the adulteress must
Heb　13: 4　for God will judge the *a*

ADULTERERS (ADULTERY)
1Co　 6: 9　idolaters nor *a* nor male prostitutes

1Ti 1:10 for murderers, for *a* and perverts,

ADULTERESS (ADULTERY)
Hos 3: 1 she is loved by another and is an *a.*

ADULTERIES (ADULTERY)
Jer 3: 8 sent her away because of all her *a.*

ADULTEROUS (ADULTERY)
Mk 8:38 in this *a* and sinful generation,
Jas 4: 4 You *a* people, don't you know that

ADULTERY (ADULTERER ADULTERERS ADULTERESS ADULTERIES ADULTEROUS)
Ex 20:14 "You shall not commit *a.*
Dt 5:18 "You shall not commit *a.*
Mt 5:27 that it was said, 'Do not commit *a.*'
     5:28 lustfully has already committed *a.*
     5:32 the divorced woman commits *a.*
     15:19 murder, *a*, sexual immorality, theft
     19: 9 marries another woman commits *a*
     19:18 do not commit *a*, do not steal,
Mk 7:21 theft, murder, *a*, greed, malice,
     10:11 marries another woman commits *a*
     10:12 another man, she commits *a.*"
     10:19 do not commit *a*, do not steal,
Lk 16:18 a divorced woman commits *a.*
     16:18 marries another woman commits *a*
     18:20 'Do not commit *a*, do not murder,
Jn 8: 4 woman was caught in the act of *a.*
Rev 18: 3 of the earth committed *a* with her,

ADULTS*
1Co 14:20 but in your thinking be *a.*

ADVANCE (ADVANCED)
Ps 18:29 With your help I can *a*
Php 1:12 has really served to *a* the gospel.

ADVANCED (ADVANCE)
Job 32: 7 *a* years should teach wisdom.'

ADVANTAGE
Ex 22:22 "Do not take *a* of a widow
Dt 24:14 Do not take *a* of a hired man who is
Ro 3: 1 What *a*, then, is there
2Co 11:20 or exploits you or takes *a* of you
1Th 4: 6 should wrong his brother or take *a*

ADVERSITY*
Pr 17:17 and a brother is born for *a.*
Isa 30:20 the Lord gives you the bread of *a*

ADVICE (ADVISERS)
1Ki 12: 8 rejected the *a* the elders
     12:14 he followed the *a* of the young men
2Ch 10: 8 rejected the *a* the elders
Pr 12: 5 but the *a* of the wicked is deceitful.
     12:15 but a wise man listens to *a.*
     19:20 Listen to *a* and accept instruction,
     20:18 Make plans by seeking *a;*

ADVISERS (ADVICE)
Pr 11:14 but many *a* make victory sure.

ADVOCATE*
Job 16:19 my *a* is on high.

AFFLICTED (AFFLICTION)
Job 2: 7 and *a* Job with painful sores
     36: 6 but gives the *a* their rights.
Ps 9:12 he does not ignore the cry of the *a.*
     9:18 nor the hope of the *a* ever perish.
     119:67 Before I was *a* I went astray,
     119:71 It was good for me to be *a*
     119:75 and in faithfulness you have *a* me.
Isa 49:13 will have compassion on his *a* ones.
     53: 4 smitten by him, and *a.*
     53: 7 He was oppressed and *a,*
Na 1:12 Although I have *a* you, O Judah,

AFFLICTION (AFFLICTED AFFLICTIONS)
Dt 16: 3 bread of *a*, because you left Egypt
Ps 107:41 he lifted the needy out of their *a*
Isa 30:20 of adversity and the water of *a,*

Isa 48:10 in the furnace of *a.*
La 3:33 For he does not willingly bring *a*
Ro 12:12 patient in *a*, faithful in prayer.

AFFLICTIONS (AFFLICTION)
Col 1:24 lacking in regard to Christ's *a,*

AFRAID (FEAR)
Ge 3:10 and I was *a* because I was naked;
     26:24 Do not be *a*, for I am with you;
Ex 2:14 Then Moses was *a* and thought,
     3: 6 because he was *a* to look at God.
Dt 1:21 Do not be *a;* do not be discouraged
     1:29 "Do not be terrified; do not be *a*
     20: 1 do not be *a* of them,
     20: 3 Do not be fainthearted or *a;*
2Ki 25:24 "Do not be *a* of the Babylonian
1Ch 13:12 David was *a* of God that day
Ps 27: 1 of whom shall I be *a?*
     56: 3 When I am *a*, / I will trust in you.
     56: 4 in God I trust; I will not be *a.*
Pr 3:24 lie down, you will not be *a;*
Isa 10:24 do not be *a* of the Assyrians,
     12: 2 I will trust and not be *a.*
     44: 8 Do not tremble, do not be *a.*
Jer 1: 8 Do not be *a* of them, for I am
Mt 8:26 You of little faith, why are you so *a*
     10:28 be *a* of the One who can destroy
     10:31 So don't be *a;* you are worth more
Mk 5:36 "Don't be *a;* just believe."
Lk 9:34 and they were *a* as they entered
Jn 14:27 hearts to be troubled and do not be *a.*
Ac 27:24 beside me and said, 'Do not be *a,*
Ro 11:20 Do not be arrogant, but be *a.*
Heb 13: 6 Lord is my helper; I will not be *a.*

AGAG (AGAGITE)
     King of Amalekites not killed by Saul (1Sa 15).

AGAGITE (AGAG)
Est 8: 3 to the evil plan of Haman the A,

AGED (AGES)
Job 12:12 Is not wisdom found among the *a?*
Pr 17: 6 children are a crown to the *a,*

AGES (AGED)
Ro 16:25 the mystery hidden for long *a* past,
Eph 2: 7 that in the coming *a* he might show
     3: 5 which for *a* past was kept hidden
Col 1:26 that has been kept hidden for *a*
Rev 15: 3 King of the *a.*

AGONY
Lk 16:24 because I am in *a* in this fire.'
Rev 16:10 Men gnawed their tongues in *a*

AGREE (AGREEMENT AGREES)
Mt 18:19 on earth *a* about anything you ask
Ro 7:16 want to do, I *a* that the law is good.
Php 4: 2 with Syntyche to *a* with each other

AGREEMENT (AGREE)
2Co 6:16 What *a* is there between the temple

AGREES* (AGREE)
Ac 7:42 This *a* with what is written
     24:14 I believe everything that *a*
1Co 4:17 which *a* with what I teach

AGRIPPA*
     Descendant of Herod; king before whom Paul pleads his case in Caesarea (Ac 25:13–26:32).

AHAB
     1. Son of Omri; king of Israel (1Ki 16:28–22:40), husband of Jezebel (1Ki 16:31). Promoted Baal worship (1Ki 16:31–33); opposed by Elijah (1Ki 17:1; 18; 21), a prophet (1Ki 20:35–43), Micaiah (1Ki 22:1–28). Defeated Ben-Hadad (1Ki 20:35–21:40). Killed for failing to kill Ben-Hadad and for murder of Naboth (1Ki 20:35–21:40).
     2. A false prophet (Jer 29:21–22).

AHAZ
     1. Son of Jotham; king of Judah, (2Ki 16; 2Ch 28). Idolatry of (2Ki 16:3–4, 10–18; 2Ch

28:1–4, 22–25). Defeated by Aram and Israel (2Ki 16:5–6; 2Ch 28:5–15). Sought help from Assyria rather than the LORD (2Ki 16:7–9; 2Ch 28:16–21; Isa 7).
     2. Benjamite, descendant of Saul (1Ch 8:35–36).

AHAZIAH
     1. Son of Ahab; king of Israel (1Ki 22:51–2Ki 1:18; 2Ch 20:35–37). Made an unsuccessful alliance with Jehoshaphat of Judah (2Ch 20:35–37). Died for seeking Baal rather than the LORD (2Ki 1).
     2. Son of Jehoram; king of Judah (2Ki 8:25–29; 9:14–29), also called Jehoahaz (2Ch 21:17–22:9; 25:23). Killed by Jehu while visiting Joram (2Ki 9:14–29; 2Ch 22:1–9).

AHIJAH
1Sa 14:18 Saul said to A, "Bring the ark
1Ki 14: 2 A the prophet is there—the one

AHIMELECH
     1. Priest who helped David in his flight from Saul (1Sa 21–22).
     2. One of David's warriors (1Sa 26:6).

AHITHOPHEL
     One of David's counselors who sided with Absalom (2Sa 15:12, 31–37; 1Ch 27:33–34); committed suicide when his advice was ignored (2Sa 16:15–17:23).

AI
Jos 7: 4 they were routed by the men of A,
     8:28 So Joshua burned A and made it

AID
Isa 38:14 troubled; O Lord, come to my *a!*"
Php 4:16 you sent me *a* again and again

AIM
1Co 7:34 Her *a* is to be devoted to the Lord
2Co 13:11 A for perfection, listen

AIR
Mt 8:20 and birds of the *a* have nests,
Lk 9:58 and birds of the *a* have nests,
1Co 9:26 not fight like a man beating the *a.*
     14: 9 You will just be speaking into the *a*
Eph 2: 2 of the ruler of the kingdom of the *a,*
1Th 4:17 clouds to meet the Lord in the *a.*

ALABASTER*
Mt 26: 7 came to him with an *a* jar
Mk 14: 3 a woman came with an *a* jar
Lk 7:37 she brought an *a* jar of perfume,

ALARM (ALARMED)
2Co 7:11 indignation, what *a*, what longing,

ALARMED (ALARM)
Mk 13: 7 and rumors of wars, do not be *a.*
2Th 2: 2 not to become easily unsettled or *a*

ALERT*
Jos 8: 4 All of you be on the *a.*
Ps 17:11 with eyes *a*, to throw me
Isa 21: 7 let him be *a*, / fully *a.*"
Mk 13:33 Be *a!* You do not know
Eph 6:18 and always keep on praying
1Th 5: 6 but let us be *a* and self-controlled.
1Pe 5: 8 Be self-controlled and *a.*

ALIEN (ALIENATED ALIENS)
Ex 22:21 "Do not mistreat an *a*
Lev 24:22 are to have the same law for the *a*
Ps 146: 9 The LORD watches over the *a*

ALIENATED (ALIEN)
Gal 5: 4 by law have been *a* from Christ;
Col 1:21 Once you were *a* from God

ALIENS (ALIEN)
Ex 23: 9 know how it feels to be *a,*
1Pe 2:11 as *a* and strangers in the world,

ALIVE (LIVE)
1Sa 2: 6 LORD brings death and makes *a;*
Lk 24:23 vision of angels, who said he was *a.*
Ac 1: 3 convincing proofs that he was *a.*
Ro 6:11 but *a* to God in Christ Jesus.
1Co 15:22 so in Christ all will be made *a.*
Eph 2: 5 made us *a* with Christ

ALMIGHTY (MIGHT)
Ge 17: 1 "I am God A; walk before me

ALPHA

Ex   6: 3   to Isaac and to Jacob as God *A*,
Ru   1:20   the *A* has made my life very bitter.
Job 11: 7   Can you probe the limits of the *A*?
        33: 4   the breath of the *A* gives me life.
Ps 89: 8   O Lᴏʀᴅ God *A*, who is like you?
        91: 1   I will rest in the shadow of the *A*.
Isa   6: 3   "Holy, holy, holy is the Lᴏʀᴅ *A*;
        45:13   says the Lᴏʀᴅ *A*."
        47: 4   the Lᴏʀᴅ *A* is his name—
        48: 2   the Lᴏʀᴅ *A* is his name;
        51:15   the Lᴏʀᴅ *A* is his name—
        54: 5   the Lᴏʀᴅ *A* is his name—
Am   5:14   the Lᴏʀᴅ God *A* will be with you,
        5:15   the Lᴏʀᴅ God *A* will have mercy
Rev   4: 8   holy is the Lord God *A*, who was,
        19: 6   For our Lord God *A* reigns.

ALPHA*

Rev   1: 8   "I am the *A* and the Omega,"
        21: 6   I am the *A* and the Omega,
        22:13   I am the *A* and the Omega,

ALTAR

Ge   8:20   Then Noah built an *a* to the Lᴏʀᴅ
        12: 7   So he built an *a* there to the Lᴏʀᴅ
        13:18   where he built an *a* to the Lᴏʀᴅ.
        22: 9   Abraham built an *a* there
        22: 9   his son Isaac and laid him on
             the *a*,
        26:25   Isaac built an *a* there and called
        35: 1   and build an *a* there to God.
Ex 17:15   Moses built an *a* and called it
        27: 1   "Build an *a* of acacia wood,
        30: 1   "Make an *a* of acacia wood
        37:25   They made the *a* of incense out
Dt 27: 5   an *a* to the Lᴏʀᴅ your God, an *a*
Jos   8:30   on Mount Ebal an *a* to the Lᴏʀᴅ,
        22:10   built an imposing *a* there
Jdg   6:24   So Gideon built an *a* to the Lᴏʀᴅ
        21: 4   the next day the people built an *a*
1Sa   7:17   he built an *a* there to the Lᴏʀᴅ.
        14:35   Then Saul built an *a* to the Lᴏʀᴅ;
2Sa 24:25   David built an *a* to the Lᴏʀᴅ
1Ki 12:33   sacrifices on the *a* he had built
        13: 2   "O *a*, *a*! This is what the Lᴏʀᴅ
        16:32   He set up an *a* for Baal
        18:30   and he repaired the *a* of the Lᴏʀᴅ
2Ki 16:11   So Uriah the priest built an *a*
1Ch 21:26   David built an *a* to the Lᴏʀᴅ
2Ch   4: 1   made a bronze *a* twenty cubits
        4:19   the golden *a*; the tables
        15: 8   He repaired the *a* of the Lᴏʀᴅ
        32:12   'You must worship before one *a*
        33:16   he restored the *a* of the Lᴏʀᴅ
Ezr   3: 2   to build the *a* of the God of Israel
Isa   6: 6   taken with tongs from the *a*.
Eze 40:47   the *a* was in front of the temple.
Mt   5:23   if you are offering your gift at
             the *a*
Ac 17:23   found an *a* with this inscription:
Heb 13:10   We have an *a* from which those
Rev   6: 9   I saw under the *a* the souls

ALTER*

Ps 89:34   or *a* what my lips have uttered.

ALWAYS

Dt 15:11   There will *a* be poor people
Ps 16: 8   I have set the Lᴏʀᴅ *a* before me.
        51: 3   and my sin is *a* before me.
Pr 23: 7   who is *a* thinking about the cost.
Mt 26:11   The poor you will *a* have with
             you,
        28:20   And surely I am with you *a*,
Mk 14: 7   The poor you will *a* have with
             you,
Jn 12: 8   You will *a* have the poor
1Co 13: 7   *a* protects, *a* trusts, *a* hopes, *a*
Php   4: 4   Rejoice in the Lord *a*.
1Pe   3:15   *A* be prepared to give an answer

AMALEKITES

Ex 17: 8   *A* came and attacked the
             Israelites
1Sa 15: 2   'I will punish the *A*

AMASA

    Nephew of David (1Ch 2:17). Commander of Absalom's forces (2Sa 17:24–27). Returned to David (2Sa 19:13). Killed by Joab (2Sa 20:4–13).

AMASSES*

Pr 28: 8   *a* it for another, who will be kind

AMAZED

Mt   7:28   the crowds were *a* at his teaching,
Mk   6: 6   And he was *a* at their lack of faith.
        10:24   The disciples were *a* at his words.
Ac   2: 7   Utterly *a*, they asked: "Are not all
        13:12   for he was *a* at the teaching about

AMAZIAH

    1. Son of Joash; king of Judah (2Ki 14; 2Ch 25). Defeated Edom (2Ki 14:7; 2Ch 25:5–13); defeated by Israel for worshiping Edom's gods (2Ki 14:8–14; 2Ch 25:14–24).
    2. Idolatrous priest who opposed Amos (Am 7:10–17).

AMBASSADOR* (AMBASSADORS)

Eph   6:20   for which I am an *a* in chains.

AMBASSADORS (AMBASSADOR)

2Co   5:20   We are therefore Christ's *a*,

AMBITION*

Ro 15:20   It has always been my *a*
Gal   5:20   fits of rage, selfish *a*, dissensions,
Php   1:17   preach Christ out of selfish *a*,
        2: 3   Do nothing out of selfish *a*
1Th   4:11   Make it your *a* to lead a quiet life,
Jas   3:14   and selfish *a* in your hearts,
        3:16   where you have envy and
             selfish *a*,

AMENDS

Pr 14: 9   Fools mock at making *a* for sin,

AMNON

    Firstborn of David (2Sa 3:2; 1Ch 3:1). Killed by Absalom for raping his sister Tamar (2Sa 13).

AMON

    1. Son of Manasseh; king of Judah (2Ki 21:18–26; 1Ch 3:14; 2Ch 33:21–25).
    2. Ruler of Samaria under Ahab (1Ki 22:26; 2Ch 18:25).

AMOS

    1. Prophet from Tekoa (Am 1:1; 7:10–17).
    2. Ancestor of Jesus (Lk 3:25).

ANAK (ANAKITES)

Nu 13:28   even saw descendants of *A* there.

ANAKITES (ANAK)

Dt   1:28   We even saw the *A* there.' "
        2:10   and numerous, and as tall as
             the *A*.
        9: 2   "Who can stand up against
             the *A*?"

ANANIAS

    1. Husband of Sapphira; died for lying to God (Ac 5:1–11).
    2. Disciple who baptized Saul (Ac 9:10–19).
    3. High priest at Paul's arrest (Ac 22:30–24:1).

ANCESTORS (ANCESTRY)

1Ki 19: 4   I am no better than my *a*."

ANCESTRY (ANCESTORS)

Ro   9: 5   from them is traced the human *a*

ANCHOR

Heb   6:19   We have this hope as an *a*

ANCIENT

Da   7: 9   and the *A* of Days took his seat.
        7:13   He approached the *A* of Days
        7:22   until the *A* of Days came

ANDREW*

    Apostle; brother of Simon Peter (Mt 4:18; 10:2; Mk 1:16–18, 29; 3:18; 13:3; Lk 6:14; Jn 1:35–44; 6:8–9; 12:22; Ac 1:13).

ANGEL (ANGELS ARCHANGEL)

Ge 16: 7   The *a* of the Lᴏʀᴅ found Hagar
        22:11   But the *a* of the Lᴏʀᴅ called out
Ex 23:20   I am sending an *a* ahead of you
Nu 22:23   When the donkey saw the *a*
Jdg   2: 1   The *a* of the Lᴏʀᴅ went up
        6:22   Gideon realized that it was the *a*
        13:15   Manoah said to the *a* of the Lᴏʀᴅ
2Sa 24:16   The *a* of the Lᴏʀᴅ was then
1Ki 19: 7   The *a* of the Lᴏʀᴅ came back
2Ki 19:35   That night the *a* of the Lᴏʀᴅ went
Ps 34: 7   The *a* of the Lᴏʀᴅ encamps
Hos 12: 4   He struggled with the *a*
Mt   2:13   an *a* of the Lord appeared
        28: 2   for an *a* of the Lord came
Lk   1:26   God sent the *a* Gabriel

Lk   2: 9   An *a* of the Lord appeared to
             them,
        22:43   An *a* from heaven appeared to
             him
Ac   6:15   his face was like the face of an *a*.
        12: 7   Suddenly an *a* of the Lord
2Co 11:14   Satan himself masquerades as
             an *a*
Gal   1: 8   or an *a* from heaven should
             preach

ANGELS (ANGEL)

Ps 91:11   command his *a* concerning you
Mt   4: 6   command his *a* concerning you,
        13:39   of the age, and the harvesters
             are *a*.
        13:49   The *a* will come and separate
        18:10   For I tell you that their *a*
        25:41   prepared for the devil and his *a*.
Lk   4:10   command his *a* concerning you
        20:36   for they are like the *a*.
1Co   6: 3   you not know that we will
             judge *a*?
        13: 1   in the tongues of men and of *a*,
Col   2:18   and the worship of *a* disqualify
             you
Heb   1: 4   as much superior to the *a*
        1: 6   "Let all God's *a* worship him."
        1: 7   "He makes his *a* winds,
        1:14   Are not all *a* ministering spirits
        2: 7   made him a little lower than
             the *a*;
        2: 9   was made a little lower than
             the *a*,
        13: 2   some people have entertained *a*
1Pe   1:12   Even *a* long to look
2Pe   2: 4   For if God did not spare *a*
Jude   6   *a* who did not keep their positions

ANGER (ANGERED ANGRY)

Ex 15: 7   You unleashed your burning *a*;
        22:24   My *a* will be aroused, and I will
             kill
        32:10   alone so that my *a* may burn
        32:11   "why should your *a* burn
        32:12   Turn from your fierce *a*; relent
        32:19   his *a* burned and he threw
        34: 6   slow to *a*, abounding in love
Lev 26:28   then in my *a* I will be hostile
Nu 14:18   slow to *a*, abounding in love
        25:11   has turned my *a* away
        32:10   Lᴏʀᴅ's *a* was aroused that day
        32:13   The Lᴏʀᴅ's *a* burned
Dt   9:19   I feared the *a* and wrath
        29:28   In furious *a* and in great wrath
Jdg 14:19   Burning with *a*, he went up
2Sa 12: 5   David burned with *a*
2Ki 22:13   Great is the Lᴏʀᴅ's *a* that burns
Ne   9:17   slow to *a* and abounding in love.
Ps 30: 5   For his *a* lasts only a moment,
        78:38   Time after time he restrained
             his *a*
        86:15   slow to *a*, abounding in love
        90: 7   We are consumed by your *a*
       103: 8   slow to *a*, abounding in love.
Pr 15: 1   but a harsh word stirs up *a*.
        29:11   A fool gives full vent to his *a*,
        30:33   so stirring up *a* produces strife."
Jnh   4: 2   slow to *a* and abounding in love,
Eph   4:26   "In your *a* do not sin": Do not let
Jas   1:20   for man's *a* does not bring about

ANGERED (ANGER)

Pr 22:24   do not associate with one easily *a*,
1Co 13: 5   it is not easily *a*, it keeps no
             record

ANGRY (ANGER)

Ps   2:12   Kiss the Son, lest he be *a*
        95:10   For forty years I was *a*
Pr 29:22   An *a* man stirs up dissension,
Mt   5:22   But I tell you that anyone who is *a*
Jas   1:19   slow to speak and slow to
             become *a*

ANGUISH

Ps 118: 5   In my *a* I cried to the Lᴏʀᴅ,
Jer   4:19   Oh, my *a*, my *a*!
Zep   1:15   a day of distress and *a*,
Lk 21:25   nations will be in *a* and perplexity
        22:44   in *a*, he prayed more earnestly,
Ro   9: 2   and unceasing *a* in my heart.

ANIMALS
Ge 1:24 wild *a*, each according to its kind."
7:16 The *a* going in were male
Dt 14:4 These are the *a* you may eat: the ox
Job 12:7 ask the *a*, and they will teach you,
Isa 43:20 The wild *a* honor me,

ANNOUNCE (ANNOUNCED)
Mt 6:2 give to the needy, do not *a* it

ANNOUNCED (ANNOUNCE)
Isa 48:5 before they happened I *a* them
Gal 3:8 and *a* the gospel in advance

ANNOYANCE*
Pr 12:16 A fool shows his *a* at once,

ANNUAL*
Ex 30:10 This *a* atonement must be made
Jdg 21:19 there is a festival of the LORD
1Sa 1:21 family to offer the *a* sacrifice
2:19 husband to offer the *a* sacrifice.
20:6 an *a* sacrifice is being made there
2Ch 8:13 New Moons and the three *a* feasts
Heb 10:3 those sacrifices are an *a* reminder

ANOINT (ANOINTED ANOINTING)
Ex 30:26 use it to *a* the Tent of Meeting,
30:30 "A Aaron and his sons
1Sa 9:16 A him leader over my people Israel
15:1 to *a* you king over his people Israel;
2Ki 9:3 what the LORD says: I *a* you king
Ps 23:5 You *a* my head with oil;
Da 9:24 prophecy and to *a* the most holy.
Jas 5:14 and *a* him with oil in the name

ANOINTED (ANOINT)
1Ch 16:22 "Do not touch my *a* ones;
Ps 105:15 "Do not touch my *a* ones;
Isa 61:1 because the LORD has *a* me
Da 9:26 the A One will be cut off
Lk 4:18 because he has *a* me
Ac 10:38 how God *a* Jesus of Nazareth

ANOINTING (ANOINT)
Lev 8:12 some of the *a* oil on Aaron's head
1Ch 29:22 *a* him before the LORD to be ruler
Ps 45:7 by *a* you with the oil of joy.
Heb 1:9 by *a* you with the oil of joy."
1Jn 2:20 you have an *a* from the Holy One,
2:27 about all things and as that *a* is real,

ANT* (ANTS)
Pr 6:6 Go to the *a*, you sluggard;

ANTICHRIST* (ANTICHRISTS)
1Jn 2:18 have heard that the *a* is coming,
2:22 a man is the *a*— he denies
4:3 of the *a*, which you have heard is
2Jn :7 person is the deceiver and the *a*.

ANTICHRISTS* (ANTICHRIST)
1Jn 2:18 even now many *a* have come.

ANTIOCH
Ac 11:26 were called Christians first at A.

ANTS* (ANT)
Pr 30:25 A are creatures of little strength,

ANXIETIES* (ANXIOUS)
Lk 21:34 drunkenness and the *a* of life,

ANXIETY (ANXIOUS)
1Pe 5:7 Cast all your *a* on him

ANXIOUS (ANXIETIES ANXIETY)
Pr 12:25 An *a* heart weighs a man down,
Php 4:6 Do not be *a* about anything,

APOLLOS*
Christian from Alexandria, learned in the Scriptures; instructed by Aquila and Priscilla (Ac 18:24–28). Ministered at Corinth (Ac 19:1; 1Co 1:12; 3; Tit 3:13).

APOLLYON*
Rev 9:11 is Abaddon, and in Greek, A.

APOSTLE (APOSTLES APOSTLES')
Ro 11:13 as I am the *a* to the Gentiles,
1Co 9:1 Am I not an *a*? Have I not seen
2Co 12:12 The things that mark an *a*— signs,
Gal 2:8 of Peter as an *a* to the Jews,
1Ti 2:7 was appointed a herald and an *a*—
2Ti 1:11 I was appointed a herald and an *a*

Heb 3:1 *a* and high priest whom we confess.

APOSTLES (APOSTLE)
See also Andrew, Bartholomew, James, John, Judas, Matthew, Matthias, Nathanael, Paul, Peter, Philip, Simon, Thaddaeus, Thomas.
Mk 3:14 twelve—designating them *a*—
Lk 11:49 'I will send them prophets and *a*,
Ac 1:26 so he was added to the eleven *a*.
2:43 signs were done by the *a*.
1Co 12:28 God has appointed first of all *a*,
15:9 For I am the least of the *a*
2Co 11:5 masquerading as *a* of Christ.
Eph 2:20 built on the foundation of the *a*
4:11 It was he who gave some to be *a*,
Rev 21:14 names of the twelve *a* of the Lamb.

APOSTLES' (APOSTLE)
Ac 5:2 the rest and put it at the *a'* feet.
8:18 at the laying on of the *a'* hands,

APPEAL
Ac 25:11 I *a* to Caesar!" After Festus had
Phm :9 yet I *a* to you on the basis of love.

APPEAR (APPEARANCE APPEARANCES APPEARED APPEARING APPEARS)
Ge 1:9 to one place, and let dry ground *a*."
Lev 16:2 I *a* in the cloud over the atonement
Mt 24:30 of the Son of Man will *a* in the sky,
Mk 13:22 false prophets will *a* and perform
Lk 19:11 of God was going to *a* at once.
2Co 5:10 we must all *a* before the judgment
Col 3:4 also will *a* with him in glory.
Heb 9:24 now to *a* for us in God's presence.
9:28 and he will *a* a second time,

APPEARANCE (APPEAR)
1Sa 16:7 Man looks at the outward *a*,
Isa 52:14 his *a* was so disfigured beyond that
53:2 in his *a* that we should desire him.
Gal 2:6 God does not judge by external *a*—

APPEARANCES* (APPEAR)
Jn 7:24 Stop judging by mere *a*,

APPEARED (APPEAR)
Nu 14:10 glory of the LORD *a* at the Tent
Mt 1:20 an angel of the Lord *a* to him
Lk 2:9 An angel of the Lord *a* to them,
1Co 15:5 and that he *a* to Peter,
Heb 9:26 now he has *a* once for all at the end

APPEARING (APPEAR)
1Ti 6:14 until the *a* of our Lord Jesus Christ,
2Ti 1:10 through the *a* of our Savior,
4:8 to all who have longed for his *a*.
Tit 2:13 the glorious *a* of our great God

APPEARS (APPEAR)
Mal 3:2 Who can stand when he *a*?
Col 3:4 When Christ, who is your life, *a*,
1Pe 5:4 And when the Chief Shepherd *a*,
1Jn 3:2 But we know that when he *a*,

APPETITE
Pr 16:26 The laborer's *a* works for him;
Ecc 6:7 yet his *a* is never satisfied.
Jer 50:19 his *a* will be satisfied

APPLES
Pr 25:11 is like *a* of gold in settings of silver.

APPLY (APPLYING)
Pr 22:17 *a* your heart to what I teach,
23:12 A your heart to instruction

APPLYING (APPLY)
Pr 2:2 and *a* your heart to understanding,

APPOINT (APPOINTED)
Ps 61:7 *a* your love and faithfulness
1Th 5:9 For God did not *a* us
Tit 1:5 and *a* elders in every town,

APPOINTED (APPOINT)
Dt 1:15 *a* them to have authority over you
Pr 8:23 I was *a* from eternity,
Da 11:27 an end will still come at the *a* time.

Hab 2:3 For the revelation awaits an *a* time;
Jn 15:16 Chose you and *a* you to go
Ro 9:9 "At the *a* time I will return,

APPROACH (APPROACHING)
Ex 24:2 but Moses alone is to *a* the LORD;
Eph 3:12 in him we may *a* God with freedom
Heb 4:16 Let us then *a* the throne of grace

APPROACHING (APPROACH)
Heb 10:25 all the more as you see the Day *a*.
1Jn 5:14 is the confidence we have in *a* God:

APPROPRIATE
1Ti 2:10 *a* for women who profess

APPROVAL (APPROVE)
Jdg 18:6 Your journey has the LORD's *a*."
Jn 6:27 the Father has placed his seal of *a*."
1Co 11:19 to show which of you have God's *a*
Gal 1:10 trying to win the *a* of men,

APPROVE (APPROVAL APPROVED APPROVES)
Ro 2:18 if you know his will and *a*
12:2 and *a* what God's will is—

APPROVED* (APPROVE)
Ro 14:18 pleasing to God and *a* by men.
16:10 Greet Apelles, tested and *a*
2Co 10:18 who commends himself who is *a*,
1Th 2:4 as men *a* by God to be entrusted
2Ti 2:15 to present yourself to God as one *a*,

APPROVES* (APPROVE)
Ro 14:22 not condemn himself by what he *a*.

APT*
Pr 15:23 A man finds joy in giving an *a* reply

AQUILA*
Husband of Priscilla; co-worker with Paul, instructor of Apollos (Ac 18; Ro 16:3; 1Co 16:19; 2Ti 4:19).

ARABIA
Gal 1:17 but I went immediately into A
4:25 Hagar stands for Mount Sinai in A

ARARAT
Ge 8:4 came to rest on the mountains of A.

ARAUNAH
2Sa 24:16 threshing floor of A the Jebusite,

ARBITER* (ARBITRATE)
Lk 12:14 who appointed me a judge or an *a*

ARBITRATE* (ARBITER)
Job 9:33 If only there were someone to *a*

ARCHANGEL* (ANGEL)
1Th 4:16 with the voice of the *a*
Jude :9 *a* Michael, when he was disputing

ARCHER
Pr 26:10 Like an *a* who wounds at random

ARCHIPPUS*
Col 4:17 Tell A: "See to it that you complete
Phm :2 to A our fellow soldier

ARCHITECT*
Heb 11:10 whose *a* and builder is God.

AREOPAGUS*
Ac 17:19 brought him to a meeting of the A,
17:22 up in the meeting of the A
17:34 of the A, also a woman named

ARGUE (ARGUMENT ARGUMENTS)
Job 13:3 and to *a* my case with God.
13:8 Will you *a* the case for God?
Pr 25:9 If you *a* your case with a neighbor,

ARGUMENT (ARGUE)
Heb 6:16 is said and puts an end to all *a*.

ARGUMENTS (ARGUE)
Isa 41:21 "Set forth your *a*," says Jacob's
Col 2:4 you by fine-sounding *a*.
2Ti 2:23 to do with foolish and stupid *a*,
Tit 3:9 and *a* and quarrels about the law,

ARK
Ge 6:14 So make yourself an *a*

Ex 25:21 and put in the *a* the Testimony,
Dt 10: 5 put the tablets in the *a* I had made,
1Sa 4:11 The *a* of God was captured,
7: 2 that the *a* remained at Kiriath
2Sa 6:17 They brought the *a* of the LORD
1Ki 8: 9 There was nothing in the *a*
1Ch 13: 9 out his hand to steady the *a*,
2Ch 35: 3 "Put the sacred *a* in the temple that
Heb 9: 4 This *a* contained the gold jar
11: 7 in holy fear built an *a*
Rev 11:19 within his temple was seen the *a*

ARM (ARMY)
Nu 11:23 "Is the LORD's *a* too short?
Dt 4:34 hand and an outstretched *a*,
7:19 mighty hand and outstretched *a*,
Ps 44: 3 it was your right hand, your *a*,
98: 1 his right hand and his holy *a*
Jer 27: 5 outstretched *a* I made the earth
1Pe 4: 1 *a* yourselves also with the same

ARMAGEDDON*
Rev 16:16 that in Hebrew is called *A.*

ARMIES (ARMY)
1Sa 17:26 Philistine that he should defy the *a*
Rev 19:14 *a* of heaven were following him,

ARMOR (ARMY)
1Ki 20:11 on his *a* should not boast like one
Jer 46: 4 put on your *a!*
Ro 13:12 deeds of darkness and put on the *a*
Eph 6:11 Put on the full *a* of God
6:13 Therefore put on the full *a* of God,

ARMS (ARMY)
Dt 33:27 underneath are the everlasting *a.*
Ps 18:32 It is God who *a* me with strength
Pr 31:17 her *a* are strong for her tasks.
31:20 She opens her *a* to the poor
Isa 40:11 He gathers the lambs in his *a*
Mk 10:16 And he took the children in his *a*,
Heb 12:12 strengthen your feeble *a*

ARMY (ARM ARMIES ARMOR ARMS)
Ps 33:16 No king is saved by the size of his *a*
Joel 2: 2 a large and mighty *a* comes,
2: 5 like a mighty *a* drawn up for battle.
2:11 thunders at the head of his *a;*
Rev 19:19 the rider on the horse and his *a.*

AROMA
Ge 8:21 The LORD smelled the pleasing *a*
Ex 29:18 a pleasing *a*, an offering made
Lev 2: 9 made by fire, a pleasing *a.*
2Co 2:15 For we are to God the *a* of Christ

AROUSE (AROUSED)
Ro 11:14 I may somehow *a* my own people

AROUSED (AROUSE)
Ps 78:58 they *a* his jealousy with their idols.

ARRANGED
1Co 12:18 But in fact God has *a* the parts

ARRAYED*
Ps 110: 3 *A* in holy majesty,
Isa 61:10 and *a* me in a robe of righteousness

ARREST
Mt 10:19 But when they *a* you, do not worry

ARROGANCE (ARROGANT)
1Sa 2: 3 or let your mouth speak such *a*,
Pr 8:13 I hate pride and *a*,
Mk 7:22 lewdness, envy, slander, *a* and folly
2Co 12:20 slander, gossip, *a* and disorder.

ARROGANT (ARROGANCE)
Ps 5: 5 The *a* cannot stand
119:78 May the *a* be put to shame
Pr 1: 7 *A* lips are unsuited to a fool—
21:24 *a* man—"Mocker" is his name;
Ro 1:30 God-haters, insolent, *a*
11:20 Do not be *a*, but be afraid.
1Ti 6:17 in this present world not to be *a*

ARROW (ARROWS)
Ps 91: 5 nor the *a* that flies by day,

Pr 25:18 Like a club or a sword or a sharp *a*

ARROWS (ARROW)
Ps 64: 3 and aim their words like deadly *a.*
64: 7 But God will shoot them with *a;*
127: 4 Like *a* in the hands of a warrior
Pr 26:18 firebrands or deadly *a*
Eph 6:16 you can extinguish all the flaming *a*

ARTAXERXES
King of Persia; allowed rebuilding of temple under Ezra (Ezr 4: 7), and of walls of Jerusalem under his cupbearer Nehemiah (Ne 2; 5:14; 13:6).

ARTEMIS
Ac 19:28 "Great is *A* of the Ephesians!"

ASA
King of Judah (1Ki 15:8–24; 1Ch 3:10; 2Ch 14–16). Godly reformer (2Ch 15); in later years defeated Israel with help of Aram, not the LORD (1Ki 15:16–22; 2Ch 16).

ASAHEL
1. Nephew of David, one of his warriors (2Sa 23:24; 1Ch 2:16; 11:26; 27:7). Killed by Abner (2Sa 2); avenged by Joab (2Sa 3:22–39).
2. Levite; teacher (2Ch 17:8).

ASAPH
1. Recorder to Hezekiah (2Ki 18:18, 37; Isa 36:3, 22).
2. Levitical musician (1Ch 6:39; 15:17–19; 16:4–7, 37). Sons of (1Ch 25; 2Ch 5:12; 20:14; 29:13; 35:15; Ezr 2:41; 3:10; Ne 7:44; 11:17; 12:27–47). Psalms of (2Ch 29:30; Ps 50; 73–83).

ASCEND* (ASCENDED ASCENDING)
Dt 30:12 "Who will *a* into heaven to get it
Ps 24: 3 Who may *a* the hill of the LORD?
Isa 14:13 "I will *a* to heaven;
14:14 I will *a* above the tops of the clouds
Jn 6:62 of Man *a* to where he was before!
Ac 2:34 For David did not *a* to heaven,
Ro 10: 6 'Who will *a* into heaven?' " (that is,

ASCENDED (ASCEND)
Ps 68:18 When you *a* on high,
Eph 4: 8 "When he *a* on high,

ASCENDING (ASCEND)
Ge 28:12 and the angels of God were *a*
Jn 1:51 and the angels of God *a*

ASCRIBE*
1Ch 16:28 *A* to the LORD, O families
16:28 *a* to the LORD glory and strength,
16:29 *a* to the LORD the glory due his
Job 36: 3 I will *a* justice to my Maker.
Ps 29: 1 *A* to the LORD, O mighty ones,
29: 1 *a* to the LORD glory and strength.
29: 2 *a* to the LORD the glory due his
96: 7 *A* to the LORD, O families
96: 7 *a* to the LORD glory and strength.
96: 8 *a* to the LORD the glory due his

ASHAMED (SHAME)
Mk 8:38 If anyone is *a* of me and my words
Lk 9:26 If anyone is *a* of me and my words,
Ro 1:16 I am not *a* of the gospel.
2Ti 1: 8 So do not be *a* to testify about our
2:15 who does not need to be *a*

ASHER
Son of Jacob by Zilpah (Ge 30:13; 35:26; 46:17; Ex 1:4; 1Ch 2:2). Tribe of blessed (Ge 49:20; Dt 33:24–25), numbered (Nu 1:40–41; 26:44–47), allotted land (Jos 10:24–31; Eze 48:2), failed to fully possess (Jdg 1:31–32), failed to support Deborah (Jdg 5:17), supported Gideon (Jdg 6:35; 7:23) and David (1Ch 12:36), 12,000 from (Rev 7:6).

ASHERAH (ASHERAHS)
Ex 34:13 and cut down their *A* poles.
1Ki 18:19 the four hundred prophets of *A,*

ASHERAHS* (ASHERAH)
Jdg 3: 7 and served the Baals and the *A.*

ASHES
Job 42: 6 and repent in dust and *a."*
Mt 11:21 ago in sackcloth and *a.*

ASHTORETHS
Jdg 2:13 and served Baal and the *A.*

1Sa 7: 4 put away their Baals and *A,*

ASLEEP (SLEEP)
1Co 15:18 who have fallen *a* in Christ are lost.
1Th 4:13 be ignorant about those who fall *a*,

ASSEMBLY
Ps 1: 5 nor sinners in the *a* of the righteous
35:18 I will give you thanks in the great *a*
82: 1 God presides in the great *a;*
149: 1 his praise in the *a* of the saints.

ASSIGNED
1Ki 7:14 and did all the work *a* to him.
Mk 13:34 with his *a* task, and tells the one
1Co 3: 5 as the Lord has *a* to each his task.
7:17 place in life that the Lord *a* to him
2Co 10:13 to the field God has *a* to us,

ASSOCIATE
Pr 22:24 do not *a* with one easily angered,
Jn 4: 9 (For Jews do not *a* with Samaritans
Ac 10:28 law for a Jew to *a* with a Gentile
Ro 12:16 but be willing to *a* with people
1Co 5: 9 to *a* with sexually immoral people
5:11 am writing you that you must not *a*
2Th 3:14 Do not *a* with him,

ASSURANCE (ASSURED)
Heb 10:22 with a sincere heart in full *a* of faith

ASSURED (ASSURANCE)
Col 4:12 the will of God, mature and fully *a.*

ASTRAY
Ps 119:67 Before I was afflicted I went *a*,
Pr 10:17 ignores correction leads others *a*.
20: 1 whoever is led *a* by them is not
Isa 53: 6 We all, like sheep, have gone *a*,
Jer 50: 6 their shepherds have led them *a*
Jn 16: 1 you so that you will not go *a*.
1Pe 2:25 For you were like sheep going *a*,
1Jn 3: 7 do not let anyone lead you *a*.

ASTROLOGERS
Isa 47:13 Let your *a* come forward,
Da 2: 2 *a* to tell him what he had dreamed.

ATE (EAT)
Ge 3: 6 wisdom, she took some and *a* it.
27:25 Jacob brought it to him and he *a;*
2Sa 9:11 Mephibosheth *a* at David's table
Ps 78:25 Men *a* the bread of angels;
Jer 15:16 When your words came, I *a* them;
Eze 3: 3 So I *a* it, and it tasted as sweet
Mt 14:20 They all *a* and were satisfied,
15:37 They all *a* and were satisfied.
Mk 6:42 They all *a* and were satisfied.
Lk 9:17 They all *a* and were satisfied,

ATHALIAH
Granddaughter of Omri; wife of Jehoram and mother of Ahaziah; encouraged their evil ways (2Ki 8:18, 27; 2Ch 22:2). At death of Ahaziah she made herself queen, killing all his sons but Joash (2Ki 11:1–3; 2Ch 22:10–12); killed six years later when Joash was revealed (2Ki 11:4–16; 2Ch 23:1–15).

ATHLETE*
2Ti 2: 5 if anyone competes as an *a*,

ATONE* (ATONEMENT)
Ex 30:15 to the LORD to *a* for your lives.
2Ch 29:24 for a sin offering to *a* for all Israel,
Da 9:24 an end to sin, to *a* for wickedness,

ATONED* (ATONEMENT)
Dt 21: 8 And the bloodshed will be *a* for.
1Sa 3:14 guilt of Eli's house will never be *a*
Pr 16: 6 faithfulness sin is *a* for;
Isa 6: 7 guilt is taken away and your sin *a*
22:14 your dying day this sin will not be *a*
27: 9 then, will Jacob's guilt be *a* for,

ATONEMENT (ATONE ATONED)
Ex 25:17 "Make an *a* cover of pure gold—
30:10 Once a year Aaron shall make *a*
Lev 17:11 it is the blood that makes *a*

Lev 23:27 this seventh month is the Day of A.
Nu 25:13 and made a for the Israelites."
Ro 3:25 presented him as a sacrifice of a,
Heb 2:17 that he might make a for the sins

ATTACK
Ps 109: 3 they a me without cause.

ATTAINED
Php 3:16 up to what we have already a.
Heb 7:11 If perfection could have been a

ATTENTION (ATTENTIVE)
Pr 4: 1 pay a and gain understanding.
4:20 My son, pay a to what I say;
5: 1 My son, pay a to my wisdom,
7:24 pay a to what I say.
22:17 Pay a and listen to the sayings
Ecc 7:21 Do not pay a to every word people
Isa 42:20 many things, but have paid no a;
Tit 1:14 and will pay no a to Jewish myths
Heb 2: 1 We must pay more careful a,

ATTENTIVE (ATTENTION)
Ne 1:11 let your ear be a to the prayer
1Pe 3:12 and his ears are a to their prayer,

ATTITUDE (ATTITUDES)
Eph 4:23 new in the a of your minds;
Php 2: 5 Your a should be the same
1Pe 4: 1 yourselves also with the same a,

ATTITUDES (ATTITUDE)
Heb 4:12 it judges the thoughts and a

ATTRACTIVE
Tit 2:10 teaching about God our Savior a.

AUDIENCE
Pr 29:26 Many seek an a with a ruler,

AUTHORITIES (AUTHORITY)
Ro 13: 1 a that exist have been established
13: 5 it is necessary to submit to the a,
13: 6 for the a are God's servants,
Eph 3:10 and a in the heavenly realms,
6:12 but against the rulers, against the a,
Col 1:16 thrones or powers or rulers or a;
2:15 having disarmed the powers and a,
Tit 3: 1 people to be subject to rulers and a,
1Pe 3:22 a and powers in submission to him.

AUTHORITY (AUTHORITIES)
Mt 7:29 because he taught as one who had a
9: 6 the Son of Man has a on earth
28:18 "All a in heaven and on earth has
Mk 1:22 he taught them as one who had a,
2:10 the Son of Man has a on earth
Lk 4:32 because his message had a.
5:24 the Son of Man has a on earth
Jn 10:18 a to lay it down and a
Ac 1: 7 the Father has set by his own a.
Ro 7: 1 that the law has a over a man only
13: 1 for there is no a except that which
13: 2 rebels against the a is rebelling
1Co 11:10 to have a sign of a on her head.
15:24 he has destroyed all dominion, a
1Ti 2: 2 for kings and all those in a,
2:12 to teach or to have a over a man;
Tit 2:15 Encourage and rebuke with all a.
Heb 13:17 your leaders and submit to their a.

AUTUMN*
Dt 11:14 both a and spring rains,
Ps 84: 6 the a rains also cover it with pools.
Jer 5:24 who gives a and spring rains
Joel 2:23 both a and spring rains, as before.
Jas 5: 7 and how patient he is for the a
Jude :12 blown along by the wind; a trees,

AVENGE (VENGEANCE)
Lev 26:25 sword upon you to a the breaking
Dt 32:35 It is mine to a; I will repay.
32:43 for he will a the blood
Ro 12:19 "It is mine to a; I will repay,"
Heb 10:30 "It is mine to a; I will repay,"
Rev 6:10 of the earth and a our blood?"

AVENGER (VENGEANCE)
Nu 35:27 the a of blood may kill the accused
Jos 20: 3 find protection from the a of blood.
Ps 8: 2 to silence the foe and the a.

AVENGES (VENGEANCE)
Ps 94: 1 O LORD, the God who a,

AVENGING (VENGEANCE)
1Sa 25:26 and from a yourself with your own
Na 1: 2 The LORD is a jealous and a God;

AVOID (AVOIDS)
Pr 4:15 A it, do not travel on it;
20: 3 It is to a man's honor to a strife,
20:19 so a a man who talks too much.
Ecc 7:18 who fears God will a all extremes.
1Th 4: 3 you should a sexual immorality;
5:22 A every kind of evil.
2Ti 2:16 A godless chatter, because those
Tit 3: 9 But a foolish controversies

AVOIDS* (AVOID)
Pr 16: 6 of the LORD a man a evil.
16:17 The highway of the upright a evil;

AWAITS (WAIT)
Pr 15:10 Stern discipline a him who leaves
28:22 and is unaware that poverty a him.

AWAKE (WAKE)
Ps 17:15 when I a, I will be satisfied
Pr 6:22 when you a, they will speak to you.

AWARD*
2Ti 4: 8 will a to me on that day—

AWARE
Ex 34:29 he was not a that his face was
Mt 24:50 and at an hour he is not a of.
Lk 12:46 and at an hour he is not a of.

AWE* (AWESOME OVERAWED)
1Sa 12:18 So all the people stood in a
1Ki 3:28 they held the king in a,
Job 25: 2 "Dominion and a belong to God;
Ps 119:120 I stand in a of your laws.
Ecc 5: 7 Therefore stand in a of God.
Isa 29:23 will stand in a of the God of Israel.
Jer 2:19 and have no a of me,"
33: 9 they will be in a and will tremble
Hab 3: 2 I stand in a of your deeds,
Mal 2: 5 and stood in a of my name.
Mt 9: 8 they were filled with a;
Lk 1:65 The neighbors were all filled with a
5:26 They were filled with a and said,
7:16 They were all filled with a
Ac 2:43 Everyone was filled with a,
Heb 12:28 acceptably with reverence and a,

AWESOME* (AWE)
Ge 28:17 and said, "How a is this place!
Ex 15:11 a in glory,
34:10 among will see how a is the work
Dt 4:34 or by great and a deeds,
7:21 is among you, is a great and a God.
10:17 the great God, mighty and a,
10:21 and a wonders you saw
28:58 revere this glorious and a name—
34:12 performed the a deeds that Moses
Jdg 13: 6 like an angel of God, very a.
2Sa 7:23 a wonders by driving out nations
1Ch 17:21 a wonders by driving out nations
Ne 1: 5 of heaven, the great and a God,
4:14 and a, and fight for your brothers,
9:32 the great, mighty and a God,
Job 10:16 again display your a power
37:22 God comes in a majesty.
Ps 45: 4 let your right hand display a deeds.
47: 2 How a is the LORD Most High,
65: 5 us with a deeds of righteousness,
66: 3 to God, "How a are your deeds!
66: 5 how a his works in man's behalf!
68:35 You are a, O God,
89: 7 he is more a than all who surround
99: 3 praise your great and a name—
106:22 and a deeds by the Red Sea.

Ps 111: 9 holy and a is his name.
145: 6 of the power of your a works,
Isa 64: 3 when you did a things that we did
Eze 1:18 Their rims were high and a,
1:22 expanse, sparkling like ice, and a.
Da 2:31 dazzling statue, a in appearance.
9: 4 "O Lord, the great and a God,
Zep 2:11 The LORD will be a to them

AX
Mt 3:10 The a is already at the root
Lk 3: 9 The a is already at the root

BAAL
Jdg 6:25 Tear down your father's altar to B
1Ki 16:32 B in the temple of B that he built
18:25 Elijah said to the prophets of B,
19:18 knees have not bowed down to B
2Ki 10:28 Jehu destroyed B worship in Israel.
Jer 19: 5 places of B to burn their sons
Ro 11: 4 have not bowed the knee to B."

BAASHA
King of Israel (1Ki 15:16–16:7; 2Ch 16:1–6).

BABBLER* (BABBLING)
Ac 17:18 "What is this b trying to say?"

BABBLING* (BABBLER)
Mt 6: 7 do not keep on b like pagans,

BABIES* (BABY)
Ge 25:22 The b jostled each other within her
Ex 2: 6 "This is one of the Hebrew b,"
Lk 18:15 also bringing b to Jesus
Ac 7:19 them to throw out their newborn b
1Pe 2: 2 Like newborn b, crave pure

BABY* (BABIES BABY'S)
Ex 2: 6 She opened it and saw the b.
2: 7 women to nurse the b for you?"
2: 9 So the woman took the b
2: 9 "Take this b and nurse him for me,
1Ki 3:17 I had a b while she was living
3:18 was born, this woman also had a b.
3:26 give her the living b! Don't kill him
3:27 Give the living b to the first woman
Isa 49:15 "Can a mother forget the b
Lk 1:41 the b leaped in her womb,
1:44 the b in my womb leaped for joy.
1:57 time for Elizabeth to have her b,
2: 6 the time came for the b to be born,
2:12 You will find a b wrapped in strips
2:16 the b, who was lying in the manger.
Jn 16:21 but when her b is born she forgets

BABY'S* (BABY)
Ex 2: 8 the girl went and got the b mother.

BABYLON
Ps 137: 1 By the rivers of B we sat and wept
Jer 29:10 seventy years are completed for B.
51:37 B will be a heap of ruins,
Rev 14: 8 "Fallen! Fallen is B the Great,
17: 5 MYSTERY B THE GREAT

BACKS
2Pe 2:21 and then to turn their b

BACKSLIDING* (BACKSLIDINGS)
Jer 2:19 your b will rebuke you.
3:22 I will cure you of b."
14: 7 For our b is great;
15: 6 "You keep on b.
Eze 37:23 them from all their sinful b,

BACKSLIDINGS* (BACKSLIDING)
Jer 5: 6 and their b many.

BALAAM
Prophet who attempted to curse Israel (Nu 22–24; Dt 23:4–5; 2Pe 2:15; Jude 11). Killed in Israel's vengeance on Midianites (Nu 31:8; Jos 13:22).

BALAK
Moabite king who hired Balaam to curse Israel (Nu 22–24; Jos 24:9).

BALDHEAD
2Ki 2:23 "Go on up, you *b!*" they said.

BALM
Jer 8:22 Is there no *b* in Gilead?

BANISH (BANISHED)
Jer 25:10 I will *b* from them the sounds of joy

BANISHED (BANISH)
Dt 30:4 Even if you have been *b*

BANNER
Ex 17:15 and called it The LORD is my *B.*
SS 2:4 and his *b* over me is love.
Isa 11:10 the Root of Jesse will stand as a *b*

BANQUET
SS 2:4 He has taken me to the *b* hall,
Lk 14:13 when you give a *b,* invite the poor,

BAPTISM* (BAPTIZE)
Mt 21:25 John's *b*— where did it come from?
Mk 1:4 and preaching a *b* of repentance
 10:38 baptized with the *b* I am baptized
 10:39 baptized with the *b* I am baptized
 11:30 John's *b*— was it from heaven,
Lk 3:3 preaching a *b* of repentance
 12:50 But I have a *b* to undergo,
 20:4 John's *b*— was it from heaven,
Ac 1:22 beginning from John's *b*
 10:37 after the *b* that John preached—
 13:24 and *b* to all the people of Israel.
 18:25 though he knew only the *b* of John.
 19:3 did you receive?" "John's *b,*"
 19:3 "Then what *b* did you receive?"
 19:4 "John's *b* was a *b* of repentance.
Ro 6:4 with him through *b* into death
Eph 4:5 one Lord, one faith, one *b;*
Col 2:12 having been buried with him in *b*
1Pe 3:21 this water symbolizes *b* that now

BAPTISMS* (BAPTIZE)
Heb 6:2 instruction about *b,* the laying

BAPTIZE* (BAPTISM BAPTISMS BAPTIZED BAPTIZING)
Mt 3:11 He will *b* you with the Holy Spirit
 3:11 "I *b* you with water for repentance.
Mk 1:8 I *b* you with water, but he will
 1:8 he will *b* you with the Holy Spirit."
Lk 3:16 He will *b* you with the Holy Spirit
 3:16 John answered them all, "I *b* you
Jn 1:25 "Why then do you *b*
 1:26 nor the Prophet?" "I *b* with water,"
 1:33 and remain is he who will *b*
 1:33 me to *b* with water told me,
1Co 1:14 I am thankful that I did not *b* any
 1:17 For Christ did not send me to *b,*

BAPTIZED* (BAPTIZE)
Mt 3:6 they were *b* by him in the Jordan
 3:13 to the Jordan to be *b* by John.
 3:14 saying, "I need to be *b* by you,
 3:16 as Jesus was *b,* he went up out
Mk 1:5 they were *b* by him in the Jordan
 1:9 and was *b* by John in the Jordan.
 10:38 or be *b* with the baptism I am
 10:38 with the baptism I am *b* with?"
 10:39 and be *b* with the baptism I am
 10:39 with the baptism I am *b* with,
 16:16 believes and is *b* will be saved,
Lk 3:7 to the crowds coming out to be *b*
 3:12 Tax collectors also came to be *b.*
 3:21 were being *b,* Jesus was *b* too.
 7:29 because they had been *b* by John.
 7:30 they had not been *b* by John.)
Jn 3:22 spent some time with them, and *b.*
 3:23 were constantly coming to be *b.*
 4:2 in fact it was not Jesus who *b,*
Ac 1:5 For John *b* with water,
 1:5 but in a few days you will be *b*
 2:38 Repent and be *b,* every one of you,
 2:41 who accepted his message were *b,*
 8:12 they were *b,* both men and women.
 8:13 Simon himself believed and was *b.*
 8:16 they had simply been *b*

Ac 8:36 Why shouldn't I be *b?*"
 8:38 into the water and Philip *b* him.
 9:18 was *b,* and after taking some food,
 10:47 people from being *b* with water?
 10:48 So he ordered that they be *b*
 11:16 what the Lord had said, 'John *b*
 11:16 you will be *b* with the Holy Spirit.'
 16:15 members of her household were *b,*
 16:33 he and all his family were *b.*
 18:8 heard him believed and were *b.*
 19:5 they were *b* into the name
 22:16 be *b* and wash your sins away,
Ro 6:3 *b* into Christ Jesus were *b*
1Co 1:13 Were you *b* into the name of Paul?
 1:15 so no one can say that you were *b*
 1:16 I also *b* the household of Stephanas
 1:16 I don't remember if I *b* anyone else
 10:2 They were all *b* into Moses
 12:13 For we were all *b* by one Spirit
 15:29 what will those do who are *b*
 15:29 why are people *b* for them?
Gal 3:27 all of you who were *b*

BAPTIZING* (BAPTIZE)
Mt 3:7 coming to where he was *b,*
 28:19 *b* them in the name of the Father
Mk 1:4 *b* in the desert region
Jn 1:28 of the Jordan, where John was *b.*
 1:31 but the reason I came *b*
 3:23 also was *b* at Aenon near Salim,
 3:26 he is *b,* and everyone is going
 4:1 and *b* more disciples than John,
 10:40 to the place where John had been *b*

BAR-JESUS*
Ac 13:6 and false prophet named *B.*

BARABBAS
Mt 27:26 Then he released *B* to them.

BARAK*
Judge who fought with Deborah against Canaanites (Jdg 4–5; 1Sa 12:11; Heb 11:32).

BARBARIAN*
Col 3:11 circumcised or uncircumcised, *b,*

BARBS*
Nu 33:55 allow to remain will become *b*

BARE
Hos 2:3 as *b* as on the day she was born;
Heb 4:13 and laid *b* before the eyes of him

BARNABAS*
Disciple, originally Joseph (Ac 4:36), prophet (Ac 13:1), apostle (Ac 14:14). Brought Paul to apostles (Ac 9:27), Antioch (Ac 11:22–29; Gal 2:1–13), on the first missionary journey (Ac 13–14). Together at Jerusalem Council, they separated over John Mark (Ac 15). Later co-workers (1Co 9:6; Col 4:10).

BARREN
Ge 11:30 Sarai was *b;* she had no children.
 29:31 her womb, but Rachel was *b.*
Ps 113:9 He settles the *b* woman
Isa 54:1 "Sing, O *b* woman,
Lk 1:7 children, because Elizabeth was *b;*
Gal 4:27 "Be glad, O *b* woman,
Heb 11:11 and Sarah herself was *b*—

BARTHOLOMEW*
Apostle (Mt 10:3; Mk 3:18; Lk 6:14; Ac 1:13). Possibly also known as Nathanael (Jn 1:45–49; 21:2).

BARUCH*
Jeremiah's secretary (Jer 32:12–16; 36; 43:1–6; 45:1–2).

BARZILLAI
 1. Gileadite who aided David during Absalom's revolt (2Sa 17:27; 19:31–39).
 2. Son-in-law of 1. (Ezr 2:61; Ne 7:63).

BASHAN
Jos 22:7 Moses had given land in *B,*
Ps 22:12 strong bulls of *B* encircle me.

BASIN
Ex 30:18 "Make a bronze *b,*

BASKET
Ex 2:3 she got a papyrus *b* for him
Ac 9:25 him in a *b* through an opening

2Co 11:33 I was lowered in a *b* from a window

BATCH*
Ro 11:16 then the whole *b* is holy;
1Co 5:6 through the whole *b* of dough?
 5:7 old yeast that you may be a new *b*
Gal 5:9 through the whole *b* of dough."

BATH (BATHING)
Jn 13:10 person who has had a *b* needs only

BATHING (BATH)
2Sa 11:2 From the roof he saw a woman *b.*

BATHSHEBA*
Wife of Uriah who committed adultery with and became wife of David (2Sa 11), mother of Solomon (2Sa 12:24; 1Ki 1–2; 1Ch 3:5).

BATTLE (BATTLES)
1Sa 17:47 for the *b* is the LORD's,
2Ch 20:15 For the *b* is not yours, but God's.
Ps 24:8 the LORD mighty in *b.*
Ecc 9:11 or the *b* to the strong,
Isa 31:4 down to do *b* on Mount Zion
Eze 13:5 in the *b* on the day of the LORD.
Rev 16:14 them for the *b* on the great day
 20:8 and Magog—to gather them for *b.*

BATTLES* (BATTLE)
1Sa 8:20 to go out before us and fight our *b.*"
 18:17 and fight the *b* of the LORD."
 25:28 because he fights the LORD's *b.*
2Ch 32:8 God to help us and to fight our *b.*"

BEAR (BEARING BEARS BIRTH BIRTHRIGHT BORE BORN CHILDBEARING CHILDBIRTH FIRSTBORN NEWBORN REBIRTH)
Ge 4:13 punishment is more than I can *b.*
Ps 38:4 like a burden too heavy to *b.*
Isa 11:7 The cow will feed with the *b,*
 53:11 and he will *b* their iniquities.
Da 7:5 beast, which looked like a *b.*
Mt 7:18 A good tree cannot *b* bad fruit,
Jn 15:2 branch that does *b* fruit he prunes
 15:8 glory, that you *b* much fruit,
 15:16 appointed you to go and *b* fruit—
Ro 7:4 in order that we might *b* fruit
 15:1 ought to *b* with the failings
1Co 10:13 tempted beyond what you can *b.*
Col 3:13 *B* with each other and forgive

BEARD
Lev 19:27 or clip off the edges of your *b.*
Isa 50:6 to those who pulled out my *b;*

BEARING (BEAR)
Eph 4:2 *b* with one another in love.
Col 1:10 *b* fruit in every good work,
Heb 13:13 outside the camp, *b* the disgrace he

BEARS (BEAR)
1Ki 8:43 house I have built *b* your Name.
Ps 68:19 who daily *b* our burdens.

BEAST (BEASTS)
Rev 13:18 him calculate the number of the *b,*
 16:2 people who had the mark of the *b*
 19:20 who had received the mark of the *b*

BEASTS (BEAST)
Da 7:3 Four great *b,* each different
1Co 15:32 If I fought wild *b* in Ephesus

BEAT (BEATEN BEATING BEATINGS)
Isa 2:4 They will *b* their swords
Joel 3:10 *b* your plowshares into swords
Mic 4:3 They will *b* their swords
1Co 9:27 I *b* my body and make it my slave

BEATEN (BEAT)
Lk 12:47 do what his master wants will be *b*
 12:48 deserving punishment will be *b*
2Co 11:25 Three times I was *b* with rods,

BEATING (BEAT)
1Co 9:26 I do not fight like a man *b* the air.
1Pe 2:20 if you receive a *b* for doing wrong

BEATINGS (BEAT)
Pr 19:29 and *b* for the backs of fools.

BEAUTIFUL* (BEAUTY)
Ge 6:2 that the daughters of men were *b,*
 12:11 "I know what a *b* woman you are.

Ge 12:14 saw that she was a very *b* woman.
    24:16 The girl was very *b*, a virgin;
    26: 7 of Rebekah, because she is *b*."
    29:17 Rachel was lovely in form, and *b*.
    49:21 that bears *b* fawns.
Nu 24: 5 "How *b* are your tents, O Jacob,
Dt 21:11 among the captives a *b* woman
Jos   7:21 saw in the plunder a *b* robe
1Sa 25: 3 was an intelligent and *b* woman,
2Sa 11: 2 The woman was very *b*,
    13: 1 the *b* sister of Absalom son
    14:27 and she became a *b* woman.
1Ki   1: 3 throughout Israel for a *b* girl
     1: 4 The girl was very *b*; she took care
Est   2: 2 for *b* young virgins for the king.
     2: 3 realm to bring all these *b* girls
Job 38:31 "Can you bind the *b* Pleiades?
    42:15 land were there found women as *b*
Ps 48: 2 It is *b* in its loftiness,
Pr 11:22 is a *b* woman who shows no
    24: 4 filled with rare and *b* treasures.
Ecc   3:11 He has made everything *b*
SS   1: 8 *Lover* If you do not know, most *b*
     1:10 Your cheeks are *b* with earrings,
     1:15 Oh, how *b!*
     1:15 *Lover* How *b* you are, my darling!
     2:10 my *b* one, and come with me.
     2:13 my *b* one, come with me."
     4: 1 How *b* you are, my darling!
     4: 1 Oh, how *b!*
     4: 7 All *b* you are, my darling;
     5: 9 most *b* of women?
     6: 1 most *b* of women?
     6: 4 *Lover* You are *b*, my darling,
     7: 1 How *b* your sandaled feet,
     7: 6 How *b* you are and how pleasing,
Isa   4: 2 of the LORD will be *b*
    28: 5 a *b* wreath
    52: 7 How *b* on the mountains
Jer   3:19 the most *b* inheritance
     6: 2 so *b* and delicate.
    11:16 with fruit *b* in form.
    46:20 "Egypt is a *b* heifer,
Eze   7:20 They were proud of their *b* jewelry
    16: 7 and became the most *b* of jewels.
    16:12 and a *b* crown on your head.
    16:13 You became very *b* and rose
    20: 6 and honey, the most *b* of all lands.
    20:15 and honey, most *b* of all lands—
    23:42 and *b* crowns on their heads.
    27:24 traded with you *b* garments,
    31: 3 with *b* branches overshadowing
    31: 9 I made it *b*
    33:32 who sings love songs with a *b* voice
Da   4:12 Its leaves were *b*, its fruit abundant
     4:21 with *b* leaves and abundant fruit,
     8: 9 to the east and toward the *B* Land.
    11:16 will establish himself in the *B* Land
    11:41 He will also invade the *B* Land.
    11:45 the seas at the *b* holy mountain.
Zec   9:17 How attractive and *b* they will be!
Mt 23:27 which look *b* on the outside
    26:10 She has done a *b* thing to me.
Mk 14: 6 She has done a *b* thing to me.
Lk 21: 5 temple was adorned with *b* stones
Ac   3: 2 carried to the temple gate called *B*,
     3:10 at the temple gate called *B*,
Ro 10:15 "How *b* are the feet
1Pe   3: 5 in God used to make themselves *b*.

BEAUTY* (BEAUTIFUL)
Est   1:11 order to display her *b* to the people
     2: 3 let *b* treatments be given to them.
     2: 9 her with her *b* treatments
     2:12 months of *b* treatments prescribed
Ps 27: 4 to gaze upon the *b* of the LORD
    37:20 LORD's enemies will be like the *b*
    45:11 The king is enthralled by your *b*;
    50: 2 From Zion, perfect in *b*,
Pr   6:25 lust in your heart after her *b*
    31:30 is deceptive, and *b* is fleeting;

Isa   3:24 instead of *b*, branding.
    28: 1 to the fading flower, his glorious *b*,
    28: 4 That fading flower, his glorious *b*,
    33:17 Your eyes will see the king in his *b*
    53: 2 He had no *b* or majesty
    61: 3 to bestow on them a crown of *b*
La   2:15 the perfection of *b*,
Eze 16:14 had given you made your *b* perfect,
    16:14 the nations on account of your *b*,
    16:15 passed by and your *b* became his.
    16:15 " 'But you trusted in your *b*
    16:25 lofty shrines and degraded your *b*,
    27: 3 "I am perfect in *b*."
    27: 4 your builders brought your *b*
    27:11 they brought your *b* to perfection.
    28: 7 draw their swords against your *b*
    28:12 full of wisdom and perfect in *b*,
    28:17 proud on account of your *b*,
    31: 7 It was majestic in *b*,
    31: 8 could match its *b*.
Jas   1:11 blossom falls and its *b* is destroyed.
1Pe   3: 3 Your *b* should not come
     3: 4 the unfading *b* of a gentle

BED (SICKBED)
Isa 28:20 The *b* is too short to stretch out on,
Lk 11: 7 and my children are with me in *b*.
    17:34 night two people will be in one *b*;
Heb 13: 4 and the marriage *b* kept pure,

BEELZEBUB*
Mt 10:25 of the house has been called *B*,
    12:24 "It is only by *B*, the prince
    12:27 And if I drive out demons by *B*,
Mk   3:22 possessed by *B!* By the prince
Lk 11:15 "By *B*, the prince of demons,
    11:18 claim that I drive out demons by *B*.
    11:19 Now if I drive out demons by *B*,

BEER
Pr 20: 1 Wine is a mocker and *b* a brawler;

BEERSHEBA
Ge 21:14 and wandered in the desert of *B*.
Jdg 20: 1 all the Israelites from Dan to *B*
1Sa   3:20 to *B* recognized that Samuel was
2Sa   3:10 and Judah from Dan to *B*."
    17:11 Let all Israel, from Dan to *B*—
    24: 2 the tribes of Israel from Dan to *B*
    24:15 of the people from Dan to *B* died.
1Ki   4:25 from Dan to *B*, lived in safety,
1Ch 21: 2 count the Israelites from *B* to Dan.
2Ch 30: 5 throughout Israel, from *B* to Dan,

BEFALLS*
Pr 12:21 No harm *b* the righteous,

BEGGING
Ps 37:25 or their children *b* bread.
Ac 16: 9 of Macedonia standing and *b* him,

BEGINNING
Ge   1: 1 In the *b* God created the heavens
Ps 102:25 In the *b* you laid the foundations
 111:10 of the LORD is the *b* of wisdom;
Pr   1: 7 of the LORD is the *b* of knowledge
     9:10 of the LORD is the *b* of wisdom,
Ecc   3:11 fathom what God has done from *b*
Isa 40:21 Has it not been told you from the *b*
    46:10 I make known the end from the *b*,
Mt 24: 8 All these are the *b* of birth pains.
Lk   1: 3 investigated everything from the *b*,
Jn   1: 1 In the *b* was the Word,
1Jn 1: 1 That which was from the *b*,
Rev 21: 6 and the Omega, the *B* and the End.
    22:13 and the Last, the *B* and the End.

BEHAVE (BEHAVIOR)
Ro 13:13 Let us *b* decently, as in the daytime.

BEHAVIOR (BEHAVE)
1Pe   3: 1 without words by the *b* of their wives,
     3:16 maliciously against your good *b*

BEHEMOTH*
Job 40:15 "Look at the *b*,

BELIEVE (BELIEVED BELIEVER BELIEVERS BELIEVES BELIEVING)
Ex   4: 1 "What if they do not *b* me
1Ki 10: 7 I did not *b* these things until I came
2Ch 9: 6 But I did not *b* what they said
Ps 78:32 of his wonders, they did not *b*.
Hab 1: 5 that you would not *b*,
Mt 18: 6 one of these little ones who *b* in me
    21:22 If you *b*, you will receive whatever
    27:42 from the cross, and we will *b* in him
Mk   1:15 Repent and *b* the good news!"
     5:36 ruler, "Don't be afraid; just *b*."
     9:24 "I do *b*; help me overcome my
     9:42 one of these little ones who *b* in me
    11:24 *b* that you have received it,
    15:32 the cross, that we may see and *b*."
    16:16 but whoever does not *b* will be
    16:17 signs will accompany those who *b*:
Lk   8:12 so that they may not *b* and be saved.
     8:13 They *b* for a while, but in the time
     8:50 just *b*, and she will be healed."
    22:67 you will not *b* me,
    24:25 to *b* all that the prophets have
Jn   1: 7 that through him all men might *b*.
     3:18 does not *b* stands condemned
     4:42 "We no longer *b* just
     5:38 for you do not *b* the one he sent.
     5:46 believed Moses, you would *b* me,
     6:29 to *b* in the one he has sent."
     6:69 We *b* and know that you are
     7: 5 his own brothers did not *b* in him.
     8:24 if you do not *b* that I am .the one I
     9:35 "Do you *b* in the Son of Man?"
     9:36 "Tell me so that I may *b* in him."
     9:38 "Lord, I *b*," and he worshiped him.
    10:26 you do not *b* because you are not
    10:37 Do not *b* me unless I do what my
    10:38 you do not *b* me, *b* the miracles,
    11:27 "I *b* that you are the Christ,
    12:37 they still would not *b* in him.
    12:39 For this reason they could not *b*,
    12:44 in me, he does not *b* in me only,
    13:19 does happen you will *b* that I am
    14:10 Don't you *b* that I am in the Father
    14:11 *B* me when I say that I am
    14:11 or at least *b* on the evidence
    16:30 This makes us *b* that you came
    16:31 "You *b* at last!" Jesus answered.
    17:21 that the world may *b* that you have
    19:35 he testifies so that you also may *b*.
    20:27 Stop doubting and *b*."
    20:31 written that you may *b* that Jesus is
Ac 16:31 They replied, "*B* in the Lord Jesus,
    19: 4 the people to *b* in the one coming
    24:14 I *b* everything that agrees
    26:27 Agrippa, do you *b* the prophets?
Ro   3:22 faith in Jesus Christ to all who *b*.
     4:11 he is the father of all who *b*
    10: 9 *b* in your heart that God raised him
    10:10 For it is with your heart that you *b*
    10:14 And how can they *b* in the one
    16:26 so that all nations might *b*
1Co 1:21 preached to save those who *b*.
Gal 3:22 might be given to those who *b*.
Php 1:29 of Christ not only to *b* on him,
1Th 4:14 We *b* that Jesus died and rose again
2Th 2:11 delusion so that they will *b* the lie
1Ti 4:10 and especially of those who *b*.
Tit 1: 6 a man whose children *b*
Heb 11: 6 comes to him must *b* that he exists
Jas   1: 6 But when he asks, he must *b*
     2:19 Even the demons *b* that—
     2:19 You *b* that there is one God.
1Pe   2: 7 to you who *b*, this stone is precious
1Jn 3:23 to *b* in the name of his Son,
     4: 1 Dear friends, do not *b* every spirit,
     5:13 things to you who *b* in the name

BELIEVED (BELIEVE)
Ge 15: 6 Abram *b* the LORD, and he
Ex 4:31 signs before the people, and they *b*.
Isa 53: 1 Who has *b* our message
Jnh 3: 5 The Ninevites *b* God.
Lk 1:45 is she who has *b* that what the Lord
Jn 1:12 to those who *b* in his name,
2:22 Then they *b* the Scripture
3:18 because he has not *b* in the name
5:46 If you *b* Moses, you would believe
7:39 whom those who *b*
11:40 "Did I not tell you that if you *b*,
12:38 "Lord, who has *b* our message
20: 8 He saw and *b*.
20:29 who have not seen and yet have *b*."
Ac 13:48 were appointed for eternal life *b*.
19: 2 the Holy Spirit when you *b*?"
Ro 4: 3 Scripture say? "Abraham *b* God,
10:14 call on the one they have not *b* in?
10:16 "Lord, who has *b* our message?"
1Co 15: 2 Otherwise, you have *b* in vain.
Gal 3: 6 Consider Abraham: "He *b* God,
2Th 2:12 who have not *b* the truth
1Ti 3:16 was *b* on in the world,
2Ti 1:12 because I know whom I have *b*,
Jas 2:23 that says, "Abraham *b* God,

BELIEVER* (BELIEVE)
1Ki 18: 3 (Obadiah was a devout *b*
Ac 16: 1 whose mother was a Jewess and a *b*
16:15 "If you consider me a *b* in the Lord
1Co 7:12 brother has a wife who is not a *b*
7:13 has a husband who is not a *b*
2Co 6:15 What does a *b* have in common
1Ti 5:16 any woman who is a *b* has widows

BELIEVERS* (BELIEVE)
Jn 4:41 of his words many more became *b*.
Ac 1:15 among the *b* (a group numbering
2:44 All the *b* were together
4:32 All the *b* were one in heart
5:12 And all the *b* used to meet together
9:41 he called the *b* and the widows
10:45 The circumcised *b* who had come
11: 2 the circumcised *b* criticized him
15: 2 along with some other *b*,
15: 5 Then some of the *b* who belonged
15:23 To the Gentile *b* in Antioch,
21:25 for the Gentile *b*, we have written
1Co 6: 5 to judge a dispute between *b*?
14:22 is for *b*, not for unbelievers.
14:22 not for *b* but for unbelievers;
Gal 6:10 who belong to the family of *b*.
1Th 1: 7 a model to all the *b* in Macedonia
1Ti 4:12 set an example for the *b* in speech,
6: 2 benefit from their service are *b*,
Jas 2: 1 *b* in our glorious Lord Jesus Christ,
1Pe 2:17 Love the brotherhood of *b*,

BELIEVES* (BELIEVE)
Pr 14:15 A simple man *b* anything,
Mk 9:23 is possible for him who *b*."
11:23 *b* that what he says will happen,
16:16 Whoever *b* and is baptized will be
Jn 3:15 that everyone who *b*
3:16 that whoever *b* in him shall not
3:18 Whoever *b* in him is not
3:36 Whoever *b* in the Son has eternal
5:24 *b* him who sent me has eternal life
6:35 and he who *b* in me will never be
6:40 and *b* in him shall have eternal life,
6:47 he who *b* has everlasting life.
7:38 Whoever *b* in me, as the Scripture
11:25 He who *b* in me will live, even
11:26 and *b* in me will never die.
12:44 Jesus cried out, "When a man *b*
12:46 so that no one who *b*
Ac 10:43 about him that everyone who *b*
13:39 him everyone who *b* is justified
Ro 1:16 for the salvation of everyone who *b*

Ro 10: 4 righteousness for everyone who *b*.
1Jn 5: 1 Everyone who *b* that Jesus is
5: 5 Only he who *b* that Jesus is the Son
5:10 Anyone who *b* in the Son

BELIEVING* (BELIEVE)
Jn 20:31 and that by *b* you may have life
Ac 9:26 not *b* that he really was a disciple.
1Co 7:14 sanctified through her *b* husband.
7:15 A *b* man or woman is not bound
9: 5 right to take a *b* wife along with us,
Gal 3: 2 or by *b* what you heard? Are you
1Ti 6: 2 Those who have *b* masters are not

BELLY
Ge 3:14 You will crawl on your *b*
Da 2:32 its *b* and thighs of bronze,
Mt 12:40 three nights in the *b* of a huge fish,

BELONG (BELONGING BELONGS)
Ge 40: 8 "Do not interpretations *b* to God?
Lev 25:55 for the Israelites *b* to me
Dt 10:14 LORD your God *b* the heavens,
29:29 The secret things *b*
Job 12:13 "To God *b* wisdom and power;
12:16 To him *b* strength and victory;
25: 2 "Dominion and awe *b* to God;
Ps 47: 9 for the kings of the earth *b* to God;
95: 4 and the mountain peaks *b* to him.
115:16 The highest heavens *b*
Jer 5:10 for these people do not *b*
Jn 8:44 You *b* to your father, the devil,
15:19 As it is, you do not *b* to the world,
Ro 1: 6 called to *b* to Jesus Christ.
7: 4 that you might *b* to another,
8: 9 of Christ, he does not *b* to Christ.
14: 8 we live or die, we *b* to the Lord.
1Co 7:39 but he must *b* to the Lord.
15:23 when he comes, those who *b*
Gal 3:29 If you *b* to Christ, then you are
5:24 Those who *b* to Christ Jesus have
1Th 5: 5 We do not *b* to the night
5: 8 But since we *b* to the day, let us be
1Jn 3:19 then is how we know that we *b*

BELONGING (BELONG)
1Pe 2: 9 a holy nation, a people *b* to God,

BELONGS (BELONG)
Lev 27:30 *b* to the LORD; it is holy
Dt 1:17 of any man, for judgment *b* to God.
Job 41:11 Everything under heaven *b* to me.
Ps 22:28 for dominion *b* to the LORD
89:18 Indeed, our shield *b* to the LORD,
111:10 To him *b* eternal praise.
Eze 18: 4 For every living soul *b* to me,
Jn 8:47 He who *b* to God hears what God
Ro 12: 5 each member *b* to all the others.
Rev 7:10 "Salvation *b* to our God,

BELOVED* (LOVE)
Dt 33:12 "Let the *b* of the LORD rest secure
SS 5: 9 How is your *b* better than others,
5: 9 Friends How is your *b* better
Jer 11:15 "What is my *b* doing in my temple

BELSHAZZAR
King of Babylon in days of Daniel (Da 5).

BELT
Ex 12:11 with your cloak tucked into your *b*,
1Ki 18:46 and, tucking his cloak into his *b*,
2Ki 4:29 "Tuck your cloak into your *b*,
9: 1 "Tuck your cloak into your *b*,
Isa 11: 5 Righteousness will be his *b*
Eph 6:14 with the *b* of truth buckled

BENEFICIAL* (BENEFIT)
1Co 6:12 for me"—but not everything is *b*.
10:23 but not everything is *b*.

BENEFIT (BENEFICIAL BENEFITS)
Job 22: 2 "Can a man be of *b* to God?
Isa 38:17 Surely it was for my *b*
Ro 6:22 the *b* you reap leads to holiness,
2Co 4:15 All this is for your *b*,

BENEFITS (BENEFIT)
Ps 103: 2 and forget not all his *b*.

Jn 4:38 you have reaped the *b* of their labor

BENJAMIN
Twelfth son of Jacob by Rachel (Ge 35:16–24; 46:19–21; 1Ch 2:2). Jacob refused to send him to Egypt, but relented (Ge 42–45). Tribe of blessed (Ge 49:27; Dt 33:12), numbered (Nu 1:37; 26:41), allotted land (Jos 18:11–28; Eze 48:23), failed to fully possess (Jdg 1:21), nearly obliterated (Jdg 20–21), sided with Ish-Bosheth (2Sa 2), but turned to David (1Ch 12:2, 29). 12,000 from (Rev 7:8).

BEREANS*
Ac 17:11 the *B* were of more noble character

BESTOWING* (BESTOWS)
Pr 8:21 *b* wealth on those who love me

BESTOWS (BESTOWING)
Ps 84:11 the LORD *b* favor and honor;

BETHANY
Mk 11: 1 and *B* at the Mount of Olives,

BETHEL
Ge 28:19 He called that place *B*,

BETHLEHEM
Ru 1:19 went on until they came to *B*.
1Sa 16: 1 I am sending you to Jesse of *B*.
2Sa 23:15 from the well near the gate of *B*!"
Mic 5: 2 "But you, *B* Ephrathah,
Mt 2: 1 After Jesus was born in *B* in Judea,
2: 6 " 'But you, *B*, in the land of Judah,

BETHPHAGE
Mt 21: 1 came to *B* on the Mount of Olives,

BETHSAIDA
Jn 12:21 who was from *B* in Galilee,

BETRAY (BETRAYED BETRAYS)
Ps 89:33 nor will I ever *b* my faithfulness.
Pr 25: 9 do not *b* another man's confidence,
Mt 10:21 "Brother will *b* brother to death,
26:21 the truth, one of you will *b* me."

BETRAYED (BETRAY)
Mt 27: 4 "for I have *b* innocent blood."

BETRAYS (BETRAY)
Pr 11:13 A gossip *b* a confidence,
20:19 A gossip *b* a confidence;

BEULAH*
Isa 62: 4 and your land *B*;

BEWITCHED*
Gal 3: 1 foolish Galatians! Who has *b* you?

BEZALEL
Judahite craftsman in charge of building the tabernacle (Ex 31:1–11; 35:30–39:31).

BIDDING*
Ps 103:20 you mighty ones who do his *b*,
148: 8 stormy winds that do his *b*,

BILDAD
One of Job's friends (Job 8; 18; 25).

BILHAH
Servant of Rachel, mother of Jacob's sons Dan and Naphtali (Ge 30:1–7; 35:25; 46:23–25).

BIND (BINDS BOUND)
Dt 6: 8 and *b* them on your foreheads.
Pr 3: 3 *b* them around your neck,
6:21 *B* them upon your heart forever;
7: 3 *B* them on your fingers;
Isa 61: 1 me to *b* up the brokenhearted,
Mt 16:19 whatever you *b* on earth will be

BINDS (BIND)
Ps 147: 3 and *b* up their wounds.
Isa 30:26 when the LORD *b* up the bruises

BIRD (BIRDS)
Pr 27: 8 Like a *b* that strays from its nest
Ecc 10:20 a *b* of the air may carry your words,

BIRDS (BIRD)
Mt 8:20 and *b* of the air have nests,
Lk 9:58 and *b* of the air have nests,

BIRTH (BEAR)
Ps 51: 5 Surely I was sinful at *b*,
58: 3 Even from *b* the wicked go astray;
Isa 26:18 but we gave *b* to wind.

Mt   1:18 This is how the *b* of Jesus Christ
     24: 8 these are the beginning of *b*
            pains.
Jn   3: 6 Flesh gives *b* to flesh, but the
            Spirit
1Pe 1: 3 great mercy he has given us
            new *b*

BIRTHRIGHT (BEAR)
Ge 25:34 So Esau despised his *b*.

BITTEN
Nu 21: 8 anyone who is *b* can look at it

BITTER (BITTERNESS EMBITTER)
Ex 12: 8 along with *b* herbs, and bread
            made
Pr 27: 7 what is *b* tastes sweet.

BITTERNESS (BITTER)
Pr 14:10 Each heart knows its own *b*,
    17:25 and *b* to the one who bore him.
Ro   3:14 full of cursing and *b*.'
Eph 4:31 Get rid of all *b*, rage and anger,

BLACK
Zec 6: 6 The one with the *b* horses is going
Rev 6: 5 and there before me was a *b*
            horse!

BLAMELESS* (BLAMELESSLY)
Ge   6: 9 *b* among the people of his time,
    17: 1 walk before me and be *b*.
Dt 18:13 You must be *b* before the LORD
2Sa 22:24 I have been *b* before him
    22:26 to the *b* you show yourself *b*,
Job 1: 1 This man was *b* and upright;
     1: 8 one on earth like him; he is *b*
     2: 3 one on earth like him; he is *b*
     4: 6 and your *b* ways your hope?
    8:20 God does not reject a *b* man
    9:20 if I were *b*, it would pronounce me
    9:21 "Although I am *b*,
    9:22 'He destroys both the *b*
    12: 4 though righteous and *b*!
    22: 3 gain if your ways were *b*?
    31: 6 and he will know that I am *b*—
Ps 15: 2 He whose walk is *b*
    18:23 I have been *b* before him
    18:25 to the *b* you show yourself *b*,
    19:13 Then will I be *b*,
    26: 1 for I have led a *b* life;
    26:11 But I lead a *b* life;
    37:18 The days of the *b* are known
    37:37 Consider the *b*, observe the
            upright
    84:11 from those whose walk is *b*.
  101: 2 I will be careful to lead a *b* life—
  101: 2 house with a *b* heart.
  101: 6 he whose walk is *b*
  119: 1 Blessed are they whose ways
            are *b*,
  119:80 May my heart be *b*
Pr   2: 7 a shield to those whose walk is *b*,
    2:21 and the *b* will remain in it;
    11: 5 of the *b* makes a straight way
    11:20 in those whose ways are *b*
    19: 1 Better a poor man whose walk
            is *b*
    20: 7 The righteous man leads a *b* life;
    28: 6 Better a poor man whose walk
    28:10 *b* will receive a good inheritance.
    28:18 He whose walk is *b* is kept safe,
Eze 28:15 You were *b* in your ways
1Co 1: 8 so that you will be *b* on the day
Eph 1: 4 world to be holy and *b* in his sight.
    5:27 any other blemish, but holy and *b*.
Php 1:10 and *b* until the day of Christ,
    2:15 so that you may become *b* and
            pure
1Th 2:10 and *b* we were among you who
    3:13 hearts so that you will be *b*
    5:23 and body be kept *b* at the coming
Tit   1: 6 An elder must be *b*, the husband
            of
     1: 7 he must be *b*— not overbearing,
Heb 7:26 *b*, pure, set apart from sinners,
2Pe 3:14 effort to be found spotless, *b*
Rev 14: 5 found in their mouths; they are *b*.

BLAMELESSLY* (BLAMELESS)
Lk   1: 6 commandments and
            regulations *b*.

BLASPHEME* (BLASPHEMED BLASPHEMER
BLASPHEMES BLASPHEMIES BLASPHEMING
BLASPHEMOUS BLASPHEMY)
Ex 22:28 "Do not *b* God or curse the ruler
Ac 26:11 and I tried to force them to *b*.
1Ti   1:20 over to Satan to be taught not
            to *b*.
2Pe 2:12 these men *b* in matters they do
            not
Rev 13: 6 He opened his mouth to *b* God,

BLASPHEMED* (BLASPHEME)
Lev 24:11 of the Israelite woman *b* the
            Name
2Ki 19: 6 of the king of Assyria have *b* me.
    19:22 Who is it you have insulted and *b*?
Isa 37: 6 of the king of Assyria have *b* me.
    37:23 Who is it you have insulted and *b*?
    52: 5 my name is constantly *b*.
Eze 20:27 your fathers *b* me by forsaking
            me:
Ac 19:37 robbed temples nor *b* our
            goddess.
Ro   2:24 name is *b* among the Gentiles

BLASPHEMER* (BLASPHEME)
Lev 24:14 "Take the *b* outside the camp.
    24:23 they took the *b* outside the camp
1Ti   1:13 I was once a *b* and a persecutor

BLASPHEMES* (BLASPHEME)
Lev 24:16 anyone who *b* the name
    24:16 native-born, when he *b* the Name,
Nu 15:30 native-born or alien, *b* the LORD,
Mk   3:29 whoever *b* against the Holy Spirit
Lk 12:10 but anyone who *b* against the
            Holy

BLASPHEMIES* (BLASPHEME)
Ne   9:18 or when they committed awful *b*.
     9:26 to you; they committed awful *b*.
Mk   3:28 and *b* of men will be forgiven
            them.
Rev 13: 5 and *b* and to exercise his
            authority

BLASPHEMING* (BLASPHEME)
Mt   9: 3 "This fellow is *b*!" Knowing their
Mk   2: 7 He's *b*! Who can forgive sins

BLASPHEMOUS* (BLASPHEME)
Rev 13: 1 and on each head a *b* name.
    17: 3 that was covered with *b* names

BLASPHEMY* (BLASPHEME)
Mt 12:31 and *b* will be forgiven men,
    12:31 the *b* against the Spirit will not be
    26:65 Look, now you have heard the *b*.
    26:65 "He has spoken *b*! Why do we
Mk 14:64 "You have heard the *b*.
Lk   5:21 "Who is this fellow who speaks *b*?
Jn 10:33 replied the Jews, "but for *b*,
    10:36 Why then do you accuse me of *b*
Ac   6:11 words of *b* against Moses

BLAST*
Ex 15: 8 By the *b* of your nostrils
    19:13 horn sounds a long *b* may they go
    19:16 and a very loud trumpet *b*.
Nu 10: 5 When a trumpet *b* is sounded,
    10: 6 At the sounding of a second *b*,
    10: 6 The *b* will be the signal
    10: 9 sound a *b* on the trumpets.
Jos 6: 5 you hear them sound a long *b*
     6:16 the priests sounded the
            trumpet *b*,
2Sa 22:16 at the *b* of breath from his
            nostrils.
Job 4: 9 at the *b* of his anger they perish.
    39:25 At the *b* of the trumpet he snorts,
Ps 18:15 the *b* of breath from your nostrils.
    98: 6 and the *b* of the ram's horn—
  147:17 Who can withstand his icy *b*?
Isa 27: 8 with his fierce *b* he drives her out,
Eze 22:20 a furnace to melt it with a fiery *b*,
Am 2: 2 tumult amid war cries and the *b*
Heb 12:19 to a trumpet *b* or to such a voice

BLEATING*
1Sa 15:14 "What then is this *b* of sheep

BLEMISH (BLEMISHES)
Lev 22:21 be without defect or *b*
Eph 5:27 or wrinkle or any other *b*,
Col 1:22 without *b* and free from
            accusation
1Pe 1:19 a lamb without *b* or defect.

BLEMISHES* (BLEMISH)
2Pe 2:13 and *b*, reveling in their pleasures
Jude :12 These men are *b* at your love
            feasts

BLESS (BLESSED BLESSES BLESSING BLESSINGS)
Ge 12: 3 I will *b* those who *b* you,
    32:26 not let you go unless you *b* me."
Dt   7:13 He will love you and *b* you
    33:11 *B* all his skills, O LORD,
Ps 72:15 and *b* him all day long.
Ro 12:14 Bless those who persecute you; *b*

BLESSED (BLESS)
Ge 1:22 God *b* them and said, "Be fruitful
     2: 3 And God *b* the seventh day
    22:18 nations on earth will be *b*,
Nu 24: 9 "May those who bless you be *b*
1Ch 17:27 have *b* it, and it will be *b* forever."
Ps   1: 1 *B* is the man
     2:12 *B* are all who take refuge in him.
    32: 2 *B* is the man
    33:12 *B* is the nation whose God is
    40: 4 *B* is the man
    41: 1 *B* is he who has regard for the
            weak
    84: 5 *B* are those whose strength is
    89:15 *B* are those who have learned
    94:12 *B* is the man you discipline,
  106: 3 *B* are they who maintain justice,
  112: 1 *B* is the man who fears the LORD,
  118:26 *B* is he who comes in the name
  119: 1 *B* are they whose ways are
  119: 2 *B* are they who keep his statutes
  127: 5 *B* is the man
Pr   3:13 *B* is the man who finds wisdom,
    8:34 *B* is the man who listens to me,
    28:20 A faithful man will be richly *b*,
    29:18 but *b* is he who keeps the law.
    31:28 Her children arise and call her *b*;
Isa 30:18 *B* are all who wait for him!
Mal 3:12 Then all the nations will call
            you *b*,
    3:15 But now we call the arrogant *b*.
Mt   5: 3 saying: "*B* are the poor in spirit,
     5: 4 *B* are those who mourn,
     5: 5 *B* are the meek,
     5: 6 *B* are those who hunger
     5: 7 *B* are the merciful,
     5: 8 *B* are the pure in heart,
     5: 9 *B* are the peacemakers,
    5:10 *B* are those who are persecuted
    5:11 "*B* are you when people insult
            you,
Lk   1:48 on all generations will call me *b*,
Jn 12:13 "*B* is he who comes in the name
Ac 20:35 'It is more *b* to give than to
            receive
Tit   2:13 while we wait for the *b* hope—
Jas   1:12 *B* is the man who perseveres
Rev 1: 3 *B* is the one who reads the words
    22: 7 *B* is he who keeps the words
    22:14 "*B* are those who wash their
            robes,

BLESSES (BLESS)
Ps 29:11 the LORD *b* his people with peace.
Ro 10:12 and richly *b* all who call on him,

BLESSING (BLESS)
Ge 27: 4 so that I may give you my *b*
Dt 23: 5 turned the curse into a *b* for you,
    33: 1 This is the *b* that Moses the man
Pr 10:22 The *b* of the LORD brings wealth,
Eze 34:26 there will be showers of *b*.

BLESSINGS (BLESS)
Dt 11:29 proclaim on Mount Gerizim the *b*,
Jos 8:34 all the words of the law—the *b*
Pr 10: 6 *B* crown the head of the
            righteous,
Ro 15:27 shared in the Jews' spiritual *b*,

BLIND (BLINDED)
Mt 15:14 *b* man leads a *b* man, both will
            fall
    23:16 "Woe to you, *b* guides! You say,
Mk 10:46 a *b* man, Bartimaeus (that is,
Lk   6:39 "Can a *b* man lead a *b* man?
Jn   9:25 I was *b* but now I see!"

BLINDED (BLIND)
Jn 12:40 elsewhere: "He has *b* their eyes
2Co 4: 4 The god of this age has *b* the
            minds

BLOOD (BLOODSHED BLOODTHIRSTY)
Ge 4:10 Your brother's *b* cries out to me
     9: 6 "Whoever sheds the *b* of man,
Ex 12:13 and when I see the *b*, I will pass
     24: 8 "This is the *b* of the covenant that
Lev 16:15 and take its *b* behind the curtain
     17:11 For the life of a creature is in the *b*,
Dt 12:23 eat the *b*, because the *b* is the life,
Ps 72:14 for precious is their *b* in his sight.
Pr   6:17 hands that shed innocent *b*,
Isa 1:11 pleasure in the *b* of bulls and lambs
Mt 26:28 This is my *b* of the covenant,
    27:24 "I am innocent of this man's *b*,"
Mk 14:24 "This is my *b* of the covenant,
Lk 22:44 drops of *b* falling to the ground.
Jn   6:53 of the Son of Man and drink his *b*,
Ac 15:20 of strangled animals and from *b*.
    20:26 innocent of the *b* of all men.
Ro   3:25 of atonement, through faith in his *b*
     5: 9 have now been justified by his *b*,
1Co 11:25 cup is the new covenant in my *b*;
Eph 1: 7 we have redemption through his *b*,
     2:13 near through the *b* of Christ.
Col 1:20 by making peace through his *b*,
Heb 9: 7 once a year, and never without *b*,
     9:12 once for all by his own *b*,
     9:20 "This is the *b* of the covenant,
     9:22 of *b* there is no forgiveness.
    12:24 word than the *b* of Abel.
1Pe 1:19 but with the precious *b* of Christ,
1Jn 1: 7 and the *b* of Jesus, his Son,
Rev 1: 5 has freed us from our sins by his *b*,
     5: 9 with your *b* you purchased men
     7:14 white in the *b* of the Lamb.
    12:11 him by the *b* of the Lamb
    19:13 He is dressed in a robe dipped in *b*,

BLOODSHED (BLOOD)
Jer 48:10 on him who keeps his sword from *b*
Eze 35: 6 did not hate *b*, *b* will pursue you.
Hab 2:12 to him who builds a city with *b*

BLOODTHIRSTY* (BLOOD)
Ps   5: 6 *b* and deceitful men
    26: 9 my life with *b* men,
    55:23 *b* and deceitful men
    59: 2 and save me from *b* men.
   139:19 Away from me, you *b* men!
Pr 29:10 *B* men hate a man of integrity

BLOSSOM
Isa 35: 1 the wilderness will rejoice and *b*.

BLOT (BLOTS)
Ex 32:32 then *b* me out of the book you have
Ps 51: 1 *b* out my transgressions.
Rev 3: 5 I will never *b* out his name

BLOTS (BLOT)
Isa 43:25 "I, even I, am he who *b* out

BLOWN
Eph 4:14 and *b* here and there by every wind
Jas 1: 6 doubts is like a wave of the sea, *b*
Jude   :12 without rain, *b* along by the wind;

BLUSH
Jer 6:15 they do not even know how to *b*.

BOAST (BOASTS)
1Ki 20:11 armor should not *b* like one who
Ps 34: 2 My soul will *b* in the LORD;
    44: 8 In God we make our *b* all day long,
Pr 27: 1 Do not *b* about tomorrow,
Jer 9:23 or the rich man *b* of his riches.
1Co 1:31 Let him who boasts *b* in the Lord."
2Co 10:17 Let him who boasts *b* in the Lord."
    11:30 I do not inwardly burn? If I must *b*,
Gal 6:14 May I never *b* except in the cross
Eph 2: 9 not by works, so that no one can *b*.

BOASTS (BOAST)
Jer 9:24 but let him who *b* boast about this:

BOAZ
Wealthy Bethlehemite who showed favor to Ruth (Ru 2), married her (Ru 4). Ancestor of David (Ru 4:18–22; 1Ch 2:12–15), Jesus (Mt 1:5–16; Lk 3:23–32).

BODIES (BODY)
Isa 26:19 their *b* will rise.
Ro 12: 1 to offer your *b* as living sacrifices,
1Co 6:15 not know that your *b* are members
Eph 5:28 to love their wives as their own *b*.

BODILY (BODY)
Col 2: 9 of the Deity lives in *b* form,

BODY (BODIES BODILY EMBODIMENT)
Zec 13: 4 What are these wounds on your *b*?'
Mt 10:28 afraid of those who kill the *b*
    26:26 saying, "Take and eat; this is my *b*
    26:41 spirit is willing, but the *b* is weak."
Mk 14:22 saying, "Take it; this is my *b*."
Lk 22:19 saying, "This is my *b* given for you;
Jn 13:10 wash his feet; his whole *b* is clean.
Ro   6:13 Do not offer the parts of your *b*
    12: 4 us has one *b* with many members,
1Co 6:19 not know that your *b* is a temple
     6:20 Therefore honor God with your *b*.
    11:24 "This is my *b*, which is for you;
    12:12 The *b* is a unit, though it is made up
    12:13 baptized by one Spirit into one *b*—
    15:44 a natural *b*, it is raised a spiritual *b*.
Eph 1:23 which is his *b*, the fullness
     4:25 for we are all members of one *b*.
     5:30 for we are members of his *b*.
Php 1:20 Christ will be exalted in my *b*,
Col 1:24 sake of his *b*, which is the church.

BOLD (BOLDNESS)
Ps 138: 3 you made me *b* and stouthearted.
Pr 21:29 A wicked man puts up a *b* front,
    28: 1 but the righteous are as *b* as a lion.

BOLDNESS* (BOLD)
Lk 11: 8 of the man's *b* he will get up
Ac   4:29 to speak your word with great *b*.

BONDAGE
Ezr 9: 9 God has not deserted us in our *b*.

BONES
Ge   2:23 "This is now bone of my *b*
Ps 22:14 and all my *b* are out of joint.
    22:17 I can count all my *b*;
Eze 37: 1 middle of a valley; it was full of *b*.
Jn 19:36 "Not one of his *b* will be broken,"

BOOK (BOOKS)
Ex 32:33 against me I will blot out of my *b*.
Jos 1: 8 Do not let this *B* of the Law depart
2Ki 22: 8 "I have found the *B* of the Law
2Ch 34:15 "I have found the *B* of the Law
Ne   8: 8 They read from the *B* of the Law
Ps 69:28 May they be blotted out of the *b*
Da 12: 1 name is found written in the *b*—
Jn 20:30 which are not recorded in this *b*.
Php 4: 3 whose names are in the *b* of life.
Rev 3: 5 never blot out his name from the *b*
    20:12 *b* was opened, which is the *b*
    20:15 was not found written in the *b*
    21:27 written in the Lamb's *b* of life.
    22:18 him the plagues described in this *b*.

BOOKS* (BOOK)
Ecc 12:12 Of making many *b* there is no end,
Da   7:10 and the *b* were opened.
    21:25 for the *b* that would be written.
Rev 20:12 the throne, and *b* were opened.
    20:12 they had done as recorded in the *b*.

BORE (BEAR)
Isa 53:12 For he *b* the sin of many,
1Pe 2:24 He himself *b* our sins in his body

BORN (BEAR)
Ecc 3: 2 a time to be *b* and a time to die,
Isa 9: 6 For to us a child is *b*,

Isa 66: 8 Can a country be *b* in a day
Lk   2:11 of David a Savior has been *b* to you
Jn   3: 3 see the kingdom of God unless he is *b* again.
     3: 4 How can a man be *b* when he is old
     3: 5 unless he is *b* of water
     3: 7 at my saying, 'You must be *b* again
     3: 8 it is with everyone *b* of the Spirit.
1Pe 1:23 For you have been *b* again,
1Jn 3: 9 because he has been *b* of God.
     4: 7 Everyone who loves has been *b*
     5: 1 believes that Jesus is the Christ is *b*
     5: 4 for everyone *b* of God overcomes
     5:18 We know that anyone *b*

BORROWER
Pr 22: 7 and the *b* is servant to the lender.

BOTHER (BOTHERING)
Lk 11: 7 one inside answers, 'Don't *b* me.

BOTHERING (BOTHER)
Lk 18: 5 yet because this widow keeps *b* me,

BOUGHT (BUY)
Ac 20:28 which he *b* with his own blood.
1Co 6:20 You are not your own; you were *b*
     7:23 You were *b* at a price; do not
2Pe 2: 1 the sovereign Lord who *b* them—

BOUND (BIND)
Is 56: 3 Let no foreigner who has *b* himself
Mt 16:19 bind on earth will be *b* in heaven,
    18:18 bind on earth will be *b* in heaven,
Ro   7: 2 by law a married woman is *b*
1Co 7:39 A woman is *b* to her husband
Jude   : 6 *b* with everlasting chains
Rev 20: 2 and *b* him for a thousand years.

BOUNDARY (BOUNDS)
Nu 34: 3 your southern *b* will start
Pr 23:10 Do not move an ancient *b* stone
Hos 5:10 who move *b* stones.

BOUNDS (BOUNDARY)
2Co 7: 4 all our troubles my joy knows no *b*.

BOUNTY*
Ge 49:26 than the *b* of the age-old hills.
Dt 28:12 heavens, the storehouse of his *b*,
1Ki 10:13 he had given her out of his royal *b*.
Ps 65:11 You crown the year with your *b*,
    68:10 from your *b*, O God, you provided
Jer 31:12 rejoice in the *b* of the LORD—
    31:14 my people will be filled with my *b*

BOW (BOWED BOWS)
Dt   5: 9 You shall not *b* down to them
1Ki 22:34 But someone drew his *b* at random
Ps   5: 7 in reverence will I *b* down
    44: 6 I do not trust in my *b*,
    95: 6 Come, let us *b* down in worship,
   138: 2 I will *b* down toward your holy
Isa 44:19 Shall I *b* down to a block of wood?"
    45:23 Before me every knee will *b*;
Ro 14:11 'every knee will *b* before me;
Php 2:10 name of Jesus every knee should *b*,

BOWED (BOW)
Ps 145:14 and lifts up all who are *b* down.
   146: 8 the LORD lifts up those who are *b*

BOWS (BOW)
Isa 44:15 he makes an idol and *b* down to it.
    44:17 he *b* down to it and worships.

BOY (BOY'S BOYS)
Ge 21:17 God heard the *b* crying,
    22:12 not lay a hand on the *b*
Jdg 13: 5 *b* is to be a Nazirite,
1Sa 2:11 ministered before the LORD.
     3: 8 the LORD was calling the *b*.
Isa 7:16 before the *b* knows enough
Mt 17:18 demon, and it came out of the *b*
Lk   2:43 the *b* Jesus stayed behind

BOY'S (BOY)
1Ki 17:22 the *b* life returned to him

2Ki 4:34 the *b* body grew warm

BOYS (BOY)
Ge 25:24 twin *b* in her womb
Ex   1:18 they let the *b* live.

BRACE*
Job 38: 3 *B* yourself like a man;
       40: 7 out of the storm: "*B* yourself like
Na   2: 1 *b* yourselves,

BRAG*
Am 4: 5 and *b* about your freewill
             offerings
Ro   2:17 *b* about your relationship to God;
       2:23 temples? You who *b* about the
             law,
Jas 4:16 As it is, you boast and *b*.

BRAIDED
1Ti 2: 9 not with *b* hair or gold or pearls
1Pe 3: 3 as *b* hair and the wearing

BRANCH (BRANCHES)
Isa   4: 2 In that day the *B* of the LORD will
Jer 23: 5 up to David a righteous *B*,
    33:15 I will make a righteous *B* sprout
Zec 3: 8 going to bring my servant, the *B*.
     6:12 is the man whose name is the *B*,
Jn 15: 2 while every *b* that does bear fruit
     15: 4 No *b* can bear fruit by itself;

BRANCHES (BRANCH)
Jn 15: 5 "I am the vine; you are the *b*.
Ro 11:21 if God did not spare the natural *b*,

BRAVE
2Sa 2: 7 Now then, be strong and *b*,
   13:28 you this order? Be strong and *b*."

BREACH (BREAK)
Ps 106:23 stood in the *b* before him

BREACHING (BREAK)
Pr 17:14 Starting a quarrel is like *b* a dam;

BREAD
Ex 12: 8 and *b* made without yeast.
    23:15 the Feast of Unleavened *B*;
    25:30 Put the *b* of the Presence
Dt   8: 3 that man does not live on *b* alone
Ps 78:25 Men ate the *b* of angels;
Pr 30: 8 but give me only my daily *b*.
Ecc 11: 1 Cast your *b* upon the waters,
Isa 55: 2 Why spend money on what is
             not *b*
Mt   4: 3 tell these stones to become *b*."
     4: 4 'Man does not live on *b* alone,
     6:11 Give us today our daily *b*.
   26:26 Jesus took *b*, gave thanks
Mk 14:22 Jesus took *b*, gave thanks
Lk   4: 3 tell this stone to become *b*."
     4: 4 'Man does not live on *b* alone.' "
     9:13 "We have only five loaves of *b*
    11: 3 Give us each day our daily *b*.
    22:19 And he took *b*, gave thanks
Jn   6:33 For the *b* of God is he who comes
     6:35 Jesus declared, "I am the *b* of life.
     6:41 "I am the *b* that came
     6:48 I am the *b* of life.
     6:51 I am the living *b* that came
     6:51 This *b* is my flesh, which I will give
    21:13 took the *b* and gave it to them,
1Co 10:16 And is not the *b* that we break
    11:23 took *b*, and when he had given
    11:26 For whenever you eat this *b*

BREAK (BREACH BREACHING BREAKERS BREAKING
BREAKS BROKE BROKEN BROKENNESS)
Nu 30: 2 he must not *b* his word
Jdg 2: 1 'I will never *b* my covenant
Pr 25:15 and a gentle tongue can *b* a bone.
Isa 42: 3 A bruised reed he will not *b*,
Mal 2:15 and do not *b* faith with the wife
Mt 12:20 A bruised reed he will not *b*,
Ac 20: 7 week we came together to *b*
             bread.
1Co 10:16 the bread that we *b* a
             participation
Rev 5: 2 "Who is worthy to *b* the seals

BREAKERS*(BREAK)
Ps 42: 7 all your waves and *b*
   93: 4 mightier than the *b* of the sea—
Jnh 2: 3 all your waves and *b*

BREAKING (BREAK)
Jos 9:20 fall on us for *b* the oath we swore
Eze 16:59 oath by *b* the covenant.

Eze 17:18 the oath by *b* the covenant.
Ac   2:42 to the *b* of bread and to prayer.
Jas 2:10 at just one point is guilty of *b* all

BREAKS (BREAK)
Jer 23:29 "and like a hammer that *b* a rock
1Jn 3: 4 Everyone who sins *b* the law;

BREASTPIECE (BREASTPLATE)
Ex 28:15 Fashion a *b* for making
             decisions—

BREASTPLATE*(BREASTPIECE)
Isa 59:17 He put on righteousness as his *b*,
Eph 6:14 with the *b* of righteousness in
             place
1Th 5: 8 putting on faith and love as a *b*,

BREASTS
La   4: 3 Even jackals offer their *b*

BREATH (BREATHED GOD-BREATHED)
Ge   2: 7 into his nostrils the *b* of life,

BREATHED (BREATH)
Ge   2: 7 *b* into his nostrils the breath of
             life,
Mk 15:37 With a loud cry, Jesus *b* his last.
Jn 20:22 And with that he *b* on them

BREEDS*
Pr 13:10 Pride only *b* quarrels,

BRIBE
Ex 23: 8 "Do not accept a *b*,
Dt 16:19 for a *b* blinds the eyes of the wise
    27:25 "Cursed is the man who accepts
             a *b*
Pr   6:35 will refuse the *b*, however great it

BRIDE
Isa 62: 5 as a bridegroom rejoices over
             his *b*,
Rev 19: 7 and his *b* has made herself ready.
    21: 2 as a *b* beautifully dressed
    21: 9 I will show you the *b*, the wife
    22:17 The Spirit and the *b* say, "Come!"

BRIDEGROOM
Ps 19: 5 which is like a *b* coming forth
Mt 25: 1 and went out to meet the *b*.
    25: 5 The *b* was a long time in coming,

BRIGHTENS*(BRIGHTNESS)
Pr 16:15 When a king's face *b*, it means
             life;
Ecc 8: 1 Wisdom *b* a man's face

BRIGHTER (BRIGHTNESS)
Pr   4:18 shining ever *b* till the full light

BRIGHTNESS*(BRIGHTENS BRIGHTER)
2Sa 22:13 Out of the *b* of his presence
    23: 4 like the *b* after rain
Ps 18:12 of the *b* of his presence clouds
Isa 59: 9 for *b*, but we walk in deep
             shadows.
    60: 3 and kings to the *b* of your dawn.
    60:19 will the *b* of the moon shine on
             you
Da 12: 3 who are wise will shine like the *b*
Am 5:20 pitch-dark, without a ray of *b*?

BRILLIANCE*(BRILLIANT)
Ac 22:11 the *b* of the light had blinded me.
Rev 1:16 was like the sun shining in all its *b*.
    21:11 its *b* was like that of a very
             precious

BRILLIANT*(BRILLIANCE)
Ecc 9:11 or wealth to the *b*
Eze 1: 4 and surrounded by *b* light.
     1:27 and *b* light surrounded him.

BRINK*
Pr   5:14 I have come to the *b* of utter ruin

BRITTLE
Da   2:42 will be partly strong and partly *b*.

BROAD
Mt   7:13 and *b* is the road that leads

BROKE (BREAK)
Mt 26:26 took bread, gave thanks and *b* it,
Mk 14:22 took bread, gave thanks and *b* it,
Ac   2:46 They *b* bread in their homes
    20:11 he went upstairs again and *b*
             bread
1Co 11:24 when he had given thanks, he *b* it

BROKEN (BREAK)
Ps 34:20 not one of them will be *b*.

Ps 51:17 The sacrifices of God are a *b*
             spirit;
Ecc 4:12 of three strands is not quickly *b*.
Lk 20:18 on that stone will be *b* to pieces,
Jn   7:23 the law of Moses may not be *b*,
    10:35 and the Scripture cannot be *b*—
    19:36 "Not one of his bones will be *b*,"
Ro 11:20 they were *b* off because of
             unbelief.

BROKENHEARTED*(HEART)
Ps 34:18 The LORD is close to the *b*
  109:16 and the needy and the *b*.
  147: 3 He heals the *b*
Isa 61: 1 He has sent me to bind up the *b*.

BROKENNESS*(BREAK)
Isa 65:14 and wail in *b* of spirit.

BRONZE
Ex 27: 2 and overlay the altar with *b*.
    30:18 "Make a *b* basin, with its *b* stand,
Nu 21: 9 So Moses made a *b* snake
Da   2:32 and thighs of *b*, its legs of iron,
    10: 6 legs like the gleam of burnished *b*,
Rev 1:15 His feet were like *b* glowing
     2:18 whose feet are like burnished *b*.

BROTHER (BROTHER'S BROTHERHOOD BROTHERLY
BROTHERS)
Pr 17:17 and a *b* is born for adversity.
    18:24 a friend who sticks closer than
             a *b*.
    27:10 neighbor nearby than a *b* far
             away.
Mt   5:24 and be reconciled to your *b*;
    18:15 "If your *b* sins against you,
Mk 3:35 Whoever does God's will is my *b*
Lk 17: 3 "If your *b* sins, rebuke him,
Ro 14:15 not by your eating destroy your *b*
    14:21 anything else that will cause
             your *b*
1Co 8:13 if what I eat causes my *b* to fall
2Th 3: 6 away from every *b* who is idle
     3:15 as an enemy, but warn him as a *b*.
Phm   :16 but better than a slave, as a
             dear *b*.
Jas 2:15 Suppose a *b* or sister is
     4:11 Anyone who speaks against his *b*
1Jn 2: 9 hates his *b* is still in the darkness.
     2:10 Whoever loves his *b* lives
     2:11 But whoever hates his *b* is
     3:10 is anyone who does not love his *b*.
     3:15 who hates his *b* is a murderer,
     3:17 material possessions and sees
             his *b*
     4:20 For anyone who does not love
             his *b*
     4:20 yet hates his *b*, he is a liar.
     4:21 loves God must also love his *b*.
     5:16 If anyone sees his *b* commit a sin

BROTHER'S (BROTHER)
Ge   4: 9 "Am I my *b* keeper?" The LORD
Mt   7: 5 remove the speck from your *b*
             eye.
Ro 14:13 or obstacle in your *b* way.

BROTHERHOOD (BROTHER)
1Pe 2:17 Love the *b* of believers, fear God,

BROTHERLY*(BROTHER)
Ro 12:10 devoted to one another in *b* love.
1Th 4: 9 Now about *b* love we do not need
2Pe 1: 7 and to godliness, *b* kindness;
     1: 7 kindness; and to *b* kindness,

BROTHERS (BROTHER)
Jos 1:14 You are to help your *b*
Ps 133: 1 is when *b* live together in unity!
Pr   6:19 who stirs up dissension among *b*.
Mt 12:49 "Here are my mother and my *b*.
    19:29 everyone who has left houses or *b*
    25:40 one of the least of these *b* of
             mine,
Mk 3:33 "Who are my mother and my *b*?"
    10:29 or *b* or sisters or mother or father
Lk 21:16 will be betrayed even by
             parents, *b*,
    22:32 turned back, strengthen your *b*."
Jn   7: 5 his own *b* did not believe in him.
Ac 15:32 to encourage and strengthen
             the *b*.
Ro   9: 3 off from Christ for the sake of
             my *b*
1Co 8:12 sin against your *b* in this way

2Co 11:26 and in danger from false *b*.
Gal 2: 4 some false *b* had infiltrated our
1Th 4:10 you do love all the *b*
     5:26 Greet all the *b* with a holy kiss.
1Ti 6: 2 for them because they are *b*.
Heb 2:11 Jesus is not ashamed to call
                them *b*.
     2:17 to be made like his *b* in every way,
    13: 1 Keep on loving each other as *b*.
1Pe 1:22 you have sincere love for your *b*,
     3: 8 be sympathetic, love as *b*,
1Jn 3:14 death to life, because we love
                our *b*.
     3:16 to lay down our lives for our *b*.
3Jn :10 he refuses to welcome the *b*.
Rev 12:10 For the accuser of our *b*,

BROW
Ge   3:19 By the sweat of your *b*

BRUISED (BRUISES)
Isa 42: 3 A *b* reed he will not break,
Mt 12:20 A *b* reed he will not break,

BRUISES (BRUISED)
Isa 30:26 when the LORD binds up the *b*

BRUTAL (BRUTE)
2Ti 3: 3 slanderous, without self-
                control, *b*,

BRUTE* (BRUTAL)
Ps 73:22 I was a *b* beast before you.
2Pe 2:12 They are like *b* beasts, creatures

BUBBLING*
Pr 18: 4 the fountain of wisdom is a *b*
                brook
Isa 35: 7 the thirsty ground *b* springs.

BUCKET*
Isa 40:15 the nations are like a drop in a *b*;

BUCKLED* (BUCKLER)
Eph 6:14 belt of truth *b* around your waist,

BUCKLER* (BUCKLED)
Ps 35: 2 Take up shield and *b*;

BUD (BUDDED)
Isa 27: 6 Israel will *b* and blossom

BUDDED (BUD)
Heb 9: 4 Aaron's staff that had *b*,

BUILD (BUILDER BUILDERS BUILDING BUILDS BUILT
REBUILD REBUILT)
2Sa 7: 5 Are you the one to *b* me a house
1Ki 6: 1 he began to *b* the temple
Ecc 3: 3 a time to tear down and a time
                to *b*,
Mt 16:18 and on this rock I will *b* my
                church,
Ac 20:32 which can *b* you up and give you
Ro 15: 2 neighbor for his good, to *b* him
                up.
1Co 14:12 excel in gifts that *b* up the church.
1Th 5:11 one another and *b* each other up,
Jude :20 *b* yourselves up in your most holy

BUILDER* (BUILD)
1Co 3:10 I laid a foundation as an expert *b*,
Heb 3: 3 the *b* of a house has greater
                honor
     3: 4 but God is the *b* of everything.
    11:10 whose architect and *b* is God.

BUILDERS (BUILD)
Ps 118:22 The stone the *b* rejected
Mt 21:42 " 'The stone the *b* rejected
Mk 12:10 " 'The stone the *b* rejected
Lk 20:17 " 'The stone the *b* rejected
Ac   4:11 " 'the stone you *b* rejected,
1Pe 2: 7 "The stone the *b* rejected

BUILDING (BUILD)
Ezr 3: 8 to supervise the *b* of the house
Ne   4:17 of Judah who were *b* the wall.
Ro 15:20 so that I would not be *b*
1Co 3: 9 you are God's field, God's *b*.
2Co 5: 1 we have a *b* from God, an eternal
    10: 8 us for *b* you up rather
    13:10 the Lord gave me for *b* you up,
Eph 2:21 him the whole *b* is joined together
     4:29 helpful for *b* others up according

BUILDS (BUILD)
Ps 127: 1 Unless the LORD *b* the house,
Pr 14: 1 The wise woman *b* her house,
1Co 3:10 one should be careful how he *b*.
     3:12 If any man *b* on this foundation

1Co 8: 1 Knowledge puffs up, but love *b*
                up.
Eph 4:16 grows and *b* itself up in love,

BUILT (BUILD)
1Ki 6:14 So Solomon *b* the temple
Mt   7:24 is like a wise man who *b* his house
Lk   6:49 is like a man who *b* a house
Ac 17:24 does not live in temples *b* by
                hands.
1Co 3:14 If what he has *b* survives, he will
2Co 5: 1 in heaven, not *b* by human hands.
Eph 2:20 *b* on the foundation of the
                apostles
     4:12 the body of Christ may be *b* up
Col 2: 7 live in him, rooted and *b* up in
                him,
1Pe 2: 5 are being *b* into a spiritual house

BULL (BULLS)
Lev 4: 3 bring to the LORD a young *b*

BULLS (BULL)
1Ki 7:25 The Sea stood on twelve *b*,
Heb 10: 4 it is impossible for the blood of *b*

BURDEN (BURDENED BURDENS BURDENSOME)
Ps 38: 4 like a *b* too heavy to bear.
Ecc 1:13 What a heavy *b* God has laid
Mt 11:30 my yoke is easy and my *b* is light."
Ac 15:28 to us not to *b* you with anything
2Co 11: 9 from being a *b* to you in any way,
    12:14 and I will not be a *b* to you,
1Th 2: 9 day in order not to be a *b* to
                anyone
2Th 3: 8 so that we would not be a *b* to
                any
Heb 13:17 not a *b*, for that would be

BURDENED* (BURDEN)
Isa 43:23 have not *b* you with grain
                offerings
    43:24 But you have *b* me with your sins
Mic 6: 3 How have I *b* you? Answer me.
Mt 11:28 all you who are weary and *b*,
2Co 5: 4 are in this tent, we groan and
                are *b*,
Gal 5: 1 do not let yourselves be *b* again
1Ti 5:16 not let the church be *b* with them,

BURDENS (BURDEN)
Ps 68:19 who daily bears our *b*.
Lk 11:46 down with *b* they can hardly
                carry,
Gal 6: 2 Carry each other's *b*,

BURDENSOME (BURDEN)
1Jn 5: 3 And his commands are not *b*,

BURIED (BURY)
Ru   1:17 die I will die, and there I will be *b*.
Ro   6: 4 *b* with him through baptism
1Co 15: 4 that he was *b*, that he was raised
Col 2:12 having been *b* with him in
                baptism

BURN (BURNING BURNT)
Dt   7: 5 and *b* their idols in the fire.
Ps 79: 5 long will your jealousy *b* like fire?
1Co 7: 9 to marry than to *b* with passion.

BURNING (BURN)
Ex 27:20 so that the lamps may be kept *b*.
Lev 6: 9 the fire must be kept *b* on the
                altar.
Ps 18:28 You, O LORD, keep my lamp *b*;
Pr 25:22 you will heap *b* coals on his head,
Ro 12:20 you will heap *b* coals on his
                head."
Rev 19:20 alive into the fiery lake of *b* sulfur.

BURNISHED*
1Ki 7:45 of the LORD were of *b* bronze.
Eze 1: 7 and gleamed like *b* bronze.
Da 10: 6 and legs like the gleam of *b*
                bronze,
Rev 2:18 and whose feet are like *b* bronze.

BURNT (BURN)
Ge   8:20 he sacrificed *b* offerings on it.
    22: 2 as a *b* offering on one
Ex 10:25 and *b* offerings to present
    18:12 brought a *b* offering and other
    40: 6 Place the altar of *b* offering in
                front
Lev 1: 3 " 'If the offering is a *b* offering
Jos 8:31 offered to the LORD *b* offerings
Jdg 6:26 offer the second bull as a *b*
                offering

Jdg 13:16 But if you prepare a *b* offering,
1Ki 3: 4 offered a thousand *b* offerings
     9:25 year Solomon sacrificed *b*
                offerings
    10: 5 and the *b* offerings he made
Ezr 3: 2 Israel to sacrifice *b* offerings on it,
Eze 43:18 for sacrificing *b* offerings

BURST
Ps 98: 4 *b* into jubilant song with music;
Isa 44:23 *B* into song, you mountains,
    49:13 *b* into song, O mountains!
    52: 9 *B* into songs of joy together,
    54: 1 *b* into song, shout for joy,
    55:12 will *b* into song before you,

BURY (BURIED)
Mt   8:22 and let the dead *b* their own
                dead."
Lk   9:60 "Let the dead *b* their own dead,

BUSH
Ex   3: 2 the *b* was on fire it did not burn
                up.
Mk 12:26 the account of the *b*, how God
                said
Lk 20:37 But in the account of the *b*,
Ac   7:35 who appeared to him in the *b*.

BUSINESS
Ecc 4: 8 a miserable *b*!
Da   8:27 and went about the king's *b*.
1Co 5:12 What *b* is it of mine to judge those
1Th 4:11 to mind your own *b* and to work
Jas 1:11 even while he goes about his *b*.

BUSY*
1Ki 18:27 Perhaps he is deep in thought,
                or *b*,
    20:40 While your servant was *b* here
Isa 32: 6 his mind is *b* with evil:
Hag 1: 9 of you is *b* with his own house.
2Th 3:11 They are not *b*; they are
Tit   2: 5 to be *b* at home, to be kind,

BUSYBODIES*
2Th 3:11 They are not busy; they are *b*.
1Ti 5:13 *b*, saying things they ought not to.

BUY (BOUGHT BUYS)
Pr 23:23 *B* the truth and do not sell it;
Isa 55: 1 Come, *b* wine and milk
Rev 13:17 so that no one could *b* or sell

BUYS (BUY)
Pr 31:16 She considers a field and *b* it;

BYWORD (WORD)
1Ki 9: 7 Israel will then become a *b*
Ps 44:14 You have made us a *b*
Joel 2:17 a *b* among the nations.

CAESAR
Mt 22:21 "Give to *C* what is Caesar's,

CAIN
Firstborn of Adam (Ge 4:1), murdered
brother Abel (Ge 4:1–16; 1Jn 3:12).

CAKE
Hos 7: 8 Ephraim is a flat *c* not turned over.

CALEB
Judahite who spied out Canaan (Nu 13:6);
allowed to enter land because of faith (Nu
13:30–14:38; Dt 1:36). Possessed Hebron (Jos
14:6–15:19).

CALF
Ex 32: 4 into an idol cast in the shape of
                a *c*,
Pr 15:17 than a fattened *c* with hatred.
Lk 15:23 Bring the fattened *c* and kill it.
Ac   7:41 made an idol in the form of a *c*.

CALL (CALLED CALLING CALLS)
1Ki 18:24 I will *c* on the name of the LORD.
2Ki 5:11 *c* on the name of the LORD his
1Ch 16: 8 to the LORD, *c* on his name;
Ps 105: 1 to the LORD, *c* on his name;
   116:13 and *c* on the name of the LORD.
   116:17 and *c* on the name of the LORD.
   145:18 near to all who *c* on him,
Pr 31:28 children arise and *c* her blessed;
Isa 5:20 Woe to those who *c* evil good
    12: 4 to the LORD, *c* on his name;
    55: 6 *c* on him while he is near.
    65:24 Before they *c* I will answer;
Jer 33: 3 'C to me and I will answer you
Zep 3: 9 that all of them may *c* on the
                name

Zec 13: 9 They will *c* on my name
Mt 9:13 come to *c* the righteous,
Mk 2:17 I have not come to *c* the
      righteous,
Lk 5:32 I have not come to *c* the
      righteous,
Ac 2:39 all whom the Lord our God will *c*.
     9:14 to arrest all who *c* on your name."
     9:21 among those who *c* on this name?
Ro 10:12 and richly blesses all who *c* on
      him,
   11:29 gifts and his *c* are irrevocable.
1Co 1: 2 with all those everywhere who *c*
1Th 4: 7 For God did not *c* us to be impure,
2Ti 2:22 along with those who *c*

CALLED (CALL)
Ge 2:23 she shall be *c* 'woman,'
     5: 2 he blessed them and *c* them "man
   12: 8 and *c* on the name of the LORD.
   21:33 and there he *c* upon the name
   26:25 and *c* on the name of the LORD.
1Sa 3: 5 and said, "Here I am; you *c* me."
2Ch 7:14 if my people, who are *c*
Ps 34: 6 This poor man *c*, and the LORD
  116: 4 Then I *c* on the name of the LORD
Isa 56: 7 for my house will be *c*
La 3:55 I *c* on your name, O LORD,
Hos 11: 1 and out of Egypt I *c* my
Mt 1:16 was born Jesus, who is *c* Christ.
     2:15 "Out of Egypt I *c* my son."
   21:13 " 'My house will be *c* a house
Mk 11:17 " 'My house will be *c*
Lk 1:32 will be the *c* the Son of the Most
      High.
     1:35 to be born will be *c* the Son of
      God.
Ro 1: 1 *c* to be an apostle and set apart
     1: 6 among those who are *c* to belong
     1: 7 loved by God and *c* to be saints:
     8:28 who have been *c* according
     8:30 And those he predestined, he
      also *c*
1Co 1: 1 *c* to be an apostle of Christ Jesus
     1: 2 in Christ Jesus and *c* to be holy,
     1:24 but to those whom God has *c*,
     1:26 of what you were when you
      were *c*.
     7:15 God has *c* us to live in peace.
     7:17 and to which God has *c* him.
Gal 1: 6 deserting the one who *c* you
     1:15 from birth and *c* me by his grace,
     5:13 You, my brothers, were *c* to be
      free
Eph 1:18 the hope to which he has *c* you,
     4: 4 as you were *c* to one hope
Col 3:15 of one body you were *c* to peace.
2Th 2:14 He *c* you to this through our
      gospel
1Ti 6:12 life to which you were *c*
2Ti 1: 9 who has saved us and *c* us
Heb 9:15 that those who are *c* may receive
1Pe 1:15 But just as he who *c* you is holy,
     2: 9 of him who *c* you out of darkness
     3: 9 to this you were *c* so that you may
     5:10 who *c* you to his eternal glory
2Pe 1: 3 of him who *c* us by his own glory
Jude : 1 To those who have been *c*,

CALLING (CALL)
Isa 40: 3 A voice of one *c*:
Mt 3: 3 "A voice of one *c* in the desert,
Mk 1: 3 "a voice of one *c* in the desert,
   10:49 Cheer up! On your feet! He's *c*
      you
Lk 3: 4 "A voice of one *c* in the desert,
Jn 1:23 I am the voice of one *c* in the
      desert
Ac 22:16 wash your sins away, *c* on his
      name
Eph 4: 1 worthy of the *c* you have received.
2Th 1:11 may count you worthy of his *c*,
2Pe 1:10 all the more eager to make your *c*

CALLOUS* (CALLOUSED)
Ps 17:10 They close up their *c* hearts,
   73: 7 From their *c* hearts comes
      iniquity;
  119:70 Their hearts are *c* and unfeeling.

CALLOUSED* (CALLOUS)
Isa 6:10 Make the heart of this people *c*;
Mt 13:15 this people's heart has become *c*;

Ac 28:27 this people's heart has become *c*;

CALLS (CALL)
Ps 147: 4 and *c* them each by name.
Isa 40:26 and *c* them each by name.
Joel 2:32 And everyone who *c*
Mt 22:43 speaking by the Spirit, *c* him 'Lord
Jn 10: 3 He *c* his own sheep by name
Ac 2:21 And everyone who *c*
Ro 10:13 "Everyone who *c* on the name
1Th 2:12 who *c* you into his kingdom
     5:24 The one who *c* you is faithful

CALM (CALMS)
Ps 107:30 They were glad when it grew *c*,
Isa 7: 4 keep *c* and don't be afraid.
Eze 16:42 I will be *c* and no longer angry.

CALMS* (CALM)
Pr 15:18 but a patient man *c* a quarrel.

CAMEL
Mt 19:24 it is easier for a *c* to go
   23:24 strain out a gnat but swallow a *c*.
Mk 10:25 It is easier for a *c* to go
Lk 18:25 It is easier for a *c* to go

CAMP (ENCAMPS)
Heb 13:13 outside the *c*, bearing the
      disgrace

CANAAN (CANAANITE CANAANITES)
Ge 10:15 *C* was the father of Sidon his
Lev 14:34 "When you enter the land of *C*,
   25:38 of Egypt to give you the land of *C*
Nu 13: 2 men to explore the land of *C*,
   33:51 'When you cross the Jordan
      into *C*,
Jdg 4: 2 a king of *C*, who reigned in Hazor.
1Ch 16:18 "To you I will give the land of *C*
Ps 105:11 "To you I will give the land of *C*
Ac 13:19 he overthrew seven nations in *C*

CANAANITE (CANAAN)
Ge 10:18 Later the *C* clans scattered
   28: 1 "Do not marry a *C* woman.
Jos 5: 1 all the *C* kings along the seacoast
Jdg 1:32 lived among the *C* inhabitants

CANAANITES (CANAAN)
Ex 33: 2 before you and drive out the *C*,

CANCEL (CANCELED)
Dt 15: 1 seven years you must *c* debts.

CANCELED (CANCEL)
Mt 18:27 pity on him, *c* the debt
Lk 7:42 so he *c* the debts of both.
Col 2:14 having *c* the written code,

CANDLESTICKS SEE LAMPSTANDS

CANOPY*
2Sa 22:12 He made darkness his *c*
2Ki 16:18 away the Sabbath *c* that had been
Ps 18:11 made darkness his covering, his *c*
Isa 4: 5 over all the glory will be a *c*.
   40:22 stretches out the heavens like a *c*,
Jer 43:10 he will spread his royal *c*

CAPERNAUM
Mt 4:13 Nazareth, he went and lived in *C*,
Jn 6:59 teaching in the synagogue in *C*.

CAPITAL
Dt 21:22 guilty of a *c* offense is put to
      death

CAPSTONE* (STONE)
Ps 118:22 has become the *c*;
Zec 4: 7 he will bring out the *c* to shouts
Mt 21:42 has become the *c*;
Mk 12:10 has become the *c*;
Lk 20:17 has become the *c*'?
Ac 4:11 which has become the *c*.'
1Pe 2: 7 has become the *c*,"

CAPTIVATE* (CAPTIVE)
Pr 6:25 or let her *c* you with her eyes,

CAPTIVATED* (CAPTIVE)
Pr 5:19 may you ever be *c* by her love.
   5:20 Why be *c*, my son, by an
      adulteress

CAPTIVE (CAPTIVATE CAPTIVATED CAPTIVES
CAPTIVITY CAPTURED)
Ac 8:23 full of bitterness and *c* to sin."
2Co 10: 5 and we take *c* every thought
Col 2: 8 See to it that no one takes you *c*
2Ti 2:26 who has taken them *c* to do his
      will.

CAPTIVES (CAPTIVE)
Ps 68:18 you led *c* in your train;
Isa 61: 1 to proclaim freedom for the *c*
Eph 4: 8 he led *c* in his train

CAPTIVITY (CAPTIVE)
Dt 28:41 because they will go into *c*.
2Ki 25:21 So Judah went into *c*, away
Jer 30: 3 Israel and Judah back from *c*
   52:27 So Judah went into *c*, away
Eze 29:14 I will bring them back from *c*

CAPTURED (CAPTIVE)
1Sa 4:11 The ark of God was *c*,
2Sa 5: 7 David *c* the fortress of Zion,
2Ki 17: 6 the king of Assyria *c* Samaria

CARCASS
Jdg 14: 9 taken the honey from the lion's *c*.
Mt 24:28 there is a *c*, there the vultures

CARE (CAREFUL CARES CARING)
Ps 8: 4 the son of man that you *c* for him?
   65: 9 You *c* for the land and water it;
  144: 3 what is man that you *c* for him,
Pr 29: 7 The righteous *c* about justice
Mk 5:26 deal under the *c* of many doctors
Lk 10:34 him to an inn and took *c* of him.
   18: 4 I don't fear God or *c* about men,
Jn 21:16 Jesus said, "Take *c* of my sheep."
1Ti 3: 5 how can he take *c* of God's church
     6:20 what has been entrusted to
      your *c*.
Heb 2: 6 the son of man that you *c* for him?
1Pe 5: 2 of God's flock that is under your *c*,

CAREFUL* (CARE)
Ge 31:24 "Be *c* not to say anything to
      Jacob,
   31:29 'Be *c* not to say anything to Jacob,
Ex 19:12 'Be *c* that you do not go up
   23:13 "Be *c* to do everything I have said
   34:12 "Be *c* not to make a treaty
   34:15 "Be *c* not to make a treaty
Lev 18: 4 and be *c* to follow my decrees.
   25:18 " 'Follow my decrees and be *c*
   26: 3 and are *c* to obey my commands,
Dt 2: 4 afraid of you, but be very *c*.
     4: 9 before you today? Only be *c*,
     4:23 Be *c* not to forget the covenant
     5:32 So be *c* to do what the LORD your
     6: 3 be *c* to obey so that it may go well
     6:12 be *c* that you do not forget
     6:25 And if we are *c* to obey all this law
     7:12 attention to these laws and are *c*
     8: 1 Be *c* to follow every command I
      am
     8:11 Be *c* that you do not forget
   11:16 Be *c*, or you will be enticed
   12: 1 and laws you must be *c* to follow
   12:13 Be *c* not to sacrifice your burnt
   12:19 Be *c* not to neglect the Levites
   12:28 Be *c* to obey all these regulations I
   12:30 be *c* not to be ensnared
   15: 5 are *c* to follow all these
      commands
   15: 9 Be *c* not to harbor this wicked
   17:10 Be *c* to do everything they direct
   24: 8 cases of leprous diseases be very *c*
Jos 1: 7 Be *c* to obey all the law my
      servant
     1: 8 so that you may be *c*
     22: 5 But be very *c* to keep
     23: 6 be *c* to obey all that is written
     23:11 be very *c* to love the LORD your
1Ki 8:25 if only your sons are *c* in all they
      do
2Ki 10:31 Yet Jehu was not *c* to keep the
      law
   17:37 You must always be *c*
   21: 8 if only they will be *c*
1Ch 22:13 if you are *c* to observe the decrees
   28: 8 Be *c* to follow all the commands
2Ch 6:16 if only your sons are *c* in all they
      do
   33: 8 if only they will be *c*
Ezr 4:22 Be *c* not to neglect this matter.
Job 36:18 Be *c* that no one entices you
Ps 101: 2 I will be *c* to lead a blameless
      life—
Pr 13:24 he who loves him is *c*
   27:23 give *c* attention to your herds;
Isa 7: 4 Be *c*, keep calm and don't be
      afraid.

2165

Jer	17:21	Be *c* not to carry a load
	17:24	But if you are *c* to obey me,
	22: 4	For if you are *c* to carry out these
Eze	11:20	will follow my decrees and be *c*
	18:19	has been *c* to keep all my decrees,
	20:19	follow my decrees and be *c*
	20:21	they were not *c* to keep my laws—
	36:27	you to follow my decrees and be *c*
	37:24	and be *c* to keep my decrees.
Mic	7: 5	be *c* of your words.
Hag	1: 5	"Give *c* thought to your ways.
	1: 7	"Give *c* thought to your ways.
	2:15	give *c* thought to this from this day
	2:18	Give *c* thought: Is there yet any
	2:18	give *c* thought to the day
Mt	2: 8	and make a *c* search for the child.
	6: 1	"Be *c* not to do your 'acts
	16: 6	"Be *c*," Jesus said to them.
Mk	8:15	"Be *c*," Jesus warned them.
Lk	21:34	Be *c*, or your hearts will be weighed
Ro	12:17	Be *c* to do what is right in the eyes
1Co	3:10	each one should be *c* how he builds
	8: 9	Be *c*, however, that the exercise
	10:12	standing firm, be *c* that you don't
Eph	5:15	Be very *c*, then, how you live—
2Ti	4: 2	great patience and *c* instruction.
Tit	3: 8	may be *c* to devote themselves
Heb	2: 1	We must pay more *c* attention,
	4: 1	let us be *c* that none

CARELESS*

Mt	12:36	for every *c* word they have spoken.

CARES* (CARE)

Dt	11:12	It is a land the LORD your God *c*
Job	39:16	she *c* not that her labor was in vain,
Ps	55:22	Cast your *c* on the LORD
	142: 4	no one *c* for my life.
Pr	12:10	A righteous man *c* for the needs
Ecc	5: 3	when there are many *c*,
Jer	12:11	because there is no one who *c*.
	30:17	Zion for whom no one *c*.'
Na	1: 7	He *c* for those who trust in him,
Jn	10:13	and *c* nothing for the sheep.
Eph	5:29	but he feeds and *c* for it, just
1Pe	5: 7	on him because he *c* for you.

CARING* (CARE)

1Th	2: 7	like a mother *c* for her little
1Ti	5: 4	practice by *c* for their own family

CARPENTER (CARPENTER'S)

Mk	6: 3	does miracles! Isn't this the *c*?

CARPENTER'S* (CARPENTER)

Mt	13:55	"Isn't this the *c* son? Isn't his

CARRIED

Ex	19: 4	and how I *c* you on eagles' wings
Dt	1:31	how the LORD your God *c* you,
Isa	53: 4	and *c* our sorrows,
	63: 9	he lifted them up and *c* them
Mt	8:17	and *c* our diseases."
Heb	13: 9	Do not be *c* away by all kinds
2Pe	1:21	as they were *c* along by the Holy
	3:17	so that you may not be *c* away

CARRIES (CARRY)

Dt	32:11	and *c* them on its pinions.
Isa	40:11	and *c* them close to his heart;

CARRY (CARRIED CARRIES CARRYING)

Lev	16:22	goat will *c* on itself all their sins
	26:15	and fail to *c* out all my commands
Isa	46: 4	I have made you and I will *c* you;
Lk	14:27	anyone who does not *c* his cross
Gal	6: 2	C each other's burdens,
	6: 5	for each one should *c* his own load.

CARRYING (CARRY)

Jn	19:17	C his own cross, he went out
1Jn	5: 2	loving God and *c* out his

CARVED

Nu	33:52	Destroy all their *c* images
Mic	5:13	I will destroy your *c* images

CARVES* (CARVED)

Dt	27:15	"Cursed is the man who *c* an image

CASE		
Pr	18:17	to present his *c* seems right,
	22:23	for the LORD will take up their *c*
	23:11	he will take up their *c* against you.
CAST	(CASTING)	
Ex	34:17	"Do not make *c* idols.
Lev	16: 8	He is to *c* lots for the two goats—
Ps	22:18	and *c* lots for my clothing.
	55:22	C your cares on the LORD
Pr	16:33	The lot is *c* into the lap,
Ecc	11: 1	C your bread upon the waters,
Jn	19:24	and *c* lots for my clothing."
1Pe	5: 7	C all your anxiety on him
CASTING	(CAST)	
Pr	18:18	C the lot settles disputes
Mt	27:35	divided up his clothes by *c* lots.
CATCH	(CATCHES CAUGHT)	
Lk	5: 4	and let down the nets for a *c*."
	5:10	from now on you will *c* men."
CATCHES	(CATCH)	
Job	5:13	He *c* the wise in their craftiness,
1Co	3:19	"He *c* the wise in their craftiness";
CATTLE		
Ps	50:10	and the *c* on a thousand hills.
CAUGHT	(CATCH)	
Ge	22:13	there in a thicket he saw a ram *c*
2Co	12: 2	who fourteen years ago was *c* up
1Th	4:17	and are left will be *c* up together with them
CAUSE	(CAUSES)	
Pr	24:28	against your neighbor without *c*,
Ecc	8: 3	Do not stand up for a bad *c*,
Mt	18: 7	of the things that *c* people to sin!
Ro	14:21	else that will *c* your brother
1Co	10:32	Do not *c* anyone to stumble,
CAUSES	(CAUSE)	
Ps	7:16	The trouble he *c* recoils on himself;
Isa	8:14	a stone that *c* men to stumble
Mt	5:29	If your right eye *c* you to sin,
	5:30	And if your right hand *c* you to sin,
	18: 6	if anyone *c* one of these little ones
	18: 8	or your foot *c* you to sin,
Ro	14:20	to eat anything that *c* someone else
1Co	8:13	if what I eat *c* my brother to fall
1Pe	2: 8	"A stone that *c* men to stumble
CAUTIOUS*		
Pr	12:26	A righteous man is *c* in friendship,
CEASE		
Ps	46: 9	He makes wars *c* to the ends
CELEBRATE*		
Ex	10: 9	we are to *c* a festival to the LORD
	12:14	generations to come you shall *c* it
	12:17	C this day as a lasting ordinance
	12:17	"C the Feast of Unleavened Bread,
	12:47	community of Israel must *c* it.
	12:48	to *c* the LORD's Passover must
	23:14	are to *c* a festival to me.
	23:15	"C the Feast of Unleavened Bread;
	23:16	"C the Feast of Harvest
	23:16	"C the Feast of Ingathering
	34:18	"C the Feast of Unleavened Bread.
	34:22	"C the Feast of Weeks
Lev	23:39	*c* the festival to the LORD
	23:41	C this as a festival to the LORD
	23:41	for the generations to come; *c* it
Nu	9: 2	"Have the Israelites *c* the Passover
	9: 3	C it at the appointed time,
	9: 4	told the Israelites to *c* the Passover,
	9: 6	of them could not *c* the Passover
	9:10	they may still *c* the LORD's
	9:11	are to *c* it on the fourteenth day
	9:12	When they *c* the Passover,
	9:13	on a journey fails to *c* the Passover,
	9:14	to *c* the LORD's Passover must do
	29:12	C a festival to the LORD
Dt	16: 1	*c* the Passover of the LORD your
	16:10	Then *c* the Feast of Weeks
	16:13	C the Feast of Tabernacles
	16:15	For seven days *c* the Feast

Jdg	16:23	to Dagon their god and to *c*,
2Sa	6:21	the LORD's people Israel—I will *c*
2Ki	23:21	"C the Passover to the LORD your
2Ch	30: 1	and *c* the Passover to the LORD,
	30: 2	decided to *c* the Passover
	30: 3	able to *c* it at the regular time
	30: 5	and *c* the Passover to the LORD,
	30:13	in Jerusalem to *c* the Feast
	30:23	to *c* the festival seven more days;
Ne	8:12	of food and to *c* with great joy,
	12:27	to *c* joyfully the dedication
Est	9:21	to have them *c* annually
Ps	145: 7	They will *c* your abundant
Isa	30:29	as on the night you *c* a holy festival
Na	1:15	C your festivals, O Judah,
Zec	14:16	and to *c* the Feast of Tabernacles.
	14:18	up to *c* the Feast of Tabernacles.
	14:19	up to *c* the Feast of Tabernacles.
Mt	26:18	I am going to *c* the Passover
Lk	15:23	Let's have a feast and *c*.
	15:24	So they began to *c*.
	15:29	goat so I could *c* with my friends.
	15:32	But we had to *c* and be glad,
Rev	11:10	will *c* by sending each other gifts,

CELESTIAL*

2Pe	2:10	afraid to slander *c* beings;
Jude	: 8	authority and slander *c* beings.

CENSER (CENSERS)

Lev	16:12	is to take a *c* full of burning coals
Rev	8: 3	Another angel, who had a golden *c*,

CENSERS (CENSER)

Nu	16: 6	Take *c* and tomorrow put fire

CENTURION

Mt	8: 5	had entered Capernaum, a *c* came
	27:54	When the *c* and those
Mk	15:39	And when the *c*, who stood there
Lk	7: 3	The *c* heard of Jesus and sent some
	23:47	The *c*, seeing what had happened,
Ac	10: 1	a *c* in what was known
	27: 1	handed over to a *c* named Julius,

CEPHAS* (PETER)

Jn	1:42	You will be called C" (which,
1Co	1:12	another, "I follow C"; still another,
	3:22	Paul or Apollos or C or the world
	9: 5	and the Lord's brothers and C?

CEREMONIAL* (CEREMONY)

Lev	14: 2	at the time of his *c* cleansing,
	15:13	off seven days for his *c* cleansing;
Mk	7: 3	they give their hands a *c* washing,
Jn	2: 6	used by the Jews for *c* washing.
	3:25	Jew over the matter of *c* washing.
	11:55	to Jerusalem for their *c* cleansing
	18:28	to avoid *c* uncleanness the Jews did
Heb	9:10	drink and various *c* washings—
	13: 9	not by *c* foods, which are

CEREMONIALLY* (CEREMONY)

Lev	4:12	outside the camp to a place *c* clean,
	5: 2	touches anything *c* unclean—
	6:11	the camp to a place that is *c* clean.
	7:19	anyone *c* clean may eat it.
	7:19	touches anything *c* unclean must
	10:14	Eat them in a *c* clean place;
	11: 4	not have a split hoof; it is *c* unclean
	12: 2	birth to a son will be *c* unclean
	12: 7	and then she will be *c* clean
	13: 3	he shall pronounce him *c* unclean.
	14: 8	with water; then he will be *c* clean.
	15:28	and after that she will be *c* clean.
	15:33	lies with a woman who is *c* unclean.
	17:15	he will be *c* unclean till evening.
	21: 1	must not make himself *c* unclean
	22: 3	of your descendants is *c* unclean
	27:11	he vowed is a *c* unclean animal—
Nu	5: 2	who is *c* unclean because of a dead
	6: 7	must not make himself *c* unclean
	8: 6	Israelites and make them *c* clean.
	9: 6	they were *c* unclean on account

Nu 9:13 But if a man who is *c* clean
   18:11 household who is *c* clean may eat
   18:13 household who is *c* clean may eat
   19: 7 but he will be *c* unclean till evening
   19: 9 and put them in a *c* clean place
   19:18 Then a man who is *c* clean is
Dt 12:15 Both the *c* unclean and the clean
   12:22 Both the *c* unclean and the clean
   14: 7 they are *c* unclean for you.
   15:22 Both the *c* unclean and the clean
1Sa 20:26 to David to make him *c* unclean—
2Ch 13:11 the bread on the *c* clean table
   30:17 for all those who were not *c* clean
Ezr 6:20 themselves and were all *c* clean.
Ne 12:30 Levites had purified themselves *c,*
Isa 66:20 of the LORD in *c* clean vessels.
Eze 22:10 period, when they are *c* unclean.
Ac 24:18 I was *c* clean when they found me
Heb 9:13 those who are *c* unclean sanctify

CEREMONY* (CEREMONIAL CEREMONIALLY)
Ge 50:11 Egyptians are holding a solemn *c*
Ex 12:25 as he promised, observe this *c.*
   12:26 'What does this *c* mean to you?'
   13: 5 are to observe this *c* in this month:

CERTAIN (CERTAINTY)
2Pe 1:19 word of the prophets made more *c,*

CERTAINTY* (CERTAIN)
Lk 1: 4 so that you may know the *c*
Jn 17: 8 They knew with *c* that I came

CERTIFICATE* (CERTIFIED)
Dt 24: 1 and writes her a *c* of divorce,
   24: 3 and writes her a *c* of divorce,
Isa 50: 1 'Where is your mother's *c*
Jer 3: 8 I gave faithless Israel her *c*
Mt 5:31 divorces his wife must give her a *c*
   19: 7 that a man give his wife a *c*
Mk 10: 4 a man to write a *c* of divorce

CERTIFIED* (CERTIFICATE)
Jn 3:33 has accepted it has *c* that God is

CHAFF
Ps 1: 4 They are like *c*
   35: 5 May they be like *c* before the wind,
Da 2:35 became like *c* on a threshing floor
Mt 3:12 up the *c* with unquenchable fire."

CHAINED (CHAINS)
2Ti 2: 9 But God's word is not *c.*

CHAINS (CHAINED)
Eph 6:20 for which I am an ambassador in *c.*
Col 4:18 Remember my *c.*
2Ti 1:16 and was not ashamed of my *c.*
Jude : 6 with everlasting *c* for judgment

CHAMPION
Ps 19: 5 like a *c* rejoicing to run his course.

CHANCE
Ecc 9:11 but time and *c* happen to them all.

CHANGE (CHANGED)
1Sa 15:29 of Israel does not lie or *c* his mind;
Ps 110: 4 and will not *c* his mind:
Jer 7: 5 If you really *c* your ways
Mal 3: 6 "I the LORD do not *c.*
Mt 18: 3 unless you *c* and become like little
Heb 7:21 and will not *c* his mind:
Jas 1:17 who does not *c* like shifting

CHANGED (CHANGE)
1Sa 10: 6 you will be *c* into a different person
Hos 11: 8 My heart is *c* within me;
1Co 15:51 but we will all be *c*— in a flash,

CHARACTER*
Ru 3:11 that you are a woman of noble *c.*
Pr 12: 4 of noble *c* is her husband's crown,
   31:10 A wife of noble *c* who can find?
Ac 17:11 noble *c* than the Thessalonians,
Ro 5: 4 perseverance, *c*; and *c,* hope.
1Co 15:33 "Bad company corrupts good *c.* "

CHARGE (CHARGES)
Job 34:13 him in *c* of the whole world?
Ro 8:33 Who will bring any *c*
1Co 9:18 the gospel I may offer it free of *c,*
2Co 11: 7 the gospel of God to you free of *c?*

2Ti 4: 1 I give you this *c:* Preach the Word;
Phm :18 or owes you anything, *c* it to me.

CHARGES (CHARGE)
Isa 50: 8 Who then will bring *c* against me?

CHARIOT (CHARIOTS)
2Ki 2:11 suddenly a *c* of fire and horses
Ps 104: 3 He makes the clouds his *c*
Ac 8:28 sitting in his *c* reading the book

CHARIOTS (CHARIOT)
2Ki 6:17 and *c* of fire all around Elisha.
Ps 20: 7 Some trust in *c* and some in horses,
   68:17 The *c* of God are tens of thousands

CHARM* (CHARMING)
Pr 17: 8 bribe is a *c* to the one who gives it;
   31:30 *C* is deceptive, and beauty is

CHARMING* (CHARM)
Pr 26:25 his speech is *c,* do not believe
SS 1:16 Oh, how *c!*

CHASE (CHASES)
Lev 26: 8 Five of you will *c* a hundred,

CHASES* (CHASE)
Pr 12:11 he who *c* fantasies lacks judgment.
   28:19 one who *c* fantasies will have his

CHASM*
Lk 16:26 and you a great *c* has been fixed,

CHATTER* (CHATTERING)
1Ti 6:20 Turn away from godless *c*
2Ti 2:16 Avoid godless *c,* because those

CHATTERING* (CHATTER)
Pr 10: 8 but a *c* fool comes to ruin.
   10:10 and a *c* fool comes to ruin.

CHEAT* (CHEATED CHEATING CHEATS)
Mal 1:14 "Cursed is the *c* who has
1Co 6: 8 you yourselves *c* and do wrong,

CHEATED* (CHEAT)
Ge 31: 7 yet your father has *c* me
1Sa 12: 3 Whom have I *c?* Whom have I
   12: 4 "You have not *c* or oppressed us,"
Lk 19: 8 if I have *c* anybody out of anything,
1Co 6: 7 Why not rather be *c?* Instead,

CHEATING* (CHEAT)
Am 8: 5 and *c* with dishonest scales,

CHEATS* (CHEAT)
Lev 6: 2 or if he *c* him, or if he finds lost

CHEEK (CHEEKS)
Mt 5:39 someone strikes you on the right *c,*
Lk 6:29 If someone strikes you on one *c,*

CHEEKS* (CHEEK)
Isa 50: 6 my *c* to those who pulled out my

CHEERFUL* (CHEERS)
Pr 15:13 A happy heart makes the face *c,*
   15:15 but the *c* heart has a continual feast
   15:30 A *c* look brings joy to the heart,
   17:22 A *c* heart is good medicine,
2Co 9: 7 for God loves a *c* giver.

CHEERS* (CHEERFUL)
Pr 12:25 but a kind word *c* him up.

CHEMOSH
2Ki 23:13 for *C* the vile god of Moab,

CHERISH (CHERISHED CHERISHES)
Ps 17:14 You still the hunger of those you *c;*

CHERISHED* (CHERISH)
Ps 66:18 If I had *c* sin in my heart,

CHERISHES* (CHERISH)
Pr 19: 8 he who *c* understanding prospers.

CHERUB* (CHERUBIM)
Ex 25:19 Make one *c* on one end
Eze 28:14 You were anointed as a guardian *c,*

CHERUBIM (CHERUB)
Ge 3:24 side of the Garden of Eden *c*
1Sa 4: 4 who is enthroned between the *c.*
2Sa 6: 2 enthroned between the *c* that are
   22:11 He mounted the *c* and flew;
1Ki 6:23 a pair of *c* of olive wood,

2Ki 19:15 of Israel, enthroned between the *c,*
1Ch 13: 6 who is enthroned between the *c*—
Ps 18:10 He mounted the *c* and flew;
   80: 1 who sit enthroned between the *c,*
   99: 1 he sits enthroned between the *c,*
Isa 37:16 of Israel, enthroned between the *c,*
Eze 10: 1 was over the heads of the *c.*

CHEST
Ex 25:10 "Have them make a *c*
2Ki 12: 9 Jehoiada the priest took a *c*
Da 2:32 its *c* and arms of silver, its belly
Rev 1:13 with a golden sash around his *c.*

CHEWS
Lev 11: 3 divided and that *c* the cud.

CHIEF
1Pe 5: 4 And when the *C* Shepherd appears,

CHILD (CHILDISH CHILDREN CHILDREN'S GRANDCHILDREN)
Pr 20:11 Even a *c* is known by his actions,
   22: 6 Train a *c* in the way he should go,
   22:15 Folly is bound up in the heart of a *c*
   23:13 not withhold discipline from a *c;*
   29:15 *c* left to himself disgraces his mother.
Isa 7:14 The virgin will be with *c*
   9: 6 For to us a *c* is born,
   11: 6 and a little *c* will lead them.
   66:13 As a mother comforts her *c,*
Mt 1:23 "The virgin will be with *c*
   18: 2 He called a little *c* and had him
Lk 1:42 and blessed is the *c* you will bear!
   1:80 And the *c* grew and became strong
1Co 13:11 When I was a *c,* I talked like a *c,*
1Jn 5: 1 who loves the father loves his *c*

CHILDBEARING (BEAR)
Ge 3:16 greatly increase your pains in *c;*

CHILDBIRTH (BEAR)
Gal 4:19 the pains of *c* until Christ is formed

CHILDISH* (CHILD)
1Co 13:11 When I became a man, I put *c* ways

CHILDREN (CHILD)
Ex 20: 5 punishing the *c* for the sin
Dt 4: 9 Teach them to your *c*
   6: 7 Impress them on your *c.*
   11: 9 them to your *c,* talking about them
   14: 1 You are the *c* of the LORD your
   24:16 nor *c* put to death for their fathers;
   30:19 so that you and your *c* may live
   32:46 so that you may command your *c*
Job 1: 5 "Perhaps my *c* have sinned
Ps 8: 2 From the lips of *c* and infants
   78: 5 forefathers to teach their *c,*
Pr 17: 6 Children's *c* are a crown
   20: 7 blessed are his *c* after him.
   31:28 Her *c* arise and call her blessed;
Joel 1: 3 Tell it to your *c,*
Mal 4: 6 the hearts of the fathers to their *c,*
Mt 7:11 how to give good gifts to your *c,*
   11:25 and revealed them to little *c.*
   18: 3 you change and become like little *c*
   19:14 "Let the little *c* come to me,
   21:16 " 'From the lips of *c* and infants
Mk 9:37 one of these little *c* in my name
   10:14 "Let the little *c* come to me,
   10:16 And he took the *c* in his arms,
   13:12 *C* will rebel against their parents
Lk 10:21 and revealed them to little *c.*
   18:16 "Let the little *c* come to me,
Jn 1:12 the right to become *c* of God—
Ac 2:39 The promise is for you and your *c*
Ro 8:16 with our spirit that we are God's *c.*
1Co 14:20 Brothers, stop thinking like *c.*
2Co 12:14 parents, but parents for their *c.*
Eph 6: 1 *C,* obey your parents in the Lord,
   6: 4 do not exasperate your *c;* instead,

Col 3:20 *C*, obey your parents in everything,
　　3:21 Fathers, do not embitter your *c*,
1Ti 3: 4 and see that his *c* obey him
　　3:12 and must manage his *c* and his
　　5:10 bringing up *c*, showing hospitality,
Heb 2:13 and the *c* God has given me."
1Jn 3: 1 that we should be called *c* of God!

CHILDREN'S (CHILD)
Isa 54:13 and great will be your *c* peace.

CHOKE
Mk 4:19 come in and *c* the word,

CHOOSE (CHOOSES CHOSE CHOSEN)
Dt 30:19 Now *c* life, so that you
Jos 24:15 then *c* for yourselves this day
Pr 8:10 *C* my instruction instead of silver,
　　16:16 to *c* understanding rather
Jn 15:16 You did not *c* me, but I chose you

CHOOSES (CHOOSE)
Mt 11:27 to whom the Son *c* to reveal him.
Lk 10:22 to whom the Son *c* to reveal him."
Jn 7:17 If anyone *c* to do God's will,

CHOSE (CHOOSE)
Ge 13:11 So Lot *c* for himself the whole plain
Ps 33:12 the people he *c* for his inheritance.
Jn 15:16 but I *c* you and appointed you to go
1Co 1:27 But God *c* the foolish things
Eph 1: 4 he *c* us in him before the creation
2Th 2:13 from the beginning God *c* you

CHOSEN (CHOOSE)
Isa 41: 8 Jacob, whom I have *c*,
Mt 22:14 For many are invited, but few are *c*
Lk 10:42 Mary has *c* what is better,
　　23:35 the Christ of God, the *C* One."
Jn 15:19 but I have *c* you out of the world.
1Pe 1:20 He was *c* before the creation
　　2: 9 But you are a *c* people, a royal

CHRIST (CHRIST'S CHRISTIANS CHRISTS)
Mt 1:16 was born Jesus, who is called *C*.
　　16:16 Peter answered, "You are the *C*,
　　22:42 "What do you think about the *C*?
Mk 1: 1 of the gospel about Jesus *C*,
　　8:29 Peter answered, "You are the *C*."
　　14:61 "Are you the *C*, the Son
Lk 9:20 Peter answered, "The *C* of God."
Jn 1:41 found the Messiah" (that is, the *C*).
　　20:31 you may believe that Jesus is the *C*,
Ac 2:36 you crucified, both Lord and *C*."
　　5:42 the good news that Jesus is the *C*.
　　9:22 by proving that Jesus is the *C*.
　　9:34 said to him, "Jesus *C* heals you.
　　17: 3 proving that the *C* had to suffer
　　18:28 the Scriptures that Jesus was the *C*.
　　26:23 that the *C* would suffer and,
Ro 1: 4 from the dead: Jesus *C* our Lord.
　　3:22 comes through faith in Jesus *C*
　　5: 1 God through our Lord Jesus *C*,
　　5: 6 we were still powerless, *C* died
　　5: 8 While we were still sinners, *C* died
　　5:11 in God through our Lord Jesus *C*,
　　5:17 life through the one man, Jesus *C*.
　　6: 4 as *C* was raised from the dead
　　6: 9 that since *C* was raised
　　6:23 life in *C* Jesus our Lord.
　　7: 4 to the law through the body of *C*,
　　8: 1 for those who are in *C* Jesus,
　　8: 9 Spirit of *C*, he does not belong to *C*.
　　8:17 heirs of God and co-heirs with *C*,
　　8:34 Who is he that condemns? *C* Jesus,
　　8:35 us from the love of *C*?
　　9: 5 is traced the human ancestry of *C*,
　　10: 4 *C* is the end of the law
　　12: 5 so in *C* we who are many form one
　　13:14 yourselves with the Lord Jesus *C*,
　　14: 9 *C* died and returned to life
　　15: 3 For even *C* did not please himself
　　15: 5 yourselves as you follow *C* Jesus,
　　15: 7 then, just as *C* accepted you,

Ro 16:18 people are not serving our Lord *C*,
1Co 1: 2 to those sanctified in *C* Jesus
　　1: 7 for our Lord Jesus *C* to be revealed.
　　1:13 Is *C* divided? Was Paul crucified
　　1:17 For *C* did not send me to baptize,
　　1:23 but we preach *C* crucified:
　　1:30 of him that you are in *C* Jesus,
　　2: 2 except Jesus *C* and him crucified.
　　3:11 one already laid, which is Jesus *C*.
　　5: 7 For *C*, our Passover lamb,
　　6:15 bodies are members of *C* himself?
　　8: 6 and there is but one Lord, Jesus *C*,
　　8:12 conscience, you sin against *C*.
　　10: 4 them, and that rock was *C*.
　　11: 1 as I follow the example of *C*.
　　11: 3 the head of every man is *C*,
　　12:27 Now you are the body of *C*,
　　15: 3 that *C* died for our sins according
　　15:14 And if *C* has not been raised,
　　15:22 so in *C* all will be made alive:
　　15:57 victory through our Lord Jesus *C*.
2Co 1: 5 as the sufferings of *C* flow
　　2:14 us in triumphal procession in *C*
　　3: 3 show that you are a letter from *C*,
　　3:14 because only in *C* is it taken away.
　　4: 4 light of the gospel of the glory of *C*,
　　4: 5 not preach ourselves, but Jesus *C*
　　4: 6 of the glory of God in the face of *C*.
　　5:10 before the judgment seat of *C*,
　　5:17 Therefore, if anyone is in *C*,
　　6:15 What harmony is there between *C*
　　10: 1 the meekness and gentleness of *C*,
　　11: 2 you to one husband, to *C*,
Gal 1: 7 are trying to pervert the gospel of *C*
　　2: 4 on the freedom we have in *C* Jesus
　　2:16 but by faith in Jesus *C*.
　　2:17 does that mean that *C* promotes sin
　　2:20 I have been crucified with *C*
　　2:21 *C* died for nothing!" You foolish
　　3:13 *C* redeemed us from the curse
　　3:16 meaning one person, who is *C*.
　　3:26 of God through faith in *C*,
　　4:19 of childbirth until *C* is formed
　　5: 1 for freedom that *C* has set us free.
　　5: 4 by law have been alienated from *C*;
　　5:24 to *C* Jesus have crucified the sinful
　　6:14 in the cross of our Lord Jesus *C*,
Eph 1: 3 with every spiritual blessing in *C*.
　　1:10 together under one head, even *C*.
　　1:20 which he exerted in *C*
　　2: 5 made us alive with *C*
　　2:10 created in *C* Jesus
　　2:12 time you were separate from *C*,
　　2:20 with *C* Jesus himself as the chief
　　3: 8 the unsearchable riches of *C*,
　　3:17 so that *C* may dwell in your hearts
　　4: 7 has been given as *C* apportioned it.
　　4:13 measure of the fullness of *C*.
　　4:15 into him who is the Head, that is, *C*
　　4:32 just as in *C* God forgave you.
　　5: 2 as *C* loved us and gave himself up
　　5:21 out of reverence for *C*.
　　5:23 as *C* is the head of the church,
　　5:25 just as *C* loved the church
Php 1:18 motives or true, *C* is preached.
　　1:21 to live is *C* and to die is gain.
　　1:23 I desire to depart and be with *C*
　　1:27 worthy of the gospel of *C*.
　　1:29 on behalf of *C* not only to believe
　　2: 5 be the same as that of *C* Jesus:
　　3: 7 now consider loss for the sake of *C*.
　　3:10 I want to know *C* and the power
　　3:18 as enemies of the cross of *C*.
　　4:19 to his glorious riches in *C* Jesus.
Col 1: 4 heard of your faith in *C* Jesus
　　1:27 which is *C* in you, the hope of glory
　　1:28 may present everyone perfect in *C*.

Col 2: 2 the mystery of God, namely, *C*,
　　2: 6 as you received *C* Jesus as Lord,
　　2: 9 For in *C* all the fullness
　　2:13 God made you alive with *C*.
　　2:17 the reality, however, is found in *C*.
　　3: 1 then, you have been raised with *C*,
　　3: 3 and your life is now hidden with *C*
　　3:15 Let the peace of *C* rule
1Th 5: 9 through our Lord Jesus *C*.
2Th 1: 2 the coming of our Lord Jesus *C*
　　2:14 in the glory of our Lord Jesus *C*.
1Ti 1:12 I thank *C* Jesus our Lord, who has
　　1:15 *C* Jesus came into the world
　　1:16 *C* Jesus might display his unlimited
　　2: 5 the man *C* Jesus, who gave himself
2Ti 1: 9 us in *C* Jesus before the beginning
　　1:10 appearing of our Savior, *C* Jesus,
　　2: 1 in the grace that is in *C* Jesus.
　　2: 3 us like a good soldier of *C* Jesus.
　　2: 8 Remember Jesus *C*, raised
　　2:10 the salvation that is in *C* Jesus,
　　3:12 life in *C* Jesus will be persecuted,
　　3:15 salvation through faith in *C* Jesus.
　　4: 1 presence of God and of *C* Jesus,
Tit 2:13 our great God and Savior, Jesus *C*,
Heb 3: 6 But *C* is faithful as a son
　　3:14 to share in *C* if we hold firmly
　　5: 5 So *C* also did not take
　　6: 1 the elementary teachings about *C*
　　9:11 When *C* came as high priest
　　9:14 more, then, will the blood of *C*,
　　9:15 For this reason *C* is the mediator
　　9:24 For *C* did not enter a man-made
　　9:26 Then *C* would have had
　　9:28 so *C* was sacrificed once
　　10:10 of the body of Jesus *C* once for all.
　　13: 8 Jesus *C* is the same yesterday
1Pe 1: 2 for obedience to Jesus *C*
　　1: 3 of Jesus *C* from the dead,
　　1:11 he predicted the sufferings of *C*
　　1:19 but with the precious blood of *C*,
　　2:21 because *C* suffered for you,
　　3:15 in your hearts set apart *C* as Lord.
　　3:18 For *C* died for sins once for all,
　　3:21 you by the resurrection of Jesus *C*,
　　4:13 participate in the sufferings of *C*,
　　4:14 insulted because of the name of *C*,
2Pe 1: 1 and Savior Jesus *C* have received
　　1:16 and coming of our Lord Jesus *C*,
1Jn 2: 1 Jesus *C*, the Righteous One.
　　2:22 man who denies that Jesus is the *C*.
　　3:16 Jesus *C* laid down his life for us.
　　3:23 in the name of his Son, Jesus *C*,
　　4: 2 that Jesus *C* has come
　　5: 1 believes that Jesus is the *C* is born
　　5:20 even in his Son Jesus *C*.
2Jn : 9 teaching of *C* does not have God;
Jude : 4 deny Jesus *C* our only Sovereign
Rev 1: 1 The revelation of Jesus *C*,
　　1: 5 from Jesus *C*, who is the faithful
　　11:15 kingdom of our Lord and of his *C*,
　　20: 4 reigned with *C* a thousand years.
　　20: 6 they will be priests of God and of *C*

CHRIST'S (CHRIST)
1Co 9:21 from God's law but am under *C* law
2Co 5:14 For *C* love compels us,
　　5:20 We are therefore *C* ambassadors,
　　12: 9 so that *C* power may rest on me.
Col 1:22 by *C* physical body through death

CHRISTIAN* (CHRIST)
Ac 26:28 you can persuade me to be a *C*?"
1Pe 4:16 as a *C*, do not be ashamed,

CHRISTIANS* (CHRIST)
Ac 11:26 the disciples were called *C* first

CHRISTS* (CHRIST)
Mt 24:24 For false *C* and false prophets will
Mk 13:22 For false *C* and false prophets will

CHURCH
Mt 16:18 and on this rock I will build my *c*,
　　18:17 if he refuses to listen even to the *c*,

Ac 20:28 Be shepherds of the *c* of God,
1Co 5:12 of mine to judge those outside the *c*
   14: 4 but he who prophesies edifies the *c*.
   14:12 to excel in gifts that build up the *c*.
   14:26 done for the strengthening of the *c*.
   15: 9 because I persecuted the *c* of God.
Gal 1:13 how intensely I persecuted the *c*
Eph 5:23 as Christ is the head of the *c*,
Col 1:18 he is the head of the body, the *c*;
   1:24 the sake of his body, which is the *c*.

CHURNING
Pr 30:33 For as *c* the milk produces butter,

CIRCLE
Isa 40:22 enthroned above the *c* of the earth,

CIRCUMCISE (CIRCUMCISED CIRCUMCISION)
Dt 10:16 *C* your hearts, therefore,

CIRCUMCISED (CIRCUMCISE)
Ge 17:10 Every male among you shall be *c*.
   17:12 who is eight days old must be *c*,
Jos 5: 3 and *c* the Israelites at Gibeath
Gal 5: 2 that if you let yourselves be *c*,

CIRCUMCISION (CIRCUMCISE)
Ro 2:25 *C* has value if you observe the law,
   2:29 and *c* is *c* of the heart, by the Spirit,
1Co 7:19 *C* is nothing and uncircumcision is

CIRCUMSTANCES
Php 4:11 to be content whatever the *c*.
1Th 5:18 continually; give thanks in all *c*,

CITIES (CITY)
Lk 19:17 small matter, take charge of ten *c*.'
   19:19 'You take charge of five *c*.'

CITIZENS (CITIZENSHIP)
Eph 2:19 but fellow *c* with God's people

CITIZENSHIP* (CITIZENS)
Ac 22:28 "I had to pay a big price for my *c*."
Eph 2:12 excluded from *c* in Israel
Php 3:20 But our *c* is in heaven.

CITY (CITIES)
Mt 5:14 A *c* on a hill cannot be hidden.
Ac 18:10 I have many people in this *c*."
Heb 13:14 here we do not have an enduring *c*,
Rev 21: 2 saw the Holy *C*, the new

CIVILIAN*
2Ti 2: 4 a soldier gets involved in *c* affairs—

CLAIM (CLAIMS RECLAIM)
Pr 25: 6 do not *c* a place among great men;
1Jn 1: 6 If we *c* to have fellowship
   1: 8 If we *c* to be without sin, we
   1:10 If we *c* we have not sinned,

CLAIMS (CLAIM)
Jas 2:14 if a man *c* to have faith
1Jn 2: 6 Whoever *c* to live in him must walk
   2: 9 Anyone who *c* to be in the light

CLANGING*
1Co 13: 1 a resounding gong or a *c* cymbal.

CLAP* (CLAPPED CLAPS)
Job 21: 5 *c* your hand over your mouth.
Ps 47: 1 *C* your hands, all you nations;
   98: 8 Let the rivers *c* their hands,
Pr 30:32 *c* your hand over your mouth!
Isa 55:12 will *c* their hands.
La 2:15 *c* their hands at you;

CLAPPED* (CLAP)
2Ki 11:12 and the people *c* their hands
Eze 25: 6 Because you have *c* your hands

CLAPS* (CLAP)
Job 27:23 It *c* its hands in derision
   34:37 scornfully he *c* his hands among us
Na 3:19 *c* his hands at your fall,

CLASSIFY*
2Co 10:12 dare to *c* or compare ourselves

CLAUDIUS
Ac 11:28 happened during the reign of *C*.)
   18: 2 because *C* had ordered all the Jews

CLAY
Isa 45: 9 Does the *c* say to the potter,
   64: 8 We are the *c*, you are the potter;
Jer 18: 6 "Like *c* in the hand of the potter,
La 2: 1 are now considered as pots of *c*,
Da 2:33 partly of iron and partly of baked *c*,
Ro 9:21 of the same lump of *c* some pottery
2Co 4: 7 we have this treasure in jars of *c*
2Ti 2:20 and *c*; some are for noble purposes

CLEAN (CLEANNESS CLEANSE CLEANSED CLEANSES CLEANSING)
Ge 7: 2 seven of every kind of *c* animal,
Lev 4:12 the camp to a place ceremonially *c*,
   16:30 you will be *c* from all your sins.
Ps 24: 4 He who has *c* hands and a pure
   51: 7 with hyssop, and I will be *c*;
Pr 20: 9 I am *c* and without sin"?
Eze 36:25 I will sprinkle *c* water on you,
Mt 8: 2 are willing, you can make me *c*."
   12:44 the house unoccupied, swept *c*
   23:25 You *c* the outside of the cup
Mk 7:19 Jesus declared all foods "*c*."
Jn 13:10 to wash his feet; his whole body is *c*
   15: 3 are already *c* because of the word
Ac 10:15 impure that God has made *c*."
Ro 14:20 All food is *c*, but it is wrong

CLEANNESS (CLEAN)
2Sa 22:25 according to my *c* in his sight.

CLEANSE (CLEAN)
Ps 51: 2 and *c* me from my sin.
   51: 7 *C* me with hyssop, and I will be
Pr 20:30 Blows and wounds *c* away evil,
Heb 9:14 *c* our consciences from acts that
   10:22 having our hearts sprinkled to *c* us

CLEANSED (CLEAN)
Heb 9:22 requires that nearly everything be *c*
2Pe 1: 9 has forgotten that he has been *c*

CLEANSES* (CLEAN)
2Ti 2:21 If a man *c* himself from the latter,

CLEANSING (CLEAN)
Eph 5:26 *c* her by the washing with water

CLEFT*
Ex 33:22 I will put you in a *c* in the rock

CLEVER
Isa 5:21 and *c* in their own sight.

CLING
Ro 12: 9 Hate what is evil; *c* to what is good.

CLINGS
Ps 63: 8 My soul *c* to you;

CLOAK
Ex 12:11 with your *c* tucked into your belt,
2Ki 4:29 "Tuck your *c* into your belt,
   9: 1 "Tuck your *c* into your belt,
Mt 5:40 let him have your *c* as well.

CLOSE (CLOSER CLOSES)
2Ki 11: 8 Stay *c* to the king wherever he goes
2Ch 23: 7 Stay *c* to the king wherever he goes
Ps 34:18 LORD is *c* to the brokenhearted
   148:14 of Israel, the people *c* to his heart.
Isa 40:11 and carries them *c* to his heart;
Jer 30:21 himself to be *c* to me?'

CLOSER (CLOSE)
Ex 3: 5 "Do not come any *c*," God said.
Pr 18:24 there is a friend who sticks *c*

CLOSES (CLOSE)
Pr 28:27 he who *c* his eyes to them receives

CLOTHE (CLOTHED CLOTHES CLOTHING)
Ps 45: 3 *c* yourself with splendor
Isa 52: 1 *c* yourself with strength.
Ro 13:14 *c* yourselves with the Lord Jesus
Col 3:12 *c* yourselves with compassion,

1Pe 5: 5 *c* yourselves with humility

CLOTHED (CLOTHE)
Ps 30:11 removed my sackcloth and *c* me
   104: 1 you are *c* with splendor
Pr 31:22 she is *c* in fine linen and purple.
   31:25 She is *c* with strength and dignity;
Isa 61:10 For he has *c* me with garments
Lk 24:49 until you have been *c* with power
Gal 3:27 into Christ have *c* yourselves

CLOTHES (CLOTHE)
Dt 8: 4 Your *c* did not wear out
Mt 6:25 the body more important than *c*?
   6:28 "And why do you worry about *c*?
   27:35 they divided up his *c* by casting lots
Jn 11:44 Take off the grave *c* and let him go

CLOTHING (CLOTHE)
Dt 22: 5 A woman must not wear men's *c*,
Job 29:14 I put on righteousness as my *c*;
Ps 22:18 and cast lots for my *c*.
Mt 7:15 They come to you in sheep's *c*,
1Ti 6: 8 But if we have food and *c*,

CLOUD (CLOUDS)
Ex 13:21 them in a pillar of *c* to guide them
1Ki 18:44 *c* as small as a man's hand is rising
   16:15 his favor is like a rain *c* in spring.
Isa 19: 1 See, the LORD rides on a swift *c*
Lk 21:27 of Man coming in a *c* with power
Heb 12: 1 by such a great *c* of witnesses,
Rev 14:14 seated on the *c* was one "like a son

CLOUDS (CLOUD)
Dt 33:26 and on the *c* in his majesty.
Ps 68: 4 extol him who rides on the *c*—
   104: 3 He makes the *c* his chariot
Pr 25:14 Like *c* and wind without rain
Da 7:13 coming with the *c* of heaven.
Mt 24:30 of Man coming on the *c* of the sky,
   26:64 and coming on the *c* of heaven."
Mk 13:26 coming in *c* with great power
1Th 4:17 with them in the *c* to meet the Lord
Rev 1: 7 Look, he is coming with the *c*,

CLUB
Pr 25:18 Like a *c* or a sword or a sharp arrow

CO-HEIRS* (INHERIT)
Ro 8:17 heirs of God and *c* with Christ,

COALS
Pr 25:22 you will heap burning *c* on his head
Ro 12:20 you will heap burning *c* on his head

COARSE*
Eph 5: 4 or *c* joking, which are out of place,

CODE*
Ro 2:27 even though you have the written *c*
   2:29 by the Spirit, not by the written *c*.
   7: 6 not in the old way of the written *c*.
Col 2:14 having canceled the written *c*,

COINS
Mt 26:15 out for him thirty silver *c*.
Lk 15: 8 suppose a woman has ten silver *c*

COLD
Pr 25:25 Like *c* water to a weary soul
Mt 10:42 if anyone gives even a cup of *c* water
   24:12 the love of most will grow *c*,

COLLECTION
1Co 16: 1 Now about the *c* for God's people:

COLT
Zec 9: 9 on a *c*, the foal of a donkey.
Mt 21: 5 on a *c*, the foal of a donkey.' "

COMB
Ps 19:10 than honey from the *c*.

COMFORT* (COMFORTED COMFORTER COMFORTERS COMFORTING COMFORTS)
Ge 5:29 "He will *c* us in the labor
   37:35 and daughters came to *c* him,
Ru 2:13 "You have given me *c*
1Ch 7:22 and his relatives came to *c* him.
Job 2:11 sympathize with him and *c* him.

Job	7:13	When I think my bed will *c* me
	16: 5	*c* from my lips would bring you
	36:16	to the *c* of your table laden
Ps	23: 4	rod and your staff, they *c* me.
	71:21	and *c* me once again.
	119:50	My *c* in my suffering is this:
	119:52	and I find *c* in them.
	119:76	May your unfailing love be my *c*,
	119:82	I say, "When will you *c* me?"
Isa	40: 1	*C*, *c* my people,
	51: 3	The Lord will surely *c* Zion
	51:19	who can *c* you?—
	57:18	I will guide him and restore *c*
	61: 2	to *c* all who mourn,
	66:13	so will I *c* you;
Jer	16: 7	food to *c* those who mourn
	31:13	I will give them *c* and joy instead
La	1: 2	there is none to *c* her.
	1: 9	there was none to *c* her.
	1:16	No one is near to *c* me,
	1:17	but there is no one to *c* her.
	1:21	but there is no one to *c* me.
	2:13	that I may *c* you,
Eze	16:54	all you have done in giving them *c*.
Na	3: 7	Where can I find anyone to *c* you?"
Zec	1:17	and the Lord will again *c* Zion
	10: 2	they give *c* in vain.
Lk	6:24	you have already received your *c*.
Jn	11:19	and Mary to *c* them in the loss
1Co	14: 3	encouragement and *c*.
2Co	1: 3	of compassion and the God of all *c*,
	1: 4	so that we can *c* those
	1: 4	with the *c* we ourselves have
	1: 5	through Christ our *c* overflows.
	1: 6	if we are comforted, it is for your *c*,
	1: 6	it is for your *c* and salvation;
	1: 7	so also you share in our *c*.
	2: 7	you ought to forgive and *c* him,
	7: 7	also by the *c* you had given him.
Php	2: 1	if any *c* from his love,
Col	4:11	and they have proved a *c* to me.

COMFORTED* (COMFORT)

Ge	24:67	Isaac was *c* after his mother's death
	37:35	comfort him, but he refused to be *c*.
2Sa	12:24	Then David *c* his wife Bathsheba,
Job	42:11	They *c* and consoled him
Ps	77: 2	and my soul refused to be *c*.
	86:17	have helped me and *c* me.
Isa	12: 1	and you have *c* me.
	52: 9	for the Lord has *c* his people,
	54:11	lashed by storms and not *c*,
	66:13	and you will be *c* over Jerusalem."
Jer	31:15	and refusing to be *c*,
Mt	2:18	and refusing to be *c*,
	5: 4	for they will be *c*.
Lk	16:25	but now he is *c* here and you are
Ac	20:12	man home alive and were greatly *c*.
2Co	1: 6	if we are *c*, it is for your comfort,
	7: 6	*c* us by the coming of Titus,

COMFORTER* (COMFORT)

Ecc	4: 1	and they have no *c*;
	4: 1	and they have no *c*.
Jer	8:18	O my *C* in sorrow,

COMFORTERS* (COMFORT)

Job	16: 2	miserable *c* are you all!
Ps	69:20	for *c*, but I found none.

COMFORTING* (COMFORT)

Isa	66:11	satisfied at her *c* breasts;
Zec	1:13	*c* words to the angel who talked
Jn	11:31	*c* her, noticed how quickly she got
1Th	2:12	*c* and urging you to live lives

COMFORTS* (COMFORT)

Job	29:25	I was like one who *c* mourners.
Isa	49:13	For the Lord *c* his people
	51:12	"I, even I, am he who *c* you.
	66:13	As a mother *c* her child,
2Co	1: 4	who *c* us in all our troubles,
	7: 6	But God, who *c* the downcast,

COMMAND (COMMANDED COMMANDING COMMANDMENT COMMANDMENTS COMMANDS)

Ex	7: 2	You are to say everything I *c* you,
Nu	14:41	are you disobeying the Lord's *c*?

Nu	24:13	to go beyond the *c* of the Lord—
Dt	4: 2	Do not add to what I *c* you
	8: 1	to follow every I am giving you
	12:32	See that you do all I *c* you;
	15:11	I *c* you to be openhanded
	30:16	For I *c* you today to love
	32:46	so that you may *c* your children
Ps	91:11	For he will *c* his angels concerning
Pr	13:13	but he who respects a *c* is rewarded
Ecc	8: 2	Obey the king's *c*, I say,
Jer	1: 7	you to and say whatever I *c* you.
	1:17	and say to them whatever I *c* you.
	7:23	Walk in all the ways I *c* you,
	11: 4	Obey me and do everything I *c* you
	26: 2	Tell them everything I *c* you;
Joel	2:11	mighty are those who obey his *c*.
Mt	4: 6	He will *c* his angels concerning you
	15: 3	why do you break the *c* of God
Lk	4:10	" 'He will *c* his angels concerning
Jn	14:15	love me, you will obey what I *c*.
	15:12	My *c* is this: Love each other
	15:14	friends if you do what I *c*.
	15:17	This is my *c*: Love each other.
1Co	14:37	writing to you is the Lord's *c*.
Gal	5:14	law is summed up in a single *c*:
1Ti	1: 5	goal of this *c* is love, which comes
	6:14	to you keep this *c* without spot
	6:17	*C* those who are rich
Heb	11: 3	universe was formed at God's *c*,
2Pe	2:21	on the sacred *c* that was passed
	3: 2	and the *c* given by our Lord
1Jn	2: 7	I am not writing you a new *c*
	3:23	this is his *c*: to believe in the name
	4:21	And he has given us this *c*:
2Jn	: 6	his *c* is that you walk in love.

COMMANDED (COMMAND)

Ge	2:16	And the Lord God *c* the man,
	7: 5	Noah did all that the Lord *c* him.
	50:12	Jacob's sons did as he had *c* them:
Ex	7: 6	did just as the Lord *c* them.
	19: 7	all the words the Lord had *c* him
Dt	4: 5	laws as the Lord my God *c* me,
	4: 5	The Lord *c* you to obey all these
Jos	1: 9	Have I not *c* you? Be strong
	1:16	Whatever you have *c* us we will do,
2Sa	5:25	So David did as the Lord *c* him,
2Ki	17:13	the entire Law that I *c* your fathers
	21: 8	careful to do everything I *c* them
2Ch	33: 8	do everything I *c* them concerning
Ps	33: 9	he *c*, and it stood firm.
	78: 5	which he *c* our forefathers
	148: 5	for he *c* and they were created.
Mt	28:20	to obey everything I have *c* you.
1Co	9:14	Lord has *c* that those who preach
1Jn	3:23	and to love one another as he *c* us.
2Jn	: 4	in the truth, just as the Father *c* us.

COMMANDING (COMMAND)

2Ti	2: 4	he wants to please his *c* officer.

COMMANDMENT* (COMMAND)

Jos	22: 5	But be very careful to keep the *c*
Mt	22:36	which is the greatest *c* in the Law?"
	22:38	This is the first and greatest *c*.
Mk	12:31	There is no *c* greater than these."
Lk	23:56	the Sabbath in obedience to the *c*.
Jn	13:34	"A new *c* I give you: Love one
Ro	7: 8	the opportunity afforded by the *c*,
	7: 9	when the *c* came, sin sprang to life
	7:10	that the very *c* that was intended
	7:11	and through the *c* put me to death.
	7:11	the opportunity afforded by the *c*,
	7:12	and the *c* is holy, righteous
	7:13	through the *c* sin might become
	13: 9	and whatever other *c* there may be,
Eph	6: 2	which is the first *c* with a promise
Heb	9:19	Moses had proclaimed every *c*

COMMANDMENTS* (COMMAND)

Ex	20: 6	who love me and keep my *c*.

Ex	34:28	of the covenant—the Ten *C*.
Dt	4:13	to you his covenant, the Ten *C*,
	5:10	who love me and keep my *c*.
	5:22	These are the *c* the Lord
	6: 6	These *c* that I give you today are
	9:10	were all the *c* the Lord
	10: 4	The Ten *C* he had proclaimed
Ecc	12:13	Fear God and keep his *c*,
Mt	5:19	one of the least of these *c*
	19:17	If you want to enter life, obey the *c*
	22:40	the Prophets hang on these two *c*."
Mk	10:19	You know the *c*: 'Do not murder,
	12:28	"Of all the *c*, which is the most
Lk	1: 6	observing all the Lord's *c*
	18:20	You know the *c*: 'Do not commit
Ro	13: 9	The *c*, "Do not commit adultery,"
Eph	2:15	in his flesh the law with its *c*
Rev	12:17	those who obey God's *c*
	14:12	part of the saints who obey God's *c*

COMMANDS (COMMAND)

Ex	24:12	and I have written for their
	25:22	give you all my *c* for the Israelites.
	34:32	gave them all the *c* the Lord had
Lev	22:31	"Keep my *c* and follow them.
Nu	15:39	and so you will remember all the *c*
Dt	7: 9	those who love him and keep his *c*.
	7:11	Therefore, take care to follow the *c*
	11: 1	decrees, his laws and his *c* always.
	11:27	the blessing if you obey the *c*
	28: 1	carefully follow all his *c* I give you
	30:10	Lord your God and keep his *c*
Jos	22: 5	to walk in all his ways, to obey his *c*
1Ki	2: 3	and keep his decrees and *c*,
	8:58	in all his ways and to keep the *c*,
	8:61	to live by his decrees and obey his *c*
1Ch	28: 7	unswerving in carrying out my *c*
	29:19	devotion to keep your *c*,
2Ch	31:21	in obedience to the law and the *c*,
Ne	1: 5	those who love him and obey his *c*,
Ps	78: 7	but would keep his *c*.
	112: 1	who finds great delight in his *c*.
	119:10	do not let me stray from your *c*
	119:32	I run in the path of your *c*,
	119:35	Direct me in the path of your *c*,
	119:47	for I delight in your *c*
	119:48	I lift up my hands to your *c*,
	119:73	me understanding to learn your *c*.
	119:86	All your *c* are trustworthy;
	119:96	but your *c* are boundless.
	119:98	Your *c* make me wiser
	119:115	that I may keep the *c* of my God!
	119:127	Because I love your *c*
	119:131	longing for your *c*.
	119:143	but your *c* are my delight.
	119:151	and all your *c* are true.
	119:172	for all your *c* are righteous.
	119:176	for I have not forgotten your *c*.
Pr	2: 1	and store up my *c* within you,
	3: 1	but keep my *c* in your heart,
	6:23	For these *c* are a lamp,
	10: 8	The wise in heart accept *c*,
Isa	48:18	you had paid attention to my *c*,
Da	9: 4	all who love him and obey his *c*,
Mt	5:19	teaches these *c* will be called great
Mk	7: 8	You have let go of the *c* of God
	7: 9	way of setting aside the *c* of God
Jn	14:21	Whoever has my *c* and obeys them,
	15:10	If you obey my *c*, you will remain
Ac	17:30	but now he *c* all people everywhere
1Co	7:19	Keeping God's *c* is what counts.
1Jn	2: 3	come to know him if we obey his *c*.
	2: 4	but does not do what he *c* is a liar,
	3:22	we obey his *c* and do what pleases
	3:24	Those who obey his *c* live in him,
	5: 2	loving God and carrying out his *c*.
	5: 3	And his *c* are not burdensome,
	5: 3	This is love for God: to obey his *c*,

2Jn : 6 that we walk in obedience to his *c*.

COMMEMORATE
Ex 12:14 "This is a day you are to *c*;

COMMEND* (COMMENDABLE COMMENDED COMMENDS)
Ps 145: 4 One generation will *c* your works
Ecc 8:15 So I *c* the enjoyment of life,
Ro 13: 3 do what is right and he will *c* you.
16: 1 I *c* to you our sister Phoebe,
2Co 3: 1 beginning to *c* ourselves again?
4: 2 the truth plainly we *c* ourselves
5:12 trying to *c* ourselves to you again,
6: 4 as servants of God we *c* ourselves
10:12 with some who *c* themselves
1Pe 2:14 and to *c* those who do right.

COMMENDABLE* (COMMEND)
1Pe 2:19 For it is *c* if a man bears up
2:20 you endure it, this is *c* before God.

COMMENDED* (COMMEND)
Ne 11: 2 The people *c* all the men who
Job 29:11 and those who saw me *c* me,
Lk 16: 8 master *c* the dishonest manager
Ac 15:40 *c* by the brothers to the grace
2Co 12:11 I ought to have been *c* by you,
Heb 11: 2 This is what the ancients were *c* for
11: 4 By faith he was *c* as a righteous
11: 5 he was *c* as one who pleased God.
11:39 These were all *c* for their faith,

COMMENDS* (COMMEND)
Pr 15: 2 of the wise *c* knowledge,
2Co 10:18 but the one whom the Lord *c*.
10:18 not the one who *c* himself who is

COMMIT (COMMITS COMMITTED)
Ex 20:14 "You shall not *c* adultery.
Dt 5:18 "You shall not *c* adultery.
1Sa 7: 3 and *c* yourselves to the LORD
Ps 31: 5 Into your hands I *c* my spirit;
37: 5 *C* your way to the LORD;
Pr 16: 3 *C* to the LORD whatever you do,
Mt 5:27 that it was said, 'Do not *c* adultery.'
5:32 causes her to *c* adultery,
19:18 do not *c* adultery, do not steal,
Mk 10:19 do not *c* adultery, do not steal,
Lk 18:20 'Do not *c* adultery, do not murder,
23:46 into your hands I *c* my spirit."
Ac 20:32 I *c* you to God and to the word
Ro 2:22 do you *c* adultery? You who abhor
2:22 that people should not *c* adultery,
13: 9 "Do not *c* adultery,"
1Co 10: 8 We should not *c* sexual immorality,
Jas 2:11 do not *c* adultery but do *c* murder,
1Pe 4:19 to God's will should *c* themselves
Rev 2:22 I will make those who *c* adultery

COMMITS (COMMIT)
Pr 6:32 man who *c* adultery lacks
29:22 a hot-tempered one *c* many sins.
Ecc 8:12 a wicked man *c* a hundred crimes
Eze 18:12 He *c* robbery.
18:14 who sees all the sins his father *c*,
18:24 from his righteousness and *c* sin,
18:26 from his righteousness and *c* sin,
22:11 you one man *c* a detestable offense
Mt 5:32 the divorced woman *c* adultery.
19: 9 marries another woman *c* adultery
Mk 10:11 marries another woman *c* adultery
10:12 another man, she *c* adultery."
Lk 16:18 a divorced woman *c* adultery.
16:18 marries another woman *c* adultery,

COMMITTED (COMMIT)
Nu 5: 7 and must confess the sin he has *c*.
1Ki 8:61 But your hearts must be fully *c*
15:14 Asa's heart was fully *c*
2Ch 16: 9 those whose hearts are fully *c*
Mt 25:8 lustfully has already *c* adultery
11:27 "All things have been *c* to me
Lk 10:22 "All things have been *c* to me
Ac 14:23 *c* them to the Lord,
14:26 where they had been *c* to the grace
1Co 9:17 I am simply discharging the trust *c*

2Co 5:19 And he has *c* to us the message
1Pe 2:22 "He *c* no sin,
Rev 17: 2 the kings of the earth *c* adultery
18: 3 of the earth *c* adultery with her,
18: 9 kings of the earth who *c* adultery

COMMON
Ge 11: 1 had one language and a *c* speech.
Lev 10:10 between the holy and the *c*,
Pr 22: 2 Rich and poor have this in *c*:
29:13 the oppressor have this in *c*:
Ac 2:44 together and had everything in *c*.
1Co 10:13 has seized you except what is *c*
2Co 6:14 and wickedness have in *c*?

COMPANION (COMPANIONS)
Ps 55:13 my *c*, my close friend,
55:20 My *c* attacks his friends;
Pr 13:20 but a *c* of fools suffers harm.
28: 7 a *c* of gluttons disgraces his father.
29: 3 *c* of prostitutes squanders his
Rev 1: 9 your brother and *c* in the suffering

COMPANIONS (COMPANION)
Ps 45: 7 your God, has set you above your *c*
Pr 18:24 A man of many *c* may come to ruin
Heb 1: 9 your God, has set you above your *c*

COMPANY
Ps 14: 5 present in the *c* of the righteous.
Pr 21:16 comes to rest in the *c* of the dead.
24: 1 do not desire their *c*,
Jer 15:17 I never sat in the *c* of revelers,
1Co 15:33 "Bad *c* corrupts good character."

COMPARE* (COMPARED COMPARING COMPARISON)
Job 28:17 Neither gold nor crystal can *c*
28:19 The topaz of Cush cannot *c* with it;
39:13 but they cannot *c* with the pinions
Ps 86: 8 no deeds can *c* with yours.
89: 6 skies above can *c* with the LORD?
Pr 3:15 nothing you desire can *c* with her.
8:11 nothing you desire can *c* with her.
Isa 40:18 To whom, then, will you *c* God?
40:18 What image will you *c* him to?
40:25 "To whom will you *c* me?
46: 5 "To whom will you *c* me
La 2:13 With what can I *c* you,
Eze 31: 8 *c* with its branches—
Da 2:31 Then *c* our appearance with that
Mt 11:16 "To what can I *c* this generation?
Lk 7:31 I *c* the people of this generation?
13:18 What shall I *c* it to? It is like
13:20 What shall I *c* the kingdom of God
2Co 10:12 and *c* themselves with themselves,
10:12 or *c* ourselves with some who

COMPARED* (COMPARE)
Jdg 8: 2 What have I accomplished *c* to you
8: 3 What was I able to do *c* to you?"
Isa 46: 5 you liken me that we may be *c*?
Eze 31: 2 Who can be *c* with you in majesty?
31:18 the trees of Eden can be *c* with you
Php 3: 8 I consider everything a loss *c*

COMPARING* (COMPARE)
Ro 8:18 present sufferings are not worth *c*
2Co 8: 8 the sincerity of your love by *c* it
Gal 6: 4 without *c* himself to somebody else

COMPARISON* (COMPARE)
2Co 3:10 now in *c* with the surpassing glory.

COMPASSION (COMPASSIONATE COMPASSIONS)
Ex 33:19 I will have *c* on whom I will have *c*.
Dt 13:17 he will show you mercy, have *c*
28:54 man among you will have no *c*
30: 3 restore your fortunes and have *c*
32:36 and have *c* on his servants
Jdg 2:18 for the LORD had *c* on them
1Ki 3:26 son was alive was filled with *c*
2Ki 13:23 and had *c* and showed concern
2Ch 30: 9 and your children will be shown *c*
Ne 9:19 of your great *c* you did not
9:27 and in your great *c* you gave them
9:28 in your *c* you delivered them time
Ps 51: 1 according to your great *c*

Ps 77: 9 Has he in anger withheld his *c*?"
90:13 Have *c* on your servants.
102:13 You will arise and have *c* on Zion,
103: 4 and crowns you with love and *c*,
103:13 As a father has *c* on his children,
103:13 so the LORD has *c*
116: 5 our God is full of *c*.
119:77 Let your *c* come to me that I may
119:156 Your *c* is great, O LORD;
135:14 and have *c* on his servants.
145: 9 he has *c* on all he has made.
Isa 13:18 will they look with *c* on children.
14: 1 The LORD will have *c* on Jacob;
27:11 so their Maker has no *c* on them,
30:18 he rises to show you *c*.
49:10 He who has *c* on them will guide
49:13 and will have *c* on his afflicted ones
49:15 and have no *c* on the child she has
51: 3 and will look with *c* on all her ruins
54: 7 with deep *c* I will bring you back.
54: 8 I will have *c* on you,"
54:10 says the LORD, who has *c* on you.
60:10 in favor I will show you *c*.
63: 7 to his *c* and many kindnesses,
63:15 and *c* are withheld from us.
Jer 12:15 I will again have *c* and will bring
13:14 *c* to keep me from destroying them
15: 6 I can no longer show *c*.
21: 7 show them no mercy or pity or *c*.'
30:18 and have *c* on his dwellings;
31:20 I have great *c* for him,
33:26 restore their fortunes and have *c*
42:12 I will show you *c* so that he will
42:12 so that he will have *c* on you
La 3:32 he brings grief, he will show *c*,
Eze 9: 5 without showing pity or *c*.
16: 5 or had *c* enough to do any
39:25 and will have *c* on all the people
Hos 2:19 in love and *c*.
11: 8 all my *c* is aroused.
13:14 "I will have no *c*,
2: 3 for in you the fatherless find *c*."
Am 1:11 stifling all *c*,
Jnh 3: 9 with *c* turn from his fierce anger
3:10 he had *c* and did not bring
Mic 7:19 You will again have *c* on us;
Zec 7: 9 show mercy and *c* to one another.
10: 6 because I have *c* on them.
Mal 3:17 as in *c* a man spares his son who
Mt 9:36 When he saw the crowds, he had *c*
14:14 he had *c* on them and healed their
15:32 "I have *c* for these people;
20:34 Jesus had *c* on them and touched
Mk 1:41 with *c*, Jesus reached out his hand
6:34 and saw a large crowd, he had *c*
8: 2 "I have *c* for these people;
Lk 15:20 and was filled with *c* for him;
Ro 9:15 and I will have *c* on whom I have *c*
2Co 1: 3 the Father of *c* and the God
Php 2: 1 and *c*, then make my joy complete
Col 3:12 clothe yourselves with *c*, kindness,
Jas 5:11 The Lord is full of *c* and mercy.

COMPASSIONATE* (COMPASSION)
Ex 22:27 out to me, I will hear, for I am *c*.
34: 6 the LORD, the *c* and gracious God
2Ch 30: 9 LORD your God is gracious and *c*.
Ne 9:17 gracious and *c*, slow to anger
Ps 86:15 O LORD, are a *c* and gracious God,
103: 8 The LORD is *c* and gracious,
111: 4 the LORD is gracious and *c*.
112: 4 the gracious and *c* and righteous
145: 8 The LORD is gracious and *c*,
La 4:10 With their own hands *c* women
Joel 2:13 for he is gracious and *c*,
Jnh 4: 2 that you are a gracious and *c* God,
Eph 4:32 Be kind and *c* to one another,
1Pe 3: 8 love as brothers, be *c* and humble.

COMPASSIONS* (COMPASSION)
La 3:22 for his *c* never fail.

COMPELLED (COMPULSION)
Ac 20:22 "And now, *c* by the Spirit,
1Co 9:16 I cannot boast, for I am *c* to preach.

COMPELS (COMPULSION)
Job 32:18 and the spirit within me *c* me;
2Co 5:14 For Christ's love *c* us, because we

COMPETENCE* (COMPETENT)
2Co 3: 5 but our *c* comes from God.

COMPETENT* (COMPETENCE)
Ro 15:14 and *c* to instruct one another.
1Co 6: 2 are you not *c* to judge trivial cases?
2Co 3: 5 Not that we are *c* in ourselves to claim
3: 6 He has made us *c* as ministers

COMPETES*
1Co 9:25 Everyone who *c* in the games goes
2Ti 2: 5 Similarly, if anyone *c* as an athlete,
2: 5 unless he *c* according to the rules.

COMPLACENCY* (COMPLACENT)
Pr 1:32 and the *c* of fools will destroy them
Eze 30: 9 ships to frighten Cush out of her *c*.

COMPLACENT* (COMPLACENCY)
Isa 32: 9 You women who are so *c*,
32:11 Tremble, you *c* women;
Am 6: 1 Woe to you who are *c* in Zion,
Zep 1:12 and punish those who are *c*,

COMPLAINING*
Php 2:14 Do everything without *c* or arguing

COMPLETE
Dt 16:15 your hands, and your joy will be *c*.
Jn 3:29 That joy is mine, and it is now *c*.
15:11 and that your joy may be *c*.
16:24 will receive, and your joy will be *c*.
17:23 May they be brought to *c* unity
Ac 20:24 *c* the task the Lord Jesus has given
Php 2: 2 then make my joy *c*
Col 4:17 to it that you *c* the work you have
Jas 1: 4 so that you may be mature and *c*,
2:22 his faith was made *c* by what he did
1Jn 1: 4 We write this to make our joy *c*.
4: 12 God's love is truly made *c* in him.
4:12 and his love is made *c* in us.
4:17 love is made *c* among us
2Jn :12 to face, so that our joy may be *c*.

COMPLIMENTS*
Pr 23: 8 and will have wasted your *c*.

COMPREHEND* (COMPREHENDED)
Job 28:13 Man does not *c* its worth;
Ecc 8:17 No one can *c* what goes
8:17 he knows, he cannot really *c* it.

COMPREHENDED* (COMPREHEND)
Job 38:18 Have you *c* the vast expanses

COMPULSION (COMPELLED COMPELS)
2Co 9: 7 not reluctantly or under *c*,

CONCEAL (CONCEALED CONCEALS)
Ps 40:10 I do not *c* your love and your truth
Pr 25: 2 It is the glory of God to *c* a matter;

CONCEALED (CONCEAL)
Jer 16:17 nor is their sin *c* from my eyes.
Mt 10:26 There is nothing *c* that will not be
Mk 4:22 and whatever is *c* is meant
Lk 8:17 nothing *c* that will not be known
12: 2 There is nothing *c* that will not be

CONCEALS* (CONCEAL)
Pr 10:18 He who *c* his hatred has lying lips,
28:13 He who *c* his sins does not prosper.

CONCEIT* (CONCEITED CONCEITS)
Isa 16: 6 her overweening pride and *c*,
Jer 48:29 her overweening pride and *c*,
Php 2: 3 out of selfish ambition or vain *c*,

CONCEITED* (CONCEIT)
1Sa 17:28 I know how *c* you are and how
Ro 11:25 brothers, so that you may not be *c*:
12:16 Do not be *c*.
2Co 12: 7 To keep me from becoming *c*
Gal 5:26 Let us not become *c*, provoking
1Ti 3: 6 or he may become *c* and fall
6: 4 he is *c* and understands nothing.
2Ti 3: 4 of the good, treacherous, rash, *c*,

CONCEITS* (CONCEIT)
Ps 73: 7 evil *c* of their minds know no

CONCEIVED (CONCEIVES)
Ps 51: 5 from the time my mother *c* me.
Mt 1:20 what is *c* in her is from the Holy
1Co 2: 9 no mind has *c*
Jas 1:15 after desire has *c*, it gives birth

CONCEIVES* (CONCEIVED)
Ps 7:14 *c* trouble gives birth

CONCERN* (CONCERNED)
Ge 39: 6 he did not *c* himself with anything
39: 8 "my master does not *c* himself
1Sa 23:21 "The LORD bless you for your *c*
2Ki 13:23 and had compassion and showed *c*
Job 9:21 I have no *c* for myself;
19: 4 my error remains my *c* alone.
Ps 131: 1 I do not *c* myself with great matters
Pr 29: 7 but the wicked have no such *c*.
Eze 36:21 I had *c* for my holy name, which
Ac 15:14 God at first showed his *c* by taking
18:17 But Gallio showed no *c* whatever.
1Co 7:32 I would like you to be free from *c*.
12:25 that its parts should have equal *c*
2Co 7: 7 your deep sorrow, your ardent *c*
7:11 what alarm, what longing, what *c*,
8:16 of Titus the same *c* I have for you.
11:28 of my *c* for all the churches.
Php 4:10 at last you have renewed your *c*

CONCERNED (CONCERN)
Ex 2:25 Israelites and was *c* about them.
Ps 142: 4 no one is *c* for me.
Jnh 4:10 "You have been *c* about this vine,
4:11 Should I not be *c* about that great
1Co 7:32 An unmarried man is *c*
9: 9 Is it about oxen that God is *c*?
Php 4:10 you have been *c*, but you had no

CONCESSION*
1Co 7: 6 I say this as a *c*, not as a command.

CONDEMN* (CONDEMNATION CONDEMNED CONDEMNING CONDEMNS)
Job 9:20 innocent, my mouth would *c* me;
10: 2 I will say to God: Do not *c* me,
34:17 Will you *c* the just and mighty One
34:29 if he remains silent, who can *c* him?
40: 8 Would you *c* me to justify yourself?
Ps 94:21 and *c* the innocent to death.
109: 7 and may his prayers *c* him.
109:31 from those who *c* him.
Isa 50: 9 Who is he that will *c* me?
Mt 12:41 with this generation and *c* it;
12:42 with this generation and *c* it;
20:18 They will *c* him to death
Mk 10:33 They will *c* him to death
Lk 6:37 Do not *c*, and you will not be
11:31 men of this generation and *c* them;
11:32 with this generation and *c* it;
Jn 3:17 Son into the world to *c* the world,
7:51 "Does our law *c* anyone
8:11 "Then neither do I *c* you,"
12:48 very word which I spoke will *c* him
Ro 2:27 yet obeys the law will *c* you who,
14: 3 everything must not *c* the man who
14:22 is the man who does not *c* himself
2Co 7: 3 this to *c* you; I have said
1Jn 3:20 presence whenever our hearts *c* us.
3:21 if our hearts do not *c* us,

CONDEMNATION* (CONDEMN)
Jer 42:18 of *c* and reproach; you will never
44:12 and horror, of *c* and reproach.
Ro 3: 8 may result"? Their *c* is deserved.
5:16 followed one sin and brought *c*,
5:18 of one trespass was *c* for all men,
8: 1 there is now no *c* for those who are
2Pe 2: 3 Their *c* has long been hanging
Jude : 4 certain men whose *c* was written

CONDEMNED* (CONDEMN)
Dt 13:17 of those *c* things shall be found
Job 32: 3 to refute Job, and yet had *c* him.
Ps 34:21 the foes of the righteous will be *c*.
34:22 be *c* who takes refuge in him.

Ps 37:33 let them be *c* when brought to trial.
79:11 preserve those *c* to die.
102:20 and release those *c* to death."
Mt 12: 7 you would not have *c* the innocent.
12:37 and by your words you will be *c*."
23:33 How will you escape being *c* to hell
27: 3 betrayed him, saw that Jesus was *c*,
Mk 14:64 They all *c* him as worthy of death.
16:16 whoever does not believe will be *c*.
Lk 6:37 condemn, and you will not be *c*.
Jn 3:18 Whoever believes in him is not *c*,
3:18 does not believe stands *c* already
5:24 has eternal life and will not be *c*;
5:29 who have done evil will rise to be *c*.
8:10 Has no one *c* you?" "No one, sir,"
16:11 prince of this world now stands *c*.
Ac 25:15 against him and asked that he be *c*.
Ro 3: 7 why am I still *c* as a sinner?"
8: 3 And so he *c* sin in sinful man,
14:23 But the man who has doubts is *c*
1Co 4: 9 like men *c* to die in the arena.
11:32 disciplined so that we will not be *c*
Gal 1: 8 let him be eternally *c*! As we have
1: 9 let him be eternally *c*! Am I now
2Th 2:12 that all will be *c* who have not
Tit 2: 8 of speech that cannot be *c*,
Heb 11: 7 By his faith he *c* the world
Jas 5: 6 You have *c* and murdered innocent
5:12 and your "No," no, or you will be *c*
2Pe 2: 6 if he *c* the cities of Sodom
Rev 19: 2 He has *c* the great prostitute

CONDEMNING* (CONDEMN)
Dt 25: 1 the innocent and *c* the guilty.
1Ki 8:32 *c* the guilty and bringing
Pr 17:15 the guilty and *c* the innocent—
Ac 13:27 yet in *c* him they fulfilled the words
Ro 2: 1 judge the other, you are *c* yourself,

CONDEMNS* (CONDEMN)
Job 15: 6 Your own mouth *c* you, not mine;
Pr 12: 2 but the LORD *c* a crafty man.
Ro 8:34 Who is he that *c*? Christ Jesus,
2Co 3: 9 the ministry that *c* men is glorious,

CONDITION
Pr 27:23 Be sure you know the *c*

CONDUCT (CONDUCTED CONDUCTS)
Pr 10:23 A fool finds pleasure in evil *c*,
20:11 by whether his *c* is pure and right.
21: 8 but the *c* of the innocent is upright.
Ecc 6: 8 how to *c* himself before others?
Jer 4:18 "Your own *c* and actions
17:10 to reward a man according to his *c*,
Eze 7: 3 I will judge you according to your *c*
Php 1:27 *c* yourselves in a manner worthy
1Ti 3:15 to *c* themselves in God's household

CONDUCTED* (CONDUCT)
2Co 1:12 testifies that we have *c* ourselves

CONDUCTS* (CONDUCT)
Ps 112: 5 who *c* his affairs with justice.

CONFESS* (CONFESSED CONFESSES CONFESSING CONFESSION)
Lev 5: 5 he must *c* in what way he has
16:21 and *c* over it all the wickedness
26:40 " 'But if they will *c* their sins
Nu 5: 7 must *c* the sin he has committed.
1Ki 8:33 back to you and *c* your name,
8:35 toward this place and *c* your name
2Ch 6:24 they turn back and *c* your name,
6:26 toward this place and *c* your name
Ne 1: 6 I *c* the sins we Israelites, including

Ps 32: 5 I said, "I will *c*
   38:18 I *c* my iniquity;
Jn 1:20 fail to *c*, but confessed freely,
   12:42 they would not *c* their faith
Ro 10: 9 That if you *c* with your mouth,
   10:10 it is with your mouth that you *c*
   14:11 every tongue will *c* to God.' "
Php 2:11 every tongue *c* that Jesus Christ is
Heb 3: 1 and high priest whom we *c*.
   13:15 the fruit of lips that *c* his name.
Jas 5:16 Therefore *c* your sins to each other
1Jn 1: 9 If we *c* our sins, he is faithful

CONFESSED* (CONFESS)
1Sa 7: 6 day they fasted and there they *c*,
Ne 9: 2 in their places and *c* their sins
Da 9: 4 to the LORD my God and *c*:
Jn 1:20 but *c* freely, "I am not the Christ."
Ac 19:18 and openly *c* their evil deeds.

CONFESSES* (CONFESS)
Pr 28:13 whoever *c* and renounces them
2Ti 2:19 and, "Everyone who *c* the name

CONFESSING* (CONFESS)
Ezr 10: 1 While Ezra was praying and *c*,
Da 9:20 *c* my sin and the sin
Mt 3: 6 C their sins, they were baptized
Mk 1: 5 C their sins, they were baptized

CONFESSION* (CONFESS)
Ezr 10:11 Now make *c* to the LORD,
Ne 9: 3 and spent another quarter in *c*
2Co 9:13 obedience that accompanies your *c*
1Ti 6:12 called when you made your good *c*
   6:13 Pontius Pilate made the good *c*,

CONFIDENCE* (CONFIDENT)
Jdg 9:26 and its citizens put their *c* in him.
2Ki 18:19 On what are you basing this *c*
2Ch 32: 8 And the people gained *c*
   32:10 On what are you basing your *c*,
Job 4: 6 Should not your piety be your *c*
Ps 71: 5 my *c* since my youth.
Pr 3:26 for the LORD will be your *c*
   3:32 but takes the upright into his *c*.
   11:13 A gossip betrays a *c*,
   20:19 A gossip betrays a *c*;
   25: 9 do not betray another man's *c*,
   31:11 Her husband has full *c* in her
Isa 32:17 will be quietness and *c* forever.
   36: 4 On what are you basing this *c*
Jer 17: 7 whose *c* is in him.
   49:31 which lives in *c*,"
Eze 29:16 a source of *c* for the people of Israel
Mic 7: 5 put no *c* in a friend.
2Co 2: 3 I had *c* in all of you, that you would
   3: 4 Such *c* as this is ours
   7: 4 I have great *c* in you; I take great
   7:16 I am glad I can have complete *c*
   8:22 so because of his great *c* in you.
Eph 3:12 God with freedom and *c*
Php 3: 3 and who put no *c* in the flesh—
   3: 4 I myself have reasons for such *c*.
   3: 4 reasons to put *c* in the flesh,
2Th 3: 4 We have *c* in the Lord that you are
Heb 3:14 till the end the *c* we had at first.
   4:16 the throne of grace with *c*,
   10:19 since we have *c* to enter the Most
   10:35 So do not throw away your *c*;
   13: 6 So we say with *c*,
1Jn 3:21 we have *c* before God and receive
   4:17 us so that we will have *c* on the day
   5:14 This is the *c* we have

CONFIDENT* (CONFIDENCE)
Job 6:20 because they had been *c*;
Ps 27: 3 even then will I be *c*.
   27:13 I am still *c* of this:
Lk 18: 9 To some who were *c*
2Co 1:15 Because I was *c* of this, I planned
   5: 6 Therefore we are always *c*
   5: 8 We are *c*, I say, and would prefer
   9: 4 ashamed of having been so *c*.
   10: 7 If anyone is *c* that he belongs
Gal 5:10 I am *c* in the Lord that you will
Php 1: 6 day until now, being *c* of this,
   2:24 I am *c* in the Lord that I myself will

Phm :21 C of your obedience, I write to you,
Heb 6: 9 we are *c* of better things
1Jn 2:28 that when he appears we may be *c*

CONFIDES*
Ps 25:14 The LORD *c* in those who fear him

CONFORM* (CONFORMED CONFORMITY CONFORMS)
Ro 12: 2 Do not *c* any longer to the pattern
1Pe 1:14 do not *c* to the evil desires you had

CONFORMED* (CONFORM)
Eze 5: 7 *c* to the standards of the nations
   11:12 but have *c* to the standards
Ro 8:29 predestined to be *c* to the likeness

CONFORMITY* (CONFORM)
Eph 1:11 in *c* with the purpose of his will,

CONFORMS* (CONFORM)
1Ti 1:11 to the sound doctrine that *c*

CONQUEROR* (CONQUERORS)
Mic 1:15 I will bring a *c* against you
Rev 6: 2 he rode out as a *c* bent on conquest.

CONQUERORS (CONQUEROR)
Ro 8:37 than *c* through him who loved us.

CONSCIENCE* (CONSCIENCE-STRICKEN CONSCIENCES CONSCIENTIOUS)
Ge 20: 5 I have done this with a clear *c*
   20: 6 I know you did this with a clear *c*
1Sa 25:31 have on his *c* the staggering burden
Job 27: 6 my *c* will not reproach me as long
Ac 23: 1 to God in all good *c* to this day."
   24:16 to keep my *c* clear before God
Ro 9: 1 my *c* confirms it in the Holy Spirit
   13: 5 punishment but also because of *c*.
1Co 4: 4 My *c* is clear, but that does not
   8: 7 since their *c* is weak, it is defiled.
   8:10 with a weak *c* sees you who have
   8:12 in this way and wound their weak *c*
   10:25 without raising questions of *c*,
   10:27 you without raising questions of *c*,
   10:28 man who told you and for *c*' sake—
   10:29 freedom be judged by another's *c*?
   10:29 the other man's *c*, I mean,
2Co 1:12 Our *c* testifies that we have
   4: 2 to every man's *c* in the sight of God
   5:11 and I hope it is also plain to your *c*.
1Ti 1: 5 and a good *c* and a sincere faith.
   1:19 holding on to faith and a good *c*.
   3: 9 truths of the faith with a clear *c*.
2Ti 1: 3 as my forefathers did, with a clear *c*
Heb 9: 9 able to clear the *c* of the worshiper.
   10:22 to cleanse us from a guilty *c*
   13:18 We are sure that we have a clear *c*
1Pe 3:16 and respect, keeping a clear *c*,
   3:21 the pledge of a good *c* toward God.

CONSCIENCE-STRICKEN* (CONSCIENCE)
1Sa 24: 5 David was *c* for having cut
2Sa 24:10 David was *c* after he had counted

CONSCIENCES* (CONSCIENCE)
Ro 2:15 their *c* also bearing witness,
1Ti 4: 2 whose *c* have been seared
Tit 1:15 their minds and *c* are corrupted.
Heb 9:14 cleanse our *c* from acts that lead

CONSCIENTIOUS* (CONSCIENCE)
2Ch 29:34 for the Levites had been more *c*

CONSCIOUS*
Ro 3:20 through the law we become *c* of sin
1Pe 2:19 of unjust suffering because he is *c*

CONSECRATE (CONSECRATED)
Ex 13: 2 "C to me every firstborn male.
   40: 9 *c* it and all its furnishings,
Lev 20: 7 " 'C yourselves and be holy,
   25:10 C the fiftieth year and proclaim
1Ch 15:12 fellow Levites are to *c* yourselves

CONSECRATED (CONSECRATE)
Ex 29:43 and the place will be *c* by my glory.
Lev 8:30 So he *c* Aaron and his garments
2Ch 7:16 *c* this temple so that my Name may
Lk 2:23 is to be *c* to the Lord"),
1Ti 4: 5 because it is *c* by the word of God

CONSENT
1Co 7: 5 except by mutual *c* and for a time,

CONSIDER (CONSIDERATE CONSIDERED CONSIDERS)
1Sa 12:24 *c* what great things he has done
   16: 7 "Do not *c* his appearance
2Ch 19: 6 "C carefully what you do,
Job 37:14 stop and *c* God's wonders.
Ps 8: 3 When I *c* your heavens,
   77:12 and *c* all your mighty deeds.
   107:43 and *c* the great love of the LORD.
   143: 5 and *c* what your hands have done.
Pr 6: 6 *c* its ways and be wise!
   20:25 and only later to *c* his vows.
Ecc 7:13 C what God has done:
Lk 12:24 C the ravens: They do not sow
   12:27 about the rest? "C how the lilies
Php 2: 3 but in humility *c* others better
   3: 8 I *c* everything a loss compared
Heb 10:24 And let us *c* how we may spur one
Jas 1: 2 C it pure joy, my brothers,

CONSIDERATE* (CONSIDER)
Tit 3: 2 to be peaceable and *c*,
Jas 3:17 then peace-loving, *c*, submissive,
1Pe 2:18 only to those who are good and *c*,
   3: 7 in the same way be *c* as you live

CONSIDERED (CONSIDER)
Job 1: 8 "Have you *c* my servant Job?
   2: 3 "Have you *c* my servant Job?
Ps 44:22 we are *c* as sheep to be slaughtered
Isa 53: 4 yet we *c* him stricken by God,
Ro 8:36 we are *c* as sheep to be slaughtered

CONSIDERS (CONSIDER)
Pr 31:16 She *c* a field and buys it;
Ro 14: 5 One man *c* one day more sacred
Jas 1:26 If anyone *c* himself religious

CONSIST (CONSISTS)
Lk 12:15 a man's life does not *c*

CONSISTS (CONSIST)
Eph 5: 9 fruit of the light *c* in all goodness,

CONSOLATION
Ps 94:19 your *c* brought joy to my soul.

CONSPIRE
Ps 2: 1 Why do the nations *c*

CONSTANT
Dt 28:66 You will live in *c* suspense,
Pr 19:13 wife is like a *c* dripping.
   3 a *c* dripping on a rainy day;
Ac 27:33 "you have been in *c* suspense
Heb 5:14 by *c* use have trained themselves

CONSTRUCTIVE*
1Co 10:23 but not everything is *c*.

CONSULT
Pr 15:12 he will not *c* the wise.
Gal 1:16 I did not *c* any man, nor did I go up

CONSUME (CONSUMES CONSUMING)
Jn 2:17 "Zeal for your house will *c* me."

CONSUMES (CONSUME)
Ps 69: 9 for zeal for your house *c* me,

CONSUMING (CONSUME)
Dt 4:24 For the LORD your God is a *c* fire,
Heb 12:29 and awe, for our "God is a *c* fire."

CONTAIN* (CONTAINED CONTAINS)
1Ki 8:27 the highest heaven, cannot *c* you.
2Ch 2: 6 the highest heavens, cannot *c* him?
   6:18 the highest heavens, cannot *c* you.
Ecc 8: 8 power over the wind to *c* it;
2Pe 3:16 His letters *c* some things that are

CONTAINED (CONTAIN)
Heb 9: 4 This ark *c* the gold jar of manna,

CONTAINS (CONTAIN)
Pr 15: 6 of the righteous *c* great treasure,

CONTAMINATES*
2Co 7: 1 from everything that *c* body

CONTEMPT
Pr 14:31 He who oppresses the poor shows *c*
17: 5 He who mocks the poor shows *c*
18: 3 When wickedness comes, so does *c*
Da 12: 2 others to shame and everlasting *c*.
Mal 1: 6 O priests, who show *c* for my name.
Ro 2: 4 Or do you show *c* for the riches
Gal 4:14 you did not treat me with *c*
1Th 5:20 do not treat prophecies with *c*.

CONTEND (CONTENDED CONTENDING CONTENTIOUS)
Ge 6: 3 "My Spirit will not *c*
Ps 35: 1 *C*, O LORD, with those who
Isa 49:25 I will *c* with those who *c* with you,
Jude : 3 you to *c* for the faith that was once

CONTENDED (CONTEND)
Php 4: 3 help these women who have *c*

CONTENDING* (CONTEND)
Php 1:27 *c* as one man for the faith

CONTENT* (CONTENTMENT)
Jos 7: 7 If only we had been *c* to stay
Pr 13:25 The righteous eat to their hearts' *c*,
19:23 one rests *c*, untouched by trouble.
Ecc 4: 8 yet his eyes were not *c*
Lk 3:14 don't accuse people falsely—be *c*
Php 4:11 to be *c* whatever the circumstances
4:12 I have learned the secret of being *c*
1Ti 6: 8 and clothing, we will be *c* with that.
Heb 13: 5 and be *c* with what you have,

CONTENTIOUS* (CONTEND)
1Co 11:16 If anyone wants to be *c* about this,

CONTENTMENT* (CONTENT)
Job 36:11 and their years in *c*.
SS 8:10 like one bringing *c*.
1Ti 6: 6 But godliness with *c* is great gain.

CONTEST*
Heb 10:32 in a great *c* in the face of suffering.

CONTINUAL (CONTINUE)
Pr 15:15 but the cheerful heart has a *c* feast.
Eph 4:19 of impurity, with a *c* lust for more.

CONTINUE (CONTINUAL CONTINUES CONTINUING)
1Ki 8:23 servants who *c* wholeheartedly
2Ch 6:14 servants who *c* wholeheartedly
Ps 36:10 *C* your love to those who know you
Ac 13:43 urged them to *c* in the grace of God
Ro 11:22 provided that you *c* in his kindness.
Gal 3:10 Cursed is everyone who does not *c*
Php 2:12 *c* to work out your salvation
Col 1:23 if you *c* in your faith, established
2: 6 received Christ Jesus as Lord, *c*
1Ti 2:15 if they *c* in faith, love and holiness
2Ti 3:14 *c* in what you have learned
1Jn 2:28 And now, dear children, *c* in him,
3: 9 born of God will *c* to sin,
5:18 born of God does not *c* to sin;
2Jn : 9 and does not *c* in the teaching
Rev 22:11 and let him who is holy *c* to be holy
22:11 let him who does right *c* to do right;

CONTINUES (CONTINUE)
Ps 100: 5 *c* through all generations.
119:90 Your faithfulness *c*
2Co 10:15 Our hope is that, as your faith *c*
1Jn 3: 6 No one who *c* to sin has

CONTINUING (CONTINUE)
Ro 13: 8 the *c* debt to love one another,

CONTRIBUTION (CONTRIBUTIONS)
Ro 15:26 pleased to make a *c* for the poor

CONTRIBUTIONS (CONTRIBUTION)
2Ch 24:10 all the people brought their *c* gladly
31:12 they faithfully brought in the *c*,

CONTRITE*
Ps 51:17 a broken and *c* heart,
Isa 57:15 also with him who is *c* and lowly
57:15 and to revive the heart of the *c*.
66: 2 he who is humble and *c* in spirit,

CONTROL (CONTROLLED CONTROLS SELF-CONTROL SELF-CONTROLLED)
Pr 29:11 a wise man keeps himself under *c*.
1Co 7: 9 But if they cannot *c* themselves,
7:37 but has *c* over his own will,
1Th 4: 4 you should learn to *c* his own body

CONTROLLED (CONTROL)
Ps 32: 9 but must be *c* by bit and bridle
Ro 8: 6 but the mind *c* by the Spirit is life
8: 8 Those *c* by the sinful nature cannot

CONTROLS* (CONTROL)
Job 37:15 you know how God *c* the clouds
Pr 16:32 a man who *c* his temper

CONTROVERSIES*
Ac 26: 3 with all the Jewish customs and *c*.
1Ti 1: 4 These promote *c* rather
6: 4 He has an unhealthy interest in *c*
Tit 3: 9 But avoid foolish *c* and genealogies

CONVERSATION
Col 4: 6 Let your *c* be always full of grace,

CONVERT
1Ti 3: 6 He must not be a recent *c*,

CONVICT (CONVICTION)
Pr 24:25 with those who *c* the guilty,
Jn 16: 8 he will *c* the world of guilt in regard
Jude : 15 and to *c* all the ungodly

CONVICTION* (CONVICT)
1Th 1: 5 the Holy Spirit and with deep *c*.

CONVINCE (CONVINCED CONVINCING)
Ac 28:23 and tried to *c* them about Jesus

CONVINCED* (CONVINCE)
Ge 45:28 "I'm *c*! My son Joseph is still alive.
Lk 16:31 will not be *c* even if someone rises
Ac 19:26 and hear how this fellow Paul has *c*
26: 9 "I too was *c* that I ought
26:26 I am *c* that none of this has escaped
28:24 Some were *c* by what he said,
Ro 2:19 if you are *c* that you are a guide
8:38 For I am *c* that neither death
14: 5 Each one should be fully *c*
14:14 I am fully *c* that no food is unclean
15:14 I myself am *c*, my brothers,
1Co 14:24 he will be *c* by all that he is a
2Co 5:14 we are *c* that one died for all,
Php 1:25 *C* of this, I know that I will remain,
2Ti 1:12 and am *c* that he is able
3:14 have learned and have become *c*

CONVINCING* (CONVINCE)
Ac 1: 3 and gave many *c* proofs that he was

COOLNESS*
Pr 25:13 Like the *c* of snow at harvest time

COPIES (COPY)
Heb 9:23 for the *c* of the heavenly things

COPY (COPIES)
Dt 17:18 for himself on a scroll a *c* of this law
Heb 8: 5 They serve at a sanctuary that is a *c*
9:24 sanctuary that was only a *c*

CORBAN*
Mk 7:11 received from me is *C*' (that is,

CORD (CORDS)
Jos 2:18 you have tied this scarlet *c*
Ecc 4:12 *c* of three strands is not quickly

CORDS (CORD)
Pr 5:22 the *c* of his sin hold him fast.
Isa 54: 2 lengthen your *c*,
Hos 11: 4 them with *c* of human kindness,

CORINTH
Ac 18: 1 Paul left Athens and went to *C*.
1Co 1: 2 To the church of God in *C*,
2Co 1: 1 To the church of God in *C*,

CORNELIUS*
Roman to whom Peter preached; first Gentile Christian (Ac 10).

CORNER (CORNERS)
Ru 3: 9 "Spread the *c* of your garment
Pr 21: 9 Better to live on a *c* of the roof
25:24 Better to live on a *c* of the roof
Ac 26:26 because it was not done in a *c*.

CORNERS (CORNER)
Mt 6: 5 on the street *c* to be seen by men.
22: 9 Go to the street *c* and invite

CORNERSTONE* (STONE)
Job 38: 6 or who laid its *c*—
Isa 28:16 a precious *c* for a sure foundation;
Jer 51:26 rock will be taken from you for a *c*,
Zec 10: 4 From Judah will come the *c*,
Eph 2:20 Christ Jesus himself as the chief *c*.
1Pe 2: 6 a chosen and precious *c*,

CORRECT* (CORRECTED CORRECTING CORRECTION CORRECTIONS CORRECTS)
Job 6:26 Do you mean to *c* what I say,
40: 2 contends with the Almighty *c* him?
Jer 10:24 *C* me, LORD, but only with justice
2Ti 4: 2 *c*, rebuke and encourage—

CORRECTED* (CORRECT)
Pr 29:19 A servant cannot be *c*

CORRECTING* (CORRECT)
2Ti 3:16 *c* and training in righteousness,

CORRECTION* (CORRECT)
Lev 26:23 things you do not accept my *c*
Job 36:10 He makes them listen to *c*
Pr 5:12 How my heart spurned *c*!
10:17 whoever ignores *c* leads others
12: 1 but he who hates *c* is stupid.
13:18 but whoever heeds *c* is honored.
15: 5 whoever heeds *c* shows prudence.
15:10 he who hates *c* will die.
15:12 A mocker resents *c*;
15:32 whoever heeds *c* gains
29:15 The rod of *c* imparts wisdom,
Jer 2:30 they did not respond to *c*.
5: 3 crushed them, but they refused *c*.
7:28 LORD its God or responded to *c*.
Zep 2: 3 she accepts no *c*.
3: 7 you will fear me / and accept *c*!'

CORRECTIONS* (CORRECT)
Pr 6:23 and the *c* of discipline

CORRECTS* (CORRECT)
Job 5:17 "Blessed is the man whom God *c*;
Pr 9: 7 Whoever *c* a mocker invites insult;

CORRUPT (CORRUPTED CORRUPTION CORRUPTS)
Ge 6:11 Now the earth was *c* in God's sight
Ps 14: 1 They are *c*, their deeds are vile;
14: 3 they have together become *c*;
Pr 4:24 keep *c* talk far from your lips.
6:12 who goes about with a *c* mouth,
19:28 A *c* witness mocks at justice,

CORRUPTED (CORRUPT)
2Co 7: 2 wronged no one, we have *c* no one.
Tit 1:15 but to those who are *c* and do not

CORRUPTION (CORRUPT)
2Pe 1: 4 escape the *c* in the world caused
2:20 If they have escaped the *c*

CORRUPTS* (CORRUPT)
Ecc 7: 7 and a bribe *c* the heart.
1Co 15:33 "Bad company *c* good character."
Jas 3: 6 It *c* the whole person, sets

COST (COSTS)
Nu 16:38 sinned at the *c* of their lives.
Pr 4: 7 Though it *c* all you have, get
7:23 little knowing it will *c* him his life.
Isa 55: 1 milk without money and without *c*.
Lk 14:28 and estimate the *c* to see
Rev 21: 6 to drink without *c* from the spring

COSTS (COST)
Pr 6:31 it *c* him all the wealth of his house.

COUNCIL
Ps 89: 7 In the *c* of the holy ones God is
107:32 and praise him in the *c* of the elders

COUNSEL (COUNSELOR COUNSELS)
1Ki 22: 5 "First seek the *c* of the LORD."
2Ch 18: 4 "First seek the *c* of the LORD."
Job 38: 2 "Who is this that darkens my *c*
42: 3 'Who is this that obscures my *c*
Ps 1: 1 walk in the *c* of the wicked
73:24 You guide me with your *c*,
107:11 despised the *c* of the Most High.
Pr 8:14 *C* and sound judgment are mine;
15:22 Plans fail for lack of *c*,
27: 9 from his earnest *c*.
Isa 28:29 wonderful in *c* and magnificent
1Ti 5:14 So I *c* younger widows to marry,
Rev 3:18 I *c* you to buy from me gold refined

COUNSELOR (COUNSEL)
Isa 9: 6 Wonderful *C*, Mighty God,
Jn 14:16 he will give you another *C* to be
14:26 But the *C*, the Holy Spirit,
15:26 "When the *C* comes, whom I will
16: 7 the *C* will not come to you;
Ro 11:34 Or who has been his *c*?"

COUNSELS (COUNSEL)
Ps 16: 7 I will praise the LORD, who *c* me;

COUNT (COUNTED COUNTING COUNTS)
Ps 22:17 I can *c* all my bones;
Ro 4: 8 whose sin the Lord will never *c*
6:11 *c* yourselves dead to sin
2Th 1:11 that our God may *c* you worthy

COUNTED (COUNT)
Ac 5:41 because they had been *c* worthy
2Th 1: 5 and as a result you will be *c* worthy

COUNTERFEIT*
2Th 2: 9 displayed in all kinds of *c* miracles,
1Jn 2:27 not *c*— just as it has taught you,

COUNTING (COUNT)
2Co 5:19 not *c* men's sins against them.

COUNTRY
Pr 28: 2 When a *c* is rebellious, it has many
29: 4 By justice a king gives a *c* stability,
Isa 66: 8 Can a *c* be born in a day
Lk 15:13 off for a distant *c* and there
Jn 4:44 prophet has no honor in his own *c*.)
2Co 11:26 in danger in the *c*, in danger at sea;
Heb 11:14 looking for a *c* of their own.

COUNTRYMEN
2Co 11:26 danger from my own *c*, in danger

COUNTS (COUNT)
Jn 6:63 The Spirit gives life; the flesh *c*
1Co 7:19 God's commands is what *c*.
Gal 5: 6 only thing that *c* is faith expressing

COURAGE* (COURAGEOUS)
Jos 2:11 everyone's *c* failed because of you,
5: 1 and they no longer had the *c*
2Sa 7: 1 he lost *c*, and all Israel became
7:27 So your servant has found *c*
1Ch 17:25 So your servant has found *c* to pray
2Ch 15: 8 son of Oded the prophet, he took *c*.
19:11 Act with *c*, and may the LORD be
Ezr 7:28 I took *c* and gathered leading men
10: 4 We will support you, so take *c*
Ps 107:26 in their peril their *c* melted away.
Eze 22:14 Will your *c* endure or your hands
Da 11:25 and *c* against the king of the South.
Mt 14:27 said to them: "Take *c*!
Mk 6:50 spoke to them and said, "Take *c*!
Ac 4:13 When they saw the *c* of Peter
23:11 "Take *c*! As you have testified
27:22 now I urge you to keep up your *c*,
27:25 So keep up your *c*, men,
1Co 16:13 stand firm in the faith; be men of *c*;
Php 1:20 will have sufficient *c* so that now

Heb 3: 6 if we hold on to our *c* and the hope

COURAGEOUS* (COURAGE)
Dt 31: 6 Be strong and *c*.
31: 7 of all Israel, "Be strong and *c*,
31:23 son of Nun: "Be strong and *c*,
Jos 1: 6 and *c*, because you will lead these
1: 7 Be strong and very *c*.
1: 9 commanded you? Be strong and *c*.
1:18 Only be strong and *c*!"
10:25 Be strong and *c*.
1Ch 22:13 Be strong and *c*.
28:20 "Be strong and *c*, and do the work.
2Ch 26:17 priest with eighty other *c* priests
32: 7 with these words: "Be strong and *c*.

COURSE
Ps 19: 5 a champion rejoicing to run his *c*.
Pr 2: 8 for he guards the *c* of the just
15:21 of understanding keeps a straight *c*.
16: 9 In his heart a man plans his *c*,
17:23 to pervert the *c* of justice.
Jas 3: 6 sets the whole *c* of his life on fire,

COURT (COURTS)
Pr 22:22 and do not crush the needy in *c*,
25: 8 do not bring hastily to *c*,
Mt 5:25 adversary who is taking you to *c*.
1Co 6: 1 judged by you or by any human *c*;

COURTS (COURT)
Ps 84:10 Better is one day in your *c*
100: 4 and his *c* with praise;
Am 5:15 maintain justice in the *c*.
Zec 8:16 and sound judgment in your *c*;

COURTYARD
Ex 27: 9 "Make a *c* for the tabernacle.

COUSIN
Col 4:10 as does Mark, the *c* of Barnabas.

COVENANT (COVENANTS)
Ge 9: 9 "I now establish my *c* with you
17: 2 I will confirm my *c* between me
Ex 19: 5 if you obey me fully and keep my *c*,
24: 7 Then he took the Book of the *C*
Dt 4:13 declared to you his *c*, the Ten
29: 1 in addition to the *c* he had made
Jdg 2: 1 'I will never break my *c* with you,
1Sa 23:18 of them made a *c* before the LORD
1Ki 8:21 in which is the *c* of the LORD that
8:23 you who keep your *c* of love
2Ki 23: 2 the words of the Book of the *C*,
1Ch 16:15 He remembers his *c* forever,
2Ch 6:14 you who keep your *c* of love
34:30 the words of the Book of the *C*,
Ne 1: 5 who keeps his *c* of love
Job 31: 1 "I made a *c* with my eyes
Ps 105: 8 He remembers his *c* forever,
Pr 2:17 ignored the *c* she made before God
Isa 42: 6 you to be a *c* for the people
61: 8 make an everlasting *c* with them.
Jer 11: 2 "Listen to the terms of this *c*
31:31 "when I will make a new *c*
31:32 It will not be like the *c*
31:33 "This is the *c* I will make
Eze 37:26 I will make a *c* of peace with them;
Da 9:27 He will confirm a *c* with many
Hos 6: 7 Like Adam, they have broken the *c*
Mal 2:14 the wife of your marriage *c*.
3: 1 of the *c*, whom you desire,
Mt 26:28 blood of the *c*, which is poured out
Mk 14:24 "This is my blood of the *c*,
Lk 22:20 "This cup is the new *c* in my blood,
1Co 11:25 "This cup is the new *c* in my blood;
2Co 3: 6 as ministers of a new *c*—
Gal 4:24 One *c* is from Mount Sinai
Heb 8: 6 as the *c* of which he is mediator is
8: 8 when I will make a new *c*
9:15 Christ is the mediator of a new *c*,
12:24 to Jesus the mediator of a new *c*,

COVENANTS (COVENANT)
Ro 9: 4 theirs the divine glory, the *c*,
Gal 4:24 for the women represent two *c*.

COVER (COVER-UP COVERED COVERING COVERINGS COVERS)
Ex 25:17 "Make an atonement *c* of pure gold
25:21 Place the *c* on top of the ark
33:22 and *c* you with my hand
Lev 16: 2 in the cloud over the atonement *c*.
Ps 32: 5 and did not *c* up my iniquity.
91: 4 He will *c* you with his feathers,
Hos 10: 8 say to the mountains, "*C* us!"
Lk 23:30 and to the hills, "*C* us!'"
1Co 11: 6 If a woman does not *c* her head,
11: 6 shaved off, she should *c* her head.
11: 7 A man ought not to *c* his head,
Jas 5:20 and *c* over a multitude of sins.

COVER-UP* (COVER)
1Pe 2:16 but do not use your freedom as a *c*

COVERED (COVER)
Ps 32: 1 whose sins are *c*.
85: 2 and *c* all their sins.
Isa 6: 2 With two wings they *c* their faces,
51:16 *c* you with the shadow of my hand
Ro 4: 7 whose sins are *c*.
1Co 11: 4 with his head *c* dishonors his head.

COVERING (COVER)
1Co 11:15 For long hair is given to her as a *c*.

COVERINGS (COVER)
Ge 3: 7 and made *c* for themselves.
Pr 31:22 She makes *c* for her bed;

COVERS (COVER)
Pr 10:12 but love *c* over all wrongs.
17: 9 He who *c* over an offense promotes
2Co 3:15 Moses is read, a veil *c* their hearts.
1Pe 4: 8 love *c* over a multitude of sins.

COVET* (COVETED COVETING COVETOUS)
Ex 20:17 You shall not *c* your neighbor's
20:17 "You shall not *c* your neighbor's
34:24 and no one will *c* your land
Dt 5:21 "You shall not *c* your neighbor's
7:25 Do not *c* the silver and gold
Mic 2: 2 They *c* fields and seize them,
Ro 7: 7 if the law had not said, "Do not *c*."
13: 9 "Do not steal," "Do not *c*,"
Jas 4: 2 *c*, but you cannot have what you

COVETED* (COVET)
Jos 7:21 weighing fifty shekels, I *c* them
Ac 20:33 I have not *c* anyone's silver or gold

COVETING
Ro 7: 7 what *c* really was if the law

COVETOUS* (COVET)
Ro 7: 8 in me every kind of *c* desire.

COWARDLY*
Rev 21: 8 But the *c*, the unbelieving, the vile,

COWS
Ge 41: 2 of the river there came up seven *c*,
Ex 25: 5 skins dyed red and hides of sea *c*;
Nu 4: 6 are to cover this with hides of sea *c*,
1Sa 6: 7 Hitch the *c* to the cart,

CRAFTINESS* (CRAFTY)
Job 5:13 He catches the wise in their *c*,
1Co 3:19 "He catches the wise in their *c*";
Eph 4:14 and *c* of men in their deceitful

CRAFTSMAN
Pr 8:30 Then I was the *c* at his side.

CRAFTY* (CRAFTINESS)
Ge 3: 1 the serpent was more *c* than any
1Sa 23:22 They tell me he is very *c*.
Job 5:12 He thwarts the plans of the *c*,
15: 5 you adopt the tongue of the *c*.
Pr 7:10 like a prostitute and with *c* intent.
12: 2 but the LORD condemns a *c* man.
14:17 and a *c* man is hated.
2Co 12:16 *c* fellow that I am, I caught you

CRAVE* (CRAVED CRAVES CRAVING CRAVINGS)
Nu 11: 4 with them began to *c* other food,

Dt 12:20 you *c* meat and say, "I would like
Pr 23: 3 Do not *c* his delicacies,
23: 6 do not *c* his delicacies;
31: 4 not for rulers to *c* beer,
Mic 7: 1 none of the early figs that I *c.*
1Pe 2: 2 newborn babies, *c* pure spiritual

CRAVED* (CRAVE)
Nu 11:34 the people who had *c* other food.
Ps 78:18 by demanding the food they *c.*
78:29 for he had given them what they *c.*
78:30 turned from the food they *c,*

CRAVES* (CRAVE)
Pr 13: 4 The sluggard *c* and gets nothing,
21:10 The wicked man *c* evil;
21:26 All day long he *c* for more,

CRAVING* (CRAVE)
Job 20:20 he will have no respite from his *c;*
Ps 106:14 In the desert they gave in to their *c;*
Pr 10: 3 but he thwarts the *c* of the wicked.
13: 2 the unfaithful have a *c* for violence.
21:25 The sluggard's *c* will be the death
Jer 2:24 sniffing the wind in her *c*—

CRAVINGS* (CRAVE)
Ps 10: 3 He boasts of the *c* of his heart;
Eph 2: 3 gratifying the *c* of our sinful nature
1Jn 2:16 in the world—the *c* of sinful man,

CRAWL
Ge 3:14 You will *c* on your belly

CREATE* (CREATED CREATES CREATING CREATION CREATOR)
Ps 51:10 *C* in me a pure heart, O God,
Isa 4: 5 Then the LORD will *c* over all
45: 7 I bring prosperity and *c* disaster;
45: 7 I form the light and *c* darkness,
45:18 he did not *c* it to be empty,
65:17 "Behold, I will *c* / new heavens
65:18 for I will *c* Jerusalem to be a delight
65:18 forever in what I will *c,*
Jer 31:22 The LORD will *c* a new thing
Mal 2:10 one Father? Did not one God *c* us?
Eph 2:15 His purpose was to *c*

CREATED* (CREATE)
Ge 1: 1 In the beginning God *c* the heavens
1:21 God *c* the great creatures of the sea
1:27 So God *c* man in his own image,
1:27 in the image of God he *c* him;
1:27 male and female he *c* them.
2: 4 and the earth when they were *c.*
5: 1 When God *c* man, he made him
5: 2 He *c* them male and female
5: 2 when they were *c,* he called them
6: 7 whom I have *c,* from the face
Dt 4:32 from the day God *c* man
Ps 89:12 You *c* the north and the south;
89:47 what futility you have *c* all men!
102:18 a people not yet *c* may praise
104:30 you send your Spirit, / they are *c,*
139:13 For you *c* my inmost being;
148: 5 for he commanded and they were *c*
Isa 40:26 Who *c* all these?
41:20 that the Holy One of Israel has *c* it.
42: 5 he who *c* the heavens and stretched
43: 1 he who *c* you, O Jacob,
43: 7 whom I *c* for my glory,
45: 8 I, the LORD, have *c* it.
45:12 and *c* mankind upon it.
45:18 he who *c* the heavens,
48: 7 They are *c* now, and not long ago;
54:16 And it is I who have *c* the destroyer
54:16 "See, it is I who *c* the blacksmith
57:16 the breath of man that I have *c.*
Eze 21:30 In the place where you were *c,*
28:13 the day you were *c* they were
28:15 ways from the day you were *c*

Mk 13:19 when God *c* the world, until now—
Ro 1:25 and served *c* things rather
1Co 11: 9 neither was man *c* for woman,
Eph 2:10 *c* in Christ Jesus to do good works,
3: 9 hidden in God, who *c* all things.
4:24 *c* to be like God in true
Col 1:16 For by him all things were *c:*
1:16 all things were *c* by him
1Ti 4: 3 which God *c* to be received
4: 4 For everything God *c* is good,
Heb 12:27 *c* things—so that what cannot be
Jas 1:18 a kind of firstfruits of all he *c.*
Rev 4:11 and by your will they were *c*
4:11 for you *c* all things,
10: 6 who *c* the heavens and all that is

CREATES* (CREATE)
Am 4:13 *c* the wind,

CREATING* (CREATE)
Ge 2: 3 the work of *c* that he had done.
Isa 57:19 *c* praise on the lips of the mourners

CREATION* (CREATE)
Hab 2:18 he who makes it trusts in his own *c;*
Mt 13:35 hidden since the *c* of the world."
25:34 for you since the *c* of the world.
Mk 10: 6 of *c* God 'made them male
16:15 and preach the good news to all *c.*
Jn 17:24 me before the *c* of the world.
Ro 1:20 For since the *c* of the world God's
8:19 The *c* waits in eager expectation
8:20 For the *c* was subjected
8:21 in hope that the *c* itself will be
8:22 that the whole *c* has been groaning
8:39 depth, nor anything else in all *c,*
2Co 5:17 he is a new *c;* the old has gone,
Gal 6:15 anything; what counts is a new *c.*
Eph 1: 4 us in him before the *c* of the world
Col 1:15 God, the firstborn over all *c.*
Heb 4: 3 finished since the *c* of the world.
4:13 Nothing in all *c* is hidden
9:11 that is to say, not a part of this *c.*
9:26 times since the *c* of the world.
1Pe 1:20 chosen before the *c* of the world,
2Pe 3: 4 as it has since the beginning of *c.*
Rev 3:14 true witness, the ruler of God's *c.*
13: 8 slain from the *c* of the world.
17: 8 life from the *c* of the world will be

CREATOR* (CREATE)
Ge 14:19 *C* of heaven and earth.
14:22 God Most High, *C* of heaven
Dt 32: 6 Is he not your Father, your *C,*
Ecc 12: 1 Remember your *C*
Isa 27:11 and their *C* shows them no favor.
40:28 The *C* of the ends of the earth.
43:15 Israel's *C,* your King."
Mt 19: 4 the beginning the *C* 'made them
Ro 1:25 created things rather than the *C*—
Col 3:10 in knowledge in the image of its *C.*
1Pe 4:19 themselves to their faithful *C*

CREATURE (CREATURES)
Lev 17:11 For the life of a *c* is in the blood,
17:14 the life of every *c* is its blood.
Ps 136:25 and who gives food to every *c.*
Eze 1:15 beside each *c* with its four faces.
Rev 4: 7 The first living *c* was like a lion,

CREATURES (CREATURE)
Ge 6:19 bring into the ark two of all living *c,*
8:21 again will I destroy all living *c,*
Ps 104:24 the earth is full of your *c.*
Eze 1: 5 was what looked like four living *c.*

CREDIT (CREDITED CREDITOR CREDITS)
Lk 6:33 what *c* is that to you? Even
Ro 4:24 to whom God will *c* righteousness
1Pe 2:20 it to your *c* if you receive a beating

CREDITED (CREDIT)
Ge 15: 6 and he *c* it to him as righteousness.
Ps 106:31 This was *c* to him as righteousness
Eze 18:20 of the righteous man will be *c*

Ro 4: 3 and it was *c* to him as righteousness
4: 4 his wages are not *c* to him as a gift,
4: 5 his faith is *c* as righteousness.
4: 9 saying that Abraham's faith was *c*
4:23 The words "it was *c*
Gal 3: 6 and it was *c* to him as righteousness
Php 4:17 for what may be *c* to your account.
Jas 2:23 and it was *c* to him as righteousness

CREDITOR (CREDIT)
Dt 15: 2 Every *c* shall cancel the loan he has

CREDITS (CREDIT)
Ro 4: 6 whom God *c* righteousness apart

CRETANS (CRETE)
Tit 1:12 "*C* are always liars, evil brutes,

CRETE (CRETANS)
Ac 27:12 harbor in *C,* facing both southwest

CRIED (CRY)
Ex 2:23 groaned in their slavery and *c* out.
14:10 They were terrified and *c* out
Nu 20:16 but when we *c* out to the LORD,
Jos 24: 7 But they *c* to the LORD for help,
Jdg 3: 9 But when they *c* out to the LORD,
3:15 Again the Israelites *c* out
4: 3 they *c* to the LORD for help.
6: 6 the Israelites that they *c* out
10:12 Maonites oppressed you and you *c*
1Sa 7: 9 He *c* out to the LORD
12: 8 they *c* to the LORD for help,
12:10 They *c* out to the LORD and said,
Ps 18: 6 I *c* to my God for help.

CRIMINALS
Lk 23:32 both *c,* were also led out with him

CRIMSON
Isa 1:18 though they are red as *c,*
63: 1 with his garments stained *c?*

CRIPPLED
2Sa 9: 3 of Jonathan; he is *c* in both feet."
Mk 9:45 better for you to enter life *c*

CRISIS*
1Co 7:26 of the present *c,* I think that it is

CRITICISM*
2Co 8:20 We want to avoid any *c*

CROOKED*
Dt 32: 5 but a warped and *c* generation.
2Sa 22:27 to the *c* you show yourself shrewd.
Ps 18:26 to the *c* you show yourself shrewd.
125: 5 But those who turn to *c* ways
Pr 2:15 whose paths are *c*
5: 6 her paths are *c,* but she knows it
8: 8 none of them is *c* or perverse.
10: 9 he who takes *c* paths will be found
Ecc 7:13 what he has made *c?*
Isa 59: 8 have turned them into *c* roads;
La 3: 9 he has made my paths *c.*
Lk 3: 5 The *c* roads shall become straight,
Php 2:15 children of God without fault in a *c*

CROP (CROPS)
Mt 13: 8 where it produced a *c*— a hundred,
21:41 share of the *c* at harvest time."

CROPS (CROP)
Pr 3: 9 with the firstfruits of all your *c;*
10: 5 He who gathers *c* in summer is
28: 3 like a driving rain that leaves no *c.*
2Ti 2: 6 the first to receive a share of the *c.*

CROSS (CROSSED CROSSING)
Dt 4:21 swore that I would not *c* the Jordan
12:10 But you will *c* the Jordan
Mt 10:38 and anyone who does not take his *c*
16:24 and take up his *c* and follow me.
Mk 8:34 and take up his *c* and follow me.

Lk	9:23	take up his *c* daily and follow me.
	14:27	anyone who does not carry his *c*
Jn	19:17	Carrying his own *c*, he went out
Ac	2:23	to death by nailing him to the *c*.
1Co	1:17	lest the *c* of Christ be emptied
	1:18	the message of the *c* is foolishness
Gal	5:11	offense of the *c* has been abolished.
	6:12	persecuted for the *c* of Christ.
	6:14	in the *c* of our Lord Jesus Christ,
Eph	2:16	both of them to God through the *c*,
Php	2: 8	even death on a *c*!
	3:18	as enemies of the *c* of Christ.
Col	1:20	through his blood, shed on the *c*.
	2:14	he took it away, nailing it to the *c*.
	2:15	triumphing over them by the *c*.
Heb	12: 2	set before him endured the *c*,

CROSSED (CROSS)

Jos	4: 7	When it *c* the Jordan, the waters
Jn	5:24	he has *c* over from death to life.

CROSSING (CROSS)

Ge	48:14	he was the younger, and *c* his arms,

CROSSROADS (ROAD)

Jer	6:16	"Stand at the *c* and look;

CROUCHING

Ge	4: 7	sin is *c* at your door; it desires

CROWD (CROWDS)

Ex	23: 2	Do not follow the *c* in doing wrong.

CROWDS (CROWD)

Mt	9:36	he saw the *c*, he had compassion

CROWED (CROWS)

Mt	26:74	the man!" Immediately a rooster *c*.

CROWN (CROWNED CROWNS)

Pr	4: 9	present you with a *c* of splendor."
	10: 6	Blessings *c* the head
	12: 4	noble character is her husband's *c*,
	16:31	Gray hair is a *c* of splendor;
	17: 6	Children's children are a *c*
Isa	35:10	everlasting joy will *c* their heads.
	51:11	everlasting joy will *c* their heads.
	61: 3	to bestow on them a *c* of beauty
	62: 3	You will be a *c* of splendor
Eze	16:12	and a beautiful *c* on your head.
Zec	9:16	like jewels in a *c*.
Mt	27:29	and then twisted together a *c* of thorns
Mk	15:17	then twisted together a *c* of thorns
Jn	19: 2	The soldiers twisted together a *c*
	19: 5	When Jesus came out wearing the *c*
1Co	9:25	it to get a *c* that will last forever.
	9:25	it to get a *c* that will not last;
Php	4: 1	and long for, my joy and *c*,
1Th	2:19	or the *c* in which we will glory
2Ti	2: 5	he does not receive the victor's *c*
	4: 8	store for me the *c* of righteousness,
Jas	1:12	he will receive the *c*
1Pe	5: 4	you will receive the *c*
Rev	2:10	and I will give you the *c* of life.
	3:11	so that no one will take your *c*.
	14:14	a son of man" with a *c* of gold

CROWNED* (CROWN)

Ps	8: 5	and *c* him with glory and honor.
Pr	14:18	the prudent are *c* with knowledge.
SS	3:11	crown with which his mother *c* him
Heb	2: 7	you *c* him with glory and honor
	2: 9	now *c* with glory and honor

CROWNS (CROWN)

Ps	103: 4	and *c* me with love and compassion
	149: 4	he *c* the humble with salvation.
Pr	11:26	blessing *c* him who is willing to sell.
Rev	4: 4	and had *c* of gold on their heads.
	4:10	They lay their *c* before the throne
	12: 3	ten horns and seven *c* on his heads.
	19:12	and on his head are many *c*.

CROWS (CROWED)

Mt	26:34	this very night, before the rooster *c*

CRUCIFIED* (CRUCIFY)

Mt	20:19	to be mocked and flogged and *c*.
	26: 2	of Man will be handed over to be *c*
	27:26	and handed him over to be *c*.
	27:35	When they had *c* him, they divided
	27:38	Two robbers were *c* with him,
	27:44	same way the robbers who were *c*
	28: 5	looking for Jesus, who was *c*.
Mk	15:15	and handed him over to be *c*.
	15:24	And they *c* him.
	15:25	the third hour when they *c* him.
	15:27	They *c* two robbers with him,
	15:32	Those *c* with him also heaped
	16: 6	for Jesus the Nazarene, who was *c*.
Lk	23:23	insistently demanded that he be *c*,
	23:33	*c* him, along with the criminals—
	24: 7	be *c* and on the third day be raised
	24:20	sentenced to death, and they *c* him;
Jn	19:16	him over to them to be *c*.
	19:18	Here they *c* him, and with him two
	19:20	for the place where Jesus was *c* was
	19:23	When the soldiers *c* Jesus,
	19:32	of the first man who had been *c*
	19:41	At the place where Jesus was *c*,
Ac	2:36	whom you *c*, both Lord and Christ
	4:10	whom you *c* but whom God raised
Ro	6: 6	For we know that our old self was *c*
1Co	1:13	Is Christ divided? Was Paul *c*
	1:23	but we preach Christ *c*: a stumbling
	2: 2	except Jesus Christ and him *c*.
	2: 8	they would not have *c* the Lord
2Co	13: 4	to be sure, he was *c* in weakness,
Gal	2:20	I have been *c* with Christ
	3: 1	Christ was clearly portrayed as *c*.
	5:24	Christ Jesus have *c* the sinful
	6:14	which the world has been *c*
Rev	11: 8	where also their Lord was *c*.

CRUCIFY* (CRUCIFIED CRUCIFYING)

Mt	23:34	Some of them you will kill and *c*;
	27:22	They all answered, "*C* him!" "Why
	27:23	they shouted all the louder, "*C* him
	27:31	Then they led him away to *c* him.
Mk	15:13	"*C* him!" they shouted.
	15:14	they shouted all the louder, "*C* him
	15:20	Then they led him out to *c* him.
Lk	23:21	they kept shouting, "*C* him! *C* him
Jn	19: 6	they shouted, "*C*! *C*!"
	19: 6	"You take him and *c* him.
	19:10	either to free you or to *c* you?"
	19:15	Crucify him!" "Shall I *c* your king
	19:15	away! Take him away! *C* him!"

CRUCIFYING* (CRUCIFY)

Heb	6: 6	to their loss they are *c* the Son

CRUSH (CRUSHED)

Ge	3:15	he will *c* your head,
Isa	53:10	it was the LORD's will to *c* him
Ro	16:20	The God of peace will soon *c* Satan

CRUSHED (CRUSH)

Ps	34:18	and saves those who are *c* in spirit.
Pr	17:22	but a *c* spirit dries up the bones.
	18:14	but a *c* spirit who can bear?
Isa	53: 5	he was *c* for our iniquities;
2Co	4: 8	not *c*; perplexed, but not in despair;

CRY (CRIED)

Ex	2:23	*c* for help because of their slavery
Ps	5: 2	Listen to my *c* for help,
	34:15	and his ears are attentive to their *c*;
	40: 1	he turned to me and heard my *c*.
	130: 1	Out of the depths I *c* to you,

Pr	21:13	to the *c* of the poor,
La	2:18	*c* out to the Lord.
Hab	2:11	The stones of the wall will *c* out,
Lk	19:40	keep quiet, the stones will *c* out."

CUNNING

2Co	11: 3	deceived by the serpent's *c*,
Eph	4:14	and by the *c* and craftiness of men

CUP

Ps	23: 5	my *c* overflows.
Isa	51:22	from that *c*, the goblet of my wrath,
	51:22	the *c* that made you stagger;
Mt	10:42	if anyone gives even a *c* of cold water
	20:22	"Can you drink the *c* I am going
	23:25	You clean the outside of the *c*
	23:26	First clean the inside of the *c*
	26:27	Then he took the *c*, gave thanks
	26:39	may this *c* be taken from me.
	26:42	possible for this *c* to be taken away
Mk	9:41	anyone who gives you a *c* of water
	10:38	"Can you drink the *c* I drink
	10:39	"You will drink the *c* I drink
	14:23	Then he took the *c*, gave thanks
	14:36	Take this *c* from me.
Lk	11:39	Pharisees clean the outside of the *c*
	22:17	After taking the *c*, he gave thanks
	22:20	after the supper he took the *c*,
	22:20	"This *c* is the new covenant
	22:42	if you are willing, take this *c*
Jn	18:11	I not drink the *c* the Father has
1Co	10:16	Is not the *c* of thanksgiving
	10:21	the *c* of the Lord and the *c*
	11:25	after supper he took the *c*, saying,
	11:25	"This *c* is the new covenant

CUPBEARER

Ge	40: 1	the *c* and the baker of the king
Ne	1:11	I was *c* to the king.

CURE (CURED)

Jer	17: 9	and beyond *c*.
	30:15	your pain that has no *c*?
Hos	5:13	But he is not able to *c* you,
Lk	9: 1	out all demons and to *c* diseases,

CURED (CURE)

Mt	11: 5	those who have leprosy are *c*,
Lk	6:18	troubled by evil spirits were *c*,

CURSE (ACCURSED CURSED CURSES CURSING)

Ge	4:11	Now you are under a *c*
	8:21	"Never again will I *c* the ground
	12: 3	and whoever curses you I will *c*;
Dt	11:26	before you today a blessing and a *c*
	11:28	the *c* if you disobey the commands
	21:23	hung on a tree is under God's *c*.
	23: 5	turned the *c* into a blessing for you,
Job	1:11	he will surely *c* you to your face."
	2: 5	he will surely *c* you to your face."
	2: 9	*C* God and die!" He replied,
Ps	109:28	They may *c*, but you will bless;
Pr	3:33	The LORD's *c* is on the house
	24:24	peoples will *c* him and nations
Mal	2: 2	and I will *c* your blessings.
Lk	6:28	bless those who *c* you, pray
Ro	12:14	persecute you; bless and do not *c*.
Gal	3:10	on observing the law are under a *c*,
	3:13	of the law by becoming a *c* for us,
Jas	3: 9	with it we *c* men, who have been
Rev	22: 3	No longer will there be any *c*.

CURSED (CURSE)

Ge	3:17	"*C* is the ground because of you;
Dt	27:15	"*C* is the man who carves an image
	27:16	"*C* is the man who dishonors his
	27:17	"*C* is the man who moves his
	27:18	"*C* is the man who leads the blind
	27:19	*C* is the man who withholds justice
	27:20	"*C* is the man who sleeps
	27:21	"*C* is the man who has sexual
	27:22	"*C* is the man who sleeps
	27:23	"*C* is the man who sleeps
	27:24	"*C* is the man who kills his
	27:25	"*C* is the man who accepts a bribe

Dt	27:26	"*C* is the man who does not uphold
Jer	17: 5	"*C* is the one who trusts in man,
Mal	1:14	"*C* is the cheat who has
Ro	9: 3	I could wish that I myself were *c*
1Co	4:12	When we are *c*, we bless;
	12: 3	"Jesus be *c*," and no one can say,
Gal	3:10	*C* is everyone who does not
	3:13	*C* is everyone who is hung on a tree

CURSES (CURSE)

Ex	21:17	"Anyone who *c* his father
Lev	20: 9	" 'If anyone *c* his father or mother,
Nu	5:23	is to write these *c* on a scroll
Jos	8:34	the blessings and the *c*— just
Pr	20:20	If a man *c* his father or mother,
	28:27	to them receives many *c*.
Mt	15: 4	and 'Anyone who *c* his father
Mk	7:10	and, 'Anyone who *c* his father

CURSING (CURSE)

Ps	109:18	He wore *c* as his garment;
Ro	3:14	"Their mouths are full of *c*
Jas	3:10	the same mouth come praise and *c*.

CURTAIN

Ex	26:31	"Make a *c* of blue, purple
	26:33	She will separate the Holy Place
Mt	27:51	At that moment the *c*
Mk	15:38	The *c* of the temple was torn in two
Lk	23:45	the *c* of the temple was torn in two.
Heb	6:19	the inner sanctuary behind the *c*,
	9: 3	Behind the second *c* was a room
	10:20	opened for us through the *c*,

CUSTOM

Job	1: 5	This was Job's regular *c*.
Mk	10: 1	and as was his *c*, he taught them.
Lk	4:16	into the synagogue, as was his *c*.
Ac	17: 2	As his *c* was, Paul went

CUT

Lev	19:27	" 'Do not *c* the hair at the sides
	21: 5	of their beards or *c* their bodies.
1Ki	3:25	"*C* the living child in two
Isa	51: 1	to the rock from which you were *c*
	53: 8	For he was *c* off from the land
Da	2:45	of the rock *c* out of a mountain,
	9:26	the Anointed One will be *c* off
Mt	3:10	not produce good fruit will be *c*
	24:22	If those days had not been *c* short,
1Co	11: 6	for a woman to have her hair *c*

CYMBAL* (CYMBALS)

1Co	13: 1	a resounding gong or a clanging *c*.

CYMBALS (CYMBAL)

1Ch	15:16	instruments: lyres, harps and *c*.
2Ch	5:12	dressed in fine linen and playing *c*,
Ps	150: 5	praise him with resounding *c*.

CYRUS

Persian king who allowed exiles to return (2Ch 36:22–Ezr 1:8), to rebuild temple (Ezr 5:13–6:14), as appointed by the LORD (Isa 44:28–45:13).

DAGON

Jdg	16:23	offer a great sacrifice to *D* their god
1Sa	5: 2	Dagon's temple and set it beside *D*.

DAMASCUS

Ac	9: 3	As he neared *D* on his journey,

DAN

1. Son of Jacob by Bilhah (Ge 30:4–6; 35:25; 46:23). Tribe of blessed (Ge 49:16–17; Dt 33:22), numbered (Nu 1:39; 26:43), allotted land (Jos 19:40–48; Eze 48:1), failed to fully possess (Jdg 1:34–35), failed to support Deborah (Jdg 5:17), possessed Laish/Dan (Jdg 18).

2. Northernmost city in Israel (Ge 14:14; Jdg 18; 20:1).

DANCE (DANCED DANCING)

Ecc	3: 4	a time to mourn and a time to *d*,
Mt	11:17	and you did not *d*;

DANCED (DANCE)

2Sa	6:14	*d* before the LORD
Mk	6:22	of Herodias came in and *d*,

DANCING (DANCE)

Ps	30:11	You turned my wailing into *d*;
	149: 3	Let them praise his name with *d*

DANGER

Pr	22: 3	A prudent man sees *d*
	27:12	The prudent see *d* and take refuge.
Mt	5:22	will be in *d* of the fire of hell.
Ro	8:35	famine or nakedness or *d* or sword?
2Co	11:26	I have been in *d* from rivers,

DANIEL

1. Hebrew exile to Babylon, name changed to Belteshazzar (Da 1:6–7). Refused to eat unclean food (Da 1:8–21). Interpreted Nebuchadnezzar's dreams (Da 2; 4), writing on the wall (Da 5). Thrown into lion's den (Da 6). Visions (Da 7–12).

2. Son of David (1Ch 3:1).

DARIUS

1. King of Persia (Ezr 4:5), allowed rebuilding of temple (Ezr 5–6).

2. Mede who conquered Babylon (Da 5:31).

DARK (DARKENED DARKENS DARKNESS)

Job	34:22	There is no *d* place, no deep
Ps	18: 9	*d* clouds were under his feet.
Pr	31:15	She gets up while it is still *d*;
SS	1: 6	Do not stare at me because I am *d*,
Jn	12:35	in the *d* does not know where he is
Ro	2:19	a light for those who are in the *d*,
2Pe	1:19	as to a light shining in a *d* place,

DARKENED (DARK)

Joel	2:10	the sun and moon are *d*,
Mt	24:29	" 'the sun will be *d*,
Ro	1:21	and their foolish hearts were *d*.
Eph	4:18	They are *d* in their understanding

DARKENS (DARK)

Job	38: 2	"Who is this that *d* my counsel

DARKNESS (DARK)

Ge	1: 2	*d* was over the surface of the deep,
	1: 4	he separated the light from the *d*.
Ex	10:22	and total *d* covered all Egypt
	20:21	approached the thick *d* where God
2Sa	22:29	the LORD turns my *d* into light.
Ps	18:28	my God turns my *d* into light.
	91: 6	the pestilence that stalks in the *d*,
	112: 4	Even in *d* light dawns
	139:12	even the *d* will not be dark to you;
Pr	4:19	the way of the wicked is like deep *d*
Isa	5:20	and light for *d*,
	42:16	I will turn the *d* into light
	45: 7	I form the light and create *d*,
	58:10	then your light will rise in the *d*,
	61: 1	and release from *d*,
Joel	2:31	The sun will be turned to *d*
Mt	4:16	the people living in *d*
	6:23	how great is that *d!* "No one can
Lk	11:34	are bad, your body also is full of *d*.
	23:44	and *d* came over the whole land
Jn	1: 5	The light shines in the *d*,
	3:19	but men loved *d* instead of light
Ac	2:20	The sun will be turned to *d*
2Co	4: 6	who said, "Let light shine out of *d*
	6:14	fellowship can light have with *d?*
Eph	5: 8	For you were once *d*, but now you
	5:11	to do with the fruitless deeds of *d*,
1Pe	2: 9	out of *d* into his wonderful light.
2Pe	2:17	Blackest *d* is reserved for them.
1Jn	1: 5	in him there is no *d* at all.
	2: 9	but hates his brother is still in the *d*.
Jude	: 6	in *d*, bound with everlasting chains
	:13	for whom blackest *d* has been

DASH

Ps	2: 9	you will *d* them to pieces like

DAUGHTER (DAUGHTERS)

Ex	2: 9	she took him to Pharaoh's *d*
Jdg	11:40	to commemorate the *d* of Jephthah
Est	2: 7	Mordecai had taken her as his own *d*

Ps	9:14	praises in the gates of the *D* of Zion
	137: 8	O *D* of Babylon, doomed
Isa	62:11	"Say to the *D* of Zion,
Zec	9: 9	Shout, *D* of Jerusalem!
Mk	5:34	"*D*, your faith has healed you.
	7:29	the demon has left your *d*.

DAUGHTERS (DAUGHTER)

Ge	6: 2	the *d* of men were beautiful,
	19:36	Lot's *d* became pregnant
Nu	36:10	Zelophehad's *d* did as the LORD
Joel	2:28	sons and *d* will prophesy,

DAVID

Son of Jesse (Ru 4:17–22; 1Ch 2:13–15), ancestor of Jesus (Mt 1:1–17; Lk 3:31). Wives and children (1Sa 18; 25:39–44; 2Sa 3:2–5; 5:13–16; 11:27; 1Ch 3:1–9). Anointed king by Samuel (1Sa 16:1–13). Musician to Saul (1Sa 16:14–23; 18:10). Killed Goliath (1Sa 17). Relation with Jonathan (1Sa 18:1–4; 19–20; 23:16–18; 2Sa 1). Disfavor of Saul (1Sa 18:6–23:29). Spared Saul's life (1Sa 24; 26). Among Philistines (1Sa 21:10–14; 27–30). Lament for Saul and Jonathan (2Sa 1). Anointed king of Judah (2Sa 2:1–11). Conflict with house of Saul (2Sa 2–4). Anointed king of Israel (2Sa 5:1–4; 1Ch 11:1–3). Conquered Jerusalem (2Sa 5:6–10; 1Ch 11:4–9). Brought ark to Jerusalem (2Sa 6; 1Ch 13; 15–16). The LORD promised eternal dynasty (2Sa 7; 1Ch 17; Ps 132). Showed kindness to Mephibosheth (2Sa 9). Adultery with Bathsheba, murder of Uriah (2Sa 11–12). Son Amnon raped daughter Tamar; killed by Absalom (2Sa 13). Absalom's revolt (2Sa 14–17); death (2Sa 18). Sheba's revolt (2Sa 20). Victories: Philistines (2Sa 5:17–25; 1Ch 14:8–17; 2Sa 21:15–22; 1Ch 20:4–8), Ammonites (2Sa 10; 1Ch 19), various (2Sa 8; 1Ch 18). Mighty men (2Sa 23:8–39; 1Ch 11–12). Punished for numbering army (2Sa 24; 1Ch 21). Appointed Solomon king (1Ki 1:28–2:9). Prepared for building of temple (1Ch 22–29). Last words (2Sa 23:1–7). Death (1Ki 2:10–12; 1Ch 29:28). Psalmist (Mt 22:43–45), musician (Am 6:5), prophet (2Sa 23:2–7; Ac 1:16; 2:30).

Psalms of: 2 (Ac 4:25), 3–32, 34–41, 51–65, 68–70, 86, 95 (Heb 4:7), 101, 103, 108–110, 122, 124, 131, 133, 138–145.

DAWN (DAWNED DAWNS)

Ps	37: 6	your righteousness shine like the *d*,
Pr	4:18	is like the first gleam of *d*,
Isa	14:12	O morning star, son of the *d!*
Am	4:13	he who turns *d* to darkness,
	5: 8	who turns blackness into *d*

DAWNED (DAWN)

Isa	9: 2	a light has *d*.
Mt	4:16	a light has *d*."

DAWNS* (DAWN)

Ps	65: 8	where morning *d* and evening
	112: 4	in darkness light *d* for the upright,
Hos	10:15	When that day *d*,
2Pe	1:19	until the day *d* and the morning

DAY (DAYS)

Ge	1: 5	God called the light "*d*,"
	1: 5	and there was morning,—the first *d*
	1: 8	there was morning,—the second *d*.
	1:13	there was morning,—the third *d*.
	1:19	there was morning,—the fourth *d*.
	1:23	there was morning,—the fifth *d*.
	1:31	there was morning,—the sixth *d*.
	2: 2	so on the seventh *d* he rested
	8:22	*d* and night
Ex	16:30	the people rested on the seventh *d*.
	20: 8	"Remember the Sabbath *d*
Lev	16:30	on this *d* atonement will be made
	23:28	because it is the *D* of Atonement,
Nu	14:14	before them in a pillar of cloud by *d*
Jos	1: 8	meditate on it *d* and night,
2Ki	7: 9	This is a *d* of good news
	25:30	*D* by *d* the king gave Jehoiachin
1Ch	16:23	proclaim his salvation *d* after *d*.
Ne	8:18	*D* after *d*, from the first *d*
Ps	84:10	Better is one *d* in your courts

Ps   96: 2 proclaim his salvation *d* after *d*.
     118:24 This is the *d* the LORD has made;
Pr   27: 1 not know what a *d* may bring
              forth.
Isa   13: 9 a cruel *d*, with wrath and fierce
Jer   46:10 But that *d* belongs to the Lord,
      50:31 "for your *d* has come,
Eze   30: 2 "Alas for that *d!*"
Joel   1:15 "Alas for that *d!*
       2:31 and dreadful *d* of the LORD.
Am   3:14 On the *d* I punish Israel for her
              sins
       5:20 Will not the *d* of the LORD be
Ob   :15 "The *d* of the LORD is near
Zep   1:14 The great *d* of the LORD is near—
Zec   2:11 joined with the LORD in that *d*
      14: 1 A *d* of the LORD is coming
      14: 7 It will be a unique *d*,
Mal   4: 5 dreadful *d* of the LORD comes.
Mt   24:38 up to the *d* Noah entered the ark;
Lk   11: 3 Give us each *d* our daily bread.
      17:24 in his *d* will be like the lightning,
Ac   5:42 *D* after *d*, in the temple courts
      17:11 examined the Scriptures every *d*
      17:17 as in the marketplace *d* by *d*
Ro   14: 5 man considers every *d* alike.
1Co   5: 5 his spirit saved on the *d* of the
              Lord
2Co   4:16 we are being renewed *d* by *d*.
      11:25 I spent a night and a *d*
1Th   5: 2 for you know very well that the *d*
       5: 4 so that this *d* should surprise you
2Th   2: 2 saying that the *d* of the Lord has
Heb   7:27 need to offer sacrifices *d* after *d*,
2Pe   3: 8 With the Lord a *d* is like
       3:10 *d* of the Lord will come like a
              thief.
Rev   6:17 For the great *d* of their wrath has
      16:14 on the great *d* of God Almighty.

DAYS (DAY)
Dt   17:19 he is to read it all the *d* of his life
      32: 7 Remember the *d* of old;
Ps   23: 6 all the *d* of my life,
      34:12 and desires to see many good *d*,
      39: 5 have made my *d* a mere
      90:10 The length of our *d* is seventy
              years
      90:12 Teach us to number our *d* aright,
     103:15 As for man, his *d* are like grass,
     128: 5 all the *d* of your life;
Pr   31:12 all the *d* of her life.
Ecc   9: 9 all the *d* of this meaningless life
      12: 1 Creator in the *d* of your youth,
Isa   38:20 all the *d* of our lives
Da   7: 9 and the Ancient of *D* took his
              seat.
       7:13 He approached the Ancient of *D*
       7:22 until the Ancient of *D* came
Hos   3: 5 and to his blessings in the last *d*.
Joel   2:29 I will pour out my Spirit in those *d*.
Mic   4: 1 In the last *d*
Lk   19:43 The *d* will come upon you
Ac   2:17 by the prophet Joel: " 'In the
              last *d*,
2Ti   3: 1 will be terrible times in the last *d*.
Heb   1: 2 in these last *d* he has spoken to us
2Pe   3: 3 that in the last *d* scoffers will
              come,

DAZZLING*
Da   2:31 *d* statue, awesome in appearance.
Mk   9: 3 His clothes became *d* white,

DEACON* (DEACONS)
1Ti   3:12 A *d* must be the husband of

DEACONS* (DEACON)
Php   1: 1 together with the overseers and *d*:
1Ti   3: 8 *D*, likewise, are to be men worthy
       3:10 against them, let them serve as *d*.

DEAD (DIE)
Lev   17:15 who eats anything found *d*
Dt   18:11 or spiritist or who consults the *d*.
Isa   8:19 Why consult the *d* on behalf
Mt   8:22 and let the *d* bury their own *d*."
      28: 7 'He has risen from the *d*
Lk   15:24 For this son of mine was *d*
      24:46 rise from the *d* on the third day,
Ro   6:11 count yourselves *d* to sin
1Co   15:29 do who are baptized for the *d*?
Eph   2: 1 you were *d* in your transgressions
1Th   4:16 and the *d* in Christ will rise first.

Jas   2:17 is not accompanied by action, is *d*.
       2:26 so faith without deeds is *d*,
Rev   14:13 Blessed are the *d* who die
      20:12 And I saw the *d*, great and small,

DEADENED* (DIE)
Jn   12:40 and *d* their hearts,

DEAR* (DEARER)
2Sa   1:26 you were very *d* to me.
Ps   102:14 For her stones are *d*
Jer   31:20 is not Ephraim my *d* son,
Jn   2: 4 "*D* woman, why do you involve
              me
      19:26 he said to his mother, "*D* woman,
Ac   15:25 to you with our *d* friends
              Barnabas
Ro   16: 5 Greet my *d* friend Epenetus.
      16: 9 in Christ, and my *d* friend Stachys.
      16:12 Greet my *d* friend Persis, another
1Co   4:14 but to warn you, as my *d* children.
      10:14 my *d* friends, flee from idolatry.
      15:58 Therefore, my *d* brothers,
2Co   7: 1 we have these promises, *d* friends,
      12:19 and everything we do, *d* friends,
Gal   4:19 My *d* children, for whom I am
Eph   6:21 the *d* brother and faithful servant
Php   2:12 my *d* friends, as you have always
       4: 1 firm in the Lord, *d* friends!
Col   1: 7 Epaphras, our *d* fellow servant,
       4: 7 He is a *d* brother, a faithful
       4: 9 our faithful and *d* brother,
       4:14 Our *d* friend Luke, the doctor,
1Th   2: 8 because you had become so *d* to
              us.
1Ti   6: 2 their service are believers, and *d*
2Ti   1: 2 To Timothy, my *d* son: Grace,
Phm   : 1 To Philemon our *d* friend
       :16 He is very *d* to me but
       :16 better than a slave, as a *d* brother.
Heb   6: 9 we speak like this, *d* friends,
Jas   1:16 Don't be deceived, my *d* brothers.
       1:19 My *d* brothers, take note of this:
       2: 5 thoughts? Listen, my *d* brothers:
1Pe   2:11 *D* friends, I urge you, as aliens
       4:12 *D* friends, do not be surprised
2Pe   3: 1 *D* friends, this is now my second
       3: 8 not forget this one thing, *d*
              friends:
       3:14 *d* friends, since you are looking
       3:15 just as our *d* brother Paul
       3:17 *d* friends, since you already know
1Jn   2: 1 My *d* children, I write this to you
       2: 7 *D* friends, I am not writing you
       2:12 I write to you, *d* children,
       2:13 I write to you, *d* children,
       2:18 *D* children, this is the last hour;
       2:28 *d* children, continue in him,
       3: 2 *D* friends, now we are children
       3: 7 *D* children, do not let anyone lead
       3:18 love of God be in him? *D* children,
       3:21 *D* friends, if our hearts do not
       4: 1 *D* friends, do not believe every
       4: 4 *d* children, are from God
       4: 7 *D* friends, let us love one another,
       4:11 *D* friends, since God so loved us,
       5:21 *D* children, keep yourselves
2Jn   : 5 *d* lady, I am not writing you a new
3Jn   : 1 The elder, To my *d* friend Gaius,
        : 2 *D* friend, I pray that you may
              enjoy
        : 5 *D* friend, you are faithful
       :11 *D* friend, do not imitate what is
              evil
Jude   : 3 *D* friends, although I was very
       :17 But, *d* friends, remember what
       :20 *d* friends, build yourselves up

DEARER* (DEAR)
Phm   :16 dear to me but even *d* to you,

DEATH (DIE)
Ex   21:12 kills him shall surely be put to *d*.
Nu   35:16 the murderer shall be put to *d*.
Dt   30:19 set before you life and *d*,
Ru   1:17 if anything but *d* separates you
2Ki   4:40 O man of God, there is *d* in the
              pot
Job   26: 6 *D* is naked before God;
Ps   23: 4 the valley of the shadow of *d*,
      44:22 for your sake we face *d* all day
              long
      89:48 What man can live and not see *d*,

Ps   116:15 is the *d* of his saints.
Pr   8:36 all who hate me love *d*."
      11:19 he who pursues evil goes to his *d*.
      14:12 but in the end it leads to *d*.
      15:11 *D* and Destruction lie open
      16:25 but in the end it leads to *d*.
      18:21 tongue has the power of life
              and *d*,
      19:18 do not be a willing party to his *d*.
      23:14 and save his soul from *d*.
Ecc   7: 2 for *d* is the destiny of every man;
Isa   25: 8 he will swallow up *d* forever.
      53:12 he poured out his life unto *d*,
Eze   18:23 pleasure in the *d* of the wicked?
      18:32 pleasure in the *d* of anyone,
      33:11 pleasure in the *d* of the wicked,
Hos   13:14 Where, O *d*, are your plagues?
Jn   5:24 he has crossed over from *d* to life.
Ro   4:25 delivered over to *d* for our sins
       5:12 and in this way *d* came to all men,
       5:14 *d* reigned from the time of Adam
       6: 3 Jesus were baptized into his *d*?
       6:23 For the wages of sin is *d*,
       7:24 me from this body of *d*?
       8:13 put to *d* the misdeeds of the body,
       8:36 your sake we face *d* all day long;
1Co   15:21 For since *d* came through a man,
      15:26 The last enemy to be destroyed
              is *d*
      15:55 Where, O *d*, is your sting?"
2Ti   1:10 who has destroyed *d* and has
Heb   2:14 him who holds the power of *d*—
1Jn   5:16 There is a sin that leads to *d*.
Rev   1:18 And I hold the keys of *d* and
              Hades
       2:11 hurt at all by the second *d*.
      20: 6 The second *d* has no power
      20:14 The lake of fire is the second *d*.
      20:14 Then *d* and Hades were thrown
      21: 4 There will be no more *d*
      21: 8 This is the second *d*."

DEBAUCHERY*
Ro   13:13 not in sexual immorality and *d*,
2Co   12:21 and *d* in which they have
              indulged.
Gal   5:19 impurity and *d*; idolatry
Eph   5:18 drunk on wine, which leads to *d*.
1Pe   4: 3 living in *d*, lust, drunkenness,

DEBORAH*
   1. Prophetess who led Israel to victory over
   Canaanites (Jdg 4–5).
   2. Rebekah's nurse (Ge 35:8).

DEBT* (DEBTOR DEBTORS DEBTS)
Dt   15: 3 must cancel any *d* your brother
      24: 6 the upper one—as security for
              a *d*,
1Sa   22: 2 or in *d* or discontented gathered
Job   24: 9 of the poor is seized for a *d*.
Mt   18:25 that he had be sold to repay
              the *d*.
      18:27 canceled the *d* and let him go.
      18:30 into prison until he could pay
              the *d*.
      18:32 'I canceled all that *d* of yours
Lk   7:43 who had the bigger *d* canceled."
Ro   13: 8 Let no *d* remain outstanding,
      13: 8 continuing *d* to love one another,

DEBTOR* (DEBT)
Isa   24: 2 for *d* as for creditor.

DEBTORS* (DEBT)
Hab   2: 7 Will not your *d* suddenly arise?
Mt   6:12 as we also have forgiven our *d*.
Lk   16: 5 called in each one of his
              master's *d*.

DEBTS* (DEBT)
Dt   15: 1 seven years you must cancel *d*.
      15: 2 time for canceling *d* has been
      15: 9 the year for canceling *d*, is near,"
      31:10 in the year for canceling *d*,
2Ki   4: 7 "Go, sell the oil and pay your *d*.
Ne   10:31 the land and will cancel all *d*.
Pr   22:26 or puts up security for *d*;
Mt   6:12 Forgive us our *d*,
Lk   7:42 so he canceled the *d* of both.

DECAY*
Ps   16:10 will you let your Holy One see *d*.
      49: 9 and not see *d*.
      49:14 their forms will *d* in the grave,

Pr 12: 4 a disgraceful wife is like *d*
Isa 5:24 so their roots will *d*
Hab 3:16 *d* crept into my bones,
Ac 2:27 will you let your Holy One see *d.*
    2:31 to the grave, nor did his body see *d.*
   13:34 never to *d*, is stated in these words:
   13:35 will not let your Holy One see *d.'*
   13:37 raised from the dead did not
Ro 8:21 liberated from its bondage to *d*

DECEIT (DECEIVE)
Ps 5: 9 with their tongue they speak *d.*
Isa 53: 9 nor was any *d* in his mouth.
Da 8:25 He will cause *d* to prosper,
Zep 3:13 nor will *d* be found in their mouths.
Mk 7:22 greed, malice, *d*, lewdness, envy,
Ac 13:10 You are full of all kinds of *d*
Ro 1:29 murder, strife, *d* and malice.
   3:13 their tongues practice *d."*
1Pe 2: 1 yourselves of all malice and all *d*,
   2:22 and no *d* was found in his mouth."

DECEITFUL (DECEIVE)
Jer 17: 9 The heart is *d* above all things
Hos 10: 2 Their heart is *d*,
2Co 11:13 men are false apostles, *d* workmen,
Eph 4:14 of men in their *d* scheming.
   4:22 is being corrupted by its *d* desires;
1Pe 3:10 and his lips from *d* speech.
Rev 21:27 who does what is shameful or *d*,

DECEITFULNESS* (DECEIVE)
Ps 119:118 for their *d* is in vain.
Mt 13:22 and the *d* of wealth choke it,
Mk 4:19 the *d* of wealth and the desires
Heb 3:13 of you may be hardened by sin's *d*.

DECEIVE (DECEIT DECEITFUL DECEITFULNESS DECEIVED DECEIVER DECEIVERS DECEIVES DECEIVING DECEPTION DECEPTIVE)
Lev 19:11 " 'Do not *d* one another.
Pr 14: 5 A truthful witness does not *d*,
   24:28 or use your lips to *d*.
Jer 37: 9 Do not *d* yourselves, thinking,
Zec 13: 4 garment of hair in order to *d*.
Mt 24: 5 'I am the Christ,' and will *d* many.
   24:11 will appear and *d* many people.
   24:24 and miracles to *d* even the elect—
Mk 13: 6 'I am he,' and will *d* many.
   13:22 and miracles to *d* the elect—
Ro 16:18 and flattery they *d* the minds
1Co 3:18 Do not *d* yourselves.
Eph 5: 6 Let no one *d* you with empty words
Col 2: 4 this so that no one may *d* you
2Th 2: 3 Don't let anyone *d* you in any way,
Jas 1:22 to the word, and so *d* yourselves.
1Jn 1: 8 we *d* ourselves and the truth is not
Rev 20: 8 and will go out to *d* the nations

DECEIVED (DECEIVE)
Ge 3:13 "The serpent *d* me, and I ate."
Lk 21: 8 "Watch out that you are not *d*.
1Co 6: 9 the kingdom of God? Do not be *d*:
2Co 11: 3 Eve was *d* by the serpent's cunning
Gal 6: 7 Do not be *d*: God cannot be
1Ti 2:14 And Adam was not the one *d*;
2Ti 3:13 to worse, deceiving and being *d*.
Tit 3: 3 *d* and enslaved by all kinds
Jas 1:16 Don't be *d*, my dear brothers.
Rev 13:14 he *d* the inhabitants of the earth.
   20:10 And the devil, who *d* them,

DECEIVER (DECEIVE)
Mt 27:63 while he was still alive that *d* said,
2Jn : 7 Any such person is the *d*

DECEIVERS* (DECEIVE)
Ps 49: 5 when wicked *d* surround me—
Tit 1:10 and *d*, especially those
2Jn : 7 Many *d*, who do not acknowledge

DECEIVES (DECEIVE)
Pr 26:19 is a man who *d* his neighbor
Mt 24: 4 "Watch out that no one *d* you.
Mk 13: 5 "Watch out that no one *d* you.
Gal 6: 3 when he is nothing, he *d* himself.

2Th 2:10 sort of evil that *d* those who are
Jas 1:26 he *d* himself and his religion is

DECEIVING* (DECEIVE)
Lev 6: 2 by *d* his neighbor about something
1Ti 4: 1 follow *d* spirits and things taught
2Ti 3:13 go from bad to worse, *d*
Rev 20: 3 him from *d* the nations anymore

DECENCY* (DECENTLY)
1Ti 2: 9 women to dress modestly, with *d*

DECENTLY* (DECENCY)
Ro 13:13 Let us behave *d*, as in the daytime,

DECEPTION (DECEIVE)
Pr 14: 8 but the folly of fools is *d.*
   26:26 His malice may be concealed by *d*,
Mt 27:64 This last *d* will be worse
2Co 4: 2 we do not use *d*, nor do we distort

DECEPTIVE
Pr 11:18 The wicked man earns *d* wages,
   31:30 Charm is *d*, and beauty is fleeting;
Jer 7: 4 Do not trust in *d* words and say,
Col 2: 8 through hollow and *d* philosophy,

DECIDED (DECISION)
2Co 9: 7 man should give what he has *d*

DECISION (DECIDED)
Ex 28:29 heart on the breastpiece of *d*
Joel 3:14 multitudes in the valley of *d!*

DECLARE (DECLARED DECLARING)
1Ch 16:24 *D* his glory among the nations,
Ps 19: 1 The heavens *d* the glory of God;
   96: 3 *D* his glory among the nations,
Isa 42: 9 and new things I *d*;

DECLARED (DECLARE)
Mk 7:19 Jesus *d* all foods "clean.")
Ro 2:13 the law who will be *d* righteous.
   3:20 no one will be *d* righteous

DECLARING (DECLARE)
Ps 71: 8 *d* your splendor all day long.
Ac 2:11 we hear them *d* the wonders

DECREE (DECREED DECREES)
Ex 15:25 There the LORD made a *d*
1Ch 16:17 He confirmed it to Jacob as a *d*,
Ps 2: 7 I will proclaim the *d* of the LORD:
   7: 6 Awake, my God; *d* justice.
   81: 4 this is a *d* for Israel,
   148: 6 he gave a *d* that will never pass
Da 4:24 and this is the *d* the Most High has
Lk 2: 1 Augustus issued a *d* that a census
Ro 1:32 know God's righteous *d* that those

DECREED (DECREE)
Ps 78: 5 He *d* statutes for Jacob
Jer 40: 2 LORD your God *d* this disaster
La 3:37 happen if the Lord has not *d* it?
Da 9:24 "Seventy 'sevens' are *d*
   9:26 and desolations have been *d*.
Lk 22:22 Son of Man will go as it has been *d*.

DECREES (DECREE)
Ge 26: 5 my commands, my *d* and my laws
Ex 15:26 to his commands and keep all his *d*,
   18:16 inform them of God's *d* and laws."
   18:20 Teach them the *d* and laws,
Lev 10:11 Israelites all the *d* the LORD has
   18: 4 and be careful to follow my *d*.
   18: 5 Keep my *d* and laws,
   18:26 you must keep my *d* and my laws.
Ps 119:12 teach me your *d*.
   119:16 I delight in your *d*;
   119:48 and I meditate on your *d*.
   119:112 My heart is set on keeping your *d*

DEDICATE (DEDICATED DEDICATION)
Nu 6:12 He must *d* himself to the LORD
Pr 20:25 for a man to *d* something rashly

DEDICATED (DEDICATE)
Lev 21:12 he has been *d* by the anointing oil
Nu 6: 9 thus defiling the hair he has *d*,
   6:18 shave off the hair that he *d*.
   18: 6 *d* to the LORD to do the work
1Ki 8:63 and all the Israelites *d* the temple
2Ch 29:31 "You have now *d* yourselves
Ne 3: 1 They *d* it and set its doors in place,

DEDICATION (DEDICATE)
Nu 6:19 shaved off the hair of his *d*,
Jn 10:22 came the Feast of *D* at Jerusalem.
1Ti 5:11 sensual desires overcome their *d*

DEED (DEEDS)
Jer 32:10 and sealed the *d*, had it witnessed,
   32:16 After I had given the *d* of purchase
Col 3:17 you do, whether in word or *d*,
2Th 2:17 and strengthen you in every good *d*

DEEDS (DEED)
Dt 3:24 or on earth who can do the *d*
   4:34 or by great and awesome *d*,
   34:12 the awesome *d* that Moses
1Sa 2: 3 and by him *d* are weighed.
1Ch 16:24 his marvelous *d* among all peoples.
Job 34:25 Because he takes note of their *d*,
Ps 26: 7 and telling of all your wonderful *d*.
   45: 4 right hand display awesome *d*;
   65: 5 with awesome *d* of righteousness,
   66: 3 "How awesome are your *d!*
   71:17 day I declare your marvelous *d*.
   72:18 who alone does marvelous *d*,
   73:28 I will tell of all your *d*.
   75: 1 men tell of your wonderful *d*.
   77:11 I will remember the *d* of the LORD
   77:12 and consider all your mighty *d*.
   78: 4 the praiseworthy *d* of the LORD,
   78: 7 and would not forget his *d*
   86: 8 no *d* can compare with yours.
   86:10 you are great and do marvelous *d*;
   88:12 or your righteous *d* in the land
   90:16 May your *d* be shown
   92: 4 For you make me glad by your *d*,
   96: 3 his marvelous *d* among all peoples.
   107: 8 and his wonderful *d* for men,
   107:15 and his wonderful *d* for men,
   107:21 and his wonderful *d* for men,
   107:24 his wonderful *d* in the deep.
   107:31 and his wonderful *d* for men.
   111: 3 Glorious and majestic are his *d*,
   145: 6 and I will proclaim your great *d*.
Jer 32:19 purposes and mighty are your *d*.
Hab 3: 2 I stand in awe of your *d*, O LORD.
Mt 5:16 that they may see your good *d*
Lk 1:51 He has performed mighty *d*
   23:41 we are getting what our *d* deserve.
Ac 26:20 prove their repentance by their *d*.
1Ti 6:18 rich in good *d*, and to be generous
Heb 10:24 on toward love and good *d*
Jas 2:14 claims to have faith but has no *d*?
   2:18 Show me your faith without *d*,
   2:20 faith without *d* is useless?
   2:26 so faith without *d* is dead.
1Pe 2:12 they may see your good *d*
Rev 2:19 I know your *d*, your love and faith,
   2:23 each of you according to your *d*.
   3: 1 I know your *d*; you have
   3: 2 I have not found your *d* complete
   3: 8 I know your *d*.
   3:15 I know your *d*, that you are neither
   14:13 for their *d* will follow them."
   15: 3 "Great and marvelous are your *d*,

DEEP (DEPTH DEPTHS)
Ge 1: 2 was over the surface of the *d*,
   8: 2 Now the springs of the *d*
Ps 42: 7 *D* calls to *d*
Lk 5: 4 to Simon, "Put out into *d* water,
1Co 2:10 all things, even the *d* things
1Ti 3: 9 hold of the *d* truths of the faith

DEER
Ps 42: 1 As the *d* pants for streams of water,

DEFAMED*
Isa 48:11 How can I let myself be *d*?

DEFEATED
1Co 6: 7 have been completely *d* already.

DEFEND (DEFENDED DEFENDER DEFENDING DEFENDS DEFENSE)
Ps 72: 4 He will *d* the afflicted
   74:22 Rise up, O God, and *d* your cause;
   82: 2 "How long will you *d* the unjust

Ps 82: 3 *D* the cause of the weak
119:154 *D* my cause and redeem me;
Pr 31: 9 *d* the rights of the poor and needy
Isa 1:17 *D* the cause of the fatherless,
1:23 They do not *d* the cause
Jer 5:28 they do not *d* the rights of the poor.
50:34 He will vigorously *d* their cause

DEFENDED (DEFEND)
Jer 22:16 He *d* the cause of the poor

DEFENDER (DEFEND)
Ex 22: 2 the *d* is not guilty of bloodshed;
Ps 68: 5 to the fatherless, a *d* of widows,
Pr 23:11 for their *D* is strong;

DEFENDING (DEFEND)
Ps 10:18 *d* the fatherless and the oppressed,
Ro 2:15 now accusing, now even *d* them.)
Php 1: 7 or *d* and confirming the gospel,

DEFENDS* (DEFEND)
Dt 10:18 He *d* the cause of the fatherless
33: 7 With his own hands he *d* his cause.
Isa 51:22 your God, who *d* his people:

DEFENSE (DEFEND)
Ps 35:23 Awake, and rise to my *d!*
Php 1:16 here for the *d* of the gospel.
1Jn 2: 1 speaks to the Father in our *d—*

DEFERRED*
Pr 13:12 Hope *d* makes the heart sick,

DEFIED
1Sa 17:45 armies of Israel, whom you have *d.*
1Ki 13:26 the man of God who *d* the word

DEFILE (DEFILED)
Da 1: 8 Daniel resolved not to *d* himself
Rev 14: 4 are those who did not *d* themselves

DEFILED (DEFILE)
Isa 24: 5 The earth is *d* by its people;

DEFRAUD
Lev 19:13 Do not *d* your neighbor or rob him.
Mk 10:19 do not *d,* honor your father

DEITY*
Col 2: 9 of the *D* lives in bodily form,

DELAY
Ecc 5: 4 vow to God, do not *d* in fulfilling it.
Isa 48: 9 my own name's sake I *d* my wrath;
Heb 10:37 is coming will come and will not *d.*
Rev 10: 6 and said, "There will be no more *d!*

DELICACIES
Ps 141: 4 let me not eat of their *d.*
Pr 23: 3 Do not crave his *d,*
23: 6 do not crave his *d;*

DELICIOUS*
Pr 9:17 food eaten in secret is *d!"*

DELIGHT* (DELIGHTED DELIGHTFUL DELIGHTING DELIGHTS)
Lev 26:31 and I will take no *d* in the pleasing
Dt 30: 9 The LORD will again *d* in you
1Sa 2: 1 for I *d* in your deliverance.
15:22 "Does the LORD *d*
Ne 1:11 the prayer of your servants who *d*
Job 22:26 Surely then you will find *d*
27:10 Will he find *d* in the Almighty?
Ps 1: 2 But his *d* is in the law of the LORD
16: 3 in whom is all my *d.*
35: 9 and *d* in his salvation.
35:27 those who *d* in my vindication
37: 4 *D* yourself in the LORD
43: 4 to God, my joy and my *d.*
51:16 You do not *d* in sacrifice,
51:19 whole burnt offerings to *d* you;
62: 4 they take *d* in lies.
68:30 Scatter the nations who *d* in war.
111: 2 by all who *d* in them.
112: 1 who finds great *d* in his commands.
119:16 I *d* in your decrees;
119:24 Your statutes are my *d;*
119:35 for there I find *d.*
119:47 for I *d* in your commands

Ps 119:70 but I *d* in your law.
119:77 for your law is my *d.*
119:92 If your law had not been my *d,*
119:143 but your commands are my *d.*
119:174 and your law is my *d.*
147:10 nor his *d* in the legs of a man;
149: 4 For the LORD takes *d*
Pr 1:22 How long will mockers *d*
2:14 who *d* in doing wrong
8:30 I was filled with *d* day after day,
11: 1 but accurate weights are his *d.*
29:17 he will bring *d* to your soul.
Ecc 2:10 My heart took *d* in all my work,
SS 1: 4 We rejoice and *d* in you;
2: 3 I *d* to sit in his shade.
Isa 5: 7 are the garden of his *d.*
11: 3 he will *d* in the fear of the LORD.
13:17 and have no *d* in gold.
32:14 the *d* of donkeys, a pasture
42: 1 my chosen one in whom I *d;*
55: 2 and your soul will *d* in the richest
58:13 if you call the Sabbath a *d*
61:10 I *d* greatly in the LORD;
62: 4 for the LORD will take *d* in you,
65:18 for I will create Jerusalem to be a *d*
65:19 and take *d* in my people;
66: 3 their souls *d* in their abominations;
66:11 *d* in her overflowing abundance."
Jer 9:24 for in these I *d,"*
15:16 they were my joy and my heart's *d,*
31:20 the child in whom I *d?*
49:25 the town in which I *d?*
Eze 24:16 away from you the *d* of your eyes.
24:21 in which you take pride, the *d*
24:25 and glory, the *d* of their eyes,
Hos 7: 3 *d* the king with their wickedness,
Mic 1:16 for the children in whom you *d;*
7:18 but *d* to show mercy.
Zep 3:17 He will take great *d* in you,
Mt 12:18 the one I love, in whom I *d;*
Mk 12:37 large crowd listened to him with *d.*
Lk 1:14 He will be a joy and *d* to you,
Ro 7:22 in my inner being I *d* in God's law;
1Co 13: 6 Love does not *d* in evil
2Co 12:10 for Christ's sake, I *d* in weaknesses,
Col 2: 5 and *d* to see how orderly you are

DELIGHTED (DELIGHT)
2Sa 22:20 he rescued me because he *d* in me.
1Ki 10: 9 who has *d* in you and placed you
2Ch 9: 8 who has *d* in you and placed you
Ps 18:19 he rescued me because he *d* in me.
Lk 13:17 but the people were *d* with all

DELIGHTFUL* (DELIGHT)
Ps 16: 6 surely I have a *d* inheritance.
SS 1: 2 for your love is more *d* than wine.
4:10 How *d* is your love, my sister,
Mal 3:12 for yours will be a *d* land,"

DELIGHTING* (DELIGHT)
Pr 8:31 and *d* in mankind.

DELIGHTS (DELIGHT)
Est 6: 6 for the man the king *d* to honor?"
Ps 22: 8 since he *d* in him."
35:27 who *d* in the well-being
36: 8 from your river of *d.*
37:23 if the LORD *d* in a man's way
147:11 the LORD *d* in those who fear him,
Pr 3:12 as a father the son he *d* in.
10:23 of understanding *d* in wisdom.
11:20 he *d* in those whose ways are
12:22 but he *d* in men who are truthful.
14:35 A king *d* in a wise servant,
18: 2 but *d* in airing his own opinions.
23:24 he who has a wise son *d* in him.
Col 2:18 Do not let anyone who *d*

DELILAH*
Woman who betrayed Samson (Jdg 16:4–22).

DELIVER (DELIVERANCE DELIVERED DELIVERER DELIVERS)
Dt 32:39 and no one can *d* out of my hand.
Ps 22: 8 Let him *d* him,

Ps 72:12 For he will *d* the needy who cry out
79: 9 *d* us and forgive our sins
109:21 of the goodness of your love, *d* me.
119:170 *d* me according to your promise.
Mt 6:13 but *d* us from the evil one.'
2Co 1:10 hope that he will continue to *d* us,

DELIVERANCE (DELIVER)
1Sa 2: 1 for I delight in your *d.*
Ps 3: 8 From the LORD comes *d.*
32: 7 and surround me with songs of *d.*
33:17 A horse is a vain hope for *d;*
Ob :17 But on Mount Zion will be *d;*

DELIVERED (DELIVER)
Ps 34: 4 he *d* me from all my fears.
107: 6 and he *d* them from their distress.
116: 8 have *d* my soul from death,
Da 12: 1 written in the book—will be *d.*
Ro 4:25 He was *d* over to death for our sins

DELIVERER* (DELIVER)
Jdg 3: 9 for them a *d,* Othniel son of Kenaz,
3:15 and he gave them a *d*— Ehud,
2Sa 22: 2 is my rock, my fortress and my *d;*
2Ki 13: 5 The LORD provided a *d* for Israel,
Ps 18: 2 is my rock, my fortress and my *d,*
40:17 You are my help and my *d;*
70: 5 You are my help and my *d;*
140: 7 O Sovereign LORD, my strong *d,*
144: 2 my stronghold and my *d,*
Ac 7:35 sent to be their ruler and *d*
Ro 11:26 "The *d* will come from Zion;

DELIVERS (DELIVER)
Ps 34:17 he *d* them from all their troubles.
34:19 but the LORD *d* him from them all
37:40 The LORD helps them and *d* them
37:40 he *d* them from the wicked

DELUSION*
2Th 2:11 God sends them a powerful *d*

DEMAND (DEMANDED)
Lk 6:30 belongs to you, do not *d* it back.

DEMANDED (DEMAND)
Lk 12:20 This very night your life will be *d*
12:48 been given much, much will be *d;*

DEMETRIUS
Ac 19:24 A silversmith named *D,* who made

DEMON* (DEMONS)
Mt 9:33 And when the *d* was driven out,
11:18 and they say, 'He has a *d.'*
17:18 Jesus rebuked the *d,* and it came
Mk 7:26 to drive the *d* out of her daughter.
7:29 the *d* has left your daughter."
7:30 lying on the bed, and the *d* gone.
Lk 4:33 there was a man possessed by a *d,*
4:35 Then the *d* threw the man
7:33 wine, and you say, 'He has a *d.'*
8:29 driven by the *d* into solitary places.
9:42 the *d* threw him to the ground
11:14 When the *d* left, the man who had
11:14 was driving out a *d* that was mute.
Jn 8:49 "I am not possessed by a *d,"*
10:21 Can a *d* open the eyes of the blind
10:21 sayings of a man possessed by a *d.*

DEMON-POSSESSED* (DEMON-POSSESSION)
Mt 4:24 those suffering severe pain, the *d,*
8:16 many who were *d* were brought
8:28 two *d* men coming
8:33 what had happened to the *d* men.
9:32 man who was *d* and could not talk
12:22 they brought him a *d* man who was
Mk 1:32 brought to Jesus all the sick and *d.*
5:16 what had happened to the *d* man—
5:18 the man who had been *d* begged
Lk 8:27 met by a *d* man from the town.
8:36 the people how the *d* man had been
Jn 7:20 "You are *d,"* the crowd answered.
8:48 that you are a Samaritan and *d?"*
8:52 "Now we know that you are *d!*
10:20 Many of them said, "He is *d*

2181

Ac 19:13 Jesus over those who were *d*.
DEMON-POSSESSION* (DEMON-POSSESSED)
Mt 15:22 is suffering terribly from *d*."
DEMONS* (DEMON)
Dt 32:17 to *d*, which are not God—
Ps 106:37 and their daughters to *d*.
Mt 7:22 and in your name drive out *d*
8:31 *d* begged Jesus, "If you drive us
9:34 prince of *d* that he drives out *d*."
10: 8 who have leprosy, drive out *d*.
12:24 of *d*, that this fellow drives out
12:24 that this fellow drives out *d*."
12:27 And if I drive out *d* by Beelzebub,
12:28 if I drive out *d* by the Spirit of God,
Mk 1:34 He also drove out many *d*,
1:34 but he would not let the *d* speak
1:39 their synagogues and driving out *d*.
3:15 to have authority to drive out *d*.
3:22 the prince of *d* he is driving out *d*."
5:12 The *d* begged Jesus, "Send us
5:15 possessed by the legion of *d*,
6:13 They drove out many *d*
9:38 "we saw a man driving out *d*
16: 9 out of whom he had driven seven *d*
16:17 In my name they will drive out *d*;
Lk 4:41 *d* came out of many people,
8: 2 from whom seven *d* had come out;
8:30 because many *d* had gone into him.
8:32 The *d* begged Jesus to let them go
8:33 When the *d* came out of the man,
8:35 from whom the *d* had gone out,
8:38 from whom the *d* had gone out
9: 1 and authority to drive out all *d*
9:49 "we saw a man driving out *d*
10:17 the *d* submit to us in your name."
11:15 the prince of *d*, he is driving out *d*."
11:18 you claim that I drive out *d*
11:19 Now if I drive out *d* by Beelzebub,
11:20 if I drive out *d* by the finger of God,
13:32 'I will drive out *d* and heal people
Ro 8:38 neither angels nor *d*, neither
1Co 10:20 of pagans are offered to *d*,
10:20 you to be participants with *d*.
10:21 the Lord and the cup of *d* too;
10:21 the Lord's table and the table of *d*.
1Ti 4: 1 spirits and things taught by *d*.
Jas 2:19 Good! Even the *d* believe that—
Rev 9:20 they did not stop worshiping *d*,
16:14 of *d* performing miraculous signs,
18: 2 She has become a home for *d*
DEMONSTRATE* (DEMONSTRATES DEMONSTRATION)
Ro 3:25 He did this to *d* his justice,
3:26 he did it to *d* his justice
DEMONSTRATES* (DEMONSTRATE)
Ro 5: 8 God *d* his own love for us in this:
DEMONSTRATION* (DEMONSTRATE)
1Co 2: 4 but with a *d* of the Spirit's power,
DEN
Da 6:16 and threw him into the lions' *d*.
Mt 21:13 you are making it a '*d* of robbers.' "
Mk 11:17 you have made it 'a *d* of robbers.' "
Lk 19:46 but you have made it 'a *d* of robbers
DENARII* (DENARIUS)
Mt 18:28 who owed him a hundred *d*.
Lk 7:41 One owed him five hundred *d*,
DENARIUS (DENARII)
Mt 20: 2 agreed to pay them a *d* for the day
Mk 12:15 Bring me a *d* and let me look at it."
DENIED (DENY)
Mt 26:70 But he *d* it before them all.
Mk 14:68 But he *d* it.
Lk 22:57 But he *d* it.
Jn 18:25 He *d* it, saying, "I am not."
1Ti 5: 8 he has *d* the faith and is worse

Rev 3: 8 my word and have not *d* my name.
DENIES (DENY)
1Jn 2:22 It is the man who *d* that Jesus is
2:23 No one who *d* the Son has
DENY (DENIED DENIES DENYING)
Ex 23: 6 "Do not *d* justice to your poor
Job 27: 5 till I die, I will not *d* my integrity.
Isa 5:23 but *d* justice to the innocent.
La 3:35 to *d* a man his rights
Am 2: 7 and *d* justice to the oppressed.
Mt 16:24 he must *d* himself and take up his
Mk 8:34 he must *d* himself and take up his
Lk 9:23 he must *d* himself and take up his
22:34 you will *d* three times that you
Ac 4:16 miracle, and we cannot *d* it.
Tit 1:16 but by their actions they *d* him.
Jas 3:14 do not boast about it or *d* the truth.
Jude : 4 *d* Jesus Christ our only Sovereign
DENYING* (DENY)
Eze 22:29 mistreat the alien, *d* them justice.
2Ti 3: 5 a form of godliness but *d* its power.
2Pe 2: 1 the sovereign Lord who bought
DEPART (DEPARTED DEPARTS DEPARTURE)
Ge 49:10 The scepter will not *d* from Judah,
Job 1:21 and naked I will *d*.
Mt 25:41 '*D* from me, you who are cursed,
Php 1:23 I desire to *d* and be with Christ,
DEPARTED (DEPART)
1Sa 4:21 "The glory has *d* from Israel"—
Ps 119:102 I have not *d* from your laws,
DEPARTS (DEPART)
Ecc 5:15 and as he comes, so he *d*.
DEPARTURE (DEPART)
Lk 9:31 spoke about his *d*, which he was
2Ti 4: 6 and the time has come for my *d*.
2Pe 1:15 after my *d* you will always be able
DEPEND
Ps 62: 7 My salvation and my honor *d*
DEPOSES*
Da 2:21 he sets up kings and *d* them.
DEPOSIT
Mt 25:27 money on *d* with the bankers,
Lk 19:23 didn't you put my money on *d*,
2Co 1:22 put his Spirit in our hearts as a *d*,
5: 5 and has given us the Spirit as a *d*,
Eph 1:14 who is a *d* guaranteeing our
2Ti 1:14 Guard the good *d* that was
DEPRAVED* (DEPRAVITY)
Eze 16:47 ways you soon became more *d*
23:11 and prostitution she was more *d*
Ro 1:28 he gave them over to a *d* mind,
Php 2:15 fault in a crooked and *d* generation,
2Ti 3: 8 oppose the truth—men of *d* minds,
DEPRAVITY* (DEPRAVED)
Ro 1:29 of wickedness, evil, greed and *d*.
2Pe 2:19 they themselves are slaves of *d*—
DEPRIVE
Dt 24:17 Do not *d* the alien or the fatherless
Pr 18: 5 or to *d* the innocent of justice.
31: 5 *d* all the oppressed of their rights.
Isa 10: 2 to *d* the poor of their rights
29:21 with false testimony *d* the innocent
La 3:36 to *d* a man of justice—
1Co 7: 5 Do not *d* each other
15: die than have anyone *d* me
DEPTH (DEEP)
Ro 8:39 any powers, neither height nor *d*,
11:33 the *d* of the riches of the wisdom
DEPTHS (DEEP)
Ps 130: 1 Out of the *d* I cry to you, O LORD;
DERIDES*
Pr 11:12 who lacks judgment *d* his neighbor,
DERIVES*
Eph 3:15 in heaven and on earth *d* its name.
DESCEND (DESCENDED DESCENDING)
Ro 10: 7 "or 'Who will *d* into the deep?' "

DESCENDED (DESCEND)
Eph 4: 9 except that he also *d* to the lower,
Heb 7:14 For it is clear that our Lord *d*
DESCENDING (DESCEND)
Ge 28:12 of God were ascending and *d* on it.
Mt 3:16 the Spirit of God *d* like a dove
Mk 1:10 and the Spirit *d* on him like a dove.
Jn 1:51 and *d* on the Son of Man."
DESECRATING*
Ne 13:17 you are doing—*d* the Sabbath day?
13:18 against Israel by *d* the Sabbath."
Isa 56: 2 who keeps the Sabbath without *d* it
56: 6 who keep the Sabbath without *d* it
Eze 44: 7 *d* my temple while you offered me
DESERT
Nu 32:13 wander in the *d* forty years,
Dt 8:16 He gave you manna to eat in the *d*,
29: 5 years that I led you through the *d*,
Ne 9:19 you did not abandon them in the *d*.
Ps 78: 19 "Can God spread a table in the *d*?
78:52 led them like sheep through the *d*.
Pr 21:19 Better to live in a *d*
Isa 32: 2 like streams of water in the *d*
32:15 and the *d* becomes a fertile field,
35: 6 and streams in the *d*.
43:20 because I provide water in the *d*
Mk 1: 3 "a voice of one calling in the *d*,
1:13 and he was in the *d* forty days,
Rev 12: 6 fled into the *d* to a place prepared
DESERTED (DESERTS)
Ezr 9: 9 our God has not *d* us
Mt 26:56 all the disciples *d* him and fled.
2Ti 1:15 in the province of Asia has *d* me,
DESERTING (DESERTS)
Gal 1: 6 are so quickly *d* the one who called
DESERTS (DESERTED DESERTING)
Zec 11:17 who *d* the flock!
DESERVE* (DESERVED DESERVES)
Ge 40:15 to *d* being put in a dungeon."
Lev 26:21 times over, as your sins *d*.
Jdg 20:10 it can give them what they *d*
1Sa 26:16 you and your men *d* to die,
1Ki 2:26 You *d* to die, but I will not put you
Ps 28: 4 bring back upon them what they *d*.
94: 2 pay back to the proud what they *d*.
103:10 he does not treat us as our sins *d*
Pr 3:27 from those who *d* it,
Ecc 8:14 men who get what the righteous *d*,
8:14 men who get what the wicked *d*,
Isa 66: 6 repaying his enemies all they *d*.
Jer 14:16 out on them the calamity they *d*.
17:10 according to what his deeds *d*."
21:14 I will punish you as your deeds *d*,
32:19 to his conduct and as his deeds *d*.
49:12 "If those who do not *d*
La 3:64 Pay them back what they *d*,
Eze 16:59 I will deal with you as you *d*,
Zec 1: 6 to us what our ways and practices *d*
Mt 8: 8 I do not *d* to have you come
22: 8 those I invited did not *d* to come.
Lk 7: 6 for I do not *d* to have you come
23:15 he has done nothing to *d* death.
23:41 for we are getting what our deeds *d*
Ro 1:32 those who do such things *d* death,
1Co 15: 9 even *d* to be called an apostle,
16:18 Such men *d* recognition.
2Co 11:15 end will be what their actions *d*.
Rev 16: 6 blood to drink as they *d*."
DESERVED* (DESERVE)
2Sa 19:28 descendants *d* nothing
Ezr 9:13 less than our sins have *d*
Job 33:27 but I did not get what I *d*.
Ac 23:29 charge against him that *d* death
Ro 3: 8 Their condemnation is *d*.

DESERVES* (DESERVE)
Nu 35:31 the life of a murderer, who *d* to die.
Dt 25: 2 If the guilty man *d* to be beaten,
    25: 2 the number of lashes his crime *d*,
Jdg 9:16 and if you have treated him as he *d*
2Sa 12: 5 the man who did this *d* to die!
Job 34:11 upon him what his conduct *d*.
Jer 51: 6 he will pay her what she *d*.
Lk 7: 4 "This man *d* to have you do this,
    10: 7 for the worker *d* his wages.
Ac 26:31 is not doing anything that *d* death
1Ti 1:15 saying that *d* full acceptance:
    4: 9 saying that *d* full acceptance
    5:18 and "The worker *d* his wages."
Heb 10:29 severely do you think a man *d*

DESIGNATED
Lk 6:13 also *d* apostles: Simon (whom he
Heb 5:10 and was *d* by God to be high priest

DESIRABLE* (DESIRE)
Ge 3: 6 and also *d* for gaining wisdom,
Pr 22: 1 A good name is more *d*
Jer 3:19 and give you a *d* land,

DESIRE* (DESIRABLE DESIRED DESIRES)
Ge 3:16 Your *d* will be for your husband,
Dt 5:21 You shall not set your *d*
1Sa 9:20 to whom is all the *d* of Israel turned
2Sa 19:38 anything you *d* from me I will do
    23: 5 and grant me my every *d*?
1Ch 29:18 keep this *d* in the hearts
2Ch 1:11 "Since this is your heart's *d*
    9: 8 and his *d* to uphold them forever,
Job 13: 3 But I *d* to speak to the Almighty
    21:14 We have no *d* to know your ways.
Ps 10:17 O LORD, the *d* of the afflicted;
    20: 4 May he give you the *d*
    21: 2 You have granted him the *d*
    27:12 me over to the *d* of my foes,
    40: 6 Sacrifice and offering you did not *d*
    40: 8 I *d* to do your will, O my God;
    40:14 may all who *d* my ruin
    41: 2 him to the *d* of his foes.
    51: 6 Surely you *d* truth
    70: 2 may all who *d* my ruin
    73:25 earth has nothing I *d* besides you
Pr 3:15 nothing you *d* can compare
    8:11 and nothing you *d* can compare
    10:24 what the righteous *d* will be
    11:23 The *d* of the righteous ends only
    12:12 The wicked *d* the plunder
    17:16 since he has no *d* to get wisdom?
    24: 1 do not *d* their company;
Ecc 12: 5 and *d* no longer is stirred.
SS 6:12 my *d* set me among the royal
    7:10 and his *d* is for me.
Isa 26: 8 are the *d* of our hearts.
    53: 2 appearance that we should *d* him.
    55:11 but will accomplish what I *d*
Eze 24:25 delight of their eyes, their heart's *d*,
Hos 6: 6 For I *d* mercy, not sacrifice,
Mic 7: 3 the powerful dictate what they *d*—
Mal 3: 1 whom you *d*, will come," says
Mt 9:13 learn what this means: 'I *d* mercy,
    12: 7 what these words mean, 'I *d* mercy,
Jn 8:44 want to carry out your father's *d*.
Ro 7: 8 in me every kind of covetous *d*.
    7:18 For I have the *d* to do what is good,
    9:16 depend on man's *d* or effort,
    10: 1 my heart's *d* and prayer to God
1Co 12:31 But eagerly *d* the greater gifts.
    14: 1 and eagerly *d* spiritual gifts,
2Co 8:10 but also to have the *d* to do so.
    8:13 Our *d* is not that others might be
Php 1:23 I *d* to depart and be with Christ,
Heb 10: 5 Sacrifice and offering you did not *d*
    10: 8 and sin offerings you did not *d*,
    13:18 *d* to live honorably in every way.
Jas 1:14 by his own evil *d*, he is dragged
    1:15 Then, after *d* has conceived,
2Pe 2:10 of those who follow the corrupt *d*

DESIRED (DESIRE)
Hag 2: 7 and the *d* of all nations will come,
Lk 22:15 "I have eagerly *d* to eat this

DESIRES* (DESIRE)
Ge 4: 7 at your door; it *d* to have you,
    41:16 will give Pharaoh the answer he *d*."
2Sa 3:21 rule over all that your heart *d*."
1Ki 11:37 rule over all that your heart *d*;
Job 17:11 and so are the *d* of my heart.
    31:16 "If I have denied the *d* of the poor
Ps 34:12 and *d* to see many good days,
    37: 4 he will give you the *d* of your heart.
    103: 5 who satisfies your *d* with good things,
    140: 8 do not grant the wicked their *d*,
    145:16 satisfy the *d* of every living thing.
    145:19 He fulfills the *d* of those who fear
Pr 11: 6 the unfaithful are trapped by evil *d*.
    13: 4 *d* of the diligent are fully satisfied.
    19:22 What a man *d* is unfailing love;
Ecc 6: 2 so that he lacks nothing his heart *d*,
SS 2: 7 or awaken love / until it so *d*.
    3: 5 or awaken love / until it so *d*.
    8: 4 or awaken love / until it so *d*.
Hab 2: 4 his *d* are not upright—
Mk 4:19 and the *d* for other things come in
Ro 1:24 over in the sinful *d* of their hearts
    6:12 body so that you obey its evil *d*.
    8: 5 set on what that nature *d*;
    8: 5 set on what the Spirit *d*.
    13:14 to gratify the *d* of the sinful nature.
Gal 5:16 and you will not gratify the *d*
    5:17 the sinful nature *d* what is contrary
    5:24 nature with its passions and *d*.
Eph 2: 3 and following its *d* and thoughts.
    4:22 being corrupted by its deceitful *d*;
Col 3: 5 impurity, lust, evil *d* and greed,
1Ti 3: 1 an overseer, he *d* a noble task.
    6: 9 their sensual *d* overcome their
    6: 9 and harmful *d* that plunge men
2Ti 2:22 Flee the evil *d* of youth,
    3: 6 are swayed by all kinds of evil *d*,
    4: 3 Instead, to suit their own *d*,
Jas 1:20 about the righteous life that God *d*.
    4: 1 from your *d* that battle within you?
1Pe 1:14 conform to the evil *d* you had
    2:11 to abstain from sinful *d*, which war
2Pe 2: 2 of his earthly life for evil human *d*,
    2:18 to the lustful *d* of sinful human
    3: 3 and following their own evil *d*.
1Jn 2:17 The world and its *d* pass away,
Jude :16 they follow their own evil *d*;
    :18 will follow their own ungodly *d*."

DESOLATE (DESOLATION)
Isa 54: 1 are the children of the *d* woman
Gal 4:27 are the children of the *d* woman

DESOLATION (DESOLATE)
Da 11:31 up the abomination that causes *d*.
    12:11 abomination that causes *d* is set up,
Mt 24:15 'the abomination that causes *d*,'

DESPAIR (DESPAIRED)
Isa 61: 3 instead of a spirit of *d*.
2Co 4: 8 perplexed, but not in *d*; persecuted,

DESPAIRED* (DESPAIR)
2Co 1: 8 ability to endure, so that we *d*

DESPERATE*
2Sa 12:18 He may do something *d*."
Ps 60: 3 have shown your people *d* times;
    79: 8 for we are in *d* need.
    142: 6 for I am in *d* need;

DESPISE (DESPISED DESPISES)
2Sa 12: 9 Why did you *d* the word
Job 5:17 so do not *d* the discipline
    36: 5 God is mighty, but does not *d* men;
    42: 6 Therefore I *d* myself

Ps 51:17 O God, you will not *d*.
    102:17 he will not *d* their plea.
Pr 1: 7 but fools *d* wisdom and discipline.
    3:11 do not *d* the LORD's discipline
    6:30 Men do not *d* a thief if he steals
    23:22 do not *d* your mother
Jer 14:21 of your name do not *d* us;
Am 5:10 and *d* him who tells the truth.
    5:21 "I hate, I *d* your religious feasts;
Mt 6:24 devoted to the one and *d* the other.
Lk 16:13 devoted to the one and *d* the other.
1Co 11:22 Or do you *d* the church of God
Tit 2:15 Do not let anyone *d* you.
2Pe 2:10 of the sinful nature and *d* authority.

DESPISED (DESPISE)
Ge 25:34 So Esau *d* his birthright.
Ps 22: 6 by men and *d* by the people.
Pr 12: 8 but men with warped minds are *d*.
Isa 53: 3 He was *d* and rejected by men,
    53: 3 he was *d*, and we esteemed him not
1Co 1:28 of this world and the *d* things—

DESPISES (DESPISE)
Pr 14:21 He who *d* his neighbor sins,
    15:20 but a foolish man *d* his mother.
    15:32 who ignores discipline *d* himself,
Zec 4:10 "Who *d* the day of small things?

DESTINED (DESTINY)
Lk 2:34 "This child is *d* to cause the falling
1Co 2: 7 and that God for our glory
Col 2:22 These are all *d* to perish with use,
1Th 3: 3 know quite well that we were *d*
Heb 9:27 Just as man is *d* to die once,
1Pe 2: 8 which is also what they were *d* for.

DESTINY* (DESTINED PREDESTINED)
Job 8:13 Such is the *d* of all who forget God;
Ps 73:17 then I understood their final *d*.
Ecc 7: 2 for death is the *d* of every man;
    9: 2 share a common *d*— the righteous
    9: 3 the sun: The same *d* overtakes all.
Isa 65:11 and fill bowls of mixed wine for D,
Php 3:19 Their *d* is destruction, their god is

DESTITUTE
Ps 102:17 to the prayer of the *d*;
Pr 31: 8 for the rights of all who are *d*.
Heb 11:37 *d*, persecuted and mistreated—

DESTROY (DESTROYED DESTROYING DESTROYS DESTRUCTION DESTRUCTIVE)
Ge 6:17 floodwaters on the earth to *d* all life
    9:11 will there be a flood to *d* the earth."
Pr 1:32 complacency of fools will *d* them;
Mt 10:28 of the One who can *d* both soul
Mk 14:58 'I will *d* this man-made temple
Lk 4:34 to *d* us? I know who you are—
Jn 10:10 only to steal and kill and *d*;
Ac 8: 3 But Saul began to *d* the church.
Rev 11:18 destroying those who *d* the earth."

DESTROYED (DESTROY)
Dt 8:19 you today that you will surely be *d*.
Job 19:26 And after my skin has been *d*,
Pr 6:15 he will suddenly be *d*—
    11: 3 the unfaithful are *d*
    21:28 listens to him will be *d* forever.
    29: 1 will suddenly be *d*—
Isa 55:13 which will not be *d*."
Da 2:44 up a kingdom that will never be *d*,
    6:26 his kingdom will not be *d*,
1Co 5: 5 so that the sinful nature may be *d*
    8:11 for whom Christ died, is *d*
    15:24 Father after he has *d* all dominion.
    15:26 The last enemy to be *d* is death.
2Co 4: 9 abandoned; struck down, but not *d*.
    5: 1 if the earthly tent we live in is *d*,
Gal 5:15 or you will be *d* by each other.
Eph 2:14 the two one and has *d* the barrier,
2Ti 1:10 who has *d* death and has brought

Heb 10: 39 of those who shrink back and
              are d,
2Pe 2: 12 born only to be caught and d,
      3: 10 the elements will be d by fire,
      3: 11 Since everything will be d
Jude : 5 later d those who did not believe.
      : 11 have been d in Korah's rebellion.

DESTROYING (DESTROY)
Jer 23: 1 "Woe to the shepherds who are d

DESTROYS (DESTROY)
Pr 6: 32 whoever does so d himself.
     11: 9 mouth the godless d his neighbor,
     18: 9 is brother to one who d.
     28: 24 he is partner to him who d.
Ecc 9: 18 but one sinner d much good.
1Co 3: 17 If anyone d God's temple,

DESTRUCTION (DESTROY)
Nu 32: 15 and you will be the cause of
            their d
Pr 16: 18 Pride goes before d,
     17: 19 he who builds a high gate
            invites d.
     24: 22 for those two will send sudden d
Hos 13: 14 Where, O grave, is your d?
Mt 7: 13 broad is the road that leads to d,
Lk 6: 49 it collapsed and its d was
            complete
Jn 17: 12 except the one doomed to d
Ro 9: 22 of his wrath—prepared for d?
Gal 6: 8 from that nature will reap d;
Php 3: 19 Their destiny is d, their god is
            their
1Th 5: 3 d will come on them suddenly,
2Th 1: 9 punished with everlasting d
      2: 3 is revealed, the man doomed to d.
1Ti 6: 9 that plunge men into ruin and d.
2Pe 2: 1 bringing swift d on themselves.
      2: 3 and their d has not been sleeping.
      3: 7 of judgment and d of ungodly
            men.
      3: 12 That day will bring about the d
      3: 16 other Scriptures, to their own d.
Rev 17: 8 out of the Abyss and go to his d.
      17: 11 to the seven and is going to his d.

DESTRUCTIVE (DESTROY)
2Pe 2: 1 will secretly introduce d heresies,

DETERMINED (DETERMINES)
Job 14: 5 Man's days are d;
Isa 14: 26 This is the plan d for the whole
Da 11: 36 for what has been d must take
            place
Ac 17: 26 and he d the times set for them

DETERMINES* (DETERMINED)
Ps 147: 4 He d the number of the stars
Pr 16: 9 but the LORD d his steps.
1Co 12: 11 them to each one, just as he d.

DETEST (DETESTABLE DETESTED DETESTS)
Lev 11: 10 in the water—you are to d.
Pr 8: 7 for my lips d wickedness.
     13: 19 but fools d turning from evil.
     16: 12 Kings d wrongdoing,
     24: 9 and men d a mocker.
     29: 27 The righteous d the dishonest;
     29: 27 the wicked d the upright.

DETESTABLE (DETEST)
Pr 6: 16 seven that are d to him:
     21: 27 The sacrifice of the wicked is d—
     28: 9 even his prayers are d.
Isa 1: 13 Your incense is d to me.
     41: 24 he who chooses you is d.
     44: 19 Shall I make a d thing
Jer 44: 4 'Do not do this d thing that I
            hate!'
Eze 8: 13 doing things that are even
            more d."
Lk 16: 15 among men is d in God's sight.
Tit 1: 16 They are d, disobedient
1Pe 4: 3 orgies, carousing and d idolatry.

DETESTED* (DETEST)
Zec 11: 8 The flock d me, and I grew weary

DETESTS* (DETEST)
Dt 22: 5 LORD your God d anyone who
     23: 18 the LORD your God d them both.
     25: 16 LORD your God d anyone who
Pr 3: 32 for the LORD d a perverse man
     11: 20 The LORD d men
     12: 22 The LORD d lying lips,

Pr 15: 8 The LORD d the sacrifice
     15: 9 The LORD d the way
     15: 26 The LORD d the thoughts
     16: 5 The LORD d all the proud of heart
     17: 15 the LORD d them both.
     20: 10 the LORD d them both.
     20: 23 The LORD d differing weights,

DEVIATE*
2Ch 8: 15 They did not d from the king's

DEVICES*
Ps 81: 12 to follow their own d.

DEVIL* (DEVIL'S)
Mt 4: 1 the desert to be tempted by
            the d.
     4: 5 the d took him to the holy city
     4: 8 d took him to a very high
            mountain
     4: 11 the d left him, and angels came
     13: 39 the enemy who sows them is
            the d.
     25: 41 the eternal fire prepared for the d
Lk 4: 2 forty days he was tempted by
            the d.
     4: 3 d said to him, "If you are the Son
     4: 5 The d led him up to a high place
     4: 9 The d led him to Jerusalem
     4: 13 When the d had finished all this
     8: 12 then the d comes and takes away
Jn 6: 70 of you is a d!" (He meant Judas,
     8: 44 You belong to your father, the d,
     13: 2 the d had already prompted Judas
Ac 10: 38 were under the power of the d,
     13: 10 "You are a child of the d
Eph 4: 27 and do not give the d a foothold.
1Ti 3: 6 under the same judgment as
            the d.
2Ti 2: 26 and escape from the trap of the d,
Heb 2: 14 the d— and free those who all
            their
Jas 3: 15 but is earthly, unspiritual, of
            the d.
      4: 7 Resist the d, and he will flee
1Pe 5: 8 Your enemy the d prowls
1Jn 3: 8 because the d has been sinning
      3: 8 who does what is sinful is of the d,
      3: 10 and who the children of the d are:
Jude : 9 with the d about the body of
            Moses
Rev 2: 10 the d will put some of you in
            prison
      12: 9 that ancient serpent called the d
      12: 12 the d has gone down to you!
      20: 2 that ancient serpent, who is the d,
      20: 10 And the d, who deceived them,

DEVIL'S* (DEVIL)
Eph 6: 11 stand against the d schemes.
1Ti 3: 7 into disgrace and into the d trap.
1Jn 3: 8 was to destroy the d work.

DEVIOUS*
Pr 2: 15 and who are d in their ways.
     14: 2 he whose ways are d despises
            him.
     21: 8 The way of the guilty is d,

DEVOTE* (DEVOTED DEVOTING DEVOTION DEVOUT)
1Ch 22: 19 Now d your heart and soul
2Ch 31: 4 Levites so they could d
Job 11: 13 "Yet if you d your heart to him
Jer 30: 21 for who is he who will d himself
Mic 4: 13 You will d their ill-gotten gains
1Co 7: 5 so that you may d yourselves
Col 4: 2 D yourselves to prayer, being
1Ti 1: 4 nor to d themselves to myths
     4: 13 d yourself to the public reading
Tit 3: 8 may be careful to d themselves
     3: 14 people must learn to d
            themselves

DEVOTED (DEVOTE)
1Ki 11: 4 and his heart was not fully d
Ezr 7: 10 For Ezra had d himself to the
            study
Ps 86: 2 Guard my life, for I am d to you.
Mt 6: 24 or he will be d to the one
Mk 7: 11 from me is Corban' (that is, a
            gift d
Ac 2: 42 They d themselves
     18: 5 Paul d himself exclusively
Ro 12: 10 Be d to one another

1Co 7: 34 Her aim is to be d to the Lord
     16: 15 and they have d themselves
2Co 7: 12 for yourselves how d to us you
            are.

DEVOTING* (DEVOTE)
1Ti 5: 10 d herself to all kinds of good
            deeds.

DEVOTION* (DEVOTE)
2Ki 20: 3 and with wholehearted d and
            have
1Ch 28: 9 and serve him with
            wholehearted d
     29: 3 in my d to the temple
     29: 19 son Solomon the wholehearted d
2Ch 32: 32 and his acts of d are written
     35: 26 of Josiah's reign and his acts of d,
Job 6: 14 despairing man should have the d
     15: 4 and hinder d to God.
Isa 38: 3 and with wholehearted d and
            have
Jer 2: 2 " 'I remember the d of your youth,
Eze 33: 31 With their mouths they express d,
1Co 7: 35 way in undivided d to the Lord.
2Co 11: 3 from your sincere and pure d

DEVOUR (DEVOURED DEVOURING DEVOURS)
2Sa 2: 26 "Must the sword d forever?
Mk 12: 40 They d widows' houses
1Pe 5: 8 lion looking for someone to d.

DEVOURED (DEVOUR)
Jer 30: 16 But all who devour you will be d;

DEVOURING (DEVOUR)
Gal 5: 15 keep on biting and d each other,

DEVOURS (DEVOUR)
2Sa 11: 25 the sword d one as well as
            another.
Pr 21: 20 but a foolish man d all he has.

DEVOUT* (DEVOTE)
1Ki 18: 3 (Obadiah was a d believer
Isa 57: 1 d men are taken away,
Lk 2: 25 Simeon, who was righteous and d.
Ac 10: 2 his family were d and God-fearing;
     10: 7 a d soldier who was one of his
            attendants
     13: 43 and d converts to Judaism
            followed
     22: 12 He was a d observer of the law

DEW
Jdg 6: 37 If there is d only on the fleece

DICTATED
Jer 36: 4 and while Jeremiah d all the
            words

DIE (DEAD DEADENED DEATH DIED DIES DYING)
Ge 2: 17 when you eat of it you will
            surely d
      3: 3 you must not touch it, or you
            will d
      3: 4 will not surely d," the serpent said
Ex 11: 5 Every firstborn son in Egypt will d,
Ru 1: 17 Where you d I will d, and there I
2Ki 14: 6 each is to d for his own sins."
Job 2: 9 Curse God and d!" He replied,
Pr 5: 23 He will d for lack of discipline.
     10: 21 but fools d for lack of judgment.
     15: 10 he who hates correction will d.
     23: 13 with the rod, he will not d.
Ecc 3: 2 a time to be born and a time to d,
Isa 22: 13 "for tomorrow we d!"
     66: 24 their worm will not d, nor will
            their
Jer 31: 30 everyone will d for his own sin;
Eze 3: 18 that wicked man will d for his sin,
      3: 19 he will d for his sin; but you will
      3: 20 block before him, he will d.
     18: 4 soul who sins is the one who
            will d.
     18: 20 soul who sins is the one who
            will d.
     18: 31 Why will you d, O house of Israel?
     33: 8 'O wicked man, you will surely d,'
Mt 26: 52 "for all who draw the sword will d
Mk 9: 48 " 'their worm does not d,
Jn 8: 21 and you will d in your sin.
     11: 26 and believes in me will never d.
Ro 5: 7 Very rarely will anyone d
     14: 8 and if we d, we d to the Lord.
1Co 15: 22 in Adam all d, so in Christ all will
     15: 31 I d every day—I mean that,

1Co 15:32 for tomorrow we *d.*"
Php 1:21 to live is Christ and to *d* is gain.
Heb 9:27 Just as man is destined to *d* once,
1Pe 2:24 so that we might *d* to sins
Rev 14:13 Blessed are the dead who *d*

DIED (DIE)
1Ki 16:18 So he *d,* because of the sins he
         had
1Ch 1:51 Hadad also *d.*
   10:13 Saul *d* because he was unfaithful
Lk 16:22 "The time came when the
         beggar *d*
Ro   5: 6 we were still powerless, Christ *d*
    5: 8 we were still sinners, Christ *d*
    6: 2 By no means! We *d* to sin;
    6: 7 anyone who has *d* has been freed
    6: 8 if we *d* with Christ, we believe
        that
   6:10 The death he, he *d* to sin once
  14: 9 Christ *d* and returned to life
  14:15 brother for whom Christ *d.*
1Co 8:11 for whom Christ *d,* is destroyed
   15: 3 that Christ *d* for our sins
        according
2Co 5:14 *d* for all, and therefore all *d.*
    5:15 he *d* for all, that those who live
Col   2:20 Since you *d* with Christ
    3: 3 For you *d,* and your life is now
1Th 4:14 We believe that Jesus *d*
    5:10 He *d* for us so that, whether we
        are
2Ti   2:11 If we *d* with him,
Heb 9:15 now that he has *d* as a ransom
    9:17 in force only when somebody
        has *d*
1Pe 3:18 For Christ *d* for sins once for all,
Rev 2: 8 who *d* and came to life again.

DIES (DIE)
Job 14:14 If a man *d,* will he live again?
Pr   11: 7 a wicked man *d,* his hope
        perishes;
   26:20 without gossip a quarrel *d* down.
Jn   11:25 in me will live, even though he *d;*
   12:24 But if it *d,* it produces many seeds.
Ro   7: 2 but if her husband *d,* she is
        released
   14: 7 and none of us *d* to himself alone.
1Co 7:39 But if her husband *d,* she is free
   15:36 does not come to life unless it *d.*

DIFFERENCE* (DIFFERENT)
2Sa 19:35 Can I tell the *d* between what is
2Ch 1: 5 so that they may learn the *d*
Eze 22:26 they teach that there is no *d*
   44:23 are to teach my people the *d*
Ro   3:22 There is no *d,* for all have sinned
   10:12 For there is no *d* between Jew
Gal   2: 6 whatever they were makes no *d*

DIFFERENCES* (DIFFERENT)
1Co 11:19 to be *d* among you to show which

DIFFERENT* (DIFFERENCE DIFFERENCES DIFFERING DIFFERS)
Lev 19:19 "'Do not mate *d* kinds of animals.
Nu 14:24 my servant Caleb has a *d* spirit
1Sa 10: 6 you will be changed into a *d*
        person
Est   1: 7 each one *d* from the other,
    3: 8 whose customs are *d* from those
Da   7: 3 Four great beasts, each *d*
    7: 7 It was *d* from all the former
        beasts,
    7:19 which was *d* from all the others
    7:23 It will be *d* from all the other
    7:24 them another king will arise, *d*
   11:29 but this time the outcome will
        be *d*
Mk 16:12 Jesus appeared in a *d* form
Ro 12: 6 We have *d* gifts, according
1Co 4: 7 For who makes you *d*
   12: 4 There are *d* kinds of gifts,
   12: 5 There are *d* kinds of service,
   12: 6 There are *d* kinds of working,
   12:10 speaking in *d* kinds of tongues,
   12:28 and those speaking in *d* kinds
2Co 11: 4 or a *d* gospel from the one you
   11: 4 or if you receive a *d* spirit
Gal   1: 6 and are turning to a *d* gospel—
    4: 1 he is no *d* from a slave,
Heb 7:13 are said belonged to a *d* tribe,
Jas   2:25 and sent them off in a *d* direction?

DIFFERING* (DIFFERENT)
Dt 25:13 Do not have two *d* weights
   25:14 Do not have two *d* measures
Pr   20:10 Differing weights and *d* measures
   20:10 *D* weights and differing measures
   20:23 The Lord detests *d* weights,

DIFFERS* (DIFFERENT)
1Co 15:41 and star *d* from star in splendor.

DIFFICULT (DIFFICULTIES)
Ex 18:22 but have them bring every *d* case
Dt 30:11 commanding you today is not
        too *d*
2Ki 2:10 "You have asked a *d* thing,"
Eze 3: 5 of obscure speech and *d*
        language,
Ac 15:19 that we should not make it *d*

DIFFICULTIES* (DIFFICULT)
Dt 31:17 and *d* will come upon them,
   31:21 when many disasters and *d* come
2Co 12:10 in hardships, in persecutions, in *d.*

DIGNITY
Pr 31:25 She is clothed with strength
        and *d;*

DIGS
Pr 26:27 If a man *d* a pit, he will fall into it;

DILIGENCE (DILIGENT)
Ezr 5: 8 The work is being carried on
        with *d*
Heb 6:11 to show this same *d* to the very
        end

DILIGENT (DILIGENCE)
Pr   10: 4 but *d* hands bring wealth.
   12:24 *D* hands will rule,
   12:27 the *d* man prizes his possessions.
   13: 4 of the *d* are fully satisfied.
   21: 5 The plans of the *d* lead to profit
1Ti   4:15 Be *d* in these matters; give
        yourself

DINAH*
    Only daughter of Jacob, by Leah (Ge 30:21;
46:15). Raped by Shechem; avenged by Simeon and Levi (Ge 34).

DINE
Pr 23: 1 When you sit to *d* with a ruler,

DIOTREPHES*
3Jn   : 9 but *D,* who loves to be first,

DIRECT (DIRECTED DIRECTIVES DIRECTS)
Ge 18:19 so that he will *d* his children
Dt 17:10 to do everything they *d* you to do.
Ps 119:35 *D* me in the path of your
  119:133 *D* my footsteps according
Jer 10:23 it is not for man to *d* his steps.
2Th 3: 5 May the Lord *d* your hearts
1Ti   5:17 The elders who *d* the affairs

DIRECTED (DIRECT)
Ge 24:51 master's son, as the Lord has *d.*"
Nu 16:40 as the Lord *d* him through Moses
Dt   2: 1 Sea, as the Lord had *d* me.
    6: 1 laws the Lord your God *d* me
Jos 11: 9 did to them as the Lord had *d:*
   11:23 just as the Lord had *d* Moses,
Pr 20:24 A man's steps are *d* by the Lord.
Jer 13: 2 as the Lord *d,* and put it
Ac   7:44 It had been made as God *d*
        Moses,
Tit   1: 5 elders in every town, as I *d* you.

DIRECTIVES* (DIRECT)
1Co 11:17 In the following *d* I have no praise

DIRECTS (DIRECT)
Ps 42: 8 By day the Lord *d* his love,
Isa 48:17 who *d* you in the way you should

DIRGE*
Mt 11:17 we sang a *d,*
Lk   7:32 we sang a *d,*

DISABLED*
Jn   5: 3 number of people used to lie—
Heb 12:13 so that the lame may not be *d.*

DISAGREEMENT*
Ac 15:39 had such a sharp *d* that they
        parted

DISAPPEAR (DISAPPEARED DISAPPEARS)
Mt   5:18 will by any means *d* from the Law
Lk 16:17 earth to *d* than for the least stroke
Heb 8:13 is obsolete and aging will soon *d.*
2Pe   3:10 The heavens will *d* with a roar;

DISAPPEARED (DISAPPEAR)
1Ki 20:40 busy here and there, the man *d."*

DISAPPEARS (DISAPPEAR)
1Co 13:10 perfection comes, the
        imperfect *d.*

DISAPPOINT* (DISAPPOINTED)
Ro   5: 5 And hope does not *d* us,

DISAPPOINTED (DISAPPOINT)
Ps 22: 5 in you they trusted and were
        not *d.*

DISAPPROVE*
Pr 24:18 or the Lord will see and *d*

DISARMED*
Col   2:15 And having *d* the powers

DISASTER
Ex 32:12 and do not bring *d* on your
        people.
Ps 57: 1 wings until the *d* has passed.
Pr   1:26 I in turn will laugh at your *d;*
    3:25 Have no fear of sudden *d*
    6:15 Therefore *d* will overtake him
   16: 4 even the wicked for a day of *d.*
   17: 5 over *d* will not go unpunished.
   27:10 house when *d* strikes you—
Isa 45: 7 I bring prosperity and create *d;*
Jer 17:17 you are my refuge in the day of *d.*
Eze 7: 5 An unheard-of *d* is coming.

DISCERN (DISCERNED DISCERNING DISCERNMENT)
Ps 19:12 Who can *d* his errors?
  139: 3 You *d* my going out and my lying
Php 1:10 you may be able to *d* what is best

DISCERNED (DISCERN)
1Co 2:14 because they are spiritually *d.*

DISCERNING (DISCERN)
1Ki 3: 9 So give your servant a *d* heart
    3:12 I will give you a wise and *d* heart,
Pr   1: 5 and let the *d* get guidance—
    8: 9 To the *d* all of them are right;
   10:13 on the lips of the *d,*
   14: 6 knowledge comes easily to the *d.*
   14:33 in the heart of the *d*
   15:14 The *d* heart seeks knowledge,
   16:21 The wise in heart are called *d,*
   17:24 A *d* man keeps wisdom in view,
   17:28 and *d* if he holds his tongue.
   18:15 heart of the *d* acquires
        knowledge;
   19:25 rebuke a *d* man, and he will gain
   28: 7 He who keeps the law is a *d* son,

DISCERNMENT (DISCERN)
Ps 119:125 I am your servant; give me *d*
Pr   3:21 preserve sound judgment and *d,*
   17:10 A rebuke impresses a man of *d*
   28:11 a poor man who has *d* sees

DISCHARGED* (DISCHARGING)
Ecc 8: 8 As no one is *d* in time of war,

DISCHARGING* (DISCHARGED)
1Co 9:17 I am simply *d* the trust committed

DISCIPLE (DISCIPLES DISCIPLES')
Mt 10:42 these little ones because he is
        my *d,*
Lk 14:26 his own life—he cannot be my *d.*
   14:27 and follow me cannot be my *d.*
   14:33 everything he has cannot be
        my *d.*
Jn 13:23 of them, the *d* whom Jesus loved,
   19:26 and the *d* whom he loved
        standing
   21: 7 Then the *d* whom Jesus loved said
   21:20 saw that the *d* whom Jesus loved

DISCIPLES (DISCIPLE)
Mt 10: 1 He called his twelve *d* to him
   26:56 Then all the *d* deserted him
   28:19 Therefore go and make *d*
Mk   3: 7 withdrew with his *d* to the lake,
   16:20 Then the *d* went out and
        preached
Lk   6:13 he called his *d* to him and chose
Jn   2:11 and his *d* put their faith in him.
    6:66 many of his *d* turned back
    8:31 to my teaching, you are really
        my *d*
   12:16 At first his *d* did not understand
        all
   13:35 men will know that you are my *d*
   15: 8 showing yourselves to be my *d.*

Jn   20:20 The *d* were overjoyed
Ac   6: 1 the number of *d* was increasing,
      11:26 The *d* were called Christians first
      14:22 strengthening the *d*
      18:23 Phrygia, strengthening all the *d*.

DISCIPLES' (DISCIPLE)
Jn   13: 5 and began to wash his *d* feet,

DISCIPLINE* (DISCIPLINED DISCIPLINES SELF-DISCIPLINE)
Dt   4:36 made you hear his voice to *d* you.
      11: 2 and experienced the *d*
      21:18 listen to them when they *d* him,
Job   5:17 so do not despise the *d*
Ps   6: 1 or *d* me in your wrath.
      38: 1 or *d* me in your wrath.
      39:11 You rebuke and *d* men for their sin;
      94:12 Blessed is the man you *d*, O LORD
Pr   1: 2 for attaining wisdom and *d*;
       1: 7 but fools despise wisdom and *d*.
       3:11 do not despise the LORD's *d*
       5:12 You will say, "How I hated *d!*
       5:23 He will die for lack of *d*,
       6:23 and the corrections of *d*
      10:17 He who heeds *d* shows the way
      12: 1 Whoever loves *d* loves knowledge,
      13:18 He who ignores *d* comes to poverty
      13:24 who loves him is careful to *d* him.
      15: 5 A fool spurns his father's *d*,
      15:10 Stern *d* awaits him who leaves
      15:32 He who ignores *d* despises himself,
      19:18 *D* your son, for in that there is hope
      22:15 the rod of *d* will drive it far
      23:13 Do not withhold *d* from a child;
      23:23 get wisdom, *d* and understanding.
      29:17 *D* your son, and he will give you
Jer   17:23 would not listen or respond to *d*.
      30:11 I will *d* you but only with justice;
      32:33 would not listen or respond to *d*.
      46:28 I will *d* you but only with justice;
Hos   5: 2 I will *d* all of them.
Heb   12: 5 do not make light of the Lord's *d*,
      12: 7 as *d;* God is treating you
      12: 8 (and everyone undergoes *d*),
      12:11 No *d* seems pleasant at the time,
Rev   3:19 Those whom I love I rebuke and *d*.

DISCIPLINED* (DISCIPLINE)
Pr   1: 3 for acquiring a *d* and prudent life,
Isa   26:16 when you *d* them,
Jer   31:18 and I have been *d*.
      31:18 'You *d* me like an unruly calf,
1Co   11:32 we are being *d* so that we will not
Tit   1: 8 upright, holy and *d*.
Heb   12: 7 For what son is not *d* by his father?
      12: 8 you are not *d* (and everyone
      12: 9 all had human fathers who *d* us
      12:10 Our fathers *d* us for a little while

DISCIPLINES* (DISCIPLINE)
Dt   8: 5 your heart that as a man *d* his son,
       8: 5 so the LORD your God *d* you.
Ps   94:10 Does he who *d* nations not punish?
Pr   3:12 the LORD *d* those he loves,
Heb   12: 6 because the Lord *d* those he loves,
      12:10 but God *d* us for our good,

DISCLOSED
Lk   8:17 is nothing hidden that will not be *d*,
Col   1:26 and generations, but is now *d*
Heb   9: 8 Holy Place had not yet been *d*

DISCORD
Gal   5:20 idolatry and witchcraft; hatred, *d*,

DISCOURAGED* (DISCOURAGEMENT)
Nu   32: 9 they *d* the Israelites
Dt   1:21 Do not be afraid; do not be *d*."
      31: 8 Do not be afraid; do not be *d*."
Jos   1: 9 Do not be terrified; do not be *d*,
       8: 1 "Do not be afraid; do not be *d*,
      10:25 "Do not be afraid; do not be *d*.
1Ch   22:13 Do not be afraid or *d*.
      28:20 or *d*, for the LORD God,
2Ch   20:15 or *d* because of this vast army.

2Ch   20:17 Do not be afraid; do not be *d*.
      32: 7 or *d* because of the king of Assyria
Job   4: 5 to you, and you are *d;*
Isa   42: 4 he will not falter or be *d*
Eph   3:13 to be *d* because of my sufferings
Col   3:21 children, or they will become *d*.

DISCOURAGEMENT* (DISCOURAGED)
Ex   6: 9 of their *d* and cruel bondage.

DISCOVERED
2Ki   23:24 book that Hilkiah the priest had *d*

DISCREDIT* (DISCREDITED)
Ne   6:13 would give me a bad name to *d*
Job   40: 8 "Would you *d* my justice?

DISCREDITED (DISCREDIT)
2Co   6: 3 so that our ministry will not be *d*.

DISCRETION*
1Ch   22:12 May the LORD give you *d*
Pr   1: 4 knowledge and *d* to the young—
       2:11 *D* will protect you,
       5: 2 that you may maintain *d*
       8:12 I possess knowledge and *d*.
      11:22 a beautiful woman who shows no *d*.

DISCRIMINATED*
Jas   2: 4 have you not *d* among yourselves

DISEASE (DISEASES)
Mt   4:23 and healing every *d* and sickness
       9:35 and healing every *d* and sickness.
      10: 1 and to heal every *d* and sickness.

DISEASES (DISEASE)
Ps   103: 3 and heals all my *d;*
Mt   8:17 and carried our *d.*"
Mk   3:10 those with *d* were pushing forward
Lk   9: 1 drive out all demons and to cure *d*,

DISFIGURE* (DISFIGURED)
Mt   6:16 for they *d* their faces

DISFIGURED (DISFIGURE)
Isa   52:14 his appearance was so *d*

DISGRACE (DISGRACEFUL DISGRACES)
Ps   44:15 My *d* is before me all day long,
      52: 1 you who are a *d* in the eyes of God?
      74:21 not let the oppressed retreat in *d;*
Pr   6:33 Blows and *d* are his lot,
      11: 2 When pride comes, then comes *d*,
      14:34 but sin is a *d* to any people.
      19:26 is a son who brings shame and *d*
Mt   1:19 want to expose her to public *d*,
Ac   5:41 of suffering *d* for the Name.
1Co   11: 6 and if it is a *d* for a woman
      11:14 it is a *d* to him, but that
1Ti   3: 7 so that he will not fall into *d*
Heb   6: 6 and subjecting him to public *d*.
      11:26 He regarded *d* for the sake
      13:13 the camp, bearing the *d* he bore.

DISGRACEFUL (DISGRACE)
Pr   10: 5 during harvest is a *d* son.
      12: 4 a *d* wife is like decay in his bones.
      17: 2 wise servant will rule over a *d* son,
1Co   14:35 for it is *d* for a woman to speak

DISGRACES (DISGRACE)
Pr   28: 7 of gluttons *d* his father.
      29:15 but a child left to himself *d* his mother

DISGUISES*
Pr   26:24 A malicious man *d* himself

DISH
Pr   19:24 sluggard buries his hand in the *d;*
Mt   23:25 the outside of the cup and *d*,

DISHONEST*
Ex   18:21 trustworthy men who hate *d* gain
Lev   19:35 "'Do not use *d* standards
1Sa   8: 3 They turned aside after *d* gain
Pr   11: 1 The LORD abhors *d* scales,
      13:11 *D* money dwindles away,
      20:23 and *d* scales do not please him.
      29:27 The righteous detest the *d;*
Jer   22:17 are set only on *d* gain,
Eze   28:18 By your many sins and *d* trade
Hos   12: 7 The merchant uses *d* scales,
Am   8: 5 and cheating with *d* scales,
Mic   6:11 Shall I acquit a man with *d* scales,

Lk   16: 8 master commended the *d* manager
      16:10 whoever is *d* with very little will
      16:10 with very little will also be *d*
1Ti   3: 8 wine, and not pursuing *d* gain.
Tit   1: 7 not violent, not pursuing *d* gain.
       1:11 and that for the sake of *d* gain.

DISHONOR* (DISHONORED DISHONORS)
Lev   18: 7 "'Do not *d* your father
      18: 8 wife; that would *d* your father.
      18:10 daughter; that would *d* you.
      18:14 "'Do not *d* your father's brother
      18:16 that would *d* your brother.
      20:19 for that would *d* a close relative;
Dt   22:30 he must not *d* his father's bed.
Pr   30: 9 and so *d* the name of my God.
Jer   14:21 do not *d* your glorious throne.
      20:11 their *d* will never be forgotten.
La   2: 2 princes down to the ground in *d*;
Eze   22:10 are those who *d* their fathers' bed;
Jn   8:49 I honor my Father and you *d* me.
Ro   2:23 do you *d* God by breaking the law?
1Co   15:43 it is sown in *d*, it is raised in glory;
2Co   6: 8 through glory and *d*, bad report

DISHONORED* (DISHONOR)
Lev   20:11 father's wife, he has *d* his father.
      20:17 He has *d* his sister and will be held
      20:20 with his aunt, he has *d* his uncle.
      20:21 of impurity; he has *d* his brother.
Dt   21:14 as a slave, since you have *d* her.
Ezr   4:14 proper for us to see the king *d*,
1Co   4:10 You are honored, we are *d!*

DISHONORS* (DISHONOR)
Dt   27:16 Cursed is the man who *d* his father
      27:20 for he *d* his father's bed."
Job   20: 3 I hear a rebuke that *d* me,
Mic   7: 6 For a son *d* his father,
1Co   11: 4 with his head covered *d* his head.
      11: 5 her head uncovered *d* her head—

DISILLUSIONMENT*
Ps   7:14 conceives trouble gives birth to *d*.

DISMAYED*
Isa   28:16 the one who trusts will never be *d*.
      41:10 do not be *d*, for I am your God.

DISOBEDIENCE* (DISOBEY)
Jos   22:22 in rebellion or *d* to the LORD,
Jer   43: 7 So they entered Egypt in *d*
Ro   5:19 as through the *d* of the one man
      11:30 mercy as a result of their *d*,
      11:32 to *d* so that he may have mercy
2Co   10: 6 ready to punish every act of *d*,
Heb   2: 2 and *d* received its just punishment,
       4: 6 go in, because of their *d*.
       4:11 fall by following their example of *d*.

DISOBEDIENT* (DISOBEY)
Ne   9:26 "But they were *d* and rebelled
Lk   1:17 and the *d* to the wisdom
Ac   26:19 I was not *d* to the vision
Ro   10:21 hands to a *d* and obstinate people."
      11:30 as you who were at one time *d*
      11:31 so they too have now become *d*.
Eph   2: 2 now at work in those who are *d*.
       5: 6 comes on those who are *d*.
       5:12 to mention what the *d* do in secret.
2Ti   3: 2 proud, abusive, *d* to their parents,
Tit   1: 6 to the charge of being wild and *d*.
       1:16 *d* and unfit for doing anything
       3: 3 At one time we too were foolish, *d*,
Heb   11:31 killed with those who were *d*.

DISOBEY* (DISOBEDIENCE DISOBEDIENT DISOBEYED DISOBEYING DISOBEYS)
Dt   11:28 the curse if you *d* the commands
2Ch   24:20 'Why do you *d* the LORD's
Est   3: 3 Why do you *d* the king's command
Jer   42:13 and so *d* the LORD your God,
Ro   1:30 they *d* their parents; they are
1Pe   2: 8 because they *d* the message—

DISOBEYED* (DISOBEY)
Nu 14:22 and in the desert but who *d* me
   27:14 both of you *d* my command
Jdg 2: 2 Yet you have *d* me.
Ne 9:29 arrogant and *d* your commands.
Isa 24: 5 they have *d* the laws,
Jer 43: 4 and all the people *d* the LORD's
Lk 15:29 for you and never *d* your orders.
Heb 3:18 rest if not to those who *d*?
1Pe 3:20 the spirits in prison who *d* long
         ago

DISOBEYING* (DISOBEY)
Nu 14:41 "Why are you *d* the LORD's

DISOBEYS* (DISOBEY)
Eze 33:12 man will not save him when he *d*,

DISORDER
1Co 14:33 For God is not a God of *d*
2Co 12:20 slander, gossip, arrogance and *d*.
Jas 3:16 there you find *d* and every evil

DISOWN (DISOWNS)
Pr 30: 9 I may have too much and *d* you
Mt 10:33 I will *d* him before my Father
   26:35 to die with you, I will never *d*
         you."
2Ti 2:12 If we *d* him,

DISOWNS (DISOWN)
Lk 12: 9 he who *d* me before men will be

DISPENSATION SEE ADMINISTRATION, TRUST

DISPLACES
Pr 30:23 a maidservant who *d* her mistress.

DISPLAY (DISPLAYED DISPLAYS)
Ps 45: 4 your right hand *d* awesome
         deeds.
Eze 39:21 I will *d* my glory among the
         nations
Ro 9:17 that I might *d* my power in you
1Co 4: 9 on *d* at the end of the procession,
1Ti 1:16 Christ Jesus might *d* his unlimited

DISPLAYED (DISPLAY)
Jn 9: 3 work of God might be *d* in his life.
2Th 2: 9 the work of Satan *d* in all kinds

DISPLAYS (DISPLAY)
Isa 44:23 he *d* his glory in Israel.

DISPLEASE (DISPLEASED)
1Th 2:15 They *d* God and are hostile

DISPLEASED (DISPLEASE)
2Sa 11:27 David had done *d* the LORD.

DISPUTABLE* (DISPUTE)
Ro 14: 1 passing judgment on *d* matters.

DISPUTE (DISPUTABLE DISPUTES DISPUTING)
Pr 17:14 before a *d* breaks out.
1Co 6: 1 If any of you has a *d* with another,

DISPUTES (DISPUTE)
Pr 18:18 Casting the lot settles *d*

DISPUTING (DISPUTE)
1Ti 2: 8 in prayer, without anger or *d*.

DISQUALIFIED*
1Co 9:27 I myself will not be *d* for the prize.

DISREPUTE*
2Pe 2: 2 will bring the way of truth into *d*.

DISSENSION* (DISSENSIONS)
Pr 6:14 he always stirs up *d*.
    6:19 and a man who stirs up *d*
   10:12 Hatred stirs up *d*,
   15:18 A hot-tempered man stirs up *d*,
   16:28 A perverse man stirs up *d*,
   28:25 A greedy man stirs up *d*,
   29:22 An angry man stirs up *d*,
Ro 13:13 debauchery, not in *d* and jealousy.

DISSENSIONS* (DISSENSION)
Gal 5:20 selfish ambition, *d*, factions

DISSIPATION*
Lk 21:34 will be weighed down with *d*,
1Pe 4: 4 with them into the same flood
         of *d*,

DISTINCTION
Ac 15: 9 He made no *d* between us

DISTINGUISH (DISTINGUISHING)
1Ki 3: 9 and to *d* between right and
         wrong.
Heb 5:14 themselves to *d* good from evil.

DISTINGUISHING
1Co 12:10 the *d* between spirits,

DISTORT
Ac 20:30 and *d* the truth in order
2Co 4: 2 nor do we *d* the word of God.
2Pe 3:16 ignorant and unstable people *d*,

DISTRACTED*
Lk 10:40 But Martha was *d* by all

DISTRESS (DISTRESSED)
2Ch 15: 4 in their *d* they turned to the LORD
Ps 18: 6 In my *d* I called to the LORD;
   81: 7 In your *d* you called and I rescued
  120: 1 I call on the LORD in my *d*,
Jnh 2: 2 "In my *d* I called to the LORD,
Mt 24:21 For then there will be great *d*,
Jas 1:27 after orphans and widows in
         their *d*

DISTRESSED (DISTRESS)
Lk 12:50 how *d* I am until it is completed!
Ro 14:15 If your brother is *d*

DIVIDE (DIVIDED DIVIDING DIVISION DIVISIONS DIVISIVE)
Ps 22:18 They *d* my garments among them

DIVIDED (DIVIDE)
Mt 12:25 household *d* against itself will not
Lk 23:34 they *d* up his clothes by casting
         lots
1Co 1:13 Is Christ *d*? Was Paul crucified

DIVIDING (DIVIDE)
Eph 2:14 destroyed the barrier, the *d* wall
Heb 4:12 it penetrates even to *d* soul

DIVINATION
Lev 19:26 " 'Do not practice *d* or sorcery.

DIVINE
Ro 1:20 his eternal power and *d* nature—
2Co 10: 4 they have *d* power
2Pe 1: 4 you may participate in the *d*
         nature

DIVISION (DIVIDE)
Lk 12:51 on earth? No, I tell you, but *d*.
1Co 12:25 so that there should be no *d*

DIVISIONS (DIVIDE)
Ro 16:17 to watch out for those who
         cause *d*
1Co 1:10 another so that there may be no *d*
   11:18 there are *d* among you,

DIVISIVE* (DIVIDE)
Tit 3:10 Warn a *d* person once,

DIVORCE* (DIVORCED DIVORCES)
Dt 22:19 he must not *d* her as long as he
         lives
   22:29 He can never *d* her as long
   24: 1 and he writes her a certificate
         of *d*,
   24: 3 and writes her a certificate of *d*,
Isa 50: 1 is your mother's certificate of *d*
Jer 3: 8 faithless Israel her certificate of *d*
Mal 2:16 "I hate *d*," says the LORD God
Mt 1:19 he had in mind to *d* her quietly.
    5:31 must give her a certificate of *d*.'
   19: 3 for a man to *d* his wife for any
   19: 7 man give his wife a certificate of *d*
   19: 8 permitted you to *d* your wives
Mk 10: 2 Is it lawful for a man to *d* his
         wife?'
   10: 4 a man to write a certificate of *d*
1Co 7:11 And a husband must not *d* his
         wife.
    7:12 to live with him, he must not *d*
         her.
    7:13 to live with her, she must not *d*
         him
    7:27 Are you married? Do not seek a *d*.

DIVORCED* (DIVORCE)
Lev 21: 7 or *d* from their husbands,
   21:14 not marry a widow, a *d* woman,
   22:13 daughter becomes a widow or
         is *d*,
Nu 30: 9 or *d* woman will be binding on
         her.
Dt 24: 4 then her first husband, who *d* her,
1Ch 8: 8 after he had *d* his wives Hushim
Eze 44:22 not marry widows or *d* women;
Mt 5:32 marries the *d* woman commits
         adultery.
Lk 16:18 who marries a *d* woman commits

DIVORCES* (DIVORCE)
Jer 3: 1 "If a man *d* his wife

Mt 5:31 'Anyone who *d* his wife must give
    5:32 tell you that anyone who *d* his
         wife,
   19: 9 tell you that anyone who *d* his
         wife,
Mk 10:11 "Anyone who *d* his wife
   10:12 And if she *d* her husband
Lk 16:18 "Anyone who *d* his wife

DOCTOR
Mt 9:12 "It is not the healthy who need
         a *d*,

DOCTRINE* (DOCTRINES)
1Ti 1:10 to the sound *d* that conforms
    4:16 Watch your life and *d* closely.
2Ti 4: 3 men will not put up with sound *d*.
Tit 1: 9 can encourage others by sound *d*
    2: 1 is in accord with sound *d*.

DOCTRINES* (DOCTRINE)
1Ti 1: 3 not to teach false *d* any longer
    6: 3 If anyone teaches false *d*

DOEG*
Edomite; Saul's head shepherd; responsible
for murder of priests at Nob (1Sa 21:7;
22:6–23; Ps 52).

DOG (DOGS)
Pr 26:11 As a *d* returns to its vomit,
Ecc 9: 4 a live *d* is better off than a dead
         lion
2Pe 2:22 "A *d* returns to its vomit," and,

DOGS (DOG)
Mt 7: 6 "Do not give *d* what is sacred;
   15:26 bread and toss it to their *d*."

DOMINION
Job 25: 2 "D and awe belong to God;
Ps 22:28 for *d* belongs to the LORD

DONKEY
Nu 22:30 *d* said to Balaam, "Am I not your
Zec 9: 9 gentle and riding on a *d*,
Mt 21: 5 gentle and riding on a *d*,
2Pe 2:16 for his wrongdoing by a *d*—

DOOR (DOORS)
Job 31:32 for my *d* was always open
Ps 141: 3 keep watch over the *d* of my lips.
Mt 6: 6 close the *d* and pray to your
         Father
    7: 7 and the *d* will be opened to you.
Ac 14:27 how he had opened the *d* of faith
1Co 16: 9 a great *d* for effective work has
2Co 2:12 found that the Lord had opened
         a *d*
Rev 3:20 I stand at the *d* and knock.

DOORFRAMES
Dt 6: 9 Write them on the *d* of your
         houses

DOORKEEPER
Ps 84:10 I would rather be a *d* in the house

DOORS (DOOR)
Ps 24: 7 be lifted up, you ancient *d*,

DORCAS
Ac 9:36 is *D*), who was always doing good

DOUBLE
2Ki 2: 9 "Let me inherit a *d* portion
1Ti 5:17 church well are worthy of *d* honor,

DOUBLE-EDGED (EDGE)
Heb 4:12 Sharper than any *d* sword,
Rev 1:16 of his mouth came a sharp *d*
         sword.
    2:12 of him who has the sharp, *d*
         sword.

DOUBLE-MINDED* (MIND)
Ps 119:113 I hate *d* men,
Jas 1: 8 he is a *d* man, unstable
    4: 8 and purify your hearts, you *d*.

DOUBT (DOUBTING DOUBTS)
Mt 14:31 he said, "why did you *d*?"
   21:21 if you have faith and do not *d*,
Mk 11:23 and does not *d* in his heart
Jas 1: 6 he must believe and not *d*,
Jude : 22 Be merciful to those who *d*;

DOUBTING* (DOUBT)
Jn 20:27 Stop *d* and believe."

DOUBTS* (DOUBT)
Lk 24:38 and why do *d* rise in your minds?
Ro 14:23 the man who has *d* is condemned
Jas 1: 6 he who *d* is like a wave of the sea,

DOVE (DOVES)
Ge 8: 8 Then he sent out a *d* to see
Mt 3:16 Spirit of God descending like a *d*

DOVES (DOVE)
Lev 12: 8 is to bring two *d* or two young
Mt 10:16 as snakes and as innocent as *d.*
Lk 2:24 "a pair of *d* or two young pigeons."

DOWNCAST
Ps 42: 5 Why are you *d*, O my soul?
2Co 7: 6 But God, who comforts the *d,*

DOWNFALL
Hos 14: 1 Your sins have been your *d!*

DRAGON
Rev 12: 7 and his angels fought against the *d,*
13: 2 The *d* gave the beast his power
20: 2 He seized the *d,* that ancient

DRAW (DRAWING DRAWS)
Mt 26:52 "for all who *d* the sword will die
Jn 12:32 up from the earth, will *d* all men
Heb 10:22 let us *d* near to God

DRAWING (DRAW)
Lk 21:28 because your redemption is *d* near

DRAWS (DRAW)
Jn 6:44 the Father who sent me *d* him,

DREAD (DREADFUL)
Ps 53: 5 they were, overwhelmed with *d,*

DREADFUL (DREAD)
Mt 24:19 How *d* it will be in those days
Heb 10:31 It is a *d* thing to fall into the hands

DREAM
Joel 2:28 your old men will *d* dreams,
Ac 2:17 your old men will *d* dreams.

DRESS
1Ti 2: 9 I also want women to *d* modestly,

DRIFT*
Heb 2: 1 so that we do not *d* away.

DRINK (DRINKING DRINKS DRUNK DRUNKARD DRUNKARD'S DRUNKARDS DRUNKENNESS)
Ex 29:40 of a hin of wine as a *d* offering.
Nu 6: 3 He must not *d* grape juice
Jdg 7: 5 from those who kneel down to *d.*"
2Sa 23:15 that someone would get me a *d*
Pr 5:15 *D* water from your own cistern,
Mt 20:22 "Can you *d* the cup I am going to *d*
26:27 saying, "*D* from it, all of you.
Mk 16:18 and when they *d* deadly poison,
Lk 12:19 Take life easy; eat, *d* and be merry
Jn 7:37 let him come to me and *d.*
18:11 Shall I not *d* the cup the Father has
1Co 10: 4 and drank the same spiritual *d;*
12:13 were all given the one Spirit to *d*
Php 2:17 being poured out like a *d* offering
2Ti 4: 6 being poured out like a *d* offering,
Rev 14:10 too, will *d* of the wine of God's fury
21: 6 to *d* without cost from the spring

DRINKING (DRINK)
Ro 14:17 God is not a matter of eating and *d,*

DRINKS (DRINK)
Isa 5:22 and champions at mixing *d,*
Jn 4:13 "Everyone who *d* this water will be
6:54 and *d* my blood has eternal life,
1Co 11:27 or *d* the cup of the Lord

DRIPPING
Pr 19:13 wife is like a constant *d.*
27:15 a constant *d* on a rainy day;

DRIVE (DRIVES)
Ex 23:30 Little by little I will *d* them out
Nu 33:52 *d* out all the inhabitants of the land
Jos 13:13 Israelites did not *d* out the people
23:13 will no longer *d* out these nations
Pr 22:10 *D* out the mocker, and out goes
Mt 10: 1 authority to *d* out evil spirits
Jn 6:37 comes to me I will never *d* away.

DRIVES (DRIVE)
Mt 12:26 If Satan *d* out Satan, he is divided
1Jn 4:18 But perfect love *d* out fear,

DROP (DROPS)
Pr 17:14 so *d* the matter before a dispute
Isa 40:15 Surely the nations are like a *d*

DROPS (DROP)
Lk 22:44 his sweat was like *d* of blood falling

DROSS
Ps 119:119 of the earth you discard like *d;*
Pr 25: 4 Remove the *d* from the silver,

DROUGHT
Jer 17: 8 It has no worries in a year of *d*

DROWNED
Ex 15: 4 are *d* in the Red Sea.
Mt 18: 6 and to be *d* in the depths of the sea.
Heb 11:29 tried to do so, they were *d.*

DROWSINESS*
Pr 23:21 and *d* clothes them in rags.

DRUNK (DRINK)
1Sa 1:13 Eli thought she was *d* and said
Ac 2:15 men are not *d,* as you suppose.
Eph 5:18 Do not get *d* on wine, which leads

DRUNKARD (DRINK)
Mt 11:19 and a *d,* a friend of tax collectors
1Co 5:11 or a slanderer, a *d* or a swindler.

DRUNKARD'S* (DRINK)
Pr 26: 9 Like a thornbush in a *d* hand

DRUNKARDS (DRINK)
Pr 23:21 for *d* and gluttons become poor,
1Co 6:10 nor the greedy nor *d* nor slanderers

DRUNKENNESS (DRINK)
Lk 21:34 weighed down with dissipation, *d*
Ro 13:13 and *d,* not in sexual immorality
Gal 5:21 factions and envy; *d,* orgies,
1Ti 3: 3 not given to *d,* not violent
1Pe 4: 3 living in debauchery, lust, *d,* orgies,

DRY
Ge 1: 9 place, and let *d* ground appear."
Ex 14:16 go through the sea on *d* ground.
Jos 3:17 the crossing on *d* ground.
Isa 53: 2 and like a root out of *d* ground.
Eze 37: 4 '*D* bones, hear the word

DULL
Isa 6:10 make their ears *d*
2Co 3:14 But their minds were made *d,*

DUST
Ge 2: 7 man from the *d* of the ground
3:19 for *d* you are
Job 42: 6 and repent in *d* and ashes."
Ps 22:15 you lay me in the *d* of death.
103:14 he remembers that we are *d.*
Ecc 3:20 all come from *d,* and to *d* all return.
Mt 10:14 shake the *d* off your feet
1Co 15:47 was of the *d* of the earth,

DUTIES (DUTY)
2Ti 4: 5 discharge all the *d* of your ministry

DUTY (DUTIES)
Ecc 12:13 for this is the whole *d* of man.
Ac 23: 1 I have fulfilled my *d* to God
1Co 7: 3 husband should fulfill his marital *d*

DWELL (DWELLING DWELLINGS DWELLS DWELT)
Ex 25: 8 for me, and I will *d* among them.
2Sa 7: 5 the one to build me a house to *d* in?
1Ki 8:27 "But will God really *d* on earth?
Ps 23: 6 I will *d* in the house of the LORD
37: 3 *d* in the land and enjoy safe pasture
61: 4 I long to *d* in your tent forever
Pr 8:12 wisdom, *d* together with prudence;
Isa 33:14 of us can *d* with the consuming fire
43:18 do not *d* on the past.
Jn 5:38 nor does his word *d* in you,
Eph 3:17 so that Christ may *d* in your hearts
Col 1:19 to have all his fullness *d* in him,
3:16 the word of Christ *d* in you richly

DWELLING (DWELL)
Lev 26:11 I will put my *d* place among you,

Dt 26:15 from heaven, your holy *d* place,
Ps 90: 1 Lord, you have been our *d* place
2Co 5: 2 to be clothed with our heavenly *d,*
Eph 2:22 to become a *d* in which God lives

DWELLINGS (DWELL)
Lk 16: 9 will be welcomed into eternal *d.*

DWELLS (DWELL)
Ps 46: 4 holy place where the Most High *d.*
91: 1 He who *d* in the shelter

DWELT (DWELL)
Dt 33:16 of him who *d* in the burning bush.

DYING (DIE)
Ro 7: 6 by *d* to what once bound us,
2Co 6: 9 yet regarded as unknown; *d,*

EAGER
Pr 31:13 and works with *e* hands.
Ro 8:19 The creation waits in *e* expectation
1Co 14:12 Since you are *e* to have spiritual
14:39 my brothers, be *e* to prophesy,
Tit 2:14 a people that are his very own, *e*
1Pe 5: 2 greedy for money, but *e* to serve;

EAGLE (EAGLE'S EAGLES)
Dt 32:11 like an *e* that stirs up its nest
Eze 1:10 each also had the face of an *e.*
Rev 4: 7 the fourth was like a flying *e.*
12:14 given the two wings of a great *e,*

EAGLE'S (EAGLE)
Ps 103: 5 your youth is renewed like the *e.*

EAGLES (EAGLE)
Isa 40:31 They will soar on wings like *e;*

EAR (EARS)
Ex 21: 6 and pierce his *e* with an awl.
Ps 5: 1 Give *e* to my words, O LORD,
Pr 2: 2 turning your *e* to wisdom
1Co 2: 9 no *e* has heard,
12:16 if the *e* should say, "Because I am
Rev 2: 7 He who has an *e,* let him hear what

EARN (EARNED EARNINGS)
2Th 3:12 down and *e* the bread they eat.

EARNED (EARN)
Pr 31:31 Give her the reward she has *e,*

EARNESTNESS
2Co 7:11 what *e,* what eagerness
8: 7 in complete *e* and in your love

EARNINGS (EARN)
Pr 31:16 out of her *e* she plants a vineyard.

EARRING (EARRINGS)
Pr 25:12 Like an *e* of gold or an ornament

EARRINGS (EARRING)
Ex 32: 2 Take off the gold *e* that your wives,

EARS (EAR)
Job 42: 5 My *e* had heard of you
Ps 34:15 and his *e* are attentive to their cry;
Pr 21:13 If a man shuts his *e* to the cry
26:17 Like one who seizes a dog by the *e*
Isa 6:10 hear with their *e,*
Mt 11:15 He who has *e,* let him hear.
2Ti 4: 3 to suit what their itching *e* want
1Pe 3:12 his *e* are attentive to their prayer,

EARTH (EARTH'S EARTHLY)
Ge 1: 1 God created the heavens and the *e.*
1: 2 Now the *e* was formless and empty,
7:24 The waters flooded the *e*
14:19 Creator of heaven and *e.*
1Ki 8:27 "But will God really dwell on *e?*
Job 26: 7 he suspends the *e* over nothing.
Ps 24: 1 *e* is the LORD's, and everything
46: 6 he lifts his voice, the *e* melts.
90: 2 or you brought forth the *e*
97: 5 before the Lord of all the *e.*
102:25 you laid the foundations of the *e,*
108: 5 and let your glory be over all the *e.*
Pr 8:26 before he made the *e* or its fields
Isa 6: 3 the whole *e* is full of his glory."
24:20 The *e* reels like a drunkard,
37:16 You have made heaven and *e.*
40:22 enthroned above the circle of the *e,*

Isa 51: 6 the *e* will wear out like a garment
54: 5 he is called the God of all the *e*.
55: 9 the heavens are higher than the *e*,
65:17 new heavens and a new *e*.
66: 1 and the *e* is my footstool.
Jer 10:10 When he is angry, the *e* trembles;
23:24 "Do not I fill heaven and *e*?"
33:25 and the fixed laws of heaven and *e*,
Hab 2:20 let all the *e* be silent before him."
Mt 5: 5 for they will inherit the *e*.
5:35 or by the *e*, for it is his footstool;
6:10 done on *e* as it is in heaven.
16:19 bind on *e* will be bound
24:35 Heaven and *e* will pass away,
28:18 and on *e* has been given to me.
Lk 2:14 on *e* peace to men
Jn 12:32 when I am lifted up from the *e*,
Ac 4:24 "you made the heaven and the *e*
7:49 and the *e* is my footstool.
1Co 10:26 The *e* is the Lord's, and everything
Eph 3:15 in heaven and on *e* derives its name
Php 2:10 in heaven and on *e* and under the *e*,
Heb 1:10 you laid the foundations of the *e*,
2Pe 3:13 to a new heaven and a new *e*,
Rev 8: 7 A third of the *e* was burned up,
12:12 But woe to the *e* and the sea,
20:11 *E* and sky fled from his presence,
21: 1 I saw a new heaven and a new *e*,
21: 1 and the first *e* had passed away,

EARTH'S (EARTH)
Job 38: 4 when I laid the *e* foundation?

EARTHENWARE
Pr 26:23 Like a coating of glaze over *e*

EARTHLY (EARTH)
Eph 4: 9 descended to the lower, *e* regions?
Php 3:19 Their mind is on *e* things.
Col 3: 2 on things above, not on *e* things.
3: 5 whatever belongs to your *e* nature:

EARTHQUAKE (EARTHQUAKES)
Eze 38:19 at that time there shall be a great *e*
Mt 28: 2 There was a violent *e*, for an angel
Rev 6:12 There was a great *e*.

EARTHQUAKES (EARTHQUAKE)
Mt 24: 7 There will be famines and *e*

EASE
Pr 1:33 and be at *e*, without fear of harm."

EASIER (EASY)
Lk 16:17 It is *e* for heaven and earth
18:25 it is *e* for a camel to go

EAST
Ge 2: 8 God had planted a garden in the *e*,
Ps 103:12 as far as the *e* is from the west,
Eze 43: 2 God of Israel coming from the *e*.
Mt 2: 1 Magi from the *e* came to Jerusalem
2: 2 We saw his star in the *e*

EASY (EASIER)
Mt 11:30 For my yoke is *e* and my burden is

EAT (ATE EATEN EATER EATING EATS)
Ge 2:16 "You are free to *e* from any tree
2:17 but you must not *e* from the tree
3:19 you will *e* your food
Ex 12:11 *E* it in haste; it is the LORD's
Lev 11: 2 these are the ones you may *e:*
17:12 "None of you may *e* blood,
Dt 8:16 He gave you manna to *e*
14: 4 These are the animals you may *e:*
Jdg 14:14 "Out of the eater, something to *e;*
2Sa 9: 7 and you will always *e* at my table."
Pr 31:27 and does not *e* the bread of idleness
Isa 55: 1 come, buy and *e!*
65:25 and the lion will *e* straw like the ox,
Eze 3: 1 *e* what is before you, *e* this scroll;
Mt 14:16 You give them something to *e.*"
15: 2 wash their hands before they *e!*"
26:26 "Take and *e;* this is my body."

Mk 14:14 where I may *e* the Passover
Lk 10: 8 and are welcomed, *e* what is set
12:19 Take life easy; *e*, drink
12:22 what you will *e;* or about your body
Jn 4:32 to *e* that you know nothing about."
6:31 bread from heaven to *e.*'"
6:52 can this man give us his flesh to *e?*"
Ac 10:13 Kill and *e.*"
Ro 14: 2 faith allows him to *e* everything,
14:15 is distressed because of what you *e*,
14:20 to *e* anything that causes someone
14:21 It is better not to *e* meat
1Co 5:11 With such a man do not even *e.*
8:13 if what I *e* causes my brother to fall
10:25 *E* anything sold in the meat market
10:27 *e* whatever is put before you
10:31 So whether you *e* or drink
11:26 For whenever you *e* this bread
2Th 3:10 man will not work, he shall not *e.*"
Rev 2: 7 the right to *e* from the tree of life,
3:20 I will come in and *e* with him,

EATEN (EAT)
Ge 3:11 Have you *e* from the tree that I
Ac 10:14 "I have never *e* anything impure
Rev 10:10 when I had *e* it, my stomach turned

EATER (EAT)
Isa 55:10 for the sower and bread for the *e*,

EATING (EAT)
Ex 34:28 and forty nights without *e* bread
Ro 14:15 not by your *e* destroy your brother
14:17 kingdom of God is not a matter of *e*
14:23 because his *e* is not from faith;
1Co 8: 4 about *e* food sacrificed to idols:
8:10 you who have this knowledge *e*
Jude :12 *e* with you without the slightest

EATS (EAT)
1Sa 14:24 "Cursed be any man who *e* food
Lk 15: 2 "This man welcomes sinners and *e*
Jn 6:51 If anyone *e* of this bread, he will live
6:54 Whoever *e* my flesh and drinks my
Ro 14: 2 faith is weak, only *e* vegetables.
14: 3 man who *e* everything must not
14: 6 He who *e* meat, *e* to the Lord,
14:23 has doubts is condemned if he *e*
1Co 11:27 whoever *e* the bread or drinks

EBAL
Dt 11:29 and on Mount *E* the curses.
Jos 8:30 Joshua built on Mount *E* an altar

EBENEZER
1Sa 7:12 He named it *E*, saying, "Thus far

EDEN
Ge 2: 8 in *E*; and there he put the man
Eze 28:13 You were in *E*,

EDGE (DOUBLE-EDGED)
Mt 9:20 and touched the *e* of his cloak.

EDICT
Heb 11:23 they were not afraid of the king's *e*.

EDIFICATION (EDIFIED EDIFIES)
Ro 14:19 leads to peace and to mutual *e*.

EDIFIED* (EDIFICATION)
1Co 14: 5 so that the church may be *e*.
14:17 but the other man is not *e*.

EDIFIES* (EDIFICATION)
1Co 14: 4 but he who prophesies *e* the church
14: 4 speaks in a tongue *e* himself,

EDOM
Ge 36: 1 the account of Esau (that is, *E*).
36: 8 *E*) settled in the hill country of Seir
Isa 63: 1 Who is this coming from *E*,
Ob :1 Sovereign LORD says about *E*—

EDUCATED*
Ac 7:22 Moses was *e* in all the wisdom

EFFECT* (EFFECTIVE)
Job 41:26 sword that reaches him has no *e*,
Isa 32:17 *e* of righteousness will be quietness
Ac 7:53 put into *e* through angels
1Co 15:10 his grace to me was not without *e*.
Gal 3:19 put into *e* through angels
Eph 1:10 put into *e* when the times will have
Heb 9:17 it never takes *e* while the one who
9:18 put into *e* without blood.

EFFECTIVE* (EFFECT)
1Co 16: 9 a great door for *e* work has opened
Jas 5:16 a righteous man is powerful and *e*.

EFFORT*
Ecc 2:19 into which I have poured my *e*
Da 6:14 and made every *e* until sundown
Lk 13:24 "Make every *e* to enter
Jn 5:44 yet make no *e* to obtain the praise
Ro 9:16 depend on man's desire or *e*,
14:19 make every *e* to do what leads
Gal 3: 3 to attain your goal by human *e*?
Eph 4: 3 Make every *e* to keep the unity
1Th 2:16 to all men in their *e* to keep us
2:17 intense longing we made every *e*
Heb 4:11 make every *e* to enter that rest,
12:14 Make every *e* to live in peace
2Pe 1: 5 make every *e* to add
1:15 And I will make every *e* to see that
3:14 make every *e* to be found spotless,

EGG
Lk 11:12 for an *e*, will give him a scorpion?

EGLON
1. Fat king of Moab killed by Ehud (Jdg 3:12–30).
2. City in Canaan (Jos 10).

EGYPT (EGYPTIANS)
Ge 12:10 went down to *E* to live there
37:28 Ishmaelites, who took him to *E*.
42: 3 went down to buy grain from *E*.
45:20 the best of all *E* will be yours.'"
46: 6 and all his offspring went to *E*.
47:27 Now the Israelites settled in *E*
Ex 3:11 and bring the Israelites out of *E*?"
12:40 lived in *E* was 430 years.
12:41 all the LORD's divisions left *E*.
32: 1 Moses who brought us up out of *E*,
Nu 11:18 We were better off in *E!*"
14: 4 choose a leader and go back to *E*."
24: 8 "God brought them out of *E*;
Dt 6:21 "We were slaves of Pharaoh in *E*,
1Ki 4:30 greater than all the wisdom of *E*.
10:28 horses were imported from *E*
11:40 but Jeroboam fled to *E*,
14:25 king of *E* attacked Jerusalem.
2Ch 35:20 Neco king of *E* went up to fight
36: 3 The king of *E* dethroned him
Isa 19:23 a highway from *E* to Assyria.
Hos 11: 1 and out of *E* I called my son.
Mt 2:15 "Out of *E* I called my son."
Heb 11:27 By faith he left *E*, not fearing
Rev 11: 8 is figuratively called Sodom and *E*,

EGYPTIANS (EGYPT)
Nu 14:13 "Then the *E* will hear about it!

EHUD
Left-handed judge who delivered Israel from Moabite king, Eglon (Jdg 3:12–30).

EKRON
1Sa 5:10 So they sent the ark of God to *E*.

ELAH
Son of Baasha; king of Israel (1Ki 16:6–14).

ELATION
Pr 28:12 righteous triumph, there is great *e;*

ELDER* (ELDERLY ELDERS)
Isa 3: 2 the soothsayer and *e*,
1Ti 5:19 an accusation against an *e*
Tit 1: 6 *e* must be blameless, the husband
1Pe 5: 1 among you, I appeal as a fellow *e*,
2Jn :1 The *e*, To the chosen lady
3Jn :1 The *e*, To my dear friend Gaius,

ELDERLY* (ELDER)
Lev 19:32 show respect for the *e*

ELDERS (ELDER)
1Ki 12: 8 rejected the advice the *e* gave him
Mt 15: 2 break the tradition of the *e*?
Mk 7: 3 holding to the tradition of the *e*.
     7: 5 to the tradition of the *e* instead
Ac 11:30 gift to the *e* by Barnabas
   14:23 and Barnabas appointed *e* for them
   15: 2 the apostles and *e* about this
   15: 4 the church and the apostles and *e*,
   15: 6 and *e* met to consider this question.
   15:22 and *e*, with the whole church,
   15:23 The apostles and *e*, your brothers,
   16: 4 and *e* in Jerusalem for the people
   20:17 to Ephesus for the *e* of the church.
   21:18 and all the *e* were present.
   23:14 They went to the chief priests and *e*
   24: 1 to Caesarea with some of the *e*
1Ti 4:14 when the body of *e* laid their hands
   5:17 The *e* who direct the affairs
Tit 1: 5 and appoint *e* in every town,
Jas 5:14 He should call the *e* of the church
1Pe 5: 1 To the *e* among you, I appeal
Rev 4: 4 seated on them were twenty-four *e*.
   4:10 the twenty-four *e* fall

ELEAZAR
Third son of Aaron (Ex 6:23–25). Succeeded Aaron as high priest (Nu 20:26; Dt 10:6). Allotted land to tribes (Jos 14:1). Death (Jos 24:33).

ELECT* (ELECTION)
Mt 24:22 the sake of the *e* those days will be
   24:24 miracles to deceive even the *e*—
   24:31 and they will gather his *e*
Mk 13:20 sake of the *e*, whom he has chosen,
   13:22 and miracles to deceive the *e*—
   13:27 gather his *e* from the four winds,
Ro 11: 7 it did not obtain, but the *e* did.
1Ti 5:21 and Christ Jesus and the *e* angels,
2Ti 2:10 everything for the sake of the *e*,
Tit 1: 1 Christ for the faith of God's *e*
1Pe 1: 1 To God's *e*, strangers in the world,

ELECTION* (ELECT)
Ro 9:11 God's purpose in *e* might stand:
   11:28 but as far as *e* is concerned,
2Pe 1:10 to make your calling and *e* sure.

ELEMENTARY* (ELEMENTS)
Heb 5:12 someone to teach you the *e* truths
   6: 1 us leave the *e* teachings about

ELEMENTS* (ELEMENTARY)
2Pe 3:10 the *e* will be destroyed by fire,
   3:12 and the *e* will melt in the heat.

ELEVATE*
2Co 11: 7 to *e* you by preaching the gospel

ELI
High priest in youth of Samuel (1Sa 1–4). Blessed Hannah (1Sa 1:12–18); raised Samuel (1Sa 2:11–26). Prophesied against because of wicked sons (1Sa 2:27–36). Death of Eli and sons (1Sa 4:11–22).

ELIHU
One of Job's friends (Job 32–37).

ELIJAH
Prophet; predicted famine in Israel (1Ki 17:1; Jas 5:17). Fed by ravens (1Ki 17:2–6). Raised Sidonian widow's son (1Ki 17:7–24). Defeated prophets of Baal at Carmel (1Ki 18:16–46). Ran from Jezebel (1Ki 19:1–9). Prophesied death of Azariah (2Ki 1). Succeeded by Elisha (1Ki 19:19–21; 2Ki 2:1–18). Taken to heaven in whirlwind (2Ki 2:11–12).
Return prophesied (Mal 4:5–6); equated with John the Baptist (Mt 17:9–13; Mk 9:9–13; Lk 1:17). Appeared with Moses in transfiguration of Jesus (Mt 17:1–8; Mk 9:1–8).

ELIMELECH
Ru 1: 3 Now *E*, Naomi's husband, died,

ELIPHAZ
1. Firstborn of Esau (Ge 36).
2. One of Job's friends (Job 4–5; 15; 22).

ELISHA
Prophet; successor of Elijah (1Ki 19:16–21); inherited his cloak (2Ki 2:1–18). Purified bad water (2Ki 2:19–22). Cursed young men (2Ki 2:23–25). Aided Israel's defeat of Moab (2Ki 3). Provided widow with oil (2Ki 4:1–7). Raised Shunammite woman's son (2Ki 4:8–37). Purified food (2Ki 4:38–41). Fed 100 men (2Ki 4:42–44). Healed Naaman's leprosy (2Ki 5). Made axhead float (2Ki 6:1–7). Captured Arameans (2Ki 6:8–23). Political adviser to Israel (2Ki 6:24–8:6; 9:1–3; 13:14–19), Damascus (2Ki 8:7–15). Death (2Ki 13:20).

ELIZABETH*
Mother of John the Baptist, relative of Mary (Lk 1:5–58).

ELKANAH
Husband of Hannah, father of Samuel (1Sa 1–2).

ELOI*
Mt 27:46 *"E, E, lama sabachthani?"*—
Mk 15:34 *"E, E, lama sabachthani?"*—

ELOQUENCE* (ELOQUENT)
1Co 2: 1 come with *e* or superior wisdom

ELOQUENT* (ELOQUENCE)
Ex 4:10 "O Lord, I have never been *e*,

ELYMAS
Ac 13: 8 *E* the sorcerer (for that is what his

EMBEDDED*
Ecc 12:11 sayings like firmly *e* nails—

EMBERS
Pr 26:21 As charcoal to *e* and as wood to fire

EMBITTER* (BITTER)
Col 3:21 Fathers, do not *e* your children,

EMBODIMENT* (BODY)
Ro 2:20 have in the law the *e* of knowledge

EMPTIED (EMPTY)
1Co 1:17 the cross of Christ be *e* of its power.

EMPTY (EMPTIED)
Ge 1: 2 Now the earth was formless and *e*,
Job 26: 7 the northern skies over *e* space;
Isa 45:18 he did not create it to be *e*,
   55:11 It will not return to me *e*,
Jer 4:23 and it was formless and *e*;
Lk 1:53 but has sent the rich away *e*.
Eph 5: 6 no one deceive you with *e* words,
1Pe 1:18 from the *e* way of life handed
2Pe 2:18 For they mouth *e*, boastful words

ENABLE (ABLE)
Lk 1:74 to *e* us to serve him without fear
Ac 4:29 *e* your servants to speak your word

ENABLED* (ABLE)
Lev 26:13 *e* you to walk with heads held high.
Ru 4:13 And the Lord *e* her to conceive,
Jn 6:65 unless the Father has *e* him."
Ac 2: 4 other tongues as the Spirit *e* them.
   7:10 and *e* him to gain the goodwill
Heb 11:11 was *e* to become a father

ENABLES* (ABLE)
Php 3:21 by the power that *e* him

ENABLING* (ABLE)
Ac 14: 3 the message of his grace by *e* them

ENCAMPS* (CAMP)
Ps 34: 7 The angel of the Lord *e*

ENCOURAGE* (ENCOURAGED ENCOURAGEMENT ENCOURAGES ENCOURAGING)
Dt 1:38 *E* him, because he will lead Israel
   3:28 and *e* and strengthen him,
2Sa 11:25 Say this to *e* Joab."
   19: 7 Now go out and *e* your men.
Job 16: 5 But my mouth would *e* you;
Ps 10:17 you *e* them, and you listen
   64: 5 They *e* each other in evil plans,
Isa 1:17 *e* the oppressed.

Jer 29: 8 to the dreams you *e* them to have.
Ac 15:32 to *e* and strengthen the brothers.
Ro 12: 8 if it is encouraging, let him *e*;
Eph 6:22 how we are, and that he may *e* you.
Col 4: 8 and that he may *e* your hearts.
1Th 3: 2 to strengthen and *e* you
   4:18 Therefore *e* each other
   5:11 Therefore *e* one another
   5:14 those who are idle, *e* the timid,
2Th 2:17 *e* your hearts and strengthen you
2Ti 4: 2 rebuke and *e*— with great patience
Tit 1: 9 so that he can *e* others
   2: 6 *e* the young men to be
   2:15 *E* and rebuke with all authority.
Heb 3:13 But *e* one another daily, as long
   10:25 but let us *e* one another—

ENCOURAGED* (ENCOURAGE)
Jdg 7:11 you will be *e* to attack the camp."
   20:22 But the men of Israel *e* one another
2Ch 22: 3 for his mother *e* him
   32: 6 and *e* them with these words:
   35: 2 and *e* them in the service
Eze 13:22 you *e* the wicked not to turn
Ac 9:31 It was strengthened; and *e*
   11:23 and *e* them all to remain true
   16:40 met with the brothers and *e* them.
   18:27 the brothers *e* him and wrote
   27:36 They were all *e* and ate some food
   28:15 men Paul thanked God and was *e*.
Ro 1:12 and I may be mutually *e*
1Co 14:31 everyone may be instructed and *e*.
2Co 7: 4 I am greatly *e*; in all our troubles
   7:13 By all this we are *e*.
Php 1:14 brothers in the Lord have been *e*
Col 2: 2 My purpose is that they may be *e*
1Th 3: 7 persecution we were *e* about you
Heb 6:18 offered to us may be greatly *e*.

ENCOURAGEMENT* (ENCOURAGE)
Ac 4:36 Barnabas (which means Son of *E*),
   13:15 a message of *e* for the people,
   20: 2 speaking many words of *e*
Ro 15: 4 *e* of the Scriptures we might have
   15: 5 and *e* give you a spirit of unity
1Co 14: 3 to men for their strengthening, *e*
2Co 7:13 to our own *e*, we were especially
Php 2: 1 If you have any *e* from being united
2Th 2:16 and by his grace gave us eternal *e*
Phm 1: 7 love has given me great joy and *e*
Heb 12: 5 word of *e* that addresses you

ENCOURAGES* (ENCOURAGE)
Isa 41: 7 The craftsman *e* the goldsmith,

ENCOURAGING* (ENCOURAGE)
Ac 14:22 *e* them to remain true to the faith.
   15:31 and were glad for its *e* message.
   20: 1 for the disciples and, after *e* them,
Ro 12: 8 if it is *e*, let him encourage:
1Th 2:12 *e*, comforting and urging you
1Pe 5:12 *e* you and testifying that this is

ENCROACH
Pr 23:10 or *e* on the fields of the fatherless,

END (ENDS)
Ps 119:33 then I will keep them to the *e*.
   119:112 to the very *e*.
Pr 1:19 Such is the *e* of all who go
   5: 4 but in the *e* she is bitter as gall,
   5:11 At the *e* of your life you will groan,
   14:12 but in the *e* it leads to death.
   14:13 and joy may *e* in grief.
   16:25 but in the *e* it leads to death.
   19:20 and in the *e* you will be wise.
   20:21 will not be blessed at the *e*.
   23:32 In the *e* it bites like a snake
   25: 8 for what will you do in the *e*
   28:23 in the *e* gain more favor
   29:21 he will bring grief in the *e*.
Ecc 3:11 done from beginning to *e*.
   7: 8 The *e* of a matter is better
   12:12 making many books there is no *e*,
Eze 7: 2 The *e*! The *e* has come
Mt 10:22 firm to the *e* will be saved.
   24:13 firm to the *e* will be saved.
   24:14 nations, and then the *e* will come.
Lk 21: 9 but the *e* will not come right away

Ro   10: 4   Christ is the *e* of the law
1Co 15:24   the *e* will come, when he hands
Rev 21: 6   Omega, the Beginning and the *E.*
     22:13   the Last, the Beginning and the *E.*

ENDS (END)
Ps   19: 4   their words to the *e* of the world.
Pr   20:17   he *e* up with a mouth full of
             gravel.
Isa 49: 6   salvation to the *e* of the earth."
     62:11   proclamation to the *e* of the
             earth:
Ac   13:47   salvation to the *e* of the earth.' "
Ro   10:18   their words to the *e* of the world."

ENDURANCE* (ENDURE)
Ro   15: 4   through *e* and the encouragement
     15: 5   May the God who gives *e*
2Co   1: 6   which produces in you patient *e*
      6: 4   in great *e*; in troubles, hardships
Col   1:11   might so that you may have
             great *e*
1Th   1: 3   and your *e* inspired by hope
1Ti   6:11   faith, love, *e*, and gentleness.
2Ti   3:10   patience, love, *e*, persecutions,
Tit   2: 2   and sound in faith, in love and
             in *e.*
Rev   1: 9   and patient *e* that are ours in
             Jesus,
     13:10   This calls for patient *e*
     14:12   This calls for patient *e* on the part

ENDURE (ENDURANCE ENDURED ENDURES
ENDURING)
Ps   72:17   May his name *e* forever;
Pr   12:19   Truthful lips *e* forever,
     27:24   for riches do not *e* forever,
Ecc   3:14   everything God does will *e*
             forever;
Da   2:44   to an end, but it will itself *e*
             forever.
Mal   3: 2   who can *e* the day of his coming?
1Co   4:12   when we are persecuted, we *e* it;
2Co   1: 8   far beyond our ability to *e*,
2Ti   2: 3   *E* hardship with us like a good
      2:10   Therefore I *e* everything
      2:12   if we *e*, / we will also reign
      4: 5   head in all situations, *e* hardship,
Heb 12: 7   *E* hardship as discipline; God is
1Pe   2:20   a beating for doing wrong and *e*
             it?
      2:20   suffer for doing good and you *e* it,
Rev   3:10   kept my command to *e* patiently,

ENDURED* (ENDURE)
Ps 123: 3   for we have *e* much contempt.
    123: 4   We have *e* much ridicule
    132: 1   and all the hardships he *e*.
Ac   13:18   and *e* their conduct forty years
2Ti   3:11   and Lystra, the persecutions I *e*.
Heb 12: 2   set before him *e* the cross,
     12: 3   him who *e* such opposition
Rev   2: 3   and have *e* hardships for my
             name,

ENDURES (ENDURE)
Ps 102:12   renown *e* through all generations.
    112: 9   his righteousness *e* forever;
    136: 1   *His love e* forever.
Da   9:15   made for yourself a name that *e*
2Co   9: 9   his righteousness *e* forever."

ENDURING (ENDURE)
2Th   1: 4   persecutions and trials you are *e*.
1Pe   1:23   through the living and *e* word

ENEMIES (ENEMY)
Ps   23: 5   in the presence of my *e*.
    110: 1   hand until I make your *e*
Pr   16: 7   his *e* live at peace with him.
Isa 59:18   wrath to his *e*
Mic   7: 6   a man's *e* are the members
Mt   5:44   Love your *e* and pray
      5:36   a man's *e* will be the members
Lk   6:27   Love your *e*, do good
      6:35   But love your *e*, do good to them,
     20:43   hand until I make your *e*
Ro   5:10   For if, when we were God's *e*,
1Co 15:25   reign until he has put all his *e*
Php   3:18   many live as *e* of the cross of
             Christ
Heb   1:13   hand until I make your *e*
     10:13   for his *e* to be made his footstool.

ENEMY (ENEMIES ENMITY)
Pr   24:17   Do not gloat when your *e* falls;

Pr   25:21   If your *e* is hungry, give him food
     27: 6   but an *e* multiplies kisses.
     29:24   of a thief is his own *e*;
Lk   10:19   to overcome all the power of
             the *e*;
Ro   12:20   "If your *e* is hungry, feed him;
1Co 15:26   The last *e* to be destroyed is
             death.
1Ti   5:14   and to give the *e* no opportunity
1Pe   5: 8   Your *e* the devil prowls

ENERGY*
Col   1:29   struggling with all his *e*, which

ENGRAVED
Isa 49:16   I have *e* you on the palms
2Co   3: 7   which was *e* in letters on stone,

ENHANCES*
Ro   3: 7   my falsehood *e* God's truthfulness

ENJOY (JOY)
Dt   6: 2   and so that you may *e* long life.
Ps   37: 3   dwell in the land and *e* safe
             pasture.
Pr   28:16   ill-gotten gain will *e* a long life.
Ecc   3:22   better for a man than to *e* his
             work,
Eph   6: 3   and that you may *e* long life
Heb 11:25   rather than to *e* the pleasures of
             sin
3Jn   : 2   I pray that you may *e* good health

ENJOYMENT (JOY)
Ecc   4: 8   and why am I depriving myself
             of *e*
1Ti   6:17   us with everything for our *e*.

ENLARGE (ENLARGES)
2Co   9:10   *e* the harvest of your
             righteousness.

ENLARGES (ENLARGE)
Dt   33:20   Blessed is he who *e* Gad's domain!

ENLIGHTENED*
Eph   1:18   that the eyes of your heart may
             be *e*
Heb   6: 4   for those who have once been *e*,

ENMITY* (ENEMY)
Ge   3:15   And I will put *e*

ENOCH
        1. Son of Cain (Ge 4:17–18).
        2. Descendant of Seth; walked with God
and taken by him (Ge 5:18–24; Heb 11:5).
Prophet (Jude 14).

ENSLAVED (SLAVE)
Gal   4: 9   Do you wish to be *e* by them all
Tit   3: 3   and *e* by all kinds of passions

ENSNARE (SNARE)
Pr   5:22   of a wicked man *e* him;
Ecc   7:26   but the sinner she will *e*.

ENSNARED* (SNARE)
Dt   7:25   for yourselves, or you will be *e* by
             it
     12:30   be careful not to be *e*
Ps   9:16   the wicked are *e* by the work
Pr   6: 2   by the words of your mouth,
     22:25   and get yourself *e*.

ENTANGLED (ENTANGLES)
2Pe   2:20   and are again *e* in it and
             overcome,

ENTANGLES* (ENTANGLED)
Heb 12: 1   and the sin that so easily *e*,

ENTER (ENTERED ENTERING ENTERS ENTRANCE)
Ps   95:11   "They shall never *e* my rest."
    100: 4   *E* his gates with thanksgiving
Pr   2:10   For wisdom will *e* your heart,
Mt   5:20   will certainly not *e* the kingdom
      7:13   "*E* through the narrow gate.
      7:21   Lord,' will *e* the kingdom of
             heaven
     18: 3   you will never *e* the kingdom
     18: 8   It is better for you to *e* life
             maimed
     19:17   to *e* life, obey the commandments
     19:23   man to *e* the kingdom of heaven.
Mk   9:43   It is better for you to *e* life
             maimed
      9:45   It is better for you to *e* life
             crippled
      9:47   for you to *e* the kingdom of God
     10:15   like a little child will never *e* it."
     10:23   is for the rich to *e* the kingdom

Lk   13:24   will try to *e* and will not be able
             to.
     13:24   "Make every effort to *e*
     18:17   like a little child will never *e* it."
     18:24   is for the rich to *e* the kingdom
Jn   3: 5   no one can *e* the kingdom of God.
Heb   3:11   'They shall never *e* my rest.' "
      4:11   make every effort to *e* that rest,

ENTERED (ENTER)
Ps   73:17   me till I *e* the sanctuary of God;
Eze   4:14   meat has ever *e* my mouth."
Ac   11: 8   or unclean has ever *e* my mouth.'
Ro   5:12   as sin *e* the world through one
             man,
Heb   9:12   but he *e* the Most Holy Place
             once

ENTERING (ENTER)
Mt   21:31   the prostitutes are *e* the kingdom
Lk   11:52   have hindered those who were *e*."
Heb   4: 1   the promise of *e* his rest still
             stands,

ENTERS (ENTER)
Mk   7:18   you see that nothing that *e* a man
Jn   10: 2   The man who *e* by the gate is

ENTERTAIN* (ENTERTAINED ENTERTAINMENT)
Jdg 16:25   "Bring out Samson to *e* us."
Mt   9: 4   "Why do you *e* evil thoughts
1Ti   5:19   Do not *e* an accusation
Heb 13: 2   Do not forget to *e* strangers,

ENTERTAINED* (ENTERTAIN)
Ac   28: 7   and for three days *e* us hospitably.
Heb 13: 2   so doing some people have *e*
             angels

ENTERTAINMENT* (ENTERTAIN)
Da   6:18   without any *e* being brought to
             him

ENTHRALLED*
Ps   45:11   The king is *e* by your beauty;

ENTHRONED* (THRONE)
1Sa   4: 4   who is *e* between the cherubim.
2Sa   6: 2   who is *e* between the cherubim
             that
2Ki 19:15   of Israel, *e* between the cherubim,
1Ch 13: 6   who is *e* between the cherubim—
Ps   2: 4   The One *e* in heaven laughs;
      9:11   to the LORD, *e* in Zion;
     22: 3   Yet you are *e* as the Holy One;
     29:10   The LORD sits *e* over the flood;
     29:10   the LORD is *e* as King forever.
     55:19   God, who is *e* forever,
     61: 7   May he be *e* in God's presence
     80: 1   who sit *e* between the cherubim,
     99: 1   he sits *e* between the cherubim,
    102:12   But you, O LORD, sit *e* forever;
    113: 5   the One who sits *e* on high,
    132:14   here I will sit *e*, for I have desired
             it
Isa 14:13   I will sit *e* on the mount
     37:16   of Israel, *e* between the cherubim,
     40:22   He sits *e* above the circle
     52: 2   rise up, sit *e*, O Jerusalem.

ENTHRONES* (THRONE)
Job 36: 7   he *e* them with kings

ENTHUSIASM*
2Co   8:17   he is coming to you with much *e*
      9: 2   and your *e* has stirred most of
             them

ENTICE* (ENTICED ENTICES)
Pr   1:10   My son, if sinners *e* you,
2Pe   2:18   they *e* people who are just
             escaping
Rev   2:14   who taught Balak to *e* the
             Israelites

ENTICED* (ENTICE)
Dt   4:19   do not be *e* into bowing
     11:16   or you will be *e* to turn away
2Ki 17:21   Jeroboam *e* Israel away
Job 31: 9   If my heart has been *e* by a
             woman,
     31:27   so that my heart was secretly *e*
Jas   1:14   desire, he is dragged away and *e*.

ENTICES* (ENTICE)
Dt   13: 6   your closest friend secretly *e* you,
Job 36:18   Be careful that no one *e* you
Pr   16:29   A violent man *e* his neighbor

ENTIRE
Gal　5:14　The *e* law is summed up

ENTRANCE (ENTER)
Mt　27:60　stone in front of the *e* to the tomb
Mk　15:46　a stone against the *e* of the tomb.
　　　16: 3　away from the *e* of the tomb?"
Jn　11:38　cave with a stone laid across
　　　　　　the *e*.
　　　20: 1　had been removed from the *e*.

ENTRUST (TRUST)
Jn　 2:24　Jesus would not *e* himself to
　　　　　　them,
2Ti　 2: 2　the presence of many witnesses *e*

ENTRUSTED (TRUST)
Jer　13:20　Where is the flock that was *e* to
　　　　　　you
Jn　 5:22　but has *e* all judgment to the Son,
Ro　 3: 2　they have been *e* with the very
　　　 6:17　of teaching to which you were *e*.
1Co　 4: 1　as those *e* with the secret things
1Th　 2: 4　by God to be *e* with the gospel.
1Ti　 1:11　of the blessed God, which he *e*
　　　 6:20　guard what has been *e* to your
　　　　　　care.
2Ti　 1:12　able to guard what I have *e* to him
　　　 1:14　Guard the good deposit that was *e*
Tit　 1: 3　light through the preaching *e* to
　　　　　　me
　　　 1: 7　Since an overseer is *e*
1Pe　 2:23　he *e* himself to him who judges
　　　 5: 3　not lording it over those *e* to you,
Jude　 : 3　once for all *e* to the saints.

ENVIES
Jas　 4: 5　spirit he caused to live in us *e*

ENVIOUS (ENVY)
Dt　32:21　I will make them *e*
Pr　24:19　or be *e* of the wicked,
Ro　10:19　"I will make you *e*

ENVOY
Pr　13:17　but a trustworthy *e* brings healing.

ENVY (ENVIOUS ENVYING)
Pr　 3:31　Do not *e* a violent man
　　　14:30　but *e* rots the bones.
　　　23:17　Do not let your heart *e* sinners,
　　　24: 1　Do not *e* wicked men,
Mk　 7:22　malice, deceit, lewdness, *e*,
　　　　　　slander
Ro　 1:29　They are full of *e*, murder, strife,
　　　11:14　arouse my own people to *e*
1Co　13: 4　It does not *e*, it does not boast,
Gal　 5:21　factions and *e*; drunkenness,
　　　　　　orgies
Php　 1:15　that some preach Christ out of *e*
1Ti　 6: 4　and quarrels about words that
　　　　　　result in *e*,
Tit　 3: 3　lived in malice and *e*, being hated
Jas　 3:14　But if you harbor bitter *e*
　　　 3:16　where you have *e* and selfish
1Pe　 2: 1　*e*, and slander of every kind.

ENVYING* (ENVY)
Gal　 5:26　provoking and *e* each other.

EPHAH
Eze　45:11　The *e* and the bath are

EPHESUS
Ac　18:19　at *E*, where Paul left Priscilla
　　　19: 1　the interior and arrived at *E*.
Eph　 1: 1　To the saints in *E*, the faithful
Rev　 2: 1　the angel of the church in *E* write:

EPHRAIM
1. Second son of Joseph (Ge 41:52; 46:20). Blessed as firstborn by Jacob (Ge 48). Tribe of numbered (Nu 1:33; 26:37), blessed (Dt 33:17), allotted land (Jos 16:4–9; Eze 48:5), failed to fully possess (Jos 16:10; Jdg 1:29).
2. Synonymous with Northern Kingdom (Isa 7:17; Hos 5).

EQUAL (EQUALITY EQUITY)
Dt　33:25　and your strength will *e* your days.
1Sa　 9: 2　without *e* among the Israelites—
Isa　40:25　who is my *e*?" says the Holy One.
　　　46: 5　you compare me or count me *e*?
Da　 1:19　and he found none to *e* Daniel,
Jn　 5:18　making himself *e* with God.
1Co　12:25　that its parts should have *e*
　　　　　　concern
2Co　 2:16　And who is *e* to such a task?

EQUALITY* (EQUAL)
2Co　 8:13　pressed, but that there might
　　　　　　be *e*.
　　　 8:14　Then there will be *e*, as it is
　　　　　　written:
Php　 2: 6　did not consider *e*

EQUIP* (EQUIPPED)
Heb　13:21　*e* you with everything good

EQUIPPED (EQUIP)
2Ti　 3:17　man of God may be thoroughly *e*

EQUITY* (EQUAL)
Ps　96:10　he will judge the peoples with *e*.
　　　98: 9　and the peoples with *e*.
　　　99: 4　you have established *e*;

ERODES*
Job　14:18　"But as a mountain *e* and
　　　　　　crumbles

ERROR (ERRORS)
Jas　 5:20　Whoever turns a sinner from the *e*
2Pe　 2:18　escaping from those who live in *e*.

ERRORS* (ERROR)
Ps　19:12　Who can discern his *e*?
Ecc　10: 4　calmness can lay great *e* to rest.

ESAU
Firstborn of Isaac, twin of Jacob (Ge 25:21–26). Also called Edom (Ge 25:30). Sold Jacob his birthright (Ge 25:29–34); lost blessing (Gen 27). Married Hittites (Ge 26:34), Ishmaelites (Ge 28:6–9). Reconciled to Jacob (Gen 33). Genealogy (Ge 36). The LORD chose Jacob over Esau (Mal 1:2–3), but gave Esau land (Dt 2:2–12). Descendants eventually obliterated (Ob 1–21; Jer 49:7–22).

ESCAPE (ESCAPED ESCAPES ESCAPING)
Ps　68:20　from the Sovereign LORD comes *e*
Pr　11: 9　through knowledge the
　　　　　　righteous *e*.
Ro　 2: 3　think you will *e* God's judgment?
1Th　 5: 3　woman, and they will not *e*.
2Ti　 2:26　and *e* from the trap of the devil,
Heb　 2: 3　how shall we *e* if we ignore such
　　　12:25　If they did not *e* when they
　　　　　　refused
2Pe　 1: 4　and *e* the corruption in the world

ESCAPED (ESCAPE)
2Pe　 2:20　If they have *e* the corruption

ESCAPES (ESCAPE)
Pr　12:13　but a righteous man *e* trouble.

ESCAPING (ESCAPE)
1Co　 3:15　only as one through the flames.
2Pe　 2:18　they entice people who are just *e*

ESTABLISH (ESTABLISHED ESTABLISHES)
Ge　 6:18　But I will *e* my covenant with you,
　　　17:21　But my covenant I will *e* with Isaac
2Sa　 7:11　the LORD himself will *e* a house
1Ki　 9: 5　I will *e* your royal throne
1Ch　28: 7　I will *e* his kingdom forever
Ps　90:17　*e* the work of our hands for us—
Isa　26:12　LORD, you *e* peace for us;
Ro　10: 3　God and sought to *e* their own,
　　　16:25　able to *e* you by my gospel
Heb　10: 9　sets aside the first to *e* the
　　　　　　second.

ESTABLISHED (ESTABLISH)
Ge　 9:17　the sign of the covenant I have *e*
Ex　 6: 4　also *e* my covenant with them
Pr　16:12　a throne is *e* through
　　　　　　righteousness.

ESTABLISHES (ESTABLISH)
Job　25: 2　he *e* order in the heights of
　　　　　　heaven.
Isa　42: 4　till he *e* justice on earth.

ESTATE
Ps　136:23　who remembered us in our low *e*

ESTEEMED
Pr　22: 1　to be *e* is better than silver or
　　　　　　gold.
Isa　53: 3　he was despised, and we *e* him
　　　　　　not.

ESTHER
Jewess, originally named Hadassah, who lived in Persia; cousin of Mordecai (Est 2:7). Chosen queen of Xerxes (Est 2:8–18). Persuaded by Mordecai to foil Haman's plan to exterminate the Jews (Est 3–4). Revealed

Haman's plans to Xerxes, resulting in Haman's death (Est 7), the Jews' preservation (Est 8–9), Mordecai's exaltation (Est 8:15; 9:4; 10). Decreed celebration of Purim (Est 9:18–32).

ETERNAL* (ETERNALLY ETERNITY)
Ge　21:33　the name of the LORD, the *E* God.
Dt　33:27　The *e* God is your refuge,
1Ki　10: 9　of the LORD's *e* love for Israel,
Ps　16:11　with *e* pleasures at your right
　　　　　　hand.
　　　21: 6　you have granted him *e* blessings
　　　111:10　To him belongs *e* praise.
　　　119:89　Your word, O LORD, is *e*;
　　　119:160　all your righteous laws are *e*.
Ecc　12: 5　Then man goes to his *e* home
Isa　26: 4　LORD, the LORD, is the Rock *e*.
　　　47: 7　the *e* queen!'
Jer　10:10　he is the living God, the *e* King.
Da　 4: 3　His kingdom is an *e* kingdom;
　　　 4:34　His dominion is an *e* dominion;
Hab　 3: 6　His ways are *e*.
Mt　18: 8　two feet and two thrown into *e* fire.
　　　19:16　good thing must I do to get *e*
　　　　　　life?"
　　　19:29　as much and will inherit *e* life.
　　　25:41　into the *e* fire prepared for the
　　　　　　devil
　　　25:46　but the righteous to *e* life."
　　　25:46　they will go away to *e*
　　　　　　punishment,
Mk　 3:29　be forgiven; he is guilty of an *e*
　　　　　　sin."
　　　10:17　"what must I do to inherit *e* life?"
　　　10:30　and in the age to come, *e* life.
Lk　10:25　"what must I do to inherit *e* life?"
　　　16: 9　will be welcomed into *e* dwellings.
　　　18:18　what must I do to inherit *e* life?"
　　　18:30　and, in the age to come, *e* life."
Jn　 3:15　believes in him may have *e* life.
　　　 3:16　him shall not perish but have *e*
　　　　　　life.
　　　 3:36　believes in the Son has *e* life,
　　　 4:14　spring of water welling up to *e*
　　　　　　life."
　　　 4:36　now he harvests the crop for *e*
　　　　　　life,
　　　 5:24　believes him who sent me has *e*
　　　　　　life
　　　 5:39　that by them you possess *e* life.
　　　 6:27　but for food that endures to *e* life,
　　　 6:40　believes in him shall have *e* life,
　　　 6:54　and drinks my blood has *e* life,
　　　 6:68　You have the words of *e* life.
　　　10:28　I give them *e* life, and they shall
　　　12:25　in this world will keep it for *e* life.
　　　12:50　that his command leads to *e* life.
　　　17: 2　all people that he might give *e* life
　　　17: 3　this is *e* life: that they may know
Ac　13:46　yourselves worthy of *e* life,
　　　13:48　were appointed for *e* life believed.
Ro　 1:20　his *e* power and divine nature—
　　　 2: 7　and immortality, he will give *e* life.
　　　 5:21　righteousness to bring *e* life.
　　　 6:22　to holiness, and the result is *e* life.
　　　 6:23　but the gift of God is *e* life
　　　16:26　by the command of the *e* God,
2Co　 4:17　for us an *e* glory that far
　　　　　　outweighs
　　　 4:18　temporary, but what is unseen
　　　　　　is *e*.
　　　 5: 1　from God, an *e* house in heaven,
Gal　 6: 8　from the Spirit will reap *e* life.
Eph　 3:11　to his *e* purpose which he
2Th　 2:16　his grace gave us *e*
　　　　　　encouragement
1Ti　 1:16　believe on him and receive *e* life.
　　　 1:17　Now to the King *e*, immortal,
　　　 6:12　Take hold of the *e* life
2Ti　 2:10　is in Christ Jesus, with *e* glory.
Tit　 1: 2　resting on the hope of *e* life,
　　　 3: 7　heirs having the hope of *e* life.
Heb　 5: 9　he became the source of *e*
　　　　　　salvation
　　　 6: 2　of the dead, and *e* judgment.
　　　 9:12　having obtained *e* redemption.
　　　 9:14　through the *e* Spirit offered
　　　　　　himself
　　　 9:15　the promised *e* inheritance—
　　　13:20　of the *e* covenant brought back
1Pe　 5:10　you to his *e* glory in Christ,

2Pe 1:11 into the *e* kingdom of our Lord
1Jn 1: 2 and we proclaim to you the *e* life,
    2:25 what he promised us—even *e* life.
    3:15 know that no murderer has *e* life
    5:11 God has given us *e* life,
    5:13 you may know that you have *e* life.
    5:20 He is the true God and *e* life.
Jude : 7 who suffer the punishment of *e* fire.
    :21 Christ to bring you to *e* life.
Rev 14: 6 and he had the *e* gospel to proclaim

ETERNALLY* (ETERNAL)
Gal 1: 8 let him be *e* condemned! As we
    1: 9 let him be *e* condemned! Am I now

ETERNITY* (ETERNAL)
Ps 93: 2 you are from all *e*.
Pr   I was appointed from *e*,
Ecc 3:11 also set *e* in the hearts of men;

ETHIOPIAN*
Jer 13:23 Can the *E* change his skin
Ac 8:27 and on his way he met an *E* eunuch

EUNUCH (EUNUCHS)
Ac 8:27 on his way he met an Ethiopian *e*,

EUNUCHS (EUNUCH)
Isa 56: 4 "To the *e* who keep my Sabbaths,
Mt 19:12 For some are *e* because they were

EUTYCHUS*
Ac 20: 9 was a young man named *E*,

EVANGELIST* (EVANGELISTS)
Ac 21: 8 stayed at the house of Philip the *e*,
2Ti 4: 5 hardship, do the work of an *e*,

EVANGELISTS* (EVANGELIST)
Eph 4:11 some to be prophets, some to be *e*,

EVE*
Ge 3:20 Adam named his wife *E*,
    4: 1 Adam lay with his wife *E*,
2Co 11: 3 as *E* was deceived by the serpent's
1Ti 2:13 For Adam was formed first, then *E*

EVEN-TEMPERED* (TEMPER)
Pr 17:27 and a man of understanding is *e*.

EVENING
Ge 1: 5 there was *e*, and there was morning

EVER (EVERLASTING FOREVER FOREVERMORE)
Ex 15:18 LORD will reign for *e* and *e*."
Dt 8:19 If you *e* forget the LORD your
1Ki 3:12 anyone like you, nor will there *e* be.
Job 4: 7 were the upright *e* destroyed?
Ps 5:11 let them *e* sing for joy.
   10:16 The LORD is King for *e* and *e*;
   21: 4 length of days, for *e* and *e*.
   25: 3 will *e* be put to shame,
   25:15 My eyes are ever on the LORD,
   26: 3 for your love is *e* before me,
   45: 6 O God, will last for *e* and *e*;
   45:17 nations will praise you for *e* and *e*.
   48:14 For this God is our God for *e* and *e*;
   52: 8 God's unfailing love for *e* and *e*.
   61: 8 will I *e* sing praise to your name
   71: 6 I will *e* praise you.
   84: 4 they are *e* praising you.
   89:33 nor will I *e* betray my faithfulness.
  111: 8 They are steadfast for *e* and *e*,
  119:44 your law, for *e* and *e*.
  119:98 for they are *e* with me.
  132:12 sit on your throne for *e* and *e*."
  145: 1 I will praise your name for *e* and *e*.
  145: 2 and extol your name for *e* and *e*.
  145:21 his holy name for *e* and *e*.
Pr 4:18 shining *e* brighter till the full light
   5:19 may you *e* be captivated
Isa 66: 8 Who has *e* heard of such a thing?
   66: 8 Who has *e* seen such things?
Jer 7: 1 I gave your forefathers for *e* and *e*.
   25: 5 and your fathers for *e* and *e*.
   31:36 the descendants of Israel *e* cease
Da 2:20 be to the name of God for *e* and *e*;
   7:18 it forever—yes, for *e* and *e*.'

Da 12: 3 like the stars for *e* and *e*.
Mic 4: 5 our God for *e* and *e*.
Mt 13:14 you will be *e* seeing but never
   13:14 "'You will be *e* hearing
Mk 4:12 *e* hearing but never understanding;
Jn 1:18 No one has *e* seen God,
Gal 1: 5 to whom be glory for *e* and *e*.
Eph 3:21 all generations, for *e* and *e*!
Php 4:20 and Father be glory for *e* and *e*.
1Ti 1:17 be honor and glory for *e* and *e*.
2Ti 4:18 To him be glory for *e* and *e*.
Heb 1: 8 O God, will last for *e* and *e*,
   13:21 to whom be glory for *e* and *e*.
1Pe 4:11 the glory and the power for *e* and *e*.
   5:11 To him be the power for *e* and *e*.
1Jn 4:12 No one has *e* seen God;
Rev 1: 6 him be glory and power for *e* and *e*!
   1:18 and behold I am alive for *e* and *e*!
  21:27 Nothing impure will *e* enter it,
  22: 5 And they will reign for *e* and *e*.

EVER-INCREASING* (INCREASE)
Ro 6:19 to impurity and to *e* wickedness,
2Co 3:18 into his likeness with *e* glory,

EVERLASTING* (EVER)
Ge 9:16 and remember the *e* covenant
   17: 7 an *e* covenant between me and you
   17: 8 I will give as an *e* possession to you
   17:13 in your flesh is to be an *e* covenant.
   17:19 an *e* covenant for his descendants
   48: 4 *e* possession to your descendants
Nu 18:19 It is an *e* covenant of salt
Dt 33:15 and the fruitfulness of the *e* hills;
   33:27 and underneath are the *e* arms.
2Sa 23: 5 made with me an *e* covenant,
1Ch 16:17 to Israel as an *e* covenant:
   16:36 from *e* to *e*.
   29:10 from *e* to *e*.
Ezr 9:12 to your children as an *e* inheritance
Ne 9: 5 your God, who is from *e* to *e*."
Ps 41:13 from *e* to *e*.
   52: 5 God will bring you down to *e* ruin:
   74: 3 toward these *e* ruins,
   78:66 he put them to *e* shame.
   90: 2 from *e* to *e* you are God.
  103:17 But from *e* to *e*
  105:10 to Israel as an *e* covenant:
  106:48 from *e* to *e*.
  119:142 Your righteousness is *e*
  139:24 and lead me in the way *e*.
  145:13 Your kingdom is an *e* kingdom,
Isa 9: 6 *E* Father, Prince of Peace.
   24: 5 and broken the *e* covenant.
   30: 8 it may be an *e* witness.
   33:14 Who of us can dwell with *e* burning
   35:10 *e* joy will crown their heads.
   40:28 The LORD is the *e* God,
   45:17 the LORD with an *e* salvation;
   45:17 to ages *e*.
   51:11 *e* joy will crown their heads.
   54: 8 but with *e* kindness
   55: 3 I will make an *e* covenant with you,
   55:13 for an *e* sign,
   56: 5 I will give them an *e* name
   60:15 I will make you the *e* pride
   60:19 for the LORD will be your *e* light,
   60:20 the LORD will be your *e* light,
   61: 7 and *e* joy will be theirs.
   61: 8 and make an *e* covenant with them.
   63:12 to gain for himself *e* renown,
Jer 5:22 an *e* barrier it cannot cross.
   23:40 I will bring upon you *e* disgrace—
   23:40 *e* shame that will not be forgotten."
   25: 9 of horror and scorn, and an *e* ruin:
   31: 3 "I have loved you with an *e* love;
   32:40 I will make an *e* covenant
   50: 5 the LORD in an *e* covenant
Eze 16:60 and I will establish an *e* covenant
   37:26 with them; it will be an *e* covenant.

Da 7:14 dominion is an *e* dominion that will
   7:27 His kingdom will be an *e* kingdom,
   9:24 to bring in *e* righteousness,
  12: 2 others to shame and *e* contempt.
  12: 2 some to *e* life, others to shame
Mic 6: 2 you *e* foundations of the earth.
Hab 1:12 O LORD, are you not from *e*?
Jn 6:47 the truth, he who believes has *e* life.
2Th 1: 9 punished with *e* destruction
Jude : 6 bound with *e* chains for judgment

EVER-PRESENT*
Ps 46: 1 an *e* help in trouble

EVIDENCE (EVIDENT)
Jn 14:11 on the *e* of the miracles themselves.
Ac 11:23 and saw the *e* of the grace of God,
2Th 1: 5 All this is *e* that God's judgment is
Jas 2:20 do you want *e* that faith

EVIDENT (EVIDENCE)
Php 4: 5 Let your gentleness be *e* to all.

EVIL (EVILDOER EVILDOERS EVILS)
Ge 2: 9 of the knowledge of good and *e*.
   3: 5 be like God, knowing good and *e*."
   6: 5 of his heart was only *e* all the time.
Ex 32:22 how prone these people are to *e*.
Jdg 2:11 Then the Israelites did *e* in the eyes
   3: 7 The Israelites did *e* in the eyes
   3:12 Once again the Israelites did *e*
   4: 1 the Israelites once again did *e*
   6: 1 Again the Israelites did *e*
  10: 6 Again the Israelites did *e*
  13: 1 Again the Israelites did *e*
1Ki 11: 6 So Solomon did *e* in the eyes
  16:25 But Omri did *e* in the eyes
2Ki 15:24 Pekahiah did *e* in the eyes
Job 1: 1 he feared God and shunned *e*.
   1: 8 a man who fears God and shuns *e*."
  34:10 Far be it from God to do *e*,
  36:21 Beware of turning to *e*,
Ps 5: 4 not a God who takes pleasure in *e*;
  23: 4 I will fear no *e*,
  34:13 keep your tongue from *e*
  34:14 Turn from *e* and do good;
  34:16 is against those who do *e*,
  37: 1 Do not fret because of *e* men
  37: 8 do not fret—it leads only to *e*.
  37:27 Turn from *e* and do good;
  49: 5 fear when *e* days come,
  51: 4 and done what is *e* in your sight,
  97:10 those who love the LORD hate *e*,
  101: 4 I will have nothing to do with *e*.
  141: 4 not my heart be drawn to what is *e*,
Pr 4:27 keep your foot from *e*.
   8:13 To fear the LORD is to hate *e*;
  10:23 A fool finds pleasure in *e* conduct,
  11:19 he who pursues *e* goes to his death.
  11:27 *e* comes to him who searches for it.
  14:16 man fears the LORD and shuns *e*,
  17:13 If a man pays back *e* for good,
  20:30 Blows and wounds cleanse away *e*,
  24:19 Do not fret because of *e* men
  24:20 for the *e* man has no future hope,
  26:23 are fervent lips with an *e* heart.
  28: 5 *E* men do not understand justice,
  29: 6 An *e* man is snared by his own sin,
Ecc 12:14 whether it is good or *e*.
Isa 5:20 Woe to those who call *e* good
  13:11 I will punish the world for its *e*,
  55: 7 and the *e* man his thoughts.
Jer 4:14 wash the *e* from your heart
  18: 8 nation I warned repents of its *e*,
  18:11 So turn from your *e* ways,
Eze 33:11 Turn! Turn from your *e* ways!
  33:13 he will die for the *e* he has done.
  33:15 and does no *e*, he will surely live;
Am 5:13 for the times are *e*.
Hab 1:13 Your eyes are too pure to look on *e*;

Zec	8:17	do not plot *e* against your neighbor.
Mt	5:45	He causes his sun to rise on the *e*
	6:13	but deliver us from the *e* one.'
	7:11	If you, then, though you are *e*,
	12:34	you who are *e* say anything good?
	12:35	and the *e* man brings *e* things out
	12:35	out of the *e* stored up in him.
	12:43	"When an *e* spirit comes out
	15:19	out of the heart come *e* thoughts,
Mk	7:21	come *e* thoughts, sexual
Lk	6:45	and the *e* man brings *e* things out
	11:13	If you then, though you are *e*,
Jn	3:19	of light because their deeds were *e*.
	3:20	Everyone who does *e* hates
	17:15	you protect them from the *e* one.
Ro	1:30	they invent ways of doing *e*;
	2:8	who reject the truth and follow *e*,
	2:9	for every human being who does *e*:
	3:8	"Let us do *e* that good may result"?
	6:12	body so that you obey its *e* desires.
	7:19	no, the *e* I do not want to do—
	7:21	to do good, *e* is right there with me.
	12:9	Hate what is *e*; cling
	12:17	Do not repay anyone *e* for *e*.
	12:21	Do not be overcome by *e*,
	14:16	good to be spoken of as *e*.
	16:19	and innocent about what is *e*.
1Co	13:6	Love does not delight in *e*
	14:20	In regard to *e* be infants,
Eph	5:16	because the days are *e*.
	6:12	forces of *e* in the heavenly realms.
	6:16	all the flaming arrows of the *e* one.
Col	3:5	impurity, lust, *e* desires and greed,
1Th	5:22	Avoid every kind of *e*.
2Th	3:3	and protect you from the *e* one.
1Ti	6:10	of money is a root of all kinds of *e*.
2Ti	2:22	Flee the *e* desires of youth,
	3:6	are swayed by all kinds of *e* desires,
	3:13	while *e* men and impostors will go
Heb	5:14	to distinguish good from *e*.
Jas	1:13	For God cannot be tempted by *e*,
	1:21	and the *e* that is so prevalent,
	3:6	a world of *e* among the parts
	3:8	It is a restless *e*, full
1Pe	2:16	your freedom as a cover-up for *e*;
	3:9	Do not repay *e* with *e* or insult
	3:10	must keep his tongue from *e*
	3:17	for doing good than for doing *e*.
1Jn	2:13	you have overcome the *e* one.
	2:14	and you have overcome the *e* one.
	3:12	who belonged to the *e* one
	5:18	and the *e* one cannot harm him.
	5:19	is under the control of the *e* one.
3Jn	:11	do not imitate what is *e*

EVILDOER* (EVIL)

2Sa	3:39	the LORD repay the *e* according
Ps	101:8	I will cut off every *e*
Mal	4:1	and every *e* will be stubble,

EVILDOERS* (EVIL)

1Sa	24:13	saying goes, 'From *e* come evil
Job	8:20	or strengthen the hands of *e*.
	34:8	He keeps company with *e*;
	34:22	where *e* can hide.
Ps	14:4	Will *e* never learn—
	14:6	You *e* frustrate the plans
	26:5	I abhor the assembly of *e*
	36:12	See how the *e* lie fallen—
	53:4	Will the *e* never learn—
	59:2	Deliver me from *e*
	64:2	from that noisy crowd of *e*.
	92:7	and all *e* flourish,
	92:9	all *e* will be scattered.
	94:4	all the *e* are full of boasting.
	94:16	will take a stand for me against *e*?
	119:115	Away from me, you *e*,
	125:5	the LORD will banish with the *e*.
	141:4	deeds with men who are *e*;
	141:5	ever against the deeds of *e*;
	141:9	from the traps set by *e*.
Pr	21:15	but terror to *e*.
Isa	1:4	a brood of *e*,
	31:2	against those who help *e*.

Jer	23:14	They strengthen the hands of *e*,
Hos	10:9	the *e* in Gibeah?
Mal	3:15	Certainly the *e* prosper, and
Mt	7:23	you *e*!' "Therefore everyone who
Lk	13:27	Away from me, all you *e*!'
	18:11	*e*, adulterers—or even like this tax

EVILS* (EVIL)

Mk	7:23	All these *e* come from inside

EWE

2Sa	12:3	one little *e* lamb he had bought.

EXACT*

Ge	43:21	the *e* weight—in the mouth
Est	4:7	including the *e* amount
Mt	2:7	from them the *e* time the star had
Jn	4:53	realized that this was the *e* time
Ac	17:26	the *e* places where they should live.
Heb	1:3	the *e* representation of his being,

EXALT* (EXALTED EXALTS)

Ex	15:2	my father's God, and I will *e* him.
Jos	3:7	begin to *e* you in the eyes
1Sa	2:10	and *e* the horn of his anointed."
1Ch	25:5	the promises of God to *e* him.
	29:12	power to *e* and give strength to all.
Job	19:5	If indeed you would *e* yourselves
Ps	30:1	I will *e* you, O LORD,
	34:3	let us *e* his name together.
	35:26	may all who *e* themselves over me
	37:34	He will *e* you to inherit the land;
	38:16	*e* themselves over me
	75:6	or from the desert can *e* a man.
	89:17	and by your favor you *e* our horn.
	99:5	*E* the LORD our God
	99:9	*E* the LORD our God
	107:32	Let them *e* him in the assembly
	118:28	you are my God, and I will *e* you.
	145:1	I will *e* you, my God the King;
Pr	4:8	Esteem her, and she will *e* you;
	25:6	Do not *e* yourself in the king's
Isa	24:15	*e* the name of the LORD, the God
	25:1	I will *e* you and praise your name,
Eze	29:15	and will never again *e* itself
Da	4:37	*e* and glorify the King of heaven,
	11:36	He will *e* and magnify himself
	11:37	but will *e* himself above them all.
Hos	11:7	he will by no means *e* them.
2Th	2:4	will *e* himself over everything that is

EXALTED* (EXALT)

Ex	15:1	for he is highly *e*.
	15:21	for he is highly *e*.
Nu	24:7	their kingdom will be *e*.
Jos	4:14	That day the LORD *e* Joshua
2Sa	5:12	and had *e* his kingdom for the sake
	22:47	*E* be God, the Rock, my Savior!
	22:49	You *e* me above my foes;
	23:1	of the man *e* by the Most High,
1Ch	14:2	that his kingdom had been highly *e*
	17:17	as though I were the most *e* of men,
	29:11	you are *e* as head over all.
	29:25	The LORD highly *e* Solomon
Ne	9:5	and may it be *e* above all blessing
Job	24:24	For a little while they are *e*,
	36:22	"God is *e* in his power.
	37:23	beyond our reach and *e* in power;
Ps	18:46	*E* be God my Savior!
	18:48	You *e* me above my foes;
	21:13	Be *e*, O LORD, in your strength;
	27:6	Then my head will be *e*
	35:27	they always say, "The LORD be *e*,
	40:16	"The LORD be *e*!"
	46:10	I will be *e* among the nations,
	46:10	I will be *e* in the earth."
	47:9	he is greatly *e*.
	57:5	Be *e*, O God, above the heavens;
	57:11	Be *e*, O God, above the heavens;
	70:4	"Let God be *e*!"
	89:13	hand is strong, your right hand is *e*.
	89:19	I have *e* a young man
	89:24	through my name his horn will be *e*
	89:27	the most *e* of the kings of the earth.
	89:42	You have *e* the right hand
	92:8	But you, O LORD, are *e* forever.

Ps	92:10	You have *e* my horn like that
	97:9	you are *e* far above all gods.
	99:2	he is *e* over all the nations.
	108:5	Be *e*, O God, above the heavens,
	113:4	The LORD is *e* over all the nations
	138:2	for you have *e* above all things
	148:13	for his name alone is *e*;
Pr	11:11	of the upright a city is *e*,
	30:32	have played the fool and *e*
Isa	2:11	the LORD alone will be *e*
	2:12	for all that is *e*
	2:17	the LORD alone will be *e*
	5:16	the LORD Almighty will be *e*
	6:1	*e*, and the train of his robe filled
	12:4	and proclaim that his name is *e*.
	24:4	the *e* of the earth languish.
	33:5	The LORD is *e*, for he dwells
	33:10	"Now will I be *e*,
	52:13	be raised and lifted up and highly *e*.
Jer	17:12	A glorious throne, *e*
La	2:17	he has *e* the horn of your foes.
Eze	21:26	The lowly will be *e* and the *e* will be
Hos	13:1	he was *e* in Israel.
Mic	6:6	and bow down before the *e* God?
Mt	23:12	whoever humbles himself will be *e*.
Lk	14:11	he who humbles himself will be *e*."
	18:14	he who humbles himself will be *e*."
Ac	2:33	to the right hand of God,
	5:31	God *e* him to his own right hand
Php	1:20	always Christ will be *e* in my body,
	2:9	Therefore God *e* him
Heb	7:26	from sinners, *e* above the heavens.

EXALTS* (EXALT)

1Sa	2:7	he humbles and he *e*.
Job	36:7	and *e* them forever.
Ps	75:7	He brings one down, he *e* another.
Pr	14:34	Righteousness *e* a nation,
Mt	23:12	For whoever *e* himself will be
Lk	14:11	For everyone who *e* himself will be
	18:14	For everyone who *e* himself will be

EXAMINE (EXAMINED EXAMINES)

Ps	11:4	his eyes *e*.
	17:3	you probe my heart and *e* me
	26:2	*e* my heart and my mind;
Jer	17:10	and *e* the mind,
	20:12	Almighty, you who *e* the righteous
La	3:40	Let us *e* our ways and test them,
1Co	11:28	A man ought to *e* himself
2Co	13:5	*E* yourselves to see whether you

EXAMINED (EXAMINE)

Job	13:9	Would it turn out well if he *e* you?
Ac	17:11	*e* the Scriptures every day to see

EXAMINES (EXAMINE)

Ps	11:5	The LORD *e* the righteous,
Pr	5:21	and he *e* all his paths.

EXAMPLE* (EXAMPLES)

2Ki	14:3	In everything he followed the *e*
Ecc	9:13	also saw under the sun this *e*
Eze	14:8	and make him an *e* and a byword,
Jn	13:15	have set you an *e* that you should
Ro	7:2	as long as he lives? For *e*,
1Co	11:1	Follow my *e*, as I follow
	11:1	as I follow the *e* of Christ.
Gal	3:15	let me take an *e* from everyday life.
Php	3:17	Join with others in following my *e*,
2Th	3:7	how you ought to follow our *e*.
1Ti	1:16	as an *e* for those who would believe
	4:12	set an *e* for the believers in speech,
Tit	2:7	In everything set them an *e*
Heb	4:11	fall by following their *e*
Jas	3:4	Or take ships as an *e*.
	5:10	an *e* of patience in the face
1Pe	2:21	leaving you an *e*, that you should
2Pe	2:6	made them an *e* of what is going
Jude	:7	as an *e* of those who suffer

EXAMPLES* (EXAMPLE)
1Co 10: 6 Now these things occurred as *e*
     10:11 as *e* and were written down
1Pe 5: 3 to you, but being *e* to the flock.

EXASPERATE*
Eph 6: 4 Fathers, do not *e* your children;

EXCEL* (EXCELLENT)
Ge 49: 4 as the waters, you will no
         longer *e,*
1Co 14:12 to *e* in gifts that build up the
         church
2Co 8: 7 But just as you *e* in everything—
     8: 7 also *e* in this grace of giving.

EXCELLENT (EXCEL)
1Co 12:31 now I will show you the most *e*
         way
Php 4: 8 if anything is *e* or praiseworthy—
1Ti 3:13 have served well gain an *e*
         standing
Tit 3: 8 These things are *e* and profitable

EXCESSIVE
Eze 18: 8 or take *e* interest.
2Co 2: 7 not be overwhelmed by *e* sorrow.

EXCHANGE (EXCHANGED)
Mt 16:26 Or what can a man give in *e*
Mk 8:37 Or what can a man give in *e*
2Co 6:13 As a fair *e*— I speak

EXCHANGED (EXCHANGE)
Ps 106:20 They *e* their Glory
Jer 2:11 But my people have *e* their Glory
Hos 4: 7 they *e* their Glory
Ro 1:23 *e* the glory of the immortal God
     1:25 They *e* the truth of God for a lie,
     1:26 their women *e* natural relations

EXCLAIM
Ps 35:10 My whole being will *e,*

EXCUSE* (EXCUSES)
Ps 25: 3 who are treacherous without *e.*
Lk 14:18 Please *e* me.'
     14:19 Please *e* me.'
Jn 15:22 they have no *e* for their sin.
Ro 1:20 so that men are without *e.*
     2: 1 You, therefore, have no *e,*

EXCUSES* (EXCUSE)
Lk 14:18 "But they all alike began to
         make *e.*

EXERTED*
Eph 1:20 which he *e* in Christ

EXHORT*
1Ti 5: 1 but *e* him as if he were your
         father.

EXILE
2Ki 17:23 taken from their homeland into *e*
     25:11 into *e* the people who remained

EXISTED* (EXISTS)
2Pe 3: 5 ago by God's word the heavens *e*

EXISTS (EXISTED)
Heb 2:10 and through whom everything *e,*
     11: 6 to him must believe that he *e*

EXPANSE
Ge 1: 7 So God made the *e* and separated
     1: 8 God called the *e* "sky."

EXPECT (EXPECTATION EXPECTED EXPECTING)
Mt 24:44 at an hour when you do not *e*
         him.
Lk 12:40 at an hour when you do not *e*
         him."
Php 1:20 I eagerly *e* and hope that I will

EXPECTATION (EXPECT)
Ro 8:19 waits in eager *e* for the sons
Heb 10:27 but only a fearful *e* of judgment

EXPECTED (EXPECT)
Pr 11: 7 all he *e* from his power comes
Hag 1: 9 "You *e* much, but see, it turned
         out

EXPECTING (EXPECT)
Lk 6:35 and lend to them without *e*

EXPEL* (EXPELLED)
1Co 5:13 *E* the wicked man from among
         you

EXPELLED (EXPEL)
Eze 28:16 and I *e* you, O guardian cherub,

EXPENSE (EXPENSIVE)
1Co 9: 7 Who serves as a soldier at his
         own *e*

EXPENSIVE* (EXPENSE)
Mt 26: 7 jar of very *e* perfume,
Mk 14: 3 jar of very *e* perfume,
Lk 7:25 those who wear *e* clothes
Jn 12: 3 a pint of pure nard, an *e* perfume;
1Ti 2: 9 or gold or pearls or *e* clothes,

EXPERT
1Co 3:10 I laid a foundation as an *e* builder,

EXPLAINING (EXPLAINS)
Ac 17: 3 and proving that the Christ had

EXPLAINS* (EXPLAINING)
Ac 8:31 he said, "unless someone *e* it to

EXPLOIT* (EXPLOITED EXPLOITING EXPLOITS)
Pr 22:22 Do not *e* the poor because they
         are
Isa 58: 3 and *e* all your workers.
2Co 12:17 Did I *e* you through any
     12:18 Titus did not *e* you, did he?
2Pe 2: 3 greed these teachers will *e* you

EXPLOITED* (EXPLOIT)
2Co 7: 2 no one, we have *e* no one.

EXPLOITING* (EXPLOIT)
Jas 2: 6 Is it not the rich who are *e* you?

EXPLOITS (EXPLOIT)
2Co 11:20 or *e* you or takes advantage of you

EXPLORE
Nu 13: 2 "Send some men to *e* the land

EXPOSE (EXPOSED)
1Co 4: 5 will *e* the motives of men's hearts.
Eph 5:11 of darkness, but rather *e* them.

EXPOSED (EXPOSE)
Jn 3:20 for fear that his deeds will be *e.*
Eph 5:13 everything *e* by the light becomes

EXPRESS (EXPRESSING)
Ro 8:26 us with groans that words
         cannot *e.*

EXPRESSING* (EXPRESS)
1Co 2:13 *e* spiritual truths in spiritual
         words.
Gal 5: 6 thing that counts is faith *e* itself

EXTENDS (EXTENT)
Pr 31:20 and *e* her hands to the needy.
Lk 1:50 His mercy *e* to those who fear
         him,

EXTENT (EXTENDS)
Jn 13: 1 he now showed them the full *e*

EXTERNAL
Gal 2: 6 judge by *e* appearance—

EXTINGUISH (EXTINGUISHED)
Eph 6:16 which you can *e* all the flaming

EXTINGUISHED (EXTINGUISH)
2Sa 21:17 the lamp of Israel will not be *e.*"

EXTOL*
Job 36:24 Remember to *e* his work,
Ps 34: 1 I will *e* the LORD at all times;
     68: 4 *e* him who rides on the clouds—
     95: 2 and *e* him with music and song.
   109:30 mouth I will greatly *e* the LORD;
   111: 1 I will *e* the LORD with all my heart
   115:18 it is we who *e* the LORD,
   117: 1 *e* him, all you peoples.
   145: 2 and *e* your name for ever and
         ever.
   145:10 your saints will *e* you.
   147:12 *E* the LORD, O Jerusalem;

EXTORT*
Lk 3:14 "Don't *e* money and don't accuse

EXTRAORDINARY*
Ac 19:11 God did *e* miracles through Paul,

EXTREME (EXTREMES)
2Co 8: 2 and their *e* poverty welled up

EXTREMES* (EXTREME)
Ecc 7:18 who fears God will avoid all *e.*

EXULT
Ps 89:16 they *e* in your righteousness.
Isa 45:25 will be found righteous and will *e.*

EYE (EYES)
Ge 3: 6 good for food and pleasing to
         the *e,*
Ex 21:24 you are to take life for life, *e* for *e,*
Dt 19:21 life for life, *e* for *e,* tooth for tooth,
Ps 94: 9 Does he who formed the *e* not
         see?
Mt 5:29 If your right *e* causes you to sin,
     5:38 '*E* for *e,* and tooth for tooth.'
     6:22 "The *e* is the lamp of the body.
     7: 3 of sawdust in your brother's *e*
1Co 2: 9 "No *e* has seen,
     12:16 I am not an *e,* I do not belong
     15:52 of an *e,* at the last trumpet.
Eph 6: 6 favor when their *e* is on you,
Col 3:22 not only when their *e* is on you
Rev 1: 7 and every *e* will see him,

EYES (EYE)
Nu 15:39 the lusts of your own hearts
         and *e.*
     33:55 remain will become barbs in
         your *e*
Dt 11:12 the *e* of the LORD your God are
     12:25 right in the *e* of the LORD.
     16:19 for a bribe blinds the *e* of the wise
Jos 23:13 on your backs and thorns in
         your *e,*
1Sa 15:17 you were once small in your
         own *e,*
1Ki 10: 7 I came and saw with my own *e.*
2Ki 9:30 heard about it, she painted her *e,*
2Ch 16: 9 For the *e* of the LORD range
Job 31: 1 "I made a covenant with my *e*
     36: 7 He does not take his *e*
Ps 25:15 My *e* are ever on the LORD,
     36: 1 God before his *e.*
   101: 6 My *e* will be on the faithful
   118:23 and it is marvelous in our *e.*
   119:18 Open my *e* that I may see
   119:37 my *e* away from worthless things;
   121: 1 I lift up my *e* to the hills—
   123: 1 I lift up my *e* to you,
   139:16 your *e* saw my unformed body.
   141: 8 But my *e* are fixed on you,
Pr 3: 7 Do not be wise in your own *e;*
     4:25 Let your *e* look straight ahead,
     15: 3 The *e* of the LORD are everywhere
     17:24 a fool's *e* wander to the ends
Isa 6: 5 and my *e* have seen the King,
     33:17 Your *e* will see the king
     42: 7 to open *e* that are blind,
Jer 24: 6 My *e* will watch over them
Hab 1:13 Your *e* are too pure to look on
         evil;
Mt 6:22 If your *e* are good, your whole
     21:42 and it is marvelous in our *e'*?
Lk 16:15 ones who justify yourselves in
         the *e*
     24:31 Then their *e* were opened
Jn 4:35 open your *e* and look at the fields!
Ac 1: 9 he was taken up before their
         very *e,*
2Co 4:18 So we fix our *e* not on what is
         seen,
     8:21 not only in the *e* of the Lord but
Eph 1:18 also that the *e* of your heart may
         be
Heb 12: 2 Let us fix our *e* on Jesus, the
         author
Jas 2: 5 poor in the *e* of the world to be
         rich
1Pe 3:12 For the *e* of the Lord are
Rev 7:17 wipe away every tear from
         their *e.*"
     21: 4 He will wipe every tear from
         their *e*

EYEWITNESSES* (WITNESS)
Lk 1: 2 by those who from the first were *e*
2Pe 1:16 but we were *e* of his majesty.

EZEKIEL*
Priest called to be prophet to the exiles
(Eze 1–3). Symbolically acted out destruction
of Jerusalem (Eze 4–5; 12; 24).

EZRA*
Priest and teacher of the Law who led a
return of exiles to Israel to reestablish temple
and worship (Ezr 7–8). Corrected intermarriage of priests (Ezr 9–10). Read Law at celebration of Feast of Tabernacles (Ne 8).
Participated in dedication of Jerusalem's walls
(Ne 12).

FACE (FACES)
Ge 32:30 "It is because I saw God *f* to *f*,
Ex 3: 6 Moses hid his *f*, because he was
    33:11 would speak to Moses *f* to *f*,
    33:20 But," he said, "you cannot see my *f*
    34:29 was not aware that his *f* was radiant
Nu 6:25 the LORD make his *f* shine
    12: 8 With him I speak *f* to *f*,
    14:14 O LORD, have been seen *f* to *f*,
Dt 5: 4 The LORD spoke to you *f* to *f* out
    31:17 I will hide my *f* from them,
    34:10 whom the LORD knew *f* to *f*,
Jdg 6:22 the angel of the LORD *f* to *f*!"
2Ki 14: 8 challenge: "Come, meet me *f* to *f*.
1Ch 16:11 seek his *f* always.
2Ch 7:14 and seek my *f* and turn
    25:17 of Israel: "Come, meet me *f* to *f*."
Ezr 9: 6 and disgraced to lift up my *f* to you,
Ps   4: 6 Let the light of your *f* shine upon us
    27: 8 Your *f*, LORD, I will seek.
    31:16 Let your *f* shine on your servant;
    44: 3 and the light of your *f*,
    44:22 Yet for your sake we *f* death all day
    51: 9 Hide your *f* from my sins
    67: 1 and make his *f* shine upon us; *Selah*
    80: 3 make your *f* shine upon us,
    105: 4 seek his *f* always.
    119:135 Make your *f* shine
SS   2:14 and your *f* is lovely.
Isa 50: 7 Therefore have I set my *f* like flint,
    50: 8 Let us *f* each other!
    54: 8 I hid my *f* from you for a moment,
Jer 32: 4 and will speak with him *f* to *f*,
    34: 3 and he will speak with you *f* to *f*.
Eze 1:10 Each of the four had the *f* of a man,
    20:35 *f* to *f*, I will execute judgment
Mt 17: 2 His *f* shone like the sun,
    18:10 angels in heaven always see the *f*
Lk   9:29 the appearance of his *f* changed,
Ro   8:36 "For your sake we *f* death all day
1Co 13:12 mirror; then we shall see *f* to *f*.
2Co 3: 7 could not look steadily at the *f*
     4: 6 the glory of God in the *f* of Christ.
    10: 1 who am "timid" when *f* to *f*
1Pe 3:12 but the *f* of the Lord is
2Jn   :12 to visit you and talk with you *f* to *f*,
3Jn   :14 see you soon, and we will talk *f* to *f*.
Rev 1:16 His *f* was like the sun shining
    22: 4 They will see his *f*, and his name

FACES (FACE)
2Co 3:18 who with unveiled *f* all reflect

FACTIONS
2Co 12:20 outbursts of anger, *f*, slander,
Gal 5:20 selfish ambition, dissensions, *f*

FADE (FADING)
Jas 1:11 the rich man will *f* away
1Pe 5: 4 of glory that will never *f* away.

FADING (FADE)
2Co 3: 7 though it was, will not
     3:11 if what was *f* away came with glory,
     3:13 at it while the radiance was *f* away.

FAIL (FAILED FAILING FAILINGS FAILS FAILURE)
Lev 26:15 and *f* to carry out all my commands
1Ki 2: 4 you will never *f* to have a man
1Ch 28:20 He will not *f* you or forsake you
2Ch 34:33 they did not *f* to follow the LORD,
Ps 89:28 my covenant with him will never *f*.
Pr 15:22 Plans *f* for lack of counsel,
Isa 51: 6 my righteousness will never *f*.
La   3:22 for his compassions never *f*.
Lk 22:32 Simon, that your faith may not f.
2Co 13: 5 unless, of course, you *f* the test?

FAILED (FAIL)
Jos 23:14 has been fulfilled; not one has *f*.
1Ki 8:56 Not one word has *f*
Ps 77: 8 Has his promise *f* for all time?

Ro   9: 6 as though God's word had *f*.
2Co 13: 6 discover that we have not *f* the test.

FAILING (FAIL)
1Sa 12:23 sin against the LORD by *f* to pray

FAILINGS (FAIL)
Ro 15: 1 ought to bear with the *f* of the weak

FAILS (FAIL)
Jer 14: 6 their eyesight *f*
Joel 1:10 the oil *f*.
1Co 13: 8 Love never *f*.

FAILURE* (FAIL)
1Th 2: 1 that our visit to you was not a *f*.

FAINT
Isa 40:31 they will walk and not be *f*.

FAINTHEARTED* (HEART)
Dt 20: 3 Do not be *f* or afraid; do not be
    20: 8 shall add, "Is any man afraid or *f*?

FAIR (FAIRNESS)
Pr   1: 3 doing what is right and just and *f*;
Col 4: 1 slaves with what is right and *f*,

FAIRNESS* (FAIR)
Pr 29:14 If a king judges the poor with *f*,

FAITH* (FAITHFUL FAITHFULLY FAITHFULNESS FAITHLESS)
Ex 21: 8 because he has broken *f* with her.
Dt 32:51 both of you broke *f* with me
Jos 22:16 'How could you break *f*
Jdg 9:16 and in good *f* when you made
     9:19 and in good *f* toward Jerub-Baal
1Sa 14:33 "You have broken *f*," he said.
2Ch 20:20 Have *f* in the LORD your God
    20:20 have *f* in his prophets and you will
Isa 7: 9 If you do not stand firm in your *f*,
    26: 2 the nation that keeps *f*.
Hab 2: 4 but the righteous will live by his *f*—
Mal 2:10 by breaking *f* with one another?
     2:11 one another? Judah has broken *f*
     2:14 because you have broken *f* with her
     2:15 and do not break *f* with the wife
     2:16 in your spirit, and do not break *f*.
Mt   6:30 O you of little *f*? So do not worry,
     8:10 anyone in Israel with such great *f*.
     8:26 He replied, "You of little *f*,
     9: 2 When Jesus saw their *f*, he said
     9:22 he said, "your *f* has healed you."
     9:29 According to your *f* will it be done
    13:58 there because of their lack of *f*.
    14:31 of little *f*," he said, "why did you
    15:28 "Woman, you have great *f*!
    16: 8 Jesus asked, "You of little *f*,
    17:20 if you have *f* as small as a mustard
    17:20 "Because you have so little *f*.
    21:21 if you have *f* and do not doubt,
    24:10 many will turn away from the *f*
Mk   2: 5 When Jesus saw their *f*, he said
     4:40 still have no *f*?" They were
     5:34 "Daughter, your *f* has healed you.
     6: 6 he was amazed at their lack of *f*.
    10:52 said Jesus, "your *f* has healed you."
    11:22 "Have *f* in God," Jesus answered.
    16:14 he rebuked them for their lack of *f*
Lk   5:20 When Jesus saw their *f*, he said,
     7: 9 I have not found such great *f*
     7:50 the woman, "Your *f* has saved you;
     8:25 "Where is your *f*?" he asked his
     8:48 "Daughter, your *f* has healed you.
    12:28 will he clothe you, O you of little *f*!
    17: 5 "Increase our *f*!" He replied,
    17: 6 "If you have *f* as small
    17:19 your *f* has made you well."
    18: 8 will he find *f* on the earth?"
    18:42 your sight; your *f* has healed you."
    22:32 Simon, that your *f* may not fail.
Jn   2:11 and his disciples put their *f* in him.
     7:31 in the crowd put their *f* in him.
     8:30 he spoke, many put their *f* in him.
    11:45 had seen what Jesus did, put their *f*
    12:11 to Jesus and putting their *f* in him.
    12:42 they would not confess their *f*
    14:12 anyone who has *f* in me will do

Ac   3:16 By *f* in the name of Jesus, this man
     3:16 *f* that comes through him that has
     6: 5 full of *f* and of the Holy Spirit;
     6: 7 of priests became obedient to the *f*.
    11:24 full of the Holy Spirit and *f*,
    13: 8 to turn the proconsul from the *f*.
    14: 9 saw that he had *f* to be healed
    14:22 them to remain true to the *f*.
    14:27 the door of *f* to the Gentiles.
    15: 9 for he purified their hearts by *f*.
    16: 5 were strengthened in the *f*
    20:21 and have *f* in our Lord Jesus.
    24:24 as he spoke about *f* in Christ Jesus.
    26:18 those who are sanctified by *f*
    27:25 for I have *f* in God that it will
Ro   1: 5 to the obedience that comes from *f*.
     1: 8 because your *f* is being reported all
     1:12 encouraged by each other's *f*.
     1:17 is by *f* from first to last,
     1:17 "The righteous will live by *f*."
     3: 3 What if some did not have *f*?
     3: 3 lack of *f* nullify God's faithfulness?
     3:22 comes through *f* in Jesus Christ
     3:25 a sacrifice of atonement, through *f*
     3:26 one who justifies those who have *f*
     3:27 the law? No, but on that of *f*.
     3:28 by *f* apart from observing the law.
     3:30 through that same *f*.
     3:31 nullify the law by this *f*? Not at all!
     4: 5 his *f* is credited as righteousness.
     4: 9 that Abraham's *f* was credited
     4:11 had by *f* while he was still
     4:12 of the *f* that our father Abraham
     4:13 the righteousness that comes by *f*.
     4:14 *f* has no value and the promise is
     4:16 Therefore, the promise comes by *f*,
     4:16 are of the *f* of Abraham.
     4:19 Without weakening in his *f*,
     4:20 but was strengthened in his *f*
     5: 1 we have been justified through *f*,
     5: 2 access by *f* into this grace
     9:30 a righteousness that is by *f*;
     9:32 Because they pursued it not by *f*
    10: 6 the righteousness that is by *f* says:
    10: 8 the word of *f* we are proclaiming:
    10:17 *f* comes from hearing the message,
    11:20 of unbelief, and you stand by *f*.
    12: 3 measure of *f* God has given you.
    12: 6 let him use it in proportion to his *f*.
    14: 1 Accept him whose *f* is weak,
    14: 2 One man's *f* allows him
    14: 2 but another man, whose *f* is weak,
    14:23 because his eating is not from *f*;
    14:23 that does not come from *f* is sin.
1Co 2: 5 so that your *f* might not rest
    12: 9 to another *f* by the same Spirit,
    13: 2 and if I have a *f* that can move
    13:13 And now these three remain: *f*,
    15:14 is useless and so is your *f*
    15:17 has not been raised, your *f* is futile;
    16:13 stand firm in the *f*; be men
2Co 1:24 Not that we lord it over your *f*,
     1:24 because it is by *f* you stand firm.
     4:13 With that same spirit of *f* we
     5: 7 We live by *f*, not by sight.
     8: 7 in *f*, in speech, in knowledge,
    10:15 as your *f* continues to grow,
    13: 5 to see whether you are in the *f*;
Gal 1:23 now preaching the *f* he once tried
     2:16 Jesus that we are justified by *f*
     2:16 but by *f* in Jesus Christ.
     2:16 have put our *f* in Christ Jesus that
     2:20 I live by *f* in the Son of God,
     3: 8 would justify the Gentiles by *f*,
     3: 9 So those who have *f* are blessed
     3: 9 along with Abraham, the man of *f*.
     3:11 "The righteous will live by *f*."
     3:12 based on *f*; on the contrary,
     3:14 by *f* we might receive the promise
     3:22 being given through *f*

Gal	3:23	Before this *f* came, we were held
	3:23	up until *f* should be revealed.
	3:24	that we might be justified by *f*.
	3:25	that *f* has come, we are no longer
	3:26	of God through *f* in Christ Jesus,
	5: 5	But by *f* we eagerly await
	5: 6	that counts is *f* expressing itself
Eph	1:15	ever since I heard about your *f*
	2: 8	through *f*— and this not
	3:12	through *f* in him we may approach
	3:17	dwell in your hearts through *f*.
	4: 5	one Lord, one *f*, one baptism;
	4:13	up until we all reach unity in the *f*
	6:16	to all this, take up the shield of *f*,
	6:23	love with *f* from God the Father
Php	1:25	for your progress and joy in the *f*
	1:27	as one man for the *f* of the gospel
	2:17	and service coming from your *f*,
	3: 9	comes from God and is by *f*.
	3: 9	that which is through *f* in Christ—
Col	1: 4	heard of your *f* in Christ Jesus
	1: 5	the *f* and love that spring
	1:23	continue in your *f*, established
	2: 5	and how firm your *f* in Christ is.
	2: 7	in the *f* as you were taught,
	2:12	him through your *f* in the power
1Th	1: 3	Father your work produced by *f*,
	1: 8	your *f* in God has become known
	3: 2	and encourage you in your *f*,
	3: 5	I sent to find out about your *f*.
	3: 6	brought good news about your *f*
	3: 7	about you because of your *f*.
	3:10	supply what is lacking in your *f*.
	5: 8	on *f* and love as a breastplate,
2Th	1: 3	because your *f* is growing more
	1: 4	and *f* in all the persecutions
	1:11	and every act prompted by your *f*.
	3: 2	evil men, for not everyone has *f*.
1Ti	1: 2	To Timothy my true son in the *f*:
	1: 4	than God's work—which is by *f*.
	1: 5	a good conscience and a sincere *f*.
	1:14	along with the *f* and love that are
	1:19	and so have shipwrecked their *f*.
	1:19	on to *f* and a good conscience.
	2: 7	of the true *f* to the Gentiles.
	2:15	if they continue in *f*, love
	3: 9	of the *f* with a clear conscience.
	3:13	assurance in their *f* in Christ Jesus.
	4: 1	later times some will abandon the *f*
	4: 6	brought up in the truths of the *f*
	4:12	in life, in love, in *f* and in purity.
	5: 8	he has denied the *f* and is worse
	6:10	have wandered from the *f*
	6:11	pursue righteousness, godliness, *f*,
	6:12	Fight the good fight of the *f*.
	6:21	so doing have wandered from the *f*.
2Ti	1: 5	been reminded of your sincere *f*,
	1:13	with *f* and love in Christ Jesus.
	2:18	and they destroy the *f* of some.
	2:22	and pursue righteousness, *f*,
	3: 8	as far as the *f* is concerned,
	3:10	my purpose, *f*, patience, love,
	3:15	wise for salvation through *f*
	4: 7	finished the race, I have kept the *f*.
Tit	1: 1	Christ for the *f* of God's elect
	1: 2	a *f* and knowledge resting
	1: 4	my true son in our common *f*:
	1:13	so that they will be sound in the *f*
	2: 2	self-controlled, and sound in *f*,
	3:15	Greet those who love us in the *f*.
Phm	: 5	because I hear about your *f*
	: 6	may be active in sharing your *f*,
Heb	4: 2	heard did not combine it with *f*.
	4:14	firmly to the *f* we profess.
	6: 1	and of *f* in God, instruction about
	6:12	but to imitate those who through *f*
	10:22	heart in full assurance of *f*,
	10:38	But my righteous one will live by *f*.
	11: 1	*f* is being sure of what we hope for
	11: 3	By *f* we understand that
	11: 4	And by *f* he still speaks, even
	11: 4	By *f* Abel offered God a better
	11: 4	By *f* he was commended
	11: 5	By *f* Enoch was taken from this life

Heb	11: 6	And without *f* it is impossible
	11: 7	By his *f* he condemned the world
	11: 7	By *f* Noah, when warned about
	11: 7	the righteousness that comes by *f*.
	11: 8	By *f* Abraham, when called to go
	11: 9	By *f* he made his home
	11:11	By *f* Abraham, even though he was
	11:13	living by *f* when they died.
	11:17	By *f* Abraham, when God tested
	11:20	By *f* Isaac blessed Jacob
	11:21	By *f* Jacob, when he was dying,
	11:22	By *f* Joseph, when his end was near
	11:23	By *f* Moses' parents hid him
	11:24	By *f* Moses, when he had grown up
	11:27	By *f* he left Egypt, not fearing
	11:28	By *f* he kept the Passover
	11:29	By *f* the people passed
	11:30	By *f* the walls of Jericho fell,
	11:31	By *f* the prostitute Rahab,
	11:33	through *f* conquered kingdoms,
	11:39	were all commended for their *f*,
	12: 2	the author and perfecter of our *f*,
	13: 7	way of life and imitate their *f*.
Jas	1: 3	of your *f* develops perseverance.
	2: 5	the eyes of the world to be rich in *f*
	2:14	has no deeds? Can such *f* save him?
	2:14	if a man claims to have *f*
	2:17	In the same way, *f* by itself,
	2:18	I will show you my *f* by what I do.
	2:18	Show me your *f* without deeds,
	2:18	"You have *f*; I have deeds."
	2:20	do you want evidence that *f*
	2:22	You see that his *f* and his actions
	2:22	and his *f* was made complete
	2:24	by what he does and not by *f* alone.
	2:26	so *f* without deeds is dead.
	5:15	in *f* will make the sick person well;
1Pe	1: 5	who through *f* are shielded
	1: 7	These have come so that your *f*—
	1: 9	you are receiving the goal of your *f*,
	1:21	and so your *f* and hope are in God.
	5: 9	Resist him, standing firm in the *f*,
2Pe	1: 1	Jesus Christ have received a *f*
	1: 5	effort to add to your *f* goodness;
1Jn	5: 4	overcome the world, even our *f*.
Jude	: 3	to contend for the *f* that was once
	:20	up in your most holy *f*
Rev	2:13	You did not renounce your *f* in me,
	2:19	your love and *f*, your service

FAITHFUL* (FAITH)

Nu	12: 7	he is *f* in all my house.
Dt	7: 9	your God is God; he is the *f* God,
	32: 4	A *f* God who does no wrong,
1Sa	2:35	I will raise up for myself a *f* priest,
2Sa	20:19	We are the peaceful and *f* in Israel.
	22:26	"To the *f* you show yourself *f*,
1Ki	3: 6	because he was *f* to you
2Ch	31:18	were *f* in consecrating themselves.
	31:20	and *f* before the LORD his God.
Ne	9: 8	You found his heart *f* to you,
Ps	12: 1	the *f* have vanished
	18:25	To the *f* you show yourself *f*,
	25:10	of the LORD are loving and *f*
	31:23	The LORD preserves the *f*,
	33: 4	he is *f* in all he does.
	37:28	and will not forsake his *f* ones.
	78: 8	whose spirits were not *f* to him.
	78:37	they were not *f* to his covenant.
	89:19	to your *f* people you said:
	89:24	My *f* love will be with him,
	89:37	the *f* witness in the sky."
	97:10	for he guards the lives of his *f* ones
	101: 6	My eyes will be on the *f* in the land,
	111: 7	The works of his hands are *f*
	145:13	The LORD is *f* to all his promises
	146: 6	the LORD, who remains *f* forever.
Pr	2: 8	and protects the way of his *f* ones.
	20: 6	but a *f* man who can find?

Pr	28:20	A *f* man will be richly blessed,
	31:26	and *f* instruction is on her tongue.
Isa	1:21	See how the *f* city has become
	1:26	the *F* City."
	49: 7	because of the LORD, who is *f*,
	55: 3	my *f* love promised to David.
Jer	42: 5	*f* witness against us if we do not act
Eze	43:11	so that they may be *f* to its design
	48:11	who were *f* in serving me
Hos	11:12	even against the *f* Holy One.
Zec	8: 8	I will be *f* and righteous to them
Mt	24:45	Who then is the *f* and wise servant,
	25:21	'Well done, good and *f* servant!
	25:21	You have been *f* with a few things;
	25:23	You have been *f* with a few things;
	25:23	'Well done, good and *f* servant!
Lk	12:42	then is the *f* and wise manager,
Ro	12:12	patient in affliction, *f* in prayer.
1Co	1: 9	his Son Jesus Christ our Lord, is *f*.
	4: 2	been given a trust must prove *f*.
	4:17	my son whom I love, who is *f*
	10:13	And God is *f*; he will not let you be
2Co	1:18	no"? But as surely as God is *f*,
Eph	1: 1	in Ephesus, the *f* in Christ Jesus:
	6:21	the dear brother and *f* servant
Col	1: 2	and *f* brothers in Christ at Colosse:
	1: 7	who is a *f* minister of Christ
	4: 7	a *f* minister and fellow servant
	4: 9	He is coming with Onesimus, our *f*
1Th	5:24	The one who calls you is *f*
2Th	3: 3	the Lord is *f*, and he will strengthen
1Ti	1:12	he considered me *f*, appointing me
	5: 9	has been *f* to her husband,
2Ti	2:13	he will remain *f*,
Heb	2:17	and *f* high priest in service to God,
	3: 2	He was *f* to the one who appointed
	3: 2	as Moses was *f* in all God's house.
	3: 5	Moses was *f* as a servant
	3: 6	But Christ is *f* as a son
	8: 9	because they did not remain *f*
	10:23	for he who promised is *f*.
	11:11	he considered him *f* who had made
1Pe	4:19	themselves to their *f* Creator
	5:12	whom I regard as a *f* brother,
1Jn	1: 9	he is *f* and just and will forgive us
3Jn	: 5	you are *f* in what you are doing
Rev	1: 5	who is the *f* witness, the firstborn
	2:10	Be *f*, even to the point of death,
	2:13	the days of Antipas, my *f* witness,
	3:14	the words of the Amen, the *f*
	14:12	commandments and remain *f*
	17:14	his called, chosen and *f* followers."
	19:11	whose rider is called *F* and True.

FAITHFULLY* (FAITH)

Dt	11:13	if you *f* obey the commands I am
Jos	2:14	*f* when the LORD gives us the land
1Sa	12:24	and serve him *f* with all your heart;
1Ki	2: 4	and if they walk *f* before me
2Ki	20: 3	how I have walked before you *f*
	22: 7	because they are acting *f*."
2Ch	19: 9	must serve *f* and wholeheartedly
	31:12	they *f* brought in the contributions,
	31:15	and Shecaniah assisted him *f*
	32: 1	all that Hezekiah had so *f* done,
	34:12	The men did the work *f*.
Ne	9:33	you have acted *f*, while we did
	13:14	so *f* done for the house of my God
Isa	38: 3	how I have walked before you *f*
Jer	23:28	one who has my word speak it *f*.
Eze	18: 9	and *f* keeps my laws.
	44:15	and who *f* carried out the duties
1Pe	4:10	*f* administering God's grace

FAITHFULNESS* (FAITH)

Ge	24:27	not abandoned his kindness and *f*
	24:49	if you will show kindness and *f*
	32:10	and *f* you have shown your servant.
	47:29	you will show me kindness and *f*.
Ex	34: 6	*f*, maintaining love to thousands,

Jos 24:14 the LORD and serve him with all *f.*
1Sa 26:23 man for his righteousness and *f.*
2Sa 2: 6 now show you kindness and *f,*
    15:20 May kindness and *f* be with you."
Ps 30: 9 Will it proclaim your *f?*
    36: 5 your *f* to the skies.
    40:10 I speak of your *f* and salvation.
    54: 5 in your *f* destroy them.
    57: 3 God sends his love and his *f.*
    57:10 your *f* reaches to the skies.
    61: 7 appoint your love and *f*
    71:22 the harp for your *f,* O my God;
    85:10 Love and *f* meet together;
    85:11 *f* springs forth from the earth,
    86:15 to anger, abounding in love and *f.*
    88:11 your *f* in Destruction?
    89: 1 mouth I will make your *f* known
    89: 2 that you established your *f*
    89: 5 your *f* too, in the assembly
    89: 8 and your *f* surrounds you.
    89:14 love and *f* go before you.
    89:33 nor will I ever betray my *f.*
    89:49 which in your *f* you swore to
        David
    91: 4 his *f* will be your shield
    92: 2 and your *f* at night,
    98: 3 and his *f* to the house of Israel;
   100: 5 *f* continues through all
   108: 4 your *f* reaches to the skies.
   111: 8 done in *f* and uprightness.
   115: 1 because of your love and *f.*
   117: 2 the *f* of the LORD endures forever.
   119:75 and in *f* you have afflicted me.
   119:90 *f* continues through all
   138: 2 name for your love and your *f,*
   143: 1 in your *f* and righteousness
Pr   3: 3 Let love and *f* never leave you;
    14:22 plan what is good find love and *f*
    16: 6 Through love and *f* sin is atoned
        for
    20:28 Love and *f* keep a king safe;
Isa 11: 5 and *f* the sash around his waist.
    16: 5 in *f* a man will sit on it—
    25: 1 for in perfect *f*
    38:18 cannot hope for your *f.*
    38:19 about your *f.*
    42: 3 In *f* he will bring forth justice;
    61: 8 In my *f* I will reward them
La   3: 3 great is your *f.*
Hos 2:20 I will betroth you in *f,*
     4: 1 "There is no *f,* no love,
Mt 23: 3 of the law—justice, mercy and *f.*
Ro   3: 3 lack of faith nullify God's *f?*
Gal 5:22 patience, kindness, goodness, *f,*
3Jn : 3 and tell about your *f* to the truth
Rev 13:10 and *f* on the part of the saints.

FAITHLESS* (FAITH)
Ps 78:57 fathers they were disloyal and *f,*
   101: 3 The deeds of *f* men I hate;
   119:158 I look on the *f* with loathing,
Pr 14:14 The *f* will be fully repaid
Jer 3: 6 you seen what *f* Israel has done?
     3: 8 I gave *f* Israel her certificate
     3:11 "*F* Israel is more righteous
     3:12 *f* Israel,' declares the LORD,
     3:14 *f* people," declares the LORD,
     3:22 "Return, *f* people;
    12: 1 Why do all the *f* live at ease?
Ro   1:31 they are senseless, *f,* heartless,
2Ti 2:13 if we are *f,*

FALL (FALLEN FALLING FALLS)
Ps 37:24 though he stumble, he will not *f,*
    55:22 he will never let the righteous *f.*
    69: 9 of those who insult you *f* on me.
   145:14 The LORD upholds all those who *f*
Pr 11:28 Whoever trusts in his riches will *f,*
Isa 40: 7 The grass withers and the
        flowers *f,*
Mt   7:25 yet it did not *f,* because it had its
Lk 10:18 "I saw Satan *f* like lightning
    11:17 a house divided against itself
        will *f.*
    23:30 say to the mountains, "*F* on us!"
Ro   3:23 and *f* short of the glory of God,
Heb 6: 6 if they *f* away, to be brought back

FALLEN (FALL)
2Sa 1:19 How the mighty have *f!*
Isa 14:12 How you have *f* from heaven,
1Co 11:30 and a number of you have *f*
        asleep.

1Co 15: 6 though some have *f* asleep.
    15:18 who have *f* asleep in Christ are
        lost.
    15:20 of those who have *f* asleep.
Gal 4: 2 you have *f* away from grace.
1Th 4:15 precede those who have *f* asleep.

FALLING (FALL)
Jude :24 able to keep you from *f*

FALLS (FALL)
Pr 11:14 For lack of guidance a nation *f,*
    24:17 Do not gloat when your enemy *f;*
    28:14 he who hardens his heart *f*
Mt 13:21 of the word, he quickly *f* away.
    21:44 He who *f* on this stone will be
Jn 12:24 a kernel of wheat *f* to the ground
Ro 14: 4 To his own master he stands or *f.*

FALSE (FALSEHOOD FALSELY)
Ex 20:16 "You shall not give *f* testimony
    23: 1 "Do not spread *f* reports.
    23: 7 Have nothing to do with a *f*
        charge
Dt   5:20 "You shall not give *f* testimony
Pr 12:17 but a *f* witness tells lies.
    13: 5 The righteous hate what is *f,*
    14: 5 but a *f* witness pours out lies.
    14:25 but a *f* witness is deceitful.
    19: 5 A *f* witness will not go
        unpunished,
    19: 9 A *f* witness will not go
        unpunished,
    21:28 A *f* witness will perish,
    25:18 is the man who gives *f* testimony
Isa 44:25 who foils the signs of *f* prophets
Jer 23:16 they fill you with *f* hopes.
Mt   7:15 "Watch out for *f* prophets.
    15:19 theft, *f* testimony, slander.
    19:18 not steal, do not give *f* testimony,
    24:11 and many *f* prophets will appear
    24:24 For *f* Christs and *f* prophets will
Mk 10:19 do not give *f* testimony, do not
    13:22 For *f* Christs and *f* prophets will
Lk   6:26 their fathers treated the *f*
        prophets.
    18:20 not steal, do not give *f* testimony,
Jn   1:47 in whom there is nothing *f.*"
1Co 15:15 found to be *f* witnesses about
        God,
2Co 11:13 For such men are *f* apostles,
    11:26 and in danger from *f* brothers.
Gal 2: 4 some *f* brothers had infiltrated
        our
Php 1:18 whether from *f* motives or true,
Col 2:18 anyone who delights in *f* humility
     2:23 their *f* humility and their harsh
1Ti 1: 3 not to teach *f* doctrines any
        longer
     6: 3 If anyone teaches *f* doctrines
2Pe 2: 1 also *f* prophets among the people,
     2: 1 there will be *f* teachers among
        you.
1Jn 4: 1 many *f* prophets have gone out
Rev 16:13 out of the mouth of the *f* prophet.
    19:20 with him the *f* prophet who had
    20:10 and the *f* prophet had been
        thrown.

FALSEHOOD* (FALSE)
Job 21:34 left of your answers but *f!*"
    31: 5 "If I have walked in *f*
Ps 52: 3 *f* rather than speaking the truth.
   119:163 I hate and abhor *f*
Pr 30: 8 Keep *f* and lies far from me;
Isa 28:15 and *f* our hiding place."
Ro   3: 7 "If my *f* enhances God's
Eph 4:25 each of you must put off *f*
1Jn 4: 6 Spirit of truth and the spirit of *f.*
Rev 22:15 everyone who loves and
        practices *f*

FALSELY (FALSE)
Lev 19:12 " 'Do not swear *f* by my name
Mt   5:11 *f* say all kinds of evil against you
Lk   3:14 and don't accuse people *f*—
1Ti 6:20 ideas of what is *f* called
        knowledge,

FALTER*
Pr 24:10 If you *f* in times of trouble,
Isa 42: 4 he will not *f* or be discouraged

FAME
Jos 9: 9 of the *f* of the LORD your God.

Isa 66:19 islands that have not heard of
        my *f*
Hab 3: 2 LORD, I have heard of your *f;*

FAMILIES (FAMILY)
Ps 68: 6 God sets the lonely in *f,*

FAMILY (FAMILIES)
Pr 15:27 greedy man brings trouble to his *f,*
    31:15 she provides food for her *f*
Mk   5:19 to your *f* and tell them how much
Lk   9:61 go back and say good-by to my *f.*"
    12:52 in one *f* divided against each
        other,
Ac 10: 2 He and all his *f* were devout
    16:33 and all his *f* were baptized.
    16:34 he and his whole *f.*
1Ti 3: 4 He must manage his own *f* well
     3: 5 how to manage his own *f,*
     5: 4 practice by caring for their own *f*
     5: 8 and especially for his immediate *f,*

FAMINE
Ge 12:10 Now there was a *f* in the land,
    26: 1 Now there was a *f* in the land—
    41:30 seven years of *f* will follow them.
Ru   1: 1 the judges ruled, there was a *f*
1Ki 18: 2 Now the *f* was severe in Samaria,
Am   8:11 but a *f* of hearing the words
Ro   8:35 or persecution or *f* or nakedness

FAN*
2Ti 1: 6 you to *f* into flame the gift of God,

FANTASIES*
Ps 73:20 you will despise them as *f.*
Pr 12:11 but he who chases *f* lacks
        judgment
    28:19 one who chases *f* will have his fill

FAST (FASTING)
Dt 10:20 Hold *f* to him and take your oaths
    11:22 in all his ways and to hold *f* to him
    13: 4 serve him and hold *f* to him.
    30:20 to his voice, and hold *f* to him.
Jos 22: 5 to hold *f* to him and to serve him
    23: 8 to hold *f* to the LORD your God,
2Ki 18: 6 He held *f* to the LORD
Ps 119:31 I hold *f* to your statutes, O LORD;
   139:10 your right hand will hold me *f.*
Mt   6:16 "When you *f,* do not look somber
1Pe 5:12 Stand *f* in it.

FASTING (FAST)
Ps 35:13 and humbled myself with *f.*
Ac 13: 2 were worshiping the Lord and *f,*
    14:23 and *f,* committed them to the
        Lord

FATHER (FATHER'S FATHERED FATHERLESS
FATHERS FOREFATHERS)
Ge   2:24 this reason a man will leave his *f*
    17: 4 You will be the *f* of many nations.
Ex 20:12 "Honor your *f* and your mother,
    21:15 "Anyone who attacks his *f*
    21:17 "Anyone who curses his *f*
Lev 18: 7 " 'Do not dishonor your *f*
    19: 3 you must respect his mother
        and *f,*
    20: 9 " 'If anyone curses his *f* or mother,
Dt   1:31 carried you, as a *f* carries his son,
     5:16 "Honor your *f* and your mother,
    21:18 son who does not obey his *f*
    32: 6 Is he not your *F,* your Creator,
2Sa 7:14 I will be his *f,* and he will be my
        son
1Ch 17:13 I will be his *f,* and he will be my
        son
    22:10 will be my son, and I will be his *f.*
    28: 6 to be my son, and I will be his *f.*
Job 38:28 Does the rain have a *f?*
Ps   2: 7 today I have become your *F.*
    27:10 Though my *f* and mother forsake
    68: 5 A *f* to the fatherless, a defender
    89:26 to me, 'You are my *F,*
   103:13 As a *f* has compassion
Pr   3:12 as a *f* the son he delights in.
    10: 1 A wise son brings joy to his *f,*
    17:21 there is no joy for the *f* of a fool.
    17:25 A foolish son brings grief to his *f*
    23:22 Listen to your *f,* who gave you life,
    23:24 *f* of a righteous man has great joy;
    28: 7 of gluttons disgraces his *f.*
    28:24 He who robs his *f* or mother
    29: 3 loves wisdom brings joy to his *f,*
Isa 9: 6 Everlasting *F,* Prince of Peace.

Isa 45: 10 Woe to him who says to his *f,*
     63: 16 But you are our *F,*
Jer   2: 27 They say to wood, 'You are my *f,'*
      3: 19 I thought you would call me *'F'*
    31: 9 because I am Israel's *f,*
Eze 18: 19 the son not share the guilt of
            his *f?'*
Mic   7: 6 For a son dishonors his *f,*
Mal   1: 6 If I am a *f,* where is the honor due
     2: 10 we not all one *F?* Did not one God
Mt   3: 9 'We have Abraham as our *f.'*
     5: 16 and praise your *F* in heaven.
     6: 9 " 'Our *F* in heaven,
     6: 26 yet your heavenly *F* feeds them.
    10: 37 "Anyone who loves his *f*
    11: 27 no one knows the *F* except the
            Son
    15: 4 'Honor your *f* and mother'
    18: 10 the face of my *F* in heaven.
    19: 5 this reason a man will leave his *f*
    19: 19 honor your *f* and mother,'
    19: 29 or brothers or sisters or *f* or
            mother
    23: 9 And do not call anyone on
            earth *'f,'*
Mk   7: 10 'Honor your *f* and your mother,'
            and,
Lk   9: 59 "Lord, first let me go and bury
            my *f*
    12: 53 *f* against son and son against *f,*
    14: 26 and does not hate his *f* and
            mother,
    18: 20 honor your *f* and mother.' "
    23: 34 Jesus said, *"F,* forgive them,
Jn   3: 35 The *F* loves the Son and has
            placed
     4: 21 you will worship the *F* neither
     5: 17 "My *F* is always at his work
     5: 18 he was even calling God his
            own *F,*
     5: 20 For the *F* loves the Son
     6: 44 the *F* who sent me draws him,
     6: 46 No one has seen the *F*
     8: 19 "You do not know me or my *F,"*
     8: 28 speak just what the *F* has taught
            me
     8: 41 The only *F* we have is God himself
     8: 42 God were your *F,* you would love
     8: 44 You belong to your *f,* the devil,
    10: 17 reason my *F* loves me is that I lay
    10: 30 I and the *F* are one."
    10: 38 and understand that the *F* is in
            me,
    14: 6 No one comes to the *F*
    14: 9 who has seen me has seen the *F.*
    14: 28 for the *F* is greater than I.
    15: 9 "As the *F* has loved me,
    15: 23 He who hates me hates my *F*
    20: 17 'I am returning to my *F* and your *F,*
Ac   13: 33 today I have become your *F.'*
Ro   4: 11 he is the *f* of all who believe
     4: 16 He is the *f* of us all.
     8: 15 And by him we cry, *"Abba, F."*
1Co   4: 15 for in Christ Jesus I became your *f*
2Co   6: 18 "I will be a *F* to you,
Eph   5: 31 this reason a man will leave his *f*
     6: 2 "Honor your *f* and mother"—
Php   2: 11 to the glory of God the *F.*
Heb   1: 5 today I have become your *F"?*
    12: 7 what son is not disciplined by
            his *f?*
1Jn   1: 3 And our fellowship is with the *F*
     2: 15 the love of the *F* is not in him.
     2: 22 he denies the *F* and the Son.

FATHER'S (FATHER)
Pr   13: 1 A wise son heeds his *f* instruction,
    15: 5 A fool spurns his *f* discipline,
    19: 13 A foolish son is his *f* ruin,
Mt   16: 27 going to come in his *F* glory
Lk   2: 49 had to be in my *F* house?"
Jn   2: 16 How dare you turn my *F* house
    10: 29 can snatch them out of my *F*
            hand.
    14: 2 In my *F* house are many rooms;
    15: 8 to my *F* glory, that you bear much

FATHERED (FATHER)
Dt   32: 18 You deserted the Rock, who *f* you;

FATHERLESS (FATHER)
Dt   10: 18 He defends the cause of the *f*
    14: 29 the *f* and the widows who live

Dt   24: 17 Do not deprive the alien or the *f*
    24: 19 Leave it for the alien, the *f*
    26: 12 the alien, the *f* and the widow,
Ps   68: 5 A father to the *f,* a defender
    82: 3 Defend the cause of the weak
            and *f*
Pr   23: 10 or encroach on the fields of the *f,*

FATHERS (FATHER)
Ex   20: 5 for the sin of the *f* to the third
Jer   31: 29 'The *f* have eaten sour grapes,
Mal   4: 6 the hearts of the children to
            their *f;*
Lk   1: 17 the hearts of the *f* to their
            children
    11: 11 "Which of you *f,* if your son asks
Jn   4: 20 Our *f* worshiped on this
            mountain,
1Co   4: 15 you do not have many *f,*
Eph   6: 4 *F,* do not exasperate your
            children;
Col   3: 21 *F,* do not embitter your children,
Heb 12: 9 all had human *f* who disciplined
            us

FATHOM* (FATHOMED)
Job   11: 7 "Can you *f* the mysteries of God?
Ps 145: 3 his greatness no one can *f.*
Ecc   3: 11 yet they cannot *f* what God has
Isa   40: 28 and his understanding no one
            can *f*
1Co   13: 2 and can *f* all mysteries and all

FATHOMED* (FATHOM)
Job   5: 9 performs wonders that cannot
            be *f,*
     9: 10 performs wonders that cannot
            be *f,*

FATTENED
Pr   15: 17 than a *f* calf with hatred.
Lk   15: 23 Bring the *f* calf and kill it.

FAULT (FAULTS)
1Sa   29: 3 I have found no *f* in him."
Mt   18: 15 and show him his *f,* just
Php   2: 15 of God without *f* in a crooked
Jas   1: 5 generously to all without finding *f,*
Jude : 24 his glorious presence without *f*

FAULTFINDERS*
Jude : 16 These men are grumblers and *f;*

FAULTLESS*
Pr   8: 9 they are *f* to those who have
Php   3: 6 as for legalistic righteousness, *f.*
Jas   1: 27 Father accepts as pure and *f* is
            this:

FAULTS* (FAULT)
Job   10: 6 that you must search out my *f*
Ps   19: 12 Forgive my hidden *f.*

FAVOR (FAVORITISM)
Ge   4: 4 The LORD looked with *f* on Abel
     6: 8 But Noah found *f* in the eyes
Ex   33: 12 and you have found *f* with me.'
    34: 9 if I have found *f* in your eyes,"
Lev   26: 9 " 'I will look on you with *f*
Nu   11: 15 if I have found *f* in your eyes—
Jdg   6: 17 "If now I have found *f* in your
            eyes,
1Sa   2: 26 in *f* with the LORD and with men.
2Sa   2: 6 and I too will show you the same *f*
2Ki   13: 4 Jehoahaz sought the LORD's *f,*
2Ch 33: 12 In his distress he sought the *f*
Est   7: 3 "If I have found *f* with you, O king,
Ps   90: 17 May the *f* of the Lord our God rest
Pr   8: 35 and receives *f* from the LORD.
    18: 22 and receives *f* from the LORD.
    19: 6 Many curry *f* with a ruler,
Isa   61: 2 proclaim the year of the LORD's *f*
Zec   11: 7 called one *F* and the other Union,
Lk   1: 30 Mary, you have found *f* with God.
     2: 14 to men on whom his *f* rests."
     2: 52 and in *f* with God and men.
     4: 19 to proclaim the year of the Lord's *f*
2Co   6: 2 now is the time of God's *f,*

FAVORITISM* (FAVOR)
Ex   23: 3 and do not show *f* to a poor man
Lev   19: 15 to the poor or *f* to the great,
Ac   10: 34 true it is that God does not show *f*
Ro   2: 11 For God does not show *f.*
Eph   6: 9 and there is no *f* with him.
Col   3: 25 for his wrong, and there is no *f.*
1Ti   5: 21 and to do nothing out of *f.*

Jas   2: 1 Lord Jesus Christ, don't show *f.*
     2: 9 But if you show *f,* you sin

FEAR (AFRAID FEARED FEARS FRIGHTENED GOD-
FEARING)
Dt   6: 13 *F* the LORD your God, serve him
    10: 12 but to *f* the LORD your God,
    31: 12 and learn to *f* the LORD your God
    31: 13 and learn to *f* the LORD your God
Jos   4: 24 you might always *f* the LORD
    24: 14 "Now *f* the LORD and serve him
1Sa 12: 14 If you *f* the LORD and serve
    12: 24 But be sure to *f* the LORD
2Sa 23: 3 when he rules in the *f* of God,
2Ch 19: 7 let the *f* of the LORD be upon you.
    26: 5 who instructed him in the *f* of
            God.
Job   1: 9 "Does Job *f* God for nothing?"
Ps   2: 11 Serve the LORD with *f*
    19: 9 The *f* of the LORD is pure,
    23: 4 I will *f* no evil,
    27: 1 whom shall I *f?*
    33: 8 Let all the earth *f* the LORD;
    34: 7 around those who *f* him,
    34: 9 *F* the LORD, you his saints,
    46: 2 Therefore we will not *f,*
    86: 11 that I may *f* your name.
    90: 11 great as the *f* that is due you.
    91: 5 You will not *f* the terror of night,
   111: 10 *f* of the LORD is the beginning
    118: 4 Let those who *f* the LORD say:
   128: 1 Blessed are all who *f* the LORD,
   145: 19 of those who *f* him;
   147: 11 delights in those who *f* him,
Pr   1: 7 *f* of the LORD is the beginning
     1: 33 and be at ease, without *f* of
            harm.
     8: 13 To *f* the LORD is to hate evil;
     9: 10 *f* of the LORD is the beginning
    10: 27 The *f* of the LORD adds length
    14: 27 The *f* of the LORD is a fountain
    15: 33 *f* of the LORD teaches a man
    16: 6 through the *f* of the LORD a man
    19: 23 The *f* of the LORD leads to life:
    22: 4 Humility and the *f* of the LORD
    29: 25 *F* of man will prove to be a snare,
    31: 21 she has no *f* for her household;
Ecc   12: 13 *F* God and keep his
Isa   11: 3 delight in the *f* of the LORD.
    33: 6 the *f* of the LORD is the key
    35: 4 "Be strong, do not *f;*
    41: 10 So do not *f,* for I am with you;
    41: 13 and says to you, Do not *f;*
    43: 1 *"F* not, for I have redeemed you;
    51: 7 Do not *f* the reproach of men
    54: 14 you will have nothing to *f.*
Jer   23: 8 It does not *f* when heat comes;
Lk   12: 5 I will show you whom you
            should *f:*
2Co   5: 11 we know what it is to *f* the Lord,
Php   2: 12 to work out your salvation with *f*
1Jn   4: 18 But perfect love drives out *f,*
Jude : 23 to others show mercy, mixed
            with *f*
Rev   14: 7 *"F* God and give him glory,

FEARED (FEAR)
Job   1: 1 he *f* God and shunned evil.
Ps   76: 7 You alone are to be *f.*
Mal   3: 16 those who *f* the LORD talked

FEARS (FEAR)
Job   1: 8 a man who *f* God and shuns evil."
     2: 3 a man who *f* God and shuns evil.
Ps   34: 4 he delivered me from all my *f.*
    112: 1 is the man who *f* the LORD,
Pr   14: 16 A wise man *f* the LORD
    14: 26 He who *f* the LORD has a secure
    31: 30 a woman who *f* the LORD is
2Co   7: 5 conflicts on the outside, *f* within.
1Jn   4: 18 The one who *f* is not made
            perfect

FEAST (FEASTING FEASTS)
Pr   15: 15 the cheerful heart has a
            continual *f.*
2Pe   2: 13 pleasures while they *f* with you.

FEASTING (FEAST)
Pr   17: 1 than a house full of *f,* with strife.

FEASTS (FEAST)
Am   5: 21 "I hate, I despise your religious *f;*
Jude : 12 men are blemishes at your love *f,*

FEATHERS
Ps   91: 4   He will cover you with his *f*,

FEEBLE
Job   4: 3   you have strengthened *f* hands.
Isa   35: 3   Strengthen the *f* hands,
Heb 12:12   strengthen your *f* arms

FEED (FEEDS)
Jn   21:15   Jesus said, "F my lambs."
       21:17   Jesus said, "F my sheep.
Ro   12:20   "If your enemy is hungry, *f* him;
Jude   :12   shepherds who *f* only themselves.

FEEDS (FEED)
Pr   15:14   but the mouth of a fool *f* on folly.
Mt   6:26   yet your heavenly Father *f* them.
Jn   6:57   so the one who *f* on me will live

FEEL
Jdg 16:26   me where I can *f* the pillars that
Ps 115: 7   they have hands, but cannot *f*,

FEET (FOOT)
Ru   3: 8   discovered a woman lying at his *f*.
Ps   8: 6   you put everything under his *f*:
       22:16   have pierced my hands and my *f*.
       40: 2   he set my *f* on a rock
       56:13   and my *f* from stumbling,
       66: 9   and kept our *f* from slipping.
       73: 2   as for me, my *f* had almost
                 slipped;
     110: 1   a footstool for your *f*."
     119:105   Your word is a lamp to my *f*
Pr   4:26   Make level paths for your *f*
Isa   52: 7   are the *f* of those who bring good
Da   2:33   its *f* partly of iron and partly
Na   1:15   the *f* of one who brings good
                 news,
Mt   10:14   shake the dust off your *f*
       22:44   enemies under your *f*.' '
Lk   1:79   to guide our *f* into the path of
                 peace
       20:43   a footstool for your *f*.' '
       24:39   Look at my hands and my *f*.
Jn   13: 5   and began to wash his disciples' *f*,
       13:14   also should wash one another's *f*.
Ro   10:15   "Their *f* are swift to shed blood;
       10:15   "How beautiful are the *f*
       16:20   will soon crush Satan under
                 your *f*.
1Co 12:21   And the head cannot say to the *f*,
       15:25   has put all his enemies under
                 his *f*.
Eph   1:22   God placed all things under his *f*
1Ti   5:10   washing the *f* of the saints,
Heb   1:13   a footstool for your *f*"?
        2: 8   and put everything under his *f*."
       12:13   "Make level paths for your *f*,"
Rev   1:15   His *f* were like bronze glowing

FELIX
     Governor before whom Paul was tried (Ac
     23:23–24:27).

FELLOWSHIP
Ex   20:24   burnt offerings and *f* offerings,
Lev   3: 1   If someone's offering is a *f*
                 offering,
1Co   1: 9   who has called you into *f*
        5: 2   out of your *f* the man who did
                 this?
2Co   6:14   what *f* can light have with
                 darkness
       13:14   and the *f* of the Holy Spirit be
Gal   2: 9   and Barnabas the right hand of *f*
Php   2: 1   if any *f* with the Spirit,
        3:10   the *f* of sharing in his sufferings,
1Jn   1: 3   And our *f* is with the Father
        1: 3   so that you also may have *f* with
                 us.
        1: 6   claim to have *f* with him yet walk
        1: 7   we have *f* with one another,

FEMALE
Ge   1:27   male and *f* he created them.
        5: 2   He created them male and *f*
Mt   19: 4   Creator 'made them male and *f*,'
Mk   10: 6   God 'made them male and *f*.'
Gal   3:28   *f*, for you are all one in Christ
                 Jesus

FEROCIOUS
Mt   7:15   but inwardly they are *f* wolves.

FERTILE (FERTILIZE)
Isa   32:15   and the desert becomes a *f* field,

FERTILIZE* (FERTILE)
Lk   13: 8   and I'll dig around it and *f* it.

FERVOR*
Ac   18:25   and he spoke with great *f*,
Ro   12:11   but keep your spiritual *f*, serving

FESTIVAL
1Co   5: 8   Therefore let us keep the *F*,
Col   2:16   or with regard to a religious *f*,

FESTUS
     Successor of Felix; sent Paul to Caesar
     (Ac 25–26).

FEVER
Job   30:30   my body burns with *f*.
Mt   8:14   mother-in-law lying in bed with
                 a *f*.
Lk   4:38   was suffering from a high *f*,
Jn   4:52   "The *f* left him yesterday
Ac   28: 8   suffering from *f* and dysentery.

FIELD (FIELDS)
Ge   4: 8   Abel, "Let's go out to the *f*."
Lev 19: 9   reap to the very edges of your *f*
       19:19   Do not plant your *f* with two kinds
Pr   31:16   She considers a *f* and buys it;
Isa   40: 6   glory is like the flowers of the *f*.
Mt   6:28   See how the lilies of the *f* grow.
        6:30   how God clothes the grass of
                 the *f*,
       13:38   *f* is the world, and the good seed
       13:44   is like treasure hidden in a *f*.
Lk   14:18   I have just bought a *f*, and I must
                 go
1Co   3: 9   you are God's *f*, God's building.
1Pe   1:24   glory is like the flowers of the *f*;

FIELDS (FIELD)
Ru   2: 2   go to the *f* and pick up the
                 leftover
Lk   2: 8   were shepherds living out in the *f*
Jn   4:35   open your eyes and look at the *f*!

FIG (FIGS SYCAMORE-FIG)
Ge   3: 7   so they sewed *f* leaves together
Jdg   9:10   "Next, the trees said to the *f* tree,
1Ki   4:25   man under his own vine and *f*
                 tree.
Pr   27:18   He who tends a *f* tree will eat its
Mic   4: 4   and under his own *f* tree,
Zec   3:10   to sit under his vine and *f* tree,'
Mt   21:19   Seeing a *f* tree by the road,
Lk   13: 6   "A man had a *f* tree, planted
Jas   3:12   brothers, can a *f* tree bear olives,
Rev   6:13   drop from a *f* tree when shaken

FIGHT (FIGHTING FIGHTS FOUGHT)
Ex   14:14   The LORD will *f* for you; you need
Dt   1:30   going before you, will *f* for you,
        3:22   the LORD your God himself will *f*
Ne   4:20   Our God will *f* for us!"
Ps   35: 1   *f* against those who *f* against me.
Jn   18:36   my servants would *f*
1Co   9:26   I do not *f* like a man beating the
                 air.
2Co 10: 4   The weapons we *f*
1Ti   1:18   them you may *f* the good *f*,
        6:12   Fight the good *f* of the faith.
2Ti   4: 7   fought the good *f*, I have finished

FIGHTING (FIGHT)
Jos   10:14   Surely the LORD was *f* for Israel!

FIGHTS (FIGHT)
Jos   23:10   the LORD your God *f* for you,
1Sa 25:28   because he *f* the LORD's battles.
Jas   4: 1   What causes *f* and quarrels

FIGS (FIG)
Lk   6:44   People do not pick *f*
Jas   3:12   grapevine bear *f*? Neither can a
                 salt

FILL (FILLED FILLING FILLS FULL FULLNESS FULLY)
Ge   1:28   and increase in number; *f* the
                 earth
Ps   16:11   you will *f* me with joy
       81:10   wide your mouth and I will *f* it.
Pr   28:19   who chases fantasies will have
                 his *f*
Hag   2: 7   and I will *f* this house with glory,'
Jn   6:26   you ate the loaves and had your *f*.
Ac   2:28   you will *f* me with joy
Ro   15:13   the God of hope *f* you with all joy

FILLED (FILL)
Ex   31: 3   I have *f* him with the Spirit of God,
       35:31   he has *f* him with the Spirit of
                 God,
Dt   34: 9   son of Nun was *f* with the spirit
1Ki   8:10   the cloud *f* the temple
        8:11   glory of the LORD *f* his temple.
2Ch   5:14   of the LORD *f* the temple of God.
        7: 1   the glory of the LORD *f* the temple
Ps   72:19   may the whole earth be *f*
     119:64   The earth is *f* with your love,
Isa   6: 4   and the temple was *f* with smoke.
Eze 10: 3   and a cloud *f* the inner court.
       10: 4   The cloud *f* the temple,
       43: 5   the glory of the LORD *f* the temple
Hab   2:14   For the earth will be *f*
        3: 3   and his praise *f* the earth.
Mt   5: 6   for they will be *f*.
Lk   1:15   and he will be *f* with the Holy
                 Spirit
        1:41   and Elizabeth was *f* with the Holy
        1:67   His father Zechariah was *f*
        2:40   and became strong; he was *f*
Jn   12: 3   the house was *f* with the
                 fragrance
Ac   2: 2   *f* the whole house where they
                 were
        2: 4   All of them were *f*
        4: 8   Then Peter, *f* with the Holy Spirit,
        4:31   they were all *f* with the Holy Spirit
        9:17   and be *f* with the Holy Spirit."
       13: 9   called Paul, *f* with the Holy Spirit,
Eph   5:18   Instead, be *f* with the Spirit.
Php   1:11   *f* with the fruit of righteousness
Rev 15: 8   And the temple was *f* with smoke

FILLING (FILL)
Eze 44: 4   the glory of the LORD *f* the temple

FILLS (FILL)
Nu   14:21   of the LORD *f* the whole earth,
Ps 107: 9   and *f* the hungry with good
                 things.
Eph   1:23   fullness of him who *f* everything

FILTH (FILTHY)
Isa   4: 4   The Lord will wash away the *f*
Jas   1:21   rid of all moral *f* and the evil that
                 is

FILTHY (FILTH)
Isa   64: 6   all our righteous acts are like *f*
                 rags;
Col   3: 8   and *f* language from your lips.
2Pe   2: 7   by the *f* lives of lawless men

FINAL (FINALITY)
Ps   73:17   then I understood their *f* destiny.

FINALITY* (FINAL)
Ro   9:28   on earth with speed and *f*."

FINANCIAL*
1Ti   6: 5   that godliness is a means to *f* gain.

FIND (FINDS FOUND)
Nu   32:23   be sure that your sin will *f* you
                 out.
Dt   4:29   you will *f* him if you look for him
1Sa 23:16   and helped him *f* strength in God.
Job 23: 3   If only I knew where to *f* him;
Ps   36: 7   *f* refuge in the shadow
       62: 5   F rest, O my soul, in God alone;
       91: 4   under his wings you will *f* refuge.
Pr   8:17   and those who seek me *f* me.
       14:22   those who plan what is good *f*
                 love
       20: 6   but a faithful man who can *f*
       24:14   if you *f* it, there is a future hope
       31:10   A wife of noble character who
                 can *f*
Jer   6:16   and you will *f* rest for your souls.
       29:13   and *f* me when you seek me
Mt   7: 7   seek and you will *f*; knock
       11:29   and you will *f* rest for your souls.
       16:25   loses his life for me will *f* it.
       22: 9   invite to the banquet anyone
                 you *f*.'
Lk   11: 9   seek and you will *f*; knock
       18: 8   will he *f* faith on the earth?"
Jn   10: 9   come in and go out, and *f* pasture.

FINDS (FIND)
Ps   62: 1   My soul *f* rest in God alone;
     112: 1   who *f* great delight
     119:162   like one who *f* great spoil.
Pr   3:13   Blessed is the man who *f* wisdom,

Pr	8:35	For whoever *f* me *f* life
	11:27	He who seeks good *f* good will,
	18:22	He who *f* a wife *f* what is good
Mt	7: 8	he who seeks *f*; and to him who
	10:39	Whoever *f* his life will lose it,
Lk	11:10	he who seeks *f*; and to him who
	12:37	whose master *f* them watching
	12:43	servant whom the master *f* doing
	15: 4	go after the lost sheep until he *f* it?
	15: 8	and search carefully until she *f* it?

FINE-SOUNDING* (SOUND)

Col	2: 4	may deceive you by *f* arguments.

FINGER

Ex	8:19	to Pharaoh, "This is the *f* of God."
	31:18	of stone inscribed by the *f* of God.
Dt	9:10	two stone tablets inscribed by the *f*
Lk	11:20	But if I drive out demons by the *f*
	16:24	to dip the tip of his *f* in water
Jn	8: 6	to write on the ground with his *f*.
	20:25	and put my *f* where the nails were,

FINISH (FINISHED)

Jn	4:34	him who sent me and to *f* his work.
	5:36	that the Father has given me to *f*,
Ac	20:24	if only I may *f* the race
2Co	8:11	Now *f* the work, so that your eager
Jas	1: 4	Perseverance must *f* its work

FINISHED (FINISH)

Ge	2: 2	seventh day God had *f* the work he
Jn	19:30	the drink, Jesus said, "It is *f*."
2Ti	4: 7	I have *f* the race, I have kept

FIRE

Ex	3: 2	in flames of *f* from within a bush.
	13:21	in a pillar of *f* to give them light,
Lev	6:12	on the altar must be kept burning;
	9:24	*F* came out from the presence
1Ki	18:38	Then the *f* of the Lᴏʀᴅ fell
2Ki	2:11	suddenly a chariot of *f*
Isa	5:24	as tongues of *f* lick up straw
	30:27	and his tongue is a consuming *f*.
Jer	23:29	my word like *f*," declares
Da	3:25	four men walking around in the *f*,
Zec	3: 2	stick snatched from the *f*?"
Mal	3: 2	For he will be like a refiner's *f*
Mt	3:11	you with the Holy Spirit and with *f*.
	3:12	the chaff with unquenchable *f*."
	5:22	will be in danger of the *f* of hell.
	18: 8	and be thrown into eternal *f*.
	25:41	into the eternal *f* prepared
Mk	9:43	where the *f* never goes out.
	9:48	and the *f* is not quenched.'
	9:49	Everyone will be salted with *f*.
Lk	3:16	you with the Holy Spirit and with *f*.
	12:49	I have come to bring *f* on the earth,
Ac	2: 3	to be tongues of *f* that separated
1Co	3:13	It will be revealed with *f*,
1Th	5:19	Do not put out the Spirit's *f*;
Heb	12:29	for our "God is a consuming *f*."
Jas	3: 5	set on *f* by a small spark.
	3: 6	also is a *f*, a world of evil
2Pe	3:10	the elements will be destroyed by *f*,
Jude	: 7	suffer the punishment of eternal *f*.
	:23	snatch others from the *f*
Rev	1:14	and his eyes were like blazing *f*.
	20:14	The lake of *f* is the second death.

FIRM*

Ex	14:13	Stand *f* and you will see
	15: 8	surging waters stood *f* like a wall;
Jos	3:17	the covenant of the Lᴏʀᴅ stood *f*
2Ch	20:17	stand *f* and see the deliverance
Ezr	9: 8	giving us a *f* place in his sanctuary,
Job	11:15	you will stand *f* and without fear.
	36: 5	he is mighty, and *f* in his purpose.
	41:23	they are *f* and immovable.
Ps	20: 8	but we rise up and stand *f*.
	30: 7	you made my mountain stand *f*;
	33: 9	he commanded, and it stood *f*.
	33:11	of the Lᴏʀᴅ stand *f* forever,
	37:23	he makes his steps *f*;

Ps	40: 2	and gave me a *f* place to stand.
	75: 3	it is I who hold its pillars *f*.
	78:13	made the water stand *f* like a wall.
	89: 2	that your love stands *f* forever,
	89: 4	and make your throne *f*
	93: 5	Your statutes stand *f*;
	119:89	it stands *f* in the heavens.
Pr	4:26	and take only ways that are *f*.
	10:25	but the righteous stand *f* forever.
	12: 7	the house of the righteous stands *f*.
Isa	7: 9	If you do not stand *f* in your faith,
	22:17	about to take *f* hold of you
	22:23	drive him like a peg into a *f* place;
	22:25	into the *f* place will give way;
Eze	2: 5	so that it will stand *f* in the battle
Zec	8:23	nations will take *f* hold of one Jew
Mt	10:22	he who stands *f* to the end will be
	24:13	he who stands *f* to the end will be
Mk	13:13	he who stands *f* to the end will be
Lk	21:19	By standing *f* you will gain life.
1Co	10:12	So, if you think you are standing *f*,
	15:58	my dear brothers, stand *f*.
	16:13	on your guard; stand *f* in the faith;
2Co	1: 7	for you is *f*, because we know that
	1:21	who makes both us and you stand *f*
	1:24	because it is by faith you stand *f*.
Gal	5: 1	Stand *f*, then, and do not let
Eph	6:14	Stand *f* then, with the belt
Php	1:27	I will know that you stand *f*
	4: 1	that is how you should stand *f*
Col	1:23	in your faith, established and *f*,
	2: 5	and how *f* your faith in Christ is.
	4:12	that you may stand *f* in all the will
1Th	3: 8	since you are standing *f* in the Lord
2Th	2:15	stand *f* and hold to the teachings
1Ti	6:19	a *f* foundation for the coming age,
2Ti	2:19	God's solid foundation stands *f*,
Heb	6:19	an anchor for the soul, *f* and secure
Jas	5: 8	You too, be patient and stand *f*,
1Pe	5: 9	Resist him, standing *f* in the faith,
	5:10	make you strong, *f* and steadfast.

FIRST

Ge	1: 5	and there was morning—the *f* day.
	13: 4	and where he had *f* built an altar.
Ex	34:19	*f* offspring of every womb belongs
1Ki	22: 5	"*F* seek the counsel of the Lᴏʀᴅ."
Pr	18:17	*f* to present his case seems right,
Isa	44: 6	I am the *f* and I am the last;
	48:12	I am the *f* and I am the last.
Mt	5:24	*F* go and be reconciled
	6:33	But seek *f* his kingdom
	7: 5	*f* take the plank out
	19:30	But many who are *f* will be last,
	20:16	last will be *f*, and the *f* will be last."
	20:27	wants to be *f* must be your slave—
	22:38	This is the *f* and greatest
	23:26	*F* clean the inside of the cup
Mk	9:35	to be *f*, he must be the very last,
	10:31	are *f* will be last, and the last *f*."
	10:44	wants to be *f* must be slave
	13:10	And the gospel must *f* be preached
Lk	13:30	*f*, and *f* who will be last."
Jn	8: 7	let him be the *f* to throw a stone
Ac	11:26	disciples were called Christians *f*
Ro	1:16	*f* for the Jew, then for the Gentile.
	1:17	is by faith from *f* to last,
	2: 9	*f* for the Jew, then for the Gentile;
	2:10	*f* for the Jew, then for the Gentile.
1Co	12:28	in the church God has appointed *f*
	15:45	"The *f* man Adam became a living
2Co	8: 5	they gave themselves *f* to the Lord
Eph	6: 2	which is the *f* commandment
1Th	4:16	and the dead in Christ will rise *f*.
1Ti	2:13	For Adam was formed *f*, then Eve.
Heb	10: 9	He sets aside the *f*
Jas	3:17	comes from heaven is *f* of all pure;
1Jn	4:19	We love because he *f* loved us.
3Jn	: 9	but Diotrephes, who loves to be *f*,
Rev	1:17	I am the *F* and the Last.
	2: 4	You have forsaken your *f* love.
	22:13	and the Omega, the *F* and the Last,

FIRSTBORN (BEAR)

Ex	11: 5	Every *f* son in Egypt will die,
	34:20	Redeem all your *f* sons.
Ps	89:27	I will also appoint him my *f*,
Lk	2: 7	and she gave birth to her *f*, a son.
Ro	8:29	that he might be the *f*
Col	1:15	image of the invisible God, the *f*
	1:18	and the *f* from among the dead,
Heb	1: 6	when God brings his *f*
	12:23	of the *f*, whose names are written
Rev	1: 5	who is the faithful witness, the *f*

FIRSTFRUITS

Ex	23:16	the Feast of Harvest with the *f*
	23:19	"Bring the best of the *f* of your soil
Ro	8:23	who have the *f* of the Spirit,
1Co	15:23	Christ, the *f*; then, when he comes,
Rev	14: 4	offered as *f* to God and the Lamb.

FISH (FISHERS)

Ge	1:26	let them rule over the *f* of the sea
Jnh	1:17	But the Lᴏʀᴅ provided a great *f*
Mt	7:10	asks for a *f*, will give him a snake?
	12:40	three nights in the belly of a huge *f*,
	14:17	loaves of bread and two *f*,"
Mk	6:38	they said, "Five—and two *f*."
Lk	5: 6	of *f* that their nets began to break.
	9:13	loaves of bread and two *f*—
Jn	6: 9	small barley loaves and two small *f*,
	21: 5	haven't you any *f*?" "No,"
	21:11	It was full of large *f*, 153, but

FISHERMEN

Mk	1:16	a net into the lake, for they were *f*.

FISHERS (FISH)

Mt	4:19	"and I will make you *f* of men."
Mk	1:17	"and I will make you *f* of men."

FISHHOOK*

Job	41: 1	pull in the leviathan with a *f*

FISTS

Mt	26:67	and struck him with their *f*.

FIT (FITTING)

Jdg	17: 6	no king; everyone did as he saw *f*.
	21:25	no king; everyone did as he saw *f*.

FITTING* (FIT)

Ps	33: 1	it is *f* for the upright to praise him.
	147: 1	how pleasant and *f* to praise him!
Pr	10:32	of the righteous know what is *f*,
	19:10	It is not *f* for a fool to live in luxury
	26: 1	honor is not *f* for a fool.
1Co	14:40	everything should be done in a *f*
Col	3:18	to your husbands, as is *f* in the Lord
Heb	2:10	sons to glory, it was *f* that God,

FIX* (FIXED)

Dt	11:18	*F* these words of mine
Job	14: 3	Do you *f* your eye on such a one?
Pr	4:25	*f* your gaze directly before you.
Isa	46: 8	"Remember this, *f* it in mind,
Am	9: 4	I will *f* my eyes upon them
2Co	4:18	we *f* our eyes not on what is seen,
Heb	3: 1	heavenly calling, *f* your thoughts
	12: 2	Let us *f* our eyes on Jesus,

FIXED* (FIX)

2Ki	8:11	stared at him with a *f* gaze
Job	38:10	when I *f* limits for it
Ps	141: 8	my eyes are *f* on you, O Sovereign
Pr	8:28	*f* securely the fountains of the deep
Jer	33:25	and night and the *f* laws of heaven
Lk	16:26	and you a great chasm has been *f*,

FLAME (FLAMES FLAMING)

2Ti	1: 6	you to fan into *f* the gift of God,

FLAMES (FLAME)

1Co	3:15	only as one escaping through the *f*.
	13: 3	and surrender my body to the *f*,

FLAMING (FLAME)

Eph	6:16	you can extinguish all the *f* arrows

FLANK

Eze	34:21	Because you shove with *f*

FLASH

1Co	15:52	in a *f*, in the twinkling of an eye,

FLATTER* (FLATTERING FLATTERS FLATTERY)
Job 32:21 nor will I f any man;
Ps 78:36 But then they would f him
Jude :16 f others for their own advantage.

FLATTERING* (FLATTER)
Ps 12: 2 their f lips speak with deception.
    12: 3 May the LORD cut off all f lips
Pr 26:28 and a f mouth works ruin.
    28:23 than he who has a f tongue.
Eze 12:24 or f divinations among the people

FLATTERS* (FLATTER)
Ps 36: 2 For in his own eyes he f himself
Pr 29: 5 Whoever f his neighbor

FLATTERY* (FLATTER)
Job 32:22 for if I were skilled in f,
Da 11:32 With f he will corrupt those who
Ro 16:18 and f they deceive the minds
1Th 2: 5 You know we never used f.

FLAWLESS*
2Sa 22:31 the word of the LORD is f.
Job 11: 4 You say to God, 'My beliefs are f
Ps 12: 6 And the words of the LORD are f,
    18:30 the word of the LORD is f.
Pr 30: 5 "Every word of God is f;
SS   5: 2 my dove, my f one.

FLEE (FLEES)
Ps 139: 7 Where can I f from your presence?
1Co 6:18 F from sexual immorality.
    10:14 my dear friends, f from idolatry.
1Ti 6:11 But you, man of God, f from all
           this
2Ti 2:22 F the evil desires of youth,
Jas 4: 7 Resist the devil, and he will f

FLEECE
Jdg 6:37 I will place a wool f

FLEES (FLEE)
Pr 28: 1 The wicked man f though no one

FLEETING*
Job 14: 2 like a f shadow, he does not
           endure
Ps 39: 4 let me know how f is my life.
    89:47 Remember how f is my life.
   144: 4 his days are like a f shadow.
Pr 21: 6 is a f vapor and a deadly snare.
    31:30 Charm is deceptive, and beauty
           is f

FLESH
Ge   2:23 and f of my f;
     2:24 and they will become one f.
2Ch 32: 8 With him is only the arm of f,
Job 19:26 yet in my f I will see God;
Eze 11:19 of stone and give them a heart
           of f.
    36:26 of stone and give you a heart of f.
Mt 19: 5 and the two will become one f'?
Mk 10: 8 and the two will become one f.
Jn   1:14 The Word became f and made his
     6:51 This bread is my f, which I will
           give
1Co 6:16 "The two will become one f."
    15:39 All f is not the same: Men have
           one
Eph 5:31 and the two will become one f."
     6:12 For our struggle is not against f
Php 3: 2 do evil, those mutilators of the f.
1Jn 4: 2 come in the f is from God,
Jude :23 the clothing stained by
           corrupted f.

FLIGHT
Dt 32:30 or two put ten thousand to f,

FLINT
Isa 50: 7 Therefore have I set my face like f.
Zec 7:12 They made their hearts as hard
           as f

FLIRTING*
Isa 3:16 f with their eyes,

FLOCK (FLOCKS)
Ps 77:20 You led your people like a f
    78:52 he brought his people out like a f;
    95: 7 the f under his care.
Isa 40:11 He tends his f like a shepherd:
Jer 10:21 and all their f is scattered.
    23: 2 "Because you have scattered my f
    31:10 watch over his f like a shepherd.'
Eze 34: 2 not shepherds take care of the f?
Zec 11:17 who deserts the f!

FLOCK (continued)
Mt 26:31 the sheep of the f will be
           scattered.'
Lk 12:32 little f, for your Father has been
Jn 10:16 shall be one f and one shepherd.
Ac 20:28 all the f of which the Holy Spirit
1Co 9: 7 Who tends a f and does not drink
1Pe 5: 2 Be shepherds of God's f that is
     5: 3 but being examples to the f.

FLOCKS (FLOCK)
Lk   2: 8 keeping watch over their f at
           night.

FLOG (FLOGGED FLOGGING)
Pr 19:25 F a mocker, and the simple will
Ac 22:25 to f a Roman citizen who hasn't

FLOGGED (FLOG)
Jn 19: 1 Pilate took Jesus and had him f.
Ac   5:40 the apostles in and had them f.
    16:23 After they had been severely f,
2Co 11:23 frequently, been f more severely,

FLOGGING (FLOG)
Heb 11:36 f, while still others were chained

FLOOD (FLOODGATES)
Ge   7: 7 ark to escape the waters of the f.
Mal 2:13 You f the LORD's altar with tears.
Mt 24:38 For in the days before the f,
2Pe 2: 5 world when he brought the f

FLOODGATES (FLOOD)
Ge   7:11 the f of the heavens were opened.
Mal 3:10 see if I will not throw open the f

FLOOR
Jas 2: 3 or "Sit on the f by my feet,"

FLOUR
Lev 2: 1 his offering is to be of fine f.
Nu   7:13 filled with fine f mixed with oil
    28: 9 of an ephah of fine f mixed with
           oil.

FLOURISH (FLOURISHES FLOURISHING)
Ps   7: 7 In his days the righteous will f;
    92: 7 and all evildoers f,
    92:12 The righteous will f like a palm
           tree
Pr 14:11 but the tent of the upright will f.

FLOURISHES (FLOURISH)
Pr 12:12 but the root of the righteous f.

FLOURISHING (FLOURISH)
Ps 52: 8 f in the house of God;

FLOW (FLOWING)
Nu 13:27 and it does f with milk and honey!
Jn   7:38 streams of living water will f

FLOWER (FLOWERS)
Job 14: 2 up like a f and withers away;
Ps 103:15 he flourishes like a f of the field;
Jas 1:10 he will pass away like a wild f.

FLOWERS (FLOWER)
Isa 40: 6 and all their glory is like the f
    40: 7 The grass withers and the f fall,
1Pe 1:24 and all their glory is like the f

FLOWING (FLOW)
Ex   3: 8 a land f with milk and honey—
     33: 3 Go up to the land f with milk
Nu 16:14 us into a land f with milk
Jos 5: 6 a land f with milk and honey.
Ps 107:33 f springs into thirsty ground,
   107:35 the parched ground into f springs;
Jer 32:22 a land f with milk and honey.
Eze 20: 6 a land f with milk and honey,
Rev 22: 1 f from the throne of God

FLUTE
Ps 150: 4 praise him with the strings and f,
Mt 11:17 " 'We played the f for you,
1Co 14: 7 that make sounds, such as the f

FOAL*
Zec 9: 9 on a colt, the f of a donkey.
Mt 21: 5 on a colt, the f of a donkey.' "

FOILS*
Ps 33:10 The LORD f the plans
Isa 44:25 who f the signs of false prophets

FOLDING* (FOLDING)
Pr   6:10 a little f of the hands to rest—
    24:33 a little f of the hands to rest—

FOLDS (FOLDING)
Ecc 4: 5 The fool f his hands

FOLLOW (FOLLOWED FOLLOWING FOLLOWS)
Ex 23: 2 Do not f the crowd in doing
           wrong.
Lev 18: 4 and be careful to f my decrees.
Dt   5: 1 Learn them and be sure to f them.
    17:19 f carefully all the words of this law
1Ki 11: 6 he did not f the LORD completely,
2Ch 34:33 they did not fail to f the LORD,
Ps 23: 6 Surely goodness and love will f me
   119:166 and I f your commands.
Mt   4:19 f me," Jesus said, "and I will make
     8:19 I will f you wherever you go."
     8:22 But Jesus told him, "F me,
    16:24 and take up his cross and f me.
    19:27 "We have left everything to f you!
Lk   9:23 take up his cross daily and f me.
     9:61 Still another said, "I will f you,
Jn 10: 4 his sheep f him because they
           know
    10: 5 But they will never f a stranger;
    10:27 I know them, and they f me.
    12:26 Whoever serves me must f me;
    21:19 Then he said to him, "F me!"
1Co 1:12 One of you says, "I f Paul";
    11: 1 F my example, as I follow
    14: 1 F the way of love and eagerly
2Th 3: 9 ourselves a model for you to f
1Pe 2:21 that you should f in his steps.
Rev 14: 4 They f the Lamb wherever he
           goes.

FOLLOWED (FOLLOW)
Nu 32:11 they have not f me
           wholeheartedly,
Dt   1:36 he f the LORD wholeheartedly."
Jos 14:14 he f the LORD, the God of Israel,
2Ch 10:14 he f the advice of the young men
Mt   4:20 once they left their nets and f
           him.
     9: 9 and Matthew got up and f him.
    26:58 But Peter f him at a distance,
Lk 18:43 he received his sight and f Jesus,

FOLLOWING (FOLLOW)
Ps 119:14 I rejoice in f your statutes
Php 3:17 Join with others in f my example,
1Ti 1:18 by f them you may fight the good

FOLLOWS (FOLLOW)
Jn   8:12 Whoever f me will never walk

FOLLY (FOOL)
Pr 14:29 a quick-tempered man displays f.
    19: 3 A man's own f ruins his life,
Ecc 10: 1 so a little f outweighs wisdom
Mk   7:22 envy, slander, arrogance and f.
2Ti 3: 9 their f will be clear to everyone.

FOOD (FOODS)
Ge   1:30 I give every green plant for f."
Pr 12: 9 to be somebody and have no f.
    12:11 his land will have abundant f,
    20:13 you will have f to spare.
    20:17 F gained by fraud tastes sweet
    21:20 of the wise are stores of choice f
    22: 9 for he shares his f with the poor.
    23: 3 for that f is deceptive.
    23: 6 Do not eat the f of a stingy man,
    25:21 If your enemy is hungry, give him f
    31:14 bringing her f from afar.
    31:15 she provides f for her family
Isa 58: 7 not to share your f with the
           hungry
Eze 18: 7 but gives his f to the hungry
Da   1: 8 to defile himself with the royal f
Mt   3: 4 His f was locusts and wild honey.
     6:25 Is not life more important than f,
Jn   4:32 "I have f to eat that you know
     4:34 have brought him f?" "My f,
     6:27 Do not work for f that spoils,
     6:55 my flesh is real f and my blood is
Ac 15:20 to abstain from f polluted by idols,
Ro 14:14 fully convinced that no f is
           unclean
1Co 8: 1 Now about f sacrificed to idols:
     8: 8 But f does not bring us near to
           God
2Co 11:27 have often gone without f;
1Ti 6: 8 But if we have f and clothing,
Heb 5:14 But solid f is for the mature,
Jas 2:15 sister is without clothes and
           daily f.

FOODS (FOOD)
Mk   7:19 Jesus declared all f "clean.")

FOOL (FOLLY FOOL'S FOOLISH FOOLISHNESS FOOLS)
1Sa 25:25 his name is *F,* and folly goes
Ps 14: 1 The *f* says in his heart,
Pr 10:10 and a chattering *f* comes to ruin.
    10:18 and whoever spreads slander is a *f.*
    12:15 The way of a *f* seems right to him,
    12:16 A *f* shows his annoyance at once,
    14:16 but a *f* is hotheaded and reckless.
    15: 5 A *f* spurns his father's discipline,
    17:12 than a *f* in his folly.
    17:16 use is money in the hand of a *f,*
    17:21 To have a *f* for a son brings grief;
    17:28 Even a *f* is thought wise
    18: 2 A *f* finds no pleasure
    20: 3 but every *f* is quick to quarrel.
    23: 9 Do not speak to a *f,*
    24: 7 Wisdom is too high for a *f;*
    26: 4 Do not answer a *f* according
    26: 5 Answer a *f* according to his folly,
    26: 7 is a proverb in the mouth of a *f.*
    26:11 so a *f* repeats his folly.
    26:12 for a *f* than for him.
    27:22 Though you grind a *f* in a mortar,
    28:26 He who trusts in himself is a *f,*
    29:11 A *f* gives full vent to his anger,
    29:20 for a *f* than for him.
Mt 5:22 But anyone who says, 'You *f!'*
Lk 12:20 "But God said to him, 'You *f!*
1Co 3:18 he should become a "*f*"
2Co 11:21 I am speaking as a *f*— I

FOOL'S (FOOL)
Pr 14: 3 A *f* talk brings a rod to his back,
    18: 7 A *f* mouth is his undoing,

FOOLISH (FOOL)
Pr 10: 1 but a *f* son grief to his mother.
    14: 1 her own hands the *f* one tears hers
    15:20 but a *f* man despises his mother.
    17:25 A *f* son brings grief to his father
    19:13 A *f* son is his father's ruin,
Mt 7:26 practice is like a *f* man who built
    25: 2 of them were *f* and five were wise.
Lk 11:40 You *f* people! Did not the one who
    24:25 He said to them, "How *f* you are,
1Co 1:20 Has not God made the wisdom
    1:27 God chose the *f* things of the world
Gal 3: 1 died for nothing!" You *f* Galatians!
Eph 5: 4 should there be obscenity, *f* talk
    5:17 Therefore do not be *f,*
Tit 3: 9 But avoid *f* controversies

FOOLISHNESS (FOOL)
1Co 1:18 of the cross is *f* to those who are
    1:21 through the *f* of what was preached
    1:23 block to Jews and *f* to Gentiles,
    1:25 For the *f* of God is wiser
    2:14 for they are *f* to him, and he cannot
    3:19 of this world is *f* in God's sight.

FOOLS (FOOL)
Pr 1: 7 but *f* despise wisdom and discipline
    3:35 but *f* he holds up to shame.
    12:23 but the heart of *f* blurts out folly.
    13:19 but *f* detest turning from evil.
    13:20 but a companion of *f* suffers harm.
    14: 9 *F* mock at making amends for sin,
    14:24 but the folly of *f* yields folly.
Ecc 7: 5 than to listen to the song of *f.*
    7: 6 so is the laughter of *f.*
    10: 6 *F* are put in many high positions,
Mt 23:17 You blind *f!* Which is greater:
Ro 1:22 they became *f* and exchanged
1Co 4:10 We are *f* for Christ, but you are

FOOT (FEET FOOTHOLD)
Jos 1: 3 every place where you set your *f,*
Ps 121: 3 He will not let your *f* slip—
Pr 3:23 and your *f* will not stumble;
    4:27 keep your *f* from evil.
    25:17 Seldom set *f* in your neighbor's
Isa 1: 6 From the sole of your *f* to the top
Mt 18: 8 or your *f* causes you to sin,
Lk 4:11 so that you will not strike your *f*
1Co 12:15 If the *f* should say, "Because I am
Rev 10: 2 He planted his right *f* on the sea

FOOTHOLD* (FOOT)
Ps 69: 2 where there is no *f.*
    73: 2 I had nearly lost my *f.*
Eph 4:27 and do not give the devil a *f.*

FOOTSTEPS (STEP)
Ps 119:133 Direct my *f* according

FOOTSTOOL
Ps 99: 5 and worship at his *f;*
    110: 1 a *f* for your feet."
Isa 66: 1 and the earth is my *f.*
Mt 5:35 for it is his *f;* or by Jerusalem,
Ac 7:49 and the earth is my *f.*
Heb 1:13 a *f* for your feet"?
    10:13 for his enemies to be made his *f,*

FORBEARANCE*
Ro 3:25 because in his *f* he had left the sins

FORBID
1Co 14:39 and do not *f* speaking in tongues.
1Ti 4: 3 They *f* people to marry

FORCE (FORCED FORCEFUL FORCES FORCING)
Jn 6:15 to come and make him king by *f,*
Ac 26:11 and I tried to *f* them to blaspheme.
Gal 2:14 that you *f* Gentiles

FORCED (FORCE)
Mt 27:32 and they *f* him to carry the cross.
Phm :14 do will be spontaneous and not *f.*

FORCEFUL* (FORCE)
Mt 11:12 forcefully advancing, and *f* men lay
2Co 10:10 "His letters are weighty and *f,*

FORCES (FORCE)
Mt 5:41 If someone *f* you to go one mile,
Eph 6:12 and against the spiritual *f* of evil

FORCING (FORCE)
Lk 16:16 and everyone is *f* his way into it.

FOREFATHERS (FATHER)
Heb 1: 1 spoke to our *f* through the prophets
1Pe 1:18 handed down to you from your *f,*

FOREHEAD (FOREHEADS)
Ex 13: 9 a reminder on your *f* that the law
    13:16 on your *f* that the LORD brought
1Sa 17:49 and struck the Philistine on the *f.*
Rev 13:16 a mark on his right hand or on his *f,*

FOREHEADS (FOREHEAD)
Dt 6: 8 hands and bind them on your *f.*
Rev 9: 4 not have the seal of God on their *f.*
    14: 1 his Father's name written on their *f*

FOREIGN (FOREIGNER FOREIGNERS)
Ge 35: 2 "Get rid of the *f* gods you have
2Ch 14: 3 He removed the *f* altars
    33:15 He got rid of the *f* gods
Isa 28:11 with *f* lips and strange tongues

FOREIGNER (FOREIGN)
Lk 17:18 give praise to God except this *f?*"
1Co 14:11 I am a *f* to the speaker,

FOREIGNERS (FOREIGN)
Eph 2:12 *f* to the covenants of the promise,
    2:19 you are no longer *f* and aliens,

FOREKNEW* (KNOW)
Ro 8:29 For those God *f* he
    11: 2 not reject his people, whom he *f.*

FOREKNOWLEDGE* (KNOW)
Ac 2:23 to you by God's set purpose and *f;*
1Pe 1: 2 to the *f* of God the Father,

FORESAW*
Gal 3: 8 Scripture *f* that God would justify

FOREST
Jas 3: 5 Consider what a great *f* is set

FOREVER (EVER)
Ge 3:22 the tree of life and eat, and live *f.*"
    6: 3 Spirit will not contend with man *f,*
Ex 3:15 This is my name *f,* the name
2Sa 7:26 so that your name will be great *f.*
1Ki 2:33 may there be the LORD's peace *f.*"
    9: 3 by putting my Name there *f.*
1Ch 16:15 He remembers his covenant *f,*
    16:34 his love endures *f.*
    16:41 "for his love endures *f.*"

1Ch 17:24 and that your name will be great *f.*
2Ch 5:13 his love endures *f.*"
    20:21 for his love endures *f.*"
Ps 9: 7 The LORD reigns *f;*
    23: 6 dwell in the house of the LORD *f.*
    28: 9 be their shepherd and carry them *f.*
    29:10 the LORD is enthroned as King *f.*
    33:11 the plans of the LORD stand firm *f,*
    37:28 They will be protected *f,*
    44: 8 and we will praise your name *f.*
    61: 4 I long to dwell in your tent *f*
    72:19 Praise be to his glorious name *f;*
    73:26 and my portion *f.*
    77: 8 Has his unfailing love vanished *f?*
    79:13 will praise you *f;*
    81:15 and their punishment would last *f.*
    86:12 I will glorify your name *f.*
    89: 1 of the LORD's great love *f;*
    92: 8 But you, O LORD, are exalted *f.*
    100: 5 is good and his love endures *f;*
    102:12 But you, O LORD, sit enthroned *f;*
    104:31 of the LORD endure *f;*
    107: 1 his love endures *f.*
    110: 4 "You are a priest *f,*
    111: 3 and his righteousness endures *f.*
    112: 6 man will be remembered *f.*
    117: 2 of the LORD endures *f.*
    118: 1 his love endures *f.*
    119:111 Your statutes are my heritage *f;*
    119:152 that you established them to last *f.*
    136: 1 *His love endures* f.
    146: 6 the LORD, who remains faithful *f.*
Pr 10:25 but the righteous stand firm *f.*
    27:24 for riches do not endure *f,*
Isa 25: 8 he will swallow up death *f.*
    26: 4 Trust in the LORD *f,*
    32:17 will be quietness and confidence *f.*
    40: 8 but the word of our God stands *f.*"
    51: 6 But my salvation will last *f,*
    51: 8 But my righteousness will last *f,*
    57:15 he who lives *f,* whose name is holy:
    59:21 from this time on and *f,*"
Jer 33:11 his love endures *f.*"
Eze 37:26 put my sanctuary among them *f.*
Da 2:44 to an end, but it will itself endure *f.*
    3: 9 live *f!* You have issued a decree,
Jn 6:51 eats of this bread, he will live *f.*
    14:16 Counselor to be with you *f*—
Ro 9: 5 who is God over all, *f* praised!
    16:27 to the only wise God be glory *f*
1Co 9:25 it to get a crown that will last *f.*
1Th 4:17 And so we will be with the Lord *f.*
Heb 5: 6 "You are a priest *f,*
    7:17 "You are a priest *f,*
    7:24 Jesus lives *f,* he has a permanent
    13: 8 same yesterday and today and *f.*
1Pe 1:25 but the word of the Lord stands *f.*"
1Jn 2:17 who does the will of God lives *f.*
2Jn : 2 lives in us and will be with us *f:*

FOREVERMORE (EVER)
Ps 113: 2 both now and *f.*

FORFEIT
Mk 8:36 the whole world, yet *f* his soul?
Lk 9:25 and yet lose or *f* his very self?

FORGAVE (FORGIVE)
Ps 32: 5 and you *f*
    65: 3 you *f* our transgressions
    78:38 you *f* their iniquities
Eph 4:32 just as in Christ God *f* you.
Col 2:13 He *f* us all our sins, having
    3:13 Forgive as the Lord *f* you.

FORGET (FORGETS FORGETTING FORGOT FORGOTTEN)
Dt 4:23 Be careful not to *f* the covenant
    6:12 that you do not *f* the LORD,
2Ki 17:38 Do not *f* the covenant I have made
Ps 9:17 all the nations that *f* God.
    10:12 Do not *f* the helpless.
    50:22 "Consider this, you who *f* God,
    78: 7 and would not *f* his deeds
    103: 2 and *f* not all his benefits.
    119: 93 I will never *f* your precepts,

Ps 137: 5 may my right hand *f* its skill.
Pr   3: 1 My son, do not *f* my teaching,
       4: 5 do not *f* my words or swerve
Isa 49:15 "Can a mother *f* the baby
   51:13 that you *f* the LORD your Maker,
Jer   2:32 Does a maiden *f* her jewelry,
   23:39 I will surely *f* you and cast you out
Heb 6:10 he will not *f* your work
   13: 2 Do not *f* to entertain strangers,
   13:16 And do not *f* to do good
2Pe   3: 8 But do not *f* this one thing,

FORGETS (FORGET)
Jn   16:21 her baby is born she *f* the anguish
Jas   1:24 immediately *f* what he looks like.

FORGETTING* (FORGET)
Php   3:13 *F* what is behind and straining
Jas   1:25 to do this, not *f* what he has
      heard,

FORGIVE* (FORGAVE FORGIVENESS FORGIVES FORGIVING)
Ge 50:17 I ask you to *f* your brothers the
      sins
   50:17 please *f* the sins of the servants
Ex   10:17 Now *f* my sin once more
   23:21 he will not *f* your rebellion,
   32:32 But now, please *f* their sin—
     34: 9 *f* our wickedness and our sin,
Nu 14:19 with your great love, *f* the sin
Dt   29:20 will never be willing to *f* him;
Jos 24:19 He will not *f* your rebellion
1Sa 15:25 *f* my sin and come back with me,
   25:28 Please *f* your servant's offense.
1Ki   8:30 place, and when you hear, *f*.
    8:34 and *f* the sin of your people Israel
    8:36 and *f* the sin of your servants,
    8:39 *F* and act; deal with each man
    8:50 *f* all the offenses they have
    8:50 *f* your people, who have sinned
2Ki   5:18 But may the LORD *f* your servant
    5:18 may the LORD *f* your servant
   24: 4 and the LORD was not willing to *f*
2Ch   6:21 place; and when you hear, *f*.
    6:25 and *f* the sin of your people Israel
    6:27 and *f* the sin of your servants,
    6:30 *F*, and deal with each man
    6:39 *f* your people, who have sinned
    7:14 will *f* their sin and will heal their
Job   7:21 and *f* my sins?
Ps   19:12 *f* my hidden faults.
   25:11 *f* my iniquity, though it is great.
   79: 9 deliver us and *f* our sins
Isa   2: 9 do not *f* them.
Jer   5: 1 I will *f* this city.
    5: 7 "Why should I *f* you?
   18:23 Do not *f* their crimes
   31:34 "For I will *f* their wickedness
   33: 8 and will *f* all their sins of rebellion
   36: 3 then I will *f* their wickedness
   50:20 for I will *f* the remnant I spare.
Da   9:19 O Lord, listen! O Lord, *f*! O Lord,
Hos   1: 6 that I should at all *f* them.
   14: 2 "*F* all our sins
Am   7: 2 *f*! How can Jacob survive?
Mt   6:12 *F* us our debts,
    6:14 For if you *f* men when they sin
    6:14 heavenly Father will also *f* you.
    6:15 But if you do not *f* men their sins,
    6:15 your Father will not *f* your sins.
    9: 6 authority on earth to *f* sins..
   18:21 many times shall I *f* my brother
   18:35 you *f* your brother from your
      heart
Mk   2: 7 Who can *f* sins but God alone?"
    2:10 authority on earth to *f* sins
   11:25 anything against anyone, *f* him,
   11:25 in heaven may *f* you your sins."
Lk   5:21 Who can *f* sins but God alone?"
    5:24 authority on earth to *f* sins..
    6:37 *F*, and you will be forgiven.
   11: 4 *f* us our sins,
   11: 4 *f* everyone who sins against us.
   17: 3 rebuke him, and if he repents, *f*
      him
   17: 4 and says, 'I repent,' *f* him."
   23:34 Jesus said, "Father, *f* them,
Jn   20:23 If you *f* anyone his sins, they are
   20:23 if you do not *f* them, they are not
Ac   8:22 Perhaps he will *f* you
2Co   2: 7 you ought to *f* and comfort him,
    2:10 If you *f* anyone, I also *f* him.

2Co   2:10 if there was anything to *f*—
   12:13 a burden to you? *F* me this wrong!
Col   3:13 and *f* whatever grievances you
      may
    3:13 *F* as the Lord forgave you.
Heb   8:12 For I will *f* their wickedness
1Jn   1: 9 and just and will *f* us our sins

FORGIVENESS* (FORGIVE)
Ps 130: 4 But with you there is *f*;
Mt   26:28 out for many for the *f* of sins.
Mk   1: 4 of repentance for the *f* of sins.
Lk   1:77 salvation through the *f* of their
      sins,
    3: 3 of repentance for the *f* of sins.
   24:47 and *f* of sins will be preached
Ac   5:31 that he might give repentance
      and *f*
   10:43 believes in him receives *f* of sins
   13:38 that through Jesus the *f*
   26:18 so that they may receive *f* of sins
Eph   1: 7 through his blood, the *f* of sins,
Col   1:14 in whom we have redemption,
      the *f*
Heb   9:22 the shedding of blood there is
      no *f*.

FORGIVES* (FORGIVE)
Ps 103: 3 He *f* all my sins
Mic   7:18 pardons sin and *f* the
      transgression
Lk   7:49 "Who is this who even *f* sins?"

FORGIVING* (FORGIVE)
Ex   34: 7 and *f* wickedness, rebellion and
      sin.
Nu 14:18 abounding in love and *f* sin
Ne   9:17 But you are a *f* God, gracious
Ps   86: 5 You are *f* and good, O Lord,
    99: 8 you were to Israel a *f* God,
Da   9: 9 The Lord our God is merciful and *f*
Eph   4:32 to one another, *f* each other,

FORGOT (FORGET)
Dt   32:18 you *f* the God who gave you birth.
Ps   78:11 They *f* what he had done,
  106:13 But they soon *f* what he had done

FORGOTTEN (FORGET)
Job 11: 6 God has even *f* some of your sin.
Ps   44:20 If we had *f* the name of our God
Isa   17:10 You have *f* God your Savior;
Hos   8:14 Israel has *f* his Maker
Lk   12: 6 Yet not one of them is *f* by God.
2Pe   1: 9 and has *f* that he has been
      cleansed

FORM (FORMED)
Isa 52:14 *f* marred beyond human
      likeness—
2Ti   3: 5 having a *f* of godliness

FORMED (FORM)
Ge   2: 7 —the LORD God *f* the man
    2:19 Now the LORD God had *f* out
Ps 103:14 for he knows how we are *f*,
Ecc 11: 5 or how the body is *f* in a mother's
Isa 29:16 Shall what is *f* say to him who *f* it,
   45:18 but *f* it to be inhabited—
   49: 5 he who *f* me in the womb
Jer   1: 5 "Before I *f* you in the womb I
      knew
Ro   9:20 "Shall what is *f* say to him who *f* it,
Gal   4:19 of childbirth until Christ is *f* in
      you,
1Ti   2:13 For Adam was *f* first, then Eve.
Heb 11: 3 understand that the universe
      was *f*
2Pe   3: 5 and the earth was *f* out of water

FORMLESS*
Ge   1: 2 Now the earth was *f* and empty,
Jer   4:23 and it was *f* and empty;

FORSAKE (FORSAKEN)
Dt   31: 6 he will never leave you nor *f* you."
Jos   1: 5 I will never leave you nor *f* you.
   24:16 "Far be it from us to *f* the LORD
2Ch 15: 2 but if you *f* him, he will *f* you.
Ps   27:10 Though my father and mother *f*
      me
   94:14 he will never *f* his inheritance.
Isa   55: 7 Let the wicked *f* his way
Heb 13: 5 never will I *f* you."

FORSAKEN (FORSAKE)
Ps   22: 1 my God, why have you *f* me?

Ps   37:25 I have never seen the righteous *f*
Mt   27:46 my God, why have you *f* me?"
Rev   2: 4 You have *f* your first love.

FORTRESS
2Sa 22: 2 "The LORD is my rock, my *f*
Ps   18: 2 The LORD is my rock, my *f*
   31: 2 a strong *f* to save me.
   59:16 for you are my *f*,
   71: 3 for you are my rock and my *f*.
Pr   14:26 who fears the LORD has a secure *f*,

FORTUNE-TELLING*
Ac 16:16 deal of money for her owners by *f*.

FORTY
Ge   7: 4 on the earth for *f* days and *f*
      nights,
   18:29 "What if only *f* are found there?"
Ex   16:35 The Israelites ate manna *f* years,
   24:18 on the mountain *f* days and *f*
      nights
Nu 14:34 For *f* years—one year for each
Jos 14: 7 I was *f* years old when Moses
1Sa   4:18 He had led Israel *f* years.
2Sa   5: 4 king, and he reigned *f* years.
1Ki 19: 8 he traveled *f* days and *f* nights
2Ki 12: 1 and he reigned in Jerusalem *f*
      years
2Ch   9:30 in Jerusalem over all Israel *f* years.
Eze 29:12 her cities will lie desolate *f* years
Jnh   3: 4 "*F* more days and Nineveh will
Mt   4: 2 After fasting *f* days and *f* nights,

FOUGHT (FIGHT)
1Co 15:32 If I *f* wild beasts in Ephesus
2Ti   4: 7 I have *f* the good fight, I have

FOUND (FIND)
2Ki 22: 8 "I have *f* the Book of the Law
1Ch 28: 9 If you seek him, he will be *f* by
      you;
2Ch 15:15 sought God eagerly, and he was *f*
Isa   55: 6 Seek the LORD while he may be *f*;
   65: 1 I was *f* by those who did not seek
Da   5:27 on the scales and *f* wanting.
Mt   1:18 she was *f* to be with child
Lk   15: 6 with me; I have *f* my lost sheep.'
   15: 9 with me; I have *f* my lost coin.'
   15:24 is alive again; he was lost and is *f*.'
Ac   4:12 Salvation is *f* in no one else,
Ro   10:20 "I was *f* by those who did not seek
Jas   2: 8 If you really keep the royal law *f*
Rev   5: 4 no one was *f* who was worthy

FOUNDATION (FOUNDATIONS FOUNDED)
Isa 28:16 a precious cornerstone for a
      sure *f*;
Mt   7:25 because it had its *f* on the rock.
Lk   14:29 For if he lays the *f* and is not able
Ro   15:20 building on someone else's *f*.
1Co   3:10 I laid a *f* as an expert builder,
    3:11 For no one can lay any *f* other
Eph   2:20 built on the *f* of the apostles
1Ti   3:15 the pillar and *f* of the truth.
2Ti   2:19 God's solid *f* stands firm,
Heb   6: 1 not laying again the *f* of
      repentance

FOUNDATIONS (FOUNDATION)
Ps 102:25 In the beginning you laid the *f*
Heb   1:10 O Lord, you laid the *f* of the earth,

FOUNDED (FOUNDATION)
Jer   10:12 he *f* the world by his wisdom
Heb   8: 6 and it is *f* on better promises.

FOUNTAIN
Ps   36: 9 For with you is the *f* of life;
Pr   14:27 The fear of the LORD is a *f* of life,
   18: 4 the *f* of wisdom is a bubbling
      brook.
Zec 13: 1 "On that day a *f* will be opened

FOX (FOXES)
Lk 13:32 He replied, "Go tell that *f*,

FOXES (FOX)
SS   2:15 the little *f*
Mt   8:20 "*F* have holes and birds

FRAGRANCE (FRAGRANT)
Ex   30:38 it to enjoy its *f* must be cut
Jn   12: 3 filled with the *f* of the perfume.
2Co   2:14 us spreads everywhere the *f*
    2:16 of death; to the other, the *f* of life.

FRAGRANT (FRAGRANCE)
Eph 5: 2 as a *f* offering and sacrifice to God.
Php 4:18 They are a *f* offering, an acceptable

FREE (FREED FREEDOM FREELY)
Ge 2:16 "You are *f* to eat from any tree
Ps 118: 5 and he answered by setting me *f.*
  119:32 for you have set my heart *f.*
  146: 7 The LORD sets prisoners *f,*
Pr 6: 3 then do this, my son, to *f* yourself,
Jn 8:32 and the truth will set you *f.*"
  8:36 if the Son sets you *f,* you will be *f*
Ro 6:18 You have been set *f* from sin
  8: 2 of life set me *f* from the law of sin
1Co 12:13 whether Jews or Greeks, slave or *f*
Gal 3:28 slave nor *f,* male nor female,
  5: 1 for freedom that Christ has set us *f.*
1Pe 2:16 *f* men, but do not use your freedom

FREED (FREE)
Ps 116:16 you have *f* me from my chains.
Ro 6: 7 anyone who has died has been *f*
Rev 1: 5 has *f* us from our sins by his blood,

FREEDOM (FREE)
Ps 119:45 I will walk about in *f,*
Isa 61: 1 to proclaim *f* for the captives
Lk 4:18 me to proclaim *f* for the prisoners
Ro 8:21 into the glorious *f* of the children
1Co 7:21 although if you can gain your *f,*
2Co 3:17 the Spirit of the Lord is, there is *f.*
Gal 2: 4 ranks to spy on the *f* we have
  5:13 But do not use your *f* to indulge
Jas 1:25 into the perfect law that gives *f,*
1Pe 2:16 but do not use your *f* as a cover-up

FREELY (FREE)
Isa 55: 7 and to our God, for he will *f* pardon
Mt 10: 8 Freely you have received, *f* give.
Ro 3:24 and are justified *f* by his grace
Eph 1: 6 which he has *f* given us

FRESH
Jas 3:11 Can both *f* water and salt water

FRET*
Ps 37: 1 Do not *f* because of evil men
  37: 7 do not *f* when men succeed
  37: 8 do not *f*— it leads only to evil.
Pr 24:19 Do not *f* because of evil men

FRICTION
1Ti 6: 5 and constant *f* between men

FRIEND (FRIENDS FRIENDSHIP)
Ex 33:11 as a man speaks with his *f.*
2Ch 20: 7 descendants of Abraham your *f?*
Pr 17:17 A *f* loves at all times,
  18:24 there is a *f* who sticks closer
  27: 6 Wounds from a *f* can be trusted
  27:10 Do not forsake your *f* and the *f*
Isa 41: 8 you descendants of Abraham my *f,*
Mt 11:19 a *f* of tax collectors and "sinners." '
Lk 11: 8 him the bread because he is his *f,*
Jn 19:12 "If you let this man go, you are no *f*
Jas 2:23 and he was called God's *f.*
  4: 4 Anyone who chooses to be a *f*

FRIENDS (FRIEND)
Pr 16:28 and a gossip separates close *f.*
  17: 9 the matter separates close *f.*
Zec 13: 6 given at the house of my *f.* '
Jn 15:13 that he lay down his life for his *f.*
  15:14 You are my *f* if you do what I

FRIENDSHIP (FRIEND)
Jas 4: 4 don't you know that *f*

FRIGHTENED (FEAR)
Php 1:28 gospel without being *f* in any way
1Pe 3:14 fear what they fear; do not be *f.* "

FROGS
Ex 8: 2 plague your whole country with *f.*
Rev 16:13 three evil spirits that looked like *f;*

FRUIT (FRUITFUL)
Jdg 9:11 'Should I give up my *f,* so good
Ps 1: 3 which yields its *f* in season
Pr 11:30 The *f* of the righteous is a tree

Pr 12:14 From the *f* of his lips a man is filled
  27:18 He who tends a fig tree will eat its *f*
Isa 11: 1 from his roots a Branch will bear *f.*
  27: 6 and fill all the world with *f.*
  32:17 The *f* of righteousness will be peace
Jer 17: 8 and never fails to bear *f.*"
Hos 10:12 reap the *f* of unfailing love,
  14: 2 that we may offer the *f* of our lips.
Am 8: 1 showed me: a basket of ripe *f.*
Mt 3: 8 Produce *f* in keeping
  3:10 does not produce good *f* will be cut
  7:16 By their *f* you will recognize them.
  7:17 good *f,* but a bad tree bears bad *f.*
  7:20 by their *f* you will recognize them.
  12:33 a tree good and its *f* will be good,
Lk 3: 9 does not produce good *f* will be cut
  6:43 nor does a bad tree bear good *f.*
  13: 6 and he went to look for *f* on it,
Jn 15: 2 branch in me that bears no *f,*
  15:16 and bear *f*— *f* that will last.
Ro 7: 4 in order that we might bear *f*
Gal 5:22 But the *f* of the Spirit is love, joy,
Php 1:11 with the *f* of righteousness that
Col 1:10 bearing *f* in every good work,
Heb 13:15 the *f* of lips that confess his name.
Jas 3:17 and good *f,* impartial and sincere.
Jude   :12 autumn trees, without *f*
Rev 22: 2 of *f,* yielding its *f* every month.

FRUITFUL (FRUIT)
Ge 1:22 "Be *f* and increase in number
  9: 1 "Be *f* and increase in number
  35:11 be *f* and increase in number.
Ex 1: 7 the Israelites were *f* and multiplied
Ps 128: 3 Your wife will be like a *f* vine
Jn 15: 2 prunes so that it will be even more *f*
Php 1:22 this will mean *f* labor for me.

FRUITLESS*
Eph 5:11 to do with the *f* deeds of darkness,

FRUSTRATION
Ro 8:20 For the creation was subjected to *f,*

FUEL
Isa 44:19 "Half of it I used for *f;*

FULFILL (FULFILLED FULFILLMENT FULFILLS)
Nu 23:19 Does he promise and not *f?*
Ps 61: 8 and *f* my vows day after day.
 116:14 I will *f* my vows to the LORD
 138: 8 The LORD will *f* his purpose.
Ecc 5: 5 than to make a vow and not *f* it.
Isa 46:11 far-off land, a man to *f* my purpose.
Jer 33:14 'when I will *f* the gracious promise
Mt 1:22 place to *f* what the Lord had said
  3:15 us to do this to *f* all righteousness."
  4:14 *f* what was said
  5:17 come to abolish them but to *f* them.
  8:17 This was to *f* what was spoken
  12:17 This was to *f* what was spoken
  21: 4 place to *f* what was spoken
  12:38 This was to *f* the word
Jn 13:18 But this is to *f* the scripture:
  15:25 But this is to *f* what is written
1Co 7: 3 husband should *f* his marital duty

FULFILLED (FULFILL)
Jos 21:45 of Israel failed; every one was *f.*
  23:14 Every promise has been *f;*
Pr 13:12 but a longing *f* is a tree of life.
  13:19 A longing *f* is sweet to the soul,
Mt 2:15 so was *f* what the Lord had said
  2:17 prophet Jeremiah was *f:*
  2:23 So was *f* what was said
  13:14 In them is the prophecy of Isaiah:
  13:35 So was *f* what was spoken
  26:54 would the Scriptures be *f* that say it
  26:56 of the prophets might be *f.*"
  27: 9 by Jeremiah the prophet was *f:*
Mk 13: 4 that they are all about to be *f?*"

Mk 14:49 But the Scriptures must be *f.*"
Lk 4:21 "Today this scripture is *f*
  18:31 about the Son of Man will be *f*
  24:44 Everything must be *f* that is
Jn 18: 9 words he had spoken would be *f:*
  19:24 the Scripture might be *f* which said,
  19:28 and so that the Scripture would be *f*
  19:36 so that the Scripture would be *f:*
Ac 1:16 to be *f* which the Holy Spirit spoke
Ro 13: 8 loves his fellowman has *f* the law.
Jas 2:23 And the scripture was *f* that says,

FULFILLMENT (FULFILL)
Ro 13:10 Therefore love is the *f* of the law.

FULFILLS (FULFILL)
Ps 57: 2 to God, who *f* his purpose for me.
 145:19 He *f* the desires of those who fear

FULL (FILL)
2Ch 24:10 them into the chest until it was *f.*
Ps 127: 5 whose quiver is *f* of them.
Pr 27: 7 He who is *f* loathes honey,
  31:11 Her husband has *f* confidence
Isa 6: 3 the whole earth is *f* of his glory."
  11: 9 for the earth will be *f*
Lk 4: 1 Jesus, *f* of the Holy Spirit,
Jn 10:10 may have life, and have it to the *f.*
Ac 6: 3 known to be *f* of the Spirit
  6: 5 a man *f* of faith and of the Holy
  7:55 But Stephen, *f* of the Holy Spirit,
  11:24 *f* of the Holy Spirit and faith,

FULL-GROWN* (GROW)
Jas 1:15 when it is *f,* gives birth to death.

FULLNESS* (FILL)
Dt 33:16 gifts of the earth and its *f*
Jn 1:16 From the *f* of his grace we have all
Ro 11:12 greater riches will their *f* bring!
Eph 1:23 the *f* of him who fills everything
  3:19 to the measure of all the *f* of God.
  4:13 to the whole measure of the *f*
Col 1:19 to have all his *f* dwell in him,
  1:25 to you the word of God in its *f*—
  2: 9 in Christ all the *f* of the Deity lives
  2:10 and you have been given *f* in Christ

FULLY (FILL)
1Ki 8:61 your hearts must be *f* committed
2Ch 16: 9 whose hearts are *f* committed
Ps 119: 4 that are to be *f* obeyed.
 119:138 they are *f* trustworthy.
Pr 13: 4 of the diligent are *f* satisfied.
Lk 6:40 everyone who is *f* trained will be
Ro 4:21 being *f* persuaded that God had
  14: 5 Each one should be *f* convinced
1Co 13:12 shall know *f,* even as I am *f* known.
  15:58 Always give yourselves *f*
2Ti 4:17 the message might be *f* proclaimed

FURIOUS (FURY)
Dt 29:28 In *f* anger and in great wrath
Jer 32:37 where I banish them in my *f* anger

FURNACE
Isa 48:10 in the *f* of affliction.
Da 3: 6 be thrown into a blazing *f.* "
Mt 13:42 will throw them into the fiery *f,*

FURY (FURIOUS)
Isa 14: 6 and in *f* subdued nations
Jer 21: 5 and a mighty arm in anger and *f*
Rev 14:10 will drink of the wine of God's *f,*
  16:19 with the wine of the *f* of his wrath.
  19:15 the winepress of the *f* of the wrath

FUTILE (FUTILITY)
Mal 3:14 You have said, 'It is *f* to serve God.
1Co 3:20 that the thoughts of the wise are *f.*"

FUTILITY (FUTILE)
Eph 4:17 in the *f* of their thinking.

FUTURE
Ps 37:37 there is a *f* for the man of peace.
Pr 23:18 There is surely a *f* hope for you,
Ecc 7:14 anything about his *f.*
  8: 7 Since no man knows the *f,*

Jer 29:11 plans to give you hope and a *f.*
    31:17 So there is hope for your *f,"*
Ro   8:38 neither the present nor the *f.*
1Co 3:22 life or death or the present or the *f*

GABRIEL*
Angel who interpreted Daniel's visions (Da 8:16–26; 9:20–27); announced births of John (Lk 1:11–20), Jesus (Lk 1:26–38).

GAD
1. Son of Jacob by Zilpah (Ge 30:9–11; 35:26; 1Ch 2:2). Tribe of blessed (Ge 49:19; Dt 33:20–21), numbered (Nu 1:25; 26:18), allotted land east of the Jordan (Nu 32; 34:14; Jos 18:7; 22), west (Eze 48:27–28), 12,000 from (Rev 7:5).
2. Prophet; seer of David (1Sa 22:5; 2Sa 24:11–19; 1Ch 29:29).

GAIN (GAINED GAINS)
Ex 14:17 And I will *g* glory through Pharaoh
Ps 60:12 With God we will *g* the victory,
Pr   4: 1 pay attention and *g* understanding.
    8: 5 You who are simple, *g* prudence;
 28:16 he who hates ill-gotten *g* will enjoy
 28:23 in the end *g* more favor
Isa 63:12 to *g* for himself everlasting renown
Da   2: 8 that you are trying to *g* time,
Mk 8:36 it for a man to *g* the whole world,
Lk   9:25 it for a man to *g* the whole world,
 21:19 standing firm you will *g* life.
1Co 13: 3 but have not love, I *g* nothing.
Php 1:21 to live is Christ and to die is *g.*
    3: 8 that I may *g* Christ and be found
1Ti 3:13 have served well *g* an excellent
    6: 5 godliness is a means to financial *g.*
    6: 6 with contentment is great *g.*

GAINED (GAIN)
Jer 32:20 have *g* the renown that is still yours
Ro   5: 2 through whom we have *g* access

GAINS (GAIN)
Pr   3:13 the man who *g* understanding,
 11:16 A kindhearted woman *g* respect,
 15:32 heeds correction *g* understanding.
 29:23 but a man of lowly spirit *g* honor.
Mt 16:26 for a man if he *g* the whole world,

GALILEE
Isa   9: 1 but in the future he will honor *G*
Mt   4:15 *G* of the Gentiles—
 26:32 I will go ahead of you into *G."*
 28:10 Go and tell my brothers to go to *G;*

GALL
Mt 27:34 mixed with *g;* but after tasting it,

GALLIO
Ac 18:12 While *G* was proconsul of Achaia,

GALLOWS
Est 7:10 Haman on the *g* he had prepared

GAMALIEL
Ac   5:34 But a Pharisee named *G,* a teacher

GAMES
1Co 9:25 in the *g* goes into strict training.

GAP
Eze 22:30 stand before me in the *g* on behalf

GAPE*
Ps 35:21 They *g* at me and say, "Aha! Aha!

GARDEN (GARDENER)
Ge   2: 8 the LORD God had planted a *g*
    2:15 put him in the *G* of Eden to work it
SS   4:12 You are a *g* locked up, my sister,
Isa 58:11 You will be like a well-watered *g,*
Jer 31:12 They will be like a well-watered *g,*
Eze 28:13 the *g* of God;
   31: 9 Eden in the *g* of God.

GARDENER (GARDEN)
Jn 15: 1 true vine, and my Father is the *g.*

GARLAND*
Pr   1: 9 They will be like a *g* to grace your head

Pr   4: 9 She will set a *g* of grace

GARMENT (GARMENTS)
Ps 102:26 they will all wear out like a *g.*
Isa 50: 9 They will all wear out like a *g;*
    51: 6 the earth will wear out like a *g*
    61: 3 and a *g* of praise
Mt   9:16 of unshrunk cloth on an old *g,*
Jn 19:23 This *g* was seamless, woven
Heb 1:11 they will all wear out like a *g.*

GARMENTS (GARMENT)
Ge   3:21 The LORD God made *g* of skin
Ex 28: 2 Make sacred *g* for your brother
Lev 16:23 and take off the linen *g* he put
 16:24 holy place and put on his regular *g.*
Isa 61:10 me with *g* of salvation
 63: 1 with his *g* stained crimson?
Joel 2:13 and not your *g.*
Zec 3: 4 and I will put rich *g* on you."
Jn 19:24 "They divided my *g* among them

GATE (GATES)
Ps 118:20 This is the *g* of the LORD
Pr 31:23 husband is respected at the city *g,*
 31:31 works bring her praise at the city *g.*
Mt   7:13 For wide is the *g* and broad is
    7:13 "Enter through the narrow *g.*
Jn 10: 1 not enter the sheep pen by the *g,*
 10: 2 enters by the *g* is the shepherd
 10: 7 "I tell you the truth, I am the *g*
 10: 9 I am the *g;* whoever enters
Heb 13:12 also suffered outside the city *g*
Rev 21:21 each *g* made of a single pearl.

GATES (GATE)
Ps 24: 7 Lift up your heads, O you *g;*
 24: 9 Lift up your heads, O you *g;*
 100: 4 Enter his *g* with thanksgiving
 118:19 Open for me the *g* of righteousness
Isa 60:11 Your *g* will always stand open,
 60:18 and your *g* Praise.
 62:10 Pass through, pass through the *g!*
Mt 16:18 the *g* of Hades will not overcome it
Rev 21:12 On the *g* were written the names
 21:21 The twelve *g* were twelve pearls,
 21:25 On no day will its *g* ever be shut,
 22:14 may go through the *g* into the city.

GATH
1Sa 17:23 the Philistine champion from *G,*
2Sa 1:20 "Tell it not in *G,*
Mic 1:10 Tell it not in *G;*

GATHER (GATHERED GATHERS)
Ps 106:47 and *g* us from the nations,
Isa 11:12 and *g* the exiles of Israel;
Jer 3:17 and all nations will *g* in Jerusalem
 23: 3 "I myself will *g* the remnant
 31:10 who scattered Israel will *g* them
Zep 2: 1 *G* together, *g* together,
    3:20 At that time I will *g* you;
Zec 14: 2 I will *g* all the nations to Jerusalem
Mt 12:30 he who does not *g* with me scatters
 13:30 then *g* the wheat and bring it
 23:37 longed to *g* your children together,
 24:31 and they will *g* his elect
 25:26 *g* where I have not scattered seed?
Mk 13:27 and *g* his elect from the four winds,
Lk 3:17 and to *g* the wheat into his barn,
 11:23 and he who does not *g* with me,
 13:34 longed to *g* your children together,

GATHERED (GATHER)
Ex 16:18 and he who *g* little did not have too
Pr 30: 4 Who has *g* up the wind
Mt 25:32 All the nations will be *g* before him
2Co 8:15 and he who *g* little did not have too
2Th 2: 1 Lord Jesus Christ and our being *g*
Rev 16:16 Then they *g* the kings together

GATHERS (GATHER)
Ps 147: 2 he *g* the exiles of Israel.
Pr 10: 5 He who *g* crops in summer is a wise
Isa 40:11 He *g* the lambs in his arms
Mt 23:37 a hen *g* her chicks under her wings,

GAVE (GIVE)
Ge 2:20 man *g* names to all the livestock,
    3: 6 She also *g* some to her husband,
 14:20 Abram *g* him a tenth of everything.
 28: 4 the land God *g* to Abraham."
 35:12 The land I *g* to Abraham
 39:23 *g* him success in whatever he did.
 47:11 *g* them property in the best part
Ex 4:11 to him, "Who *g* man his mouth?
 31:18 he *g* him the two tablets
Dt 2:12 did in the land the LORD *g* them
    2:36 The LORD our God *g* us all
    3:12 I *g* the Reubenites and the Gadites
    3:13 I *g* to the half tribe of Manasseh.
    3:15 And I *g* Gilead to Makir.
    3:16 Gadites I *g* the territory extending
    8:16 He *g* you manna to eat in the desert
 26: 9 us to this place and *g* us this land,
 32: 8 the Most High *g* the nations their
Jos 11:23 and he *g* it as an inheritance
 13:14 tribe of Levi he *g* no inheritance,
 14:13 *g* him Hebron as his inheritance.
 21:44 The LORD *g* them rest
 24:13 I *g* you a land on which you did not
1Sa 27: 6 So on that day Achish *g* him Ziklag
2Sa 12: 8 I *g* you the house of Israel
1Ki 4:29 God *g* Solomon wisdom
    5:12 The LORD *g* Solomon wisdom,
Ezr 2:69 According to their ability they *g*
Ne 9:15 In their hunger you *g* them bread
    9:20 You *g* your good Spirit
    9:22 You *g* them kingdoms and nations,
    9:27 compassion you *g* them deliverers,
Job 1:21 LORD *g* and the LORD has taken
 42:10 prosperous again and *g* him twice
Ps 69:21 and *g* me vinegar for my thirst.
 135:12 he *g* their land as an inheritance,
Ecc 12: 7 the spirit returns to God who *g* it.
Eze 3: 2 and he *g* me the scroll to eat.
Mt 1:25 And he *g* him the name Jesus.
 25:35 and you *g* me something to drink,
 25:42 and you *g* me nothing to drink,
 26:26 Jesus took bread, *g* thanks
 27:50 in a loud voice, he *g* up his spirit.
Mk 6: 7 *g* them authority over evil spirits.
Jn 1:12 he *g* the right to become children
    3:16 so loved the world that he *g* his one
 17: 4 by completing the work you *g* me
 17: 6 you *g* them to me and they have
 19:30 bowed his head and *g* up his spirit.
Ac 1: 3 *g* many convincing proofs that he
    2:45 they *g* to anyone as he had need.
 11:17 *g* them the same gift as he *g* us,
Ro 1:24 Therefore God *g* them
    1:26 God *g* them over to shameful lusts.
    1:28 he *g* them over to a depraved mind,
    8:32 not spare his own Son, but *g* him up
2Co 5:18 *g* us the ministry of reconciliation:
    8: 3 For I testify that they *g* as much
    8: 5 they *g* themselves first to the Lord
Gal 1: 4 who *g* himself for our sins
    2:20 who loved me and *g* himself for me
Eph 4: 8 and *g* gifts to men."
    5: 2 as Christ loved us and *g* himself up
    5:25 and *g* himself up for her
2Th 2:16 and by his grace *g* us eternal
1Ti 2: 6 who *g* himself as a ransom
Tit 2:14 who *g* himself for us to redeem us
1Jn 3:24 We know it by the Spirit he *g* us.

GAZE
Ps 27: 4 to *g* upon the beauty of the LORD
Pr   4:25 fix your *g* directly before you.

GEDALIAH
Governor of Judah appointed by Nebuchadnezzar (2Ki 25:22–26; Jer 39–41).

GEHAZI*
Servant of Elisha (2Ki 4:12–5:27; 8:4–5).

GENEALOGIES
1Ti 1: 4 themselves to myths and endless *g.*
Tit 3: 9 avoid foolish controversies and *g*

GENERATION (GENERATIONS)
Ex   3:15 am to be remembered from *g* to *g.*
Nu 32:13 until the whole *g* of those who had
Dt   1:35 of this evil *g* shall see the good land
Jdg 2:10 After that whole *g* had been
Ps 24: 6 Such is the *g* of those who seek him
    48:13 tell of them to the next *g.*
    71:18 I declare your power to the next *g.*
    78: 4 we will tell the next *g*
    102:18 Let this be written for a future *g,*
    112: 2 the *g* of the upright will be blessed
    145: 4 One *g* will commend your works
La   5:19 your throne endures from *g* to *g.*
Da   4: 3 his dominion endures from *g* to *g.*
     4:34 his kingdom endures from *g* to *g.*
Joel 1: 3 and their children to the next *g.*
Mt 12:39 adulterous *g* asks for a miraculous
    17:17 "O unbelieving and perverse *g,*"
    23:36 all this will come upon this *g.*
    24:34 this *g* will certainly not pass away
Mk   9:19 "O unbelieving," Jesus replied,
    13:30 this *g* will certainly not pass away
Lk   1:50 who fear him, from *g* to *g.*
    11:29 Jesus said, "This is a wicked *g.*
    11:30 will the Son of Man be to this *g.*
    11:50 Therefore this *g* will be held
    21:32 this *g* will certainly not pass away
Ac   2:40 Save yourselves from this corrupt *g.*
Php 2:15 fault in a crooked and depraved *g,*

GENERATIONS (GENERATION)
Ge   9:12 a covenant for all *g* to come:
    17: 7 after you for the *g* to come.
    17: 9 after you for the *g* to come.
Ex 20: 6 a thousand *g* of those
    31:13 and you for the *g* to come,
Dt   7: 9 covenant of love to a thousand *g*
    32: 7 consider the *g* long past.
1Ch 16:15 he commanded, for a thousand *g,*
Job 8: 8 "Ask the former *g*
Ps 22:30 future *g* will be told about the Lord
    33:11 of his heart through all *g.*
    45:17 your memory through all *g;*
    89: 1 faithfulness known through all *g.*
    90: 1 throughout all *g.*
    100: 5 continues through all *g.*
    102:12 your renown endures through all *g.*
    105: 8 he commanded, for a thousand *g,*
    119:90 continues through all *g;*
    135:13 renown, O LORD, through all *g.*
    145:13 dominion endures through all *g.*
    146:10 your God, O Zion, for all *g.*
Pr 27:24 and a crown is not secure for all *g.*
Isa 41: 4 forth the *g* from the beginning?
    51: 8 my salvation through all *g.*"
Lk   1:48 now on all *g* will call me blessed,
Eph 3: 5 not made known to men in other *g*
     3:21 in Christ Jesus throughout all *g,*
Col 1:26 been kept hidden for ages and *g,*

GENEROSITY* (GENEROUS)
2Co 8: 2 poverty welled up in rich *g.*
     9:11 and through us your *g* will result
     9:13 and for your *g* in sharing with them

GENEROUS* (GENEROSITY)
Ps 37:26 They are always *g* and lend freely;
    112: 5 Good will come to him who is *g*

Pr 11:25 A *g* man will prosper;
    22: 9 A *g* man will himself be blessed,
Mt 20:15 Or are you envious because I am *g*
2Co 9: 5 Then it will be ready as a *g* gift,
     9: 5 for the *g* gift you had promised.
     9:11 way so that you can be *g*
1Ti 6:18 and to be *g* and willing to share.

GENTILE (GENTILES)
Ac 21:25 As for the *G* believers, we have
Ro   1:16 first for the Jew, then for the *G.*
     2: 9 first for the Jew, then for the *G;*
     2:10 first for the Jew, then for the *G.*
    10:12 difference between Jew and *G*—

GENTILES (GENTILE)
Isa 42: 6 and a light for the *G,*
    49: 6 also make you a light for the *G,*
    49:22 "See, I will beckon to the *G,*
Lk   2:32 a light for revelation to the *G*
    21:24 on by the *G* until the times
Ac   9:15 to carry my name before the *G*
    10:45 been poured out even on the *G.*
    11:18 granted even the *G* repentance unto
    13:16 and you *G* who worship God,
    13:46 of eternal life, we now turn to the *G*
    13:47 I have made you a light for the *G,*
    14:27 opened the door of faith to the *G.*
    15:14 by taking from the *G* a people
    18: 6 From now on I will go to the *G.*"
    22:21 I will send you far away to the *G.*'"
    26:20 and in all Judea, and to the *G* also,
    28:28 salvation has been sent to the *G,*
Ro   2:14 when *G,* who do not have the law,
     3: 9 and *G* alike are all under sin.
     3:29 Is he not the God of *G* too? Yes,
     9:24 from the Jews but also from the *G?*
    11:11 to the *G* to make Israel envious.
    11:12 their loss means riches for the *G,*
    11:13 as I am the apostle to the *G,*
    15: 9 I will praise you among the *G;*
    15: 9 so that the *G* may glorify God
1Co 1:23 block to Jews and foolishness to *G,*
Gal 1:16 I might preach him among the *G,*
     2: 2 gospel that I preach among the *G.*
     2: 8 my ministry as an apostle to the *G.*
     2: 9 agreed that we should go to the *G,*
     3: 8 that God would justify the *G*
     3:14 to the *G* through Christ Jesus,
Eph 3: 6 the gospel the *G* are heirs together
     3: 8 to the *G* the unsearchable riches
Col 1:27 among the *G* the glorious riches
1Ti 2: 7 a teacher of the true faith to the *G.*
2Ti 4:17 and all the *G* might hear it.

GENTLE* (GENTLENESS)
Dt 28:54 Even the most *g* and sensitive man
    28:56 The most *g* and sensitive woman
    28:56 and *g* that she would not venture
2Sa 18: 5 Be *g* with the young man Absalom
1Ki 19:12 And after the fire came a *g* whisper
Job 41: 3 Will he speak to you with *g* words?
Pr 15: 1 A *g* answer turns away wrath,
    25:15 and a *g* tongue can break a bone.
Jer 11:19 I had been like a *g* lamb led
Zec 9: 9 *g* and riding on a donkey,
Mt 11:29 for I am *g* and humble in heart,
    21: 5 *g* and riding on a donkey,
Ac 27:13 When a *g* south wind began
1Co 4:21 or in love and with a *g* spirit?
Eph 4: 2 Be completely humble and *g;*
1Th 2: 7 but we were *g* among you,
1Ti 3: 3 not violent but *g,* not quarrelsome,
1Pe 3: 4 the unfading beauty of a *g*

GENTLENESS* (GENTLE)
2Co 10: 1 By the meekness and *g* of Christ,

Gal 5:23 faithfulness, *g* and self-control.
Php 4: 5 Let your *g* be evident to all.
Col 3:12 kindness, humility, *g* and patience.
1Ti 6:11 faith, love, endurance and *g.*
1Pe 3:15 But do this with *g* and respect,

GENUINE*
2Co 6: 8 *g,* yet regarded as impostors;
Php 2:20 who takes a *g* interest
1Pe 1: 7 may be proved *g* and may result

GERIZIM
Dt 27:12 on Mount *G* to bless the people:

GERSHOM
Ex   2:22 and Moses named him *G,* saying,

GETHSEMANE*
Mt 26:36 disciples to a place called *G,*
Mk 14:32 They went to a place called *G,*

GHOST SEE ALSO SPIRIT
Lk 24:39 a *g* does not have flesh and bones,

GIBEON
Jos 10:12 "O sun, stand still over *G,*

GIDEON*
Judge, also called Jerub-Baal; freed Israel from Midianites (Jdg 6–8; Heb 11:32). Given sign of fleece (Jdg 6:36–40).

GIFT (GIFTED GIFTS)
Pr 18:16 A *g* opens the way for the giver
    21:14 A *g* given in secret soothes anger,
Ecc 3:13 in all his toil—this is the *g* of God.
Mt   5:23 if you are offering your *g*
Jn   4:10 "If you knew the *g* of God
Ac   1: 4 wait for the *g* my Father promised,
     2:38 And you will receive the *g*
    11:17 So if God gave them the same *g*
Ro   6:23 but the *g* of God is eternal life
    12: 6 If a man's *g* is prophesying,
1Co 7: 7 each man has his own *g* from God;
2Co 8:12 the *g* is acceptable according
     9:15 be to God for his indescribable *g!*
Eph 2: 8 it is the *g* of God—not by works,
1Ti 4:14 not neglect your *g,* which was
2Ti 1: 6 you to fan into flame the *g* of God,
Heb 6: 4 who have tasted the heavenly *g,*
Jas 1:17 and perfect *g* is from above,
1Pe 3: 7 with you of the gracious *g* of life,
     4:10 should use whatever *g* he has
Rev 22:17 let him take the free *g* of the water

GIFTED* (GIFT)
1Co 14:37 he is a prophet or spiritually *g,*

GIFTS (GIFT)
Ps 76:11 bring *g* to the One to be feared.
    112: 9 He has scattered abroad his *g*
Pr 25:14 of *g* he does not give.
Mt   2:11 and presented him with *g* of gold
     7:11 Father in heaven give good *g*
     7:11 to give good *g* to your children,
Lk 11:13 to give good *g* to your children,
Ac 10: 4 and *g* to the poor have come up
Ro 11:29 for God's *g* and his call are
    12: 6 We have different *g,* according
1Co 12: 1 Now about spiritual *g,* brothers,
    12: 4 There are different kinds of *g,*
    12:28 those with *g* of administration,
    12:30 all work miracles? Do all have *g*
    12:31 But eagerly desire the greater *g.*
    14: 1 and eagerly desire spiritual *g,*
    14:12 eager to have spiritual *g,*
    14:12 excel in *g* that build up the church.
2Co 9: 9 "He has scattered abroad his *g*
Eph 4: 8 and gave *g* to men."
Heb 2: 4 and *g* of the Holy Spirit distributed
     9: 9 indicating that the *g* and sacrifices

GILEAD
1Ch 27:21 the half-tribe of Manasseh in *G:*
Jer 8:22 Is there no balm in *G?*
    46:11 "Go up to *G* and get balm,

GILGAL
Jos 5: 9 So the place has been called *G*

GIRD*
Ps 45: 3 *G* your sword upon your side,

GIRL
Ge 24:16 *g* was very beautiful, a virgin;
2Ki 5: 2 a young *g* from Israel.
Mk 5:41 Little *g*, I say to you, get up!

GIVE (GAVE GIVEN GIVER GIVES GIVING LIFE-GIVING)
Ge 28: 4 you and your descendants the blessing *g* to Abraham
28:22 that you *g* me I will *g* you a tenth."
Ex 20:16 "You shall not *g* false testimony
30:15 The rich are not to *g* more
Nu 6:26 and *g* you peace." '
Dt 5:20 "You shall not *g* false testimony
15:10 *G* generously to him and do
15:14 *G* to him as the LORD your God
1Sa 1:11 then I will *g* him to the LORD
1:28 So now I *g* him to the LORD.
2Ch 15: 7 be strong and do not *g* up,
Pr 21:26 but the righteous *g* without sparing
23:26 My son, *g* me your heart
25:21 if he is thirsty, *g* him water to drink
30: 8 but *g* me only my daily bread.
31:31 *G* her the reward she has earned,
Ecc 3: 6 a time to search and a time to *g* up,
Isa 42: 8 I will not *g* my glory to another
Eze 36:26 I will *g* you a new heart
Mt 6:11 *G* us today our daily bread.
7:11 know how to *g* good gifts
10: 8 Freely you have received, freely *g*.
16:19 I will *g* you the keys
22:21 "*G* to Caesar what is Caesar's,
Mk 8:37 Or what can a man *g* in exchange
10:19 not steal, do not *g* false testimony,
Lk 6:38 *G*, and it will be given to you.
11: 3 *G* us each day our daily bread.
11:13 Father in heaven *g* the Holy Spirit
14:33 who does not *g* up everything he
Jn 10:28 I *g* them eternal life, and they shall
13:34 "A new commandment I *g* you:
14:16 he will *g* you another Counselor
14:27 I do not *g* to you as the world gives.
14:27 leave with you; my peace I *g* you.
17: 2 people that he might *g* eternal life
Ac 20:35 blessed to *g* than to receive.' "
Ro 2: 7 immortality, he will *g* eternal life.
8:32 with him, graciously *g* us all things
12: 8 let him *g* generously;
13: 7 *G* everyone what you owe him:
14:12 each of us will *g* an account
2Co 9: 7 Each man should *g* what he has
Gal 2: 5 We did not *g* in to them
6: 9 reap a harvest if we do not *g* up.
Heb 10:25 Let us not *g* up meeting together,
Rev 14: 7 "Fear God and *g* him glory,

GIVEN* (GIVE)
Nu 8:16 are to be *g* wholly to me.
Dt 26:11 things the LORD your God has *g*
Job 3:23 Why is life *g* to a man
Ps 115:16 but the earth he has *g* to man.
Isa 9: 6 to us a son is *g*,
Mt 6:33 and all these things will be *g* to you
7: 7 "Ask and it will be *g* to you;
13:12 Whoever has will be *g* more,
22:30 people will neither marry nor be *g*
25:29 everyone who has will be *g* more,
Lk 6:38 Give, and it will be *g* to you.
8:10 kingdom of God has been *g* to you,
11: 9 Ask and it will be *g* to you;
22:19 saying, "This is my body *g* for you;
Jn 3:27 man can receive only what is *g* him
15: 7 you wish, and it will be *g* you.
17:24 I want those you have *g* me to be
17:24 the glory you have *g* me
18:11 the cup the Father has *g* me?"
Ac 5:32 whom God has *g* to those who
20:24 the task the Lord Jesus has *g* me—
Ro 5: 5 the Holy Spirit, whom he has *g* us.
1Co 4: 2 those who have been *g* a trust must

1Co 11:24 and when he had *g* thanks,
12:13 we were all *g* the one Spirit to drink
2Co 5: 5 and has *g* us the Spirit as a deposit,
Eph 1: 6 which he has freely *g* us
4: 7 to each one of us grace has been *g*
1Ti 4:14 was *g* you through a prophetic
1Jn 4:13 because he has *g* us of his Spirit.

GIVER* (GIVE)
Pr 18:16 A gift opens the way for the *g*
2Co 9: 7 for God loves a cheerful *g*.

GIVES (GIVE)
Job 35:10 who *g* songs in the night,
Ps 119:130 The unfolding of your words *g* light;
Pr 3:34 but *g* grace to the humble.
11:24 One man *g* freely, yet gains
14:30 A heart at peace *g* life to the body,
15:30 good news *g* health to the bones.
19: 6 of a man who *g* gifts.
25:26 is a righteous man who *g* way
28:27 He who *g* to the poor will lack
29: 4 justice a king *g* a country stability,
Isa 40:29 He *g* strength to the weary
Hab 2:15 "Woe to him who *g* drink
Mt 10:42 if anyone *g* even a cup of cold water
Jn 5:21 even so the Son *g* life to whom he is
6:63 The Spirit *g* life; the flesh counts
1Co 15:57 He *g* us the victory
2Co 3: 6 the letter kills, but the Spirit *g* life.
1Th 4: 8 who *g* you his Holy Spirit.
Jas 1:25 into the perfect law that *g* freedom,
4: 6 but *g* grace to the humble."
1Pe 5: 5 but *g* grace to the humble."

GIVING (GIVE)
Ne 8: 8 *g* the meaning so that the people
Est 9:19 a day for *g* presents to each other.
Ps 19: 8 *g* joy to the heart.
Pr 15:23 A man finds joy in *g* an apt reply—
Mt 6: 4 so that your *g* may be in secret.
24:38 marrying and *g* in marriage,
Ac 15: 8 them by *g* the Holy Spirit to them,
2Co 8: 7 also excel in this grace of *g*.
Php 4:15 shared with me in the matter of *g*

GLAD* (GLADDENS GLADNESS)
Ex 4:14 his heart will be *g* when he sees you
Jos 22:33 They were *g* to hear the report
Jdg 8:25 "We'll be *g* to give them."
18:20 household?" Then the priest was *g*.
1Sa 19: 5 and you saw it and were *g*.
2Sa 1:20 daughters of the Philistines be *g*,
1Ki 8:66 *g* in heart for all the good things
1Ch 16:31 heavens rejoice, let the earth be *g*;
2Ch 7:10 and *g* in heart for the good things
Ps 5:11 let all who take refuge in you be *g*;
9: 2 I will be *g* and rejoice in you;
14: 7 let Jacob rejoice and Israel be *g*!
16: 9 Therefore my heart is *g*
21: 6 made him *g* with the joy
31: 7 I will be *g* and rejoice in your love,
32:11 Rejoice in the LORD and be *g*,
40:16 rejoice and be *g* in you;
45: 8 music of the strings makes you *g*.
46: 4 whose streams make *g* the city
48:11 the villages of Judah are *g*
53: 6 let Jacob rejoice and Israel be *g*!
58:10 The righteous will be *g*
67: 4 May the nations be *g* and sing
68: 3 But may the righteous be *g*
69:32 The poor will see and be *g*—
70: 4 rejoice and be *g* in you;
90:14 for joy and be *g* all our days.
90:15 Make us *g* for as many days
92: 4 For you make me *g* by your deeds,
96:11 heavens rejoice, let the earth be *g*;
97: 1 LORD reigns, let the earth be *g*;

Ps 97: 8 and the villages of Judah are *g*
105:38 Egypt was *g* when they left,
107:30 They were *g* when it grew calm,
118:24 let us rejoice and be *g* in it.
149: 2 of Zion be *g* in their King.
Pr 23:15 then my heart will be *g*;
23:25 May your father and mother be *g*;
29: 6 a righteous one can sing and be *g*.
Ecc 8:15 sun than to eat and drink and be *g*.
Isa 25: 9 let us rejoice and be *g*
35: 1 and the parched land will be *g*;
65:18 But be *g* and rejoice forever
66:10 with Jerusalem and be *g* for her,
Jer 20:15 who made him very *g*, saying,
31:13 Then maidens will dance and be *g*,
41:13 were with him, they were *g*.
50:11 "Because you rejoice and are *g*,
La 4:21 be *g*, O Daughter of Edom,
Joel 2:21 be *g* and rejoice.
2:23 Be *g*, O people of Zion,
Hab 1:15 and so he rejoices and is *g*.
Zep 3:14 Be *g* and rejoice with all your heart
Zec 2:10 and be *g*, O Daughter of Zion.
8:19 will become joyful and *g* occasions
10: 7 their hearts will be *g* as with wine.
Mt 5:12 be *g*, because great is your reward
Lk 15:32 But we had to celebrate and be *g*,
Jn 4:36 and the reaper may be *g* together.
8:56 my day; he saw it and was *g*."
11:15 for your sake I am *g* I was not there
14:28 you would be *g* that I am going
Ac 2:26 Therefore my heart is *g*
2:46 together with *g* and sincere hearts,
11:23 he was *g* and encouraged them all
13:48 they were *g* and honored the word
15: 3 news made all the brothers very *g*.
15:31 were *g* for its encouraging message.
1Co 16:17 was *g* when Stephanas, Fortunatus
2Co 2: 2 who is left to make me *g*
7:16 I am *g* I can have complete
13: 9 We are *g* whenever we are weak
Gal 4:27 "Be *g*, O barren woman,
Php 2:17 I am *g* and rejoice with all of you.
2:18 So you too should be *g* and rejoice
2:28 you see him again you may be *g*
Rev 19: 7 Let us rejoice and be *g*

GLADDENS* (GLAD)
Ps 104:15 wine that *g* the heart of man,

GLADNESS* (GLAD)
2Ch 29:30 So they sang praises with *g*
Est 8:16 a time of happiness and joy, *g*
8:17 there was joy and *g*
Job 3:22 who are filled with *g*
Ps 35:27 shout for joy and *g*;
45:15 They are led in with joy and *g*;
51: 8 Let me hear joy and *g*;
65:12 the hills are clothed with *g*.
100: 2 Worship the LORD with *g*;
Ecc 5:20 God keeps him occupied with *g*
9: 7 Go, eat your food with *g*,
Isa 16:10 *g* are taken away from the orchards
35:10 *G* and joy will overtake them,
51: 3 Joy and *g* will be found in her,
51:11 *G* and joy will overtake them,
61: 3 the oil of *g* / instead of mourning,
Jer 7:34 and *g* and to the voices of bride
16: 9 and *g* and to the voices of bride
25:10 from them the sounds of joy and *g*,
31:13 I will turn their mourning into *g*;
33:11 once more the sounds of joy and *g*,
48:33 Joy and *g* are gone
Joel 1:16 joy and *g*

GLAZE*
Pr 26:23 of *g* over earthenware

GLEAM*
Pr   4:18 of the righteous is like the first *g*
Da 10: 6 legs like the *g* of burnished bronze,

GLOAT (GLOATS)
Pr 24:17 Do not *g* when your enemy falls;

GLOATS* (GLOAT)
Pr 17: 5 whoever *g* over disaster will not go

GLORIES* (GLORY)
1Pe 1:11 and the *g* that would follow.

GLORIFIED* (GLORY)
Isa 66: 5 'Let the Lord be *g*,
Eze 39:13 day I am *g* will be a memorable day
Da 4:34 and *g* him who lives forever.
Jn 7:39 since Jesus had not yet been *g*.
    11: 4 glory so that God's Son may be *g*
    12:16 after Jesus was *g* did they realize
    12:23 come for the Son of Man to be *g*.
    12:28 "I have *g* it, and will glorify it again
    13:31 Son of Man *g* and God is *g* in him.
    13:32 If God is *g* in him, God will glorify
Ac 3:13 our fathers, has *g* his servant Jesus.
Ro 1:21 they neither *g* him as God
    8:30 those he justified, he also *g*.
2Th 1:10 comes to be *g* in his holy people
    1:12 of our Lord Jesus may be *g* in you,
1Pe 1:11 him from the dead and *g* him,

GLORIFIES* (GLORY)
Lk 1:46 My soul *g* the Lord
Jn 8:54 as your God, is the one who *g* me.

GLORIFY* (GLORY)
Ps 34: 3 *G* the Lord with me;
    63: 3 my lips will *g* you.
    69:30 and *g* him with thanksgiving.
    86:12 I will *g* your name forever.
Isa 60:13 and I will *g* the place of my feet.
Da 4:37 and exalt and *g* the King of heaven,
Jn 8:54 Jesus replied, "If I *g* myself,
    12:28 glorified it, and will *g* it again."
    12:28 *g* your name!" Then a voice came
    13:32 God will *g* the Son in himself,
    13:32 in himself, and will *g* him at once.
    17: 1 *G* your Son, that your Son may
    17: 1 your Son, that your Son may *g* you.
    17: 5 *g* me in your presence
    21:19 death by which Peter would *g* God.
Ro 15: 6 and mouth you may *g* the God
    15: 9 so that the Gentiles may *g* God
1Pe 2:12 and *g* God on the day he visits us.
Rev 16: 9 they refused to repent and *g* him.

GLORIFYING* (GLORY)
Lk 2:20 *g* and praising God

GLORIOUS* (GLORY)
Dt 28:58 not revere this *g* and awesome
    33:29 and your *g* sword.
1Ch 29:13 and praise your *g* name.
Ne 9: 5 "Blessed be your *g* name,
Ps 16: 3 they are the *g* ones
    45:13 All *g* is the princess
    66: 2 make his praise *g*.
    72:19 Praise be to his *g* name forever;
    87: 3 *G* things are said of you,
    111: 3 *G* and majestic are his deeds,
    145: 5 of the *g* splendor of your majesty,
    145:12 the *g* splendor of your kingdom.
Isa 3: 8 defying his *g* presence.
    4: 2 the Lord will be beautiful and *g*,
    11:10 and his place of rest will be *g*.
    12: 5 for he has done *g* things;
    28: 1 to the fading flower, his *g* beauty,
    28: 4 That fading flower, his *g* beauty,
    28: 5 will be a *g* crown,
    42:21 to make his law great and *g*.
    60: 7 and I will adorn my *g* temple.
    63:12 who sent his *g* arm of power
    63:14 to make for yourself a *g* name.
    63:15 from your lofty throne, holy and *g*.
    64:11 *g* temple, where our fathers praised
Jer 13:18 for your *g* crowns
    14:21 do not dishonor your *g* throne.

Jer 17:12 A *g* throne, exalted
    48:17 how broken the *g* staff!'
Mt 19:28 the Son of Man sits on his *g* throne,
Lk 9:31 appeared in *g* splendor, talking
Ac 2:20 of the great and *g* day of the Lord.
Ro 8:21 and brought into the *g* freedom
2Co 3: 8 of the Spirit be even more *g*?
    3: 9 how much more *g* is the ministry
    3: 9 ministry that condemns men is *g*,
    3:10 For what was *g* has no glory now
Eph 1: 6 to the praise of his *g* grace,
    1:17 *g* Father, may give you the Spirit
    1:18 the riches of his *g* inheritance
    3:16 of his *g* riches he may strengthen
Php 3:21 so that they will be like his *g* body.
    4:19 to his *g* riches in Christ Jesus.
Col 1:11 all power according to his *g* might
    1:27 among the Gentiles the *g* riches
1Ti 1:11 to the *g* gospel of the blessed God,
Tit 2:13 the *g* appearing of our great God
Jas 2: 1 believers in our *g* Lord Jesus Christ
1Pe 1: 8 with an inexpressible and *g* joy,
Jude :24 before his *g* presence without fault

GLORIOUSLY* (GLORY)
Isa 24:23 and before its elders, *g*.

GLORY (GLORIES GLORIFIED GLORIFIES GLORIFY GLORIFYING GLORIOUS GLORIOUSLY)
Ex 14: 4 But I will gain *g* for myself
    14:17 And I will gain *g* through Pharaoh
    15:11 awesome in *g*,
    16:10 and there was the *g* of the Lord
    24:16 and the *g* of the Lord settled
    33:18 Moses said, "Now show me your *g*
    40:34 and the *g* of the Lord filled
Nu 14:21 the *g* of the Lord fills the whole
Dt 5:24 Lord our God has shown us his *g*
Jos 7:19 "My son, give *g* to the Lord,
1Sa 4:21 "The *g* has departed from Israel"—
1Ch 16:10 *G* in his holy name;
    16:24 Declare his *g* among the nations,
    16:28 ascribe to the Lord *g*
    29:11 and the *g* and the majesty
Ps 8: 1 You have set your *g*
    8: 5 and crowned him with *g* and honor
    19: 1 The heavens declare the *g* of God;
    24: 7 that the King of *g* may come in.
    26: 8 the place where your *g* dwells.
    29: 1 ascribe to the Lord *g*
    29: 9 And in his temple all cry, "*G!*"
    57: 5 let your *g* be over all the earth.
    66: 2 Sing the *g* of his name;
    72:19 the whole earth be filled with his *g*.
    96: 3 Declare his *g* among the nations,
    102:15 of the earth will revere your *g*.
    108: 5 and let your *g* be over all the earth.
    149: 9 This is the *g* of all his saints.
Pr 19:11 it is to his *g* to overlook an offense.
    25: 2 It is the *g* of God to conceal
Isa 4: 5 over all the *g* will be a canopy.
    6: 3 the whole earth is full of his *g*."
    24:16 "*G* to the Righteous One."
    26:15 You have gained *g* for yourself;
    35: 2 they will see the *g* of the Lord,
    40: 5 the *g* of the Lord will be revealed
    42: 8 I will not give my *g* to another
    42:12 Let them give *g* to the Lord
    43: 7 whom I created for my *g*,
    44:23 he displays his *g* in Israel.
    48:11 I will not yield my *g* to another.
    66:18 and they will come and see my *g*.
    66:19 They will proclaim my *g*
Eze 1:28 the likeness of the *g* of the Lord.
    10: 4 the radiance of the *g* of the Lord.
    43: 2 and the land was radiant with his *g*.
    44: 4 and saw the *g* of the Lord filling
Hab 2:14 knowledge of the *g* of the Lord,
    3: 3 His *g* covered the heavens
Zec 2: 5 'and I will be its *g* within.'
Mt 16:27 in his Father's *g* with his angels,

Mt 24:30 of the sky, with power and great *g*.
    25:31 sit on his throne in heavenly *g*.
    25:31 the Son of Man comes in his *g*,
Mk 8:38 in his Father's *g* with the holy
    13:26 in clouds with great power and *g*.
Lk 2: 9 and the *g* of the Lord shone
    2:14 saying, "*G* to God in the highest,
    9:26 and in the *g* of the Father
    9:26 of him when he comes in his *g*
    9:32 they saw his *g* and the two men
    19:38 in heaven and *g* in the highest!"
    21:27 in a cloud with power and great *g*.
    24:26 these things and then enter his *g*?"
Jn 1:14 We have seen his *g*, the *g* of the One
    2:11 He thus revealed his *g*,
    8:50 I am not seeking *g* for myself;
    8:54 myself, my *g* means nothing.
    11: 4 for God's *g* so that God's Son may
    11:40 you would see the *g* of God?"
    12:41 he saw Jesus' *g* and spoke about
    14:13 so that the Son may bring *g*
    15: 8 is to my Father's *g*, that you bear
    16:14 He will bring *g* to me by taking
    17: 4 I have brought you *g* on earth
    17: 5 presence with the *g* I had with you
    17:10 *g* has come to me through them.
    17:22 given them the *g* that you gave
    17:24 to see my *g*, the *g* you have given
Ac 7: 2 The God of *g* appeared
    7:55 up to heaven and saw the *g* of God,
Ro 1:23 exchanged the *g* of the immortal
    2: 7 by persistence in doing good seek *g*
    2:10 then for the Gentile; but *g*,
    3: 7 truthfulness and so increases his *g*,
    3:23 and fall short of the *g* of God,
    4:20 in his faith and gave *g* to God,
    8:17 that we may also share in his *g*.
    8:18 with the *g* that will be revealed
    9: 4 theirs the divine *g*, the covenants,
    9:23 riches of his *g* known to the objects
    9:23 whom he prepared in advance for *g*
    11:36 To him be the *g* forever! Amen.
    15:17 Therefore I *g* in Christ Jesus
    16:27 to the only wise God be *g* forever
1Co 2: 7 for our *g* before time began.
    10:31 whatever you do, do it all for the *g*
    11: 7 but the woman is the *g* of man.
    11: 7 since he is the image and *g* of God;
    11:15 it is her *g*? For long hair is given
    15:43 it is raised in *g*; it is sown
2Co 1:20 spoken by us to the *g* of God.
    3: 7 in letters on stone, came with *g*,
    3: 7 the face of Moses because of its *g*,
    3:10 comparison with the surpassing *g*.
    3:10 what was glorious has no *g* now
    3:11 how much greater is the *g*
    3:11 what was fading away came with *g*,
    3:18 faces all reflect the Lord's *g*,
    3:18 likeness with ever-increasing *g*,
    4: 4 of the gospel of the *g* of Christ,
    4: 6 of the knowledge of the *g* of God
    4:15 to overflow to the *g* of God.
    4:17 us an eternal *g* that far outweighs
Gal 1: 5 to whom be *g* for ever and ever.
Eph 1:12 might be for the praise of his *g*.
    1:14 to the praise of his *g*.
    3:13 for you, which are your *g*.
    3:21 to him be *g* in the church
Php 1:11 to the *g* and praise of God.
    2:11 to the *g* of God the Father.
    3: 3 of God, who *g* in Christ Jesus,
    4:20 and Father be *g* for ever and ever.
Col 1:27 Christ in you, the hope of *g*.
    3: 4 also will appear with him in *g*.
1Th 2:12 you into his kingdom and *g*.
    2:19 in which we will *g* in the presence
    2:20 Indeed, you are our *g* and joy.
2Th 2:14 in the *g* of our Lord Jesus Christ.
1Ti 1:17 be honor and *g* for ever and ever.

1Ti 3:16 was taken up in *g*.
2Ti 2:10 is in Christ Jesus, with eternal *g*.
4:18 To him be *g* for ever and ever.
Heb 1:3 The Son is the radiance of God's *g*
2:7 you crowned him with *g* and honor
2:9 now crowned with *g* and honor
2:10 In bringing many sons to *g*,
5:5 take upon himself the *g*
9:5 the ark were the cherubim of the G,
13:21 to whom be *g* for ever and ever.
1Pe 1:7 *g* and honor when Jesus Christ is
1:24 and all their *g* is like the flowers
4:11 To him be the *g* and the power
4:13 overjoyed when his *g* is revealed.
4:14 for the Spirit of *g* and of God rests
5:1 will share in the *g* to be revealed:
5:4 of *g* that will never fade away.
5:10 you to his eternal *g* in Christ,
2Pe 1:3 of him who called us by his own *g*
1:17 and *g* from God the Father
1:17 came to him from the Majestic G,
3:18 To him be *g* both now and forever!
Jude :25 to the only God our Savior be *g*,
Rev 1:6 to him be *g* and power for ever
4:9 the living creatures give *g*,
4:11 to receive *g* and honor and power,
5:12 and honor and *g* and praise!"
5:13 and honor and *g* and power,
7:12 Praise and *g*
11:13 and gave *g* to the God of heaven.
14:7 "Fear God and give him *g*,
15:4 and bring *g* to your name?
15:8 with smoke from the *g* of God
19:1 *g* and power belong to our God,
19:7 and give him *g*!
21:11 It shone with the *g* of God,
21:23 for the *g* of God gives it light,
21:26 *g* and honor of the nations will be

GLOWING
Eze 8:2 was as bright as *g* metal.
Rev 1:15 His feet were like bronze *g*

GLUTTONS* (GLUTTONY)
Pr 23:21 for drunkards and *g* become poor,
28:7 of *g* disgraces his father.
Tit 1:12 always liars, evil brutes, lazy *g*."

GLUTTONY* (GLUTTONS)
Pr 23:2 throat if you are given to *g*.

GNASHING
Mt 8:12 where there will be weeping and *g*

GNAT* (GNATS)
Mt 23:24 You strain out a *g* but swallow

GNATS (GNAT)
Ex 8:16 of Egypt the dust will become *g*."

GOADS
Ecc 12:11 The words of the wise are like *g*,
Ac 26:14 hard for you to kick against the *g*.'

GOAL*
Lk 13:32 on the third day I will reach my *g*.'
2Co 5:9 So we make it our *g* to please him,
Gal 3:3 to attain your *g* by human effort?
Php 3:14 on toward the *g* to win the prize
1Ti 1:5 The *g* of this command is love,
1Pe 1:9 for you are receiving the *g*

GOAT (GOATS SCAPEGOAT)
Ge 15:9 "Bring me a heifer, a *g* and a ram,
30:32 and every spotted or speckled *g*.
37:31 slaughtered a *g* and dipped
Ex 26:7 Make curtains of *g* hair for the tent
Lev 16:9 shall bring the *g* whose lot falls
Nu 7:16 one male *g* for a sin offering;
Isa 11:6 the leopard will lie down with the *g*
Da 8:5 suddenly a *g* with a prominent

GOATS (GOAT)
Nu 7:17 five male *g* and five male lambs
Mt 25:32 *separates the sheep from the g.*
Heb 10:4 of bulls and *g* to take away sins.

GOD (GOD'S GODLINESS GODLY GODS)
Ge 1:1 In the beginning G created
1:2 the Spirit of G was hovering
1:3 And G said, "Let there be light,"
1:7 So G made the expanse

Ge 1:9 And G said, "Let the water
1:11 Then G said, "Let the land produce
1:20 And G said, "Let the water teem
1:21 So G created the great creatures
1:25 G made the wild animals according
1:26 Then G said, "Let us make man
1:27 So G created man in his own image
1:31 G saw all that he had made,
2:3 And G blessed the seventh day
2:7 And the LORD G formed the man
2:8 the LORD G had planted a garden
2:18 The LORD G said, "It is not good
2:22 Then the LORD G made a woman
3:1 to the woman, "Did G really say,
3:5 you will be like G, knowing good
3:8 from the LORD G among the trees
3:9 But the LORD G called to the man
3:21 The LORD G made garments
3:22 LORD G said, "The man has now
3:23 So the LORD G banished him
5:1 When G created man, he made him
5:22 Enoch walked with G 300 years
5:24 because G took him away.
6:2 sons of G saw that the daughters
6:9 of his time, and he walked with G.
6:12 G saw how corrupt the earth had
8:1 But G remembered Noah
9:1 Then G blessed Noah and his sons,
9:6 for in the image of G
9:16 everlasting covenant between G
14:18 He was priest of G Most High,
14:19 Blessed be Abram by G Most High,
16:13 "You are the G who sees me,"
17:1 "I am G Almighty; walk before me
17:7 to be your G and the G
21:4 him, as G commanded him.
21:6 "G has brought me laughter,
21:20 G was with the boy as he grew up.
21:22 G is with you in everything you do.
21:33 name of the LORD, the Eternal G.
22:1 Some time later G tested Abraham.
22:8 "G himself will provide the lamb
22:12 Now I know that you fear G,
25:11 Abraham's death, G blessed his
28:12 and the angels of G were ascending
28:17 other than the house of G;
31:42 But G has seen my hardship
31:50 remember that G is a witness
32:1 and the angels of G met him.
32:28 because you have struggled with G
32:30 "It is because I saw G face to face,
33:11 for G has been gracious to me
35:1 and build an altar there to G,
35:5 and the terror of G fell
35:10 G said to him, "Your name is Jacob
35:11 G said to him, "I am G Almighty;
41:51 G has made me forget all my
41:52 G has made me fruitful in the land
50:20 but G intended it for good
50:24 But G will surely come to your aid
Ex 2:24 G heard their groaning
3:5 "Do not come any closer," G said.
3:6 because he was afraid to look at G.
3:12 And G said, "I will be with you.
3:14 what shall I tell them?" G said.
4:27 he met Moses at the mountain of G
6:7 own people, and I will be your G.
8:10 is no one like the LORD our G.
10:16 sinned against the LORD your G
13:18 So G led the people
15:2 He is my G, and I will praise him,
16:12 that I am the LORD your G.'"
17:9 with the staff of G in my hands."
18:5 camped near the mountain of G.
19:3 Then Moses went up to G,
20:1 And G spoke all these words:
20:2 the LORD your G, who brought
20:5 the LORD your G, am a jealous G,

Ex 20:7 the name of the LORD your G,
20:10 a Sabbath to the LORD your G.
20:12 the LORD your G is giving you.
20:19 But do not have G speak to us
20:20 the fear of G will be with you
22:20 "Whoever sacrifices to any *g* other
22:28 "Do not blaspheme G
23:19 to the house of the LORD your G.
31:18 inscribed by the finger of G.
34:6 the compassionate and gracious G,
34:14 name is Jealous, is a jealous G.
Lev 2:13 salt of the covenant of your G out
11:44 the LORD your G; consecrate
18:21 not profane the name of your G.
19:2 the LORD your G, am holy.
20:7 because I am the LORD your G.
21:6 They must be holy to their G
22:33 out of Egypt to be your G.
26:12 walk among you and be your G,
Nu 15:40 and will be consecrated to your G.
22:18 the command of the LORD my G.
22:38 I must speak only what G puts
23:19 G is not a man, that he should lie,
25:13 zealous for the honor of his G
Dt 1:17 for judgment belongs to G.
1:21 the LORD your G has given you
1:30 The LORD your G, who is going
3:22 LORD your G himself will fight
3:24 For what *g* is there in heaven
4:24 is a consuming fire, a jealous G.
4:29 there you seek the LORD your G,
4:31 the LORD your G is a merciful G;
4:39 heart this day that the LORD is G
5:9 the LORD your G, am a jealous G,
5:11 the name of the LORD your G,
5:12 the LORD your G has commanded
5:14 a Sabbath to the LORD your G.
5:15 the LORD your G brought you out
5:16 the LORD your G has commanded
5:16 the LORD your G is giving you.
5:24 LORD our G has shown us his
5:26 of the living G speaking out of fire,
6:2 them may fear the LORD your G
6:4 LORD our G, the LORD is one.
6:5 Love the LORD your G
6:13 the LORD your G, serve him only
6:16 Do not test the LORD your G.
7:6 holy to the LORD your G.
7:9 your G is G; he is the faithful G,
7:12 the LORD your G will keep his
7:19 LORD your G will do the same
7:21 is a great and awesome G.
8:5 the LORD your G disciplines you.
8:11 do not forget the LORD your G,
8:18 But remember the LORD your G,
9:10 inscribed by the finger of G.
10:12 but to fear the LORD your G,
10:14 the LORD your G belong
10:17 For the LORD your G is G of gods
10:21 He is your praise; he is your G,
11:1 Love the LORD your G
11:13 to love the LORD your G
12:12 rejoice before the LORD your G,
12:28 in the eyes of the LORD your G.
13:3 The LORD your G is testing you
13:4 the LORD your G you must
15:6 the LORD your G will bless you
15:19 the LORD your G every firstborn
16:11 rejoice before the LORD your G
16:17 the LORD your G has blessed you.
18:13 before the LORD your G.
18:15 The LORD your G will raise up
19:9 to love the LORD your G
22:5 the LORD your G detests anyone
23:5 the LORD your G loves you.
23:14 the LORD your G moves about
23:21 a vow to the LORD your G,
25:16 the LORD your G detests anyone
26:5 declare before the LORD your G:
29:13 that he may be your G
29:29 belong to the LORD our G,
30:2 return to the LORD your G
30:4 the LORD your G will gather you
30:6 The LORD your G will circumcise
30:16 today to love the LORD your G,
30:20 you may love the LORD your G,
31:6 for the LORD your G goes
32:3 Oh, praise the greatness of our G!
32:4 A faithful G who does no wrong,

Dt 33:27 The eternal *G* is your refuge,
Jos 1: 9 for the LORD your *G* will be
     14: 8 the LORD my *G* wholeheartedly.
     14: 9 the LORD my *G* wholeheartedly.'
     14:14 the *G* of Israel, wholeheartedly.
     22: 5 to love the LORD your *G*,
     22:22 The Mighty One, *G*, the LORD!
     22:34 Between Us that the LORD our *G*
     23: 8 to hold fast to the LORD your *G*.
     23:11 careful to love the LORD your *G*.
     23:14 the LORD your *G* gave you has
     23:15 of the LORD your *G* has come true
     24:19 He is a holy *G*; he is a jealous *G*.
     24:23 to the LORD, the *G* of Israel."
Jdg 5: 3 to the LORD, the *G* of Israel.
     16:28 O *G*, please strengthen me just
Ru   1:16 be my people and your *G* my *G*.
     2:12 by the LORD, the *G* of Israel,
1Sa 2: 2 there is no Rock like our *G*.
     2: 3 for the LORD is a *G* who knows,
     2:25 another man, *G* may mediate
     10:26 men whose hearts *G* had
            touched.
     12:12 the LORD your *G* was your king.
     16:15 spirit from *G* is tormenting you.
     17:26 defy the armies of the living *G*?"
     17:36 defied the armies of the living *G*.
     17:45 the *G* of the armies of Israel,
     17:46 world will know that there is a *G*
     23:16 and helped him find strength in *G*.
     28:15 and *G* has turned away from me.
     30: 6 strength in the LORD his *G*.
2Sa 7:22 and there is no *G* but you,
     7:23 on earth that *G* went out to
            redeem
     14:14 But *G* does not take away life;
     21:14 *G* answered prayer in behalf
     22: 3 my *G* is my rock, in whom I take
     22:31 "As for *G*, his way is perfect;
     22:32 And who is the Rock except our *G*
     22:33 It is *G* who arms me with strength
     22:47 Exalted be *G*, the Rock, my Savior!
1Ki 2: 3 what the LORD your *G* requires:
     4:29 *G* gave Solomon wisdom
     5: 5 for the Name of the LORD my *G*,
     8:23 there is no *G* like you in heaven
     8:27 "But will *G* really dwell on earth?
     8:60 may know that the LORD is *G*
     8:61 committed to the LORD our *G*,
     10:24 to hear the wisdom *G* had put
     15:30 he provoked the LORD, the *G*
     18:21 If the LORD is *G*, follow him;
     18:36 it be known today that you are *G*
     18:37 are *G*, and that you are turning
     20:28 a *g* of the hills and not a *g*
2Ki 5:15 "Now I know that there is no *G*
     18: 5 in the LORD, the *G* of Israel.
     19:15 *G* of Israel, enthroned
     19:19 Now, O LORD our *G*, deliver us
1Ch 12:18 for your *G* will help you."
     13: 2 if it is the will of the LORD our *G*,
     16:35 Cry out, "Save us, O *G* our Savior;
     17:20 and there is no *G* but you,
     17:24 the *G* over Israel, is Israel's *G*!'
     21: 8 said to *G*, "I have sinned greatly
     22: 1 house of the LORD *G* is to be here,
     22:19 soul to seeking the LORD your *G*.
     28: 2 for the footstool of our *G*,
     28: 9 acknowledge the *G* of your father,
     28:20 for the LORD *G*, my *G*, is with you
     29: 1 not for man but for the LORD *G*.
     29: 2 provided for the temple of
            my *G*—
     29: 3 of my *G* I now give my personal
     29:10 *G* of our father Israel,
     29:13 Now, our *G*, we give you thanks,
     29:16 O LORD our *G*, as for all this
     29:17 my *G*, that you test the heart
     29:18 *G* of our fathers Abraham,
2Ch 2: 4 for the Name of the LORD my *G*
     5:14 of the LORD filled the temple of *G*
     6: 4 be to the LORD, the *G* of Israel,
     6:14 there is no *G* like you in heaven
     6:18 "But will *G* really dwell on earth
     10:15 for this turn of events was from *G*,
     13:12 *G* is with us; he is our leader.
     15: 3 was without the true *G*,
     15:12 the *G* of their fathers,
     15:15 They sought *G* eagerly,
     18:13 I can tell him only what my *G* says

2Ch 19: 3 have set your heart on
            seeking *G*."
     19: 7 with the LORD our *G* there is no
     20: 6 are you not the *G* who is in
            heaven?
     20:20 Have faith in the LORD your *G*
     25: 8 for *G* has the power to help
     26: 5 sought the LORD, *G* gave him
     30: 9 for the LORD your *G* is gracious
     30:19 who sets his heart on seeking *G*—
     31:21 he sought his *G* and worked
     32:31 *G* left him to test him
     33:12 the favor of the LORD his *G*
     34:33 fail to follow the LORD, the *G*
Ezr 6:21 to seek the LORD, the *G* of Israel.
     7:18 accordance with the will of
            your *G*.
     7:23 Whatever the *G* of heaven has
     8:22 "The gracious hand of our *G* is
     8:31 The hand of our *G* was on us,
     9: 6 "O my *G*, I am too ashamed
     9: 9 our *G* has not deserted us
     9:13 our *G*, you have punished us less
     9:15 *G* of Israel, you are righteous!
Ne   1: 5 the great and awesome *G*,
     1: 5 fear of our *G* to avoid the
            reproach
     5:15 for I did not act like that.
     7: 2 feared *G* more than most men do.
     8: 8 from the Book of the Law of *G*,
     8:18 from the Book of the Law of *G*.
     9: 5 and praise the LORD your *G*,
     9:17 But you are a forgiving *G*,
     9:31 you are a gracious and merciful *G*.
     9:32 the great, mighty and awesome *G*,
     10:29 oath to follow the Law of *G* given
     10:39 not neglect the house of our *G*."
     12:43 *G* had given them great joy.
     13:11 Why is the house of *G*
            neglected?"
     13:26 He was loved by his *G*,
     13:31 Remember me with favor,
            O my *G*
Job 1: 1 he feared *G* and shunned evil.
     1:22 by charging *G* with wrongdoing.
     2:10 Shall we accept good from *G*,
     4:17 a mortal be more righteous
            than *G*?
     5:17 is the man whom *G* corrects;
     8: 3 Does *G* pervert justice?
     8:20 "Surely *G* does not reject
     9: 2 a mortal be righteous before *G*?
     11: 7 Can you fathom the mysteries
            of *G*
     12:13 "To *G* belong wisdom and power;
     16: 7 Surely, O *G*, you have worn me
            out
     19:26 yet in my flesh I will see *G*;
     21:19 '*G* stores up a man's punishment
     21:22 Can anyone teach knowledge
            to *G*,
     22:12 "Is not *G* in the heights of heaven?
     22:13 Yet you say, 'What does *G* know?
     22:21 "Submit to *G* and be at peace
     25: 2 "Dominion and awe belong to *G*;
     25: 4 can a man be righteous before *G*?
     26: 6 Death is naked before *G*;
     30:20 O *G*, but you do not answer;
     31: 6 let *G* weigh me in honest scales
     31:14 do when *G* confronts me?
     32:13 let *G* refute him, not man.'
     33: 6 I am just like you before *G*;
     33:14 For *G* does speak—now one way,
     33:26 He prays to *G* and finds favor
     34:10 Far be it from *G* to do evil,
     34:12 is unthinkable that *G* would do
     34:23 *G* has no need to examine men
     34:33 Should *G* then reward you
     36: 5 "*G* is mighty, but does not despise
     36:26 is *G*— beyond our understanding!
     37:22 *G* comes in awesome majesty.
Ps   5: 4 You are not a *G* who takes
            pleasure
     7:11 *G* is a righteous judge,
     10:14 O *G*, do see trouble and grief;
     14: 5 for *G* is present in the company
     18: 2 my *G* is my rock, in whom I take
     18:28 my *G* turns my darkness into light.
     18:30 As for *G*, his way is perfect;
     18:31 And who is the Rock except our *G*
     18:32 It is *G* who arms me with strength

Ps   18:46 Exalted be *G* my Savior!
     19: 1 The heavens declare the glory
            of *G*;
     22: 1 *G*, my *G*, why have you forsaken
     22:10 womb you have been my *G*.
     27: 9 O *G* my Savior.
     29: 3 the *G* of glory thunders,
     31: 5 redeem me, O LORD, the *G*
     31:14 I say, "You are my *G*."
     33:12 the nation whose *G* is the LORD,
     35:24 righteousness, O LORD my *G*;
     37:31 The law of his *G* is in his heart;
     40: 3 a hymn of praise to our *G*.
     40: 8 I desire to do your will, O my *G*;
     42: 1 so my soul pants for you, O *G*.
     42: 2 thirsts for *G*, for the living *G*.
     42: 5 Put your hope in *G*,
     42: 8 a prayer to the *G* of my life.
     42:11 Put your hope in *G*,
     43: 4 to *G*, my joy and my delight.
     44: 8 In *G* we make our boast all day
     45: 6 O *G*, will last for ever and ever;
     45: 7 therefore *G*, your *G*, has set you
     46: 1 is our refuge and strength,
     46: 5 *G* will help her at break of day.
     46:10 "Be still, and know that I am *G*;
     47: 1 shout to *G* with cries of joy.
     47: 6 Sing praises to *G*, sing praises;
     47: 7 For *G* is the King of all the earth;
     48: 9 Within your temple, O *G*,
     49: 7 or give to *G* a ransom for him—
     50: 2 *G* shines forth.
     50: 3 Our *G* comes and will not be
            silent;
     51: 1 Have mercy on me, O *G*,
     51:10 Create in me a pure heart, O *G*,
     51:17 O *G*, you will not despise.
     53: 2 any who seek *G*.
     54: 4 Surely *G* is my help;
     55:19 *G*, who is enthroned forever,
     56: 4 In *G*, whose word I praise,
     56:10 In *G*, whose word I praise,
     56:13 that I may walk before *G*
     57: 3 *G* sends his love and his
     57: 7 My heart is steadfast, O *G*,
     59:17 are my fortress, my loving *G*.
     62: 1 My soul finds rest in *G* alone;
     62: 7 my honor depend on *G*;
     62: 8 for *G* is our refuge.
     62:11 One thing *G* has spoken,
     63: 1 O *G*, you are my *G*,
     65: 5 O *G* our Savior,
     66: 1 Shout with joy to *G*, all the earth!
     66: 3 Say to *G*, "How awesome are your
     66: 5 Come and see what *G* has done,
     66:16 listen, all you who fear *G*;
     66:20 Praise be to *G*,
     68: 4 Sing to *G*, sing praise to his name,
     68: 6 *G* sets the lonely in families,
     68:20 Our *G* is a *G* who saves;
     68:24 has come into view, O *G*,
     68:35 You are awesome, O *G*,
     69: 5 You know my folly, O *G*;
     70: 1 Hasten, O *G*, to save me;
     70: 4 "Let *G* be exalted!"
     70: 5 come quickly to me, O *G*.
     71: 7 my youth, O *G*, you have taught
     71:18 do not forsake me, O *G*,
     71:19 reaches to the skies, O *G*,
     71:22 harp for your faithfulness,
            O my *G*;
     73:17 me till I entered the sanctuary
            of *G*;
     73:26 but *G* is the strength of my heart
     76:11 Make vows to the LORD your *G*
     77:13 What *g* is so great as our God?
     77:14 You are the *G* who performs
     78:19 Can *G* spread a table in the
            desert?
     79: 9 Help us, O *G* our Savior,
     81: 1 Sing for joy to *G* our strength;
     82: 1 *G* presides in the great assembly;
     84: 2 out for the living *G*.
     84:10 a doorkeeper in the house of
            my *G*
     84:11 For the LORD *G* is a sun
     86:12 O Lord my *G*, with all my heart;
     86:15 a compassionate and gracious *G*,
     87: 3 O city of *G*: *Selah*
     89: 7 of the holy ones *G* is greatly
            feared;

Ps 90: 2 to everlasting you are *G.*
91: 2 my *G,* in whom I trust."
94:22 my *G* the rock in whom I take
95: 7 for he is our *G*
99: 8 you were to Israel a forgiving *G,*
99: 9 Exalt the Lord our *G*
100: 3 Know that the Lord is *G.*
108: 1 My heart is steadfast, O *G;*
113: 5 Who is like the Lord our *G,*
115: 3 Our *G* is in heaven;
116: 5 our *G* is full of compassion.
123: 2 look to the Lord our *G,*
136: 2 Give thanks to the *G* of gods.
136:26 Give thanks to the *G* of heaven.
139:17 to me are your thoughts, O *G!*
139:23 Search me, O *G,* and know my
143:10 for you are my *G;*
144: 2 He is my loving *G* and my fortress,
147: 1 is to sing praises to our *G,*
Pr 3: 4 in the sight of *G* and man.
14:31 to the needy honors *G.*
25: 2 of *G* to conceal a matter;
30: 5 "Every word of *G* is flawless;
Ecc 2:26 *G* gives wisdom, knowledge
3:11 cannot fathom what *G* has done
3:13 in all his toil—this is the gift of *G.*
3:14 *G* does it so that men will revere him.
5: 4 When you make a vow to *G,*
5:19 in his work—this is a gift of *G.*
8:12 who are reverent before *G.*
11: 5 cannot understand the work of *G,*
12: 7 the spirit returns to *G* who gave it.
12:13 Fear *G* and keep his
Isa 5:16 the holy *G* will show himself holy
9: 6 Wonderful Counselor, Mighty *G,*
12: 2 Surely *G* is my salvation;
25: 9 "Surely this is our *G;*
28:11 *G* will speak to this people,
29:23 will stand in awe of the *G* of Israel.
30:18 For the Lord is a *G* of justice.
35: 4 your *G* will come,
37:16 you alone are *G* over all
40: 1 says your *G.*
40: 3 a highway for our *G.*
40: 8 the word of our *G* stands forever."
40:18 then, will you compare *G?*
40:28 The Lord is the everlasting *G,*
41:10 not be dismayed, for I am your *G.*
41:13 For I am the Lord, your *G,*
43:10 Before me no *g* was formed,
44: 6 apart from me there is no *G.*
44:15 he also fashions a *g* and worships it;
45:18 he is *G;*
48:17 "I am the Lord your *G,*
52: 7 "Your *G* reigns!"
52:12 *G* of Israel will be your rear guard.
55: 7 to our *G,* for he will freely pardon.
57:21 says my *G,* "for the wicked."
59: 2 you from your *G;*
60:19 and your *G* will be your glory.
61: 2 and the day of vengeance of our *G,*
61:10 my soul rejoices in my *G.*
62: 5 so will your *G* rejoice over you.
Jer 7:23 I will be your *G* and you will be my
10:10 But the Lord is the true *G;*
10:12 But *G* made the earth by his power;
23:23 "Am I only a *G* nearby,"
23:36 distort the words of the living *G,*
31:33 I will be their *G,*
32:27 "I am the Lord, the *G*
42: 6 for we will obey the Lord our *G.* "
51:10 what the Lord our *G* has done.'
51:56 For the Lord is a *G* of retribution
Eze 28:13 the garden of *G;*
34:31 and I am your *G,* declares
Da 2:28 there is a *G* in heaven who reveals
3:17 the *G* we serve is able to save us
3:29 for no other *g* can save in this way
6:16 "May your *G,* whom you serve
9: 4 O Lord, the great and awesome *G,*
10:12 to humble yourself before your *G,*
11:36 things against the *G* of gods.
Hos 1: 9 my people, and I am not your *G.*
1:10 be called 'sons of the living *G.*'

Hos 4: 6 you have ignored the law of your *G*
6: 6 acknowledgment of *G* rather
9: 8 The prophet, along with my *G,*
12: 6 and wait for your *G* always.
Joel 2:13 Return to the Lord your *G,*
2:23 rejoice in the Lord your *G,*
Am 4:12 prepare to meet your *G,* O Israel."
4:13 the Lord *G* Almighty is his name
Jnh 1: 6 Get up and call on your *g!*
4: 2 a gracious and compassionate *G,*
Mic 6: 8 and to walk humbly with your *G.*
7: 7 I wait for *G* my Savior;
7:18 Who is a *G* like you,
Na 1: 2 Lord is a jealous and avenging *G;*
Hab 3:18 I will be joyful in *G* my Savior.
Zep 3:17 The Lord your *G* is with you,
Zec 14: 5 Then the Lord my *G* will come,
Mal 2:10 Father? Did not one *G* create us?
2:16 says the Lord *G* of Israel,
3: 8 Will a man rob *G?* Yet you rob me.
Mt 1:23 which means, "*G* with us."
4: 4 comes from the mouth of *G.* ' "
4: 7 'Do not put the Lord your *G*
4:10 'Worship the Lord your *G,*
5: 8 for they will see *G.*
6:24 You cannot serve both *G*
19: 6 Therefore what *G* has joined
19:26 but with *G* all things are possible."
22:21 and to *G* what is God's."
22:32 He is not the *G* of the dead
22:37 " 'Love the Lord your *G*
27:46 which means, "My *G,* my *G,*
Mk 2: 7 Who can forgive sins but *G* alone?"
7:13 Thus you nullify the word of *G*
10: 6 of creation *G* 'made them male
10: 9 Therefore what *G* has joined
10:18 "No one is good—except *G* alone.
10:27 all things are possible with *G.* "
11:22 "Have faith in *G,*" Jesus answered.
12:17 and to *G* what is God's."
12:29 the Lord our *G,* the Lord is one.
12:30 Love the Lord your *G*
15:34 which means, "My *G,* my *G,*
16:19 and he sat at the right hand of *G.*
Lk 1:30 Mary, you have found favor with *G*
1:37 For nothing is impossible with *G.* "
1:47 my spirit rejoices in *G* my Savior,
2:14 "Glory to *G* in the highest,
2:52 and in favor with *G* and men.
4: 8 'Worship the Lord your *G*
5:21 Who can forgive sins but *G* alone?"
8:39 tell how much *G* has done for you."
10: 9 'The kingdom of *G* is near you.'
10:27 " 'Love the Lord your *G*
13:18 "What is the kingdom of *G* like?
13:19 "No one is good—except *G* alone.
18:27 with men is possible with *G.* "
20:25 and to *G* what is God's."
20:38 He is not the *G* of the dead,
22:69 at the right hand of the mighty *G.* "
Jn 1: 1 was with *G,* and the Word was *G.*
1:18 ever seen *G,* but *G* the One and Only,
1:29 Lamb of *G,* who takes away the sin
3:16 "For *G* so loved the world that he
3:34 the one whom *G* has sent speaks
4:24 *G* is spirit, and his worshipers must
5:44 praise that comes from the only *G?*
6:29 answered, "The work of *G* is this:
7:17 my teaching comes from *G* or
8:42 to them, "If *G* were your Father,
8:47 belongs to *G* hears what *G* says.
11:40 you would see the glory of *G?*"
13: 3 from *G* and was returning to *G;*
13:31 of Man glorified and *G* is glorified
14: 1 Trust in *G;* trust also in me.
17: 3 the only true *G,* and Jesus Christ,
20:17 your Father, to my *G* and your *G*
20:28 "My Lord and my *G!*"
20:31 the Son of *G,* and that
Ac 2:11 wonders of *G* in our own tongues!"

Ac 2:24 But *G* raised him from the dead,
2:33 Exalted to the right hand of *G,*
2:36 *G* has made this Jesus, whom you
3:15 but *G* raised him from the dead.
3:19 Repent, then, and turn to *G,*
4:31 and spoke the word of *G* boldly.
5: 4 You have not lied to men but to *G*
5:29 "We must obey *G* rather than men!
5:31 *G* exalted him to his own right
5:32 whom *G* has given
7:55 to heaven and saw the glory of *G,*
8:21 your heart is not right before *G.*
11: 9 anything impure that *G* has made
13:24 But the word of *G* continued
13:32 What *G* promised our fathers he
15:10 to test *G* by putting on the necks
17:23 TO AN UNKNOWN *G.*
17:30 In the past *G* overlooked such
20:27 to you the whole will of *G.*
20:32 "Now I commit you to *G*
24:16 keep my conscience clear before *G*
Ro 1:16 the power of *G* for the salvation
1:17 a righteousness from *G* is revealed,
1:18 The wrath of *G* is being revealed
1:24 Therefore *G* gave them
1:26 *G* gave them over to shameful lusts
2:11 For *G* does not show favoritism.
2:16 when *G* will judge men's secrets
3: 4 Let *G* be true, and every man a liar.
3:19 world held accountable to *G.*
3:23 and fall short of the glory of *G,*
3:29 Is *G* the *G* of Jews only? Is he not
4: 3 say? "Abraham believed *G,*
4: 6 to whom *G* credits righteousness
4:17 the *G* who gives life to the dead
4:24 to whom *G* will credit
5: 1 we have peace with *G*
5: 5 because *G* has poured out his love
5: 8 *G* demonstrates his own love for us
6:22 and have become slaves to *G,*
6:23 but the gift of *G* is eternal life
8: 7 the sinful mind is hostile to *G.*
8:17 heirs of *G* and co-heirs with Christ,
8:28 in all things *G* works for the good
9:14 What then shall we say? Is *G* unjust
9:18 Therefore *G* has mercy
10: 9 in your heart that *G* raised him
11: 2 *G* did not reject his people,
11:22 the kindness and sternness of *G:*
11:32 For *G* has bound all men
13: 1 exist have been established by *G.*
14:12 give an account of himself to *G.*
16:20 of peace will soon crush Satan
1Co 1:18 are being saved it is the power of *G.*
1:20 Has not *G* made foolish
1:25 For the foolishness of *G* is wiser
1:27 But *G* chose the foolish things
2: 9 what *G* has prepared
2:11 of *G* except the Spirit of *G.*
3: 6 watered it, but *G* made it grow.
3:17 God's temple, *G* will destroy
6:20 Therefore honor *G* with your body.
7: 7 each man has his own gift from *G;*
7:15 *G* has called us to live in peace.
7:20 was in when *G* called him.
7:24 each man, as responsible to *G,*
8: 3 man who loves *G* is known by *G.*
8: 8 food does not bring us near to *G;*
10:13 *G* is faithful; he will not let you be
10:31 do it all for the glory of *G.*
12:24 But *G* has combined the members
14:33 For *G* is not a *G* of disorder
15:24 over the kingdom to *G* the Father
15:28 so that *G* may be all in all.
15:34 some who are ignorant of *G*—
15:57 be to *G!* He gives us the victory
2Co 1: 9 rely on ourselves but on *G,*
2:14 be to *G,* who always leads us
2:15 For we are to *G* the aroma of Christ
2:17 we do not peddle the word of *G*

2Co 3: 5 but our competence comes from G.
4: 2 nor do we distort the word of G.
4: 7 this all-surpassing power is from G
5: 5 Now it is G who has made us
5:19 that G was reconciling the world
5:20 though G were making his appeal
5:21 G made him who had no sin
6:16 we are the temple of the living G.
9: 7 for G loves a cheerful giver.
9: 8 G is able to make all grace abound
10:13 to the field G has assigned to us,
Gal 2: 6 G does not judge by external
3: 5 Does G give you his Spirit
3: 6 Abraham: "He believed G,
3:11 justified before G by the law,
3:26 You are all sons of G through faith
6: 7 not be deceived: G cannot be
Eph 1:22 G placed all things under his feet
2: 8 it is the gift of G— not by works,
2:10 which G prepared in advance for us
2:22 in which G lives by his Spirit.
4: 6 one baptism; one G and Father
4:24 to be like G in true righteousness
5: 1 Be imitators of G, therefore,
6: 6 doing the will of G from your heart.
Php 2: 6 Who, being in very nature G,
2: 9 Therefore G exalted him
2:13 for it is G who works in you to will
4: 7 peace of G, which transcends all
4:19 And my G will meet all your needs
Col 1:19 For G was pleased
2:13 G made you alive with Christ.
1Th 2: 4 trying to please men but G,
2:13 but as it actually is, the word of G,
3: 9 How can we thank G enough
4: 7 For G did not call us to be impure,
4: 9 taught by G to love each other.
5: 9 For G did not appoint us
1Ti 2: 5 one mediator between G and men,
4: 4 For everything G created is good,
5: 4 for this is pleasing to G.
2Ti 1: 6 you to fan into flame the gift of G,
Tit 1: 2 which G, who does not lie,
2:13 glorious appearing of our great G
Heb 1: 1 In the past G spoke
3: 4 but G is the builder of everything.
4: 4 "And on the seventh day G rested
4:12 For the word of G is living
6:10 G is not unjust; he will not forget
6:18 in which it is impossible for G to lie
7:19 by which we draw near to G.
7:25 come to G through him,
10:22 draw near to G with a sincere heart
10:31 to fall into the hands of the living G
11: 5 commended as one who pleased G.
11: 6 faith it is impossible to please G,
12: 7 as discipline; G is treating you
12:10 but G disciplines us for our good,
12:29 for our "G is a consuming fire."
13:15 offer to G a sacrifice of praise—
Jas 1:12 crown of life that G has promised
1:13 For G cannot be tempted by evil,
1:27 Religion that G our Father accepts
2:19 You believe that there is one G.
2:23 "Abraham believed G,
4: 4 the world becomes an enemy of G.
4: 6 "G opposes the proud
4: 8 Come near to G and he will come
1Pe 1:23 the living and enduring word of G.
2:20 this is commendable before G.
3:18 the unrighteous, to bring you to G.
4:11 it with the strength G provides,
5: 5 because, "G opposes the proud
2Pe 1:21 but men spoke from G
2: 4 For if G did not spare angels
1Jn 1: 5 G is light; in him there is no
2:17 the will of G lives forever.
3: 1 we should be called children of G!
3: 1 born of G will continue to sin,
3: 9 born of G will continue to sin,

1Jn 3:10 we know who the children of G are
3:20 For G is greater than our hearts,
4: 7 for love comes from G.
4: 8 not know G, because G is love.
4: 9 This is how G showed his love
4:11 Dear friends, since G so loved us,
4:12 No one has ever seen G;
4:15 G lives in him and he in G.
4:16 G is love.
4:20 "I love G," yet hates his brother,
4:21 Whoever loves G must
5: 2 that we love the children of G:
5: 3 love for G: to obey his commands.
5: 4 born of G overcomes the world.
5:10 does not believe G has made him
5:14 have in approaching G:
5:18 born of G does not continue to sin;
Rev 4: 8 holy is the Lord G Almighty,
7:12 be to our G for ever and ever.
7:17 G will wipe away every tear
11:16 fell on their faces and worshiped G,
15: 3 Lord G Almighty.
17:17 For G has put it into their hearts
19: 6 For our Lord G Almighty reigns.
21: 3 Now the dwelling of G is with men,
21:23 for the glory of G gives it light,

GOD-BREATHED* (BREATH)
2Ti 3:16 All Scripture is G and is useful

GOD-FEARING* (FEAR)
Ecc 8:12 that it will go better with G men,
Ac 2: 5 staying in Jerusalem G Jews
10: 2 all his family were devout and G;
10:22 He is a righteous and G man,
13:26 of Abraham, and you G Gentiles,
13:50 But the Jews incited the G women
17: 4 as did a large number of G Greeks
17:17 with the Jews and the G Greeks,

GOD-HATERS* (HATE)
Ro 1:30 They are gossips, slanderers, G,

GOD'S (GOD)
2Ch 20:15 For the battle is not yours, but G
Job 37:14 stop and consider G wonders.
Ps 52: 8 I trust in G unfailing love
69:30 I will praise G name in song
Mk 3:35 Whoever does G will is my brother
Jn 7:17 If anyone chooses to do G will,
10:36 'I am G Son'? Do not believe me
Ro 2: 3 think you will escape G judgment?
2: 4 not realizing that G kindness leads
3: 3 lack of faith nullify G faithfulness?
7:22 in my inner being I delight in G law
9:16 or effort, but on G mercy.
11:29 for G gifts and his call are
12: 2 and approve what G will is—
12:13 Share with G people who are
13: 6 for the authorities are G servants,
1Co 7:19 Keeping G commands is what
2Co 6: 2 now is the time of G favor,
Eph 1: 7 riches of G grace that he lavished
1Th 4: 3 It is G will that you should be sanctified:
5:18 for this is G will for you
1Ti 6: 1 so that G name and our teaching
2Ti 2:19 G solid foundation stands firm,
Tit 1: 7 overseer is entrusted with G work,
Heb 1: 3 The Son is the radiance of G glory
9:24 now to appear for us in G presence.
11: 3 was formed at G command,
1Pe 2:15 For it is G will that
3: 4 which is of great worth in G sight.
1Jn 2: 5 G love is truly made complete

GODLESS
Job 20: 5 the joy of the g lasts but a moment.
1Ti 6:20 Turn away from g chatter

GODLINESS (GOD)
1Ti 2: 2 and quiet lives in all g and holiness.
4: 8 but g has value for all things,
6: 5 and who think that g is a means
6: 6 g with contentment is great gain.

1Ti 6:11 and pursue righteousness, g, faith,
2Pe 1: 6 and to perseverance, g;

GODLY (GOD)
Ps 4: 3 that the Lord has set apart the g
2Co 7:10 G sorrow brings repentance that
11: 2 jealous for you with a g jealousy.
2Ti 3:12 everyone who wants to live a g life
2Pe 3:11 You ought to live holy and g lives

GODS (GOD)
Ex 20: 3 "You shall have no other g
Dt 5: 7 "You shall have no other g
1Ch 16:26 For all the g of the nations are idols
Ps 82: 6 "I said, 'You are "g";
Jn 10:34 have said you are g'? If he called
Ac 19:26 He says that man-made g are no g

GOG
Eze 38:18 When G attacks the land of Israel,
Rev 20: 8 G and Magog—to gather them

GOLD
1Ki 20: 3 'Your silver and g are mine,
Job 22:25 then the Almighty will be your g,
23:10 tested me, I will come forth as g.
28:15 cannot be bought with the finest g,
31:24 "If I have put my trust in g
Ps 19:10 They are more precious than g,
119:127 more than g, more than pure g,
Pr 3:14 and yields better returns than g
22: 1 esteemed is better than silver or g.
Hag 2: 8 The silver is mine and the g is mine
Mt 2:11 and presented him with gifts of g
Rev 3:18 to buy from me g refined in the fire,

GOLGOTHA*
Mt 27:33 to a place called G (which means
Mk 15:22 to the place called G (which means
Jn 19:17 (which in Aramaic is called G).

GOLIATH
Philistine giant killed by David (1Sa 17; 21:9).

GOMORRAH
Ge 19:24 sulfur on Sodom and G—
Mt 10:15 and G on the day of judgment
2Pe 2: 6 and G by burning them to ashes,
Jude 7 G and the surrounding towns gave

GOOD
Ge 1: 4 God saw that the light was g,
1:10 And God saw that it was g.
1:12 And God saw that it was g.
1:18 And God saw that it was g.
1:21 And God saw that it was g.
1:25 And God saw that it was g.
1:31 he had made, and it was very g.
2: 9 and the tree of the knowledge of g
2: 9 pleasing to the eye and g for food.
2:18 "It is not g for the man to be alone.
3:22 become like one of us, knowing g
50:20 but God intended it for g
2Ch 7: 3 "He is g; / his love endures
31:20 doing what was g and right
Job 2:10 Shall we accept g from God,
Ps 14: 1 there is no one who does g.
34: 8 Taste and see that the Lord is g;
34:14 Turn from evil and do g;
37: 3 Trust in the Lord and do g;
37:27 Turn from evil and do g;
52: 9 for your name is g.
53: 1 there is no one who does g,
84:11 no g thing does he withhold
86: 5 You are forgiving and g, O Lord
100: 5 For the Lord is g and his love
103: 5 satisfies your desires with g things,
112: 5 G will come to him who is
119:68 You are g, and what you do is g;
133: 1 How g and pleasant it is
145: 9 The Lord is g to all;
147: 1 How g it is to sing praises
Pr 3: 4 you will win favor and a g name
3:27 Do not withhold g
11:27 He who seeks g finds g will,

2213

Pr 13:22 A *g* man leaves an inheritance
14:22 those who plan what is *g* find love
15: 3 on the wicked and the *g*.
15:23 and how *g* is a timely word!
15:30 *g* news gives health to the bones.
17:22 A cheerful heart is *g* medicine,
18:22 He who finds a wife finds what is *g*
19: 2 It is not *g* to have zeal
22: 1 A *g* name is more desirable
31:12 She brings him *g*, not harm,
Ecc 12:14 whether it is *g* or evil.
Isa 5:20 Woe to those who call evil *g*
40: 9 You who bring *g* tidings
52: 7 the feet of those who bring *g* news,
61: 1 me to preach *g* news to the poor.
Jer 6:16 ask where the *g* way is,
13:23 Neither can you do *g*
32:39 the *g* of their children after them.
Eze 34:14 I will tend them in a *g* pasture,
Mic 6: 8 has showed you, O man, what is *g*.
Na 1:15 the feet of one who brings *g* news,
Mt 5:45 sun to rise on the evil and the *g*,
7:11 Father in heaven give *g* gifts
7:17 Likewise every *g* tree bears *g* fruit,
7:18 A *g* tree cannot bear bad fruit,
12:35 The *g* man brings *g* things out
13: 8 Still other seed fell on *g* soil,
13:24 is like a man who sowed *g* seed
13:48 and collected the *g* fish in baskets,
19:17 "There is only One who is *g*.
22:10 both *g* and bad, and the wedding
25:21 'Well done, *g* and faithful servant!
Mk 1:15 Repent and believe the *g* news!"
3: 4 lawful on the Sabbath: to do *g*
4: 8 Still other seed fell on *g* soil.
8:36 What *g* is it for a man
10:18 "No one is *g*— except God alone.
16:15 preach the *g* news to all creation.
Lk 2:10 I bring you *g* news
3: 9 does not produce *g* fruit will be
6:27 do *g* to those who hate you,
6:43 nor does a bad tree bear *g* fruit.
6:45 The *g* man brings *g* things out
8: 8 Still other seed fell on *g* soil.
9:25 What *g* is it for a man
14:34 "Salt is *g*, but if it loses its saltiness,
18:19 "No one is *g*— except God alone.
19:17 " 'Well done, my *g* servant!'
Jn 10:11 "I am the *g* shepherd.
Ro 3:12 there is no one who does *g*,
7:12 is holy, righteous and *g*.
7:16 want to do, I agree that the law is *g*.
7:18 I have the desire to do what is *g*,
8:28 for the *g* of those who love him,
10:15 feet of those who bring *g* news!"
12: 2 his *g*, pleasing and perfect will.
12: 9 Hate what is evil; cling to what is *g*.
13: 4 For he is God's servant to do you *g*
16:19 you to be wise about what is *g*,
1Co 7: 1 It is *g* for a man not to marry.
10:24 should seek his own *g*, but the *g*
15:33 Bad company corrupts *g* character
2Co 9: 8 you will abound in every *g* work.
Gal 4:18 provided the purpose is *g*,
6: 9 us not become weary in doing *g*,
6:10 as we have opportunity, let us do *g*
Eph 2:10 in Christ Jesus to do *g* works,
6: 8 everyone for whatever *g* he does,
Php 1: 6 that he who began a *g* work
Col 1:10 bearing fruit in every *g* work,
1Th 5:21 Hold on to the *g*.
1Ti 3: 7 have a *g* reputation with outsiders.
4: 4 For everything God created is *g*,
6:12 Fight the *g* fight of the faith.
6:18 them to do *g*, to be rich in *g* deeds,
2Ti 3:17 equipped for every *g* work.
4: 7 I have fought the *g* fight, I have
Tit 1: 8 loves what is *g*, who is
2: 7 an example by doing what is *g*.

Tit 2:14 his very own, eager to do what is *g*.
Heb 5:14 to distinguish *g* from evil.
10:24 on toward love and *g* deeds.
12:10 but God disciplines us for our *g*,
13:16 do not forget to do *g* and to share
Jas 4:17 who knows the *g* he ought to do
1Pe 2: 3 you have tasted that the Lord is *g*.
2:12 Live such *g* lives among the pagans
2:18 not only to those who are *g*
3:17 to suffer for doing *g*

GOODS
Ecc 5:11 As *g* increase,

GORGE
Pr 23:20 or *g* themselves on meat,

GOSHEN
Ge 45:10 You shall live in the region of *G*
Ex 8:22 differently with the land of *G*,

GOSPEL
Ro 1:16 I am not ashamed of the *g*,
15:16 duty of proclaiming the *g* of God,
15:20 to preach the *g* where Christ was
1Co 1:17 to preach the *g*— not with words
9:12 rather than hinder the *g* of Christ.
9:14 who preach the *g* should receive
9:16 Woe to me if I do not preach the *g*!
15: 1 you of the *g* I preached to you,
15: 2 By this *g* you are saved,
2Co 4: 4 light of the *g* of the glory of Christ,
9:13 your confession of the *g*
Gal 1: 7 a different *g*— which is really no *g*
Eph 6:15 comes from the *g* of peace.
Php 1:27 in a manner worthy of the *g*
Col 1:23 This is the *g* that you heard
1Th 2: 4 by God to be entrusted with the *g*.
2Th 1: 8 do not obey the *g* of our Lord Jesus
2Ti 1:10 immortality to light through the *g*.
Rev 14: 6 he had the eternal *g* to proclaim

GOSSIP*
Pr 11:13 A *g* betrays a confidence,
16:28 and a *g* separates close friends.
18: 8 of a *g* are like choice morsels;
20:19 A *g* betrays a confidence;
26:20 without a *g* a quarrel dies down.
26:22 of a *g* are like choice morsels;
2Co 12:20 slander, *g*, arrogance and disorder.

GOVERN (GOVERNMENT)
Ge 1:16 the greater light to *g* the day
Job 34:17 Can he who hates justice *g*?
Ro 12: 8 it is leadership, let him *g* diligently;

GOVERNMENT (GOVERN)
Isa 9: 6 and the *g* will be on his shoulders.

GRACE* (GRACIOUS)
Ps 45: 2 lips have been anointed with *g*,
Pr 1: 9 will be a garland to *g* your head
3:22 an ornament to *g* your neck.
3:34 but gives *g* to the humble.
4: 9 She will set a garland of *g*
Isa 26:10 Though *g* is shown to the wicked,
Jnh 2: 8 forfeit the *g* that could be theirs.
Zec 12:10 of Jerusalem a spirit of *g*
Lk 2:40 and the *g* of God was upon him.
Jn 1:14 who came from the Father, full of *g*
1:16 of his *g* we have all received one
1:17 *g* and truth came through Jesus
Ac 4:33 and much *g* was upon them all.
6: 8 a man full of God's *g* and power,
11:23 saw the evidence of the *g* of God,
13:43 them to continue in the *g* of God.
14: 3 message of his *g* by enabling them
14:26 they had been committed to the *g*
15:11 We believe it is through the *g*
15:40 by the brothers to the *g* of the Lord
18:27 to those who by *g* had believed.
20:24 testifying to the gospel of God's *g*.
20:32 to God and to the word of his *g*,
Ro 1: 5 we received *g* and apostleship
1: 7 *G* and peace to you
3:24 and are justified freely by his *g*
4:16 be by *g* and may be guaranteed

Ro 5: 2 access by faith into this *g*
5:15 came by the *g* of the one man,
5:15 how much more did God's *g*
5:17 God's abundant provision of *g*
5:20 where sin increased, *g* increased all
5:21 also *g* might reign
6: 1 on sinning so that *g* may increase?
6:14 you are not under law, but under *g*.
6:15 we are not under law but under *g*?
11: 5 there is a remnant chosen by *g*,
11: 6 if by *g*, then it is no longer by works
11: 6 if it were, *g* would no longer be *g*.
12: 3 For by the *g* given me I say
12: 6 according to the *g* given us,
15:15 because of the *g* God gave me
16:20 The *g* of our Lord Jesus be
1Co 1: 3 *G* and peace to you
1: 4 of his *g* given you in Christ Jesus.
3:10 By the *g* God has given me,
15:10 But by the *g* of God I am what I am
15:10 but the *g* of God that was with me
15:10 his *g* to me was not without effect.
16:23 The *g* of the Lord Jesus be with you
2Co 1: 2 *G* and peace to you
1:12 wisdom but according to God's *g*.
4:15 so that the *g* that is reaching more
6: 1 not to receive God's *g* in vain.
8: 1 to know about the *g* that God has
8: 6 also to completion this act of *g*
8: 7 also excel in this *g* of giving.
8: 9 For you know the *g*
9: 8 able to make all *g* abound to you,
9:14 of the surpassing *g* God has given
12: 9 "My *g* is sufficient for you,
13:14 May the *g* of the Lord Jesus Christ,
Gal 1: 3 *G* and peace to you
1: 6 the one who called you by the *g*
1:15 from birth and called me by his *g*,
2: 9 when they recognized the *g* given
2:21 I do not set aside the *g* of God,
3:18 God in his *g* gave it to Abraham
5: 4 you have fallen away from *g*.
6:18 The *g* of our Lord Jesus Christ be
Eph 1: 2 *G* and peace to you
1: 6 to the praise of his glorious *g*,
1: 7 riches of God's *g* that he lavished
2: 5 it is by *g* you have been saved.
2: 7 the incomparable riches of his *g*,
2: 8 For it is by *g* you have been saved,
3: 2 of God's *g* that was given to me
3: 7 by the gift of God's *g* given me
3: 8 God's people, this *g* was given me:
4: 7 to each one of us *g* has been given
6:24 *G* to all who love our Lord Jesus
Php 1: 2 *G* and peace to you
1: 7 all of you share in God's *g* with me.
4:23 The *g* of the Lord Jesus Christ be
Col 1: 2 *G* and peace to you
1: 6 understood God's *g* in all its truth.
4: 6 conversation be always full of *g*,
4:18 *G* be with you.
1Th 1: 1 and the Lord Jesus Christ: *G*
5:28 The *g* of our Lord Jesus Christ be
2Th 1: 2 *G* and peace to you
1:12 according to the *g* of our God
2:16 and by his *g* gave us eternal
3:18 The *g* of our Lord Jesus Christ be
1Ti 1: 2 my true son in the faith: *G*,
1:14 The *g* of our Lord was poured out
6:21 *G* be with you.
2Ti 1: 2 To Timothy, my dear son: *G*,
1: 9 This *g* was given us in Christ Jesus
1: 9 because of his own purpose and *g*.
2: 1 be strong in the *g* that is
4:22 *G* be with you.
Tit 1: 4 *G* and peace from God the Father
2:11 For the *g* of God that brings
3: 7 having been justified by his *g*,

Tit 3:15 *G* be with you all.
Phm : 3 *G* to you and peace
: 25 The *g* of the Lord Jesus Christ be
Heb 2: 9 that by the *g* of God he might taste
4:16 find *g* to help us in our time of need
4:16 the throne of *g* with confidence,
10:29 and who has insulted the Spirit of *g*
12:15 See to it that no one misses the *g*
13: 9 hearts to be strengthened by *g*,
13:25 *G* be with you all.
Jas 4: 6 but gives *g* to the humble."
4: 6 But he gives us more *g*. That is why
1Pe 1: 2 *G* and peace be yours in abundance
1:10 who spoke of the *g* that was
1:13 fully on the *g* to be given you
4:10 faithfully administering God's *g*
5: 5 but gives *g* to the humble."
5:10 the God of all *g*, who called you
5:12 and testifying that this is the true *g*
2Pe 1: 2 *G* and peace be yours in abundance
3:18 But grow in the *g* and knowledge
2Jn : 3 and will be with us forever: *G*,
Jude : 4 who change the *g* of our God
Rev 1: 4 *G* and peace to you
22:21 The *g* of the Lord Jesus be

GRACIOUS (GRACE)
Ex 34: 6 the compassionate and *g* God,
Nu 6:25 and be *g* to you;
Ne 9:17 But you are a forgiving God, *g*
Ps 67: 1 May God be *g* to us and bless us
Pr 22:11 a pure heart and whose speech is *g*
Isa 30:18 Yet the LORD longs to be *g* to you

GRAIN
Lev 2: 1 When someone brings a *g* offering
Lk 17:35 women will be grinding *g* together;
1Co 9: 9 ox while it is treading out the *g*."

GRANDCHILDREN (CHILD)
1Ti 5: 4 But if a widow has children or *g*,

GRANDMOTHER (MOTHER)
2Ti 1: 5 which first lived in your *g* Lois

GRANT (GRANTED)
Ps 20: 5 May the LORD *g* all your requests
51:12 *g* me a willing spirit, to sustain me.

GRANTED (GRANT)
Pr 10:24 what the righteous desire will be *g*.
Mt 15:28 great faith! Your request is *g*."
Php 1:29 For it has been *g* to you on behalf

GRAPES
Nu 13:23 branch bearing a single cluster of *g*.
Jer 31:29 'The fathers have eaten sour *g*,
Eze 18: 2 " 'The fathers eat sour *g*,
Mt 7:16 Do people pick *g* from thornbushes
Rev 14:18 and gather the clusters of *g*

GRASPED
Php 2: 6 with God something to be *g*,

GRASS
Ps 103:15 As for man, his days are like *g*,
Isa 40: 6 "All men are like *g*,
Mt 6:30 If that is how God clothes the *g*
1Pe 1:24 "All men are like *g*,

GRASSHOPPERS
Nu 13:33 We seemed like *g* in our own eyes,

GRATIFY* (GRATITUDE)
Ro 13:14 think about how to *g* the desires
Gal 5:16 and you will not *g* the desires

GRATITUDE (GRATIFY)
Col 3:16 and spiritual songs with *g*

GRAVE (GRAVES)
Nu 19:16 who touches a human bone or a *g*,
Dt 34: 6 day no one knows where his *g* is.

Ps 5: 9 Their throat is an open *g*;
49:15 will redeem my life from the *g*;
Pr 7:27 Her house is a highway to the *g*,
Hos 13:14 Where, O *g*, is your destruction?
Jn 11:44 "Take off the *g* clothes
Ac 2:27 you will not abandon me to the *g*,

GRAVES (GRAVE)
Eze 37:12 I am going to open your *g*
Jn 5:28 are in their *g* will hear his voice
Ro 3:13 "Their throats are open *g*;

GRAY
Pr 16:31 *G* hair is a crown of splendor;
20:29 *g* hair the splendor of the old.

GREAT (GREATER GREATEST GREATNESS)
Ge 12: 2 I will make your name *g*,
12: 2 "I will make you into a *g* nation
Ex 32:11 out of Egypt with *g* power
Nu 14:19 In accordance with your *g* love,
Dt 4:32 so *g* as this ever happened,
10:17 the *g* God, mighty and awesome,
29:28 in *g* wrath the LORD uprooted
Jos 7: 9 do for your own *g* name?"
Jdg 16: 5 you the secret of his *g* strength
2Sa 7:22 "How *g* you are, O Sovereign
22:36 you stoop down to make me *g*.
24:14 for his mercy is *g*; but do not let me
1Ch 17:19 made known all these *g* promises.
Ps 18:35 you stoop down to make me *g*.
19:11 in keeping them there is *g* reward.
47: 2 the *g* King over all the earth!
57:10 For *g* is your love, reaching
68:11 and *g* was the company
89: 1 of the LORD's *g* love forever;
103:11 so *g* is his love for those who fear
107:43 consider the *g* love of the LORD.
108: 4 For *g* is your love, higher
117: 2 For *g* is his love toward us,
119:165 *G* peace have they who love your
145: 3 *G* is the LORD and most worthy
Pr 22: 1 is more desirable than *g* riches;
23:24 of a righteous man has *g* joy;
Isa 42:21 to make his law *g* and glorious.
Jer 27: 5 With my *g* power and outstretched
32:19 *g* are your purposes and mighty are
La 3:23 *g* is your faithfulness.
Da 9: 4 "O Lord, the *g* and awesome God,
Joel 2:11 The day of the LORD is *g*;
2:20 Surely he has done *g* things.
Zep 1:14 "The *g* day of the LORD is near—
Mal 1:11 My name will be *g*
4: 5 the prophet Elijah before that *g*
Mt 20:26 whoever wants to become *g*
Mk 10:43 whoever wants to become *g*
Lk 6:23 because *g* is your reward in heaven.
6:35 Then your reward will be *g*,
21:27 in a cloud with power and *g* glory.
Eph 1:19 and his incomparably *g* power
2: 4 But because of his *g* love for us,
1Ti 6: 6 with contentment is *g* gain.
Tit 2:13 glorious appearing of our *g* God
Heb 2: 3 if we ignore such a *g* salvation?
1Jn 3: 1 How *g* is the love the Father has
Rev 6:17 For the *g* day of their wrath has
20:11 Then I saw a *g* white throne

GREATER (GREAT)
Mt 11:11 there has not risen anyone *g*
12: 6 I tell you that one *g*
12:41 and now one *g* than Jonah is here.
12:42 now one *g* than Solomon is here.
Mk 12:31 There is no commandment *g*
Jn 1:50 You shall see *g* things than that."
3:30 He must become *g*; I must become
14:12 He will do even *g* things than these
15:13 *G* love has no one than this,
1Co 12:31 But eagerly desire the *g* gifts.
2Co 3:11 how much *g* is the glory
Heb 3: 3 the builder of a house has *g* honor
3: 3 worthy of *g* honor than Moses,
7: 7 lesser person is blessed by the *g*.
11:26 as of *g* value than the treasures
1Jn 3:20 For God is *g* than our hearts,
4: 4 is in you is *g* than the one who is

GREATEST (GREAT)
Mt 22:38 is the first and *g* commandment.
23:11 *g* among you will be your servant.
Lk 9:48 least among you all—he is the *g*."
1Co 13:13 But the *g* of these is love.

GREATNESS* (GREAT)
Ex 15: 7 In the *g* of your majesty
Dt 3:24 to show to your servant your *g*
32: 3 Oh, praise the *g* of our God!
1Ch 29:11 O LORD, is the *g* and the power
2Ch 9: 6 half the *g* of your wisdom was told
Est 10: 2 account of the *g* of Mordecai
Ps 145: 3 his *g* no one can fathom.
150: 2 praise him for his surpassing *g*.
Isa 63: 1 forward in the *g* of his strength?
Eze 38:23 I will show my *g* and my holiness.
Da 4:22 your *g* has grown until it reaches
5:18 and *g* and glory and splendor.
7:27 and *g* of the kingdoms
Mic 5: 4 will live securely, for then his *g*
Lk 9:43 And they were all amazed at the *g*
Php 3: 8 compared to the surpassing *g*

GREED (GREEDY)
Lk 12:15 on your guard against all kinds of *g*
Ro 1:29 kind of wickedness, evil, *g*
Eph 5: 3 or of any kind of impurity, or of *g*,
Col 3: 5 evil desires and *g*, which is idolatry
2Pe 2:14 experts in *g*— an accursed brood!

GREEDY (GREED)
Pr 15:27 A *g* man brings trouble
1Co 6:10 nor thieves nor the *g* nor drunkards
Eph 5: 5 No immoral, impure or *g* person—
1Pe 5: 2 not *g* for money, but eager to serve;

GREEK (GREEKS)
Gal 3:28 There is neither Jew nor *G*,
Col 3:11 Here there is no *G* or Jew,

GREEKS (GREEK)
1Co 1:22 miraculous signs and *G* look

GREEN
Ps 23: 2 makes me lie down in *g* pastures,

GREW (GROW)
Lk 1:80 And the child *g* and became strong
2:52 And Jesus *g* in wisdom and stature,
Ac 9:31 by the Holy Spirit, it *g* in numbers,
16: 5 in the faith and *g* daily in numbers.

GRIEF (GRIEFS GRIEVANCES GRIEVE GRIEVED)
Ps 10:14 O God, do see trouble and *g*;
Pr 10: 1 but a foolish son to his mother.
14:13 and joy may end in *g*.
17:21 To have a fool for a son brings *g*;
Ecc 1:18 the more knowledge, the more *g*.
La 3:32 Though he brings *g*, he will show
Jn 16:20 but your *g* will turn to joy.
1Pe 1: 6 had to suffer *g* in all kinds of trials.

GRIEFS* (GRIEF)
1Ti 6:10 pierced themselves with many *g*.

GRIEVANCES* (GRIEF)
Col 3:13 forgive whatever *g* you may have

GRIEVE (GRIEF)
Eph 4:30 do not *g* the Holy Spirit of God,
1Th 4:13 or to *g* like the rest of men,

GRIEVED (GRIEF)
Isa 63:10 and *g* his Holy Spirit.

GRINDING
Lk 17:35 women will be *g* grain together;

GROAN (GROANING GROANS)
Ro 8:23 inwardly as we wait eagerly
2Co 5: 4 For while we are in this tent, we *g*

GROANING (GROAN)
Ex 2:24 God heard their *g* and he
Eze 21: 7 'Why are you *g*?' you shall say,
Ro 8:22 that the whole creation has been *g*

GROANS (GROAN)
Ro 8:26 with *g* that words cannot express.

GROUND
Ge	1:10	God called the dry *g* "land,"
	3:17	"Cursed is the *g* because of you;
	4:10	blood cries out to me from the *g.*
Ex	3: 5	where you are standing is holy *g.*"
	15:19	walked through the sea on dry *g.*
Isa	53: 2	and like a root out of dry *g.*
Mt	10:29	fall to the *g* apart from the will
	25:25	and hid your talent in the *g.*
Jn	8: 6	to write on the *g* with his finger.
Eph	6:13	you may be able to stand your *g,*

GROW (FULL-GROWN GREW GROWING GROWS)
Pr	13:11	by little makes it *g.*
	20:13	not love sleep or you will *g* poor;
Isa	40:31	they will run and not *g* weary,
Mt	6:28	See how the lilies of the field *g.*
1Co	3: 6	watered it, but God made it *g.*
2Pe	3:18	But *g* in the grace and knowledge

GROWING (GROW)
Col	1: 6	this gospel is bearing fruit and *g,*
	1:10	*g* in the knowledge of God,
2Th	1: 3	your faith is *g* more and more,

GROWS (GROW)
Eph	4:16	*g* and builds itself up in love,
Col	2:19	*g* as God causes it to grow.

GRUMBLE (GRUMBLED GRUMBLERS GRUMBLING)
1Co	10:10	And do not *g,* as some of them did
Jas	5: 9	Don't *g* against each other,

GRUMBLED (GRUMBLE)
Ex	15:24	So the people *g* against Moses,
Nu	14:29	and who has *g* against me.

GRUMBLERS* (GRUMBLE)
Jude	:16	These men are *g* and faultfinders;

GRUMBLING (GRUMBLE)
Jn	6:43	"Stop *g* among yourselves,"
1Pe	4: 9	to one another without *g.*

GUARANTEE (GUARANTEEING)
Heb	7:22	Jesus has become the *g*

GUARANTEEING* (GUARANTEE)
2Co	1:22	as a deposit, *g* what is to come.
	5: 5	as a deposit, *g* what is to come.
Eph	1:14	who is a deposit *g* our inheritance

GUARD (GUARDS)
1Sa	2: 9	He will *g* the feet of his saints,
Ps	141: 3	Set a *g* over my mouth, O Lᴏʀᴅ;
Pr	2:11	and understanding will *g* you.
	4:13	*g* it well, for it is your life.
	4:23	Above all else, *g* your heart,
	7: 2	*g* my teachings as the apple
Isa	52:12	the God of Israel will be your rear *g.*
Mk	13:33	Be on *g!* Be alert! You do not know
Lk	12: 1	"Be on your *g* against the yeast
	12:15	Be on your *g* against all kinds
Ac	20:31	So be on your *g!* Remember that
1Co	16:13	Be on your *g;* stand firm in the faith
Php	4: 7	will *g* your hearts and your minds
1Ti	6:20	*g* what has been entrusted
2Ti	1:14	*G* the good deposit that was

GUARDS (GUARD)
Pr	13: 3	He who *g* his lips *g* his life,
	19:16	who obeys instructions *g* his life,
	21:23	He who *g* his mouth and his tongue
	22: 5	he who *g* his soul stays far

GUIDANCE (GUIDE)
Pr	1: 5	and let the discerning get *g—*
	11:14	For lack of *g* a nation falls,
	24: 6	for waging war you need *g,*

GUIDE (GUIDANCE GUIDED GUIDES)
Ex	13:21	of cloud to *g* them on their way
	15:13	In your strength you will *g* them
Ne	9:19	cease to *g* them on their path,
Ps	25: 5	*g* me in your truth and teach me,
	43: 3	let them *g* me;
	48:14	he will be our *g* even to the end.
	67: 4	and *g* the nations of the earth.
	73:24	You *g* me with your counsel,
	139:10	even there your hand will *g* me,
Pr	4:11	I *g* you in the way of wisdom
	6:22	When you walk, they will *g* you;
Isa	58:11	The Lᴏʀᴅ will *g* you always;
Jn	16:13	comes, he will *g* you into all truth.

GUIDED (GUIDE)
Ps	107:30	he *g* them to their desired haven.

GUIDES (GUIDE)
Ps	23: 3	He *g* me in paths of righteousness
	25: 9	He *g* the humble in what is right
Pr	11: 3	The integrity of the upright *g* them,
	16:23	A wise man's heart *g* his mouth,
Mt	23:16	"Woe to you, blind *g!* You say,
	23:24	You blind *g!* You strain out a gnat

GUILT (GUILTY)
Lev	5:15	It is a *g* offering.
Ps	32: 5	the *g* of my sin.
	38: 4	My *g* has overwhelmed me
Isa	6: 7	your *g* is taken away and your sin
Jer	2:22	the stain of your *g* is still before me
Eze	18:19	'Why does the son not share the *g*

GUILTY (GUILT)
Ex	34: 7	does not leave the *g* unpunished;
Mk	3:29	Spirit will never be forgiven; he is *g*
Jn	8:46	Can any of you prove me *g* of sin?
1Co	11:27	in an unworthy manner will be *g*
Heb	10: 2	and would no longer have felt *g*
	10:22	to cleanse us from a *g* conscience
Jas	2:10	at just one point is *g* of breaking all

HABAKKUK*
Prophet to Judah (Hab 1:1; 3:1).

HABIT
1Ti	5:13	they get into the *h* of being idle
Heb	10:25	as some are in the *h* of doing,

HADAD
Edomite adversary of Solomon (1Ki 11:14–25).

HADES*
Mt	16:18	the gates of *H* will not overcome it.
Rev	1:18	And I hold the keys of death and *H*
	6: 8	*H* was following close behind him.
	20:13	and *H* gave up the dead that were
	20:14	*H* were thrown into the lake of fire.

HAGAR
Servant of Sarah, wife of Abraham, mother of Ishmael (Ge 16:1–6; 25:12). Driven away by Sarah while pregnant (Ge 16:5–16); after birth of Isaac (Ge 21:9–21; Gal 4:21–31).

HAGGAI*
Post-exilic prophet who encouraged rebuilding of the temple (Ezr 5:1; 6:14; Hag 1–2).

HAIL
Ex	9:19	the *h* will fall on every man
Rev	8: 7	and there came *h* and fire mixed

HAIR (HAIRS HAIRY)
Lev	19:27	" 'Do not cut the *h* at the sides
Nu	6: 5	he must let the *h* of his head grow
Pr	16:31	Gray *h* is a crown of splendor;
	20:29	gray *h* the splendor of the old.
Lk	7:44	and wiped them with her *h.*
	21:18	But not a *h* of your head will perish
Jn	11: 2	and wiped his feet with her *h.*
	12: 3	and wiped his feet with her *h.*
1Co	11: 6	for a woman to have her *h* cut
	11: 6	she should have her *h* cut off;
	11:14	that if a man has long *h,*
	11:15	For long *h* is given to her
	11:15	but that if a woman has long *h,*
1Ti	2: 9	not with braided *h* or gold or pearls
1Pe	3: 3	as braided *h* and the wearing
Rev	1:14	and *h* were white like wool,

HAIRS (HAIR)
Mt	10:30	even the very *h* of your head are all
Lk	12: 7	the very *h* of your head are all

HAIRY (HAIR)
Ge	27:11	"But my brother Esau is a *h* man,

HALF
Ex	30:13	This *h* shekel is an offering
Jos	8:33	*H* of the people stood in front
1Ki	3:25	give *h* to one and *h* to the other."

1Ki	10: 7	Indeed, not even *h* was told me;
Est	5: 3	Even up to *h* the kingdom,
Da	7:25	him for a time, times and *h* a time.
Mk	6:23	up to *h* my kingdom."

HALF-TRIBE (TRIBE)
Nu	32:33	and the *h* of Manasseh son

HALLELUJAH*
Rev	19: 1,	3, 4, 6.

HALLOWED* (HOLY)
Mt	6: 9	*h* be your name,
Lk	11: 2	*h* be your name,

HALT
Job	38:11	here is where your proud waves *h*'?

HALTER*
Pr	26: 3	for the horse, a *h* for the donkey,

HAM
Son of Noah (Ge 5:32; 1Ch 1:4), father of Canaan (Ge 9:18; 10:6–20; 1Ch 1:8–16). Saw Noah's nakedness (Ge 9:20–27).

HAMAN
Agagite nobleman honored by Xerxes (Est 3:1–2). Plotted to exterminate the Jews because of Mordecai (Est 3:3–15). Forced to honor Mordecai (Est 5–6). Plot exposed by Esther (Est 5:1–8; 7:1–8). Hanged (Est 7:9–10).

HAMPERED*
Pr	4:12	you walk, your steps will not be *h;*

HAND (HANDED HANDFUL HANDS OPENHANDED)
Ge	24: 2	"Put your *h* under my thigh.
	47:29	put your *h* under my thigh
Ex	13: 3	out of it with a mighty *h.*
	15: 6	Your right *h,* O Lᴏʀᴅ,
	33:22	and cover you with my *h*
Dt	12: 7	in everything you have put your *h*
1Ki	8:42	your mighty *h* and your
	13: 4	But the *h* he stretched out
1Ch	29:14	you only what comes from your *h.*
	29:16	it comes from your *h,* and all
2Ch	6:15	with your *h* you have fulfilled it—
Ne	4:17	materials did their work with one *h*
Job	40: 4	I put my *h* over my mouth.
Ps	16: 8	Because he is at my right *h,*
	32: 4	your *h* was heavy upon me;
	37:24	the Lᴏʀᴅ upholds him with his *h.*
	44: 3	it was your right *h,* your arm,
	45: 9	at your right *h* is the royal bride
	63: 8	your right *h* upholds me.
	75: 8	In the *h* of the Lᴏʀᴅ is a cup
	91: 7	ten thousand at your right *h,*
	98: 1	his right *h* and his holy arm
	109:31	at the right *h* of the needy one,
	110: 1	"Sit at my right *h*
	137: 5	may my right *h* forget .its skill.
	139:10	even there your *h* will guide me,
	145:16	You open your *h*
Pr	27:16	or grasping oil with the *h.*
Ecc	5:15	that he can carry in his *h.*
	9:10	Whatever your *h* finds to do,
Isa	11: 8	the young child put his *h*
	40:12	the waters in the hollow of his *h,*
	41:13	who takes hold of your right *h*
	44: 5	still another will write on his *h,*
	48:13	My own *h* laid the foundations
	64: 8	we are all the work of your *h.*
La	3: 3	he has turned his *h* against me
Da	10:10	*h* touched me and set me trembling
Jnh	4:11	people who cannot tell their right *h*
Hab	3: 4	rays flashed from his *h,*
Mt	5:30	if your right *h* causes you to sin,
	6: 3	know what your right *h* is doing,
	12:10	a man with a shriveled *h* was there.
	18: 8	If your *h* or your foot causes you
	22:44	"Sit at my right *h*
	26:64	at the right *h* of the Mighty One
Mk	3: 1	a man with a shriveled *h* was there.
	9:43	If your *h* causes you to sin, cut it off
	12:36	"Sit at my right *h*
	16:19	and he sat at the right *h* of God.
Lk	6: 6	there whose right *h* was shriveled.
	20:42	"Sit at my right *h*
	22:69	at the right *h* of the mighty God."

Jn 10:28 one can snatch them out of my *h.*
   20:27 Reach out your *h* and put it
Ac 7:55 Jesus standing at the right *h* of God
1Co 12:15 I am not a *h,* I do not belong
Heb 1:13 "Sit at my right *h*
Rev 13:16 to receive a mark on his right *h*

HANDED (HAND)
Da 7:25 The saints will be *h* over to him
1Ti 1:20 whom I have *h* over to Satan

HANDFUL (HAND)
Ecc 4:6 Better one *h* with tranquillity

HANDLE (HANDLES)
Col 2:21 "Do not *h!* Do not taste! Do not

HANDLES (HANDLE)
2Ti 2:15 who correctly *h* the word of truth.

HANDS (HAND)
Ge 27:22 but the *h* are the *h* of Esau."
Ex 17:11 As long as Moses held up his *h,*
   29:10 his sons shall lay their *h* on its head
Dt 6:8 Tie them as symbols on your *h*
Jdg 7:6 lapped with their *h* to their mouths.
2Ki 11:12 and the people clapped their *h*
2Ch 6:4 who with his *h* has fulfilled what he
Ps 22:16 they have pierced my *h*
   24:4 He who has clean *h* and a pure
   31:5 Into your *h* I commit my spirit;
   31:15 My times are in your *h;*
   47:1 Clap your *h,* all you nations;
   63:4 and in your name I will lift up my *h*
Pr 10:4 Lazy *h* make a man poor,
   21:25 because his *h* refuse to work.
   31:13 and works with eager *h.*
   31:20 and extends her *h* to the needy.
Ecc 10:18 if his *h* are idle, the house leaks.
Isa 35:3 Strengthen the feeble *h,*
   49:16 you on the palms of my *h;*
   55:12 will clap their *h.*
   65:2 All day long I have held out my *h*
La 3:41 Let us lift up our hearts and our *h*
Lk 23:46 into your *h* I commit my spirit."
Ac 6:6 who prayed and laid their *h*
   8:18 at the laying on of the apostles' *h,*
   13:3 they placed their *h* on them
   19:6 When Paul placed his *h* on them,
   28:8 placed his *h* on him and healed him
1Th 4:11 and to work with your *h,*
1Ti 2:8 to lift up holy *h* in prayer,
   4:14 body of elders laid their *h* on you.
   5:22 hasty in the laying on of *h,*
2Ti 1:6 you through the laying on of my *h.*
Heb 6:2 the laying on of *h,* the resurrection

HANDSOME*
Ge 39:6 Now Joseph was well-built and *h,*
1Sa 16:12 a fine appearance and *h* features.
   17:42 ruddy and *h,* and he despised him.
2Sa 14:25 praised for his *h* appearance
1Ki 1:6 also very *h* and was born next
SS 1:16 *Beloved* How *h* you are, my lover!
Eze 23:6 all of them *h* young men,
   23:12 horsemen, all *h* young men.
   23:23 with them, *h* young men,
Da 1:4 without any physical defect, *h,*
Zec 11:13 the *h* price at which they priced me

HANG (HANGED HANGING HUNG)
Mt 22:40 and the Prophets *h* on these two

HANGED (HANG)
Mt 27:5 Then he went away and *h* himself.

HANGING (HANG)
Ac 10:39 They killed him by *h* him on a tree,

HANNAH*
Wife of Elkanah, mother of Samuel (1Sa 1).
Prayer at dedication of Samuel (1Sa 2:1–10).
Blessed (1Sa 2:18–21).

HAPPIER (HAPPY)
Mt 18:13 he is *h* about that one sheep
1Co 7:40 she is *h* if she stays as she is—

HAPPINESS* (HAPPY)
Dt 24:5 bring *h* to the wife he has married.
Est 8:16 For the Jews it was a time of *h*
Job 7:7 my eyes will never see *h* again.
Ecc 2:26 gives wisdom, knowledge and *h,*
Mt 25:21 Come and share your master's *h!*
   25:23 Come and share your master's *h!'*

HAPPY* (HAPPIER HAPPINESS)
Ge 30:13 The women will call me *h.*"
   30:13 Then Leah said, "How *h* I am!
1Ki 4:20 they drank and they were *h.*
   10:8 How *h* your men must be!
   10:8 men must be! How *h* your officials,
2Ch 9:7 How *h* your men must be!
   9:7 men must be! How *h* your officials,
Est 5:9 Haman went out that day *h*
   5:14 the king to the dinner and be *h.*"
Ps 10:6 I'll always be *h* and never have
   68:3 may they be *h* and joyful.
   113:9 as a *h* mother of children.
   137:8 *h* is he who repays you
Pr 15:13 A *h* heart makes the face cheerful,
Ecc 2:12 better for men than to be *h*
   5:19 to accept his lot and be *h*
   7:14 When times are good, be *h;*
   11:9 Be *h,* young man, while you are
Jnh 4:6 Jonah was very *h* about the vine.
Zec 8:19 and glad occasions and *h* festivals
1Co 7:30 those who are *h,* as if they were not
2Co 7:9 yet now I am *h,* not because you
   7:13 delighted to see how *h* Titus was,
Jas 5:13 Is anyone *h?* Let him sing songs

HARD (HARDEN HARDENED HARDENING HARDENS HARDER HARDSHIP HARDSHIPS)
Ge 18:14 Is anything too *h* for the LORD?
1Ki 10:1 came to test him with *h* questions.
Pr 14:23 All *h* work brings a profit,
Jer 32:17 Nothing is too *h* for you.
Zec 7:12 They made their hearts as *h* as flint
Mt 19:23 it is *h* for a rich man
Mk 10:5 your hearts were *h* that Moses
Jn 6:60 disciples said, "This is a *h* teaching.
Ac 20:35 of *h* work we must help the weak,
   26:14 It is *h* for you to kick
Ro 16:12 woman who has worked very *h*
1Co 4:12 We work *h* with our own hands.
2Co 6:5 imprisonments and riots; in *h* work
1Th 5:12 to respect those who work *h*
Rev 2:2 your *h* work and your

HARDEN (HARD)
Ex 4:21 I will *h* his heart so that he will not
Ps 95:8 do not *h* your hearts as you did
Ro 9:18 he hardens whom he wants to *h.*
Heb 3:8 do not *h* your hearts

HARDENED (HARD)
Ex 10:20 But the LORD *h* Pharaoh's heart,

HARDENING* (HARD)
Ro 11:25 Israel has experienced a *h* in part
Eph 4:18 in them due to the *h* of their hearts.

HARDENS* (HARD)
Pr 28:14 he who *h* his heart falls into trouble
Ro 9:18 and he *h* whom he wants to harden.

HARDER (HARD)
1Co 15:10 No, I worked *h* than all of them—
2Co 11:23 I have worked much *h,* been

HARDHEARTED* (HEART)
Dt 15:7 do not be *h* or tightfisted

HARDSHIP (HARD)
Ro 8:35 Shall trouble or *h* or persecution
2Ti 2:3 Endure *h* with us like a good
   4:5 endure *h,* do the work
Heb 12:7 Endure *h* as discipline; God is

HARDSHIPS (HARD)
Ac 14:22 go through many *h* to enter
2Co 6:4 in troubles, *h* and distresses;

2Co 12:10 in insults, in *h,* in persecutions,
Rev 2:3 and have endured *h* for my name,

HARM (HARMS)
1Ch 16:22 do my prophets no *h.*"
Ps 105:15 do my prophets no *h.*"
   121:6 the sun will not *h* you by day,
Pr 3:29 not plot *h* against your neighbor,
   12:21 No *h* befalls the righteous,
   31:12 She brings him good, not *h,*
Jer 10:5 they can do no *h*
   29:11 to prosper you and not to *h* you,
Ro 13:10 Love does no *h* to its neighbor.
1Co 11:17 for your meetings do more *h*
1Jn 5:18 the evil one cannot *h* him.

HARMONY*
Zec 6:13 there will be *h* between the two.'
Ro 12:16 Live in *h* with one another.
2Co 6:15 What *h* is there between Christ
1Pe 3:8 live in *h* with one another;

HARMS* (HARM)
Pr 8:36 whoever fails to find me *h* himself;

HARP (HARPS)
Ge 4:21 the father of all who play the *h*
1Sa 16:23 David would take his *h* and play.
Ps 33:2 Praise the LORD with the *h;*
   98:5 with the *h* and the sound of singing
   150:3 praise him with the *h* and lyre,
Rev 5:8 Each one had a *h* and they were

HARPS (HARP)
Ps 137:2 we hung our *h,*

HARSH
Pr 15:1 but a *h* word stirs up anger.
Col 2:23 and their *h* treatment of the body,
   3:19 and do not be *h* with them.
1Pe 2:18 but also to those who are *h.*
Jude 15 of all the *h* words ungodly sinners

HARVEST (HARVESTERS)
Ge 8:22 seedtime and *h,*
Ex 23:16 the Feast of *H* with the firstfruits
Dt 16:15 God will bless you in all your *h*
Pr 10:5 during *h* is a disgraceful son.
Jer 8:20 "The *h* is past,
Joel 3:13 for the *h* is ripe.
Mt 9:37 *h* is plentiful but the workers are
Lk 10:2 He told them, "The *h* is plentiful,
Jn 4:35 at the fields! They are ripe for *h.*
1Co 9:11 if we reap a material *h* from you?
2Co 9:10 the *h* of your righteousness.
Gal 6:9 at the proper time we will reap a *h*
Heb 12:11 it produces a *h* of righteousness
Jas 3:18 in peace raise a *h* of righteousness.
Rev 14:15 for the *h* of the earth is ripe."

HARVESTERS (HARVEST)
Ru 2:3 to glean in the fields behind the *h.*

HASTE (HASTEN HASTY)
Ex 12:11 it in *h;* it is the LORD's Passover.
Pr 21:5 as surely as *h* leads to poverty.
   29:20 Do you see a man who speaks in *h?*

HASTEN (HASTE)
Ps 70:1 *H,* O God, to save me;
   119:60 I will *h* and not delay

HASTY* (HASTE)
Pr 19:2 nor to be *h* and miss the way.
Ecc 5:2 do not be *h* in your heart
1Ti 5:22 Do not be *h* in the laying

HATE (GOD-HATERS HATED HATES HATING HATRED)
Lev 19:17 " 'Do not *h* your brother
Ps 5:5 you *h* all who do wrong.
   36:2 too much to detect or *h* his sin.
   45:7 righteousness and *h* wickedness;
   97:10 those who love the LORD *h* evil,
   119:104 therefore I *h* every wrong path.
   119:163 I *h* and abhor falsehood
   139:21 Do I not *h* those who *h* you,
Pr 8:13 To fear the LORD is to *h* evil;
   9:8 rebuke a mocker or he will *h* you;
   13:5 The righteous *h* what is false,
   25:17 too much of you, and he will *h* you.
   29:10 Bloodthirsty men *h* a man
Ecc 3:8 a time to love and a time to *h,*
Isa 61:8 I *h* robbery and iniquity.
Eze 35:6 Since you did not *h* bloodshed,

HATED

Am 5:15 *H* evil, love good;
Mal 2:16 "I *h* divorce," says the LORD God
Mt 5:43 your neighbor and *h* your enemy.'
   10:22 All men will *h* you because of me,
Lk 6:22 Blessed are you when men *h* you,
   6:27 do good to those who *h* you,
   14:26 does not *h* his father and mother,
Ro 12: 9 *H* what is evil; cling to what is good

HATED (HATE)
Mal 1: 3 loved Jacob, but Esau I have *h,*
Jn 15:18 keep in mind that it *h* me first.
Ro 9:13 "Jacob I loved, but Esau I *h.*"
Eph 5:29 no one ever *h* his own body,
Heb 1: 9 righteousness and *h* wickedness;

HATES (HATE)
Pr 6:16 There are six things the LORD *h,*
   13:24 He who spares the rod *h* his son,
   15:27 but he who *h* bribes will live.
   26:28 A lying tongue *h* those it hurts,
Jn 3:20 Everyone who does evil *h* the light,
   12:25 while the man who *h* his life
1Jn 2: 9 *h* his brother is still in the darkness.
   4:20 "I love God," yet *h* his brother,

HATING (HATE)
Jude : 23 *h* even the clothing stained

HATRED (HATE)
Pr 10:12 *H* stirs up dissension,
   15:17 than a fattened calf with *h.*
Jas 4: 4 with the world is *h* toward God?

HAUGHTY
Pr 6:17 detestable to him: / *h* eyes,
   16:18 a *h* spirit before a fall.

HAVEN
Ps 107:30 he guided them to their desired *h.*

HAY
1Co 3:12 costly stones, wood, *h* or straw,

HEAD (HEADS HOTHEADED)
Ge 3:15 he will crush your *h,*
Nu 6: 5 no razor may be used on his *h.*
Jdg 16:17 If my *h* were shaved, my strength
1Sa 9: 2 a *h* taller than any of the others.
2Sa 18: 9 Absalom's *h* got caught in the tree.
Ps 23: 5 You anoint my *h* with oil;
   133: 2 is like precious oil poured on the *h,*
Pr 10: 6 Blessings crown the *h*
   25:22 will heap burning coals on his *h,*
Isa 59:17 and the helmet of salvation on his *h*
Eze 33: 4 his blood will be on his own *h.*
Mt 8:20 of Man has no place to lay his *h.*"
Jn 19: 2 crown of thorns and put it on his *h.*
Ro 12:20 will heap burning coals on his *h.*"
1Co 11: 3 and the *h* of Christ is God.
   11: 5 her *h* uncovered dishonors her *h*—
   12:21 And the *h* cannot say to the feet,
Eph 1:22 him to be *h* over everything
   5:23 For the husband is the *h* of the wife
Col 1:18 And he is the *h* of the body,
2Ti 4: 5 keep your *h* in all situations,
Rev 14:14 with a crown of gold on his *h*
   19:12 and on his *h* are many crowns.

HEADS (HEAD)
Lev 26:13 you to walk with *h* held high.
Ps 22: 7 they hurl insults, shaking their *h:*
   24: 7 Lift up your *h,* O you gates;
Isa 35:10 everlasting joy will crown their *h.*
   51:11 everlasting joy will crown their *h.*
Mt 27:39 shaking their *h* and saying,
Lk 21:28 stand up and lift up your *h,*
Ac 18: 6 "Your blood be on your own *h!*
Rev 4: 4 and had crowns of gold on their *h.*

HEAL* (HEALED HEALING HEALS)
Nu 12:13 please *h* her!" The LORD replied
Dt 32:39 I have wounded and I will *h,*
2Ki 20: 5 and seen your tears; I will *h* you.
   20: 8 the sign that the LORD will *h* me
2Ch 7:14 their sin and will *h* their land.
Job 5:18 he injures, but his hands also *h.*

Ps 6: 2 *h* me, for my bones are in agony.
   41: 4 *h* me, for I have sinned against you
Ecc 3: 3 a time to kill and a time to *h,*
Isa 19:22 he will strike them and *h* them.
   19:22 respond to their pleas and *h* them.
   57:18 seen his ways, but I will *h* him;
   57:19 "And I will *h* them."
Jer 17:14 *H* me, O LORD, and I will be
   30:17 and *h* your wounds,'
   33: 6 I will *h* my people and will let them
La 2:13 Who can *h* you?
Hos 5:13 not able to *h* your sores.
   6: 1 but he will *h* us;
   7: 1 whenever I would *h* Israel,
   14: 4 "I will *h* their waywardness
Na 3:19 Nothing can *h* your wound;
Zec 11:16 or seek the young, or *h* the injured,
Mt 8: 7 said to him, "I will go and *h* him."
   10: 1 to *h* every disease and sickness.
   10: 8 *H* the sick, raise the dead,
   12:10 "Is it lawful to *h* on the Sabbath?"
   13:15 and turn, and I would *h* them.'
   17:16 but they could not *h* him."
Mk 3: 2 if he would *h* him on the Sabbath.
   6: 5 on a few sick people and *h* them.
Lk 4:23 to me: 'Physician, *h* yourself!
   5:17 present for him to *h* the sick.
   6: 7 to see if he would *h* on the Sabbath.
   7: 3 him to come and *h* his servant.
   8:43 years, but no one could *h* her.
   9: 2 kingdom of God and to *h* the sick.
   9: 2 *H* the sick who are there
   13:32 and *h* people today and tomorrow,
   14: 3 "Is it lawful to *h* on the Sabbath
Jn 4:47 begged him to come and *h* his son,
   12:40 nor turn—and I would *h* them."
Ac 4:30 Stretch out your hand to *h*
   28:27 and turn, and I would *h* them.'

HEALED* (HEAL)
Ge 20:17 to God, and God *h* Abimelech,
Ex 21:19 and see that he is completely *h.*
Lev 13:37 hair has grown in it, the itch is *h,*
   14: 3 If the person has been *h*
Jos 5: 8 were in camp until they were *h.*
1Sa 6: 3 you will be *h,* and you will know
2Ki 2:21 LORD says: 'I have *h* this water.
2Ch 30:20 heard Hezekiah and *h* the people.
Ps 30: 2 and you *h* me.
   107:20 He sent forth his word and *h* them;
Isa 6:10 and turn and be *h.*"
   53: 5 and by his wounds we are *h.*
Jer 14:19 us so that we cannot be *h?*
   17:14 Heal me, O LORD, and I will be *h;*
   51: 8 perhaps she can be *h.*
   51: 9 but she cannot be *h;*
   51: 9 " 'We would heal Babylon,
Eze 34: 4 the weak or *h* the sick
Hos 11: 3 it was I who *h* them.
Mt 4:24 and the paralyzed, and he *h* them.
   8: 8 the word, and my servant will be *h.*
   8:13 his servant was *h* at that very hour.
   8:16 with a word and *h* all the sick.
   9:21 If I only touch his cloak, I will be *h*
   9:22 he said, "your faith has *h* you."
   9:22 woman was *h* from that moment.
   12:15 him, and he *h* all their sick,
   12:22 Jesus *h* him, so that he could both
   14:14 on them and *h* their sick.
   14:36 and all who touched him were *h.*
   15:28 And her daughter was *h*
   15:30 laid them at his feet; and he *h* them
   17:18 and he was *h* from that moment.
   19: 2 followed him, and he *h* them there.
   21:14 to him at the temple, and he *h* them
Mk 1:34 and Jesus *h* many who had various
   3:10 For he had *h* many, so that those

Mk 5:23 hands on her so that she will be *h*
   5:28 If I just touch his clothes, I will be *h*
   5:34 "Daughter, your faith has *h* you.
   6:13 people with oil and *h* them.
   6:56 and all who touched him were *h.*
   10:52 said Jesus, "your faith has *h* you."
Lk 4:40 hands on each one, he *h* them.
   5:15 and to be *h* of their sicknesses.
   6:18 and to be *h* of their diseases.
   7: 7 the word, and my servant will be *h.*
   8:47 and how she had been instantly *h.*
   8:48 "Daughter, your faith has *h* you.
   8:50 just believe, and she will be *h.*"
   9:11 and *h* those who needed healing.
   9:42 *h* the boy and gave him back
   13:14 Jesus had *h* on the Sabbath,
   13:14 So come and be *h* on those days,
   14: 4 he *h* him and sent him away.
   17:15 when he saw he was *h,* came back,
   18:42 your sight; your faith has *h* you."
   22:51 touched the man's ear and *h* him.
Jn 5:10 said to the man who had been *h,*
   5:13 man who was *h* had no idea who it
Ac 4: 9 and are asked how he was *h,*
   4:10 stands before you *h.*
   4:14 who had been *h* standing there
   4:22 man who was miraculously *h* was
   5:16 evil spirits, and all of them were *h.*
   8: 7 paralytics and cripples were *h.*
   14: 9 saw that he had faith to be *h*
   28: 8 placed his hands on him and *h* him.
Heb 12:13 may not be disabled, but rather *h.*
Jas 5:16 for each other so that you may be *h*
1Pe 2:24 by his wounds you have been *h.*
Rev 13: 3 but the fatal wound had been *h.*
   13:12 whose fatal wound had been *h.*

HEALING* (HEAL)
2Ch 28:15 food and drink, and *h* balm.
Pr 12:18 but the tongue of the wise brings *h.*
   13:17 but a trustworthy envoy brings *h.*
   15: 4 The tongue that brings *h* is a tree
   16:24 sweet to the soul and *h* to the bones
Isa 58: 8 and your *h* will quickly appear;
Jer 8:15 for a time of *h*
   8:22 Why then is there no *h*
   14:19 for a time of *h*
   30:12 your injury beyond *h.*
   30:13 no *h* for you.
   33: 6 I will bring health and *h* to it;
   46:11 there is no *h* for you.
Eze 30:21 It has not been bound up for *h*
   47:12 for food and their leaves for *h.*"
Mal 4: 2 rise with *h* in its wings.
Mt 4:23 and *h* every disease and sickness
   9:35 and *h* every disease and sickness.
Lk 6:19 coming from him and *h* them all.
   9: 6 gospel and *h* people everywhere.
   9:11 and healed those who needed *h.*
Jn 7:23 angry with me for *h* the whole man
Ac 3:16 him that has given this complete *h*
   10:38 all who were under the power
1Co 12: 9 to another gifts of *h*
   12:28 also those having gifts of *h,*
   12:30 Do all have gifts of *h?* Do all speak
Rev 22: 2 are for the *h* of the nations.

HEALS* (HEAL)
Ex 15:26 for I am the LORD, who *h* you."
Lev 13:18 a boil on his skin and it *h,*
Ps 103: 3 and *h* all your diseases;
   147: 3 He *h* the brokenhearted
Isa 30:26 and *h* the wounds he inflicted.
Ac 9:34 said to him, "Jesus Christ *h* you.

HEALTH* (HEALTHIER HEALTHY)
1Sa 25: 6 And good *h* to all that is yours!
   25: 6 Good *h* to you and your household
Ps 38: 3 of your wrath there is no *h*
   38: 7 there is no *h* in my body.
Pr 3: 8 This will bring *h* to your body
   4:22 and *h* to a man's whole body.

Pr   15:30   and good news gives *h* to the bones
Isa   38:16   You restored me to *h*
Jer   30:17   But I will restore you to *h*
     33: 6   I will bring *h* and healing to it;
3Jn   : 2   I pray that you may enjoy good *h*

HEALTHIER* (HEALTH)
Da   1:15   end of the ten days they looked *h*

HEALTHY* (HEALTH)
Ge   41: 5   Seven heads of grain, *h* and good,
     41: 7   of grain swallowed up the seven *h*,
Ps   73: 4   their bodies are *h* and strong.
Zec   11:16   or heal the injured, or feed the *h*,
Mt   9:12   "It is not the *h* who need a doctor,
Mk   2:17   "It is not the *h* who need a doctor,
Lk   5:31   "It is not the *h* who need a doctor,

HEAP
Pr   25:22   you will *h* burning coals
Ro   12:20   you will *h* burning coals

HEAR (HEARD HEARING HEARS)
Ex   15:14   The nations will *h* and tremble;
     22:27   I will *h*, for I am compassionate.
Nu   14:13   Then the Egyptians will *h* about it!
Dt   1:16   *H* the disputes between your
     4:36   heaven he made you *h* his voice
     6: 4   *H*, O Israel: The Lord our God,
     19:20   The rest of the people will *h* of this
     31:13   must *h* it and learn
Jos   7: 9   of the country will *h* about this
1Ki   8:30   *H* the supplication of your servant
2Ki   19:16   O Lord, and *h*; open your eyes,
2Ch   7:14   then will I *h* from heaven
Job   31:35   ("Oh, that I had someone to *h* me!
Ps   94: 9   he who implanted the ear not *h*?
     95: 7   Today, if you *h* his voice,
Ecc   7:21   or you may *h* your servant cursing
Isa   21: 3   I am staggered by what I *h*,
     29:18   that day the deaf will *h* the words
     30:21   your ears will *h* a voice behind you,
     51: 7   *H* me, you who know what is right,
     59: 1   nor his ear too dull to *h*.
     65:24   while they are still speaking I will *h*
Jer   5:21   who have ears but do not *h*:
Eze   33: 7   so *h* the word I speak and give
     37: 4   'Dry bones, *h* the word
Mt   11: 5   the deaf *h*, the dead are raised,
     11:15   He who has ears, let him *h*.
     13:17   and to *h* what you *h* but did not *h* it
Mk   12:29   answered Jesus, "is this: 'H,
Lk   7:22   the deaf *h*, the dead are raised,
Jn   8:47   reason you do not *h* is that you do
Ac   4: 7   he wanted to *h* the word of God.
     13:44   gathered to *h* the word of the Lord.
     17:32   "We want to *h* you again
Ro   2:13   is not those who *h* the law who are
     10:14   they *h* without someone preaching
2Ti   4: 3   what their itching ears want to *h*.
Heb   3: 7   "Today, if you *h* his voice,
Rev   1: 3   and blessed are those who *h* it

HEARD (HEAR)
Ex   2:24   God *h* their groaning and he
Dt   4:32   has anything like it ever been *h*
2Sa   7:22   as we have *h* with our own ears.
Job   42: 5   My ears had *h* of you
Isa   40:21   Have you not *h*?
     40:28   Have you not *h*?
     66: 8   Who has ever *h* of such a thing?
Jer   18:13   Who has ever *h* anything like this?
Da   10:12   your words were *h*, and I have
     12: 8   I *h*, but I did not understand.
Hab   3:16   I *h* and my heart pounded,
Mt   5:21   "You have *h* that it was said
     5:27   "You have *h* that it was said,
     5:33   you have *h* that it was said,
     5:38   "You have *h* that it was said,
     5:43   "You have *h* that it was said,
Lk   12: 3   in the dark will be *h* in the daylight,

Jn   8:26   and what I have *h* from him I tell
Ac   2: 6   because each one *h* them speaking
1Co   2: 9   no ear has *h*,
2Co   12: 4   He *h* inexpressible things,
1Th   2:13   word of God, which you *h* from us,
2Ti   1:13   What you *h* from me, keep
Jas   1:25   not forgetting what he has *h*,
Rev   22: 8   am the one who *h* and saw these

HEARING (HEAR)
Isa   6: 9   Be ever *h*, but never understanding
Mt   13:14   will be ever *h* but never
Mk   4:12   ever *h* but never understanding;
Ac   28:26   will be ever *h* but never
Ro   10:17   faith comes from *h* the message,
1Co   12:17   where would the sense of *h* be?

HEARS (HEAR)
Jn   5:24   whoever *h* my word and believes
1Jn   5:14   according to his will, he *h* us.
Rev   3:20   If anyone *h* my voice and opens

HEART (BROKENHEARTED FAINT-HEARTED HARDHEARTED HEART'S HEARTACHE HEARTS KINDHEARTED SIMPLEHEARTED STOUTHEARTED WHOLEHEARTED WHOLEHEARTEDLY)
Ge   6: 5   of his *h* was only evil all the time.
Ex   4:21   But I will harden his *h*
     25: 2   each man whose *h* prompts him
     35:21   and whose *h* moved him came
Lev   19:17   Do not hate your brother in your *h*.
Dt   4: 9   or let them slip from your *h* as long
     4:29   if you look for him with all your *h*
     6: 5   Lord your God with all your *h*
     10:12   Lord your God with all your *h*
     11:13   and to serve him with all your *h*
     13: 3   you love him with all your *h*
     15:10   and do so without a grudging *h*;
     26:16   observe them with all your *h*
     29:18   you today whose *h* turns away
     30: 2   and obey him with all your *h*
     30: 6   you may love him with all your *h*
     30:10   Lord your God with all your *h*
Jos   22: 5   and to serve him with all your *h*
     23:14   You know with all your *h*
1Sa   10: 9   God changed Saul's *h*,
     12:20   serve the Lord with all your *h*.
     12:24   serve him faithfully with all your *h*;
     13:14   sought out a man after his own *h*
     14: 7   I am with you *h* and soul."
     16: 7   but the Lord looks at the *h*."
     17:32   "Let no one lose *h* on account
1Ki   2: 4   faithfully before me with all their *h*
     3: 9   So give your servant a discerning *h*
     3:12   give you a wise and discerning *h*,
     8:48   back to you with all their *h*
     9: 3   and my *h* will always be there.
     9: 4   walk before me in integrity of *h*
     10:24   the wisdom God had put in his *h*.
     11: 4   and his *h* was not fully devoted
     14: 8   and followed me with all his *h*,
2Ki   22:19   Because your *h* was responsive
     23: 3   with all his *h* and all his soul,
1Ch   28: 9   for the Lord searches every *h*
2Ch   6:38   back to you with all their *h*
     7:16   and my *h* will always be there.
     15:12   of their fathers, with all their *h*
     15:17   Asa's *h* was fully committed
     17: 6   His *h* was devoted to the ways
     22: 9   sought the Lord with all his *h*."
     34:31   with all his *h* and all his soul,
     36:13   stiff-necked and hardened his *h*
Ezr   1: 5   everyone whose *h* God had moved
Ne   4: 6   the people worked with all their *h*.
Job   19:27   How my *h* yearns within me!
     22:22   and lay up his words in your *h*.
     37: 1   "At this my *h* pounds
Ps   9: 1   you, O Lord, with all my *h*;
     14: 1   The fool says in his *h*,
     16: 9   Therefore my *h* is glad
     19:14   and the meditation of my *h*
     20: 4   he give you the desire of your *h*

Ps   24: 4   who has clean hands and a pure *h*,
     26: 2   examine my *h* and my mind;
     37: 4   will give you the desires of your *h*.
     37:31   The law of his God is in his *h*;
     44:21   since he knows the secrets of the *h*
     45: 1   My *h* is stirred by a noble theme
     51:10   Create in me a pure *h*, O God,
     51:17   a broken and contrite *h*,
     53: 1   The fool says in his *h*,
     66:18   If I had cherished sin in my *h*,
     73: 1   to those who are pure in *h*.
     73:26   My flesh and my *h* may fail,
     86:11   give me an undivided *h*,
     90:12   that we may gain a *h* of wisdom.
     97:11   and joy on the upright in *h*.
     108: 1   My *h* is steadfast, O God;
     109:22   and my *h* is wounded within me.
     111: 1   will extol the Lord with all my *h*
     112: 7   his *h* is steadfast, trusting
     112: 8   His *h* is secure, he will have no fear
     119: 2   and seek him with all their *h*.
     119:10   I seek you with all my *h*;
     119:11   I have hidden your word in my *h*
     119:30   I have set my *h* on your laws.
     119:32   for you have set my *h* free.
     119:34   and obey it with all my *h*.
     119:36   Turn my *h* toward your statutes
     119:58   sought your face with all my *h*;
     119:69   I keep your precepts with all my *h*.
     119:111   they are the joy of my *h*.
     119:112   My *h* is set on keeping your
     119:145   I call with all my *h*; answer me,
     125: 4   to those who are upright in *h*.
     138: 1   you, O Lord, with all my *h*;
     139:23   Search me, O God, and know my *h*
Pr   2: 2   applying your *h* to understanding,
     3: 1   but keep my commands in your *h*,
     3: 3   write them on the tablet of your *h*.
     3: 5   Trust in the Lord with all your *h*
     4: 4   hold of my words with all your *h*;
     4:21   keep them within your *h*;
     4:23   Above all else, guard your *h*,
     6:21   Bind them upon your *h* forever;
     7: 3   write them on the tablet of your *h*.
     10: 8   The wise in *h* accept commands,
     13:12   Hope deferred makes the *h* sick,
     14:13   Even in laughter the *h* may ache,
     14:30   A *h* at peace gives life to the body,
     15:13   A happy *h* makes the face cheerful,
     15:15   the cheerful *h* has a continual feast.
     15:28   *h* of the righteous weighs its
     15:30   A cheerful look brings joy to the *h*,
     16:23   A wise man's *h* guides his mouth,
     17:22   A cheerful *h* is good medicine,
     20: 9   can say, "I have kept my *h* pure;
     22:11   He who loves a pure *h*
     22:17   apply your *h* to what I teach,
     22:18   when you keep them in your *h*
     23:15   My son, if your *h* is wise,
     23:19   and keep your *h* on the right path.
     23:26   My son, give me your *h*
     24:17   stumbles, do not let your *h* rejoice,
     27:19   so a man's *h* reflects the man.
Ecc   5: 2   do not be hasty in your *h*
     8: 5   wise *h* will know the proper time
     11:10   banish anxiety from your *h*
SS   3: 1   I looked for the one my *h* loves;
     4: 9   You have stolen my *h*, my sister,
     5: 2   *Beloved* I slept but my *h* was awake
     5: 4   my *h* began to pound for him.
     8: 6   Place me like a seal over your *h*,
Isa   6:10   Make the *h* of this people calloused
     40:11   and carries them close to his *h*;
     57:15   and to revive the *h* of the contrite.
     66:14   you see this, your *h* will rejoice
Jer   3:15   give you shepherds after my own *h*,
     4:14   wash the evil from your *h*

Jer   9:26   of Israel is uncircumcised in *h*."
      17: 9   The *h* is deceitful above all things
      20: 9   is in my *h* like a fire,
      24: 7   I will give them a *h* to know me,
      29:13   when you seek me with all your *h*.
      32:39   I will give them singleness of *h*
      32:41   them in this land with all my *h*
      51:46   Do not lose *h* or be afraid
Eze 11:19   I will give them an undivided *h*
      18:31   and get a new *h* and a new spirit.
      36:26   I will give you a new *h*
      44: 7   foreigners uncircumcised in *h*
Da   7: 4   and the *h* of a man was given to it.
Joel   2:12   "return to me with all your *h*,
      2:13   Rend your *h*
Zep   3:14   Be glad and rejoice with all
           your *h*,
Mt   5: 8   Blessed are the pure in *h*,
      5:28   adultery with her in his *h*.
      6:21   treasure is, there your *h* will be
     11:29   for I am gentle and humble in *h*,
     12:34   of the *h* the mouth speaks.
     13:15   For this people's *h* has become
     15:18   out of the mouth come from
           the *h*,
     15:19   For out of the *h* come evil
           thoughts
     18:35   forgive your brother from your *h*."
     22:37   the Lord your God with all your *h*
Mk 11:23   and does not doubt in his *h*
     12:30   the Lord your God with all your *h*
     12:33   To love him with all your *h*,
Lk   2:19   and pondered them in her *h*.
      2:51   treasured all these things in her *h*.
      6:45   out of the good stored up in his *h*
      6:45   overflow of his *h* his mouth
           speaks.
      8:15   for those with a noble and good *h*,
     10:27   the Lord your God with all your *h*
     12:34   treasure is, there your *h* will be
Jn   12:27   "Now my *h* is troubled,
Ac   1:24   "Lord, you know everyone's *h*.
      2:37   they were cut to the *h*
      4:32   All the believers were one in *h*
      8:21   your *h* is not right before God.
     15: 8   who knows the *h*, showed that he
     16:14   The Lord opened her *h* to respond
     28:27   For this people's *h* has become
Ro   1: 9   with my whole *h* in preaching
      2:29   is circumcision of the *h*,
     10: 9   in your *h* that God raised him
     10:10   is with your *h* that you believe
     15: 6   with one *h* and mouth you may
1Co 14:25   the secrets of his *h* will be laid
           bare.
2Co   2: 4   anguish of *h* and with many tears,
      4: 1   this ministry, we do not lose *h*.
      4:16   Therefore we do not lose *h*.
      9: 7   give what he has decided in his *h*
Eph   1:18   eyes of your *h* may be
           enlightened
      5:19   make music in your *h* to the Lord,
      6: 5   and with sincerity of *h*, just
      6: 6   doing the will of God from your *h*.
Php   1: 7   since I have you in my *h*; for
Col   2: 2   is that they may be encouraged
           in *h*
      3:22   but with sincerity of *h*
      3:23   work at it with all your *h*,
1Ti   1: 5   which comes from a pure *h*
      3: 1   If anyone sets his *h*
2Ti   2:22   call on the Lord out of a pure *h*.
Phm   : 12   who is my very *h*— back to you.
      : 20   in the Lord; refresh my *h* in Christ.
Heb   4:12   the thoughts and attitudes of
           the *h*.
1Pe   1:22   one another deeply, from the *h*.

HEART'S* (HEART)
2Ch   1:11   "Since this is your *h* desire
Jer   15:16   they were my joy and my *h*
           delight,
Eze 24:25   delight of their eyes, their *h*
           desire,
Ro   10: 1   my *h* desire and prayer to God

HEARTACHE* (HEART)
Pr   15:13   but *h* crushes the spirit.

HEARTLESS*
La   4: 3   but my people have become *h*
Ro   1:31   they are senseless, faithless, *h*,

HEARTS (HEART)
Lev 26:41   their uncircumcised *h* are
           humbled
Dt   6: 6   are to be upon your *h*.
     10:16   Circumcise your *h*, therefore,
     11:18   Fix these words of mine in your *h*
     30: 6   your God will circumcise your *h*
Jos 11:20   himself who hardened their *h*
     24:23   and yield your *h* to the LORD,
1Sa   7: 3   to the LORD with all your *h*
     10:26   valiant men whose *h* God had
2Sa 15: 6   and so he stole the *h* of the men
1Ki   8:39   for you alone know the *h* of all
           men
      8:61   your *h* must be fully committed
     18:37   are turning their *h* back again."
1Ch 29:18   and keep their *h* loyal to you.
2Ch   6:30   (for you alone know the *h* of
           men),
     11:16   tribe of Israel who set their *h*
     29:31   all whose *h* were willing brought
Ps   7: 9   who searches minds and *h*,
     33:21   In him our *h* rejoice,
     62: 8   pour out your *h* to him,
     95: 8   do not harden your *h* as you did
Ecc   3:11   also set eternity in the *h* of men;
Isa   26: 8   are the desire of our *h*.
     29:13   but their *h* are far from me.
     35: 4   say to those with fearful *h*,
     51: 7   people who have my law in
           your *h*:
     63:17   harden our *h* so we do not revere
     65:14   out of the joy of their *h*,
Jer   4: 4   circumcise your *h*,
      12: 2   but far from their *h*.
      17: 1   on the tablets of their *h*
     31:33   and write it on their *h*.
Mal   4: 6   He will turn the *h* of the fathers
Mt   15: 8   but their *h* are far from me.
Mk   6:52   the loaves; their *h* were hardened.
      7: 6   but their *h* are far from me.
      7:21   out of men's *h*, come evil
           thoughts,
Lk   1:17   to turn the *h* of the fathers
     16:15   of men, but God knows your *h*.
     24:32   "Were not our *h* burning within us
Jn   5:42   not have the love of God in
           your *h*.
     14: 1   "Do not let your *h* be troubled.
     14:27   Do not let your *h* be troubled
Ac   7:51   with uncircumcised *h* and ears!
     11:23   true to the Lord with all their *h*.
     15: 9   for he purified their *h* by faith.
     28:27   understand with their *h*
Ro   1:21   and their foolish *h* were darkened.
      2:15   of the law are written on their *h*,
      5: 5   love into our *h* by the Holy Spirit,
      8:27   who searches our *h* knows
1Co   4: 5   will expose the motives of
           men's *h*.
2Co   1:22   put his Spirit in our *h* as a deposit,
      3: 2   written on our *h*, known
      3: 3   but on tablets of human *h*.
      4: 6   shine in our *h* to give us the light
      6:11   and opened wide our *h* to you.
      6:13   to my children—open wide your *h*
      7: 2   Make room for us in your *h*.
Gal   4: 6   the Spirit of his Son into our *h*,
Eph   3:17   dwell in your *h* through faith.
Php   4: 7   will guard your *h* and your minds
Col   3: 1   set your *h* on things above,
      3:15   the peace of Christ rule in your *h*,
      3:16   with gratitude in your *h* to God.
1Th   2: 4   men but God, who tests our *h*.
      3:13   May he strengthen your *h*
2Th   2:17   encourage your *h* and strengthen
Phm   : 7   have refreshed the *h* of the saints.
Heb   3: 8   do not harden your *h*
      8:10   and write them on their *h*.
     10:16   I will put my laws in their *h*,
     10:22   having our *h* sprinkled
Jas   4: 8   purify your *h*, you double-minded.
2Pe   1:19   the morning star rises in your *h*.
1Jn   3:20   For God is greater than our *h*.

HEAT
Ps   19: 6   nothing is hidden from its *h*.
2Pe   3:12   and the elements will melt in
           the *h*.

HEAVEN (HEAVENLY HEAVENS HEAVENWARD)
Ge   14:19   Creator of *h* and earth.

Ge   28:12   with its top reaching to *h*,
Ex   16: 4   rain down bread from *h* for you.
     20:22   that I have spoken to you from *h*:
Dt   26:15   from *h*, your holy dwelling place,
     30:12   "Who will ascend into *h* to get it
1Ki   8:27   the highest *h*, cannot contain you.
      8:30   Hear from *h*, your dwelling place,
     22:19   the host of *h* standing around him
2Ki   2: 1   up to *h* in a whirlwind,
     19:15   You have made *h* and earth.
2Ch   7:14   then will I hear from *h*
Isa   14:12   How you have fallen from *h*,
     66: 1   "*H* is my throne,
Da   7:13   coming with the clouds of *h*.
Mt   3: 2   for the kingdom of *h* is near."
      3:16   At that moment *h* was opened,
      4:17   for the kingdom of *h* is near."
      5:12   because great is your reward in *h*,
      5:19   great in the kingdom of *h*.
      6: 9   " 'Our Father in *h*,
      6:10   done on earth as it is in *h*.
      6:20   up for yourselves treasures in *h*,
      7:21   Lord,' will enter the kingdom of *h*,
     16:19   bind on earth will be bound in *h*,
     18: 3   will never enter the kingdom of *h*.
     18:18   bind on earth will be bound in *h*,
     19:14   the kingdom of *h* belongs to such
     19:21   and you will have treasure in *h*.
     19:23   man to enter the kingdom of *h*.
     23:13   the kingdom of *h* in men's faces.
     24:35   *H* and earth will pass away,
     26:64   and coming on the clouds of *h*."
     28:18   "All authority in *h*
Mk   1:10   he saw *h* being torn open
     10:21   and you will have treasure in *h*.
     13:31   *H* and earth will pass away,
     14:62   and coming on the clouds of *h*."
     16:19   he was taken up into *h*
Lk   3:21   *h* was opened and the Holy Spirit
     10:18   saw Satan fall like lightning
           from *h*.
     10:20   that your names are written in *h*."
     12:33   in *h* that will not be exhausted,
     15: 7   in *h* over one sinner who repents
     18:22   and you will have treasure in *h*.
     21:33   *H* and earth will pass away,
     24:51   left them and was taken up into *h*.
Jn   3:13   No one has ever gone into *h*
      6:38   down from *h* not to do my will
     12:28   Then a voice came from *h*,
Ac   1:11   has been taken from you into *h*,
      7:49   the prophet says: " '*H* is my
      7:55   looked up to *h* and saw the glory
      9: 3   a light from *h* flashed around him.
     26:19   disobedient to the vision from *h*.
Ro   10: 6   'Who will ascend into *h*?' " (that
           is,
1Co 15:47   the earth, the second man from *h*.
2Co   5: 1   an eternal house in *h*, not built
      12: 2   ago was caught up to the third *h*
Eph   1:10   to bring all things in *h*
Php   2:10   *h* and on earth and under the
           earth,
      3:20   But our citizenship is in *h*
Col   1:16   things in *h* and on earth, visible
      4: 1   that you also have a Master in *h*.
1Th   1:10   and to wait for his Son from *h*,
      4:16   himself will come down from *h*,
Heb   1: 3   hand of the Majesty in *h*.
      8: 5   and shadow of what is in *h*.
      9:24   he entered itself, now to appear
     12:23   whose names are written in *h*.
1Pe   1: 4   spoil or fade—kept in *h* for you,
      3:22   who has gone into *h* and is
2Pe   3:13   we are looking forward to a new *h*
Rev   5:13   Then I heard every creature in *h*
     11:19   God's temple in *h* was opened,
     12: 7   And there was war in *h*.
     15: 5   this I looked and in *h* the temple,
     19: 1   of a great multitude in *h* shouting:
     19:11   I saw *h* standing open and there
     21: 1   Then I saw a new *h* and a new
           earth
     21:10   coming down out of *h* from God.

HEAVENLY (HEAVEN)
Ps   8: 5   him a little lower than the *h*
           beings
2Co   5: 2   to be clothed with our *h* dwelling,
Eph   1: 3   in the *h* realms with every
           spiritual

Eph 1:20 at his right hand in the *h* realms,
2Ti 4:18 bring me safely to his *h* kingdom.
Heb 12:22 to the *h* Jerusalem, the city

HEAVENS (HEAVEN)
Ge 1: 1 In the beginning God created the *h*
   11: 4 with a tower that reaches to the *h*,
Dt 33:26 who rides on the *h* to help you
1Ki 8:27 The *h*, even the highest heaven,
2Ch 2: 6 since the *h*, even the highest
Ezr 9: 6 and our guilt has reached to the *h*.
Ne 9: 6 You made the *h*, even the highest
Job 11: 8 They are higher than the *h*—
   38:33 Do you know the laws of the *h*?
Ps 8: 3 When I consider your *h*,
   19: 1 The *h* declare the glory of God;
   33: 6 of the LORD were the *h* made,
   57: 5 Be exalted, O God, above the *h*;
   102:25 the *h* are the work of your hands.
   103:11 as high as the *h* are above the earth,
   108: is your love, higher than the *h*;
   115:16 The highest *h* belong to the LORD
   119:89 it stands firm in the *h*.
   135: 6 in the *h* and on the earth,
   139: 8 If I go up to the *h*, you are there;
   148: 1 Praise the LORD from the *h*,
Isa 40:26 Lift your eyes and look to the *h*:
   45: 8 "You *h* above, rain
   51: 6 Lift up your eyes to the *h*,
   55: 9 "As the *h* are higher than the earth,
   65:17 new *h* and a new earth.
Jer 31:37 if the *h* above can be measured
   32:17 you have made the *h* and the earth
Eze 1: 1 *h* were opened and I saw visions
Da 12: 3 shine like the brightness of the *h*,
Joel 2:30 I will show wonders in the *h*
Mt 24:31 from one end of the *h* to the other.
Mk 13:27 of the earth to the ends of the *h*.
Eph 4:10 who ascended higher than all the *h*,
Heb 4:14 priest who has gone through the *h*,
   7:26 from sinners, exalted above the *h*.
2Pe 3: 5 ago by God's word the *h* existed
   3:10 The *h* will disappear with a roar;

HEAVENWARD (HEAVEN)
Php 3:14 for which God has called me *h*

HEAVIER (HEAVY)
Pr 27: 3 provocation by a fool is *h* than both

HEAVY (HEAVIER)
1Ki 12: 4 and the *h* yoke he put on us,
Ecc 1:13 What a *h* burden God has laid
Isa 47: 6 you laid a very *h* yoke.
Mt 23: 4 They tie up *h* loads and put them

HEBREW (HEBREWS)
Ge 14:13 and reported this to Abram the *H*.
2Ki 18:26 speak to us in *H* in the hearing
Php 3: 5 tribe of Benjamin, a *H* of Hebrews;

HEBREWS (HEBREW)
Ex 9: 1 of the *H*, says: "Let my people go,
2Co 11:22 Are they *H*? So am I.

HEBRON
Ge 13:18 near the great trees of Mamre at *H*,
   23: 2 died at Kiriath Arba (that is, *H*)
Jos 14:13 and gave him *H* as his inheritance.
   20: 7 *H*) in the hill country of Judah.
   21:13 the priest they gave *H* (a city
2Sa 2:11 king in *H* over the house

HEDGE
Job 1:10 "Have you not put a *h* around him

HEED (HEEDS)
Ecc 7: 5 It is better to *h* a wise man's rebuke

HEEDS (HEED)
Pr 13: 1 wise son *h* his father's instruction,
   13:18 whoever *h* correction is honored.
   15: 5 whoever *h* correction shows
   15:32 whoever *h* correction gains

HEEL
Ge 3:15 and you will strike his *h*."

HEIR (INHERIT)
Gal 4: 7 God has made you also an *h*.
Heb 1: 2 whom he appointed *h* of all things,

HEIRS (INHERIT)
Ro 8:17 then we are *h*— of God
Gal 3:29 and according to the promise.
Eph 3: 6 gospel the Gentiles are *h* together
1Pe 3: 7 as *h* with you of the gracious gift

HELD (HOLD)
Ex 17:11 As long as Moses *h* up his hands,
Dt 4: 4 but all of you who *h* fast
2Ki 3: 3 He *h* fast to the LORD
SS 3: 4 I *h* him and would not let him go
Isa 65: 2 All day long I have *h* out my hands
Ro 10:21 day long I have *h* out my hands
Col 2:19 and *h* together by its ligaments

HELL*
Mt 5:22 will be in danger of the fire of *h*.
   5:29 body to be thrown into *h*.
   5:30 for your whole body to go into *h*.
   10:28 destroy both soul and body in *h*.
   18: 9 and be thrown into the fire of *h*.
   23:15 as much a son of *h* as you are.
   23:33 you escape being condemned to *h*?
Mk 9:43 than with two hands to go into *h*,
   9:45 have two feet and be thrown into *h*.
   9:47 two eyes and be thrown into *h*,
Lk 12: 5 has power to throw you into *h*.
   16:23 In *h*, where he was in torment,
Jas 3: 6 and is itself set on fire by *h*.
2Pe 2: 4 but sent them to *h*, putting them

HELMET
Isa 59:17 and the *h* of salvation on his head;
Eph 6:17 Take the *h* of salvation
1Th 5: 8 and the hope of salvation as a *h*.

HELP (HELPED HELPER HELPFUL HELPING HELPLESS HELPS)
Ex 23: 5 leave it there; be sure you *h* him
Lev 25:35 *h* him as you would an alien
Dt 33:26 who rides on the heavens to *h* you
2Ch 16:12 even in his illness he did not seek *h*
Ps 18: 6 I cried to my God for *h*.
   30: 2 my God, I called to you for *h*
   33:20 he is our *h* and our shield.
   46: 1 an ever-present *h* in trouble.
   72:12 the afflicted who have no one to *h*.
   79: 9 *H* us, O God our Savior,
   108:12 for the *h* of man is worthless.
   115: 9 he is their *h* and shield.
   121: 1 where does my *h* come from?
Ecc 4:10 his friend can *h* him up.
Isa 41:10 I will strengthen you and *h* you;
Jnh 2: 2 depths of the grave I called for *h*,
Mk 9:24 *h* me overcome my unbelief!"
Lk 11:46 will not lift one finger to *h* them.
Ac 16: 9 Come over to Macedonia and *h* us
   18:27 he was a great *h* to those who
   20:35 of hard work we must *h* the weak,
   26:22 I have had God's *h* to this very day,
1Co 12:28 those able to *h* others, those
2Co 9: 2 For I know your eagerness to *h*,
1Ti 5:16 she should *h* them and not let

HELPED (HELP)
1Sa 7:12 "Thus far has the LORD *h* us."

HELPER (HELP)
Ge 2:18 I will make a *h* suitable for him."
Ps 10:14 you are the *h* of the fatherless.
Heb 13: 6 Lord is my *h*; I will not be afraid.

HELPFUL (HELP)
Eph 4:29 only what is *h* for building others

HELPING (HELP)
Ac 9:36 always doing good and *h* the poor.
1Ti 5:10 *h* those in trouble and devoting

HELPLESS (HELP)
Ps 10:12 Do not forget the *h*.
Mt 9:36 because they were harassed and *h*,

HELPS (HELP)
Ro 8:26 the Spirit *h* us in our weakness.

HEN
Mt 23:37 as a *h* gathers her chicks
Lk 13:34 as a *h* gathers her chicks

HERALD
1Ti 2: 7 for this purpose I was appointed a *h*
2Ti 1:11 of this gospel I was appointed a *h*

HERBS
Ex 12: 8 with bitter *h*, and bread made

HERITAGE (INHERIT)
Ps 61: 5 you have given me the *h*
   119:111 Your statutes are my *h* forever;
   127: 3 Sons are a *h* from the LORD,

HEROD
1. King of Judea who tried to kill Jesus (Mt 2; Lk 1:5).
2. Son of 1. Tetrarch of Galilee who arrested and beheaded John the Baptist (Mt 14:1–12; Mk 6:14–29; Lk 3:1, 19–20; 9:7–9); tried Jesus (Lk 23:6–15).
3. Grandson of 1. King of Judea who killed James (Ac 12:2); arrested Peter (Ac 12:3–19). Death (Ac 12:19–23).

HERODIAS
Wife of Herod the Tetrarch who persuaded her daughter to ask for John the Baptist's head (Mt 14:1–12; Mk 6:14–29).

HEWN
Isa 51: 1 the quarry from which you were *h*;

HEZEKIAH
King of Judah. Restored the temple and worship (2Ch 29–31). Sought the LORD for help against Assyria (2Ki 18–19; 2Ch 32:1–23; Isa 36–37). Illness healed (2Ki 20:1–11; 2Ch 32:24–26; Isa 38). Judged for showing Babylonians his treasures (2Ki 20:12–21; 2Ch 32:31; Isa 39).

HID (HIDE)
Ge 3: 8 and they *h* from the LORD God
Ex 2: 2 she *h* him for three months.
Jos 6:17 because she *h* the spies we sent.
1Ki 18:13 I *h* a hundred of the LORD's
2Ch 22:11 she *h* from Athaliah
Isa 54: 8 I *h* my face from you for a moment,
Mt 13:44 When a man found it, he *h* it again,
   25:25 and *h* your talent in the ground.
Heb 11:23 By faith Moses' parents *h* him

HIDDEN (HIDE)
1Sa 10:22 has *h* himself among the baggage."
Job 28:11 and brings *h* things to light.
Ps 19:12 Forgive my *h* faults.
   78: 2 I will utter *h* things, things from of old—
   119:11 I have *h* your word in my heart
Pr 2: 4 and search for it as for *h* treasure,
   27: 5 rebuke than *h* love.
Isa 59: 2 your sins have *h* his face from you,
Da 2:22 He reveals deep and *h* things;
Mt 5:14 A city on a hill cannot be *h*.
   10:26 or *h* that will not be made known.
   11:25 because you have *h* these things
   13:35 I will utter things *h*
   13:44 of heaven is like treasure *h*
Mk 4:22 For whatever is *h* is meant
Ro 16:25 of the mystery *h* for long ages past,
1Co 2: 7 a wisdom that has been *h*
Eph 3: 9 for ages past was kept *h* in God,
Col 1:26 the mystery that has been kept *h*
   2: 3 in whom are *h* all the treasures
   3: 3 and your life is now *h* with Christ

HIDE (HID HIDDEN HIDING)
Dt 31:17 I will *h* my face from them,
Ps 17: 8 *h* me in the shadow of your wings
   27: 5 he will *h* me in the shelter
   143: 9 for I *h* myself in you.
Isa 53: 3 one from whom men *h* their faces

HIDING (HIDE)
Ps 32: 7 You are my *h* place;
Pr 28:12 to power, men go into *h*.

HIGH

Ge 14:18 He was priest of God Most *H*,
 14:22 God Most *H*, Creator of heaven
Ps 21: 7 the unfailing love of the Most *H*
 82: 6 you are all sons of the Most *H*.'
Isa 14:14 I will make myself like the Most *H*
Da 4:17 know that the Most *H* is sovereign
Mk 5: 7 Jesus, Son of the Most *H* God?
Heb 7: 1 and priest of God Most *H*.

HIGHWAY

Isa 40: 3 a *h* for our God.

HILL (HILLS)

Ps 24: 3 ascend the *h* of the LORD?
Isa 40: 4 every mountain and *h* made low;
Mt 5:14 A city on a *h* cannot be hidden.
Lk 3: 5 every mountain and *h* made low.

HILLS (HILL)

1Ki 20:23 "Their gods are gods of the *h*.
Ps 50:10 and the cattle on a thousand *h*.
 121: 1 I lift up my eyes to the *h*—
Hos 10: 8 and to the *h*, "Fall on us!"
Lk 23:30 and to the *h*, "Cover us!" '
Rev 17: 9 The seven heads are seven *h*

HINDER (HINDERED HINDERS)

1Sa 14: 6 Nothing can *h* the LORD
Mt 19:14 come to me, and do not *h* them,
1Co 9:12 anything rather than *h* the gospel
1Pe 3: 7 so that nothing will *h* your
 prayers.

HINDERED (HINDER)

Lk 11:52 and you have *h* those who were

HINDERS (HINDER)

Heb 12: 1 let us throw off everything that *h*

HINT*

Eph 5: 3 even a *h* of sexual immorality,

HIP

Ge 32:32 socket of Jacob's *h* was touched

HIRAM

King of Tyre; helped David build his palace
(2Sa 5:11–12; 1Ch 14:1); helped Solomon
build the temple (1Ki 5; 2Ch 2) and his navy
(1Ki 9:10–27; 2Ch 8).

HIRED

Lk 15:15 and *h* himself out to a citizen
Jn 10:12 *h* hand is not the shepherd who

HOARDED (HOARDS)

Ecc 5:13 wealth *h* to the harm of its owner,
Jas 5: 3 You have *h* wealth in the last days.

HOARDS (HOARDED)

Pr 11:26 People curse the man who *h*
 grain,

HOLD (HELD HOLDS)

Ex 20: 7 LORD will not *h* anyone guiltless
Lev 19:13 " 'Do not *h* back the wages
Dt 5:11 LORD will not *h* anyone guiltless
 11:22 in all his ways and to *h* fast to him
 13: 4 serve him and *h* fast to him.
 30:20 listen to his voice, and *h* fast to
 him
Jos 22: 5 to *h* fast to him and to serve him
2Ki 4:16 "you will *h* a son in your arms."
Ps 18:16 from on high and took *h* of me;
 73:23 you *h* me by my right hand.
Pr 4: 4 "Lay *h* of my words
Isa 41:13 who takes *h* of your right hand
 54: 2 do not *h* back;
Eze 3:18 and I will *h* you accountable
 3:20 and I will *h* you accountable
 33: 6 I will *h* the watchman accountable
Zec 8:23 nations will take firm *h* of one Jew
Mk 11:25 if you *h* anything against anyone,
Jn 20:17 Jesus said, "Do not *h* on to me,
Php 2:16 as you *h* out the word of life—
 3:12 but I press on to take *h* of that
Col 1:17 and in him all things *h* together.
1Th 5:21 *H* on to the good.
1Ti 6:12 Take *h* of the eternal life
Heb 10:23 Let us *h* unswervingly

HOLDS (HOLD)

Pr 10:19 but he who *h* his tongue is wise.
 17:28 and discerning if he *h* his tongue.

HOLES

Hag 1: 6 to put them in a purse with *h* in
 it."
Mt 8:20 "Foxes have *h* and birds

HOLINESS* (HOLY)

Ex 15:11 majestic in *h*,
Dt 32:51 because you did not uphold my *h*
1Ch 16:29 the LORD in the splendor of his *h*.
2Ch 20:21 him for the splendor of his *h*
Ps 29: 2 in the splendor of his *h*.
 89:35 Once for all, I have sworn by my *h*
 93: 5 *h* adorns your house
 96: 9 in the splendor of his *h*;
Isa 29:23 they will acknowledge the *h*
 35: 8 it will be called the Way of *H*.
Eze 36:23 I will show the *h* of my great
 name,
 38:23 I will show my greatness and
 my *h*,
Am 4: 2 LORD has sworn by his *h*:
Lk 1:75 fear in *h* and righteousness
Ro 1: 4 the Spirit of *h* was declared
 6:19 to righteousness leading to *h*.
 6:22 the benefit you reap leads to *h*,
1Co 1:30 our righteousness, *h*
2Co 1:12 in the *h* and sincerity that are
 7: 1 perfecting *h* out of reverence
Eph 4:24 God in true righteousness and *h*.
1Ti 2: 2 quiet lives in all godliness and *h*.
 2:15 love and *h* with propriety.
Heb 12:10 that we may share in his *h*.
 12:14 without *h* no one will see the
 Lord.

HOLY (HALLOWED HOLINESS)

Ge 2: 3 the seventh day and made it *h*,
Ex 3: 5 you are standing is *h* ground."
 16:23 a *h* Sabbath to the LORD.
 19: 6 kingdom of priests and a *h*
 nation.'
 20: 8 the Sabbath day by keeping it *h*.
 26:33 Place from the Most *H* Place.
 26:33 curtain will separate the *H* Place
 28:36 seal: *H* TO THE LORD.
 29:37 Then the altar will be most *h*,
 30:10 It is most *h* to the LORD."
 30:29 them so they will be most *h*,
 31:13 I am the LORD, who makes you *h*.
 40: 9 all its furnishings, and it will be *h*.
Lev 10: 3 I will show myself *h*;
 10:10 must distinguish between the *h*
 10:13 in a *h* place, because it is your
 share
 11:44 and be *h*, because I am *h*.
 11:45 therefore be *h*, because I am *h*.
 19: 2 'Be *h* because I, the LORD your
 19: 8 he has desecrated what is *h*
 19:24 the fourth year all its fruit will
 be *h*,
 20: 3 and profaned my *h* name.
 20: 7 " 'Consecrate yourselves and
 be *h*,
 20: 8 I am the LORD, who makes you *h*.
 20:26 You are to be *h* to me because I,
 21: 6 They must be *h* to their God
 21: 8 Consider them *h*, because I
 22: 9 am the LORD, who makes them *h*.
 22:32 Do not profane my *h* name.
 25:12 For it is a jubilee and is to be *h*
 27: 9 given to the LORD becomes *h*.
Nu 4:15 they must not touch the *h* things
 6: 5 He must be *h* until the period
 20:12 as *h* in the sight of the Israelites,
 20:13 and where he showed himself *h*
Dt 5:12 the Sabbath day by keeping it *h*,
 23:14 Your camp must be *h*,
 26:15 from heaven, your *h* dwelling
 place
 33: 2 He came with myriads of *h* ones
Jos 5:15 place where you are standing
 is *h*.
 24:19 He is a *h* God; he is a jealous God.
1Sa 2: 2 "There is no one *h* like the LORD;
 6:20 of the LORD, this *h* God?
 21: 5 even on missions that are not *h*.
2Ki 4: 9 often comes our way is a *h* man
1Ch 16:10 Glory in his *h* name;
 16:35 may give thanks to your *h* name,
 29: 3 I have provided for this *h* temple:
2Ch 30:27 heaven, his *h* dwelling place.
Ezr 9: 2 and have mingled the *h* race
Ne 11: 1 the *h* city, while the remaining
 nine
Job 6:10 not denied the words of the *H*
 One.

Ps 2: 6 King on Zion, my *h* hill."
 11: 4 The LORD is in his *h* temple;
 16:10 will you let your *H* One see decay.
 22: 3 you are enthroned as the *H* One;
 24: 3 Who may stand in his *h* place?
 30: 4 praise his *h* name.
 77:13 Your ways, O God, are *h*.
 78:54 to the border of his *h* land,
 99: 3 he is *h*.
 99: 5 he is *h*.
 99: 9 for the LORD our God is *h*.
 105: 3 Glory in his *h* name;
 111: 9 *h* and awesome is his name.
Pr 9:10 of the *H* One is understanding.
Isa 5:16 the *h* God will show himself *h*
 6: 3 *H, h, h*, is the LORD Almighty;
 8:13 is the one you are to regard as *h*,
 29:23 they will keep my name *h*;
 40:25 who is my equal?" says the *H*
 One.
 43: 3 the *H* One of Israel, your Savior;
 54: 5 *H* One of Israel is your Redeemer;
 57:15 who lives forever, whose name
 is *h*:
 58:13 and the LORD's *h* day honorable,
Jer 17:22 but keep the Sabbath day *h*,
Eze 20:41 I will show myself *h* among you
 22:26 to my law and profane my *h*
 things;
 28:22 and show myself *h* within her.
 28:25 I will show myself *h* among them
 36:20 nations they profaned my *h* name,
 38:16 when I show myself *h* through you
 44:23 the difference between the *h*
Da 9:24 prophecy and to anoint the
 most *h*.
Hab 2:20 But the LORD is in his *h* temple;
Zec 14: 5 and all the *h* ones with him.
 14:20 On that day *H* TO THE LORD
Mt 24:15 in the *h* place 'the abomination
Mk 1:24 the *H* One of God!" "Be quiet!"
Lk 1:35 the *h* one to be born will be called
 1:49 *h* is his name.
 4:34 the *H* One of God!" "Be quiet!"
Jn 6:69 and know that you are the *H* One
Ac 2:27 will you let your *H* One see decay.
 13:35 will not let your *H* One see decay.'
Ro 1: 2 prophets in the *H* Scriptures
 7:12 and the commandment is *h*,
 11:16 if the root is *h*, so are the
 branches.
 12: 1 as living sacrifices, *h* and pleasing
1Co 1: 2 in Christ Jesus and called to be *h*,
 7:14 be unclean, but as it is, they are *h*.
Eph 1: 4 the creation of the world to be *h*
 2:21 and rises to become a *h* temple
 3: 5 by the Spirit to God's *h* apostles
 5: 3 improper for God's *h* people.
 5:26 up for her to make her *h*,
Col 1:22 death to present you *h* in his
 sight,
1Th 2:10 and so is God, of how *h*,
 3:13 and *h* in the presence of our God
 3:13 comes with all his *h* ones.
 4: 7 us to be impure, but to live a *h*
 life.
2Th 1:10 to be glorified in his *h* people
1Ti 2: 8 to lift up *h* hands in prayer,
2Ti 1: 9 saved us and called us to a *h*
 life—
 2:21 for noble purposes, made *h*,
 3:15 you have known the *h* Scriptures,
Tit 1: 8 upright, *h* and disciplined.
Heb 2:11 Both the one who makes men *h*
 7:26 one who is *h*, blameless, pure,
 10:10 we have been made *h*
 10:14 those who are being made *h*.
 10:19 to enter the Most *H* Place
 12:14 in peace with all men and to be *h*;
 13:12 gate to make the people *h*
1Pe 1:15 But just as he who called you is *h*,
 1:16 is written: "Be *h*, because I am *h*."
 2: 5 house to be a *h* priesthood,
 2: 9 a royal priesthood, a *h* nation,
 3: 5 For this is the way the *h* women
2Pe 3:11 You ought to live *h* and godly lives
Jude :14 upon thousands of his *h* ones
Rev 3: 7 are the words of him who is *h*
 4: 8 "*H, h, h* is the Lord God
 15: 4 For you alone are *h*.
 20: 6 and *h* are those who have part

Rev 22:11   let him who is *h* continue to
         be *h.*"

HOME (HOMES)
Dt   6: 7   Talk about them when you sit at *h*
   11:19   about them when you sit at *h*
   20: 5   Let him go *h*, or he may die
   24: 5   is to be free to stay at *h*
Ru   1:11   "Return *h*, my daughters.
2Sa   7:10   them so that they can have a *h*
1Ch 16:43   and David returned *h* to bless his
Ps   84: 3   Even the sparrow has found a *h*,
   113: 9   settles the barren woman in her *h*
Pr   3:33   but he blesses the *h* of the
         righteous
   27: 8   is a man who strays from his *h.*
Ecc 12: 5   Then man goes to his eternal *h*
Eze 36: 8   for they will soon come *h.*
Mic   2: 2   They defraud a man of his *h*,
Mt   1:24   and took Mary *h* as his wife.
Mk 10:29   "no one who has left *h* or
         brothers
Lk 10:38   named Martha opened her *h*
Jn 14:23   to him and make our *h* with him.
   19:27   this disciple took her into his *h.*
Ac 16:15   baptized, she invited us to her *h.*
Tit   2: 5   to be busy at *h*, to be kind,

HOMELESS*
1Co   4:11   we are brutally treated, we are *h.*

HOMES (HOME)
Ne   4:14   daughters, your wives and
         your *h.*"
Isa 32:18   in secure *h*,
Mk 10:30   as much in this present age (*h*,
1Ti   5:14   to manage their *h* and to give

HOMETOWN
Mt 13:57   "Only in his *h*
Lk   4:24   "no prophet is accepted in his *h.*

HOMOSEXUAL*
1Co   6: 9   male prostitutes nor *h* offenders

HONEST (HONESTY)
Lev 19:36   Use *h* scales and *h* weights,
Dt 25:15   and *h* weights and measures,
Job 31: 6   let God weigh me in *h* scales
Pr 12:17   truthful witness gives *h* testimony,

HONESTY (HONEST)
2Ki 12:15   they acted with complete *h.*

HONEY (HONEYCOMB)
Ex   3: 8   a land flowing with milk and *h*—
Jdg 14: 8   a swarm of bees and some *h*,
1Sa 14:26   they saw the *h* oozing out,
Ps 19:10   than *h* from the comb.
   119:103   sweeter than *h* to my mouth!
Pr 25:16   If you find *h*, eat just enough—
SS   4:11   milk and *h* are under your tongue.
Isa   7:15   and *h* when he knows enough
Eze   3: 3   it tasted as sweet as *h* in my
         mouth.
Mt   3: 4   His food was locusts and wild *h.*
Rev 10: 9   mouth it will be as sweet as *h.*"

HONEYCOMB (HONEY)
SS   4:11   Your lips drop sweetness as the *h*,
   5: 1   I have eaten my *h* and my honey;

HONOR (HONORABLE HONORABLY HONORED
HONORS)
Ex 20:12   "*H* your father and your mother,
Nu 20:12   trust in me enough to *h* me
   25:13   he was zealous for the *h* of his
         God
Dt   5:16   "*H* your father and your mother,
Jdg   4: 9   going about this, the *h* will not be
1Sa   2: 8   and has them inherit a throne
         of *h.*
   2:30   Those who *h* me I will *h*,
1Ch 29:12   Wealth and *h* come from you;
2Ch   1:11   or *h*, nor for the death
   18: 1   had great wealth and *h*,
Est   6: 6   for the man the king delights to *h*
Ps   8: 5   and crowned him with glory
         and *h.*
   45:11   *h* him, for he is your lord.
   84:11   the LORD bestows favor and *h*;
Pr   3: 9   *H* the LORD with your wealth,
   3:35   The wise inherit *h*,
   15:33   and humility comes before *h.*
   18:12   but humility comes before *h.*
   20: 3   It is to a man's *h* to avoid strife,

Pr 25:27   is it honorable to seek one's
         own *h.*
Isa 29:13   and *h* me with their lips,
Jer 33: 9   and *h* before all nations
Mt 13:57   own house is a prophet
         without *h.*"
   15: 4   '*H* your father and mother'
   15: 8   These people *h* me with their lips,
   19:19   *h* your father and mother,'
   23: 6   they love the place of *h* at
         banquets
Mk   6: 4   own house is a prophet
         without *h.*"
Lk 14: 8   do not take the place of *h*,
Jn   5:23   that all may *h* the Son just
   7:18   does so to gain *h* for himself,
   12:26   My Father will *h* the one who
Ro 12:10   *H* one another above yourselves.
1Co   6:20   Therefore *h* God with your body.
Eph   6: 2   "*H* your father and mother"—
1Ti   5:17   well are worthy of double *h*,
Heb   2: 7   you crowned him with glory and *h*
Rev   4: 9   *h* and thanks to him who sits

HONORABLE (HONOR)
1Th   4: 4   body in a way that is holy and *h*,

HONORABLY (HONOR)
Heb 13:18   and desire to live *h* in every way.

HONORED (HONOR)
Ps 12: 8   when what is vile is *h* among
         men.
Pr 13:18   but whoever heeds correction
         is *h.*
Da   4:34   and glorified him who lives
1Co 12:26   if one part is *h*, every part rejoices
Heb 13: 4   Marriage should be *h* by all,

HONORS (HONOR)
Ps 15: 4   but *h* those who fear the LORD,
Pr 14:31   to the needy *h* God.

HOOF
Ex 10:26   not a *h* is to be left behind.

HOOKS
Isa   2: 4   and their spears into pruning *h.*
Joel   3:10   and your pruning *h* into spears.
Mic   4: 3   and their spears into pruning *h.*

HOPE (HOPES)
Job 13:15   Though he slay me, yet will I *h*
Ps 25: 3   No one whose *h* is in you
   33:17   A horse is a vain *h* for deliverance;
   33:18   on those whose *h* is
   42: 5   Put your *h* in God,
   62: 5   my *h* comes from him.
   119:74   for I have put my *h* in your word.
   130: 5   and in his word I put my *h.*
   130: 7   O Israel, put your *h* in the LORD,
   146: 5   whose *h* is in the LORD his God,
   147:11   who put their *h* in his unfailing
         love
Pr 13:12   *H* deferred makes the heart sick,
   23:18   There is surely a future *h* for you,
Isa 40:31   but those who *h* in the LORD
Jer 29:11   plans to give you *h* and a future.
La   3:21   and therefore I have *h:*
Zec   9:12   to your fortress, O prisoners of *h*;
Ro   5: 4   character; and character, *h.*
   8:20   in *h* that the creation itself will be
   8:24   But *h* that is seen is no *h* at all.
   8:25   if we *h* for what we do not yet
         have,
   12:12   Be joyful in *h*, patient in affliction,
   15: 4   of the Scriptures we might have *h.*
   15:13   May the God of *h* fill you
1Co 13:13   now these three remain: faith, *h*
   15:19   for this life we have *h* in Christ,
Eph   2:12   without *h* and without God
Col   1:27   Christ in you, the *h* of glory.
1Th   1: 3   and your endurance inspired by *h*
   5: 8   and the *h* of salvation as a helmet.
1Ti   4:10   that we have put our *h*
   1: 1   but to put their *h* in God,
Tit   1: 2   resting on the *h* of eternal life,
   2:13   while we wait for the blessed *h*—
Heb   6:19   We have this *h* as an anchor
   10:23   unswervingly to the *h* we profess,
   11: 1   faith is being sure of what we *h*
         for
1Jn   3: 3   Everyone who has this *h*

HOPES (HOPE)
1Co 13: 7   always *h*, always perseveres.

HORN (HORNS)
Ex 19:13   when the ram's *h* sounds a long
   27: 2   Make a *h* at each of the four
Da   7: 8   This *h* had eyes like the eyes

HORNS (HORN)
Da   7:24   ten *h* are ten kings who will come
Rev   5: 6   He had seven *h* and seven eyes,
   12: 3   and ten *h* and seven crowns
   13: 1   He had ten *h* and seven heads,
   17: 3   and had seven heads and ten *h.*

HORRIBLE (HORROR)
Jer   5:30   "A *h* and shocking thing

HORROR (HORRIBLE)
Jer   2:12   and shudder with great *h*,"

HORSE
Ps 147:10   not in the strength of the *h*,
Pr 26: 3   A whip for the *h*, a halter
Zec   1: 8   before me was a man riding a
         red *h*
Rev   6: 2   and there before me was a
         white *h!*
   6: 4   Come!" Then another *h* came out,
   6: 5   and there before me was a
         black *h!*
   6: 8   and there before me was a pale *h!*
   19:11   and there before me was a
         white *h*,

HOSANNA
Mt 21: 9   "*H* in the highest!"
Mk 11: 9   "*H!*"
Jn 12:13   "*H!*"

HOSEA
Prophet whose wife and family pictured the
unfaithfulness of Israel (Hos 1–3).

HOSHEA (JOSHUA)
  1. Original name of Joshua (Nu 13:16).
  2. Last king of Israel (2Ki 15:30; 17:1–6).

HOSPITABLE* (HOSPITALITY)
1Ti   3: 2   self-controlled, respectable, *h*,
Tit   1: 8   Rather he must be *h*, one who
         loves

HOSPITABLY* (HOSPITALITY)
Ac 28: 7   and for three days entertained
         us *h.*

HOSPITALITY* (HOSPITABLE HOSPITABLY)
Ro 12:13   Practice *h.*
   16:23   whose *h* I and the whole church
1Ti   5:10   as bringing up children,
         showing *h*,
1Pe   4: 9   Offer *h* to one another
3Jn   : 8   therefore to show *h* to such men

HOSTILE (HOSTILITY)
Ro   8: 7   the sinful mind is *h* to God.

HOSTILITY (HOSTILE)
Eph   2:14   wall of *h*, by abolishing
   2:16   by which he put to death their *h.*

HOT
1Ti   4: 2   have been seared as with a *h* iron.
Rev   3:15   that you are neither cold nor *h.*

HOT-TEMPERED (TEMPER)
Pr 15:18   A *h* man stirs up dissension,
   19:19   A *h* man must pay the penalty;
   22:24   Do not make friends with a *h*
         man,
   29:22   and a *h* one commits many sins.

HOTHEADED (HEAD)
Pr 14:16   but a fool is *h* and reckless.

HOUR
Ecc   9:12   knows when his *h* will come:
Mt   6:27   you by worrying can add a
         single *h*
Lk 12:40   the Son of Man will come at an *h*
Jn 12:23   The *h* has come for the Son of
         Man
   12:27   for this very reason I came to
         this *h*

HOUSE (HOUSEHOLD HOUSEHOLDS HOUSES
STOREHOUSE)
Ex 12:22   the door of his *h* until morning.
   20:17   shall not covet your neighbor's *h.*
Nu 12: 7   he is faithful in all my *h.*
Dt   5:21   desire on your neighbor's *h*
2Sa   7:11   LORD himself will establish a *h*
1Ch 17:23   and his *h* be established forever.
Ne 10:39   "We will not neglect the *h*

Ps 23: 6 I will dwell in the *h* of the LORD
27: 4 dwell in the *h* of the LORD
69: 9 for zeal for your *h* consumes me.
84:10 a doorkeeper in the *h* of my God
122: 1 "Let us go to the *h* of the LORD."
127: 1 Unless the LORD builds the *h*.
Pr 7:27 Her *h* is a highway to the grave,
21: 9 than share a *h* with a quarrelsome
Isa 56: 7 a *h* of prayer for all nations."
Jer 7:11 Has this *h*, which bears my Name,
18: 2 "Go down to the potter's *h*,
Eze 33: 7 made you a watchman for the *h*
Joel 3:18 will flow out of the LORD's *h*
Zec 13: 6 given at the *h* of my friends.'
Mt 7:24 is like a wise man who built his *h*
10:11 and stay at his *h* until you leave.
12:29 can anyone enter a strong man's *h*
21:13 My *h* will be called a *h* of prayer,'
Mk 3:25 If a *h* is divided against itself,
11:17 " 'My *h* will be called
Lk 6:48 He is like a man building a *h*,
10: 7 Do not move around from *h* to *h*.
11:17 a *h* divided against itself will fall.
11:24 'I will return to the *h* I left.'
15: 8 sweep the *h* and search carefully
19: 9 Today salvation has come to this *h*,
Jn 2:16 How dare you turn my Father's *h*
2:17 "Zeal for your *h* will consume me."
12: 3 the *h* was filled with the fragrance
14: 2 In my Father's are many rooms;
Ac 20:20 you publicly and from *h* to *h*.
Ro 16: 5 the church that meets at their *h*.
Heb 3: 3 the builder of a *h* has greater honor
1Pe 2: 5 built into a spiritual *h* to be a holy

HOUSEHOLD (HOUSE)
Ex 12: 3 lamb for his family, one for each *h*.
Jos 24:15 my *h*, we will serve the LORD."
Pr 31:21 it snows, she has no fear for her *h*;
31:27 over the affairs of her *h*
Mic 7: 6 are the members of his own *h*.
Mt 10:36 will be the members of his own *h*.'
12:25 or *h* divided against itself will not
Ac 16:31 you will be saved—you and your *h*
Eph 2:19 people and members of God's *h*,
1Ti 3:12 manage his children and his *h* well.
3:15 to conduct themselves in God's *h*,

HOUSEHOLDS (HOUSE)
Tit 1:11 because they are ruining whole *h*

HOUSES (HOUSE)
Ex 12:27 passed over the *h* of the Israelites
Mt 19:29 everyone who has left *h* or brothers

HOVERING* (HOVERS)
Ge 1: 2 of God was *h* over the waters.
Isa 31: 5 Like birds *h* overhead,

HOVERS* (HOVERING)
Dt 32:11 and *h* over its young,

HULDAH*
Prophetess inquired by Hilkiah for Josiah
(2Ki 22; 2Ch 34:14–28).

HUMAN (HUMANITY)
Lev 24:17 If anyone takes the life of a *h* being,
Isa 52:14 his form marred beyond *h* likeness
Jn 8:15 You judge by *h* standards;
Ro 1: 3 as to his *h* nature was a descendant
9: 5 from them is traced the *h* ancestry
1Co 1:17 not with words of *h* wisdom,
1:26 of you were wise by *h* standards;
2:13 not in words taught us by *h* wisdom
2Co 3: 3 of stone but on tablets of *h* hearts.
Gal 3: 3 to attain your goal by *h* effort?
2Pe 2:18 lustful desires of sinful *h* nature,

HUMANITY* (HUMAN)
Heb 2:14 he too shared in their *h* so that

HUMBLE (HUMBLED HUMBLES HUMILIATE HUMILIATED HUMILITY)
Nu 12: 3 (Now Moses was a very *h* man,

2Ch 7:14 will *h* themselves and pray
Ps 18:27 You save the *h*
25: 9 He guides the *h* in what is right
149: 4 he crowns the *h* with salvation.
Pr 3:34 but gives grace to the *h*.
Isa 66: 2 he who is *h* and contrite in spirit,
Mt 11:29 for I am gentle and *h* in heart,
Eph 4: 2 Be completely *h* and gentle;
Jas 4: 6 but gives grace to the *h*."
4:10 *H* yourselves before the Lord,
1Pe 5: 5 but gives grace to the *h*."
5: 6 *H* yourselves,

HUMBLED (HUMBLE)
Mt 23:12 whoever exalts himself will be *h*,
Lk 14:11 who exalts himself will be *h*,
Php 2: 8 he *h* himself

HUMBLES* (HUMBLE)
1Sa 2: 7 he *h* and he exalts.
Isa 26: 5 He *h* those who dwell on high,
Mt 18: 4 whoever *h* himself like this child is
23:12 whoever *h* himself will be exalted.
Lk 14:11 he who *h* himself will be exalted."
18:14 he who *h* himself will be exalted."

HUMILIATE* (HUMBLE)
Pr 25: 7 than for him to *h* you
1Co 11:22 and *h* those who have nothing?

HUMILIATED (HUMBLE)
Jer 31:19 I was ashamed and *h*
Lk 14: 9 *h*, you will have to take the least

HUMILITY* (HUMBLE)
Ps 45: 4 of truth, *h* and righteousness;
Pr 11: 2 but with *h* comes wisdom.
15:33 and *h* comes before honor.
18:12 but *h* comes before honor.
22: 4 and the fear of the LORD
Zep 2: 3 Seek righteousness, seek *h*;
Ac 20:19 I served the Lord with great *h*
Php 2: 3 but in *h* consider others better
Col 2:18 let anyone who delights in false *h*
2:23 their false *h* and their harsh
3:12 *h*, gentleness and patience.
Tit 3: 2 and to show true *h* toward all men.
Jas 3:13 in the *h* that comes from wisdom.
1Pe 5: 5 clothe yourselves with *h*

HUNG (HANG)
Dt 21:23 anyone who is *h* on a tree is
Mt 18: 6 him to have a large millstone *h*
Lk 19:48 all the people *h* on his words.
Gal 3:13 "Cursed is everyone who is *h*

HUNGER (HUNGRY)
Ne 9:15 In their *h* you gave them bread
Pr 6:30 to satisfy his *h* when he is starving.
Mt 5: 6 Blessed are those who *h*
Lk 6:21 Blessed are you who *h* now,
2Co 6: 5 sleepless nights and *h*; in purity,
11:27 I have known *h* and thirst
Rev 7:16 Never again will they *h*;

HUNGRY (HUNGER)
Job 24:10 carry the sheaves, but still go *h*.
Ps 107: 9 and fills the *h* with good things.
146: 7 and gives food to the *h*.
Pr 19:15 and the shiftless man goes *h*.
25:21 If your enemy is *h*, give him food
27: 7 to the *h* even what is bitter tastes
Isa 58: 7 not to share your food with the *h*
58:10 spend yourselves in behalf of the *h*
Eze 18: 7 but gives his food to the *h*
18:16 but gives his food to the *h*
Mt 15:32 I do not want to send them away *h*,
25:35 For I was *h* and you gave me
25:42 For I was *h* and you gave me
Lk 1:53 He has filled the *h* with good things
Jn 6:35 comes to me will never go *h*,
Ro 12:20 "If your enemy is *h*, feed him;
1Co 4:11 To this very hour we go *h*
Php 4:12 whether well fed or *h*,

HUR
Ex 17:12 Aaron and *H* held his hands up—

HURL
Mic 7:19 *h* all our iniquities into the depths

HURT (HURTS)
Ecc 8: 9 it over others to his own *h*.

Mk 16:18 deadly poison, it will not *h* them
Rev 2:11 He who overcomes will not be *h*

HURTS* (HURT)
Ps 15: 4 even when it *h*,
Pr 26:28 A lying tongue hates those it *h*,

HUSBAND (HUSBAND'S HUSBANDS)
Pr 31:11 Her *h* has full confidence in her
31:23 Her *h* is respected at the city gate,
31:28 her *h* also, and he praises her:
Isa 54: 5 For your Maker is your *h*—
Jer 3:14 the LORD, "for I am your *h*.
3:20 like a woman unfaithful to her *h*,
Jn 4:17 "I have no *h*," she replied.
Ro 7: 2 a married woman is bound to her *h*
1Co 7: 2 and each woman her own *h*.
7: 3 The *h* should fulfill his marital duty
7:10 wife must not separate from her *h*.
7:11 And a *h* must not divorce his wife.
7:13 And if a woman has a *h* who is not
7:14 For the unbelieving *h* has been
7:39 A woman is bound to her *h* as long
7:39 But if her *h* dies, she is free
2Co 11: 2 I promised you to one *h*, to Christ,
Gal 4:27 woman than of her who has a *h*."
Eph 5:23 For the *h* is the head of the wife
5:33 and the wife must respect her *h*.
1Ti 3: 2 the *h* of but one wife, temperate,
3:12 A deacon must be the *h* of
5: 9 has been faithful to her *h*,
Tit 1: 6 An elder must be blameless, the *h*

HUSBANDMAN SEE GARDENER

HUSBAND'S (HUSBAND)
Dt 25: 5 Her *h* brother shall take her
Pr 12: 4 of noble character is her *h* crown,
1Co 7: 4 the *h* body does not belong

HUSBANDS (HUSBAND)
Eph 5:22 submit to your *h* as to the Lord.
5:25 *H*, love your wives, just
5:28 *h* ought to love their wives
Col 3:18 submit to your *h*, as is fitting
3:19 *H*, love your wives and do not be
Tit 2: 4 the younger women to love their *h*
2: 5 and to be subject to their *h*,
1Pe 3: 1 same way be submissive to your *h*
3: 7 *H*, in the same way be considerate

HUSHAI
Wise man of David who frustrated
Ahithophel's advice and foiled Absalom's
revolt (2Sa 15:32–37; 16:15–17:16; 1Ch 27:33).

HYMN* (HYMNS)
Ps 40: 3 a *h* of praise to our God.
Mt 26:30 they had sung a *h*, they went out
Mk 14:26 they had sung a *h*, they went out
1Co 14:26 everyone has a *h*, or a word

HYMNS* (HYMN)
Ac 16:25 Silas were praying and singing *h*
Ro 15: 9 I will sing *h* to your name."
Eph 5:19 to one another with psalms, *h*
Col 3:16 *h* and spiritual songs with gratitude

HYPOCRISY* (HYPOCRITE HYPOCRITES HYPOCRITICAL)
Mt 23:28 but on the inside you are full of *h*
Mk 12:15 we?" But Jesus knew their *h*.
Lk 12: 1 yeast of the Pharisees, which is *h*.
Gal 2:13 The other Jews joined him in his *h*,
2:13 by their *h* even Barnabas was led
1Pe 2: 1 *h*, envy, and slander of every kind.

HYPOCRITE* (HYPOCRISY)
Mt 7: 5 You *h*, first take the plank out
Lk 6:42 You *h*, first take the plank out

HYPOCRITES* (HYPOCRISY)
Ps 26: 4 nor do I consort with *h*;
Mt 6: 2 as the *h* do in the synagogues
6: 5 when you pray, do not be like the *h*
6:16 do not look somber as the *h* do,
15: 7 You *h*! Isaiah was right
22:18 their evil intent, said, "You *h*,
23:13 of the law and Pharisees, you *h*!

Mt   23:15   of the law and Pharisees, you *h*!
     23:23   of the law and Pharisees, you *h*!
     23:25   of the law and Pharisees, you *h*!
     23:27   you *h*! You are like whitewashed
     23:29   of the law and Pharisees, you *h*!
     24:51   and assign him a place with the *h*,
Mk   7: 6   when he prophesied about you *h*;
Lk   12:56   *H*! You know how
     13:15   The Lord answered him, "You *h*!

HYPOCRITICAL* (HYPOCRISY)
1Ti   4: 2   teachings come through *h* liars,

HYSSOP
Ex   12:22   Take a bunch of *h*, dip it
Ps   51: 7   with *h*, and I will be clean;
Jn   19:29   the sponge on a stalk of the *h* plant,

ICHABOD
1Sa   4:21   She named the boy *I*, saying,

IDLE* (IDLENESS IDLERS)
Dt   32:47   They are not just *i* words for you—
Job   11: 3   Will your *i* talk reduce men
Ecc   10:18   if his hands are *i*, the house leaks.
     11: 6   at evening let not your hands be *i*,
Isa   58:13   as you please or speaking *i* words,
Col   2:18   mind puffs him up with *i* notions.
1Th   5:14   those who are *i*, encourage
2Th   3: 6   away from every brother who is *i*
     3: 7   We were not *i* when we were
     3:11   We hear that some among you are *i*
1Ti   5:13   they get into the habit of being *i*

IDLENESS* (IDLE)
Pr   31:27   and does not eat the bread of *i*.

IDLERS* (IDLE)
1Ti   5:13   And not only do they become *i*,

IDOL (IDOLATER IDOLATERS IDOLATRY IDOLS)
Ex   20: 4   make for yourself an *i* in the form
     32: 4   made it into an *i* cast in the shape
Isa   40:19   As for an *i*, a craftsman casts it,
     41: 7   He nails down the *i*
     44:15   he makes an *i* and bows down to it.
     44:17   From the rest he makes a god, his *i*;
Hab   2:18   "Of what value is an *i*,
1Co   8: 4   We know that an *i* is nothing at all

IDOLATER* (IDOL)
1Co   5:11   an *i* or a slanderer, a drunkard
Eph   5: 5   greedy person—such a man is an *i*

IDOLATERS* (IDOL)
1Co   5:10   or the greedy and swindlers, or *i*.
     6: 9   Neither the sexually immoral nor *i*

IDOLATRY (IDOL)
1Sa   15:23   and arrogance like the evil of *i*.
1Co   10:14   my dear friends, flee from *i*.
Gal   5:20   and debauchery; *i* and witchcraft;
Col   3: 5   evil desires and greed, which is *i*.
1Pe   4: 3   orgies, carousing and detestable *i*.

IDOLS (IDOL)
Dt   32:16   angered him with their detestable *i*.
Ps   78:58   aroused his jealousy with their *i*.
Isa   44: 9   All who make *i* are nothing,
Eze   23:39   sacrificed their children to their *i*,
Ac   15:20   to abstain from food polluted by *i*,
     21:25   abstain from food sacrificed to *i*,
1Co   8: 1   Now about food sacrificed to *i*:
1Jn   5:21   children, keep yourselves from *i*.
Rev   2:14   to sin by eating food sacrificed to *i*

IGNORANT (IGNORE)
1Co   15:34   for there are some who are *i* of God
Heb   5: 2   to deal gently with those who are *i*
1Pe   2:15   good you should silence the *i* talk
2Pe   3:16   which *i* and unstable people distort

IGNORE (IGNORANT IGNORED IGNORES)
Dt   22: 1   do not *i* it but be sure
Ps   9:12   he does not *i* the cry of the afflicted
Heb   2: 3   if we *i* such a great salvation?

IGNORED (IGNORE)
Hos   4: 6   you have *i* the law of your God,

1Co   14:38   he ignores this, he himself will be *i*.

IGNORES* (IGNORE)
Pr   10:17   whoever *i* correction leads others
     13:18   He who *i* discipline comes
     15:32   He who *i* discipline despises
1Co   14:38   If he *i* this, he himself will be

ILL (ILLNESS)
Mt   4:24   brought to him all who were *i*

ILL-GOTTEN
Pr   1:19   the end of all who go after *i* gain;
     10: 2   *I* treasures are of no value,

ILL-TEMPERED* (TEMPER)
Pr   21:19   than with a quarrelsome and *i* wife.

ILLEGITIMATE
Heb   12: 8   then you are *i* children

ILLNESS (ILL)
2Ki   8: 9   'Will I recover from this *i*?' "
2Ch   16:12   even in his *i* he did not seek help
Ps   41: 3   and restore him from his bed of *i*.
Isa   38: 9   king of Judah after his *i*

ILLUMINATED*
Rev   18: 1   and the earth was *i* by his splendor.

IMAGE (IMAGES)
Ge   1:26   "Let us make man in our *i*,
     1:27   So God created man in his own *i*,
     9: 6   for in the *i* of God
Dt   27:15   "Cursed is the man who carves an *i*
Isa   40:18   What *i* will you compare him to?
Da   3: 1   King Nebuchadnezzar made an *i*
1Co   11: 7   since he is the *i* and glory of God;
2Co   4: 4   glory of Christ, who is the *i* of God.
Col   1:15   He is the *i* of the invisible God,
     3:10   in knowledge in the *i* of its Creator.
Rev   13:14   them to set up an *i* in honor

IMAGES (IMAGE)
Ps   97: 7   All who worship *i* are put to shame,
Jer   10:14   His *i* are a fraud;
Ro   1:23   of the immortal God for *i* made

IMAGINATION (IMAGINE)
Eze   13: 2   who prophesy out of their own *i*:

IMAGINE (IMAGINATION)
Eph   3:20   more than all we ask or *i*,

IMITATE (IMITATORS)
1Co   4:16   Therefore I urge you to *i* me.
Heb   6:12   but to *i* those who through faith
     13: 7   of their way of life and *i* their faith.
3Jn   :11   do not *i* what is evil but what is

IMITATORS* (IMITATE)
Eph   5: 1   Be *i* of God, therefore,
1Th   1: 6   You became *i* of us and of the Lord
     2:14   became *i* of God's churches

IMMANUEL*
Isa   7:14   birth to a son, and will call him *I*.
     8: 8   O *I*!"
Mt   1:23   and they will call him *I*"—

IMMORAL* (IMMORALITY)
Pr   6:24   keeping you from the *i* woman,
1Co   5: 9   to associate with sexually *i* people
     5:10   the people of this world who are *i*,
     5:11   but is sexually *i* or greedy,
     6: 9   Neither the sexually *i* nor idolaters
Eph   5: 5   No *i*, impure or greedy person—
Heb   12:16   See that no one is sexually *i*,
     13: 4   the adulterer and all the sexually *i*.
Rev   21: 8   the murderers, the sexually *i*,
     22:15   the sexually *i*, the murderers,

IMMORALITY* (IMMORAL)
Nu   25: 1   in sexual *i* with Moabite women,
Jer   3: 9   Because Israel's *i* mattered so little
Mt   15:19   murder, adultery, sexual *i*, theft,
Mk   7:21   sexual *i*, theft, murder, adultery,
Ac   15:20   from sexual *i*, from the meat
     15:29   animals and from sexual *i*.
     21:25   animals and from sexual *i*."

Ro   13:13   not in sexual *i* and debauchery,
1Co   5: 1   reported that there is sexual *i*
     6:13   The body is not meant for sexual *i*,
     6:18   Flee from sexual *i*.
     7: 2   But since there is so much *i*,
     10: 8   We should not commit sexual *i*,
Gal   5:19   sexual *i*, impurity and debauchery;
Eph   5: 3   must not be even a hint of sexual *i*,
Col   3: 5   sexual *i*, impurity, lust, evil desires
1Th   4: 3   that you should avoid sexual *i*;
Jude   : 4   grace of our God into a license for *i*
     : 7   gave themselves up to sexual *i*
Rev   2:14   and by committing sexual *i*.
     2:20   misleads my servants into sexual *i*
     2:21   given her time to repent of her *i*,
     9:21   their sexual *i* or their thefts.

IMMORTAL* (IMMORTALITY)
Ro   1:23   glory of the *i* God for images made
1Ti   1:17   Now to the King eternal, *i*,
     6:16   who alone is *i* and who lives

IMMORTALITY* (IMMORTAL)
Pr   12:28   along that path is *i*.
Ro   2: 7   honor and *i*, he will give eternal life
1Co   15:53   and the mortal with *i*.
     15:54   with *i*, then the saying that is
2Ti   1:10   and *i* to light through the gospel.

IMPARTIAL*
Jas   3:17   and good fruit, *i* and sincere.

IMPARTS*
Pr   29:15   The rod of correction *i* wisdom,

IMPERFECT*
1Co   13:10   perfection comes, the *i* disappears.

IMPERISHABLE
1Co   15:42   it is raised *i*; it is sown in dishonor,
     15:50   nor does the perishable inherit the *i*
1Pe   1:23   not of perishable seed, but of *i*,

IMPLANTED*
Ps   94: 9   Does he who *i* the ear not hear?

IMPLORE*
Mal   1: 9   "Now *i* God to be gracious to us.
2Co   5:20   We *i* you on Christ's behalf:

IMPORTANCE* (IMPORTANT)
1Co   15: 3   passed on to you as of first *i*:

IMPORTANT (IMPORTANCE)
Mt   6:25   Is not life more *i* than food,
     23:23   have neglected the more *i* matters
Mk   12:29   "The most *i* one," answered Jesus,
     12:33   as yourself is more *i* than all burnt
Php   1:18   The *i* thing is that in every way,

IMPOSSIBLE
Mt   17:20   Nothing will be *i* for you."
     19:26   "With man this is *i*,
Mk   10:27   "With man this is *i*, but not
Lk   1:37   For nothing is *i* with God."
     18:27   "What is *i* with men is possible
Ac   2:24   it was *i* for death to keep its hold
Heb   6: 4   It is *i* for those who have once been
     6:18   things in which it is *i* for God to lie,
     10: 4   because it is *i* for the blood of bulls
     11: 6   without faith it is *i* to please God,

IMPOSTORS
2Ti   3:13   and *i* will go from bad to worse,

IMPRESS* (IMPRESSES)
Dt   6: 7   *I* them on your children.

IMPRESSES* (IMPRESS)
Pr   17:10   A rebuke *i* a man of discernment

IMPROPER*
Eph   5: 3   these are *i* for God's holy people.

IMPURE (IMPURITY)
Ac   10:15   not call anything *i* that God has
Eph   5: 5   No immoral, *i* or greedy person—
1Th   2: 3   spring from error or *i* motives,
     4: 7   For God did not call us to be *i*,
Rev   21:27   Nothing *i* will ever enter it,

IMPURITY (IMPURE)

Ro   1:24   hearts to sexual *i* for the degrading
Gal 5:19   sexual immorality, *i*
Eph 4:19   as to indulge in every kind of *i*,
      5: 3   or of any kind of *i*, or of greed,
Col   3: 5   *i*, lust, evil desires and greed,

INCENSE

Ex 30: 1   altar of acacia wood for burning *i*.
    40: 5   Place the gold altar of *i* in front
Ps 141: 2   my prayer be set before you like *i*;
Mt   2:11   him with gifts of gold and of *i*
Heb 9: 4   which had the golden altar of *i*
Rev 5: 8   were holding golden bowls full of *i*,
     8: 4   The smoke of the *i*, together

INCLINATION (INCLINES)

Ge   6: 5   and that every *i* of the thoughts

INCLINES* (INCLINATION)

Ecc 10: 2   The heart of the wise *i* to the right,

INCOME

Ecc 5:10   wealth is never satisfied with his *i*
1Co 16: 2   sum of money in keeping with his *i*,

INCOMPARABLE*

Eph 2: 7   ages he might show the *i* riches

INCREASE (EVER-INCREASING INCREASED INCREASES INCREASING)

Ge   1:22   "Be fruitful and *i* in number
    3:16   "I will greatly *i* your pains
    8:17   be fruitful and *i* in number upon it
Ps 62:10   though your riches *i*,
Pr 22:16   oppresses the poor to *i* his wealth
Isa   9: 7   Of the *i* of his government
Mt 24:12   Because of the *i* of wickedness,
Lk 17: 5   said to the Lord, "*I* our faith!"
Ac 12:24   But the word of God continued to *i*
Ro   5:20   added so that the trespass might *i*.
1Th 3:12   May the Lord make your love *i*

INCREASED (INCREASE)

Ac   6: 7   of disciples in Jerusalem *i* rapidly,
Ro   5:20   But where sin *i*, grace *i* all the more

INCREASES (INCREASE)

Pr 24: 5   and a man of knowledge *i* strength;

INCREASING (INCREASE)

Ac   6: 1   when the number of disciples was *i*,
2Th 1: 3   one of you has for each other is *i*.
2Pe 1: 8   these qualities in *i* measure,

INCREDIBLE*

Ac 26: 8   of you consider it *i* that God raises

INDECENT

Ro   1:27   Men committed *i* acts

INDEPENDENT*

1Co 11:11   however, woman is not *i* of man,
    11:11   of man, nor is man *i* of woman.

INDESCRIBABLE*

2Co 9:15   Thanks be to God for his *i* gift!

INDESTRUCTIBLE*

Heb 7:16   on the basis of the power of an *i* life

INDIGNANT

Mk 10:14   When Jesus saw this, he was *i*.

INDISPENSABLE*

1Co 12:22   seem to be weaker are *i*,

INEFFECTIVE*

2Pe 1: 8   they will keep you from being *i*

INEXPRESSIBLE*

2Co 12: 4   He heard *i* things, things that man
1Pe 1: 8   are filled with an *i* and glorious joy,

INFANCY* (INFANTS)

2Ti 3:15   *from i you have known the holy*

INFANTS (INFANCY)

Ps   8: 2   From the lips of children and *i*
Mt 21:16   " 'From the lips of children and *i*
1Co 3: 1   but as worldly—mere *i* in Christ.
    14:20   In regard to evil be *i*,
Eph 4:14   Then we will no longer be *i*,

INFIRMITIES*

Isa 53: 4   Surely he took up our *i*
Mt   8:17   "He took up our *i*

INFLAMED

Ro   1:27   were *i* with lust for one another.

INFLUENTIAL*

1Co 1:26   not many were *i*; not many were

INHABITANTS (INHABITED)

Nu 33:55   " 'But if you do not drive out the *i*
Rev 8:13   Woe! Woe to the *i* of the earth,

INHABITED (INHABITANTS)

Isa 45:18   but formed it to be *i*—

INHERIT (CO-HEIRS HEIR HEIRS HERITAGE INHERITANCE)

Dt   1:38   because he will lead Israel to *i* it.
Jos   1: 6   people to *i* the land I swore
Ps 37:11   But the meek will *i* the land
    37:29   the righteous will *i* the land
Zec 2:12   The Lord will *i* Judah
Mt   5: 5   for they will *i* the earth.
    19:29   as much and will *i* eternal life.
Mk 10:17   "what must I do to *i* eternal life?"
Lk 10:25   "what must I do to *i* eternal life?"
    18:18   what must I do to *i* eternal life?"
1Co 6: 9   the wicked will not *i* the kingdom
    15:50   blood cannot *i* the kingdom of God
Rev 21: 7   He who overcomes will *i* all this,

INHERITANCE (INHERIT)

Lev 20:24   I will give it to you as an *i*,
Dt   4:20   to be the people of his *i*,
    10: 9   the Lord is their *i*, as the Lord
Jos 14: 3   two-and-a-half tribes their *i* east
Ps   16: 6   surely I have a delightful *i*.
    33:12   the people he chose for his *i*.
  136:21   and gave their land as an *i*,
Pr 13:22   A good man leaves an *i*
Mt 25:34   blessed by my Father; take your *i*,
Eph 1:14   who is a deposit guaranteeing our *i*
    5: 5   has any *i* in the kingdom of Christ
Col   1:12   you to share in the *i* of the saints
    3:24   you know that you will receive an *i*
Heb 9:15   receive the promised eternal *i*—
1Pe 1: 4   and into an *i* that can never perish,

INIQUITIES (INIQUITY)

Ps 78:38   he forgave their *i*
  103:10   or repay us according to our *i*.
Isa 53: 5   he was crushed for our *i*;
    53:11   and he will bear their *i*.
    59: 2   But your *i* have separated
Mic 7:19   and hurl all our *i* into the depths

INIQUITY (INIQUITIES)

Ps 25:11   forgive my *i*, though it is great.
    32: 5   and did not cover up my *i*.
    51: 2   Wash away all my *i*
    51: 9   and blot out all my *i*.
Isa 53: 6   the *i* of us all.

INJURED

Eze 34:16   will bind up the *i* and strengthen
Zec 11:16   or heal the *i*, or feed the healthy,

INJUSTICE

2Ch 19: 7   the Lord our God there is no *i*

INK

2Co 3: 3   not with *i* but with the Spirit

INN*

Lk   2: 7   there was no room for them in the *i*
    10:34   took him to an *i* and took care

INNOCENT

Ex 23: 7   do not put an *i* or honest person
Dt 25: 1   acquitting the *i* and condemning
Pr   6:17   hands that shed *i* blood,
    17:26   It is not good to punish an *i* man,
Mt 10:16   shrewd as snakes and as *i* as doves.
    27: 4   "for I have betrayed *i* blood."
    27:24   I am *i* of this man's blood," he said.
Ac 20:26   declare to you today that I am *i*
Ro 16:19   what is good, and *i* about what is
1Co 4: 4   but that does not make me *i*.

INQUIRE

Isa   8:19   should not a people *i* of their God?

INSCRIPTION

Mt 22:20   And whose *i*?" "Caesar's,"
2Ti 2:19   with this *i*: "The Lord knows those

INSIGHT

1Ki 4:29   Solomon wisdom and very great *i*,
Ps 119:99   I have more *i* than all my teachers,
Pr   5: 1   listen well to my words of *i*,
    21:30   There is no wisdom, no *i*, no plan
Php 1: 9   more in knowledge and depth of *i*,
2Ti 2: 7   for the Lord will give you *i*

INSOLENT

Ro   1:30   God-haters, *i*, arrogant

INSPIRED*

Hos 9: 7   the *i* man a maniac.
1Th 1: 3   and your endurance *i* by hope

INSTALLED

Ps   2: 6   "I have *i* my King

INSTINCT* (INSTINCTS)

2Pe 2:12   are like brute beasts, creatures of *i*,
Jude : 10   things they do understand by *i*,

INSTINCTS* (INSTINCT)

Jude : 19   who follow mere natural *i*

INSTITUTED

Ro 13: 2   rebelling against what God has *i*,
1Pe 2:13   to every authority *i* among men:

INSTRUCT (INSTRUCTED INSTRUCTION INSTRUCTIONS INSTRUCTOR)

Ps 32: 8   I will *i* you and teach you
  105:22   to *i* his princes as he pleased
Pr   9: 9   *I* a wise man and he will be wiser
Ro 15:14   and competent to *i* one another.
1Co 2:16   that he may *i* him?"
    14:19   to *i* others than ten thousand words
2Ti 2:25   who oppose him he must gently *i*,

INSTRUCTED (INSTRUCT)

2Ch 26: 5   who *i* him in the fear of God.
Pr 21:11   a wise man is *i*, he gets knowledge.
Isa 50: 4   Lord has given me an *i* tongue;
Mt 13:52   who has been *i* about the kingdom
1Co 14:31   in turn so that everyone may be *i*

INSTRUCTION (INSTRUCT)

Pr   1: 8   Listen, my son, to your father's *i*
    4: 1   Listen, my sons, to a father's *i*;
    4:13   Hold on to *i*, do not let it go;
    8:10   Choose my *i* instead of silver,
    8:33   Listen to my *i* and be wise;
    13: 1   A wise son heeds his father's *i*,
    13:13   He who scorns *i* will pay for it,
    16:20   Whoever gives heed to *i* prospers,
    16:21   and pleasant words promote *i*.
    19:20   Listen to advice and accept *i*,
    23:12   Apply your heart to *i*
1Co 14: 6   or prophecy or word of *i*?
    14:26   or a word of *i*, a revelation,
Eph 6: 4   up in the training and *i* of the Lord.
1Th 4: 8   he who rejects this *i* does not reject
2Th 3:14   If anyone does not obey our *i*
1Ti 1:18   I give you this *i* in keeping
    6: 3   to the sound *i* of our Lord Jesus
2Ti 4: 2   with great patience and careful *i*.

INSTRUCTIONS (INSTRUCT)

1Ti 3:14   I am writing you these *i* so that,

INSTRUCTOR (INSTRUCT)

Gal 6: 6   share all good things with his *i*.

INSTRUMENT* (INSTRUMENTS)

Eze 33:32   beautiful voice and plays an *i* well,
Ac   9:15   This man is my chosen *i*
2Ti 2:21   he will be an *i* for noble purposes,

INSTRUMENTS (INSTRUMENT)

Ro   6:13   as *i* of wickedness, but rather offer

INSULT (INSULTED INSULTS)

Pr   9: 7   corrects a mocker invites *i*;
    12:16   but a prudent man overlooks an *i*.
Mt   5:11   Blessed are you when people *i* you,
Lk   6:22   when they exclude you and *i* you

1Pe 3: 9 evil with evil or *i* with *i*,

INSULTED (INSULT)
Heb 10:29 and who has *i* the Spirit of grace?
Jas   2: 6 love him? But you have *i* the poor.
1Pe 4:14 If you are *i* because of the name

INSULTS (INSULT)
Ps 22: 7 they hurl *i*, shaking their heads;
      69: 9 the *i* of those who insult you fall
Pr 22:10 quarrels and *i* are ended.
Mk 15:29 passed by hurled *i* at him,
Jn   9:28 Then they hurled *i* at him and said,
Ro 15: 3 "The *i* of those who insult you have
2Co 12:10 in *i*, in hardships, in persecutions,
1Pe 2:23 When they hurled their *i* at him,

INTEGRITY*
Dt   9: 5 or your *i* that you are going
1Ki 9: 4 if you walk before me in *i* of heart
1Ch 29:17 the heart and are pleased with *i*.
Ne   7: 2 because he was a man of *i*
Job   2: 3 And he still maintains his *i*,
       2: 9 "Are you still holding on to your *i*?
      6:29 reconsider, for my *i* is at stake.
    27: 5 till I die, I will not deny my *i*.
Ps   7: 8 according to my *i*, O Most High.
    25:21 May *i* and uprightness protect me,
    41:12 In my *i* you uphold me
    78:72 David shepherded them with *i*
Pr 10: 9 The man of *i* walks securely,
    11: 3 The *i* of the upright guides them,
    13: 6 Righteousness guards the man of *i*,
    17:26 or to flog officials for their *i*.
    29:10 Bloodthirsty men hate a man of *i*
Isa 45:23 my mouth has uttered in all *i*
    59: 4 no one pleads his case with *i*.
Mt 22:16 "we know you are a man of *i*
Mk 12:14 we know you are a man of *i*.
Tit   2: 7 your teaching show *i*, seriousness

INTELLIGENCE (INTELLIGENT)
Isa 29:14 the *i* of the intelligent will vanish."
1Co 1:19 *i* of the intelligent I will frustrate."

INTELLIGENT (INTELLIGENCE)
Isa 29:14 the intelligence of the *i* will vanish

INTELLIGIBLE*
1Co 14:19 I would rather speak five *i* words

INTENDED
Ge 50:20 place of God? You *i* to harm me,

INTENSE
1Th 2:17 out of our *i* longing we made every
Rev 16: 9 They were seared by the *i* heat

INTERCEDE (INTERCEDES INTERCEDING INTERCESSION INTERCESSOR)
Heb 7:25 he always lives to *i* for them.

INTERCEDES* (INTERCEDE)
Ro 8:26 but the Spirit himself *i* for us
    8:27 because the Spirit *i* for the saints

INTERCEDING* (INTERCEDE)
Ro 8:34 hand of God and is also *i* for us.

INTERCESSION* (INTERCEDE)
Isa 53:12 and made *i* for the transgressors.
1Ti 2: 1 *i* and thanksgiving to be made

INTERCESSOR* (INTERCEDE)
Job 16:20 My *i* is my friend

INTEREST (INTERESTS)
Lev 25:36 Do not take *i* of any kind from him,
Dt 23:20 You may charge a foreigner *i*,
Mt 25:27 would have received it back with *i*.
Php 2:20 who takes a genuine *i*

INTERESTS (INTEREST)
1Co 7:34 his wife—and his *i* are divided.
Php 2: 4 only to your own *i*, but also to
    2:21 everyone looks out for his own *i*,

INTERFERE*
Ezr 6: 7 Do not *i* with the work

INTERMARRY (MARRY)
Dt   7: 3 Do not *i* with them.
Ezr 9:14 and *i* with the peoples who commit

INTERPRET (INTERPRETATION INTERPRETER INTERPRETS)
Ge 41:15 "I had a dream, and no one can *i* it.
Mt 16: 3 you cannot *i* the signs of the times.
1Co 12:30 Do all *i*? But eagerly desire
    14:13 pray that he may *i* what he says.
    14:27 one at a time, and someone must *i*.

INTERPRETATION (INTERPRET)
1Co 12:10 and to still another the *i* of tongues.
    14:26 a revelation, a tongue or an *i*.
2Pe 1:20 about by the prophet's own *i*.

INTERPRETER (INTERPRET)
1Co 14:28 If there is no *i*, the speaker should

INTERPRETS (INTERPRET)
1Co 14: 5 he *i*, so that the church may be

INVADED
2Ki 17: 5 king of Assyria *i* the entire land,
    24: 1 king of Babylon *i* the land,

INVENT* (INVENTED)
Ro 1:30 boastful; they *i* ways of doing evil;

INVENTED* (INVENT)
2Pe 1:16 We did not follow cleverly *i* stories

INVESTIGATED
Lk   1: 3 I myself have carefully *i* everything

INVISIBLE*
Ro 1:20 of the world God's *i* qualities—
Col 1:15 He is the image of the *i* God,
    1:16 and on earth, visible and *i*,
1Ti 1:17 immortal, *i*, the only God,
Heb 11:27 because he saw him who is *i*.

INVITE (INVITED INVITES)
Mt 22: 9 *i* to the banquet anyone you find.'
    25:38 did we see you a stranger and *i* you
Lk 14:12 do not *i* your friends, your brothers
    14:13 you give a banquet, *i* the poor,

INVITED (INVITE)
Zep 1: 7 he has consecrated those he has *i*.
Mt 22:14 For many are *i*, but few are chosen
    25:35 I was a stranger and you *i* me in,
Lk 14:10 But when you are *i*, take the lowest
Rev 19: 9 'Blessed are those who are *i*

INVITES (INVITE)
Pr 18: 6 and his mouth *i* a beating.
1Co 10:27 If some unbeliever *i* you to a meal

INVOLVED
2Ti 2: 4 a soldier gets *i* in civilian affairs—

IRON
2Ki 6: 6 threw it there, and made the *i* float.
Ps   2: 9 will rule them with an *i* scepter;
Pr 27:17 As *i* sharpens *i*,
Da 2:33 and thighs of bronze, its legs of *i*,
1Ti 4: 2 have been seared as with a hot *i*.
Rev 2:27 He will rule them with an *i* scepter;
    12: 5 all the nations with an *i* scepter.
    19:15 He will rule them with an *i* scepter

IRRELIGIOUS*
1Ti 1: 9 and sinful, the unholy and *i*;

IRREVOCABLE*
Ro 11:29 for God's gifts and his call are *i*.

ISAAC
  Son of Abraham by Sarah (Ge 17:19; 21:1–7; 1Ch 1:28). Abrahamic covenant perpetuated through (Ge 17:21; 26:2–5). Offered up by Abraham (Ge 22; Heb 11:17–19). Rebekah taken as wife (Ge 24). Inherited Abraham's estate (Ge 25:5). Fathered Esau and Jacob (Ge 25:19–26; 1Ch 1:34). Nearly lost Rebekah to Abimelech (Ge 26:1–11). Covenant with Abimelech (Ge 26:12–31). Tricked into blessing Jacob (Ge 27). Death (Ge 35:27–29). Father of Israel (Ex 3:6; Dt 29:13; Ro 9:10).

ISAIAH
  Prophet to Judah (Isa 1:1). Called by the LORD (Isa 6). Announced judgment to Ahaz (Isa 7), deliverance from Assyria to Hezekiah (2Ki 19; Isa 36–37), deliverance from death to Hezekiah (2Ki 20:1–11; Isa 38). Chronicler of Judah's history (2Ch 26:22; 32:32).

ISH-BOSHETH*
  Son of Saul who attempted to succeed him as king (2Sa 2:8–4:12; 1Ch 8:33).

ISHMAEL
  Son of Abraham by Hagar (Ge 16; 1Ch 1:28). Blessed, but not son of covenant (Ge 17:18–21; Gal 4:21–31). Sent away by Sarah (Ge 21:8–21). Children (Ge 25:12–18; 1Ch 1:29–31). Death (Ge 25:17).

ISLAND
Rev 1: 9 was on the *i* of Patmos
    16:20 Every *i* fled away

ISRAEL (ISRAEL'S ISRAELITE ISRAELITES)
  1. Name given to Jacob (see JACOB).
  2. Corporate name of Jacob's descendants; often specifically Northern Kingdom.
Ex 28:11 Engrave the names of the sons of *I*
    28:29 of the sons of *I* over his heart
Nu 24:17 a scepter will rise out of *I*.
Dt   6: 4 Hear, O *I*: The LORD our God,
    10:12 O *I*, what does the LORD your
Jos 4:22 *I* crossed the Jordan on dry ground
Jdg 17: 6 In those days *I* had no king;
Ru 2:12 of *I*, under whose wings you have
1Sa 3:20 *I* from Dan to Beersheba
    4:21 "The glory has departed from *I*"—
   14:23 So the LORD rescued *I* that day,
   15:26 has rejected you as king over *I*"
   17:46 will know that there is a God in *I*.
   18:16 But all *I* and Judah loved David,
2Sa 5: 2 'You will shepherd my people *I*,
    5: 3 they anointed David king over *I*.
   14:25 In all *I* there was not a man
1Ki 1:35 I have appointed him ruler over *I*
   10: 9 of the LORD's eternal love for *I*,
   18:17 "Is that you, you troubler of *I*?"
   19:18 Yet I reserve seven thousand in *I*—
2Ki 5: 8 know that there is a prophet in *I*."
1Ch 17:22 made your people *I* your very own
   21: 1 incited David to take a census of *I*.
   29:25 Solomon in the sight of all *I*
2Ch 9: 8 of the love of your God for *I*
Ps 73: 1 Surely God is good to *I*,
    81: 8 if you would but listen to me, O *I*!
    98: 3 his faithfulness to the house of *I*;
    99: 8 you were to *I* a forgiving God,
Isa 11:12 and gather the exiles of *I*;
    27: 6 *I* will bud and blossom
   44:21 O *I*, I will not forget you.
   46:13 my splendor to *I*.
Jer 2: 3 *I* was holy to the LORD,
   23: 6 and *I* will live in safety.
   31: 2 I will come to give rest to *I*."
   31:10 'He who scattered *I* will gather
   31:31 covenant with the house of *I*
   33:17 sit on the throne of the house of *I*,
Eze 3:17 you a watchman for the house of *I*;
   33: 7 you a watchman for the house of *I*;
   34: 2 prophesy against the shepherds of *I*
   37:28 that I the LORD make *I* holy,
   39:23 of *I* went into exile for their sin,
Da 9:20 my sin and the sin of my people *I*
Hos 11: 1 "When *I* was a child, I loved him,
Am 4:12 prepare to meet your God, O *I*."
    7:11 and *I* will surely go into exile,
    8: 2 "The time is ripe for my people *I*;
    9:14 I will bring back my exiled people *I*
Mic 5: 2 one who will be ruler over *I*,
Zep 3:13 The remnant of *I* will do no wrong;
Zec 11:14 brotherhood between Judah and *I*.
Mal 1: 5 even beyond the borders of *I*!'
Mt 2: 6 be the shepherd of my people *I*.' "
   10: 6 Go rather to the lost sheep of *I*.
   15:24 only to the lost sheep of *I*."

Mk 12:29 'Hear, O *l*, the Lord our God,
Lk 22:30 judging the twelve tribes of *l*.
Ac 1: 6 going to restore the kingdom
to *l*?"
    9:15 and before the people of *l*.
Ro 9: 4 of my own race, the people of *l*.
    9: 6 all who are descended from *l*
are *l*.
    9:31 but *l*, who pursued a law
  11: 7 What *l* sought so earnestly it did
  11:26 And so all *l* will be saved,
Gal 6:16 who follow this rule, even to the *l*
Eph 2:12 excluded from citizenship in *l*
    3: 6 Gentiles are heirs together with *l*,
Heb 8: 8 covenant with the house of *l*.
Rev 7: 4 144,000 from all the tribes of *l*.
  21:12 the names of the twelve tribes
of *l*.

ISRAEL'S (ISRAEL)
Jdg 10:16 he could bear *l* misery no longer.
2Sa 23: 1 *l* singer of songs;
Isa 44: 6 *l* King and Redeemer, the LORD
Jer 3: 9 Because *l* immorality mattered
  31: 9 because I am *l* father,
Jn 3:10 "You are *l* teacher," said Jesus,

ISRAELITE (ISRAEL)
Ex 16: 1 The whole *l* community set out
  35:29 All the *l* men and women who
Nu 8:16 offspring from every *l* woman.
  20: 1 the whole *l* community arrived
  20:22 The whole *l* community set out
Jn 1:47 "Here is a true *l*, in whom there is
Ro 11: 1 I am an *l* myself, a descendant

ISRAELITES (ISRAEL)
Ex 1: 7 the *l* were fruitful and multiplied
   2:23 The *l* groaned in their slavery
   3: 9 the cry of the *l* has reached me,
 12:35 The *l* did as Moses instructed
 12:37 The *l* journeyed from Rameses
 14:22 and the *l* went through the sea
 16:12 I have heard the grumbling of
the *l*.
 16:35 The *l* ate manna forty years,
 24:17 To the *l* the glory of the LORD
 28:30 decisions for the *l* over his heart
 29:45 Then I will dwell among the *l*
 31:16 The *l* are to observe the Sabbath,
 33: 5 "Tell the *l*, 'You are a stiff-necked
 39:42 The *l* had done all the work just
Lev 22:32 be acknowledged as holy by the *l*.
 25:46 rule over your fellow *l* ruthlessly.
 25:55 for the *l* belong to me as servants.
Nu 2:32 These are the *l*, counted
according
  6:23 'This is how you are to bless the *l*.
  9: 2 "Have the *l* celebrate the
Passover
  9:17 the *l* set out; wherever the cloud
 10:12 Then the *l* set out from the Desert
 14: 2 All the *l* grumbled against Moses
 20:12 as holy in the sight of the *l*,
 21: 6 they bit the people and many *l*
died
 26:65 had told those *l* they would surely
 27:12 and see the land I have given
the *l*.
 33: 3 The *l* set out from Rameses
 35:10 "Speak to the *l* and say to them:
Dt 33: 1 on the *l* before his death.
Jos 1: 2 about to give to them—to the *l*.
  5: 6 The *l* had moved about
  7: 1 the *l* acted unfaithfully in regard
  8:32 There in the presence of the *l*,
 18: 1 of the *l* gathered at Shiloh
 21: 3 the *l* gave the Levites the
following
 22: 9 of Manasseh left the *l* at Shiloh
Jdg 2:11 Then the *l* did evil in the eyes
  3:12 Once again the *l* did evil
  4: 1 the *l* once again did evil in the
eyes
  6: 1 Again the *l* did evil in the eyes
 10: 6 Again the *l* did evil in the eyes
 13: 1 Again the *l* did evil in the eyes
1Sa 17: 2 Saul and the *l* assembled
1Ki 8:63 and all the *l* dedicated the temple
  9:22 did not make slaves of any of
the *l*;
 12: 1 for all the *l* had gone there
 12:17 But as for the *l* who were living

2Ki 17:24 towns of Samaria to replace the *l*.
1Ch 9: 2 in their own towns were some *l*,
 10: 1 fought against Israel; the *l* fled
 11: 4 and all the *l* marched to
Jerusalem,
2Ch 7: 6 and all the *l* were standing.
Ne 1: 6 the sins we *l*, including myself
Jer 16:14 who brought the *l* up out of
Egypt,'
Hos 1:10 "Yet the *l* will be like the sand
  3: 1 Love her as the LORD loves the *l*,
Am 4: 5 boast about them, you *l*,
Mic 5: 3 return to join the *l*.
Ro 9:27 the number of the *l* be like the
sand
 10: 1 for the *l* is that they may be saved.
 10:16 But not all the *l* accepted the
good
2Co 11:22 Are they *l*? So am I.

ISSACHAR
Son of Jacob by Leah (Ge 30:18; 35:23; 1Ch
2:1). Tribe of blessed (Ge 49:14–15; Dt
33:18–19), numbered (Nu 1:29; 26:25), allotted land (Jos 19:17–23; Eze 48:25), assisted
Deborah (Jdg 5:15), 12,000 from (Rev 7:7).

ISSUING*
Da 9:25 From the *i* of the decree to restore

ITALY
Ac 27: 1 decided that we would sail for *I*,
Heb 13:24 from *I* send you their greetings.

ITCHING*
2Ti 4: 3 to say what their *i* ears want to
hear

ITHAMAR
Son of Aaron (Ex 6:23; 1Ch 6:3). Duties at
tabernacle (Ex 38:21; Nu 4:21–33; 7:8).

ITTAI
2Sa 15:19 The king said to *l* the Gittite,

IVORY
1Ki 10:22 silver and *i*, and apes and
baboons.
 22:39 the palace he built and inlaid
with *i*

JABBOK
Ge 32:22 and crossed the ford of the *J*.
Dt 3:16 and out to the *J* River,

JABESH
1Sa 11: 1 And all the men of *J* said to him,
 31:12 wall of Beth Shan and went to *J*,
1Ch 10:12 and his sons and brought them
to *J*.

JABESH GILEAD
Jdg 21: 8 that no one from *J* had come to
2Sa 2: 4 the men of *J* who had buried Saul,
1Ch 10:11 the inhabitants of *J* heard

JACOB
Second son of Isaac, twin of Esau (Ge
26:21–26; 1Ch 1:34). Bought Esau's birthright
(Ge 26:29–34); tricked Isaac into blessing him
(Ge 27:1–37). Fled to Haran (Ge 28:1–5).
Abrahamic covenant perpetuated through (Ge
28:13–15; Mal 1:2). Vision at Bethel (Ge
28:10–22). Served Laban for Rachel and Leah
(Ge 29:1–30). Children (Ge 29:31–30:24;
35:16–26; 1Ch 2–9). Flocks increased (Ge
30:25–43). Returned to Canaan (Ge 31). Wres-
tled with God; name changed to Israel (Ge
32:22–32). Reconciled to Esau (Ge 33).
Returned to Bethel (Ge 35:1–15). Favored
Joseph (Ge 37:3). Sent sons to Egypt during
famine (Ge 42–43). Settled in Egypt (Ge 46).
Blessed Ephraim and Manasseh (Ge 48).
Blessed sons (Ge 49:1–28; Heb 11:21). Death
(Ge 49:29–33). Burial (Ge 50:1–14).

JAEL*
Woman who killed Canaanite general, Sisera (Jdg 4:17–22; 5:24–27).

JAIR
Judge from Gilead (Jdg 10:3–5).

JAIRUS*
Synagogue ruler whose daughter Jesus
raised (Mk 5:22–43; Lk 8:41–56).

JAMES
1. Apostle; brother of John (Mt 4:21–22;
10:2; Mk 3:17; Lk 5:1–10). At transfiguration

(Mt 17:1–13; Mk 9:1–13; Lk 9:28–36). Killed by
Herod (Ac 12:2).
2. Apostle; son of Alphaeus (Mt 10:3; Mk
3:18; Lk 6:15).
3. Brother of Jesus (Mt 13:55; Mk 6:3; Lk
24:10; Gal 1:19) and Judas (Jude 1). With
believers before Pentecost (Ac 1:13). Leader
of church at Jerusalem (Ac 12:17; 15; 21:18;
Gal 2:9, 12). Author of epistle (Jas 1:1).

JAPHETH
Son of Noah (Ge 5:32; 1Ch 1:4–5). Blessed
(Ge 9:18–28). Sons of (Ge 10:2–5).

JAR (JARS)
Ge 24:14 let down your *j* that I may have
1Ki 17:14 'The *j* of flour will not be used up
Jer 19: 1 "Go and buy a clay *j* from a potter.
Lk 8:16 hides it in a *j* or puts it under a
bed.

JARS (JAR)
Jn 2: 6 Nearby stood six stone water *j*,
2Co 4: 7 we have this treasure in *j* of clay

JASPER
Ex 28:20 row a chrysolite, an onyx and a *j*.
Eze 28:13 chrysolite, onyx and *j*,
Rev 4: 3 sat there had the appearance of *j*
 21:19 The first foundation was *j*,

JAVELIN
1Sa 17:45 me with sword and spear and *j*,

JAWBONE
Jdg 15:15 Finding a fresh *j* of a donkey,

JEALOUS (JEALOUSY)
Ex 20: 5 the LORD your God, am a *j* God,
 34:14 whose name is Jealous, is a *j* God.
Dt 4:24 God is a consuming fire, a *j* God.
  6:15 is a *j* God and his anger will burn
 32:21 They made me *j* by what is no god
Jos 24:19 He is a holy God; he is a *j* God.
Eze 16:38 of my wrath and *j* anger.
 16:42 my *j* anger will turn away from
you
 23:25 I will direct my *j* anger against
you,
 36: 6 in my *j* wrath because you have
Joel 2:18 the LORD will be *j* for his land
Na 1: 2 LORD is a *j* and avenging God;
Zep 3: 8 consumed by the fire of my *j*
anger.
Zec 1:14 I am very *j* for Jerusalem and
Zion,
  8: 2 "I am very *j* for Zion; I am burning
2Co 11: 2 I am *j* for you with a godly
jealousy

JEALOUSY (JEALOUS)
Ps 79: 5 How long will your *j* burn like fire?
Pr 6:34 for *j* arouses a husband's fury,
 27: 4 but who can stand before *j*?
SS 8: 6 its *j* unyielding as the grave.
Zep 1:18 In the fire of his *j*
Zec 8: 2 I am burning with *j* for her."
Ro 13:13 debauchery, not in dissension
and *j*
1Co 3: 3 For since there is *j* and quarreling
 10:22 trying to arouse the Lord's *j*?
2Co 11: 2 I am jealous for you with a godly *j*.
 12:20 *j*, outbursts of anger, factions,
Gal 5:20 hatred, discord, *j*, fits of rage,

JEERS*
Heb 11:36 Some faced *j* and flogging,

JEHOAHAZ
1. Son of Jehu; king of Israel (2Ki 13:1–9).
2. Son of Josiah; king of Judah (2Ki
23:31–34; 2Ch 36:1–4).

JEHOASH
1. See JOASH.
2. Son of Jehoahaz; king of Israel. Defeat of
Aram prophesied by Elisha (2Ki 13:10–25).
Defeated Amaziah in Jerusalem (2Ki 14:1–16;
2Ch 25:17–24).

JEHOIACHIN
Son of Jehoiakim; king of Judah exiled by
Nebuchadnezzar (2Ki 24:8–17; 2Ch 36:8–10;
Jer 22:24–30; 24:1). Raised from prisoner sta-
tus (2Ki 25:27–30; Jer 52:31–34).

JEHOIADA
Priest who sheltered Joash from Athaliah
(2Ki 11–12; 2Ch 22:11–24:16).

JEHOIAKIM
Son of Josiah; made king of Judah by Pharaoh Neco (2Ki 23:34–24:6; 2Ch 36:4–8; Jer 22:18–23). Burned scroll of Jeremiah's prophecies (Jer 36).

JEHORAM
1. Son of Jehoshaphat; king of Judah (2Ki 8:16–24). Prophesied against by Elijah; killed by the Lord (2Ch 21).
2. See JORAM.

JEHOSHAPHAT
Son of Asa; king of Judah. Strengthened his kingdom (2Ch 17). Joined with Ahab against Aram (2Ki 22; 2Ch 18). Established judges (2Ch 19). Joined with Joram against Moab (2Ki 3; 2Ch 20).

JEHU
1. Prophet against Baasha (2Ki 16:1–7).
2. King of Israel. Anointed by Elijah to obliterate house of Ahab (1Ki 19:16–17); anointed by servant of Elisha (2Ki 9:1–13). Killed Joram and Ahaziah (2Ki 9:14–29; 2Ch 22:7–9), Jezebel (2Ki 9:30–37), relatives of Ahab (2Ki 10:1–17), ministers of Baal (2Ki 10:18–29). Death (2Ki 10:30–36).

JEPHTHAH
Judge from Gilead who delivered Israel from Ammon (Jdg 10:6–12:7). Made rash vow concerning his daughter (Jdg 11:30–40).

JEREMIAH
Prophet to Judah (Jer 1:1–3). Called by the Lord (Jer 1). Put in stocks (Jer 20:1–3). Threatened for prophesying (Jer 11:18–23; 26). Opposed by Hananiah (Jer 28). Scroll burned (Jer 36). Imprisoned (Jer 37). Thrown into cistern (Jer 38). Forced to Egypt with those fleeing Babylonians (Jer 43).

JERICHO
Nu 22: 1 along the Jordan across from *J.*
Jos 3:16 the people crossed over opposite *J.*
      5:10 camped at Gilgal on the plains of *J,*
Lk 10:30 going down from Jerusalem to *J,*
Heb 11:30 By faith the walls of *J* fell,

JEROBOAM
1. Official of Solomon; rebelled to become first king of Israel (1Ki 11:26–40; 12:1–20; 2Ch 10). Idolatry (1Ki 12:25–33); judgment for (1Ki 13–14; 2Ch 13).
2. Son of Jehoash; king of Israel (1Ki 14:23–29).

JERUSALEM
Jos 10: 1 of *J* heard that Joshua had taken Ai
      15: 8 of the Jebusite city (that is, *J*).
Jdg 1: 8 The men of Judah attacked *J* also
1Sa 17:54 head and brought it to *J,*
2Sa 5: 5 and in *J* he reigned over all Israel
       5: 6 and his men marched to *J*
       9:13 And Mephibosheth lived in *J,*
      11: 1 But David remained in *J.*
      15:29 took the ark of God back to *J*
      24:16 stretched out his hand to destroy *J.*
1Ki 3: 1 the Lord, and the wall around *J.*
       9:15 the wall of *J,* and Hazor, Megiddo
       9:19 whatever he desired to build in *J,*
      10:26 cities and also with him in *J.*
      10:27 as common in *J* as stones,
      11: 7 of *J,* Solomon built a high place
      11:13 my servant and for the sake of *J,*
      11:36 always have a lamp before me in *J,*
      11:42 Solomon reigned in *J*
      12:27 at the temple of the Lord in *J,*
      14:21 and he reigned seventeen years in *J*
      14:25 Shishak king of Egypt attacked *J.*
      15: 2 and he reigned in *J* three years.
      15:10 and he reigned in *J* forty-one years.
      22:42 he reigned in *J* twenty-five years.
2Ki 8:17 and he reigned in *J* eight years.
       8:26 and he reigned in *J* one year.
      12: 1 and he reigned in *J* forty years.
      12:17 Then he turned to attack *J.*
      14: 2 he reigned in *J* twenty-nine years.

2Ki 14:13 Then Jehoash went to *J*
      15: 2 and he reigned in *J* fifty-two years.
      15:33 and he reigned in *J* sixteen years.
      16: 2 and he reigned in *J* sixteen years.
      16: 5 Israel marched up to fight against *J*
      18: 2 he reigned in *J* twenty-nine years.
      18:17 Lachish to King Hezekiah at *J.*
      19:31 For out of *J* will come a remnant,
      21: 1 and he reigned in *J* fifty-five years.
      21:12 going to bring such disaster on *J*
      21:19 and he reigned in *J* two years.
      22: 1 he reigned in *J* thirty-one years.
      23:27 and I will reject *J,* the city I chose,
      23:31 and he reigned in *J* three months.
      23:36 and he reigned in *J* eleven years.
      24: 8 and he reigned in *J* three months.
      24:10 king of Babylon advanced on *J*
      24:14 He carried into exile all *J:*
      24:18 and he reigned in *J* eleven years.
      24:20 anger that all this happened to *J*
      25: 1 king of Babylon marched against *J*
      25: 9 royal palace and all the houses
1Ch 11: 4 and all the Israelites marched to *J,*
      21:16 sword in his hand extended over *J*
2Ch 1: 4 he had pitched a tent for it in *J.*
       3: 1 the Lord in *J* on Mount Moriah,
       6: 6 now I have chosen *J* for my Name
       9: 1 she came to *J* to test him
      20:15 and all who live in Judah and *J!*
      20:27 and *J* returned joyfully to *J.*
      29: 8 Lord has fallen on Judah and *J;*
      36:19 and broke down the wall of *J;*
Ezr 1: 2 a temple for him at *J* in Judah.
       2: 1 to Babylon (they returned to *J*
       3: 1 people assembled as one man in *J.*
       4: 1 up to us from you have gone to *J*
       4:24 of God in *J* came to a standstill
       6:12 or to destroy this temple in *J.*
       7: 8 Ezra arrived in *J* in the fifth month
       9: 9 a wall of protection in Judah and *J.*
      10: 7 for all the exiles to assemble in *J.*
Ne   1: 2 the exile, and also about *J.*
       1: 3 The wall of *J* is broken down,
       2:11 to *J,* and after staying there three days
       2:17 Come, let us rebuild the wall of *J,*
       2:20 you have no share in *J* or any claim
       3: 8 They restored *J* as far as the Broad
       4: 8 fight against *J* and stir up trouble
      11: 1 leaders of the people settled in *J,*
      12:27 At the dedication of the wall of *J,*
      12:43 in *J* could be heard far away.
Ps 51:18 build up the walls of *J.*
      79: 1 they have reduced *J* to rubble.
     122: 2 in your gates, O *J.*
     122: 3 is built like a city
     122: 6 Pray for the peace of *J:*
     125: 2 As the mountains surround *J,*
     128: 5 may you see the prosperity of *J,*
     137: 5 If I forget you, O *J,*
     147: 2 The Lord builds up *J.*
     147:12 Extol the Lord, O *J;*
SS   6: 4 lovely as *J,*
Isa 1: 1 and *J* that Isaiah son of Amoz saw
       2: 1 saw concerning Judah and *J:*
       3: 1 is about to take from *J* and Judah
       3: 8 *J* staggers,
       4: 3 recorded among the living in *J.*
       8:14 And for the people of *J* he will be
      27:13 Lord on the holy mountain in *J.*
      31: 5 the Lord Almighty will shield *J;*
      33:20 your eyes will see *J,*
      40: 2 Speak tenderly to *J,*
      40: 9 You who bring good tidings to *J,*
      52: 1 O *J,* the holy city.
      52: 2 rise up, sit enthroned, O *J.*
      62: 6 on your walls, O *J;*
      62: 7 give him no rest till he establishes *J*
      65:18 for I will create *J* to be a delight
Jer 2: 2 and proclaim in the hearing of *J:*
       3:17 time they will call *J* The Throne
       4: 5 and proclaim in *J* and say:
       4:14 O *J,* wash the evil from your heart

Jer 5: 1 "Go up and down the streets of *J,*
       6: 6 and build siege ramps against *J.*
       8: 5 Why does *J* always turn away?
       9:11 "I will make *J* a heap of ruins,
      13:27 Woe to you, O *J!*
      23:14 And among the prophets of *J*
      24: 1 into exile from *J* to Babylon
      26:18 *J* will become a heap of rubble,
      32: 2 of Babylon was then besieging *J,*
      33:10 the streets of *J* that are deserted,
      39: 1 This is how *J* was taken: In
      51:50 and think on *J.*"
      52:14 broke down all the walls around *J.*
La   1: 7 *J* remembers all the treasures
Eze 14:21 send against *J* my four dreadful
      16: 2 confront *J* with her detestable
Da   6:10 the windows opened toward *J.*
       9: 2 of *J* would last seventy years.
       9:12 done like what has been done to *J.*
       9:25 and rebuild *J* until the Anointed
Joel 3: 1 restore the fortunes of Judah and *J,*
       3:16 and thunder from *J;*
       3:17 *J* will be holy;
Am   2: 5 will consume the fortresses of *J.*"
Ob   :11 and cast lots for *J,*
Mic 1: 5 Is it not *J?*
       4: 2 the word of the Lord from *J.*
Zep 3:16 On that day they will say to *J,*
Zec 1:14 'I am very jealous for *J* and Zion,
       1:17 comfort Zion and choose *J.*' "
       2: 2 He answered me, "To measure *J,*
       2: 4 '*J* will be a city without walls
       8: 3 I will return to Zion and dwell in *J.*
       8: 8 I will bring them back to live in *J;*
       8:15 determined to do good again to *J*
       8:22 powerful nations will come to *J*
       9: 9 Shout, Daughter of *J!*
       9:10 and the war-horses from *J,*
      12: 3 I will make *J* an immovable rock
      12:10 the inhabitants of *J* a spirit of grace
      14: 2 the nations to *J* to fight against it;
      14: 8 living water will flow out from *J,*
      14:16 that have attacked *J* will go up
Mt 16:21 to his disciples that he must go to *J*
      20:18 said to them, "We are going up to *J*
      21:10 When Jesus entered *J,* the whole
      23:37 "O *J, J,* you who kill the prophets
Mk 10:33 "We are going up to *J,*" he said,
Lk   2:22 Mary took him to *J* to present him
       2:41 Every year his parents went to *J*
       2:43 the boy Jesus stayed behind in *J,*
       4: 9 The devil led him to *J*
       9:31 about to bring to fulfillment at *J.*
       9:51 Jesus resolutely set out for *J,*
      13:34 die outside *J!* "O *J, J,*
      18:31 told them, "We are going up to *J,*
      19:41 As he approached *J* and saw
      21:20 "When you see *J* being surrounded
      21:24 *J* will be trampled
      24:47 name to all nations, beginning at *J.*
Jn   4:20 where we must worship is in *J.*"
Ac   1: 4 this command: "Do not leave *J,*
       1: 8 and you will be my witnesses in *J,*
       6: 7 of disciples in *J* increased rapidly,
      20:22 by the Spirit, I am going to *J,*
      23:11 As you have testified about me in *J*
Ro 15:19 So from *J* all the way
Gal 4:25 corresponds to the present city of *J*
       4:26 But the *J* that is above is free,
Heb 12:22 to the heavenly *J,* the city
Rev 3:12 the new *J,* which is coming
      21: 2 I saw the Holy City, the new *J,*
      21:10 and showed me the Holy City, *J,*

JESSE
Father of David (Ru 4:17–22; 1Sa 16; 1Ch 2:12–17).

JESUS
LIFE: Genealogy (Mt 1:1–17; Lk 3:21–37). Birth announced (Mt 1:18–25; Lk 1:26–45). Birth (Mt 2:1–12; Lk 2:1–40). Escape to Egypt (Mt 2:13–23). As a boy in the temple (Lk

2:41–52). Baptism (Mt 3:13–17; Mk 1:9–11; Lk 3:21–22; Jn 1:32–34). Temptation (Mt 4:1–11; Mk 1:12–13; Lk 4:1–13). Ministry in Galilee (Mt 4:12–18:35; Mk 1:14–9:50; Lk 4:14–13:9; Jn 1:35–2:11; 4; 6), Transfiguration (Mt 17:1–8; Mk 9:2–8; Lk 9:28–36), on the way to Jerusalem (Mt 19–20; Mk 10; Lk 13:10–19:27), in Jerusalem (Mt 21–25; Mk 11–13; Lk 19:28–21:38; Jn 2:12–3:36; 5; 7–12). Last supper (Mt 26:17–35; Mk 14:12–31; Lk 22:1–38; Jn 13–17). Arrest and trial (Mt 26:36–27:31; Mk 14:43–15:20; Lk 22:39–23:25; Jn 18:1–19:16). Crucifixion (Mt 27:32–66; Mk 15:21–47; Lk 23:26–55; Jn 19:28–42). Resurrection and appearances (Mt 28; Mk 16; Lk 24; Jn 20–21; Ac 1:1–11; 7:56; 9:3–6; 1Co 15:1–8; Rev 1:1–20).

MIRACLES. Healings: official's son (Jn 4:43–54), demoniac in Capernaum (Mk 1:23–26; Lk 4:33–35), Peter's mother-in-law (Mt 8:14–17; Mk 1:29–31; Lk 4:38–39), leper (Mt 8:2–4; Mk 1:40–45; Lk 5:12–16), paralytic (Mt 9:1–8; Mk 2:1–12; Lk 5:17–26), cripple (Jn 5:1–9), shriveled hand (Mt 12:10–13; Mk 3:1–5; Lk 6:6–11), centurion's servant (Mt 8:5–13; Lk 7:1–10), widow's son raised (Lk 7:11–17), demoniac (Mt 12:22–23; Lk 11:14), Gadarene demoniacs (Mt 8:28–34; Mk 5:1–20; Lk 8:26–39), woman's bleeding and Jairus' daughter (Mt 9:18–26; Mk 5:21–43; Lk 8:40–56), blind man (Mt 9:27–31), mute man (Mt 9:32–33), Canaanite woman's daughter (Mt 15:21–28; Mk 7:24–30), deaf man (Mk 7:31–37), blind man (Mk 8:22–26), demoniac boy (Mt 17:14–18; Mk 9:14–29; Lk 9:37–43), ten lepers (Lk 17:11–19), man born blind (Jn 9:1–7), Lazarus raised (Jn 11), crippled woman (Lk 13:11–17), man with dropsy (Lk 14:1–6), two blind men (Mt 20:29–34; Mk 10:46–52; Lk 18:35–43), Malchus' ear (Lk 22:50–51). Other Miracles: water to wine (Jn 2:1–11), catch of fish (Lk 5:1–11), storm stilled (Mt 8:23–27; Mk 4:37–41; Lk 8:22–25), 5,000 fed (Mt 14:15–21; Mk 6:35–44; Lk 9:10–17; Jn 6:1–14), walking on water (Mt 14:25–33; Mk 6:48–52; Jn 6:15–21), 4,000 fed (Mt 15:32–39; Mk 8:1–9), money from fish (Mt 17:24–27), fig tree cursed (Mt 21:18–22; Mk 11:12–14), catch of fish (Jn 21:1–14).

MAJOR TEACHING: Sermon on the Mount (Mt 5–7; Lk 6:17–49), to Nicodemus (Jn 3), to Samaritan woman (Jn 4), Bread of Life (Jn 6:22–59), at Feast of Tabernacles (Jn 7–8), woes to Pharisees (Mt 23; Lk 11:37–54), Good Shepherd (Jn 10:1–18), Olivet Discourse (Mt 24–25; Mk 13; Lk 21:5–36), Upper Room Discourse (Jn 13–16).

PARABLES: Sower (Mt 13:3–23; Mk 4:3–25; Lk 8:5–18), seed's growth (Mk 4:26–29), wheat and weeds (Mt 13:24–30, 36–43), mustard seed (Mt 13:31–32; Mk 4:30–32), yeast (Mt 13:33; Lk 13:20–21), hidden treasure (Mt 13:44), valuable pearl (Mt 13:45–46), net (Mt 13:47–51), house owner (Mt 13:52), good Samaritan (Lk 10:25–37), unmerciful servant (Mt 18:15–35), lost sheep (Mt 18:10–14; Lk 15:4–7), lost coin (Lk 15:8–10), lost son (Lk 15:11–32), dishonest manager (Lk 16:1–13), rich man and Lazarus (Lk 16:19–31), persistent widow (Lk 18:1–8), Pharisee and tax collector (Lk 18:9–14), payment of workers (Mt 20:1–16), tenants and the vineyard (Mt 21:28–46; Mk 12:1–12; Lk 20:9–19), wedding banquet (Mt 22:1–14), faithful servant (Mt 24:45–51), ten virgins (Mt 25:1–13), talents (Mt 25:14–30; Lk 19:12–27).

DISCIPLES see APOSTLES. Call of (Jn 1:35–51; Mt 4:18–22; 9:9; Mk 1:16–20; 2:13–14; Lk 5:1–11, 27–28). Named Apostles (Mk 3:13–19; Lk 6:12–16). Twelve sent out (Mt 10; Mk 6:7–11; Lk 9:1–5). Seventy sent out (Lk 10:1–24). Defection of (Jn 6:60–71; Mt 26:56; Mk 14:50–52). Final commission (Mt 28:16–20; Jn 21:15–23; Ac 1:3–8).

Ac 2:32 God has raised this *J* to life,
    9:5 "I am *J*, whom you are persecuting
    9:34 said to him, "*J* Christ heals you.
    15:11 of our Lord *J* that we are saved,
    16:31 "Believe in the Lord *J*,

Ac 20:24 the task the Lord *J* has given me—
Ro 3:24 redemption that came by Christ *J*.
    5:17 life through the one man, *J* Christ.
    8:1 for those who are in Christ *J*,
1Co 1:7 for our Lord *J* Christ to be revealed
    2:2 except *J* Christ and him crucified.
    6:11 in the name of the Lord *J* Christ
    8:6 and there is but one Lord, *J* Christ,
    12:3 and no one can say, "*J* is Lord,"
2Co 4:5 not preach ourselves, but *J* Christ
    13:5 Do you not realize that Christ *J* is
Gal 2:16 but by faith in *J* Christ.
    3:28 for you are all one in Christ *J*.
    5:6 in Christ *J* neither circumcision
    6:17 bear on my body the marks of *J*.
Eph 1:5 as his sons through *J* Christ,
    2:10 created in Christ *J*
    2:20 with Christ *J* himself as the chief
Php 1:6 until the day of Christ *J*.
    2:5 be the same as that of Christ *J*:
    2:10 name of *J* every knee should bow,
Col 3:17 do it all in the name of the Lord *J*,
1Th 1:10 whom he raised from the dead—*J*,
    4:14 We believe that *J* died
    5:23 at the coming of our Lord *J* Christ.
2Th 1:7 when the Lord *J* is revealed
    2:1 the coming of our Lord *J* Christ
1Ti 1:15 Christ *J* came into the world
2Ti 1:10 appearing of our Savior, Christ *J*,
    2:3 us like a good soldier of Christ *J*.
    3:12 life in Christ *J* will be persecuted,
Tit 2:13 our great God and Savior, Christ *J*,
Heb 2:9 But we see *J*, who was made a little
    2:11 So *J* is not ashamed to call them
    3:1 fix your thoughts on *J*, the apostle
    3:3 *J* has been found worthy
    4:14 through the heavens, *J* the Son
    6:20 where *J*, who went before us,
    7:22 *J* has become the guarantee
    7:24 but because *J* lives forever,
    8:6 But the ministry *J* has received is
    12:2 Let us fix our eyes on *J*, the author
    12:24 to *J* the mediator of a new
1Pe 1:3 the resurrection of *J* Christ
2Pe 1:16 and coming of our Lord *J* Christ,
1Jn 1:7 and the blood of *J*, his Son,
    2:1 *J* Christ, the Righteous One.
    2:6 to live in him must walk as *J* did.
    4:15 anyone acknowledges that *J* is
Rev 1:1 The revelation of *J* Christ,
    22:16 *J*, have sent my angel
    22:20 Come, Lord *J*.

JETHRO
Father-in-law and adviser of Moses (Ex 3:1; 18). Also known as Reuel (Ex 2:18).

JEW (JEWS JEWS' JUDAISM)
Est 2:5 of Susa a *J* of the tribe of Benjamin,
Zec 8:23 of one *J* by the hem of his robe
Ac 21:39 "I am a *J*, from Tarsus in Cilicia,
Ro 1:16 first for the *J*, then for the Gentile.
    2:28 A man is not a *J* if he is only one
    10:12 there is no difference between *J*
1Co 9:20 To the Jews I became like a *J*,
Gal 2:14 "You are a *J*, yet you live like
    3:28 There is neither *J* nor Greek,
Col 3:11 Here there is no Greek or *J*,

JEWEL (JEWELRY JEWELS)
Pr 20:15 that speak knowledge are a rare *j*.
SS 4:9 with one *j* of your necklace.
Rev 21:11 that of a very precious *j*,

JEWELRY (JEWEL)
Ex 35:22 and brought gold *j* of all kinds:
Jer 2:32 Does a maiden forget her *j*,
Eze 16:11 you with *j*: I put bracelets
1Pe 3:3 wearing of gold *j* and fine clothes.

JEWELS (JEWEL)
Isa 54:12 your gates of sparkling *j*,
    61:10 as a bride adorns herself with her *j*.
Zec 9:16 like *j* in a crown.

JEWS (JEW)
Ne 4:1 He ridiculed the *J*,

Est 3:13 kill and annihilate all the *J*—
    4:14 and deliverance for the *J* will arise
Mt 2:2 who has been born king of the *J*?
    27:11 "Are you the king of the *J*?" "Yes,
Jn 4:9 (For *J* do not associate
    4:22 for salvation is from the *J*.
    19:3 saying, "Hail, king of the *J*!"
Ac 20:21 I have declared to both *J*
Ro 3:29 Is God the God of *J* only?
    9:24 not only from the *J* but
    15:27 they owe it to the *J* to share
1Co 1:22 *J* demand miraculous signs
    9:20 To the *J* I became like a Jew,
    12:13 whether *J* or Greeks, slave or free
Gal 2:8 of Peter as an apostle to the *J*,
Rev 2:9 slander of those who say they are *J*
    3:9 claim to be *J* though they are not,

JEWS' (JEW)
Ro 15:27 shared in the *J* spiritual blessings,

JEZEBEL
Sidonian wife of Ahab (1Ki 16:31). Promoted Baal worship (1Ki 16:32–33). Killed prophets of the LORD (1Ki 18:4, 13). Opposed Elijah (1Ki 19:1–2). Had Naboth killed (1Ki 21). Death prophesied (1Ki 21:17–24). Killed by Jehu (2Ki 9:30–37).

JEZREEL
2Ki 9:36 at *J* dogs will devour Jezebel's flesh
    10:7 and sent them to Jehu in *J*.
Hos 1:4 house of Jehu for the massacre at *J*,

JOAB
Nephew of David (1Ch 2:16). Commander of his army (2Sa 8:16). Victorious over Ammon (2Sa 10; 1Ch 19), Rabbah (2Sa 11; 1Ch 20), Jerusalem (1Ch 11:6), Absalom (2Sa 18), Sheba (2Sa 20). Killed Abner (2Sa 3:22–39), Amasa (2Sa 20:1–13). Numbered David's army (2Sa 24; 1Ch 21). Sided with Adonijah (1Ki 1:17, 19). Killed by Benaiah (1Ki 2:5–6, 28–35).

JOASH
Son of Ahaziah; king of Judah. Sheltered from Athaliah by Jehoiada (2Ki 11; 2Ch 22:10–23:21). Repaired temple (2Ki 12; 2Ch 24).

JOB
Wealthy man from Uz; feared God (Job 1:1–5). Righteousness tested by disaster (Job 1:6–22), personal affliction (Job 2). Maintained innocence in debate with three friends (Job 3–31), Elihu (Job 32–37). Rebuked by the LORD (Job 38–41). Vindicated and restored to greater stature by the LORD (Job 42). Example of righteousness (Eze 14:14, 20).

JOCHEBED*
Mother of Moses and Aaron (Ex 6:20; Nu 26:59).

JOEL
Prophet (Joel 1:1; Ac 2:16).

JOHN
1. Son of Zechariah and Elizabeth (Lk 1). Called the Baptist (Mt 3:1–12; Mk 1:2–8). Witness to Jesus (Mt 3:11–12; Mk 1:7–8; Lk 3:15–18; Jn 1:6–35; 3:27–30; 5:33–36). Doubts about Jesus (Mt 11:2–6; Lk 7:18–23). Arrest (Mt 4:12; Mk 1:14). Execution (Mt 14:1–12; Mk 6:14–29; Lk 9:7–9). Ministry compared to Elijah (Mt 11:7–19; Mk 9:11–13; Lk 7:24–35).
2. Apostle; brother of James (Mt 4:21–22; 10:2; Mk 3:17; Lk 5:1–10). At transfiguration (Mt 17:1–13; Mk 9:1–13; Lk 9:28–36). Desire to be greatest (Mk 10:35–45). Leader of church at Jerusalem (Ac 4:1–3; Gal 2:9). Elder who wrote epistles (2Jn 1; 3Jn 1). Prophet who wrote Revelation (Rev 1:1; 22:8).
3. Cousin of Barnabas, co-worker with Paul, (Ac 12:12–13:13; 15:37), see MARK.

JOIN (JOINED JOINS)
Ne 10:29 all these now *j* their brothers
Pr 23:20 Do not *j* those who drink too much
    24:21 and do not *j* with the rebellious,
Jer 3:18 of Judah will *j* the house of Israel,
Eze 37:17 *J* them together into one stick
Da 11:34 who are not sincere will *j* them.

Ro   15: 30 to *j* me in my struggle by praying
2Ti   1: 8 *j* with me in suffering for the
             gospel

JOINED (JOIN)
Zec   2: 11 "Many nations will be *j*
Mt   19: 6 Therefore what God has *j*
             together,
Mk   10: 9 Therefore what God has *j*
             together,
Ac   1: 14 They all *j* together constantly
Eph   2: 21 him the whole building is *j*
             together
      4: 16 *j* and held together

JOINS (JOIN)
1Co 16: 16 and to everyone who *j* in the
             work,

JOINT (JOINTS)
Ps   22: 14 and all my bones are out of *j*.

JOINTS (JOINT)
Heb   4: 12 even to dividing soul and spirit, *j*

JOKING*
Ge   19: 14 his sons-in-law thought he was *j*.
Pr   26: 19 and says, "I was only *j!*"
Eph   5: 4 or coarse *j*, which are out of place,

JONAH
     Prophet in days of Jeroboam II (2Ki 14:25).
Called to Nineveh; fled to Tarshish (Jnh
1:1–3). Cause of storm; thrown into sea (Jnh
1:4–16). Swallowed by fish (Jnh 1:17). Prayer
(Jnh 2). Preached to Nineveh (Jnh 3). Attitude
reproved by the LORD (Jnh 4). Sign of (Mt
12:39–41; Lk 11:29–32).

JONATHAN
     Son of Saul (1Sa 13:16; 1Ch 8:33). Valiant
warrior (1Sa 13–14). Relation to David (1Sa
18:1–4; 19–20; 23:16–18). Killed at Gilboa (1Sa
31). Mourned by David (2Sa 1).

JOPPA
Ezr   3: 7 logs by sea from Lebanon to *J*,
Jnh   1: 3 to *J*, where he found a ship bound
Ac   9: 43 Peter stayed in *J* for some time

JORAM
     1. Son of Ahab; king of Israel. Fought with
Jehoshaphat against Moab (2Ki 3). Killed with
Ahaziah by Jehu (2Ki 8:25–29; 9:14–26; 2Ch
22:5–9).
     2. See JEHORAM.

JORDAN
Ge   13: 10 plain of the *J* was well watered,
Nu   22: 1 and camped along the *J*
     34: 12 boundary will go down along
             the *J*
Dt   3: 27 you are not going to cross this *J*.
Jos   1: 2 get ready to cross the *J* River
      3: 11 go into the *J* ahead of you.
      3: 17 ground in the middle of the *J*,
      4: 22 Israel crossed the *J* on dry
             ground.'
2Ki   2: 7 and Elisha had stopped at the *J*.
      2: 13 and stood on the bank of the *J*.
      5: 10 wash yourself seven times in
             the *J*,
      6: 4 They went to the *J* and began
Ps 114: 3 the *J* turned back;
Isa   9: 1 along the *J*— The people walking
Jer 12: 5 manage in the thickets by the *J*?
Mt   3: 6 baptized by him in the *J* River.
      4: 15 the way to the sea, along the *J*,
Mk   1: 9 and was baptized by John in
             the *J*.

JOSEPH
     1. *Son of Jacob by Rachel* (Ge 30:24; 1Ch
2:2). Favored by Jacob, hated by brothers (Ge
37:3–4). Dreams (Ge 37:5–11). Sold by brothers (Ge 37:12–36). Served Potiphar; imprisoned by false accusation (Ge 39). Interpreted
dreams of Pharaoh's servants (Ge 40), of
Pharaoh (Ge 41:4–40). Made greatest in Egypt
(Ge 41:41–57). Sold grain to brothers (Ge
42–45). Brought Jacob and sons to Egypt (Ge
46–47). Sons Ephraim and Manasseh blessed
(Ge 48). Blessed (Ge 49:22–26; Dt 33:13–17).
Death (Ge 50:22–26; Ex 13:19; Heb 11:22).
12,000 from (Rev 7:8).
     2. Husband of Mary, mother of Jesus (Mt
1:16–24; 2:13–19; Lk 1:27; 2; Jn 1:45).

     3. Disciple from Arimathea, who gave his
tomb for Jesus' burial (Mt 27:57–61; Mk
15:43–47; Lk 24:50–52).
     4. Original name of Barnabas (Ac 4:36).

JOSHUA (HOSHEA)
     1. Son of Nun; name changed from Hoshea
(Nu 13:8, 16; 1Ch 7:27). Fought Amalekites
under Moses (Ex 17:9–14). Servant of Moses
on Sinai (Ex 24:13; 32:17). Spied Canaan (Nu
13). With Caleb, allowed to enter land (Nu
14:6, 30). Succeeded Moses (Dt 1:38; 31:1–8;
34:9).
     Charged Israel to conquer Canaan (Jos 1).
Crossed Jordan (Jos 3–4). Circumcised sons of
wilderness wanderings (Jos 5). Conquered
Jericho (Jos 6), Ai (Jos 7–8), five kings at
Gibeon (Jos 10:1–28), southern Canaan (Jos
10:29–43), northern Canaan (Jos 11–12).
Defeated at Ai (Jos 7). Deceived by
Gibeonites (Jos 9). Renewed covenant (Jos
8:30–35; 24:1–27). Divided land among tribes
(Jos 13–22). Last words (Jos 23). Death (Jos
24:28–31).
     2. High priest during rebuilding of temple
(Hag 1–2; Zec 3:1–9; 6:11).

JOSIAH
     Son of Amon; king of Judah (2Ki 21:26; 1Ch
3:14). Prophesied (1Ki 13:2). Book of Law discovered during his reign (2Ki 22; 2Ch
34:14–31). Reforms (2Ki 23:1–25; 2Ch 34:1–13;
35:1–19). Killed by Pharaoh Neco (2Ki
23:29–30; 2Ch 35:20–27).

JOTHAM
     1. Son of Gideon (Jdg 9).
     2. Son of Azariah (Uzziah); king of Judah
(2Ki 15:32–38; 2Ch 26:21–27:9).

JOURNEY
Dt   1: 33 who went ahead of you on your *j*,
      2: 7 over your *j* through this vast
             desert
Jdg 18: 6 Your *j* has the LORD's approval."
Ezr   8: 21 and ask him for a safe *j* for us
Job 16: 22 before I go on the *j* of no return.
Isa 35: 8 The unclean will not *j* on it;
Mt   25: 14 it will be like a man going on a *j*,
Ro   15: 24 to have you assist me on my *j*
             there

JOY* (ENJOY ENJOYMENT JOYFUL JOYOUS
OVERJOYED REJOICE REJOICES REJOICING)
Ge   31: 27 so I could send you away with *j*
Lev   9: 24 shouted for *j* and fell facedown.
Dt   16: 15 and your *j* will be complete.
Jdg   9: 19 may Abimelech be your *j*,
1Ch 12: 40 and sheep, for there was *j* in
             Israel.
     16: 27 strength and *j* in his dwelling
             place.
     16: 33 sing for *j* before the LORD,
     29: 17 with *j* how willingly your people
     29: 22 drank with great *j* in the presence
2Ch 30: 26 There was great *j* in Jerusalem.
Ezr   3: 12 while many others shouted for *j*.
      3: 13 of the shouts of *j* from the sound
      6: 16 of the house of God with *j*.
      6: 22 with *j* by changing the attitude
      6: 22 *j* the Feast of Unleavened Bread,
Ne   8: 10 for the *j* of the LORD is your
      8: 12 and to celebrate with great *j*,
      8: 17 And their *j* was very great.
     12: 43 God had given them great *j*.
Est   8: 16 a time of happiness and *j*,
      8: 17 there was *j* and gladness
      9: 17 and made it a day of feasting
             and *j*.
      9: 18 and made it a day of feasting
             and *j*.
      9: 19 as a day of *j* and feasting,
      9: 22 and *j* and giving presents of food
      9: 22 their sorrow was turned into *j*
Job   3: 7 may no shout of *j* be heard in it.
      6: 10 my *j* in unrelenting pain—
      8: 21 and your lips with shouts of *j*.
      9: 25 they fly away without a glimpse
             of *j*
     10: 20 from me so I can have a
             moment's *j*
     20: 5 the *j* of the godless lasts
     33: 26 he sees God's face and shouts
             for *j*;

Job 38: 7 and all the angels shouted for *j*?
Ps   4: 7 have filled my heart with greater *j*
      5: 11 let them ever sing for *j*.
     16: 11 me with *j* in your presence,
     19: 8 giving *j* to the heart.
     20: 5 We will shout for *j*
     21: 1 How great is his *j* in the victories
     21: 6 with the *j* of your presence.
     27: 6 will I sacrifice with shouts of *j*;
     28: 7 My heart leaps for *j*
     30: 11 sackcloth and clothed me with *j*,
     33: 3 play skillfully, and shout for *j*.
     35: 27 shout for *j* and gladness;
     42: 4 with shouts of *j* and thanksgiving
     43: 4 to God, my *j* and my delight.
     45: 7 by anointing you with the oil of *j*.
     45: 15 They are led in with *j* and
             gladness;
     47: 1 shout to God with cries of *j*.
     47: 5 God has ascended amid shouts
             of *j*,
     48: 2 the *j* of the whole earth.
     51: 8 Let me hear *j* and gladness;
     51: 12 to me the *j* of your salvation
     65: 8 you call forth songs of *j*.
     65: 13 they shout for *j* and sing.
     66: 1 Shout with *j* to God, all the earth!
     67: 4 the nations be glad and sing for *j*,
     71: 23 My lips will shout for *j*
     81: 1 Sing for *j* to God our strength;
     86: 4 Bring *j* to your servant,
     89: 12 Hermon sing for *j* at your name.
     90: 14 for *j* and be glad all our days.
     92: 4 I sing for *j* at the works
     94: 19 your consolation brought *j*
     95: 1 let us sing for *j* to the LORD;
     96: 12 the trees of the forest will sing
             for *j*;
     97: 11 and *j* on the upright in heart.
     98: 4 for *j* to the LORD, all the earth,
     98: 6 shout for *j* before the LORD,
     98: 8 the mountains sing together for *j*;
    100: 1 for *j* to the LORD, all the earth.
    105: 43 his chosen ones with shouts of *j*;
    106: 5 share in the *j* of your nation
    107: 22 and tell of his works with songs
             of *j*
    118: 15 Shouts of *j* and victory
    119:111 they are the *j* of my heart.
    126: 2 our tongues with songs of *j*.
    126: 3 and we are filled with *j*.
    126: 5 will reap with songs of *j*.
    126: 6 will return with songs of *j*,
    132: 9 may your saints sing for *j*."
    132: 16 and her saints will ever sing for *j*.
    137: 3 tormentors demanded songs of *j*;
    137: 6 my highest *j*.
    149: 5 and sing for *j* on their beds.
Pr   10: 1 A wise son brings *j* to his father,
     10: 28 The prospect of the righteous is *j*,
     11: 10 wicked perish, there are shouts
             of *j*.
     12: 20 but *j* for those who promote
             peace.
     14: 10 and no one else can share its *j*.
     14: 13 and *j* may end in grief.
     15: 20 A wise son brings *j* to his father,
     15: 23 A man finds *j* in giving an apt
             reply
     15: 30 A cheerful look brings *j*
     17: 21 there is no *j* for the father of a
             fool.
     21: 15 it brings *j* to the righteous
     23: 24 of a righteous man has great *j*;
     27: 9 incense bring *j* to the heart,
     27: 11 my son, and bring *j* to my heart;
     29: 3 A man who loves wisdom brings *j*
Ecc   8: 15 Then *j* will accompany him
     11: 9 let your heart give you *j* in the
             days
Isa   9: 3 and increased their *j*;
     12: 3 With *j* you will draw water
     12: 6 Shout aloud and sing for *j*,
     16: 9 shouts of *j* over your ripened fruit
     16: 10 *J* and gladness are taken away
     22: 13 But see, there is *j* and revelry,
     24: 11 all *j* turns to gloom,
     24: 14 raise their voices, they shout for *j*;
     26: 19 wake up and shout for *j*.
     35: 2 will rejoice greatly and shout for *j*.
     35: 6 the mute tongue shout for *j*.

Isa	35:10	Gladness and *j* will overtake them,
	35:10	everlasting *j* will crown their heads
	42:11	Let the people of Sela sing for *j*;
	44:23	Sing for *j*, O heavens,
	48:20	Announce this with shouts of *j*
	49:13	Shout for *j*, O heavens;
	51: 3	*J* and gladness will be found in her,
	51:11	Gladness and *j* will overtake them,
	51:11	everlasting *j* will crown their heads
	52: 8	together they shout for *j*,
	52: 9	Burst into songs of *j* together,
	54: 1	burst into song, shout for *j*,
	55:12	You will go out in *j*
	56: 7	give them *j* in my house of prayer.
	58:14	then you will find your *j*
	60: 5	heart will throb and swell with *j*;
	60:15	and the *j* of all generations.
	61: 7	and everlasting *j* will be theirs.
	65:14	out of the *j* of their hearts,
	65:18	and its people a *j*.
	66: 5	that we may see your *j*!'
Jer	7:34	will bring an end to the sounds of *j*
	15:16	they were my *j* and my heart's
	16: 9	will bring an end to the sounds of *j*
	25:10	banish from them the sounds of *j*
	31: 7	"Sing with *j* for Jacob;
	31:12	shout for *j* on the heights of Zion;
	31:13	give them comfort and *j* instead
	33: 9	this city will bring me renown, *j*,
	33:11	be heard once more the sounds of *j*
	48:33	*J* and gladness are gone
	48:33	no one treads them with shouts of *j*
	48:33	they are not shouts of *j*.
	51:48	will shout for *j* over Babylon,
La	2:15	the *j* of the whole earth?"
	5:15	*J* is gone from our hearts;
Eze	7: 7	not *j*, upon the mountains.
	24:25	their *j* and glory, the delight
Joel	1:12	Surely the *j* of mankind
	1:16	*j* and gladness
Mt	13:20	and at once receives it with *j*.
	13:44	in his *j* went and sold all he had
	28: 8	afraid yet filled with *j*,
Mk	4:16	and at once receive it with *j*.
Lk	1:14	He will be a *j* and delight to you,
	1:44	the baby in my womb leaped for *j*.
	1:58	great mercy, and they shared her *j*,
	2:10	news of great *j* that will be
	6:23	"Rejoice in that day and leap for *j*,
	8:13	the word with *j* when they hear it,
	10:17	The seventy-two returned with *j*
	10:21	full of *j* through the Holy Spirit,
	24:41	still did not believe it because of *j*
	24:52	returned to Jerusalem with great *j*.
Jn	3:29	That *j* is mine, and it is now
	3:29	full of *j* when he hears
	15:11	and that your *j* may be complete.
	15:11	this so that my *j* may be in you
	16:20	but your grief will turn to *j*.
	16:21	because of her *j* that a child is born
	16:22	and no one will take away your *j*.
	16:24	and your *j* will be complete.
	17:13	measure of my *j* within them.
Ac	2:28	with *j* in your presence.'
	8: 8	So there was great *j* in that city.
	13:52	And the disciples were filled with *j*
	14:17	and fills your hearts with *j*."
	16:34	he was filled with *j* because he had come
Ro	14:17	peace and *j* in the Holy Spirit,
	15:13	the God of hope fill you with all *j*
	15:32	will I may come to you with *j*
	16:19	so I am full of *j* over you;
2Co	1:24	but we work with you for your *j*,
	2: 3	that you would all share my *j*.
	7: 4	our troubles my *j* knows no
	7: 7	so that my *j* was greater than ever.
	8: 2	their overflowing *j* and their
Gal	4:15	What has happened to all your *j*?
	5:22	*j*, peace, patience, kindness,
Php	1: 4	I always pray with *j*

Php	1:25	for your progress and *j* in the faith,
	1:26	being with you again your *j*
	2: 2	then make my *j* complete
	2:29	him in the Lord with great *j*,
1Th	4: 1	and long for, my *j* and crown,
	1: 6	with the *j* given by the Holy Spirit.
	2:19	For what is our hope, our *j*,
	2:20	Indeed, you are our glory and *j*.
	3: 9	you in return for all the *j* we have
2Ti	1: 4	so that I may be filled with *j*.
Phm	: 7	Your love has given me great *j*
Heb	1: 9	by anointing you with the oil of *j*."
	12: 2	for the *j* set before him endured
	13:17	them so that their work will be a *j*,
Jas	1: 2	Consider it pure *j*, my brothers,
	4: 9	to mourning and your *j* to gloom.
1Pe	1: 8	with an inexpressible and glorious *j*
1Jn	1: 4	this to make our *j* complete.
2Jn	: 4	It has given me great *j* to find some
	:12	so that our *j* may be complete.
3Jn	: 3	It gave me great *j* to have some
	: 4	I have no greater *j*
Jude	:24	without fault and with great *j*—

JOYFUL* (JOY)

Dt	16:14	Be *j* at your Feast—you, your sons
1Sa	18: 6	with *j* songs and with tambourines
1Ki	8:66	*j* and glad in heart
1Ch	15:16	as singers to sing *j* songs,
2Ch	7:10	*j* and glad in heart
Ps	68: 3	may they be happy and *j*.
	100: 2	come before him with *j* songs.
Ecc	9: 7	and drink your wine with a *j* heart,
Isa	24: 8	the *j* harp is silent.
Jer	31: 4	and go out to dance with the *j*.
Hab	3:18	I will be *j* in God my Savior.
Zec	8:19	and tenth months will become *j*
	10: 7	Their children will see it and be *j*;
Ro	12:12	Be *j* in hope, patient in affliction,
1Th	5:16	Be *j* always; pray continually;
Heb	12:22	thousands of angels in *j* assembly,

JOYOUS* (JOY)

Est	8:15	the city of Susa held a *j* celebration.

JUBILANT

Ps	96:12	let the fields be *j*, and everything
	98: 4	burst into *j* song with music;

JUBILEE

Lev	25:11	The fiftieth year shall be a *j* for you;

JUDAH (JUDEA)

1. Son of Jacob by Leah (Ge 29:35; 35:23; 1Ch 2:1). Did not want to kill Joseph (Ge 37:26–27). Among Canaanites, fathered Perez by Tamar (Ge 38). Tribe of blessed as ruling tribe (Ge 49:8–12; Dt 33:7), numbered (Nu 1:27; 26:22), allotted land (Jos 15; Eze 48:7), failed to fully possess (Jos 15:63; Jdg 1:1–20).
2. Name used for people and land of Southern Kingdom.

Ru	1: 7	take them back to the land of *J*.
2Sa	2: 4	king over the house of *J*.
Isa	1: 1	The vision concerning *J*.
	3: 8	*J* is falling;
Jer	13:19	All *J* will be carried into exile,
	30: 3	bring my people Israel and *J* back
Hos	1: 7	I will show love to the house of *J*;
Zec	10: 4	From *J* will come the cornerstone,
Mt	2: 6	least among the rulers of *J*;
Heb	7:14	that our Lord descended from *J*,
	8: 8	and with the house of *J*.
Rev	5: 5	of the tribe of *J*, the Root of David,

JUDAISM (JEW)

Ac	13:43	devout converts to *J* followed Paul
Gal	1:13	of my previous way of life in *J*,
	1:14	advancing in *J* beyond many Jews

JUDAS

1. Apostle; son of James (Lk 6:16; Jn 14:22; Ac 1:13). Probably also called Thaddaeus (Mt 10:3; Mk 3:18).
2. Brother of James and Jesus (Mt 13:55; Mk 6:3), also called Jude (Jude 1).
3. Christian prophet (Ac 15:22–32).

4. Apostle, also called Iscariot, who betrayed Jesus (Mt 10:4; 26:14–56; Mk 3:19; 14:10–50; Lk 6:16; 22:3–53; Jn 6:71; 12:4; 13:2–30; 18:2–11). Suicide of (Mt 27:3–5; Ac 1:16–25).

JUDEA (JUDAH)

Mt	2: 1	born in Bethlehem in *J*,
	24:16	are in *J* flee to the mountains.
Lk	3: 1	Pontius Pilate was governor of *J*,
Ac	1: 8	and in all *J* and Samaria,
	9:31	Then the church throughout *J*,
1Th	2:14	imitators of God's churches in *J*,

JUDGE (JUDGED JUDGES JUDGING JUDGMENT JUDGMENTS)

Ge	16: 5	May the LORD *j* between you
	18:25	Will not the *J* of all the earth do
Lev	19:15	but *j* your neighbor fairly.
Dt	1:16	between your brothers and *j* fairly,
	17:12	man who shows contempt for the *j*
	32:36	The LORD will *j* his people
Jdg	2:18	Whenever the LORD raised up a *j*
1Sa	3:10	the LORD will *j* the ends
	3:13	that I would *j* his family forever
	7:15	*j* over Israel all the days of his life.
	24:12	May the LORD *j* between you
1Ki	8:32	*J* between your servants,
1Ch	16:33	for he comes to *j* the earth.
2Ch	6:23	*J* between your servants, repaying
	19: 7	*J* carefully, for with the LORD our
Job	9:15	plead with my *J* for mercy.
Ps	7: 8	*J* me, O LORD, according
	7: 8	let the LORD *j* the peoples.
	7:11	God is a righteous *j*,
	9: 8	He will *j* the world in righteousness
	50: 6	for God himself is *j*.
	51: 4	and justified when you *j*.
	75: 2	it is I who *j* uprightly.
	76: 9	when you, O God, rose up to *j*,
	82: 8	Rise up, O God, *j* the earth,
	94: 2	Rise up, O *J* of the earth!
	96:10	he will *j* the peoples with equity.
	96:13	He will *j* the world in righteousness
	98: 9	He will *j* the world in righteousness
	110: 6	He will *j* the nations, heaping up
Pr	31: 9	Speak up and *j* fairly;
Isa	2: 4	He will *j* between the nations
	3:13	he rises to *j* the people.
	11: 3	He will not *j* by what he sees
	33:22	For the LORD is our *j*,
Jer	11:20	Almighty, you who *j* righteously
Eze	7: 3	I will *j* you according
	7:27	by their own standards I will *j* them
	18:30	O house of Israel, I will *j* you,
	20:36	so I will *j* you, declares
	22: 2	"Son of man, will you *j* her?
	34:17	I will *j* between one sheep
Joel	3:12	sit to *j* all the nations on every side.
Mic	3:11	Her leaders *j* for a bribe,
	4: 3	He will *j* between many peoples
Mt	7: 1	Do not *j*, or you too will be judged.
Lk	6:37	"Do not *j*, and you will not be
	18: 2	there was a *j* who neither feared
Jn	5:27	And he has given him authority to *j*
	5:30	By myself I can do nothing; I *j* only
	8:16	But if I do *j*, my decisions are right,
	12:47	For I did not come to *j* the world,
	12:48	There is a *j* for the one who rejects
Ac	10:42	as *j* of the living and the dead.
	17:31	a day when he will *j* the world
Ro	2:16	day when God will *j* men's secrets
	3: 6	how could God *j* the world?
	14:10	then, why do you *j* your brother?
1Co	4: 3	indeed, I do not even *j* myself.
	4: 5	Therefore *j* nothing
	6: 2	and if you are to *j* the world,
	6: 2	that the saints will *j* the world?
Gal	2: 6	not *j* by external appearance—
Col	2:16	Therefore do not let anyone *j* you
2Ti	4: 1	who will *j* the living and the dead,

2Ti 4:8 which the Lord, the righteous J,
Heb 10:30 "The Lord will j his people."
12:23 come to God, the j of all men,
13:4 for God will j the adulterer
Jas 4:12 There is only one Lawgiver and J,
4:12 who are you to j your neighbor?
1Pe 4:5 to him who is ready to j the living
Rev 20:4 who had been given authority to j.

JUDGED (JUDGE)
Mt 7:1 "Do not judge, or you too will be j.
1Co 4:3 I care very little if I am j by you
10:29 For why should my freedom be j
11:31 But if we j ourselves, we would not
14:24 all that he is a sinner and will be j
Jas 3:1 who teach will be j more strictly.
Rev 20:12 The dead were j according

JUDGES (JUDGE)
Jdg 2:16 Then the LORD raised up j,
Job 9:24 he blindfolds its j.
Ps 58:11 there is a God who j the earth."
75:7 But it is God who j:
Pr 29:14 If a king j the poor with fairness,
Jn 5:22 Moreover, the Father j no one,
1Co 4:4 It is the Lord who j me.
Heb 4:12 it j the thoughts and attitudes
1Pe 1:17 on a Father who j each man's work
2:23 himself to him who j justly.
Rev 19:11 With justice he j and makes war.

JUDGING (JUDGE)
Ps 9:4 on your throne, j righteously.
Pr 24:23 To show partiality in j is not good:
Isa 16:5 one who in j seeks justice
Mt 19:28 j the twelve tribes of Israel.
Jn 7:24 Stop j by mere appearances,

JUDGMENT (JUDGE)
Nu 33:4 for the LORD had brought j
Dt 1:17 of any man, for j belongs to God.
32:41 and my hand grasps it in j,
1Sa 25:33 May you be blessed for your good j
Ps 1:5 the wicked will not stand in the j,
9:7 he has established his throne for j.
76:8 From heaven you pronounced j,
82:1 he gives j among the "gods":
119:66 Teach me knowledge and good j,
143:2 Do not bring your servant into j,
Pr 3:21 preserve sound j and discernment,
6:32 man who commits adultery lacks j;
8:14 Counsel and sound j are mine;
10:21 but fools die for lack of j.
11:12 man who lacks j derides his
12:11 but he who chases fantasies lacks j.
17:18 A man lacking in j strikes hands
18:1 he defies all sound j.
28:16 A tyrannical ruler lacks j,
Ecc 12:14 God will bring every deed into j,
Isa 3:14 The LORD enters into j
28:6 justice to him who sits in j,
53:8 By oppression and j he was taken
66:16 the LORD will execute j,
Jer 2:35 But I will pass j on you
25:31 he will bring j on all mankind
51:18 when their j comes, they will
Eze 11:10 and I will execute j on you
Da 7:22 pronounced j in favor of the saints
Am 7:4 Sovereign LORD was calling for j
Zec 8:16 and sound j in your courts;
Mal 3:5 "So I will come near to you for j.
Mt 5:21 who murders will be subject to j.'
5:22 with his brother will be subject to j.
10:15 on the day of j than for that town.
11:24 on the day of j than for you."
12:36 have to give account on the day of j
12:41 up at the j with this generation
Jn 5:22 but has entrusted all j to the Son,
5:30 as I hear, and my j is just,
7:24 appearances, and make a right j."
8:26 "I have much to say in j of you.
9:39 "For j I have come into this world,

Jn 12:31 Now is the time for j on this world;
16:8 to sin and righteousness and j:
16:11 in regard to j, because the prince
Ac 24:25 self-control and the j to come,
Ro 2:1 you who pass j on someone else,
2:1 Now we know that God's j
5:16 The j followed one sin
12:3 rather think of yourself with sober j
14:10 stand before God's j seat.
14:13 Therefore let us stop passing j
1Co 7:40 In my j, she is happier if she stays
11:29 body of the Lord eats and drinks j
2Co 5:10 appear before the j seat of Christ,
2Th 1:5 is evidence that God's j is right,
1Ti 3:6 fall under the same j as the devil.
5:12 Thus they bring j on themselves,
Heb 6:2 of the dead, and eternal j.
9:27 to die once, and after that to face j,
10:27 but only a fearful expectation of j
Jas 2:13 j without mercy will be shown
4:11 are not keeping it, but sitting in j
1Pe 4:11 For it is time for j to begin
2Pe 2:9 the unrighteous for the day of j,
3:7 being kept for the day of j
1Jn 4:17 have confidence on the day of j,
Jude :6 bound with everlasting chains for j
Rev 14:7 because the hour of his j has come.

JUDGMENTS (JUDGE)
Jer 1:16 I will pronounce my j on my people
Da 9:11 and sworn j written in the Law
Hos 6:5 my j flashed like lightning
Ro 11:33 How unsearchable his j,
1Co 2:15 spiritual man makes j about all
Rev 16:7 true and just are your j."

JUG
1Sa 26:12 and water j near Saul's head,
1Ki 17:12 of flour in a jar and a little oil in a j.

JUST* (JUSTICE JUSTIFICATION JUSTIFIED JUSTIFIES JUSTIFY JUSTIFYING JUSTLY)
Ge 18:19 LORD by doing what is right and j,
Dt 2:12 j as Israel did in the land
6:3 j as the LORD, the God
27:3 and honey, j as the LORD,
30:9 j as he delighted in your fathers,
32:4 and all his ways are j.
32:4 upright and j is he.
32:47 They are not j idle words for you—
32:50 j as your brother Aaron died
2Sa 8:15 doing what was j and right
1Ch 18:14 doing what was j and right
2Ch 12:6 and said, "The LORD is j."
Ne 9:13 and laws that are j and right,
9:33 you have been j; you have acted
Job 34:17 Will you condemn the j?
35:2 Elihu said: "Do you think this is j?
Ps 37:28 For the LORD loves the j
37:30 and his tongue speaks what is j.
99:4 what is j and right.
111:7 of his hands are faithful and j;
119:121 I have done what is righteous and j;
Pr 1:3 doing what is right and j and fair;
2:9 will understand what is right and j
8:8 All the words of my mouth are j;
8:15 and rulers make laws that are j;
12:5 The plans of the righteous are j,
21:3 To do what is right and j
Isa 32:7 even when the plea of the needy is j
58:2 They ask me for j decisions
Jer 4:2 if in a truthful, j and righteous way
22:3 what the LORD says: Do what is j
22:15 He did what was right and j,
23:5 do what is j and right in the land.
33:15 he will do what is j and right
Eze 18:5 who does what is j and right.
18:19 Since the son has done what is j
18:21 and does what is j and right,
18:25 'The way of the Lord is not j.'
18:27 and does what is j and right,
18:29 'The way of the Lord is not j.'

Eze 33:14 and does what is j and right—
33:16 He has done what is j and right;
33:17 But it is their way that is not j.
33:17 'The way of the Lord is not j.'
33:19 and does what is j and right,
33:20 'The way of the Lord is not j.'
45:9 and oppression and do what is j
Da 4:37 does is right and all his ways are j.
Jn 5:30 as I hear, and my judgment is j,
Ro 3:26 as to be j and the one who justifies
2Th 1:6 God is j: He will pay back trouble
Heb 2:2 received its j punishment,
1Jn 1:9 and j and will forgive us our sins
Rev 15:3 J and true are your ways,
16:5 "You are j in these judgments,
16:7 true and j are your judgments."
19:2 for true and j are his judgments.

JUSTICE* (JUST)
Ge 49:16 "Dan will provide j for his people
Ex 23:2 do not pervert j by siding
23:6 "Do not deny j to your poor people
Lev 19:15 "'Do not pervert j; do not show
Dt 16:19 Do not pervert j or show partiality.
16:20 Follow j and j alone,
24:17 the alien or the fatherless of j,
27:19 Cursed is the man who withholds j
1Sa 8:3 accepted bribes and perverted j.
2Sa 15:4 and I would see that he gets j."
15:6 came to the king asking for j,
1Ki 3:11 for discernment in administering j,
3:28 wisdom from God to administer j.
7:7 the Hall of J, where he was to judge
10:9 to maintain j and righteousness."
2Ch 9:8 to maintain j and righteousness.
Ezr 7:25 and judges to administer j
Est 1:13 experts in matters of law and j,
Job 8:3 Does God pervert j?
9:19 matter of j, who will summon him?
19:7 though I call for help, there is no j.
27:2 as God lives, who has denied me j,
29:14 j was my robe and my turban.
31:13 "If I have denied j
34:5 but God denies me j.
34:12 that the Almighty would pervert j.
34:17 Can he who hates j govern?
36:3 I will ascribe j to my Maker.
36:17 j have taken hold of you.
37:23 in his j and great righteousness,
40:8 "Would you discredit my j?
Ps 7:6 Awake, my God; decree j.
9:8 he will govern the peoples with j.
9:16 The LORD is known by his j;
11:7 he loves j;
33:5 LORD loves righteousness and j;
36:6 your j like the great deep.
37:6 j of your cause like the noonday
45:6 a scepter of j will be the scepter
72:1 Endow the king with your j, O God
72:2 your afflicted ones with j.
89:14 j are the foundation of your throne;
97:2 j are the foundation of his throne.
99:4 The King is mighty, he loves j—
101:1 I will sing of your love and j;
103:6 and j for all the oppressed.
106:3 Blessed are they who maintain j,
112:5 who conducts his affairs with j.
140:12 I know that the LORD secures j
Pr 8:20 along the paths of j,
16:10 and his mouth should not betray j.
17:23 to pervert the course of j.
18:5 or to deprive the innocent of j.
19:28 A corrupt witness mocks at j,
21:15 When j is done, it brings joy
28:5 Evil men do not understand j,
29:4 By j a king gives a country stability
29:7 The righteous care about j
29:26 from the LORD that man gets j.
Ecc 3:16 place of j— wickedness was there.
5:8 poor oppressed in a district, and j
Isa 1:17 Seek j,
1:21 She once was full of j;

Isa 1:27 Zion will be redeemed with *j*,
    5: 7 he looked for *j*, but saw
        bloodshed;
    5:16 Almighty will be exalted by his *j*,
    5:23 but deny *j* to the innocent.
    9: 7 it with *j* and righteousness
    10: 2 and withhold *j* from the
        oppressed of
    11: 4 with *j* he will give decisions
    16: 5 one who in judging seeks *j*
    28: 6 He will be a spirit of *j*
    28:17 I will make *j* the measuring line
    29:21 deprive the innocent of *j*.
    30:18 For the LORD is a God of *j*.
    32: 1 and rulers will rule with *j*.
    32:16 *J* will dwell in the desert
    33: 5 with *j* and righteousness.
    42: 1 and he will bring *j* to the nations.
    42: 3 In faithfulness he will bring forth *j*;
    42: 4 till he establishes *j* on earth.
    51: 4 my *j* will become a light
    51: 5 my arm will bring *j* to the nations.
    56: 1 "Maintain *j*
    59: 4 No one calls for *j*;
    59: 8 there is no *j* in their paths.
    59: 9 So *j* is far from us,
    59:11 We look for *j*, but find none;
    59:14 So *j* is driven back,
    59:15 that there was no *j*.
    61: 8 "For I, the LORD, love *j*;
Jer 9:24 *j* and righteousness on earth.
    10:24 Correct me, LORD, but only with *j*
    12: 1 speak with you about your *j*:
    21:12 " 'Administer *j* every morning;
    30:11 I will discipline you but only
        with *j*;
    46:28 I will discipline you but only
        with *j*;
La 3:36 to deprive a man of *j*—
Eze 22:29 mistreat the alien, denying them *j*.
    34:16 I will shepherd the flock with *j*.
Hos 2:19 you in righteousness and *j*,
    12: 6 maintain love and *j*,
Am 2: 7 and deny *j* to the oppressed.
    5: 7 You who turn *j* into bitterness
    5:12 and you deprive the poor of *j*
    5:15 maintain *j* in the courts.
    5:24 But let *j* roll on like a river,
    6:12 But you have turned *j* into poison
Mic 3: 1 Should you not know *j*,
    3: 8 and with *j* and might,
    3: 9 who despise *j*
Hab 1: 4 and *j* never prevails.
    1: 4 so that *j* is perverted.
Zep 3: 5 by morning he dispenses his *j*,
Zec 7: 9 'Administer true *j*; show mercy
Mal 2:17 or "Where is the God of *j*?"
    3: 5 and deprive aliens of *j*,
Mt 12:18 he will proclaim *j* to the nations.
    12:20 till he leads *j* to victory.
    23:23 important matters of the law—*j*,
Lk 11:42 you neglect *j* and the love of God.
    18: 3 'Grant me *j* against my adversary.'
    18: 5 I will see that she gets *j*,
    18: 7 And will not God bring about *j*
    18: 8 he will see that they get *j*,
Ac 8:33 humiliation he was deprived of *j*.
    17:31 with *j* by the man he has
        appointed.
    28: 4 *J* has not allowed him to live."
Ro 3:25 He did this to demonstrate his *j*,
    3:26 it to demonstrate his *j*
2Co 7:11 what readiness to see *j* done.
Heb 11:33 administered *j*, and gained what
Rev 19:11 With *j* he judges and makes war.

JUSTIFICATION* (JUST)
Eze 16:52 for you have furnished some *j*
Ro 4:25 and was raised to life for our *j*.
    5:16 many trespasses and brought *j*.
    5:18 of righteousness was *j* that brings

JUSTIFIED* (JUST)
Ps 51: 4 and *j* when you judge.
Lk 18:14 rather than the other, went home *j*
Ac 13:39 from everything you could not
        be *j*
    13:39 him everyone who believes is *j*
Ro 3:24 and are *j* freely by his grace
    3:28 For we maintain that a man is *j*
    4: 2 If, in fact, Abraham was *j* by
        works,

Ro 5: 1 since we have been *j* through
        faith,
    5: 9 Since we have now been *j*
    8:30 those he called, he also *j*; those
        he *j*,
    10:10 heart that you believe and are *j*,
1Co 6:11 you were *j* in the name
Gal 2:16 in Christ Jesus that we may be *j*
    2:16 observing the law no one will be *j*.
    2:16 sinners' know that a man is not *j*
    2:17 "If, while we seek to be *j* in Christ,
    3:11 Clearly no one is *j* before God
    3:24 to Christ that we might be *j* by
        faith
    5: 4 to be *j* by law have been alienated
Tit 3: 7 so that, having been *j* by his
        grace,
Jas 2:24 You see that a person is *j*

JUSTIFIES* (JUST)
Ro 3:26 one who *j* those who have faith
    4: 5 but trusts God who *j* the wicked,
    8:33 God has chosen? It is God who *j*.

JUSTIFY* (JUST)
Est 7: 4 such distress would *j* disturbing
Job 40: 8 you condemn me to *j* yourself?
Isa 53:11 my righteous servant will *j* many,
Lk 10:29 But he wanted to *j* himself,
    16:15 "You are the ones who *j*
        yourselves
Ro 3:30 who will *j* the circumcised by faith
Gal 3: 8 that God would *j* the Gentiles

JUSTIFYING* (JUST)
Job 32: 2 angry with Job for *j* himself rather

JUSTLY* (JUST)
Ps 58: 1 Do you rulers indeed speak *j*?
    67: 4 for you rule the peoples *j*
Jer 7: 5 and deal with each other *j*,
Mic 6: 8 To act *j* and to love mercy
Lk 23:41 We are punished *j*,
1Pe 2:23 himself to him who judges *j*.

KADESH
Nu 20: 1 of Zin, and they stayed at *K*.
Dt 1:46 And so you stayed in *K* many days

KADESH BARNEA
Nu 32: 8 I sent them from *K* to look over

KEBAR
Eze 1: 1 among the exiles by the *K* River,

KEDORLAOMER
Ge 14:17 Abram returned from defeating *K*

KEEP (KEEPER KEEPING KEEPS KEPT)
Ge 31:49 "May the LORD *k* watch
Ex 15:26 his commands and *k* all his
    20: 6 and *k* my commandments,
Lev 15:31 You must *k* the Israelites separate
Nu 6:24 and *k* you;
Dt 4: 2 but *k* the commands of the LORD
    6:17 Be sure to *k* the commands
    7: 9 who love him and *k* his
        commands.
    7:12 your God will *k* his covenant
    11: 1 your God and *k* his requirements,
    13: 4 *K* his commands and obey him;
    30:10 your God and *k* his commands
    30:16 and to *k* his commands, decrees
Jos 22: 5 careful to *k* the commandment
1Ki 8:58 and to *k* the commands,
2Ki 17:19 Judah did not *k* the commands
    23: 3 the LORD and *k* his commands,
1Ch 29:18 and *k* their hearts loyal to you.
2Ch 6:14 you who *k* your covenant of love
    34:31 the LORD and *k* his commands,
Job 14:16 but not *k* track of my sin.
Ps 18:28 You, O LORD, *k* my lamp burning
    19:13 *K* your servant also from willful
    78:10 they did not *k* God's covenant
    119: 2 Blessed are they who *k* his
        statutes
    119: 9 can a young man *k* his way pure?
    121: 7 The LORD will *k* you
    141: 3 *k* watch over the door of my lips.
Pr 4:21 *k* them within your heart;
    4:24 corrupt talk far from your lips.
    30: 8 *K* falsehood and lies far from me;
Ecc 3: 6 a time to *k* and a time
    12:13 and *k* his commandments,
Isa 26: 3 You will *k* in perfect peace
    42: 6 I will *k* you and will make you
    58:13 "If you *k* your feet

Jer 16:11 forsook me and did not *k* my law.
Eze 20:19 and be careful to *k* my laws.
Mt 10:10 for the worker is worth his *k*.
Lk 12:35 and *k* your lamps burning,
    17:33 tries to *k* his life will lose it,
Jn 10:24 How long will you *k* us in
        suspense
    12:25 in this world will *k* it for eternal
        life
Ac 2:24 for death to *k* its hold on him.
    18: 9 "Do not be afraid; *k* on speaking,
Ro 7:19 want to do—this I *k* on doing.
    12:11 but *k* your spiritual fervor,
    14:22 you believe about these things *k*
    16:17 *K* away from them.
1Co 1: 8 He will *k* you strong to the end,
2Co 12: 7 To *k* me from becoming conceited
Gal 5:25 let us *k* in step with the Spirit.
Eph 4: 3 Make every effort to *k* the unity
2Th 3: 6 to *k* away from every brother who
1Ti 5:22 *K* yourself pure.
2Ti 4: 5 *k* your head in all situations,
Heb 9:20 God has commanded you to *k*."
    13: 5 *K* your lives free from the love
Jas 1:26 and yet does not *k* a tight rein
    2: 8 If you really *k* the royal law found
    3: 2 able to *k* his whole body in check.
2Pe 1: 8 will *k* you from being ineffective
Jude :21 *K* yourselves in God's love
    :24 able to *k* you from falling
Rev 3:10 also *k* you from the hour
    22: 9 of all who *k* the words of this
        book.

KEEPER (KEEP)
Ge 4: 9 I my brother's *k*?" The LORD

KEEPING (KEEP)
Ex 20: 8 the Sabbath day by *k* it holy.
Dt 5:12 the Sabbath day by *k* it holy,
    13:18 *k* all his commands that I am
Ps 19:11 in *k* them there is great reward.
    119:112 My heart is set on *k* your decrees
Pr 15: 3 *k* watch on the wicked
Mt 3: 8 Produce fruit in *k* with
        repentance.
Lk 2: 8 *k* watch over their flocks at night.
1Co 7:19 *K* God's commands is what
        counts.
2Co 8: 5 and then to us in *k* with God's
        will.
Jas 4:11 you are not *k* it, but sitting
1Pe 3:16 and respect, *k* a clear conscience,
2Pe 3: 9 Lord is not slow in *k* his promise,

KEEPS (KEEP)
Ne 1: 5 who *k* his covenant of love
Ps 15: 4 who *k* his oath
Pr 12:23 A prudent man *k* his knowledge
    15:21 of understanding *k* a straight
    17:28 a fool is thought wise if he *k*
        silent,
    29:11 a wise man *k* himself under
        control
Isa 56: 2 who *k* the Sabbath
Da 9: 4 who *k* his covenant of love
Am 5:13 Therefore the prudent man *k*
        quiet
Jn 7:19 Yet not one of you *k* the law.
    8:51 if anyone *k* my word, he will never
1Co 13: 5 is not easily angered, it *k* no
        record
Jas 2:10 For whoever *k* the whole law
Rev 22: 7 Blessed is he who *k* the words

KEILAH
1Sa 23:13 that David had escaped from *K*,

KEPT (KEEP)
Ex 12:42 Because the LORD *k* vigil that
Dt 7: 8 and *k* the oath he swore
2Ki 18: 6 he *k* the commands the LORD had
Ne 9: 8 You have *k* your promise
Ps 130: 3 If you, O LORD, *k* a record of sins,
Isa 38:17 In your love you *k* me
Mt 19:20 these I have *k*," the young man
2Co 11: 9 I have *k* myself from being
2Ti 4: 7 finished the race, I have *k* the
        faith.
1Pe 1: 4 spoil or fade—*k* in heaven for you,

KERNEL
Mk 4:28 then the full *k* in the head.
Jn 12:24 a *k* of wheat falls to the ground

KEY (KEYS)
Isa 33: 6 the fear of the LORD is the k
Rev 20: 1 having the k to the Abyss

KEYS* (KEY)
Mt 16:19 I will give you the k of the
          kingdom
Rev 1:18 And I hold the k of death

KICK*
Ac 26:14 for you to k against the goads.'

KILL (KILLED KILLS)
Ecc 3: 3 a time to k and a time to heal,
Mt 10:28 k the body but cannot k the soul.
   17:23 They will k him, and on the third
Mk 9:31 will k him, and after three days
   10:34 spit on him, flog him and k him.

KILLED (KILL)
Ge 4: 8 his brother Abel and k him.
Ex 2:12 he k the Egyptian and hid him
   13:15 the LORD k every firstborn
Nu 35:11 who has k someone accidentally
1Sa 17:50 down the Philistine and k him.
Ne 9:26 They k your prophets, who had
Hos 6: 5 I k you with the words
Lk 11:48 they k the prophets, and you
          build
Ac 3:15 You k the author of life,

KILLS (KILL)
Ex 21:12 k him shall surely be put to death.
Lev 24:21 but whoever k a man must be put
2Co 3: 6 for the letter k, but the Spirit gives

KIND (KINDNESS KINDNESSES KINDS)
Ge 1:24 animals, each according to its k."
2Ch 10: 7 "If you will be k to these people
Pr 11:17 A k man benefits himself,
   12:25 but a k word cheers him up.
   14:21 blessed is he who is k to the
          needy.
   14:31 whoever is k to the needy honors
   19:17 He who is k to the poor lends
Da 4:27 by being k to the oppressed.
Lk 6:35 because he is k to the ungrateful
1Co 13: 4 Love is patient, love is k.
   15:35 With what k of body will they
Eph 4:32 Be k and compassionate
1Th 5:15 but always try to be k to each
          other
2Ti 2:24 instead, he must be k to
          everyone,
Tit 2: 5 to be busy at home, to be k,

KINDHEARTED* (HEART)
Pr 11:16 A k woman gains respect,

KINDNESS (KIND)
Ge 24:12 and show k to my master
          Abraham
   32:10 I am unworthy of all the k
   39:21 he showed him k and granted him
Jdg 8:35 failed to show k to the family
Ru 2:20 has not stopped showing his k
2Sa 9: 3 to whom I can show God's k?"
   22:51 he shows unfailing k
Ps 18:50 he shows unfailing k
   141: 5 righteous man strike me—it is a k;
Isa 54: 8 but with everlasting k
Jer 9:24 I am the LORD, who exercises k,
Hos 11: 4 I led them with cords of human k,
Ac 14:17 He has shown k by giving you rain
Ro 11:22 Consider therefore the k
2Co 6: 6 understanding, patience and k;
Gal 5:22 peace, patience, k, goodness,
Eph 2: 7 expressed in his k to us
Col 3:12 yourselves with compassion, k,
Tit 3: 4 But when the k and love
2Pe 1: 7 brotherly k; and to brotherly k,

KINDNESSES* (KIND)
Ps 106: 7 did not remember your many k,
Isa 63: 7 I will tell of the k of the LORD,
   63: 7 to his compassion and many k.

KINDS (KIND)
Ge 1:12 bearing seed according to their k
1Co 12: 4 There are different k of gifts,
1Ti 6:10 of money is a root of all k of evil.
1Pe 1: 6 had to suffer grief in all k of trials.

KING (KING'S KINGDOM KINGDOMS KINGS)
   1. Kings of Judah and Israel: see Saul, David, Solomon.
   2. Kings of Judah: see Rehoboam, Abijah, Asa, Jehoshaphat, Jehoram, Ahaziah, Athaliah

(Queen), Joash, Amaziah, Azariah (Uzziah), Jotham, Ahaz, Hezekiah, Manasseh, Amon, Josiah, Jehoahaz, Jehoiakim, Jehoiachin, Zedekiah.
   3. Kings of Israel: see Jeroboam I, Nadab, Baasha, Elah, Zimri, Tibni, Omri, Ahab, Ahaziah, Joram, Jehu, Jehoahaz, Jehoash, Jeroboam II, Zechariah, Shallum, Menahem, Pekah, Pekahiah, Hoshea.
Ex 1: 8 a new k, who did not know about
Dt 17:14 "Let us set a k over us like all
Jdg 17: 6 In those days Israel had no k;
1Sa 8: 5 now appoint a k to lead us,
   11:15 as k in the presence of the LORD.
   12:12 the LORD your God was your k.
2Sa 2: 4 and there they anointed David k
1Ki 1:30 Solomon your son shall be k
Ps 2: 6 "I have installed my K
   24: 7 that the K of glory may come in.
   44: 4 You are my K and my God,
   47: 7 For God is the K of all the earth;
Isa 32: 1 See, a k will reign in righteousness
Jer 30: 9 and David their k,
Hos 3: 5 their God and David their k.
Mic 2:13 k will pass through before them,
Zec 9: 9 See, your k comes to you,
Mt 2: 2 is the one who has been born k
   27:11 "Are you the k of the Jews?" "Yes,
Lk 19:38 "Blessed is the k who comes
   23: 3 "Are you the k of the Jews?" "Yes,
   23:38 THE K OF THE JEWS.
Jn 1:49 of God; you are the K of Israel."
   12:13 "Blessed is the K of Israel!"
Ac 17: 7 saying that there is another k,
1Ti 1:17 Now to the K eternal, immortal,
   6:15 the K of kings and Lord of lords,
Heb 7: 1 This Melchizedek was k of Salem
1Pe 2:13 to the k, as the supreme
          authority,
   2:17 of believers, fear God, honor
          the k.
Rev 15: 3 K of the ages.
   17:14 he is Lord of lords and K of
          kings—
   19:16 K OF KINGS AND LORD

KING'S (KING)
Pr 21: 1 The k heart is in the hand
Ecc 8: 3 in a hurry to leave the k presence.

KINGDOM (KING)
Ex 19: 6 you will be for me a k of priests
Dt 17:18 When he takes the throne of his k,
2Sa 7:12 body, and I will establish his k.
1Ki 11:31 to tear the k out of Solomon's
          hand
1Ch 17:11 own sons, and I will establish
          his k.
   29:11 Yours, O LORD, is the k;
Ps 45: 6 justice will be the scepter of
          your k.
   103:19 and his k rules over all.
   145:11 They will tell of the glory of your k
Eze 29:14 There they will be a lowly k.
Da 2:39 "After you, another k will rise,
   4: 3 His k is an eternal k;
   7:27 His k will be an everlasting k,
Ob :21 And the k will be the LORD's.
Mt 3: 2 Repent, for the k of heaven is near
   4:17 Repent, for the k of heaven is near
   4:23 preaching the good news of the k,
   5: 3 for theirs is the k of heaven.
   5:10 for theirs is the k of heaven.
   5:19 great in the k of heaven.
   5:19 least in the k of heaven,
   5:20 you will certainly not enter the k
   6:10 your k come,
   6:33 But seek first his k and his
   7:21 Lord,' will enter the k of heaven,
   8:11 Isaac and Jacob in the k of
          heaven.
   8:12 the subjects of the k will be
          thrown
   9:35 preaching the good news of the k
   10: 7 preach this message: 'The k
   11:11 least in the k of heaven is greater
   11:12 the k of heaven has been
          forcefully
   12:25 "Every k divided against itself will
   12:26 How then can his k stand?
   12:28 then the k of God has come
   13:11 knowledge of the secrets of the k

Mt 13:19 hears the message about the k
   13:24 "The k of heaven is like a man
          who
   13:31 k of heaven is like a mustard seed,
   13:33 "The k of heaven is like yeast that
   13:38 stands for the sons of the k.
   13:41 of his k everything that causes sin
   13:43 the sun in the k of their Father.
   13:44 k of heaven is like treasure hidden
   13:45 the k of heaven is like a merchant
   13:47 k of heaven is like a net that was
          let
   13:52 has been instructed about the k
   16:19 the keys of the k of heaven;
   16:28 the Son of Man coming in his k."
   18: 1 the greatest in the k of heaven?"
   18: 3 you will never enter the k
   18: 4 the greatest in the k of heaven.
   18:23 the k of heaven is like a king who
   19:12 because of the k of heaven.
   19:14 for the k of heaven belongs to
          such
   19:23 man to enter the k of heaven.
   19:24 for a rich man to enter the k of
          God
   20: 1 "For the k of heaven is like
   20:21 the other at your left in your k."
   21:31 the prostitutes are entering the k
   21:43 "Therefore I tell you that the k
   22: 2 "The k of heaven is like a king
          who
   23:13 You shut the k of heaven
   24: 7 rise against nation, and k
          against k.
   24:14 gospel of the k will be preached
   25: 1 "At that time the k
   25:34 the k prepared for you
   26:29 anew with you in my Father's k."
Mk 1:15 "The k of God is near.
   3:24 If a k is divided against itself,
   3:24 against itself, that k cannot stand.
   4:11 "The secret of the k
   4:26 "This is what the k of God is like.
   4:30 "What shall we say the k
   6:23 I will give you, up to half my k."
   9: 1 before they see the k of God
          come
   9:47 better for you to enter the k of
          God
   10:14 for the k of God belongs to such
   10:15 anyone who will not receive the k
   10:23 for the rich to enter the k of
          God!"
   10:24 how hard it is to enter the k of
          God
   10:25 for a rich man to enter the k of
          God
   11:10 "Blessed is the coming k
   12:34 "You are not far from the k of God
   13: 8 rise against nation, and k
          against k.
   14:25 day when I drink it anew in the k
   15:43 who was himself waiting for the k
Lk 1:33 Jacob forever; his k will never
   4:43 of the k of God to the other towns
   6:20 for yours is the k of God.
   7:28 in the k of God is greater than
          he."
   8: 1 proclaiming the good news of
          the k
   8:10 knowledge of the secrets of the k
   9: 2 out to preach the k of God
   9:11 spoke to them about the k of God,
   9:27 before they see the k of God."
   9:60 you go and proclaim the k of God
   9:62 fit for service in the k of God."
   10: 9 'The k of God is near you.'
   10:11 sure of this: The k of God is near.'
   11: 2 your k come.
   11:17 "Any k divided against itself will
   11:18 himself, how can his k stand?
   11:20 then the k of God has come to
          you.
   12:31 seek his k, and these things will
          be
   12:32 has been pleased to give you
          the k.
   13:18 "What is the k of God like?
   13:20 What shall I compare the k of God
   13:28 all the prophets in the k of God,
   13:29 places at the feast in the k of God.

Lk 14:15 eat at the feast in the *k* of God."
16:16 the good news of the *k*
17:20 when the *k* of God would come,
17:20 *k* of God does not come with careful
17:21 because the *k* of God is within you
18:16 for the *k* of God belongs to such
18:17 anyone who will not receive the *k*
18:24 for the rich to enter the *k* of God!
18:25 for a rich man to enter the *k* of God
18:29 for the sake of the *k* of God will fail
19:11 and the people thought that the *k*
21:10 rise against nation, and *k* against *k*.
21:31 you know that the *k* of God is near.
22:16 until it finds fulfillment in the *k*
22:18 the vine until the *k* of God comes."
22:29 And I confer on you a *k*, just
22:30 and drink at my table in my *k*
23:42 me when you come into your *k*."
23:51 he was waiting for the *k* of God.
Jn 3:3 no one can see the *k* of God.
3:5 no one can enter the *k* of God.
18:36 now my *k* is from another place."
18:36 "My *k* is not of this world.
Ac 1:3 and spoke about the *k* of God.
1:6 going to restore the *k* to Israel?"
8:12 he preached the good news of the *k*
14:22 hardships to enter the *k* of God,"
19:8 arguing persuasively about the *k*
20:25 about preaching the *k* will ever see
28:23 and declared to them the *k* of God
28:31 hindrance he preached the *k*
Ro 14:17 For the *k* of God is not a matter
1Co 4:20 For the *k* of God is not a matter
6:9 the wicked will not inherit the *k*
6:10 swindlers will inherit the *k* of God.
15:24 hands over the *k* to God the Father
15:50 blood cannot inherit the *k* of God,
Gal 5:21 live like this will not inherit the *k*
Eph 2:2 and of the ruler of the *k* of the air,
5:5 has any inheritance in the *k*
Col 1:12 of the saints in the *k* of light.
1:13 and brought us into the *k*
4:11 among my fellow workers for the *k*
1Th 2:12 who calls you into his *k* and glory.
2Th 1:5 will be counted worthy of the *k*
2Ti 4:1 in view of his appearing and his *k*,
4:18 bring me safely to his heavenly *k*.
Heb 1:8 will be the scepter of your *k*.
12:28 we are receiving a *k* that cannot be
Jas 2:5 to inherit the *k* he promised those
2Pe 1:11 into the eternal *k* of our Lord
Rev 1:6 has made us to be a *k* and priests
1:9 companion in the suffering and *k*
5:10 You have made them to be a *k*
11:15 of the world has become the *k*
11:15 "The *k* of the world has become
12:10 the power and the *k* of our God,
16:10 his *k* was plunged into darkness.
17:12 who have not yet received a *k*,

KINGDOMS (KING)
2Ki 19:15 God over all the *k* of the earth.
19:19 so that all *k* on earth may know
2Ch 20:6 rule over all the *k* of the nations.
Ps 68:32 Sing to God, O *k* of the earth,
Isa 37:16 God over all the *k* of the earth.
37:20 so that all *k* on earth may know
Eze 29:15 It will be the lowliest of *k*
37:22 or be divided into two *k*.
Da 4:17 Most High is sovereign over the *k*
7:17 great beasts are four *k* that will rise
Zep 3:8 to gather the *k*

KINGS (KING)
Ps 2:2 The *k* of the earth take their stand
47:9 for the *k* of the earth belong to God
68:29 *k* will bring you gifts.

Ps 72:11 All *k* will bow down to him
110:5 he will crush *k* on the day
149:8 to bind their *k* with fetters,
Pr 16:12 *K* detest wrongdoing,
Isa 24:21 and the *k* on the earth below.
52:15 and *k* will shut their mouths
60:11 their *k* led in triumphal procession.
Da 2:21 he sets up *k* and deposes them.
7:24 ten horns are ten *k* who will come
Lk 21:12 and you will be brought before *k*
1Co 4:8 You have become *k*—
1Ti 2:2 for *k* and all those in authority,
6:15 the King of *k* and Lord of lords,
Rev 1:5 and the ruler of the *k* of the earth.
17:14 he is Lord of lords and King of *k*—
19:16 KING OF *K* AND LORD

KINSMAN-REDEEMER (REDEEM)
Ru 3:9 over me, since you are a *k*."
4:14 day has not left you without a *k*.

KISS (KISSED KISSES)
Ps 2:12 *K* the Son, lest he be angry
Pr 24:26 is like a *k* on the lips.
SS 1:2 *Beloved* Let him *k* me
8:1 I would *k* you,
Lk 22:48 the Son of Man with a *k*?"
Ro 16:16 Greet one another with a holy *k*.
1Co 16:20 Greet one another with a holy *k*.
2Co 13:12 Greet one another with a holy *k*.
1Th 5:26 Greet all the brothers with a holy *k*
1Pe 5:14 Greet one another with a *k* of love.

KISSED (KISS)
Mk 14:45 Judas said, "Rabbi!" and *k* him.
Lk 7:38 *k* them and poured perfume

KISSES* (KISS)
Pr 27:6 but an enemy multiplies *k*.
SS 1:2 with the *k* of his mouth—

KNEE (KNEES)
Isa 45:23 Before me every *k* will bow;
Ro 14:11 'every *k* will bow before me;
Php 2:10 name of Jesus every *k* should bow,

KNEEL (KNELT)
Est 3:2 But Mordecai would not *k* down
Ps 95:6 let us *k* before the LORD our
Eph 3:14 For this reason I *k*

KNEES (KNEE)
1Ki 19:18 all whose *k* have not bowed
Isa 35:3 steady the *k* that give way;
Da 6:10 times a day he got down on his *k*
Lk 5:8 he fell at Jesus' *k* and said,
Heb 12:12 your feeble arms and weak *k*.

KNELT* (KNEEL)
1Ki 1:16 Bathsheba bowed low and *k*
2Ch 6:13 and then *k* down before the whole
7:3 they *k* on the pavement
29:29 everyone present with him *k* down
Est 3:2 officials at the king's gate *k* down
Mt 8:2 and *k* before him and said,
9:18 a ruler came and *k* before him
15:25 The woman came and *k* before him
17:14 a man approached Jesus and *k*
27:29 *k* in front of him and mocked him.
Lk 22:41 *k* down and prayed, "Father,
Ac 20:36 he *k* down with all of them
21:5 there on the beach we *k* to pray.

KNEW (KNOW)
2Ch 33:13 Manasseh *k* that the LORD is God
Job 23:3 If only I *k* where to find him;
Pr 24:12 "But we *k* nothing about this,"
Jer 1:5 you in the womb I *k* you,
Jnh 4:2 I *k* that you are a gracious
Mt 7:23 tell them plainly, 'I never *k* you.
12:25 Jesus *k* their thoughts
Jn 2:24 himself to them, for he *k* all men.
14:7 If you really *k* me, you would know

KNIFE
Ge 22:10 and took the *k* to slay his son.
Pr 23:2 and put a *k* to your throat

KNOCK* (KNOCKS)
Mt 7:7 *k* and the door will be opened

Lk 11:9 *k* and the door will be opened
Rev 3:20 I am! I stand at the door and *k*.

KNOCKS (KNOCK)
Mt 7:8 and to him who *k*, the door will be

KNOW (FOREKNEW FOREKNOWLEDGE KNEW KNOWING KNOWLEDGE KNOWN KNOWS)
Ge 22:12 Now I *k* that you fear God,
Ex 7:5 you will *k* that I am the LORD
14:4 and the Egyptians will *k* that I am
33:13 teach me your ways so I may *k* you
Dt 7:9 *K* therefore that the LORD your
18:21 "How can we *k* when a message
Jos 4:24 of the earth might *k* that the hand
23:14 You *k* with all your heart
1Sa 17:46 the whole world will *k* that there is
1Ki 8:39 heart (for you alone *k* the hearts
Job 11:6 *K* this: God has even forgotten
19:25 I *k* that my Redeemer lives,
42:3 things too wonderful for me to *k*.
Ps 46:10 Those who *k* your name will trust
46:10 "Be still, and *k* that I am God;
100:3 *K* that the LORD is God.
139:1 and you *k* me.
139:23 Search me, O God, and *k* my heart;
145:12 so that all men may *k*
Pr 27:1 for you do not *k* what a day may
30:4 Tell me if you *k*!
Ecc 8:5 wise heart will *k* the proper time
Isa 29:15 "Who sees us? Who will *k*?"
40:21 Do you not *k*?
Jer 6:15 they do not even *k* how to blush.
22:16 Is that not what it means to *k* me?"
24:7 I will give them a heart to *k* me,
31:34 his brother, saying, '*K* the LORD,'
33:3 unsearchable things you do not *k*.
Eze 2:5 they will *k* that a prophet has been
6:10 they will *k* that I am the LORD;
Da 11:32 people who *k* their God will firmly
Mt 6:3 let your left hand *k* what your right
7:11 *k* how to give good gifts
9:6 But so that you may *k* that the Son
22:29 you do not *k* the Scriptures
24:42 you do not *k* on what day your
26:74 "I don't *k* the man!" Immediately
Mk 12:24 you do not *k* the Scriptures
Lk 1:4 so that you may *k* the certainty
11:13 *k* how to give good gifts
12:48 But the one who does not *k*
13:25 'I don't *k* you or where you come
21:31 you *k* that the kingdom of God is
23:34 for they do not *k* what they are
Jn 1:26 among you stands one you do not *k*
3:11 we speak of what we *k*,
4:22 we worship what we do *k*,
4:42 and we *k* that this man really is
6:69 and *k* that you are the Holy One
7:28 You do not *k* him, but I *k* him
8:14 for I *k* where I came from
8:19 "You do not *k* me or my Father,"
8:32 Then you will *k* the truth,
8:55 Though you do not *k* him, I *k* him.
9:25 One thing I do *k*.
10:4 him because they *k* his voice.
10:14 I *k* my sheep and my sheep *k* me—
10:27 I *k* them, and they follow me.
12:35 the dark does not *k* where he is
13:17 Now that you *k* these things,
13:35 all men will *k* that you are my
14:17 you *k* him, for he lives with you
15:21 for they do not *k* the One who sent
16:30 we can see that you *k* all things
17:3 that they may *k* you, the only true
17:23 to let the world *k* that you sent me
21:15 he said, "you *k* that I love you."
21:24 We *k* that his testimony is true.
Ac 1:7 "It is not for you to *k* the times
1:24 "Lord, you *k* everyone's heart.

Ro	3:17	and the way of peace they do not *k*
	6:3	Or don't you *k* that all
	6:6	For we *k* that our old self was
	6:16	Don't you *k* that when you offer
	7:14	We *k* that the law is spiritual;
	7:18	I *k* that nothing good lives in me,
	8:22	We *k* that the whole creation has
	8:26	We do not *k* what we ought to pray
	8:28	we *k* that in all things God works
1Co	1:21	through its wisdom did not *k* him,
	2:2	For I resolved to *k* nothing
	3:16	Don't you *k* that you yourselves
	5:6	Don't you *k* that a little yeast
	6:2	Do you not *k* that the saints will
	6:15	Do you not *k* that your bodies are
	6:16	Do you not *k* that he who unites
	6:19	Do you not *k* that your body is
	7:16	How do you *k*, wife, whether you
	8:2	does not yet *k* as he ought to *k*.
	9:13	Don't you *k* that those who work
	9:24	Do you not *k* that
	13:9	For we *k* in part and we prophesy
	13:12	Now I *k* in part; then I shall *k* fully,
	15:58	because you *k* that your labor
2Co	5:1	we *k* that if the earthly tent we live
	5:11	we *k* what it is to fear the Lord,
	8:9	For you *k* the grace
Gal	1:11	you to *k*, brothers, that the gospel I
	2:16	not 'Gentile sinners' *k* that a man
Eph	1:17	so that you may *k* him better.
	1:18	in order that you may *k* the hope
	6:8	you *k* that the Lord will reward
	6:9	since you *k* that he who is both
Php	3:10	I want to *k* Christ and the power
	4:12	I *k* what it is to be in need,
Col	2:2	order that they may *k* the mystery
	4:1	because you *k* that you
	4:6	so that you may *k* how
1Th	3:3	You *k* quite well that we were
	5:2	for you *k* very well that the day
2Th	1:8	punish those who do not *k* God
1Ti	1:7	they do not *k* what they are talking
	3:5	(If anyone does not *k* how
	3:15	you will *k* how people ought
2Ti	1:12	because I *k* whom I have believed,
	2:23	you *k* they produce quarrels.
	3:14	you *k* those from whom you
Heb	8:11	because they will all *k* me,
	11:8	he did not *k* where he was going.
Jas	1:3	because you *k* that the testing
	3:1	you *k* that we who teach will be
	4:4	don't you *k* that friendship
	4:14	what will happen tomorrow.
1Pe	1:18	For you *k* that it was not
2Pe	1:12	even though you *k* them
1Jn	2:3	We *k* that we have come
	2:4	The man who says, "I *k* him,"
	2:5	This is how we *k* we are in him:
	2:11	he does not *k* where he is going,
	2:20	and all of you *k* the truth.
	2:29	you *k* that everyone who does
	3:1	not *k* us is that it did not *k* him.
	3:2	But we *k* that when he appears,
	3:10	This is how we *k* who the children
	3:14	We *k* that we have passed
	3:16	This is how we *k* what love is:
	3:19	then is how we *k* that we belong
	3:24	We *k* it by the Spirit he gave us.
	4:8	does not love does not *k* God,
	4:13	We *k* that we live in him
	4:16	so we *k* and rely on the love God
	5:2	This is how we *k* that we love
	5:13	so that you may *k* that you have
	5:15	And if we *k* that he hears us—
	5:18	We *k* that anyone born
	5:20	We *k* also that the Son
Rev	2:2	I *k* your deeds, your hard work
	2:9	I *k* your afflictions and your
	2:19	I *k* your deeds, your love and faith,
	3:3	you will not *k* at what time I will
	3:15	I *k* your deeds, that you are neither

KNOWING (KNOW)

Ge	3:5	and you will be like God, *k* good

Ge	3:22	now become like one of us, *k* good
Jn	19:28	*k* that all was now completed,
Php	3:8	of *k* Christ Jesus my Lord,
Phm	:21	*k* that you will do even more
Heb	13:2	entertained angels without *k* it.

KNOWLEDGE (KNOW)

Ge	2:9	the tree of the *k* of good and evil.
	2:17	eat from the tree of the *k* of good
2Ch	1:10	and *k*, that I may lead this people,
Job	21:22	"Can anyone teach *k* to God,
	38:2	counsel with words without *k*?
	42:3	obscures my counsel without *k*?'
Ps	19:2	night after night they display *k*.
	73:11	Does the Most High have *k*?"
	94:10	Does he who teaches man lack *k*?
	119:66	Teach me *k* and good judgment,
	139:6	Such *k* is too wonderful for me,
Pr	1:4	*k* and discretion to the young—
	1:7	of the LORD is the beginning of *k*,
	2:5	and find the *k* of God.
	2:6	from his mouth come *k*
	2:10	and *k* will be pleasant to your soul.
	3:20	by his *k* the deeps were divided,
	8:10	*k* rather than choice gold,
	8:12	I possess *k* and discretion.
	9:10	*k* of the Holy One is understanding
	10:14	Wise men store up *k*,
	12:1	Whoever loves discipline loves *k*,
	12:23	A prudent man keeps his *k*
	13:16	Every prudent man acts out of *k*,
	14:6	*k* comes easily to the discerning.
	15:7	The lips of the wise spread *k*;
	15:14	The discerning heart seeks *k*,
	17:27	A man of *k* uses words
	18:15	heart of the discerning acquires *k*;
	19:2	to have zeal without *k*,
	19:25	discerning man, and he will gain *k*.
	20:15	lips that speak *k* are a rare jewel.
	23:12	and your ears to words of *k*.
	24:4	through its rooms are filled
Ecc	7:12	but the advantage of *k* is this:
Isa	11:2	the Spirit of *k* and of the fear
	11:9	full of the *k* of the LORD
	40:14	Who was it that taught him *k*
Jer	3:15	who will lead you with *k*
Hos	4:6	are destroyed from lack of *k*.
Hab	2:14	filled with the *k* of the glory
Mal	2:7	lips of a priest ought to preserve *k*,
Mt	13:11	The *k* of the secrets of the kingdom
Lk	8:10	The *k* of the secrets of the kingdom
	11:52	you have taken away the key to *k*.
Ac	18:24	with a thorough *k* of the Scriptures
Ro	1:28	worthwhile to retain the *k* of God,
	10:2	but their zeal is not based on *k*.
	11:33	riches of the wisdom and *k* of God!
1Co	8:1	*K* puffs up, but love builds up.
	8:11	Christ died, is destroyed by your *k*.
	12:8	to another the message of *k*
	13:2	can fathom all mysteries and all *k*,
	13:8	where there is *k*, it will pass away.
2Co	2:14	everywhere the fragrance of the *k*
	4:6	light of the *k* of the glory of God
	8:7	in *k*, in complete earnestness
	11:6	a trained speaker, but I do have *k*.
Eph	3:19	to know this love that surpasses *k*
	4:13	and in the *k* of the Son of God
Php	1:9	and more in *k* and depth of insight,
Col	1:9	God to fill you with the *k* of his will
	1:10	every good work, growing in the *k*
	2:3	all the treasures of wisdom and *k*.
	3:10	which is being renewed in *k*
1Ti	2:4	and to come to a *k* of the truth.
	6:20	ideas of what is falsely called *k*,
Tit	1:1	and the *k* of the truth that leads
Heb	10:26	after we have received the *k*
2Pe	1:5	and to goodness, *k*; and to *k*,
	3:18	grow in the grace and *k* of our Lord

KNOWN (KNOW)		
Ex	6:3	the LORD I did not make myself *k*
Ps	16:11	You have made *k* to me the path
	89:1	I will make your faithfulness *k*
	98:2	LORD has made his salvation *k*
	105:1	make *k* among the nations what he
	119:168	for all my ways are *k* to you.
Pr	20:11	Even a child is *k* by his actions,
Isa	12:4	make *k* among the nations what he
	46:10	*k* the end from the beginning,
	61:9	Their descendants will be *k*
Eze	38:23	I will make myself *k* in the sight
	39:7	" 'I will make *k* my holy name
Mt	10:26	or hidden that will not be made *k*.
	24:43	of the house had *k* at what time
Lk	19:42	had only *k* on this day what would
Jn	15:15	from my Father I have made *k*
	16:14	from what is mine and making it *k*
	17:26	I have made you *k* to them,
Ac	2:28	You have made *k* to me the paths
Ro	1:19	since what may be *k* about God is
	3:21	apart from law, has been made *k*,
	9:22	his wrath and make his power *k*,
	11:34	"Who has *k* the mind of the Lord?
	15:20	the gospel where Christ was not *k*,
	16:26	and made *k* through the prophetic
1Co	2:16	"For who has *k* the mind
	8:3	But the man who loves God is *k*
	13:12	know fully, even as I am fully *k*.
2Co	3:2	written on our hearts, *k*
Gal	4:9	or rather are *k* by God—
Eph	3:5	which was not made *k* to men
	6:19	will fearlessly make *k* the mystery
2Ti	3:15	infancy you have *k* the holy
2Pe	2:21	than to have *k* it and then

KNOWS (KNOW)		
1Sa	2:3	for the LORD is a God who *k*,
Est	4:14	And who *k* but that you have come
Job	23:10	But he *k* the way that I take;
Ps	44:21	since he *k* the secrets of the heart?
	94:11	The LORD *k* the thoughts of man;
	103:14	for he *k* how we are formed,
Ecc	8:7	Since no man *k* the future,
	8:17	Even if a wise man claims he *k*,
	9:12	no man *k* when his hour will come:
Isa	29:16	"He *k* nothing"?
Jer	9:24	that he understands and *k* me,
Mt	6:8	for your Father *k* what you need
	11:27	No one *k* the Son
	24:36	"No one *k* about that day or hour,
Lk	12:47	"That servant who *k* his master's
	16:15	of men, but God *k* your hearts.
Ac	15:8	who *k* the heart, showed that he
Ro	8:27	who searches our hearts *k* the mind
1Co	2:11	who among men *k* the thoughts
	8:2	who thinks he *k* something does
2Ti	2:19	The Lord *k* those who are his," and
Jas	4:17	who *k* the good he ought to do
1Jn	4:6	and whoever *k* God listens to us;
	4:7	born of God and *k* God.

KOHATHITE (KOHATHITES)		
Nu	3:29	The *K* clans were to camp
KOHATHITES (KOHATHITES)		
Nu	3:28	The *K* were responsible
	4:15	*K* are to carry those things that are

KORAH
Levite who led rebellion against Moses and Aaron (Nu 16; Jude 11).

KORAZIN

Mt	11:21	"Woe to you, *K*! Woe to you,

LABAN
Brother of Rebekah (Ge 24:29), father of Rachel and Leah (Ge 29:16). Received Abraham's servant (Ge 24:29–51). Provided daughters as wives for Jacob in exchange for Jacob's service (Ge 29:1–30). Provided flocks for Jacob's service (Ge 30:25–43). After Jacob's departure, pursued and covenanted with him (Ge 31).

LABOR (LABORING)
Ex   1:11 to oppress them with forced *l*,
      20: 9 Six days you shall *l* and do all your
Dt   5:13 Six days you shall *l* and do all your
Ps 127: 1 its builders *l* in vain.
    128: 2 You will eat the fruit of your *l*;
Pr   12:24 but laziness ends in slave *l*.
Isa 54: 1 you who were never in *l*;
     55: 2 and your *l* on what does not
             satisfy
Mt   6:28 They do not *l* or spin.
Jn   4:38 have reaped the benefits of
             their *l*."
1Co   3: 8 rewarded according to his own *l*.
     15:58 because you know that your *l*
Gal   4:11 you who have no *l* pains;
Php   2:16 day of Christ that I did not run or *l*
Rev 14:13 "they will rest from their *l*,

LABORING* (LABOR)
2Th   3: 8 *l* and toiling so that we would not

LACK (LACKED LACKING LACKS)
Ps   34: 9 for those who fear him *l* nothing.
Pr   5:23 He will die for *l* of discipline,
     10:21 but fools die for *l* of judgment.
     11:14 For *l* of guidance a nation falls,
     15:22 Plans fail for *l* of counsel,
     28:27 to the poor will *l* nothing,
Mk   6: 6 he was amazed at their *l* of faith.
     16:14 he rebuked them for their *l* of
             faith
Ro   3: 1 Will their *l* of faith nullify God's
1Co   1: 7 you do not *l* any spiritual gift
      7: 5 because of your *l* of self-control.
Col   2:23 *l* any value in restraining sensual

LACKED (LACK)
Dt   2: 7 and you have not *l* anything.
Ne   9:21 them in the desert; they *l* nothing,
1Co 12:24 honor to the parts that *l* it,

LACKING (LACK)
Pr   17:18 A man *l* in judgment strikes hands
Ro   12:11 Never be *l* in zeal, but keep your
Jas   1: 4 and complete, not *l* anything.

LACKS (LACK)
Pr   6:32 who commits adultery *l* judgment;
     11:12 man who *l* judgment derides his
     12:11 he who chases fantasies *l*
             judgment
     15:21 delights a man who *l* judgment,
     24:30 of the man who *l* judgment;
     25:28 is a man who *l* self-control.
     28:16 A tyrannical ruler *l* judgment,
     31:11 and *l* nothing of value.
Eze 34: 8 because my flock *l* a shepherd
Jas   1: 5 any of you *l* wisdom, he should
             ask

LAID (LAY)
Isa 53: 6 and the LORD has *l* on him
Mk   6:29 took his body and *l* it in a tomb.
Lk   6:48 and *l* the foundation on rock.
Ac   6: 6 and *l* their hands on them.
1Co   3:11 other than the one already *l*,
1Ti   4:14 body of elders *l* their hands on
             you.
1Jn   3:16 Jesus Christ *l* down his life for us.

LAKE
Mt   8:24 a furious storm came up on the *l*,
     14:25 out to them, walking on the *l*
Mk   4: 1 into a boat and sat in it out on
             the *l*,
Lk   8:33 down the steep bank into the *l*
Jn   6:25 him on the other side of the *l*,
Rev 19:20 into the fiery *l* of burning sulfur.
     20:14 The *l* of fire is the second death.

LAMB (LAMB'S LAMBS)
Ge   22: 8 "God himself will provide the *l*
Ex   12:21 and slaughter the Passover *l*.
Nu   9:11 are to eat the *l*, together
2Sa 12: 4 he took the ewe *l* that belonged
Isa 11: 6 The wolf will live with the *l*,
     53: 7 he was led like a *l* to the
             slaughter.
Mk   14:12 to sacrifice the Passover *l*,
Jn   1:29 *L* of God, who takes away the sin
Ac   8:32 as a *l* before the shearer is silent,
1Co   5: 7 our Passover *l*, has been
             sacrificed.
1Pe   1:19 a *l* without blemish or defect.
Rev   5: 6 Then I saw a *L*, looking

Rev   5:12 "Worthy is the *L*, who was slain,
      7:14 white in the blood of the *L*.
     14: 4 They follow the *L* wherever he
     15: 3 of God and the song of the *L*:
     17:14 but the *L* will overcome them
     19: 9 to the wedding supper of the *L!*' "
     21:23 gives it light, and the *L* is its lamp.

LAMB'S (LAMB)
Rev 21:27 written in the *L* book of life.

LAMBS (LAMB)
Lk   10: 3 I am sending you out like *l*
Jn   21:15 Jesus said, "Feed my *l*."

LAME
Isa 33:23 even the *l* will carry off plunder.
     35: 6 Then will the *l* leap like a deer,
Mt   11: 5 The blind receive sight, the *l* walk,
     15:31 the *l* walking and the blind seeing.
Lk   14:21 the crippled, the blind and the *l*.'

LAMENT
2Sa   1:17 took up this *l* concerning Saul
Eze 19: 1 Take up a *l* concerning the princes

LAMP (LAMPS LAMPSTAND LAMPSTANDS)
2Sa 22:29 You are my *l*, O LORD;
Ps   18:28 You, O LORD, keep my *l* burning;
    119:105 Your word is a *l* to my feet
    132:17 and set up a *l* for my anointed
             one.
Pr   6:23 For these commands are a *l*,
     20:27 *l* of the LORD searches the spirit
     31:18 and her *l* does not go out at night.
Mt   6:22 "The eye is the *l* of the body.
Lk   8:16 "No one lights a *l* and hides it
Rev 21:23 gives it light, and the Lamb is its *l*.
     22: 5 They will not need the light of a *l*

LAMPS (LAMP)
Mt   25: 1 be like ten virgins who took their *l*
Lk   12:35 for service and keep your *l*
             burning,
Rev   4: 5 the throne, seven *l* were blazing.

LAMPSTAND (LAMP)
Ex   25:31 "Make a *l* of pure gold
Zec   4: 2 "I see a solid gold *l* with a bowl
      4: 2 on the right and the left of the *l*?"
Heb   9: 2 In its first room were the *l*,
Rev   2: 5 and remove your *l* from its place.

LAMPSTANDS (LAMP)
2Ch   4: 7 He made ten gold *l* according
Rev   1:12 when I turned I saw seven
             golden *l*,
      1:20 and of the seven golden *l* is this:

LAND (LANDS)
Ge   1:10 God called the dry ground "*l*,"
      1:11 "Let the *l* produce vegetation:
      1:24 "Let the *l* produce living creatures
     12: 1 and go to the *l* I will show you.
     12: 7 To your offspring I will give this *l*."
     13:15 All the *l* that you see I will give
     15:18 "To your descendants I give this *l*,
     50:24 out of this *l* to the *l* he promised
Ex   3: 8 a *l* flowing with milk and honey—
      6: 8 to the *l* I swore with uplifted hand
     33: 3 Go up to the *l* flowing with milk
Lev 25:23 I must not be sold permanently,
Nu   14: 8 us into that *l*, a *l* flowing with milk
     35:33 Do not pollute the *l* where you
             are.
Dt   1: 8 See, I have given you this *l*.
      8: 7 God is bringing you into a
             good *l*—
     11:10 The *l* you are entering to take
     28:21 you from the *l* you are entering
     29:19 will bring disaster on the
             watered *l*
     34: 1 LORD showed him the whole *l*—
Jos 13: 2 "This is the *l* that remains:
     14: 4 Levites received no share of the *l*
     14: 9 *l* on which your feet have walked
2Sa 21:14 answered prayer in behalf of the *l*.
2Ki 17: 5 of Assyria invaded the entire *l*
     24: 1 king of Babylon invaded the *l*.
     25:21 into captivity, away from her *l*.
2Ch   7:14 their sin and will heal their *l*.
      7:20 then I will uproot Israel from my *l*,
     36:21 The *l* enjoyed its sabbath rests;
Ezr   9:11 entering to possess is a *l* polluted
Ne   9:36 in the *l* you gave our forefathers
Ps   37:11 But the meek will inherit the *l*
     37:29 the righteous will inherit the *l*

Ps 136:21 and gave their *l* as an inheritance,
    142: 5 my portion in the *l* of the living."
Pr   2:21 For the upright will live in the *l*,
     12:11 who works his *l* will have
             abundant
Isa   6:13 though a tenth remains in the *l*,
     53: 8 cut off from the *l* of the living;
Jer   2: 7 But you came and defiled my *l*
Eze 36:24 and bring you back into your
             own *l*.

LANDS (LAND)
Ps 111: 6 giving them the *l* of other nations.
Eze 20: 6 honey, the most beautiful of all *l*.
Zec 10: 9 in distant *l* they will remember
             me.

LANGUAGE (LANGUAGES)
Ge   11: 1 Now the whole world had one *l*
     11: 9 there the LORD confused the *l*
Ps   19: 3 There is no speech or *l*
Jn   8:44 When he lies, he speaks his
             native *l*,
Ac   2: 6 heard them speaking in his own *l*.
Col   3: 8 slander, and filthy *l* from your lips.
Rev   5: 9 from every tribe and *l* and people
      7: 9 every nation, tribe, people and *l*,
     14: 6 to every nation, tribe, *l* and
             people.

LANGUAGES (LANGUAGE)
Zec   8:23 "In those days ten men from all *l*

LAODICEA
Rev   3:14 the angel of the church in *L* write:

LAP
Jdg   7: 5 "Separate those who *l* the water

LASHES
Pr   17:10 more than a hundred *l* a fool.
2Co 11:24 from the Jews the forty *l* minus
             one

LAST (LASTING LASTS LATTER)
Ex   14:24 During the *l* watch of the night
2Sa 23: 1 These are the *l* words of David:
Isa   2: 2 and Jerusalem: In the *l* days
     41: 4 and with the *l*—I am he."
     44: 6 I am the first and I am the *l*;
     48:12 I am the first and I am the *l*.
Hos   3: 5 and to his blessings in the *l* days.
Mic   4: 1 In the *l* days
Mt   19:30 But many who are first will be *l*,
     20: 8 beginning with the *l* ones hired
     21:37 *L* of all, he sent his son to them.
Mk   9:35 must be the very *l*, and the
             servant
     10:31 are first will be *l*, and the *l* first."
     15:37 a loud cry, Jesus breathed his *l*.
Jn   6:40 and I will raise him up at the *l*
             day."
     15:16 and bear fruit—fruit that will *l*.
Ac   2:17 " 'In the *l* days, God says,
Ro   1:17 is by faith from first to *l*,
1Co 15:26 enemy to be destroyed is death.
     15:52 of an eye, at the *l* trumpet.
2Ti   3: 1 will be terrible times in the *l* days.
2Pe   3: 3 in the *l* days scoffers will come,
Jude   :18 "In the *l* times there will be
Rev   1:17 I am the First and the *L*.
     22:13 the First and the *L*, the Beginning

LASTING (LAST)
Ex   12:14 to the LORD—a *l* ordinance.
Lev 24: 8 of the Israelites, as a *l* covenant.
Nu   25:13 have a covenant of a *l* priesthood,
Heb 10:34 had better and *l* possessions.

LASTS (LAST)
Ps   30: 5 For his anger *l* only a moment,
2Co   3:11 greater is the glory of that
             which *l*!

LATTER (LAST)
Job 42:12 The LORD blessed the *l* part
Mt   23:23 You should have practiced the *l*,
Php   1:16 *l* do so in love, knowing that I am

LAUGH (LAUGHED LAUGHS LAUGHTER)
Ps   59: 8 But you, O LORD, *l* at them;
Pr   31:25 she can *l* at the days to come.
Ecc   3: 4 a time to weep and a time to *l*,
Lk   6:21 for you will *l*
      6:25 Woe to you who *l* now,

LAUGHED (LAUGH)
Ge   17:17 Abraham fell facedown; he *l*

Ge 18:12 So Sarah *l* to herself as she
         thought,

LAUGHS (LAUGH)
Ps   2: 4 The One enthroned in heaven *l;*
   37:13 but the Lord *l* at the wicked,

LAUGHTER (LAUGH)
Ge 21: 6 Sarah said, "God has brought
         me *l,*
Ps 126: 2 Our mouths were filled with *l,*
Pr 14:13 Even in their *l* may ache,
Jas   4: 9 Change your *l* to mourning

LAVISHED
Eph 1: 8 of God's grace that he *l* on us
1Jn 3: 1 great is the love the Father has *l*

LAW (LAWFUL LAWGIVER LAWS)
Lev 24:22 are to have the same *l* for the
         alien
Nu   6:13 " 'Now this is the *l* for the Nazirite
Dt   1: 5 Moses began to expound this *l,*
    6:25 to obey all this *l* before the Lord
   27:26 of this *l* by carrying them out."
   31:11 you shall read this *l* before them
   31:26 "Take this Book of the *L*
Jos 1: 7 to obey all the *l* my servant Moses
    1: 8 of the *L* depart from your mouth;
   22: 5 and the *l* that Moses the servant
2Ki 22: 8 of the *L* in the temple of the Lord
2Ch 6:16 walk before me according to my *l,*
   17: 9 the Book of the *L* of the Lord;
   34:14 of the *L* of the Lord that had
Ezr 7: 6 versed in the *L* of Moses,
Ne   8: 2 Ezra the priest brought the *L*
    8: 8 from the Book of the *L* of God,
Ps   1: 2 and on his *l* he meditates day
   19: 7 The *l* of the Lord is perfect,
   37:31 The *l* of his God is in his heart;
   40: 8 your *l* is within my heart."
  119:18 wonderful things in your *l.*
  119:70 but I delight in your *l.*
  119:72 *l* from your mouth is more
         precious
  119:77 for your *l* is my delight.
  119:97 Oh, how I love your *l!*
  119:163 but I love your *l,*
  119:165 peace have they who love your *l,*
Pr 28: 9 If anyone turns a deaf ear to the *l,*
   29:18 but blessed is he who keeps the *l.*
Isa   2: 3 The *l* will go out from Zion,
   8:20 To the *l* and to the testimony!
   42:21 to make his *l* great and glorious.
Jer   2: 8 deal with the *l* did not know me;
    8: 8 for we have the *l* of the Lord,"
   31:33 "I will put my *l* in their minds
Mic 4: 2 The *l* will go out from Zion,
Hab 1: 7 they are a *l* to themselves
Zec 7:12 as flint and would not listen to
         the *l*
Mt   5:17 that I have come to abolish the *L*
   7:12 sums up the *L* and the Prophets.
   22:36 greatest commandment in the *L?*"
   22:40 All the *L* and the Prophets hang
   23:23 more important matters of the *l—*
Lk 11:52 "Woe to you experts in the *l,*
   16:17 stroke of a pen to drop out of
         the *L.*
   24:44 me in the *L* of Moses,
Jn   1:17 For the *l* was given through
         Moses;
Ac 13:39 justified from by the *l* of Moses.
Ro   2:12 All who sin apart from the *l* will
    2:15 of the *l* are written on their
         hearts,
    2:20 you have in the *l* the embodiment
    2:25 value if you observe the *l,*
    3:19 we know that whatever the *l* says,
    3:20 in his sight by observing the *l;*
    3:21 apart from *l,* has been made
         known
    3:28 by faith apart from observing
         the *l.*
    3:31 Not at all! Rather, we uphold
         the *l.*
    4:13 It was not through *l* that Abraham
    4:15 worthless, because *l* brings wrath.
    4:16 not only to those who are of the *l*
    5:13 for before the *l* was given,
    5:20 *l* was added so that the trespass
    6:14 because you are not under *l,*

Ro   6:15 we are not under *l* but under
         grace?
    7: 1 that the *l* has authority
    7: 4 also died to the *l* through the
         body
    7: 5 aroused by the *l* were at work
    7: 6 released from the *l* so that we
         serve
    7: 7 then? Is the *l* sin? Certainly not!
    7: 8 For apart from *l,* sin is dead.
   7:12 *l* is holy, and the commandment is
   7:14 We know that the *l* is spiritual;
   7:22 my inner being I delight in God's *l;*
   7:25 in my mind am a slave to God's *l,*
    8: 2 because through Christ Jesus the *l*
    8: 3 For what the *l* was powerless to
         do
    8: 4 of the *l* might be fully met in us,
    8: 7 It does not submit to God's *l,*
    9: 4 covenants, the receiving of the *l,*
    9:31 who pursued a *l* of righteousness,
   10: 4 Christ is the end of the *l*
   13: 8 his fellowman has fulfilled the *l.*
   13:10 love is the fulfillment of the *l.*
1Co 6: 6 goes to *l* against another—
    9: 9 For it is written in the *L* of Moses:
   9:20 the *l* I became like one under the *l*
   9:21 I became like one not having the *l*
   15:56 and the power of sin is the *l.*
Gal 2:16 justified by observing the *l,*
    2:19 For through the *l* I died to the *l*
    3: 2 the Spirit by observing the *l,*
    3: 5 you because you observe the *l,*
    3:10 on observing the *l* are under a
         curse
    3:11 justified before God by the *l,*
    3:13 curse of the *l* by becoming a curse
    3:17 The *l,* introduced 430 years later,
    3:19 then, was the purpose of the *l?*
    3:21 Is the *l,* therefore, opposed
    3:23 we were held prisoners by the *l,*
    3:24 So the *l* was put in charge to lead
         us
    4:21 you who want to be under the *l,*
    5: 3 obligated to obey the whole *l.*
    5: 4 justified by *l* have been alienated
    5:14 The entire *l* is summed up
    5:18 by the Spirit, you are not under *l.*
    6: 2 and in this way you will fulfill the *l*
Eph 2:15 flesh the *l* with its
         commandments
Php 3: 9 of my own that comes from the *l,*
1Ti 1: 8 We know that the *l* is good
Heb 7:12 there must also be a change of
         the *l.*
    7:19 (for the *l* made nothing perfect),
   10: 1 The *l* is only a shadow
Jas   1:25 intently into the perfect *l* that
         gives
    2: 8 If you really keep the royal *l* found
   2:10 For whoever keeps the whole *l*
   4:11 or judges him speaks against the *l*
1Jn 3: 4 Everyone who sins breaks the *l;*

LAWFUL (LAW)
Mt 12:12 Therefore it is *l* to do good

LAWGIVER* (LAW)
Isa 33:22 the Lord is our *l*
Jas   4:12 There is only one *L* and Judge,

LAWLESS (LAWLESSNESS)
2Th 2: 8 And then the *l* one will be
         revealed
Heb 10:17 "Their sins and *l* acts

LAWLESSNESS* (LAWLESS)
2Th 2: 3 and the man of *l* is revealed,
    2: 7 power of *l* is already at work;
1Jn 3: 4 sins breaks the law; in fact, sin is *l.*

LAWS (LAW)
Ex 21: 1 "These are the *l* you are to set
Lev 25:18 and be careful to obey my *l,*
Dt   4: 1 and I *l* am about to teach you.
   30:16 decrees and *l;* then you will live
Ps 119:30 I have set my heart on your *l.*
  119:43 for I have put my hope in your *l.*
  119:120 I stand in awe of your *l.*
  119:164 for your righteous *l.*
  119:175 and may your *l* sustain me.
Eze 36:27 and be careful to keep my *l.*
Heb 8:10 I will put my *l* in their minds
   10:16 I will put my *l* in their hearts,

LAWSUITS
Hos 10: 4 therefore *l* spring up
1Co 6: 7 The very fact that you have *l*

LAY (LAID LAYING LAYS)
Ex 29:10 and his sons shall *l* their hands
Lev 1: 4 He is to *l* his hand on the head
    4:15 the community are to *l* their
         hands
Nu   8:10 the Israelites are to *l* their hands
   27:18 whom is the spirit, and *l* your
         hand
1Sa 26: 9 Who can *l* a hand on the Lord's
Job 1:12 on the man himself do not *l* a
         finger
   22:22 and *l* up his words in your heart.
Ecc 10: 4 calmness can *l* great errors to rest.
Isa 28:16 "See, I *l* a stone in Zion,
Mt   8:20 of Man has no place to *l* his
         head."
   28: 6 Come and see the place where
         he *l.*
Mk 6: 5 *l* his hands on a few sick people
Lk   9:58 of Man has no place to *l* his
         head."
Jn 10:15 and I *l* down my life for the sheep.
   10:18 but I *l* it down of my own accord.
   15:13 that he *l* down his life
Ac   8:19 on whom I *l* my hands may
         receive
Ro   9:33 I *l* in Zion a stone that causes men
1Co 3:11 no one can *l* any foundation other
1Pe 2: 6 "See, I *l* a stone in Zion,
1Jn 3:16 And we ought to *l* down our lives
Rev 4:10 They *l* their crowns

LAYING (LAY)
Lk   4:40 and *l* his hands on each one,
Ac   8:18 at the *l* on of the apostles' hands,
1Ti 5:22 Do not be hasty in the *l* on of
         hands
2Ti 1: 6 is in you through the *l*
Heb 6: 1 not *l* again the foundation
    6: 2 instruction about baptisms, the *l*

LAYS (LAY)
Jn 10:11 The good shepherd *l* down his life

LAZARUS
   1. Poor man in Jesus' parable (Lk 16:19–31).
   2. Brother of Mary and Martha whom Jesus
raised from the dead (Jn 11:1–12:19).

LAZINESS* (LAZY)
Pr 12:24 but *l* ends in slave labor.
   19:15 *L* brings on deep sleep,

LAZY* (LAZINESS)
Ex   5: 8 They are *l;* that is why they are
    5:17 Pharaoh said, "*L,* that's what you
    5:17 "Lazy, that's what you are—*l!*
Pr 10: 4 *L* hands make a man poor,
   12:27 The *l* man does not roast his
         game,
   26:15 he is too *l* to bring it back
Ecc 10:18 If a man is *l,* the rafters sag;
Mt 25:26 replied, 'You wicked, *l* servant!
Tit 1:12 liars, evil brutes, *l* gluttons."
Heb 6:12 We do not want you to become *l,*

LEAD (LEADER LEADERS LEADERSHIP LEADS LED)
Ex 15:13 "In your unfailing love you will *l*
Nu 14: 8 with us, he will *l* us into that land,
Dt 31: 2 and I am no longer able to *l* you.
Jos 1: 6 because you will *l* these people
1Sa 8: 5 now appoint a king to *l* us,
2Ch 1:10 knowledge, that I may *l* this
         people
Ps 27:11 *l* me in a straight path
   61: 2 *l* me to the rock that is higher
  139:24 and *l* me in the way everlasting.
  143:10 *l* me on level ground.
Pr   4:11 and *l* you along straight paths.
Ecc 5: 6 Do not let your mouth *l* you
Isa 11: 6 and a little child will *l* them.
   49:10 and *l* them beside springs of
         water.
Da 12: 3 those who *l* many to
         righteousness,
Mt   6:13 And *l* us not into temptation,
Lk 11: 4 And *l* us not into temptation.' "
Gal 3:24 So the law was put in charge to *l*
         us
1Th 4:11 it your ambition to *l* a quiet life,
1Jn 3: 7 do not let anyone *l* you astray.

Rev   7: 17   he will / them to springs

LEADER (LEAD)
1Sa   7:   6   Samuel was / of Israel at Mizpah.
     10:   1   Has not the LORD anointed you /
     12:   2   I have been your / from my youth
     13: 14   and appointed him / of his people,

LEADERS (LEAD)
Heb 13:   7   Remember your /, who spoke
     13: 17   Obey your / and submit

LEADERSHIP* (LEAD)
Nu   33:   1   by divisions under the / of Moses
Ps 109:   8   may another take his place of /.
Ac   1: 20   " 'May another take his place of /.'
Ro   12:   8   if it is /, let him govern diligently;

LEADS (LEAD)
Dt   27: 18   is the man who / the blind astray
Ps   23:   2   he / me beside quiet waters,
     37:   8   do not fret—it / only to evil.
     68:   6   he / forth the prisoners
Pr   2: 18   For her house / down to death
     10: 17   ignores correction / others astray.
     14: 23   but mere talk / only to poverty.
     16: 25   but in the end it / to death.
     19: 23   The fear of the LORD / to life:
     20:   7   righteous man / a blameless life;
     21:   5   as surely as haste / to poverty.
Isa   40: 11   he gently / those that have young.
Mt   7: 13   and broad is the road that /
     12: 20   till he / justice to victory.
     15: 14   If a blind man / a blind man,
Jn   10:   3   sheep by name and / them out.
Ro   6: 16   which / to death, or to obedience,
     6: 22   the benefit you reap / to holiness,
     14: 19   effort to do what / to peace
2Co   2: 14   always / us in triumphal
          procession
     7: 10   sorrow brings repentance that /
Tit   1:   1   of the truth that / to godliness—

LEAH
     Wife of Jacob (Ge 29:16–30); bore six sons and one daughter (Ge 29:31–30:21; 34:1; 35:23).

LEAN (LEANED)
Pr   3:   5   / not on your own understanding;

LEANED (LEAN)
Ge   47: 31   as he / on the top of his staff.
Jn   21: 20   (This was the one who had / back
Heb 11: 21   as he / on the top of his staff.

LEAP (LEAPED LEAPS)
Isa   35:   6   Then will the lame / like a deer,
Mal   4:   2   / like calves released from the
          stall.
Lk   6: 23   "Rejoice in that day and / for joy,

LEAPED (LEAP)
Lk   1: 41   heard Mary's greeting, the baby /

LEAPS (LEAP)
Ps   28:   7   My heart / for joy

LEARN (LEARNED LEARNING LEARNS)
Dt   4: 10   so that they may / to revere me
     5:   1   L them and be sure to follow
          them.
     31: 12   and / to fear the LORD your God
Ps 119:   7   as I / your righteous laws.
Isa   1: 17   / to do right!
     26:   9   of the world / righteousness.
Mt   11: 29   yoke upon you and / from me,
Jn   14: 31   world must / that I love the Father
1Th   4:   1   that each of you should /
1Ti   2: 11   A woman should / in quietness
     5:   4   these should / first of all

LEARNED (LEARN)
Ps 119:152   Long ago I / from your statutes
Mt   11: 25   things from the wise and /,
Php   4:   9   Whatever you have / or received
     4: 11   for I have / to be content
          whatever
2Ti   3: 14   continue in what you have /
Heb   5:   8   he / obedience from what he

LEARNING (LEARN)
Pr   1:   5   let the wise listen and add to
          their /,
     9:   9   man and he will add to his /.
Isa   44: 25   who overthrows the / of the wise
Jn   7: 15   "How did this man get such /
2Ti   3:   7   always / but never able

LEARNS (LEARN)
Jn   6: 45   and / from him comes to me.

LEATHER
2Ki   1:   8   and with a / belt around his
          waist."
Mt   3:   4   and he had a / belt around his
          waist

LEAVES
Ge   3:   7   so they sewed fig / together
Eze   47: 12   for food and their / for healing."
Rev   22:   2   the / of the tree are for the
          healing

LEBANON
Dt   11: 24   from the desert to L,
1Ki   4: 33   from the cedar of L

LED (LEAD)
Ex   3:   1   and he / the flock to the far side
Dt   8:   2   the LORD your God / you all
1Ki   11:   3   and his wives / him astray.
2Ch   26: 16   his pride / to his downfall.
Ne   13: 26   he was / into sin by foreign
          women.
Ps   68: 18   you / captives in your train;
     78: 52   he / them like sheep
Pr   7: 21   persuasive words she / him astray;
     20:   1   whoever is / astray
Isa   53:   7   he was / like a lamb to the
          slaughter
Jer   11: 19   I had been like a gentle lamb /
Am   2: 10   and I / you forty years in the
          desert
Mt   4:   1   Then Jesus was / by the Spirit
     27: 31   they / him away to crucify him.
Lk   4:   1   was / by the Spirit in the desert,
Ac   8: 32   "He was / like a sheep
Ro   8: 14   those who are / by the Spirit
2Co   7:   9   your sorrow / you to repentance.
Gal   5: 18   But if you are / by the Spirit,
Eph   4:   8   he / captives in his train

LEEKS*
Nu   11:   5   melons, /, onions and garlic.

LEFT
Dt   28: 14   or to the /, following other gods
Jos   1:   7   turn from it to the right or to the /,
     23:   6   aside to the right or to the /.
2Ki   22:   2   aside to the right or to the /.
Pr   4: 27   Do not swerve to the right or
          the /;
Isa   30: 21   turn to the right or to the /,
Mt   6:   3   do not let your / hand know what
     25: 33   on his right and the goats on his /.

LEGALISTIC*
Php   3:   6   as for / righteousness, faultless.

LEGION
Mk   5:   9   "My name is L," he replied,

LEND (LENDER LENDS MONEYLENDER)
Lev   25: 37   You must not / him money
Dt   15:   8   freely / him whatever he needs.
Ps   37: 26   are always generous and / freely;
Eze   18:   8   He does not / at usury
Lk   6: 34   if you / to those from whom you

LENDER (LEND)
Pr   22:   7   and the borrower is servant to
          the /.
Isa   24:   2   for borrower as for /,

LENDS (LEND)
Ps   15:   5   who / his money without usury
   112:   5   to him who is generous and /
          freely,
Pr   19: 17   to the poor / to the LORD,

LENGTH (LONG)
Ps   90: 10   The / of our days is seventy
          years—
Pr   10: 27   The fear of the LORD adds / to life

LENGTHY* (LONG)
Mk   12: 40   and for a show make / prayers.
Lk   20: 47   and for a show make / prayers.

LEOPARD
Isa   11:   6   the / will lie down with the goat,
Da   7:   6   beast, one that looked like a /
Rev   13:   2   The beast I saw resembled a /,

LEPROSY (LEPROUS)
Nu   12: 10   toward her and saw that she
          had /;
2Ki   5:   1   was a valiant soldier, but he had /.
     7:   3   men with / at the entrance

2Ch   26: 21   King Uzziah had /
Mt   11:   5   those who have / are cured,
Lk   17: 12   ten men who had / met him.

LEPROUS (LEPROSY)
Ex   4:   6   and when he took it out, it was /,

LETTER (LETTERS)
Mt   5: 18   not the smallest /, not the least
2Co   3:   2   You yourselves are our /, written
     3:   6   for the / kills, but the Spirit gives
2Th   3: 14   not obey our instruction in this /,

LETTERS (LETTER)
2Co   3:   7   which was engraved in / on stone,
     10: 10   "His / are weighty and forceful,
2Pe   3: 16   His / contain some things that are

LEVEL
Ps 143: 10   lead me on / ground.
Pr   4: 26   Make / paths for your feet
Isa   26:   7   The path of the righteous is /;
     40:   4   the rough ground shall become /,
Jer   31:   9   on a / path where they will not
Heb 12: 13   "Make / paths for your feet,"

LEVI (LEVITE LEVITES LEVITICAL)
     1. Son of Jacob by Leah (Ge 29:34; 46:11; 1Ch 2:1). With Simeon avenged rape of Dinah (Ge 34). Tribe of blessed (Ge 49:5–7; Dt 33:8–11), chosen as priests (Nu 3–4), numbered (Nu 3:39; 26:62), allotted cities, but not land (Nu 18; 35; Dt 10:9; Jos 13:14; 21), land (Eze 48:8–22), 12,000 from (Rev 7:7).
     2. See MATTHEW.

LEVIATHAN
Job   41:   1   pull in the / with a fishhook
Ps   74: 14   you who crushed the heads of L
Isa   27:   1   L the gliding serpent,

LEVITE (LEVI)
Dt   26: 12   you shall give it to the L, the alien,
Jdg   19:   1   a L who lived in a remote area

LEVITES (LEVI)
Nu   1: 53   The L are to be responsible
     3: 12   "I have taken the L
     8:   6   "Take the L from among the other
     18: 21   I give to the L all the tithes in
          Israel
     35:   7   must give the L forty-eight towns,
2Ch   31:   2   assigned the priests and L
Mal   3:   3   he will purify the L and refine
          them

LEVITICAL (LEVI)
Heb   7: 11   attained through the L priesthood

LEWDNESS
Mk   7: 22   malice, deceit, /, envy, slander,

LIAR* (LIE)
Dt   19: 18   and if the witness proves to be a /,
Job   34:   6   I am considered a /;
Pr   17:   4   / pays attention to a malicious
     19: 22   better to be poor than a /.
     30:   6   will rebuke you and prove you a /.
Mic   2: 11   If a / and deceiver comes and says,
Jn   8: 44   for he is a / and the father of lies.
     8: 55   I did not, I would be a / like you,
Ro   3:   4   Let God be true, and every man
          a /.
1Jn   1: 10   we make him out to be a /
     2:   4   not do what he commands is a /,
     2: 22   Who is the /? It is the man who
     4: 20   yet hates his brother, he is a /.
     5: 10   God has made him out to be a /

LIARS* (LIE)
Ps   63: 11   the mouths of / will be silenced.
   116: 11   "All men are /."
Isa   57:   4   the offspring of /?
Mic   6: 12   her people are /
1Ti   1: 10   for slave traders and / and
          perjurers
     4:   2   come through hypocritical /,
Tit   1: 12   "Cretans are always /, evil brutes,
Rev   3:   9   though they are not, but are /—
     21:   8   magic arts, the idolaters and
          all /—

LIBERATED*
Ro   8: 21   that the creation itself will be /

LICENSE
Jude   :   4   of our God into a / for immorality

LICK
Ps   72:   9   and his enemies will / the dust.
Isa   49: 23   they will / the dust at your feet.

Mic 7:17 They will / dust like a snake,
LIE (LIAR LIARS LIED LIES LYING)
Lev 18:22 " 'Do not / with a man
19:11 " 'Do not /.
Nu 23:19 God is not a man, that he
should /,
Dt 6: 7 when you / down and when you
get
25: 2 the judge shall make him / down
1Sa 15:29 the Glory of Israel does not /
Ps 4: 8 I will / down and sleep in peace,
23: 2 me / down in green pastures,
89:35 and I will not / to David—
Pr 3:24 when you / down, you will not be
Isa 11: 6 leopard will / down with the goat,
28:15 for we have made a / our refuge
Jer 9: 5 They have taught their tongues
to /
23:14 They commit adultery and live a /.
Eze 13: 6 are false and their divinations a /.
34:14 they will / down in good grazing
Ro 1:25 exchanged the truth of God for
a /,
Col 3: 9 Do not / to each other,
2Th 2:11 so that they will believe the /
Tit 1: 2 which God, who does not /,
Heb 6:18 which it is impossible for God to /,
1Jn 2:21 because no / comes from the
truth.
Rev 14: 5 No / was found in their mouths;
LIED (LIE)
Ac 5: 4 You have not / to men but to
God."
LIES (LIE)
Lev 6: 3 finds lost property and / about it,
Ps 5: 6 You destroy those who tell /;
10: 7 His mouth is full of curses and /
12: 2 Everyone / to his neighbor;
34:13 and your lips from speaking /.
58: 3 they are wayward and speak /.
144: 8 whose mouths are full of /.
Pr 6:19 a false witness who pours out /
12:17 but a false witness tells /.
19: 5 he who pours out / will not go
free.
19: 9 and he who pours out / will
perish.
29:12 If a ruler listens to /,
30: 8 Keep falsehood and / far from me;
Isa 59: 3 Your lips have spoken /,
Jer 5:31 The prophets prophesy /,
9: 3 like a bow, to shoot /;
14:14 "The prophets are prophesying /
Hos 11:12 Ephraim has surrounded me
with /,
Jn 8:44 for he is a liar and the father of /.
LIFE (LIVE)
Ge 1:30 everything that has the breath of /
2: 7 into his nostrils the breath of /,
2: 9 of the garden were the tree of /
6:17 to destroy all / under the heavens,
9: 5 for the / of his fellow man.
9:11 Never again will all / be cut
Ex 21: 6 Then he will be his servant for /.
21:23 you are to take / for /, eye for eye,
23:26 I will give you a full / span.
Lev 17:14 the / of every creature is its blood.
24:17 " 'If anyone takes the /
24:18 must make restitution—/ for /.
Nu 35:31 a ransom for the / of a murderer,
Dt 4:42 one of these cities and save his /.
12:23 because the blood is the /,
19:21 Show no pity: / for /, eye for eye,
30:15 I set before you today /
30:19 Now choose /, so that you
30:20 For the LORD is your /,
32:39 I put to death and I bring to /,
32:47 words for you—they are your /.
1Sa 19: 5 He took his / in his hands
Job 2: 6 hands; but you must spare his /."
33: 4 of the Almighty gives me /.
33:30 that the light of / may shine on
him.
Ps 16:11 known to me the path of /;
17:14 this world whose reward is in
this /.
23: 6 all the days of my /,
27: 1 LORD is the stronghold of my /—
34:12 Whoever of you loves /

Ps 36: 9 For with you is the fountain of /;
39: 4 let me know how fleeting is my /.
41: 2 will protect him and preserve
his /;
49: 7 No man can redeem the /
49: 8 the ransom for a / is costly,
63: 3 Because your love is better than /,
69:28 they be blotted out of the book
of /
91:16 With long / will I satisfy him
104:33 I will sing to the LORD all my /;
119:25 preserve my / according to your
word
Pr 1: 3 a disciplined and prudent /,
3: 2 will prolong your / many years
3:18 of / to those who embrace her;
4:23 for it is the wellspring of /.
6:23 are the way to /,
6:26 adulteress preys upon your very /.
7:23 little knowing it will cost him his /.
8:35 For whoever finds me finds /
10:11 of the righteous is a fountain of /,
10:27 of the LORD adds length to /,
11:30 of the righteous is a tree of /,
13: 3 He who guards his lips guards
his /,
13:12 but a longing fulfilled is a tree of /.
13:14 of the wise is a fountain of /,
14:27 of the LORD is a fountain of /,
15: 4 that brings healing is a tree of /
16:22 Understanding is a fountain of /
19: 3 A man's own folly ruins his /,
19:23 The fear of the LORD leads to /:
21:21 finds /, prosperity and honor.
Isa 53:10 LORD makes his / a guilt offering,
53:11 he will see the light .of /
53:12 he poured out his / unto death,
Jer 10:23 that a man's / is not his own;
La 3:58 you redeemed my /.
Eze 18:27 and right, he will save his /.
37: 5 enter you, and you will come to /.
Da 12: 2 some to everlasting /, others
Jnh 2: 6 you brought my / up from the pit,
Mal 2: 5 a covenant of / and peace,
Mt 6:25 Is not / more important than food,
7:14 and narrow the road that leads
to /,
10:39 Whoever finds his / will lose it,
16:21 and on the third day be raised
to /.
16:25 wants to save his / will lose it,
18: 8 better for you to enter / maimed
19:16 thing must I do to get eternal /?"
19:29 as much and will inherit eternal /.
20:28 to give his / as a ransom for
many."
25:46 but the righteous to eternal /."
Mk 8:35 but whoever loses his / for me
9:43 better for you to enter / maimed
10:17 "what must I do to inherit
eternal /
10:30 and in the age to come, eternal /.
10:45 to give his / as a ransom for
many."
Lk 6: 9 to save / or to destroy it?"
9:22 and on the third day be raised
to /."
9:24 wants to save his / will lose it,
12:15 a man's / does not consist
12:22 do not worry about your /,
12:25 can add a single hour to his /?
14:26 even his own /— he cannot be my
17:33 tries to keep his / will lose it,
21:19 standing firm you will gain /.
Jn 1: 4 In him was /, and that /was
3:15 believes in him may have
eternal /.
3:36 believes in the Son has eternal /,
4:14 of water welling up to eternal /."
5:21 raises the dead and gives them /,
5:24 him who sent me has eternal /
5:26 For as the Father has / in himself,
5:39 that by them you possess
eternal /.
5:40 refuse to come to me to have /.
6:27 for food that endures to eternal /,
6:33 down from heaven and gives /
6:35 Jesus declared, "I am the bread
of /
6:40 believes in him shall have
eternal /,

Jn 6:47 he who believes has everlasting /.
6:48 I am the bread of /.
6:51 give for the / of the world."
6:53 and drink his blood, you have no /
6:63 The Spirit gives /; the flesh counts
6:68 You have the words of eternal /.
8:12 but will have the light of /."
10:10 I have come that they may have /,
10:15 and I lay down my / for the sheep.
10:17 loves me is that I lay down my /—
10:28 I give them eternal /, and they
shall
11:25 "I am the resurrection and the /.
12:25 The man who loves his / will lose
it,
12:50 his command leads to eternal /.
13:37 I will lay down my / for you."
14: 6 am the way and the truth and
the /.
15:13 lay down his / for his friends.
17: 2 people that he might give
eternal /
17: 3 Now this is eternal /: that they
may
20:31 that by believing you may have /
Ac 2:32 God has raised this Jesus to /,
3:15 You killed the author of /,
11:18 the Gentiles repentance unto /."
13:48 appointed for eternal / believed.
Ro 2: 7 immortality, he will give eternal /.
4:25 was raised to / for our
justification.
5:10 shall we be saved through his /!
5:18 was justification that brings /
5:21 righteousness to bring eternal /
6: 4 the Father, we too may live a
new /.
6:13 have been brought from death
to /;
6:22 holiness, and the result is
eternal /.
6:23 but the gift of God is eternal /
8: 6 mind controlled by the Spirit is /
8:11 also give / to your mortal bodies
8:38 convinced that neither death
nor /,
1Co 15:19 If only for this / we have hope
15:36 What you sow does not come to /
2Co 2:16 to the other, the fragrance of /.
3: 6 letter kills, but the Spirit gives /.
4:10 so that the / of Jesus may
5: 4 is mortal may be swallowed up
by /.
Gal 2:20 The / I live in the body, I live
3:21 had been given that could
impart /,
6: 8 from the Spirit will reap eternal /.
Eph 4: 1 I urge you to live a / worthy
Php 2:16 as you hold out the word of /—
4: 3 whose names are in the book of /.
Col 1:10 order that you may live a / worthy
3: 3 your / is now hidden with Christ
1Th 4:12 so that your daily / may win
1Ti 1:16 on him and receive eternal /.
4: 8 for both the present / and the /
4:12 in /, in love, in faith and in purity.
4:16 Watch your / and doctrine closely.
6:12 Take hold of the eternal /
6:19 hold of the / that is truly /.
2Ti 1: 9 saved us and called us to a
holy /—
1:10 destroyed death and has brought /
3:12 to live a godly / in Christ Jesus will
Tit 1: 2 resting on the hope of eternal /,
3: 7 heirs having the hope of eternal /.
Heb 7:16 of the power of an
indestructible /.
Jas 1:12 crown of / that God has promised
3:13 Let him show it by his good /,
1Pe 3: 7 with you of the gracious gift of /,
3:10 "Whoever would love /
4: 2 rest of his earthly / for evil human
2Pe 1: 3 given us everything we need for /
1Jn 1: 1 proclaim concerning the Word
of /.
2:25 he promised us—even eternal /.
3:14 we have passed from death to /,
3:16 Jesus Christ laid down his / for us.
5:11 has given us eternal /, and this / is
5:20 He is the true God and eternal /.
Jude : 21 Christ to bring you to eternal /.

Rev　2:　7　the right to eat from the tree of *l*.
　　2:　8　who died and came to / again.
　　2:10　and I will give you the crown of *l*.
　　3:　5　name from the book of *l*.
　　13:　8　written in the book of / belonging
　　17:　8　in the book of / from the creation
　　20:12　was opened, which is the book of *l*.
　　20:15　not found written in the book of *l*.
　　21:　6　from the spring of the water of *l*.
　　21:27　written in the Lamb's book of *l*.
　　22:　1　me the river of the water of *l*,
　　22:　2　side of the river stood the tree of *l*.
　　22:14　may have the right to the tree of *l*
　　22:17　take the free gift of the water of *l*.
　　22:19　from him his share in the tree of *l*

LIFE-GIVING (GIVE)
Pr　15:31　He who listens to a / rebuke
1Co　15:45　being"; the last Adam, a / spirit.

LIFETIME (LIVE)
Ps　30:　5　but his favor lasts a *l*;
Lk　16:25　in your / you received your good

LIFT (LIFTED LIFTING LIFTS)
Ps　3:　3　you bestow glory on me and *l*
　　28:　2　as I / up my hands
　　63:　4　in your name I will / up my hands.
　　91:12　they will / you up in their hands,
　　121:　1　I / up my eyes to the hills—
　　123:　1　I / up my eyes to you,
　　134:　2　*L* up your hands in the sanctuary
　　143:　8　for to you I / up my soul.
Isa　40:　9　*l* up your voice with a shout,
La　2:19　*L* up your hands to him
　　3:41　Let us / up our hearts and our
Mt　4:　6　they will / you up in their hands,
Lk　21:28　stand up and / up your heads,
1Ti　2:　8　everywhere to / up holy hands
Jas　4:10　the Lord, and he will / you up.
1Pe　5:　6　that he may / you up in due time.

LIFTED (LIFT)
Ne　8:　6　and all the people / their hands
Ps　24:　7　be / up, you ancient doors,
　　40:　2　He / me out of the slimy pit,
　　41:　9　has / up his heel against me.
Isa　52:13　/ up and highly exalted.
　　63:　9　he / them up and carried them
Jn　3:14　Moses / up the snake in the desert,
　　8:28　"When you have / up the Son
　　12:32　when I am / up from the earth,
　　12:34　'The Son of Man must be / up'?
　　13:18　shares my bread has / up his heel

LIFTING (LIFT)
Ps　141:　2　may the / up of my hands be like

LIFTS (LIFT)
Ps　113:　7　and / the needy from the ash heap;

LIGAMENT* (LIGAMENTS)
Eph　4:16　held together by every supporting /

LIGAMENTS* (LIGAMENT)
Col　2:19　held together by its / and sinews,

LIGHT (ENLIGHTENED LIGHTS)
Ge　1:　3　"Let there be *l*," and there was *l*.
Ex　13:21　in a pillar of fire to give them *l*,
　　25:37　it so that they / the space in front
2Sa　22:29　Lord turns my darkness into *l*.
Job　38:19　"What is the way to the abode of *l*?
Ps　4:　6　Let the / of your face shine upon us
　　18:28　my God turns my darkness into *l*.
　　19:　8　giving / to the eyes.
　　27:　1　Lord is my / and my salvation—
　　36:　9　in your / we see *l*.
　　56:13　God in the / of life.
　　76:　4　You are resplendent with *l*,
　　89:15　who walk in the / of your presence,
　　104:　2　He wraps himself in *l*
　　119:105　and a / for my path.
　　119:130　The unfolding of your words gives *l*;
　　139:12　for darkness is as / to you.
Pr　4:18　till the full / of day.
Isa　2:　5　let us walk in the / of the Lord.
　　9:　2　have seen a great *l*;

Isa　42:　6　and a / for the Gentiles,
　　45:　7　I form the / and create darkness,
　　49:　6　also make you a / for the Gentiles,
　　53:11　he will see the *l*, of life,
　　60:　1　"Arise, shine, for your / has come,
　　60:19　Lord will be your everlasting *l*,
Eze　1:27　and brilliant / surrounded him.
Mic　7:　8　the Lord will be my *l*.
Mt　4:16　have seen a great *l*;
　　5:14　"You are the / of the world.
　　5:15　it gives / to everyone in the house.
　　5:16　let your / shine before men,
　　6:22　your whole body will be full of *l*.
　　11:30　yoke is easy and my burden is *l*."
　　17:　2　his clothes became as white as the *l*.
　　24:29　and the moon will not give its *l*;
Mk　13:24　and the moon will not give its *l*;
Lk　2:32　a / for revelation to the Gentiles
　　8:16　those who come in can see the *l*.
　　11:33　those who come in may see the *l*.
Jn　1:　4　and that life was the / of men.
　　1:　5　The / shines in the darkness,
　　1:　7　witness to testify concerning that *l*.
　　1:　9　The true / that gives *l*
　　3:19　but men loved darkness instead of *l*.
　　3:20　Everyone who does evil hates the *l*,
　　8:12　he said, "I am the / of the world.
　　9:　5　in the world, I am the / of the world
　　12:35　Walk while you have the *l*,
　　12:46　I have come into the world as a *l*,
Ac　13:47　" 'I have made you a *l*'
Ro　13:12　darkness and put on the armor of *l*.
2Co　4:　6　made his / shine in our hearts
　　6:14　Or what fellowship can / have
　　11:14　masquerades as an angel of *l*.
Eph　5:　8　but now you are / in the Lord.
1Th　5:　5　You are all sons of the *l*
1Ti　6:16　and who lives in unapproachable *l*,
1Pe　2:　9　of darkness into his wonderful *l*.
2Pe　1:19　as to a / shining in a dark place,
1Jn　1:　5　God is *l*; in him there is no
　　1:　7　But if we walk in the *l*,
　　2:　9　Anyone who claims to be in the *l*
Rev　21:23　for the glory of God gives it *l*,
　　22:　5　for the Lord God will give them *l*.

LIGHTNING
Ex　9:23　and / flashed down to the ground.
　　20:18　and / and heard the trumpet
Ps　18:12　with hailstones and bolts of *l*.
Eze　1:13　it was bright, and / flashed out of it.
Da　10:　6　his face like *l*, his eyes like flaming
Mt　24:27　For as the / that comes from the east
　　28:　3　His appearance was like *l*,
Lk　10:18　"I saw Satan fall like / from heaven.
Rev　4:　5　From the throne came flashes of *l*,

LIGHTS (LIGHT)
Ge　1:14　"Let there be / in the expanse
Lk　8:16　No one / a lamp and hides it in a jar

LIKE-MINDED* (MIND)
Php　2:　2　make my joy complete by being *l*,

LIKENESS
Ge　1:26　man in our image, in our *l*,
Ps　17:15　I will be satisfied with seeing your *l*
Isa　52:14　his form marred beyond human *l*—
Ro　8:　3　Son in the / of sinful man
　　8:29　to be conformed to the / of his Son,
2Co　3:18　his / with ever-increasing glory,
Php　2:　7　being made in human *l*.
Jas　3:　9　who have been made in God's *l*.

LILIES (LILY)
Lk　12:27　"Consider how the / grow.

LILY (LILIES)
SS　2:　1　a / of the valleys.
　　2:　2　*Lover* Like a / among thorns

LIMIT
Ps　147:　5　his understanding has no *l*.
Jn　3:34　for God gives the Spirit without *l*.

LINEN
Lev　16:　4　He is to put on the sacred / tunic,
Pr　31:22　she is clothed in fine / and purple.
　　31:24　She makes / garments
Mk　15:46　So Joseph bought some / cloth,
Jn　20:　6　He saw the strips of / lying there,
Rev　4:　7　shining / and wore golden sashes
　　19:　8　Fine *l*, bright and clean,

LINGER
Hab　2:　3　Though it *l*, wait for it;

LION (LION'S LIONS')
Jdg　14:　6　power so that he tore the / apart
1Sa　17:34　When a / or a bear came
Isa　11:　7　and the / will eat straw like the ox.
　　65:25　and the / will eat straw like the ox,
Eze　1:10　right side each had the face of a *l*,
　　10:14　the third the face of a *l*,
Da　7:　4　"The first was like a *l*,
1Pe　5:　8　around like a roaring / looking
Rev　4:　7　The first living creature was like a *l*
　　5:　5　See, the *L* of the tribe of Judah,

LION'S (LION)
Ge　49:　9　You are a / cub, O Judah;

LIONS' (LION)
Da　6:　7　shall be thrown into the / den.

LIPS
Ps　8:　2　From the / of children and infants
　　34:　1　his praise will always be on my *l*.
　　40:　9　I do not seal my *l*,
　　63:　3　my / will glorify you.
　　119:171　May my / overflow with praise,
　　140:　3　the poison of vipers is on their *l*.
　　141:　3　keep watch over the door of my *l*.
Pr　10:13　on the / of the discerning,
　　10:18　who conceals his hatred has lying *l*,
　　10:32　/ of the righteous know what is
　　12:22　The Lord detests lying *l*,
　　13:　3　He who guards his / guards his life,
　　14:　7　will not find knowledge on his *l*.
　　24:26　is like a kiss on the *l*.
　　26:23　are fervent / with an evil heart.
　　27:　2　someone else, and not your own *l*.
Isa　6:　5　For I am a man of unclean *l*,
　　28:11　with foreign / and strange tongues
　　29:13　and honor me with their *l*,
Mal　2:　7　"For the / of a priest ought
Mt　15:　8　These people honor me with their *l*,
　　21:16　" 'From the / of children
Lk　4:22　words that came from his *l*.
Ro　3:13　"The poison of vipers is on their *l*."
Col　3:　8　and filthy language from your *l*.
Heb　13:15　the fruit of / that confess his name.
1Pe　3:10　and his / from deceitful speech.

LISTEN (LISTENED LISTENING LISTENS)
Dt　18:15　You must / to him.
　　30:20　to his voice, and hold fast to him.
1Ki　4:34　came to / to Solomon's wisdom,
2Ki　21:　9　But the people did not *l*.
Pr　1:　5　let the wise / and add
Ecc　5:　1　Go near to / rather
Eze　2:　5　And whether they / or fail to *l*—
Mt　12:42　earth to / to Solomon's wisdom,
Mk　9:　7　*L* to him!" Suddenly,
Jn　10:27　My sheep / to my voice; I know
Ac　3:22　you must / to everything he tells
Jas　1:19　Everyone should be quick to *l*,
　　1:22　Do not merely / to the word,
1Jn　4:　6　not from God does not / to us.

LISTENED (LISTEN)
Ne　8:　3　And all the people / attentively
Isa　66:　4　when I spoke, no one *l*.
Da　9:　6　We have not / to your servants

LISTENING (LISTEN)
1Sa　3:　9　Speak, Lord, for your servant is *l*
Pr　18:13　He who answers before *l*—
Lk　10:39　at the Lord's feet / to what he said.

2242

LISTENS (LISTEN)
Pr 12:15 but a wise man / to advice.
Lk 10:16 "He who / to you /
1Jn 4: 6 and whoever knows God / to us;

LIVE (ALIVE LIFE LIFETIME LIVES LIVING)
Ge 3:22 tree of life and eat, and / forever."
Ex 20:12 so that you may / long
33:20 for no one may see me and /."
Nu 21: 8 who is bitten can look at it and /."
Dt 5:24 we have seen that a man can /
6: 2 as you / by keeping all his decrees
8: 3 to teach you that man does not /
Job 14:14 If a man dies, will he / again?
Ps 15: 1 Who may / on your holy hill?
24: 1 the world, and all who / in it;
26: 8 I love the house where you /,
119:175 Let me / that I may praise you,
Pr 21: 9 Better to / on a corner of the roof
21:19 Better to / in a desert
Ecc 9: 4 a / dog is better off than a dead lion
Isa 26:19 But your dead will /;
55: 3 hear me, that your soul may /.
Eze 17:19 LORD says: As surely as I /,
20:11 for the man who obeys them will /
37: 3 can these bones /?" I said,
Am 5: 6 Seek the LORD and /,
Hab 2: 4 but the righteous will / by his faith
Zec 2:11 I will / among you and you will
Mt 4: 4 'Man does not / on bread alone,
Lk 4: 4 'Man does not / on bread alone.' "
Jn 14:19 Because I /, you also will /.
Ac 17:24 does not / in temples built by hands
17:28 'For in him we / and move
Ro 1:17 "The righteous will / by faith."
2Co 5: 7 We / by faith, not by sight.
6:16 "I will / with them and walk
Gal 2:20 The life I / in the body, I / by faith
3:11 "The righteous will / by faith."
5:25 Since we / by the Spirit, let us keep
Eph 4:17 that you must no longer /
Php 1:21 to / is Christ and to die is gain.
Col 1:10 order that you may / a life worthy
1Th 4: 1 we instructed you how to / in order
5:13 L in peace with each other.
1Ti 2: 2 that we may / peaceful
2Ti 3:12 who wants to / a godly life
Tit 2:12 and to / self-controlled, upright
Heb 10:38 But my righteous one will / by faith
12:14 Make every effort to / in peace
1Pe 1:17 / your lives as strangers here
3: 8 / in harmony with one another;

LIVES (LIVE)
Ge 45: 7 and to save your / by a great
Job 19:25 I know that my Redeemer /,
Pr 1:19 it takes away the /
Isa 57:15 he who / forever, whose name is
Da 3:28 to give up their / rather than serve
Jn 14:17 for he / with you and will be in you.
Ro 6:10 but the life he /, he / to God.
7:18 I know that nothing good in me,
8: 9 if the Spirit of God / in you.
14: 7 For none of us / to himself alone
1Co 3:16 and that God's Spirit / in you?
Gal 2:20 I no longer live, but Christ / in me.
1Th 2: 8 only the gospel of God but our /
1Ti 2: 2 quiet / in all godliness and holiness.
Tit 2:12 and godly / in this present age,
Heb 7:24 but because Jesus / forever,
13: 5 Keep your / free from the love
1Pe 3: 2 the purity and reverence of your /.
2Pe 3:11 You ought to live holy and godly /
1Jn 3:16 to lay down our / for our brothers.
4:16 Whoever / in love in God,

LIVING (LIVE)
Ge 2: 7 and the man became a / being.
1Sa 17:26 defy the armies of the / God?"
Isa 53: 8 cut off from the land of the /;
Jer 2:13 the spring of / water,
Eze 1: 5 what looked like four / creatures.
Zec 14: 8 On that day / water will flow out
Mt 22:32 the God of the dead but of the /."
Jn 4:10 he would have given you / water."
6:51 I am the / bread that came

Jn 7:38 streams of / water will flow
Ro 8:11 Jesus from the dead is / in you,
12: 1 to offer your bodies as / sacrifices,
1Co 9:14 the gospel should receive their /
Heb 4:12 For the word of God is / and active.
10:20 and / way opened for us
10:31 to fall into the hands of the / God.
1Pe 1:23 through the / and enduring word
Rev 1:18 I am the L One; I was dead,
4: 6 the throne, were four / creatures,
7:17 to springs of / water.

LOAD (LOADS)
Gal 6: 5 for each one should carry his own /.

LOADS (LOAD)
Mt 23: 4 They tie up heavy / and put them

LOAF (LOAVES)
1Co 10:17 for we all partake of the one /.

LOAVES (LOAF)
Mk 6:41 Taking the five / and the two fish
8: 6 When he had taken the seven /
Lk 11: 5 'Friend, lend me three / of bread,

LOCKED
Jn 20:26 the doors were /, Jesus came
Gal 3:23 / up until faith should be revealed.

LOCUSTS
Ex 10: 4 I will bring / into your country
Joel 2:25 you for the years the / have eaten—
Mt 3: 4 His food was / and wild honey.
Rev 9: 3 And out of the smoke / came

LOFTY
Ps 139: 6 too / for me to attain.
Isa 57:15 is what the high and / One says—

LONELY
Ps 68: 6 God sets the / in families,
Lk 5:16 Jesus often withdrew to / places

LONG (LENGTH LENGTHY LONGED LONGING LONGINGS LONGS)
Ex 17:11 As / as Moses held up his hands,
Nu 6: 5 the hair of his head grow /.
1Ki 18:21 "How / will you waver
Ps 119:97 I meditate on it all day /.
119:174 I / for your salvation, O LORD,
Hos 7:13 I / to redeem them
Am 5:18 Why do you / for the day
Mt 25: 5 The bridegroom was a / time
Jn 9: 4 As / as it is day, we must do
1Co 11:14 that if a man has / hair,
Eph 3:18 to grasp how wide and / and high
Php 1: 8 God can testify how I / for all
1Pe 1:12 Even angels to / look

LONGED (LONG)
Mt 13:17 righteous men / to see what you see
23:37 how often I have /
Lk 13:34 how often I have /
2Ti 4: 8 to all who have / for his appearing.

LONGING* (LONG)
Dt 28:65 with /, and a despairing heart.
Job 7: 2 Like a slave / for the evening
Ps 119:20 My soul is consumed with /
119:81 with / for your salvation,
119:131 / for your commands.
143: 7 my spirit faints with /.
Pr 13:12 but a / fulfilled is a tree of life.
13:19 A / fulfilled is sweet to the soul,
Eze 23:27 look on these things with /
Lk 16:21 and / to eat what fell from the rich
Ro 15:23 since I have been / for many years
2Co 5: 2 / to be clothed with our heavenly
7: 7 He told us about your / for me,
7:11 what alarm, what /, what concern,
1Th 2:17 out of our intense / we made every
Heb 11:16 they were / for a better country—

LONGINGS* (LONG)
Ps 38: 9 All my / lie open before you,
112:10 the / of the wicked will come

LONGS* (LONG)
Ps 63: 1 my body / for you,
Isa 26: 9 in the morning my spirit / for you.
30:18 Yet the LORD / to be gracious
Php 2:26 For he / for all of you and is

LOOK (LOOKED LOOKING LOOKS)
Ge 19:17 "Flee for your lives! Don't / back,
Ex 3: 6 because he was afraid to / at God.
Nu 21: 8 anyone who is bitten can / at it
32: 8 Kadesh Barnea to / over the land.
Dt 4:29 you will find him if you / for him
1Sa 16: 7 The LORD does not /
Job 31: 1 not to / lustfully at a girl.
Ps 34: 5 Those who / to him are radiant;
105: 4 L to the LORD and his strength;
113: 6 who stoops down to /
123: 2 As the eyes of slaves / to the hand
Pr 1:28 they will / for me but will not find
4:25 Let your eyes / straight ahead,
15:30 A cheerful / brings joy to the heart,
Isa 17: 7 In that day men will /
31: 1 do not / to the Holy One of Israel,
40:26 Lift your eyes and / to the heavens;
60: 5 Then you will / and be radiant,
Jer 3: 3 Yet you have the brazen /
6:16 "Stand at the crossroads and /;
Eze 34:11 for my sheep and / after them.
Zec 12:10 They will / on me, the one they
Mt 18:10 "See that you do not / down on one
18:12 go to / for the one that wandered
23:27 which / beautiful on the outside
Mk 13:21 'L, here is the Christ!' or, 'L,
Lk 6:41 "Why do you / at the speck
24:39 L at my hands and my feet.
Jn 1:36 he said, "L, the Lamb of God!"
4:35 open your eyes and / at the fields!
19:37 "They will / on the one they have
Ro 14:10 why do you / down on your brother
Php 2: 4 Each of you should / not only
1Ti 4:12 Don't let anyone / down on you
Jas 1:27 to / after orphans and widows
1Pe 1:12 long to / into these things.
2Pe 3:12 as you / forward to the day of God

LOOKED (LOOK)
Ge 19:26 Lot's wife / back, and she became
Ex 2:25 So God / on the Israelites
1Sa 6:19 because they had / into the ark
SS 3: 1 I / for the one my heart loves;
Eze 22:30 "I / for a man among them who
34: 6 and no one searched or / for them.
44: 4 I / and saw the glory
Da 7: 9 "As I /,
10: 5 I / up and there before me was
Hab 3: 6 he /, and made the nations tremble.
Mt 25:36 I was sick and you / after me,
Lk 18: 9 and / down on everybody else,
22:61 The Lord turned and / straight
1Jn 1: 1 which we have / at and our hands

LOOKING (LOOK)
Ps 69: 3 / for my God.
119:82 My eyes fail, / for your promise;
119:123 My eyes fail, / for your salvation,
Mk 16: 6 "You are / for Jesus the Nazarene,
2Co 10: 7 You are / only on the surface
Php 4:17 Not that I am / for a gift,
1Th 2: 6 We were not / for praise from men,
2Pe 3:13 with his promise we are / forward
Rev 5: 6 I saw a Lamb, / as if it had been

LOOKS (LOOK)
1Sa 16: 7 Man / at the outward appearance,
Ezr 8:22 is on everyone who / to him,
Ps 104:32 who / at the earth, and it trembles;
138: 6 on high, he / upon the lowly,
Pr 27:18 he who / after his master will be
Eze 34:12 As a shepherd / after his scattered
Mt 5:28 But I tell you that anyone who /
16: 4 and adulterous generation /
Lk 9:62 and / back is fit for service
Jn 6:40 Father's will is that everyone who /
12:45 When he / at me, he sees the one
Php 2:21 For everyone / out
Jas 1:25 But the man who / intently

LOOSE
Isa 33:23 Your rigging hangs /:

Mt 16:19 and whatever you *l* on earth will be
18:18 and whatever you *l* on earth will be

LORD† (LORD'S† LORDED LORDING)
Ge 18:27 been so bold as to speak to the *L,*
Ex 15:17 O *L,* your hands established.
Nu 16:13 now you also want to *l* it over us?
Dt 10:17 God of gods and *L* of lords,
Jos 3:13 the *L* of all the earth—set foot
1Ki 3:10 *L* was pleased that Solomon had
Ne 4:14 Remember the *L,* who is great
Job 28:28 'The fear of the *L—* that is wisdom,
Ps 37:13 but the *L* laughs at the wicked,
38:22 O *L* my Savior.
54: 4 the *L* is the one who sustains me.
62:12 and that you, O *L,* are loving.
69: 6 O *L,* the LORD Almighty;
86: 5 You are forgiving and good, O *L,*
86: 8 gods there is none like you, O *L;*
89:49 O *L,* where is your former great
110: 1 The LORD says to my *L:*
110: 5 The *L* is at your right hand;
130: 3 O *L,* who could stand?
135: 5 that our *L* is greater than all gods.
136: 3 Give thanks to the *L* of lords:
147: 5 Great is our *L* and mighty in power
Isa 6: 1 I saw the *L* seated on a throne,
Da 2:47 and the *L* of kings and a revealer
9: 4 "O *L,* the great and awesome God,
9: 7 "L, you are righteous,
9: 9 The *L* our God is merciful
9:19 O *L,* listen! O *L,* forgive! O *L,*
Mt 3: 3 'Prepare the way for the *L,*
4: 7 'Do not put the *L* your God
4:10 'Worship the *L* your God,
7:21 "Not everyone who says to me, '*L,*
9:38 Ask the *L* of the harvest, therefore,
12: 8 Son of Man is *L* of the Sabbath."
20:25 of the Gentiles *l* it over them,
21: 9 comes in the name of the *L!*"
22:37 " 'Love the *L* your God
22:44 For he says, " 'The *L* said to my *L:*
23:39 comes in the name of the *L.* ' "
Mk 1: 3 'Prepare the way for the *L,*
1:11 the *L* has done this,
12:29 the *L* our God, the *L* is one.
12:30 Love the *L* your God
Lk 2: 9 glory of the *L* shone around them,
6: 5 The Son of Man is *L* of the Sabbath
6:46 "Why do you call me, '*L, L,*'
10:27 " 'Love the *L* your God
11: 1 one of his disciples said to him, "*L,*
24:34 The *L* has risen and has appeared
Jn 1:23 'Make straight the way for the *L.* ' "
Ac 2:21 on the name of the *L* will be saved.'
2:25 " 'I saw the *L* always before me.
2:34 " 'The *L* said to my *L:*
8:16 into the name of the *L* Jesus.
9: 5 "Who are you, *L?*" Saul asked.
10:36 through Jesus Christ, who is *L*
11:23 true to the *L* with all their hearts.
16:31 replied, "Believe in the *L* Jesus,
Ro 4:24 in him who raised Jesus our *L*
5:11 in God through our *L* Jesus Christ,
6:23 life in Christ Jesus our *L.*
8:39 of God that is in Christ Jesus our *L.*
10: 9 with your mouth, "Jesus is *L,*"
10:13 on the name of the *L* will be saved
10:16 *L,* who has believed our message?"
11:34 Who has known the mind of the *L?*
12:11 your spiritual fervor, serving the *L.*
13:14 yourselves with the *L* Jesus Christ,
14: 4 for the *L* is able to make him stand.
14: 8 we live to the *L;* and if we die,
1Co 1:31 Let him who boasts boast in the *L.*"
3: 5 the *L* has assigned to each his task.

1Co 4: 5 time; wait till the *L* comes.
6:13 for the *L,* and the *L* for the body.
6:14 By his power God raised the *L*
7:32 affairs—how he can please the *L.*
7:34 to be devoted to the *L* in both body
7:35 in undivided devotion to the *L.*
7:39 but he must belong to the *L.*
8: 6 and there is but one *L,* Jesus Christ,
10: 9 We should not test the *L,*
11:23 For I received from the *L* what I
12: 3 "Jesus is *L,*" except by the Holy
15:57 victory through our *L* Jesus Christ.
15:58 fully to the work of the *L,*
16:22 If anyone does not love the *L—*
2Co 1:24 Not that we *l* it over your faith,
2:12 found that the *L* had opened a door
3:17 Now the *L* is the Spirit,
4: 5 but Jesus Christ as *L,* and ourselves
5: 6 in the body we are away from the *L*
8: 5 they gave themselves first to the *L*
8:21 not only in the eyes of the *L* but
10:17 Let him who boasts boast in the *L.*"
10:18 but the one whom the *L* commends
13:10 the authority the *L* gave me
Gal 6:14 in the cross of our *L* Jesus Christ,
Eph 4: 5 one *L,* one faith, one baptism;
5: 8 but now you are light in the *L.*
5:10 and find out what pleases the *L.*
5:19 make music in your heart to the *L,*
5:22 submit to your husbands as to the *L*
6: 1 obey your parents in the *L,*
6: 7 as if you were serving the *L,*
6: 8 know that the *L* will reward
6:10 in the *L* and in his mighty power.
Php 2:11 confess that Jesus Christ is *L,*
3: 1 my brothers, rejoice in the *L!*
3: 8 of knowing Christ Jesus my *L,*
4: 1 you should stand firm in the *L,*
4: 4 Rejoice in the *L* always.
4: 5 The *L* is near.
Col 1:10 you may live a life worthy of the *L*
2: 6 as you received Christ Jesus as *L,*
3:13 Forgive as the *L* forgave you.
3:17 do it all in the name of the *L* Jesus,
3:18 your husbands, as is fitting in the *L.*
3:20 in everything, for this pleases the *L.*
3:23 as working for the *L,* not for men,
3:24 It is the *L* Christ you are serving.
3:24 receive an inheritance from the *L*
4:17 work you have received in the *L.*"
1Th 3: 8 since you are standing firm in the *L*
3:12 May the *L* make your love increase
4: 1 and urge you in the *L* Jesus
4: 6 The *L* will punish men
4:15 who are left till the coming of the *L*
5: 2 day of the *L* will come like a thief
5:23 at the coming of our *L* Jesus Christ.
2Th 1: 7 when the *L* Jesus is revealed
1:12 of our *L* Jesus may be glorified
2: 1 the coming of our *L* Jesus Christ
2: 8 whom the *L* Jesus will overthrow
3: 3 *L* is faithful, and he will strengthen
3: 5 May the *L* direct your hearts
1Ti 6:15 the King of kings and *L* of lords,
2Ti 1: 8 ashamed to testify about our *L,*
2:19 "The *L* knows those who are his,"
4: 8 which the *L,* the righteous Judge,
4:17 But the *L* stood at my side
Heb 1:10 O *L,* you laid the foundations
10:30 "The *L* will judge his people."
12:14 holiness no one will see the *L.*
13: 6 *L* is my helper; I will not be afraid.
Jas 3: 9 With the tongue we praise our *L*
4:10 Humble yourselves before the *L,*
5:11 The *L* is full of compassion
1Pe 1:25 the word of the *L* stands forever."

1Pe 2: 3 you have tasted that the *L* is good.
3:12 eyes of the *L* are on the righteous
3:15 in your hearts set apart Christ as *L.*
2Pe 1:11 into the eternal kingdom of our *L*
1:16 and coming of our *L* Jesus Christ,
2: 1 the sovereign *L* who bought
2: 9 then the *L* knows how
3: 9 The *L* is not slow in keeping his
3:18 and knowledge of our *L* and Savior
Jude : 14 the *L* is coming with thousands
Rev 4: 8 holy, holy is the *L* God Almighty,
4:11 "You are worthy, our *L* and God,
11:15 has become the kingdom of our *L*
17:14 he is *L* of lords and King of kings—
19:16 KINGS AND *L* OF LORDS.
22: 5 for the *L* God will give them light.
22:20 Come, *L* Jesus.

LORD'S† (LORD†)
Lk 1:38 "I am the *L* servant," Mary
Ac 11:21 The *L* hand was with them,
21:14 and said, "The *L* will be done."
1Co 7:32 is concerned about the *L* affairs—
10:26 "The earth is the *L,* and everything
11:26 you proclaim the *L* death
2Co 3:18 faces all reflect the *L* glory,
Eph 5:17 but understand what the *L* will is.
2Ti 2:24 And the *L* servant must not quarrel
Heb 12: 5 light of the *L* discipline,
Jas 4:15 you ought to say, "If it is the *L* will,
5: 8 because the *L* coming is near.
1Pe 2:13 Submit yourselves for the *L* sake

LORDED* (LORD†)
Ne 5:15 Their assistants also *l* it

LORDING* (LORD†)
1Pe 5: 3 not *l* it over those entrusted to you,

LORD‡ (LORD'S‡)
2: 4 When the *L* God made the earth
2: 7 the *L* God formed the man
2:22 Then the *L* God made a woman
3:21 The *L* God made garments of skin
3:23 So the *L* God banished him
4: 4 The *L* looked with favor on Abel
4:26 began to call on the name of the *L.*
6: 7 So the *L* said, "I will wipe mankind
7:16 Then the *L* shut him in.
9:26 Blessed be the *L,* the God of Shem!
11: 9 there the *L* confused the language
12: 1 *L* had said to Abram, "Leave your
15: 6 Abram believed the *L,*
15:18 On that day the *L* made a covenant
17: 1 the *L* appeared to him and said,
18: 1 The *L* appeared to Abraham
18:14 Is anything too hard for the *L?*
18:19 way of the *L* by doing what is right
21: 1 Now the *L* was gracious to Sarah
22:14 that place The *L* Will Provide.
24: 1 the *L* had blessed him in every way
26: 2 The *L* appeared to Isaac and said,
28:13 There above it stood the *L,*
31:49 "May the *L* keep watch
39: 2 The *L* was with Joseph
39:21 in the prison, the *L* was with him;
Ex 3: 2 the angel of the *L* appeared to him
4:11 Is it not I, the *L?* Now go;
4:31 heard that the *L* was concerned
6: 2 also said to Moses, "I am the *L.*
9:12 the *L* hardened Pharaoh's heart
12:27 'It is the Passover sacrifice to the *L,*
12:43 The *L* said to Moses and Aaron,
13: 9 For the *L* brought you out of Egypt
13:21 By day the *L* went ahead of them
14:13 the deliverance the *L* will bring
14:30 That day the *L* saved Israel
15: 3 The *L* is a warrior;
15:11 among the gods is like you, O *L?*
15:26 for I am the *L,* who heals you."

For the explanation of the articles LORD†, LORD'S†, LORD‡ and LORD'S‡, see the introduction on page 2150.

Ex 16:12 know that I am the L your God.' "
16:23 day of rest, a holy Sabbath to the L.
17:15 and called it The L is my Banner.
19:8 will do everything the L has said."
19:20 The L descended to the top
20:2 "I am the L your God, who
20:5 the L your God, am a jealous God,
20:7 for the L will not hold anyone
20:10 a Sabbath to the L your God.
20:11 in six days the L made the heavens
20:12 in the land the L your God is giving
23:25 Worship the L your God,
24:3 "Everything the L has said we will
24:12 The L said to Moses, "Come up
24:16 and the glory of the L settled
25:1 The L said to Moses, "Tell
28:36 HOLY TO THE L.
30:11 Then the L said to Moses,
31:13 so you may know that I am the L,
31:18 When the L finished speaking
33:11 The L would speak to Moses face
33:19 And the L said, "I will cause all my
34:1 I said to Moses, "Chisel out two
34:6 proclaiming, "The L, the L,
34:10 awesome is the work that I, the L,
34:29 because he had spoken with the L.
40:34 glory of the L filled the tabernacle.
40:38 So the cloud of the L was

Lev 8:36 did everything the L commanded
9:23 and the glory of the L appeared
10:2 and they died before the L.
19:2 'Be holy because I, the L your God,
20:8 I am the L, who makes you holy.
20:26 to be holy to me because I, the L,
23:40 and rejoice before the L your God

Nu 6:24 Say to them: " ' "The L bless you
8:5 L said to Moses: "Take the Levites
11:1 hardships in the hearing of the L,
14:14 O L, have been seen face to face,
14:18 you have declared: 'The L is slow
14:21 glory of the L fills the whole earth,
21:6 Then the L sent venomous snakes
22:31 Then the L opened Balaam's eyes,
23:12 "Must I not speak what the L puts
30:2 When a man makes a vow to the L
32:12 followed the L wholeheartedly.'

Dt 1:21 and take possession of it as the L,
2:7 forty years the L your God has
4:29 there you seek the L your God,
5:6 And he said: "I am the L your God,
5:9 the L your God, am a jealous God,
6:4 The L our God, the L is one.
6:5 Love the L your God
6:16 Do not test the L your God
6:25 law before the L our God,
7:1 When the L your God brings you
7:6 holy to the L your God.
7:8 But it was because the L loved you
7:9 that the L your God is God;
7:12 then the L your God will keep his
8:5 so the L your God disciplines you.
9:10 The L gave me two stone tablets
10:12 but to fear the L your God,
10:14 To the L your God belong
10:17 For the L your God is God of gods
10:20 Fear the L your God and serve him
10:22 now the L your God has made you
11:1 Love the L your God and keep his
11:13 to love the L your God
16:1 the Passover of the L your God,
17:15 the king the L your God chooses.
28:1 If you fully obey the L your God
28:15 if you do not obey the L your God
29:1 covenant the L commanded Moses
29:29 things belong to the L our God,
30:4 from there the L your God will
30:6 L your God will circumcise your
30:10 if you obey the L your God
30:16 today to love the L your God,
30:20 For the L is your life, and he will
31:6 for the L your God goes with you;

Dt 34:5 of the L died there in Moab,

Jos 10:14 a day when the L listened to a man.
22:5 to love the L your God, to walk
23:11 careful to love the L your God.
24:15 my household, we will serve the L
24:18 We too will serve the L,

Jdg 2:12 They forsook the L, the God

Ru 1:8 May the L show kindness to you,
4:13 And the L enabled her to conceive,

1Sa 1:11 him to the L for all the days
1:15 I was pouring out my soul to the L.
1:28 So now I give him to the L.
2:2 "There is no one holy like the L;
2:25 but if a man sins against the L,
2:26 in favor with the L and with men.
3:9 L, for your servant is listening.' "
3:19 The L was with Samuel
7:12 "Thus far has the L helped us."
9:17 sight of Saul, the L said to him,
11:15 as king in the presence of the L.
12:18 all the people stood in awe of the L
12:22 his great name the L will not reject
12:24 But be sure to fear the L
13:14 the L has sought out a man
14:6 Nothing can hinder the L
15:22 "Does the L delight
16:13 Spirit of the L came upon David
17:45 you in the name of the L Almighty,

2Sa 6:14 danced before the L
7:22 How great you are, O Sovereign L!
8:6 L gave David victory everywhere
12:7 This is what the L, the God
22:2 "The L is my rock, my fortress
22:29 You are my lamp, O L;
22:31 the word of the L is flawless.

1Ki 1:30 today what I swore to you by the L,
2:3 and observe what the L your God
3:7 O L my God, you have made your
5:5 for the Name of the L my God,
5:12 The L gave Solomon wisdom,
8:11 the glory of the L filled his temple.
8:23 toward heaven and said: "O L,
8:61 fully committed to the L our God,
9:3 The L said to him: "I have heard
10:9 Praise be to the L your God,
15:14 committed to the L all his life.
18:21 If the L is God, follow him;
18:36 "O L, God of Abraham, Isaac
18:39 "The L— he is God! The L—
21:23 also concerning Jezebel the L says:

2Ki 13:23 But the L was gracious to them
17:18 So the L was very angry with Israel
18:5 Hezekiah trusted in the L,
19:1 and went into the temple of the L.
20:11 L made the shadow go back the ten
21:12 Therefore this is what the L,
22:2 right in the eyes of the L
22:8 of the Law in the temple of the L."
23:3 to follow the L and keep his
23:21 the Passover to the L your God,
23:25 a king like him who turned to the L
24:2 The L sent Babylonian, Aramean,
24:4 and the L was not willing to forgive

1Ch 10:13 because he was unfaithful to the L;
11:3 with them at Hebron before the L,
11:9 the L Almighty was with him.
13:6 from there the ark of God the L, who
16:8 Give thanks to the L, call
16:11 Look to the L and his strength;
16:14 He is the L our God;
16:23 Sing to the L, all the earth;
17:1 covenant of the L is under a tent."
21:24 take for the L what is yours,
22:5 to be built for the L should be
22:11 build the house of the L your God,
22:13 and laws that the L gave Moses
22:16 Now begin the work, and the L be

1Ch 22:19 soul to seeking the L your God.
25:7 and skilled in music for the L—
28:9 for the L searches every heart
28:20 for the L God, my God, is with you
29:1 not for man but for the L God.
29:11 O L, is the greatness and the power
29:18 O L, God of our fathers Abraham,
29:25 The L highly exalted Solomon

2Ch 1:1 for the L his God was with him
5:13 to give praise and thanks to the L.
5:14 the glory of the L filled the temple
6:16 "Now L, God of Israel, keep
6:41 O L God, and come
6:42 O L God, do not reject your
7:1 the glory of the L filled the temple.
7:12 the L appeared to him at night
7:21 'Why has the L done such a thing
9:8 as king to rule for the L your God.
13:12 do not fight against the L.
14:2 right in the eyes of the L his God.
15:14 to the L with loud acclamation,
16:9 of the L range throughout the earth
17:9 the Book of the Law of the L;
18:13 said, "As surely as the L lives,
19:6 judging for man but for the L.
19:9 wholeheartedly in the fear of the L.
20:15 This is what the L says to you:
20:20 Have faith in the L your God
20:21 appointed men to sing to the L
26:5 As long as he sought the L,
26:16 He was unfaithful to the L his God,
29:30 to praise the L with the words
30:9 for the L your God is gracious
31:20 and faithful before the L his God.
32:8 with us is the L our God to help us
34:14 Law of the L that had been given
34:31 to follow the L and keep his

Ezr 3:10 foundation of the temple of the L,
7:6 for the hand of the L his God was
7:10 observance of the Law of the L,
9:5 hands spread out to the L my God
9:8 the L our God has been gracious
9:15 O L, God of Israel, you are

Ne 1:5 Then I said: "O L, God of heaven,
8:1 which the L had commanded
9:6 You alone are the L.

Job 1:6 to present themselves before the L,
1:21 L gave and the L has taken away;
38:1 the L answered Job out
42:9 and the L accepted Job's prayer.
42:12 The L blessed the latter part

Ps 1:2 But his delight is in the law of the L
1:6 For the L watches over the way
4:6 of your face shine upon us, O L.
4:8 for you alone, O L,
5:3 In the morning, O L,
6:1 O L, do not rebuke me
8:1 O L, our Lord,
9:9 The L is a refuge for the oppressed;
9:19 Arise, O L, let not man triumph;
10:16 The L is King for ever and ever;
12:6 And the words of the L are flawless
16:5 L, you have assigned me my
16:8 I have set the L always before me.
18:1 I love you, O L, my strength.
18:6 In my distress I called to the L;
18:30 the word of the L is flawless.
19:7 The law of the L is perfect,
19:14 O L, my Rock and my Redeemer.
20:5 May the L grant all your requests.
20:7 in the name of the L our God.
22:8 let the L rescue him.
23:1 The L is my shepherd, I shall
23:6 I will dwell in the house of the L
24:3 Who may ascend the hill of the L?
24:8 The L strong and mighty,
25:10 All the ways of the L are loving
27:1 The L is my light and my salvation
27:4 to gaze upon the beauty of the L
27:6 I will sing and make music to the L.
29:1 Ascribe to the L, O mighty ones,

For the explanation of the articles LORD†, LORD'S†, LORD‡ and LORD'S‡, see the introduction on page 2150.

2245

Ps 29: 4 The voice of the *L* is powerful;
30: 4 Sing to the *L*, you saints of his;
31: 5 redeem me, O *L*, the God of truth.
32: 2 whose sin the *L* does not count
33: 1 joyfully to the *L*, you righteous;
33: 6 of the *L* were the heavens made,
33:12 is the nation whose God is the *L*,
33:18 But the eyes of the *L* are
34: 1 I will extol the *L* at all times;
34: 3 Glorify the *L* with me;
34: 4 I sought the *L*, and he answered me
34: 7 The angel of the *L* encamps
34: 8 Taste and see that the *L* is good;
34: 9 Fear the *L*, you his saints,
34:15 The eyes of the *L* are
34:18 The *L* is close to the brokenhearted
37: 4 Delight yourself in the *L*
37: 5 Commit your way to the *L*;
39: 4 "Show me, O *L*, my life's end
40: 1 I waited patiently for the *L*;
40: 5 Many, O *L* my God,
46: 8 Come and see the works of the *L*,
47: 2 How awesome is the *L* Most High,
48: 1 Great is the *L*, and most worthy
50: 1 The Mighty One, God, the *L*,
55:22 Cast your cares on the *L*
59: 8 But you, O *L*, laugh at them;
68: 4 his name is the *L*—
68:18 O *L* God, might dwell there.
68:20 from the Sovereign *L* comes escape
69:31 This will please the *L* more
72:18 Praise be to the *L* God, the God
75: 8 In the hand of the *L* is a cup
78: 4 the praiseworthy deeds of the *L*,
84: 8 my prayer, O *L* God Almighty;
84:11 For the *L* God is a sun and shield;
85: 7 Show us your unfailing love, O *L*,
86:11 Teach me your way, O *L*,
87: 2 the *L* loves the gates of Zion
89: 5 heavens praise your wonders, O *L*,
89: 8 O *L* God Almighty, who is like you
91: 2 I will say of the *L*, "He is my refuge
92: 1 It is good to praise the *L*
92: 4 by your deeds, O *L*;
92:13 planted in the house of the *L*,
93: 1 The *L* reigns, he is robed in majesty
93: 5 house for endless days, O *L*.
94: 1 O *L*, the God who avenges,
94:12 is the man you discipline, O *L*,
94:18 your love, O *L*, supported me.
95: 1 Come, let us sing for joy to the *L*;
95: 3 For the *L* is the great God,
95: 6 let us kneel before the *L* our Maker
96: 1 Sing to the *L* a new song;
96: 5 but the *L* made the heavens.
96: 8 to the *L* the glory due his name;
96: 9 Worship the *L* in the splendor
96:13 they will sing before the *L*,
97: 1 The *L* reigns, let the earth be glad;
97: 9 O *L*, are the Most High
98: 1 Sing to the *L* a new song,
98: 2 *L* has made his salvation known
98: 4 Shout for joy to the *L*, all the earth,
99: 1 The *L* reigns,
99: 2 Great is the *L* in Zion;
99: 5 Exalt the *L* our God
99: 9 Exalt the *L* our God
100: 1 Shout for joy to the *L*, all the earth.
100: 2 Worship the *L* with gladness;
100: 3 Know that the *L* is God.
100: 5 For the *L* is good and his love
101: 1 to you, O *L*, I will sing praise.
102:12 But you, O *L*, sit enthroned forever
103: 1 Praise the *L*, O my soul;
103: 8 The *L* is compassionate
103:19 The *L* has established his throne
104: 1 O *L* my God, you are very great;
104:24 How many are your works, O *L*!
104:33 I will sing to the *L* all my life;
105: 4 Look to the *L* and his strength;
105: 7 He is the *L* our God;
106: 2 proclaim the mighty acts of the *L*

Ps 107: 1 Give thanks to the *L*, for he is good
107: 8 to the *L* for his unfailing love
107:21 to the *L* for his unfailing love
107:43 and consider the great love of the *L*
108: 3 I will praise you, O *L*,
109:26 Help me, O *L* my God,
110: 1 The *L* says to my Lord:
110: 4 The *L* has sworn
111: 2 Great are the works of the *L*;
111: 4 *L* is gracious and compassionate.
111:10 The fear of the *L* is the beginning
112: 1 Blessed is the man who fears the *L*,
113: 1 Praise, O servants of the *L*,
113: 2 Let the name of the *L* be praised,
113: 4 *L* is exalted over all the nations,
113: 5 Who is like the *L* our God,
115: 1 Not to us, O *L*, not to us
115:18 it is we who extol the *L*,
116:12 How can I repay the *L*
116:15 Precious in the sight of the *L*
117: 1 Praise the *L*, all you nations;
118: 1 Give thanks to the *L*, for he is good
118: 5 In my anguish I cried to the *L*,
118: 8 It is better to take refuge in the *L*
118:18 The *L* has chastened me severely,
118:23 the *L* has done this,
118:24 This is the day the *L* has made;
118:26 comes in the name of the *L*.
119: 1 to the law of the *L*.
119:64 with your love, O *L*;
119:89 Your word, O *L*, is eternal;
119:126 It is time for you to act, O *L*;
119:159 O *L*, according to your love.
120: 1 I call on the *L* in my distress,
121: 2 My help comes from the *L*,
121: 5 The *L* watches over you—
121: 8 the *L* will watch over your coming
122: 1 "Let us go to the house of the *L*."
123: 2 so our eyes look to the *L* our God,
124: 1 If the *L* had not been on our side—
124: 8 Our help is in the name of the *L*,
125: 2 so the *L* surrounds his people
126: 3 The *L* has done great things for us,
126: 4 Restore our fortunes, O *L*,
127: 1 Unless the *L* builds the house,
127: 3 Sons are a heritage from the *L*,
128: 1 Blessed are all who fear the *L*,
130: 1 O *L*; O Lord, hear my voice.
130: 3 If you, O *L*, kept a record of sins,
130: 5 I wait for the *L*, my soul waits,
131: 3 O Israel, put your hope in the *L*
132: 1 O *L*, remember David
132:13 For the *L* has chosen Zion,
133: 3 For there the *L* bestows his
134: 3 May the *L*, the Maker of heaven
135: 4 For the *L* has chosen Jacob
135: 6 The *L* does whatever pleases him,
136: 1 Give thanks to the *L*, for he is good
137: 4 How can we sing the songs of the *L*
138: 1 I will praise you, O *L*,
138: 8 The *L* will fulfill his purpose.
139: 1 O *L*, you have searched me
140: 1 Rescue me, O *L*, from evil men;
141: 1 O *L*, I call to you; come quickly
141: 3 Set a guard over my mouth, O *L*;
142: 5 I cry to you, O *L*;
143: 9 Rescue me from my enemies, O *L*,
144: 3 O *L*, what is man that you care
145: 3 Great is the *L* and most worthy
145: 8 *L* is gracious and compassionate,
145: 9 The *L* is good to all;
145:17 The *L* is righteous in all his ways
145:18 The *L* is near to all who call on him
146: 5 whose hope is in the *L* his God,
146: 7 The *L* sets prisoners free,
147: 2 The *L* builds up Jerusalem;
147: 7 Sing to the *L* with thanksgiving;
147:11 *L* delights in those who fear him,
147:12 Extol the *L*, O Jerusalem;
148: 1 Praise the *L* from the heavens,
148: 7 Praise the *L* from the earth,
149: 4 For the *L* takes delight

Ps 150: 1 Praise the *L*.
150: 6 that has breath praise the *L*.
Pr 1: 7 The fear of the *L* is the beginning
1:29 and did not choose to fear the *L*,
2: 5 will understand the fear of the *L*
2: 6 For the *L* gives wisdom,
3: 5 Trust in the *L* with all your heart
3: 7 fear the *L* and shun evil.
3: 9 Honor the *L* with your wealth,
3:12 the *L* disciplines those he loves,
3:19 By wisdom the *L* laid the earth's
5:21 are in full view of the *L*,
6:16 There are six things the *L* hates,
8:13 To fear the *L* is to hate evil;
9:10 "The fear of the *L* is the beginning
10:27 The fear of the *L* adds length to life
11: 1 The *L* abhors dishonest scales,
12:22 The *L* detests lying lips,
14: 2 whose walk is upright fears the *L*,
14:26 He who fears the *L* has a secure
14:27 The fear of the *L* is a fountain
15: 3 The eyes of the *L* are everywhere,
15:16 Better a little with the fear of the *L*
15:33 of the *L* teaches a man wisdom,
16: 2 but motives are weighed by the *L*.
16: 3 Commit to the *L* whatever you do,
16: 4 The *L* works out everything
16: 5 The *L* detests all the proud of heart
16: 9 but the *L* determines his steps.
16:33 but its every decision is from the *L*.
18:10 The name of the *L* is a strong tower
18:22 and receives favor from the *L*.
19:14 but a prudent wife is from the *L*.
19:17 to the poor lends to the *L*,
19:23 The fear of the *L* leads to life:
20:10 the *L* detests them both.
21: 2 but the *L* weighs the heart.
21: 3 to the *L* than sacrifice.
21:30 that can succeed against the *L*.
21:31 but victory rests with the *L*.
22: 2 The *L* is the Maker of them all.
22:23 for the *L* will take up their case
23:17 for the fear of the *L*.
24:18 or the *L* will see and disapprove
24:21 Fear the *L* and the king, my son,
25:22 and the *L* will reward you.
28:14 is the man who always fears the *L*,
29:26 from the *L* that man gets justice.
30: 7 "Two things I ask of you, O *L*;
31:30 a woman who fears the *L* is
Isa 2: 3 up to the mountain of the *L*,
2:10 the ground from dread of the *L*,
3:17 the *L* will make their scalps bald."
4: 2 of the *L* will be beautiful
5:16 the *L* Almighty will be exalted
6: 3 holy, holy is the *L* Almighty;
9: 7 The zeal of the *L* Almighty
11: 2 The Spirit of the *L* will rest on him
11: 9 full of the knowledge of the *L*
12: 2 The *L*, the *L*, is my strength
18: 7 of the Name of the *L* Almighty.
24: 1 the *L* is going to lay waste the earth
25: 1 O *L*, you are my God;
25: 6 this mountain the *L* Almighty will
25: 8 The Sovereign *L* will wipe away
26: 4 Trust in the *L* forever,
26: 8 *L*, walking in the way of your laws,
26:13 O *L*, our God, other lords
26:21 the *L* is coming out of his dwelling
27: 1 the *L* will punish with his sword,
27:12 In that day the *L* will thresh
28: 5 In that day the *L* Almighty
29: 6 the *L* Almighty will come
29:15 to hide their plans from the *L*,
30:18 For the *L* is a God of justice.
30:26 when the *L* binds up the bruises
30:27 the Name of the *L* comes from afar
30:30 The *L* will cause men
33: 2 O *L*, be gracious to us;
33: 6 the fear of the *L* is the key
33:22 For the *L* is our judge,
34: 2 The *L* is angry with all nations;
35: 2 they will see the glory of the *L*,
35:10 the ransomed of the *L* will return.

Isa 38: 7 to you that the *L* will do what he
40: 3 the way for the *L;*
40: 5 the glory of the *L* will be revealed,
40: 7 the breath of the *L* blows on them.
40: 10 the Sovereign *L* comes with power,
40: 14 Whom did the *L* consult
40: 28 The *L* is the everlasting God,
40: 31 but those who hope in the *L*
41: 14 will help you," declares the *L,*
41: 20 that the hand of the *L* has done this
42: 6 the *L,* have called you
42: 8 "I am the *L;* that is my name!
42: 13 The *L* will march out like a mighty
42: 21 It pleased the *L*
43: 3 For I am the *L,* your God,
43: 11 I, even I, am the *L.*
44: 6 "This is what the *L* says—
44: 24 I am the *L,*
45: 5 I am the *L,* and there is no other;
45: 7 I, the *L,* do all these things.
45: 21 Was it not I, the *L?*
48: 17 "I am the *L* your God,
50: 4 Sovereign *L* has given me
50: 10 Who among you fears the *L*
51: 1 and who seek the *L:*
51: 11 The ransomed of the *L* will return.
51: 15 the *L* Almighty is his name.
53: 1 the arm of the *L* been revealed?
53: 6 and the *L* has laid on him
53: 10 and the will of the *L* will prosper
54: 5 the *L* Almighty is his name—
55: 6 Seek the *L* while he may be found;
55: 7 to the *L,* and he will have mercy
56: 6 who bind themselves to the *L*
58: 8 of the *L* will be your rear guard.
58: 11 The *L* will guide you always;
59: 1 the arm of the *L* is not too short
60: 1 the glory of the *L* rises upon you.
60: 16 Then you will know that I, the *L,*
60: 20 the *L* will be your everlasting light,
61: 1 Spirit of the Sovereign *L* is on me,
61: 3 a planting of the *L*
61: 10 I delight greatly in the *L;*
61: 11 so the Sovereign *L* will make
62: 4 for the *L* will take delight in you,
63: 7 I will tell of the kindnesses of the *L,*
64: 8 Yet, O *L,* you are our Father.
66: 15 See, the *L* is coming with fire,

Jer 1: 9 Then the *L* reached out his hand
2: 19 when you forsake the *L* your God,
3: 25 sinned against the *L* our God,
4: 4 Circumcise yourselves to the *L,*
8: 7 the requirements of the *L.*
9: 24 I am the *L,* who exercises kindness,
10: 6 No one is like you, O *L;*
10: 10 But the *L* is the true God;
12: 1 You are always righteous, O *L,*
14: 7 O *L,* do something for the sake
14: 20 O *L,* we acknowledge our
16: 15 will say, 'As surely as the *L* lives,
16: 19 O *L,* my strength and my fortress,
17: 7 is the man who trusts in the *L,*
17: 10 "I the *L* search the heart
20: 11 *L* is with me like a mighty warrior;
23: 6 The *L* Our Righteousness.
24: 7 heart to know me, that I am the *L.*
28: 9 as one truly sent by the *L* only
31: 11 For the *L* will ransom Jacob
31: 22 The *L* will create a new thing
31: 34 his brother, saying, 'Know the *L,*'
32: 27 I am the *L,* the God of all mankind.
33: 16 The *L* Our Righteousness.'
36: 6 the words of the *L* that you wrote
40: 3 now the *L* has brought it about;
42: 3 Pray that the *L* your God will tell
42: 4 I will tell you everything the *L* says
42: 6 we will obey the *L* our God,
50: 4 go in tears to seek the *L* their God.
51: 10 " 'The *L* has vindicated us;
51: 56 For the *L* is a God of retribution;

La 3: 24 to myself, "The *L* is my portion;
3: 25 *L* is good to those whose hope is
3: 40 and let us return to the *L.*

Eze 1: 3 the word of the *L* came
1: 28 of the likeness of the glory of the *L.*
4: 14 Sovereign *L!* I have never defiled
10: 4 Then the glory of the *L* rose
15: 7 you will know that I am the *L.*
30: 3 the day of the *L* is near—
36: 23 nations will know that I am the *L,*
37: 4 'Dry bones, hear the word of the *L!*
43: 4 glory of the *L* entered the temple
44: 4 *L*ord filling the temple of the *L,*

Da 9: 2 to the word of the *L* given

Hos 1: 7 horsemen, but by the *L* their God."
2: 20 and you will acknowledge the *L.*
3: 1 as the *L* loves the Israelites,
3: 5 They will come trembling to the *L*
6: 1 "Come, let us return to the *L.*
6: 3 Let us acknowledge the *L;*
10: 12 for it is time to seek the *L,*
12: 5 the *L* is his name of renown!
14: 1 O Israel, to the *L* your God.

Joel 1: 1 The word of the *L* that came
1: 15 For the day of the *L* is near;
2: 1 for the day of the *L* is coming.
2: 11 The day of the *L* is great;
2: 13 Return to the *L* your God,
2: 23 rejoice in the *L* your God,
2: 31 the great and dreadful day of the *L.*
2: 32 on the name of the *L* will be saved;
3: 14 For the day of the *L* is near
3: 16 the *L* will be a refuge for his people,

Am 4: 13 the *L* God Almighty is his name.
5: 6 Seek the *L* and live,
5: 15 Perhaps the *L* God Almighty will
5: 18 long for the day of the *L?*
7: 15 *L* took me from tending the flock
8: 12 searching for the word of the *L,*
9: 5 The Lord, the *L* Almighty,

Ob :15 "The day of the *L* is near

Jnh 1: 3 But Jonah ran away from the *L*
1: 4 the *L* sent a great wind on the sea,
1: 17 But the *L* provided a great fish
2: 9 Salvation comes from the *L.*"
4: 2 He prayed to the *L,* "O *L,*
4: 6 Then the *L* God provided a vine

Mic 1: 1 The word of the *L* that came to Micah
4: 2 up to the mountain of the *L,*
5: 4 flock in the strength of the *L,*
6: 2 For the *L* has a case
6: 8 And what does the *L* require of you
7: 7 as for me, I watch in hope for the *L,*

Na 1: 2 The *L* takes vengeance on his foes
1: 3 The *L* is slow to anger

Hab 2: 14 knowledge of the glory of the *L,*
2: 20 But the *L* is in his holy temple;
3: 2 I stand in awe of your deeds, O *L.*

Zep 1: 1 The word of the *L* that came
1: 7 for the day of the *L* is near.
3: 17 The *L* your God is with you,

Hag 1: 1 the word of the *L* came
1: 8 and be honored," says the *L.*
2: 23 that day,' declares the *L* Almighty,

Zec 1: 1 the word of the *L* came
1: 17 and the *L* will again comfort Zion
3: 1 standing before the angel of the *L,*
4: 6 by my Spirit,' says the *L* Almighty.
6: 12 and build the temple of the *L.*
8: 21 the *L* and seek the *L* Almighty.
9: 16 The *L* their God will save them
14: 5 Then the *L* my God will come,
14: 9 The *L* will be king
14: 16 the *L* Almighty, and to celebrate

Mal 1: 1 The word of the *L* to Israel
3: 6 "I the *L* do not change.
4: 5 and dreadful day of the *L* comes.

Ex 4: 14 the *L* anger burned against Moses
12: 11 Eat it in haste; it is the *L* Passover.
34: 34 he entered the *L* presence

Lev 23: 4 " 'These are the *L* appointed feasts,

Nu 9: 23 At the *L* command they encamped
14: 41 you disobeying the *L* command?
32: 13 The *L* anger burned against Israel

Dt 6: 18 is right and good in the *L* sight,
10: 13 and to observe the *L* commands
32: 9 For the *L* portion is his people,

Jos 21: 45 Not one of all the *L* good promises

1Sa 24: 10 because he is the *L* anointed.'

1Ki 10: 9 Because of the *L* eternal love

Ps 24: 1 The earth is the *L,* and everything
32: 10 but the *L* unfailing love
89: 1 of the *L* great love forever;
103: 17 *L* love is with those who fear him,
118: 15 "The *L* right hand has done mighty

Pr 3: 11 do not despise the *L* discipline
19: 21 but it is the *L* purpose that prevails.

Isa 24: 14 west they acclaim the *L* majesty.
30: 9 to listen to the *L* instruction.
49: 4 Yet what is due me is in the *L* hand
53: 10 Yet it was the *L* will to crush him
55: 13 This will be for the *L* renown,
61: 2 to proclaim the year of the *L* favor
62: 3 of splendor in the *L* hand,

Jer 25: 17 So I took the cup from the *L* hand
48: 10 lax in doing the *L* work!
51: 7 was a gold cup in the *L* hand;

La 3: 22 of the *L* great love we are not

Eze 7: 19 them in the day of the *L* wrath.

Joel 3: 18 will flow out of the *L* house

Ob :21 And the kingdom will be the *L.*

Mic 4: 1 of the *L* temple will be established
6: 2 O mountains, the *L* accusation;

Hab 2: 16 from the *L* right hand is coming

Zep 2: 3 sheltered on the day of the *L* anger.

LOSE (LOSES LOSS LOST)
Dt 1: 28 Our brothers have made us *l* heart.

1Sa 17: 32 "Let no one *l* heart on account

Isa 7: 4 Do not *l* heart because of these two

Mt 10: 39 Whoever finds his life will *l* it,
and yet *l* or forfeit his very self?

Lk 9: 25 and yet *l* or forfeit his very self?

Jn 6: 39 that I shall *l* none of all that he has

2Co 4: 1 this ministry, we do not *l* heart.
4: 16 Therefore we do not *l* heart.

Heb 12: 3 will not grow weary and *l* heart.
12: 5 do not *l* heart when he rebukes you

2Jn :8 that you do not *l* what you have

LOSES (LOSE)
Mt 5: 13 But if the salt *l* its saltiness,
Lk 15: 4 you has a hundred sheep and *l* one
15: 8 has ten silver coins and *l* one.

LOSS (LOSE)
Ro 11: 12 and their *l* means riches
1Co 3: 15 he will suffer *l;* he himself will be
Php 3: 8 I consider everything a *l* compared

LOST (LOSE)
Ps 73: 2 I had nearly *l* my foothold.
Jer 50: 6 "My people have been *l* sheep;
Eze 34: 4 the strays or searched for the *l.*
34: 16 for the *l* and bring back the strays.
Mt 18: 14 any of these little ones should be *l.*
Lk 15: 4 go after the *l* sheep until he finds it?
15: 6 with me; I have found my *l* sheep.'
15: 9 with me; I have found my *l* coin.'
15: 24 is alive again; he was *l* and is found
19: 10 to seek and to save what was *l.*"
Php 3: 8 for whose sake I have *l* all things.

LOT (LOTS)
Nephew of Abraham (Ge 11:27; 12:5).
Chose to live in Sodom (Ge 13). Rescued from
four kings (Ge 14). Rescued from Sodom (Ge
19:1–29; 2Pe 2:7). Fathered Moab and Ammon
by his daughters (Ge 19:30–38).
Est 3: 7 the *l*) in the presence of Haman
9: 24 the *l*) for their ruin and destruction.

Pr 16:33 The *l* is cast into the lap,
18:18 Casting the *l* settles disputes
Ecc 3:22 his work, because that is his *l.*
Ac 1:26 Then they cast lots, and the *l* fell

LOTS (LOT)
Jos 18:10 Joshua then cast *l* for them
Ps 22:18 and cast *l* for my clothing.
Joel 3: 3 They cast *l* for my people
Ob :11 and cast *l* for Jerusalem,
Mt 27:35 divided up his clothes by casting *l.*
Ac 1:26 Then they cast *l,* and the lot fell

LOVE* (BELOVED LOVED LOVELY LOVER'S
LOVERS LOVES LOVING LOVING-KINDNESS)
Ge 20:13 'This is how you can show your *l*
22: 2 your only son, Isaac, whom you *l,*
29:18 Jacob was in *l* with Rachel and said
29:20 days to him because of his *l* for her.
29:32 Surely my husband will *l* me now."
Ex 15:13 "In your unfailing *l* you will lead
20: 6 showing *l* to a thousand generations
20: 6 of those who *l* me
21: 5 'I *l* my master and my wife
34: 6 abounding in *l* and faithfulness,
34: 7 maintaining *l* to thousands,
Lev 19:18 but *l* your neighbor as yourself.
19:34 *L* him as yourself,
Nu 14:18 abounding in *l* and forgiving sin
14:19 In accordance with your great *l,*
Dt 5:10 showing *l* to a thousand generations
5:10 of those who *l* me
6: 5 *L* the LORD your God
7: 9 generations of those who *l* him
7: 9 keeping his covenant of *l*
7:12 God will keep his covenant of *l*
7:13 He will *l* you and bless you
10:12 to walk in all his ways, to *l* him,
10:19 you are to *l* those who are aliens,
11: 1 *L* the LORD your God
11:13 to *l* the LORD your God,
11:22 to *l* the LORD your God,
13: 3 you *l* him with all your heart
13: 6 wife you *l,* or your closest friend
19: 9 to *l* the LORD your God
21:15 the son of the wife he does not *l,*
21:16 the son of the wife he does not *l.*
30: 6 so that you may *l* him
30:16 today to *l* the LORD your God,
30:20 and that you may *l* the LORD your
33: 3 Surely it is you who *l* the people;
Jos 22: 5 to *l* the LORD your God, to walk
23:11 careful to *l* the LORD your God.
Jdg 5:31 may they who *l* you be like the sun
14:16 You hate me! You don't really *l* me
16: 4 he fell in *l* with a woman
16:15 "How can you say, 'I *l* you,'
1Sa 18:20 Saul's daughter Michal was in *l*
20:17 had David reaffirm his oath out of *l*
2Sa 1:26 Your *l* for me was wonderful,
7:15 But my *l* will never be taken away
13: 1 son of David fell in *l* with Tamar,
13: 4 said to him, "I'm in *l* with Tamar,
16:17 "Is this the *l* you show your friend?
19: 6 You *l* those who hate you
19: 6 hate you and hate those who *l* you.
1Ki 3: 3 Solomon showed his *l*
8:23 you who keep your covenant of *l*
10: 9 of the LORD's eternal *l* for Israel,
11: 2 Solomon held fast to them in *l.*
1Ch 16:34 his *l* endures forever.
16:41 "for his *l* endures forever."
17:13 I will never take my *l* away
2Ch 5:13 his *l* endures forever."
6:14 you who keep your covenant of *l*
6:42 Remember the great *l* promised
7: 3 his *l* endures forever."
7: 6 saying, "His *l* endures forever."
9: 8 Because of the *l* of your God
19: 2 and *l* those who hate the LORD?
20:21 for his *l* endures forever."
Ezr 3:11 his *l* to Israel endures forever."
Ne 1: 5 covenant of *l* with those who *l* him

Ne 9:17 slow to anger and abounding in *l.*
9:32 who keeps his covenant of *l.*
13:22 to me according to your great *l.*
Job 15:34 of those who *l* bribes.
19:19 those I *l* have turned against me.
37:13 or to water his earth and show his *l.*
Ps 4: 2 How long will you *l* delusions
5:11 that those who *l* your name may
6: 4 save me because of your unfailing *l.*
11: 5 wicked and those who *l* violence
13: 5 But I trust in your unfailing *l;*
17: 7 Show the wonder of your great *l,*
18: 1 I *l* you, O LORD, my strength.
21: 7 through the unfailing *l*
23: 6 Surely goodness and *l* will follow
25: 6 O LORD, your great mercy and *l,*
25: 7 according to your *l* remember me,
26: 3 for your *l* is ever before me,
26: 8 I *l* the house where you live,
31: 7 I will be glad and rejoice in your *l,*
31:16 save me in your unfailing *l.*
31:21 for he showed his wonderful *l*
31:23 *L* the LORD, all his saints!
32:10 but the LORD's unfailing *l*
33: 5 the earth is full of his unfailing *l.*
33:18 whose hope is in his unfailing *l,*
33:22 May your unfailing *l* rest upon us,
36: 5 Your *l,* O LORD, reaches
36: 7 How priceless is your unfailing *l!*
36:10 Continue your *l* to those who know
40:10 I do not conceal your *l*
40:11 may your *l* and your truth always
40:16 may those who *l* your salvation
42: 8 By day the LORD directs his *l,*
44:26 of your unfailing *l.*
45: 7 You *l* righteousness and hate
48: 9 we meditate on your unfailing *l.*
51: 1 according to your unfailing *l;*
52: 3 You *l* evil rather than good,
52: 4 You *l* every harmful word,
52: 8 I trust in God's unfailing *l*
57: 3 God sends his *l* and his faithfulness
57:10 For great is your *l,* reaching
59:16 in the morning I will sing of your *l;*
60: 5 that those who *l* may be delivered.
61: 7 appoint your *l* and faithfulness
63: 3 Because your *l* is better than life,
66:20 or withheld his *l* from me!
69:13 in your great *l,* O God,
69:16 out of the goodness of your *l;*
69:36 and those who *l* his name will dwell
70: 4 may those who *l* your salvation
77: 8 Has his unfailing *l* vanished forever
85: 7 Show us your unfailing *l,* O LORD
85:10 *L* and faithfulness meet together;
86: 5 abounding in *l* to all who call
86:13 For great is your *l* toward me;
86:15 abounding in *l* and faithfulness.
88:11 Is your *l* declared in the grave,
89: 1 of the LORD's great *l* forever;
89: 2 declare that your *l* stands firm
89:14 *l* and faithfulness go before you.
89:24 My faithful *l* will be with him,
89:28 I will maintain my *l* to him forever,
89:33 but I will not take my *l* from him,
89:49 where is your former great *l,*
90:14 with your unfailing *l,*
92: 2 to proclaim your *l* in the morning
94:18 your *l,* O LORD, supported me.
97:10 Let those who the LORD hate
98: 3 He has remembered his *l*
100: 5 is good and his *l* endures forever;
101: 1 I will sing of your *l* and justice;
103: 4 crowns you with *l* and compassion.
103: 8 slow to anger, abounding in *l.*
103:11 so great is his *l* for those who fear
103:17 LORD's *l* is with those who fear
106: 1 his *l* endures forever.
106:45 and out of his great *l* he relented.
107: 1 his *l* endures forever.
107: 8 to the LORD for his unfailing *l*
107:15 to the LORD for his unfailing *l*
107:21 to the LORD for his unfailing *l*
107:31 to the LORD for his unfailing *l*

Ps 107:43 consider the great *l* of the LORD.
108: 4 For great is your *l,* higher
108: 6 that those you *l* may be delivered.
109:21 out of the goodness of your *l,*
109:26 save me in accordance with your *l.*
115: 1 because of your *l* and faithfulness,
116: 1 I *l* the LORD, for he heard my
117: 2 For great is his *l* toward us,
118: 1 his *l* endures forever.
118: 2 "His *l* endures forever."
118: 3 "His *l* endures forever."
118: 4 "His *l* endures forever."
118:29 his *l* endures forever.
119:41 May your unfailing *l* come to me,
119:47 because I *l* them.
119:48 to your commands, which I *l,*
119:64 The earth is filled with your *l,*
119:76 May your unfailing *l* be my
119:88 my life according to your *l,*
119:97 Oh, how I *l* your law!
119:113 but I *l* your law.
119:119 therefore I *l* your statutes.
119:124 your servant according to your *l*
119:127 Because I *l* your commands
119:132 to those who *l* your name.
119:149 in accordance with your *l;*
119:159 O LORD, according to your *l.*
119:159 See how I *l* your precepts;
119:163 but I *l* your law.
119:165 peace have they who *l* your law,
119:167 for I *l* them greatly.
122: 6 "May those who *l* you be secure.
130: 7 for with the LORD is unfailing *l*
136: 1 -26 His *l* endures forever.
138: 2 for your *l* and your faithfulness,
138: 8 your *l,* O LORD, endures forever
143: 8 of your unfailing *l,*
143:12 In your unfailing *l,* silence my
145: 8 slow to anger and rich in *l.*
145:20 over all who *l* him,
147:11 who put their hope in his unfailing *l*
Pr 1:22 you simple ones *l* your simple
3: 3 Let *l* and faithfulness never leave
4: 6 *l* her, and she will watch over you.
5:19 you ever be captivated by her *l.*
7:18 let's drink deep of *l* till morning;
7:18 let's enjoy ourselves with *l!*
8:17 I *l* those who *l* me,
8:21 wealth on those who *l* me
8:36 all who hate me *l* death."
9: 8 rebuke a wise man and he will *l* you
10:12 but *l* covers over all wrongs.
14:22 those who plan what is good find *l*
15:17 of vegetables where there is *l*
16: 6 Through *l* and faithfulness sin is
17: 9 over an offense promotes *l,*
18:21 and those who *l* it will eat its fruit.
19:22 What a man desires is unfailing *l;*
20: 6 claims to have unfailing *l,*
20:13 Do not *l* sleep or you will grow
20:28 *L* and faithfulness keep a king safe;
20:28 through *l* his throne is made secure
21:21 who pursues righteousness and *l*
27: 5 rebuke than hidden *l.*
Ecc 3: 8 a time to *l* and a time to hate,
9: 1 but no man knows whether *l*
9: 6 Their *l,* their hate
9: 9 life with your wife, whom you *l,*
SS 1: 2 for your *l* is more delightful
1: 3 No wonder the maidens *l* you!
1: 4 we will praise your *l* more
1: 7 you whom I *l,* where you graze
2: 4 and his banner over me is *l.*
2: 5 for I am faint with *l.*
2: 7 Do not arouse or awaken *l*
3: 5 Do not arouse or awaken *l*
4:10 How delightful is your *l,* my sister,
4:10 How much more pleasing is your *l*
5: 8 Tell him I am faint with *l.*
7: 6 O *l,* with your delights!
7:12 there I will give you my *l.*
8: 4 Do not arouse or awaken *l*
8: 6 for *l* is as strong as death,
8: 7 Many waters cannot quench *l;*
8: 7 all the wealth of his house for *l,*
Isa 1:23 they all *l* bribes

Isa 5: 1 I will sing for the one I /
16: 5 In / a throne will be established;
38:17 In your / you kept me
43: 4 and because I / you,
54:10 yet my unfailing / for you will not
55: 3 my faithful / promised to David.
56: 6 to / the name of the LORD,
56:10 they / to sleep.
57: 8 a pact with those whose beds you /,
61: 8 "For I, the LORD, / justice;
63: 9 In his / and mercy he redeemed
66:10 all you who / her;
Jer 2:25 I / foreign gods,
2:33 How skilled you are at pursuing /!
5:31 and my people / it this way.
12: 7 I will give the one I /
14:10 "They greatly / to wander;
16: 5 my / and my pity from this people
31: 3 you with an everlasting /;
32:18 You show / to thousands
33:11 his / endures forever."
La 3:22 of the LORD's great / we are not
3:32 so great is his unfailing /.
Eze 16: 8 saw that you were old enough for /,
23:17 of /, and in their lust they defiled
33:32 more than one who sings / songs
Da 9: 4 covenant of / with all who / him
Hos 1: 6 for I will no longer show /
1: 7 Yet I will show / to the house
2: 4 I will not show my / to her children
2:19 in / and compassion.
2:23 I will show my / to the one I called
3: 1 Go, show your / to your wife again,
3: 1 and / the sacred raisin cakes."
3: 1 L her as the LORD loves
4: 1 "There is no faithfulness, no /,
4:18 their rulers dearly / shameful ways.
6: 4 Your / is like the morning mist,
9: 1 you / the wages of a prostitute
9:15 I will no longer / them;
10:12 reap the fruit of unfailing /,
11: 4 with ties of /;
12: 6 maintain / and justice,
14: 4 and / them freely,
Joel 2:13 slow to anger and abounding in /,
Am 4: 5 for this is what you / to do,"
5:15 Hate evil, / good;
Jnh 4: 2 slow to anger and abounding in /,
Mic 3: 2 you who hate good and / evil;
6: 8 To act justly and to / mercy
Zep 3:17 he will quiet you with his /,
Zec 8:17 and do not / to swear falsely.
8:19 Therefore / truth and peace."
Mt 3:17 "This is my Son, whom I /;
5:43 'L your neighbor and hate your
5:44 L your enemies and pray
5:46 you / those who / you, what reward
6: 5 for they / to pray standing
6:24 he will hate the one and / the other,
12:18 the one I /, in whom I delight;
17: 5 "This is my Son, whom I /;
19:19 and '/ your neighbor as yourself.' "
22:37 " 'L the Lord your God
22:39 'L your neighbor as yourself.'
23: 6 they / the place of honor
23: 7 they / to be greeted
24:12 the / of most will grow cold,
Mk 1:11 "You are my Son, whom I /;
9: 7 "This is my Son, whom I /.
12:30 L the Lord your God
12:31 'L your neighbor as yourself.'
12:33 To / him with all your heart,
12:33 and to / your neighbor
Lk 3:22 "You are my Son, whom I /;
6:27 you who hear me: L your enemies,
6:32 Even 'sinners' / those who / them.
6:32 you / those who / you, what credit
6:35 / your enemies, do good to them,
7:42 which of them will / him more?"
10:27 and, '/ your neighbor as yourself
10:27 " 'L the Lord your God
11:42 you neglect justice and the / of God

Lk 11:43 you / the most important seats
16:13 he will hate the one and / the other,
20:13 whom I /; perhaps they will respect
20:46 / to be greeted in the marketplaces
Jn 5:42 I know that you do not have the /
8:42 were your Father, you would / me,
11: 3 "Lord, the one you / is sick."
13: 1 them the full extent of his /.
13:34 I give you: L one another.
13:34 so you must / one another.
13:35 disciples, if you / one another."
14:15 "If you / me, you will obey what I
14:21 I too will / him and show myself
14:23 My Father will / him, and we will
14:24 He who does not / me will not obey
14:31 world must learn that I / the Father
15: 9 Now remain in my /.
15:10 commands and remain in his /.
15:10 you will remain in my /,
15:12 L each other as I have loved you.
15:13 Greater / has no one than this,
15:17 This is my command: L each other.
15:19 to the world, it would / you
17:26 known in order that the / you have
21:15 do you truly / me more than these
21:15 he said, "you know that I / you."
21:16 Yes, Lord, you know that I / you."
21:16 do you truly / me?" He answered,
21:17 all things; you know that I / you."
21:17 "Do you / me?" He said, "Lord,
21:17 "Simon son of John, do you / me?"
Ro 5: 5 because God has poured out his /
5: 8 God demonstrates his own / for us
8:28 for the good of those who / him,
8:35 us from the / of Christ?
8:39 us from the / of God that is
12: 9 L must be sincere.
12:10 to one another in brotherly /.
13: 8 continuing debt to / one another,
13: 9 "L your neighbor as yourself."
13:10 Therefore / is the fulfillment
13:10 L does no harm to its neighbor.
14:15 you are no longer acting in /.
15:30 and by the / of the Spirit,
16: 8 Greet Ampliatus, whom I /
1Co 2: 9 prepared for those who / him"—
4:17 my son whom I /, who is faithful
4:21 or in / and with a gentle spirit?
8: 1 Knowledge puffs up, but / builds up
13: 1 have not /, I am only a resounding
13: 2 but have not /, I am nothing.
13: 3 but have not /, I gain nothing.
13: 4 Love is patient, / is kind.
13: 4 L is patient, love is kind.
13: 6 L does not delight in evil
13: 8 L never fails.
13:13 But the greatest of these is /.
13:13 three remain: faith, hope and /.
14: 1 way of / and eagerly desire spiritual
16:14 Do everything in /.
16:22 If anyone does not / the Lord—
16:24 My / to all of you in Christ Jesus.
2Co 2: 4 to let you know the depth of my /
2: 8 therefore, to reaffirm your / for him
5:14 For Christ's / compels us,
6: 6 in the Holy Spirit and in sincere /;
8: 7 complete earnestness and in your /
8: 8 sincerity of your / by comparing it
8:24 show these men the proof of your /
11:11 Why? Because I do not / you?
12:15 If I / you more, will you / me less?
13:11 And the God of / and peace will be
13:14 of the Lord Jesus Christ, and the /
Gal 5: 6 is faith expressing itself through /.
5:13 rather, serve one another in /.
5:14 "L your neighbor as yourself."
5:22 But the fruit of the Spirit is /, joy,
Eph 1: 4 In / he predestined us

Eph 1:15 and your / for all the saints,
2: 4 But because of his great / for us,
3:17 being rooted and established in /,
3:18 and high and deep is the / of Christ,
3:19 and to know this / that surpasses
4: 2 bearing with one another in /.
4:15 Instead, speaking the truth in /,
4:16 grows and builds itself up in /,
5: 2 loved children and live a life of /,
5:25 / your wives, just as Christ loved
5:28 husbands ought to / their wives
5:33 each one of you also must / his wife
6:23 / with faith from God the Father
6:24 Christ with an undying /.
6:24 to all who / our Lord Jesus Christ
Php 1: 9 that your / may abound more
1:16 so in /, knowing that I am put here
2: 1 from his /, if any fellowship
2: 2 having the same /, being one
4: 1 you whom I / and long for,
Col 1: 4 of the / you have for all the saints—
1: 5 / that spring from the hope that is
1: 8 also told us of your / in the Spirit.
2: 2 in heart and united in /,
3:14 And over all these virtues put on /,
3:19 / your wives and do not be harsh
1Th 1: 3 your labor prompted by /,
3: 6 good news about your faith and /.
3:12 May the Lord make your / increase
4: 9 about brotherly / we do not need
4: 9 taught by God to / each other.
4:10 you do / all the brothers
5: 8 on faith and / as a breastplate,
5:13 them in the highest regard in /
2Th 1: 3 and the / every one of you has
2:10 because they refused to / the truth
3: 5 direct your hearts into God's /
1Ti 1: 5 The goal of this command is /,
1:14 and / that are in Christ Jesus.
2:15 / and holiness with propriety.
4:12 in life, in /, in faith and in purity.
6:10 For the / of money is a root
6:11 faith, /, endurance and gentleness.
2Ti 1: 7 of power, of / and of self-discipline.
1:13 with faith and / in Christ Jesus.
2:22 and pursue righteousness, faith, /,
3: 3 unholy, without /, unforgiving,
3:10 faith, patience, /, endurance,
Tit 2: 2 in faith, in / and in endurance.
2: 4 women to / their husbands
3: 4 and / of God our Savior appeared,
3:15 Greet those who / us in the faith.
Phm : 5 and your / for all the saints.
: 7 Your / has given me great joy
: 9 yet I appeal to you on the basis of /.
Heb 6:10 and the / you have shown him
10:24 may spur one another on toward /
13: 5 free from the / of money
Jas 1:12 promised to those who / him.
2: 5 he promised those who / him?
2: 8 "L your neighbor as yourself,"
1Pe 1: 8 you have not seen him, you / him;
1:22 the truth so that you have sincere /
1:22 / one another deeply,
2:17 L the brotherhood of believers,
3: 8 be sympathetic, / as brothers,
3:10 "Whoever would / life
4: 8 Above all, / each other deeply,
4: 8 / covers over a multitude of sins.
5:14 Greet one another with a kiss of /.
2Pe 1: 7 and to brotherly kindness, /.
1:17 "This is my Son, whom I /;
1Jn 2: 5 God's / is truly made complete
2:15 Do not / the world or anything
2:15 the / of the Father is not in him.
3: 1 How great is the / the Father has
3:10 anyone who does not / his brother.
3:11 We should / one another.
3:14 Anyone who does not / remains
3:14 because we / our brothers.
3:16 This is how we know what / is:
3:17 how can the / of God be in him?

1Jn 3:18 let us not / with words or tongue
3:23 to / one another as he commanded
4: 7 Dear friends, let us / one another,
4: 7 for / comes from God.
4: 8 Whoever does not / does not know
4: 8 not know God, because God is *l*.
4: 9 This is how God showed his *l*
4:10 This is *l*: not that we loved God,
4:11 we also ought to / one another.
4:12 seen God; but if we / one another,
4:12 and his / is made complete in us.
4:16 God is *l*.
4:16 Whoever lives in / lives in God,
4:16 and rely on the / God has for us.
4:17 / is made complete among us
4:18 But perfect / drives out fear,
4:18 There is no fear in *l*.
4:18 who fears is not made perfect in *l*.
4:19 We / because he first loved us.
4:20 If anyone says, "I / God,"
4:20 anyone who does not / his brother,
4:20 whom he has seen, cannot / God,
4:21 loves God must also / his brother.
5: 2 we know that we / the children
5: 3 This is / for God: to obey his
2Jn : 1 whom I / in the truth—
: 3 will be with us in truth and *l*.
: 5 I ask that we / one another.
: 6 his command is that you walk in *l*.
: 6 this is *l*: that we walk in obedience
3Jn : 1 To my dear friend Gaius, whom I /
: 6 have told the church about your *l*.
Jude : 2 peace and / be yours in abundance.
:12 men are blemishes at your / feasts,
:21 Keep yourselves in God's *l*
Rev 2: 4 You have forsaken your first *l*.
2:19 I know your deeds, your / and faith
3:19 Those whom I / I rebuke
12:11 they did not / their lives so much

LOVED* (LOVE)
Ge 24:67 she became his wife, and he / her;
25:28 / Esau, but Rebekah / Jacob.
29:30 and he / Rachel more than Leah.
29:31 the LORD saw that Leah was not *l*,
29:33 the LORD heard that I am not *l*,
34: 3 and he / the girl and spoke tenderly
37: 3 Now Israel / Joseph more than any
37: 4 saw that their father / him more
Dt 4:37 Because he / your forefathers
7: 8 But it was because the LORD / you
10:15 on your forefathers and / them,
1Sa 1: 5 a double portion because he / her,
18: 1 in spirit with David, and he / him
18: 3 with David because he / him
18:16 But all Israel and Judah / David,
18:28 that his daughter Michal / David,
20:17 because he / him as he / himself.
2Sa 1:23 in life they were / and gracious,
12:24 The LORD / him; and
12:25 and because the LORD / him,
13:15 hated her more than he had / her.
1Ki 11: 1 / many foreign women
2Ch 11:21 Rehoboam / Maacah daughter
26:10 in the fertile lands, for he / the soil.
Ne 13:26 He was / by his God, and God
Ps 44: 3 light of your face, for you / them.
47: 4 the pride of Jacob, whom he *l*.
78:68 Mount Zion, which he *l*.
88:18 taken my companions and / ones
109:17 He / to pronounce a curse—
Isa 5: 1 My / one had a vineyard
Jer 2: 2 how as a bride you / me
8: 2 which they have / and served
31: 3 "I have / you with an everlasting
Eze 16:37 those you / as well as those you
Hos 2: 1 and of your sisters, 'My / one.'
2:23 to the one I called 'Not my / one.'
3: 1 though she is / by another
9:10 became as vile as the thing they *l*.
11: 1 "When Israel was a child, I / him,

Mal 1: 2 "But you ask, 'How have you / us?'
1: 2 "I have / you," says the LORD.
1: 2 "Yet I have / Jacob, but Esau I
Mk 10:21 Jesus looked at him and / him.
12: 6 left to send, a son, whom he /
Lk 7:47 been forgiven—for she / much.
16:14 The Pharisees, who / money,
Jn 3:16 so / the world that he gave his one
3:19 but men / darkness instead of light
11: 5 Jesus / Martha and her sister
11:36 "See how he / him!" But some
12:43 for they / praise from men more
13: 1 Having / his own who were
13:23 the disciple whom Jesus *l*,
13:34 As I have / you, so you must love
14:21 He who loves me will be /
14:28 If you / me, you would be glad that
15: 9 the Father has / me, so have I / you.
15:12 Love each other as I have / you.
16:27 loves you because you have / me
17:23 have / them even as you have / me.
17:24 you / me before the creation
19:26 the disciple whom he / standing
20: 2 one Jesus /, and said, "They have
21: 7 the disciple whom Jesus / said
21:20 whom Jesus / was following
Ro 1: 7 To all in Rome who are / by God
8:37 conquerors through him who / us.
9:13 "Jacob I /, but Esau I hated."
9:25 her 'my / one' who is not my / one,"
11:28 they are / on account
Gal 2:20 who / me and gave himself for me.
Eph 5: 1 as dearly / children and live a life
5: 2 as Christ / us and gave himself up
5:25 just as Christ / the church
Col 3:12 and dearly /, clothe yourselves
1Th 1: 4 For we know, brothers / by God,
2: 8 We / you so much that we were
2Th 2:13 for you, brothers / by the Lord,
2Ti 4:10 for Demas, because he / this world,
Heb 1: 9 You have / righteousness
2Pe 2:15 who / the wages of wickedness.
1Jn 4:10 This is love: not that we / God,
4:10 but that he / us and sent his Son
4:19 Dear friends, since God so / us,
4:19 We love because he first / us.
Jude : 1 who are / by God the Father
Rev 3: 9 and acknowledge that I have / you.

LOVELY* (LOVE)
Ge 29:17 but Rachel was / in form,
Est 1:11 and nobles, for she was / to look at.
2: 7 was / in form and features,
Ps 84: 1 How / is your dwelling place,
SS 1: 5 Dark am I, yet *l*,
2:14 and your face is *l*.
4: 3 your mouth is *l*.
5:16 he is altogether *l*.
6: 4 / as Jerusalem,
Am 8:13 / young women and strong young
Php 4: 8 whatever is *l*, whatever is

LOVER* (LOVE)
SS 1:13 My / is to me a sachet of myrrh
1:14 My / is to me a cluster
1:16 How handsome you are, my *l*!
2: 3 is my / among the young men.
2: 8 Listen! My *l*!
2: 9 My / is like a gazelle or a young
2:10 My / spoke and said to me,
2:16 *Beloved* My / is mine and I am his;
2:17 turn, my *l*,
4:16 Let my / come into his garden
5: 2 Listen! My / is knocking:
5: 4 My / thrust his hand
5: 5 I arose to open for my *l*,
5: 6 I opened for my *l*,
5: 6 but my / had left; he was gone.
5: 8 if you find my *l*,
5:10 *Beloved* My / is radiant and ruddy,
5:16 This is my *l*, this my friend,
6: 1 Where has your / gone,
6: 1 Which way did your / turn,

SS 6: 2 *Beloved* My / has gone
6: 3 I am my lover's and my / is mine;
7: 9 May the wine go straight to my *l*,
7:10 I belong to my *l*,
7:11 my *l*, let us go to the countryside,
7:13 that I have stored up for you, my *l*.
8: 5 leaning on her *l*?
8:14 *Beloved* Come away, my *l*,
1Ti 3: 3 not quarrelsome, not a / of money.

LOVER'S* (LOVE)
SS 6: 3 I am my / and my lover is mine;

LOVERS* (LOVE)
SS 5: 1 drink your fill, O *l*.
Jer 3: 1 as a prostitute with many /—
3: 2 the roadside you sat waiting for *l*,
4:30 Your / despise you;
La 1: 2 Among all her /,
Eze 16:33 but you give gifts to all your *l*,
16:36 in your promiscuity with your *l*,
16:37 I am going to gather all your *l*,
16:39 Then I will hand you over to your *l*,
16:41 and you will no longer pay your *l*,
23: 5 she lusted after her *l*, the Assyrians
23: 9 I handed her over to her *l*,
23:20 There she lusted after her *l*,
23:22 I will stir up your / against you,
Hos 2: 5 She said, 'I will go after my *l*,
2: 7 She will chase after her /
2:10 lewdness before the eyes of her *l*;
2:12 she said were her pay from her *l*;
2:13 and went after her *l*,
8: 9 Ephraim has sold herself to *l*.
2Ti 3: 2 People will be / of themselves,
3: 2 / of money, boastful, proud,
3: 3 without self-control, brutal, not /
3: 4 / of pleasure rather than / of God—

LOVES* (LOVE)
Ge 44:20 sons left, and his father / him.'
Dt 10:18 and / the alien, giving him food
15:16 because he / you and your family
21:15 and he / one but not the other,
21:16 son of the wife he / in preference
23: 5 because the LORD your God / you
28:54 wife he / or his surviving children
28:56 will begrudge the husband she /
33:12 and the one the LORD / rests
Ru 4:15 who / you and who is better to you
2Ch 2:11 "Because the LORD / his people,
Ps 11: 7 he / justice;
33: 5 The LORD / righteousness
34:12 Whoever of you / life
37:28 For the LORD / the just
87: 2 the LORD / the gates of Zion
91:14 Because he / me," says the LORD,
99: 4 The King is mighty, he / justice—
119:140 and your servant / them.
127: 2 for he grants sleep to those he *l*.
146: 8 the LORD / the righteous.
Pr 3:12 the LORD disciplines those he *l*,
12: 1 Whoever / discipline / knowledge,
13:24 he who / him is careful
15: 9 he / those who pursue
17:17 A friend / at all times,
17:19 He who / a quarrel / sin;
19: 8 He who gets wisdom / his own soul
21:17 He who / pleasure will become
21:17 whoever / wine and oil will never
22:11 He who / a pure heart and whose
29: 3 A man who / wisdom brings joy
Ecc 5:10 Whoever / money never has
5:10 whoever / wealth is never satisfied
SS 3: 1 I looked for the one my heart *l*;
3: 2 I will search for the one my heart *l*.
3: 3 "Have you seen the one my heart *l*?"
3: 4 when I found the one my heart *l*.
Hos 3: 1 as the LORD / the Israelites,
10:11 that / to thresh;
12: 7 he / to defraud.
Mal 2:11 the sanctuary the LORD /,
Mt 10:37 anyone who / his son or daughter
10:37 "Anyone who / his father
Lk 7: 5 because he / our nation

Lk	7:47	has been forgiven little / little."
Jn	3:35	Father / the Son and has placed
	5:20	For the Father / the Son
	10:17	reason my Father / me is that I lay
	12:25	The man who / his life will lose it,
	14:21	He who / me will be loved
	14:21	obeys them, he is the one who / me.
	14:23	Jesus replied, "If anyone / me,
	16:27	the Father himself / you
Ro	13:8	for he who / his fellowman has
1Co	8:3	But the man who / God is known
2Co	9:7	for God / a cheerful giver.
Eph	1:6	has freely given us in the One he l.
	5:28	He who / his wife / himself.
	5:33	must love his wife as he / himself,
Col	1:13	us into the kingdom of the Son he l,
Tit	1:8	one who / what is good, who is
Heb	12:6	the Lord disciplines those he l,
1Jn	2:10	Whoever / his brother lives
	2:15	If anyone / the world, the love
	4:7	Everyone who / has been born
	4:21	Whoever / God must also love his
	5:1	who / the father / his child
3Jn	:9	but Diotrephes, who / to be first,
Rev	1:5	To him who / us and has freed us
	20:9	camp of God's people, the city he l.
	22:15	and everyone who / and practices

LOVING* (LOVE)
Ps	25:10	All the ways of the Lord are l
	59:10	my l God.
	59:17	O God, are my fortress, my l God.
	62:12	and that you, O Lord, are l.
	144:2	He is my l God and my fortress,
	145:13	and l toward all he has made.
	145:17	and l toward all he has made.
Pr	5:19	A l doe, a graceful deer—
Heb	13:1	Keep on l each other as brothers.
1Jn	5:2	by l God and carrying out his

LOVING-KINDNESS* (LOVE)
Jer	31:3	I have drawn you with l.

LOWER
Ps	8:5	You made him a little l
2Co	11:7	a sin for me to l myself in order
Heb	2:7	You made him a little l

LOWING
1Sa	15:14	What is this l of cattle that I hear?"

LOWLY
Job	5:11	The l he sets on high,
Ps	138:6	on high, he looks upon the l,
Pr	29:23	but a man of l spirit gains honor.
Isa	57:15	also with him who is contrite and l
Eze	21:26	l will be exalted and the exalted
1Co	1:28	He chose the l things of this world

LOYAL
1Ch	29:18	and keep their hearts l to you.
Ps	78:8	whose hearts were not l to God,

LUKE*
Co-worker with Paul (Col 4:14; 2Ti 4:11; Phm 24).

LUKEWARM*
Rev	3:16	So, because you are l— neither hot

LUST (LUSTED LUSTS)
Pr	6:25	Do not l in your heart
Eze	20:30	and l after their vile images?
Col	3:5	sexual immorality, impurity, l,
1Th	4:5	not in passionate l like the heathen,
1Pe	4:3	in debauchery, l, drunkenness,
1Jn	2:16	the l of his eyes and the boasting

LUSTED (LUST)
Eze	23:5	she l after her lovers, the Assyrians

LUSTS* (LUST)
Nu	15:39	yourselves by going after the l
Ro	1:26	God gave them over to shameful l.

LUXURY
Jas	5:5	You have lived on earth in l

LYDIA'S*
Ac	16:40	went to L house, where they met

LYING (LIE)
Pr	6:17	a l tongue,
	12:22	The Lord detests l lips,
	21:6	A fortune made by a l tongue
	26:28	A l tongue hates those it hurts,

MACEDONIA
Ac	16:9	"Come over to M and help us."

MAD
Dt	28:34	The sights you see will drive you m

MADE (MAKE)
Ge	1:7	So God m the expanse
	1:16	God m two great lights—
	1:16	He also m the stars.
	1:25	God m the wild animals according
	1:31	God saw all that he had m,
	2:22	Then the Lord God m a woman
	6:6	was grieved that he had m man
	9:6	has God m man.
	15:18	that day the Lord m a covenant
Ex	20:11	six days the Lord m the heavens
	20:11	the Sabbath day and m it holy.
	24:8	the covenant that the Lord has m
	32:4	m it into an idol cast in the shape
Lev	16:34	Atonement is to be m once a year
Dt	32:6	who m you and formed you?
Jos	24:25	On that day Joshua m a covenant
2Ki	19:15	You have m heaven and earth.
2Ch	2:12	the God of Israel, who m heaven
Ne	9:6	You m the heavens,
	9:10	You m a name for yourself,
Ps	33:6	of the Lord were the heavens m,
	95:5	The sea is his, for he m it,
	96:5	but the Lord m the heavens.
	100:3	It is he who m us, and we are his;
	118:24	This is the day the Lord has m;
	136:7	who m the great lights—
	139:14	I am fearfully and wonderfully m,
Ecc	3:11	He has m everything beautiful
Isa	43:7	whom I formed and m."
	45:12	It is I who m the earth
	45:18	he who fashioned and m the earth,
	66:2	Has not my hand m all these things
Jer	10:12	But God m the earth by his power;
	27:5	and outstretched arm I m the earth
	32:17	you have m the heavens
	33:2	Lord says, he who m the earth,
	51:15	"He m the earth by his power;
Eze	3:17	I have m you a watchman
	33:7	I have m you a watchman
Am	5:8	(he who m the Pleiades and Orion,
Jnh	1:9	who m the sea and the land."
Mk	2:27	"The Sabbath was m for man,
Jn	1:3	Through him all things were m;
Ac	17:24	"The God who m the world
1Co	3:6	watered it, but God m it grow.
Heb	1:2	through whom he m the universe.
Jas	3:9	who have been m in God's likeness
Rev	14:7	Worship him who m the heavens,

MAGDALENE
Lk	8:2	Mary (called M) from whom seven

MAGI
Mt	2:1	M from the east came to Jerusalem

MAGIC (MAGICIANS)
Eze	13:20	I am against your m charms
Rev	21:8	those who practice m arts,
	22:15	those who practice m arts,

MAGICIANS (MAGIC)
Ex	7:11	the Egyptian m also did the same
Da	2:2	So the king summoned the m,

MAGNIFICENCE* (MAGNIFICENT)
1Ch	22:5	for the Lord should be of great m

MAGNIFICENT (MAGNIFICENCE)
1Ki	8:13	I have indeed built a m temple
Isa	28:29	in counsel and m in wisdom.
Mk	13:1	stones! What m buildings!"

MAGOG
Eze	38:2	of the land of M, the chief prince
	39:6	I will send fire on M

Rev	20:8	and M— to gather them for battle.

MAIDEN (MAIDENS)
Pr	30:19	and the way of a man with a m.
Isa	62:5	As a young man marries a m,
Jer	2:32	Does a m forget her jewelry,

MAIDENS (MAIDEN)
SS	1:3	No wonder the m love you!

MAIMED
Mt	18:8	It is better for you to enter life m

MAINTAIN (MAINTAINING)
Ps	82:3	m the rights of the poor
	106:3	Blessed are they who m justice,
Hos	12:6	m love and justice,
Am	5:15	m justice in the courts.
Ro	3:28	For we m that a man is justified

MAINTAINING* (MAINTAIN)
Ex	34:7	faithfulness, m love to thousands,

MAJESTIC* (MAJESTY)
Ex	15:6	was m in power.
	15:11	m in holiness.
Job	37:4	he thunders with his m voice.
Ps	8:1	how m is your name in all the earth
	8:9	how m is your name in all the earth
	29:4	the voice of the Lord is m.
	68:15	of Bashan are m mountains;
	76:4	more m than mountains rich
	111:3	Glorious and m are his deeds,
SS	6:4	m as troops with banners.
	6:10	m as the stars in procession?
Isa	30:30	men to hear his m voice
Eze	31:7	It was m in beauty,
2Pe	1:17	came to him from the M Glory,

MAJESTY* (MAJESTIC)
Ex	15:7	In the greatness of your m
Dt	5:24	has shown us his glory and his m,
	11:2	his m, his mighty hand, his
	33:17	In m he is like a firstborn bull;
	33:26	and on the clouds in his m.
1Ch	16:27	Splendor and m are before him;
	29:11	and the m and the splendor,
Est	1:4	the splendor and glory of his m.
	7:3	if it pleases your m, grant me my
Job	37:22	God comes in awesome m.
	40:10	and clothe yourself in honor and m
Ps	21:5	on him splendor and m.
	45:3	with splendor and m.
	45:4	In your m ride forth victoriously
	68:34	whose m is over Israel,
	93:1	The Lord reigns, he is robed in m
	93:1	the Lord is robed in m
	96:6	Splendor and m are before him;
	104:1	clothed with splendor and m.
	110:3	Arrayed in holy m,
	145:5	of the glorious splendor of your m,
Isa	2:10	and the splendor of his m!
	2:19	and the splendor of his m,
	2:21	and the splendor of his m,
	24:14	west they acclaim the Lord's m.
	26:10	and regard not the m of the Lord.
	53:2	or m to attract us to him,
Eze	31:2	can be compared with you in m?
	31:18	with you in splendor and m?
Da	4:30	and for the glory of my m?"
Mic	5:4	in the m of the name
Zec	6:13	and he will be clothed with m
Ac	19:27	will be robbed of her divine m."
	25:26	to write to His M about him.
2Th	1:9	and from the m of his power
Heb	1:3	hand of the M in heaven.
	8:1	of the throne of the M in heaven,
2Pe	1:16	but we were eyewitnesses of his m.
Jude	:25	only God our Savior be glory, m,

MAKE (MADE MAKER MAKERS MAKES MAKING MAN-MADE)
Ge	1:26	"Let us m man in our image,
	2:18	I will m a helper suitable for him."
	6:14	m yourself an ark of cypress wood;
	12:2	"I will m you into a great nation
Ex	22:3	thief must certainly m restitution,
	25:9	M this tabernacle and all its
	25:40	See that you m them according

Nu	6:25	the LORD *m* his face shine
2Sa	7: 9	Now I will *m* your name great,
Job	7:17	"What is man that you *m* so much
Ps	4: 8	*m* me dwell in safety.
	20: 4	and *m* all your plans succeed.
	108: 1	*m* music with all my soul.
	110: 1	hand until I *m* your enemies
	119:165	and nothing can *m* them stumble.
Pr	3: 6	and he will *m* your paths straight.
	4:26	*M* level paths for your feet
	20:18	*M* plans by seeking advice;
Isa	14:14	I will *m* myself like the Most High
	29:16	"He did not *m* me"?
	55: 3	I will *m* an everlasting covenant
	61: 8	and *m* an everlasting covenant
Jer	31:31	"when I will *m* a new covenant
Eze	37:26	I will *m* a covenant of peace
Mt	3: 3	*m* straight paths for him.' "
	28:19	and *m* disciples of all nations,
Mk	1:17	"and I will *m* you fishers of men."
Lk	13:24	"*M* every effort to enter
	14:23	country lanes and *m* them come in,
Ro	14:19	*m* every effort to do what leads
2Co	5: 9	So we *m* it our goal to please him,
Eph	4: 3	*M* every effort to keep the unity
Col	4: 5	*m* the most of every opportunity.
1Th	4:11	*M* it your ambition
Heb	4:11	*m* every effort to enter that rest,
	8: 5	it that you *m* everything according
	12:14	*M* every effort to live in peace
2Pe	1: 5	*m* every effort to add
	3:14	*m* every effort to be found spotless,

MAKER* (MAKE)

Job	4:17	Can a man be more pure than his *M*
	9: 9	He is the *M* of the Bear and Orion,
	32:22	my *M* would soon take me away.
	35:10	no one says, 'Where is God my *M*,
	36: 3	I will ascribe justice to my *M*.
	40:19	yet his *M* can approach him
Ps	95: 6	kneel before the LORD our *M*;
	115:15	the *M* of heaven and earth.
	121: 2	the *M* of heaven and earth.
	124: 8	the *M* of heaven and earth.
	134: 3	the *M* of heaven and earth,
	146: 6	the *M* of heaven and earth,
	149: 2	Let Israel rejoice in their *M*;
Pr	14:31	poor shows contempt for their *M*,
	17: 5	poor shows contempt for their *M*;
	22: 2	The LORD is the *M* of them all.
Ecc	11: 5	the *M* of all things.
Isa	17: 7	that day men will look to their *M*
	27:11	so their *M* has no compassion
	45: 9	to him who quarrels with his *M*,
	45:11	the Holy One of Israel, and its *M*:
	51:13	that you forget the LORD your *M*,
	54: 5	For your *M* is your husband—
Jer	10:16	for he is the *M* of all things,
	51:19	for he is the *M* of all things,
Hos	8:14	Israel has forgotten his *M*

MAKERS* (MAKE)

Isa	45:16	All the *m* of idols will be put

MAKES (MAKE)

Ps	23: 2	*m* me lie down in green pastures,
Pr	13:12	Hope deferred *m* the heart sick,
1Co	3: 7	but only God, who *m* things grow.

MAKING (MAKE)

Ps	19: 7	*m* wise the simple.
Ecc	12:12	Of *m* many books there is no end,
Jn	5:18	*m* himself equal with God.
Eph	5:16	*m* the most of every opportunity,

MALACHI*

Mal	1: 1	of the LORD to Israel through *M*.

MALE

Ge	1:27	*m* and female he created them.
Ex	13: 2	to me every firstborn *m*.
Nu	3:40	the first *m* offspring
Mt	19: 4	the Creator 'made them *m*
Gal	3:28	slave nor free, *m* nor female,

MALICE (MALICIOUS)

Mk	7:22	adultery, greed, *m*, deceit,
Ro	1:29	murder, strife, deceit and *m*.
1Co	5: 8	the yeast of *m* and wickedness,
Eph	4:31	along with every form of *m*.
Col	3: 8	*m*, slander, and filthy language

1Pe	2: 1	rid yourselves of all *m*

MALICIOUS (MALICE)

Pr	26:24	A *m* man disguises himself
1Ti	3:11	not *m* talkers but temperate
	6: 4	*m* talk, evil suspicions

MALIGN

Tit	2: 5	so that no one will *m* the word

MAN (MAN'S MANKIND MEN MEN'S WOMAN WOMEN)

Ge	1:26	"Let us make *m* in our image,
	2: 7	God formed the *m* from the dust
	2: 8	*m* became a living being
	2:15	God took the *m* and put
	2:18	for the *m* to be alone
	2:20	*m* gave names to all the
	2:23	she was taken out of *m*.
	2:25	*m* and his wife were both
	3: 9	God called to the *m*,
	3:22	*m* has now become like
	4: 1	I have brought forth a *m*.
	6: 3	not contend with *m* forever,
	6: 6	grieved that he had made *m*
	9: 6	Whoever sheds the blood of *m*,
Dt	8: 3	*m* does not live on bread
1Sa	13:14	a *m* after his own heart
	15:29	he is not a *m* that he
	16: 7	at the things *m* looks at.
Job	14: 1	*M* born of woman is of few
	14:14	If a *m* dies, will he live
Ps	1: 1	Blessed is the *m* who does
	8: 4	what is *m* that you are
	32: 2	Blessed is the *m* whose sin
	40: 4	Blessed is the *m* who makes
	84:12	blessed is the *m* who trusts
	103:15	As for *m*, his days are
	112: 1	Blessed is the *m* who fears
	119: 9	can a young *m* keep his
	127: 5	Blessed is the *m* whose quiver
	144: 3	what is *m* that you care
Pr	3:13	Blessed is the *m* who finds
	9: 8	Instruct a wise *m*
	14:12	that seems right to a *m*,
	30:19	way of a *m* with a maiden.
Isa	53: 3	a *m* of sorrows,
Jer	17: 5	the one who trusts in *m*,
	17: 7	blessed is the *m* who trusts
Eze	22:30	I looked for a *m*
Mt	4: 4	*M* does not live on bread
	19: 5	a *m* will leave his father
Mk	8:36	What good is it for a *m*
Lk	4: 4	'*M* does not live on bread
Ro	5:12	entered the world through one *m*
1Co	2:15	spiritual *m* makes judgments
	3:12	If any *m* builds on this
	7: 1	good for a *m* not to marry.
	7: 2	each *m* should have his own
	11: 3	head of every *m* is Christ,
	11: 3	head of woman is *m*
	13:11	When I became a *m*,
	15:21	death came through a *m*,
	15:45	first *m* Adam became a
	15:47	the second *m* from heaven
2Co	12: 2	I know a *m* in Christ
Eph	2:15	create in himself one new *m*
	5:31	a *m* will leave his father
Php	2: 8	found in appearance as a *m*,
1Ti	2: 5	the *m* Christ Jesus,
	2:12	have authority over a *m*;
2Ti	3:17	that the *m* of God may be
Heb	2: 6	what is *m* that you are
	9:27	as *m* is destined to die

MAN'S (MAN)

Pr	20:24	A *m* steps are directed by
Jer	10:23	a *m* life is not his own;
1Co	1:25	is wiser than *m* wisdom,

MAN-MADE (MAKE)

Heb	9:11	perfect tabernacle that is not *m*,
	9:24	not enter a *m* sanctuary that was

MANAGE (MANAGER)

Jer	12: 5	how will you *m* in the thickets
1Ti	3: 4	He must *m* his own family well
	3:12	one wife and must *m* his children
	5:14	to *m* their homes and to give

MANAGER (MANAGE)

Lk	12:42	Who then is the faithful and wise *m*
	16: 1	a rich man whose *m* was accused

MANASSEH

1. Firstborn of Joseph (Ge 41:51; 46:20). Blessed by Jacob but not firstborn (Ge 48). Tribe of blessed (Dt 33:17), numbered (Nu 1:35; 26:34), half allotted land east of Jordan (Nu 32; Jos 13:8–33), half west (Jos 17; Eze 48:4), failed to fully possess (Jos 17:12–13; Jdg 1:27), 12,000 from (Rev 7:6).

2. Son of Hezekiah; king of Judah (2Ki 21:1–18; 2Ch 33:1–20). Judah exiled for his detestable sins (2Ki 21:10–15). Repentance (2Ch 33:12–19).

MANDRAKES

Ge	30:14	give me some of your son's *m*."

MANGER

Lk	2:12	in strips of cloth and lying in a *m*."

MANIFESTATION*

1Co	12: 7	to each one the *m* of the Spirit is

MANKIND (MAN)

Ge	6: 7	I will wipe *m*, whom I have created
Ps	33:13	and sees all *m*;
Pr	8:31	and delighting in *m*.
Ecc	7:29	God made *m* upright,
Isa	40: 5	and all *m* together will see it.
	45:12	and created *m* upon it.
Jer	32:27	"I am the LORD, the God of all *m*.
Zec	2:13	Be still before the LORD, all *m*,
Lk	3: 6	And all *m* will see God's salvation

MANNA

Ex	16:31	people of Israel called the bread *m*.
Dt	8:16	He gave you *m* to eat in the desert.
Jn	6:49	Your forefathers ate the *m*
Rev	2:17	I will give some of the hidden *m*.

MANNER

1Co	11:27	in an unworthy *m* will be guilty
Php	1:27	conduct yourselves in a *m* worthy

MANSIONS*

Ps	49:14	far from their princely *m*.
Isa	5: 9	the fine *m* left without occupants.
Am	3:15	and the *m* will be demolished,"
	5:11	though you have built stone *m*,

MARCH

Jos	6: 4	*m* around the city seven times,
Isa	42:13	LORD will *m* out like a mighty

MARITAL* (MARRY)

Ex	21:10	of her food, clothing and *m* rights.
Mt	5:32	except for *m* unfaithfulness,
	19: 9	except for *m* unfaithfulness,
1Co	7: 3	husband should fulfill his *m* duty

MARK (MARKS)

Cousin of Barnabas (Col 4:10; 2Ti 4:11; Phm 24; 1Pe 5:13), see JOHN.

Ge	4:15	Then the LORD put a *m* on Cain
Rev	13:16	to receive a *m* on his right hand

MARKET (MARKETPLACE MARKETPLACES)

Jn	2:16	turn my Father's house into a *m*!"

MARKETPLACE (MARKET)

Lk	7:32	are like children sitting in the *m*

MARKETPLACES (MARKET)

Mt	23: 7	they love to be greeted in the *m*

MARKS (MARK)

Jn	20:25	Unless I see the nail *m* in his hands
Gal	6:17	bear on my body the *m* of Jesus.

MARRED

Isa	52:14	his form *m* beyond human likeness

MARRIAGE (MARRY)

Mt	22:30	neither marry nor be given in *m*;
	24:38	marrying and giving in *m*,
Ro	7: 2	she is released from the law of *m*.
Heb	13: 4	by all, and the *m* bed kept pure,

MARRIED (MARRY)

Dt	24: 5	happiness to the wife he has *m*.
Ezr	10:10	you have *m* foreign women,
Pr	30:23	an unloved woman who is *m*,
Mt	1:18	pledged to be *m* to Joseph,
Mk	12:23	since the seven were *m* to her?"
Ro	7: 2	by law a *m* woman is bound
1Co	7:27	Are you *m*? Do not seek a divorce.
	7:33	But a *m* man is concerned about
	7:36	They should get *m*.

MARRIES (MARRY)
Mt   5:32 anyone who m the divorced
                woman
     19: 9 and m another woman commits
Lk 16:18 the man who m a divorced
                woman

MARROW
Heb 4:12 joints and m; it judges the
                thoughts

MARRY (INTERMARRY MARITAL MARRIAGE
MARRIED MARRIES)
Dt 25: 5 brother shall take her and m her
Mt 22:30 resurrection people will neither m
1Co 7: 1 It is good for a man not to m.
      7: 9 control themselves, they
                should m,
      7:28 if you do m, you have not sinned;
1Ti   4: 3 They forbid people to m
      5:14 So I counsel younger widows
                to m,

MARTHA*
    Sister of Mary and Lazarus (Lk 10:38–42; Jn
11; 12:2).

MARVELED* (MARVELOUS)
Lk   2:33 mother m at what was said about
2Th 1:10 and to be m at among all those
                who

MARVELING* (MARVELOUS)
Lk   9:43 While everyone was m

MARVELOUS* (MARVELED MARVELING)
1Ch 16:24 his m deeds among all peoples.
Job 37: 5 God's voice thunders in m ways;
Ps 71:17 to this day I declare your m deeds.
     72:18 who alone does m deeds.
     86:10 For you are great and do m deeds;
     96: 3 his m deeds among all peoples.
     98: 1 for he has done m things;
    118:23 and it is m in our eyes.
Isa 25: 1 you have done m things,
Zec 8: 6 but will it seem m to me?"
      8: 6 "It may seem m to the remnant
Mt 21:42 and it is m in our eyes'?
Mk 12:11 and it is m in our eyes'?"
Rev 15: 1 in heaven another great and m
                sign
     15: 3 "Great and m are your deeds,

MARY
    1. Mother of Jesus (Mt 1:16–25; Lk 1:27–56;
2:1–40). With Jesus at temple (Lk 2:41–52), at
the wedding in Cana (Jn 2:1–5), questioning
his sanity (Mk 3:21), at the cross (Jn
19:25–27). Among disciples after Ascension
(Ac 1:14).
    2. Magdalene; former demoniac (Lk 8:2).
Helped support Jesus' ministry (Lk 8:1–3). At
the cross (Mt 27:56; Mk 15:40; Jn 19:25), burial (Mt 27:61; Mk 15:47). Saw angel after resurrection (Mt 28:1–10; Mk 16:1–9; Lk 24:1–12);
also Jesus (Jn 20:1–18).
    3. Sister of Martha and Lazarus (Jn 11).
Washed Jesus' feet (Jn 12:1–8).

MASQUERADES*
2Co 11:14 for Satan himself m as an angel

MASTER (MASTER'S MASTERED MASTERS
MASTERY)
Ge   4: 7 to have you, but you must m it."
Hos 2:16 you will no longer call me 'my m.'
Mal 1: 6 If I am a m, where is the respect
Mt 10:24 nor a servant above his m.
     23: 8 for you have only one M
     24:46 that servant whose m finds him
     25:21 "His m replied, 'Well done,
     25:23 "His m replied, 'Well done,
Ro   6:14 For sin shall not be your m,
     14: 4 To his own m he stands or falls.
Col   4: 1 you know that you also have a M
2Ti   2:21 useful to the M and prepared

MASTER'S (MASTER)
Mt 25:21 Come and share your m
                happiness

MASTERED* (MASTER)
1Co 6:12 but I will not be m by anything.
2Pe 2:19 a slave to whatever has m him.

MASTERS (MASTER)
Pr 25:13 he refreshes the spirit of his m.
Mt   6:24 "No one can serve two m.
Lk 16:13 "No servant can serve two m.

Eph 6: 5 obey your earthly m with respect
      6: 9 And m, treat your slaves
Col   3:22 obey your earthly m in
                everything;
      4: 1 M, provide your slaves
1Ti   6: 1 should consider their m worthy
      6: 2 who have believing m are not
Tit   2: 9 subject to their m in everything,
1Pe 2:18 to your m with all respect,

MASTERY* (MASTER)
Ro   6: 9 death no longer has m over him.

MAT
Mk   2: 9 'Get up, take your m and walk'?
Ac   9:34 Get up and take care of your m."

MATCHED*
2Co 8:11 do it may be m by your
                completion

MATTHEW*
    Apostle; former tax collector (Mt 9:9–13;
10:3; Mk 3:18; Lk 6:15; Ac 1:13). Also called
Levi (Mk 2:14–17; Lk 5:27–32).

MATTHIAS
Ac   1:26 the lot fell to M; so he was added

MATURE* (MATURITY)
Lk   8:14 and pleasures, and they do not m.
1Co 2: 6 a message of wisdom among
                the m,
Eph 4:13 of the Son of God and become m,
Php 3:15 of us who are m should take such
Col   4:12 firm in all the will of God, m
Heb 5:14 But solid food is for the m,
Jas   1: 4 work so that you may be m

MATURITY* (MATURE)
Heb 6: 1 about Christ and go on to m,

MEAL
Pr 15:17 Better a m of vegetables where
1Co 10:27 some unbeliever invites you to
                a m
Heb 12:16 for a single m sold his inheritance

MEANING
Ne   8: 8 and giving the m so that the
                people

MEANINGLESS
Ecc 1: 2 "M! M!" says the Teacher.
1Ti   1: 6 from these and turned to m talk.

MEANS
1Co 9:22 by all possible m I might save
                some

MEASURE (MEASURED MEASURES)
Ps 71:15 though I know not its m.
Eze 45: 3 In the sacred district,
Zec 2: 2 He answered me, "To m
                Jerusalem
Lk   6:38 A good m, pressed
Eph 3:19 to the m of all the fullness of God.
      4:13 to the whole of the fullness
Rev 11: 1 "Go and m the temple of God

MEASURED (MEASURE)
Isa 40:12 Who has m the waters
Jer 31:37 if the heavens above can be m

MEASURES (MEASURE)
Dt 25:14 Do not have two differing m
Pr 20:10 Differing weights and differing m

MEAT
Pr 23:20 or gorge themselves on m,
Ro 14: 6 He who eats m, eats to the Lord,
     14:21 It is better not to eat m
1Co 8:13 I will never eat m again,
     10:25 m market without raising
                questions

MEDDLER* (MEDDLES)
1Pe 4:15 kind of criminal, or even as a m.

MEDDLES* (MEDDLER)
Pr 26:17 is a passer-by who m

MEDIATOR
1Ti   2: 5 and one m between God and
                men,
Heb 8: 6 of which he is m is superior
      9:15 For this reason Christ is the m
     12:24 to Jesus the m of a new covenant,

MEDICINE*
Pr 17:22 A cheerful heart is good m,

MEDITATE* (MEDITATED MEDITATES MEDITATION)
Ge 24:63 out to the field one evening to m,

Jos   1: 8 from your mouth; m on it day
Ps 48: 9 we m on your unfailing love.
     77:12 I will m on all your works
    119:15 I m on your precepts
    119:23 your servant will m
    119:27 then I will m on your wonders.
    119:48 and I m on your decrees.
    119:78 but I will m on your precepts.
    119:97 I m on it all day long.
    119:99 for I m on your statutes.
    119:148 that I may m on your promises.
    143: 5 I m on all your works
    145: 5 I will m on your wonderful works.

MEDITATED* (MEDITATE)
Ps 39: 3 and as I m, the fire burned;

MEDITATES* (MEDITATE)
Ps   1: 2 and on his law he m day and
                night.

MEDITATION* (MEDITATE)
Ps 19:14 of my mouth and the m of my
                heart
    104:34 May my m be pleasing to him,

MEDIUM
Lev 20:27 " 'A man or woman who is a m

MEEK* (MEEKNESS)
Ps 37:11 But the m will inherit the land
Zep 3:12 the m and humble,
Mt   5: 5 Blessed are the m,

MEEKNESS* (MEEK)
2Co 10: 1 By the m and gentleness of Christ,

MEET (MEETING MEETINGS MEETS)
Ps 42: 2 When can I go and m with God?
     85:10 Love and faithfulness m together;
Am   4:12 prepare to m your God, O Israel."
1Co 11:34 when you m together it may not
1Th 4:17 them in the clouds to m the Lord

MEETING (MEET)
Ex 40:34 the cloud covered the Tent of M,
Heb 10:25 Let us not give up m together,

MEETINGS* (MEET)
1Co 11:17 for your m do more harm

MEETS (MEET)
Heb 7:26 Such a high priest m our need—

MELCHIZEDEK
Ge 14:18 M king of Salem brought out
                bread
Ps 110: 4 in the order of M."
Heb 7:11 in the order of M, not in the order

MELT (MELTS)
2Pe 3:12 and the elements will m in the
                heat.

MELTS (MELT)
Am   9: 5 he who touches the earth and
                it m,

MEMBER (MEMBERS)
Ro 12: 5 each m belongs to all the others.

MEMBERS (MEMBER)
Mic 7: 6 a man's enemies are the m
Mt 10:36 a man's enemies will be the m
Ro   7:23 law at work in the m of my body,
     12: 4 of us has one body with many m,
1Co 6:15 not know that your bodies are m
     12:24 But God has combined the m
Eph 3: 6 m together of one body,
      4:25 for we are all m of one body.
      5:30 for we are m of his body.
Col   3:15 as m of one body you were called

MEMORABLE* (MEMORY)
Eze 39:13 day I am glorified will be a m day

MEMORIES* (MEMORY)
1Th 3: 6 us that you always have
                pleasant m

MEMORY (MEMORABLE MEMORIES)
Pr 10: 7 m of the righteous will be
Mt 26:13 she has done will also be told,
                in m

MEN (MAN)
Ge   6: 2 daughter of m were beautiful,
      6: 4 heroes of old, m of renown
Ps   9:20 nations know they are but m.
     11: 4 He observes the sons of m;
Mt   4:19 will make you fishers of m
      5:16 your light shine before m
      6:14 if you forgive m when
     10:32 acknowledges me before m

Mt 12:31 blasphemy will be forgiven *m*,
   12:36 *m* will have to give account
   23: 5 is done for *m* to see:
Mk 7: 7 are but rules taught by *m*.
Lk 6:22 Blessed are you when *m*
    6:26 Woe to you when all *m*
Jn 1: 4 life was the light of *m*.
    2:24 for he knew all *m*.
    3:19 *m* loved darkness instead
   12:32 will draw all *m* to myself
   13:35 all *m* will know that you
Ac 5:29 obey God rather than *m*!
Ro 1:18 wickedness of *m*
    1:27 indecent acts with other *m*,
    5:12 death came to all *m*,
1Co 2:11 among *m* knows the thoughts
    3: 3 acting like mere *m*?
    3:21 no more boasting about *m*!
    9:22 all things to all *m*
   13: 1 tongues of *m* and of angels
   16:13 be *m* of courage;
   16:18 Such *m* deserve recognition.
2Co 5:11 we try to persuade *m*.
    8:21 but also in the eyes of *m*.
Gal 1: 1 sent not from *m* nor
    1:10 to win approval of *m*, or
Eph 4: 8 and gave gifts to *m*.
1Th 2: 4 as *m* approved by God
    2:13 not as the word of *m*,
1Ti 2: 4 wants all *m* to be saved
    2: 6 as a ransom for all *m*—
    4:10 the Savior of all *m*
    5: 2 younger *m* as brothers
2Ti 2: 2 entrust to reliable *m*
Tit 2:11 has appeared to all *m*.
Heb 5: 1 is selected from among *m*
    7:28 high priests *m* who are weak;
2Pe 1:21 but *m* spoke from God
Rev 21: 3 dwelling of God is with *m*,

MEN'S (MAN)
2Ki 19:18 fashioned by *m* hands.
2Ch 32:19 the work of *m* hands.
1Co 2: 5 not rest on *m* wisdom,

MENAHEM*
King of Israel (2Ki 15:17–22).

MENE
Da 5:25 that was written: *M, M,*

MEPHIBOSHETH
Son of Jonathan shown kindness by David (2Sa 4:4; 9; 21:7). Accused of siding with Absalom (2Sa 16:1–4; 19:24–30).

MERCHANT
Pr 31:14 She is like the *m* ships,
Mt 13:45 of heaven is like a *m* looking

MERCIFUL (MERCY)
Dt 4:31 the LORD your God is a *m* God;
Ne 9:31 for you are a gracious and *m* God.
Ps 77: 9 Has God forgotten to be *m*?
   78:38 Yet he was *m*;
Jer 3:12 for I am *m*,' declares the LORD,
Da 9: 9 The Lord our God is *m*
Mt 5: 7 Blessed are the *m*,
Lk 1:54 remembering to be *m*
    6:36 Be *m*, just as your Father is *m*.
Heb 2:17 in order that he might become a *m*
Jas 2:13 to anyone who has not been *m*.
Jude :22 Be *m* to those who doubt; snatch

MERCY (MERCIFUL)
Ex 33:19 *m* on whom I will have *m*,
2Sa 24:14 of the LORD, for his *m* is great;
1Ch 21:13 for his *m* is very great;
Ne 9:31 But in your great *m* you did not put
Ps 25: 6 O LORD, your great *m* and love,
   28: 6 for he has heard my cry for *m*.
   57: 1 Have *m* on me, O God, have *m*
Pr 28:13 renounces them finds *m*.
Isa 63: 9 and *m* he redeemed them;
Da 9:18 but because of your great *m*.
Hos 6: 6 For I desire *m*, not sacrifice,
Am 5:15 LORD God Almighty will have *m*
Mic 6: 8 To act justly and to love *m*
    7:18 but delight to show *m*.
Hab 3: 2 in wrath remember *m*.
Zec 7: 9 show *m* and compassion
Mt 5: 7 for they will be shown *m*.
    9:13 learn what this means: 'I desire *m*,

Mt 12: 7 'I desire *m*, not sacrifice,' you
   18:33 Shouldn't you have had *m*
   23:23 justice, *m* and faithfulness.
Lk 1:50 His *m* extends to those who fear
Ro 9:15 "I will have *m* on whom I have *m*,
    9:18 Therefore God has *m*
   11:32 so that he may have *m* on them all.
   12: 1 brothers, in view of God's *m*,
   12: 8 if it is showing *m*, let him do it
Eph 2: 4 who is rich in *m*, made us alive
1Ti 1:13 I was shown *m* because I acted
    1:16 for that very reason I was shown *m*
Tit 3: 5 we had done, but because of his *m*.
Heb 4:16 so that we may receive *m*
Jas 2:13 judgment without *m* will be
    2:13 *M* triumphs over judgment!
    3:17 submissive, full of *m* and good fruit
    5:11 full of compassion and *m*.
1Pe 1: 3 In his great *m* he has given us new
    2:10 once you had not received *m*,
Jude :23 to others show *m*, mixed with fear

MERRY
Lk 12:19 Take life easy; eat, drink and be *m*

MESHACH
Hebrew exiled to Babylon; name changed from Mishael (Da 1:6–7). Refused defilement by food (Da 1:8–20). Refused to worship idol (Da 3:1–18); saved from furnace (Da 3:19–30).

MESSAGE (MESSENGER)
Isa 53: 1 Who has believed our *m*
Jn 12:38 "Lord, who has believed our *m*
Ac 5:20 "and tell the people the full *m*
   10:36 You know the *m* God sent
   17:11 for they received the *m*
Ro 10:16 who has believed our *m*?"
   10:17 faith comes from hearing the *m*,
1Co 1:18 For the *m* of the cross is
    2: 4 My *m* and my preaching were not
2Co 5:19 to us the *m* of reconciliation.
2Th 3: 1 pray for us that the *m*
Tit 1: 9 firmly to the trustworthy *m*
Heb 4: 2 the *m* they heard was of no value
1Pe 2: 8 because they disobey the *m*—

MESSENGER (MESSAGE)
Pr 25:13 is a trustworthy *m*
Mal 3: 1 I will send my *m*, who will prepare
Mt 11:10 " 'I will send my *m* ahead of you,
2Co 12: 7 a *m* of Satan, to torment me.

MESSIAH*
Jn 1:41 "We have found the *M*" (that is,
    4:25 "I know that *M*" (called Christ) "is

METHUSELAH
Ge 5:27 Altogether, *M* lived 969 years,

MICAH
1. Idolater from Ephraim (Jdg 17–18).
2. Prophet from Moresheth (Jer 26:18–19; Mic 1:1).

MICAIAH
Prophet of the LORD who spoke against Ahab (1Ki 22:1–28; 2Ch 18:1–27).

MICHAEL
Archangel (Jude 9); warrior in angelic realm, protector of Israel (Da 10:13, 21; 12:1; Rev 12:7).

MICHAL
Daughter of Saul, wife of David (1Sa 14:49; 18:20–28). Warned David of Saul's plot (1Sa 19). Saul gave her to Paltiel (1Sa 25:44); David retrieved her (2Sa 3:13–16). Criticized David for dancing before the ark (2Sa 6:16–23); 1Ch 15:29).

MIDIAN
Ex 2:15 Pharaoh went to live in *M*,
Jdg 7: 2 me to deliver *M* into their hands.

MIDWIVES
Ex 1:17 The *m*, however, feared God

MIGHT (ALMIGHTY MIGHTIER MIGHTY)
Jdg 16:30 Then he pushed with all his *m*,
2Sa 6: 5 with all their *m* before the LORD,
    6:14 before the LORD with all his *m*,
2Ch 20: 6 Power and *m* are in your hand,

Ps 21:13 we will sing and praise your *m*.
   54: 1 vindicate me by your *m*.
Isa 63:15 Where are your zeal and your *m*?
Mic 3: 8 and with justice and *m*,
Zec 4: 6 'Not by *m* nor by power,
Col 1:11 power according to his glorious *m*
1Ti 6:16 To him be honor and *m* forever.

MIGHTIER (MIGHT)
Ps 93: 4 *M* than the thunder

MIGHTY (MIGHT)
Ge 49:24 of the hand of the *M* One of Jacob,
Ex 6: 1 of my *m* hand he will drive them
   13: 3 out of it with a *m* hand.
Dt 5:15 out of there with a *m* hand
    7: 8 he brought you out with a *m* hand
   10:17 the great God, *m* and awesome,
   34:12 one has ever shown the *m* power
2Sa 1:19 How the *m* have fallen!
   23: 8 the names of David's *m* men:
Ne 9:32 the great, *m* and awesome God,
Job 36: 5 God is *m*, but does not despise men
Ps 24: 8 The LORD strong and *m*,
   45: 3 upon your side, O *m* one;
   50: 1 The *M* One, God, the LORD,
   62: 7 he is my rock, my refuge.
   68:33 who thunders with *m* voice.
   71:16 proclaim your *m* acts,
   77:12 and consider all your *m* deeds.
   77:15 With your *m* arm you redeemed
   89: 8 You are *m*, O LORD,
   93: 4 the LORD on high is *m*.
   99: 4 The King is *m*, he loves justice—
  110: 2 LORD will extend your *m* scepter
  118:15 right hand has done *m* things!
  136:12 with a *m* hand and outstretched
  145: 4 they will tell of your *m* acts.
  145:12 all men may know of your *m* acts
  147: 5 Great is our Lord and *m* in power;
SS 8: 6 like a *m* flame.
Isa 9: 6 Wonderful Counselor, *M* God,
   60:16 your Redeemer, the *M* One
   63: 1 *m* to save."
Jer 10: 6 and your name is *m* in power.
   20:11 with me like a *m* warrior;
   32:19 your purposes and *m* are your
Eze 20:33 I will rule over you with a *m* hand
Zep 3:17 he is *m* to save.
Mt 26:64 at the right hand of the *M* One
Eph 1:19 like the working of his *m* strength,
    6:10 in the Lord and in his *m* power.
1Pe 5: 6 therefore, under God's *m* hand,

MILE*
Mt 5:41 If someone forces you to go one *m*,

MILK
Ex 3: 8 a land flowing with *m* and honey—
   23:19 a young goat in its mother's *m*.
Pr 30:33 as churning the *m* produces butter,
Isa 55: 1 Come, buy wine and *m*
1Co 3: 2 I gave you *m*, not solid food,
Heb 5:12 You need *m*, not solid food!
1Pe 2: 2 babies, crave pure spiritual *m*,

MILLSTONE (STONE)
Lk 17: 2 sea with a *m* tied around his neck

MIND (DOUBLE-MINDED LIKE-MINDED MINDED MINDFUL MINDS)
Nu 23:19 that he should change his *m*.
Dt 28:65 LORD will give you an anxious *m*,
1Sa 15:29 Israel does not lie or change his *m*;
1Ch 28: 9 devotion and with a willing *m*,
2Ch 30:12 the people to give them unity of *m*
Ps 26: 2 examine my heart and my *m*;
  110: 4 and will not change his *m*:
Isa 26: 3 him whose *m* is steadfast,
Jer 17:10 and examine the *m*,
Mt 22:37 all your soul and with all your *m*.'
Mk 12:30 with all your *m* and with all your
Lk 10:27 with all your strength and with all your *m*';
Ac 4:32 believers were one in heart and *m*.
Ro 1:28 he gave them over to a depraved *m*

Ro   7:25   I myself in my *m* am a slave
     8: 6   The *m* of sinful man is death,
     8: 7   the sinful man is hostile to God.
   12: 2   by the renewing of your *m*.
   14:13   make up your *m* not
1Co   1:10   you may be perfectly united in *m*
   2: 9   no *m* has conceived
   14:14   spirit prays, but my *m* is unfruitful.
2Co   1:15   be of one *m*, live in peace.
Php   3:19   Their *m* is on earthly things.
Col   2:18   and his unspiritual *m* puffs him up
1Th   4:11   to *m* your own business
Heb   7:21   and will not change his *m:*

MINDED* (MIND)
1Pe   4: 7   be clear *m* and self-controlled

MINDFUL* (MIND)
Ps   8: 4   what is man that you are *m* of him,
Lk   1:48   God my Savior, for he has been *m*
Heb   2: 6   What is man that you are *m* of him,

MINDS (MIND)
Dt   11:18   of mine in your hearts and *m;*
Ps   7: 9   who searches *m* and hearts,
Jer   31:33   "I will put my law in their *m*
Lk   24:38   and why do doubts rise in your *m?*
   24:45   Then he opened their *m*
Ro   8: 5   to the sinful nature have their *m* set
2Co   4: 4   god of this age has blinded the *m*
Eph   4:23   new in the attitude of your *m;*
Col   3: 2   Set your *m* on things above,
Heb   8:10   I will put my laws in their *m*
   10:16   and I will write them on their *m.* "
1Pe   1:13   prepare your *m* for action;
Rev   2:23   I am he who searches hearts and *m,*

MINISTER (MINISTERING MINISTERS MINISTRY)
Ps   101: 6   will *m* to me.
1Ti   4: 6   you will be a good *m*

MINISTERING (MINISTER)
Heb   1:14   Are not all angels *m* spirits sent

MINISTERS (MINISTER)
2Co   3: 6   as *m* of a new covenant—

MINISTRY (MINISTER)
Ac   6: 4   to prayer and the *m* of the word."
Ro   11:13   I make much of my *m*
2Co   4: 1   God's mercy we have this *m,*
   5:18   gave us the *m* of reconciliation:
   6: 3   so that our *m* will not be
   6: 2   who was at work in the *m* of Peter
2Ti   4: 5   discharge all the duties of your *m.*
Heb   8: 6   But the *m* Jesus has received is

MIRACLE* (MIRACLES MIRACULOUS)
Ex   7: 9   'Perform a *m*,' then say to Aaron,
Mk   9:39   "No one who does a *m*
Lk   23: 8   hoped to see him perform some *m.*
Jn   7:21   "I did one *m*, and you are all
Ac   4:16   they have done an outstanding *m,*

MIRACLES* (MIRACLE)
1Ch   16:12   his *m*, and the judgments he
Ne   9:17   to remember the *m* you performed
Job   5: 9   *m* that cannot be counted.
   9:10   *m* that cannot be counted.
Ps   77:11   I will remember your *m* of long ago
   77:14   You are the God who performs *m;*
   78:12   He did *m* in the sight
   105: 5   his *m*, and the judgments he
   106: 7   they gave no thought to your *m;*
   106:22   *m* in the land of Ham
Mt   7:22   out demons and perform many *m?*'
   11:20   most of his *m* had been performed,
   11:21   If the *m* that were performed
   11:23   If the *m* that were performed
   13:58   And he did not do many *m* there
   24:24   and perform great signs and *m*
Mk   6: 2   does *m!* Isn't this the carpenter?
   6: 5   He could not do any *m* there,
   13:22   and *m* to deceive the elect—
Lk   10:13   For if the *m* that were performed
   19:37   for all the *m* they had seen:
Jn   7: 3   disciples may see the *m* you do.
   10:25   *m* I do in my Father's name speak

Jn   10:32   "I have shown you many great *m*
   10:38   do not believe me, believe the *m*
   14:11   the evidence of the *m* themselves.
   15:24   But now they have seen these *m.*
Ac   2:22   accredited by God to you by *m,*
   8:13   by the great signs and *m* he saw.
   19:11   God did extraordinary *m*
Ro   15:19   by the power of signs and *m,*
1Co   12:28   third teachers, then workers of *m,*
   12:29   Are all teachers? Do all work *m?*
2Co   12:12   and *m—* were done among you
Gal   3: 5   work *m* among you because you
2Th   2: 9   in all kinds of counterfeit *m,*
Heb   2: 4   it by signs, wonders and various *m,*

MIRACULOUS (MIRACLE)
Dt   13: 1   and announces to you a *m* sign
Mt   12:39   generation asks for a *m* sign!
   13:54   this wisdom and these *m* powers?"
Jn   2:11   This, the first of his *m* signs,
   2:23   people saw the *m* signs he was
   3: 2   could perform the *m* signs you are
   4:48   "Unless you people see *m* signs
   7:31   will he do more *m* signs
   9:16   "How can a sinner do such *m* signs
   12:37   Jesus had done all these *m* signs
   20:30   Jesus did many other *m* signs
Ac   2:43   *m* signs were done by the apostles.
   5:12   apostles performed many *m* signs
1Co   1:22   Jews demand *m* signs and Greeks
   12:10   to another *m* powers;

MIRE
Ps   40: 2   out of the mud and *m;*
Isa   57:20   whose waves cast up *m* and mud.

MIRIAM
Sister of Moses and Aaron (Nu 26:59). Led dancing at Red Sea (Ex 15:20–21). Struck with leprosy for criticizing Moses (Nu 12). Death (Nu 20:1).

MIRROR
1Co   13:12   but a poor reflection as in a *m;*
Jas   1:23   a man who looks at his face in a *m*

MISDEEDS*
Ps   99: 8   though you punished their *m.*
Ro   8:13   put to death the *m* of the body,

MISERY
Ex   3: 7   "I have indeed seen the *m*
Jdg   10:16   he could bear Israel's *m* no longer.
Hos   5:15   in their *m* they will earnestly seek
Ro   3:16   ruin and *m* mark their ways,
Jas   5: 1   of the *m* that is coming upon you.

MISFORTUNE
Ob   : 12   brother in the day of his *m,*

MISLEAD (MISLED)
Isa   47:10   wisdom and knowledge *m* you

MISLED (MISLEAD)
1Co   15:33   Do not be *m:* "Bad company

MISS (MISSES)
Pr   19: 2   nor to be hasty and *m* the way.

MISSES (MISS)
Heb   12:15   See to it that no one *m* the grace

MIST
Hos   6: 4   Your love is like the morning *m,*
Jas   4:14   You are a *m* that appears for a little

MISTREAT (MISTREATED)
Ex   22:21   "Do not *m* an alien or oppress him,
Eze   22:29   and needy and *m* the alien,
Lk   6:28   pray for those who *m* you.

MISTREATED (MISTREAT)
Eze   22: 7   *m* the fatherless and the widow.
Heb   11:25   to be *m* along with the people
   11:37   destitute, persecuted and *m—*
   13: 3   who are *m* as if you yourselves

MISUSE* (MISUSES)
Ex   20: 7   "You shall not *m* the name
Dt   5:11   "You shall not *m* the name
Ps   139:20   your adversaries *m* your name.

MISUSES* (MISUSE)
Ex   20: 7   anyone guiltless who *m* his name.
Dt   5:11   anyone guiltless who *m* his name.

MIXED (MIXING)
Da   2:41   even as you saw iron *m* with clay.

MIXING (MIXED)
Isa   5:22   and champions at *m* drinks,

MOAB (MOABITESS)
Ge   19:37   she named him *M*; he is the father
Dt   34: 6   He buried him in *M*, in the valley
Ru   1: 1   live for a while in the country of *M.*
Isa   15: 1   An oracle concerning *M:*
Jer   48:16   "The fall of *M* is at hand;
Am   2: 1   "For three sins of *M,*

MOABITESS (MOAB)
Ru   1:22   accompanied by Ruth the *M,*

MOAN
Ps   90: 9   we finish our years with a *m.*

MOCK (MOCKED MOCKER MOCKERS MOCKING MOCKS)
Ps   22: 7   All who see me *m* me;
   119:51   The arrogant *m* me
Pr   1:26   I will *m* when calamity overtakes
   14: 9   Fools *m* at making amends for sin,
Mk   10:34   who will *m* him and spit on him,

MOCKED (MOCK)
Ps   89:51   with which they have *m* every step
Mt   27:29   knelt in front of him and *m* him.
   27:41   of the law and the elders *m* him.
Gal   6: 7   not be deceived: God cannot be *m.*

MOCKER (MOCK)
Pr   9: 7   corrects a *m* invites insult;
   9:12   if you are a *m*, you alone will suffer
   20: 1   Wine is a *m* and beer a brawler;
   22:10   Drive out the *m*, and out goes strife

MOCKERS (MOCK)
Ps   1: 1   or sit in the seat of *m.*
Pr   29: 8   *M* stir up a city,

MOCKING (MOCK)
Isa   50: 6   face from *m* and spitting.

MOCKS (MOCK)
Pr   17: 5   He who *m* the poor shows
   30:17   "The eye that *m* a father,

MODEL*
Eze   28:12   " 'You were the *m* of perfection,
1Th   1: 7   And so you became a *m*
2Th   3: 9   to make ourselves a *m* for you

MODESTY*
1Co   12:23   are treated with special *m,*

MOLDED*
Job   10: 9   Remember that you *m* me like clay

MOLDY
Jos   9: 5   of their food supply was dry and *m.*

MOLECH
Lev   20: 2   of his children to *M* must be put
1Ki   11:33   and *M* the god of the Ammonites,

MOMENT (MOMENTARY)
Job   20: 5   the joy of the godless lasts but a *m.*
Ps   2:12   for his wrath can flare up in a *m.*
   30: 5   For his anger lasts only a *m,*
Pr   12:19   but a lying tongue lasts only a *m.*
Isa   54: 7   "For a brief *m* I abandoned you,
   66: 8   or a nation be brought forth in a *m?*
Gal   2: 5   We did not give in to them for a *m,*

MOMENTARY* (MOMENT)
2Co   4:17   and *m* troubles are achieving

MONEY
Pr   13:11   Dishonest *m* dwindles away,
Ecc   5:10   Whoever loves *m* never has *m*
Isa   55: 1   and you who have no *m,*
Mt   6:24   You cannot serve both God and *M.*
   27: 5   Judas threw the *m* into the temple
Lk   3:14   "Don't extort *m* and don't accuse
   9: 3   no bread, no *m*, no extra tunic.
   16:13   You cannot serve both God and *M*
Ac   5: 2   part of the *m* for himself,

1Co	16: 2	set aside a sum of *m* in keeping
1Ti	3: 3	not quarrelsome, not a lover of *m*.
	6:10	For the love of *m* is a root
2Ti	3: 2	lovers of *m*, boastful, proud,
Heb	13: 5	free from the love of *m*
1Pe	5: 2	not greedy for *m*, but eager to serve

MONEYLENDER* (LEND)

Ex	22:25	not be like a *m*; charge him no
Lk	7:41	men owed money to a certain *m*.

MONTH (MONTHS)

Ex	12: 2	"This *m* is to be for you the first
Eze	47:12	Every *m* they will bear,
Rev	22: 2	of fruit, yielding its fruit every *m*.

MONTHS (MONTH)

Gal	4:10	and *m* and seasons and years!
Rev	11: 2	trample on the holy city for 42 *m*.
	13: 5	his authority for forty-two *m*.

MOON

Jos	10:13	and the *m* stopped,
Ps	8: 3	the *m* and the stars,
	74:16	you established the sun and *m*.
	89:37	be established forever like the *m*,
	104:19	The *m* marks off the seasons,
	121: 6	nor the *m* by night.
	136: 9	the *m* and stars to govern the night;
	148: 3	Praise him, sun and *m*,
SS	6:10	fair as the *m*, bright as the sun,
Joel	2:31	and the *m* to blood
Hab	3:11	and *m* stood still in the heavens
Mt	24:29	and the *m* will not give its light;
Ac	2:20	and the *m* to blood
1Co	15:41	*m* another and the stars another;
Col	2:16	a New *M* celebration or a Sabbath
Rev	6:12	the whole *m* turned blood red,
	21:23	city does not need the sun or the *m*

MORAL*

Jas	1:21	rid of all *m* filth and the evil that is

MORDECAI

Benjamite exile who raised Esther (Est 2:5–15). Exposed plot to kill Xerxes (Est 2:19–23). Refused to honor Haman (Est 3:1–6; 5:9–14). Charged Esther to foil Haman's plot against the Jews (Est 4). Xerxes forced Haman to honor Mordecai (Est 6). Mordecai exalted (Est 8–10). Established Purim (Est 9:18–32).

MORIAH*

Ge	22: 2	and go to the region of *M*.
2Ch	3: 1	LORD in Jerusalem on Mount *M*,

MORNING

Ge	1: 5	and there was *m*— the first day.
Dt	28:67	In the *m* you will say, "If only it
2Sa	23: 4	he is like the light of *m* at sunrise
Ps	5: 3	In the *m*, O LORD,
Pr	27:14	blesses his neighbor early in the *m*,
Isa	14:12	O *m* star, son of the dawn!
La	3:23	They are new every *m*;
2Pe	1:19	and the *m* star rises in your hearts.
Rev	2:28	I will also give him the *m* star.
	22:16	of David, and the bright *M* Star."

MORTAL

Ge	6: 3	for he is *m*; his days will be
Job	10: 4	Do you see as a *m* sees?
Ro	8:11	also give life to your *m* bodies
1Co	15:53	and the *m* with immortality.
2Co	5: 4	that what is *m* may be swallowed

MOSES

Levite; brother of Aaron (Ex 6:20; 1Ch 6:3). Put in basket into Nile; discovered and raised by Pharaoh's daughter (Ex 2:1–10). Fled to Midian after killing Egyptian (Ex 2:11–15). Married to Zipporah, fathered Gershom (Ex 2:16–22).

Called by the LORD to deliver Israel (Ex 3–4). Pharaoh's resistance (Ex 5). Ten plagues (Ex 7–11). Passover and Exodus (Ex 12–13). Led Israel through Red Sea (Ex 14). Song of deliverance (Ex 15:1–21). Brought water from rock (Ex 17:1–7). Raised hands to defeat Amalekites (Ex 17:8–16). Delegated judges (Ex 18; Dt 1:9–18).

Received Law at Sinai (Ex 19–23; 25–31; Jn 1:17). Announced Law to Israel (Ex 19:7–8; 24;

35). Broke tablets because of golden calf (Ex 32; Dt 9). Saw glory of the LORD (Ex 33–34). Supervised building of tabernacle (Ex 36–40). Set apart Aaron and priests (Lev 8–9). Numbered tribes (Nu 1–4; 26). Opposed by Aaron and Miriam (Nu 12). Sent spies into Canaan (Nu 13). Announced forty years of wandering for failure to enter land (Nu 14). Opposed by Korah (Nu 16). Forbidden to enter land for striking rock (Nu 20:1–13; Dt 1:37). Lifted bronze snake for healing (Nu 21:4–9; Jn 3:14). Final address to Israel (Dt 1–33). Succeeded by Joshua (Nu 27:12–23; Dt 34). Death (Dt 34:5–12).

"Law of Moses" (1Ki 2:3; Ezr 3:2; Mk 12:26; Lk 24:44). "Book of Moses" (2Ch 25:12; Ne 13:1). "Song of Moses" (Ex 15:1–21; Rev 15:3). "Prayer of Moses" (Ps 90).

MOTH

Mt	6:19	where *m* and rust destroy,

MOTHER (GRANDMOTHER MOTHER-IN-LAW MOTHER'S)

Ge	2:24	and *m* and be united to his wife,
	3:20	because she would become the *m*
Ex	20:12	"Honor your father and your *m*,
Lev	20: 9	" 'If anyone curses his father or *m*,
Dt	5:16	"Honor your father and your *m*,
	21:18	who does not obey his father and *m*
	27:16	who dishonors his father or his *m*."
Jdg	5: 7	arose a *m* in Israel.
1Sa	2:19	Each year his *m* made him a little
Ps	113: 9	as a happy *m* of children.
Pr	10: 1	but a foolish son grief to his *m*.
	23:22	do not despise your *m*
	23:25	May your father and *m* be glad;
	29:15	a child left to himself disgraces his *m*.
	30:17	that scorns obedience to a *m*,
	31: 1	an oracle his *m* taught him:
Isa	49:15	"Can a *m* forget the baby
	66:13	As a *m* comforts her child,
Jer	20:17	with my *m* as my grave,
Mic	7: 6	a daughter rises up against her *m*,
Mt	10:35	a daughter against her *m*,
	10:37	or *m* more than me is not worthy
	12:48	He replied to him, "Who is my *m*,
	15: 4	'Honor your father and *m*'
	19: 5	and *m* and be united to his wife,
	19:19	honor your father and *m*,'
Mk	7:10	'Honor your father and your *m*,' and,
	10:19	honor your father and *m*.' "
Lk	11:27	"Blessed is the *m* who gave you
	12:53	daughter and daughter against *m*,
	18:20	honor your father and *m*.' "
Jn	19:27	to the disciple, "Here is your *m*."
Gal	4:26	is above us free, and she is our *m*.
Eph	5:31	and *m* and be united to his wife,
	6: 2	"Honor your father and *m*"—
1Th	2: 7	like a *m* caring for her little
2Ti	1: 5	and in your *m* Eunice and,

MOTHER-IN-LAW (MOTHER)

Ru	2:19	Ruth told her *m* about the one
Mt	10:35	a daughter-in-law against her *m*—

MOTHER'S (MOTHER)

Job	1:21	"Naked I came from my *m* womb,
Pr	1: 8	and do not forsake your *m* teaching
Ecc	5:15	from his *m* womb,
	11: 5	the body is formed in a *m* womb,
Jn	3: 4	time into his *m* womb to be born!"

MOTIVE* (MOTIVES)

1Ch	28: 9	and understands every *m*

MOTIVES* (MOTIVE)

Pr	16: 2	but *m* are weighed by the LORD.
1Co	4: 5	will expose the *m* of men's hearts.
Php	1:18	whether from false *m* or true,
1Th	2: 3	spring from error or impure *m*,
Jas	4: 3	because you ask with wrong *m*,

MOUNT (MOUNTAIN MOUNTAINS MOUNTAINTOPS)

Ps	89: 9	when its waves *m* up, you still them
Isa	14:13	enthroned on the *m* of assembly,
Eze	28:14	You were on the holy *m* of God;
Zec	14: 4	stand on the *M* of Olives,

MOUNTAIN (MOUNT)

Ge	22:14	"On the *m* of the LORD it will be
Ex	24:18	And he stayed on the *m* forty days
Dt	5: 4	face to face out of the fire on the *m*.
Job	14:18	"But as a *m* erodes and crumbles
Ps	48: 1	in the city of our God, his holy *m*.
Isa	40: 4	every *m* and hill made low;
Mic	4: 2	let us go up to the *m* of the LORD,
Mt	4: 8	the devil took him to a very high *m*
	17:20	say to this *m*, 'Move from here
Mk	9: 2	with him and led them up a high *m*,
Lk	3: 5	every *m* and hill made low.
Jn	4:21	the Father neither on this *m*
2Pe	1:18	were with him on the sacred *m*.

MOUNTAINS (MOUNT)

Ps	36: 6	righteousness is like the mighty *m*,
	46: 2	the *m* fall into the heart of the sea,
	90: 2	Before the *m* were born
Isa	52: 7	How beautiful on the *m*
	54:10	Though the *m* be shaken
	55:12	the *m* and hills
Eze	34: 6	My sheep wandered over all the *m*
Mt	24:16	are in Judea flee to the *m*.
Lk	23:30	they will say to the *m*, "Fall on us!"
1Co	13: 2	if I have a faith that can move *m*,
Rev	6:16	They called to the *m* and the rocks,

MOUNTAINTOPS (MOUNT)

Isa	42:11	let them shout from the *m*.

MOURN (MOURNING MOURNS)

Ecc	3: 4	a time to *m* and a time to dance,
Isa	61: 2	to comfort all who *m*,
Mt	5: 4	Blessed are those who *m*,
Ro	12:15	*m* with those who *m*.

MOURNING (MOURN)

Isa	61: 3	instead of *m*,
Jer	31:13	I will turn their *m* into gladness;
Rev	21: 4	There will be no more death or *m*

MOURNS (MOURN)

Zec	12:10	as one *m* for an only child,

MOUTH (MOUTHS)

Nu	22:38	only what God puts in my *m*."
Dt	8: 3	comes from the *m* of the LORD.
	18:18	I will put my words in his *m*,
	30:14	it is in your *m* and in your heart
Jos	1: 8	of the Law depart from your *m*;
2Ki	4:34	*m* to *m*, eyes to eyes, hands
Ps	10: 7	His *m* is full of curses and lies
	17: 3	resolved that my *m* will not sin.
	19:14	May the words of my *m*
	37:30	*m* of the righteous man utters
	40: 3	He put a new song in my *m*,
	71: 8	My *m* is filled with your praise,
	119:103	sweeter than honey to my *m*!
	141: 3	Set a guard over my *m*, O LORD;
Pr	2: 6	and from his *m* come knowledge
	4:24	Put away perversity from your *m*;
	10:11	The *m* of the righteous is a fountain
	10:31	*m* of the righteous brings forth
	16:23	A wise man's heart guides his *m*,
	26:28	and a flattering *m* works ruin.
	27: 2	praise you, and not your own *m*;
Ecc	5: 2	Do not be quick with your *m*,
SS	1: 2	with the kisses of his *m*—
	5:16	His *m* is sweetness itself;
Isa	29:13	come near to me with their *m*
	40: 5	For the *m* of the LORD has spoken
	45:23	my *m* has uttered in all integrity
	51:16	I have put my words in your *m*
	53: 7	so he did not open his *m*.
	55:11	my word that goes out from my *m*:
	59:21	*m* will not depart from your *m*
Eze	3: 2	So I opened my *m*, and he gave me
Mal	2: 7	and from his *m* men should seek
Mt	4: 4	comes from the *m* of God.' "
	12:34	overflow of the heart the *m* speaks.
	15:11	into a man's *m* does not make him
	15:18	out of the *m* come from the heart,

Lk   6:45   overflow of his heart his *m* speaks.
Ro   10: 9   That if you confess with your *m*,
     15: 6   and *m* you may glorify the God
1Pe   2:22   and no deceit was found in
         his *m*."
Rev   1:16   and out of his *m* came a sharp
     2:16   them with the sword of my *m*.
     3:16   I am about to spit you out of
         my *m*.
   19:15   Out of his *m* comes a sharp sword

MOUTHS (MOUTH)
Ps   78:36   would flatter him with their *m*,
Eze   33:31   With their *m* they express
         devotion
Ro   3:14   "Their *m* are full of cursing
Eph   4:29   talk come out of your *m*,
Jas   3: 3   bits into the *m* of horses

MOVE (MOVED MOVES)
Dt   19:14   Do not *m* your neighbor's
Pr   23:10   Do not *m* an ancient boundary
Ac   17:28   and *m* and have our being.'
1Co   13: 2   have a faith that can *m*
         mountains,
   15:58   Let nothing *m* you.

MOVED (MOVE)
Ex   35:21   and whose heart *m* him came
2Ch   36:22   the LORD *m* the heart
Ezr   1: 5   everyone whose heart God had *m*
Ps   93: 1   it cannot be *m*.
Jn   11:33   he was deeply *m* in spirit
Col   1:23   not *m* from the hope held out

MOVES (MOVE)
Dt   23:14   For the LORD your God *m* about

MUD (MUDDIED)
Ps   40: 2   out of the *m* and mire;
Isa   57:20   whose waves cast up mire and *m*.
Jn   9: 6   made some *m* with the saliva,
2Pe   2:22   back to her wallowing in the *m*."

MUDDIED (MUD)
Pr   25:26   Like a *m* spring or a polluted well
Eze   32:13   or *m* by the hoofs of cattle.

MULBERRY*
Lk   17: 6   you can say to this *m* tree,

MULTITUDE (MULTITUDES)
Isa   31: 1   who trust in the *m* of their
         chariots
Jas   5:20   and cover over a *m* of sins.
1Pe   4: 8   love covers over a *m* of sins.
Rev   7: 9   me was a great *m* that no one
         could
     19: 1   of a great *m* in heaven shouting:

MULTITUDES (MULTITUDE)
Ne   9: 6   and the *m* of heaven worship you.
Da   12: 2   *M* who sleep in the dust
Joel   3:14   *M*, *m* in the valley of decision!

MURDER (MURDERED MURDERER MURDERERS)
Ex   20:13   "You shall not *m*.
Dt   5:17   "You shall not *m*.
Pr   28:17   A man tormented by the guilt
         of *m*
Mt   5:21   'Do not *m*, and anyone who
     15:19   *m*, adultery, sexual immorality,
Ro   1:29   *m*, strife, deceit and malice.
     13: 9   "Do not *m*," "Do not steal,"
Jas   2:11   adultery," also said, "Do not *m*."

MURDERED (MURDER)
Mt   23:31   of those who *m* the prophets.
Ac   7:52   now you have betrayed and *m*
         him
1Jn   3:12   to the evil one and *m* his brother.

MURDERER (MURDER)
Nu   35:16   he is a *m*; the *m* shall be put
Jn   8:44   He was a *m* from the beginning,
1Jn   3:15   who hates his brother is a *m*,

MURDERERS (MURDER)
1Ti   1: 9   for *m*, for adulterers and perverts,
Rev   21: 8   the *m*, the sexually immoral,
     22:15   the sexually immoral, the *m*,

MUSIC* (MUSICAL MUSICIAN MUSICIANS)
Ge   31:27   singing to the *m* of tambourines
Jdg   5: 3   I will make *m* to the LORD,
1Ch   6:31   put in charge of the *m* in the
         house
     6:32   They ministered with *m*
     25: 6   fathers for the *m* of the temple
     25: 7   and skilled in *m* for the LORD—

Ne   12:27   and with the *m* of cymbals,
Job   21:12   They sing to the *m* of tambourine
Ps   27: 6   and make *m* to the LORD.
     33: 2   make *m* to him on the ten-
         stringed
     45: 8   the *m* of the strings makes you
         glad
     57: 7   I will sing and make *m*.
     81: 2   Begin the *m*, strike the
         tambourine,
     87: 7   As they make *m* they will sing,
     92: 1   and make *m* to your name,
     92: 3   to the *m* of the ten-stringed lyre
     95: 2   and extol him with *m* and song.
     98: 4   burst into jubilant song with *m*;
     98: 5   make *m* to the LORD
   108: 1   make *m* with all my soul.
   144: 9   the ten-stringed lyre I will make *m*
   147: 7   make *m* to our God on the harp.
   149: 3   make *m* to him with tambourine
Isa   30:32   will be to the *m* of tambourines
La   5:14   young men have stopped their *m*.
Eze   26:13   *m* of your harps will be heard no
Da   3: 5   lyre, harp, pipes and all kinds
         of *m*,
     3: 7   and all kinds of *m*, all the peoples,
     3:10   and all kinds of *m* must fall down
     3:15   lyre, harp, pipes and all kinds
         of *m*,
Am   5:23   to the *m* of your harps.
Hab   3:19   For the director of *m*.
Lk   15:25   came near the house, he heard *m*
Eph   5:19   make *m* in your heart to the Lord,
Rev   18:22   The *m* of harpists and musicians,

MUSICAL* (MUSIC)
1Ch   15:16   accompanied by *m* instruments:
     23: 5   with the *m* instruments I have
2Ch   7: 6   with the LORD's *m* instruments,
     23:13   with *m* instruments were leading
     34:12   skilled in playing *m* instruments—
Ne   12:36   with *m* instruments prescribed
Am   6: 5   and improvise on *m* instruments.

MUSICIAN* (MUSIC)
1Ch   6:33   Heman, the *m*, the son of Joel,

MUSICIANS* (MUSIC)
1Ki   10:12   to make harps and lyres for the *m*.
1Ch   9:33   Those who were *m*, heads
     15:19   The *m* Heman, Asaph
2Ch   5:12   All the Levites who were *m*—
     9:11   to make harps and lyres for the *m*.
     35:15   The *m*, the descendants of Asaph,
Ps   68:25   are the singers, after them the *m*;
Rev   18:22   The music of harpists and *m*,

MUSTARD
Mt   13:31   kingdom of heaven is like a *m*
         seed,
     17:20   you have faith as small as a *m*
         seed,
Mk   4:31   It is like a *m* seed, which is

MUTILATORS*
Php   3: 2   those men who do evil, those *m*

MUTUAL* (MUTUALLY)
Ro   14:19   leads to peace and to *m*
         edification.
1Co   7: 5   by *m* consent and for a time,

MUTUALLY* (MUTUAL)
Ro   1:12   and I may be *m* encouraged

MUZZLE*
Dt   25: 4   Do not *m* an ox while it is treading
Ps   39: 1   I will put a *m* on my mouth
1Co   9: 9   "Do not *m* an ox while it is
1Ti   5:18   "Do not *m* the ox while it is

MYRRH
Ps   45: 8   All your robes are fragrant with *m*
SS   1:13   My lover is to me a sachet of *m*
Mt   2:11   of gold and of incense and of *m*.
Mk   15:23   offered him wine mixed with *m*,
Jn   19:39   Nicodemus brought a mixture
         of *m*
Rev   18:13   of incense, *m* and frankincense,

MYSTERIES* (MYSTERY)
Job   11: 7   "Can you fathom the *m* of God?
Da   2:28   a God in heaven who reveals *m*.
     2:29   of *m* showed you what is going
     2:47   Lord of kings and a revealer of *m*,
1Co   13: 2   can fathom all *m* and all
         knowledge

1Co   14: 2   he utters *m* with his spirit.

MYSTERY* (MYSTERIES)
Da   2:18   God of heaven concerning this *m*,
     2:19   the night the *m* was revealed
     2:27   to the king the *m* he has asked
     2:30   this *m* has been revealed to me,
     2:47   for you were able to reveal
         this *m*."
     4: 9   and no *m* is too difficult for you.
Ro   11:25   you to be ignorant of this *m*,
     16:25   to the revelation of the *m* hidden
1Co   15:51   I tell you a *m*: We will not all
         sleep,
Eph   1: 9   to us the *m* of his will according
     3: 3   the *m* made known to me
     3: 4   insight into the *m* of Christ,
     3: 6   This *m* is that through the gospel
     3: 9   the administration of this *m*,
     5:32   This is a profound *m*—
     6:19   I will fearlessly make known the *m*
Col   1:26   the *m* that has been kept hidden
     1:27   the glorious riches of this *m*,
     2: 2   in order that they may know
         the *m*
     4: 3   so that we may proclaim the *m*
1Ti   3:16   the *m* of godliness is great:
Rev   1:20   *m* of the seven stars that you saw
     10: 7   the *m* of God will be
         accomplished,
     17: 5   written on her forehead: *M*
     17: 7   explain to you the *m* of the
         woman

MYTHS*
1Ti   1: 4   nor to devote themselves to *m*
     4: 7   Have nothing to do with
         godless *m*
2Ti   4: 4   from the truth and turn aside
         to *m*.
Tit   1:14   will pay no attention to Jewish *m*

NAAMAN
     Aramean general whose leprosy was
cleansed by Elisha (2Ki 5).

NABAL
     Wealthy Carmelite the LORD killed for refusing to help David (1Sa 25). David married Abigail, his widow (1Sa 25:39–42).

NABOTH*
     Jezreelite killed by Jezebel for his vineyard (1Ki 21). Ahab's family destroyed for this (1Ki 21:17–24; 2Ki 9:21–37).

NADAB
     1. Firstborn of Aaron (Ex 6:23); killed with Abihu for offering unauthorized fire (Lev 10; Nu 3:4).
     2. Son of Jeroboam I; king of Israel (1Ki 15:25–32).

NAHUM
     Prophet against Nineveh (Na 1:1).

NAIL* (NAILING)
Jn   20:25   "Unless I see the *n* marks

NAILING* (NAIL)
Ac   2:23   him to death by *n* him to the
         cross.
Col   2:14   he took it away, *n* it to the cross.

NAIVE
Ro   16:18   they deceive the minds of *n*
         people.

NAKED
Ge   2:25   The man and his wife were
         both *n*,
Job   1:21   *N* I came from my mother's
         womb,
Isa   58: 7   when you see the *n*, to clothe
         him,
2Co   5: 3   are clothed, we will not be
         found *n*.

NAME (NAMES)
Ge   2:19   man to see what he would *n*
         them;
     4:26   to call on the *n* of the LORD.
     11: 4   so that we may make a *n*
     12: 2   I will make your *n* great,
     32:29   Jacob said, "Please tell me
         your *n*."
Ex   3:15   This is my *n* forever, the *n*
     20: 7   "You shall not misuse the *n*
     34:14   for the LORD, whose *n* is Jealous,

Lev 24:11 Israelite woman blasphemed
the N
Dt 5:11 "You shall not misuse the n
12:11 choose as a dwelling for his N—
18: 5 minister in the LORD's n always.
25: 6 carry on the n of the dead brother
28:58 this glorious and awesome n—
Jos 7: 9 do for your own great n?"
Jdg 13:17 "What is your n, so that we may
1Sa 12:22 of his great n the LORD will not
2Sa 6: 2 which is called by the N, the

7: 9 Now I will make your n great,
1Ki 5: 5 will build the temple for my N.'
8:29 you said, 'My N shall be there,'
1Ch 17: 8 I will make your n like the names
2Ch 7:14 my people, who are called by
my n,
Ne 9:10 You made a n for yourself,
Ps 8: 1 how majestic is your n
9:10 Those who know your n will trust
20: 7 in the n of the LORD our God.
29: 2 to the LORD the glory due his n;
34: 3 let us exalt his n together.
44:20 If we had forgotten the n
66: 2 Sing the glory of his n;
68: 4 Sing to God, sing praise to his n,
79: 9 for the glory of your n;
96: 8 to the LORD the glory due his n;
103: 1 my inmost being, praise his
holy n.
115: 1 but to your n be the glory,
138: 2 your n and your word.
145: 1 I will praise your n for ever
147: 4 and calls them each by n.
Pr 10: 7 you will win favor and a good n
18:10 n of the LORD is a strong tower;
22: 1 A good n is more desirable
30: 4 What is his n, and the n of his
son?
Ecc 7: 1 A good n is better
SS 1: 3 your n is like perfume poured out.
Isa 12: 4 thanks to the LORD, call on his n;
26: 8 your n and renown
40:26 and calls them each by n.
42: 8 "I am the LORD; that is my n!
56: 5 I will give them an everlasting n
57:15 who lives forever, whose n is holy:
63:14 to make for yourself a glorious n.
Jer 14: 7 do something for the sake of
your n

15:16 for I bear your n,
Eze 20: 9 of my n I did what would keep it
20:14 of my n I did what would keep it
20:22 of my n I did what would keep it
Da 12: 1 everyone whose n is found
written
Hos 12: 5 the LORD is his n of renown!
Joel 2:32 on the n of the LORD will be saved
Mic 5: 4 in the majesty of the n
Zep 3: 9 call on the n of the LORD
Zec 6:12 is the man whose n is the Branch,
14: 9 one LORD, and his n the only n.
Mal 1: 6 O priests, who show contempt for
my n.
Mt 1:21 and you are to give him the n
Jesus,
6: 9 hallowed be your n,
18:20 or three come together in my n,
24: 5 For many will come in my n,
28:19 them in the n of the Father
Mk 9:41 gives you a cup of water in my n
Lk 11: 2 hallowed be your n,
Jn 10: 3 He calls his own sheep by n
14:13 I will do whatever you ask in
my n,
16:24 asked for anything in my n.
Ac 2:21 on the n of the Lord will be
saved.'

4:12 for there is no other n
Ro 10:13 "Everyone who calls on the n
Php 2: 9 him the n that is above every n,
2:10 at the n of Jesus every knee
should
Col 3:17 do it all in the n of the Lord Jesus,
Heb 1: 4 as the n he has inherited is
superior
Jas 5:14 him with oil in the n of the Lord.
1Jn 5:13 believe in the n of the Son of God
Rev 2:17 stone with a new n written on it,
3: 5 I will never blot out his n

Rev 3:12 I will also write on him my new n.
19:13 and his n is the Word of God.
20:15 If anyone's n was not found
written

NAMES (NAME)
Ex 28: 9 engrave on them the n of the sons
Lk 10:20 but rejoice that your n are written
Php 4: 3 whose n are in the book of life.
Heb 12:23 whose n are written in heaven.
Rev 21:27 but only those whose n are
written

NAOMI
Wife of Elimelech, mother-in-law of Ruth
(Ru 1:2, 4). Left Bethlehem for Moab during
famine (Ru 1:1). Returned a widow, with Ruth
(Ru 1:6–22). Advised Ruth to seek marriage
with Boaz (Ru 2:17–3:4). Cared for Ruth's son
Obed (Ru 4:13–17).

NAPHTALI
Son of Jacob by Bilhah (Ge 30:8; 35:25; 1Ch
2:2). Tribe of blessed (Ge 49:21; Dt 33:23),
numbered (Nu 1:43; 26:50), allotted land (Jos
19:32–39; Eze 48:3), failed to fully possess (Jdg
1:33), supported Deborah (Jdg 4:10; 5:18),
David (1Ch 12:34), 12,000 from (Rev 7:6).

NARROW
Mt 7:13 "Enter through the n gate.
7:14 and n the road that leads to life,

NATHAN
Prophet and chronicler of Israel's history
(1Ch 29:29; 2Ch 9:29). Announced the Davidic
covenant (2Sa 7; 1Ch 17). Denounced David's
sin with Bathsheba (2Sa 12). Supported
Solomon (1Ki 1).

NATHANAEL*
Apostle (Jn 1:45–49; 21:2). Probably also
called Bartholomew (Mt 10:3).

NATION (NATIONS)
Ge 12: 2 "I will make you into a great n
Ex 19: 6 a kingdom of priests and a holy n.'
Dt 4: 7 What other n is so great
Jos 5: 8 And after the whole n had been
2Sa 7:23 one n on earth that God went out
Ps 33:12 Blessed is the n whose God is
Pr 11:14 For lack of guidance a n falls,
14:34 Righteousness exalts a n,
Isa 2: 4 N will not take up sword
26: 2 that the righteous n may enter,
60:12 For the n or kingdom that will not
65: 1 To a n that did not call on my
name
66: 8 a n be brought forth in a
moment?
Mic 4: 3 N will not take up sword
Mt 24: 7 N will rise against n,
Mk 13: 8 N will rise against n,
1Pe 2: 9 a royal priesthood, a holy n,
Rev 5: 9 and language and people and n.
7: 9 from every n, tribe, people
14: 6 to every n, tribe, language

NATIONS (NATION)
Ge 17: 4 You will be the father of many n.
18:18 and all n on earth will be blessed
Ex 19: 5 of all n you will be my treasured
Lev 20:26 apart from the n to be my own.
Dt 1: 7 drives out before you many n—
15: 6 You will rule over many n
Jdg 3: 1 These are the n the LORD left
2Ch 20: 6 rule over all the kingdoms of
the n.
Ne 1: 8 I will scatter you among the n,
Ps 2: 1 Why do the n conspire
2: 8 I will make the n your inheritance,
9: 5 You have rebuked the n
22:28 and he rules over the n.
46:10 I will be exalted among the n,
47: 8 God reigns over the n;
66: 7 his eyes watch the n—
67: 2 your salvation among all n.
68:30 Scatter the n who delight in war.
72:17 All n will be blessed through him,
96: 3 Declare his glory among the n,
99: 2 he is exalted over all the n.
106:35 but they mingled with the n
110: 6 He will judge the n, heaping up
113: 4 The LORD is exalted over all the n
Isa 2: 2 and all n will stream to it.
11:10 the n will rally to him,

Isa 12: 4 among the n what he has done,
40:15 Surely the n are like a drop
42: 1 and he will bring justice to the n.
51: 4 justice will become a light to
the n.
52:15 so will he sprinkle many n,
56: 7 a house of prayer for all n."
60: 3 N will come to your light,
66:18 and gather all n and tongues,
Jer 1: 5 you as a prophet to the n."
3:17 and all n will gather in Jerusalem
31:10 "Hear the word of the LORD, O n;
33: 9 and honor before all n
46:28 I completely destroy all the n
Eze 22: 4 you an object of scorn to the n
34:13 I will bring them out from the n
36:23 n will know that I am the LORD,
37:22 and they will never again be
two n
39:21 I will display my glory among
the n
Hos 7: 8 "Ephraim mixes with the n;
Joel 2:17 a byword among the n.
3: 2 I will gather all n
Am 9:12 and all the n that bear my name,"
Zep 3: 8 I have decided to assemble the n,
Hag 2: 7 and the desired of all n will come,
Zec 8:13 an object of cursing among the n,
8:23 n will take firm hold of one Jew
9:10 He will proclaim peace to the n.
14: 2 I will gather all the n to Jerusalem
Mt 12:18 he will proclaim justice to the n.
24: 9 and you will be hated by all n
24:14 whole world as a testimony to
all n,
25:32 All the n will be gathered
28:19 and make disciples of all n,
Mk 11:17 a house of prayer for all n'?
Ac 4:25 " 'Why do the n rage
Ro 15:12 who will arise to rule over the n;
Gal 3: 8 All n will be blessed through you."
1Ti 3:16 was preached among the n,
Rev 15: 4 All n will come
21:24 The n will walk by its light,
22: 2 are for the healing of the n.

NATURAL (NATURE)
Ro 6:19 you are weak in your n selves.
1Co 15:44 If there is a n body, there is

NATURE (NATURAL)
Ro 1:20 his eternal power and divine n—
7:18 lives in me, that is, in my sinful n.
8: 4 do not live according to the
sinful n
8: 5 to the sinful n have their minds
set
8: 8 by the sinful n cannot please God.
13:14 to gratify the desires of the
sinful n.
Gal 5:13 freedom to indulge the sinful n;
5:19 The acts of the sinful n are
obvious:
5:24 Jesus have crucified the sinful n
Php 2: 6 Who, being in very n God,
Col 3: 5 whatever belongs to your
earthly n
2Pe 1: 4 you may participate in the
divine n

NAZARENE* (NAZARETH)
Mt 2:23 prophets: "He will be called a N."
Mk 14:67 "You also were with that N,
Jesus,"
16: 6 "You are looking for Jesus the N,
Ac 24: 5 He is a ringleader of the N sect
and

NAZARETH (NAZARENE)
Mt 4:13 Leaving N, he went and lived
Lk 4:16 to N, where he had been brought
Jn 1:46 "N! Can anything good come

NAZIRITE
Nu 6: 2 of separation to the LORD as a N,
Jdg 13: 7 because the boy will be a N of
God

NEBO
Dt 34: 1 Then Moses climbed Mount N

NEBUCHADNEZZAR
Babylonian king. Subdued and exiled Judah
(2Ki 24–25; 2Ch 36; Jer 39). Dreams interpret-

ed by Daniel (Da 2; 4). Worshiped God (Da 3:28–29; 4:34–37).

NECESSARY*
Ac	1:21	Therefore it is *n* to choose one
Ro	13:5	it is *n* to submit to the authorities,
2Co	9:5	I thought it *n* to urge the brothers
Php	1:24	it is more *n* for you that I remain
	2:25	But I think it is *n* to send back
Heb	8:3	and so it was *n* for this one
	9:16	it is *n* to prove the death
	9:23	It was *n*, then, for the copies

NECK (STIFF-NECKED)
Pr	3:22	an ornament to grace your *n*.
	6:21	fasten them around your *n*.
Mt	18:6	a large millstone hung around his *n*

NECO
Pharaoh who killed Josiah (2Ki 23:29–30; 2Ch 35:20–22), deposed Jehoahaz (2Ki 23:33–35; 2Ch 36:3–4).

NEED (NEEDS NEEDY)
1Ki	8:59	Israel according to each day's *n*,
Ps	79:8	for we are in desperate *n*.
	116:6	when I was in great *n*, he saved me.
	142:6	for I am in desperate *n*;
Mt	6:8	for your Father knows what you *n*
Lk	15:14	country, and he began to be in *n*.
Ac	2:45	they gave to anyone as he had *n*.
Ro	12:13	with God's people who are in *n*.
1Co	12:21	say to the hand, "I don't *n* you!"
Eph	4:28	something to share with those in *n*.
1Ti	5:3	to those widows who are really in *n*
Heb	4:16	grace to help us in our time of *n*.
1Jn	3:17	sees his brother in *n* but has no pity

NEEDLE
| Mt | 19:24 | go through the eye of a *n* |

NEEDS (NEED)
Isa	58:11	he will satisfy your *n*
Php	2:25	sent to take care of my *n*.
	4:19	God will meet all your *n* according
Jas	2:16	does nothing about his physical *n*,

NEEDY (NEED)
Dt	15:11	toward the poor and *n* in your land.
1Sa	2:8	and lifts the *n* from the ash heap;
Ps	35:10	and *n* from those who rob them."
	69:33	The LORD hears the *n*
	72:12	he will deliver the *n* who cry out,
	140:12	and upholds the cause of the *n*.
Pr	14:21	blessed is he who is kind to the *n*.
	14:31	to the *n* honors God.
	22:22	and do not crush the *n* in court,
	31:9	defend the rights of the poor and *n*
	31:20	and extends her hands to the *n*.
Mt	6:2	"So when you give to the *n*,

NEGLECT* (NEGLECTED)
Dt	12:19	Be careful not to *n* the Levites
	14:27	And do not *n* the Levites living
Ezr	4:22	Be careful not to *n* this matter.
Ne	10:39	We will not *n* the house of our God
Est	6:10	Do not *n* anything you have
Ps	119:16	I will not *n* your word.
Lk	11:42	you *n* justice and the love of God.
Ac	6:2	for us to *n* the ministry of the word
1Ti	4:14	Do not *n* your gift, which was

NEGLECTED (NEGLECT)
| Mt | 23:23 | But you have the more important |

NEHEMIAH
Cupbearer of Artaxerxes (Ne 2:1); governor of Israel (Ne 8:9). Returned to Jerusalem to rebuild walls (Ne 2–6). With Ezra, reestablished worship (Ne 8). Prayer confessing nation's sin (Ne 9). Dedicated wall (Ne 12).

NEIGHBOR (NEIGHBOR'S)
Ex	20:16	give false testimony against your *n*.
	20:17	or anything that belongs to your *n*
Lev	19:13	Do not defraud your *n* or rob him.
	19:17	Rebuke your *n* frankly

Lev	19:18	but love your *n* as yourself.
Ps	15:3	who does him *n* wrong
Pr	3:29	Do not plot harm against your *n*,
	11:12	who lacks judgment derides his *n*,
	14:21	He who despises his *n* sins,
	16:29	A violent man entices his *n*
	24:28	against your *n* without cause,
	25:18	gives false testimony against his *n*.
	27:10	better a *n* nearby than a brother far
	27:14	If a man loudly blesses his *n*
	29:5	Whoever flatters his *n*
Jer	31:34	No longer will a man teach his *n*,
Zec	8:17	do not plot evil against your *n*,
Mt	5:43	Love your *n* and hate your enemy.'
	19:19	and 'love your *n* as yourself.' "
Mk	12:31	The second is this: 'Love your *n*
Lk	10:27	and, 'Love your *n* as yourself.' "
	10:29	who is my *n*?" In reply Jesus said:
Ro	13:9	"Love your *n* as yourself."
	13:10	Love does no harm to its *n*.
	15:2	Each of us should please his *n*
Gal	5:14	"Love your *n* as yourself."
Eph	4:25	and speak truthfully to his *n*,
Heb	8:11	No longer will a man teach his *n*,
Jas	2:8	"Love your *n* as yourself,"

NEIGHBOR'S (NEIGHBOR)
Ex	20:17	You shall not covet your *n* wife,
Dt	5:21	not set your desire on your *n* house
	19:14	not move your *n* boundary stone
	27:17	who moves his *n* boundary stone."
Pr	25:17	Seldom set foot in your *n* house—

NESTS
| Mt | 8:20 | and birds of the air have *n*, |

NET (NETS)
Pr	1:17	How useless to spread a *n*
Hab	1:15	he catches them in his *n*,
Mt	13:47	of heaven is like a *n* that was let
Jn	21:6	"Throw your *n* on the right side

NETS (NET)
Ps	141:10	Let the wicked fall into their own *n*
Mt	4:20	At once they left their *n*
Lk	5:4	and let down the *n* for a catch."

NEVER-FAILING*
| Am | 5:24 | righteousness like a *n* stream! |

NEW
Ps	40:3	He put a *n* song in my mouth,
	98:1	Sing to the LORD a *n* song,
Ecc	1:9	there is nothing *n* under the sun.
Isa	42:9	and *n* things I declare;
	62:2	you will be called by a *n* name
	65:17	*n* heavens and a *n* earth.
	66:22	"As the *n* heavens and the *n* earth
Jer	31:31	"when I will make a *n* covenant
La	3:23	They are *n* every morning;
Eze	11:19	undivided heart and put a *n* spirit
	18:31	and get a *n* heart and a *n* spirit.
	36:26	give you a *n* heart and put a *n* spirit
Zep	3:5	and every *n* day he does not fail,
Mt	9:17	Neither do men pour *n* wine
Mk	16:17	they will speak in *n* tongues;
Lk	5:39	after drinking old wine wants the *n*
	22:20	"This cup is the *n* covenant
Jn	13:34	"A *n* commandment I give you:
Ac	5:20	the full message of this *n* life."
Ro	6:4	the Father, we too may live a *n* life.
1Co	5:7	old yeast that you may be a *n* batch
	11:25	"This cup is the *n* covenant
2Co	3:6	as ministers of a *n* covenant—
	5:17	he is a *n* creation; the old has
Gal	6:15	what counts is a *n* creation.
Eph	4:23	to be made *n* in the attitude
	4:24	and to put on the *n* self, created
Col	3:10	and have put on the *n* self,
Heb	8:8	when I will make a *n* covenant
	9:15	is the mediator of a *n* covenant,
	10:20	by a *n* and living way opened for us
	12:24	Jesus the mediator of a *n* covenant,

1Pe	1:3	great mercy he has given us *n* birth
2Pe	3:13	to a *n* heaven and a *n* earth,
1Jn	2:8	Yet I am writing you a *n* command;
Rev	2:17	stone with a *n* name written on it,
	3:12	the *n* Jerusalem, which is coming
	21:1	I saw a *n* heaven and a *n* earth,

NEWBORN (BEAR)
| 1Pe | 2:2 | Like *n* babies, crave pure spiritual |

NEWS
2Ki	7:9	This is a day of good *n*
Ps	112:7	He will have no fear of bad *n*;
Pr	15:30	good *n* gives health to the bones.
	25:25	is good *n* from a distant land.
Isa	52:7	the feet of those who bring good *n*,
	61:1	me to preach good *n* to the poor.
Na	1:15	the feet of one who brings good *n*,
Mt	4:23	preaching the good *n*
	9:35	preaching the good *n*
	11:5	the good *n* is preached to the poor.
Mk	1:15	Repent and believe the good *n*!"
	16:15	preach the good *n* to all creation.
Lk	1:19	and to tell you this good *n*.
	2:10	I bring you good *n*
	3:18	and preached the good *n* to them.
	4:43	"I must preach the good *n*
	8:1	proclaiming the good *n*
	16:16	the good *n* of the kingdom
Ac	5:42	proclaiming the good *n* that Jesus
	10:36	telling the good *n* of peace
	14:7	continued to preach the good *n*.
	14:21	They preached the good *n*
	17:18	preaching the good *n* about Jesus
Ro	10:15	feet of those who bring good *n*!"

NICODEMUS*
Pharisee who visited Jesus at night (Jn 3). Argued fair treatment of Jesus (Jn 7:50–52). With Joseph, prepared Jesus for burial (Jn 19:38–42).

NIGHT (NIGHTS NIGHTTIME)
Ge	1:5	and the darkness he called "*n*.
	1:16	and the lesser light to govern the *n*.
Ex	13:21	and by *n* in a pillar of fire
	14:24	During the last watch of the *n*.
Dt	28:66	filled with dread both *n* and day,
Jos	1:8	and *n*, so that you may be careful
Job	35:10	who gives songs in the *n*,
Ps	1:2	on his law he meditates day and *n*.
	19:2	*n* after *n* they display knowledge.
	42:8	at *n* his song is with me—
	63:6	of you through the watches of the *n*
	77:6	I remembered my songs in the *n*.
	90:4	or like a watch in the *n*.
	91:5	You will not fear the terror of *n*,
	119:148	through the watches of the *n*,
	121:6	nor the moon by *n*.
	136:9	the moon and stars to govern the *n*;
Pr	31:18	her lamp does not go out at *n*.
Isa	21:11	Watchman, what is left of the *n*?"
	58:10	and your *n* will become like
Jer	33:20	and my covenant with the *n*,
Lk	2:8	watch over their flocks at *n*,
	6:12	and spent the *n* praying to God.
Jn	3:2	He came to Jesus at *n* and said,
	9:4	*N* is coming, when no one can work
1Th	5:2	Lord will come like a thief in the *n*.
	5:5	We do not belong to the *n*
Rev	21:25	for there will be no *n* there.

NIGHTS (NIGHT)
Jnh	1:17	the fish three days and three *n*.
Mt	4:2	After fasting forty days and forty *n*
	12:40	three *n* in the belly of a huge fish,
2Co	6:5	in hard work, sleepless *n*

NIGHTTIME* (NIGHT)
| Zec | 14:7 | or *n*— a day known to the LORD. |

NIMROD
| Ge | 10:9 | "Like *N*, a mighty hunter |

2259

NINEVEH

Jnh 1: 2 "Go to the great city of *N*
Na   1: 1 An oracle concerning *N.*
Mt 12:41 The men of *N* will stand up

NOAH

Righteous man (Eze 14:14, 20) called to build ark (Ge 6–8; Heb 11:7; 1Pe 3:20; 2Pe 2:5). God's covenant with (Ge 9:1–17). Drunkenness of (Ge 9:18–23). Blessed sons, cursed Canaan (Ge 9:24–27).

NOBLE

Ru   3:11 you are a woman of *n* character.
Ps   45: 1 My heart is stirred by a *n* theme
Pr   12: 4 of *n* character is her husband's
     31:10 A wife of *n* character who can find?
     31:29 "Many women do *n* things,
Isa 32: 8 But the *n* man makes *n* plans,
Lk   8:15 good soil stands for those with a *n*
Ro   9:21 of clay some pottery for *n* purposes
Php 4: 8 whatever is *n,* whatever is right,
2Ti 2:20 some are for *n* purposes

NOSTRILS

Ge   2: 7 and breathed into his *n* the breath
Ex 15: 8 By the blast of your *n*
Ps 18:15 at the blast of breath from your *n.*

NOTE

Ac   4:13 and they took *n* that these men had
Php 3:17 take *n* of those who live according

NOTHING

2Sa 24:24 offerings that cost me *n.*"
Ne   9:21 in the desert; they lacked *n,*
Ps 73:25 earth has *n* I desire besides you
Jer 32:17 *N* is too hard for you
Jn 15: 5 apart from me you can do *n.*

NOURISH

Pr 10:21 The lips of the righteous *n* many,

NULLIFY

Mt 15: 6 Thus you *n* the word of God
Ro   3:31 Do we, then, *n* the law by this faith

OATH

Ex 33: 1 up to the land I promised on *o*
Nu 30: 2 or takes an *o* to obligate himself
Dt   6:18 promised on *o* to your forefathers,
     7: 8 and kept the *o* he swore
   29:12 you this day and sealing with an *o.*
Ps 95:11 So I declared on *o* in my anger,
  119:106 I have taken an *o* and confirmed it,
  132:11 The LORD swore an *o* to David,
Ecc 8: 2 because you took an *o* before God.
Mt   5:33 'Do not break your *o,* but keep
Heb 7:20 And it was not without an *o!*

OBADIAH

1. Believer who sheltered 100 prophets from Jezebel (1Ki 18:1–16).

2. Prophet against Edom (Ob 1).

OBEDIENCE* (OBEY)

Ge 49:10 and the *o* of the nations is his.
Jdg 2:17 of *o* to the LORD's commands.
1Ch 21:19 So David went up in *o*
2Ch 31:21 in *o* to the law and the commands,
Pr 30:17 that scorns *o* to a mother,
Lk 23:56 Sabbath in *o* to the commandment.
Ac 21:24 but that you yourself are living in *o*
Ro   1: 5 to the *o* that comes from faith.
     5:19 also through the *o* of the one man
     6:16 to *o,* which leads to righteousness?
   16:19 Everyone has heard about your *o,*
2Co 9:13 for the *o* that accompanies your
   10: 6 once your *o* is complete.
Phm :21 Confident of your *o,* I write to you,
Heb 5: 8 he learned *o* from what he suffered
1Pe 1: 2 for *o* to Jesus Christ and sprinkling
2Jn   : 6 that we walk in *o* to his commands.

OBEDIENT* (OBEY)

Dt 30:17 heart turns away and you are not *o,*
Isa 1:19 If you are willing and *o,*
Lk   2:51 with them and was *o* to them.
Ac   6: 7 of priests became *o* to the faith.
2Co 2: 9 if you would stand the test and be *o*
     7:15 he remembers that you were all *o,*
   10: 5 thought to make it *o* to Christ.
Php 2: 8 and became *o* to death—
Tit   3: 1 to be *o,* to be ready
1Pe 1:14 As *o* children, do not conform

OBEY (OBEDIENCE OBEDIENT OBEYED OBEYING OBEYS)

Ex 12:24 "*O* these instructions as a lasting
   19: 5 Now if you *o* me fully and keep my
   24: 7 the LORD has said; we will *o.*"
Lev 18: 4 You must *o* my laws and be careful
   25:18 and be careful to *o* my laws,
Nu 15:40 remember to *o* all my commands
Dt   5:27 We will listen and *o.*"
     6: 3 careful to *o* so that it may go well
     6:24 us to *o* all these decrees
   11:13 if you faithfully *o* the commands I
   12:28 to *o* all these regulations I am
   13: 4 Keep his commands and *o* him;
   21:18 son who does not *o* his father
   28: 1 If you fully *o* the LORD your God
   28:15 if you do not *o* the LORD your
   30: 2 and *o* him with all your heart
   30:10 if you *o* the LORD your God
   30:14 and in your heart so you may *o* it.
   32:46 children to *o* carefully all the words
Jos 1: 7 to *o* all the law my servant Moses
   22: 5 in all his ways, to *o* his commands,
   24:24 the LORD our God and *o* him."
1Sa 15:22 To *o* is better than sacrifice,
1Ki 8:61 by his decrees and *o* his commands
2Ki 17:13 that I commanded your fathers to *o*
2Ch 34:31 and to *o* the words of the covenant
Ne   1: 5 who love him and *o* his commands,
Ps 103:18 and remember to *o* his precepts.
  103:20 who *o* his word.
  119:17 I will *o* your word.
  119:34 and *o* it with all my heart.
  119:57 I have promised to *o* your words.
  119:67 but now I *o* your word.
  119:100 for I *o* your precepts.
  119:129 therefore I *o* them.
  119:167 I *o* your statutes.
Pr   5:13 I would not *o* my teachers
Jer 7:23 I gave them this command: *O* me,
   11: 4 '*O* me and do everything I
   11: 7 and again, saying, "*O* me."
   42: 6 we will *o* the LORD our God,
Da   9: 4 who love him and *o* his commands,
Mt   8:27 the winds and the waves *o* him!"
   19:17 to enter life, *o* the commandments
   28:20 to *o* everything I have commanded
Lk 11:28 hear the word of God and *o* it."
Jn 14:15 you will *o* what I command.
   14:23 loves me, he will *o* my teaching.
   14:24 not love me will not *o* my teaching.
   15:10 If you *o* my commands, you will
Ac   5:29 "We must *o* God rather than men!
    5:32 given to those who *o* him."
Ro   2:13 it is those who *o* the law who will
    6:12 body so that you *o* its evil desires.
    6:16 slaves to the one whom you *o*—
    6:16 yourselves to someone to *o* whom
   15:18 in leading the Gentiles to *o* God
   16:26 nations might believe and *o* him—
Gal 5: 3 obligated to *o* the whole law.
Eph 6: 1 *o* your parents in the Lord,
    6: 5 *o* your earthly masters with respect
Col 3:20 *o* your parents in everything,

Col 3:22 *o* your earthly masters
2Th 3:14 anyone does not *o* our instruction
1Ti   3: 4 and see that his children *o* him
Heb 5: 9 eternal salvation for all who *o* him
   13:17 *O* your leaders and submit
1Pe 4:17 for those who do not *o* the gospel
1Jn 3:24 Those who *o* his commands live
    5: 3 love for God: to *o* his commands.
Rev 12:17 those who *o* God's commandments
   14:12 the saints who *o* God's

OBEYED (OBEY)

Ge 22:18 blessed, because you have *o* me."
Jos 1:17 we fully *o* Moses, so we will obey
Ps 119: 4 that are to be fully *o.*
Da   9:10 we have not *o* the LORD our God
Jnh 3: 3 Jonah *o* the word of the LORD
Mic 5:15 the nations that have not *o* me."
Jn 15:10 as I have *o* my Father's commands
   15:20 If they *o* my teaching, they will
   17: 6 and they have *o* your word.
Ac   7:53 through angels but have not *o* it."
Ro   6:17 you wholeheartedly *o* the form
Php 2:12 as you have always *o*— not only
Heb 11: 8 *o* and went, even though he did not
1Pe 3: 6 who *o* Abraham and called him her

OBEYING (OBEY)

1Sa 15:22 as in *o* the voice of the LORD?
Ps 119: 5 steadfast in *o* your decrees!
Gal 5: 7 and kept you from *o* the truth?
1Pe 1:22 purified yourselves by *o* the truth

OBEYS (OBEY)

Lev 18: 5 for the man who *o* them will live
Pr 19:16 He who *o* instructions guards his
Eze 20:11 for the man who *o* them will live
Jn 14:21 has my commands and *o* them,
Ro   2:27 and yet *o* the law will condemn you
1Jn 2: 5 if anyone *o* his word, God's love is

OBLIGATED (OBLIGATION)

Ro   1:14 I am *o* both to Greeks
Gal 5: 3 himself be circumcised that he is *o*

OBLIGATION (OBLIGATED)

Ro   8:12 Therefore, brothers, we have an *o*

OBSCENITY*

Eph 5: 4 Nor should there be *o,* foolish talk

OBSCURES*

Job 42: 3 'Who is this that *o* my counsel

OBSERVE (OBSERVING)

Ex 31:13 'You must *o* my Sabbaths.
Lev 25: 2 the land itself must *o* a sabbath
Dt   4: 6 *O* them carefully, for this will show
    5:12 "*O* the Sabbath day
    8: 6 *O* the commands of the LORD
   11:22 If you carefully *o* all these
   26:16 carefully *o* them with all your heart
Ps 37:37 the blameless, *o* the upright;

OBSERVING (OBSERVE)

Ro   3:27 principle? On that of *o* the law?
Gal 2:16 a man is not justified by *o* the law,
    3: 2 you receive the Spirit by *o* the law,
    3:10 All who rely on *o* the law are

OBSOLETE

Heb 8:13 he has made the first one *o;*

OBSTACLE* (OBSTACLES)

Ro 14:13 or *o* in your brother's way.

OBSTACLES (OBSTACLE)

Ro 16:17 put *o* in your way that are contrary

OBSTINATE

Isa 65: 2 hands to an *o* people,
Ro 10:21 to a disobedient *o* people."

OBTAIN (OBTAINED OBTAINS)

Ro 11: 7 sought so earnestly it did not *o,*
2Ti 2:10 they too may *o* the salvation that

OBTAINED (OBTAIN)

Ro   9:30 not pursue righteousness, have *o* it,
Php 3:12 Not that I have already *o* all this,
Heb 9:12 having *o* eternal redemption.

OBTAINS* (OBTAIN)
Pr   12: 2 A good man *o* favor

OBVIOUS*
Mt   6: 18 so that it will not be *o*
Gal   5: 19 The acts of the sinful nature are *o:*
1Ti   5: 24 The sins of some men are *o,*
          5: 25 In the same way, good deeds
             are *o,*

OCCASIONS
Eph   6: 18 in the Spirit on all *o* with all kinds

OFFENDED (OFFENSE)
Pr   18: 19 An *o* brother is more unyielding

OFFENDERS* (OFFENSE)
1Co   6: 9 nor homosexual *o* nor thieves

OFFENSE (OFFENDED OFFENDERS OFFENSES
OFFENSIVE)
Pr   17: 9 over an *o* promotes love,
          19: 11 it is to his glory to overlook an *o.*
Gal   5: 11 In that case the *o* of the cross has

OFFENSES (OFFENSE)
Isa   44: 22 swept away your *o* like a cloud,
          59: 12 For our *o* are many in your sight,
Eze   18: 30 Repent! Turn away from all
             your *o;*
          33: 10 "Our *o* and sins weigh us down,

OFFENSIVE (OFFENSE)
Ps 139: 24 See if there is any way in me,

OFFER (OFFERED OFFERING OFFERINGS OFFERS)
Ps   4: 5 *O* right sacrifices
Ro   6: 13 Do not *o* the parts of your body
          12: 1 to *o* your bodies as living
             sacrifices,
Heb   9: 25 he enter heaven to *o* himself
             again
          13: 15 therefore, let us continually *o*

OFFERED (OFFER)
Isa   50: 6 I *o* my back to those who beat me,
1Co   9: 13 share in what is *o* on the altar?
          10: 20 of pagans are *o* to demons,
Heb   7: 27 once for all when he *o* himself.
          9: 14 the eternal Spirit *o* himself
          11: 4 By faith Abel *o* God a better
          11: 17 when God tested him, *o* Isaac
Jas   5: 15 prayer *o* in faith will make the sick

OFFERING (OFFER)
Ge   4: 3 of the soil as an *o* to the LORD.
          22: 2 a burnt *o* on one of the mountains
             I
          22: 8 provide the lamb for the burnt *o,*
Ex   29: 18 before the LORD as a wave *o.*
          29: 40 quarter of a hin of wine as a
             drink *o.*
Lev   1: 3 If the *o* is a burnt *o* from the herd,
          2: 4 " 'If you bring a grain *o* baked
          3: 1 " 'If someone's *o* is a fellowship *o,*
          4: 3 a sin *o* for the sin he has
             committed
          5: 15 It is a guilt *o.*
          7: 37 ordination *o* and the fellowship *o,*
          9: 24 and consumed the burnt *o*
          22: 18 to fulfill a vow or as a freewill *o,*
          22: 21 a special vow or as a freewill *o,*
1Sa   13: 9 And Saul offered up the burnt *o.*
1Ch   21: 26 from heaven on the altar of
             burnt *o.*
2Ch   7: 1 and consumed the burnt *o*
Ps   40: 6 Sacrifice and *o* you did not desire,
          116: 17 I will sacrifice a thank *o* to you
Isa   53: 10 the LORD makes his life a guilt *o,*
Mt   5: 23 if you are *o* your gift at the altar
Ro   8: 3 likeness of sinful man to be a
             sin *o.*
Eph   5: 2 as a fragrant *o* and sacrifice to
             God.
Php   2: 17 I am being poured out like a
             drink *o*
          4: 18 are a fragrant *o,* an acceptable
2Ti   4: 6 being poured out like a drink *o,*
Heb   10: 5 "Sacrifice and *o* you did not
             desire,
1Pe   2: 5 *o* spiritual sacrifices acceptable

OFFERINGS (OFFER)
1Sa   15: 22 Does the LORD delight in burnt *o*
2Ch   35: 7 and goats for the Passover *o.*
Isa   1: 13 Stop bringing meaningless *o!*
Hos   6: 6 of God rather than burnt *o.*
Mal   3: 8 do we rob you?' "In tithes and *o.*

Mk   12: 33 is more important than all burnt *o*
Heb   10: 8 First he said, "Sacrifices and *o,*

OFFERS (OFFER)
Heb   10: 11 and again he *o* the same
             sacrifices,

OFFICER (OFFICIALS)
2Ti   2: 4 wants to please his
             commanding *o.*

OFFICIALS (OFFICER)
Ex   5: 21 a stench to Pharaoh and his *o.*
Pr   17: 26 or to flog *o* for their integrity.
          29: 12 all his *o* become wicked.

OFFSPRING
Ge   3: 15 and between your *o* and hers;
          12: 7 "To your *o* I will give this land."
          13: 16 I will make your *o* like the dust
          26: 4 and through your *o* all nations
          28: 14 blessed through you and your *o.*
Ex   13: 2 The first *o* of every womb
Ru   4: 12 Through the *o* the LORD gives
Isa   44: 3 I will pour out my Spirit on your *o,*
          53: 10 he will see his *o* and prolong his
Ac   3: 25 'Through your *o* all peoples
          17: 28 own poets have said, 'We are
             his *o.*'
          17: 29 "Therefore since we are God's *o,*
Ro   4: 18 said to him, "So shall your *o* be."
          9: 8 who are regarded as Abraham's *o.*

OG
Nu   21: 33 *O* king of Bashan and his whole
Ps   136: 20 and *O* king of Bashan—

OIL
Ex   29: 7 Take the anointing *o* and anoint
          30: 25 It will be the sacred anointing *o.*
Dt   14: 23 tithe of your grain, new wine
             and *o,*
1Sa   10: 1 Then Samuel took a flask of *o*
          16: 13 So Samuel took the horn of *o*
1Ki   17: 16 and the jug of *o* did not run dry,
2Ki   4: 6 Then the *o* stopped flowing.
Ps   23: 5 You anoint my head with *o;*
          45: 7 by anointing you with the *o* of joy.
          104: 15 *o* to make his face shine,
          133: 2 It is like precious *o* poured
Pr   21: 17 loves wine and *o* will never be
Isa   1: 6 or soothed with *o.*
          61: 3 the *o* of gladness
Mt   25: 3 but did not take any *o* with them.
Heb   1: 9 by anointing you with the *o* of
             joy."

OLIVE (OLIVES)
Ge   8: 11 beak was a freshly plucked *o* leaf!
Jdg   9: 8 said to the *o* tree, 'Be our king.'
Jer   11: 16 LORD called you a thriving *o* tree
Zec   4: 3 Also there are two *o* trees by it,
Ro   11: 17 and you, though a wild *o* shoot,
          11: 24 of an *o* tree that is wild by nature,
Rev   11: 4 These are the two *o* trees

OLIVES (OLIVE)
Zec   14: 4 stand on the Mount of *O,*
Mt   24: 3 sitting on the Mount of *O,*
Jas   3: 12 a fig tree bear *o,* or a grapevine
             bear

OMEGA*
Rev   1: 8 "I am the Alpha and the *O,*"
          21: 6 I am the Alpha and the *O,*
          22: 13 I am the Alpha and the *O,*

OMIT*
Jer   26: 2 I command you; do not *o* a word.

OMRI
King of Israel (1Ki 16:21–26).

ONESIMUS*
Col   4: 9 He is coming with *O,* our faithful
Phm   : 10 I appeal to you for my son *O,*

ONESIPHORUS*
2Ti   1: 16 mercy to the household of *O,*
          4: 19 Aquila and the household of *O.*

ONIONS*
Nu   11: 5 melons, leeks, *o* and garlic.

ONYX
Ex   28: 9 "Take two *o* stones and engrave
          28: 20 in the fourth row a chrysolite,
             an *o*

OPENHANDED* (HAND)
Dt   15: 8 Rather be *o* and freely lend him
          15: 11 you to be *o* toward your brothers

OPINIONS*
1Ki   18: 21 will you waver between two *o?*
Pr   18: 2 but delights in airing his own *o.*

OPPONENTS (OPPOSE)
Pr   18: 18 and keeps strong *o* apart.

OPPORTUNE (OPPORTUNITY)
Lk   4: 13 he left him until an *o* time.

OPPORTUNITY* (OPPORTUNE)
1Sa   18: 21 "Now you have a second *o*
Jer   46: 17 he has missed his *o.*'
Mt   26: 16 watched for an *o* to hand him
             over.
Mk   14: 11 So he watched for an *o* to hand
             him
Lk   22: 6 and watched for an *o* to hand
             Jesus
Ac   25: 16 and has had an *o* to defend
             himself
Ro   7: 8 seizing the *o* afforded
          7: 11 seizing the *o* afforded
1Co   16: 12 but he will go when he has the *o.*
2Co   5: 12 are giving you an *o* to take pride
          11: 12 from under those who want an *o*
Gal   6: 10 as we have *o,* let us do good
Eph   5: 16 making the most of every *o,*
Php   4: 10 but you had no *o* to show it.
Col   4: 5 make the most of every *o.*
1Ti   5: 14 to give the enemy no *o* for
             slander.
Heb   11: 15 they would have had *o* to return.

OPPOSE (OPPONENTS OPPOSED OPPOSES
OPPOSING OPPOSITION)
Ex   23: 22 and will *o* those who *o* you.
1Sa   2: 10 those who *o* the LORD will be
Job   23: 13 he stands alone, and who can *o*
             him
Ac   11: 17 I to think that I could *o* God?"
2Ti   2: 25 Those who *o* him he must gently
Tit   1: 9 doctrine and refute those who *o*
             it.
          2: 8 so that those who *o* you may be

OPPOSED (OPPOSE)
Gal   2: 11 to Antioch, I *o* him to his face,
          3: 21 therefore, *o* to the promises of
             God

OPPOSES (OPPOSE)
Jas   4: 6 "God *o* the proud
1Pe   5: 5 because, "God *o* the proud

OPPOSING (OPPOSE)
1Ti   6: 20 of *o* ideas of what is falsely
             called

OPPOSITION (OPPOSE)
Heb   12: 3 Consider him who endured such *o*

OPPRESS (OPPRESSED OPPRESSES OPPRESSION
OPPRESSOR)
Ex   1: 11 masters over them to *o* them
          22: 21 "Do not mistreat an alien or *o*
             him,
Isa   3: 5 People will *o* each other—
Eze   22: 29 they *o* the poor and needy
Da   7: 25 the Most High and *o* his saints
Am   5: 12 You *o* the righteous and take
             bribes
Zec   7: 10 Do not *o* the widow
Mal   3: 5 who *o* the widows

OPPRESSED (OPPRESS)
Jdg   2: 18 as they groaned under those
Ps   9: 9 The LORD is a refuge for the *o,*
          82: 3 the rights of the poor and *o.*
          146: 7 He upholds the cause of the *o*
Pr   16: 19 in spirit and among the *o*
          31: 5 and deprive all the *o* of their
             rights.
Isa   1: 17 encourage the *o.*
          53: 7 He was *o* and afflicted,
          58: 10 and satisfy the needs of the *o,*
Zec   10: 2 *o* for lack of a shepherd.
Lk   4: 18 to release the *o,*

OPPRESSES (OPPRESS)
Pr   14: 31 He who *o* the poor shows
             contempt
          22: 16 He who *o* the poor
Eze   18: 12 He *o* the poor and needy.

OPPRESSION (OPPRESS)
Ps   12: 5 "Because of the *o* of the weak
          72: 14 He will rescue them from *o*

Ps 119:134 Redeem me from the *o* of men,
Isa 53: 8 By *o* and judgment he was taken
 58: 9 "If you do away with the yoke
 of *o*,

OPPRESSOR (OPPRESS)
Ps 72: 4 he will crush the *o*.
Isa 51:13 For where is the wrath of the *o*?
Jer 22: 3 hand of his *o* the one who has
 been

ORDAINED
Ps 8: 2 you have *o* praise
 111: 9 he *o* his covenant forever—
 139:16 All the days *o* for me
Eze 28:14 for so I *o* you.
Hab 1:12 you have *o* them to punish.
Mt 21:16 you have *o* praise'?"

ORDER (ORDERLY ORDERS)
Nu 9:23 They obeyed the LORD's *o*,
Ps 110: 4 in the *o* of Melchizedek."
Heb 5:10 priest in the *o* of Melchizedek.
 9:10 until the time of the new *o*.
Rev 21: 4 for the old *o* of things has passed

ORDERLY (ORDER)
1Co 14:40 done in a fitting and *o* way.
Col 2: 5 and delight to see how *o* you are

ORDERS (ORDER)
Mk 1:27 He even gives *o* to evil spirits
 3:12 But he gave them strict *o* not
 9: 9 Jesus gave them *o* not

ORDINARY
Ac 4:13 that they were unschooled, *o*
 men,

ORGIES*
Ro 13:13 not in *o* and drunkenness,
Gal 5:21 drunkenness, *o*, and the like.
1Pe 4: 3 *o*, carousing and detestable

ORIGIN (ORIGINATE ORIGINS)
2Pe 1:21 For prophecy never had its *o*

ORIGINATE* (ORIGIN)
1Co 14:36 Did the word of God *o* with you?

ORIGINS* (ORIGIN)
Mic 5: 2 whose *o* are from of old,

ORNAMENT* (ORNAMENTED)
Pr 3:22 an *o* to grace your neck.
 25:12 of gold or an *o* of fine gold

ORNAMENTED (ORNAMENT)
Ge 37: 3 and he made a richly *o* robe for
 him

ORPHAN* (ORPHANS)
Ex 22:22 advantage of a widow or an *o*.

ORPHANS (ORPHAN)
Jn 14:18 will not leave you as *o*; I will come
Jas 1:27 to look after *o* and widows

OTHNIEL
 Nephew of Caleb (Jos 15:15–19; Jdg
1:12–15). Judge who freed Israel from Aram
(Jdg 3:7–11).

OUTBURSTS*
2Co 12:20 jealousy, *o* of anger, factions,

OUTCOME
Heb 13: 7 Consider the *o* of their way of life
1Pe 4:17 what will the *o* be for those who
 do

OUTNUMBER
Ps 139:18 they would *o* the grains of sand.

OUTSIDERS*
Col 4: 5 wise in the way you act toward *o*;
1Th 4:12 daily life may win the respect of *o*
1Ti 3: 7 also have a good reputation
 with *o*,

OUTSTANDING
SS 5:10 *o* among ten thousand.
Ro 13: 8 no debt remain *o*,

OUTSTRETCHED
Ex 6: 6 and will redeem you with an *o*
 arm
Dt 4:34 by a mighty hand and an *o* arm,
 5:15 with a mighty hand and an *o* arm.
1Ki 8:42 your mighty hand and your *o* arm
Ps 136:12 with a mighty hand and *o* arm;
Jer 27: 5 and *o* arm I made the earth
 32:17 by your great power and *o* arm.
Eze 20:33 an *o* arm and with outpoured
 wrath

OUTWEIGHS (WEIGH)
2Co 4:17 an eternal glory that far *o* them
 all.

OUTWIT*
2Co 2:11 in order that Satan might not *o* us.

OVERAWED* (AWE)
Ps 49:16 Do not be *o* when a man grows
 rich

OVERBEARING*
Tit 1: 7 not *o*, not quick-tempered,

OVERCAME (OVERCOME)
Rev 3:21 as I *o* and sat down with my
 Father
 12:11 They *o* him

OVERCOME (OVERCAME OVERCOMES)
Mt 16:18 and the gates of Hades will not *o*
 it.
Mk 9:24 I do believe; help me *o* my
 unbelief
Lk 10:19 to *o* all the power of the enemy;
Jn 16:33 But take heart! I have *o* the
 world."
Ro 12:21 Do not be *o* by evil, but *o* evil
2Pe 2:20 and are again entangled in it
 and *o*,
1Jn 2:13 because you have *o* the evil one.
 4: 4 are from God and have *o* them,
 5: 4 is the victory that has *o* the world,
Rev 17:14 but the Lamb will *o* them

OVERCOMES* (OVERCOME)
1Jn 5: 4 born of God *o* the world.
 5: 5 Who is it that *o* the world?
Rev 2: 7 To him who *o*, I will give the right
 2:11 He who *o* will not be hurt at all
 2:17 To him who *o*, I will give some
 2:26 To him who *o* and does my will
 3: 5 He who *o* will, like them, be
 3:12 Him who *o* I will make a pillar
 3:21 To him who *o*, I will give the right
 21: 7 He who *o* will inherit all this,

OVERFLOW (OVERFLOWING OVERFLOWS)
Ps 65:11 and your carts *o* with abundance.
 119:171 May my lips *o* with praise,
La 1:16 and my eyes *o* with tears.
Mt 12:34 out of the *o* of the heart the
 mouth
Lk 6:45 out of the *o* of his heart his mouth
Ro 5:15 Jesus Christ, *o* to the many!
 Again,
 15:13 so that you may *o* with hope
2Co 4:15 to *o* to the glory of God.
1Th 3:12 *o* for each other and for everyone

OVERFLOWING (OVERFLOW)
Pr 3:10 then your barns will be filled to *o*,
2Co 8: 2 their *o* joy and their extreme
 9:12 *o* in many expressions of thanks
Col 2: 7 as you were taught, and *o*

OVERFLOWS* (OVERFLOW)
Ps 23: 5 my cup *o*
2Co 1: 5 also through Christ our comfort *o*.

OVERJOYED* (JOY)
Da 6:23 The king was *o* and gave orders
Mt 2:10 they saw the star, they were *o*.
Jn 20:20 The disciples were *o*
Ac 12:14 she was so *o* she ran back
1Pe 4:13 so that you may be *o*

OVERLOOK
Pr 19:11 it is to his glory to *o* an offense.

OVERSEER* (OVERSEERS)
Pr 6: 7 no *o* or ruler,
1Ti 3: 1 anyone sets his heart on being
 an *o*,
 3: 2 Now the *o* must be above
 reproach,
Tit 1: 7 Since an *o* is entrusted
1Pe 2:25 returned to the Shepherd and O

OVERSEERS* (OVERSEER)
Ac 20:28 the Holy Spirit has made you *o*.
Php 1: 1 together with the *o* and deacons:
1Pe 5: 2 as *o*— not because you must,

OVERSHADOW* (OVERSHADOWING)
Lk 1:35 power of the Most High will *o*
 you.

OVERSHADOWING (OVERSHADOW)
Ex 25:20 wings spread upward, *o* the cover
Heb 9: 5 the glory, *o* the atonement cover.

OVERTHROW (OVERTHROWS)
2Th 2: 8 whom the Lord Jesus will *o*

OVERTHROWS (OVERTHROW)
Pr 13: 6 but wickedness *o* the sinner.
Isa 44:25 who *o* the learning of the wise

OVERWHELMED (OVERWHELMING)
2Sa 22: 5 the torrents of destruction *o* me.
1Ki 10: 5 temple of the LORD, she was *o*.
Ps 38: 4 My guilt has *o* me
 65: 3 When we were *o* by sins,
Mt 26:38 "My soul is *o* with sorrow
Mk 7:37 People were *o* with amazement.
 9:15 they were *o* with wonder
2Co 2: 7 so that he will not be *o*

OVERWHELMING (OVERWHELMED)
Pr 27: 4 Anger is cruel and fury *o*,
Isa 10:22 *o* and righteous.
 28:15 When an *o* scourge sweeps by,

OWE
Ro 13: 7 If you *o* taxes, pay taxes; if
 revenue
Phm :19 to mention that you *o* me your
 very

OWNER'S (OWNERSHIP)
Isa 1: 3 the donkey his *o* manger,

OWNERSHIP* (OWNER'S)
2Co 1:22 He anointed us, set his seal of *o*

OX (OXEN)
Dt 25: 4 Do not muzzle an *o*
Isa 11: 7 and the lion will eat straw like
 the *o*
Eze 1:10 and on the left the face of an *o*;
Lk 13:15 of you on the Sabbath untie his *o*
1Co 9: 9 "Do not muzzle an *o*
1Ti 5:18 "Do not muzzle the *o*
Rev 4: 7 second was like an *o*, the third
 had

OXEN (OX)
1Ki 19:20 Elisha then left his *o* and ran
Lk 14:19 'I have just bought five yoke of *o*,

PAGAN (PAGANS)
Mt 18:17 as you would a *p* or a tax
 collector.
Lk 12:30 For the *p* world runs

PAGANS* (PAGAN)
Isa 2: 6 and clasp hands with *p*.
Mt 5:47 Do not even *p* do that? Be
 perfect,
 6: 7 do not keep on babbling like *p*,
 6:32 For the *p* run after all these
 things,
1Co 5: 1 that does not occur even
 among *p*:
 10:20 but the sacrifices of *p* are offered
 12: 2 You know that when you were *p*,
1Pe 2:12 such good lives among the *p* that,
 4: 3 in the past doing what *p* choose
3Jn : 7 receiving no help from the *p*.

PAID (PAY)
Isa 40: 2 that her sin has been *p* for,
Zec 11:12 So they *p* me thirty pieces of
 silver.

PAIN (PAINFUL PAINS)
Ge 3:16 with *p* you will give birth
 6: 6 and his heart was filled with *p*.
Job 6:10 my joy in unrelenting *p*—
 33:19 may be chastened on a bed of *p*
Jer 4:19 I writhe in *p*.
 15:18 Why is my *p* unending
Mt 4:24 suffering severe *p*,
Jn 16:21 woman giving birth to a child
 has *p*
1Pe 2:19 up under the *p* of unjust suffering
Rev 21: 4 or mourning or crying or *p*,

PAINFUL (PAIN)
Ge 3:17 through *p* toil you will eat of it
 5:29 and *p* toil of our hands caused
Job 6:25 How *p* are honest words!
Eze 28:24 neighbors who are *p* briers
2Co 2: 1 I would not make another *p* visit
Heb 12:11 seems pleasant at the time, but *p*.
1Pe 4:12 at the *p* trial you are suffering,

PAINS (PAIN)
Ge 3:16 "I will greatly increase your *p*
Mt 24: 8 these are the beginning of birth *p*.
Ro 8:22 as in the *p* of childbirth right up

PAIRS

Gal   4: 19   again in the *p* of childbirth
1Th   5: 3   as labor *p* on a pregnant woman,

PAIRS

Ge   7: 8   *P* of clean and unclean animals,

PALACE (PALACES)

2Sa   7: 2   "Here I am, living in a *p* of cedar,
Jer 22: 6   is what the LORD says about the *p*
      22: 13   "Woe to him who builds his *p*

PALACES (PALACE)

Mt 11: 8   wear fine clothes are in kings' *p.*
Lk   7: 25   and indulge in luxury are in *p.*

PALE

Isa 29: 22   no longer will their faces grow *p.*
Jer 30: 6   every face turned deathly *p?*
Da 10: 8   my face turned deathly *p*
Rev   6: 8   and there before me was a *p* horse!

PALM (PALMS)

Jn 12: 13   They took *p* branches and went out
Rev   7: 9   and were holding *p* branches

PALMS (PALM)

Isa 49: 16   you on the *p* of my hands;

PAMPERS*

Pr 29: 21   If a man *p* his servant from youth,

PANIC

Dt 20: 3   or give way to *p* before them.
1Sa 14: 15   It was a *p* sent by God.
Eze   7: 7   there is *p*, not joy,
Zec 14: 13   by the LORD with great *p.*

PANTS

Ps 42: 1   As the deer *p* for streams of water,

PARABLES

See also JESUS: PARABLES
Ps 78: 2   I will open my mouth in *p.*
Mt 13: 35   "I will open my mouth in *p,*
Lk   8: 10   but to others I speak in *p*, so that,

PARADISE*

Lk 23: 43   today you will be with me in *p."*
2Co 12: 4   God knows—was caught up to *p.*
Rev   2: 7   of life, which is in the *p* of God.

PARALYTIC

Mt   9: 2   Some men brought to him a *p,*
Mk   2: 3   bringing to him a *p*, carried by four
Ac   9: 33   a *p* who had been bedridden

PARCHED

Ps 143: 6   my soul thirsts for you like a *p* land.

PARCHMENTS*

2Ti   4: 13   and my scrolls, especially the *p.*

PARDON* (PARDONED PARDONS)

2Ch 30: 18   *p* everyone who sets his heart
Job   7: 21   Why do you not *p* my offenses
Isa 55: 7   and to our God, for he will freely *p.*
Joel   3: 21   I will *p.*"

PARDONED* (PARDON)

Nu 14: 19   as you have *p* them from the time
Joel   3: 21   bloodguilt, which I have not *p,*

PARDONS* (PARDON)

Mic   7: 18   who *p* sin and forgives

PARENTS

Pr 17: 6   and *p* are the pride of their children
     19: 14   wealth are inherited from *p,*
Mt 10: 21   children will rebel against their *p*
Lk 18: 29   left home or wife or brothers or *p*
     21: 16   You will be betrayed even by *p*, brothers,
Jn   9: 3   Neither this man nor his *p* sinned,"
Ro   1: 30   they disobey their *p*; they are
2Co 12: 14   for their *p*, but *p* for their children.
Eph   6: 1   Children, obey your *p* in the Lord,
Col   3: 20   obey your *p* in everything,
1Ti   5: 4   repaying their *p* and grandparents,
2Ti   3: 2   disobedient to their *p*, ungrateful,

PARTAKE*

1Co 10: 17   for we all *p* of the one loaf.

PARTIAL* (PARTIALITY)

Pr 18: 5   It is not good to be *p* to the wicked

PARTIALITY (PARTIAL)

Lev 19: 15   do not show *p* to the poor
Dt   1: 17   Do not show *p* in judging;
     10: 17   who shows no *p* and accepts no
     16: 19   Do not pervert justice or show *p.*
2Ch 19: 7   our God there is no injustice or *p*
Job 32: 21   I will show *p* to no one,
     34: 19   who shows no *p* to princes
Pr 24: 23   To show *p* in judging is not good:
Mal   2: 9   have shown *p* in matters of the law
Lk 20: 21   and that you do not show *p*
1Ti   5: 21   keep these instructions without *p,*

PARTICIPANTS (PARTICIPATE)

1Co 10: 20   you to be *p* with demons.

PARTICIPATE (PARTICIPANTS PARTICIPATION)

1Pe   4: 13   rejoice that you *p* in the sufferings
2Pe   1: 4   that through them you may *p*

PARTICIPATION (PARTICIPATE)

1Co 10: 16   is not the bread that we break a *p*

PARTNER (PARTNERS PARTNERSHIP)

Pr   2: 17   who has left the *p* of her youth
Mal   2: 14   though she is your *p*, the wife
1Pe   3: 7   them with respect as the weaker *p*

PARTNERS (PARTNER)

Eph   5: 7   Therefore do not be *p* with them.

PARTNERSHIP* (PARTNER)

Php   1: 5   because of your *p* in the gospel

PASS (PASSED PASSER-BY PASSING)

Ex 12: 13   and when I see the blood, I will *p*
     33: 19   goodness to *p* in front of you,
1Ki   9: 8   all who *p* by will be appalled
     19: 11   for the LORD is about to *p* by."
Ps 90: 10   for they quickly *p*, and we fly away.
    105: 19   till what he foretold came to *p,*
Isa 31: 5   he will '*p* over' it and will rescue it
     43: 2   When you *p* through the waters,
     62: 10   *P* through, *p* through the gates!
Jer 22: 8   "People from many nations will *p*
La   1: 12   to you, all you who *p* by?
Da   7: 14   dominion that will not *p* away,
Am   5: 17   for I will *p* through your midst,"
Mt 24: 34   will certainly not *p* away
     24: 35   Heaven and earth will *p* away,
Mk 13: 31   Heaven and earth will *p* away,
Lk 21: 33   Heaven and earth will *p* away,
1Co 13: 8   there is knowledge, it will *p* away.
Jas   1: 10   he will *p* away like a wild flower.
1Jn   2: 17   The world and its desires *p* away,

PASSED (PASS)

Ge 15: 17   a blazing torch appeared and *p*
Ex 33: 22   you with my hand until I have *p* by.
2Ch 21: 20   *p* away, to no one's regret,
Ps 57: 1   wings until the disaster has *p.*
Lk 10: 32   saw him, *p* by on the other side.
1Co 15: 3   For what I received I *p* on to you
Heb 11: 29   By faith the people *p*

PASSER-BY* (PASS)

Pr 26: 10   is he who hires a fool or any *p.*
     26: 17   is a *p* who meddles

PASSING (PASS)

1Co   7: 31   world in its present form is *p* away.
1Jn   2: 8   because the darkness is *p*

PASSION* (PASSIONATE PASSIONS)

Hos   7: 6   Their *p* smolders all night;
1Co   7: 9   better to marry than to burn with *p.*

PASSIONATE* (PASSION)

1Th   4: 5   not in *p* lust like the heathen,

PASSIONS* (PASSION)

Ro   7: 5   the sinful *p* aroused
Gal   5: 24   crucified the sinful nature with its *p*
Tit   2: 12   to ungodliness and worldly *p,*
      3: 3   and enslaved by all kinds of *p*

PASSOVER

Ex 12: 11   Eat it in haste; it is the LORD's *P.*
Nu   9: 2   Have the Israelites celebrate the *P*
Dt 16: 1   celebrate the *P* of the LORD your
Jos   5: 10   the Israelites celebrated the *P.*
2Ki 23: 21   "Celebrate the *P* to the LORD
Ezr   6: 19   the exiles celebrated the *P.*
Mk 14: 12   customary to sacrifice the *P* lamb,
Lk 22: 1   called the *P*, was approaching,
1Co   5: 7   our *P* lamb, has been sacrificed.
Heb 11: 28   he kept the *P* and the sprinkling

PAST

Isa 43: 18   do not dwell on the *p.*
     65: 16   For the *p* troubles will be forgotten
Ro 15: 4   in the *p* was written to teach us,
     16: 25   the mystery hidden for long ages *p,*
Eph   3: 9   which for ages *p* was kept hidden
Heb   1: 1   In the *p* God spoke

PASTORS*

Eph   4: 11   and some to be *p* and teachers,

PASTURE (PASTURES)

Ps 37: 3   dwell in the land and enjoy safe *p.*
     95: 7   and we are the people of his *p,*
   100: 3   we are his people, the sheep of his *p*
Jer 50: 7   against the LORD, their true *p,*
Eze 34: 13   I will *p* them on the mountains
Zec 11: 4   "*P* the flock marked for slaughter.
Jn 10: 9   come in and go out, and find *p.*

PASTURES (PASTURE)

Ps 23: 2   He makes me lie down in green *p,*

PATCH

Jer 10: 5   Like a scarecrow in a melon *p,*
Mt   9: 16   No one sews a *p* of unshrunk cloth

PATH (PATHS)

Ps 16: 11   known to me the *p* of life;
     27: 11   lead me in a straight *p*
   119: 32   I run in the *p* of your commands,
   119: 105   and a light for my *p.*
Pr   2: 9   and fair—every good *p.*
     12: 28   along that *p* is immortality.
     15: 10   awaits him who leaves the *p;*
     15: 19   the *p* of the upright is a highway.
     15: 24   The *p* of life leads upward
     21: 16   from the *p* of understanding
Isa 26: 7   The *p* of the righteous is level;
Jer 31: 9   on a level *p* where they will not
Mt 13: 4   fell along the *p*, and the birds came
Lk   1: 79   to guide our feet into the *p* of peace
2Co   6: 3   no stumbling block in anyone's *p,*

PATHS (PATH)

Ps 23: 3   He guides me in *p* of righteousness
     25: 4   teach me your *p;*
Pr   2: 13   who leave the straight *p*
      3: 6   and he will make your *p* straight.
      4: 11   and lead you along straight *p.*
      4: 26   Make level *p* for your feet
      5: 21   and he examines all his *p.*
      8: 20   along the *p* of justice,
     22: 5   In the *p* of the wicked lie thorns
Isa   2: 3   so that we may walk in his *p.*"
Jer   6: 16   ask for the ancient *p,*
Mic   4: 2   so that we may walk in his *p.*"
Mt   3: 3   make straight *p* for him.' "
Ac   2: 28   to me the *p* of life;
Ro 11: 33   and his *p* beyond tracing out!
Heb 12: 13   "Make level *p* for your feet,"

PATIENCE* (PATIENT)

Pr 19: 11   A man's wisdom gives him *p;*
     25: 15   Through *p* a ruler can be persuaded
Ecc   7: 8   and *p* is better than pride.
Isa   7: 13   Is it not enough to try the *p* of men?
      7: 13   Will you try the *p* of my God also?
Ro   2: 4   and *p*, not realizing that God's
      9: 22   bore with great *p* the objects
2Co   6: 6   understanding, and *p*; kindness;
Gal   5: 22   joy, peace, *p*, kindness, goodness,
Col   1: 11   may have great endurance and *p,*
      3: 12   humility, gentleness and *p.*
1Ti   1: 16   Jesus might display his unlimited *p*
2Ti   3: 10   my purpose, faith, *p*, love,
      4: 2   with great *p* and careful instruction

Heb 6:12 *p* inherit what has been promised.
Jas 5:10 as an example of *p* in the face
2Pe 3:15 that our Lord's *p* means salvation,

PATIENT* (PATIENCE PATIENTLY)
Ne   9:30 For many years you were *p*
Job 6:11 What prospects, that I should
           be *p*?
Pr   14:29 A *p* man has great understanding,
     15:18 but a *p* man calms a quarrel.
     16:32 Better a *p* man than a warrior,
Mt   18:26 'Be *p* with me,' he begged,
     18:29 'Be *p* with me, and I will pay you
Ro   12:12 Be joyful in hope, *p* in affliction,
1Co 13: 4 Love is *p*, love is kind.
2Co   1: 6 produces in you *p* endurance
Eph   4: 2 humble and gentle; be *p*,
1Th   5:14 help the weak, be *p* with
           everyone.
Jas   5: 7 Be *p*, then, brothers,
      5: 7 and how *p* he is for the autumn
      5: 8 You too, be *p* and stand firm,
2Pe   3: 9 He is *p* with you, not wanting
Rev   1: 9 *p* endurance that are ours in
           Jesus,
     13:10 This calls for *p* endurance
     14:12 This calls for *p* endurance

PATIENTLY* (PATIENT)
Ps   37: 7 still before the LORD and wait *p*
     40: 1 I waited *p* for the LORD;
Isa 38:13 I waited *p* till dawn,
Hab   3:16 Yet I will wait *p* for the day
Ac   26: 3 I beg you to listen to me *p*
Ro   8:25 we do not yet have, we wait for
           it *p*.
Heb   6:15 after waiting *p*, Abraham received
1Pe   3:20 ago when God waited *p* in the
           days
Rev   3:10 kept my command to endure *p*,

PATTERN
Ex   25:40 according to the *p* shown you
Ro   5:14 who was a *p* of the one to come.
     12: 2 longer to the *p* of this world,
2Ti   1:13 keep as the *p* of sound teaching,
Heb   8: 5 according to the *p* shown you

PAUL
    Also called Saul (Ac 13:9). Pharisee from
Tarsus (Ac 9:11; Php 3:5). Apostle (Gal 1). At
stoning of Stephen (Ac 8:1). Persecuted
Church (Ac 9:1–2; Gal 1:13). Vision of Jesus on
road to Damascus (Ac 9:4–9; 26:12–18). In
Arabia (Gal 1:17). Preached in Damascus;
escaped death through the wall in a basket
(Ac 9:19–25). In Jerusalem; sent back to Tarsus (Ac 9:26–30).
    Brought to Antioch by Barnabas (Ac
11:22–26). First missionary journey to Cyprus
and Galatia (Ac 13–14). Stoned at Lystra (Ac
14:19–20). At Jerusalem council (Ac 15). Split
with Barnabas over Mark (Ac 15:36–41).
    Second missionary journey with Silas (Ac
16–20). Called to Macedonia (Ac 16:6–10).
Freed from prison in Philippi (Ac 16:16–40). In
Thessalonica (Ac 17:1–9). Speech in Athens
(Ac 17:16–33). In Corinth (Ac 18). In Ephesus
(Ac 19). Return to Jerusalem (Ac 20). Farewell
to Ephesian elders (Ac 20:13–38). Arrival in
Jerusalem (Ac 21:1–26). Arrested (Ac
21:27–36). Addressed crowds (Ac 22), Sanhedrin (Ac 23:1–11). Transferred to Caesarea
(Ac 23:12–35). Trial before Felix (Ac 24), Festus (Ac 25:1–12). Before Agrippa (Ac
25:13–26:32). Voyage to Rome; shipwreck (Ac
27). Arrival in Rome (Ac 28).
    Epistles: Romans, 1 and 2 Corinthians, Gala-
tians, Ephesians, Philippians, Colossians, 1 and
2 Thessalonians, 1 and 2 Timothy, Titus, Philemon.

PAVEMENT
Jn   19:13 as the Stone P (which

PAY (PAID PAYMENT PAYS REPAID REPAY
REPAYING)
Lev 26:43 They will *p* for their sins
Dt   7:12 If you *p* attention to these laws
Pr   4: 1 *p* attention and gain
           understanding
      4:20 My son, *p* attention to what I say;
      5: 1 My son, *p* attention to my
           wisdom,

Pr   6:31 if he is caught, he must *p*
           sevenfold,
     19:19 man must *p* the penalty;
     22:17 P attention and listen
     24:29 I'll *p* that man back for what he
           did
Eze 40: 4 and *p* attention to everything I am
Zec 11:12 give me my *p*; but if not, keep it."
Mt   20: 2 He agreed to *p* them a denarius
     22:16 you *p* no attention to who they
           are.
     22:17 Is it right to *p* taxes to Caesar
Lk   3:14 falsely—be content with your *p*."
     19: 8 I will *p* back four times the
           amount
Ro   13: 6 This is also why you *p* taxes,
2Pe   1:19 you will do well to *p* attention to
           it,

PAYMENT (PAY)
Ps   49: 8 no *p* is ever enough—
Php   4:18 I have received full *p* and

PAYS (PAY)
Pr   17:13 If a man *p* back evil for good,
1Th   5:15 sure that nobody *p* back wrong

PEACE (PEACEABLE PEACEFUL PEACEMAKERS)
Lev 26: 6 " 'I will grant *p* in the land,
Nu   6:26 and give you *p*.' "
     25:12 him I am making my covenant of *p*
Dt   20:10 make its people an offer of *p*.
Jdg   3:11 So the land had *p* for forty years.
      3:30 and the land had *p* for eighty
           years.
      5:31 Then the land had *p* forty years.
      6:24 and called it The LORD is P.
      8:28 the land enjoyed *p* forty years.
1Sa   7:14 And there was *p* between Israel
2Sa 10:19 they made *p* with the Israelites
1Ki   2:33 may there be the LORD's *p* forever
     22:44 also at *p* with the king of Israel.
2Ki   9:17 come in *p*?' " The horseman rode
1Ch 19:19 they made *p* with David
     22: 9 and I will grant Israel *p*
2Ch 14: 1 and in his days the country was
           at *p*
     20:30 kingdom of Jehoshaphat was at *p*,
Job   3:26 I have no *p*, no quietness;
     22:21 to God and be at *p* with him;
Ps   29:11 LORD blesses his people with *p*.
     34:14 seek *p* and pursue it.
     37:11 and enjoy great *p*.
     37:37 there is a future for the man of *p*.
     85:10 righteousness and *p* kiss each
           other
    119:165 Great *p* have they who love your
    120: 7 I am a man of *p*;
    122: 6 Pray for the *p* of Jerusalem:
    147:14 He grants *p* to your borders
Pr   12:20 but joy for those who promote *p*.
     14:30 A heart at *p* gives life to the body,
     16: 7 his enemies live at *p* with him.
     17: 1 Better a dry crust with *p* and
           quiet
Ecc   3: 8 a time for war and a time for *p*.
Isa   9: 6 Everlasting Father, Prince of P.
     14: 7 All the lands are at rest and at *p*;
     26: 3 You will keep in perfect *p*
     32:17 The fruit of righteousness will
           be *p*;
     48:18 your *p* would have been like a
           river,
     48:22 "There is no *p*," says the LORD.
     52: 7 who proclaim *p*,
     53: 5 punishment that brought us *p* was
     54:10 nor my covenant of *p* be
           removed,"
     55:12 and be led forth in *p*;
     57: 2 enter into *p*;
     57:19 P, *p*, to those far and near,"
     57:21 "There is no *p*," says my God,
     59: 8 The way of *p* they do not know;
Jer   6:14 'P, *p*,' they say,
      6:14 'P, *p*,' . . . there is no *p*.
     30:10 Jacob will again have *p*
     46:27 Jacob will again have *p*
Eze 13:10 "P," when there is no *p*,
     34:25 " 'I will make a covenant of *p*
     37:26 I will make a covenant of *p*
Mic   5: 5 And he will be their *p*.
Zec   8:19 Therefore love truth and *p*."
      9:10 He will proclaim *p* to the nations.

Mal   2: 5 a covenant of life and *p*,
      2: 6 He walked with me in *p*
Mt   10:34 I did not come to bring *p*,
Mk   9:50 and be at *p* with each other."
Lk   1:79 to guide our feet into the path
           of *p*
      2:14 on earth *p* to men on whom his
     19:38 "P in heaven and glory
Jn   14:27 P I leave with you; my *p*
     16:33 so that in me you may have *p*.
Ro   1: 7 and *p* to you from God our Father
      2:10 and *p* for everyone who does
           good:
      5: 1 we have *p* with God
      8: 6 by the Spirit is life and *p*;
     12:18 on you, live at *p* with everyone.
     14:19 effort to do what leads to *p*
1Co   7:15 God has called us to live in *p*.
     14:33 a God of disorder but of *p*.
2Co 13:11 be of one mind, live in *p*.
Gal   5:22 joy, *p*, patience, kindness,
Eph   2:14 he himself is our *p*, who has made
      2:15 thus making *p*, and in this one
           body
      2:17 and *p* to those who were near.
      6:15 comes from the gospel of *p*.
Php   4: 7 the *p* of God, which transcends all
Col   1:20 by making *p* through his blood,
      3:15 Let the *p* of Christ rule
      3:15 of one body you were called to *p*.
1Th   5: 3 While people are saying, "P
      5:13 Live in *p* with each other.
      5:23 the God of *p*, sanctify you through
2Th   3:16 the Lord of *p* himself give you *p*
2Ti   2:22 righteousness, faith, love and *p*,
Heb   7: 2 "king of Salem" means "king
           of *p*,
     12:11 *p* for those who have been trained
     12:14 effort to live in *p* with all men
     13:20 May the God of *p*, who
1Pe   3:11 he must seek *p* and pursue it.
2Pe   3:14 blameless and at *p* with him.
Rev   6: 4 power to take *p* from the earth

PEACEABLE* (PEACE)
Tit   3: 2 to slander no one, to be *p*

PEACEFUL (PEACE)
1Ti   2: 2 that we may live *p* and quiet lives

PEACE-LOVING
Jas   3:17 then *p*, considerate

PEACEMAKERS* (PEACE)
Mt   5: 9 Blessed are the *p*,
Jas   3:18 P who sow in peace raise a
           harvest

PEARL* (PEARLS)
Rev 21:21 each gate made of a single *p*.

PEARLS (PEARL)
Mt   7: 6 do not throw your *p* to pigs.
     13:45 like a merchant looking for fine *p*.
1Ti   2: 9 or gold or *p* or expensive clothes,
Rev 21:21 The twelve gates were twelve *p*,

PEDDLE*
2Co   2:17 we do not *p* the word of God

PEG
Jdg   4:21 She drove the *p* through his
           temple

PEKAH
    King of Israel (2Ki 15:25–31; Isa 7:1).

PEKAHIAH*
    Son of Menahem; king of Israel (2Ki
15:22–26).

PEN
Ps   45: 1 my tongue is the *p*
Mt   5:18 letter, not the least stroke of a *p*,
Jn   10: 1 who does not enter the sheep *p*

PENETRATES*
Heb   4:12 it *p* even to dividing soul and
           spirit,

PENNIES* (PENNY)
Lk   12: 6 not five sparrows sold for two *p*?

PENNY* (PENNIES)
Mt   5:26 out until you have paid the last *p*.
     10:29 Are not two sparrows sold for a *p*?
Mk   12:42 worth only a fraction of a *p*.
Lk   12:59 out until you have paid the
           last *p*."

PENTECOST*
Ac 2: 1 of *P* came, they were all together
   20:16 if possible, by the day of *P.*
1Co 16: 8 I will stay on at Ephesus until *P,*

PEOPLE (PEOPLES)
Ge 11: 6 as one *p* speaking the same
Ex 5: 1 Let my *p* go,
    6: 7 take you as my own *p,*
    8:23 between my *p* and your *p.*
   15:13 the *p* you have redeemed.
   19: 8 The *p* all responded together,
   24: 3 Moses went and told the *p*
   32: 1 When the *p* saw that Moses
   32: 9 they are a stiff-necked *p.*
   33:13 this nation is your *p.*
Lev 9: 7 for yourself and the *p.;*
   16:24 the burnt offering for the *p,*
   26:12 and you will be my *p.*
Nu 11:11 burden of all these *p* on
   14:11 *p* treat me with contempt?
   14:19 forgive the sin of these *p,*
   22: 5 A *p* has come out of Egypt
Dt 4: 6 a wise and understanding *p.*
    4:20 the *p* of his inheritance,
    5:28 what this *p* said to you.
    7: 6 a *p* holy to the LORD
   26:18 that you are his *p,*
   31: 7 you must go with this *p*
   31:16 these *p* will soon prostitute
   32: 9 the LORD's portion is his *p,*
   32:43 atonement for his land and *p.*
   33:29 a *p* saved by the LORD?
Jos 1: 6 you will lead this *p*
   24:24 the *p* said to Joshua,
Jdg 2: 7 *p* served the LORD throughout
Ru 1:16 Your *p* will be my *p*
1Sa 8: 7 the *p* are saying to you;
   12:22 LORD will not reject his *p,*
2Sa 5: 2 will shepherd my *p* Israel
    7:10 provide a place for my *p*
1Ki 3: 8 among the *p* you have chosen,
    8:30 your *p* Israel when they pray
    8:56 has given rest to his *p*
   18:39 when all the *p* saw this,
2Ki 23: 3 all the *p* pledged themselves
1Ch 17:21 to redeem *p* for himself
   29:17 how willingly your *p* who are
2Ch 2:11 Because the LORD loves his *p,*
    7: 5 *p* dedicated the temple
    7:14 if my *p,* who are called
   30: 6 "*P* of Israel, return to
   36:16 was aroused against his *p*
Ezr 2: 1 These are the *p* of the
    3: 1 *p* assembled as one man
Ne 1:10 your *p,* whom you redeemed
    4: 6 *p* worked with all their heart
    8: 1 *p* assembled as one man
Est 3: 6 to destroy all Mordecai's *p,*
Job 12: 2 Doubtless you are the *p;*
Ps 29:11 gives strength to his *p;*
   33:12 *p* he chose for his inheritance
   50: 4 that he may judge his *p*
   53: 6 restores the fortunes of his *p,*
   81:13 If my *p* would but listen
   94:14 LORD will not reject his *p;*
   95: 7 we are the *p* of his pasture,
   95:10 a *p* whose hearts go astray,
  125: 2 the LORD surrounds his *p*
  135:14 LORD will vindicate his *p*
  144:15 *p* whose God is the LORD.
Pr 14:34 sin is a disgrace to any *p.*
   29: 2 righteous thrive, the *p* rejoice
   29:18 the *p* cast off restraint
Isa 1: 3 my *p* do not understand.
    1: 4 a *p* loaded with guilt,
    5:13 my *p* will go into exile
    6:10 the heart of this *p* calloused;
    9: 2 the *p* walking in darkness
   12:12 will assemble the scattered *p*
   19:25 Blessed be Egypt my *p,*
   25: 8 remove the disgrace of his *p*
   29:13 These *p* come near to me
   40: 1 Comfort, comfort my *p*
   40: 7 Surely the *p* are grass.
   42: 6 a covenant for the *p*
   49:13 the LORD comforts his *p*
   51: 4 "Listen to me, my *p;*
   52: 6 my *p* will know my name;
   53: 8 for the transgression of my *p*
   60:21 will all your *p* be righteous

Isa 62:12 will be called the Holy *P,*
   65:23 they will be a *p* blessed
Jer 2:11 my *p* have exchanged their
    2:13 *p* have committed two sins:
    2:32 my *p* have forgotten me,
    4:22 My *p* are fools;
    5:14 Because the *p* have spoken
    5:31 my *p* love it this way
    7:16 do not pray for this *p*
    7:23 you will be my *p,*
   18:15 my *p* have forgotten me;
   30: 3 I will bring my *p* Israel
Eze 13:23 I will save my *p* from
   36: 8 fruit for my *p* Israel,
   36:28 you will be my *p,*
   36:38 be filled with flocks of *p.*
   37:13 Then you, my *p,* will know
   38:14 *p* Israel are living in safety
   39: 7 name among my *p* Israel.
Da 7:27 saints, the *p* of the Most High.
    8:24 mighty men and the holy *p.*
    9:19 your *p* bear your name
    9:24 are decreed for your *p*
   10:14 will happen to your *p*
   11:32 *p* who know their God will
   12: 1 prince who protects your *p.*
Hos 1:10 'You are not my *p,'*
    2:23 'You are my *p';*
    4:14 a *p* without understanding
Joel 2:18 and take pity on his *p.*
    3:16 be a refuge for his *p,*
Am 9:14 back my exiled *p* Israel;
Mic 6: 2 a case against his *p;*
    7:14 Shepherd your *p* with
Hag 1:12 remnant of the *p* obeyed
Zec 2:11 and will become my *p.*
    8: 7 I will save my *p*
   13: 9 will say, 'They are my *p.'*
Mk 7: 6 *p* honor me with their lips
    8:27 "Who do *p* say I am?"
Lk 1:17 make ready a *p* prepared
    1:68 and has redeemed his *p.*
    2:10 joy that will be for all the *p.*
   21:23 and wrath against this *p.*
Jn 11:50 one man die for the *p*
   18:14 if one man died for the *p,*
Ac 15:14 from the Gentiles a *p.*
   18:10 have many *p* in this city.
Ro 9:25 will call them 'my *p.'*
   11: 1 Did God reject his *p?*
   15:10 O Gentiles, with his *p.* "
2Co 6:16 and they will be my *p.* "
Tit 2:14 a *p* that are his very own,
Heb 2:17 for the sins of the *p.*
    4: 9 a Sabbath-rest for the *p*
    5: 3 for the sins of the *p.*
   10:30 Lord will judge his *p.*
   11:25 mistreated along with the *p*
   13:12 to make the *p* holy
1Pe 2: 9 you are a chosen *p,*
    2:10 Once you were not a *p,*
    2:10 you are the *p* of God;
2Pe 2: 1 false prophets among the *p,*
    3:11 kind of *p* ought you to be?
Rev 18: 4 "Come out of her, my *p,*
   21: 3 They will be his *p,*

PEOPLES (PEOPLE)
Ge 17:16 kings of *p* will come from her
   25:23 two *p* from within you will
   27:29 and *p* bow down to you
   28: 3 become a community of *p.*
   48: 4 you a community of *p.*
Dt 14: 2 of all the *p* on the face of
   28:10 Then all the *p* on earth
   32: 8 set up boundaries for the *p*
Jos 4:24 all the *p* of the earth might
1Ki 8:43 all the *p* of the earth may
2Ch 7:20 of ridicule among all *p.*
Ps 8: 9 he will govern the *p*
   67: 5 may all the *p* praise you.
   87: 6 in the register of the *p:*
   96:10 he will judge the *p*
Isa 2: 4 settle disputes for many *p.*
   17:12 Oh, the uproar of the *p*—
   25: 6 of rich food for all *p,*
   34: 1 pay attention, you *p!*
   55: 4 him a witness to the *p,*
Jer 10: 3 customs of the *p* are worthless
Da 7:14 all *p,* nations and men

Mic 4: 1 and *p* will stream to it.
    4: 3 will judge between many *p*
    5: 7 in the midst of many *p*
Zep 3: 9 purify the lips of the *p,*
    3:20 among all the *p* of the
Zec 8:20 Many *p* and the inhabitants
   12: 2 all the surrounding *p* reeling.
Rev 10:11 prophesy again about many *p,*
   17:15 the prostitute sits, are *p,*

PEOR
Nu 25: 3 joined in worshiping the Baal of *P.*
Dt 4: 3 who followed the Baal of *P,*

PERCEIVE (PERCEIVING)
Ps 139: 2 you *p* my thoughts from afar.
Pr 24:12 not he who weighs the heart *p* it?

PERCEIVING* (PERCEIVE)
Isa 6: 9 be ever seeing, but never *p.'*
Mt 13:14 you will be ever seeing but
                never *p.*
Mk 4:12 may be ever seeing but never *p.*
Ac 28:26 you will be ever seeing but
                never *p*

PERFECT* (PERFECTER PERFECTING PERFECTION)
Dt 32: 4 He is the Rock, his works are *p,*
2Sa 22:31 "As for God, his way is *p;*
   22:33 and makes my way *p.*
Job 36: 4 one *p* in knowledge is with you.
   37:16 of him who is *p* in knowledge?
Ps 18:30 As for God, his way is *p;*
   18:32 and makes my way *p.*
   19: 7 The law of the LORD is *p,*
   50: 2 From Zion, *p* in beauty,
   64: 6 "We have devised a *p* plan!"
SS 6: 9 but my dove, my *p* one, is unique,
Isa 25: 1 for in *p* faithfulness
   26: 3 You will keep in *p* peace
Eze 16:14 had given you made your
                beauty *p,*
   27: 3 "I am *p* in beauty."
   28:12 full of wisdom and *p* in beauty.
Mt 5:48 Do not even pagans do that?
                Be *p,*
    5:48 as your heavenly Father is *p.*
   19:21 answered, "If you want to be *p,*
Ro 12: 2 his good, pleasing and *p* will.
2Co 12: 9 for my power is made *p*
Php 3:12 or have already been made *p,*
Col 1:28 so that we may present
                everyone *p*
    3:14 binds them all together in *p* unity.
Heb 2:10 the author of their salvation *p*
    5: 9 what he suffered and, once
                made *p,*
    7:19 useless (for the law made
                nothing *p*
    7:28 who has been made *p* forever.
    9:11 and more *p* tabernacle that is not
   10: 1 make *p* those who draw
   10:14 he has made *p* forever those who
   11:40 with us would they be made *p.*
   12:23 spirits of righteous men made *p,*
Jas 1:17 Every good and *p* gift is from
                above
    1:25 into the *p* law that gives freedom,
    3: 2 he is a *p* man, able
1Jn 4:18 But *p* love drives out fear,
    4:18 The one who fears is not made *p*

PERFECTER* (PERFECT)
Heb 12: 2 the author and *p* of our faith,

PERFECTING* (PERFECT)
2Co 7: 1 *p* holiness out of reverence for
                God

PERFECTION* (PERFECT)
Ps 119:96 To all *p* I see a limit;
La 2:15 the *p* of beauty,
Eze 27: 4 builders brought your beauty to *p.*
   27:11 they brought your beauty to *p.*
   28:12 " 'You were the model of *p,*
1Co 13:10 but when *p* comes, the imperfect
2Co 13: 9 and our prayer is for your *p.*
   13:11 Aim for *p,* listen to my appeal,
Heb 7:11 If *p* could have been attained

PERFORM (PERFORMED PERFORMS)
Ex 3:20 with all the wonders that I will *p*
2Sa 7:23 to *p* great and awesome wonders
Jn 3: 2 no one could *p* the miraculous

PERFORMED (PERFORM)
Mt 11:21 If the miracles that were *p*

Jn 10:41 John never *p* a miraculous

PERFORMS (PERFORM)
Ps 77:14 You are the God who *p* miracles;

PERFUME
Ecc 7: 1 A good name is better than fine *p*,
SS   1: 3 your name is like *p* poured out.
Mk 14: 3 jar of very expensive *p*,

PERIL
2Co 1:10 us from such a deadly *p*,

PERISH (PERISHABLE PERISHED PERISHES PERISHING)
Ge   6:17 Everything on earth will *p*.
Est 4:16 And if I *p*, I *p*."
Ps   1: 6 but the way of the wicked will *p*.
    37:20 But the wicked will *p*:
    73:27 Those who are far from you will *p*;
   102:26 They will *p*, but you remain;
Pr 11:10 when the wicked *p*, there are
    19: 9 and he who pours out lies will *p*
    21:28 A false witness will *p*,
    28:28 when the wicked *p*, the righteous
Isa 1:28 who forsake the LORD will *p*.
    29:14 the wisdom of the wise will *p*,
    60:12 that will not serve you will *p*;
Zec 11: 9 the dying die, and the perishing *p*.
Lk 13: 3 unless you repent, you too will all *p*
    13: 5 unless you repent, you too will all *p*
    21:18 But not a hair of your head will *p*.
Jn   3:16 whoever believes in him shall not *p*
    10:28 eternal life, and they shall never *p*;
Ro   2:12 apart from the law will also *p* apart
Col 2:22 These are all destined to *p* with use,
2Th 2:10 They *p* because they refused
Heb 1:11 They will *p*, but you remain;
1Pe 1: 4 into an inheritance that can never *p*
2Pe 3: 9 not wanting anyone to *p*,

PERISHABLE (PERISH)
1Co 15:42 The body that is sown is *p*,
1Pe 1:18 not with *p* things such
     1:23 not of *p* seed, but of imperishable,

PERISHED (PERISH)
Ps 119:92 I would have *p* in my affliction.

PERISHES (PERISH)
Job 8:13 so *p* the hope of the godless.
1Pe 1: 7 which *p* even though refined by fire

PERISHING (PERISH)
1Co 1:18 foolishness to those who are *p*,
2Co 2:15 being saved and those who are *p*.
     4: 3 it is veiled to those who are *p*.

PERJURERS* (PERJURY)
Mal 3: 5 and *p*, against those who defraud
1Ti 1:10 for slave traders and liars and *p*—

PERJURY* (PERJURERS)
Jer 7: 9 murder, commit adultery and *p*,

PERMANENT
Heb 7:24 lives forever, he has a *p* priesthood.

PERMISSIBLE (PERMIT)
1Co 6:12 "Everything is *p* for me"—
    10:23 "Everything is *p*"—but not

PERMIT (PERMISSIBLE PERMITTED)
Hos 5: 4 "Their deeds do not *p* them
1Ti 2:12 I do not *p* a woman to teach

PERMITTED (PERMIT)
Mt 19: 8 Moses *p* you to divorce your wives
2Co 12: 4 things that man is not *p* to tell.

PERSECUTE (PERSECUTED PERSECUTION PERSECUTIONS)
Ps 119:86 for men *p* me without cause.
Mt   5:11 *p* you and falsely say all kinds
     5:44 and pray for those who *p* you,
Jn 15:20 they persecuted me, they will *p* you
Ac   9: 4 why do you *p* me?" "Who are you,
Ro 12:14 Bless those who *p* you; bless

PERSECUTED (PERSECUTE)
Mt   5:10 Blessed are those who are *p*

Mt   5:12 same way they *p* the prophets who
Jn 15:20 If they *p* me, they will persecute
1Co 4:12 when we are *p*, we endure it;
    15: 9 because I *p* the church of God.
2Co 4: 9 in despair; *p*, but not abandoned;
1Th 3: 4 kept telling you that we would be *p*.
2Ti 3:12 life in Christ Jesus will be *p*,
Heb 11:37 destitute, *p* and mistreated—

PERSECUTION (PERSECUTE)
Mt 13:21 When trouble or *p* comes
Ro   8:35 or hardship or *p* or famine

PERSECUTIONS (PERSECUTE)
Mk 10:30 and with them, *p*) and in the age
2Co 12:10 in hardships, in *p*, in difficulties.
2Th 1: 4 faith in all the *p* and trials you are
2Ti 3:11 love, endurance, *p*, sufferings—

PERSEVERANCE* (PERSEVERE)
Ro   5: 3 we know that suffering produces *p*;
     5: 4 *p*, character; and character, hope.
2Co 12:12 were done among you with great *p*.
2Th 1: 4 churches we boast about your *p*
     3: 5 into God's love and Christ's *p*.
Heb 12: 1 run with *p* the race marked out
Jas 1: 3 the testing of your faith develops *p*.
     1: 4 *P* must finish its work
     5:11 You have heard of Job's *p*
2Pe 1: 6 *p*; and to *p*, godliness;
Rev 2: 2 your hard work and your *p*.
     2:19 and faith, your service and *p*,

PERSEVERE* (PERSEVERANCE PERSEVERED PERSEVERES PERSEVERING)
1Ti 4:16 *P* in them, because if you do,
Heb 10:36 You need to *p* so that

PERSEVERED* (PERSEVERE)
Heb 11:27 he *p* because he saw him who is
Jas 5:11 consider blessed those who have *p*.
Rev 2: 3 You have *p* and have endured

PERSEVERES* (PERSEVERE)
1Co 13: 7 trusts, always hopes, always *p*.
Jas 1:12 Blessed is the man who *p*

PERSEVERING* (PERSEVERE)
Lk   8:15 retain it, and by *p* produce a crop.

PERSIANS
Da   6:15 law of the Medes and *P* no decree

PERSISTENCE*
Ro   2: 7 To those who by *p*

PERSUADE (PERSUADED PERSUASIVE)
Ac 18: 4 trying to *p* Jews and Greeks.
2Co 5:11 is to fear the Lord, we try to *p* men.

PERSUADED (PERSUADE)
Ro   4:21 being fully *p* that God had power

PERSUASIVE (PERSUADE)
1Co 2: 4 not with wise and *p* words,

PERVERSION* (PERVERT)
Lev 18:23 sexual relations with it; that is a *p*.
    20:12 What they have done is a *p*;
Ro   1:27 the due penalty for their *p*.
Jude   7 up to sexual immorality and *p*.

PERVERT (PERVERSION PERVERTED PERVERTS)
Ex 23: 2 do not *p* justice by siding
Dt 16:19 Do not *p* justice or show partiality.
Job 34:12 that the Almighty would *p* justice.
Pr 17:23 to *p* the course of justice.
Gal 1: 7 are trying to *p* the gospel of Christ.

PERVERTED (PERVERT)
1Sa 8: 3 and accepted bribes and *p* justice.

PERVERTS* (PERVERT)
1Ti 1:10 for murderers, for adulterers and *p*,

PESTILENCE (PESTILENCES)
Ps 91: 6 nor the *p* that stalks in the darkness

PESTILENCES (PESTILENCE)
Lk 21:11 famines and *p* in various places,

PETER
     Apostle, brother of Andrew, also called
     Simon (Mt 10:2; Mk 3:16; Lk 6:14; Ac 1:13),
     and Cephas (Jn 1:42). Confession of Christ (Mt
     16:13–20; Mk 8:27–30; Lk 9:18–27). At transfig-
     uration (Mt 17:1–8; Mk 9:2–8; Lk 9:28–36; 2Pe
     1:16–18). Caught fish with coin (Mt 17:24–27).
     Denial of Jesus predicted (Mt 26:31–35; Mk
     14:27–31; Lk 22:31–34; Jn 13:31–38). Denied
     Jesus (Mt 26:69–75; Mk 14:66–72; Lk 22:54–62;
     Jn 18:15–27). Commissioned by Jesus to shep-
     herd his flock (Jn 21:15–23).
        Speech at Pentecost (Ac 2). Healed beggar
     (Ac 3:1–10). Speech at temple (Ac 3:11–26),
     before Sanhedrin (Ac 4:1–22). In Samaria (Ac
     8:14–25). Sent by vision to Cornelius (Ac 10).
     Announced salvation of Gentiles in Jerusalem
     (Ac 11; 15). Freed from prison (Ac 12). Incon-
     sistency at Antioch (Gal 2:11–21). At
     Jerusalem Council (Ac 15).
        Epistles: 1–2 Peter.

PETITION (PETITIONS)
1Ch 16: 4 to make *p*, to give thanks,
Php 4: 6 by prayer and *p*, with thanksgiving,

PETITIONS (PETITION)
Heb 5: 7 he offered up prayers and *p*

PHANTOM*
Ps 39: 6 Man is a mere *p* as he goes to

PHARAOH (PHARAOH'S)
Ge 12:15 her to *P*, and she was taken
    41:14 So *P* sent for Joseph, and he was
Ex 14: 4 glory for myself through *P*
    14:17 And I will gain glory through *P*

PHARAOH'S (PHARAOH)
Ex   7: 3 But I will harden *P* heart, and

PHARISEE (PHARISEES)
Ac 23: 6 brothers, I am a *P*, the son of a *P*.
Php 3: 5 in regard to the law, a *P*; as for zeal,

PHARISEES (PHARISEE)
Mt   5:20 surpasses that of the *P*
    16: 6 guard against the yeast of the *P*
    23:13 of the law and *P*, you hypocrites!
Jn   3: 1 a man of the *P* named Nicodemus,

PHILADELPHIA
Rev 3: 7 the angel of the church in *P* write:

PHILEMON*
Phm   1 To *P* our dear friend and fellow

PHILIP
     1. Apostle (Mt 10:3; Mk 3:18; Lk 6:14; Jn
     1:43–48; 14:8; Ac 1:13).
     2. Deacon (Ac 6:1–7); evangelist in Samaria
     (Ac 8:4–25), to Ethiopian (Ac 8:26–40).

PHILIPPI
Ac 16:12 From there we traveled to *P*,
Php 1: 1 To all the saints in Christ Jesus at *P*

PHILISTINE (PHILISTINES)
Jos 13: 3 of the five *P* rulers in Gaza,
1Sa 14: 1 let's go over to the *P* outpost
    17:26 is this uncircumcised *P* that he
    17:37 me from the hand of this *P*."

PHILISTINES (PHILISTINE)
Jdg 10: 7 them into the hands of the *P*
    13: 1 the hands of the *P* for forty years.
    16: 5 The rulers of the *P* went to her
1Sa 4: 1 at Ebenezer, and the *P* at Aphek.
     5: 8 together all the rulers of the *P*
    13:23 a detachment of *P* had gone out
    17: 1 the *P* gathered their forces for war
    23: 1 the *P* are fighting against Keilah
    27: 1 is to escape to the land of the *P*.
    31: 1 Now the *P* fought against Israel;
2Sa 5:17 When the *P* heard that David had
     8: 1 David defeated the *P* and subdued
    21:15 there was a battle between the *P*
2Ki 18: 8 he defeated the *P*, as far as Gaza
Am   1: 8 Ekron till the last of the *P* is dead,"

PHILOSOPHER* (PHILOSOPHY)
1Co 1:20 Where is the *p* of this age?

PHILOSOPHY* (PHILOSOPHER)
Col 2: 8 through hollow and deceptive *p*,

PHINEHAS
Nu 25: 7 When *P* son of Eleazar, the son
Ps 106:30 But *P* stood up and intervened,

PHOEBE*
Ro 16: 1 I commend to you our sister *P,*

PHYLACTERIES*
Mt 23: 5 They make their *p* wide

PHYSICAL
Ro   2:28 merely outward and *p.*
Col 1:22 by Christ's *p* body through death
1Ti 4: 8 For *p* training is of some value,
Jas 2:16 but does nothing about his *p*
          needs,

PICK (PICKED)
Mk 16:18 they will *p* up snakes

PICKED (PICK)
Lk 14: 7 noticed how the guests *p* the
          places
Jn   5: 9 he *p* up his mat and walked.

PIECE (PIECES)
Jn 19:23 woven in one *p* from top to
          bottom.

PIECES (PIECE)
Ge 15:17 and passed between the *p.*
Jer 34:18 and then walked between its *p.*
Zec 11:12 So they paid me thirty *p* of silver.
Mt 14:20 of broken *p* that were left over.

PIERCE (PIERCED)
Ex 21: 6 and *p* his ear with an awl.
Pr 12:18 Reckless words *p* like a sword,
Lk   2:35 a sword will *p* your own soul too."

PIERCED (PIERCE)
Ps 22:16 they have *p* my hands and my
          feet.
      40: 6 but my ears you have *p;*
Isa 53: 5 But he was *p* for our
          transgressions,
Zec 12:10 look on me, the one they have *p,*
Jn 19:37 look on the one they have *p."*
Rev 1: 7 even those who *p* him;

PIG'S (PIGS)
Pr 11:22 Like a gold ring in a *p* snout

PIGEONS
Lev 5:11 afford two doves or two young *p,*
Lk   2:24 "a pair of doves or two young *p."*

PIGS (PIG'S)
Mt   7: 6 do not throw your pearls to *p.*
Mk   5:11 A large herd of *p* was feeding on

PILATE
          Governor of Judea. Questioned Jesus (Mt
      27:1–26; Mk 15:15; Lk 22:66–23:25; Jn
      18:28–19:16); sent him to Herod (Lk 23:6–12);
      consented to his crucifixion when crowds
      chose Barabbas (Mt 27:15–26; Mk 15:6–15; Lk
      23:13–25; Jn 19:1–10).

PILLAR (PILLARS)
Ge 19:26 and she became a *p* of salt.
Ex 13:21 ahead of them in a *p* of cloud
1Ti 3:15 the *p* and foundation of the truth.
Rev 3:12 who overcomes I will make a *p*

PILLARS (PILLAR)
Gal 2: 9 and John, those reputed to be *p,*

PINIONS
Dt 32:11 and carries them on its *p.*

PISGAH
Dt   3:27 Go up to the top of *P* and look
          west

PIT
Ps   7:15 falls into the *p* he has made.
      40: 2 He lifted me out of the slimy *p,*
   103: 4 who redeems your life from the *p*
Pr 23:27 for a prostitute is a deep *p*
    26:27 If a man digs a *p,* he will fall into
          it;
Isa 24:17 Terror and *p* and snare await you,
    38:17 me from the *p* of destruction;
Mt 15:14 a blind man, both will fall into
          a *p."*

PITCH
Ge   6:14 and coat it with *p* inside and out.
Ex   2: 3 and coated it with tar and *p.*

PITIED (PITY)
1Co 15:19 we are to be *p* more than all men.

PITY (PITIED)
Ps 72:13 He will take *p* on the weak
Ecc 4:10 But *p* the man who falls
Lk 10:33 when he saw him, he took *p* on
          him

PLAGUE (PLAGUED PLAGUES)
2Ch 6:28 "When famine or *p* comes
Ps 91: 6 nor the *p* that destroys at midday.

PLAGUED* (PLAGUE)
Ps 73: 5 they are not *p* by human ills.
    73:14 All day long I have been *p;*

PLAGUES (PLAGUE)
Hos 13:14 Where, O death, are your *p?*
Rev 21: 9 full of the seven last *p* came
    22:18 to him the *p* described in this
          book.

PLAIN
Isa 40: 4 the rugged places a *p.*
Ro   1:19 what may be known about God
          is *p*

PLAN (PLANNED PLANS)
Ex 26:30 according to the *p* shown you
Job 42: 2 no *p* of yours can be thwarted.
Pr 14:22 those who *p* what is good find
          love
    21:30 is no wisdom, no insight, no *p*
Am 3: 7 nothing without revealing his *p*
Eph 1:11 predestined according to the *p*

PLANK
Mt   7: 3 attention to the *p* in your own
          eye?
Lk   6:41 attention to the *p* in your own
          eye?

PLANNED (PLAN)
Ps 40: 5 The things you *p* for us
Isa 14:24 "Surely, as I have *p,* so it will be,
    23: 9 The LORD Almighty *p* it,
    46:11 what I have *p,* that will I do.
Heb 11:40 God had *p* something better for
          us

PLANS (PLAN)
Ps 20: 4 and make all your *p* succeed.
    33:11 *p* of the LORD stand firm forever,
Pr 15:22 *P* fail for lack of counsel,
    16: 3 and your *p* will succeed.
    19:21 Many are the *p* in a man's heart,
    20:18 Make *p* by seeking advice;
Isa 29:15 to hide their *p* from the LORD,
    30: 1 those who carry out *p* that are not
    32: 8 But the noble man makes noble *p,*
2Co 1:17 Or do I make my *p* in a worldly

PLANT (PLANTED PLANTING PLANTS)
Am 9:15 I will *p* Israel in their own land,
Mt 15:13 "Every *p* that my heavenly Father

PLANTED (PLANT)
Ge   2: 8 the LORD God had *p* a garden
Ps   1: 3 He is like a tree *p* by streams
Jer 17: 8 He will be like a tree *p* by the
          water
Mt 15:13 Father has not *p* will be pulled
    21:33 was a landowner who *p* a
          vineyard.
Lk 13: 6 "A man had a fig tree, *p*
1Co 3: 6 I *p* the seed, Apollos watered it,
Jas 1:21 humbly accept the word *p* in you,

PLANTING (PLANT)
Isa 61: 3 a *p* of the LORD

PLANTS (PLANT)
Pr 31:16 out of her earnings she *p* a
          vineyard
1Co 3: 7 So neither he who *p* nor he who
    9: 7 Who *p* a vineyard and does not
          eat

PLATTER
Mk   6:25 head of John the Baptist on a *p."*

PLAY (PLAYED)
1Sa 16:23 David would take his harp and *p.*
Isa 11: 8 The infant will *p* near the hole

PLAYED (PLAY)
Lk   7:32 " 'We *p* the flute for you,
1Co 14: 7 anyone know what tune is being *p*

PLEA (PLEAD PLEADED PLEADS)
1Ki 8:28 to your servant's prayer and his *p*
Ps 102:17 he will not despise their *p.*
La   3:56 You heard my *p:* "Do not close

PLEAD (PLEA)
Isa 1:17 *p* the case of the widow.

PLEADED (PLEA)
2Co 12: 8 Three times I *p* with the Lord

PLEADS (PLEA)
Job 16:21 on behalf of a man he *p* with God

PLEASANT (PLEASE)
Ge 49:15 and how *p* is his land,
Ps 16: 6 for me in *p* places;
   133: 1 How good and *p* it is
   135: 3 sing praise to his name, for that
          is *p*
   147: 1 how *p* and fitting to praise him!
Pr   2:10 knowledge will be *p* to your soul.
    3:17 Her ways are *p* ways,
    16:21 and *p* words promote instruction.
    16:24 *P* words are a honeycomb,
Isa 30:10 Tell us *p* things,
1Th 3: 6 that you always have *p* memories
Heb 12:11 No discipline seems *p* at the time,

PLEASANTNESS* (PLEASE)
Pr 27: 9 the *p* of one's friend springs

PLEASE (PLEASANT PLEASANTNESS PLEASED
PLEASES PLEASING PLEASURE PLEASURES)
Ps 69:31 This will *p* the LORD more
Pr 20:23 and dishonest scales do not *p*
          him.
Isa 46:10 and I will do all that I *p.*
Jer   6:20 your sacrifices do not *p* me."
    27: 5 and I give it to anyone I *p.*
Jn   5:30 for I seek not to *p* myself
Ro   8: 8 by the sinful nature cannot *p* God.
    15: 1 of the weak and not to *p*
          ourselves.
    15: 2 Each of us should *p* his neighbor
1Co 7:32 affairs—how he can *p* the Lord.
    10:33 I try to *p* everybody in every way.
2Co 5: 9 So we make it our goal to *p* him,
Gal 1:10 or of God? Or am I trying to *p*
          men
    6: 8 the one who sows to *p* the Spirit,
Col 1:10 and may *p* him in every way:
1Th 2: 4 We are not trying to *p* men
    4: 1 how to live in order to *p* God,
2Ti 2: 4 wants to *p* his commanding
          officer.
Tit   2: 9 to try to *p* them, not to talk back
Heb 11: 6 faith it is impossible to *p* God,

PLEASED (PLEASE)
Dt 28:63 as it *p* the LORD to make you
1Sa 12:22 LORD was *p* to make you his own.
1Ki 3:10 The Lord was *p* that Solomon had
1Ch 29:17 that you test the heart and are *p*
Mic 6: 7 Will the LORD be *p*
Mal 1:10 I am not *p* with you," says
Mt   3:17 whom I love; with him I am well *p*
    17: 5 whom I love; with him I am well *p.*
Mk   1:11 whom I love; with you I am well *p*
Lk   3:22 whom I love; with you I am well *p*
1Co 1:21 God was *p* through the
          foolishness
Col 1:19 For God was *p* to have all his
Heb 10: 6 you were not *p.*
    10: 8 nor were you *p* with them"
    10:38 I will not be *p* with him."
    11: 5 commended as one who *p* God.
    13:16 for with such sacrifices God is *p.*
2Pe 1:17 whom I love; with him I am well *p*

PLEASES (PLEASE)
Job 23:13 He does whatever he *p.*
Ps 115: 3 he does whatever *p* him.
   135: 6 The LORD does whatever *p* him,
Pr 15: 8 but the prayer of the upright *p*
          him.
    21: 1 it like a watercourse wherever
          he *p.*
Ecc 2:26 To the man who *p* him, God gives
    7:26 man who *p* God will escape her,
Da   4:35 He does as he *p*
Jn   3: 8 The wind blows wherever it *p.*
    8:29 for I always do what *p* him."
Eph 5:10 truth) and find out what *p* the
          Lord
Col 3:20 in everything, for this *p* the Lord.
1Ti 2: 3 This is good, and *p* God our
          Savior,
1Jn 3:22 his commands and do what *p* him.

PLEASING (PLEASE)
Ge 2: 9 trees that were *p* to the eye
Lev 1: 9 an aroma *p* to the LORD.
Ps 19:14 be *p* in your sight,
    104:34 May my meditation be *p* to him,
Pr 15:26 but those of the pure are *p* to him.
    16: 7 When a man's ways are *p*
SS 1: 3 *P* is the fragrance of your perfumes
     4:10 How much more *p* is your love
     7: 6 How beautiful you are and how *p*,
Ro 12: 1 *p* to God—this is your spiritual
    14:18 Christ in this way is *p* to God
Php 4:18 an acceptable sacrifice, *p* to God.
1Ti 5: 4 grandparents, for this is *p* to God.
Heb 13:21 may he work in us what is *p* to him,

PLEASURE (PLEASE)
Ps 5: 4 You are not a God who takes *p*
    51:16 you do not take *p* in burnt offerings
    147:10 His *p* is not in the strength
Pr 10:23 A fool finds *p* in evil conduct,
    18: 2 A fool finds no *p* in understanding
    21:17 He who loves *p* will become poor;
Isa 1:11 I have no *p*
Jer 6:10 they find no *p* in it.
Eze 18:23 Do I take any *p* in the death
    18:32 For I take no *p* in the death
    33:11 I take no *p* in the death
Lk 10:21 Father, for this was your good *p*.
Eph 1: 5 in accordance with his *p* and will—
     1: 9 of his will according to his good *p*,
1Ti 5: 6 the widow who lives for *p* is dead
2Ti 3: 4 lovers of *p* rather than lovers
2Pe 2:13 Their idea of *p* is to carouse

PLEASURES* (PLEASE)
Ps 16:11 with eternal *p* at your right hand.
Lk 8:14 and *p*, and they do not mature.
Tit 3: 3 by all kinds of passions and *p*
Heb 11:25 rather than to enjoy the *p* of sin
Jas 4: 3 may spend what you get on your *p*.
2Pe 2:13 reveling in their *p* while they feast

PLEDGE
Dt 24:17 take the cloak of the widow as a *p*.
1Pe 3:21 but the *p* of a good conscience

PLEIADES
Job 38:31 "Can you bind the beautiful *P?*
Am 5: 8 (he who made the *P* and Orion,

PLENTIFUL (PLENTY)
Mt 9:37 harvest is *p* but the workers are
Lk 10: 2 harvest is *p*, but the workers are

PLENTY (PLENTIFUL)
2Co 8:14 the present time your *p* will supply
Php 4:12 whether living in *p* or in want.

PLOT (PLOTS)
Est 2:22 Mordecai found out about the *p*
Ps 2: 1 and the peoples *p* in vain?
Pr 3:29 not *p* harm against your neighbor,
Zec 8:17 do not *p* evil against your neighbor,
Ac 4:25 and the peoples *p* in vain?

PLOTS (PLOT)
Pr 6:14 who *p* evil with deceit in his heart

PLOW (PLOWMAN PLOWSHARES)
Lk 9:62 "No one who puts his hand to the *p*

PLOWMAN (PLOW)
1Co 9:10 because when the *p* plows

PLOWSHARES (PLOW)
1Sa 13:20 to the Philistines to have their *p*,
Isa 2: 4 They will beat their swords into *p*
Joel 3:10 Beat your *p* into swords
Mic 4: 3 They will beat their swords into *p*

PLUCK
Mk 9:47 your eye causes you to sin, *p* it out.

PLUNDER (PLUNDERED)
Ex 3:22 And so you will *p* the Egyptians."
Est 3:13 of Adar, and to *p* their goods.
     8:11 to *p* the property of their enemies.

Est 9:10 did not lay their hands on the *p*.
Pr 22:23 and will *p* those who *p* them.
Isa 3:14 the *p* from the poor is

PLUNDERED (PLUNDER)
Eze 34: 8 lacks a shepherd and so has been *p*

PLUNGE
1Ti 6: 9 and harmful desires that *p* men
1Pe 4: 4 think it strange that you do not *p*

PODS
Lk 15:16 with the *p* that the pigs were eating,

POINT
Mt 4: 5 on the highest *p* of the temple.
    26:38 with sorrow to the *p* of death,
Jas 2:10 yet stumbles at just one *p* is guilty
Rev 2:10 Be faithful, even to the *p* of death,

POISON
Ps 140: 3 the *p* of vipers is on their lips.
Mk 16:18 and when they drink deadly *p*,
Ro 3:13 "The *p* of vipers is on their lips."
Jas 3: 8 It is a restless evil, full of deadly *p*.

POLE (POLES)
Nu 21: 8 "Make a snake and put it up on a *p*;
Dt 16:21 not set up any wooden Asherah *p*

POLES (POLE)
Ex 25:13 Then make *p* of acacia wood

POLISHED
Isa 49: 2 he made me into a *p* arrow

POLLUTE* (POLLUTED POLLUTES)
Nu 35:33 " 'Do not *p* the land where you are.
Jude : 8 these dreamers *p* their own bodies,

POLLUTED* (POLLUTE)
Ezr 9:11 entering to possess is a land *p*
Pr 25:26 Like a muddied spring or a *p* well
Ac 15:20 to abstain from food *p* by idols,
Jas 1:27 oneself from being *p* by the world.

POLLUTES* (POLLUTE)
Nu 35:33 Bloodshed *p* the land,

PONDER (PONDERED)
Ps 64: 9 and *p* what he has done.
    119:95 but I will *p* your statutes.

PONDERED (PONDER)
Ps 111: 2 they are *p* by all who delight
Lk 2:19 up all these things and *p* them

POOR (POVERTY)
Lev 19:10 Leave them for the *p* and the alien.
    23:22 Leave them for the *p* and the alien.
    27: 8 If anyone making the vow is too *p*
Dt 15: 4 there should be no *p* among you,
    15: 7 is a *p* man among your brothers
    15:11 There will always be *p* people
    24:12 If the man is *p*, do not go to sleep
    24:14 advantage of a hired man who is *p*
Job 5:16 So the *p* have hope,
    24: 4 force all the *p* of the land
Ps 14: 6 frustrate the plans of the *p*,
    34: 6 This *p* man called, and the LORD
    35:10 You rescue the *p* from those too
    40:17 Yet I am *p* and needy;
    68:10 O God, you provided for the *p*.
    82: 3 maintain the rights of the *p*
    112: 9 scattered abroad his gifts to the *p*,
    113: 7 He raises the *p* from the dust
    140:12 the LORD secures justice for the *p*
Pr 10: 4 Lazy hands make a man *p*,
    13: 7 to be *p*, yet has great wealth.
    14:20 The *p* are shunned
    14:31 oppresses the *p* shows contempt
    17: 5 who mocks the *p* shows contempt
    19: 1 Better a *p* man whose walk is
    19:17 to the *p* lends to the LORD,
    19:22 better to be *p* than a liar.
    20:13 not love sleep or you will grow *p*;
    21:13 to the cry of the *p*,
    21:17 who loves pleasure will become *p*;
    22: 2 Rich and *p* have this in common:
    22: 9 for he shares his food with the *p*
    22:22 not exploit the *p* because they are *p*
    28: 6 Better a *p* man whose walk is

Pr 28:27 to the *p* will lack nothing,
    29: 7 care about justice for the *p*,
    31: 9 defend the rights of the *p*
    31:20 She opens her arms to the *p*
Ecc 4:13 Better a *p* but wise youth
Isa 3:14 the plunder from the *p* is
    10: 2 to deprive the *p* of their rights
    14:30 of the *p* will find pasture.
    25: 4 You have been a refuge for the *p*,
    32: 7 schemes to destroy the *p* with lies.
    61: 1 me to preach good news to the *p*.
Jer 22:16 He defended the cause of the *p*
Eze 18:12 He oppresses the *p* and needy.
Am 2: 7 They trample on the heads of the *p*
     4: 1 you women who oppress the *p*
     5:11 You trample on the *p*
Zec 7:10 or the fatherless, the alien or the *p*.
Mt 5: 3 saying: "Blessed are the *p* in spirit,
    11: 5 the good news is preached to the *p*.
    19:21 your possessions and give to the *p*,
    26:11 The *p* you will always have
Mk 12:42 But a *p* widow came and put
    14: 7 The *p* you will always have
Lk 4:18 me to preach good news to the *p*.
     6:20 "Blessed are you who are *p*,
    11:41 is inside the dish, to the *p*,
    14:13 invite the *p*, the crippled, the lame,
    21: 2 also saw a *p* widow put
Jn 12: 8 You will always have the *p*
Ac 9:36 doing good and helping the *p*.
    10: 4 and gifts to the *p* have come up
    24:17 to bring my people gifts for the *p*
Ro 15:26 for the *p* among the saints
1Co 13: 3 If I give all I possess to the *p*
2Co 6:10 sorrowful, yet always rejoicing; *p*,
     8: 9 yet for your sakes he became *p*,
Gal 2:10 continue to remember the *p*,
Jas 2: 2 and a *p* man in shabby clothes
     2: 5 not God chosen those who are *p*
     2: 6 But you have insulted the *p*.

POPULATION*
Pr 14:28 A large *p* is a king's glory,

PORTION
Nu 18:29 as the LORD's *p* the best
Dt 32: 9 For the LORD's *p* is his people,
1Sa 1: 5 But to Hannah he gave a double *p*
2Ki 2: 9 "Let me inherit a double *p*
Ps 73:26 and my *p* forever.
    119:57 You are my *p*, O LORD;
Isa 53:12 Therefore I will give him a *p*
Jer 10:16 He who is the *P* of Jacob is not like
La 3:24 to myself, "The LORD is my *p*;
Zec 2:12 LORD will inherit Judah as his *p*

PORTRAIT
Lk 20:24 Whose *p* and inscription are on it?"

PORTRAYED
Gal 3: 1 very eyes Jesus Christ was clearly *p*

POSITION (POSITIONS)
Ro 12:16 to associate with people of low *p*.
Jas 1: 9 ought to take pride in his high *p*.
2Pe 3:17 and fall from your secure *p*.

POSITIONS (POSITION)
2Ch 20:17 Take up your *p*; stand firm
Jude : 6 the angels who did not keep their *p*

POSSESS (POSSESSED POSSESSING POSSESSION POSSESSIONS)
Nu 33:53 for I have given you the land to *p*.
Dt 4:14 you are crossing the Jordan to *p*.
Pr 8:12 I *p* knowledge and discretion.
Jn 5:39 that by them you *p* eternal life.

POSSESSED (POSSESS)
Jn 10:21 the sayings of a man *p* by a demon.

POSSESSING* (POSSESS)
2Co 6:10 nothing, and yet *p* everything.

POSSESSION (POSSESS)
Ge 15: 7 to give you this land to take *p* of it

Ex   6: 8   I will give it to you as a *p.*
    19: 5   nations you will be my treasured *p.*
Nu 13:30   "We should go up and take *p*
Dt   7: 6   to be his people, his treasured *p.*
Jos   1:11   take *p* of the land the LORD your
Ps   2: 8   the ends of the earth your *p.*
    135: 4   Israel to be his treasured *p.*
Eph   1:14   of those who are God's *p*—

POSSESSIONS (POSSESS)
Mt 19:21   go, sell your *p* and give to the poor,
Lk 11:21   guards his own house, his *p* are safe
    12:15   consist in the abundance of his *p.*"
    19: 8   now I give half of my *p* to the poor,
Ac   4:32   any of his *p* was his own,
2Co 12:14   what I want is not your *p* but you.
Heb 10:34   yourselves had better and lasting *p.*
1Jn   3:17   If anyone has material *p*

POSSIBLE
Mt 19:26   but with God all things are *p.*"
    26:39   if it is *p*, may this cup be taken
Mk   9:23   "Everything is *p* for him who
    10:27   all things are *p* with God."
    14:35   prayed that if *p* the hour might pass
Ro 12:18   If it is *p*, as far as it depends on you,
1Co   6: 5   Is it *p* that there is nobody
    9:19   to everyone, to win as many as *p.*
    9:22   by all *p* means I might save some.

POT (POTSHERD POTTER POTTER'S POTTERY)
2Ki   4:40   there is death in the *p!*"
Jer 18: 4   But the *p* he was shaping

POTIPHAR*
Egyptian who bought Joseph (Ge 37:36), set him over his house (Ge 39:1–6), sent him to prison (Ge 39:7–30).

POTSHERD (POT)
Isa 45: 9   a *p* among the potsherds

POTTER (POT)
Isa 29:16   Can the pot say of the *p,*
    45: 9   Does the clay say to the *p,*
    64: 8   We are the clay, you are the *p;*
Jer 18: 6   "Like clay in the hand of the *p,*
Zec 11:13   it to the *p*"— the handsome price
Ro   9:21   Does not the *p* have the right

POTTER'S (POT)
Mt 27: 7   to use the money to buy the *p* field

POTTERY (POT)
Ro   9:21   of clay some *p* for noble purposes

POUR (POURED POURS)
Ps 62: 8   *p* out your hearts to him,
Isa 44: 3   I will *p* out my Spirit
Eze 20: 8   So I said I would *p* out my wrath
    39:29   for I will *p* out my Spirit
Joel   2:28   I will *p* out my Spirit on all people.
Zec 12:10   I will *p* out on the house of David
Mal   3:10   *p* out so much blessing that you
Ac   2:17   I will *p* out my Spirit on all people.

POURED (POUR)
Ps 22:14   I am *p* out like water,
Isa 32:15   till the Spirit is *p* upon us
Mt 26:28   which is *p* out for many
Lk 22:20   in my blood, which is *p* out for you.
Ac   2:33   and has *p* out what you now see
    10:45   of the Holy Spirit had been *p* out
Ro   5: 5   because God has *p* out his love
Php   2:17   even if I am being *p* out like a drink
2Ti   4: 6   I am already being *p* out like
Tit   3: 6   whom he *p* out on us generously
Rev 16: 2   and *p* out his bowl on the land,

POURS (POUR)
Lk   5:37   And no one *p* new wine

POVERTY* (POOR)
Dt 28:48   and thirst, in nakedness and dire *p,*
1Sa   2: 7   The LORD sends *p* and wealth;
Pr   6:11   *p* will come on you like a bandit
    10:15   but *p* is the ruin of the poor.

Pr 11:24   withholds unduly, but comes to *p.*
    13:18   who ignores discipline comes to *p*
    14:23   but mere talk leads only to *p.*
    21: 5   as surely as haste leads to *p.*
    22:16   to the rich—both come to *p.*
    24:34   *p* will come on you like a bandit
    28:19   fantasies will have his fill of *p.*
    28:22   and is unaware that *p* awaits him.
    30: 8   give me neither *p* nor riches,
    31: 7   let them drink and forget their *p*
Ecc   4:14   born in *p* within his kingdom.
Mk 12:44   out of her *p*, put in everything—
Lk 21: 4   she out of her *p* put in all she had
2Co   8: 2   and their extreme *p* welled up
    8: 9   through his *p* might become rich.
Rev   2: 9   I know your afflictions and your *p*

POWER (POWERFUL POWERS)
Ex 15: 6   was majestic in *p.*
    32:11   out of Egypt with great *p*
Dt   8:17   "My *p* and the strength
    34:12   one has ever shown the mighty *p*
1Sa 10: 6   LORD will come upon you in *p,*
    10:10   Spirit of God came upon him in *p,*
    11: 6   Spirit of God came upon him in *p,*
    16:13   the LORD came upon David in *p.*
1Ch 29:11   LORD, is the greatness and the *p*
2Ch 20: 6   *P* and might are in your hand,
    32: 7   for there is a greater *p* with us
Job   9: 4   wisdom is profound, his *p* is vast.
    36:22   "God is exalted in his *p.*
    37:23   beyond our reach and exalted in *p;*
Ps 20: 6   with the saving *p* of his right hand.
    63: 2   and beheld your *p* and your glory.
    66: 3   So great is your *p*
    68:34   Proclaim the *p* of God,
    77:14   you display your *p*
    89:13   Your arm is endued with *p;*
    145: 6   of the *p* of your awesome works,
    147: 5   Great is our Lord and mighty in *p;*
    150: 2   Praise him for his acts of *p;*
Pr   3:27   when it is in your *p* to act.
    18:21   The tongue has the *p* of life
    24: 5   A wise man has great *p,*
Isa 11: 2   the Spirit of counsel and of *p,*
    40:10   the Sovereign LORD comes with *p*
    40:26   of his great *p* and mighty strength,
    63:12   who sent his glorious arm of *p*
Jer 10: 6   and your name is mighty in *p.*
    10:12   But God made the earth by his *p;*
    27: 5   With my great *p* and outstretched
    32:17   and the earth by your great *p*
Hos 13:14   from the *p* of the grave;
Na   1: 3   to anger and great in *p;*
Zec   4: 6   nor by *p*, but by my Spirit,'
Mt 22:29   do not know the Scriptures or the *p*
    24:30   on the clouds of the sky, with *p*
Lk   1:35   and the *p* of the Most High will
    4:14   to Galilee in the *p* of the Spirit,
    9: 1   he gave them *p* and authority
    10:19   to overcome all the *p* of the enemy;
    24:49   clothed with *p* from on high."
Ac   1: 8   you will receive *p* when the Holy
    4:28   They did what your *p* and will had
    4:33   With great *p* the apostles
    10:38   with the Holy Spirit and *p,*
    26:18   and from the *p* of Satan to God,
Ro   1:16   it is the *p* of God for the salvation
    1:20   his eternal *p* and divine nature—
    4:21   fully persuaded that God had *p*
    9:17   that I might display my *p* in you
    15:13   overflow with hope by the *p*
    15:19   through the *p* of the Spirit.
1Co   1:17   cross of Christ be emptied of its *p.*
    1:18   to us who are being saved it is the *p*
    2: 4   a demonstration of the Spirit's *p,*
    6:14   By his *p* God raised the Lord
    15:24   all dominion, authority and *p.*
    15:56   of death is sin, and the *p*
2Co   4: 7   to show that this all-surpassing *p* is
    6: 7   in truthful speech and in the *p*
    10: 4   they have divine *p*
    12: 9   for my *p* is made perfect
    13: 4   weakness, yet he lives by God's *p.*
Eph   1:19   and his incomparably great *p*

Eph   3:16   you with *p* through his Spirit
    3:20   according to his *p* that is at work
    6:10   in the Lord and in his mighty *p.*
Php   3:10   and the *p* of his resurrection
    3:21   by the *p* that enables him
Col   1:11   strengthened with all *p* according
    2:10   who is the head over every *p*
1Th   1: 5   also with *p*, with the Holy Spirit
2Ti   1: 7   but a spirit of *p*, of love
    3: 5   form of godliness but denying its *p.*
Heb   2:14   might destroy him who holds the *p*
    7:16   of the *p* of an indestructible life.
1Pe   1: 5   by God's *p* until the coming
2Pe   1: 3   His divine *p* has given us
Jude   :25   *p* and authority, through Jesus
Rev   4:11   to receive glory and honor and *p,*
    5:12   to receive *p* and wealth
    11:17   you have taken your great *p*
    19: 1   and glory and *p* belong to our God,
    20: 6   The second death has no *p*

POWERFUL (POWER)
2Ch 27: 6   Jotham grew *p* because he walked
Est   9: 4   and he became more and more *p.*
Ps 29: 4   The voice of the LORD is *p;*
Jer 32:18   *p* God, whose name is the LORD
Zec   8:22   *p* nations will come to Jerusalem
Mk   1: 7   "After me will come one more *p*
Lk 24:19   *p* in word and deed before God
2Th   1: 7   in blazing fire with his *p* angels.
Heb   1: 3   sustaining all things by his *p* word.
Jas   5:16   The prayer of a righteous man is *p*

POWERLESS
Ro   5: 6   when we were still *p*, Christ died
    8: 3   For what the law was *p* to do

POWERS (POWER)
Da   4:35   pleases with the *p* of heaven
Ro   8:38   nor any *p*, neither height nor depth
1Co 12:10   to another miraculous *p,*
Eph   6:12   against the *p* of this dark world
Col   1:16   whether thrones or *p* or rulers
    2:15   And having disarmed the *p*
Heb   6: 5   and the *p* of the coming age,
1Pe   3:22   and *p* in submission to him.

PRACTICE (PRACTICED PRACTICES)
Lev 19:26   " 'Do not *p* divination or sorcery.
Ps 119:56   This has been my *p:*
Eze 33:31   but they do not put them into *p.*
Mt   7:24   into *p* is like a wise man who built
    23: 3   for they do not *p* what they preach.
Lk   8:21   hear God's word and put it into *p.*"
Ro 12:13   *P* hospitality.
Php   4: 9   or seen in me—put it into *p.*
1Ti   5: 4   to put their religion into *p* by caring

PRACTICED (PRACTICE)
Mt 23:23   You should have *p* the latter,

PRACTICES (PRACTICE)
Ps 101: 7   No one who *p* deceit
Mt   5:19   but whoever *p* and teaches these
Col   3: 9   taken off your old self with its *p*

PRAISE (PRAISED PRAISES PRAISEWORTHY PRAISING)
Ex 15: 2   He is my God, and I will *p* him,
Dt 10:21   He is your *p;* he is your God,
    26:19   declared that he will set you in *p,*
    32: 3   Oh, *p* the greatness of our God!
Ru   4:14   said to Naomi: "*P* be to the LORD,
2Sa 22: 4   to the LORD, who is worthy of *p,*
    22:47   The LORD lives! *P* be to my Rock
1Ch 16:25   is the LORD and most worthy of *p;*
    16:35   that we may glory in your *p.*"
    23: 5   four thousand are to *p* the LORD
    29:10   "*P* be to you, O LORD,
2Ch   5:13   they raised their voices in *p*
    20:21   and to *p* him for the splendor
    29:30   to *p* the LORD with the words
Ezr   3:10   took their places to *p* the LORD,
Ne   9: 5   and *p* the LORD your God,
Ps   8: 2   you have ordained *p*
    9: 1   I will *p* you, O LORD,
    16: 7   I will *p* the LORD, who counsels
    26: 7   proclaiming aloud your *p*

Ps	30: 4	*p* his holy name.
	33: 1	it is fitting for the upright to *p* him.
	34: 1	his *p* will always be on my lips.
	40: 3	a hymn of *p* to our God.
	42: 5	for I will yet *p* him,
	43: 5	for I will yet *p* him,
	45: 17	the nations will *p* you for ever
	47: 7	sing to him a psalm of *p*.
	48: 1	the LORD, and most worthy of *p*.
	51: 15	and my mouth will declare your *p*.
	56: 4	In God, whose word I *p*,
	57: 9	I will *p* you, O Lord,
	63: 4	I will *p* you as long as I live,
	65: 1	*P* awaits you, O God, in Zion;
	66: 2	make his *p* glorious.
	66: 8	*P* our God, O peoples,
	68: 19	*P* be to the Lord, to God our Savior
	68: 26	*p* the LORD in the assembly
	69: 30	I will *p* God's name in song
	69: 34	Let heaven and earth *p* him,
	71: 8	My mouth is filled with your *p*,
	71: 14	I will *p* you more and more.
	71: 22	I will *p* you with the harp
	74: 21	the poor and needy *p* your name.
	86: 12	I will *p* you, O Lord my God,
	89: 5	The heavens *p* your wonders,
	92: 1	It is good to *p* the LORD
	96: 2	Sing to the LORD, *p* his name;
	100: 4	and his courts with *p*;
	101: 1	to you, O LORD, I will sing *p*.
	102: 18	not yet created may *p* the LORD:
	103: 1	*P* the LORD, O my soul;
	103: 20	*P* the LORD, you his angels,
	104: 1	*P* the LORD, O my soul.
	105: 2	Sing to him, sing *p* to him;
	106: 1	*P* the LORD.
	108: 3	I will *p* you, O LORD,
	111: 1	*P* the LORD.
	113: 1	*P* the LORD.
	117: 1	*P* the LORD, all you nations;
	119:175	Let me live that I may *p* you,
	135: 1	*P* the LORD.
	135: 20	you who fear him, *p* the LORD.
	138: 1	I will *p* you, O LORD,
	139: 14	I *p* you because I am fearfully
	144: 1	*P* be to the LORD my Rock,
	145: 3	is the LORD and most worthy of *p*;
	145: 10	All you have made will *p* you,
	145: 21	Let every creature *p* his holy name
	146: 1	*P* the LORD, O my soul.
	147: 1	how pleasant and fitting to *p* him!
	148: 1	*P* the LORD from the heavens,
	148: 13	Let them *p* the name of the LORD,
	149: 1	his *p* in the assembly of the saints.
	149: 6	May the *p* of God be
	149: 9	*P* the LORD.
	150: 2	*p* him for his surpassing greatness.
	150: 6	that has breath *p* the LORD.
Pr	27: 2	Let another *p* you, and not your
	27: 21	man is tested by the *p* he receives.
	31: 31	let her works bring her *p*
SS	1: 4	we will *p* your love more than wine
Isa	12: 1	"I will *p* you, O LORD.
	42: 10	his *p* from the ends of the earth,
	61: 3	and a garment of *p*
Jer	33: 9	*p* and honor before all nations
Da	2: 20	"*P* be to the name of God for ever
	4: 37	*p* and exalt and glorify the King
Mt	21: 9	and *p* your Father in heaven.
	21: 16	you have ordained *p*'?"
Lk	19: 37	to *p* God in loud voices
Jn	5: 44	effort to obtain the *p* that comes
	12: 43	for they loved *p* from men more
Ro	2: 29	Such a man's *p* is not from men,
	15: 7	in order to bring *p* to God.
2Co	1: 3	*P* be to the God and Father
Eph	1: 3	*P* be to the God and Father
	1: 6	to the *p* of his glorious grace,
	1: 12	might be for the *p* of his glory.
	1: 14	*to the p of his glory.*
1Th	2: 6	We were not looking for *p*
Heb	13: 15	offer to God a sacrifice of *p*—
Jas	3: 9	With the tongue we *p* our Lord
	5: 13	happy? Let him sing songs of *p*.
Rev	5: 13	be *p* and honor and glory
	7: 12	*P* and glory

PRAISED (PRAISE)

1Ch	29: 10	David *p* the LORD in the presence
Ne	8: 6	Ezra *p* the LORD, the great God;
Job	1: 21	may the name of the LORD be *p*."
Ps	113: 2	Let the name of the LORD be *p*,
Pr	31: 30	who fears the LORD is to be *p*.
Isa	63: 7	the deeds for which he is to be *p*,
Da	2: 19	Then Daniel *p* the God of heaven
	4: 34	Then I *p* the Most High; I honored
Lk	18: 43	the people saw it, they also *p* God.
	23: 47	seeing what had happened, *p* God
Ro	9: 5	who is God over all, forever *p*!
Gal	1: 24	And they *p* God because of me.
1Pe	4: 11	that in all things God may be *p*

PRAISES (PRAISE)

2Sa	22: 50	I will sing *p* to your name.
Ps	18: 49	I will sing *p* to your name.
	47: 6	Sing *p* to God, sing *p*;
	147: 1	How good it is to sing *p* to our God,
Pr	31: 28	her husband also, and he *p* her:
1Pe	2: 9	that you may declare the *p*

PRAISEWORTHY* (PRAISE)

Ps	78: 4	the *p* deeds of the LORD.
Php	4: 8	if anything is excellent or *p*—

PRAISING (PRAISE)

Lk	2: 13	*p* God and saying, "Glory to God
	2: 20	*p* God for all the things they had
Ac	2: 47	*p* God and enjoying the favor
	10: 46	speaking in tongues and *p* God.
1Co	14: 16	If you are *p* God with your spirit,

PRAY (PRAYED PRAYER PRAYERS PRAYING PRAYS)

Dt	4: 7	is near us whenever we *p* to him?
1Sa	12: 23	the LORD by failing to *p* for you.
1Ki	8: 30	when they *p* toward this place.
2Ch	7: 14	will humble themselves and *p*
Ezr	6: 10	and *p* for the well-being of the king
Job	42: 8	My servant Job will *p* for you,
Ps	5: 2	for to you I *p*.
	32: 6	let everyone who is godly *p*
	122: 6	*P* for the peace of Jerusalem:
Jer	29: 7	*P* to the LORD for it,
	29: 12	upon me and come and *p* to me,
	42: 3	*P* that the LORD your God will
Mt	5: 44	and *p* for those who persecute you,
	6: 5	"And when you *p*, do not be like
	6: 9	"This, then, is how you should *p*:
	14: 23	up on a mountainside by himself to *p*.
	19: 13	hands on them and *p* for them.
	26: 36	Sit here while I go over there and *p*."
Lk	6: 28	*p* for those who mistreat you.
	11: 1	us to *p*, just as John taught his
	18: 1	them that they should always *p*
	22: 40	"*P* that you will not fall
Jn	17: 20	*p* also for those who will believe
Ro	8: 26	do not know what we ought to *p* for,
1Co	14: 13	in a tongue should *p* that he may
Eph	1: 18	I *p* also that the eyes
	3: 16	I *p* that out of his glorious riches he
	6: 18	And *p* in the Spirit on all occasions
Col	1: 10	we *p* this in order that you may live
	4: 3	*p* for us, too, that God may open
1Th	5: 17	Be joyful always; *p* continually;
2Th	1: 11	in mind, we constantly *p* for you,
Jas	5: 13	one of you in trouble? He should *p*.
	5: 16	*p* for each other so that you may be
1Pe	4: 7	self-controlled so that you can *p*.
Jude	: 20	up in your most holy faith and *p*

PRAYED (PRAY)

1Sa	1: 27	I *p* for this child, and the LORD
1Ki	18: 36	Elijah stepped forward and *p*:
	19: 4	under it and *p* that he might die.
2Ki	6: 17	And Elisha *p*, "O LORD.
2Ch	30: 18	But Hezekiah *p* for them, saying,
Ne	4: 9	we *p* to our God and posted a guard
Job	42: 10	After Job had *p* for his friends,
Da	6: 10	got down on his knees and *p*,

Da	9: 4	I *p* to the LORD my God
Jnh	2: 1	From inside the fish Jonah *p*
Mt	26: 39	with his face to the ground and *p*,
Mk	1: 35	off to a solitary place, where he *p*.
	14: 35	*p* that if possible the hour might
Lk	22: 41	knelt down and *p*, "Father,
Jn	17: 1	he looked toward heaven and *p*:
Ac	4: 31	After they *p*, the place where they
	6: 6	who *p* and laid their hands on them
	8: 15	they *p* for them that they might
	13: 3	So after they had fasted and *p*,

PRAYER (PRAY)

2Ch	30: 27	for their *p* reached heaven,
Ezr	8: 23	about this, and he answered our *p*.
Ps	4: 1	be merciful to me and hear my *p*.
	6: 9	The LORD accepts my *p*.
	17: 1	Give ear to my *p*—
	17: 6	give ear to me and hear my *p*.
	65: 2	O you who hear *p*,
	66: 20	who has not rejected my *p*
	86: 6	Hear my *p*, O LORD;
Pr	15: 8	but the *p* of the upright pleases him
	15: 29	but he hears the *p* of the righteous.
Isa	56: 7	a house of *p* for all nations."
Mt	21: 13	house will be called a house of *p*,'
	21: 22	receive whatever you ask for in *p*."
Mk	9: 29	This kind can come out only by *p*."
	11: 24	whatever you ask for in *p*,
Jn	17: 15	My *p* is not that you take them out
Ac	1: 14	all joined together constantly in *p*,
	2: 42	to the breaking of bread and to *p*.
	6: 4	and will give our attention to *p*
	10: 31	has heard your *p* and remembered
	16: 13	expected to find a place of *p*.
Ro	12: 12	patient in affliction, faithful in *p*.
1Co	7: 5	you may devote yourselves to *p*.
2Co	13: 9	and our *p* is for your perfection.
Php	1: 9	this is my *p*: that your love may
	4: 6	but in everything, by *p* and petition
Col	4: 2	yourselves to *p*, being watchful
1Ti	2: 8	to lift up holy hands in *p*,
	4: 5	by the word of God and *p*.
Jas	5: 15	*p* offered in faith will make the sick
1Pe	3: 12	and his ears are attentive to their *p*,

PRAYERS (PRAY)

1Ch	5: 20	He answered their *p*, because they
Isa	1: 15	even if you offer many *p*,
Mk	12: 40	and for a show make lengthy *p*.
2Co	1: 11	as you help us by your *p*.
Eph	6: 18	on all occasions with all kinds of *p*
1Ti	2: 1	then, first of all, that requests, *p*,
1Pe	3: 7	so that nothing will hinder your *p*.
Rev	5: 8	which are the *p* of the saints.
	8: 3	with the *p* of all the saints,

PRAYING (PRAY)

Ge	24: 45	"Before I finished *p* in my heart,
1Sa	1: 12	As she kept on *p* to the LORD,
Mk	11: 25	And when you stand *p*,
Lk	3: 21	as he was *p*, heaven was opened
	6: 12	and spent the night *p* to God.
	9: 29	As he was *p*, the appearance
Jn	17: 9	I am not *p* for the world,
Ac	9: 11	from Tarsus named Saul, for he is *p*
	16: 25	and Silas were *p* and singing hymns
Ro	15: 30	in my struggle by *p* to God for me.
Eph	6: 18	always keep on *p* for all the saints.

PRAYS (PRAY)

1Co	14: 14	my spirit *p*, but my mind is

PREACH (PREACHED PREACHING)

Isa	61: 1	me to *p* good news to the poor.
Mt	10: 7	As you go, *p* this message:
	23: 3	they do not practice what they *p*.
Mk	16: 15	and *p* the good news to all creation.
Lk	4: 18	me to *p* good news to the poor.

Ac   9:20 At once he began to *p*
    16:10 us to *p* the gospel to them.
Ro   1:15 am so eager to *p* the gospel
  10:15 how can they *p* unless they are
           sent
  15:20 to *p* the gospel where Christ was
1Co 1:17 to *p* the gospel—not with words
   1:23 wisdom, but we *p* Christ crucified:
   9:14 that those who *p* the gospel
           should
   9:16 Woe to me if I do not *p* the
           gospel!
2Co 4:5 For we do not *p* ourselves,
  10:16 so that we can *p* the gospel
Gal   1:8 from heaven should *p* a gospel
2Ti   4:2 I give you this charge: *P* the Word;

PREACHED (PREACH)
Mt 24:14 gospel of the kingdom will be *p*
Mk   6:12 and *p* that people should repent.
  13:10 And the gospel must first be *p*
  14:9 wherever the gospel is *p*
Ac   8:4 had been scattered *p* the word
  28:31 hindrance he *p* the kingdom
1Co 9:27 so that after I have *p* to others,
  15:1 you of the gospel I *p* to you,
2Co 11:4 other than the Jesus we *p*,
Gal   1:8 other than the one we *p* to you,
Eph 2:17 *p* peace to you who were far away
Php 1:18 false motives or true, Christ is *p*.
1Ti   3:16 was *p* among the nations,
1Pe   1:25 this is the word that was *p* to you.
   3:19 and *p* to the spirits in prison who

PREACHING (PREACH)
Lk   9:6 *p* the gospel and healing people
Ac 18:5 devoted himself exclusively to *p*,
Ro 10:14 hear without someone to *p* to them?
1Co 2:4 and my *p* were not with wise
   9:18 in *p* the gospel I may offer it free
Gal   1:9 If anybody is *p* to you a gospel
1Ti   4:13 the public reading of Scripture,
           to *p*
   5:17 especially those whose work is *p*

PRECEDE*
1Th 4:15 will certainly not *p* those who
          have

PRECEPTS*
Dt 33:10 He teaches your *p* to Jacob
Ps 19:8 The *p* of the LORD are right,
 103:18 and remember to obey his *p*.
 105:45 that they might keep his *p*
 111:7 all his *p* are trustworthy.
 111:10 who follow his *p* have good
 119:4 You have laid down *p*
 119:15 I meditate on your *p*
 119:27 understand the teaching of
           your *p*;
 119:40 How I long for your *p*!
 119:45 for I have sought out your *p*.
 119:56 I obey your *p*.
 119:63 to all who follow your *p*.
 119:69 I keep your *p* with all my heart.
 119:78 but I will meditate on your *p*.
 119:87 but I have not forsaken your *p*.
 119:93 I will never forget your *p*,
 119:94 I have sought out your *p*.
 119:100 for I obey your *p*.
 119:104 I gain understanding from your *p*;
 119:110 but I have not strayed from
           your *p*.
 119:128 because I consider all your *p* right,
 119:134 that I may obey your *p*.
 119:141 I do not forget your *p*.
 119:159 See how I love your *p*;
 119:168 I obey your *p* and your statutes,
 119:173 for I have chosen your *p*.

PRECIOUS
Ps 19:10 They are more *p* than gold,
 72:14 for *p* is their blood in his sight.
 116:15 *P* in the sight of the LORD
 119:72 from your mouth is more *p* to me
 139:17 How *p* to me are your thoughts,
Pr   8:11 for wisdom is more *p* than rubies,
Isa 28:16 a *p* cornerstone for a sure
1Pe   1:19 but with the *p* blood of Christ,
   2:4 but chosen by God and *p* to
           him—
   2:6 a chosen and *p* cornerstone,
2Pe   1:1 Christ have received a faith as *p*
   1:4 us his very great and *p* promises,

PREDESTINED* (DESTINY)
Ro   8:29 *p* to be conformed to the likeness
   8:30 And those he *p*, he also called;
Eph   1:5 In love he *p* us to be adopted
   1:11 having been *p* according

PREDICTED (PREDICTION)
1Sa 28:17 The LORD has done what he *p*
Ac   7:52 killed those who *p* the coming
1Pe   1:11 when he *p* the sufferings of Christ

PREDICTION* (PREDICTED PREDICTIONS)
Jer 28:9 only if his *p* comes true."

PREDICTIONS (PREDICTION)
Isa 44:26 and fulfills the *p* of his
          messengers,

PREGNANT
Ex 21:22 who are fighting hit a *p* woman
Mt 24:19 be in those days for *p* women
1Th   5:3 as labor pains on a *p* woman,

PREPARE (PREPARED)
Ps 23:5 You *p* a table before me
Isa 25:6 the LORD Almighty will *p*
  40:3 "In the desert *p*
Am   4:12 *p* to meet your God, O Israel."
Mal   3:1 who will *p* the way before me.
Mt   3:3 '*P* the way for the Lord,
Jn 14:2 there to *p* a place for you.
Eph   4:12 to *p* God's people for works
1Pe   1:13 Therefore, *p* your minds for
          action;

PREPARED (PREPARE)
Ex 23:20 to bring you to the place I have *p*.
Mt 25:34 the kingdom *p* for you
Ro   9:22 of his wrath—*p* for destruction?
1Co 2:9 what God has *p* for those who
          love
Eph   2:10 which God *p* in advance for us
2Ti   2:21 and *p* to do any good work.
   4:2 be *p* in season and out of season;
1Pe   3:15 Always be *p* to give an answer

PRESCRIBED
Ezr   7:23 Whatever the God of heaven
          has *p*,

PRESENCE (PRESENT)
Ex 25:30 Put the bread of the *P* on this
          table
  33:14 The LORD replied, "My *P* will go
Nu   4:7 "Over the table of the *P* they are
1Sa   6:20 in the *p* of the LORD, this
  21:6 of the *P* that had been removed
2Sa 22:13 Out of the brightness of his *p*
2Ki 17:23 LORD removed them from his *p*,
  23:27 also from my *p* as I removed
          Israel,
Ezr   9:15 one of us can stand in your *p*."
Ps 16:11 you will fill me with joy in your *p*,
  21:6 with the joy of your *p*.
  23:5 in the *p* of my enemies.
  31:20 the shelter of your *p* you hide
          them
  41:12 and set me in your *p* forever.
  51:11 Do not cast me from your *p*
  52:9 in the *p* of your saints.
  89:15 who walk in the light of your *p*,
  90:8 our secret sins in the light of
          your *p*
 114:7 O earth, at the *p* of the Lord,
 139:7 Where can I flee from your *p*?
Isa 26:17 so were we in your *p*, O LORD.
Jer   5:22 "Should you not tremble in my *p*
Eze 38:20 of the earth will tremble at my *p*.
Hos   6:2 that we may live in his *p*.
Na   1:5 The earth trembles at his *p*,
Mal   3:16 in his *p* concerning those who
Ac   2:28 you will fill me with joy in your *p*.'
1Th   3:9 have in the *p* of our God
   3:13 and holy in the *p* of our God
2Th   1:9 and shut out from the *p* of the
          Lord
Heb   9:24 now to appear for us in God's *p*.
1Jn   3:19 rest in his *p* whenever our hearts
Jude   :24 before his glorious *p* without fault

PRESENT (PRESENCE)
1Co   3:22 life or death or the *p* or the
          future—
   7:26 of the *p* crisis, I think that it is
          good
2Co 11:2 so that I might *p* you as a pure
Eph   5:27 and to *p* her to himself

1Ti   4:8 holding promise for both the *p* life
2Ti   2:15 Do your best to *p* yourself to God
Jude   :24 and to *p* you before his glorious

PRESERVE
Lk 17:33 and whoever loses his life will *p* it.

PRESERVES
Ps 119:50 Your promise *p* my life.

PRESS (PRESSED PRESSURE)
Php   3:12 but I *p* on to take hold of that
   3:14 I *p* on toward the goal

PRESSED (PRESS)
Lk   6:38 *p* down, shaken together

PRESSURE (PRESS)
2Co   1:8 We were under great *p*, far
  11:28 I face daily the *p* of my concern

PRETENDED
1Sa 21:13 So he *p* to be insane

PREVAILS
1Sa   2:9 "It is not by strength that one *p*;
Pr 19:21 but it is the LORD's purpose that *p*

PRICE (PRICELESS)
Job 28:18 the *p* of wisdom is beyond rubies.
1Co   6:20 your own; you were bought at a *p*.
   7:23 bought at a *p*; do not become
          slaves

PRICELESS* (PRICE)
Ps 36:7 How *p* is your unfailing love!

PRIDE (PROUD)
Pr   8:13 I hate *p* and arrogance,
  11:2 When *p* comes, then comes
  13:10 *P* only breeds quarrels,
  16:18 *P* goes before destruction,
  29:23 A man's *p* brings him low,
Isa 25:11 God will bring down their *p*
Da   4:37 And those who walk in *p* he is
          able
Am   8:7 The LORD has sworn by the *P*
2Co   5:12 giving you an opportunity to
          take *p*
   7:4 in you; I take great *p* in you.
   8:24 and the reason for our *p* in you,
Gal   6:4 Then he can take *p* in himself,
Jas   1:9 ought to take *p* in his high
          position.

PRIEST (PRIESTHOOD PRIESTLY PRIESTS)
Ge 14:18 he was *p* of God Most High,
Nu   5:10 to the *p* will belong to the *p*.'"
2Ch 13:9 and seven rams may become a *p*
Ps 110:4 "You are a *p* forever,
Heb   2:17 faithful high *p* in service to God,
   3:1 and high *p* whom we confess.
   4:14 have a great high *p* who has gone
   4:15 do not have a high *p* who is
          unable
   5:6 "You are a *p* forever,
   6:20 He has become a high *p* forever,
   7:3 Son of God he remains a *p*
          forever.
   7:15 clear if another *p* like
          Melchizedek
   7:26 Such a high *p* meets our need—
   8:1 We do have such a high *p*,
  10:11 Day after day every *p* stands
  13:11 The high *p* carries the blood

PRIESTHOOD (PRIEST)
Heb   7:24 lives forever, he has a
          permanent *p*.
1Pe   2:5 into a spiritual house to be a
          holy *p*,
   2:9 you are a chosen people, a
          royal *p*,

PRIESTLY (PRIEST)
Ro 15:16 to the Gentiles with the *p* duty

PRIESTS (PRIEST)
Ex 19:6 you will be for me a kingdom of *p*
Lev 21:1 "Speak to the *p*, the sons of
          Aaron,
Eze 42:13 where the *p* who approach
  46:2 *p* are to sacrifice his burnt offering
Mal   1:6 O *p*, who show contempt for my
          name.
Rev   5:10 to be a kingdom and *p*
  20:6 but they will be *p* of God

PRIME
Isa 38:10 recovery: I said, "In the *p* of my
          life

PRINCE (PRINCES PRINCESS)
Isa   9: 6 Everlasting Father, *P* of Peace.
Eze 34:24 and my servant David will be *p*
      37:25 my servant will be their *p* forever.
Da   8:25 stand against the *P* of princes.
Jn   12:31 now the *p* of this world will be
Ac   5:31 as *P* and Savior that he might give

PRINCES (PRINCE)
Ps   118: 9 than to trust in *p*.
     148:11 you *p* and all rulers on earth,
Isa   40:23 He brings *p* to naught

PRINCESS* (PRINCE)
Ps   45:13 All glorious is the *p*

PRISCILLA*
    Wife of Aquila; co-worker with Paul (Ac 18;
Ro 16:3; 1Co 16:19; 2Ti 4:19); instructor of
Apollos (Ac 18:24–28).

PRISON (PRISONER PRISONERS)
Ps   66:11 You brought us into *p*
     142: 7 Set me free from my *p*,
Isa   42: 7 to free captives from *p*
Mt   25:36 I was in *p* and you came to visit
              me
2Co 11:23 been in *p* more frequently,
Heb 11:36 others were chained and put in *p*.
      13: 3 Remember those in *p*
1Pe   3:19 spirits in *p* who disobeyed long
              ago
Rev   20: 7 Satan will be released from his *p*

PRISONER (PRISON)
Ro   7:23 and making me a *p* of the law of
              sin
Gal   3:22 declares that the whole world is
              a *p*
Eph   3: 1 the *p* of Christ Jesus for the sake

PRISONERS (PRISON)
Ps   68: 6 he leads forth the *p* with singing;
      79:11 groans of the *p* come before you;
     107:10 *p* suffering in iron chains,
     146: 7 The LORD sets *p* free,
Zec   9:12 to your fortress, O *p* of hope;
Lk   4:18 me to proclaim freedom for the *p*
Gal   3:23 we were held *p* by the law,

PRIVILEGE*
2Co   8: 4 pleaded with us for the *p* of
              sharing

PRIZE*
1Co   9:24 Run in such a way as to get the *p*.
       9:24 but only one gets the *p*? Run
       9:27 will not be disqualified for the *p*.
Php   3:14 on toward the goal to win the *p*
Col   2:18 of angels disqualify you for the *p*.

PROBE
Job   11: 7 Can you *p* the limits
Ps   17: 3 Though you *p* my heart

PROCEDURE
Ecc   8: 6 For there is a proper time and *p*

PROCESSION
Ps   68:24 Your *p* has come into view,
              O God,
     118:27 boughs in hand, join in the
              festal *p*
1Co   4: 9 on display at the end of the *p*,
2Co   2:14 us in triumphal *p* in Christ

PROCLAIM (PROCLAIMED PROCLAIMING
PROCLAIMS PROCLAMATION)
Ex   33:19 and I will *p* my name, the LORD,
Lev   25:10 and *p* liberty throughout the land
Dt   30:12 and *p* it to us so we may obey it?"
2Sa   1:20 *p* it not in the streets of Ashkelon,
1Ch 16:23 *p* his salvation day after day.
Ne   8:15 and that they should *p* this word
Ps   2: 7 I will *p* the decree of the LORD:
       9:11 *p* among the nations what he has
      19: 1 the skies *p* the work of his hands.
      22:31 They will *p* his righteousness
      40: 9 I *p* righteousness in the great
      50: 6 the heavens *p* his righteousness,
      64: 9 they will *p* the works of God
      68:34 *P* the power of God,
      71:16 I will come and *p* your mighty
              acts,
      92: 2 to *p* your love in the morning
      96: 2 *p* his salvation day after day.
      97: 6 The heavens *p* his righteousness,
     106: 2 Who can *p* the mighty acts
     118:17 will *p* what the LORD has done.

Ps   145: 6 and I will *p* your great deeds.
Isa   12: 4 and *p* that his name is exalted.
      42:12 and *p* his praise in the islands.
      52: 7 who *p* salvation,
      61: 1 to *p* freedom for the captives
      66:19 They will *p* my glory
Jer   7: 2 house and there *p* this message:
      50: 2 lift up a banner and *p* it;
Hos   5: 9 I *p* what is certain.
Zec   9:10 He will *p* peace to the nations.
Mt   10:27 in your ear, *p* from the roofs.
      12:18 and he will *p* justice to the
              nations.
Lk   4:18 me to *p* freedom for the prisoners
       9:60 you go and *p* the kingdom of
              God."
Ac   17:23 unknown I am going to *p*
      20:27 hesitated to *p* to you the whole
              will
1Co   11:26 you *p* the Lord's death
Col   1:28 We *p* him, admonishing
       4: 4 Pray that I may *p* it clearly,
1Jn   1: 1 this we *p* concerning the Word

PROCLAIMED (PROCLAIM)
Ex   9:16 and that my name might be *p*
      34: 5 there with him and *p* his name,
Ps   68:11 was the company of those who *p*
              it:
Ro   15:19 I have fully *p* the gospel of Christ.
Col   1:23 that has been *p* to every creature
2Ti   4:17 me the message might be fully *p*

PROCLAIMING (PROCLAIM)
Ps   26: 7 *p* aloud your praise
      92:15 *p*, "The LORD is upright;
Ac   5:42 and *p* the good news that Jesus is
Ro   10: 8 the word of faith we are *p*:

PROCLAIMS (PROCLAIM)
Dt   18:22 If what a prophet *p* in the name

PROCLAMATION (PROCLAIM)
Isa   62:11 The LORD has made *p*

PRODUCE (PRODUCES)
Mt   3: 8 *P* fruit in keeping with
              repentance.
       3:10 tree that does not *p* good fruit will

PRODUCES (PRODUCE)
Pr   30:33 so stirring up anger *p* strife."
Ro   5: 3 that suffering *p* perseverance;
Heb 12:11 it *p* a harvest of righteousness

PROFANE (PROFANED)
Lev   19:12 and so *p* the name of your God.
      22:32 Do not *p* my holy name.
Mal   2:10 Why do we *p* the covenant

PROFANED (PROFANE)
Eze   36:20 the nations they *p* my holy name,

PROFESS*
1Ti   2:10 for women who *p* to worship God.
Heb   4:14 let us hold firmly to the faith
              we *p*.
      10:23 unswervingly to the hope we *p*,

PROFIT (PROFITABLE)
Pr   14:23 All hard work brings a *p*,
      21: 5 The plans of the diligent lead to *p*
Isa   44:10 which can *p* him nothing?
2Co   2:17 not peddle the word of God for *p*.
Php   3: 7 was to my *p* I now consider loss

PROFITABLE* (PROFIT)
Pr   3:14 for she is more *p* than silver
      31:18 She sees that her trading is *p*,
Tit   3: 8 These things are excellent and *p*

PROFOUND
Job   9: 4 His wisdom is *p*, his power is vast.
Ps   92: 5 how *p* your thoughts!
Eph   5:32 This is a *p* mystery—but I am

PROGRESS
Php   1:25 continue with all of you for your *p*
1Ti   4:15 so that everyone may see your *p*.

PROLONG*
Dt   5:33 *p* your days in the land that you
Ps   85: 5 Will you *p* your anger
Pr   3: 2 for they will *p* your life many
              years
Isa   53:10 will see his offspring and *p* his
              days,
La   4:22 he will not *p* your exile.

PROMISE (PROMISED PROMISES)
Nu   23:19 Does he *p* and not fulfill?

Jos   23:14 Every *p* has been fulfilled;
2Sa   7:25 keep forever the *p* you have made
1Ki   8:20 The LORD has kept the *p* he made
       8:24 You have kept your *p*
Ne   5:13 man who does not keep this *p*.
       9: 8 have kept your *p* because you are
Ps   77: 8 Has his *p* failed for all time?
     119:41 your salvation according to
              your *p*;
     119:50 Your *p* preserves my life.
     119:58 to me according to your *p*.
     119:162 I rejoice in your *p*
Ac   2:39 The *p* is for you and your children
Ro   4:13 offspring received the *p* that he
       4:20 unbelief regarding the *p* of God,
Gal   3:14 that by faith we might receive
              the *p*
Eph   2:12 foreigners to the covenants of
              the *p*
1Ti   4: 8 holding *p* for both the present life
Heb   6:13 When God made his *p* to
              Abraham
      11:11 him faithful who had made the *p*.
2Pe   3: 9 Lord is not slow in keeping his *p*,
       3:13 with his *p* we are looking forward

PROMISED (PROMISE)
Ge   21: 1 did for Sarah what he had *p*.
      24: 7 who spoke to me and *p* me on
              oath,
Ex   3:17 And I have *p* to bring you up out
Nu   10:29 for the LORD has *p* good things
Dt   15: 6 your God will bless you as he
              has *p*,
      26:18 his treasured possession as he *p*,
      27: 3 and you have *p* these good things
2Sa   7:28 and you have *p* these good things
1Ki   9: 5 I *p* David your father when I said,
2Ch   6:15 with your mouth you have *p*
Ps   119:57 I have *p* to obey your words.
Lk   24:49 to send you what my Father
              has *p*;
Ac   1: 4 but wait for the gift my Father *p*,
      13:32 What God *p* our fathers he has
Ro   4:21 power to do what he had *p*.
Tit   1: 2 *p* before the beginning of time,
Heb 10:23 for he who *p* is faithful.
      10:36 you will receive what he has *p*.
Jas   1:12 the crown of life that God has *p*
       2: 5 the kingdom he *p* those who love
2Pe   3: 4 "Where is this 'coming' he *p*?
1Jn   2:25 And this is what he *p* us—

PROMISES (PROMISE)
Jos   21:45 one of all the LORD's good *p*
      23:14 of all the good *p* the LORD your
1Ki   8:56 failed of all the good *p* he gave
1Ch 17:19 and made known all these
              great *p*.
Ps   85: 8 he *p* peace to his people, his
              saints
     106:12 Then they believed his *p*
     119:140 Your *p* have been thoroughly
     119:148 that I may meditate on your *p*.
     145:13 The LORD is faithful to all his *p*
Ro   9: 4 the temple worship and the *p*.
2Co   1:20 matter how many *p* God has
              made,
       7: 1 Since we have these *p*, dear
              friends,
Heb   8: 6 and it is founded on better *p*.
2Pe   1: 4 us his very great and precious *p*,

PROMOTE (PROMOTES)
Pr   12:20 but joy for those who *p* peace.
      16:21 and pleasant words *p* instruction.
1Ti   1: 4 These *p* controversies rather

PROMOTES (PROMOTE)
Pr   17: 9 over an offense *p* love,

PROMPTED
1Th   1: 3 your labor *p* by love, and your
2Th   1:11 and every act *p* by your faith.

PRONOUNCE (PRONOUNCED)
1Ch 23:13 to *p* blessings in his name forever.

PRONOUNCED (PRONOUNCE)
1Ch 16:12 miracles, and the judgments he *p*,

PROOF (PROVE)
Ac   17:31 He has given *p* of this to all men
2Co   8:24 Therefore show these men the *p*

PROPER
Ps   104:27 give them their food at the *p* time.
     145:15 give them their food at the *p* time.

Ecc 5:18 Then I realized that it is good
                and *p*
      8: 5 the wise heart will know the *p*
                time
Mt 24:45 give them their food at the *p*
                time?
Lk   1:20 which will come true at their *p*
                time
1Co 11:13 Is it *p* for a woman to pray to God
Gal 6: 9 at the *p* time we will reap a
                harvest
1Ti 2: 6 the testimony given in its *p* time.
1Pe 2:17 Show *p* respect to everyone:

PROPERTY
Heb 10:34 the confiscation of your *p*,

PROPHECIES (PROPHESY)
1Co 13: 8 where there are *p*, they will cease;
1Th 5:20 do not treat *p* with contempt.

PROPHECY (PROPHESY)
Da   9:24 to seal up vision and *p*
1Co 12:10 miraculous powers, to another *p*,
      13: 2 of *p* and can fathom all mysteries
      14: 1 gifts, especially the gift of *p*.
      14: 6 or *p* or word of instruction?
      14:22 *p*, however, is for believers,
2Pe 1:20 you must understand that no *p*
Rev 22:18 the words of the *p* of this book:

PROPHESIED (PROPHESY)
Nu 11:25 the Spirit rested on them, they *p*,
1Sa 19:24 and also *p* in Samuel's presence.
Jn 11:51 that year he *p* that Jesus would
Ac 19: 6 and they spoke in tongues and *p*.
      21: 9 four unmarried daughters who *p*.

PROPHESIES (PROPHESY)
Jer 28: 9 the prophet who *p* peace will be
Eze 12:27 and he *p* about the distant future.'
1Co 11: 4 *p* with his head covered dishonors
      14: 3 But everyone who *p* speaks to
                men

PROPHESY (PROPHECIES PROPHECY PROPHESIED
PROPHESIES PROPHESYING PROPHET PROPHET'S
PROPHETESS PROPHETS)
1Sa 10: 6 and you will *p* with them;
Eze 13: 2 Say to those who *p* out
      13:17 daughters of your people who *p*
                out
      34: 2 *p* against the shepherds of Israel;
      37: 4 "*P* to these bones and say to
                them,
Joel 2:28 Your sons and daughters will *p*,
Mt   7:22 Lord, did we not *p* in your name,
Ac   2:17 Your sons and daughters will *p*,
1Co 13: 9 know in part and we *p* in part,
      14:39 my brothers, be eager to *p*,
Rev 11: 3 and they will *p* for 1,260 days,

PROPHESYING (PROPHESY)
1Ch 25: 1 and Jeduthun for the ministry
                of *p*,
Ro 12: 6 If a man's gift is *p*, let him use it

PROPHET (PROPHESY)
Ex   7: 1 your brother Aaron will be your *p*.
Nu 12: 6 "When a *p* of the LORD is
Dt 13: 1 If a *p*, or one who foretells
      18:18 up for them a *p* like you
      18:22 If what a *p* proclaims in the name
1Sa 3:20 that Samuel was attested as a *p*
      9: 9 because the *p* of today used
1Ki 1: 8 son of Jehoiada, Nathan the *p*,
      18:36 the *p* Elijah stepped forward
2Ki 5: 8 and he will know that there is a *p*
      6:12 "but Elisha, the *p* who is in Israel,
      20: 1 The *p* Isaiah son of Amoz went
2Ch 35:18 since the days of the *p* Samuel;
      36:12 himself before Jeremiah the *p*,
Ezr 5: 1 Haggai the *p* and Zechariah the *p*,
Eze 2: 5 they will know that a *p* has been
      33:33 they will know that a *p* has been
Hos 9: 7 the *p* is considered a fool,
Am   7:14 "I was neither a *p* nor a prophet's
Hab 1: 1 that Habakkuk the *p* received.
Hag 1: 1 came through the *p* Haggai
Zec 1: 1 to the *p* Zechariah son of
                Berekiah,
      13: 4 that day every *p* will be ashamed
Mal 4: 5 I will send you the *p* Elijah
Mt 10:41 Anyone who receives a *p*
      11: 9 what did you go out to see? A *p*?
      12:39 except the sign of the *p* Jonah.

Lk   1:76 will be called a *p* of the Most
                High;
      4:24 "no *p* is accepted in his
                hometown.
      7:16 A great *p* has appeared among
                us,"
      24:19 "He was a *p*, powerful in word
Jn   1:21 "Are you the P?" He answered,
Ac   7:37 'God will send you a *p* like me
      21:10 a *p* named Agabus came
1Co 14:37 If anybody thinks he is a *p*
Rev 16:13 and out of the mouth of the
                false *p*.

PROPHET'S (PROPHESY)
2Pe 1:20 about by the *p* own
                interpretation.

PROPHETESS (PROPHESY)
Ex 15:20 Then Miriam the *p*, Aaron's sister,
Jdg 4: 4 a *p*, the wife of Lappidoth,
Isa 8: 3 I went to the *p*, and she conceived
Lk   2:36 a *p*, Anna, the daughter of
                Phanuel,

PROPHETS (PROPHESY)
Nu 11:29 that all the LORD's people were *p*
1Sa 10:11 Is Saul also among the *p*?"
      28: 6 him by dreams or Urim or *p*.
1Ki 19:10 put your *p* to death with the
                sword.
1Ch 16:22 do my *p* no harm."
Ps 105:15 do my *p* no harm."
Jer 23: 9 Concerning the *p*:
      23:30 "I am against the *p* who steal
Eze 13: 2 prophesy against the *p*
Mt   5:17 come to abolish the Law or the P;
      7:12 for this sums up the Law and
                the P.
      7:15 "Watch out for false *p*.
      22:40 and the P hang on these two
      23:37 you who kill the *p* and stone
                those
      24:24 false Christs and false *p* will
                appear
      26:56 of the *p* might be fulfilled."
Lk 10:24 For I tell you that many *p*
      11:49 'I will send them *p* and apostles,
      24:25 believe all that the *p* have spoken!
      24:44 me in the Law of Moses, the P
Ac   3:24 "Indeed, all the *p* from Samuel on,
      10:43 All the *p* testify about him that
      13: 1 the church at Antioch there
                were *p*
      26:22 nothing beyond what the *p*
      28:23 the Law of Moses and from the P.
Ro   1: 2 through his *p* in the Holy
      3:21 to which the Law and the P
                testify.
      11: 3 they have killed your *p*
1Co 12:28 second *p*, third teachers, then
      12:29 Are all *p*? Are all teachers?
      14:32 The spirits of *p* are subject
Eph 2:20 foundation of the apostles and *p*,
      3: 5 Spirit to God's holy apostles
                and *p*.
      4:11 some to be *p*, some
Heb 1: 1 through the *p* at many times
1Pe 1:10 Concerning this salvation, the *p*,
2Pe 1:19 word of the *p* made more certain,
      3: 2 spoken in the past by the holy *p*
1Jn 4: 1 because many false *p* have gone
                out
Rev 11:10 these two *p* had tormented those
      18:20 Rejoice, saints and apostles and *p*!

PROPORTION
Dt 16:10 by giving a freewill offering in *p*
      16:17 Each of you must bring a gift in *p*

PROPRIETY*
1Ti 2: 9 with decency and *p*,
      2:15 in faith, love and holiness with *p*.

PROSPECT*
Pr 10:28 The *p* of the righteous is joy,

PROSPER (PROSPERED PROSPERITY PROSPEROUS
PROSPERS)
Dt   5:33 so that you may live and *p*
      28:63 pleased the LORD to make you *p*
      29: 9 that you may *p* in everything you
1Ki 2: 3 so that you may *p* in all you do
Ezr 6:14 and *p* under the preaching
Pr 11:10 When the righteous *p*, the city

Pr 11:25 A generous man will *p*;
      17:20 A man of perverse heart does
                not *p*
      28:13 who conceals his sins does not *p*,
      28:25 he who trusts in the LORD will *p*.
Isa 53:10 of the LORD will *p* in his hand.
Jer 12: 1 Why does the way of the
                wicked *p*?

PROSPERED (PROSPER)
Ge 39: 2 was with Joseph and he *p*,
2Ch 14: 7 So they built and *p*.
      31:21 And so he *p*.

PROSPERITY (PROSPER)
Dt 28:11 will grant you abundant *p*—
      30:15 I set before you today life and *p*,
Job 36:11 will spend the rest of their days
                in *p*
Ps 73: 3 when I saw the *p* of the wicked.
      122: 9 I will seek your *p*.
      128: 2 blessings and *p* will be yours.
Pr   3: 2 and bring you *p*.
      13:21 but *p* is the reward of the
                righteous.
      21:21 finds life, *p* and honor.
Isa 45: 7 I bring *p* and create disaster;

PROSPEROUS (PROSPER)
Dt 30: 9 your God will make you most *p*
Jos 1: 8 Then you will be *p* and successful.
Job 42:10 the LORD made him *p* again

PROSPERS (PROSPER)
Ps   1: 3 Whatever he does *p*.
Pr 16:20 gives heed to instruction *p*,
      19: 8 he who cherishes
                understanding *p*.

PROSTITUTE (PROSTITUTES PROSTITUTION)
Lev 20: 6 and spiritists to *p* himself
Nu 15:39 and not *p* yourselves by going
Jos 2: 1 the house of a *p* named Rahab
Pr   6:26 for the *p* reduces you to a loaf
      7:10 like a *p* and with crafty intent.
      23:27 for a *p* is a deep pit
Eze 16:15 and used your fame to become
                a *p*.
      23: 7 a *p* to all the elite of the Assyrians
Hos 3: 3 you must not be a *p* or be
                intimate
1Co 6:15 of Christ and unite them with a *p*?
      6:16 with a *p* is one with her in body?
Rev 17: 1 you the punishment of the
                great *p*,

PROSTITUTES (PROSTITUTE)
Pr 29: 3 of *p* squanders his wealth.
Mt 21:31 and the *p* are entering the
                kingdom
Lk 15:30 property with *p* comes home,
1Co 6: 9 male *p* nor homosexual offenders

PROSTITUTION (PROSTITUTE)
Eze 16:16 where you carried on your *p*.
      23: 3 engaging in *p* from their youth.
Hos 4:10 engage in *p* but not increase,

PROSTRATE
Dt   9:18 again I fell *p* before the LORD
1Ki 18:39 they fell *p* and cried, "The LORD

PROTECT (PROTECTED PROTECTION PROTECTS)
Dt 23:14 about in your camp to *p* you
Ps 25:21 integrity and uprightness *p* me,
      32: 7 you will *p* me from trouble
      40:11 your truth always *p* me.
      41: 2 The LORD will *p* him
      91:14 I will *p* him, for he acknowledges
      140: 1 *p* me from men of violence,
Pr   2:11 Discretion will *p* you,
      4: 6 forsake wisdom, and she will *p*
                you;
Jn 17:11 *p* them by the power of your
                name
      17:15 that you *p* them from the evil one.
2Th 3: 3 and *p* you from the evil one.

PROTECTED (PROTECT)
Jos 24:17 us on our entire journey
1Sa 30:23 He has *p* us and handed
Ps 37:28 He has *p* us and handed
Jn 17:12 I *p* them and kept them safe

PROTECTION (PROTECT)
Ezr 9: 9 he has given us a wall of *p* in
                Judah
Ps   5:11 Spread your *p* over them,

PROTECTS (PROTECT)
Ps 116: 6 The LORD *p* the simplehearted;
Pr   2: 8 and *p* the way of his faithful ones.
1Co 13: 7 It always *p*, always trusts,

PROUD (PRIDE)
Ps 31:23 but the *p* he pays back in full.
    101: 5 has haughty eyes and a *p* heart,
    138: 6 but the *p* he knows from afar.
Pr   3:34 He mocks *p* mockers
    16: 5 The LORD detests all the *p*
    16:19 than to share plunder with the *p*.
    18:12 his downfall a man's heart is *p*,
    21: 4 Haughty eyes and a *p* heart,
Isa   2:12 store for all the *p* and lofty,
Ro 12:16 Do not be *p*, but be willing
1Co 13: 4 it does not boast, it is not *p*.
2Ti   3: 2 lovers of money, boastful, *p*,
Jas   4: 6 "God opposes the *p*
1Pe   5: 5 because, "God opposes the *p*

PROVE (PROOF PROVED PROVING)
Pr 29:25 Fear of man will *p* to be a snare,
Jn   8:46 Can any of you *p* me guilty of sin?
Ac 26:20 *p* their repentance by their deeds.
1Co   4: 2 been given a trust must *p* faithful.

PROVED (PROVE)
Ps 51: 4 so that you are *p* right
Mt 11:19 wisdom is *p* right by her actions."
Ro   3: 4 "So that you are *p* right
1Pe   1: 7 may be *p* genuine and may result

PROVIDE (PROVIDED PROVIDES PROVISION)
Ge 22: 8 "God himself will *p* the lamb
    22:14 that place "The LORD will P."
Isa 43:20 because I *p* water in the desert
    61: 3 and *p* for those who grieve in
              Zion
1Co 10:13 *p* a way out so that you can stand
1Ti   5: 8 If anyone does not *p*
Tit   3:14 in order that they may *p*

PROVIDED (PROVIDE)
Ps 68:10 O God, you *p* for the poor.
    111: 9 He *p* redemption for his people;
Jnh   1:17 But the LORD *p* a great fish
    4: 6 Then the LORD God *p* a vine
    4: 7 dawn the next day God *p* a worm,
    4: 8 God *p* a scorching east wind,
Gal   4:18 to be zealous, *p* the purpose is
              good
Heb   1: 3 After he had *p* purification for
              sins,

PROVIDES (PROVIDE)
Ps 111: 5 He *p* food for those who fear him;
Pr 31:15 she *p* food for her family
Eze 18: 7 and *p* clothing for the naked.
1Ti   6:17 who richly *p* us with everything
1Pe   4:11 it with the strength God *p*,

PROVING* (PROVE)
Ac   9:22 by *p* that Jesus is the Christ.
    17: 3 and *p* that the Christ had to suffer
    18:28 *p* from the Scriptures that Jesus

PROVISION (PROVIDE)
Ro   5:17 who receive God's abundant *p*

PROVOKED
Ecc   7: 9 Do not be quickly *p* in your spirit,
Jer 32:32 Judah have *p* me by all the evil
              they

PROWLS
1Pe   5: 8 Your enemy the devil *p*

PRUDENCE* (PRUDENT)
Pr   1: 4 for giving *p* to the simple,
    8: 5 You who are simple, gain *p*;
    8:12 "I, wisdom, dwell together with *p*;
    15: 5 whoever heeds correction
              shows *p*.
    19:25 and the simple will learn *p*;

PRUDENT* (PRUDENCE)
Pr   1: 3 acquiring a disciplined and *p* life,
    12:16 but a *p* man overlooks an insult.
    12:23 A *p* man keeps his knowledge
    13:16 Every *p* man acts out of
              knowledge
    14: 8 *The wisdom of the p is*
    14:15 a *p* man gives thought to his
              steps.
    14:18 the *p* are crowned with
              knowledge.
    19:14 but a *p* wife is from the LORD.
    22: 3 *p* man sees danger and takes

Pr 27:12 The *p* see danger and take refuge,
Jer 49: 7 Has counsel perished from the *p*?
Am   5:13 Therefore the *p* man keeps quiet

PRUNES (PRUNING)
Jn 15: 2 that does bear fruit he *p*

PRUNING (PRUNES)
Isa   2: 4 and their spears into *p* hooks.
Joel 3:10 and your *p* hooks into spears.

PSALMS
Eph   5:19 Speak to one another with *p*,
Col   3:16 and as you sing *p*, hymns

PUBLICLY
Ac 20:20 have taught you *p* and from house
1Ti   5:20 Those who sin are to be
              rebuked *p*,

PUFFS
1Co   8: 1 Knowledge *p* up, but love builds
              up

PULLING
2Co 10: 8 building you up rather than *p* you

PUNISH (PUNISHED PUNISHES PUNISHMENT)
Ge 15:14 But I will *p* the nation they serve
Ex 32:34 I will *p* them for their sin."
Pr 17:26 It is not good to *p* an innocent
              man,
    23:13 if you *p* him with the rod, he will
Isa 13:11 I will *p* the world for its evil,
Jer   2:19 Your wickedness will *p* you;
    21:14 I will *p* you as your deeds deserve,
Zep   1:12 and *p* those who are complacent,
Ac   7: 7 But I will *p* the nation they serve
2Th   1: 8 He will *p* those who do not know
1Pe   2:14 by him to *p* those who do wrong

PUNISHED (PUNISH)
Ezr   9:13 you have *p* us less than our sins
Ps 99: 8 though you *p* their misdeeds.
La   3:39 complain when *p* for his sins?
Mk 12:40 Such men will be *p* most
              severely."
Lk 23:41 the same sentence? We are *p*
              justly,
2Th   1: 9 be *p* with everlasting destruction
Heb 10:29 to be *p* who has trampled the Son

PUNISHES (PUNISH)
Heb 12: 6 and he *p* everyone he accepts

PUNISHMENT (PUNISH)
Isa 53: 5 the *p* that brought us peace was
Jer   4:18 This is your *p*.
Mt 25:46 Then they will go away to
              eternal *p*
Lk 12:48 and does things deserving *p* will
              be
    21:22 For this is the time of *p*
Ro 13: 4 wrath to bring *p* on the
              wrongdoer.
Heb   2: 2 disobedience received its just *p*,
2Pe   2: 9 while continuing their *p*.

PURCHASED
Ps 74: 2 Remember the people you *p* of
              old,
Rev   5: 9 with your blood you *p* men for
              God

PURE (PURIFICATION PURIFIED PURIFIES PURIFY PURITY)
2Sa 22:27 to the *p* you show yourself *p*,
Job 14: 4 Who can bring what is *p*
Ps 19: 9 The fear of the LORD is *p*,
    24: 4 who has clean hands and a *p*
              heart,
    51:10 Create in me a *p* heart, O God,
    119: 9 can a young man keep his way *p*?
Pr 15:26 those of the *p* are pleasing to him.
    20: 9 can say, "I have kept my heart *p*;
Isa 52:11 Come out from it and be *p*,
Hab   1:13 Your eyes are too *p* to look on
              evil;
Mt   5: 8 Blessed are the *p* in heart,
2Co 11: 2 I might present you as a *p* virgin
Php   4: 8 whatever is *p*, whatever is lovely,
1Ti   1: 5 which comes from a *p* heart
    5:22 Keep yourself *p*.
2Ti   2:22 call on the Lord out of a *p* heart.
Tit   1:15 To the *p*, all things are *p*,
    2: 5 to be self-controlled and *p*,
Heb   7:26 blameless, *p*, set apart from
              sinners
    13: 4 and the marriage bed kept *p*,

Jas   1:27 that God our Father accepts as *p*
    3:17 comes from heaven is first of all *p*;
1Jn   3: 3 him purifies himself, just as he
              is *p*.

PURGE
Pr 20:30 and beatings *p* the inmost being.

PURIFICATION (PURE)
Heb   1: 3 After he had provided *p* for sins,

PURIFIED (PURE)
Ac 15: 9 for he *p* their hearts by faith.
1Pe   1:22 Now that you have *p* yourselves

PURIFIES* (PURE)
1Jn   1: 7 of Jesus, his Son, *p* us from all sin.
    3: 3 who has this hope in him *p*
              himself,

PURIFY (PURE)
Nu 19:12 He must *p* himself with the water
2Co   7: 1 us *p* ourselves from everything
              that
Tit   2:14 to *p* for himself a people that are
Jas   4: 8 you sinners, and *p* your hearts,
1Jn   1: 9 and *p* us from all unrighteousness.

PURIM
Est   9:26 Therefore these days were
              called P

PURITY* (PURE)
Hos   8: 5 long will they be incapable of *p*?
2Co   6: 6 in *p*, understanding, patience
1Ti   4:12 in life, in love, in faith and in *p*.
    5: 2 as sisters, with absolute *p*.
1Pe   3: 2 when they see the *p* and
              reverence

PURPLE
Pr 31:22 she is clothed in fine linen and *p*.
Mk 15:17 They put a *p* robe on him, then

PURPOSE (PURPOSED PURPOSES)
Ex   9:16 I have raised you up for this
              very *p*,
Job 36: 5 he is mighty, and firm in his *p*.
Pr 19:21 but it is the LORD's *p* that prevails
Isa 46:10 I say: My *p* will stand,
    55:11 and achieve the *p* for which I sent
              it
Ac   2:23 handed over to you by God's set *p*
Ro   8:28 have been called according to
              his *p*.
    9:11 in order that God's *p*
    9:17 "I raised you up for this very *p*,
1Co   3: 8 the man who waters have one *p*,
2Co   5: 5 who has made us for this very *p*
Gal   4:18 be zealous, provided the *p* is
              good,
Eph   1:11 in conformity with the *p* of his
              will,
    3:11 according to his eternal *p* which
              he
Php   2: 2 love, being one in spirit and *p*.
    2:13 and to act according to his
              good *p*.
2Ti   1: 9 but because of his own *p* and
              grace.

PURPOSED (PURPOSE)
Isa 14:24 and as I have *p*, so it will stand.
    14:27 For the LORD Almighty has *p*,
Eph   1: 9 which he *p* in Christ, to be put

PURPOSES (PURPOSE)
Ps 33:10 he thwarts the *p* of the peoples.
Jer 23:20 the *p* of his heart.
    32:19 great are your *p* and mighty are

PURSE (PURSES)
Hag   1: 6 to put them in a *p* with holes in
              it."
Lk 10: 4 Do not take a *p* or bag or sandals;
    22:36 "But now if you have a *p*, take it,

PURSES (PURSE)
Lk 12:33 Provide *p* for yourselves that will

PURSUE (PURSUES)
Ps 34:14 seek peace and *p* it.
Pr 15: 9 he loves those who *p*
              righteousness
Ro   9:30 who did not *p* righteousness,
1Ti   6:11 and *p* righteousness, godliness,
2Ti   2:22 and *p* righteousness, faith,
1Pe   3:11 he must seek peace and *p* it.

PURSUES (PURSUE)
Pr 21:21 He who *p* righteousness and love

Pr 28: 1 wicked man flees though no
           one p,

QUAIL
Ex 16:13 That evening q came and covered
Nu 11:31 and drove q in from the sea.

QUALITIES* (QUALITY)
Da   6: 3 by his exceptional q that the king
Ro   1:20 of the world God's invisible q—
2Pe 1: 8 For if you possess these q

QUALITY (QUALITIES)
1Co 3:13 and the fire will test the q

QUARREL (QUARRELING QUARRELS QUARRELSOME)
Pr 15:18 but a patient man calms a q.
    17:14 Starting a q is like breaching a
           dam;
    17:19 He who loves a q loves sin;
    20: 3 but every fool is quick to q.
    26:17 in a q not his own.
    26:20 without gossip a q dies down.
2Ti 2:24 And the Lord's servant must
           not q;
Jas 4: 2 You q and fight.

QUARRELING (QUARREL)
1Co 3: 3 For since there is jealousy and q
2Ti 2:14 before God against q about
           words;

QUARRELS (QUARREL)
Pr 13:10 Pride only breeds q,
Isa 45: 9 Woe to him who q with his Maker,
2Ti 2:23 because you know they
           produce q.
Jas 4: 1 What causes fights and q

QUARRELSOME (QUARREL)
Pr 19:13 a q wife is like a constant
           dripping.
    21: 9 than share a house with a q wife.
    26:21 so is a q man for kindling strife.
1Ti 3: 3 not violent but gentle, not q,

QUEEN
1Ki 10: 1 When the q of Sheba heard about
2Ch 9: 1 When the q of Sheba heard
Mt 12:42 The Q of the South will rise

QUENCH (QUENCHED)
SS   8: 7 Many waters cannot q love;

QUENCHED (QUENCH)
Isa 66:24 nor will their fire be q,
Mk   9:48 and the fire is not q.'

QUICK-TEMPERED* (TEMPER)
Pr 14:17 A q man does foolish things,
    14:29 but a q man displays folly.
Tit 1: 7 not q, not given to drunkenness,

QUIET (QUIETNESS)
Ps 23: 2 he leads me beside q waters,
Pr 17: 1 Better a dry crust with peace
           and q
Ecc 9:17 The q words of the wise are more
Am   5:13 Therefore the prudent man
           keeps q
Zep 3:17 he will q you with his love,
Lk 19:40 he replied, "if they keep q,
1Th 4:11 it your ambition to lead a q life,
1Ti 2: 2 we may live peaceful and q lives
1Pe 3: 4 beauty of a gentle and q spirit,

QUIETNESS (QUIET)
Isa 30:15 in q and trust is your strength,
    32:17 the effect of righteousness will
           be q
1Ti 2:11 A woman should learn in q

QUIVER
Ps 127: 5 whose q is full of them.

RACE
Ecc 9:11 The r is not to the swift
Ac 20:24 if only I may finish the r
1Co 9:24 that in a r all the runners run,
Gal 2: 2 that I was running or had run my r
     5: 7 You were running a good r.
2Ti 4: 7 I have finished the r, I have kept
Heb 12: 1 perseverance the r marked out

RACHEL
    Daughter of Laban (Ge 29:16); wife of Jacob
(Ge 29:28); bore two sons (Ge 30:22–24;
35:16–24; 46:19). Stole Laban's gods (Ge 31:19,
32–35). Death (Ge 35:19–20).

RADIANCE (RADIANT)
Eze 1:28 so was the r around him.

Heb 1: 3 The Son is the r of God's glory

RADIANT (RADIANCE)
Ex 34:29 he was not aware that his face
           was r
Ps 34: 5 Those who look to him are r;
SS   5:10 Beloved My lover is r and ruddy,
Isa 60: 5 Then you will look and be r,
Eph 5:27 her to himself as a r church,

RAGE
Ac   4:25 " 'Why do the nations r
Col 3: 8 r, malice, slander, and filthy

RAGS
Isa 64: 6 our righteous acts are like filthy r;

RAHAB
    Prostitute of Jericho who hid Israelite spies
(Jos 2; 6:22–25; Heb 11:31; Jas 2:25). Mother
of Boaz (Mt 1:5).

RAIN (RAINBOW)
Ge   7: 4 from now I will send r on the
           earth
1Ki 17: 1 nor r in the next few years
    18: 1 and I will send r on the land."
Mt   5:45 and sends r on the righteous
Jas 5:17 it did not r on the land for three
Jude   12 They are clouds without r,

RAINBOW (RAIN)
Ge   9:13 I have set my r in the clouds,

RAISE (RISE)
Jn   6:39 but r them up at the last day.
1Co 15:15 he did not r him if in fact the dead

RAISED (RISE)
Isa 52:13 he will be r and lifted up
Mt 17:23 on the third day he will be r to life
Lk   7:22 the deaf hear, the dead are r,
Ac   2:24 But God r him from the dead,
Ro   4:25 was r to life for our justification.
     6: 4 as Christ was r from the dead
     8:11 And if the Spirit of him who r
           Jesus
    10: 9 in your heart that God r him
1Co 15: 4 that he was r on the third day
    15:20 But Christ has indeed been r

RALLY*
Isa 11:10 the nations will r to him,

RAM (RAMS)
Ge 22:13 there in a thicket he saw a r
           caught
Da   8: 3 before me was a r with two horns,

RAMPART*
Ps 91: 4 will be your shield and r.

RAMS (RAM)
1Sa 15:22 to heed is better than the fat of r.
Mic 6: 7 pleased with thousands of r,

RAN (RUN)
Jnh 1: 3 But Jonah r away from the LORD

RANSOM (RANSOMED)
Isa 50: 2 Was my arm too short to r you?
Hos 13:14 "I will r them from the power
Mt 20:28 and to give his life as a r for
           many."
Mk 10:45 and to give his life as a r for
           many."
1Ti 2: 6 who gave himself as a r for all
           men
Heb 9:15 as a r to set them free

RANSOMED (RANSOM)
Isa 35:10 and the r of the LORD will return.

RARE
Pr 20:15 that speak knowledge are a r
           jewel.

RAVEN (RAVENS)
Ge   8: 7 made in the ark and sent out a r,
Job 38:41 Who provides food for the r

RAVENS (RAVEN)
1Ki 17: 6 The r brought him bread
Ps 147: 9 and for the young r when they
           call.
Lk 12:24 Consider the r: They do not sow

READ (READING READS)
Dt 17:19 he is to r it all the days of his life
Jos 8:34 Joshua r all the words of the
           law—
2Ki 23: 2 He r in their hearing all the words
Ne   8: 8 They r from the Book of the Law
Jer 36: 6 and r to the people from the scroll

2Co 3: 2 known and r by everybody.

READING (READ)
1Ti 4:13 to the public r of Scripture,

READS (READ)
Rev 1: 3 Blessed is the one who r the
           words

REAFFIRM
2Co 2: 8 therefore, to r your love for him.

REAL* (REALITIES REALITY)
Jn   6:55 is r food and my blood is r drink.
1Jn 2:27 all things and as that anointing
           is r,

REALITIES* (REAL)
Heb 10: 1 are coming—not the r
           themselves.

REALITY* (REAL)
Col 2:17 the r, however, is found in Christ.

REALM (REALMS)
Hab 2: 9 "Woe to him who builds his r

REALMS (REALM)
Eph 1: 3 the heavenly r with every spiritual
     2: 6 in the heavenly r in Christ Jesus,

REAP (REAPER REAPS)
Job 4: 8 and those who sow trouble r it.
Ps 126: 5 will r with songs of joy.
Hos 8: 7 and r the whirlwind.
    10:12 r the fruit of unfailing love,
Jn   4:38 you to r what you have not
           worked
Ro   6:22 the benefit you r leads to
           holiness,
2Co 9: 6 generously will also r generously.
Gal 6: 8 from that nature will r
           destruction;

REAPER (REAP)
Jn   4:36 and the r may be glad together.

REAPS (REAP)
Pr 11:18 who sows righteousness r a sure
    22: 8 He who sows wickedness r
           trouble,
Gal 6: 7 A man r what he sows.

REASON (REASONED)
Ge   2:24 For this r a man will leave his
Isa 1:18 "Come now, let us r together,"
Mt 19: 5 'For this r a man will leave his
Jn 12:27 it was for this very r I came
    15:25 'They hated me without r.'
1Pe 3:15 to give the r for the hope that you
2Pe 1: 5 For this very r, make every effort

REASONED (REASON)
1Co 13:11 thought like a child, I r like a child.

REBEKAH
    Sister of Laban, secured as bride for Isaac
(Ge 24). Mother of Esau and Jacob (Ge
25:19–26). Taken by Abimelech as sister of
Isaac; returned (Ge 26:1–11). Encouraged
Jacob to trick Isaac out of blessing (Ge
27:1–17).

REBEL (REBELLED REBELLION REBELS)
Nu 14: 9 Only do not r against the LORD.
1Sa 12:14 and do not r against his
           commands,
Mt 10:21 children will r against their
           parents

REBELLED (REBEL)
Ps 78:56 and r against the Most High;
Isa 63:10 Yet they r

REBELLION (REBEL)
Ex 34: 7 and forgiving wickedness, r and
           sin
Nu 14:18 in love and forgiving sin and r.
1Sa 15:23 For r is like the sin of divination,
2Th 2: 3 will not come, until the r occurs

REBELS (REBEL)
Ro 13: 2 he who r against the authority is
1Ti 1: 9 but for lawbreakers and r,

REBIRTH* (BEAR)
Tit 3: 5 us through the washing of r

REBUILD (BUILD)
Ezr 5: 2 set to work to r the house of God
Ne   2:17 let us r the wall of Jerusalem,
Ps 102:16 For the LORD will r Zion
Da   9:25 and r Jerusalem until the
           Anointed

Am   9:14   they will *r* the ruined cities
Ac   15:16   Its ruins I will *r*,
REBUILT (BUILD)
Zec   1:16   and there my house will be *r*.
REBUKE (REBUKED REBUKES REBUKING)
Lev   19:17   *R* your neighbor frankly
Ps   141: 5   let him *r* me—it is oil on my head.
Pr   3:11   and do not resent his *r*,
     9: 8   *r* a wise man and he will love you.
     15:31   He who listens to a life-giving *r*
     17:10   A *r* impresses a man
     19:25   *r* a discerning man, and he will gain
     25:12   is a wise man's *r* to a listening ear.
     27: 5   Better is open *r*
     30: 6   or he will *r* you and prove you a liar
Ecc   7: 5   It is better to heed a wise man's *r*
Isa   54: 9   never to *r* you again.
Jer   2:19   your backsliding will *r* you.
Lk   17: 3   "If your brother sins, *r* him,
1Ti   5: 1   Do not *r* an older man harshly,
2Ti   4: 2   correct, *r* and encourage—
Tit   1:13   Therefore, *r* them sharply,
     2:15   Encourage and *r* with all authority.
Rev   3:19   Those whom I love I *r*
REBUKED (REBUKE)
Mk   16:14   he *r* them for their lack of faith
1Ti   5:20   Those who sin are to be *r* publicly,
REBUKES (REBUKE)
Job   22: 4   "Is it for your piety that he *r* you
Pr   28:23   He who *r* a man will
     29: 1   remains stiff-necked after many *r*
Heb   12: 5   do not lose heart when he *r* you,
REBUKING (REBUKE)
2Ti   3:16   *r*, correcting and training
RECEIVE (RECEIVED RECEIVES)
Mt   10:41   a righteous man will *r* a righteous
Mk   10:15   anyone who will not *r* the kingdom
Jn   20:22   and said, "*R* the Holy Spirit.
Ac   1: 8   you will *r* power when the Holy
     2:38   you will *r* the gift of the Holy Spirit
     19: 2   "Did you *r* the Holy Spirit
     20:35   'It is more blessed to give than to *r*
1Co   9:14   the gospel should *r* their living
2Co   6:17   and I will *r* you."
1Ti   1:16   believe on him and *r* eternal life.
Jas   1: 7   should not think he will *r* anything
2Pe   1:11   and you will *r* a rich welcome
1Jn   3:22   and *r* from him anything we ask,
Rev   4:11   to *r* glory and honor and power,
     5:12   to *r* power and wealth and wisdom
RECEIVED (RECEIVE)
Mt   6: 2   they have *r* their reward in full.
     10: 8   Freely you have *r*, freely give.
Mk   11:24   believe that you have *r* it,
Jn   1:12   Yet to all who *r* him,
     1:16   his grace we have all *r* one blessing
Ac   8:17   and they *r* the Holy Spirit.
     10:47   They have *r* the Holy Spirit just
Ro   8:15   but you *r* the Spirit of sonship.
1Co   11:23   For I *r* from the Lord what I
2Co   1: 4   the comfort we ourselves have *r*
Col   2: 6   just as you *r* Christ Jesus as Lord,
1Pe   4:10   should use whatever gift he has *r*
RECEIVES (RECEIVE)
Pr   18:22   and *r* favor from the LORD.
     27:21   but man is tested by the praise he *r*.
Mt   7: 8   everyone who asks *r*; he who seeks
     10:40   he who *r* me *r* the one who sent me.
     10:40   "He who *r* you *r* me, and he who
Ac   10:43   believes in him *r* forgiveness of sins
RECITE
Ps   45: 1   as I *r* my verses for the king;
RECKLESS
Pr   12:18   *R* words pierce like a sword,
     14:16   but a fool is hotheaded and *r*.

RECKONING
Isa   10: 3   What will you do on the day of *r*,
Hos   9: 7   the days of *r* are at hand.
RECLAIM* (CLAIM)
Isa   11:11   time to *r* the remnant that is left
RECOGNITION (RECOGNIZE)
1Co   16:18   Such men deserve *r*.
1Ti   5: 3   Give proper *r* to those widows who
RECOGNIZE (RECOGNITION RECOGNIZED)
Mt   7:16   By their fruit you will *r* them.
1Jn   4: 2   This is how you can *r* the Spirit
     4: 6   This is how we *r* the Spirit of truth
RECOGNIZED (RECOGNIZE)
Mt   12:33   for a tree is *r* by its fruit.
Ro   7:13   in order that sin might be *r* as sin,
RECOMPENSE*
Isa   40:10   and his *r* accompanies him.
     62:11   and his *r* accompanies him.' "
RECONCILE* (RECONCILED RECONCILIATION RECONCILING)
Ac   7:26   He tried to *r* them by saying, 'Men,
Eph   2:16   in this one body to *r* both of them
Col   1:20   him to *r* to himself all things,
RECONCILED* (RECONCILE)
Mt   5:24   First go and be *r* to your brother;
Lk   12:58   try hard to be *r* to him on the way,
Ro   5:10   how much more, having been *r*,
     5:10   we were *r* to him through the death
1Co   7:11   or else be *r* to her husband.
2Co   5:18   who *r* us to himself through Christ
     5:20   you on Christ's behalf: Be *r* to God.
Col   1:22   he has *r* you by Christ's physical
RECONCILIATION* (RECONCILE)
Ro   5:11   whom we have now received *r*.
     11:15   For if their rejection is the *r*
2Co   5:18   and gave us the ministry of *r*:
     5:19   committed to us the message of *r*.
RECONCILING* (RECONCILE)
2Co   5:19   that God was *r* the world to himself
RECORD (RECORDED)
Ps   130: 3   If you, O LORD, kept a *r* of sins,
Hos   13:12   his sins are kept on *r*.
1Co   13: 5   is not easily angered, it keeps no *r*
RECORDED (RECORD)
Job   19:23   "Oh, that my words were *r*,
Jn   20:30   which are not *r* in this book.
RECOUNT*
Ps   40: 5   no one can *r* to you;
     79:13   we will *r* your praise.
     119:13   With my lips I *r*
RED
Ex   15: 4   are drowned in the *R* Sea.
Ps   106: 9   He rebuked the *R* Sea,
Pr   23:31   Do not gaze at wine when it is *r*,
Isa   1:18   though they are *r* as crimson,
REDEEM (KINSMAN-REDEEMER REDEEMED REDEEMER REDEEMS REDEMPTION)
Ex   6: 6   will *r* you with an outstretched arm
2Sa   7:23   on earth that God went out to *r*
Ps   44:26   *r* us because of your unfailing love.
     49: 7   No man can *r* the life of another
     49:15   God will *r* my life from the grave;
     130: 8   He himself will *r* Israel
Hos   13:14   I will *r* them from death.
Gal   4: 5   under law, to *r* those under law,
Tit   2:14   for us to *r* us from all wickedness
REDEEMED (REDEEM)
Job   33:28   He *r* my soul from going
Ps   71:23   I, whom you have *r*.
     107: 2   Let the *r* of the LORD say this—
Isa   35: 9   But only the *r* will walk there,
     63: 9   In his love and mercy he *r* them;
Gal   3:13   Christ *r* us from the curse
1Pe   1:18   or gold that you were *r*
REDEEMER (REDEEM)
Job   19:25   I know that my *R* lives,
Ps   19:14   O LORD, my Rock and my *R*.
Isa   44: 6   and *R*, the LORD Almighty:
     48:17   your *R*, the Holy One of Israel:

Isa   59:20   "The *R* will come to Zion,
REDEEMS (REDEEM)
Ps   34:22   The LORD *r* his servants;
     103: 4   he *r* my life from the pit
REDEMPTION (REDEEM)
Ps   130: 7   and with him is full *r*.
Lk   21:28   because your *r* is drawing near."
Ro   3:24   grace through the *r* that came
     8:23   as sons, the *r* of our bodies.
1Co   1:30   our righteousness, holiness and *r*.
Eph   1: 7   In him we have *r* through his blood
     1:14   until the *r* of those who are God's
     4:30   you were sealed for the day of *r*.
Col   1:14   in whom we have *r*, the forgiveness
Heb   9:12   having obtained eternal *r*.
REED
Isa   42: 3   A bruised *r* he will not break,
Mt   12:20   A bruised *r* he will not break,
REFINE*
Jer   9: 7   "See, I will *r* and test them,
Zec   13: 9   I will *r* them like silver
Mal   3: 3   and *r* them like gold and silver.
REFLECT (REFLECTS)
2Co   3:18   unveiled faces all *r* the Lord's
REFLECTS (REFLECT)
Pr   27:19   As water *r* a face,
REFRESH (REFRESHED REFRESHING)
Phm   : 20   in the Lord; *r* my heart in Christ.
REFRESHED (REFRESH)
Pr   11:25   refreshes others will himself be *r*.
REFRESHING* (REFRESH)
Ac   3:19   that times of *r* may come
REFUGE
Nu   35:11   towns to be your cities of *r*,
Dt   33:27   The eternal God is your *r*,
Jos   20: 2   to designate the cities of *r*,
Ru   2:12   wings you have come to take *r*."
2Sa   22: 3   God is my rock, in whom I take *r*.
     22:31   a shield for all who take *r* in him.
Ps   2:12   Blessed are all who take *r* in him.
     5:11   But let all who take *r* in you be glad
     9: 9   The LORD is a *r* for the oppressed,
     16: 1   for in you I take *r*
     17: 7   those who take *r* in you
     18: 2   God is my rock, in whom I take *r*,
     31: 2   be my rock of *r*,
     34: 8   blessed is the man who takes *r*
     36: 7   find *r* in the shadow of your wings.
     46: 1   God is our *r* and strength,
     62: 8   for God is our *r*.
     71: 1   In you, O LORD, I have taken *r*;
     91: 2   "He is my *r* and my fortress,
     144: 2   my shield, in whom I take *r*,
Pr   14:26   and for his children it will be a *r*.
     30: 5   a shield to those who take *r* in him.
Na   1: 7   a *r* in times of trouble.
REFUSE (REFUSED)
Jn   5:40   yet you *r* to come to me to have life
REFUSED (REFUSE)
2Th   2:10   because they *r* to love the truth
Rev   16: 9   but they *r* to repent and glorify him
REGARD (REGARDS)
1Th   5:13   Hold them in the highest *r* in love
REGARDS (REGARD)
Ro   14:14   But if anyone *r* something
REGRET
2Co   7:10   leads to salvation and leaves no *r*,
REHOBOAM
Son of Solomon (1Ki 11:43; 1Ch 3:10).
Harsh treatment of subjects caused divided kingdom (1Ki 12:1–24; 14:21–31; 2Ch 10–12).
REIGN (REIGNED REIGNS)
Ex   15:18   The LORD will *r*
Ps   68:16   mountain where God chooses to *r*,
Isa   9: 7   He will *r* on David's throne
     24:23   for the LORD Almighty will *r*
     32: 1   See, a king will *r* in righteousness

Jer 23: 5 a King who will *r* wisely
Lk 1:33 and he will *r* over the house
Ro 6:12 Therefore do not let sin *r*
1Co 15:25 For he must *r* until he has put all
2Ti 2:12 we will also *r* with him.
Rev 11:15 and he will *r* for ever and ever."
20: 6 will *r* with him for a thousand
years
22: 5 And they will *r* for ever and ever.

REIGNED (REIGN)
Ro 5:21 so that, just as sin *r* in death,
Rev 20: 4 and *r* with Christ a thousand
years.

REIGNS (REIGN)
Ps 9: 7 The LORD *r* forever;
47: 8 God *r* over the nations;
93: 1 The LORD *r*, he is robed
96:10 among the nations, "The LORD *r*
97: 1 The LORD *r*, let the earth be glad;
99: 1 The LORD *r*, / let the nations
tremble;
146:10 The LORD *r* forever,
Isa 52: 7 "Your God *r*!"
Rev 19: 6 For our Lord God Almighty *r*.

REIN
Jas 1:26 and yet does not keep a tight *r*

REJECT (REJECTED REJECTION REJECTS)
Ps 94:14 For the LORD will not *r* his people
Ro 11: 1 I ask then: Did God *r* his people?

REJECTED (REJECT)
1Sa 8: 7 it is not you they have *r*,
1Ki 19:10 The Israelites have *r* your
covenant
2Ki 17:15 They *r* his decrees
Ps 66:20 who has not *r* my prayer
118:22 The stone the builders *r*
Isa 5:24 for they have *r* the law
41: 9 chosen you and have not *r* you.
53: 3 He was despised and *r* by men,
Jer 8: 9 Since they have *r* the word
Mt 21:42 " 'The stone the builders *r*
1Ti 4: 4 nothing is to be *r* if it is received
1Pe 2: 4 *r* by men but chosen by God
2: 7 "The stone the builders *r*

REJECTION* (REJECT)
Ro 11:15 For if their *r* is the reconciliation

REJECTS (REJECT)
Lk 10:16 but he who *r* me *r* him who sent
me
Jn 3:36 whoever *r* the Son will not see
life,
1Th 4: 8 he who *r* this instruction does not

REJOICE (JOY)
Dt 12: 7 shall *r* in everything you have put
1Ch 16:10 of those who seek the LORD *r*.
16:31 Let the heavens *r*, let the earth be
with trembling.
Ps 2:11 and *r* with trembling.
5:11 those who love your name may *r*
9:14 and there *r* in your salvation.
34: 2 let the afflicted hear and *r*.
63:11 But the king will *r* in God;
66: 6 come, let us *r* in him.
68: 3 and *r* before God;
105: 3 of those who seek the LORD *r*.
118:24 let us *r* and be glad in it.
119:14 I *r* in following your statutes
119:162 I *r* in your promise
149: 2 Let Israel *r* in their Maker;
Pr 5:18 may you *r* in the wife of your
youth
23:25 may she who gave you birth *r*!
24:17 stumbles, do not let your heart *r*,
Isa 9: 3 as men *r*
35: 1 the wilderness will *r* and blossom.
61: 7 they will *r* in their inheritance.
62: 5 so will your God *r* over you.
Jer 31:12 they will *r* in the bounty
Zep 3:17 he will *r* over you with singing."
Zec 9: 9 *R* greatly, O Daughter of Zion!
Lk 6:23 "*R* in that day and leap for joy,
10:20 but *r* that your names are written
15: 6 '*R* with me; I have found my lost
15: 9 '*R* with me; I have found my lost
Ro 5: 2 And we *r* in the hope of the glory
12:15 Rejoice with those who *r*; mourn
Php 2:17 I am glad and *r* with all of you.
3: 1 Finally, my brothers, *r* in the Lord!
4: 4 *R* in the Lord always.

1Pe 4:13 But *r* that you participate
Rev 19: 7 Let us *r* and be glad

REJOICES (JOY)
Ps 13: 5 my heart *r* in your salvation.
16: 9 my heart is glad and my tongue *r*;
Isa 61:10 my soul *r* in my God.
62: 5 as a bridegroom *r* over his bride,
Lk 1:47 and my spirit *r* in God my Savior,
Ac 2:26 my heart is glad and my tongue *r*;
1Co 12:26 if one part is honored, every part *r*
13: 6 delight in evil but *r* with the truth.

REJOICING (JOY)
2Sa 6:12 to the City of David with *r*.
Ne 12:43 *r* because God had given them
Ps 30: 5 but *r* comes in the morning.
Lk 15: 7 in the same way there will be
more *r*
Ac 5:41 because they had been counted
2Co 6:10 sorrowful, yet always *r*; poor,

RELATIVES
Pr 19: 7 A poor man is shunned by all his *r*
Mk 6: 4 among his *r* and in his own house
is
Lk 21:16 betrayed even by parents,
brothers, *r*
1Ti 5: 8 If anyone does not provide for
his *r*

RELEASE (RELEASED)
Isa 61: 1 and *r* from darkness,
Lk 4:18 to *r* the oppressed,

RELEASED (RELEASE)
Ro 7: 6 we have been *r* from the law
Rev 20: 7 Satan will be *r* from his prison

RELENTED (RELENTS)
Ex 32:14 the LORD *r* and did not bring
Ps 106:45 and out of his great love he *r*.

RELENTS* (RELENTED)
Joel 2:13 and he *r* from sending calamity.
Jnh 4: 2 a God who *r* from sending
calamity

RELIABLE (RELY)
Pr 22:21 teaching you true and *r* words,
Jn 8:26 But he who sent me is *r*,
2Ti 2: 2 witnesses entrust to *r* men who
will

RELIANCE* (RELY)
Pr 25:19 is *r* on the unfaithful in times

RELIED (RELY)
2Ch 13:18 were victorious because they *r*
16: 8 Yet when you *r* on the LORD,
Ps 71: 6 From birth I have *r* on you;

RELIEF
Job 35: 9 they plead for *r* from the arm
Ps 94:13 you grant him *r* from days
143: 1 come to my *r*.
La 3:49 without *r*,
3:56 to my cry for *r*."
2Th 1: 7 and give *r* to you who are
troubled,

RELIGION* (RELIGIOUS)
Ac 25:19 dispute with him about their
own *r*
26: 5 to the strictest sect of our *r*,
1Ti 5: 4 all to put their *r* into practice
Jas 1:26 himself and his *r* is worthless.
1:27 *R* that God our Father accepts

RELIGIOUS (RELIGION)
Jas 1:26 If anyone considers himself *r*

RELY (RELIABLE RELIANCE RELIED)
Isa 50:10 and *r* on his God.
Eze 33:26 you then possess the land? You *r*
2Co 1: 9 this happened that we might not *r*
Gal 3:10 All who *r* on observing the law are
1Jn 4:16 and *r* on the love God has for us.

REMAIN (REMAINS)
Nu 33:55 allow to *r* will become barbs
Ps 102:27 But you *r* the same,
Jn 1:32 from heaven as a dove and *r* on
him
15: 4 *R* in me, and I will *r* in you.
15: 7 If you *r* in me and my words
15: 9 Now *r* in my love.
Ro 13: 8 Let no debt *r* outstanding,
1Co 13:13 And now these three *r*: faith,
2Ti 2:13 he will *r* faithful,
Heb 1:11 They will perish, but you *r*;

1Jn 2:27 just as it has taught you, *r* in him.

REMAINS (REMAIN)
Ps 146: 6 the LORD, who *r* faithful forever.
Heb 7: 3 Son of God he *r* a priest forever.

REMEDY
Isa 3: 7 "I have no *r*.

REMEMBER (REMEMBERED REMEMBERS
REMEMBRANCE)
Ge 9:15 I will *r* my covenant between me
Ex 20: 8 "*R* the Sabbath day
33:13 *R* that this nation is your people."
Dt 5:15 *R* that you were slaves in Egypt
1Ch 16:12 *R* the wonders he has done,
Job 36:24 *R* to extol his work,
Ps 25: 6 *R*, O LORD, your great mercy
63: 6 On my bed I *r* you;
74: 2 *R* the people you purchased of
old,
77:11 I will *r* the deeds of the LORD;
Ecc 12: 1 *R* your Creator
Isa 46: 8 "*R* this, fix it in mind,
Jer 31:34 and will *r* their sins no more."
Hab 3: 2 in wrath *r* mercy.
Lk 1:72 and to *r* his holy covenant,
Gal 2:10 we should continue to *r* the poor,
Php 1: 3 I thank my God every time I *r* you.
2Ti 2: 8 *R* Jesus Christ, raised
Heb 8:12 and will *r* their sins no more."

REMEMBERED (REMEMBER)
Ex 2:24 he *r* his covenant with Abraham,
3:15 am to be *r* from generation
Ps 98: 3 He has *r* his love
106:45 for their sake he *r* his covenant
111: 4 He has caused his wonders to
be *r*;
136:23 to the One who *r* us
Isa 65:17 The former things will not be *r*,
Eze 18:22 offenses he has committed will
be *r*
33:13 things he has done will be *r*;

REMEMBERS (REMEMBER)
Ps 103:14 he *r* that we are dust.
111: 5 he *r* his covenant forever.
Isa 43:25 and your sins no more.

REMEMBRANCE (REMEMBER)
Lk 22:19 given for you; do this in *r* of me."
1Co 11:24 which is for you; do this in *r* of me
11:25 whenever you drink it, in *r* of me."

REMIND
Jn 14:26 will *r* you of everything I have said
2Pe 1:12 I will always *r* you of these things,

REMNANT
Ezr 9: 8 has been gracious in leaving us a *r*
Isa 11:11 time to reclaim the *r* that is left
Jer 23: 3 "I myself will gather the *r*
Zec 8:12 inheritance to the *r* of this people.
Ro 11: 5 the present time there is a *r*
chosen

REMOVED
Ps 30:11 you *r* my sackcloth and clothed
me
103:12 so far has he *r* our transgressions
Jn 20: 1 and saw that the stone had been *r*

REND
Joel 2:13 *R* your heart

RENEW (RENEWAL RENEWED RENEWING)
Ps 51:10 and *r* a steadfast spirit within me.
Isa 40:31 will *r* their strength.

RENEWAL (RENEW)
Isa 57:10 You found *r* of your strength,
Tit 3: 5 of rebirth and *r* by the Holy Spirit,

RENEWED (RENEW)
Ps 103: 5 that your youth is *r* like the
eagle's.
2Co 4:16 yet inwardly we are being *r* day

RENEWING* (RENEW)
Ro 12: 2 transformed by the *r* of your
mind.

RENOUNCE (RENOUNCED RENOUNCES)
Da 4:27 *R* your sins by doing what is right,

RENOUNCED (RENOUNCE)
2Co 4: 2 we have *r* secret and shameful

RENOUNCES (RENOUNCE)
Pr 28:13 confesses and *r* them finds

RENOWN*
Ge 6: 4 were the heroes of old, men of *r.*
Ps 102:12 *r* endures through all generations.
135:13 *r,* O LORD, through all
Isa 26: 8 your name and *r*
55:13 This will be for the LORD's *r,*
63:12 to gain for himself everlasting *r,*
Jer 13:11 to be my people for my *r* and praise
32:20 have gained the *r* that is still yours.
33: 9 Then this city will bring me *r,* joy,
49:25 the city of *r* not been abandoned.
Eze 26:17 How you are destroyed, O city of *r,*
Hos 12: 5 the LORD is his name of *r!*

REPAID (PAY)
Lk 6:34 to 'sinners,' expecting to be *r* in full
14:14 you will be *r* at the resurrection
Col 3:25 Anyone who does wrong will be *r*

REPAY (PAY)
Dt 7:10 But those who hate him he will *r*
32:35 It is mine to avenge; I will *r.*
Ru 2:12 May the LORD *r* you
Ps 103:10 or *r* us according to our iniquities.
116:12 How can I *r* the LORD
Jer 25:14 I will *r* them according
Ro 12:17 Do not *r* anyone evil for evil.
12:19 "It is mine to avenge; I will *r,"*
1Pe 3: 9 Do not *r* evil with evil

REPAYING (PAY)
2Ch 6:23 *r* the guilty by bringing
1Ti 5: 4 so *r* their parents and grandparents

REPEATED
Heb 10: 1 the same sacrifices *r* endlessly year

REPENT (REPENTANCE REPENTED REPENTS)
1Ki 8:47 *r* and plead with you in the land
Job 36:10 commands them to *r* of their evil.
42: 6 and *r* in dust and ashes."
Jer 15:19 "If you *r,* I will restore you
Eze 18:30 *R!* Turn away from all your
18:32 *R* and live! "Take up a lament
Mt 3: 2 "*R,* for the kingdom of heaven is
4:17 "*R,* for the kingdom of heaven is
Mk 6:12 and preached that people should *r.*
Lk 13: 3 unless you *r,* you too will all perish.
Ac 2:38 Peter replied, "*R* and be baptized,
3:19 *R,* then, and turn to God,
17:30 all people everywhere to *r.*
26:20 also, I preached that they should *r*
Rev 2: 5 *R* and do the things you did at first.

REPENTANCE (REPENT)
Isa 30:15 "In *r* and rest is your salvation,
Mt 3: 8 Produce fruit in keeping with *r.*
Mk 1: 4 a baptism of *r* for the forgiveness
Lk 3: 8 Produce fruit in keeping with *r.*
5:32 call the righteous, but sinners to *r.*"
24:47 and *r* and forgiveness of sins will be
Ac 20:21 that they must turn to God in *r*
26:20 and prove their *r* by their deeds.
Ro 2: 4 kindness leads you toward *r?*
2Co 7:10 Godly sorrow brings *r* that leads
2Pe 3: 9 but everyone to come to *r.*

REPENTED (REPENT)
Mt 11:21 they would have *r* long ago

REPENTS (REPENT)
Lk 15: 7 in heaven over one sinner who *r*
15:10 of God over one sinner who *r.*"
17: 3 rebuke him, and if he *r,* forgive him

REPORTS
Ex 23: 1 "Do not spread false *r.*

REPOSES*
Pr 14:33 Wisdom *r* in the heart

REPRESENTATION*
Heb 1: 3 and the exact *r* of his being,

REPROACH
Job 27: 6 my conscience will not *r* me
Isa 51: 7 Do not fear the *r* of men

1Ti 3: 2 Now the overseer must be above *r,*

REPUTATION
1Ti 3: 7 also have a good *r* with outsiders,

REQUESTS
Ps 20: 5 May the LORD grant all your *r.*
Php 4: 6 with thanksgiving, present your *r*

REQUIRE (REQUIRED REQUIRES)
Mic 6: 8 And what does the LORD *r* of you

REQUIRED (REQUIRE)
1Co 4: 2 it is *r* that those who have been

REQUIRES (REQUIRE)
1Ki 2: 3 what the LORD your God *r:*
Heb 9:22 the law *r* that nearly everything be

RESCUE (RESCUED RESCUES)
Ps 22: 8 let the LORD *r* him.
31: 2 come quickly to my *r;*
69:14 *R* me from the mire.
91:14 says the LORD, "I will *r* him;
143: 9 *R* me from my enemies, O LORD,
Da 6:20 been able to *r* you from the lions?"
Ro 7:24 Who will *r* me from this body
Gal 1: 4 himself for our sins to *r* us
2Pe 2: 9 how to *r* godly men from trials

RESCUED (RESCUE)
Ps 18:17 He *r* me from my powerful enemy,
Pr 11: 8 The righteous man is *r*
Col 1:13 For he has *r* us from the dominion

RESCUES (RESCUE)
Da 6:27 He *r* and he saves;
1Th 1:10 who *r* us from the coming wrath.

RESENT* (RESENTFUL RESENTS)
Pr 3:11 and do not *r* his rebuke,

RESENTFUL* (RESENT)
2Ti 2:24 to everyone, able to teach, not *r.*

RESENTS* (RESENT)
Pr 15:12 A mocker *r* correction;

RESERVE (RESERVED)
1Ki 19:18 Yet I *r* seven thousand in Israel—

RESERVED (RESERVE)
Ro 11: 4 "I have *r* for myself seven

RESIST (RESISTED RESISTS)
Da 11:32 know their God will firmly *r* him.
Mt 5:39 I tell you, Do not *r* an evil person.
Lk 21:15 of your adversaries will be able to *r*
Jas 4: 7 *R* the devil, and he will flee
1Pe 5: 9 *R* him, standing firm in the faith,

RESISTED (RESIST)
Job 9: 4 Who has *r* him and come out

RESISTS* (RESIST)
Ro 9:19 For who *r* his will?" But who are

RESOLVED
Ps 17: 3 I have *r* that my mouth will not sin.
Da 1: 8 But Daniel *r* not to defile himself
1Co 2: 2 For I *r* to know nothing while I was

RESOUNDING*
Ps 150: 5 praise him with *r* cymbals.
1Co 13: 1 I am only a *r* gong or a clanging

RESPECT (RESPECTABLE RESPECTED RESPECTS)
Lev 19: 3 " 'Each of you must *r* his mother
19:32 show *r* for the elderly and revere
Pr 11:16 A kindhearted woman gains *r,*
Mal 1: 6 where is the *r* due me?" says
Eph 5:33 and the wife must *r* her husband.
6: 5 obey your earthly masters with *r*
1Th 4:12 so that your daily life may win the *r*
5:12 to *r* those who work hard
1Ti 3: 4 children obey him with proper *r.*
3: 8 are to be men worthy of *r,* sincere,
3:11 are to be women worthy of *r,*
6: 1 their masters worthy of full *r,*
Tit 2: 2 worthy of *r,* self-controlled,
1Pe 2:17 Show proper *r* to everyone:
3: 7 them with *r* as the weaker partner
3:16 But do this with gentleness and *r,*

RESPECTABLE* (RESPECT)
1Ti 3: 2 self-controlled, *r,* hospitable,

RESPECTED (RESPECT)
Pr 31:23 Her husband is *r* at the city gate,

RESPECTS (RESPECT)
Pr 13:13 he who *r* a command is rewarded.

RESPLENDENT*
Ps 76: 4 You are *r* with light,
132:18 but the crown on his head will be *r*

RESPOND
Ps 102:17 He will *r* to the prayer
Hos 2:21 "I will *r* to the skies,

RESPONSIBILITY (RESPONSIBLE)
Ac 18: 6 your own heads! I am clear of my *r.*

RESPONSIBLE (RESPONSIBILITY)
Nu 1:53 The Levites are to be *r* for the care
1Co 7:24 Brothers, each man, as *r* to God,

REST (RESTED RESTS SABBATH-REST)
Ex 31:15 the seventh day is a Sabbath of *r,*
33:14 go with you, and I will give you *r.*"
Lev 25: 5 The land is to have a year of *r.*
Dt 31:16 going to *r* with your fathers,
Jos 14:15 Then the land had *r* from war.
21:44 The LORD gave them *r*
1Ki 5: 4 The LORD my god has given me *r*
1Ch 22: 9 who will be a man of peace and *r,*
Job 3:17 and there the weary are at *r.*
Ps 16: 9 my body also will *r* secure,
33:22 May your unfailing love *r* upon us,
62: 1 My soul finds *r* in God alone;
62: 5 Find *r,* O my soul, in God alone;
90:17 of the LORD our God *r* upon us;
91: 1 will *r* in the shadow
95:11 "They shall never enter my *r.*"
Pr 6:10 a little folding of the hands to *r*—
Isa 11: 2 Spirit of the LORD will *r* on him—
11:10 and his place of *r* will be glorious.
30:15 "In repentance and *r* is your
32:18 in undisturbed places of *r.*
57:20 which cannot *r,*
Jer 6:16 and you will find *r* for your souls.
47: 6 'how long till you *r?*
Mt 11:28 and burdened, and I will give you *r.*
2Co 12: 9 so that Christ's power may *r* on me
Heb 3:11 'They shall never enter my *r.*'"
4: 3 'They shall never enter my *r.*'"
4:10 for anyone who enters God's *r*
Rev 14:13 "they will *r* from their labor,

RESTED (REST)
Ge 2: 2 so on the seventh day he *r*
Heb 4: 4 "And on the seventh day God *r*

RESTITUTION
Ex 22: 3 "A thief must certainly make *r,*
Lev 6: 5 He must make *r* in full, add a fifth
Nu 5: 8 the *r* belongs to the LORD

RESTORE (RESTORES)
Ps 51:12 *R* to me the joy of your salvation
80: 3 *R* us, O God;
126: 4 *R* our fortunes, O LORD,
Jer 31:18 *R* me, and I will return,
La 5:21 *R* us to yourself, O LORD,
Da 9:25 From the issuing of the decree to *r*
Na 2: 2 The LORD will *r* the splendor
Gal 6: 1 are spiritual should *r* him gently.
1Pe 5:10 will himself *r* you and make you

RESTORES (RESTORE)
Ps 23: 3 he *r* my soul.

RESTRAINED (RESTRAINT)
Ps 78:38 Time after time he *r* his anger

RESTRAINING (RESTRAINT)
Pr 27:16 *r* her is like *r* the wind
Col 2:23 value in *r* sensual indulgence.

RESTRAINT (RESTRAINED RESTRAINING)
Pr 17:27 of knowledge uses words with *r,*
23: 4 have the wisdom to show *r.*
29:18 no revelation, the people cast off *r;*

RESTS (REST)
Dt 33:12 and the one the LORD loves *r*
Pr 19:23 one *r* content, untouched
Lk 2:14 to men on whom his favor *r.*"

RESULT

Lk	21:13	This will *r* in your being witnesses
Ro	6:22	to holiness, and the *r* is eternal life.
	11:31	as a *r* of God's mercy to you.
2Co	3: 3	from Christ, the *r* of our ministry,
2Th	1: 5	as a *r* you will be counted worthy
1Pe	1: 7	may be proved genuine and may *r*

RESURRECTION*

Mt	22:23	who say there is no *r,* came to him
	22:28	at the *r,* whose wife will she be
	22:30	At the *r* people will neither marry
	22:31	But about the *r* of the dead—
	27:53	and after Jesus' *r* they went
Mk	12:18	who say there is no *r,* came to him
	12:23	At the *r* whose wife will she be,
Lk	14:14	repaid at the *r* of the righteous."
	20:27	who say there is no *r,* came to Jesus
	20:33	at the *r* whose wife will she be,
	20:35	in the *r* from the dead will neither
	20:36	since they are children of the *r.*
Jn	11:24	again in the *r* at the last day."
	11:25	Jesus said to her, "I am the *r*
Ac	1:22	become a witness with us of his *r.*
	2:31	he spoke of the *r* of the Christ,
	4: 2	in Jesus the *r* of the dead.
	4:33	to testify to the *r* of the Lord Jesus,
	17:18	good news about Jesus and the *r.*
	17:32	When they heard about the *r*
	23: 6	of my hope in the *r* of the dead."
	23: 8	Sadducees say that there is no *r,*
	24:15	that there will be a *r*
	24:21	'It is concerning the *r*
Ro	1: 4	Son of God by his *r* from the dead:
	6: 5	also be united with him in his *r.*
1Co	15:12	some of you say that there is no *r*
	15:13	If there is no *r* of the dead,
	15:21	the *r* of the dead comes
	15:29	if there is no *r,* what will those do
	15:42	So will it be with the *r* of the dead.
Php	3:10	power of his *r* and the fellowship
	3:11	to attain to the *r* from the dead.
2Ti	2:18	say that the *r* has already taken
Heb	6: 2	on of hands, the *r* of the dead,
	11:35	so that they might gain a better *r.*
1Pe	1: 3	hope through the *r* of Jesus Christ
	3:21	It saves you by the *r* of Jesus Christ
Rev	20: 5	This is the first *r.*
	20: 6	those who have part in the first *r.*

RETALIATE*

1Pe	2:23	he did not *r;* when he suffered,

RETRIBUTION

Ps	69:22	may it become *r* and a trap.
Jer	51:56	For the LORD is a God of *r;*
Ro	11: 9	a stumbling block and a *r* for them.

RETURN (RETURNED RETURNS)

Ge	3:19	and to dust you will *r.*"
2Sa	12:23	go to him, but he will not *r* to me."
2Ch	30: 9	If you *r* to the LORD, then your
Ne	1: 9	but if you *r* to me and obey my
Job	10:21	joy before I go to the place of no *r,*
	16:22	before I go on the journey of no *r.*
	22:23	If you *r* to the Almighty, you will
Ps	80:14	*R* to us, O God Almighty!
	126: 6	will *r* with songs of joy,
Isa	10:21	A remnant will *r,* a remnant
	35:10	the ransomed of the LORD will *r.*
	55:11	It will not *r* to me empty,
Jer	24: 7	for they will *r* to me
	31: 8	a great throng will *r.*
La	3:40	and let us *r* to the LORD.
Hos	6: 1	"Come, let us *r* to the LORD.
	12: 6	But you must *r* to your God;
	14: 1	*R,* O Israel, to the LORD your
Joel	2:12	"*r* to me with all your heart,
Zec	1: 3	'*R* to me,' declares the LORD
	10: 9	and they will *r.*

RETURNED (RETURN)

Ps	35:13	When my prayers *r*
Am	4: 6	yet you have not *r* to me,"
1Pe	2:25	now you have *r* to the Shepherd

RETURNS (RETURN)

Pr	3:14	and yields better *r* than gold.
Isa	52: 8	When the LORD *r* to Zion,
Mt	24:46	finds him doing so when he *r.*

REUBEN

Firstborn of Jacob by Leah (Ge 29:32; 46:8; 1Ch 2:1). Attempted to rescue Joseph (Ge 37:21–30). Lost birthright for sleeping with Bilhah (Ge 35:22; 49:4). Tribe of blessed (Ge 49:3–4; Dt 33:6), numbered (Nu 1:21; 26:7), allotted land east of Jordan (Nu 32; 34:14; Jos 13:15), west (Eze 48:6), failed to help Deborah (Jdg 5:15–16), supported David (1Ch 12:37), 12,000 from (Rev 7:5).

REVEAL (REVEALED REVEALS REVELATION REVELATIONS)

Mt	11:27	to whom the Son chooses to *r* him.
Gal	1:16	was pleased to *r* his Son in me

REVEALED (REVEAL)

Dt	29:29	but the things *r* belong to us
Isa	40: 5	the glory of the LORD will be *r,*
	43:12	I have *r* and saved and proclaimed
	53: 1	the arm of the LORD been *r?*
	65: 1	I *r* myself to those who did not ask
Mt	11:25	and *r* them to little children.
Jn	12:38	the arm of the Lord been *r?*"
	17: 6	"I have *r* you to those whom you
Ro	1:17	a righteousness from God is *r,*
	8:18	with the glory that will be *r* in us.
	10:20	I *r* myself to those who did not ask
	16:26	but now *r* and made known
1Co	2:10	but God has *r* it to us by his Spirit.
2Th	1: 7	happen when the Lord Jesus is *r*
	2: 3	and the man of lawlessness is *r,*
1Pe	1: 5	and honor when Jesus Christ is *r.*
	1:20	but was *r* in these last times
	4:13	overjoyed when his glory is *r.*

REVEALS* (REVEAL)

Nu	23: 3	Whatever he *r* to me I will tell you
Job	12:22	He *r* the deep things of darkness
Da	2:22	He *r* deep and hidden things;
	2:28	a God in heaven who *r* mysteries.
Am	4:13	and *r* his thoughts to man,

REVELATION* (REVEAL)

2Sa	7:17	David all the words of this entire *r.*
1Ch	17:15	David all the words of this entire *r.*
Pr	29:18	Where there is no *r,* the people cast
Da	10: 1	a *r* was given to Daniel (who was
Hab	2: 2	"Write down the *r*
	2: 3	For the *r* awaits an appointed time;
Lk	2:32	a light for *r* to the Gentiles
Ro	16:25	according to the *r*
1Co	14: 6	I bring you some *r* or knowledge
	14:26	a *r,* a tongue or an interpretation.
	14:30	And if a *r* comes to someone who is
Gal	1:12	I received it by *r* from Jesus Christ.
	2: 1	I went in response to a *r*
Eph	1:17	you the Spirit of wisdom and *r,*
	3: 3	mystery made known to me by *r,*
Rev	1: 1	of Jesus Christ, which God gave

REVELATIONS* (REVEAL)

2Co	12: 1	on to visions and *r* from the Lord.
	12: 7	of these surpassingly great *r,*

REVELED* (REVELRY)

Ne	9:25	they *r* in your great goodness.

REVELRY (REVELED)

Ex	32: 6	drink and got up to indulge in *r.*
1Co	10: 7	and got up to indulge in pagan *r.*"

REVENGE (VENGEANCE)

Lev	19:18	"'Do not seek *r* or bear a grudge
Ro	12:19	Do not take *r,* my friends,

REVERE* (REVERENCE REVERENT REVERING)

Lev	19:32	for the elderly and *r* your God.
Dt	4:10	so that they may learn to *r* me
	13: 4	must follow, and him you must *r.*
	14:23	to *r* the LORD your God always.
	17:19	learn to *r* the LORD his God
	28:58	and do not *r* this glorious
Job	37:24	Therefore, men *r* him,
Ps	22:23	*R* him, all you descendants
	33: 8	let all the people of the world *r* him
	102:15	of the earth will *r* your glory.

Ecc	3:14	God does it so that men will *r* him.
Isa	25: 3	cities of ruthless nations will *r* you.
	59:19	of the sun, they will *r* his glory.
	63:17	hearts so we do not *r* you?
Jer	10: 7	Who should not *r* you,
Hos	10: 3	because we did not *r* the LORD.
Mal	4: 2	But for you who *r* my name,

REVERENCE (REVERE)

Lev	19:30	and have *r* for my sanctuary.
Ne	5:15	of *r* for God I did not act like that.
Ps	5: 7	in *r* will I bow down
Da	6:26	people must fear and *r* the God
2Co	7: 1	perfecting holiness out of *r* for God
Eph	5:21	to one another out of *r* for Christ.
Col	3:22	of heart and *r* for the Lord.
1Pe	3: 2	when they see the purity and *r*
Rev	11:18	and those who *r* your name,

REVERENT* (REVERE)

Ecc	8:12	with God-fearing men, who are *r*
Tit	2: 3	women to be *r* in the way they live,
Heb	5: 7	because of his *r* submission.
1Pe	1:17	as strangers here in *r* fear.

REVERING* (REVERE)

Dt	8: 6	walking in his ways and *r* him.
Ne	1:11	who delight in *r* your name.

REVERSE*

Isa	43:13	When I act, who can *r* it?"

REVIVE* (REVIVING)

Ps	80:18	*r* us, and we will call on your name.
	85: 6	Will you not *r* us again,
Isa	57:15	and to *r* the heart of the contrite.
	57:15	to *r* the spirit of the lowly
Hos	6: 2	After two days he will *r* us;

REVIVING* (REVIVE)

Ps	19: 7	*r* the soul.

REVOKED

Isa	45:23	a word that will not be *r:*

REWARD (REWARDED REWARDING REWARDS)

Ge	15: 1	your very great *r.*"
1Sa	24:19	May the LORD *r* you well
Ps	19:11	in keeping them there is great *r.*
	62:12	Surely you will *r* each person
	127: 3	children a *r* from him.
Pr	25: 2	are wise, your wisdom will *r* you;
	11:18	sows righteousness reaps a sure *r.*
	13:21	prosperity is the *r* of the righteous.
	19:17	he will *r* him for what he has done.
	25:22	and the LORD will *r* you.
	31:31	Give her the *r* she has earned,
Isa	40:10	See, his *r* is with him,
	49: 4	and my *r* is with my God."
	61: 8	In my faithfulness I will *r* them
	62:11	See, his *r* is with him,
Jer	17:10	to *r* a man according to his conduct
	32:19	you *r* everyone according
Mt	5:12	because great is your *r* in heaven,
	6: 1	you will have no *r*
	6: 5	they have received their *r* in full.
	10:41	a prophet will receive a prophet's *r,*
	16:27	and then he will *r* each person
Lk	6:23	because great is your *r* in heaven.
	6:35	Then your *r* will be great,
1Co	3:14	built survives, he will receive his *r.*
Eph	6: 8	know that the Lord will *r* everyone
Col	3:24	an inheritance from the Lord as a *r.*
Heb	11:26	he was looking ahead to his *r.*
Rev	22:12	I am coming soon! My *r* is with me

REWARDED (REWARD)

Ru	2:12	May you be richly *r* by the LORD,
2Sa	22:21	of my hands he has *r* me.
2Ch	15: 7	for your work will be *r.*"
Ps	18:24	The LORD has *r* me according
Pr	13:13	he who respects a command is *r.*
	14:14	and the good man *r* for his.
Jer	31:16	for your work will be *r,*"
1Co	3: 8	and each will be *r* according
Heb	10:35	your confidence; it will be richly *r.*

2Jn : 8 but that you may be *r* fully.

REWARDING* (REWARD)
Rev 11:18 for *r* your servants the prophets

REWARDS (REWARD)
1Sa 26:23 The LORD *r* every man
Pr 12:14 the work of his hands *r* him.
Heb 11: 6 that he *r* those who earnestly seek

RIBS
Ge 2:21 he took one of the man's *r*

RICH (RICHES RICHEST)
Job 34:19 does not favor the *r* over the poor,
Ps 49:16 overawed when a man grows *r*,
145: 8 slow to anger and in love.
Pr 21:17 loves wine and oil will never be *r*.
22: 2 *R* and poor have this in common:
23: 4 Do not wear yourself out to get *r*;
28: 6 than a *r* man whose ways are
28:20 to get *r* will not go unpunished.
28:22 A stingy man is eager to get *r*
Ecc 5:12 but the abundance of a *r* man
Isa 33: 6 a *r* store of salvation and wisdom
53: 9 and with the *r* in his death,
Jer 9:23 or the *r* man boast of his riches,
Zec 9: 4 and I will put *r* garments on you."
Mt 19:23 it is hard for a *r* man
Lk 1:53 but has sent the *r* away empty.
6:24 "But woe to you who are *r*,
12:21 for himself but is not *r* toward God
16: 1 "There was a *r* man whose
21: 1 Jesus saw the *r* putting their gifts
2Co 6:10 yet making many *r*; having nothing
8: 2 poverty welled up in *r* generosity.
8: 9 he was *r*, yet for your sakes he
9:11 You will be made *r* in every way
Eph 2: 4 love for us, God, who is *r* in mercy,
1Ti 6: 9 want to get *r* fall into temptation
6:17 Command those who are *r*
6:18 to do good, to be *r* in good deeds,
Jas 1:10 the one who is *r* should take pride
2: 5 the eyes of the world to be *r* in faith
5: 1 you *r* people, weep and wail
Rev 2: 9 and your poverty—yet you are *r*!
3:18 you can become *r*; and white

RICHES (RICH)
Job 36:18 that no one entices you by *r*;
Ps 49: 6 and boast of their great *r*?
49:12 despite his *r*, does not endure;
62:10 though your *r* increase,
119:14 as one rejoices in great *r*.
Pr 3:16 in her left hand are *r* and honor.
11:28 Whoever trusts in his *r* will fall,
22: 1 is more desirable than great *r*;
27:24 for *r* do not endure forever,
30: 8 give me neither poverty nor *r*,
Isa 10: 3 Where will you leave your *r*?
60: 5 to you the *r* of the nations will
Jer 9:23 or the rich man boast of his *r*,
Lk 8:14 *r* and pleasures, and they do not
Ro 9:23 to make the *r* of his glory known
11:33 the depth of the *r* of the wisdom
Eph 2: 7 he might show the incomparable *r*
3: 8 to the Gentiles the unsearchable *r*
Col 1:27 among the Gentiles the glorious *r*
2: 2 so that they may have the full *r*

RICHEST (RICH)
Isa 55: 2 and your soul will delight in the *r*

RID
Ge 21:10 "Get *r* of that slave woman
1Co 5: 7 Get *r* of the old yeast that you may
Gal 4:30 "Get *r* of the slave woman

RIDE (RIDER RIDING)
Ps 45: 4 In your majesty *r* forth victoriously

RIDER (RIDE)
Rev 6: 2 was a white horse! Its *r* held a bow,
19:11 whose *r* is called Faithful and True.

RIDING (RIDE)
Zec 9: 9 gentle and *r* on a donkey,
Mt 21: 5 gentle and *r* on a donkey,

RIGGING
Isa 33:23 Your *r* hangs loose:

RIGHT (RIGHTS)
Ge 4: 7 But if you do not do what is *r*,
18:19 of the LORD by doing what is *r*
18:25 the Judge of all the earth do *r*?"
48:13 on his left toward Israel's *r* hand,
Ex 15: 6 Your *r* hand, O LORD,
15:26 and do what is *r* in his eyes,
Dt 5:32 do not turn aside to the *r*
6:18 Do what is *r* and good
13:18 and doing what is *r* in his eyes.
Jos 1: 7 do not turn from it to the *r*
1Sa 12:23 you the way that is good and *r*.
1Ki 3: 9 to distinguish between *r* and wrong
15: 5 For David had done what was *r*
2Ki 7: 9 to each other, "We're not doing *r*.
Ne 9:13 and laws that are just and *r*,
Ps 16: 8 Because he is at my *r* hand,
16:11 eternal pleasures at your *r* hand.
17: 7 you who save by your *r* hand
18:35 and your *r* hand sustains me;
19: 8 The precepts of the LORD are *r*,
25: 9 He guides the humble in what is *r*
33: 4 For the word of the LORD is *r*
44: 3 it was your *r* hand, your arm,
45: 4 let your *r* hand display awesome
51: 4 so that you are proved *r*
63: 8 your *r* hand upholds me.
73:23 you hold me by my *r* hand.
91: 7 ten thousand at your *r* hand,
98: 1 his *r* hand and his holy arm
106: 3 who constantly do what is *r*.
110: 1 "Sit at my *r* hand
118:15 LORD's *r* hand has done mighty
119:144 Your statutes are forever *r*;
137: 5 may my *r* hand forget its skill.
139:10 your *r* hand will hold me fast.
Pr 1: 3 doing what is *r* and just and fair;
4:27 Do not swerve to the *r* or the left;
14:12 There is a way that seems *r*
18:17 The first to present his case seems *r*
Ecc 7:20 who does what is *r* and never sins.
SS 1: 4 How *r* they are to adore you!
Isa 1:17 learn to do *r*!
7:15 reject the wrong and choose the *r*.
30:10 us no more visions of what is *r*!
30:21 Whether you turn to the *r*
41:10 you with my righteous *r* hand.
41:13 who takes hold of your *r* hand
48:13 my *r* hand spread out the heavens;
64: 5 to the help of those who gladly do *r*
Jer 23: 5 and do what is just and *r* in the land
Eze 18: 5 who does what is just and *r*.
18:21 and does what is just and *r*,
33:14 and does what is just and *r*—
Hos 14: 9 The ways of the LORD are *r*;
Mt 5:29 If your *r* eye causes you to sin,
6: 3 know what your *r* hand is doing,
22:44 "Sit at my *r* hand
25:33 He will put the sheep on his *r*
Jn 1:12 he gave the *r* to become children
Ac 2:34 "Sit at my *r* hand
7:55 Jesus standing at the *r* hand of God
Ro 4: 2 "So that you may be proved *r*
8:34 is at the *r* hand of God and is
9:21 Does not the potter have the *r*
12:17 careful to do what is *r* in the eyes
1Co 9: 4 Don't we have the *r* to food
2Co 8:21 we are taking pains to do what is *r*,
Eph 1:20 and seated him at his *r* hand
6: 1 parents in the Lord, for this is *r*.
Php 4: 8 whatever is *r*, whatever is pure,
2Th 3:13 never tire of doing what is *r*.
Heb 1: 3 down at the *r* hand of the Majesty
Jas 2: 8 as yourself," you are doing *r*.
1Pe 3:14 if you should suffer for what is *r*,
1Jn 2:29 who does what is *r* has been born
Rev 2: 7 I will give the *r* to eat from the tree
3:21 I will give the *r* to sit with me
22:11 let him who does *r* continue to do *r*

RIGHTEOUS (RIGHTEOUSLY RIGHTEOUSNESS)
Ge 6: 9 Noah was a *r* man, blameless
18:23 "Will you sweep away the *r*
Nu 23:10 Let me die the death of the *r*,
Ne 9: 8 your promise because you are *r*.
Job 36: 7 He does not take his eyes off the *r*;
Ps 1: 5 nor sinners in the assembly of the *r*.
5:12 O LORD, you bless the *r*;
11: 7 For the LORD is *r*,
15: 2 and who does what is *r*,
34:15 The eyes of the LORD are on the *r*
37:16 Better the little that the *r* have
37:21 but the *r* give generously;
37:25 yet I have never seen the *r* forsaken
37:30 of the *r* man utters wisdom,
55:22 he will never let the *r* fall.
64:10 Let the *r* rejoice in the LORD
68: 3 But may the *r* be glad
112: 4 compassionate and *r* man.
118:20 through which the *r* may enter.
119: 7 as I learn your *r* laws.
119:137 *R* are you, O LORD,
140:13 Surely the *r* will praise your name
143: 2 for no one living is *r* before you.
145:17 The LORD is *r* in all his ways
Pr 3:33 but he blesses the home of the *r*.
4:18 of the *r* is like the first gleam
10: 7 of the *r* will be a blessing,
10:11 The mouth of the *r* is a fountain
10:16 The wages of the *r* bring them life,
10:20 The tongue of the *r* is choice silver,
10:24 what the *r* desire will be granted.
10:28 The prospect of the *r* is joy,
10:32 of the *r* know what is fitting,
11:23 The desire of the *r* ends only
11:30 The fruit of the *r* is a tree of life,
12:10 A *r* man cares for the needs
12:21 No harm befalls the *r*,
13: 9 The light of the *r* shines brightly,
15:28 of the *r* weighs its answers,
15:29 but he hears the prayer of the *r*.
16:31 it is attained by a *r* life.
18:10 the *r* run to it and are safe.
20: 7 The *r* man leads a blameless life;
21:15 justice is done, it brings joy to the *r*
23:24 The father of a *r* man has great joy;
28: 1 but the *r* are as bold as a lion.
29: 6 but a *r* one can sing and be glad.
29: 7 The *r* care about justice
29:27 The *r* detest the dishonest;
Ecc 7:20 There is not a *r* man on earth
Isa 26: 7 The path of the *r* is level;
41:10 you with my *r* right hand.
45:21 a *r* God and a Savior;
53:11 his knowledge my *r* servant will
64: 6 and all our *r* acts are like filthy rags
Jer 23: 5 up to David a *r* Branch,
Eze 3:20 when a *r* man turns
18: 5 "Suppose there is a *r* man
18:20 of the *r* man will be credited
33:12 The *r* man, if he sins, will not be
Da 9:18 requests of you because we are *r*,
Hab 2: 4 but the *r* will live by his faith—
Zec 9: 9 *r* and having salvation,
Mal 3:18 see the distinction between the *r*
Mt 5:45 rain on the *r* and the unrighteous.
9:13 For I have not come to call the *r*,
10:41 and anyone who receives a *r* man
13:43 Then the *r* will shine like the sun
13:49 and separate the wicked from the *r*
25:37 "Then the *r* will answer him, 'Lord,
25:46 to eternal punishment, but the *r*
Ac 24:15 will be a resurrection of both the *r*
Ro 1:17 as it is written: "The *r* will live
2: 5 when his judgment will be
2:13 the law who will be declared *r*.
3:10 "There is no one *r*, not even one;
3:20 Therefore no one will be declared *r*
5:19 one man the many will be made *r*.
Gal 3:11 because, "The *r* will live by faith."
1Ti 1: 9 that law is made not for the *r*

2Ti 4: 8 which the Lord, the *r* Judge,
Tit 3: 5 because of *r* things we had done,
Heb 10:38 But my *r* one will live by faith.
Jas 5:16 The prayer of a *r* man is powerful
1Pe 3:12 the eyes of the Lord are on the *r*
     3:18 the *r* for the unrighteous,
     4:18 "If it is hard for the *r* to be saved,
1Jn 2: 1 defense—Jesus Christ, the *R* One.
     3: 7 does what is right is *r*, just as he
            is *r*.
Rev 19: 8 stands for the *r* acts of the saints.)

RIGHTEOUSLY* (RIGHTEOUS)
Ps   9: 4 on your throne, judging *r*.
Isa 33:15 He who walks *r*
Jer 11:20 Lord Almighty, you who judge *r*

RIGHTEOUSNESS (RIGHTEOUS)
Ge 15: 6 and he credited it to him as *r*.
Dt   9: 4 of this land because of my *r*."
1Sa 26:23 Lord rewards every man for his *r*
1Ki 10: 9 to maintain justice and *r*."
Job 37:23 great *r*, he does not oppress.
Ps   7:17 to the Lord because of his *r*
     9: 8 He will judge the world in *r*;
    17:15 And I—in *r* I will see your face;
    23: 3 He guides me in paths of *r*
    33: 5 The Lord loves *r* and justice.
    35:28 My tongue will speak of your *r*
    36: 6 Your *r* is like the mighty
    37: 6 He will make your *r* shine like
    40: 9 I proclaim *r* in the great assembly;
    45: 4 in behalf of truth, humility and *r*;
    45: 7 You love *r* and hate wickedness;
    48:10 your right hand is filled with *r*.
    65: 5 us with awesome deeds of *r*,
    71: 2 Rescue me and deliver me in
            your *r*
    71:15 My mouth will tell of your *r*,
    71:19 Your *r* reaches to the skies,
            O God,
    85:10 *r* and peace kiss each other.
    89:14 *R* and justice are the foundation
    96:13 He will judge the world in *r*
    98: 9 He will judge the world in *r*
   103: 6 The Lord works *r*
   103:17 his *r* with their children's children
   106:31 This was credited to him as *r*
   111: 3 and his *r* endures forever.
   118:19 Open for me the gates of *r*;
   132: 9 May your priests be clothed
            with *r*;
   145: 7 and joyfully sing of your *r*.
Pr 11: 5 *r* of the blameless makes a
            straight
    11:18 he who sows *r* reaps a sure
            reward.
    13: 6 *R* guards the man of integrity,
    14:34 *R* exalts a nation,
    16: 8 Better a little with *r*
    16:12 a throne is established through *r*.
    21:21 He who pursues *r* and love
Isa 5:16 will show himself holy by his *r*.
     9: 7 it with justice and *r*
    11: 4 but with *r* he will judge the needy,
    16: 5 and speeds the cause of *r*.
    26: 9 the people of the world learn *r*.
    32:17 The fruit of *r* will be peace;
    42: 6 "I, the Lord, have called you in *r*;
    42:21 the Lord for the sake of his *r*
    45: 8 "You heavens above, rain down *r*;
    51: 1 "Listen to me, you who pursue *r*
    51: 6 my *r* will never fail.
    51: 8 But my *r* will last forever,
    58: 8 then your *r* will go before you,
    59:17 He put on *r* as his breastplate,
    61:10 and arrayed me in a robe of *r*,
    63: 1 "It is I, speaking in *r*,
Jer 9:24 justice and *r* on earth,
    23: 6 The Lord Our *R*.
Eze 3:20 a righteous man turns from his *r*
    14:20 save only themselves by their *r*.
    18:20 The *r* of the righteous man will be
    33:12 *r* of the righteous man will not
            save
Da   9:24 to bring in everlasting *r*,
    12: 3 and those who lead many to *r*,
Hos 10:12 Sow for yourselves in *r*,
Am   5:24 *r* like a never-failing stream!
Mic 7: 9 I will see his *r*.
Zep 2: 3 Seek *r*, seek humility;
Mal 4: 2 the sun of *r* will rise with healing

Mt   5: 6 those who hunger and thirst for *r*,
     5:10 who are persecuted because of *r*,
     5:20 unless your *r* surpasses that
     6: 1 to do your 'acts of *r*' before men,
     6:33 But seek first his kingdom and
            his *r*
Jn 16: 8 world of guilt in regard to sin
            and *r*
Ac 24:25 Paul discoursed on *r*, self-control
Ro   1:17 For in the gospel a *r* from God is
     3: 5 brings out God's *r* more clearly,
     3:22 This *r* from God comes
     4: 3 and it was credited to him as *r*."
     4: 5 wicked, his faith is credited as *r*.
     4: 6 man to whom God credits *r* apart
     4: 9 faith was credited to him as *r*.
     4:13 through the *r* that comes by faith.
     4:22 why "it was credited to him as *r*."
     5:18 of *r* was justification that brings
            life
     6:13 body to him as instruments of *r*.
     6:16 or to obedience, which leads to *r*?
     6:18 and have become slaves to *r*.
     6:19 in slavery to *r* leading to holiness.
     8:10 yet your spirit is alive because
            of *r*.
     9:30 did not pursue *r*, have obtained it,
    10: 3 they did not know the *r* that
            comes
    14:17 but of *r*, peace and joy
1Co 1:30 our *r*, holiness and redemption.
2Co 3: 9 is the ministry that brings *r*!
     5:21 that in him we might become
            the *r*
     6: 7 with weapons of *r* in the right
            hand
     6:14 For what do *r* and wickedness
            have
     9: 9 his *r* endures forever."
Gal 2:21 for if *r* could be gained
     3: 6 and it was credited to him as *r*."
     3:21 then *r* would certainly have come
Eph 4:24 created to be like God in true *r*
     5: 9 *r* and truth) and find out what
     6:14 with the breastplate of *r* in place,
Php 1:11 filled with the fruit of *r* that comes
     3: 6 as for legalistic *r*, faultless.
     3: 9 not having a *r* of my own that
1Ti 6:11 and pursue *r*, godliness, faith,
            love,
2Ti 2:22 and pursue *r*, faith, love and
            peace,
     3:16 correcting and training in *r*,
     4: 8 is in store for me the crown of *r*,
Heb 1: 8 and *r* will be the scepter
     5:13 with the teaching about *r*.
     7: 2 his name means "king of *r*";
    11: 7 became heir of the *r* that comes
    12:11 it produces a harvest of *r*
Jas 2:23 and it was credited to him as *r*,"
     3:18 sow in peace raise a harvest of *r*.
1Pe 2:24 die to sins and live for *r*;
2Pe 2:21 not to have known the way of *r*,
     3:13 and a new earth, the home of *r*.

RIGHTS (RIGHT)
Ps 82: 3 maintain the *r* of the poor
Pr 31: 8 for the *r* of all who are destitute.
Isa 10: 2 to deprive the poor of their *r*
La   3:35 to deny a man his *r*
Gal 4: 5 that we might receive the full *r*

RING
Pr 11:22 Like a gold *r* in a pig's snout
Lk 15:22 Put a *r* on his finger and sandals

RIOTS
2Co 6: 5 imprisonments and *r*; in hard
            work,

RIPE
Joel 3:13 for the harvest is *r*.
Am   8: 1 showed me: a basket of *r* fruit.
Jn   4:35 at the fields! They are *r* for
            harvest.
Rev 14:15 for the harvest of the earth is *r*."

RISE (RAISE RAISED RISEN ROSE)
Lev 19:32 " '*R* in the presence of the aged,
Nu 24:17 a scepter will *r* out of Israel.
Isa 26:19 their bodies will *r*.
Mal 4: 2 of righteousness will *r* with
            healing
Mt 27:63 'After three days I will *r* again.'

Mk   8:31 and after three days *r* again.
Lk 18:33 On the third day he will *r* again."
Jn   5:29 those who have done good will *r*
    20: 9 had to *r* from the dead.
Ac 17: 3 had to suffer and *r* from the dead.
1Th 4:16 and the dead in Christ will *r* first.

RISEN (RISE)
Mt 28: 6 He is not here; he has *r*, just
Mk 16: 6 He has *r*! He is not here.
Lk 24:34 The Lord has *r* and has appeared

RIVER (RIVERS)
Ps 46: 4 There is a *r* whose streams make
Isa 66:12 "I will extend peace to her like a *r*,
Eze 47:12 grow on both banks of the *r*.
Rev 22: 1 Then the angel showed me the *r*

RIVERS (RIVER)
Ps 137: 1 By the *r* of Babylon we sat

ROAD (CROSSROADS ROADS)
Mt   7:13 and broad is the *r* that leads

ROADS (ROAD)
Lk   3: 5 crooked *r* shall become straight,

ROARING
1Pe 5: 8 prowls around like a *r* lion looking

ROB (ROBBERS ROBBERY ROBS)
Mal 3: 8 "Will a man *r* God? Yet you *r* me.

ROBBERS (ROB)
Jer 7:11 become a den of *r* to you?
Mk 15:27 They crucified two *r* with him,
Lk 19:46 but you have made it 'a den
            of *r*.' "
Jn 10: 8 came before me were thieves
            and *r*,

ROBBERY (ROB)
Isa 61: 8 I hate *r* and iniquity,

ROBE (ROBED ROBES)
Ge 37: 3 and he made a richly
            ornamented *r*
Isa 6: 1 the train of his *r* filled the temple.
    61:10 arrayed me in a *r* of
            righteousness,
Rev 6:11 each of them was given a white *r*,

ROBED (ROBE)
Ps 93: 1 the Lord is *r* in majesty
Isa 63: 1 Who is this, *r* in splendor,

ROBES (ROBE)
Ps 45: 8 All your *r* are fragrant with myrrh
Rev 7:13 "These in white *r*— who are they,

ROBS* (ROB)
Pr 19:26 He who *r* his father and drives out
    28:24 He who *r* his father or mother

ROCK
Ge 49:24 of the Shepherd, the *R* of Israel,
Ex 17: 6 Strike the *r*, and water will come
Nu 20: 8 Speak to that *r* before their eyes
Dt 32: 4 He is the *R*, his works are perfect,
    32:13 him with honey from the *r*,
2Sa 22: 2 "The Lord is my *r*, my fortress
Ps 18: 2 The Lord is my *r*, my fortress
    19:14 O Lord, my *R* and my Redeemer
    40: 2 he set my feet on a *r*
    61: 2 lead me to the *r* that is higher
    92:15 he is my *R*, there is no
Isa 26: 4 the Lord, is the *R* eternal.
    51: 1 to the *r* from which you were cut
Da   2:34 you were watching, a *r* was cut
            out,
Mt   7:24 man who built his house on the *r*.
    16:18 and on this *r* I will build my
            church
Ro   9:33 and a *r* that makes them fall,
1Co 10: 4 the spiritual *r* that accompanied
1Pe 2: 8 and a *r* that makes them fall."

ROD (RODS)
2Sa 7:14 I will punish him with the *r* of
            men,
Ps 23: 4 your *r* and your staff,
Pr 13:24 He who spares the *r* hates his son,
    22:15 the *r* of discipline will drive it far
    23:13 if you punish him with the *r*,
    29:15 *r* of correction imparts wisdom,
Isa 11: 4 the earth with the *r* of his mouth;

RODS (ROD)
2Co 11:25 Three times I was beaten with *r*,

ROLL (ROLLED)
Mk 16: 3 "Who will *r* the stone away

ROLLED (ROLL)
Lk 24: 2 They found the stone *r* away

ROMAN
Ac 16:37 even though we are *R* citizens,
    22:25 you to flog a *R* citizen who hasn't

ROOF (ROOFS)
Pr 21: 9 Better to live on a corner of the *r*

ROOFS
Mt 10:27 in your ear, proclaim from the *r*.

ROOM (ROOMS)
Mt   6: 6 But when you pray, go into your *r*,
Mk 14:15 He will show you a large upper *r*,
Lk   2: 7 there was no *r* for them in the inn.
Jn   8:37 because you have no *r* for my
            word
    21:25 the whole world would not have *r*
2Co 7: 2 Make *r* for us in your hearts.

ROOMS (ROOM)
Jn 14: 2 In my Father's house are many *r*;

ROOSTER
Mt 26:34 this very night, before the *r* crows,

ROOT (ROOTED ROOTS)
Isa 11:10 In that day the *R* of Jesse will
            stand
    53: 2 and like a *r* out of dry ground.
Mt   3:10 already at the *r* of the trees,
    13:21 But since he has no *r*, he lasts only
Ro 11:16 if the *r* is holy, so are the
            branches.
    15:12 "The *R* of Jesse will spring up,
1Ti 6:10 of money is a *r* of all kinds of evil.
Rev 5: 5 the *R* of David, has triumphed.
    22:16 I am the *R* and the Offspring

ROOTED (ROOT)
Eph 3:17 being *r* and established in love,

ROOTS (ROOT)
Isa 11: 1 from his *r* a Branch will bear fruit.

ROSE (RISE)
SS   2: 1 I am a *r* of Sharon,
1Th 4:14 believe that Jesus died and *r*
            again

ROTS
Pr 14:30 but envy *r* the bones.

ROUGH
Isa 42:16 and make the *r* places smooth.
Lk   3: 5 the *r* ways smooth.

ROUND
Ecc 1: 6 *r* and *r* it goes,

ROYAL
Ps 45: 9 at your right hand is the *r* bride
Da   1: 8 not to defile himself with the *r*
            food
Jas 2: 8 If you really keep the *r* law found
1Pe 2: 9 a *r* priesthood, a holy nation,

RUBBISH*
Php 3: 8 I consider them *r*, that I may gain

RUBIES
Job 28:18 the price of wisdom is beyond *r*.
Pr   3:15 She is more precious than *r*;
     8:11 for wisdom is more precious
            than *r*,
    31:10 She is worth far more than *r*.

RUDDER*
Jas 3: 4 by a very small *r* wherever the
            pilot

RUDDY
1Sa 16:12 He was *r*, with a fine appearance
SS   5:10 *Beloved* My lover is radiant and *r*,

RUDE*
1Co 13: 5 It is not *r*, it is not self-seeking,

RUIN (RUINED RUINING RUINS)
Pr 10: 8 but a chattering fool comes to *r*.
    10:10 and a chattering fool comes to *r*.
    10:14 but the mouth of a fool invites *r*.
    10:29 but it is the *r* of those who do evil.
    18:24 many companions may come to *r*,
    19:13 A foolish son is his father's *r*,
    26:28 and a flattering mouth works *r*.
SS   2:15 that *r* the vineyards,
Eze 21:27 A *r*! A *r*! I will make it a *r*!
1Ti 6: 9 desires that plunge men into *r*

RUINED (RUIN)
Isa 6: 5 "I am *r*! For I am a man
Mt   9:17 and the wineskins will be *r*.

RUINING* (RUIN)
Tit 1:11 they are *r* whole households

RUINS (RUIN)
Pr 19: 3 A man's own folly *r* his life,
Ecc 4: 5 and *r* himself.
2Ti 2:14 and only *r* those who listen.

RULE (RULER RULERS RULES)
Ge   1:26 let them *r* over the fish of the sea
     3:16 and he will *r* over you."
Jdg 8:22 said to Gideon, "*R* over us—
1Sa 12:12 'No, we want a king to *r* over
Ps   2: 9 You will *r* them with an iron
    67: 4 for you the peoples justly
    119:133 let no sin *r* over me.
Pr 17: 2 A wise servant will *r*
Isa 28:10 *r* on *r*, *r* on *r*;
Eze 20:33 I will *r* over you with a mighty
Zec 6:13 and will sit and *r* on his throne.
     9:10 His *r* will extend from sea to sea
Ro 13: 9 are summed up in this one *r*:
    15:12 arise to *r* over the nations;
1Co 7:17 This is the *r* I lay down in all
Gal 6:16 and mercy to all who follow this *r*,
Eph 1:21 far above all *r* and authority,
Col 3:15 the peace of Christ *r* in your
            hearts,
2Th 3:10 we gave you this *r*: "If a man will
Rev 2:27 He will *r* them with an iron
            scepter;
    12: 5 who will *r* all the nations
    19:15 He will *r* them with an iron
            scepter

RULER (RULE)
Ps   8: 6 You made him *r* over the works
Pr 19: 6 Many curry favor with a *r*,
    23: 1 When you sit to dine with a *r*,
    25:15 Through patience a *r* can be
    29:26 Many seek an audience with a *r*,
Isa 60:17 and righteousness your *r*.
Da   9:25 the *r*, comes, there will be seven
Mic 5: 2 one who will be *r* over Israel,
Mt   2: 6 for out of you will come a *r*
Eph 2: 2 of the *r* of the kingdom of the air,
1Ti 6:15 God, the blessed and only *R*,
Rev 1: 5 and the *r* of the kings of the earth.

RULERS (RULE)
Ps   2: 2 and the *r* gather together
    119:161 *R* persecute me without cause,
Isa 40:23 reduces the *r* of this world
Da   7:27 and all *r* will worship and obey
            him
Mt 20:25 "You know that the *r*
Ac 13:27 and their *r* did not recognize
            Jesus,
Ro 13: 3 For *r* hold no terror
1Co 2: 6 of this age or of the *r* of this age,
Eph 3:10 should be made known to the *r*
     6:12 the *r*, against the authorities,
Col 1:16 or powers or *r* or authorities;

RULES (RULE)
Nu 15:15 is to have the same *r* for you
2Sa 23: 3 when he *r* in the fear of God,
Ps 22:28 and he *r* over the nations.
    66: 7 He *r* forever by his power,
    103:19 and his kingdom *r* over all.
Isa 29:13 is made up only of *r* taught by
            men.
    40:10 and his arm *r* for him.
Mt 15: 9 their teachings are but *r* taught
Lk 22:26 one who *r* like the one who
            serves.
2Ti 2: 5 he competes according to the *r*.

RUMORS
Jer 51:46 afraid when *r* are heard in the
            land;
Mt 24: 6 You will hear of wars and *r* of
            wars,

RUN (RAN RUNNERS RUNNING RUNS)
Ps 19: 5 champion rejoicing to *r* his course.
Pr   4:12 when you *r*, you will not stumble.
    18:10 the righteous *r* to it and are safe.
Isa 10: 3 To whom will you *r* for help?
    40:31 they will *r* and not grow weary,
Joel 3:18 ravines of Judah will *r* with water.
Hab 2: 2 so that a herald may *r* with it.

Mt 12:25 divided against itself will be *r*,

Mt 12:25 divided against itself will be *r*,

1Co 9:24 *R* in such a way as to get the
            prize.
Gal 2: 2 that I was running or had *r* my
            race
Php 2:16 on the day of Christ that I did
            not *r*
Heb 12: 1 let us *r* with perseverance the
            race

RUNNERS* (RUN)
1Co 9:24 that in a race all the *r* run,

RUNNING (RUN)
Ps 133: 2 *r* down on Aaron's beard,
Lk 17:23 Do not go *r* off after them.
1Co 9:26 I do not run like a man *r* aimlessly;
Gal 5: 7 You were *r* a good race.

RUNS (RUN)
Jn 10:12 he abandons the sheep and *r*
            away.

RUSH
Pr   1:16 for their feet *r* into sin,
     6:18 feet that are quick to *r* into evil,
Isa 59: 7 Their feet *r* into sin;

RUST
Mt   6:19 where moth and *r* destroy,

RUTH*
    Moabitess; widow who went to Bethlehem
    with mother-in-law Naomi (Ru 1). Gleaned in
    field of Boaz; shown favor (Ru 2). Proposed
    marriage to Boaz (Ru 3). Married (Ru 4:1–12);
    bore Obed, ancestor of David (Ru 4:13–22),
    Jesus (Mt 1:5).

RUTHLESS
Pr 11:16 but *r* men gain only wealth.
Ro   1:31 are senseless, faithless,
            heartless, *r*.

SABBATH (SABBATHS)
Ex 20: 8 "Remember the *S* day
    31:14 " 'Observe the *S*, because it is
            holy
Lev 25: 2 the land itself must observe a *s*
Dt   5:12 "Observe the *S* day
Isa 56: 2 keeps the *S* without desecrating
            it,
    56: 6 all who keep the *S*
    58:13 if you call the *S* a delight
Jer 17:21 not to carry a load on the *S* day
Mt 12: 1 through the grainfields on the *S*.
Lk 13:10 On a *S* Jesus was teaching in one
Col 2:16 A New Moon celebration or a *S*
            day

SABBATH-REST* (REST)
Heb 4: 9 then, a *S* for the people of God;

SABBATHS (SABBATH)
2Ch 2: 4 evening and on *S* and New Moons
Eze 20:12 Also I gave them my *S*

SACKCLOTH
Ps 30:11 you removed my *s* and clothed
            me
Da   9: 3 in fasting, and in *s* and ashes.
Mt 11:21 would have repented long ago in *s*

SACRED
Lev 23: 2 are to proclaim as *s* assemblies.
Mt   7: 6 "Do not give dogs what is *s*;
Ro 14: 5 One man considers one day
            more *s*
1Co 3:17 for God's temple is *s*, and you are
2Pe 1:18 were with him on the *s* mountain.
    on the *s* command that was

SACRIFICE (SACRIFICED SACRIFICES)
Ge 22: 2 *S* him there as a burnt offering
Ex 12:27 'It is the Passover *s* to the LORD,
1Sa 15:22 To obey is better than *s*,
1Ki 18:38 the LORD fell and burned up the *s*,
1Ch 21:24 or *s* a burnt offering that costs me
Ps 40: 6 *S* and offering you did not desire,
    50:14 *S* thank offerings to God,
    51:16 You do not delight in *s*,
    54: 6 I will *s* a freewill offering to you;
    107:22 Let them *s* thank offerings
    141: 2 of my hands be like the evening *s*.
Pr 15: 8 The LORD detests the *s*
    21: 3 to the LORD than *s*.
Da   9:27 the 'seven' he will put an end to *s*
    12:11 time that the daily *s* is abolished
Hos 6: 6 For I desire mercy, not *s*,
Mt   9:13 this means: 'I desire mercy, not *s*.'

Ro   3:25 God presented him as a s
Eph   5: 2 as a fragrant offering and s to
            God.
Php   4:18 an acceptable s, pleasing to God.
Heb   9:26 away with sin by the s of himself.
     10: 5 "S and offering you did not desire,
     10:10 holy through the s of the body
     10:14 by one s he has made perfect
     10:18 there is no longer any s for sin.
     11: 4 faith Abel offered God a better s
     13:15 offer to God a s of praise—
1Jn   2: 2 He is the atoning s for our sins,
      4:10 as an atoning s for our sins.

SACRIFICED (SACRIFICE)
Ac   15:29 are to abstain from food s to idols,
1Co   5: 7 our Passover lamb, has been s.
      8: 1 Now about food s to idols:
Heb   7:27 He s for their sins once for all
      9:28 so Christ was s once

SACRIFICES (SACRIFICE)
Ps   51:17 The s of God are a broken spirit;
Mk   12:33 than all burnt offerings and s."
Ro   12: 1 to offer your bodies as living s,
Heb   9:23 with better s than these.
     13:16 for with such s God is pleased.
1Pe   2: 5 offering spiritual s acceptable

SAD
Lk   18:23 he heard this, he became very s,

SADDUCEES
Mt   16: 6 the yeast of the Pharisees and S."
Mk   12:18 S, who say there is no
            resurrection,
Ac   23: 8 S say that there is no resurrection,

SAFE (SAVE)
Ps   27: 5 he will keep me s in his dwelling;
     37: 3 in the land and enjoy s pasture.
Pr   18:10 the righteous run to it and are s.
     28:26 he who walks in wisdom is kept s.
     29:25 in the LORD is kept s.
Jer 12: 5 If you stumble in s country,
Jn   17:12 kept them s by that name you
            gave
1Jn   5:18 born of God keeps him s,

SAFETY (SAVE)
Ps   4: 8 make me dwell in s.
Hos   2:18 so that all may lie down in s.
1Th   5: 3 people are saying, "Peace and s,"

SAINTS
1Sa   2: 9 He will guard the feet of his s,
Ps   16: 3 As for the s who are in the land,
     30: 4 Sing to the LORD, you s of his;
     31:23 Love the LORD, all his s!
     34: 9 Fear the LORD, you his s,
    116:15 is the death of his s.
    149: 1 his praise in the assembly of the s.
    149: 5 Let the s rejoice in this honor
Da   8:13 the s of the Most High will receive
Ro   8:27 intercedes for the s in accordance
1Co   6: 2 not know that the s will judge
Eph   1:15 Jesus and your love for all the s,
      1:18 of his glorious inheritance in the s,
      6:18 always keep on praying for all
            the s
Phm   : 7 have refreshed the hearts of the s.
Rev   5: 8 which are the prayers of the s.
     19: 8 for the righteous acts of the s.)

SAKE (SAKES)
1Sa 12:22 For the s of his great name
Ps   23: 3 righteousness for his name's s.
     44:22 Yet for your s we face death all
            day
    106: 8 Yet he saved them for his
            name's s,
Isa 42:21 for the s of his righteousness
     43:25 your transgressions, for my own s,
     48: 9 For my own name's s I delay my
     48:11 For my own s, for my own s,
Jer 14: 7 for the s of your name.
     14:21 For the s of your name do not
Eze 20: 9 But for the s of my name I did
            what
     20:14 But for the s of my name I did
            what
     20:22 and for the s of my name I did
            what
     36:22 but for the s of my holy name,
Da   9:17 For your s, O Lord, look with favor
Mt   10:39 life for my s will find it.

Mt   19:29 for my s will receive a hundred
1Co   9:23 I do all this for the s of the gospel,
2Co 12:10 for Christ's s, I delight
Php   3: 7 loss for the s of Christ.
Heb 11:26 He regarded disgrace for the s
1Pe   2:13 for the Lord's s to every authority
3Jn   : 7 was for the s of the Name that
            they

SAKES* (SAKE)
2Co   8: 9 yet for your s he became poor,

SALEM
Ge   14:18 king of S brought out bread
Heb   7: 2 "king of S" means "king of peace."

SALT
Ge   19:26 and she became a pillar of s.
Nu   18:19 covenant of s before the LORD
Mt   5:13 "You are the s of the earth.
Col   4: 6 with s, so that you may know how
Jas   3:11 s water flow from the same
            spring?

SALVATION* (SAVE)
Ex   15: 2 he has become my s.
2Sa 22: 3 my shield and the horn of my s.
     23: 5 Will he not bring to fruition my s
1Ch 16:23 proclaim his s day after day.
2Ch   6:41 O LORD God, be clothed with s,
Ps   9:14 and there rejoice in your s.
     13: 5 my heart rejoices in your s.
     14: 7 that s for Israel would come out
     18: 2 is my shield and the horn of my s,
     27: 1 The LORD is my light and my s—
     28: 8 a fortress of s for his anointed
            one.
     35: 3 "I am your s."
     35: 9 and delight in his s.
     37:39 The s of the righteous comes
     40:10 I speak of your faithfulness and s.
     40:16 those who love your s always say,
     50:23 way so that I may show him the s
     51:12 Restore to me the joy of your s
     53: 6 that s for Israel would come out
     62: 1 my s comes from him.
     62: 2 He alone is my rock and my s;
     62: 6 He alone is my rock and my s;
     62: 7 My s and my honor depend
     67: 2 your s among all nations.
     69:13 answer me with your sure s.
     69:27 do not let them share in your s.
     69:29 may your s, O God, protect me.
     70: 4 those who love your s always say,
     71:15 of your s all day long,
     74:12 you bring s upon the earth.
     85: 7 and grant us your s.
     85: 9 Surely his s is near those who fear
     91:16 and show him my s."
     95: 1 to the Rock of our s.
     96: 2 proclaim his s day after day.
     98: 1 have worked s for him.
     98: 2 The LORD has made his s known
     98: 3 the s of our God.
    116:13 I will lift up the cup of s
    118:14 he has become my s.
    118:21 you have become my s.
    119:41 your s according to your promise;
    119:81 with longing for your s,
    119:123 My eyes fail, looking for your s,
    119:155 S is far from the wicked,
    119:166 I wait for your s, O LORD,
    119:174 I long for your s, O LORD,
    132:16 I will clothe her priests with s,
    149: 4 he crowns the humble with s.
Isa 12: 2 Surely God is my s;
     12: 2 he has become my s."
     12: 3 from the wells of s.
     25: 9 let us rejoice and be glad in his s."
     26: 1 God makes s
     26:18 We have not brought s to the
            earth;
     30:15 "In repentance and rest is your s,
     33: 2 our s in time of distress.
     33: 6 a rich store of s and wisdom
     45: 8 let s spring up,
     45:17 the LORD with an everlasting s;
     46:13 I will grant s to Zion,
     46:13 and my s will not be delayed.
     49: 6 that you may bring my s
     49: 8 and in the day of s I will help you;
     51: 5 my s is on the way,
     51: 6 But my s will last forever,

Isa 51: 8 my s through all generations."
     52: 7 who proclaim s,
     52:10 the s of our God.
     56: 1 for my s is close at hand
     59:16 so his own arm worked s for him,
     59:17 and the helmet of s on his head;
     60:18 but you will call your walls S
     61:10 me with garments of s
     62: 1 her s like a blazing torch.
     63: 5 so my own arm worked s for me,
Jer   3:23 is the s of Israel.
La   3:26 quietly for the s of the LORD.
Jnh   2: 9 S comes from the LORD."
Zec   9: 9 righteous and having s,
Lk   1:69 He has raised up a horn of s for us
      1:71 of long ago), s from our enemies
      1:77 give his people the knowledge
            of s
      2:30 For my eyes have seen your s,
      3: 6 And all mankind will see God's s
     19: 9 "Today s has come to this house,
Jn   4:22 for s is from the Jews.
Ac   4:12 S is found in no one else,
     13:26 message of s has been sent.
     13:47 that you may bring s to the ends
     28:28 to know that God's s has been
            sent
Ro   1:16 for the s of everyone who
            believes:
     11:11 s has come to the Gentiles
     13:11 because our s is nearer now
2Co   1: 6 it is for your comfort and s;
      6: 2 and in the day of s I helped you."
      7:10 of God's favor, now is the day of s.
      7:10 brings repentance that leads to s
Eph   1:13 word of truth, the gospel of
            your s.
      6:17 Take the helmet of s and the
            sword
Php   2:12 to work out your s with fear
1Th   5: 8 and the hope of s as a helmet.
      5: 9 to receive s through our Lord
            Jesus
2Ti   2:10 they too may obtain the s that is
      3:15 wise for s through faith
Tit   2:11 of God that brings s has appeared
Heb   1:14 to serve those who will inherit s?
      2: 3 This s, which was first announced
      2: 3 escape if we ignore such a great s?
      2:10 of their s perfect through
            suffering.
      5: 9 of eternal s for all who obey him
      6: 9 case—things that accompany s.
      9:28 to bring s to those who are
            waiting
1Pe   1: 5 the coming of the s that is ready
      1: 9 of your faith, the s of your souls.
      1:10 Concerning this s, the prophets,
      2: 2 by it you may grow up in your s,
2Pe   3:15 that our Lord's patience means s,
Jude   : 3 to write to you about the s we
            share
Rev   7:10 "S belongs to our God,
     12:10 have come the s and the power
     19: 1 S and glory and power belong

SAMARIA (SAMARITAN)
1Ki 16:24 He bought the hill of S
2Ki 17: 6 the king of Assyria captured S
Jn   4: 4 Now he had to go through S.
      4: 5 came to a town in S called Sychar,

SAMARITAN (SAMARIA)
Lk   10:33 But a S, as he traveled, came
            where
     17:16 and thanked him—and he was
            a S.
Jn   4: 7 When a S woman came

SAMSON
Danite judge. Birth promised (Jdg 13). Married to Philistine, but wife given away (Jdg 14). Vengeance on Philistines (Jdg 15). Betrayed by Delilah (Jdg 16:1–22). Death (Jdg 16:23–31). Feats of strength: killed lion (Jdg 14:6), 30 Philistines (Jdg 14:19), 1,000 Philistines with jawbone (Jdg 15:13–17), carried off gates of Gaza (Jdg 16:3), pushed down temple of Dagon (Jdg 16:25–30).

SAMUEL
Ephraimite judge and prophet (Heb 11:32). Birth prayed for (1Sa 1:10–18). Dedicated to

temple by Hannah (1Sa 1:21–28). Raised by Eli (1Sa 2:11, 18–26). Called as prophet (1Sa 3). Led Israel to victory over Philistines (1Sa 7). Asked by Israel for a king (1Sa 8). Anointed Saul as king (1Sa 9–10). Farewell speech (1Sa 12). Rebuked Saul for sacrifice (1Sa 13). Announced rejection of Saul (1Sa 15). Anointed David as king (1Sa 16). Protected David from Saul (1Sa 19:18–24). Death (1Sa 25:1). Returned from dead to condemn Saul (1Sa 28).

SANBALLAT
Led opposition to Nehemiah's rebuilding of Jerusalem (Ne 2:10, 19; 4; 6).

SANCTIFIED* (SANCTIFY)
Jn   17:19   that they too may be truly s.
Ac   20:32   among all those who are s.
     26:18   among those who are s by faith
Ro   15:16   to God, s by the Holy Spirit.
1Co   1: 2   to those s in Christ Jesus
     6:11   But you were washed, you were s,
     7:14   and the unbelieving wife has been s
     7:14   the unbelieving husband has been s
1Th   4: 3   It is God's will that you should be s
Heb 10:29   blood of the covenant that s him,

SANCTIFY* (SANCTIFIED SANCTIFYING)
Jn   17:17   S them by the truth; your word is
     17:19   For them I s myself, that they too
1Th   5:23   s you through and through.
Heb   9:13   are ceremonially unclean s them

SANCTIFYING* (SANCTIFY)
2Th   2:13   through the s work of the Spirit
1Pe   1: 2   through the s work of the Spirit,

SANCTUARY
Ex   25: 8   "Then have them make a s for me,
Lev 19:30   and have reverence for my s,
Ps   15: 1   LORD, who may dwell in your s?
     63: 2   I have seen you in the s
     68:24   of my God and King into the s.
     68:35   are awesome, O God, in your s;
     73:17   me till I entered the s of God;
     102:19   looked down from his s on high,
     134: 2   Lift up your hands in the s
     150: 1   Praise God in his s;
Eze 37:26   I will put my s among them forever
     41: 1   the man brought me to the outer s
Da   9:26   will destroy the city and the s.
Heb   6:19   It enters the inner s
     8: 2   in the s, the true tabernacle set up
     8: 5   They serve at a s that is a copy
     9:24   enter a man-made s that was only

SAND
Ge   22:17   and as the s on the seashore.
Mt   7:26   man who built his house on s.

SANDAL (SANDALS)
Ru   4: 7   one party took off his s

SANDALS (SANDAL)
Ex   3: 5   off your s, for the place where you
Dt   25: 9   take off one of his s, spit in his face
Jos   5:15   off your s, for the place where you
Mt   3:11   whose s I am not fit to carry.

SANG (SING)
Ex   15: 1   and the Israelites s this song
     15:21   Miriam s to them:
Nu   21:17   Then Israel s this song:
Jdg   5: 1   Barak son of Abinoam s this song:
1Sa 18: 7   As they danced, they s:
2Sa 22: 1   David s to the LORD the words
2Ch   5:13   in praise to the LORD and s:
     29:30   So they s praises with gladness
Ezr   3:11   thanksgiving they s to the LORD:
Job 38: 7   while the morning stars s together
Ps   106:12   and s his praise.
Rev   5: 9   And they s a new song:
     5:12   In a loud voice they s:
     14: 3   they s a new song before the throne
     15: 3   and s the song of Moses the servant

SAP
Ro   11:17   share in the nourishing s

SAPPHIRA*
Ac   5: 1   together with his wife S,

SARAH
Wife of Abraham, originally named Sarai; barren (Ge 11:29–31; 1Pe 3:6). Taken by Pharaoh as Abraham's sister; returned (Ge 12:10–20). Gave Hagar to Abraham; sent her away in pregnancy (Ge 16). Name changed; Isaac promised (Ge 17:15–21; 18:10–15; Heb 11:11). Taken by Abimelech as Abraham's sister; returned (Ge 20). Isaac born; Hagar and Ishmael sent away (Ge 21:1–21; Gal 4:21–31). Death (Ge 23).

SARDIS
Rev   3: 1   the angel of the church in S write:

SASH (SASHES)
Rev   1:13   with a golden s around his chest.

SASHES (SASH)
Rev 15: 6   wore golden s around their chests.

SAT (SIT)
Ps   137: 1   By the rivers of Babylon we s
Mk 16:19   and he s at the right hand of God.
Lk   10:39   who s at the Lord's feet listening
Heb   1: 3   he s down at the right hand
     8: 1   who s down at the right hand
     10:12   he s down at the right hand of God.
     12: 2   and s down at the right hand

SATAN
Job   1: 6   and S also came with them.
Zec   3: 2   said to S, "The LORD rebuke you,
Mt   12:26   If S drives out S, he is divided
     16:23   S! You are a stumbling block to me;
Mk   4:15   S comes and takes away the word
Lk   10:18   "I saw S fall like lightning
     22: 3   S entered Judas, called Iscariot,
Ro   16:20   The God of peace will soon crush S
1Co   5: 5   is present, hand this man over to S,
2Co 11:14   for S himself masquerades
     12: 7   a messenger of S, to torment me.
1Ti   1:20   handed over to S to be taught not
Rev 12: 9   serpent called the devil, or S,
     20: 2   or S, and bound him for a thousand
     20: 7   S will be released from his prison

SATISFIED (SATISFY)
Ps   17:15   I will be s with seeing your likeness
     22:26   The poor will eat and be s;
     63: 5   My soul will be s as with the richest
     104:28   they are s with good things.
     105:40   s them with the bread of heaven.
Pr   13: 4   the desires of the diligent are fully s
     30:15   are three things that are never s,
Ecc   5:10   whoever loves wealth is never s
Isa   53:11   he will see the light of life, and be s
Mt   14:20   They all ate and were s,
Lk   6:21   for you will be s.

SATISFIES* (SATISFY)
Ps 103: 5   who s your desires with good things,
     107: 9   for he s the thirsty
     147:14   and s you with the finest of wheat.

SATISFY (SATISFIED SATISFIES)
Ps   90:14   S us in the morning
     145:16   the desires of every living thing.
Pr   5:19   may her breasts s you always,
Isa   55: 2   and your labor on what does not s?
     58:10   and s the needs of the oppressed,

SAUL
1. Benjamite; anointed by Samuel as first king of Israel (1Sa 9–10). Defeated Ammonites (1Sa 11). Rebuked for offering sacrifice (1Sa 13:1–15). Defeated Philistines (1Sa 14). Rejected as king for failing to annihilate Amalekites (1Sa 15). Soothed from evil spirit by David (1Sa 16:14–23). Sent David against Goliath (1Sa 17). Jealousy and attempted murder of David (1Sa 18:1–11). Gave David Michal as wife (1Sa 18:12–30). Second attempt to kill David (1Sa 19). Anger at Jonathan (1Sa 20:26–34). Pursued David: killed priests at Nob (1Sa 22), went to Keilah and Ziph (1Sa 23), life spared by David at En Gedi (1Sa 24) and in his tent (1Sa 26). Rebuked by Samuel's spirit for consulting witch at Endor (1Sa 28). Wounded by Philistines; took his own life (1Sa 31; 1Ch 10). Lamented by David (2Sa 1:17–27). Children (1Sa 14:49–51; 1Ch 8).
2. See PAUL

SAVAGE
Ac   20:29   s wolves will come in among you

SAVE (SAFE SAFETY SALVATION SAVED SAVES SAVIOR)
Ge   45: 5   to s lives that God sent me ahead
1Ch 16:35   Cry out, "S us, O God our Savior;
Job 40:14   that your own right hand can s you.
Ps   17: 7   you who s by your right hand
     18:27   You s the humble
     28: 9   S your people and bless your
     31:16   s me in your unfailing love.
     69:35   for God will s Zion
     71: 2   turn your ear to me and s me.
     72:13   and s the needy from death.
     89:48   or s himself from the power
     91: 3   Surely he will s you
     109:31   to s his life from those who
     146: 3   in mortal men, who cannot s.
Pr   2:16   will s you also from the adulteress,
Isa   35: 4   he will come to s you."
     38:20   The LORD will s me,
     46: 7   it cannot s him from his troubles.
     59: 1   of the LORD is not too short to s,
     63: 1   mighty to s."
Jer   17:14   s me and I will be saved,
Eze   3:18   ways in order to s his life,
     7:19   able to s them in the day
     14:14   they could s only themselves
     33:12   of the righteous man will not s him
     34:22   I will s my flock, and they will no
Da   3:17   the God we serve is able to s us
Hos   1: 7   and I will s them—not by bow,
Zep   1:18   will be able to s them
     3:17   he is mighty to s.
Zec   8: 7   "I will s my people
Mt   1:21   he will s his people from their sins
     16:25   wants to s his life will lose it,
Lk   19:10   to seek and to s what was lost."
Jn   3:17   but to s the world through him.
     12:47   come to judge the world, but to s it.
Ro   11:14   people to envy and s some of them.
1Co   7:16   whether you will s your husband?
1Ti   1:15   came into the world to s sinners—
Heb   7:25   to s completely those who come
Jas   5:20   of his way will s him from death
Jude : 23   others from the fire and s them;

SAVED (SAVE)
Ps   22: 5   They cried to you and were s;
     33:16   No king is s by the size of his army;
     34: 6   he s him out of all his troubles.
     106:21   They forgot the God who s them,
     116: 6   when I was in great need, he s me.
Isa   25: 9   we trusted in him, and he s us.
     45:22   "Turn to me and be s,
     64: 5   How then can we be s?
Jer   4:14   from your heart and be s.
     8:20   and we are not s."
Eze   3:19   but you will have s yourself.
     33: 5   warning, he would have s himself.
Joel   2:32   on the name of the LORD will be s;
Mt   10:22   firm to the end will be s.
     24:13   firm to the end will be s.
Mk   13:13   firm to the end will be s.
     16:16   believes and is baptized will be s,
Jn   10: 9   enters through me will be s.
Ac   2:21   on the name of the Lord will be s.'
     2:47   daily those who were being s.
     4:12   to men by which we must be s."
     15:11   of our Lord Jesus that we are s,
     16:30   do to be s?" They replied,
Ro   5: 9   how much more shall we be s

Ro   9:27 only the remnant will be s.
     10: 1 the Israelites is that they may
            be s.
     10: 9 him from the dead, you will be s.
     10:13 on the name of the Lord will
            be s.”
     11:26 so all Israel will be s, as it is
            written:
1Co 1:18 to us who are being s it is the
            power
     3:15 will suffer loss; he himself will
            be s,
     5: 5 his spirit on the day of the Lord.
    10:33 of many, so that they may be s.
     15: 2 By this gospel you are s,
Eph 2: 5 it is by grace you have been s.
     2: 8 For it is by grace you have been s,
2Th 2:13 you to be s through the
            sanctifying
1Ti 2: 4 who wants all men to be s
     2:15 But women will be s
2Ti 1: 9 who has s us and called us
Tit   3: 5 He s us through the washing
Heb 10:39 but of those who believe and
            are s.

SAVES (SAVE)
Ps   7:10 who s the upright in heart.
   68:20 Our God is a God who s;
 145:19 he hears their cry and s them.
1Pe 3:21 It s you by the resurrection

SAVIOR* (SAVE)
Dt 32:15 and rejected the Rock his S.
2Sa 22: 3 stronghold, my refuge and my s—
   22:47 Exalted be God, the Rock, my S!
1Ch 16:35 Cry out, “Save us, O God our S;
Ps 18:46 Exalted be God my S!
   24: 5 and vindication from God his S.
   25: 5 for you are God my S,
   27: 9 O God my S.
   38:22 O Lord my S.
   42: 5 my S and
   42:11 my S and my God.
   43: 5 my S and my God.
   65: 5 O God our S,
   68:19 Praise be to the Lord, to God
            our S,
   79: 9 Help us, O God our S,
   85: 4 Restore us again, O God our S,
   89:26 my God, the Rock my S.’
Isa 17:10 You have forgotten God your S;
   19:20 he will send them a s and
            defender,
   43: 3 the Holy One of Israel, your S;
   43:11 and apart from me there is no s.
   45:15 O God and S of Israel.
   45:21 a righteous God and a S;
   49:26 that I, the LORD, am your S,
   60:16 know that I, the LORD, am your S,
   62:11 ‘See, your S comes!’
   63: 8 and so he became their S.
Jer 14: 8 its S in times of distress,
Hos 13: 4 no S except me.
Mic 7: 7 I wait for God my S;
Hab 3:18 I will be joyful in God my S.
Lk   1:47 and my spirit rejoices in God
            my S,
   2:11 of David a S has been born to
            you;
Jn   4:42 know that this man really is the S
Ac   5:31 S that he might give repentance
   13:23 God has brought to Israel the S
Eph 5:23 his body, of which he is the S.
Php 3:20 we eagerly await a S from there,
1Ti 1: 1 by the command of God our S
   2: 3 This is good, and pleases God
            our S
   4:10 who is the S of all men,
2Ti 1:10 through the appearing of our S,
Tit   1: 3 me by the command of God our S
   1: 4 the Father and Christ Jesus our S.
   2:10 about God our S attractive.
   2:13 appearing of our great God and S,
   3: 4 and love of God our S appeared,
   3: 6 through Jesus Christ our S,
2Pe 1: 1 S Jesus Christ have received a
            faith
   1:11 eternal kingdom of our Lord and S
   2:20 and S Jesus Christ and are again
   3: 2 and S through your apostles.
   3:18 and knowledge of our Lord and S

1Jn 4:14 Son to be the S of the world.
Jude :25 to the only God our S be glory,

SCALE (SCALES)
Ps 18:29 with my God I can s a wall.

SCALES (SCALE)
Lev 11: 9 may eat any that have fins and s.
   19:36 Use honest s and honest weights,
Pr 11: 1 The LORD abhors dishonest s,
Da 5:27 You have been weighed on the s
Rev 6: 5 Its rider was holding a pair of s

SCAPEGOAT (GOAT)
Lev 16:10 by sending it into the desert as
            a s.

SCARECROW*
Jer 10: 5 Like a s in a melon patch,

SCARLET
Jos 2:21 she tied the s cord in the window.
Isa 1:18 “Though your sins are like s,
Mt 27:28 They stripped him and put a s
            robe

SCATTER (SCATTERED SCATTERS)
Dt   4:27 The LORD will s you
Ne   1: 8 I will s you among the nations,
Jer 9:16 I will s them among nations that
   30:11 the nations among which I s you,
Zec 10: 9 I s them among the peoples,

SCATTERED (SCATTER)
Isa 11:12 he will assemble the s people
Jer 31:10 ‘He who s Israel will gather them
Zec 2: 6 “for I have s you to the four winds
   13: 7 and the sheep will be s,
Mt 26:31 and the sheep of the flock will
            be s.’
Jn 11:52 but also for the s children of God,
Ac   8: 4 who had been s preached the
            word
Jas 1: 1 To the twelve tribes s
1Pe 1: 1 s throughout Pontus, Galatia,

SCATTERS (SCATTER)
Mt 12:30 he who does not gather with
            me s.

SCEPTER
Ge 49:10 The s will not depart from Judah,
Nu 24:17 a s will rise out of Israel.
Ps   2: 9 You will rule them with an iron s;
   45: 6 a s of justice will be the s
Heb 1: 8 and righteousness will be the s
Rev 2:27 ‘He will rule them with an iron s;
   12: 5 rule all the nations with an iron s.
   19:15 “He will rule them with an iron s.”

SCHEMES
Pr   6:18 a heart that devises wicked s,
   24: 9 The s of folly are sin,
2Co 2:11 For we are not unaware of his s.
Eph 6:11 stand against the devil’s s.

SCHOLAR*
1Co 1:20 Where is the s? Where is

SCOFFERS
2Pe 3: 3 that in the last days s will come,

SCORN (SCORNED SCORNING SCORNS)
Ps 69: 7 For I endure s for your sake,
   69:20 S has broken my heart
   89:41 he has become the s
  109:25 I am an object of s to my accusers;
  119:22 Remove from me s and contempt,
Mic 6:16 you will bear the s of the nations.”

SCORNED (SCORN)
Ps 22: 6 s by men and despised

SCORNING (SCORN)
Heb 12: 2 him endured the cross, s its
            shame,

SCORNS (SCORN)
Pr 13:13 He who s instruction will pay for
            it,
   30:17 that s obedience to a mother,

SCORPION
Lk 11:12 will give him a s? If you then,
Rev 9: 5 sting of a s when it strikes a man.

SCOUNDREL
Pr   6:12 A s and villain,

SCRIPTURE (SCRIPTURES)
Jn   2:22 Then they believed the S
   7:42 Does not the S say that the Christ
  10:35 and the S cannot be broken—
Ac   8:32 was reading this passage of S:

1Ti 4:13 yourself to the public reading of S,
2Ti 3:16 All S is God-breathed
2Pe 1:20 that no prophecy of S came about

SCRIPTURES (SCRIPTURE)
Mt 22:29 because you do not know the S
Lk 24:27 said in all the S concerning
            himself.
   24:45 so they could understand the S.
Jn   5:39 These are the S that testify about
Ac 17:11 examined the S every day to see
2Ti 3:15 you have known the holy S,
2Pe 3:16 as they do the other S,

SCROLL
Ps 40: 7 it is written about me in the s.
Isa 34: 4 and the sky rolled up like a s;
Eze 3: 1 eat what is before you, eat this s;
Heb 10: 7 it is written about me in the s—
Rev 6:14 The sky receded like a s, rolling
            up,
   10: 8 take the s that lies open in the
            hand

SCUM
1Co 4:13 this moment we have become
            the s

SEA (SEASHORE)
Ex 14:16 go through the s on dry ground.
Dt 30:13 “Who will cross the s to get it
1Ki 7:23 He made the S of cast metal,
Job 11: 9 and wider than the s.
Ps 93: 4 mightier than the breakers of
            the s
   95: 5 The s is his, for he made it,
Ecc 1: 7 All streams flow into the s,
Isa 57:20 the wicked are like the tossing s,
Jnh 1: 4 LORD sent a great wind on the s,
Mic 7:19 iniquities into the depths of the s.
Hab 2:14 as the waters cover the s.
Zec 9:10 His rule will extend from s to s
Mt 18: 6 drowned in the depths of the s.
1Co 10: 1 that they all passed through the s.
Jas 1: 6 who doubts is like a wave of the s,
Jude :13 They are wild waves of the s,
Rev 10: 2 He planted his right foot on the s
   13: 1 I saw a beast coming out of the s.
   20:13 The s gave up the dead that were
   21: 1 and there was no longer any s.

SEAL (SEALED SEALS)
Ps 40: 9 I do not s my lips,
SS   8: 6 Place me like a s over your heart,
Da 12: 4 and s the words of the scroll
Jn   6:27 God the Father has placed his s
1Co 9: 2 For you are the s of my
            apostleship
2Co 1:22 set his s of ownership on us,
Eph 1:13 you were marked in him with a s,
Rev 6: 3 the Lamb opened the second s,
   6: 5 When the Lamb opened the
            third s,
   6: 7 the Lamb opened the fourth s,
   6: 9 When he opened the fifth s,
   6:12 I watched as he opened the
            sixth s,
   8: 1 When he opened the seventh s,
   9: 4 people who did not have the s
   22:10 “Do not s up the words

SEALED (SEAL)
Eph 4:30 with whom you were s for the day
2Ti 2:19 solid foundation stands firm, s
Rev 5: 1 on both sides and s with seven
            seals

SEALS (SEAL)
Rev 5: 2 “Who is worthy to break the s
   6: 1 opened the first of the seven s.

SEAMLESS*
Jn 19:23 This garment was s, woven

SEARCH (SEARCHED SEARCHES SEARCHING)
Ps   4: 4 s your hearts and be silent.
  139:23 S me, O God, and know my heart;
Pr   2: 4 and s for it as for hidden treasure,
   25: 2 to s out a matter is the glory
SS   3: 2 I will s for the one my heart loves.
Jer 17:10 “I the LORD s the heart
Eze 34:11 myself will s for my sheep
   34:16 I will s for the lost and bring back
Lk 15: 8 and s carefully until she finds it?

SEARCHED (SEARCH)
Ps 139: 1 O LORD, you have s me

Ecc 12:10 The Teacher *s* to find just the
right
1Pe 1:10 *s* intently and with the greatest

SEARCHES (SEARCH)
1Ch 28: 9 for the LORD *s* every heart
Ps 7: 9 who *s* minds and hearts,
Pr 11:27 but evil comes to him who *s* for it.
20:27 The lamp of the LORD *s* the spirit
Ro 8:27 And he who *s* our hearts knows
1Co 2:10 The Spirit *s* all things,
Rev 2:23 will know that I am he who *s*
hearts

SEARCHING (SEARCH)
Jdg 5:15 there was much *s* of heart.
Am 8:12 *s* for the word of the LORD.

SEARED
1Ti 4: 2 whose consciences have been *s*

SEASHORE (SEA)
Jos 11: 4 as numerous as the sand on the *s.*
1Ki 4:29 as measureless as the sand on
the *s.*

SEASON (SEASONED SEASONS)
Lev 26: 4 I will send you rain in its *s,*
Ps 1: 3 which yields its fruit in *s*
2Ti 4: 2 be prepared in *s* and out of *s;*

SEASONED* (SEASON)
Col 4: 6 full of grace, *s* with salt,

SEASONS (SEASON)
Ge 1:14 signs to mark *s* and days and
years,
Gal 4:10 and months and *s* and years!

SEAT (SEATED SEATS)
Ps 1: 1 or sit in the *s* of mockers.
Pr 31:23 where he takes his *s*
Da 7: 9 and the Ancient of Days took
his *s.*
Lk 14: 9 say to you, 'Give this man your *s.'*
2Co 5:10 before the judgment *s* of Christ,

SEATED (SEAT)
Ps 47: 8 God is *s* on his holy throne.
Isa 6: 1 I saw the Lord on a throne,
Lk 22:69 of Man will be *s* at the right hand
Eph 1:20 and *s* him at his right hand
2: 6 and *s* us with him in the heavenly
Col 3: 1 where Christ is *s* at the right hand
Rev 14:14 *s* on the cloud was one "like a son
20:11 white throne and him who was *s*

SEATS (SEAT)
Lk 11:43 you love the most important *s*

SECLUSION*
Lk 1:24 and for five months remained in *s.*

SECRET (SECRETLY SECRETS)
Dt 29:29 The *s* things belong
Jdg 16: 6 Tell me the *s* of your great
strength
Ps 90: 8 our *s* sins in the light
139:15 when I was made in the *s* place.
Pr 11:13 but a trustworthy man keeps a *s.*
21:14 A gift given in *s* soothes anger,
Jer 23:24 Can anyone hide in *s* places
Mt 6: 4 so that your giving may be in *s.*
6:18 who sees what is done in *s,*
Mk 4:11 "The *s* of the kingdom
1Co 2: 1 No, we speak of God's *s* wisdom,
4: 1 entrusted with the *s* things of
God.
2Co 4: 2 we have renounced *s* and
shameful
Eph 5:12 what the disobedient do in *s.*
Php 4:12 I have learned the *s*

SECRETLY (SECRET)
2Pe 2: 1 They will *s* introduce destructive
Jude : 4 about long ago have *s* slipped

SECRETS (SECRET)
Ps 44:21 since he knows the *s* of the heart?
Ro 2:16 day when God will judge men's *s*
1Co 14:25 the *s* of his heart will be laid bare.
Rev 2:24 Satan's so-called deep *s* (I will not

SECURE (SECURITY)
Dt 33:12 beloved of the LORD rest *s* in him,
Ps 16: 5 you have made my lot *s.*
16: 9 my body also will rest *s,*
112: 8 His heart is *s,* he will have no fear;
Pr 14:26 fears the LORD has a *s* fortress,
Heb 6:19 an anchor for the soul, firm and *s.*
2Pe 3:17 and fall from your *s* position.

SECURITY (SECURE)
Job 31:24 or said to pure gold, 'You are
my *s,'*

SEED (SEEDS SEEDTIME)
Ge 1:11 on the land that bear fruit with *s*
Isa 55:10 so that it yields *s* for the sower
Mt 13: 3 "A farmer went out to sow his *s.*
13:31 of heaven is like a mustard *s,*
17:20 have faith as small as a mustard *s,*
Lk 8:11 of the parable: The *s* is the word
1Co 3: 6 I planted the *s,* Apollos watered it,
2Co 9:10 he who supplies *s* to the sower
Gal 3:29 then you are Abraham's *s,*
1Pe 1:23 not of perishable *s,*
1Jn 3: 9 because God's *s* remains in him;

SEEDS (SEED)
Jn 12:24 But if it dies, it produces many *s.*
Gal 3:16 Scripture does not say "and to *s,"*

SEEDTIME* (SEED)
Ge 8:22 *s* and harvest,

SEEK (SEEKING SEEKS SELF-SEEKING SOUGHT)
Lev 19:18 Do not *s* revenge or bear a grudge
Dt 4:29 if from there you *s* the LORD your
1Ki 22: 5 "First *s* the counsel of the LORD."
1Ch 28: 9 If you *s* him, he will be found
2Ch 7:14 themselves and pray and *s* my
face
15: 2 If you *s* him, he will be found
Ps 34:10 those who *s* the LORD lack no
105: 3 of those who *s* the LORD rejoice.
105: 4 *s* his face always.
119: 2 and *s* him with all their heart.
119:10 I *s* you with all my heart;
119:176 *S* your servant,
Pr 8:17 and those who *s* me find me.
18:15 the ears of the wise *s* it out.
25:27 is it honorable to *s* one's own
honor
28: 5 those who *s* the LORD understand
Isa 55: 6 *S* the LORD while he may be
65: 1 found by those who did not *s* me.
Jer 29:13 You will *s* me and find me
Hos 10:12 for it is time to *s* the LORD,
Am 5: 4 "*S* me and live;
Zep 2: 3 *S* the LORD, all you humble
Mt 6:33 But *s* first his kingdom
7: 7 and it will be given to you; *s*
Lk 12:31 *s* his kingdom, and these things
will
19:10 For the Son of Man came to *s*
Jn 5:30 for I *s* not to please myself
Ro 10:20 found by those who did not *s* me;
1Co 7:27 you married? Do not *s* a divorce.
10:24 Nobody should *s* his own good,
Heb 11: 6 rewards those who earnestly *s*
him.
1Pe 3:11 he must *s* peace and pursue it.

SEEKING (SEEK)
2Ch 30:19 who sets his heart on *s* God—
Pr 20:18 Make plans by *s* advice;
Mal 3: 1 the Lord you are *s* will come
Jn 8:50 I am not *s* glory for myself;
1Co 10:33 For I am not *s* my own good

SEEKS (SEEK)
Pr 11:27 He who *s* good finds good will,
Mt 7: 8 he who *s* finds; and to him who
Jn 4:23 the kind of worshipers the
Father *s.*
Ro 3:11 no one who *s* God.

SEER
1Sa 9: 9 of today used to be called a *s.)*

SELF-CONTROL* (CONTROL)
Pr 25:28 is a man who lacks *s.*
Ac 24:25 *s* and the judgment to come,
1Co 7: 5 you because of your lack of *s.*
Gal 5:23 faithfulness, gentleness and *s.*
2Ti 3: 3 slanderous, without *s,* brutal,
2Pe 1: 6 and to knowledge, *s;* and to *s,*

SELF-CONTROLLED* (CONTROL)
1Th 5: 6 are asleep, but let us be alert
and *s.*
5: 8 let us be *s,* putting on faith and
love
1Ti 3: 2 *s,* respectable, hospitable,
Tit 1: 8 who is *s,* upright and holy
2: 2 worthy of respect, *s,* and sound
2: 5 to be *s* and pure, to be busy at
home

Tit 2: 6 encourage the young men to be *s.*
2:12 to live *s,* upright and godly lives
1Pe 1:13 prepare your minds for action;
be *s;*
4: 7 and *s* so that you can pray.
5: 8 Be *s* and alert.

SELF-DISCIPLINE* (DISCIPLINE)
2Ti 1: 7 a spirit of power, of love and of *s.*

SELF-INDULGENCE*
Mt 23:25 inside they are full of greed and *s.*
Jas 5: 5 lived on earth in luxury and *s.*

SELF-SEEKING* (SEEK)
Ro 2: 8 But for those who are *s*
1Co 13: 5 it is not *s,* it is not easily angered,

SELFISH*
Ps 119:36 and not toward *s* gain.
Pr 18: 1 An unfriendly man pursues *s*
ends;
Gal 5:20 fits of rage, *s* ambition,
dissensions,
Php 1:17 preach Christ out of *s* ambition,
2: 3 Do nothing out of *s* ambition
Jas 3:14 and *s* ambition in your hearts,
3:16 you have envy and *s* ambition,

SELL (SELLING SELLS SOLD)
Ge 25:31 "First *s* me your birthright."
Mk 10:21 *s* everything you have
Rev 13:17 or *s* unless he had the mark,

SELLING (SELL)
Lk 17:28 buying and *s,* planting and
building

SELLS (SELL)
Pr 31:24 makes linen garments and *s* them,

SEND (SENDING SENDS SENT)
Ps 43: 3 *S* forth your light and your truth,
Isa 6: 8 *S* me!" He said, "Go and tell this
Mal 3: 1 "See, I will *s* my messenger,
Mt 9:38 to *s* out workers into his harvest
24:31 And he will *s* his angels
Mk 1: 2 I will *s* my messenger ahead of
Lk 20:13 I will *s* my son, whom I love;
Jn 3:17 For God did not *s* his Son
16: 7 but if I go, I will *s* him to you.
1Co 1:17 For Christ did not *s* me to baptize,

SENDING (SEND)
Mt 10:16 I am *s* you out like sheep
Jn 20:21 Father has sent me, I am *s* you."
Ro 8: 3 God did by *s* his own Son

SENDS (SEND)
Ps 57: 3 God *s* his love and his faithfulness.

SENNACHERIB
Assyrian king whose siege of Jerusalem was
overthrown by the LORD following prayer of
Hezekiah and Isaiah (2Ki 18:13–19:37; 2Ch
32:1–21; Isa 36–37).

SENSES*
Lk 15:17 "When he came to his *s,* he said,
1Co 15:34 Come back to your *s* as you
ought,
2Ti 2:26 and that they will come to their *s*

SENSITIVITY*
Eph 4:19 Having lost all *s,* they have given

SENSUAL* (SENSUALITY)
Col 3: 5 value in restraining *s* indulgence.
1Ti 5:11 For when their *s* desires overcome

SENSUALITY* (SENSUAL)
Eph 4:19 have given themselves over to *s*

SENT (SEND)
Ex 3:14 to the Israelites: 'I AM has *s* me
Isa 55:11 achieve the purpose for which I *s*
it.
61: 1 He has *s* me to bind up
Jer 28: 9 as one truly *s* by the LORD only
Mt 10:40 me receives the one who *s* me.
Mk 6: 7 he *s* them out two by two
Lk 4:18 He has *s* me to proclaim freedom
9: 2 and he *s* them out to preach
10:16 rejects me rejects him who *s* me."
Jn 1: 6 There came a man who was *s*
4:34 "is to do the will of him who *s* me
5:24 believes him who *s* me has
8:16 I stand with the Father, who *s* me.
9: 4 must do the work of him who *s*
me.

Jn 16: 5 "Now I am going to him who *s*
            me,
      17: 3 and Jesus Christ, whom you
            have *s.*
      17:18 As you *s* me into the world,
      20:21 As the Father has *s* me, I am
Ro 10:15 can they preach unless they are *s?*
Gal   4: 4 God *s* his Son, born of a woman,
1Jn 4:10 but that he loved us and *s* his Son

SENTENCE
2Co 1: 9 in our hearts we felt the *s* of
            death.

SEPARATE (SEPARATED SEPARATES SEPARATION)
Mt 19: 6 has joined together, let man
            not *s.*"
Ro   8:35 Who shall *s* us from the love
1Co 7:10 wife must not *s* from her husband.
2Co 6:17 and be *s,* says the Lord.
Eph 2:12 at that time you were *s* from
            Christ,

SEPARATED (SEPARATE)
Isa 59: 2 But your iniquities have *s*
Eph 4:18 in their understanding and *s*

SEPARATES (SEPARATE)
Pr 16:28 and a gossip *s* close friends.
      17: 9 repeats the matter *s* close friends.
Mt 25:32 as a shepherd *s* the sheep

SEPARATION (SEPARATE)
Nu 6: 2 a vow of *s* to the LORD

SERAPHS*
Isa   6: 2 Above him were *s,* each
       6: 6 Then one of the *s* flew to me

SERIOUSNESS*
Tit   2: 7 *s* and soundness of speech that

SERPENT (SERPENT'S)
Ge   3: 1 the *s* was more crafty than any
Isa 27: 1 Leviathan the coiling *s;*
Rev 12: 9 that ancient *s* called the devil
      20: 2 that ancient *s,* who is the devil,

SERPENT'S (SERPENT)
2Co 11: 3 Eve was deceived by the *s*
            cunning,

SERVANT (SERVANTS)
Ex 14:31 trust in him and in Moses his *s.*
      21: 2 "If you buy a Hebrew *s,* he is
1Sa 3:10 "Speak, for your *s* is listening."
2Sa 7:19 the future of the house of your *s.*
1Ki 20:40 While your *s* was busy here
Job 1: 8 "Have you considered my *s* Job?
Ps 19:11 By them is your *s* warned;
      19:13 Keep your *s* also from willful sins;
      31:16 Let your face shine on your *s;*
      89: 3 I have sworn to David my *s,*
Pr 14:35 A king delights in a wise *s,*
      17: 2 wise *s* will rule over a disgraceful
      22: 7 and the borrower is *s* to the
            lender.
      31:15 and portions for her *s* girls.
Isa 41: 8 "But you, O Israel, my *s,*
      49: 3 He said to me, "You are my *s,*
      53:11 my righteous *s* will justify
Zec   3: 8 going to bring my *s,* the Branch.
Mal 1: 6 his father, and a *s* his master.
Mt   8:13 his *s* was healed at that very hour.
      20:26 great among you must be your *s,*
      24:45 Who then is the faithful and
            wise *s,*
      25:21 'Well done, good and faithful *s!*
Lk 1:38 I am the Lord's *s,*" Mary answered.
      16:13 "No *s* can serve two masters.
Jn 12:26 and where I am, my *s* also will be.
Ro 1: 1 a *s* of Christ Jesus, called
      13: 4 For he is God's *s* to do you good.
Php 2: 7 taking the very nature of a *s,*
Col 1:23 of which I, Paul, have become a *s.*
2Ti 2:24 And the Lord's *s* must not quarrel;

SERVANTS (SERVANT)
Lev 25:55 for the Israelites belong to me
            as *s.*
2Ki 17:13 to you through my *s* the
            prophets."
Ezr 5:11 "We are the *s* of the God of
            heaven
Ps 34:22 The LORD redeems his *s;*
  103:21 you his *s* who do his will.
  104: 4 flames of fire his *s.*
Isa 44:26 who carries out the words of his *s*

Isa 65: 8 so will I do in behalf of my *s;*
      65:13 my *s* will drink,
Lk 17:10 should say, 'We are unworthy *s;*
Jn 15:15 longer call you *s,* because a
            servant
Ro 13: 6 for the authorities are God's *s,*
1Co 3: 5 And what is Paul? Only *s,*
Heb 1: 7 his *s* flames of fire."

SERVE (SERVED SERVES SERVICE SERVING)
Dt 10:12 to *s* the LORD your God
      11:13 and to *s* him with all your heart
      13: 4 *s* him and hold fast to him.
      28:47 you did not *s* the LORD your
Jos 22: 5 and to *s* him with all your heart
      24:15 this day whom you will *s,*
      24:18 We too will *s* the LORD,
1Sa 7: 3 to the LORD and *s* him only,
      12:20 but *s* the LORD with all your heart
      12:24 *s* him faithfully with all your heart;
2Ch 19: 9 "You must *s* faithfully
Job 36:11 If they obey and *s* him,
Ps 2:11 *S* the LORD with fear
Da 3:17 the God we *s* is able to save us
Mt 4:10 Lord your God, and *s* him only.' "
      6:24 "No one can *s* two masters.
      20:28 but to *s,* and to give his life
Ro 12: 7 If it is serving, let him *s;*
Gal 5:13 rather, *s* one another in love.
Eph 6: 7 *S* wholeheartedly,
1Ti 6: 2 they are to *s* them even better,
Heb 9:14 so that we may *s* the living God!
1Pe 4:10 gift he has received to *s* others,
      5: 2 greedy for money, but eager to *s;*
Rev 5:10 kingdom and priests to *s* our God,

SERVED (SERVE)
Mt 20:28 Son of Man did not come to be *s,*
Jn 12: 2 Martha *s,* while Lazarus was
Ac 17:25 And he is not *s* by human hands,
Ro 1:25 and *s* created things rather
1Ti 3:13 Those who have *s* well gain

SERVES (SERVE)
Lk 22:26 one who rules like the one who *s.*
      22:27 But I am among you as one who *s.*
Jn 12:26 Whoever *s* me must follow me;
Ro 14:18 because anyone who *s* Christ
1Pe 4:11 If anyone *s,* he should do it

SERVICE (SERVE)
Lk 9:62 fit for *s* in the kingdom
      12:35 "Be dressed ready for *s*
Ro 15:17 in Christ Jesus in my *s* to God.
1Co 12: 5 There are different kinds of *s,*
      16:15 themselves to the *s* of the saints.
2Co 9:12 This *s* that you perform is not only
Eph 4:12 God's people for works of *s,*
Rev 2:19 and faith, your *s* and
            perseverance,

SERVING (SERVE)
Jos 24:15 if *s* the LORD seems undesirable
2Ch 12: 8 learn the difference between *s* me
Ro 12: 7 If it is *s,* let him serve;
      12:11 your spiritual fervor, *s* the Lord.
      16:18 people are not *s* our Lord Christ,
Eph 6: 7 as if you were *s* the Lord, not men,
Col 3:24 It is the Lord Christ you are *s.*
2Ti 2: 4 No one *s* as a soldier gets involved

SETH
Ge 4:25 birth to a son and named him *S,*

SETTLE
Mt 5:25 "*S* matters quickly
2Th 3:12 in the Lord Jesus Christ to *s* down

SEVEN (SEVENS SEVENTH)
Ge 7: 2 Take with you *s* of every kind
Jos 6: 4 march around the city *s* times,
1Ki 19:18 Yet I reserve *s* thousand in
            Israel—
Pr 6:16 *s* that are detestable to him:
      24:16 a righteous man falls *s* times,
Isa 4: 1 In that day *s* women
Da 9:25 comes, there will be *s* 'sevens,'
Mt 18:21 Up to *s* times?" Jesus answered,
Lk 11:26 takes *s* other spirits more wicked
Ro 11: 4 for myself *s* thousand who have
            not
Rev 1: 4 To the *s* churches in the province
      6: 1 opened the first of the *s* seals.
      8: 2 and to them were given *s*
            trumpets.
      10: 4 And when the *s* thunders spoke,

Rev 15: 7 to the *s* angels *s* golden bowls
            filled

SEVENS* (SEVEN)
Da 9:24 "Seventy '*s*' are decreed
      9:25 will be seven '*s,*' and sixty-two '*s.*'
      9:26 the sixty-two '*s,*' the Anointed

SEVENTH (SEVEN)
Ge 2: 2 By the *s* day God had finished
Ex 20:10 but the *s* day is a Sabbath
      23:11 but during the *s* year let the land
            lie
      23:12 but on the *s* day do not work,
Heb 4: 4 "And on the *s* day God rested

SEVERE
2Co 8: 2 Out of the most *s* trial, their
1Th 1: 6 of the Lord; in spite of *s* suffering,

SEWED (SEWS)
Ge 3: 7 so they *s* fig leaves together

SEWS (SEWED)
Mt 9:16 No one *s* a patch of unshrunk
            cloth

SEXUAL (SEXUALLY)
Ex 22:19 "Anyone who has *s* relations
Lev 18: 6 relative to have *s* relations.
      18: 7 father by having *s* relations
      18:20 Do not have *s* relations with
Mt 15:19 murder, adultery, *s* immorality,
Ac 15:20 by idols, from *s* immorality,
1Co 5: 1 reported that there is *s* immorality
      6:13 body is not meant for *s*
            immorality,
      6:18 Flee from *s* immorality,
      10: 8 should not commit *s* immorality,
2Co 12:21 *s* sin and debauchery
Gal 5:19 *s* immorality, impurity
Eph 5: 3 even a hint of *s* immorality,
Col 3: 5 *s* immorality, impurity, lust,
1Th 4: 3 that you should avoid *s*
            immorality

SEXUALLY (SEXUAL)
1Co 5: 9 to associate with *s* immoral
            people
      6: 9 Neither the *s* immoral nor
            idolaters
      6:18 he who sins *s* sins against his own
Heb 12:16 See that no one is *s* immoral,
      13: 4 the adulterer and all the *s*
            immoral.
Rev 21: 8 the murderers, the *s* immoral,

SHADE
Ps 121: 5 the LORD is your *s*
Isa 25: 4 and a *s* from the heat.

SHADOW
Ps 17: 8 hide me in the *s* of your wings
      23: 4 through the valley of the *s* of
            death,
      36: 7 find refuge in the *s* of your wings.
      91: 1 will rest in the *s* of the Almighty.
Isa 51:16 covered you with the *s* of my
            hand
Col 2:17 These are a *s* of the things that
Heb 8: 5 and *s* of what is in heaven.
      10: 1 The law is only a *s*

SHADRACH
    Hebrew exiled to Babylon; name changed
from Hananiah (Da 1:6–7). Refused defilement
by food (Da 1:8–20). Refused to worship idol
(Da 3:1–18); saved from furnace (Da 3:19–30).

SHAKE (SHAKEN SHAKING)
Ps 64: 8 all who see them will *s* their
            heads
      99: 1 let the earth *s.*
Hag 2: 6 I will once more *s* the heavens
Heb 12:26 "Once more I will *s* not only

SHAKEN (SHAKE)
Ps 16: 8 I will not be *s.*
      30: 6 "I will never be *s.*"
      62: 2 he is my fortress, I will never be *s.*
    112: 6 surely he will never be *s.*
Isa 54:10 Though the mountains be *s*
Mt 24:29 and the heavenly bodies will be *s.*'
Lk 6:38 *s* together and running over,
Ac 2:25 I will not be *s.*
Heb 12:27 that what cannot be *s* may
            remain.

SHAKING* (SHAKE)
Ps   22: 7 they hurl insults, *s* their heads:
Mt   27:39 insults at him, *s* their heads
Mk 15:29 *s* their heads and saying, "So!

SHALLUM
King of Israel (2Ki 15:10–16).

SHAME (ASHAMED SHAMED SHAMEFUL)
Ps   25: 3 will ever be put to *s*,
       34: 5 their faces are never covered
               with *s*
       69: 6 not be put to *s* because of me,
Pr   13:18 discipline comes to poverty and *s*,
       18:13 that is his folly and his *s*.
Jer   8: 9 The wise will be put to *s*;
         8:12 No, they have no *s* at all;
Ro   9:33 trusts in him will never be put
               to *s*."
       10:11 trusts in him will never be put
               to *s*."
1Co   1:27 things of the world to *s* the wise,
Heb 12: 2 endured the cross, scorning its *s*,

SHAMED (SHAME)
Jer   10:14 every goldsmith is *s* by his idols.
Joel   2:26 never again will my people be *s*.

SHAMEFUL (SHAME)
2Co   4: 2 have renounced secret and *s*
               ways;
2Pe   2: 2 Many will follow their *s* ways
Rev 21:27 nor will anyone who does what
               is *s*

SHAMGAR
Judge; killed 600 Philistines (Jdg 3:31).

SHAPE (SHAPES SHAPING)
Job 38:14 The earth takes *s* like clay

SHAPES (SHAPE)
Isa   44:10 Who *s* a god and casts an idol,

SHAPING (SHAPE)
Jer   18: 4 the pot he was *s* from the clay was

SHARE (SHARED SHARERS SHARES SHARING)
Ge   21:10 that slave woman's son will
               never *s*
Lev   19:17 frankly so you will not *s* in his
               guilt.
Dt   10: 9 That is why the Levites have no *s*
1Sa   30:24 All will *s* alike."
Eze   18:20 The son will not *s* the guilt
Mt   25:21 and *s* your master's happiness!'
Lk   3:11 "The man with two tunics
               should *s*
Ro   8:17 if indeed we *s* in his sufferings,
       12:13 *S* with God's people who are
2Co   1: 7 as you *s* in our sufferings,
Gal   4:30 the slave woman's son will never *s*
         6: 6 in the word must *s* all good things
Eph   4:28 something to *s* with those in
               need.
Col   1:12 you to *s* in the inheritance
2Th   2:14 that you might *s* in the glory
1Ti   5:22 and do not *s* in the sins of others.
         6:18 and to be generous and willing
               to *s*.
2Ti   2: 6 the first to receive a *s* of the
               crops.
Heb 12:10 that we may *s* in his holiness.
       13:16 to do good and to *s* with others,
Rev 22:19 from him his *s* in the tree of life

SHARED (SHARE)
Ps   41: 9 he who *s* my bread,
Ac   4:32 but they *s* everything they had.
Heb   2:14 he too *s* in their humanity so that

SHARERS* (SHARE)
Eph   3: 6 and *s* together in the promise

SHARES (SHARE)
Pr   22: 9 for he *s* his food with the poor.
Jn   13:18 'He who *s* my bread has lifted up

SHARING (SHARE)
1Co   9:10 so in the hope of *s* in the harvest.
2Co   9:13 for your generosity in *s* with them
Php   3:10 the fellowship of *s* in his
               sufferings,
Phm   : 6 you may be active in *s* your faith,

SHARON
SS   2: 1 I am a rose of *S*,

SHARP (SHARPENED SHARPENS SHARPER)
Pr   5: 4 *s* as a double-edged sword.
Isa   5:28 Their arrows are *s*,

Rev   1:16 came a *s* double-edged sword.
       19:15 Out of his mouth comes a *s* sword

SHARPENED (SHARP)
Eze   21: 9 *s* and polished—

SHARPENS* (SHARP)
Pr   27:17 As iron *s* iron,
       27:17 so one man *s* another.

SHARPER* (SHARP)
Heb   4:12 *S* than any double-edged sword,

SHATTER (SHATTERED SHATTERS)
Jer   51:20 with you I *s* nations,

SHATTERED (SHATTER)
1Sa   2:10 who oppose the Lord will be *s*.
Job 16:12 All was well with me, but he *s* me;
       17:11 days have passed, my plans are *s*,
Ecc 12: 6 before the pitcher is *s* at the
               spring,

SHATTERS (SHATTER)
Ps   46: 9 he breaks the bow and *s* the
               spear,

SHAVED
Jdg   16:17 my head were *s*, my strength
               would
1Co 11: 5 it is just as though her head
               were *s*.

SHEAF (SHEAVES)
Lev   23:11 is to wave the *s* before the Lord

SHEARER* (SHEARERS)
Ac   8:32 and as a lamb before the *s* is
               silent,

SHEARERS (SHEARER)
Isa   53: 7 and as a sheep before her *s* is
               silent,

SHEAVES (SHEAF)
Ge   37: 7 while your *s* gathered around
               mine
Ps   126: 6 carrying *s* with him.

SHEBA
1. Benjamite who rebelled against David
(2Sa 20).
2. See QUEEN.

SHECHEM
1. Raped Jacob's daughter Dinah; killed by
Simeon and Levi (Ge 34).
2. City where Joshua renewed the covenant
(Jos 24).

SHED (SHEDDING SHEDS)
Ge   9: 6 by man shall his blood be *s*;
Pr   6:17 hands that *s* innocent blood,
Ro   3:15 "Their feet are swift to *s* blood;
Col   1:20 through his blood, *s* on the cross.

SHEDDING (SHED)
Heb   9:22 without the *s* of blood there is no

SHEDS (SHED)
Ge   9: 6 "Whoever *s* the blood of man,

SHEEP (SHEEP'S SHEEPSKINS)
Nu   27:17 Lord's people will not be like *s*
Dt   17: 1 a *s* that has any defect or flaw in
               it,
1Sa   15:14 "What then is this bleating of *s*
Ps   44:22 we are considered as *s*
       78:52 led them like *s* through the
               desert.
      100: 3 we are his people, the *s*
      119:176 I have strayed like a lost *s*.
SS   4: 2 teeth are like a flock of *s* just
               shorn,
Isa   53: 6 We all, like *s*, have gone astray,
       53: 7 as a *s* before her shearers is silent,
Jer   50: 6 "My people have been lost *s*;
Eze   34:11 I myself will search for my *s*
Zec   13: 7 and the *s* will be scattered,
Mt   9:36 helpless, like *s* without a
               shepherd.
       10:16 I am sending you out like *s*
       12:11 "If any of you has a *s* and it falls
       18:13 he is happier about that one *s*
       25:32 as a shepherd separates the *s*
Jn   10: 1 man who does not enter the *s* pen
       10: 3 He calls his own *s* by name
       10: 7 the truth, I am the gate for the *s*.
       10:15 and I lay down my life for the *s*.
       10:27 My *s* listen to my voice; I know
       21:17 Jesus said, "Feed my *s*.
1Pe   2:25 For you were like *s* going astray,

SHEEP'S* (SHEEP)
Mt   7:15 They come to you in *s* clothing,

SHEEPSKINS* (SHEEP)
Heb 11:37 They went about in *s* and
               goatskins

SHEKEL
Ex   30:13 This half *s* is an offering

SHELTER
Ps   27: 5 me in the *s* of his tabernacle
       31:20 In the *s* of your presence you hide
       55: 8 I would hurry to my place of *s*,
       61: 4 take refuge in the *s* of your wings.
       91: 1 in the *s* of the Most High
Ecc   7:12 Wisdom is a *s*
Isa   4: 6 It will be a *s* and shade
       25: 4 a *s* from the storm
       32: 2 Each man will be like a *s*
       58: 7 the poor wanderer with *s*—

SHEM
Son of Noah (Ge 5:32; 6:10). Blessed (Ge
9:26). Descendants (Ge 10:21–31; 11:10–32).

SHEPHERD (SHEPHERDS)
Ge   48:15 the God who has been my *s*
       49:24 because of the *S*, the Rock of
               Israel
Nu   27:17 will not be like sheep without
               a *s*."
2Sa   7: 7 commanded to *s* my people Israel,
1Ki   22:17 on the hills like sheep without a *s*,
Ps   23: 1 Lord is my *s*, I shall not be in
               want.
       28: 9 be their *s* and carry them forever.
       80: 1 Hear us, O *S* of Israel,
Isa   40:11 He tends his flock like a *s*:
Jer   31:10 will watch over his flock like a *s*.'
Eze   34: 5 scattered because there was no *s*,
       34:12 As a *s* looks after his scattered
Zec   11: 7 and said, "I will not be your *s*.
       11:17 "Woe to the worthless *s*,
       13: 7 "Strike the *s*,
Mt   2: 6 who will be the *s* of my people
         9:36 and helpless, like sheep without
               a *s*.
       26:31 " 'I will strike the *s*,
Jn   10:11 The good *s* lays down his life
       10:14 "I am the good *s*; I know my
               sheep
       10:16 there shall be one flock and one *s*.
Heb 13:20 that great *S* of the sheep, equip
               you
1Pe   5: 4 And when the Chief *S* appears,
Rev   7:17 of the throne will be their *s*;

SHEPHERDS (SHEPHERD)
Jer   23: 1 "Woe to the *s* who are destroying
       50: 6 their *s* have led them astray
Eze   34: 2 prophesy against the *s* of Israel;
Lk   2: 8 there were *s* living out in the
               fields
Ac   20:28 Be *s* of the church of God,
1Pe   5: 2 Be *s* of God's flock that is
Jude   :12 *s* who feed only themselves.

SHIBBOLETH*
Jdg   12: 6 No," they said, "All right, say '*S*.' "

SHIELD (SHIELDED SHIELDS)
Ge   15: 1 I am your *s*,
2Sa   22: 3 my *s* and the horn of my salvation.
       22:36 You give me your *s* of victory;
Ps   3: 3 But you are a *s* around me,
         5:12 with your favor as with a *s*.
         7:10 My *s* is God Most High,
       18: 2 He is my *s* and the horn
       28: 7 Lord is my strength and my *s*;
       33:20 he is our help and our *s*.
       84:11 For the Lord God is a sun and a *s*;
       91: 4 his faithfulness will be your *s*
      115: 9 he is their help and *s*.
      119:114 You are my refuge and my *s*;
      144: 2 my *s*, in whom I take refuge,
Pr   2: 7 he is a *s* to those whose walk is
       30: 5 he is a *s* to those who take refuge
Eph   6:16 to all this, take up the *s* of faith,

SHIELDED (SHIELD)
1Pe   1: 5 through faith are *s* by God's
               power

SHIELDS (SHIELD)
Dt   33:12 for he *s* him all day long,

SHIFTLESS*
Pr   19:15   and the *s* man goes hungry.

SHIMEI
Cursed David (2Sa 16:5–14); spared (2Sa 19:16–23). Killed by Solomon (1Ki 2:8–9, 36–46).

SHINE (SHINES SHINING SHONE)
Nu   6:25   the LORD make his face *s*
Job 33:30   that the light of life may *s* on him.
Ps   4: 6   Let the light of your face *s* upon us,
      37: 6   make your righteousness *s* like
      67: 1   and make his face *s* upon us; *Selah*
      80: 1   between the cherubim, *s* forth
     118:27   and he has made his light *s* upon us.
Isa   60: 1   "Arise, *s*, for your light has come,
Da   12: 3   are wise will *s* like the brightness
Mt   5:16   let your light *s* before men,
     13:43   the righteous will *s* like the sun
2Co   4: 6   made his light *s* in our hearts
Eph   5:14   and Christ will *s* on you."
Php   2:15   in which you *s* like stars

SHINES (SHINE)
Ps   50: 2   God *s* forth.
Pr   13: 9   The light of the righteous *s* brightly
Jn   1: 5   The light *s* in the darkness,

SHINING (SHINE)
Pr   4:18   s ever brighter till the full light
2Pe   1:19   as to a light *s* in a dark place,
Rev   1:16   His face was like the sun *s*

SHIPS
Pr   31:14   She is like the merchant *s*,

SHIPWRECKED*
2Co 11:25   I was stoned, three times I was *s*,
1Ti   1:19   and so have *s* their faith.

SHISHAK
1Ki 14:25   S king of Egypt attacked Jerusalem
2Ch 12: 2   S king of Egypt attacked Jerusalem

SHOCKING*
Jer   5:30   "A horrible and *s* thing

SHONE (SHINE)
Mt   17: 2   His face *s* like the sun,
Lk   2: 9   glory of the Lord *s* around them,
Rev 21:11   It *s* with the glory of God,

SHOOT
Isa   53: 2   up before him like a tender *s*,
Ro   11:17   and you, though a wild olive *s*,

SHORE
Lk   5: 3   asked him to put out a little from *s*.

SHORT (SHORTENED)
Nu   11:23   "Is the LORD's arm too *s*?
Isa   50: 2   Was my arm too *s* to ransom you?
     59: 1   of the LORD is not too *s* to save,
Mt   24:22   If those days had not been cut *s*,
Ro   3:23   and fall *s* of the glory of God,
1Co   7:29   brothers, is that the time is *s*.
Heb   4: 1   of you be found to have fallen *s* of it
Rev 20: 3   he must be set free for a *s* time.

SHORTENED (SHORT)
Mt   24:22   of the elect those days will be *s*.

SHOULDER (SHOULDERS)
Zep   3: 9   and serve him *s* to *s*.

SHOULDERS (SHOULDER)
Dt   33:12   LORD loves rests between his *s*."
Isa   9: 6   and the government will be on his *s*
Lk   15: 5   he joyfully puts it on his *s*

SHOUT (SHOUTED)
Ps   47: 1   s to God with cries of joy.
     66: 1   S with joy to God, all the earth!
     95: 1   let us *s* aloud to the Rock
     98: 4   S for joy to the LORD, all the earth
    100: 1   S for joy to the LORD, all the earth
Isa   12: 6   S aloud and sing for joy, people
     26:19   wake up and *s* for joy.
     35: 6   the mute tongue *s* for joy.
     40: 9   lift up your voice with a *s*,
     42: 2   He will not *s* or cry out,
     44:23   s aloud, O earth beneath.

Isa   54: 1   burst into song, *s* for joy,
Zec   9: 9   S, Daughter of Jerusalem!

SHOUTED (SHOUT)
Job 38: 7   and all the angels *s* for joy?

SHOW (SHOWED)
Ex   18:20   and *s* them the way to live
     33:18   Moses said, "Now *s* me your glory
2Sa 22:26   the faithful you *s* yourself faithful,
1Ki   2: 2   "So be strong, *s* yourself a man,
Ps   17: 7   S the wonder of your great love,
     25: 4   S me your ways, O LORD,
     39: 4   "S me, O LORD, my life's end
     85: 7   S us your unfailing love, O LORD,
    143: 8   S me the way I should go,
Pr   23: 4   have the wisdom to *s* restraint.
SS   2:14   s me your face,
Isa   5:16   the holy God will *s* himself holy
     30:18   he rises to *s* you compassion.
Eze 28:25   I will *s* myself holy among them
Joel   2:30   I will *s* wonders in the heavens
Zec   7: 9   s mercy and compassion
Ac   2:19   I will *s* wonders in the heaven
     10:34   it is that God does not *s* favoritism
1Co 12:31   now I will *s* you the most excellent
Eph   2: 7   ages he might *s* the incomparable
Tit   2: 7   In your teaching *s* integrity,
Jas   2:18   I will *s* you my faith by what I do.
Jude   : 23   to others *s* mercy, mixed with fear

SHOWED (SHOW)
1Ki   3: 3   Solomon *s* his love for the LORD
Lk   24:40   he *s* them his hands and feet.
1Jn   4: 9   This is how God *s* his love

SHOWERS
Eze 34:26   in season; there will be *s* of blessing
Hos 10:12   and *s* righteousness on you.

SHREWD
2Sa 22:27   to the crooked you show yourself *s*.
Mt   10:16   Therefore be as *s* as snakes and

SHRINK (SHRINKS)
Heb 10:39   But we are not of those who *s* back

SHRINKS* (SHRINK)
Heb 10:38   And if he *s* back,

SHRIVEL
Isa   64: 6   we all *s* up like a leaf,

SHUDDER
Eze 32:10   and their kings will *s* with horror

SHUHITE
Job   2:11   Bildad the S and Zophar

SHUN* (SHUNS)
Job 28:28   and to *s* evil is understanding.' "
Pr   3: 7   fear the LORD and *s* evil.

SHUNS (SHUN)
Job   1: 8   a man who fears God and *s* evil."
Pr   14:16   man fears the LORD and *s* evil,

SHUT
Ge   7:16   Then the LORD *s* him in.
Isa   22:22   what he opens no one can *s*,
     60:11   they will never be *s*, day or night,
Da   6:22   and he *s* the mouths of the lions.
Heb 11:33   who *s* the mouths of lions,
Rev   3: 7   no one can *s*, and what he shuts
     21:25   On no day will its gates ever be *s*,

SICK (SICKNESS)
Pr   13:12   Hope deferred makes the heart *s*,
Eze 34: 4   or healed the *s* or bound up
Mt   9:12   who need a doctor, but the *s*.
     10: 8   Heal the *s*, raise the dead, cleanse
     25:36   I was *s* and you looked after me,
1Co 11:30   many among you are weak and *s*,
Jas   5:14   of you *s*? He should call the elders

SICKBED* (BED)
Ps   41: 3   LORD will sustain him on his *s*

SICKLE
Joel   3:13   Swing the *s*,
Rev 14:14   gold on his head and a sharp *s*

SICKNESS (SICK)
Mt   4:23   and healing every disease and *s*

SIDE (SIDES)
Ps   91: 7   A thousand may fall at your *s*,
    124: 1   If the LORD had not been on our *s*
Jn   18:37   Everyone on the *s* of truth listens

Jn   20:20   he showed them his hands and *s*.
2Ti   4:17   But the Lord stood at my *s*
Heb 10:33   at other times you stood *s* by *s*

SIDES (SIDE)
Nu   33:55   in your eyes and thorns in your *s*.

SIFT
Lk   22:31   Satan has asked to *s* you as wheat.

SIGHING
Isa   35:10   and sorrow and *s* will flee away.

SIGHT
Ps   51: 4   and done what is evil in your *s*,
     90: 4   For a thousand years in your *s*
    116:15   Precious in the *s* of the LORD
Pr   3: 4   in the *s* of God and man.
Mt   11: 5   The blind receive *s*, the lame walk,
Ac   4:19   right in God's *s* to obey you rather
1Co   3:19   this world is foolishness in God's *s*.
2Co   5: 7   We live by faith, not by *s*.
1Pe   3: 4   which is of great worth in God's *s*.

SIGN (SIGNS)
Ge   9:12   "This is the *s* of the covenant I am
     17:11   and it will be the *s* of the covenant
Isa   7:14   the Lord himself will give you a *s*:
     55:13   for an everlasting *s*,
Eze 20:12   I gave them my Sabbaths as a *s*
Mt   12:38   to see a miraculous *s* from you."
     24: 3   what will be the *s* of your coming
     24:30   "At that time the *s* of the Son
Lk   2:12   This will be a *s* to you: You will
     11:29   It asks for a miraculous *s*,
Ro   4:11   he received the *s* of circumcision,
1Co 11:10   to have a *s* of authority on her head
     14:22   are a *s*, not for believers

SIGNS (SIGN)
Ge   1:14   let them serve as *s* to mark seasons
Ps   78:43   day he displayed his miraculous *s*
    105:27   They performed his miraculous *s*
Da   6:27   he performs *s* and wonders
Mt   24:24   and perform great *s* and miracles
Mk   16:17   these *s* will accompany those who
Jn   3: 2   perform the miraculous *s* you are
     20:30   Jesus did many other miraculous *s*
Ac   2:19   and *s* on the earth below,
1Co   1:22   Jews demand miraculous *s*
2Co 12: 1   s, wonders and miracles—
2Th   2: 9   s and wonders, and in every sort

SIHON
Nu   21:21   to say to S king of the Amorites:
Ps   136:19   S king of the Amorites

SILAS*
Prophet (Ac 15:22–32); co-worker with Paul on second missionary journey (Ac 16–18; 2Co 1:19). Co-writer with Paul (1Th 1:1; 2Th 1:1); Peter (1Pe 5:12).

SILENCE (SILENCED SILENT)
1Pe   2:15   good you should *s* the ignorant talk
Rev   8: 1   there was *s* in heaven

SILENCED (SILENCE)
Ro   3:19   so that every mouth may be *s*
Tit   1:11   They must be *s*, because they are

SILENT (SILENCE)
Est   4:14   For if you remain *s* at this time,
Ps   30:12   to you and not be *s*.
     32: 3   When I kept *s*,
     39: 2   But when I was *s* and still,
Pr   17:28   a fool is thought wise if he keeps *s*,
Ecc   3: 7   a time to be *s* and a time to speak,
Isa   53: 7   as a sheep before her shearers is *s*,
     62: 1   For Zion's sake I will not keep *s*,
Hab   2:20   let all the earth be *s* before him."
Ac   8:32   and as a lamb before the shearer is *s*
1Co 14:34   women should remain *s*
1Ti   2:12   over a man; she must be *s*.

SILVER
Ps   12: 6   like *s* refined in a furnace of clay,
     66:10   you refined us like *s*.

Pr 2: 4 and if you look for it as for s
    3: 14 for she is more profitable than s
    8: 10 Choose my instruction instead
            of s,
   22: 1 to be esteemed is better than s
   25: 4 Remove the dross from the s,
   25: 11 is like apples of gold in settings
            of s.
Isa 48: 10 I have refined you, though not
            as s;
Eze 22: 18 They are but the dross of s.
Da 2: 32 its chest and arms of s, its belly
Hag 2: 8 'The s is mine and the gold is
            mine,'
Zec 13: 9 I will refine them like s
Ac 3: 6 Peter said, "S or gold I do not
            have,
1Co 3: 12 s, costly stones, wood, hay or
            straw
1Pe 1: 18 not with perishable things such
            as s

SILVERSMITH
Ac 19: 24 A s named Demetrius, who made

SIMEON
    Son of Jacob by Leah (Ge 29:33; 35:23; 1Ch
2:1). With Levi killed Shechem for rape of
Dinah (Ge 34:25–29). Held hostage by Joseph
in Egypt (Ge 42:24–43:23). Tribe of blessed
(Ge 49:5–7), numbered (Nu 1:23; 26:14), allotted land (Jos 19:1–9; Eze 48:24), 12,000 from
(Rev 7:7).

SIMON
    1. See PETER.
    2. Apostle, called the Zealot (Mt 10:4; Mk
3:18; Lk 6:15; Ac 1:13).
    3. Samaritan sorcerer (Ac 8:9–24).

SIMPLE
Ps 19: 7 making wise the s.
   119:130 it gives understanding to the s.
Pr 8: 5 You who are s, gain prudence;
   14: 15 A s man believes anything,

SIMPLEHEARTED* (HEART)
Ps 116: 6 The LORD protects the s;

SIN (SINFUL SINNED SINNER SINNERS SINNING
SINS)
Ge 4: 7 s is crouching at your door;
Ex 32: 32 please forgive their s— but if not,
Nu 5: 7 and must confess the s he has
   32: 23 be sure that your s will find you
Dt 24: 16 each is to die for his own s.
1Sa 12: 23 it from me that I should s
   15: 23 For rebellion is like the s
1Ki 8: 46 for there is no one who does not s
2Ch 7: 14 and will forgive their s and will
            heal
Job 1: 22 Job did not s by charging God
Ps 4: 4 In your anger do not s;
   17: 3 resolved that my mouth will not s.
   32: 2 whose s the LORD does not count
   32: 5 Then I acknowledged my s to you
   36: 2 too much to detect or hate his s.
   38: 18 I am troubled by my s.
   39: 1 and keep my tongue from s;
   51: 2 and cleanse me from my s.
   66: 18 If I had cherished s in my heart,
   119: 11 that I might not s against you.
   119:133 let no s rule over me.
Pr 5: 22 the cords of his s hold him fast.
   10: 19 words are many, s is not absent,
   14: 9 Fools mock at making amends
            for s,
   16: 6 faithfulness s is atoned for;
   17: 19 He who loves a quarrel loves s;
   20: 9 I am clean and without s "?
Isa 3: 9 they parade their s like Sodom;
    6: 7 is taken away and your s atoned
   64: 5 But when we continued to s;
Jer 31: 30 everyone will die for his own s;
Eze 3: 18 that wicked man will die for his s,
   18: 26 his righteousness and commits s,
   33: 8 that wicked man will die for his s,
Am 4: 4 "Go to Bethel and s;
Mic 6: 7 of my body for the s of my soul?
    7: 18 who pardons s and forgives
Zec 3: 4 "See, I have taken away your s,
Mt 18: 6 little ones who believe in me to s,
Mk 3: 29 he is guilty of an eternal s."
    9: 43 If your hand causes you to s,
Lk 17: 1 people to s are bound to come,

Jn 1: 29 who takes away the s of the
            world!
    8: 7 "If any one of you is without s,
    8: 34 everyone who sins is a slave to s.
    8: 46 Can any of you prove me guilty
            of s
Ro 2: 12 All who s apart from the law will
    5: 12 as s entered the world
    5: 20 where s increased, grace
            increased
    6: 2 By no means! We died to s;
    6: 11 count yourselves dead to s
    6: 14 For s shall not be your master,
    6: 23 For the wages of s is death,
    7: 7 I would not have known what s
            was
    7: 25 sinful nature a slave to the law
            of s.
   14: 23 that does not come from faith is s.
1Co 8: 12 When you s against your brothers
   15: 56 The sting of death is s,
2Co 5: 21 God made him who had no s to
            be s
Gal 6: 1 if someone is caught in a s,
1Ti 5: 20 Those who s are to be rebuked
Heb 4: 15 just as we are—yet was without s.
    9: 26 to do away with s by the sacrifice
   11: 25 the pleasures of s for a short time.
   12: 1 and the s that so easily entangles,
Jas 1: 15 it gives birth to s; and s,
1Pe 2: 22 "He committed no s,
1Jn 1: 7 his Son, purifies us from all s.
    1: 8 If we claim to be without s,
    2: 1 But if anybody does s, we have
            one
    3: 4 in fact, s is lawlessness.
    3: 5 And in him is no s.
    3: 6 No one who continues to s has
    3: 9 born of God will continue to s,
    5: 16 There is a s that leads to death.
    5: 17 All wrongdoing is s, and there is s
    5: 18 born of God does not continue
            to s;

SINAI
Ex 19: 20 descended to the top of Mount S
   31: 18 speaking to Moses on Mount S,
Ps 68: 17 from S into his sanctuary.

SINCERE* (SINCERITY)
Da 11: 34 many who are not s will join
            them.
Ac 2: 46 ate together with glad and s
            hearts,
Ro 12: 9 Love must be s.
2Co 6: 6 in the Holy Spirit and in s love;
   11: 3 somehow be led astray from
            your s
1Ti 1: 5 a good conscience and a faith.
    3: 8 s, not indulging in much wine,
2Ti 1: 5 have been reminded of your s
            faith,
Heb 10: 22 near to God with a s heart
Jas 3: 17 and good fruit, impartial and s.
1Pe 1: 22 the truth so that you have s love

SINCERITY* (SINCERE)
1Co 5: 8 bread without yeast, the bread
            of s
2Co 1: 12 in the holiness and s that are
    2: 17 speak before God with s,
    8: 8 but I want to test the s of your
            love
Eph 6: 5 and with s of heart, just
Col 3: 22 but with s of heart and reverence

SINFUL (SIN)
Ps 51: 5 Surely I was s at birth,
   51: 5 s from the time my mother
Lk 5: 8 from me, Lord; I am a s man!"
Ro 7: 5 we were controlled by the s
            nature,
    7: 18 lives in me, that is, in my s nature.
    7: 25 but in the s nature a slave to the
            law
    8: 3 Son in the likeness of s man
    8: 4 not live according to the s nature
    8: 7 the s mind is hostile to God.
    8: 8 by the s nature cannot please
            God.
    8: 9 are controlled not by the s nature
    8: 13 if you live according to the s
            nature

Ro 13: 14 to gratify the desires of the s
            nature
1Co 5: 5 so that the s nature may be
Gal 5: 13 freedom to indulge the s nature;
    5: 16 gratify the desires of the s nature.
    5: 19 The acts of the s nature are
            obvious
    5: 24 Jesus have crucified the s nature
    6: 8 sows to please his s nature,
Col 2: 11 in the putting off of the s nature,
Heb 3: 12 brothers, that none of you has a s,
1Pe 2: 11 abstain from s desires, which war
1Jn 3: 8 He who does what is s is

SING (SANG SINGER SINGING SINGS SONG SONGS
SUNG)
Ex 15: 1 "I will s to the LORD,
Ps 5: 11 let them ever s for joy.
   13: 6 I will s to the LORD,
   30: 4 S to the LORD, you saints of his;
   33: 1 S joyfully to the LORD, you
   47: 6 S praises to God, s praises;
   57: 7 I will s and make music.
   59: 16 But I will s of your strength,
   63: 7 I s in the shadow of your wings.
   66: 2 S to the glory of his name;
   89: 1 I will s of the LORD's great love
   95: 1 Come, let us s for joy to the LORD
   96: 1 S to the LORD a new song;
   98: 1 S to the LORD a new song,
   101: 1 I will s of your love and justice;
   108: 1 I will s and make music
   137: 3 "S us one of the songs of Zion!"
   147: 1 is to s praises to our God,
   149: 1 S to the LORD a new song,
Isa 54: 1 "S, O barren woman,
1Co 14: 15 also pray with my mind; I will s
Eph 5: 19 S and make music in your heart
Col 3: 16 and as you s psalms, hymns
Jas 5: 13 Is anyone happy? Let him s songs

SINGER* (SING)
2Sa 23: 1 Israel's s of songs:

SINGING (SING)
Ps 63: 5 with s lips my mouth will praise
   68: 6 he leads forth the prisoners
            with s;
   98: 5 with the harp and the sound of s,
Isa 35: 10 They will enter Zion with s;
Zep 3: 17 he will rejoice over you with s."
Ac 16: 25 Silas were praying and s hymns
Rev 5: 13 on the sea, and all that is in
            them, s:

SINGLE
Ex 23: 29 I will not drive them out in a s
            year,
Mt 6: 27 you by worrying can add a s hour
Gal 5: 14 law is summed up in a s
            command:

SINGS (SING)
Eze 33: 32 more than one who s love songs

SINNED (SIN)
Lev 5: 5 confess in what way he has s
1Sa 15: 24 Then Saul said to Samuel, "I
            have s
2Sa 12: 13 "I have s against the LORD."
   24: 10 I have s greatly in what I have
            done
2Ch 6: 37 'We have s, we have done wrong
Job 1: 5 "Perhaps my children have s
   33: 27 'I s, and perverted what was right,
Ps 51: 4 Against you, you only, have I s
Jer 2: 35 because you say, 'I have not s.'
   14: 20 we have indeed s against you.
Da 9: 5 we have s and done wrong.
Mic 7: 9 Because I have s against him,
Mt 27: 4 "I have s," he said,
Lk 15: 18 I have s against heaven
Ro 3: 23 for all have s and fall short
    5: 12 all s— for before the law was
            given,
2Pe 2: 4 did not spare angels when they s,
1Jn 1: 10 claim we have not s, we make him

SINNER (SIN)
Ecc 9: 18 but one s destroys much good.
Lk 15: 7 in heaven over one s who repents
   18: 13 'God, have mercy on me, a s.'
1Co 14: 24 convinced by all that he is a s
Jas 5: 20 Whoever turns a s from the error

1Pe 4:18 become of the ungodly and
           the s?"

SINNERS (SIN)
Ps   1: 1 or stand in the way of s
     37:38 But all s will be destroyed;
Pr   1:10 My son, if s entice you,
     23:17 Do not let your heart envy s,
Mt   9:13 come to call the righteous, but s."
Ro   5: 8 While we were still s, Christ died
Gal   2:17 evident that we ourselves are s,
1Ti   1:15 came into the world to save s—
Heb   7:26 set apart from s, exalted

SINNING (SIN)
Ex   20:20 be with you to keep you from s."
1Co 15:34 stop s; for there are some who are
Heb 10:26 If we deliberately keep on s
1Jn   3: 6 No one who lives in him keeps
           on s
      3: 9 go on s, because he has been
           born

SINS (SIN)
Lev   5: 1 " 'If a person s because he does
           not
     16:30 you will be clean from all your s.
     26:40 " 'But if they will confess their s
Nu   15:30 " 'But anyone who s defiantly,
1Sa   2:25 If a man s against another man,
2Ki 14: 6 each is to die for his own s."
Ezr   9: 6 our s are higher than our heads
      9:13 less than our s have deserved
Ps   19:13 your servant also from willful s;
     32: 1 whose s are covered.
     51: 9 Hide your face from my s
     79: 9 deliver us and forgive our s
     85: 2 and covered all their s.
    103: 3 who forgives all your s
    103:10 does not treat us as our s deserve
    130: 3 O LORD, kept a record of s,
Pr   14:21 He who despises his neighbor s,
     28:13 who conceals his s does not
     29:22 one commits many s.
Ecc   7:20 who does what is right and
           never s.
Isa   1:18 "Though your s are like scarlet,
     38:17 you have put all my s
     43:25 and remembers your s no more.
     59: 2 your s have hidden his face
     64: 6 like the wind our s sweep us away.
Jer 31:34 and will remember their s no
           more
La   3:39 complain when punished for
           his s?
Eze 18: 4 soul who s is the one who will die.
     33:10 Our offenses and s weigh us
           down,
     36:33 day I cleanse you from all your s,
Hos 14: 1 Your s have been your downfall!
Mt   1:21 he will save his people from
           their s
      6:15 if you do not forgive men their s,
      9: 6 authority on earth to forgive s.....'
     18:15 "If your brother s against you,
     26:28 for many for the forgiveness of s.
Lk   5:24 authority on earth to forgive s.....'
     11: 4 Forgive us our s,
     17: 3 "If your brother s, rebuke him,
Jn   8:24 you will indeed die in your s."
     20:23 If you forgive anyone his s,
Ac   2:38 for the forgiveness of your s.
      3:19 so that your s may be wiped out,
     10:43 forgiveness of s through his
           name."
     22:16 be baptized and wash your s
           away,
     26:18 they may receive forgiveness of s
Ro   4: 7 whose s are covered.
      4:25 delivered over to death for our s
1Co 15: 3 died for our s according
2Co   5:19 not counting men's s against
           them.
Gal   1: 4 himself for our s to rescue us
Eph   2: 1 dead in your transgressions and s,
Col   1:14 us all our s, having canceled
1Ti   5:22 and do not share in the s of
           others.
Heb   1: 3 he had provided purification for s,
      2:17 atonement for the s of the people.
      7:27 He sacrificed for their s once for
           all

Heb   8:12 and will remember their s no
           more
      9:28 to take away the s of many
           people;
     10: 4 of bulls and goats to take away s.
     10:12 for all time one sacrifice for s,
     10:26 of the truth, no sacrifice for s is
           left,
Jas   4:17 ought to do and doesn't do it, s.
      5:16 Therefore confess your s
      5:20 and cover over a multitude of s.
1Pe   2:24 He himself bore our s in his body
      3:18 For Christ died for s once for all,
      4: 8 love covers over a multitude of s.
1Jn   1: 9 If we confess our s, he is faithful
      2: 2 He is the atoning sacrifice for
           our s,
      3: 5 so that he might take away our s.
      4:10 as an atoning sacrifice for our s.
Rev   1: 5 has freed us from our s by his
           blood

SISERA
Jdg   4: 2 The commander of his army
           was S,
      5:26 She struck S, she crushed his
           head,

SISTER (SISTERS)
Lev 18: 9 have sexual relations with your s,
Mk   3:35 does God's will is my brother
           and s

SISTERS (SISTER)
Mt   19:29 or brothers or s or father or
           mother
1Ti   5: 2 as s, with absolute purity.

SIT (SAT SITS SITTING)
Dt   6: 7 them when you s at home
1Ki   8:25 fail to have a man to s before me
Ps   1: 1 or s in the seat of mockers.
     26: 5 and refuse to s with the wicked.
     80: 1 you who s enthroned
    110: 1 "S at my right hand
    139: 2 You know when I s and when I
           rise
SS   2: 3 I delight to s in his shade,
Isa 16: 5 in faithfulness a man will s on it—
Mic   4: 4 Every man will s under his own
Mt   20:23 to s at my right or left is not for
           me
     22:44 "S at my right hand
Lk   22:30 in my kingdom and s on thrones,
Heb   1:13 "S at my right hand
Rev   3:21 right to s with me on my throne,

SITS (SIT)
Ps   99: 1 s enthroned between the
           cherubim,
Isa 40:22 He s enthroned above the circle
Mt   19:28 of Man s on his glorious throne,
Rev   4: 9 thanks to him who s on the
           throne

SITTING (SIT)
Est   2:19 Mordecai was s at the king's gate.
Mt   26:64 the Son of Man s at the right hand
Rev   4: 2 in heaven with someone s on it.

SITUATION (SITUATIONS)
1Co   7:24 remain in the s God called him
Php   4:12 of being content in any and
           every s,

SITUATIONS* (SITUATION)
2Ti   4: 5 head in all s, endure hardship,

SKIES (SKY)
Ps   19: 1 the s proclaim the work
     71:19 Your righteousness reaches to
           the s
    108: 4 your faithfulness reaches to the s.

SKILL (SKILLED SKILLFUL)
Ps 137: 5 may my right hand forget its s..
Ecc 10:10 but s will bring success.

SKILLED (SKILL)
Pr   22:29 Do you see a man s in his work?

SKILLFUL (SKILL)
Ps   45: 1 my tongue is the pen of a s writer.
     78:72 with s hands he led them.

SKIN (SKINS)
Job 19:20 with only the s of my teeth.
     19:26 And after my s has been
           destroyed,

Jer 13:23 Can the Ethiopian change his s

SKINS (SKIN)
Ex   25: 5 ram s dyed red and hides
Lk   5:37 the new wine will burst the s,

SKULL
Mt   27:33 (which means The Place of the S).

SKY (SKIES)
Ge   1: 8 God called the expanse "s."
Pr   30:19 the way of an eagle in the s,
Isa   4: 4 and the s rolled up like a scroll;
Jer 33:22 stars of the s and as measureless
Mt   24:29 the stars will fall from the s,
     24:30 coming on the clouds of the s,
Rev 20:11 Earth and s fled from his
           presence,

SLACK*
Pr   18: 9 One who is s in his work

SLAIN (SLAY)
1Sa 18: 7 "Saul has s his thousands,
Eze 37: 9 into these s, that they may live.' "
Rev   5: 6 as if it had been s, standing
      5:12 "Worthy is the Lamb, who was s,
      6: 9 the souls of those who had been s

SLANDER (SLANDERED SLANDERER SLANDERERS
SLANDEROUS)
Lev 19:16 " 'Do not go about spreading s
Ps   15: 3 and has no s on his tongue,
Pr   10:18 and whoever spreads s is a fool.
2Co 12:20 outbursts of anger, factions, s,
Eph   4:31 rage and anger, brawling and s,
1Ti   5:14 the enemy no opportunity for s.
Tit   3: 2 to s no one, to be peaceable
1Pe   3:16 in Christ may be ashamed of
           their s
2Pe   2:10 afraid to s celestial beings;

SLANDERED (SLANDER)
1Co   4:13 when we are s, we answer kindly.

SLANDERER (SLANDER)
1Co   5:11 an idolater or a s, a drunkard

SLANDERERS (SLANDER)
Ro   1:30 They are gossips, s, God-haters,
1Co   6:10 nor the greedy nor drunkards
           nor s
Tit   2: 3 not to be s or addicted

SLANDEROUS (SLANDER)
2Ti   3: 3 unforgiving, s, without self-control
2Pe   2:11 do not bring s accusations

SLAUGHTER (SLAUGHTERED)
Isa 53: 7 he was led like a lamb to the s,
Jer 11:19 been like a gentle lamb led to
           the s;
Ac   8:32 "He was led like a sheep to the s,

SLAUGHTERED (SLAUGHTER)
Ps   44:22 we are considered as sheep to
           be s.
Ro   8:36 we are considered as sheep to
           be s

SLAVE (ENSLAVED SLAVERY SLAVES)
Ge   21:10 "Get rid of that s woman
Mt   20:27 wants to be first must be your s—
Jn   8:34 everyone who sins is a s to sin.
Ro   7:14 I am unspiritual, sold as a s to sin.
1Co   7:21 Were you a s when you were
           called
     12:13 whether Jews or Greeks, s or free
Gal   3:28 s nor free, male nor female,
      4: 7 So you are no longer a s, but a
           son;
      4:30 Get rid of the s woman and her
           son
Col   3:11 barbarian, Scythian, s or free,
1Ti   1:10 for s traders and liars and
           perjurers
Phm   :16 no longer as a s, but better than
           a s,
2Pe   2:19 a man is a s to whatever has

SLAVERY (SLAVE)
Ex   2:23 The Israelites groaned in their s
Ro   6:19 parts of your body in s to impurity
Gal   4: 3 were in s under the basic
           principles
1Ti   6: 1 of s should consider their masters

SLAVES (SLAVE)
Ps 123: 2 As the eyes of s look to the hand
Ecc 10: 7 I have seen s on horseback,

Ro 6: 6 that we should no longer be *s* to sin
6:16 you are *s* to sin, which leads
6:22 and have become *s* to God,
Gal 2: 4 in Christ Jesus and to make us *s*.
4: 8 you were *s* to those who
Eph 6: 5 *S*, obey your earthly masters
Col 3:22 *S*, obey your earthly masters
4: 1 provide your *s* with what is right
Tit 2: 9 Teach *s* to be subject

SLAY (SLAIN)
Job 13:15 Though he *s* me, yet will I hope

SLEEP (ASLEEP SLEEPER SLEEPING SLEEPS)
Ge 2:21 the man to fall into a deep *s;*
15:12 Abram fell into a deep *s,*
28:11 it under his head and lay down to *s.*
Ps 4: 8 I will lie down and *s* in peace,
121: 4 will neither slumber nor *s.*
127: 2 for he grants *s* to those he loves.
Pr 6: 9 When will you get up from your *s?*
Ecc 5:12 The *s* of a laborer is sweet,
1Co 15:51 We will not all *s,* but we will all be
1Th 5: 7 For those who *s,* *s* at night,

SLEEPER (SLEEP)
Eph 5:14 "Wake up, O *s,*

SLEEPING (SLEEP)
Mk 13:36 suddenly, do not let him find you *s.*

SLEEPLESS*
2Co 6: 5 in hard work, *s* nights and hunger;

SLEEPS (SLEEP)
Pr 10: 5 he who *s* during harvest is

SLIMY
Ps 40: 2 He lifted me out of the *s* pit,

SLING
1Sa 17:50 over the Philistine with a *s*

SLIP (SLIPPING)
Dt 4: 9 let them *s* from your heart as long
Ps 121: 3 He will not let your foot *s—*

SLIPPING (SLIP)
Ps 66: 9 and kept our feet from *s.*

SLOW
Ex 34: 6 and gracious God, *s* to anger,
Jas 1:19 *s* to speak and *s* to become angry,
2Pe 3: 9 The Lord is not *s* in keeping his

SLUGGARD
Pr 6: 6 Go to the ant, you *s;*
13: 4 The *s* craves and gets nothing,
20: 4 A *s* does not plow in season;
26:15 The *s* buries his hand in the dish;

SLUMBER
Ps 121: 3 he who watches over you will not *s;*
Pr 6:10 A little sleep, a little *s,*
Ro 13:11 for you to wake up from your *s,*

SLUR
Ps 15: 3 and casts no *s* on his fellow man,

SMELL
Ecc 10: 1 As dead flies give perfume a bad *s,*
2Co 2:16 To the one we are the *s* of death;

SMITTEN
Isa 53: 4 *s* by him, and afflicted.

SMOKE
Ex 19:18 Mount Sinai was covered with *s,*
Ps 104:32 touches the mountains, and they *s.*
Isa 6: 4 and the temple was filled with *s.*
Joel 2:30 blood and fire and billows of *s.*
Ac 2:19 blood and fire and billows of *s.*
Rev 15: 8 filled with *s* from the glory

SMYRNA
Rev 2: 8 the angel of the church in *S* write:

SNAKE (SNAKES)
Nu 21: 8 "Make a *s* and put it up on a pole;
Pr 23:32 In the end it bites like a *s*
Jn 3:14 Moses lifted up the *s* in the desert,

SNAKES (SNAKE)
Mt 10:16 as shrewd as *s* and as innocent
Mk 16:18 they will pick up *s* with their hands;

SNARE (ENSNARE ENSNARED SNARED)
Dt 7:16 for that will be a *s* to you.
Ps 69:22 before them become a *s;*
91: 3 from the fowler's *s*
Pr 29:25 Fear of man will prove to be a *s,*
Ro 11: 9 "May their table become a *s*

SNARED (SNARE)
Pr 3:26 will keep your foot from being *s.*

SNATCH
Jn 10:28 no one can *s* them out of my hand.
Jude :23 *s* others from the fire and save

SNOUT
Pr 11:22 Like a gold ring in a pig's *s*

SNOW
Ps 51: 7 and I will be whiter than *s.*
Isa 1:18 they shall be as white as *s;*

SNUFF (SNUFFED)
Isa 42: 3 a smoldering wick he will not *s* out.
Mt 12:20 a smoldering wick he will not *s* out,

SNUFFED (SNUFF)
Pr 13: 9 but the lamp of the wicked is *s* out.

SOAP
Mal 3: 2 a refiner's fire or a launderer's *s.*

SOAR (SOARED)
Isa 40:31 They will *s* on wings like eagles;

SOARED (SOAR)
2Sa 22:11 he *s* on the wings of the wind.

SOBER
Ro 12: 3 think of yourself with *s* judgment,

SODOM
Ge 13:12 and pitched his tents near *S.*
19:24 rained down burning sulfur on *S*
Isa 1: 9 we would have become like *S,*
Lk 10:12 on that day for *S* than for that town
Ro 9:29 we would have become like *S,*
Rev 11: 8 which is figuratively called *S*

SOIL
Ge 4: 2 kept flocks, and Cain worked the *s.*
Mt 13:23 on good *s* is the man who hears

SOLD (SELL)
1Ki 21:25 who *s* himself to do evil in the eyes
Mt 10:29 Are not two sparrows *s* for a penny
13:44 then in his joy went and *s* all he had
Ro 7:14 I am unspiritual, *s* as a slave to sin.

SOLDIER
1Co 9: 7 as a *s* at his own expense?
2Ti 2: 3 with us like a good *s* of Christ Jesus

SOLE
Dt 28:65 place for the *s* of your foot.
Isa 1: 6 From the *s* of your foot to the top

SOLID
2Ti 2:19 God's *s* foundation stands firm,
Heb 5:12 You need milk, not *s* food!

SOLOMON
Son of David by Bathsheba; king of Judah (2Sa 12:24; 1Ch 3:5, 10). Appointed king by David (1Ki 1); adversaries Adonijah, Joab, Shimei killed by Benaiah (1Ki 2). Asked for wisdom (1Ki 3; 2Ch 1). Judged between two prostitutes (1Ki 3:16–28). Built temple (1Ki 5–7; 2Ch 2–5); prayer of dedication (1Ki 8; 2Ch 6). Visited by Queen of Sheba (1Ki 10; 2Ch 9). Wives turned his heart from God (1Ki 11:1–13). Jeroboam rebelled against (1Ki 11:26–40). Death (1Ki 11:41–43; 2Ch 9:29–31). Proverbs of (1Ki 4:32; Pr 1:1; 10:1; 25:1); psalms of (Ps 72; 127); song of (SS 1:1).

SON (SONS SONSHIP)
Ge 17:19 your wife Sarah will bear you a *s,*
21:10 rid of that slave woman and her *s,*
22: 2 "Take your *s,* your only *s,* Isaac,
Ex 11: 5 Every firstborn *s* in Egypt will die,
Dt 1:31 father carries his *s,* all the way you
6:20 In the future, when your *s* asks you,

Dt 8: 5 as a man disciplines his *s,*
21:18 rebellious *s* who does not obey his
2Sa 7:14 be his father, and he will be my *s.*
1Ki 3:20 and put her dead *s* by my breast.
Ps 2: 7 He said to me, "You are my *S;*
2:12 Kiss the *S,* lest he be angry
8: 4 the *s* of man that you care for him?
Pr 3:12 as a father the *s* he delights in.
6:20 My *s,* keep your father's
10: 1 A wise *s* brings joy to his father,
13:24 He who spares the rod hates his *s,*
29:17 Discipline your *s,* and he will give
Isa 7:14 with child and will give birth to a *s,*
Eze 18:20 The *s* will not share the guilt
Da 3:25 the fourth looks like a *s* of the gods
7:13 before me was one like a *s* of man,
Hos 11: 1 and out of Egypt I called my *s.*
Am 7:14 neither a prophet nor a prophet's *s,*
Mt 1: 1 of Jesus Christ the *s* of David,
1:21 She will give birth to a *s,*
2:15 "Out of Egypt I called my *s.*"
3:17 "This is my *S,* whom I love;
4: 3 "If you are the *S* of God, tell these
8:20 but the *S* of Man has no place
11:27 one knows the *S* except the Father,
12: 8 For the *S* of Man is Lord
12:32 a word against the *S* of Man will be
12:40 so the *S* of Man will be three days
13:41 *S* of Man will send out his angels,
13:55 "Isn't this the carpenter's *s?*
14:33 "Truly you are the *S* of God."
16:16 "You are the Christ, the *S*
16:27 For the *S* of Man is going to come
17: 5 "This is my *S,* whom I love;
19:28 when the *S* of Man sits
20:18 and the *S* of Man will be betrayed
20:28 as the *S* of Man did not come
21: 9 "Hosanna to the *S* of David!"
22:42 Whose *s* is he?" "The *s* of David,"
24:27 so will be the coming of the *S*
24:30 They will see the *S* of Man coming
24:44 the *S* of Man will come at an hour
25:31 "When the *S* of Man comes
26:63 if you are the Christ, the *S* of God."
27:54 "Surely he was the *S* of God!"
28:19 and of the *S* and of the Holy Spirit,
Mk 1:11 "You are my *S,* whom I love;
2:28 So the *S* of Man is Lord
8:38 the *S* of Man will be ashamed
9: 7 "This is my *S,* whom I love.
10:45 even the *S* of Man did not come
13:32 nor the *S,* but only the Father.
14:62 you will see the *S* of Man sitting
Lk 1:32 and will be called the *S*
2: 7 she gave birth to her firstborn, a *s.*
3:22 "You are my *S,* whom I love;
9:35 This is my *S,* whom I have chosen;
9:58 but the *S* of Man has no place
12: 8 the *S* of Man will also acknowledge
15:20 he ran to his *s,* threw his arms
18: 8 when the *S* of Man comes,
18:31 written by the prophets about the *S*
19:10 For the *S* of Man came to seek
Jn 1:34 I testify that this is the *S* of God."
3:14 so the *S* of Man must be lifted up,
3:16 that he gave his one and only *S,*
3:36 believes in the *S* has eternal life,
5:19 the *S* can do nothing by himself;
6:40 is that everyone who looks to the *S*
11: 4 so that God's *S* may be glorified
17: 1 Glorify your *S,* that your *S* may
Ac 7:56 the *S* of Man standing
13:33 " 'You are my *S;*
Ro 1: 4 with power to be the *S* of God
5:10 to him through the death of his *S,*
8: 3 did by sending his own *S*
8:29 conformed to the likeness of his *S,*
8:32 He who did not spare his own *S,*

1Co 15:28 then the *S* himself will be made
Gal 2:20 I live by faith in the *S* of God,
     4: 4 God sent his *S*, born of a woman,
     4:30 rid of the slave woman and her *s*,
1Th 1:10 and to wait for his *S* from heaven,
Heb 1: 2 days he has spoken to us by his *S*,
     1: 5 "You are my *S*;
     2: 6 the *s* of man that you care for him?
     4:14 Jesus the *S* of God, let us hold
     5: 5 "You are my *S*;
     7:28 appointed the *S*, who has been
    10:29 punished who has trampled the *S*
    12: 6 everyone he accepts as a *s*."
2Pe 1:17 saying, "This is my *S*, whom I love;
1Jn 1: 3 is with the Father and with his *S*,
     1: 7 his *S*, purifies us from all sin.
     2:23 whoever acknowledges the *S* has
     3: 8 reason the *S* of God appeared was
     4: 9 only *S* into the world that we might
     4:14 that the Father has sent his *S*
     5: 5 he who believes that Jesus is the *S*
     5:11 eternal life, and this life is in his *S*.
Rev 1:13 lampstands was someone "like a *s*
    14:14 on the cloud was one "like a *s*

SONG (SING)
Ex 15: 2 LORD is my strength and my *s*;
Ps 40: 3 He put a new *s* in my mouth,
    69:30 I will praise God's name in a *s*
    96: 1 Sing to the LORD a new *s*;
    98: 4 burst into jubilant *s* with music;
   119:54 Your decrees are the theme of my *s*
   149: 1 Sing to the LORD a new *s*,
Isa 49:13 burst into *s*, O mountains!
    55:12 will burst into *s* before you,
Rev 5: 9 And they sang a new *s*:
    15: 3 and sang the *s* of Moses the servant

SONGS (SING)
2Sa 23: 1 Israel's singer of *s*:
Job 35:10 who gives *s* in the night,
Ps 100: 2 come before him with joyful *s*.
   126: 6 will return with *s* of joy,
   137: 3 "Sing us one of the *s* of Zion!"
Eph 5:19 with psalms, hymns and spiritual *s*.
Jas 5:13 Is anyone happy? Let him sing *s*

SONS (SON)
Ge   6: 2 the *s* of God saw that the daughters
    10:20 These are the *s* of Ham
Ru   4:15 who is better to you than seven *s*,
Ps 127: 3 *S* are a heritage from the LORD,
   132:12 if your *s* keep my covenant
Hos 1:10 they will be called *s*
Joel 2:28 Your *s* and daughters will prophesy
Mt   5: 9 for they will be called *s* of God.
Lk   6:35 and you will be *s* of the Most High;
Jn 12:36 so that you may become *s* of light."
Ro   8:14 by the Spirit of God are *s* of God.
     9:26 they will be called '*s*
2Co 6:18 and you will be my *s* and daughters
Gal 3:26 You are all *s* of God through faith
     4: 5 we might receive the full rights of *s*.
     4: 6 Because you are *s*, God sent
Heb 12: 7 discipline; God is treating you as *s*.

SONSHIP* (SON)
Ro   8:15 but you received the Spirit of *s*.

SORCERY
Lev 19:26 " 'Do not practice divination or *s*.

SORROW (SORROWS)
Ps   6: 7 My eyes grow weak with *s*;
   116: 3 I was overcome by trouble and *s*.
Isa 60:20 and your days of *s* will end.
Jer 31:12 and they will *s* no more.
Ro   9: 2 I have great *s* and unceasing
2Co 7:10 Godly *s* brings repentance that

SORROWS (SORROW)
Isa 53: 3 a man of *s*, and familiar

SOUGHT (SEEK)
2Ch 26: 5 As long as he *s* the LORD,
    31:21 he *s* his God and worked
Ps 34: 4 I *s* the LORD, and he answered me
   119:58 I have *s* your face with all my heart;

SOUL (SOULS)
Dt   6: 5 with all your *s* and with all your
    10:12 all your heart and with all your *s*,
    30: 6 all your heart and with all your *s*,
Jos 22: 5 with all your heart and all your *s*."
2Ki 23:25 and with all his *s* and with all his
Ps 23: 3 he restores my *s*.
    34: 2 My *s* will boast in the LORD;
    42: 1 so my *s* pants for you, O God.
    42:11 Why are you downcast, O my *s*?
    62: 5 Find rest, O my *s*, in God alone;
    63: 8 My *s* clings to you;
    94:19 consolation brought joy to my *s*.
   103: 1 Praise the LORD, O my *s*;
Pr 13:19 A longing fulfilled is sweet to the *s*,
    16:24 sweet to the *s* and healing
    22: 5 he who guards his *s* stays far
Isa 55: 2 your *s* will delight in the richest
La   3:20 and my *s* is downcast within me.
Eze 18: 4 For every living *s* belongs to me,
Mt 10:28 kill the body but cannot kill the *s*.
    16:26 yet forfeits his *s*? Or what can
    22:37 with all your *s* and with all your
Heb 4:12 even to dividing *s* and spirit,
3Jn   : 2 even as your *s* is getting along well.

SOULS (SOUL)
Pr 11:30 and he who wins *s* is wise.
Jer 6:16 and you will find rest for your *s*.
Mt 11:29 and you will find rest for your *s*.

SOUND (FINE-SOUNDING)
Ge   3: 8 and his wife heard the *s*
Pr   3:21 preserve *s* judgment
Eze 3:12 I heard behind me a loud rumbling *s*
Jn   3: 8 You hear its *s*, but you cannot tell
Ac   2: 2 Suddenly a *s* like the blowing
1Co 14: 8 if the trumpet does not *s* a clear call
    15:52 the trumpet will *s*, the dead will
1Ti 1:10 to the *s* doctrine that conforms
2Ti 4: 3 men will not put up with *s* doctrine.
Tit 1: 9 can encourage others by *s* doctrine
     2: 1 is in accord with *s* doctrine.

SOUR
Eze 18: 2 " 'The fathers eat *s* grapes,

SOURCE
Heb 5: 9 became the *s* of eternal salvation

SOVEREIGN (SOVEREIGNTY)
Ge 15: 2 But Abram said, "O S LORD,
2Sa 7:18 O S LORD, and what is my family,
Ps 71:16 your mighty acts, O S LORD;
Isa 25: 8 S LORD will wipe away the tears
    40:10 the S LORD comes with power,
    50: 4 S LORD has given me
    61: 1 The Spirit of the S LORD is on me,
    61:11 so the S LORD will make
Jer 32:17 to the LORD: "Ah, S LORD,
Eze 12:28 fulfilled, declares the S LORD,' "
Da   4:25 that the Most High is *s*
2Pe 2: 1 denying the *s* Lord who bought
Jude : 4 and deny Jesus Christ our only S

SOVEREIGNTY (SOVEREIGN)
Da   7:27 Then the *s*, power and greatness

SOW (SOWER SOWN SOWS)
Job 4: 8 and those who *s* trouble reap it.
Ps 126: 5 Those who *s* in tears
Hos 8: 7 "They *s* the wind
    10:12 S for yourselves righteousness,
Mt   6:26 they do not *s* or reap or store away
    13: 3 "A farmer went out to *s* his seed.
1Co 15:36 What you *s* does not come to life
Jas 3:18 Peacemakers who *s*
2Pe 2:22 and, "A *s* that is washed goes back

SOWER (SOW)
Isa 55:10 so that it yields seed for the *s*
Mt 13:18 to what the parable of the *s* means:

Jn   4:36 so that the *s* and the reaper may be
2Co 9:10 Now he who supplies seed to the *s*

SOWN (SOW)
Mt 13: 8 sixty or thirty times what was *s*.
Mk   4:15 along the path, where the word is *s*.
1Co 15:42 The body that is is *s* is perishable,

SOWS (SOW)
Pr 11:18 he who *s* righteousness reaps a sure
    22: 8 He who *s* wickedness reaps trouble
2Co 9: 6 Whoever *s* sparingly will
Gal 6: 7 A man reaps what he *s*.

SPARE (SPARES SPARING)
Est 7: 3 *s* my people—this is my request.
Ro   8:32 He who did not *s* his own Son,
    11:21 natural branches, he will not *s* you
2Pe 2: 4 For if God did not *s* angels
     2: 5 if he did not *s* the ancient world

SPARES (SPARE)
Pr 13:24 He who *s* the rod hates his son,

SPARING (SPARE)
Pr 21:26 but the righteous give without *s*.

SPARKLE
Zec 9:16 They will *s* in his land

SPARROW (SPARROWS)
Ps 84: 3 Even the *s* has found a home,

SPARROWS (SPARROW)
Mt 10:29 Are not two *s* sold for a penny?

SPEAR (SPEARS)
1Sa 19:10 as Saul drove the *s* into the wall.
Ps 46: 9 breaks the bow and shatters the *s*,

SPEARS (SPEAR)
Isa 2: 4 and their *s* into pruning hooks.
Joel 3:10 and your pruning hooks into *s*.
Mic 4: 3 and their *s* into pruning hooks.

SPECIAL
Jas 2: 3 If you show *s* attention

SPECK
Mt   7: 3 look at the *s* of sawdust

SPECTACLE
1Co 4: 9 We have been made a *s*
Col 2:15 he made a public *s* of them,

SPEECH
Ps 19: 3 There is no *s* or language
Pr 22:11 pure heart and whose *s* is gracious
2Co 8: 7 in faith, in *s*, in knowledge,
1Ti 4:12 set an example for the believers in *s*

SPEND (SPENT)
Pr 31: 3 do not *s* your strength on women,
Isa 55: 2 Why *s* money on what is not bread,
2Co 12:15 So I will very gladly *s*

SPENT (SPEND)
Mk   5:26 many doctors and had *s* all she had,
Lk   6:12 and *s* the night praying to God.
    15:14 After he had *s* everything,

SPIN
Mt   6:28 They do not labor or *s*.

SPIRIT (SPIRIT'S SPIRITS SPIRITUAL SPIRITUALLY)
Ge   1: 2 and the *S* of God was hovering
     6: 3 "My S will not contend
Ex 31: 3 I have filled him with the *S* of God,
Nu 11:25 and put the *S* on the seventy elders.
Dt 34: 9 filled with the *S* of wisdom
Jdg 6:34 Then the *S* of the LORD came
    11:29 Then the *S* of the LORD came
    13:25 and the *S* of the LORD began
1Sa 10:10 the *S* of God came upon him
    16:13 day on the *S* of the LORD came
    16:14 the *S* of the LORD had departed
2Sa 23: 2 "The *S* of the LORD spoke
2Ki 2: 9 inherit a double portion of your *s*,"
Ne   9:20 You gave your good S
     9:30 By your *S* you admonished them
Job 33: 4 The *S* of God has made me;

Ps   31: 5   Into your hands I commit my *s*;
      34:18   saves those who are crushed in *s*.
      51:10   and renew a steadfast *s* within
              me.
      51:11   or take your Holy *S* from me.
      51:17   sacrifices of God are a broken *s*;
     106:33   rebelled against the *S* of God,
     139: 7   Where can I go from your *S*?
     143:10   may your good *S*
Isa   11: 2   The *S* of the LORD will rest
      30: 1   an alliance, but not by my *S*,
      32:15   till the *S* is poured upon us
      44: 3   I will pour out my *S*
      57:15   him who is contrite and lowly in *s*,
      61: 1   The *S* of the Sovereign LORD is
      63:10   and grieved his Holy *S*.
Eze   11:19   an undivided heart and put a
              new *s*
      13: 3   prophets who follow their own *s*
      36:26   you a new heart and put a new *s*
Da   4: 8   and the *s* of the holy gods is in
              him
Joel   2:28   I will pour out my *S* on all people.
Zec   4: 6   but by my *S*,' says the LORD
Mt   1:18   to be with child through the
              Holy *S*
       3:11   will baptize you with the Holy *S*
       3:16   he saw the *S* of God descending
       4: 1   led by the *S* into the desert
       5: 3   saying: "Blessed are the poor in *s*,
      10:20   but the *S* of your Father speaking
      12:31   against the *S* will not be forgiven.
      26:41   *s* is willing, but the body is weak."
      28:19   and of the Son and of the Holy *S*,
Mk   1: 8   he will baptize you with the
              Holy *S*
Lk   1:35   "The Holy *S* will come upon you;
       1:80   child grew and became strong
              in *s*;
       3:16   will baptize you with the Holy *S*
       4:18   "The *S* of the Lord is on me,
      11:13   Father in heaven give the Holy *S*
      23:46   into your hands I commit my *s*."
Jn   1:33   who will baptize with the Holy *S*.'
       3: 5   a man is born of water and the *S*,
       4:24   God is *s*, and his worshipers must
       6:63   The *S* gives life; the flesh counts
       7:39   Up to that time the *S* had not
              been
      14:26   But the Counselor, the Holy *S*,
      16:13   But when he, the *S* of truth,
              comes,
      20:22   and said, "Receive the Holy *S*.
Ac   1: 5   will be baptized with the Holy *S*."
       1: 8   when the Holy *S* comes on you;
       2: 4   of them were filled with the
              Holy *S*
       2:17   I will pour out my *S* on all people.
       2:38   will receive the gift of the Holy *S*.
       4:31   they were all filled with the Holy *S*
       5: 3   that you have lied to the Holy *S*
       6: 3   who are known to be full of the *S*
       8:15   that they might receive the
              Holy *S*,
       9:17   and be filled with the Holy *S*."
      11:16   will be baptized with the Holy *S*.'
      13: 2   and fasting, the Holy *S* said,
      19: 2   "Did you receive the Holy *S*
Ro   8: 4   nature but according to the *S*.
       8: 5   set on what the *S* desires.
       8: 9   And if anyone does not have the *S*
       8:13   but if by the *S* you put
       8:16   The *S* himself testifies
       8:23   who have the firstfruits of the *S*,
       8:26   the *S* helps us in our weakness.
1Co   2:10   God has revealed it to us by his *S*.
       2:14   man without the *S* does not
              accept
       5: 3   present, I am with you in *s*.
       6:19   body is a temple of the Holy *S*,
      12:13   baptized by one *S* into one
              body—
2Co   1:22   and put his *S* in our hearts
       3: 3   but with the *S* of the living God,
       3: 6   the letter kills, but the *S* gives life.
       3:17   Now the Lord is the *S*,
       5: 5   and has given us the *S* as a
              deposit.
       7: 1   that contaminates body and *s*,
Gal   3: 2   Did you receive the *S*
       5:16   by the *S*, and you will not gratify

Gal   5:22   But the fruit of the *S* is love, joy,
       5:25   let us keep in step with the *S*.
       6: 8   from the *S* will reap eternal life.
Eph   1:13   with a seal, the promised Holy *S*,
       2:22   in which God lives by his *S*.
       4: 4   There is one body and one *S*—
       4:30   do not grieve the Holy *S* of God,
       5:18   Instead, be filled with the *S*.
       6:17   of salvation and the sword of
              the *S*,
Php   2: 2   being one in *s* and purpose.
1Th   5:23   May your whole *s*, soul
2Th   2:13   the sanctifying work of the *S*
1Ti   3:16   was vindicated by the *S*,
2Ti   1: 7   For God did not give us a *s*
Heb   2: 4   of the Holy *S* distributed
              according
       4:12   even to dividing soul and *s*,
      10:29   and who has insulted the *S* of
              grace
1Pe   3: 4   beauty of a gentle and quiet *s*,
2Pe   1:21   carried along by the Holy *S*.
1Jn   3:24   We know it by the *S* he gave us.
       4: 1   Dear friends, do not believe
              every *s*
       4:13   because he has given us of his *S*.
Jude   :20   holy faith and pray in the Holy *S*.
Rev   2: 7   let him hear what the *S* says

SPIRIT'S* (SPIRIT)
1Co   2: 4   a demonstration of the *S* power,
       5:19   not put out the *S* fire; do not treat

SPIRITS (SPIRIT)
1Co   12:10   to another distinguishing
              between *s*,
      14:32   The *s* of prophets are subject
1Jn   4: 1   test the *s* to see whether they are

SPIRITUAL (SPIRIT)
Ro   12: 1   to God—this is your *s* act of
              worship.
      12:11   but keep your *s* fervor, serving
1Co   2:13   expressing *s* truths in *s* words.
       3: 1   I could not address you as *s* but
      12: 1   Now about *s* gifts, brothers,
      14: 1   of love and eagerly desire *s* gifts,
      15:44   a natural body, it is raised a *s*
              body.
Gal   6: 1   you who are *s* should restore him
Eph   1: 3   with every *s* blessing in Christ.
       5:19   with psalms, hymns and *s* songs.
       6:12   and against the *s* forces of evil
1Pe   2: 2   newborn babies, crave pure *s*
              milk,
       2: 5   are being built into a *s* house

SPIRITUALLY (SPIRIT)
1Co   2:14   because they are *s* discerned.

SPIT
Mt   27:30   They *s* on him, and took the staff
Rev   3:16   I am about to *s* you out

SPLENDOR
1Ch   16:29   the LORD in the *s* of his holiness.
      29:11   the glory and the majesty and
              the *s*,
Job   37:22   of the north he comes in golden *s*;
Ps   29: 2   in the *s* of his holiness.
      45: 3   clothe yourself with *s* and
              majesty.
      96: 6   *S* and majesty are before him;
      96: 9   in the *s* of his holiness;
     104: 1   you are clothed with *s* and
              majesty.
     145: 5   of the glorious *s* of your majesty,
     145:12   and the glorious *s* of your
              kingdom.
     148:13   his *s* is above the earth
Pr   4: 9   and present you with a crown
              of *s*."
      16:31   Gray hair is a crown of *s*;
      20:29   gray hair the *s* of the old.
Isa   55: 5   for he has endowed you with *s*."
      60:21   for the display of my *s*.
      61: 3   the LORD for the display of his *s*.
      63: 1   Who is this, robed in *s*,
Hab   3: 4   His *s* was like the sunrise;
Mt   6:29   in all his *s* was dressed like one
Lk   9:31   appeared in glorious *s*, talking
2Th   2: 8   and destroy by the *s* of his
              coming.

SPOIL (SPOILS)
Ps   119:162 like one who finds great *s*.

SPOILS (SPOIL)
Isa   53:12   he will divide the *s* with the
              strong,
Jn   6:27   Do not work for food that *s*,

SPONTANEOUS*
Phm   :14   so that any favor you do will be *s*

SPOTLESS
2Pe   3:14   make every effort to be found *s*,

SPOTS (SPOTTED)
Jer   13:23   or the leopard its *s*?

SPOTTED (SPOTS)
Ge   30:32   and every *s* or speckled goat.

SPREAD (SPREADING SPREADS)
Ps   78:19   "Can God *s* a table in the desert?
Ac   6: 7   So the word of God *s*.
      12:24   of God continued to increase
              and *s*.
      13:49   of the Lord *s* through the whole
      19:20   the word of the Lord *s* widely
2Th   3: 1   message of the Lord may *s* rapidly

SPREADING (SPREAD)
Pr   29: 5   is *s* a net for his feet.
1Th   3: 2   God's fellow worker in *s* the
              gospel

SPREADS (SPREAD)
Pr   10:18   and whoever *s* slander is a fool.

SPRING (SPRINGS WELLSPRING)
Jer   2:13   the *s* of living water,
Jn   4:14   in him a *s* of water welling up
Jas   3:12   can a salt *s* produce fresh water.

SPRINGS (SPRING)
2Pe   2:17   These men are *s* without water

SPRINKLE (SPRINKLED SPRINKLING)
Lev   16:14   and with his finger *s* it on the
              front

SPRINKLED (SPRINKLE)
Heb   10:22   having our hearts *s* to cleanse us

SPRINKLING (SPRINKLE)
1Pe   1: 2   to Jesus Christ and *s* by his blood:

SPROUT
Pr   23: 5   for they will surely *s* wings
Jer   33:15   I will make a righteous Branch *s*

SPUR*
Heb   10:24   how we may *s* one another

SPURNS*
Pr   15: 5   A fool *s* his father's discipline,

SPY
Gal   2: 4   ranks to *s* on the freedom we
              have

SQUANDERED* (SQUANDERS)
Lk   15:13   there *s* his wealth in wild living.

SQUANDERS* (SQUANDERED)
Pr   29: 3   of prostitutes *s* his wealth.

SQUARE
Rev   21:16   The city was laid out like a *s*,

STABILITY*
Pr   29: 4   By justice a king gives a country *s*,

STAFF
Ge   49:10   the ruler's *s* from between his
              feet,
Ex   7:12   Aaron's *s* swallowed up their
              staffs.
Nu   17: 6   and Aaron's *s* was among them.
Ps   23: 4   your rod and your *s*,

STAIN (STAINED)
Eph   5:27   without *s* or wrinkle or any other

STAINED (STAIN)
Isa   63: 1   with his garments *s* crimson?

STAKES
Isa   54: 2   strengthen your *s*.

STAND (STANDING STANDS STOOD)
Ex   14:13   *S* firm and you will see
Jos   10:12   "O sun, *s* still over Gibeon,
2Ch   20:17   *s* firm and see the deliverance
Job   19:25   in the end he will *s* upon the
              earth.
Ps   1: 1   or *s* in the way of sinners
       1: 5   Therefore the wicked will not *s*
      24: 3   Who may *s* in his holy place?
      33:11   of the LORD *s* firm forever,

Ps 40: 2 and gave me a firm place to *s*.
76: 7 Who can *s* before you
93: 5 Your statutes *s* firm;
119:120 I *s* in awe of your laws.
130: 3 O Lord, who could *s*?
Ecc 5: 7 Therefore *s* in awe of God.
Isa 7: 9 If you do not *s* firm in your faith,
29:23 will *s* in awe of the God of Israel.
Eze 22:30 *s* before me in the gap on behalf
Hab 3: 2 I *s* in awe of your deeds, O LORD.
Zec 14: 4 On that day his feet will *s*
Mal 3: 2 Who can *s* when he appears?
Mt 12:25 divided against itself will not *s*.
Ro 14: 4 for the Lord is able to make him *s*.
14:10 we will all *s* before God's
judgment
1Co 10:13 out so that you can *s* up under it.
15:58 Therefore, my dear brothers, *s*
firm
16:13 Be on your guard; *s* firm in the
faith
Gal 5: 1 *S* firm, then, and do not let
Eph 6:14 *S* firm then, with the belt
2Th 2:15 *s* firm and hold to the teachings
we
Jas 5: 8 You too, be patient and *s* firm,
Rev 3:20 Here I am! I *s* at the door

STANDING (STAND)
Ex 3: 5 where you are *s* is holy ground."
Jos 5:15 the place where you are *s* is holy."
Ru 2: 1 a man of *s*, whose name was
Boaz.
4:11 May you have *s* in Ephrathah
Lk 21:19 By *s* firm you will gain life.
1Ti 3:13 have served well gain an
excellent *s*
1Pe 5: 9 Resist him, *s* firm in the faith,

STANDS (STAND)
Ps 89: 2 that your love *s* firm forever,
119:89 it *s* firm in the heavens.
Pr 12: 7 the house of the righteous *s* firm.
Isa 40: 8 but the word of our God *s*
forever."
Mt 10:22 but he who *s* firm to the end will
be
2Ti 2:19 God's solid foundation *s* firm,
1Pe 1:25 but the word of the Lord *s* forever

STAR (STARS)
Nu 24:17 A *s* will come out of Jacob;
Isa 14:12 O morning *s*, son of the dawn!
Mt 2: 2 We saw his *s* in the east
2Pe 1:19 the morning *s* rises in your hearts.
Rev 2:28 I will also give him the morning *s*.
22:16 and the bright Morning *S*."

STARS (STAR)
Ge 1:16 He also made the *s*.
Job 38: 7 while the morning *s* sang together
Da 12: 3 like the *s* for ever and ever.
Php 2:15 in which you shine like *s*

STATURE
1Sa 2:26 boy Samuel continued to grow
in *s*
Lk 2:52 And Jesus grew in wisdom and *s*,

STATUTES
Ps 19: 7 *s* of the LORD are trustworthy,
93: 5 Your *s* stand firm;
119: 2 Blessed are they who keep his *s*
119:14 I rejoice in following your *s*
119:24 Your *s* are my delight;
119:36 Turn my heart toward your *s*
119:99 for I meditate on your *s*.
119:111 Your *s* are my heritage forever;
119:125 that I may understand your *s*.
119:129 Your *s* are wonderful;
119:138 The *s* you have laid
119:152 Long ago I learned from your *s*
119:167 I obey your *s*,

STEADFAST*
Ps 51:10 and renew a *s* spirit within me.
57: 7 My heart is *s*, O God,
57: 7 my heart is *s*;
108: 1 My heart is *s*, O God;
111: 8 They are *s* for ever and ever,
112: 7 his heart is *s*, trusting in the LORD
119: 5 Oh, that my ways were *s*
Isa 26: 3 him whose mind is *s*,
1Pe 5:10 and make you strong, firm and *s*.

STEADY
Isa 35: 3 *s* the knees that give way;

STEAL (STOLEN)
Ex 20:15 "You shall not *s*.
Lev 19:11 "'Do not *s*.
Dt 5:19 "You shall not *s*.
Mt 19:18 do not *s*, do not give false
Ro 13: 9 "Do not *s*," "Do not covet,"
Eph 4:28 has been stealing must *s* no
longer,

STEP (FOOTSTEPS STEPS)
Job 34:21 he sees their every *s*.
Gal 5:25 let us keep in *s* with the Spirit.

STEPHEN
Deacon (Ac 6:5). Arrested (Ac 6:8–15).
Speech to Sanhedrin (Ac 7). Stoned (Ac
7:54–60; 22:20).

STEPS (STEP)
Ps 37:23 he makes his *s* firm;
Pr 14:15 prudent man gives thought to
his *s*.
16: 9 but the LORD determines his *s*.
20:24 A man's *s* are directed
Jer 10:23 it is not for man to direct his *s*.
1Pe 2:21 that you should follow in his *s*.

STERN (STERNNESS)
Pr 15:10 *S* discipline awaits him who leaves

STERNNESS* (STERN)
Ro 11:22 and *s* of God: *s* to those who fell,

STICKS
Pr 18:24 there is a friend who *s* closer

STIFF-NECKED (NECK)
Ex 34: 9 Although this is a *s* people,
Pr 29: 1 A man who remains *s*

STILL
Jos 10:13 So the sun stood *s*,
Ps 37: 7 Be *s* before the LORD
46:10 "Be *s*, and know that I am God;
89: 9 its waves mount up, you *s* them.
Zec 2:13 Be *s* before the LORD, all mankind
Mk 4:39 said to the waves, "Quiet! Be *s*!"

STIMULATE*
2Pe 3: 1 as reminders to *s* you

STING*
1Co 15:55 Where, O death, is your *s*?"

STINGY
Pr 28:22 A *s* man is eager to get rich

STIRRED (STIRS)
Ps 45: 1 My heart is *s* by a noble theme

STIRS (STIRRED)
Pr 6:19 and a man who *s* up dissension
10:12 Hatred *s* up dissension,
15: 1 but a harsh word *s* up anger.
15:18 hot-tempered man *s* up
dissension,
16:28 A perverse man *s* up dissension,
28:25 A greedy man *s* up dissension,
29:22 An angry man *s* up dissension,

STOLEN (STEAL)
Lev 6: 4 he must return what he has *s*
SS 4: 9 You have *s* my heart, my sister,

STOMACH
1Co 6:13 Food for the *s* and the *s* for
food"—
Php 3:19 their god is their *s*, and their glory

STONE (CAPSTONE CORNERSTONE MILLSTONE
STONED STONES)
Ex 24: 4 set up twelve *s* pillars
representing
28:10 on one *s* and the remaining six
34: 1 "Chisel out two *s* tablets like
Dt 4:13 then wrote them on two *s* tablets.
19:14 your neighbor's boundary *s* set up
1Sa 17:50 the Philistine with a sling and a *s*;
Ps 91:12 will not strike your foot against
a *s*.
118:22 The *s* the builders rejected
Pr 22:28 not move an ancient boundary *s*
Isa 8:14 a *s* that causes men to stumble
28:16 "See, I lay a *s* in Zion,
Eze 11:19 remove from them their heart of *s*
36:26 remove from you your heart of *s*
Mt 7: 9 will give him a *s*? Or if he asks
21:42 "'The *s* the builders rejected
24: 2 not one *s* here will be left

STRANGE (STRANGER STRANGERS)
Mk 16: 3 "Who will roll the *s* away
Lk 4: 3 tell this *s* to become bread."
Jn 8: 7 the first to throw a *s* at her."
Ac 4:11 "'the *s* you builders rejected,
Ro 9:32 stumbled over the "stumbling *s*."
2Co 3: 3 not on tablets of *s* but on tablets
1Pe 2: 6 "See, I lay a *s* in Zion,
Rev 2:17 also give him a white *s*

STONED (STONE)
2Co 11:25 once I was *s*, three times I was
Heb 11:37 They were *s*; they were sawed

STONES (STONE)
Ex 28:21 are to be twelve *s*, one for each
Jos 4: 3 to take up twelve *s* from the
middle
1Sa 17:40 chose five smooth *s*
Mt 3: 9 out of these *s* God can raise up
1Co 3:12 silver, costly *s*, wood, hay or straw,
1Pe 2: 5 also, like living *s*, are being built

STOOD (STAND)
Jos 10:13 So the sun *s* still,
Lk 22:28 You are those who have *s* by me
2Ti 4:17 But the Lord *s* at my side
Jas 1:12 because when he has *s* the test,

STOOP (STOOPS)
2Sa 22:36 you *s* down to make me great.

STOOPS (STOOP)
Ps 113: 6 who *s* down to look

STOP
Job 37:14 *s* and consider God's wonders.
Isa 1:13 *S* bringing meaningless offerings!
1:16 *S* doing wrong,
2:22 *S* trusting in man,
Jer 32:40 I will never *s* doing good to them,
Mk 9:39 "Do not *s* him," Jesus said.
Jn 6:43 "*S* grumbling among yourselves,"
7:24 *S* judging by mere appearances,
20:27 *S* doubting and believe."
Ro 14:13 Therefore let us *s* passing
judgment
1Co 14:20 Brothers, *s* thinking like children.

STORE (STORED)
Pr 2: 1 and *s* up my commands within
you,
7: 1 and *s* up my commands within
you.
10:14 Wise men *s* up knowledge,
Isa 33: 6 a rich *s* of salvation and wisdom
Mt 6:19 not *s* up for yourselves treasures
6:26 or reap or *s* away in barns,
2Ti 4: 8 Now there is in *s* for me the
crown

STORED (STORE)
Lk 6:45 out of the good *s* up in his heart,
Col 1: 5 from the hope that is *s* up for you

STOREHOUSE (HOUSE)
Mal 3:10 Bring the whole tithe into the *s*,

STORIES*
2Pe 1:16 did not follow cleverly invented *s*
2: 3 you with *s* they have made up.

STORM
Job 38: 1 LORD answered Job out of the *s*.
Ps 107:29 He stilled the *s* to a whisper;
Lk 8:24 the *s* subsided, and all was calm.

STOUTHEARTED* (HEART)
Ps 138: 3 you made me bold and *s*.

STRAIGHT
Ps 27:11 lead me in a *s* path
107: 7 He led them by a *s* way
Pr 2:13 who leave the *s* paths
3: 6 and he will make your paths *s*.
4:11 and lead you along *s* paths.
4:25 Let your eyes look *s* ahead,
11: 5 of the blameless makes a *s* way
15:21 of understanding keeps a *s*
course.
Isa 40: 3 make *s* in the wilderness
Mt 3: 3 make *s* paths for him.'"
Jn 1:23 'Make *s* the way for the Lord.'"
2Pe 2:15 They have left the *s* way

STRAIN (STRAINING)
Mt 23:24 You *s* out a gnat but swallow

STRAINING (STRAIN)
Php 3:13 and *s* toward what is ahead,

STRANGE (STRANGER STRANGERS)
Isa 28:11 with foreign lips and *s* tongues

1Co 14:21 "Through men of *s* tongues
1Pe 4: 4 They think it *s* that you do not
STRANGER (STRANGE)
Ps 119:19 I am a *s* on earth;
Mt 25:35 I was a *s* and you invited me in,
Jn 10: 5 But they will never follow a *s;*
STRANGERS (STRANGE)
Heb 13: 2 Do not forget to entertain *s,*
1Pe 2:11 as aliens and *s* in the world,
STRAW
Isa 11: 7 and the lion will eat *s* like the ox.
1Co 3:12 silver, costly stones, wood, hay
        or *s*
STRAYED (STRAYS)
Ps 119:176 I have *s* like a lost sheep.
Jer 31:19 After I *s,*
STRAYS (STRAYED)
Pr 21:16 A man who *s* from the path
Eze 34:16 for the lost and bring back the *s.*
STREAM (STREAMS)
Am   5:24 righteousness like a never-
        failing *s!*
STREAMS (STREAM)
Ps   1: 3 He is like a tree planted by *s*
     46: 4 is a river whose *s* make glad
Ecc 2: 7 All *s* flow into the sea,
Jn   7:38 *s* of living water will flow
STREET
Mt   6: 5 on the *s* corners to be seen by
        men.
     22: 9 Go to the *s* corners and invite
Rev 21:21 The great *s* of the city was of pure
        gold,
STRENGTH (STRONG)
Ex 15: 2 The LORD is my *s* and my song;
Dt   4:37 by his Presence and his great *s,*
     6: 5 all your soul and with all your *s.*
Jdg 16:15 told me the secret of your
        great *s.*"
2Sa 22:33 It is God who arms me with *s*
2Ki 23:25 with all his soul and with all his *s,*
1Ch 16:11 Look to the LORD and his *s;*
     16:28 ascribe to the LORD glory and *s,*
     29:12 In your hands are *s* and power
Ne   8:10 for the joy of the LORD is your *s.*"
Ps 18: 1 I love you, O LORD, my *s.*
     21:13 Be exalted, O LORD, in your *s;*
     28: 7 The LORD is my *s* and my shield;
     29:11 The LORD gives *s* to his people;
     33:16 no warrior escapes by his great *s.*
     46: 1 God is our refuge and *s,*
     59:17 O my *S,* I sing praise to you;
     65: 6 having armed yourself with *s,*
     73:26 but God is the *s* of my heart
     84: 5 Blessed are those whose *s* is in
        you,
     96: 7 ascribe to the LORD glory and *s.*
    105: 4 Look to the LORD and his *s;*
    118:14 The LORD is my *s* and my song;
    147:10 not in the *s* of the horse,
Pr 24: 5 a man of knowledge increases *s;*
     30:25 Ants are creatures of little *s,*
Isa 12: 2 the LORD is my *s* and my song;
     31: 1 and in the great *s* of their
        horsemen
     40:26 of his great power and mighty *s,*
     40:31 will renew their *s.*
     63: 1 forward in the greatness of his *s?*
Jer 9:23 or the strong man boast of his *s*
Mic 5: 4 flock in the *s* of the LORD,
Hab 3:19 The Sovereign LORD is my *s;*
Mk 12:30 all your mind and with all your *s.*'
1Co 1:25 of God is stronger than man's *s.*
Eph 1:19 is like the working of his mighty *s,*
Php 4:13 through him who gives me *s.*
Heb 11:34 whose weakness was turned to *s;*
1Pe 4:11 it with the *s* God provides.
STRENGTHEN (STRONG)
2Ch 16: 9 to *s* those whose hearts are fully
Ps 119:28 *s* me according to your word.
Isa 35: 3 *S* the feeble hands,
     41:10 I will *s* you and help you;
Lk 22:32 have turned back, *s* your
        brothers.
Eph 3:16 of his glorious riches he may *s* you
1Th 3:13 May he *s* your hearts
2Th 2:17 and *s* you in every good deed

Heb 12:12 *s* your feeble arms and weak
        knees.
STRENGTHENED (STRONG)
Col 1:11 being *s* with all power according
Heb 13: 9 good for our hearts to be *s* by
        grace,
STRENGTHENING (STRONG)
1Co 14:26 done for the *s* of the church.
STRETCHES
Ps 104: 2 he *s* out the heavens like a tent
STRICKEN (STRIKE)
Isa 53: 8 of my people he was *s.*
STRICT
1Co 9:25 in the games goes into *s* training.
STRIFE (STRIVE)
Pr 17: 1 than a house full of feasting,
        with *s.*
     20: 3 It is to a man's honor to avoid *s,*
     22:10 out the mocker, and out goes *s;*
     30:33 so stirring up anger produces *s.*"
1Ti 6: 4 *s,* malicious talk, evil suspicions
STRIKE (STRIKES STROKE)
Ge   3:15 and you will *s* his heel."
Zec 13: 7 "*S* the shepherd,
Mt   4: 6 so that you will not *s* your foot
     26:31 " 'I will *s* the shepherd,
STRIKES (STRIKE)
Mt   5:39 If someone *s* you on the right
STRIPS
Lk   2:12 You will find a baby wrapped in *s*
Jn 20: 5 in at the *s* of linen lying there
STRIVE* (STRIFE)
Ac 24:16 I *s* always to keep my conscience
1Ti 4:10 (and for this we labor and *s),*
STROKE (STRIKE)
Mt   5:18 the smallest letter, not the least *s*
STRONG (STRENGTH STRENGTHEN STRENGTHENED
STRENGTHENING STRONGER)
Dt   3:24 your greatness and your *s* hand.
     31: 6 Be *s* and courageous,
Jos 1: 6 "Be *s* and courageous,
Jdg 5:21 March on, my soul; be *s!*
2Sa 10:12 Be *s* and let us fight bravely
1Ki 2: 2 "So be *s,* show yourself a man,
1Ch 28:20 "Be *s* and courageous,
2Ch 32: 7 them with these words: "Be *s*
Ps 24: 8 The LORD *s* and mighty,
     31: 2 a *s* fortress to save me.
     62:11 that you, O God, are *s,*
Pr 18:10 The name of the LORD is a *s* tower
     31:17 her arms are *s* for her tasks.
Ecc 9:11 or the battle to the *s,*
SS   8: 6 for love is as *s* as death,
Isa 35: 4 "Be *s,* do not fear;
     53:12 he will divide the spoils with
        the *s.*
Jer 9:23 or the *s* man boast of his strength
     50:34 Yet their Redeemer is *s;*
Hag 2: 4 Be *s,* all you people of the land,'
Mt 12:29 can anyone enter a *s* man's house
Lk   2:40 And the child grew and became *s;*
Ro 15: 1 We who are *s* ought to bear
1Co 1: 8 He will keep you *s* to the end,
     1:27 things of the world to shame
        the *s.*
     16:13 in the faith; be men of courage;
        be *s*
2Co 12:10 For when I am weak, then I am *s.*
Eph 6:10 be *s* in the Lord and in his mighty
2Ti 2: 1 be *s* in the grace that is
1Pe 5:10 restore you and make you *s,*
STRONGER (STRONG)
Dt   4:38 before you nations greater and *s*
1Co 1:25 of God is *s* than man's strength.
STRONGHOLD (STRONGHOLDS)
2Sa 22: 3 He is my *s,* my refuge and my
Ps   9: 9 a *s* in times of trouble.
     18: 2 the horn of my salvation, my *s.*
     27: 1 The LORD is the *s* of my life—
    144: 2 my *s* and my deliverer,
STRONGHOLDS (STRONGHOLD)
Zep 3: 6 their *s* are demolished.
2Co 10: 4 have divine power to demolish *s.*
STRUGGLE (STRUGGLED STRUGGLING)
Ro 15:30 me in my *s* by praying to God
Eph 6:12 For our *s* is not against flesh

Heb 12: 4 In your *s* against sin, you have not
STRUGGLED (STRUGGLE)
Ge 32:28 because you have *s* with God
STRUGGLING* (STRUGGLE)
Col 1:29 To this end I labor, *s*
     2: 1 to know how much I am *s* for you
STUDENT (STUDY)
Mt 10:24 "A *s* is not above his teacher,
STUDY (STUDENT)
Ezr 7:10 Ezra had devoted himself to the *s*
Ecc 12:12 and much *s* wearies the body.
Jn   5:39 You diligently *s* the Scriptures
STUMBLE (STUMBLES STUMBLING)
Ps 37:24 though he *s,* he will not fall,
    119:165 and nothing can make them *s.*
Pr   3:23 and your foot will not *s;*
Isa 8:14 a stone that causes men to *s*
Jer 13:16 before your feet *s*
     31: 9 a level path where they will not *s,*
Eze 7:19 for it has made them *s* into sin.
Hos 14: 9 but the rebellious *s* in them.
Mal 2: 8 teaching have caused many to *s;*
Jn 11: 9 A man who walks by day will
        not *s,*
Ro   9:33 in Zion a stone that causes men
        to *s*
     14:20 that causes someone else to *s.*
1Co 10:32 Do not cause anyone to *s,*
Jas 3: 2 We all *s* in many ways.
1Pe 2: 8 and, "A stone that causes men
        to *s*
1Jn 2:10 nothing in him to make him *s.*
STUMBLES (STUMBLE)
Pr 24:17 when he *s,* do not let your heart
Jn 11:10 is when he walks by night that
        he *s,*
Jas 2:10 and yet *s* at just one point is guilty
STUMBLING
Lev 19:14 put a *s* block in front of the blind,
Ps 56:13 and my feet from *s,*
Mt 16:23 Satan! You are a *s* block to me;
Ro   9:32 They stumbled over the "*s* stone."
     11: 9 a *s* block and a retribution for
        them
     14:13 up your mind not to put any *s*
        block
1Co 1:23 a *s* block to Jews and foolishness
     8: 9 freedom does not become a *s*
        block
2Co 6: 3 We put no *s* block in anyone's
        path,
STUMP
Isa 6:13 so the holy seed will be the *s*
     11: 1 up from the *s* of Jesse;
STUPID
Pr 12: 1 but he who hates correction is *s.*
2Ti 2:23 to do with foolish and *s*
        arguments,
STUPOR
Ro 11: 8 "God gave them a spirit of *s,*
SUBDUE (SUBDUED)
Ge   1:28 in number; fill the earth and *s* it.
SUBDUED (SUBDUE)
Jos 10:40 So Joshua *s* the whole region,
Ps 47: 3 He *s* nations under us,
SUBJECT (SUBJECTED)
Mt   5:22 angry with his brother will be *s*
1Co 14:32 of prophets are *s* to the control
     15:28 then the Son himself will be
        made *s*
Tit 2: 5 and to be *s* to their husbands,
     2: 9 slaves to be *s* to their masters
     3: 1 Remind the people to be *s* to
        rulers
SUBJECTED (SUBJECT)
Ro   8:20 For the creation was *s*
SUBMISSION (SUBMIT)
1Co 14:34 but must be in *s,* as the Law says.
1Ti 2:11 learn in quietness and full *s.*
SUBMISSIVE (SUBMIT)
Jas 3:17 then peace-loving, considerate,
1Pe 3: 1 in the same way be *s*
     5: 5 in the same way be *s*
SUBMIT (SUBMISSION SUBMISSIVE SUBMITS)
Ro 13: 1 Everyone must *s* himself

Ro 13: 5 necessary to *s* to the authorities,
1Co 16:16 to *s* to such as these
Eph 5:21 *S* to one another out of reverence
Col 3:18 Wives, *s* to your husbands,
Heb 12: 9 How much more should we *s*
     13:17 Obey your leaders and *s*
Jas 4: 7 *S* yourselves, then, to God.
1Pe 2:18 *s* yourselves to your masters

SUBMITS* (SUBMIT)
Eph 5:24 Now as the church *s* to Christ,

SUBTRACT*
Dt 4: 2 what I command you and do not *s*

SUCCEED (SUCCESS SUCCESSFUL)
Ps 20: 4 and make all your plans *s*.
Pr 15:22 but with many advisers they *s*.
     16: 3 and your plans will *s*.
     21:30 that can *s* against the LORD.

SUCCESS (SUCCEED)
Ge 39:23 and gave him *s* in whatever he did.
1Sa 18:14 In everything he did he had great *s*,
1Ch 12:18 *S, s* to you, and *s*
     22:13 you will have *s* if you are careful
2Ch 26: 5 the LORD, God gave him *s*.
Ecc 10:10 but skill will bring *s*.

SUCCESSFUL (SUCCEED)
Jos 1: 7 that you may be *s* wherever you go.
2Ki 18: 7 he was *s* in whatever he undertook.
2Ch 20:20 in his prophets and you will be *s*."

SUFFER (SUFFERED SUFFERING SUFFERINGS SUFFERS)
Job 36:15 those who *s* he delivers
Isa 53:10 to crush him and cause him to *s,*
Mk 8:31 the Son of Man must *s* many things
Lk 24:26 the Christ have to *s* these things
     24:46 The Christ will *s* and rise
2Co 1: 6 of the same sufferings we *s.*
Php 1:29 to *s* for him, since you are going
Heb 9:26 would have had to *s* many times
1Pe 3:17 to *s* for doing good
     4:16 However, if you *s* as a Christian,

SUFFERED (SUFFER)
Heb 2: 9 and honor because he *s* death,
     2:18 Because he himself *s*
1Pe 3:18 Christ *s* for you, leaving you
     4: 1 he who has *s* in his body is done

SUFFERING (SUFFER)
Job 36:15 who suffer he delivers in their *s;*
Ps 22:24 the *s* of the afflicted one;
Isa 53: 3 of sorrows, and familiar with *s.*
     53:11 After the *s* of his soul,
La 1:12 Is any *s* like my *s*
Ac 5:41 worthy of *s* disgrace for the Name.
Ro 5: 3 know that *s* produces
2Ti 1: 8 But join with me in *s* for the gospel,
Heb 2:10 of their salvation perfect through *s.*
     13: 3 as if you yourselves were *s.*
1Pe 4:12 at the painful trial you are *s,*

SUFFERINGS (SUFFER)
Ro 5: 3 but we also rejoice in our *s,*
     8:17 share in his *s* in order that we may
     8:18 that our present *s* are not worth
2Co 1: 5 as the *s* of Christ flow
Php 3:10 the fellowship of sharing in his *s,*
1Pe 4:13 rejoice that you participate in the *s*
     5: 9 are undergoing the same kind of *s.*

SUFFERS (SUFFER)
Pr 13:20 but a companion of fools *s* harm.
1Co 12:26 If one part *s,* every part *s* with it;

SUFFICIENT
2Co 12: 9 said to me, "My grace is *s* for you,

SUITABLE
Ge 2:18 I will make a helper *s* for him."

SUMMED* (SUMS)
Ro 13: 9 there may be, are *s* up
Gal 5:14 The entire law is *s* up

SUMMONS
Ps 50: 1 speaks and *s* the earth
Isa 45: 3 God of Israel, who *s* you by name.

SUMS* (SUMMED)
Mt 7:12 for this *s* up the Law

SUN (SUNRISE)
Jos 10:13 So the *s* stood still,
Jdg 5:31 may they who love you be like the *s*
Ps 84:11 For the LORD God is a *s*
     121: 6 the *s* will not harm you by day,
     136: 8 the *s* to govern the day,
Ecc 1: 9 there is nothing new under the *s.*
Isa 60:19 The *s* will no more be your light
Mal 4: 2 the *s* of righteousness will rise
Mt 5:45 He causes his *s* to rise on the evil
     13:43 the righteous will shine like the *s*
     17: 2 His face shone like the *s,*
Lk 23:45 for the *s* stopped shining.
Eph 4:26 Do not let the *s* go
Rev 1:16 His face was like the *s* shining
     21:23 The city does not need the *s*

SUNG (SING)
Mt 26:30 When they had a *s* a hymn, they

SUNRISE (SUN)
2Sa 23: 4 he is like the light of morning at *s*
Hab 3: 4 His splendor was like the *s;*

SUPERIOR
Heb 1: 4 he became as much *s* to the angels
     8: 6 ministry Jesus has received is as *s*

SUPERVISION
Gal 3:25 longer under the *s* of the law.

SUPPER
Lk 22:20 after the *s* he took the cup, saying,
1Co 11:25 after *s* he took the cup,
Rev 19: 9 to the wedding *s* of the Lamb!' "

SUPPLIED (SUPPLY)
Ac 20:34 of mine have *s* my own needs
Php 4:18 and even more; I am amply *s,*

SUPPLY (SUPPLIED SUPPLYING)
2Co 8:14 your plenty will *s* what they need,
1Th 3:10 and *s* what is lacking in your faith.

SUPPLYING* (SUPPLY)
2Co 9:12 you perform is not only *s* the needs

SUPPORT (SUPPORTED SUPPORTING)
Ps 18:18 but the LORD was my *s.*
Ro 11:18 consider this: You do not *s* the root
1Co 9:12 If others have this right of *s*

SUPPORTED (SUPPORT)
Ps 94:18 your love, O LORD, *s* me.
Col 2: 9 *s* and held together by its ligaments

SUPPORTING (SUPPORT)
Eph 4:16 held together by every *s* ligament,

SUPPRESS*
Ro 1:18 wickedness of men who *s* the truth

SUPREMACY* (SUPREME)
Col 1:18 in everything he might have the *s.*

SUPREME (SUPREMACY)
Pr 4: 7 Wisdom is *s;* therefore get wisdom.

SURE
Nu 28:31 Be *s* the animals are without defect
     32:23 you may be *s* that your sin will find
Dt 6:17 Be *s* to keep the commands
     14:22 Be *s* to set aside a tenth
     29:18 make *s* there is no root
Jos 23:13 then you may be *s* that the LORD
1Sa 12:24 But be *s* to fear the LORD
Ps 19: 9 The ordinances of the LORD are *s*
     132:11 a *s* oath that he will not revoke:
Pr 27:23 Be *s* you know the condition
Isa 28:16 cornerstone for a *s* foundation;
Eph 5: 5 of this you can be *s:* No immoral,
Heb 11: 1 faith is being *s* of what we hope for
2Pe 1:10 to make your calling and election *s.*

SURFACE
2Co 10: 7 You are looking only on the *s*

SURPASS* (SURPASSED SURPASSES SURPASSING)
Pr 31:29 but you *s* them all."

SURPASSED* (SURPASS)
Jn 1:15 'He who comes after me has *s* me
     1:30 man who comes after me has *s* me

SURPASSES* (SURPASS)
Pr 8:19 what I yield *s* choice silver.
Mt 5:20 unless your righteousness *s* that
Eph 3:19 to know this love that *s* knowledge

SURPASSING* (SURPASS)
Ps 150: 2 praise him for his *s* greatness.
2Co 3:10 in comparison with the *s* glory.
     9:14 of the *s* grace God has given you.
Php 3: 8 the *s* greatness of knowing Christ

SURPRISE (SURPRISED)
1Th 5: 4 that this day should *s* you like

SURPRISED (SURPRISE)
1Pe 4:12 do not be *s* at the painful trial you
1Jn 3:13 Do not be *s,* my brothers,

SURRENDER
1Co 13: 3 and *s* my body to the flames,

SURROUND (SURROUNDED SURROUNDS)
Ps 5:12 you *s* them with your favor
     32: 7 and *s* me with songs of deliverance.
     89: 7 awesome than all who *s* him.
     125: 2 As the mountains *s* Jerusalem,
Jer 31:22 a woman will *s* a man."

SURROUNDED (SURROUND)
Heb 12: 1 since we are *s* by such a great cloud

SURROUNDS (SURROUND)
Ps 32:10 *s* the man who trusts in him.
     89: 8 and your faithfulness *s* you.
     125: 2 so the LORD *s* his people

SUSA
Ezr 4: 9 and Babylon, the Elamites of *S,*
Ne 1: 1 while I was in the citadel of *S,*

SUSPENDS*
Job 26: 7 he *s* the earth over nothing.

SUSPICIONS*
1Ti 6: 4 evil *s* and constant friction

SUSTAIN (SUSTAINING SUSTAINS)
Ps 55:22 and he will *s* you;
Isa 46: 4 I am he, I am he who will *s* you.

SUSTAINING* (SUSTAIN)
Heb 1: 3 *s* all things by his powerful word.

SUSTAINS (SUSTAIN)
Ps 18:35 and your right hand *s* me;
     146: 9 and *s* the fatherless and the widow,
     147: 6 The LORD *s* the humble
Isa 50: 4 to know the word that *s* the weary.

SWALLOW (SWALLOWED)
Isa 25: 8 he will *s* up death forever.
Jnh 1:17 provided a great fish to *s* Jonah,
Mt 23:24 You strain out a gnat but *s* a camel.

SWALLOWED (SWALLOW)
1Co 15:54 "Death has been *s* up in victory."
2Co 5: 4 so that what is mortal may be *s* up

SWAYED
Mt 11: 7 A reed *s* by the wind? If not,
     22:16 you aren't *s* by men, because you
2Ti 3: 6 are *s* by all kinds of evil desires,

SWEAR (SWORE SWORN)
Lev 19:12 " 'Do not *s* falsely by my name
Ps 24: 4 or *s* by what is false.
Isa 45:23 by me every tongue will *s.*
Mt 5:34 Do not *s* at all: either by heaven,
Jas 5:12 Above all, my brothers, do not *s*—

SWEAT*
Ge 3:19 By the *s* of your brow
Lk 22:44 his *s* was like drops of blood falling

SWEET (SWEETER SWEETNESS)
Job 20:12 "Though evil is *s* in his mouth
Ps 119:103 How *s* are your words
Pr 9:17 "Stolen water is *s;*

Pr 13:19   A longing fulfilled is *s* to the soul,
     16:24   *s* to the soul and healing
     20:17   by fraud tastes *s* to a man,
     24:14   also that wisdom is *s* to your soul;
Ecc 5:12   The sleep of a laborer is *s*,
Isa 5:20   and *s* for bitter.
Eze 3:3   it tasted as *s* as honey in my mouth.
Rev 10:10   It tasted as *s* as honey in my mouth

SWEETER (SWEET)
Ps 19:10   they are *s* than honey,
     119:103   *s* than honey to my mouth!

SWEETNESS* (SWEET)
SS 4:11   Your lips drop *s* as the honeycomb,
     5:16   His mouth is *s* itself;

SWEPT
Mt 12:44   finds the house unoccupied, *s* clean

SWERVE*
Pr 4:5   do not forget my words or *s*
     4:27   Do not *s* to the right or the left;

SWIFT
Pr 1:16   they are *s* to shed blood.
Ecc 9:11   The race is not to the *s*
Isa 59:7   they are *s* to shed innocent blood.
Ro 3:15   "Their feet are *s* to shed blood;
2Pe 2:1   bringing *s* destruction

SWINDLER* (SWINDLERS)
1Co 5:11   or a slanderer, a drunkard or a *s*.

SWINDLERS* (SWINDLER)
1Co 5:10   or the greedy and *s*, or idolaters.
     6:10   *s* will inherit the kingdom of God.

SWORD (SWORDS)
Ge 3:24   and a flaming *s* flashing back
Dt 32:41   when I sharpen my flashing *s*
Jos 5:13   of him with a drawn *s* in his hand.
1Sa 17:45   "You come against me with *s*
     17:47   here will know that it is not by *s*
     31:4   so Saul took his own *s* and fell on it.
2Sa 12:10   therefore, the *s* will never depart
Ps 44:6   my *s* does not bring me victory;
     45:3   Gird your *s* upon your side,
Pr 12:18   Reckless words pierce like a *s*,
Isa 2:4   Nation will not take up *s*
Mic 4:3   Nation will not take up *s*
Mt 10:34   come to bring peace, but a *s*.
     26:52   all who draw the *s* will die by the *s*.
Lk 2:35   a *s* will pierce your own soul too."
Ro 13:4   for he does not bear the *s*
Eph 6:17   of salvation and the *s* of the Spirit,
Heb 4:12   Sharper than any double-edged *s*,
Rev 1:16   came a sharp double-edged *s*.
     19:15   Out of his mouth comes a sharp *s*

SWORDS (SWORD)
Ps 64:3   who sharpen their tongues like *s*
Isa 2:4   They will beat their *s*
Joel 3:10   Beat your plowshares into *s*

SWORE (SWEAR)
Heb 6:13   for him to swear by, he *s* by himself

SWORN (SWEAR)
Ps 110:4   The LORD has *s*
Eze 20:42   the land I had *s* with uplifted hand
Heb 7:21   "The Lord has *s*

SYCAMORE-FIG (FIG)
Am 7:14   and I also took care of *s* trees.
Lk 19:4   and climbed a *s* tree to see him,

SYMBOLIZES*
1Pe 3:21   this water *s* baptism that now saves

SYMPATHETIC* (SYMPATHY)
1Pe 3:8   in harmony with one another; be *s*,

SYMPATHIZED* (SYMPATHY)
Heb 10:34   You *s* with those in prison

SYMPATHY (SYMPATHETIC SYMPATHIZED)
Ps 69:20   I looked for *s*, but there was none,

SYNAGOGUE
Lk 4:16   the Sabbath day he went into the *s*,
Ac 17:2   custom was, Paul went into the *s*,

TABERNACLE (TABERNACLES)
Ex 40:34   the glory of the LORD filled the *t*.
Heb 8:2   the true *t* set up by the Lord,
     9:11   and more perfect *t* that is not
     9:21   sprinkled with the blood both the *t*
Rev 15:5   that is, the *t* of the Testimony,

TABERNACLES (TABERNACLE)
Lev 23:34   the LORD's Feast of *T* begins,
Dt 16:16   Feast of Weeks and the Feast of *T*.
Zec 14:16   and to celebrate the Feast of *T*.

TABLE (TABLES)
Ex 25:23   "Make a *t* of acacia wood—
Ps 23:5   You prepare a *t* before me

TABLES (TABLE)
Jn 2:15   changers and overturned their *t*.
Ac 6:2   word of God in order to wait on *t*.

TABLET (TABLETS)
Pr 3:3   write them on the *t* of your heart.
     7:3   write them on the *t* of your heart.

TABLETS (TABLET)
Ex 31:18   he gave him the two *t*
Dt 10:5   and put the *t* in the ark I had made,
2Co 3:3   not on *t* of stone but on *t*

TAKE (TAKEN TAKES TAKING TOOK)
Ge 15:7   land to *t* possession of it."
     22:17   Your descendants will *t* possession
Ex 3:5   "*T* off your sandals,
     21:23   you are to *t* life for life, eye for eye,
     22:22   "Do not *t* advantage of a widow
Lev 10:17   given to you to *t* away the guilt
     25:14   do not *t* advantage of each other.
Nu 13:30   and *t* possession of the land,
Dt 1:8   and *t* possession of the land that
     12:32   do not add to it or *t* away from it.
     31:26   "*T* this Book of the Law
1Sa 8:11   He will *t* your sons and make them
1Ch 17:13   I will never *t* my love away
Job 23:10   But he knows the way that I *t*;
Ps 2:12   Blessed are all who *t* refuge in him.
     25:18   and *t* away all my sins.
     27:14   be strong and *t* heart
     31:24   Be strong and *t* heart,
     49:17   for he will *t* nothing with him
     51:11   or *t* your Holy Spirit from me.
     73:24   afterward you will *t* me into glory.
     118:8   It is better to *t* refuge in the LORD
Pr 22:23   for the LORD will *t* up their case
Isa 62:1   for the LORD will *t* delight in you,
Eze 3:10   and *t* to heart all the words I speak
     33:11   I *t* no pleasure in the death
Mt 10:38   anyone who does not *t* his cross
     11:29   *T* my yoke upon you and learn
     16:24   deny himself and *t* up his cross
     26:26   saying, "*T* and eat; this is my body
Mk 14:36   *T* this cup from me.
1Ti 6:12   *T* hold of the eternal life

TAKEN (TAKE)
Ge 2:23   for she was *t* out of man."
Lev 6:4   must return what he has stolen or *t*
Nu 8:16   I have *t* them as my own in place
     19:3   it is to be *t* outside the camp
Ecc 3:14   added to and nothing *t* from it.
Isa 6:7   your guilt is *t* away and your sin
Zec 3:4   "See, I have *t* away your sin,
Mt 13:12   even what he has will be *t* from him
     24:40   one will be *t* and the other left.
     26:39   may this cup be *t* from me.
Mk 16:19   he was *t* up into heaven
Ac 1:9   he was *t* up before their very eyes,
Ro 5:13   But sin is not *t* into account
1Ti 3:16   was *t* up in glory.

TAKES (TAKE)
1Ki 20:11   should not boast like one who *t* it
Ps 5:4   You are not a God who *t* pleasure
     34:8   blessed is the man who *t* refuge
Lk 6:30   and if anyone *t* what belongs to you
Jn 1:29   who *t* away the sin of the world!
     10:18   No one *t* it from me, but I lay it
Rev 22:19   And if anyone *t* words away

TAKING (TAKE)
Ac 15:14   by *t* from the Gentiles a people
Php 2:7   *t* the very nature of a servant,

TALENT
Mt 25:15   to another one *t*, each according

TALES*
1Ti 4:7   with godless myths and old wives' *t*

TALL
1Sa 17:4   He was over nine feet *t*.
1Ch 11:23   who was seven and a half feet *t*.

TAMAR
     1. Wife of Judah's sons Er and Onan (Ge 38:1–10). Tricked Judah into fathering children when he refused her his third son (Ge 38:11–30).
     2. Daughter of David, raped by Amnon (2Sa 13).

TAMBOURINE
Ps 150:4   praise him with *t* and dancing,

TAME* (TAMED)
Jas 3:8   but no man can *t* the tongue.

TAMED* (TAME)
Jas 3:7   the sea are being *t* and have been *t*

TARSHISH
Jnh 1:3   from the LORD and headed for *T*.

TARSUS
Ac 9:11   ask for a man from *T* named Saul,

TASK (TASKS)
1Ch 29:1   The *t* is great, because this palatial
Mk 13:34   each with his assigned *t*,
Ac 20:24   complete the *t* the Lord Jesus has
1Co 3:5   the Lord has assigned to each his *t*.
2Co 2:16   And who is equal to such a *t*?
1Ti 3:1   an overseer, he desires a noble *t*.

TASKS (TASK)
Pr 31:17   her arms are strong for her *t*.

TASTE (TASTED TASTY)
Ps 34:8   *T* and see that the LORD is good;
     119:103   sweet are your words to my *t*,
Pr 24:13   from the comb is sweet to your *t*.
SS 2:3   and his fruit is sweet to my *t*.
Col 2:21   Do not *t*! Do not touch!"?
Heb 2:9   the grace of God he might *t* death

TASTED (TASTE)
Eze 3:3   it *t* as sweet as honey in my mouth.
1Pe 2:3   now that you have *t* that the Lord
Rev 10:10   It *t* as sweet as honey in my mouth,

TASTY (TASTE)
Ge 27:4   Prepare me the kind of *t* food I like

TATTOO*
Lev 19:28   or put *t* marks on yourselves.

TAUGHT (TEACH)
1Ki 4:33   He also *t* about animals and birds,
2Ki 17:28   *t* them how to worship the LORD.
2Ch 17:9   *t* throughout Judah,
Ps 119:102   for you yourself have *t* me.
Pr 4:4   he *t* me and said,
     31:1   an oracle his mother *t* him:
Isa 29:13   is made up only of rules *t* by men.
     50:4   ear to listen like one being *t*.
Mt 7:29   he *t* as one who had authority,
     15:9   their teachings are but rules *t*
Lk 4:15   he *t* in their synagogues,
Ac 20:20   have *t* you publicly and from house
1Co 2:13   but in words *t* by the Spirit,
Gal 1:12   nor was I *t* it; rather, I received it
1Ti 1:20   to Satan to be *t* not to blaspheme.
1Jn 2:27   just as it has *t* you, remain in him.

TAX (TAXES)
Mt 11:19   a friend of *t* collectors and "sinners
     17:24   of the two-drachma *t* came to Peter

TAXES (TAX)
Mt 22:17   Is it right to pay *t* to Caesar or not
Ro 13:7   If you owe *t*, pay *t*; if revenue,

TEACH (TAUGHT TEACHER TEACHERS TEACHES TEACHING TEACHINGS)

Ex	4:12	and will *t* you what to say."
	18:20	*T* them the decrees and laws,
	33:13	*t* me your ways so I may know you
Lev	10:11	and you must *t* the Israelites all
Dt	4:9	*T* them to your children
	6:1	me to *t* you to observe
	8:3	to *t* you that man does not live
	11:19	*T* them to your children, talking
1Sa	12:23	I will *t* you the way that is good
1Ki	8:36	*T* them the right way to live,
Job	12:7	ask the animals, and they will *t* you
Ps	32:8	*t* you in the way you should go;
	34:11	I will *t* you the fear of the LORD.
	51:13	I will *t* transgressors your ways,
	78:5	forefathers to *t* their children,
	90:12	*T* us to number our days aright,
	119:33	*T* me, O LORD, to follow your
	143:10	*T* me to do your will,
Pr	9:9	*t* a righteous man and he will add
Jer	31:34	No longer will a man *t* his neighbor
Mic	4:2	He will *t* us his ways,
Lk	11:1	said to him, "Lord, *t* us to pray,
	12:12	for the Holy Spirit will *t* you
Jn	14:26	will *t* you all things and will remind
Ro	2:21	who *t* others, do you not *t* yourself?
	15:4	in the past was written to *t* us,
1Ti	2:12	I do not permit a woman to *t*
	3:2	respectable, hospitable, able to *t*,
2Ti	2:2	also be qualified to *t* others.
	2:24	kind to everyone, able to *t*,
Tit	2:1	You must *t* what is in accord
	2:15	then, are the things you should *t*.
Heb	8:11	No longer will a man *t* his neighbor
Jas	3:1	know that we who *t* will be judged
1Jn	2:27	you do not need anyone to *t* you.

TEACHER (TEACH)

Ecc	1:1	The words of the *T*, son of David,
Mt	10:24	"A student is not above his *t*,
	13:52	"Therefore every *t*
	23:10	Nor are you to be called '*t*,'
Lk	6:40	A student is not above his *t*,
Jn	3:2	we know you are a *t* who has come
	13:14	and *T*, have washed your feet,

TEACHERS (TEACH)

Ps	119:99	I have more insight than all my *t*,
Pr	5:13	I would not obey my *t*
Lk	20:46	"Beware of the *t* of the law.
1Co	12:28	third *t*, then workers of miracles,
Eph	4:11	and some to be pastors and *t*,
2Ti	4:3	around them a great number of *t*
Heb	5:12	by this time you ought to be *t*,
Jas	3:1	of you should presume to be *t*,
2Pe	2:1	as there will be false *t* among you.

TEACHES (TEACH)

Ps	25:9	and *t* them his way.
	94:10	Does he who *t* man lack
Pr	15:33	of the LORD *t* a man wisdom,
Isa	48:17	who *t* you what is best for you,
Mt	5:19	*t* these commands will be called
1Ti	6:3	If anyone *t* false doctrines
Tit	2:12	It *t* us to say "No" to ungodliness
1Jn	2:27	his anointing *t* you about all things

TEACHING (TEACH)

Ezr	7:10	to *t* its decrees and laws in Israel.
Pr	1:8	and do not forsake your mother's *t*.
	3:1	My son, do not forget my *t*,
	6:23	this *t* is a light,
Mt	28:20	*t* them to obey everything I have
Jn	7:17	whether my *t* comes from God or
	8:31	to my *t*, you are really my disciples.
	14:23	loves me, he will obey my *t*.
Ac	2:42	themselves to the apostles' *t*
Ro	12:7	let him serve; if it is *t*, let him teach;
Eph	4:14	and there by every wind of *t*
2Th	3:6	to the *t* you received from us.
1Ti	4:13	of Scripture, to preaching and to *t*.
	5:17	whose work is preaching and *t*.
	6:3	Lord Jesus Christ and to godly *t*,
2Ti	3:16	is God-breathed and is useful for *t*,
Tit	1:11	by *t* things they ought not
	2:7	In your *t* show integrity,
Heb	5:13	with the *t* about righteousness.
2Jn	9	and does not continue in the *t*

TEACHINGS (TEACH)

Pr	7:2	guard my *t* as the apple of your eye.
2Th	2:15	hold to the *t* we passed on to you,
Heb	6:1	leave the elementary *t* about Christ

TEAR (TEARS)

Rev	7:17	God will wipe away every *t*
	21:4	He will wipe every *t*

TEARS (TEAR)

Ps	126:5	Those who sow in *t*
Isa	25:8	LORD will wipe away the *t*
Jer	31:16	and your eyes from *t*,
	50:4	in *t* to seek the LORD their God.
Lk	7:38	she began to wet his feet with her *t*.
2Co	2:4	anguish of heart and with many *t*,
Php	3:18	and now say again even with *t*,

TEETH (TOOTH)

Job	19:20	with only the skin of my *t*.
Ps	35:16	they gnashed their *t* at me.
Jer	31:29	and the children's *t* are set on edge
Mt	8:12	will be weeping and gnashing of *t*."

TEMPER (EVEN-TEMPERED HOT-TEMPERED ILL-TEMPERED QUICK-TEMPERED)

Pr	16:32	a man who controls his *t*

TEMPERANCE SEE SELF-CONTROL

TEMPERATE*

1Ti	3:2	*t*, self-controlled, respectable,
	3:11	not malicious talkers but *t*
Tit	2:2	Teach the older men to be *t*,

TEMPEST

Ps	50:3	and around him a *t* rages.
	55:8	far from the *t* and storm."

TEMPLE (TEMPLES)

1Ki	6:1	began to build the *t* of the LORD.
	6:38	the *t* was finished in all its details
	8:10	the cloud filled the *t* of the LORD.
	8:27	How much less this *t* I have built!
2Ch	36:19	They set fire to God's *t*
	36:23	me to build a *t* for him at Jerusalem
Ezr	6:14	finished building the *t* according
Ps	27:4	and to seek him in his *t*.
Isa	6:1	and the train of his robe filled the *t*.
Eze	10:4	cloud filled the *t*, and the court was
	43:4	glory of the LORD entered the *t*
Hab	2:20	But the LORD is in his holy *t*;
Mt	12:6	that one greater than the *t* is here.
	26:61	'I am able to destroy the *t* of God
	27:51	of the *t* was torn in two from top
Lk	21:5	about how the *t* was adorned
Jn	2:14	In the *t* courts he found men selling
1Co	3:16	that you yourselves are God's *t*
	6:19	you not know that your body is a *t*
2Co	6:16	For we are the *t* of the living God.
Rev	21:22	I did not see a *t* in the city,

TEMPLES (TEMPLE)

Ac	17:24	does not live in *t* built by hands.

TEMPORARY

2Co	4:18	what is seen is *t*, but what is unseen

TEMPT* (TEMPTATION TEMPTED TEMPTER TEMPTING)

1Co	7:5	again so that Satan will not *t* you
Jas	1:13	does he *t* anyone; but each one is

TEMPTATION* (TEMPT)

Mt	6:13	And lead us not into *t*,
	26:41	pray so that you will not fall into *t*.
Mk	14:38	pray so that you will not fall into *t*.
Lk	11:4	And lead us not into *t*.'"
	22:40	"Pray so that you will not fall into *t*."

Lk	22:46	pray so that you will not fall into *t*
1Co	10:13	No *t* has seized you except what is
1Ti	6:9	want to get rich fall into *t*

TEMPTED* (TEMPT)

Mt	4:1	into the desert to be *t* by the devil.
Mk	1:13	was in the desert forty days, being *t*
Lk	4:2	for forty days he was *t* by the devil.
1Co	10:13	But when you are *t*, he will
	10:13	he will not let you be *t*
Gal	6:1	yourself, or you also may be *t*.
1Th	3:5	way the tempter might have *t* you
Heb	2:18	able to help those who are being *t*.
	2:18	he himself suffered when he was *t*,
	4:15	but we have one who has been *t*
Jas	1:13	For God cannot be *t* by evil,
	1:13	When *t*, no one should say,
	1:14	each one is *t* when, by his own evil

TEMPTER* (TEMPT)

Mt	4:3	The *t* came to him and said,
1Th	3:5	some way the *t* might have

TEMPTING* (TEMPT)

Lk	4:13	the devil had finished all this *t*,
Jas	1:13	no one should say, "God is *t* me."

TEN (TENTH TITHE TITHES)

Ex	34:28	covenant—the *T* Commandments.
Lev	26:8	of you will chase *t* thousand,
Dt	4:13	covenant, the *T* Commandments,
	10:4	The *T* Commandments he had
Ps	91:7	*t* thousand at your right hand,
Da	7:24	*t* horns are *t* kings who will come
Mt	25:1	will be like *t* virgins who took
	25:28	it to the one who has the *t* talents.
Lk	15:8	suppose a woman has *t* silver coins
Rev	12:3	and *t* horns and seven crowns

TENANTS

Mt	21:34	servants to the *t* to collect his fruit.

TEND

Jer	23:2	to the shepherds who *t* my people:
Eze	34:14	I will *t* them in a good pasture,

TENDERNESS*

Isa	63:15	Your *t* and compassion are
Php	2:1	fellowship with the Spirit, if any *t*

TENT (TENTMAKER TENTS)

Ex	27:21	In the *T* of Meeting,
	40:2	"Set up the tabernacle, the *T*
Isa	54:2	"Enlarge the place of your *t*,
2Co	5:1	that if the earthly *t* we live
2Pe	1:13	as long as I live in the *t* of this body,

TENTH (TEN)

Ge	14:20	Abram gave him a *t* of everything.
Nu	18:26	you must present a *t* of that tithe
Dt	14:22	Be sure to set aside a *t*
1Sa	8:15	He will take a *t* of your grain
Lk	11:42	you give God a *t* of your mint,
	18:12	I fast twice a week and give a *t*
Heb	7:4	patriarch Abraham gave him a *t*

TENTMAKER* (TENT)

Ac	18:3	and because he was a *t* as they were

TENTS (TENT)

Ge	13:12	and pitched his *t* near Sodom.
Ps	84:10	than dwell in the *t* of the wicked.

TERAH

Ge	11:31	*T* took his son Abram, his

TERRIBLE (TERROR)

2Ti	3:1	There will be *t* times

TERRIFIED (TERROR)

Dt	7:21	Do not be *t* by them,
	20:3	do not be *t* or give way to panic
Ps	90:7	and *t* by your indignation.
Mt	14:26	walking on the lake, they were *t*.
	17:6	they fell facedown to the ground, *t*.

Mt 27:54	they were *t*, and exclaimed,
Mk 4:41	They were *t* and asked each other,

TERRIFYING (TERROR)
Heb 12:21 The sight was so *t* that Moses said,

TERRITORY
2Co 10:16 done in another man's *t*.

TERROR (TERRIBLE TERRIFIED TERRIFYING)
Dt 2:25 very day I will begin to put the *t*
28:67 of the *t* that will fill your hearts
Job 9:34 so that his *t* would frighten me no
Ps 91:5 You will not fear the *t* of night,
Pr 21:15 but *t* to evildoers.
Isa 13:8 *T* will seize them,
24:17 *T* and pit and snare await you,
51:13 live in constant *t* every day
54:14 *T* will be far removed;
Lk 21:26 Men will faint from *t*, apprehensive
Ro 13:3 For rulers hold no *t*

TEST (TESTED TESTING TESTS)
Dt 6:16 Do not *t* the LORD your God
Jdg 3:1 to *t* all those Israelites who had not
1Ki 10:1 came to *t* him with hard questions.
1Ch 29:17 that you *t* the heart and are pleased
Ps 26:2 *T* me, O LORD, and try me,
78:18 They willfully put God to the *t*
106:14 wasteland they put God to the *t*.
139:23 *t* me and know my anxious
Jer 11:20 and *t* the heart and mind,
Lk 4:12 put the Lord your God to the *t*.' "
Ac 5:9 How could you agree to *t* the Spirit
Ro 12:2 Then you will be able to *t*
1Co 3:13 and the fire will *t* the quality
10:9 We should not *t* the Lord,
2Co 13:5 unless, of course, you fail the *t*?
1Th 5:21 *T* everything.
Jas 1:12 because when he has stood the *t*,
1Jn 4:1 *t* the spirits to see whether they are

TESTED (TEST)
Ge 22:1 Some time later God *t* Abraham.
Job 23:10 when he has *t* me, I will come forth
34:36 that Job might be *t* to the utmost
Ps 66:10 For you, O God, *t* us;
Pr 27:21 man is *t* by the praise he receives.
Isa 28:16 a *t* stone,
48:10 I have *t* you in the furnace
1Ti 3:10 They must first be *t*; and then
Heb 11:17 By faith Abraham, when God *t* him

TESTIFIES (TESTIFY)
Jn 5:32 There is another who *t* in my favor,
Ro 8:16 The Spirit himself *t*

TESTIFY (TESTIFIES TESTIMONY)
Pr 24:28 Do not *t* against your neighbor
Jn 1:7 a witness to *t* concerning that light,
1:34 and I *t* that this is the Son of God."
5:39 are the Scriptures that *t* about me,
7:7 because I *t* that what it does is evil.
15:26 he will *t* about me. And you
Ac 4:33 continued to *t* to the resurrection
10:43 All the prophets *t* about him that
2Ti 1:8 ashamed to *t* about our Lord,
1Jn 4:14 *t* that the Father has sent his Son
5:7 For there are three that *t*: the Spirit

TESTIMONY (TESTIFY)
Ex 20:16 "You shall not give false *t*
31:18 gave him the two tablets of the *T*,
Nu 35:30 only on the *t* of witnesses.
Dt 19:18 giving false *t* against his brother,
Pr 12:17 A truthful witness gives honest *t*,
Isa 8:20 and to the *T*! If they do not speak
Mt 15:19 sexual immorality, theft, false *t*,
24:14 preached in the whole world as a *t*
Lk 18:20 not give false *t*, honor your father

Jn 2:25	He did not need man's *t* about man
21:24	We know that his *t* is true.
1Jn 5:9	but God's *t* is greater because it is
Rev 12:11	and by the word of their *t*;

TESTING (TEST)
Lk 8:13 but in the time of *t* they fall away.
Heb 3:8 during the time of *t* in the desert,
Jas 1:3 because you know that the *t*

TESTS (TEST)
Pr 17:3 but the LORD *t* the heart.
1Th 2:4 but God, who *t* our hearts.

THADDAEUS
Apostle (Mt 10:3; Mk 3:18); probably also known as Judas son of James (Lk 6:16; Ac 1:13).

THANK (THANKFUL THANKFULNESS THANKS THANKSGIVING)
Php 1:3 I *t* my God every time I remember
1Th 3:9 How can we *t* God enough for you

THANKFUL (THANK)
Col 3:15 And be *t*.
Heb 12:28 let us be *t*, and so worship God

THANKFULNESS (THANK)
1Co 10:30 If I take part in the meal with *t*,
Col 2:7 taught, and overflowing with *t*.

THANKS (THANK)
1Ch 16:8 Give *t* to the LORD, call
Ne 12:31 assigned two large choirs to give *t*.
Ps 7:17 I will give *t* to the LORD
28:7 and I will give *t* to him in song.
30:12 my God, I will give you *t* forever.
35:18 I will give you *t* in the great
75:1 we give *t*, for your Name is near;
100:4 give *t* to him and praise his name.
107:1 Give *t* to the LORD, for he is good;
118:28 are my God, and I will give you *t*;
136:1 Give *t* to the LORD, for he is good.
Ro 1:21 as God nor gave *t* to him,
1Co 11:24 when he had given *t*, he broke it
15:57 *t* be to God! He gives us the victory
2Co 2:14 *t* be to God, who always leads us
9:15 *T* be to God for his indescribable
1Th 5:18 give *t* in all circumstances,
Rev 4:9 and *t* to him who sits on the throne

THANKSGIVING (THANK)
Ps 95:2 Let us come before him with *t*
100:4 Enter his gates with *t*
1Co 10:16 cup of *t* for which we give thanks
Php 4:6 by prayer and petition, with *t*,
1Ti 4:3 created to be received with *t*

THEFT (THIEF)
Mt 15:19 sexual immorality, *t*, false

THEFTS* (THIEF)
Rev 9:21 their sexual immorality or their *t*.

THEME*
Ps 45:1 My heart is stirred by a noble *t*
119:54 Your decrees are the *t* of my song

THIEF (THEFT THEFTS THIEVES)
Ex 22:3 A *t* must certainly make restitution
Pr 6:30 Men do not despise a *t* if he steals
Lk 12:39 at what hour the *t* was coming,
1Th 5:2 day of the Lord will come like a *t*
1Pe 4:15 or *t* or any other kind of criminal,
Rev 16:15 I come like a *t*! Blessed is he who

THIEVES (THIEF)
Mt 6:19 and where *t* break in and steal.
Jn 10:8 who ever came before me were *t*
1Co 6:10 nor homosexual offenders nor *t*

THINK (THINKING THOUGHT THOUGHTS)
Ps 63:6 I *t* of you through the watches
Isa 44:19 No one stops to *t*,
Mt 22:42 "What do you *t* about the Christ?
Ro 12:3 Do not *t* of yourself more highly
Php 4:8 praiseworthy—*t* about such things

THINKING (THINK)
Pr 23:7 who is always *t* about the cost.
1Co 14:20 Brothers, stop *t* like children.
2Pe 3:1 to stimulate you to wholesome *t*.

THIRST (THIRSTS THIRSTY)
Ps 69:21 and gave me vinegar for my *t*.

Mt 5:6	Blessed are those who hunger and *t*
Jn 4:14	the water I give him will never *t*.
2Co 11:27	I have known hunger and *t*
Rev 7:16	never again will they *t*.

THIRSTS (THIRST)
Ps 42:2 My soul *t* for God,

THIRSTY (THIRST)
Ps 107:9 for he satisfies the *t*
Pr 25:21 if he is *t*, give him water to drink.
Isa 55:1 "Come, all you who are *t*,
Mt 25:35 I was *t* and you gave me something
Jn 7:37 "If anyone is *t*, let him come to me
Ro 12:20 if he is *t*, give him something
Rev 21:6 To him who is *t* I will give to drink
22:17 Whoever is *t*, let him come;

THOMAS
Apostle (Mt 10:3; Mk 3:18; Lk 6:15; Jn 11:16; 14:5; 21:2; Ac 1:13). Doubted resurrection (Jn 20:24–28).

THONGS
Mk 1:7 *t* of whose sandals I am not worthy

THORN (THORNBUSHES THORNS)
2Co 12:7 there was given me a *t* in my flesh,

THORNBUSHES (THORN)
Lk 6:44 People do not pick figs from *t*,

THORNS (THORN)
Ge 3:18 It will produce *t* and thistles
Nu 33:55 in your eyes and *t* in your sides.
Mt 13:7 fell among *t*, which grew up
27:29 and then twisted together a crown of *t*
Heb 6:8 But land that produces *t*

THOUGHT (THINK)
Pr 14:15 a prudent man gives *t* to his steps.
21:29 an upright man gives *t* to his ways.
1Co 13:11 I talked like a child, I *t* like a child,

THOUGHTS (THINK)
1Ch 28:9 every motive behind the *t*.
Ps 94:11 The LORD knows the *t* of man;
139:23 test me and know my anxious *t*.
Isa 55:8 "For my *t* are not your *t*,
Mt 15:19 For out of the heart come evil *t*,
1Co 2:11 among men knows the *t* of a man
Heb 4:12 it judges the *t* and attitudes

THREE
Ge 6:10 Noah had *t* sons: Shem, Ham
Ex 23:14 "*T* times a year you are
Dt 19:15 the testimony of two or *t* witnesses.
2Sa 23:8 a Tahkemonite, was chief of the *T*;
Pr 30:15 "There are *t* things that are never
30:18 "There are *t* things that are too
30:21 "Under *t* things the earth trembles,
30:29 "There are *t* things that are stately
Ecc 4:12 of *t* strands is not quickly broken.
Da 3:24 "Weren't there *t* men that we tied up
Am 1:3 "For *t* sins of Damascus,
Jnh 1:17 inside the fish *t* days and *t* nights.
Mt 12:40 so the Son of Man will be *t* days
12:40 *t* nights in the belly of a huge fish,
12:40 *t* nights in the heart of the earth.
17:4 I will put up *t* shelters—one
18:20 or *t* come together in my name,
26:34 you will disown me *t* times."
26:75 you will disown me *t* times."
27:63 'After *t* days I will rise again.'
Mk 8:31 and after *t* days rise again.
9:5 Let us put up *t* shelters—one
14:30 yourself will disown me *t* times."
2:19 and I will raise it again in *t* days."
1Co 13:13 And now these *t* remain: faith,
14:27 or at the most *t*— should speak,
2Co 13:1 testimony of two or *t* witnesses."
1Jn 5:7 For there are *t* that testify:

THRESHER* (THRESHING)
1Co 9:10 plowman plows and the *t* threshes,

THRESHING (THRESHER)
Ru 3:6 So she went down to the *t* floor
2Sa 24:18 an altar to the LORD on the *t* floor

Lk   3:17 is in his hand to clear his *t* floor

THREW (THROW)
Da   6:16 and *t* him into the lions' den.
Jnh 1:15 took Jonah and *t* him overboard,

THRIVE
Pr 29: 2 When the righteous *t*, the people

THROAT (THROATS)
Ps   5: 9 Their *t* is an open grave;
Pr 23: 2 and put a knife to your *t*

THROATS (THROAT)
Ro   3:13 "Their *t* are open graves;

THROB*
Isa 60: 5 your heart will *t* and swell with joy;

THRONE (ENTHRONED ENTHRONES THRONES)
2Sa 7:16 your *t* will be established forever
1Ch 17:12 and I will establish his *t* forever.
Ps 11: 4 The LORD is on his heavenly *t*.
     45: 6 Your *t*, O God, will last for ever
     47: 8 God is seated on his holy *t*.
    89:14 justice are the foundation of your *t*;
Isa   6: 1 I saw the Lord seated on a *t*,
    66: 1 "Heaven is my *t*,
Eze 28: 2 I sit on the *t* of a god
Da   7: 9 His *t* was flaming with fire,
Mt 19:28 Son of Man sits on his glorious *t*,
Ac   7:49 prophet says: " 'Heaven is my *t*,
Heb 1: 8 "Your *t*, O God, will last for ever
     4:16 Let us then approach the *t* of grace
    12: 2 at the right hand of the *t* of God.
Rev 3:21 sat down with my Father on his *t*.
     3:21 the right to sit with me on my *t*,
     4: 2 there before me was a *t* in heaven
     4:10 They lay their crowns before the *t*
   20:11 Then I saw a great white *t*,
    22: 3 *t* of God and of the Lamb will be

THRONES (THRONE)
Mt 19:28 me will also sit on twelve *t*,
Rev 4: 4 throne were twenty-four other *t*,

THROW (THREW)
Jn   8: 7 the first to *t* a stone at her."
Heb 10:35 So do not *t* away your confidence;
    12: 1 let us *t* off everything that hinders

THUNDER (THUNDERS)
Ps 93: 4 Mightier than the *t*
Mk   3:17 which means Sons of *T*); Andrew,

THUNDERS (THUNDER)
Job 37: 5 God's voice *t* in marvelous ways;
Ps 29: 3 the God of glory *t*,
Rev 10: 3 the voices of the seven *t* spoke.

THWART* (THWARTED)
Isa 14:27 has purposed, and who can *t* him?

THWARTED (THWART)
Job 42: 2 no plan of yours can be *t*.

THYATIRA
Rev 2:18 the angel of the church in *T* write:

TIBNI
King of Israel (1Ki 16:21–22).

TIDINGS
Isa 40: 9 You who bring good *t* to Jerusalem
    52: 7 who bring good *t*,

TIES
Hos 11: 4 with *t* of love;
Mt 12:29 unless he first *t* up the strong man?

TIGHT*
Jas 1:26 and yet does not keep a *t* rein

TIGHTFISTED*
Dt 15: 7 or *t* toward your poor brother.

TIME (TIMES)
Est 4:14 come to royal position for such a *t*
Ecc 3: 1 There is a *t* for everything,
     8: 5 wise heart will know the proper *t*
Da   7:25 to him for a *t*, times and half a *t*.
    12: 7 "It will be for a *t*, times and half a *t*.
Hos 10:12 for it is *t* to seek the LORD,
Jn   2: 4 Jesus replied, "My *t* has not yet
    17: 1 prayed: "Father, the *t* has come.
Ro   9: 9 "At the appointed *t* I will return,
   13:11 understanding the present *t*.
1Co 7:29 brothers, is that the *t* is short.

2Co 6: 2 now is the *t* of God's favor,
2Ti 1: 9 Jesus before the beginning of *t*,
Tit 1: 2 promised before the beginning of *t*,
Heb 9:28 and he will appear a second *t*,
   10:12 for all *t* one sacrifice for sins,
1Pe 4:17 For it is *t* for judgment to begin

TIMES (TIME)
Ps   9: 9 a stronghold in *t* of trouble.
   31:15 My *t* are in your hands;
   62: 8 Trust in him at all *t*, O people;
Pr 17:17 A friend loves at all *t*,
Isa 46:10 from ancient *t*, what is still to come
Am 5:13 for the *t* are evil.
Mt 16: 3 cannot interpret the signs of the *t*.
   18:21 how many *t* shall I forgive my
Ac   1: 7 "It is not for you to know the *t*
Rev 12:14 *t* and half a time, out

TIMID (TIMIDITY)
1Th 5:14 encourage the *t*, help the weak,

TIMIDITY* (TIMID)
2Ti 1: 7 For God did not give us a spirit of *t*

TIMOTHY
Believer from Lystra (Ac 16:1). Joined Paul on second missionary journey (Ac 16–20). Sent to settle problems at Corinth (1Co 4:17; 16:10). Led church at Ephesus (1Ti 1:3). Co-writer with Paul (1Th 1:1; 2Ti 1:1; Phm 1).

TIP
Job 33: 2 my words are on the *t* of my tongue

TIRE (TIRED)
2Th 3:13 never *t* of doing what is right.

TIRED (TIRE)
Ex 17:12 When Moses' hands grew *t*,
Isa 40:28 He will not grow *t* or weary,

TITHE (TEN)
Lev 27:30 " 'A *t* of everything from the land,
Dt 12:17 eat in your own towns the *t*
Mal 3:10 the whole *t* into the storehouse,

TITHES (TEN)
Nu 18:21 give to the Levites all the *t* in Israel
Mal 3: 8 'How do we rob you?' "In *t*

TITUS*
Gentile co-worker of Paul (Gal 2:1–3; 2Ti 4:10); sent to Corinth (2Co 2:13; 7–8; 12:18), Crete (Tit 1:4–5).

TODAY
Ps   2: 7 *t* I have become your Father.
   95: 7 *T*, if you hear his voice,
Mt   6:11 Give us *t* our daily bread.
Lk   2:11 *T* in the town of David a Savior has
   23:43 *t* you will be with me in paradise."
Ac 13:33 *t* I have become your Father.'
Heb 1: 5 *t* I have become your Father"?
     3: 7 "*T*, if you hear his voice,
     3:13 daily, as long as it is called *T*,
     5: 5 *t* I have become your Father."
    13: 8 Christ is the same yesterday and *t*

TOIL (TOILED TOILING)
Ge   3:17 through painful *t* you will eat of it

TOILED (TOIL)
2Co 11:27 and *t* and have often gone

TOILING (TOIL)
2Th 3: 8 *t* so that we would not be a burden

TOLERANCE* (TOLERATE)
Ro   2: 4 for the riches of his kindness, *t*

TOLERATE (TOLERANCE)
Hab 1:13 you cannot *t* wrong.
Rev 2: 2 that you cannot *t* wicked men,

TOMB
Mt 27:65 make the *t* as secure as you know
Lk 24: 2 the stone rolled away from the *t*,

TOMORROW
Pr 27: 1 Do not boast about *t*,
Isa 22:13 "for *t* we die!"
Mt   6:34 Therefore do not worry about *t*,
1Co 15:32 for *t* we die."
Jas 4:13 "Today or *t* we will go to this

TONGUE (TONGUES)
Ex   4:10 I am slow of speech and *t*."
Job 33: 2 my words are on the tip of my *t*.
Ps   5: 9 with their *t* they speak deceit.
   34:13 keep your *t* from evil
   37:30 and his *t* speaks what is just.
   39: 1 and keep my *t* from sin;
   51:14 my *t* will sing of your righteousness
   52: 4 O you deceitful *t*!
   71:24 My *t* will tell of your righteous acts
  119:172 May my *t* sing of your word,
  137: 6 May my *t* cling to the roof
  139: 4 Before a word is on my *t*
Pr   6:17 a lying *t*,
   10:19 but he who holds his *t* is wise.
   12:18 but the *t* of the wise brings healing.
   15: 4 The *t* that brings healing is a tree
   17:20 he whose *t* is deceitful falls
   21:23 He who guards his mouth and his *t*
   25:15 and a gentle *t* can break a bone.
   26:28 A lying *t* hates those it hurts,
   28:23 than he who has a flattering *t*.
   31:26 and faithful instruction is on her *t*.
SS   4:11 milk and honey are under your *t*.
Isa 32: 4 and the stammering *t* will be fluent
   45:23 by me every *t* will swear.
   50: 4 has given me an instructed *t*,
   59: 3 and your *t* mutters wicked things.
Lk 16:24 of his finger in water and cool my *t*,
Ro 14:11 every *t* will confess to God.' "
1Co 14: 2 speaks in a *t* does not speak to men
   14: 4 He who speaks in a *t* edifies himself
   14: 9 intelligible words with your *t*,
   14:13 in a *t* should pray that he may
   14:19 than ten thousand words in a *t*.
   14:26 revelation, a *t* or an interpretation.
   14:27 If anyone speaks in a *t*, two—
Php 2:11 every *t* confess that Jesus Christ is
Jas 1:26 does not keep a tight rein on his *t*,
    3: 5 Likewise the *t* is a small part
    3: 8 but no man can tame the *t*.
1Jn 3:18 or *t* but with actions and in truth.

TONGUES (TONGUE)
Ps   12: ? "We will triumph with our *t*;
  126: 2 our *t* with songs of joy.
Isa 28:11 with foreign lips and strange *t*
   66:18 and gather all nations and *t*,
Jer 23:31 the prophets who wag their own *t*
Mk 16:17 in new *t*; they will pick up snakes
Ac   2: 3 to be *t* of fire that separated
    2: 4 and began to speak in other *t*
   10:46 For they heard them speaking in *t*
   19: 6 and they spoke in *t* and prophesied
Ro   3:13 their *t* practice deceit."
1Co 12:10 still another the interpretation of *t*.
   12:28 speaking in different kinds of *t*.
   12:30 Do all speak in *t*? Do all interpret?
   13: 1 If I speak in the *t* of men
   13: 8 where there are *t*, they will be
   14: 5 greater than one who speaks in *t*,
   14:18 speak in *t* more than all of you.
   14:21 "Through men of strange *t*
   14:39 and do not forbid speaking in *t*.

TOOK (TAKE)
Isa 53: 4 Surely he *t* up our infirmities
Mt   8:17 "He *t* up our infirmities
   26:26 they were eating, Jesus *t* bread,
   26:27 Then he *t* the cup, gave thanks
1Co 11:23 the night he was betrayed, *t* bread,
   11:25 after supper he *t* the cup, saying,
Php 3:12 for which Christ Jesus *t* hold of me.

TOOTH (TEETH)
Ex 21:24 eye for eye, *t* for *t*, hand for hand,
Mt   5:38 'Eye for eye, and *t* for *t*.'

TOP
Dt 28:13 you will always be at the *t*,

Isa 1: 6 of your foot to the *t* of your head
Mt 27:51 torn in two from *t* to bottom.

TORMENT (TORMENTED TORMENTORS)
Lk 16:28 also come to this place of *t*.'
2Co 12: 7 a messenger of Satan, to *t* me.

TORMENTED (TORMENT)
Rev 20:10 They will be *t* day and night

TORMENTORS (TORMENT)
Ps 137: 3 our *t* demanded songs of joy;

TORN
Gal 4:15 you would have *t* out your eyes
Php 1:23 I do not know! I am *t*

TORTURED*
Mt 18:34 turned him over to the jailers to be *t*.
Heb 11:35 Others were *t* and refused

TOSSED (TOSSING)
Eph 4:14 *t* back and forth by the waves,
Jas 1: 6 of the sea, blown and *t* by the wind.

TOSSING (TOSSED)
Isa 57:20 But the wicked are like the *t* sea,

TOUCH (TOUCHED TOUCHES)
Ge 3: 3 you must not *t* it, or you will die.'
Ex 19:12 go up the mountain or *t* the foot
Ps 105:15 "Do not *t* my anointed ones;
Mt 9:21 If I only *t* his cloak, I will be healed
Lk 18:15 babies to Jesus to have him *t* them.
    24:39 It is I myself! *T* me and see;
2Co 6:17 *T* no unclean thing,
Col 2:21 Do not taste! Do not *t*!"?

TOUCHED (TOUCH)
1Sa 10:26 men whose hearts God had *t*.
Isa 6: 7 With it he *t* my mouth and said,
Mt 14:36 and all who *t* him were healed.
Lk 8:45 "Who *t* me?" Jesus asked.
1Jn 1: 1 looked at and our hands have *t*—

TOUCHES (TOUCH)
Ex 19:12 Whoever *t* the mountain shall
Zec 2: 8 for whoever *t* you *t* the apple

TOWER
Ge 11: 4 with a *t* that reaches to the heavens
Pr 18:10 of the LORD is a strong *t*;

TOWN (TOWNS)
Mt 2:23 and lived in a *t* called Nazareth.

TOWNS (TOWN)
Nu 35: 2 to give the Levites *t* to live
    35:15 These six *t* will be a place of refuge
Jer 11:13 as many gods as you have *t*,
Mt 9:35 Jesus went through all the *t*

TRACING*
Ro 11:33 and his paths beyond *t* out!

TRACK
Job 14:16 but not keep *t* of my sin.

TRADERS (TRADING)
1Ti 1:10 for slave *t* and liars and perjurers—

TRADING (TRADERS)
1Ki 10:22 The king had a fleet of *t* ships at sea
Pr 31:18 She sees that her *t* is profitable,

TRADITION (TRADITIONS)
Mt 15: 2 "Why do your disciples break the *t*
    15: 6 word of God for the sake of your *t*.
Mk 7:13 by your *t* that you have handed
Col 2: 8 which depends on human *t*

TRADITIONS (TRADITION)
Mk 7: 8 are holding on to the *t* of men."
Gal 1:14 zealous for the *t* of my fathers.

TRAIL
1Ti 5:24 the sins of others *t* behind them.

TRAIN* (TRAINED TRAINING)
Ps 68:18 you led captives in your *t*;
Pr 22: 6 *T* a child in the way he should go,
Isa 2: 4 nor will they *t* for war anymore.
    6: 1 the *t* of his robe filled the temple.
Mic 4: 3 nor will they *t* for war anymore.
Eph 4: 8 he led captives in his *t*
1Ti 4: 7 rather, *t* yourself to be godly.

Tit 2: 4 they can *t* the younger women

TRAINED (TRAIN)
Lk 6:40 everyone who is fully *t* will be like
Ac 22: 3 Under Gamaliel I was thoroughly *t*
2Co 11: 6 I may not be a *t* speaker,
Heb 5:14 by constant use have *t* themselves
    12:11 for those who have been *t* by it.

TRAINING* (TRAIN)
1Co 9:25 in the games goes into strict *t*.
Eph 6: 4 up in the *t* and instruction
1Ti 4: 8 For physical *t* is of some value,
2Ti 3:16 correcting and *t* in righteousness,

TRAITOR (TRAITORS)
Lk 6:16 and Judas Iscariot, who became a *t*.
Jn 18: 5 Judas the *t* was standing there

TRAITORS (TRAITOR)
Ps 59: 5 show no mercy to wicked *t*.

TRAMPLE (TRAMPLED)
Joel 3:13 Come, *t* the grapes,
Am 2: 7 They *t* on the heads of the poor
    5:11 You *t* on the poor
    8: 4 Hear this, you who *t* the needy
Mt 7: 6 they may *t* them under their feet,
Lk 10:19 I have given you authority to *t*

TRAMPLED (TRAMPLE)
Isa 63: 6 I *t* the nations in my anger;
Lk 21:24 Jerusalem will be *t*
Heb 10:29 to be punished who has *t* the Son
Rev 14:20 They were *t* in the winepress

TRANCE*
Ac 10:10 was being prepared, he fell into a *t*.
    11: 5 and in a *t* I saw a vision.
    22:17 into a *t* and saw the Lord speaking.

TRANQUILLITY*
Ecc 4: 6 Better one handful with *t*

TRANSACTIONS*
Ru 4: 7 method of legalizing *t* in Israel.)

TRANSCENDS*
Php 4: 7 which *t* all understanding,

TRANSFIGURED*
Mt 17: 2 There he was *t* before them.
Mk 9: 2 There he was *t* before them.

TRANSFORM* (TRANSFORMED)
Php 3:21 will *t* our lowly bodies

TRANSFORMED (TRANSFORM)
Ro 12: 2 be *t* by the renewing of your mind.
2Co 3:18 are being *t* into his likeness

TRANSGRESSED* (TRANSGRESSION)
Da 9:11 All Israel has *t* your law

TRANSGRESSION* (TRANSGRESSED
TRANSGRESSIONS TRANSGRESSORS)
Ps 19:13 innocent of great *t*.
Isa 53: 8 for the *t* of my people he was
Da 9:24 and your holy city to finish *t*,
Mic 1: 5 All this is because of Jacob's *t*,
    1: 5 What is Jacob's *t*?
    3: 8 to declare to Jacob his *t*,
    6: 7 Shall I offer my firstborn for my *t*,
    7:18 who pardons sin and forgives the *t*
Ro 4:15 where there is no law there is no *t*.
    11:11 Rather, because of their *t*,
    11:12 if their *t* means riches for the world

TRANSGRESSIONS* (TRANSGRESSION)
Ps 32: 1 whose *t* are forgiven,
    32: 5 my *t* to the LORD"—
    39: 8 Save me from all my *t*;
    51: 1 blot out my *t*.
    51: 3 For I know my *t*,
    65: 3 you forgave our *t*.
    103:12 so far has he removed our *t* from us
Isa 43:25 your *t*, for my own sake,
    50: 1 of your *t* your mother was sent
    53: 5 But he was pierced for our *t*,
Mic 1:13 for the *t* of Israel
Ro 4: 7 whose *t* are forgiven,
Gal 3:19 because of *t* until the Seed to whom
Eph 2: 1 you were dead in your *t* and sins,
    2: 5 even when we were dead in *t*—

TRANSGRESSORS* (TRANSGRESSION)
Ps 51:13 Then I will teach *t* your ways,
Isa 53:12 and made intercession for the *t*.
    53:12 and was numbered with the *t*.
    22:37 'And he was numbered with the *t*';

TRAP (TRAPPED TRAPS)
Ps 69:22 may it become retribution and a *t*.
Pr 20:25 a *t* for a man to dedicate something
    28:10 will fall into his own *t*,
Isa 8:14 a *t* and a snare.
Mt 22:15 and laid plans to *t* him in his words.
Lk 21:34 close on you unexpectedly like a *t*.
Ro 11: 9 their table become a snare and a *t*,
1Ti 3: 7 into disgrace and into the devil's *t*.
    6: 9 and a *t* and into many foolish
2Ti 2:26 and escape from the *t* of the devil,

TRAPPED (TRAP)
Pr 6: 2 if you have been *t* by what you said
    12:13 An evil man is *t* by his sinful talk,

TRAPS (TRAP)
Jos 23:13 they will become snares and *t*
La 4:20 was caught in their *t*.

TRAVEL (TRAVELER)
Pr 4:15 Avoid it, do not *t* on it;
Mt 23:15 You *t* over land and sea

TRAVELER (TRAVEL)
Job 31:32 door was always open to the *t*—
Jer 14: 8 like a *t* who stays only a night?

TREACHEROUS (TREACHERY)
Ps 25: 3 who are *t* without excuse.
2Ti 3: 4 not lovers of the good, *t*, rash,

TREACHERY (TREACHEROUS)
Isa 59:13 rebellion and *t* against the LORD,

TREAD (TREADING TREADS)
Ps 91:13 You will *t* upon the lion

TREADING (TREAD)
Dt 25: 4 an ox while it is *t* out the grain.
1Co 9: 9 an ox while it is *t* out the grain."
1Ti 5:18 the ox while it is *t* out the grain,"

TREADS (TREAD)
Rev 19:15 He *t* the winepress of the fury

TREASURE (TREASURED TREASURES TREASURY)
Pr 2: 4 and search for it as for hidden *t*,
Isa 33: 6 of the LORD is the key to this *t*.
Mt 6:21 For where your *t* is, there your
    13:44 of heaven is like *t* hidden in a field.
Lk 12:33 a *t* in heaven that will not be
2Co 4: 7 But we have this *t* in jars of clay
1Ti 6:19 In this way they will lay up *t*

TREASURED (TREASURE)
Ex 19: 5 you will be my *t* possession.
Dt 7: 6 to be his people, his *t* possession.
    26:18 his *t* possession as he promised,
Job 23:12 I have *t* the words
Mal 3:17 when I make up my *t* possession.
Lk 2:19 But Mary *t* up all these things
    2:51 But his mother *t* all these things

TREASURES (TREASURE)
1Ch 29: 3 my God I now give my personal *t*
Pr 10: 2 Ill-gotten *t* are of no value,
Mt 6:19 up for yourselves *t* on earth,
    13:52 out of his storeroom new *t*
Col 2: 3 in whom are hidden all the *t*
Heb 11:26 of greater value than the *t* of Egypt,

TREASURY (TREASURE)
Mk 12:43 more into the *t* than all the others.

TREAT (TREATED TREATING TREATMENT)
Lev 22: 2 sons to *t* with respect the sacred
Ps 103:10 he does not *t* us as our sins deserve
Mt 18:17 *t* him as you would a pagan
    18:35 my heavenly Father will *t* each
Eph 6: 9 *t* your slaves in the same way.
1Th 5:20 do not *t* prophecies with contempt.
1Ti 5: 1 *T* younger men as brothers,
1Pe 3: 7 and *t* them with respect

TREATED (TREAT)
Lev 19:34 The alien living with you must be *t*
25:40 He is to be *t* as a hired worker
1Sa 24:17 "You have *t* me well, but I have
Heb 10:29 who has *t* as an unholy thing

TREATING (TREAT)
Ge 18:25 *t* the righteous and the wicked
Heb 12: 7 as discipline; God is *t* you as sons.

TREATMENT (TREAT)
Col 2:23 and their harsh *t* of the body,

TREATY
Ex 34:12 not to make a *t* with those who live
Dt 7: 2 Make no *t* with them, and show
23: 6 Do not seek a *t* of friendship with them

TREE (TREES)
Ge 2: 9 and the *t* of the knowledge of good
2: 9 of the garden were the *t* of life
Dt 21:23 hung on a *t* is under God's curse.
2Sa 18: 9 Absalom's head got caught in the *t*.
1Ki 14:23 and under every spreading *t*.
Ps 1: 3 He is like a *t* planted by streams
52:12 But I am like an olive *t*
92:12 righteous will flourish like a palm *t*,
Pr 3:18 She is a *t* of life to those who
11:30 of the righteous is a *t* of life,
27:18 He who tends a fig *t* will eat its fruit
Isa 65:22 For as the days of a *t*,
Jer 17: 8 He will be like a *t* planted
Eze 17:24 I the LORD bring down the tall *t*
Da 4:10 before me stood a *t* in the middle
Mic 4: 4 and under his own fig *t*,
Zec 3:10 to sit under his vine and fig *t*, '
Mt 3:10 every *t* that does not produce good
12:33 for a *t* is recognized by its fruit.
Lk 19: 4 climbed a sycamore-fig *t* to see him
Ac 5:30 killed by hanging him on a *t*.
Ro 11:24 be grafted into their own olive *t!*
Gal 3:13 is everyone who is hung on a *t*."
Jas 3:12 My brothers, can a fig *t* bear olives,
1Pe 2:24 sins in his body on the *t*,
Rev 2: 7 the right to eat from the *t* of life,
22: 2 side of the river stood the *t* of life,
22:14 they may have the right to the *t*
22:19 from him his share in the *t* of life

TREES (TREE)
Jdg 9: 8 One day the *t* went out
Ps 96:12 Then all the *t* of the forest will sing
Isa 55:12 and all the *t* of the field
Mt 3:10 The ax is already at the root of the *t*
Mk 8:24 they look like *t* walking around."
Jude :12 autumn *t*, without fruit

TREMBLE (TREMBLED TREMBLES TREMBLING)
Ex 15:14 The nations will hear and *t;*
1Ch 16:30 *T* before him, all the earth!
Ps 114: 7 *T*, O earth, at the presence
Jer 5:22 "Should you not *t* in my presence?
Eze 38:20 of the earth will *t* at my presence.
Joel 2: 1 Let all who live in the land *t,*
Hab 3: 6 he looked, and made the nations *t*.

TREMBLED (TREMBLE)
Ex 19:16 Everyone in the camp *t*.
20:18 in smoke, they *t* with fear.
2Sa 22: 8 "The earth *t* and quaked,
Ac 7:32 Moses *t* with fear and did not dare

TREMBLES (TREMBLE)
Ps 97: 4 the earth sees and *t*.
104:32 he who looks at the earth, and it *t*,
Isa 66: 2 and *t* at my word.
Jer 10:10 When he is angry, the earth *t;*
Na 1: 5 The earth *t* at his presence,

TREMBLING (TREMBLE)
Ps 2:11 and rejoice with *t*.
Da 10:10 set me *t* on my hands and knees.
Php 2:12 out your salvation with fear and *t,*

TRESPASS (TRESPASSES)
Heb 12:21 terrifying that Moses said, "I am *t*

TRESPASS* (TRESPASSES)
Ro 5:15 But the gift is not like the *t*.
5:15 died by the *t* of the one man,
5:17 For if, by the *t* of the one man,
5:18 result of one *t* was condemnation
5:20 added so that the *t* might increase.

TRESPASSES* (TRESPASS)
Ro 5:16 but the gift followed many *t*

TRIAL (TRIALS)
Ps 37:33 condemned when brought to *t*.
Mk 13:11 you are arrested and brought to *t,*
2Co 8: 2 most severe *t*, their overflowing
Jas 1:12 is the man who perseveres under *t,*
1Pe 4:12 at the painful *t* you are suffering,
Rev 3:10 you from the hour of *t* that is going

TRIALS* (TRIAL)
Dt 7:19 saw with your own eyes the great *t,*
29: 3 own eyes you saw those great *t,*
Lk 22:28 who have stood by me in my *t.*
1Th 3: 3 one would be unsettled by these *t*.
2Th 1: 4 the persecutions and *t* you are
Jas 1: 2 whenever you face *t* of many kinds,
1Pe 1: 6 had to suffer grief in all kinds of *t*.
2Pe 2: 9 how to rescue godly men from *t*

TRIBE (HALF-TRIBE TRIBES)
Heb 7:13 no one from that *t* has ever served
Rev 5: 5 See, the Lion of the *t* of Judah,
5: 9 God from every *t* and language
11: 9 men from every people, *t,*
14: 6 to every nation, *t,* language

TRIBES (TRIBE)
Ge 49:28 All these are the twelve *t* of Israel,
Mt 19:28 judging the twelve *t* of Israel.

TRIBULATION*
Rev 7:14 who have come out of the great *t;*

TRICKERY*
Ac 13:10 full of all kinds of deceit and *t*.
2Co 12:16 fellow that I am, I caught you by *t!*

TRIED (TRY)
Ps 73:16 When I *t* to understand all this,
95: 9 where your fathers tested and *t* me,
Heb 3: 9 where your fathers tested and *t* me

TRIES (TRY)
Lk 17:33 Whoever *t* to keep his life will lose

TRIMMED
Mt 25: 7 virgins woke up and *t* their lamps.

TRIUMPH (TRIUMPHAL TRIUMPHED TRIUMPHING TRIUMPHS)
Ps 25: 2 nor let my enemies *t* over me.
54: 7 my eyes have looked in *t*
112: 8 in the end he will look in *t*
118: 7 I will look in *t* on my enemies.
Pr 28:12 When the righteous *t,* there is great
Isa 42:13 and will *t* over his enemies.

TRIUMPHAL* (TRIUMPH)
Isa 60:11 their kings led in *t* procession.
2Co 2:14 us in *t* procession in Christ

TRIUMPHED (TRIUMPH)
Rev 5: 5 of Judah, the Root of David, has *t*.

TRIUMPHING* (TRIUMPH)
Col 2:15 of them, *t* over them by the cross.

TRIUMPHS* (TRIUMPH)
Jas 2:13 Mercy *t* over judgment! What

TROUBLE (TROUBLED TROUBLES)
Ge 41:51 God has made me forget all my *t*
Jos 7:25 Why have you brought this *t* on us?
Job 5:10 good from God, and not *t*?"
5: 7 Yet man is born to *t*
14: 1 is of few days and full of *t*.
42:11 him over all the *t* the LORD had
Ps 7:14 conceives *t* gives birth
7:16 The *t* he causes recoils on himself;
9: 9 a stronghold in times of *t*.

Ps 10:14 But you, O God, do see *t* and grief;
22:11 for *t* is near
27: 5 For in the day of *t*
32: 7 you will protect me from *t*
37:39 he is their stronghold in time of *t*.
41: 1 LORD delivers him in times of *t*.
46: 1 an ever-present help in *t*.
50:15 and call upon me in the day of *t;*
59:16 my refuge in times of *t*.
66:14 spoke when I was in *t*.
86: 7 In the day of my *t* I will call to you,
91:15 I will be with him in *t,*
107: 6 to the LORD in their *t,*
107:13 they cried to the LORD in their *t,*
116: 3 I was overcome by *t* and sorrow.
119:143 *T* and distress have come upon me,
138: 7 Though I walk in the midst of *t,*
143:11 righteousness, bring me out of *t*.
Pr 11: 8 righteous man is rescued from *t,*
11:17 a cruel man brings *t* on himself
11:29 He who brings *t* on his family will
12:13 but a righteous man escapes *t*.
12:21 but the wicked have their fill of *t*.
15:27 A greedy man brings *t* to his family
19:23 one rests content, untouched by *t*.
22: 8 He who sows wickedness reaps *t,*
24:10 If you falter in times of *t,*
25:19 on the unfaithful in times of *t*.
28:14 he who hardens his heart falls into *t*
Jer 30: 7 It will be a time of *t* for Jacob,
Na 1: 7 a refuge in times of *t*.
Zep 1:15 a day of *t* and ruin,
Mt 6:34 Each day has enough *t* of its own.
13:21 When *t* or persecution comes
Jn 16:33 In this world you will have *t*.
Ro 8:35 Shall *t* or hardship or persecution
2Co 1: 4 those in any *t* with the comfort we
2Th 1: 6 *t* to those who you
Jas 5:13 one of you in *t*? He should pray.

TROUBLED (TROUBLE)
Ps 38:18 I am *t* by my sin.
Isa 38:14 I am *t;* O Lord, come to my aid!"
Mk 14:33 began to be deeply distressed and *t*.
Jn 14: 1 "Do not let your hearts be *t*.
14:27 Do not let your hearts be *t*
2Th 1: 7 and give relief to you who are *t,*

TROUBLES (TROUBLE)
Ps 34: 6 he saved him out of all his *t*.
34:17 he delivers them from all their *t*.
34:19 A righteous man may have many *t,*
40:12 For *t* without number surround me
54: 7 he has delivered me from all my *t,*
1Co 7:28 those who marry will face many *t*
2Co 1: 4 who comforts us in all our *t,*
4:17 and momentary *t* are achieving
6: 4 in *t,* hardships and distresses;
7: 4 in all our *t* my joy knows no bounds
Php 4:14 good of you to share in my *t*.

TRUE (TRUTH)
Nu 11:23 not what I say will come *t* for you."
12: 7 this is not *t* of my servant Moses;
Dt 18:22 does not take place or come *t,*
Jos 23:15 of the LORD your God has come *t*
1Sa 9: 6 and everything he says comes *t*.
1Ki 10: 6 and your wisdom is *t*.
2Ch 6:17 your servant David come *t*.
15: 3 was without the *t* God,
Ps 33: 4 of the LORD is right and *t;*
119:142 and your law is *t*.
119:151 and all your commands are *t*.
119:160 All your words are *t;*
Pr 8: 7 My mouth speaks what is *t,*
22:21 teaching you *t* and reliable words,
Jer 10:10 But the LORD is the *t* God;
28: 9 only if his prediction comes *t*."
Eze 33:33 "When all this comes *t*—
Lk 16:11 who will trust you with *t* riches?
Jn 1: 9 The *t* light that gives light
4:23 when the *t* worshipers will worship

Jn 6:32 Father who gives you the *t* bread
7:28 on my own, but he who sent me is *t*
15: 1 "I am the *t* vine, and my Father is
17: 3 the only *t* God, and Jesus Christ,
19:35 testimony, and his testimony is *t*.
21:24 We know that his testimony is *t*.
Ac 10:34 "I now realize how *t* it is that God
11:23 all to remain *t* to the Lord
14:22 them to remain *t* to the faith.
17:11 day to see if what Paul said was *t*.
Ro 3: 4 Let God be *t*, and every man a liar.
Php 4: 8 whatever is *t*, whatever is noble,
1Jn 2: 8 and the *t* light is already shining.
5:20 He is the *t* God and eternal life.
Rev 19: 9 "These are the *t* words of God."
22: 6 These words are trustworthy and *t*.

TRUMPET (TRUMPETS)
Isa 27:13 And in that day a great *t* will sound
Eze 33: 5 Since he heard the sound of the *t*
Zec 9:14 Sovereign Lord will sound the *t*;
Mt 24:31 send his angels with a loud *t* call,
1Co 14: 8 if the *t* does not sound a clear call,
15:52 For the *t* will sound, the dead will
1Th 4:16 and with the *t* call of God,
Rev 8: 7 The first angel sounded his *t*,

TRUMPETS (TRUMPET)
Jdg 7:19 They blew their *t* and broke the jars
Rev 8: 2 and to them were given seven *t*.

TRUST* (ENTRUST ENTRUSTED TRUSTED TRUSTFULLY TRUSTING TRUSTS TRUSTWORTHY)
Ex 14:31 put their *t* in him and in Moses his
19: 9 and will always put their *t* in you."
Nu 20:12 "Because you did not *t*
Dt 1:32 you did not *t* in the Lord your
9:23 You did not *t* him or obey him.
28:52 walls in which you *t* fall down.
Jdg 11:20 did not *t* Israel to pass
2Ki 17:14 who did not *t* in the Lord their
18:30 to *t* in the Lord when he says,
1Ch 9:22 to their positions of *t* by David
Job 4:18 If God places no *t* in his servants,
15:15 If God places no *t* in his holy ones,
31:24 "If I have put my *t* in gold
39:12 Can you *t* him to bring
Ps 4: 5 and *t* in the Lord.
9:10 Those who know your name will *t*
13: 5 But I *t* in your unfailing love;
20: 7 Some *t* in chariots and some
20: 7 we *t* in the name of the Lord our
22: 4 In you our fathers put their *t*;
22: 9 you made me *t* in you
25: 2 I lift up my soul; in you I *t*,
31: 6 I *t* in the Lord.
31:14 But I *t* in you, O Lord;
33:21 for we *t* in his holy name.
37: 3 *T* in the Lord and do good;
37: 5 *t* in him and he will do this:
40: 3 and put their *t* in the Lord.
40: 4 who makes the Lord his *t*,
44: 6 I do not *t* in my bow,
49: 6 those who *t* in their wealth
49:13 of those who *t* in themselves,
52: 8 I *t* in God's unfailing love
55:23 But as for me, I *t* in you.
56: 3 I will *t* in you.
56: 4 in God I *t*; I will not be afraid.
56:11 in God I *t*; I will not be afraid.
62: 8 *T* in him at all times, O people;
62:10 Do not *t* in extortion
78: 7 Then they would put their *t* in God
78:22 or *t* in his deliverance.
91: 2 my God, in whom I *t*."
115: 8 and so will all who *t* in them.
115: 9 O house of Israel, *t* in the Lord—
115:10 O house of Aaron, *t* in the Lord
115:11 You who fear him, *t* in the Lord
118: 8 than to *t* in man.
118: 9 than to *t* in princes.
119:42 for I *t* in your word.
125: 1 Those who *t* in the Lord are like
135:18 and so will all who *t* in them.
143: 8 for I have put my *t* in you.
146: 3 Do not put your *t* in princes,
Pr 3: 5 *T* in the Lord with all your heart
21:22 the stronghold in which they *t*.

Pr 22:19 So that your *t* may be in the Lord
Isa 8:17 I will put my *t* in him.
12: 2 I will *t* and not be afraid.
26: 4 *T* in the Lord forever,
30:15 in quietness and *t* is your strength,
31: 1 who *t* in the multitude
36:15 to *t* in the Lord when he says,
42:17 But those who *t* in idols,
50:10 *t* in the name of the Lord
Jer 2:37 Lord has rejected those you *t*;
5:17 the fortified cities in which you *t*.
7: 4 Do not *t* in deceptive words
7:14 the temple you *t* in, the place I gave
9: 4 do not *t* your brothers.
12: 6 Do not *t* them,
28:15 you have persuaded this nation to *t*
39:18 you *t* in me, declares the Lord.' "
48: 7 Since you *t* in your deeds
49: 4 you *t* in your riches and say,
49:11 Your widows too can *t* in me."
Mic 7: 5 Do not *t* a neighbor;
Na 1: 7 He cares for those who *t* in him,
Zep 3: 2 She does not *t* in the Lord,
3:12 who *t* in the name of the Lord.
Lk 16:11 who will *t* you with true riches?
Jn 12:36 Put your *t* in the light
14: 1 *T* in God; *t* also in me.
Ac 14:23 Lord, in whom they had put their *t*.
Ro 15:13 you with all joy and peace as you *t*
1Co 4: 2 been given a *t* must prove faithful.
9:17 discharging the *t* committed
2Co 13: 6 I *t* that you will discover that we
Heb 2:13 "I will put my *t* in him."

TRUSTED* (TRUST)
1Sa 27:12 Achish *t* David and said to himself,
2Ki 18: 5 Hezekiah *t* in the Lord, the God
1Ch 5:20 their prayers, because they *t*
Job 12:20 He silences the lips of *t* advisers
Ps 5: 9 from their mouth can be *t*;
22: 4 they *t* and you delivered them.
22: 5 in you they *t* and were not
26: 1 I have *t* in the Lord
41: 9 Even my close friend, whom I *t*,
52: 7 but *t* in his great wealth
Isa 20: 5 Those who *t* in Cush and boasted
25: 9 This is the Lord, we *t* in him;
25: 9 we *t* in him, and he saved us.
47:10 You have *t* in your wickedness
Jer 13:25 and *t* in false gods.
38:22 those *t* friends of yours.
48:13 ashamed when they *t* in Bethel.
Eze 16:15 " 'But you *t* in your beauty
Da 3:28 They *t* in him and defied the king's
6:23 because he had *t* in his God.
Lk 11:22 the armor in which the man *t*
16:10 *t* with very little can also be *t*
Ac 12:20 a *t* personal servant of the king,
Tit 2:10 but to show that they can be fully *t*,
3: 8 so that those who have *t*

TRUSTFULLY* (TRUST)
Pr 3:29 who lives *t* near you.

TRUSTING* (TRUST)
Job 15:31 by *t* what is worthless,
Ps 112: 7 his heart is steadfast, *t*
Isa 2:22 Stop *t* in man,
Jer 7: 8 you are *t* in deceptive words that

TRUSTS* (TRUST)
Job 8:14 What he *t* in is fragile;
Ps 21: 7 For the king *t* in the Lord;
22: 8 "He *t* in the Lord;
28: 7 my heart *t* in him, and I am helped.
32:10 surrounds the man who *t* in him
84:12 blessed is the man who *t* in you.
86: 2 who *t* in you.
Pr 11:28 Whoever *t* in his riches will fall,
16:20 blessed is he who *t* in the Lord.
28:25 he who *t* in the Lord will prosper.
28:26 He who *t* in himself is a fool,
29:25 whoever *t* in the Lord is kept safe
Isa 26: 3 because he *t* in you.

Isa 28:16 one who *t* will never be dismayed.
Jer 17: 5 "Cursed is the one who *t* in man,
17: 7 blessed is the man who *t*
Eze 33:13 but then he *t* in his righteousness
Hab 2:18 For he who makes it *t*
Mt 27:43 He *t* in God.
Ro 4: 5 but *t* God who justifies the wicked,
9:33 one who *t* in him will never be put
10:11 "Anyone who *t* in him will never
1Co 13: 7 always protects, always *t*,
1Pe 2: 6 and the one who *t* in him

TRUSTWORTHY* (TRUST)
Ex 18:21 *t* men who hate dishonest gain—
2Sa 7:28 you are God! Your words are *t*,
Ne 13:13 these men were considered *t*.
Ps 19: 7 The statutes of the Lord are *t*,
111: 7 all his precepts are *t*.
119:86 All your commands are *t*;
119:138 they are fully *t*.
Pr 11:13 but a *t* man keeps a secret.
13:17 but a *t* envoy brings healing.
25:13 is a *t* messenger to those who send
Da 2:45 and the interpretation is *t*."
6: 4 he was *t* and neither corrupt
Lk 16:10 So if you have not been *t*
16:12 And if you have not been *t*
19:17 'Because you have been *t*
1Co 7:25 one who by the Lord's mercy is *t*.
1Ti 1:15 Here is a *t* saying that deserves full
3: 1 Here is a *t* saying: If anyone sets his
3:11 but temperate and *t* in everything.
4: 9 This is a *t* saying that deserves full
2Ti 2:11 Here is a *t* saying:
Tit 1: 9 must hold firmly to the *t* message
3: 8 This is a *t* saying.
Rev 21: 5 for these words are *t* and true."
22: 6 "These words are *t* and true.

TRUTH* (TRUE TRUTHFUL TRUTHFULNESS TRUTHS)
Ge 42:16 tested to see if you are telling the *t*.
1Ki 17:24 Lord from your mouth is the *t*."
22:16 the *t* in the name of the Lord?"
2Ch 18:15 the *t* in the name of the Lord?"
Ps 15: 2 who speaks the *t* from his heart
25: 5 guide me in your *t* and teach me,
26: 3 and I walk continually in your *t*.
31: 5 redeem me, O Lord, the God of *t*
40:10 do not conceal your love and your *t*
40:11 your *t* always protect me.
43: 3 Send forth your light and your *t*,
45: 4 victoriously in behalf of *t*, humility
51: 6 Surely you desire *t*
52: 3 than speaking the *t*.
86:11 and I will walk in your *t*;
96:13 and the peoples in his *t*.
119:30 I have chosen the way of *t*;
119:43 of *t* from my mouth,
145:18 to all who call on him in *t*.
Pr 16:13 they value a man who speaks the *t*.
23:23 Buy the *t* and do not sell it;
Isa 45:19 I, the Lord, speak the *t*;
48: 1 but not in *t* or righteousness—
59:14 *t* has stumbled in the streets,
59:15 *T* is nowhere to be found,
65:16 will do so by the God of *t*;
65:16 will swear by the God of *t*
Jer 5: 1 who deals honestly and seeks the *t*,
5: 3 do not your eyes look for *t*?
7:28 *T* has perished; it has vanished
9: 3 it is not by *t*
9: 5 and no one speaks the *t*.
26:15 for in *t* the Lord has sent me
Da 8:12 and *t* was thrown to the ground.
9:13 and giving attention to your *t*.
10:21 what is written in the Book of *T*.
11: 2 "Now then, I tell you the *t*:
Am 5:10 and despise him who tells the *t*
Zec 8: 3 will be called the City of *T*,
8:16 are to do: Speak the *t* to each other,
8:19 Therefore love *t* and peace."
Mt 5:18 I tell you the *t*, until heaven

Mt	5: 26	I tell you the *t*, you will not get out
	6: 2	I tell you the *t*, they have received
	6: 5	I tell you the *t*, they have received
	6: 16	I tell you the *t*, they have received
	8: 10	"I tell you the *t*, I have not found
	10: 15	I tell you the *t*, it will be more
	10: 23	I tell you the *t*, you will not finish
	10: 42	I tell you the *t*, he will certainly not
	11: 11	I tell you the *t*: Among those born
	13: 17	For I tell you the *t*, many prophets
	16: 28	I tell you the *t*, some who are
	17: 20	I tell you the *t*, if you have faith
	18: 3	And he said: "I tell you the *t*,
	18: 13	And if he finds it, I tell you the *t*,
	18: 18	"I tell you the *t*, whatever you bind
	19: 23	to his disciples, "I tell you the *t*,
	19: 28	"I tell you the *t*, at the renewal
	21: 21	Jesus replied, "I tell you the *t*,
	21: 31	Jesus said to them, "I tell you the *t*,
	22: 16	of God in accordance with the *t*.
	23: 36	I tell you the *t*, all this will come
	24: 2	"I tell you the *t*, not one stone here
	24: 34	I tell you the *t*, this generation will
	24: 47	I tell you the *t*, he will put him
	25: 12	'I tell you the *t*, I don't know you.'
	25: 40	The King will reply, 'I tell you the *t*
	25: 45	"He will reply, 'I tell you the *t*,
	26: 13	tell you the *t*, wherever this gospel
	26: 21	"I tell you the *t*, one
	26: 34	"I tell you the *t*," Jesus answered,
Mk	3: 28	I tell you the *t*, all the sins
	5: 33	with fear, told him the whole *t*.
	8: 12	I tell you the *t*, no sign will be given
	9: 1	he said to them, "I tell you the *t*,
	9: 41	I tell you the *t*, anyone who gives
	10: 15	I tell you the *t*, anyone who will not
	10: 29	"I tell you the *t*," Jesus replied,
	11: 23	"I tell you the *t*, if anyone says
	12: 14	of God in accordance with the *t*.
	12: 43	Jesus said, "I tell you the *t*,
	13: 30	I tell you the *t*, this generation will
	14: 9	I tell you the *t*, wherever the gospel
	14: 18	"I tell you the *t*, one
	14: 25	"I tell you the *t*, I will not drink
	14: 30	"I tell you the *t*," Jesus answered,
Lk	4: 24	"I tell you the *t*," he continued,
	9: 27	I tell you the *t*, some who are
	12: 37	I tell you the *t*, he will dress himself
	12: 44	I tell you the *t*, he will put him
	18: 17	I tell you the *t*, anyone who will not
	18: 29	I tell you the *t*," Jesus said to them,
	20: 21	of God in accordance with the *t*.
	21: 3	"I tell you the *t*," he said, "this
	21: 32	tell you the *t*, this generation will
	23: 43	answered him, "I tell you the *t*,
Jn	1: 14	from the Father, full of grace and *t*.
	1: 17	and *t* came through Jesus Christ.
	1: 51	"I tell you the *t*, you shall see
	3: 3	"I tell you the *t*, no one can see
	3: 5	Jesus answered, "I tell you the *t*,
	3: 11	I tell you the *t*, we speak
	3: 21	But whoever lives by the *t* comes
	4: 23	worship the Father in spirit and *t*,
	4: 24	must worship in spirit and in *t*."
	5: 19	"I tell you the *t*, the Son can do
	5: 24	"I tell you the *t*, whoever hears my
	5: 25	I tell you the *t*, a time is coming
	5: 33	and he has testified to the *t*.
	6: 26	"I tell you the *t*, you are looking
	6: 32	Jesus said to them, "I tell you the *t*,
	6: 47	I tell you the *t*, he who believes has
	6: 53	Jesus said to them, "I tell you the *t*,
	7: 18	the one who sent him is a man of *t*;

Jn	8: 32	Then you will know the *t*,
	8: 32	and the *t* will set you free."
	8: 34	Jesus replied, "I tell you the *t*,
	8: 40	who has told you the *t* that I heard
	8: 44	to the *t*, for there is no *t* in him.
	8: 45	I tell the *t*, you do not believe me!
	8: 46	I am telling the *t*, why don't you
	8: 51	I tell you the *t*, if anyone keeps my
	8: 58	"I tell you the *t*," Jesus answered,
	10: 1	"I tell you the *t*, the man who does
	10: 7	"I tell you the *t*, I am the gate
	12: 24	I tell you the *t*, unless a kernel
	13: 16	I tell you the *t*, no servant is greater
	13: 20	tell you the *t*, whoever accepts
	13: 21	"I tell you the *t*, one of you is going
	13: 38	I tell you the *t*, before the rooster
	14: 6	I am the way and the *t* and the life.
	14: 12	I tell you the *t*, anyone who has
	14: 17	with you forever—the Spirit of *t*.
	15: 26	the Spirit of *t* who goes out
	16: 7	But I tell you the *t*: It is
	16: 13	But when he, the Spirit of *t*, comes,
	16: 13	comes, he will guide you into all *t*.
	16: 20	I tell you the *t*, you will weep
	16: 23	I tell you the *t*, my Father will give
	17: 17	them by the *t*; your word is *t*.
	18: 23	if I spoke the *t*, why did you strike
	18: 37	into the world, to testify to the *t*.
	18: 37	on the side of *t* listens to me."
	18: 38	"What is *t*?" Pilate asked.
	19: 35	He knows that he tells the *t*,
	21: 18	I tell you the *t*, when you were
Ac	20: 30	and distort the *t* in order
	21: 24	everybody will know there is no *t*
	21: 34	commander could not get at the *t*
	24: 8	able to learn the *t* about all these
	28: 25	"The Holy Spirit spoke the *t*
Ro	1: 18	of men who suppress the *t*
	1: 25	They exchanged the *t* of God
	2: 2	who do such things is based on *t*.
	2: 8	who reject the *t* and follow evil,
	2: 20	embodiment of knowledge and *t*—
	9: 1	I speak the *t* in Christ—I am not
	15: 8	of the Jews on behalf of God's *t*,
1Co	5: 8	the bread of sincerity and *t*.
	13: 6	in evil but rejoices with the *t*.
2Co	4: 2	setting forth the *t* plainly we
	11: 10	As surely as the *t* of Christ is in me,
	12: 6	because I would be speaking the *t*.
	13: 8	against the *t*, but only for the *t*.
Gal	2: 5	so that the *t* of the gospel might
	2: 14	in line with the *t* of the gospel,
	4: 16	enemy by telling you the *t*?
	5: 7	and kept you from obeying the *t*?
Eph	1: 13	when you heard the word of *t*,
	4: 15	Instead, speaking the *t* in love,
	4: 21	him in accordance with the *t* that is
	5: 9	and *t*) and find out what pleases
	6: 14	with the belt of *t* buckled
Col	1: 5	heard about in the word of *t*,
	1: 6	understood God's grace in all its *t*.
2Th	2: 10	because they refused to love the *t*
	2: 12	who have not believed the *t*
	2: 13	and through belief in the *t*.
1Ti	2: 4	to come to a knowledge of the *t*.
	2: 7	I am telling the *t*, I am not lying—
	3: 15	the pillar and foundation of the *t*.
	4: 3	who believe and who know the *t*.
	6: 5	who have been robbed of the *t*
2Ti	2: 15	correctly handles the word of *t*.
	2: 18	have wandered away from the *t*.
	2: 25	them to a knowledge of the *t*,
	3: 7	never able to acknowledge the *t*.
	3: 8	so also these men oppose the *t*—
	4: 4	will turn their ears away from the *t*
Tit	1: 1	the knowledge of the *t* that leads
	1: 14	of those who reject the *t*.
Heb	10: 26	received the knowledge of the *t*,
Jas	1: 18	birth through the word of *t*,

Jas	3: 14	do not boast about it or deny the *t*.
	5: 19	of you should wander from the *t*
1Pe	1: 22	by obeying the *t* so that you have
2Pe	1: 12	established in the *t* you now have.
	2: 2	the way of *t* into disrepute.
1Jn	1: 6	we lie and do not live by the *t*.
	1: 8	deceive ourselves and the *t* is not
	2: 4	commands is a liar, and the *t* is not
	2: 8	its *t* is seen in him and you,
	2: 20	and all of you know the *t*.
	2: 21	because no lie comes from the *t*.
	2: 21	because you do not know the *t*,
	3: 18	or tongue but with actions and in *t*.
	3: 19	we know that we belong to the *t*,
	4: 6	is how we recognize the Spirit of *t*
	5: 6	testifies, because the Spirit is the *t*.
2Jn	: 1	whom I love in the *t*—
	: 2	who know the *t*— because of the *t*,
	: 3	will be with us in *t* and love.
	: 4	of your children walking in the *t*,
3Jn	: 1	friend Gaius, whom I love in the *t*.
	: 3	how you continue to walk in the *t*.
	: 3	tell about your faithfulness to the *t*
	: 4	my children are walking in the *t*.
	: 8	we may work together for the *t*.
	: 12	everyone—and even by the *t* itself.

TRUTHFUL* (TRUTH)
Pr	12: 17	A *t* witness gives honest testimony,
	12: 19	*T* lips endure forever,
	12: 22	but he delights in men who are *t*.
	14: 5	A *t* witness does not deceive,
	14: 25	A *t* witness saves lives,
Jer	4: 2	and if in a *t*, just and righteous way
Jn	3: 33	it has certified that God is in *t*.
2Co	6: 7	in *t* speech and in the power

TRUTHFULNESS* (TRUTH)
Ro	3: 7	"If my falsehood enhances God's *t*

TRUTHS* (TRUTH)
1Co	2: 13	expressing spiritual *t*
1Ti	3: 9	hold of the deep *t* of the faith
	4: 6	brought up in the *t* of the faith
Heb	5: 12	to teach you the elementary *t*

TRY (TRIED TRIES TRYING)
Ps	26: 2	Test me, O LORD, and *t* me,
Isa	7: 13	enough to try the patience of men?
Lk	12: 58	*t* hard to be reconciled to him
	13: 24	will *t* to enter and will not be able
1Co	10: 33	even as I *t* to please everybody
	14: 12	*t* to excel in gifts that build up
1Th	5: 11	is to fear the Lord, we *t*
	5: 15	always *t* to be kind to each other
Tit	2: 9	to *t* to please them, not to talk back

TRYING (TRY)
2Co	5: 12	We are not *t* to commend ourselves
Gal	1: 10	If I were still *t* to please men,
1Th	2: 4	We are not *t* to please men but God
1Pe	1: 11	*t* to find out the time
1Jn	2: 26	things to you about those who are *t*

TUMORS
1Sa	5: 6	them and afflicted them with *t*.

TUNE
1Co	14: 7	anyone know what *t* is being

TUNIC (TUNICS)
Lk	6: 29	do not stop him from taking your *t*.

TUNICS (TUNIC)
Lk	3: 11	"The man with two *t* should share

TURMOIL
Ps	65: 7	and the *t* of the nations.
Pr	15: 16	than great wealth with *t*.

TURN (TURNED TURNING TURNS)
Ex	32: 12	*T* from your fierce anger; relent
Nu	32: 15	If you *t* away from following him,
Dt	5: 32	do not *t* aside to the right

Dt 28:14 Do not *t* aside from any
   30:10 and *t* to the LORD your God
Jos 1: 7 do not *t* from it to the right
1Ki 8:58 May he *t* our hearts to him,
2Ch 7:14 and *t* from their wicked ways,
   30: 9 He will not *t* his face from you
Job 33:30 to *t* back his soul from the pit,
Ps 28: 1 do not *t* a deaf ear to me.
   34:14 *T* from evil and do good;
   51:13 and sinners will *t* back to you.
   78: 6 they in *t* would tell their children.
   119:36 *T* my heart toward your statutes
   119:132 *T* to me and have mercy on me,
Pr 22: 6 when he is old he will not *t* from
      it.
Isa 17: 7 *t* their eyes to the Holy One
   28: 6 to those who *t* back the battle
   29:16 You *t* things upside down,
   30:21 Whether you *t* to the right
   45:22 "*T* to me and be saved,
   55: 7 Let him *t* to the LORD,
Jer 31:13 I will *t* their mourning
Eze 33: 9 if you do warn the wicked man
      to *t*
   33:11 *T! T* from your evil ways!
Jnh 3: 9 and with compassion *t*
Mal 4: 6 He will *t* the hearts of the fathers
Mt 5:39 you on the right cheek, *t*
   10:35 For I have come to *t*
Lk 1:17 to *t* the hearts of the fathers
Jn 12:40 nor *t*— and I would heal them."
   16:20 but your grief will *t* to joy.
Ac 3:19 Repent, then, and *t* to God,
   26:18 and *t* them from darkness to light,
1Co 14:31 For you can all prophesy in *t*
   15:23 But each in his own *t*: Christ,
1Ti 6:20 *T* away from godless chatter
1Pe 3:11 He must *t* from evil and do good;

TURNED (TURN)
Dt 23: 5 *t* the curse into a blessing for you,
1Ki 11: 4 his wives *t* his heart
2Ch 15: 4 But in their distress they *t*
Est 9: 1 but now the tables were *t*
   9:22 when their sorrow was *t* into joy
Ps 14: 3 All have *t* aside,
   30:11 You *t* my wailing into dancing;
   40: 1 he *t* to me and heard my cry.
Isa 9:12 for all this, his anger is not *t* away,
   53: 6 each of us has *t* to his own way;
Hos 7: 8 Ephraim is a flat cake not *t* over.
Joel 2:31 The sun will be *t* to darkness
Lk 22:32 And when you have *t* back,
Ro 3:12 All have *t* away,

TURNING (TURN)
2Ki 21:13 wiping it and *t* it upside down.
Pr 2: 2 *t* your ear to wisdom
   14:27 *t* a man from the snares of death.

TURNS (TURN)
2Sa 22:29 the LORD *t* my darkness into light
Pr 15: 1 A gentle answer *t* away wrath,
Isa 44:25 and *t* it into nonsense,
Jas 5:20 Whoever *t* a sinner from the error

TWELVE
Ge 35:22 Jacob had *t* sons: The sons of
      Leah:
   49:28 All these are the *t* tribes of Israel.
Mt 10: 1 He called his *t* disciples to him
Lk 9:17 the disciples picked up *t*
      basketfuls
Rev 21:12 the names of the *t* tribes of Israel.
   21:14 of the *t* apostles of the Lamb.

TWIN (TWINS)
Ge 25:24 there were *t* boys in her womb.

TWINKLING*
1Co 15:52 in a flash, in the *t* of an eye,

TWINS (TWIN)
Ro 9:11 before the *t* were born

TWISTING* (TWISTS)
Pr 30:33 and as *t* the nose produces blood,

TWISTS (TWISTING)
Ex 23: 8 and *t* the words of the righteous.

TYRANNICAL*
Pr 28:16 A *t* ruler lacks judgment,

TYRE
Eze 28:12 a lament concerning the king of *T*
Mt 11:22 it will be more bearable for *T*

UNAPPROACHABLE*
1Ti 6:16 immortal and who lives in *u* light,

UNASHAMED*
1Jn 2:28 and *u* before him at his coming.

UNBELIEF* (UNBELIEVER UNBELIEVERS
UNBELIEVING)
Mk 9:24 help me overcome my *u*!"
Ro 4:20 through *u* regarding the promise
   11:20 they were broken off because
      of *u*
   11:23 And if they do not persist in *u*,
1Ti 1:13 because I acted in ignorance
      and *u*.
Heb 3:19 able to enter, because of their *u*.

UNBELIEVER* (UNBELIEF)
1Co 7:15 But if the *u* leaves, let him do so.
   10:27 If some *u* invites you to a meal
   14:24 if an *u* or someone who does not
2Co 6:15 have in common with an *u*?
1Ti 5: 8 the faith and is worse than an *u*.

UNBELIEVERS* (UNBELIEF)
Lk 12:46 and assign him a place with the *u*.
Ro 15:31 rescued from the *u* in Judea
1Co 6: 6 another—and this in front of *u*!
   14:22 however, is for believers, not
      for *u*.
   14:22 not for believers but for *u*;
   14:23 do not understand or some *u*
      come
2Co 4: 4 this age has blinded the minds
      of *u*,
   6:14 Do not be yoked together with *u*.

UNBELIEVING* (UNBELIEF)
Mt 17:17 "O *u* and perverse generation,"
Mk 9:19 "O *u* generation," Jesus replied,
Lk 9:41 "O *u* and perverse generation,"
1Co 7:14 For the *u* husband has been
   7:14 and the *u* wife has been sanctified
Heb 3:12 *u* heart that turns away
Rev 21: 8 But the cowardly, the *u*, the vile,

UNBLEMISHED*
Heb 9:14 the eternal Spirit offered himself *u*

UNCEASING
Ro 9: 2 and *u* anguish in my heart.

UNCERTAIN*
1Ti 6:17 which is so *u*, but to put their
      hope

UNCHANGEABLE* (UNCHANGING)
Heb 6:18 by two *u* things in which it is

UNCHANGING* (UNCHANGEABLE)
Heb 6:17 wanted to make the *u* nature

UNCIRCUMCISED
Lev 26:41 when their *u* hearts are humbled
1Sa 17:26 Who is this *u* Philistine that he
Jer 9:26 house of Israel is *u* in heart."
Ac 7:51 stiff-necked people, with *u* hearts
Ro 4:11 had by faith while he was *u*
1Co 7:18 Was a man *u* when he was called?
Col 3:11 circumcised or *u*, barbarian,

UNCIRCUMCISION
1Co 7:19 is nothing and *u* is nothing.
Gal 5: 6 neither circumcision nor *u* has any

UNCLEAN
Ge 7: 2 and two of every kind of *u* animal,
Lev 10:10 between the *u* and the clean,
   11: 4 it is ceremonially *u* for you.
   17:15 he will be ceremonially *u* till
      evening.
Isa 6: 5 ruined! For I am a man of *u* lips,
   52:11 Touch no *u* thing!
Mt 15:11 mouth does not make him '*u*,'
Ac 10:14 never eaten anything impure
      or *u*."
Ro 14:14 fully convinced that no food is *u*
2Co 6:17 Touch no *u* thing,

UNCLOTHED*
2Co 5: 4 because we do not wish to be *u*

UNCONCERNED*
Eze 16:49 were arrogant, overfed and *u*;

UNCOVERED
Ru 3: 7 Ruth approached quietly, *u* his
      feet
1Co 11: 5 with her head *u* dishonors her
      head
   11:13 to pray to God with her head *u*?
Heb 4:13 Everything is *u* and laid bare

UNDERGOES* (UNDERGOING)
Heb 12: 8 (and everyone *u* discipline),

UNDERGOING* (UNDERGOES)
1Pe 5: 9 the world are *u* the same kind

UNDERSTAND (UNDERSTANDING UNDERSTANDS
UNDERSTOOD)
Ne 8: 8 the people could *u* what was
      being
Job 38: 4 Tell me, if you *u*.
   42: 3 Surely I spoke of things I did
      not *u*,
Ps 14: 2 men to see if there are any who *u*,
   73:16 When I tried to *u* all this,
   119:27 Let me *u* the teaching
   119:125 that I may *u* your statutes.
Pr 2: 5 then you will *u* the fear
   2: 9 Then you will *u* what is right
   30:18 four that I do not *u*:
Ecc 7:25 to *u* the stupidity of wickedness
   11: 5 so you cannot *u* the work of God,
Isa 6:10 *u* with their hearts,
   44:18 know nothing, they *u* nothing;
   52:15 they have not heard, they will *u*.
Jer 17: 9 Who can *u* it?
   31:19 after I came to *u*,
Da 9:25 and *u* this: From the issuing
Hos 14: 9 Who is discerning? He will *u*
      them.
Mt 13:15 *u* with their hearts
   24:15 Daniel—let the reader *u*—
Lk 24:45 so they could *u* the Scriptures.
Ac 8:30 "Do you *u* what you are reading?"
Ro 7:15 I do not *u* what I do.
   15:21 those who have not heard will *u*."
1Co 2:12 that we may *u* what God has
      freely
   2:14 and he cannot *u* them,
   14:16 those who do not *u* say "Amen"
Eph 5:17 but *u* what the Lord's will is.
Heb 11: 3 By faith we *u* that the universe
      was
2Pe 1:20 you must *u* that no prophecy
   3: 3 you must *u* that in the last days
   3:16 some things that are hard to *u*,

UNDERSTANDING (UNDERSTAND)
1Ki 4:29 and a breadth of *u* as measureless
Job 12:12 Does not long life bring *u*?
   28:12 Where does *u* dwell?
   28:28 and to shun evil is *u*.' "
   32: 8 of the Almighty, that gives him *u*.
   36:26 How great is God—beyond our *u*!
   37: 5 he does great things beyond
      our *u*.
Ps 111:10 follow his precepts have good *u*.
   119:34 Give me *u*, and I will keep your
      law
   119:100 I have more *u* than the elders,
   119:104 I gain *u* from your precepts;
   119:130 it gives *u* to the simple.
   136: 5 who by his *u* made the heavens,
   147: 5 his *u* has no limit.
Pr 2: 2 and applying your heart to *u*,
   2: 6 his mouth come knowledge
      and *u*.
   3: 5 and lean not on your own *u*;
   3:13 the man who gains *u*,
   4: 5 Get wisdom, get *u*;
   4: 7 Though it cost all you have, get *u*.
   7: 4 and call *u* your kinsman,
   9:10 knowledge of the Holy One is *u*.
   10:23 but a man of *u* delights in
      wisdom.
   11:12 but a man of *u* holds his tongue.
   14:29 A patient man has great *u*,
   15:21 a man of *u* keeps a straight
      course.
   15:32 whoever heeds correction gains *u*.
   16:16 to choose *u* rather than silver!
   16:22 *U* is a fountain of life
   17:27 and a man of *u* is even-tempered.
   18: 2 A fool finds no pleasure in *u*,
   19: 8 he who cherishes *u* prospers.
   20: 5 but a man of *u* draws them out.
   23:23 get wisdom, discipline and *u*.
Isa 11: 2 the Spirit of wisdom and of *u*,
   40:28 and his *u* no one can fathom.
   56:11 They are shepherds who lack *u*;
Jer 3:15 you with knowledge and *u*.
   10:12 stretched out the heavens by
      his *u*.

Da 5: 12 a keen mind and knowledge and u,
10: 12 that you set your mind to gain u
Hos 4: 11 which take away the u
Mk 4: 12 and ever hearing but never u;
12: 33 with all your u and with all your
Lk 2: 47 who heard him was amazed at his u
2Co 6: 6 in purity, u, patience and kindness;
Eph 1: 8 on us with all wisdom and u.
Php 4: 7 of God, which transcends all u,
Col 1: 9 through all spiritual wisdom and u.
2: 2 have the full riches of complete u,
1Jn 5: 20 God has come and has given us u,

UNDERSTANDS (UNDERSTAND)
1Ch 28: 9 and u every motive
Jer 9: 24 that he u and knows me,
Mt 13: 23 man who hears the word and u it.
Ro 3: 11 there is no one who u
1Ti 6: 4 he is conceited and u nothing.

UNDERSTOOD (UNDERSTAND)
Ne 8: 12 they now u the words that had
Ps 73: 17 then I u their final destiny.
Isa 40: 13 Who has u the mind of the LORD,
40: 21 Have you not u since the earth was
Jn 1: 5 but the darkness has not u it.
Ro 1: 20 being u from what has been made,

UNDESIRABLE*
Jos 24: 15 But if serving the LORD seems u

UNDIVIDED*
1Ch 12: 33 to help David with u loyalty—
Ps 86: 11 give me an u heart,
Eze 11: 19 I will give them an u heart
1Co 7: 35 way in u devotion to the Lord.

UNDOING
Pr 18: 7 A fool's mouth is his u,

UNDYING*
Eph 6: 24 Lord Jesus Christ with an u love.

UNEQUALED*
Mt 24: 21 u from the beginning of the world
Mk 13: 19 of distress u from the beginning,

UNFADING*
1Pe 3: 4 the u beauty of a gentle

UNFAILING*
Ex 15: 13 "In your u love you will lead
1Sa 20: 14 But show me u kindness like that
2Sa 22: 51 he shows u kindness
Ps 6: 4 save me because of your u love.
13: 5 But I trust in your u love;
18: 50 he shows u kindness
21: 7 through the u love
31: 16 save me in your u love.
32: 10 but the LORD's u love
33: 5 the earth is full of his u love,
33: 18 those whose hope is in his u love,
33: 22 May your u love rest upon us,
36: 7 How priceless is your u love!
44: 26 redeem us because of your u love.
48: 9 we meditate on your u love.
51: 1 according to your u love;
52: 8 I trust in God's u love
77: 8 Has his u love vanished forever?
85: 7 Show us your u love, O LORD,
90: 14 in the morning with your u love,
107: 8 thanks to the LORD for his u love
107: 15 thanks to the LORD for his u love
107: 21 to the LORD for his u love
107: 31 to the LORD for his u love
119: 41 May your u love come to me,
119: 76 May your u love be my comfort,
130: 7 for with the LORD is u love
143: 8 bring me word of your u love,
143: 12 In your u love, silence my enemies;
147: 11 who put their hope in his u love,
Pr 19: 22 What a man desires is u love;
20: 6 Many a man claims to have u love,
Isa 54: 10 yet my u love for you will not be
La 3: 32 so great is his u love.
Hos 10: 12 reap the fruit of u love,

UNFAITHFUL (UNFAITHFULNESS)
Lev 6: 2 is u to the LORD by deceiving his
Nu 5: 6 and so is u to the LORD,

1Ch 10: 13 because he was u to the LORD;
Pr 11: 6 the u are trapped by evil desires.
13: 2 the u have a craving for violence.
13: 15 but the way of the u is hard.
22: 12 but he frustrates the words of the u.
23: 28 and multiplies the u among men.
25: 19 is reliance on the u in times
Jer 3: 20 But like a woman u to her husband,

UNFAITHFULNESS (UNFAITHFUL)
1Ch 9: 1 to Babylon because of their u.
Mt 5: 32 except for marital u, causes her
19: 9 for marital u, and marries another

UNFIT*
Tit 1: 16 and u for doing anything good.

UNFOLDING
Ps 119:130 the u of your words gives light;

UNFORGIVING*
2Ti 3: 3 unholy, without love, u, slanderous

UNFRIENDLY*
Pr 18: 1 An u man pursues selfish ends;

UNFRUITFUL
1Co 14: 14 my spirit prays, but my mind is u.

UNGODLINESS (UNGODLY)
Tit 2: 12 It teaches us to say "No" to u

UNGODLY (UNGODLINESS)
Ro 5: 6 powerless, Christ died for the u.
1Ti 1: 9 the u and sinful, the unholy
2Ti 2: 16 in it will become more and more u.
2Pe 2: 6 of what is going to happen to the u;
Jude : 15 and to convict all the u

UNGRATEFUL*
Lk 6: 35 he is kind to the u and wicked.
2Ti 3: 2 disobedient to their parents, u,

UNHOLY*
1Ti 1: 9 and sinful, the u and irreligious;
2Ti 3: 2 ungrateful, u, without love,
Heb 10: 29 as an u thing the blood

UNINTENTIONALLY
Lev 4: 2 'When anyone sins u and does
Nu 15: 22 " 'Now if you u fail to keep any
Dt 4: 42 flee if he had u killed his neighbor

UNIT
1Co 12: 12 body is a u, though it is made up

UNITE (UNITED UNITY)
1Co 6: 15 and u them with a prostitute?

UNITED (UNITE)
Ge 2: 24 and mother and be u to his wife,
Mt 19: 5 and mother and be u to his wife,
Ro 6: 5 If we have been u with him like this
Eph 5: 31 and mother and be u to his wife,
Php 2: 1 from being u with Christ,
Col 2: 2 encouraged in heart and u in love,

UNITY* (UNITE)
2Ch 30: 12 the people to give them u of mind
Ps 133: 1 is when brothers live together in u!
Jn 17: 23 May they be brought to complete u
Ro 15: 5 a spirit of u among yourselves
Eph 4: 3 effort to keep the u of the Spirit
4: 13 up until we all reach u in the faith
Col 3: 14 them all together in perfect u.

UNIVERSE*
1Co 4: 9 made a spectacle to the whole u,
Eph 4: 10 in order to fill the whole u.)
Php 2: 15 which you shine like stars in the u
Heb 1: 2 and through whom he made the u.
11: 3 understand that the u was formed

UNJUST
Ro 3: 5 That God is u in bringing his wrath
9: 14 What then shall we say? Is God u?
1Pe 2: 19 up under the pain of u suffering

UNKNOWN
Ac 17: 23 TO AN U GOD.

UNLEAVENED
Ex 12: 17 "Celebrate the Feast of U Bread,
Dt 16: 16 at the Feast of U Bread, the Feast

UNLIMITED*
1Ti 1: 16 Jesus might display his u patience

UNLOVED
Pr 30: 23 an u woman who is married,

UNMARRIED
1Co 7: 8 It is good for them to stay u,
7: 27 Are you u? Do not look for a wife.
7: 32 An u man is concerned about

UNPLOWED
Ex 23: 11 the seventh year let the land lie u
Hos 10: 12 and break up your u ground;

UNPRODUCTIVE
Tit 3: 14 necessities and not live u lives.
2Pe 1: 8 and u in your knowledge

UNPROFITABLE
Tit 3: 9 because these are u and useless.

UNPUNISHED
Ex 34: 7 Yet he does not leave the guilty u;
Pr 6: 29 no one who touches her will go u.
11: 21 of this: The wicked will not go u,
19: 5 A false witness will not go u,

UNQUENCHABLE
Lk 3: 17 he will burn up the chaff with u fire

UNREPENTANT*
Ro 2: 5 stubbornness and your u heart,

UNRIGHTEOUS*
Zep 3: 5 yet the u know no shame.
Mt 5: 45 rain on the righteous and the u.
1Pe 3: 18 the righteous for the u, to bring you
2Pe 2: 9 and to hold the u for the day

UNSEARCHABLE
Ro 11: 33 How u his judgments,
Eph 3: 8 preach to the Gentiles the u riches

UNSEEN*
Mt 6: 6 and pray to your Father, who is u.
6: 18 who is u; and your Father,
2Co 4: 18 on what is seen, but on what is u.
4: 18 temporary, but what is u is eternal.

UNSETTLED*
1Th 3: 3 so that no one would be u
2Th 2: 2 not to become easily u

UNSHRUNK
Mt 9: 16 patch of u cloth on an old garment,

UNSPIRITUAL*
Ro 7: 14 but I am u, sold as a slave to sin.
Col 2: 18 and his u mind puffs him up
Jas 3: 15 down from heaven but is earthly, u,

UNSTABLE*
Jas 1: 8 he is a double-minded man, u
2Pe 2: 14 they seduce the u; they are experts
3: 16 ignorant and u people distort,

UNTHINKABLE*
Job 34: 12 It is u that God would do wrong,

UNTIE
Mk 1: 7 worthy to stoop down and u.
Lk 13: 15 each of you on the Sabbath u his ox

UNVEILED*
2Co 3: 18 with u faces all reflect the Lord's

UNWHOLESOME*
Eph 4: 29 Do not let any u talk come out

UNWISE
Eph 5: 15 how you live—not as u but as wise,

UNWORTHY*
Ge 32: 10 I am u of all the kindness
Job 40: 4 "I am u— how can I reply to you?
Lk 17: 10 should say, 'We are u servants;
1Co 11: 27 Lord in an u manner will be guilty

UPHOLD (UPHOLDS)
Isa 41: 10 I will u you with my righteous right
Ro 3: 31 Not at all! Rather, we u the law.

UPHOLDS* (UPHOLD)
Ps 37: 17 but the LORD u the righteous.
37: 24 for the LORD u him with his hand.

Ps 63: 8 your right hand *u* me.
   140:12 and *u* the cause of the needy.
   145:14 The Lord *u* all those who fall
   146: 7 He *u* the cause of the oppressed

UPRIGHT
Dt 32: 4 *u* and just is he.
Job 1: 1 This man was blameless and *u;*
Ps 7:10 who saves the *u* in heart.
   11: 7 *u* men will see his face.
   25: 8 Good and *u* is the Lord;
   33: 1 it is fitting for the *u* to praise him.
   64:10 let all the *u* in heart praise him!
   92:15 proclaiming, "The Lord is *u;*
   97:11 and joy on the *u* in heart.
  119: 7 I will praise you with an *u* heart
Pr 2: 7 He holds victory in store for the *u,*
   3:32 but takes the *u* into his confidence.
   14: 2 whose walk is *u* fears the Lord,
   15: 8 but the prayer of the *u* pleases him.
   21:29 an *u* man gives thought to his ways.
Isa 26: 7 O *u* One, you make the way
Tit 1: 8 who is self-controlled, *u,* holy
   2:12 *u* and godly lives in this present

UPROOTED
Dt 28:63 You will be *u* from the land you are
Jer 31:40 The city will never again be *u*
Jude :12 without fruit and *u*— twice dead.

UPSET
Lk 10:41 are worried and *u* about many

URIAH
Hittite husband of Bathsheba, killed by David's order (2Sa 11).

USEFUL
Eph 4:28 doing something *u*
2Ti 2:21 *u* to the Master and prepared
   3:16 Scripture is God-breathed and is *u*
Phm :11 now he has become *u* both to you

USELESS
1Co 15:14 our preaching is *u*
Tit 3: 9 these are unprofitable and *u.*
Phm :11 Formerly he was *u* to you,
Heb 7:18 *u* (for the law made nothing perfect
Jas 2:20 faith without deeds is *u?*

USURY
Ne 5:10 But let the exacting of *u* stop!
Ps 15: 5 who lends his money without *u*

UTMOST
Job 34:36 that Job might be tested to the *u*

UTTER (UTTERS)
Ps 78: 2 I will *u* hidden things, things from of old—
Mt 13:35 I will *u* things hidden

UTTERS (UTTER)
1Co 14: 2 he *u* mysteries with his spirit.

UZZIAH
Son of Amaziah; king of Judah also known as Azariah (2Ki 15:1–7; 1Ch 6:24; 2Ch 26). Struck with leprosy because of pride (2Ch 26:16–23).

VAIN
Ps 33:17 A horse is a *v* hope for deliverance;
   73:13 in *v* have I kept my heart pure;
  127: 1 its builders labor in *v.*
Isa 65:23 They will not toil in *v*
1Co 15: 2 Otherwise, you have believed in *v.*
   15:58 labor in the Lord is not in *v.*
2Co 6: 1 not to receive God's grace in *v.*
Gal 2: 2 running or had run my race in *v.*

VALIANT
1Sa 10:26 by *v* men whose hearts God had

VALID
Jn 8:14 my own behalf, my testimony is *v,*

VALLEY (VALLEYS)
Ps 23: 4 walk through the *v* of the shadow
Isa 40: 4 Every *v* shall be raised up,
Joel 3:14 multitudes in the *v* of decision!

VALLEYS (VALLEY)
SS 2: 1 a lily of the *v.*

VALUABLE (VALUE)
Lk 12:24 And how much more *v* you are

VALUE (VALUABLE VALUED)
Lev 27: 3 set the *v* of a male between the ages
Pr 16:13 they *v* a man who speaks the truth.
   31:11 and lacks nothing of *v.*
Mt 13:46 When he found one of great *v,*
1Ti 4: 8 For physical training is of some *v,*
Heb 11:26 as of greater *v* than the treasures

VALUED (VALUE)
Lk 16:15 What is highly *v* among men is

VANISHES
Jas 4:14 appears for a little while and then *v.*

VASHTI*
Queen of Persia replaced by Esther (Est 1–2).

VAST
Ge 2: 1 completed in all their *v* array.
Dt 1:19 of the Amorites through all that *v*
   8:15 He led you through the *v*
Ps 139:17 How *v* is the sum of them!

VEGETABLES
Pr 15:17 of *v* where there is love
Ro 14: 2 whose faith is weak, eats only *v.*

VEIL
Ex 34:33 to them, he put a *v* over his face.
2Co 3:14 for to this day the same *v* remains

VENGEANCE (AVENGE AVENGER AVENGES AVENGING REVENGE)
Nu 31: 3 to carry out the Lord's *v* on them
Isa 34: 8 For the Lord has a day of *v,*
Na 1: 2 The Lord takes *v* on his foes

VERDICT
Jn 3:19 This is the *v:* Light has come

VICTOR'S* (VICTORY)
2Ti 2: 5 he does not receive the *v* crown

VICTORIES* (VICTORY)
2Sa 22:51 He gives his king great *v;*
Ps 18:50 He gives his king great *v;*
   21: 1 great is his joy in the *v* you give!
   21: 5 Through the *v* you gave, his glory is
   44: 4 who decrees *v* for Jacob.

VICTORIOUS (VICTORY)
Ps 20: 5 for joy when you are *v*

VICTORIOUSLY* (VICTORY)
Ps 45: 4 In your majesty ride forth *v*

VICTORY (VICTOR'S VICTORIES VICTORIOUS VICTORIOUSLY)
2Sa 8: 6 gave David *v* wherever he
Ps 44: 6 my sword does not bring me *v;*
   60:12 With God we will gain the *v,*
  129: 2 they have not gained the *v* over me.
Pr 11:14 but many advisers make *v* sure.
1Co 15:54 "Death has been swallowed up in *v*
   15:57 He gives us the *v* through our Lord
1Jn 5: 4 This is the *v* that has overcome

VIEW
Pr 5:21 are in full *v* of the Lord,
2Ti 4: 1 and in *v* of his appearing

VILLAGE
Mk 6: 6 went around teaching from *v* to *v.*

VINDICATED (VINDICATION)
Job 13:18 I know I will be *v.*
1Ti 3:16 was *v* by the Spirit,

VINDICATION (VINDICATED)
Ps 24: 5 and *v* from God his Savior.

VINE (VINEYARD)
Ps 128: 3 Your wife will be like a fruitful *v*
Isa 36:16 one of you will eat from his own *v*
Jnh 4: 6 Jonah was very happy about the *v.*
Jn 15: 1 "I am the true *v,* and my Father is

VINEGAR
Pr 10:26 As *v* to the teeth and smoke
Mk 15:36 filled a sponge with wine *v,*

VINEYARD (VINE)
1Ki 21: 1 an incident involving a *v* belonging
Pr 31:16 out of her earnings she plants a *v.*
SS 1: 6 my own *v* I have neglected.
Isa 5: 1 My loved one had a *v*
1Co 9: 7 Who plants a *v* and does not eat

VIOLATION
Heb 2: 2 every *v* and disobedience received

VIOLENCE (VIOLENT)
Ge 6:11 in God's sight and was full of *v.*
Isa 53: 9 though he had done no *v,*
   60:18 No longer will *v* be heard
Eze 45: 9 Give up your *v* and oppression
Joel 3:19 of *v* done to the people of Judah.
Jnh 3: 8 give up their evil ways and their *v.*

VIOLENT (VIOLENCE)
Eze 18:10 "Suppose he has a *v* son, who sheds
1Ti 1:13 and a persecutor and a *v* man,
   3: 3 not *v* but gentle, not quarrelsome,
Tit 1: 7 not *v,* not pursuing dishonest gain.

VIPERS
Ps 140: 3 the poison of *v* is on their lips.
Lk 3: 7 "You brood of *v!* Who warned you
Ro 3:13 "The poison of *v* is on their lips."

VIRGIN (VIRGINS)
Dt 22:15 shall bring proof that she was a *v*
Isa 7:14 The *v* will be with child
Mt 1:23 "The *v* will be with child
Lk 1:34 I am a *v?*" The angel answered,
2Co 11: 2 that I might present you as a pure *v*

VIRGINS (VIRGIN)
Mt 25: 1 will be like ten *v* who took their
1Co 7:25 Now about *v:* I have no command

VIRTUES*
Col 3:14 And over all these *v* put on love,

VISIBLE
Eph 5:13 exposed by the light becomes *v,*
Col 1:16 and on earth, *v* and invisible,

VISION (VISIONS)
Da 9:24 to seal up *v* and prophecy
Ac 26:19 disobedient to the *v* from heaven.

VISIONS (VISION)
Nu 12: 6 I reveal myself to him in *v,*
Joel 2:28 your young men will see *v,*
Ac 2:17 your young men will see *v,*

VOICE
Dt 30:20 listen to his *v,* and hold fast to him.
1Sa 15:22 as in obeying the *v* of the Lord?
Job 40: 9 and can your *v* thunder like his?
Ps 19: 4 Their *v* goes out into all the earth,
   29: 3 The *v* of the Lord is
   66:19 and heard my *v* in prayer.
   95: 7 Today, if you hear his *v,*
Pr 8: 1 Does not understanding raise her *v*
Isa 30:21 your ears will hear a *v* behind you,
   40: 3 A *v* of one calling:
Mk 1: 3 "a *v* of one calling in the desert,
Jn 5:28 are in their graves will hear his *v*
   10: 3 and the sheep listen to his *v.*
Ro 10:18 "Their *v* has gone out
Heb 3: 7 "Today, if you hear his *v,*
Rev 3:20 If anyone hears my *v* and opens

VOMIT
Lev 18:28 it will *v* you out as it vomited out
Pr 26:11 As a dog returns to its *v,*
2Pe 2:22 "A dog returns to its *v,*" and,

VOW (VOWS)
Nu 6: 2 a *v* of separation to the Lord
   30: 2 When a man makes a *v*
Jdg 11:30 Jephthah made a *v* to the Lord:

VOWS (VOW)
Ps 116:14 I will fulfill my *v* to the Lord
Pr 20:25 and only later to consider his *v.*

VULTURES
Mt 24:28 is a carcass, there the *v* will gather.

WAGE (WAGES WAGING)
2Co 10: 3 we do not *w* war as the world does.

WAGES (WAGE)
Mal 3: 5 who defraud laborers of their w,
Lk 10: 7 for the worker deserves his w.
Ro 4: 4 his w are not credited to him
    6:23 For the w of sin is death,
1Ti 5:18 and "The worker deserves his w."

WAGING (WAGE)
Ro 7:23 w war against the law of my mind

WAILING
Ps 30:11 You turned my w into dancing;

WAIST
2Ki 1: 8 and with a leather belt around
        his w.
Mt 3: 4 he had a leather belt around
        his w.

WAIT (AWAITS WAITED WAITING WAITS)
Ps 27:14 W for the LORD;
  130: 5 I w for the LORD, my soul waits,
Isa 30:18 Blessed are all who w for him!
Ac 1: 4 w for the gift my Father promised,
Ro 8:23 as we w eagerly for our adoption
1Th 1:10 and to w for his Son from heaven,
Tit 2:13 while we w for the blessed
        hope—

WAITED (WAIT)
Ps 40: 1 I w patiently for the LORD;

WAITING (WAIT)
Heb 9:28 to those who are w for him.

WAITS (WAIT)
Ro 8:19 creation w in eager expectation

WAKE (AWAKE WAKENS)
Eph 5:14 "W up, O sleeper,

WAKENS* (WAKE)
Isa 50: 4 He w me morning by morning,
    50: w my ear to listen like one being

WALK (WALKED WALKING WALKS)
Lev 26:12 I will w among you and be your
Dt 5:33 W in all the way that the LORD
    6: 7 and when you w along the road,
  10:12 to w in all his ways, to love him,
  11:19 and when you w along the road,
  11:22 to w in all his ways and to hold
        fast
  26:17 and that you will w in his ways,
Jos 22: 5 to w in all his ways,
Ps 1: 1 who does not w in the counsel
  15: 2 He whose w is blameless
  23: 4 Even though I w
  84:11 from those whose w is blameless.
  89:15 who w in the light of your
        presence
  119:45 I will w about in freedom,
Pr 4:12 When you w, your steps will not
        be
  6:22 When you w, they will guide you;
Isa 2: 3 so that we may w in his paths."
  2: 5 let us w in the light of the LORD.
  30:21 saying, "This is the way; w in it."
  40:31 they will w and not be faint.
  57: 2 Those who w uprightly
Jer 6:16 ask where the good way is, and w
Da 4:37 And those who w in pride he is
        able
Am 3: 3 Do two w together
Mic 4: 5 All the nations may w
  6: 8 and to w humbly with your God.
Mk 2: 9 'Get up, take your mat and w'?
Jn 8:12 Whoever follows me will never w
1Jn 1: 6 with him yet w in the darkness,
  1: 7 But if we w in the light,
2Jn : 6 his command is that you w in
        love.

WALKED (WALK)
Ge 5:24 Enoch w with God; then he was
        no
Jos 14: 9 which your feet have w will be
        your
Mt 14:29 w on the water and came toward
        Jesus.

WALKING (WALK)
1Ki 3: 3 love for the LORD by w according
Da 3:25 I see four men w around in the
        fire,
2Jn : 4 of your children w in the truth,

WALKS (WALK)
Pr 10: 9 The man of integrity w securely,

Pr 13:20 He who w with the wise grows
        wise
Isa 33:15 He who w righteously
Jn 11: 9 A man who w by day will not

WALL (WALLS)
Jos 6:20 w collapsed; so every man
        charged
Ne 2:17 let us rebuild the w of Jerusalem,
Eph 2:14 the dividing w of hostility,
Rev 21:12 It had a great, high w

WALLOWING
2Pe 2:22 back to her w in the mud."

WALLS (WALL)
Isa 58:12 be called Repairer of Broken W,
  60:18 but you will call your w Salvation
Heb 11:30 By faith the w of Jericho fell,

WANDER (WANDERED)
Nu 32:13 he made them w in the desert
        forty
Jas 5:19 one of you should w from the
        truth

WANDERED (WANDER)
Eze 34: 6 My sheep w over all the
        mountains
Mt 18:12 go to look for the one that w off?
1Ti 6:10 have w from the faith and pierced
2Ti 2:18 who have w away from the truth.

WANT (WANTED WANTING WANTS)
1Sa 8:19 "We w a king over us.
Mt 19:21 Jesus answered, "If you w
Lk 19:14 'We don't w this man to be our
        king
Ro 7:15 For what I w to do I do not do,
  13: 3 Do you w to be free from fear
2Co 12:14 what I w is not your possessions
Php 3:10 I w to know Christ and the power

WANTED (WANT)
1Co 12:18 of them, just as he w them to be.
Heb 6:17 Because God w to make

WANTING (WANT)
Da 5:27 weighed on the scales and
        found w.
2Pe 3: 9 with you, not w anyone to perish,

WANTS (WANT)
Mt 5:42 from the one who w to borrow
  20:26 whoever w to become great
Mk 8:35 For whoever w to save his life will
  10:43 whoever w to become great
Ro 9:18 he hardens whom he w to harden.
1Ti 2: 4 who w all men to be saved
1Pe 5: 2 you are willing, as God w you to
        be;

WAR (WARRIOR WARS)
Jos 11:23 Then the land had rest from w.
1Sa 15:18 make w on them until you have
Ps 68:30 the nations who delight in w.
  120: 7 but when I speak, they are for w.
  144: 1 who trains my hands for w,
Isa 2: 4 nor will they train for w anymore.
Da 9:26 W will continue until the end,
Ro 7:23 waging w against the law
2Co 10: 3 we do not wage w as the world
        does
1Pe 2:11 which w against your soul.
Rev 12: 7 And there was w in heaven.
  19:11 With justice he judges and
        makes w

WARN* (WARNED WARNING WARNINGS)
Ex 19:21 w the people so they do not force
Nu 24:14 let me w you of what this people
1Sa 8: 9 but w them solemnly and let
        them
1Ki 2:42 swear by the LORD and w you,
2Ch 19:10 you are to w them not to sin
Ps 81: 8 O my people, and I will w you—
Jer 42:19 I w you today that you made a
        fatal
Eze 3:18 and you do not w him or speak
        out
  3:19 But if you do w the wicked man
  3:20 Since you did not w him, he will
        die
  3:21 if you do w the righteous man not
  33: 3 blows the trumpet to w the
        people,
  33: 6 blow the trumpet to w the people

Eze 33: 9 if you do w the wicked man to
        turn
Lk 16:28 Let him w them, so that they will
Ac 4:17 we must w these men
1Co 4:14 but to w you, as my dear children.
Gal 5:21 I w you, as I did before, that those
1Th 5:14 brothers, w those who are idle,
2Th 3:15 an enemy, but w him as a brother.
2Ti 2:14 W them before God
Tit 3:10 and then w him a second time.
  3:10 W a divisive person once,
Rev 22:18 I w everyone who hears the words

WARNED (WARN)
2Ki 17:13 The LORD w Israel and Judah
Ps 19:11 By them is your servant w;
Jer 22:21 I w you when you felt secure,
Mt 3: 7 Who w you to flee
1Th 4: 6 have already told you and w you.
Heb 11: 7 when w about things not yet
        seen,
  12:25 they refused him who w them

WARNING (WARN)
Jer 6: 8 Take w, O Jerusalem,
1Ti 5:20 so that the others may take w.

WARNINGS (WARN)
1Co 10:11 and were written down as w for
        us,

WARRIOR (WAR)
Ex 15: 3 The LORD is a w;
1Ch 28: 3 you are a w and have shed blood.'
Pr 16:32 Better a patient man than a w,

WARS (WAR)
Ps 46: 9 He makes w cease to the ends
Mt 24: 6 You will hear of w and rumors
        of w,

WASH (WASHED WASHING)
Ps 51: 7 w me, and I will be whiter
Jer 4:14 w the evil from your heart
Jn 13: 5 and began to w his disciples' feet,
Ac 22:16 be baptized and w your sins away,
Jas 4: 8 W your hands, you sinners,
Rev 22:14 Blessed are those who w their
        robes

WASHED (WASH)
Ps 73:13 in vain have I w my hands
1Co 6:11 you were w, you were sanctified,
Heb 10:22 and having our bodies w
2Pe 2:22 and, "A sow that is w goes back
Rev 7:14 they have w their robes

WASHING (WASH)
Eph 5:26 cleansing her by the w with water
1Ti 5:10 showing hospitality, w the feet
Tit 3: 5 us through the w of rebirth

WASTED (WASTING)
Jn 6:12 Let nothing be w."

WASTING (WASTED)
2Co 4:16 Though outwardly we are w away,

WATCH (WATCHER WATCHES WATCHING WATCHMAN)
Ge 31:49 "May the LORD keep w
Ps 90: 4 or like a w in the night.
  141: 3 keep w over the door of my lips.
Pr 4: 6 love her, and she will w over you.
  6:22 when you sleep, they will w
Jer 31:10 will w over his flock like a
        shepherd
Mic 7: 7 I w in hope for the LORD,
Mt 24:42 "Therefore keep w, because you
        do
  26:41 W and pray so that you will not
        fall
Mk 13:35 "Therefore keep w because you
        do
Lk 2: 8 keeping w over their flocks at
        night
1Ti 4:16 W your life and doctrine closely.
Heb 13:17 They keep w over you

WATCHER* (WATCH)
Job 7:20 O w of men?

WATCHES* (WATCH)
Nu 19: 5 While he w, the heifer is
Job 24:15 The eye of the adulterer w for
        dusk;
Ps 1: 6 For the LORD w over the way
  33:14 from his dwelling place he w
  63: 6 of you through the w of the night.

Ps 119:148 through the *w* of the night,
   121: 3 he who *w* over you will not
          slumber
   121: 4 indeed, he who *w* over Israel
   121: 5 The LORD *w* over you—
   127: 1 Unless the LORD *w* over the city,
   145:20 LORD *w* over all who love him,
   146: 9 The LORD *w* over the alien
Pr 31:27 She *w* over the affairs
Ecc 11: 4 Whoever *w* the wind will not
          plant;
La   2:19 as the *w* of the night begin;
     4:16 he no longer *w* over them.

WATCHING (WATCH)
Lk 12:37 whose master finds them *w*

WATCHMAN (WATCH)
Eze 3:17 I have made you a *w* for the house
     33: 6 but I will hold the *w* accountable

WATER (WATERED WATERING WATERS WELL-
WATERED)
Ex   7:20 all the *w* was changed into blood.
     17: 1 but there was no *w* for the people
Nu 20: 2 there was no *w* for the
          community,
Ps   1: 3 like a tree planted by streams
          of *w*,
     22:14 I am poured out like *w*,
     42: 1 As the deer pants for streams
          of *w*,
Pr 25:21 if he is thirsty, give him *w* to drink.
Isa 12: 3 With joy you will draw *w*
     30:20 of adversity and the *w* of
          affliction,
     32: 2 like streams of *w* in the desert
     49:10 and lead them beside springs
          of *w*.
Jer 2:13 broken cisterns that cannot
          hold *w*.
     17: 8 will be like a tree planted by
          the *w*
     31: 9 I will lead them beside streams
Eze 36:25 I will sprinkle clean *w* on you,
Zec 14: 8 On that day living *w* will flow out
Mt 14:29 walked on the *w* and came toward
          Jesus.
Mk   9:41 anyone who gives you a cup of *w*
Lk   5: 4 to Simon, "Put out into deep *w*,
Jn   3: 5 unless he is born of *w* and the
          Spirit.
     4:10 he would have given you
          living *w*."
     7:38 streams of living *w* will flow
Eph 5:26 washing with *w* through the word,
Heb 10:22 our bodies washed with pure *w*.
1Pe 3:21 this *w* symbolizes baptism that
          now
2Pe 2:17 These men are springs without *w*
1Jn 5: 6 This is the one who came by *w*
     5: 6 come by *w* only, but by *w*
     5: 8 the Spirit, the *w* and the blood;
Rev 7:17 to springs of living *w*.
     21: 6 cost from the spring of the *w* of
          life.

WATERED (WATER)
1Co 3: 6 I planted the seed, Apollos *w* it,

WATERING (WATER)
Isa 55:10 it without *w* the earth

WATERS (WATER)
Ps 23: 2 he leads me beside quiet *w*,
Ecc 11: 1 Cast your bread upon the *w*,
SS   8: 7 Many *w* cannot quench love;
Isa 11: 9 as the *w* cover the sea.
     43: 2 When you pass through the *w*,
     55: 1 come to the *w*;
     58:11 like a spring whose *w* never fail.
Hab 2:14 as the *w* cover the sea.
1Co 3: 7 plants nor he who *w* is anything,

WAVE (WAVES)
Lev 23:11 He is to *w* the sheaf
Jas 1: 6 he who doubts is like a *w* of the
          sea,

WAVER*
1Ki 18:21 "How long will you *w*
Ro   4:20 Yet he did not *w* through unbelief

WAVES (WAVE)
Isa 57:20 whose *w* cast up mire and mud.

Mt   8:27 Even the winds and the *w* obey
          him
Eph 4:14 tossed back and forth by the *w*,

WAY (WAYS)
Ex 13:21 of cloud to guide them on their *w*
     18:20 and show them the *w* to live
Dt   1:33 to show you the *w* you should go.
     32: 6 Is this the *w* you repay the LORD,
1Sa 12:23 I will teach you the *w* that is good
2Sa 22:31 "As for God, his *w* is perfect;
1Ki 8:23 wholeheartedly in your *w*.
Job 23:10 But he knows the *w* that I take;
Ps   1: 1 or stand in the *w* of sinners
     32: 8 teach you in the *w* you should go;
     37: 5 Commit your *w* to the LORD;
     86:11 Teach me your *w*, O LORD,
     119: 9 can a young man keep his *w* pure?
     139:24 See if there is any offensive *w* in
          me
Pr   4:11 I guide you in the *w* of wisdom
     12:15 The *w* of a fool seems right to
          him,
     14:12 There is a *w* that seems right
     16:17 he who guards his *w* guards his
          life.
     19: 2 nor to be hasty and miss the *w*.
     22: 6 Train a child in the *w* he should
          go,
     30:19 and the *w* of a man with a
          maiden.
Isa 30:21 saying, "This is the *w*; walk in it."
     35: 8 it will be called the *W* of Holiness.
     40: 3 the *w* for the LORD;
     48:17 you in the *w* you should go.
     53: 6 each of us has turned to his
          own *w*;
     55: 7 Let the wicked forsake his *w*
Jer 5:31 and my people love it this *w*.
Mal 3: 1 who will prepare the *w* before me.
Mt   3: 3 'Prepare the *w* for the Lord,
Lk   7:27 who will prepare your *w* before
          you
Jn 14: 6 "I am the *w* and the truth
Ac   1:11 in the same *w* you have seen him
          go
     9: 2 any there who belonged to the *W*,
     24:14 of the *W*, which they call a sect.
1Co 10:13 also provide a *w* out so that you
          can
     12:31 will show you the most
          excellent *w*.
     14: 1 Follow the *w* of love and eagerly
Col 1:10 and may please him in every *w*:
Tit 2:10 that in every *w* they will make
Heb 4:15 who has been tempted in
          every *w*,
     9: 8 was showing by this that the *w*
     10:20 and living *w* opened for us
     13:18 desire to live honorably in
          every *w*.

WAYS (WAY)
Ex 33:13 teach me your *w* so I may know
Dt 10:12 to walk in all his *w*, to love him,
     26:17 and that you will walk in his *w*,
     30:16 in his *w*, and to keep his
          commands
     32: 4 and all his *w* are just.
Jos 22: 5 in all his *w*, to obey his
          commands,
2Ch 11:17 walking in the *w* of David
Job 34:21 "His eyes are on the *w* of men;
Ps 25: 4 Show me your *w*, O LORD;
     25:10 All the *w* of the LORD are loving
     37: 7 fret when men succeed in their *w*
     51:13 I will teach transgressors your *w*,
     77:13 Your *w*, O God, are holy.
     119:59 I have considered my *w*
     139: 3 you are familiar with all my *w*.
     145:17 The LORD is righteous in all his *w*
Pr   3: 6 in all your *w* acknowledge him,
     4:26 and take only *w* that are firm.
     5:21 For a man's *w* are in full view
     16: 2 All a man's *w* seem innocent
     21: 2 When a man's *w* are pleasing
Isa 2: 3 He will teach us his *w*,
     55: 8 neither are your *w* my *w*,"
Eze 28:15 You were blameless in your *w*
     33: 8 out to dissuade him from his *w*,
Hos 14: 9 The *w* of the LORD are right;

Ro   1:30 they invent *w* of doing evil;
Jas 3: 2 We all stumble in many *w*.

WEAK (WEAKER WEAKNESS WEAKNESSES)
Ps 41: 1 is he who has regard for the *w*;
     72:13 He will take pity on the *w*
     82: 3 Defend the cause of the *w*
Eze 34: 4 You have not strengthened the *w*
Mt 26:41 spirit is willing, but the body is *w*."
Ac 20:35 of hard work we must help the *w*,
Ro 14: 1 Accept him whose faith is *w*,
     15: 1 to bear with the failings of the *w*
1Co 1:27 God chose the *w* things
     8: 9 become a stumbling block to
          the *w*.
     9:22 To the *w* I became *w*, to win
          the *w*.
     11:30 That is why many among you
          are *w*
2Co 12:10 For when I am *w*, then I am
          strong.
1Th 5:14 help the *w*, be patient
Heb 12:12 your feeble arms and *w* knees.

WEAK-WILLED (WILL)
2Ti 3: 6 and gain control over *w* women,

WEAKER* (WEAK)
2Sa 3: 1 the house of Saul grew *w* and *w*.
1Co 12:22 seem to be *w* are indispensable,
1Pe 3: 7 them with respect as the *w*
          partner

WEAKNESS* (WEAK)
La   1: 6 in *w* they have fled
Ro   8:26 the Spirit helps us in our *w*.
1Co 1:25 and the *w* of God is stronger
     2: 3 I came to you in *w* and fear,
     15:43 it is sown in *w*, it is raised in
          power;
2Co 11:30 boast of the things that show
          my *w*.
     12: 9 for my power is made perfect in *w*
     13: 4 he was crucified in *w*, yet he lives
Heb 5: 2 since he himself is subject to *w*.
     11:34 whose *w* was turned to strength;

WEAKNESSES* (WEAK)
2Co 12: 5 about myself, except about my *w*.
     12: 9 all the more gladly about my *w*,
     12:10 I delight in *w*, in insults,
Heb 4:15 unable to sympathize with our *w*,

WEALTH
Dt   8:18 gives you the ability to produce *w*,
2Ch 1:11 and you have not asked for *w*,
Ps 39: 6 he heaps up *w*, not knowing who
Pr   3: 9 Honor the LORD with your *w*,
     10: 4 but diligent hands bring *w*.
     11: 4 *W* is worthless in the day of
          wrath,
     13: 7 to be poor, yet has great *w*.
     15:16 than great *w* with turmoil.
     22: 4 bring *w* and honor and life.
Ecc 5:10 whoever loves *w* is never satisfied
     5:13 *w* hoarded to the harm of its
          owner,
SS   8: 7 all the *w* of his house for love,
Mt 13:22 and the deceitfulness of *w* choke
          it,
Mk 10:22 away sad, because he had
          great *w*.
     12:44 They all gave out of their *w*; but
          she
Lk 15:13 and there squandered his *w*
1Ti 6:17 nor to put their hope in *w*,
Jas 5: 2 Your *w* has rotted, and moths
          have
     5: 3 You have hoarded *w*

WEAPON (WEAPONS)
Ne   4:17 work with one hand and held a *w*

WEAPONS (WEAPON)
Ecc 9:18 Wisdom is better than *w* of war,
2Co 6: 7 with *w* of righteousness
     10: 4 The *w* we fight with are not

WEAR (WEARING)
Dt   8: 4 Your clothes did not *w* out
     22: 5 nor a man *w* women's clothing,
Ps 102:26 they will all *w* out like a garment.
Pr 23: 4 Do not *w* yourself out to get rich;
Isa 51: 6 the earth will *w* out like a
          garment
Heb 1:11 they will all *w* out like a garment.
Rev 3:18 and white clothes to *w*,

WEARIES (WEARY)
Ecc 12:12 and much study w the body.

WEARING (WEAR)
Jn 19: 5 When Jesus came out w the crown
Jas 2: 3 attention to the man w fine clothes
1Pe 3: 3 as braided hair and the w
Rev 7: 9 They were w white robes

WEARY (WEARIES)
Isa 40:28 He will not grow tired or w,
 40:31 they will run and not grow w,
 50: 4 know the word that sustains the w.
Mt 11:28 all you who are w and burdened,
Gal 6: 9 Let us not become w in doing good,
Heb 12: 3 so that you will not grow w
Rev 2: 3 my name, and have not grown w.

WEDDING
Mt 22:11 who was not wearing w clothes.
Rev 19: 7 For the w of the Lamb has come,

WEEDS
Mt 13:25 and sowed w among the wheat,

WEEK
Mt 28: 1 at dawn on the first day of the w,
1Co 16: 2 On the first day of every w,

WEEP (WEEPING WEPT)
Ecc 3: 4 a time to weep and a time to laugh,
Lk 6:21 Blessed are you who w now,
 23:28 w for yourselves and for your

WEEPING (WEEP)
Ps 30: 5 w may remain for a night,
 126: 6 He who goes out w,
Jer 31:15 Rachel w for her children
Mt 2:18 Rachel w for her children
 8:12 where there will be w and gnashing

WEIGH (OUTWEIGHS WEIGHED WEIGHS WEIGHTIER WEIGHTS)
1Co 14:29 others should w carefully what is

WEIGHED (WEIGH)
Job 28:15 nor can its price be w in silver.
Da 5:27 You have been w on the scales
Lk 21:34 or your hearts will be w

WEIGHS (WEIGH)
Pr 12:25 An anxious heart w a man down,
 15:28 of the righteous w its answers,
 21: 2 but the LORD w the heart.
 24:12 not he who w the heart perceive

WEIGHTIER* (WEIGH)
Jn 5:36 "I have testimony w than that

WEIGHTS (WEIGH)
Lev 19:36 Use honest scales and honest w,
Dt 25:13 Do not have two differing w
Pr 11: 1 but accurate w are his delight.

WELCOME (WELCOMES)
Mk 9:37 welcomes me does not w me
2Pe 1:11 and you will receive a rich w

WELCOMES (WELCOME)
Mt 18: 5 whoever w a little child like this
2Jn :11 Anyone who w him shares

WELL (WELLED WELLING WELLS)
Mt 15:31 crippled made w, the lame walking
Lk 14: 5 falls into a w on the Sabbath day,
 17:19 your faith has made you w."
Jas 5:15 in faith will make the sick person w

WELL-WATERED (WATER)
Isa 58:11 You will be like a w garden,

WELLED* (WELL)
2Co 8: 2 and their extreme poverty w up

WELLING* (WELL)
Jn 4:14 of water w up to eternal life."

WELLS (WELL)
Isa 12: 3 from the w of salvation.

WELLSPRING* (SPRING)
Pr 4:23 for it is the w of life.

WEPT (WEEP)
Ps 137: 1 of Babylon we sat and w
Lk 22:62 And he went outside and w bitterly
Jn 11:35 Jesus w.

WEST
Ps 103:12 as far as the east is from the w,
 107: 3 from east and w, from north

WHEAT
Mt 3:12 gathering his w into the barn
 13:25 and sowed weeds among the w,
Lk 22:31 Satan has asked to sift you as w.
Jn 12:24 a kernel of w falls to the ground

WHEELS
Eze 1:16 appearance and structure of the w:

WHIRLWIND (WIND)
2Ki 2: 1 to take Elijah up to heaven in a w,
Hos 8: 7 and reap the w.
Na 1: 3 His way is in the w and the storm,

WHISPER (WHISPERED)
1Ki 19:12 And after the fire came a gentle w.
Job 26:14 how faint the w we hear of him!
Ps 107:29 He stilled the storm to a w;

WHISPERED (WHISPER)
Mt 10:27 speak in the daylight; what is w

WHITE (WHITER)
Isa 1:18 they shall be as w as snow;
Da 7: 9 His clothing was as w as snow;
 7: 9 the hair of his head was w like wool
Mt 28: 3 and his clothes were w as snow.
Rev 1:14 hair were w like wool, as w as snow,
 3: 4 dressed in w, for they are worthy.
 6: 2 and there before me was a w horse!
 7:13 "These in w robes—who are they,
 19:11 and there before me was a w horse,
 20:11 Then I saw a great w throne

WHITER (WHITE)
Ps 51: 7 and I will be w than snow.

WHOLE
Ge 1:29 plant on the face of the w earth
 2: 6 and watered the w surface
 11: 1 Now the w world had one language
Ex 12:47 The w community
 19: 5 Although the w earth is mine,
Lev 16:17 and the w community of Israel.
Nu 14:21 of the LORD fills the w earth,
 32:13 until the w generation
Dt 13:16 w burnt offering to the LORD your
 18: 8 gives you the w land he promised
Jos 2: 3 come to spy out the w land."
1Sa 1:28 For his w life he will be given
 17:46 the w world will know that there is
1Ki 10:24 The w world sought audience
2Ki 21: 8 and will keep the w Law that my
Ps 72:19 may the w earth be filled
Pr 4:22 and health to a man's w body.
 8:31 rejoicing in his w world
Ecc 12:13 for this is the w duty of man.
Isa 1: 5 Your w head is injured,
 6: 3 the w earth is full of his glory."
 14:26 plan determined for the w world;
Eze 34: 6 were scattered over the w earth,
 37:11 these bones are the w house
Da 2:35 mountain and filled the w earth.
Zep 1:18 the w world will be consumed,
Zec 14: 9 will be king over the w earth.
Mal 3:10 the w tithe into the storehouse,
Mt 5:29 than for your w body to be thrown
 6:22 your w body will be full of light.
 16:26 for a man if he gains the w world,
 24:14 will be preached in the w world
Lk 21:35 live on the face of the w earth.
Jn 12:19 Look how the w world has gone
 13:10 to wash his feet; his w body is clean
 21:25 the w world would not have room
Ac 17:26 they should inhabit the w earth,
 20:27 proclaim to you the w will of God.
Ro 1: 9 whom I serve with my w heart
 3:19 and the w world held accountable
 8:22 know that the w creation has been
1Co 4: 9 made a spectacle to the w universe,

1Co 12:17 If the w body were an ear,
Gal 3:22 declares that the w world is
 5: 3 obligated to obey the w law.
Eph 4:10 in order to fill the w universe.)
 4:13 attaining to the w measure
1Th 5:23 May your w spirit, soul
Jas 2:10 For whoever keeps the w law
1Jn 2: 2 but also for the sins of the w world.
Rev 3:10 going to come upon the w world

WHOLEHEARTED* (HEART)
2Ki 20: 3 you faithfully and with w devotion
1Ch 28: 9 and serve him with w devotion
 29:19 my son Solomon the w devotion
Isa 38: 3 you faithfully and with w devotion

WHOLEHEARTEDLY* (HEART)
Nu 14:24 a different spirit and follows me w,
 32:11 they have not followed me w,
 32:12 for they followed the LORD w.'
Dt 1:36 because he followed the LORD w
Jos 14: 8 followed the LORD my God w.
 14: 9 followed the LORD my God w.'
 14:14 the LORD, the God of Israel, w.
1Ki 8:23 with your servants who continue w
1Ch 29: 9 for they had given freely and w
2Ch 6:14 with your servants who continue w
 15:15 oath because they had sworn it w.
 19: 9 and w in the fear of the LORD.
 25: 2 in the eyes of the LORD, but not w
 31:21 he sought his God and worked w.
Ro 6:17 you obeyed the form of teaching
Eph 6: 7 Serve w, as if you were serving

WHOLESOME*
2Ki 2:22 And the water has remained w
2Pe 3: 1 to stimulate you to w thinking.

WICK
Isa 42: 3 a smoldering w he will not snuff out
Mt 12:20 a smoldering w he will not snuff out

WICKED (WICKEDNESS)
Ge 13:13 Now the men of Sodom were w
 39: 9 How then could I do such a w thing
Ex 23: 1 Do not help a w man
Nu 14:35 things to this whole w community,
Dt 15: 9 not to harbor this w thought:
Jdg 19:22 some of the w men
1Sa 2:12 Eli's sons were w men; they had no
 15:18 completely destroy those w people,
 25:17 He is such a w man that no one can
2Sa 13:12 in Israel! Don't do this w thing.
2Ki 21: 8 They did w things that provoked
2Ch 7:14 and turn from their w ways,
 19: 2 "Should you help the w
Ne 13:17 "What is this w thing you are doing
Ps 1: 1 walk in the counsel of the w
 1: 5 Therefore the w will not stand
 7: 9 to an end the violence of the w
 10:13 Why does the w man revile God?
 11: 5 the w and those who love violence
 12: 8 The w freely strut about
 26: 5 and refuse to sit with the w.
 32:10 Many are the woes of the w,
 36: 1 concerning the sinfulness of the w:
 37:13 but the Lord laughs at the w,
 49: 5 when w deceivers surround me—
 50:16 But to the w, God says:
 58: 3 Even from birth the w go astray;
 73: 3 when I saw the prosperity of the w.
 82: 2 and show partiality to the w? Selah
 112:10 the longings of the w will come
 119:61 Though the w bind me with ropes,
 119:155 Salvation is far from the w,
 140: 8 do not grant the w their desires,
 141:10 Let the w fall into their own nets,

Ps 146: 9 but he frustrates the ways of the *w*.
Pr 2:12 you from the ways of *w* men,
     4:14 Do not set foot on the path of the *w*
     6:18 a heart that devises *w* schemes,
     9: 7 whoever rebukes a *w* man incurs
     10:20 the heart of the *w* is of little value.
     10:28 the hopes of the *w* come to nothing
     11: 5 *w* are brought down by their own
     11:10 when the *w* perish, there are shouts
     11:21 The *w* will not go unpunished,
     12: 5 but the advice of the *w* is deceitful.
     12:10 the kindest acts of the *w* are cruel.
     14:19 the *w* at the gates of the righteous.
     15: 3 keeping watch on the *w*
     15:26 detests the thoughts of the *w*,
     21:10 The *w* man craves evil;
     21:29 A *w* man puts up a bold front,
     28: 1 *w* man flees though no one pursues,
     28: 4 who forsake the law praise the *w*,
     29: 7 but the *w* have no such concern.
     29:16 When the *w* thrive, so does sin,
     29:27 the *w* detest the upright.
Isa 11: 4 breath of his lips he will slay the *w*.
     13:11 the *w* for their sins.
     26:10 Though grace is shown to the *w*,
     48:22 says the LORD, "for the *w*."
     53: 9 He was assigned a grave with the *w*
     55: 7 Let the *w* forsake his way
     57:20 But the *w* are like the tossing sea,
Jer 35:15 of you must turn from your *w* ways
Eze 3:18 that *w* man will die for his sin,
     3:22 you encouraged the *w* not to turn
     14: 7 and puts a *w* stumbling block
     18:21 "But if a *w* man turns away
     18:23 pleasure in the death of the *w*?
     21:25 " 'O profane and *w* prince of Israel,
     33: 8 When I say to the *w*, 'O *w* man,
     33:11 pleasure in the death of the *w*,
     33:14 to the *w* man, 'You will surely die,'
     33:19 And if a *w* man turns away
Da 12:10 but the *w* will continue to be *w*.
Mt 12:39 *w* and adulterous generation asks
     12:45 be with this *w* generation."
     12:45 with it seven other spirits more *w*
Lk 6:35 he is kind to the ungrateful and *w*.
Ac 2:23 and you, with the help of *w* men,
Ro 4: 5 but trusts God who justifies the *w*,
1Co 5:13 "Expel the *w* man from among you
     6: 9 not know that the *w* will not inherit
Rev 2: 2 that you cannot tolerate *w* men,

WICKEDNESS (WICKED)
Ge 6: 5 The LORD saw how great man's *w*
Ex 34: 7 and forgiving *w*, rebellion and sin.
Lev 16:21 and confess over it all the *w*
     19:29 to prostitution and be filled with *w*.
Dt 9: 4 it is on account of the *w*
Ne 9: 2 and confessed their sins and the *w*
Ps 45: 7 You love righteousness and hate *w*;
     92:15 he is my Rock, and there is no *w*
Pr 13: 6 but *w* overthrows the sinner.
Jer 3: 2 land with your prostitution and *w*.
     8: 6 No one repents of his *w*,
     14:20 O LORD, we acknowledge our *w*
Eze 18:20 the *w* of the wicked will be charged
     28:15 created till *w* was found in you.
     33:19 *wicked man turns away from his w*
Da 4:27 and your *w* by being kind
     9:24 to atone for *w*, to bring
Jnh 1: 2 its *w* has come up before me."
Mt 24:12 Because of the increase of *w*,
Lk 11:39 inside you are full of greed and *w*.
Ac 1:18 (With the reward he got for his *w*,

Ro 1:18 who suppress the truth by their *w*,
1Co 5: 8 the yeast of malice and *w*,
2Co 6:14 what do righteousness and *w* have
2Ti 2:19 of the Lord must turn away from *w*
Tit 2:14 for us to redeem us from all *w*
Heb 1: 9 loved righteousness and hated *w*;
     8:12 For I will forgive their *w*
2Pe 2:15 who loved the wages of *w*.

WIDE
Ps 81:10 Open *w* your mouth and I will fill it
Isa 54: 2 stretch your tent curtains *w*,
Mt 7:13 For *w* is the gate and broad is
2Co 6:13 my children—open *w* your hearts
Eph 3:18 to grasp how *w* and long and high

WIDOW (WIDOWS)
Ex 22:22 "Do not take advantage of a *w*
Dt 10:18 cause of the fatherless and the *w*,
Ps 146: 9 sustains the fatherless and the *w*,
Isa 1:17 plead the case of the *w*.
Lk 21: 2 saw a poor *w* put in two very small
1Ti 5: 4 But if a *w* has children

WIDOWS (WIDOW)
Ps 68: 5 to the fatherless, a defender of *w*,
Ac 6: 1 their *w* were being overlooked
1Co 7: 8 to the unmarried and the *w* I say:
1Ti 5: 3 to those who are really *w*
Jas 1:27 look after orphans and *w*

WIFE (WIVES WIVES')
Ge 2:24 and mother and be united to his *w*,
     19:26 But Lot's *w* looked back,
     24:67 she became his *w*, and he loved her;
Ex 20:17 shall not covet your neighbor's *w*,
Lev 20:10 adultery with another man's *w*—
Dt 5:21 shall not covet your neighbor's *w*,
     24: 5 happiness to the *w* he has married.
Ru 4:13 took Ruth and she became his *w*.
Pr 5:18 in the *w* of your youth.
     12: 4 *w* of noble character is her
     18:22 He who finds a *w* finds what is
     19:13 quarrelsome *w* is like a constant
     31:10 *w* of noble character who can find?
Hos 1: 2 take to yourself an adulterous *w*
Mal 2:14 the witness between you and your *w*,
Mt 1:20 to take Mary home as your *w*,
     19: 3 for a man to divorce his *w* for any
Lk 17:32 Remember Lot's *w*! Whoever tries
     18:29 or *w* or brothers or parents
1Co 7: 2 each man should have his own *w*,
     7:33 how he can please his *w*—
Eph 5:23 the husband is the head of the *w*
     5:33 must love his *w* as he loves himself,
1Ti 3: 2 husband of but one *w*, temperate,
Rev 21: 9 I will show you the bride, the *w*

WILD
Ge 1:25 God made the *w* animals according
     8: 1 Noah and all the *w* animals
Lk 15:13 squandered his wealth in *w* living.
Ro 11:17 and you, though a *w* olive shoot,

WILL (WEAK-WILLED WILLFUL WILLING WILLINGNESS)
Ps 40: 8 I desire to do your *w*, O my God;
     143:10 Teach me to do your *w*,
Isa 53:10 Yet it was the LORD's *w*
Mt 6:10 your *w* be done
     7:21 who does the *w* of my Father
     10:29 apart from the *w* of your Father.
     12:50 does the *w* of my Father
     26:39 Yet not as I *w*, but as you *w*."
     26:42 I drink it, may your *w* be done."
Jn 6:38 but to do the *w* of him who sent me.
     7:17 If anyone chooses to do God's *w*,
Ac 20:27 to you the whole *w* of God.
Ro 12: 2 and approve what God's *w* is—
1Co 7:37 but has control over his own *w*,
Eph 5:17 understand what the Lord's *w* is.
Php 2:13 for it is God who works in you to *w*

1Th 4: 3 God's *w* that you should be sanctified:
     5:18 for this is God's *w* for you
2Ti 2:26 has taken them captive to do his *w*.
Heb 2: 4 distributed according to his *w*.
     9:16 In the case of a *w*, it is necessary
     10: 7 I have come to do your *w*, O God
     13:21 everything good for doing his *w*,
Jas 4:15 "If it is the Lord's *w*,
1Pe 3:17 It is better, if it is God's *w*,
     4: 2 but rather for the *w* of God.
2Pe 1:21 never had its origin in the *w*
1Jn 5:14 we ask anything according to his *w*,
Rev 4:11 and by your *w* they were created

WILLFUL (WILL)
Ps 19:13 Keep your servant also from *w* sins;

WILLING (WILL)
1Ch 28: 9 devotion and with a *w* mind,
     29: 5 who is *w* to consecrate himself
Ps 51:12 grant me a *w* spirit, to sustain me.
Da 3:28 were *w* to give up their lives rather
Mt 18:14 Father in heaven is not *w* that any
     23:37 her wings, but you were not *w*.
     26:41 The spirit is *w*, but the body is weak
1Ti 6:18 and to be generous and *w* to share.
1Pe 5: 2 but because you are *w*,

WILLINGNESS* (WILL)
2Co 8:11 so that your eager *w*
     8:12 For if the *w* is there, the gift is

WIN (WINS WON)
1Co 9:19 myself a slave to everyone, to *w*
Php 3:14 on toward the goal to *w* the prize
1Th 4:12 your daily life may *w* the respect

WIND (WHIRLWIND WINDS)
Ps 1: 4 that the *w* blows away.
Ecc 2:11 meaningless, a chasing after the *w*;
Hos 8: 7 "They sow the *w*
Mk 4:41 Even the *w* and the waves obey
Jn 3: 8 The *w* blows wherever it pleases.
Eph 4:14 and there by every *w* of teaching
Jas 1: 6 blown and tossed by the *w*.

WINDOW
Jos 2:21 she tied the scarlet cord in the *w*.
Ac 20: 9 in a *w* was a young man named
2Co 11:33 in a basket from a *w* in the wall

WINDS (WIND)
Ps 104: 4 He makes *w* his messengers,
Mt 24:31 gather his elect from the four *w*,
Heb 1: 7 "He makes his angels *w*,

WINE
Ps 104:15 *w* that gladdens the heart of man,
Pr 20: 1 *W* is a mocker and beer a brawler;
     23:20 join those who drink too much *w*
     23:31 Do not gaze at *w* when it is red,
     31: 6 *w* to those who are in anguish;
SS 1: 2 your love is more delightful than *w*.
Isa 28: 7 And these also stagger from *w*
     55: 1 Come, buy *w* and milk
Mt 9:17 Neither do men pour new *w*
Lk 23:36 They offered him *w* vinegar
Jn 2: 3 When the *w* was gone, Jesus'
Ro 14:21 not to eat meat or drink *w*
Eph 5:18 on *w*, which leads to debauchery.
1Ti 5:23 a little *w* because of your stomach
Rev 16:19 with the *w* of the fury of his wrath.

WINEPRESS
Isa 63: 2 like those of one treading the *w*?
Rev 19:15 He treads the *w* of the fury

WINESKINS
Mt 9:17 do men pour new wine into old *w*.

WINGS
Ex 19: 4 and how I carried you on eagles' *w*
Ru 2:12 under whose *w* you have come
Ps 17: 8 hide me in the shadow of your *w*
     91: 4 under his *w* you will find refuge;
Isa 6: 2 him were seraphs, each with six *w*:

Isa 40:31 They will soar on *w* like eagles;
Eze 1: 6 of them had four faces and four *w*.
Zec 5: 9 in their *w*! They had *w* like those
Mal 4: 2 rise with healing in its *w*.
Lk 13:34 hen gathers her chicks under her *w*,
Rev 4: 8 the four living creatures had six *w*

WINS (WIN)
Pr 11:30 and he who *w* souls is wise.

WINTER
Mk 13:18 that this will not take place in *w*,

WIPE (WIPED)
Isa 25: 8 The Sovereign LORD will *w* away
Rev 7:17 God will *w* away every tear
21: 4 He will *w* every tear

WIPED (WIPE)
Lk 7:38 Then she *w* them with her hair,
Ac 3:19 so that your sins may be *w* out,

WISDOM (WISE)
Ge 3: 6 and also desirable for gaining *w*,
1Ki 4:29 God gave Solomon *w* and very
2Ch 1:10 Give me *w* and knowledge,
Ps 51: 6 you teach me *w* in the inmost place
111:10 of the LORD is the beginning of *w*;
Pr 2: 6 For the LORD gives *w*,
3:13 Blessed is the man who finds *w*,
4: 7 *W* is supreme; therefore get
8:11 for *w* is more precious than rubies,
11: 2 but with humility comes *w*.
13:10 *w* is found in those who take advice
23:23 get *w*, discipline and understanding
29: 3 A man who loves *w* brings joy
29:15 The rod of correction imparts *w*,
31:26 She speaks with *w*,
Isa 11: 2 Spirit of *w* and of understanding,
28:29 in counsel and magnificent in *w*.
Jer 10:12 he founded the world by his *w*
Mic 6: 9 and to fear your name is *w*—
Mt 11:19 But *w* is proved right by her actions
Lk 2:52 And Jesus grew in *w* and stature,
Ac 6: 3 known to be full of the Spirit and *w*.
Ro 11:33 the depth of the riches of the *w*
1Co 1:17 not with words of human *w*,
1:30 who has become for us *w* from God
12: 8 through the Spirit the message of *w*
Eph 1:17 may give you the Spirit of *w*
Col 2: 3 are hidden all the treasures of *w*
2:23 indeed have an appearance of *w*.
Jas 1: 5 of you lacks *w*, he should ask God,
3:13 in the humility that comes from *w*.
Rev 5:12 and wealth and *w* and strength

WISE (WISDOM WISER)
1Ki 3:12 give you a *w* and discerning heart,
Job 5:13 He catches the *w* in their craftiness
Ps 19: 7 making *w* the simple.
Pr 3: 7 Do not be *w* in your own eyes;
9: 8 rebuke a *w* man and he will love
10: 1 A *w* son brings joy to his father,
11:30 and he who wins souls is *w*.
13: 1 A *w* son heeds his father's
13:20 He who walks with the *w* grows *w*,
16:23 A *w* man's heart guides his mouth,
17:28 Even a fool is thought *w*
Ecc 9:17 The quiet words of the *w* are more
Jer 9:23 "Let not the *w* man boast
Eze 28: 6 " 'Because you think you are *w*,
Da 2:21 He gives wisdom to the *w*
12: 3 Those who are *w* will shine like
Mt 11:25 hidden these things from the *w*
25: 2 them were foolish and five were *w*.
1Co 1:19 I will destroy the wisdom of the *w*;
1:27 things of the world to shame the *w*;
3:19 He catches the *w* in their craftiness

Eph 5:15 but as *w*, making the most
2Ti 3:15 able to make you *w* for salvation
Jas 3:13 Who is *w* and understanding

WISER (WISE)
Pr 9: 9 a wise man and he will be *w* still;
1Co 1:25 of God is *w* than man's wisdom,

WISH (WISHES)
Jn 15: 7 ask whatever you *w*, and it will be
Ro 9: 3 For I could *w* that I myself were
Rev 3:15 I *w* you were either one

WISHES (WISH)
Rev 22:17 let him come; and whoever *w*,

WITCHCRAFT
Dt 18:10 engages in *w*, or casts spells,
Gal 5:20 idolatry and *w*; hatred, discord,

WITHDREW
Lk 5:16 But Jesus often *w* to lonely places

WITHER (WITHERS)
Ps 1: 3 and whose leaf does not *w*.
37:19 In times of disaster they will not *w*;

WITHERS (WITHER)
Isa 40: 7 The grass *w* and the flowers fall,
1Pe 1:24 the grass *w* and the flowers fall,

WITHHELD (WITHHOLD)
Ge 22:12 you have not *w* from me your son,

WITHHOLD (WITHHELD WITHHOLDS)
Ps 84:11 no good thing does he *w*
Pr 23:13 Do not *w* discipline from a child;

WITHHOLDS (WITHHOLD)
Dt 27:19 "Cursed is the man who *w* justice

WITNESS (EYEWITNESSES WITNESSES)
Pr 12:17 truthful *w* gives honest testimony,
19: 9 A false *w* will not go unpunished,
Jn 1: 8 he came only as a *w* to the light.

WITNESSES (WITNESS)
Dt 19:15 by the testimony of two or three *w*.
Mt 18:16 by the testimony of two or three *w*.'
Ac 1: 8 and you will be my *w* in Jerusalem,

WIVES (WIFE)
Eph 5:22 *W*, submit to your husbands
5:25 love your *w*, just as Christ loved
1Pe 3: 1 words by the behavior of their *w*,

WIVES' (WIFE)
1Ti 4: 7 with godless myths and old *w* tales

WOE
Isa 6: 5 "*W* to me!" I cried.
Eze 34: 2 *W* to the shepherds
Mt 18: 7 "*W* to the world
23:13 "*W* to you, teachers of the law
Jude :11 *W* to them! They have taken

WOLF (WOLVES)
Isa 65:25 *w* and the lamb will feed together,

WOLVES (WOLF)
Mt 10:16 you out like sheep among *w*.

WOMAN (MAN)
Ge 2:22 God made a *w* from
2:23 she shall be called '*w*,'
3: 6 *w* saw that the fruit
3:12 The *w* you put here with
3:15 between you and the *w*,
3:16 To the *w* he said,
12:11 a beautiful *w* you are.
20: 3 because of the *w* you have
24: 5 if the *w* is unwilling
Ex 2: 1 married a Levite *w*
3:22 Every *w* is to ask her
21:10 If he marries another *w*
21:22 hit a pregnant *w*
Lev 12: 2 *w* who becomes pregnant
15:19 *w* has her regular flow
15:25 a *w* has a discharge
18:17 sexual relations with both a *w*
20:13 as one lies with a *w*,
Nu 5:29 when a *w* goes astray
30: 3 young *w* still living in
30: 9 by a widow or divorced *w*
30:10 *w* living with her husband
Dt 20: 7 become pledged to a *w*
21:11 the captives a beautiful *w*
22: 5 *w* must not wear men's

Dt 22:13 married this *w* but when
Jdg 4: 9 hand Sisera over to a *w*.
13: 6 the *w* went to her husband
14: 2 have seen a Philistine *w*
16: 4 he fell in love with a *w*
20: 4 husband of the murdered *w*
Ru 3:11 a *w* of noble character
1Sa 1:15 a *w* who is deeply troubled
25: 3 intelligent and beautiful *w*,
28: 7 a *w* who is a medium,
2Sa 11: 2 he saw a *w* bathing
13:17 "Get this *w* out of here
14: 2 had a wise *w* brought
20:16 a wise *w* called from
1Ki 3:18 this *w* also had a baby.
17:24 the *w* said to Elijah,
2Ki 4: 8 a well-to-do *w* was there,
8: 1 Elisha had said to the *w*
9:34 "Take care of that cursed *w*,"
Job 14: 1 Man born of *w* is of few
Pr 11:16 A kindhearted *w* gains respect,
11:22 a beautiful *w* who shows no
14: 1 a wise *w* builds her house,
30:23 unloved *w* who is married,
31:30 a *w* who fears the LORD
Isa 54: 1 O barren *w*, you who never
Mt 5:28 looks at a *w* lustfully
9:20 a *w* who had been subject
15:28 *W* you have great faith!
26: 7 a *w* came to him with
Mk 5:25 a *w* was there who had
7:25 a *w* whose little daughter
Lk 7:39 what kind of a *w* she is
10:38 a *w* named Martha opened
13:12 "*W*, you are set free
15: 8 suppose a *w* has ten silver
Jn 2: 4 *w*, why do you involve
4: 7 a Samaritan *w* came
8: 3 a *w* caught in adultery.
19:26 *w*, here is your son,"
20:15 *W*, 'he said, "Why are you crying?
Ac 9:40 Turning toward the dead *w*,
16:14 was a *w* named Lydia,
Ro 7: 2 a married *w* is bound to
1Co 7: 2 each *w* her own husband
7:15 a believing man or *w* is
7:34 an unmarried *w* or virgin
7:39 *w* is bound to her husband
11: 3 the head of the *w* is man,
11: 7 the *w* is the glory of man
11:13 a *w* to pray to God with
Gal 4: 4 his Son, born of a *w*,
4:31 not children of the slave *w*,
1Ti 2:11 A *w* should learn in
5:16 any *w* who is a believer
Rev 2:20 You tolerate that *w* Jezebel,
12: 1 a *w* clothed with the sun
12:13 he pursued the *w* who had
17: 3 a *w* sitting on a scarlet

WOMEN (MAN)
Mt 11:11 among those born of *w*,
28: 5 The angel said to the *w*,
Mk 15:41 Many other *w* who had come
Lk 1:42 Blessed are you among *w*,
8: 2 also some *w* who had been
23:27 *w* who mourned and wailed
24:11 they did not believe the *w*,
Ac 1:14 along with the *w* and Mary
16:13 speak to the *w* who had
17: 4 not a few prominent *w*.
Ro 1:26 *w* exchanged natural relations
1Co 14:34 *w* should remain silent in
Php 4: 3 help these *w* who have
1Ti 2: 9 want *w* to dress modestly
5: 2 older *w* as mothers,
Tit 2: 3 teach the older *w* to be
2: 4 train the younger *w* to love
Heb 11:35 *W* received back their dead
1Pe 3: 5 the holy *w* of the past

WOMB
Job 1:21 Naked I came from my mother's *w*,
Ps 139:13 in my mother's *w*.
Pr 31: 2 "O my son, O son of my *w*,
Jer 1: 5 you in the *w* I knew you,
Lk 1:44 the baby in my *w* leaped for joy.
Jn 3: 4 into his mother's *w* to be born!"

WON (WIN)
1Pe 3: 1 they may be *w* over without words

WONDER (WONDERFUL WONDERS)
Ps   17: 7 Show the *w* of your great love,
SS   1: 3 No *w* the maidens love you!

WONDERFUL* (WONDER)
2Sa   1:26 Your love for me was *w*,
       1:26 more *w* than that of women.
1Ch 16: 9 tell of all his *w* acts.
Job 42: 3 things too *w* for me to know.
Ps   26: 7 and telling of all your *w* deeds.
      31:21 for he showed his *w* love to me
      75: 1 men tell of your *w* deeds.
     105: 2 tell of all his *w* acts.
     107: 8 and his *w* deeds for men,
     107:15 and his *w* deeds for men,
     107:21 and his *w* deeds for men,
     107:24 his *w* deeds in the deep.
     107:31 and his *w* deeds for men,
     119:18 *w* things in your law.
     119:129 Your statutes are *w*;
     131: 1 or things too *w* for me.
     139: 6 Such knowledge is too *w* for me,
     139:14 your works are *w*,
     145: 5 I will meditate on your *w* works.
Isa   9: 6 *W* Counselor, Mighty God,
      28:29 *w* in counsel and magnificent
Mt   21:15 of the law saw the *w* things he did
Lk   13:17 with all the *w* things he was
             doing.
1Pe   2: 9 out of darkness into his *w* light.

WONDERS (WONDER)
Ex   3:20 with all the *w* that I will perform
Dt   10:21 and awesome *w* you saw
2Sa   7:23 awesome *w* by driving out nations
Job   37:14 stop and consider God's *w*.
Ps   9: 1 I will tell of all your *w*.
      89: 5 The heavens praise your *w*,
     119:27 then I will meditate on your *w*.
Joel   2:30 I will show *w* in the heavens
Ac   2:11 we hear them declaring the *w*
       2:19 I will show *w* in the heaven above
       5:12 many miraculous signs and *w*
2Co   12:12 that mark an apostle—signs,
2Th   2: 9 and *w*, and in every sort
Heb   2: 4 also testified to it by signs,

WOOD
Isa   44:19 Shall I bow down to a block of *w*?"
1Co   3:12 costly stones, *w*, hay or straw,

WOOL
Pr   31:13 She selects *w* and flax
Isa   1:18 they shall be like *w*.
Da   7: 9 hair of his head was white like *w*.
Rev   1:14 and hair were white like *w*,

WORD (BYWORD WORDS)
Nu   30: 2 he must not break his *w*
Dt   8: 3 but on every *w* that comes
2Sa   22:31 the *w* of the LORD is flawless.
Ps   56: 4 In God, whose *w* I praise,
      119: 9 By living according to your *w*.
     119:11 I have hidden your *w* in my heart
     119:105 Your *w* is a lamp to my feet
Pr   12:25 but a kind *w* cheers him up.
      15: 1 but a harsh *w* stirs up anger.
      25:11 A *w* aptly spoken
      30: 5 "Every *w* of God is flawless;
Isa   55:11 so is my *w* that goes out
Jer   23:29 "Is not my *w* like fire," declares
Mt   4: 4 but on every *w* that comes
      12:36 for every careless *w* they have
      15: 6 Thus you nullify the *w* of God
Mk   4:14 parable? The farmer sows the *w*.
Jn   1: 1 was the *W*, and the *W* was
       1: 1 The *W* became flesh and made
             his
      17:17 them by the truth; your *w* is truth.
Ac   6: 4 and the ministry of the *w*."
2Co   2:17 we do not peddle the *w* of God
       4: 2 nor do we distort the *w* of God.
Eph   6:17 of the Spirit, which is the *w* of
             God.
Php   2:16 as you hold out the *w* of life—
Col   3:16 Let the *w* of Christ dwell
2Ti   2:15 and who correctly handles the *w*
Heb   4:12 For the *w* of God is living
Jas   1:22 Do not merely listen to the *w*,
2Pe   1:19 And we have the *w* of the
             prophets

WORDS (WORD)
Dt   11:18 Fix these *w* of mine in your hearts
Ps   12: 6 the *w* of the LORD are flawless,

Ps   119:103 How sweet are your *w* to my
             taste,
     119:130 The unfolding of your *w* gives
             light;
     119:160 All your *w* are true;
Pr   2: 1 My son, if you accept my *w*
      10:19 When *w* are many, sin is not
             absent
      16:24 Pleasant *w* are a honeycomb,
      30: 6 Do not add to his *w*.
Ecc   12:11 The *w* of the wise are like goads,
Jer   15:16 When your *w* came, I ate them;
Mt   24:35 but my *w* will never pass away.
Lk   6:47 and hears my *w* and puts them
Jn   6:68 You have the *w* of eternal life.
      15: 7 in me and my *w* remain in you,
1Co   2:13 but in *w* taught by the Spirit,
      14:19 rather speak five intelligible *w*
Rev   22:19 And if anyone takes *w* away

WORK (WORKED WORKER WORKERS WORKING WORKMAN WORKMANSHIP WORKS)
Ge   2: 2 day he rested from all his *w*.
Ex   23:12 "Six days do your *w*,
Nu   8:11 ready to do the *w* of the LORD.
Dt   5:14 On it you shall not do any *w*,
Ps   19: 1 the skies proclaim the *w*
Ecc   5:19 his lot and be happy in his *w*—
Jer   48:10 lax in doing the LORD's *w*!
Mt   20: 1 to hire men to *w* in his vineyard.
Jn   6:27 Do not *w* for food that spoils,
       9: 4 we must do the *w* of him who
             sent
Ac   13: 2 for the *w* to which I have called
1Co   3:13 test the quality of each man's *w*.
       4:12 We *w* hard with our own hands.
Eph   4:16 up in love, as each part does its *w*.
Php   1: 6 that he who began a good *w*
       2:12 continue to *w* out your salvation
Col   3:23 Whatever you do, *w* at it
1Th   4:11 and to *w* with your hands,
       5:12 to respect those who *w* hard
2Th   3:10 If a man will not *w*, he shall not
             eat
2Ti   3:17 equipped for every good *w*.
Heb   6:10 he will not forget your *w*
2Jn   :11 him shares in his wicked *w*.
3Jn   : 8 men so that we may *w* together

WORKED (WORK)
1Co   15:10 No, I *w* harder than all of them—
2Th   3: 8 On the contrary, we *w* night

WORKER (WORK)
Lk   10: 7 for the *w* deserves his wages.
1Ti   5:18 and "The *w* deserves his wages."

WORKERS (WORK)
Mt   9:37 is plentiful but the *w* are few.
1Co   3: 9 For we are God's fellow *w*;

WORKING (WORK)
Col   3:23 as *w* for the Lord, not for men,

WORKMAN (WORK)
2Ti   2:15 a *w* who does not need

WORKMANSHIP* (WORK)
Eph   2:10 For we are God's *w*, created

WORKS (WORK)
Ps   66: 5 how awesome his *w* in man's
             behalf
     145: 6 of the power of your awesome *w*,
Pr   8:22 As the first of his *w*,
      31:31 let her *w* bring her praise
Ro   4: 2 in fact, Abraham was justified
             by *w*
       8:28 in all things God *w* for the good
Eph   2: 9 not by *w*, so that no one can
             boast.
       4:12 to prepare God's people for *w*

WORLD (WORLDLY)
Ps   9: 8 He will judge the *w*
      50:12 for the *w* is mine, and all that is in
      96:13 He will judge the *w*
Pr   8:23 before the *w* began.
Isa   13:11 I will punish the *w* for its evil,
Zep   1:18 the whole *w* will be consumed,
Mt   5:14 "You are the light of the *w*.
      16:26 for a man if he gains the whole *w*,
Mk   16:15 into all the *w* and preach the good
Jn   1:29 who takes away the sin of the *w*!
       3:16 so loved the *w* that he gave his
             one

Jn   8:12 he said, "I am the light of the *w*.
      15:19 As it is, you do not belong to
             the *w*,
      16:33 In this *w* you will have trouble.
      17: 5 had with you before the *w* began.
      17:14 not of the *w* any more than I am
      18:36 "My kingdom is not of this *w*.
Ac   17:24 "The God who made the *w*
Ro   3:19 and the whole *w* held
             accountable
      10:18 their words to the ends of the *w*."
1Co   1:27 things of the *w* to shame the
             strong.
       3:19 the wisdom of this *w* is foolishness
       6: 2 that the saints will judge the *w*?
2Co   5:19 that God was reconciling the *w*
      10: 3 For though we live in the *w*,
1Ti   6: 7 For we brought nothing into
             the *w*,
Heb   11:38 the *w* was not worthy of them.
Jas   2: 5 poor in the eyes of the *w* to be
             rich
       4: 4 with the *w* is hatred toward God?
1Pe   1:20 before the creation of the *w*,
1Jn   2: 2 but also for the sins of the
             whole *w*.
       2:15 not love the *w* or anything in
             the *w*.
       5: 4 born of God overcomes the *w*.
Rev   13: 8 slain from the creation of the *w*.

WORLDLY (WORLD)
1Co   3: 1 address you as spiritual but
             as *w*—
Tit   2:12 to ungodliness and *w* passions,

WORM
Mk   9:48 " 'their *w* does not die,

WORRY (WORRYING)
Mt   6:25 I tell you, do not *w* about your
             life,
      10:19 do not *w* about what to say

WORRYING (WORRY)
Mt   6:27 of you by *w* can add a single hour

WORSHIP (WORSHIPED WORSHIPS)
Jos   22:27 that we will *w* the LORD
2Ki   17:36 arm, is the one you must *w*.
1Ch   16:29 *w* the LORD in the splendor
Ps   95: 6 Come, let us bow down in *w*,
     100: 2 *w* the LORD with gladness;
Zec   14:17 up to Jerusalem to *w* the King,
Mt   2: 2 and have come to *w* him."
       4: 9 "if you will bow down and *w* me."
Jn   4:24 and his worshipers must *w* in
             spirit
Ro   12: 1 to God—this is your spiritual act
             of *w*.
Heb   10: 1 perfect those who draw near to *w*.

WORSHIPED (WORSHIP)
2Ch   29:30 and bowed their heads and *w*.
Mt   28: 9 clasped his feet and *w* him.

WORSHIPS (WORSHIP)
Isa   44:15 But he also fashions a god and *w*
             it;

WORTH (WORTHY)
Job   28:13 Man does not comprehend its *w*;
Pr   31:10 She is *w* far more than rubies.
Mt   10:31 are *w* more than many sparrows.
Ro   8:18 sufferings are not *w* comparing
1Pe   1: 7 of greater *w* than gold,
       3: 4 which is of great *w* in God's sight.

WORTHLESS
Pr   11: 4 Wealth is *w* in the day of wrath,
Jas   1:26 himself and his religion is *w*.

WORTHY (WORTH)
1Ch   16:25 For great is the LORD and most *w*
Mt   10:37 more than me is not *w* of me;
Lk   15:19 I am no longer *w* to be called your
Eph   4: 1 to live a life *w* of the calling you
Php   1:27 in a manner *w* of the gospel
Col   1:10 in order that you may live a life *w*
1Ti   3: 8 are to be men of respect,
             sincere,
Heb   3: 3 Jesus has been found *w*
3Jn   : 6 on their way in a manner *w* of
             God.
Rev   5: 2 "Who is *w* to break the seals

WOUND (WOUNDS)
1Co   8:12 and *w* their weak conscience,

2314

WOUNDS (WOUND)
Pr 27: 6 *w* from a friend can be trusted
Isa 53: 5 and by his *w* we are healed.
Zec 13: 6 'What are these *w* on your body?'
1Pe 2:24 by his *w* you have been healed.

WRAPS
Ps 104: 2 He *w* himself in light

WRATH
2Ch 36:16 scoffed at his prophets until the *w*
Ps   2: 5 and terrifies them in his *w*, saying,
     76:10 Surely your *w* against men brings
Pr 15: 1 A gentle answer turns away *w*,
Isa 13:13 at the *w* of the LORD Almighty,
     51:17 the cup of his *w*,
Jer 25:15 filled with the wine of my *w*
Eze 5:13 my *w* against them will subside,
     20: 8 So I said I would pour out my *w*
Am 1: 1 I will not turn back from my *w*,
Na 1: 2 maintains his *w* against his
           enemies
Zep 1:15 That day will be a day of *w*,
Jn 3:36 for God's *w* remains on him."
Ro 1:18 The *w* of God is being revealed
      2: 5 you are storing up *w*
      5: 9 saved from God's *w* through him!
      9:22 choosing to show his *w*
1Th 5: 9 God did not appoint us to suffer *w*
Rev 6:16 and from the *w* of the Lamb!
     19:15 the fury of the *w* of God Almighty.

WRESTLED
Ge 32:24 and a man *w* with him till
           daybreak

WRITE (WRITER WRITING WRITTEN WROTE)
Dt 6: 9 *W* them on the doorframes
     10: 2 I will *w* on the tablets the words
Pr 7: 3 *w* them on the tablet of your
           heart.
Jer 31:33 and *w* it on their hearts.
Heb 8:10 and *w* them on their hearts.
Rev 3:12 I will also *w* on him my new name.

WRITER* (WRITE)
Ps 45: 1 my tongue is the pen of a
           skillful *w*.

WRITING (WRITE)
1Co 14:37 him acknowledge that what I
           am *w*

WRITTEN (WRITE)
Dt 28:58 which are *w* in this book,
Jos 1: 8 careful to do everything *w* in it.
     23: 6 to obey all that is *w* in the Book
Ps 40: 7 it is *w* about me in the scroll.
Da 12: 1 everyone whose name is found *w*
Mal 3:16 A scroll of remembrance was *w*
Lk 10:20 but rejoice that your names are *w*
     24:44 must be fulfilled that is *w* about
           me
Jn 20:31 these are *w* that you may believe
     21:25 for the books that would be *w*.
Ro 15: 4 of the law are *w* on their hearts,
1Co 4: 6 "Do not go beyond what is *w*."
     10:11 as examples and were *w* down
2Co 3: 3 *w* not with ink but with the Spirit
Col 2:14 having canceled the *w* code,
Heb 10: 7 it is *w* about me in the scroll—
     12:23 whose names are *w* in heaven.
Rev 21:27 but only those whose names
           are *w*

WRONG (WRONGDOING WRONGED WRONGS)
Ex 23: 2 Do not follow the crowd in
           doing *w*
Nu 5: 7 must make full restitution for
           his *w*,
Dt 32: 4 A faithful God who does no *w*,
Job 34:12 unthinkable that God would do *w*,
Ps 5: 5 you hate all who do *w*.
Gal 2:11 to his face, because he was clearly
           in the *w*.
1Th 5:15 that nobody pays back *w* for *w*,

WRONGDOING (WRONG)
Job 1:22 sin by charging God with *w*.
1Jn 5:17 All *w* is sin, and there is sin that

WRONGED (WRONG)
1Co 6: 7 not rather be *w*? Why not rather

WRONGS (WRONG)
Pr 10:12 but love covers over all *w*.
1Co 13: 5 angered, it keeps no record of *w*.

WROTE (WRITE)
Ex 34:28 And he *w* on the tablets the
           words
Jn 5: 46 for he *w* about me.
      8: 8 down and *w* on the ground.

XERXES
King of Persia, husband of Esther. Deposed Vashti; replaced her with Esther (Est 1–2). Sealed Haman's edict to annihilate the Jews (Est 3). Honored Mordecai (Est 6). Hanged Haman (Est 7). Issued edict allowing Jews to defend themselves (Est 8). Exalted Mordecai (Est 8:1–2, 15; 9:4; 10).

YEAR (YEARS)
Ex 34:23 Three times a *y* all your men are
Lev 16:34 to be made once a *y* for all the
           sins
     25: 4 But in the seventh *y* the land is
     25:11 The fiftieth *y* shall be a jubilee
Heb 10: 1 repeated endlessly *y* after *y*,

YEARS (YEAR)
Ge 1:14 to mark seasons and days and *y*,
Ex 12:40 lived in Egypt was 430 *y*.
     16:35 The Israelites ate manna forty *y*,
Job 36:26 of his *y* is past finding out.
Ps 90: 4 For a thousand *y* in your sight
     90:10 The length of our days is
           seventy *y*
Pr 3: 2 they will prolong your life many *y*
Lk 3:23 Jesus himself was about thirty *y*
           old
2Pe 3: 8 the Lord a day is like a
           thousand *y*,
Rev 20: 2 and bound him for a thousand *y*.

YEAST
Ex 12:15 are to eat bread made without *y*.
Mt 16: 6 guard against the *y* of the
           Pharisees
1Co 5: 6 you know that a little *y* works

YESTERDAY
Heb 13: 8 Jesus Christ is the same *y*

YOKE (YOKED)
1Ki 12: 4 and the heavy *y* he put on us,
Mt 11:29 Take my *y* upon you and learn
Gal 5: 1 be burdened again by a *y*

YOKED (YOKE)
2Co 6:14 Do not be *y* together

YOUNG (YOUNGER YOUTH)
2Ch 10:14 he followed the advice of the *y*
           men
Ps 37:25 I was *y* and now I am old,
     119: 9 How can a *y* man keep his way
Pr 20:29 The glory of *y* men is their
           strength
Isa 40:11 he gently leads those that have *y*.
Joel 2:28 your *y* men will see visions.
Ac 2:17 your *y* men will see visions,
      7:58 at the feet of a *y* man named Saul.
1Ti 4:12 down on you because you are *y*,
Tit 2: 6 encourage the *y* men
1Pe 5: 5 *Y* men, in the same way be
1Jn 2:13 I write to you, *y* men,

YOUNGER (YOUNG)
1Ti 5: 1 Treat *y* men as brothers, older
Tit 2: 4 Then they can train the *y* women

YOUTH (YOUNG)
Ps 103: 5 so that your *y* is renewed like
Ecc 12: 1 Creator in the days of your *y*,

2Ti 2:22 Flee the evil desires of *y*,

ZACCHAEUS
Lk 19: 2 A man was there by the name
           of *Z*;

ZEAL (ZEALOUS)
Ps 69: 9 for *z* for your house consumes
           me,
Pr 19: 2 to have *z* without knowledge,
Isa 59:17 and wrapped himself in *z*
Jn 2:17 "*Z* for your house will consume
           me
Ro 10: 2 their *z* is not based on knowledge.
     12:11 Never be lacking in *z*,

ZEALOUS (ZEAL)
Nu 25:13 he was *z* for the honor of his God
Pr 23:17 always be *z* for the fear
Eze 39:25 and I will be *z* for my holy name.
Gal 4:18 fine to be *z*, provided the purpose
           is

ZEBULUN
Son of Jacob by Leah (Ge 30:20; 35:23; 1Ch 2:1). Tribe of blessed (Ge 49:13; Dt 33:18–19), numbered (Nu 1:31; 26:27), allotted land (Jos 19:10–16; Eze 48:26), failed to fully possess (Jdg 1:30), supported Deborah (Jdg 4:6–10; 5:14, 18), David (1Ch 12:33), 12,000 from (Rev 7:8).

ZECHARIAH
1. Son of Jeroboam II; king of Israel (2Ki 15:8–12).
2. Post-exilic prophet who encouraged rebuilding of temple (Ezr 5:1; 6:14; Zec 1:1).
3. Father of John the Baptist (Lk 1:13; 3:2).

ZEDEKIAH
1. False prophet (1Ki 22:11–24; 2Ch 18:10–23).
2. Mattaniah, son of Josiah (1Ch 3:15), made king of Judah by Nebuchadnezzar (2Ki 24:17–25:7; 2Ch 36:10–14; Jer 37–39; 52:1–11).

ZEPHANIAH
Prophet; descendant of Hezekiah (Zep 1:1).

ZERUBBABEL
Descendant of David (1Ch 3:19; Mt 1:3). Led return from exile (Ezr 2:2; Ne 7:7). Governor of Israel; helped rebuild altar and temple (Ezr 3; Hag 1–2; Zec 4).

ZILPAH
Servant of Leah, mother of Jacob's sons Gad and Asher (Ge 30:9–12; 35:26, 46:16–18).

ZIMRI
King of Israel (1Ki 16:9–20).

ZION
2Sa 5: 7 David captured the fortress of *Z*,
Ps   2: 6 King on *Z*, my holy hill."
      9:11 to the LORD, enthroned in *Z*;
     74: 2 Mount *Z*, where you dwelt.
     87: 2 the LORD loves the gates of *Z*
    102:13 and have compassion on *Z*,
    137: 3 "Sing us one of the songs of *Z*!"
Isa 2: 3 The law will go out from *Z*,
     28:16 "See, I lay a stone in *Z*,
     51:11 They will enter *Z* with singing;
     52: 8 When the LORD returns to *Z*,
Jer 50: 5 They will ask the way to *Z*
Joel 3:21 The LORD dwells in *Z*!
Am 6: 1 to you who are complacent in *Z*,
Mic 4: 2 The law will go out from *Z*,
Zec 9: 9 Rejoice greatly, O Daughter of *Z*!
Ro 9:33 I lay in *Z* a stone that causes men
     11:26 "The deliverer will come from *Z*;
Heb 12:22 But you have come to Mount *Z*,
Rev 14: 1 standing on Mount *Z*,

ZIPPORAH*
Daughter of Reuel; wife of Moses (Ex 2:21–22; 4:20–26; 18:1–6).

ZOPHAR
One of Job's friends (Job 11; 20).

Faith in Action Study Bible

General Editor	**Terry C. Muck**
Project Management and Editorial	**Donna L. Huisjen**
Editorial Development	**Denise Cavinee Koenig, Natalie J. Block**
Theological Review	**Andrew Sloan, Tim Dearborn, Mike Klassen, Brian Sellers-Petersen**
Production Management	**Phil Herich**
Art Direction and Cover Design	**Jamie DeBruyn**
Interior Design	**Sharon VanLoozenoord, Belmont, MI**
Interior Proofreading	**Peachtree Editorial and Proofreading Service, Atlanta, GA**
Interior Typesetting	**Blue Heron Bookcraft, Battle Ground, WA**

The World in the 21st Century

Understanding today's world

Putting your faith into action in today's world requires an understanding of the needs around the globe. This section of the *Faith in Action Study Bible* will give you insight into the daily life of billions of people. You'll also gain a new perspective on your place in this world.

There are more than 6 billion people in the world.

One in two lives on less than $2 a day
One in three claims to be a Christian
One in four is under 14 years old
One in five is Chinese
One in six does not have access to health care
One in seven does not get enough to eat

How the world worships

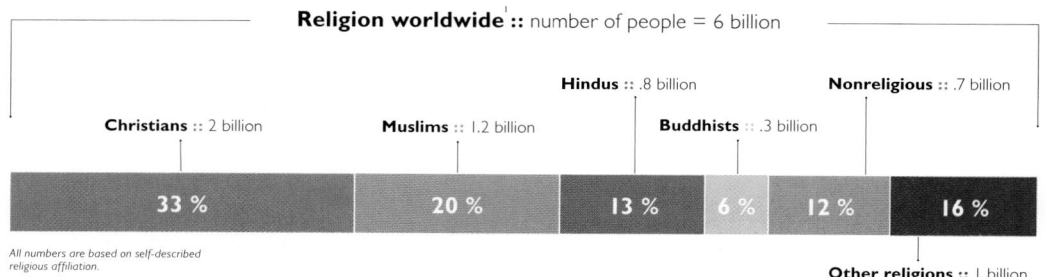

Religion worldwide[1] :: number of people = 6 billion

Hindus :: .8 billion

Nonreligious :: .7 billion

Christians :: 2 billion

Muslims :: 1.2 billion

Buddhists :: .3 billion

| 33 % | 20 % | 13 % | 6 % | 12 % | 16 % |

All numbers are based on self-described religious affiliation.

Other religions :: 1 billion

To the ends of the earth

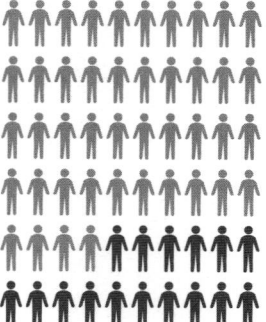

Of the 6 billion people in the world, 1.6 billion have never heard the gospel.[2]

Where Christians live[1,3]

In the 125-year period shown below, the growth of the church is rapidly shifting from north to south of the Equator, and from the West to East Asia.

Total number of Christians

■ = **in 1900 ::** 558 million

■ = **today ::** 2.0 billion

■ = **in 2025 ::** est. 2.6 billion

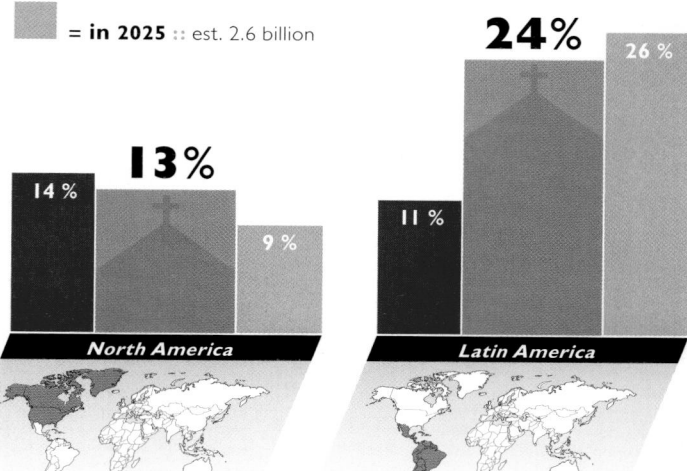

13%

14 %   9 %

North America

24%

11 %   26 %

Latin America

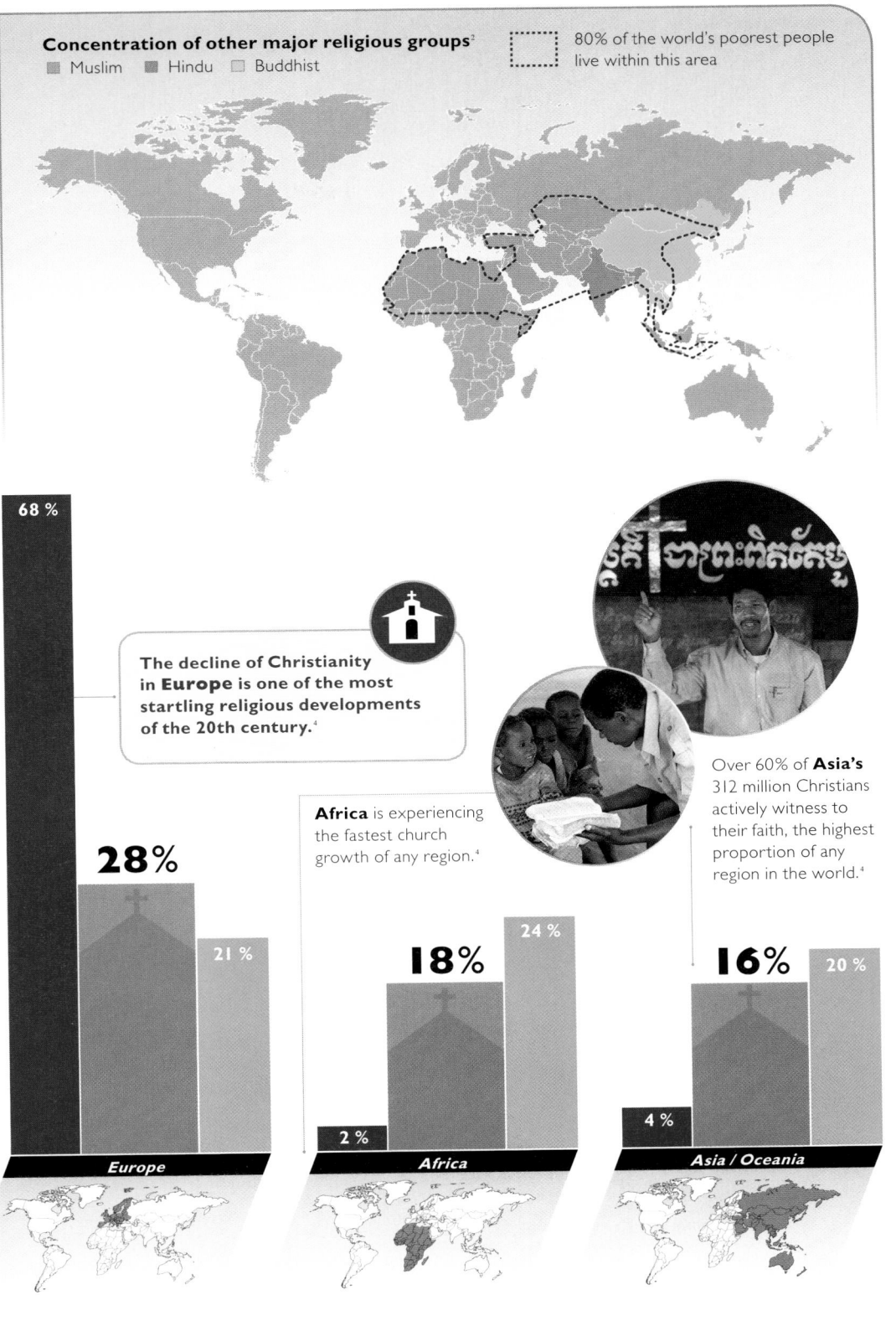

Concentration of other major religious groups[2]
▪ Muslim ▪ Hindu ▫ Buddhist

80% of the world's poorest people live within this area

68 %

The decline of **Christianity** in **Europe** is one of the most startling religious developments of the 20th century.[4]

Over 60% of **Asia's** 312 million Christians actively witness to their faith, the highest proportion of any region in the world.[4]

28%

21 %

Africa is experiencing the fastest church growth of any region.[4]

18%

24 %

2 %

16%

20 %

4 %

Europe

Africa

Asia / Oceania

Wealth and poverty around the globe

Population[5]

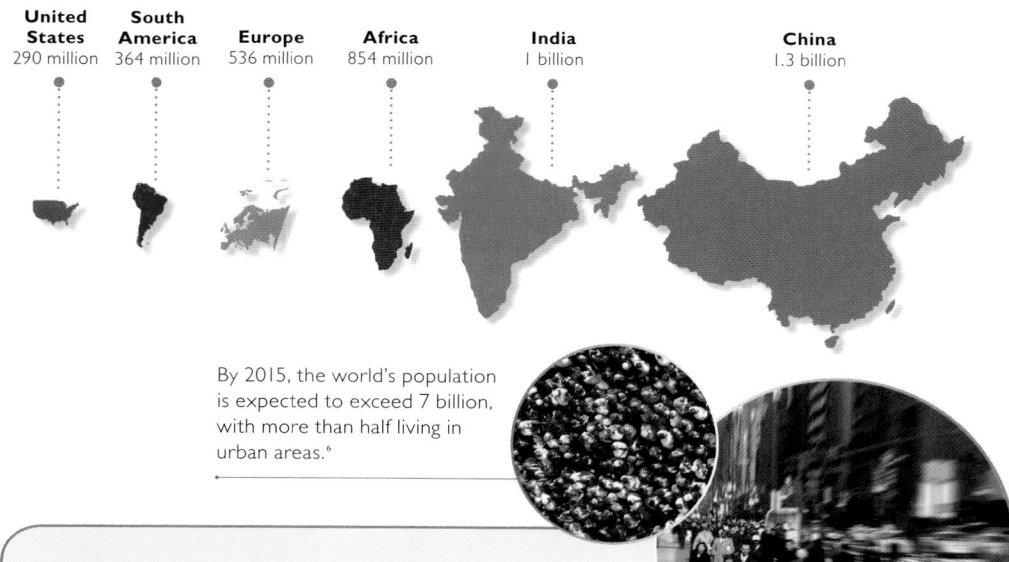

United States	South America	Europe	Africa	India	China
290 million	364 million	536 million	854 million	1 billion	1.3 billion

By 2015, the world's population is expected to exceed 7 billion, with more than half living in urban areas.[6]

Helping other countries in need

Among 22 of the most developed nations, the United States ranks last in percentage of financial assistance provided for developing nations as compared to **gross domestic product (GDP)**, one of the broadest measures of economic health.

Countries, by wealth :: (GDP, per capita)[7]

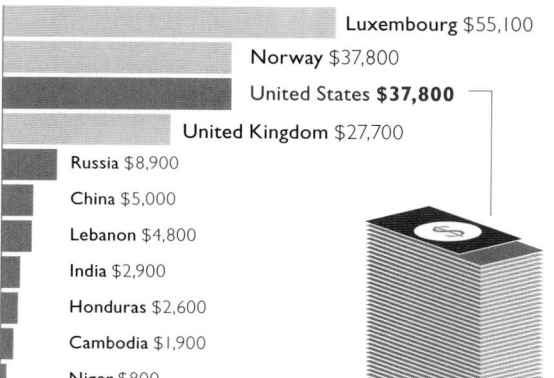

Country	GDP per capita
Luxembourg	$55,100
Norway	$37,800
United States	**$37,800**
United Kingdom	$27,700
Russia	$8,900
China	$5,000
Lebanon	$4,800
India	$2,900
Honduras	$2,600
Cambodia	$1,900
Niger	$800
Afghanistan	$700
Sierra Leone	$500

$0 $60,000

Industrialized countries, by generosity :: (per capita foreign aid)[5]

Country	Per capita foreign aid
Luxembourg	$352.30
Norway	$307.95
Denmark	$302.72
Sweden	$191.48
France	$104.68
Switzerland	$150.30
United Kingdom	$74.88
Japan	$71.53
Portugal	$26.82
United States	$23.76

$23.76
($0.06 per $100)

Listings throughout this section may include selected countries only. All monetary figures are in U.S. dollars.

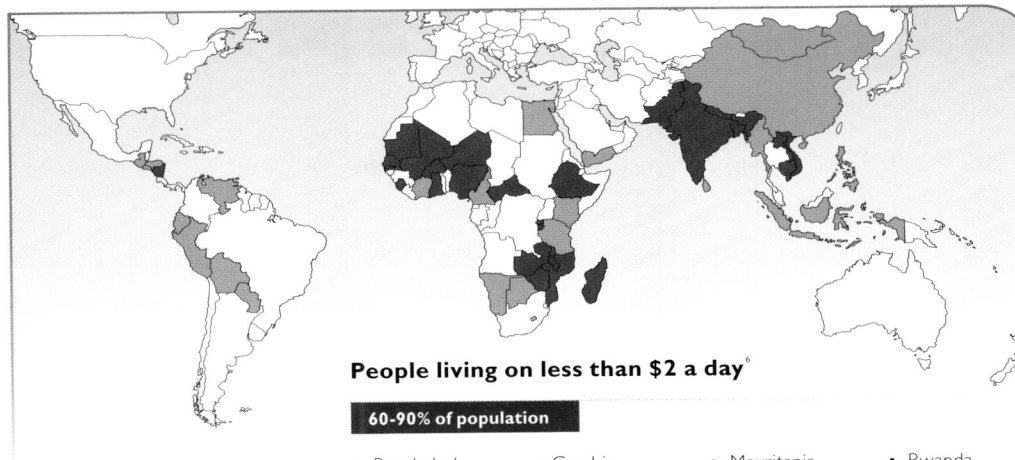

People living on less than $2 a day[6]

60-90% of population

- Bangladesh
- Burkina Faso
- Burundi
- Cambodia
- Central African Republic
- Ethiopia
- Gambia
- Ghana
- India
- Laos
- Madagascar
- Malawi
- Mali
- Mauritania
- Mozambique
- Nepal
- Nicaragua
- Niger
- Nigeria
- Pakistan
- Rwanda
- Senegal
- Sierra Leone
- Vietnam
- Zambia
- Zimbabwe

30-59% of population

- Bolivia
- Botswana
- Cameroon
- China
- Cote d'Ivoire
- Ecuador
- Egypt
- El Salvador
- Guatemala
- Honduras
- Indonesia
- Kenya
- Lesotho
- Mongolia
- Namibia
- Paraguay
- Peru
- Philippines
- Sri Lanka
- Tanzania
- Thailand
- Trinidad & Tobago
- Venezuela
- Yemen

Nearly 3 billion people—half of the world's population—live on less than $2 a day.[10]

More than 1 billion people live on less than $1 a day; of these, 46 percent live in sub-Saharan Africa.[10]

Unemployment[8, 9]

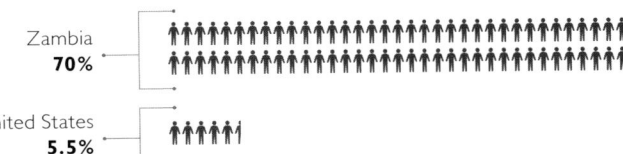

Zambia
70%

United States
5.5%

Technical divide

Cellular phone subscribers
(per 1,000 people in 2002)[11]

Italy	939
Japan	637
United States	488
China	161
India	12
Ethiopia	1

Internet users
(per 1,000 people)[11]

Sweden	573
United States	551
Australia	481
Argentina	112
Haiti	10
Albania	4

Television owners
(per 1,000 people)[5]

United States	754
Canada	668
Germany	623
Cambodia	7
Afghanistan	3
Chad	1

Access to food and water

Proportion of undernourished (%) [12]   **Number of undernourished** (millions) [12]

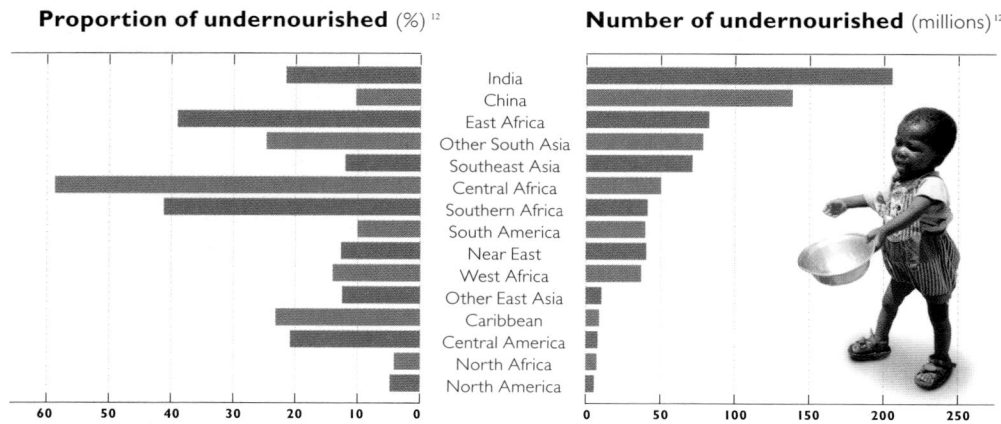

India
China
East Africa
Other South Asia
Southeast Asia
Central Africa
Southern Africa
South America
Near East
West Africa
Other East Asia
Caribbean
Central America
North Africa
North America

Food-challenged regions :: Percentage of population lacking sufficient food [13]

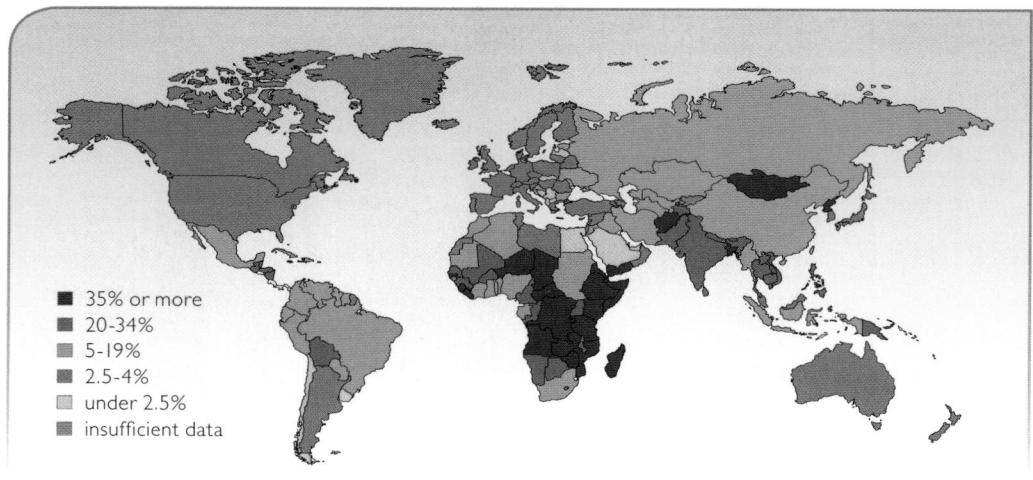

- ■ 35% or more
- ■ 20-34%
- ■ 5-19%
- ■ 2.5-4%
- □ under 2.5%
- ■ insufficient data

Every day 799 million people in developing countries—about one of every seven people worldwide—go hungry. [16]

Every 5 seconds a child dies because he or she was hungry. [18]

Americans spend an estimated $20 billion annually on ice cream, an amount that could feed 83 million hungry children for an entire year. [17, 9]

Water-challenged regions :: Percentage of population lacking access to safe drinking water [14, 15]

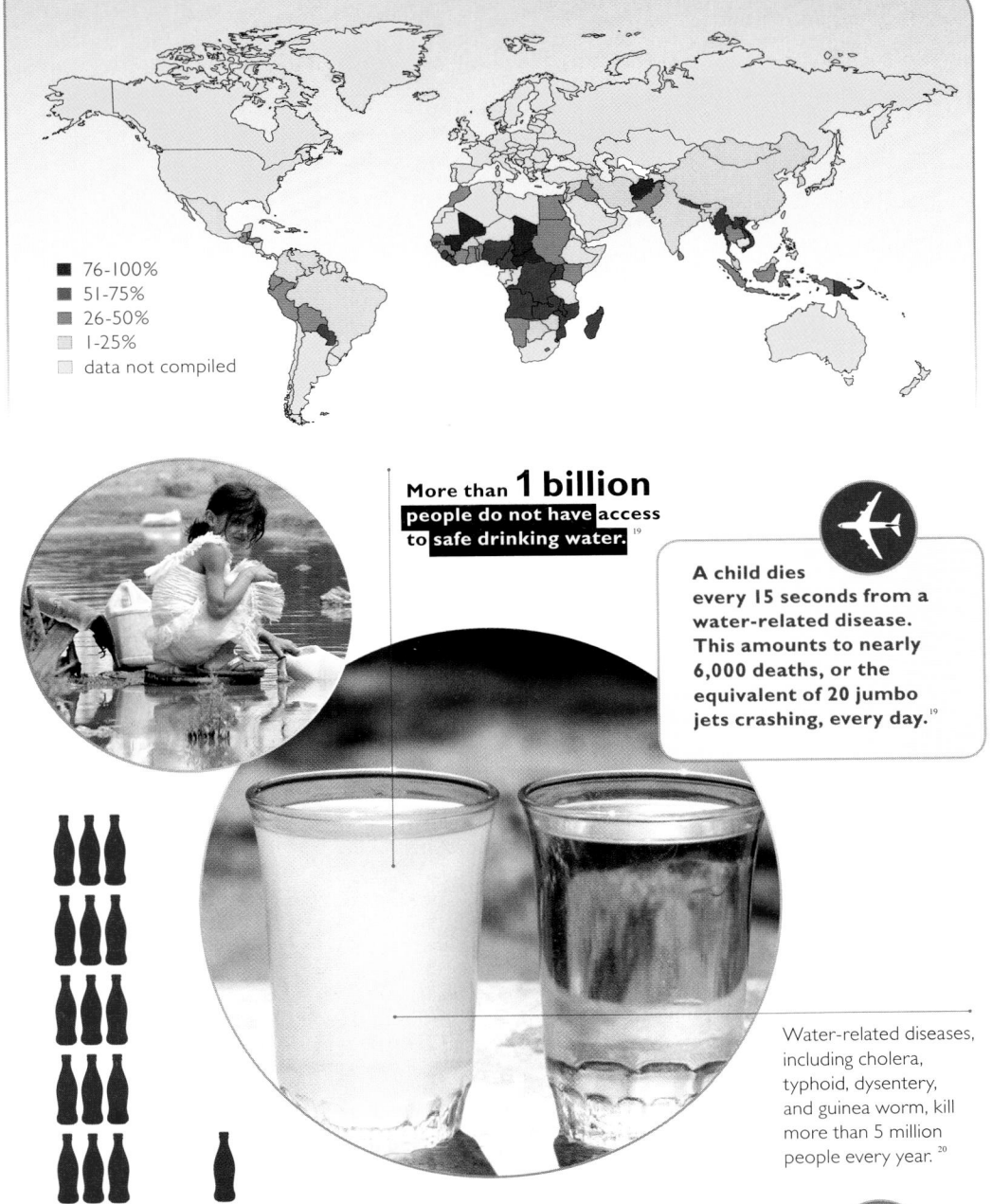

- ■ 76-100%
- ■ 51-75%
- ■ 26-50%
- ■ 1-25%
- □ data not compiled

More than **1 billion** people do not have access to safe drinking water. [19]

A child dies every 15 seconds from a water-related disease. This amounts to nearly 6,000 deaths, or the equivalent of 20 jumbo jets crashing, every day. [19]

Water-related diseases, including cholera, typhoid, dysentery, and guinea worm, kill more than 5 million people every year. [20]

soft drink spending   USAID budget

Americans spend more than $61 billion on soft drinks every year—15 times the budget of the United States Agency for International Development (USAID), the U.S. government's humanitarian assistance agency. [22, 23]

H2O

The average American uses 170 gallons of water every day. [21]

The health divide

**Every 15 seconds,
five children die—most from
preventable disease or malnutrition.
Of these, one dies due to diarrhea.**[24, 25]

Dying young :: children who die before their fifth birthday (per 1,000 live births)[6]

The majority of these children die of preventable causes, including diarrhea,
malnutrition, measles, and malaria.[10]

Sierra Leone **284**

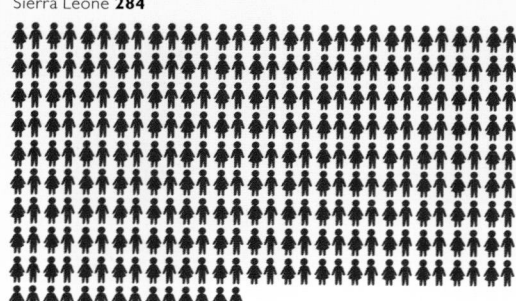

Angola **260**

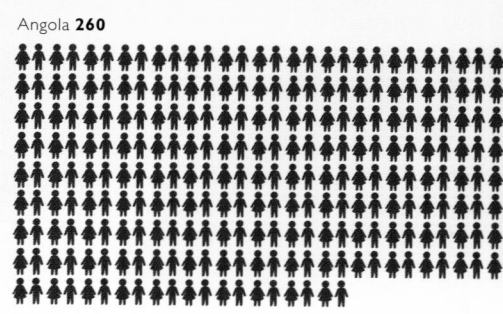

Bolivia **71**

Guatemala **49**

Chad **200**

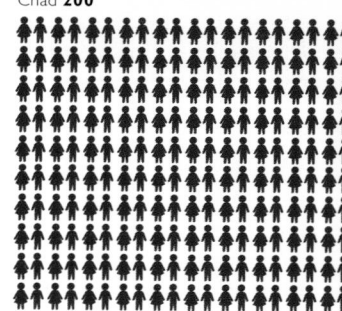

Killers of adults worldwide :: annual deaths

**One-third of the
world's population
is infected with tuberculosis.**[29]

AIDS   Tuberculosis   Malaria   Lung Cancer

**Worldwide every year, AIDS kills 2.9 million
people, tuberculosis more than 2 million,
and malaria around 1 million.**[26, 27]

In the U.S., yearly deaths due to lung cancer
average just over 150,000.[28]

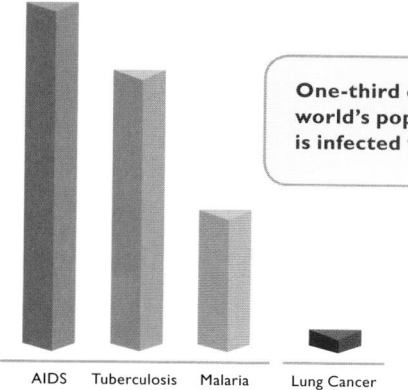

Dying to give birth :: maternal deaths per 100,000 live births[6]

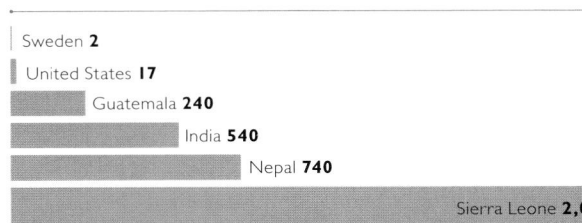

Sweden **2**

United States **17**

Guatemala **240**

India **540**

Nepal **740**

Sierra Leone **2,000**

Cambodia **138**

Azerbaijan **105**

Lebanon **32**

India **93**

Saudi Arabia **28**

United States **8**   Japan **5**   Germany **5**   Sweden **3**

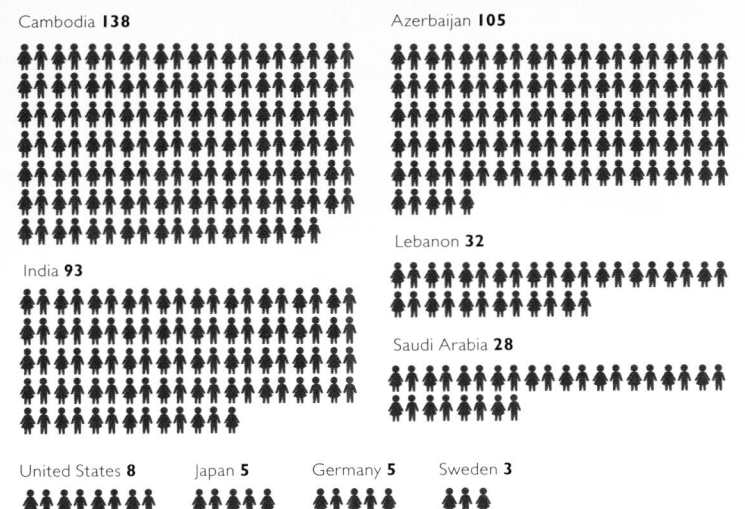

Worldwide, **every 60 seconds a woman dies** of complications related to pregnancy or childbirth. In sub-Saharan Africa, 1 of every 100 live births results in the mother's death.[16]

There is only 1 physician for every 100,000 people in Burundi compared to 607 for every 100,000 people in Italy.[6]

Budgeting for health :: per capita annual health expenditures[6]

United States **$4,887**

Jordan **$412**

China **$224**

Ukraine **$176**

Honduras **$153**

Burundi **$19**

Japan

Sweden

United States

Cambodia

Haiti

Zambia

Birth ● — **33** — **49** — **57** — **77 80 81** — **100**

Life expectancy at birth :: in years[6]

AIDS:

The pandemic of our century

Projected HIV/AIDS hot spots

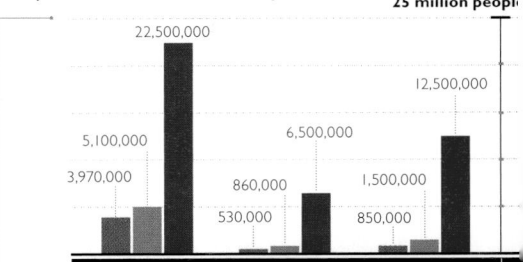

25 million people

Number of people living with HIV/AIDS[26, 30]

- ■ in 2001
- ■ today
- ■ by 2010

	India	Russia	China
	3,970,000	530,000	850,000
	5,100,000	860,000	1,500,000
	22,500,000	6,500,000	12,500,000

By 2010, a child born in Botswana, Africa, can expect to live only 27 years due to the AIDS pandemic.

Since it was discovered, AIDS has killed 28.2 million people— more than three times the population of Sweden.[26]

HIV/AIDS cases by region[26]

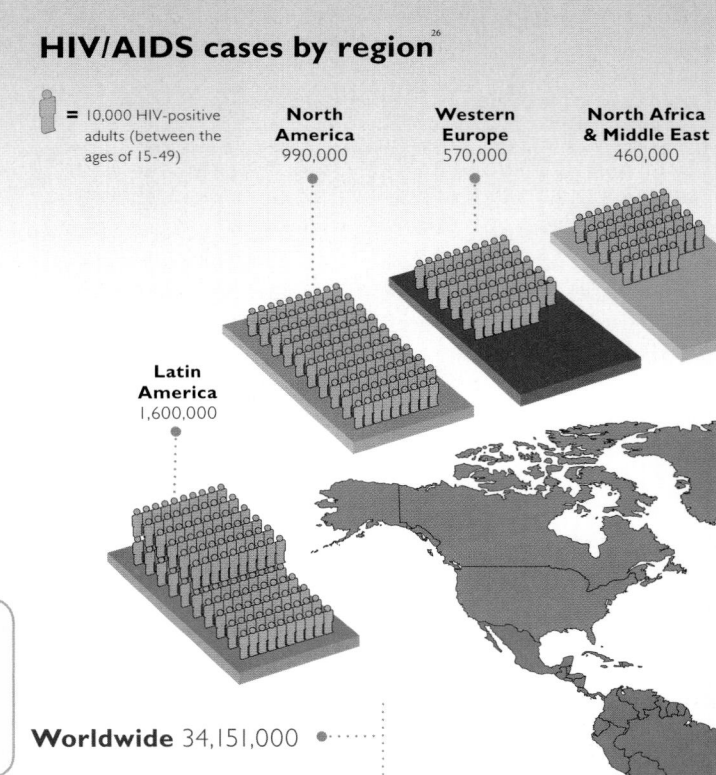

= 10,000 HIV-positive adults (between the ages of 15-49)

North America 990,000

Western Europe 570,000

North Africa & Middle East 460,000

Latin America 1,600,000

Worldwide 34,151,000

% of total HIV cases[26]

East Asia	3%
Eastern Europe & Central Asia	4%
Latin America	5%
North Africa & Middle East	1%
Oceania	less than 1%
North America	3%
South & Southeast Asia	18%
Sub-Saharan Africa	64%
Western Europe	2%

HIV-positive adults
countries with highest prevalences[26]

Botswana	37.3%
Zimbabwe	24.6%
Swaziland	38.8%
Lesotho	28.9%

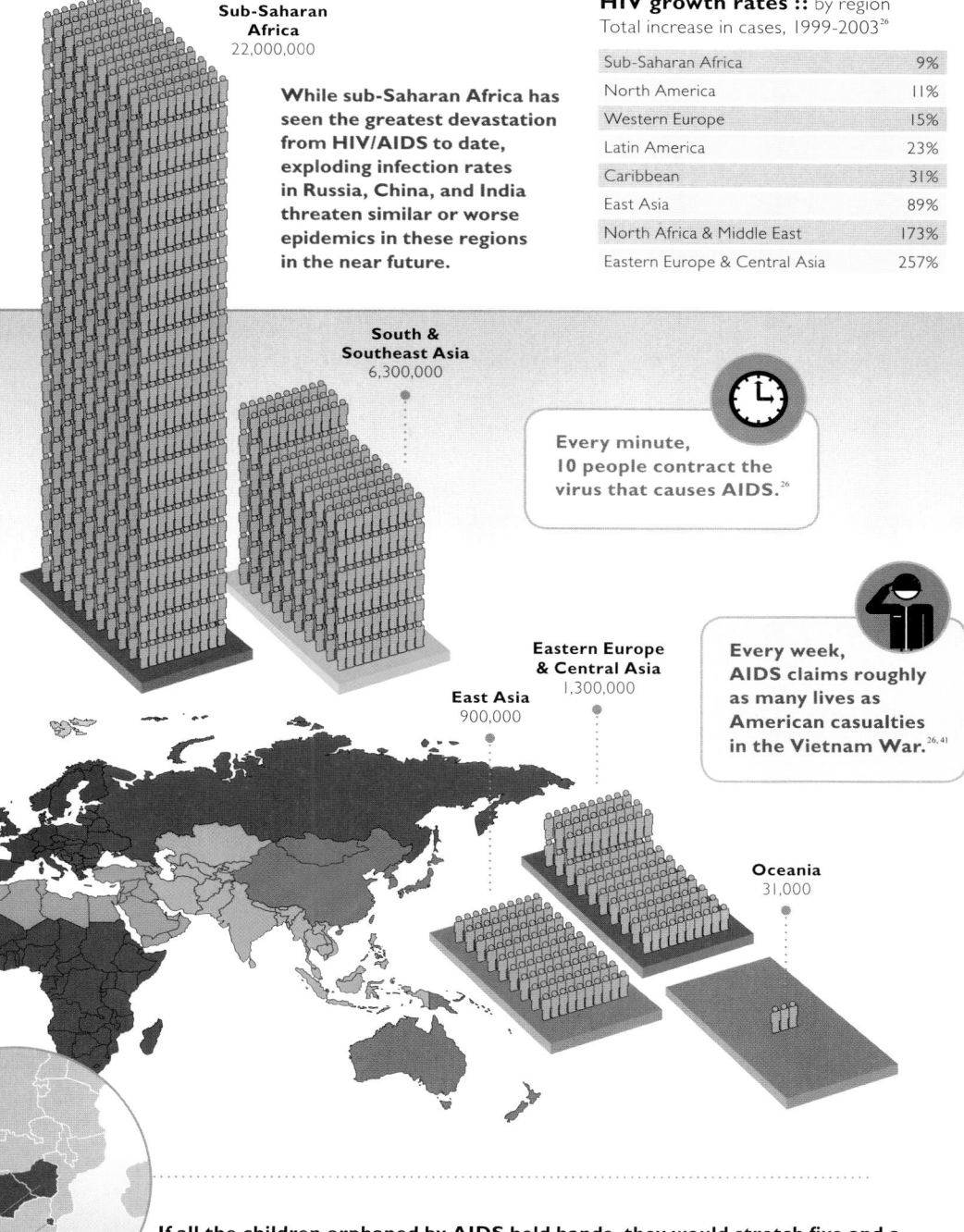

Sub-Saharan Africa
22,000,000

While sub-Saharan Africa has seen the greatest devastation from HIV/AIDS to date, exploding infection rates in Russia, China, and India threaten similar or worse epidemics in these regions in the near future.

HIV growth rates :: by region
Total increase in cases, 1999-2003[26]

Sub-Saharan Africa	9%
North America	11%
Western Europe	15%
Latin America	23%
Caribbean	31%
East Asia	89%
North Africa & Middle East	173%
Eastern Europe & Central Asia	257%

South & Southeast Asia
6,300,000

Every minute, 10 people contract the virus that causes AIDS.[26]

Eastern Europe & Central Asia
1,300,000

Every week, AIDS claims roughly as many lives as American casualties in the Vietnam War.[26, 41]

East Asia
900,000

Oceania
31,000

If all the children orphaned by AIDS held hands, they would stretch five and a half times across the United States (or more than halfway around the globe). By 2011, this virtual chain will reach around the world.[26, 32, 42]

Education and literacy

Illiteracy rates by country [33]

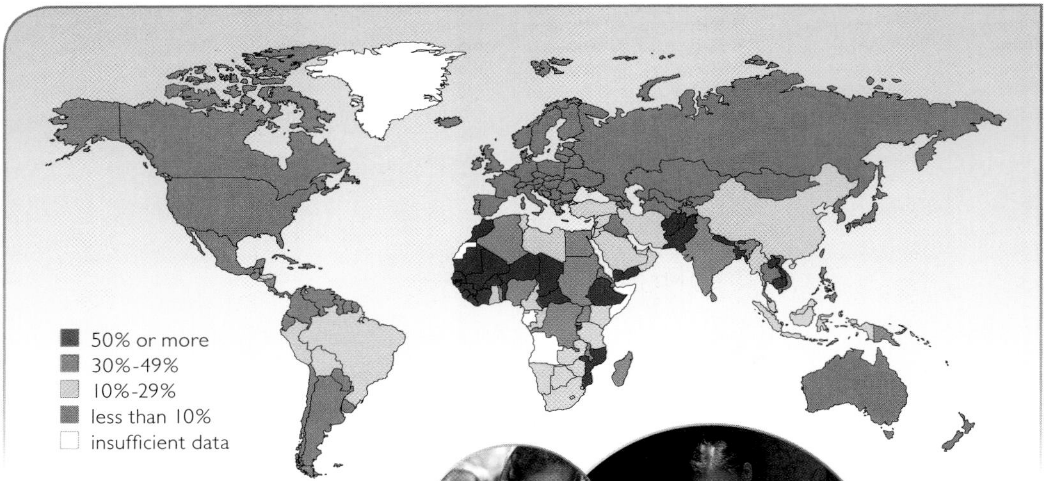

- ■ 50% or more
- ■ 30%-49%
- ■ 10%-29%
- ■ less than 10%
- □ insufficient data

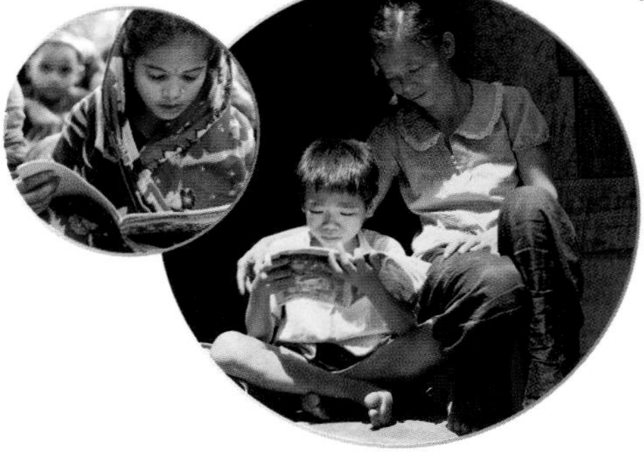

> **One-quarter of adults in the developing world cannot read or write.** [16]

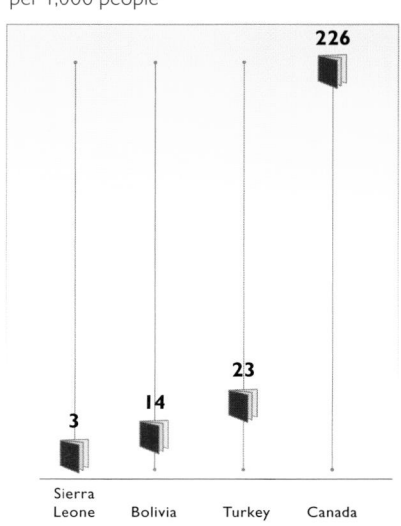

Estimated world illiteracy rates :: by region and gender [33]

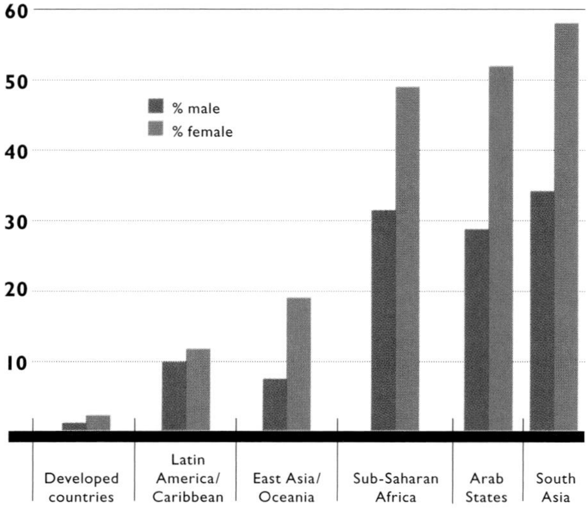

- ■ % male
- ■ % female

	Developed countries	Latin America/ Caribbean	East Asia/ Oceania	Sub-Saharan Africa	Arab States	South Asia

Number of library books
per 1,000 people [33]

Sierra Leone	Bolivia	Turkey	Canada
3	14	23	226

Primary school-age girls not in school [34]

Somalia **94%**

Ethiopia **84%**

Haiti **74%**

India **39%**

Venezuela **10%**

United States less than **1%**

Nearly half of the children who start primary school do not finish. [16]

In some school districts in Kenya, a single teacher may have up to 250 students. Many of these students fail, due to both hunger (which makes it difficult to concentrate) and lack of instruction. [35]

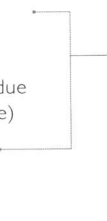

Average student-teacher ratio [36, 37]

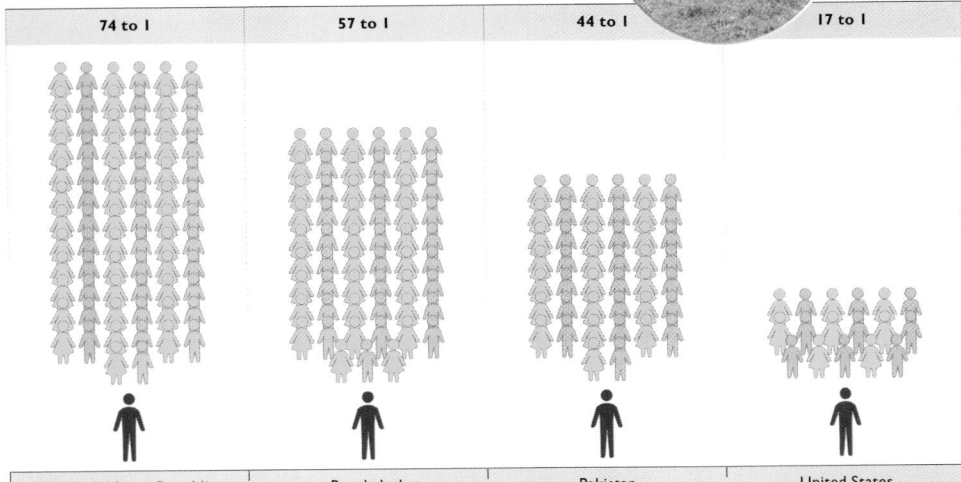

74 to 1	57 to 1	44 to 1	17 to 1
Central African Republic	Bangladesh	Pakistan	United States

The gender gap

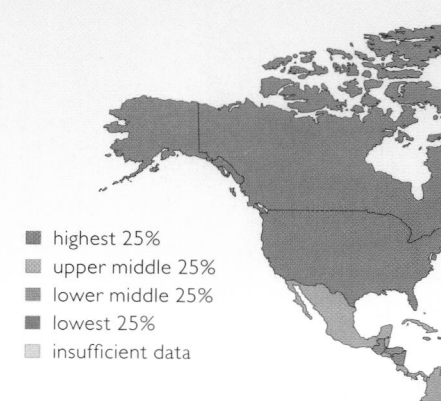

Development index for women [38]

The Gender Development Index measures average achievement in the areas of long and healthy life, knowledge, and decent standard of living—adjusted to account for inequalities between women and men.

- ■ highest 25%
- ▨ upper middle 25%
- ■ lower middle 25%
- ■ lowest 25%
- ☐ insufficient data

Gender gap in the developing world :: female as a percent of male [38, 39]

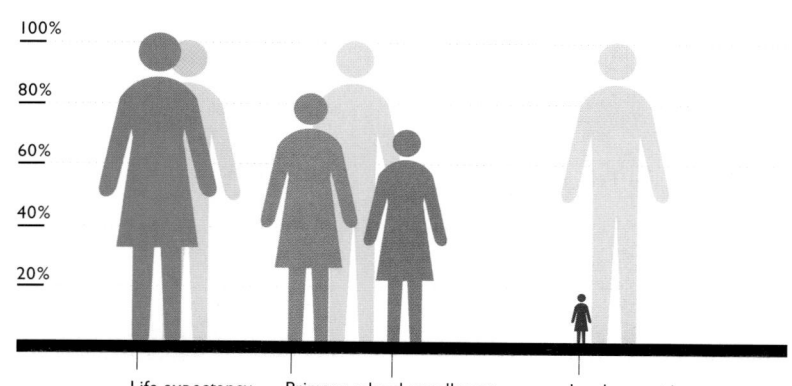

100%
80%
60%
40%
20%

Life expectancy   Primary school enrollment   Involvement in government
| Secondary school enrollment

Women work two out of every three of the world's total working hours. [40]

Women earn 10% of the world's income. [40]

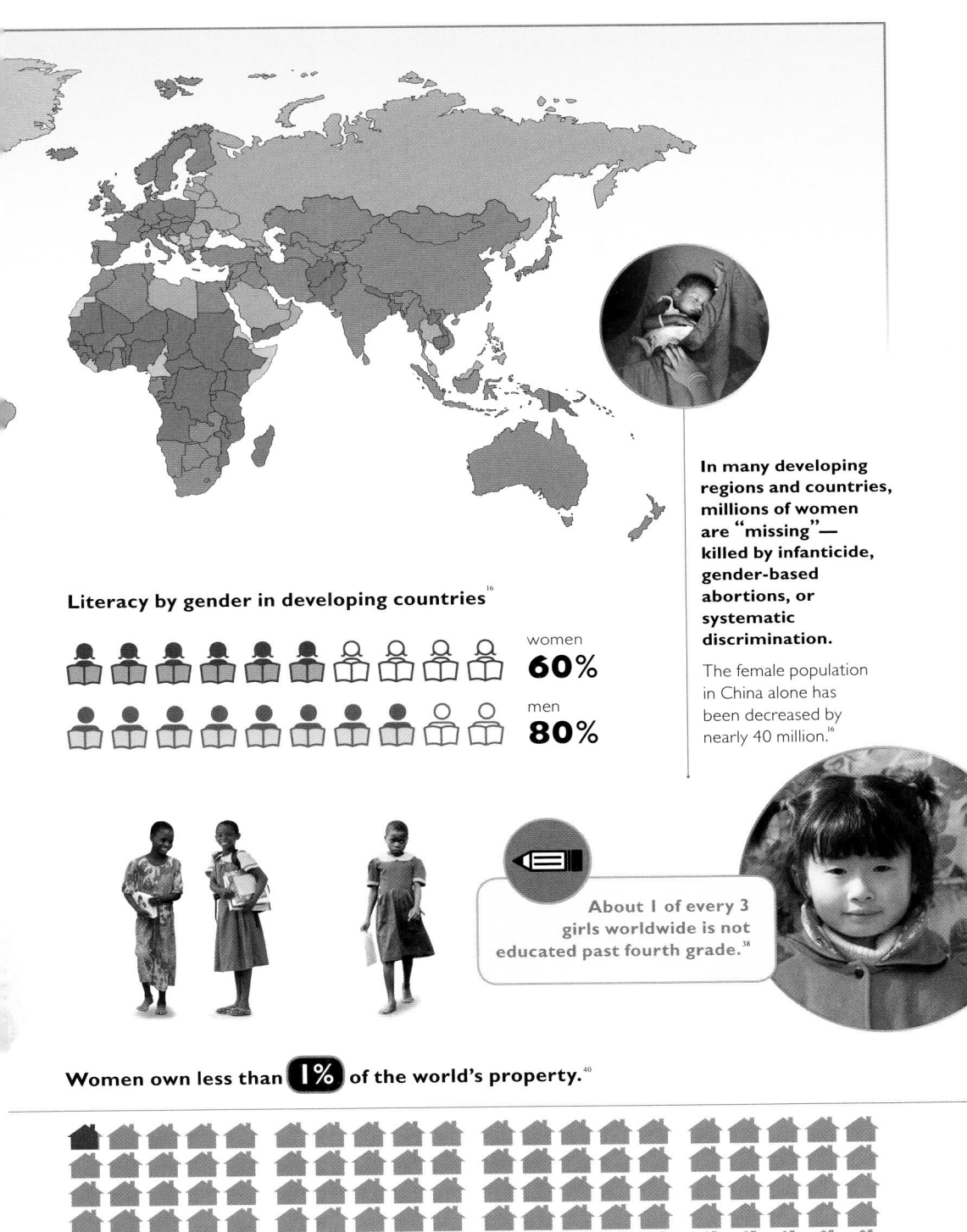

Literacy by gender in developing countries[16]

women
60%

men
80%

In many developing regions and countries, millions of women are "missing"— killed by infanticide, gender-based abortions, or systematic discrimination.

The female population in China alone has been decreased by nearly 40 million.[16]

About 1 of every 3 girls worldwide is not educated past fourth grade.[38]

Women own less than 1% of the world's property.[40]

"And God will wipe away every tear"

"I looked and there before me was a great multitude that no one could count, from every nation, tribe, people and language, standing before the throne and in front of the Lamb . . . He will wipe away every tear from their eyes. There will be no more death or mourning or crying or pain, for the old order of things has passed away."

—Revelation 7:9;21:4

Source references

1. World Christian Database, 2004
2. World Christian Encyclopedia, 2001
3. Operation World, 2001
4. Exploring World Mission, Bryant Myers. World Vision International, 2003
5. CIA World Factbook, 2003
6. United Nations Human Development Report 2004
7. CIA World Factbook, 2004
8. U.S. Department of Labor, Bureau of Labor Statistics, October 2004
9. World Vision
10. World Bank, 2004
11. International Telecommunication Union, March 2004
12. Undernourishment Around the World, Food and Agriculture Organization, 2003
13. State of Food Insecurity in the World, Food and Agriculture Organization, 2001
14. The World's Water, The Biennial Report on Freshwater Resources (Gleick 1998)
15. www.worldwater.org
16. United Nations Human Development Report 2003
17. State of the World 2004, Worldwatch Institute
18. State of Food Insecurity in the World, Food and Agriculture Organization, 2003
19. World Health Organization, 2004
20. UN World Water Development Report, 2003
21. Environmental Protection Agency, 2004
22. Center for Science in the Public Interest, 2004
23. USAID, 2004
24. State of the World's Children, UNICEF, 2004
25. www.oneworldhealth.org
26. UNAIDS (2004 Report on the Global AIDS Epidemic, www.unaids.org)
27. Centers for Disease Control and Prevention, 2003
28. National Vital Statistics Reports, 2003
29. Centers for Disease Control and Prevention, 2004
30. National Intelligence Council of the United States, 2003
31. USAID, 2002
32. Children on the Brink, UNICEF, 2002
33. UNESCO Institute for Statistics, 2000 and 2002 data
34. Household survey data, net enrollment data from UNESCO, and data from UNICEF country offices (data available at www.nationmaster.com)
35. "Educational nourishment feeding children in Africa," New York Times, October 24, 2004
36. UNESCO (data available at www.nationmaster.com)
37. Washington Research Council, 2004
38. United Nations Human Development Report 2001
39. State of the Future, 2002
40. State of the World Index, 2000
41. Every day, 8,000 people die of AIDS. The Vietnam War claimed 58,200 American casualties.
42. Worldwide, there are currently 15 million orphans due to AIDS. By 2010 this number is expected to exceed 25,000.

For more information, visit the following Web sites:
www.cia.gov/cia/publications/factbook
  (Central Intelligence Agency Factbook)
www.un.org (United Nations)
www.worldvision.org

World Vision
Building a better world for children

World Vision is a Christian relief and development organization dedicated to helping children and their communities worldwide reach their full potential by tackling the causes of poverty. Motivated by our faith in Jesus, we serve the world's poor—regardless of a person's religion, race, ethnicity, or gender—as a demonstration of God's unconditional love for all people.